SCHOOL DICTIONARY 2

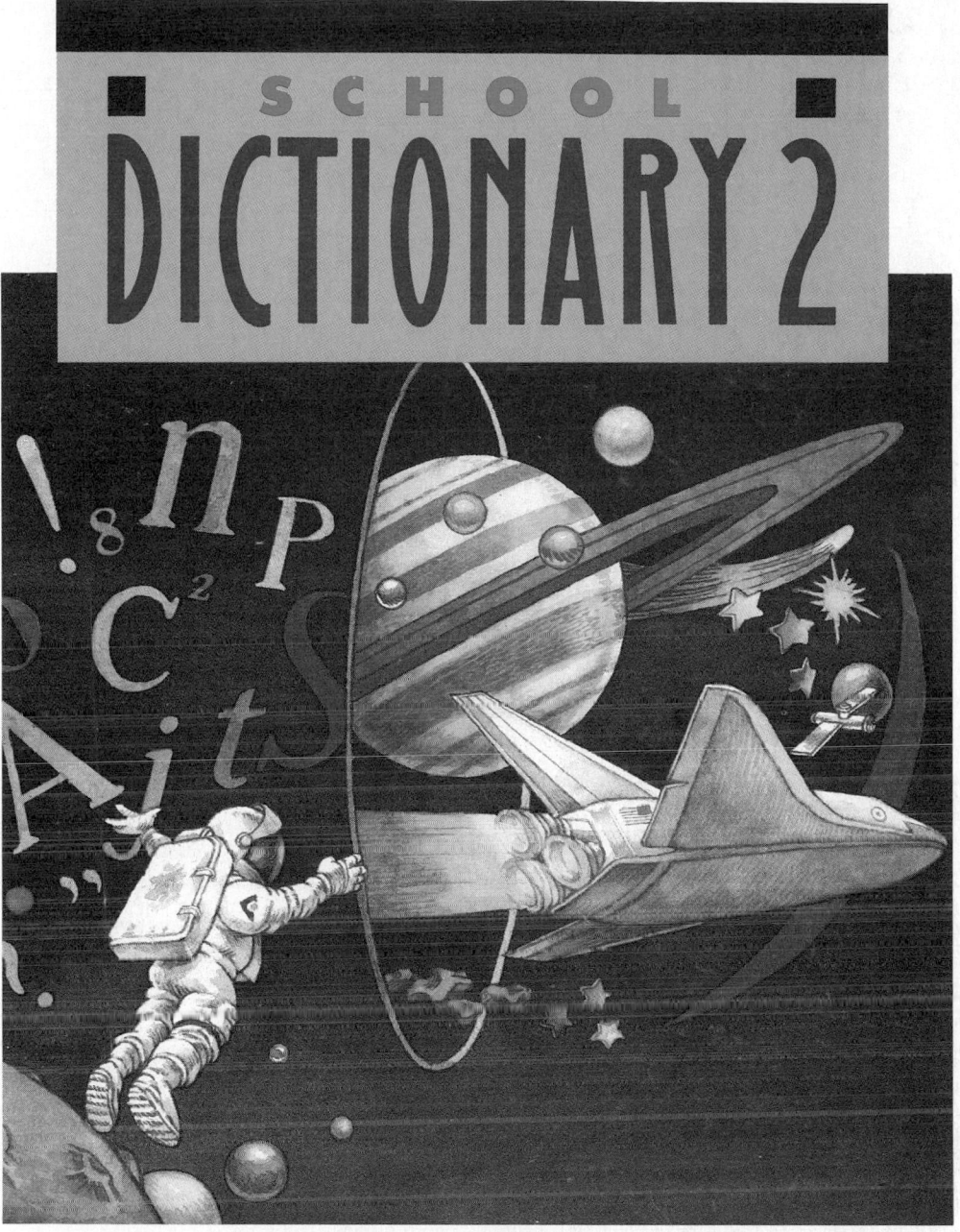

The images on the cover of this book focus on the exploration of space—an enterprise made possible because of the letters and numbers that make up the languages of mathematics, science, and technology.

MACMILLAN

Macmillan Publishing Company
New York

Collier Macmillan Publishers
London

Macmillan Publishing Company
866 Third Avenue
New York, New York 10022
Collier Macmillan Canada, Inc.

Printed in the United States of America
ISBN 0-02-195004-0/6-8
9 8

Editorial Staff

Editor in Chief	Judith S. Levey
Managing Editor	Helen Adele Chumbley
Senior Editor	Michael E. Agnes
Editors	Frank R. Abate, Ronald J. Bogus, Carol G. Braham, William C. Hale (etymologies), Bonny Hart (life sciences), Archie Hobson, Paul G. Lagassé, Edward J. Moran (physical sciences), Gloria Mihályi Solomon (pronunciation)
Contributing Editors	Kathleen Derzipilski (biographies), Eden Eskin, Lora Goldman (geography), Hal B. Grossman (law), Robert K. Haycraft, Susan R. Norton (art), Peggy Seeger
Production Manager	Karen L. Tates
Editorial Production	Robert B. Gampert, Milica Govich, John Mariano, Nick Scelsi, Patricia Clements Shuldiner
Proofreaders	Patricia Bonder, Mary Louise Byrd, Jerilyn Famighetti, Emily Garlin, Honora Horan, Mary Ann Maderer, Ezra Maurer, Dana M. Schwartz, John F. Scorza, Stephanie Sweeney
Production Assistants	Margot A. Bonelli, Joseph D. Henry

Consultants

Lexicographic Consultant	Sidney I. Landau
Area Consultants	Judith Bloch, *Collier's Encyclopedia,* geography Lona Greenhouse, teacher of mathematics, mathematics Susan J. Lacerte, Brooklyn Botanic Garden, botany Dr. Alan Oppenheim, physical sciences Dr. Marissa M. Seligman, medicine, pharmacology

Art Staff

Design Director	Zelda Haber
Associate Design Director	Joan Gampert
Senior Designer	Marvin Friedman
Designers	Norman Dane, Lee Goldstein, Anna Sabin
Photo Research	Omni-Photo Communications, Inc.
Artists	Erni Barth; Bertrick Associates; Ann Brewster; James Calvin; Eva Cellini; Howard Friedman; Amy Horowitz; Ken Longtemps; Tina Mercie; Maria Mizzaro; Greg Purdon; Frank Schwartz; Judy Skorpil
Cover Design	Barnett-Brandt Design
Cover Art	Fred Winkowski
Frontmatter/Backmatter Design	MKR Design

Illustrations: Frontmatter: Fred Winkowski; Backmatter: Time Line, R29–R32, Joel Snyder; Birds, flowers, flags, R33–R45, Alex Bloch; Maps, R52–R56, R. R. Donnelley Cartographic Services; Math art, R56–R59, Simon Galkin; Math technical art, R60, Tom Cardamone Associates; Solar System, R61, Deborah Morse; Inside the Earth, R64, Deborah Morse

Acknowledgments

The publisher gratefully acknowledges permission to reproduce the following copyrighted materials:

For photograph of the cover of the 1989 WORLD ALMANAC: THE WORLD ALMANAC & BOOK OF FACTS, 1989 edition, copyright © Newspaper Enterprise Association, Inc. 1988, New York, NY 10166. Used by permission.

For photograph of the cover of the 1989 INFORMATION PLEASE ALMANAC and photograph of page 696 from above volume: From INFORMATION PLEASE ALMANAC 1989. Copyright © 1988 by Houghton Mifflin Company. Reprinted by permission of Houghton Mifflin Company.

Photograph of covers/spines of *Collier's Encyclopedia* and photograph of pages 90–91 in Volume 10 of above: Reprinted with permission from *Collier's Encyclopedia* © 1984 Macmillan Educational Company.

Photograph of page 53 in *Rand McNally Road Atlas*: From ROAD ATLAS © Copyright 1989 Rand McNally & Company, R.L. 89-S-S.

Photo Credits (A-Z Section): aardvark: Charles R. Belinky/Photo Researchers; **abstract:** "Les Masques" by Alexander Calder/Geoffrey Clements/Whitney Museum of American Art; **accordion:** Alan Becker/Image Bank; **adapted:** Bob & Clara Calhoun/Bruce Coleman; **adobe:** Jack Parsons/OPC; **agate:** Louise K. Broman/Photo Researchers; **Alaskan malamute:** Stephen J. Krasemann/Photo Researchers; **alpenhorn:** H.R. Uthoff/Image Bank; **amphibian:** Eric Simmons/Stock, Boston; **angelfish:** Tom McHugh/Photo Researchers; **arabesque:** Jack Vartoogian; **armadillo:** Patti Murray/Animals Animals; **art nouveau:** Tiffany Studios/The Metropolitan Museum of Art, Gift of Hugh J. Grant, 1974; **asymmetry:** Stephen Krasemann/Peter Arnold; **automated teller machine:** Alvis Upitis/Image Bank; **baboon:** John S. Flannery/Bruce Coleman; **balloon:** George Hall/Woodfin Camp; **barge:** Mark E. Gibson/Stock Market; **basket:** Lee Boltin; **bazaar:** Mark Bernheim/Woodfin Camp; **beekeeper:** Gordon Wiltsie/Bruce Coleman; **beret:** Elliott Erwitt/Magnum; **billow:** C. Seghers/Photo Researchers; **binocular:** Karen R. Preuss/Taurus; **blast-off:** NASA; **blue jay:** Ralph A. Reinhold/Animals Animals; **bobsled:** Gerard Champlong/Image Bank; **border:** Scala/Art Resource; **braille:** Georges Tourdjman/Image Bank; **bricklayer:** Richard Hutchings/Photo Researchers; **Brussels sprouts:** Lee Foster/Bruce Coleman; **bullet train:** Brian Brake/Rapho, Photo Researchers; **burnoose:** Frank Siteman/Stock, Boston; **cactus:** Eric Chrichton/Bruce Coleman; **camcorder:** Tibor Bognar/Stock Market; **canyon:** Judith S. Levey; **cardinal:** John H. Hoffman/Bruce Coleman; **cascade:** Susan Norton; **castle:** Harold Scind/Image Bank; **cattle:** Margot Conte/Animals Animals; **cello:** Lou Jones/Image Bank; **chairlift:** Marcel Isy-Schwart/Image Bank; **chess:** Beth Ullman/Taurus; **chip:** Joel Greenstein/OPC; **chopsticks:** William Hubbell/Woodfin Camp; **citizen:** Sachs/Sygma; **cliff dwelling:** Susan Norton; **cockpit:** Chris Sorensen/Stock Market; **collaborate:** Michal Heron/Woodfin Camp; **columbine:** Michael E. Agnes; **commencement:** Jan Halaska/Photo Researchers; **compact disc:** Barry Seidman/Stock Market; **computer:** Michal Heron/Woodfin Camp; **conductor:** Cecile Brunswick/Peter Arnold; **construction:** J. Barry O'Rourke/Stock Market; **control tower:** Michael L. Abramson/Woodfin Camp; **coral reef:** Shirley Richards/Photo Researchers; **cotton:** Bruce Roberts/Rapho, Photo Researchers; **courtroom:** William Hubbell/Woodfin Camp; **crater:** NASA; **crop-dusting:** Jeff Smith/Image Bank; **cubism:** "Three Musicians" by Santi Visalle/Image Bank; **date palm:** Paolo Koch/Photo Researchers; **decoy:** Michael Manheim/Stock Market; **delphinium:** E.R. Degginger/Earth Scenes; **derail:** F. Poincet/Sygma; **desolate:** Richard Weiss; **dialogue:** Lenore Weber/Omni-Photo Communications, Inc.; **dig:** Marty Cooper/Peter Arnold; **disc jockey:** Lou Jones/Image Bank; **dish:** Pete Salovtos/Stock Market; **disrepair:** C.B. Jones/Taurus; **dolphin:** William Curtsinger/Photo Researchers; **double-decker:** DPI; **drawbridge:** David Brownell/Image Bank; **drum:** Guy Gillette/Photo Researchers; **Dutch door:** Erik Leigh Simmons/Image Bank; **egret:** Jeff Simon/Bruce Coleman; **embroidery:** Luis Villota/Stock Market; **encrust:** Granger Collection; **envelop:** J. Alex Langley/DPI; **erosion:** Judith S. Levey; **everglade:** Breck P. Kent/Earth Scenes; **expedition:** David Hiser/Image Bank; **extravaganza:** Al Satterwhite/Image Bank; **fairy tale:** Little Red Riding Hood/Culver; **fanlight:** Tim Bieber/Image Bank; **fawn:** Leonard Lee Rue III/Photo Researchers; **ferryboat:** Sil Strung/Stock Market; **fireboat:** Mark E. Gibson/Stock Market; **fjord:** Mike Yamashita/Woodfin Camp; **floppy disk:** Martin Dohrn/Science Photo Library-Photo Researchers; **flute:** Pam Hasagawa/Taurus; **folk dance:** L. Villota/Stock Market; **forklift:** Paul Steel/Stock Market; **free fall:** Laurence Hughes/Image Bank; **gable:** Jawitz/Image Bank; **gaucho:** Isy-Schwart/Image Bank; **geometric:** Herbert W. Franke/Peter Arnold; **glacier:** Charlie Ott/Photo Researchers; **goalkeeper:** Peeters/Focus on Sports; **gondola:** Cecile Brunswick/Peter Arnold; **grandfather clock:** D. Bassil/Photo Source; **greenhouse:** Frank Siteman/Omni-Photo Communications, Inc.; **ground crew:** Brett H. Froomer/Image Bank; **guide dog:** Baron Wolman/Woodfin Camp; **gymnastics:** David Madison; **hammock:** Shelley Rotner/Omni-Photo Communications, Inc.; **hang gliding:** Guido Alberto Rossi/Image Bank; **hatch:** Zig Lescynski/Animals Animals; **headdress:** Chie Nishio/Omni-Photo Communications, Inc.; **helicopter:** Joe Azzara/Image Bank; **hibiscus:** Wardene Weisser/Bruce Coleman; **hogan:** Judith S. Levey; **honeycomb:** Timothy Eagan/Woodfin Camp; **houseboat:** John Blaustein/Woodfin Camp; **hurdle:** Ann Hagen Griffiths/Omni-Photo Communications, Inc.; **ice-skate:** Focus on

Sports; **igloo:** C. Bonington/Daily Telegraph Magazine/Woodfin Camp; **immobilize:** Charles Krebs/Stock Market; **impressionism:** "Terrace at Ste Adresse" by Claude Monet/Metropolitan Museum of Art; **incubator:** Kay Chernush/Image Bank; **inflatable:** R. Rowan/Photo Researchers; **inlay:** Scala/Art Resource; **integrated circuit:** G.V. Faint/Image Bank; **intricate:** John Banagan/Image Bank; **iris:** Bob & Clara Calhoun/Bruce Coleman; **jackhammer:** Sylvia Johnson/Woodfin Camp; **jockey:** Mel DiGiacomo/Image Bank; **jump:** Focus on Sports; **karate:** Michal Heron/Woodfin Camp; **kiwi:** Erwin & Peggy Bauer/Bruce Coleman; **laboratory:** Michal Heron/Woodfin Camp; **larva:** E.R. Degginger/Animals Animals; **lava:** Eric Meola/Image Bank; **leg warmers:** Roy Morsch/Stock Market; **Liberty Bell:** Joseph Nettis/Photo Researchers; **lighthouse:** Philip Ashwood/Stock Market; **llama:** Francisco Erize/Bruce Coleman; **loom:** Shelly Rotner/Omni-Photo Communications, Inc.; **lumbering:** Arthur d'Arazien/Image Bank; **macaw:** E.R. Degginger/Bruce Coleman; **magnify:** Dr. Jeremy Burgess/Science Photo Library/Photo Researchers; **mangrove:** C.B. Frith/Bruce Coleman; **marathon:** Jeffrey D. Smith/Woodfin Camp; **mask (1):** Museum of the American Indian; **mask (2):** M & E Bernheim/Woodfin Camp; **Mayflower:** Pilgrim Society; **memorial:** Roy Morsch/Stock Market; **mesa:** Jeff Hunter/Image Bank; **microscope:** Michal Heron/Woodfin Camp; **migration:** Frank Whitney/Image Bank; **minaret:** J. Alex Langley/DPI; **mobile:** "Lobster Trap and Fish Tail" by Alexander Calder (1939), Hanging mobile: painted steel wire and sheet aluminum about 8'6" x 9'6". Collection, The Museum of Modern Art, New York; **monarch:** Patti Murray/Animals Animals; **mosaic:** Tom McHugh/Photo Researchers; **national park:** Betsy Lee/Taurus; **neon:** Roy Morsch/Stock Market; **nomad:** Alexander Low/Woodfin Camp; **noted:** Charles Krebs/Stock Market; **obi:** Greg David/Stock Market; **offshore:** B. Gelberg/Image Bank; **optical fiber:** John Walsh/Science Photo Library/Photo Researchers; **origami:** Michal Heron/Woodfin Camp; **outboard motor:** Sonya Jacobs/Stock Market; **oxygen mask:** George Hall/Woodfin Camp; **paddy:** V. Engelbert/Photo Researchers; **pantomime:** Karen R. Preuss/Taurus; **Parthenon:** J. Alex Langley/DPI; **patchwork:** William Strode/Woodfin Camp; **peacock:** Peter Davey/Bruce Coleman; **pepper:** Thomas Braise/Stock Market; **perspective:** Patti McConville/Image Bank; **phlox:** M.J. Manuel/Photo Researchers; **picket line:** Wesley Bocxe/Photo Researchers; **pineapple:** Paola Koch/Photo Researchers; **plaza:** Victor Engelbert/Photo Researchers; **poinsettia:** Mark N. Boulton National Audubon Society/Photo Researchers; **poncho:** Loren McIntyre/Woodfin Camp; **potter's wheel:** Ken Karp/Omni-Photo Communications, Inc.; **prefabricate:** Bernard Gotfryd/Woodfin Camp; **prickly pear:** Bruce Coleman, Inc.; **procession:** Martha Cooper/Peter Arnold; **protective coloration:** Doug Wechsler/Animals Animals; **pueblo:** Adam Woolfitt/Woodfin Camp; **puppet:** Ken Karp/Omni-Photo Communications, Inc.; **pyramid:** Stephen Frink/Stock Market; **quetzal:** Michael Fogden/Animals Animals; **race:** Lawrence Migdale/Photo Researchers; **rapids:** John Blaustein/Woodfin Camp; **reaper:** Dick Durrance II/Woodfin Camp; **refuel:** George Hall/Woodfin Camp; **relief:** George Holton/Photo Researchers; **replica:** Van Bucher/Photo Researchers; **restoration:** Brownie Harris/Stock Market; **rhododendron:** Neville Fox-Davies/Bruce Coleman; **robot:** D. Goldberg/Sygma; **runway:** Adam Gesar/Image Bank; **safety belt:** G. Anderson/Taurus; **sampan:** R. Thompson/Taurus; **Saturn:** NASA/OPC; **schooner:** Jim Raycroft/Stock Market; **screech owl:** Tom Edwards/Animals Animals; **scuba diving:** Donna McLaughlin/Stock Market; **seine:** Keith Gunnar/Bruce Coleman; **sequoia:** Zelda Haber; **shako:** Gabe Palmer/Stock Market; **shear:** Robert Frerck/Woodfin Camp; **shrike:** Edgar T. Jones/Bruce Coleman; **sign language:** Ken Karp/Omni-Photo Communications, Inc.; **skiing:** Stowe Ski Area; **sleek:** J. Alex Langley/DPI; **smudge pot:** Eric Kroll/Taurus Photos; **snow leopard:** Zig Lescynski/Animals Animals; **solar panel:** Robert Phillip/Image Bank; **sousaphone:** Gerry Souter/Photo Researchers; **spacewalk:** NASA; **sphinx:** Luis Villota/Stock Market; **spoonbill:** J.L. Lepore/Photo Researchers; **stained glass:** Hans Halbertstadt/Photo Researchers; **statue:** Lea/Omni-Photo Communications, Inc.; **stethoscope:** Michal Heron/Woodfin Camp; **stonemason:** Robert McElroy/Woodfin Camp; **straw:** Lowell Georgia/Photo Researchers; **stunt:** Patrick Harbron/Sygma; **subway:** Jim Anderson/Woodfin Camp; **sundial:** John V.A.F. Neal/Photo Researchers; **sushi:** Whitney Lane/Image Bank; **synthesizer:** David Burnett/Woodfin Camp; **tackle:** Harold W. Hoffman/Photo Researchers; **tap:** Roy Morsch/Stock Market; **telescope:** Douglas Kirkland/Woodfin Camp; **thatch:** Richard Weiss; **thistle:** Stephen P. Parker/Photo Researchers; **tiger:** Lawrence Migdale/Photo Researchers; **toboggan:** Catherine Ursillo/Photo Researchers; **totem pole:** Alon Reininger/Contact Camp; **trampoline:** Richard Hutchings/Photo Researchers; **treadmill:** Ken Karp/Omni-Photo Communications, Inc.; **tripod:** Art Wolfe/Image Bank; **tuba:** Thomas Braise/Stock Market; **turban:** Lisl Dennis/Image Bank; **twilight:** Bob Hahn/Taurus Photos; **unadorned:** Chris Tortora/Woodfin Camp; **underpass:** Craig Aurness/Woodfin Camp; **unicycle:** G. Lloyd/Taurus; **uproot:** Betsy Blass/Photo Researchers; **vat:** Gary Gladstone/Image Bank; **vault:** Charles West/Stock Market; **versatile:** Roy Morsch/Stock Market; **viaduct:** Blair Seitz/Photo Researchers; **volcano:** F. Salmoiraghi/Stock Market; **walkie-talkie:** Will McIntyre/Photo Researchers; **waterfall:** Kunio Owaki/Stock Market; **web:** John Lemker/Animals Animals; **wharf:** Sally Myers/Taurus; **whittle:** Linda Bartlett/Photo Researchers; **wok:** William Hubbell/Woodfin Camp; **workshop:** Michal Heron/Woodfin Camp; **yucca:** Anthony Mercieca/Photo Researchers; **zebra:** Eric Dragesco/Bruce Coleman

Contents

REFERENCE SECTION

LANGUAGE ARTS AND READING

SOCIAL STUDIES

MATHEMATICS AND SCIENCE

Introduction

TO STUDENTS

Words are marvelous things. Every word has its own special history, its own meaning or meanings, and its own place in our language. This dictionary can be a wonderfully helpful guide to the words we use.

The *Macmillan School Dictionary II* is a book designed especially to help you learn about the English language and to use it more effectively. It contains many special features intended to make words come alive and help you enjoy learning about them and using them.

All of the words in the *Macmillan School Dictionary* have been carefully selected to make this dictionary helpful to you. The editors studied and selected vocabulary from many different sources. Among the most important sources were the current textbooks of all major publishers and works of literature—the novels, essays, poems, and plays that you might be likely to read. The editors have also searched computerized texts of contemporary magazines and newspapers. Terms and expressions commonly used in everyday conversation have been included as well.

In addition, the *Macmillan School Dictionary* offers many other kinds of information. The entries for many words contain an etymology, or word history, which explains where the word comes from. Thousands of entries explain the meanings of idioms, or common expressions, and give examples of their use. Notes on usage help you choose the right word and use it correctly. You will also find features called Word Families, Language Notes, and Words From Other Languages.

The front and back sections of the *Macmillan School Dictionary* contain many other special features. The pages in the front section explain how to use the dictionary and describe what you will find in it. Activities, called "Your Turn," are included to help you become familiar with the dictionary. The back section provides resources and reference materials that will make this book helpful to you in your studies. These materials are organized by subject matter: Language Arts and Reading, Social Studies, and Mathematics and Science. Among other useful tools, you will find a thesaurus, a description of library resources, maps, a time line, facts about United States Presidents and all fifty states, a table of weights and measures, and information about the solar system.

The *Macmillan School Dictionary* is a valuable reference tool that you will appreciate more and more as you use it. By using it often, you will learn a great deal about words and how to use them. Such knowledge will help you communicate more effectively with others.

TO PARENTS AND TEACHERS

A school dictionary should be a useful reference tool as well as a real source of excitement about language and learning. The *Macmillan School Dictionary II* is designed to meet both of these needs.

The dictionary editors have carefully selected the words listed in this dictionary by studying grade-level textbooks from all major publishers, literature, computerized texts of periodicals, and other materials relevant to students in this age group. The dictionary also includes dozens of entries for words that have only recently entered our language.

The definitions of the words have been written carefully to make sure they are clear and understandable to students. And the special features of this dictionary are designed not only to provide information for students but also to excite their interest in learning more about language. The front section of this book explains the various features of the dictionary in clear, concise language. A series of exercises is included to help students develop and practice their dictionary skills. The back section of this dictionary provides reference materials and resources related to Language Arts and Reading, Social Studies, and Mathematics and Science to help make this reference book even more valuable.

The *Macmillan School Dictionary* provides clear, understandable answers to questions students have about words and how to use them. It also provides two kinds of illustration: example sentences to show how words are used and pictures to illustrate and clarify meanings. As students become increasingly familiar with this dictionary, a new world of language will open up to them.

Dictionary Preview

MAIN ENTRY

dace (dās) *n., pl.* **dace** or **dac·es.** any of various minnows commonly found in small streams of North America and Europe.

SYLLABLE DIVISION

dai·sy (dā′zē) *n., pl.* **dai·sies.** **1.** a flower usually having pink, yellow, or white petallike florets surrounding a yellow center. **2.** the plant bearing this flower.

PARTS OF SPEECH

dap·ple (dap′ əl) *adj.* having spots; spotted: *a dapple horse.* Also, **dap·pled** (dap′əld). —*n.* **1.** a spot or dot, as on an animal's skin or coat. **2.** an animal having a spotted coat.

PRONUNCIATION

dart (därt) *n.* **1.** a long, slender, pointed object resembling an arrow, used in the playing of certain games. **2. darts.** a game in which these objects are thrown at a target. **3.** a slender, pointed weapon to be thrown by hand or shot from a blowgun.

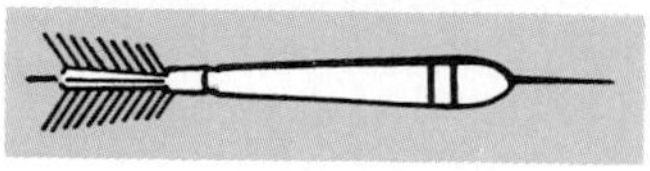

dart (*n. def. 1*)

DEFINITION

da·ta·base (dā′tə bās′, dat′ə bās′) *n.* a collection of data that is organized by categories so that information can be retrieved logically and easily, as by a computer.

CROSS-REFERENCE

daw (dô) *n.* see **jackdaw.**

INFLECTED FORMS

daze (dāz) *v.t.,* **dazed, daz·ing.** to stun or confuse, as by a blow; bewilder: *The punch dazed the boxer.* —*n.* a dazed state or condition: *The auto accident left the driver in a daze.* —**daz·ed·ly** (dā′ zid lē), *adv.*

PREFIX

de- *prefix* **1. a.** to remove (something) from: *defrost.* **b.** to remove from (something): *dethrone.* **2.** to lower: *devalue.* **3.** to do the opposite of, reverse, or undo: *decode.*

ILLUSTRATIVE PHRASE

deft (deft) *adj.* skillful and nimble; adroit: *the deft fingers of a pianist.* Your deft handling of the difficult situation prevented a crisis. —**deft′ly,** *adv.* —**deft′ness,** *n.*

RUN-ON ENTRIES

den·si·ty (den′si tē) *n., pl.* **den·si·ties.** **1.** the quality or condition of being closely packed together; thickness; compactness: *The density of the tall grass made walking difficult.* **2.** *Physics.* the ratio of the mass of a substance to its volume: *Iron has a greater density than wood.* **3.** quantity per unit of area, volume, length, or time: *The density of population in that country is very high.* **4.** *Informal.* stupidity.

SUBJECT LABEL

USAGE LABEL

der·i·va·tion (der′ə vā′shən) *n.* **1.** the act of deriving or the state of being derived. **2.** a source or origin: *This legend is of Irish derivation.* **3.** something derived; derivative: *This custom is a derivation from an earlier English one.* **4.** the process of tracing the origin and development of a word. **5.** a statement of the history of a word; etymology. **6.** the formation of a new word from an existing word, root, or stem, especially by the addition of a prefix or suffix, such as *kindness* from *kind.*

ILLUSTRATIVE SENTENCES

Language Note

In language, **derivation** usually refers to the formation of a word by the addition of a prefix or a suffix to an existing word. . . . If you take *friend* as a root word, you can make the common words *friendly, friendliness, friendless, friendship, befriend, unfriendly,* and *unfriendliness.*

LANGUAGE NOTE

GUIDE WORDS

USAGE NOTE

dint (dint) *n.* **1.** force; power. ▲ now used chiefly in the phrase *by dint of: by dint of argument, by dint of effort.*

doc·tor (dok′tər) *n.* **1.** a person who is licensed to practice any of various branches of medicine, such as pediatrics or psychiatry; physician or surgeon. **2.** a person who is licensed to practice any of various related sciences.

Word Family

The meanings of words often change over time. This is evident from the meanings of most of the English words derived from the Latin word *docere,* meaning ''to teach.'' Today, the word **doctor** most often refers to a person trained in medicine, someone who may not teach at all. Tools for teaching include **documents,** which contain important facts, and the **documentary.**

WORD FAMILY

SUFFIX

-dom *suffix* (used to form nouns) **1.** office, rank, or realm of: *earldom, kingdom.* **2.** the state of being: *freedom, wisdom.* **3.** all of those who are: *officialdom.*

COMPOUND

double bass (bās) the largest and deepest-toned instrument of the violin family, usually having four strings, and played in an upright position. Also, **bass viol, contrabass.**

VARIANT TERMS

VARIANT SPELLING

dread·nought (dred′nôt′) *also,* **dread·naught.** *n.* a battleship with heavy armor and very large guns.

dress·er¹ (dres′ər) *n.* **1.** a person who dresses something: *a window dresser.* **2.** a person who assists another in dressing, as for the stage. **3.** a person who dresses in a particular way: *a fancy dresser.* [*Dress + -er¹.*]

HOMOGRAPHS

dress·er² (dres′ər) *n.* **1.** a chest of drawers, often with a mirror; bureau. **2.** a sideboard or set of shelves for holding dishes and kitchen utensils. [From the Old French word *dreceor* meaning ''a sideboard.'']

ETYMOLOGY

SUBENTRY

Dutch (duch) *adj.* of or relating to the Netherlands, its people, or their language. —*n.* **1. the Dutch.** the people of the Netherlands. **2.** the language of the Netherlands.

IDIOM

• **to go Dutch.** *Informal.* to have each person pay for himself or herself, as on a date.

Words From Other Languages

... Because the Dutch were noted sailors, many Dutch words borrowed into English are sailing terms.
boom the arm of a derrick or support for a sail
sloop a sailboat with one mast
WORDS FROM OTHER LANGUAGES **yacht** a small ship for racing or pleasure

ABBREVIATION

dz., dozen; dozens.

at; āpe; fär; câre; end; mē; it; īce; pîrce; hot; ōld; sông; fôrk; oil; out; up; ūse; rüle; pùll; tûrn; chin; sing; shop; thin; this; hw in white; zh in treasure. The symbol ə stands for the unstressed vowel sound in about, taken, pencil, lemon, and circus.

PRONUNCIATION KEY

A11

*L*ocating Words in the Dictionary

MAIN ENTRY WORDS: Words Listed in the Dictionary

Think of a dictionary as a long list of words. Each word in the list is called a **main entry**. Main entries are printed in heavy black type, and they are found at the left-hand margin of each column.

Information about a main entry follows in lighter type. The main entry and the information about it make up an **entry**. In the example below, each word in heavy type at the left-hand margin is a main entry: **give-and-take, giveaway, given, given name, gizmo, gizzard**. Notice that some main entries are made up of more than one word.

> **give-and-take** (giv′ən tāk′) *n.* **1.** a mutual yielding or concession; compromise. **2.** a good-natured exchange of talk; banter.
>
> **give·a·way** (giv′ə wā′) *n. Informal.* **1.** the revealing of something, such as a secret, accidentally; exposure. **2.** something given away or sold at a very low price, as to promote sales.
>
> **giv·en** (giv′ən) *v.* the past participle of **give**. —*adj.* **1.** inclined; disposed; prone; *a person given to spreading gossip.* **2.** stated; specified: *to do something at a given time.*
>
> **given name,** the name given to a person at birth or baptism; first name.
>
> **giz·mo** (giz′mō) *n. pl.* **giz·mos.** *Slang.* a gadget or object, especially one whose name is not known or remembered: *We really need one of those gizmos for punching holes in paper.*
>
> **giz·zard** (giz′ərd) *n.* the muscular second part of the stomach of a bird, in which partially digested food from the first part of the stomach is finely ground.

ALPHABETICAL ORDER: How Words Are Listed

Main entries are arranged in alphabetical order. All the entries under each letter of the alphabet are arranged in alphabetical order, too, letter by letter. All the words in the **a** section of the dictionary start with the same first letter, so the remaining letters, beginning with the second letter, determine the order of the words.

about   **act**   **adult**   **after**

About comes before *act* because **b** comes before **c** in the alphabet.

Often the second, third, and even the fourth letters in words are the same. Then you have to look for the first letters that are different to determine the correct alphabetical order.

A B C D E

YOUR TURN 1

Read the words in each column below. On your own paper, arrange the words in each column in alphabetical order.

1. fling	**2.** frill	**3.** forty
flat	friend	forth
flute	frizzy	fortune
fleet	fright	fortress

4. Now arrange all these words in one longer list as they should appear in the dictionary.

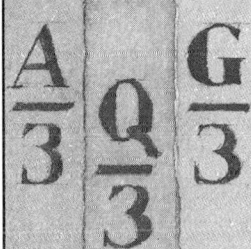

DICTIONARY SECTIONS: Three Thirds

Main entries can be fairly easy to find in the *Macmillan School Dictionary* when you know how to use alphabetical order. If you want to look up a word that begins with **a**, you know you open the dictionary near the beginning. If the word begins with **z**, you open the dictionary near the end. But suppose you want to look up the word *regalia*. You know that you have to look in the section of the dictionary with all the **r** words. But do you know how to open the book to the **r** section, or at least to a nearby letter? Would you find the **r** words closer to the front of the dictionary or to the back? Open the book to where you think **r** is. Were you correct?

Here is a way to help you open the book and quickly find the section you want. Think of the dictionary as being divided into three parts: the first third, the middle third, and the last third. About one third of the pages are in each part. Here is how the letters of the alphabet are grouped when the book is divided into thirds:

First Third	Middle Third	Last Third
A – F	G – P	Q – Z

You can use these thirds as guides to help direct you to the part of the dictionary you want.

The *Macmillan School Dictionary* has a special feature designed to make it even easier to find words by using thirds. If you look at the side of the book, you will notice three bright color bars: blue, red, and green. There is a different color for each third of the dictionary. If you want to find a word in the first third, you would look in the section with the blue bar. The middle third has a red bar, and the last third has a green bar.

GUIDE WORDS: The First and Last Main Entries on a Page

You can open this dictionary fairly close to the letter section you want by thinking of the dictionary as being divided into thirds. However, suppose you are looking for the word *harpsichord*, and you open to the **g** words instead of the **h** words. You know that **h** words come just after **g** words, so you would just turn ahead a few pages. But, once you find the **h** words, what should your next step be?

This dictionary provides another kind of signpost to help you find the word you are looking for. You do not have to search through every page in the **h** section to find *harpsichord*. Look at the top outer corner of each page in the dictionary. There you will find a pair of words such as the following:

headlight/heather   handsaw/hansom   harness/hasn't

These pairs of words are **guide words**. The first guide word on a page tells you the first main entry that appears on that page. The other guide word tells you the last main entry that appears on the page. Look at the guide words **headlight/heather**. *Headlight* is the first main entry on the page, and *heather* is the last. *Harpsichord* cannot be on that page because *harpsichord* comes before *headlight* in alphabetical order, so you must look closer to the beginning of the **h** words.

Next, look at the guide words **handsaw/hansom**. *Harpsichord* cannot be on this page either. *Harpsichord* comes after *hansom* in alphabetical order. You will find *harpsichord* on the page with the guide words **harness/hasn't**. *Harpsichord* comes between these two entries in alphabetical order. Once you find the correct page by using the guide words, look through the main entries on the page. Use alphabetical order to find the word.

Now look in the dictionary for *harpsichord*. Use the "thirds" plan and the guide words to find it quickly. On what page does *harpsichord* appear?

Look up each of the following main entries in this dictionary. Write each word on your own paper. Next to it write the guide words for the page.

1. **ginseng**   2. **rubicund**   3. **distaff**
4. **vaquero**   5. **Mogul**   6. **euphoria**

Verifying Spellings

If you can spell a main entry, you should be able to find it in the *Macmillan School Dictionary*. But finding a word that you do not know how to spell can be a problem. The Table of English Spellings can help. The story below shows how.

One day, Polly was standing in the kitchen making a sandwich. She happened to overhear her mother talking about her on the telephone.

"Oh yes, she has *charisma,* that one," said Polly's mom.

"Charisma?" Polly thought. Well, she wasn't sure she liked the sound of that. She hoped it wasn't a disease! So she decided she should look up the word in the dictionary.

Polly went and got the dictionary, but then she realized that she didn't know how to spell the word. It sounded like "karizma," so she looked under **k**. But the word wasn't there. Then she remembered that the dictionary had a Table of English Spellings, so she turned to that page.

She found a table that listed all the sounds in English words and most of the different ways they might be spelled. So she looked under **k** and discovered that the **k** sound can be spelled in several different ways.

Sound	Spelling	Example
k	**c, k, ck, ch, cc, qu,**	cat, key, ta**ck**, **ch**ord,
	q, cq, cu, que	a**cc**ount, liquor, Iraq,
		ac**qu**aint, bis**c**uit,
		bis**que**

Polly wrote down the **k** sounds, and then she thought about the rest of the word that sounded like "karizma." She knew she would need to find ways to spell at least the first and second sounds. Then she could start looking for the word. She wrote down the spellings of the first two sounds in different ways. Here are some of the ways she spelled the beginning of word: *ca, ka, cha, qua, ke, che, que, cu, chu, ku.* She looked up each of these beginning spellings until she found a word that looked like the right one: **charisma**, "a rare personal quality that attracts the loyalty and devotion of a large following of people."

Well, that's not bad, she thought. The next time she saw her mom, she smiled and said "Thanks." Her mother told her she was welcome, but she never found out what Polly was thanking her for.

When you need to look up a word but you're not sure how to spell it, you can use the Table of English Spellings as Polly did. Think about how each part of the word sounds, and then look up the sounds you need in the table. You will find the table on pages A46–A47 of this book.

Here's another example. Suppose you want to know something about gyroscopes. *Gyroscope* begins with a **j** sound, so you might look for the word in the **j** section. You could try *jiroscope, jyroskope,* or *jyroscope,* but you would not find the word you want.

Turn to the Table of English Spellings on pages A46–A47 of this dictionary. The table matches the sounds of English with all the letters that can stand for the sounds. The first sound in *gyroscope* is **j**, so find this sound first. You will find several spellings of this sound: **g, j, dg, d, gg, di**. Make a list of these spellings. The long **i** is the next sound, so list the possible spellings for this sound. Then start your search. Check the words you make against the words in the dictionary to see what the correct spelling is.

In the Table of English Spellings, the most common spellings for each sound are listed first. Since you have already looked in the **j**'s, you should next look under the **g**'s. In this way, you will find the correct spelling.

YOUR TURN 3

Use this dictionary to check the spellings of the words below. If a word is not spelled correctly, use the Table of English Spellings to find the correct spelling. Then on your own paper, write the number of the word and its correct spelling.

1. squeleton
2. orchid
3. biceps
4. gnome
5. mashine
6. sellafane
7. filatelly
8. kurrage
9. awtograff
10. seenery
11. arkiteckt
12. hite

Kinds of Main Entries

Most of the words in this dictionary are single words, such as *igloo*, *gold*, and *parallel*. You have already learned how these words are alphabetized, and you have learned how to find them easily. But some entries are made up of more than one word, and others are only parts of words. Here are some of these other kinds of main entries.

COMPOUNDS: Main Entries Made Up of Two or More Words

A **compound** is a word made up of two or more words. The new compound word has its own special meaning. You may not know the meaning of the compound even if you know the meanings of the words that make it up.

If someone said, "I have used the last straw in the box for my milk," you would have no trouble understanding what the phrase **last straw** means.

But if someone said, "Leaving the lawn mower out in the rain was the last straw!" you might need a dictionary to learn the special meaning of **last straw**.

> **last straw,** the added factor that finally makes something impossible to bear or endure.

You usually need to look up a compound to learn its meaning. You also need to look it up to find out how it is written.

Some compounds are written as one word. Examples of these are *bunkhouse* and *frogman*. Others are written with a hyphen between the words. Some examples are *sister-in-law* and *light-footed*. Still other compounds, like *cliff dweller* and *ground swell* are written as separate words with spaces between them.

Some compounds are written differently depending on how they are used in a sentence. For example, you may have a **short circuit** in your electrical wiring, but if you plug in the toaster, heater, and broiler all at once, you may **short-circuit** the entire system.

No matter how the compound is written, it does not always mean what its separate parts say. A **blue blood** is not blue, and it is not blood. A **coat of arms** is not a coat, and it does not have arms.

Compound entries are alphabetized as if they were just one word with no spaces in between.

P Q r s U

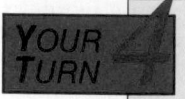
YOUR TURN 4

Read each question below. Use this dictionary to find the meaning of each underlined phrase. Then on your own paper, write the answer to each question. Give a reason for each answer by explaining what the underlined phrase means.

1. Do <u>sacred cows</u> live on farms?
2. Do people eat toast at a <u>jam session</u>?
3. Would you go to a plumbing shop to get a <u>pipe dream</u>?
4. Does a <u>sacrifice fly</u> have wings?
5. Would you find a <u>county seat</u> in a furniture store?
6. Do you have to be a member to go into a <u>club car</u>?
7. Does a musician play a <u>horn of plenty</u>?
8. Can a <u>clay pigeon</u> fly?
9. Is it dark in a <u>black market</u>?
10. Is a person sick if he or she has a <u>green thumb</u>?

BIOGRAPHICAL ENTRIES: Names of People

Also in the back of this dictionary, you will find a section called **Biographical Names**. This section is a list of **biographical entries**. It lists the names of many famous people: presidents, authors, inventors, historical figures, and the like. If you come across the name of a famous person you are not familiar with, you could look up the name in this section.

In the **Biography** section, most people are listed alphabetically under their family names. For example, Benjamin Franklin is listed under **Franklin, Benjamin**, and Indira Gandhi is listed under **Gandhi, Indira**.

If two or more people with the same family name are listed, they are listed in alphabetical order under the family name that they share. For example, under **Washington**, you would find **1. Booker T.**, **2. George**, and **3. Martha**.

GEOGRAPHICAL ENTRIES: Names of Places

In the back of this dictionary, you will find a section called **Geographical Names**. This section is a list of **geographical entries**. It lists the names of all countries and many cities, mountains, rivers, lakes, and such. If you wanted to find out about a well-known place, you would look it up in this section.

Geographical entries are listed alphabetically under their actual names. Do not look for them under words such as *Mount*, *Cape*, or *Lake*. Words such as these tell you what things are. Look them up under their particular names. For example, Lake Victoria is listed under **Victoria, Lake**. Mount Sinai is listed under **Sinai, Mount**.

ABBREVIATIONS: Short Forms of Words

Sometimes a writer shortens a word. For example, **Oct.** stands for *October*, and **Dr.** stands for *doctor*. These shortened forms of words are **abbreviations**.

You may see abbreviations in many places, but especially in addresses, in advertisements, and on signs. Most abbreviations are followed by a period. This period indicates a shortened form.

If you do not know the meaning of an abbreviation, you can look it up in the dictionary. Abbreviations are alphabetized in the dictionary just as whole words are.

When you look up an abbreviation, you will find an entry like this:

    oz. *pl.* **ozs.** ounce.

This means that the abbreviation **oz.** stands for the word *ounce*. If you do not know what the word *ounce* means, then you would look up *ounce* in the dictionary.

Suppose you are reading an advertisement, for example, and the ad says "Call and ask for supt." If you did not know what the abbreviation **supt.** stood for, then you would not be able to ask for anyone. To find out what **supt.** means, you could look up the abbreviation in the dictionary. You would find this entry: **Supt.**, superintendent.

Now you know that **supt.** stands for *superintendent*. If you look up the word, you would find that a **superintendent** is "a person who manages and is responsible for the maintenance of an apartment building or office building."

Although most abbreviations are followed by a period, some abbreviations do not have periods. In particular, abbreviations for metric measurements and postal abbreviations are not written with periods. Look at these examples.

100 meter = 100 m	**CA = California**
50 grams = 50 gm	**GA = Georgia**

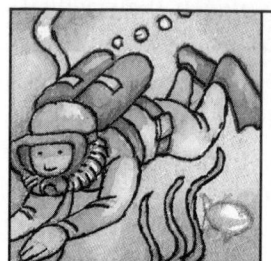

ACRONYMS: Words Formed With Letters From Other Words

Like abbreviations, **acronyms** are shortened forms of words or phrases. However, there are important differences. An acronym is treated as a word, and it is usually pronounced as a word. It is formed by combining the first letters or syllables of a series of other words, and it does not require a period. The word **scuba**, for example, is an acronym formed from the first letters of the words **s**elf-**c**ontained **u**nderwater **b**reathing **a**pparatus.

If you want to know the meaning of an acronym, you can look it up in the dictionary. Acronyms are alphabetized just like words. In many cases, all of the letters in the acronym are capitalized. For example, **NATO** is an acronym for **N**orth **A**tlantic **T**reaty **O**rganization. **NATO** is pronounced as a word (nā′tō). Some acronyms are pronounced by saying each letter (as in **UFO**, which stands for "**u**nidentified **f**lying **o**bject").

YOUR TURN 5

Read the list of abbreviations and acronyms below. Look up each one in this dictionary. Decide whether it is an abbreviation or an acronym. Write the word on your own paper. If it is an abbreviation, write the word that it stands for. If it is an acronym, write the words from which the acronym was formed.

1. atty.	**2. laser**	**3. sonar**
4. NAACP	**5. kg**	**6. dept.**
7. SWAT	**8. COBOL**	**9. ZIP**
10. misc.	**11. ed.**	**12. assn.**

PREFIXES AND SUFFIXES:
Words Parts Added to Form New Words

Some main entries are not words at all. They are prefixes and suffixes, or parts of words. A word part that is added to the beginning of a word is called a **prefix**. A word part that is added to the end of a word is called a **suffix**. You will find prefixes and suffixes in the dictionary because they help to form new words. Many of our words are formed by adding word parts to other words.

Fg I J

Often you will not find a word formed with a prefix or suffix in the dictionary. Yet you can use the dictionary to figure out the meaning of such a word. Look up the meaning of the prefix or suffix and the meaning of the word to which it is attached. For example, you might read something about "preholiday preparations" and wonder what the word *preholiday* means. This word does not appear in your dictionary, but the parts, **pre-** and **holiday**, do. You can look them up.

> **pre-** *prefix* **1.** before in place, time, or rank: *prewar, prehistoric.* **2.** in preparation for: *preschool.* [From the Old French prefix *pre-*, going back to the Latin word *prae* meaning "before, in front of."]
> **holiday** (hol′i dā′) *n.* a day on which most people do not work, especially a day that is fixed by custom or law to celebrate a special event . . .

From these two entries, you can figure out that *preholiday* means "before the holiday."

Find the meaning of each word below by looking up the meaning of the base word and the meaning of the prefix or suffix. Write a definition for each word on your own paper.

1. **antimodern**   2. **pregraduation**   3. **reorder**
4. **scoreless**   5. **post depression**   6. **misconclude**

HOMOGRAPHS: Words That Are Spelled Alike

Many words in English are spelled exactly the same way as other words. But they have different meanings and have come into our language in different ways. These words are called **homographs**.

Suppose you read this sentence in a story: "She turned the pitcher upside down, but nothing came out." You might find this sentence confusing if you think of *pitcher* as the baseball player who throws the ball. That meaning of *pitcher* does not fit here. When you check the dictionary, you will find two main entries for *pitcher*.

> **pitch·er¹** (pich′ər) *n.* **1.** a vessel with a handle and a lip or spout, used chiefly for holding and pouring liquids. **2.** the amount contained by a pitcher. [From the Old French word *pichier* meaning this container, from the Medieval Latin word *bicarius* "a goblet," from the Greek word *bikos* "a drinking bowl."]
> **pitch·er²** (pich′ər) *n.* a person who pitches, especially the player on a baseball team who throws the ball to the batter. [*Pitch¹ + -er¹.*]

The meaning of the first main entry for *pitcher* fits the context of the sentence.

In this dictionary, homographs have separate main entries. Each homograph has a small number above and to the right of the main entry word. This is called a **superscript** number. (*Superscript* means "written above.") There will be at least two main entries in each group of homographs.

Homographs have the same spelling, and most homographs are pronounced the same way. Some homographs, however, are pronounced differently even though they are spelled alike.

YOUR TURN 7

Read each sentence below. The underlined word in each sentence is a homograph. Look up the underlined word and, on your own paper, write the definition of the word as it is used in the sentence.

1. Use this tool to <u>bore</u> a hole in the wood.
2. He thinks the shirt and tie are a good <u>match</u>.
3. Mr. Braun put a new roof on his <u>cot</u> last summer.
4. Louis wants to learn how to play <u>bridge</u>.
5. Juan spent two days camping in the <u>desert</u>.
6. Sherry tried to <u>console</u> her grief-stricken brother.
7. The oriole had a twig in its <u>bill</u>.
8. We finished off the whole bowl of <u>dates</u>.

Kinds of Secondary Entries

The preceding section of this book explained the kinds of main entries found in the *Macmillan School Dictionary*. Words that are *related to* main entries are often included in the information that follows the main entry. Such words are called **secondary entries**. They are printed in heavy black type that is slightly smaller than the type used for main entries. This section describes different kinds of secondary entries.

INFLECTED FORMS OF WORDS:
Nouns, Adjectives, Verbs, and Adverbs

In English, changes in the meaning of a word are often shown by changes in the form of the word. For example, to speak of more than one story, we change the word to *stories*. These changed forms of a word are called **inflected forms**. The main word that is changed is called the **base word**. Four kinds of words may be inflected: nouns, adjectives, verbs, and adverbs. The inflected forms are secondary entries.

NOUNS

A **noun** is a word that names or denotes something, such as a person, animal, place, thing, action, or quality. A noun that names one person, place, or thing such as *father*, *meadow*, or *toy* is called a **singular noun**. If you want to name more than one, you usually use the plural form of the noun: *fathers*, *meadows*, or *toys*. These are **plural nouns**.

Most nouns form the plural by adding **-s** to the singular form. These nouns follow the regular pattern of the English language, so they are called **regular plurals**. Regular plurals are not shown in the dictionary.

Some nouns do not add the regular **-s** ending. The plural of *coach*, for example, is *coaches*, and the plural of *mouse* is *mice*. These plurals are not regular, so they are called **irregular plurals**. The irregular plurals of nouns are listed in the dictionary as secondary entries.

> **ber·ry** (ber′ē) *n.*, *pl.* **ber·ries.**
> **elf** (elf) *n. pl.* **elves.**

In some cases, you may find two forms of the plural listed. Either form is correct, but the first form listed is usually the most common.

> **in·dex** (in′deks′) *n.*, *pl.* **in·dex·es** or **in·di·ces.**

YOUR TURN 8

On your own paper, write the plural of each noun below. Check the dictionary. If you don't find an inflected form listed for a noun, just add **-s** to make it plural.

1. shelf
2. radius
3. box
4. clove
5. turkey
6. ox
7. gadfly
8. handful
9. dervish
10. sergeant at arms
11. salmon
12. moss

ADJECTIVES

Adjectives are words that modify nouns or pronouns. Adjectives have two kinds of inflected forms. One kind gives the idea of "more" in comparing two things. This kind is called a **comparative**. The comparative of *small* is *smaller* (which means "more small"): Danny's feet are *smaller* than Sally's feet. The second kind of inflected form of adjectives gives the idea of "most" in comparing more than two things. This kind is called a **superlative**. The superlative of *small* is *smallest* (which means "most small"): Peter's feet are the *smallest* of all.

The regular way of forming comparatives in English is by adding the ending **-er**. The regular way of forming superlatives is by adding **-est**. The spelling of the base word does not change in regular comparatives and superlatives. For example, **small + -er** forms the comparative **smaller**. **Small + -est** forms the superlative **smallest**. These **-er** and **-est** forms are **regular**. They are not listed in the dictionary.

Often the spelling of a word changes when a comparative or superlative ending is added to it. If the spelling changes, the inflected forms of the word are listed in the dictionary.

> sad . . . sad·der, sad·dest
> fun·ny . . . fun·ni·er, fun·ni·est

When forming the comparative or superlative of the word *sad*, the **d** at the end is doubled: *sadder*, *saddest*. When forming the comparative or superlative of *funny*, the **y** changes to **i**: *funnier*, *funniest*.

For a few adjectives, the comparative and superlative forms are quite different from the base word. When this is the case, the forms are always given in the dictionary.

good...bet·ter, best
bad...worse, worst

There is another way to show the idea of "more" or "most." Many words, especially long words of three or more syllables, sound awkward if you add **er** or **-est**. Instead, you put the word **more** or **most** in front of the word. You say "**more humorous**," not "humorouser." You say "**most capable**," not "capablest." You can usually tell when to do this by thinking how the possible inflected forms will sound.

Check this dictionary for the comparative and superlative forms of each adjective below. Write them on your own paper. If you don't find an inflected form listed, add **-er** and **-est**, or use **more** and **most**.

1. young	2. wide	3. clever
4. great	5. drab	6. narrow
7. chilly	8. ambitious	9. frothy
10. usual	11. many	12. interesting

VERBS

Verbs are words that show action, existence, or occurrence. Their form changes to show differences in time. If something is happening in the present, the simple present tense may be used. For example: I *like* apples. You *look* worried. If something happened in the past, the simple past tense may be used. For example: I *liked* that movie. You *looked* wonderful. These changed forms are called **inflections**.

Verbs are usually listed in a dictionary in their uninflected, or infinitive, form. Most verbs form their inflections according to a regular pattern. The ending **-ed** is added to form the past tense and the past participle. I *wanted* more applesauce. They have *searched* everywhere for the book. The ending **-ing** is added to form the present participle. What are you *reading*? When the dictionary does not list inflections, it means that the verb is a regular verb and follows this pattern.

Some verbs are irregular and form their inflections in unpredictable ways. For example: I *threw* the baseball over the fence. You have *done* well on the test. The dictionary lists inflections for the past tense, past participle, and present participle for all irregular verbs. If the past tense and past participle have the same form, they are not listed separately.

> **trade . . . trad · ed, trad · ing**
> **throw . . . threw, thrown, throw · ing**
> **scur · ry . . . scur · ried, scur · ry · ing**
> **think . . . thought, think · ing**
> **give . . . gave, giv · en, giv · ing**

YOUR TURN 10

On your own paper, write the past tense, past participle, and present participle of each verb below. Check this dictionary. If you don't find inflected forms listed, add **-ed** to form the past tense and past participle and **-ing** to form the present participle.

1. exclaim	2. annul	3. cling
4. go	5. take	6. reach
7. teach	8. sweep	9. drive
10. eschew	11. answer	12. bring

ADVERBS

Adverbs are words that modify verbs, adjectives, or other adverbs. Like adjectives, adverbs have two kinds of inflected forms. One kind gives the idea of "more" in comparing two things. This kind is called a **comparative**. The comparative of *soon* is *sooner* (which means "more soon"): Dennis will arrive *sooner* than Harriet. The second kind of inflected form of adjectives gives the idea of "most" in comparing more than two things. This kind is called a **superlative**. The superlative of *soon* is *soonest* (which means "most soon"): Frankie will arrive *soonest* of all.

The regular way of forming comparatives in English is by adding the ending **-er**. The regular way of forming superlatives is by adding **-est**. The spelling of the base word does not change in regular adverbs. For example, **soon** + **-er** forms the comparative **sooner**. **Soon** + **-est** forms the superlative **soonest**. These **-er** and **-est** forms are **regular**. They are not listed in the dictionary.

Some adverbs in English, however, are irregular. Sometimes the spelling of a word changes when a comparative or superlative ending is added to it. When the spelling changes, the inflected forms of the word are listed in the dictionary.

> **late . . . lat·er, lat·est**

When forming the comparative or superlative of the word *late*, the **e** at the end is dropped: *later*, *latest*.

For a few adverbs, the comparative and superlative forms are quite different from the base word. When this is true, the forms are always given in this dictionary.

> **well . . . bet·ter, best**

There is also another way to show the idea of "more" or "most." Many adverbs end in **-ly**, as in *rapidly*, *slowly*, *angrily*. Instead of adding **-er** or **-est** to these words, you put the word **more** or **most** in front of the word. You say "**more rapidly**," not "rapidlier." You say "**most angrily**," not "angriliest." You can usually tell when to do this by thinking about how possible inflected forms of an adverb would sound.

DERIVED WORDS: Words Formed From Other Words

As you learned earlier, suffixes can be added to base words to form new words. For example, when the suffix *-ly* is added to *slow*, another word, *slowly*, is formed. The word *slowly* comes from, or is derived from, the word *slow*. So it is called a **derived word**. Derived words often appear as **run-on entries** in this dictionary. They are added at the end of an entry. The run-on entry also has a label to show its part of speech.

> **slow** (slō) *adj.* **1.** acting, moving, or happening with little speed; not fast or quick . . . **—slow'ly,** *adv.*
> **—slow'ness,** *n.*

The meaning of a derived word can usually be understood from the meaning of the base word plus the meaning of the suffix. The base word *stargaze*, for example, means "to gaze at or study the stars." The suffix **-er** means "a person who does (something)." So you know that a *stargazer* is a person who gazes at or studies the stars. This derived word is not listed as a main entry. It is placed at the end of the entry for *stargaze*.

> **star·gaze** (stär′gāz′) *v.i.* **star·gazed, star·gaz·ing.**
> **1.** to gaze at or study the stars. **2.** to daydream.
> —**star′gaz′er,** *n.*

Derived words have separate main entries if they have special meanings or if the meaning is not simply the meaning of the base word plus the meaning of the suffix. A *pointer*, for example, is not just "a person who points."

> **point·er** (poin′tər) *n.* **1.** a long stick used to point out things, as on a blackboard, chart, or map. **2.** any of a breed of short-haired dogs having long ears and a long, tapering tail. Pointers hunt game birds by scent and point to their location. **3.** a needle or similar device, as on a scale or meter, showing a measurement. **4.** *Informal.* a piece of information or advice; hint; suggestion: *The teacher gave me some good pointers on how to write the composition.* **5.** a person or thing that points.

When you want to find a derived word, first look for it as a main entry. If you do not find it as a main entry, look at the word carefully and figure out what the base word is. Then find the base word as a main entry and look for the derived word as a run-on at the end of an entry. To find *slowly*, for example, look under *slow*. To find *seriousness*, look under *serious*.

YOUR TURN 11

Read the derived words listed below. Find each one in this dictionary. On your own paper, write the word, and next to the word, write "run-on entry" or "main entry." Then tell what the word means.

1. shyness	2. invisibility	3. liveliness
4. realization	5. kindness	6. sander
7. likely	8. royally	9. bicycler
10. carder	11. frailty	12. legislation

SUBENTRIES: Different Forms of Main Entries

Sometimes a word is closely related to a main entry but is different in form. The different form may be a **subentry**. The subentry is printed in heavy black type that is smaller than that of the main entry. The subentry has a special meaning different from that of the main entry.

A subentry may be the plural form of a main entry (**jack/jacks,** for example). A subentry may also be the capitalized form of a main entry. In this case, you may need to read the definitions carefully to decide which form of the word to use in a given sentence.

> **der·by** (dûr′bē; *esp. for def. 2a,* där′bē)   *n.   pl.,*   **der·bies.**   **1.** a hard, round hat with a narrow rolled brim.   **2. Derby. a.** a race for three-year-old horses, held annually near London, England.   **b.** any similar horse race: *the Kentucky Derby.*   **3.** any large race or contest.

In this entry, **derby** (beginning with a lowercase letter) refers to a hat or a race; **Derby** (beginning with a capital letter) refers to one specific race held in England. A man may wear a *derby,* but he would not wear a *Derby.* A subentry may also be the lower-case form of a main entry that begins with a capital letter. It may be one word or more than one word.

Find the main entry for each subentry listed below. On your own paper, write the main entry.

1. **Dominion**   2. **Parliament**
3. **the South**   4. **baths**
5. **moneys**   6. **khakis**
7. **jeans**   8. **Revolutionary**

VARIANT SPELLINGS: More Than One Correct Spelling

Some words have more than one correct spelling; for example, *theater* and *theatre.* In this dictionary, the more widely used spelling appears as the main entry. The other spelling or spellings are called **variant spellings.** They appear as secondary entries. The word *also* always comes before the variant spelling.

V W X Y Z

the·a·ter (thē′ ə tər) *also,* the·a·tre.
pol·li·wog (pol′ ē wog′) *also,* pol·ly·wog.

YOUR TURN 13

Find one or more variant spellings for each of these words. Write all spellings on your own paper.

1. archaeology
2. inward
3. karat
4. ameba
5. Mahican
6. hostler
7. chamomile
8. calorie

VARIANT TERMS: Different Words for the Same Thing

Sometimes two or more words have exactly the same meaning. *Hayrick* and *haystack*, for example, or *historic* and *historical*. The word that is used most often is the main entry. The less commonly used word or words appear as secondary entries. Such words are called **variant terms**. A variant term appears at the end of an entry or at the end of a definition. The word *Also* always comes before a variant term.

Po·lar·is (pō lar′ is) *n.* a star located in the northern sky. It is the outermost star in the handle of the Little Dipper. Also, **North Star, polestar.**

In most cases, the variant term is also listed as a main entry, followed by the words "another word [*or* term *or* name] for . . .". If you looked up **North Star**, for example, you would find this entry.

North Star, another term for **Polaris.**

This means you should look under **Polaris** to find the main entry. This kind of note is called a **cross reference.**

CROSS REFERENCES: How to Find the Main Entry

Full information about an entry is often given under another main entry. A **cross reference** in heavy black type shows you the main entry you must find to get all the information you want. There are several kinds of cross references, as you can see from the examples below. Some cross references appear after the main entry word, some appear after the definition, and some appear as separate definitions.

> **baking soda,** another term for **sodium bicarbonate.**
> **English** . . . See **Old English** for further information.
> **Norse** . . . 2. another word for **Norwegian.**

YOUR TURN 11

Look up each entry listed below. On your own paper, write the cross reference for each word. Under that main entry you will find full information.

1. nacre
2. colour
3. soft coal
4. baleen
5. oleomargarine
6. northern lights
7. puma
8. ambuscade
9. Olympics
10. pianoforte
11. polliwog
12. photo

IDIOMS: Phrases Having Special Meanings

Another kind of secondary entry is the **idiom.** An idiom is a group of words having a meaning different from the meanings of the separate words. If you say that someone "drives you up a wall," for example, the phrase does not mean that someone actually gives you a ride up a wall in a car. It means that the person bothers or irritates you.

An idiom is listed separately at the end of the entry for its most important, or key, word. For example, you might read that "Joey **was all ears.**" In the phrase **to be all ears,** the key word is *ears.* If you look under *ear,* you would find an explanation of the idiom **to be all ears.**

> **ear¹** (ir) *n.* **1.** the organ of the body by which people and animals hear...
> • **to be all ears.** to listen eagerly: *We were all ears when we heard the scout leader mention a camping trip.*
> • **to go in one ear and out the other.** to leave no impression; be heard but not remembered.
> • **to play by ear.** to play (a musical instrument) without following written music.

Idioms appear in heavy type at the end of an entry. If there are two or more idioms in an entry, they appear in alphabetical order.

Read the underlined idiom in each sentence below. Decide what the key word is in each idiom, and look up that word. On your own paper, write the key word and another sentence using the idiom.

1. Pam arranged the whole party <u>behind his back</u>.
2. The baby is the <u>apple of his eye</u>.
3. The basketball game was <u>nip and tuck</u> up until the last second.
4. Mel tried to <u>jazz up</u> his presentation by using music.
5. We <u>counted on</u> Shirley to do the job.
6. She took up the <u>gauntlet</u> and ran for mayor.
7. Beth <u>nailed down</u> the job when she described her college studies.
8. Mr. Drake has looked rather <u>down and out</u> lately.

The Dictionary as a Resource

You have learned about the kinds of words that can be found in the *Macmillan School Dictionary*—how to find them and how to spell them. Next you will find out what other kinds of information your dictionary gives about these words.

SYLLABLE DIVISIONS: Separating Words Into Parts

When you are writing or typing, you may need to divide a word into smaller parts, or **syllables**, because the entire word won't fit on a line. Most main entries in your dictionary are divided into syllables by black dots.

ar·roy·o   e·las·tic   de·moc·ra·cy

Syllable divisions tell you where to divide a word that will not fit on one line. Suppose you are writing **democracy**. You discover that you must write part of the word on one line and the rest of it on the next line. You may break off **democracy** after **de-**, **democ-**, or **democra-**. Where you divide the word depends on how much space you have at the end of the line. Be sure to put a hyphen (-) after the syllable at the end of a line to show that there is more of the word to come. Never break up a word so that only one letter is left on a line. For example, do not divide **elastic** after **e-** or **arroyo** after **arroy-**.

Many words in the dictionary are not divided by dots at all. Words such as *make*, *house*, and *strength* are not divided. These are words of only one syllable. They should never be broken up at all when you are writing.

On your own paper, write the words below with syllable divisions just as they appear in the main entries or secondary entries in this dictionary.

1. scarab
2. vagaries
3. microwave
4. jerboa
5. stickleback
6. undulation
7. corvette
8. mesmerize
9. witticism
10. desperado
11. onionskin
12. integument

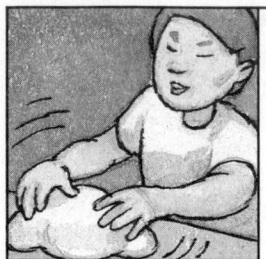

PRONUNCIATION RESPELLINGS: How to Say Words

The dictionary can be a great help when you want to know how to pronounce a word. Suppose you are helping your brother make bread. The directions say "**Knead** the dough. . . ." You would like to tell your brother to "**knead** the dough," since it is tiring work, but you don't know how to pronounce the word *knead.* Look up *knead* and find the pronunciation. It is shown in parentheses right after the main entry word.

knead (nēd)

The pronunciation (nēd) is a **respelling** of *knead.* A main entry spelling often does not help you pronounce the word because the alphabet has 26 letters, but these letters and combinations of them can stand for nearly twice as many different sounds. A single letter may be used for different sounds in different words. For example, **o** has one sound in **hot**, another sound in **some**, and another in **roll**. The different sounds represented by the alphabet can be spelled in about 250 different ways.

The first sound in **knead** can be spelled **n, gn, kn, nn, pn,** or **mn.** So the way a word is spelled may not tell you how to say it. For this reason, the *Macmillan School Dictionary* respells words, using a special alphabet. These respellings help you match the sound of a word to its spelling.

The Pronunciation Key on page A48 shows these respellings. Look at the left-hand column of the key. Each letter symbol stands for only one sound. In the right-hand column are common words in which the sound is heard. The sample words help you understand the sound of the letter symbol.

You will find a shorter pronunciation key at the bottom of each right-hand page of the dictionary. It contains the most important respellings for sounds and the respellings that usually give the most trouble.

at: āpe; fär; câre; end; mē; it; īce; pîerce; hot; ōld; sông, fôrk; oil; out; up; ūse; rüle; pull; tûrn; chin; sing; shop; thin; <u>th</u>is; hw in white; zh in treasure. The symbol ə stands for the unstressed vowel sound in about, taken, pencil, lemon, and circus.

If you do not find a certain sound in the short pronunciation key on the right-hand page, you will find it in the Pronunciation Key on page A48.

To figure out the pronunciation of a word, use the respelling and the pronunciation key. For example, the respelling of **knead** (nēd) begins with the **n** sound in **not**. It is followed by the **e** sound in **me**. It ends with the **d** sound in **bad**. When you put these sounds together in the correct order, you can pronounce **knead**.

Different people sometimes say words in different ways. So some words have more than one pronunciation.

> **aunt** (ant, änt)
> **har·ass** (har′əs, hə ras′)

Usually the first pronunciation listed is the most common one, but sometimes other pronunciations are used just as often. All of the pronunciations given in this dictionary are considered correct English.

YOUR TURN 17

On your own paper, write the respelling for each of the words as it is given in this dictionary. Check the pronunciation. Then think of a common word that rhymes with each one and write the rhyming word.

1. height	2. tough	3. yeast
4. weigh	5. though	6. break
7. straight	8. through	9. dread
10. laugh	11. caught	12. yearn

I SAY, IS THAT A dong′kē OR A dong kē′?

ACCENTS: **Stressing Syllables**

For words with more than one syllable, pronunciations are divided into syllables, which are separated by spaces or accents. The syllables help you figure out the pronunciation part by part.

When you say a word with more than one syllable, you do not say each syllable in exactly the same way. You say some syllables with more **stress**, or emphasis, than others. When you say *rabbit*, for example, you

A35

put more stress on the second syllable. In the pronunciation listed in your dictionary, an accent mark follows a syllable that is stressed.

> **rab·bit** (rab′ it)
> **gi·raffe** (jə raf′)

In some words, more than one syllable is stressed. Usually one syllable receives more stress than others. We say that this syllable receives the **primary stress**. A stressed syllable spoken with less emphasis receives the **secondary stress**. Your dictionary shows the primary stress with a heavy **accent mark** (′) and the secondary stress with a lighter accent mark (′).

> **demi·i·john** (dem′ē jon′)
> **de·mo·bi·lize** (dē mō′ bə liz′)
> **de·part·men·tal** (dē′ pärt men′təl)

In some cases, two syllables in the same word will receive the same stress, as in **der·ring-do** (der′ ing dü′).

Words of only one syllable have no accent marks.

The pronunciation key in this dictionary has only one symbol that does not use an actual letter of the alphabet. That symbol is called a **schwa** (shwä). It looks like an upside-down **e** (ə). The schwa can stand for any one of the five vowels or for combinations of vowels when the sound of that vowel or vowel combination is not stressed. That is why the schwa is sometimes called the "unstressed vowel sound." Think of the way you say the vowel **a** in **about**, **e** in **taken**, **i** in **pencil**, **o** in **lemon**, and **u** in **circus**. Think also of the vowel sound underlined in fou<u>n</u>tain, nat<u>io</u>n, and jeal<u>ou</u>s. That is what the schwa sounds like.

PRONUNCIATION SYLLABLES: **Sound Breaks**

The syllables of the pronunciation are not always the same as the syllables of the main entry. Syllables in the respelling are divided according to how a word is spoken, not according to how it is divided in writing.

> **cha·me·leon** (kə mēl′ yən)
> **las·si·tude** (las′ i tüd′)
> **lab·o·ra·to·ry** (lab′ rə tôr′ ē)

When you want to divide a word in writing, use the syllable divisions in the main entry. When you want to know how to say a word, use the syllable divisions in the pronunciation.

YOUR TURN 18

Say each word below aloud. Think about the way you stress different syllables. Decide where primary and secondary stress marks should be placed in the pronunciation. Copy the pronunciations on your own paper and add the stress marks. Check your work with the pronunciations given in this dictionary.

1. **des·sert (di zûrt)**
2. **guar·an·tee (gar ən tē)**
3. **ex·ag·ger·ate (eg zaj ə rāt)**
4. **re·pub·li·can (ri pub li kən)**
5. **how·ev·er (hou ev ər)**
6. **sen·sa·tion (sen sā shən)**
7. **des·ti·na·tion (des tə nā shən)**
8. **tan·ge·rine (tan jə rēn)**

CLASSIFYING WORDS: Parts of Speech

Words can be grouped, or classified, according to how they are used. The way a word is used in a sentence determines its **part of speech**. This dictionary uses twelve parts of speech: **noun**, **pronoun**, **verb**, **auxiliary verb**, **adjective**, **definite article**, **indefinite article**, **adverb**, **preposition**, **conjunction**, **contraction**, and **interjection**. In addition, verbs are classified as **transitive** and **intransitive**. A transitive verb has a direct object: She **wrote** a letter. An intransitive verb does not have a direct object: I **wrote** all morning. Many verbs can be either transitive or intransitive.

See! We waited patiently at the depot, but the express train never came.

| PRONOUN | ADVERB | PREPOSITION | NOUN | | ADJECTIVE | NOUN | ADVERB | VERB |

VERB   DEFINITE   CONJUNCTION
                ARTICLE

INTERJECTION   DEFINITE
                                    ARTICLE

The following abbreviations are used for the parts of speech.

n.	noun	**adv.**	adverb
pron.	pronoun	**prep.**	preposition
v.	verb	**conj.**	conjunction
v.t.	transitive verb	**interj.**	interjection
v.i.	intransitive verb	**contr.**	contraction
adj.	adjective		

When a main entry has only one part of speech, the abbreviation for that part of speech follows the pronunciation. Often, however, a main entry can be used as more than one part of speech. Then the abbreviation for each part of speech is listed before the meaning or meanings given for that part of speech. A dash (—) comes before each different part-of-speech abbreviation to separate the groups of meanings. The abbreviation for the part of speech of a run-on entry is given after the run-on word.

> **win·ter** (win′ tər) *n.* the season of the year coming between fall and spring. In the Northern Hemisphere it extends from about December 22 to about March 21. —*adj.* of, relating to, or suitable for winter: *winter sports, winter clothes, a winter vacation.* —*v.i.* to spend or pass the winter: *to winter in Florida.*

DEFINING WORDS: What Words Mean

The dictionary can help you learn the meaning of words in two important ways. It can help you learn the meaning of new words, and it can help you learn new meanings for words you already know.

You will find some words in your dictionary that have only one meaning, or definition.

> **red·cap** (red′kap′) *n.* a porter who handles baggage, especially at a railroad station.

Most words have more than one meaning. When a word has more than one meaning for a part of speech, the definitions are numbered within the entry. The most common meaning is placed first. The second most common meaning is placed second, and so on. When there is only one meaning for each part of speech, a dash (—) and the abbreviation for the part of speech separate the meanings.

> **grain** (grān) *n.* **1.** the seed of various cereal grasses, such as rye, wheat, oats, or corn. **2.** the plants bearing such seeds. **3.** a tiny, hard particle: *a grain of sand, a grain of sugar.* **4.** the markings or patterns in wood, stone, cloth or other materials caused by the arrangement of fibers or layers. **5.** a very small unit of weight, equal to 64.8 milligrams. **6.** the smallest possible amount; tiny bit: *There isn't a grain of truth in what they said.*

Suppose you read this sentence: "I don't get a **grain** of respect around here," cried Mr. O'Casey. Which definition of *grain* fits?

If you chose definition 6, you were correct. The context helped you choose the correct meaning of the word *grain*. The **context** is the sentence, paragraph, or situation in which the word is found. When you want to be sure that you have chosen the right definition for a sentence, put the definition, or part of it, in place of the word in the context sentence. See if the sentence makes sense.

ILLUSTRATIVE SENTENCES AND ILLUSTRATIVE PHRASES

At the end of many definitions in this dictionary, you will find an **illustrative sentence** or **illustrative phrase**. These are examples that show how the entry word is actually used.

> **drape** . . . *v.t.* . . . **3.** to arrange, spread, or let fall casually or carelessly: *She draped her feet over the chair.*
> **fer·ret** . . . *v.t.* **2.** to bring to light; search; hunt: *to ferret out the facts.*

ILLUSTRATIONS

Pictures can often add to the understanding that you get from a definition. The following examples show how your knowledge of a word can be increased by an illustration.

> **claw** . . . *n.* **1.a.** a sharp, usually curved nail on the foot of a bird or animal. **b.** a foot with such a nail or nails. **2.** one of the pincers of a shellfish, such as a lobster or crab.
> **hermit crab,** any of a group of soft-bodied, mostly ocean-dwelling crabs that occupy the empty shells of snails and similar animals for protection.

How is a cat's **claw** different from a lobster **claw**? Where do **hermit crabs** live? Look at the illustrations that follow. You can probably give a more complete answer to these questions now.

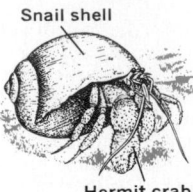

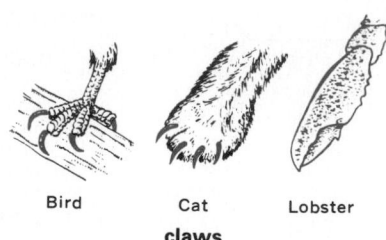

Snail shell

Hermit crab

Bird   Cat   Lobster

claws

YOUR TURN 19

Look up each underlined word in the sentences below. On your own paper, write the part of speech and the meaning of the word as it is used in the sentence.

1. Thus, a new chapter in American politics has begun.
2. The cook labored in the kitchen all day long.
3. Dad thinks that his stockbroker is an oracle.
4. Lani will show me how to wattle a new roof.
5. Pedro staggered the tiles as he laid them on the floor.

USING WORDS: Special Uses of Words

The *Macmillan School Dictionary* uses two kinds of special labels to give you extra information about many words and their definitions.

SUBJECT LABELS

One kind of label that this dictionary uses is the **subject label**. Subject labels such as *Music, Mathematics, Greek Mythology,* and *Astronomy* tell you what field of knowledge a word belongs to. The subject label indicates that a word is used in a certain field or there is a special meaning of the main entry word within a certain field.

> **base¹** (bās) *n.*   **1.** the part on which a thing rests or stands . . . **9.** *Chemistry.* a compound that reacts with an acid to form a salt. A base has a bitter taste in a water solution and turns red litmus paper blue.
> **Ganymede** (gan′ə mēd′) *n. Greek Mythology.* a beautiful youth who was the favorite of Zeus and cupbearer to the Olympian gods.
> **rook²** (rŭk) *n. Chess.* any of the four pieces, two to each player, that may move any number of spaces parallel to the sides of the board . . .

YOUR TURN 20

Look up each entry listed below and find the subject label. On your own paper, write the field of knowledge to which the word or definition belongs.

1. divide, v.t. 6
2. mute, adj. 3
3. flat¹, n. 5
4. slice, n. 3
5. pinnacle, n. 3
6. Cupid, n. 1
7. work, n. 11
8. developer, n. 2
9. pin, n. 5
10. Oedipus
11. pianissimo
12. draft, n. 14

USAGE LABELS

The other kind of special label used in this dictionary is the **usage label**. Some words that were common many years ago are rarely used today. Other words are not usually used in all forms of speaking and writing. Such words have usage labels in your dictionary. These labels tell you when it would be better to use a different word in your own speech or writing. When a word or meaning does not have a usage label, you may use it in any kind of speech or writing.

Here are some of the usage labels you will find in this dictionary.

• **Archaic** words or definitions are ones that were used long ago, but they are not common today. Archaic words are included in dictionaries to help you understand them if you see them when reading stories, plays, and poems written long ago. In many cases, the illustrative sentence for an archaic word is a quotation from a literary work. You would generally not want to use these words in your own speech or writing.

> **twain** ...*Archaic. adj.* two —*n.* two; pair: *Oh, East is East, and West is West, and never the twain shall meet* (Rudyard Kipling).
> **do·eth** (dü′ith) *Archaic.* the present indicative, third person singular, of **do¹.**

• **Informal** words are often used in everyday speech, but they are not used in formal writing, such as term papers and legal contracts.

> **belt** (belt)... —*v.t.* **1.** to encircle or fasten with a belt ... **3.** *Informal.* to strike forcefully: *The batter belted the ball into the bleachers.*

• **Slang** words and phrases are very informal, but they are often colorful. We use them for special effect when talking with friends, for example. However, slang would normally not be used in writing.

> **ball**² (bôl) *n.* **1.** a large, formal dance. **2.** *Slang.* a very enjoyable time: *We had a ball at the Christmas party.*

• The label **British** shows that a word, meaning, or spelling is common in Great Britain but is not used often by Americans.

> **fla·vor** (flā′vər) *also, British,* **fla·vour.**
> **gaol** (jāl) *n. British.* another spelling of jail.
> —**gaol′er,** *n.*
> **lor·ry** (lôr′ē, lor′ē) *n. pl.* **lor·ries. 1.** a long, flat wagon without sides, drawn by a horse. **2.** *British.* a truck.

There are usage labels for other dialects and languages in this dictionary also. These labels indicate words or expressions that may be widely known in America, but they would not generally be used in American speech or writing.

> **bon·jour** (bōn zhùr′) *French.* good morning; good day.
> **Ge·sund·heit** (gə zúnt′hīt′) *interj. German.* used to wish good health to someone who has just sneezed.

• In addition, you may see the label **Trademark** following some words in this dictionary. This label means that when the word is used in writing, it must always be capitalized because it is a proper name for the products of a particular company, such as *Lucite* and *Xerox.*

YOUR TURN 21

Look up each entry listed below and find out if it is informal, slang, archaic, British, or a dialect or another language. Write each word and its usage label on your own paper.

1. **metre**	2. **brae**	3. **softy**
4. **shenanigans**	5. **cool,** adj. 5	6. **scrounge**
7. **thine**	8. **pram**	9. **bowler**²
10. **sooth**	11. **whilom**	12. **wacky**

Fg I J

CHOOSING WORDS: Using Special Words

Usage labels tell you special uses of words in particular situations and fields of knowledge. **Usage notes** tell you how educated speakers and writers use certain words. Usage notes are introduced by a red triangle (▲).

> **ain't** (ănt) **1.** am not. **2.** is not; are not. **3.** has not; have not. ▲ **Ain't** is not considered good English by most people. Careful speakers try to avoid using *ain't*.

Other kinds of usage notes explain the difference between words that are easily confused.

> **af·fect¹** (ə fekt′) *v.t.*   **1.** to produce an effect in; act upon; influence: *That drug affects the nervous system. The long strike affected the local economy.* **2.** to influence the emotions of; move: *The photographs of the flood victims affected us deeply.* [From the Latin word *affectus*, past participle of *afficere* meaning "to influence, produce a physical effect on."]
> ▲ **Affect** and **effect** are close in sound, but they belong to different parts of speech and should not be confused. **Affect** is a verb: *Daily exercise will affect your health.* **Effect** is most commonly used as a noun: *Daily exercise will have a good effect on your health.*

EXPLORING WORDS: Where Words Come From

Studying the origins of words can be fascinating. Brief histories telling where many words come from are included in this dictionary. These histories are called **etymologies**. Etymologies appear in brackets [ ] at the ends of entries.

> **brake²** (brāk) *n.* an area overgrown with shrubs, bushes, or briers; thicket. [Probably from the Middle Low German word *brake* meaning "thicket."]

Special Information About Words

This dictionary contains special articles with information on words and language. You will find these articles printed beneath colored banners throughout the dictionary.

LANGUAGE NOTES: How Words Are Used

Language notes are short essays on language. They discuss individual languages, points of grammar and language use, and how language works. They are printed beneath a blue banner. For example, you will find information on individual languages at the entries for the words *Greek*, *Latin*, and *French*. Language Notes at the entries for *dictionary* and *lexicography* will tell you much about dictionaries and how they are made. Points of grammar and usage are discussed at entries for *function word*, *idiom*, *noun*, and *part of speech*. There are more than sixty Language Notes in this dictionary.

What was the English language like hundreds of years ago? You will find answers in the Language Notes at the entries for *Old English* and *Middle English*. If you want to know more about slang, you will find information in the Language Notes at the entry for *slang*.

WORD FAMILIES: Words That Are Related

Word Families are special essays that present groups of words that have entered the English language from a single word or root in Latin or Greek. Word Families are printed beneath a red banner. You will have fun reading about these words and discovering for yourself how their meanings are related. For example, the words *doctor* and *document* both come from the Latin word for "to teach." You will find other words that come from the same source in the Word Family at the entry *doctor*. There is a Word Family at the entry *sign* that tells you how the words *sign*, *significant*, and *signal* are all related.

What do the words *manual*, *manufacture*, and *mannerism* have in common? Read the Word Family at the entry *manual*. How are the words *voice* and *vowel* related? You will find the answer in the Word Family at the entry *voice*.

and Language

WORDS FROM OTHER LANGUAGES:
Borrowed Words

English is such a rich language partly because it has freely borrowed words from other languages. Some of these words have been used in English for so many years that you would expect that they have always been a part of our language. Lists of borrowed words are printed in this dictionary beneath green banners with the title "Words From Other Languages." For example, did you know that the words *chipmunk* and *chocolate* were originally American Indian words? These and other words borrowed from the languages of American Indians are listed at the entry for *American Indian*. The words *piano* and *umbrella* seem so common that it may come as a surprise to learn they were borrowed from Italian. Check the Words From Other Languages at the entry *Italian*. Would you have guessed that *mosquito* and *ranch* were borrowed into English from Spanish? Read Words From Other Languages at the entry *Spanish*.

Look up the entries for the languages *Arabic* and *Chinese*. What words have these two languages contributed to English?

Answer each of the questions below by reading the Language Note, Word Family, or Words From Other Languages feature for the words in parentheses. Write the answers on your own paper.

1. What words in our language have been borrowed from Australia? (**Australian**)
2. How did Alfred the Great help make English a widely used language? (**vernacular**)
3. Where did the words *brunch*, *smog*, and *telecast* come from? (**blend**)
4. What does the name *Oklahoma* mean, and where did it come from? (**Oklahoma**)
5. What words are related to the word *captain*? (**captain**)

Table of English Spellings

SOUND	SPELLING	EXAMPLE
a	a, au, ai	hand, laugh, plaid
ä	a, e, ea, ua	father, sergeant, heart, guard
ā	a, a-consonant-e, ai, ay, eigh, et, ea, ei, ey, au	paper, rate, rain, pay, eight, ballet, steak, veil, obey, gauge
âr	are, air, ayer, ere, ear, eir	care, fair, prayer, there, bear, heir
b	b, bb	bit, rabbit
ch	ch, t, tch, ti, c	chin, nature, batch, mention, cello
d	d, dd, ed	dive, ladder, failed
e	e, ea, a, ai, ie, eo, u, ae, ay, ei, ue	met, weather, many, said, friend, jeopardy, bury, aesthetic, says, heifer, guess
ē	e, y, ee, ea, e-consonant-e, i-consonant-e, ie, ei, ey, ae, ay, oe, eo	he, city, bee, beach, cede, machine, field, deceive, key, Caesar, quay, amoeba, people
f	f, ph, ff, gh	fine, physical, off, laugh
g	g, gg, gue, gh	go, stagger, catalogue, ghost
h	h, wh	how, whole
hw	wh	wheel
i	i, i-consonant-e, a-consonant-e, y, ie, ui, ei, ia, e, ee, u, o	sit, give, damage, myth, sieve, build, counterfeit, carriage, pretty, been, busy, women
ī	i-consonant-e, i, y, igh, ie, ei, eigh, uy, ai, ey, ye, eye	fine, tiger, try, high, tie, stein, height, buy, aisle, geyser, dye, eye
îr	ear, eer, ere, er, ier, ir, yr	near, deer, here, imperial, fierce, delirious, Syria
j	g, j, dg, d, gg, di	magic, jump, ledger, graduate, exaggerate, soldier
k	c, k, ck, ch, cc, qu, q, cq, cu, que	cat, key, tack, chord, account, liquor, Iraq, acquaint, biscuit, bisque
l	l, ll	line, hall
m	m, mm, mb, mn	mine, hammer, climb, hymn
n	n, nn, kn, gn, pn	nice, funny, knee, gnome, pneumonia
ng	ng, n, ngue	sing, link, tongue
o	o, a	lock, watch

SOUND	SPELLING	EXAMPLE
ō	o, o-consonant-e, oa, ow, ou, ough, oe, au, eau, oo, ew, oh	so, bone, boat, know, soul, though, foe, mauve, beau, brooch, sew, oh
ô	o, a, au, aw, ough, augh, oa	toss, fall, author, jaw, bought, caught, broad
ôr	or, ore, orr, oar, aur, our	order, more, horrible, soar, aural, four
oi	oi, oy, uoy	foil, toy, buoy
ou	ou, ow, ough	out, now, bough
p	p, pp	pill, happy
r	r, rr, wr, rh	ray, parrot, wrong, rhyme
s	s, ss, c, sc, ps, st, sch	song, mess, city, scene, psychology, listen, schism
sh	ti, sh, ci, ssi, si, ss, ch, s, sci, ce, sch	nation, shin, special, mission, expansion, tissue, machine, sugar, conscience, ocean, schist
t	t, tt, ed, pt, th	ten, bitter, topped, ptomaine, thyme
th	th	thin
th̲	th	them, bathe
u	u, o, ou, o-consonant-e, oo, oe	sun, son, touch, come, flood, does
u̇	u, oo, ou, o	full, look, should, wolf
ü	oo, u, o, u-consonant-e, ou, ew, ue, o-consonant-e, ui, eu, oe	tool, luminous, who, flute, soup, jewel, true, lose, fruit, maneuver, canoe
ū	u, u-consonant-e, ew, eu, ue, iew, eau, ieu, ueue	music, use, new, feud, cue, view, beautiful, adieu, queue
ûr	er, or, ur, ir, yr, our, ear, err, eur, yrrh	fern, worst, turn, thirst, myrtle, courage, earth, err, amateur, myrrh
v	v, f	vine, of
w	w, u, o	we, queen, choir
y	i, y, j	onion, yes, hallelujah
z	s, z, x, zz, ss	has, zoo, xylophone, fuzz, scissors
zh	si, s, g, z, zi	division, treasure, mirage, azure, brazier
ə	o, a, i, e, ou, u, y, ai	lemon, about, pencil, taken, furious, circus, analysis, bargain

Pronunciation Key

a	at, bad	d	dear, soda, bad
ā	ape, pain, day, break	f	five, defend, leaf, off, cough, elephant
ä	father, car, heart	g	game, ago, fog, egg
âr	care, pair, bear, their, where	h	hat, ahead
e	end, pet, said, heaven, friend	hw	white, whether, which
ē	equal, me, feet, team, piece, key	j	joke, enjoy, gem, page, edge
i	it, big, English, hymn	k	kite, bakery, seek, tack, cat
ī	ice, fine, lie, my	l	lid, sailor, feel, ball, allow
îr	ear, deer, here, pierce	m	man, family, dream
o	odd, hot, watch	n	not, final, pan, knife
ō	old, oat, toe, low	ng	long, singer, pink
ô	coffee, all, taught, law, fought	p	pail, repair, soap, happy
ôr	order, fork, horse, story, pour	r	ride, parent, wear, more, marry
oi	oil, toy	s	sit, aside, pets, cent, pass
ou	out, now	sh	shoe, washer, fish, mission, nation
u	up, mud, love, double	t	tag, pretend, fat, button, dressed
ū	use, mule, cue, feud, few	th	thin, panther, both
ü	rule, true, food	th	this, mother, smooth
u̇	put, wood, should	v	very, favor, wave
ûr	burn, hurry, term, bird, word, courage	w	wet, weather, reward
ə	about, taken, pencil, lemon, circus	y	yes, onion
b	bat, above, job	z	zoo, lazy, jazz, rose, dogs, houses
ch	chin, such, match	zh	vision, treasure, seizure

Abbreviations

A.D.	Anno Domini (after Chirst)	mi.	miles
adj.	adjective	n.	noun
adv.	adverb	pl.	plural
approx.	approximately	pop.	population
b.	born	prep.	preposition
B.C.	before Christ	pron.	pronoun
conj.	conjunction	sing.	singular
contr.	contraction	sq. km.	square kilometers
d.	died	sq. mi.	square miles
def., defs.	definition, definitions	St.	Saint
est.	estimated	UN	United Nations
fl.	flourished	U.S.	United States
ft.	feet	v.	verb
interj.	interjection	v.i.	intransitive verb
km.	kilometers	v.t.	transitive verb
m.	meters		

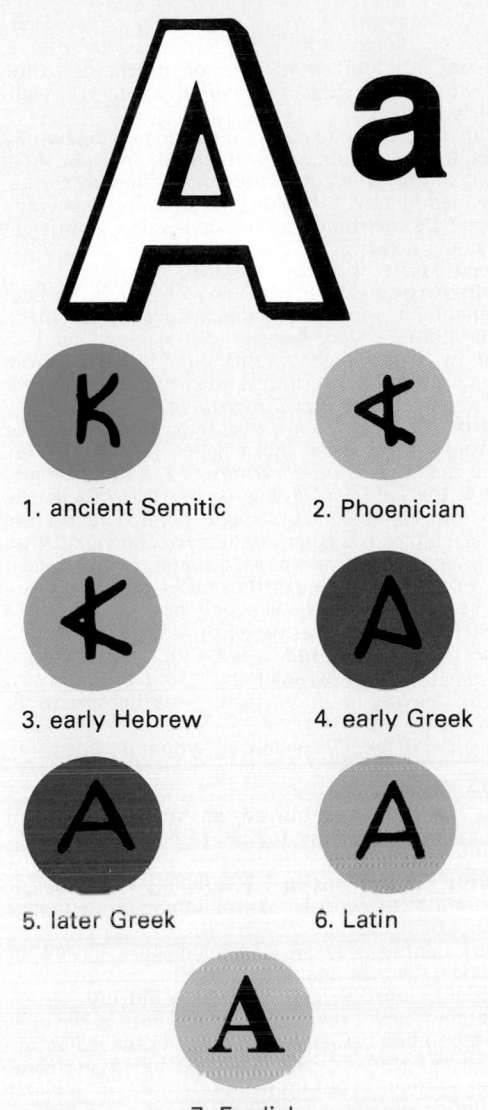

1. ancient Semitic
2. Phoenician
3. early Hebrew
4. early Greek
5. later Greek
6. Latin
7. English

A is the first letter of the English alphabet. Since about 4,000 years ago, the alphabet of every language that developed from ancient Semitic (1) has begun with a letter that looked something like our modern capital **A.** In the Phoenician (2) and early Hebrew (3) alphabets, this letter was a consonant called *aleph,* meaning "ox." The Greeks borrowed the form of *aleph,* reversed its design, and used it to represent a vowel called *alpha* (4). By the eighth century B.C., the Greeks were writing *alpha* (5) almost exactly the way we write the capital letter **A** today. Because it is the first letter of the alphabet, **A** is often used to show the first or highest quality or rank, as in marking schoolwork or for grading food. The Romans borrowed this letter about 2,700 years ago (6), and from it English (7) and other European languages derived their initial letters.

a, A (ā) *n., pl.* **a's, A's. 1.** the first letter of the English alphabet. **2.** the shape of this letter. **3.** the first item in a series or group. **4.** the highest rating as a mark of excellence: *to get an A in history.* **5.** *Music.* the sixth note of the scale of C major.

a[1] (ə; *stressed* ā) *indefinite article.* **1.** any; no particular one: *A dog would love that bone.* **2.** one: *We won a hundred dollars.* **3.** one single: *There was not a person in sight.* **4.** one of a particular class or group: *The orange is a fruit.* ▲ used before words that begin with a consonant sound: *a cat, a house, a youngster.* [Short for the Old English numeral *ān* meaning "one."]

a[2] (ə; *stressed* ā) *prep.* to, in, or for each; per: *three times a year, two dollars a pound.* [Short for the Old English preposition *an* meaning "on, in, to."]

a– *prefix* in; on; to; at: *atop, aboard, afoot, abed, afield.*

a. 1. about. **2.** acre; acres. **3.** *Sports.* assist.

A 1. angstrom. **2.** answer. **3.** argon.

A–1 *also,* **A-one, A number 1.** *adj. Informal.* of the highest rate or class; excellent: *The house was in A-1 shape.* [From the rating *A-1* given by the British insurance company Lloyd's to ships in the best possible condition.]

AA 1. Alcoholics Anonymous. **2.** antiaircraft.

AAA, American Automobile Association.

aard·vark (ärd′värk′) *n.* a burrowing mammal having a long, sticky tongue and powerful claws, native to southern and east-central Africa. It feeds on ants and termites.

aardvark

AB, postal abbreviation for Alberta.

ab– *prefix* from; departing from; away from: *abduct, abnormal.*

A.B., Bachelor of Arts. Also, **B.A.**

ab·a·ca (ab′ə kä′) *n.* **1.** a large tropical plant bearing leaves from which Manila hemp is made. **2.** another word for **Manila hemp.**

a·back (ə bak′) *adv.* **taken aback.** suddenly surprised or startled: *I was taken aback by the angry reply to my question.*

ab·a·cus (ab′ə kəs) *n., pl.* **ab·a·cus·es** or **ab·a·ci** (ab′-ə sī′). a device consisting of a frame with balls or beads that slide back and forth in grooves or on wires, used especially for adding and subtracting. Abacuses have been used since ancient times and are still widely used in the Far East.

abacus

a·baft (ə baft′) *prep.* to the stern or rear of: *abaft the funnels. —adv.* at or toward the stern of a ship.

ab·a·lo·ne (ab′ə lō′nē) *n.* any of a group of sea snails that can be eaten, having an ear-shaped shell that is lined with mother-of-pearl and perforated along part of the outer rim.

1

a·ban·don (ə ban′dən) *v.t.* **1.** to go away from without intending to return; forsake completely; leave behind: *The crew abandoned the sinking ship.* **2.** to give up (something) completely: *I abandoned hope of making the team.* **3.** to surrender (oneself) completely, as to an emotion or influence: *to abandon oneself to grief.* —*n.* complete surrender to one's impulses or emotions: *We played with abandon all afternoon. The crowd cheered with abandon when the home team won.* —**a·ban′don·ment,** *n.*

a·ban·doned (ə ban′dənd) *adj.* **1.** left behind or alone; deserted; forsaken: *We spent the afternoon exploring an abandoned house.* **2.** lacking, or showing no respect for, morals; wicked: *an abandoned life.*

a·base (ə bās′) *v.t.,* **a·based, a·bas·ing.** to lower in rank, position, or reputation; humiliate; humble: *They refused to abase themselves by begging.* —**a·base′ment,** *n.*

a·bash (ə bash′) *v.t.* to make embarrassed or ashamed; disconcert: *I was abashed by my error.*

a·bate (ə bāt′) *v.t., v.i.,* **a·bat·ed, a·bat·ing.** to make or become less in force, intensity, or amount: *The gale winds abated. Nothing could abate their anger over the closing of the school.* —**a·bate′ment,** *n.*

ab·at·toir (ab′ə twär′) *n.* another word for **slaughterhouse.**

ab·bé (ab′ā) *n. French.* a member of the clergy, especially a priest. ▲ used as a title of respect.

ab·bess (ab′is) *n., pl.* **ab·bess·es.** a woman who is the head of a community of nuns.

ab·bey (ab′ē) *n., pl.* **ab·beys. 1.** a monastery under the rule of an abbot. **2.** a convent under the rule of an abbess. **3.** a group of monks or nuns living in a monastery or convent. **4.** a church or other building or group of buildings that is or was an abbey or part of an abbey.

ab·bot (ab′ət) *n.* a man who is the head of a community of monks.

abbr., abbreviation. Also, **abbrev.**

ab·bre·vi·ate (ə brē′vē āt′) *v.t.,* **ab·bre·vi·at·ed, ab·bre·vi·at·ing. 1.** to shorten (a word or phrase) so that one or more letters stand for the whole, such as *Feb.* for *February, pt.* for *pint,* or *UK* for *United Kingdom.* **2.** to make shorter; shorten: *to abbreviate a speech.*

ab·bre·vi·a·tion (ə brē′vē ā′shən) *n.* **1.** one or more letters standing for the whole of a word or phrase. **2.** the act of abbreviating. ▲ Many **abbreviations** may be written either with or without periods. An abbreviation that is made up of the first letter of two or more words is often written without periods: *PTA* (Parent-Teacher Association), *UN* (United Nations), *mph* (miles per hour). An abbreviation that includes more than just the first letter of a word generally has a period: *wt.* (weight), *pres.* (president), *sq. yd.* (square yard or square yards). See **acronym** for an additional usage note.

ABC's (ā′bē′sēz′) *also,* **ABC.** *pl. n.* **1.** the alphabet. **2.** the simplest or basic facts of a subject: *the ABC's of chemistry.*

ab·di·cate (ab′di kāt′) *v.,* **ab·di·cat·ed, ab·di·cat·ing.** —*v.t.* to give up or renounce formally (power, rights, or responsibility): *to abdicate an influential role.* —*v.i.* to give up or renounce power, rights, or responsibility, such as a throne: *King Edward VIII of Great Britain abdicated in 1936.* —**ab′di·ca′tion,** *n.* —**ab′di·ca′tor,** *n.*

ab·do·men (ab′də mən, ab dō′mən) *n.* **1.** the largest of the body cavities of humans and other animals with backbones; belly. It is located between the chest and the pelvis and contains many vital organs, such as the stomach, the intestines, the kidneys, and the liver. **2.** the rear section of the body of an insect, spider, or crustacean.

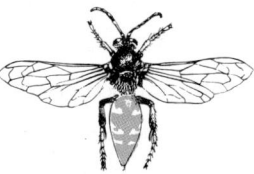

abdomen of an insect

ab·dom·i·nal (ab dom′ə nəl) *adj.* of or relating to the abdomen: *abdominal pain, abdominal surgery.* —**ab·dom′i·nal·ly,** *adv.*

ab·duct (ab dukt′) *v.t.* to carry off (someone) unlawfully by force or trickery; kidnap: *to abduct people and hold them as hostages.* —**ab·duc′tion,** *n.* —**ab·duc′tor,** *n.*

a·beam (ə bēm′) *adv.* **1.** alongside a ship, especially directly opposite the middle of a ship's side. **2.** at right angles to a ship's keel.

a·bed (ə bed′) *adv.* in bed: *to lie abed.*

Ab·er·deen Angus (ab′ər dēn′) any of a breed of beef cattle originating in Scotland, having a stocky body, black hair, and no horns. Also, **Angus.**

ab·er·rant (ə ber′ənt, ab′ər ənt) *adj.* differing from what is usual, normal, or correct; abnormal: *an aberrant pattern of growth, an aberrant heartbeat.*

ab·er·ra·tion (ab′ə rā′shən) *n.* **1.** a going away or differing from what is usual, normal, or correct: *The shy child's loud talking was an aberration.* **2.** a slight mental disorder. **3.** the failure of a lens or mirror to focus the light rays from an object at a single point, causing the formation of a blurred or otherwise imperfect image. **4.** an apparent change in the position of a heavenly body, caused by the movement of the earth that takes place between the time when light leaves the heavenly body and the time when it reaches the observer on earth.

a·bet (ə bet′) *v.t.,* **a·bet·ted, a·bet·ting.** to encourage or help, especially in wrongdoing: *Someone abetted the thief by leaving a door open.* —**a·bet′ment,** *n.* —**a·bet′tor;** *also,* **a·bet′ter,** *n.*

a·bey·ance (ə bā′əns) *n.* a state of temporary inactivity or suspension: *Hold the decision in abeyance until we learn all the facts.*

ab·hor (ab hôr′) *v.t.,* **ab·horred, ab·hor·ring.** to feel disgust or hatred for; detest; loathe: *I abhor rats.* —**ab·hor′rer,** *n.*

ab·hor·rence (ab hôr′əns) *n.* **1.** a feeling of disgust or hatred: *an abhorrence of war.* **2.** something disgusting or loathsome.

ab·hor·rent (ab hôr′ənt) *adj.* causing disgust, hatred, or loathing; detestable: *an abhorrent crime.*

a·bide (ə bīd′) *v.,* **a·bid·ed** or **a·bode, a·bid·ing.** —*v.i.* **1.** to continue to live or dwell; reside: *to abide in the city.* **2.** to continue to be; last; endure: *True courage will abide even in the worst of times.* **3.** to continue to stay; remain. —*v.t.* to bear patiently; put up with; tolerate: *The teacher would not abide rudeness in the classroom.* —**a·bid′er,** *n.*

·**to abide by. a.** to accept and obey: *to abide by the rules of a game.* **b.** to do or perform; carry out; fulfill: *to abide by a promise.*

a·bid·ing (ə bī′ding) *adj.* continuing; lasting; enduring: *to have abiding trust in someone.* —**a·bid′ing·ly,** *adv.*

a·bil·i·ty (ə bil′i tē) *n., pl.* **a·bil·i·ties. 1.** the power to do or act: *Ostriches do not have the ability to fly.* **2.** talent or skill: *to show great ability as a carpenter.*

–ability *suffix* (used to form nouns) capability of being: *predictability, manageability.*

a·bi·ot·ic (ā′bī ot′ik) *adj.* of, relating to, or characterized by the absence of life or living things: *an abiotic planet.*

ab·ject (ab′jekt, ab jekt′) *adj.* **1.** in or of a low, hopeless condition; miserable: *abject poverty, abject refugees.* **2.** low in, or showing lowness of, character; base: *an abject liar, abject cowardice.* —**ab′ject·ly,** *adv.* —**ab′ject·ness,** *n.*

ab·jure (ab jùr′) *v.t.,* **ab·jured, ab·jur·ing.** to give up on oath; renounce: *to abjure allegiance to a political party.* —**ab′ju·ra′tion,** *n.* —**ab·jur′er,** *n.*

ab·la·tion (ab lā′shən) *n.* a process in which a special protective coating on the nose cone of a spacecraft slowly melts away as the spacecraft reenters the earth's atmosphere in order to carry off excessive heat.

ab·la·tive (ab′lə tiv) *n.* a grammatical case in Latin and certain other languages that indicates movement or direction away from, source, cause, or the like.

a·blaze (ə blāz′) *adj.* **1.** in flames; on fire: *The house was ablaze when the firemen arrived.* **2.** brilliantly lit; gleaming: *The store windows were ablaze with lights.*

a·ble (ā′bəl) *adj.,* **a·bler, a·blest. 1.** having enough power, skill, or means to do something: *The child was able to read and write at an early age. An ostrich is not able to fly.* **2.** having or showing unusual ability, talent, or intelligence: *an able pianist, an able performance.*

–able *suffix* **1.** (used to form adjectives from verbs) **a.** capable of being: *eatable, tolerable.* **b.** worthy of being: *believable, laudable, commendable.* **c.** likely to: *perishable.* **2.** (used to form adjectives from nouns) **a.** worthy of or able to cause: *objectionable, comfortable.* **b.** tending toward: *peaceable.*

a·ble–bod·ied (ā′bəl bod′ēd) *adj.* having a strong, healthy body; capable of physical work.

able–bodied seaman, an experienced and skilled sailor in the merchant marine who has passed an examination testing ability as a seaman. Also, **able seaman.**

a·bloom (ə blüm′) *adj.* in bloom; flowering.

ab·lu·tion (ə blü′shən) *also,* **ablutions.** *n.* a washing or cleansing of one's body or a part of it, especially as part of a religious ceremony.

a·bly (ā′blē) *adv.* in an able manner; skillfully.

ABM, antiballistic missile.

ab·ne·gate (ab′ni gāt′) *v.t.,* **ab·ne·gat·ed, ab·ne·gat·ing.** to deny (something) to oneself; give up or abandon: *to abnegate the pleasures of life, to abnegate responsibility.* **—ab′ne·ga′tor,** *n.*

ab·ne·ga·tion (ab′ni gā′shən) *n.* a giving up of one's rights, desires, or interests; self-denial.

ab·nor·mal (ab nôr′məl) *adj.* different from what is normal, usual, or average; unusual: *This chilly weather is abnormal for July.* **—ab·nor′mal·ly,** *adv.*

ab·nor·mal·i·ty (ab′nôr mal′i tē) *n., pl.* **ab·nor·mal·i·ties. 1.** the state of being abnormal. **2.** something that is abnormal.

a·board (ə bôrd′) *adv.* in, on, or into a ship, train, airplane, or other vehicle: *That passenger came aboard in Chicago.* **—prep.** in, on, or into (a ship, train, airplane, or other vehicle): *Load these bags aboard the boat.*

‎ **·all aboard.** get in; get on. ▲ a call used to warn passengers that a ship, train, or other vehicle is about to depart.

a·bode (ə bōd′) *v.* a past tense and past participle of **abide. —***n.* the place where one lives; dwelling; home.

a·bol·ish (ə bol′ish) *v.t.* to put an end to; do away with completely: *to abolish an unfair law.*

ab·o·li·tion (ab′ə lish′ən) *n.* **1.** the act of abolishing or the state of being abolished. **2.** *also,* **Abolition.** the abolishing of slavery in the United States.

ab·o·li·tion·ist (ab′ə lish′ə nist) *n.* **1.** a person who is in favor of abolishing something. **2.** *also,* **Abolitionist.** a person who favored the abolition of slavery in the United States before the Civil War.

A–bomb (ā′bom′) *n.* another word for **atomic bomb.**

a·bom·i·na·ble (ə bom′ə nə bəl) *adj.* **1.** deserving or causing hate; loathsome; detestable: *Slavery is an abominable practice.* **2.** very unpleasant, disagreeable, or distasteful: *abominable table manners.* **—a·bom′i·na·bly,** *adv.*

abominable snowman, a creature that supposedly lives in the Himalayas, often believed to resemble a bear, ape, or primitive human. There is no generally accepted proof that it exists. Also, **yeti.**

a·bom·i·nate (ə bom′ə nāt′) *v.t.,* **a·bom·i·nat·ed, a·bom·i·nat·ing. 1.** to feel disgust, hatred, or loathing for; abhor; detest: *All the nations said that they abominated war.* **2.** to dislike strongly: *I abominate driving in heavy traffic.*

a·bom·i·na·tion (ə bom′ə nā′shən) *n.* **1.** something disgusting, hateful, or loathsome. **2.** a strong feeling of disgust, hatred, or loathing.

ab·o·rig·i·nal (ab′ə rij′ə nəl) *adj.* **1.** living or existing in a place from the earliest known time; native: *aboriginal plants, aboriginal peoples.* **2.** of or relating to aborigines: *The boomerang was an Australian aboriginal weapon.* **—***n.* an aboriginal person, plant, or animal.

ab·o·rig·i·ne (ab′ə rij′ə nē) *n.* **1.** one of the original or earliest known inhabitants of a country: *The aborigines of Australia are not known to be related to any other group of people.* **2.** any of the original plants or animals of a region.

a·bort (ə bôrt′) *v.i.* **1.** to bring forth or expel a fetus or embryo before it has developed enough to be able to live. **2.** to end something, such as a mission or project, before completion: *The pilots were given orders to abort because their plane developed engine trouble.* **—v.t. 1.** to cause an abortion of. **2.** to end before completion: *to abort a space mission.*

a·bor·tion (ə bôr′shən) *n.* **1.** the bringing forth or expulsion of a fetus or embryo before it has developed enough to be able to live. Abortions may be due to miscarriage or may be carried out intentionally. **2.** something that fails to develop completely or succeed, such as a mission or project.

a·bor·tive (ə bôr′tiv) *adj.* **1.** failing to succeed; fruitless: *Until 1953 all attempts to climb Mount Everest were abortive.* **2.** *Medicine.* causing or relating to an abortion: *abortive drugs.* **3.** not fully formed or developed. **—a·bor′tive·ly,** *adv.* **—a·bor′tive·ness,** *n.*

a·bound (ə bound′) *v.i.* to exist in great quantity or large numbers; be plentiful: *Bison used to abound on the western plains. Humor abounded during the party.*

‎ **·to abound with** or **to abound in.** to be rich in; to be filled with: *The Amazon rain forest abounds with rare flowers.*

a·bout (ə bout′) *prep.* **1.** relating to; having to do with: *That book is about Abraham Lincoln. There is something strange about that house.* **2.** on every side of; around: *A moat runs about the castle.* **3.** on the point of; ready. ▲ followed by an infinitive: *We are about to start on our trip.* **4.** around or over the parts of; here and there; in or on: *Wind scattered the leaves about the yard.* **—adv. 1.** not exactly; approximately: *There were about a thousand people in the crowd.* **2.** almost; nearly: *We are about ready to go.* **3.** in several directions; all around: *to look about.* **4.** here and there; to and fro: *to wander about.* **5.** in or to the opposite direction: *Hearing my name called I turned about.* **—adj.** moving around; on the move; astir: *The patient was up and about two days after the operation.*

a·bout–face (*n.,* ə bout′fās′; *v.,* ə bout′fās′) *n.* **1.a.** the act of turning around and facing in the opposite direction, as in a military drill. **b.** the act of turning and going in the opposite direction. **2.** a change from one attitude or opinion to its opposite: *The results of the poll led to an about-face in government policy.* **—v.i.,** **a·bout-faced, a·bout-fac·ing.** to turn and face or go in the opposite direction.

a·bove (ə buv′) *adv.* **1.** in, at, or to a higher place or position; overhead: *Stars glittered above.* **2.** in an earlier part of a book or other piece of writing: *See the examples*

---

at; āpe; fär; câre; end; mē; it; īce; pîerce; hot; ōld; sông, fôrk; oil; out; up; ūse; rüle; pùll; tûrn; chin; sing; shop; thin; this; hw in white; zh in treasure. The symbol ə stands for the unstressed vowel sound heard in about, taken, pencil, lemon, and circus.

given above. —*prep.* **1.** over or higher than; rising beyond: *The building towered above the city. I could hear birds above the noise of the waterfall.* **2.** superior to the influence of; not likely to stoop to: *to be above cheating on a test.* **3.** superior to in rank, position, or importance: *A captain is above a lieutenant in the army.* **4.** in preference to: *This above all, to thine own self be true* (Shakespeare, *Hamlet*). **5.** more than; over: *Anything above fifty dollars will be too expensive.* **6.a.** farther than, especially when measured by a higher number: *The park is above 59th Street.* **b.** upstream from: *The city lies above the rapids.* **c.** north of: *Pennsylvania is above the Mason-Dixon line.* —*adj.* written or mentioned earlier: *the above explanation, the above example.* —*n.* something that is written or mentioned earlier: *The above will be used to illustrate this theory.*

a·bove·board (ə buv′bôrd′) *adv., adj.* without deception, dishonesty, or concealment: *Their dealings with us have been open and aboveboard.*

ab·ra·ca·dab·ra (ab′rə kə dab′rə) *n.* **1.** a secret word or words supposed to have magic power. **2.** meaningless talk; mumbo jumbo. —*interj.* used in performance of a magic trick, supposedly as to effect the magic.

a·brade (ə brād′) *v.t.,* **a·brad·ed, a·brad·ing.** to wear off or away by rubbing or scraping: *to abrade the skin on one's elbow against a rough surface.*

a·bra·sion (ə brā′zhən) *n.* **1.** the act or process of wearing off or away by rubbing or scraping. **2.** a scraped area or spot: *to suffer abrasions from a fall.*

a·bra·sive (ə brā′siv, ə brā′ziv) *n.* a substance used for cleaning, grinding, or polishing: *Sandpaper is an abrasive.* —*adj.* **1.** wearing away by rubbing or scraping; causing or capable of causing abrasion: *Sandpaper has an abrasive surface.* **2.** harsh or irritating in manner: *an abrasive person, an abrasive remark.* —**a·bra′sive·ly,** *adv.* —**a·bra′sive·ness,** *n.*

a·breast (ə brest′) *adv., adj.* side by side and facing or moving in the same direction: *The seniors marched two abreast to graduation.*

·**abreast of** or **abreast with. a.** aware of; up on: *to keep abreast of new ideas.* **b.** parallel to or alongside of: *The ship was abreast of the shore.*

a·bridge (ə brij′) *v.t.,* **a·bridged, a·bridg·ing. 1.** to shorten, especially by leaving out less important parts; condense: *to abridge a book.* **2.** to make less; lessen, restrict: *The dictator abridged the people's rights.*

a·bridg·ment (ə brij′ment) *also,* **a·bridge·ment.** *n.* **1.** a shortened version of a book or other written work: *There was an abridgment of that novel in a magazine.* **2.** the act of abridging or the state of being abridged: *an abridgment of freedom of the press.*

a·broad (ə brôd′) *adv.* **1.** out of one's country; in or to a foreign land: *to travel abroad. We lived abroad for several years.* **2.** going around; current: *Rumors of victory were abroad.* **3.** over a large area; far and wide: *The news spread abroad quickly.*

ab·ro·gate (ab′rə gāt′) *v.t.,* **ab·ro·gat·ed, ab·ro·gat·ing.** to put an end to by authority; abolish; annul: *to abrogate a law.* —**ab′ro·ga′tion,** *n.*

a·brupt (ə brupt′) *adj.* **1.** happening quickly or without warning; sudden; unexpected: *The bus made an abrupt stop on the highway.* **2.** impolite or blunt: *to be abrupt in speaking.* **3.** steep: *The road makes an abrupt descent at the edge of town.* [From the Latin word *abruptus,* past participle of *abrumpere* meaning "to break off" or "interrupt," from the prefix *ab-* "from, away" + *rumpere* "to break."] —**a·brupt′ly,** *adv.* —**a·brupt′ness,** *n.*

ab·scess (ab′ses) *n., pl.* **ab·scess·es.** a collection of pus resulting from an infection in the tissues of some part of the body.

ab·scessed (ab′sest) *adj.* having an abscess: *an abscessed tooth.*

ab·scis·sa (ab sis′ə) *n., pl.* **ab·scis·sas** or **ab·scis·sae** (ab sis′ē). **1.** on a graph, the distance of a point from the vertical axis measured parallel to the horizontal axis, used to define the point in the Cartesian coordinate system. The abscissa is frequently called the *x* coordinate. **2.** the line, number, or algebraic expression representing this distance.

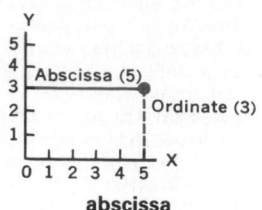

abscissa

ab·scond (ab skond′) *v.i.* to go away secretly and conceal oneself, especially to avoid arrest: *The treasurer absconded with the company's funds.*

ab·sence (ab′səns) *n.* **1.** the state of being away or not being present: *The star's absence disappointed the audience.* **2.** a period of being away: *The soldier came home after an absence of three years.* **3.** the state of being without; lack: *The absence of light in the room made reading impossible.*

ab·sent (*adj.,* ab′sənt; *v.,* ab sent′) *adj.* **1.** not in a certain place at a given time; not present; away: *to be absent from school because of illness.* **2.** not existing; lacking: *Gills are absent in an adult frog.* **3.** not showing any interest or attention; preoccupied: *to have an absent expression on one's face.* —*v.t.* to take or keep (oneself) away: *They absented themselves from the conference.* —**ab′sent·ly,** *adv.*

ab·sen·tee (ab′sən tē′) *n.* a person who is absent, as from work or school.

absentee ballot, a ballot that enables a voter who cannot be present at the polls to vote by mail.

ab·sen·tee·ism (ab′sən tē′iz əm) *n.* habitual or repeated absence, as from work or school.

absentee landlord, a person who owns and rents land or buildings but lives elsewhere.

ab·sent-mind·ed (ab′sənt mīn′did) *adj.* **1.** not alert to or aware of one's surroundings or actions; lost in thought; preoccupied: *to stare out a window in an absent-minded way.* **2.** likely to forget; forgetful: *I'm so absent-minded I'm always misplacing my keys.* —**ab′sent-mind′ed·ly,** *adv.* —**ab′sent-mind′ed·ness,** *n.*

ab·sinthe (ab′sinth) *n.* a bitter, green liqueur with a licorice taste, flavored with wormwood and anise.

ab·so·lute (ab′sə lüt′) *adj.* **1.** complete or perfect: *absolute purity.* **2.** free from all restrictions or limitations: *The emperor had absolute power over the people.* **3.** without doubt; positive: *absolute proof for a theory.* —**ab′so·lute′ness,** *n.*

absolute alcohol, ethyl alcohol that is at least 99% pure.

ab·so·lute·ly (ab′sə lüt′lē, ab′sə lüt′lē) *adv.* **1.** to the fullest extent or highest degree; completely: *The room was absolutely empty.* **2.** without doubt; definitely: *Are you absolutely sure of your answer?*

absolute pitch, the ability to identify or sing any tone heard or specified. Also, **perfect pitch.**

absolute temperature, temperature measured from absolute zero.

absolute value, the positive numerical value of a given number, whether the number is positive or negative. The absolute value of both 2 and -2 is 2.

absolute zero, theoretically, the temperature at which all motion of molecules in a substance would stop and it would have no heat whatsoever. Absolute zero is 0 degrees on the Kelvin temperature scale and is equal to -273.15 degrees Celsius, or -459.67 degrees Fahrenheit.

ab·so·lu·tion (ab′sə lü′shən) *n.* **1.** formal forgiveness of sins, especially by a priest. **2.** forgiveness of or freedom from obligation, guilt, or penalty.

ab·so·lut·ism (ab′sə lü tiz′əm) *n.* a system of government in which the power of the ruler or ruling group is unlimited.

ab·solve (ab zolv′, ab solv′) *v.t.*, **ab·solved, ab·solv·ing.** **1.** to free from guilt or blame: *The thief's confession absolved the original suspect in the case.* **2.** to set (someone) free, as from an obligation, duty, or responsibility. **3.** to forgive the sins of: *The priest absolved the people who had confessed their sins.* —**ab·solv′er,** *n.*

ab·sorb (ab sôrb′, ab zôrb′) *v.t.* **1.** to take into oneself or soak up (liquid): *A sponge absorbs water.* **2.** to take up all the attention of; engross: *The fascinating book absorbed me.* **3.** to take in and make part of oneself: *The Roman Empire absorbed many territories.* **4.** to take in (light, sound, or heat) without reflection or echo: *The walls of this building absorb sound.*

ab·sorbed (ab sôrbd′, ab zôrbd′) *adj.* very interested; preoccupied; rapt: *I was so absorbed in this book that I didn't hear you come into the room.*

ab·sorb·en·cy (ab sôr′bən sē, ab zôr′bən sē) *n.* the state or degree of being absorbent.

ab·sorb·ent (ab sôr′bənt, ab zôr′bənt) *adj.* absorbing or capable of absorbing: *absorbent cotton.* —*n.* a material that absorbs: *Blotting paper is an absorbent.*

ab·sorb·ing (ab sôr′bing, ab zôr′bing) *adj.* very interesting; engrossing: *an absorbing film.* —**ab·sorb′ing·ly,** *adv.*

ab·sorp·tion (ab sôrp′shən, ab zôrp′shən) *n.* **1.** the act or process of absorbing: *Digested food passes from the intestines into the blood by means of absorption.* See **adsorption** for illustration. **2.** complete attention; engrossment.

ab·stain (ab stān′) *v.i.* **1.** to keep oneself from doing something; hold oneself back; refrain: *I abstained from eating dessert as part of my diet.* **2.** to choose not to vote: *In the vote on new membership rules, three club members abstained.* —**ab·stain′er,** *n.*

ab·ste·mi·ous (ab stē′mē əs) *adj.* moderate or sparing, especially in the use of food and drink: *The stomach illness made me more abstemious.* —**ab·ste′mi·ous·ly,** *adv.*

ab·sten·tion (ab sten′shən) *n.* **1.** the act or practice of abstaining: *an abstention from smoking.* **2.** the act or fact of not voting: *There were eight votes in favor, six against, and three abstentions.*

ab·sti·nence (ab′stə nəns) *n.* the act or practice of doing without certain foods, drink, or pleasures.

an **abstract** painting

ab·stract (*adj.*, ab′strakt, ab strakt′; *v.*, *defs.* 1, 3 ab-strakt′, *def.* 2 ab′strakt; *n.*, ab′strakt) *adj.* **1.** expressing a quality that can be thought of apart from any particular thing having that quality: *"Goodness" and "beauty" are abstract nouns.* **2.** not concerned with real or practical examples or instances; general: *abstract science.* **3.** relating to or designating a style of art that does not represent real objects directly, but uses lines, shapes, and colors to express emotions or ideas: *an abstract painting.*

—*v.t.* **1.** to separate (a quality) from particular things having that quality: *to abstract the idea of coldness from cold objects.* **2.** to make a brief account of (a book, speech, or the like); summarize. **3.** to take away; remove: *to abstract gold from ore.* —*n.* **1.** a summary of a book, speech, or other work. **2.** a work of art in the abstract style: *The painter did an abstract for the exhibition.* [From the Latin word *abstractus,* past participle of *abstrahere* meaning "to draw away," from the prefix *ab–* "from, away" + *trahere* "to draw, pull."] —**ab·stract′ly,** *adv.* —**ab·stract′ness,** *n.*

·**in the abstract.** without reference to particular examples or instances; in theory: *to know poverty only in the abstract.*

ab·stract·ed (ab strak′tid) *adj.* lost in thought; preoccupied. —**ab·stract′ed·ly,** *adv.*

ab·strac·tion (ab strak′shən) *n.* **1.** the act or process of separating a quality from particular things having that quality. **2.** an idea formed in this way: *Wealth, redness, and anger are abstractions.* **3.** an abstract work of art. **4.** the act of withdrawing or removing; separation. **5.** the state of being abstracted; preoccupation.

ab·struse (ab strüs′) *adj.* hard to understand: *an abstruse poem, an abstruse theory.* —**ab·struse′ly,** *adv.* —**ab·struse′ness,** *n.*

ab·surd (ab sûrd′, ab zûrd′) *adj.* **1.** contrary to reason, common sense, or truth; ridiculous: *It is absurd to believe that the earth is flat.* **2.** *Informal.* ridiculous because inappropriate or in poor taste: *What an absurd color that house is!* —**ab·surd′ly,** *adv.* —**ab·surd′ness,** *n.*

ab·surd·i·ty (ab sûr′di tē, ab zûr′di tē) *n., pl.* **ab·surd·i·ties.** **1.** the state or quality of being absurd; foolishness. **2.** something absurd: *The play was supposed to be serious, but it was full of absurdities.*

a·bun·dance (ə bun′dəns) *n.* a quantity that is more than enough; plentiful or overflowing supply: *an abundance of food. The book contained an abundance of information.*

a·bun·dant (ə bun′dənt) *adj.* more than enough; plentiful: *The campers had an abundant supply of food.* —**a·bun′dant·ly,** *adv.*

·**abundant in.** having in great quantity: *The lake was abundant in fish.*

a·buse (*v.,* ə būz′; *n.,* ə būs′) *v.t.* **a·bused, a·bus·ing.** **1.** to use improperly or wrongly; misuse: *Some politicians abuse their authority by giving important jobs to friends.* **2.** to hurt by treating wrongly; mistreat; injure: *The owner of the zoo was arrested for abusing the animals.* **3.** to attack with harsh or insulting language. —*n.* **1.** wrong or improper use; misuse: *a dictator's abuse of power.* **2.** cruel or rough treatment; injury: *During the trip over the mountains our car took much abuse.* **3.** a practice or custom that is unfair or that does harm. **4.** harsh or insulting language.

a·bu·sive (ə bū′siv, ə bū′ziv) *adj.* **1.** having or using harsh or insulting language: *an abusive political speech.* **2.** wrongly or improperly used; corrupt: *Searching the building without a warrant was an abusive exercise of police power.* **3.** involving cruel or rough treatment; injurious: *Abusive handling ruined the camera.* —**a·bu′sive·ly,** *adv.* —**a·bu′sive·ness,** *n.*

a·but (ə but′) *v.i., v.t.,* **a·but·ted, a·but·ting.** to touch at one end or side; adjoin; border: *Our land abuts on the forest. A wall abuts the lawn.*

---

at; āpe; fär; câre; end; mē; it; īce; pîerce; hot; ōld; sông, fôrk; oil; out; up; ūse; rüle; pull; tûrn; chin; sing; shop; thin; this; hw in white; zh in treasure. The symbol ə stands for the unstressed vowel sound heard in about, taken, pencil, lemon, and circus.

a·but·ment (ə but′mənt) *n.* **1.** a structure on either end of an arch or bridge, used to support weight or resist pressure. **2.** something that abuts on something else.

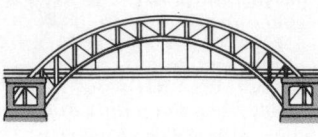

abutments

a·bys·mal (ə biz′məl) *adj.* **1.** too deep or great to be measured; like an abyss; immeasurable: *an abysmal crevice in a glacier, abysmal sorrow at the death of a friend.* **2.** extremely poor or bad; wretched; miserable: *abysmal conditions in slums.* —**a·bys′mal·ly,** *adv.*

a·byss (ə bis′) *n., pl.* **a·byss·es. 1.** an immeasurably deep or apparently bottomless pit or opening in the surface of the earth; chasm. **2.** anything too deep or great to be measured: *the abyss of outer space.*

Ac, the symbol for actinium.

AC, A.C., a.c., alternating current.

a·ca·cia (ə kā′shə) *n.* **1.** any of a group of trees or shrubs found in warm regions throughout the world, many of which bear delicate, fernlike leaves and clusters of white, yellow, or orange flowers. Some species yield useful products, such as gum arabic or tannic acid. **2.** any of several other trees, especially certain locust trees. **3.** another word for **gum arabic.**

acad. 1. academic. **2.** academy.

ac·a·dem·ic (ak′ə dem′ik) *adj.* **1.** of or relating to an academy, school, or college: *an academic degree, academic studies.* **2.** relating to liberal or general education, especially to studies that prepare a student for college: *to take an academic course in high school.* **3.** not practical; theoretical: *Who invented the wheel is an academic question.* Also, **ac·a·dem·i·cal** (ak′ə dem′i kəl). —**ac′a·dem′i·cal·ly,** *adv.*

academic freedom, the freedom of a teacher or student to teach, study, or discuss any subject without fear of interference.

a·cad·e·my (ə kad′ə mē) *n., pl.* **a·cad·e·mies. 1.** a school giving instruction or training in a particular field: *a military academy, an academy of music.* **2.** a private high school. **3.** a society or institution for the encouragement and advancement of literature, science, or the arts. [From the French word *académie* meaning "a place of learning," going back to the Greek word *Akadēmeia,* the grove near Athens where Plato had his school.]

Academy Award, another term for **Oscar.**

A·ca·di·an (ə kā′dē ən) *adj.* of or relating to Acadia, its people, or their culture. —*n.* **1.** an inhabitant of Acadia. **2.** see **Cajun.**

a·can·thus (ə kan′thəs) *n., pl.* **a·can·thus·es** or **a·can·thi** (ə kan′thī). **1.** any of a group of plants native to the Mediterranean region, bearing large spiny leaves and clusters of white or colored flowers. **2.** a design in art or architecture representing an acanthus leaf, used especially as decorations on Corinthian columns.

Acanthus leaf

In Greek architecture

acanthus

a cap·pel·la (ä′ kə pel′ə) *adv., adj. Music.* without instrumental accompaniment: *to sing a cappella, an a cappella arrangement.*

acc. 1. accusative. **2.** account.

ac·cede (ak sēd′) *v.i.,* **ac·ced·ed, ac·ced·ing. 1.** to give consent or approval; agree: *The judge acceded to the request for a recess in the trial.* **2.** to gain control or possession of something, such as an office, title, or position: *The new monarch acceded to the throne in 1952.*

accel., accelerando.

ac·ce·le·ran·do (ak sel′ə rän′dō) *adv., adj. Music.* gradually increasing in speed.

ac·cel·er·ate (ak sel′ə rāt′) *v.,* **ac·cel·er·at·ed, ac·cel·er·at·ing.** —*v.t.* **1.** to increase the speed of; cause to go faster: *to accelerate an automobile. Running up stairs accelerates a person's heartbeat.* **2.** to cause to happen sooner; hasten: *The bad weather accelerated our departure.* **3.** *Physics.* to change the speed or direction of (a moving body). —*v.i.* to increase in speed; go faster: *The car accelerated as it went down the hill.*

ac·cel·er·a·tion (ak sel′ə rā′shən) *n.* **1.** the act of accelerating or the state of being accelerated: *The hiring of additional workers caused an acceleration in the rate of production.* **2.** *Physics.* **a.** a change in the speed or direction of a moving body. **b.** the rate of such a change per unit of time. The acceleration of a falling object is approximately 32 feet per second per second (9.8 meters per second per second).

ac·cel·er·a·tor (ak sel′ə rā′tər) *n.* **1.** a device for increasing the speed of a machine, especially the foot pedal that controls the speed of an automobile engine. **2.** *Physics.* any of various devices that accelerate subatomic particles to high speeds and high energies, such as a cyclotron or a synchrotron. Also, **atom smasher.**

ac·cel·er·om·e·ter (ak sel′ə rom′i tər) *n.* a device that is used to measure acceleration, as in an aircraft or spacecraft.

ac·cent (*n.,* ak′sent; *v.,* ak′sent, ak sent′) *n.* **1.** greater force or emphasis given to a particular syllable or word in speech. In the word *access,* the accent is on the first syllable; in the word *accept,* the accent is on the second syllable. **2.** a mark used in writing and printing to indicate a syllable that is spoken with greater force or emphasis. In this dictionary the mark ′ is used to show a strong or primary accent, and the mark ′ is used to show a weaker or secondary accent, as seen in the word *ac·cen·tu·ate* (ak sen′chü āt′). **3.** any of various marks used in certain languages to show how a particular letter is pronounced. In the French word *consommé,* the accent over the *e* indicates that it is pronounced as (ā). **4.** a special manner of pronouncing words that is characteristic of a certain part of a country, or of a person speaking a foreign language: *a New York accent. My grandparents speak English with a German accent.* **5.** stress or importance given something; emphasis: *a biology course with an accent on laboratory work.* **6.** stress on certain words or syllables marking the rhythm of a line of verse. **7.** *Music.* **a.** stress or emphasis given to certain notes or chords. **b.** a mark used to indicate this. —*v.t.* **1.** to pronounce (a syllable, word, or words) with particular stress or emphasis: *to accent the first syllable of the word "accident."* **2.** to mark with a written or printed accent. **3.** to stress or emphasize; accentuate.

accent mark, see **accent** (*defs. 2, 3*).

ac·cen·tu·ate (ak sen′chü āt′) *v.t.,* **ac·cen·tu·at·ed, ac·cen·tu·at·ing. 1.** to increase the effect of; point up; emphasize; stress: *Your height accentuates your thinness.* **2.** to mark or pronounce with an accent. —**ac·cen′-tu·a′tion,** *n.*

ac·cept (ak sept′) *v.t.* **1.** to agree to take (something offered): *to accept a present, to accept an honor.* **2.** to receive with favor or approval: *The students quickly accepted their new teacher.* **3.** to agree or consent to; adjust oneself to; submit to: *to accept the facts. The team accepted the referee's decision.* **4.** to answer yes to: *to accept an invitation, to accept an offer.* **5.** to receive or regard as true, satisfactory, or sufficient; believe in: *The scientific community accepted the new theory slowly.* **6.** to take upon oneself; assume; undertake: *I accepted the responsibility of feeding the dog.* —*v.i.* to take something offered.

ac·cept·a·ble (ak sep′tə bəl) *adj.* **1.** good enough to be accepted; satisfactory: *Their work was acceptable, but* *not outstanding.* **2.** pleasing, welcome, or agreeable: *The plan for the picnic was acceptable to the whole group.* —**ac·cept′a·bil′i·ty,** *n.* —**ac·cept′a·bly,** *adv.*

ac·cept·ance (ak sep′ təns) *n.* **1.** the act of taking something that is offered: *the acceptance of a present.* **2.** a favorable reception; approval: *The new product gained wide acceptance among the public.* **3.** a believing something to be true: *the acceptance of a scientific theory.*

ac·cess (ak′ses) *n., pl.* **ac·cess·es.** **1.** the right or permission to approach, enter, or use: *Foreign visitors were denied access to the missile base.* **2.** a way of approaching; means of approach: *The only access to the farm was a dirt road.* **3.** *Computers.* the ability to retrieve data from a file or from memory. —*v.t. Computers.* to retrieve (data) from a file or from memory.

access code, a combination of letters, numbers, or other symbols that a person must enter into a computer or other device so that it will respond to further commands.

ac·ces·si·ble (ak ses′ə bəl) *adj.* **1.** able to be reached, entered, or approached: *When the new highway is finished, the airport will be accessible from all directions.* **2.** able to be acquired; obtainable; attainable: *The information you want is not readily accessible.* —**ac·ces′si·bil′i·ty,** *n.* —**ac·ces′si·bly,** *adv.*

ac·ces·sion (ak sesh′ən) *n.* **1.** the act of coming into control or possession of something, such as an office, title, or position: *the accession of a monarch to the throne.* **2.** an increase by the addition of something: *The library collection was enlarged by the accession of fifty volumes.* **3.** something that is added: *The new books were a valuable accession.*

ac·ces·so·ry (ak ses′ə rē) *also,* **ac·ces·sa·ry.** *n., pl.* **ac·ces·so·ries.** **1.** something that is not necessary but adds to appearance or usefulness; extra thing that is helpful in a secondary way: *A radio is a car accessory. The gloves, hat, purse, and other accessories match the dress.* **2.** a person who, without being present at the scene of a crime, helps another in committing the crime or in escaping from the law after the crime. —*adj.* contributing in a secondary way; additional; extra: *Including a map of zip codes is an accessory function of a telephone directory.*

ac·ci·dent (ak′si dənt) *n.* **1.** something that happens unexpectedly or without apparent cause or reason: *The discovery of oil under the farm was a happy accident.* **2.** an unfortunate event that is not expected or intended, usually causing harm or injury; mishap: *a traffic accident.* **3.** chance; fortune: *I found that missing watch by accident while cleaning out my desk.*

ac·ci·den·tal (ak′si den′təl) *adj.* happening by chance; unexpected; not intended: *The European discovery of America was accidental.* —*n. Music.* a sign, such as a flat, sharp, or natural, that does not appear in the key signature and changes the pitch of the note or notes it goes before.

ac·ci·den·tal·ly (ak′si den′tə lē, ak′sə dent′lē) *adv.* by chance: *I met my friends accidentally on the bus.*

ac·claim (ə klām′) *v.t.* **1.** to greet or welcome with loud or enthusiastic approval; hail; applaud: *The crowd acclaimed the astronauts.* **2.** to announce or declare with strong approval: *The judges acclaimed our team the winner.* —*n.* enthusiastic praise or welcome.

ac·cla·ma·tion (ak′lə mā′shən) *n.* **1.** an enthusiastic show of approval: *The victorious team was received with acclamation by its fans.* **2.** a vote by voice, especially an enthusiastic or unanimous vote of approval: *The motion was passed by acclamation.*

ac·cli·mate (ak′lə māt′, ə klī′mit) *v.,* **ac·cli·mat·ed, ac·cli·mat·ing.** —*v.t.* to adjust or adapt to a new place or situation, or to new surroundings: *We quickly acclimated ourselves to the cold weather.* —*v.i.* to become adjusted or adapted to a new place or situation, or to new surroundings: *The fish acclimated easily to their new tank.* —**ac′cli·ma′tion,** *n.*

ac·cli·ma·tize (ə klī′mə tīz′) *v.t., v.i.,* **ac·cli·ma·tized, ac·cli·ma·tiz·ing.** to acclimate. —**ac·cli·ma·ti·za′tion,** *n.*

ac·co·lade (ak′ə lād′) *n.* **1.** something given as an award or honor: *The scientist received many accolades for the new theory.* **2.** the ceremony used in making someone a knight, usually a tap on the shoulder with a sword.

ac·com·mo·date (ə kom′ə dāt′) *v.,* **ac·com·modat·ed, ac·com·mo·dat·ing.** —*v.t.* **1.** to have or make room for; hold: *This car can accommodate five passengers.* **2.** to furnish with a place to stay or sleep: *That motel can accommodate 200 guests.* **3.** to do a favor or service for; help; oblige: *When we asked for directions, the farmer was happy to accommodate us.* **4.** to make fit or suitable; adapt; adjust: *Accommodate yourself to the new situation.* —*v.i.* to come into adjustment; become adjusted: *The lens of the eye accommodates in order to see objects at different distances.*

ac·com·mo·dat·ing (ə kom′ə dā′ting) *adj.* ready or willing to help; helpful; obliging: *The accommodating police officer directed us to our destination.* —**ac·com′mo·dat′ing·ly,** *adv.*

ac·com·mo·da·tion (ə kom′ə dā′shən) *n.* **1.** the act of accommodating or the state of being accommodated; adjustment; adaptation. **2.** often, **accommodations.** a place to stay or sleep, often with food: *accommodations at a motel, tourist accommodations on an airplane.* **3.** aid, comfort, or convenience: *These rest areas are for the accommodation of travelers.* **4.** something that fills a need or is helpful, such as a loan. **5.** the automatic adjustment of the lens of the eye for seeing objects at different distances.

ac·com·pa·ni·ment (ə kum′pə ni mənt) *n.* **1.** a thing that goes along with something else: *We had stuffing and cranberry sauce as accompaniments to our turkey.* **2.** a musical part that provides a background for a main part: *a violin piece with piano accompaniment.*

ac·com·pa·nist (ə kum′pə nist) *n.* a person who performs a musical accompaniment.

ac·com·pa·ny (ə kum′pə nē) *v.t.,* **ac·com·pa·nied, ac·com·pa·ny·ing.** **1.** to go along or in company with; act as a companion or escort to: *I'll accompany you to the theater.* **2.** to be or happen in connection or combination with: *Slides accompanied the lecture.* **3.** to perform a musical accompaniment for or to: *to accompany a violinist on the piano.*

ac·com·plice (ə kom′plis) *n.* a person who knowingly helps another in committing a crime or in other wrongdoing: *The driver of the car used in the escape was an accomplice of the robber.*

ac·com·plish (ə kom′plish) *v.t.* to succeed in completing or carrying out; perform: *We accomplished the cleaning of the house in two hours. Did you accomplish everything you wanted?*

ac·com·plished (ə kom′plisht) *adj.* **1.** successfully completed; done: *an accomplished task.* **2.** skilled; expert: *an accomplished drummer.*

ac·com·plish·ment (ə kom′plish mənt) *n.* **1.** the act of accomplishing or the state of being accomplished; completion: *The accomplishment of our goal will be difficult.* **2.** something done successfully; achievement: *The defeat of smallpox was a great accomplishment.* **3.** a skill, art, or ability, especially one that is acquired through training: *a person of many accomplishments.*

---

at; āpe; fär; câre; end; mē; it; īce; pîerce; hot; ōld;
sông, fôrk; oil; out; up; ūse; rüle; pull; tûrn; chin;
sing; shop; thin; this; hw in white; zh in treasure.
The symbol ə stands for the unstressed vowel sound
heard in about, taken, pencil, lemon, and circus.

ac·cord (ə kôrd′) *n.* **1.** the state of being in agreement; harmony: *The decision was in accord with the wishes of the people.* **2.** an agreement between parties, especially one between nations. —*v.t.* to grant or give as earned or due; concede: *to be accorded praise for one's achievements.* —*v.i.* to be in harmony or agreement: *My opinions on politics accord with yours.*
 •**of one's own accord** or **on one's own accord.** by a person's own choice or will; voluntarily: *The children cleaned their room of their own accord.*

ac·cord·ance (ə kôr′dəns) *n.* **1.** the state of being in agreement; harmony: *in accordance with the rules. The two groups acted in accordance.* **2.** the act of according, granting, or giving.

ac·cord·ing (ə kôr′ding) *adj.* in harmony; agreeing.
 •**according to. a.** in agreement with: *to go according to plan.* **b.** in proportion to; in relation to: *to be paid according to the work done.* **c.** as stated by or in; on the authority of: *According to the radio, it will snow today.*

ac·cord·ing·ly (ə kôr′ding lē) *adv.* **1.** in a fitting or suitable manner: *The dance is informal, so dress accordingly.* **2.** as a result; therefore.

ac·cor·di·on (ə kôr′dē ən) *n.* a portable musical wind instrument with keys, metal reeds, and a bellows. It produces tones when the player squeezes or expands the bellows, forcing air through the reeds. —*adj.* resembling the folds of the bellows of an accordion: *a skirt with accordion pleats.*

accordion

ac·cost (ə kôst′) *v.t.* to approach boldly and speak to: *The movie star was accosted by a group of dedicated fans seeking autographs.*

ac·count (ə kount′) *n.* **1.** a spoken or written statement; report; description: *The witness gave a detailed account of the accident. I read an account of the fire in the newspaper.* **2.** a statement of reasons, causes, or grounds; explanation: *Give us an account of your strange behavior.* **3.** a record or statement of business or financial dealings: *household accounts.* **4.** a sum of money deposited with a bank; bank account. **5.** a firm or company that is a client or customer: *That advertising agency has two new accounts.* **6.** worth; importance: *a matter of no account.* —*v.t.* to consider to be: *I account them honest.*
 •**on account. a.** as partial payment of a larger amount. **b.** on credit: *We bought the television on account.*
 •**on account of. a.** because of: *a game delayed on account of rain.* **b.** for the sake of; in consideration of.
 •**on no account.** under no circumstances; never: *On no account should you leave the baby at home alone.*
 •**on one's account.** for one's sake or benefit: *Don't leave the party early on my account.*
 •**to account for. a.** to give a satisfactory explanation for: *How do you account for your lateness?* **b.** to be the reason for: *The heavy snowfall accounts for the large number of traffic accidents.* **c.** to be responsible for: *The salesperson had to account for all the money lost.*
 •**to call to account. a.** to demand an explanation from:

They were called to account for their lateness. **b.** to scold; reprimand; rebuke.
 •**to give a good account of oneself.** to behave or perform well.
 •**to take account of** or **to take into account. a.** to consider as an element or factor; allow for: *Take into account the delays we've had.* **b.** to take note of: *History will take account of their achievements.*

ac·count·a·ble (ə koun′tə bəl) *adj.* **1.** liable to be called to account; responsible: *You must be held accountable for your actions.* **2.** capable of being explained: *Their lateness was accountable; they had a flat tire on the way.* —**ac·count′a·bil′i·ty,** *n.* —**ac·count′a·bly,** *adv.*

ac·count·ant (ə koun′tənt) *n.* a person whose job is recording, managing, or examining financial records or accounts, as for a business firm.

ac·count·ing (ə koun′ting) *n.* **1.** the system, practice, or occupation of recording, managing, or examining financial records or accounts. **2.** a formal report or statement, as of business dealings.

ac·cou·ter (ə kü′tər) *v.t.* to furnish with clothing or equipment: *to accouter an expedition to explore the jungle.*

ac·cou·ter·ments (ə kü′tər mənts) *also,* **ac·cou·tre·ments.** *pl. n.* **1.** personal equipment or accessories: *a camera, a guidebook, and the other accouterments of a tourist.* **2.** the equipment of a soldier other than weapons and clothing.

ac·cou·tre (ə kü′tər) *v.t.,* **ac·cou·tred, ac·cou·tring.** another spelling of **accouter.**

ac·cred·it (ə kred′it) *v.t.* **1.** to consider to belong to; ascribe or attribute; credit: *Scientists accredit the discovery of radium to Pierre and Marie Curie.* **2.** to send or provide with official authority or credentials: *to accredit an ambassador.* **3.** to certify as meeting certain official standards or requirements: *to accredit a college.* **4.** to accept as true; believe. —**ac·cred′i·ta′tion,** *n.*

ac·cre·tion (ə krē′shən) *n.* **1.** an increase in size by natural growth or by an outside addition. **2.** something that is added; outside addition.

ac·cru·al (ə krü′əl) *n.* **1.** the act or process of accruing. **2.** an amount accrued.

ac·crue (ə krü′) *v.i.,* **ac·crued, ac·cru·ing. 1.** to come as a result of natural growth or addition: *Many benefits accrued to the community from the construction of new housing.* **2.** to grow in amount; accumulate: *Interest on this savings account accrues from the day of deposit.*

acct., account; accountant.

ac·cu·mu·late (ə kū′myə lāt′) *v.,* **ac·cu·mu·lat·ed, ac·cu·mu·lat·ing.** —*v.t.* to gather or pile up (something); collect; amass: *to accumulate a large collection of books.* —*v.i.* to grow in size, quantity, or number; increase gradually: *A pile of papers had accumulated on my desk.*

ac·cu·mu·la·tion (ə kyü′myə lā′shən) *n.* **1.** the act or process of accumulating: *the accumulation of evidence.* **2.** something that is accumulated or has accumulated; mass; collection: *an accumulation of dust in a corner.*

ac·cu·ra·cy (ak′yər ə sē) *n.* freedom from errors or mistakes; correctness; exactness: *Can you describe with accuracy what happened?*

ac·cu·rate (ak′yər it) *adj.* **1.** making few or no errors or mistakes; exact; precise: *an accurate typist, an accurate watch.* **2.** without errors or mistakes; correct; truthful: *The early reports of the battle were not accurate.* —**ac′cu·rate·ly,** *adv.* —**ac′cu·rate·ness,** *n.*

ac·curs·ed (ə kûr′sid, ə kûrst′) *also,* **ac·curst** (ə kûrst′). *adj.* **1.** under a curse; doomed; ill-fated. **2.** worthy of curses; hateful. —**ac·curs′ed·ly,** *adv.* —**ac·curs′ed·ness,** *n.*

accus., accusative.

ac·cu·sa·tion (ak′yə zā′shən) *n.* **1.** a statement that a person has committed a crime or offense; charge of wrongdoing: *The accusation is that the defendant robbed the* *bank.* **2.** the act of accusing or the state of being accused.

ac·cu·sa·tive (ə kū′zə tiv) *n.* **1.** a grammatical case in Latin, Greek, and certain other languages that shows the direct object of a verb or the object of certain prepositions. It corresponds to the objective case in English. **2.** a word or construction in this case. *—adj.* relating to this case.

ac·cuse (ə kūz′) *v.t.,* **ac·cused, ac·cus·ing. 1.** to charge with a crime or offense; bring charges against: *The police accused them of rioting.* **2.** to find at fault or in error; blame: *My boss accused me of doing careless work.* **—ac·cus′er,** *n.*

ac·cused (ə kūzd′) *adj.* charged with a crime or offense. *—n.* a person or persons who are charged with a crime or offense, especially the defendant in a criminal case.

ac·cus·tom (ə kus′təm) *v.t.* to make familiar by use, custom, or habit: *Years as an actor had accustomed the candidate to public speaking.*

ac·cus·tomed (ə kus′təmd) *adj.* established by custom or habit; usual; customary; habitual: *The dog lay in its accustomed place by the fire.*

·**accustomed to.** in the habit of; used to: *I'm accustomed to sleeping late on Saturdays.*

ace (ās) *n.* **1.** a playing card having a single symbol of the suit it represents. **2.** a person who is an expert at something: *to be an ace at baseball.* **3.** a combat pilot who has destroyed five or more enemy planes in the air. **4.** in tennis and other racket games, a serve that the opponent fails to touch. *—adj.* performing at, or capable of performing at, the highest level; expert: *an ace pitcher.* *—v.t.* **1.** to make a serve that cannot be touched to: *The winner aced the loser five times.* **2.** *Informal.* to do very well on or in (a test or course): *I aced the math exam.*

·**within an ace of.** at the very point of; very close to.

ac·e·tate (as′i tāt′) *n.* **1.** a salt or ester of acetic acid. **2.** cellulose acetate or any of its products, especially a cellulose acetate fabric, fiber, or yarn.

a·ce·tic (ə sē′tik) *adj.* relating to or producing vinegar or acetic acid.

acetic acid, a colorless, liquid acid having a strong odor and a sour taste. It is the acid in vinegar and is widely used in the production of textile fibers, plastics, and drugs.

a·cet·y·lene (ə set′ə lēn′) *n.* a colorless, highly flammable gas that is widely used in combination with oxygen in the cutting and welding of metals.

a·ce·tyl·sal·i·cyl·ic acid (ə sē′təl sal′ə sil′ik) another name for **aspirin.**

ache (āk) *v.i.,* **ached, ach·ing. 1.** to have or be in pain, especially dull or continuous pain: *My teeth ached from the cold. The runner's whole body ached after the marathon.* **2.** *Informal.* to be eager; long; yearn: *The homesick sailor ached to return home.* *—n.* continuous, usually dull, pain: *an ache in one's back.*

a·chieve (ə chēv′) *v.t.,* **a·chieved, a·chiev·ing. 1.** to do or reach successfully; accomplish: *to achieve one's goals. We achieved all that we set out to do.* **2.** to have or get through effort; attain: *to achieve fame, to achieve the position of vice president.* **—a·chiev′er,** *n.*

a·chieve·ment (ə chēv′mənt) *n.* **1.** something achieved, especially by unusual effort or skill; accomplishment: *The invention of the telephone was a great achievement.* **2.** the act of achieving: *Achievement of a cure for the disease will involve much work and money.*

achievement test, a test measuring how much a person has learned in a particular subject over a certain period of time.

A·chil·les (ə kil′ēz) *n. Greek Legend.* a Greek warrior in the Trojan War. Achilles was killed by Paris, who wounded him in his heel, the only spot where he could be injured.

Achilles' heel, a weak or vulnerable point: *Math has always been my Achilles' heel.* [From the legendary Greek hero *Achilles,* who was vulnerable to injury only on his heel.]

Achilles' tendon, the tendon that joins the muscles of the calf to the bone of the heel.

ach·ro·mat·ic (ak′rə mat′ik) *adj.* **1.** without color. **2.** refracting white light without separating it into the colors of the spectrum: *Most windows are achromatic.*

ach·y (ā′kē) *adj.,* **ach·i·er, ach·i·est.** having or feeling an ache: *I felt achy all over when I had the flu.*

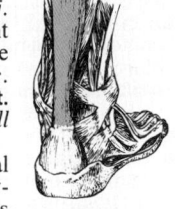

Achilles' tendon

ac·id (as′id) *n.* any of a class of chemical compounds containing hydrogen and having a sour taste in a water solution. Acids react with bases to form salts and turn blue litmus paper red. *—adj.* **1.** of, relating to, containing, or like an acid. **2. a.** sharp and biting to the taste. **b.** sour to the taste, as fermented milk. **3.** sharp, as in tone or manner; ill-tempered; biting: *acid remarks.* **—ac′id·ly,** *adv.* **—ac′id·ness,** *n.*

a·cid·ic (ə sid′ik) *adj.* containing or forming acid.

a·cid·i·fy (ə sid′ə fī′) *v.t., v.i.,* **a·cid·i·fied, a·cid·i·fy·ing.** to make acid or become acid.

a·cid·i·ty (ə sid′i tē) *n., pl.* **a·cid·i·ties. 1.** the quality or state of being or containing acid; sourness; tartness. **2.** the degree of being acid or the degree of acid contained: *The acidity of this soil is very high.*

acid rain, rain, sleet, or other water vapor polluted with sulfuric, nitric, or other acids formed from chemicals in the exhaust of automobiles, the smoke of some manufacturing plants, and various other sources, such as the by-products of coal-burning power plants.

acid rock, a type of rock music characterized by a hypnotic beat and long, slow instrumental solos. The music and lyrics sometimes suggest the taking of drugs or psychedelic experiences.

acid test, something that tests the real quality, character, or worth of a person or thing: *This election will be the acid test of that politician's popularity.* [From the use of acid as a test for gold.]

ac·knowl·edge (ak nol′ij) *v.t.,* **ac·knowl·edged, ac·knowl·edg·ing. 1.** to admit the truth or fact of; concede: *to acknowledge an error.* **2.** to recognize the authority, rights, or claims of: *The tribe acknowledged a new chief.* **3.** to show or express appreciation or gratitude for: *I acknowledged the gift by sending a note of thanks.* **4.** to show or make known that one has received or noticed (something): *The company acknowledged the letter of complaint with a prompt reply.*

ac·knowl·edg·ment (ak nol′ij mənt) *also,* **ac·knowl·edge·ment.** *n.* **1.** the act of admitting or conceding: *an acknowledgment of one's mistakes.* **2.** recognition, as of authority, rights, or claims: *acknowledgment of a court's jurisdiction.* **3.** a thing given, sent, or done to show that one has received something: *Their letter was an acknowledgment of the shipment.* **4.** an expression of gratitude, recognition, or appreciation: *an acknowledgment of a gift for graduation.*

ac·me (ak′mē) *n.* the highest point; peak; zenith: *Winning the Nobel Prize was the acme of the writer's career.*

ac·ne (ak′nē) *n.* a skin condition characterized by pimples or other blemishes on the face, back, or chest. It results from excessive secretion of oil by glands at the base of hair follicles. The oil and pus formed by invading bacteria build up and clog the pore that opens from the follicle to the skin.

at; āpe; fär; câre; end; mē; it; īce; pîerce; hot; ōld; sông, fôrk; oil; out; up; ūse; rüle; pùll; tûrn; chin; sing; shop; thin; this; hw in white; zh in treasure. The symbol ə stands for the unstressed vowel sound heard in about, taken, pencil, lemon, and circus.

A

ac·o·lyte (ak′ə līt′) *n.* **1.** a person who helps a minister or priest at certain religious services. **2.** any attendant or assistant; follower.

ac·o·nite (ak′ə nīt′) *n.* **1.** any of a group of mostly poisonous plants of the Northern Hemisphere, bearing blue, white, purple, or yellow hood-shaped flowers. Also, **wolfsbane, monkshood. 2.** a drug obtained from these plants, formerly used to relieve pain.

a·corn (ā′kôrn, ā′kərn) *n.* the nut of the oak tree.

a·cous·tic (ə küs′tik) *adj.* **1.** relating to the sense or organs of hearing, to sound, or to the science of sound: *An auditorium should have good acoustic qualities.* **2.** used to absorb and deaden sound: *acoustic tile.* **3.** (of musical instruments) not using or requiring electronic modification of sound: *an acoustic guitar.* Also, **a·cous·ti·cal** (ə küs′ti kəl). **—a·cous′ti·cal·ly,** *adv.*

a·cous·tics (ə küs′tiks) *n.* **1.** the qualities of a room, theater, auditorium, or the like that determine how well sound is carried and heard in it. ▲ used with a plural verb. **2.** the science that deals with sound. ▲ used with a singular verb.

ac·quaint (ə kwānt′) *v.t.* **1.** to make familiar: *Acquaint yourself with the new rules.* **2.** to let know; inform: *Shall we acquaint them with our decision before going on?*

ac·quaint·ance (ə kwān′təns) *n.* **1.** a person whom one knows, but who is not a close friend. **2.** a relationship between people who are not close friends; the state of being acquainted: *We had a brief acquaintance with them one summer.* **3.** knowledge of something, especially as a result of personal experience or contact; familiarity: *Two months in Dakar gave me an acquaintance with western Africa.*
·**to make someone's acquaintance.** to get to know someone.

ac·quaint·ance·ship (ə kwān′təns ship′) *n.* the state of being acquainted.

ac·quaint·ed (ə kwān′tid) *adj.* **1.** known to one, or each other, but not close friends: *Are you two acquainted?* **2.** familiar: *I have been one acquainted with the night* (Robert Frost).

ac·qui·esce (ak′wē es′) *v.i.,* **ac·qui·esced, ac·qui·esc·ing.** to consent or agree by remaining silent or by not raising objections; submit quietly: *In 1938 France and England acquiesced to Germany's occupation of Czechoslovakia.*

ac·qui·es·cence (ak′wē es′əns) *n.* the act of acquiescing; agreement without protest: *The rebels overthrew the government with the acquiescence of the army.*

ac·qui·es·cent (ak′wē es′ənt) *adj.* consenting or agreeing without protest: *They were acquiescent to our plan.* **—ac′qui·es′cent·ly,** *adv.*

ac·quire (ə kwīr′) *v.t.,* **ac·quired, ac·quir·ing.** to get possession of; gain or obtain as one's own: *to acquire wealth and property, to acquire an education, to acquire the ability to speak a foreign language.*

ac·quire·ment (ə kwīr′mənt) *n.* **1.** the act of acquiring: *the acquirement of wealth.* **2.** something acquired; attainment; accomplishment.

ac·qui·si·tion (ak′wə zish′ən) *n.* **1.** the act of acquiring: *Acquisition of Alaska by the United States took place in 1867.* **2.** something received or acquired: *The museum displayed its recent acquisitions.*

ac·quis·i·tive (ə kwiz′i tiv) *adj.* eager or inclined to acquire things; grasping: *a greedy and acquisitive person.* **—ac·quis′i·tive·ly,** *adv.* **—ac·quis′i·tive·ness,** *n.*

ac·quit (ə kwit′) *v.t.,* **ac·quit·ted, ac·quit·ting. 1.** to free or clear from an accusation or charge of crime; declare not guilty; exonerate: *The jury acquitted the defendant after reviewing the evidence.* **2.** to conduct (oneself); behave: *The team acquitted itself well in its first game.*

ac·quit·tal (ə kwit′əl) *n.* a setting free from a criminal charge by a verdict of not guilty: *The jury voted for acquittal of the defendant.*

a·cre (ā′kər) *n.* **1.** a measure of land equal to 43,560 square feet (1.61 hectares), or 160 square rods. **2. acres.** lands; property.

a·cre·age (ā′kər ij) *n.* an area of land measured in acres: *How much acreage does that farmer own?*

ac·rid (ak′rid) *adj.* **1.** burning, biting, or irritating to the taste, smell, or eyes: *the acrid smell of smoke.* **2.** biting or cutting in manner, temper, or tone: *The critic made acrid comments about the new play.* **—ac′rid·ly,** *adv.* **—ac′rid·ness,** *n.*

ac·ri·mo·ni·ous (ak′rə mō′nē əs) *adj.* bitter or sarcastic in temper, manner, or tone; caustic: *The book is an acrimonious attack on the present administration.* **—ac′ri·mo′ni·ous·ly,** *adv.* **—ac′ri·mo′ni·ous·ness,** *n.*

ac·ri·mo·ny (ak′rə mō′nē) *n.* sharpness or bitterness in temper, manner, or tone: *the acrimony of a victim's remarks.*

ac·ro·bat (ak′rə bat′) *n.* a person who performs or can perform feats or stunts requiring great physical strength, control, and agility, such as swinging on a trapeze or walking on a tightrope.

ac·ro·bat·ic (ak′rə bat′ik) *adj.* relating to or like an acrobat or acrobatics: *an acrobatic leap.* **—ac′ro·bat′i·cal·ly,** *adv.*

ac·ro·bat·ics (ak′rə bat′iks) *pl. n.* **1.** the stunts or skills of an acrobat. **2.** any display of great skill or agility: *The pianist performed musical acrobatics.*

ac·ro·nym (ak′rə nim′) *n.* a word formed by combining the first letters or syllables of a series of other words. *Radar* is an acronym for *r*adio *d*etecting *a*nd *r*anging.
▲ Acronyms are short forms of longer terms, as are **abbreviations.** Although there are no specific rules for determining which short forms become acronyms and which become abbreviations, there are certain differences between them. **Acronyms** are words and are therefore pronounced in the same way as other words. The word *scuba* is an acronym formed from *s*elf-contained *u*nderwater *b*reathing *a*pparatus. **Abbreviations** are not independent words and are not pronounced as full words, but are spoken by naming the individual letters. *C.O.D.* is the abbreviation of *c*ash *o*n *d*elivery. Sometimes an abbreviation becomes an acronym. For example, the abbreviation *a.w.o.l.,* meaning *a*bsent *w*ithout *l*eave (from military duty), is now usually written as a word, *AWOL,* and pronounced (ā′wôl).

a·crop·o·lis (ə krop′ə lis) *n., pl.* **a·crop·o·lis·es. 1.** a strongly fortified place in an ancient Greek city, usually built on the highest part. **2. Acropolis.** a fortified place on the highest hill in ancient Athens, famous for its temples and monuments, including the Parthenon.

Acropolis

a·cross (ə krôs′) *adv.* **1.** from one side to the other: *We came across in a boat.* **2.** on or to the other side: *We'll soon be across.* **—prep. 1.** from one side of to the other;

over: *We drove across the bridge.* **2.** on the other side of; beyond: *They live in the house across the street.* **3.** in a direction so as to cross: *The cat walked across our path.*

·**to come across** or **to run across.** to come into contact with or find unexpectedly: *I came across some old coins when I cleaned the attic.*

a·cros·tic (ə krôs′tik) *n.* a poem or other arrangement of words in which the first, last, or certain other letters in each line, taken in order, form a word or a phrase.

a·cryl·ic (ə kril′-ik) *n.* **1.** see a- crylic fiber. **2.** see acrylic resin. **3.** a paint that contains an acrylic resin. —*adj.* of or containing an acrylic fiber or acrylic resin. [Formed from the Latin word *acer* meaning "sharp," the Greek word *hylē* meaning "matter," and the English suffix *–ic*.]

```
Few plants grow when it is cold,
Locked up in the ground's stronghold.
Over them the snowflakes fall,
Winter white till April's call.
Earth wakes up, it's almost May,
Rain brings blossoms every day.
```

acrostic

acrylic fiber, any of a group of synthetic textile fibers made from acrylic resins. When woven, they make a long-wearing, lightweight fabric that is resistant to wrinkles.

acrylic resin, any of a group of synthetic polymers used especially in paints and textiles.

act (akt) *n.* **1.** something done; deed: *Saving the child was an act of bravery.* **2.** the process of doing something: *The burglars were caught in the act of opening the safe.* **3.** a formal decision or law, as of a legislature: *The United States can declare war only by an act of Congress.* **4.** one of the main divisions of a play or opera: *"Hamlet" has five acts.* **5.** a short performance that is usually one of several on a program: *The magician's act follows the intermission.* **6.** a show of false or insincere behavior; pretense: *All their concern was just an act.* —*v.i.* **1.** to do or perform something: *The doctor acted quickly to save the injured child.* **2.** to conduct oneself; behave: *If you act like adults we'll let you in.* **3.** to be an actor; play a part: *The star has acted in several recent films.* **4.** to have or produce an effect: *The drug acted quickly.* **5.** to pretend to be: *I acted calm, although I was very worried.* **6.** to serve or function: *This box will act as a table.* —*v.t.* **1.** to behave in a manner that is suitable for: *Act your age.* **2.** to play the part of; perform: *The star acts the lead with great passion.* **3.** to pretend to be or behave like: *to act the fool.*

·**to act on** or **to act upon.** to behave according to; follow: *Act quickly on this order.*

·**to act up.** *Informal.* **a.** to behave mischievously or playfully: *The twins are acting up again.* **b.** to cause trouble: *The car's engine acted up on the highway.*

ACTH, a hormone that is produced by the pituitary gland and stimulates the adrenal gland to secrete its hormones. It can be obtained from the pituitary gland of hogs and other animals for use in the treatment of certain diseases, such as arthritis, rheumatic fever, and asthma. It is also manufactured synthetically.

act·ing (ak′ting) *adj.* temporarily performing the duties of another: *The council president served as the acting mayor.* —*n.* the act, art, or occupation of performing as an actor.

ac·tin·ic (ak tin′ik) *adj.* relating to or having actinism: *actinic rays.*

ac·tin·ism (ak′tə niz′əm) *n.* the property of ultraviolet rays, X rays, and other forms of radiant energy that enables them to produce chemical changes.

ac·tin·i·um (ak tin′ē əm) *n.* a rare, silver-white, poisonous, radioactive metallic element found in pitchblende and other uranium ores. Symbol: **Ac** [Formed from the

Greek word *aktis* meaning "ray." The radioactivity of actinium causes it to glow in the dark.]

ac·tion (ak′shən) *n.* **1.** the process of acting or doing: *The action of throwing a ball involves many different muscles.* **2.** great movement or activity: *The stadium was bustling with action.* **3.** a thing that is done; act; deed: *Actions speak louder than words.* **4. actions.** behavior; conduct: *We couldn't understand our guest's strange actions at the party.* **5.** force or influence: *The action of waves wears away rock.* **6.** a way of moving or operating: *a washing machine with gentle action.* **7.** a mechanism by which something operates: *the action of a rifle.* **8.** battle; combat. **9.** the events in a story, play, or the like. **10.** a lawsuit. **11.** tendency to act forcefully or quickly: *a person of action.*

·**in action.** in a state of activity; at work; in operation.

·**to take action.** to become active; start to act: *The police took action immediately to find the criminal.*

action verb, a verb that expresses action. Action verbs can be transitive, as *radiate* in *The sun radiates light and warmth,* or intransitive, as *overslept* in *Yesterday I overslept and was late for work.*

ac·ti·vate (ak′tə vāt′) *v.t.,* **ac·ti·vat·ed, ac·ti·vat·ing.** **1.** to cause to work or operate; put into action; make active: *Turning this switch activates the machine. The general activated a reserve unit.* **2.** *Physics.* to make radioactive. **3.** *Chemistry.* to cause a reaction in; make more reactive. —**ac′ti·va′tion,** *n.*

ac·tive (ak′tiv) *adj.* **1.** full of action or movement; busy: *an active child.* **2.** having or showing energy; lively; vigorous: *an active mind.* **3.** taking part in an action; participating: *Everyone must take an active part in decorating for the dance.* **4.** acting or capable of acting; functioning: *an active volcano.* **5.** *Grammar.* relating to or designating the voice of a verb whose subject is shown as performing the action expressed by the verb. In the sentences *My parents bought a car* and *I live in Ohio* the verbs *bought* and *live* are in the active voice. —*n.* **1.** the active voice. **2.** a verb form in this voice. —**ac′tive·ly,** *adv.* —**ac′tive·ness,** *n.*

active duty, full-time military service.

ac·tiv·ist (ak′tə vist) *n.* a person who believes in and actively supports a cause: *a civil rights activist.*

ac·tiv·i·ty (ak tiv′i tē) *n., pl.* **ac·tiv·i·ties.** **1.** the quality or state of being active; movement: *the activity of the mind.* **2.** brisk or vigorous action; energy; liveliness: *There was little activity in the quiet town.* **3.** a thing done or to be done: *The activity of insects damaged the tree. I am involved in many school activities.*

act of God, an occurrence or event that is caused by the forces of nature and could not have been foreseen or prevented by humans, such as an earthquake.

ac·tor (ak′tər) *n.* **1.** a person who plays a role or performs, as in a play, motion picture, television program, or the like. **2.** a person who acts; doer; participant.

ac·tress (ak′tris) *n., pl.* **ac·tress·es.** a woman or girl who plays a role or performs, as in a play, motion picture, television program, or the like.

Acts (akts) *n.* a book of the New Testament, thought to have been written by the apostle Luke. Also, **Acts of the Apostles.**

ac·tu·al (ak′chü əl) *adj.* existing or happening, as opposed to imagined or possible; real: *The actual result differed from what we had expected.*

A

at; āpe; fär; câre; end; mē; it; īce; pîerce; hot; ōld; sông; fôrk; oil; out; up; ūse; rüle; pull; tûrn; chin; sing; shop; thin; this; hw in white; zh in treasure. The symbol ə stands for the unstressed vowel sound heard in about, taken, pencil, lemon, and circus.

ac·tu·al·i·ty (ak′chü al′i tē) *n., pl.* **ac·tu·al·i·ties.**
1. the state or quality of being actual; reality. **2.** an actual condition or circumstance; fact.

ac·tu·al·ly (ak′chü ə lē) *adv.* in reality or fact; really.

ac·tu·ate (ak′chü āt′) *v.t.,* **ac·tu·at·ed, ac·tu·at·ing.**
1. to put into action or motion: *A spring actuates the trap.*
2. to incite or influence to act; motivate: *to be actuated by a desire for fame.* —**ac′tu·a′tion,** *n.* —**ac′·tu·a′tor,** *n.*

a·cu·i·ty (ə kū′i tē) *n.* acuteness of perception; keenness; sharpness: *Safe driving requires visual and mental acuity at all times.*

a·cu·men (ə kū′mən) *n.* keenness of mind or judgment: *business acumen.*

ac·u·punc·ture (ak′yü pungk′chər) *n.* the practice, originally Chinese, of inserting needles into various parts of the body in order to treat diseases or to serve as an anesthetic during surgery. [Formed from the Latin word *acus* meaning "needle" + the English word *puncture.*]

a·cute (ə kūt′) *adj.* **1.** having or showing quickness and keenness in seeing and understanding: *an acute mind.*
2. very sensitive; keen: *acute hearing.* **3.** sharp; intense: *acute pain.* **4.** (of a disease) developing and reaching a crisis quickly: *acute appendicitis.* **5.** very serious; crucial: *an acute need for funds.* **6.** high in pitch; shrill: *Dogs can hear acute sounds that people cannot hear.*
[From the Latin word *acutus* meaning "sharp, severe," going back to the word *acus* "needle."] —**a·cute′ly,** *adv.* —**a·cute′ness,** *n.*

acute accent, a mark used in certain languages to indicate such things as the sound of a vowel, as in French *été,* or the syllable that receives the accent, as in Spanish *corazón.*

acute angle, an angle whose measure is between 0 and 90 degrees.

ad (ad) *n.* another word for **advertisement.**

ad– *prefix* used to express motion toward or nearness to: *advance, adjoin.*

A.D., in the (given) year since the birth of Jesus. ▲ used before a number in expressing dates: *Nero became emperor of Rome in* A.D. *54.* [Abbreviation of the Latin phrase *anno Domini* meaning "in the year of the Lord."]

ad·age (ad′ij) *n.* an old and familiar saying that is believed to be true; proverb. For example: *The early bird catches the worm.*

a·da·gi·o (ə dä′ zhē ō′, ə dä′ jē o′)*Music. adv.* slowly. —*adj.* slow. —*n., pl.* **a·da·gi·os. 1.** a musical composition, movement, or part in adagio tempo. **2.** a ballet dance in slow tempo.

ad·a·mant (ad′ə mənt, ad′ə mant′) *adj.* not changing position at all; totally unyielding: *The child was adamant in refusing to join in the game.* —*n.* in old legends, a substance so hard that it could not be cut or broken. [From the Old French word *adamant* meaning "hardest metal," going back to the Greek word *adamas,* with the same meaning.] —**ad′a·mant·ly,** *adv.*

Ad·am's apple (ad′əmz) a lump in the throat just below the chin, formed by the largest cartilage of the larynx.

a·dapt (ə dapt′) *v.t.* **1.** to change to meet new requirements or to fit new uses; modify; alter: *Can we adapt this machine to run on batteries?* **2.** to adjust (oneself) to new conditions or surroundings. —*v.i.* to become adjusted: *Mastodons probably became extinct because they could not adapt to changes in the environment.*
▲ **Adapt** and **adopt** have different meanings, but they are often confused because they are spelled and pronounced in somewhat the same way. **Adapt** means to change something so that it can be used for another purpose: *The writer adapted the novel for television.* **Adopt** means to take something for one's own: *The school adopted the name "Wildcats" for its football team.*

a·dapt·a·ble (ə dapt′ə bəl) *adj.* capable of being adapted or of adapting. —**a·dapt′a·bil′i·ty,** *n.* —**a·dapt′a·ble·ness,** *n.*

ad·ap·ta·tion (ad′əp tā′shən) *n.* **1.** the act of adapting or the state of being adapted. **2.** a thing produced by adapting: *This story is an adaptation of an old folk tale.*
3. a change in a plant or animal so that it is better suited to survive in its environment.

a·dapt·ed (ə dap′tid) *adj.* changed for new or different conditions; suited; fitted.

a·dapt·er (ə dap′tər) *n.* **1.** a person who adapts something. **2.** a device for modi-

adapted
The hummingbird's bill is ideally adapted for reaching nectar.

fying an apparatus for a new use. **3.** a device for connecting two pieces of equipment that would not otherwise operate together.

a·dap·tive (ə dap′tiv) *adj.* capable of or resulting from adaptation: *The long beak of a hummingbird is an adaptive trait.*

add (ad) *v.t.* **1.** to put (something) together with another or others of the same kind: *I added a new stamp to my collection.* **2.** to join together or combine with: *to add cream to coffee, to add a porch to a house.* **3.** to find the result of putting numbers together: *to add a column of figures.* **4.** to say or write further: *Do you wish to add anything to what has been said?* —*v.i.* **1.** to find the sum of numbers; perform addition: *Most people learn to add before they learn to multiply.* **2.** to make or serve as another; contribute something more: *The balloons added to the party atmosphere. Don't add to our problems by complaining.*
•**to add up.** to be meaningful or reasonable; make sense: *The facts don't add up in this case.*
•**to add up to.** to amount to: *Their actions added up to a deliberate violation of the rules.*

ad·dend (ad′end, ə dend′) *n.* any number or quantity that is to be added to another. In the example 8 + 4 = 12, 8 and 4 are the addends.

ad·den·dum (ə den′dəm) *n., pl.* **ad·den·da** (ə den′də). something that is added; addition.

ad·der (ad′ər) *n.* **1.** a poisonous snake of northern Europe and Asia, having a brown skin with black markings. **2.** the hognose snake of North America. **3.** any of various snakes of Africa, especially the puff adder. [From the Middle English word *naddre* meaning "a viper," from the Old English word *nǣdre.* The form *adder* developed from the Middle English phrase *a naddre* when it was mistakenly divided as *an addre.*]

ad·dict (*n.,* ad′ikt; *v.,* ə dikt′) *n.* **1.** a person who has a strong and constant need for some substance, especially a drug: *a cocaine addict.* **2.** a person who is strongly devoted to some activity or pleasure. —*v.t.* to cause (someone) to become an addict.

ad·dict·ed (ə dik′tid) *adj.* **1.** unable to do without some substance: *to be addicted to a drug.* **2.** inclined by strong habit or preference: *to be addicted to watching television.*

ad·dic·tion (ə dik′shən) *n.* the condition of being addicted, especially complete dependence on a drug.

ad·dic·tive (ə dik′tiv) *adj.* causing addiction: *Heroin is an addictive drug.*

adding machine, a machine consisting of a set of keys that, when struck, print numbers on a roll of paper. Adding machines can add, and some can also subtract, multiply, and divide.

ad·di·tion (ə dish′ən) *n.* **1.** the act or process of adding: *The addition of seasoning improved the flavor of the stew.*

2. the process of finding the amount made by two or more numbers together. $9 + 2 + 5 = 16$ is an example of addition. **3.** something that is added: *to build an addition to the museum.*
　·in addition or **in addition to.** something more (than); as well; also; besides: *In addition to cleaning, this machine can spray paint.*

ad·di·tion·al (ə dish′ə nəl) *adj.* more; added; further: *to make additional money by working nights.* —**ad·di′tion·al·ly,** *adv.*

ad·di·tive (ad′i tiv) *n.* a substance added in small quantities to improve, change, or preserve another substance or thing: *a gasoline additive, an additive put in a food to prevent spoiling.* —*adj.* relating to or involving addition.

additive identity, a number that, when added to another number, produces a sum equal to that other number. Zero is the additive identity, since $0 + 5 = 5$ and $¾ + 0 = ¾$.

additive inverse, either one of a pair of numbers whose sum is zero, such as 5 and −5 or ¾ and −¾.

ad·dle (ad′əl) *v.,* **ad·dled, ad·dling.** *v.t.* **1.** to make confused. **2.** to cause (as an egg) to become rotten. —*v.i.* to become addled.

ad·dress (*n.,* ə dres′, ad′res; *v.,* ə dres′) *n., pl.* **ad·dress·es. 1.** a formal speech: *The president's address to the nation will be on television.* **2.** the place at which a person lives or an organization is located: *Our address is 90 Pine Lane. That store's address is 545 Main Street.* **3.** the writing on a letter, package, or other item indicating where it is to be delivered. **4.** personal manner in conversation: *to have the poise and address of a diplomat.* **5. Computers.** a location in the memory of a computer where specific information can be found. —*v.t.* **1.** to speak formally to: *to address a convention.* **2.** to direct (writing or speech): *The judge addressed some remarks to the jury.* **3.** to direct (oneself) in speech or writing: *I addressed myself to the crowd.* **4.** to write the destination on (a letter, package, or other item to be delivered.) **5.** to use proper form in speaking or writing to: *You should address the judge as "Your Honor."* **6.** to direct one's energies or attention; apply (oneself): *I'll address myself to the hardest job first.*

ad·dress·ee (ad′re sē′) *n.* a person to whom a letter, package, or other item is addressed.

ad·duce (ə düs′, ə dūs′) *v.t.,* **ad·duced, ad·duc·ing.** to present as proof, reason, or example: *The speaker adduced a great many facts to support the proposition.*

ad·e·nine (ad′ə nēn′) *n.* a purine base that is an essential constituent of DNA and RNA.

ad·e·noi·dal (ad′ə noi′dəl) *adj.* relating to the adenoids.

ad·e·noids (ad′ə noidz′) *pl. n.* a mass of glandular tissue in the upper part of the throat, behind the nose. This tissue sometimes becomes swollen enough to make speaking and breathing difficult.

a·dept (*adj.,* ə dept′; *n.,* ad′ept) *adj.* highly skilled; expert; proficient. —*n.* a person who is highly skilled; an expert. —**a·dept′ly,** *adv.* —**a·dept′ness,** *n.*

ad·e·qua·cy (ad′i kwə sē) *n.* the state of being adequate.

ad·e·quate (ad′i kwit) *adj.* **1.** as much as is needed for a certain purpose; sufficient; enough: *In order for crops to grow, there must be adequate rainfall.* **2.** good enough; satisfactory: *Your work is adequate if not outstanding.* —**ad′e·quate·ly,** *adv.* —**ad′e·quate·ness,** *n.*

ad·here (ad hîr′) *v.i.,* **ad·hered, ad·her·ing. 1.** to stick or hold fast: *The gum adhered to my shoe.* **2.** to hold

adenoids

faithfully or firmly; remain attached or devoted; follow closely: *to adhere to a plan.*

ad·her·ence (ad hîr′əns) *n.* **1.** the act or the state of adhering. **2.** firm attachment; faithful support: *adherence to a cause, adherence to a belief.*

ad·her·ent (ad hîr′ənt) *n.* a person who believes in or follows a cause, leader, organization, or the like; firm supporter; advocate: *an adherent of car safety laws.* —*adj.* sticking or holding fast; adhering.

ad·he·sion (ad hē′zhən) *n.* **1.** the act or the state of sticking or holding fast. **2.** faithful attachment; adherence. **3.** the abnormal growing together of organs or parts that are normally separate.

ad·he·sive (ad hē′siv) *adj.* **1.** tending to stick or hold fast; clinging: *Paste and glue have adhesive properties.* **2.** having a sticky surface that will hold fast to something; gummed: *an adhesive label.* —*n.* **1.** an adhesive substance: *Glue is an adhesive.* **2.** see **adhesive tape.** —**ad·he′sive·ness,** *n.*

adhesive tape, a tape coated on one side with a sticky substance.

ad hoc (ad hok′) for a specific and limited purpose: *an ad hoc committee.* [From the Latin phrase *ad hoc* meaning "to this."]

a·dieu (ə dü′, ə dū′) *interj.* good-by; farewell. —*n., pl.* **a·dieus** or **a·dieux** (ə düz′, ə dūz′). good-by; farewell. [From the Old French expression *adieu,* from the words *a* (from Latin *ad*) meaning "to" + *dieu* meaning "God" (from the Latin word *deus* "god.")]

ad in·fi·ni·tum (ad′ in′fə nī′təm) without limit; endlessly. [From the Latin phrase *ad infinitum* meaning "to the endless."]

a·di·os (ä′dē ōs′) *interj.* good-by; farewell. —*n., pl.* **a·di·os·es.** good-by; farewell. [From the Spanish expression *adiós,* from the words *a* (from Latin *ad*) meaning "to" + *diós* meaning "God" (from the Latin word *deus* "god").]

ad·i·pose (ad′ə pōs′) *adj.* relating to animal fat; fatty: *adipose tissue.*

adj., adjective.

ad·ja·cent (ə jā′sənt) *adj.* lying next to or near; adjoining: *the field adjacent to the house.* —**ad·ja′cent·ly,** *adv.*

adjacent angle, in geometry, either of two angles having the same vertex and a common side.

ad·jec·ti·val (aj′ik tī′vəl) *adj.* **1.** of or relating to an adjective: *The suffixes "-ous" and "-ful" are adjectival endings.* **2.** functioning as an adjective. In the sentence "The freight handling office is closed," *freight handling* is an adjectival phrase. —**ad′jec·ti′val·ly,** *adv.*

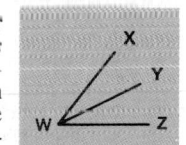

adjacent angles
XWY and *YWZ*
are adjacent
angles

ad·jec·tive (aj′ik tiv) *n.* a word that modifies a noun or pronoun. An adjective may describe the word it modifies (the *red* car, a *sad* song, the tree is *tall*) or in some way limit the word (*their* bat, *many* books, *three* dogs). Adjectives may appear next to the word they modify, or they may be used after a noun and the verb "seem" (The dog seems *hungry*) or after a noun and the verb "to be" (The baby is *asleep*). —*adj.* relating to or used as an adjective.

ad·join (ə join′) *v.t.* to be very close to or touch on; be next to: *The garage adjoins the house.* —*v.i.* to be close together or touching: *The two farms adjoin.*

at; āpe; fär; câre; end; mē; it; īce; pîerce; hot; ōld; sông, fôrk; oil; out; up; ūse; rüle; pùll; tûrn; chin; sing; shop; thin; this; hw in white; zh in treasure. The symbol ə stands for the unstressed vowel sound heard in about, taken, pencil, lemon, and circus.

ad·join·ing (ə joi′ning) *adj.* being next to; adjacent: *The school has an adjoining playground.*

ad·journ (ə jûrn′) *v.t.* to put off to a later time; postpone; defer: *to adjourn a meeting. The judge adjourned the trial until the following week.* —*v.i.* **1.** to stop work or proceedings until a later time: *The Senate adjourned for the summer.* **2.** *Informal.* to go from one place to another: *Since we've finished eating, let's adjourn to the living room.*

ad·journ·ment (ə jûrn′mənt) *n.* **1.** the act of adjourning or the state of being adjourned: *The chair called for a vote on adjournment.* **2.** the time during which a group or formal body is not in session: *a month's adjournment.*

ad·judge (ə juj′) *v.t.,* **ad·judged, ad·judg·ing. 1.** to decide or settle by law: *The defendant was adjudged guilty of the crime.* **2.** to award or grant by law: *The money was adjudged to the plaintiff.* **3.** to judge to be; deem; consider.

ad·ju·di·cate (ə jü′di kāt′) *v.t.,* **ad·ju·di·cat·ed, ad·ju·di·cat·ing.** to consider and decide by law: *to adjudicate a case.* —**ad·ju′di·ca′tion,** *n.*

ad·junct (aj′ungkt) *n.* something added to another thing but not a necessary part of it; less important or secondary thing: *A dial indicating the day and month is an adjunct to a wristwatch.*

ad·jure (ə jür′) *v.t.,* **ad·jured, ad·jur·ing. 1.** to order (especially someone under oath) solemnly: *The judge adjured the witness to testify truthfully.* **2.** to urge (someone) seriously; request earnestly: *to adjure a skydiver to be careful.* —**ad′jura′tion,** *n.*

ad·just (ə just′) *v.t.* **1.** to change or arrange to fit a need or demand; make suitable: *to adjust the length of a skirt.* **2.** to move or arrange the parts of so as to put in proper working order; regulate: *to adjust the brakes of an automobile.* **3.** to bring into the proper state or condition; arrange satisfactorily; settle: *to adjust an insurance claim.* —*v.i.* to become accustomed; adapt oneself: *We found it hard to adjust to our new surroundings.* —**ad·just′a·ble,** *adj.*

ad·just·er (ə jus′tər) *also,* **ad·jus·tor.** *n.* **1.** a thing that is used to make an adjustment. **2.** a person who adjusts, especially a person who adjusts insurance claims.

ad·just·ment (ə just′mənt) *n.* **1.** the act of adjusting or the state of being adjusted: *a perfect adjustment of a bus seat.* **2.** a method or device by which something is adjusted: *the adjustments on a microscope.* **3.** the process of determining or settling something: *the adjustment of an insurance claim.*

ad·ju·tant (aj′ə tənt) *n.* **1.** a military officer who acts as an administrative assistant to a commanding officer. **2.** an aide; assistant. **3.** see **adjutant stork.**

adjutant stork, a very large stork found in India and Africa. Also, **adjutant, adjutant bird.**

ad–lib (ad′lib′) *v.,* **ad–libbed, ad–lib·bing.** —*v.t.* to make up on the spur of the moment; improvise: *to ad-lib a speech. The pianist ad-libbed an accompaniment to the singer.* —*v.i.* to do or say something without previous preparation: *I lost my notes and had to ad-lib.* —*n.* an improvised remark, joke, song, or the like; something ad-libbed. —*adj.* made up on the spur of the moment; improvised: *an ad-lib remark.* —*adv.* in an improvised way. [Short for the Latin phrase *ad libitum* meaning "at one's pleasure."]

Adm., Admiral.

ad·min·is·ter (ad min′ə stər) *v.t.* **1.** to control the operation of; manage; direct: *to administer a college, to administer a department of the government.* **2.** to give out, especially while directing the use or choosing the target of; dispense; distribute: *to administer medicine. The Red Cross administers aid in disaster areas.* **3.** to give or offer formally: *The judge administered the oath to the witness.* —*v.i.* to be of service; contribute: *to administer to the well-being of the community.*

ad·min·is·trate (ad min′ə strāt′) *v.t., v.i.,* **ad·min·is·trat·ed, ad·min·is·trat·ing.** to administer.

ad·min·is·tra·tion (ad min′ə strā′shən) *n.* **1.** the act or method of managing or directing a business, organization, government, or the like. **2.** a group of people having the power to manage or direct something: *a school administration.* **3.** the executive branch of a government. **4. the Administration.** the president of the United States, together with the cabinet and the other officials who make up the executive branch of the government. **5.** the period during which a chief executive holds office. **6.** the act of administering something: *the administration of an oath, the administration of justice.*

ad·min·is·tra·tive (ad min′ə strā′tiv, ad min′ə strə-tiv) *adj.* of or relating to administration or management: *A business executive must have administrative skill.* —**ad·min′is·tra′tive·ly,** *adv.*

ad·min·is·tra·tor (ad min′ə strā′tər) *n.* **1.** a person who administers. **2.** a person appointed by a court of law to manage or settle the estate of a dead person.

ad·mi·ra·ble (ad′mər ə bəl) *adj.* deserving admiration; excellent: *an admirable person, an admirable quality.* —**ad′mi·ra·ble·ness,** *n.* —**ad′mi·ra·bly,** *adv.*

ad·mi·ral (ad′mər əl) *n.* **1.** a naval officer of the highest rank. **2.** in the U.S. Navy: **a.** an officer ranking above a vice admiral and below a fleet admiral. **b.** any other officer ranking above a captain. See **fleet admiral, rear admiral,** and **vice admiral. 3.** either of two species of brightly colored butterflies.

ad·mi·ral·ty (ad′mər əl tē) *n., pl.* **ad·mi·ral·ties. 1.a.** the branch of law that deals with matters involving ships and shipping. **b.** the court in which such matters are heard: *The dispute was taken to admiralty.* **2. Admiralty.** the department of the British government that has charge of naval affairs.

ad·mi·ra·tion (ad′mə rā′shən) *n.* **1.** a feeling of high regard or esteem: *We all felt admiration for the speaker's honesty.* **2.** the act of viewing something with appreciation and delight: *admiration of a beautiful painting.*

ad·mire (ad mīr′) *v.t.,* **ad·mired, ad·mir·ing. 1.** to feel high regard or esteem for: *to admire a person's character. I admire your way of dealing with people.* **2.** to regard with appreciation and delight: *to admire a painting, to admire a friend's new coat.* —**ad·mir′er,** *n.* —**ad·mir′ing·ly,** *adv.*

ad·mis·si·ble (ad mis′ə bəl) *adj.* **1.** that can be allowed or properly considered; allowable: *Illness is an admissible reason for absence from school.* **2.** that can be admitted: *Children are not admissible to that film.* —**ad·mis′si·bil′i·ty,** *n.* —**ad·mis′si·bly,** *adv.*

ad·mis·sion (ad mish′ən) *n.* **1.** the act of letting in or being let in; entrance; granting or being granted admitting: *the admission of water into a newly dug pond.* **2.** the privilege or right to enter or use: *admission to college, to have admission to a club.* **3.** a fee required to enter: *The admission to this game is two dollars.* **4.** the act of agreeing that something is true or relevant, especially if it goes against one's interest; acknowledgment; confession: *an admission of guilt, the admission of an argument in debate.*

ad·mit (ad mit′) *v.,* **ad·mit·ted, ad·mit·ting.** —*v.t.* **1.** to grant entrance to; allow to enter; let in: *The ushers admitted only one person at a time.* **2.** to agree that (something) is true; acknowledge; confess; grant: *to admit one's guilt. I'll admit you're right.* **3.** to recognize as valid or relevant: *to admit evidence in a trial.* **4.** to be the means of entrance for: *This pass will admit you to the show.* **5.** to have the room to hold; accommodate: *The auditorium admits 500 people.* —*v.i.* **1.** to allow the possibility: *Their outrageous behavior admits of no apology.* **2.** to provide access; open: *That door admits to the engine room.*

ad·mit·tance (ad mit′əns) *n.* **1.** permission to enter;

privilege of entrance: *Show your ticket to gain admittance.* **2.** the act of admitting or the state of being admitted.

ad·mit·ted·ly (ad mit′id lē) *adv.* by one's own admission or by common agreement: *I am admittedly a very poor swimmer.*

ad·mix (ad miks′) *v.t., v.i.* to mix into something else; blend.

ad·mix·ture (ad miks′chər) *n.* **1.** something added in mixing. **2.** the act of mixing. **3.** something formed by mixing; mixture.

ad·mon·ish (ad mon′ish) *v.t.* **1.** to caution against some action; warn: *They were admonished not to cut class again.* **2.** to scold or rebuke mildly: *The lifeguard admonished them for running near the pool.* —**ad·mon′ish·ment,** *n.*

ad·mo·ni·tion (ad′mə nish′ən) *n.* **1.** the act of admonishing; warning. **2.** a mild reprimand.

ad·mon·i·to·ry (ad mon′i tôr′ē) *adj.* cautioning; warning: *The police officer spoke in an admonitory tone of voice.*

a·do (ə dü′) *n.* fuss; bustle; difficulty.

a·do·be (ə dō′bē) *n.* **1.** a brick made by baking clay in the sun, used as a building material. **2.** a building made of such bricks. **3.** the clay from which such bricks are made. —*adj.* constructed or made of adobe: *an adobe house.*

adobe *(def. 2)*

ad·o·les·cence (ad′ə les′əns) *n.* **1.** the period of life between childhood and adulthood; youth. **2.** the state of being adolescent.

ad·o·les·cent (ad′ə les′ənt) *n.* a person between childhood and adulthood, especially one between the ages of twelve and eighteen. —*adj.* of or relating to adolescence or an adolescent; youthful; immature: *adolescent behavior.*

A·don·is (ə don′is, ə dō′nis) *n.* **1.** *Greek Mythology.* a handsome youth who was loved by Aphrodite. **2.** any handsome young man.

a·dopt (ə dopt′) *v.t.* **1.** to take (a child of other parents) into one's family to raise as one's own: *The young couple adopted the orphan.* **2.** to take and use as one's own: *The tune of a British song was adopted for "The Star-Spangled Banner."* **3.** to accept or approve, especially by formal vote: *The board adopted the proposal after much debate.* ▲ See **adapt** for usage note.

a·dopt·ee (ə dop tē′) *n.* a person who is adopted.

a·dop·tion (ə dop′shən) *n.* **1.** the act of adopting or the state of being adopted: *the adoption of a child.* **2.** acceptance or approval: *the adoption of a proposal.*

a·dop·tive (ə dop′tiv) *adj.* related by adoption: *adoptive parents, an adoptive family.*

a·dor·a·ble (ə dôr′ə bəl) *adj.* **1.** delightful; lovable; charming: *an adorable child.* **2.** worthy of adoration. —**a·dor′a·ble·ness,** *n.* —**a·dor′a·bly,** *adv.*

ad·o·ra·tion (ad′ə rā′shən) *n.* **1.** the act of honoring or worshiping as divine: *the adoration of idols.* **2.** deep love and devotion for: *a grandparent's adoration of a child.*

a·dore (ə dôr′) *v.t.,* **a·dored, a·dor·ing. 1.** to have love and admiration for; idolize: *The children adored the old teacher.* **2.** to honor as divine; worship. **3.** *Informal.* to have a great liking for: *I adore your new hat.* —**a·dor′er,** *n.* —**a·dor′ing·ly,** *adv.*

a·dorn (ə dôrn′) *v.t.* to add something beautiful to; make beautiful; ornament; decorate: *to adorn a room with flowers. That model's face has adorned many magazine covers.* —**a·dorn′er,** *n.*

a·dorn·ment (ə dôrn′mənt) *n.* **1.** something that adorns; ornament; decoration. **2.** the act of adorning.

ad·re·nal (ə drē′nəl) *adj.* **1.** located near or on the kidneys. **2.** relating to or from the adrenal glands. —*n.* see **adrenal gland.**

adrenal gland, one of a pair of small glands above the kidneys. The adrenal glands secrete adrenaline and several other hormones. Also, **suprarenal gland.**

ad·ren·a·line (ə dren′ə lin) *n.* a hormone secreted by the adrenal glands, especially under conditions of excitement, danger, or stress. Adrenaline makes the heart beat faster, quickens the rate of breathing, and produces other changes that enable the body to deal more effectively with an emergency. Adrenaline can also be produced synthetically. Also, **epinephrine.**

a·drift (ə drift′) *adv., adj.* **1.** moving with the current or wind; without being anchored or steered; floating freely: *The campers accidentally set the canoe adrift.* **2.** without direction or aim: *I was adrift in the city for a few weeks until I found a job.*

a·droit (ə droit′) *adj.* smoothly skillful; deft; clever: *The department's adroit handling of the problem prevented a crisis.* —**a·droit′ly,** *adv.* —**a·droit′ness,** *n.*

ad·sorb (ad sôrb′, ad zôrb′) *v.t.* to retain (a gas, liquid, or dissolved substance) on the surface instead of absorbing it: *A window pane adsorbs moisture during a rainstorm.*

ad·sorp·tion (ad sôrp′shən, ad zôrp′shən) *n.* the process of adsorbing: *the adsorption of gases by a charcoal filter.*

ad·u·la·tion (aj′ə lā′shən) *n.* lavish praise or flattery; too much praise: *The politician's speech was filled with adulation for the leading candidate.*

ad·u·la·to·ry (aj′ə lə tôr′ē) *adj.* lavishly praising or flattering: *an adulatory speech.*

a·dult (ə dult′, ad′ult) *n.* **1.** a grown man or woman; mature person. **2.** a plant or animal that has reached full growth. **3.** a person who is legally of age, usually a person more than twenty-one years old. —*adj.* **1.** having reached full size and strength; fully grown; mature: *an adult wolf.* **2.** relating to or for adults: *adult education.*

a·dul·ter·ant (ə dul′tər ənt) *n.* a substance or element that adulterates something.

a·dul·ter·ate (ə dul′tə rāt′) *v.t.,* **a·dul·ter·at·ed, a·dul·ter·at·ing.** to lessen the quality of (something) by including in it inferior or inappropriate substances: *to adulterate milk with water. The writer felt that the addition*

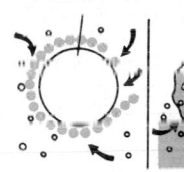

Charcoal particle   Sponge

Adsorption of   Absorption
gas molecules   of water

adsorption

---

at; āpe; fär; câre; end; mē; it; īce; pîerce; hot; ōld; sông, fôrk; oil; out; up; ūse; rüle; pùll; tûrn; chin; sing; shop; thin; this; hw in white; zh in treasure. The symbol ə stands for the unstressed vowel sound heard in about, taken, pencil, lemon, and circus.

of many new slang terms had adulterated the language.

a·dul·ter·a·tion (ə dul′tə rā′shən) *n.* **1.** the process of adulterating. **2.** an adulterated substance or product: *Wine thinned with water is an adulteration.*

a·dul·ter·er (ə dul′tər ər) *n.* a person who commits adultery.

a·dul·ter·ess (ə dul′tər is, ə dul′tris) *n., pl.* **a·dul·ter·ess·es.** a woman who commits adultery.

a·dul·ter·ous (ə dul′tər əs) *adj.* **1.** guilty of adultery: *an adulterous spouse.* **2.** relating to adultery: *adulterous behavior.*

a·dul·ter·y (ə dul′tə rē) *n., pl.* **a·dul·ter·ies.** sexual relationship between a married person and someone who is not the person's spouse.

a·dult·hood (ə dult′hŭd′) *n.* the state or time of being an adult.

adv. **1.** adverb. **2.** advertisement.

ad·vance (ad vans′) *v.,* **ad·vanced, ad·vanc·ing.** —*v.t.* **1.** to move (something) forward: *to advance the hands on a clock. The football team advanced the ball ten yards.* **2.** to help the progress of; further: *Charles Darwin's work advanced the science of biology.* **3.** to offer; propose: *to advance a new theory.* **4.** to raise to a higher or more favorable position or rank. **5.** to make earlier, as a time, date, or event: *to advance a wedding from June 30 to June 12.* **6.a.** to pay (an amount) before due or promised. **b.** to lend: *The bank advanced us $1,000.* —*v.i.* **1.** to move forward; proceed: *The army advanced to the gates of the city.* **2.** to move up in position, rank, or esteem; progress: *to advance rapidly in a job.* **3.** to increase in price, rate, or value: *Railroad stocks advanced two points.* —*n.* **1.** movement forward: *The troops made a steady advance.* **2.** development toward a better state; progress; improvement: *The discovery of a polio vaccine was an advance in medical knowledge.* **3.a.** a payment given before due: *I got an advance on next month's salary.* **b.** a loan. **4. advances.** attempts to gain the friendship or approval of someone: *Your cold manner discourages all advances.* —*adj.* **1.** situated in front: *an advance position.* **2.** ahead of time: *advance information, advance notice, an advance showing of a film.*

ad·vanced (ad vanst′) *adj.* **1.** ahead of others; modern; progressive: *an advanced theory, advanced techniques of manufacturing.* **2.** past the beginning or elementary stage; not primary: *advanced algebra, an advanced swimmer.* **3.** near the end in development or time: *The famous painter was advanced in age.*

ad·vance·ment (ad vans′mənt) *n.* **1.** movement toward a better state; progress or improvement: *scientific advancement.* **2.** a promotion to a higher rank or position: *This job has opportunities for advancement.* **3.** movement forward.

ad·van·tage (ad van′tij) *n.* **1.** a useful or helpful circumstance, factor, or event; something of benefit; asset: *Height is a great advantage in basketball.* **2.** benefit; gain: *More practice will be to your advantage.* [From the Old French word *avantage* meaning "advance, head start."]

> **·to advantage.** so as to make or show the best of (something or someone): *to display a painting to advantage.*

> **·to take advantage of. a.** to use profitably: *to take advantage of an opportunity.* **b.** to use unfairly; exploit: *to take advantage of someone's patience.*

ad·van·ta·geous (ad′vən tā′jəs) *adj.* giving an advantage or benefit; favorable; helpful: *Cold winters are advantageous for some kinds of farming.* —**ad′van·ta′geous·ly,** *adv.* —**ad′van·ta′geous·ness,** *n.*

ad·vent (ad′vent) *n.* **1.** a coming into being; arrival: *the advent of spring, the advent of old age.* **2. Advent. a.** the birth of Jesus. **b.** a period of religious observance including the four Sundays before Christmas.

Ad·vent·ist (ad′ven tist) *n.* a member of a Christian denomination believing that the Second Coming of Jesus will soon occur.

ad·ven·ti·tious (ad′ven tish′əs) *adj.* **1.** added by accident from outside; not inherent or essential. **2.** (of part of a plant or animal) appearing in an unusual or abnormal place, such as buds growing from the roots of a plant. —**ad′ven·ti′tious·ly,** *adv.* —**ad′ven·ti′tious·ness,** *n.*

ad·ven·ture (ad ven′chər) *n.* **1.** a difficult and dangerous undertaking in which risk is involved: *In the sixteenth century any voyage to the New World was a great adventure.* **2.** dangerous or exciting activity: *a spirit of adventure, a life filled with adventure.* **3.** a thrilling or unusual experience: *A day in the city was always an adventure for us.* —*v.,* **ad·ven·tured, ad·ven·tur·ing.** *v.i.* to have hazardous or thrilling experiences. —*v.t.* to risk; venture.

ad·ven·tur·er (ad ven′chər ər) *n.* **1.** a person who seeks or has adventures. **2.** a person who uses deceitful, dishonest methods to make money or to get ahead.

ad·ven·ture·some (ad ven′chər səm) *adj.* eager for adventure; adventurous.

ad·ven·tur·ess (ad ven′chər is) *n., pl.* **ad·ven·tur·ess·es.** a woman who schemes or uses her charms to obtain wealth or social position.

ad·ven·tur·ous (ad ven′chər əs) *adj.* **1.** eager for adventure; willing to encounter danger: *an adventurous traveler.* **2.** full of danger; hazardous: *an adventurous voyage.* —**ad·ven′tur·ous·ly,** *adv.* —**ad·ven′tur·ous·ness,** *n.*

ad·verb (ad′vûrb′) *n.* a word that modifies a verb, adjective, or another adverb. An adverb may indicate such ideas as manner (He walked *slowly*), time (She is *rarely* angry), place (The boat sailed *away*), or degree (I am *very* tired). Most adverbs are formed by adding the suffix *-ly* to an adjective or participle, such as "sad*ly*," "clever*ly*," or "excited*ly*."

ad·ver·bi·al (ad vûr′bē əl) *adj.* **1.** of or relating to an adverb: *The suffix "-ly" is an adverbial ending.* **2.** functioning as an adverb. In the sentence "They ran as fast as they could," *as fast as they could* is an adverbial phrase. —**ad·ver′bi·al·ly,** *adv.*

ad·ver·sar·y (ad′vər ser′ē) *n., pl.* **ad·ver·sar·ies.** a person or group that is hostile toward or competing with another; opponent or enemy: *The two politicians have been adversaries for years.*

ad·verse (ad vûrs′, ad′vûrs) *adj.* **1.** unfavorable to one's interests or to what is desired: *adverse circumstances. The game was played under adverse weather conditions.* **2.** unfriendly; antagonistic; hostile: *an adverse attitude, adverse criticism.* **3.** acting in an opposite or contrary direction, especially so as to hinder: *The ship met adverse winds.* —**ad·verse′ly,** *adv.* —**ad·verse′ness,** *n.*

ad·ver·si·ty (ad vûr′si tē) *n., pl.* **ad·ver·si·ties.** **1.** a condition of misfortune, hardship, or suffering: *to show courage in the face of adversity.* **2.** an instance of misfortune; unfavorable event: *They became successful despite many adversities.*

ad·vert (ad vûrt′) *v.i.* to call attention; refer: *The candidate adverted to the accusations made in the newspapers.*

ad·ver·tise (ad′vər tīz′) *v.,* **ad·ver·tised, ad·ver·tis·ing.** —*v.t.* **1.** to make a public announcement describing the qualities of (a product, service, cause, idea, or the like) in such a way as to make people want to buy it or support it: *to advertise medicine, to advertise a new television series.* **2.** to make known publicly: *to advertise a political rally.* —*v.i.* **1.** to inquire about or seek something by public notice (with *for*): *They advertised for a baby-sitter in the newspaper.* **2.** to present advertisements: *That company advertises frequently on television.* —**ad′ver·tis′er,** *n.*

ad·ver·tise·ment (ad′vər tīz′mənt, ad vûr′tis mənt) *n.* a public announcement, usually printed or broadcast, especially one that promotes a product or service: *This magazine contains many advertisements for the new fashions.*

ad·ver·tis·ing (ad′vər tī′zing) *n.* **1.** the use of public announcements to promote the sale of a product or the success of something: *The drugstore chose radio advertising to introduce its new line of cosmetics.* **2.** the business of preparing and placing advertisements, especially in newspapers and magazines or on television or radio: *Many people in this city work in advertising.* **3.** advertisements: *A newspaper earns most of its profit from advertising.*

ad·vice (ad vīs′) *n.* **1.** an opinion offered to help someone decide what course of action should be followed; counsel: *I asked my teacher for advice in choosing a college.* **2.** *also,* **advices.** information; news: *We received advice on the closing of the bridge.*

ad·vis·a·ble (ad vī′zə bəl) *adj.* that would be good advice; worth recommending; wise; sensible: *It is advisable to drive at a slower speed on wet roads.* —**ad·vis′a·bly,** *adv.*

ad·vis·a·bil·i·ty (ad vī′zə bil′i tē) *n.* the quality of being advisable; suitability; propriety.

ad·vise (ad vīz′) *v.,* **ad·vised, ad·vis·ing.** —*v.t.* **1.** to give advice to; counsel: *I advise you not to buy that coat. An older friend advised me on looking for work.* **2.** to suggest as a sound course; recommend: *I advise caution in dealing with wild dogs.* **3.** to give notice to; notify; inform: *The letter advised me that I had been chosen for the position.* —*v.i.* **1.** to give advice: *I'll do as you advise.* **2.** to meet with and discuss; confer: *I'll advise with the others before making a final plan.*

ad·vis·ed·ly (ad vī′zid lē) *adv.* after thinking about it; deliberately: *In describing their actions, I use the term "dangerous" advisedly.*

ad·vise·ment (ad vīz′mənt) *n.* serious thought or consultation: *The manager took the workers' complaints under advisement.*

ad·vis·er (ad vī′zər) *also,* **ad·vi·sor.** *n.* **1.** a person who advises: *The president has several economic advisers.* **2.** a teacher or professor who advises students about their studies, choice of career, and the like.

ad·vis·o·ry (ad vī′zə rē) *adj.* **1.** having the power or duty to advise: *The mayor appointed an advisory panel.* **2.** giving advice: *an advisory report.* —*n.* a bulletin giving current information: *a traffic advisory.*

ad·vo·ca·cy (ad′və kə sē) *n.* the act of advocating; support.

ad·vo·cate (*v.,* ad′və kāt′; *n.,* ad′və kit) *v.t.,* **ad·vo·cat·ed, ad·vo·cat·ing.** to plead in favor of; urge; support: *to advocate prison reform. The council advocated a change of policy.* —*n.* **1.** a person who publicly speaks for a cause or policy: *an advocate of nonviolence.* **2.** a person who pleads the cause of another, especially a lawyer.

advt., advertisement.

adz (adz) *also,* **adze.** *n.* a tool resembling an ax, used for trimming and shaping timber. It has a blade like a chisel set at right angles to the handle and curving inward.

ae·gis (ē′jis) *also,* **e·gis.** *n.* **1.** official sponsorship or support: *The relief program was carried out under the aegis of the federal government.* **2.** protection; guard.

Ae·ne·as (i nē′əs) *n. Greek and Roman Legend.* the Trojan warrior who was the hero of Virgil's *Aeneid,* whose descendants are said to have founded Rome.

Ae·ne·id (i nē′id) *n.* a Latin epic poem by Virgil, describing the travels and adventures of Aeneas.

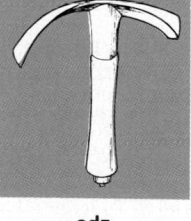

adz

Ae·o·lus (ē′ə ləs) *n. Greek Mythology.* the god of the winds.

ae·on (ē′ən, ē′on) another spelling of **eon.**

aer·ate (âr′āt) *v.t.,* **aer·at·ed, aer·at·ing. 1.** to mix with air; to expose to air: *to aerate drinking water, to aerate soil by plowing.* **2.** to charge or fill (a liquid) with gas: *Soda is aerated with carbon dioxide.* **3.** to expose to the chemical action of oxygen; oxygenate: *The blood is aerated in respiration.* —**aer′a·tion,** *n.* —**aer′a·tor,** *n.*

aer·i·al (âr′ē əl) *adj.* **1.** of or in the air: *aerial acrobatics, an aerial ascent in a balloon.* **2.** like air; light and thin. **3.** for, from, or relating to aircraft: *aerial photography.* **4.** growing in the air rather than in soil or water: *a plant with aerial roots.* —*n.* a radio or television antenna. —**aer′i·al·ly,** *adv.*

aer·i·a·list (âr′ē ə list) *n.* an acrobat who performs in the air, as on a trapeze or high wire.

ae·rie (âr′ē, îr′ē, îr′ē) *also,* **ey·rie, ey·ry.** *n.* **1.** a nest built high on a cliff or mountainside by an eagle, hawk, or other bird of prey. **2.** a building in a high, remote place.

aero– *combining form* of the air; air: *aerodynamics.*

aer·obe (âr′ōb) *n.* a microorganism that requires oxygen for life.

aer·o·bic (â rō′bik) *adj.* **1.** living only in the presence of oxygen: *aerobic bacteria.* **2.** relating to or produced by microorganisms requiring oxygen. **3.** relating to exercise designed to improve the body's intake and use of oxygen: *aerobic dancing.*

aer·o·bics (â rō′biks) *pl. n.* physical exercises designed to improve the body's ability to use oxygen, especially by strengthening the heart and lungs. [*Aero-* + *bi(o)-* + *-ics.*]

aer·o·drome (âr′ə drōm′) *n. British.* another word for **airdrome.**

aer·o·dy·nam·ic (âr′ō dī nam′ik) *adj.* pertaining to or based on aerodynamics: *aerodynamic analysis, an automobile with aerodynamic lines.* —**aer′o·dy·nam′i·cal·ly,** *adv.*

aer·o·dy·nam·ics (âr′ō dī nam′iks) *n.* **1.** the branch of physics that deals with the laws of motion of air and other gases, and with the forces exerted by such gases on bodies moving in them. ▲ used with a singular verb. **2.** the way an object moving through air or another gas behaves. ▲ used with a plural verb: *The aerodynamics of the experimental plane are being tested.*

aer·ol·o·gy (â rol′ə je) *n.* the branch of meteorology that deals with the study of air, especially in the upper atmosphere.

aer·o·nau·tic (âr′ə nô′tik) *adj.* of or relating to aeronautics. Also, **aer·o·nau·ti·cal** (âr′ə nô′ti kəl). —**aer′o·nau′ti·cal·ly,** *adv.*

aer·o·nau·tics (âr′ə nô′tiks) *n.* **1.** the science or art of flight. **2.** the branch of engineering concerned with designing, making, and flying aircraft. ▲ used with a singular verb in both definitions.

aer·o·pause (âr′ō pôz′) *n.* the region where outer space is considered to begin and where the atmosphere will not support aircraft.

aer·o·plane (âr′ə plān′) *n. British.* another word for **airplane.**

aer·o·sol (âr′ə sôl′) *n.* **1.** a mass of very fine solid or liquid particles suspended in a gas. Smoke, fog, and smog are aerosols. **2.** see **aerosol can.**

at; āpe; fär; câre; end; mē; it; īce; pîerce; hot; ōld; sông, fôrk; oil; out; up; ūse; rüle; pull; tûrn; chin; sing; shop; thin; <u>th</u>is; hw in white; zh in treasure. The symbol ə stands for the unstressed vowel sound heard in about, taken, pencil, lemon, and circus.

aerosol can, a container from which a liquid sealed under pressure with a gas can be released in the form of a fine mist or spray, used for dispensing insecticide, paint, and other materials. Also, **aerosol, aerosol bomb.**

aer·o·space (âr′ō spās′) *n.* the earth's atmosphere and outer space, considered as the region in which aircraft or spacecraft are operated. —*adj.* relating to aerospace and all aspects of human activity in or for this region: *aerospace medicine, the aerospace industry.*

aes·thete (es′thēt) *also,* **es·thete.** *n.* **1.** a person who is particularly sensitive to and appreciative of art and beauty. **2.** a person who pretends to be sensitive to art and beauty.

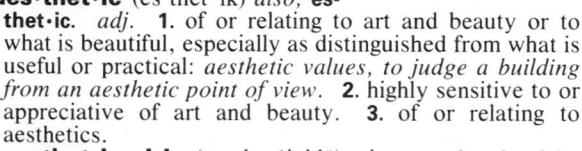

aerosol can

aes·thet·ic (es thet′ik) *also,* **es·thet·ic.** *adj.* **1.** of or relating to art and beauty or to what is beautiful, especially as distinguished from what is useful or practical: *aesthetic values, to judge a building from an aesthetic point of view.* **2.** highly sensitive to or appreciative of art and beauty. **3.** of or relating to aesthetics.

aes·thet·i·cal·ly (es thet′i klē) *also,* **es·thet·i·cal·ly.** *adv.* **1.** according to aesthetic standards. **2.** in an aesthetic manner: *The room was decorated aesthetically.*

aes·thet·ics (es thet′iks) *also,* **es·thet·ics.** *n.* the branch of philosophy that studies beauty in art and nature. ▲ used with a singular verb.

AF, Air Force. Also, **A.F.**

a·far (ə fär′) *adv.* at or to a distance; far away. ·**from afar.** from a distance.

af·fa·ble (af′ə bəl) *adj.* easy to approach and speak to; pleasant; friendly. —**af′fa·bil′i·ty,** *n.* —**af′fa·bly,** *adv.*

af·fair (ə fâr′) *n.* **1.** a matter or business done or to be done: *Moving to a new home can be a tiring affair.* **2. affairs.** the practical matters with which a person or group is involved: *The affairs of business left me little time to spend with my family.* **3.** a private or personal concern: *That's none of your affair.* **4.** a romantic relationship between two people, especially a brief one. **5.** a social gathering or party: *The wedding was a lovely affair.* **6.** *Informal.* a thing or object: *The first cake I baked was a sad affair.*

af·fect[1] (ə fekt′) *v.t.* **1.** to produce an effect in; act upon; influence: *That drug affects the nervous system. The long strike affected the local economy.* **2.** to influence the emotions of; move: *The photographs of the flood victims affected us deeply.* [From the Latin word *affectus,* past participle of *afficere* meaning "to influence, produce a physical effect on."]

▲ **Affect** and **effect** are close in sound, but they belong to different parts of speech and should not be confused. **Affect** is a verb: *Daily exercise will affect your health.* **Effect** is most commonly used as a noun: *Daily exercise will have a good effect on your health.*

af·fect[2] (ə fekt′) *v.t.* **1.** to put on a false show of; pretend to have or feel: *The dog affected boldness although it was really frightened.* **2.** to prefer to have, use, or wear; have a liking for: *Some people who care about style affect casual clothes.* [From the Latin word *affectare* meaning "to attempt something, strive for something" and "to pretend to have."]

af·fec·ta·tion (af′ek tā′shən) *n.* an artificial manner of acting or speaking, usually to impress or deceive others: *an affectation of innocence. My roommate's interest in modern art is an affectation.*

af·fect·ed[1] (ə fek′tid) *adj.* **1.** acted upon or influenced: *The proposed highway was opposed by the affected landowners.* **2.** influenced emotionally; moved. **3.** impaired; afflicted. [From *affect*[1].]

af·fect·ed[2] (ə fek′tid) *adj.* **1.** assumed for show; artificial: *affected behavior, an affected British accent.* **2.** assuming or displaying an artificial manner of acting or speaking: *an affected person.* [From *affect*[2].] —**af·fect′ed·ly,** *adv.* —**af·fect′ed·ness,** *n.*

af·fect·ing (ə fek′ting) *adj.* emotionally moving; stirring: *The drama contained several affecting scenes.* —**af·fect′ing·ly,** *adv.*

af·fec·tion (ə fek′shən) *n.* **1.** tender feeling or fondness; warm attachment: *the affection of a dog for its master, to have a great affection for one's grandparents.* **2.** a disease or diseased condition.

af·fec·tion·ate (ə fek′shə nit) *adj.* full of, expressing, or displaying affection; loving; tender: *an affectionate friend, an affectionate smile, an affectionate message.* —**af·fec′tion·ate·ly,** *adv.*

af·fer·ent (af′ər ənt) *adj.* leading or conducting to a central organ or point: *afferent nerve fibers.*

af·fi·ance (ə fī′əns) *v.t.,* **af·fi·anced, af·fi·anc·ing.** to pledge to be married; betroth: *to become affianced to each other.*

af·fi·da·vit (af′i dā′vit) *n.* a written declaration made by a person who swears under oath that it is true, usually before a judge or other recognized authority.

af·fil·i·ate (*v.,* ə fil′ē āt′; *n.,* ə fil′ē it) *v.,* **af·fil·i·at·ed, af·fil·i·at·ing.** —*v.t.* **1.** to join in close association; connect; unite: *The merger affiliates two large companies.* **2.** to associate (oneself) as a member or supporter: *The mayor is not affiliated with any political party. I chose not to affiliate myself with that club.* —*v.i.* to join or associate oneself. —*n.* **1.** an organization or group that is closely connected with a larger organization: *Our local television station is an affiliate of the national network.* **2.** a person who is affiliated; associate.

af·fil·i·a·tion (ə fil′ē ā′shən) *n.* the state of being affiliated; association; connection: *Our club has an affiliation with a national organization.*

af·fin·i·ty (ə fin′i tē) *n., pl.* **af·fin·i·ties. 1.** a natural attraction or liking: *The young couple had a great affinity for each other.* **2.** a close relation or similarity: *the affinity between the Spanish and Italian languages.* **3.** *Chemistry.* the force of attraction by which the atoms of certain elements unite with those of certain others to form compounds.

af·firm (ə fûrm′) *v.t.* **1.** to state positively; declare firmly: *The senators affirmed their support for the bill.* **2.** to give formal approval to; confirm; ratify: *The higher court affirmed the trial court's decision.*

af·fir·ma·tion (af′ər mā′shən) *n.* **1.** the act of stating positively; firm declaration. **2.** a statement of approval or agreement; confirmation; ratification, as of a legal decision.

af·firm·a·tive (ə fûr′mə tiv) *adj.* stating that something is true or valid; saying "yes"; assenting: *A nod is usually an affirmative response.* —*n.* **1.** a word or expression of assent or agreement, such as "yes." **2.** the side that argues in favor of the proposition in a debate. —**af·firm′a·tive·ly,** *adv.* ·**in the affirmative.** in agreement; saying yes.

affirmative action, preferential treatment of minority groups and women in employment and education, designed to compensate for past discrimination against these groups.

af·fix (*v.,* ə fiks′; *n.,* af′iks) *v.t.* **1.** to fix to something; attach; fasten: *to affix stamps to an envelope.* **2.** to add at the end; append: *The witnesses affixed their names to the document.* —*n., pl.* **af·fix·es.** a syllable or group of syllables added to the beginning or end of a word to change its meaning or to make another word; a prefix or suffix. The forms *anti-, pre-, -ment,* and *-ly* are affixes.

af·flict (ə flikt′) *v.t.* to cause great suffering and pain to; distress severely: *Poison ivy afflicted the campers with itching and rashes.*

af·flic·tion (ə flik′shən) *n.* **1.** the state of being afflicted; misery; suffering. **2.** any cause of pain or suffering; misfortune: *Blindness is a severe affliction.*

af·flu·ence (af′lü əns) *n.* **1.** a large amount of money, goods, or property; great material wealth. **2.** any abundant supply; profusion: *an affluence of emotion.*

af·flu·ent (af′lü ənt) *adj.* **1.** having much money or property; wealthy; prosperous; rich: *an affluent society.* **2.** in abundance; plentiful; profuse: *The poet received affluent praise.* —**af′flu·ent·ly,** *adv.*

af·ford (ə fôrd′) *v.t.* **1.** to be able to bear the expense of; have the money for: *Can you afford a new coat?* **2.** to be able to spare or give: *I can't afford the time to help you.* **3.** to be able to do without harm: *Since we know the train will be late, you can afford to make that phone call.* **4.** to yield or supply; give; provide: *The holiday afforded us a chance to rest.*

af·fray (ə frā′) *n.* a noisy brawl or quarrel; public disturbance.

af·front (ə frunt′) *n.* an insulting act or remark, especially one that is open and deliberate: *Your rude comments about my home were an affront to me.* —*v.t.* to insult openly; offend deliberately: *The audience affronted the actors by jeering loudly throughout the play.* [From the Old French word *afronter* meaning "to strike in the face, insult," going back to the Latin words *ad* "to, toward" and *frons* "forehead, face."]

Af·ghan (af′gan, af′gən) *n.* **1.** a person who was born in or is a citizen of Afghanistan. **2.** a tall, long-headed dog of a breed originally from Afghanistan, having a coat of long, silky, usually tan hair, large, drooping ears, and a long tail. **3. afghan.** a knitted or crocheted wool blanket or shawl, made in colored squares, stripes, or other patterns. —*adj.* of or relating to Afghanistan, its people, or their culture.

Afghan (def. 2)

a·fi·ci·o·na·do (ə fē′sē ə nä′dō, ə fish′ē ə nä′dō) *n., pl.* **a·fi·ci·o·na·dos.** an enthusiastic supporter; devotee; fan: *an aficionado of the ballet.* [From the Spanish word *aficionado* meaning "fan," from the past participle of *aficionar* "to inspire affection," going back to the Latin word *affectio* meaning "feeling, affection."]

a·field (ə fēld′) *adv.* **1.** off the correct or usual path or course: *The irrelevant comments led the discussion far afield.* **2.** away from home; abroad. **3.** on, in, or to the field.

a·fire (ə fīr′) *adv., adj.* **1.** on fire: *to set a log afire. The old ship was afire.* **2.** as if on fire: *The crew was afire with a spirit of mutiny.*

a·flame (ə flām′) *adv., adj.* **1.** flaming; on fire; burning. **2.** as if on fire: *The skater's cheeks were aflame from the frosty air.*

a·float (ə flōt′) *adv., adj.* **1.** floating on water: *That is the largest ship afloat.* **2.** on board ship; at sea. **3.** in circulation: *There are strange rumors afloat.* **4.** covered by water; flooded: *The deck was afloat.* **5.** out of difficulty, especially financial difficulty: *to keep a business afloat.*

a·flut·ter (ə flut′ər) *adv., adj.* **1.** fluttering: *The leaves were aflutter in the strong breeze.* **2.** nervously confused or agitated; excited: *The children were all aflutter as vacation drew nearer.*

a·foot (ə füt′) *adv., adj.* **1.** by walking; on foot: *We proceeded afoot.* **2.** in progress or motion; stirring: *There's an evil plot afoot.*

a·fore (ə fôr′) *adv., prep., conj.* another word for **before.**

a·fore·men·tioned (ə fôr′men′shənd) *adj.* mentioned before: *The aforementioned rules apply to everyone.*

a·fore·said (ə fôr′sed′) *adj.* said or mentioned before.

a·fore·thought (ə fôr′thôt′) *adj.* thought of or planned beforehand; premeditated: *to commit a crime with malice aforethought.*

a·foul (ə foul′) *adv., adj.* fouled or tangled; snarled; in collision: *a sailboat with its lines afoul.*
　·to run afoul of. to become entangled with; get into trouble with: *The forgers finally ran afoul of the law.*

Afr., Africa; African.

a·fraid (ə frād′) *adj.* **1.** feeling fear; frightened: *Are you afraid of snakes?* **2.** feeling unhappiness or regret; sorry: *I'm afraid I won't be able to meet you tonight.*

A-frame (ā′ frām′) *n.* a house shaped like a triangle, with sides that slant inward from the ground and meet at the top, forming the roof.

a·fresh (ə fresh′) *adv.* as from the beginning; anew; again: *When the water washed our sand castle away, we started afresh.*

Af·ri·can (af′ri kən) *adj.* of or relating to Africa, its people, or their languages or culture. —*n.* a person who was born in Africa or is a citizen of an African nation.

Words From Other Languages

The continent of Africa is home to approximately 1,300 different languages, more than are spoken on any other continent. Most of the words that English has borrowed from languages spoken in Africa are names of animals and plants found on the continent.

baobab	a tree with a broad trunk
bongos	a pair of small drums played with the hands
canary	a small yellow songbird
chimpanzee	an ape known for its intelligence
gorilla	the largest ape in the world
okra	a plant whose pods are eaten as a vegetable
tsetse	the African fly that carries sleeping sickness
yam	a plant root eaten as a vegetable
zebra	a striped animal closely related to the horse

Af·ri·can–A·mer·i·can (af′ri kən ə mer′i kən) *adj.* of or relating to American blacks, especially as influenced by African culture. —*n.* an American black.

African violet, any of a group of plants usually grown as houseplants for their pink, violet, and white flowers and velvety leaves.

Af·ri·kaans (af′ri käns′) *n.* an official language of South Africa. Afrikaans developed from the Dutch spoken by the seventeenth-century settlers.

Af·ri·ka·ner (af′ri kä′nər) *n.* a South African who is of European descent, especially one of Dutch descent.

Af·ro (af′rō) *n., pl.* **Af·ros.** a hair style in which naturally wiry hair is worn in a high, rounded mass. [Short for *Afro-American.*]

at; āpe; fär; câre; end; mē; it; īce; pîerce; hot; ōld; sông, fôrk; oil; out; up; ūse; rüle; pull; tûrn; chin; sing; shop; thin; this; hw in white; zh in treasure. The symbol ə stands for the unstressed vowel sound heard in about, taken, pencil, lemon, and circus.

Af·ro–A·mer·i·can (af'rō ə mer'i kən) *adj.* **1.** of or relating to American blacks. **2.** relating to the culture of American blacks, especially as influenced by African culture. —*n.* an American black.

aft (aft) *adv., adj.* at, near, or toward the rear of a ship or an aircraft: *the aft cabin. Go aft to see the ship's wake.*

af·ter (af'tər) *prep.* **1.** in or at the rear of; behind: *The chicks walked after the hen.* **2.** in pursuit or search of: *The hounds ran after the fox. The prospector set out after gold.* **3.** following in time; later than: *It is ten minutes after three o'clock. We arrived shortly after dark.* **4.** as a result of; because of: *After that remark, you'll have to apologize.* **5.** in spite of; regardless of: *After all we've said, are you still willing to try it?* **6.** concerning; about: *My cousin inquired after your health.* **7.** in imitation of; in the style of: *a building designed after the Parthenon.* **8.** with a name like: *to be named after a grandparent.* **9.** below in rank, order, or importance: *After the president, the treasurer has the highest salary in the company.* —*adv.* **1.** in the rear; behind: *to follow after.* **2.** later; subsequently: *I arrived on Sunday, and the snow came two days after.* —*conj.* following the time that: *It happened after you left.* —*adj.* **1.** later; subsequent: *in after years.* **2.** toward the rear or stern of a ship.

af·ter·birth (af'tər bûrth') *n.* the mass of matter expelled from the uterus after the birth of a child, consisting chiefly of the placenta.

af·ter·burn·er (af'tər bûr'nər) *n.* a device that injects fuel into the hot exhaust of a jet engine, thereby creating additional thrust.

af·ter·deck (af'tər dek') *n.* a deck at a ship's stern.

af·ter·ef·fect (af'tər i fekt') *n.* an effect that occurs some time after its cause; delayed effect: *aftereffects from a drug. Germany's economic depression of the 1920s was an aftereffect of World War I.*

af·ter·glow (af'tər glō') *n.* **1.** a glow remaining after the light that caused it has gone, as in the western sky after sunset. **2.** a good feeling lingering after a pleasant experience.

af·ter·im·age (af'tər im'ij) *n.* an image that continues to be seen after the light that caused it is no longer there. If you look at a bright neon sign and then close your eyes, you will see an afterimage.

af·ter·life (af'tər līf') *n.* life after death.

af·ter·math (af'tər math') *n.* a situation that results; consequence or consequences: *the aftermath of a hurricane, the aftermath of an epidemic.* [From the word *after* + the earlier English word *math* meaning "a mowing." The original meaning was "a second mowing of grass from the same field in one season."]

af·ter·noon (af'tər nün') *n.* the part of the day from noon until evening.

af·ter·shock (af'tər shok') *n.* a small earthquake or tremor that follows a larger one.

af·ter·taste (af'tər tāst') *n.* a taste that remains after what caused it is gone: *The medicine left an unpleasant aftertaste.*

af·ter·thought (af'tər thôt') *n.* a later or second thought or idea: *His name was added to the list as an afterthought.*

af·ter·ward (af'tər wərd) *also,* **af·ter·wards.** *adv.* at a later time; subsequently: *We swam for an hour, and afterward we rested.*

Ag, the symbol for silver. [Abbreviation of the Latin word *argentum* meaning "silver."]

a·gain (ə gen') *adv.* **1.** once more; another time: *Our first attempt failed, so we tried again.* **2.** looking at it from another viewpoint; on the other hand: *We might go, and again we might not.* **3.** looking at it one more time; moreover; besides; furthermore: *Again, we should consider the risks involved.* **4.** in or to a former position or state: *The dog ran to the corner and then back again.*

　•**again and again.** many times; often.

　•**now and again.** not often; occasionally; sometimes: *We visit the city now and again.*

a·gainst (ə genst') *prep.* **1.** not in favor of; in opposition to: *Five representatives voted against the bill.* **2.** not the same way; in the opposite direction to: *The salmon swam against the current.* **3.a.** in contact with: *to lean a bicycle against a tree.* **b.** so as to strike or come into contact with: *to drive one's fist against the wall.* **4.** as a protection or defense from; in preparation for: *to save against an emergency.* **5.** on a background of; in contrast with: *The painting shows a blue vase against a yellow wall.* **6.** as a charge upon: *an advance against next week's salary.*

Ag·a·mem·non (ag'ə mem'non) *n. Greek Legend.* a king of Mycenae who led the Greeks in the Trojan War.

a·gape (ə gāp') *adj., adv.* with the mouth wide open, especially in wonder or disbelief: *We all stared agape at the mysterious figure in the shadows.*

a·gar (ä'gär, ag'ər) *also,* **a·gar-a·gar** (ä'gär ä'gär, ag'ər ag'ər). *n.* **1.** a jellylike product obtained from certain seaweeds, used especially as a medium for growing bacteria in a laboratory. **2.** a medium for growing bacteria that contains agar.

ag·ate (ag'it) *n.* **1.** a semiprecious variety of quartz, usually having variously colored layers or bands. **2.** a playing marble that is made of or looks like agate.

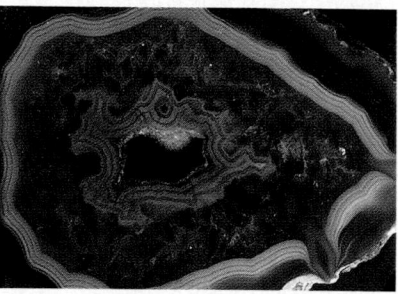
agate *(def. 1)*

a·ga·ve (ə gä'vē) *n.* any of a group of desert plants of the Western Hemisphere, having long flower stalks and thick, fleshy leaves. The most familiar is the century plant.

age (āj) *n.* **1.** the length of time that a person, animal, or thing has existed: *That tree's age is ten years. Many workers retire at the age of sixty-five.* **2.** a particular period or stage of life: *middle age.* **3.a.** the effects of becoming older: *With age, one's physical abilities lessen.* **b.** the latter part of life: *In age, the old couple began to look alike.* **4.** a particular period of history: *the atomic age, the age of mammals.* **5.** *also,* **ages.** *Informal.* a long time: *I haven't heard from them in ages.* —*v.,* **aged, ag·ing** *or* **age·ing.** —*v.t.* **1.** to cause to seem or look older: *Years of ill health aged my neighbor prematurely.* **2.** to allow to mature or ripen with time: *to age wine, to age beef.* —*v.i.* **1.** to become old or mature: *The wine aged for two years.* **2.** to appear older: *You have aged noticeably since your illness.*

　•**of age.** having reached the age when full adult rights and responsibilities apply, usually eighteen or twenty-one years.

–age *suffix* (used to form nouns) **1.** the act or process of: *breakage.* **2.** the condition or the state of: *wreckage.* **3.** a collection of: *wordage.* **4.** the amount of: *acreage.* **5.** the fee for or cost of: *postage.* **6.** a home or place of: *orphanage.*

a·ged (*adj., def. 1* ā'jid; *defs. 2, 3* ājd; *n.,* ā'jid) *adj.* **1.** grown old; old: *aged grandparents.* **2.** having the age of: *a child aged three.* **3.** having a desired quality as the result of aging: *aged cheese.* —*n.* **the aged.** old people as a group: *medical care for the aged.*

age·ism (ā'jiz əm) *n.* discrimination or prejudice against a particular age group, especially older people.

age·less (āj'lis) *adj.* **1.** not showing signs of age. **2.** not ending; eternal: *the ageless majesty of the ocean.*

a·gen·cy (ā′jən sē) *n., pl.* **a·gen·cies.** **1.** a company or person that has the power to do business for others: *An insurance agency can arrange insurance guaranteed by its parent company.* **2.** the office or place of business of such a company or person. **3.** an administrative department of government. **4.** the means, action, or power by or through which a thing is done: *The hostages were set free through the agency of their ambassador.*

a·gen·da (ə jen′də) *n.* a list of things to be done: *The committee prepared the agenda for the meeting.*

a·gent (ā′jənt) *n.* **1.** a person or organization having the power to represent or act for another: *an insurance agent. My agent represented me during the contract negotiations.* **2.** something that produces or is used to produce a certain effect: *Soap is a cleansing agent.* **3.** an officer of a government agency, especially a law enforcement agency: *an agent of the FBI.*

a·gent pro·vo·ca·teur (ā′jənt prə vok′ə tûr′) *n., pl.* **a·gents pro·vo·ca·teurs** (ā′jənts prə vok′ə tûr′). a person secretly placed in a group to provoke illegal acts for which the group can then be blamed.

ag·er·a·tum (aj′ə rā′təm) *n.* any of various ornamental plants related to the chrysanthemum, having clusters of blue, white, or pink flowers.

ag·glom·er·ate (*v.,* ə glom′ə rāt′; *n., adj.,* ə glom′-ər it) *v.t., v.i.,* **ag·glom·er·at·ed, ag·glom·er·at·ing.** to gather in a mass or cluster. —*n.* **1.** a group of things gathered together in a mass or cluster. **2.** a rock formed of a mass of volcanic fragments fused together. —*adj.* gathered together in a mass or cluster: *an agglomerate whole.* —**ag·glom′er·a′tion,** *n.*

ag·glu·ti·nate (*v.,* ə glü′tə nāt′; *adj.,* ə glü′tə nit) *v.t., v.i.,* **ag·glu·ti·nat·ed, ag·glu·ti·nat·ing.** **1.** to unite with or as if with glue; stick together. **2.** to clump together, as bacteria or blood cells. —*adj.* joined with or as if with glue.

ag·glu·ti·na·tion (ə glü′tə nā′shən) *n.* **1.** the process of sticking together or the state of being stuck together. **2.** a clumping together of bacteria or blood cells in the body due to the presence of an antibody. **3.** a collection of parts stuck together.

ag·glu·tin·in (ə glü′tə nin) *n.* a substance that causes agglutination, such as an antibody.

ag·gran·dize (ə gran′dīz, ag′rən dīz′) *v.t.,* **ag·gran·dized, ag·gran·diz·ing.** to make greater, larger, or more important, as in power, wealth, or rank: *The empire sought always to aggrandize itself.* —**ag·gran′dize·ment,** *n.* —**ag·gran′diz′er,** *n.*

ag·gra·vate (ag′rə vāt′) *v.t.,* **ag·gra·vated, ag·gra·vat·ing.** **1.** to make worse or more severe: *The chilly, damp weather aggravated my cold. Violence at the border aggravated the tension between the two countries.* **2.** to annoy; irritate: *Your constant complaining aggravates me.* —**ag′gra·vat′ing·ly,** *adv.* —**ag′gra·va′tor,** *n.*

ag·gra·va·tion (ag′rə vā′shən) *n.* **1.** making worse or more severe: *the aggravation of a wound by infection.* **2.** state of being annoyed; irritation: *The passengers expressed their aggravation at the delay.* **3.** something that aggravates.

ag·gre·gate (*adj., n.,* ag′ri git; *v.,* ag′ri gāt′) *adj.* composed of parts gathered together: *The aggregate number of marathon runners from all towns was 194.* —*n.* **1.** a whole composed of separate parts; mass or group of individual things: *Our team's victory was the outcome of an aggregate of many different efforts.* **2.** a sum total: *The aggregate of receipts from all sources was $1,000.* **3.** *Geology.* a mixture of different mineral substances. —*v.t.,* **ag·gre·gat·ed, ag·gre·gat·ing.** **1.** to collect or gather into a mass or group. **2.** to amount to; total. —**ag′gre·gate·ly,** *adv.* —**ag′gre·gate·ness,** *n.* **·in the aggregate.** taken together; as a whole.

ag·gre·ga·tion (ag′ri gā′shən) *n.* **1.** the collecting of individual things into a single mass or whole. **2.** such a group or collection: *The variety show featured an aggregation of talented performers.*

ag·gres·sion (ə gresh′ən) *n.* **1.** a hostile or unprovoked attack or assault: *A country that invades the territory of its neighbor is guilty of aggression.* **2.** the habit or policy of making assaults or attacks; hostile behavior.

ag·gres·sive (ə gres′iv) *adj.* **1.** relating to or showing aggression: *a nation with an aggressive foreign policy.* **2.** acting with energy; forceful; bold: *an aggressive salesperson, an aggressive advertising campaign.* —**ag·gres′sive·ly,** *adv.* —**ag·gres′sive·ness,** *n.*

ag·gres·sor (ə gres′ər) *n.* a person, nation, or group that engages in aggression.

ag·grieve (ə grēv′) *v.t.,* **ag·grieved, ag·griev·ing.** to cause grief, trouble, or injury to; distress: *The mayor's dishonesty aggrieved the citizens.*

a·ghast (ə gast′) *adj.* filled with fear, shock, or amazement: *We were aghast at the suggestion that we break into the building.*

ag·ile (aj′əl, aj′īl) *adj.* **1.** able to move quickly and easily; nimble: *A deer is an agile animal.* **2.** able to think quickly: *A debater must have an agile mind.* —**ag′ile·ly,** *adv.* —**ag′ile·ness,** *n.*

a·gil·i·ty (ə jil′i tē) *n.* quickness and ease in motion or thought; nimbleness: *The acrobat displayed great agility.*

ag·i·tate (aj′i tāt′) *v.,* **ag·i·tat·ed, ag·i·tat·ing.** —*v.t.* **1.** to move or shake roughly or irregularly; stir up: *The wind agitated the trees.* **2.** to move to and fro with a regular motion: *A washing machine agitates clothes.* **3.** to disturb the feelings of; stir up; perturb; excite: *The rude behavior of the teenagers agitated the neighborhood.* —*v.i.* to seek to arouse public interest, especially in an effort to bring about change: *The students agitated for a greater role in school policy by picketing the dean's office.* —**ag′i·tat′ed·ly,** *adv.*

ag·i·ta·tion (aj′i tā′shən) *n.* **1.** the act of agitating. **2.** the state of being emotionally upset or shaken. **3.** an effort to arouse public interest in some matter.

ag·i·ta·tor (aj′i tā′tər) *n.* **1.** a person who seeks to arouse interest or support for a cause, especially a political one. **2.** a device for shaking or stirring.

a·gleam (ə glēm′) *adv., adj.* gleaming: *The lights of the Christmas tree were all agleam.*

a·glit·ter (ə glit′ər) *adv., adj.* glittering.

a·glow (ə glō′) *adv., adj.* glowing.

ag·nos·tic (ag nos′tik) *n.* a person who believes that nothing is known or can be known about the existence of God. —*adj.* relating to agnostics or their beliefs. ▲ See **atheist** for usage note.

ag·nos·ti·cism (ag nos′tə siz əm) *n.* the belief of or philosophical position taken by agnostics.

Ag·nus De·i (ag′nəs dā′ē) **1.** a prayer in the Mass starting with the words "Agnus Dei" or "Lamb of God." **2.** the music for this prayer. **3.** an image of a lamb representing Jesus, especially one with a halo and the banner of the Cross. [Latin *Agnus Deī* Lamb of God.]

a·go (ə gō′) *adj.* before now; past: *They left ten minutes ago.* —*adv.* in the past: *Dinosaurs lived long ago.*

a·gog (ə gog′) *adj., adv.* in a state of excitement or eager expectation: *The crowd was agog as the game began.*

ag·o·nize (ag′ə nīz′) *v.,* **ag·o·nized, ag·o·niz·ing.** —*v.i.* to feel great discomfort, anguish, or pain; suffer greatly: *We agonized over the terrible choice we were*

at; āpe; fär; câre; end; mē; it; īce; pierce; hot; ōld; sông; fôrk; oil; out; up; ūse; rüle; pùll; tûrn; chin; sing; shop; thin; this; hw in white; zh in treasure. The symbol ə stands for the unstressed vowel sound heard in about, taken, pencil, lemon, and circus.

A

faced with. —*v.t.* to cause to suffer great discomfort, anguish, or pain. —**ag'o·niz'ing·ly,** *adv.*

ag·o·ny (ag'ə nē) *n., pl.* **ag·o·nies.** **1.** great pain, suffering, or anguish of mind or body: *to be in agony from a toothache. They suffered agony at the death of their friend.* **2.** violent movements of the body resembling a struggle, especially those preceding death.

a·gou·ti (ə gü'tē) *n., pl.* **a·gou·tis.** a burrowing rodent found in the West Indies and Central and South America, related to the guinea pig. It is about the size of a rabbit.

a·grar·i·an (ə grâr'ē ən) *adj.* **1.** relating to farmland, its use, or its ownership: *agrarian practices.* **2.** relating to farmers or farming interests; agricultural: *an agrarian movement.*

agouti

a·gree (ə grē') *v.,* **a·greed, a·gree·ing.** —*v.i.* **1.** to have the same opinion or feeling; concur: *All the others wanted to go to the beach, but my cousins didn't agree.* **2.** to consent: *They agreed to wait for us after the movie.* **3.** to reach an understanding; come to terms: *The car dealer and my parents agreed on a price. The two sides finally agreed on the terms of the treaty.* **4.** to be in harmony; coincide: *Your description of the robbery agrees with the official report.* **5.** *Grammar.* to correspond in case, number, gender, or person. In the sentence *These books are new,* the words *these* and *are* agree with the subject *books.* —*v.t.* to acknowledge or accept; admit; grant: *I agree that the delay was my fault.*
·**to agree with.** to produce no ill effect in; be good or healthful for; suit: *Greasy food doesn't agree with me.*

a·gree·a·ble (ə grē'ə bəl) *adj.* **1.** to one's liking; pleasant: *an agreeable personality.* **2.** willing to consent: *Are you agreeable to my suggestion?* —**a·gree'a·ble·ness,** *n.* —**a·gree'a·bly,** *adv.*

a·gree·ment (ə grē'mənt) *n.* **1.** an understanding reached by two or more persons or groups, such as a treaty or contract: *a trade agreement between two nations. By agreement, neither of us ever mentioned the incident again.* **2.** the state of agreeing; harmony; accord: *My views on the subject are in agreement with yours.* **3.** *Grammar.* the correspondence of words in case, number, gender, or person. The phrases *that coat* and *those women* are in agreement, but *this men* is not in agreement.

ag·ri·busi·ness (ag'rə biz'nis) *n.* farming combined with businesses connected with farming, such as the manufacturing of farm equipment and the processing and distribution of farm products.

agric. 1. agricultural. **2.** agriculture.

ag·ri·cul·tur·al (ag'ri kul'chər əl) *adj.* relating to farms or farming; of agriculture: *agricultural research, an agricultural college.* —**ag'ri·cul'tur·al·ly,** *adv.*

ag·ri·cul·tur·al·ist (ag'ri kul'chər ə list) *n.* another word for **agriculturist.**

ag·ri·cul·ture (ag'ri kul'chər) *n.* the science, art, or business of cultivating the soil, producing crops, and raising livestock; farming.

ag·ri·cul·tur·ist (ag'ri kul'chər ist) *n.* **1.** a farmer. **2.** an expert in the science of agriculture.

a·gron·o·mist (ə gron'ə mist) *n.* a student of or an expert in agronomy.

a·gron·o·my (ə gron'ə mē) *n.* the branch of scientific agriculture concerned with crop production, including the cultivation of farmland and conservation and improvement of soil.

a·ground (ə ground') *adv., adj.* on or onto the shore or bottom; stranded, as in shallow water: *The boat ran aground on the sandbar.*

agt., agent.

a·gue (ā'gū) *n.* **1.** a malarial fever marked by regularly recurring cold, hot, and sweating stages. **2.** any fit of shivering; chill.

ah (ä) *interj.* used to show any of various feelings, such as pain, sorrow, joy, admiration, or surprise: *Ah, what a beautiful sunset!*

a·ha (ä hä') *interj.* used to show any of various feelings, such as triumph, satisfaction, discovery, surprise, or scorn.

A·hab (ā'hab) in Herman Melville's novel *Moby Dick,* a whaling captain intent on his pursuit of a white whale.

a·head (ə hed') *adv.* **1.** in front: *Walk ahead of me. The American runner was now ahead in the race.* **2.** forward; onward: *Go ahead with your plan.* **3.** toward the future; in advance: *to plan ahead. Set the clock ahead one hour.* **4.** having as a profit or advantage: *The home team is two goals ahead.*
·**to get ahead.** to advance one's position; succeed: *to get ahead in the business world.*

a·hem (ə hem') *interj.* a sound made by clearing the throat, used especially to attract attention or to give warning.

a·hoy (ə hoi') *interj.* used as a greeting or to attract attention, especially by sailors in hailing another ship.

AI, artificial intelligence.

aid (ād) *v.t.* to give help or support to; assist: *A research team aided the scientist in the experiment. The local police aided the federal agents.* —*v.i.* to give help: *Two teenagers aided in the rescue.* —*n.* **1.** help or support; assistance: *to walk with the aid of a cane.* **2.** a person or thing that is helpful: *to use the dictionary as an aid in writing a composition.*

aide (ād) *n.* **1.** a helper or assistant: *a nurse's aide, an aide to the president.* **2.** another word for **aide-de-camp.**

aide–de–camp (ād'də kamp') *n., pl.* **aides-de-camp.** a military officer who serves as an assistant to a superior officer, especially a general.

AIDS (ādz) *n.* a disease that severely damages the body's immune system, making the body more susceptible to other infections and diseases. AIDS is caused by a type of virus called a retrovirus and is transmitted by sexual intercourse or by exposure to infected blood. An infected woman who is pregnant can also transmit the disease to the fetus. [Abbreviation of A(cquired) I(mmune) D(eficiency) S(yndrome).]

ai·grette (ā'gret, ā gret') *n.* **1.** a plume or tuft of feathers, especially the feathers of the egret, worn as an ornament on hats and helmets. **2.** ornamental jewelry imitating such feathers.

ai·ki·do (ī kē'dō) *n.* a Japanese system of unarmed self-defense related to jujitsu. It uses various holds and throws to unbalance and overcome an opponent.

ail (āl) *v.t.* to cause illness, trouble, or discomfort to: *What ails you?* —*v.i.* to be ill or indisposed: *My elderly cousin has been ailing for years.*

ai·lan·thus (ā lan'thəs) *n., pl.* **ai·lan·thus·es.** a tree bearing featherlike leaves and clusters of small, greenish flowers. Also, **tree of heaven.**

ai·le·ron (ā'lə ron') *n.* a movable section on the rear edge of an airplane wing, used to control movement of the plane in flight.

ail·ment (āl'mənt) *n.* an illness or affliction: *to suffer from many ailments.*

aim (ām) *v.t.* **1.** to point or direct (a weapon or blow) for the purpose of hitting a target: *to aim a rifle. The boxer aimed a punch at the opponent's jaw.*

ailanthus

2. to direct (something) toward or intend for: *The police aim their campaign to reduce traffic accidents.* —*v.i.* **1.** to point or direct a weapon or blow: *to aim at a target.* **2.** to have as a goal; intend: *They aim to become professional musicians.* —*n.* **1.** the act of pointing or directing a weapon or blow at a target. **2.** the ability to hit a target: *to have good aim.* **3.** what one wants or wants to do; purpose; intention; goal: *My aim is good grades.*

aim·less (ām′lis) *adj.* without purpose or direction: *aimless wanderings, aimless remarks.* —**aim′less·ly,** *adv.* —**aim′less·ness,** *n.*

ain't (ānt) **1.** am not. **2.** is not; are not. **3.** has not; have not. ▲ **Ain't** is not considered good English by most people. Careful speakers try to avoid using *ain't.*

Ai·nu (ī′nü) *n., pl.* **Ai·nu** or **Ai·nus. 1.** a member of an aboriginal race of northern Japan, having light skin and dark hair. **2.** the language of the Ainus, not known to be related to any other language.

air (âr) *n.* **1.** the mixture of gases that surrounds and envelops the earth, forming its atmosphere. Air is invisible, odorless, and tasteless, and it consists chiefly of nitrogen and oxygen, with small amounts of argon, carbon dioxide, neon, and other gases. **2.** the open space above the earth; sky: *I threw the ball into the air.* **3.** a moving current of air; light wind. **4.** fresh air: *Please open the window and let in some air.* **5.** the impression, mood, or feeling given by a person or thing: *an air of mystery.* **6. airs.** haughty or affected manners assumed to impress others: *to put on airs.* **7.** a melody or tune. —*v.t.* **1.** to freshen, cool, or dry by exposing to air; ventilate: *to air a room. I aired my winter clothing after taking it out of the trunk.* **2.** to bring to public notice; express publicly: *The workers aired their complaints.* **3.** to broadcast by radio or television: *to air a special program.*

· **in the air.** going around; in circulation: *Rumors of a strike were in the air.*
· **off the air.** not broadcasting or being broadcasted.
· **on the air.** broadcasting or being broadcast.
· **to clear the air.** to remove tension or disagreements, as through discussion.
· **to walk on air.** to be very happy.
· **up in the air.** unsettled; undecided: *The date of the concert is still up in the air.*

air bag, a plastic bag mounted under an automobile dashboard or in front of a passenger, designed to inflate automatically in a collision to protect the driver or passenger from injury.

air base, a place from which military airplanes operate.

air bladder 1. a sac filled with air or another gas, found in most fish. It aids in maintaining buoyancy in the water. Also, **swim bladder. 2.** any air-filled sac, as in a bird or plant.

air·borne (âr′bôrn′) *adj.* **1.** carried by the air: *airborne pollen.* **2.** transported by airplanes or gliders: *airborne artillery.* **3.** off the ground; in flight: *By midnight we were airborne.*

air brake, a brake that is operated by the action of compressed air against a piston or pistons, used especially in trains, trucks, and buses.

air·brush (âr′brush′) *n., pl.* **air·brush·es.** an atomizer operated by compressed air, used to spray paint or other liquids on a surface. —*v.t.* to paint, embellish, or alter with an airbrush: *to airbrush a photograph.*

air-con·di·tion (âr′kən dish′ən) *v.t.* to provide with or ventilate by air conditioning: *to air-condition a room.*

air-con·di·tioned (âr′kən dish′ənd) *adj.* having air conditioning.

air conditioner, a machine that is used for air conditioning.

air conditioning, a system for controlling the temperature, humidity, purity, and circulation of the air in an enclosed area, such as a building, room, or vehicle.

air-cooled (âr′küld′) *adj.* cooled by circulating air: *an air-cooled automobile engine.*

air·craft (âr′kraft′) *n., pl.* **air·craft.** any machine designed for flight in the air, including airplanes, airships, gliders, and balloons. An aircraft may be supported by the action of air across its wings or may float because it is lighter than air.

aircraft carrier, a warship that serves as a base for aircraft, having a large, flat deck designed so that airplanes can take off from and land on it.

air·drome (âr′drōm′) *n.* another word for **airport.**

air·drop (âr′drop′) *v.t.,* **air·dropped, air·drop·ping.** to drop (food, supplies, or personnel) by parachute from aircraft in flight. —*n.* the act of dropping something by parachute from aircraft in flight.

Aire·dale (âr′dāl′) *n.* the largest breed of terrier, having a wiry tan coat with dark markings on the back and shoulders.

air·field (âr′fēld′) *n.* **1.** the landing field of an airport. **2.** an airport, especially a small one.

air·foil (âr′foil′) *n.* **1.** any part, such as a wing, aileron, or rudder, designed to help generate lift or control an aircraft by directing the flow of air over or around its surface. **2.** any body or surface that serves to control the direction of a flow of air.

air force 1. the branch of a country's armed forces in charge of aircraft and air warfare. **2. Air Force.** the air force of the United States.

air gun, a rifle or pistol using compressed air to propel its bullet or other projectile.

air hammer, an automatic hammer driven by compressed air.

air hole 1. a hole through which air is permitted to pass in or out. **2.** a natural opening in the ice on a river, pond, or the like.

air·i·ly (âr′ə lē) *adv.* in an airy manner; lightly; gaily.

air·i·ness (âr′ē nis) *n.* the quality or state of being airy.

air·ing (âr′ing) *n.* **1.** exposure to air for the purpose of drying or freshening: *to give a blanket an airing.* **2.** exposure to public knowledge or discussion: *The students' grievances received a thorough airing at the meeting.* **3.** a walk or ride in the open air.

air lane, a route used regularly by aircraft.

air·less (âr′lis) *adj.* **1.** without air. **2.** without fresh air; stuffy. **3.** without any wind; still.

air letter 1. a letter sent by airmail. **2.** a lightweight sheet of paper designed to fold into the form of an envelope, used for writing a letter to be sent by airmail.

air·lift (âr′lift′) *n.* an emergency system of transporting people or supplies by aircraft when roads or other land approaches to a place are closed. —*v.t.* to transport (something) by airlift: *to airlift food to a town cut off by a blizzard.*

air·line (âr′līn′) *n.* **1.** a system and equipment for transporting people and goods by aircraft. **2.** a business organization owning and managing such a system. **3.** a route used by such a system.

air·lin·er (âr′lī′nər) *n.* a large passenger airplane operated by an airline.

air lock 1. an airtight chamber in which air pressure can be varied, allowing passage between two places that do not have the same air pressures. **2.** a blockage in a pipe or other vessel, created by an air bubble.

air·mail (âr′māl′) *n.* **1.** mail carried by aircraft. **2.** a

A

at; āpe; fär; câre; end; mē; it; īce; pîerce; hot; ōld;
sông, fôrk; oil; out; up; ūse; rüle; pùll; tûrn; chin;
sing; shop; thin; this; hw in white; zh in treasure.
The symbol ə stands for the unstressed vowel sound
heard in about, taken, pencil, lemon, and circus.

system of transporting mail by aircraft. —*v.t.* to send by airmail. —*adj.* of or relating to airmail: *an airmail letter.* —*adv.* by means of airmail.

air·man (âr′mən) *n., pl.* **air·men** (âr′mən). **1.** a pilot or other member of the crew of an aircraft. **2.** in the U.S. Air Force, an enlisted person of either of the two lowest grades.

airman first class, in the U.S. Air Force, an enlisted person ranking below a sergeant and above an airman.

air mass, a widespread body of air that has approximately the same temperature, humidity, and pressure throughout: *A cold air mass arrived yesterday.*

air mile, a unit of distance in air navigation, equal to approximately 6,076 feet (1,852 meters).

air piracy, the act of hijacking an airplane in flight; skyjacking.

air·plane (âr′plān′) *n.* an aircraft that is heavier than air, is supported in flight by the action of air across its wings, and is driven by an engine or engines. Also, **aeroplane, plane.**

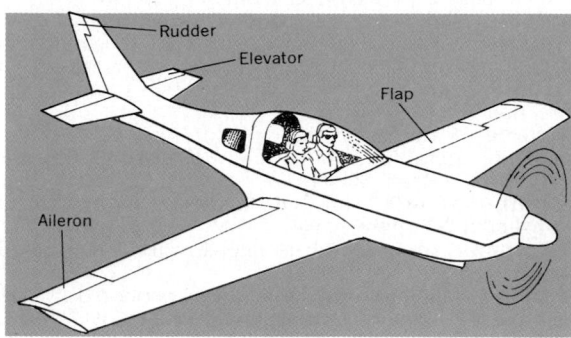

airplane

air plant, a plant that grows on another plant for support; epiphyte.

air pocket, a downward current of air causing an airplane to drop suddenly.

air·port (âr′pôrt′) *n.* an area equipped with facilities necessary for the landing, takeoff, repair, and storage of aircraft and for the loading and discharge of passengers and cargo. Also, **airdrome.**

air pressure, the pressure exerted in all directions by a mass of air.

air pump, a machine for compressing air in, or removing air from, a container, or for forcing air through pipes or other apparatus.

air raid, an attack by aircraft, especially the dropping of bombs on populated or industrial areas by organized groups of airplanes.

air rifle, a rifle powered by compressed air, especially one that shoots BB's.

air rights, the legal rights to own and use the space above a tract of land or any piece of property.

air sac 1. in birds, one of a number of air-filled pouches throughout the body that are connected to the lungs. **2.** see **alveolus** (*def.* 3).

air shaft, a passage to permit fresh air to flow into a mine, building, or the like.

air·ship (âr′ship′) *n.* any aircraft that is lighter than air, driven by a motor, and steered.

air·sick (âr′sik′) *adj.* sick as a result of the motion of an aircraft. —**air′sick′ness,** *n.*

air·space (âr′spās′) *n.* the space above some part of the earth, especially the space above a country, considered as subject to certain laws of that country.

air speed, the speed of an aircraft relative to the air through which it is moving rather than to the ground.

air·strip (âr′strip′) *n.* a paved or cleared area where aircraft can land and take off.

air·tight (âr′tīt′) *adj.* **1.** so tight as to prevent air or gas from entering or escaping. **2.** free of weak points that could easily be attacked, proved wrong, or criticized: *The prosecutor's airtight case convinced the jury.*

air·time (âr′tīm′) *n.* **1.** the time at which a radio or television broadcast begins: *Airtime of the show is 9 A.M.* **2.** the amount of time devoted to a broadcast: *The candidate bought two minutes of airtime on a local station.*

air–to–air (âr′tü âr′, âr′tə âr′) *adj.* launched from an aircraft and directed at an airborne target: *an air-to-air guided missile.*

air·waves (âr′ wāvz′) *pl. n.* the media through which radio and television broadcast signals are sent: *The concert was sent over the airwaves.*

air·way (âr′wā′) *n.* **1.** a route for aircraft; air lane. **2.** a passage used to permit a flow of fresh air, as in a mine.

air·wor·thy (âr′wûr′<u>th</u>ē) *adj.* (of an aircraft) in good or safe condition for flying. —**air′wor′thi·ness,** *n.*

air·y (âr′ē) *adj.,* **air·i·er, air·i·est.** **1.** light as air in appearance or movement; delicate or graceful: *an airy gown.* **2.** lighthearted; gay: *an airy tune.* **3.** open to the flow of air; breezy: *an airy apartment.* **4.** having no more substance than air does; unreal; imaginary: *an airy scheme for earning money.*

aisle (īl) *n.* **1.** a passageway between sections of seats in a place of assembly, such as a theater or stadium. **2.** any similar passageway: *an aisle between counters in a department store.* **3.** a side division of a church, set off from the main part by pillars or arches.

a·jar¹ (ə jär′) *adj., adv.* partly open: *The door was left ajar.* [From the Middle English phrase *on char* meaning "slightly open," going back to the Old English words *on* "in" and *cyrr* "a turning."]

a·jar² (ə jär′) *adv., adj.* out of harmony; in disorder: *My nerves are all ajar since the accident.* [A- + *jar²*.]

A·jax (ā′jaks) *n. Greek Legend.* a Greek hero in the Trojan War, known for his great bravery.

AK, postal abbreviation for Alaska.

a·kim·bo (ə kim′bō) *adj., adv.* with the hands on the hips and elbows out: *to stand with arms akimbo.*

a·kin (ə kin′) *adj.* **1.** belonging to the same family; related by blood. **2.** similar in character or properties; of the same kind: *Love and friendship are akin.*

–al¹ *suffix* (used to form adjectives) of, relating to, or characterized by: *medicinal, musical.* [Originally from the Latin suffix -*alis* with the same meaning as the English suffix.]

–al² *suffix* (used to form nouns from verbs) the act, process, or result: *recital, denial, arrival.* [Originally from the Latin suffix -*alia* with the same meaning as the English suffix.]

Al, the symbol for aluminum.

AL, postal abbreviation for Alabama.

Ala., Alabama.

al·a·bas·ter (al′ə bas′tər) *n.* **1.** a smooth, whitish stone used especially in sculpture. Alabaster is a fine-grained, translucent variety of gypsum. **2.** a calcite of a semi-translucent, hard variety, often having bandlike markings. —*adj.* resembling alabaster; smooth, translucent, and pale: *a person with alabaster skin.*

a la carte (ä′ lə kärt′) also, **à la carte.** with a separate price for each item on the menu, rather than one price for a complete meal.

a·lack (ə lak′) *interj.* an exclamation expressing regret, dismay, or disappointment.

a·lac·ri·ty (ə lak′ri tē) *n.* **1.** eager willingness: *I accepted the job with alacrity.* **2.** swiftness; liveliness: *to move with alacrity.*

A·lad·din (ə lad′in) *n.* in the *Arabian Nights,* a youth who obtains a magic lamp and a magic ring with which he is able to summon a genie to obey his commands.

a la king (ä′ lə king′) also, **à la king.** cooked in cream sauce with mushrooms and pimentos or green peppers: *chicken a la king.*

al·a·me·da (al′ə mē′də, al′ə mā′də) *n.* a shaded public walk lined with poplar or other trees.

Al·a·mo (al′ə mō′) *n.* a fortified mission in San Antonio, Texas, that was attacked and captured by Mexican troops in 1836. All of its defenders were killed.

a la mode (ä′ lə mōd′) *also,* **à la mode. 1.** served with ice cream: *apple pie a la mode.* **2.** braised with vegetables and served with a rich brown sauce: *beef a la mode.* **3.** in style; fashionable. [From the French phrase *à la mode* meaning "according to the fashion" or "in the manner (of)."]

a·larm (ə lärm′) *n.* **1.** a sudden fear of danger: *The clap of thunder filled the child with alarm.* **2.** a warning of danger: *Give the alarm.* **3.** a device or signal that warns, rouses, or calls to action: *a burglar alarm.* —*v.t.* **1.** to cause to feel sudden fear: *Reports of an approaching storm alarmed the ship's passengers.* **2.** to warn of danger. [From the old French word *alarme* meaning "alarm," from the old Italian call to arms *all'arme!* meaning "to the weapons!" or "to arms!"]

alarm clock, a clock that can be set to ring, buzz, or sound at any given time in order to wake a person.

a·larm·ing (ə lär′ming) *adj.* causing fear and excitement; disturbing: *alarming news.* —**a·larm′ing·ly,** *adv.*

a·larm·ist (ə lär′mist) *n.* a person who is inclined to become alarmed or to alarm others needlessly or on slight grounds.

a·lar·um (ə lar′əm) *n. Archaic.* a call to action or to arms.

a·las (ə las′) *interj.* an exclamation expressing disappointment, sorrow, or regret.

Alas., Alaska.

A·las·kan mal·a·mute (ə las′kən mal′ə mūt′) *n.* a wolflike dog of a breed native to northwestern Alaska, having a thick, coarse coat.

A·las·ka Standard Time (ə las′kə) the local time used in all of Alaska except the western Aleutian Islands. It is 9 hours behind Greenwich Time.

alb (alb) *n.* a white linen robe that is worn by Roman Catholic and some Anglican priests at the Mass and other ceremonies.

al·ba·core (al′bə kôr′) *n., pl.* **al·ba·core** or **al·ba·cores.** an important food and game fish that is related to the tuna. It is found mostly in warm seas and is distinguished from other tunas by its long pectoral fins.

Alaskan malamutes

Al·ba·ni·an (al bā′nē ən) *n.* **1.** a person who was born in or is a citizen of Albania. **2.** the language of Albania. —*adj.* of or relating to Albania, its people, their language, or culture.

al·ba·tross (al′bə trôs′) *n., pl.* **al·ba·tross·es. 1.** any of various web-footed seabirds, found chiefly in the southern oceans, having a long, hooked beak. An albatross is capable of very long flights. One species has a wingspan of up to 11 feet (3.3 meters), the largest of any living bird. **2.** a burden; millstone: *The unfinished work had become an albatross around my neck.*

al·be·it (ôl bē′it) *conj.* even though; although: *We had an enjoyable, albeit rather tiring, day at the zoo.*

al·bi·nism (al′bə niz′əm) *n.* the state of being an albino.

al·bi·no (al bī′nō) *n., pl.* **al·bi·nos. 1.** a person born with a lack of normal coloring, having pale, milky skin, very light hair, and pink eyes. **2.** any plant or animal with a lack of normal coloring.

Al·bi·on (al′bē ən) *n.* another name for **England.** ▲ used chiefly in literature.

al·bum (al′bəm) *n.* **1.** a book with blank pages in which to keep collected items: *a stamp album, a photograph album.* **2.** a holder for a phonograph record or records. **3.** a long-playing phonograph record, or a set of records sold as a unit.

al·bu·men (al bū′mən) *n.* **1.** the white of an egg. **2.** another word for **albumin.**

al·bu·min (al bū′mən) *n.* a protein that dissolves in water and is found in the whites of eggs, blood, and other plant and animal tissues and fluids.

al·che·mist (al′kə mist) *n.* a person who studied or practiced alchemy.

al·che·my (al′kə mē) *n.* a system of chemistry practiced during the Middle Ages. It was chiefly concerned with attempts to turn common metals into gold and with the search for a substance that would prolong life and cure all diseases. [From the Old French word *alkemie* meaning "alchemy," from the Medieval Latin word *alchemia,* from the Arabic word *al-kīmiyā,* from *al* meaning "the" + *kīmiyā* meaning "alchemy." The Arabic word *kīmiyā* comes from the Late Greek word *chēmia* meaning "transmutation of metals, chemistry."]

al·co·hol (al′kə hôl′) *n.* **1.** an odorless, flammable liquid that evaporates quickly and is produced synthetically or by fermenting grain, fruit, or other starchy or sugary substances. It is the substance in liquor that causes drunkenness and is used widely in the manufacture of drugs and other chemicals. Also, **ethanol, ethyl alcohol, grain alcohol. 2.** any drink containing this liquid, such as gin or bourbon. **3.** *Chemistry.* any of a group of colorless, flammable, organic compounds, such as wood alcohol.

al·co·hol·ic (al′kə hô′lik) *adj.* **1.** of, containing, or caused by alcohol. **2.** suffering from alcoholism. —*n.* a person who suffers from alcoholism.

Alcoholics Anonymous, an organization of men and women who are addicted or have been addicted to alcohol and who meet regularly to support each other in their efforts to recover.

al·co·hol·ism (al′kə hô liz′əm) *n.* a chronic illness in which a person feels a strong urge to drink large amounts of alcoholic beverages. Untreated alcoholism can lead to severe physical and mental illness.

al·cove (al′kōv) *n.* **1.** a small room or recess opening off a larger room. **2.** any closed-off space or area that is set back or apart: *an alcove in a garden.*

Al·deb·a·ran (al deb′ər ən) *n.* a giant red star in Taurus, one of the brightest stars in the sky.

al·der (ôl′dər) *n.* any of a group of trees or shrubs growing in cool, moist re-

alder

---

at; āpe; fär; câre; end; mē; it; īce; pîerce; hot; ōld; sông, fôrk; oil; out; up; ūse; rüle; pùll; tûrn; chin; sing; shop; thin; **th**is; hw in white; zh in treasure. The symbol ə stands for the unstressed vowel sound heard in about, taken, pencil, lemon, and circus.

gions of the Northern Hemisphere. Most alders have scaly bark and oval leaves.

al·der·man (ôl′dər mən) *n., pl.* **al·der·men** (ôl′dər mən). a member of the governing body or council of a city or town, often representing a certain ward or district.

ale (āl) *n.* an alcoholic drink made from hops and malt. It is similar to beer, but heavier and more bitter.

a·lee (ə lē′) *adv., adj.* on or toward the lee side of a ship; away from the wind.

a·lert (ə lûrt′) *adj.* 1. paying quick and close attention; keenly watchful: *An alert guard is needed for sentry duty.* 2. quick to act or learn; lively; active: *an alert mind.* —*n.* 1. a signal that warns of possible danger; alarm. 2. the period during which danger is possible: *They hid in the cellar during the alert.* —*v.t.* 1. to warn to be ready: *The coast guard alerted the town about the approaching hurricane.* 2. to make aware of: *They alerted the town to the fact that the water supply was running low.* —**a·lert′ly,** *adv.* —**a·lert′ness,** *n.*

·**on the alert.** on the lookout; watchful: *to be on the alert for any sign of danger.*

A·leut (ə lüt′) *n., pl.* **Aleut** or **Aleuts.** *n.* 1. a member of a Mongoloid race of people living in southwestern Alaska, the Aleutian Islands, and islands off the coast of Siberia. 2. the language spoken by these people, related to Eskimo. —*adj.* of or relating to the Aleut, their language, or their culture. Also, **A·leu·tian** (ə lü′shən)

ale·wife (āl′wīf′) *n., pl.* **ale·wives** (āl′wīvz′). a small bony fish found along the Atlantic coast of the United States. It swims upstream in large numbers to spawn.

Al·ex·an·dri·an (al′ig zan′drē ən) *adj.* 1. of ancient Alexandria. 2. of Alexander the Great or his reign.

al·fal·fa (al fal′fə) *n.* any of a group of plants resembling clover, many of which are widely grown as food for cattle and other livestock.

al·fres·co (al fres′kō) *also,* **al fres·co.** *adv., adj.* in the open air; outdoor or outdoors.

alg., algebra.

al·gae (al′jē) *pl. n., sing.* **al·ga** (al′gə). a large group of plants that lack true roots and flowers, including scums formed in ponds and most kinds of seaweed. Algae range in size from microscopic, one-celled organisms to giant seaweeds and kelps. The best-known kinds have chlorophyll and are found in water.

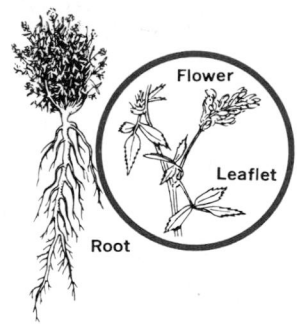

alfalfa

al·ge·bra (al′jə brə) *n.* the branch of mathematics in which quantities and the relationships between them are shown by letters, numerals, and abstract symbols. For example: *If 2x + y = 7, and x = 3, then y = 1.*

al·ge·bra·ic (al′jə brā′ik) *adj.* relating to or used in algebra: *2x + y = 7 is an algebraic equation.* Also, **al·ge·bra·i·cal** (al′jə brā′i kəl). —**al′ge·bra′i·cal·ly,** *adv.*

Al·gon·qui·an (al gong′kē ən, al gong′kwē ən) *n., pl.* **Al·gon·qui·an** or **Al·gon·qui·ans** 1. a family of North American Indian languages, including Cree, Delaware, Shawnee, Ojibwa, Blackfoot, and Cheyenne. 2. a member of any tribe that spoke one of these languages. —*adj.* of or relating to this family of languages.

Al·gon·quin (al gong′kin, al gong′kwin) *n., pl.* **Al·gon·quin** or **Al·gon·quins.** 1. a member of an Indian tribe that spoke an Algonquian language and lived along the Ottawa and St. Lawrence rivers in southeastern Canada. 2. the language spoken by this tribe.

al·go·rithm (al′gə rith′əm) *n.* a set of rules for solving a mathematical or computer problem, such as adding numbers or doing long division.

Al·ham·bra (al ham′brə) *n.* a palace in Granada, Spain, built by Moorish princes in the thirteenth century.

a·li·as (ā′lē əs) *n., pl.* **a·li·as·es.** a false name used to conceal one's real identity. *William H. Bonney's alias was Billy the Kid.* —*adv.* also known as; otherwise called: *Martha Jane Burk, alias Calamity Jane.*

al·i·bi (al′ə bī′) *n., pl.* **al·i·bis.** 1. a claim or proof of having been somewhere else when a crime or other act was committed: *Part of the thief's plan was to establish an alibi ahead of time.* 2. an excuse: *Do you have any alibi for not arriving on time?* —*v.i.,* **al·i·bied, al·i·bi·ing.** to offer an excuse: *My friends alibied for me.*

al·ien (āl′yən, ā′lē ən) *n.* 1. a person who is not a citizen of the country in which he or she is living. 2. a being from outer space. —*adj.* 1. of or belonging to another country or people; foreign. 2. not familiar or natural; strange; unfamiliar: *an alien pattern of behavior.* 3. not compatible; opposed: *Censorship of the press is alien to democracy.*

al·ien·ate (āl′yə nāt′, ā′lē ə nāt′) *v.t.,* **al·ien·at·ed, al·ien·at·ing.** 1. to cause (someone) to feel unfriendly, indifferent, or hostile: *Your thoughtless conduct alienated the whole family.* 2. to cause to be withdrawn or isolated: *Government scandals alienate some young people from society.* —**al′ien·a′tion,** *n.*

a·light¹ (ə līt′) *v.i.,* **a·light·ed** or **a·lit, a·light·ing.** 1. to step down from; get off: *The rider alighted from the pony.* 2. to land from flight: *The bee alighted on the flower.* [From the Old English word *ālīhtan* meaning "to descend" or "come down from," from the word *līhtan* "to remove a weight from."]

a·light² (ə līt′) *adv., adj.* 1. lighted up; aglow: *a restaurant alight with candles, a face alight with joy.* 2. on fire; burning. [From the past participle of the obsolete word *alight* meaning "to light up," from the Old English word *ālīhtan* "to enlighten, light up," going back to the word *lēoht* "light."]

a·lign (ə līn′) *also,* **a·line.** *v.t.* 1. to bring into line: *to align a golf club with the ball.* 2. to ally (oneself) with others for a common cause: *In the voting the Republicans aligned themselves with the Southern Democrats.* 3. to adjust (the wheels of a vehicle) to their proper position. 4. to adjust (the parts of a machine or device) for proper functioning. —*v.i.* to fall into line.

a·lign·ment (ə līn′mənt) *also,* **a·line·ment.** *n.* 1. the act of aligning or the state of being aligned: *The wheels of the car are out of alignment.* 2. a line or lines formed by aligning. 3. the act or policy of allying with others.

a·like (ə līk′) *adv.* in the same way; similarly: *The twins often dress alike.* —*adj.* like one another; similar: *No two people have fingerprints that are alike.*

al·i·men·ta·ry (al′ə men′tə rē, al′ə men′trē) *adj.* of or relating to food and nutrition.

alimentary canal, a continuous tube extending from the mouth to the anus, through which food passes as it is digested, then absorbed, and finally eliminated as waste matter.

al·i·mo·ny (al′ə mō′nē) *n.* a fixed sum of money that a court may order one spouse to pay to support the other after they are divorced or legally separated.

a·line (ə līn′) *v.t., v.i.,* **a·lined, a·lin·ing.** another spelling of **align.** —**a·line′ment,** *n.*

a·lit (ə lit′) a past tense and past participle of **alight¹.**

a·live (ə līv′) *adj.* 1. having life; living: *If you don't put those flowers in water, they won't be alive much longer.* 2. in force or operation; active: *to keep alive a child's belief in Santa Claus.* 3. full of life; animated; lively: *We were alive with excitement on the night of the dance.* 4. of all living: *the proudest grandparents alive.* —**a·live′ness,** *n.*

·**alive with.** filled or swarming with: *The porch was alive with mosquitoes.*

al·ka·li (al′kə lī′) *n., pl.* **al·ka·lis** or **al·ka·lies.** 1. any of a group of strong bases that dissolve in water, or the salts formed when these bases react with acids. Ammonia and lye are common alkalis. **2.** any mineral salt that dissolves in water, or a mixture of such salts. Alkalis are found in soils, especially desert soil.

al·ka·li metal, any of a group of soft, metallic elements. The alkali metals are lithium, sodium, potassium, rubidium, cesium, and francium.

al·ka·line (al′kə līn′) *adj.* of, like, or containing an alkali. —**al·ka·lin·i·ty** (al′kə lin′i tē), *n.*

al·ka·line–earth metal (al′kə līn′ûrth′) any of a group of metallic elements. The alkaline-earth metals are beryllium, magnesium, calcium, strontium, barium, and radium.

al·ka·lize (al′kə līz′) *v.*, **al·ka·lized, al·ka·liz·ing.** —*v.t.* to make (something) alkaline. —*v.i.* to become alkaline.

al·ka·loid (al′kə loid′) *n.* any of a group of alkaline substances, including morphine, caffeine, and quinine. Alkaloids are obtained chiefly from certain plants and are widely used in medicine.

all (ôl) *adj.* **1.** the whole of; every part of: *I finished all the work you gave me. We ate all the ice cream.* **2.** the entire number of: *Delegates from all states attended the convention.* **3.** the greatest possible: *Come home with all speed.* **4.** any whatever: *The crisis has gone beyond all hope.* **5.** nothing but; only: *This is all nonsense.* —*n.* **1.** everything one has: *The runners gave their all when they saw the finish line.* **2.** everything: *All is lost.* —*pron.* **1.** the whole quantity, amount, or number: *All of the cake is gone.* **2.** every one; each: *All answered yes.* —*adv.* **1.** wholly; completely; entirely: *Your figures are all wrong.* **2.** each; apiece: *The score at the half was seven all.*

• **above all.** before everything else; most importantly: *Above all, a lifeguard must be a good swimmer.*

• **after all.** considering everything; despite everything: *Even though some people couldn't come, it was, after all, a good party.*

• **all but.** not quite completely: *The family business was all but ruined during the depression.*

• **all in.** *Informal.* exhausted; weary.

• **all in all.** everything considered; on the whole.

• **all of.** no less than: *I am all of sixty years old.*

• **all out.** *Informal.* with the greatest effort possible: *We went all out to help catch the runaway horse.*

• **all over.** **a.** finished; ended. **b.** many places; everywhere: *We searched for the dog all over.* **c.** *Informal.* in every way; typically: *That's my cousin all over.*

• **at all.** **a.** in any way: *I can't sing at all.* **b.** under any circumstances. *They say they won't come here at all.*

• **for all** or **for all that. a.** in spite of: *For all their kind words, they're still not to be trusted.* **b.** as far as: *For all we know, the weather may change this afternoon.*

• **in all.** altogether: *In all, about fifty people attended.*

Al·lah (al′ə, ä′lə) *n.* in the Muslim religion, God.

all–A·mer·i·can (ôl′ə mer′i kən) *adj.* **1.** typical of the United States: *an all-American teenager.* **2.a.** selected as the best of his or her type in the United States: *an all-American halfback.* **b.** made up of people so selected: *an all-American team.* **c.** made up entirely of Americans or American parts: *an all-American expedition.* —*n.* an all-American player or athlete.

all–a·round (ôl′ə round′) *adj.* **1.** good at many things: *an all-around athlete.* **2.** good for many purposes: *an all-around education.* Also, **all-round.**

al·lay (ə lā′) *v.t.*, **al·layed, al·lay·ing. 1.** to put to rest; quiet; calm: *The veterinarian allayed the child's fears about the sick dog.* **2.** to make less severe: *The ice pack allayed the pain in my ankle.*

all clear, a signal indicating that an air raid or other danger is over.

al·le·ga·tion (al′i gā′shən) *n.* a statement or declaration, especially one made without proof.

al·lege (ə lej′) *v.t.*, **al·leged, al·leg·ing. 1.** to state or declare, especially without proof: *The state alleged that they had not paid taxes.* **2.** to give as an excuse or reason: *They alleged that a flat tire had made them late.* —**al·lege′a·ble,** *adj.* —**al·leg′er,** *n.*

al·leged (ə lejd′) *adj.* declared to be so, but without proof: *The alleged murderer was later proven to be innocent.* —**al·leg·ed·ly** (ə lej′id lē), *adv.*

al·le·giance (ə lē′jəns) *n.* **1.** loyalty or faithfulness to a government, country, or ruler: *to pledge allegiance to the United States.* **2.** loyalty or devotion to a person, cause, or thing: *The workers felt great allegiance to their union.*

al·le·gor·i·cal (al′i gôr′i kəl) *adj.* relating to or containing an allegory: *an allegorical poem.* Also, **al·le·gor·ic** (al′ə gôr′ik). —**al′le·gor′i·cal·ly,** *adv.*

al·le·go·ry (al′i gôr′ē) *n.*, *pl.* **al·le·go·ries.** a story that teaches a lesson or shows something about life by having the characters and events stand for ideas, people, or moral principles. Aesop's fables are examples of allegories.

al·le·gret·to (al′i gret′ō) *Music. adj., adv.* slower than allegro, but rather lively. —*n.*, *pl.* **al·le·gret·tos.** a piece, movement, or passage in a rather lively tempo.

al·le·gro (ə lā′grō, ə leg′rō) *Music. adj., adv.* faster than allegretto but slower than presto; lively; fast. —*n.*, *pl.* **al·le·gros.** a piece, movement, or passage in a fast tempo.

al·lele (ə lēl′) *n.*, *pl.* **al·leles.** any of the possible forms of a gene that determines a particular inherited trait, such as hair or eye color.

al·le·lu·ia (al′ə lü′yə) *interj.* another word for **hallelujah.** —*n.* a hymn or other musical composition based on the word *alleluia.*

al·ler·gen (al′ər jən) *n.* a substance that causes allergy.

al·ler·gen·ic (al′ər jen′ik) *adj.* causing allergy.

al·ler·gic (ə lûr′jik) *adj.* **1.** of or caused by allergy: *A rash is sometimes an allergic reaction.* **2.** having an allergy: *I'm allergic to chocolate.* **3.** *Informal.* having a strong dislike (with *to*): *to be allergic to hard work.*

al·ler·gy (al′ər jē) *n.*, *pl.* **al·ler·gies.** an abnormal reaction of the body to a certain substance that is harmless to most people, such as pollen, dust, animal hair, wool, or certain foods. Allergies result in symptoms such as hives, rashes, sneezing, and asthma.

al·le·vi·ate (ə lē′vē āt′) *v.t.*, **al·le·vi·at·ed, al·le·vi·at·ing.** to make easier to bear; relieve; lessen: *The pill alleviated the pain.* —**al·le·vi·a′tion,** *n.*

al·ley¹ (al′ē) *n.*, *pl.* **al·leys. 1.** a narrow street or passageway, especially one at the rear of a row of buildings. **2.** see **bowling alley. 3.** a path or walk bordered by trees or shrubbery. [From the Old French word *alee* meaning "a passage, a walk," from the word *aler* meaning "to go," from the Latin word *ambulare* "to walk, to go."]

• **up one's alley.** *Slang.* to one's liking; suited to one's talents: *This job should be right up your alley.*

al·ley² (al′ē) *n.*, *pl.* **al·leys.** a large playing marble, used to shoot at other marbles. [Short for *alabaster.* The best marbles were originally made from alabaster.]

al·ley·way (al′ē wā′) *n.* a narrow or short passageway between buildings.

All Fools' Day, another name for **April Fools' Day.**

All·hal·lows (ôl hal′ōz) *n.*, *pl.* **All·hal·lows.** another name for **All Saints' Day.**

al·li·ance (ə lī′əns) *n.* **1.** a formal agreement between two or more nations to cooperate closely, as in fighting a

at; āpe; fär; câre; end; mē; it; īce; pîerce; hot; ōld; sông, fôrk; oil; out; up; ūse; rüle; pull; tûrn; chin; sing; shop; thin; this; hw in white; zh in treasure. The symbol ə stands for the unstressed vowel sound heard in about, taken, pencil, lemon, and circus.

war or trading goods. **2.** any similar agreement in which persons or groups join together for a common cause: *Government and business formed an alliance to bolster the economy.* **3.** the persons, nations, or groups taking part in such an agreement.

al·lied (ə līd′, al′īd) *adj.* **1.** united by treaty or agreement for a common purpose: *allied nations, allied labor unions.* **2.** related or similar: *Painting and sculpture are allied arts.* **3. Allied.** of or relating to the Allies.

Al·lies (al′īz, ə līz′) *pl. n.* **1.** the nations allied against the Axis in World War II, especially the United States, Great Britain, and the Soviet Union. **2.** the nations allied against the Central Powers in World War I, especially Great Britain, Russia, France, and the United States.

al·li·ga·tor (al′i gā′tər) *n.* **1.** a large reptile with a thick, tough skin, similar to the crocodile but having a broader snout. Alligators are found in the United States and China. **2.** leather made from the skin of an alligator. [Spanish *el lagarto* the lizard, from Latin *lacertus* a lizard.]

alligator pear, another term for **avocado.**

all–im·por·tant (ôl′ im pôr′tənt) *adj.* making the difference, as between success and failure; essential: *Water is all-important in the desert.*

al·lit·er·a·tion (ə lit′ə rā′shən) *n.* the repetition of the same initial letter, sound, or group of sounds in a series of words. For example: *tender torrents of tears.*

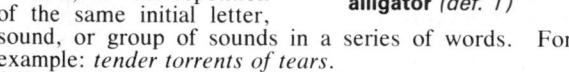

Alligator

Crocodile

alligator *(def. 1)*

al·lit·er·a·tive (ə lit′ə rā′tiv, ə lit′ər ə tiv) *adj.* of or characterized by alliteration: *an alliterative song.*

al·lo·cate (al′ə kāt′) *v.t.,* **al·lo·cat·ed, al·lo·cat·ing.** to set aside or divide for a specific purpose: *to allocate funds for public housing.* —**al′lo·ca′tion,** *n.*

al·lot (ə lot′) *v.t.,* **al·lot·ted, al·lot·ting.** to give out or assign as a share: *The teacher allotted five minutes to each question on the test.*

al·lot·ment (ə lot′mənt) *n.* **1.** the act or process of allotting. **2.** an amount allotted.

al·lot·ro·py (ə lot′rə pē) *n.* the existence of a chemical element in two or more forms that have different structures.

all–out (ôl′ out′) *adj.* using all one's energy or resources: *an all-out effort to win a race.*

all·o·ver (ôl′ō′vər) *adj.* covering the whole surface: *A dress with an allover pattern of polka dots.*

al·low (ə lou′) *v.t.* **1.** to grant permission to or for; permit: *My parents allow me to drive the car. Smoking is not allowed in this theater.* **2.** to let have; give: *They allow me ten dollars a week for lunch money.* **3.** to take into account or make provision for; set aside: *You must allow extra time for the trip because of the traffic.* **4.** to accept as true or valid: *to allow a point in a argument.*

　·**to allow for.** to think of and plan for; make provision for: *We allowed for medical expenses in planning our budget.*

　·**to allow of.** to have as possible; permit: *This problem allows of only one solution.*

al·low·a·ble (ə lou′ə bəl) *adj.* that can be allowed; not forbidden. —**al·low′a·bly,** *adv.*

al·low·ance (ə lou′əns) *n.* **1.** a quantity granted or set apart, especially a sum of money given regularly or for a particular purpose: *an allowance of one dollar a week, a travel allowance.* **2.** a reduction in price given in return for something: *The dealer gave us an allowance of $600*

on our old car when we traded it in for a new one. **3.** the act of allowing or conceding; acceptance: *the court's allowance of a claim.*

　·**to make allowance for** or **to make allowances for.** to think of and plan for; take into consideration: *They made allowance for the tides and arrived at the island on time.*

al·loy (*n.,* al′oi, ə loi′; *v.,* ə loi′) *n.* **1.** a metal formed by fusing two or more metals, or a metal and another substance: *Brass is an alloy of copper and zinc.* Alloys tend to be harder, stronger, and more resistant to heat than the substances of which they are made. **2.** a less valuable metal mixed with a more valuable one. **3.** something that lessens the purity or value of another thing. —*v.t.* **1.** to combine (two or more metals) so as to form an alloy. **2.** to make less pure or valuable by mixing: *Their pleasure in eating the stolen pie was alloyed with guilt.*

all–pur·pose (ôl′pûr′pəs) *adj.* useful for many purposes: *an all-purpose detergent, an all-purpose flour.*

all right **1.** satisfactory; acceptable: *His work is all right. It's all right with me if you go.* **2.** safe; uninjured; well: *Are you all right?* **3.** yes; agreed: *All right, I'll do it.* **4.** satisfactorily: *I'm doing all right.* **5.** without fail; certainly: *I'll be there, all right.* ▲ See **alright** for usage note.

all–round (ôl′ round′) another word for **all-around.**

All Saints' Day, a Christian festival celebrated in honor of all the saints. It falls on November 1. Also, **Allhallows, Hallowmas.**

All Souls' Day, in the Roman Catholic Church, a day of services and prayer for the souls in purgatory. It falls on November 2.

all·spice (ôl′spīs′) *n.* **1.** a spice made from dried and ground berries of the pimento tree. Its flavor resembles a blend of cinnamon, nutmeg, and cloves. **2.** the berry or tree itself.

all–star (ôl′stär′) *adj.* made up of exceptional or star players or performers: *an all-star baseball team.* —*n.* someone who is or should be chosen for an all-star group.

al·lude (ə lüd′) *v.i.,* **al·lud·ed, al·lud·ing.** to refer to indirectly; mention casually or in passing: *Don't even allude to our errors in yesterday's game.*

al·lure (ə lür′) *v.t.,* **al·lured, al·lur·ing.** to fascinate or attract with something tempting or desirable. —*n.* the power to allure; fascination; attractiveness: *the allure of traveling to faraway countries.* —**al·lur′er,** *n.*

al·lure·ment (ə lür′mənt) *n.* **1.** something that allures: *The scholarship was a powerful allurement.* **2.** the power to allure: *the allurement of the sea.*

al·lur·ing (ə lür′ing) *adj.* very attractive or tempting: *an alluring smile, an alluring offer.*

al·lu·sion (ə lü′zhən) *n.* **1.** a mention made indirectly or in passing; something alluded to: *This novel contains many allusions to the works of Shakespeare.* **2.** the act of alluding.

al·lu·vi·al (ə lü′vē əl) *adj.* of, relating to, or composed of alluvium: *an alluvial deposit.* —*n.* alluvial material.

al·lu·vi·um (ə lü′vē əm) *n., pl.* **al·lu·vi·ums** or **al·lu·vi·a** (ə lü′vē ə). mud, sand, or other material carried and deposited by a river or other flowing water.

al·ly (*v.,* ə lī′, al′ī; *n.,* al′ī, ə lī′) *v.t.,* **al·lied, al·ly·ing. 1.** to unite or associate (oneself) with for a common purpose: *The United States allied itself with England and Canada during World War II.* **2.** to connect by some similarity or common feature; relate. *n., pl.* **al·lies.** a person, nation, or group united with another for a common purpose: *France was an ally of the American colonies during the Revolutionary War.*

al·ma ma·ter (äl′mə mä′tər) *also,* **Al·ma Ma·ter. 1.** the school, college, or university that a person has attended: *John F. Kennedy's alma mater was Harvard University.* **2.** the official song of a school, college, or

A

university. [From the Latin phrase *alma mater* meaning "nourishing mother." Students thought of their school as a mother who brought them up and nourished them.]

al·ma·nac (ôl′mə nak′) *n.* **1.** a reference book that is compiled every year, containing general information and important statistics on many different subjects. **2.** a book arranged by days, weeks, and months, containing facts and forecasts about the weather, the tides, and the rising and setting of the sun.

al·might·y (ôl mī′tē) *adj.* having limitless power; all-powerful. —*n.* **the Almighty.** God.

al·mond (ä′mənd, am′ənd) *n.* **1.** the edible, oval-shaped nut of a tree growing in warm regions. The sweet variety of almond is widely used in desserts, candy, and cooking. **2.** the tree that bears this fruit.

al·mond–eyed (ä′mənd īd′, am′ənd īd′) *adj.* having narrow, oval-shaped eyes.

al·mon·er (al′mə nər, ä′mə nər) *n.* a person who gives out alms as an official duty, as for a church or royal court.

al·most (ôl′mōst) *adv.* nearly but not completely: *The skater almost fell on the ice, but recovered just in time. The job is almost done.*

alms (ämz) *n.* money or gifts for the poor. ▲ used with a singular or plural verb.

alms·house (ämz′hous′) *n., pl.* **alms·hous·es** (ämz′hou′ziz). a home for people too poor to support themselves; poorhouse.

al·oe (al′ō) *n., pl.* **al·oes. 1.** any of a group of succulent plants native mostly to dry parts of Africa. Most aloes have thick, fleshy leaves with spiny edges and red or yellow flowers growing at the top of tall, leafless stalks. **2. aloes.** a bitter drug made from the juice of this plant's leaves. ▲ used with a singular verb. **3.** the century plant of North America.

a·loft (ə lôft′) *adv.* **1.** in or to a place far above the ground; high up. **2.** or in toward the rigging of a ship; far above the deck.

a·lo·ha (ə lō′ə, ä lō′hä) *n., interj.* **1.** greetings; hello. **2.** good-bye; farewell. [From the Hawaiian word *aloha* meaning "love," used either as a greeting or farewell.]

a·lone (ə lōn′) *adj.* **1.** apart from anyone or anything else: *The orphan was all alone in the world.* **2.** excluding all other persons or things; only; solely: *Congress alone can declare a war.* ▲ used after the word or words it modifies in definition 2. —*adv.* without anyone or anything else: *I will be traveling alone.*

　•**let alone.** not to mention: *I can't even make toast, let alone cook an entire meal.*

　•**to leave alone** or **to let alone.** to leave undisturbed; not bother or interfere with: *I'm busy right now, so leave me alone.*

　•**to leave well enough alone** or **to let well enough alone.** to be content with things the way they are; to not disturb things.

a·long (ə lông′) *prep.* over the length of: *Flowers grew along the path. We walked along the highway.* —*adv.* **1.** onward; forward: *The car moved along swiftly.* **2.** near or on one's person; with one: *Bring your umbrella along.*

　•**all along.** from the start: *The enemy knew about the plan all along.*

　•**along with. a.** together with: *Let me go along with you to the market.* **b.** in addition to.

a·long·side (ə lông′sīd′) *adv.* close to or by the side: *They brought the rescue boat alongside.* —*prep.* by or at the side of; beside: *Park the car alongside the curb.*

　•**alongside of.** side by side with; next to: *The soldiers stood at attention alongside of each other.*

a·loof (ə lüf′) *adv.* at a distance in position or feeling; apart: *They kept aloof from their neighbors.* —*adj.* not warm or friendly; reserved; distant: *an aloof manner.* —**a·loof′ly,** *adv.* —**a·loof′ness,** *n.*

a·loud (ə loud′) *adv.* **1.** with the voice; so as to be heard:

All the students will read their reports aloud to the class. **2.** loudly: *The child shouted aloud.*

alp (alp) *n.* a high mountain or mountain peak.

al·pac·a (al pak′ə) *n.* **1.** a South American animal closely related to the llama, raised in the Andes Mountains for its fine, silky wool. **2.** the wool of this animal. **3.** a silky, lightweight fabric woven from or containing this wool, used especially for coats and suits.

al·pen·horn (al′pən hôrn′) *n.* a long, slightly curved, wooden horn, used by herders in the Alps.

al·pen·stock (al′pən stok′) *n.* a strong staff having an iron point, used in mountain climbing.

al·pha (al′fə) *n.* **1.** the first letter of the Greek alphabet (A, α) corresponding to the English letter A, a. **2.** the first in a group or series; beginning.

alpha and omega, the beginning and the end; the first and the last. [From the names of the first and last letters of the Greek alphabet.]

alpenhorns

al·pha·bet (al′fə bet′) *n.* **1.** a series of letters or characters used to write a language, arranged in an established order. **2.** any system of characters or symbols representing sounds or words: *In this dictionary pronunciation is shown by a phonetic alphabet.* [From the Late Latin word *alphabetum* meaning "the letters of a language," from the Greek word *alphabetos,* from *alpha* and *bēta,* the names of the first two letters in the Greek alphabet.]

Language Note

The **alphabet** that we use today is one of about fifty alphabets used in the modern world. Although these alphabets may differ in the number and design of their letters, they are all based on the idea of using symbols to represent the sound of language.

The first alphabets appeared about 4,000 years ago in what we now call the Middle East. These early alphabets, which included the ancient Semitic, early Hebrew, and early Phoenician alphabets, were most probably based on ancient Egyptian picture writing, known as hieroglyphics. North Semitic alphabets contained 22 letters which were placed in a fixed order that could be memorized and recited. Each letter had a name, the first sound of the

at; āpe; fär; câre; end; mē; it; īce; pîerce; hot; ōld; sông, fôrk; oil; out; up; ūse; rüle; pull; tûrn; chin; sing; shop; thin; **this**; hw in white; zh in treasure. The symbol ə stands for the unstressed vowel sound heard in about, taken, pencil, lemon, and circus.

name being the sound that the letter represented. For example, the second letter of these alphabets was called *beth*, which, like our letter *B*, stood for a *b* sound. Unlike our modern alphabet, these ancient alphabets had no symbols for vowels.

The North Semitic alphabets spread westward along the north coast of the Mediterranean, probably by way of the Phoenicians, who were great seafarers and traders and were the source of the ancient Greek alphabet, which appeared about 3,000 years ago. The names of the letters, such as *beth*, which became *beta*, were only slightly changed by the Greeks. For the most part, the shape of the North Semitic letters was also used. The Greeks added several new letters to stand for speech sounds in Greek that were not represented in the North Semitic alphabets. They also used some of the North Semitic letters to stand for vowel sounds, which had not previously been represented. The Greek alphabet, in turn, was the source of the Etruscan alphabet. The Etruscans, who settled north of Rome before the eighth century B.C., used the twenty-two North Semitic letters and four additional Greek letters in their alphabet. In the seventh century B.C., the Latin alphabet was developed, using the shape and sound of the Etruscan letters with only minor changes. In later years, certain Greek and Etruscan letters were dropped from the Latin alphabet and a new letter, *G*, was added. By about the first century A.D., the Latin alphabet consisted of twenty-three letters, lacking only the modern letters *W*, *U*, and *J*, which were added to certain Western alphabets during the Middle Ages. Our modern English alphabet is a direct descendant of the Latin alphabet.

al·pha·bet·i·cal (al'fə bet'i kəl) *adj.* **1.** in the order of the letters of the alphabet: *words in alphabetical order.* **2.** relating to or using an alphabet. Also, **al·pha·bet·ic** (al'fə bet'ik). —**al'pha·bet'i·cal·ly,** *adv.*

al·pha·bet·ize (al'fə bi tīz') *v.t.,* **al·pha·bet·ized, al·pha·bet·iz·ing.** to arrange in alphabetical order: *The publisher alphabetized the list of names.* —**al·pha·bet·i·za·tion** (al'fə bet'ə zā'shən), *n.* —**al'pha·bet·i'zer,** *n.*

al·pha·nu·mer·ic (al'fə nü mer'ik) *adj.* of or relating to a set of symbols, especially computer characters, that include both letters of the alphabet and numerals. A, B, C and 1, 2, 3 are alphanumeric characters.

alpha particle, a positively charged particle that is identical to the nucleus of an atom of helium. It consists of two protons and two neutrons. Alpha particles are given off by certain radioactive substances.

alpha ray, a stream of alpha particles.

al·pine (al'pīn) *adj.* **1.** of, like, or situated in high mountains: *alpine flowers.* **2. Alpine.** of or relating to the Alps. —*n.* a plant of a type that grows primarily in high mountains.

al·read·y (ôl red'ē) *adv.* **1.** before or by this time; previously: *They've already left. The job has already been done.* **2.** so soon: *Are you finished already?*
▲ The adverb **already** should not be confused with the two words **all ready. Already** means "previously" and "so soon." **All ready** means "completely ready": *I was all ready to go at eight o'clock.*

al·right (ôl rīt') another spelling of **all right.** ▲ The form *alright* is not considered to be a correct spelling of the phrase **all right,** and careful writers avoid using it.

Al·sa·tian (al sā'shən) *n.* **1.** a person who was born in or is a citizen of Alsace. **2.** another name for **German shepherd.** —*adj.* of or relating to Alsace or its people.

al·so (ôl'sō) *adv.* in addition; as well; too: *Australia is a country and also a continent.*

al·so–ran (ôl'sō ran') *n. Informal.* **1.** a horse that fails to finish in first, second, or third place in a race. **2.** a person who loses in a competition, especially one who finishes far behind the winner.

alt., altitude.

Alta., Alberta.

al·tar (ôl'tər) *n.* **1.** a raised structure or place where religious services are performed, as, in some Christian churches, the table where Communion services are held. **2.** a place where sacrifices are offered to a god.

altar boy, a boy or man who aids a priest during religious services, as during Mass.

al·tar·piece (ôl'tər pēs') *n.* a decorative drapery or panel behind or above an altar.

al·ter (ôl'tər) *v.t.* **1.** to make different; change: *The tailor altered the dress to fit me.* **2.** to castrate or spay (an animal). —*v.i.* to become different; change: *My attitude toward schoolwork has altered in the past year.* —**al'ter·a·ble,** *adj.* —**al'ter·a·bly,** *adv.*

al·ter·a·tion (ôl'tə rā'shən) *n.* **1.** the act of altering or the state of being altered: *Alteration of the coat will take at least one day.* **2.** the result of altering; change: *There's been an alteration in our plans.*

al·ter·ca·tion (ôl'tər kā'shən) *n.* a loud or angry dispute.

al·ter e·go (ôl'tər ē'gō) *n.* **1.** a constant companion or very close friend. **2.** another side of one's personality.

al·ter·nate (*v.,* ôl'tər nāt'; *adj., n.,* ôl'tər nit) *v.,* **al·ter·nat·ed, al·ter·nat·ing.** —*v.i.* **1.** to take turns: *The teenagers alternate at washing the car.* **2.** to follow each other by turns; happen or appear in turn: *Red squares alternate with black ones on this checkerboard.* **3.** to pass back and forth from one condition, action, or place to another. —*v.t.* **1.** to do or perform by turns: *The entertainer alternated singing and dancing.* **2.** to cause to follow one another by turns. —*adj.* **1.** occurring or following by turns: *alternate layers of cake and icing.* **2.** following each other but with an exception between every two; every other: *I have piano lessons on alternate Mondays.* **3.** taking the place of another; substitute; alternative: *The club sent an alternate delegate to the convention.* —*n.* a person who takes the place of another; substitute. —**al'ter·nate·ly,** *adv.* —**al'ter·na'tion,** *n.*

alternate angles, two angles that are not adjacent to each other and are formed on opposite sides of a line that crosses two other lines.

alternating current, an electric current in which the electrons flow regularly first in one direction and then in the other, as contrasted with direct current.

al·ter·na·tive (ôl tûr'nə tiv) *n.* **1.** a choice between two or more things: *the alternative of a quick airplane ride or a longer, scenic trip by car.* **2.** one of the things that may be chosen: *I chose the alternative of driving.* **3.** other or remaining choice: *You have no alternative but to admit the truth.* —*adj.* being or giving a choice between two or more things.

al·ter·na·tor (ôl'tər nā'tər) *n.* a generator that produces alternating electric current.

al·though (ôl thō') also, **al·tho.** *conj.* in spite of the fact that; even though; though: *Although I ate a big dinner, I was hungry soon afterward.*

al·tim·e·ter (al tim'i tər, al'tə mē'tər) *n.* an instrument for measuring altitude above sea level or the ground, used chiefly in aircraft.

al·ti·tude (al'ti tüd', al'ti tūd') *n.* **1.** the elevation above any given point, especially above the earth's surface or sea level: *The plane flew at an altitude of 20,000 feet.* **2. altitudes.** great heights; high places: *Frostbite is common in some mountain altitudes.* **3.** *Geometry.* the perpendicular distance from the base of a figure to its highest point. **4.** *Astronomy.* the angle of elevation of a celestial body above the horizon.

al·to (al'tō) *n., pl.* **al·tos. 1.** the lowest female voice; contralto. **2.** the highest adult male voice; countertenor. **3.** a singer who has such a voice. **4.** a musical instrument that has a similar range. **5.** a musical part for such a voice

A

or instrument. —*adj.* **1.** able to sing or play alto: *an alto voice, an alto recorder.* **2.** for an alto: *an alto solo.*

al·to·cu·mu·lus (al'tō kū'myə ləs) *n., pl.* **al·to·cu·mu·lus** or **al·to·cu·mu·li** (al'tō kū'myə lī'). a middle-level cloud, grayer on the bottom, consisting of large, oval-shaped masses often separated by clear sky. See **cloud** (*def. 1.*).

al·to·geth·er (ôl'tə geth'ər) *adv.* **1.** entirely; wholly; completely: *The arrow missed the target altogether.* **2.** with everything included; in all: *There were twelve of us at the meeting altogether.* **3.** on the whole; considering everything: *Altogether, it was a good party.*

al·to·stra·tus (al'tō strā'təs, al'tō strat'əs) *n., pl.* **al·to·stra·tus** or **al·to·stra·ti** (al'tō strā'tī, al'tō strat'ī). a middle-level cloud appearing as a bluish or grayish white, uniform sheet and covering all or most of the sky. See **cloud** (*def. 1.*).

al·tru·ism (al'trü iz'əm) *n.* an unselfish concern for the welfare of other people.

al·tru·ist (al'trü ist) *n.* a person who is unselfishly concerned about the welfare of other people. —**al'tru·is'tic,** *adj.* —**al'tru·is'ti·cal·ly,** *adv.*

al·um (al'əm) *n.* any of a group of mineral salts, especially a salt of potassium and aluminum that is used in dyeing and tanning, in medicine, and in water purification.

a·lu·mi·num (ə lü'mə nəm) *n.* a light, soft, silver-white metallic element that is obtained from bauxite. Aluminum is the most abundant metal in the earth's crust. It is an excellent conductor of heat and electricity, and is highly resistant to corrosion. Aluminum alloys are durable and have a wide range of uses. Symbol: **Al** Also, *British,* **a·lu·min·i·um** (al'yə min'ē əm). [Formed from the Latin word *alumen* meaning "alum." Alum contains aluminum compounds.]

a·lum·na (ə lum'nə) *n., pl.* **a·lum·nae** (ə lum'nē). a female graduate or former student of a school, college, or university.

a·lum·nus (ə lum'nəs) *n., pl.* **a·lum·ni** (ə lum'nī). a graduate or former student of a school, college, or university, especially a male graduate.

al·ve·o·lus (al vē'ə ləs) *n., pl.* **al·ve·o·li** (al vē'ə lī'). **1.** a small cavity or pit in the body. **2.** a socket in the jawbone in which a tooth fits. **3.** one of the tiny, thin-walled sacs in the lungs in which gas exchange between inhaled air and the blood occurs.

al·ways (ôl'wāz, ôl'wēz) *adv.* **1.** at all times; on every occasion: *I always brush my teeth in the morning.* **2.** all the time: *The weather is always cold at the North Pole.* **3.** throughout all time; forever: *I'll remember you always.* **4.** *Informal.* in any case: *If there are no seats left, we can always stand.*

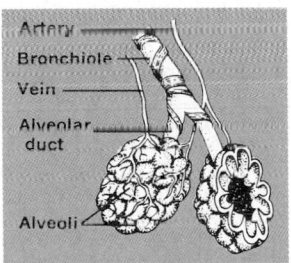

alveolus *(def. 3)*

Labels on figure: Artery; Bronchiole; Vein; Alveolar duct; Alveoli

a·lys·sum (ə lis'əm) *n.* any of a group of low, branching plants of the mustard family, bearing clusters of small white or yellow flowers.

Alz·hei·mer's disease (älts'hī mərz) a disease of the brain cells that causes confusion and progressive loss of memory and mental ability. [From the German physician Alois *Alzheimer* (1864–1915), who described this disease.]

am (am, əm) the first person singular, present tense, of **be**: *I am going to the store.*

Am, the symbol for americium.

Am., America; American.

AM **1.** a method of radio broadcasting by which a signal is transmitted over radio waves by altering the amplitude of the waves. **2.** a broadcasting system using this method. **3.** relating to or using an AM broadcasting system: *an AM radio, an AM station.* [Abbreviation of *amplitude modulation.*]

A.M. **1.** the time from midnight to noon: *We left for school at 7 A.M.* Also, **a.m.** [Abbreviation of the Latin phrase *ante meridiem* meaning "before noon."] **2.** Master of Arts; M.A.

AMA, American Medical Association.

a·mal·gam (ə mal'gəm) *n.* **1.** an alloy of mercury with another metal or metals. Silver amalgam is used for filling teeth. **2.** any mixture or combination: *The population of New York City is an amalgam of many nationalities.*

a·mal·ga·mate (ə mal'gə māt') *v.,* **a·mal·ga·mat·ed, amal·ga·mat·ing.** —*v.t.* **1.** to put together so as to form a whole; merge: *The city decided to amalgamate several school districts into one.* **2.** to combine (a metal or metals) with mercury. —*v.i.* to unite together; merge: *The two labor unions amalgamated.* —**a·mal'ga·ma'tion,** *n.*

am·a·ni·ta (am'ə nī'tə) *n.* any of a group of mushrooms with gills on the underside of the cap and usually with a cup at the base of the stalk. Some amanitas are deadly poisonous, but the edibility of most species is not known.

a·man·u·en·sis (ə man'ū en'sis) *n., pl.* **a·man·u·en·ses** (ə man'ū en'sēz). a person employed to write down what another person says or to copy what another person has written.

am·a·ranth (am'ə ranth') *n.* **1.** any of a group of weeds and garden plants, some of which are grown for their colorful leaves or showy flowers. **2.** an imaginary flower that never fades or wilts.

am·a·ryl·lis (am'ə ril'is) *n., pl.* **am·a·ryl·lis·es.** any of a group of plants found chiefly in tropical America, bearing large, bright-colored, lilylike flowers.

amaryllis

a·mass (ə mas') *v.t.* to collect (a great quantity); gather; accumulate: *The movie star amassed great wealth.*

am·a·teur (am'ə chər, am'ə tər) *n.* **1.** a person who does something as a pastime or for pleasure, rather than as a profession or for money: *to be a gifted amateur at the violin.* **2.** a person who does something without experience or professional skill: *The clear fingerprints left by the thief show that the crime was the work of an amateur.* **3.** an athlete who has never competed for money or earned money through athletic skills. —*adj.* **1.** done by or relating to amateurs: *amateur sports.* **2.** being an amateur: *an amateur actor.* **3.** characteristic of an amateur or amateurs; amateurish: *an amateur attempt at writing a novel.*

am·a·teur·ish (am'ə chûr'ish, am'ə tûr'ish) *adj.* performed as though by an amateur or amateurs; not expert: *an amateurish production of a play.* —**am'a·teur'ish·ly,** *adv.* —**am'a·teur'ish·ness,** *n.*

am·a·to·ry (am'ə tôr'ē) *adj.* relating to or expressing love: *an amatory letter.*

a·maze (ə māz') *v.t.,* **a·mazed, a·maz·ing.** to overwhelm with wonder or surprise; astound: *The magician's tricks amazed the audience.* —**a·maz·ed·ly** (ə mā'zid-lē), *adv.*

---

at; āpe; fär; câre; end; mē; it; īce; pîerce; hot; ōld; sông, fôrk; oil; out; up; ūse; rüle; púll; tûrn; chin; sing; shop; thin; **th**is; hw in white; zh in treasure. The symbol ə stands for the unstressed vowel sound heard in about, taken, pencil, lemon, and circus.

a·maze·ment (ə māz′mənt) *n.* overwhelming wonder or surprise; astonishment.

a·maz·ing (ə mā′zing) *adj.* causing amazement; wonderful; astonishing: *an amazing sight, an amazing event.* —**a·maz′ing·ly,** *adv.*

Am·a·zon (am′ə zon′) *n.* **1.** *Greek Legend.* one of a race of female warriors, said to have lived near the Black Sea. **2.** *also,* **amazon.** any large or powerful woman.

Am·a·zo·ni·an (am′ə zō′nē ən) *adj.* **1.** of or relating to the Amazon River or the region it drains. **2.** *also,* **amazonian.** relating to or characteristic of an Amazon.

Amb., Ambassador.

am·bas·sa·dor (am bas′ə dər) *n.* **1.** a diplomat of the highest rank. Some ambassadors are sent as official representatives to a foreign country or government and live in that country. Other ambassadors are given special assignments to represent their country in the United Nations or another international body. **2.** any representative or messenger: *Those dancers are ambassadors of goodwill for their country.* —**am·bas·sa·dor·i·al** (am-bas′ə dôr′ē əl), *adj.*

am·bas·sa·dor-at-large (am bas′ə dər at lärj′) *n., pl.* **am·bas·sa·dors-at-large.** an ambassador assigned to no particular country or specific task.

am·bas·sa·dor·ship (am bas′ə dər ship′) *n.* the position, rank, or term of office of an ambassador.

am·ber (am′bər) *n.* **1.** a hard, translucent, yellowish orange or yellowish brown material used especially for jewelry, carvings, and electrical insulation. Amber is a fossil formed from the resin of pine trees that grew millions of years ago. **2.** the color of amber; yellowish orange or yellowish brown. —*adj.* **1.** made of amber. **2.** having the color amber.

am·ber·gris (am′bər grēs′, am′bər gris) *n.* a grayish, waxy substance formed in the intestines of sperm whales, used in making perfume.

am·bi·dex·trous (am′bi dek′strəs) *adj.* able to use both hands equally well. —**am′bi·dex′trous·ly,** *adv.* **am′bi·dex′trous·ness,** *n.*

am·bi·ence (am′bē əns) *also,* **am·bi·ance.** *n.* surroundings and atmosphere. *The room had a cozy ambience.*

am·bi·ent (am′bē ənt) *adj.* surrounding on all sides; encircling; encompassing: *ambient temperature.*

am·bi·gu·i·ty (am′bi gū′i tē) *n., pl.* **am·bi·gu·i·ties.** **1.** the condition of having more than one possible meaning; vagueness of purpose or meaning: *I don't know what the policy is because of the ambiguity of the official statements.* **2.** something that is unclear or vague, or that has more than one meaning.

am·big·u·ous (am big′ū əs) *adj.* **1.** having more than one possible meaning. The sentence *Tom told Bill that his dog bit Mary* is ambiguous because we cannot be sure from the word "his" whether the dog belongs to Tom or to Bill. **2.** unclear; vague: *an ambiguous attitude.* —**am·big′u·ous·ly,** *adv.* —**am·big′u·ous·ness,** *n.*

am·bi·tion (am bish′ən) *n.* **1.** a strong desire or drive to succeed or to achieve something: *to be filled with ambition.* **2.** the object of such a desire: *My ambition is to be a doctor.* [From the Latin word *ambitio* meaning "a going about to gather votes," from *ambitus,* past participle of *ambire* "to go around after, to canvass," from the prefix *ambi-* "around, about" + *ire* "to go."]

am·bi·tious (am bish′əs) *adj.* **1.** full of or showing ambition: *an ambitious politician.* **2.** strongly desirous; eager: *to be ambitious to win a contest, to be ambitious of fame.* **3.** requiring great ability or effort: *The governor proposed an ambitious program to end water pollution.* —**am·bi′tious·ly,** *adv.* —**am·bi′tious·ness,** *n.*

am·biv·a·lence (am biv′ə ləns) *n.* the quality or state of being ambivalent: *You can tell my ambivalence toward the plan from my not giving you a definite "yes" or "no."*

am·biv·a·lent (am biv′ə lənt) *adj.* having or showing conflicting feelings about an object, person, or idea: *I'd like to take a trip, but I'm ambivalent because it will cost a lot of money.* —**am·biv′a·lent·ly,** *adv.*

am·ble (am′bəl) *v.i.,* **am·bled, am·bling.** **1.** to walk at a relaxed, leisurely pace: *We ambled through the park, looking at the flowers and statues.* **2.** (of a horse) to move at a slow, easy pace by lifting both legs on the same side together. —*n.* **1.** a slow, leisurely pace in walking. **2.** a leisurely stroll or walk: *to take an amble down the boardwalk.* **3.** the ambling pace of a horse. —**am′bler,** *n.*

am·bro·sia (am brō′zhə) *n.* **1.** *Greek and Roman Mythology.* the food of the gods, capable of making anyone who ate it immortal. **2.** something particularly delicious or delightful to the taste or smell.

am·bro·sial (am brō′zhəl) *adj.* of or like ambrosia; particularly delicious or delightful.

am·bu·lance (am′byə ləns) *n.* a specially equipped vehicle that is used for carrying persons who are sick, injured, or wounded.

am·bu·la·tory (am′byə lə tôr′ē) *adj.* **1.** able to walk; not confined to bed: *an ambulatory patient.* **2.** of or relating to walking: *ambulatory exercise.*

am·bus·cade (am′bə skād′) *n., v.,* **am·bus·cad·ed, am·bus·cad·ing.** another word for **ambush.**

am·bush (am′bŭsh) *n., pl.* **am·bush·es.** **1.** a surprise attack from a hidden position: *The patrol moved cautiously for fear of an ambush.* **2.** a hidden position for surprise attack: *The bandits waited in ambush over the top of the hill.* —*v.t.* to make a surprise attack on from a hidden position. —**am′bush·er,** *n.*

a·me·ba (ə mē′bə) *also,* **a·moe·ba.** *n., pl.* **a·me·bas** or **a·me·bae** (ə-mē′bē). a tiny organism consisting of a single cell. An ameba moves and takes in food by sending out projections, called pseudopods, that are constantly in motion, so that it is always changing shape. Amebas are found in fresh or salt water, in moist earth, or as parasites in animals. They are members of the protist kingdom.

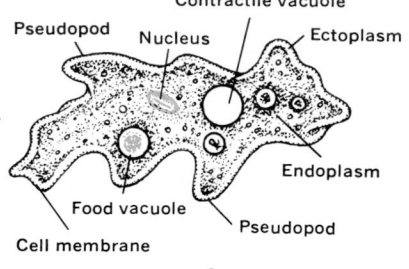

Contractile vacuole
Pseudopod
Nucleus
Ectoplasm
Endoplasm
Food vacuole
Pseudopod
Cell membrane

ameba

a·me·bic (ə mē′bik) *also,* **a·moe·bic.** *adj.* **1.** of or relating to an ameba. **2.** caused by an ameba or amebas: *an amebic disease.*

a·me·lio·rate (ə mēl′yə rāt′) *v.,* **a·me·lio·rat·ed, a·me·lio·rat·ing.** —*v.t.* to make (something) better; improve: *The union wanted to ameliorate working conditions in the factory.* —*v.i.* to grow or become better. —**a·mel′io·ra′tion,** *n.*

a·men (ā′men′, ä′men′) *interj.* may it be so; so be it. ▲ said after a prayer or after other statements to express agreement or approval. —*n.* an uttering of this word: *The congregation responded to the prayer with a hearty "Amen!"* [From the Old English word *amen,* from Latin *amen,* from Greek *amēn,* from the Hebrew word *āmēn* meaning "verily, truly." From its earliest occurrences in Hebrew, *amen* has been used as a closing affirmation.]

A·men (ä′mən) *also,* **A·mon, Am·mon.** *n.* one of the gods worshiped in ancient Egypt.

a·me·na·ble (ə mē′nə bəl, ə men′ə bəl) *adj.* **1.** willing to accept or pay attention to; open to: *our boss is always amenable to suggestions for new projects.* **2.** within the power of some authority; answerable: *Citizens are amenable to the laws of their country.* **3.** able to be acted on in some way: *This problem is amenable to solution.*

—**a·me·na·bil·i·ty, a·me·na·ble·ness,** *n.* —**a·me'na·bly,** *adv.*

a·mend (ə mend′) *v.t.* **1.** to change formally: *In 1865 the Constitution was amended to outlaw slavery.* **2.** to change for the better; improve; correct.

a·mend·ment (ə mend′mənt) *n.* **1.** the act of amending or the state of being amended. **2.** the result of amending; a change. **3.** a formal change made by parliamentary or constitutional procedure: *Women were given the right to vote in all states by an amendment to the Constitution.*

a·mends (ə mendz′) *pl. n.* **to make amends.** to make up for (loss, injury, or insult): *I tried to make amends for my rude behavior by sending a letter of apology.*

a·men·i·ty (ə men′i tē) *n., pl.* **a·men·i·ties. 1. amenities. a.** polite social actions or behavior, especially certain standard or accepted ones. **b.** agreeable features; pleasant qualities: *all the amenities of a luxurious hotel.* **2.** pleasantness; agreeableness: *the amenity of good manners.*

Amer., America; American.

Am·er·a·sian (am′ə rā′zhən) *n.* a person of mixed American and Asian parentage. —*adj.* of mixed American and Asian parentage: *an Amerasian child.*

A·mer·i·can (ə mer′i kən) *adj.* **1.** of, relating to, or characteristic of the United States or its people: *the American flag.* **2.** of, relating to, or characteristic of the Americas or their people: *The coyote is an American animal.* —*n.* **1.** a person who was born in or is a citizen of the United States. **2.** a person who was born in or is a citizen of any country in the Americas.

A·mer·i·ca·na (ə mer′i kan′ə, ə mer′i kä′nə) *n.* **1.** books, documents, and other materials that relate to American history or culture. ▲ often used with a plural verb: *These pamphlets are valuable Americana.* **2.** items, customs, or the like, typical of American culture.

American cheese, any of several mild white or yellow cheddar or process cheeses.

American eagle, the North American bald eagle, the national emblem of the United States.

American English, the English language as spoken and written in the United States.

Language Note

American English began to emerge as a separate variety of English as soon as the first colonists from England arrived in the New World. The colonists needed new words to describe the many unfamiliar things they found in America, so they often borrowed native American Indian words. The word *canoe,* for example, was not used in England, but appears in a book written in 1608 by Captain John Smith. These new additions to vocabulary soon set American English apart from its British parent.

Not only have Americans borrowed Indian words, but they also now use different English words for the same thing. For example, an *elevator* in the United States is called a *lift* in England. Sometimes the same word means different things in the two varieties of English: for example, the British *billion* (a million million) is a thousand times larger than the American *billion* (which is a thousand million).

Another feature distinguishing American English from British English is its pronunciation. In the United States, the same word is likely to be pronounced differently in different regions, as we recognize when we speak of a "Southern drawl," "Western twang," or "New England accent." And although England, too, has its own regional dialects, no one would be likely to confuse any of these with the sounds of American speech.

During colonial times, most writers and critics in both England and America thought that American English was inferior to British English. But after the Revolutionary War, Americans wanted to be independent of British influence in language, just as they had become politically independent. So American English came to be considered completely acceptable in this country. Writers such as James Fenimore Cooper began using American expressions in their books. With the publication of Noah Webster's dictionary, American spellings for words gained wide acceptance: *centre* became *center,* and *colour* became *color.*

In England, however, American English was long considered an "impure" form of the language. American words such as *lengthy, reliable, talented,* and *influential* were attacked as "vile" and "barbarous" by prominent English writers, although all these terms were derived from words commonly used in England. It was not until after the Civil War, when writers such as Mark Twain became popular in England, that American English really became accepted in Great Britain. Today, with television programs and movies produced in and readily available to both nations, the differences between American and British English remain, but each group is more accepting of the other's use of the language.

American Indian *n.* a member of one of the tribes of people inhabiting North and South America before Europeans arrived there. —*adj.* of or relating to American Indians. Also, **Amerind, Amerindian, Indian, Native American.**

Words From Other Languages

American Indian languages spoken in North and South America have contributed a wealth of words to English.

avocado	a pear-shaped, green tropical fruit
cashew	an edible nut shaped like a *C*
chili	a hot spice made from red peppers
chipmunk	a small rodent with stripes on its back
chocolate	a food made from cacao seeds
cocoa	a powder made from cacao seeds
condor	a large vulture with huge wings
hickory	a tall tree that bears an edible nut
llama	a mammal related to the camel
moccasin	an Indian slipper
moose	a type of large deer with heavy antlers
opossum	a mammal that holds its young in a pouch
pecan	a type of nut with a thin, brittle shell
petunia	a flower shaped like a funnel
poncho	a cape that slips over the head
raccoon	a small mammal with a ringed tail
squash	a vegetable that grows in many shapes
tapioca	a starchy food used in pudding
toboggan	a type of long sled without runners
tomahawk	a light Indian ax
tomato	a green vegetable that ripens to red
woodchuck	a small mammal that burrows in the ground

at; āpe; fär; câre; end; mē; it; īce; pîerce; hot; ōld; sông, fôrk; oil; out; up; ūse; rüle; pull; tûrn; chin; sing; shop; thin; this; hw in white; zh in treasure. The symbol ə stands for the unstressed vowel sound heard in about, taken, pencil, lemon, and circus.

A·mer·i·can·ism (ə mer′i kə niz′əm) *n.* **1.** a word, phrase, or expression originating in the United States or found mainly in American English. *Hamburger, canyon, flunk,* and *OK* are Americanisms. **2.** a custom, trait, or belief peculiar to the United States. **3.** devotion to or support of the United States, its institutions, and its traditions.

A·mer·i·can·ize (ə mer′i kə nīz′) *v.t., v.i.,* **A·mer·i·can·ized, A·mer·i·can·iz·ing.** to make or become American, as in habits, customs, beliefs, or manners. —**A·mer′i·can·i·za′tion,** *n.*

American plan, in hotels, a system of charging guests at a fixed rate that includes both room and all meals.

American Revolution, a war fought from 1775 to 1783 between Great Britain and its American colonies, in which the colonies gained their independence. Also, **Revolutionary War.**

am·er·i·ci·um (am′ə rish′ē əm) *n.* a silver-white metallic element produced artificially from uranium and plutonium. It is the only radioactive element known to be superconductive. Symbol: **Am** [From *America.*]

Am·er·ind (am′ə rind′) *n., adj.* see **American Indian.** Also, **Am·er·in·di·an** (am′ə rin′dē ən).

am·e·thyst (am′ə thist) *n.* **1.** a purple or violet quartz, used as a gem. **2.** a purple or violet color.

a·mi·a·ble (ā′mē ə bəl) *adj.* having a pleasing and kindly disposition; good-natured; friendly: *It is easy to like someone as amiable as you.* —**a′mi·a·bil′i·ty,** *n.* —**a′mi·a·bly,** *adv.*

am·i·ca·ble (am′i kə bəl) *adj.* characterized by friendliness and good will; peaceable: *After an amicable discussion the dispute was settled.* —**am′i·ca·bil′i·ty,** *n.* —**am′i·ca·bly,** *adv.*

a·mid (ə mid′) *prep.* in the middle or midst of; surrounded by; among: *The house stood amid pine trees.* Also, **amidst, midst.**

a·mid·ships (ə mid′ships′) *adv.* in or toward the middle of a ship. Also, **midships.**

a·midst (ə midst′) *prep.* another word for **amid.**

a·mi·go (ə mē′gō) *n., pl.* **a·mi·gos.** friend. [From the Spanish word *amigo,* from the Latin word *amicus* meaning "friend."]

a·mi·no acid (ə mē′nō, am′ə nō′) any of a group of organic acids composed of carbon, hydrogen, oxygen, and nitrogen. Amino acids are needed by organisms to make proteins.

Am·ish (ä′mish, am′ish) *pl. n.* a Protestant religious denomination, closely related to the Mennonites. It was founded in Switzerland in the seventeenth century. Most members now live in the United States. —*adj.* of, belonging to, or relating to this sect.

a·miss (ə mis′) *adj.* not as it should be; out of order; wrong: *We knew that something was amiss when we found the door open.* —*adv.* not in the proper manner or order; improperly; wrongly.
   ·to take amiss. to take offense at; resent.

am·i·ty (am′i tē) *n., pl.* **am·i·ties.** peaceful and friendly relations; friendship: *The conference aimed at achieving amity among the nations.*

am·me·ter (am′mē′tər) *n.* an instrument used for measuring the strength of an electric current in amperes.

am·mo (am′ō) *n. Informal.* ammunition.

Am·mon (am′ən) *n.* another spelling for the name of the god **Amen.**

am·mo·nia (ə mōn′yə) *n.* **1.** a colorless, gaseous compound of nitrogen and hydrogen having a highly pungent odor. Ammonia is used especially in fertilizers and in the production of other chemicals. **2.** a solution of ammonia in water, used as a household cleaner.

am·mo·ni·um (ə mō′nē əm) *n.* a chemical ion consisting of four atoms of hydrogen bound to a single nitrogen atom.

am·mu·ni·tion (am′yə nish′ən) *n.* **1.** bullets, shells, and other projectiles for use in firearms and artillery.

2. any type of explosive weapon, such as a grenade or bomb. **3.** anything used in attack or defense, as in debate: *The scandal provided new ammunition for the senator's political opponents.*

am·ne·sia (am nē′zhə) *n.* partial or total loss of memory, especially as the result of brain injury, mental illness, disease, or shock.

am·nes·ty (am′nə stē) *n., pl.* **am·nes·ties.** a general pardon given, often before any prosecution has begun, to prisoners, outlaws, or rebels who have committed offenses against a government: *At the end of the war the president granted amnesty to those who had refused to serve in the army.*

am·ni·o·cen·te·sis (am′nē ō sen tē′sis) *n.* a medical test for pregnant women in which a sample of the fluid surrounding the fetus is obtained and analyzed in a laboratory. Amniocentesis is used for detecting genetic disorders in the fetus, such as Down syndrome.

am·ni·on (am′nē ən) *n., pl.* **am·ni·ons** or **am·ni·a** (am′nē ə). a membrane that forms a fluid-filled sac surrounding the embryo in reptiles, birds, and mammals.

am·ni·ot·ic (am′nē ot′ik) *adj.* of or relating to the fluid-filled sac surrounding the embryo in reptiles, birds, and mammals.

a·moe·ba (ə mē′bə) *n., pl.* **a·moe·bas** or **a·moe·bae** (ə mē′bē). another spelling of **ameba.**

a·moe·bic (ə mē′bik) another spelling of **amebic.**

a·mok (ə muk′, ə mok′) *also,* **a·muck.** *adv.* **to run amuck.** to lose control of oneself and run about wildly, especially with intent to attack or kill.

A·mon (ä′mən) *n.* another spelling for the name of the god **Amen.**

a·mong (ə mung′) *prep.* **1.** in the midst of; surrounded by: *The campers pitched their tent among the trees.* **2.** in the company of: *The relief workers lived among the poor.* **3.** in the number or class of: *Among trees, the redwood is the tallest.* **4.** by, with, or through many or all of: *a candidate popular among college students.* **5.** in shares for each of: *to divide a prize among the winners.* **6.** by the combined or joint action of: *Among us, we can raise the money.* ▲ See **between** for usage note.

a·mongst (ə mungst′) *prep.* another word for **among.**

a·mor·al (ā môr′əl, ā mor′əl) *adj.* not having or interested in moral standards; neither moral nor immoral: *Science is amoral.* —**a·mor·al·i·ty** (ā′mə ral′i tē), *n.* —**a·mor′al·ly,** *adv.*

am·o·rous (am′ər əs) *adj.* **1.** inclined to love or to fall in love: *Don Juan's amorous disposition.* **2.** produced by or showing love: *an amorous glance.* **3.** of or relating to love. —**am′o·rous·ly,** *adv.* —**am′o·rous·ness,** *n.*

a·mor·phous (ə môr′fəs) *adj.* **1.** without definite form or shape; shapeless: *an amorphous fog.* **2.** of no particular kind or character; unorganized: *The people opposed to that policy are an amorphous group.* **3.** *Chemistry.* (of a solid) not formed of crystals: *Glass is amorphous.* —**a·mor′phous·ly,** *adv.* —**a·mor′phous·ness,** *n.*

am·or·tize (am′ər tīz′) *v.t.,* **am·or·tized, am·or·tiz·ing.** to pay (a debt), usually by making payments of equal amounts over a period of time. —**am′or·ti·za′tion,** *n.*

A·mos (ā′məs) *n.* a book of the Old Testament containing the prophecies of the Hebrew reformer Amos.

a·mount (ə mount′) *n.* **1.** numerical quantity; sum: *We paid the full amount of the bill.* **2.** any quantity or measure: *I have a large amount of work to do. No amount of criticism could persuade them that they were wrong.* —*v.i.* **1.** to equal in number or quantity; add up: *The bill amounts to ten dollars.* **2.** to be equal in value, significance, or effect: *That remark amounts to a threat.* **3.** (of a person) to develop into; become: *A lazy worker will never amount to anything.*

▲ **Amount** and **number** both refer to a quantity. **Amount** is usually used when a quantity is considered as a whole and its separate units cannot be counted: *There is a great amount of information in books.* **Number** is usually used when the separate units that make up the quantity can be counted: *I read a large number of books during the past year.*

a·mour (ə mu̇r′) *n.* a love affair, especially one that is secret.

amp. 1. ampere; amperes. 2. amperage.

am·per·age (am′pər ij) *n.* the strength of an electric current measured in amperes.

am·pere (am′pîr) *n.* the standard unit for measuring the strength of an electric current. It is equal to the amount of current produced by one volt acting through a resistance of one ohm. [From André Marie *Ampère*, 1775–1836, a French physicist.]

am·per·sand (am′pər sand′) *n.* the symbol (&) representing the word ''and'': *Smith & Company.*

am·phet·a·mine (am fet′ə mēn′, am fet′ə min) *n.* a drug that stimulates the central nervous system. It acts to deaden the appetite and combat sleepiness.

am·phib·i·an (am fib′ē ən) *n.* 1. any of a class of cold-blooded animals with backbones, including frogs, toads, and salamanders, usually living in or near water and having moist, scaleless skin. Their eggs are usually laid in water or moist places and hatch into legless larvae with gills, which develop into adults with lungs and two pairs of legs. 2. any animal or plant that lives both on land and in water, such as an alligator or a seal. 3. an aircraft that is designed to take off from and land on either water or land. 4. a tank or other vehicle that can travel on both land and water. —*adj.* 1. of, relating to, or characteristic of the class of amphibians. 2. another word for **amphibious.**

amphibian *(def. 3)*

am·phib·i·ous (am fib′ē əs) *adj.* 1. capable of living both on land and in water. 2. adapted or suitable for use on land or water: *an amphibious airplane.* 3. carried out by the action of both land and naval forces: *an amphibious attack.*

am·phi·the·a·ter (am′fi thē′ə tər) *also,* **am·phi·the·a·tre.** *n.* 1. an oval or circular structure with rising rows of seats around a central open space. 2. a room having rising rows of seats arranged around a central area, such as a classroom or an operating room in a hospital. 3. a level area of ground that is completely surrounded by rising slopes, either natural or artificial.

am·pho·ra (am′fər ə) *n., pl.* **am·pho·ras** or **am·pho·rae** (am′fə rē′). a two-handled jar or vase with a narrow neck, broad body, and tapering base. It was used by the ancient Greeks and Romans.

am·ple (am′pəl) *adj.,* **am·pler, am·plest.** 1. large in size or extent; roomy: *The car has an ample trunk.* 2. more than enough; abundant: *We have ample time to finish the*

job. 3. as much as needed; enough; sufficient; adequate: *We have ample money for our trip.* —**am′ple·ness,** *n.* —**am′ply,** *adv.*

am·pli·fi·ca·tion (am′plə fi kā′shən) *n.* 1. the act of amplifying or the state of being amplified. 2. something used to amplify; additional matter. 3. an increase in the strength of an electronic signal.

am·pli·fi·er (am′plə fī′ər) *n.* 1. a device for increasing the strength of an electronic signal. 2. the part of a sound-reproduction system that contains such a device. 3. a person or thing that amplifies.

am·pli·fy (am′plə fī′) *v.t.,* **am·pli·fied, am·pli·fy·ing.** 1. to add to or expand; enlarge on: *The official amplified the statement by providing explanatory details.* 2. to increase the strength of (an electronic signal).

am·pli·tude (am′pli tüd′, am′pli tūd′) *n.* 1. the state or quality of being ample; largeness; abundance; fullness. 2. the distance that a vibrating body, such as a pendulum, moves in either direction from a central position. 3. the highest strength reached by an alternating electric current during a complete cycle.

amplitude modulation, see AM.

am·pu·tate (am′pyə tāt′) *v.t.,* **am·pu·tat·ed, am·pu·tat·ing.** to cut off, especially to remove (a limb) by means of surgery: *Because of the infection, the doctor was forced to amputate the patient's finger.* —**am′pu·ta′tion,** *n.*

am·pu·tee (am′pyə tē′) *n.* a person who has had a limb or limbs amputated.

amt., amount

a·muck (ə muk′) another spelling of **amok.**

am·u·let (am′yə lit) *n.* an object worn as a protection against disease, bad luck, or evil; a charm.

a·muse (ə mūz′) *v.t.,* **a·mused, a·mus·ing.** 1. to cause to laugh or smile; please the sense of humor of: *Your jokes amused all of us.* 2. to keep pleasantly busy or interested; entertain: *I amused the children by reading.*

a·mused (ə mūzd′) *adj.* feeling or showing happiness or enjoyment: *an amused audience, an amused look.* —**a·mus·ed·ly** (ə mū′zid lē), *adv.*

a·muse·ment (ə mūz′mənt) *n.* 1. the state of being amused; enjoyment. 2. something that amuses or entertains.

amusement park, a park or other area containing various games, rides, and other forms of amusement, such as a Ferris wheel, merry-go-round, or roller coaster.

a·mus·ing (ə mū′zing) *adj.* causing laughter, happiness, or enjoyment. —**a·mus′ing·ly,** *adv.*

am·yl·ase (am′ə lās′) *n.* an enzyme produced by the pancreas that breaks down starch into sugar during digestion.

an (an; *unstressed* ən) *indefinite article* the form of the word **a** used before words that begin with a vowel sound: *an apple, an hour.*

–an *suffix* 1. (used to form nouns) **a.** a person who was born in or is a citizen of (a country, state, or the like): *Mexican, Texan.* **b.** a person belonging to or associated with (an organization, system of thought, or the like): *Republican, Lutheran.* **c.** a person skilled or expert in: *mathematician, magician.* 2. (used to form adjectives) of, relating to, belonging to, or characteristic of: *Shakespearean, American.* [From the Old French suffix *-ien* meaning ''relating to,'' from the Latin suffix *-ianus* with the same meaning.]

a·nab·o·lism (ə nab′ə liz′əm) *n.* the phase of metabo-

at; āpe; fär; câre; end; mē; it; īce; pîerce; hot; ōld; sông, fôrk; oil; out; up; ūse; rüle; pu̇ll; tûrn; chin; sing; shop; thin; this; hw in white; zh in treasure. The symbol ə stands for the unstressed vowel sound heard in about, taken, pencil, lemon, and circus.

lism in which energy is used to build proteins from food molecules.

a·nach·ro·nism (ə nak′rə niz′əm) *n.* **1.** something or someone that is out of or past its proper time: *A suit of armor worn in battle today would be an anachronism.* **2.** the placement of something in a time to which it does not belong: *To speak of Shakespeare using a typewriter is an anachronism.* [Going back to the Greek prefix *ana-* meaning "back, again" and *chronos* "time."]

a·nach·ro·nis·tic (ə nak′rə nis′tik) *adj.* containing or involving an anachronism. —**a·nach′ro·nis′ti·cal·ly,** *adv.*

an·a·con·da (an′ə kon′də) *n.* a very large snake that squeezes and suffocates its prey in its coils and is native to tropical South America. It feeds mostly on fish, water birds, and small animals.

anaconda

a·nae·mi·a (ə nē′mē ə) another spelling of **anemia.**

a·nae·mic (ə nē′mik) another spelling of **anemic.**

an·aer·obe (an âr′ōb, an′ə-rōb′) *n.* a microorganism that is able to live without oxygen.

an·aer·o·bic (an′â rō′bik, an′ə rō′bik) *adj.* **1.** able to live or grow without oxygen, such as certain kinds of bacteria. **2.** caused by a lack of air or oxygen. **3.** pertaining to or caused by anaerobes.

an·aes·the·sia (an′əs thē′zhə) another spelling of **anesthesia.**

an·aes·the·si·ol·o·gist (an′əs thē′zē ol′ə jist) another spelling of **anesthesiologist.**

an·aes·the·si·ol·o·gy (an′əs thē′zē ol′ə jē) another spelling of **anesthesiology.**

an·aes·thet·ic (an′əs thet′ik) another spelling of **anesthetic.** —**an′aes·thet′i·cal·ly,** *adv.*

an·aes·the·tist (ə nes′thi tist) another spelling of **anesthetist.**

an·aes·the·tize (ə nes′thi tīz′) another spelling of **anesthetize.**

an·a·gram (an′ə gram′) *n.* **1.** a word or phrase made by changing the order of the letters of another word or phrase. The word *veil* is an anagram of the word *live.* **2. anagrams.** a game in which the players form words by changing the order of letters or by adding letters.

a·nal (ā′nəl) *adj.* of, relating to, or near the anus.

an·al·ge·si·a (an′əl jē′zē ə, an′əl jē′sē ə) *n.* the lack of a sense of pain, without the loss of consciousness.

an·al·ge·sic (an′əl jē′zik, an′əl jē′sik) *adj.* relieving or removing pain: *an analgesic drug.* —*n.* a remedy that is used to relieve or remove pain: *Aspirin is a common analgesic.*

an·a·log (an′ə lôg′, an′ə log′) *adj.* (of an automatic device) representing or processing information by measuring or displaying continuous information about a physical variable, as the hands of a clock show time or the level of a mercury thermometer shows temperature. [From the French word *analogue* meaning "something similar," going back to the Greek word *analogos* "in proper proportion."]

analog computer, a computer in which numbers directly represent physical quantities, such as weight, length, temperature, or voltage. A slide rule is a simple form of analog computer.

a·nal·o·gous (ə nal′ə gəs) *adj.* alike or similar in certain ways; comparable: *The gills of a fish are analogous to the lungs of an animal.* —**a·nal′o·gous·ly,** *adv.*

a·nal·o·gy (ə nal′ə jē) *n.*, *pl.* **a·nal·o·gies.** **1.** a likeness in certain ways between things that are otherwise unlike; partial similarity: *There is an analogy between the gills of a fish and the lungs of an animal.* **2.** any comparison or parallel: *The historian drew an analogy between the current war and one that took place in ancient times.*

Language Note

In language, the word **analogy** means "the process of changing or forming a word according to rules or general patterns." Analogy can help to simplify writing and speaking, but because English spelling and pronunciation often do not follow rules and patterns, analogy can also lead to natural mistakes. A child or an adult just beginning to learn English will know the general rule that by adding an *-s* to the end of a noun, such as *hand* or *boy,* you form its plural. But forming the plural of *foot* or *child* according to analogy would lead this person incorrectly to write or say "foots" and "childs," instead of the correct *feet* and *children.* The only way to learn the correct spelling and pronunciation of English words is to learn the rules and patterns of our language and then to memorize the many words that are exceptions to the rules.

Analogy, which really represents a "common sense" way of writing and speaking, has helped to remove some of the confusing, irregular words from our language. English, which has developed over the last 1,500 years, once had many more irregular words than it has now. An example of this is the plural of the noun *cow,* which originally was *kine.* This was simplified to *cows* by analogy with the *-s* ending that English nouns normally have in the plural.

At times a regular word can become an irregular word by false analogy. For example, the verb *dig* originally had the past tense and past participle *digged.* The past participle form *dug* appeared about 400 years ago, on the pattern of *stick/stuck,* and it later replaced the form *digged* as both past participle and past tense.

Analogy helps language to grow by allowing us to invent new words that are patterned after older ones. A word such as *finalize,* which has only recently come into our language, is the result of analogy. It is derived from the adjective *final* and is based on a pattern that appears quite often in English, as in the words *civil/civilize* and *familiar/familiarize.* Analogy also produces new words that come directly from older words. The word *skyjack,* which was invented in the late 1960s when airplane hijacking first became common, was formed by analogy with the older word *hijack.* The Latin word meaning "to hear" was first used in English as the prefix *audio-.* Later this prefix became the adjective *audio* and the noun *audio.* By analogy, the same thing happened to the Latin word meaning "to see," and the word *video* was created.

a·nal·y·sis (ə nal′ə sis) *n.*, *pl.* **a·nal·y·ses** (ə nal′ə-sēz′). **1.** a method of finding out the nature of something by separating it into parts: *An analysis of the lake water indicated that it was polluted. An analysis of the testimony shows that the witness did not tell the truth.* **2.** a statement of the results of such an examination. **3.** any careful and detailed examination: *an analysis of an election.* **4.** another word for **psychoanalysis.**

an·a·lyst (an′ə list′) *n.* **1.** a person who analyzes or is skilled in analysis: *an experienced political analyst.* **2.** another word for **psychoanalyst.**

an·a·lyt·i·cal (an′ə lit′i kəl) *adj.* of, relating to, or using analysis: *Physics requires an analytical mind.* Also, **an·a·lyt·ic** (an′ə lit′ik). —**an′a·lyt′i·cal·ly,** *adv.*

analytic geometry, a branch of mathematics in which geometric figures are described and analyzed in terms of algebra and plotted in space by means of coordinates.

an·a·lyze (an′ə līz′) *v.t.,* **an·a·lyzed, an·a·lyz·ing.** **1.** to find out the nature of (something) by separating it into parts: *to analyze a chemical solution.* **2.** to examine carefully and in detail: *The jury analyzed the evidence in the case.*

A

an·a·pest (an'ə pest') *n.* **1.** in poetry, a metrical foot consisting of two unaccented or short syllables followed by an accented or long syllable. The line *And the sheen of their spears was like stars on the sea* (Lord Byron) contains four anapests. **2.** a line of verse made up of this.

an·ar·chic (an är'kik) *adj.* of, like, or causing anarchy. Also, **an·ar·chi·cal** (an är'ki kəl). —**an·ar'chi·cal·ly**, *adv.*

an·ar·chism (an'ər kiz'əm) *n.* the political theory that all forms of government and governmental restraint violate liberty and must be abolished.

an·ar·chist (an'ər kist) *n.* **1.** a person who believes in or supports anarchy or anarchism. **2.** a person who promotes anarchy or stirs up revolt against government. —**an'ar·chis'tic,** *adj.*

an·ar·chy (an'ər kē) *n.* **1.** the total absence of government and law. **2.** a state of complete disorder and confusion; chaos.

a·nath·e·ma (ə nath'ə mə) *n., pl.* **a·nath·e·mas. 1.** in certain churches, the formal denunciation of a person or the condemnation of a practice or doctrine. **2.** any strong denunciation or curse. **3.** a person or thing that is cursed, denounced, or hated.

an·a·tom·i·cal (an'ə tom'i kəl) *adj.* of or relating to anatomy. Also, **an·a·tom·ic** (an'ə tom'ik). —**an'a·tom'i·cal·ly,** *adv.*

a·nat·o·mist (ə nat'ə mist) *n.* a person who is an expert in anatomy.

a·nat·o·mize (ə nat'ə mīz') *v.t.,* **a·nat·o·mized, a·nat·o·miz·ing. 1.** to dissect (an animal or plant) in order to study the structure and relationships of its parts. **2.** to analyze (something) closely. —**a·nat'o·mi·za'tion,** *n.*

a·nat·o·my (ə nat'ə mē) *n., pl.* **a·nat·o·mies. 1.** the branch of science that deals with the structure of animals or plants and the relationships of their parts. **2.** the structure of an animal or plant or any of its parts. **3.** the dissection of animals or plants in order to study their structure. **4.** a detailed examination; analysis: *the anatomy of a crime.*

–ance *suffix* **1.** (used to form nouns from verbs) **a.** the process or action of: *disturbance, utterance.* **b.** the state, quality, or condition of: *resemblance, continuance.* **c.** the result of an action: *contrivance.* **d.** an agent of: *conveyance.* **2.** (used to form nouns from adjectives ending in *ant*) the state, quality, or condition of being: *ignorance, brilliance, vigilance.* [From the Old French suffix *-ance,* from the Latin suffix *-antia* meaning "the state of."]

an·ces·tor (an'ses tər) *n.* **1.** a person from whom one is descended: *My ancestors came to this country from France.* **2.** something from which another thing is developed or descended: *The Wright brothers' plane is an ancestor of modern aircraft.*

an·ces·tral (an ses'trəl) *adj.* of, relating to, or inherited from ancestors: *an ancestral home, an ancestral trait.* —**an·ces'tral·ly,** *adv.*

an·ces·try (an'ses trē) *n., pl.* **an·ces·tries. 1.** the line of persons from whom one is descended; lineage. **2.** ancestors as a group: *Most of my ancestry lived in New England.*

an·chor (ang'kər) *n.* **1.** a device for preventing a boat or ship from drifting. An anchor usually grips the bottom and is attached to the

types of **anchors**

vessel by a chain or cable. **2.** any device that holds something in place. **3.** something that gives support or security: *Hope was the castaways' anchor.* **4.** another word for **anchorman** or **anchorwoman.** —*v.t.* **1.** to hold (a boat or ship) in place by an anchor. **2.** to fasten in place; fix firmly: *Anchor the shelf to the wall.* **3.** to be the anchorman or anchorwoman for: *That new reporter now anchors the morning news.* —*v.i.* to lower the anchor overboard and remain held fast: *We anchored in the bay.*

·**at anchor.** held fast by an anchor: *The ship was at anchor.*

·**to cast anchor** or **to drop anchor.** to lower an anchor overboard.

·**to ride at anchor.** to be held fast by an anchor.

·**to weigh anchor.** to take up an anchor.

an·chor·age (ang'kər ij) *n.* **1.** a place for anchoring. **2.** something that fastens or holds securely: *The ropes were used as anchorage for the crates.*

an·cho·rite (ang'kə rīt') *n.* a person who lives completely apart from society, especially for religious reasons; hermit.

an·chor·man (ang'kər man') *n., pl.* **an·chor·men** (ang'-kər men'). **1.** a man who is the main announcer on and coordinates a news broadcast. **2.** a man who is the last runner in a relay race.

an·chor·per·son (ang'kər pûr'sən) *n.* an anchorman or anchorwoman.

an·chor·wom·an (ang'kər wŭm'ən) *n., pl.* **an·chor·wom·en** (ang'kər wim'ən). **1.** a woman who is the main announcer on and coordinates a news broadcast. **2.** a woman who is the last runner in a relay race.

an·cho·vy (an'chō vē, an chō'vē) *n., pl.* **an·cho·vies.** any of various small saltwater and freshwater fish, closely related to the herring. Anchovies are canned and made into a paste.

an·cient (ān'shənt) *adj.* **1.** of or relating to times long past, especially before the fall of the Western Roman Empire in A.D. 476: *Greek culture was a dominant force in the ancient world.* **2.** of great age; very old: *Marriage is an ancient tradition.* —*n.* **1.** a very old person. **2. the ancients.** civilized peoples of long ago, especially the ancient Greeks and Romans: *Slavery was a common practice among the ancients.* —**an'cient·ly,** *adv.* —**an'cient·ness,** *n.*

ancient history, history from the beginning of recorded events to the fall of the Western Roman Empire in A.D. 476.

an·cil·lar·y (an'sə ler'ē) *adj.* that helps or supports in a secondary way; supplementary; auxiliary: *In addition to a raise in salary, the new contract contains ancillary benefits.*

–ancy, another form of the suffix **-ance,** as in *vacancy.*

and (and; *unstressed* ənd, ən) *conj.* **1.** as well as; also; moreover: *A bear is big and strong. St. Louis and Minneapolis are on the Mississippi.* **2.** added to; plus: *Two and two make four.* **3.** as a result or consequence; then: *Treat me fairly and I'll be fair with you.* **4.** *Informal.* to: *Try and finish the work today.*

an·dan·te (än dän'tā, an dan'tē) *Music. adv., adj.* slower than moderato but faster than adagio; moderately slow. —*n.* a composition, movement, or part in such a tempo.

Ring
Stock
Shank
Fluke
Common anchor
Grapnel anchor
Stockless anchor
Mushroom anchor

at; āpe; fär; câre; end; mē; it; īce; pîerce; hot; ōld; sông, fôrk; oil; out; up; ūse; rüle; pull; tûrn; chin; sing; shop; thin; <u>th</u>is; hw in white; zh in treasure. The symbol ə stands for the unstressed vowel sound heard in about, taken, pencil, lemon, and circus.

An·de·an (an dē′ən, an′dē ən) *adj.* of or relating to the Andes.

and·i·ron (and′ī′ərn) *n.* either of two metal supports for holding wood in a fireplace. Also, **firedog.**

and/or, both or either. ▲ The expression **and/or** is used to show that either the word *and* or the word *or* may be used to connect two parts of a sentence, depending upon what is meant. *I hope to play on the basketball team and/or the baseball team* means that I hope to play on both of the teams or on either one of them.

andirons

An·dro·cles (an′drə klēz′) also, **An·dro·clus** (an′drə kləs). *n.* *Roman Legend.* a slave spared in the arena by a lion because he had once removed a thorn from its paw.

an·dro·gen (an′drə jən) *n.* any of various hormones that control and stimulate the development of masculine characteristics.

an·droid (an′droid) *n.* a robot with the shape of a human being. [Formed from the Greek words *anēr* meaning "man, male" and *oeidēs* meaning "-oid."]

An·drom·a·che (an drom′ə kē) *n.* *Greek Legend.* the wife of Hector.

An·drom·e·da (an drom′i də) *n.* **1.** *Greek Mythology.* an Ethiopian princess whom Perseus rescued from a sea monster and then took as his wife. **2.** a constellation in the northern sky, thought to resemble the shape of a woman with outstretched arms.

an·ec·do·tal (an′ik dō′təl) *adj.* **1.** relating to or consisting of anecdotes: *an anecdotal history.* **2.** consisting of a number of examples, but not proven scientifically: *There is only anecdotal evidence of the effectiveness of this new drug.* —**an′ec·do′tal·ly,** *adv.*

an·ec·dote (an′ik dōt′) *n.* a short account of some incident or event, especially one intended to amuse or illustrate: *We heard several anecdotes about George Washington.*

a·ne·mi·a (ə nē′mē ə) also, **a·nae·mi·a.** *n.* a condition in which the blood does not have enough hemoglobin or red blood cells. It is characterized by paleness, weakness, and fatigue.

a·ne·mic (ə nē′mik) also, **a·nae·mic.** *adj.* **1.** relating to, having, or characteristic of anemia. **2.** lacking vitality or spirit: *The city's anemic attempt to deal with the parking problem failed.*

an·e·mom·e·ter (an′ə mom′i tər) *n.* an instrument for measuring the speed of the wind.

a·nem·o·ne (ə nem′ə nē′) *n.* **1.** any of various plants having slender stems, lobed or notched leaves, and small white or colored flowers. Also, **windflower. 2.** see sea anemone.

a·nent (ə nent′) *prep.* regarding; concerning; about.

an·er·oid barometer (an′ə roid′) a barometer in which the flexible top of a metal box containing a partial vacuum contracts and expands according to

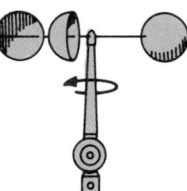

anemometer

changes in air pressure. When the box contracts or expands, it moves a spring attached to a pointer that shows the change.

an·es·the·sia (an′əs thē′zhə) also, **an·aes·the·sia.** *n.* a loss of sensation in the body, especially of the sense of pain. In medicine, anesthesia is induced by drugs; it may affect only part of the body (local anesthesia), or it may render the patient unconscious (general anesthesia).

an·es·the·si·ol·o·gist (an′əs thē′zē ol′ə jist) also, **an·aes·the·si·ol·o·gist.** *n.* a physician who specializes in anesthesiology.

an·es·the·si·ol·o·gy (an′əs thē′zē ol′ə jē) *also,* **an·aes·the·si·ol·o·gy.** *n.* the branch of medicine that deals with anesthesia.

an·es·thet·ic (an′əs thet′ik) also, **an·aes·thet·ic.** *n.* a drug or other substance that causes anesthesia: *Ether is an anesthetic.* —*adj.* **1.** causing anesthesia. **2.** relating to anesthesia. —**an′es·thet′i·cal·ly,** *adv.*

a·nes·the·tist (ə nes′thi tist) also, **a·naes·the·tist.** *n.* a person who is trained and licensed to give anesthetics.

a·nes·the·tize (ə nes′thi tīz′) also, **a·naes·the·tize.** *v.t.,* **a·nes·the·tized, a·nes·the·tiz·ing.** to make insensible, especially to pain: *to anesthetize a patient before surgery.* —**a·nes′the·ti·za′tion,** *n.*

an·eu·rysm (an′yə riz′əm) also, **an·eu·rism.** *n.* a sac formed by the dilation of the wall of an artery weakened by disease, injury, or infection.

a·new (ə nü′, ə nū′) *adv.* **1.** in a new or different way: *The first attempt failed, so we started anew with a different approach.* **2.** over again: *to begin a song anew.*

an·gel (ān′jəl) *n.* **1.** in Judaism, Christianity, Islam, and certain other religions, one of the group of immortal, spiritual beings who are believed to serve as the attendants and messengers of God. **2.** an attendant or guardian spirit: *My good angel must have been watching over me.* **3.** a person thought of as like an angel in goodness, beauty, or kindliness. **4.** *Informal.* a person who provides funds for something, especially a theatrical production.

an·gel·fish (ān′jəl fish′) *n., pl.* **an·gel·fish** or **an·gel·fish·es.** **1.** any of various silvery South American freshwater fish that have long upper and lower fins shaped something like wings. **2.** any of various colorful fish that live in tropical salt waters.

angelfish *(def. 2)*

an·gel·ic (an jel′ik) *adj.* **1.** like or characteristic of an angel; good, beautiful, and kindly: *an angelic face, an angelic disposition.* **2.** of or relating to angels. Also, **an·gel·i·cal** (an jel′i kəl). —**an·gel′i·cal·ly,** *adv.*

An·ge·lus (an′jə ləs) also, **an·ge·lus.** *n., pl.* **An·ge·lus·es. 1.** in the Roman Catholic Church, a prayer said in celebration of the Annunciation. **2.** a bell rung at morning, noon, and evening to announce the time for saying this prayer.

an·ger (ang′gər) *n.* a strong feeling of not being pleased or happy with a person or thing that opposes, annoys, harms, or mistreats one; rage; wrath: *In anger the child threw the broken toy into the wastebasket.* —*v.t.* to make angry: *The student's rudeness angered the teacher.* —*v.i.* to become angry.

an·gi·na (an jī′nə, an′jə nə) *n.* sudden, severe pain spreading across the chest and often down the left arm. It results from too little blood getting to the muscle of the heart and is usually caused by heart disease.

an·gi·o·sperm (an′jē ə spûrm′) *n.* another word for **flowering plant.**

A

an·gle¹ (ang′gəl) *n.* **1.** the figure formed by two lines extending from the same point or by two planes extending from the same straight line. **2.** the space between these lines or planes. **3.** the amount of divergence between such lines or planes, measured in degrees: *The rocket was launched at a 90° angle to the ground.* **4.** a sharp corner: *an angle of a building.* **5.** a point of view; aspect: *We must consider the problem from every angle.* —*v.*, **an·gled**, **an·gling.** —*v.t.* to cause to move or turn at an angle: *to angle a billiard ball into a corner pocket.* —*v.i.* to move or bend at an angle: *The road angles to the left.* [From the Old French word *angle*, from the Latin word *angulus* meaning "a corner."]

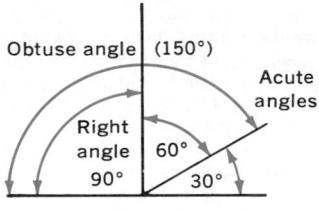

types of **angles**

an·gle² (ang′gəl) *v.i.*, **an·gled**, **an·gling.** to fish with a hook and line. [From the Old English word *angel* meaning "a fishhook."]

·**to angle for.** to use tricks or schemes to try to get something: *Some eager fans angled for seats near the front of the auditorium.*

angle of incidence, the angle that a ray, as of light, striking a surface forms with a line perpendicular to that surface at the point of striking.

angle of reflection, the angle that a ray, as of light, reflected from a surface forms with a line perpendicular to that surface at the point of reflection.

an·gler (ang′glər) *n.* **1.** a person who fishes with a hook and line. **2.** see **anglerfish.**

an·gler·fish (ang′glər fish′) *n., pl.* **an·gler·fish** or **an·gler·fish·es.** a saltwater fish having a large head, a wide mouth, and a rod that looks like a worm extending from the head, which lures its prey toward it.

An·gles (ang′gəlz) *pl. n.* a Germanic tribe that settled in Britain in the fifth and sixth centuries A.D., at the same time as other Germanic tribes, the Saxons and the Jutes, were settling there.

an·gle·worm (ang′gəl wûrm′) *n.* another word for **earthworm.**

An·gli·can (ang′gli kən) *adj.* of or relating to the Church of England or to any of the churches related to it. —*n.* a member of the Church of England or any of the churches related to it.

An·gli·can·ism (ang′gli kə niz′əm) *n.* the body of beliefs and practices of the Church of England.

An·gli·cize (ang′glə sīz′) *v.t.*, **An·gli·cized, An·gli·ciz·ing. 1.** to adopt (a foreign word or phrase) into English, sometimes with a slight change in pronunciation, form, or meaning. *Chauffeur* is a French word that has been Anglicized. **2.** to cause to adapt to or acquire English traits, institutions, or beliefs. —**An′gli·ci·za′tion,** *n.*

an·gling (ang′gling) *n.* the act or sport of fishing with a hook and line.

An·glo (ang′glō) *n., pl.* **An·glos.** a white inhabitant of the United States who is not of Hispanic descent. —*adj.* of, having to do with, or characteristic of Anglos.

Anglo– *combining form* English: *Anglo-Norman, Anglo-American.*

An·glo–A·mer·i·can (ang′glō ə mer′i kən) *adj.* **1.** English and American: *an Anglo-American trade agreement.* **2.** of or relating to Anglo-Americans. —*n.* an American of English birth or descent.

An·glo–French (ang′glō french′) *adj.* English and French. —*n.* see **Anglo-Norman** (*def. 2*).

An·glo–Nor·man (ang′glō nôr′mən) *n.* **1.** one of the Normans who settled in England after the Norman Conquest in 1066. **2.** a dialect of Old French spoken by the Norman conquerors and the upper classes in England

from the Norman Conquest through the fourteenth century. —*adj.* of or relating to the Anglo-Normans, their language, or their culture.

An·glo–Sax·on (ang′glō sak′sən) *n.* **1.** a member or descendant of one of the Germanic tribes that invaded England in the fifth and sixth centuries A.D. **2.** any English person of the period from the fifth century to the Norman Conquest in 1066. **3.** any person of English descent. **4.** the language of the Anglo-Saxons; Old English. —*adj.* of or relating to the Anglo-Saxons, their language, or their culture.

An·go·ra (ang gôr′ə) *n.* **1. a.** see **Angora cat. b.** see **Angora goat. c.** see **Angora rabbit. 2.** *also,* **angora. a.** another name for **mohair. b.** yarn or knitted fabric made from the hair of the Angora rabbit or Angora goat.

Angora cat, any domestic cat with long, silky hair.

Angora goat, a goat of a breed that originated in Asia Minor, raised for its long, silky hair, which is called mohair.

Angora rabbit, a domestic rabbit bred for its long, silky hair.

Angora goat

an·gos·tu·ra (ang′gə stûr′ə, ang′gə styûr′ə) *n.* the aromatic, bitter bark of certain South American trees, used especially for making a kind of bitters.

an·gry (ang′grē) *adj.*, **an·gri·er, an·gri·est. 1.** feeling or showing anger: *an angry look. I was angry with them for ruining my party.* **2.** threatening and raging, as if in anger: *an angry sea.* **3.** painfully inflamed: *an angry rash.* —**an′gri·ly,** *adv.* —**an′gri·ness,** *n.*

ang·strom (ang′strəm) *also,* **Ang·strom.** *n.* a unit of measurement equal to $\frac{1}{100,000,000}$ of a centimeter, used to express the wavelength of light or other radiation. [From the Swedish physicist Anders J. Ångström (1814–1874).]

an·guish (ang′gwish) *n.* great suffering of body or mind; agony: *We were in anguish over the missing dog.*

an·guished (ang′gwisht) *adj.* feeling or showing anguish: *an anguished mourner, an anguished moan.*

an·gu·lar (ang′gyə lər) *adj.* **1.** having or forming an angle or angles; sharp-cornered: *an angular piece of rock.* **2.** measured by an angle: *angular distance.* **3.** having prominent bones; gaunt: *an angular face.* —**an′gu·lar·ly,** *adv.*

an·gu·lar·i·ty (ang′gyə lar′i tē) *n., pl.* **an·gu·lar·i·ties. 1.** the quality or state of being angular. **2.** an angular part or form.

An·gus (ang′gəs) *n.* another word for **Aberdeen Angus.**

an·hy·dride (an hī′drīd) *n.* an oxide that forms an acid or base when it is added to water.

an·hy·drous (an hī′drəs) *adj.* (of a chemical compound) having no water, especially water of crystallization.

an·i·line (an′ə lin) *also,* **an·i·lin.** *n.* an oily, poisonous liquid used in making rubber, dyes, and drugs. —*adj.* made of, derived from, or relating to aniline.

aniline dye 1. any of a number of dyes made from aniline. **2.** any synthetic dye.

---

at; āpe; fär; câre; end; mē; it; īce; pîerce; hot; ōld; sông, fôrk; oil; out; up; ūse; rüle; pùll; tûrn; chin; sing; shop; thin; this; hw in white; zh in treasure. The symbol ə stands for the unstressed vowel sound heard in about, taken, pencil, lemon, and circus.

an·i·mad·ver·sion (an'ə mad vûr'zhən) *n.* **1.** an unfavorable remark. **2.** criticism.

an·i·mal (an'ə məl) *n.* **1.** any of a large kingdom of living things that are made of many cells, have a well-defined shape, can move about by themselves, and can respond quickly to stimuli. Unlike plants, animals cannot make their own food. Wolves, snakes, starfish, flies, goldfish, and human beings are all animals. **2.** any animal except human beings; beast. **3.** a person who acts like a beast; coarse, brutish person. —*adj.* of, relating to, or derived from animals: *animal fats, animal instincts.*

animal husbandry, the branch of agriculture dealing with the breeding, raising, and care of livestock.

an·i·mate (*v.,* an'ə māt'; *adj.,* an'ə mit) *v.t.,* **an·i·mat·ed, an·i·mat·ing. 1.** to give life, vividness, or interest to; enliven: *Delight animated the faces of the audience.* **2.** to move to action; inspire; incite: *Curiosity animated them as they began their project.* —*adj.* having life; alive: *An animal is an animate being.*

an·i·mat·ed (an'ə mā'tid) *adj.* **1.** full of life, activity, or spirit; lively; vivacious: *The animated speaker easily held the attention of the audience.* **2.** made to move as if alive: *animated puppets.* —**an'i·mat'ed·ly,** *adv.*

animated cartoon, a motion picture consisting of a series of drawings, each of which shows a slight change from the drawing before it. When the drawings are photographed and projected in rapid succession, the figures seem to move.

an·i·ma·tion (an'ə mā'shən) *n.* **1.** the state of being full of life; vigor; spirit: *The old sailor told the story with great animation.* **2.** the act of animating or the state of being animated. **3. a.** the process and technique of preparing animated cartoons. **b.** the product of this process: *The animation in this film was done by a famous cartoonist.*

a·ni·ma·to (ä'nə mä'tō) *adj. Music.* lively; animated. —*adv.* in a spirited, lively manner.

an·i·mism (an'ə miz'əm) *n.* the belief that inanimate things and forces, such as trees, rocks, and winds, have souls or spirits.

an·i·mos·i·ty (an'ə mos'i tē) *n., pl.* **an·i·mos·i·ties.** strong or open hostility or hatred; enmity.

an·i·mus (an'ə məs) *n.* **1.** strong or open hostility or hatred; enmity; animosity. **2.** an animating spirit, force, or purpose.

an·i·on (an'ī'ən) *n.* a negatively charged ion of an electrolyte, attracted to the anode in electrolysis.

an·ise (an'is) *n.* **1.** a plant related to parsley, widely cultivated in the Mediterranean region, India, and South America. **2.** another word for **aniseed.**

an·i·seed (an'i sēd', an'is sēd') *n.* the fragrant seed of the anise, having a spicy, licoricelike taste, used as a flavoring and in some medicines.

an·kle (ang'kəl) *n.* **1.** the joint that connects the foot and the leg. **2.** the part of the leg that is located at and just above this joint.

an·kle·bone (ang'kəl bōn') *n.* the bone of the ankle. Also, **talus.**

an·klet (ang'klit) *n.* **1.** a short sock reaching just above the ankle. **2.** an ornamental band or chain worn around the ankle.

an·nals (an'əlz) *pl. n.* **1.** written accounts of events recorded year by year. **2.** any historical record or chronicle; history: *the annals of crime, the annals of football.*

an·neal (ə nēl') *v.t.* to heat and then slowly cool (metal or glass) to make less brittle.

an·ne·lid (an'ə lid) *n.* any of various worms whose bodies are made up of ringlike segments, such as the earthworm.

an·nex (*v.,* ə neks'; *n.,* an'eks) *v.t.* to add or attach, as to something larger: *The city annexed the suburb to itself.* —*n., pl.* **an·nex·es.** a building used as an addition to another: *The school built an annex because of the increased enrollment.* —**an'nex·a'tion,** *n.*

an·ni·hi·late (ə nī'ə lāt') *v.t.,* **an·ni·hi·lat·ed, an·ni·hi·lat·ing.** to destroy totally; reduce to nothing: *The bombers annihilated the city.* —**an·ni'hi·la'tion,** *n.*

an·ni·ver·sa·ry (an'ə vûr'sə rē) *n., pl.* **an·ni·ver·sa·ries. 1.** the yearly return of the date on which some important event occurred in an earlier year: *My grandparents celebrated their fiftieth wedding anniversary.* **2.** a celebration of the return of such an event. —*adj.* of or relating to an anniversary: *an anniversary gift.*

an·no Dom·i·ni (an'ō dom'ə nī', an'ō dom'ə nē') *Latin.* in the year of the Lord. Abbreviation, **A.D.** ▲ used to indicate dates occurring since the birth of Jesus.

an·no·tate (an'ə tāt') *v.t.,* **an·no·tat·ed, an·no·tat·ing.** to provide with critical or explanatory notes: *Many scholars have annotated the plays of Shakespeare.* —**an'no·ta'tor,** *n.*

an·no·ta·tion (an'ə tā'shən) *n.* **1.** a critical or explanatory note or comment. **2.** the act of annotating or the state of being annotated.

an·nounce (ə nouns') *v.,* **an·nounced, an·nounc·ing.** —*v.t.* **1.** to make known publicly or officially; proclaim: *The radio announced that the school would be closed because of the blizzard.* **2.** to make known the approach, arrival, or presence of: *The conductor announced each station as the train stopped.* **3.** to make known; indicate: *The disease announced itself with a rash.* **4.** to serve as the announcer for: *to announce a basketball game.* —*v.i.* to serve as a radio or television announcer.

an·nounce·ment (ə nouns'mənt) *n.* **1.** the act of announcing or the state of being announced. **2.** a public statement that makes something known: *The president will make an important announcement tonight.* **3.** a written or printed notice of an event: *a wedding announcement.*

an·nounc·er (ə noun'sər) *n.* **1.** a person on radio or television who introduces programs and performers, identifies the station, or presents advertisements, bulletins, or news items. **2.** any person who announces something.

an·noy (ə noi') *v.t.* to be troublesome or irritating to; vex; bother: *Carelessness annoys me. We were annoyed by the unnecessary delay.* —**an·noy'er,** *n.*

an·noy·ance (ə noi'əns) *n.* **1.** a person or thing that annoys; nuisance: *Your constant teasing is a great annoyance.* **2.** the act of annoying or the state of being annoyed: *I couldn't hide my annoyance.*

an·noy·ing (ə noi'ing) *adj.* troublesome; irritating; vexing: *an annoying delay.* —**an·noy'ing·ly,** *adv.*

an·nu·al (an'ū əl) *adj.* **1.** relating to or measured by the year: *a child's annual growth, a person's annual salary.* **2.** happening or returning once a year; yearly: *That store has an annual sale of clothing.* **3.** done during a year: *The earth makes an annual course around the sun.* **4.** (of a plant) living or lasting for only one year or season: *Corn, wheat, and cucumbers are annual plants.* —*n.* **1.** a journal or other publication issued once a year. **2.** a plant that lives or lasts for only one year or season. —**an'nu·al·ly,** *adv.*

annual ring, any of the rings seen in the cross section of a tree trunk or other woody plant stem. Each ring represents a year's growth.

an·nu·i·ty (ə nü'i tē, ə nū'i tē) *n., pl.* **an·nu·i·ties. 1.** a specified amount of money paid yearly or at other fixed intervals. **2.** the right to receive or obligation to pay such an amount of money. **3.** an investment, usually made with an insurance company, by which a fixed income is paid during the investor's lifetime or for a number of years.

annual rings

an·nul (ə nul′) *v.t.*, **an·nulled, an·nul·ling**. to declare void or nonexistent; do away with; declare invalid: *to annul a marriage, to annul an agreement*. **—an·nul′ment,** *n.*

an·nu·lar (an′yə lər) *adj*. relating to, made up of, or shaped like a ring or rings.

annular eclipse, a solar eclipse in which a portion of the sun is visible as a ring surrounding the dark body of the moon.

an·num (an′əm) *n. Latin.* a year.

an·nun·ci·a·tion (ə nun′sē ā′shən) *n.* **1. the Annunciation.** in the Bible, the announcement by the angel Gabriel to the Virgin Mary that she was to give birth to Jesus. **2. Annunciation.** the church festival commemorating this announcement. It falls on March 25.

an·ode (an′ōd) *n.* **1.** an electrode through which electrons leave an electrical device or medium. When electricity is used to produce a chemical reaction, the positive electrode is the anode. When a chemical reaction is used to produce electricity, the negative electrode is the anode. **2.** in electrolysis, an electrode that has a comparative lack of electrons and is positively charged. Negatively charged ions are oxidized at the anode. **3.** in an electron tube, an electrode or plate that attracts electrons.

an·o·dyne (an′ə dīn′) *n.* **1.** a medicine or treatment that relieves pain. **2.** anything that soothes or calms.

a·noint (ə noint′) *v.t.* **1.** to cover or smear with oil or an oily substance; apply ointment to. **2.** to put oil on as an act of consecration: *to anoint a monarch*. **—a·noint′ment,** *n.*

a·nom·a·lous (ə nom′ə ləs) *adj*. different from the usual or normal; irregular; abnormal. **—a·nom′a·lous·ly,** *adv.* **—a·nom′a·lous·ness,** *n.*

a·nom·a·ly (ə nom′ə lē) *n., pl.* **a·nom·a·lies.** something different from the usual or normal; irregularity; abnormality: *Snow in Florida is an anomaly*.

a·non (ə non′) *adv. Archaic.* **1.** in a little while; soon. **2.** at another time; again.
·**ever and anon.** again and again; now and then.

anon., anonymous.

an·o·nym·i·ty (an′ə nim′i tē) *n.* the condition of being anonymous: *In free elections, one votes in anonymity*.

a·non·y·mous (ə non′ə məs) *adj*. **1.** of unknown authorship or origin; without any name given: *an anonymous book, an anonymous telephone call*. **2.** not giving one's name; not known by name: *The author of the book on organized crime chose to remain anonymous*. **—anon′y·mous·ly,** *adv.*

a·noph·e·les (ə nof′ə lēz′) *n., pl.* **a·noph·e·les.** any of a group of mosquitoes that includes varieties that can transmit malaria to humans by their bite.

an·o·rex·i·a (an′ə rek′sē ə) *n.* a serious eating disorder that occurs mainly in young women. It is characterized by a great fear of gaining weight and by uncontrolled dieting, resulting in malnutrition. Also, **anorexia ner·vo·sa** (nər vō′sə). [From the Greek word *anorexia* meaning "lack of appetite," from the prefix *a-* "not" and the word *orexis* "appetite."]

an·oth·er (ə nuth′ər) *adj*. **1.** one more; an additional: *Do you want another glass of juice?* **2.** different: *Let's try another place to eat today*. **3.** similar or the same in character or achievements: *My cousins think their house is so beautiful it's another Taj Mahal*. **—pron.** **1.** one more; an additional one: *I finished the sandwich and then ordered another*. **2.** a different person or thing: *That plan didn't work, so we'll use another*.

an·ox·i·a (an ok′sē ə) *n.* a condition in which the body cells fail to receive or to use enough oxygen.

ans., answer.

an·swer (an′sər) *n.* **1.** something spoken or written as a reply: *No one could give an answer to the teacher's question. Did you receive an answer to your letter?* **2.** something done in reply or return: *The dog came in answer to my whistle*. **3.** the solution to a problem: *To*

find the correct answer, multiply by two. **4.** any solution or explanation: *The answer to our engine trouble was new spark plugs*. **—v.t.** **1.** to speak or write in reply to: *The company never answered my letter*. **2.** to act in response to: *I ran to answer the telephone*. **3.** to be suitable or enough for; serve: *This money should answer your needs*. **—v.i.** **1.** to give an answer: *When you hear your name, answer in a loud and clear voice*. **2.** to be responsible or accountable: *You will have to answer for the broken goods*. **3.** to agree or conform: *This car answers to the description of the one that was stolen*.
·**to answer back.** *Informal.* to reply rudely; talk back: *Don't answer back when your mother scolds you!*

an·swer·a·ble (an′sər ə bəl) *adj.* **1.** able to be held responsible; accountable: *The club treasurer is answerable for the financial records*. **2.** that can be answered.

answering machine, a tape recorder that automatically answers the telephone and records messages from callers.

answering service, a company that accepts telephone calls for its clients in their absence and gives messages to them on their return.

ant (ant) *n.* any of a group of small insects related to bees and wasps. Ants are found in all temperate and tropical regions of the world. They live in colonies that may contain as few as several dozen individuals or as many as 1,500,000.

-ant *suffix* **1.** (used to form adjectives) doing or being: *defiant, radiant*. **2.** (used to form nouns) a person or thing that does: *servant, lubricant*. [Originally from the Latin suffix *-ant*, the participial suffix of some verbs.]

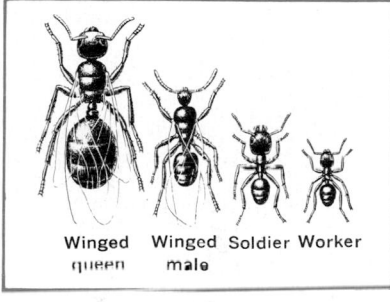

Winged queen   Winged male   Soldier   Worker

types of **ants**

ant., antonym.

ant·ac·id (ant as′id) *n.* a chemical substance that neutralizes acids, especially a remedy for excess stomach acidity. **—adj.** that can neutralize acids.

an·tag·o·nism (an tag′ə niz′əm) *n.* active opposition or strong feeling against; hostility: *The rival political groups felt great antagonism toward each other*.

an·tag·o·nist (an tag′ə nist) *n.* a person, group, or force that opposes, fights, or competes with another; adversary.

an·tag·o·nis·tic (an tag′ə nis′tik) *adj*. acting or being in opposition; hostile. **—an·tag′o·nis′ti·cal·ly,** *adv.*

an·tag·o·nize (an tag′ə nīz′) *v.t.*, **an·tag·o·nized, an·tag·o·niz·ing.** to provoke dislike or hostility in; make unfriendly: *Their nasty comments about my family antagonized me*.

ant·arc·tic (ant ärk′tik, ant är′tik) *adj*. of or relating to the South Pole or to the south polar regions. **—n. the Antarctic.** another name for **Antarctica.**

Antarctic Circle, an imaginary line around the earth running parallel to the equator at 66°33′ south latitude, or about 1,600 miles (2,575 kilometers) from the South Pole.

---

at; āpe; fär; câre; end; mē; it; īce; pîerce; hot; ōld; sông; fôrk; oil; out; up; ūse; rüle; pull; tûrn; chin; sing; shop; thin; this; hw in white; zh in treasure. The symbol ə stands for the unstressed vowel sound heard in about, taken, pencil, lemon, and circus.

ant bear, a gray anteater of tropical Central and South America. It is the largest kind of anteater.

an·te (an′tē) *n.* **1.** in poker, a stake that each player must pay before receiving a hand or drawing new cards. **2.** *Slang.* any amount required as a share. *v.,* **an·ted** or **an·teed, an·te·ing.** —*v.t.* (often

ant bear

followed by *up*) to pay (an ante): *Each of us anted a dime.* —*v.i.* (often followed by *up*) to pay an ante: *We anted up and started the next hand.*

ante– *prefix* **1.** before in time; prior to: *antebellum.* **2.** before in position; in front of: *antechamber.*

ant·eat·er (ant′ē′tər) *n.* any of various toothless mammals of tropical Central and South America that feed on ants and termites. They have long narrow heads, long, sticky tongues, and powerful front claws.

an·te·bel·lum (an′tē bel′əm) *adj.* before or existing since before the war, especially the American Civil War: *the antebellum South, an antebellum plantation.*

an·te·ced·ent (an′tə sē′dənt) *n.* **1.** a thing or event that occurs before another: *A drop in air pressure is often an antecedent to a storm.* **2.** *Grammar.* a noun or clause to which a pronoun refers. In the sentence *I bought a new hat but left it on the bus,* the noun *hat* is the antecedent of the pronoun *it.* **3. antecedents. a.** the previous events or influences in a person's life. **b.** a person's ancestors. —*adj.* occurring or existing before; preceding; prior: *the conditions antecedent to the Industrial Revolution.* —**an′te·ced′ent·ly,** *adv.*

an·te·cham·ber (an′tē chām′bər) *n.* another word for **anteroom.**

an·te·date (an′ti dāt′) *v.t.,* **an·te·dat·ed, an·te·dat·ing.** **1.** to be or happen earlier than; precede in time: *Propeller-driven planes antedated jet planes.* **2.** to give (something) a date earlier than the correct one: *to antedate a check.*

an·te·di·lu·vi·an (an′tē də lü′vē ən) *adj.* **1.** of or relating to the period before the Biblical Flood. **2.** very old or old-fashioned: *antediluvian social attitudes.* —*n.* **1.** a person who lived before the Biblical Flood. **2.** a very old or old-fashioned person.

an·te·lope (ant′ə lōp′) *n., pl.* **an·te·lope** or **an·te·lopes.** **1.** any of various cud-chewing animals that are closely related to goats, having unbranched horns and cloven hoofs. Antelopes are native to Africa and southern Asia. **2.** another name for **pronghorn.**

an·te me·rid·i·em (an′tē mə rid′ē əm) from midnight up to, but not including, noon. Abbreviation, **A.M.** [From the Latin phrase *ante meridiem* meaning "before noon."]

an·ten·na (an ten′ə) *n., pl.* **an·ten·nas** (*def. 1*) or **an·ten·nae** (an ten′ē) (*def. 2*). **1.** a metal structure, wire, or set of wires used to receive or transmit radio or television signals; aerial. **2.** one of a pair of jointed sense organs, or feelers, on the head of an insect or crustacean.

antelope
(def. 1)

an·te·pe·nult (an′tē pē′nult) *n.* the third-to-last syllable in a word. In the word *port·fo·li·o,* the syllable *fo* is the antepenult.

an·te·ri·or (an tîr′ē ər) *adj.* **1.** at or toward the front or head: *the anterior lobe of the brain.* **2.** earlier in time.

an·te·room (an′tē rüm′, an′tē rüm′) *n.* a room serving as a waiting room or entrance to a larger or main room. Also, **antechamber.**

an·them (an′thəm) *n.* **1.** a song of gladness, praise, devotion, or patriotism: *"The Star-Spangled Banner" is the national anthem of the United States.* **2.** a piece of sacred choral music with words usually taken from a Biblical passage.

an·ther (an′thər) *n.* in a flower, the pollen-bearing part of the stamen.

ant·hill (ant′hil′) *n.* a mound of dirt or other material heaped up by ants around the entrance to their underground nest.

an·thol·o·gist (an thol′ə jist) *n.* a person who collects material for an anthology.

an·thol·o·gy (an thol′ə jē) *n., pl.* **an·thol·o·gies.** a collection of written works or passages, often by different authors, within a single book or set: *an anthology of French poetry.*

an·thra·cite (an′thrə sīt′) *n.* a very hard, glossy black coal with a high carbon content. It burns with a low, smokeless flame. Also, **hard coal.**

an·thrax (an′thraks) *n.* a highly infectious, usually fatal disease of animals, especially cows and sheep, that can be transmitted to humans. It is caused by a bacterium.

an·thro·poid (an′thrə poid′) *adj.* **1.** resembling a human being: *A gorilla is an anthropoid ape.* **2.** resembling an ape. —*n.* any of several tailless apes that resemble humans in form, such as gorillas and chimpanzees.

an·thro·pol·o·gist (an′thrə pol′ə gist) *n.* a student of or an expert in anthropology.

an·thro·pol·o·gy (an′thrə pol′ə jē) *n.* the science that deals with the physical, cultural, and social development of humans, including their origin, evolution, behavior, and geographic distribution from prehistoric times to the present. —**an·thro·po·log·i·cal** (an′thrə pə loj′i kəl), *adj.* —**an′thro·po·log′i·cal·ly,** *adv.*

anti– *prefix* **1.** opposed to; against: *antitrust, anticlerical.* **2.** expressing the opposite or reverse of: *anticlimax.* **3.** operating against; counteracting: *antifreeze, antiaircraft.*

an·ti·air·craft (an′tē âr′kraft′) *adj.* used or for use against aircraft in flight: *an antiaircraft missile.*

an·ti·bal·lis·tic missile (an′tē bə lis′tik) guided missile launched to search out and destroy a ballistic missile before it reaches its target.

an·ti·bi·ot·ic (an′tē bī ot′ik) *n.* any of a group of substances, such as penicillin or erythromycin, produced by molds, bacteria, and other microorganisms. Antibiotics are used in medicine to kill or slow the growth of disease-causing bacteria or fungi. —*adj.* of or relating to antibiotics.

an·ti·bod·y (an′ti bod′ē) *n., pl.* **an·ti·bod·ies.** any of various proteins in the blood produced by the body as a normal function or in response to the presence of a foreign substance. Antibodies neutralize or destroy germs and can give immunity against certain diseases. Antibodies are also involved in allergic reactions.

an·tic (an′tik) *n.* a silly or comical action; caper; prank: *the antics of a clown, the antics of a puppy.* —*adj.* grotesque; bizarre; ludicrous.

An·ti·christ (an′ti krīst′) *n.* **1.** in early Christian prophecy, the great enemy or opponent of Jesus Christ. **2.** *also,* **antichrist.** anyone who does not believe in Jesus Christ or is an opponent of Christianity.

an·tic·i·pate (an tis′ə pāt′) *v.t.,* **an·tic·i·pat·ed, an·tic·i·pat·ing.** **1.** to look forward to; expect: *I do not anticipate any trouble. We anticipate their arrival at four o'clock.* **2.** to foresee and deal with in advance: *They anticipated my objections to the idea.* **3.** to be before (another) in doing something; precede: *The Vikings are believed to have anticipated Columbus in the discovery of America.* —**an·tic′i·pa′tor,** *n.*

an·tic·i·pa·tion (an tis′ə pā′shən) *n.* **1.** the act of anticipating or the state of being anticipated. **2.** a feeling of excited expectation.

an·ti·cler·i·cal (an′tē kler′i kəl) *adj.* opposed to the influence and activities of the church or clergy.

an·ti·cli·mac·tic (an′ti klī mak′tic) *adj.* of, having, or like an anticlimax. —**an′ti·cli·mac′ti·cal·ly**, *adv.*

an·ti·cli·max (an′ti klī′maks) *n., pl.* **an·ti·cli·max·es.** **1.** an unexpected, sudden change from something important or dignified to something trivial or absurd. In the sentence *My house burned down, my wallet was stolen, and I didn't have time to eat lunch,* the phrase *and I didn't have time to eat lunch* is an anticlimax. **2.** anything that is much less important or interesting than what has come before it.

an·ti·cline (an′ti klīn′) *n.* a geologic formation in which a layer of folded rock inclines downward on both sides of the center of the fold. —**an′ti·cli′nal,** *adj.*

an·ti·co·a·gu·lant (an′tē kō ag′yə lənt) *n.* a drug that slows or stops clotting of the blood.

an·ti·cy·clone (an′ti sī′klōn) *n.* an atmospheric condition consisting of a mass of air currents rotating about a center of high barometric pressure.

an·ti·do·tal (an′ti dō′təl) *adj.* of, like, or acting as an antidote.

an·ti·dote (an′ti dōt′) *n.* **1.** a medicine or other remedy to counteract the effects of a poison. **2.** any remedy: *An interesting book is an antidote to boredom.*

an·ti·freeze (an′ti frēz′) *n.* any substance added to a liquid to lower its freezing point, especially an alcohol mixture added to the fluid in automobile radiators to prevent it from freezing in cold weather.

an·ti·gen (an′ti jən) *n.* a substance that causes the body to produce antibodies, such as a toxin, bacterium, or drug.

An·tig·o·ne (an tig′ə nē′) *n. Greek Legend.* the daughter of Oedipus. She was condemned to death for giving her brother a proper burial against the command of Creon, her uncle.

an·ti·he·ro (an′tē hir′ō) *n., pl.* **an·ti·he·roes.** a main character, as in a play, motion picture, or novel, who lacks the positive characteristics traditionally associated with a hero.

an·ti·her·o·ine (an′tē her′ō in) *n.* a main character, as in a play, motion picture, or novel, who lacks the positive characteristics traditionally associated with a heroine.

an·ti·his·ta·mine (an′ti his′tə mēn′) *n.* any of several drugs that counteract the effect of histamine in the body. Antihistamines are used chiefly in the treatment of colds and such allergic reactions as hives, hay fever, and asthma.

an·ti·knock (an′tē nok′) *n.* a chemical substance that is added to gasoline to reduce knocking in an automobile engine.

an·ti·log·a·rithm (an′ti lô′gə rith′əm, an′ti log′ə-rith′əm) *n.* the number corresponding to a given logarithm. In the expression $2^3 = 8$, the logarithm is 3 and the antilogarithm is 8.

an·ti·ma·cas·sar (an′ti mə kas′ər) *n.* a small covering put over the back and arms of a chair, to protect against soiling and as a decoration.

an·ti·mat·ter (an′tē mat′ər) *n. Physics.* a theoretical form of matter consisting of antiparticles.

an·ti·mis·sile (an tē mis′əl) *adj.* designed or used for defense against ballistic and guided missiles.

an·ti·mo·ny (an′tə mō′nē) *n.* a silver or bluish white crystalline metallic element used in alloys to increase their

Anticline

Syncline

anticline
cross section of
stratified rock

hardness. Symbol: **Sb** [From the Medieval Latin word *antimonium* meaning "antimony," perhaps of Greek origin.]

an·ti·neu·tron (an′tē nū′tron, an′tē nū′tron) *n. Physics.* the antiparticle of the neutron.

an·ti·par·ti·cle (an′tē pär′ti kəl) *n. Physics.* any of a group of subatomic particles, each of which corresponds to one of the particles that make up ordinary matter but has opposite magnetic properties to its corresponding particle and, in the case of charged particles, opposite charge. When a particle and its antiparticle collide, they destroy each other and their combined mass is changed into energy.

an·ti·pas·to (an′ti päs′tō) *n., pl.* **an·ti·pas·tos.** an Italian dish consisting of small portions of various foods, served as appetizers.

an·tip·a·thy (an tip′ə thē) *n., pl.* **an·tip·a·thies.** **1.** a feeling of strong dislike; distaste; aversion: *an antipathy to violence.* **2.** a person or thing that arouses such dislike.

an·ti·per·spi·rant (an′tē pûr′spər ənt) *n.* a preparation applied to the skin to reduce or prevent perspiration.

an·tip·o·dal (an tip′ə dəl) *adj.* of or relating to antipodes; on opposite sides of the earth.

an·tip·o·des (an tip′ə dēz′) *pl. n.* **1.** two places on the earth's surface that are exactly opposite one another: *The North Pole and the South Pole are antipodes.* **2.** two opposite or contrary things: *Love and hate are antipodes.* **3.** *British.* Australia and New Zealand.

an·ti·pov·er·ty (an′tē pov′ər tē) *adj.* intended to relieve or eliminate poverty: *antipoverty programs.*

an·ti·pro·ton (an′tē prō′ton) *n. Physics.* the antiparticle of the proton.

an·ti·quar·i·an (an′ti kwâr′ē ən) *adj.* of or relating to antiquities. —*n.* another word for **antiquary.**

an·ti·quar·y (an′ti kwer′ē) *n., pl.* **an·ti·quar·ies.** a person who collects, studies, or deals in antiquities.

an·ti·quate (an′ti kwāt′) *v.t.,* **an·ti·quat·ed, an·ti·quat·ing.** to cause to become old-fashioned; make out-of-date.

an·ti·quat·ed (an′ti kwā′tid) *adj.* **1.** no longer in fashion; out-of-date: *antiquated ideas, an antiquated style of dress.* **2.** no longer in use or no longer suited for use: *an antiquated piece of machinery.*

an·tique (an tēk′) *adj.* **1.** of, belonging to, or in the style of times long ago: *antique furniture, an antique watch.*

antiques on display in a shop

at; āpe; fär; câre; end; mē; it; īce; pîerce; hot; ōld; sông, fôrk; oil; out; up; ūse; rüle; pull; tûrn; chin; sing; shop; thin; <u>th</u>is; hw in white; zh in treasure. The symbol ə stands for the unstressed vowel sound heard in about, taken, pencil, lemon, and circus.

2. of, belonging to, or in the style of ancient Greece or Rome: *an antique temple.* —*n.* **1.** something made very long ago. **2.** a work of art or craftsmanship that is valued for its age, especially one that is more than one hundred years old. —*v.t.,* **an·tiqued, an·ti·quing.** to make (something) appear old: *to antique a chair.*

an·tiq·ui·ty (an tik′wi tē) *n., pl.* **an·tiq·ui·ties. 1.** the early ages of history, especially the period before the Middle Ages; ancient times. **2.** the people and cultures of ancient times. **3.** the quality of being ancient; great age: *a gold necklace that is valued for its antiquity.* **4. antiquities.** objects belonging to or remaining from ancient times.

an·ti–Se·mit·ic (an′tē sə mit′ik) *adj.* prejudiced or discriminating against Jews.

an·ti–Sem·i·tism (an′tē sem′i tiz′əm) *n.* prejudice or discrimination against Jews.

an·ti·sep·tic (an′ti sep′tik) *n.* a substance that kills or stops the growth of germs. Alcohol, iodine, and hydrogen peroxide are common antiseptics. —*adj.* **1.** preventing infection or decay by killing or stopping the growth of germs. **2.** free from germs; sterilized. —**an′ti·sep′ti·cal·ly,** *adv.*

an·ti·so·cial (an′tē sō′shəl) *adj.* **1.** not liking companionship or the society of others; unsociable: *an antisocial person.* **2.** opposed to the general good of society: *Murder is an antisocial act.* —**an′ti·so′cial·ly,** *adv.*

an·tith·e·sis (an tith′ə sis) *n., pl.* **an·tith·e·ses** (an-tith′ə sēz′). **1.** the exact opposite: *Hope is the antithesis of despair.* **2.** a state of opposition; contrast: *The antithesis of bravery and cowardice was the theme of the story.* **3.** the contrast of strongly opposed ideas in speech or writing: *''Ask not what your country can do for you—ask what you can do for your country''* (John F. Kennedy) is an example of antithesis.

an·ti·tox·in (an′ti tok′sin) *n.* **1.** an antibody formed in the body that provides protection against a specific poison released by invading bacteria. **2.** a serum containing such an antibody, obtained from the blood of horses or other animals that have been injected with a toxin.

an·ti·trades (an′ti trādz′) *pl. n.* winds that blow above, and in a direction opposite to, the trade winds.

an·ti·trust (an′tē trust′) *adj.* opposed to or regulating monopolies, trusts, or other business combinations or practices that interfere with competition: *antitrust laws, an antitrust lawyer.*

an·ti·vi·ral (an′tē vī′rəl) *adj.* killing or slowing the growth of viruses: *an antiviral medicine.* —*n.* a drug that kills or slows the growth of viruses.

ant·ler (ant′lər) *n.* **1.** one of the branched horns of deer, elk, moose, and other related animals. Antlers are shed each year and replaced by new ones. **2.** any of the branches of such a horn.

ant lion, an insect whose larva feeds on ants and other wingless insects, which it catches by digging a pit into which the prey falls and is trapped.

an·to·nym (an′tə nim′) *n.* a word that has the opposite meaning of another word. *Young* and *old, up* and *down,* and *left* and *right* are antonyms.

Language Note

An **antonym** is a word that has exactly the opposite meaning of another word. A word that has exactly the same meaning as another word is called a synonym. Our language contains very few real synonyms because it is of little use to have two or more words that stand for exactly the same thing. The meaning of the word *happy,* for example, is very similar to the meaning of the words *cheerful* and *joyful.* But each word has a shade of meaning that distinguishes it from the other two, which keeps them from being true synonyms.

There are, however, many real antonyms in English because it is often useful to be able to express the opposite of the meaning of a word. When we want to express the opposite of *happy,* we use the word *sad,* which is its antonym.

ants·y (ant′sē) *adj.,* **ants·i·er, ants·i·est.** *Informal.* very eager, anxious, or restless: *Waiting for the train was making us antsy. The children were antsy to leave the beach.*

A·nu·bis (ə nü′bis, ə nū′bis) *n. Egyptian Mythology.* the son of Osiris and a god of the underworld, represented as a man with the head of a jackal.

A number 1, another term for **A-1.**

a·nus (ā′nəs) *n., pl.* **a·nus·es.** an opening at the lower end of the alimentary canal, through which solid waste products pass from the body.

an·vil (an′vəl) *n.* **1.** an iron or steel block on which heat-softened metals are hammered into desired shapes. **2.** another term for **incus.**

anx·i·e·ty (ang zī′i tē) *n., pl.* **anx·i·e·ties. 1.** a feeling of fearful uneasiness or worry about what may happen: *Our anxiety became deeper as the hours passed and the children did not return.* **2.** something that causes this feeling: *Lack of money is my chief anxiety.* **3.** an earnest and eager desire: *anxiety to please a new employer.*

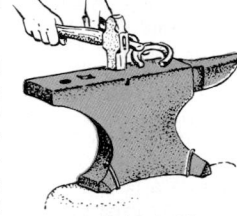

anvil *(def. 1)*

anx·ious (angk′shəs, ang′shəs) *adj.* **1.** uneasy, worried, and fearful about what may happen: *I am always anxious when a friend of mine is on an airplane.* **2.** showing, causing, or resulting from anxiety: *an anxious look, an anxious moment.* **3.** earnestly and eagerly desiring: *to be anxious to make friends at a new school.* —**anx′ious·ly,** *adv.* —**anx′ious·ness,** *n.*

an·y (en′ē) *adj.* **1.** one, no matter which; some, whatever kind: *Take any seat. Any information will help.* **2.** some, in whatever quantity or number: *Have you any apples?* **3.** every: *Any child can do this problem.* **4.** at all: *I haven't any change.* —*pron.* any one or ones; any quantity or number: *We haven't any left. You scored higher than any of the others.* —*adv.* to any extent or degree: *Stop before you go any farther.*

an·y·bod·y (en′ē bod′ē, en′ē bud′ē) *pron.* any person whatever; anyone: *Has anybody seen the cat?* —*n.* a person of importance: *Everybody who is anybody was at the party.* ▲ **Anybody** and **anyone** are both singular. In writing and formal speech, they are used with a singular pronoun: *Anyone who wants to tell the class about his or her hobby may speak tomorrow.* In conversation, they are often used with a plural pronoun: *If anybody asks for me, tell them* (rather than *him* or *her) I've gone home for the day.*

an·y·how (en′ē hou′) *adv.* **1.** in any case; at any rate; nevertheless: *I didn't really want to go anyhow. The movie was half over, but we went in anyhow.* **2.** in any way whatever: *Anyhow you go, you'll have to pay a lot.*

an·y·more (en′ē môr′) *adv.* at the present time or from now on: *Let's not fight anymore.*

an·y·one (en′ē wun′) *pron.* any person whatever; anybody. ▲ The pronoun **anyone** and the two words **any one** are spelled alike, but they do not mean the same thing. **Anyone** means ''any person'': *Anyone may attend the meeting.* **Any one** means ''any of a group'' and is followed by *of: Any one of these books will help you.* See **anybody** for an additional usage note.

an·y·place (en′ē plās′) *adv. Informal.* anywhere.

an·y·thing (en′ē thing′) *pron.* any thing whatever: *I'll do anything you say. I didn't have anything to eat all*

A

day. —*adv.* to any extent; at all: *You aren't anything like your brothers and sisters.*
· **anything but.** by no means; not at all: *The train station was anything but quiet.*

an·y·time (en′ē tīm′) *adv.* at any time: *Come anytime you like.*

an·y·way (en′ē wā′) *adv.* **1.** in any case; at any rate; nevertheless: *Anyway, I am glad it happened. It began to rain, but we finished the game anyway.* **2.** in any manner or way: *I'm too careful to do this work just anyway.*

an·y·where (en′ē hwâr′, en′ē wâr′) *adv.* **1.** in, at, or to any place: *Just put it down anywhere.* **2.** *Informal.* to any extent; at all: *Did I come anywhere near the right answer?*

an·y·wise (en′ē wīz′) *adv.* in any way; to any degree; at all.

A-OK (ā′ō kā′) *also,* **A-o·kay.** *adj., adv., interj. Informal.* excellent; perfect: *Everything is working A-OK.*

A-one (ā′wun′) another word for **A-1.**

a·or·ta (ā ôr′tə) *n., pl.* **a·or·tas** or **a·or·tae** (ā ôr′tē). the main artery of the body. It carries the blood from the left ventricle of the heart to all parts of the body except the lungs.

a·pace (ə pās′) *adv.* swiftly; quickly; rapidly: *Great weeds do grow apace* (Shakespeare, *Richard III*).

A·pach·e (ə pach′ē) *n., pl.* **A·pach·e** or **A·pach·es.** **1.** a member of an Indian tribe living in the southwestern United States. **2.** the language spoken by these people. **3.** a ruffian, gangster, or thug of Paris. —*adj.* of or relating to the Apaches, their language, or their culture.

a·part (ə pärt′) *adv.* **1.** away from one another; separated in space or time: *The houses are 50 feet apart. The two trains left three hours apart.* **2.** into two or more parts; in or to pieces: *The pigs tore the sack apart. The mechanic took the engine apart.* **3.** at a distance; aside: *I sat apart from the others.* **4.** as a separate consideration; independently: *Viewed apart, the matter becomes clearer.*
· **apart from.** other than; besides: *Apart from the loud, boring music, the movie was very good.*
· **to take apart. a.** to separate into its various parts: *to take an engine apart.* **b.** to criticize severely: *to take someone apart because of a bad mistake.*
· **to tell apart.** to see the differences between: *Can you tell the twins apart?*

a·part·heid (ə pär′tīd, ə pärt′hāt) *n.* racial segregation, especially as an official policy in South Africa.

a·part·ment (ə pärt′mənt) *n.* a room or set of rooms to live in, usually in a large building.

apartment house, a building divided into a number of apartments. Also, **apartment building.**

ap·a·thet·ic (ap′ə thet′ik) *adj.* **1.** having or showing little interest, concern, or desire to act; indifferent: *The speaker tried to arouse emotions, but the crowd was apathetic.* **2.** having or showing little or no feeling or emotion: *The apathetic patient recovered slowly.* —**ap′a·thet′i·cal·ly,** *adv.*

ap·a·to·sau·rus (ap′ə tō sôr′əs) *n., pl.* **ap·a·to·sau·rus.** another term for **brontosaurus.**

ap·a·thy (ap′ə thē) *n.* **1.** a lack of interest, concern, or desire to act; indifference: *to view politics with apathy.* **2.** a lack of feeling or emotion.

ape (āp) *n.* **1.** any of several primates that have a somewhat human form and brain structure and that are able to stand or walk nearly erect, including the chimpanzee, gibbon, gorilla, and orangutan. **2.** any monkey. **3.** a person who imitates; mimic. —*v.t.,* **aped, ap·ing.** to imitate; mimic. —**ape′like′,** *adj.* —**ap′er,** *n.*

ap·er·ture (ap′ər chər) *n.* **1.** a hole, gap, or other opening. **2.** an opening through which light passes into a camera or other optical instrument.

a·pex (ā′peks) *n., pl.* **a·pex·es** or **ap·i·ces.** **1.** the highest point; tip: *the apex of a triangle, the apex of a mountain.*

2. the highest achievement: *This novel was the apex of the writer's career.*

a·pha·sia (ə fā′zhə) *n.* total or partial loss of the ability to use or understand spoken or written language. It is a symptom of brain disease or injury.

a·phe·li·on (ə fē′lē ən) *n., pl.* **a·phe·li·a** (ə fē′lē ə). the point in the orbit of a planet or other heavenly body at which it is farthest away from the sun.

a·phid (ā′fid, af′id) *n.* any of a group of small insects that live by sucking juices from the stems and leaves of plants; plant louse.

aph·o·rism (af′ə riz′əm) *n.* a short statement expressing a general truth. For example: *A little learning is a dangerous thing* (Alexander Pope).

aph·ro·dis·i·ac (af′rə diz′ē ak′) *n.* a drug or food that arouses sexual drive. —*adj.* stimulating sexual desire.

Aph·ro·di·te (af′rə dī′tē) *n. Greek Mythology.* the goddess of love and beauty. In Roman mythology she was called Venus.

a·pi·ar·y (ā′pē er′ē) *n., pl.* **a·pi·ar·ies.** a place where colonies of bees are kept; collection of beehives.

ap·i·ces (ap′ə sēz′, ā′pə sēz′) a plural of **apex.**

a·piece (ə pēs′) *adv.* for or to each one; each: *These peaches are fifteen cents apiece. Give the dogs two biscuits apiece.*

ap·ish (ā′pish) *adj.* **1.** like an ape. **2.** stupid or foolish in behavior. **3.** stupidly imitative. —**ap′ish·ly,** *adv.* —**ap′ish·ness,** *n.*

a·plen·ty (ə plen′tē) *adj.* enough or more than enough: *We had trouble aplenty when our cellar flooded.* ▲ see the usage note at **galore.**

a·plomb (ə plom′, ə plum′) *n.* complete control of oneself or self-confidence; poise: *The emergency medical worker handled the difficult problem with aplomb.*

APO, Army Post Office. ▲ used in military addresses.

a·poc·a·lypse (ə pok′ə lips′) *n.* **1.** a prophecy or revelation, especially one about the end of the world. **2. Apocalypse.** the last book of the New Testament. Also, **Revelation. 3.** the end of the world; doomsday.

A·poc·ry·pha (ə pok′rə fə) *pl. n.* **1.** fourteen books that form an appendix to the Old Testament in certain versions of the Bible. Eleven of these books are accepted by Roman Catholics, but none of the fourteen is regarded as authentic by Protestants and Jews. **2.** various early Christian writings of uncertain origin, rejected as part of the New Testament. **3. apocrypha.** writings or statements of doubtful authorship or authenticity.

a·poc·ry·phal (ə pok′rə fəl) *adj.* **1.** of doubtful authenticity; probably false: *Many stories told about George Washington are apocryphal.* **2. Apocryphal.** of or relating to the Apocrypha.

ap·o·gee (ap′ə jē′) *n.* the point in the orbit of the moon or an artificial earth satellite at which it is farthest away from the earth.

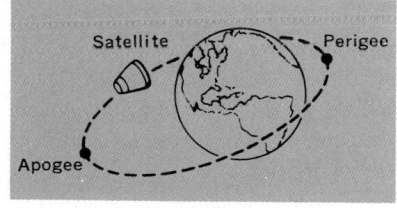

apogee

A·pol·lo (ə pol′ō) *n., pl.* **A·pol·los.** **1.** *Greek and Roman Mythology.* the god of manly beauty, poetry, music, prophecy,

at; āpe; fär; câre; end; mē; it; īce; pîerce; hot; ōld; sông, fôrk; oil; out; up; ūse; rüle; pùll; tûrn; chin; sing; shop; thin; **this**; hw in white; zh in treasure. The symbol ə stands for the unstressed vowel sound heard in about, taken, pencil, lemon, and circus.

and healing. He was also considered to be the god of the sun and, as such, was god of light and truth. **2.** *also,* **apollo.** a very handsome young man.

a·pol·o·get·ic (ə pol'ə jet'ik) *adj.* making or willing to make an apology; feeling or expressing regret: *an apologetic note, to be apologetic because you missed an appointment.* —**a·pol'o·get'i·cal·ly,** *adv.*

a·pol·o·gist (ə pol'ə jist) *n.* a person who speaks or writes in defense of another person or a cause, faith, or idea: *an apologist for government policy.*

a·pol·o·gize (ə pol'ə jīz') *v.i.,* **a·pol·o·gized, a·pol·o·giz·ing.** **1.** to acknowledge and express regret for a fault, error, or offense: *I apologized to my parents for being rude.* **2.** to speak or write in defense of another person or a cause, faith, or idea.

a·pol·o·gy (ə pol'ə jē) *n., pl.* **a·pol·o·gies.** **1.** an expression of regret for a fault, error, or offense: *Please accept my apology for being late.* **2.** something spoken or written in defense of a person, cause, or idea. **3.** a poor substitute; makeshift: *The old raft was a sad apology for a boat.*

ap·o·plec·tic (ap'ə plek'tik) *adj.* **1.** of, relating to, or causing apoplexy: *an apoplectic seizure.* **2.** suffering from apoplexy: *an apoplectic patient.* **3.** seemingly on the verge of having a stroke; violently excited: *apoplectic with rage.* —*n.* a person suffering from apoplexy. —**ap'o·plec'ti·cal·ly,** *adv.*

ap·o·plex·y (ap'ə plek'sē) *n., pl.* **ap·o·plex·ies.** a sudden weakness or paralysis, with or without loss of consciousness, caused by a rupture or blockage of blood vessels in the brain; stroke.

a·pos·ta·sy (ə pos'tə sē) *n., pl.* **a·pos·ta·sies.** a desertion or renunciation of one's religion, cause, political party, or principles.

a·pos·tate (ə pos'tāt) *n.* a person who deserts or renounces his or her religion, cause, political party, or principles.

a·pos·tle (ə pos'əl) *n.* **1. Apostle.** an early disciple of Jesus, especially one of the twelve originally chosen by Jesus to preach his gospel. **2.** any early Christian leader or missionary. **3.** a leader or early advocate of any movement or cause: *an apostle of disarmament.*

Apostles' Creed, a formal statement of Christian faith that affirms the teachings of the Apostles. It begins with the statement ''I believe in God the Father Almighty.''

ap·os·tol·ic (ap'ə stol'ik) *adj.* **1.** of or relating to the Apostles, their times, or their teachings: *apostolic tradition.* **2.** *also,* **Apostolic.** of or relating to the pope; papal: *an apostolic pronouncement.*

a·pos·tro·phe[1] (ə pos'trə fē) *n.* a punctuation mark (') used in the following ways: **1.** to indicate the omission of one or more letters in a word or phrase, as in *you're* for *you are,* or *e'er* for *ever.* **2.** to indicate the possessive case of nouns and indefinite pronouns, as in *the student's desk, anyone's concern, the children's room, the dogs' tails.* **3.** to indicate the plural of letters and figures, as in *the three R's, five 6's.* [From the French word *apostrophe,* from the Late Latin word *apostrophus,* the name for this punctuation mark, going back to the Greek word *apostrophos* meaning ''turned away'' or ''left out.'' The apostrophe is used when a letter has been left out.]

a·pos·tro·phe[2] (ə pos'trə fē) *n.* a figure of speech in which a thing or person, often absent or imaginary, is directly addressed as if present. For example: *Freedom, we cherish you!* [From the Latin *apostrophe,* the name for this figure of speech, from the Greek word *apostrophē* meaning ''a turning away.'']

apothecaries' measure, a system of liquid measure used in pharmacy.

apothecaries' weight, a system of weights used in pharmacy.

a·poth·e·car·y (ə poth'ə ker'ē) *n., pl.* **a·poth·e·car·ies.** a person who prepares and sells drugs and medicines; druggist; pharmacist.

ap·o·thegm (ap'ə them') *n.* a short, instructive saying; maxim. For example: *Live and let live.*

a·poth·e·o·sis (ə poth'ē ō'sis) *n., pl.* **a·poth·e·o·ses** (ə poth'ē ō'sēz). **1.** the act of raising a human being to the rank of a god; deification. **2.** a glorified ideal; perfect example: *The explorer was regarded as the apotheosis of courage.*

app. 1. apparent; apparently. **2.** appendix. **3.** appointed.

ap·pall (ə pôl') *also,* **ap·pal.** *v.t.,* **ap·palled, ap·pall·ing.** to fill with horror or dismay; terrify or shock: *We were appalled by the news of the flood.*

ap·pall·ing (ə pô'ling) *adj.* causing horror or dismay; shocking; dreadful. —**ap·pall'ing·ly,** *adv.*

ap·pa·rat·us (ap'ə rat'əs, ap'ə rā'təs) *n., pl.* **ap·pa·rat·us** or **ap·pa·rat·us·es.** **1.** a device or mechanism used for a particular purpose: *an apparatus for breathing underwater.* **2.** an organized set of instruments, materials, or equipment designed for a particular use. **3.** a group of bodily organs working together to perform a particular function: *The intestines are part of the digestive apparatus.*

ap·par·el (ə par'əl) *n.* clothing or garments; attire. —*v.t.,* **ap·par·eled, ap·par·el·ing;** *also, British,* **ap·par·elled, ap·par·el·ling.** to clothe; dress: *The students were appareled in green uniforms.*

ap·par·ent (ə par'ənt) *adj.* **1.** easily seen or understood; plainly visible; evident: *Your black eye is apparent even behind those dark glasses. It was apparent that the bus would be late.* **2.** appearing or seeming real or true, although not necessarily so: *The apparent size of a star in the sky is much smaller than its real size.* —**ap·par'ent·ly,** *adv.*

ap·pa·ri·tion (ap'ə rish'ən) *n.* **1.** something supernatural that appears; a ghost; phantom. **2.** something strange, startling, or unexpected that comes suddenly into view.

ap·peal (ə pēl') *n.* **1. a.** an earnest request or call, as for help or sympathy: *The prisoner made an appeal for mercy.* **b.** a request to someone to decide something in one's favor: *When one parent refused the children's request, they made an appeal to the other.* **2.** the power or ability to attract, charm, or interest: *Birds have great appeal to our cat.* **3.** *Law.* **a.** the action of bringing a case before a higher court to be heard again. **b.** a request for this. —*v.i.* **1.** to make an earnest request: *to appeal for aid after a flood.* **2.** to be attractive, charming, or interesting: *This food doesn't appeal to me.* **3.** to address someone in an effort to gain support or acceptance: *The president appealed to the people for their support.* **4.** *Law.* to bring a case, or request that a case be brought, before a higher court to be heard again. —*v.t.* *Law.* to start proceedings for the appeal of (a case).

ap·peal·ing (ə pē'ling) *adj.* attractive, charming, or interesting. —**ap·peal'ing·ly,** *adv.*

ap·pear (ə pîr') *v.i.* **1.** to come into view; become visible: *The snowy mountain peaks appeared in the distance.* **2.** to give the impression of being; seem: *The listener appeared interested, but was actually bored.* **3.** to be or become clear or plain to the mind: *It appears that you were mistaken.* **4.** to come or be presented before the public: *to appear on the stage. The book appeared in May.* **5.** to come formally before an authoritative body: *I appeared as a witness at the trial.*

ap·pear·ance (ə pîr'əns) *n.* **1.** the act of appearing or coming into view: *the appearance of the sun above the horizon.* **2.** outward look or aspect: *The shabby appearance of the poor neighborhood.* **3.** outward show: *In spite of their troubles, they gave the appearance of being happy.* **4.** the act of coming before the public: *This was the band's first appearance on the stage.* **5. appearances.** outward signs.

 •**to keep up appearances.** to maintain the outward signs of what is normal or proper.

 •**to put in an appearance.** to appear briefly; attend for a short time.

ap·pease (ə pēz′) *v.t.*, **ap·peased, ap·peas·ing. 1.** to cause to be satisfied: *to appease one's hunger.* **2.** to bring to a state of peace or quiet: *to appease someone's anger.* **3.** to pacify by giving in to demands or making concessions: *I appeased my parents by promising to study harder.* —**ap·peas′er,** *n.*

ap·pease·ment (ə pēz′mənt) *n.* **1.** the act of appeasing or the state of being appeased. **2.** a policy of trying to avoid war with an aggressive nation by giving in to its demands.

ap·pel·lant (ə pel′ənt) *n.* a person who appeals, especially to a higher court. —*adj.* of or relating to legal appeals; appellate.

ap·pel·late (ə pel′it) *adj.* **1.** relating to legal appeals. **2.** having the power to hear and rule on legal appeals: *an appellate court.*

appellate court, a court that has the power to hear legal appeals and to review the decisions of lower courts. The Supreme Court is the highest appellate court in the federal court system of the United States.

ap·pel·la·tion (ap′ə lā′shən) *n.* **1.** a descriptive name or title: In *Catherine the Great,* the appellation of Catherine is *the Great.* **2.** the act of naming.

ap·pend (ə pend′) *v.t.* to add or attach as a subordinate or extra part: *The author appended explanatory notes at the end of the text.*

ap·pend·age (ə pen′dij) *n.* **1.** something appended; addition. **2.** a subordinate part attached to and extending from the main part of the body of a plant or animal. Legs, wings, branches, and horns are appendages.

ap·pen·dec·to·my (ap′ən dek′tə mē) *n., pl.* **ap·pen·dec·to·mies.** removal of the appendix by means of surgery.

ap·pen·di·ces (ə pen′də sēz′) a plural of **appendix.**

ap·pen·di·ci·tis (ə pen′də sī′tis) *n.* an inflammation of the appendix, especially when accompanied by swelling, severe abdominal pain, and the danger of a ruptured appendix.

ap·pen·dix (ə pen′diks) *n., pl.* **ap·pen·dix·es** or **ap·pen·di·ces. 1.** a thin, saclike structure attached to the upper part of the large intestine. In humans, it is two to three inches in length, is located in the lower right abdomen, and has no apparent function. Also, **vermiform appendix. 2.** any of various outgrowths or projections of bodily organs **3.** a section of additional related material at the end of a book or other piece of writing: *This mathematics book has an appendix containing logarithms.*

ap·per·tain (ap′ər tān′) *v.i.* to belong as a part; relate: *A number of responsibilities appertain to the office of president.*

ap·pe·tite (ap′i tīt′) *n.* **1.** a desire for food: *Growing children usually have large appetites.* **2.** a natural or strong desire; craving: *to have an appetite for adventure and excitement.*

ap·pe·tiz·er (ap′i tī′zər) *n.* food or drink served as a first course or before a meal, usually to stimulate the appetite.

ap·pe·tiz·ing (ap′i tī′zing) *adj.* appealing to the appetite; stimulating or arousing desire: *the food was so appetizing we couldn't wait to start eating.* —**ap′pe·tiz′ing·ly,** *adv.*

ap·plaud (ə plôd′) *v.t.* **1.** to show approval or enjoyment of by clapping the hands: *The audience applauded me when I finished the song.* **2.** to approve; praise: *The citizens applauded the mayor's plan for reform.* —*v.i.* to show approval or enjoyment by clapping the hands: *The audience kept applauding long after the curtain came down.*

ap·plause (ə plôz′) *n.* **1.** a clapping of the hands to show approval or enjoyment: *Loud applause greeted the star's appearance on stage.* **2.** any show of approval or appreciation; praise: *The novel received the applause of the critics.*

ap·ple (ap′əl) *n.* **1.** a roundish fruit with red, yellow, or green skin, and a firm, edible outer part surrounding a core with small seeds. **2.** any of numerous cultivated trees bearing this fruit.
•**apple of one's eye.** a person or thing that is most precious or dear.

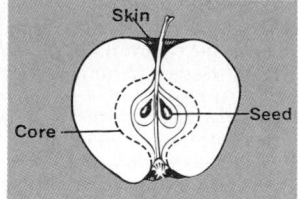

cross section of an **apple**

apple butter, a thick, brown, spiced applesauce, used as a spread for bread.

ap·ple·jack (ap′əl jak′) *n.* **1.** an alcoholic beverage made by freezing apple cider that has fermented. **2.** a brandy made by distilling apple cider that has fermented.

ap·ple·sauce (ap′əl sôs′) *n.* a food consisting of apples stewed to a pulp and sweetened.

ap·pli·ance (ə plī′əns) *n.* a machine or piece of equipment for a particular use, especially one for household use: *Electric irons and dishwashers are appliances.*

ap·pli·ca·ble (ap′li kə bəl) *adj.* that can be applied; suitable; relevant: *That law is not applicable in this case.* —**ap′pli·ca·bil′i·ty,** *n.*

ap·pli·cant (ap′li kənt) *n.* a person who asks or applies for something; candidate: *There were ten applicants for the job.*

ap·pli·ca·tion (ap′li kā′shən) *n.* **1.** the act of putting to use: *the application of scientific discoveries to the needs of industry.* **2.** the act of putting on: *the application of ointment to a burn.* **3.** something put on or applied: *This application will soothe the sore area.* **4.** a way of being applied or used: *This rule has many applications.* **5.** a request made personally or in writing: *an application for a transfer.* **6.** a written form used in making such a request: *I filled out the application for the job.* **7.** close or careful attention: *application to one's studies.*

ap·pli·ca·tor (ap′li kā′tər) *n.* a device for applying something, such as shoe polish, paint, or medicine.

ap·plied (ə plīd′) *adj.* used to solve practical problems; put to practical use: *applied science, applied mathematics.*

ap·pli·qué (ap′li kā′) *n.* a design or decoration made of one material and then sewed or otherwise fastened to the background of another. —*adj.* decorated in this way. —*v.t.,* **ap·pli·quéd, ap·pli·qué·ing.** to decorate with or apply as appliqué.

ap·ply (ə plī′) *v.,* **ap·plied, ap·ply·ing.** —*v.t.* **1.** to put into use or practice; employ: *to apply force to pry open a locked door.* **2.** to bring into contact with; put on: *to apply paint to a wall.* **3.** to use (a word or statement) to refer to a particular person or thing: *My classmates applied the nickname "Red" to me because of the color of my hair.* **4.** to devote (oneself) fully: *You'll have to apply yourself to the job to get it done in time.* —*v.i.* **1.** to make a request; ask: *I applied for a scholarship. They applied for jobs as technicians.* **2.** to be suitable or related: *The rule that nouns form their plural by adding "s" does not apply to the word "mouse."* [From the Old French word *aplier* meaning "to apply," from the Latin word *applicare* meaning "to place near to, join together."]

ap·point (ə point′) *v.t.* **1.** to name to or select for an office or position: *We must appoint someone to be treas-*

at; āpe; fär; câre; end; mē; it; īce; pierce; hot; ōld; sông, fôrk; oil; out; up; ūse; rüle; pull; tûrn; chin; sing; shop; thin; <u>th</u>is; hw in white; zh in treasure. The symbol ə stands for the unstressed vowel sound heard in about, taken, pencil, lemon, and circus.

urer. *Members of the Supreme Court are appointed by the president.* **2.** to arrange or decide on by authority or agreement; fix: *The judge appointed the trial date.* **3.** to furnish; equip. ▲ in definition 3, often used in combination in the past participle: *a well-appointed boat.*

ap·point·ee (ə poin'tē') *n.* a person named to an office or position.

ap·poin·tive (ə poin'tiv) *adj.* relating to or filled by appointment rather than election: *The office of secretary of state is appointive.*

ap·point·ment (ə point'mənt) *n.* **1.** the act of naming someone to an office or position, or the state of having been named: *The vacancy in the council was filled by appointment. My appointment to office made my parents proud.* **2.** an office or position so filled: *a high appointment in government.* **3.** an arrangement to meet or see someone at a certain time and place; engagement: *I have a doctor's appointment at ten o'clock.* **4. appointments.** furnishings; equipment.

ap·por·tion (ə pôr'shən) *v.t.* to divide and give out in portions or according to a rule or plan; distribute proportionally: *They apportioned the money they raised at the fair to three charities.*

ap·por·tion·ment (ə pôr'shən mənt) *n.* **1.** the act of apportioning or the state of being apportioned; distribution according to a rule or plan. **2.** the distribution of seats in a legislative body to states or other areas, as according to population.

ap·po·site (ap'ə zit) *adj.* suited to the matter at hand; appropriate; pertinent: *an opposite remark.*

ap·po·si·tion (ap'ə zish'ən) *n.* *Grammar.* **1.** the placing of a noun or a noun phrase after another noun or noun phrase so that the second explains and has the same grammatical construction as the first. **2.** the relationship existing between such words. In the sentence *I read a book about Marie Curie, the scientist,* the phrase *the scientist* is in apposition to the phrase *Marie Curie.* —**ap'po·si'tion·al,** *adj.* —**ap'po·si'tion·al·ly,** *adv.*

ap·pos·i·tive (ə poz'i tiv) *n.* a word, phrase, or clause that is in apposition. —*adj.* relating to or placed in apposition.

ap·prais·al (ə prā'zəl) *n.* **1.** the act of appraising or the state of being appraised. **2.** a price or value assigned in appraising; estimate.

ap·praise (ə prāz') *v.t.,* **ap·praised, ap·prais·ing.** **1.** to estimate the value of; fix a price for: *to appraise land, to appraise a diamond ring.* **2.** to estimate the quality or significance of; judge: *to appraise a situation, to appraise someone's character.* —**ap·prais'er,** *n.*

ap·pre·cia·ble (ə prē'shə bəl) *adj.* enough to be felt or noticed; perceptible: *Your work has shown an appreciable improvement.* —**ap·pre'cia·bly,** *adv.*

ap·pre·ci·ate (ə prē'shē āt') *v.,* **ap·pre·ci·at·ed, ap·pre·ci·at·ing.** —*v.t.* **1.** to recognize the value or quality of; value or regard highly: *The public did not appreciate Vincent Van Gogh's paintings until after his death.* **2.** to be grateful for: *I appreciate your help.* **3.** to be aware of or sensitive to: *We appreciate the dangers involved in such an experiment.* **4.** to raise in value: *The repairs we made will appreciate our house.* —*v.i.* to rise in value: *The value of land has appreciated in this area.*

ap·pre·ci·a·tion (ə prē'shē ā'shən) *n.* **1.** the act of recognizing value or quality: *Their appreciation of my efforts gratified me.* **2.** sensitive understanding: *to have a keen appreciation of music.* **3.** gratitude: *I express my deep appreciation for your help.* **4.** an increase in value.

ap·pre·cia·tive (ə prē'shə tiv, ə prē'shē ā'tiv) *adj.* feeling or showing appreciation. —**ap·pre'cia·tive·ly,** *adv.*

ap·pre·hend (ap'ri hend') *v.t.* **1.** to seize and take into custody; arrest; capture: *The police apprehended the burglar.* **2.** to grasp with the mind; understand: *Do you*

fully apprehend the meaning of these words? **3.** to look forward to with fear; dread: *The soldier apprehended the next day's combat.*

ap·pre·hen·sion (ap'ri hen'shən) *n.* **1.** a fear of what may happen: *The thought of going to the hospital filled me with apprehension.* **2.** a seizing; arrest; capture: *the apprehension of a criminal.* **3.** understanding.

ap·pre·hen·sive (ap'ri hen'siv) *adj.* fearful about what may happen; uneasy; worried: *Are you apprehensive about today's test?* —**ap'pre·hen'sively,** *adv.* —**ap'pre·hen'sive·ness,** *n.*

ap·pren·tice (ə pren'tis) *n.* **1.** a person who works for a skilled worker in order to learn a trade or art. In earlier times, apprentices were bound by contract to work for their masters for a definite period of time in return for training. **2.** any learner or beginner. —*v.t.,* **ap·pren·ticed, ap·pren·tic·ing.** to take on or place as an apprentice.

ap·pren·tice·ship (ə pren'tis ship') *n.* **1.** the condition of being an apprentice. **2.** the period of time during which a person works as an apprentice.

ap·prise (ə prīz') *v.t.,* **ap·prised, ap·pris·ing.** to give notice to; inform: *The bulletin apprised motorists of the hazardous driving conditions.*

ap·proach (ə prōch') *v.i.* to come near: *The car approached swiftly. The hour of decision is approaching.* —*v.t.* **1.** to come near or close to, as in time, place, or quality: *It is approaching midnight. We approached the house.* **2.** to go to with a plan or request: *They approached the planning board to request permission to build.* **3.** to deal with: *We should approach the problem from this angle.* —*n., pl.* **ap·proach·es.** **1.** the act of coming near: *the approach of spring.* **2.** a method of dealing with or doing something: *a new approach to the pollution problem.* **3.** a way of reaching a place or person: *The only approach to the town was blocked by snow.*

ap·proach·a·ble (ə prō'chə bəl) *adj.* **1.** possible to approach; accessible: *The town was approachable from only one direction.* **2.** easy to approach or talk to; friendly: *an approachable person.* —**ap·proach'a·bil'i·ty,** *n.*

ap·pro·ba·tion (ap'rə bā'shən) *n.* expression of a favorable opinion; approval, acceptance, or praise: *The approbation of other artists was important to the painter. The senate gave its approbation to the bill.*

ap·pro·pri·ate (*adj.,* ə prō'prē it; *v.,* ə prō'prē āt') *adj.* suitable for an occasion; fitting; proper: *Is this hat appropriate for the party?* —*v.t.,* **ap·pro·pri·at·ed, ap·pro·pri·at·ing.** **1.** to set apart for a particular use: *Congress appropriated funds for health care.* **2.** to take for oneself, especially without permission: *They appropriated my oars without asking.* —**ap·pro'pri·ate·ly,** *adv.* —**ap·pro'pri·ate·ness,** *n.*

ap·pro·pri·a·tion (ə prō'prē ā'shən) *n.* **1.** something appropriated, especially a sum of public money set aside for a particular use. **2.** the act of appropriating.

ap·prov·al (ə prü'vəl) *n.* **1.** favorable opinion; acceptance: *The mayor's actions were looked on with approval by most people.* **2.** official consent; permission: *to reprint an article with the author's approval.*

·on approval. for a customer to try or examine before deciding whether to buy: *These records will be sent to you on approval.*

ap·prove (ə prüv') *v.,* **ap·proved, ap·prov·ing.** —*v.t.* **1.** to say yes to; think well of: *My parents approved my plans for the summer.* **2.** to consent to officially: *Congress approved the annual budget.* —*v.i.* to have or give a favorable opinion (often with *of*): *I don't approve of that television program.* —**ap·prov'ing·ly,** *adv.*

approx. **1.** approximate. **2.** approximately.

ap·prox·i·mate (*adj.,* ə prok'sə mit; *v.,* ə prok'sə māt') *adj.* nearly correct or exact: *The approximate value of this clock is fifty dollars.* —*v.t.,* **ap·prox·i·mat·ed, ap·prox·i·mat·ing.** **1.** to come near or close to:

Your calculation approximates the actual width of the room. **2.** to estimate: *Approximate the time it will take you to finish the job.* —**ap·prox·i·mate·ly,** *adv.*

ap·prox·i·ma·tion (ə prok′sə mā′shən) *n.* **1.** the act of approximating. **2.** something that is nearly correct, as an estimated amount; close estimate: *The figure 7,500,000 is an approximation of the population of New York City.*

ap·pur·te·nance (ə pûr′tə nəns) *n.* something that goes along with another more important thing; accessory: *The farm is for sale with its machinery, tools, and other appurtenances.*

Apr., April.

a·pri·cot (ā′pri kot′, ap′ri kot′) *n.* **1.** an orange-colored fruit resembling a small peach. **2.** the tree this fruit grows on. **3.** a pale orange-yellow color. —*adj.* having the color apricot.

A·pril (ā′prəl) *n.* the fourth month of the year, having thirty days. [From the Old French name for this month *Avril,* from the Latin name *Aprilis.* The Latin name may go back to the Greek name *Aphroditē,* who was the goddess of love.]

apricots

April Fools' Day, a day when tricks and practical jokes are often played on people. It falls on April 1. Also, **All Fools' Day.**

a·pron (ā′prən) *n.* **1.** a garment worn over the front of the body to protect one's clothes. **2.** a hard-surfaced area in front of an airplane hangar or terminal. **3.** the part of a stage in front of the curtain.

ap·ro·pos (ap′rə pō′) *adj.* suitable for an occasion; to the point; fitting: *Your jokes are not apropos to a serious discussion.* —*adv.* at the right time; appropriately.
  •**apropos of.** with regard to; in relation to: *My question is apropos of the letter you sent me.*

apse (aps) *n.* in a building, a usually semicircular recess with a domed or arched ceiling, especially one at the east end of a church.

apt (apt) *adj.* **1.** having a good chance; likely; inclined: *You're apt to have an accident if you don't drive more carefully.* **2.** appropriate; suitable: *an apt reply.* **3.** quick to learn: *an apt student of mathematics.* **apt′ly,** *adv.* —**apt′ness,** *n.*

apt. *pl.* **apts.** apartment.

ap·ti·tude (ap′ti tüd′, ap′ti tūd′) *n.* **1.** a natural ability or talent: *an aptitude for learning languages.* **2.** quickness in learning or understanding: *a pupil of great aptitude.*

aptitude test, a test given to determine a person's ability to learn to do certain kinds of work or to acquire certain skills.

aq·ua (ak′wə) *n., pl.* **aq·uae** (ak′wē) or **aq·uas. 1.** water. **2.** a solution formed of some substance dissolved in water. **3.** a light greenish blue color. —*adj.* of the color aqua; light greenish blue.

aq·ua·cul·ture (ak′wə kul′chər) *also* **aq·ui·cul·ture.** *n.* the raising of aquatic animals and plants, such as shellfish or seaweed, for food; underwater agriculture.

aq·ua·lung (ak′wə lung′) *n.* a device for breathing underwater, having a valve that supplies air according to the needs of the diver; scuba. Trademark: **Aqua-Lung.**

aq·ua·ma·rine (ak′wə mə rēn′) *n.* **1.** a transparent stone having a pale blue or bluish green color, used as a gem. **2.** a bluish green color. —*adj.* having the color aquamarine.

aq·ua·plane (ak′wə plān′) *n.* a board on which a person can stand and ride across the surface of the water while being towed by a motorboat. —*v.i.* **aqua·planed, aq·ua·plan·ing.** to ride an aquaplane.

aq·ua re·gi·a (ak′wə rē′jē ə) a chemical in liquid form composed of nitric acid and hydrochloric acid. It is used to dissolve gold and platinum.

a·quar·i·um (ə kwâr′ē əm) *n., pl.* **a·quar·i·ums** or **a·quar·i·a** (ə kwâr′ē ə). **1.** a tank, bowl, or similar container, partly of glass or other transparent material, in which living fish, water animals, or water plants are kept and observed. **2.** a building where collections of such animals and plants are exhibited or studied.

A·quar·i·us (ə kwâr′ē əs) *n.* **1.** a constellation thought to resemble a man pouring water out of a vase. **2.** the eleventh sign of the zodiac.

a·quat·ic (ə kwat′ik, ə kwot′ik) *adj.* **1.** (of a plant or animal) growing or living in or on water. **2.** performed in or on water: *Swimming and skin diving are aquatic sports.*

aq·ue·duct (ak′wə dukt′) *n.* **1.** a pipe or artificial channel for carrying water, especially over long distances. **2.** a structure supporting such a pipe or channel.

a·que·ous (ā′kwē əs, ak′wē əs) *adj.* of, like, or containing water; watery: *an aqueous solution.*

aqueous humor, in the eye, the clear, watery fluid filling the space between the cornea and the lens.

aq·ui·cul·ture (ak′wə kul′chər) *n.* another spelling of **aquaculture.**

aq·ui·fer (ak′wə fər) *n.* an underground bed of rock, sand, or gravel that holds ground water or conducts it elsewhere, especially to springs or wells. [From the Latin words *aqua* meaning "water" and *ferre* meaning "to bear, carry."]

aq·ui·line (ak′wə līn′, ak′wə lin) *adj.* **1.** curved like an eagle's beak: *an aquiline nose.* **2.** of or like an eagle.

Ar, the symbol for argon.

AR, postal abbreviation for Arkansas.

aqueduct *(def. 2)*

Ar·ab (ar′əb) *n.* **1.** a member of a Semitic people inhabiting southwestern Asia and North Africa. **2.** a person who was born in or is a citizen of an Arabian country. **3.** another word for **Arabian horse.** —*adj.* of or relating to the Arabs or their culture, or to Arabia: *Arab tribes, Arab customs, the Arab world.*

ar·a·besque (ar′ə besk′) *n.* **1.** an elaborate design consisting of intertwined patterns of scrollwork, flowers, leaves, or other figures. **2.** a position in ballet in which the dancer stands on one leg with the other ex-

arabesque *(def. 2)*

at; āpe; fär; câre; end; mē; it; īce; pîerce; hot; ōld; sông, fôrk; oil; out; up; ūse; rüle; pùll; tûrn; chin; sing; shop; thin; *this*; hw in white; zh in treasure. The symbol ə stands for the unstressed vowel sound heard in about, taken, pencil, lemon, and circus.

tended straight backward. —*adj.* relating to or done in the style of arabesque.

A·ra·bi·an (ə rā′bē ən) *adj.* of or relating to Arabia, its people, or their culture. —*n.* another word for **Arab**.

Arabian horse, any of a breed of horses native to Arabia, noted for their speed, grace, and intelligence.

Arabian Nights, a collection of stories of adventure and romance from Arabia, Persia, and India, dating from the tenth century A.D.

Ar·a·bic (ar′ə bik) *adj.* of or relating to the Arabs, their language, or their culture. —*n.* the Semitic language of the Arabs, spoken in most of the Middle East and North Africa.

Words From Other Languages

Arabic has contributed many words to the English language, particularly in mathematics and astronomy.

admiral	a high-ranking officer in a navy
alfalfa	an important plant for feeding livestock
algebra	a branch of mathematics
coffee	a drink made from coffee beans and water
cotton	the plant from which cotton fabric is made
sherbet	a frozen dessert flavored with fruit juice
sofa	furniture for seating two or more people
zenith	a point in the sky directly overhead
zero	the number zero

Arabic numerals, the number symbols 1, 2, 3, 4, 5, 6, 7, 8, 9, and 0. This numbering system is believed to have been developed in India about 2,000 years ago. The numerals are called *Arabic* because they were traditionally believed to have been introduced to Western Europe by Arab scholars.

ar·a·ble (ar′ə bəl) *adj.* (of land) fit for plowing or cultivation.

a·rach·nid (ə rak′nid) *n.* any of a large group of animals without backbones having four pairs of legs, no wings or antennae, and a body divided into two parts. Spiders, mites, scorpions, and ticks are arachnids.

Ar·a·ma·ic (ar′ə mā′ik) *n.* an ancient Semitic language spoken throughout the Middle East in biblical times. It was spoken by Jesus.

A·rap·a·ho (ə rap′ə hō′) *n., pl.* **A·rap·a·ho** or **A·rap·a·hos.** **1.** a member of a North American Indian tribe that lived in Wyoming and Colorado. **2.** the Algonquian language of this tribe. —*adj.* of or relating to the Arapaho, their language, or their culture.

Ar·au·ca·ni·an (ar′ô kā′nē ən) *n.* **1.** a member of a South American Indian tribe living in Chile. **2.** the language spoken by this tribe. —*adj.* of or relating to the Araucanians or their language or culture.

Ar·a·wak (ar′ə wak′) *n., pl.* **Ar·a·wak** or **Ar·a·waks.** **1.** a member of a Central American and South American Indian tribe that formerly lived in the West Indies, Venezuela, and Colombia. **2.** the language spoken by the Arawak.

ar·bi·ter (är′bi tər) *n.* **1.** a person chosen to settle a dispute; arbitrator. **2.** a person or organization whose opinion or decision is final: *an arbiter of taste*.

ar·bi·trar·y (är′bi trer′ē) *adj.* **1.** based on someone's personal opinion or will rather than on rule, law, or reason: *The decision of a judge must not be arbitrary*. **2.** relying only on personal judgment or will rather than on the guidance of rules or law; despotic: *an arbitrary ruler, arbitrary government*. **3.** based on whim or chance, rather than calculation: *an arbitrary choice*. —**ar′bi·trar′i·ly,** *adv.* —**ar′bi·trar′i·ness,** *n.*

ar·bi·trate (är′bi trāt′) *v.,* **ar·bi·trat·ed, ar·bi·trat·ing.**

—*v.t.* **1.** to decide as an arbitrator; settle: *I was chosen to arbitrate the differences between the two groups*. **2.** to submit to arbitration: *Neither the union nor the company would arbitrate their dispute*. —*v.i.* **1.** to act as an arbitrator. **2.** to submit a dispute to arbitration.

ar·bi·tra·tion (är′bi trā′shən) *n.* a method of settling a dispute in which an impartial person or group is called in to make the final decision: *Labor and management agreed to submit to arbitration in the contract negotiations*.

ar·bi·tra·tor (är′bi trā′tər) *n.* **1.** a person chosen by the parties in a dispute to settle or decide their differences. **2.** a person who has the power to make final decisions; arbiter: *The referee is the arbitrator in a football game*.

ar·bor (är′bər) *n.* an area covered and shaded by trees, shrubs, or a vine-covered trellis, especially such an area in a garden.

Arbor Day, a day set aside in many states for planting trees. The date varies from state to state but is usually in the spring.

ar·bo·re·al (är bôr′ē əl) *adj.* **1.** of, like, or relating to trees. **2.** living in trees: *Squirrels are arboreal animals*.

ar·bo·re·tum (är′bə rē′təm) *n., pl.* **ar·bo·re·tums** or **ar·bo·re·ta** (är′bə rē′tə). a garden where trees and shrubs are grown for study or exhibition.

ar·bor·vi·tae (är′bər vī′tē) *n.* any of various evergreen shrubs or trees having scalelike leaves. Many varieties are grown as ornamental trees or as hedges.

ar·bu·tus (är bū′təs) *n., pl.* **ar·bu·tus·es. 1.** a trailing evergreen plant found in North America, bearing fragrant pink or white flowers in early spring. **2.** any of various evergreen shrubs or trees related to the heath.

arc (ärk) *n.* **1.** a continuous curved line between any two points on a circle; part of the circumference of a circle. **2. a.** any line curving in this way. **b.** anything in this shape: *We saw the arc of a rainbow*. **3.** a hot and bright electric current flowing in a curved path between two electrodes separated by a small space. —*v.i.,* **arced** or **arcked, arc·ing** or **arck·ing. 1.** to move in a curved line. **2.** to form an electric arc.

ar·cade (är kād′) *n.* **1.** a passageway covered by an arched roof. **2.** any covered passageway, street, or area opening onto a street, especially one with shops along its sides. **3.** a row of arches with their supporting columns. **4.** a building, room, or space filled with coin-operated game machines.

Ar·ca·di·a (är kā′dē ə) *n. also,* **arcadia.** a place of ideal calm, pleasantness, and simplicity. —**Ar·ca′di·an** *also,* ar·ca′di·an, *adj., n.*

Arc de Tri·omphe (ärk də trē ônf′) an arch in Paris, begun as a monument by Napoleon Bonaparte to celebrate the victories of his troops. Also, **Arch of Triumph**.

arch¹ (ärch) *n., pl.* **arch·es 1.** a curved structure that

arch¹ *(def. 2)*

spans a doorway, window, or similar space, usually made up of wedge-shaped blocks fitted together in a semicircle or similar shape. It is generally built to support the weight of material above it, but may be merely ornamental. **2.** a monument consisting of an arch or arches. **3.** a curved line or shape: *the arch of an eyebrow.* **4.** anything like an arch in shape or function. **5.** the raised, curved part of the foot between the ball and the heel. **6.** see **archway.** —*v.t.* **1.** to form (something) into an arch: *The cat arched its back.* **2.** to force (something) into an arch: *Heavy snow arched the trees over the lawn.* **3.** to cover or span with an arch: *A small bridge arched the stream.* —*v.i.* to have the form of an arch: *Two huge trees arched over the roof of the house.* [From the Old French word *arche* meaning "a curved structure," going back to the Latin word *arcus* "a bow" or "arc."]

arch² (ärch) *adj.* **1.** sly and playful; mischievous: *an arch smile.* **2.** chief; leading: *the arch criminal.* [From the prefix *arch-.*] —**arch′ly,** *adv.* —**arch′ness,** *n.*

arch– *prefix* chief; principal: *archbishop, archangel, archenemy.* [Originally from the Greek prefix *arch-* with the same meaning, from the word *archein* meaning "to begin," "to take the lead," "to rule."]

ar·chae·o·log·i·cal (är′kē ə loj′i kəl) *also,* **ar·che·o·log·i·cal,** *adj.* of or relating to archaeology. —**ar′chae·o·log′i·cal·ly,** *adv.*

ar·chae·ol·o·gist (är′kē ol′ə jist) *also,* **ar·che·ol·o·gist.** *n.* a student of or an expert in archaeology.

ar·chae·ol·o·gy (är′kē ol′ə jē) *also,* **ar·che·ol·o·gy.** *n.* the scientific study of the way people lived in the past. Archaeologists dig up the remains of ancient cities, towns, and tombs and then study the tools, weapons, pottery, monuments, and other things that they find.

ar·chae·op·ter·yx (är′kē op′tə riks) *n.* an extinct, primitive bird that lived during the Jurassic Period. It had many features of a reptile, such as teeth, as well as wings and feathers.

ar·cha·ic (är kā′ik) *adj.* **1.** no longer in common use in speech or writing: *"Thou" is an archaic form of "you."* **2.** of an earlier time; out-of-date: *archaic customs.* —**ar·cha′i·cal·ly,** *adv.*

Language Note

In this dictionary, the term **Archaic** means that a word or meaning was once common in English, but is not used very often today. You might ask: "If a word isn't used in today's language, why put it in the dictionary at all?" The reason is that not all the words you read, either in or out of school, are modern words. For example, many words that are no longer used can still be found in some translations of the Bible or in the works of great writers of the past, such as William Shakespeare. You need to know the meanings of archaic words like *shalt, hast, wouldst,* and *methinks* when you read the plays of Shakespeare. Therefore such words are included in this dictionary.

ar·cha·ism (är′kē iz′əm) *n.* something archaic, especially an archaic word or phrase.

arch·an·gel (ärk′ān′jəl) *n.* an angel of high rank.

arch·bish·op (ärch′bish′əp) *n.* a bishop of the highest rank.

arch·di·o·cese (ärch′dī′ə sis, ärch′dī′ə sēz′) *n., pl.* **arch·di·o·ces·es** (ärch′dī′ə sēz′, ärch′dī′ə sis′iz). a church district consisting of several dioceses. An archdiocese is governed by an archbishop.

arch·duch·ess (ärch′duch′is) *n., pl.* **arch·duch·ess·es.** **1.** the wife or widow of an archduke. **2.** a princess of the former royal family of Austria.

arch·duke (ärch′dük′, ärch′dūk′) *n.* a prince of the former royal family of Austria.

arched (ärcht) *adj.* **1.** having the form of an arch. **2.** covered with or having an arch or arches.

arch·en·e·my (ärch′en′ə mē) *n., pl.* **arch·en·e·mies.** a chief or principal enemy.

ar·che·o·log·i·cal (är′kē ə loj′i kəl) another spelling of **archaeological.**

ar·che·ol·o·gist (är′kē ol′ə jist) another spelling of **archaeologist.**

ar·che·ol·o·gy (är′kē ol′ə jē) another spelling of **archaeology.**

arch·er (är′chər) *n.* a person who shoots with a bow and arrow.

arch·er·y (är′chə rē) *n.* **1.** the practice, skill, or sport of shooting with a bow and arrow. **2.** a group or company of archers.

ar·che·type (är′ki tīp′) *n.* the original or ideal model or pattern from which all other things of the same type are developed or copied: *Alexander Graham Bell's invention is the archetype of all modern telephones.*

ar·chi·pel·a·go (är′kə pel′i gō′) *n., pl.* **ar·chi·pel·a·goes** or **ar·chi·pel·a·gos.** **1.** a large group of islands. **2.** a large body of water having many islands.

ar·chi·tect (är′ki tekt′) *n.* **1.** a person whose profession is to design, draw plans for, and often supervise the construction of buildings or other structures. **2.** the creator, maker, or designer of anything: *the architects of the United States Constitution.*

ar·chi·tec·ture (är′ki tek′chər) *n.* **1.** the science, art, or profession of designing, planning, and constructing buildings or other structures. **2.** a particular style or method of designing or constructing buildings: *modern architecture.* **3.** architectural work or works: *We saw some outstanding architecture on our trip to Rome.* **4.** the construction or design of anything: *the architecture of a motion picture or novel; the elegant architecture of a computer system.* —**ar′chi·tec′tur·al,** *adj.* —**ar′chi·tec′tur·al·ly,** *adv.*

ar·chi·trave (är′ki trāv′) *n.* in architecture, a beam or stone resting directly on top of a column of a building.

ar·chive (är′kīv) *n.* **1. archives.** public records, papers, or documents, as of a government or institution. **2. archives.** the place where such records, papers, or documents are kept. **3.** a collection of documents. —**ar·chi′val,** *adj.*

Arch of Triumph, another name for **Arc de Triomphe.**

arch·way (ärch′wā′) *n.* **1.** an entrance or passage under an arch. **2.** an arch over a passage.

arc lamp, a lamp in which intense light is produced by an electric arc between two carbon electrodes surrounded by a gas. Also, **arc light.**

arc·tic (ärk′tik, är′tik) *adj.* **1.** of or relating to the North Pole or the north polar regions. **2.** extremely cold; frigid. —*n.* **arctics.** warm, waterproof overshoes.

Arctic Circle, an imaginary line around the earth running parallel to the equator at 66°33′ north latitude, or about 1,600 miles (2,575 kilometers) from the North Pole.

Arc·tu·rus (ärk tûr′əs, ärk tyūr′əs) *n.* a giant orange star, one of the brightest in the sky and the brightest in the constellation Boötes.

ar·dent (är′dənt) *adj.* full of or showing eagerness, enthusiasm, or passion: *an ardent supporter of a candidate, ardent applause.* —**ar′dent·ly,** *adv.*

at; āpe; fär; câre; end; mē; it; īce; pîerce; hot; ōld; sông, fôrk; oil; out; up; ūse; rüle; pùll; tûrn; chin; sing; shop; thin; this; hw in white; zh in treasure. The symbol ə stands for the unstressed vowel sound heard in about, taken, pencil, lemon, and circus.

ar·dor (är′dər) *n.* great enthusiasm; strong passion: *The ardor of the fans was obvious in their cheers.*

ar·du·ous (är′jü əs) *adj.* requiring great effort or energy; difficult; strenuous: *an arduous task.* —**ar′du·ous·ly,** *adv.* —**ar′du·ous·ness,** *n.*

are (är) **1.** the second person singular of **be**: *You are late.* **2.** the present plural of **be**: *We are glad that they are coming.*

ar·e·a (âr′ē ə) *n.* **1.** the amount of surface within a given set of limits, especially as measured in square units: *The area of our yard is 400 square feet.* **2.** a particular space, section, or region: *a slum area. That part of the country is a farming area.* **3.** a section of a place set aside for a particular use: *a picnic area, the dining area of a house.* **4.** a field of interest or activity: *studies in the area of science. I don't have much knowledge in that area.*

area code, a combination of three numbers that represents one of the geographic areas into which the United States, Canada, and many other areas are divided for the purpose of communication by telephone: *The area code for the state of Colorado is 303.* These numbers are dialed before the local number in calling from one area to another.

area rug, a rug for covering part of a floor.

ar·e·a·way (âr′ē ə wā′) *n.* **1.** a sunken space or passage in front of the windows or entrance of a cellar or basement. **2.** a passageway between buildings.

a·re·na (ə rē′nə) *n.* **1.** in ancient Rome, the central part of an amphitheater, used for contests involving gladiators or for other performances. **2.** any similar place, now usually inside a building, used for public meetings or entertainment: *a boxing arena.* **3.** a scene or area of conflict or activity: *the arena of politics.* [From the Latin word *arena* meaning "sand" or "sandy place." Sand was used to cover the ground of the Roman amphitheater.]

aren't (ärnt, är′ənt) *contr.* **1.** are not: *These shoes aren't new.* **2.** am not. ▲ used in asking questions: *Aren't I allowed to come along?*

Ar·es (âr′ēz) *n. Greek Mythology.* the god of war. In Roman mythology he was called Mars.

ar·gent (är′jənt) *adj. Archaic.* **1.** made of silver. **2.** silvery white.

Ar·gen·tine (är′jən tēn′, är′jən tīn′) *adj.* of or relating to Argentina or its people. —*n.* a person who was born in or is a citizen of Argentina. Also, **Ar·gen·tin·e·an** (är′jən tin′ē ən).

ar·gon (är′gon) *n.* a colorless, inert gaseous element that makes up about one percent of the earth's atmosphere. It is used in a certain kind of welding and to fill electric light bulbs. Symbol: **Ar** [Formed from the Greek word *argon* meaning "lazy," from the prefix *a-* "not" + *ergon* "work." The name refers to the inert nature of this gas.]

Ar·go·naut (är′gə nôt′) *n. Greek Legend.* any of the men who sailed with Jason in search of the Golden Fleece.

ar·go·sy (är′gə sē) *n., pl.* **ar·go·sies. 1.** a large merchant ship. **2.** a fleet of such ships.

ar·got (är′gō, är′gət) *n.* the special idiom or slang used by a particular group or class, especially the secret language of thieves.

ar·gue (är′gū) *v.,* **ar·gued, ar·gu·ing.** —*v.i.* **1.** to have a discussion and disagree; dispute: *My parents and their friends often argue about politics.* **2.** to give reasons for or against something: *I argued against the plan.* —*v.t.* **1.** to give reasons for or against; debate: *Let's not argue the matter.* **2.** to persuade (someone) by giving reasons: *My friends tried to argue me out of leaving the team.* **3.** to try to establish (something) by giving reasons; maintain; contend: *to argue that a theory is wrong.* **4.** to show; indicate: *Your accent argues that you were raised in New York City.* —**ar′gu·a·ble,** *adj.* —**ar′gu·er,** *n.*

ar·gu·ment (är′gyə mənt) *n.* **1.** a discussion of a disputed subject; debate: *They had an argument over whose turn it was to wash the dishes.* **2.** a reason or reasons given to support or oppose something: *What are the arguments for accepting the proposal?* **3.** a process or line of reasoning: *I couldn't follow the speaker's argument.* **4.** a summary, often given at the beginning, of the chief points of a book, poem, or other literary work.

ar·gu·men·ta·tion (är′gyə men tā′shən) *n.* **1.** the process of forming and giving reasons and of developing conclusions from them. **2.** argument; debate.

ar·gu·men·ta·tive (är′gyə men′tə tiv) *adj.* fond of arguing or full of arguments; quarrelsome: *an argumentative student, an argumentative book.* —**ar′gu·men′ta·tive·ly,** *adv.* —**ar′gu·men′ta·tive·ness,** *n.*

Ar·gus (är′gəs) *n., pl.* **Ar·gus·es. 1.** *Greek Mythology.* a giant with a hundred eyes. **2.** a very watchful or alert person.

ar·gyle (är′gīl) also, **Ar·gyle.** *n.* **1.** a diamond-shaped pattern of contrasting colors, used especially in knitting. **2.** a sock having this pattern. —*adj.* having this pattern.

a·ri·a (är′ē ə, âr′ē ə) *n.* a musical composition for one voice with instrumental accompaniment, as in an opera.

Ar·i·ad·ne (ar′ē ad′nē) *n. Greek Legend.* the daughter of King Minos of Crete. She gave Theseus the ball of thread by which he found his way out of the Labyrinth.

ar·id (ar′id) *adj.* **1.** having little rainfall; dry; parched: *an arid wasteland.* **2.** without interest; lifeless: *an arid book.* —**a·rid·i·ty** (ə rid′ə tē), **ar′id·ness,** *n.* —**ar′id·ly,** *adv.*

Ar·ies (âr′ēz) *n.* **1.** a constellation in the northern sky, thought to resemble a ram in shape. **2.** the first sign of the zodiac.

a·right (ə rīt′) *adv.* correctly; rightly: *Report me and my cause aright* (Shakespeare, *Hamlet*).

a·rise (ə rīz′) *v.i.,* **a·rose, a·ris·en, a·ris·ing. 1.** to come into being; appear; originate: *Questions often arise as we read. They dealt with each problem as it arose.* **2.** to get up; stand up: *The audience arose cheering.* **3.** to move upward; rise; ascend: *Smoke arose from the fire.*

ar·is·toc·ra·cy (ar′ə stok′rə sē) *n. pl.* **ar·is·toc·ra·cies. 1.** a class of persons inheriting a high social position by birth; nobility. **2.** a government in which such a class has control. **3.** a government in which control is held by a privileged or superior class. **4.** any group of persons superior or outstanding because of wealth, intelligence, or culture: *the cultural aristocracy of a country.*

a·ris·to·crat (ə ris′tə krat′) *n.* **1.** a member of an aristocracy; nobleman or noblewoman. **2.** a person who has attitudes associated with the aristocracy. **3.** a person who favors government by the aristocracy.

a·ris·to·crat·ic (ə ris′tə krat′ik) *adj.* **1.** characteristic of or suiting an aristocrat: *an aristocratic manner, aristocratic attitudes.* **2.** of or belonging to the aristocracy: *an aristocratic family.* **3.** relating to or supporting government by aristocracy. —**a·ris′to·crat′i·cal·ly,** *adv.*

Ar·is·to·te·li·an (ar′ə stə tē′lē ən, ə ris′tə tē′lē ən) *adj.* relating to or characteristic of Aristotle or his philosophy: *Aristotelian logic.* —*n.* a follower of Aristotle or his philosophy.

arith. 1. arithmetic. **2.** arithmetical.

a·rith·me·tic (*n.,* ə rith′mə tik′; *adj.,* ar′ith met′ik) *n.* **1.** the science and technique of computing with numbers. Arithmetic deals with four basic operations: addition, subtraction, multiplication, and division. **2.** an act of calculation using one or more of these operations: *You must have made a mistake in your arithmetic.* —*adj. also,* **ar·ith·met·i·cal** (ar′ith met′i cal). of, relating to, or according to the rules of arithmetic: *arithmetic calculations.* —**ar′ith·met′i·cal·ly,** *adv.*

a·rith·me·ti·cian (ə rith′mə tish′ən) *n.* a student of or an expert in arithmetic.

arithmetic mean a value that is obtained by dividing the sum of a set of quantities by the number of quantities;

average.   The arithmetic mean of 2, 4, 11, and 7 is 6, because $(2 + 4 + 11 + 7) \div 4 = 6$.

arithmetic progression a series of numbers in which the difference between any two successive numbers is the same.   1, 3, 5, 7, 9 and 10, 17, 24, 31, 38 are arithmetic progressions.

Ariz., Arizona.

ark (ärk) *n.*   **1.** a large, flat-bottomed, clumsy boat.   **2.** in the Bible, the large boat built by Noah.   **3.** see **Ark of the Covenant.**

Ark., Arkansas.

Ark of the Covenant.   1. a sacred chest in which the ancient Hebrews kept the two stone tablets containing the Ten Commandments.   **2.** a cabinet in a synagogue in which the scrolls of the Torah and other sacred books are kept.

arm¹ (ärm) *n.*   **1.** either of the two upper limbs of the human body, especially the part between the shoulder and the wrist.   **2.** the forelimb of any animal.   **3.** something used to support or cover the human arm: *the arm of a chair, the arm of a coat.*   **4.** anything shaped like an arm or branching out from a larger body: *an arm of the sea, the arm of a phonograph.*   **5.** a branch or part of an organization: *The Coast Guard is an arm of the government.*   **6.** an extension of authority; power: *the arm of the law.*   [From the Old English word *earm* meaning "arm."]

 ·**arm in arm.** with arms linked: *We walked arm in arm.*
 ·**at arm's length.** on a formal, rather than friendly, basis; at a distance.
 ·**to twist someone's arm.** to convince or try to convince someone (to do something) by using or threatening force or by persuasion that is hard to resist.
 ·**with open arms.** with an eager welcome; cordially.

arm² (ärm) *n.* any weapon, especially a firearm. See also **arms.**   —*v.t.* **1.** to provide with weapons: *to arm troops for war.*   **2.** to provide with something that protects or strengthens: *the porcupine is armed with quills.*   **3.** to prepare; equip: *College armed them with a good education.*   **4.** to set or prepare to explode or detonate: *to arm a bomb, to arm a missile.*   —*v.i.* to prepare for war or conflict, especially by equipping oneself with weapons: *The country armed for war.*   [From the English word *arms,* from the Old French word *armes* meaning "arms," from the Latin word *arma* "weapons."]

ar·ma·da (är mä′də) *n.*   **1.** a large fleet of warships.   **2.** the Armada. see **Spanish Armada.**

ar·ma·dil·lo (är′mə dil′ō) *n., pl.* **ar·ma·dil·los.** any of several insect-eating, burrowing mammals having an armorlike shell of bony plates, a long snout, strong, sharp claws, and a long tail. Armadillos are found in South America and parts of the southern United States. [From the Spanish word *armadillo* meaning "armadillo," earlier "little armored creature."]

armadillo

Ar·ma·ged·don (är′mə ged′ən) *n.*   **1.** in the Bible, the site of the world's great and final battle between the forces of good and evil.   **2.** any great and decisive battle.

ar·ma·ment (är′mə mənt) *n.*   **1. armaments.** military forces, equipment, and supplies, especially considered as the entire military strength of a nation.   **2.** *also,* **armaments.** the weapons with which a military unit, ship, or plane is equipped.   **3.** the process of arming: *The country's armament took two months.*

ar·ma·ture (är′mə chər) *n.*   **1.** a rotating part of an electric motor or dynamo, consisting of an iron core with coils of wire around it.   **2.** a piece of soft iron placed across the poles of a magnet to preserve magnetic power.   **3.** a vibrating iron part of an electric buzzer or relay.   **4.** a part or organ of an animal or plant that functions as a protective covering, such as the shell of a turtle.   **5.** any protective covering; armor.   **6.** a framework used to support clay or other material that is being made into a sculpture.

arm·band (ärm′band′) *n.* a band worn around the upper part of the arm as a badge or symbol: *The victim's family wore black armbands as a sign of mourning.*

arm·chair (ärm′châr′) *n.* a chair with supports at each side for one's arms or elbows.   —*adj.* dealing with problems indirectly or without actual experience: *an armchair detective with a library of mystery novels.*

armed (ärmd) *adj.*   **1.** having, bearing, or supported by arms or weapons: *armed troops, an armed conflict.*   **2.** prepared; equipped: *We went to the meeting armed with facts and figures.*   **3.** having an arm or arms.   ▲ usually used in combination: *one-armed, long-armed.*

armed forces, all of the military forces of a nation, considered as a whole.   The armed forces of the United States include the Army, Navy, Marine Corps, Air Force, and Coast Guard.

Ar·me·ni·an (är mē′nē ən, är mēn′yən) *adj.* of or relating to Armenia, its people, their language, or culture.   —*n.*   **1.** an inhabitant of the region of Armenia.   **2.** a person who was born in or is a citizen of the Soviet republic of Armenia.   **3.** the language of the Armenians.

arm·ful (ärm′fül′) *n., pl.* **arm·fuls.** as much as one arm or both arms can hold: *an armful of packages.*

arm·hole (ärm′hōl′) *n.* an opening in a garment for the arm.

ar·mi·stice (är′mə stis) *n.* a temporary stop of fighting by mutual agreement; truce.

Armistice Day, see **Veterans Day.**

ar·mor (är′mər) *also,* British, **ar·mour.** *n.*   **1.** a covering, as of metal, formerly worn to protect the body in battle.   **2.** a protective metal covering used on tanks, warships, or other military vehicles and equipment.   **3.** armored military vehicles.   **4.** any protective covering, such as that of an armadillo.   —*v.t.* to cover or furnish with armor.   —**ar′mor·like′,** *adj.*

ar·mored (är′mərd) *also,* British, **ar·moured.** *adj.*   **1.** protected by armor: *an armored ship.*   **2.** equipped

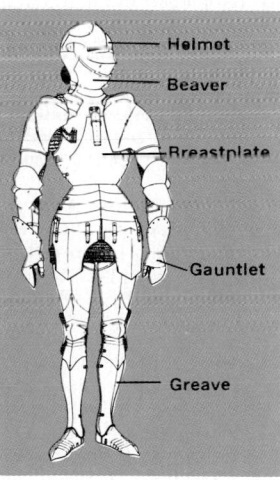

armor *(def. 1)*

at; āpe; fär; câre; end; mē; it; īce; pîerce; hot; ōld; sông, fôrk; oil; out; up; ūse; rüle; pull; tûrn; chin; sing; shop; thin; <u>th</u>is; hw in white; zh in treasure. The symbol ə stands for the unstressed vowel sound heard in about, taken, pencil, lemon, and circus.

with armored vehicles: *armored troops.*

armored car, a vehicle covered with armor plate, often used to transport money or other valuable cargo.

ar·mor·er (är′mər ər) *also, British,* **ar·mour·er.** *n.*
1. a person who makes or repairs armor. **2.** a soldier or other person who has charge of firearms. **3.** a person or company that makes weapons.

ar·mo·ri·al (är môr′ē əl) *adj.* relating to heraldry.

armor plate, specially hardened steel used as a protective covering, as on a tank or warship.

ar·mor·y (är′mə rē) *n., pl.* **ar·mor·ies. 1.** a building that is the headquarters and training center of a National Guard or other military reserve unit. **2.** a place where weapons are kept; arsenal. **3.** a place where weapons are manufactured.

ar·mour (är′mər) *British.* another spelling of **armor.**

arm·pit (ärm′pit′) *n.* the hollow under the arm at the shoulder.

arm·rest (ärm′rest′) *n.* a support for the arm or elbow, as on an armchair.

arms (ärmz) *pl. n.* **1.** weapons, especially firearms: *The defeated troops laid down their arms.* **2.** see **coat of arms.**
·**to bear arms. a.** to possess or carry weapons. **b.** to serve in the armed forces.
·**to take up arms.** to prepare to fight.
·**under arms.** furnished with weapons; ready for war: *That country has half its youth under arms.*
·**up in arms.** ready to fight; hostile; indignant: *The residents were up in arms over the planned highway.*

ar·my (är′mē) *n., pl.* **ar·mies. 1.** a large, organized body of soldiers armed and trained for combat on land: *The ancient Romans had a powerful army.* **2.** *also,* **Army.** the branch of the military forces of a nation trained chiefly for land operations. In some countries it also includes the air force. **3.** in the U.S. Army, the largest military unit, consisting of two or more corps. **4.** a large body of persons organized for a common cause: *An army of protesters marched to the White House.* **5.** any large group; multitude: *an army of ants, an army of motorists on their way to the beach.*

Army Post Office, see **APO.**

ar·ni·ca (är′ni kə) *n.* **1.** any of a group of plants bearing clusters of yellow flowers. **2.** a medicinal liquid made from the dried flowers and roots of several of these plants.

a·ro·ma (ə rō′mə) *n.* a pleasant or agreeable odor; fragrance.

ar·o·mat·ic (ar′ə mat′ik) *adj.* having an aroma; fragrant. —**ar′o·mat′i·cal·ly,** *adv.*

a·rose (ə rōz′) the past tense of **arise:** *I arose before dawn.*

a·round (ə round′) *prep.* **1.** in a circle about: *I wore a scarf around my neck.* **2.** along the circumference or outer edge of: *to walk around the block.* **3.** so as to surround or envelop: *There is a lawn around the house.* **4.** on all sides of: *Around us lay the ruins of the city.* **5.** here and there in: *The tourists wandered around the city.* **6.** somewhere in or near: *Please stay around the house.* **7.** somewhat near, as in time or amount; about: *I'll meet you around six o'clock.* **8.** on another side of: *Their house is around the corner from mine.* —*adv.* **1.** in a circle or circular course: *The wheel spun around and around.* **2.** in circumference: *The pole measures two feet around.* **3.** on all sides; in various directions: *We looked around for a policeman.* **4.** here and there; about: *We saw tools lying around in the yard.* **5.** *Informal.* somewhere nearby; *Why not stay around for a few minutes?* **6.** to a particular place: *Come around again tomorrow.* **7.** in or to the opposite direction: *The cat spun around quickly.* **8.** close to in number; approximately: *Around a hundred people signed the petition.*
▲ See **round** for usage note.

around–the–clock (ə round′ thə klok′) *adj.* going on for 24 hours without interruption; continuous: *Around-*

the-clock negotiations helped to settle the strike. Also, **round–the–clock.**

a·rous·al (ə rou′zəl) *n.* the act of arousing or the state of being aroused.

a·rouse (ə rouz′) *v.t.,* **a·roused, a·rous·ing. 1.** to stir up; excite: *The angry speech aroused the crowd. Something different in the room aroused my suspicion.* **2.** to awaken: *Our friends aroused us for breakfast.*

ar·peg·gio (är pej′ē ō′) *n., pl.* **ar·peg·gi·os.** *Music.* **1.** the playing of the notes of a chord in succession rather than together. **2.** a chord played in this way.

ar·que·bus (är′kwə bəs) *n., pl.* **ar·que·bus·es.** another spelling of **harquebus.**

ar·raign (ə rān′) *v.t.* **1.** to state formally the charge against (someone) before a judge, and record an answer to the charge. **2.** to charge with or criticize for something: *Public opinion arraigned the creators of the eyesore.* —**ar·raign′ment,** *n.*

ar·range (ə rānj′) *v.,* **ar·ranged, ar·rang·ing.** —*v.t.* **1.** to put in proper, convenient, or pleasing order: *to arrange a list of names in alphabetical order, to arrange the furniture in a room.* **2.** to help to bring about; prepare for; make plans for: *Who arranged the meeting?* **3.** to make certain or formal; determine: *to arrange the terms of a contract.* **4.** to adapt (a musical composition) for instruments or voices for which it was not originally written. —*v.i.* **1.** to make plans or preparations: *Can you arrange to meet us tonight?* **2.** to come to an agreement: *I'll arrange with them about the tickets.* —**ar·rang′er,** *n.*

ar·range·ment (ə rānj′mənt) *n.* **1.** the act of putting in order or the state of being put in order: *Arrangement of furniture for the party took two hours.* **2.** the result of arranging or ordering; something arranged in a particular way: *a flower arrangement.* **3.** the style or manner in which something is ordered: *a diagram showing the arrangement of electrons in an atom.* **4. arrangements.** plans; preparations: *to make arrangements for a dance.* **5.** the act of settling or the state of being settled; adjustment: *The arrangement of the dispute pleased us all.* **6. a.** adaptation of a musical composition for instruments or voices for which it was not originally written. **b.** any musical work so adapted.

ar·rant (ar′ənt) *adj.* complete; out-and-out; downright: *an arrant fool.*

ar·ras (ar′əs) *n., pl.* **ar·ras. 1.** a type of tapestry with a rich design. **2.** any screen or wall hanging of tapestry. [From *Arras,* the city in northern France where this tapestry was made.]

ar·ray (ə rā′) *n.* **1.** an orderly grouping or arrangement, as of troops for battle. **2.** a large, imposing collection; display: *an array of jewels.* **3.** persons or things on display or in order: *The movie features an array of famous stars.* **4.** clothing, especially fine clothing; attire: *to be dressed in rich array.* —*v.t.* **1.** to place in order: *to array troops.* **2.** to dress, especially in fine clothing; adorn: *The couple were arrayed like royalty.*

ar·rears (ə rîrz′) *pl. n.* money that is due but has not been paid.
·**in arrears.** behind in payments, duties, or obligations.

ar·rest (ə rest′) *v.t.* **1.** to seize or take into custody by authority of the law: *The police arrested the criminal.* **2.** to stop; check: *to arrest the progress of a disease.* **3.** to catch and hold; engage: *This story arrested my attention.* —*n.* **1.** a seizure by authority of the law; the act of taking into custody. **2.** the act of stopping.
·**under arrest.** held by authority of the law.

ar·rest·ing (ə res′ting) *adj.* holding the attention; striking.

ar·riv·al (ə rī′vəl) *n.* **1.** the act of arriving: *Reporters were awaiting the arrival of the president.* **2.** a person or thing that arrives or has arrived: *Recent arrivals to the zoo include two rare hawks.*

ar·rive (ə rīv′) *v.i.*, **ar·rived, ar·riv·ing. 1.** to reach a place by traveling: *We will arrive in Denver at midnight.* **2.** (of time) to be at hand; come: *The week of exams has arrived.* **3.** to become successful or famous: *After writing for years, my cousin finally arrived as a novelist.*
·to arrive at. to come to or reach: *We arrived at the decision after much discussion.*

ar·ri·ve·der·ci (ä′rē və dâr′chē) *interj.* until we meet again; good-bye for now. [From the Italian farewell salutation *arrivederci!*]

ar·ro·gance (ar′ə gəns) *n.* too much pride or confidence mixed with a lack of respect for other people; conceit; haughtiness.

ar·ro·gant (ar′ə gənt) *adj.* feeling or showing too much pride and a lack of respect for other people; conceited and haughty: *an arrogant person, an arrogant way of talking.* —**ar′ro·gant·ly,** *adv.*

ar·ro·gate (ar′ə gāt′) *v.t.*, **ar·ro·gat·ed, ar·ro·gat·ing.** to claim or seize without right: *The dictator arrogated powers that belonged to the people.* —**ar′ro·ga′tion,** *n.*

ar·row (ar′ō) *n.* **1.** a slender shaft, usually pointed at one end and having feathers at the other, made to be shot from a bow. **2.** a symbol in the shape of an arrow, used to indicate direction or position, as on a road sign. **3.** something like an arrow in shape or use: *An arrow of light came through the blinds.*

ar·row·head (ar′ō hed′) *n.* the pointed tip or head of an arrow.

ar·row·root (ar′ō rüt′, ar′ō rut′) *n.* **1.** an easily digestible starch made from the roots of a tropical American plant, used as a thickening agent in cooking. **2.** the plant itself, widely grown in the West Indies and other tropical regions. It has long, pointed leaves and small, white flowers.

ar·roy·o (ə roi′ō) *n., pl.* **ar·roy·os. 1.** a dry bed of a stream; gully. **2.** a small river or stream.

ar·rhyth·mi·a (ə rith′mē ə) *n.* a heart rhythm that is not normal.

ar·se·nal (är′sə nəl) *n.* **1.** a place for storing or making arms and ammunition. **2.** a collection of firearms or other weapons. **3.** a store or collection: *an arsenal of facts and figures to support an argument.*

ar·se·nic (är′sə nik) *n.* **1.** an element, usually in the form of silver-gray or blackish crystals with metallic luster, used in alloys and poisonous compounds. **2.** a white, tasteless, highly poisonous compound of this element and oxygen, used in rat, insect, and weed poisons. Symbol: **As** [From the Old French word *arsenic,* from the Latin word *arsenicum,* from the Greek word *arsenikon,* from the Persian word *zarnīk,* all meaning "arsenic."]

ar·son (är′sən) *n.* the crime of deliberately setting fire to a dwelling or other property.

ar·son·ist (är′sə nist) *n.* a person who commits arson.

art¹ (ärt) *n.* **1.** the creation or study of the beautiful or the meaningful, as in painting, music, literature, dance, or drama. **2.** a particular activity carried on for the purpose of creating something beautiful or meaningful. Painting, sculpture, and literature are forms of art. **3.** the works produced by creative activity: *an exhibit of Indian art.* **4.** a special skill; knack: *There's an art to dressing well.* **5.** a skilled craft or occupation: *the navigator's art, the art of diplomacy.* **6. the arts. a.** the different forms of creative activity thought of as a group. **b.** the branches of learning that are not sciences; liberal arts; humanities. **7.** a branch of learning or study: *a course in language arts.* **8.** human skill or effort, as distinguished from the work of nature. **9.** sly cleverness; cunning. [From the Old French word *art* meaning "skill," from the Latin word *ars* "skill," "art," "science."]

art² (ärt) *Archaic.* the second person singular, present indicative of **be:** *Thou art not for the fashion of these times* (Shakespeare). [From the Old English word *eart* meaning "(you) [singular] are."]

art de·co (dek′ō) *also,* **Art De·co.** a style of decorative design introduced in the 1920s, characterized by geometric shapes and bold colors, and by the use of new materials, such as chrome and plastic.

Ar·te·mis (är′tə mis) *n. Greek Mythology.* the goddess of the hunt and of the moon, and twin sister of Apollo. In Roman mythology she was called Diana.

ar·te·ri·al (är tîr′ē əl) *adj.* **1.** of, relating to, or like an artery or arteries. **2.** of, relating to, or designating the blood in the arteries. Arterial blood becomes bright red when it mixes with oxygen as it passes through the lungs. **3.** serving as a major path or route: *an arterial road.*

ar·te·ri·ole (är tîr′ē ōl′) *n.* any of the very small blood vessels located at the ends of the arteries and serving to carry blood from the arteries to the capillaries.

ar·te·ri·o·scle·ro·sis (är tîr′ē ō sklə rō′sis) *n.* a disease in which the walls of the arteries thicken and harden, thus making it difficult for the blood to circulate.

ar·ter·y (är′tə rē) *n., pl.* **ar·ter·ies. 1.** one of the tubes carrying blood away from the heart to all parts of the body. **2.** a main road or channel, as of communication or transportation.

ar·te·sian well (är tē′zhən) a deep well in which water usually rises to the surface from a porous layer of rock without pumping. The porous layer is overlaid by impermeable rock through which a hole is bored, allowing the water to reach the surface.

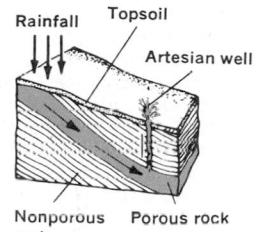

artesian well

art·ful (ärt′fəl) *adj.* **1.** showing cunning or deceit; crafty: *The burglar had artful ways of avoiding capture by the police.* **2.** done with or showing art or skill: *The actor's performance was artful.* —**art′ful·ly,** *adv.* —**art′ful·ness,** *n.*

ar·thrit·ic (är thrit′ik) *adj.* of, relating to, or afflicted with arthritis. —*n.* a person who is afflicted with arthritis.

ar·thri·tis (är thrī′tis) *n.* a painful inflammation of a joint or joints of the body.

ar·thro·pod (är′thrə pod′) *n.* any of a large group of animals without backbones that have jointed legs and bodies and an external skeleton, including insects, spiders, centipedes, and crabs.

ar·thro·scope (är′thrə skōp′) *n.* a medical instrument that is inserted inside a joint to examine or treat injuries and abnormalities. —**ar′thro·scop′ic,** *adj.*

Ar·thur (är′thər) *n.* a legendary king of ancient Britain and the leader of the knights of the Round Table. The real King Arthur was probably a military chieftain who led the Britons against the Saxons early in the sixth century A.D.

Ar·thu·ri·an (är thûr′ē ən) *adj.* relating to King Arthur or to the legends about him and his knights.

ar·ti·choke (är′ti chōk′) *n.* **1.** a thistlelike plant belonging to the composite family. **2.** the immature yel-

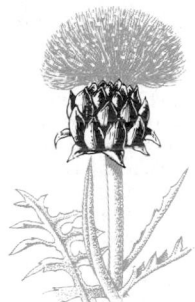

artichoke

A

lowish green flower head of this plant, cooked and eaten as a vegetable.

ar·ti·cle (är′ti kəl) *n.* **1.** a piece of writing on a particular subject, forming part of a larger publication, such as a newspaper, magazine, or encyclopedia: *The professor wrote an article on water pollution for the magazine.* **2.** a particular thing or object; item: *articles of clothing. Several articles were stolen from the house.* **3.** a separate clause or section of a formal document, such as a treaty, constitution, or contract: *Article I of the U.S. Constitution deals with the powers of Congress.* **4.** *Grammar.* any one of the words *a, an,* or *the,* used before a noun or noun phrase, as in *a house, an art show, the mayor. A* and *an* are indefinite articles and *the* is the definite article.

Articles of Confederation, the first constitution of the United States, adopted by the thirteen colonies in 1781. It was replaced by the present Constitution in 1788.

ar·tic·u·late (*adj.,* är tik′yə lit; *v.,* är tik′yə lāt′) *adj.* **1.** spoken clearly in distinct syllables and words: *When you mumble, what you say is not articulate enough to be understood.* **2.** able to speak: *The baby was not yet articulate.* **3.** able to express one's thoughts clearly and effectively: *The senator was an articulate advocate of civil rights.* **4.** said or presented clearly and effectively: *The lawyer won the case with an articulate plea to the jury.* **5.** having joints; segmented: *an articulate animal.* —*v.,* **ar·ti·cu·lat·ed, ar·ti·cu·lat·ing.** —*v.t.* **1.** to pronounce clearly. **2.** to put into words; express effectively: *I found it hard to articulate my feelings toward them.* —*v.i.* **1.** to pronounce syllables and words clearly: *An actor must be able to articulate.* **2.** to form a joint or connection: *The bones of the arm articulate at the elbow.* —**ar·tic′u·late·ly,** *adv.* —**ar·tic′u·late·ness,** *n.* —**ar·tic′u·la′tion,** *n.*

ar·ti·fact (är′tə fakt′) *n.* anything made or changed by human beings, especially a tool, weapon, or other simple object used in ancient times.

ar·ti·fice (är′tə fis) *n.* **1.** a clever or cunning trick: *The prisoner escaped from jail by an artifice.* **2.** trickery; deception: *The swindler relied on artifice.*

ar·tif·i·cer (är tif′ə sər) *n.* a skilled worker; craftsman or craftswoman.

ar·ti·fi·cial (är′tə fish′əl) *adj.* **1.** not natural; made by human beings: *an artificial lake.* **2.** made in imitation of something natural or real: *artificial flowers.* **3.** not sincere or genuine; affected: *artificial manners, an artificial show of sympathy.* —**ar′ti·fi′cial·ly,** *adv.*

artificial intelligence 1. the ability of a computer to perform operations that seem to imitate human reasoning and logic in such applications as designing objects, analyzing problems, or diagnosing illnesses. **2.** a branch of computer science concerned with studying and developing this ability in computer systems.

ar·ti·fi·ci·al·i·ty (är′tə fish′ē al′i tē) *n., pl.* **ar·ti·fi·ci·al·i·ties. 1.** the quality of being artificial. **2.** something that is artificial.

artificial respiration, the forcing of air into and out of the lungs of a person who has stopped breathing or is having great difficulty in breathing.

ar·til·ler·y (är til′ə rē) *n.* **1.** large, heavy, mounted firearms, such as cannons, howitzers, and mortars. **2.** the part of an army that uses such firearms.

ar·til·ler·y·man (är til′ə rē mən) *n., pl.* **ar·til·lery·men** (är til′ə rē mən). a soldier in the artillery.

ar·ti·san (är′tə zən) *n.* a person who is skilled in a particular craft; craftsman or craftswoman.

art·ist (är′tist) *n.* **1.** a person who is skilled in or whose work is one or more of the arts, especially a painter or sculptor. **2.** a skilled public performer: *Singers, dancers, and other artists performed in the park.* **3.** a person who shows talent or skill in work or occupation: *an artist at repairing cars.*

ar·tis·tic (är tis′tik) *adj.* **1.** of or relating to art or artists.

2. skillfully and tastefully done: *an artistic performance.* —**ar·tis′ti·cal·ly,** *adv.*

art·ist·ry (är′tə strē) *n.* artistic quality, methods, skill, or workmanship.

art·less (ärt′lis) *adj.* **1.** without trickery or deceit; sincere; naive: *the artless questions of a child.* **2.** not artificial; simple; natural: *The dancer moved with artless grace.* **3.** lacking skill or knowledge; ignorant. —**art′less·ly,** *adv.* —**art′less·ness,** *n.*

art nou·veau (nü vō′) *also,* **Art Nou·veau.** a style of decorative design and architecture characterized by flowing lines and shapes suggestive of plants and flowers. Art nouveau flourished from 1890 to 1910.

art·work (ärt′wûrk′) *n.* **1.** the production of works of art or craft, especially when done by hand. **2.** any work of art or craft. **3.** the decorative or illustrative material in a book or other printed matter.

ar·um (âr′əm) *n.* **1.** any of a group of small plants that have a cluster of tiny flowers on a spike surrounded by a large, flowerlike leaf. **2.** any of several similar plants, such as the calla.

art nouveau lamp

–ary *suffix* **1.** (used to form nouns) a person or thing connected with: *missionary, revolutionary.* **2.** (used to form adjectives) being or relating to: *secondary, honorary.*

Ar·y·an (âr′ē ən, är′ē ən) *n.* **1.** a member of a group of prehistoric wandering people who spoke an Indo-European language. **2.** a former name for the Indo-European family of languages. **3.** in the doctrine of the Nazis: **a.** a member of the Nordic race, supposedly superior to other racial groups. **b.** any non-Jewish Caucasian. —*adj.* of or relating to Aryans.

as (az) *adv.* **1.** to the same amount or degree; equally: *The first movie was exciting, but the second was not as good.* **2.** for example; for instance: *I have outfits in several colors, as red and blue.* —*conj.* **1.** to the same degree or extent that: *They were proud as they could be.* **2.** in the same way or manner that: *That tribe lives as people did in the Stone Age.* **3.** at the same time that; while: *I arrived as they were leaving.* **4.** because; since: *As you are not ready, we will wait for you.* **5.** that the result is or was: *You were so insulting as to offend everyone.* **6.** though: *Late as it was, we decided to visit our friends.* —*prep.* in the manner or role of: *I speak as a friend.* —*pron.* **1.** that; which: *They go to the same school as I do.* **2.** a fact that: *That book belongs to me, as you well know.*

•**as for** or **as to.** with respect to; concerning: *As for vacations, I prefer the beach to the country.*

•**as if** or **as though.** as it would be if: *The rude children behaved as if they had no manners.*

•**as is.** in the present condition; just as it is: *The house will be sold as is.*

•**as of.** beginning at or on (a certain time or date): *As of January 6, you will be old enough to drive a car.*

•**as yet.** up to this time; so far: *The repair crew has not as yet finished the work.*

As, the symbol for arsenic.

AS, postal abbreviation for American Samoa.

as·a·fet·i·da (as′ə fet′i də) *also,* **as·a·foet·i·da.** *n.* a brown gum resin that smells like garlic, obtained from the roots of various central Asian plants of the parsley family. It was formerly used in medicines.

as·bes·tos (as bes′təs, az bes′təs) *n.* any of several varieties of a grayish mineral whose fibers may be woven or pressed into material that does not burn, is resistant to heat and chemical action, and does not conduct electricity. Such material was formerly used in insulating buildings or for fireproofing, but is now regarded as a cause of diseases including cancer.

as·cend (ə send′) *v.i.* **1.** to move upward; rise: *The elevator ascended slowly.* **2.** to move upward to a higher condition, rank, or level: *to ascend to the rank of vice president.* —*v.t.* **1.** to go up (something); climb: *to ascend a mountain.* **2.** to come to occupy; succeed to: *to ascend the throne.*

as·cen·dan·cy (ə sen′dən sē) *also,* **as·cen·den·cy.** *n.* the quality or state of having power or control; domination: *British ascendancy in Asia ended after World War II.*

as·cen·dant (ə sen′dənt) *also,* **as·cen·dent.** *adj.* **1.** moving upward; ascending; rising. **2.** holding power; dominant: *an ascendant position in public life.* —*n.* a position of power or control.
   ·in the ascendant. in or coming to a dominant, influential, or superior position.

as·cen·sion (ə sen′shən) *n.* **1.** the act or process of ascending. **2. Ascension.** in the Bible, the passing of Jesus from earth to heaven after his resurrection.

Ascension Day, in the Christian Church, the day on which Jesus passed from earth to heaven, celebrated on the fortieth day after Easter. Also, **Ascension Thursday.**

as·cent (ə sent′) *n.* **1.** a movement upward; rise: *the ascent of a balloon filled with helium.* **2.** the act of climbing or going up: *Snow made an ascent of the mountain impossible.* **3.** a place or way that one ascends; upward slope: *a steep ascent.* **4.** a movement upward in condition, rank, or level: *the rapid ascent of a secretary to the position of editor.*

as·cer·tain (as′ər tān′) *v.t.* to find out with certainty; determine: *Have you ascertained the identity of the person who wrote the letter?* —**as′cer·tain′a·ble,** *adj.* —**as′cer·tain′a·bly,** *adv.* —**as′cer·tain′ment,** *n.*

as·cet·ic (ə set′ik) *n.* a person who lives simply and with few of the material comforts and pleasures of life, especially for religious reasons. —*adj.* relating to or characteristic of ascetics or asceticism: *an ascetic hut, an ascetic style of life.* —**as·cet′i·cal·ly,** *adv.*

as·cet·i·cism (ə set′ə siz′əm) *n.* the way of life of an ascetic; extreme self-denial.

ASCII (as′kē) a standard computer code of binary numbers that correspond to a standard set of letters, numbers and other characters. [Abbreviation of *A(merican) S(tandard) C(ode) for I(nformation) I(nterchange).*]

a·scor·bic acid (ə skôr′bik) see **vitamin C.**

as·cot (as′kət, as′kot) *n.* a necktie or scarf worn with one broad end placed over the other. [From *Ascot,* a racetrack in England where this neckwear was fashionable.]

as·cribe (ə skrīb′) *v.t.,* **as·cribed, as·crib·ing. 1.** to regard (something) as coming from a particular cause or source: *They ascribed the fire to lightning.* **2.** to think of (something) as belonging to: *to ascribe selfishness to other people.* —**as·crib′a·ble,** *adj.*

ascot

as·crip·tion (ə skrip′shən) *n.* **1.** the act of ascribing. **2.** an expression or statement that ascribes.

a·sep·tic (ə sep′tik, ā sep′tik) *adj.* free from disease-causing germs. —**a·sep′ti·cal·ly,** *adv.*

a·sex·u·al (ā sek′shü əl) *adj. Biology.* **1.** without sex or distinct sexual organs. **2.** not involving the union of male and female germ cells. The cell division of amebas is a form of asexual reproduction. —**a·sex′u·al·ly,** *adv.*

As·gard (as′gärd) *n. Norse Mythology.* the home of the gods and of heroes killed in battle.

ash¹ (ash) *n.* **1.** a gray-white, powdery substance left after something has been burned. See also **ashes. 2.** fine particles of lava. [From the Old English word *asce* meaning ''ash.'']

ash² (ash) *n., pl.* **ash·es. 1.** any of a group of shade trees related to the olive, usually having winged seeds. **2.** the wood of any of these trees, used for timber. [From the Old English word *æsc* meaning this tree.]

a·shamed (ə shāmd′) *adj.* **1.** feeling shame, as when one realizes that one's actions or thoughts are foolish or improper: *I was ashamed that I lost my temper.* **2.** unwilling through fear or shame: *to be ashamed to admit a mistake in public.* —**a·sham·ed·ly** (ə shā′mid-lē), *adv.*

ash·can (ash′kan′) *n.* a can or similar receptacle for ashes or trash.

ash·en¹ (ash′ən) *adj.* **1.** ash-colored; pale. **2.** consisting of ashes. [*Ash¹* + *-en².*]

ash·en² (ash′ən) *adj.* made of the wood of the ash tree. [*Ash²* + *-en².*]

ash·es (ash′iz) *pl. n.* **1.** a gray-white powdery substance left after something has been burned. **2.** this substance together with partially burned material, as in a fireplace. **3.** the remains of a dead body after it has been cremated or has decayed. **4.** the remains of something that has been destroyed; ruins: *Their hopes were turned to ashes by the crushing defeat.*

a·shore (ə shôr′) *adv., adj.* **1.** on or to the shore. **2.** on land.

ash·tray (ash′trā′) *n.* a receptacle for tobacco ashes.

Ash Wednesday, the first day of Lent. It falls on the seventh Wednesday before Easter. [From the custom of placing *ashes* on the foreheads of churchgoers as a symbol of repentance on this day.]

ash·y (ash′ē) *adj.,* **ash·i·er, ash·i·est. 1.** of, resembling, or covered with ashes. **2.** ash-colored; pale.

A·sian (ā′zhən) *adj.* of or relating to Asia, its peoples, or its cultures. —*n.* a person who was born in or is a citizen of an Asian country. ▲ See **Asiatic** for usage note.

A·si·at·ic (ā′zhē at′ik) *n., adj.* another word for **Asian.** ▲ **Asiatic** is now generally considered offensive; **Asian** is preferred.

a·side (ə sīd′) *adv.* **1.** on or to one side; out of the way; away: *Step aside, please.* **2.** out of thought or use: *Mountain climbing is enjoyable if you can put aside your fear of heights.* **3.** in reserve; in keeping: *The librarian promised to keep that book aside for me.* —*n.* a remark not intended to be heard by all those who are present, especially an actor's remark intended for the audience but not the other characters.
   ·aside from. a. apart from; independent of; not relevant to: *Your comment is aside from the argument.* **b.** except for: *I have done all the housework aside from washing the dishes.*

as·i·nine (as′ə nīn′) *adj.* stupid; silly. **as′i·nine′ly,** *adv.*

as·i·nin·i·ty (as′ə nin′i tē) *n., pl.* **as·i·nin·i·ties. 1.** the quality of being asinine; silliness. **2.** something that is asinine, such as a remark.

ask (ask) *v.t.* **1.** to put a question about; inquire about: *We asked the way to town.* **2.** to put a question to; inquire of: *Ask the teacher if you're not sure what the word means.* **3.** to call for the answer to: *to ask a question.* **4. a.** to make a request of: *We asked a farmer for directions.*

at; āpe; fär; câre; end; mē; it; īce; pîerce; hot; ōld; sông, fôrk; oil; out; up; ūse; rüle; püll; tûrn; chin; sing; shop; thin; <u>th</u>is; hw in white; zh in treasure. The symbol ə stands for the unstressed vowel sound heard in about, taken, pencil, lemon, and circus.

A

b. to make a request for: *to ask a favor.* **5.** to invite: *I asked twenty people to the party.* **6.** to set as a price; demand: *to ask a high price for an old car.* **7.** to require: *The company asks too much from new workers.* —*v.i.* **1.** to make inquiries: *Everyone asked about you last week.* **2.** to make a request: *The child asked for another piece of cake.*

a·skance (ə skans') *adv.* **1.** with a side glance; sideways. **2.** with disapproval or suspicion: *We all looked askance at their explanation for the delay.*

a·skew (ə skū') *adv., adj.* on or to one side; out of the proper position: *The painting hung askew until straightened.*

a·slant (ə slant') *adv.* in a slanting direction; on a slant. —*adj.* slanting. —*prep.* slantingly across or over: *sunlight aslant an opening in the trees.*

a·sleep (ə slēp') *adj.* **1.** in a state of sleep; sleeping: *The baby is asleep.* **2.** (of an arm, leg, or other body part) without feeling; numb: *My foot was asleep because I sat in the same position for so long.* —*adv.* into a state of sleep: *Please wake me if I fall asleep.*

asp (asp) *n.* **1.** a kind of cobra native to Egypt. **2.** any of several other poisonous snakes, especially a viper native to Europe.

as·par·a·gus (ə spar'ə gəs) *n.* **1.** the young green or white spears of a plant of the lily family. It is cooked and eaten as a vegetable. The spears grow from underground stems and bear scalelike leaves at the tip. **2.** the plant itself. It is raised in most parts of the world.

as·par·tame (as'pər tām', ə spär'tām) *n.* a sweet-tasting white powder manufactured from amino acids and used as a low-calorie sweetener.

as·pect (as'pekt) *n.* **1.** any of the ways in which something can be viewed by the mind: *aspects of a problem. Looked at from this aspect, the situation doesn't seem as serious.* **2.** appearance; look: *the striking aspect of the mountains.* **3.** facial expression; countenance: *The minister had a somber aspect.* **4.** the direction in which something faces; exposure: *This room has southern and western aspects.*

as·pen (as'pən) *n.* any of several poplar trees found in the Northern Hemisphere, bearing small, rounded leaves that tremble in the slightest breeze.

as·per·i·ty (a sper'i tē) *n., pl.* **as·per·i·ties.** **1.** harshness of manner or temper; bitterness; severity: *I was so angry that I answered their question with great asperity.* **2.** difficult conditions; hardship: *The asperities of the frontier made life hard for the pioneers.*

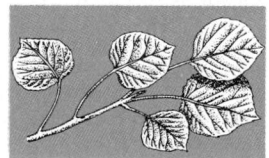

aspen leaves

as·per·sion (ə spûr'zhən) *n.* **1.** a damaging or untrue statement; slander: *to cast aspersions on a person's good name.* **2.** the act of slandering; defaming.

as·phalt (as'fôlt) *n.* **1.** a brown or black tarlike substance, occurring in nature and also obtained as a by-product of petroleum refining. **2.** a mixture of this substance with gravel or sand, used especially for paving roads. —*v.t.* to pave or cover with asphalt: *to asphalt dirt and gravel roads.*

as·pho·del (as'fə del') *n.* any of several plants of the lily family, having trumpet-shaped white or yellow flowers on a spike.

as·phyx·i·a (as fik'sē ə) *n.* a state of unconsciousness caused by a lack of oxygen and an increase of carbon dioxide in the blood and body tissues.

as·phyx·i·ate (as fik'sē āt') *v.,* **as·phyx·i·at·ed, as·phyx·i·at·ing.** —*v.t.* to cause to die or become unconscious because of lack of oxygen. —*v.i.* to die or become unconscious because of lack of oxygen. —**as·phyx·i·a'tion,** *n.*

as·pic (as'pik) *n.* a jelly made from meat, poultry, fish, or vegetable juices, chilled and often served as a molded salad dish.

as·pi·rant (as'pər ənt, ə spīr'ənt) *n.* a person who aspires to or seeks something, such as advancement, a high position, or honors.

as·pi·rate (*v.,* as'pə rāt'; *n., adj.,* as'pər it) *v.t.,* **as·pi·rat·ed, as·pi·rat·ing.** **1.** to begin the pronunciation of (a word or syllable) with a puff of breath or with an *h* sound. In the pronunciation of the word *when,* when the *wh* is aspirated, the word is pronounced *hwen.* **2.** to follow (the pronunciation of a consonant) with a puff of breath. The letters *p, t,* and *k* are aspirated when followed by a vowel, as in *palm, ton,* and *kid.* **3.** to remove (something) by means of suction. —*n.* **1.** the sound of the letter *h.* **2.** a consonant whose pronunciation is followed by a puff of breath. —*adj.* pronounced with an aspirate or followed by a puff of breath.

as·pi·ra·tion (as'pə rā'shən) *n.* **1.** a strong desire to attain a goal; high ambition: *to have aspirations to become a writer.* **2.** the object of such desire or ambition: *Being a doctor is my aspiration.* **3.** the act of breathing in; a breath. **4.** the pronunciation of an aspirate. **5.** the removal of something, such as a fluid or gas from a body cavity, by the use of suction.

as·pi·ra·tor (as'pə rā'tər) *n.* **1.** any machine or device that uses suction to remove gases, liquids, or grainy solids. **2.** a medical instrument that removes fluids and gases from a body cavity by the use of suction.

as·pire (ə spīr') *v.i.,* **as·pired, as·pir·ing.** to seek ambitiously to attain something; aim: *The young soldier aspired after glory. The senator aspired to the presidency.*

as·pi·rin (as'pər in, as'prin) *n.* **1.** a white, crystalline substance derived from salicylic acid, used in tablet form as a medicine to relieve pain and fever. Also, **acetylsalicylic acid.** **2.** a tablet of aspirin.

ass (as) *n., pl.* **ass·es.** **1.** a long-eared animal of the horse family; donkey. **2.** a stupid person; fool.

as·sa·gai (as'ə gī') also, **as·se·gai.** *n., pl.* **as·sa·gais.** a slender spear made of hard wood, used by some tribes of southern Africa.

as·sail (ə sāl') *v.t.* **1.** to attack with physical violence. **2.** to attack vigorously with arguments or abuse: *The townspeople assailed the mayor for raising taxes.* —**as·sail'a·ble,** *adj.* —**as·sail'er,** *n.*

as·sail·ant (ə sā'lənt) *n.* a person who assails; attacker: *The police rescued the couple from their assailant.*

as·sas·sin (ə sas'in) *n.* a murderer, especially someone who kills an important or famous person, as for political reasons.

as·sas·si·nate (ə sas'ə nāt') *v.t.,* **as·sas·si·nat·ed, as·sas·si·nat·ing.** to murder (someone, especially an important or famous person), as for political reasons. —**as·sas'si·na'tion,** *n.* —**as·sas'si·na'tor,** *n.*

as·sault (ə sôlt') *n.* **1.** a violent or vigorous attack: *an assault on a fort, an assault on someone's honor through lies and rumors.* **2.** *Law.* an unlawful attempt or threat to do physical violence to a person. —*v.t.* to make an assault on; attack: *The soldiers assaulted the enemy's fort.*

assault and battery *Law.* a threat to commit violence against a person combined with some act of physically touching that person.

as·say (*v.,* ə sā'; *n.,* ə sā', as'ā) *v.t.* **1.** to test (an ore, mineral, alloy, or the like) by chemical means to determine the nature or quality of its ingredients: *They assayed the ore to find out how much gold was in it.* **2.** to put to trial; test: *We assayed the wind before launching the model plane.* **3.** to try to do; attempt: *to assay a difficult task.* —*n.* **1.** a chemical analysis of an ore, mineral, alloy, or the like, to determine the nature or quality of its ingredients. **2.** any substance so analyzed. —**as·say'er,** *n.*

as·se·gai (as′i gī′) *n., pl.* **as·se·gais.** another spelling of **assagai.**

as·sem·blage (ə sem′blij) *n.* **1.** a group of persons or things gathered together; collection: *The entire assemblage wished me a happy birthday.* **2.** the act of putting or fitting parts together to construct something: *the assemblage of a model plane.* **3.** the act of assembling or the state of being assembled.

as·sem·ble (ə sem′bəl) *v.,* **as·sem·bled, as·sem·bling.** —*v.t.* **1.** to gather or bring together; collect: *The students assembled a large stamp collection.* **2.** to put or fit together: *to assemble cars in a factory. The parts of the bicycle had to be assembled before I could ride it.* —*v.i.* to meet or come together; convene: *A crowd assembled outside the theater.* —**as·sem′bler,** *n.*

as·sem·bly (ə sem′blē) *n., pl.* **as·sem·blies. 1.** a group of people gathered together for a common purpose. **2.** a body of lawmakers. **3. Assembly.** in certain states of the United States, the lower house of the legislature. **4.** the act or process of fitting together parts to make a whole. **5.** a group of parts that fit or work together. **6.** the act of assembling or the state of being assembled: *The assembly of the model airplane took several days.*

assembly line, a line of workers and machines along which a product is moved to be put together. Each worker or machine adds something to the product in turn until it is assembled completely.

as·sem·bly·man (ə sem′blē mən) *n., pl.* **as·sem·bly·men** (ə sem′blē mən). a person who is a member of a legislative assembly, especially of the lower house of a state legislature.

as·sem·bly·wom·an (ə sem′blē wùm′ən) *n., pl.* **as·sem·bly·wom·en** (ə sem′blē wim′ən). a woman who is a member of a legislative assembly, especially of the lower house of a state legislature.

as·sent (ə sent′) *v.i.* to express agreement; concur: *I thought the plan was foolish and refused to assent to it.* —*n.* agreement; consent: *The committee gave their assent to our idea.*

as·sert (ə sûrt′) *v.t.* **1.** to state firmly and clearly; affirm: *The witness asserted that the defendant had been at the scene of the crime.* **2.** to insist upon recognition of: *to assert one's rights by demanding to be treated fairly.* —**as·sert′er,** *n.*
▸**to assert oneself.** to put forward or defend one's own position or rights in a bold manner.

as·ser·tion (ə sûr′shən) *n.* **1.** a positive statement; declaration: *That assertion was later proven to be false.* **2.** the act of putting forward or maintaining.

as·ser·tive (ə sûr′tiv) *adj.* bold and forward in manner; asserting oneself; aggressive: *an assertive person who always wants to control things.* —**as·ser′tive·ly,** *adv.* —**as·ser′tive·ness,** *n.*

as·sess (ə ses′) *v.t.* **1.** to set the official value of (property) for taxation. **2.** to fix the amount of (a tax, fine, or damages): *The judge assessed a fine of fifty dollars.* **3.** to tax or charge (a person or property): *The club assesses each member five dollars for dues.* **4.** to evaluate: *The coach assessed the ability of each player who tried out for the team.*

as·sess·ment (ə ses′mənt) *n.* **1.** the act of assessing. **2.** the amount or value assessed. **3.** an estimation; evaluation: *What is your assessment of the situation?*

as·ses·sor (ə ses′ər) *n.* a person who assesses property for taxation.

as·set (as′et) *n.* **1.** something valuable or useful; advantage: *Being tall is a great asset for a basketball player.* **2. assets.** the property and resources of a business or person that have a cash value and can be used to pay the owner's debts.

as·sev·er·ate (ə sev′ə rāt′) *v.t.,* **as·sev·er·at·ed, as·sev·er·at·ing.** to declare solemnly or positively; affirm. —**as·sev′er·a′tion,** *n.*

as·si·du·i·ty (as′i dü′i tē, as′i dū′i tē) *n.* constant or careful attention and hard work; diligence.

as·sid·u·ous (ə sij′ü əs) *adj.* constantly attentive; diligent: *They were assiduous students who always worked hard.* —**as·sid′u·ous·ly,** *adv.* —**as·sid′u·ous·ness,** *n.*

as·sign (ə sīn′) *v.t.* **1.** to give out; distribute; allot: *The teacher assigned a different project to each student.* **2.** to select for a duty or office; appoint: *A new principal was assigned to the school.* **3.** to set or fix definitely; designate: *The president of the club assigned a date for the next meeting.* **4.** *Law.* to transfer (a right, property, or interest): *When the farmers couldn't pay their debts, they had to assign the land to their creditors.* —**as·sign′a·ble,** *adj.* —**as·sign′er,** *n.*

as·sign·ee (ə sī nē′) *n.* a person to whom something is assigned, especially one to whom a right, property, or interest is legally transferred.

as·sign·ment (ə sīn′mənt) *n.* **1.** something that is assigned, such as a task or job: *Our homework assignment included ten multiplication problems. The reporter's assignment was to write a story about the election.* **2.** the act of assigning or the state of being assigned: *My assignment to the new position meant that I had to get up very early in the morning.* **3.** *Law.* **a.** the transfer of a right, property, or interest. **b.** a document by which such a transfer is made.

as·sim·i·late (ə sim′ə lāt′) *v.,* **as·sim·i·lat·ed, as·sim·i·lat·ing** —*v.t.* **1.** to take in and make part of oneself: *to assimilate knowledge. The drawings were assimilated into a display covering the entire wall.* **2.** to absorb and convert into living tissue: *In the human body, food is assimilated in the small intestine.* **3.** to absorb (a social group) into a larger or more dominant culture: *The United States has assimilated immigrants from many nations.* —*v.i.* to be or become assimilated. —**as·sim′i·la′tor,** *n.*

as·sim·i·la·tion (ə sim′ə lā′shən) *n.* **1.** the act of assimilating or the state of being assimilated. **2.** a process in which a social group gradually takes on the characteristics of a larger or more dominant culture. **3.** the process by which digested food is absorbed and converted into living tissue. **4.** in language, a process in which a sound changes to become similar to another nearby sound.

As·sin·i·boin (ə sin′ə boin′) *also,* **As·sin·i·boine.** *n., pl.* **As·sin·i·boin** or **As·sin·i·boins. 1.** a member of a North American Indian tribe formerly living in the northern Great Plains. **2.** the Siouan language spoken by this tribe. —*adj.* of or relating to the Assiniboin or their language or culture.

as·sist (ə sist′) *v.t.* to give help or aid to: *We assisted our neighbors when they moved in.* —*v.i.* to help; aid: *to assist in choosing the site for a new building.* —*n.* **1.** the act of helping; aid: *I got the job with an assist from my teacher.* **2.** in baseball, a throwing or handling of the ball that helps a teammate to put out a base runner. **3.** in ice hockey or basketball, a pass that helps a teammate to score a goal.

as·sist·ance (ə sis′təns) *n.* the act of assisting; aid or support.

as·sist·ant (ə sis′tənt) *n.* a person who assists; helper; aide: *My assistant took charge of the office while I was away.* —*adj.* serving in a position under another person: *The assistant principal helps the principal in running the school.*

---

at; āpe; fär; câre; end; mē; it; īce; pîerce; hot; ōld; sông, fôrk; oil; out; up; ūse; rüle; pùll; tûrn; chin; sing; shop; thin; <u>th</u>is; hw in white; zh in treasure. The symbol ə stands for the unstressed vowel sound heard in about, taken, pencil, lemon, and circus.

as·siz·es (ə sī′ziz) *pl. n.* in England, court sessions held periodically in each county to try cases by jury.

assn., association.

assoc. 1. associate. 2. association.

as·so·ci·ate (*v.*, ə sō′shē āt′, ə sō′sē āt′; *n., adj.*, ə sō′shē it, ə sō′sē it) *v.*, **as·so·ci·at·ed, as·so·ci·at·ing.** —*v.t.* 1. to connect in one's mind: *Because the children associated darkness with danger, they were afraid to turn out the light.* 2. to join or connect (oneself) as a friend, companion, or partner: *I associated myself with the tenants' organization.* —*v.i.* 1. to keep company as a friend, companion, or partner; be friendly: *Do you associate with your fellow workers on weekends?* 2. to form a union or combination; unite: *Hydrogen associates freely with oxygen.* —*n.* 1. a person who is frequently in the company of another; companion; friend. 2. a person who is connected with another or others in some business or action; partner; colleague. —*adj.* having secondary membership, status, or privileges: *an associate professor.*

as·so·ci·a·tion (ə sō′sē ā′shən, ə sō′shē ā′shən) *n.* 1. an organized group of people with common interests; society: *a local medical association.* 2. the act of associating or the state of being associated; relationship; connection. 3. a connection made in the mind between one thought or feeling and another: *the association between "red" and "blood."* 4. such a thought or feeling: *This house has many happy associations for me.*

as·so·ci·a·tive (ə sō′shē ā′tiv, ə sō′sē ā′tiv) *adj.* 1. relating to or resulting from association. 2. *Mathematics.* relating to or designating a law stating that the sum or product of two or more quantities will be the same regardless of the way in which they are grouped. For example: (6 + 12) + 5 is the same as 6 + (12 + 5) and a × (b × c) is the same as (a × b) × c.

as·so·nance (as′ə nəns) *n.* 1. similarity or repetition of sounds, as in poetry. 2. a form of partial rhyme in which the stressed vowel sounds are alike but the consonant sounds are different, as in *same* and *take* or *labor* and *haven.*

as·sort (ə sôrt′) *v.t.* to put into groups or categories; sort: *Assort these cards by color.* —**as·sort′er,** *n.*

as·sort·ed (ə sôr′tid) *adj.* of various kinds: *a pound of assorted cookies.*

as·sort·ment (ə sôrt′mənt) *n.* 1. a collection of various kinds of things: *an assortment of cheeses.* 2. the act of assorting or the state of being assorted.

asst., assistant.

as·suage (ə swāj′) *v.t.*, **as·suaged, as·suag·ing.** 1. to make less severe; ease: *The drug assuaged the pain of the sprained ankle.* 2. to calm; pacify: *Someone who is really angry may be difficult to assuage.* 3. to satisfy: *The meal assuaged our appetites.* —**as·suage′ment,** *n.*

as·sume (ə süm′) *v.t.*, **as·sumed, as·sum·ing.** 1. to take for granted as true; suppose as a fact: *I assume we'll arrive on time if we leave now.* 2. to take upon oneself; undertake: *We assumed responsibility for feeding the dog.* 3. to take on; adopt: *to assume a new name.* 4. to take for oneself; seize: *The dictator assumed control of the country.* 5. to put on a show of; pretend: *I assumed indifference whenever your name was mentioned.*

as·sumed (ə sümd′) *adj.* 1. pretended; false: *an assumed name.* 2. taken for granted as true: *That is an assumed fact.*

as·sum·ing (ə sü′ming) *adj.* taking things for granted in an arrogant manner; bold.

as·sump·tion (ə sump′shən) *n.* 1. the act of assuming or the state of being assumed. 2. something taken for granted: *The scientist's assumption proved to be wrong.* 3. **the Assumption. a.** in Roman Catholic dogma, the taking up into heaven of the body and soul of the Virgin Mary after her death. **b.** a church festival celebrating this event. It falls on August 15.

as·sur·ance (ə shu̇r′əns) *n.* 1. the act of assuring or the state of being assured: *In my assurance that I would get the job, I bought a new suit.* 2. a positive declaration intended to give confidence; guarantee: *We had their assurance that they would pay for the damage.* 3. freedom from doubt; certainty: *to have assurance of someone's friendship.* 4. confidence in oneself; aplomb: *Despite being new at the job, the teacher had great assurance.* 5. *British.* another word for **insurance.**

as·sure (ə shu̇r′) *v.t.*, **as·sured, as·sur·ing.** 1. to state positively to; tell positively: *I assure you that they will come.* 2. to make certain; guarantee: *Your hard work assured the success of the project.* 3. to make certain; convince: *They assured us of their good intentions.* 4. to give confidence to; reassure: *to assure a frightened child.* 5. to make safe or secure: *I assured a position in the firm.* 6. *British.* to insure.

as·sured (ə shu̇rd′) *adj.* 1. made certain; guaranteed: *an assured victory.* 2. confident in oneself; self-possessed: *an assured manner and way of speaking.* —**as·sur·ed·ly** (ə shu̇r′id lē, ə shu̇rd′lē), *adv.*

as·ta·tine (as′tə tēn′) *n.* a radioactive element, usually produced artificially from bismuth. It is the heaviest element of the halogen group. Symbol: **At** [Formed from the Greek word *astatos* meaning "unsteady," going back to the prefix *a-* "not" and *histanai* "to stand." Astatine is radioactive and has no stable isotopes.]

as·ter (as′tər) *n.* 1. the daisylike flower head of any of a large group of plants that bloom in the fall. 2. a plant bearing such flowers. [From the Latin word *aster* meaning "star" and "aster," from the Greek word *astēr* "star." The array of this flower's head resembles a star.]

as·ter·isk (as′tə risk′) *n.* a star-shaped mark (*) used in printing or writing to point out a reference or a footnote, or to show that something is missing from the text. —*v.t.* to mark with an asterisk.

a·stern (ə stûrn′) *adv.* 1. at or toward the rear of a ship. 2. behind a ship. 3. backward.

asters

as·ter·oid (as′tə roid′) *n.* any of thousands of small, rocky bodies that revolve around the sun, chiefly between the orbits of Mars and Jupiter. Also, **planetoid.**

asth·ma (az′mə) *n.* a chronic disease that is usually caused by an allergic reaction. It is characterized by attacks of difficult breathing, wheezing, and coughing.

asth·mat·ic (az mat′ik) *adj.* relating to or having asthma. —*n.* a person who has asthma.

a·stig·ma·tism (ə stig′mə tiz′əm) *n.* a defect in a lens, as the lens of the eye, in which light rays coming from a single point are not focused at a single point. Astigmatism causes blurred vision or unclear images. —**a·stig·mat·ic** (as′tig mat′ik), *adj.*

a·stir (ə stûr′) *adj.* 1. in motion; stirring; active. 2. out of bed.

as·ton·ish (ə ston′ish) *v.t.* to surprise greatly; amaze: *The news astonished us.*

as·ton·ish·ing (ə ston′ə shing) *adj.* causing astonishment; amazing. —**as·ton′ish·ing·ly,** *adv.*

as·ton·ish·ment (ə ston′ish mənt) *n.* 1. a state of being astonished; surprise; amazement: *I stared in astonishment at the talking dog.* 2. something that causes amazement or surprise.

as·tound (ə stound′) *v.t.* to surprise so much as to stun; amaze: *The announcement that I had won the raffle astounded me.* —**as·tound′ing·ly,** *adv.*

a·strad·dle (ə strad′əl) *adj., adv., prep.* another word for **astride.**

as·tra·khan (as′trə kən) *n.* 1. the curly fur of young lambs, originally from the region of Astrakhan. It is a grade of karakul wool. **2.** a cloth woven to resemble this.

as·tral (as′trəl) *adj.* relating to or from the stars.

a·stray (ə strā′) *adj., adv.* off the right path or track: *Two cows have been astray since last night. Poor advice led us astray.*

a·stride (ə strīd′) *adj., adv.* with one leg on each side. —*prep.* with one leg on each side of: *to sit astride a fence.* Also, **astraddle.**

as·trin·gen·cy (ə strin′jən sē) *n.* the state of being astringent.

as·trin·gent (ə strin′jənt) *n.* a substance that shrinks the tissues of the body. Astringents are used to stop the flow of blood from a wound or cut. —*adj.* **1.** causing the tissues of the body to shrink: *an astringent lotion.* **2.** stern, severe, or harsh. —**as·trin′gent·ly,** *adv.*

as·tro·labe (as′trə lāb′) *n.* an instrument formerly used for measuring the positions of the stars, planets, and other heavenly bodies. It has been replaced by the sextant.

as·trol·o·ger (ə strol′ə jər) *n.* a person who practices astrology.

as·trol·o·gy (ə strol′ə jē) *n.* the study of the influence that the stars and planets supposedly have on people and events. —**as·tro·log·i·cal** (as′trə loj′i kəl), *adj.* —**as′tro·log′i·cal·ly,** *adv.*

astron. 1. astronomer. **2.** astronomical. **3.** astronomy.

as·tro·naut (as′trə nôt′) *n.* a person who is trained to fly in or navigate a spacecraft.

as·tro·naut·ics (as′trə nô′tiks) *n.* the science that deals with the design, construction, and operation of spacecraft. ▲ used with a singular verb. —**as·tro·naut·ic** (as′trə nô′tik); *also,* **as′tro·naut′i·cal,** *adj.*

as·tron·o·mer (ə stron′ə mər) *n.* a student of or an expert in astronomy.

as·tro·nom·i·cal (as′trə nom′i kəl) *adj.* **1.** of or relating to astronomy. **2.** very great; unbelievably large: *The dealer set an astronomical price on the diamond.* Also, **as·tro·nom·ic** (as′trə nom′ik). —**as′tro·nom′i·cal·ly,** *adv*

astronomical unit, a unit of length used to measure distances in astronomy. One unit is equal to the distance between the earth and the sun, or about 93 million miles (150 million kilometers).

astronomical year, see **year** (*def. 2*).

as·tron·o·my (ə stron′ə mē) *n.* the science that deals with the planets, stars, and other heavenly bodies, including the study of their size, position, motion, and physical characteristics.

as·tro·phys·ics (as′trō fiz′iks) *n.* the branch of astronomy that deals with the physical and chemical nature of the stars, planets, and other heavenly bodies. ▲ used with a singular verb. —**as·tro·phys·i·cal** (as′trō fiz′i kəl), *adj.*

As·tro·turf (as′trə tûrf′) *n. Trademark.* an artificial ground cover of vinyl and nylon made to resemble grass, used especially on the playing area of sports stadiums.

as·tute (ə stüt′, ə stūt′) *adj.* having or showing a keen mind; shrewd: *an astute judge of character, an astute essay.* —**as·tute′ly,** *adv.* —**as·tute′ness,** *n.*

a·sun·der (ə sun′dər) *adv.* **1.** into pieces or separate parts: *The wall was torn asunder by the blast.* **2.** apart from each other: *The wind scattered the leaves asunder.*

As·wan High Dam (as′wän) a large dam in southeastern Egypt, on the Nile.

a·sy·lum (ə sī′ləm) *n.* **1.** a place that provides care for helpless people, such as orphans or the insane. **2.** shelter or protection, such as that sought by a fugitive. Some countries grant asylum to political fugitives from other countries. **3.** a place that provides safety or protection, such as a church.

a·sym·met·ri·cal (ā′si met′ri kəl) *adj.* not the same on either side of a central line; not symmetrical. Also, **a·sym·met·ric** (ā′si met′rik). —**a′symmet′ri·cal·ly,** *adv.*

a·sym·me·try (ā sim′ə trē) *n.* a lack of symmetry.

at (at) *prep.* **1.** in, on, or by: *to stand at someone's side. The race started at the top of the hill.* **2.** to or toward: *Look at this picture.* **3.** in a place, state, or condition of; engaged in: *at home. The children are at play.* **4.** near or during the age or time of: *We ate at noon. The poet died at seventy.* **5.** because of: *The children cried at the thought of leaving.* **6.** in the rate, order, or position of: *to travel at 60 miles per hour.* **7.** in the amount of; for: *The dress was sold at half price.* **8.** in the method or manner of: *The teams were chosen at random.* **9.** by way of; through: *I entered at the back door.*

asymmetry in the claws of the fiddler crab

At, the symbol for astatine.

at·a·vism (at′ə viz′əm) *n.* the reappearance, usually after several generations, of a physical trait of an ancestor. —**at·a·vis′tic,** *adj.*

at·a·vis·tic (at′ə vis′tik) *adj.* of, relating to, or characterized by atavism: *an atavistic feature.*

a·tax·i·a (ə tak′sē ə) *n.* lack of coordination of the voluntary muscles. —**a·tax′ic,** *adj.*

ate (āt) the past tense of **eat.**

–ate *suffix* **1.** (used to form adjectives from nouns) relating to or having: *affectionate, collegiate.* **2.** (used to form certain verbs) **a.** to become: *evaporate.* **b.** to cause to become: *activate.* **c.** to combine or treat with: *chlorinate.* **3.** (used to form nouns) **a.** an office or function: *directorate, delegate.* **b.** the object or result of an action: *syndicate.*

at·el·ier (at′əl yā′) *n.* a workshop or studio, especially that of an artist.

a tem·po (ä tem′pō) *Music.* a direction telling the performer to go back to the original tempo.

Ath·a·pas·can (ath′ə pas′kən) *n.* a family of languages spoken by various Indian tribes of northwestern Canada and Alaska and the western United States, including the Apache and Navaho languages. —*adj.* of or relating to this family of languages.

a·the·ism (ā′thē iz′əm) *n.* the belief that there is no God.

a·the·ist (ā′thē ist) *n.* a person who does not believe in the existence of God. ▲ Atheist is sometimes confused with **agnostic,** but they do not have the same meaning. An **atheist** believes that there is no God. An **agnostic** is not sure whether or not God exists, and believes that there is no way to know.

a·the·is·tic (ā′thē is′tik) *adj.* of or relating to atheism or atheists.

A·the·na (ə thē′nə) *also,* **A·the·ne** (ə thē′nē). *n. Greek Mythology.* the goddess of wisdom and the arts and

at; āpe; fär; câre; end; mē; it; īce; pîerce; hot; ōld; sông, fôrk; oil; out; up; ūse; rüle; pull; tûrn; chin; sing; shop; thin; **this;** hw in white; zh in treasure. The symbol ə stands for the unstressed vowel sound heard in about, taken, pencil, lemon, and circus.

crafts. In Roman mythology she was called Minerva. Also, **Pallas, Pallas Athena.**

A·the·ni·an (ə thē′nē ən) *adj.* of or relating to Athens, especially ancient Athens, its people, or their culture. —*n.* **1.** a person who was born in or is a citizen of Athens. **2.** a person who lived in ancient Athens.

ath·er·o·scle·ro·sis (ath′ə rō sklə rō′sis) *n.* a disease in which fatty substances, such as cholesterol, build up on the inside walls of arteries. It is the most common form of arteriosclerosis.

a·thirst (ə thûrst′) *adj.* **1.** having a strong desire; eager: *The warriors were athirst for battle.* **2.** thirsty.

ath·lete (ath′lēt) *n.* **1.** a person who has ability or training in sports, games, or other activities requiring physical strength, skill, and endurance. **2.** a person who takes part in sports, especially competitive sports.

athlete's foot, a contagious infection with a fungus, marked by itching and scaling skin between the toes and on the soles; ringworm of the foot.

ath·let·ic (ath let′ik) *adj.* **1.** relating to, like, or for an athlete or athletics: *athletic equipment, an athletic journal.* **2.** physically active and strong: *an athletic youth.* —**ath·let′i·cal·ly,** *adv.*

ath·let·ics (ath let′iks) *n.* **1.** games, sports, or activities involving physical strength, skill, or endurance. ▲ usually used with a plural verb. **2.** the practice or principles of such activities or physical training. ▲ used with a singular verb.

athletic supporter, another term for **jockstrap.**

a·thwart (ə thwôrt′) *adv.* from side to side; crosswise. —*prep.* **1.** from side to side of; across. **2.** in opposition to; against. **3.** across the line or course of: *The tugboat was athwart the bow of the schooner.*

–ation *suffix* (used to form nouns) **1.** the action or process of: *education.* **2.** the condition or state of being: *isolation.* **3.** the result of: *degradation.*

–ative *suffix* (used to form adjectives) **1.** tending to: *talkative.* **2.** of or relating to: *quantitative.*

At·lan·tic Standard Time (at lan′tik) the local time used in Puerto Rico, the U.S. Virgin Islands, and much of eastern coastal Canada. It is 4 hours behind Greenwich Time.

At·lan·tis (at lan′tis) *n.* a legendary island or continent in the Atlantic that supposedly sank into the sea.

At·las (at′ləs) *n. Greek Mythology.* a giant condemned by Zeus to hold the heavens on his shoulders forever.

at·las (at′ləs) *n.* a book of maps. [Such books in the sixteenth century often contained a picture of the giant *Atlas* holding up the earth.]

ATM, automated teller machine.

at·mos·phere (at′məs fîr′) *n.* **1.** the mass of gases surrounding the earth or any heavenly body. The earth's atmosphere is made up of air. **2.** the air in a particular place: *the stifling atmosphere of a crowded subway train.* **3.** a feeling or mood, as of a place: *the cheerful atmosphere of a party, a restaurant with a quiet atmosphere.* **4.** a unit of pressure equal to atmospheric pressure at sea level, or 14.69 pounds per square inch.

at·mos·pher·ic (at′məs fer′ik) *adj.* of, in, or relating to the atmosphere. —**at′mos·pher′i·cal·ly,** *adv.*

atmospheric pressure, the pressure produced by the weight of the earth's atmosphere. At sea level it is equal to 14.69 pounds per square inch. Also, **barometric pressure.**

at. no., atomic number.

at·oll (at′ôl, ə tôl′, at′ōl, ə tōl′) *n.* a ring-shaped coral island or string of islands surrounding a lagoon.

at·om (at′əm) *n.* **1.** the smallest particle of a chemical element that has the chemical properties of that element. It is made up of a central nucleus containing protons and neutrons around which electrons travel in circular or elliptical paths. **2.** any very small particle; tiny bit: *There's not an atom of proof for that claim.* [From the Latin

word *atomos* meaning "the smallest particle," going back to the Greek word *atomos* "indivisible," from the prefix *a-* "not" + *temnein* "to divide." It was formerly thought that such small particles could not be divided.]

atom bomb, another term for **atomic bomb.**

a·tom·ic (ə tom′ik) *adj.* **1.** of or relating to an atom or atoms: *an atomic reaction.* **2.** using atomic energy: *an atomic submarine, a missile with an atomic warhead.* **3.** very small; minute. —**a·tom′i·cal·ly,** *adv.*

atomic age, the period of history characterized by the existence of the atomic bomb and the use of atomic energy; the present age.

atomic bomb, a nuclear bomb whose great force is produced by the energy released from the splitting of atoms of heavy elements, such as uranium or plutonium. Also, **atom bomb, A-bomb.**

atomic clock, an extremely accurate electric clock that is regulated by the movements within atoms or molecules.

atomic energy, another term for **nuclear energy.**

atomic mass, the mass of an atom, usually expressed in atomic mass units.

atomic mass unit, a unit of mass equal to $1/12$ of the mass of the most common kind of carbon atom.

atomic number, the number of protons in the nucleus of an atom of an element.

atomic pile, another term for **nuclear reactor.**

atomic power, another term for **nuclear power.**

atomic reactor, another term for **nuclear reactor.**

atomic theory, the theory that all matter in the universe is composed of atoms.

atomic weight, the average weight of an atom of a chemical element, measured against the standard of an atom of carbon, whose weight is set at 12.

at·om·ize (at′ə mīz′) *v.t.,* **at·om·ized, at·om·iz·ing. 1.** to break up into atoms or very small particles. **2.** to make (a liquid) into a fine spray. —**at′om·i·za′tion,** *n.*

at·om·iz·er (at′ə mī′zər) *n.* a device that turns a liquid into a fine spray: *a perfume atomizer.*

atom smasher, see **accelerator** *(def. 2).*

a·ton·al (ā tō′nəl) *adj. Music.* not written in a key or organized around a central tone. —**a·to·nal·i·ty** (ā′tō nal′i tē), *n.* —**a·ton′al·ly,** *adv.*

a·tone (ə tōn′) *v.i.,* **a·toned, a·ton·ing.** to make up, as for a wrong; make amends: *to atone for a mistake by doing the work over.*

atomizer

a·tone·ment (ə tōn′mənt) *n.* **1.** something done to make up for a wrong or injury; amends. **2. the Atonement.** in Christianity, the redemption of humanity through the life, sufferings, and death of Jesus.

a·top (ə top′) *prep.* on the top of.

A·tre·us (ā′trē əs) *n. Greek Legend.* a king who was the father of Agamemnon and Menelaus.

a·tri·um (ā′trē əm) *n., pl.* **a·tri·a** (ā′trē ə) or **a·tri·ums. 1.** the main room or entrance hall of an ancient Roman house, having an opening in the roof. **2.** either of the two upper chambers of the heart; auricle. The atria receive blood from the veins and send it to the ventricles.

a·tro·cious (ə trō′shəs) *adj.* **1.** very cruel, brutal, or wicked: *an atrocious crime.* **2.** *Informal.* very bad; distasteful; offensive: *Your table manners are atrocious.* —**a·tro′cious·ly,** *adv.* —**a·tro′cious·ness,** *n.*

a·troc·i·ty (ə tros′i tē) *n., pl.* **a·troc·i·ties. 1.** something that is atrocious, as a cruel or brutal act: *atrocities committed during a war.* **2.** the state or quality of being atrocious: *the atrocity of the crime.* **3.** *Informal.* something that is very bad: *That film is an atrocity.*

at·ro·phy (at'rə fē) *n.* **1.** a wasting away of the body or any of its parts: *A complete lack of physical activity can cause atrophy of the muscles.* **2.** any wasting away; decay: *the atrophy of the power of a great nation.* —*v.*, **at·ro·phied, at·ro·phy·ing.** —*v.i.* to waste away. —*v.t.* to cause to waste away.

at·ro·pine (at'rə pēn') *n.* a poisonous drug made synthetically or obtained from belladonna and similar plants. It is used in medicine in very small doses to relieve spasms and to dilate the pupil of the eye.

at·tach (ə tach') *v.t.* **1.** to fasten to or on; join; connect: *to attach a sign to a building.* **2.** to add at the end; affix; append: *to attach a clause to a contract.* **3.** to bind by ties of affection, gratitude, or loyalty: *I am attached to my dog.* **4.** to consider (something) as belonging to; attribute: *We attached much importance to the advice.* **5.** to appoint or assign officially, usually on a temporary basis: *The training sergeant was attached to the battalion of recruits.* **6.** to take (property) by legal authority: *to attach someone's salary to collect a debt.* —*v.i.* to belong; adhere: *A broad range of responsibilities attach to this job.* —**at·tach'a·ble,** *adj.*

at·ta·ché (at'ə shā') *n.* a person who is assigned to a diplomatic staff, especially one who is a specialist in a particular field: *a press attaché.* [From the French word *attaché,* from the past participle of *attacher* meaning "to attach."]

attaché case, a slim briefcase for carrying papers.

at·tach·ment (ə tach'mənt) *n.* **1.** the act of attaching or the state of being attached. **2.** warm feelings binding one to someone or something; affection; devotion: *The children showed strong attachment to their classmates.* **3.** a part or device that is connected to a machine or implement for a special purpose: *The movie camera had an attachment for filming indoors.* **4.** a part that connects two things or holds them together; fastening. **5.** the act of taking property by legal authority.

at·tack (ə tak') *v.t.* **1.** to go against with force or arms; assault: *The soldiers attacked the fort.* **2.** to write or speak against: *The candidate attacked the governor's policies.* **3.** to start to work on vigorously: *We attacked the problem with enthusiasm.* **4.** to act on or affect harmfully: *A plant disease attacked the elms in our yard.* —*v.i.* to make an attack: *The enemy attacked without warning.* —*n.* **1.** the act of attacking: *The attack on the fort will begin at dawn.* **2.** a sudden coming on, as of a disease: *an attack of asthma.* —**at·tack'er,** *n.*

at·tain (ə tān') *v.t.* **1.** to achieve or gain (something) through work or effort: *Marie Curie attained fame by discovering radium.* **2.** to arrive at; reach: *The basketball player attained a height of 6 feet at the age of fourteen.* —**at·tain'a·ble,** *adj.*

at·tain·der (ə tān'dər) *n.* the taking away of all civil rights from a person who has been sentenced to death or declared an outlaw.

at·tain·ment (ə tān'mənt) *n.* **1.** the act of attaining: *The attainment of success is often difficult.* **2.** something attained; accomplishment: *Albert Einstein was given a Nobel Prize for his attainments in physics.*

at·taint (ə tānt') *v.t.* to take away all civil rights from (a person sentenced to death or outlawed).

at·tar (at'ər) *n.* an oil obtained from the petals of flowers, especially roses, used in making perfume.

at·tempt (ə tempt') *v.t.* to make an effort to do (something); try: *I have never even attempted to learn to ski.* —*n.* **1.** a putting forth of effort to do something: *They made an attempt to climb the mountain.* **2.** an assault or attack: *to make an attempt on a person's life.*

at·tend (ə tend') *v.t.* **1.** to be present at: *to attend a meeting, to attend church.* **2.** to take care of or wait on: *The doctor attended the patient.* **3.** to be with (another) so as to provide service or companionship: *Two bodyguards attended the ambassador.* **4.** to occur with or

result from: *Fever attends many diseases.* —*v.i.* **1.** to be present: *I enjoy the theater, but I do not attend often.* **2.** to take care of: *The nurse attended to the oldest patients. Please attend to this matter today.* **3.** to pay attention; give heed: *Attend to what the doctor tells you.*

at·ten·dance (ə ten'dəns) *n.* **1.** the act or the state of being present: *Attendance at the lecture is required.* **2.** the number of persons present: *The attendance at the concert was over 300.* **3.** a record of persons present: *The teacher took attendance.* **4.** the act or the state of taking care of a person or thing: *In addition to the patient's own doctor, a specialist was in attendance.*

at·ten·dant (ə ten'dənt) *n.* **1.** a person who takes care of or waits on another: *a parking lot attendant.* **2.** a person who is with another so as to provide service or companionship: *a medical attendant.* **3.** a person who is present. —*adj.* **1.** occurring at the same time or as a result; accompanying: *war and its attendant evils.* **2.** providing care or service: *an attendant nurse.*

at·ten·tion (ə ten'shən) *n.* **1.** the act or power of watching, listening, or fixing one's thoughts on something: *The speaker had our whole attention.* **2.** careful thought; consideration: *This matter will receive my immediate attention.* **3. attentions.** acts of courtesy, thoughtfulness, or devotion. **4.** a military position in which a person stands erect, with arms at sides, feet together, and eyes straight ahead: *The soldiers stood at attention when the general entered the room.* —*interj.* a command to take this position.

at·ten·tive (ə ten'tiv) *adj.* **1.** paying attention: *an attentive audience.* **2.** having or showing regard for others; courteous; considerate; thoughtful: *an attentive host.* —**at·ten'tive·ly,** *adv.* —**at·ten'tive·ness,** *n.*

at·ten·u·ate (ə ten'ū āt') *v.t.*, **at·ten·u·at·ed, at·ten·u·at·ing.** **1.** to make thin or slender: *You can attenuate a rubber band by stretching it.* **2.** to lessen or reduce; weaken: *The effect of the illness was attenuated by the drug.* —**at·ten'u·a'tion,** *n.*

at·test (ə test') *v.t.* **1.** to give evidence of or be a witness to (something); declare to be true or genuine: *to attest a will. The witness attested the truth of the defendant's story.* **2.** to be proof of; show clearly: *Your high grades attest your good study habits.* —*v.i.* to bear witness; to attest to the validity of a document.

at·tic (at'ik) *n.* the space directly below the roof of a house or other building.

at·tire (ə tīr') *v.t.*, **at·tired, at·tir·ing.** to dress especially in fine or costly garments: *to attire oneself in one's best clothes.* —*n.* clothes; apparel: *elegant attire.*

at·ti·tude (at'i tüd', at'i tūd') *n.* **1.** a manner of thinking, acting, or feeling: *A good attitude toward life helps keep one healthy.* **2.** a position of the body that suggests an emotion or condition: *to stand in an attitude of watchfulness.* **3.** the position of an aircraft or spacecraft in relation to some point of reference, such as the earth.

at·tor·ney (ə tûr'nē) *n.*, *pl.* **at·tor·neys. 1.** a person whose profession is representing people in lawsuits or in court, and advising them of their rights; lawyer. **2.** a person who has been given the power to act in another person's place, especially in a legal matter.

attorney at law *pl.* **attorneys at law.** a lawyer.

attorney general *pl.* **attorneys general** or **attorney generals.** the chief law officer of a national or state government.

---

at; āpe; fär; câre; end; mē; it; īce; pîerce; hot; ōld; sông, fôrk; oil; out; up; ūse; rüle; pull; tûrn; chin; sing; shop; thin; this; hw in white; zh in treasure. The symbol ə stands for the unstressed vowel sound heard in about, taken, pencil, lemon, and circus.

at·tract (ə trakt') *v.t.* **1.** to draw the attention or interest of; be appealing to; fascinate: *The scenery in these mountains attracts many tourists.* **2.** to draw to oneself or itself by physical force: *The north pole of one magnet attracts the south pole of another magnet.* —**at·tract'er;** *also,* **at·trac'tor,** *n.*

at·trac·tion (ə trak'shən) *n.* **1.** the act or power of attracting: *the attraction of a magnet.* **2.** a person or thing that attracts: *The magician was the main attraction at the children's party.* **3.** the quality of something or someone that attracts: *The main attraction of the coast for me is the fresh air.*

at·trac·tive (ə trak'tiv) *adj.* **1.** having an appealing quality; pleasing: *an attractive dress. Your friend is an attractive person.* **2.** having the power of attracting: *Gravity is an attractive force.* —**at·trac'tive·ly,** *adv.* —**at·trac'tive·ness,** *n.*

at·trib·ute (*v.,* ə trib'ūt; *n.,* at'rə būt') *v.t.,* **at·trib·ut·ed, at·trib·ut·ing.** to consider (something) as belonging to, produced by, or resulting from: *We attribute our good health to eating properly. Scholars attributed the painting to Rembrandt.* —*n.* **1.** something that is thought of as belonging to a person or thing, such as a quality or characteristic: *One of my cousin's attributes is friendliness.* **2.** an object used as a symbol, as of a god: *A hunter's bow was one of the attributes of the goddess Diana.* —**at·trib'ut·a·ble,** *adj.* —**at'tri·bu'tion,** *n.*

at·trib·u·tive (ə trib'yə tiv) *adj.* relating to an adjective, or a noun used as an adjective, that modifies a noun and usually comes before it. In the phrase *school bus,* the noun *school* is an attributive word. —*n.* an attributive word. In the phrase *green jacket, green* is an attributive. —**at·trib'u·tive·ly,** *adv.*

at·tri·tion (ə trish'ən) *n.* **1.** a wearing away by friction. **2.** a gradual wearing down or weakening: *a war of attrition exhausted the enemies.*

at·tune (ə tün', ə tūn') *v.t.,* **at·tuned, at·tun·ing.** to bring into harmony or accord: *My mind was soon attuned to the peace and quiet of country life.*

atty., attorney.

at. wt, atomic weight.

a·typ·i·cal (ā tip'i kəl) *adj.* not like most; not typical: *A bird that cannot fly is atypical.* —**a·typ'i·cal·ly,** *adv.*

Au, the symbol for gold. [Abbreviation of the Latin word *aurum* meaning "gold."]

au·burn (ô'bərn) *n.* a reddish brown color. —*adj.* having the color auburn; reddish brown.

auc·tion (ôk'shən) *n.* a public sale at which articles or property are sold to the highest bidder. —*v.t.* to sell at an auction: *He auctioned his collection of paintings.*

auc·tion·eer (ôk'shə nîr') *n.* a person who conducts sales by auction.

au·da·cious (ô dā'shəs) *adj.* **1.** not showing any fear; recklessly bold: *The audacious explorer went alone into the jungle.* **2.** not showing respect; impudent: *to be shocked by someone's audacious behavior.* —**au·da'cious·ly,** *adv.* —**au·da'cious·ness,** *n.*

au·dac·i·ty (ô das'i tē) *n.* **1.** boldness or courage; daring. **2.** shameless boldness; impudence.

au·di·ble (ô'də bəl) *adj.* loud enough to be heard: *The radio was barely audible in the next room. n. Football.* a play that is called at the line of scrimmage rather than in the huddle. —**au'di·bil'i·ty,** *n.* —**au'di·bly,** *adv.*

au·di·ence (ô'dē əns) *n.* **1.** a group of people gathered to hear and see something, such as a play. **2.** a group of people who give attention to something: *The television program reached an audience of millions.* **3.** people who appreciate and support something: *Hockey has a growing audience in this country.* **4.** a formal meeting with a person of rank or position: *an audience with the pope.* **5.** an opportunity to be heard; hearing: *an audience with a committee.*

au·di·o (ô'dē ō') *adj.* **1.** of or relating to sound. **2.** of or relating to the reproduction, transmission, or reception of sound. —*n.* the portion of a television broadcast, motion picture, or videotape recording that carries sound.

audio frequency, any frequency at which a sound wave can be heard by a person with normal hearing, ranging from about 15 cycles to 20,000 cycles per second.

au·di·om·e·ter (ô'dē om'i tər) *n.* an instrument that produces controlled sounds, used for testing a person's hearing.

au·di·o·vis·u·al (ô'dē ō vizh'ü əl) *adj.* **1.** of or relating to hearing and sight. **2.** relating to or using such teaching materials as films, recordings, television, and photographs.

au·dit (ô'dit) *v.t.* **1.** to examine (financial accounts and records) to make sure they are correct. **2.** to attend (a college course) as a listener, without receiving credit for attendance. —*v.i.* to examine financial accounts and records. —*n.* **1.** an examination of financial accounts and records. **2.** a statement of the financial accounts and records that have been examined.

au·di·tion (ô dish'ən) *n.* a short performance that tests the abilities of a singer, musician, actor, or other performer. —*v.t.* to give an audition to (a performer): *The director auditioned three actors for the part.* —*v.i.* to perform in an audition: *Eighteen performers auditioned for the leading role.*

au·di·tor (ô'di tər) *n.* **1.** a person who audits financial accounts and records. **2.** a hearer; listener.

au·di·to·ri·um (ô'di tôr'ē əm) *n., pl.* **au·di·to·ri·ums.** **1.** a large room in a church, school, theater, or other building for public gatherings. **2.** a building used for public gatherings.

au·di·to·ry (ô'di tôr'ē) *adj.* of or relating to hearing.

auditory nerve, the nerve carrying impulses from the inner ear to the brain.

auf Wie·der·seh·en (ouf vē'dər zā'ən) *German.* until we meet again; good-bye for now.

Aug., August.

au·ger (ô'gər) *n.* a tool or drill for boring holes in wood or in the earth.

aught¹ (ôt) *also,* **ought.** *n.* anything; any part. —*adv.* in any way; at all. [From the Old English word *āwiht* meaning "anything."]

aught² (ôt) *also,* **ought.** *n.* **1.** zero. **2.** nothing; naught. [From *naught,* from the Old English word *nāwiht* meaning "nothing." The phrase *a naught* was incorrectly written as *an aught.*]

augers

aug·ment (ôg ment') *v.t.* to make greater; increase; enlarge: *The museum augmented its collection by buying two new paintings.* —*v.i.* to become greater; increase; grow. —**aug·ment'a·ble,** *adj.* —**aug'men·ta'tion,** *n.*

au grat·in (ō grä'tən, ō grat'ən) covered with bread crumbs and grated cheese and baked or grilled until brown. [From the French phrase *au gratin* meaning "with burnt (bread) crumbs."]

au·gur (ô'gər) *n.* **1.** any of a group of priests of ancient Rome who predicted future events from signs or omens. **2.** any fortuneteller; soothsayer. —*v.t.* **1.** to predict (something) from signs or omens. **2.** to be a sign or omen of; give promise of. —*v.i.* to predict from signs or omens.

  ·**to augur ill.** to be a bad sign or omen: *Our captain's injury augurs ill for our chances of winning the championship.*

  ·**to augur well.** to be a good sign or omen.

au·gu·ry (ô'gyə rē) *n., pl.* **au·gu·ries.** **1.** the art or practice of predicting future events from signs or omens. **2.** a sign or omen.

au·gust (ô gust′) *adj.* **1.** inspiring awe, reverence, or admiration; magnificent; majestic; imposing: *the august Capitol building in Washington.* **2.** dignified; eminent: *an august assembly.* —**au·gust′ly,** *adv.* —**au·gust′ness,** *n.*

Au·gust (ô′gəst) *n.* the eighth month of the year, having thirty-one days. [From *Augustus,* the Latin name of this month, from the first Roman emperor, *Augustus* Caesar (63 B.C.–A.D. 14).]

au jus (ō jüs′) *French.* (of meat) served with the gravy that forms naturally from the juices of the meat while it is cooking: *roast beef au jus.*

auk (ôk) *n.* any of several diving birds found in arctic waters, having webbed feet, short wings, and black and white feathers.

au lait (ō lā′) *French.* with milk.

auld lang syne (ôld′ lang zīn′) the days of long ago; the good old days. [From the Scottish phrase *auld lang syne* meaning "old long ago."]

aunt (ant, änt) *n.* **1.** the sister of one's father or mother. **2.** the wife of one's uncle.

auk

au·ra (ôr′ə) *n., pl.* **au·ras.** the distinctive character or atmosphere arising from and surrounding a person or thing: *an aura of mystery about someone. There was an aura of peace in the cathedral.*

au·ral (ôr′əl) *adj.* of or relating to the ear or to the sense of hearing. —**au′ral·ly,** *adv.*

au·re·ole (ôr′ē ōl′) *n.* **1.** in art, a circle of light surrounding the head of a sacred person. **2.** a bright area around the sun or moon, especially when seen through fog.

Au·re·o·my·cin (ôr′ē ō mī′sin) *n. Trademark.* an antibiotic drug used against certain infections caused by bacteria and fungi.

au re·voir (ō rə vwär′) *French.* until we meet again; good-bye.

au·ri·cle (ôr′i kəl) *n.* **1.** the external ear. **2.** an atrium of the heart.

au·ric·u·lar (ô rik′yə lər) *adj.* **1.** of or relating to the ear or to the sense of hearing. **2.** of or relating to an auricle of the heart.

au·rochs (ôr′oks) *n., pl.* **au·rochs.** an extinct wild ox of Europe, believed to be the direct ancestor of modern domestic cattle.

Au·ro·ra (ə rôr′ə) *n.* **1.** *Roman Mythology.* the goddess of the dawn. **2. aurora.** shining bands or streamers of light appearing in the night sky.

au·ro·ra aus·tra·lis (ə rôr′ə ôs trā′lis) the aurora seen in the Southern Hemisphere. Also, **southern lights.**

au·ro·ra bo·re·al·is (ə rôr′ə bôr′ē al′is) the aurora seen in the Northern Hemisphere. Also, **northern lights.**

aus·pic·es (ôs′pə siz) *pl. n.* **1.** signs or omens, especially those that indicate success. **2.** support or guidance; patronage: *The tour was conducted under the auspices of the school board.* [From the Latin word *auspicium* meaning "a prediction made from watching birds."]

aus·pi·cious (ô spish′əs) *adj.* showing promise of success; favorable: *The victory was an auspicious beginning for the team's season.* —**aus·pi′cious·ly,** *adv.* —**aus·pi′cious·ness,** *n.*

aus·tere (ô stîr′) *adj.* **1.** severe or stern, as in manner or appearance: *an austere person who rarely smiled.* **2.** severely simple; unadorned: *The austere room contained only a chair and table.* **3.** lacking comforts or pleasures; frugal or harsh: *the austere life of pioneers.* —**aus·tere′ly,** *adv.* —**aus·tere′ness,** *n.*

aus·ter·i·ty (ô ster′i tē) *n., pl.* **aus·ter·i·ties.** **1.** the quality or condition of being austere. **2.** *also,* **austerities.** austere and self-denying behavior or practices: *the austerities of a monastery.*

Aus·tra·lian (ô strāl′yən) *adj.* of or relating to Aus-

tralia, its people, their languages, or their culture. —*n.* **1.** a person who was born in or is a citizen of Australia. **2.** a member of the ethnic group native to Australia; Australian aborigine. **3.** any of the languages spoken by the aborigines of Australia.

Words From Other Languages

Many of the words that English has borrowed from Australian languages are names of animals found only in Australia.

boomerang	a curved stick thrown as a weapon
dingo	a kind of wild dog
kangaroo	a mammal that hops on its hind legs
koala	a small mammal that lives in trees
wallaby	a mammal resembling the kangaroo
wombat	a burrowing animal active at night

Australian ballot, a ballot containing the names of all candidates in an election. It is marked in secrecy by the voter. It was first used in Australia.

au·then·tic (ô then′tik) *adj.* **1.** that can be accepted as true; reliable; trustworthy: *The eyewitness gave an authentic account of the accident.* **2.** being what it appears or claims to be; genuine; real: *an authentic Indian arrowhead.* —**au·then′ti·cal·ly,** *adv.*

au·then·ti·cate (ô then′ti kāt′) *v.t.,* **au·then·ti·cat·ed, au·then·ti·cat·ing.** to show to be authentic: *The signature was authenticated by comparing it with one in a letter.* —**au·then′ti·ca′tion,** *n.*

au·then·tic·i·ty (ô′then tis′i tē) *n.* the state or quality of being authentic: *The art critic questioned the authenticity of the painting.*

au·thor (ô′thər) *n.* **1.** the writer of a book, story, play, poem, or other written work: *Charles Dickens and Jane Austen were authors of many novels.* **2.** a person who originates or begins something; creator: *the author of a plan.* —*v.t.* to be the author of: *to author a book.*

au·thor·i·tar·i·an (ə thôr′i târ′e ən) *adj.* **1.** in favor of total obedience to authority and opposed to individual freedom: *an authoritarian personality.* **2.** based on or operating by these impulses: *The dictator set up an authoritarian government.* —*n.* an authoritarian person. —**au·thor′i·tar′i·an·ism,** *n.*

au·thor·i·ta·tive (ə thôr′i tā′tiv) *adj.* **1.** worthy of acceptance or belief; reliable: *The reporter got the story from an authoritative source.* **2.** coming from or having authority: *The mayor made an authoritative statement.* **3.** showing authority: *The officer had an authoritative manner.* —**au·thor′i·ta′tive·ly,** *adv.* —**au·thor′i·ta′tive·ness,** *n.*

au·thor·i·ty (ə thôr′i tē) *n., pl.* **au·thor·i·ties.** **1.** the ability to act, command, enforce obedience, or make decisions: *The dictator had absolute authority. The captain had authority over the ships.* **2.** a person or group having such ability: *a city housing authority. Report this incident to the authorities.* **3.** a trustworthy source of expert information or advice: *The encyclopedia is an authority on many subjects.* **4.** an expert on a particular subject: *That professor is an authority on lake pollution.*

at; āpe; fär; câre; end; mē; it; īce; pîerce; hot; ōld; sông, fôrk; oil; out; up; ūse; rüle; pu̇ll; tûrn; chin; sing; shop; thin; <u>th</u>is; hw in white; zh in treasure. The symbol ə stands for the unstressed vowel sound heard in about, taken, pencil, lemon, and circus.

A

au·thor·i·za·tion (ô′thər ə zā′shən) *n.* **1.** the act of authorizing. **2.** legal right or power: *The writer gave the magazine authorization to publish the story.*

au·thor·ize (ô′thə rīz′) *v.t.,* **au·thor·ized, au·thor·iz·ing. 1.** to give authority to: *I was authorized by the treasurer to sign the contract.* **2.** to approve officially: *to authorize the appointment of a new police chief.*

au·thor·ized (ô′thə rīzd′) *adj.* having authority: *an authorized agent.*

Authorized Version, another term for **King James Version.**

au·thor·ship (ô′thər ship′) *n.* the origin or source of a written work: *This book is of unknown authorship.*

au·tism (ô′tiz əm) *n.* a brain disorder that impairs development in children, often characterized by absence of speech or response to it, an inability to relate to other people, and sometimes rigid, rocking body movements. [From the Greek word *autos* "self" or "same" + the English suffix *-ism.*]

au·to (ô′tō) *n., pl.* **au·tos.** see **automobile.**

au·to·bi·og·ra·phy (ô′tə bī og′rə fē) *n., pl.* **au·to·bi·og·ra·phies.** the story of a person's own life written by himself or herself. **—au·to·bi·og·ra·pher** (ô′tə bī og′rə fər), *n.* **—au·to·bi·o·graph·ic** (ô′tə bī′ə graf′ik); *also,* **au′to·bi′o·graph′i·cal,** *adj.* **—au′to·bi′o·graph′i·cal·ly,** *adv.*

au·to·clave (ô′tə klāv′) *n.* **1.** a vessel in which medical instruments are sterilized by high-pressure steam. **2.** a vessel in which chemical reactions are carried out under high pressure.

au·toc·ra·cy (ô tok′rə sē) *n., pl.* **au·toc·ra·cies. 1.** a form of government in which one person holds absolute power. **2.** a country ruled by an autocrat.

au·to·crat (ô′tə krat′) *n.* **1.** a ruler who has absolute power. **2.** a person who is arrogant and domineering toward other people.

au·to·crat·ic (ô′tə krat′ik) *adj.* of or like an autocrat or an autocracy: *The president's autocratic actions.* **—au′to·crat′i·cal·ly,** *adv.*

au·to·graph (ô′tə graf′) *n.* **1.** a person's own signature. **2.** something written in a person's own handwriting. **—v.t. 1.** to write one's signature in or on: *The writer autographed a copy of the book for me.* **2.** to write in one's own handwriting. **—au′to·graph′ic;** *also,* **au′to·graph′i·cal,** *adj.*

au·to·im·mune (ô′tō i mūn′) *adj.* of or relating to the production by an organism of antibodies that attack the organism's own tissues or cells.

au·to·mat (ô′tə mat′) *n.* a cafeteria in which food is obtained from small compartments whose doors open when the proper coins are put in the slots.

au·to·mate (ô′tə māt′) *v.t., v.i.,* **au·to·mat·ed, au·to·mat·ing.** to convert to or operate by automation: *to automate the printing of a newspaper. The office automated this summer.*

automated teller machine *also,* **automatic teller ma-**

automated teller machine

chine. a computerized machine that allows bank customers to deposit or withdraw money and make other transactions without the help of a teller. Also, **cash machine.**

au·to·mat·ic (ô′tə mat′ik) *adj.* **1.** acting, moving, or operating by itself: *an automatic washing machine.* **2.** done without a person's control: *Breathing is an automatic action of the body during sleep.* **3.** (of a firearm) capable of firing and reloading continuously until the trigger is released: *an automatic rifle.* **—n.** an automatic firearm. **—au′to·mat′i·cal·ly,** *adv.*

automatic pilot, a device that steers an aircraft, ship, or other vehicle automatically by means of a computer controlled by one or more gyroscopes.

au·to·ma·tion (ô′tə mā′shən) *n.* the development and use of machines or systems of machines that are self-operating or are operated by other machines rather than by people.

au·tom·a·ton (ô tom′ə ton′) *n.* **1.** a machine that acts, moves, or operates by itself. **2.** a person whose behavior is mechanical.

au·to·mo·bile (ô′tə mə bēl′, ô′tə mə bēl′) *n.* a passenger vehicle usually having four wheels and driven by an engine powered by gasoline; car. **—adj.** of or for automobiles.

au·to·mo·tive (ô′tə mō′tiv) *adj.* **1.** of, relating to, or for an automobile or automobiles: *automotive engineering, the automotive industry.* **2.** moving by itself; self-propelled.

au·to·nom·ic (ô′tə nom′ik) *adj.* of or relating to the autonomic nervous system.

autonomic nervous system, the part of the nervous system that controls and regulates the involuntary actions of the body, such as the beating of the heart.

au·ton·o·mous (ô ton′ə məs) *adj.* free from outside rule or control; self-governing; independent. **—au·ton′o·mous·ly,** *adv.*

au·ton·o·my (ô ton′ə mē) the quality, condition, or right of being autonomous; self-government: *The former colony won its autonomy from the parent country.*

au·top·sy (ô′top sē) *n., pl.* **au·top·sies.** a medical examination of a dead body, especially in order to find the cause of death; post-mortem.

au·tumn (ô′təm) *n.* the season of the year coming between summer and winter; fall. **—adj.** relating to or characteristic of autumn.

au·tum·nal (ô tum′nəl) *adj.* relating to or characteristic of autumn: *apples and other autumnal fruit.*

autumnal equinox, the equinox that takes place on or about September 23. It marks the beginning of autumn in the Northern Hemisphere.

aux·il·ia·ry (ôg zil′yə rē, ôg zil′ə rē) *adj.* **1.** giving aid or support; helping: *The sailboat has an auxiliary engine.* **2.** more or other than the regular; additional; supplementary: *auxiliary police.* **—n., pl.** **aux·il·ia·ries. 1.** something that is attached to give aid or support. **2.** a group that is a subsidiary of a larger group: *an auxiliary to a civic club.* **3.** see **auxiliary verb. 4. auxiliaries.** foreign troops in the service of a nation at war.

auxiliary verb, a verb used before the main verb in a verb phrase to express the tense, mood, or voice of the main verb. In the sentence *They will go,* the word *will* is an auxiliary verb.

av. 1. avenue. **2.** average. **3.** avoirdupois.

A.V., Authorized Version.

a·vail (ə vāl′) *v.t.* to be of advantage or worth to: *My help will not avail you now.* **—v.i.** to be of use or value; help. **—n.** use; help; advantage: *Our efforts were of no avail.*

·to avail oneself of. to take advantage of; make use of: *Avail yourself of the books in the library.*

a·vail·a·bil·i·ty (ə vā′lə bil′i tē) *n., pl.* **a·vail·a·bil·i·ties.** the state or quality of being available.

a·vail·a·ble (ə vā′lə bəl) *adj.* **1.** that can be had; obtainable: *This dress is available in all sizes.* **2.** that can be used: *The telephone is now available.* —**a·vail′a·bly**, *adv.*

av·a·lanche (av′ə lanch′) *n.* **1.** the swift, sudden fall of a mass of snow, ice, earth, or rocks down a mountain slope. **2.** anything like an avalanche: *I was overwhelmed by an avalanche of work.*

a·vant–garde (ə vänt′gärd′) *n.* a group of people who use or experiment with new, daring, or extreme styles or ideas, especially in the arts. —*adj.* new, daring, or extreme in styles or ideas: *an avant-garde movie.* [From the French word *avant-garde* meaning "advance guard" or "vanguard."]

av·a·rice (av′ər is) *n.* an intense desire to acquire money and keep it; greed for wealth or possessions.

av·a·ri·cious (av′ə rish′əs) *adj.* greedy for wealth or possessions: *The avaricious merchants charged inflated prices.* —**av′a·ri′cious·ly**, *adv.* —**av′a·ri′cious·ness**, *n.*

a·vast (ə vast′) *interj.* stop; stay; cease. ▲ used as a command on board a ship.

a·vaunt (ə vônt′) *interj. Archaic.* go away; begone.

ave., avenue.

A·ve Ma·ri·a (ä′vä mə rē′ə) another term for **Hail Mary**.

a·venge (ə venj′) *v.t.,* **a·venged, a·veng·ing.** to get revenge for: *to avenge a friend's murder.* —**a·veng′er**, *n.*

av·e·nue (av′ə nū′, av′ə nü′) *n.* **1.** a street or thoroughfare, especially a wide one. **2.** a road or walk lined with trees. **3.** a way of reaching or accomplishing something: *Hard work is an avenue to success.*

a·ver (ə vûr′) *v.t.,* **a·verred, a·ver·ring.** to declare positively; assert.

av·er·age (av′rij, av′ər ij) *n.* **1.** a number found by dividing the sum of two or more quantities by the total number of quantities: *The average of 2, 4, 6, and 8 is 5.* **2.** the typical, ordinary, or usual amount or kind: *This year's rainfall came close to the average.* —*adj.* **1.** found by figuring an average: *the average yield of a crop, the average speed of a car.* **2.** usual; typical; ordinary: *a person of average height, an average American.* —*v.,* **av·er·aged, av·er·ag·ing.** —*v.t.* **1.** to find the average of: *We averaged our incomes to see how much we could save.* **2.** to do, have, or amount to as an average: *That basketball player averages 20 points per game.* —*v.i.* to be or amount to an average.

 ·on the average. considered from the basis of an average: *On the average, it rains more in Boston than it does in Phoenix.*

a·verse (ə vûrs′) *adj.* strongly against; unwilling (with *to*): *I would not be averse to altering our plans.* —**a·verse′ly**, *adv.* —**a·verse′ness**, *n.*

a·ver·sion (ə vûr′zhən) *n.* **1.** a strong opposition or dislike; antipathy: *an aversion to insects.* **2.** a cause of dislike or opposition: *Spiders are my chief aversion.*

a·vert (ə vûrt′) *v.t.* **1.** to turn away or aside: *We averted our eyes from the glare of the sun.* **2.** to keep from happening; prevent: *The driver narrowly averted a crash by slamming on the brakes.* —**a·vert′i·ble**, *adj.*

avg., average.

a·vi·an (ā′vē ən) *adj.* of or relating to birds.

a·vi·ar·y (ā′vē er′ē) *n., pl.* **a·vi·ar·ies.** a large cage, building, or enclosure for birds.

a·vi·a·tion (ā′vē ā′shən, av′ē ā′shən) *n.* **1.** the science or art of flying in heavier-than-air aircraft. **2.** the production and design of heavier-than-air aircraft. **3.** the business of flying such aircraft.

a·vi·a·tor (ā′vē ā′tər, av′ē ā′tər) *n.* a person who flies an airplane or other heavier-than-air aircraft.

av·id (av′id) *adj.* **1.** very eager or enthusiastic: *an avid sports fan, an avid reader of mystery stories.* **2.** having a great desire; greedy: *to be avid for wealth.* —**av′id·ly**, *adv.* —**av′id·ness**, *n.*

a·vid·i·ty (ə vid′i tē) *n.* great eagerness or greed.

av·o·ca·do (av′ə kä′dō) *n., pl.* **av·o·ca·dos.** **1.** a pear-shaped tropical fruit having a large, single seed and pulp with a buttery texture and a nutty flavor. It is eaten raw in salads, desserts, and other dishes. Also, **alligator pear. 2.** the evergreen tree bearing this fruit.

halved **avocado**

av·o·ca·tion (av′ə kā′shən) *n.* an interest or pastime that a person has in addition to a regular occupation; hobby: *Our family doctor's avocation is collecting antique clocks.* —**av′o·ca′tion·al**, *adj.*

a·void (ə void′) *v.t.* to keep away from; shun; evade: *Please try to avoid trouble.* —**a·void′a·ble**, *adj.* —**a·void′a·bly**, *adv.*

a·void·ance (ə voi′dəns) *n.* the act of avoiding something: *The avoidance of war is one of the goals of the United Nations.*

av·oir·du·pois (av′ər də poiz′) *n.* **1.** *Informal.* body weight: *The boxer needed to train to lose some avoirdupois.* **2.** see **avoirdupois weight.**

avoirdupois weight, a system of weights based on a pound that contains sixteen ounces. It is used in the United States, Great Britain, and Canada for weighing all goods except drugs and precious metals.

a·vouch (ə vouch′) *v.t.* **1.** to declare positively; assert; affirm. **2.** to vouch for; guarantee.

a·vow (ə vou′) *v.t.* to declare frankly or openly; admit; acknowledge: *to avow one's failure.*

a·vow·al (ə vou′əl) *n.* a frank or open declaration, admission, or acknowledgment: *an avowal of one's true feelings.*

a·vowed (ə voud′) *adj.* openly declared or acknowledged: *an avowed enemy.* —**a·vow·ed·ly** (ə vou′id lē, ə voud′lē), *adv.*

a·vun·cu·lar (ə vung′kyə lər) *adj.* of, relating to, or like an uncle: *avuncular affection.*

a·wait (ə wāt′) *v.t.* **1.** to wait for; anticipate: *We had long awaited the day of the party.* **2.** to be ready or in store for: *Many surprises await you in your career.*

a·wake (ə wāk′) *v.,* **a·woke** or **a·waked, awaked** or **awoken, a·wak·ing.** —*v.t.* **1.** to rouse from sleep; wake. **2.** to make active; stir up or excite: *The startling testimony awoke new interest in the case.* —*v.i.* **1.** to cease to sleep: *I awoke at dawn.* **2.** to become active or aroused: *People are now awaking to the need to conserve natural resources.* —*adj.* **1.** not asleep: *I lay awake listening to the wind.* **2.** conscious; alert; aware: *to be awake to the risks involved in a plan.*

a·wak·en (ə wā′kən) *v.t., v.i.* to awake; wake up: *The barking dog awakened us. The film awakened memories of our trip to Paris. I awakened at six.*

a·wak·en·ing (ə wā′kə ning) *n.* **1.** the act of waking. **2.** a becoming aware; realization. —*adj.* arousing; growing; increasing: *As I grew older, I had an awakening sense of the society I lived in.*

a·ward (ə wôrd′) *v.t.* **1.** to give after careful consideration, especially as deserved or due: *to be awarded a medal for bravery. The judges awarded me first prize for my essay.* **2.** to grant by judicial decision: *The jury awarded damages to the plaintiff.* —*n.* **1.** something that is

at; āpe; fär; câre; end; mē; it; īce; pîerce; hot; ōld; sông; fôrk; oil; out; up; ūse; rüle; pull; tûrn; chin; sing; shop; thin; <u>th</u>is; hw in white; zh in treasure. The symbol ə stands for the unstressed vowel sound heard in about, taken, pencil, lemon, and circus.

A

awarded: *The newspaper received many awards for its well-written, informative reports.* **2.** a decision or finding, as of a judge or arbitrator.

a·ware (ə wâr′) *adj.* knowing or realizing; conscious: *We were aware that someone was in the house.* —**a·ware′ness,** *n.*

a·wash (ə wôsh′, ə wosh′) *adv., adj.* **1.** covered with or washed over by water: *The decks of the ship were awash during the storm.* **2.** set floating: *After the rain, leaves were awash in the gutter.*

a·way (ə wā′) *adv.* **1.** from this or that place; off: *The ship sailed away into the sunset.* **2.** at a distance: *They stood several feet away from us.* **3.** in another place; absent: *to be away from one's desk.* **4.** in another direction; aside: *We turned away from the sun when it became so bright we couldn't see.* **5.** from or out of one's possession or use: *Throw away that old coat.* **6.** at or to an end; out of existence: *The old plant withered away.* **7.** without interruption; continuously: *We worked away for three hours.* **8.** without hesitation or delay; directly: *Fire away!* —*adj.* **1.** distant; far: *The school is three miles away.* **2.** absent; gone: *The ship has been away for two weeks.*

　·**to do away with. a.** to put an end or stop to; get rid of: *The new club president did away with all the old rules.* **b.** to kill.

awe (ô) *n.* great wonder combined with fear or reverence: *We stood in awe of the great poet.* —*v.t.,* **awed, aw·ing.** to inspire or fill with awe: *We were awed by the fury of the storm.*

a·weigh (ə wā′) *adj.* (of an anchor) raised clear of the bottom.

awe·some (ô′səm) *adj.* **1.** inspiring awe: *The polar bear is an awesome creature.* **2.** showing awe: *an awesome look.* —**awe′some·ly,** *adv.* —**awe′some·ness,** *n.*

awe·struck (ô′struk′) *adj.* filled with awe. Also, **awe·strick·en** (ô′strik′ən).

aw·ful (ô′fəl) *adj.* **1.** causing fear, dread, or awe; terrible: *an awful disaster.* **2.** *Informal.* very bad, distasteful, or ugly: *awful handwriting.* **3.** *Informal.* very large; great: *That's an awful lot of money.* —*adv. Informal.* extremely; terribly: *I'm awful glad to see you.* —**aw′ful·ness,** *n.*

aw·ful·ly (ô′fə lē, ô′flē) *adv.* **1.** so as to cause awe or dread; terribly: *The lion roared awfully.* **2.** *Informal.* very; extremely: *It's awfully nice to see you again.*

a·while (ə hwīl′, ə wīl′) *adv.* for a short time: *After the long walk, they sat down and rested awhile.*

awk·ward (ôk′wərd) *adj.* **1.** lacking or showing lack of ease, skill, or grace in movement or bearing: *The dancer gave an awkward performance.* **2.** difficult or embarrassing: *Having to make excuses for my friend's rudeness was awkward.* **3.** difficult to use, manage, or handle: *The large cabinet was awkward to move.* —**awk′ward·ly,** *adv.* —**awk′ward·ness,** *n.*

awl (ôl) *n.* a pointed tool used for making small holes and for working designs into the surface of leather or wood.

aw·ning (ô′ning) *n.* a rooflike cover of canvas or other material, as over a door or window, used as a shelter from the sun or rain.

a·woke (ə wōk′) the past tense and past participle of **awake.**

AWOL (ā′wôl′) *adv., adj.* absent from one's military post or duties without official leave. [*A*(bsent) *W*(ith) *O*(ut) *L*(eave).]

a·wry (ə rī′) *adv., adj.* **1.** twisted or turned to one side; askew. **2.** off the

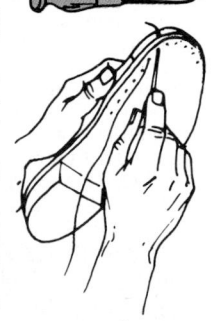

awl

right course; wrong; amiss: *Something went awry in our plans.*

ax (aks) *also,* **axe.** *n., pl.* **ax·es.** a tool consisting of a metal blade attached to a handle, used especially for cutting down trees and chopping wood. —*v.t.* to chop or cut with an ax.

axe (aks) *n., v.t.,* **axed, ax·ing.** another spelling of **ax.**

ax·es[1] (ak′siz) the plural of **ax.**

ax·es[2] (ak′sēz) the plural of **axis.**

ax·i·al (ak′sē əl) *adj.* of, relating to, or forming an axis.

ax·il (ak′səl) *n.* the upper angle formed where a leafstalk or stem joins the stem on which it grows.

ax·i·om (ak′sē əm) *n.* **1.** a statement or principle accepted as true without proof; self-evident or universally accepted truth. For example: *The shortest distance between two points is a straight line.* **2.** an established principle, rule, or law.

ax·i·o·mat·ic (ak′sē ə mat′ik) *adj.* of, relating to, or like an axiom; self-evident: *It is axiomatic that night follows day.* —**ax′i·o·mat′i·cal·ly,** *adv.*

ax·is (ak′sis) *n., pl.* **ax·es** (ak′sēz). **1.** a real or imaginary straight line around which an object or body, such as the earth, rotates or seems to rotate. **2.** a straight, central line around which the parts of a plane or solid figure are symmetrically arranged. **3.** another word for **number line. 4. the Axis.** the World War II alliance between Germany, Italy, and, later, Japan and other nations.

ax·le (ak′səl) *n.* a shaft or bar on which a wheel or wheels turn.

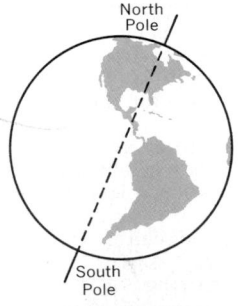

axis *(def. 1)*

ax·le·tree (ak′səl trē′) *n.* a fixed axle connecting a pair of wheels, as on a cart or wagon. Each end of the axletree has a spindle or bearings on which the wheel turns.

ax·o·lotl (ak′sə lot′əl) *n.* any of various salamanders found in Mexico and the western United States that do not usually undergo metamorphosis into an adult form, but keep the characteristics of the larval form throughout life.

ax·on (ak′son) *also,* **ax·one** (ak′sōn). *n.* a long, slender extension of a nerve cell that carries impulses away from the body of the cell. See **neuron** for illustration.

a·ya·tol·lah (ä′yə tō′lə) *n.* among Shiite Muslims, a religious leader of the highest rank. ▲ Used as a title of respect.

aye (ī) *also,* **ay.** *n.* an affirmative vote or voter. —*adv.* yes; yea.

Ay·ma·ra (ī′mä rä′) *n., pl.* **Ay·ma·ra** or **Ay·ma·ras. 1.** a member of a South American Indian tribe living in Bolivia and southern Peru. **2.** the language spoken by this tribe. —**Ay·ma·ran** (ī′mä rän′), *adj.*

Ayr·shire (âr′shər) *n.* one of a breed of hardy, long-horned dairy cattle that originated in Scotland, varying in color from red to dark brown with white blotches.

AZ, postal abbreviation for Arizona.

a·za·lea (ə zāl′yə) *n.* any of a group of shrubs related to the rhododendron, bearing clusters of funnel-shaped flowers.

Az·tec (az′tek) *n., pl.* **Az·tec** or **Az·tecs. 1.** a member of a large group of Indian tribes having a well-developed civilization and controlling an empire in central Mexico at the time of the Spanish conquest in 1519. **2.** another word for **Nahuatl.** —*adj.* of or relating to the Aztecs, their language, or their culture. —**Az′tec·an,** *adj.*

az·ure (azh′ər) *n.* a clear sky-blue color. —*adj.* having the color azure; sky-blue.

Bb

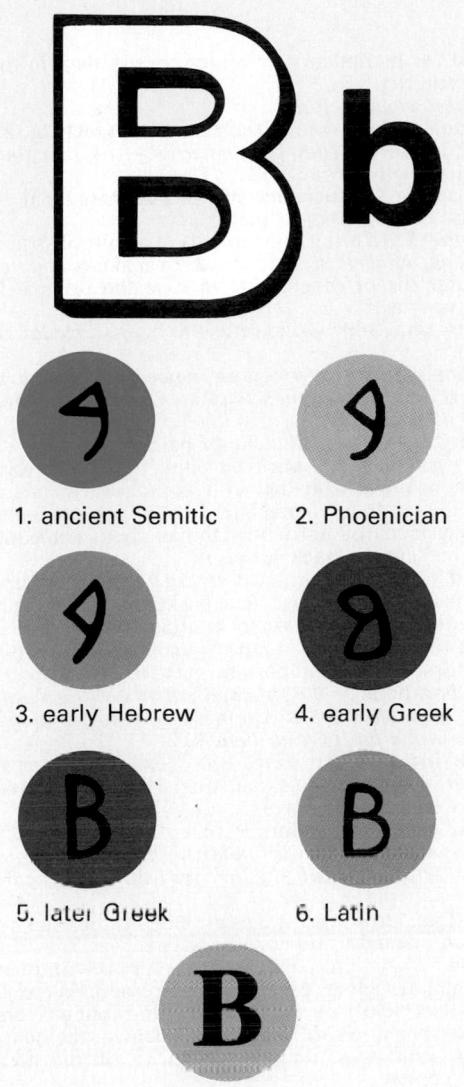

1. ancient Semitic
2. Phoenician
3. early Hebrew
4. early Greek
5. later Greek
6. Latin
7. English

B is the second letter of the English alphabet. The earliest ancestor of our modern letter **B** was a symbol used as the second letter of the ancient Semitic alphabet (1). In the Phoenician (2) and early Hebrew (3) alphabets, this letter was called *beth,* meaning "house." The Greeks borrowed *beth* about 3,000 years ago and called it *beta.* The English word *alphabet* comes from a combination of *alpha* and *beta,* the names of the first two letters of the Greek alphabet. By about 2,800 years ago, the Greeks were writing *beta* (4) very much like a modern capital letter **B** that has been turned around. Several hundred years later, the Greeks reversed *beta* (5), and it was in this form that it was borrowed and used in the Latin alphabet (6). From Roman times until the present (7), there have been almost no changes in the way that the capital letter **B** is written.

b, B (bē) *n., pl.* **b's, B's. 1.** the second letter of the English alphabet. **2.** the second item in a series or group. **3.** *Music.* the seventh note of the scale of C major.

B, the symbol for boron.

b. 1. base. **2.** bass. **3.** book. **4.** born.

B. 1. Bay. **2.** Bible. **3.** British.

Ba, the symbol for barium.

B.A., Bachelor of Arts. Also, **A.B.**

baa (bä) *n.* the sound that is made by a sheep; bleat. —*v.i.,* **baaed, baa·ing.** to make such a sound; bleat.

Ba·al (bā'əl) *n., pl.* **Ba·al·im** (bā'ə lim). **1.** any of various gods of the ancient Semites, especially the Canaanites and Phoenicians. **2.** a false god; idol.

Bab·bitt metal (bab'it) any of various alloys having a lead or tin base and smaller amounts of antimony or copper, used to reduce friction, as in bearings. [From the American inventor Isaac *Babbitt* (1799–1862.]

bab·ble (bab'əl) *v.,* **bab·bled, bab·bling.** —*v.i.* **1.** to make sounds that are unclear or meaningless: *The baby gurgled and babbled.* **2.** to talk foolishly or too much; chatter. **3.** to make a continuous murmuring sound: *The brook babbled.* —*v.t.* **1.** to say in an unclear or meaningless way: *to babble in one's sleep.* **2.** to say or reveal without thinking; blab: *to babble a secret.* —*n.* **1.** unclear or meaningless sounds or talk. **2.** foolish talk; chatter. **3.** a continuous murmuring sound. —**bab'bler,** *n.*

babe (bāb) *n.* **1.** a baby or young child. **2.** a naive, inexperienced, or helpless person.

Ba·bel (bā'bəl, bab'əl) *n.* **1.** in the Old Testament, a tower begun in the city of Babylon by the descendants of Noah in order to reach heaven. God kept them from finishing the tower by changing their language into many different languages so that they could not understand each other. **2.** *also,* **babel.** a confused mixture of many voices or languages.

bab·ka (bäb'kə) *n.* a cake leavened with yeast and containing raisins, often glazed and flavored with rum. [From the Polish word *babka,* from the word *baba* "old woman."]

ba·boon (ba bün') *n.* a large, social African monkey that has a dog-like face, cheek pouches for storing food, front and back legs of almost the same length, and usually a short tail.

ba·bush·ka (ba bùsh'ka) *n.* a kerchief, usually folded in the shape of a triangle, worn over the head and tied under the chin. [From the Russian word *babushka* meaning "little grandmother," "little old woman." Old women in Russia often wore such kerchiefs.]

baboon

ba·by (bā'bē) *n., pl.* **ba·bies. 1.** a newborn or very young child. **2.** the youngest member of a family or group. **3.** a person who behaves like a child; childish person. **4.** a newborn or very young animal. —*adj.* **1.** for a baby: *a baby blanket.* **2.** of or like a baby: *a baby face.* **3.** very young or small: *a baby rabbit.* —*v.t.,* **ba·bied, ba·by·ing.** to treat like a baby; pamper; coddle: *to baby a sick child.*

baby boom, an unusual increase in a population's birth rate, especially in the United States after World War II.

baby boom·er (bü′mər) a person born during a baby boom.

baby carriage, a small, four-wheeled carriage for a baby, usually with a folding top. Also, **baby buggy.**

ba·by·hood (bā′bē hůd′) n. **1.** the state of being a baby. **2.** the time during which a person is a baby.

ba·by·ish (bā′bē ish) adj. like a baby; childish. —**ba·by·ish·ly,** adv. —**ba·by·ish·ness,** n.

Bab·y·lo·ni·an (bab′ə lō′nē ən) adj. of or relating to Babylon or Babylonia. —n. **1.** a person who lived in Babylonia. **2.** the Semitic language of Babylonia.

ba·by's–breath (bā′bēz breth′) n. a plant bearing thick clusters of tiny white or pink flowers.

ba·by–sit (bā′bē sit′) v.i., **ba·by–sat** (bā′bē sat′), **ba·by–sit·ting.** to take care of a young child or children while the parents are away temporarily. —**ba′by–sit′ter,** n.

baby tooth pl. **baby teeth.** in humans, a milk tooth.

bac·ca·lau·re·ate (bak′ə lôr′ē it) n. **1.** another word for **bachelor's degree. 2.** a sermon or address delivered to a graduating class at commencement.

Bac·chus (bak′əs) n. Roman Mythology. the god of wine. In Greek mythology he was called Dionysus.

bach·e·lor (bach′ə lər) n. **1.** a man who has not married. **2.** a person who has earned a bachelor's degree. [From the Old French word bacheler meaning ''young man'' or ''squire,'' from the Medieval Latin word baccalarius ''farmer,'' ''squire,'' and later ''advanced student.'']

Bachelor of Arts, a bachelor's degree in the liberal arts or social sciences.

Bachelor of Science, a bachelor's degree in science or mathematics.

bach·e·lor's–but·ton (bach′ə lərz but′ən) n. **1.** a plant bearing many slender branching stems and showy flowers. **2.** any of several plants with button-shaped flowers.

bachelor's degree, an undergraduate degree given by a college or university to a person who has completed a four-year program or its equivalent. Also, **baccalaureate, bachelor's.**

ba·cil·lus (bə sil′əs) n., pl. **ba·cil·li** (bə sil′ī). **1.** any bacterium shaped like a rod. **2.** any bacterium.

back (bak) n. **1.** the rear part of the human body, from the neck to the end of the spine. **2.** the upper part of the body of an animal corresponding to the human back. **3.** the spinal column; backbone. **4.** the part opposite to or farthest from the front; rear part: the back of a closet, the back of the classroom. **5.** the part or side that is not normally used; reverse: Sign the back of the check. **6.** the part of an object that supports or covers the human back: the back of a chair, the back of a jacket. **7.a.** a player whose regular position is behind that of players in the front line, as in football. **b.** the position occupied by such a player. —v.t. **1.** to support or help (often with up): to back a candidate, to back up an argument with facts. **2.** to cause to move backward (often with up): to back a car into a garage, to back up a truck. **3.** to provide with a backing; strengthen at the back: to back a picture with cardboard. —v.i. to move backward: to back away from a growling dog. —adj. **1.** at or in the back or rear: a back door. **2.** belonging to the past; not current: a back copy of a magazine. **3.** in a backward direction: a back somersault. **4.** distant from a center of population; remote: back settlements, a back road. **5.** overdue: back taxes, back pay. —adv. **1.** at, to, or toward the rear; backward: Please step back so that I may pass. **2.** in, to, or toward a former place or position: Put the box back on the shelf. **3.** in, to, or toward a former condition or state: My cold has come back. **4.** in or into the past: The earthquake happened back in 1906. **5.** in reply or return: to hit someone back. **6.** in check; under control: The dam held back the floodwaters.

·**back and forth.** first in one direction and then in the other; to and fro.

·**back of.** Informal. behind.

·**behind one's back.** without a person's knowledge or approval; in secret: They pretend to like you, but they criticize you behind your back.

·**to back out** or **to back out of.** to withdraw from an agreement, undertaking, or the like.

·**to back up. 1.** to bring (movement) to a halt; obstruct: The accident backed up traffic. **2.** to make a copy of (a computer file or other data) in case the original is damaged or erased.

·**to go back on.** Informal. to refuse to keep (a pledge or promise.)

·**to turn one's back on.** to ignore, neglect, or abandon: My parents never turned their back on me when I needed help.

back·ache (bak′āk′) n. an ache or pain in one's back.

back·bite (bak′bīt′) v. **back·bit** (bak′bit′), **back·bit·ten** (bak′bit′ən), **back·bit·ing.** —v.t. to say mean or unfriendly things about (someone who is not present). —v.i. to say mean or unfriendly things about someone who is not present. —**back′bit′er,** n.

back·board (bak′bôrd′) n. **1.** a board forming or supporting the back of something. **2.** in basketball, the raised, upright board to which the basket is attached.

back·bone (bak′bōn′) n. **1.** the spinal column; spine. **2.** the strongest or most important part: Brave pioneers formed the backbone of the first settlements in the West. **3.** strength of character or firmness of will: It takes backbone to stand up for your beliefs.

back·break·ing (bak′brā′king) adj. calling for great strength or effort; physically exhausting: Moving the piano upstairs was backbreaking work.

back burner. on the back burner. in a state of temporary delay or suspension: Plans to build the library were put on the back burner until the needed money became available.

back·drop (bak′drop′) n. a curtain hung at the back of a stage, often painted to represent a scene.

back·er (bak′ər) n. a person who supports another person or an undertaking, especially by providing money.

back·field (bak′fēld′) n. Football. **1.** the four players whose regular positions are behind the linemen; the quarterback, two halfbacks, and the fullback. **2.** the area behind the linemen.

back·fire (bak′fīr′) n. **1.** an explosion in the cylinder of an internal combustion engine that occurs when fuel is ignited too soon. **2.** a fire built to stop an advancing forest or prairie fire by burning off an area in its path, thus depriving it of fuel. —v.i., **back·fired, back·firing. 1.** to have a backfire: The truck backfired as it switched into gear. **2.** to bring about results that are opposite to those hoped for or expected: Our plan to make money backfired, and we went bankrupt.

back–for·ma·tion (bak′fôr mā′shən) n. **1.** a word formed by removing the end part of an existing, longer word, as greed from greedy, or edit from editor. **2.** the formation of such a word.

back·gam·mon (bak′gam′ən) n. a game for two people played on a special board with dice and fifteen pieces for each player. The throw of the dice determines how the pieces may be moved.

back·ground (bak′ground′) n. **1.** the part of a picture or scene that is, or appears to be, furthest from the viewer's eye: The artist painted a waterfall in the background of the picture. **2.** a surface around or behind objects or designs: The kitchen wallpaper has yellow tulips on a white background. **3.** past events or facts that help to explain some later event or situation: the background of World War II. **4.** a person's past experience and education: You have the right kind of background for the job.

background music, music that accompanies the speech or action in a play, motion picture, or broadcast.

back·hand (bak′hand′) *n.* **1.** a stroke in tennis and similar games, made with the arm drawn across the body and the back of the hand turned outward. **2.** handwriting that slants toward the left. —*adj.* backhanded. —*adv.* with a backhand stroke.

back·hand·ed (bak′han′did) *adj.* **1.** done or made with the back of the hand, or with the back of the hand turned outward: *a backhanded tennis stroke.* **2.** slanting to the left: *backhanded handwriting.* **3.** criticizing while seeming to praise; insincere: *The statement ''You're not as fat as you used to be'' is a backhanded compliment.* —**back′hand′ed·ly,** *adv.* —**back′hand′ed·ness,** *n.*

back·ing (bak′ing) *n.* **1.** approval or assistance; support: *We got the principal's backing for a new gymnasium.* **2.** supporters or backers as a group. **3.** something used to support, form, or strengthen a back: *The picture has a cardboard backing.*

back·lash (bak′lash′) *n., pl.* **back·lash·es. 1.** a sudden, forceful backward motion. **2.** negative reaction, as to some social or political event, development, or movement: *The rise in crime caused a backlash against prison reforms.*

back·log (bak′lôg′, bak′log′) *n.* **1.** a large amount, as of unfinished work or unfilled orders. **2.** a large log at the back of a fireplace to keep the fire going.

back·pack (bak′pak′) *n.* a bag for hiking or camping supplies carried on the back and often supported by a metal frame. —*v.i.* to go hiking or camping using a backpack. —**back′pack′er,** *n.*

back·rest (bak′rest′) *n.* a support for the back.

back·seat (bak′sēt′) *n.* a seat in the back, especially of a vehicle. Also, **back seat.**

·**to take a backseat.** *Informal.* to occupy a less important position: *new employees take a backseat to more experienced workers.*

backseat driver *Informal.* a person who offers unwanted advice, especially a passenger in a car who advises or criticizes the driver.

back·side (bak′sīd′) *n.* **1.** the back or rear part. **2.** the rump; buttocks.

back·slide (bak′slīd′) *v.i.,* **back·slid** (bak′slid′), **back·slid·ing.** to return to bad habits or practices, especially in religious matters. —**back′slid′er,** *n.*

back·spin (bak′spin′) *n.* a backward spin given to a ball to reverse or stop its forward movement.

back·stage (bak′stāj′) *adj.* **1.** relating to, located, or happening in the area of a theater behind the proscenium. **2.** behind the scenes; private; secret: *backstage negotiations for a contract.* —*adv.* in, to, or toward the backstage area of a theater.

back·stop (bak′stop′) *n.* **1.** a fence, screen, or wall used in sports to stop the ball from going too far beyond the playing area. **2.** *Baseball.* the catcher.

back·stroke (bak′strōk′) *n.* a stroke in swimming that is made by lying on the back and moving the arms alternately up and back into the water, while kicking the feet rapidly.

back talk, a reply that is rude or disrespectful.

back·track (bak′trak′) *v.i.* **1.** to return by the same route or path; retrace one's course. **2.** to reverse or retreat from one's position or stand: *You just backtracked on the story you told me yesterday.*

back·up (bak′up′) *n.* **1.** a standby or reserve: *The hospital installed a generator in the basement as a backup in case of power failures.* **2.** a backing up; buildup: *The clog in the pipe caused a backup of drainage water.* **3.** the copying of a file or other set of computer data onto another tape, diskette, or the like, to provide a reserve copy of the information in case the original is lost or damaged. —*adj.* **1.** serving as a standby or reserve: *a backup supply of food.* **2.** of or relating to a backup of data: *a backup file.*

back·ward (bak′wərd) *adv. also,* **back·wards. 1.** toward the back; to the rear: *Swing your arms up and then backward.* **2.** with the back first: *I was walking backward and fell.* **3.** opposite to the usual or right way; in reverse: *to recite the alphabet backward.* **4.** toward or into the past: *Look backward in time and imagine life in 1800.* **5.** toward a worse state or condition: *Under the last administration, the city moved backward.* —*adj.* **1.** directed or turned toward the back or rear: *a backward glance, backward movement.* **2.** behind in growth or development: *a backward area.* **3.** done or performed backward: *a backward dive.* **4.** shy; bashful. —**back′ward·ly,** *adv.* —**back′ward·ness,** *n.* ▲ Both **backward** and **backwards** may be used as adverbs: *The car rolled backward (or backwards) in the parking lot.* Only **backward** may be used as an adjective: *a backward step* (not a *backwards step*).

back·wash (bak′wôsh′, bak′wosh′) *n.* **1.** water moved backward by the force of an object moving through it. **2.** a backward current of air from an airplane propeller. **3.** the aftereffect of an event or condition.

back·wa·ter (bak′wô′tər) *n.* **1.** water turned or held back by an obstruction, tide, or opposing current. **2.** a place or condition thought of as dull or backward.

back·woods (bak′wùdz′) *pl. n.* **1.** heavily wooded areas far from cities or towns. **2.** any remote, thinly settled area, especially one considered culturally backward.

back·woods·man (bak′wùdz′mən) *n., pl.* **back·woods·men** (bak′wùdz′mən). a person who lives in or comes from the backwoods.

back·yard (bak′yärd′) *n.* a yard behind a house or other building.

ba·con (bā′kən) *n.* salted and smoked meat from the back and sides of a hog.

bac·te·ri·a (bak tîr′ē ə) *pl. n., sing.* **bac·te·ri·um.** one-celled organisms that are so small that they can be seen only through a microscope. Bacteria are found in air, soil, and water, and in and on all plants and animals. Some kinds of bacteria cause diseases. Others are useful in cheese-making, brewing, and sewage disposal. [Formed from the Greek word *baktērion* meaning ''little rod,'' ''stick.'' When these microorganisms were first seen under the microscope, they appeared to resemble little rods or bars.]

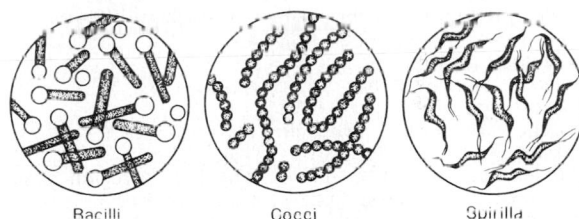

Bacilli   Cocci   Spirilla

three types of **bacteria**
as seen under a microscope

bac·te·ri·al (bak tîr′ē əl) *adj.* of, relating to, or produced by bacteria: *a bacterial stomach infection.*

bac·te·ri·o·log·i·cal (bak tîr′ē ə loj′i kəl) *adj.* of or relating to bacteriology: *a bacteriological study of water samples.* Also, **bac·te·ri·o·log′ic.** —**bac·te·ri·o·log′i·cal·ly,** *adv.*

at; āpe; fär; câre; end; mē; it; īce; pîerce; hot; ōld; sông, fôrk; oil; out; up; ūse; rüle; pùll; tûrn; chin; sing; shop; thin; **th**is; hw in white; zh in treasure. The symbol ə stands for the unstressed vowel sound heard in about, taken, pencil, lemon, and circus.

B

bac·te·ri·ol·o·gist (bak tîr′ē ol′ə jist) *n.* a specialist in bacteriology.

bac·te·ri·ol·o·gy (bak tîr′ē ol′ə jē) *n.* the science that deals with bacteria.

bac·te·ri·um (bak tîr′ē əm) the singular of **bacteria.**

Bac·tri·an camel (bak′trē ən) a two-humped camel of central Asia.

bad (bad) *adj.,* **worse, worst.** **1.** having little quality or worth; below standard; poor: *a bad student, a bad movie.* **2.a.** evil; wicked; immoral: *the bad deeds of infamous criminals.* **b.** naughty; mischievous; disobedient: *We won't tolerate bad behavior.* **3.** severe or violent: *a bad storm, a bad fall, a bad cough.* **4.** having errors; incorrect; faulty: *bad spelling.* **5.** not pleasant; disagreeable: *a bad smell, bad weather.* **6.** having a harmful effect; damaging: *Polluted air is bad for your lungs.* **7.** distressing; unfavorable; unfortunate: *We were sorry to hear the bad news.* **8.** regretful; sorry; distressed: *I felt bad about causing so much trouble.* **9.** in poor health; sick: *to feel bad after overeating.* **10.** rotten or spoiled: *Milk turns bad if it is not kept cool.* **11.** *Slang.* very good, excellent; outstanding: *a real bad blues singer.* —*n.* something that is bad: *The good outweighed the bad in the mayor's record.* —*adv. Informal.* badly. —**bad′ness,** *n.*

·**not bad** or **not half bad.** *Informal.* fairly good; acceptable.

·**to be in bad.** *Informal.* to be in disfavor: *I'm in bad with my parents because I was late for dinner every day last week.*

▲ The adjective **bad,** not the adverb **badly,** has traditionally been used in careful writing and speech with linking verbs such as *look, smell,* and *feel: Those tomatoes smell bad. I felt bad about losing my wallet.* The adverb *badly* is now often used in place of *bad,* especially with the verb *feel.*

bad blood, hatred or hostility: *There has always been bad blood between the two families.*

bade (bad, bād) a past tense of **bid.**

badge (baj) *n.* an emblem or other symbol worn to show rank, membership, or achievement: *a sheriff's badge.*

badg·er (baj′ər) *n.* **1.** any of a group of mammals having a heavy body, short legs, long claws, and a short, thick tail. Badgers live in holes in the ground, which they have burrowed, and they usually feed at night. **2.** the yellowish gray fur of a badger. —*v.t.* to harass or annoy in a persistent way; pester: *The district attorney badgered the witness with questions.*

badger *(def. 1)*

bad·lands (bad′landz′) *pl. n.* any barren region characterized by numerous ridges, mesas, and peaks cut by erosion.

bad·ly (bad′lē) *adv.* **1.** in a bad manner: *The engine of the car runs badly. Our plans turned out badly.* **2.** very much: *I need new shoes badly.* ▲ See usage note under **bad.**

bad·min·ton (bad′min tən) *n.* a game in which players use light rackets to hit a shuttlecock back and forth over a high net. [From *Badminton,* the name of an English duke's estate where the game was introduced.]

bad–mouth (bad′mouth′, bad′mouth′) *v.t., v.i. Informal.* to speak ill of someone; malign; slander.

bad–tem·pered (bad′tem′pərd) *adj.* cross or quarrelsome; irritable.

baf·fle (baf′əl) *v.t.,* **baf·fled, baf·fling.** **1.** to bewilder or puzzle greatly; confuse; perplex: *The magician's escape from a locked box baffled the audience.* **2.** to control or change the progress or flow of. —*n.* a partition or other device for controlling or changing the flow of fluids or sound waves: *a baffle on a loudspeaker.* —**baf′fle·ment,** *n.* —**baf′fler,** *n.*

bag (bag) *n.* **1.** a container made of paper, cloth, plastic, or other flexible material. **2.** the amount that a bag can hold: *I ate a bag of popcorn at the movie.* **3.** something that hangs loosely or is like a bag in shape: *This sweater has bags at the elbows.* **4.** a purse; handbag. **5.** a suitcase or satchel; valise: *Have you packed your bags yet?* **6.** the amount of game killed or captured in hunting. **7.** a base in baseball. **8.** *Slang.* Something that one is interested in or does well: *Tennis is not my bag.* —*v.,* **bagged, bag·ging.** —*v.t.* **1.** to kill or capture (game) in hunting: *The hunter bagged three birds.* **2.** *Informal.* to seize or capture; trap: *The police officer bagged the thief.* **3.** to put into a bag: *The cashier bagged my apples.* —*v.i.* to hang loosely; sag: *My slacks bagged at the knees.* —**bag′like′,** *adj.*

·**holding the bag.** *Informal.* taking full blame or responsibility unwillingly: *After we broke the window, my friends ran away and left me holding the bag.*

bag·a·telle (bag′ə tel′) *n.* something of little value or importance; trifle.

ba·gel (bā′gəl) *n.* a doughnut-shaped roll made of leavened dough, cooked in simmering water and then baked. [From the Yiddish word *beygel* meaning "bagel," going back to the Old High German word *boug* "ring."]

bag·gage (bag′ij) *n.* **1.** suitcases, bags, and other containers used to carry one's belongings when traveling; luggage. **2.** portable equipment and supplies of an army, such as tents, bedding, and cooking utensils.

bag·gy (bag′ē) *adj.,* **bag·gi·er, bag·gi·est.** hanging loosely; bulging: *baggy trousers.* —**bag′gi·ness,** *n.*

bag lady, a homeless woman who roams a city carrying her possessions in a shopping bag or bags.

bag·pipe (bag′pīp′) *also,* **bag·pipes,** *n.* a shrill-toned musical instrument, used especially in Scotland, consisting of a leather bag into which air is blown by the mouth or by a bellows and several pipes that are made to sound when air in the bag is forced through them.

bah (bä) *interj.* an exclamation of contempt or disbelief.

Ba·ha'i (bə hī′, bə hä′ē) *n., pl.* **Ba·ha'is.** **1.** a religion that originated in Iran in the nineteenth century. It stresses that all religions are to be respected, that all peoples share a common bond, and that men and women are equal. **2.** a follower of this religion. —*adj.* of or having to do with this religion.

bagpipe

bail¹ (bāl) *n.* **1.** security, especially money, deposited with a court to obtain the temporary release of a person under arrest and to guarantee that person's appearance for trial at a specified time. **2.** the state of temporary release so obtained. **3.** a person or persons providing bail. —*v.t.* to obtain the temporary release of (a person under arrest) by providing bail (often with *out*). [From the Middle French word *bail* meaning "custody."]

·**to bail out.** to help (a person) in a financial crisis or other emergency: *Whenever they're out of money, they come to me to bail them out.*

·**to go bail** or **to stand bail.** to supply bail.

·**to jump bail.** to run away while free on bail.

bail² (bāl) *n.* the curved handle of a kettle, pail, or similar container. [Probably of Scandinavian origin.]

bail³ (bāl) *v.t.* **1.** to remove (water) from a boat with a pail or similar container. **2.** to clear (a boat) of water with a pail or similar container (often with *out*): *to bail* *out a sinking canoe.* —*v.i.* to bail water: *We bailed desperately for an hour, but the boat sank anyway.* [From the Middle English word *baille* meaning "bucket," from the Middle French word *baille* "bucket."]

·**to bail out.** to parachute from an aircraft, especially in an emergency.

bail·iff (bā′lif) *n.* **1.** a court officer with various duties, such as the maintenance of order in a courtroom during a trial. **2.** an assistant to a sheriff. **3.** in England, a person who manages an estate for the owner; steward.

bail·i·wick (bā′lə wik′) *n.* **1.** the office, jurisdiction, or district of a bailiff. **2.** a field in which a person has special or superior knowledge, interest, or authority: *American history is my bailiwick.*

bails·man (bālz′mən) *n., pl.* **bails·men** (bālz′mən). a person who gives bail or serves as security for another.

bairn (bârn) *n. Scottish.* a son or daughter; child.

bait (bāt) *n.* **1.** food or any other lure used to attract fish or other animals so that they may be caught: *Worms make good bait for many fish.* **2.** anything that tempts or attracts: *Money was the bait that attracted me to the job.* —*v.t.* **1.** to place food or any other lure on or in: *to bait a mousetrap with cheese.* **2.** to torment or annoy, especially with insulting remarks; harass: *Children may bait each other by calling silly names.* **3.** to incite or goad dogs into attacking (an animal) for sport: *In the Middle Ages people used to bait bears.*

baize (bāz) *n.* a thick woolen or cotton fabric made to resemble felt, used especially to cover billiard tables.

bake (bāk) *v.,* **baked, bak·ing.** —*v.t.* **1.** to cook (food) by dry indirect heat, especially in an oven: *to bake a cake.* **2.** to dry or harden by heating: *The potter baked the bowls in a kiln.* —*v.i.* **1.** to cook food by baking: *I like to bake on weekends.* **2.** to become baked: *The potatoes baked slowly.*

baked Alaska, a dessert consisting of a piece of cake covered with ice cream and topped with meringue. It is baked briefly to brown the meringue.

bak·er (bā′kər) *n.* **1.** a person who bakes, especially one whose job is to make and sell bread and other baked goods. **2.** a small portable oven.

baker's dozen, a dozen plus one; thirteen. [From a former custom among *bakers* of adding an extra roll to each *dozen* as protection against the penalties for giving too few.]

bak·er·y (bā′kə rē) *n., pl.* **bak·er·ies.** a place where bread and other baked goods are made or sold.

bak·ing (bā′king) *n.* **1.** the act of baking. **2.** the amount or batch baked at one time.

baking powder, a fine, white powder consisting of baking soda, starch, and an acid-forming substance, used in baking to make dough or batter rise.

baking soda, another term for **sodium bicarbonate.**

ba·kla·va (bä′klə vä′, bä′klə vä′) *n.* a dessert made of many layers of very thin dough, chopped nuts, and honey. [From the Turkish word *baklava* meaning "lozenge."]

bal., balance.

bal·ance (bal′əns) *n.* **1.** a condition of equality between opposing or interacting elements: *to maintain a balance between work and play.* **2.** the ability to keep one's body in a steady, upright position: *I lost my balance and fell off my bike.* **3.** a state of bodily steadiness: *The tightrope walker's balance was off.* **4.** a pleasing or harmonious arrangement of parts: *the balance between light and dark colors in a painting.* **5.** an instrument for weighing, especially an instrument consisting of a horizontal bar having a pan hung from either end, that pivots on a central point as weights are placed in the pans. **6.** the part that is left over; remainder: *I will finish the balance of my homework later.* **7.** something that counterbalances or offsets something else: *A fruit dessert is a good balance for a heavy meal.* **8.** mental or emotional steadiness; sound mental condition: *to maintain one's*

balance in an emergency. **9.** *Bookkeeping.* **a.** an equality between the debit and credit sides of an account. **b.** the difference between the debit and credit sides of an account. **10.** see **balance wheel.** —*v.,* **bal·anced, bal·anc·ing.** —*v.t.* **1.** to put or keep in a steady state, condition, or position: *I balanced a tray of dishes on one hand.* **2.** to compare or estimate the value, weight, or importance of: *The jury balanced the testimony of the two witnesses in deciding the case.* **3.** to make up for; offset: *Do the advantages of the plan balance the disadvantages?* **4.** to place or keep in proportion; equalize: *We can't balance the seesaw because you are heavier than I am.* **5.** to be equal or in proportion to: *The white balances the black in the wallpaper.* **6.** *Bookkeeping.* **a.** to find the difference between the debit and credit sides of (an account). **b.** to make the debit and credit sides of (an account) equal. **c.** to settle (an account) by paying the amount due. —*v.i.* **1.** to be in or come into a steady state, condition, or position: *The acrobat balanced on the wire.* **2.** to be equal: *income and expenses balanced this month.* **3.** *Bookkeeping.* (of an account) to have the debit and credit sides equal to each other: *Our checking account doesn't balance.* [From the Old French word *balance* meaning "a weighing instrument," going back to the Late Latin word *bilanx* meaning "having two scales," from the Latin prefix *bi-* "two" and *lanx* "scale."]

·**in the balance.** uncertain or undecided: *The decision on the new gym hung in the balance after the school board met.*

balance beam 1. a long, narrow wooden beam raised about 4 feet (1.2 meters) from the floor, used to demonstrate balancing feats in gymnastics. **2.** a women's competitive event in which the balance beam is used.

balanced diet, a diet that includes the proper amounts of vitamins, minerals, carbohydrates, fats, and proteins needed for the body to grow or remain healthy.

balance of payments, the difference between the total payments made by one country to all foreign countries and their total payments to that country in any given period.

balance of power, a distribution of military or economic power among nations or groups of nations that is maintained to prevent domination by any one nation or group of nations.

balance of trade, the difference in value between the exports and imports of a nation.

balance wheel, a wheel that regulates the rate of motion, as of the hands of a watch or clock.

bal·brig·gan (bal brig′ən) *n.* a knitted cotton cloth, used especially for hosiery or underwear. [From the Irish town of *Balbriggan,* where it was first made.]

bal·co·ny (bal′kə nē) *n., pl.* **bal·co·nies.** **1.** a platform projecting from the wall of a building and enclosed by a low wall or railing. **2.** a gallery that projects over the main floor in a theater, auditorium, or other place of assembly.

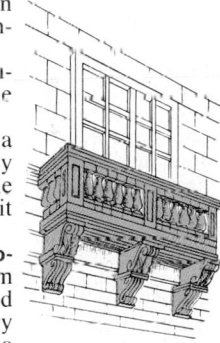

balcony *(def. 1)*

bald (bôld) *adj.* **1.** having little or no hair on the head. **2.** without usual or natural covering: *a bald mountain*

at; āpe; fär; câre; end; mē; it; īce; pîerce; hot; ōld; sông; fôrk; oil; out; up; ūse; rüle; pull; tûrn; chin; sing; shop; thin; **th**is; hw in white; zh in treasure. The symbol ə stands for the unstressed vowel sound heard in about, taken, pencil, lemon, and circus.

peak. **3.** not disguised; simple: *the bald truth.* **4.** (of animals) having white on the face or head: *a bald horse.* —*v.i.* to lose one's hair; become bald: *I am balding rapidly.* —**bald′ness,** *n.*

bald eagle, a large eagle of North America that is brown with a white head, neck, and tail. It is the national symbol of the United States. Also, **American eagle.**

bal·der·dash (bôl′dər dash′) *n., interj.* nonsense; foolishness.

bal·dric (bôl′drik) *n.* a belt, often richly ornamented, worn over one shoulder and across the chest, used to hold a sword or bugle.

bale (bāl) *n.* a large bundle of bulky goods compressed, tightly tied, or otherwise prepared for shipping or storage: *a bale of hay.* —*v.t.,* **baled, bal·ing.** to make into a bale or bales: *to bale cotton.* —**bal′er,** *n.*

ba·leen (bə lēn′) *n.* another word for **whalebone.**

bale·ful (bāl′fəl) *adj.* full of evil or danger; sinister: *a baleful look.* —**bale′ful·ly,** *adv.* —**bale′ful·ness,** *n.*

Ba·li·nese (bä′lə nēz′, bä′lə nēs′, bal′ə nēz′, bal′ə nēs′) *n., pl.* **Ba·li·nese. 1.** a person who was born or is living in Bali. **2.** the language of Bali. —*adj.* of or relating to Bali, its people, their language, or their culture.

balk (bôk) *v.i.* **1.** to stop short and refuse to proceed: *The horse balked when it approached the fence.* **2.** *Baseball.* (of a pitcher) to make an illegal motion, especially to fail to complete a pitching motion when one or more runners are on base. —*v.t.* to keep from going on; hinder: *The rain balked our plans to go camping.* —*n.* **1.** something that hinders or obstructs. **2.** *Baseball.* an act of balking.
  ·**to balk at.** to draw away from; refuse: *I balked at the thought of going to the party alone.*

Bal·kan (bôl′kən) *adj.* of or relating to the Balkan Peninsula, the Balkan Mountains, or the Balkan States, or their inhabitants.

balk·y (bô′kē) *adj.,* **balk·i·er, balk·i·est.** given to balking; stubborn: *a balky horse.*

ball[1] (bôl) *n.* **1.** any round or roundish body; globe: *a ball of string.* **2.** a round or roundish object used in various sports and games, such as baseball, tennis, or golf. **3.** any game played with such an object, especially baseball. **4.** a ball put into motion or play in a specified manner: *a high ball, a curve ball.* **5.** a rounded, protruding part of something: *the ball of the foot.* **6.** *Baseball.* a pitch that fails to pass through the strike zone and that is not swung at by the batter. **7.** a solid, usually round, projectile that is fired from a cannon or other firearm. —*v.t., v.i.* to form into a ball. [From the Old Norse word *böllr* meaning "ball, globe."] —**ball′like′,** *adj.*

ball[2] (bôl) *n.* **1.** a large, formal dance. **2.** *Slang.* a very enjoyable time: *We had a ball at the party.* [From the French word *bal* meaning "dance," going back to the Late Latin word *ballare* "to dance."]

bal·lad (bal′əd) *n.* **1.** a poem that tells a story in simple verse and short stanzas, often intended to be sung to a repeated melody. **2.** the music to such a poem. **3.** a slow popular song with romantic or sentimental lyrics.

ball-and-sock·et joint (bôl′ən sok′it) a joint, as that of the hip or shoulder, formed by a ball or knob in a socket, permitting some rotary movement in nearly every direction.

bal·last (bal′əst) *n.* **1.** a heavy material placed in a ship to steady it or in a balloon to control its altitude. **2.** anything that gives steadiness, especially to a person: *Common sense can serve as a ballast in times of crisis.* **3.** gravel or crushed rock used as a bed for the ties of a railroad. —*v.t.* to fill, provide, or steady with ballast: *to ballast a ship.*

ball bearing **1.** a bearing consisting of a number of metal balls on which the moving parts of a machine turn. **2.** any of these metal balls.

bal·le·ri·na (bal′ə rē′nə) *n.* a female ballet dancer, especially one who is a principal dancer in a ballet company.

bal·let (ba lā′, bal′ā) *n.* **1.** a form of dancing, usually set to music, that combines formal steps and positions in continuous, flowing movement. **2.** a theatrical presentation in which a story or theme is presented by such dancing. **3.** a group or company of dancers who perform in a ballet. **4.** music for a ballet. [From the French word *ballet,* from the Italian word *balletto* meaning "a little dance," from *ballare* "to dance."]

ballet master, a man who trains and rehearses the dancers of a ballet company.

ballet mistress, a woman who trains and rehearses the dancers of a ballet company.

ball·game (bôl′gām′) *n.* **1.** a game played with a ball, such as baseball. **2.** *Informal.* a set of conditions or circumstances; situation: *With the sudden rise in prices, consumers found themselves in a whole new ballgame.*

bal·lis·tic (bə lis′tik) *adj.* of or relating to ballistics or projectiles.

ballistic missile, a self-propelled missile that is controlled as it rises, but is a free-falling object in its descent.

bal·lis·tics (bə lis′tiks) *n.* the science that deals with the motion of projectiles, such as bombs or bullets, and the conditions that affect their motion. ▲ used with a singular verb.

bal·loon (bə lün′) *n.* **1.** a rubber bag, often brightly colored, that is filled with air or gas and used as a toy or decoration. **2.** an airtight bag made of tough, light material, filled with a gas that is lighter than air and designed to rise and float in the atmosphere. A basket or container is often attached to its bottom for carrying scientific instruments or passengers. —*v.i.* to swell out or expand like a balloon: *The parachute ballooned as soon as the jumper pulled the rip cord.*

bal·loon·ist (bə-lü′nist) *n.* a person who operates or rides in balloons as a sport.

balloon *(def. 2)*

bal·lot (bal′ət) *n.* **1.** a sheet of paper or ticket used to cast a secret vote. **2.** the system or act of secret voting by ballots or voting machines. **3.** the list of candidates running in an election: *There were six names on the ballot.* —*v.i.* to cast a ballot or ballots; vote. **4.** the total number of votes cast in an election: *The ballot was recorded after the polls closed.* [From the Italian word *ballotta* meaning "a little ball." Italian citizens placed small balls in a container to register their votes. A white ball indicated approval, and a black ball indicated disapproval.]

ballot box, a box into which ballots are put.

ball·park (bôl′pärk′) *n.* a stadium for playing baseball. —*adj. Informal.* not exact; approximate: *The mechanic gave me a ballpark figure on the cost of repairing my car.*

·**in the ballpark.** *Informal.* within a reasonable or acceptable range: *That price is high, but it's still in the ballpark.*

ball·play·er (bôl′plā′ər) *n.* a person who plays ball, especially one who plays baseball.

ball·point pen (bôl′point′) a pen whose point is a small metal ball that rolls ink from a cartridge onto the writing surface. Also, **ballpoint.**

ball·room (bôl′rüm′, bôl′rùm′) *n.* a large room for dances or other social gatherings.

bal·ly·hoo (*n.,* bal′ē hü′; *v.,* bal′ē hü′, bal′ē hü′) *Informal. n., pl.* **bal·ly·hoos. 1.** exaggerated or sensational advertising or publicity. **2.** an uproar; clamor. —*v.t.,* **bal·ly·hooed, bal·ly·hoo·ing.** to advertise or promote (someone or something) with ballyhoo.

balm (bäm) *n.* **1.** a fragrant oily or gummy resin obtained from certain trees or shrubs, often used as a salve; balsam. **2.** any fragrant ointment or oil that heals or soothes. **3.** anything that heals or soothes: *Sleep was a balm to my troubled mind.*

balm·y (bä′mē) *adj.,* **balm·i·er, balm·i·est. 1.** mild and soothing: *balmy spring weather.* **2.** fragrant. —**balm′·i·ly,** *adv.* —**balm′i·ness,** *n.*

ba·lo·ney (bə lō′nē) *n.* **1.** another spelling of **bologna. 2.** *Slang.* nonsense; foolishness.

bal·sa (bôl′sə) *n.* **1.** a strong, lightweight wood used especially for making airplane or boat models and in rafts and floats. **2.** any of a group of tropical American trees from which this wood is obtained.

bal·sam (bôl′səm) *n.* **1.** any of a group of fragrant, oily or gummy resins obtained from certain trees or shrubs, used in cough drops, candies, and medicine, in products for the hair, and in making a soothing salve. **2.** a tree yielding such resins, as the balsam fir. **3.** a bushy plant that is widely cultivated for its showy flowers.

balsam fir 1. a North American evergreen tree of the pine family. **2.** the wood of this tree, used especially to make boxes, crates, and paper pulp.

Bal·tic (bôl′tik) *adj.* of or relating to the Baltic or the Baltic States.

Bal·ti·more oriole (bôl′tə môr′) a North American songbird closely related to the meadowlark and blackbird. The male has brilliant markings of orange and black. It is now considered to be a subspecies.

bal·us·ter (bal′ə stər) *n.* one of the small posts that support the railing of a staircase, parapet, or similar structure.

bal·us·trade (bal′ə strād′) *n.* a row of balusters and the handrail they support, as on a staircase.

Baluster   Balustrade

bam·bi·no (bam bē′nō) *n., pl.* **bam·bi·nos** or **bam·bi·ni** (bam bē′nē) **1.** a baby or child. **2.** a figure of the baby Jesus. [From the Italian word *bambino* meaning "little baby," from the word *bambo* "baby."]

bam·boo (bam bü′) *n., pl.* **bam·boos. 1.** the hollow, jointed, woody stems of any of a large group of plants of the grass family, used to make furniture, window shades, canes, and fishing poles. **2.** a plant bearing these stems, having slender branches and sword-shaped leaves. Some bamboo plants may reach a height of 120 feet (36.6 meters).

bam·boo·zle (bam bü′zəl) *v.t.,* **bam·boo·zled, bam·boo·zling.** *Informal.* to deceive or cheat by tricking or confusing: *Our neighbors bamboozled us into buying their worthless car.*

ban (ban) *v.t.,* **banned, ban·ning.** to forbid officially; prohibit: *to ban smoking in a theater.* —*n.* **1.** the official or formal forbidding of something: *a ban on the testing of nuclear weapons.* **2.** an official condemnation by church authorities.

ba·nal (bā′nəl, bə nal′) *adj.* dull or boring from having been used or said very often; trite; commonplace: *a speech full of banal comments.* —**ba′nal·ly,** *adv.*

ba·nal·i·ty (bā nal′i tē, bə nal′i tē) *n., pl.* **ba·nal·i·ties. 1.** a banal remark or idea. **2.** the quality of being banal.

ba·nan·a (bə nan′ə) *n.* **1.** a narrow, slightly curved fruit having a sweet, creamy flesh and yellow or red skin. **2.** the treelike plant bearing this fruit, having a high, thick stalk and large, deep green leaves. It is found in nearly all tropical regions of the world.

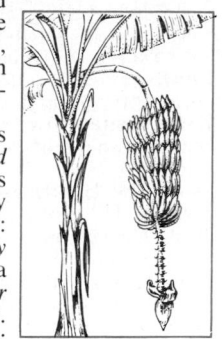

banana plant

band[1] (band) *n.* **1.** a group of persons or animals: *a band of thieves, a band of gorillas.* **2.** a group of musicians organized to play together, especially on wind and percussion instruments: *The marching band plays at every football game.* —*v.i.* to unite in a group: *The citizens banded together to oppose the new highway.* —*v.t.* to unite (persons or things) in a group: *The residents banded themselves together to clean up the block.* [From the Middle French word *bande* meaning "band, group."]

band[2] (band) *n.* **1.** a flat strip of metal, fabric, or other flexible material used for binding or trimming: *There were iron bands around the barrel to strengthen it. I tied a red band around my hat.* **2.** a strip of another color or material; stripe: *bands of white and red around a barber pole.* **3.** a particular range of wavelengths or frequencies in radio broadcasting. —*v.t.* to mark or provide with a band or bands: *The game warden banded the pigeon's leg for identification.* [From the Old French word *bande* meaning "strip," of Germanic origin.]

band·age (ban′dij) *n.* a strip of cloth or other material used in covering or binding a wound or injury. —*v.t.,* **band·aged, band·ag·ing.** to bind or cover with a bandage.

Band–Aid (band′ād′) *n. Trademark.* an adhesive bandage with a gauze pad in the center to cover minor cuts and wounds.

ban·dan·na (ban dan′ə) *also,* **ban·dan·a.** *n.* a large handkerchief, usually brightly colored and patterned: *Rodeo riders often wear bandannas around their necks.*

band·box (band′boks′) *n., pl.* **band·box·es.** a box of cardboard or other light material used for holding hats and other articles of apparel.

ban·deau (ban dō′) *n., pl.* **ban·deaux** (ban dōz′) or **ban·deaus** a narrow band, especially one worn about the hair.

ban·di·coot (ban′di küt′) *n.* **1.** a large rat of India and Sri Lanka that may grow to over a foot in length and often damages gardens and rice fields. **2.** any of a group of small animals native to Australia and neighboring islands that resemble rats and have large ears and a pointed snout. They are marsupials.

bandicoot *(def. 2)*

ban·dit (ban′dit) *n., pl.* **ban·dits** or **ban·dit·ti** (ban dit′ē). a robber or outlaw.

ban·dit·ry (ban′di trē) *n.* the actions of bandits; robbing and plundering.

band·mas·ter (band′mas′tər) *n.* the conductor of a musical band.

ban·do·leer (ban′də lîr′) *also,* **ban·do·lier.** *n.* a broad belt worn over the shoulder and across the chest, with loops or small pockets used for carrying ammunition and other small articles.

band saw, a saw consisting of an endless saw-toothed steel belt running over pulleys.

band shell, a bandstand with a back wall that curves toward the audience to reflect sound.

band·stand (band′stand′) *n.* a platform for a band or orchestra, often having a roof when situated outdoors.

band·wag·on (band′wag′ən) *n.* a decorated wagon that carries a band of musicians in a parade or similar procession.
  •**on the bandwagon** or **aboard the bandwagon.** *Informal.* on the successful or popular side: *The candidate's victory in the primary was so impressive that everyone climbed on the bandwagon.*

ban·dy (ban′dē) *v.t.,* **ban·died, ban·dy·ing.** **1.** to throw or knock back and forth: *to bandy a ball over a net.* **2.** to give and take; exchange: *to bandy insults, to bandy blows.* **3.** to mention or discuss in a casual or careless way (often with *about*): *The mayor's name was bandied about in our discussion of politics.* —*adj.* (of legs) bent or curved outward; bowed.

ban·dy-leg·ged (ban′dē leg′id) *adj.* with the legs bent or curved outward; bowlegged.

bane (bān) *n.* a cause of death, ruin, or injury: *Drought and blight were the bane of the farmers.*

bane·ber·ry (bān′ber′ē, bān′bə rē) *n., pl.* **bane·ber·ries.** **1.** a plant bearing clusters of small white flowers and white or red berries. **2.** the poisonous berry of this plant.

bane·ful (bān′fəl) *adj.* causing death, ruin, or injury: *a baneful influence.* —**bane′ful·ly,** *adv.* —**bane′ful·ness,** *n.*

bang¹ (bang) *n.* **1.** a loud, sudden, or explosive noise: *The door shut with a bang.* **2.** a heavy, noisy blow; thump; whack: *The cupboard door flew open and I got a terrible bang on my head.* **3.** *Informal.* a sudden burst of energy or activity: *The race started off with a bang.* **4.** *Slang.* a feeling of pleasure or excitement; thrill; kick: *to get a bang out of riding on a roller coaster.* —*v.t.* **1.** to strike or hit (something) noisily or violently: *to bang a drum, to bang one's ankle on the leg of a chair.* **2.** to close (something) noisily; slam: *to bang a window shut.* —*v.i.* **1.** to make a loud, sudden, or explosive noise: *The shutters banged in the wind.* **2.** to strike or bump noisily or violently: *I banged into my desk as I looked for the light switch in the dark.* —*adv. Informal.* suddenly and violently: *The baseball player ran bang into the fence while trying to catch the ball.* [Of Scandinavian origin.]
  •**to bang up.** to do damage to (something): *to bang up a car in a crash.*

bang² (bang) *n. usually,* **bangs.** front hair cut short and straight across the forehead. —*v.t.* to cut (front hair) short and straight across the forehead. [Short for *bangtail* meaning "a racehorse with a short tail."]

ban·gle (bang′gəl) *n.* **1.** a circular band worn as an ornament around the wrist, arm, or ankle. **2.** a small ornament that hangs loosely, as on a bracelet.

bang-up (bang′up′) *adj. Slang.* exceptionally good; excellent: *You did a bang-up job of waxing the car.*

ban·ian (ban′yən) another spelling of **banyan.**

ban·ish (ban′ish) *v.t.* **1.** to force by authority to leave a country or place: *The new rulers banished their enemies.* **2.** to force to depart; drive away: *to banish my fears of being lonely.* —**ban′ish·ment,** *n.*

ban·is·ter (ban′ə stər) *n.* **1.** another word for **baluster.** **2.** a handrail and its upright supports along the edge of a staircase; balustrade.

ban·jo (ban′jō) *n., pl.* **ban·jos** or **ban·joes.** a musical instrument with a long neck and a round body, having four or five strings that are strummed or plucked.

bank¹ (bangk) *n.* **1.** a mound, pile, or mass: *a bank of clouds, a bank of dirt.* **2.** the rising ground bordering a body of water. **3.** a steep slope: *The mountain road has a bank to the left around the bend.* **4.** a rise in the sea floor or bed of a river over which the water is shallow. **5.** a tilt to one side made by an airplane in turning. —*v.t.* **1.** to border with a bank; raise a bank around: *They banked the river with sandbags in case of a flood.* **2.** to form into a bank; pile: *The plow banked the snow along the side of the street.* **3.** to cover (a fire) with ashes, earth, or fuel so that it will burn slowly: *The workers banked the fire before closing time at the steel factory.* **4.** to slope so that the outer edge is higher: *The tractors banked the road.* **5.** to tilt (an airplane) when making a turn so that one wing is higher than the other. —*v.i.* **1.** to lie or form in banks: *Fallen leaves banked on the lawn.* **2.** to tilt an airplane when turning: *The pilot banked sharply to the left.* [Of Scandinavian origin.]

bank² (bangk) *n.* **1.** a place of business that safeguards, lends, exchanges, and issues money and carries on a number of other financial dealings. **2.** a small closed container, often with a slot, into which money may be placed for saving. **3.** a reserve supply held ready for use when needed. **4.** a place that stores such a supply. —*v.t.* to deposit in a bank: *I banked twenty dollars this week.* —*v.i.* to do business or have an account with a bank: *We bank downtown.* [Originally from the Italian word *banca* meaning "bench or counter (of a money-changer)," of Germanic origin.]
  •**to bank on.** *Informal.* to depend on; be sure about: *You can bank on our going, so buy us tickets.*

bank³ (bangk) *n.* **1.** a group or set of similar things arranged in a line or row: *a bank of spotlights, a bank of elevators.* **2.a.** a bench for rowers in a galley. **b.** a row or tier of oars. **3.** a row of keys on an organ. —*v.t.* to arrange in a bank. [From the Old French word *banc* meaning "bench," of Germanic origin.]

bank account, money deposited in a bank that is credited to and may be withdrawn by the depositor.

bank·book (bangk′buk′) *n.* a book held by a person, in which the deposits, withdrawals, and balance relating to his or her bank account are shown. Also, **passbook.**

bank·card (bangk′kärd′) *also,* **bank card.** *n.* **1.** a credit card issued by a bank. **2.** a coded card used for identification at an automated teller machine: *to use a bankcard for making deposits or withdrawing cash.*

bank·er (bang′kər) *n.* a person who owns or has an executive position in a bank.

bank·ing (bang′king) *n.* the business carried on by a bank or by a banker.

bank note, a promissory note issued by a bank that can be exchanged for or used as money.

bank·roll (bangk′rōl′) *n.* a supply of money; funds. —*v.t.* to provide money for; finance: *to bankroll a new business.*

bank·rupt (bangk′rupt) *n.* a person who is declared unable to pay his or her debts by a court of law, and whose property is divided among the people to whom the debts are owed. —*adj.* **1.** unable to pay one's debts. **2.** lacking or destitute (often with *in* or *of*): *bankrupt in sound judgment, bankrupt of compassion.* —*v.t.* to make bankrupt: *Heavy debts and bad management bankrupted the company.* [Originally from the old Italian word *bancarotta* meaning "broken bench" or "bankruptcy," going back to the Italian word *banca* "bench" and the Latin word *rumpere* "to break." If a moneylender could no longer carry on business, his bench was "broken up" or removed.]

bank·rupt·cy (bangk′rupt sē, bangk′rəp sē) *n., pl.* **bank·rupt·cies.** **1.** the state of being bankrupt; financial ruin. **2.** total ruin or failure: *The rebels' plan to overthrow the government ended in bankruptcy.*

ban·ner (ban′ər) *n.* **1.** a piece of cloth with some emblem or motto on it. **2.** a flag. **3.** a headline extending across the top of a newspaper page. —*adj.* leading or outstanding: *a banner year for our championship team.*

banns (banz) *pl. n.* a public announcement in church that a man and woman are to be married.

ban·quet (bang′kwit) *n.* **1.** a large, elaborate meal; lavish feast. **2.** a formal or ceremonial dinner, often followed by speeches: *a banquet honoring a crew of astronauts.* —*v.t.* to entertain at a banquet: *The embassy banqueted the visiting ambassador.* —*v.i.* to attend a banquet.

ban·quette (bang ket′) *n.* a long upholstered bench, as along a wall in a restaurant.

ban·shee (ban′shē) *also,* **ban·shie.** *n.* in Irish and Scottish folklore, a female spirit whose appearance or wailing warns the members of a family that one of them will soon die. [From the Scottish Gaelic word *bean-sīth* meaning "the banshee."]

ban·tam (ban′təm) *n.* **1.** *also,* **Bantam.** a small chicken of any of various breeds. Some of the males are known for their fighting ability. **2.** a small person who is cocky or quarrelsome. —*adj.* small. [From *Bantam,* a city in Java from which such chickens were supposedly imported.]

ban·tam·weight (ban′təm wāt′) *n.* an athlete competing in the next-to-lowest weight class in boxing or wrestling or the lowest weight class in weightlifting.

ban·ter (ban′tər) *n.* good-natured, playful teasing or joking: *the banter of teammates after a game.* —*v.i.* to exchange good-natured, playful remarks.

Ban·tu (ban′tü) *n., pl.* **Ban·tu** or **Ban·tus.** **1.** a member of any of numerous Negroid tribes in central and southern Africa. **2.** any of the languages spoken by these tribes. —*adj.* of or relating to the Bantu, their languages, or their culture.

ban·yan (ban′yən) *also,* **ban·ian.** *n.* any of several large trees of Asia, whose branches send down roots that enter the ground and develop into new trunks. One tree will often cover a large area of ground.

banyan

ban·zai (bän′zī′) *interj.* a Japanese battle cry, patriotic cheer, or greeting. [From the Japanese exclamation *banzai!* meaning "May you live ten thousand years!"]

ba·o·bab (bā′ō bab′) *n.* a tree found mostly in tropical Africa, having a broad trunk, thick spreading branches, and a fruit resembling a gourd.

bap·tism (bap′tiz əm) *n.* **1.** a religious ceremony in which a person is sprinkled with or dipped into water as a sign of the cleansing away of sin and of admission to a Christian church. **2.** a new and often difficult experience or trial.

bap·tis·mal (bap tiz′ məl) *adj.* of or relating to baptism.

Bap·tist (bap′tist) *n.* **1.** a member of a Protestant church that baptizes believers by dipping them completely in water. **2. the Baptist.** John the Baptist. —*adj.* of or relating to the Baptists, their doctrines, or their practices.

bap·tis·ter·y (bap′tə strē) *n., pl.* **bap·tis·ter·ies.** a part of a church, or a separate building, in which baptism is performed.

bap·tis·try (bap′tə strē) *n., pl.* **bap·tis·tries.** another spelling of **baptistery.**

bap·tize (bap tīz′, bap′tīz) *v.t.,* **bap·tized, bap·tiz·ing.** **1.** to ceremonially admit (a person) into a Christian church by baptism. **2.** to give a name to; christen: *The twins were baptized Kim and Lee.* —**bap·tiz′er,** *n.*

bar (bär) *n.* **1.** a piece of metal, wood, or other material, longer than it is wide or thick, used as a barrier, fastening, lever, or support: *The prison cell had bars across the window.* **2.** an oblong piece of solid material: *a bar of soap, a bar of gold.* **3.** anything that hinders or blocks progress; obstacle; barrier: *Lack of education can be a bar to business success.* **4.** a bank of sand or other material blocking navigation or the flow of water, as at the mouth of a river. **5.** a stripe or band: *The football jersey had bars of red and gold on it.* **6.a.** a counter where food or drinks, especially alcoholic drinks, are served. **b.** a place containing such a counter. **7.** the railing in a courtroom that encloses the area occupied by judges, attorneys, defendants, and witnesses. **8.** a court of law. **9.a.** the profession of a lawyer: *to be admitted to the bar.* **b.** lawyers as a group. **10.** *Music.* **a.** a vertical line placed on a staff to mark the division between two measures. **b.** a unit of music contained between two such lines; measure. **c.** two parallel vertical lines marking the end of a section or composition. Also, **double bar.** **11.** another spelling of **barre.** —*v.t.,* **barred, bar·ring.** **1.** to fasten with a bar: *Bar the door.* **2.** to hinder or block: *Armed guards barred the way into the building.* **3.** to prevent; prohibit: *Talking was barred in the halls.* **4.** to keep out; exclude: *Those under eighteen were barred from the club.* **5.** to mark or provide with stripes or bands. —*prep.* except; excluding: *This is the best bowling alley in town, bar none.*

bar *(n., def. 10)*

barb (bärb) *n.* **1.** a sharp point that extends out and backward from the main part or tip, as of an arrow: *The barb of the fishhook hooked onto the fish's mouth. My sleeve ripped on the barbs of the wire fence.* **2.** something that hurts, especially an unkind remark. —*v.t.* to furnish with a barb or barbs: *to barb an arrow.*

bar·bar·i·an (bär bâr′ē ən) *n.* **1.** a member of a people whose way of life is considered uncivilized or savage. **2.** a crude, coarse, or brutal person. **3.** a person who lacks understanding or appreciation of literature or the arts. —*adj.* of, relating to, or characteristic of a barbarian: *barbarian customs, barbarian tastes.*

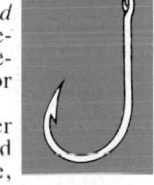

barb

bar·bar·ic (bär bar′ik) *adj.* **1.** of, relating to, or characteristic of barbarians; uncivilized or savage: *barbaric tribes.* **2.** crude or wild in style or manner: *barbaric art.*

bar·ba·rism (bär′bə riz′əm) *n.* **1.** the state of existence of uncivilized or savage people: *Cave dwellers lived in barbarism for centuries.* **2.** an act, custom, or quality characteristic of such a condition: *Beating a child is a barbarism.* **3.** a word or phrase that is not approved or accepted in the usage of a language. *Drownded* is a barbarism for *drowned.*

bar·bar·i·ty (bär bar′i tē) *n., pl.* **bar·bar·i·ties.** **1.** savage or brutal cruelty. **2.** an act of savage or brutal cruelty. **3.** crudeness or coarseness, as in taste, style, or manner.

bar·ba·rize (bär′bə rīz′) *v.t., v.i.,* **bar·ba·rized, bar·ba·riz·ing.** to make or become barbarous: *Brutal treatment and long imprisonment barbarized the captives.*

bar·ba·rous (bär′bər əs) *adj.* **1.** not civilized; savage:

at; āpe; fär; câre; end; mē; it; īce; pîerce; hot; ōld; sông, fôrk; oil; out; up; ūse; rüle; pull; tûrn; chin; sing; shop; thin; this; hw in white; zh in treasure. The symbol ə stands for the unstressed vowel sound heard in about, taken, pencil, lemon, and circus.

In ancient times barbarous tribes inhabited many parts of the world. **2.** brutally harsh or cruel: *barbarous living conditions in the slums of a large city.* **3.** crude; coarse: *barbarous behavior.* **4.** characterized by or using words or phrases not in accepted use. [From the Latin word *barbarus* meaning "strange," "foreign," or "wild," from the Greek word *barbaros* "foreign."]

Bar·ba·ry States (bär′bə rē) Morocco, Algeria, Tunisia, and the region of Tripoli when under Turkish control, used as a refuge by pirates from the sixteenth to the early nineteenth century.

bar·be·cue (bär′bi kū′) also, **bar·be·que.** *n.* **1.** a gathering, usually outdoors, at which meat, chicken, or other foods are roasted over an open fire. **2.** a spit, grill, or pit used for roasting food. **3.** a whole animal or other meat roasted over an open fire, especially with a highly seasoned sauce. —*v.t.,* **bar·be·cued, bar·be·cu·ing.** to cook (meat or other foods) over an open fire or by direct heat, especially with a highly seasoned sauce.

barbed (bärbd) *adj.* **1.** having a barb or barbs: *We used barbed fishhooks to catch the trout.* **2.** sharp or sarcastic; cutting: *barbed remarks.*

barbed wire, a wire or set of twisted wires to which barbs are attached at short intervals, used for fences.

bar·bel (bär′bəl) *n.* **1.** a threadlike growth hanging from the mouth of certain fish, as the catfish, used as a feeler. **2.** any of various freshwater fish having such feelers.

bar·bell (bär′bel′) *n.* a bar to which weights are attached at both ends, used for exercise and in weightlifting.

Barbels

bar·ber (bär′bər) *n.* a person whose business is cutting hair and shaving or trimming beards. —*v.t.* to trim or cut the hair or beard of. —*v.i.* to work as a barber. [From the Anglo-Norman word *barber,* going back to the Latin word *barba* meaning "beard."]

bar·ber·ry (bär′ber′ē, bär′bə rē) *n., pl.* **bar·ber·ries. 1.** any of a group of shrubs usually having small thorns, fragrant yellow to red flowers, and sour red or purple berries. **2.** the berry itself.

bar·ber·shop (bär′bər shop′) *n.* **1.** a barber's place of business. **2.** a type of American vocal music characterized by the performance of traditional or popular songs in close, four-part harmony.

bar·bi·can (bär′bi kən) *n.* a tower or other fortification at a bridge or gate leading into a castle or city.

bar·bi·tu·rate (bär bich′ər it, bär bich′ə rāt′) *n.* any of a group of drugs used chiefly for bringing on sleep and as tranquilizers. Barbiturates are often habit-forming.

bar·ca·role (bär′kə rōl′) *also,* **bar·ca·rolle.** *n.* **1.** a song sung by Venetian gondoliers. **2.** music having the style and rhythm of this song.

bard (bärd) *n.* **1.** in ancient times, a person who composed and sang poems about heroes and heroic deeds. **2.** any poet. **3. the Bard.** William Shakespeare.

bare¹ (bâr) *adj.,* **bar·er, bar·est. 1.** without covering or clothing; naked: *In winter the trees are bare. It's fun to walk in the sand with bare feet.* **2.** without contents, furnishings, or decoration; empty: *The cupboard was bare. There were no pictures to brighten the bare walls.* **3.** without disguise or adornment; plain: *The bare facts are that the money is missing and one of our employees took it.* **4.** just enough; mere: *The poor family could afford only the bare necessities of life.* —*v.t.,* **bared, bar·ing.** to make bare; uncover; expose: *The dog bared its fangs. You can bare your feelings to me.* [From the Old English word *bær* meaning "bare, naked."] —**bare′ness,** *n.*

·**to lay bare.** to open to view; uncover; expose: *The lawyer laid bare the witness's motives at the trial.*

bare² (bâr) *Archaic.* a past tense of **bear¹.**

bare·back (bâr′bak′) *adj.* on the unsaddled back of a horse or other animal: *a bareback rider.* —*adv.* without a saddle: *to ride bareback.*

bare·faced (bâr′fāst′) *adj.* without concealment or embarrassment; shameless; bold: *a barefaced lie.*

bare·foot (bâr′fůt′) *adj., adv.* with the feet bare: *a barefoot child, to walk barefoot on the beach.* Also, **bare·foot·ed** (bâr′fůt′id)

bare·hand·ed (bâr′han′did) *adv., adj.* **1.** with the hands unprotected or uncovered, as by a glove: *to box barehanded, to make a barehanded catch.* **2.** without tools, weapons, or other means; with the hands alone: *to catch a fish barehanded.*

bare·head·ed (bâr′hed′id) *adj., adv.* with the head uncovered.

bare·leg·ged (bâr′leg′id) *adj., adv.* with the legs bare.

bare·ly (bâr′lē) *adv.* **1.** hardly; scarcely: *There was barely enough food to go around.* **2.** in a bare way; poorly: *a barely furnished room.*

bar·gain (bär′gin) *n.* **1.** something bought or offered at a low price; something worth more than the price paid for it: *At only fifty dollars this bicycle is a bargain.* **2.** an agreement on the terms of a business deal or other arrangement: *The twins and I made a bargain that I would wash the dishes if they would dry them.* **3.** the terms of such an agreement: *You did not meet your part of the bargain.* —*v.i.* to discuss or argue over the terms of a bargain: *In some countries, buyers and sellers always bargain before they agree on a price.*

·**in the bargain** or **into the bargain.** in addition; besides: *I broke my leg, and lost a ski in the bargain.*

·**to bargain for** or **to bargain on.** to be prepared for; count on; expect: *Cleaning out the attic was more work than I bargained for.*

·**to strike a bargain.** to reach an agreement: *We discussed the price of the bike and struck a bargain.*

barge (bärj) *n.* **1.** a flat-bottomed boat for carrying freight on rivers, canals, and other inland waterways: *a coal barge.* **2.** a large boat, often highly decorated, used for recreation, pageants, or formal ceremonies. —*v.,* **barged, barg·ing.** —*v.i.* **1.** to move clumsily and abruptly: *to barge out of a room.* **2.** to enter rudely or heedlessly: *to barge into a meeting, to barge in on a conversation.* **3.** to bump or collide: *I apologize for barging into you.* —*v.t.* to transport (freight) by barge.

barge being pushed by a tugboat

bar graph, a graph in which different quantities are represented by rectangles of lengths that are proportional to the quantities.

bar·i·tone (bar′i tōn′) *n.* **1.** a male singing voice with a range that is lower than tenor and higher than bass. **2.** a singer who has such a voice. **3.** a musical instrument that has a similar range. **4.** a musical part for such a voice or instrument. —*adj.* **1.** able to sing or play the baritone: *a baritone voice, a baritone saxophone.* **2.** for the baritone. [From the Italian word *baritone* meaning "a baritone," from the Greek word *barytonos* "deep-toned," from *barys* "heavy, deep" + *tonos* "tone."]

bar·i·um (bar′ē əm) *n.* a soft, silver-white metallic element, used in alloys, vacuum tubes, X-ray examinations, and white pigments. Symbol: **Ba** [Formed from the Greek word *barys* meaning "heavy." The mineral compounds of barium are dense and heavy.]

bark¹ (bärk) *n.* the outer covering of the branches, stems, trunks, and roots of trees and other woody plants. —*v.t.* **1.** to strip the bark off. **2.** to rub the skin off; scrape: *to bark one's shins.* [From the Old Norse word *börkr* with the same meaning.]

bark² (bärk) *n.* **1.** the sharp, abrupt cry made by a dog, seal, and certain other animals. **2.** a cry or sound like this: *The bark of a gun could be heard from deep within the woods.* —*v.i.* **1.** to make this sound: *The dog barked when the robber entered the house.* **2.** to speak loudly and sharply: *The teacher barked at us when we slammed the door.* —*v.t.* to utter in a loud, sharp tone: *The sergeant barked orders at the soldiers.* [From the Old English word *beorcan* meaning "to bark²."]

bark³ (bärk) *also,* **barque.** *n.* **1.** a ship with three or more masts, all square-rigged except for an after mast, which is fore-and-aft-rigged. **2.** *Archaic.* a sailing ship, especially a small one. [From the Middle French word *barque* meaning this sort of ship, going back to the Late Latin word *barca* "a small sailing ship."]

bar·keep·er (bär′kē′pər) *n.* **1.** a person who owns or manages a bar where alcoholic drinks are served. **2.** a bartender. *Also,* **bar·keep** (bär′kēp′).

bar·ken·tine (bär′kən tēn′) *also,* **bar·quen·tine.** *n.* a ship with three or more masts, the foremast square-rigged and the other masts fore-and-aft-rigged.

bark·er (bär′kər) *n.* **1.** an animal or person that makes a barking sound. **2.** a person who stands outside a show, as at a carnival, and urges customers to go in by lively, loud talking.

bar·ley (bär′lē) *n.* **1.** the grain of a hollow-stemmed plant of the grass family. It is used mainly as animal feed, but is often made into malt and used for flavoring cereals and beverages, such as beer. **2.** the plant bearing this grain, having short, spear-shaped leaves.

bar·ley·corn (bär′lē kôrn′) *n.* a grain of barley.

bar magnet, a magnet shaped like a bar.

bar·maid (bär′mād′) *n.* a woman who serves customers in a bar; bartender.

bar·man (bär′mən) *n., pl.* **bar·men** (bär′mən). a man who serves customers in a bar; bartender.

bar mitz·vah (bär mits′və) **1.** a ceremony held for a Jewish boy when he becomes thirteen, marking his assumption of religious responsibilities. **2.** a boy for whom this ceremony is held. [From the Hebrew phrase *bar mitzvāh* meaning "son of the commandment," from the words *bar* "son" + *mitzvāh* "law, commandment."]

barn (bärn) *n.* a building for storing hay, grain, and other farm produce, and for housing farming equipment and cows and other livestock.

bar·na·cle (bär′nə kəl) *n.* any of various small marine shellfish that attach themselves to underwater objects, such as ship bottoms, rocks, and wharves.

barn dance, a party, usually held in a barn, at which square dances or other folk dances are done.

barn·storm (bärn′stôrm′) *v.i.* **1.** to tour rural or outlying areas, making brief

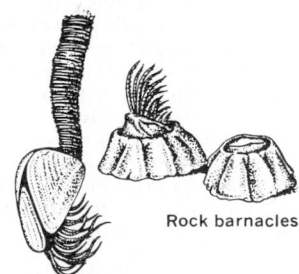

Rock barnacles

Goose barnacle

stops, as to give campaign speeches or lectures or to present plays: *The presidential candidate barnstormed through five states.* **2.** to tour rural or outlying areas as a pilot, taking people on short airplane rides or giving exhibitions of stunt flying. —*v.t.* to tour (an area) in such a manner: *to barnstorm the Southwest.* —**barn′storm′er,** *n.*

barn swallow, a swallow that has a long, forked tail and usually builds mud nests in chimneys or on the rafters inside barns.

barn·yard (bärn′yärd′) *n.* a yard next to a barn, often fenced in to hold poultry or livestock.

bar·o·gram (bar′ə gram′) *n.* a record traced by a barograph.

bar·o·graph (bar′ə graf′) *n.* an aneroid barometer that automatically records its readings.

ba·rom·e·ter (bə rom′i tər) *n.* **1.** an instrument for measuring atmospheric pressure, used in weather forecasting and to determine height above sea level. **2.** anything that indicates changes: *The stock market is a barometer of business activity.* [Formed from the Greek word *baros* meaning "weight" + the English combining form *-meter* meaning "measuring device."]

bar·o·met·ric (bar′ə met′rik) *adj.* of or indicated by a barometer. *Also,* **bar·o·met·ri·cal** (bar′ə met′ri kəl). —**bar′o·met′ri·cal·ly,** *adv.*

barometric pressure, another term for **atmospheric pressure.**

bar·on (bar′ən) *n.* **1.** a British nobleman of the lowest rank. **2.** a nobleman of certain European countries or of Japan, having a similar rank. **3.** in the Middle Ages, a lord who held lands as a vassal of a king or other high-ranking nobleman. **4.** a person who has great power or influence, especially in business or industry: *an oil baron.*

bar·on·ess (bar′ə nis) *n., pl.* **bar·on·ess·es. 1.** the wife or widow of a baron. **2.** a noblewoman holding the rank of baron in her own right.

bar·on·et (bar′ə nit) *n.* in Great Britain, a person holding a hereditary title of honor and ranking lower than a baron but higher than a knight.

ba·ro·ni·al (bə rō′nē əl) *adj.* **1.** of or relating to a baron or a barony. **2.** suiting a baron; stately; magnificent: *a baronial mansion, baronial splendor.*

bar·o·ny (bar′ə nē) *n., pl.* **bar·o·nies. 1.** the land held by a baron. **2.** the rank or title of a baron.

ba·roque (bə rōk′) *adj.* **1.** characteristic of or resembling a very ornate style of art and architecture that is marked by the use of curved rather than straight lines. **2.** characteristic of or resembling a very ornate style of music that is marked by strong, complex rhythms. **3.** showy or ornate in an extreme or grotesque way. **4.** (of pearls) irregular in shape. —*n.* the baroque style, or the period when such a style was popular. [From the French word *baroque,* from the Italian word *barocco* meaning "baroque," probably going back to the Provençal word *barroca* "irregular, mountainous terrain."]

ba·rouche (bə rüsh′) *n.* a large four-wheeled carriage with a driver's seat, a folding top, and two double seats facing each other.

barque (bärk) another spelling of **bark³.**

B

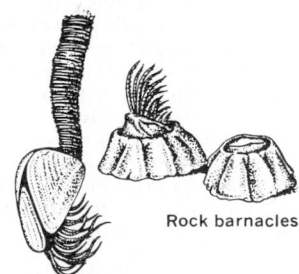
barometer
(def. 1)

at; āpe; fär; câre; end; mē; it; īce; pîerce; hot; ōld; sông, fôrk; oil; out; up; ūse; rüle; pull; tûrn; chin; sing; shop; thin; <u>th</u>is; hw in white; zh in treasure. The symbol ə stands for the unstressed vowel sound heard in about, taken, pencil, lemon, and circus.

79

bar·quen·tine (bär′kən tēn′) another spelling of **barken-tine**.

bar·racks (bar′əks) *pl. n.* **1.** a building or set of buildings for housing soldiers or other military personnel. **2.** any plain structure that provides temporary housing, as for workers.

bar·ra·cu·da (bar′ə kü′də) *n., pl.* **bar·ra·cu·da** or **bar·ra·cu·das.** any of a group of ferocious fish found in warm seas throughout the world, having a long and narrow body, a large mouth, and sharp teeth. Barracuda have been known to attack swimmers.

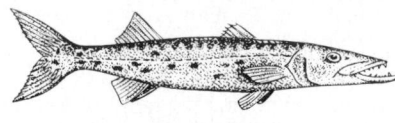

barracuda

bar·rage (bə räzh′) *n.* **1.** a heavy amount of artillery fire to check the advance of enemy troops or to protect one's own troops. **2.** any large or overwhelming amount: *The reporters met the president with a barrage of questions.* —*v.t.,* **bar·raged, bar·rag·ing.** to attack or confront with a barrage: *The movie star was barraged with requests for autographs.*

barre (bär) *n.* a round, horizontal bar in a ballet class-room, used by ballet dancers for support during exercises.

bar·rel (bar′əl) *n.* **1.** a large wooden container shaped like a cylinder, having bulging sides and round, flat ends. Barrels are usually made up of boards bound together by metal hoops. **2.** any container resembling this: *a trash barrel.* **3.** the amount that a barrel can hold: *The family packed four barrels of dishes when they moved.* **4.** any of various measures of weight or quantity. The standard U.S. barrel for liquids holds 31½ gallons (119.2 liters). **5.** the tube-shaped part of a gun through which the bullet or shell is shot. **6.** any part shaped like a cylinder or tube: *the barrel of a fountain pen.* **7.** *Informal.* a large quantity: *a barrel of fun, a barrel of money.* —*v.,* **bar·reled, bar·rel·ing;** also, British, **bar·relled, bar·rel·ling.** —*v.t.* to put or pack in barrels. —*v.i. Informal.* to move rapidly: *A car barreled past us.*

barrel organ, another term for **hand organ.**

bar·ren (bar′ən) *adj.* **1.** having little or no plant life; not productive: *barren soil.* **2.** not able to produce offspring: *a barren animal, a barren fruit tree.* **3.** not leading to any results or gain: *The barren talks with the union failed to prevent a strike.* **4.** without interest, charm, or hopefulness; empty; dreary: *Life must seem barren for people with no friends or family.* —*n.* also, **barrens.** an area of barren land. —**bar′ren·ness,** *n.*

bar·rette (bə ret′) *n.* a clasp or clip, often in the shape of a bar, for holding the hair in place.

bar·ri·cade (bar′i kād′) *n.* **1.** a hastily made barrier for defense: *The rebels built barricades against the approaching army.* **2.** any barrier that blocks passage: *The police barricades kept the crowds back.* —*v.t.,* **bar·ri·cad·ed, bar·ri·cad·ing.** **1.** to block; obstruct: *Fallen trees barricaded the road.* **2.** to prevent access to with or as if with a barricade: *The guerrillas barricaded themselves in an old warehouse.*

bar·ri·er (bar′ē ər) *n.* **1.** something that blocks the way; an obstruction, as a fence or wall. **2.** something that hinders, divides, or keeps apart: *Language differences can be a barrier between people.*

barrier reef, a long coral reef that is parallel to a shoreline and separated from it by a lagoon.

bar·ring (bär′ing) *prep.* with the exception of; except for: *Barring delays, we will arrive on Wednesday.*

bar·ri·o (bär′ē ō, bar′ē ō) *n., pl.* **bar·ri·os.** in the United States, a neighborhood or section of a city inhabited mainly by Spanish-speaking people. [From the Spanish word *barrio,* from the Arabic word *barrī* meaning "open country."]

bar·ris·ter (bar′ə stər) *n.* in Great Britain, a lawyer who argues cases in court.

bar·room (bär′rüm′, bär′rum′) *n.* a room or place having a bar where alcoholic drinks are sold.

bar·row¹ (bar′ō) *n.* **1.** see **wheelbarrow. 2.** see **handbarrow.** [From the Old English word *bearwe* meaning "wheelbarrow."]

bar·row² (bar′ō) *n.* a mound of earth or stones marking an ancient grave. [From the Old English word *beorg* with the same meaning.]

bar sinister, a diagonal stripe on a coat of arms, supposed to indicate illegitimate birth.

Bart., Baronet.

bar·tend·er (bär′ten′dər) *n.* a person who makes and serves alcoholic drinks at a bar.

bar·ter (bär′tər) *v.t.* to trade (goods) for other goods without using money: *The early settlers bartered seed for animal skins with the Indians.* —*v.i.* to barter goods. —*n.* **1.** the act or practice of bartering: *Among these tribes trade is carried on by barter.* **2.** something bartered.

Bart·lett pear (bärt′lit) a large, yellow, juicy pear. [From Enoch *Bartlett,* a merchant who popularized it in the United States.]

ba·sal (bā′səl, bā′zəl) *adj.* **1.** of or at the base; forming the base. **2.** fundamental; basic.

basal metabolism, the amount of energy used up by an animal or plant when it is completely at rest. Basal metabolism is measured by the amount of heat given off in a given time.

ba·salt (bə sôlt′) *n.* a dark, usually fine-grained volcanic rock.

bas·cule bridge (bas′kül) a drawbridge hinged at the bank so that it may be raised to allow ships to pass under it.

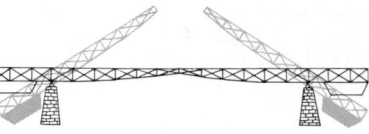

bascule bridge

base¹ (bās) *n., pl.* **bas·es.** **1.** the part on which a thing rests or stands: *The base of the statue was a marble block.* **2.** the underlying part that supports something; foundation: *That political party has a broad base among the working people.* **3.** the lowest part; bottom: *the base of a mountain.* **4.** the chief or essential part of a thing; main element: *This paint has an oil base.* **5.** a military area and facilities where supplies are kept or from which operations are started: *an air force base, a missile base.* **6.** any center or starting point of activity: *the base of a mountain-climbing expedition.* **7.** a station, goal, or safety area in certain games. **8.** any of the four corners of a baseball diamond. **9.** *Chemistry.* a compound that reacts with an acid to form a salt. A base has a bitter taste in a water solution and turns red litmus paper blue. **10.** *Mathematics.* **a.** the number in a numerical system that marks the point in counting when a new digit is added at the left and counting begins again. Simple arithmetic is usually done in the decimal system, whose base is 10. According to this system, the numeral 40 represents 4 times the base of 10. Computers use the binary system, whose base is 2. According to this system, the numeral 10 represents 1 times the base of 2. **b.** a line or plane in a geometrical figure on which it is thought to rest: *the base of a triangle.* **c.** in a trapezoid, either of the two parallel sides. **11.** a word or part of a word to which other parts may be added; stem; root. —*v.t.,* **based, bas·ing.** **1.** to place on a basis or foundation: *to base a house on concrete, to base an opinion on facts, to base a movie on a novel.* **2.** to locate; station: *These troops have been based in Europe for two years.* [From the Old French word *base,* from the Latin word *basis* meaning "foundation, base," from the Greek word *basis* "pedestal, base."]

B

·off base. *Informal.* not accurate; mistaken: *Your guess was really off base.*

base² (bās) *adj.*, **bas·er, bas·est.** **1.** having or showing a lack of decency or bravery; morally low; dishonorable: *Betraying one's country is a base act.* **2.** menial; degrading: *base labor.* **3.** low in value in comparison to something else: *Iron is a base metal.* [From the Middle French word *base,* from the Medieval Latin word *bassus* meaning ''low, short.'']

base·ball (bās′bôl′) *n.* **1.** a game played with a ball and bat between two teams of nine players each, on a field having four bases that form a diamond. A player of the team at bat tries to reach all four bases to score a run. The team in the field tries to put the player out. Each team is allowed three outs per inning, and a game consists of nine innings. **2.** the hard ball used in this game.

base·board (bās′bôrd′) *n.* a strip of board, molding, or similar material at the bottom of a wall, for covering the line where the wall meets the floor.

base·born (bās′bôrn′) *adj.* **1.** of humble birth or origin. **2.** born out of wedlock; illegitimate.

base hit, the hitting of a pitched baseball in a way that allows the batter to get on base without benefit of an opponent's error and without forcing out a runner already on base.

base·less (bās′lis) *adj.* having no basis in fact: *The story was just a baseless rumor.*

base·line (bās′līn′) *n.* **1.** a line serving as a base. **2.** *Baseball.* an area within which a base runner must stay while running from one base to another. **3.** a line marking the back ends of the playing area in tennis.

base·man (bās′mən) *n., pl.* **base·men** (bās′mən), a baseball player stationed near first, second, or third base. ▲ used only in the compounds *first baseman, second baseman,* and *third baseman.*

base·ment (bās′mənt) *n.* the lowest story of a building, below or partly below the ground.

ba·sen·ji (bə sen′jē) *n.* a short-haired dog of a breed that originated in central Africa, usually having a reddish-brown or black coat with white markings. It does not bark, but makes a sound similar to a chuckle or a whine.

base runner, a member of a baseball team at bat who is on base or trying to reach a base.

bas·es¹ (bā′siz) the plural of **base¹.**

ba·ses² (bā′sēz) the plural of **ba·sis.**

bash (bash) *v.t. Informal.* to strike with a smashing blow (often with *in*): *The force from the collision bashed in the side of the car.* —*n., pl.* **bash·es** **1.** *Informal.* such a blow. **2.** *Slang.* an exciting, lively party.

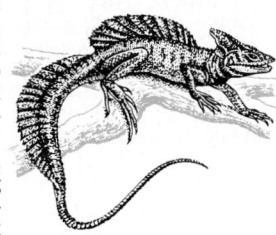

basenji

bash·ful (bash′fəl) *adj.* uncomfortable in the presence of strangers; shy, timid. —**bash′ful·ly,** *adv.* —**bash′ful·ness,** *n.*

ba·sic (bā′sik) *adj.* **1.** of, at, or forming the base; fundamental: *Food is a basic human need. The basic difference between your bicycle and mine is that mine has gears.* **2.** *Chemistry.* **a.** of or containing a base. **b.** alkaline. —*n. usually,* **basics.** something that is basic: *to learn the basics of cooking.*

BASIC (bā′sik) *n.* a programming language that uses simple English words to represent computer commands designed especially for beginners. [Short for *B(eginner's) A(ll-purpose) S(ymbolic) I(nstruction) C(ode).*]

ba·si·cal·ly (bā′si kə lē, bā′si klē) *adv.* in a basic way; essentially; fundamentally: *Human beings are basically dependent on one another.*

basic training, the initial period of military training for

a person who has been inducted into the armed forces.

bas·il (baz′əl, bā′zəl) *n.* **1.** a sweet-smelling plant of the mint family whose leaves are used for seasoning food. **2.** the leaves themselves.

ba·sil·i·ca (bə sil′i kə) *n.* **1.** a public building in ancient Rome, usually a rectangular hall with rows of columns on either side and a broad central aisle ending in a semicircular area. Basilicas were used chiefly as courtrooms and for public meeting places. **2.** an early Christian church built on the model of the Roman building.

bas·i·lisk (bas′ə lisk′) *n.* **1.** a mythical monster resembling a lizard, whose breath and gaze were said to be deadly. **2.** a tropical American lizard related to the iguana, able to run very quickly on its hind legs and dash across the surface of water.

basilisk *(def. 2)*

ba·sin (bā′sin) *n.* **1.** a shallow, round container with sloping sides, used especially for holding liquids. **2.** the amount that such a container will hold. **3.** a bowl or sink for washing, as in a bathroom. **4.** the entire region drained by a river and its tributaries: *the Nile basin.* **5.** an enclosed place containing water: *The harbor has a boat basin.*

ba·sis (bā′sis) *n., pl.* **ba·ses** (bā′sēz). **1.** a fundamental part on which a thing rests or depends; foundation; support: *the basis for a belief.* **2.** the main part or chief ingredient: *the basis of a sauce.*

bask (bask) *v.i.* **1.** to lie in or expose oneself to pleasant warmth: *The cat basked in the sun.* **2.** to take pleasure: *to bask in someone's praise.*

bas·ket (bas′kit) *n.* **1.** a container made by weaving together twigs, rushes, straw, cane, strips of wood, or the like, and usually having a handle or handles: *a clothes basket.* **2.** something resembling a basket in shape or use: *a wire basket on the handlebars of a bicycle.* **3.** the amount that a basket will hold: *a basket of pears.* **4.** *Basketball.* **a.** a metal hoop having a circular net open at the bottom, through which the ball is thrown to score. **b.** a score made by tossing the ball through the basket.

basket *(def. 1)*

bas·ket·ball (bas′kit bôl′) *n.* **1.** a game played with a large, round, air-filled ball on a rectangular court between two teams of five players each. To score, a player must toss the ball through a raised basket at the opponent's end of the court. **2.** the ball used in this game.

bas·ket·ry (bas′ki trē) *n.* **1.** the art of weaving baskets. **2.** baskets as a group.

basket weave, a weave in cloth made by alternately lacing two or more weft yarns over and under the same number of warp yarns.

at; āpe; fär; câre; end; mē; it; īce; pîerce; hot; ōld; sông, fôrk; oil; out; up; ūse; rüle; pùll; tûrn; chin; sing; shop; thin; this; hw in white; zh in treasure. The symbol ə stands for the unstressed vowel sound heard in about, taken, pencil, lemon, and circus.

bas·mitz·vah (bäs mits′və) see **bat mitzvah**.

Basque (bask) n.   1. a member of a people living in the Pyrenees in southwestern France and northern Spain. 2. the language of the Basque people, apparently having no relation to any other known language. —adj. of or relating to the Basques, their language, or their culture.

bas-re·lief (bä′ri lēf′, bä′ri lēf′) n. a carving or sculpture on a flat surface, such as a wall or door, in which the figures stand out only slightly from the background. Also, **low relief**.

bass[1] (bās) n., pl. **bass·es**.   1. a male singing voice with the lowest range, below baritone.   2. a singer who has such a voice.   3. a musical instrument that has a similar range.   4. a musical part for such a voice or instrument. —adj.   1. able to sing or play the bass: a bass voice, a bass clarinet.   2. for the bass. [A form of base[2], influenced in spelling by the Italian word basso meaning "low."]

bass[2] (bas) n., pl. **bass** or **bass·es**. any of various freshwater or saltwater food and game fish of North America. [From earlier barse meaning this fish, from the Old English word bærs "perch."]

bass[3] (bas) n.   1. basswood.   2. bast. [A form of bast.]

bass clef (bās) a clef placed on the fourth line of a musical staff, indicating that this line corresponds to the note F below middle C. Also, **F clef**. See **clef** for illustration.

bass drum (bās) the largest type of drum. It gives off a deep, booming sound and is usually held so that both sides can be struck.

bas·set (bas′it) n. a short-legged dog with a long body, drooping ears, and usually a black, tan, and white coat. Also, **basset hound**.

bass horn (bās) another term for **tuba**.

bas·si·net (bas′ə net′) n. a basketlike bed for a baby, often with a hood at one end.

bas·so (bas′ō, bä′sō) n., pl. **bas·sos**. a bass singer, especially one who sings in operas.

bas·soon (bə sün′) n. a wind instrument with a low range. It consists of a long, doubled wooden tube and a curved metal mouthpiece which contains a double reed.

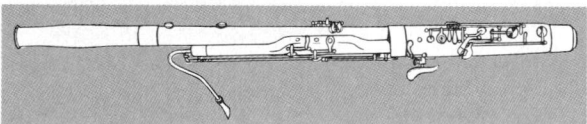

bassoon

bass vi·ol (bās′vī′əl) another term for **double bass**.

bass·wood (bas′wùd′) n.   1. a linden tree that grows in North America.   2. its soft, light wood, widely used in cabinetmaking.

bast (bast) n.   1. the strong, flexible fibers obtained from the inner bark of certain trees and from the stems or leaves of certain plants, used especially in making cloth, rope, and heavy paper.   2. another word for **phloem**.

bas·tard (bas′tərd) n. a child born to parents who are not married to each other.

baste[1] (bāst) v.t., **bast·ed, bast·ing**. to apply melted butter, gravy, fat, or other liquid to (food) while cooking: to baste a turkey with a large spoon. [Of uncertain origin.]

baste[2] (bāst) v.t., **bast·ed, bast·ing**. to sew with long, loose stitches that are usually pulled out after the final sewing: to baste a hem. [From the Middle French word bastir meaning "to sew loosely," of Germanic origin.]

baste[3] (bāst) v.t., **bast·ed, bast·ing**. to beat soundly; thrash. [From the Old Norse word beysta meaning "to beat."]

Bas·tille (bas tēl′) n. a fortress in Paris used as a prison before the French Revolution. Its destruction on July 14, 1789, was one of the opening acts of the revolution. The anniversary of this date, **Bastille Day**, is celebrated as a national holiday in France.

bas·ti·na·do (bas′tə nā′dō) n., pl. **bas·ti·na·does**. 1. a blow or beating with a stick, especially on the soles of the feet.   2. a stick; cudgel.

bast·ing[1] (bā′sting) n.   1. the application of melted fat, butter, or other liquid over food being cooked.   2. the liquid used in basting food. [From baste[1].]

bast·ing[2] (bā′sting) n.   1. the act of sewing with long, loose, temporary stitches.   2. the thread used to make such stitches.   3. **bastings**. the stitches made in basting. [From baste[2].]

bas·tion (bas′chən) n.   1. a part of a rampart or fortification projecting from the main part, that allows the defenders a wider firing range.   2. any fortified or firmly established place or position; stronghold: That country is a bastion of freedom.

bat[1] (bat) n.   1. a wooden stick or club, especially one used for hitting the ball in baseball and other games.   2. the right or turn to bat.   3. a hard blow.   4. Slang. a spree; binge. —v., **bat·ted, bat·ting**. —v.i.   1. to use a bat in baseball and other games.   2. to take a turn at bat: Our team bats next. —v.t.   1. to hit with or as if with a bat: to bat a ball, to bat a fly.   2. to have a batting average of (a certain figure): to bat .319 for the season. [From the Old English word batt meaning "a club, stick."]

   •**at bat**. in the act or position of batting.

   •**right off the bat**. Informal. at once; immediately: I knew the answer right off the bat.

   •**to go to bat for**. Informal. to defend; support: My best friend went to bat for me when I was in trouble.

bat[2] (bat) n. a small animal with a furry body like that of a mouse and wings of thin skin stretched over a framework of elongated bones. Bats are active at night and are the only mammals that can fly. Many species use a kind of natural radar by which the echo of their cries indicates the size and position of an object. [From the Middle English word bakke meaning this animal, probably of Scandinavian origin.]

bat²

bat[3] (bat) v.t., **bat·ted, bat·ting**. to flutter; wink: to bat one's eyelashes. [From the earlier bate meaning "to flap" or "to beat the wings," from the Old French word batre "to beat," from the Latin word battuere "to beat."]

   •**not bat an eye** or **not bat an eyelash**. to fail to show any emotion or surprise.

batch (bach) n., pl. **batch·es**.   1. a number of persons or things taken together; group: a batch of papers to be graded.   ,2. a quantity of material prepared at one time or needed for one operation: a batch of dough, a batch of cement.   3. an amount baked at one time: a batch of apple dumplings.   4. computers. a group of operations processed as a unit by a computer.

bate (bāt) v.t., v.i., **bat·ed, bat·ing**. Archaic. to diminish or lessen; abate.

   •**with bated breath**. with breath checked or held because of wonder, fear, or excitement: The crowd waited for the astronauts' landing with bated breath.

ba·teau (ba tō′) n., pl. **ba·teaux** (ba tōz′). any of various lightweight, flat-bottomed boats used chiefly in the United States and Canada.

bath (bath) n., pl. **baths** (bathz, baths).   1. a washing or dipping of something, especially the body, in water or other liquid: I gave the dog a bath.   2. the water or other liquid used for bathing: The bath was too hot.   3. a container for such liquid, as a bathtub: Clean out the bath when you're done.   4. a room equipped for bathing; bathroom.   5. also, **baths**. a set of rooms or a building

used for bathing: *the public baths of the ancient Romans.*
6. a solution or other preparation in which something is washed or dipped for chemical treatment: *an acid bath.*

bathe (bāth) *v.*, **bathed, bath·ing.** —*v.i.* **1.** to take a bath. **2.** to go into a body of water to swim or to cool oneself; go swimming: *to bathe in the ocean.* —*v.t.* **1.** to give a bath to: *to bathe a baby.* **2.** to wash or moisten with water or other liquid to cleanse, soothe, or heal: *to bathe the eyes, to bathe a wound.* **3.** to make wet; moisten: *Sweat bathed my forehead.* **4.** to cover or envelop as if with liquid: *The room was bathed in light.* —**bath′er**, *n.*

bath·house (bath′hous′) *n.*, *pl.* **bath·hous·es** (bath′-hou′ziz). **1.** a building equipped for bathing. **2.** a building having dressing rooms for swimmers.

bathing suit, a garment worn while swimming.

bath mat **1.** a mat or rug used to stand on when getting in or out of a bathtub or shower. **2.** a mat, especially of rubber, placed on the bottom of a bathtub to prevent a person from slipping.

ba·thos (bā′thos, bā′thōs) *n.* a sudden and ridiculous descent from a lofty style to one that is commonplace or trivial in speech or writing. For example: *The senator pledged to oppose war, fight poverty, and name a new state flower.*

bath·robe (bath′rōb′) *n.* a loose, coatlike garment worn before and after bathing or for lounging.

bath·room (bath′rüm′, bath′rum′) *n.* **1.** a room with a bathtub or shower and usually a toilet and sink. **2.** a room containing a toilet and a sink.

bath·tub (bath′tub′) *n.* a tub in which to bathe, now usually one permanently fixed in a bathroom and having faucets and a drain.

bath·y·scaphe (bath′ə skāf′) *also,* **bath·y·scaph** (bath′ə-skaf′). *n.* a small submersible vessel used for undersea exploration, usually including a spherical observation chamber.

bath·y·sphere (bath′ə sfîr′) *n.* a hollow, watertight steel globe that has observation windows, used for undersea exploration. A bathysphere is suspended by cables from a surface vessel and cannot move independently.

ba·tik (bə tēk′) *n.* **1.** a method of hand printing colored designs on cloth by putting a wax coating on those parts that are not to be dyed. **2.** cloth decorated by this method. [From the Javanese word *mbatik* meaning "wax painting."]

ba·tiste (bə tēst′) *n.* a fine, soft, sheer fabric made of one of several fibers, as cotton or linen.

bat mitz·vah (bät mits′və) **1.** a ceremony held for a Jewish girl of about thirteen, marking her assumption of religious responsibilities. **2.** a girl for whom this ceremony is held. Also, **bas mitzvah.**

ba·ton (bə ton′) *n.* **1.** a slender rod used by a conductor to direct the performance of an orchestra or band. **2.** a rod with a knob at one or both ends, carried by a drum major or drum majorette and twirled in a showy manner. **3.** a short staff used as a symbol of office, command, or authority: *a field marshal's baton.* **4.** a short stick that is handed from one runner to the next in a relay race.

ba·tra·chi·an (bə trā′kē ən) *n.* a tailless amphibian, such as a frog or toad.

bats·man (bats′mən) *n.*, *pl.* **bats·men** (bats′mən). a batter in cricket.

bat·tal·ion (bə tal′yən) *n.* **1.** a military unit usually made up of two or more companies or batteries and a head-quarters and forming part of a brigade or regiment. **2.** any large group of persons or things; host: *Battalions of volunteers searched for the lost child.*

bat·ten[1] (bat′ən) *n.* **1.** a piece of sawed timber used especially for flooring. **2.** a light strip of wood used in building, especially to cover or reinforce a joint between boards. **3.** a narrow strip of wood or metal used for various purposes on a ship, as to fasten canvas over a

hatch or to stiffen the edges of a sail. —*v.t.* to fasten, furnish, or strengthen with battens: *to batten a sail. The crew battened down the hatches of the ship as the storm was about to break.* [From the French word *baton* meaning "a small stick," going back to the Late Latin word *bastum* meaning 'stick.'']

bat·ten[2] (bat′ən) *Archaic.* *v.i.* to grow fat by feeding well; thrive, as cattle. —*v.t.* to make fat. [From the Old Norse word *batna* meaning "to get better.'']

bat·ter[1] (bat′ər) *v.t.* **1.** to strike or beat with heavy, repeated blows: *The champion battered the young boxer.* **2.** to break or damage by rough treatment: *Driving on bad roads has battered our car.* —*v.i.* to strike or beat heavily and repeatedly; pound; hammer: *The fire fighters battered away at the door of the burning house.* [*Bat*[1] + the obsolete suffix *-er* indicating repeated action.]

bat·ter[2] (bat′ər) *n.* a thin mixture of flour, liquid, and other ingredients beaten together for use in cooking: *pancake batter.* [Probably from *batter*[1].]

bat·ter[3] (bat′ər) *n.* a player who is batting or whose turn it is to bat in baseball, softball, or cricket. [*Bat*[1] + *-er*[1].]

battering ram **1.** a device used in ancient warfare for battering down walls or gates. It had a heavy wooden beam with a mass of metal at one end that was sometimes shaped like a ram's head. **2.** any heavy beam, log, or bar used to knock down a door or wall.

bat·ter·y (bat′ə rē) *n.*, *pl.* **bat·ter·ies.** **1.** a group of two or more electric cells that can produce electric current by means of chemical action. Batteries provide the electricity for flashlights, portable radios, hearing aids, and auto-mobiles. **2.** any group of similar or related things used or thought of as a unit: *A battery of bright lights shone on the stage.* **3.** a set of two or more heavy guns or other weapons used as a unit. **4.** a unit of soldiers in the artillery, corresponding to a company in the infantry. **5.** *Law.* an unlawful attack on another person by beating or by touching the person in a threatening or offensive manner. **6.** *Baseball.* a team's pitcher and catcher, considered as a unit.

bat·ting (bat′ing) *n.* **1.** the act or manner of using a bat, especially in a game. **2.** cotton, wool, or synthetic fibers that have been pressed into sheets or layers, used espe-cially in bandaging wounds or as padding for upholstery or quilts.

batting average **1.** a mathematical average indicating the batting ability of a baseball player, obtained by dividing the number of hits the player has made by the number of times the player has officially batted. A player who has batted 500 times and has 150 hits has a batting average of .300. **2.** *Informal.* a level of accomplishment or achieve-ment in any activity: *a great batting average in landing new accounts for an ad agency.*

bat·tle (bat′əl) *n.* **1.** a fight between opposing armed forces on land, at sea, or in the air: *A decisive battle of the Civil War was fought at Gettysburg.* **2.** fighting; warfare; combat: *to die in battle.* **3.** any fight or contest; conflict; struggle: *Life in the Arctic is a constant battle against the elements. There was a battle for the cham-pionship between the two teams.* —*v.*, **bat·tled, bat·tling.** —*v.i.* to fight or struggle: *The armies battled for three days. The two players battled for possession of the ball.* —*v.t.* to fight or struggle against: *The ship battled the high waves.* —**bat′tler**, *n.*

bat·tle–ax (bat′əl aks′) *also,* **bat·tle–axe.** *n.*, *pl.* **bat-**

at; āpe; fär; câre; end; mē; it; īce; pîerce; hot; ōld; sông; fôrk; oil; out; up; ūse; rüle; pùll; tûrn; chin; sing; shop; thin; this; hw in white; zh in treasure. The symbol ə stands for the unstressed vowel sound heard in about, taken, pencil, lemon, and circus.

tle·ax·es. a heavy, wide-bladed ax, formerly used as a weapon in war.

battle cry **1.** a shout or cry of troops in battle. **2.** a motto or slogan used in any contest or conflict: *"Down with poverty" was the organization's battle cry.*

bat·tle·dore (bat′əl dôr′) *n.* a small racket used in the game of battledore and shuttlecock.

battledore and shuttlecock, an ancient game from which the modern game of badminton was developed.

bat·tle·field (bat′əl fēld′) *n.* a place where a battle is fought or was once fought.

bat·tle·front (bat′əl frunt′) *n.* a place where a battle is being fought; front.

bat·tle·ground (bat′əl ground′) *n.* a battlefield.

bat·tle·ment (bat′əl mənt) *n.* **1.** a low wall formerly built along the top of a fort or tower, having a series of openings through which soldiers could shoot at the enemy. **2.** a similar wall built for decoration.

battle royal *pl.* **battles royal.** **1.** a fight or struggle involving many people; riot: *The police and the protesters had quite a battle royal.* **2.** a loud, heated argument: *The discussion between the umpire and the players soon became a battle royal.*

bat·tle·ship (bat′əl ship′) *n.* a type of large warship, having the most powerful guns and the heaviest armor of any naval vessel.

bat·ty (bat′ē) *adj.,* **bat·ti·er, bat·ti·est.** *Slang.* crazy.

bau·ble (bô′bəl) *n.* a showy, worthless trinket: trifle: *The peddler sold cheap bracelets and other baubles.*

baux·ite (bôk′sīt) *n.* a claylike substance made up of several different minerals. It is the chief ore of aluminum. [From the French word *bauxite,* from Les *Baux,* the French town where it was first found.]

bawd·y (bô′dē) *adj.,* **bawd·i·er, bawd·i·est.** indecent or lewd; obscene. —**bawd′i·ly,** *adv.* —**bawd′i·ness,** *n.*

bawl (bôl) *v.i.* **1.** to weep or sob loudly; wail: *The colicky baby bawled through the night.* **2.** to shout or yell; bellow. —*v.t.* to call out noisily; shout: *to bawl orders.* —*n.* a loud shout or outcry: *a bawl of anger.*

 ·**to bawl out.** *Informal.* to scold or reprimand severely: *The boss bawled them out for coming in late.*

bay[1] (bā) *n.* an arm of a sea or lake extending into the land; broad inlet. A bay is usually smaller than a gulf and is widest at its mouth. [From the Old French word *baie* meaning "inlet," from the Spanish word *bahia* meaning "bay[1]."]

bay[2] (bā) *n.* **1.** a space or section of a wall or building between two columns, beams, pillars, or the like. **2.** an outward projection in a wall containing a window or set of windows. **3.** see **bay window. 4.** a compartment or area, as in an aircraft, that is used for a particular purpose: *a cargo bay.* [From the Old French word *baée* meaning "opening," from the word *baer* meaning "to stand open."]

bay[3] (bā) *n.* **1.** a deep, long barking or howling, as of a dog: *the bay of hounds chasing a rabbit.* **2.** the position of a cornered animal or person forced to turn and face pursuers: *The big lion had turned at bay* (Ernest Hemingway). *The police brought the escaped prisoner to bay.* **3.** the position of an animal, person, or thing being checked or held back: *trying to keep poverty at bay by creating new jobs.* being held or kept off: *The bronco kept the cowboys at bay.* —*v.i.* to bark with a deep, long howl: *The campers heard a wolf baying at the moon.* [From the Old French word *abiier* meaning "to bark, bay[3]."]

bay[4] (bā) *n.* **1.** any of various evergreen

bay[2] *(def. 1)*

trees or shrubs having stiff, smooth leaves and small berries; laurel. **2.** any of various shrubs or trees resembling the laurel. [From the Middle French word *baie* meaning "berry," from the Latin word *baca* "berry."]

bay[5] (bā) *n.* **1.** a reddish brown color. **2.** a horse or other animal of this color. —*adj.* having the color bay; reddish brown. [From the Old French word *bai* meaning "bay-colored," from the Latin word *badius* with the same meaning.]

bay·ber·ry (bā′ber′ē, bā′bə rē) *n., pl.* **bay·ber·ries.** **1.** a North American shrub having fragrant leaves and pale-blue berries coated with wax. **2.** the small, round berry itself, used for making scented soaps and fragrant candles. **3.** a tropical American tree having large leathery leaves that yield a fragrant oil used in making bay rum.

bay leaf, the dried, spicy leaf of a bay tree, used as a seasoning in cooking.

bay·o·net (bā′ə nit, bā′ə net′) *n.* a large knife or dagger that can be attached to the muzzle of a rifle and used for stabbing or slashing in hand-to-hand fighting. —*v.t.,* **bay·o·net·ed, bay·o·net·ing.** to stab or slash with a bayonet. [From the French word *baïonnette* meaning "bayonet," from *Bayonne,* the French city where bayonets were first made.]

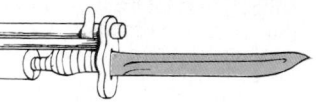
bayonet

bay·ou (bī′ü, bī′ō) *n., pl.* **bay·ous.** a marshy, sluggish, sometimes stagnant inlet or outlet of a river, lake, or gulf, especially in the southern United States. [From the word *bayou* in the French dialect spoken in Louisiana, from the Choctaw word *bayuk* meaning "stream."]

bay rum, a fragrant liquid used in cosmetics and medicines, originally made from the leaves of the bayberry tree, but now prepared from a mixture of certain oils, alcohol, and water.

bay window, a window or set of windows projecting outward from the wall of a building and forming an alcove or recess in the room within.

ba·zaar (bə zär′) *also,* **ba·zar.** *n.* **1.** a sale of various things for some special purpose: *a charity bazaar.* **2.** a place for the sale of various kinds of goods. **3.** in Middle Eastern and Far Eastern countries, a marketplace or street lined with shops or stalls. [Originally from the Persian word *bāzār* meaning "market."]

bazaar *(def. 3)*

ba·zoo·ka (bə zü′kə) *n.* a portable tube-shaped weapon for firing rockets at tanks.

BB *pl.* **BB's.** a very small lead shot, used especially in a type of air rifle.

BBC, British Broadcasting Corporation.

BB gun, an air rifle that uses BB's.

bbl. *pl.* **bbls.** barrel.

BC, postal abbreviation for British Columbia.

B.C. **1.** before Christ. ▲ used in expressing dates: *The Athenians defeated the Persians at Marathon in 490 B.C.* **2.** British Columbia.

bd. **1.** board. **2.** bond.

bd. ft., board foot; board feet.

be (bē) *v.* **been, be·ing.** Present tense: *sing.,* first person **am;** second **are;** third **is;** *pl.* **are.** Past tense: *sing.,* first person **was;** second **were;** third **was;** *pl.* **were.** —*v.i.* **1.** to have reality; exist or live: *To be, or not to be* (Shakespeare, *Hamlet*). *There are 120 tenants in that apartment building.* **2.a.** used as a linking verb to connect the subject with a noun: *My cousin is an engineer. They are my parents.* **b.** used as a linking verb to connect the subject with an adjective: *That car is blue. I am so tired. The work is done. Be still!* **3.** to take place; happen; occur: *The wedding was last month.* **4.** to occupy a place, position, or situation: *Your coat is on the chair.* **5.** to come or go: *Have you ever been to California?* **6.** to stay, as in the same place: *I have been in the house all day.* **7.** to remain or continue, as in the same condition: *Let me be.* —*auxiliary verb.* **1.** used with the present participle of a verb to show continuous action: *I am studying for a history test.* **2.** used with the past participle of a transitive verb to form the passive: *Were you injured in the game?* **3.** used with *to* and the infinitive of a verb to indicate the future or obligation: *They are to join us later. You are to wash the dishes.*

Be, the symbol for beryllium.

be– *prefix* **1.** throughout; all around; all over: *besiege, besprinkle.* **2.** about: *bemoan.* **3.** make; cause to be: *betroth, bedazzle.* **4.** furnish with: *bejewel, bespeckled.*

beach (bēch) *n., pl.* **beach·es.** the gently sloping shore of an ocean or other body of water, especially that part covered by sand or pebbles. —*v.t.* to run or haul (a boat) onto a beach.

beach buggy, another term for **dune buggy.**

beach·comb·er (bēch′kō′mər) *n.* **1.** a person who lives as a vagrant on the seashore, especially one living on an island in the South Pacific. **2.** a long wave that rolls in from the ocean and onto the beach.

beach·head (bēch′hed′) *n.* **1.** an area on an enemy shore seized and held by the advance troops of an invading force. **2.** an advance position or foothold: *a vaccine that established a beachhead in the fight against polio.*

bea·con (bē′kən) *n.* **1.** a guiding or warning signal, especially a light or fire. **2.** a lighthouse, buoy, or other object placed so as to guide or warn ships. **3.** a radio transmitter that sends out special signals to assist aircraft and ships in determining their position and course. **4.** anything that warns, signals, or guides.

bead (bēd) *n.* **1.** a small, usually round ball or piece of glass, wood, metal, or other material, having a hole through it so that it can be strung on a thread or wire with other objects of the same kind. **2. beads. a.** a necklace of beads. **b.** a rosary. **3.** any small, roundish body: *beads of sweat.* **4.** a small, metal knob on the muzzle of a gun, used in aiming. —*v.t.* to furnish or decorate with beads or beading: *to bead moccasins.* —*v.i.* to collect in beads or drops: *Water beaded on the side of the glass.* [From the Middle English word *bede* meaning ''prayer,'' probably from the Old English word *gebed* ''prayer.'' In the medieval church, prayers were often recited while using a rosary. The meaning of *bead* shifted from ''prayer'' to ''the rosary,'' and then to the small beads which make up a rosary.] —**bead′like′,** *adj.*

   •**to draw a bead on.** to aim carefully at.

   •**to tell one's beads** or **to say one's beads.** to say prayers with a rosary.

bead·ing (bē′ding) *n.* **1.** decorative work made of beads. **2.** material consisting of or decorated with beads. **3.** lace or embroidered trimming having openwork through which ribbon may be run.

bea·dle (bē′dəl) *n.* a minor church official having such duties as ushering and keeping order during services.

bead·work (bēd′wûrk′) *n.* decorative work made of beads.

bead·y (bē′dē) *adj.,* **bead·i·er, bead·i·est.** small, round, and glittering: *The bird had beady eyes.*

bea·gle (bē′gəl) *n.* a small, smooth-coated hound having short legs, drooping ears, and usually white, tan, and black markings, used in hunting rabbits.

beak (bēk) *n.* **1.** the horny, projecting mouth part of a bird; bill. **2.** a similar projecting part in other animals, such as the horny jaws of turtles. **3.** something resembling a bird's beak, such as the spout of a pitcher. **4.** a pointed projection at the prow of an ancient warship, used to ram or pierce enemy ships. —**beak′like′,** *adj.*

beak·er (bē′kər) *n.* **1.** a large, open container of glass or other material, often having a lip for pouring, used especially in laboratories. **2.** a large drinking cup or goblet with a wide mouth. **3.** the contents of a beaker.

beaks *(def. 1)*

beam (bēm) *n.* **1.** a long, heavy piece of wood, steel, or other material, used in building. **2.** one of the main horizontal supports of a building or ship. **3.** the widest part of a ship. **4.** the horizontal bar of a balance from which the pans are suspended. **5.** a ray or shaft, as of light: *the beams of a searchlight.* **6.** a continuous radio signal transmitted in one direction, to guide aircraft or ships. **7.** a suggestion or hint; gleam: *a beam of hope.* —*v.t.* **1.** to send out in beams or rays. **2.** to direct or transmit (a broadcast or radio signal) in a certain direction: *That radio program is beamed to our troops overseas.* —*v.i.* **1.** to shine brightly; radiate: *The sun beamed down.* **2.** to smile radiantly or joyfully: *to beam with delight.*

   •**off the beam. a.** not following the course indicated by a radio beam. **b.** *Informal.* wrong; incorrect.

   •**on the beam. a.** following the course indicated by a radio beam. **b.** *Informal.* right; correct.

beam·ing (bē′ming) *adj.* bright; shining; radiant: *a beaming smile, a beaming child.* —**beam′ing·ly,** *adv.*

bean (bēn) *n.* **1.** a smooth seed of any of various plants, eaten as a vegetable, such as the string bean, lima bean, and kidney bean. **2.** the long, narrow pod containing such seeds. The pods of some varieties are cooked and eaten with the seed still inside. **3.** any of the plants that produce these seeds and pods. **4.** a similar seed of any of various unrelated plants: *a coffee bean.* —**bean′like′,** *adj.*

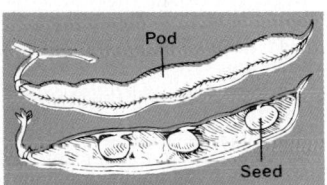

bean (string bean)

bean·bag (bēn′bag′) *n.* a small cloth bag filled with beans and used in certain games.

bean curd, another term for **tofu.**

at; āpe; fär; câre; end; mē; it; īce; pîerce; hot; ōld; sông, fôrk; oil; out; up; ūse; rüle; pull; tûrn; chin; sing; shop; thin; <u>th</u>is; hw in white; zh in treasure. The symbol ə stands for the unstressed vowel sound heard in about, taken, pencil, lemon, and circus.

bean·ie (bē′nē) *n.* a small cap without a brim.

bean sprout, the sprout of certain beans, especially the mung bean, used as a vegetable in salads and in cooking.

bean·stalk (bēn′stôk′) *n.* the main stem of a bean plant.

bear[1] (bâr) *v.,* **bore, borne** or **born, bear·ing.** —*v.t.* **1.** to hold up; support: *Beams bear the weight of the roof.* **2.** to carry; transport: *to bear gifts.* **3.** to have as a visible feature or characteristic; show; display: *twins who bear a strong resemblance to a grandparent, a book bearing the autograph of its author.* **4.** to give birth to: *to bear a child.* **5.** to bring forth; produce: *The apple tree bore fruit.* **6.** to hold in the mind or emotions: *I bear no grudge against you.* **7.** to carry or behave (oneself): *The dancers bore themselves gracefully.* **8.** to put up with; endure or tolerate: *I can't bear their rudeness.* **9.** to accept, acknowledge; assume: *to bear the blame, to bear the expense.* —*v.i.* **1.** to lean or press; weigh: *The sadness of our dog's death bore heavily on us.* **2.** to lie or move in a particular direction: *Bear left at the intersection to reach the town.* **3.** to bring forth fruit: *The pear tree did not bear this year.* [From the Old English word *beran* meaning "to carry."]

·**to bear down. a.** to press or weigh down: *The heavy bundle bore me down.* **b.** to make a strong effort: *The runner bore down near the finish line.*

·**to bear down on** or **to bear down upon. a.** to make a great effort towards: *to bear down on the task at hand.* **b.** to put pressure on; press hard: *I bore down on the pencil and broke the point.* **c.** to approach rapidly.

·**to bear on** or **to bear upon.** to be relevant to; relate to: *This evidence bears on the crime.*

·**to bear out.** to confirm or support; prove to be right: *The facts bear out my story.*

·**to bear up.** to support a weight or strain; endure: *The fabric bore up well during testing.*

·**to bear with.** to be patient or tolerant toward: *Bear with my faults.*

bear[2] (bâr) *n.* **1.** a large, heavy mammal with coarse, thick fur, powerful legs and claws, and a short, stumpy tail, such as the grizzly bear, polar bear, black bear, or brown bear. Bears are the largest meat-eating land animals, and are found in North and South America, Asia, Europe, and the Arctic. **2.** a rough, rude, or surly person. **3.** a person or business that believes prices on the stock market are going to fall, especially one that sells stock with the hope of buying it back later at a lower price. —*adj.* marked by or relating to falling prices, such as those of stocks: *to lose money in a bear market.* [From the Old English word *bera* meaning "a bear."] —**bear′like′,** *adj.*

bear·a·ble (bâr′ə bəl) *adj.* able to be borne or endured; tolerable: *The amusing comments of his friend made the boring movie bearable.* —**bear′a·bly,** *adv.*

bear·bait·ing (bâr′bā′ting) *n.* the former sport of setting dogs to attack a chained bear.

beard (bîrd) *n.* **1.** a growth of hair on the cheeks, chin, and throat of a man. **2.** any growth resembling a beard, such as the hair on the chin of a goat, the bristles near the beak of certain birds, or the hairlike tuft on the head of a stalk of wheat. —*v.t.* to face or defy boldly (an opponent or difficulty): *to beard a lion in its den.*

beard·ed (bîr′did) *adj.* having a beard.

beard·less (bîrd′lis) *adj.* having no beard.

bear·er (bâr′ər) *n.* **1.** a person or thing that carries, supports, or brings: *a flag bearer, a bearer of good news.* **2.** a person who holds or presents a check or other order for payment of money.

bear hug, a tight, vigorous hug.

bear·ing (bâr′ing) *n.* **1.** a way of carrying or behaving oneself: *a regal bearing.* **2.** connection or relation in thought: *Your comments have no bearing on this matter.* **3.** position or direction in relation to another point or to the points of the compass. **4. bearings.** knowledge or understanding of one's position or direction: *to lose one's bearings in a storm.* **5.** a part of a machine that holds or supports a moving part and allows it to move with less friction. **6.** the act or power of producing or bringing forth: *That fruit tree is past bearing.*

bear·ish (bâr′ish) *adj.* **1.** rough or rude; surly. **2.** expecting a decline in the price of stock. —**bear′ish·ly,** *adv.* —**bear′ish·ness,** *n.*

bear·skin (bâr′skin′) *n.* **1.** the skin of a bear. **2.** a coat, rug, or robe made from this skin. **3.** a tall, black fur cap, such as that worn by some soldiers or drum majors.

beast (bēst) *n.* **1.** any animal other than a human being, especially a large four-footed animal. **2.** a person who is coarse, brutal, or cruel.

beast·ly (bēst′lē) *adj.,* **beast·li·er, beast·li·est. 1.** brutal or coarse; like a beast. **2.** *Informal.* very bad; disagreeable; unpleasant: *beastly weather.* —*adv. Informal.* very: *It's beastly hot today.* —**beast′li·ness,** *n.*

beast of burden, an animal used for carrying or pulling loads.

beat (bēt) *v.,* **beat, beat·en** or **beat, beat·ing.** —*v.t.* **1.** to strike or hit again and again; pound: *to beat a rug to clean it, to beat a table with one's fists.* **2.** to defeat or outdo: *I beat him at checkers. The runner beat the record.* **3.** to flap repeatedly: *The bird beat its wings against the cage.* **4.** to shape or flatten by hammering: *to beat gold into thin sheets.* **5.** to stir or mix vigorously: *to beat egg whites.* **6.** to mark or measure (time or rhythm), as with a baton, by tapping the foot, or by waving the hand. **7.** to hunt through in order to find a person or thing: *The hunters beat the brush for the quail.* **8.** to make (a path) by repeated walking: *to beat a trail through the woods.* **9.** *Informal.* to bewilder or baffle: *It beats me how you get such high marks without studying.* —*v.i.* **1.** to strike or pound repeatedly: *The waves beat against the shore. Torrents of rain beat down on the roof.* **2.** to glare steadily and intensely: *The tropical sun beat down on us.* **3.** to throb: *The heart beats rhythmically.* **4.** to make a sound when struck: *The drums beat slowly.* **5.** to sail against the wind in a zigzag course: *The boat beat along the coast.* —*n.* **1.** a stroke or blow, especially one made again and again: *the beat of a drum.* **2.** a throb: *the beat of the heart.* **3.** a regular route taken or area covered: *a police officer's beat. That reporter's beat is city hall.* **4.** *Music.* **a.** the basic unit of time or accent. **b.** a movement used to show this, as with a baton or the hand. —*adj. Informal.* very tired; exhausted.

·**to beat around the bush.** *Informal.* to approach a matter in a roundabout way; avoid coming to the point.

·**to beat back** or **to beat off.** to drive back by force: *The villagers beat back the approaching fire.*

·**to beat down.** to force (a seller) to lower a price.

·**to beat it.** *Slang.* to leave hurriedly.

·**to beat up.** *Informal.* to give a beating to; thrash.

beat·en (bē′tən) *v.* a past participle of **beat.** —*adj.* **1.** formed or shaped by blows; hammered: *a necklace made of beaten gold.* **2.** worn by use; commonly used: *a beaten path.* **3.** thwarted or vanquished; defeated: *a beaten mayoral candidate.* **4.** mixed by vigorous stirring: *a beaten egg.*

beat·er (bē′tər) *n.* **1.** a person or thing that beats, especially a device or appliance used for beating. **2.** a person who drives game out from hiding for a hunter.

be·a·tif·ic (bē′ə tif′ik) *adj.* showing great happiness or blessedness; blissful: *a beatific smile.* —**be′a·tif′i·cal·ly,** *adv.*

be·at·i·fi·ca·tion (bē at′ə fi kā′shən) *n.* the act of beatifying or the condition of being beatified.

be·at·i·fy (bē at′ə fī′) *v.t.,* **be·at·i·fied, be·at·i·fy·ing. 1.** to make extremely happy. **2.** in the Roman Catholic Church, to declare that (a deceased person) is one of the blessed in heaven and is entitled to public veneration.

beat·ing (bē′ting) *n.* **1.** the act of a person or thing that

B

beats. **2.** punishment by a series of blows; thrashing. **3.** a throbbing, as of the heart. **4.** a defeat or setback: *They gave our team quite a beating.* **5.** a punishing or damaging experience: *The car got a beating on those old roads.*

be·at·i·tude (bē at′i tūd′, bē a′ti tūd′) *n.* **1.** great happiness or blessedness; bliss. **2. the Beatitudes.** in the New Testament, the pronouncements on blessedness made by Jesus in the Sermon on the Mount. Each begins with the words "Blessed are."

beat·nik (bēt′nik) *n.* a person of the 1950s who rebelled against the values of middle-class society and was characterized by unconventional behavior and clothing.

beat–up (bēt′up′) *adj. Informal.* worn out from overuse or abuse; shabby: *a beat-up sofa with broken springs.*

beau (bō) *n., pl.* **beaux** or **beaus** (bōz). **1.** a sweetheart or boyfriend of a girl or woman. **2.** a man who cares too much about his clothes and appearance; dandy.

Beau·fort Scale (bō′fərt) a scale of wind velocities, ranging from zero for speeds of less than 1 mile per hour (1.61 kilometers per hour) to seventeen for speeds above 75 miles per hour (120.7 kilometers per hour). [From the British admiral Sir Francis *Beaufort* (1774–1857), who introduced this scale.]

beau·te·ous (bū′tē əs) *adj.* beautiful. —**beau′te·ous·ly**, *adv.* —**beau′te·ous·ness**, *n.*

beau·ti·cian (bū tish′ən) *n.* a person skilled in the cosmetic services offered in a beauty parlor, as a hairdresser.

beau·ti·ful (bū′tə fəl) *adj.* having qualities that please the senses or mind; full of beauty: *the beautiful fragrance of roses, beautiful long hair, a beautiful piece of music.* —**beau′ti·ful·ly**, *adv.* —**beau′ti·ful·ness**, *n.*

beau·ti·fy (bū′tə fī′) *v.t.*, **beau·ti·fied, beau·ti·fy·ing.** to make beautiful; add beauty to. —**beau′ti·fi·ca′tion**, *n.* —**beau′ti·fi′er**, *n.*

beau·ty (bū′tē) *n., pl.* **beau·ties. 1.** a quality or combination of qualities that please the senses or mind: *the beauty of the English countryside.* **2.** a person or thing that is beautiful: *That yacht is a beauty.* **3.** an outstanding or very pleasing feature or part: *The beauty of this recipe is that it's so easy to follow.* [From the Old French word *hiauté* meaning "beauty," going back to the Latin word *bellus* meaning "pretty."]

beauty mark, a mole or other small mark on the skin.

beauty parlor, a place that offers cosmetic services, as hairdressing and manicuring. Also, **beauty salon, beauty shop**

beaux (bōz) a plural of **beau.**

bea·ver¹ (bē′vər) *n.* **1.** a mammal related to the rat, having sharp front teeth, grayish brown fur, and a broad, flat tail and webbed hind feet that help it to swim. It builds its den in or on the banks of shallow streams and builds a dam of branches, stones, and mud to protect this den. **2.** the fur of this animal. **3.** a man's top hat, originally made of beaver fur. [From the Old English word *beofor* meaning this animal.]

beaver *(def. 1)*

bea·ver² (bē′vər) *n.* a movable piece of armor attached to a helmet in order to protect the mouth and chin. [From the Old French word *baviere* meaning "beaver of a helmet" or "bib."]

bea·ver·board (bē′vər bôrd′) *n.* a light, stiff material made of compressed wood fibers, used for ceilings and temporary structures. Trademark: **Beaverboard.**

be·calmed (bi kämd′) *adj.* kept motionless by lack of wind: *The sailboat was becalmed in the bay.*

be·came (bi kām′) the past tense of **become.**

be·cause (bi kôz′, bi kuz′) *conj.* **1.** for the reason that; due to the fact that; since: *We took the bus because it was raining.* **2.** *Informal.* the fact that: *The reason we're late is because there was very heavy traffic on the road.*

•**because of.** by reason of; on account of: *I went swimming because of the heat.*

beck (bek) *Archaic. n.* a nod or other gesture given as a call or command. —*v.t., v.i.* to beckon.

•**at one's beck and call.** subject to one's slightest wish; ready to do one's bidding: *to be at your employer's beck and call.*

beck·on (bek′ən) *v.t.* **1.** to signal, summon, or direct (someone) by a sign or gesture: They beckoned me to come closer. **2.** to be inviting to; attract: *The beautiful, deserted beach beckoned us.* —*v.i.* **1.** to signal or summon: *to beckon to a waiter.* **2.** to be inviting or attractive.

be·cloud (bi kloud′) *v.t.* to hide or obscure with or as if with clouds: *Angry arguments beclouded the real issue.*

be·come (bi kum′) *v.*, **be·came, be·come, be·com·ing.** —*v.i.* to come or grow to be: *The tired child became cranky. Tadpoles become frogs.* —*v.t.* **1.** to look attractive on; suit: *That blue shirt becomes you.* **2.** to be suitable or appropriate for: *Such impolite behavior does not become them.*

•**to become of.** to happen to: *What became of my hat?*

be·com·ing (bi kum′ing) *adj.* **1.** looking well on; flattering; attractive: *a becoming color.* **2.** suitable to; appropriate to: *conduct not becoming an officer.* —**be·com′ing·ly**, *adv.*

bed (bed) *n.* **1.** a piece of furniture for sleeping or resting, usually consisting of a mattress and springs and a supporting framework. **2.** any place or thing used for sleeping or resting: *A pillow was the kitten's bed.* **3.** something resembling a bed in shape or function: *a bed of leaves.* **4.** the use of a bed for the night; lodging. **5.** a piece of ground used for planting: *beds of roses and tulips.* **6.** the ground at the bottom of a body of water: *The stream had a bed of sand and pebbles.* **7.** a part or surface serving as a foundation or support: *The road was built on a bed of gravel.* **8.** a layer; stratum: *to drill through beds of sand and clay.* —*v.*, **bed·ded, bed·ding.** —*v.t.* **1.** to provide with a place to sleep: *to bed guests in a spare room.* **2.** to put or take to bed: *to bed a sleepy baby.* **3.** to set or plant in the ground: *rose bushes bedded by the front door.*

•**to bed down. a.** to provide with a place to sleep: *to bed down cattle.* **b.** to go to bed; sleep.

be·daub (bi dôb′) *v.t.* **1.** to smear with something dirty. **2.** to ornament in a gaudy or excessive way.

be·daz·zle (bi daz′əl) *v.t.*, **be·daz·zled, be·daz·zling. 1.** to cause to be confused or blinded: *The glare of the headlights bedazzled us.* **2.** to impress greatly; overwhelm: *Audiences were bedazzled by the singer's performance.*

bed·bug (bed′bug′) *n.* a small, flat, wingless, bloodsucking insect that often infests beds and upholstery.

bed·cham·ber (bed′chām′bər) *n.* a bedroom.

bed·clothes (bed′klōz′, bed′klōthz′) *pl. n.* coverings used on a bed, such as sheets and blankets.

bedbug

at; āpe; fär; câre; end; mē; it; īce; pîerce; hot; ōld; sông, fôrk; oil; out; up; ūse; rüle; pull; tûrn; chin; sing; shop; thin; this; hw in white; zh in treasure. The symbol ə stands for the unstressed vowel sound heard in about, taken, pencil, lemon, and circus.

bed·ding (bed′ing) *n.* **1.** bedclothes. **2.** materials for a bed: *We used straw for the bedding for the oxen.* **3.** a bottom layer; foundation: *a bedding of gravel for a road.*

be·deck (bi dek′) *v.t.* to cover with ornaments; adorn: *a royal robe bedecked with jewels.*

be·dev·il (bi dev′əl) *v.t.,* **be·dev·iled, be·dev·il·ing;** *also, British,* **be·dev·illed, be·dev·il·ling.** **1.** to worry or harass; plague; torment: *bedeviled by debts.* **2.** to possess with or as if with a devil; bewitch. —**be·dev′il·ment,** *n.*

be·dew (bi dü′, bi dū′) *v.t.* to wet with or as with dew: *Raindrops bedewed the window.* ▲ used in literature.

bed·fast (bed′fast′) *adj.* bedridden.

bed·fel·low (bed′fel′ō) *n.* **1.** a person who shares a bed with another. **2.** a companion or ally; associate: *Politics makes strange bedfellows.*

be·dim (bi dim′) *v.t.,* **be·dimmed, be·dim·ming.** to make dim; darken or obscure.

be·di·zen (bi dī′zən, bi diz′ən) *v.t.* *Archaic.* to dress or adorn gaudily.

bed·lam (bed′ləm) *n.* **1.** a place or condition of wild uproar and confusion: *It was bedlam at the department store during the sale.* **2.** *Archaic.* an insane asylum. [A form of *Bethlehem* in the name *Hospital of St. Mary of Bethlehem,* an insane asylum in London.]

Bed·ou·in (bed′ü in) *n.* **1.** a member of a large group of nomadic Arab tribes living in the deserts of North Africa, Arabia, Israel, and Syria. **2.** any wanderer or nomad. —*adj.* of, relating to, or like the Bedouins.

bed·pan (bed′pan′) *n.* a shallow container designed for use as a toilet by a person who is confined to bed.

bed·post (bed′pōst′) *n.* one of the vertical supports at the corners of certain beds.

be·drag·gled (bi drag′əld) *adj.* **1.** wet, dirty, and limp, as though drenched with rain. **2.** messy or soiled, as though dragged through mire.

bed·rid·den (bed′rid′ən) *adj.* confined to bed for a long time, as by illness or injury.

bed·rock (bed′rok′) *n.* **1.** the solid rock that lies under the soil and other loose materials of the earth's surface. **2.** a foundation; basis: *The theory was built on a bedrock of careful research.* **3.** the lowest point or level; bottom.

bed·roll (bed′rōl′) *n.* a sleeping bag, blankets, or other bedding that can be rolled up and carried, usually used for sleeping outdoors.

bed·room (bed′rüm′, bed′rùm′) *n.* a room for sleeping.

bed·side (bed′sīd′) *n.* the space beside a bed, especially of a sick person: *We hurried to our friend's bedside.*

bed·sore (bed′sôr′) *n.* an ulcer in the skin caused by prolonged pressure against a bed. People who are bedridden for long periods of time often get bedsores.

bed·spread (bed′spred′) *n.* a covering placed on a bed for decoration or protection.

bed·stead (bed′sted′) *n.* a framework that supports the springs and mattress of a bed.

bed·time (bed′tīm′) *n.* the time when one usually goes to bed: *The child's bedtime is usually seven o'clock.*

bed–wet·ting (bed′wet′ing) *n.* uncontrolled urination in bed, usually occurring while a person is asleep.

bee (bē) *n.* **1.** any of a group of winged, often stinging, insects that have a thick, hairy body and feed on nectar and pollen. Bees are related to wasps and ants. Some bees, such as the honeybee, live in colonies, or hives, of many thousands and are often raised for the honey and beeswax they make. **2.** a gathering of people for a specific purpose, as to work together or engage in an amicable competition, as a quilting bee or spelling bee.

bee·bread (bē′bred′) *n.* a mixture of pollen and honey or nectar, made by bees to feed their larvae or young.

beech (bēch) *n., pl.* **beech·es.** **1.** any of a group of trees found in cooler regions of the Northern Hemisphere, having light gray bark and small nuts that may be eaten. **2.** the wood of this tree.

beech·nut (bēch′nut′) *n.* the nut of the beech tree, used to make cooking oil and flavorings.

beef (bēf) *n., pl.* **beeves** (*def. 2*) or **beefs** (*def. 3*). **1.** the meat of a full-grown steer, cow, or bull. **2.** a full-grown steer, cow, or bull that is raised for meat. **3.** *Slang.* a complaint. —*v.i.* *Slang.* to complain: *to beef about having to wash the dishes.* [From the old French word *buef* meaning "ox, beef," from the Latin word *bos* "ox, head of cattle."]

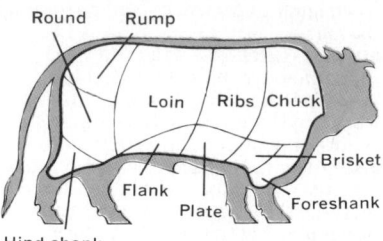
cuts of **beef**

·**to beef up.** *Informal.* to add force or vigor to; strengthen: *to beef up an army by drafting more soldiers.*

beef cattle, cattle raised for meat.

beef·steak (bēf′stāk′) *n.* a slice of beef for broiling or frying.

beef·y (bē′fē) *adj.,* **beef·i·er, beef·i·est.** strong and muscular; brawny: *a beefy athlete.* —**beef′i·ness,** *n.*

bee·hive (bē′hīv′) *n.* **1.** hive for a colony of bees. **2.** a busy, crowded place: *The store was a beehive of activity during the sale.*

bee·keep·er (bē′kē′pər) *n.* a person who raises bees.

bee·line (bē′līn′) *n.* a direct line or course, as the course a bee follows to its hive.

·**to make a beeline for.** to go directly to: *They made a beeline for the swimming pool.*

Be·el·ze·bub (bē·el′zə bub′) *n.* the Devil; Satan.

been (bin) the past participle of **be.**

beep (bēp) *n.* a brief sound, as that made by the horn of an automobile or by an electronic device, used as a warning or signal. —*v.i., v.t.* to make or cause to make such a sound: *The clock radio beeped rapidly. I beeped the car horn as a warning.*

beekeeper

beep·er (bē′pər) *n.* **1.** a small electronic device that beeps a signal to summon the person carrying it. It is controlled by radio from some central location. Also, **pager.** **2.** an electronic device that emits a beep, often built into watches, clocks, telephones, or computers to alert the user to the time, a message, an error, or the like.

beer (bir) *n.* **1.** an alcoholic drink usually made from water, malt, hops, and other ingredients. **2.** any of various carbonated or fermented beverages with flavorings from the roots or leaves of a plant, as ginger.

bees·wax (bēz′waks′) *n.* the yellow wax secreted by

honeybees to make their honeycombs. Beeswax is used in such products as candles, cosmetics, and floor wax.

beet (bēt) *n.* **1.** the fleshy root of any of a group of leafy plants, especially the common red beet, which is cooked and eaten as a vegetable. **2.** the plant bearing this root, having leaves that may be eaten cooked or raw. **3.** see **sugar beet.** —**beet′like′,** *adj.*

bee·tle[1] (bē′təl) *n.* **1.** any insect having biting mouth parts and hard, sheathlike front wings that, when folded back, cover the thin, delicate hind wings. **2.** any insect resembling a beetle, such as a cockroach. [From the Old English word *bitela* meaning ''biting insect,'' from the word *bītan* ''to bite.'']

bee·tle[2] (bē′təl) *n.* a heavy hammering or ramming tool, usually having a wooden head. —*v.t.,* **bee·tled, bee·tling.** to use a beetle on. [From the Old English word *bīetel* meaning ''hammer,'' from the word *bēatan* ''to beat.'']

bee·tle[3] (bē′təl) *v.i.,* **bee·tled, bee·tling.** to stick out; jut out: *The cliffs beetled over the shore.* —*adj.* (of eyebrows) sticking out. [From the word *beetle-browed.*]

bee·tle–browed (bē′təl broud′) *adj.* **1.** having eyebrows that stick out. **2.** scowling; frowning.

beet sugar, sugar obtained from the sugar beet.

beeves (bēvz) a plural of **beef.**

be·fall (bi fôl′) *v.,* **be·fell** (bi fel′), **be·fall·en, be·fall·ing.** —*v.t.* to happen to: *The shipwrecked passengers told about the misfortune that befell them.* —*v.i.* to happen, as by chance; occur: *No matter what befalls, we'll succeed.*

be·fit (bi fit′) *v.t.,* **be·fit·ted, be·fit·ting.** to be suitable or appropriate for: *to be treated with the dignity that befits one's rank.*

be·fit·ting (bi fit′ing) *adj.* suitable; fitting; proper: *to treat a visitor with befitting courtesy.*

be·fog (bi fôg′, bi fog′) *v.t.,* **be·fogged, be·fog·ging.** **1.** to surround or obscure with or as if with fog: *Mist befogged the skyline.* **2.** to confuse: *The speaker rambled and befogged the audience.*

be·fore (bi fôr′) *prep.* **1.** in front of; ahead of: *Two people stood before me in line.* **2.** earlier than: *The guests arrived before dinner.* **3.** rather than: *to choose one thing before another.* **4.** in the presence or sight of: *to appear before a large crowd.* **5.** in an earlier or more important position than: *A comes before B. The parents put the welfare of their child before all else.* **6.** under the consideration of: *We must deal with the problem before us.* —*adv.* **1.** in front; in advance; ahead: *In the procession, the younger children went before.* **2.** at an earlier time; previously: *They have been to my house before.* **3.** earlier; sooner: *I'll phone at six o'clock, not before.* —*conj.* **1.** previous to the time when: *They spoke to me before they left.* **2.** rather than; sooner than: *I would walk away before I would fight.*

be·fore·hand (bi fôr′hand′) *adv., adj.* ahead of time; in advance.

be·foul (bi foul′) *v.t.* to make dirty or foul; soil: *Oil had befouled the beach.*

be·friend (bi frend′) *v.t.* to act as a friend to; assist: *to befriend a stranger.*

be·fud·dle (bi fud′əl) *v.t.,* **be·fud·dled, be·fud·dling.** to confuse or bewilder completely: *The complicated instructions befuddled me.*

beg (beg) *v.,* **begged, beg·ging.** —*v.t.* **1.** to ask for as charity: *to beg food and clothes.* **2.** to ask earnestly or courteously: *to beg someone for help. I beg your pardon.* —*v.i.* **1.** to ask for alms or charity: *to beg for a meal.* **2.** to ask earnestly or humbly: *to beg for mercy.* **·to beg off.** to ask to be excused from a promise: *They said they would go, but then begged off.*

be·gan (bi gan′) the past tense of **begin.**

be·get (bi get′) *v.t.,* **be·got,** or (*archaic*) **be·gat** (bi

gat′), **be·got·ten** or **be·got, be·get·ting.** **1.** to sire; father. **2.** to give rise to; produce: *Jealousy begets hatred.* —**be·get′ter,** *n.*

beg·gar (beg′ər) *n.* **1.** a person who asks for charity, especially a person who does so for a living. **2.** a very poor person; pauper. **3.** a fellow; rascal. —*v.t.* **1.** to make very poor. **2.** to outdo; surpass: *wealth that beggars description.*

beg·gar·ly (beg′ər lē) *adj.* fit for or like a beggar; poor; inadequate: *a torn, beggarly coat.* —**beg′gar·li·ness,** *n.*

beg·gar·y (beg′ə rē) *n.* **1.** extreme poverty. **2.** beggars as a group.

be·gin (bi gin′) *v.,* **be·gan, be·gun, be·gin·ning.** —*v.i.* **1.** to do or be the first part of something; start: *The actors began an hour ago.* **2.** to have the first part undertaken, performed, or the like: *The movie begins soon.* **3.** to come into being; arise: *The epidemic began last month.* —*v.t.* **1.** to do the first part of; start to do: *They began their homework.* **2.** to bring into being; originate: *Who began this business?*

be·gin·ner (bi gin′ər) *n.* **1.** a person who is just beginning to do or learn something: *a beginner at skating.* **2.** a person who begins or originates something.

be·gin·ning (bi gin′ing) *n.* **1.** the first part: *The beginning of the movie was dull.* **2.** the time at which something begins: *A gun signaled the beginning of the race.* **3.** the act of starting: *to make a good beginning on your homework.* **4.** a first cause; source; origin: *The beginning of their quarrel is unknown.* **5.** *also,* **beginnings.** the first or basic stage: *a book about the beginnings of the United States.*

be·gone (bi gôn′, bi gon′) *interj.* go away; depart. ▲ used in literature.

be·gon·ia (bi gōn′yə) *n.* **1.** the large flower of certain tropical plants. The flowers may be white, yellow, red, orange, or pink. **2.** the plant bearing this flower.

be·got (bi got′) the past tense and a past participle of **beget.**

be·got·ten (bi got′ən) a past participle of **beget.**

be·grime (bi grīm′) *v.t.,* **be·grimed, be·grim·ing.** to make grimy; soil: *a face begrimed with mud.*

be·grudge (bi gruj′) *v.t.,* **be·grudged, be·grudg·ing.** **1.** to envy (someone) the possession or pleasure of: *to begrudge the opposing team its victory.* **2.** to give or allow reluctantly: *The scientists begrudged every minute they had to spend away from their experiment.* —**be·grudg′ing·ly,** *adv.*

be·guile (bi gīl′) *v.t.,* **be·guiled, be·guil·ing.** **1.** to trick by guile; mislead; deceive: *to beguile someone into buying a product that is not needed.* **2.** to amuse or delight; charm: *to beguile children with amusing stories.* **3.** to pass (time) pleasantly. —**be·guile′ment,** *n.* —**be·guil′er,** *n.*

be·gun (bi gun′) the past participle of **begin.**

be·half (bi haf′) *n.* **1.** **in behalf of** or **on behalf of.** **a.** in the interest of; for the benefit of: *a fair planned in behalf of an orphanage.* **b.** in the name of: *The minister accepted the contribution on behalf of his congregation.* **2.** **in someone's behalf** or **on someone's behalf.** in the interest or aid of: *The lawyer spoke in the defendant's behalf.*

be·have (bi hāv′) *v.,* **be·haved, be·hav·ing.** —*v.i.* **1.** to act, react, or function in a particular way: *to behave bravely, a car engine that behaves badly in cold weather.* **2.** to act properly: *Did the students behave when the*

---

at; āpe; fär; câre; end; mē; it; īce; pîerce; hot; ōld; sông, fôrk; oil; out; up; ūse; rüle; pùll; tûrn; chin; sing; shop; thin; this; hw in white; zh in treasure. The symbol ə stands for the unstressed vowel sound heard in about, taken, pencil, lemon, and circus.

B

teacher was gone? —*v.t.* to conduct (oneself) in a particular way: *They behaved themselves badly.* **2.** to conduct (oneself) properly: *Will you please keep quiet and behave yourself.*

be·hav·ior (bi hāv′yər) *also,* British, **be·hav·iour.** *n.* **1.** a manner of behaving or acting; conduct: *disgraceful behavior.* **2.** the manner in which something acts under given circumstances: *The scientist studied the behavior of air under pressure.*

be·hav·ior·al (bi hāv′yər əl) *adj.* having to do with behavior. —**be·hav·ior·al·ly,** *adv.*

be·head (bi hed′) *v.t.* to cut off the head of; decapitate.

be·held (bi held′) the past tense and past participle of behold.

be·he·moth (bi hē′məth) *n* **1.** in the Bible, an enormous animal that may have been the hippopotamus. **2.** any creature or thing of enormous size or power. [From the Hebrew word *behēmōth,* meaning this animal.]

be·hest (bi hest′) *n.* a command or urgent request: *The teacher acted at the principal's behest.*

be·hind (bi hīnd′) *prep.* **1.** at or toward the back of; in the rear of: *I sat behind someone tall.* **2.** at or on the farther side of; beyond: *The path runs behind those hedges.* **3.** later than; after: *Our train was behind schedule.* **4.** less advanced than; inferior to: *to be behind friends in one's schoolwork.* **5.** hidden by: *Fear lay behind their show of bravery.* **6.** causing or helping to cause: *the reason behind an action.* **7.** in support of; supporting; backing: *to be behind your team.* **8.** in a place, time, or condition that has been left or passed by: *Put your cares behind you.* —*adv.* **1.** in a place, time, or condition that has been left or passed: *to leave one's umbrella behind.* **2.** at or toward the back; in the rear: *You go first; I'll walk behind.* **3.** in or into a condition of being late: *Because of the extended holiday, a lot of offices got behind in their work. The steelworkers who were laid off got behind in their car and house payments.* —*n. Informal.* the buttocks; backside.

be·hind·hand (bi hīnd′hand′) *adv., adj.* late: *behindhand with the rent.*

be·hold (bi hōld′) *v.t.,* **be·held, be·hold·ing.** to look at; gaze upon; see: *The travelers beheld a beautiful valley.* —*interj.* look; see. —**be·hold′er,** *n.*

be·hold·en (bi hōl′dən) *adj.* obligated; indebted: *I am beholden to you for your helpful advice.*

be·hoove (bi hüv′) *v.t.,* **be·hooved, be·hoov·ing.** to be necessary, right, or advantageous: *It behooves you to be honest.*

beige (bāzh) *n.* a pale brown or grayish tan color. —*adj.* having the color beige.

be·ing (bē′ing) *n.* **1.** existence; life: *Those mountains came into being millions of years ago.* **2.** a living creature, especially a person: *a human being.* **3.** something thought of as having existence: *beings from outer space.*

be·jew·el (bi jü′əl) *v.t.,* **be·jew·eled, be·jew·el·ing;** *also,* British, **be·jew·elled, be·jew·el·ling.** to ornament with jewels: *to bejewel a crown.*

bel (bel) *n. Physics.* a unit for measuring the loudness of sounds. One bel is equal to ten decibels. [From Alexander Graham *Bell* (1847–1922), American inventor of the telephone.]

be·la·bor (bi lā′bər) *also,* British, **be·la·bour.** *v.t.* **1.** to beat soundly; thrash. **2.** to attack with words: *to belabor a friend for being late.* **3.** to deal with (something) for too long a time: *The speaker belabored the point long after the audience had lost interest.*

be·lat·ed (bi lā′tid) *adj.* delayed; late: *a belated birthday present, a belated arrival at a party.* —**be·lat′ed·ly,** *adv.* —**be·lat′ed·ness,** *n.*

be·lay (bi lā′) *v.t.,* **be·layed, be·lay·ing.** *Nautical.* **1.** to fasten (a rope) by winding it around a belaying pin, cleat, or similar object. **2.** *Informal.* to stop; hold. ▲ used chiefly as a command.

belaying pin *Nautical.* a removable pin around which ropes can be fastened.

belch (belch) *v.i.* **1.** to let out gas suddenly and noisily from the stomach through the mouth. **2.** pour out in violent spasms; spurt; gush: *Flames belched from the windows of the burning house.* —*v.t.* to send forth in violent spasms: *The chimney belched smoke and sparks.* —*n., pl.* **belch·es.** the act of belching.

bel·dam (bel′dəm) *also,* **bel·dame** (bel′dəm, bel′dām′). *n.* an old woman, especially one who is ugly; hag.

be·lea·guer (bi lē′gər) *v.t.* **1.** to surround or shut in with troops; besiege: *The soldiers beleaguered the castle.* **2.** to surround or harass; beset: *To be constantly beleaguered by creditors, a candidate beleaguered by reporters.*

belaying pins

bel·fry (bel′frē) *n., pl.* **bel·fries.** **1.** a tower in which a bell or bells are hung, especially one attached to a church or other structure. **2.** the part of a steeple or tower in which a bell or bells are hung.

Bel·gian (bel′jən) *n.* a person who was born in or is a citizen of Belgium. —*adj.* of or relating to Belgium, its people, or their culture.

Be·li·al (bē′lē əl, bēl′yəl) *n.* in the New Testament, the Devil.

be·lie (bi lī′) *v.t.,* **be·lied, be·ly·ing.** **1.** to give a false idea of; disguise: *a smile that belied the child's sadness.* **2.** to show to be false; contradict: *Your kindness belies your reputation for nastiness.*

be·lief (bi lēf′) *n.* **1.** acceptance of the truth or reality of something: *The defendant's testimony is not worthy of belief.* **2.** something that is believed; opinion; conviction: *a belief that all people are created equal.* **3.** confidence, especially in another person; faith; trust: *children's belief in their parents.* ▲ See **faith** for usage note.

belfry

be·lieve (bi lēv′) *v.,* **be·lieved, be·liev·ing.** —*v.t.* **1.** to accept as true or real: *I believe your story.* **2.** to think (somebody) is telling the truth: *I believe you because you've never lied to me.* **3.** to have the opinion; think; suppose: *I believe they went shopping.* —*v.i.* to have faith or trust: *to believe in democracy, to believe in regular exercise.* —**be·liev′a·ble,** *adj.* —**be·liev′er,** *n.*

·**to make believe.** to imagine; pretend: *The twins made believe that they were pioneers.*

be·lit·tle (bi lit′əl) *v.t.,* **be·lit·tled, be·lit·tling.** to cause to seem small or not important; disparage: *to belittle someone you envy.*

bell (bel) *n.* **1.** a hollow instrument, usually cup-shaped and made of metal, that makes a ringing sound when struck by a clapper, hammer, or similar object. **2.** the sounding or sound of a bell. **3.** something that is like a bell in shape or use, such as a doorbell or the flared lower end of a trumpet. **4.** *Nautical.* **a.** a sounding of a bell aboard ship to mark each half hour during the watches, which begin at 4:00, 8:00, and 12:00. One bell signals the end of the first half hour, and an additional bell is struck for every half hour that follows. **b.** a half-hour interval marked by these bells. —*v.t.* **1.** to put a bell on: *to bell cows.* **2.** to cause to flare out like a bell.

bel·la·don·na (bel′ə don′ə) *n.* **1.** a poisonous plant of Europe and Asia, having purple-brown flowers and black berries. Also, **deadly nightshade.** **2.** a drug made from this plant; atropine. [From the Italian name for this plant, *bella donna*, meaning "beautiful lady."]

bell–bot·tom (bel′bot′əm) *also,* **bell-bot·tomed.** *adj.* (of trousers) gradually flaring from below the knee to the bottom of each leg.

bell·bot·toms (bel′bot′əmz) *pl. n.* bell-bottom trousers.

bell·boy (bel′boi′) *n.* a bellhop.

bell buoy, a buoy having a bell that is rung by the motion of the waves.

belle (bel) *n.* **1.** a beautiful woman or girl. **2.** the most beautiful, popular, or admired woman or girl: *the belle of the ball.*

Bel·ler·o·phon (bə ler′ə fon′) *n. Greek Legend.* the hero who killed the monster Chimera with the help of the winged horse Pegasus.

bell·flow·er (bel′flou′ər) *n.* **1.** a bell-shaped flower of any of a large group of plants found throughout the Northern Hemisphere, ranging in color from lavender to blue, white, or pink. **2.** a plant bearing this flower, having narrow, scalloped or toothed leaves.

bell·hop (bel′hop′) *n.* a person employed in a hotel or club to assist guests, as by carrying luggage, and to run errands.

bel·li·cose (bel′i kōs′) *adj.* showing a willingness or eagerness to fight; warlike: *a bellicose nation.* —**bel·li·cos·i·ty** (bel′i kos′i tē), *n.*

bel·lig·er·ence (bə lij′ər əns) *n.* **1.** the condition or quality of being belligerent: *The bully's belligerence frightened everyone.* **2.** fighting; warfare.

bel·lig·er·en·cy (bə lij′ər ən sē) *n.* **1.** the condition of being at war. **2.** belligerence.

bel·lig·er·ent (bə lij′ər ənt) *adj.* **1.** eager or willing to fight; hostile. **2.** engaged in warfare; at war: *belligerent countries.* —*n.* a country or person engaged in warfare or fighting. —**bel·lig′er·ent·ly,** *adv.*

bell jar, a bell-shaped glass container, used especially in laboratories to cover objects, to contain gases, or to create a vacuum.

bel·low (bel′ō) *v.i.* **1.** to make a loud, deep sound; roar: *The bull bellowed.* **2.** to cry out in a loud, deep voice: *to bellow with pain.* —*v.t.* to utter loudly and deeply: *to bellow an order.* —*n.* **1.** a loud, deep sound; roar: *the bellow of a foghorn.* **2.** any loud, deep outcry.

bel·lows (bel′ōz) *pl. n.* **1.** a device for producing a strong air current, used for such purposes as making a fire burn faster or sounding a musical instrument. A bellows consists of an air chamber that can be expanded to draw air into it and contracted to force air out. **2.** anything that is like a bellows, such as the collapsible part of some cameras.

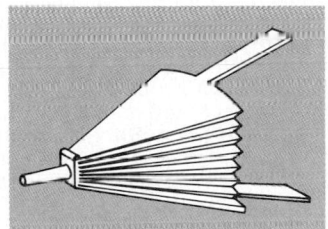

bellows *(def. 1)*

bell·weth·er (bel′weth′ər) *n.* **1.** a castrated male sheep that leads the flock, usually having a bell around its neck. **2.** a person or thing that leads or marks a trend: *The state of Maine has been called a bellwether in presidential elections.*

bel·ly (bel′ē) *n., pl.* **bel·lies.** **1.** the front part of the human body between the chest and pelvis; abdomen. **2.** the underside of the body of an animal. **3.** the stomach. **4.** the inside or interior of something: *the belly of a ship.* **5.** a curved or bulging surface or part: *The belly of a bottle holds more liquid than the neck.* **6.** the front or under surface of anything: *The airplane landed on its belly.* —*v.,* **bel·lied, bel·ly·ing.** —*v.i.* to swell or billow out; bulge: *The ship's sails bellied.* —*v.t.* to cause (something) to swell or billow out.

bel·ly·ache (bel′ē āk′) *n.* a pain in the abdomen, especially in the stomach. —*v.i.,* **bel·ly·ached, bel·ly·ach·ing.** *Slang.* to complain peevishly; grumble: *to bellyache about having to wash the car.* —**bel′ly·ach′er,** *n.*

bel·ly·band (bel′ē band′) *n.* a strap that forms part of a harness and goes under an animal's belly.

bel·ly·but·ton (bel′ē but′ən) *n. Informal.* the navel.

bel·ly·flop (bel′ē flop′) *Informal. n.* a dive in which the front of the diver's body lands flat against the surface of the water. —*v.i.* **bel·ly-flopped, bel·ly-flop·ping.** to make a bellyflop.

bel·ly–land (bel′ē land′) *v.i., v.t. Informal.* to land (an aircraft) without using the landing gear.

belly laugh *Informal.* a loud, deep, hearty laugh.

be·long (bi lông′) *v.i.* to have a proper place; be suitable or right: *The lamp belongs on that table.*
 ·**to belong to. a.** to be the property of: *This book belongs to me.* **b.** to be a part of; be connected with: *a vest that belongs to a suit.* **c.** to be a member of.

be·long·ings (bi lông′ingz) *pl. n.* personal property; possessions: *We packed our belongings before we moved.*

be·lov·ed (bi luv′id, bi luvd′) *adj.* much loved. —*n.* a person who is much loved.

be·low (bi lō′) *adv.* **1.** in or to a lower place: *From the roof we could see cars in the street below.* **2.** on or to a lower floor or deck: *The sailors stowed the cargo below.* **3.** in a later part of a book or other piece of writing: *the incidents described below.* **4.** less than zero on the temperature scale: *It was five below this morning.* —*prep.* **1.** in a lower place or position than: *a hem that is below the knee.* **2.** lower in rank, degree, or amount than; less than: *five degrees below zero, a shirt on sale for five dollars below the original price.* **3.** unworthy of; beneath: *It is below you to be dishonest.*

belt (belt) *n.* **1.** a strip or band of leather or other material worn around the waist. Belts are used to support clothing, tools, or weapons or as an ornament. **2.** any strip or band: *A belt of highways surrounded the city.* **3.** a region or zone having distinctive characteristics: *Most of the nation's wheat is grown in the wheat belt.* **4.** *Mechanics.* **a.** an endless flexible band that passes around two or more wheels or pulleys, used to transmit power or motion from one to the other. **b.** see conveyor belt. **5.** *Informal.* a strong or powerful blow. —*v.t.* **1.** to encircle or fasten with a belt: *to belt slacks.* **2.** to beat or strike with a belt or strap. **3.** *Informal.* to strike forcefully: *The batter belted the ball into the bleachers.*
 ·**below the belt. a.** in boxing, below the waist. **b.** unfair; unfairly: *The nasty criticism of the candidate's family was below the belt.*
 ·**to tighten one's belt.** to live in a more thrifty way.

belt·ing (bel′ting) *n.* **1.** material used for belts. **2.** *Informal.* a beating; thrashing.

be·lu·ga (bə lü′gə) *n.* **1.** a freshwater sturgeon of the Black Sea, Caspian Sea, and Volga River, whose eggs are eaten as caviar. **2.** a white whale living in the shallow coastal waters of Arctic seas.

be·moan (bi mōn′) *v.t.* to grieve over; lament: *to bemoan one's fate.*

be·mused (bi mūzd′) *adj.* **1.** lost in thought; preoccupied. **2.** confused; bewildered.

bench (bench) *n., pl.* **bench·es.** **1.** a long, often backless seat. **2.** a sturdy table for doing work with tools: *a cobbler's bench.* **3.a.** the seat for a judge in a court of

at; āpe; fär; câre; end; mē; it; īce; pêrce; hot; ōld; sông, fôrk; oil; out; up; ūse; rüle; pull; tûrn; chin; sing; shop; thin; <u>th</u>is; hw in white; zh in treasure. The symbol ə stands for the unstressed vowel sound heard in about, taken, pencil, lemon, and circus.

B

law. **b.** the office or position of a judge: *to be appointed to the bench.* **c.** a judge or judges who preside in a court of law. —*v.t. Sports.* to keep or take (a player) out of a game.

•**on the bench. a.** serving as a judge in a court of law. **b.** *Sports.* (of a player) not playing in a game: *The substitute was on the bench until the captain was hurt.*

bench mark 1. a surveyor's mark made on a rock or other permanent object whose elevation is known, used as a reference point in surveying and tidal observation. **2. benchmark.** something that serves as a standard or reference by which something else can be measured or compared.

bend (bend) *v.*, **bent, bend·ing.** —*v.t.* **1.** to change the shape of (something), especially by making it crooked or curved: *to bend a wire hanger, to bend one's knees.* **2.** to cause to yield; make submissive: *to bend an animal to one's will.* **3.** to direct or turn: *The hikers bent their steps toward home. The couple bent all their energies toward building their business.* —*v.i.* **1.** to become curved or crooked: *The branch bent under the weight of its fruit.* **2.** to take a stooping position; bow: *to bend over to tie your shoe.* **3.** to turn in a particular direction: *The river bends westward.* **4.** to give in; submit; yield: *They bent to their parents' wishes.* —*n.* **1.** a thing that is curved or bent; crook: *a bend in a river.* **2.** any of several knots used to join two ropes or to fasten a rope to something else. **3. the bends.** a painful condition caused by nitrogen gas bubbles in the body; caisson disease. It is caused by a rapid decrease in pressure of air or water on the body, such as when a deep-sea diver rises to the surface of the water too quickly.

•**to bend over backward** or **to bend over backwards.** to make a great effort; do one's best: *to bend over backward to help a friend.*

be·neath (bi nēth′) *prep.* **1.** lower than; below: *We stood beneath the stars.* **2.** directly under; underneath: *After the boat trip I was glad to feel the earth beneath my feet.* **3.** not fitting the dignity of; unworthy of: *Telling a lie is beneath you.* —*adv.* below; underneath: *Look beneath.*

Ben·e·dic·tine (ben′i dik′tin, ben′i dik′tēn) *n.* a monk or nun belonging to the order founded by Saint Benedict in the sixth century. —*adj.* of or relating to Saint Benedict or his religious order.

ben·e·dic·tion (ben′i dik′shən) *n.* a blessing, especially one given at the close of a religious service. [From the Late Latin word *benedictio* meaning "a benediction," from the Latin word *benedicere* meaning "to speak well of, praise," from the Latin words *bene* "well" and *dicere* "to say, to speak."]

ben·e·fac·tion (ben′ə fak′shən) *n.* a charitable gift or act, especially a donation of money.

ben·e·fac·tor (ben′ə fak′tər) *n.* a person who gives help or financial aid; patron: *This opera company has many benefactors.* —**ben′e·fac′tress,** *n.*

ben·e·fice (ben′ə fis) *n.* a church office, as that of a rector or vicar, and the income that comes with it.

be·nef·i·cence (bə nef′ə səns) *n.* **1.** doing good; kindness or generosity; charity. **2.** a charitable gift or act.

be·nef·i·cent (bə nef′ə sənt) *adj.* doing or causing good; being charitable. —**be·nef′i·cent·ly,** *adv.*

ben·e·fi·cial (ben′ə fish′əl) *adj.* having a good effect; advantageous; helpful: *Some insects are beneficial to plants.* —**ben′e·fi′cial·ly,** *adv.*

ben·e·fi·ci·ar·y (ben′ə fish′ē er′ē) *n., pl.* **ben·e·fi·ci·ar·ies. 1.** a person who receives anything as a benefit: *to be the beneficiary of a generous scholarship.* **2.** a person named to receive money or property, as from a will, trust, or insurance policy.

ben·e·fit (ben′ə fit) *n.* **1.** something that helps or betters a person or thing; advantage: *the benefits of a good education.* **2.** *usually,* **benefits.** money or other services given by an insurance company, government agency, or other institution, as to sick, disabled, or aged persons: *health insurance benefits.* **3.** a social or theatrical event held to raise money for some charity or cause. —*v.t.* to be useful or helpful to: *Rain will benefit the crops.* —*v.i.* to gain or profit; receive help: *to benefit from a teacher's knowledge.*

be·nev·o·lence (bə nev′ə ləns) *n.* **1.** the desire to do good; kindliness; generosity: *Their benevolence was shown by their many hours of work on the charity bazaar.* **2.** an act of kindness or a charitable gift.

be·nev·o·lent (bə nev′ə lənt) *adj.* doing or desiring to do good; kindly; generous: *The benevolent family donated much money to charity.* —**be·nev′o·lent·ly,** *adv.*

Ben·ga·li (ben gô′lē, ben gä′lē) *adj.* of or relating to Bengal, its people, or their culture. —*n., pl.* **Ben·ga·li.** a person who was born or is living in Bengal. Also, **Ben·ga·lese** (ben′gə lēz′, ben′gə lēs′).

be·night·ed (bi nī′tid) *adj.* **1.** mentally or morally ignorant: *a benighted people given to superstitions.* **2.** overtaken by darkness or night: *A blanket whiteness of benighted snow* (Robert Frost).

be·nign (bi nīn′) *adj.* **1.** having or showing a kindly disposition; gracious: *a benign monarch, a benign smile.* **2.** favorable; beneficial: *the benign climate of a tropical island.* **3.** not seriously threatening to life or health; not malignant: *a benign tumor.*

be·nig·nant (bi nig′nənt) *adj.* **1.** kindly toward others: *a benignant ruler.* **2.** favorable; beneficial. —**be·nig′nan·cy,** *n.* —**be·nig′nant·ly,** *adv.*

be·nig·ni·ty (bi nig′ni tē) *n., pl.* **be·nig·ni·ties. 1.** the quality or condition of being benign. **2.** a kind act.

ben·i·son (ben′ə zən) *n.* a blessing; benediction.

bent (bent) *v.* the past tense and past participle of **bend.** —*adj.* **1.** crooked or curved: *a bent wire.* **2.** firmly determined; set: *I was bent on going camping.* —*n.* a leaning or ability: *You have a natural bent for sports.*

be·numb (bi num′) *v.t.* to make numb.

ben·zene (ben′zēn) *n.* a colorless liquid that catches fire easily. It is obtained mainly from coal tar and is used as a solvent and in the manufacture of chemicals. Also, **benzol.**

ben·zine (ben′zēn) *n.* a colorless liquid that catches fire easily. It is obtained by distilling petroleum and is used as a solvent and as a motor fuel.

ben·zo·ic acid (ben zō′ik) a colorless or white acid found in certain plants and also made synthetically. It is used in dyes, cosmetics, and medicine.

ben·zo·in (ben′zō in, ben′zoin) *n.* a fragrant resin obtained from a tree found in southeastern Asia, used in medicine and perfume.

ben·zol (ben′zōl) *n.* another word for **benzene.**

be·queath (bi kwēth′, bi kwēth′) *v.t.* **1.** to give or leave (property) by will: *to bequeath money to a charity.* **2.** to hand down: *The pioneers bequeathed a heritage of independence to us.*

be·quest (bi kwest′) *n.* **1.** something bequeathed; legacy: *a bequest of money.* **2.** the act of bequeathing.

be·rate (bi rāt′) *v.t.,* **be·rat·ed, be·rat·ing.** to find fault with sharply; scold severely.

Ber·ber (bûr′bər) *n.* **1.** a member of one of a group of Muslim tribes living in northern Africa. **2.** any of several languages spoken by the Berbers. —*adj.* of or relating to the Berbers or their language.

be·reave (bi rēv′) *v.t.,* **be·reaved** or **be·reft, be·reav·ing.** to deprive and make desolate, usually by the death of a loved one: *The children were bereaved by the death of their dog.*

be·reave·ment (bi rēv′mənt) *n.* the condition of being bereaved.

be·reft (bi reft′) *v.* a past tense and past participle of **bereave.** —*adj.* deprived: *The shipwreck left them bereft of their belongings.*

be·ret (bə rā′) *n.* a soft, round cap, usually without a brim.

beret
two bicyclists wearing **berets**

berg (bûrg) *n.* see **iceberg.**

ber·i·ber·i (ber′ē ber′ē) *n.* a disease affecting the heart, muscles, and nervous system, caused by a lack of vitamin B₁.

ber·ke·li·um (bər kē′lē əm) *n.* a radioactive element artificially produced from americium. Symbol: **Bk** [From *Berkeley*, California, where it was first isolated.]

ber·lin (bər lin′, bûr′lin) *n.* a closed, four-wheeled carriage with a raised front seat for the driver.

berm (bûrm) *n.* **1.** an almost level part of a beach, back from the part near the water, formed by sand deposited by waves. **2.** a bank of earth pushed up against a building to protect it from extreme temperatures.

Ber·mu·da shorts (bər mū′də) shorts reaching almost to the knees. Also, **Ber·mu·das** (bər mū′dəz). [From *Bermuda*, where American tourists had tailors make them shorts patterned after those worn by British soldiers stationed there.]

ber·ry (ber′ē) *n., pl.* **ber·ries.** **1.** any small, pulpy fruit with many seeds, such as the raspberry or strawberry. **2.** any fleshy fruit with a skin around it, usually containing many seeds, such as the tomato, grape, or cranberry. —**ber′ry·like′,** *adj.*

ber·serk (bər sûrk′, bər zûrk′) *adj.* in a wild or violent rage. —*adv.* into a wild or violent rage: *The bull went berserk when it saw the bullfighter's cape.* [From the Old Norse word *berserkr* meaning "a frenzied Scandinavian warrior." According to legend, when the warrior was in a berserk state, he was invulnerable.]

berth (bûrth) *n.* **1.** a bed or bunk on a train or ship. **2.** a place for a ship to anchor or dock. **3.** a job or position: *to get a berth as a doctor in a hospital.* —*v.t.* **1.** to bring (a ship) into a berth. **2.** to provide with a berth. —*v.i.* to come into a berth: *The ship berthed in the harbor.*

  ·to give a wide berth to. to keep away from; avoid: *We give a wide berth to our neighbor's unfriendly dog.*

ber·yl (ber′əl) *n.* a hard mineral found in various colors, especially green or greenish blue. Emeralds and aquamarines are varieties of beryl.

be·ryl·li·um (bə ril′ē əm) *n.* a rare, strong, light, gray, poisonous element. This metal is

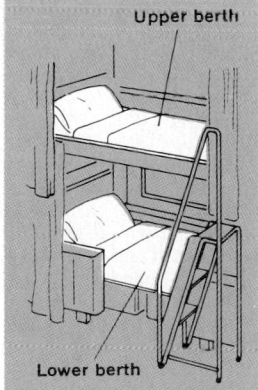

Upper berth

Lower berth

berth *(n., def. 1)*

used in alloys and nuclear reactors. Symbol: **Be** [Formed from the Greek word *bēryllion* meaning "little beryl," from the word *bēryllos* "beryl." This element was first discovered in beryl.]

be·seech (bi sēch′) *v.t.,* **be·sought** or **be·seeched, be·seech·ing.** **1.** to ask (someone) earnestly; implore; beg: *I beseech you, help us.* **2.** to ask for earnestly; plead for: *to beseech mercy of a judge.* —**be·seech′ing·ly,** *adv.*

be·seem (bi sēm′) *v.t. Archaic.* to be suitable or fitting for; suit.

be·set (bi set′) *v.t.,* **be·set, be·set·ting.** **1.** to attack from all sides: *beset by a gang of robbers.* **2.** to hem in; surround: *Enemy troops beset the camp under cover of night.* **3.** to trouble constantly; harass: *Many problems beset the new teacher.*

be·set·ting (bi set′ing) *adj.* constantly attacking; always present: *Poverty is a besetting problem.*

be·shrew (bi shrū′) *v.t. Archaic.* to curse: *Beshrew me, if I would do such a wrong* (Shakespeare, *Othello*).

be·side (bi sīd′) *prep.* **1.** at or by the side of; near: *Sit beside me.* **2.** in comparison with: *My grades seem awful beside yours.* **3.** see **besides. 4.** not relevant to; not connected with: *What you said was quite beside the point.* —*adv.* see **besides.**

  ·beside oneself. out of one's senses: *to be beside oneself with anger.*

be·sides (bi sīdz′) *adv.* **1.** moreover; furthermore: *I don't want to go; besides, it's too late.* **2.** in addition; also: *I have a pet cat and dog, and a pony besides.* —*prep.* **1.** in addition to; as well as: *I play the trumpet besides the piano.* **2.** other than: *Besides you, no one else is coming to lunch.* Also, **beside.**

be·siege (bi sēj′) *v.t.,* **be·sieged, be·sieg·ing.** **1.** to surround with armed forces in order to capture: *to besiege a fort.* **2.** to crowd around: *Autograph seekers besieged the famous singer.* **3.** to overwhelm or harass: *The store manager was besieged with complaints.* —**be·sieg′er,** *n.*

be·smear (bi smîr′) *v.t.* to smear.

be·smirch (bi smûrch′) *v.t.* to soil; sully: *to besmirch a person's reputation.*

be·sought (bi sôt′) a past tense and a past participle of beseech.

be·spake (bi spāk′) *Archaic.* a past tense of **bespeak.**

be·span·gle (bi spang′gəl) *v.t.,* **be·span·gled, be·span·gling.** to decorate or cover with spangles.

be·spat·ter (bi spat′ər) *v.t.* to spatter, as with mud; soil; sully.

be·speak (bi spēk′) *v.t.,* **be·spoke** or *(archaic)* **be·spake, be·spo·ken** or **be·spoke, be·speak·ing. 1.** to give evidence of; show: *expensive clothes that bespeak great wealth.* **2.** to arrange for in advance; reserve.

be·spec·ta·cled (bi spek′tə kəld) *adj.* wearing eyeglasses.

be·spoke (bi spōk′) a past tense and a past participle of bespeak.

be·spo·ken (bi spō′kən) a past participle of bespeak.

be·sprin·kle (bi spring′kəl) *v.t.,* **be·sprin·kled, be·sprin·kling.** to sprinkle.

Bes·se·mer converter (bes′ə mər) a pear-shaped steel vessel with air inlets at the bottom, used in the Bessemer process. [From the English industrialist Sir Henry *Bessemer* (1813–1898), who invented it.]

Bessemer process, a method of making steel in which

at; āpe; fär; câre; end; mē; it; īce; pîerce; hot; ōld; sông, fôrk; oil; out; up; ūse; rüle; pùll; tûrn; chin; sing; shop; thin; **th**is; hw in white; zh in treasure. The symbol ə stands for the unstressed vowel sound heard in about, taken, pencil, lemon, and circus.

a blast of air is blown through molten iron to oxidize and remove the carbon and impurities in the iron. [From the English industrialist Sir Henry *Bessemer* (1813–1898), who developed this process.]

best (best) *adj.* superlative of **good. 1.** of the highest quality; superior to all others: *the best speller in the class.* **2.** most desirable, satisfactory, or suitable: *the best way to get home.* **3.** largest; greatest: *The trip took the best part of the day.* —*adv.* superlative of **well¹. 1.** in the most excellent way; most successfully: *I work best when I work by myself.* **2.** in or to the highest degree; most fully: *I like this dress best.* —*n.* **1.** something of the highest quality or excellence: *Is this stereo the best that you sell?* **2.** a person or persons with the highest reputation or greatest ability: *That outfielder is the best on the team.* **3.** one's greatest effort or degree of excellence: *Do your best on the exam.* —*v.t.* to outdo; defeat: *to best someone at wrestling.*
 •**at best.** under the most favorable circumstances: *At best I can't possibly finish this job before Tuesday.*
 •**had best.** would be wise to; ought to: *You had best get home before midnight.*
 •**to get the best of** or **to have the best of.** to defeat: *My cousin got the best of me in the chess game.*
 •**to make the best of.** to cope with as well as possible: *We made the best of the tiresome bus ride.*
bes·tial (bes′chəl) *adj.* having the qualities of a beast; savage; brutish. —**bes′tial·ly,** *adv.*
bes·ti·al·i·ty (bes′chē al′i tē) *n., pl.* **bes·ti·al·i·ties. 1.** the quality, character, or nature of a beast. **2.** a bestial act.
be·stir (bi stûr′) *v.t.,* **be·stirred, be·stir·ring.** to rouse to action: *to bestir oneself early in the morning.*
best man, the chief attendant of the bridegroom at a wedding.
be·stow (bi stō′) *v.t.* to present as a gift or honor; give; confer: *to bestow a trophy on the winner of a race.* —**be·stow′al,** *n.*
be·strew (bi strü′) *v.t.,* **be·strewed, be·strewed** or **be·strewn, be·strew·ing. 1.** to scatter over (a surface): *to bestrew the floor with toys.* **2.** to scatter (something) around: *They carelessly bestrewed trash on the sidewalk.* **3.** to lie scattered over: *Litter bestrewed the street.*
be·stride (bi strīd′) *v.t.,* **be·strode** (bi strōd′) or **be·strid** (be strid′), **be·strid·den** (bi strid′ən) or **be·strid, be·strid·ing.** to sit on or stand over (something) with one leg on each side; straddle: *to bestride a fence.*
best·sell·er (best′sel′ər) also, **best seller, best-sell·er.** —*n.* a book that sells in very large quantities.
bet (bet) *n.* **1.** an agreement, usually between two parties, that one will pay or give something to the other, depending on the outcome of a contest or uncertain event; wager: *My cousin and I made a small bet on who would win the election.* **2.** the amount of money or the thing risked in a bet: *a bet of a dollar.* **3.** something on which such an agreement is made: *That horse is a good bet in the first race.* —*v.,* **bet** or **bet·ted, bet·ting.** —*v.t.* **1.** to agree to give or pay (something) in a bet. **2.** to say confidently: *I bet they will be late.* —*v.i.* to make a bet.
be·ta (bā′tə, bē′tə) *n.* the second letter of the Greek alphabet (B, β).
be·take (bi tāk′) *v.t.,* **be·took, be·tak·en, be·tak·ing.** to cause (oneself) to go: *They betook themselves on a great voyage.*
beta particle, an electron ejected from the atomic nucleus of an element that is radioactive.
beta ray, a stream of beta particles.
be·ta·tron (bā′tə tron′) *n.* a device in which electrons are accelerated to high speeds by a varying magnetic field.
be·tel (bē′təl) *n.* a climbing pepper plant found in Asia.
Be·tel·geuse (bē′təl jüz′) *n.* a bright giant red star that is the brightest star in the constellation Orion.
bête noire (bāt′nwär′) a person or thing that is particu-

larly dreaded or disliked; bugbear. [From the French phrase *bête noire* meaning "black beast," going back to the Latin words *bestia* "beast" and *niger* "black."]
be·think (bi thingk′) *v.t.,* **be·thought** (bi thôt′), **be·think·ing.** to remind (oneself): *The old couple bethought themselves of their younger days.*
be·tide (bi tīd′) *v.t., v.i.,* **be·tid·ed, be·tid·ing.** to happen (to); befall.
be·times (bi tīmz′) *adv.* early: *to wake betimes.*
be·to·ken (bi tō′kən) *v.t.* to be a sign or token of: *This gift betokens my affection for you.*
be·took (bi tůk′) the past tense of **betake.**
be·tray (bi trā′) *v.t.* **1.** to aid the enemy of; be a traitor to: *to betray one's country.* **2.** to be unfaithful or false to: *to betray a friend's trust.* **3.** to reveal or disclose: *The traitor betrayed the secret plans to the enemy. A blush betrayed the child's embarrassment.* **4.** to make known; indicate; show: *The sound of muffled gunfire betrayed the approach of enemy troops.* —**be·tray′al,** *n.* —**be·tray′er,** *n.*
be·troth (bi trōth′, bi trôth′) *v.t.* to promise to give in marriage. —**be·troth′al,** *n.*
be·trothed (bi trōthd′, bi trôtht′) *n.* a person who is engaged to be married. —*adj.* engaged to be married.
bet·ter¹ (bet′ər) *adj.* comparative of **good. 1.** of higher quality or excellence: *You are a better skater than I am.* **2.** more suitable, satisfactory, or desirable: *Copper is a better conductor of heat than iron.* **3.** improved in health: *I'm feeling much better today.* **4.** larger; greater: *to spend the better part of one's salary on rent.* —*adv.* comparative of **well¹. 1.** in a more excellent way; more successfully: *Cactuses grow better in a hot, dry climate.* **2.** to a higher degree; more fully: *Your dog is better trained than mine.* **3.** more: *The trip took better than an hour.* —*n.* **1.** something of a higher quality or excellence: *Which is the better of the two books?* **2.** also, **betters.** a person's superior, as in position or power: *Listen to your betters.* —*v.t.* **1.** to make better; improve: *to better oneself by studying harder.* **2.** to outdo; surpass: *to better one's former record in a marathon.* [From the Old English word *betera,* comparative of the word *gōd* "good."]
 •**better off.** in a better position or condition: *We'd be better off staying right here until the rain stops.*
 •**had better.** would be wise to; ought to: *You had better start studying if you want to pass the test.*
 •**to get the better of** or **to have the better of.** to defeat.
 •**to think better of.** to think again and more wisely of: *I thought better of sending the letter after rereading it.*
bet·ter² (bet′ər) also, **bet·tor.** *n.* a person who bets. [*Bet + -er¹.*]
bet·ter·ment (bet′ər mənt) *n.* the act of bettering or the condition of being bettered; improvement.
be·tween (bi twēn′) *prep.* **1.** in the space, time, or range separating: *a table between two chairs. to eat between meals.* **2.** joining; connecting: *a bridge between the island and the mainland.* **3.** involving: *a discussion between students and teachers.* **4.** by the joint action of: *Between them, the two friends mowed the lawn in an hour.* **5.** one or the other of: *to choose between two books.* —*adv.* in the space, time, or range separating: *two houses with a vacant lot between.*
 •**between you and me.** in confidence: *This secret is between you and me.*
 •**in between.** in a middle position: *The apartment has two rooms with a hall in between.*
 ▲ **Between** and **among** should not be confused. **Between** is usually used for two persons or things and **among** is usually used for three or more: *You and I can split the pizza between us.* **Between** is also used with three or more when each item is considered separately: *The teacher explained the difference between ducks, geese, and swans.*
be·twixt (bi twikst′) *prep., adv.* between.
 •**betwixt and between.** in a middle position.

Bev (bev) *also,* **bev.** *n.* a unit of energy equal to one billion electron volts. [Short for *B(illion) e(lectron) v(olts).*]

bev·a·tron (bev′ə tron′) *n.* a machine that accelerates protons to energies in the billions of electron volts.

bev·el (bev′əl) *n.* **1.** a slanting edge, such as on a ruler, mirror, or piece of plate glass. **2.** the angle formed by such an edge. **3.** an adjustable tool used to measure the angle of surfaces that are to be set at a slant. Also, **bevel square.** *—v.t.,* **bev·eled, bev·el·ing;** *also, British,* **bev·elled, bev·el·ling.** to shape or cut a slanting edge on (something). *—adj.* slanting; oblique; sloping.

bevel gear, a gear fitting into another in such a way that the shafts are not parallel.

bev·er·age (bev′ər ij, bev′rij) *n.* a liquid for drinking; drink.

bev·y (bev′ē) *n., pl.* **bev·ies. 1.** a group, especially of girls or women. **2.** a group of birds or animals, especially a flock of quail.

be·wail (bi wāl′) *v.t.* to feel or express deep sorrow for; mourn; lament: *to bewail one's fate.*

be·ware (bi wâr′) *v.i.* to be wary or careful: *Beware of the dog!* *—v.t.* to be wary or careful of: *Beware the oncoming storm!*

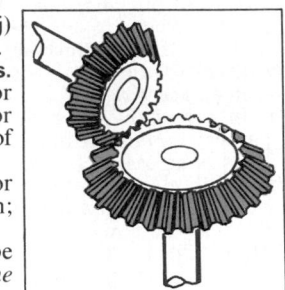

bevel gears

be·wil·der (bi wil′dər) *v.t.* to confuse or puzzle completely. **—be·wil·der·ment,** *n.*

be·witch (bi wich′) *v.t.* **1.** to cast a spell over by witchcraft or magic: *In the fairy tale the children were bewitched by a wicked fairy.* **2.** to charm; fascinate.

be·witch·ing (bi wich′ing) *adj.* charming; fascinating: *a bewitching smile.* **—be·witch′ing·ly,** *adv.*

bey (bā) *n.* in the Ottoman Empire, a governor of a province.

be·yond (bē ond′, bi yond′) *prep.* **1.** on or to the other or far side of; farther on than: *The camp is beyond those hills.* **2.** later than: *to be up beyond one's bedtime.* **3.** out of the reach or understanding of: *socks so worn that they're beyond mending, a math problem that's beyond me.* **4.** more than: *jewels priced far beyond their worth.* *—adv.* farther on or away: *Beyond is the ocean.* *—n.* **the beyond** or **the great beyond.** life after death.

bi– *prefix* **1.** having or involving two: *bicycle, bilateral.* **2.** twice; doubly: *biconvex.* **3.** coming or occurring every two: *bimonthly, biweekly.* [From the Latin prefix *bi–* meaning "two," "doubly," or "twice."]

Bi, the symbol for bismuth.

bi·a·ly (bē ä′lē, byä′lē) *n., pl.* **bi·a·lys.** a flat roll with a depressed center covered with onion flakes. [Short for the Yiddish phrase *Bialystoker kuchen* meaning "a roll from *Bialystok,* Poland."]

bi·an·nu·al (bī an′ū əl) *adj.* happening twice a year; semiannual: *a biannual publication, a biannual trip.* **—bi·an′nu·al·ly,** *adv.*

▲ **Biannual** should not be confused with **biennial,** which means "occurring every two years."

bi·as (bī′əs) *n., pl.* **bi·as·es. 1.** a tendency to favor one side or point of view; prejudice: *A good judge never shows bias.* **2.** a slanting line cutting across the threads of a fabric: *cloth cut on the bias.* *—adj.* slanting across the threads of the fabric: diagonal. *—v.t.,* **bi·ased, bi·as·ing;** *also, British,* **bi·assed, bi·as·sing.** to cause to have a bias: *Their lies have biased me against them.*

bi·ath·lon (bī ath′lon) *n.* an athletic competition that combines cross-country skiing and rifle marksmanship.

bib (bib) *n.* **1.** a piece of cloth or plastic tied under the chin, especially of a baby, to protect the clothing from spilled food or drink. **2.** the upper front part of an apron or overalls.

Bi·ble (bī′bəl) *n.* **1.** the sacred writings of the Christian religion contained in the Old and New Testaments. **2.** the sacred writings of the Jewish religion corresponding to the Christian Old Testament. **3.** a book or writings sacred to any religion. **4. bible.** any book used or accepted as an authority: *This book is a bible for baseball fans.* [From the Old French word *bible,* from the Medieval Latin word *biblia* meaning "bible," from the Greek word *biblia* meaning "the books," from the word *biblos* "a papyrus scroll" or "book."]

bib·li·cal (bib′li kəl) *also,* **Bib·li·cal.** *adj.* of, relating to, or found in the Bible: *a biblical scholar, biblical names.* **—bib′li·cal·ly,** *adv.*

bib·li·og·ra·pher (bib′lē og′rə fər) *n.* a person who compiles bibliographies.

bib·li·og·ra·phy (bib′lē og′rə fē) *n., pl.* **bib·li·og·ra·phies. 1.** a list of books on a particular subject or person, or by a particular author. **2.** the history, description, comparison, and classification of books and other writings. **—bib·li·o·graph·i·cal** (bib′lē ə graf′i kəl), *adj.* **—bib′·li·o·graph′i·cal·ly,** *adv.*

bib·li·o·phile (bib′lē ə fīl′) *n.* a person who loves books.

bi·cam·er·al (bī kam′ər əl) *adj.* having or consisting of two legislative chambers or houses: *The United States Congress is a bicameral legislature.* [Formed from the prefix *bi–* meaning "two" + the Latin word *camera* meaning "chamber."]

bi·car·bo·nate (bī kär′bə nit) *n.* any salt containing the radical HCO₃, such as sodium bicarbonate.

bicarbonate of soda, another term for **sodium bicarbonate.**

bi·cen·ten·ni·al (bī′sen ten′ē əl) *adj.* happening once every 200 years. *—n.* a 200th anniversary or its celebration.

bi·ceps (bī′seps) *n., pl.* **bi·ceps** or **bi·ceps·es.** the large muscle in the front of the upper arm that serves to bend the arm.

bi·chlo·ride (bī klôr′īd) *n.* **1.** a compound that contains two atoms of chlorine; dichloride. **2.** see **bichloride of mercury.**

bichloride of mercury, a very poisonous white compound, used in photography.

bick·er (bik′ər) *v.i.* to quarrel noisily, especially about something unimportant: *The two friends bickered over who would ride the bicycle.* *—n.* a quarrel.

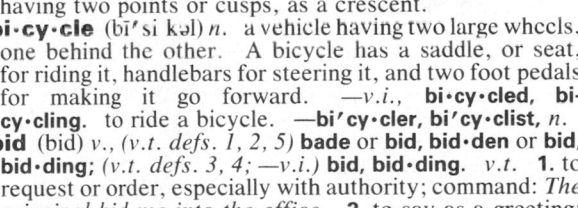

biceps

bi·con·cave (bī′kon kāv′) *adj.* concave on both sides: *a biconcave lens.*

bi·con·vex (bī′kon veks′) *adj.* convex on both sides: *a biconvex lens.*

bi·cus·pid (bī kus′pid) *n.* a tooth having two points; premolar. Human adults have eight bicuspids. *—adj.* having two points or cusps, as a crescent.

bi·cy·cle (bī′si kəl) *n.* a vehicle having two large wheels, one behind the other. A bicycle has a saddle, or seat, for riding it, handlebars for steering it, and two foot pedals for making it go forward. *—v.i.,* **bi·cy·cled, bi·cy·cling.** to ride a bicycle. **—bi′cy·cler, bi′cy·clist,** *n.*

bid (bid) *v., (v.t. defs. 1, 2, 5)* **bade** or **bid, bid·den** or **bid, bid·ding; (v.t. defs. 3, 4; —v.i.)** **bid, bid·ding.** *v.t.* **1.** to request or order, especially with authority; command: *The principal bid me into the office.* **2.** to say as a greeting:

at; āpe; fär; câre; end; mē; it; īce; pîerce; hot; ōld; sông, fôrk; oil; out; up; ūse; rüle; pùll; tûrn; chin; sing; shop; thin; *this;* hw in white; zh in treasure. The symbol ə stands for the unstressed vowel sound heard in about, taken, pencil, lemon, and circus.

We bade good-bye to our friends. **3.** to offer (an amount of money) as a price: *We bid fifty dollars for the lamp at the auction.* **4.** to state (the number of tricks or points) that one will try to make in return for declaring what is trump in a card game, such as bridge. **5.** to invite: *The host bade us to enter.* —*v.i.* to make an offer of an amount of money for something: *to bid on a painting at an auction.* —*n.* **1.** an offer of an amount of money for something: *Did you make a bid at the auction?* **2.** the amount offered: *a bid of ten dollars.* **3.** an attempt to win or get: *to make a bid for the presidency.* **4.a.** the number of tricks or points a player tries to make in return for declaring what is trump in a card game, such as bridge. **b.** a player's turn to bid. **5.** an invitation. —**bid'der,** *n.*

bid·ding (bid'ing) *n.* **1.** an order or command: *I closed my book at the teacher's bidding.* **2.** invitation: *We came to the party at our friend's bidding.* **3.** the making of a bid or bids: *The bidding at the auction was slow.*

bide (bīd) *v.t.,* **bid·ed** or **bode, bid·ed, bid·ing.** to wait. **·to bide one's time.** to wait patiently for the right moment or opportunity.

bi·en·ni·al (bī en'ē əl) *adj.* **1.** happening once every two years: *a biennial election.* **2.** living for two years: *a biennial plant.* —*n.* **1.** a plant that lives for two years, usually producing flowers, fruit, and seeds in the second year. **2.** an event that happens once every two years. —**bi·en'ni·al·ly,** *adv.* ▲ See **biannual** for usage note.

bier (bîr) *n.* a stand on which a dead body or the coffin containing it is placed before burial.

bi·fo·cal (bī fō'kəl) *adj.* (of an eyeglass lens) having two parts, one for seeing close objects and one for seeing distant objects. —*n.* **1.** a lens ground with two parts. **2. bifocals.** a pair of eyeglasses having bifocal lenses.

big (big) *adj.,* **big·ger, big·gest. 1.** of great size, extent, amount, or degree; large: *a big ranch with many acres.* **2.** of great importance: *a big banker, a big problem.* **3.** grown-up; mature: *to act like a big girl or big boy.* **4.** loud: *a big voice.* **5.** proud and boastful: *to be a big talker.* **6.** kind or generous: *to have a big heart.* —*adv. Informal.* boastfully: *to talk big.* —**big'ness,** *n.*

big·a·mist (big'ə mist) *n.* a person who commits bigamy.

big·a·my (big'ə mē) *n.* the crime of marrying a person while being married to someone else.

big bang theory, the theory that the universe began billions of years ago as the result of a huge cosmic explosion of a dense mass of material.

Big Dipper, a group of seven stars in the constellation Ursa Major, forming the outline of a dipper.

big game, large animals, such as elephants, lions, and tigers, hunted for sport.

big·heart·ed (big'här'tid) *adj.* having or showing kindness or generosity.

big·horn (big'hôrn') *n., pl.* **big·horn** or **big·horns.** a wild sheep of the Rocky Mountains, having large, tightly curled horns. Also, **Rocky Mountain sheep.**

bight (bīt) *n.* **1.** a bend or curve, as in a river or coastline. **2.** a bay formed by such a bend in a coastline. **3.** a loop of a rope.

big league 1. another term for **major league. 2.** Usually, **big leagues.** *Informal.* a group made up of the leading people or organizations engaged in a particular activity: *Our computer company has grown a lot, and now it's in the big leagues.* —**big-league,** *adj.*

bighorn

big·ot (big'ət) *n.* a person who is excessively intolerant, as of any race, religion, belief, or opinion differing from his or her own.

big·ot·ed (big'ə tid) *adj.* characteristic of a bigot; intolerant; prejudiced.

big·ot·ry (big'ə trē) *n., pl.* **big·ot·ries.** a belief, attitude, or action characteristic of a bigot.

big shot *Slang.* a person of importance.

big time *Informal.* the highest level of achievement, as in some profession or activity: *an actor who hasn't yet made the big time.*

big top 1. the main tent of a circus. **2.** the circus.

big·wig (big'wig') *n. Informal.* a person of importance or influence. [From the large wigs worn by men of importance during the eighteenth century.]

bike (bīk) *Informal. n.* **1.** a bicycle. **2.** a motorcycle. **3.** a motorbike. —*v.i.,* **biked, bik'ing.** to ride a bicycle, motorcycle, or motorbike.

bi·ki·ni (bi kē'nē) *n.* a scanty two-piece bathing suit for women and girls.

bi·lat·er·al (bī lat'ər əl) *adj.* **1.** affecting two sides or parties: *a bilateral agreement.* **2.** arranged on opposite sides of an axis. **3.** having two sides.

bile (bīl) *n.* **1.** a bitter yellow or greenish liquid secreted by the liver to aid digestion, especially the digestion of fats. **2.** bad temper; anger.

bilge (bilj) *n.* **1.** the lowest inner part of the hull of a ship. **2.** see **bilge water. 3.** the bulging part of a cask or barrel. **4.** *Informal.* nonsense; foolishness.

bilge water, stagnant water that collects in the bilge of a ship.

bi·lin·gual (bī ling'gwəl) *adj.* **1.** able to speak two languages, especially with equal or nearly equal skill and ease. **2.** expressed or written in two languages: *a bilingual dictionary.* —**bi·lin'gual·ly,** *adv.*

bil·ious (bil'yəs) *adj.* **1.** bad-tempered; cross. **2.** of or relating to bile. **3.** caused by or having a disorder of the liver. —**bil'ious·ly,** *adv.* —**bil'ious·ness,** *n.*

bilk (bilk) *v.t.* to cheat; swindle: *The dishonest mechanic bilked us of $150.*

bill[1] (bil) *n.* **1.** a statement of money owed for things supplied, services performed, or work done: *a grocery bill, a dentist's bill, a bill for repairs on a car.* **2.** a piece of paper money: *a five-dollar bill.* **3.** a printed advertisement or public notice; poster: *Do not post bills on the walls of this building.* **4.** a performance or concert offered by a theater: *a good bill at the movie theater.* **5.** the draft of a proposed law: *Congress sent several bills to the president to be signed.* —*v.t.* **1.** to send (to someone) a statement of money owed: *The store billed us for the furniture we bought.* **2.** to announce or advertise by bills or posters: *A band was billed as the main attraction.* [From the Medieval Latin word *billa,* a form of the word *bulla* meaning "seal" or "document with a seal," from the Latin word *bulla* "bubble, knob."] **·to fill the bill.** to satisfy or meet the needs: *If you want an interesting book, this novel will fill the bill.*

bill[2] (bil) *n.* **1.** the horny beak of a bird. **2.** an animal's beak resembling a bird's bill: *the bill of a turtle.* —*v.i.* (of birds) to join or touch bills. [From the Old English word *bile* meaning "beak."] **·to bill and coo.** to kiss and speak lovingly.

bill·board (bil'bôrd') *n.* a large panel usually placed outdoors for posting advertisements or announcements.

bil·let[1] (bil'it) *n.* **1.** an order to provide lodging for a member of the armed forces, as in a private home. **2.** the lodging assigned by such an order. —*v.t.* **1.** to assign lodging by a billet. **2.** to provide lodging for. [From the Old French word *billette* meaning "letter of safe conduct," going back to the Medieval Latin word *billa,* a form of the word *bulla* "document with a seal."]

bil·let[2] (bil'it) *n.* **1.** a small, thick stick of wood, especially one used for fuel. **2.** a bar of iron or steel. [From the French word *billette* meaning "billet of wood," from the word *bille* meaning "wood log."]

bil·let–doux (bil'ā dü', bil'ē dü') *n., pl.* **bil·lets-doux**

(bil´ā düz´, bil´ē düz´). a love letter. [From the French phrase *billet doux* meaning "sweet letter," going back to the Medieval Latin word *billa* "document" and the Latin word *dulcis* "sweet."]

bill·fold (bil´fōld´) *n.* a folding case for paper money; wallet.

bil·liards (bil´yərdz) *n.* **1.** a game played with three hard balls that are hit with a long stick called a cue. It is played on a cloth-covered rectangular table with cushions along the edges. **2.** any of several similar games such as pool. ▲ used with a singular verb in both definitions.

bill·ing (bil´ing) *n.* **1.** advertising or publicity, as for a performer or product: *The movie didn't live up to its advance billing.* **2.** the position occupied by the name of a performer or act in a program or advertisement: *Which performer had top billing at the concert?*

bil·lings·gate (bil´ingz gāt´) *n.* language that is vulgar and insulting. [From the London fish market at *Billingsgate,* known for its vulgar language.]

bil·lion (bil´yən) *n.* **1.a.** in the United States, the cardinal number that is one thousand times one million. **b.** the symbol representing this number; 1,000,000,000. **2.a.** in Great Britain, the cardinal number that is one million times one million. **b.** the symbol representing this number: 1,000,000,000,000. —*adj.* numbering one billion.

bil·lion·aire (bil´yə nâr´) *n.* a person who has a billion or more dollars, pounds, francs, or other kind of currency.

bil·lionth (bil´yənth) *adj.* **1.** (the ordinal of billion) being last in a series of one billion. **2.** being one of a billion equal parts. —*n.* **1.** something that is last in a series of one billion. **2.** one of a billion equal parts.

bill of exchange, a written order to pay to a designated person a specified sum of money.

bill of fare, a list of the foods served at a restaurant; menu.

bill of health, a certificate given to the captain of a ship indicating the presence or absence of infectious diseases on board the ship and in the port at the time the ship departs.

·**clean bill of health.** *Informal.* a favorable report.

bill of lading, a receipt given by a carrier, as a shipping firm or railroad, for goods accepted for transportation by the carrier.

bill of rights **1. Bill of Rights.** the first ten amendments to the Constitution of the United States, guaranteeing certain basic rights and liberties for all citizens, such as freedom of speech and freedom of religion. **2.** any declaration of the rights and liberties guaranteed to the citizens of a country.

bill of sale, a written statement transferring property from the person who sells it to the person who buys it.

bil·low (bil´ō) *n.* **1.** a great wave or swell of a body of water: *Ocean billows tossed the ship.* **2.** any great or surging mass: *billows of smoke from a burning house.* —*v.i.* **1.** to rise or roll in billows; surge; swell. **2.** to swell out: *The sail billowed in the wind.* —*v.t.* to cause to swell out: *Wind billowed the flag.*

bil·low·y (bil´ō ē) *adj.,* **bil·low·i·er, bil·low·i·est.** full of or characterized by billows; surging: *a billowy sea.*

bil·ly (bil´ē) *n., pl.* **bil·lies.** a short, heavy club or stick, especially one carried by a police officer. Also, **billy club.**

billy goat *Informal.* a male goat.

bi·month·ly (bī munth´lē) *adj.* **1.** happening every two months. **2.** happening twice a month; semimonthly. —*n., pl.* **bi·month·lies.** a bimonthly publication. —*adv.* **1.** every two months. **2.** twice a month; semimonthly.

▲ Although the adjective **bimonthly** has two different definitions, it is usually used to mean "happening every two months." If "happening twice a month" is meant, it is clearer to use the word **semimonthly,** which has only this meaning.

bin (bin) *n.* a receptacle or enclosed place for holding or storing something, such as grain or coal. —*v.t.,* **binned, bin·ning.** to store in a bin.

bi·na·ry (bī´nə rē, bī´ner ē) *adj.* **1.** consisting of, involving, or characterized by two things or parts. **2.** using or based on the binary system: *a binary numeral.* —*n., pl.* **bi·na·ries.** see **binary star.**

binary star, a pair of stars revolving around a common center of gravity.

binary system, a number system with a base of two, in which any number may be expressed by 0 or 1 or by some combination of these. Digital computers use the binary system.

bin·au·ral (bī nôr´əl, bin ôr´əl) *adj.* **1.** involving both ears: *binaural hearing.* **2.** another word for **stereophonic.**

bind (bīnd) *v.,* **bound, bind·ing.** —*v.t.* **1.** to tie, as with a rope; fasten together; secure: *to bind a package with twine, to bind wheat into bundles.* **2.** to fasten or wrap around; encircle: *to bind one's hair with a bandanna.* **3.** to bandage (often with *up*): *to bind up a wound.* **4.** to force or obligate; compel: *The contract binds the workers to stay with the company for a year.* **5.** to hamper or restrain; limit: *to be bound by tight clothing.* **6.** to cause to stick together: *Water binds particles of dirt to form mud.* **7.** to bring or hold together, as by ties of love, gratitude, or loyalty: *team members bound together by their desire for victory.* **8.** to strengthen or ornament by a border or edge: *to bind the hem of a blanket.* **9.** to fasten or enclose between covers: *to bind a book.* —*v.i.* **1.** to have the power to obligate or compel: *a promise that binds.* **2.** to hamper or restrain someone or something: *My jeans shrank so much that they bind.* **3.** to stick together; cohere: *Water made the mixture bind.* —*n. Informal.* a difficult situation: *Receiving two invitations for the same night really put me in a bind.*

bind·er (bīn´dər) *n.* **1.** a person who binds, especially a bookbinder. **2.** anything that binds, such as string or glue. **3.** a removable cover that holds sheets of paper or other material together. **4.** a machine that reaps grain and ties it into bundles.

bind·er·y (bīn´də rē) *n., pl.* **bind·er·ies.** a place where books are bound.

bind·ing (bīn´ding) *n.* **1.** anything that binds. **2.** a cloth tape used to protect or finish raw edges, as of a garment, carpet, or blanket. **3.** a cover and backing holding together

billow *(v., def. 2)*
sails **billowing** in the wind

at; āpe; fär; câre; end; mē; it; īce; pîerce; hot; ōld; sông; fôrk; oil; out; up; ūse; rüle; pull; tûrn; chin; sing; shop; thin; this; hw in white; zh in treasure. The symbol ə stands for the unstressed vowel sound heard in about, taken, pencil, lemon, and circus.

and enclosing the pages of a book. **4.** the act of binding. —*adj.* having the power to obligate or compel; obligatory: *a binding agreement to pay back a loan.*

bind·weed (bīnd′wēd′) *n.* a trailing or climbing plant with showy, trumpet-shaped flowers.

binge (binj) *n. Informal.* a period of unrestrained or extreme indulgence in some activity, such as eating, drinking, or spending money; spree.

bin·go (bing′gō) *n.* a game in which each player covers numbers on a card as they are called out. The winner is the first player to cover a row of five numbers.

bin·na·cle (bin′ə kəl) *n.* a case or stand containing a ship's compass, usually placed near the helm.

bi·noc·u·lar (bə nok′yə lər, bī nok′yə lər) *adj.* **1.** for use by both eyes: *a binocular microscope.* **2.** using both eyes: *binocular vision.* —*n.* **binoculars.** an optical instrument consisting of two small telescopes joined together. Field glasses and opera glasses are binoculars.

binoculars

bi·no·mi·al (bī nō′mē əl) *adj.* consisting of two terms. *x − y* is a binomial expression. —*n.* **1.** a mathematical expression consisting of two terms joined by a plus or minus sign. The expressions *3x + 7y* and *8 + 2* are binomials. **2.** the scientific name for an animal or plant consisting of two terms. *Canis lupus,* the scientific name for the wolf, is a binomial.

bio- *combining form* of life or living things: *biology, biography.* [Originally from the Greek word *bios* meaning "life."]

bi·o·chem·i·cal (bī′o kem′i kəl) *adj.* of or relating to biochemistry. —**bi′o·chem′i·cal·ly,** *adv.*

bi·o·chem·ist (bī′ō kem′ist) *n.* an expert in biochemistry.

bi·o·chem·is·try (bī′ō kem′ə strē) *n.* the science dealing with the chemical structure and processes of living things.

bi·o·de·grad·a·ble (bī′ō di grā′də bəl) *adj.* capable of decaying naturally into products that can be absorbed by the environment: *Paper is biodegradable, but most plastics are not.*

bi·o·e·lec·tric·i·ty (bī′ō i lek tris′i tē) *n.* electricity occurring naturally in living organisms, as in the electric eel.

bi·o·en·gi·neer·ing (bī′ō en′jə nîr′ing) *n.* the use of engineering principles and equipment to understand and solve problems in biology and medicine, as in the development of artificial organs and limbs. Also, **biomedical engineering.**

bi·o·eth·ics (bī′ō eth′iks) *n.* a field of study concerned with ethical questions raised by new biological and medical procedures, such as prolonging life by artificial means and transplanting organs. ▲ used with a singular verb. —**bi′o·eth′i·cal,** *adj.*

bi·o·feed·back (bī′ō fēd′bak′) *n.* a method by which a person can learn to control a body function that is usually considered to be involuntary, such as blood pressure or heart rate.

bi·o·gen·e·sis (bī′ō jen′ə sis) *n.* **1.** the theory that life can develop only from living organisms. **2.** the development of living organisms from other living organisms.

bi·og·ra·pher (bī og′rə fər) *n.* a person who writes biographies.

bi·o·graph·i·cal (bī′ə graf′i kəl) *adj.* **1.** of or relating to a person's life: *a biographical novel.* **2.** of, relating to, or containing biography: *biographical writings.* Also, **bi·o·graph·ic** (bī′ə graf′ik). —**bi′o·graph′i·cal·ly,** *adv.*

bi·og·ra·phy (bī og′rə fē) *n., pl.* **bi·og·ra·phies.** an account of a person's life.

bi·o·log·i·cal (bī′ə loj′i kəl) *adj.* of or relating to biology: *a biological experiment.* Also, **bi·o·log·ic** (bī′ə loj′ik). —**bi′o·log′i·cal·ly,** *adv.*

biological clock, an internal timing mechanism in plants and animals that directs certain natural rhythms and cycles of behavior, such as sleep and wakefulness.

biological warfare, warfare in which disease-producing microorganisms or their toxins are used against people, livestock, or crops. Also, **germ warfare.**

bi·ol·o·gist (bī ol′ə jist) *n.* an expert in biology.

bi·ol·o·gy (bī ol′ə jē) *n.* the science of living organisms and their processes. Botany, zoology, and ecology are branches of biology. [From the German word *biologie* meaning "biology," formed from the Greek word *bios* "life" and *logos* "word," "explanation," "reckoning."]

bi·o·lu·mi·nes·cence (bī′ō lü′mə nes′əns) *n.* a giving off of light by living organisms, such as fireflies.

bi·o·mass (bī′ō mas′) *n.* **1.** *Ecology.* the weight or volume of living material, including plants, animals, and bacteria, in a certain habitat: *The scientists carefully measured the biomass of the pond.* **2.** organic material, especially discarded matter such as cornstalks or scrap paper, that can be used as fuel or as a source of fuel: *Biomass may be an important source of energy in the future.*

bi·ome (bī′ōm) *n.* **1.** a complex community of plants and animals living in a particular geographical area with a particular climate: *Deserts and rain forests are two vastly different biomes.* **2.** the area occupied by such a community. [From *bio-* + the Latin suffix *-oma* meaning "a mass."]

bi·o·med·i·cal engineering (bī′ō med′i kəl) another term for **bioengineering.**

bi·o·met·rics (bī′ō met′riks) *n.* the science that uses statistical methods in the study of biological and medical problems. ▲ used with a singular verb. Also, **biometry.**

bi·on·ic (bī on′ik) *adj.* having to do with or being a mechanical device that replaces or strengthens a part of the human body: *a bionic arm.*

bi·on·ics (bī on′iks) *n.* the study of the parts of the bodies of human beings and other animals in order to make new mechanical or electronic devices or to improve old ones. The design of computers and artificial legs and arms is based on bionics. ▲ used with a singular verb.

bi·o·phys·i·cist (bī′ō fiz′ə sist) *n.* an expert in biophysics.

bi·o·phys·ics (bī′ō fiz′iks) *n.* the science that applies the principles and methods of physics to the study of biological organisms and processes. ▲ used with a singular verb.

bi·op·sy (bī′op sē) *n., pl.* **bi·op·sies.** the surgical removal of a small amount of tissue from a living person or animal for microscopic examination. It is often used to diagnose the presence or absence of cancer.

bi·o·rhythm (bī′ō rith′əm) *n.* an inborn cycle in certain biological functions, occurring in living organisms: *The cycle of sleep and wakefulness in animals is a daily biorhythm.*

bi·o·sphere (bī′ə sfîr′) *n.* the part of the earth, its waters, and its atmosphere where life is found.

bi·o·tech·nol·o·gy (bī′ō tek nol′ə jē) *n.* the use of living organisms in solving practical problems. For example, gene-splicing has been used to develop bacteria that can be used in the manufacture of insulin.

bi·ot·ic (bī ot′ik) *adj.* of, relating to, or characterized by life or living organisms: *The desert is a complex biotic community.*

bi·o·tin (bī′ə tin) *n.* a vitamin necessary for metabolism and growth, part of the vitamin B complex group; formerly called vitamin H.

bi·par·ti·san (bī pär′tə zən) *adj.* composed of, representing, or supported by two parties, especially the Republican and Democratic parties: *a bipartisan bill.*

bi·par·tite (bī pär′tīt) *adj.* **1.** of or relating to two groups, nations, or the like: *a bipartite trade agreement.* **2.** consisting of two parts, especially two corresponding parts, as a leaf.

bi·ped (bī′ped) *n.* an animal having two feet. Human beings and birds are bipeds. —*adj.* two-footed.

bi·plane (bī′plān′) *n.* an airplane with two sets of main wings, one above the other.

birch (bûrch) *n., pl.* **birch·es. 1.** any of a group of trees and shrubs bearing saw-toothed leaves. The pale or white bark of one kind of birch is easily peeled in thin papery strips and was used by American Indians to make canoes. **2.** the hard, close-grained wood of this tree. **3.** a branch or bundle of twigs from this tree, used as a whip.

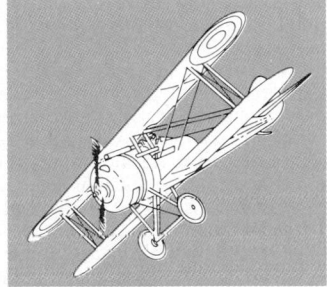
biplane

bird (bûrd) *n.* **1.** any of a class of warm-blooded, egg-laying animals that have two legs, feathers, and wings. **2.** another word for **shuttlecock**. **3.** *Informal.* a person: *Our neighbor is an odd bird.* **4.** *Informal.* an aircraft, spacecraft, rocket, or guided missile. —**bird′like**′, *adj.*

bird·bath (bûrd′bath′) *n., pl.* **bird·baths** (bûrd′bathz′, bûrd′baths′). a shallow basin filled with water for birds to bathe in and drink.

bird call 1. the sound made by a bird; song of a bird. **2.** a sound imitating that made by a bird. **3.** a device for imitating the sound made by a bird.

bird dog, any of various dogs specially trained to hunt and retrieve game birds.

bird·er (bûr′dər) *n.* another word for **bird watcher.**

bird·house (bûrd′hous′) *n., pl.* **bird·hous·es** (bûrd′-hou′ziz). a small box in which birds may nest, often resembling a house.

bird·ie (bûr′dē) *n.* **1.** a small bird. **2.** in golf, a score of one stroke under par on a hole.

bird·ing (bûr′ding) *n.* another word for **bird-watching.**

bird·lime (bûrd′līm′) *n.* a sticky substance that is smeared on twigs to catch small birds.

bird of paradise, a songbird of Australia, New Guinea, and neighboring islands. The male of the species is noted for its brilliant feathers.

bird of passage 1. any bird that migrates with the seasons. **2.** a person who does not stay in one place for long.

bird of prey, any of various birds that feed on other birds and animals. Eagles, hawks, and owls are birds of prey.

bird·seed (bûrd′sēd′) *n.* a mixture of small seeds fed chiefly to caged birds.

bird's–eye (bûrdz′ī′) *adj.* **1.** seen from above: *a bird's-eye view of the town from an airplane.* **2.** having markings somewhat resembling birds' eyes: *a desk made of bird's-eye maple.*

bird watcher, a person who observes and studies wild birds in their natural surroundings. Also, **birder.**

bird–watch·ing (bûrd′woch′ing) *n.* the observation and study of wild birds in their natural surroundings. Also, **birding.**

bi·ret·ta (bə ret′ə) *n.* a stiff, square cap worn by members of the Roman Catholic clergy and by some members of the Anglican clergy. Its color is black for priests, purple for bishops, and red for cardinals.

birth (bûrth) *n.* **1.** the act or fact of being born. **2.** the act of bringing forth offspring. **3.** the beginning of anything; origin: *the birth of an idea, the birth of a nation.* **4.** descent; lineage; ancestry: *of noble birth.*

·**to give birth to. a.** to bring forth (offspring): *The cat gave birth to six kittens.* **b.** to bring forth (anything); be the cause of: *The artist's work gave birth to a new style of painting.*

birth control, the control of the number of offspring born, especially by the prevention of conception.

birth·day (bûrth′dā′) *n.* **1.** the day of a person's birth. **2.** the anniversary of this day.

birth defect, any physical or mental deformity or disorder present at birth.

birth·mark (bûrth′märk′) *n.* a mark or blemish on the skin that is present at birth.

birth·place (bûrth′plās′) *n.* **1.** the place of a person's birth. **2.** any place or origin: *Greece is often considered to be the birthplace of democracy.*

birth·rate (bûrth′rāt′) *also,* **birth rate.** *n.* the number of births occurring in a given population within a specified time. It is often expressed in terms of the number of births of live offspring per thousand of the population.

birth·right (bûrth′rīt′) *n.* a right, privilege, or possession that a person is entitled to by birth: *Freedom of religion is the birthright of everyone born in the United States.*

birth·stone (bûrth′stōn′) *n.* a gem associated with a particular month of the year, supposed to bring good luck when it is worn by a person whose birthday falls in that month.

bis·cuit (bis′kit) *n., pl.* **bis·cuits** or **bis·cuit. 1.** a small baked cake made of bread dough, usually raised with baking powder or soda. **2.** *British.* a cracker or thin cookie. [From the Old French word *bescoit* meaning "biscuit," from the phrase *(pain) bescoit* "twice-baked (bread)."]

bi·sect (bī sekt′, bī′sekt) *v.t.* **1.** to divide (a geometrical figure) into two equal parts: *to bisect a circle.* **2.** to cut in two. —**bi·sec·tion** (bī sek′shən), *n.* —**bi·sec′tor,** *n.*

bi·sex·u·al (bī sek′chōō əl) *adj.* having both male and female reproductive organs; hermaphroditic. —**bi·sex′u·al·ly,** *adv.*

bish·op (bish′əp) *n.* **1.** a high-ranking member of the clergy who is usually the head of a church diocese. **2.** one of the pieces in the game of chess. It may be moved diagonally across any number of squares.

bish·op·ric (bish′ə prik) *n.* **1.** the office or rank of a bishop. **2.** a diocese administered by a bishop.

bis·muth (biz′məth) *n.* a brittle, gray metallic element with a reddish tinge. It melts at low temperatures, and its alloys are used in fire alarms and sprinkler systems. Bismuth is also used in drugs.

bishop
(def. 2)

at; āpe; fär; câre; end; mē; it; īce; pîerce; hot; ōld; sông, fôrk; oil; out; up; ūse; rüle; pull; tûrn; chin; sing; shop; thin; **this**; hw in white; zh in treasure. The symbol ə stands for the unstressed vowel sound heard in about, taken, pencil, lemon, and circus.

Symbol: **Bi** [From the scientific Latin word *bismutum* meaning this element, from the obsolete German word *Wismut* "bismuth," of uncertain origin.]

bi·son (bī′sən, bī′zən) *n., pl.* **bi·son.** an animal of North America, resembling the ox and having a large head, short horns, humped shoulders, and a brown coat; buffalo.

bisque (bisk) *n.* a thick, creamy soup: *tomato bisque.*

bis·tro (bis′trō, bē′strō) *n., pl.* **bis·tros.** a small bar, nightclub, or café. [From the French word *bistro* meaning "tavern, wineshop."]

bison

bit¹ (bit) *n.* **1.** the metal piece of a bridle that goes into the horse's mouth. **2.a.** a boring or drilling part that fits into a brace, drill, or similar tool. **b.** the cutting part of a tool, such as the blade of a knife or ax. **3.** the part of a key that enters the lock and moves the bolt and tumblers. [From the Old English word *bite* meaning "a bite."]

bit² (bit) *n.* **1.** a small piece, part, or quantity: *bits of a broken plate, a bit of bread.* **2.** a short while: *Wait a bit.* **3.** *Informal.* an amount equal to twelve and a half cents. ▲ used only in multiples of two, as *two bits, four bits.* —*adj.* small; insignificant: *a bit part in a play.* [From the Old English word *bita* meaning "morsel" or "piece bitten off."]

·**a bit.** somewhat: *to be a bit tired.*

·**bit by bit.** little by little; gradually.

bit³ (bit) the past tense and a past participle of **bite**.

bit⁴ (bit) *n.* *Computers.* a single unit of information processed by a computer. A bit can have a value of either 0 or 1. [Short for *bi(nary) (digi)t*.]

bitch (bich) *n., pl.* **bitch·es.** the female of the dog, wolf, or other related animals.

bite (bīt) *v.*, **bit, bit·ten** or **bit, bit·ing.** —*v.t.* **1.** to cut, pierce, or seize with the teeth: *to bite a sandwich.* **2.** to remove with the teeth; cut or tear: *to bite a piece of an apple.* **3.** to pierce the skin of with teeth, fangs, or similar parts: *a mosquito bit me.* **4.** to cause to smart or sting: *The icy wind bit our faces.* **5.** to take a firm hold on; grip: *The chains enabled the tires to bite the snow.* —*v.i.* **1.** to cut, pierce, seize, or grip something: *The teeth of the saw bit into the wood.* **2.** to pierce the skin with teeth, fangs, or similar parts: *Does the dog bite?* **3.** to cause smarting or stinging. *That wind really bites.* **4.** (of fish) to take the bait: *When the fish bites, pull back on the line.* —*n.* **1.** the act of biting. **2.** a wound made by biting or stinging: *a mosquito bite.* **3.** a piece bitten off; mouthful: *Do you want a bite of my apple?* **4.** *Informal.* a small meal; snack: *Let's have a bite at the cafeteria.* **5.** the effect or quality of biting; sting: *the bite of food that's too spicy.* **6.** the manner in which the upper and lower teeth meet: *to need braces to correct a faulty bite.* —**bi′ter,** *n.*

bit·ing (bī′ting) *adj.* **1.** sharp; stinging: *biting cold.* **2.** sarcastic; cutting: *a writer's biting wit.* —**bit′ing·ly,** *adv.*

bit·ten (bit′ən) a past participle of **bite**.

bit·ter (bit′ər) *adj.* **1.** having a sharp, biting, unpleasant taste: *a bitter medicine.* **2.** unpleasant or difficult to accept or bear: *the bitter truth, a bitter loss.* **3.** harsh or biting; sarcastic: *bitter humor.* **4.** causing or showing pain, misery, or discomfort: *the bitter cold, bitter tears.* **5.** having or showing intense anger, ill will, or hatred: *a bitter quarrel, bitter enemies.* **6.** full of resentment; unforgiving: *to be bitter about not making the team two years in a row.* —**bit′ter·ly,** *adv.* —**bit′ter·ness,** *n.*

bit·tern (bit′ərn) *n.* any of several marsh birds closely related to, but smaller than, the heron, and having a loud, booming cry.

bit·ter·root (bit′ər rŭt′, bit′ər rŭt′) *n.* a low-growing plant having a circle of fleshy leaves at its base and a single white or rose-colored flower at the top, found in the northern Rocky Mountain region.

bit·ters (bit′ərz) *pl. n.* a usually alcoholic liquid made from bitter herbs, roots, or bark, used to flavor drinks or as an ingredient in medicine.

bittern

bit·ter·sweet (bit′ər swēt′) *n.* **1.** a poisonous, climbing, woody plant of Europe, northern Africa, and Asia, bearing drooping clusters of violet flowers that ripen into scarlet berries. **2.** a climbing shrub of North America, bearing clusters of small, greenish flowers that ripen into yellow and orange fruits. —*adj.* **1.** both bitter and sweet: *bittersweet chocolate.* **2.** both pleasant and painful: *bittersweet memories of one's first trip away from home and family.*

bi·tu·men (bī tü′mən, bī tyü′mən) *n.* any of various dark brown or black substances that burn easily and are composed chiefly of hydrocarbons, such as asphalt, bituminous coal, or crude petroleum.

bi·tu·mi·nous (bī tü′mə nəs, bī tyü′mə nəs) *adj.* made of, containing, or like bitumen.

bituminous coal, a black coal that burns with a smoky flame and has a low carbon content. Also, **soft coal.**

bi·va·lent (bī vā′lənt) *adj.* having a valence of two.

bi·valve (bī′valv′) *n.* a mollusk whose shell consists of two parts, or valves, hinged together, such as the oyster or clam. —*adj.* having two shells hinged together.

biv·ou·ac (biv′ü ak′) *n.* a temporary camp, especially one made by soldiers in the field, often without tents or other shelter. —*v.i.*, **biv·ou·acked, biv·ou·ack·ing.** to camp out in a bivouac.

bi·week·ly (bī wēk′lē) *adj.* **1.** happening every two weeks. **2.** happening twice a week; semiweekly. —*n., pl.* **bi·week·lies.** a biweekly publication. —*adv.* **1.** every two weeks. **2.** twice a week; semiweekly.

▲ Although the adjective **biweekly** has two different definitions, it is usually used to mean "happening every two weeks." If "happening twice a week" is meant, it is clearer to use the word **semiweekly,** which has only this meaning.

bi·year·ly (bī yîr′lē) *adj.* **1.** happening every two years. **2.** happening twice a year. —*adv.* **1.** every two years. **2.** twice a year; semiannually.

bi·zarre (bi zär′) *adj.* very odd or strange, as in manner or appearance; fantastic; grotesque.

Bk, the symbol for berkelium.

blab (blab) *v.*, **blabbed, blab·bing.** —*v.t.* to tell or reveal thoughtlessly: *to blab a secret.* —*v.i.* **1.** to chatter thoughtlessly. **2.** to tell or reveal a secret.

blab·ber (blab′ər) *v.i.* to chatter thoughtlessly, foolishly, or excessively. —*n.* **1.** a person who blabs. **2.** thoughtless or foolish chatter.

blab·ber·mouth (blab′ər mouth′) *n., pl.* **blab·ber·mouths** (blab′ər mouthz′, blab′ər mouths′). *Informal.* a person who talks thoughtlessly or excessively.

black (blak) *adj.* **1.** having the darkest of all colors; having the color of coal; opposite of white: *a black car.* **2.** having no light; in darkness; dark: *the black depths of the ocean.* **3.** of, relating to, or belonging to a dark-skinned people, especially of African descent. **4.** gloomy; dismal: *The unemployed workers faced a black future.* **5.** angry; sullen: *to give someone a black look.* **6.** dirty; soiled: *a shirt collar black with grime.* **7.** morally evil; wicked: *a black deed.* —*n.* **1.** the darkest of all colors, reflecting no light; the opposite of white. Black is the color of coal. **2.** a black dye, paint, or the like.

3. something black, as a black piece in a game of checkers. 4. a member of a dark-skinned people, especially of African descent. 5. dark clothes, especially those worn for mourning: *to dress in black for a funeral.* —*v.t.* 1. to make black; blacken: *Storm clouds blacked the sky.* 2. to polish with blacking: *to black shoes.* —*v.i.* to become black. —**black′ly,** *adv.* —**black′ness,** *n.*
·**to black out. a.** to lose consciousness temporarily. **b.** to turn off or cover lights in, especially as a protection against air raids: *to black out a city.*

black–and–blue (blak′ən blü′) *adj.* discolored as a result of ruptured blood vessels under the skin; bruised.

black·ball (blak′bôl′) *v.t.* to vote against, especially to vote against letting (a person) become a member of some organization. —*n.* a vote against a person or thing. [From the ancient custom of putting a small black ball in a container to indicate a negative vote.]

black bear, a North American bear having black or reddish brown fur.

black belt 1. the highest rank awarded in judo and karate. 2. a person who has attained such a rank.

black·ber·ry (blak′ber′ē, blak′bə rē) *n., pl.* **black·ber·ries. 1.** the sweet black fruit of any of several bramble bushes of the rose family. 2. a thorny bush that bears this fruit.

black·bird (blak′bûrd′) *n.* 1. any of various American birds that are all or mostly black or dark in color in the male or in both sexes. 2. a black or dark brown thrush of Europe.

black·board (blak′bôrd′) *n.* a hard, smooth, usually dark surface of slate or other material for writing or drawing on with chalk.

blackberries

black·bod·y (blak′bod′ē) *n., pl.* **black·bod·ies.** a theoretical surface or body capable of absorbing all radiation falling on it and reflecting none.

black book, a book containing a blacklist.

black box 1. a mechanical or electronic device for performing intricate automatic functions, especially one that can be installed or removed as a unit. 2. any device or system whose function is known but whose structure or workings are not known or understood. 3. another term for **flight recorder.**

black·damp (blak′damp′) *n.* a suffocating gaseous mixture consisting mostly of carbon dioxide, produced by explosions or fires in mines.

Black Death, an extremely destructive plague that spread through Europe and much of Asia in the fourteenth century. [From the black swellings caused by this disease.]

black·en (blak′ən) *v.t.* 1. to make black; darken: *Smoke blackened the walls of the building.* 2. to speak evil of; defame: *to blacken someone's reputation.* —*v.i.* to become black or dark: *The sky blackened.*

black eye 1. a bruise on the skin around the eye, usually caused by a blow. 2. *Informal.* a damaged or bad reputation: *The rumors about corruption in the city government gave the mayor a black eye.*

black–eyed pea (blak′īd′) a kind of cowpea.

black–eyed Su·san (sü′zən) a flower having yellow petals surrounding a dark brown center, found in eastern Canada and the United States.

black·fish (blak′fish′) *n., pl.* **black·fish** or **black·fish·es. 1.** any of various dark-colored saltwater fish, such as the sea bass. 2. any of several small, dark, toothed whales. 3. a freshwater fish of the swamps and bogs of Alaska and Siberia that can survive in freezing water for a short period of time, valued as a food fish.

black flag, see **Jolly Roger.**

Black·foot (blak′fŭt′) *n., pl.* **Black·feet** or **Black·foot. 1.** a member of a tribe of plains Indians who lived east of the Rocky Mountains in Alberta, Saskatchewan, and Montana. 2. the Algonquian language of the Blackfeet. [A translation of the Blackfoot word *Siksika,* possibly referring to their custom of blackening their moccasins.]

black·guard (blag′ärd) *n.* a low, dishonorable person; scoundrel. —**black′guard·ly,** *adj.*

black·head (blak′hed′) *n.* a collection of oil and dead skin cells plugging a pore in the skin.

black hole, an object in outer space whose gravitational pull is so strong that not even light can escape from it. The existence of black holes has not been conclusively proven.

black·ing (blak′ing) *n.* a black polish, as for shoes.

black·jack (blak′jak′) *n.* 1. a small club with a flexible handle, used as a weapon. 2. a pirate's black flag. 3. a card game in which the players play against the dealer, the winner being the person whose cards bear numbers adding up to twenty-one or to the closest number below that. If both the dealer and another player have twenty-one, the dealer wins. Also, **twenty-one.** —*v.t.* to strike with a blackjack.

black·list (blak′list) *n.* a list of persons or organizations that are regarded as suspect, or to be boycotted or punished in some way. —*v.t.* to place on a blacklist: *to be blacklisted because of one's political beliefs.*

black lung, an occupational disease of the lungs that affects coal miners. It is caused by the constant inhaling of coal dust.

black magic, magic used for evil purposes; witchcraft.

black·mail (blak′māl′) *n.* 1. the act of obtaining money or something else of value from a person by threat, especially the threat to reveal information that would harm him or her in some way. 2. something of value obtained in this way. —*v.t.* to subject (someone) to blackmail: *to blackmail a politician who had secretly misappropriated funds.* [From *black* + the Scottish word *mail* meaning "rent" or "tribute," from the Old Norse word *māl* "agreement" or "speech." The usage can be traced to the payment of cattle or grain made by farmers along the Scottish and English borders to robbers and other outlaws in return for protection. *Black mail* was distinguished from *white mail,* which was paid in silver.] —**black′mail′er,** *n.*

black mark, something unfavorable or disgraceful on a person's record.

black market 1. the selling of goods illegally, especially in violation of price controls or rationing. 2. a place where such selling is carried on.

Black Muslim, a member of a chiefly black American sect of Islam.

black·out (blak′out′) *n.* 1. a temporary loss of consciousness, sight, or memory. 2. the temporary stopping or interruption of electric service in a certain area: *The power blackout was caused by a generator that failed.* 3. the turning out or covering of lights as a protection against enemy air raids. 4. a turning off of all lights on the stage of a theater, especially to mark a separation between scenes. 5. a deliberate withholding of information: *a news blackout.*

black pepper, a hot, pungent spice made from the dried, ground berries of the pepper plant.

black power *also,* **Black Power. 1.** the power of Amer-

at; āpe; fär; câre; end; mē; it; īce; pîerce; hot; ōld; sông, fôrk; oil; out; up; ūse; rüle; pull; tûrn; chin; sing; shop; thin; <u>th</u>is; hw in white; zh in treasure. The symbol ə stands for the unstressed vowel sound heard in about, taken, pencil, lemon, and circus.

ican blacks as a group to exert political, social, and economic pressure to achieve such goals as racial equality. **2.** a movement of American blacks that sought to use such power to achieve such goals as racial equality.

black sheep, a person who is regarded as a disgrace or discredit by the other members of the person's family or group.

black·smith (blak′smith′) *n.* a person who works with iron by heating it in a forge and then hammering it into shape on an anvil.

black·snake (blak′snāk′) *n.* a nonpoisonous snake of the eastern United States, having dull black scales.

black·thorn (blak′thôrn′) *n.* a thorny shrub of the rose family, found in Europe and Asia, bearing white flowers and deep blue fruit. Also, **sloe.**

black tie 1. a black bow tie, worn with a formal jacket or a tuxedo. **2.** semiformal evening wear for men.

black·top (blak′top′) *n.* **1.** asphalt or similar material used to pave roads. **2.** a road paved with such a material. —*v.t.*, **black·topped, black·top·ping.** to pave with blacktop.

black widow, a glossy black spider commonly found in Central America and in southern and western parts of the United States. The female is poisonous, has a red hour glass-shaped marking on the underside of its abdomen, and is more than twice the size of the male. [From the color of this spider and the female's practice of devouring its mate.]

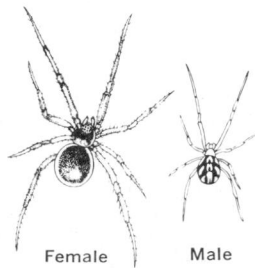

Female   Male

black widows

blad·der (blad′ər) *n.* **1.** a small, elastic sac in the body that stores urine received from the kidneys. **2.** something resembling a bladder, such as the inner bag of a football.

blade (blād) *n.* **1.** the flat, sharp-edged part of a tool, instrument, or weapon that cuts: *the blade of a knife, the blade of a sword.* **2.** a leaf, as of grass. **3.** the broad part of a leaf or petal. **4.** a broad, flat part or surface, as of an oar, propeller, or fan. **5.** a sword. **6.** the sharp runner of an ice skate. **7.** a dashing young man. —**blade′like′,** *adj.*

blame (blām) *v.t.*, **blamed, blam·ing. 1.** to find fault with; censure: *I don't blame you for losing your temper.* **2.** to hold (someone or something) responsible: *Don't blame me for your mistakes.* —*n.* **1.** responsibility for something wrong or bad: *to take the blame for an error.* **2.** the act of finding fault; censure: *Such serious misbehavior is deserving of blame.* —**blam′a·ble,** *adj.*

•**to be to blame.** to be at fault: *It was an accident, so no one is to blame.*

blame·less (blām′lis) *adj.* not deserving blame; innocent. —**blame′less·ly,** *adv.* —**blame′less·ness,** *n.*

blame·wor·thy (blām′wûr′thē) *adj.* deserving blame: *Everyone who was involved in the affair is blameworthy.*

blanch (blanch) *v.i.* to become white; turn pale: *to blanch with fear during a scary movie.* —*v.t.* **1.** to remove color from; bleach. **2.** to make pale, as from fear or sickness. **3.** to remove the skin of by scalding: *to blanch almonds.* **4.** to scald or parboil, as in preparation for further cooking or for freezing.

bland (bland) *adj.* **1.** lacking excitement, interest, or distinction; dull: *a bland book.* **2.** not irritating; soothing; mild: *a bland diet, a bland climate.* **3.** smoothly agreeable or pleasant: *a bland smile.* —**bland′ly,** *adv.* —**bland′ness,** *n.*

blan·dish (blan′dish) *v.t.* to coax with flattery.

blan·dish·ment (blan′dish mənt) *n.* a coaxing or flattering speech or action; coaxing; flattery.

blank (blangk) *adj.* **1.** not written or printed upon; unmarked: *a blank sheet of paper.* **2.** having spaces to be filled out: *a blank questionnaire.* **3.** lacking interest or thought; empty: *My mind is blank.* **4.** showing a lack of interest or thought; expressionless; vacant: *a blank stare.* —*n.* **1.** an empty space to be filled in, as in a printed form: *Fill in the blank with your name and address.* **2.** a form or document containing such spaces: *an application blank.* **3.** a place where something is lacking or missing: *My mind was a blank.* **4.** a cartridge containing powder, but no bullet. —*v.t.* to keep (an opponent) from scoring in a game: *Our baseball team was blanked for four games in a row.* —**blank′ly,** *adv.* —**blank′ness,** *n.*

blank check 1. a bank check that has been signed to be cashed but that has the amount left blank to be filled in by the bearer. **2.** freedom to act without control; carte blanche: *Because our parents trusted us, they gave us a blank check to plan our party.*

blan·ket (blang′kit) *n.* **1.** a covering made of wool or other woven fabric, used to keep people or animals warm. **2.** something that covers like a blanket: *a blanket of fog, a blanket of snow.* —*v.t.* to cover with or as if with a blanket. —*adj.* covering a wide range of topics, items, or conditions: *to give a blanket approval.*

blank verse 1. unrhymed verse written in iambic pentameter. Much of Shakespeare's work is written in blank verse. **2.** any unrhymed verse.

blare (blâr) *v.*, **blared, blar·ing.** —*v.i.* to make a loud, harsh sound: *The horns blared.* —*v.t.* to proclaim loudly and harshly: *The radio blared the news.* —*n.* a loud, harsh sound.

blar·ney (blär′nē) *n.* smooth, flattering talk. —*v.t.* to influence or try to influence with blarney; coax; wheedle. [From the *Blarney Stone.*]

Blarney Stone, a stone block in a wall of Blarney Castle in Ireland, said to give skill in flattery and coaxing to those who kiss it.

bla·sé (blä zā′) *adj.* bored or wearied, as from too much of a pleasant experience.

blas·pheme (blas fēm′) *v.*, **blas·phemed, blas·phem·ing.** —*v.t.* to speak of (God or anything sacred) with contempt or disrespect. —*v.i.* to speak with contempt or disrespect. —**blas·phem′er,** *n.*

blas·phe·mous (blas′fə məs) *adj.* characterized by or using blasphemy; irreverent: *a blasphemous statement.* —**blas′phe·mous·ly,** *adv.*

blas·phe·my (blas′fə mē) *n.,* pl. **blas·phe·mies.** an expression of contempt or disrespect for God or anything sacred.

blast (blast) *n.* **1.** a strong rush of wind; gust: *the chilling blasts of winter.* **2.** a loud, explosive sound, as that made by a horn: *the blast of trumpets, the blast of a radio.* **3.** an explosion, as of dynamite. **4.** the amount of explosive used to produce such an explosion. **5.** a strong current of air, steam, or gas, as the air forced into a blast furnace to aid combustion during smelting. —*v.t.* **1.** to blow up or shatter with an explosive. **2.** to cause to be damaged or ruined; wither: *The rain blasted our hopes for a successful picnic.* **3.** to cause to sound loudly. **4.** *Informal.* to criticize or scold severely: *The newspaper editorial blasted the factory for ignoring safety guidelines.* —*v.i.* to sound loudly or harshly: *The loudspeakers blasted.*

•**at full blast.** at the highest degree, as of speed, volume, or operation: *to have a radio on at full blast.*

•**to blast off.** (of a rocket or missile) to take off; begin flight.

blast furnace, a furnace used in smelting in which an intense heat is produced by a continuous blast of preheated air.

blas·to·coele (blas′tə sēl′) *also,* **blas·to·coel, blas·to·cele.** *n.* the cavity of a blastula.

blas·to·derm (blas′tə dûrm′) *n.* a layer of cells forming the wall of the blastula.

blast-off (blast'-ôf') *also*, **blast·off**. *n*. the launching of a rocket or missile: *The blast-off took place at 6:00 A.M.*

blas·tu·la (blas'-chə lə) *n.*, *pl.* **blas·tu·lae** (blas'chə-lē'). an early stage in the development of an animal embryo, usually consisting of a single layer of cells forming a hollow sphere.

bla·tant (blā'-tənt) *adj.* **1.** impossible to overlook; conspicuous; very obvious: *blatant lies, blatant errors.* **2.** noisy in a coarse or vulgar way. —**bla'tan·cy**, *n.* —**bla'tant·ly**, *adv.*

blast-off

blaze[1] (blāz) *n.* **1.** a bright, intense flame or fire: *The blaze destroyed a block of buildings.* **2.** a bright, intense light or glow: *the blaze of the sun.* **3.** a brilliant or striking display: *The parade was a blaze of color.* **4.** a strong, sudden outburst: *a blaze of fury.* —*v.i.*, **blazed, blaz·ing. 1.** to burn brightly: *Torches blazed through the night.* **2.** to shine brilliantly; be bright: *The city streets blazed with light.* **3.** to show strong feeling: *eyes that blaze with anger.* [From the Old English word *blæse* meaning "flame, torch."]

blaze[2] (blāz) *n.* **1.** a light-colored marking on the face of an animal, such as a horse or a cow. **2.** a mark made on a tree to show a trail or boundary, as by chipping off a piece of bark. —*v.t.*, **blazed, blaz·ing. 1.** to mark with blazes: *to blaze a tree, to blaze a trail.* **2.** to open up or take the lead in: *to blaze the way in medical research.* [Probably from the Middle Low German word *bles* meaning "white spot."]

blaze[3] (blāz) *v.t.*, **blazed, blaz·ing.** to make known; proclaim. [From the Old Norse word *blāsa* meaning "to blow."]

blaz·er (blā'zər) *n.* a sports jacket, usually having a solid color or bright stripes.

bla·zon (blā'zən) *v.t.* **1.** to make public; proclaim. **2.** to decorate with bright colors or displays; adorn. **3.** to describe or picture (a coat of arms) accurately. —*n.* a coat of arms.

bldg. *pl.* **bldgs.** building.

bleach (blēch) *v.t.* to make (something) white or colorless by exposing it to the sun or by the use of chemicals: *The harsh sun bleached the curtains.* —*n.*, *pl.* **bleach·es. 1.** something used for bleaching, such as a chemical. **2.** the act or process of bleaching: *Those clothes need another bleach.*

bleach·er (blē'chər) *n.* **1.** a person or thing that bleaches. **2. bleachers.** a group of tiered seats or benches, usually without a roof over them, for spectators at public events, especially outdoor events, such as parades and baseball games.

bleaching powder 1. a powder that bleaches. **2.** another name for **chloride of lime.**

bleak (blēk) *adj.* **1.** open and exposed to the wind; bare: *a bleak, barren desert.* **2.** cold; chilling: *a bleak December day.* **3.** not cheerful or hopeful; gloomy: *Our team's* prospects for winning were bleak. —**bleak'ly**, *adv.* —**bleak'ness**, *n.*

blear (blîr) *adj.* dimmed or blurred; bleary. —*v.t.* to make dim with or as if with tears; blur.

blear·y (blîr'ē) *adj.*, **blear·i·er, blear·i·est.** dimmed or blurred: *eyes bleary from fatigue, a bleary old snapshot.* —**blear'i·ness**, *n.*

blear·y-eyed (blîr'ē īd') *adj.* having bleary eyes.

bleat (blēt) *n.* **1.** the cry of a sheep, goat, or calf. **2.** any sound like a bleat. —*v.i.* **1.** to utter the cry of a sheep, goat, or calf. **2.** to make a sound like a bleat. —*v.t.* to utter with a bleat or a sound like a bleat. —**bleat'er**, *n.*

bleed (blēd) *v.*, **bled** (bled), **bleed·ing.** —*v.i.* **1.** to lose or shed blood: *My cut finger bled.* **2.** to suffer wounds or die: *We honor those who bled on the battlefields.* **3.** to feel pity or sympathy: *My heart bled for the lost child.* **4.** to ooze sap or other fluid from an opening or cut. **5.** (of a dye or paint) to run or become mixed: *When I washed the shirt, its colors bled.* —*v.t.* **1.** to take blood from as a treatment for illness. **2.** to ooze (a fluid) from an opening or a cut: *The trees bled sap.* **3.** to drain or draw off a liquid or gas from: *to bleed a tire.*

bleed·er (blē'dər) *n.* a person who bleeds excessively, especially a hemophiliac.

blem·ish (blem'ish) *n.*, *pl.* **blem·ish·es.** something that spoils beauty or perfection: *skin blemishes, a character without blemish.* —*v.t.* to spoil the beauty or perfection of; stain; mar: *to blemish a good reputation.*

blench (blench) *v.i.* to shrink away; flinch.

blend (blend) *v.t.* **1.** to mix together thoroughly; combine so that the original ingredients cannot be separated: *We blended flour, milk, and eggs to make the pancake batter.* **2.** to make a mixture of different varieties or grades of: *to blend several teas.* —*v.i.* **1.** to mingle together; mix: *voices that blend in a choir.* **2.** to pass or shade gradually into each other; merge: *Sea and sky seemed to blend on the horizon.* **3.** to fit together; harmonize: *The rug blends with the other colors in the room.* —*n.* **1.** a thorough mixture: *a new blend of coffee.* **2.** a word formed by combining separate words or parts of separate words.

Language Note

In language, a **blend** is a word that is formed by combining separate words or parts of separate words. Blends are sometimes used to create new words that combine the meanings of the original words that are blended. Our word *brunch* is a combination of the words *breakfast* and *lunch* and as a meal is a combination of the two.

Blends are also formed when we need to describe something for which there has not previously been a word. Air pollution in cities is often called *smog*, which is a blend of the words *smoke* and *fog*. After television was invented, the blend *telecast* was coined, combining the words *television* and *broadcast*.

blend·er (blen'dər) *n.* **1.** an appliance that performs various operations on food and liquids, as chopping, mixing, and blending. **2.** a person or thing that blends.

bless (bles) *v.t.*, **blessed** (blest) or **blest, bless·ing. 1.** to make or declare holy; consecrate: *to bless a new chapel.*

at; āpe; fär; câre; end; mē; it; īce; pîerce; hot; ōld; sông, fôrk; oil; out; up; ūse; rüle; pull; tûrn; chin; sing; shop; thin; this; hw in white; zh in treasure. The symbol ə stands for the unstressed vowel sound heard in about, taken, pencil, lemon, and circus.

2. to ask God's favor or protection for: *to bless a congregation.* **3.** to endow: *to be blessed with good looks.* **4.** to praise or glorify: *to bless God in prayer.* **5.** to make the sign of the cross over.

bless·ed (bles′id; blest) *also,* **blest.** *adj.* **1.** made holy by a religious rite; sacred. **2.** worthy of adoration or worship: *the blessed saints.* **3.** enjoying great happiness; fortunate. **4.** bringing happiness or pleasure: *the blessed relief of knowing that a lost child had been found.* —**bless′ed·ly,** *adv.* —**bless′ed·ness,** *n.*

Bless·ed Virgin (bles′id) Mary; the mother of Jesus.

bless·ing (bles′ing) *n.* **1.** a prayer asking for God's favor. **2.** a prayer of thanks, usually made before or after a meal. **3.** something that brings happiness or pleasure: *Good friends are a blessing.* **4.** approval; consent: *My parents gave their blessings to my plan to get married.* **5.** a wish for good fortune or success: *We send our blessings for the New Year.*

blest (blest) *v.* a past tense and past participle of **bless.** —*adj.* another spelling of **blessed.**

blew (blü) the past tense of **blow²** and **blow³.**

blight (blīt) *n.* **1.** any of several diseases that wither or kill plants. **2.** the bacterium, fungus, or virus that causes such a disease. **3.** something that damages, ruins, or destroys: *These slums are a blight on our city.* —*v.t.* **1.** to cause to wither or decay: *Too much rain blighted the corn.* **2.** to damage, ruin, or destroy: *Lack of money blighted their hopes for a new home.*

blimp (blimp) *n. Informal.* a small airship whose body is not supported by a rigid framework.

blind (blīnd) *adj.* **1.** unable to see; sightless. **2.a.** not easily seen; hidden from view: *a blind driveway.* **b.** not easily seen around: *a blind curve.* **3.** done without the help of sight: *In my blind groping in the dark room, I knocked over a lamp.* **4.** done by using instruments only: *blind flying, a blind landing.* **5.** unable to notice or understand (often with *to*): *to be blind to one's faults.* **6.** lacking thought, control, or good judgment; reckless: *The cattle stampeded in blind terror after the gunshots.* **7.** not based on reason or intelligence: *a people's blind faith in an untried but charismatic politician.* **8.** closed at one end: *a blind hole in a block of wood.* —*n.* **1.** something that blocks sight or keeps out light: *Please shut the blinds.* **2.** a person, thing, or action used to conceal or mislead: *The job in the embassy was a blind for the spy.* **3.** a hiding place for hunters. —*v.t.* **1.** to make sightless permanently or temporarily: *to be blinded in an explosion, to be blinded by bright lights.* **2.** to take away the power to understand or judge well: *to be blinded by jealousy.* —*adv.* with little or no power of sight: *to fly blind through a storm.* —**blind′ly,** *adv.* —**blind′ness,** *n.*

blind alley, any activity or undertaking that leads nowhere; a fruitless course of action.

blind date, a date between two people who have never met before.

blind·er (blīn′dər) *n.* either of a pair of flaps attached to a horse's bridle to prevent the horse from seeing sideways. Also, **blinker.**

blind·fold (blīnd′fōld′) *v.t.* to cover the eyes of, especially with a cloth. —*n.* a cover for the eyes. —*adj.* having the eyes covered.

blind·man's buff (blīnd′-manz′ buf′) a game in which a blindfolded player tries to catch and identify one of several other players. Also, **blindman's bluff.**

blind spot **1.** a very small point on the retina of the

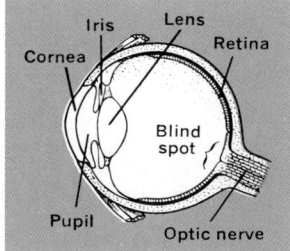

blind spot (def. 1)

eye that is not sensitive to light because the optic nerve enters there. **2.** an area or subject about which a person is prejudiced, ignorant, or unappreciative: *Politics is one of my blind spots. Your one blind spot is sports.* **3.** an area where sight is hindered or obscured: *a blind spot in a car's rearview mirror.*

blink (blingk) *v.i.* **1.** to close and open the eyes rapidly, often without meaning to: *to blink when a flashbulb goes off.* **2.** to flash on and off; glimmer, twinkle: *A star blinked in the sky.* —*v.t.* **1.** to close and open (the eyes) rapidly. **2.** to cause to flash on and off: *to blink the car lights.* —*n.* **1.** a rapid closing and opening of the eye. **2.** a sudden glimmer of light; twinkle.

·**on the blink.** *Slang.* not working properly; out of order: *The radio is on the blink.*

·**to blink at.** to deliberately overlook or ignore: *The manager blinked at the mistakes the new employee made during the first week.*

blink·er (bling′kər) *n.* **1.** a blinder. **2.** a light that blinks on and off, used to send messages or as a warning signal.

blintze (blints, blint′sə) *also,* **blintz** (blints). *n.* a thin pancake rolled around a filling, as of cheese or fruit.

blip (blip) *n.* an image on a radar screen that indicates the presence of an object.

bliss (blis) *n.* great happiness or joy.

bliss·ful (blis′fəl) *adj.* full of, characterized by, or causing great happiness or joy: *a blissful marriage.* —**bliss′ful·ly,** *adv.* —**bliss′ful·ness,** *n.*

blis·ter (blis′tər) *n.* **1.** a swelling of the skin that resembles a small bubble and is filled with watery matter. It is usually caused by rubbing or by a burn. **2.** any similar swelling, as on a plant, a painted surface, or molded plastic. —*v.t.* to raise a blister or blisters on: *Sunburn blistered our faces.* —*v.i.* to have or develop a blister or blisters: *The paint blistered from the heat of the flames.* —**blis′ter·y,** *adj.*

blithe (blīth, blīth) *adj.* **1.** full of joy or gaiety; cheerful; lighthearted: *the blithe laughter of children playing.* **2.** showing no concern, interest, or responsibility; thoughtless: *a blithe disregard for the rights of other people.* —**blithe′ly,** *adv.* —**blithe′ness,** *n.*

blithe·some (blīth′səm, blīth′səm) *adj.* gay; cheerful; lighthearted. —**blithe′some·ly,** *adv.* —**blithe′some·ness,** *n.*

blitz (blits) *n., pl.* **blitz·es.** **1.** see **blitzkrieg.** **2.** any sudden overwhelming attack: *a blitz of publicity for a new product.* —*v.t.* to attack with or overwhelm by a blitz.

blitz·krieg (blits′krēg′) *n.* warfare using sudden, violent, and overwhelming attacks, usually by combined air and ground forces, intended to defeat the enemy quickly. [From the German word *Blitzkrieg* meaning "lightning war," from the words *Blitz* "lightning" + *Krieg* "war."]

bliz·zard (bliz′ərd) *n.* **1.** a strong windstorm marked by intense cold and blowing snow. **2.** a severe, heavy snowstorm marked by a very strong wind. **3.** a great quantity arriving, happening, or the like at one time: *The representatives received a blizzard of letters objecting to the law.*

bloat (blōt) *v.t.* to cause to swell or expand: *Too much food bloated my stomach.* —*v.i.* to become swollen or expanded.

blob (blob) *n.* a drop or lump of a thick, soft, or sticky substance: *a blob of paint.*

bloc (blok) *n.* a combination of persons, groups, or nations united to promote a common interest or purpose: *the farm bloc in Congress.*

block (blok) *n.* **1.** a solid piece of wood, stone, or other material, often having one or more flat surfaces. **2.a.** a usually rectangular area enclosed by four streets:

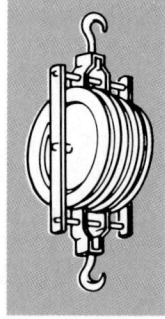

block
(n., def. 8)

a walk around the block. **b.** the length of a side of such an area: *to park a car a block away from a store.* **3.** the buildings in such an area. **4.** a number of things of the same kind, taken as a unit: *a block of seats at the theater.* **5.** anything that stops movement or progress, or hinders: *a mental block about driving a car after an accident.* **6.** a mold or form upon which something is shaped or displayed: *a hat block.* **7.** a platform or stand where things are put up for sale at an auction. **8.** a pulley or system of pulleys mounted in a frame. —*v.t.* **1.** to hinder or stop movement or progress through (often with *up*): *After the storm, fallen trees blocked the road.* **2.** to stand in the way of; hinder: *You're blocking my view.* **3.** to shape with a block: *to block a sweater after finishing knitting it.* **4.** *Sports.* to interfere with (an opponent's movement or play). —*v.i.* *Sports.* to interfere with an opponent's movement. —
  ·to block out or **to block in.** to plan or outline roughly: *The author blocked out a new novel.*

block·ade (blo kād') *n.* **1.** a shutting off of an area by troops or ships to prevent people or supplies from going into or out of it. **2.** the forces that carry on a blockade. **3.** something that shuts off or obstructs; obstacle. —*v.t.,* **block·ad·ed, block·ad·ing.** to subject to a blockade. —**block·ad'er,** *n.*
  ·to run the blockade. to go through a blockade.

block·ade–run·ner (blo kād'run'ər) *n.* a person or ship that tries to go through a blockade.

block·age (blok'ij) *n.* The act of blocking or the state of being blocked; obstruction: *the blockage of a road by snow.*

block and tackle, an arrangement of pulley blocks and ropes, used for lifting or hauling.

block·bust·er (blok'bus'tər) *n.* *Informal.* **1.** a large aerial bomb. **2.** a person or thing that is remarkably impressive or successful: *The novel was a blockbuster and sold millions of copies.*

block·head (blok'hed') *n.* a stupid or foolish person.
block·house (blok'hous') *n., pl.* **block·hous·es** (blok'hou'ziz). **1.** a fortified building of former times, made of timber or logs, having loopholes from which to fire weapons and an upper story built out over the lower one. **2.** a small building of concrete or other heavy material. **3.** a building made of strong, heavy material, serving as an observation and control center near the launching pad of a rocket or missile.

blockhouse *(def. 1)*

bloke (blōk) *n. British. Slang.* a fellow; man.
blond (blond) *adj.* **1.** (of hair) having some shade of light yellow as its main color. **2.** (of a person) having such hair, often with light-colored skin and eyes. **3.** light-colored: *blond furniture, a blond complexion.* —*n.* a blond person. —**blond'ish,** *adj.* —**blond'ness,** *n.*
blonde (blond) *adj.* **blond·er, blond·est.** (of a woman or girl) having blond hair. —*n.* a blonde woman or girl. —**blonde'ness,** *n.*
blood (blud) *n.* **1.** the red fluid pumped by the heart through the arteries, veins, and capillaries, bringing oxygen and nourishment to all parts of the body and carrying away waste materials. **2.** descent from a common ancestor; kinship: *a cousin related by blood, not by marriage.* **3.** parental or ancestral origin or heritage: *to be of noble blood, a person with Indian blood.* **4.** state of mind or temperament; disposition: *a person of hot blood.*
  ·in cold blood. deliberately and without feeling or compassion: *to kill someone in cold blood.*

blood bank **1.** a place where whole blood and parts of blood are collected and stored for future use in giving transfusions. **2.** the reserve of blood so stored.
blood bath, the merciless slaughter of many people; massacre.
blood count, a count of the number of red and white blood cells and platelets in a given sample of blood, used chiefly as a test to help diagnose or treat a disease.
blood·cur·dling (blud'kûrd'ling) *adj.* causing great horror or fear; terrifying: *a bloodcurdling scream.*
blood·ed (blud'id) *adj.* (of horses and other livestock) of pure blood or stock; thoroughbred.
blood group, one of the groups into which blood is classified according to the presence or absence of certain substances on red blood cells that either allow or prevent mixing with other groups of blood. The four major blood groups are A, B, AB, and O. Also, **blood type.**
blood·hound (blud'hound') *n.* a hunting dog having long, drooping ears, a wrinkled face, and a smooth coat, noted for its keen sense of smell. Bloodhounds are often used to track criminals or lost persons.
blood·less (blud'lis) *adj.* **1.** without bleeding or bloodshed: *a bloodless victory.* **2.** lacking blood; pale: *The frightened child had bloodless lips.* **3.** lacking spirit or energy. **4.** lacking warmth; cold-hearted. —**blood'less·ly,** *adv.* —**blood'less·ness,** *n.*
blood·let·ting (blud'let'ing) *n.* **1.** the act of removing blood by opening a vein. **2.** bloodshed.
blood·line (blud'līn') *n.* a line of direct descent, especially of an animal.
blood·mo·bile (blud'mə bēl') *n.* a vehicle equipped for the collection of blood from donors.
blood poisoning, a diseased condition of the blood caused by the presence of bacteria or bacterial toxins.
blood pressure, the force exerted by the blood against the inner walls of the arteries and other blood vessels. It is created by the pumping action of the heart and varies according to age, health, and other conditions.
blood·root (blud'rüt', blud'rùt') *n.* a plant related to the poppy, having white or rose flowers and a root that yields a red sap.
blood·shed (blud'shed') *n.* the shedding of blood, especially the slaughter of human beings
blood·shot (blud'shot') *adj.* (of the eye) inflamed or marked with reddish streaks from the widening of the blood vessels
blood·stain (blud'stān') *n.* a spot or stain caused by blood. —**blood'stained',** *adj.*
blood·stream (blud'strēm') *n.* the blood as it flows through the body.
blood·suck·er (blud'suck'ər) *n.* any animal that sucks blood, especially a leech.
blood test, an analysis of a sample of a person's blood, often used to determine the condition of a person's health.
blood·thirst·y (blud'thûr'stē) *adj.* eager to shed blood; murderous; brutal: *a bloodthirsty pirate.* —**blood'thirst'i·ly,** *adv.* —**blood'thirst'i·ness,** *n.*
blood type, another term for **blood group.**
blood vessel, any of the flexible tubes through which the blood flows, such as an artery, vein, or capillary.
blood·y (blud'ē) *adj.,* **blood·i·er, blood·i·est.** **1.** stained or covered with blood: *a bloody knife.* **2.** losing blood; bleeding: *a bloody wound.* **3.** involving much bloodshed:

at; āpe; fär; câre; end; mē; it; īce; pîerce; hot; ōld; sông, fôrk; oil; out; up; ūse; rüle; pùll; tûrn; chin; sing; shop; thin; this; hw in white; zh in treasure. The symbol ə stands for the unstressed vowel sound heard in about, taken, pencil, lemon, and circus.

a bloody battle. **4.** eager to shed blood; bloodthirsty. —*v.t.,* **blood·ied, blood·y·ing.** to stain or cover with blood; make bloody: *to bloody one's nose in a fall.* —**blood'i·ly,** *adv.* —**blood'i·ness,** *n.*

bloom (blüm) *n.* **1.** the flower of a plant. **2.** the condition or time of flowering: *The roses are in bloom.* **3.** a condition or time of great freshness, beauty, or vigor: *an artist whose talent is in bloom.* **4.** a rosy glow of the cheeks or skin suggesting health or vigor. **5.** a powdery coating on certain fruits, leaves, stems, or other parts of a plant: *the bloom on a peach.* —*v.i.* **1.** to produce blossoms; flower: *Cherry trees bloom in the spring.* **2.** to be at or come to a condition or time of greatest health, beauty, or vigor; flourish. **3.** to glow with health, beauty, or vigor. —**bloom'er,** *n.*

bloom·ers (blü'mərz) *pl. n.* **1.** loose, baggy pants gathered at the knee, formerly worn by women or girls, chiefly for sports. **2.** women's underpants resembling these. [From the American feminist Amelia J. *Bloomer* (1818–1894), who promoted this costume.]

bloom·ing (blü'ming) *adj.* **1.** in flower; blossoming. **2.** full of health, beauty, or vigor: *blooming complexion.* **3.** *British. Slang.* complete; utter: *a blooming fool.*

blos·som (blos'əm) *n.* **1.** a flower, especially of a plant or tree that produces fruit: *an apple blossom.* **2.** the state or time of flowering; bloom: *a peach tree in blossom.* —*v.i.* **1.** to put forth blossoms; bloom: *All the trees in the garden are blossoming.* **2.** to develop into maturity or prosperity: *In the story the ugly duckling blossomed into a beautiful swan.*

blot (blot) *n.* **1.** a spot or stain, especially of ink. **2.** something that spoils or mars; blemish: *These billboards are a blot on the countryside.* —*v.,* **blot·ted, blot·ting.** —*v.t.* **1.** to spot or stain with or as if with ink. **2.** to dry or absorb with blotting paper: *I blotted every line I wrote so the ink wouldn't smear.* —*v.i.* **1.** to make blots: *The ink blotted.* **2.** to become stained or marked with a blot.
·**to blot out. a.** to cover up completely: *The clouds blotted out the moon.* **b.** to destroy completely; put an end to: *The pleasant evening blotted out our memory of the morning's problems.*

blotch (bloch) *n., pl.* **blotch·es. 1.** a spot or stain, especially one that is large and irregular in shape: *The jelly left a blotch on the tablecloth.* **2.** a blemished or discolored patch on the skin: *The horse is light brown with some darker blotches.* —*v.t.* to mark or cover with blotches. —**blotch'y,** *adj.*

blot·ter (blot'ər) *n.* **1.** a piece or pad of blotting paper. **2.** a book in which transactions or events are recorded in the order of their occurrence, such as a record of arrests and charges kept in a police station.

blotting paper, soft, absorbent paper used to soak up excess ink.

blouse (blous, blouz) *n.* **1.** a garment that resembles a loose, light shirt and extends to the waist or below. **2.** a smock worn chiefly by certain European peasants and workers. **3.** a jacket or tunic worn as part of the U.S. Army uniform.

blow[1] (blō) *n.* **1.** a forceful, heavy stroke with the fist, a weapon, or some object: *a blow to the jaw.* **2.** a sudden, severe shock: *The bad news came as quite a blow to us.* **3.** a sudden, forceful attack, action, or effort: *The raid was a blow against the criminals.* [From the Middle English word *blaw* with the same meaning, of Germanic origin.]
·**at one blow** or **at a blow.** by a single action or effort.
·**to come to blows.** to begin fighting: *The arguing children came to blows.*

blow[2] (blō) *v.,* **blew, blown, blow·ing.** —*v.i.* **1.** (of wind or air) to be in motion;

blouse
(def. 2)

move with speed or force: *The wind blew against the sails.* **2.** to produce or send forth a current of air: *The fan was blowing. Blow on your hands to warm them.* **3.** to move or be carried by a current of air or wind: *The laundry blew in the breeze.* **4.** to produce sound by a blast of air: *The whistle blows at noon.* **5.** to break and expel air; burst (often with *out*): *As we drove down the street a tire blew.* **6.** to stop working in some way: *The fuse blew.* **7.** (of a whale) to exhale air and water vapor through a blowhole: *The lookouts saw two whales blow on the port side.* —*v.t.* **1.** to cause to move by a current of air: *The wind blew the leaves across the yard.* **2.** to cause to sound by directing a blast of air: *to blow a trumpet.* **3.** to form or shape by a current of air: *to blow bubbles.* **4.** to break, burst, or destroy, as by an explosion: *The dynamite blew the rock to pieces.* **5.** to clear or empty by forcing air into or through: *to blow one's nose.* **6.** to melt or disable (a fuse). **7.** *Slang.* to handle awkwardly or unsuccessfully: *You blew your chance to get that job when you were rude at the interview.* —*n.* **1.** the act of producing or directing a current of air. **2.** a sound resulting from producing or directing a blast of air. **3.** a strong wind; gale: *Yesterday's big blow knocked down the telephone wires.* [From the Old English word *blāwan* meaning "to blow[2]."]
·**to blow hot and cold.** to change one's mind frequently: *to blow hot and cold on an issue.*
·**to blow in.** *Informal.* to arrive; appear.
·**to blow off steam.** *Informal.* to release pent-up feelings noisily or violently.
·**to blow out.** to put out or be put out by a gust of air: *to blow out candles. The lantern blew out during the storm.*
·**to blow over. a.** to pass by or over; subside: *The storm finally blew over.* **b.** to be forgotten: *The scandal blew over quickly.*
·**to blow the whistle on.** to reveal wrongdoing by (a person or persons); inform on; expose: *A secretary blew the whistle on the boss's embezzlement.*
·**to blow up. a.** to explode or destroy with an explosion: *to blow up a bridge. The barrel of gas blew up when the fire reached it.* **b.** to fill with air or gas: *to blow up a balloon.* **c.** *Informal.* to lose one's temper: *I apologized for blowing up over the minor mistake.* **d.** to arise: *A storm blew up last night.* **e.** to enlarge (a photograph).

blow[3] (blō) *v.i.,* **blew, blown, blow·ing.** *Archaic.* to blossom. ▲ Although the verb is archaic, the past participle **blown** is used, especially in the phrase *full-blown.* [From the Old English word *blōwan* meaning "to blossom."]

blow–dry (blō'drī') *v.t.,* **blow-dried, blow-dry·ing.** to dry or style (hair) with a blow dryer.

blow dryer, a portable electric device that blows a stream of warmed air, used for drying and styling a person's hair.

blow·er (blō'ər) *n.* **1.** a machine for producing a current of air or for forcing air into a particular area: *We need blowers to keep this kitchen cool.* **2.** a person or thing that blows.

blow·fly (blō'flī') *n., pl.* **blow·flies.** any of various flies that deposit their larvae on the wounds, wastes, or flesh of animals.

blow·gun (blō'gun') *n.* a tube through which a person blows darts or other similar missiles. Also, **blowpipe, blowtube.**

blow·hole (blō'hōl') *n.* **1.** a breathing hole of certain whales, dolphins, and other similar animals, often located at the top of the head. **2.** an escape vent for gas or air, as in mines. **3.** a hole in the ice to which underwater animals, such as whales or seals, come to the surface in order to breathe.

blown (blōn) *v.* the past participle of **blow**[2] and **blow**[3].

blow·out (blō′out′) *n.* **1.** a sudden bursting of an automobile tire. **2.** a melting of an electric fuse caused by too much current in the circuit.

blow·pipe (blō′pīp′) *n.* **1.** a tube for blowing air or gas into a flame to increase its heat. **2.** another word for **blowgun**. **3.** another word for **blowtube** (*def. 1*).

blows·y (blou′zē) *adj.*, **blows·i·er, blows·i·est.** another spelling of **blowzy**.

blow·torch (blō′tôrch′) *n.* a device that produces and shoots out a very hot flame under pressure, used especially in melting and soldering metals and in removing paint.

blow·tube (blō′tūb′, blō′tūb′) *n.* **1.** a long metal tube used to shape molten glass. Also, **blowpipe**. **2.** another word for **blowgun**.

blowtorch

blow·up (blō′up′) *n.* **1.** an explosion. **2.** *Informal.* an outburst of temper; quarrel. **3.** an enlargement, as of a snapshot.

blowz·y (blou′zē) *also,* **blows·y.** *adj.,* **blowz·i·er, blowz·i·est. 1.** red-faced and coarse. **2.** not clean, neat, or tidy; messy; slovenly.

BLT, a bacon, lettuce, and tomato sandwich.

blub·ber (blub′ər) *n.* **1.** a layer of fat under the skin of whales and certain other sea animals, used especially as a source of oil. **2.** a noisy weeping. —*v.i.* to weep and sob noisily. —**blub′ber·er,** *n.*

blub·ber·y (blub′ə rē) *adj.* of or like blubber; fat.

bludg·eon (bluj′ən) *n.* a short club, often heavier or thicker at one end. —*v.t.* to strike with a bludgeon.

blue (blū) *n.* **1.** the color of the clear sky in the daytime; the color between green and violet in the spectrum. **2.** a blue dye or paint. **3.** *also,* **Blue.** a Union soldier in the Civil War. **4. the blue. a.** the sky. **b.** the sea. **5.** something, as clothing, having the color blue: *I wore blue to the dance.* —*adj.,* **blu·er, blu·est. 1.** having the color blue: *blue eyes.* **2.** (of skin) of a bluish purple color; discolored: *to be blue from the cold.* **3.** unhappy and low in spirits; sad; melancholy: *I felt lonely and blue when most of my friends went away to camp.* —*v.t.,* **blued, blu·ing** or **blue·ing. 1.** to treat with bluing. **2.** make blue. —**blue′ness,** *n.*
· **out of the blue.** suddenly and unexpectedly.

blue baby, a baby born with a defect of the heart that prevents enough oxygen from entering the blood, resulting in a bluish color of the skin.

blue·bell (blū′bel′) *n.* any of various plants with blue flowers shaped like bells, such as the harebell of Scotland.

blue·ber·ry (blū′ber′ē, blū′bə rē) *n., pl.* **blue·ber·ries. 1.** a small, dark blue, sweet berry with tiny seeds that grows on any of several shrubs. **2.** any of the shrubs bearing this berry.

blue·bird (blū′bûrd′) *n.* any of several songbirds of North America that have mainly blue feathers and are related to the thrush.

blue blood 1. aristocratic or royal descent. **2.** a person of such descent; aristocrat. [A translation of the Spanish phrase *sangre azul,* from the idea that the blood of aristocrats had a blue tint.]

blue·bon·net (blū′bon′it) *n.* any of several plants of North America having clusters of blue flowers, especially a lupine that is the state flower of Texas.

blue·bot·tle (blū′bot′əl) *n.* a large blowfly with a blue abdomen and hairy body.

blue–col·lar (blū′kol′ər) *adj.* of or relating to workers who do mostly physical labor. [From the traditional blue shirts worn by many workers.]

blue·fish (blū′fish′) *n., pl.* **blue·fish** or **blue·fish·es.** a saltwater food and game fish having a bluish and silver body, found in coastal waters in various parts of the world.

blue flag, an iris with blue or purple flowers.

blue·grass (blū′gras′) *n., pl.* **blue·grass·es.** a popular name for any of various grasses with bluish green stems, widely raised as hay for pastures and as grass for lawns.

blue–green algae (blū′grēn′) a group of one-celled organisms having some characteristics of both plants and bacteria.

blue·ing (blū′ing) another spelling of **bluing**.

blue·jack·et (blū′jak′it) *n.* a sailor in the navy.

blue jay *also,* **blue·jay** (blū′jā′). a jay of eastern North America that has a crest and is mainly blue above and white below with black and white markings.

blue jays

blue jeans, pants or overalls, usually made of blue denim.

blue law 1. one of the strict laws passed in colonial New England, forbidding recreation or business on Sunday. **2.** any law regulating Sunday activities.

blue·print (blū′print′) *n.* **1.** a photographic print, usually showing white lines on a blue background, used especially for copying architectural plans and mechanical drawings. **2.** any detailed outline or plan of action: *The legislature must create a blueprint for dealing with the housing shortage.* —*v.t.* to make a blueprint of.

blue racer, a bluish green blacksnake, found in the central and south-central United States.

blue ribbon, the highest honor or award in a contest or competition; first prize.

blues (blūz) *pl. n.* **1. the blues.** *Informal.* low spirits; melancholy: *to have the blues because a friend moved away.* **2.** *also,* **the blues.** an American music originating with often melancholy songs sung by Southern blacks. The blues are an important element in jazz and rock music.

blu·ets (blū′its) *n., pl.* **blu·ets.** a low-growing plant of North America, bearing light blue, white, or violet flowers with yellowish centers.

blue whale, a migratory whale of the oceans and seas of the Southern Hemisphere having grayish blue skin with light spots. It grows to a length of 100 feet (30.5 meters) and is the largest mammal ever known.

bluff¹ (bluf) *n.* a high, broad bank or cliff. —*adj.* **1.** rising with or having a flat, broad front: *bluff cliffs.* **2.** blunt or abrupt in a good-natured way; rough and hearty: *Our guide's bluff manner gave us confidence.* [Possibly

---

at; āpe; fär; câre; end; mē; it; īce; pîerce; hot; ōld; sông, fôrk; oil; out; up; ūse; rüle; pull; tûrn; chin; sing; shop; thin; this; hw in white; zh in treasure. The symbol ə stands for the unstressed vowel sound heard in about, taken, pencil, lemon, and circus.

from the Middle Dutch word *blaf* meaning "broad, flat."]
—**bluff′ly**, *adv.* —**bluff′ness**, *n.*

bluff² (bluf) *v.t.* **1.** to fool or deceive (someone) by putting on a false front of confidence or bravery: *You bluffed your friends into thinking you knew what you were doing.* **2.** to gain or succeed with (something) by using deception or a false front: *I bluffed my way into the party even though I hadn't been invited.* —*v.i.* to deceive by putting on a false front: *I was only bluffing when I said I knew all the answers.* —*n.* **1.** the act of bluffing. **2.** a person who bluffs. [Possibly from the Dutch word *bluffen* meaning "to boast."] —**bluff′er**, *n.*

·**to call someone's bluff.** to challenge someone's statements or actions when it seems that he or she is bluffing.

blu·ing (blü′ing) *also,* **blue·ing.** *n.* a blue liquid or powder used in laundering to keep white fabrics from turning yellow.

blu·ish (blü′ish) *adj.* somewhat blue.

blun·der (blun′dər) *n.* a careless or stupid mistake: *Forgetting my friend's birthday was an awful blunder.* —*v.i.* **1.** to make a careless or stupid mistake: *The mayor blundered by raising taxes just before the election.* **2.** to move or act blindly or clumsily: *The lost campers blundered through the woods.* —**blun′der·er**, *n.*

blun·der·buss (blun′dər bus′) *n., pl.* **blun·der·buss·es.** a short gun with a wide, flared muzzle for scattering shot at close range. It is no longer used. [From the Dutch word *donderbus* meaning "blunderbuss," from the words *donder* "thunder" + *bus* "gun." This gun was so inaccurate that the first part of the word was changed to the rhyming English word *blunder*.]

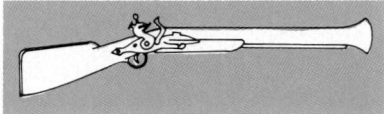
blunderbuss

blunt (blunt) *adj.* **1.** having a dull edge or point; not sharp: *a blunt point on a pencil.* **2.** direct and frank in speech or manner; outspoken; abrupt: *Being too blunt can hurt someone's feelings.* —*v.t.* to make less sharp or keen; dull: *to blunt scissors by using them to cut wire.* —*v.i.* to become blunt or dull. —**blunt′ly**, *adv.* —**blunt′ness**, *n.*

blur (blûr) *v.,* **blurred, blur·ring.** —*v.t.* **1.** to make less clear or distinct in form or outline: *Fog blurred the skyline of the city.* **2.** to cause to smudge or smear: *to blur the paints in a watercolor.* **3.** to make dim: *Age had blurred the old jeweler's eyesight.* —*v.i.* **1.** to become less clear or distinct in form or outline: *The road ahead blurred in the rain.* **2.** to smudge or smear: *The ink blurred from contact with my wet hands.* **3.** to dim: *The mourners' eyes blurred with tears.* —*n.* **1.** something indistinct or dim: *the blur of the landscape from a speeding train.* **2.** a smudge or smear; stain. —**blur′ry**, *adj.*

blurb (blûrb) *n. Informal.* a brief advertisement or description: *The blurb on the book jacket tells all about the author.*

blurt (blûrt) *v.t.* to say suddenly or without thinking (often with *out*): *to blurt out a secret.*

blush (blush) *v.i.* **1.** to become red in the face from shame, embarrassment, or modesty: *to blush when praised by the teacher.* **2.** to be ashamed or embarrassed (often with *at* or *for*): *to blush at a silly mistake.* —*n., pl.* **blush·es.** **1.** a reddening of the face from shame, embarrassment, or modesty. **2.** a rosy color: *the first blush of dawn.*

blush·er (blush′ər) *n.* **1.** a person who blushes. **2.** a cosmetic that is used to give a rosy tint to the face, especially to the cheekbones.

blus·ter (blus′tər) *v.i.* **1.** to blow with noise or stormy violence: *The storm blustered outside the house.* **2.** to

talk in a noisy or threatening way. —*n.* **1.** a noisy, stormy blowing, as of the wind. **2.** noisy, threatening talk. —**blus′ter·er**, *n.* —**blus′ter·y**, *adj.*

blvd., boulevard.

bo·a (bō′ə) *n.* **1.** any of various nonpoisonous snakes found in tropical and temperate regions, that kill their prey by squeezing it in their coils and suffocating it. **2.** a long scarf of fur or feathers.

boa constrictor, a large boa of Mexico and Central and South America, having light brown skin with dark brown marks on its back.

boa constrictor

boar (bôr) *n.* **1.** a male pig or hog. **2.** see **wild boar.**

board (bôrd) *n.* **1.** a thin piece of sawed wood longer than it is wide. **2.** a flat piece of wood or other material used for some particular purpose: *a board for playing checkers.* **3.** a group of persons who direct or supervise an activity: *the board of directors of a bank.* **4.** meals provided regularly for pay: *The fee covered my room and board.* ▲ usually used in the phrase *room and board.* **5.** a panel or similar surface on which information and notices may be posted: *Please check the board for all arrivals and departures.* —*v.t.* **1.** to cover or close with boards (often with *up* or *over*): *They boarded up the windows of the cabin each fall.* **2.** to provide with meals, or with lodging and meals, for pay. **3.** to get on (a ship, plane, or train): *We boarded the bus at the terminal.* —*v.i.* to get meals, or lodging and meals, for pay: *I boarded with a farm family last summer.*

·**on board.** on or in a ship, plane, or train; aboard.

board·er (bôr′dər) *n.* a person who gets meals, or meals and lodging, at another's house for pay.

board foot *pl.* **board feet.** a unit of measure for logs and lumber, equal to the volume of a board 1 foot square and 1 inch thick; 144 cubic inches (929 cubic centimeters).

board·ing (bôr′ding) *n.* wooden boards.

boarding house, a house at which meals, or lodging and meals, are furnished for pay.

boarding school, a school where the pupils live during the school year.

board of education, a committee responsible for setting the policies of a school system.

board·walk (bôrd′wôk′) *n.* a wide walk or promenade along a beach, usually made of boards.

boast (bōst) *v.i.* to speak with too much pride or with exaggeration about oneself or one's possessions; brag: *When you boast about your new car you become boring.* —*v.t.* **1.** to speak about or assert with too much pride or with exaggeration: *They boasted that their team was the best in the league.* **2.** to be proud of having: *The library boasts 500 new volumes.* —*n.* **1.** a bragging statement: *Your boast that you are the best player on the team is not true.* **2.** something boasted of; cause for pride: *A new gymnasium is that school's boast.* —**boast′er**, *n.*

boast·ful (bōst′fəl) *adj.* characterized by or given to boasting; bragging: *a boastful story, a boastful youth.* —**boast′ful·ly**, *adv.* —**boast′ful·ness**, *n.*

boat (bōt) *n.* **1.** a small vessel for use on water, moved by oars, sails, or a motor. **2.** a vessel of any size; ship: *They took a boat to South America.* **3.** an open dish shaped like a boat, as for gravy. —*v.i.* to travel in

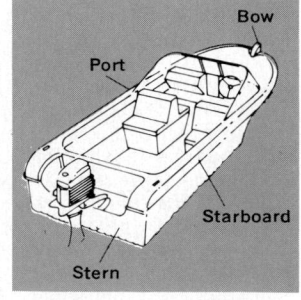
boat *(n., def. 1)*

a boat: *We boated across the lake to see our friends.* —*v.t.* to put or carry in a boat.

   ·in the same boat. in the same situation or condition: *Neither of us has any money, so we're in the same boat.*

   ·to miss the boat. to fail to make use of an opportunity: *to miss the boat by not buying a coat during a sale.*

   ▲ In common usage, **boat** can refer to a vessel of any size. In nautical usage, **boat** means only a small vessel; **ship** applies to a larger vessel, such as an ocean liner.

boat·house (bōt'hous') *n., pl.* **boat·hous·es** (bōt'hou'ziz). a building near the water's edge for sheltering or storing boats.

boat·ing (bō'ting) *n.* the act or practice of using a boat, especially for pleasure: *We enjoy boating on the lake.*

boat·man (bōt'mən) *n., pl.* **boat·men** (bōt'mən). a person who operates, works on, or deals with boats.

boat·swain (bō'sən, bōt'swān') *also,* **bo's'n, bo·sun.** *n.* an officer on a ship who has charge of the rigging and anchors and directs the work of the crew.

bob[1] (bob) *v.,* **bobbed, bob·bing.** —*v.i.* **1.** to move up and down, or to and fro, with a short, jerky motion: *The cork bobbed in the water.* **2.** to try to snatch floating or dangling objects with the teeth: *to bob for apples.* —*v.t.* to move (something) up and down with a short, jerky motion: *to bob one's head in time to music.* —*n.* a short, jerky motion. [Of uncertain origin.]

bob[2] (bob) *n.* **1.** a short haircut for a woman or child. **2.** a small, hanging weight, as at the end of a pendulum or plumb line. **3.** a float or cork for a fishing line. —*v.,* **bobbed, bob·bing.** —*v.t.* to cut short, as hair or a tail. —*v.i.* to fish with a bob. [From the Middle English word *bobbe* meaning "a bunch."]

bob[3] (bob) *n., pl.* **bob.** *British. Informal.* shilling. [Possibly from the name *Bob,* a form of *Robert.*]

bob·bin (bob'in) *n.* **1.** a spool around which thread or yarn is wound, used in weaving, machine sewing, or spinning. **2.** something resembling a bobbin in shape or use, such as a reel around which wire is coiled.

bob·ble (bob'əl) *v.* **bob·bled, bob·bling.** —*v.i.* **1.** to move with a continuous or repeated bobbing. **2.** *Informal.* to make a mistake; blunder. —*v.t. Baseball.* to fumble or mishandle (a ball). —*n. Informal.* a mistake; blunder.

bob·by (bob'e) *n., pl.* **bob·bies.** *British. Informal.* a police officer. [From the British statesman Sir *Robert Peel* (1788–1850), who reorganized the London police force.]

bobby pin, a flat hairpin with prongs that press together to hold hair tightly.

bobby socks *Informal.* ribbed, often heavy, socks, usually folded just above the ankle.

bob·cat (bob'kat') *n.* a North American lynx having a reddish brown coat with dark spots. Also, **wildcat.**

bob·o·link (bob'ə lingk') *n.* a songbird of North and South America, related to the blackbird. Also, **reedbird, ricebird.**

bob·sled (bob'sled') *n.* **1.** a long racing sled with two

bobsled *(def. 1)*

sets of runners, a steering wheel, and a brake. **2.a.** a long sled made by attaching one short sled behind another. **b.** either of the short sleds so joined. —*v.i.,* **bob·sled·ded, bob·sled·ding.** to ride on a bobsled.

bob·tail (bob'tāl') *n.* **1.** a tail that is cut short. **2.** an animal having such a tail. —*v.t.* to cut the tail of: *to bobtail a horse.* —*adj.* having a bobtail.

bob·white (bob'hwīt', bob'wīt') *n.* an American quail that has a reddish brown body with markings of white, black, and buff.

bock beer (bok) a strong, dark beer, usually brewed in the cold months and sold in the spring. Also, **bock.**

bode[1] (bōd) *v.t.,* **bod·ed, bod·ing.** to be an omen or sign of: *The dark sky boded a storm.*

   ·to bode ill. to be a bad omen or sign: *The breakdown in negotiations boded ill for an early end to the dispute.*

   ·to bode well. to be a good omen or sign: *Your good work bodes well for your future in the business.*

bode[2] (bōd) a past tense of **bide.**

bo·de·ga (bō dā'gə) *n.* in a Spanish-speaking community, a small grocery store. [From the Spanish word *bodega,* from the Latin word *apotheca* "storehouse," from the Greek word *apothēkē* "storehouse," from the word *apotithenai* "to put away, store."]

bod·ice (bod'is) *n.* **1.** the part of a dress from the neckline to the waistline. **2.** a vest that laces up the front, worn over a dress or blouse.

bod·i·less (bod'ē lis) *adj.* having no body.

bod·i·ly (bod'ə lē) *adj.* of or relating to the body: *to escape bodily harm in an accident.* —*adv.* **1.** in the flesh; in person. **2.** as a single body: *The audience rose bodily to applaud the singer.*

bod·kin (bod'kin) *n.* **1.** a small, pointed tool used for making holes in cloth. **2.** a long, ornamental hairpin. **3.** a large, blunt needle for pulling tape or other material through a hem. **4.** *Archaic.* a dagger.

bod·y (bod'ē) *n., pl.* **bod·ies.** **1.** the whole physical structure and material of a human being, animal, or plant. **2.** the main portion of a human being or animal without the head and limbs; trunk. **3.** the main or central part of anything: *the body of an automobile, the body of a letter.* **4.** a dead person; corpse. **5.** a group of persons or things considered as a whole: *a student body, a legislative body.* **6.** a distinct mass; portion of matter: *a body of water, a body of cold air.* **7.** the quality of having substance; density: *This soup has very little body.*

bod·y·build·er (bod'ē bil'dər) *n.* a person who engages in bodybuilding.

bod·y·build·ing (bod'ē bil'ding) *n.* development of the human body by a program of diet and exercise that often includes weightlifting to build the muscles.

bod·y·guard (bod'ē gärd') *n.* a person or persons responsible for protecting someone from physical danger or attack.

body language, the body movements, gestures, postures, and facial expressions by which a person communicates, often unconsciously, with others.

Boer (bôr) *n.* a South African of Dutch descent. —*adj.* of or relating to the Boers.

Boer War, the war between Great Britain and the Boers, from 1899 to 1902, in which the Boers were defeated.

bog (bog) *n.* wet, spongy ground made up chiefly of decayed plant material; marsh; swamp. —*v.,* **bogged,**

at; āpe; fär; câre; end; mē; it; īce; pîerce; hot; ōld; sông, fôrk; oil; out; up; ūse; rüle; pull; tûrn; chin; sing; shop; thin; <u>th</u>is; hw in white; zh in treasure. The symbol ə stands for the unstressed vowel sound heard in about, taken, pencil, lemon, and circus.

bog·ging. —*v.t.* to cause to become stuck in or as if in a bog (often with *down*): *Don't let all this work bog you down.* —*v.i.* to sink or stick in or as if in a bog (often with *down*): *to be bogged down in money problems.* —**bog'gy,** *adj.*

bo·gey¹ (bō'gē) *n., pl.* **bo·geys.** another spelling of **bogy.**

bo·gey² (bō'gē) *n., pl.* **bo·geys.** in golf, one stroke over par for a hole. [Probably from *bogy.* Par is represented as the score of an imaginary partner.]

bo·gey·man (bùg'ē man', bü'gē man') *n., pl.* **bo·gey·men** (bùg'ē men', bü'gē men') a frightening imaginary figure, especially one described to children to threaten them.

bog·gle (bog'əl) *v.,* **bog·gled, bog·gling.** —*v.i.* **1.** to make a startled movement, as from fright or astonishment. **2.** to hesitate, as from doubt or confusion (with *at*): *to boggle at the thought of so much work.* —*v.t.* to confuse and overwhelm; astound: *the tiny size of an atom boggles the mind.*

bo·gie¹ (bō'gē) another spelling of **bogy.**

bo·gie² (bō'gē) *also,* **bo·gy.** *n.* **1.** a four-wheeled support under a railroad car. **2.** one of the wheels supporting the tread of a tractor or tank. [Of uncertain origin.]

bo·gus (bō'gəs) *adj.* not genuine; counterfeit; sham.

bo·gy (bō'gē) *also,* **bo·gey, bo·gie.** *n., pl.* **bo·gies.** **1.** an evil spirit; goblin. **2.** a frightening or dreaded person or thing; specter.

Bo·he·mi·an (bō hē'mē ən) *n.* **1.** a person who was born or is living in Bohemia. **2.** *also,* **bohemian.** a person who leads an unconventional life, especially an artist or writer. —*adj.* **1.** of or relating to Bohemia or its people. **2.** *also,* **bohemian.** characteristic of or relating to a bohemian: *a bohemian life.*

boil¹ (boil) *v.i.* **1.** (of a liquid) to form bubbles that escape as steam or vapor due to heating. **2.** to contain a boiling liquid: *The pot is boiling.* **3.** to reach the boiling point: *Turn off the flame as soon as the water boils.* **4.** to be stirred up or angry: *Left out of the game, the child boiled with rage.* **5.** to be in motion like boiling water; seethe: *The floodwaters boiled over the river's banks.* —*v.t.* **1.** to bring to the boiling point: *to boil water for tea.* **2.** to cook or prepare in boiling liquid: *to boil potatoes.* —*n.* the act or state of boiling: *Bring the water to a boil.* [From the Old French word *boillir* meaning "to boil," from the Latin word *bullire* "to be bubbling," from the word *bulla* "a bubble."]
   ·**to boil down. a.** to reduce or lessen by boiling. **b.** to shorten or be shortened: *to boil down a long report to a brief outline.*
   ·**to boil over. a.** to overflow during boiling. **b.** to lose one's temper; show anger: *I boiled over at the insult.*

boil² (boil) *n.* a painful, pus-filled swelling in the skin, formed around a hard core. It is caused by bacterial infection. [From the Old English word *bӯl* meaning "a skin blotch."]

boil·er (boi'lər) *n.* **1.** a large container with a system of tubes in which water or other liquid is changed into steam for heating a building or running an engine. **2.** a container in which something is heated or boiled. **3.** a tank in which water is heated or hot water is stored.

boiling point 1. the temperature at which a liquid begins to boil. The boiling point of water at sea level is 212 degrees Fahrenheit, or 100 degrees Celsius. **2.** *Informal.* the point at which a person loses his or her temper: *My cousin has a low boiling point.*

bois·ter·ous (boi'stər-əs) *adj.* noisy and lively: *a boisterous party.* —**bois'ter·ous·ly,** *adv.* —**bois'ter·ous·ness,** *n.*

bo·la (bō'lə) *n.* a weapon

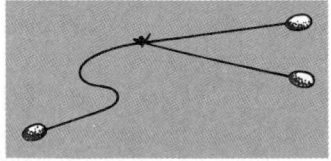

bola

used chiefly in South America, consisting of heavy balls tied to the ends of a cord. It is thrown at cattle or game to capture them by entangling their legs.

bold (bōld) *adj.* **1.** having courage; fearless: *a bold explorer.* **2.** showing or requiring spirit or courage; daring: *Rescuing the child from the burning house was a bold deed.* **3.** very free or too free in speech or manner; forward; impudent: *Your bold behavior annoyed the boss.* **4.** standing out prominently; distinct and striking: *a dress with bold red stripes.* —**bold'ly,** *adv.* —**bold'ness,** *n.*

bold·face (bōld'fās') *n.* a kind of printing type with heavy thick lines that make it stand out clearly. **This sentence is printed in boldface.**

bole (bōl) *n.* the trunk of a tree.

bo·le·ro (bə lâr'ō) *n., pl.* **bo·le·ros. 1.** a lively Spanish dance in ¾ time that is usually accompanied by castanets. **2.** the music for this dance. **3.** a short, open jacket ending at or above the waistline.

boll (bōl) *n.* a rounded seed pod of a plant, as of cotton or flax.

boll weevil, a beetle with a long snout, whose larva lives in and causes damage to cotton bolls.

bo·lo (bō'lō) *n., pl.* **bo·los.** a long, single-edged knife, used in the Philippines for cutting through brush.

bo·lo·gna (bə lō'nə, bə lō'nē) *also,* **ba·lo·ney, bo·lo·ney** (bə lō'nē). *n.* a smoked sausage made of beef, veal, and pork. [Short for *Bologna sausage,* from *Bologna,* the city in Italy where it originated.]

Bol·she·vik (bōl'shə vik) *also,* **bol·she·vik.** *n.* **1.** a member of the radical faction of the Socialist party in czarist Russia that in 1917, led by Lenin and Trotsky, gained control of the government. In 1918 the Bolsheviks formed the Communist Party of the Soviet Union. **2.** any extreme radical. —*adj.* **1.** relating to or characteristic of the Bolsheviks or Bolshevism. **2.** extremely radical.

Bol·she·vism (bōl'shə viz'əm) *also,* **bol·she·vism.** *n.* **1.** the doctrines and policies of the Bolsheviks. **2.** extreme radicalism.

Bol·she·vist (bōl'shə vist) *also,* **bol·she·vist.** *n., adj.* another name for **Bolshevik.**

bol·ster (bōl'stər) *n.* **1.** a long, narrow pillow or cushion. **2.** any cushion, pad, or pillow. —*v.t.* to support or strengthen: *The timbers bolstered the roof of the cabin. The good news bolstered our spirits.*

bolt¹ (bōlt) *n.* **1.** a pin or rod used for holding things together, usually with a head at one end and threads for a nut to be attached on the other end. **2.** a sliding bar for fastening a door or gate. **3.** the part of a lock that is moved out or withdrawn by turning the key. **4.** a sudden spring or start: *to make a bolt for an exit.* **5.** a stroke of lightning; thunderbolt. **6.** a roll of

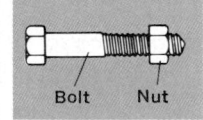

Bolt   Nut

bolt¹ *(n., def. 1)*

cloth or paper. **7.** a short, stout arrow, used with a crossbow. —*v.t.* **1.** to fasten or secure with a bolt: *We bolted the door for the night.* **2.** to swallow (food) quickly or without chewing; gulp: *They bolted their dinner and ran out to play.* **3.** to break away from: *The mayor bolted the party and ran as an independent candidate.* —*v.i.* **1.** to spring or move suddenly: *to bolt up the stairs.* **2.** to break away from control; start and run off: *The horse bolted and threw its rider.* [From the Old English word *bolt* meaning "arrow."]
   ·**bolt upright.** stiffly straight and erect: *At the clap of thunder, I sat bolt upright in bed.*

bolt² (bōlt) *v.t.* to sift through a cloth or sieve: *to bolt flour.* [From the Old French word *buleter* meaning "to sift."]

bomb (bom) *n.* **1.** a container filled with an explosive, incendiary, or chemical substance, that is set off by dropping or throwing, by a fuse, or by a timing device.

2. a container whose contents are stored under pressure for release as a fine spray or foam: *an insecticide bomb.* **3.** *Slang.* a total failure: *That play was a real bomb.* —*v.t.* to attack or destroy with a bomb or bombs: *to bomb a village.*

bom·bard (bom bärd′) *v.t.* **1.** to attack with artillery or bombs: *The advancing army bombarded the fort.* **2.** to keep on attacking vigorously: *The reporters bombarded the mayor with questions.* **3.** *Physics.* to subject (atomic nuclei) to a stream of high-speed subatomic particles. —**bom·bard′ment,** *n.*

bom·bar·dier (bom′bər dîr′) *n.* the crew member of a bomber who works the bombsight and releases the bombs.

bom·bast (bom′bast) *n.* speech or writing that sounds important but has little meaning; pompous language: *The candidate's political bombast fooled many people.*

bom·bas·tic (bom bas′tik) *adj.* characterized by high-sounding or pompous speech or writing: *a bombastic speaker.* —**bom·bas′ti·cal·ly,** *adv.*

bomb bay, the section in a bomber in which bombs are carried and from which they are dropped.

bomb·er (bom′ər) *n.* **1.** a military airplane used for dropping bombs. **2.** a person who drops or sets off bombs.

bomb·proof (bom′prüf′) *adj.* safe from damage by bombs: *a bombproof shelter.*

bomb·shell (bom′shel′) *n.* **1.** a bomb. **2.** a person or thing that has a startling or overwhelming effect: *The news that the mayor had been bribed was a political bombshell.*

bomb shelter, a place, usually underground, where people may take refuge from an air raid.

bomb·sight (bom′sīt′) *n.* an instrument in a bomber used to sight the target and help the bombardier drop bombs accurately.

bo·na fide (bō′nə fīd′) **1.** in good faith; without fraud or deception: *They made a bona fide offer for the property.* **2.** genuine; authentic: *bona fide Swiss watches.*

bo·nan·za (bə nan′zə) *n.* **1.** a rich mine or mass of ore. **2.** any source of great wealth or profit. [From the Spanish word *bonanza* meaning "fair weather, prosperity," going back to the Latin word *bonus* "good."]

bon·bon (bon′bon′) *n.* a piece of candy, especially one with a chocolate coating and a smooth, creamy center.

bond (bond) *n.* **1.** something that binds, fastens, or holds together: *The prisoner's bonds were made of rope.* **2.** a binding or uniting force or influence; tie: *the bond of friendship.* **3.** a certificate issued by a government or corporation, promising to pay back a specified amount of money with interest at a fixed future date: *The state issued bonds to pay for the new highway.* **4.** *Law.* **a.** an obligation to pay a specified sum of money if certain acts, such as appearing for a trial, are or are not performed. **b.** the amount of money so specified: *The prisoner was released on $50,000 bond.* **5.** the storage of imported goods in a warehouse until taxes upon them are paid. **6.** an insurance policy covering an employer's losses caused by the acts of an employee. **7.** *Chemistry.* the force of attraction that holds together the atoms of a molecule. The type of bond depends on the arrangement of the electrons in the individual atoms. —*v.t.* **1.** to place in or under bond. **2.** to furnish bond for: *to bond a prisoner.* **3.** to bind together; unite. —*v.i.* to be held together.

bond·age (bon′dij) *n.* the condition of being under another's control against one's will; slavery; serfdom.

bond·ed (bon′did) *adj.* guaranteed by a bond or bonds: *a bonded security guard.*

bond·hold·er (bond′hōl′dər) *n.* the owner of a bond issued by a government or corporation.

bond·man (bond′mən) *n., pl.* **bond·men** (bond′mən). a slave or serf.

bonds·man (bondz′mən) *n., pl.* **bonds·men** (bondz′-mən). **1.** a person who takes responsibility for another by furnishing a bond. **2.** another word for **bondman.**

bond·wom·an (bond′wùm′ən) *n., pl.* **bond·wom·en** (bond′wim′ən). a female slave or serf.

bone (bōn) *n.* **1.** one of the parts of the skeleton of an animal with a backbone. **2.** the hard porous substance of which such parts are composed. **3.** a substance resembling bone, such as ivory or whalebone. **4.** **bones.** the body, living or dead. —*v.t.,* **boned, bon·ing.** to remove the bones from: *to bone a fish.* —**bone′less,** *adj.* —**bone′like′,** *adj.*

·**to feel in one's bones.** to feel certain of something for no apparent reason.

·**to have a bone to pick.** to have something to argue or complain about.

·**to make no bones about.** to be direct or blunt about: *I make no bones about my dislike of snakes.*

Marrow cavity

cross section of a **bone**

bone–chill·ing (bōn′chil′ing) *adj.* very frightening; terrifying.

bone–dry (bōn′drī′) *adj.* very dry.

bone meal, crushed or ground animal bones, used as fertilizer or feed.

bon·er (bō′nər) *n.* *Informal.* a foolish mistake: *Mailing that letter without addressing it was a real boner.*

bon·fire (bon′fīr′) *n.* a large fire built in the open air. [From the Middle English word *bonefire* meaning "a fire (made) from bones."]

bon·go drums (bong′gō) a pair of small drums, each with a different pitch, played with the hands while being held between the knees. Also, **bon·gos** (bong′gōz).

bo·ni·to (bə nē′tō) *n., pl.* **bo·ni·tos.** any of various saltwater food fish closely related to the tuna and mackerel.

bon jour (bōn zhùr′) *French.* good morning; good day.

bongo drums

bon·net (bon′it) *n.* **1.** a hat enclosing both the sides and the back of the head and tied under the chin, worn especially by women and girls. **2.** a ceremonial headdress of feathers worn by some North American Indians. **3.** a cap worn by men and boys in Scotland.

bon·ny (bon′ē) also, **bon·nie.** *adj.,* **bon·ni·er, bon·ni·est.** *Scottish.* **1.** pleasing in appearance; handsome or pretty. **2.** fine; pleasant: *a bonny day.* —**bon′ni·ly,** *adv.* —**bon′ni·ness,** *n.*

bon·sai (bon sī′, bon′sī) *n., pl.* **bon·sai.** **1.** the art of growing miniature plants that have been dwarfed and shaped by special methods, including pruning roots and stems and wiring branches. **2.** a plant developed using these methods.

bo·nus (bō′nəs) *n., pl.* **bo·nus·es.** something given in addition to what is usual or due; something extra: *Every employee received a Christmas bonus.*

bon vo·yage (bon′ voi äzh′) pleasant trip; good-bye. [From the French interjection *bon voyage!* meaning "(Have a) good journey!"]

bon·y (bō′nē) *adj.,* **bon·i·er, bon·i·est. 1.** relating to or like bone: *a bony growth.* **2.** having many bones: *a bony fish.* **3.** having prominent bones; thin: *a bony person.* —**bon′i·ness,** *n.*

boo (bü) *interj.* used to show dislike or disapproval, or to frighten. —*n., pl.* **boos.** a shout of "boo." —*v.,*

at; āpe; fär; câre; end; mē; it; īce; pîerce; hot; ōld; sông, fôrk; oil; out; up; ūse; rüle; pùll; tûrn; chin; sing; shop; thin; <u>th</u>is; hw in white; zh in treasure. The symbol ə stands for the unstressed vowel sound heard in about, taken, pencil, lemon, and circus.

booed, boo·ing. —*v.t.* to show disapproval of by making this sound: *The crowd booed the umpire.* —*v.i.* to make this sound.

boob (büb) *n.* *Slang.* a stupid or foolish person; dunce.

boob tube *Slang.* **the boob tube.** television.

boo·by (bü′bē) *n., pl.* **boo·bies.** **1.** *Informal.* a stupid or foolish person; dunce. **2.** any of several large tropical sea birds having a long, straight bill and long, pointed wings.

booby prize, a prize, often a funny one, given to the person who has done the worst in a competition or game.

booby trap 1. a bomb set to explode when a harmless-looking object attached to it is moved or touched by an unsuspecting victim. **2.** any trick or device for causing someone harm unexpectedly.

boog·ie-woog·ie (bŭg′ē wŭg′ē) *n.* a form of blues played chiefly on the piano, with repeated patterns in the bass.

boo·hoo (bü′hü′) *v.i.,* **boo·hooed, boo·hoo·ing.** to weep noisily; blubber. —*n., pl.* **boo·hoos.** a noisy sob; loud weeping.

book (bŭk) *n.* **1.** a written or printed work of some length, especially on sheets bound together between two covers. **2.** a set of blank or ruled sheets of paper bound together: *an address book.* **3.** a section of a literary work: *a book of the Bible.* **4.** a set of things bound together like a book: *a book of matches, a book of stamps.* **5.** the words or text of an opera or musical play. **6. books.** business accounts or records. **7. the Book.** the Bible. —*v.t.* **1.** to arrange for; engage; reserve: *to book a hotel room, to book an act into a theater.* **2.** to enter charges against (someone) in a police record.

·**the book.** the correct or accepted way of doing something: *to do something by the book.*

·**to know like a book.** to know completely and thoroughly: *I know my old friend like a book.*

·**to throw the book at.** *Slang.* **a.** to make all possible legal charges against (an accused person). **b.** to punish severely: *The judge threw the book at the lawbreaker.*

book·bind·er (bŭk′bīn′dər) *n.* a person whose business is binding books.

book·case (bŭk′kās′) *n.* a cabinet or set of shelves for holding books.

book club, a business organization that sells selected books by mail to its subscribers, usually at a discount.

book·end (bŭk′end′) *n.* a support placed at the end of a row of books to hold them upright.

book·ie (bŭk′ē) *n.* *Informal.* see **bookmaker** (*def. 1*).

book·ish (bŭk′ish) *adj.* **1.** fond of reading or study; studious. **2.** depending more on knowledge from books than on practical experience. **3.** too formal or scholarly in writing or speaking; stilted. —**book′ish·ly,** *adv.* —**book′ish·ness,** *n.*

book·keep·er (bŭk′kē′pər) *n.* a person who keeps records of business accounts or transactions.

book·keep·ing (bŭk′kē′ping) *n.* the work or system of keeping records of business accounts or transactions.

book·let (bŭk′lit) *n.* a small, thin book, especially one with paper covers; pamphlet.

book·mak·er (bŭk′mā′kər) *n.* **1.** a person who makes a business of taking bets, as on horse races and other sports events. Also, **bookie. 2.** a person who prints or binds books.

book·mark (bŭk′märk′) *n.* an object inserted between the pages of a book to mark the reader's place.

book·mo·bile (bŭk′mə bēl′) *n.* a truck equipped to carry books and serve as a traveling library.

Book of Common Prayer, the book of services and prayers of the Church of England.

book·plate (bŭk′plāt′) *n.* a printed label pasted in a book to show who owns it.

book·sell·er (bŭk′sel′ər) *n.* a person whose business is selling books.

book·shelf (bŭk′shelf′) *n., pl.* **book·shelves** (bŭk′-shelvz′). a shelf for books.

book·stall (bŭk′stôl′) *n.* a stall or stand, often outdoors, where books are sold.

book·store (bŭk′stôr′) *n.* a store where books are sold. Also, **book·shop** (bŭk′shop′).

book·worm (bŭk′wûrm′) *n.* **1.** any of various insect larvae that feed on the bindings or pages of books. **2.** a person who devotes a great deal of time or too much time to reading and studying.

Bool·e·an algebra (bü′lē ən) algebra that deals with relationships among sets, such as the sum of two sets. For example, the set of positive integers belongs to the set of positive numbers and to the set of all integers. Boolean algebra is used to design computer programs. [From George *Boole,* 1815–64, British mathematician.]

boom[1] (büm) *n.* **1.** a deep, hollow, resonant sound: *the boom of crashing waves.* **2.** a period of rapid economic growth and prosperity: *That town is having a boom since the factory moved there.* **3.** a great or sudden increase, as in growth, importance, or popularity: *a boom in automobile sales.* —*v.i.* **1.** to make a deep, hollow resonant sound: *The cannon boomed in the distance.* **2.** to increase or grow suddenly and rapidly; flourish: *Business has been booming this year.* —*v.t.* **1.** to utter with a booming sound (often with *out*): *to boom out an order.* **2.** to promote the growth, importance, or popularity of: *The party is booming the mayor for governor.* —*adj.* caused by a boom: *boom prices.* [Representation of this sound.]

boom[2] (büm) *n.* **1.** a long pole or beam used to extend the bottom of certain sails or to aid in handling cargo. **2.** the movable arm of a crane or derrick, from which the object to be moved is suspended. **3.** a long adjustable pole used to support a microphone. **4.** a chain, cable, or connection of timbers in a waterway, used to keep logs from floating away. [From the Dutch word *boom* meaning "tree" or "pole."]

boom box *Slang.* a large portable radio, often combined with a cassette player.

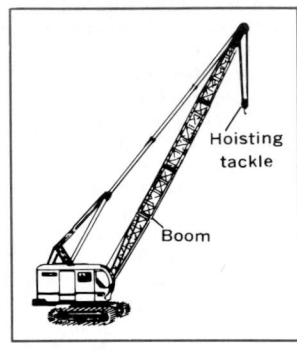

boom[2] *(def. 2)*

boom·er·ang (bü′mə rang′) *n.* **1.** a flat curved piece of wood that can be thrown so as to return to the thrower. It is used as a weapon by Australian natives and some Africans. **2.** something that returns to harm its originator. —*v.i.* to act as a boomerang: *Lies about other people can boomerang and hurt the liar.*

boom town, a town that has grown rapidly because of sudden increased activity in a business or industry: *a mining boom town.*

boon[1] (bün) *n.* **1.** a great benefit; blessing: *Your help was a boon.* **2.** *Archaic.* something asked for as a favor. [From the Old Norse word *bōn* meaning "a petition."]

boon[2] (bün) *adj.* jolly; merry: *a boon companion.* [From the Old French word *bon* meaning "good," from the Latin word *bonus* "good."]

boon·docks (bün′doks′) *pl. n.* *Informal.* a remote or backwoods area. [From the Tagalog word *bundok* meaning "mountain."]

boon·dog·gle (bün′dog′əl) *v.i.,* **boon·dog·gled, boon·dog·gling.** to do useless or unnecessary work, usually resulting in a waste of time or money. —*n.* useless or unnecessary work, usually resulting in a waste of time or money. —**boon′dog′gler,** *n.*

boor (bür) *n.* a crude, bad-mannered, or awkward person.

boor·ish (bur′ish) *adj.* crude, bad-mannered, or awkward: *Their boorish behavior on the bus offended everyone.* —**boor′ish·ly**, *adv.* —**boor′ish·ness**, *n.*

boost (büst) *n.* **1.** an upward shove or push: *Give me a boost over the wall.* **2.** something that supports, aids, or encourages: *The president's optimistic speech was intended to be a boost to public morale.* **3.** an increase or rise: *a tax boost.* —*v.t.* **1.** to lift by pushing from below. **2.** to give support or aid to; promote or encourage: *to boost someone's spirits with praise.* **3.** to raise; increase.

boost·er (bü′stər) *n.* **1.** an enthusiastic supporter: *Boosters paid for the candidate's campaign.* **2.** something that increases or reinforces power or effectiveness, such as an amplifier for a radio or television receiver. **3.** a first-stage engine of a rocket providing thrust for the launching and initial part of the flight.

booster shot, an additional inoculation of a vaccine or serum, given to prolong or reinforce immunity.

boot¹ (büt) *n.* **1.** a covering for the foot and part or much of the leg, usually made of leather or rubber. **2.** a blow with the foot or feet; kick: *With two boots I sent the ball all the way across the field.* **3.** something like a boot in shape or function. **4.** a thick patch put on the inner surface of an automobile tire. **5.** *British.* the trunk of an automobile. —*v.t.* **1.** to give a kick to: *to boot a football.* **2.** to put boots on. **3.a.** to start up a computer by loading the operating system. **b.** to start a computer by loading the first few instructions. [From the Old French word *bote* meaning "a leather foot covering."]

boot² (büt) *Archaic.* *v.t.* to be of use to. —*v.i.* to be useful. [From the Old English word *bōt* meaning "assistance" or "remedy."]
·**to boot.** in addition; besides: *On my birthday I received a baseball glove and a bat to boot.*

boot·black (büt′blak′) *n.* a person whose work is polishing shoes and boots.

boot camp, a military camp for training new recruits.

boot·ee (bü′tē) *n.* an infant's soft shoe.

Bo·ö·tes (bō ō′tēz) *n.* a constellation in the northern sky containing the bright star Arcturus.

booth (büth) *n., pl.* **booths** (büthz, büths). **1.** a small, enclosed space designed for a particular use: *a voting booth, a telephone booth, a ticket booth.* **2.** a small, partly enclosed space with a table and a seat or set of seats, as in a restaurant. **3.** a stall for the display or sale of goods: *a refreshment booth at a fair.*

boot·jack (büt′jak′) *n.* a device to hold a boot while the foot is pulled out.

boot·leg (büt′leg′) *v.*, **boot·legged**, **boot·leg·ging.** —*v.t.* to make, sell, or transport (liquor or other goods) illegally. —*v.i.* to bootleg liquor or other goods. —*adj.* made, sold, or transported illegally: *bootleg whiskey.* —*n.* a bootlegged article, especially liquor. [From the practice of smuggling products, especially liquor, in the *legs* of *boots.*] —**boot′leg′ger**, *n.*

boot·less (büt′lis) *adj.* not helping or producing a desired result; unprofitable; useless.

boot·lick (büt′lik′) *Informal.* *v.t., v.i.* to try to gain favor with (someone) by flattery or by acting in a servile manner. —**boot′lick′er**, *n.*

boo·ty (bü′tē) *n., pl.* **boo·ties.** **1.** goods taken from an enemy in war. **2.** goods seized by violence and robbery; plunder: *a pirate's booty.* **3.** any rich prize or gain.

booze (büz) *Informal.* *n.* any alcoholic drink. —*v.i.*, **boozed, booz·ing.** to drink heavily. —**booz′er**, *n.*

bop (bop) *v.t.* **bopped, bop·ping.** *Informal. v.t.* to hit or punch. —*n.* a blow or punch.

bo·rax (bôr′aks) *n.* a compound of sodium, boron, and oxygen in the form of white or colorless crystals, used especially in soaps and cleansing powders. [From the Old French word *boras* meaning "borax," from the Medieval Latin word *borax*, from the Arabic word *būraq*, from the Persian word *būrah*, all meaning "borax."]

Bor·deaux (bôr dō′) *n.* any of several red or white wines produced in the region around Bordeaux, France.

bor·der (bôr′dər) *n.* **1.** a boundary line of a territory, country, or state: *A traveler must go through customs in order to cross the border.* **2.** a strip along an edge of anything, especially one that is ornamental: *a blue border on a dress.* **3.** an edge of anything, or the part near it; margin: *a path along the border of the river.* —*v.t.* **1.** to lie on or form the edge of; bound: *Montana borders Idaho.* **2.** to put a border or edging on.
·**to border on** or **to border upon. a.** to be next to or adjoining: *Their land borders on ours.* **b.** to come close to: *That scheme borders on madness.*

border *(n., def. 2)*
a marble **border** surrounding an inlaid design

bor·der·land (bôr′dər land′) *n.* **1.** land lying near or at a border. **2.** an indefinite or vague region or area: *the borderland between science and fantasy.*

bor·der·line (bôr′dər līn′) *n.* a dividing line; boundary: *the borderline between East Germany and Poland.* —*adj.* **1.** on or near a border or boundary: *a borderline river.* **2.** not completely clear or evident; uncertain; debatable: *a borderline case of flu.*

bore¹ (bôr) *v.*, **bored, bor·ing.** —*v.t.* **1.** to make (a hole or passage) by drilling or digging: *The highway crew bored a tunnel through the mountain.* **2.** to make a hole in or through, as with a rotating tool: *to bore the ground for oil.* —*v.i.* **1.** to make a hole or passage: *The turtle bored into the sand.* **2.** to be drilled by an instrument: *This wood bores easily.* —*n.* **1.** a hole made by boring. **2.** the long, hollow space inside a tube, pipe, or gun barrel. **3.** the diameter of a hole or the inside of a tube, pipe, or gun barrel: *a three-inch bore.* [From the Old English word *borian* meaning "to make a hole."]

bore² (bôr) *v.t.*, **bored, bor·ing.** to make weary by being dull or monotonous: *My cousin always bores me by telling the same jokes over and over again.* —*n.* a person or thing that bores: *That television program was a bore.* [Of uncertain origin.]

bore³ (bôr) the past tense of **bear¹.**

bore⁴ (bôr) *n.* a high wave or wall of tidal water that forms in a shallow bay or estuary and moves upstream with great force. [From the Old Norse word *bāra* "a wave."]

bore·dom (bôr′dəm) *n.* the state of being bored or uninterested: *My boredom with my job caused me to quit.*

bor·er (bôr′er) *n.* **1.** a tool for boring holes. **2.** an insect

at; āpe; fär; câre; end; mē; it; īce; pîerce; hot; ōld; sông, fôrk; oil; out; up; ūse; rüle; pùll; tûrn; chin; sing; shop; thin; **this**; hw in white; zh in treasure. The symbol ə stands for the unstressed vowel sound heard in about, taken, pencil, lemon, and circus.

or its wormlike larva that bores into wood, fruit, or other parts of plants.

bor·ic acid (bôr′ik) a compound of hydrogen, boron, and oxygen in the form of odorless white granules or colorless crystals, used as a mild antiseptic, especially for the eyes, and in manufacturing.

born (bôrn) *v.* a past participle of **bear**[1]. —*adj.* **1.** brought into life or existence. **2.** by birth or nature; innate: *a born artist, a born comedian.*

born–a·gain (bôrn′ə gen′) *adj.* **1.** of, relating to, or being a person who establishes or renews a commitment to faith in Jesus as a personal savior, especially after an intense religious experience: *a born-again Christian.* **2.** characterized by or having a renewal of interest, conviction, or activity: *I used to exercise daily, and then I gave it up, but now I'm a born-again jogger.* [From the statement in the Gospel of John that a person "must be born again" (John 3:3).]

borne (bôrn) a past participle of **bear**[1].

bo·ron (bôr′on) *n.* a nonmetallic element that occurs in the form of yellowish brown crystals or a dark brown powder, obtained from borax. It is used in alloys and in nuclear reactors, and to make transistors. Symbol: **B** [From *borax.*]

bor·ough (bûr′ō, bur′ō) *n.* **1.** in some states of the United States, an incorporated municipality smaller than a city. **2.** one of the five administrative divisions of New York City. **3.** In Great Britain, an urban district entitled to send a representative to Parliament.

bor·row (bôr′ō, bor′ō) *v.t.* **1.** to take or get (something) with the understanding that it must be returned: *to borrow a book from the library.* **2.** to take or adopt from another source and use as one's own: *The English word "debris" was borrowed from French.* **3.** in subtraction, to take 1 from a position in the minuend and add it as 10 to the position of the next lower denomination. To subtract 17 from 93, you borrow 1 from 90 and add it as 10 to the 3, so that the subtraction in the first column is 7 from 13. —**bor′row·er**, *n.*

borscht (bôrsht) *also,* **borsch** (bôrsh). *n.* a beet soup of Russian origin, eaten hot or cold.

bor·zoi (bôr′zoi) *n.* a dog having a narrow head, a long, curving tail, and a coat of long, silky hair. Borzois were originally raised in Russia for hunting wolves. Also, **Russian wolfhound.**

bosh (bosh) *n., interj. Informal.* foolish talk; nonsense.

bosk·y (bos′kē) *adj.,* **bosk·i·er,** **bosk·i·est.** **1.** wooded. **2.** shaded by trees or shrubs: *a bosky lane.*

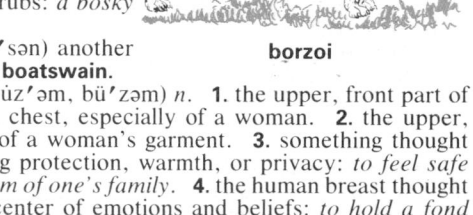
borzoi

bo's'n (bō′sən) another spelling of **boatswain.**

bos·om (bùz′əm, bü′zəm) *n.* **1.** the upper, front part of the human chest, especially of a woman. **2.** the upper, front part of a woman's garment. **3.** something thought of as giving protection, warmth, or privacy: *to feel safe in the bosom of one's family.* **4.** the human breast thought of as the center of emotions and beliefs: *to hold a fond memory close to one's bosom.* —*adj.* close and dear: *a bosom friend.*

boss[1] (bôs) *n., pl.* **boss·es.** **1.** a person who hires or supervises workers; employer or supervisor. **2.** a politician who controls a political organization, as in a certain city. —*v.t.* **1.** to be boss of: *to boss a work crew.* **2.** to order, especially in an arrogant manner (usually with *around*): *to boss someone around.* [From the Dutch word *baas* meaning "master, boss."]

boss[2] (bôs) *n., pl.* **boss·es.** a raised ornamental knob or part on a flat surface, as on silver, ivory, or leather. —*v.t.* to ornament with bosses; emboss. [From the Middle French word *boce* meaning "a raised ornament."]

boss·y (bô′sē) *adj.,* **boss·i·er,** **boss·i·est.** fond of bossing people around; domineering: *My bossy friend is always telling me what to do.*

Bos·ton terrier (bôs′tən) any of a breed of small, short-haired dogs having a smooth, black or brindled coat with white markings. Also, **Boston bull.**

bo·sun (bō′sən) another spelling of **boatswain.**

bo·tan·i·cal (bə tan′i kəl) *adj.* of or relating to plants or botany. [From the French word *botanique* meaning "botanical" or "botany," from the Greek word *botanikos* "of herbs," from *botanē* "plant, herb."] Also, **bo·tan·ic** (bə tan′ik). —**bo·tan′i·cal·ly,** *adv.*

botanical garden, a garden or collection of gardens, often including greenhouses, for the study, culture, and display of plants. Also, **botanic garden.**

bot·a·nist (bot′ə nist) *n.* a specialist in botany.

bot·a·ny (bot′ə nē) *n.* the science or study of plants. Botany deals with the origin, development, structure, function, and distribution of all forms of plant life.

botch (boch) *v.t.* to do or make in a poor or clumsy way; bungle: *to botch a job and have to do it again.* —*n., pl.* **botch·es.** a poor piece of work.

both (bōth) *adj.* the two; the one and the other: *Both twins have blue eyes.* —*pron.* one and the other: *Why not invite both to the party?* —*conj.* alike; equally; as well: *London is both the capital and largest city of Great Britain.*

both·er (both′ər) *v.t.* **1.** to give trouble to; pester; annoy: *Stop bothering me.* **2.** to make uneasy or anxious: *Meeting new people bothers my shy friend.* —*v.i.* to take trouble; concern oneself: *Don't bother to see me to the door.* —*n.* a troublesome or annoying person or thing: *Buttoning all these buttons is a real bother.*

both·er·some (both′ər səm) *adj.* causing trouble or worry; annoying: *a bothersome noise, bothersome gnats.*

bot·tle (bot′əl) *n.* **1.** a container for holding liquids, having a narrow neck or mouth that can be capped or stopped. Bottles are usually made of glass or plastic. **2.** the amount held by a bottle: *We drank a whole bottle of milk.* —*v.t.,* **bot·tled, bot·tling.** to put into a bottle or bottles. —**bot′tler,** *n.*
  ·**to bottle up.** to hold in or back; restrain: *to bottle up one's feelings.*

bot·tle·neck (bot′əl nek′) *n.* **1.** a narrow opening or passageway. **2.** a situation or thing that hinders progress: *The accident caused a bottleneck that slowed traffic.*

bot·tom (bot′əm) *n.* **1.** the lowest part of anything: *The snowball rolled to the bottom of the hill. Roots are at the bottom of a tree.* **2.** the part on which something rests or stands: *the bottom of a plate.* **3.** the ground beneath a body of water, such as the ocean or a lake or river. **4.** *also,* **bottoms.** low land near a river. **5.** the seat of a chair. **6.** *Informal.* the buttocks. **7.** the fundamental or essential part of something; basis; foundation: *The detective tried to get to the bottom of the mystery.* **8.** the part of a ship's hull below the surface of the water. —*adj.* at or on the bottom: *the bottom drawer of a dresser.*

bot·tom·less (bot′əm lis′) *adj.* **1.** having no bottom. **2.** seeming to have no bottom; very, very deep: *a bottomless well.*

Bosses

bosses
on a Chinese bell

B

bottom line 1. the line at the end of a financial statement of a business, showing its profit or loss. 2. a final result or consequence; upshot; outcome: *The other team played very well, but the bottom line was a win for our team.* 3. the essential point or most important consideration; crux: *The illustrations in a book can be interesting and helpful, but the bottom line is the quality of the text.*

bot·u·lism (boch′ə liz′əm) *n.* a food poisoning caused by toxins produced by certain bacteria that grow very rapidly in places where there is no air, such as in improperly canned foods. Botulism affects the nervous system and can cause death.

bou·doir (büd′wär) *n.* a woman's bedroom, dressing room, or private sitting room. [From the French word *boudoir* meaning "a lady's private room," from the word *bouder* "to sulk."]

bouf·fant (bü fänt′) *adj.* puffed out: *a bouffant skirt, a bouffant hairdo.*

bough (bou) *n.* a branch of a tree, especially a large or main branch.

bought (bôt) a past tense and past participle of **buy**.

bouil·la·baisse (bül′yə bās′, bül′yə bās′) *n.* a chowder made of fish and shellfish, vegetables, wine, and seasonings such as garlic and saffron.

bouil·lon (bül′yon) *n.* a clear, thin soup or broth, usually made from chicken or beef.

boul·der (bōl′dər) *n.* a large, rounded rock, especially one lying on the surface of the ground.

Boulder Dam, see **Hoover Dam.**

boul·e·vard (bül′ə värd′) *n.* a broad city street, often lined with trees.

bounce (bouns) *v.,* **bounced, bounc·ing.** —*v.i.* 1. to spring back from a surface; rebound: *The rubber ball bounced off the sidewalk.* 2. to move or walk in a springy or lively way: *The happy children bounced down the street.* 3. *Informal.* (of a check) to be rejected for payment by a bank because the person who wrote it does not have enough money in his or her account to pay for it. —*v.t.* 1. to cause (something) to spring back or rebound: *to bounce a ball.* 2. *Slang.* to force (someone) to leave: *The restaurant owner bounced the noisy customer.* —*n.* 1. a springing back; rebound: *I caught the ball on the second bounce.* 2. the ability to spring back or rebound: *This old tennis ball has lost its bounce.* 3. liveliness; energy: *Those dancers have a lot of bounce.*

•**to bounce back,** to recover, as from a blow or defeat: *After losing the first game, the team bounced back to win the second.*

bounc·er (boun′sər) *n.* 1. something that bounces. 2. *Slang.* a person employed to make disorderly persons leave a public place, such as a nightclub or bar.

bounc·ing (boun′sing) *adj.* big or strong; healthy; strapping: *a bouncing baby.*

bound¹ (bound) *v.* a past tense and past participle of **bind.** —*adj.* 1. made fast; tied: *a bound prisoner.* 2. certain; sure: *You are bound to fail the test if you don't study.* 3. under obligation; obliged: *to feel bound by a promise.* 4. having a binding or cover: *a bound volume of poetry.* 5. in language, designating a form that does not occur by itself as a separate word. The *-ly* in *gladly* and the *pre-* in *preschool* are bound forms. 6. *Informal.* determined; resolved: *They are bound on getting their way.* [From the Middle English *bounden,* past participle of *binden* meaning "to bind," from the Old English word *bindan* "to bind."]

•**bound up in** or **bound up with. a.** closely connected with. **b.** deeply devoted to: *Scientists are often bound up in their work.*

bound² (bound) *v.i.* 1. to move by a series of leaps; spring; jump. *The children went bounding over the hill.* 2. to spring back from a surface; rebound: *The ball bounded off the wall.* —*n.* 1. a long or high leap: *With one bound the deer cleared the stream.* 2. a springing back; rebound:

the bound of a ball. [From the Middle French word *bondir* meaning "to leap."]

bound³ (bound) *n.* also, **bounds.** 1. a limiting line; boundary: *the bounds of a park.* 2. an area near or within a boundary: *the vast bounds of a cattle ranch.* —*v.t.* 1. to form the boundary of: *A river bounds this land on the north.* 2. to name the boundaries of: *Can you bound your state?* —*v.i.* to have a boundary with another country or state. [From the Old French word *bodne* meaning "boundary."]

•**out of bounds. a.** beyond the boundary or limits, as of a playing field. **b.** not allowed; prohibited.

bound⁴ (bound) *adj.* going or intending to go; on the way: *The train is bound for California. I'm homeward bound.* [From the Old Norse word *būinn* meaning "ready," from *būinn,* past participle of *būa* "to dwell."]

bound·a·ry (boun′də rē, bound′rē) *n., pl.* **bound·a·ries.** a line or thing that limits or marks a separation; border: *The boundary between Illinois and Iowa is the Mississippi River.*

bound·en (boun′dən) *adj.* able to bind; obligatory; binding: *bounden duty.*

bound·less (bound′lis) *adj.* having or seeming to have no bounds or limits; vast: *the boundless expanse of the universe, the boundless energy of children.* —**bound′less·ly,** *adv.* —**bound′less·ness,** *n.*

boun·te·ous (boun′tē əs) *adj.* 1. existing in plenty; abundant: *a bounteous crop.* 2. giving or given freely; generous: *a bounteous supporter of the hospital fund, bounteous donations.* —**boun′te·ous·ly,** *adv.* —**boun′te·ous·ness,** *n.*

boun·ti·ful (boun′tə fəl) *adj.* 1. existing in plenty; abundant: *a bountiful supply.* 2. giving freely; generous: *A bountiful friend helped the homeless family.* —**boun′ti·ful·ly,** *adv.* —**boun′ti·ful·ness,** *n.*

boun·ty (boun′tē) *n., pl.* **boun·ties.** 1. a reward or premium, especially one given by a government for the killing of certain animals or the raising of certain crops: *That state has a bounty on wolves.* 2. generosity in giving: *The museum is dependent on your bounty.* 3. a gift generously given.

bou·quet (bō kā′, bü kā′) *n.* 1. a bunch of picked flowers. 2. fragrance or aroma, especially of a wine.

bour·bon (bûr′bən) also, **Bour·bon.** *n.* a whiskey distilled mainly from corn. [From *Bourbon* County, Kentucky, where it was first distilled.]

bour·geois (bür zhwä′) *adj.* 1. of or relating to the bourgeoisie or middle class. 2. having the views and characteristics of the middle class: *a bourgeois custom.* 3. having a narrow-minded and materialistic view of life: *a bourgeois greed for social standing and possessions.* [From the French word *bourgeois,* from the Old French word *borjois* meaning "citizen of a town," from the word *borc* "town," from a Germanic word meaning "fortified place."] —*n., pl.* **bour·geois.** a member of the middle class.

bour·geoi·sie (bür′zhwä zē′) *n.* 1. the social class between the working class and the rich; middle class. 2. in the political theory of Karl Marx, the capitalist class, as opposed to the proletariat.

bourn¹ (bôrn) also, **bourne.** *n.* a small stream; brook. [From the Old English word *burn* meaning "a stream."]

bourn² (bôrn, bürn) also, **bourne.** *n. Archaic.* 1. a boundary; limit. 2. goal; destination. [From the French

at; āpe; fär; câre; end; mē; it; īce; pierce; hot; ōld; sông; fôrk; oil; out; up; ūse; rüle; pull; tûrn; chin; sing; shop; thin; this; hw in white; zh in treasure. The symbol ə stands for the unstressed vowel sound heard in about, taken, pencil, lemon, and circus.

115

word *borne* meaning "boundary marker, limit," going back to the Old French word *bodne* meaning "boundary."]

bour·rée (bù rā′) *n.* **1.** an old French dance similar to the gavotte, usually in quick time. **2.** the music for this dance.

bourse (bùrs) *n.* any of various stock exchanges, especially in some European cities.

bout (bout) *n.* **1.** a trial of strength or skill; contest; match: *a boxing bout, a fencing bout.* **2.** a spell or period to be endured: *a bout of mumps, a bout of hot weather.*

bou·tique (bü tēk′) *n.* a small shop, especially one selling clothing and accessories.

bou·ton·niere (bü tən yâr′) *n.* a flower worn in the buttonhole of a lapel.

bo·vine (bō′vīn) *adj.* **1.** of or relating to an ox or cow. **2.** like an ox or cow; dull, sluggish, or stupid. —*n.* an ox, cow, or other related animal.

bow¹ (bou) *v.i.* **1.** to bend the head or upper part of the body forward in respect, submission, or greeting: *The diplomat bowed in greeting.* **2.** to give in; submit; yield: *The company bowed to the demands of the workers.* **3.** to bend, as under a weight: *The trees bowed in the wind.* —*v.t.* **1.** to cause to stoop or be bent: *Age has bowed my back.* **2.** to cause to bend forward in respect, submission, or greeting: *to bow one's head in prayer.* **3.** to show by bowing: *to bow a welcome.* —*n.* a forward bending of the head or upper part of the body in respect, submission, or greeting: *a graceful bow.* [From the Old English word *būgan* meaning "to bend, bow."]

·**to bow and scrape.** to be too polite or submissive: *The headwaiter bowed and scraped when the movie star came to the restaurant.*

·**to bow out.** to withdraw: *We were both entered in the race, but then my friend bowed out.*

·**to take a bow.** to acknowledge applause.

bow² (bō) *n.* **1.** a weapon for shooting arrows, consisting of a strip of flexible wood or other material that is bent and held by a taut string connecting the two ends. **2.** a knot with two or more loops extending from it: *a bow of ribbon.* **3.** a slender rod having horsehairs or similar fibers stretched tautly from one end to the other, used in playing the violin and related stringed instruments. **4.** something curved or bent, such as a rainbow. —*v.t.* **1.** to bend in the shape of a bow: *The hurricane bowed the trees.* **2.** to play by means of a bow: *to bow a cello.* —*v.i.* **1.** to curve in the shape of a bow: *to have legs that bow out.* **2.** to play a stringed instrument with a bow. [From the Old English word *boga* meaning this weapon.] —**bow′like′,** *adj.*

bow³ (bou) *n.* **1.** the forward end of a boat, ship, or aircraft. **2.** the rower nearest the bow of a boat. [Probably from either the Middle Low German word *boog* or the Dutch word *boeg*, both meaning "bow of a ship."]

bowd·ler·ize (bōd′lə rīz′, boud′lə rīz′) *v.t.,* **bowd·ler·ized, bowd·ler·iz·ing.** to edit by taking out words and passages considered to be obscene or otherwise objectionable. [From the English editor Thomas *Bowdler* (1754–1825), who published an expurgated version of Shakespeare's plays.]

bow·el (bou′əl) *n.* **1.** a part of the intestines. **2.** *usually,* **bowels.** intestines; entrails. **3. bowels.** the inner or deepest part of something: *the bowels of the earth.*

bow·er (bou′ər) *n.* a shelter of leafy branches; arbor.

bow·fin (bō′fin′) *n.* a large fish found in fresh waters of the eastern United States. It is the only surviving species of an ancient order of fish.

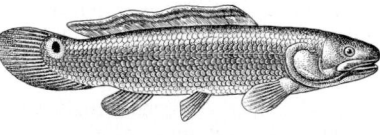
bowfin

bow·ie knife (bō′ē, bü′ē) a long, single-edged hunting knife. [From the American frontiersman Colonel James *Bowie* (1796–1836), for whom this knife was designed.]

bowie knife

bowl¹ (bōl) *n.* **1.** a deep, rounded dish used for holding food or liquid: *a salad bowl, a mixing bowl.* **2.** the amount such a container can hold; contents of a bowl: *a bowl of soup.* **3.** something shaped like a bowl; hollow, rounded thing or part: *the bowl of a spoon, a natural bowl in the side of a hill.* **4.** a stadium or other structure having the shape of a bowl. **5.** a football game played after the regular season between two specially selected teams. [From the Old English word *bolla* meaning this vessel.]

bowl² (bōl) *n.* **1.** a wooden ball that is weighted or shaped so that it will curve when rolled, used in the game of bowls. **2.** the act of rolling the ball in bowling or in bowls. —*v.i.* **1.** to take part in a game of bowls or bowling. **2.** to roll a ball in bowls or bowling. **3.** to move with a rapid and easy motion: *The truck bowled along on the open road.* —*v.t.* **1.** to roll (a ball or a bowl). **2.** to make (a certain score) in bowling: *I bowled 175 in the last game.* [From the Middle French word *boule* meaning "a ball," going back to the Latin word *bulla* "a bubble."]

·**to bowl over. a.** to knock over: *The swimmer was bowled over by the surging waves.* **b.** *Informal.* to confuse or overwhelm: *to be bowled over by shocking news.*

bow·leg (bō′leg′) *n.* a leg that curves outward.

bow·leg·ged (bō′leg′id) *adj.* having legs that curve outward at the knee, coming together again at the ankle; having bowlegs: *The rodeo champion was bowlegged from years of riding.*

bowl·er¹ (bō′lər) *n.* a person who bowls. [*Bowl²* + -*er¹*.]

bowl·er² (bō′lər) *n. British.* a derby hat. [Probably from *bowl¹* + -*er¹*.]

bow·line (bō′lin′) *n.* a knot used in making a loop that will not slip.

bowl·ing (bō′ling) *n.* **1.** a game in which ten wooden pins are set up at one end of a narrow lane and a player standing at the opposite end rolls a large, heavy ball at the pins in an attempt to knock them all down; tenpins. **2.** a similar game, such as duckpins and candlepins. **3.** see **bowls. 4.** the act of playing any of these games.

bowling alley 1. the long, narrow lane along which the ball is rolled in bowling. **2.** a building containing a number of these alleys.

bowling green, a smooth, level lawn for the game of bowls.

bowls (bōlz) *n.* a game played on a level lawn by rolling a weighted or slightly flattened wooden ball toward a smaller stationary ball. The object of the game is to roll the ball so that it stops as close as possible to the stationary ball. ▲ used with a singular verb. Also, **lawn bowling.**

bow·man (bō′mən) *n., pl.* **bow·men** (bō′mən). a person who shoots with a bow and arrow.

bow·sprit (bou′sprit′) *n.* a large pole or spar projecting forward from the bow of a sailing ship, to which lines steadying or holding sails are attached.

bow·string (bō′string′) *n.* a strong cord connecting the two ends of a bow.

bow tie (bō) a necktie tied in a bow.

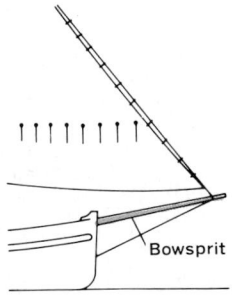
Bowsprit

box¹ (boks) *n., pl.* **box·es. 1.** a

container to hold or carry things, made of wood, card-board, or some other stiff material, and usually having four sides, a bottom, and a lid or cover. **2.** the amount such a container can hold; contents of a box: *A box of crayons lasts me a month. We used a box of raisins in the recipe.* **3.** anything that resembles a box, such as a stall for a horse or a shelter for a sentry. **4.** an enclosed or separated area for one or more persons: *a jury box, a press box, a theater box.* **5.** any of certain designated areas on a baseball field, such as the marked-off space where the batter stands. —*v.t.* to place or pack in a box: *to box fruit.* [From the Old English word *box* meaning this container, from the Late Latin word *buxis* meaning "a box, container," going back to the Greek word *pyxis* "box, container."] —**box'like'**, *adj.*
    ·to box in or **to box up.** to keep in; confine.
box² (boks) *n., pl.* **box·es.** a blow struck with the open hand or the fist, especially on the ear or side of the head. —*v.t.* **1.** to strike with the hand or fist: *to box someone's ears.* **2.** to fight (someone) with the fists as a sport: *The champion boxed the challenger with great skill.* —*v.i.* to fight with the fists as a sport. [From the Middle English word *box* meaning "a blow, stroke."]
box³ (boks) *n., pl.* **box·es.** any of various evergreen trees or shrubs with small, oval, leathery leaves. Boxes are often used as hedges. [From the Old English word *box* meaning "boxwood" or "boxwood tree," from the Latin word *buxum* "boxwood," from the Greek word *pyxos* "box tree."]
box·car (boks'kär') *n.* a railroad freight car that is completely enclosed, usually with a sliding door in the side.
box elder, a North American tree related to the maple, having low, spreading branches.
box·er (bok'sər) *n.* **1.** a person who boxes; prizefighter; pugilist. **2.** a medium-sized, short-haired dog having a smooth, tan or brindled coat, often with white markings, and a square, black muzzle.
box·ing (bok'sing) *n.* the act or sport of fighting with the fists.
Boxing Day, the first weekday after Christmas, observed as a holiday in the United Kingdom, Canada, and several other countries.
boxing glove, a padded leather glove worn for boxing.

boxer *(def. 2)*

box office, a booth or window where admission tickets are sold, as in a theater, stadium, or the like.
box score, a summary of an athletic contest, as a baseball or basketball game, arranged in the form of a table listing a statistical record of each player's performance.
box seat, a seat in a box, as at a theater or stadium.
box spring, a boxlike frame containing rows of coiled springs, used as a support for a mattress.
box·wood (boks'wŭd') *n.* **1.** the hard, close-grained wood of the box tree or shrub. **2.** the tree or shrub itself.
boy (boi) *n.* **1.** a male child from birth to the time he is a young man. **2.** *Informal.* any man; fellow: *The boys at work gave a party for me.* **3.** a male servant.
boy·cott (boi'kot) *v.t.* **1.** to join with others in refusing to do business or have contact with (a person, group, or country): *The public boycotted the grocery store because its prices were too high.* **2.** to refuse to buy, sell, or use: *The American colonists sometimes boycotted British goods.* —*n.* a planned and organized refusal to have anything to do with a person, group, or nation: *The strikers called for a boycott of the company's products.* [From the English land agent Captain Charles *Boycott* (1832–1897). When he refused to reduce rents in Ireland, the tenants refused to have anything to do with him.]

boy·friend (boi'frend') *n. Informal.* **1.** a male friend. **2.** a male sweetheart.
boy·hood (boi'hŭd') *n.* **1.** the time or state of being a boy: *My father spent his boyhood in Virginia.* **2.** boys as a group.
boy·ish (boi'ish) *adj.* of, relating to, or fit for boys or boyhood: *boyish pranks, boyish enthusiasm.* —**boy'ish·ly,** *adv.* —**boy'ish·ness,** *n.*
boy scout, a member of the Boy Scouts.
Boy Scouts, a worldwide organization for boys that aims to promote physical fitness and outdoor skills, to develop qualities of leadership and good citizenship, and to encourage usefulness to others.
boy·sen·ber·ry (boi'zən ber'ē, boi'zən bə rē) *n., pl.* **boy·sen·ber·ries. 1.** a large, soft, dark red or purple berry resembling a blackberry. **2.** the plant on which it grows. [From the American botanist Rudolph *Boysen* (d. 1950), who developed this plant.]
Br, the symbol for bromine.
bra (brä) *n.* see **brassiere.**
brace (brās) *n.* **1.** something that holds parts together or in place; thing that steadies or supports, such as a beam for strengthening a part of a building or a metal device for supporting a weak part of the body. **2.** pair; couple: *a brace of pheasants, a brace of pistols.* **3.** a tool resembling a handle, used for holding

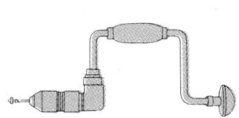

brace *(n., def. 3)*

and turning a bit or drill. **4.** either of two curved lines, {}, used in writing and printing to enclose words, letters, figures, staffs in music, or the members of a mathematical set. **5. braces.** metal wires used to straighten crooked teeth. **6. braces.** another word for **suspenders.** —*v.t.,* **braced, brac·ing. 1.** to make strong, firm, or steady; support: *to brace a tree with wires.* **2.** to prepare to meet some form of shock: *Brace yourself for the bad news.* **3.** to give vigor and energy to; invigorate.
brace and bit, a tool for drilling or boring, consisting of a drill (the *bit*) fitted into a removable handle (the *brace*).
brace·let (brās'lit) *n.* an ornamental band or chain worn around the wrist or arm. [From the Old French word *bracelet* meaning "a little arm" or "bracelet," from the Latin word *bracchium* "arm," from the Greek word *brachiōn* "arm."]
bra·chi·o·pod (brā'kē ə pod') *n.* any of a large group of mollusklike sea animals having a shell with a top and bottom half. Brachiopods have a pair of tentacles covered with cilia near the mouth, used in feeding.
brac·ing (brā'sing) *adj.* giving vigor and energy; refreshing; stimulating: *a bracing sea breeze.*
brack·en (brak'ən) *n.* another word for **brake³.**
brack·et (brak'it) *n.* **1.** a piece of wood, metal, or stone projecting from a wall, used as a support for a shelf or other object. **2.** a support joined or bent at an angle, especially at a right angle. **3.** a shelf supported by brackets. **4.** either of two symbols, [], used to enclose words, letters, or figures. **5.** a grouping or classification: *a high income tax bracket.* —*v.t.* **1.** to supply or support with a bracket or brackets: *to bracket a shelf.* **2.** to enclose within brackets: *to bracket a word.* **3.** to group or classify together: *The employer bracketed job applicants according to years of schooling.*
brack·ish (brak'ish) *adj.* **1.** somewhat salty; briny:

at; āpe; fär; câre; end; mē; it; īce; pîerce; hot; ōld; sông; fôrk; oil; out; up; ūse; rüle; pùll; tûrn; chin; sing; shop; thin; **th**is; hw in white; zh in treasure. The symbol ə stands for the unstressed vowel sound heard in about, taken, pencil, lemon, and circus.

B

brackish water, a brackish pond. **2.** having an unpleasant taste; distasteful; nauseating. —**brack′ish·ness,** *n.*

bract (brakt) *n.* a leaf at or near the base of a flower or flower cluster. Some bracts, such as those of the poinsettia, are very showy and are frequently mistaken for flower petals.

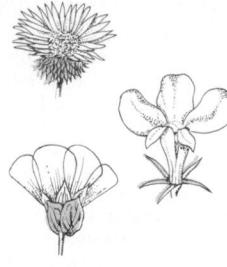

bracts

brad (brad) *n.* a thin nail with a small head.

brae (brā) *n. Scottish.* slope; hillside. [Old Norse *brā* eyelash (suggesting "the brow of a hill.")]

brag (brag) *v.i., v.t.,* **bragged, brag·ging.** to praise oneself or one's possessions; boast: *to brag about how much money you have.* —*n.* a boast; boastful talk; bragging. —**brag′ger,** *n.*

brag·ga·do·ci·o (brag′ə dō′shē ō′) *n., pl.* **brag·ga·do·ci·os. 1.** empty boasting or bragging. **2.** a person who boasts; braggart.

brag·gart (brag′ərt) *n.* a person who brags a great deal; boaster. —*adj.* bragging; boastful.

Brah·ma (brä′mə) *n.* **1.** in the Hindu religion, the god who created the universe. **2.** another word for **Brahman** *(def. 2).*

Brah·man (brä′mən) *also,* **Brah·min.** *n., pl.* **Brah·mans. 1.** a member of the highest, priestly caste of Hinduism. **2.** any of a breed of cattle native to India, now raised widely in hot or tropical regions. It has a prominent hump over the shoulder and a deep fold of drooping skin under the throat.

Brah·man·ism (brä′mə niz′əm) *n.* the religious and social system of the Brahmans.

Brah·min (brä′min) *n., pl.* **Brah·min. 1.** another spelling of **Brahman. 2.** a cultivated member of the upper class, especially in New England.

braid (brād) *n.* **1.** a ropelike strip or band in which several strands of hair, straw, leather, or the like are woven together. **2.** a band of fabric woven in this way, used for trimming or binding: *a band uniform trimmed with gold braid.* —*v.t.* **1.** to weave together several strands of (hair, straw, leather, or the like). **2.** to make (something) by such weaving: *to braid a belt out of thongs.* **3.** to trim or bind with braid. —**braid′er,** *n.*

braille (brāl) *also,* **Braille.** *n.* a system of writing and printing for the blind, in which the letters are represented by raised dots in patterns that may be recognized and read by touching them. [From the French teacher Louis *Braille* (1809–1852), who developed this system for his blind students.]

reading **braille**

brain (brān) *n.* **1.** the main organ of the nervous system in humans and other animals with backbones. It is enclosed in the skull and located at the upper end of the spinal cord. The brain is composed of a complex mass of nerves and supporting tissue and is divided into several different parts having different functions. The brain controls all the voluntary actions of the body and many of the involuntary actions, such as breathing, and in humans it is the center of thought, memory, learning, and the emotions. **2.** *also,* **brains.** mind; intelligence: *That student has real brains.* **3.** *also,* **brains.** *Informal.* the part of a machine or computer that controls all of its functions. **4.** *Informal.* a very intelligent person. —*v.t.* **1.** to kill by smashing the skull of. **2.** *Informal.* to hit on the head.

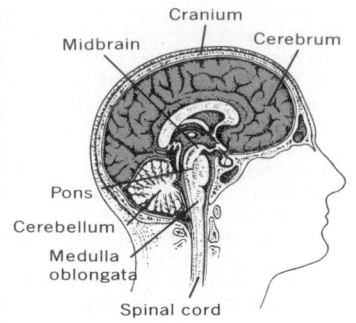

brain *(n., def. 1)*

·**to rack one's brains** or **to cudgel one's brains.** to try hard to remember, understand, or solve something.

brain·child (brān′chīld′) *n., pl.* **brain·chil·dren** (brān′chil′drən). *Informal.* a product of one's imagination; an invention, discovery, or original idea.

brain-dead (brān′ded′) *adj.* (of a person) showing no brain activity.

brain·less (brān′lis) *adj.* without intelligence; foolish; stupid. —**brain′less·ly,** *adv.* —**brain′less·ness,** *n.*

brain·stem (brān′stem′) *n.* the part of the spinal cord that extends into the brain, consisting of the pons, the medulla oblongata, and the midbrain.

brain·storm (brān′stôrm′) *n. Informal.* a sudden inspiration or idea.

brain·wash (brān′wôsh′, brān′wosh′) *v.t.* **1.** to indoctrinate (a person) so thoroughly that his or her beliefs, ideals, or way of acting are completely changed: *The captured soldier was brainwashed into accepting the political beliefs of the enemy.* **2.** to persuade (someone) by subtle or high-pressure methods: *The salesclerk tried to brainwash me into buying the most expensive model.*

brain·wash·ing (brān′wô′shing, brān′wosh′ing) *n.* the action or process by which a person is brainwashed.

brain wave, a series of electrical signals produced by brain cells. Recordings of brain waves are used to study brain activity and diagnose brain disorders.

brain·y (brā′nē) *adj.,* **brain·i·er, brain·i·est.** *Informal.* very intelligent; bright; clever. —**brain′i·ness,** *n.*

braise (brāz) *v.t.,* **braised, brais·ing.** to cook (meat or vegetables) by browning quickly on all sides in fat and then simmering in a covered pot or pan with a little liquid.

brake¹ (brāk) *n.* a device for slowing or stopping the motion of a wheel or vehicle, especially by means of friction. —*v.,* **braked, brak·ing.** —*v.t.* to cause to slow up or stop by applying a brake: *to brake a bicycle, to brake an automobile.* —*v.i.* to apply a brake: *The driver braked when a deer crossed the road.* [Of uncertain origin.]

brake² (brāk) *n.* an area overgrown with shrubs, bushes, or briers; thicket. [Probably from the Middle Low German word *brake* meaning "thicket."]

brake³ (brāk) *n.* a large, coarse fern. *Also,* **bracken.** [Probably from the Middle English word *bracken* with the same meaning, of Scandinavian origin.]

brake band, a flexible band with a friction lining, extending partially around a wheel or drum and exerting a braking force when tightened against the wheel or drum.

B

brake drum, a metal cylinder on the hub of a wheel, to which a brake band is applied in order to stop the wheel's motion.

brake·man (brāk′mən) *n., pl.* **brake·men** (brāk′mən). a member of a train crew who assists the conductor and who formerly operated the brakes.

bram·ble (bram′bəl) *n.* any of a large group of shrubs and plants having thorny stems, such as the blackberry.

bram·bly (bram′blē) *adj.,* **bram·bli·er, bram·bli·est. 1.** full of brambles. **2.** like a bramble; thorny.

bran (bran) *n.* the ground husks of wheat, rye, or other cereal grains, separated from the flour by sifting. Bran is used to feed livestock and in breakfast cereals and some other foods.

branch (branch) *n., pl.* **branch·es. 1.** a woody part of a tree, shrub, or bush, growing out and away from the trunk or main stem, or from a main limb. **2.** anything that extends out or away from a main part: *a branch of a deer's antlers, a branch of a river, a branch of a railroad line.* **3.** any part or division of a main body: *a branch of the government, a branch of a family. Algebra is a branch of mathematics.* **4.** a part of an organization located apart from the main unit: *a neighborhood branch of a library, a suburban branch of a store.* —*v.i.* **1.** to put forth branches; spread in branches. **2.** to separate or divide from a main route or body: *Turn left at the point where the path branches.*

  ·**to branch off.** to go off in a different direction or directions: *The trail branches off west of the stream.*
  ·**to branch out. a.** to give forth branches. **b.** to extend or enlarge one's activities, interests, or the like: *The bicycle company branched out and began making sailboats.*

brand (brand) *n.* **1.** the kind, quality, or make of a product: *a good brand of clothing, a new brand of soap.* **2.** a manufacturer's mark identifying a product; trademark. **3.** a mark burned on the skin of cattle or other livestock with a hot iron to show who owns them. **4.** the iron used for this purpose. **5.** in former times, a mark burned on the skin of criminals. **6.** a mark of disgrace; stigma: *to bear the brand of a traitor.* **7.** a burning or partly burned piece of wood. —*v.t.* **1.** to mark with a brand: *to brand cattle.* **2.** to put a mark of disgrace on: *Their actions in support of the enemy branded them as traitors.* —**brand′er,** *n.*

bran·dish (bran′dish) *v.t.* to wave, shake, or swing in a threatening way: *to brandish a club at an intruder.*

brand name, another term for **trade name** (def. 1).

brand–new (brand′nü′, brand′nū′) *adj.* entirely new; newly made or acquired; unused: *a brand-new car, a brand-new house.*

bran·dy (bran′dē) *n., pl.* **bran·dies.** an alcoholic beverage distilled from wine or fermented fruit juice. —*v.t.,* **bran·died, bran·dy·ing.** to treat, flavor, or preserve with brandy: *The cook brandied apples and pears to accompany the roast pork.* [From the earlier form *brandywine,* from the Dutch word *brandewijn* meaning "brandy," from the word *brant* "burnt, distilled" + *wijn* "wine."]

brant (brant) *n., pl.* **brants** or **brant.** a small, dark wild goose that breeds in arctic regions.

brash (brash) *adj.* **1.** not respectful; rudely bold; impudent: *a brash youth.* **2.** too hasty; rash; reckless: *a brash decision.* —**brash′ly,** *adv.* —**brash′ness,** *n.*

brass (bras) *n., pl.* **brass·es. 1.** a yellow metal that is an alloy of copper and zinc. **2.** objects made of brass, such as utensils or ornaments. **3.** *also,* **brasses.** musical wind instruments made of brass or other metal, such as the trombone, trumpet, or tuba. **4.** *Informal.* extreme boldness or rudeness; impudence: *I can't believe you had the brass to borrow my bicycle without asking me.* **5.** *also,* **the brass.** *Informal.* persons of high rank or position, especially high-ranking military officers. —*adj.* made of brass: *a brass tray.*

bras·siere (brə zîr′) *n.* a woman's undergarment worn to support the breasts. Also, **bra.**

brass tacks *Informal.* basic or essential facts: *Let's get down to brass tacks.*

brass·y (bras′ē) *adj.,* **brass·i·er, brass·i·est. 1.** made of or resembling brass. **2.** harsh and loud in tone: *a brassy voice.* **3.** *Informal.* rude and bold; impudent. —**brass′i·ly,** *adv.* —**brass′i·ness,** *n.*

brat (brat) *n.* a boy or girl who misbehaves or is ill-mannered; spoiled, rude child.

bra·va (brä′vä) *interj.* well done! good! excellent! ▲ used to express enthusiastic approval of a female performer. —*n., pl.* **bra·vas.** a shout of "brava!"

bra·va·do (brə vä′dō) *n.* a showy display of boldness or confidence to hide a true feeling of fear or uncertainty: *The rookie pitcher started the game with considerable bravado.*

brave (brāv) *adj.,* **brav·er, brav·est.** willing to face danger, pain, or difficulty; having or showing courage: *a brave explorer, brave deeds. The brave captain did not leave the burning ship until all the passengers were in lifeboats.* —*n.* a North American Indian warrior. —*v.t.,* **braved, brav·ing.** to face without showing fear, or despite fear; meet courageously; defy: *The teenagers braved the icy water to rescue their drowning friend* —**brave′ly,** *adv.* —**brave′ness,** *n.*

brav·er·y (brā′və rē) *n.* the quality of being brave; courage: *to show bravery in the face of danger.*

bra·vo (brä′vō) *interj.* well done! good! excellent! *n., pl.* **bra·vos** or **bravoes.** a shout of "bravo!"

bra·vu·ra (brə vyùr′ə, brə vùr′ə) *n.* **1.** a musical piece or passage requiring great technical skill and power on the part of the performer. **2.** a display of daring; a show of boldness or spirit.

brawl (brôl) *n.* a noisy, rough fight or quarrel: *The game was marred by a brawl among the players.* —*v.i.* to fight or quarrel noisily. —**brawl′er,** *n.*

brawn (brôn) *n.* **1.** muscular strength: *a person with more brawn than brains.* **2.** large, strong muscles.

brawn·y (brô′nē) *adj.,* **brawn·i·er, brawn·i·est.** robust and muscular; strong: *a brawny weightlifter.* —**brawn′i·ness,** *n.*

bray (brā) *n.* **1.** a loud, harsh cry made by a donkey or mule. **2.** any sound resembling such a cry: *the bray of trumpets.* —*v.i.* to make a loud, harsh cry or sound. —*v.t.* to make (a cry or sound) in loud, harsh tones: *The sergeant brayed out orders.*

bra·zen (brā′zən) *adj.* **1.** without shame; bold and impudent: *brazen behavior, a brazen lie.* **2.** loud; harsh. **3.** made of or resembling brass. —**bra′zen·ly,** *adv.* —**bra′zen·ness,** *n.*

  ·**to brazen it out** or **to brazen it through.** to face a situation boldly and without shame; behave defiantly: *The thief brazened it out and refused to confess despite the evidence.*

bra·zier (brā′zhər) *n.* a metal container to hold burning charcoal or other coals, used for heating or lighting, or when furnished with a grill, for cooking food.

Bra·zil·ian (brə zil′yən) *n.* a person who was born in or is a citizen of Brazil. —*adj.* of or relating to Brazil, its people, or their culture.

---

at; āpe; fär; câre; end; mē; it; īce; pîerce; hot; ōld; sông, fôrk; oil; out; up; ūse; rüle; pùll; tûrn; chin; sing; shop; thin; this; hw in white; zh in treasure. The symbol ə stands for the unstressed vowel sound heard in about, taken, pencil, lemon, and circus.

Bra·zil nut (brə zil′) a large, oily nut with a dark, hard shell and a triangular, cream-colored kernel. It is the seed of a large evergreen tree native to Brazil.

bra·zil·wood (brə zil′wůd′) *n.* a deep red wood of any of several tropical trees native to Brazil. It yields red and purple dyes and is also used in making violin bows and furniture.

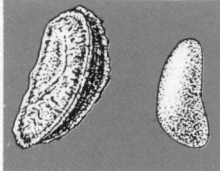

Brazil nut
shell and nut

breach (brēch) *n., pl.* **breach·es.**
1. a break or gap made in something solid: *Water gushed forth through a breach in the dam.* **2.** a violation of or failure to live up to a law, promise, or obligation: *a breach of duty, to sue a person for breach of contract.* **3.** a breaking of friendly relations; quarrel: *a breach between members of a family.* —*v.t.* to break through; make a gap in: *The attackers breached the enemy lines.*

breach of promise, a breaking of a promise, especially a promise to marry.

bread (bred) *n.* **1.** food made by mixing flour or meal with water or other liquid and then kneading and baking it. **2.** the means of living; livelihood: *to earn one's bread by writing.* —*v.t.* to cover with bread crumbs before cooking: *to bread cutlets.*
·to break bread. to eat, especially with someone else.

bread–and–but·ter (bred′ən but′ər) *adj. Informal.*
1. relating to basic needs, such as making a living: *The union members were worried about the bread-and-butter issues of wages and promotions.* **2.** basic or major; staple: *The company relied on its bread-and-butter products to make most of its profits.*

bread and butter *Informal.* means of earning a living; livelihood: *Selling used cars is my bread and butter.*

bread·bas·ket (bred′bas′kit) *n.* **1.** a basket for holding bread or rolls. **2.** a region that produces much grain: *The Middle West is sometimes referred to as the breadbasket of the nation.* **3.** *Slang.* the stomach.

bread·fruit (bred′früt′) *n.* **1.** a round, starchy fruit of a tropical tree, native to southern Asia and Polynesia. When baked, it looks and tastes somewhat like bread. **2.** the tree bearing this fruit, having leathery, glossy green leaves and yellow flowers.

bread line, a line of needy people waiting to receive food distributed by a charity or by the government.

bread·stick (bred′stik′) *n.* a long, slender roll of very crisp bread, sometimes covered with sesame seeds.

bread·stuff (bred′stuf′) *n.* the grain, flour, or meal for making bread.

breadth (bredth) *n.* **1.** the measure of a thing from side to side; width: *The breadth of the rug is six feet.* **2.** something having a definite and regular width: *a breadth of silk.* **3.** spaciousness; largeness: *the breadth of the ocean.* **4.** freedom from narrowness in attitude or outlook: *Breadth of understanding is an aim of education.*

bread·win·ner (bred′win′ər) *n.* a person who provides support for a family or other dependents.

break (brāk) *v.,* **broke, bro·ken, break·ing.** —*v.t.*
1.a. to make come apart by force; cause to separate into pieces: *I dropped a plate and broke it.* **b.** to crack or split; fracture: *How did you break your arm?* **2.** to open the surface of: *to break ground, to break the skin.* **3.** to put out of order by damaging; make useless: *You probably broke the typewriter by hitting the keys too hard.* **4.** to destroy the order or completeness of: *The troops broke formation.* **5.** to fail to obey or keep; violate: *to break the law by driving too fast, to break a promise.* **6.** to escape from: *The prisoner broke jail.* **7.** to weaken the force or effect of; lessen: *The pile of leaves broke my fall.* **8.** to cause to end; end: *A scream broke the silence.* **9.** to lower in rank; demote: *The captain broke the soldier from sergeant to corporal.* **10.** to train to obey; tame: *to break a wild horse.* **11.** to overwhelm with grief or sorrow; crush: *to break a person's heart.* **12.** to go beyond; surpass; excel: *The runners will try to break the school record in the mile.* **13.** to make known; disclose: *I broke the news of the accident to the family.* **14.** to cause (someone) to stop a habit: *to break someone of smoking.* **15.** to divide (a bill or coin) into smaller units: *Can you break a five-dollar bill?* **16.** to bring into financial difficulty; ruin: *The losses from the fire broke the shopkeeper.*
—*v.i.* **1.** to come apart by force; separate into pieces: *The mirror broke when I dropped it.* **2.** to become useless because of damage: *The clock broke.* **3.** to move suddenly: *The runners broke from the starting line. The water broke through the dam.* **4.** to divide up or scatter: *The clouds broke and the sun shone again.* **5.** to take place, come into being, or become known: *The day is breaking. The story broke in the morning newspapers.* **6.** to change or fall off suddenly and abruptly: *At mention of the disaster, the speaker's voice broke.* **7.** to become overwhelmed with sorrow: *The children's hearts broke when the dog died.* **8.** (of a pitched baseball) to curve near or over home plate.
—*n.* **1.** the result of breaking; broken place; crack: *a break in a fence.* **2.** the act of breaking. **3.** a sudden rush or dash: *The prisoner made a break for freedom.* **4.** beginning; start: *the break of day.* **5.** a sudden change or interruption: *a break in the weather, a break in peaceful relations between countries.* **6.** a brief rest period; pause: *After an hour of practice the band took a ten-minute break.* **7.** *Slang.* a stroke of luck; chance: *a lucky break, a bad break.*
·to break away. a. to escape suddenly; get away: *One of the prisoners broke away.* **b.** to change, as by ceasing some activity: *to break away from habit.*
·to break down. a. to fail to work properly; stop working: *The car broke down and we had to walk.* **b.** to have a physical or mental collapse; become ill. **c.** to give way to emotion: *to break down and cry.* **d.** to separate or divide into smaller or simpler parts; analyze: *to break down a chemical compound.*
·to break in. a. to make ready for use or work: *to break in a new pair of shoes. The grocer broke in the new cashier.* **b.** to enter by force: *A thief broke in by the back door.* **c.** to interrupt: *It is rude to break in while I am talking.*
·to break into. a. to enter by force: *The burglars broke into the apartment.* **b.** to interrupt: *The announcer broke into the regular program with a news bulletin.* **c.** to burst forth with: *to break into laughter.*
·to break off. a. to stop suddenly: *to break off in the middle of a sentence.* **b.** to stop being friendly: *to break off with old friends after moving away.*
·to break out. a. to start suddenly and unexpectedly: *A fire broke out.* **b.** to become covered with a rash or pimples: *My hands broke out from poison ivy.* **c.** to make an escape: *to break out of jail.*
·to break up. a. to separate or scatter: *The ice on the pond is breaking up.* **b.** to put an end to; stop: *The police broke up the fight.* **c.** to make or become upset: *The sad news broke us up.* **d.** to end a relationship: *The partnership broke up.* **e.** *Informal.* to laugh or cause to laugh: *Your jokes always break me up.*
·to break with. to stop being friendly with: *The two friends broke with each other after their quarrel.*

break·a·ble (brā′kə bəl) *adj.* that can be broken: *a breakable glass.* —*n.* something that is easily broken.

break·age (brā′kij) *n.* **1.** the act of breaking. **2.** something broken. **3.** damage caused by breaking: *The store charged me for the breakage when I accidentally dropped the cups.* **4.** the cost for such damage.

break dance, to engage in break dancing.

break danc·ing, a style of dancing characterized by acrobatic movements, such as spinning and jumping, improvisation, and pantomime.

break·down (brāk′doun′) *n.* **1.** a failure to work properly: *After the breakdown, our car had to be towed away.* **2.** a collapse of one's physical or mental health: *to suffer a breakdown because of great stress.* **3.** a separation of something into smaller or simpler parts; analysis: *The reporters were given a breakdown of the facts that the police had about the case.*

break·er (brā′kər) *n.* **1.** a large wave that foams as it breaks on the rocks or shore. **2.** a person or thing that breaks.

break·fast (brek′fəst) *n.* the first meal of the day, usually eaten in the morning. —*v.i.* to eat breakfast. [*Break* + *fast*². This meal *breaks* the night's *fast.*]

break·neck (brāk′nek′) *adj.* extremely dangerous: *The racer drove at a breakneck speed in order to win.*

break·through (brāk′thrü′) *n.* an important development, achievement, or discovery that helps to further progress in any field of knowledge or activity: *The invention of the microscope was a breakthrough in science.*

break·up (brāk′up′) *n.* **1.** a separation or breaking into smaller parts: *The warm weather caused the breakup of ice on the river.* **2.** a stopping or ending: *the breakup of a friendship.*

break·wa·ter (brāk′wô′tər) *n.* a wall or barrier that protects an area from the force of waves.

bream (brēm) *n., pl.* **breams** or **bream.** **1.** any of various freshwater fish of Europe related to the carp. **2.** a freshwater sunfish of the southeastern United States.

breast (brest) *n.* **1.** the front part of the human body between the neck and the abdomen; chest. **2.** the corresponding upper, front part of an animal's body. **3.** either of the two milk glands of women. **4.** something like the breast: *the breast of a hill.* **5.** the breast thought of as the center of emotions: *Pride filled their breasts.* —*v.t.* to struggle against; oppose: *The lifeguard breasted the waves in an attempt to reach the drowning child.*

·**to make a clean breast of.** to make complete confession of.

breast·bone (brest′bōn′) *n.* the flat, narrow bone in the center of the breast to which the ribs are joined; sternum.

breast–feed (brest′fēd′) *v.t.,* **breast-fed** (brest′fed′), **breast-feed·ing.** to feed (a baby) with milk from a mother's breast; nurse; suckle.

breast·plate (brest′plāt′) *n.* a piece of armor worn to protect the chest.

breast·stroke (brest′strōk′) a stroke in swimming made while face down, in which both arms go out in front of the head and then are swept in an arc to the sides and back.

breast·work (brest′wûrk′) *n.* a low, hastily built wall for defense.

breath (breth) *n.* **1.** air drawn into and forced out of the lungs in breathing. **2.** the act or process of breathing; respiration: *to hold your breath while swimming under water.* **3.** a single act or instance of breathing: *When I was sick my chest hurt with every breath I took.* **4.** the ability to breathe freely and easily: *to get one's breath back after running.* **5.** air forced out from the lungs, especially in the form of vapor: *We saw our breath in the cold air.* **6.** a slight current of air: *There is not a breath of air in this hot room.* **7.** a whisper or hint; suggestion: *the first breath of spring.*

·**in the same breath** or **in the next breath.** at almost the same time; immediately afterward.

·**to catch one's breath. a.** to stop or pause for breath; rest; relax. **b.** to gasp.

·**to take one's breath away.** to leave one breathless; overwhelm or stun: *The view from the mountaintop took our breath away.*

·**under** or **below one's breath.** in a very low voice; in a whisper: *Are you mumbling complaints under your breath?*

breathe (brēth) *v.,* **breathed, breath·ing.** —*v.i.* **1.** to draw air into the lungs and force it out: *It is sometimes hard to breathe in the high altitude of the mountains.* **2.** to be alive; live. **3.** to stop or pause for breath; rest; relax. **4.** to send out a fragrance or impression: *The field breathed of newly mowed hay. His manner breathed of self-confidence.* —*v.t.* **1.** to draw into and force out from the lungs, as air. **2.** to give out or instill: *The volunteer's enthusiasm breathed new life into our work.* **3.** to send out by breathing: *We breathed a sigh of relief when the lost child was found.* **4.** to whisper or say confidentially: *Don't breathe a word of what I tell you.* **5.** to allow to rest or recover breath: *The jockey breathed the horse after the race.*

·**to breathe one's last.** to die.

breath·er (brē′thər) *n.* **1.** *Informal.* a short rest period: *Stop studying for ten minutes and take a breather.* **2.** a person who breathes, especially in a particular way.

breathing space (brē′thing) a space or span of time in which a person can breathe or move freely: *There was no breathing space in the crowded room.*

breath·less (breth′lis) *adj.* **1.** out of breath: *to be breathless after climbing a mountain.* **2.** in a state of fear or excitement; tense: *The children were breathless as they watched the lion-taming act.* —**breath′less·ly,** *adv.* —**breath′less·ness,** *n.*

breath·tak·ing (breth′tā′king) *adj.* causing great excitement or pleasure; thrilling; overwhelming: *the breathtaking beauty of sunset over the water.*

bred (bred) the past tense and past participle of **breed.**

breech (brēch) *n., pl.* **breech·es** (brē′chiz). **1.** the part of a gun or other firearm behind or at the rear of the barrel. **2.** the lower, rear part of the body; buttocks.

breech·cloth (brēch′klôth′) *n., pl.* **breech·cloths** (brēch′klôthz′, brēch′klôths′). a piece of cloth worn to cover the loins; loincloth.

breech·clout (brēch′klout′) *n.* another word for **breech-cloth.**

breech·es (brich′iz) *also,* **britch·es.** *pl. n.* **1.** trousers reaching to or just below the knees. **2.** *Informal.* any trousers.

breech·es buoy (brich′iz) a device for rescuing or transporting a person while at sea, consisting of a pair of short canvas pants suspended from a life preserver. It is hung from a pulley that slides along a rope strung between two ships or between a ship and a shore point.

breech·load·er (brēch′lō′dər) *n.* a firearm that is loaded at the breech instead of at the muzzle.

breech·load·ing (brēch′lō′ding) *adj.* (of a firearm) loading at the breech instead of at the muzzle.

breed (brēd) *v.,* **bred, breed·ing.** —*v.t.* **1.** to raise (plants or animals), especially in order to develop new or improved kinds: *a ranch that breeds cattle.* **2.** to give rise to; cause; produce: *War and famine breed human misery.* **3.** to bring up or train; rear: *The members of that family were bred to be leaders.* **4.** to mate: *They bred the stallion with the mare.* —*v.i.* **1.** to mate and produce young: *Certain animals breed once a year.* **2.** to come into being; develop: *Disease breeds in poor living conditions.* —*n.* **1.** a particular strain or variety of a species of plant or animal, produced and maintained by controlled breeding: *Beagles are a breed of dog.* **2.** a kind or sort of anything; type: *The pioneers of the American West were a hardy breed.*

---

at; āpe; fär; câre; end; mē; it; īce; pîerce; hot; ōld; sông, fôrk; oil; out; up; ūse; rüle; pull; tûrn; chin; sing; shop; thin; this; hw in white; zh in treasure. The symbol ə stands for the unstressed vowel sound heard in about, taken, pencil, lemon, and circus.

breed·er (brē′dər) *n.* **1.** a person who breeds plants or animals. **2.** a plant or animal that produces young, especially a plant or animal kept for this purpose.

breeder reactor, a nuclear reactor that produces at least as much fissionable material as it consumes. Also, **breeder pile.**

breed·ing (brē′ding) *n.* **1.** the bringing up or training of the young, especially as shown in a person's manners or behavior: *to show good breeding by being polite.* **2.** the act of producing young. **3.** the reproduction of plants or animals, usually to bring about improvements in the young.

breeze (brēz) *n.* **1.** a light current of air; soft, gentle wind. **2.** *Informal.* something easy to do: *That English test was a breeze.* —*v.i.*, **breezed, breez·ing.** *Informal.* to move in a relaxed or brisk manner: *to breeze into a room.*

·**to breeze through.** to do or complete easily and quickly: *I breezed through my first job interview.*

breeze·way (brēz′wā′) *n.* a roofed passageway, open at the sides, between two buildings or structures, as between a house and a garage.

breez·y (brē′zē) *adj.*, **breez·i·er, breez·i·est. 1.** having gentle winds: *breezy shores, a breezy day.* **2.** lively or carefree; cheerful: *a breezy manner of speaking.* —**breez′i·ly,** *adv.* —**breez′i·ness,** *n.*

breth·ren (breth′rən) a plural of **brother.** ▲ used chiefly for people who belong to the same organization, especially a religious order or a fraternal society.

Bret·on (bret′ən) *n.* **1. a.** a person who was born in or is a citizen of Brittany. **b.** one of the people who have inhabited Brittany since ancient times and who speak a Celtic language. **2.** the Celtic language spoken by Bretons. —*adj.* of or relating to Brittany, its people, their language, or culture.

breve (brēv, brev) *n.* a mark (˘) placed over a vowel or syllable to show that it has a short sound.

bre·vi·ar·y (brē′vē er′ē) *n.*, *pl.* **bre·vi·ar·ies.** in the Roman Catholic and certain other churches, a book or books containing prayers, lessons, hymns, and special readings to be recited each day by priests and members of certain religious orders.

brev·i·ty (brev′i tē) *n.* shortness or briefness, especially in speech or writing.

brew (brü) *v.t.* **1.** to make (beer, ale, or a similar beverage) by steeping, boiling, and fermenting malt and hops. **2.** to prepare (a nonalcoholic beverage, such as tea or coffee) by steeping, boiling, or mixing. **3.** to plan or bring about; plot: *to brew trouble.* —*v.i.* **1.** to be brewed. **2.** to form or develop: *There is a storm brewing in the west.* —*n.* **1.** a drink prepared by brewing. **2.** the amount that is brewed at one time.

brew·er (brü′ər) *n.* a person who brews, especially one whose business or trade is the brewing of beer or ale.

brewer's yeast, a type of yeast used in brewing and sometimes consumed as a source of vitamins in the vitamin B complex.

brew·er·y (brü′ə rē) *n.*, *pl.* **brew·er·ies.** a place where beer, ale, or other similar beverages are brewed.

brew·ing (brü′ing) *n.* **1.** the process by which beer, ale, or similar beverages are made. **2.** the amount brewed at one time.

bri·ar¹ (brī′ər) *also,* **bri·er.** *n.* **1.** another word for **tree heath. 2.** the root of the tree heath, used for making tobacco pipes. **3.** a tobacco pipe made from this root. [From the French word *bruyère* meaning this plant, of Celtic origin.]

bri·ar² (brī′ər) another spelling of **brier¹.**

bri·ar·root (brī′ər rüt′, brī′ər rút′) *also,* **bri·er·root.** *n.* another word for **briarwood.**

bri·ar·wood (brī′ər wüd′) *also,* **bri·er·wood.** *n.* **1.** the wood of the root of the tree heath, used in making tobacco pipes. **2.** a tobacco pipe made from this wood.

bribe (brīb) *n.* **1.** money or gifts given or offered to a person in a position of trust or responsibility to persuade him or her to do something illegal or dishonest: *The speeder offered the police officer a bribe to avoid a ticket.* **2.** anything that influences or persuades. —*v.t.,* **bribed, brib·ing. 1.** to give or offer a bribe to: *The gangster tried to bribe the judge before the trial began.* **2.** to influence or persuade with a bribe.

brib·er·y (brī′bə rē) *n.*, *pl.* **brib·er·ies.** the act or practice of giving, offering, or accepting a bribe.

bric–a–brac (brik′ə brak′) *n.* small decorative objects; knickknacks.

brick (brik) *n.* **1.** a molded, usually rectangular, block of clay baked by fire in a kiln or oven, or by the sun, used in building and paving. **2.** bricks as a material for building: *a fireplace made of brick.* **3.** something shaped like a brick: *a brick of gold.* —*v.t.* **1.** to enclose, cover or wall with bricks: *to brick up a doorway.* **2.** to build or pave with bricks. —*adj.* made of brick: *a brick house.*

brick·bat (brik′bat′) *n.* **1.** a piece of brick or other material, especially when thrown at someone. **2.** *Informal.* an insulting or critical remark.

brick·lay·er (brik′lā′ər) *n.* a person whose business or trade is building with bricks.

bricklayer

brick·lay·ing (brik′lā′ing) *n.* the act or business of building with bricks.

brick·work (brik′wûrk′) *n.* work made of bricks.

brick·yard (brik′yärd′) *n.* a place where bricks are made or sold.

brid·al (brī′dəl) *adj.* of or relating to a bride or wedding: *a bridal bouquet, a bridal suite.*

bride (brīd) *n.* a woman newly married or about to be married.

bride·groom (brīd′grüm′, brīd′grúm′) *n.* a man newly married or about to be married.

brides·maid (brīdz′mād′) *n.* a woman who attends a bride at her wedding.

bridge¹ (brij) *n.* **1. a.** any structure built over a river, railroad track, highway, or other obstacle or gap to allow passage for people or vehicles. **b.** something that provides a connection between two places, processes, eras, or the like: *a bridge between two cultures.* **2.** the upper, bony ridge of the nose. **3.** the curved part of a pair of eyeglasses that joins the two lenses and rests on the bridge of the nose. **4.** one or more false teeth in a mounting fastened to the adjacent natural teeth. **5.** a raised structure on a deck of a ship, from which the ship is navigated and steered. **6.** in certain string instruments, such as violins and cellos, a thin piece of wood or other material over which the strings are stretched. —*v.t.,* **bridged, bridg·ing. 1.** to build a bridge or bridges over: *to bridge a river.* **2.** to go over or across; span: *An overpass bridged the highway.* **3.** to serve as a way of overcoming: *Setting up* a student exchange program may help to bridge the gap in understanding between the two countries. [From the Old English word *brycg* meaning this structure.]

·**to burn one's bridges behind one** or **to burn one's bridges.** to destroy all ways or chances for return or retreat from a course of action.

bridge² (brij) *n.* a card game played by four players in teams of two. [From the earlier word *biritch* meaning this game, of uncertain origin.]

bridge·head (brij'hed') *n.* a military position established on enemy territory to which personnel and supplies may be sent so that further advance may be made.

bridge·work (brij'wûrk') *n.* a dental bridge or bridges.

bri·dle (brī'dəl) *n.* **1.** the part of a horse's harness that fits over the head, including the bit and reins, used to guide or control the animal. **2.** anything that restrains or controls. —*v.*, **bri·dled, bri·dling.** —*v.t.* **1.** to put a bridle on. **2.** to restrain or control; curb: *to bridle one's anger.* —*v.i.* to throw back the head and draw in the chin to show anger, indignation, or scorn: *to bridle at an insult.*

bridle path, a path for horseback riding.

brief (brēf) *adj.* **1.** short in time; ending quickly: *a brief interruption of a program for a news bulletin. We paused only for a brief moment.* **2.** using few words; concise: *The teacher asked me to give a brief summary of the story.* —*n.* **1.** a summary of the facts, points of law, and other material important to a case, prepared by a lawyer as the basis for arguing a case in court. **2. briefs.** short, close-fitting underpants. —*v.t.* to give important details to: *The scout leader briefed us before the camping trip.* —**brief′ly,** *adv.* —**brief′ness,** *n.*

·**in brief.** in a few words; in short: *In brief, we had a wonderful time.*

brief·case (brēf'kās') *n.* a flat case with a handle, used especially for carrying papers and books.

bri·er¹ (brī'ər) *also,* **bri·ar.** *n.* **1.** any thorny shrub or plant, especially the wild rose. **2.** a thorny stem or a thorn on such a stem. [From the Old English word *brēr* meaning this plant.]

bri·er² (brī'ər) another spelling of **briar¹.**

bri·er·root (brī'ər rüt', brī'ər rùt') another spelling of **briarroot.**

bri·er·wood (brī'ər wùd') another spelling of **briarwood.**

brig (brig) *n.* **1.** a two masted ship with square mainsails. **2.** a place on a ship for confining prisoners. **3.** a naval prison.

Brig. 1. Brigade. **2.** Brigadier.

bri·gade (bri gād') *n.* **1.** a military unit that is made up of two or more battalions and that forms part of a division. **2.** a group of people organized for a particular purpose or a specific function: *a fire brigade.*

brig *(def. 1)*

brig·a·dier (brig'ə dîr') *n.* see **brigadier general.**

brigadier general, a commissioned officer in the U.S. Army, Air Force, or Marines, ranking above a colonel and below a major general.

brig·and (brig'ənd) *n.* a robber or bandit, especially one who is a member of a band of roving outlaws.

brig·an·tine (brig'ən tēn') *n.* a two-masted ship having a square-rigged foremast, but, unlike a brig, a fore-and-aft-rigged mainmast.

bright (brīt) *adj.* **1.** giving or reflecting much light; filled with light; shining: *The sun was so bright it hurt your eyes when you looked out* (Ernest Hemingway). *The waxed floor had a bright finish.* **2.** of brilliant color; vivid: *a bright yellow dress.* **3.** having or showing much intelligence; quick-witted; clever: *a bright child, a bright reply.*

4. favorable or hopeful: *a bright future.* **5.** lively; cheerful: *The children were bright and gay at the party.* —*adv.* in a bright manner; brightly: *The stars shone bright.* —**bright′ly,** *adv.* —**bright′ness,** *n.*

bright·en (brī'tən) *v.t.* to make bright or brighter: *Painting the walls white brightened the room.* —*v.i.* to become bright or brighter: *The day brightened after the rain.*

bril·liance (bril'yəns) *n.* the state or quality of being brilliant. Also, **bril·lian·cy** (bril'yən sē).

bril·liant (bril'yənt) *adj.* **1.** shining or sparkling with light or luster: *brilliant spotlights, brilliant stars.* **2.** done in an outstanding way; magnificent: *The team played a brilliant game to win the championship.* **3.** having or showing much intelligence, ability, or talent: *a brilliant painter.* **4.** very rich in color; vivid: *Brilliant flags flew in the breeze.* —*n.* a gem, especially a diamond, cut with many facets to increase its sparkle. —**bril′liant·ly,** *adv.*

brim (brim) *n.* **1.** the upper edge or rim of a cup, bowl, or similar object: *My glass is filled to the brim.* **2.** a projecting edge or rim: *the brim of a hat.* **3.** the edge or rim of a space, as a canyon. —*v.i.*, **brimmed, brimming.** to be full to the brim; be about to overflow: *a brimming bowlful. My eyes brimmed with tears.*

brim·ful (brim'fùl') *adj.* full to the brim; completely full: *a glass brimful of milk.*

brim·stone (brim'stōn') *n.* another word for **sulfur.**

brin·dle (brin'dəl) *adj.* brindled. —*n.* **1.** a brindled color. **2.** an animal having a brindled color.

brin·dled (brin'dəld) *adj.* gray or brownish yellow with irregular, dark streaks or spots: *a brindled cow.*

brine (brīn) *n.* **1.** water that is salted heavily, used especially for pickling or preserving food. **2.** the sea or its water.

bring (bring) *v.t.*, **brought, bring·ing. 1.** to carry or cause (someone or something) to come with oneself: *I brought two friends home from school with me. Bring all your books home.* **2.** to cause to come; attract; draw: *What brings you here? The news brought tears to their eyes.* **3.** to cause to reach a particular state or condition: *Bring the water to a boil. The crew quickly brought the fire under control.* **4.** to cause to come about or happen; result in; produce: *The floods brought disaster to the town.* **5.** to cause (someone or oneself) to adopt a course of action or belief; persuade: *We couldn't bring them to give up their objections.* **6.** to sell for: *The car brought a high price.*

·**to bring about.** to cause to happen; cause; accomplish: *Moving to a new town brought about many changes in our lives.*

·**to bring around** or **to bring round. a.** to cause (someone) to adopt a course of action or belief; convince; persuade. **b.** to bring back to consciousness; revive.

·**to bring forth. a.** to produce (young or fruit). **b.** to make known; reveal: *The next witness brought forth new evidence.*

·**to bring forward.** to introduce; present: *The committee brought arguments forward in support of the plan.*

·**to bring in. a.** to produce, as profits: *The newspaper stand brings in about $100 a day.* **b.** to give or submit, as a verdict: *The jury brought in a verdict of "not guilty."*

·**to bring off.** to accomplish successfully: *to bring off a business deal.*

at; āpe; fär; câre; end; mē; it; īce; pîerce; hot; ōld; sông, fôrk; oil; out; up; ūse; rüle; pùll; tûrn; chin; sing; shop; thin; this; hw in white; zh in treasure. The symbol ə stands for the unstressed vowel sound heard in about, taken, pencil, lemon, and circus.

·**to bring on.** to lead to; cause: *Not getting enough rest brought on my cold.*

·**to bring out. a.** to make clear or evident; reveal: *Enlarging the photograph brought out more details.* **b.** to introduce or present to the public: *to bring out a new movie.*

·**to bring to.** to bring back to consciousness; revive.

·**to bring up. a.** to take care of during childhood; rear or educate: *I was brought up in the city.* **b.** to introduce to notice or consideration: *May I bring up an important question?* **c. to bring up short.** to cause to pause or stop: *The rudeness of the clerk's reply brought me up short.*

▲ **Bring** and **take** both mean "to carry from one place to another." **Bring** usually describes carrying something *into* a place or *to* a person; **take** usually describes carrying something *away* from a place or *from* a person: *Please take these books back to the library and bring me some new ones.*

brink (bringk) *n.* **1.** the top edge or margin of a steep place, as of a cliff or the bank of a river. **2.** the point at which something is likely to happen or begin; verge: *The lost child was on the brink of tears.*

brin·y (brī′nē) *adj.*, **brin·i·er, brin·i·est.** of or like brine; salty.

bri·quette (bri ket′) *also,* **bri·quet.** *n.* a molded block of coal dust or other material, used for fuel: *We bought charcoal briquettes for the hibachi.*

brisk (brisk) *adj.***1.** quick and lively; energetic; vigorous: *The hikers walked at a brisk pace. The writer has a brisk intelligence.* **2.** keen and bracing; invigorating: *a brisk autumn wind.* —**brisk′ly,** *adv.* —**brisk′ness,** *n.*

bris·ket (bris′kit) *n.* **1.** a cut of meat from the breast of an animal, especially a cow or steer. **2.** the breast of an animal.

bris·ling (briz′ling) *n.* a kind of small herring of the northeastern Atlantic.

bris·tle (bris′əl) *n.* **1.** a coarse, short, stiff hair, especially of a hog: *a brush made of hog bristles.* **2.** something resembling this: *My toothbrush has nylon bristles.* —*v.,* **bris·tled, bris·tling.** —*v.i.* **1.** to have the hairs on the back rise stiffly, as in fear, anger, excitement: *The cat bristled at the sight of the dog.* **2.** to show anger or irritation: *The speaker bristled at the crowd's jeers.* **3.** to rise stiffly: *The dog's hair bristled as we approached.* —*v.t.* **1.** to cause to rise stiffly: *The porcupine bristled its quills.* **2.** to furnish with bristles.

·**to bristle with.** to be thick with or full of: *The shore bristled with boats. The audience bristled with excitement.*

bris·tly (bris′lē) *adj.,* **bris·tli·er, bris·tli·est. 1.** like bristles: *The goat had bristly hairs on its chin.* **2.** easily angered or irritated: *a bristly personality.*

Brit., Britain; British.

Bri·tan·ni·a (bri tan′ē ə, bri tan′yə) *n.* **1.** the ancient Roman name for Great Britain. **2.** the British Empire. **3.** a female figure symbolic of Great Britain or the British Empire.

britch·es (brich′iz) *pl.n. Informal.* another spelling of **breeches.**

Brit·i·cism (brit′ə siz′əm) *n.* a word, phrase, or idiom used only or mainly by the British. *Petrol* is a Briticism for *gasoline.*

Brit·ish (brit′ish) *adj.* of, relating to, or characteristic of Great Britain or its people. —*n.* **1. the British.** the people of Great Britain. **2.** see **British English.**

British Commonwealth of Nations, see **Commonwealth of Nations.**

British Empire, formerly, all the countries, colonies, dependencies, and protectorates controlled by Great Britain.

British English, the English language as spoken and written in Great Britain.

The famous writer George Bernard Shaw once said, "England and America are two countries separated by the same language." He meant that, although they speak the same language, people from England and people from the United States sometimes have trouble understanding each other. Words in **British English** and American English sometimes differ in spelling, pronunciation, meaning, or usage. If you have ever read a book from Great Britain, you may have noticed such words as *honour, centre,* or *traveller.* You were probably able to guess that these were the British spellings of *honor, center,* and *traveler.*

The pronunciation of British English differs from the pronunciation of American English in various ways. The most obvious difference is the broad *a,* as in *brass, can't, bath,* and *dance.* Other differences in British pronunciation appear in such words as *clerk* and *derby,* in which the *er* is said like the *ar* in *car,* and in the word *schedule,* which begins with an *sh* sound rather than the *sk* sound that American speakers use.

Most words have the same meaning in Britain that they have in the United States. Most words that are not common to both British and American speakers are words that were created after the American Revolution, especially those words that describe industrial or scientific inventions or processes. In England, an elevator is called a *lift,* the hood of a car is called the *bonnet,* the trunk of a car is called the *boot,* and gasoline is called *petrol.*

The differences in grammar in British and American English are very slight. One very obvious difference is in the British use of a plural verb with a singular collective noun, as in *Manchester are confident of winning the soccer match.*

Despite these differences, if you were to pick up a British newspaper there would probably be only a few words or phrases that you could not understand. In the last seventy years there has been increased communication between speakers of American English and British English. This greater communication, caused by the exchange of books, movies, popular music, and television shows, the stationing of American soldiers in Britain in wartime, and increased trade and travel between the two countries, has helped to make each group more familiar with the other's form of English.

Brit·ish·er (brit′i shər) *n.* a person who was born in or is a citizen of Great Britain, especially someone from England.

British thermal unit, a unit of measurement equal to the amount of heat needed to raise the temperature of one pound of water one degree Fahrenheit.

Brit·on (brit′ən) *n.* **1.** a person who was born in or who is a citizen of Great Britain; Britisher. **2.** a member of an ancient Celtic people who lived in southern Britain at the time of the Roman invasion.

brit·tle (brit′əl) *adj.* likely to break or snap; easily broken: *brittle twigs, brittle glass.*

bro., brother.

broach (brōch) *n., pl.* **broach·es.** a pointed cutting tool driven or pulled through rough holes to enlarge or shape them. —*v.t.* **1.** to mention or suggest for the first time; introduce: *to broach an unpleasant subject.* **2.** to make a hole in so as to draw out a liquid; tap: *to broach a keg of wine.* —*v.i.* to come up to and break the surface of water: *The whale broached right in front of us.*

broad (brôd) *adj.* **1.** large from one side to the other; wide: *The broad highway had four traffic lanes.* **2.** large in size; spacious: *the broad plains of the Midwest.* **3.** ready to accept a wide range of thoughts, opinions, or

B

the like; open-minded; tolerant: *a broad outlook on life.*
4. having a wide range; not limited or narrow: *a broad
knowledge of rocketry.* **5.** concerning the main parts or
features; not detailed; general: *a broad description of a
movie.* **6.** easy to understand; clear; obvious: *to give
someone a broad hint that you know a secret.* **7.** clear
and open: *broad daylight.* **8.** (of vowel sounds) formed
with the mouth wide open and the back of the tongue
in a low, flat position. The *a* in *father* is broad.
—broad′ly, *adv.* **—broad′ness,** *n.*

broad·ax (brôd′aks′) *also,* **broad·axe.** *n., pl.* **broad·
ax·es.** **1.** an ax with a broad blade, used especially to cut
and shape timbers. **2.** an ancient weapon with a wide
blade.

broad·cast (brôd′kast′) *v.,* **broad·cast** or **broad·cast·
ed, broad·cast·ing.** **—v.t.** **1.** to send out (information or
entertainment) by radio or television. **2.** to make widely
known or spread: *to broadcast a rumor all over town.*
3. to scatter over a large area: *to broadcast seed.* **—v.i.**
to send out by radio or television: *That television channel
does not broadcast early in the morning.* **—n.** **1.** something that is broadcast by radio or television, especially a
program: *a news broadcast.* **2.** the act of broadcasting,
especially by radio or television. **—adj.** **1.** relating to or
sent by radio or television broadcast. **2.** scattered over a
large area: *broadcast seed.* **—adv.** by scattering over a
large area: *to sow broadcast.* **—broad′cast·er,** *n.*

broad·cloth (brôd′klôth′) *n.* **1.** a smooth, closely woven
cotton or silk fabric, used especially in making shirts,
pajamas, and dresses. **2.** a closely woven woolen fabric,
used especially in suits and coats.

broad·en (brôd′ən) *v.t.* to make broad or broader: *to
broaden a road by adding new lanes.* **—v.i.** to become
broad or broader: *My views of how other people live
broadened after I traveled for a year.*

broad jump, another term for **long jump.**

broad·loom (brôd′lüm′) *n.* a carpet woven on a wide
loom, usually in widths ranging from 6 feet (1.8 meters)
to 18 feet (5.5 meters). **—adj.** woven in this way.

broad–mind·ed (brôd′mīn′did) *adj.* tolerant of views,
beliefs, and behavior that are unconventional or different
from one's own; liberal; not bigoted: *to be broad-minded
about the political views of others.* **—broad–′mind′-
ed·ly,** *adv.* **—broad′–mind′ed·ness,** *n.*

broad·side (brôd′sīd′) *n.* **1.** the whole side of a boat or
ship above the water line. **2.** the firing of all the guns on
one side of a ship at the same time. **3.** a written or spoken
attack against someone or something: *a broadside against
an opponent for office.* **—adv.** with the side turned; on
the side; sideward: *The wave caught the boat broadside,
almost capsizing it.*

broad·sword (brôd′sôrd′) *n.* a sword with a broad, flat
blade, made for cutting rather than thrusting.

Broad·way (brôd′wā′) *n.* the American theater industry.
[From *Broadway*, a street in New York City with many
theaters.]

bro·cade (brō kād′) *n.* a heavy fabric woven with raised
designs. **—v.t.,** **bro·cad·ed, bro·
cad·ing.** to weave (fabric) with a
raised design.

broc·co·li (brok′ə lē) *n.* **1.** the
thick green stems and flower buds
of a plant related to the cabbage,
eaten as a vegetable. **2.** the plant
itself.

bro·chette (brō shet′) *n.* a small
skewer or spit on which pieces of
food are placed for broiling or
roasting.

bro·chure (brō shùr′) *n.* a small
pamphlet; booklet: *an advertising
brochure.*

bro·gan (brō′gən) *n.* a heavy,

broccoli

sturdy shoe, especially one that reaches to the ankle.

brogue¹ (brōg) *n.* a thick or rough accent in the pronunciation of English, especially an Irish accent. [Of uncertain origin.]

brogue² (brōg) *n.* **1.** a heavy, sturdy shoe of untanned
hide, formerly worn in Ireland and Scotland. **2.** a shoe
similar to an oxford, usually decorated with perforations.
[From the Irish and Scottish Gaelic word *brōg* meaning
''shoe.'']

broil (broil) *v.t.* **1.** to cook by flame or direct heat; grill:
to broil chicken on a charcoal grill. **2.** to make very hot;
scorch. **—v.i.** **1.** to be cooked by direct heat: *The meat
broiled quickly.* **2.** to become very hot: *We broiled under
the hot sun at the beach.* **—n.** something broiled,
especially meat.

broil·er (broi′lər) *n.* **1.** a pan, rack, or part of a stove
used for broiling food. **2.** a chicken, usually young and
tender, for broiling.

broke (brōk) *v.* the past tense of **break.** **—adj.** *Informal.*
having little or no money.

bro·ken (brō′kən) *v.* the past participle of **break.**
—adj. **1.** separated into pieces by force: *a broken window,
a broken dish.* **2.** marked by interruptions; not complete:
a broken electrical circuit. **3.** not smooth or even; rough:
We rode over miles of broken ground. **4.** not kept or
fulfilled: *a broken promise.* **5.** not working; damaged: *a
broken television set.* **6.** overwhelmed by grief or sorrow;
crushed, as in spirit or strength: *Many years of hardship
left the family broken.* **7.** (of a language) imperfectly
spoken: *The foreign visitors spoke broken English.*
8. trained to obey; tamed: *a broken horse.* **—bro′ken·ly,**
adv.

bro·ken–down (brō′kən doun′) *adj.* **1.** not functioning
or operating; out of order: *a broken-down car.* **2.** in poor
condition, as from ill health or old age: *a broken-down
horse.*

bro·ken·heart·ed (brō′kən här′tid) *adj.* crushed by
grief or disappointment. **—bro′ken·heart′ed·ly,** *adv.*

bro·ker (brō′kər) *n.* a person who arranges for the buying
or selling of stocks, bonds, real estate, or other property,
or handles business affairs for another person, receiving
a fee for these services: *an insurance broker.*

bro·ker·age (brō′kər ij) *n.* **1.** the business of a broker.
2. the fees charged by a broker.

bro·mide (brō′mīd) *n.* **1.** a compound of bromine and
another element or radical. **2.** *Informal.* a commonplace
or often-repeated saying; platitude.

bro·mine (brō′mēn) *n.* a reddish brown nonmetallic
liquid element of the halogen group. It has a disagreeable
odor and poisonous fumes and causes chemical burns on
contact. It is used in gasoline, drugs, dyes, and photographic chemicals. Symbol: **Br** [From the French word
brome meaning ''bromine,'' from the Greek word *brōmos*
''bad smell.'' The element has a pungent odor.]

bron·chi (brong′kī) the plural of **bronchus.**

bron·chi·a (brong′kē ə) *pl.n.* the larger tubes that are
branches or subdivisions of the bronchi.

bron·chi·al (brong′kē əl) *adj.* of or relating to the bronchi, bronchia, or bronchioles.

bronchial tubes, the passages through which air flows
to and from the lungs, consisting of the bronchi and their
branching tubes.

bron·chi·ole (brong′kē ōl′) *n.* the smallest subdivision
of a bronchus.

at; āpe; fär; câre; end; mē; it; īce; pîerce; hot; ōld;
sông, fôrk; oil; out; up; ūse; rüle; pùll; tûrn; chin;
sing; shop; thin; this; hw in white; zh in treasure.
The symbol ə stands for the unstressed vowel sound
heard in about, taken, pencil, lemon, and circus.

bron·chi·tis (brong kī′tis) *n.* an inflammation of the bronchial tubes.

bron·cho (brong′kō) *n., pl.* **bron·chos.** another spelling of **bronco.**

bron·cho·scope (brong′kə skōp′) *n.* a medical instrument for looking into the upper part of the respiratory tract. It usually consists of an illuminated, flexible tube inserted through the mouth.

bron·chus (brong′kəs) *n., pl.* **bron·chi.** either of the two main divisions of the windpipe that allow the passage of air into the lungs.

bron·co (brong′kō) *also,* **bron·cho.** *n., pl.* **bron·cos.** an untamed or partly tamed horse of the western United States.

bron·to·sau·rus (bron′tə sôr′əs) ′*n., pl.* **bron·to·sau·rus·es** or **bron·to·sau·ri** (bron′tə sôr′ī) or **bron·to·sau·rus.** a plant-eating dinosaur that lived during the Jurassic period. It was one of the largest land animals, growing to a length of 80 feet (24.4 meters) and weighing up to 35 tons (31.8 metric tons). Also, **apatosaurus.** [Formed from the Greek words *brontē* meaning ''thunder'' + *sauros* ''lizard.'']

brontosaurus

bronze (bronz) *n.* **1.** a strong, hard alloy of copper and tin. **2.** an alloy of copper and a metal other than tin, such as aluminum. **3.** a work of art made of bronze, as a bust or statue. **4.** a brownish color like that of bronze. —*adj.* **1.** made of bronze. —*v.,* **bronzed, bronz·ing.** —*v.t.* to give a bronze color or appearance to; brown. —*v.i.* to become bronze in color; turn brown; tan.

Bronze Age, a stage in the development of civilization, from the end of the Stone Age to the Iron Age, characterized by the widespread use of bronze in making tools and weapons.

brooch (brōch, brüch) *n., pl.* **brooch·es.** an ornamental pin fastened by a clasp, usually worn at the neck or breast.

brood (brüd) *n.* **1.** the young of a bird, hatched or cared for at the same time: *a brood of chicks.* **2.** all of the children in one family. —*v.i.* **1.** to sit on eggs in order to hatch them; incubate: *The hens are brooding.* **2.** to think in a worried or moody manner, especially for a long time: *to brood over a bad test score.* —*v.t.* to sit on (eggs) until they hatch; incubate.

brood·er (brü′dər) *n.* **1.** a heated structure for keeping newly hatched chicks. **2.** a hen that hatches eggs and cares for newly hatched chicks. **3.** a person who broods.

brook¹ (brůk) *n.* a small stream. [From the Old English word *brōc* meaning ''brook, stream.'']

brook² (brůk) *v.t.* to put up with; endure; tolerate: *a teacher who brooks no nonsense from students.* [From the Old English word *brūcan* meaning ''to use.'']

brook·let (brůk′lit) *n.* a small brook.

brook trout, a game fish of eastern North America, having speckles on its back. Also, **speckled trout.**

broom (brüm, brům) *n.* **1.** a device for sweeping consisting of a bundle of stiff bristles or straw at the end of a long handle. **2.** a tree and shrub having long, slender branches and small leaves and bearing yellow, white, or purple flowers.

broom·corn (brüm′kôrn′, brům′kôrn′) *n.* a grassy plant whose grain grows on long, strawlike stems that are used for making brooms.

broom·stick (brüm′stik′, brům′stik′) *n.* the long handle of a broom.

bros., brothers.

broth (brôth) *n., pl.* **broths** (brôths, brôthz). a thin soup made by boiling meat, fish, or vegetables in water.

broth·er (bruth′ər) *n., pl.* **broth·ers** or (*defs. 3, 4*) **breth·ren. 1.** a boy or man having the same parents as another person of either sex. **2.** a fellow human being. **3.** a man who is a fellow member of a church, profession, or fraternal order. **4.** a man who is a member of a religious order, but who is not a priest.

broth·er·hood (bruth′ər hůd′) *n.* **1.** the state or quality of being a brother or brothers; brotherly relationship. **2.** all the men who are members of a church, profession, or fraternal order.

broth·er·in–law (bruth′ər in lô′) *n., pl.* **bro·thers-in-law. 1.** the brother of one's husband or wife. **2.** the husband of one's sister. **3.** the husband of the sister of one's wife or husband.

broth·er·ly (bruth′ər lē) *adj.* relating to, characteristic of, or befitting a brother; kind; affectionate: *There was a warm brotherly feeling between the two boys.* —**broth′er·li·ness,** *n.*

brougham (brüm, brü′əm, brō′əm) *n.* **1.** a closed, four-wheeled, horse-drawn carriage for two or four passengers having an uncovered, raised seat outside for the driver. **2.** an automobile having an enclosed passenger compartment, with the driver's seat outside. [From the Scottish statesman Baron *Brougham* (1778–1868), who designed this type of carriage.]

brought (brôt) the past tense and past participle of **bring.**

brow (brou) *n.* **1.** the part of the face above the eyes; forehead. **2.** an arch of hair over the eye; eyebrow. **3.** the edge of a steep place: *the brow of a hill.*

brow·beat (brou′bēt′) *v.t.,* **brow·beat, brow·beat·en, brow·beat·ing.** to frighten or coerce with stern looks or words; bully: *to browbeat someone into doing a distasteful chore.*

brown (broun) *n.* a color like that of chocolate and coffee. —*adj.* **1.** having the color brown: *brown hair.* **2.** dark-complexioned; tanned. —*v.t.* to make brown: *to brown meat in an oven.* —*v.i.* to become brown: *We browned in the sun.* —**brown′ish,** *adj.* —**brown′ness,** *n.*

brown–bag (broun′bag′) *v.i., v.t.* **brown-bagged, brown-bag·ging.** to take (one's lunch) to work or school, often in a brown paper bag. —**brown′-bag′ger,** *n.*

brown bear, any of various bears native to North America, Europe, and Asia, having fur that ranges from yellowish brown to very dark brown.

brown coal, another word for **lignite.**

brown·ie (brou′nē) *n.* **1.** in folklore, an elf or goblin that does good deeds. **2.** a small, flat, sweet cake, usually chocolate, sometimes made with nuts or topped with frosting. **3. Brownie.** a girl between the ages of six and eight who belongs to the junior division of the Girl Scouts.

brown·out (broun′out′) *n.* a temporary reduction in electric power, especially because of a shortage.

brown rice, rice with the hulls removed, but with the layers of bran still intact.

brown·stone (broun′stōn′) *n.* **1.** reddish brown sandstone, used as a building material. **2.** a house having its outer walls made of brownstone.

brown sugar, partly refined sugar that still has traces of molasses, which gives it a dark or golden brown color.

browse (brouz) *v.,* **browsed, brows·ing.** —*v.i.* **1.** to glance through or look at something in a slow, casual manner: *to browse through a magazine, browsing in a shop.* **2.** to feed or nibble on grass, leaves, or twigs. —*v.t.* to cause to feed or nibble on grass, leaves, or twigs: *to browse cattle.* —*n.* grass, leaves, or twigs on which certain animals, such as cattle or deer, feed.

bru·in (brü′in) *n.* a bear, especially a brown bear.

bruise (brüz) *n.* **1.** an injury, as from a fall or blow, that discolors but does not break the surface of the skin. **2.** a discoloration on the outer surface of a fruit, vegetable, or plant caused by a similar injury. —*v.,* **bruised, bruis·ing.** —*v.t.* **1.** to cause a bruise on the surface of: *to bruise one's arm on the edge of a table. The bananas were bruised in shipping.* **2.** to injure, offend, or hurt slightly: *The critics' comments bruised the actor's feelings.* —*v.i.* to become bruised: *My skin bruises easily.*

bruit (brüt) *v.t.* to spread a rumor or news of: *Reports of victory were bruited about.*

brunch (brunch) *n., pl.* **brunch·es.** a meal combining breakfast and lunch, usually eaten late in the morning. —*v.i.* to eat brunch. [A blend of *br*(eakfast) and (l)*unch*.]

bru·nette (brü net´) *also,* **bru·net.** *adj.* **1.** (of hair) having some shade of brown or brownish black as its main color. **2.** (of a person) having such hair, often with dark-colored skin and eyes. **3.** dark-colored: *a brunette complexion.* —*n.* a brunette person.

brunt (brunt) *n.* the worst or heaviest part: *The village bore the brunt of the storm.*

brush¹ (brush) *n., pl.* **brush·es.** **1.** an implement having bristles, hairs, or wires set into a stiff back or attached to a handle, used especially for smoothing, scrubbing, painting, or cleaning: *a hair brush, a paint brush, a clothes brush.* **2.** the act of using a brush: *Give the dog a good brush.* **3.** anything resembling a brush, such as the bushy tail of an animal. **4.** an electrical conductor that serves to make contact between fixed and moving parts of an electric motor or generator. **5.** a growth of shrubs, small trees, and bushes; thicket. **6.** cut or broken twigs or branches. **7.** thinly settled country; backwoods. —*v.t.* **1.** to use a brush on, as in smoothing, scrubbing, painting, or cleaning: *to brush one's hair.* **2.** to remove with or as with a brush: *to brush crumbs from a table.* [From the Middle English word *brushe* meaning both "bushes, brush-wood" and "a brush," from the Old French word *broce* "bushes, brushwood."] —**brush'y,** *adj.*

•**to brush aside.** to pay little or no attention to; disregard: *The coach brushed aside all criticism of the team.*

•**to brush off.** to get rid of abruptly or ignore completely.

•**to brush up** or **to brush up on.** to go over again in order to refresh one's memory: *I'm going to brush up on French verbs for the test.*

brush² (brush) *n., pl.* **brush·es.** **1.** a light touch in passing: *I felt a brush against my leg when the cat went by.* **2.** a brief encounter or fight; *I had a brush with some bullies outside the playground.* —*v.t.* to touch (something) lightly in passing: *Leaves brushed my face as I walked through the woods.* —*v.i.* to touch lightly in passing: *to brush against a chair in the dark.* [From the Middle English word *brushen* meaning "to hasten," "rush into battle," probably from the Old French *brosser* "travel (through the woods)."]

brush·off (brush'ôf') *n.* Informal. an abrupt dismissal: *I thought I had the job, but then they gave me the brush-off.*

brush·wood (brush'wüd') *n.* **1.** cut or broken twigs or branches. **2.** a dense growth of shrubs, small trees, or bushes.

brusque (brusk) *adj.* blunt or rude in manner or speech: *a brusque person, a brusque reply.* —**brusque'ly,** *adv.* —**brusque'ness,** *n.*

Brus·sels sprouts (brus'əlz sprouts') **1.** buds resembling small cabbages that grow on

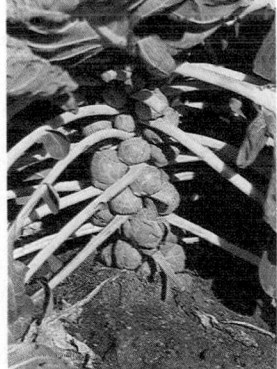

Brussels sprouts

the stalk of a leafy plant, cooked and eaten as a vegetable. **2.** the plant bearing these buds.

bru·tal (brü'təl) *adj.* of or like a savage animal; cruel; inhuman. —**bru'tal·ly,** *adv.*

bru·tal·i·ty (brü tal'i tē) *n., pl.* **bru·tal·i·ties.** **1.** brutal behavior; cruelty; inhumanity. **2.** a brutal act.

bru·tal·ize (brü'tə līz') *v.,* **bru·tal·ized, bru·tal·iz·ing.** —*v.t.* to make brutal: *Harsh treatment brutalized the captured soldiers.* —*v.i.* to become brutal. —**bru'tal·i·za'tion,** *n.*

brute (brüt) *n.* **1.** any animal. **2.** a brutal person. —*adj.* **1.** powerful, but without reason or feeling: *the brute forces of nature.* **2.** like the power of a large animal: *brute strength.* **3.** brutal in character.

brut·ish (brü'tish) *adj.* of or like an animal that cannot reason; stupid and savage. —**brut'ish·ly,** *adv.* —**brut'ish·ness,** *n.*

bry·o·phyte (brī'ə fīt') *n.* any of a group of small plants including the mosses and liverworts.

b.s., bill of sale.

B.S., Bachelor of Science. Also, **B.Sc.**

btl., bottle.

btry., battery.

BTU, British thermal unit.

bu., bushel; bushels.

bub·ble (bub'əl) *n.* **1.** a thin film of liquid having the shape of a ball, filled with air or other gas: *The children blew soap bubbles with a pipe.* **2.** a small area in a solid or liquid that is round in shape and filled with air or another gas: *The glass is marred by bubbles. There are bubbles in carbonated drinks.* —*v.i.,* **bub·bled, bub·bling.** **1.** to rise in or form bubbles: *The boiling water bubbled rapidly.* **2.** to flow with or make a gurgling sound: *The creek bubbled along.* **3.** to show emotion in a bright, happy manner: *to bubble with joy.* —**bub'bly,** *adj.*

•**to bubble over.** to show great excitement or enthusiasm.

bubble chamber, a device filled with a very hot liquid through which atomic particles leave trails of bubbles. By this means, the particles can be studied and identified.

bub·ble·gum (bub'əl gum') *n.* chewing gum that can be blown into large bubbles.

bu·bon·ic plague (bū bon'ik, bü bon'ik) a very serious and dangerous disease marked by a high fever and swelling of the lymph glands. It is carried to humans by fleas, usually from infected rats.

buc·ca·neer (buk'ə nîr') *n.* **1.** a pirate. **2.** any of a group of pirates of the seventeenth and eighteenth centuries who attacked and robbed Spanish ships and settlements in America.

buck¹ (buk) *n.* **1.** the male of certain animals, especially the deer, antelope, rabbit, or goat. **2.** the act of jumping or kicking upward in order to throw off a rider or load. —*v.i.* to jump or kick upward with the back arched, in order to throw off a rider or load: *The donkey bucked.* —*v.t.* **1.** to throw by bucking. **2.** to make a charge at or against, especially with the head down: *The football player bucked the opposing line.* **3.** *Informal.* to oppose or resist stubbornly: *to buck the rules, to buck a trend.* [From the Old English words *buc* meaning "a male deer" and *bucca* meaning "a male goat."]

•**to buck up.** *Informal.* to cheer up: *Buck up; examinations are almost over.*

buck² (buk) *n. Slang.* a dollar. [Of uncertain origin.]

at; āpe; fär; câre; end; mē; it; īce; pîerce; hot; ōld; sông; fôrk; oil; out; up; ūse; rüle; pull; tûrn; chin; sing; shop; thin; *th*is; hw in white; zh in treasure. The symbol ə stands for the unstressed vowel sound heard in about, taken, pencil, lemon, and circus.

·to pass the buck. *Informal.* to shift the blame or responsibility to someone else.

buck·board (buk′bôrd′) *n.* an open, four-wheeled carriage with the seat resting on a platform of long, flexible boards instead of on springs.

buckboard

buck·et (buk′it) *n.* **1.** a round, hollow container with a flat bottom, used for carrying or holding water, sand, or other things; pail. **2.** anything like this, such as a scooplike device on a steam shovel. **3.** the amount that a bucket can hold; bucketful.

buck·et·ful (buk′it fůl′) *n., pl.* **buck·et·fuls.** the amount that a bucket can hold: *a bucketful of sand.*

bucket seat, a low, padded seat for one person, as in some cars.

buck·eye (buk′ī′) *n.* **1.** a North American shrub or tree related to the horse chestnut, bearing showy clusters of yellow, white, or red flowers. **2.** the shiny brown nutlike seed of this tree.

Buck·ing·ham Palace (buk′ing əm) the official London residence of British kings and queens.

buck·le (buk′əl) *n.* **1.** a clasp used to fasten together two loose ends, such as the ends of a belt or strap. **2.** something that resembles this, such as an ornament on a shoe. **3.** a bend or sag in a surface: *a buckle in the counter top.* —*v.,* **buck·led, buck·ling.** —*v.t.* **1.** to fasten with a buckle. **2.** to cause (something) to sag or bend, especially from strain or heat. —*v.i.* **1.** to be fastened or joined by a buckle. **2.** to sag or bend: *A beam supporting the roof buckled.*

·to buckle down or **to buckle down to.** to begin working hard on: *to buckle down and finish a job.*

buck·ler (buk′lər) *n.* a small, round shield.

buck·ram (buk′rəm) *n.* a coarse cloth that has been stiffened with glue, used in bookbinding.

buck·saw (buk′sô′) *n.* a saw set in a frame, used especially for sawing logs.

buck·shot (buk′shot′) *n.* large metal pellets for shotgun shells, used in hunting game.

buck·skin (buk′skin′) *n.* **1.** a strong, soft, yellowish tan leather, made from the skins of deer or sheep. **2.** **buckskins.** clothing made of buckskin.

buck·tooth (buk′tüth′) *n., pl.* **buck·teeth** (buk′tēth′). a projecting upper front tooth. —**buck′toothed′,** *adj.*

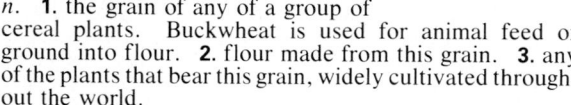
bucksaw

buck·wheat (buk′hwēt′, buk′wēt′) *n.* **1.** the grain of any of a group of cereal plants. Buckwheat is used for animal feed or ground into flour. **2.** flour made from this grain. **3.** any of the plants that bear this grain, widely cultivated throughout the world.

buckwheat cake, a pancake made of buckwheat flour.

bu·col·ic (bū kol′ik) *adj.* **1.** of or relating to shepherds; pastoral. **2.** relating to country life; rustic; rural. —*n.* a poem dealing with rural life.

bud (bud) *n.* **1.** a small swelling on a plant that will later grow into a flower, stem, leaf, or branch. **2.** a flower that has not completely blossomed. **3.** a small swelling on certain simple animals or fungi that later grows into a new organism. **4.** the state or time of budding; early development: *The cherry trees are in bud. This is only the bud of a complete plan.* —*v.i.,* **bud·ded, bud·ding.** **1.** to put forth buds: *The apple trees have started to bud.* **2.** to begin to grow or develop.

·to nip in the bud. to stop (something) just as it is beginning: *to nip a brush fire in the bud.*

Bud·dhism (bůd′iz əm, bü′diz əm) *n.* a religion originating in India that is based on the teachings of Buddha. It teaches that pain and evil are caused by desire and that to conquer desire is to attain a state of bliss, or nirvana.

Bud·dhist (bůd′ist, bü′dist) *n.* a person who adheres to Buddhism. —*adj.* of or relating to Buddha or Buddhism.

bud·dy (bud′ē) *n., pl.* **bud·dies.** *Informal.* a close friend; pal.

budge (buj) *v.,* **budged, budg·ing.** —*v.i.* to move slightly or give way: *the dog wouldn't budge from the hammock.* —*v.t.* to cause to move slightly or give way: *We could not budge the heavy chest.*

budg·et (buj′it) *n.* a plan that shows an amount of money to be spent for specific purposes in a given period of time: *a budget for household expenses. The cost of building roads is a part of the budget of a state.* —*v.t.,* **budg·et·ed, budg·et·ing.** **1.** to plan for the spending of: *to budget one's salary very carefully.* **2.** to plan for in a budget: *to budget a week's vacation this year.* —**budg·et·ar·y** (buj′i ter′ē), *adj.*

buff[1] (buf) *n.* **1.** a soft, sturdy, yellowish brown leather with a fuzzy surface, usually made from the hide of a buffalo or ox. **2.** a yellowish brown color. **3.** a wheel or stick covered with leather, used for polishing. —*adj.* having the color buff; yellowish brown. —*v.t.* to polish or clean, as with a wheel or stick covered with leather: *to buff shoes.* [From the French word *buffle* meaning "buffalo, wild ox," from the Italian word *bufalo* "ox," going back to the Greek word *boubalos* "antelope," from the word *bous* "a head of cattle."]

buff[2] (buf) *n.* a person who is an enthusiastic follower of something; fan; enthusiast: *a football buff, a movie buff.* [From *buff*[1]; because nineteenth-century New York City volunteer firemen wore *buff* coats and were known as "fire buffs."]

buf·fa·lo (buf′ə lō′) *n., pl.* **buf·fa·loes** or **buf·fa·los** or **buf·fa·lo.** **1.** the bison of North America. **2.** any of various wild or domesticated oxen of Europe, Asia, and Africa, such as the water buffalo.

buff·er[1] (buf′ər) *n.* a person or thing that comes between two other persons or things to lessen or soften the force or shock of a conflict or collision: *the rubber padding acted as a buffer; to be a buffer between two angry people.* [From the earlier word *buff* meaning "to soften a blow" + *-er*[1].]

buff·er[2] (buf′ər) *n.* **1.** a person who polishes. **2.** a wheel, stick, or other object covered with a soft cloth or leather, used for polishing. [*Buff*[1] + *-er*[1].]

buffer state, a small country lying between two larger countries that may be rivals or enemies, helping to reduce tensions or prevent conflicts between them.

buf·fet[1] (buf′it) *v.t.* **1.** to beat or strike with the hand or fist. **2.** to knock about: *The rough water buffeted the raft.* —*n.* **1.** a blow with the hand or fist. **2.** something that hits with the force of a blow; violent shock: *the buffet of a hurricane or a tornado.* [From the Old French word *buffet,* a form of *buffe* meaning "a blow."]

buf·fet[2] (bə fā′, bů fā′) *n.* **1.** a piece of furniture with a flat surface for serving food and with cabinets for storing dishes, silver, and table linen; sideboard. **2.** a meal laid out on a buffet or table so that guests may serve themselves. **3.** a counter where refreshments or light meals are served. [From the French word *buffet* meaning "sideboard" or "light meal."]

buf·foon (bə fün′) *n.* a person who amuses others with pranks and jokes, especially crude or undignified ones.

bug (bug) *n.* **1.** any of a group of insects with or without wings, having beaklike sucking mouth parts, as a bedbug. **2.** any insect that crawls, such as an ant, spider, or cockroach. **3.** *Informal.* a germ that causes a disease: *a flu bug.* **4.** *Informal.* a defect or difficulty in a machine, computer, or computer program: *There is a bug in the television set.* **5.** *Slang.* a small hidden microphone used to overhear or record conversations. **6.** *Informal.* **a.** a person who is enthusiastic about something; fan or hobbyist. **b.** an extreme enthusiasm or obsession: *My friend has the fitness bug.* —*v.t.,* **bugged, bug·ging. 1.** *Slang.* to place a small hidden microphone in: *The spy bugged the conference room.* **2.** *Slang.* to annoy, bother, or worry (someone): *Their constant complaining really bugs me.* —**bug'like',** *adj.*

bug·a·boo (bug'ə bü') *n., pl.* **bug·a·boos.** a real or imaginary thing that a person fears. Also, **bugbear.**

bug·bear (bug'bâr') *n.* **1.** an annoying problem. **2.** another word for **bugaboo.**

bug·gy (bug'ē) *n., pl.* **bug·gies. 1.** a light, four-wheeled carriage with one large seat, and, sometimes, a top. **2.** a baby's carriage.

bu·gle (bū'gəl) *n.* a brass wind instrument usually without keys or valves, used especially in the armed forces to give signals or calls, such as reveille or taps. *v.i.,* **bu·gled, bu·gling.** to sound or play a bugle. —**bu'gler,** *n.*

build (bild) *v.,* **built, build·ing.** —*v.t.* **1.** to make (something) by putting materials or parts together; construct: *to build a house, to build a bridge, to build an argument point by point.* **2.** to form over a length of time: *The druggist built a successful business.* —*v.i.* to construct a building: *The company will build on that vacant lot.* —*n.* the way in which someone or something is formed: *an athlete with a sturdy build.*

  ·**to build up. a.** to increase or make stronger or better: *to build up one's muscles by exercising. The dentist built up a good practice.* **b.** to fill with buildings or houses: *That area has been built up in recent years.* **c.** to grow or develop, as toward a climax: *A storm was building up in the east.*

build·er (bil'dər) *n.* **1.** a person who builds. **2.** a person whose work or business is constructing buildings.

build·ing (bil'ding) *n.* **1.** something built, especially to live or work in, or for similar purposes. **2.** the act, process, or business of building.

build·up (bild'up') also, **build-up.** *n.* **1.** an increasing, strengthening, developing, or improving: *a buildup of weapons, a buildup of suspense in a detective story.* **2.** publicity or praise to make someone or something famous: *The lawyer was given a big buildup in the newspapers.*

built (bilt) a past tense and past participle of **build.**

built-in (bilt'in') *adj.* built or designed as a permanent part of something; not removable: *a room with built-in book shelves, a plan with built-in safeguards.*

bulb (bulb) *n.* **1.** a usually rounded, underground bud of some plants, such as the onion or the lily, from which the plant grows. **2.** an underground stem resembling a bulb, as a corm or tuber. **3.** any rounded object or part resembling this: *an electric light bulb, a thermometer bulb.* —**bulb'like',** *adj.*

bulb·ous (bul'bəs) *adj.* **1.** growing from bulbs: *Tulips are bulbous plants.* **2.** shaped like a bulb; round or swollen: *The clown had a bulbous nose.*

Bul·gar·i·an (bul gâr'ē ən, bùl gâr'ē ən) *n.* **1.** a person who was born in or is a citizen of Bulgaria. **2.** the language of Bulgaria. —*adj.* of or relating to Bulgaria, its people, their language, or culture.

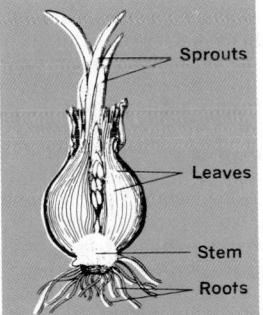

cross section of
a hyacinth **bulb**

Sprouts

Leaves

Stem

Roots

bulge (bulj) *n.* a rounded part that swells out; swelling: *The pillow made a bulge under the bedspread.* —*v.i.* **bulged, bulg·ing.** to swell out: *The bag bulged with groceries.*

bul·gur (bul'gər, bùl'gər) *n.* cracked wheat that has been parboiled and dried.

bu·lim·i·a (bū lim'ē ə, bü lē'mē ə, bü lim'ē ə, bü lē'mē ə) *n.* a serious eating disorder, mainly affecting young women. It is characterized by the consumption of large amounts of food followed by deliberate vomiting or the excessive use of laxatives to prevent weight gain. [From the Greek word *boulimia* meaning ''extreme hunger.'']

bulk (bulk) *n.* **1.** large size: *The bulk, not the weight, of the package made it hard to carry.* **2.** the largest or main part: *The bulk of the land was cultivated. The wealthy couple left the bulk of their estate to charity.*

  ·**in bulk. a.** not packaged; loose: *to sell fruit in bulk.* **b.** in large quantities: *The bakery buys flour in bulk.*

bulk·head (bulk'hed') *n.* **1.** one of the walls that divide a ship into compartments in order to hold in check or prevent the spread of flood or fire. **2.** a wall or partition built, as in a mine, to hold back earth, water, or gases.

bulk·y (bul'kē) *adj.,* **bulk·i·er, bulk·i·est. 1.** of great bulk; large. **2.** difficult to handle; clumsy: *The piano is too bulky to move.* —**bulk'i·ly,** *adv.* —**bulk'i·ness,** *n.*

bull¹ (bùl) *n.* **1.** the mature male of any animal of the bovine family. **2.** the male of certain other large animals, such as the elephant, moose, whale, or seal. **3.** a person or business that believes that prices on the stock market are going to rise, especially one that buys stock with the hope of selling it back later at a higher price. —*adj.* marked by or relating to rising prices, such as those of stocks: *a bull market.* [From the Old English word *bula* meaning this animal.]

bull² (bùl) *n.* a document containing an official pronouncement from the pope. [From the Medieval Latin word *bulla* meaning ''seal'' or ''document,'' from the Latin word *bulla* ''a bubble'' or ''a knob,'' from the large wax seal bearing the pope's insignia on this document.]

bull·dog (bùl'dôg') *n.* a heavily built dog having a large head, square jaws, short bowed legs, and a smooth coat. —*v.t.,* **bull·dogged, bull·dog·ging.** to wrestle (a steer) to the ground by taking hold of its horns and twisting its neck. —*adj.* characteristic of a bulldog: *bulldog courage, a bulldog grip.* [*Bull¹* + *dog.* These dogs were bred to harass bulls.]

bulldog

bull·doze (bùl'dōz') *v.t.,* **bull·dozed, bull·doz·ing. 1.** to move, clear, or level by using a bulldozer: *to bulldoze earth for a road.* **2.** to bully.

bull·doz·er (bùl'dō'zər) *n.* a tractor with a powerful motor and a heavy metal blade mounted in front, used for moving earth and clearing land.

bul·let (bùl'it) *n.* a piece of rounded or pointed metal that is shot from a firearm.

bul·le·tin (bùl'i tin) *n.* **1.** a short account, statement, or report of news: *We heard a bulletin on the radio about an approaching storm.* **2.** a newspaper or magazine published regularly by a society, church, or other organization.

bulletin board, a board for posting notices, announcements, and pictures.

at; āpe; fär; câre; end; mē; it; īce; pîerce; hot; ōld; sông, fôrk; oil; out; up; ūse; rüle; pùll; tûrn; chin; sing; shop; thin; **th**is; hw in white; zh in treasure. The symbol **ə** stands for the unstressed vowel sound heard in about, taken, pencil, lemon, and circus.

bul·let·proof (bŭl′it prüf′) *adj.* able to keep a bullet from passing through, or to lessen or absorb its shock: *a bulletproof vest, bulletproof glass.*

bullet train

bullet train, a high-speed passenger train, especially such a train operated in Japan.

bull·fight (bŭl′fīt′) *n.* a sport in which a bull is fought, and often killed, in an arena. Bullfights are popular in Spain, Portugal, and Latin America. —**bull′fight′er,** *n.* —**bull′fight′ing,** *n.*

bull·finch (bŭl′finch′) *n., pl.* **bull·finch·es.** a songbird of Europe and Asia with a rose-colored breast, related to the cardinal and often kept as a pet.

bull·frog (bŭl′frôg′, bŭl′frog′) *n.* a type of frog that makes a loud, bellowing croak. It is the largest frog in the United States.

bull·head (bŭl′hed′) *n.* any of a group of freshwater catfish of eastern North America, having a large head and thin feelers around the mouth.

bull·head·ed (bŭl′hed′id) *adj.* foolishly stubborn. —**bull′head′ed·ness,** *n.*

bull·horn (bŭl′hôrn′) *n.* a portable electric device resembling a megaphone, used to increase or direct the sound of the voice.

bull·ion (bŭl′yən) *n.* gold, silver, or other precious metal, especially in the form of bars.

bull·ish (bŭl′ish) *adj.* **1.** like a bull. **2.** expecting a rise in the price of stocks. —**bull′ish·ly,** *adv.* —**bull′ish·ness,** *n.*

bull·ock (bŭl′ək) *n.* **1.** a castrated bull. **2.** a young bull.

bull's-eye (bŭlz′ī′) *n.* **1.** the central circle of a target. **2.** a shot that hits this circle. **3.** a round piece of thick glass set in a floor or ship's deck to let in light. **4.a.** a lens that curves outward. **b.** a lantern having such a lens.

bull terrier, a strong, medium-sized dog having a broad, pointed snout, pointed ears, and a white or brindled coat.

bul·ly (bŭl′ē) *n., pl.* **bul·lies.** a quarrelsome person who frightens, threatens, or hurts smaller or weaker people. —*v.t.,* **bul·lied, bul·ly·ing.** to frighten (someone) into doing something by threats. —*adj. Informal.* very good: *That's a bully idea.* —*interj. Informal.* well done; good.

bul·rush (bŭl′rush′) *n., pl.* **bul·rush·es.** any of a group of coarse, relatively tall plants, having grasslike leaves. They grow in wet ground along shores, or in quiet, shallow water.

bul·wark (bŭl′wərk) *n.* **1.** a wall of earth, stone, or other material built for defense. **2.** any means of defense or protection. **3.** a breakwater for protection against the force of waves. **4.** *also,* **bulwarks.** the part of a ship's side above the deck.

bum (bum) *n. Informal.* a person who is lazy or worthless; loafer; tramp. —*v.,* **bummed, bum·ming.** —*v.i.* **1.** to live or be like a bum; loaf. **2.** to live at the expense of others. —*v.t.* to get (something) by begging: *to bum a ride.* —*adj.,* **bum·mer, bum·mest.** not functioning properly; worthless; bad: *bum luck, a bum leg.* —**bum′mer,** *n.*

bum·ble·bee (bum′bəl bē′) *n.* any of several species of thick-bodied, hairy bees closely related to honeybees. Bumblebees make a loud humming sound as they fly.

bump (bump) *v.i.* **1.** to strike or knock suddenly; collide: *The two cars bumped into each other.* **2.** to move with a bump or series of bumps: *The wagon bumped down the dirt road.* —*v.t.* to hit suddenly; knock against: *to bump your knee on a chair.* —*n.* **1.** a heavy blow or jolt; thump: *to get a bump on the leg.* **2.** a swelling or lump, usually resulting from a blow: *There's a bump on my head where the ball hit.* **3.** any uneven part that rises above the surrounding surface: *a bump in a road.*
·**to bump into.** to meet by chance.

bump·er (bum′pər) *n.* **1.** a device in the shape of a bar or strip attached to the front and rear ends of a car or truck to protect the body of the vehicle against damage or shock. **2.** a cup or glass filled to the brim, especially when drunk as a toast. —*adj.* very large or abundant: *a bumper crop of wheat.*

bumper sticker, a sticker bearing a printed message or slogan for display on the bumper of a vehicle.

bump·kin (bump′kin) *n.* a simple or awkward person from the country.

bump·tious (bump′shəs) *adj.* unpleasantly bold or conceited: *several bumptious youths.* —**bump′tious·ly,** *adv.* —**bump′tious·ness,** *n.*

bump·y (bum′pē) *adj.,* **bump·i·er, bump·i·est.** having or causing bumps; full of bumps: *a bumpy piece of wood, a bumpy road.* —**bump′i·ly,** *adv.* —**bump′i·ness,** *n.*

bun (bun) *n.* **1.** a roll made of bread, variously shaped, sometimes sweetened or containing small pieces of fruit, such as raisins: *a breakfast bun.* **2.** a knot or roll of hair worn on the top or back of the head.

bunch (bunch) *n., pl.* **bunch·es. 1.** a number of things of the same kind growing, fastened, or grouped together; collection: *a bunch of bananas, a bunch of letters.* **2.** *Informal.* a group of people: *A bunch of us went to the movies.* —*v.i.* to form a bunch or bunches; gather together: *The kittens bunched together to keep warm.* —*v.t.* to place or form into a bunch or bunches.

bun·dle (bun′dəl) *n.* **1.** a number of things tied, wrapped, or bound together: *a bundle of old newspapers.* **2.** a package; parcel. —*v.,* **bun·dled, bun·dling.** —*v.t.* **1.** to wrap or bind together; make into a bundle: *to bundle sheets for the laundry.* **2.** *Informal.* to send hastily: *to bundle the children off to school.* —*v.i.* to go hastily; hurry.

bung (bung) *n.* **1.** a stopper for closing the bunghole in a barrel or cask. **2.** another word for **bunghole.**

bun·ga·low (bung′gə lō′) *n.* a small house or cottage, usually of one story. [Originally from the Hindi word *banglā* meaning "(house) in the Bengalese style."]

bun·gee cord (bun′jē) *also,* **bungee.** an elastic cord with a hook at each end, used as a fastener, for example, to secure packages to a luggage rack.

bung·hole (bung′hōl′) *n.* a hole in a barrel or cask through which it is filled or emptied.

bun·gle (bung′gəl) *v.,* **bun·gled, bun·gling.** —*v.t.* to do or make (something) in a poor or clumsy way; botch: *to bungle a job by working carelessly.* —*v.i.* to work or act in a poor or clumsy way. —*n.* a poor or clumsy performance, job, or piece of work. —**bun′gler,** *n.*

bun·ion (bun′yən) *n.* a painful inflammation in the joint at the base of the big toe.

bunk¹ (bungk) *n.* **1.** a narrow bed that is built into or against a wall, sometimes one of two or more arrayed vertically. **2.** any narrow bed. **3.** any place to sleep. —*v.i. Informal.* **1.** to sleep in a bunk. **2.** to sleep anywhere: *We bunked on the floor.* [Short for *bunker.*]

bunk² (bungk) *n. Informal.* empty, foolish talk; nonsense; humbug. [Short for *bunkum,* another spelling of *buncombe.* In 1820, the congressman from *Buncombe* County, North Carolina, gave a long-winded, pointless

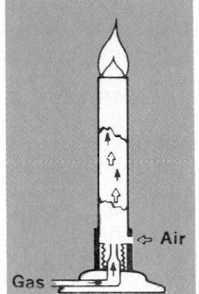

speech which he explained was intended not for Congress but for Buncombe.]

bunk·bed (bungk′bed′) *n.* **1.** a piece of furniture consisting of two single beds, one above the other. **2.** either of the two beds that make up such a piece of furniture.

bunk·er (bung′kər) *n.* **1.** a fortification built below ground and having walls usually of steel and concrete. **2.** an obstacle on a golf course, such as a sand trap or barrier of earth. **3.** a storage bin, such as for coal on a ship.

bunk·house (bungk′hous′) *n., pl.* **bunk·hous·es** (bungk′-hou′ziz). a building with sleeping quarters or bunks for workers or campers.

bun·ny (bun′ē) *n., pl.* **bun·nies.** *Informal.* a rabbit.

Bun·sen burner (bun′sən) a gas burner with a very hot blue flame, used in laboratories. Openings at the base allow air to enter and mix with the gas. [From the German chemist Robert W. *Bunsen* (1811–1899), who invented it.]

bunt (bunt) *v.t.* **1.** to tap (a pitched baseball) so that it goes only a short distance into the infield. **2.** to strike or push with the head or horns; butt. —*v.i.* **1.** to tap a pitched baseball. **2.** to strike or push with the head or horns. —*n.* **1.** the act of bunting. **2.** a ball hit by bunting. **3.** a push; butt. —**bunt′er,** *n.*

bun·ting¹ (bun′ting) *n.* **1.** a blanket or wrapper for babies, made of wool, cotton, or other soft material. **2.** a light cloth used in making flags. **3.** banners or drapes printed with colors or symbols, usually of a country's flag. [Perhaps from the earlier word *bunt* meaning ''to sift.'' Possibly because bunting was used to sift flour.]

bun·ting² (bun′ting) *n.* any of various songbirds related to and resembling the sparrow. [Of uncertain origin.]

Bun·yan, Paul (bun′yən) see **Paul Bunyan.**

bu·oy (bü′ē, boi) *n.* **1.** a floating device that is anchored and used to warn ships of sandbars, wrecks, or other hazards, or to show the way through a channel. **2.** see **life buoy.** —*v.t.* **1.** to keep afloat. **2.** to raise: *to buoy up a friend's morale with praise.*

Caption: **Bunsen burner**

Caption: Lighted buoy   Spar buoy   Can buoy   Nun buoy   types of **buoys**

buoy·an·cy (boi′ən sē) *n.* **1.** the power of something to float or rise in water: *Cork has great buoyancy.* **2.** the power of a liquid or gas to keep something afloat: *Salt water has much greater buoyancy than fresh water.* **3.** resiliency of spirit; cheerfulness.

buoy·ant (boi′ənt) *adj.* **1.** able to float or rise in water: *buoyant soap.* **2.** able to keep something afloat: *Salt water is buoyant.* **3.** resilient in spirit; cheerful: *a buoyant personality.*

bur (bûr) *also,* **burr¹.** *n.* **1.** a prickly seed case covered with tiny barbs that cause it to stick to cloth or fur. **2.** any plant bearing burs, especially a weed.

bur·ble (bûr′bəl) *v.i.,* **bur·bled, bur·bling.** to make a bubbling sound; gurgle: *a burbling brook.*

bur·den¹ (bûr′dən) *n.* **1.** something that is carried; load: *The mule carried the burden easily.* **2.** something very difficult to bear: *the burden of a long illness.* —*v.t.* to put a heavy load on; load too heavily; oppress: *Debts burdened the poor family.* [From the Old English word *byrthen* meaning ''load.'']

bur·den² (bûr′dən) *n.* **1.** the main topic, theme, or idea of something written or spoken: *the burden of an essay.* **2.** a refrain or chorus of a song or ballad. [From the Old

French word *bourdon* meaning ''a drone'' or ''the bass line of a song.'']

burden of proof, the obligation of proving a statement or charge in court or in a dispute.

bur·den·some (bûr′dən səm) *adj.* heavy or oppressive; hard to bear: *burdensome responsibilities, burdensome financial obligations.*

bur·dock (bûr′dok) *n.* any of a small group of plants with coarse leaves and burs.

bu·reau (byŭr′ō) *n., pl.* **bu·reaus** or **bu·reaux** (byŭr′ōz). **1.** a chest of drawers, especially for clothes, sometimes with a mirror. **2.** a department or agency of a government: *to work for the bureau of motor vehicles.* **3.** an office or agency: *a credit bureau, a travel bureau.*

bu·reauc·ra·cy (byŭ rok′rə sē) *n., pl.* **bu·reauc·ra·cies.** **1. a.** a government by bureaus and by the many officials who are appointed to direct or work in them. **b.** a government, or part of a government, operating in this way. **2.** government officials as a group. **3.** too strict attention to rules and routine, often resulting in delay and inefficiency.

bu·reau·crat (byŭr′ə krat′) *n.* **1.** an official in a bureaucracy. **2.** an official in a government or business who pays too much attention to rules and routine.

bu·reau·crat·ic (byŭr′ə krat′ik) *adj.* of or relating to bureaucracy, a bureaucracy, or a bureaucrat. —**bu′reau·crat′i·cal·ly,** *adv.*

burg (bûrg) *n.* *Informal.* a small town or city.

bur·geon (bûr′jən) *v.i.* **1.** to put forth new leaves, buds, or shoots; sprout. **2.** to grow rapidly; flourish: *New factories and apartment buildings have burgeoned on what was once farmland.*

burg·er (bûr′gər) *n.* *Informal.* a hamburger.

bur·gess (bûr′jis) *n., pl.* **bur·gess·es.** a member of the House of Burgesses, the popularly elected lower house of the legislature in colonial Virginia or Maryland.

burgh·er (bûr′gər) *n.* a citizen of a town, especially a merchant city in feudal times.

bur·glar (bûr′glər) *n.* a person who commits burglary.

bur·glar·ize (bûr′glə rīz′) *v.t.,* **bur·glar·ized, bur·glar·iz·ing.** to commit burglary: *to burglarize a gas station.*

bur·glar·y (bûr′glə rē) *n., pl.* **bur·glar·ies.** the act of breaking into and entering a building or home in order to steal or commit some other crime.

bur·go·mas·ter (bûr′gə mas′tər) *n.* the mayor of a town in the Netherlands, Flanders, Germany, or Austria.

Bur·gun·di·an (bər gun′dē ən) *adj.* of or relating to Burgundy or its people. —*n.* a person who was born in or is a citizen of Burgundy.

Bur·gun·dy (bûr′gən de) *n., pl.* **Bur·gun·dies.** a red or white wine first produced in Burgundy, France.

bur·i·al (ber′ē əl) *n.* the act of putting a dead body in the earth, a tomb, or the sea. —*adj.* of or relating to burying: *a burial ceremony. In the park there is an Indian burial mound.*

bur·ied (ber′ēd) the past tense and past participle of **bury.**

bur·lap (bûr′lap) *n.* a coarse cloth made from jute or hemp, used for making sacks, curtains, and wall coverings.

bur·lesque (bər lesk′) *n.* **1.** the comic treatment of a serious subject or the serious treatment of an unimportant or trivial subject: *The novel* Don Quixote *by Cervantes is a burlesque of medieval ideas of chivalry and romance.* **2.** a stage show with often indecent dancing, songs, and

at; āpe; fär; câre; end; mē; it; īce; pîerce; hot; ōld; sông; fôrk; oil; out; up; ūse; rüle; pull; tûrn; chin; sing; shop; thin; this; hw in white; zh in treasure. The symbol ə stands for the unstressed vowel sound heard in about, taken, pencil, lemon, and circus.

131

jokes. —*v.t.*, **bur·lesqued, bur·les·quing.** to make (something) appear comic or ridiculous, especially by imitating it.

bur·ly (bûr′lē) *adj.*, **bur·li·er, bur·li·est.** big, strong, and sturdy: *a burly lumberjack.* —**bur′li·ness,** *n.*

Bur·mese (bər mēz′, bər mēs′) *n., pl.* **Bur·mese. 1.** a person who was born in or is a citizen of Burma. **2.** the language of Burma. —*adj.* of or relating to Burma, its people, their language, or their culture.

burn¹ (bûrn) *v.*, **burned** or **burnt, burn·ing.** —*v.t.* **1.** to set on fire; consume by fire: *to burn a pile of leaves.* **2.** to hurt, change, damage, or destroy by fire, heat, or acid: *to burn one's hand on a hot stove.* **3.** to make by fire, heat, or acid: *A cigarette spark burned a hole in the dress.* **4.** to cause a sensation of heat in: *The chili burned my mouth.* **5.** to use for fuel, to create light or heat: *Our furnace burns oil.* **6.** *Chemistry.* to cause to undergo combustion. —*v.i.* **1.** to be on fire: *The candles burned very slowly.* **2.** to be hurt, changed, or destroyed by fire, heat, or acid: *The steak burned on the grill.* **3.** to give off light or heat: *The street lights burned all night.* **4.** to feel or seem to be hot: *The child burned with a fever.* **5.** to be filled with a strong emotion, such as love or anger. **6.** *Chemistry.* to undergo combustion. —*n.* an injury, change, or destruction caused by or as if by burning: *I got a burn on my finger from the toaster. The burn on the rug is from a cigarette.* [Partly from the Old English word *beornan* meaning ''to be on fire'' and partly from the Old English word *bærnan* meaning ''to set on fire.''] —**burn′a·ble,** *adj.*

  •**to burn down.** to destroy or be destroyed by fire: *to burn down a building.*

  •**to burn up. a.** to destroy or be destroyed by fire. **b.** *Slang.* to make or become angry: *Their yelling really burns me up.*

burn² (bûrn) *n. Scottish.* a stream. [From the Old English word *burn* meaning ''a stream.'']

burn·er (bûr′nər) *n.* the part of a stove, furnace, or other device from which the flame comes.

bur·nish (bûr′nish) *v.t.* to make smooth and shiny; polish: *to burnish a metal tray.* —*n.* a polish; gloss.

bur·noose (bər nüs′, bûr′nüs) *also,* **bur·nous.** *n.* a cloak with a hood, such as that worn by Arabs.

burnoose

burnt (bûrnt) a past tense and past participle of **burn¹.**

burp (bûrp) *n.* a belch. —*v.i.* to belch. —*v.t.* to cause or help (a baby) to belch.

burr (bûr) *also,* **bur.** *n.* **1.** see **bur. 2.** a rough or sharp edge left on metal by a cutting or drilling tool. **3.** any of several small cutting heads used on dentists' drills. **4.** a rough, trilled pronunciation of *r*, as heard in Scotland and northern England. **5.** a humming or whirring sound. —*v.t.* to pronounce (something) with a burr. —*v.i.* **1.** to speak with a burr. **2.** to make a humming or whirring sound.

bur·ri·to (bə rē′tō) *n., pl.* **bur·ri·tos.** a tortilla wrapped around a filling of meat, cheese, or beans. [From the Spanish word *burrito* meaning ''little donkey'' and used as the name of this food, from the word *burro* ''burro.'']

bur·ro (bûr′ō, bùr′ō) *n., pl.* **bur·ros.** a small donkey.

bur·row (bûr′ō) *n.* a hole dug in the ground by an animal, such as a rabbit or fox, for living or hiding in. —*v.i.* **1.** to live or hide in a burrow. **2.** to dig a burrow or burrows. **3.** to hunt; search: *Burrow into your desk and find a pencil.* —**bur′row·er,** *n.*

bur·sa (bûr′sə) *n., pl.* **bur·sae** (bûr′sē) or **bur·sas.** a small sac in the body, especially one that is at a joint and filled with a lubricating fluid.

bur·sar (bûr′sər, bûr′sär) *n.* a treasurer, especially of a college.

bur·si·tis (bər sī′tis) *n.* a very painful condition resulting from inflammation of a bursa.

burst (bûrst) *v.*, **burst, burst·ing.** —*v.i.* **1.** to fly apart or break open suddenly and violently, especially from pressure inside; explode: *The buds on the tree were ready to burst into bloom. The overstuffed grocery bag burst.* **2.** to be full to the point of overflowing: *a closet bursting with clothes.* **3.** to come in or appear suddenly: *to burst into a room.* **4.** to give in suddenly to an emotion: *to burst into tears.* —*v.t.* to cause to fly apart or break open suddenly and violently: *to burst a balloon with a pin.* —*n.* **1.** a sudden explosion; bursting; outbreak: *a burst of gunfire, a burst of enthusiasm.* **2.** a sudden effort or action; spurt; *a burst of speed.*

bur·y (ber′ē) *v.t.*, **bur·ied, bur·y·ing. 1.** to put (a dead body) in the earth, a tomb, or the sea. **2.** to cover up or hide: *to bury a bone, to bury your face in your hands.* **3.** to plunge by force: *I buried the ax in the tree trunk.* **4.** to interest (oneself) in completely: *to bury yourself in a book.* **5.** to put out of one's mind; forget: *to bury your anger.*

bus (bus) *n., pl.* **bus·es** or **bus·ses.** a motor vehicle with rows of seats for many passengers. —*v.*, **bused** or **bussed, bus·ing** or **bus·sing.** —*v.t.* **1.** to carry by bus. **2.** to transport by bus to a school outside a neighborhood in order to help the school maintain a racial balance of students. —*v.i.* to travel by bus: *We bused to the city.* [Shortened from the earlier word *omnibus*, from the French word *omnibus* meaning ''a large public vehicle,'' from the Latin word *omnibus* ''for all,'' from the word *omnis* ''all.'']

bus·boy (bus′boi′) *also,* **bus boy.** *n.* a waiter's or waitress's assistant who sets and clears the table, fills glasses with water, and performs other duties.

bush (bùsh) *n., pl.* **bush·es. 1.** a woody plant smaller than a tree and having many stems that branch at or near the ground; shrub. **2.** a clump of shrubs or small trees; thicket. **3.** wild, uncultivated or unsettled land covered with shrubby growth: *The explorer crossed the Australian bush.* —*v.i.* to be or become thick or bushy; resemble a bush: *hair that bushes out.*

  •**to beat around the bush.** to speak or write around a subject without coming to the point: *Stop beating around the bush and tell the truth.*

bush·el (bùsh′əl) *n.* **1.** a unit of dry measure equal to 4 pecks, or 32 quarts (35.24 liters). It is used for fruit, vegetables, grain, and other products. **2.** a container holding a bushel.

bush·ing (bùsh′ing) *n.* a removable metal lining used in a machine to lessen friction and wear to a part.

Bush·man (bùsh′mən) *n., pl.* **Bush·men** (bùsh′mən) a member of a group of wandering people living in the desert regions of southern Africa.

bush·mas·ter (bùsh′mas′tər) *n.* a large poisonous snake found in Central and South America.

bush pilot, a pilot who provides passenger and cargo service for areas that are unsettled or only partly settled.

bush·whack (bùsh′hwak′, bùsh′wak′) *v.t.* to attack from ambush. —*v.i.* to cut one's way through rough, overgrown terrain. —**bush′whack·er,** *n.*

bush·y (bùsh′ē) *adj.*, **bush·i·er, bush·i·est. 1.** like a bush; thick and spreading; *bushy eyebrows.* **2.** full of or overgrown with bushes: *bushy land.* —**bush′i·ness,** *n.*

bus·i·ly (biz′ə lē) *adv.* in a busy manner.

busi·ness (biz′nis) *n., pl.* **busi·ness·es. 1.** work or activity that is a person's source of livelihood: *My business* *is raising cattle.* **2.** a store, factory, or other commercial or industrial enterprise: *The druggist sold the business and retired.* **3.** the buying and selling of goods; trade: *Business was bad at the store.* **4. a.** something done or about to be done; matter; affair: *Moving to a new house can be a tiresome business.* **b.** something to be concerned about: *This business of noisy traffic has the neighborhood upset.* **5.** private or personal concern or responsibility: *What business is it of yours how they dress?* —*adj.* of or relating to business: *Business hours in this office are from nine to five.* —**busi′ness·like′,** *adj.*

·**to mean business.** *Informal.* to be in earnest: *When the coaches say the team must practice every day, they mean business.*

busi·ness·man (biz′nis man′) *n., pl.* **busi·ness·men** (biz′nis men′). a man who owns, manages, or works in a business.

busi·ness·wom·an (biz′nis wûm′ən) *n., pl.* **busi·ness·wom·en** (biz′nis wim′ən). a woman who owns, manages, or works in a business.

bus·ing (bus′ing) *also,* **bus·sing.** *n.* the transportation of children by buses to schools outside their neighborhoods in order to help the schools maintain a racial balance of students.

bus·kin (bus′kin) *n.* **1.** a laced boot usually reaching to the middle of the calf. **2.** a thick-soled boot worn by actors in tragedies during Greek and Roman times.

buss (bus) *Archaic. n., pl.* **buss·es.** a kiss. —*v.t.* to kiss (someone).

bust[1] (bust) *n.* **1.** a piece of sculpture depicting a person's head, shoulders, and breast. **2.** the bosom of a woman. [From the French word *buste* with the same meaning, from the Italian word *busto* with the same meaning.]

bust[2] (bust) *Slang. v.t.* **1.** to cause to come apart; burst or break. **2.** to hit; punch; sock. **3.** to apprehend for a crime. **4.** to demote in military rank. —*v.i.* **1.** to burst or break. **2.** to fail after great effort: *The team's attitude was "Win or bust."* —*n.* **1.** a complete failure; flop. **2.** a blow; hit. [A form of *burst.*]

bus·tard (bus′tərd) *n.* a game bird related to the crane, having long legs, a large, heavy body, and a long neck, living in Australia and parts of the Old World.

bus·tle[1] (bus′əl) *v.i.,* **bus·tled, bus·tling.** to move in a quick, excited, or noisy manner: *to bustle about, getting ready for company.* —*n.* excited activity; stir: *the noise and bustle of the city.* [Possibly from the earlier word *buskle* meaning "to prepare," from the Old Norse word *būask* "to prepare oneself."]

bustard

bus·tle[2] (bus′əl) *n.* a pad or frame formerly worn by women to add fullness to the back part of a skirt. [Of uncertain origin.]

bus·y (biz′ē) *adj.,* **bus·i·er, bus·i·est.** **1.** doing something; active: *to be busy making plans for vacation.* **2.** full of activity: *Tomorrow is going to be a busy day.* **3.** in use: *When we phoned, the line was busy.* —*v.t.,* **bus·ied, bus·y·ing.** to make or keep busy; occupy (oneself): *to busy oneself cleaning out closets.*

bus·y·bod·y (biz′ē bod′ē) *n., pl.* **bus·y·bod·ies.** a person who meddles in other people's affairs.

but (but) *conj.* **1.** on the other hand; in contrast: *One is tall, but the other is short.* **2.** in spite of all; nevertheless: *It is early May, but it has begun snowing.* **3.** other than; except: *There was no direct route but through the center of town.* **4.** that: *There is no doubt but the patient will recover.* —*prep.* other than; except: *Everyone has signed but you.* —*adv.* only; merely; just: *I saw them but a few minutes ago.*

bu·ta·di·ene (bū′tə dī′ēn) *n.* a colorless gas obtained from petroleum, used in making rocket fuels.

bu·tane (bū′tān) *n.* a colorless gas that burns easily, used as a fuel and in making synthetic rubber.

butch·er (bùch′ər) *n.* **1.** a person who kills animals and prepares their meat for market. **2.** a person who cuts up and sells meat. **3.** a person who kills in a cruel or bloody manner. —*v.t.* **1.** to kill and prepare (animals) for market or for food. **2.** to kill in a cruel or bloody manner. **3.** to spoil by bad work; botch: *to butcher a job.* [From the Old French word *bochier* meaning "butcher," from the word *boc* "he-goat." Originally, a butcher was one who sold goat-meat.]

butch·er·y (bùch′ə rē) *n., pl.* **butch·er·ies.** cruel or bloody killing; carnage.

but·ler (but′lər) *n.* a male servant, usually the head servant in a household.

butt[1] (but) *n.* **1.** the end of something, especially the thicker or larger end: *a rifle butt, the butt of a spear.* **2.** a leftover end, especially of a cigar or cigarette; stub. [Probably of Germanic origin.]

butt[2] (but) *n.* a person or thing that is the object of ridicule or jokes: *The fat child was the butt of their teasing.* [Probably from the Old French word *but* meaning "goal."]

butt[3] (but) *v.i.* to push or strike with the head or horns: *The goat butted at the gate.* —*v.t.* to strike or push (something) with the head or horns; ram. —*n.* a push or blow with the head or horns. [From the Anglo-Norman word *buter* meaning "to push."]

·**to butt in.** *Informal.* to interrupt or meddle.

butte (būt) *n.* a steep mountain or hill standing alone, usually having a flat top.

but·ter (but′ər) *n.* **1.** the yellowish fatty food obtained from cream or milk by churning, used especially as a spread or as a flavoring in cooking. **2.** any of various other foods used as spreads, such as peanut butter. —*v.t.* **1.** to spread with butter: *to butter bread.* **2.** *Informal.* to flatter (usually with up): *If we butter up the teacher we may be able to leave early.*

but·ter·cup (but′ər kup′) *n.* **1.** a usually yellow flower having the shape of a cup. **2.** any of a number of plants bearing these flowers.

but·ter·fat (but′ər fat′) *n.* the yellowish fat in milk from which butter is made.

but·ter·fin·gers (but′ər ting′gərz) *n. Informal.* a person who drops things easily or frequently.

but·ter·fish (but′ər fish′) *n., pl.* **but·ter·fish** or **but·ter·fish·es.** a saltwater fish having a silvery blue body and a deeply forked tail, valued as a food fish.

but·ter·fly (but′ər flī′) *n., pl.* **but·ter·flies.** **1.** any of various insects having a slender body and four large, usually bright-colored wings. **2.** a stroke in swimming performed face down, in which the arms move together in a circular motion. [From the Old English word *buttorflēoge* meaning this insect, from the words *buttor* "butter" + *flēoge* "a fly." People used to believe that witches, in the form of butterflies, stole butter and milk.]

but·ter·milk (but′ər milk′) *n.* the liquid that remains after cream or milk has been churned to make butter.

but·ter·nut (but′ər nut′) *n.* **1.** the oily nut of a tree of the walnut family. **2.** the tree bearing this nut.

but·ter·scotch (but′ər skoch′) *n.* **1.** a candy or flavoring made from brown sugar, butter, and corn syrup. —*adj.* made or flavored with butterscotch.

at; āpe; fär; câre; end; mē; it; īce; pîerce; hot; ōld; sông, fôrk; oil; out; up; ūse; rüle; pùll; tûrn; chin; sing; shop; thin; this; hw in white; zh in treasure. The symbol ə stands for the unstressed vowel sound heard in about, taken, pencil, lemon, and circus.

B

but·ter·y (but′ə rē) *adj.* **1.** having the look or taste of butter. **2.** spread with or containing butter.

but·tock (but′ək) *n.* **1.** either of the two fleshy hind parts of the body on which a person sits. **2. buttocks.** the rump.

but·ton (but′ən) *n.* **1.** a small disk or knob made of any of various materials, used to fasten or ornament clothing. **2.** anything resembling a button and worn on the clothing, as for ornament: *a campaign button.* **3.** a disk or knob that is turned or pushed to make something work: *Press the elevator button.* —*v.t.* to fasten with a button or buttons: *to button a jacket.* —*v.i.* to be capable of being fastened with a button or buttons: *This shirt buttons up the front.*

but·ton·hole (but′ən hōl′) *n.* a hole or slit through which a button passes. —*v.t.,* **but·ton·holed, but·ton·hol·ing. 1.** to make buttonholes in. **2.** to make a person stop and listen to you as if by seizing the buttonhole of his or her coat.

but·ton·wood (but′ən wůd′) *n.* the plane tree of North America; sycamore.

but·tress (but′ris) *n., pl.* **but·tress·es.** a strong or heavy structure built against a wall to strengthen or support it. —*v.t.* to strengthen or support with, or as if with, a buttress: *to buttress an argument with facts.*

bux·om (buk′səm) *adj.* (of a woman) plump; full-bosomed. —**bux′om·ness,** *n.*

buy (bī) *v.,* **bought, buy·ing.** —*v.t.* **1.** to get (something) by giving money in return; purchase: *I bought a book for a dollar.* **2.** to serve as proper payment for; be a means of buying: *Money cannot buy health.* **3.** to bribe: *No one could buy our candidate with money or support.* —*v.i.* to make a purchase. —*n. Informal.* something bought at a lower price than usual; bargain: *That car was a good buy.*

·**to buy off.** to bribe: *to attempt to buy off a judge.*

·**to buy out.** to buy all the shares, rights, or interests of: *to buy out a business partner.*

·**to buy up.** to buy the entire supply of: *to buy up all the fresh strawberries in the store.*

buy·er (bī′ər) *n.* **1.** a person who buys; purchaser. **2.** a person who buys merchandise for a business, as for a store.

buzz (buz) *n., pl.* **buzz·es. 1.** a continuous humming sound, such as that made by a bee. **2.** a low sound such as that made by many people talking: *The buzz of conversation in the theater stopped when the play began.* —*v.i.* to make a continuous humming sound: *A mosquito buzzed in my ear.* **2.** to talk or gossip excitedly, especially in low tones: *The entire village buzzed with the news.* —*v.t.* **1.** to signal with a buzzer: *to buzz someone into an apartment building.* **2.** to fly an airplane fast and low over: *The pilot buzzed the bridge.*

buz·zard (buz′ərd) *n.* **1.** any of various large birds of prey, such as vultures and certain hawks.

buzz·er (buz′ər) *n.* an electrical device used as a signal.

buzz saw, a power saw with a circular blade.

by (bī) *prep.* **1.** close to; near; beside: *A table is by the bed.* **2.** up to and beyond; past: *The bus sped by us.* **3.** through the means, action, or use of: *I came by train. The house was destroyed by fire. This book was written by Charles Dickens.* **4.** according to; in terms of: *to buy milk by the gallon, to always play by the rules.* **5.** by way of; through: *We came by the northern route.* **6.** during the course of: *These animals hunt by night.* **7.** not later than: *Be here by eight o'clock.* **8.** after: *The children went into the room one by one.* **9.** in or to the extent or amount of: *to be older than a friend by six months.* **10.** combined

in multiplication or measurement with: *Multiply 3 by 4. The rug measures nine feet by twelve feet.* —*adv.* **1.** close at hand; near: *a house that is close by.* **2.** past: *Many years have gone by since we last met.* **3.** at or in another's house: *Stop by on your way to the store.* From the adverb *by.*]

·**by and by.** at some future time; before long.

·**by and large.** on the whole: *By and large, you did a good job.*

·**by the way** or **by the by.** incidentally: *By the way, where is the book I lent you?*

by– *prefix* **1.** of less importance: *by-product.* **2.** near by: *bystander.* **3.** aside: *byway.* [From the adverb *by.*]

by–and–by (bī′ən bī′) *n.* a future time.

Bye·lo·rus·sian (byel′ō rush′ən, bel′ō rush′ən) *n.* **1.** a person who was born in or is a citizen of Byelorussia. **2.** the language of Byelorussia. —*adj.* of or relating to Byelorussia, its people, their language, or culture. Also, **White Russian.**

by·gone (bī′gôn′, bī′gon′) *adj.* gone by; past; former: *The theater was decorated in the style of a bygone era.* —*n.,* usually **bygones.** something gone by or past.

·**to let bygones be bygones.** to let past disagreements or hatreds be forgotten.

by·law (bī′lô′) *n.* a law or rule that is made by an organization, such as a corporation or club, to regulate its own affairs.

by·line (bī′līn′) *n.* a line at the beginning of an article in a newspaper or magazine giving the writer's name.

by·pass (bī′pas′) *n., pl.* **by·pass·es. 1.** a road that turns off the main road, especially one that goes around the center of a city. **2.** a pipe or channel for carrying a flow of a liquid or gas away from a main pipe or around an obstacle. **3.** a surgical operation in which a diseased part, such as a blocked artery, is circumvented. —*v.t.* to go around or avoid: *to bypass a traffic jam by taking another road.*

by·path (bī′path′) *n., pl.* **by·paths** (bī′pathz′, bī′paths′). a side path.

by·play (bī′plā′) *n.* an action that takes place apart from or is not a direct part of the main action, especially in a stage production.

by–prod·uct (bī′prod′əkt) *n.* something useful that results from the manufacture of something else. Buttermilk is a by-product of the making of butter. Also **byproduct.**

by·road (bī′rōd′) *n.* a road that is out of the way or rarely used; side road.

by·stand·er (bī′stan′dər) *n.* a person who is present but does not take an active part: *Several bystanders watched the demonstration.*

byte (bīt) *n. Computers.* **1.** a group of eight bits treated as a unit. One byte can store a single alphabetical character or numerical symbol. **2.** a memory cell that can store eight bits of information.

by·way (bī′wā′) *n.* a road that is out of the way or rarely used; side road.

by·word (bī′wûrd′) *n.* **1.** a common saying or proverb. **2.** an object of contempt or scorn: *That shopkeeper became a byword for dishonesty.* **3.** something or someone thought of or spoken of as representing a particular quality: *The company's name has become a byword for quality.*

Byz·an·tine (biz′ən tēn′) *adj.* **1.** of or relating to Byzantium, the Byzantine Empire, or its art or culture. **2.** of or relating to a style of architecture developed in the Byzantine Empire, characterized by round arches, domes, and rich mosaic decorations. —*n.* a person who lived in Byzantium.

Byzantine Empire, the eastern part of the Roman Empire dating from A.D. 395, when the eastern and western parts were permanently divided, and lasting until 1453, when the capital, Constantinople, fell to the Ottoman Turks. Also, **Eastern Roman Empire.**

buttress

Cc

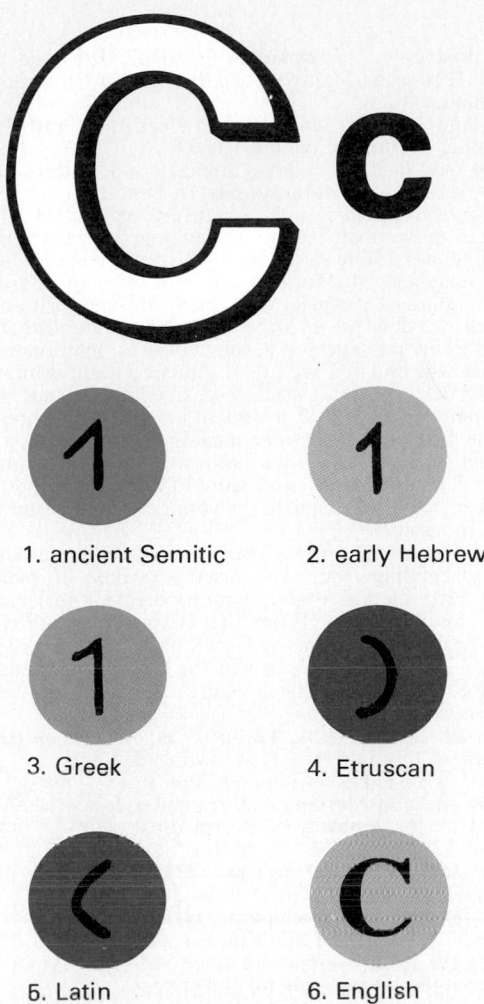

1. ancient Semitic
2. early Hebrew
3. Greek
4. Etruscan
5. Latin
6. English

C is the third letter of the English alphabet. Its earliest ancestor was *gimel,* meaning "camel" (1), the third letter of the ancient Semitic alphabets. The early Hebrew form (2) was borrowed by the Greeks, who called it *gamma* (3). Both gimel and gamma stood for the hard *g* sound, as in *game.* About 400 B.C., the Etruscans used a form of *gamma* (4) for both the hard *g* and *k* sounds. The Romans borrowed the Etruscan alphabet, using this letter in the same way. The Latin letter **C** (5) came to be used mostly for the language's more common *k* sound. For about 2,300 years, the capital letter **C** has been written almost exactly as we write it today (6).

When the Anglo-Saxons adopted the Latin alphabet, they continued to use **C** for the *k* sound, with some **C**'s later pronounced *ch.* The sound of *c* in grace became part of Middle English when certain French words were adopted. Thus, the Modern English **C** can represent all of these pronunciations.

---

c, C (sē) *n., pl.* **c's, C's.** **1.** the third letter of the English alphabet. **2.** something having the shape of this letter. **3.** the third item in a series or group. **4.** the Roman numeral for 100. **5.** *Music.* the first note of the scale of C major.

C, the symbol for carbon.

c. **1.** cent; cents. **2.** centimeter. **3.** century. **4.** circa; approximately; about. **5.** copyright. **6.** cubit.

C. **1.** Catholic. **2.** Celsius. **3.** Centigrade. **4.** Conservative.

Ca, the symbol for calcium.

CA, postal abbreviation for California.

ca., circa; approximately; about. [Short for the Latin word *circa* meaning "around."]

cab (kab) *n.* **1.** see **taxicab.** **2.** any of various horse-drawn carriages for hire with a driver, such as a hansom. **3.** the enclosed or covered part of a truck, locomotive, steam shovel, or the like, where the controls and operator are housed.

ca·bal (kə bal') *n.* **1.** a small group of people secretly united to create or further some scheme. **2.** a secret scheme developed by such a group; plot.

cab·al·le·ro (kab'əl yâr'ō, kab'ə lâr'ō) *n., pl.* **cab·al·le·ros.** **1.** a Spanish gentleman or knight; cavalier. **2.** a horseman. **3.** a lady's escort or admirer. [From the Spanish word *caballero* meaning "knight" or "horse-man," from the Late Latin word *caballarius* "hostler," from the Latin word *caballus* "inferior horse, nag."]

ca·ba·na (kə ban'ə) *n.* **1.** a small shelter at a swimming area, used as a bathhouse. **2.** a small cabin.

cab·a·ret (kab'ə rā') *n.* a restaurant or café providing food and drink, dancing, and entertainment; nightclub.

cab·bage (kab'ij) *n.* a plant having thick, green or reddish purple leaves that grow in a head and are eaten as a vegetable.

cab·by (kab'ē) also, **cab·bie.** *n., pl.* **cab·bies.** *Informal.* cabdriver.

cab·driv·er (kab'drī'vər) *n.* the driver of a taxicab.

cab·in (kab'in) *n.* **1.** a small, simply constructed house, usually having only one story. **2.** a room or compartment serving as living or working quarters on a ship. **3.** a compartment on a small boat, providing living quarters or shelter. **4.** an enclosed space for passengers, crew, or cargo in an aircraft or spacecraft.

cabin boy, a boy who waits on the officers and passengers of a ship.

cabin cruiser, a motorboat having a cabin equipped for living on board, used for pleasure cruises.

cab·i·net (kab'ə nit) *n.* **1.** a piece of furniture with shelves or drawers and often having doors, used for storing or displaying objects: *a kitchen cabinet, a china cabinet.* **2.** *also,* **Cabinet.** the council that advises the chief executive or sovereign of a nation, usually made up of the heads of various departments of the government.

cab·i·net·mak·er (kab'ə nit mā'kər) *n.* a person who makes or repairs fine furniture and woodwork.

ca·ble (kā'bəl) *n.* **1.** a strong, thick rope, especially one made of wires twisted together. **2.** a bundle of wires enclosed in a protective covering, used to carry electric current. **3.** see **cablegram.** **4.** see **cable TV.** —*adj.* transmitted by cable TV: *cable movies.* —*v.,* **ca·bled, ca·bling.** —*v.t.* **1.** to transmit (a message) by underwater cable. **2.** to send a cablegram to: *Cable the hotel for reservations.* —*v.i.* to transmit a message by underwater cable.

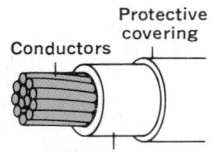

cable *(def. 2)*

cable car, a car drawn by an overhead cable or pulled along rails by an underground cable, used to carry passengers or cargo up and down steep grades.

ca·ble·gram (kā'bəl gram') *n.* a message sent by underwater telegraph cable.

135

cable TV, a system for transmitting television programs by cable to the individual sets of subscribers who pay for such a service. Also, **cable television.**

ca·boose (kə büs') *n.* a railroad car, usually at the rear of a freight train, used by the crew of the train.

cab·ri·o·let (kab′rē ə lā′) *n.* a light, one-horse carriage, usually two-wheeled, with a folding top.

ca·ca·o (kə ka′ō, kə kā′ō) *n., pl.* **ca·ca·os.** **1.** the seed of a tropical American evergreen tree, valued as the source of cocoa, chocolate, and cocoa butter. **2.** the tree that bears this seed.

cac·cia·to·re (kach′ə tôr′ē, kä′chə tôr′ē) *adj.* cooked with tomatoes, herbs and spices, and often dry white wine: *veal cacciatore, chicken cacciatore.* [From the Italian word *cacciatore* meaning "hunter." This was the traditional way a hunter would prepare food.]

cach·a·lot (kash′ə lot′) *n.* another word for **sperm whale.**

cache (kash) *n.* **1.** a hiding place, especially for provisions or treasure. **2.** something hidden or stored in such a place. —*v.t.,* **cached, cach·ing.** to hide or store in a cache.

ca·chet (ka shā′) *n.* **1.** a seal or stamp, as on an official letter or document. **2.** a distinguishing feature or quality, especially one indicating desirability: *expensive leather luggage with the cachet of exclusiveness.*

cack·le (kak′əl) *v.i.,* **cack·led, cack·ling.** **1.** to utter a shrill, broken cry, like the sound a hen makes after laying an egg. **2.** to laugh or talk with such a sound. —*n.* **1.** the act or sound of cackling. **2.** chatter.

ca·coph·o·ny (kə kof′ə nē) *n., pl.* **ca·coph·o·nies.** a harsh or unpleasant sound; dissonance; discord. —**ca·coph′o·nous,** *adj.*

cac·tus (kak′təs) *n., pl.* **cac·ti** (kak′tī) or **cac·tus·es** or **cac·tus.** any of a large group of North and South American plants found chiefly in desert regions, usually having a central woody stem surrounded by thick, pulpy tissue, a leathery skin, and spines or scales instead of leaves. Many species bear showy flowers and fruit that can be eaten.

cad (kad) *n.* a man who does not behave like a gentleman; ill-bred or ill-mannered man. —**cad′dish,** *adj.* —**cad′dish·ness,** *n.*

CAD, computer-aided design.

cacti

ca·dav·er (kə dav′ər) *n.* a dead body, especially a corpse prepared or used for dissection.

ca·dav·er·ous (kə dav′ər əs) *adj.* like a corpse; pale; ghastly; gaunt.

cad·die (kad′ē) *also,* **cad·dy.** *n.* a person who assists a golfer, as by carrying his or her golf clubs. —*v.i.,* **cad·died, cad·dy·ing.** to act as a caddie.

cad·dis·fly (kad′is flī′) *n., pl.* **cad·dis·flies.** a small, mothlike insect whose larva lives in fresh water.

Cad·do (kad′ō) *n., pl.* **Cad·do** or **Cad·dos.** a member of an American Indian tribe that lived in what is now southwestern Arkansas, Louisiana, and eastern Texas.

cad·dy¹ (kad′ē) *n., pl.* **cad·dies.** a small box used to hold tea. [From the Malay word *kati* meaning "a weight of 1⅓ pounds."]

cad·dy² (kad′ē) *n., pl.* **cad·dies,** *v.i.,* **cad·died, cad·dy·ing.** another spelling of **caddie.**

ca·dence (kā′dəns) *n.* **1.** a rhythmic flow or pattern, as in poetry, speech, or natural sounds; rhythm: *the cadence of the windshield wipers.* **2.** a measure or beat of any rhythmical movement, such as dancing or marching. **3.** the rising and falling of a sound, as of the voice at the end of a sentence. **4.** *Music.* a series of tones or chords that ends a phrase, passage, movement, or composition.

ca·den·za (kə den′zə) *n. Music.* an elaborate and technically difficult passage for a solo voice or instrument, usually near the end of a section of a musical composition.

ca·det (kə det′) *n.* **1.** a student in a military academy training to be an officer. **2.** a student in a military school. [From the French word *cadet* meaning "younger son" and "cadet," going back to the Latin word *caput* meaning "head." Since the eldest son would inherit his father's land, it became traditional for a younger son to find a career in the army.]

cad·mi·um (kad′mē əm) *n.* a soft, bluish white metallic element resembling zinc. It is used especially to plate steel and other metals to give them a corrosion-resistant surface. Symbol: **Cd** [From the Latin word *cadmia* meaning "calamine," from the Greek phrase *kadmia (gē)* "(earth) of Thebes." *Kadmos* was the legendary founder of the Greek city of Thebes, where cadmium ore was found with calamine.]

ca·du·ce·us (kə dü′sē əs, kə dū′sē əs) *n., pl.* **ca·du·ce·i** (kə dü′sē ī′, kə dū′sē ī′). **1.** a winged staff with two snakes twined around it, carried by the god Mercury. **2.** a similar staff used as the emblem of the medical profession.

caduceus
(def. 2)

cae·cum (sē′kəm) *n., pl.* **cae·ca** (sē′kə). another spelling of **cecum.**

Cae·sar (sē′zər) *n.* any emperor, tyrant, or dictator. [From the Latin title *Caesar,* applied to the Roman emperors since Augustus, from the Roman general and statesman Gaius Julius *Caesar* (100?–44 B.C.).]

cae·sar·e·an (si zâr′ē ən) *also,* **cae·sar·i·an.** *n.* see **cesarean section.** —*adj.* **Caesarean** *also,* **Caesarian.** of or relating to Julius Caesar or the Caesars.

caesarean section, another spelling of **cesarean section.** [From the Roman statesman Julius *Caesar* (100?–44 B.C.), who was once thought to have been born this way.]

cae·si·um (sē′zē əm) another spelling of **cesium.**

cae·su·ra (si zhūr′ə) *n., pl.* **cae·su·ras** or **cae·su·rae** (si zhūr′ē). a pause or break in a line of verse.

ca·fé (ka fā′) *also,* **ca·fe.** *n.* **1.** a coffeehouse or restaurant. **2.** a barroom, cabaret, or nightclub.

caf·e·te·ri·a (kaf′i tîr′ē ə) *n.* a restaurant where customers buy food at a counter and seat themselves.

caf·feine (ka fēn′, kaf′ēn) *also,* **caf·fein.** *n.* an odorless, bitter, white substance found especially in coffee, tea, and many soft drinks. It is used as a stimulant.

cage (kāj) *n.* **1.** a boxlike structure or enclosure, usually having bars or made of wire mesh, used for confining birds or animals. **2.** anything like a cage, such as a cashier's window having bars. **3.** anything that confines or imprisons; prison. —*v.t.,* **caged, cag·ing.** to put or confine in a cage: *to cage a wild animal.*

cag·ey (kā′jē) *also,* **cag·y.** *adj.,* **cag·i·er, cag·i·est.** *Informal.* wary of being tricked; shrewd; cautious: *The cagey general was not fooled by the enemy's seeming retreat.* —**cag′i·ly,** *adv.* —**cag′i·ness,** *n.*

ca·hoots (kə hüts′) *n.* **in cahoots.** *Slang.* in partnership, especially to plot secretly: *The ruler's most trusted friends were in cahoots with the rebels.*

CAI, computer-aided instruction.

cai·man (kā′mən) *also,* **cay·man**. *n.* a large reptile of Central and South America, closely resembling the alligator.

Cain (kān) *n.* **to raise Cain.** *Slang.* to make a great disturbance. [From *Cain,* son of Adam and Eve, who murdered his brother, Abel, in the book of Genesis.]

caiman

cairn (kârn) *n.* a mound of stones piled up as a memorial or landmark.

cais·son (kā′sən, kā′son) *n.* **1.** a large, boxlike or cylindrical watertight structure in which building or construction work can be carried on under water. See **pneumatic caisson** for illustration. **2.** a watertight container that is attached to a sunken ship and filled with air. The buoyancy of the caisson helps to raise the ship to the surface. **3.** a two-wheeled ammunition wagon.

caisson disease, another name for **the bends** (see **bend**).

ca·jole (kə jōl′) *v.t.,* **ca·joled, ca·jol·ing.** to coax or persuade by flattery, soothing words, or false promises; wheedle: *The clerk tried to cajole us into buying a new vacuum cleaner.*

ca·jol·er·y (kə jō′lə rē) *n., pl.* **ca·jol·er·ies.** persuasion by flattery, soothing words, or false promises.

Ca·jun (kā′jən) *n.* a descendant of the French who formerly lived in Acadia and settled in Louisiana in the eighteenth century. —*adj.* of or relating to the Cajuns: *Cajun music, Cajun cooking.* [A variant of *Acadian.*]

cake (kāk) *n.* **1.** a baked mixture of various ingredients, such as flour, sugar, eggs, and flavoring, often covered with icing: *a chocolate cake.* **2.** a flat, thin portion of dough or batter that is baked or fried, as a pancake. **3.** any flat mass of food. **4.** a shaped, flattened, or compressed mass: *a cake of soap.* —*v.i.,* **caked, cak·ing.** to form into a hardened mass: *The wax caked where it had been applied too thickly.*

cake·walk (kāk′wôk′) *n.* **1.** formerly, a march or promenade originated by American blacks in which a cake was awarded to the person or couple who performed the most original and intricate steps. **2.** a dance developed from this promenade. **3.** the music for this dance. —*v.i.* to participate in a cakewalk.

Cal., California.

cal·a·bash (kal′ə bash′) *n., pl.* **cal·a·bash·es. 1.** another word for **gourd. 2.** the dried fruit of a tropical American tree, used to make bowls, dippers, and water jugs. **3.** something made from this fruit, such as a bowl or tobacco pipe. **4.** the tree bearing this fruit.

cal·a·boose (kal′ə büs′) *n. Informal.* jail.

cal·a·mine (kal′ə mīn′) *n.* an odorless pink powder made from a mixture of zinc oxide and ferric oxide, used in skin lotions and ointments.

cal·am·i·tous (kə lam′i təs) *adj.* marked by or causing calamity; disastrous. —**cal·am′i·tous·ly,** *adv.*

cal·am·i·ty (kə lam′i tē) *n., pl.* **cal·am·i·ties. 1.** an event that causes great misfortune; disaster: *Fire, flood, and other calamities nearly destroyed the village.* **2.** great suffering or distress; misery.

cal·car·e·ous (kal kâr′ē əs) *adj.* consisting of or containing calcium, calcium carbonate, or lime; chalky.

cal·ci·fi·ca·tion (kal′sə fi kā′shən) *n.* **1.** the process of calcifying, especially the depositing of calcium salts in body tissue. **2.** a calcified formation or structure.

cal·ci·fy (kal′sə fī′) *v.t., v.i.,* **cal·ci·fied, cal·ci·fy·ing.** to make or become hard or stony by the deposit of calcium salts.

cal·ci·mine (kal′sə mīn′) *n.* a white or colored powder used especially to decorate plastered ceilings and walls.

—*v.t.,* **cal·ci·mined, cal·ci·min·ing.** to cover with calcimine.

cal·cine (kal′sīn) *v.,* **cal·cined, cal·cin·ing.** —*v.t.* to cause (a substance) to lose moisture or impurities, or to be oxidized or reduced, by heating it to a high temperature. Limestone is calcined to make lime. —*v.i.* to become calcined. —**cal′ci·na′tion,** *n.*

cal·cite (kal′sīt) *n.* a very common mineral that is made up of calcium carbonate and is the chief component of limestone, chalk, and marble.

cal·ci·um (kal′sē əm) *n.* a soft, silver-white metallic element found in chalk, limestone, and marble. It is essential for the bones, teeth, blood, and muscles, as well as for plant growth. Symbol: **Ca** [Formed from the Latin word *calx* meaning "lime, limestone." Lime is made up mostly of calcium.]

calcium carbonate, a compound of calcium, carbon, and oxygen that occurs as a white powder or as colorless crystals in its pure state and, in nature, as chalk, limestone, marble, and several other mineral forms. It is used in medicines, baking powder, tooth powders, and cement.

cal·cu·la·ble (kal′kyə lə bəl) *adj.* able to be calculated.

cal·cu·late (kal′kyə lāt′) *v.,* **cal·cu·lat·ed, cal·cu·lat·ing.** —*v.t.* **1.** to determine by using mathematics; compute: *The scientists calculated the time required for a trip to the moon.* **2.** to figure out beforehand by reasoning; estimate: *The athletes calculated their chances of winning the tournament.* **3.** *Informal.* to plan; intend: *The speech was calculated to win votes.* —*v.i.* **1.** to perform a mathematical process; compute. **2.** to rely or count (with *on* or *upon*): *The farmers were calculating on good weather.* [From the Late Latin word *calculatus,* past participle of *calculare* meaning "to count, compute," from the Latin word *calculus* "a pebble." Pebbles were used for calculating in ancient times.]

cal·cu·lat·ed (kal′kyə lā′tid) *adj.* **1.** done or attempted after estimating the probable results: *The attack on the enemy stronghold was a calculated risk.*

cal·cu·lat·ing (kal′kyə lā′ting) *adj.* **1.** given to careful or shrewd consideration of one's own interests. **2.** selfish; scheming. **3.** able to perform mathematical operations: *a calculating machine.*

cal·cu·la·tion (kal′kyə lā′shən) *n.* **1.** the act or process of calculating. **2.** the product or result of calculating. **3.** careful or shrewd planning.

cal·cu·la·tor (kal′kyə lā′tər) *n.* **1.** a person who calculates. **2.** a machine for performing mathematical operations mechanically.

cal·cu·lus (kal′kyə ləs) *n., pl.* **cal·cu·li** (kal′kyə lī′) or **cal·cu·lus·es. 1.** a method of calculation in advanced mathematics that uses a special system of algebraic symbols to solve problems. **2.** an abnormal hard mass of mineral matter formed in the body. Kidney stones are calculi.

cal·dron (kôl′drən) another spelling of **cauldron.**

cal·en·dar (kal′ən dər) *n.* **1.** a table showing the days, weeks, and months of a given year. **2.** a method of dividing time into fixed intervals, especially with reference to the beginning, length, and division of the year. **3.** a list, register, or schedule arranged in chronological order, such as a list of cases to be tried in court or of bills to be considered by a legislature. [Originally from the Medieval Latin word *kalendarium* meaning "calendar," from the Latin word *calendarium* "account book," from *calendae,*

at; āpe; fär; câre; end; mē; it; īce; pîerce; hot; ōld; sông, fôrk; oil; out; up; ūse; rüle; pull; tûrn; chin; sing; shop; thin; this; hw in white; zh in treasure. The symbol ə stands for the unstressed vowel sound heard in about, taken, pencil, lemon, and circus.

the name of the first day of the month in the ancient Roman calendar.]

calendar month, see **month** *(def. 1).*

calendar year, see **year** *(def. 1).*

cal·en·der (kal′ən dər) *n.* a machine consisting of a number of rollers through which cloth, paper, or other material is passed in order to produce a desired finish or a uniform thickness. —*v.t.* to press in a calender.

calf[1] (kaf) *n., pl.* **calves. 1.** a young cow or bull. **2.** the young of various other mammals, such as the elephant, whale, and seal. **3.** see **calfskin.** [From the Old English word *cealf* meaning "young cow."]

calf[2] (kaf) *n., pl.* **calves.** the fleshy, muscular part of the back of the leg between the knee and ankle. [From the Old Norse word *kālfi* meaning "calf of the leg."]

calf·skin (kaf′skin′) *n.* **1.** the skin or hide of a calf. **2.** leather made from it.

cal·i·ber (kal′ə bər) *also,* **cal·i·bre.** *n.* **1.** the diameter of the inside of a hollow tube. **2.a.** the diameter of the bore of a gun. **b.** the diameter of a bullet or shell. **3.** a degree of merit or ability; quality: *The job requires someone of high caliber.*

cal·i·brate (kal′ə brāt′) *v.t.,* **cal·i·brat·ed, cal·i·brat·ing. 1.** to determine, check, correct, or mark the scale of (a thermometer or similar measuring instrument). **2.** to determine the caliber of, as the interior of a thermometer tube. —**cal′i·bra′tion,** *n.*

cal·i·co (kal′i kō′) *n., pl.* **cal·i·coes** or **cal·i·cos.** a cotton fabric printed with small, usually brightly colored designs. —*adj.* **1.** made of calico. **2.** resembling calico; spotted: *a calico cat.* [From *Calicut,* the port of India from which this fabric was first imported.]

ca·lif (kā′lif) another spelling of **caliph.**

Calif., California.

cal·i·for·ni·um (kal′ə fôr′nē əm) *n.* a radioactive element produced artificially from curium. Symbol: **Cf** [From *California,* where the element was discovered.]

cal·i·pers (kal′ə pərz) *also,* **cal·li·pers.** *pl. n.* a hinged instrument resembling a pair of tongs, used especially to measure the internal or external dimensions of a small object.

cal·iph (kā′lif) *also,* **ca·lif.** *n.* formerly, the title given to the successors of Muhammad as the religious and secular heads of Islam.

ca·liph·ate (kā′lə fāt′) *n.* the office, reign, or government of a caliph or the land under a caliph's rule.

cal·is·then·ics (kal′əs then′iks) *also,* **cal·lis·then·ics.** *pl. n.* **1.** light gymnastic exercises designed to develop strength and grace and to promote good health: *We did calisthenics to keep in shape.* **2.** the science or practice of such exercises. ▲ used with a singular verb in definition 2. —**cal′is·then′ic,** *adj.* [Formed from the Greek words *kallos* meaning "beauty" and *sthenos* meaning "strength."]

calk[1] (kôk) another spelling of **caulk.**

calk[2] (kôk) *n.* **1.** one of the projecting pieces of a horseshoe that grips the ground and prevents the horse from slipping. **2.** a sharp, projecting piece of metal on the bottom of the heel or toe of a shoe or boot to prevent slipping. —*v.t.* to furnish with calks. [Short for the earlier word *calkin* with the same meaning, from the Norman French word *calcain* meaning "heel," going back to the Latin word *calx* "heel."]

calk·er (kô′kər) another spelling of **caulker.**

call (kôl) *v.t.* **1.** to utter in a loud voice; proclaim; announce: *The teacher called my name.* **2.** to command, request, or cause to come; summon: *I was called to testify*

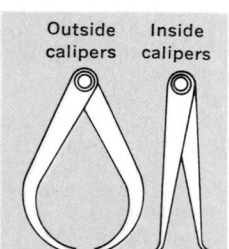

Outside calipers   Inside calipers

calipers

in the case. I'll call a cab for us.* **3.** to cause to assemble or begin officially: *to call a meeting, to call a strike.* **4.** to summon to a special duty, office, or activity: *They were called to serve in the army.* **5.** to arouse from sleep; waken: *Call me for breakfast at seven o'clock.* **6.** to make a telephone call to: *Call us from the airport when you arrive.* **7.** to give a name to; name: *Let's call the puppy "Daisy."* **8.** to describe or characterize in some way: *That's what I call a dirty trick.* **9.** to stop or suspend: *The game was called on account of darkness.* **10.** *Sports.* **a.** to rule, as a pitch or a player's action: *The umpire called the pitch a strike.* **b.** to choose and signal (a particular play): *The quarterback called a short pass.* —*v.i.* **1.** to speak loudly; cry; shout: *Did you hear someone call a minute ago?* **2.** to make a short visit or stop: *We called yesterday, but you weren't home.* **3.** to make a telephone call: *Try to call before midnight.* —*n.* **1.** the act of calling; shout; cry. **2.a.** a characteristic sound or cry made by a bird or animal. **b.** a device that produces an imitation of such a sound in order to lure birds or animals. **3.** a summons; invitation: *The fiery speech was a call to revolution.* **4.** a signal or summons played on a drum or bugle: *Reveille is the first call of the day.* **5.** a need; occasion; cause: *There was no call for you to contribute so generously.* **6.** the act or instance of communicating by telephone: *Did I receive any calls while I was out?* **7.** *Sports.* a ruling by an official. **8.** a short visit. **9.** an urge or feeling that one should do something: *I felt the call to help them.*

• **close call.** a narrow escape: *The skier had many close calls with injury.*

• **on call. a.** available when summoned; ready: *The doctor is on call all night.* **b.** payable on demand.

• **to call back. a.** to summon (a person) to return; bring back. **b.** to telephone again or in return.

• **to call for. a.** to go and get; stop to obtain: *We called for the package at the post office.* **b.** to require or demand; need: *This problem calls for careful thinking.*

• **to call forth.** to bring into action; evoke.

• **to call in. a.** to withdraw from circulation, as currency. **b.** to summon or invite, as for assistance or consultation: *The farmer called in a geologist to evaluate the land.* **c.** to demand repayment of: *to call in a loan.*

• **to call off. a.** to cancel: *to call off a trip, to call off an investigation.* **b.** to make go away: *Call off your dog.* **c.** to read aloud: *The judge called off the names of the winners.*

• **to call on** or **to call upon. a.** to make a brief visit to. **b.** to appeal to: *The senator called on the voters for support.*

• **to call out. a.** to utter or cry out in a loud voice. **b.** to order into action: *to call out the army reserves.*

• **to call up. a.** to telephone. **b.** to bring or summon into action or service: *They were called up for military duty.* **c.** to bring to mind: *The old letter called up pleasant memories.* **d.** to display on the screen of a computer: *to call up a file.*

cal·la (kal′ə) *n.* any of several plants that bear tiny flowers on a spike inside a showy, usually white or yellow spathe. Also, **calla lily.**

call·er (kô′lər) *n.* **1.** a person who makes a short visit. **2.** a person or thing that calls. **3.** a person who calls directions to dancers during a square dance.

cal·lig·ra·phy (kə lig′rə fē) *n.* **1.** beautiful or elegant handwriting. **2.** handwriting; penmanship.

call·ing (kô′ling) *n.* **1.** a vocation; profession. **2.** a strong impulse or urge to follow a certain course of action, especially of a religious nature: *The student felt a calling to join the ministry.* **3.** the act of a person or thing that calls, especially crying or shouting aloud.

calling card, a small card with one's name on it, used for social calls or business purposes. Also, **visiting card.**

cal·li·o·pe (kə lī′ə pē′) *n.* **1.** a musical instrument consisting of a series of steam whistles, played by means of a keyboard. **2. Calliope.** *Greek Mythology.* the Muse of eloquence and epic poetry.

cal·li·pers (kal′ə pərz) another spelling of **calipers.**

cal·lis·then·ics (kal′əs then′iks) another spelling of **calisthenics.**

call letters, the letters that identify a radio or television station.

call number, a number and letter code used in a library to classify books according to their subjects and their location on the shelves.

cal·lous (kal′əs) *adj.* **1.** thickened and hardened, as a callus on the skin. **2.** hardened in mind or feelings; unfeeling; insensitive: *to be callous about the troubles of other people.* —*v.t., v.i.* to make or become callous. —**cal′lous·ly,** *adv.* —**cal′lous·ness,** *n.*

cal·low (kal′ō) *adj.* **1.** inexperienced; immature: *a callow youth who knew nothing of life.* **2.** (of young birds) not having enough feathers for flight. —**cal′low·ness,** *n.*

cal·lus (kal′əs) *n., pl.* **cal·lus·es.** a hardened and thickened area of the skin.

calm (käm) *adj.* **1.** without or nearly without wind or motion; not stormy: *a calm sea.* **2.** free from excitement, nervousness, or strong feeling; quiet; serene: *The crowd remained calm during the blackout.* —*n.* **1.** the condition or period of being without motion or wind; stillness: *There was an eerie calm before the tornado hit the town.* **2.** freedom from excitement, nervousness, or strong feeling; tranquillity; serenity. —*v.t.* to make calm or quiet: *The nurse calmed the child.* —*v.i.* to become calm or quiet (often with *down*): *The children calmed down after their fight.* —**calm′ly,** *adv.* —**calm′ness,** *n.*

cal·o·mel (kal′ə mel′) *n.* a compound of mercury and chlorine in the form of a white, tasteless powder. It is used as an insecticide, antiseptic, and laxative.

ca·lor·ic (kə lôr′ik) *adj.* relating to heat or calories.

cal·o·rie (kal′ə rē) *also,* **cal·o·ry.** *n., pl.* **cal·o·ries.** **1.** the quantity of heat required to raise the temperature of 1 gram of water 1 degree centigrade. Also, **small calorie.** **2.** the quantity of heat, equal to 1,000 small calories, required to raise the temperature of 1 kilogram of water 1 degree centigrade. Also, **large calorie.** **3.** a unit equal to the large calorie, used to measure the heat output of organisms or the energy-producing value of food. **4.** a quantity of food having such an energy-producing value. [From the French word *calorie* meaning "small calorie," from the Latin word *calor* "heat."]

cal·o·rif·ic (kal′ə rif′ik) *adj.* relating to or producing heat.

cal·o·rim·e·ter (kal′ə rim′i tər) *n.* an apparatus for measuring the amount of heat given off or absorbed by a substance.

cal·u·met (kal′yə met′) *n.* another word for **peace pipe.**

ca·lum·ni·ate (kə lum′nē āt′) *v.t.,* **ca·lum·ni·at·ed, ca·lum·ni·at·ing.** to make false and harmful statements or accusations about; slander. —**ca·lum′ni·a′tion,** *n.* —**ca·lum′ni·a′tor,** *n.*

ca·lum·ni·ous (kə lum′nē əs) *adj.* containing or characterized by calumny; slanderous. —**ca·lum′ni·ous·ly,** *adv.*

cal·um·ny (kal′əm nē) *n., pl.* **cal·um·nies.** a false and harmful statement or accusation intended to damage another person's reputation; slander.

calve (kav) *v.i.,* **calved, calv·ing.** to give birth to a calf.

calves (kavz) the plural of **calf.**

Cal·vin·ism (kal′və niz′əm) *n.* the religious teachings of John Calvin, particularly predestination and salvation through God's grace alone.

Cal·vin·ist (kal′və nist) *n.* a person who believes in Calvinism.

ca·ly·ces (kal′ə sēz′, kā′lə sēz′) a plural of **calyx.**

ca·lyp·so (kə lip′sō) *n., pl.* **ca·lyp·sos.** an improvised song, originally from the British West Indies, usually on subjects that are humorous or of current interest.

ca·lyx (kā′liks, kal′iks) *n., pl.* **ca·lyx·es** or **ca·ly·ces.** the outer circle of protective leaves, or sepals, that surround an unopened flower and usually fold back beneath the petals when the bud opens.

cal·zo·ne (kal zō′nā, kal zōn′) *n.* a triangular-shaped pastry made of pizza dough, with a cheese, meat, or other filling. [From the Italian word *calzone* meaning "trouser leg" and used as the name of this food.]

cam (kam) *n.* the projection on a rotating shaft that changes a circular motion into motion back and forth.

CAM, computer-aided manufacture.

ca·ma·ra·de·rie (kä′mə rä′də rē, kam′ə rad′ə rē) *n.* friendliness and loyalty among comrades; fellowship.

cam·bi·um (kam′bē əm) *n.* a layer of growth tissue between the bark and the wood of trees and woody plants. It gives rise to cells for new bark and new wood.

Cam·bo·di·an (kam bō′dē ən) *adj.* of or relating to Cambodia, its people, their language, or their culture. —*n.* **1.** a person who was born in or is a citizen of Cambodia. **2.** another word for **Khmer** (*def. 2*). Also, **Kampuchean.**

Cam·bri·an (kam′brē ən) *n.* the first geological period of the Paleozoic era. —*adj.* of or relating to this period.

cam·bric (kām′brik) *n.* a soft, lightweight linen or cotton fabric.

cambric tea, a drink made with water, milk, sugar, and usually a little tea.

cam·cord·er (kam′kôr′dər) *n.* a portable television camera and videotape recorder in a single unit.

came (kām) the past tense of **come.**

cam·el (kam′əl) *n.* a cud-chewing animal of the desert regions of Africa, Asia, Asia Minor, and Arabia, having a humped back, a sandy white to deep brown coat, and cloven hoofs. Camels are used for riding, as beasts of burden, and as a source of meat, milk, and leather. There are two species of camels: the dromedary, with one hump, and the Bactrian camel, with two humps.

camcorder

ca·mel·ia (kə mēl′yə) *n.* **1.** the waxy flower of any of a group of shrubs and trees, widely grown in warm, damp regions and having white, red, or pink petals. **2.** the woody plant bearing this flower.

---

at; āpe; fär; câre; end; mē; it; īce; pîerce; hot; ōld; sông, fôrk; oil; out; up; ūse; rüle; pull; tûrn; chin; sing; shop; thin; this; hw in white; zh in treasure. The symbol ə stands for the unstressed vowel sound heard in about, taken, pencil, lemon, and circus.

C

139

Cam·e·lot (kam′ə lot′) *n.* the legendary British site of King Arthur's court.

camel's hair, a soft fabric made of the hair of camels or of this hair in combination with wool. It usually has a distinctive tan color, and is used for coats, suits, and sweaters.

Cam·em·bert (kam′əm bâr′) *n.* a rich, creamy, soft cheese. [From *Camembert,* the town in northern France where this cheese was first produced.]

cam·e·o (kam′ē ō′) *n., pl.* **cam·e·os.** a piece of jewelry made from a precious or semiprecious stone or a shell, having a carved, raised design on it. The stone often consists of different colored layers so that the darker layer can serve as a background for a figure, usually the head of a woman, that is carved in relief from the lighter part.

cam·er·a (kam′ər ə, kam′rə) *n., pl.* **cam·er·as.** **1.** a device for taking photographs, consisting of a lightproof box with a lens and shutter through which light is admitted and the image is focused on a film or plate that is sensitive to light. **2.** *Television.* a device that changes an image into electrical impulses for transmission. [Short for the Latin phrase *camera obscura* meaning "dark chamber," the earlier name for this device.]

cam·er·al (kam′ər əl, kam′rəl) *adj.* of or relating to a legislature or a judge's chambers.

cam·er·a·man (kam′ər ə man′, kam′rə man′) *n., pl.* **cam·er·a·men** (kam′ər ə men′, kam′rə men′). a person whose occupation is operating a motion picture or television camera.

cam·er·a–shy (kam′ər ə shī′, kam′rə shī′) *adj.* embarrassed or unwilling to be photographed.

cam·i·on (kam′ē ən) *n.* **1.** a heavy wagon or cart; dray. **2.** a truck, especially one used to carry military supplies or artillery.

cam·i·sole (kam′ə sōl′) *n.* a woman's undergarment that looks like the top of a slip, often trimmed with lace or ribbons.

cam·o·mile (kam′ə mīl′, kam′ə mēl′) another spelling of **chamomile.**

cam·ou·flage (kam′ə fläzh′) *n.* **1.** *Military.* the act or process of disguising or changing the appearance of troops, equipment, or installations in order to conceal them from the enemy, especially by using paint, nets, or foliage to make them blend into the surroundings. **2.** any disguise, appearance, or behavior that serves to conceal or deceive, such as the protective coloring of an animal. —*v.t.,* **cam·ou·flaged, cam·ou·flag·ing.** to disguise or conceal by means of camouflage: *The soldiers camouflaged the tank by covering it with branches.*

camp (kamp) *n.* **1.** an outdoor site, often with tents, huts, or other structures, where people live or sleep temporarily, especially while traveling or marching: *We established a camp near the mountains.* **2.** a place, usually in the country, that provides supervised activities and is attended for a fixed period of time: *This summer I'm going to a camp for musicians.* **3.** a group of permanent structures in which a number of persons may be sheltered or confined: *a prisoner-of-war camp.* **4.** an area employed for or occupied by a camp. —*v.i.* to set up or live in a camp (often with *out*): *to camp in the wilderness, to camp out by a lake.*

· **to break camp.** to pack up camping equipment.

· **to make camp.** to lay out camping equipment and establish a camp.

cam·paign (kam pān′) *n.* **1.** a series of related military operations carried on to accomplish a specific goal: *The campaign was designed to gain control of the enemy's territory.* **2.** an organized series of actions carried on for a particular purpose or toward a particular goal: *an election campaign, a fund-raising campaign.* —*v.i.* to carry on or serve in a campaign: *The candidate campaigned here last week. Volunteers campaigned for the mayor.* —**cam·paign′er,** *n.*

cam·pa·ni·le (kam′pə nē′lē) *n., pl.* **cam·pa·ni·les** or **cam·pa·ni·li** (kam′pə nē′lē). a bell tower, especially one that stands separately from any other building.

camp·er (kam′pər) *n.* **1.** a person who stays at, goes to, or lives in a camp. **2.** a vehicle or trailer built or designed for camping.

camp·fire (kamp′fīr′) *n.* **1.** an outdoor fire in a camp, used for warmth or cooking. **2.** a social gathering or meeting, as around such a fire.

Camp Fire, a national organization for girls and boys of ages seven through eighteen that encourages participation in outdoor activities, sports, arts, and community service.

camp·ground (kamp′ground′) *n.* a place for a camp or a camp meeting.

cam·phor (kam′fər) *n.* a white crystalline compound with a strong odor, used in mothballs, some medicines, and in the manufacture of plastics. Camphor is obtained from the wood of a kind of evergreen tree or made synthetically.

camp·ing (kam′ping) *n.* the practice or pastime of living outdoors, at a camp, or in a camper. —*adj.* relating to or used in camping: *camping gear.*

campanile

camp meeting, a religious gathering, usually lasting several days, held outdoors or in a tent.

camp·site (kamp′sīt′) *n.* an area reserved for camping, usually having facilities for cooking and eating.

camp·stool (kamp′stül′) *n.* a light, portable, folding seat.

cam·pus (kam′pəs) *n., pl.* **cam·pus·es.** the grounds, including buildings, of a school, college, or university. —*adj.* of or relating to a school, college, or university or to its students: *campus politics.* [From the Latin word *campus* meaning "field." The word *campus* was first used to refer to the grounds of a college about 200 years ago.]

can¹ (kan; *unstressed* kən) *auxiliary verb.* Present tense: *sing.,* first person, **can;** second, **can** or (*archaic*) **canst;** third, **can;** *pl.,* **can.** Past tense: **could** or (*archaic*) **couldest** or **couldst.** **1.** to be able to: *I can run faster than you. The car can hold five passengers.* **2.** to know how to: *I can speak French. Can you dance the waltz?* **3.** to have the right to: *Only the general can give that order.* **4.** *Informal.* to be permitted to; may: *Our parents say we can go to the movies.* [From the Old English word *can,* third person singular form of *cunnan* meaning "to know, know how to be, be able."]

▲ In formal usage, **can** means to be able to do something, and **may** to be allowed to do it. In informal usage, *can* is often used in place of *may.*

can² (kan) *n.* **1.** a metal container: *a garbage can.* **2.** a container, usually made of iron coated with tin or of aluminum, in which food or other products are sealed for preservation. **3.** the contents of a can: *The recipe calls for a can of tomatoes.* **4.** *Slang.* jail. —*v.t.,* **canned, can·ning.** **1.** to put or preserve in a can or jar: *to can peaches.* **2.** *Slang.* to fire from a job; discharge: *The boss canned two workers for being late too often.* [From the Old English word *canne* meaning "a container, a can."]

Can. 1. Canada. 2. Canadian.

Ca·naan·ite (kā′nə nīt′) *n.* a member of the Semitic people who lived in Canaan before its conquest by the Hebrews.

Can·a·da Day (kan′ə də) a national holiday of Canada, celebrated on July 1. It commemorates the formation of the Dominion of Canada in 1867. It was formerly called Dominion Day.

Canada goose, a wild goose native to arctic and temperate regions of North America, having a black head and neck, white patches on the face, and a brownish gray body.

ca·nal (kə nal′) *n.* 1. a waterway built across land to carry water for navigation, irrigation, drainage, or power. 2. a tubelike passage in a plant or in the body of an animal. 3. any of the long, faint, narrow markings on the planet Mars, as seen through a telescope.

can·a·pé (kan′ə pā′, kan′ə pē′) *n.* a cracker or thin piece of bread topped with cheese, meat, fish, or a seasoned spread and served hot or cold as an appetizer.

Canada goose

ca·nard (kə närd′) *n.* a false or exaggerated story, report, or rumor; hoax.

ca·nar·y (kə nâr′ē) *n., pl.* **ca·nar·ies.** 1. a small yellow songbird, popular as a pet. 2. see **canary yellow.** —*adj.* having the color canary yellow.

canary yellow, a light, bright yellow color.

ca·nas·ta (kə nas′tə) *n.* a form of rummy for two to six players, usually using two decks of fifty-two cards and four jokers.

can·can (kan′kan′) *n.* a dance that originated in Paris in the early nineteenth century, marked by high kicking.

can·cel (kan′səl) *v.,* **can·celed, can·cel·ing;** *also, British,* **can·celled, can·cel·ling.** —*v.t.* 1. to do away with, withdraw, or stop; call off: *to cancel an appointment.* 2. to cross out or mark with a line or lines, especially to mark (a postage stamp) so that it cannot be used again. 3. to make up for; balance; offset: *A vote for and a vote against a candidate cancel each other.* 4. *Mathematics.* to eliminate (a common factor) from the numerator and denominator of a fraction or from both sides of an equation. —*v.i.* to offset each other (with *out*).

can·cel·la·tion (kan′sə lā′shən) *n.* 1. the act of canceling or the state of being canceled: *Rain caused the cancellation of the baseball game.* 2. the marks used in canceling. 3. something that is canceled.

can·cer (kan′sər) *n.* 1. any of a group of diseases characterized by abnormal growth of cells that destroys healthy tissues and organs. 2. any malignant tumor. 3. any destructive or spreading evil. 4. **Cancer. a.** see **Tropic of Cancer. b.** a constellation located in the northern sky and thought to resemble a crab in shape. **c.** the fourth sign of the zodiac. —**can′cer·ous,** *adj.*

can·de·la (kan dē′lə) *n.* a unit for measuring the intensity of light.

can·de·la·bra (kan′də lä′brə, kan′də lā′brə) *n., pl.* **can·de·la·bras.** another word for **candelabrum.**

can·de·la·brum (kan′də lä′brəm, kan′də lā′brəm) *n., pl.* **can·de·la·bra** or **can·de·la·brums.** a large ornamental candlestick having several branches for holding candles. Also, **candelabra.**

candelabrum

can·did (kan′did) *adj.* 1. honest and straightforward; frank; sincere: *a candid opinion.* 2. not posed; informal: *a candid photograph.* —**can′did·ly,** *adv.* —**can′did·ness,** *n.*

can·di·da·cy (kan′di də sē) *n., pl.* **can·di·da·cies.** the state or fact of being a candidate.

can·di·date (kan′di dāt′) *n.* a person who seeks, or is put forward by others for, an office or honor: *The senator will not be a presidential candidate.* [From the Latin word *candidatus* meaning "a person dressed in white" and "candidate," from the word *candidus* meaning "white." In ancient Rome, candidates for office wore white togas while soliciting votes.]

can·died (kan′dēd) *adj.* 1. cooked in or coated with sugar: *candied yams.* 2. wholly or partially crystallized into sugar.

can·dle (kan′dəl) *n.* 1. a mass of wax, tallow, or other solid fat formed around a wick, burned to give light or low heat. 2. another word for **candela.** —*v.t.* **can·dled, can·dling.** to examine (eggs) for freshness and quality by holding in front of a light.
 ·**to hold a candle to.** to compare favorably with; be as good as: *As a musician, I can't hold a candle to you.*

can·dle·hold·er (kan′dəl hōl′dər) *n.* another word for **candlestick.**

can·dle·light (kan′dəl līt′) *n.* 1. the light given by a candle or candles. 2. the time to light candles; dusk.

Can·dle·mas (kan′dəl məs) *n.* a Christian festival celebrating the purification of Mary, the mother of Jesus, during which candles for sacred use are blessed. It falls on February 2.

can·dle·pin (kan′dəl pin′) *n.* 1. a cylindrical wooden pin tapering slightly at the top and bottom, used in the game of candlepins. 2. **candlepins.** a bowling game using ten of these pins, in which three balls are bowled in each frame and the pins that are knocked down are not removed until each frame is over. ▲ used with a singular verb.

can·dle·pow·er (kan′dəl pou′ər) *n.* a measure of the intensity of a source of light, based on the light given off in a particular direction from that source. Candlepower is expressed in candelas.

can·dle·stick (kan′dəl stik′) *n.* a holder with a cup or spike for a candle.

can·dle·wick (kan′dəl wik′) *n.* the wick of a candle.

can·dor (kan′dər) *n.* 1. frankness, as of speech; honesty; openness. 2. freedom from prejudice; fairness.

can·dy (kan′dē) *n., pl.* **can·dies.** 1. a sweet food made chiefly of sugar or syrup combined with other ingredients, such as chocolate, milk, nuts, or fruit. 2. a piece of this. —*v.,* **can·died, can·dy·ing.** —*v.t.* 1. to preserve by cooking or coating with sugar. 2. to cover with or as with sugar crystals. —*v.i.* to turn into or become covered with sugar.

candy striper, a young person who works in a hospital as a volunteer nurse's aide. [From the striped uniforms originally worn by such aides, suggesting the stripes on some candy sticks.]

can·dy·tuft (kan′dē tuft′) *n.* a plant of the mustard family, having narrow leaves and clusters of small white, purple, or pink flowers.

cane (kān) *n.* 1. a stick or staff, usually made of wood, used as an aid in walking. 2. the slender, woody, jointed stem of certain tall grasses, such as bamboo, reed, and rattan. 3. any plant having such a stem. 4. a material

at; āpe; fär; câre; end; mē; it; īce; pîerce; hot; ōld; sông, fôrk; oil; out; up; ūse; rüle; pull; tûrn; chin; sing; shop; thin; <u>th</u>is; hw in white; zh in treasure. The symbol ə stands for the unstressed vowel sound heard in about, taken, pencil, lemon, and circus.

made of such stems, used in making furniture and wickerwork. **5.** see **sugarcane.** —*v.t.,* **caned, can·ing. 1.** to beat or flog with a cane. **2.** to make or repair with cane. —*adj.* made of cane: *cane chairs.*

cane·brake (kān′brāk) *n.* a thicket of cane.

cane sugar, sugar obtained from sugarcane.

ca·nine (kā′nīn) *adj.* **1.** of, resembling, or relating to a dog. **2.** of or relating to the dog family, which includes dogs, foxes, wolves, coyotes, and jackals. —*n.* **1.** a domestic dog. **2.** any member of the dog family. **3.** see **canine tooth.**

canine tooth, one of the four sharp-pointed teeth located between the incisors and the bicuspids in the upper and lower jaw. Also, **cuspid.**

can·is·ter (kan′ə stər) *n.* a small box, can, or other container, usually made of metal, used especially for holding coffee, sugar, flour, or other dry foods.

can·ker (kang′kər) *n.* **1.** an open sore, especially on the mouth or lip. **2.** anything that corrupts or destroys.

can·ker·ous (kang′kər əs) *adj.* **1.** of or like a canker. **2.** causing a canker.

can·ker·worm (kang′kər wûrm′) *n.* any of several caterpillars that are very destructive to shade and fruit trees.

can·na (kan′ə) *n.* **1.** a red or yellow flower of a tropical plant. **2.** the plant bearing this flower, having large, oblong leaves.

canned (kand) *adj.* **1.** preserved in a can or jar: *canned fruit.* **2.** *Informal.* recorded: *a television comedy with canned laughter.*

can·ner (kan′ər) *n.* a person who cans food.

can·ner·y (kan′ə rē) *n., pl.* **can·ner·ies.** a factory where foods are canned.

can·ni·bal (kan′ə bəl) *n.* **1.** a person who eats human flesh. **2.** an animal that eats its own kind. —*adj.* **1.** of or relating to cannibals. **2.** given to cannibalism.

can·ni·bal·ism (kan′ə bə liz′əm) *n.* the act or practice of eating the flesh of one's own kind. —**can′ni·bal·is′tic,** *adj.*

can·ni·bal·ize (kan′ə bə līz′) *v.t.,* **can·ni·bal·ized, can·ni·bal·iz·ing.** to take parts from (something) to build, repair, or strengthen one or more other things: *They built a hot rod by cannibalizing abandoned cars.*

can·ning (kan′ing) *n.* the act, process, or business of preserving food by sealing it in airtight containers.

can·no·li (kə nō′lē) *n., pl.* **can·no·li.** a tube-shaped pastry filled with sweetened ricotta cheese, often flavored with citron, chocolate, and the like. [From the Italian word *cannoli,* meaning "little tubes," going back to the Greek word *kanna* "reed, cane."]

can·non (kan′ən) *n., pl.* **can·nons** or **can·non.** a large gun that is mounted on a base.

can·non·ade (kan′ə nād′) *n.* **1.** a continuous firing of artillery. **2.** an attack with artillery. —*v.t.,* **can·non·ad·ed, can·non·ad·ing.** to attack with artillery.

can·non·ball (kan′ən bôl′) *n.* a heavy metal ball designed to be fired from a cannon.

can·non·eer (kan′ə nîr′) *n.* a soldier in the artillery; gunner.

can·not (kan′ot, ka not′) can not.

can·ny (kan′ē) *adj.,* **can·ni·er, can·ni·est.** shrewd and cautious; wary. —**can′ni·ly,** *adv.* —**can′ni·ness,** *n.*

ca·noe (kə nü′) *n.* a light, narrow boat, usually pointed at both ends, propelled with a paddle. —*v.,* **ca·noed, ca·noe·ing.** —*v.i.* to paddle or go in a canoe. —*v.t.* to transport by canoe. —**ca·noe′ist,** *n.*

can of worms *Informal.* a situation that produces unexpected problems.

can·on¹ (kan′ən) *n.* **1.** a law, rule, or decree of a church. **2.** a general rule, fundamental principle, or standard: *to be guided by the canons of good behavior.* **3.** a collection or list of the books of the Bible accepted by a church as genuine and divinely inspired. **4.** a list of saints officially recognized by the Roman Catholic Church and certain

other churches. **5.** a musical composition in which a melody is begun and continued by different voices in succession. [From the Late Latin word *canon* meaning "a rule of the church," from the Latin word *canon* "rule, standard," from the Greek word *kanōn* with the same meaning.]

can·on² (kan′ən) *n.* **1.** a member of the clergy serving in a cathedral. **2.** in the Middle Ages, a Roman Catholic clergyman living according to certain rules, or canons, of the church. [From the Old French word *canonie* meaning "a priest serving in the cathedral," from the Late Latin word *canonicus* "someone living according to a rule," going back to the Greek word *kanōn* "rule, standard."]

ca·ñon (can′yən) another spelling of **canyon.**

ca·non·i·cal (kə non′i kəl) *adj.* **1.** relating to, established by, or conforming to church law or rule. **2.** of or contained in the canon of the Bible.

canonical hours, the seven periods of the day fixed by church canon for prayer and devotion.

can·on·ize (kan′ə nīz′) *v.t.,* **can·on·ized, can·on·iz·ing.** to declare (a deceased person) a saint; place in the canon of saints: *The missionary was canonized in the eighteenth century.* —**can′on·i·za′tion,** *n.*

canon law, in a Christian church, the body of law governing matters of faith and discipline.

can·o·py (kan′ə pē) *n., pl.* **can·o·pies. 1.** a covering of cloth or other material, hung over a bed, throne, or entrance of a building, or supported on poles over a person or sacred object. **2.** anything that acts or seems to act as an overhanging shelter or covering: *the canopy of the stars.* **3.** a transparent, sliding covering over an airplane cockpit. —*v.t.,* **can·o·pied, can·o·py·ing.** to cover with a canopy.

canopy *(def. 1)*

canst (kanst) *Archaic.* the present second person singular of **can.** ▲ used with **thou.**

cant¹ (kant) *n.* **1.** talk that is insincere or trite, especially hypocritical religious or moral statements. **2.** words or language peculiar to a particular profession, class, or group: *The will was written in the cant of attorneys.* [From the earlier verb *to cant* meaning "to beg in a whining or singsong voice," going back to the Latin word *cantare* "to sing."]

cant² (kant) *n.* **1.** a slant or slope; tilt. **2.** a sudden movement that tilts or overturns something. —*v.t.* **1.** to put or set at an angle; slant; tilt. **2.** to give a sloping edge to; bevel. —*v.i.* to tilt, slant, or slope. [From the Middle Dutch word *cant* meaning "edge" or "corner."]

can't (kant) *contr.* can not.

can·ta·loupe (kan′tə lōp′) *also,* **can·ta·loup.** *n.* a kind of muskmelon, having a coarse, pale green or yellow rind and sweet, usually yellowish orange flesh.

can·tan·ker·ous (kan tang′kər əs) *adj.* ill-tempered and ready to quarrel. —**can·tan′ker·ous·ly,** *adv.* —**can·tan′ker·ous·ness,** *n.*

can·ta·ta (kən tä′tə) *n.* a musical composition in which a story is sung by a chorus and soloists but not acted.

can·teen (kan tēn′) *n.* **1.** a small metal container for carrying water or other liquids. **2.** a place run by civilian volunteers where free food, beverages, and, usually, entertainment are provided for members of the armed forces. **3.** another word for **post exchange. 4.** a place providing food and beverages, such as a snack bar at a factory.

can·ter (kan′tər) *n.* an easy gait faster than a trot but slower than a full gallop. —*v.t., v.i.* to move or ride at a canter. [Short for *Canterbury pace,* the slow pace used by pilgrims to approach the shrine at Canterbury.]

Can·ter·bur·y bell (kan′tər ber′ē) a plant with tall stalks of bell-shaped flowers having white, pink, or blue-violet petals.

cant hook, a pole with a movable hooked arm at or near one end, used to grip and turn over logs or poles.

can·ti·cle (kan′ti kəl) *n.* a short hymn whose words are usually taken directly from the Bible.

can·ti·le·ver (kan′tə lē′vər, kan′tə lev′ər) *n.* a projecting bracket, beam, or slab that is supported only at one end.

cantilever bridge, a bridge formed by two cantilevers whose projecting ends meet but do not support each other.

can·tle (kan′təl) *n.* the part of the seat of certain saddles that curves up at the back.

can·to (kan′tō) *n., pl.* **can·tos.** one of the main divisions of a long poem.

can·ton (kan′tən, kan′ton) *n.* a small territorial district or political division of a country, especially one of the twenty-two states of the Swiss confederation.

cant hook

Can·ton·ese (kan′tə nēz′, kan′tə nēs′) *n., pl.* **Can·ton·ese.** **1.** a person who was born or lives in or near Canton, China. **2.** a Chinese dialect spoken in and around Canton, China. —*adj.* of or relating to Canton, China, its people, their dialect, or their culture.

can·ton·ment (kan tōn′mənt, kan ton′mənt) *n.* **1.** a military installation that includes quarters for soldiers and their families. **2.** temporary housing for troops.

can·tor (kan′tər) *n.* **1.** the chief singer of the liturgy in a synagogue. **2.** the singer who leads a choir or congregation.

Ca·nuck (kə nuk′) *n. Slang.* **1.** Canadian. **2.** French Canadian. ▲ sometimes considered offensive.

can·vas (kan′vəs) *n., pl.* **can·vas·es.** **1.** a strong, heavy cloth made of cotton, flax, or hemp, used for such items as tents, sails, and awnings. **2.** a piece of canvas on which a painting, especially an oil painting, is done. **3.** an oil painting done on canvas: *an artist's favorite canvas.* —*adj.* made of canvas: *a canvas screen.*

can·vas·back (kan′vəs bak′) *n.* a wild duck of North America. The male has black and brown feathers on most of its body and white feathers on its back.

can·vass (kan′vəs) *v.t.* **1.** to go through (a place) or among (people) trying to get votes, opinions, orders, or contributions: *The candidate's supporters canvassed the neighborhood.* **2.** to examine or discuss carefully or thoroughly: *to canvass a legal problem.* —*v.i.* to go about trying to get votes, opinions, orders, or contributions. —*n., pl.* **can·vass·es.** **1.** the act of canvassing. **2.** an examination; discussion. —**can′vass·er,** *n.*

can·yon (kan′yən) *also,* **cañon.** *n.* a deep valley with steep sides, usually with a stream running through it.

canyon

caou·tchouc (kou chük′) *n.* a natural rubber, especially in its crude form.

cap (kap) *n.* **1.** a soft, close-fitting head covering, usually without a brim or with a visor. **2.** a special head covering worn to show rank, membership, or occupation: *a nurse's cap.* **3.** something resembling a cap in shape, position, or use: *a bottle cap.* **4.** a paper wrapping or covering containing a small quantity of explosive, used in toy guns. **5.** see **percussion cap.** —*v.t.,* **capped, cap·ping.** **1.** to put a cap on; cover: *to cap a bottle.* **2.** to form or serve as a cap, cover, or top for; lie on top of: *Clouds capped the mountains.* **3.** to follow with something equal to or better than; match; surpass: *I capped my friend's story with an even funnier one.*

cap. **1.** capital. **2.** *pl.* **caps.** capital letter.

ca·pa·bil·i·ty (kā′pə bil′i tē) *n., pl.* **ca·pa·bil·i·ties.** **1.** the quality of being capable; ability; capacity: *Your capability as a leader is beyond question.* **2.** a quality or ability that may be used or developed; potentiality: *the capabilities of modern technology to improve life.*

ca·pa·ble (kā′pə bəl) *adj.* having or showing ability; able; efficient; competent: *a capable doctor, a capable performance.* —**ca′pa·bly,** *adv.*

·**capable of. a.** having the capacity, ability, or quality needed for: *I think that our team is capable of winning the championship.* **b.** open or subject to: *The speaker made several statements that were capable of misunderstanding.*

ca·pa·cious (kə pā′shəs) *adj.* able to hold or contain much; roomy; spacious: *a capacious auditorium.* —**ca·pa′cious·ly,** *adv.* —**ca·pa′cious·ness,** *n.*

ca·pac·i·tance (kə pas′i təns) *n.* the ratio of the amount of electric charge stored in a capacitor to the voltage across its terminals. Capacitance is measured in farads.

ca·pac·i·tor (kə pas′i tər) *n.* a device for receiving and storing an electric charge, usually made of two metallic plates separated by a nonconductor. Also, **condenser.**

ca·pac·i·ty (kə pas′i tē) *n., pl.* **ca·pac·i·ties.** **1.** the ability to receive or contain: *The auditorium has a very small seating capacity.* **2.** the maximum amount that can be held or contained in a space; content: *This car's gas tank has a capacity of twelve gallons.* **3.** the ability or power to do something: *the capacity to do good or evil.* **4.** mental ability: *a scholar of great capacity.* **5.** a specific position, occupation, or function: *Who represents the company in the capacity of district manager?*

cap and bells, a cap trimmed with bells, worn by a court jester.

cap and gown, a flat cap and loose gown, worn by teachers and students at academic functions, especially at graduation ceremonies.

ca·par·i·son (kə par′ə sən) *n.* **1.** an ornamental covering for a horse. **2.** rich clothing. —*v.t.* **1.** to cover (a horse) with a caparison. **2.** to dress with rich clothing.

cape[1] (kāp) *n.* an outer garment without sleeves, which falls loosely over the shoulders and is worn in place of or attached to a jacket or coat. [Originally from the Late Latin word *cappa* meaning "cloak" or "garment that covers the head."]

caparison *(def. 1)*

at; āpe; fär; câre; end; mē; it; īce; pîerce; hot; ōld; sông, fôrk; oil; out; up; ūse; rüle; pùll; tûrn; chin; sing; shop; thin; this; hw in white; zh in treasure. The symbol ə stands for the unstressed vowel sound heard in about, taken, pencil, lemon, and circus.

cape² (kāp) *n.* a point of land extending out from the coastline into the sea, a lake, or another large body of water. [From the Middle French word *cap* meaning "headland" or "cape²," going back to the Latin word *caput* "head."]

ca·per¹ (kā′pər) *v.i.* to leap or jump about in a playful manner; prance. —*n.* **1.** a playful leap, skip, or jump. **2.** a prank; antic. **3.** *Slang.* an illegal act, such as a robbery or burglary. [From the Middle French word *capriole* meaning "a leap," from the Italian word *capriola* "a leap like that of a goat," going back to the Latin word *caper* "a male goat."]

ca·per² (kā′pər) *n.* **1.** the green flower bud of a Mediterranean shrub, pickled and used as a seasoning. **2.** the spiny shrub bearing this flower bud. [From the Latin word *capparis* meaning this shrub, from the Greek word *kapparis* with the same meaning.]

cap·il·lar·i·ty (kap′ə lar′i tē) *n.* another word for **capillary action.**

cap·il·lar·y (kap′ə ler′ē) *n., pl.* **cap·il·lar·ies. 1.** any of the smallest blood vessels of the circulatory system, connecting the arteries and veins. **2.** a tube with a small, very narrow opening. —*adj.* **1.** of or like a hair; fine; slender. **2.** having a very small opening, as a tube. **3.** relating to or taking place in a capillary or capillaries.

capillary action, the rising or falling of a liquid where it touches a solid. When a lump of sugar is dipped into coffee, capillary action causes the coffee to rise in the lump. The tendency of liquids to rise in this way is called **capillary attraction;** the tendency to fall is called **capillary repulsion.** Also, **capillarity.**

cap·i·tal¹ (kap′i təl) *n.* **1.** a city or town in which the official seat of government of a country, state, or other political division is located: *Albany is the capital of New York State.* **2.** see **capital letter. 3.** the total amount of money or property owned or used by a corporation or individual. **4.** wealth in any form used or available for use in the production of more wealth. —*adj.* **1.** main, principal, or chief. **2.** being the official seat of government: *Madrid is Spain's capital city.* **3.** excellent; first-rate: *a capital idea.* **4.** punishable by or involving the death penalty: *a capital offense.* **5.** of or relating to capital or wealth: *capital investments.* [From the Old French word *capital* meaning "chief," from the Latin word *capitalis* "at or of the head" or "first, chief," from the word *caput* "head."]

·**to make capital of.** to use to one's advantage.

▲ **Capital** is sometimes confused with **capitol. Capital** means the city in which a government is located: *Washington, D.C. is the capital of the United States.* A **capitol** is the building in which a legislature meets: *The U.S. Congress meets in the Capitol.*

cap·i·tal² (kap′i təl) *n.* the top part of a column or pillar. [From the Norman French word *capitel* meaning "head of a column," from the Late Latin word *capitellum* with the same meaning, going back to the Latin word *caput* "head."]

capital gain, the profit resulting from the sale of capital investments, such as stocks, bonds, or real estate.

cap·i·tal·ism (kap′i tə liz′əm) *n.* an economic system in which the means of production, such as land and factories, are privately owned and operated for profit. Competition between producers and the level of demand by consumers determine the price of goods.

cap·i·tal·ist (kap′i tə list) *n.* **1.** a person who has capital, especially capital that is available for, or being used in, some business activity. **2.** a supporter of capitalism. **3.** any wealthy or financially successful person. —**cap′i·tal·is′tic,** *adj.* —**cap′i·tal·is′ti·cal·ly,** *adv.*

cap·i·tal·i·za·tion (kap′i tə lə zā′shən) *n.* **1.** the act or process of capitalizing. **2.** the total amount of capital used in a business.

cap·i·tal·ize (kap′i tə līz′) *v.,* **cap·i·tal·ized, cap·i·tal-**

iz·ing. —*v.t.* **1.** to write or print with a capital letter or letters, or begin with a capital letter: *Always capitalize proper nouns.* **2.** to change into or use as capital. **3.** to provide capital for; finance. —*v.i.* to use to one's advantage; take advantage of.

capital letter, a large form of a letter of the alphabet, used as the first letter of a sentence or proper noun.

Capital letters as we know them today have been used for only a relatively short period of time. There were letters called capitals in early Greek and Latin writing, but they were not used in combination with small letters. These early capital letters were used for a separate style of writing, just as we use script and printing for different styles today. The modern use of capitals first developed in the Middle Ages, when the first letter of a paragraph was made large and ornate. About two hundred years ago, most English writers tended to capitalize all nouns, as you can see if you look at a reproduction of the *Declaration of Independence.* Now, only proper nouns, proper adjectives, and nouns used in the abstract, like *Beauty* and *Truth,* are capitalized. Only later did people begin using two distinct styles of letters: capitals at the beginning of sentences and small letters everywhere else.

cap·i·tal·ly (kap′i tə lē) *adv.* in a capital manner; excellently; admirably.

capital punishment, the death penalty for a crime.

capital ship, a large warship, formerly a heavily armed sailing ship, now usually an aircraft carrier or battleship.

Cap·i·tol (kap′i təl) *n.* **1.** the building in which the U.S. Congress meets, in Washington, D.C. **2.** *also,* **capitol.** a building in which a state legislature meets. ▲ See **capital¹** for usage note.

ca·pit·u·late (kə pich′ə lāt′) *v.i.,* **ca·pit·u·lat·ed, ca·pit·u·lat·ing.** to surrender or yield, especially on certain terms or conditions.

ca·pit·u·la·tion (kə pich′ə lā′shən) *n.* **1.** surrender, especially on certain terms or conditions. **2.** a statement of the main points of a subject; summary.

cap·let (kap′lit) *n.* an oval-shaped tablet of medicine, coated to make it easier to swallow. Trademark, **Caplet.**

ca·pon (kā′pon) *n.* a young, castrated rooster.

cap·puc·ci·no (kap′ə chē′nō, kä′pə chē′no) *n., pl.* **cap·puc·ci·nos.** a drink made with espresso and hot milk, usually flavored with cinnamon. [From the Italian word *cappuccino* meaning "Capuchin monk" and used as the name of this form of coffee. The color of cappuccino resembles that of the Capuchin habit.]

ca·price (kə prēs′) *n.* **1.** a sudden change of mind for no good or apparent reason; whim. **2.** a tendency to change one's mind in this way; capriciousness.

ca·pri·cious (kə prish′əs) *adj.* tending to change suddenly, unexpectedly, and for no apparent reason; guided by or as if by whim or fancy; unpredictable: *a capricious child, capricious weather.* —**ca·pri′cious·ly,** *adv.* —**ca·pri′cious·ness,** *n.*

Cap·ri·corn (kap′ri kôrn′) *n.* **1.** see **Tropic of Capricorn. 2.** a constellation in the southern sky, thought to resemble a goat in shape. **3.** the tenth sign of the zodiac.

caps., capital letters.

cap·si·cum (kap′si kəm) *n.* any of a group of plants widely grown for their red or green pods containing sharp-tasting seeds. Peppers, pimientos, and chilies are kinds of capsicum.

cap·size (kap′sīz, kap sīz′) *v.,* **cap·sized, cap·siz·ing.** —*v.t.* to cause to overturn: *Rough waves capsized the boat.* —*v.i.* to overturn: *The boat capsized in the hurricane.*

cap·stan (kap′stən) *n.* a device with an upright spindle that is turned by hand or by motor to wind up a rope or cable, as in hoisting an anchor.

cap·su·lar (kap′sə lər) *adj.* of, in, or resembling a capsule.

cap·sule (kap′səl) *n.* **1.** a small soluble case enclosing a dose of medicine. **2.** a detachable, sealed compartment of a spacecraft, designed to support life during flight and to be recovered after flight. **3.** a dry seedcase that opens when ripe. The seeds of the iris, azalea, and poppy develop in capsules. **4.** any membrane or membranous sac enclosing an organ or body part. —*adj.* in a brief form; concise: *a capsule summary of a novel's plot.*

Capt., Captain.

cap·tain (kap′tən) *n.* **1.** a person who is in charge of, has authority over, or has been chosen to lead others; leader; chief: *the captain of a team.* **2.** a person in command of a boat or ship. **3.** in the U.S. Navy and Coast Guard, an officer ranking below a commodore or rear admiral and above a commander. **4.** in the U.S. Army, Air Force, and Marine Corps, an officer ranking below a major and above a first lieutenant. —*v.t.* to act as captain of; lead: *to captain a basketball team.*

Word Family

The Latin word *caput,* meaning "head" or "first, most important" has been the source of many English words. A **captain** who "heads" a group of soldiers may have started out as a **cadet** (a word that comes from an Old French word meaning "little head"). A country's **capital** is its most important city, and its **per capita** income is the average income for each "head," or person. The crimes of treason and murder are often considered **capital** crimes that call for **capital** punishment. In a few countries such punishment still means **decapitation**. A person might wear a **cape**, which at one time meant "head covering," but many more wear **caps**. If we wanted to cover the material under this heading a second time, we would **recapitulate** it, but instead we can move on to another **chapter,** or "heading."

The Old French word *chief* evolved from the Latin word *caput*. From Old French come the words **chief,** the head of a tribe, and **chef,** the head cook. A **kerchief** may be used to cover the head, and we may move "toward the head" and **achieve** some goal, unless we become sidetracked by **mischief**.

---

cap·tain·cy (kap′tən sē) *n., pl.* **cap·tain·cies.** the rank, authority, or period of authority of a captain.

cap·tion (kap′shən) *n.* **1.** a title or written description for a picture: *The funny photograph needed no caption.* **2.** a title or heading, as at the beginning of a chapter, page, or article. —*v.t.* to furnish with a caption.

cap·tious (kap′shəs) *adj.* **1.** inclined to make much of unimportant faults or defects; difficult to please: *a captious critic.* **2.** designed to entrap or confuse: *a captious question.* —**cap′tious·ly,** *adv.* —**cap′tious·ness,** *n.*

cap·ti·vate (kap′tə vāt′) *v.t.,* **cap·ti·vat·ed, cap·ti·vat·ing.** to capture and hold the attention or affection of, as by beauty or excellence; charm; fascinate; enchant: *The audience was captivated by the singer's performance.* —**cap′ti·va′tion,** *n.*

cap·tive (kap′tiv) *n.* a person or animal captured and held in confinement; prisoner: *The enemy captives were brought to the commanding officer for questioning.* —*adj.* **1.** taken or kept prisoner: *captive soldiers.* **2.** kept under control; restrained; confined: *a captive balloon.*

cap·tiv·i·ty (kap tiv′i tē) *n., pl.* **cap·tiv·i·ties.** the state of being a captive: *Animals in a zoo live in captivity.*

cap·tor (kap′tər) *n.* a person who captures someone or something.

cap·ture (kap′chər) *v.t.,* **cap·tured, cap·tur·ing. 1.** to take or seize by force, surprise, or skill: *to capture an enemy gunboat, to capture a lion, to capture an opponent's pawn in chess.* **2.** to attract or catch: *The exciting novel captured my interest.* **3.** to represent in permanent form; reproduce: *The artist tried to capture the scene on canvas.* —*n.* **1.** the act of capturing. **2.** a person or thing that is captured. [From the French word *capture,* going back to the Latin word *captus,* past participle of *capere* meaning "to take."]

cap·u·chin (kap′yə chin, kap′yə shin) *n.* **1.** any of various tree-dwelling monkeys of Central and South America having black or brown fur and a long tail that is used for grasping. Some have black hair on their head that resembles a monk's hood. **2. Capuchin.** a member of one of the branches of the Franciscan religious order of the Roman Catholic Church.

capuchin *(def. 1)*

A Capuchin monk usually is bearded and wears sandals and a brown habit with a long, pointed hood.

cap·y·ba·ra (kap′ə bär′ə) *n.* a South American rodent resembling a large guinea pig, and having a coarse coat of brownish, bristly hair. It grows to a length of three to four feet and is the largest living rodent.

car (kär) *n.* **1.** another word for **automobile. 2.** a vehicle designed to move on rails: *a railroad car.* **3.** any vehicle that moves on wheels. **4.** the part of an elevator that carries the passengers or cargo.

car·a·bao (kär′ə bä′ō, kär′ə bou′) *n., pl.* **car·a·ba·os.** a water buffalo of the Philippines.

car·a·cul (kar′ə kəl) *n.* the loosely curled fur of very young karakul lambs. Also, **karakul.**

ca·rafe (kə raf′) *n.* a glass bottle for water, wine, or other beverages; decanter.

car·a·mel (kar′ə məl, kär′məl) *n.* **1.** burnt sugar used for coloring and flavoring foods. **2.** a chewy candy made mainly from sugar, cream, and corn syrup, usually in the form of small squares.

car·a·pace (kar′ə pās′) *n.* the hard or bony covering on the back of some animals, such as turtles or lobsters.

car·at (kar′ət) *n.* **1.** a unit of weight equal to ⅕ of a gram (0.007 ounce), used chiefly in measuring the weight of gems. **2.** another spelling of **karat.**

car·a·van (kar′ə van′) *n.* **1.** a company of travelers, merchants, or pilgrims traveling together for safety and security, especially through deserts or dangerous regions. **2.** a number of vehicles traveling together: *The caravan of trucks stopped to refuel.* **3.** *British.* a home on wheels; trailer.

car·a·van·sa·ry (kar′ə van′sə rē) *also,* **car·a·van·se·rai** (kar′ə van′sə rī′) *n., pl.* **car·a·van·sar·ies. 1.** in certain Asian and African countries, an inn with a large central court, in which caravans can stay. **2.** any large inn or hotel.

car·a·vel (kar′ə vel′) *n.* any of several types of small, fast sailing ships developed in Portugal and Spain in the

---

at; āpe; fär; câre; end; mē; it; īce; pîerce; hot; ōld; sông; fôrk; oil; out; up; ūse; rüle; pùll; tûrn; chin; sing; shop; thin; this; hw in white; zh in treasure. The symbol ə stands for the unstressed vowel sound heard in about, taken, pencil, lemon, and circus.

C

fifteenth century. Two of Christopher Columbus' ships were caravels.

car·a·way (kar′ə wā′) *n.* **1.** the fragrant, spicy seeds of a plant related to carrots and parsley, used as a spice. **2.** the plant bearing these seeds.

car·bide (kär′bīd) *n.* any of a large group of compounds that contain carbon and one other element, usually a metal.

car·bine (kär′bīn, kär′bēn) *n.* a lightweight automatic or semiautomatic rifle.

car·bo·hy·drate (kär′bō hī′drāt) *n.* a compound of carbon, hydrogen, and oxygen produced by green plants in the process of photosynthesis. Carbohydrates are used by animals as a source of energy. Cellulose, sugars, and starches are carbohydrates.

car·bo·lat·ed (kär′bə lā′tid) *adj.* containing or treated with carbolic acid, or phenol.

car·bol·ic acid (kär bol′ik) *n.* another term for **phenol.**

car·bon (kär′bən) *n.* **1.** a common nonmetallic element that occurs in crystalline forms, such as diamond and graphite, and in uncrystallized forms, such as charcoal. Carbon is essential to all forms of life. It is present in all organic compounds and in many inorganic compounds. Symbol: C **2.** a piece of carbon paper. **3.** see **carbon copy.** [From the French word *carbone* meaning this element, from the Latin word *carbo* "a coal, charcoal, ember."]

carbon 12, the most common isotope of carbon, now used instead of oxygen as the standard for determining the atomic weight of chemical elements.

carbon 14, a radioactive isotope of carbon, used in radiocarbon dating.

car·bo·na·ceous (kär′bə nā′shəs) *adj.* of, relating to, or containing carbon.

car·bon·ate (*n.*, kär′bə nāt′, kär′bə nit; *v.*, kär′bə nāt′) *n.* a salt or ester of carbonic acid. —*v.t.,* **car·bon·at·ed, car·bon·at·ing.** to charge or treat (a substance) with carbon dioxide, especially to dissolve carbon dioxide in (a liquid) to make it effervescent.

car·bon·a·tion (kär′bə nā′shən) *n.* treatment or saturation with carbon dioxide, especially in manufacturing soda water.

carbon copy 1. a copy, as of a letter, made by using carbon paper. **2.** a close or exact replica; duplicate: *This cabin is a carbon copy of the one next door.*

carbon dating, another term for **radiocarbon dating.**

carbon dioxide, a colorless, odorless gas, made up of carbon and oxygen, that is present in the atmosphere. It is used commercially in soft drinks, in fire extinguishers, and, in the form of dry ice, as a refrigerating agent. Carbon dioxide is exhaled by animals as a waste product and is absorbed by green plants as part of photosynthesis. Formula: CO_2

car·bon·ic (kär bon′ik) *adj.* of, containing, or obtained from carbon.

carbonic acid, a weak acid formed when carbon dioxide is dissolved in water.

Car·bon·if·er·ous (kär′bə nif′ər əs) *n.* the geological period of the Paleozoic era during which most of the coal-forming tropic forests flourished. —*adj.* **1.** of, relating to, or characteristic of this period. **2. carboniferous.** containing carbon or coal.

car·bon·ize (kär′bə nīz′) *v.t.,* **car·bon·ized, car·bon·iz·ing. 1.** to change (a substance) into carbon, as by burning. **2.** to cover, treat, or combine (something) with carbon. —**car′bon·i·za′tion,** *n.*

carbon monoxide, a colorless, odorless, very poisonous gas that is formed when carbon burns in an atmosphere not having enough oxygen for complete combustion. Carbon monoxide is found in the exhaust gases of automobiles. Formula: CO

carbon paper, a thin paper coated on one side with a preparation of carbon or another dark coloring substance.

Carbon paper is placed between two sheets of paper to reproduce on the lower sheet any marks made by pressure, as of writing or typing, on the top sheet.

carbon tet·ra·chlo·ride (tet′rə klôr′īd) a colorless, poisonous, nonflammable liquid made from carbon and chlorine. It is used in refrigerants and propellants, in fire extinguishers, and as a cleaning fluid.

Car·bo·run·dum (kär′bə run′dəm) *n. Trademark.* an abrasive made of silicon carbide, used in grinding and polishing.

car·bun·cle (kär′bung kəl) *n.* **1.** a hard, painful, pus-filled sore under the skin that resembles a boil, but is larger and more severe. Carbuncles are often accompanied by fever, headache, and loss of appetite. **2.** a smooth, deep red garnet or other jewel.

car·bu·re·tor (kär′bə rā′tər, kär′byə rā′tər) *also, British,* **car·bu·ret·tor** (kär′byə-ret′ər). *n.* a device in an internal-combustion engine that mixes a fine spray of gasoline with air to form a mixture that can be burned in the cylinders of the engine.

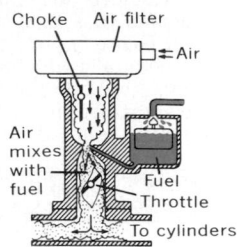
carburetor

car·cass (kär′kəs) *n., pl.* **car·cass·es. 1.** the dead body of an animal. **2.** *Informal.* the body of a human being. **3.** decaying or worthless remains, such as the ruined framework of a structure: *All that was left of the farm was the carcass of an old barn.*

car·cin·o·gen (kär sin′ə jən) *n.* any of various substances that are capable of causing or helping to cause cancer. —**car·cin·o·gen·ic** (kär′sə nə jen′ik) *adj.*

car·ci·no·ma (kär′sə nō′mə) *n., pl.* **car·ci·no·mas** or **car·ci·no·ma·ta** (kär′sə nō′mə tə). cancer, especially cancer arising in the cells that cover the inner and outer surfaces of the body. [From the Latin word *carcinoma* meaning "cancerous ulcer," from the Greek word *karkinōma* "cancerous ulcer," from the word *karkinos* "cancer."]

card¹ (kärd) *n.* **1.** a flat, usually rectangular piece of stiff paper or thin cardboard, used for any of various purposes, such as for identifying the owner of something: *a membership card.* **2.** one of a set of such cards, marked with pictures, numbers, or symbols, used in playing various games; playing card. **3. cards. a.** a game played with such cards, such as poker or bridge. **b.** the playing of such a game: *I usually lose at cards.* **4.** a piece of stiff paper or cardboard, usually decorated and bearing a message or greeting; greeting card: *a birthday card, a Christmas card.* **5.** see **postcard** (def. 1). **6.** *Informal.* an amusing or witty person. [From the Middle French word *carte* meaning "a piece of paper" or "playing card," going back to the Latin word *charta* "a piece of papyrus," from the Greek word *chartēs* "a piece of papyrus."]

·**in the cards.** likely to happen.

·**to put one's cards on the table** or **to lay one's cards on the table.** to be frank and open, as about one's intentions; be completely straightforward.

card² (kärd) *n.* a comb, brush, or similar device having metal or wire teeth, used to separate, comb, or straighten fibers, as of wool or cotton, before spinning. —*v.t.* to use a card on: *to card wool.* [From the Middle French word *carde* meaning this instrument, going back to the Latin word *carduus* "thistle."] —**card′er,** *n.*

car·da·mom (kär′də məm) *n.* **1.** the aromatic fruit of a plant used whole or ground as a spice in foods and beverages, as in curries and spicy wines. It is also used in medicines and for chewing. **2.** the plant bearing these fruits in a small, greenish brown capsule.

card·board (kärd′bôrd′) *n.* a thin pasteboard or other stiff material made of paper pulp. Cardboard is used to make such items as boxes and cards.

card catalog, an index of cards listing various types of information, especially an alphabetical file indicating the books and other items in a library's collection.

car·di·ac (kär′dē ak′) *adj.* of, relating to, or near the heart: *cardiac disease, a cardiac patient.*

car·di·gan (kär′di gən) *n.* a sweater that opens down the front and usually has no collar. [From the Earl of *Cardigan* (1797–1868), British army officer.]

car·di·nal (kär′də nəl) *n.* **1.** in the Roman Catholic Church, one of a number of high officials ranking immediately below the pope and appointed by him. When he dies, the cardinals meet to elect a new pope. **2.** a crested American songbird. The male cardinal has bright red feathers with a black patch around the bill. **3.** a deep, rich red color. —*adj.* **1.** of greatest importance; chief; principal. **2.** having the color cardinal; deep, rich red: *Cardinal leaves covered the hillsides in autumn.*

cardinal *(n., def. 2)*

cardinal flower **1.** the usually bright red flower of a plant that grows wild in damp regions of eastern and central North America. **2.** the plant bearing this flower.

cardinal number, a number that expresses how many, such as zero, one, two, three, and so forth.

▲ A **cardinal number** shows the number or total of something: *twelve boxes.* An **ordinal number** indicates the number that something is in a series: *the twelfth box.*

cardinal points, the four main directions of the compass; north, south, east, and west.

card·ing (kär′ding) *n.* the process of preparing textile fibers, such as wool, cotton, or flax, for spinning. During carding, the raw material is passed through rollers and brushes to clean, untangle, and straighten the fibers.

car·di·o·gram (kär′dē ə gram′) *n.* see **electrocardiogram.**

car·di·o·graph (kär′dē ə graf′) *n.* see **electrocardiograph.**

car·di·ol·o·gist (kär′dē ol′ə jist) *n.* a doctor who specializes in disorders and diseases of the heart.

car·di·ol·o·gy (kär′dē ol′ə jē) *n.* the study of the heart and its diseases.

car·di·o·pul·mo·nar·y resuscitation (kar′dē ō pul′- mə ner′ē) see **CPR.**

car·di·o·vas·cu·lar (kär′dē ō vas′kyə lər) *adj.* of or relating to the heart and the blood vessels: *the cardiovascular system.*

care (kâr) *n.* **1.** a troubled state of mind, such as that arising from anxiety, doubt, or concern; worry; distress. **2.** the cause of such a state of mind: *You act as though you didn't have a care in the world.* **3.** close and serious attention: *The scientist used great care in handling the chemical.* **4.** keeping or charge; supervision; custody: *The sick child was under a doctor's care.* —*v.,* **cared, car·ing.** —*v.i.* **1.** to have or show interest; be anxious

or concerned: *I care a great deal about the future of this business.* **2.** to have or feel a liking, fondness, or affection: *I don't care for spinach. They care very much about their grandparents.* **3.** to want or wish; like: *Would you care to go to the movies this evening?* **4.** to have an objection; mind: *Do you care if I borrow the book?* —*v.t.* to feel interest, concern, or distress about; pay attention to: *I don't care what people think.* —**car′er,** *n.*

·**in care of.** at the address of: *The letter was sent to me in care of my former roommate.*

·**to care for.** to look after or provide for; take care of.

·**to take care.** to be careful: *Take care crossing the street.*

·**to take care of. a.** to look after or provide for; tend: *A nurse took care of the patient.* **b.** to attend to; deal with; finish: *Take care of the most important tasks first.*

ca·reen (kə rēn′) *v.i.* **1.** to sway from side to side while moving quickly; lurch: *The speeding car careened around the corner.* **2.** to lean to one side: *The ship careened as its sails caught the wind.* —*v.t.* to turn (a ship) over on its side in order to clean or repair the bottom.

ca·reer (kə rir′) *n.* **1.** an occupation or profession: *to choose acting as a career.* **2.** the course or progress of a person's life: *I've met many interesting people in my career.* **3.** a swift or rushing movement or course; speed: *The horse galloped across the field in full career.* —*v.i.* to move or run with a swift, headlong motion: *The train careered down the tracks.*

care·free (kâr′frē′) *adj.* free from care or worry; untroubled; lighthearted: *We spent a carefree day in the country.*

care·ful (kâr′fəl) *adj.* **1.** showing caution and close attention; watchful; cautious: *Be careful not to trip on that last step. I was careful not to say anything about the surprise party.* **2.** done or made with great care or thoroughness; painstaking: *careful research.* **3.** taking pains with or being attentive to one's work: *Careful writers check their spelling.* —**care′ful·ly,** *adv.* —**care′ful·ness,** *n.*

care·less (kâr′lis) *adj.* **1.** not paying enough attention; not cautious or watchful; negligent: *The careless guest spilled the soup.* **2.** caused by or done with a lack of care, attentiveness, or thoughtfulness: *Copying the address wrong was a careless mistake.* **3.** free from care or worry; carefree: *a simple and careless life.* —**care′less·ly,** *adv.* —**care′less·ness,** *n.*

ca·ress (kə res′) *v.t.* to touch or stroke gently and lovingly; pet: *The child caressed the new puppy.* —*n., pl.* **1.** a gentle, loving touch or stroke. **2.** a light, soothing touch: *the soft caress of a summer breeze.*

car·et (kar′it) *n.* a mark (‸) used in editing to indicate where something should be inserted.

care·tak·er (kâr′tā′kər) *n.* a person who takes care of a person, place, or thing, especially the custodian of a building or estate.

care·worn (kâr′wôrn′) *adj.* showing the effects of worry or distress: *The beggar's face was wrinkled and careworn.*

car·fare (kär′fâr′) *n.* the amount a passenger must pay to ride on a bus, subway, or the like.

car·go (kär′gō) *n., pl.* **car·goes** or **car·gos.** the goods or merchandise carried by a ship, plane, or vehicle: *The freighter carried a cargo of rice.*

car·hop (kär′hop′) *n.* a person who waits on customers at a drive-in restaurant.

Car·ib (kar'ib) *n.* **1.** a member of one of several Indian tribes in the West Indies and northeastern South America. **2.** the family of South American Indian languages spoken chiefly in the West Indies and northeastern parts of South America.

Words From Other Languages

The Carib languages are native to the West Indies and northeastern South America and were spoken there when Columbus arrived.

barbecue	food roasted over an open fire
cannibal	a person who eats human flesh
canoe	a narrow, lightweight boat
hammock	a bed made from a piece of cloth or netting hung from both ends
hurricane	a violent, windy rainstorm
maize	corn that is used as food
mangrove	a kind of tropical evergreen tree
potato	a starchy vegetable from a tuber
tobacco	a plant whose leaves are made into cigars, cigarettes, and snuff

car·i·bou (kar'ə bü') *n., pl.* **car·i·bou** or **car·i·bous.** any of a group of large deer that live in the northern regions of the world, having a heavy coat and large antlers.

car·i·ca·ture (kar'i kə chùr') *n.* **1.** a picture or description that ridiculously exaggerates or distorts the characteristics, peculiarities, or striking features of a person or thing. **2.** the art or process of making such pictures or descriptions. —*v.t.,* **car·i·ca·tured, car·i·ca·tur·ing.** to make a caricature of.

car·i·ca·tur·ist (kar'i kə chùr'ist) *n.* a person who makes caricatures.

car·ies (kâr'ēz) *n.* decay of the teeth, often resulting in a cavity. ▲ used with a singular verb.

car·il·lon (kar'ə lon') *n.* a set of bells usually played by means of a keyboard.

car·load (kär'lōd') *n.* the amount that a car can hold.

Car·mel·ite (kär'mə līt') *n.* a member of a religious order of friars and nuns founded in the twelfth century. —*adj.* of or relating to the Carmelites or their order.

car·mine (kär'mən, kär'mīn) *n.* **1.** a deep red or purplish red color; crimson. **2.** the crimson pigment obtained from the dye cochineal. —*adj.* having the color carmine; deep red or purplish red.

car·nage (kär'nij) a great and bloody slaughter, as in battle: *The war caused terrible carnage.*

car·nal (kär'nəl) *adj.* **1.** relating to the passions and appetites of the body; fleshly; sensual: *carnal pleasures.* **2.** not spiritual; worldly. —**car'nal·ly,** *adv.*

car·na·tion (kär nā'shən) *n.* **1.** a fragrant, usually red, white, or pink flower, grown commercially and as a garden flower. **2.** the plant bearing this flower, having grayish green leaves that look like grass. **3.** a light red color. —*adj.* having the color carnation; light red.

car·nel·ian (kär nēl'yən) *n.* a semiprecious stone that is red to reddish orange in color.

car·ni·val (kär'nə vəl) *n.* **1.** a public amusement show, usually one that travels, having rides, sideshows, games, and refreshments. **2.** any merrymaking or festival, such as an organized program of entertainment or sports. **3.** *also,* **Carnival.** the period of feasting and merrymaking that comes just before Lent.

carnation
(def. 1)

car·ni·vore (kär'nə vôr') *n.* **1.** an animal or plant that feeds chiefly on flesh. Sharks, eagles, dogs, and Venus's-flytraps are carnivores. **2.** any of a group of flesh-eating mammals having long, sharp teeth, such as dogs, seals, and lions.

car·niv·o·rous (kär niv'ər əs) *adj.* feeding chiefly on flesh; flesh-eating: *Flytraps are carnivorous plants.* —**car·niv'o·rous·ly,** *adv.* —**car·niv'o·rous·ness,** *n.*

car·ob (kar'əb) *n.* an evergreen tree native to the eastern Mediterranean but cultivated in many warm regions for the sweet pulp contained in its pods.

car·ol (kar'əl) *n.* a song of joy or praise, especially a Christmas song or hymn. —*v.,* **car·oled, car·ol·ing;** *also,* British, **car·olled, car·ol·ling.** —*v.i.* to sing joyously, especially to sing Christmas carols: *We carol every Christmas Eve.* —*v.t.* to sing (a song, carol, or the like) joyously. —**car'ol·er;** *also,* British, **car'ol·ler,** *n.*

car·om (kar'əm) *also,* **car·rom.** *n.* **1.** the act of striking and rebounding. **2.** in various sports and games, a bounce off a wall. —*v.i.* to strike and rebound: *The baseball caromed off the wall.*

car·o·tene (kar'ə tēn') *n.* an orange or yellow substance found in egg yolks, butter, and certain vegetables such as carrots. It is used by the liver to manufacture vitamin A.

ca·rot·id (kə rot'id) *n.* either of two large arteries located on each side of the neck which carry blood to the head. Also, **carotid artery.** —*adj.* of, relating to, or near these arteries.

ca·rous·al (kə rou'zəl) *n.* a noisy, jovial drinking party.

ca·rouse (kə rouz') *v.i.,* **ca·roused, ca·rous·ing.** to drink freely and heavily, especially at a party; take part in a carousal. —*n.* a carousal. —**ca·rous'er,** *n.*

car·ou·sel (kar'ə sel') *also,* **car·rou·sel.** *n.* see **merry-go-round** *(def.1).*

carp[1] (kärp) *v.i.* to find fault or complain, especially unreasonably or repeatedly: *The boss carps at every small error.* [From the Old Norse word *karpa* meaning "to brag."]

carp[2] (kärp) *n., pl.* **carp** or **carps.** a large freshwater fish used as food. [From the Middle French word *carpe* meaning this fish, from the Late Latin word *carpa* "carp[2]," probably of Germanic origin.]

car·pal (kär'pəl) *adj.* of, relating to, or near the wrist. —*n.* a bone of the wrist. See **hand** for illustration.

car·pel (kär'pəl) *n.* the pistil of a flower, or one unit of a compound pistil.

car·pen·ter (kär'pən tər) *n.* a person who builds and repairs wooden structures and parts, as of houses.

car·pen·try (kär'pən trē) *n.* the business, trade, or work of a carpenter.

car·pet (kär'pit) *n.* **1.** a floor covering made of heavy, often woven fabric. **2.** the fabric used for such covering. **3.** any covering or surface resembling a carpet: *a carpet of snow.* —*v.t.* to cover or furnish with a carpet.
   •**on the carpet.** before an authority for a scolding or reprimand: *The supervisor called the employee on the carpet for doing poor work.*

car·pet·bag (kär'pit bag') *n.* a satchel or traveling bag, especially one made of carpeting.

car·pet·bag·ger (kär'pit bag'ər) *n.* a Northerner who went to the South after the Civil War, especially one who tried to gain political or other advantages from the disorganized situation in the Southern states. [Many of these people went South carrying all their belongings in a *carpetbag.*]

car·pet·ing (kär'pi ting) *n.* **1.** the fabric used for carpets. **2.** a carpet or carpets: *wall-to-wall carpeting.*

car pool **1.** an arrangement among a group of car owners in which each member of the group takes a turn driving the others or their children, as to and from work or school. **2.** the people belonging to such a group.

car·port (kär'pôrt') *n.* a shelter for an automobile, usually a roof projecting from the side of a building.

car·pus (kär′pəs) *n., pl.* **car·pi** (kär′pī). the wrist, or the group of bones that make up the wrist.

car·riage (kar′ij) *n.* **1.** a wheeled vehicle for transporting people, usually drawn by a horse or horses. **2.** a light, wheeled vehicle for a baby, designed to be pushed by a person on foot. **3.** a manner of carrying or holding the head and body: *The conductor had a stately carriage.* **4.** a movable part of a machine that supports or carries some other part: *the carriage of a typewriter.* **5.** a wheeled support for a gun or cannon. **6.** the act of carrying or transporting. **7.** the cost or price of transportation.

car·ri·er (kar′ē ər) *n.* **1.** a person or organization whose business it is to carry or transport something. Railroads, trucking companies, and shipping lines are carriers. **2.** a commercial or military vehicle used to carry or transport something: *a troop carrier.* **3.** a medium or device by which something is carried: *the blood serves as a carrier of oxygen to the cells.* **4.** any living thing that carries or transmits an infectious disease. A carrier may be immune to the disease transmitted. **5.** a person who has a gene for a disease or trait that can be passed on to offspring even though the person does not suffer from the disease or exhibit the trait. **6.** see **carrier wave. 7.** see **aircraft carrier.**

carrier pigeon, a homing pigeon used to carry messages.

carrier wave, an electromagnetic wave that can be modulated and carries signals to be transmitted, as through a radio system.

car·ri·on (kar′ē ən) *n.* dead and decaying flesh.

car·rom (kar′əm) another spelling of **carom.**

car·rot (kar′ət) *n.* **1.** the fleshy, orange-colored root of a plant related to parsley, eaten as a vegetable. **2.** the plant bearing this root.

car·rou·sel (kar′ə sel′) another spelling of **carousel.**

car·ry (kar′ē) *v.,* **car·ried, car·ry·ing.** —*v.t.* **1.** to bear or hold while moving, especially in order to transport or convey: *Carry the suitcase upstairs.* **2.** to act or serve as a means of conveying or transmitting: *This pipe carries oil. Air carries sound waves. Some insects carry diseases.* **3.** to have on one's person: *I always carry a pen.* **4.** to have as a characteristic, property, or consequence: *The senator's opinion carried great weight in Congress.* **5.** to bear the weight of; sustain: *to carry the heavy burden of responsibility.* **6.** to extend or continue: *You carried your teasing too far.* **7.** to keep in stock for sale; deal in: *That store carries household supplies.* **8.** to pass or adopt (a motion or bill): *The motion was carried by a wide margin.* **9.** to be successful or victorious in; win or capture: *Our candidate carried the county.* **10.** to transfer and add, as a number or total from one column or page to another. **11.** to cause to go or come: *The hurricane carried the ship off course.* **12.** to sing (a melody or part) correctly: *I can't carry a tune.* **13.** to hold (one's body or part of it) in a certain way: *The young deer carried itself gracefully.* —*v.i.* **1.** to go or travel for a distance: *The arrow carried for thirty yards. The singer's voice carries to the back of the theater.* **2.** to be approved by vote: *The proposed bill carried by a large majority.* **3.** to act as a bearer or carrier. —*n., pl.* **car·ries. 1.** the range or distance covered or traveled by something, such as a gun or projectile. **2.** a portage between two bodies of water. **3.** the act of carrying: *The halfback gained sixty yards in ten carries.*

·**to carry away.** to arouse strong feeling in: *The audience was carried away by the musician's performance.*

·**to carry off. a.** to win, as a prize or honor. **b.** to complete successfully; accomplish: *to carry off a plan.* **c.** to cause the death of; kill.

·**to carry on. a.** to keep going; continue: *After the interruption we carried on with our work.* **b.** to engage in; conduct: *to carry on a debate.* **c.** *Informal.* to behave in a wild, foolish, or silly manner.

·**to carry out. a.** to obey; follow: *The soldier carried out orders promptly.* **b.** to bring to completion; accomplish: *to carry out a plan.*

car·ry·all[1] (kar′ē ôl′) *n.* a lightweight, covered, one-horse carriage for several persons. [From the French word *carriole* meaning this type of carriage, going back to the Latin word *carrus* meaning a kind of wagon.]

car·ry·all[2] (kar′ē ôl′) *n.* a large bag, basket, or handbag. [*Carry + all.*]

car·ry·on (kar′ē ôn′, kar′ē on′) *adj.* small enough for a passenger to carry aboard an airplane and store beneath a seat or in an overhead compartment: *carry-on luggage.* —*n.* a suitcase or other piece of luggage this small.

car·ry·out (kar′ē out′) *adj.* another word for **take-out.**

car·ry·o·ver (kar′ē ō′vər) *n.* something retained or remaining: *My interest in model trains is a carry-over from childhood.*

car·sick (kär′sik′) *adj.* nauseated from riding in a car, bus, or other vehicle. —**car′sick′ness,** *n.*

cart (kärt) *n.* **1.** a sturdy, two-wheeled vehicle for carrying heavy loads, usually drawn by horses or mules. **2.** a small, wheeled vehicle moved by hand; pushcart. **3.** a light, two-wheeled carriage. —*v.t.* to carry in a cart.

cart·age (kär′tij) *n.* **1.** the act of carting or transporting. **2.** the rate charged for this.

carte blanche (kärt′ blänch′) *pl.* **cartes blanches** (kärts′ blänch′). the complete authority or freedom to act as one wishes or thinks best. [From the French phrase *carte blanche* meaning ''a blank card'' (to be filled in as someone wishes).]

car·tel (kär tel′) *n.* a group of companies or businesses, formed to establish a monopoly by controlling prices and production.

Car·te·sian coordinate system (kär tē′zhən) *Mathematics.* a system of coordinates that locates a point in a plane by its distance from each of two perpendicular lines at right angles to each other.

Car·tha·gin·i·an (kär′thə jin′ē ən) *adj.* of or relating to Carthage, its people, or its civilization. —*n.* a person who lived in Carthage.

Car·thu·sian (kär thü′zhən) *n.* a member of a religious order of monks and nuns, founded in France in 1084.

car·ti·lage (kär′tə lij) *n.* **1.** the tough, flexible connective tissue in the skeleton of humans and other animals with backbones; gristle. **2.** a part or structure formed of cartilage.

car·ti·lag·i·nous (kär′tə laj′ə nəs) *adj.* **1.** of or resembling cartilage. **2.** having a skeleton consisting mostly of cartilage, as the shark or manta.

car·tog·ra·pher (kär tog′rə fər) *n.* a person who makes maps or charts.

car·tog·ra·phy (kär tog′rə fē) *n.* the art of science of making maps or charts.

car·ton (kär′tən) *n.* **1.** a container made of any of various materials, such as cardboard, wood, or plastic: *an egg carton, a milk carton.* **2.** the amount that a carton holds.

car·toon (kär tün′) *n.* **1.** a sketch or drawing, as in a magazine or newspaper, that shows an amusing situation, makes fun of some person or subject, or illustrates an opinion. **2.** see **animated cartoon. 3.** see **comic strip. 4.** the preliminary drawing of a design or picture, to be copied in a mosaic, tapestry, mural painting, or the like.

car·toon·ist (kär tü′nist) *n.* a person who draws cartoons, especially one who draws cartoons as a profession.

---

at; āpe; fär; câre; end; mē; it; īce; pîerce; hot; ōld; sông, fôrk; oil; out; up; ūse; rüle; püll; tûrn; chin; sing; shop; thin; this; hw in white; zh in treasure. The symbol ə stands for the unstressed vowel sound heard in about, taken, pencil, lemon, and circus.

car·tridge (kär′trij) *n.* **1.** a cylindrical case, usually made of metal or cardboard and containing a percussion cap, a propelling charge of gunpowder, and a bullet. **2.** a roll of camera film enclosed in a protective case that fits into a camera as a unit. **3.** a device that holds a phonograph needle and transforms its vibrations into an electric current as the needle

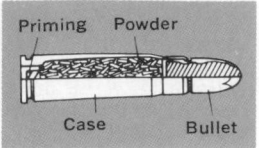

cartridge (def. 1)

follows the groove of a record. **4.** another word for **cassette** *(def. 2).* **5.** a small container designed for easy replacement as a unit: *an ink cartridge for a pen.* **6.** a small case that holds the electronic circuits that make up a computer program or video game.

cart·wheel (kärt′hwēl′, kärt′wēl′) *n.* **1.** the wheel of a cart. **2.** a sideways handspring in which the weight is put first on one hand and then on the other.

carve (kärv) *v.,* **carved, carv·ing.** —*v.t.* **1.** to cut (meat) into slices or pieces: *to carve a turkey.* **2.** to make or shape by or as if by cutting (often with *out*): *to carve a doll from a block of wood. The pioneers carved a new town out of the wilderness.* **3.** to decorate by cutting figures or designs: *The old chest was carved with many strange designs.* —*v.i.* to cut meat into slices or pieces. —**carv′er,** *n.*

carv·ing (kär′ving) *n.* **1.** a carved work, such as a figure or design: *a wood carving of a dog.* **2.** the act or art of a person who carves.

carving knife, a knife used for carving, especially one used for carving meat.

car·y·at·id (kar′ē at′id) *n., pl.* **car·y·at·ids** or **car·y·at·i·des** (kar′ē at′i dēz′). a statue of a draped female figure, serving as a column.

ca·sa·ba (kə sä′bə) *also,* **cas·sa·ba.** *n.* a melon having a creamy white pulp and a wrinkled rind.

cas·cade (kas kād′) *n.* **1.** a small waterfall or a series of small waterfalls. **2.** anything resembling this: *a cascade of ruffles down the front of a blouse.* —*v.i.* **cas·cad·ed, cas·cad·ing.** to fall or flow in a cascade: *Water cascaded over the rocks. Long vines cascaded down over the branches.*

cas·car·a (kas kâr′ə) *n.* **1.** a North American tree having reddish brown bark. **2.** a laxative made from dried strips of bark of this tree.

case¹ (kās) *n.* **1.** a specific example or occurrence; instance: *The fire was an obvious case of carelessness.* **2.** the ac-

cascade (def. 1)

tual state of affairs or circumstances: *If that's the case, there is nothing we can do.* **3.** an instance of a disease or injury: *a case of the flu.* **4.** a person who has a disease or injury; patient. **5.** a statement or presentation, as of arguments or reasons: *The senator made a case for the proposed law.* **6.** a matter or problem, especially one

under investigation: *The police were baffled by the case of the stolen painting.* **7. a.** an action or suit brought before a court of law for decision: *The judge found it difficult to rule on the case.* **b.** a statement of facts or circumstances presented for consideration in a court of law: *The attorney stated the case simply.* **8.** *Grammar.* one of the various forms of a noun, pronoun, or adjective, used to show its relation to other words in a sentence by means of its ending or its position in the sentence. [From the Old French word *cas* meaning "occurrence, event" or "circumstances," from the Latin word *casus* "chance" or "fall," going back to the Latin word *cadere* "to fall."]

 ·in any case. no matter what happens; anyhow; regardless.

 ·in case. in the event that; if: *In case anything happens, call me immediately.*

 ·in case of. in the event of: *In case of rain, we'll go to the movies instead of playing baseball.*

case² (kās) *n.* **1.** something designed to contain, enclose, or protect; box or other container: *The camera comes with a leather case.* **2.** the amount that a case can hold: *We ordered three cases of detergent.* **3.** *Printing.* a shallow tray divided into compartments, used for holding type. —*v.t.,* **cased, cas·ing.** **1.** to put in or cover with a case; encase. **2.** *Informal.* to look over carefully, especially with criminal intent: *The thieves cased the building before breaking in.* [From the Norman French word *casse* meaning "a box, container," from the Latin word *capsa* "box, chest."]

case history, a collection of facts about a person, group, or thing, gathered for the purpose of studying or dealing with some physical, mental, or social condition.

ca·sein (kā′sēn) *n.* the main protein present in milk, and the chief ingredient of cheese. Casein is also used in the manufacture of paints, plastics, fabrics, and adhesives.

case·ment (kās′mənt) *n.* **1.** the frame of a window that opens on hinges. **2.** a window having such a frame.

case·work (kās′wûrk′) *n.* the work done by a caseworker.

case·work·er (kās′wûr′kər) *n.* a social worker who is assigned to interview and give guidance and advice to an individual or family with social, psychological, or economic problems.

cash (kash) *n.* **1.** money in the form of coins or bills. **2.** money or its equivalent, such as a check, paid at the time of buying something: *Instead of charging the suit, I paid cash.* —*v.t.* to give or get cash for: *to cash a check.*

 ·to cash in on. *Informal.* to use to one's advantage; take advantage of: *The explorers cashed in on their fame by writing a book.*

cash crop, a crop grown for sale in a market rather than for use on a farm. Cotton is a cash crop.

cash·ew (kash′ü) *n.* **1.** a kidney-shaped nut that can be eaten. **2.** the tropical evergreen tree bearing this nut.

cash·ier¹ (ka shîr′) *n.* a person who is in charge of taking in and paying out money, as in a bank or business. [From the French word *caissier* meaning "someone in charge of money," from the word *caisse* "money box," going back to the Latin word *capsa* "box, chest."]

cash·ier² (ka shîr′) *v.t.* to dismiss from service in disgrace: *The officer was cashiered for cowardice.* [From the Dutch word *casseren* meaning "to discharge, dismiss," from the Middle French word *casser* "to dismiss" or "to break," going back to the Latin word *quatere* "to shake."]

cashier's check, a check drawn by a bank on its own funds and signed by its cashier.

cash machine, another term for **automated teller machine.**

cash·mere (kazh′mîr, kash′mîr) *n.* **1.** a fine, soft wool from the silky hair of a breed of goats of Kashmir. It is used to make coats, suits, and sweaters. **2.** a rare and expensive cloth made from this hair. —*adj.* made from cashmere: *a cashmere sweater.* [Another form of *Kash-*

mir, the area on the India-Pakistan border where this fabric was originally made.]

cash on delivery, immediate payment in cash upon delivery of merchandise.

cash register, a machine that automatically shows and records the amount of a sale, usually having a drawer for money.

cas·ing (kā′sing) *n.* **1.** something that covers, encloses, or protects, such as the outer covering of an automobile tire. **2.** a frame, especially of a door or window.

ca·si·no (kə sē′no) *n., pl.* **ca·si·nos. 1.** a building or room for public entertainment, especially for gambling. **2.** *also,* **cassino.** a card game for two, three, or four persons in which the player with the most points for cards taken is the winner.

cask (kask) *n.* **1.** a large wooden barrel, usually used to hold liquids. **2.** the amount contained in a cask.

cas·ket (kas′kit) *n.* **1.** a box of wood or metal, in which a dead body is placed for burial; coffin. **2.** a small box or chest, as for jewels.

casque (kask) *n.* a medieval helmet.

cas·sa·ba (kə sä′bə) another spelling of **casaba.**

Cas·san·dra (kə san′drə) *n. Greek Legend.* a daughter of King Priam of Troy. Apollo, who was in love with her, gave her the gift of prophecy. When she refused to love him in return, he decreed that no one should believe her prophecies. Her warnings against the Trojan Horse were ignored.

cas·sa·va (kə sä′və) *n.* **1.** a bushy shrub widely grown in tropical regions for its roots, which can be eaten. **2.** a nutritious starch obtained from these roots, from which tapioca and bread are made. Also, **manioc.**

cas·se·role (kas′ə rōl′) *n.* **1.** a deep baking dish, often of glass or earthenware, in which food can be cooked and served. **2.** any food prepared and served in a casserole.

cas·sette (kə set′) *n.* **1.** another word for **cartridge** (def. 2). **2.** a small case designed to hold magnetic tape for easy insertion into a tape recorder or player.

cas·sia (kash′ə, kas′ē ə) *n.* **1.** the bark of an Asian tree, used as a substitute for cinnamon. **2.** the tree bearing this bark, having glossy, oblong leaves.

cas·si·no (kə sē′nō) another spelling of **casino** (def. 2).

Cas·si·o·pe·ia (kas′e ə pē′ə) *n.* **1.** *Greek Legend.* the mother of Andromeda. **2.** a constellation in the northern sky, thought to resemble the seated figure of Cassiopeia.

cas·sock (kas′ək) *n.* an ankle-length garment worn by the clergy in the Roman Catholic and certain other churches. In the Roman Catholic Church the cassocks of priests are black, those of bishops violet, those of cardinals red, and that of the pope white.

cas·so·war·y (kas′ə wer′ē) *n., pl.* **cas·so·war·ies.** any of several large birds of Australia and New Guinea that cannot fly. Cassowaries resemble ostriches and have long legs, a featherless head and neck, and a bony crest.

cast (kast) *v.,* **cast, casting.** —*v.t.* **1.** to throw through the air; hurl; fling: *I cast a handful of pebbles into the lake.* **2.** to cause to fall upon: *The statue cast a long shadow on the ground.* **3.** to direct or turn: *The teacher cast a glance in my direction.* **4.** to deposit or register: *to cast a vote.*
5.a. to assign the parts of (a play, motion picture, or the like) to the actors: *to cast a new movie.* **b.** to select (an actor) for a particular part: *The director cast me in the leading role.* **6.a.** to shape (a substance) by pouring it into a mold to harden. **b.** to make (something) by this process: *to cast a statue.* **7.** to throw off; shed: *The snake cast its skin.* —*v.i.* **1.** to throw something, especially a fishing line. **2.** to take shape in a mold.—*n.* **1.** the act or manner of throwing. **2.** the distance a thing is thrown.

cassock

3. something that is formed or shaped in a mold. **4.** the actors in a play, motion picture, or the like: *The cast is composed entirely of children.* **5.** a stiff, molded form, usually made of gauze soaked in plaster of Paris, used to keep a broken bone or badly sprained joint motionless while it heals. **6.** an impression formed by molding; mold: *a cast of a dinosaur's footprints.* **7.** a tinge of color: *The sky had a bluish cast.* **8.** the form, appearance, or shape of something, such as physical features: *The officer's face had a stern cast.* **9.** a twist or turn to one side; squint: *to have a cast in one eye.*
•**to cast about for.** to search for; look for: *We cast about for an explanation of the mystery.*
•**to cast aside.** to discard, dismiss, or ignore: *The daring pilot cast caution aside.*
•**to cast off.** to let loose; release: *The crew cast off the boat from its moorings.*

cas·ta·net (kas′tə net′) *n.* one of a pair of small, shell-shaped pieces, usually made of wood or ivory. Castanets are held in the hand and clicked together rhythmically, and are used especially as an accompaniment to certain Spanish music and dancing. [From the Spanish word *castañeta* meaning "castanet," from the word *castaña* "chestnut," going back to the Greek word *kastanea* "chestnut, chestnut tree."]

cast·a·way (kast′ə wā′) *n.* **1.** a person who is shipwrecked or set adrift at sea. **2.** an outcast. —*adj.* **1.** shipwrecked or set adrift at sea. **2.** thrown away; discarded.

caste (kast) *n.* **1.** one of the hereditary social classes into which Hindus are traditionally divided. **2.** any social system or set of principles that divides a society into classes on the basis of birth, wealth, rank, or religion. **3.** an exclusive social or professional group.
•**to lose caste.** to lose one's position or rank, as in society.

cas·tel·lat·ed (kas′tə la′tid) *adj.* having turrets and battlements like those of a castle.

cast·er (kas′tər) *n.* **1.** a person or thing that casts. **2.** *also,* **castor.** one of a set of wheels or rollers placed or fitted under a piece of furniture or other large, heavy object to make it easier to move. **3.** *also,* **castor. a.** a bottle for holding salt, mustard, vinegar, or the like; cruet. **b.** a stand for such bottles.

cas·ti·gate (kas′ti gāt′) *v.t.,* **cas·ti·gat·ed, cas·ti·gat·ing.** to criticize severely; rebuke; punish. —**cas′ti·ga′tion,** *n.* —**cas′ti·ga′tor,** *n.*

Cas·tile soap (kas tēl′) a fine, hard soap made with olive oil.

Cas·til·ian (kas til′yən) *adj.* of or relating to Castile, its people, or their language. —*n.* **1.** the standard European form of the Spanish language, based on the dialect of Castile. **2.** a person who was born or is living in Castile.

cast·ing (kas′ting) *n.* **1.** something that is shaped in a mold; cast. **2.** the act or process of a person or thing that casts: *The casting for the play has been completed. Casting in bronze is an ancient art.*

cast–i·ron (kast′ī′ərn) *adj.* **1.** made of cast iron. **2.** unyielding; inflexible: *cast-iron rules.* **3.** hardy; strong: *You have to have a cast-iron stomach to eat such spicy food.*

cast iron, a hard, brittle form of iron that contains a large amount of carbon and is shaped by casting.

---

at; āpe; fär; câre; end; mē; it; īce; pîerce; hot; ōld; sông; fôrk; oil; out; up; ūse; rüle; pull; tûrn; chin; sing; shop; thin; this; hw in white; zh in treasure. The symbol ə stands for the unstressed vowel sound heard in about, taken, pencil, lemon, and circus.

castle *(def. 1)*

cas·tle (kas′əl) *n.* **1.** a large fortified building or group of buildings serving as a stronghold or residence, as of a medieval prince or noble. **2.** any large, imposing house. **3.** *Chess.* another word for **rook²**. —*v.t., v.i.,* **cas·tled, cas·tling.** *Chess.* to move (the king) two squares to the left or right and move the rook to the square passed over by the king.
· **castle in the air.** something that is wished for but is not likely to happen; daydream.

cast·off (kast′ôf′) *adj.* discarded or abandoned; thrown away: *The charity collected castoff clothing to give to poor families.* —*n.* a person or thing that has been discarded or abandoned.

cas·tor¹ (kas′tər) another spelling of **caster** *(defs. 2 and 3).*

cas·tor² (kas′tər) *n.* an oily, strong-smelling substance produced by certain glands in beavers, used in making perfume. [From the Latin word *castor* meaning "beaver," from the Greek word *kastōr* "beaver."]

Cas·tor and Pol·lux (kas′tər; pol′əks) *Greek and Roman Mythology.* the twin brothers usually regarded as sons of Leda and Zeus. Castor was traditionally thought to be mortal, and Pollux immortal.

castor bean, the oval bean of the castor-oil plant.

castor oil, a pale yellow or colorless oil obtained from castor beans, used as a strong laxative, as a lubricant, and in the preparation of such products as paints and soaps.

cas·tor–oil plant (kas′tər oil′) a wide-leaved tropical plant whose beans yield castor oil.

cas·trate (kas′trāt) *v.t.,* **cas·trat·ed, cas·trat·ing.** to remove the testicles of; emasculate. —**cas·tra′tion,** *n.*

cas·u·al (kazh′ü əl) *adj.* **1.** without serious intention or thought; offhand: *a casual remark.* **2.** happening by chance; unexpected; accidental: *a casual meeting.* **3.** designed for informal wear: *We wore casual clothes to the party.* **4.** unconcerned or indifferent; nonchalant: *a casual attitude toward work.* **5.** temporary or irregular: *The farmer hired casual labor to help pick the crops.* —**cas′u·al·ly,** *adv.* —**cas′u·al·ness,** *n.*

cas·u·al·ty (kazh′ü əl tē) *n., pl.* **cas·u·al·ties. 1.** a per-

son who has been wounded, killed, captured, or is missing in combat. **2.** a person who is injured or killed in an accident. **3.** an accident, especially one involving a death. **4.** something that is damaged or destroyed by fighting, an accident, or the like: *the big tree was the first casualty in the hurricane.*

cas·u·ist (kazh′ü ist) *n.* a person who reasons cleverly but falsely.

cas·u·ist·ry (kazh′ü ə strē) *n., pl.* **cas·u·ist·ries.** clever but false or misleading reasoning; sophistry.

cat (kat) *n.* **1.** a small, furry animal commonly kept as a pet or for catching mice and rats. **2.** any of a group of animals of the same family as the domestic cat, such as the lion, tiger, or leopard; feline. —*adj.* of, relating to, or for a cat or cats: *cat food, the cat family.*
·**to let the cat out of the bag.** to reveal a secret: *My cousin let the cat out of the bag by telling everyone about the surprise anniversary celebration we had planned for our grandparents.*

ca·tab·o·lism (kə tab′ə liz′əm) *n.* the phase of metabolism in which complex substances such as digested food and stored fat are broken down into simpler substances and release energy.

cat·a·clysm (kat′ə kliz′əm) *n.* **1.** a violent and sudden change in the ordinary processes of nature, such as a flood or earthquake. **2.** any violent change or sudden upheaval, such as a revolution or war. —**cat′a·clys′mic,** *adj.*

cat·a·combs (kat′ə kōmz′) *pl. n.* an underground cemetery made up of rooms and passages with recesses in the walls for tombs.

Cat·a·lan (kat′ə lan′, kat′ə lan′) *n.* **1.** a person who was born in or is a citizen of Catalonia. **2.** a Romance language of Catalonia, Valencia, Andorra, the Balearic Islands, and some parts of southern France. —*adj.* of or relating to Catalonia, its people, or their language.

cat·a·log (kat′ə lôg′, kat′ə log′) *also,* **cat·a·logue.** *n.* **1.** a list of books, names, subjects, or other items, often in alphabetical order, that identifies and often describes each item. **2.** a publication containing such a list: *The store sent us a catalog of furniture.* —*v.t.* to make a catalog of; enter in a catalog: *to catalog the paintings in a museum.* —**cat′a log′er,** *n.*

cat·a·logue (kat′ə lôg′, kat′ə log′) *n., v.t.,* **cat·a·logued, cat·a·logu·ing.** another spelling of **catalog.** —**cat′a·logu′er,** *n.*

ca·tal·pa (kə tal′pə) *n.* **1.** a tree found in North America and Asia, having large, heart-shaped leaves, white, pink, or yellow flowers, and pods that resemble beans. It is planted as a shade tree. **2.** the coarse-grained, durable wood of this tree.

ca·tal·y·sis (kə tal′ə sis) *n., pl.* **ca·tal·y·ses** (kə tal′ə sēz′). the speeding up of a chemical reaction by the presence of a substance that undergoes no permanent chemical change itself.

cat·a·lyst (kat′ə list) *n.* **1.** a substance that causes the speeding up of a chemical reaction while remaining chemically unchanged itself. **2.** a person or thing that brings about or hastens a change: *The students' protests were a catalyst for reform.*

cat·a·lyt·ic (kat′ə lit′ik) *adj.* relating to catalysis.

catalytic converter, a device on a motor vehicle that converts harmful carbon monoxide and hydrocarbons in the exhaust gases of an internal-combustion engine into carbon dioxide and water vapor.

cat·a·ma·ran (kat′ə mə ran′) *n.* **1.** a sailboat or other boat having two hulls connected side by side by poles or by a platform that serves as a deck. **2.** a raft made of logs lashed together in the shape of a boat hull.

cat·a·mount (kat′ə mount′) *n.* any of several wild animals of the cat family, such as the cougar.

cat·a·pult (kat′ə pult′) *n.* **1.** an ancient military weapon used to shoot or hurl stones, arrows, or other projectiles. **2.** a device for launching an airplane from the deck of a ship. **3.** *British.* another word for **slingshot.** —*v.t.* to hurl or shoot (something) from a catapult. —*v.i.* to move quickly or suddenly; leap; spring: *At the sound of the explosion we catapulted out of our chairs.*

cat·a·ract (kat′ə rakt′) *n.* **1.** a high, steep waterfall. **2. cataracts.** steep rapids in a river. **3.** a violent flood or downpour of water. **4.** a clouding of the lens of the eye, resulting in partial or total blindness.

ca·tarrh (kə tär′) *n.* an inflammation of a mucous membrane, especially that of the nose or throat, causing excessive production of mucus. —**ca·tarrh′al,** *adj.*

ca·tas·tro·phe (kə tas′trə fē′) *n.* a great and sudden disaster or misfortune: *The plane crash was a catastrophe.*

cat·a·stroph·ic (kat′ə strof′ik) *adj.* of, relating to, or resulting in a catastrophe; disastrous: *a catastrophic explosion, a catastrophic decision.* —**cat′a·stroph′i·cal·ly,** *adv.*

cat·a·to·ni·a (kat′ə tō′nē ə) *n.* an abnormal mental and physical state characterized by a rigid body and a complete loss of the ability to feel or perceive. [From the German word *katatonie* meaning "catatonia," formed from the Greek word *kata* "down" or "through" and the Latin word *tonus* "tension" or "tone."]

cat·a·ton·ic (kat′ə ton′ik) *adj.* **1.** caused by catatonia: *a catatonic stupor.* **2.** suffering from catatonia: *a catatonic patient.*

cat·bird (kat′bûrd′) *n.* a slate-gray songbird of North and Central America, related to the mockingbird and having a call that sounds like the mewing of a cat.

cat·boat (kat′bōt′) *n.* a sailboat with a single mast set well forward and a mainsail but no jib.

cat·call (kat′kôl′) *n.* a shrill cry or whistle expressing disapproval, scorn, or impatience: *The politician was showered with catcalls from the audience.* —*v.i.* to make catcalls: *The angry audience hissed and catcalled.*

catch (kach) *v.,* **caught, catch·ing.** —*v.t.* **1.** to capture or seize, as after a chase or search: *The police caught the thief. We caught three fish.* **2.** to take or get hold of; grasp: *The woman caught my arm as I was leaving. The outfielder caught the ball.* **3.** to stop or prevent the motion or action of: *We used a pail to catch the water from the leaking roof. I caught myself about to say something rude.* **4.** to be in time for boarding; get aboard: *We will have to hurry to catch the train.* **5.** to cause to become stuck, entangled, or hooked: *I caught my sweater on a branch.* **6.** to hit; strike: *The bullet caught the robber in the leg.* **7.** to come upon suddenly or unexpectedly; surprise or discover: *They were caught in the act of stealing.* **8.** to take or get suddenly or momentarily: *We caught a glimpse of the moose going into the woods.* **9.** to become infected with: *to catch a cold.* **10.** to attract: *The bright dress caught my eye.* —*v.i.* **1.** to become stuck, entangled, or hooked: *The fabric caught in the zipper.* **2.** to become fastened or take hold: *The bolt on the door didn't catch.* **3.** to become lighted; start to burn. **4.** to act as a catcher in baseball. —*n., pl.* **catch·es. 1.** the act of catching: *The shortstop made a great catch.* **2.** a device that catches or fastens: *a catch on a door.* **3.** something that is caught; amount caught: *a crabber's catch.* **4.** a game in which an object, usually a ball, is thrown back and forth between players. **5.** a break in the voice, especially as a result of emotion. **6.** *Informal.* a hidden condition; trick or trap: *The offer seems too good; there must be a catch.*

·**to catch on.** *Informal.* **a.** to understand: *They had to explain the problem three times before I caught on.* **b.** to become fashionable or popular: *That style caught on very quickly.*

·**to catch up.** to come from behind so as to be even.

·**to catch up on.** to get or become up to date: *I spent the evening trying to catch up on my reading.*

·**to catch up to.** to come from behind so as to be even with or overtake: *Our captain caught up to the leader near the end of the race.*

·**to catch up with. a.** to come up to or overtake; catch up to. **b.** to get up to date; catch up on.

catch·all (kach′ôl′) *n.* **1.** anything that serves as a place to keep odds and ends: *The closet was a catchall.* **2.** a word or phrase used to cover various conditions or situations.

catch·er (kach′ər) *n.* **1.** a person or thing that catches. **2.** *Baseball.* the player who is positioned behind home plate to catch pitched balls.

catch·ing (kach′ing) *adj.* contagious; infectious: *Many diseases are catching.*

catch·up (kech′əp, kach′əp) another spelling of **ketchup.**

catch·word (kach′wûrd′) *n.* a word or phrase used repeatedly for effect, as by a political group; slogan.

catch·y (kach′ē) *adj.,* **catch·i·er, catch·i·est. 1.** catching the attention and easy to remember: *I keep humming that catchy tune.* **2.** tricky; deceptive: *a catchy question.*

cat·e·chism (kat′i kiz′əm) *n.* **1.** a small book or manual in which the principles of a religion are set forth in the form of questions and answers. **2.** a similar book or manual about any subject. **3.** a series of questions used as an examination.

cat·e·chize (kat′i kīz′) *v.t.,* **cat·e·chized, cat·e·chiz·ing. 1.** to instruct by questions and answers. **2.** to question closely.

cat·e·gor·i·cal (kat′i gôr′i kəl) *adj.* without conditions or qualifications; absolute: *a categorical denial.* —**cat′e·gor′i·cal·ly,** *adv.*

cat·e·go·rize (kat′i gə rīz′) *v.t.,* **cat·e·go·rized, cat·e·go·riz·ing.** to put into a category or categories; classify: *Categorize the books you read by author and subject.*

cat·e·go·ry (kat′i gôr′ē) *n., pl.* **cat·e·go·ries.** a group or division in a system of classification; class.

ca·ter (kā′tər) *v.i.* **1.** to provide food, supplies, and related services: *This restaurant caters for large private parties.* **2.** to provide what is needed or desired: *That shop caters only to very wealthy people.* —*v.t.* to provide with food, supplies, and related services.

cat·er·cor·ner (kat′ər kôr′nər) *also,* **cat·ty·cor·ner, cat·ty·cor·nered, kit·ty·cor·ner, kit·ty·cor·nered.** *adj.* placed in or having a diagonal position. —*adv.* diagonally. *Also,* **cat·er·cor·nered** (kat′ər kôr′nərd)

ca·ter·er (kā′tər ər) *n.* a person or business that caters, especially one that provides food and other services, as for a party.

cat·er·pil·lar (kat′ər pil′ər) *n.* the wormlike larva of a butterfly or moth. Caterpillars can be smooth or furry and are sometimes brightly colored. [From Norman French *catepelose* meaning "hairy cat" or "caterpillar."]

cat·er·waul (kat′ər wôl′) *v.i.* to howl or screech like a cat. —*n.* such a howl or screech.

cat·fish (kat′fish′) *n., pl.* **cat·fish** or **cat·fish·es.** any of several

caterpillar

usually scaleless fish having long feelers around the mouth that look like a cat's whiskers.

at; āpe; fär; câre; end; mē; it; īce; pîerce; hot; ōld; sông, fôrk; oil; out; up; ūse; rüle; pùll; tûrn; chin; sing; shop; thin; this; hw in white; zh in treasure. The symbol ə stands for the unstressed vowel sound heard in about, taken, pencil, lemon, and circus.

cat·gut (kat′gut′) *n.* a tough string or cord that is made from the dried and twisted intestines of sheep and certain other animals. Catgut is used for surgical sutures and for stringing musical instruments and tennis rackets.

ca·thar·tic (kə thär′tik) *n.* a medicine that causes movement of the bowels; laxative. —*adj.* causing bowel movement; laxative.

ca·the·dral (kə thē′drəl) *n.* **1.** the official church of a bishop, containing the bishop's throne. **2.** any large or important church.

cath·e·ter (kath′i tər) *n.* a thin, hollow tube inserted into a vessel or duct in the body in order to drain or inject fluids.

cath·ode (kath′ōd) *n.* **1.** an electrode through which electrons enter an electrical device or medium. When electricity is used to produce a chemical reaction, the negative electrode is the cathode, but when a chemical reaction is used to produce electricity, the positive electrode is the cathode. **2.** in electrolysis, an electrode that has an excess of electrons and is negatively charged. Positively charged ions are reduced at the cathode. **3.** an electrode from which electrons are given off.

cathode ray, a stream of electrons given off by the cathode in a vacuum tube.

cath·ode–ray tube (kath′ōd rā′) a vacuum tube in which a visible glowing pattern is produced on a luminescent screen by a cathode ray given off from an electron gun at the back of the tube. It is used in television sets, computer monitors, oscilloscopes, and radar sets.

Cath·o·lic (kath′ə lik) *adj.* **1.** of or relating to the Christian church under the authority of the pope; Roman Catholic. **2.** of or relating to the ancient undivided Christian church, or those churches claiming unbroken descent from it, as the Roman, Orthodox, Eastern, and Anglican. **3.** **catholic.** of universal interest, extent, or use; broad: *to have a catholic taste in art.* —*n.* a member of a Catholic Church, especially the Roman Catholic Church.

Ca·thol·i·cism (kə thol′ə siz′əm) *n.* the beliefs, practices, and government of the Roman Catholic Church.

cat·i·on (kat′ī′ən) *n.* a positively charged ion of an electrolyte, attracted to the cathode in electrolysis.

cat·kin (kat′kin) *n.* a fuzzy spike of tiny flowers without petals growing on certain trees, such as willows or birches. [From the obsolete Dutch word *katteken* "little cat," from the word *katte* "cat." The spike resembles a cat's tail.]

cat·nap (kat′nap′) *n.* a short nap. —*v.i.*, **cat·napped, cat·nap·ping.** to take a short nap.

cat·nip (kat′nip′) *n.* **1.** the dried leaves and stems of a plant of the mint family, used as a stuffing for cats' toys because cats are stimulated and attracted by its strong aroma. **2.** the strong-smelling plant that bears these leaves and stems.

cat-o′-nine-tails (kat′ə nīn′tālz′) *n.*, *pl.* **cat-o′-nine-tails.** a whip usually consisting of nine knotted cords fastened to a handle.

CAT scan (kat) an X ray study made by a computerized machine providing views of cross-sections of different parts of the body. CAT scans are used to diagnose various types of disease. [Abbreviation for *C(omputerized) A(xial) T(omography)*.]

cat's cradle, a children's game in which a string is looped over the fingers of both hands in such a way as to form different patterns.

cat's-paw (kats′pô′) *also,* **cats-paw.** *n.* **1.** a person used by another to do something difficult, dangerous, or unlawful; dupe. **2.** a light breeze that ruffles the surface of calm water.

cat·sup (kat′səp, kech′əp) another spelling of **ketchup.**

cat·tail (kat′tāl′) *n.* a tall marsh plant bearing long, narrow leaves and brown flowers clustered in a spike that turns velvety brown when mature.

cat·tle (kat′əl) *pl. n.* animals of the ox family, such as cows, bulls, and steers, raised for meat and dairy products.
▲ **Cattle** is a plural noun that has no true singular form. If one animal is meant, the name of the particular kind of cattle is usually used, for example, *bull* or *cow.*

cattle

cat·tle·man (kat′əl mən) *n.*, *pl.* **cat·tle·men** (kat′əl-mən). a person who owns, raises, or deals in cattle.

cat·ty (kat′ē) *adj.*, **cat·ti·er, cat·ti·est. 1.** slyly malicious; spiteful: *a catty remark.* **2.** relating to or resembling a cat or cats. —**cat′ti·ly,** *adv.* —**cat′ti·ness,** *n.*

cat·ty-cor·ner (kat′ē kôr′nər) *adj.*, *adv.* another word for **catercorner.** Also, **cat·ty·cor·nered** (kat′ē kôr′nərd).

cat·walk (kat′wôk′) *n.* a narrow walking space or platform, as along a bridge.

Cau·ca·sian (kô kā′zhən) *n.* **1.** a member of one of the major divisions of the human race, often referred to as the white race, with skin color ranging from pale pink to dark brown, and hair color from blond to dark brown. **2.** a person who was born or is living in Caucasia. —*adj.* **1.** of or relating to Caucasians. **2.** of or relating to Caucasia or its people.

cau·cus (kô′kəs) *n.*, *pl.* **cau·cus·es.** a meeting of the members of a political party to choose party leaders, nominate candidates, and determine party policy. —*v.i.* to meet in or hold a caucus.

cau·dal (kô′dəl) *adj.* **1.** of, relating to, or near the tail: *the caudal fin of a fish.* **2.** like or resembling a tail.

caught (kôt) the past tense and past participle of **catch.**

caul·dron (kôl′drən) *also,* **cal·dron.** *n.* a large kettle or boiler. [From the Anglo-Norman word *caudron* meaning "cauldron," going back to the Latin word *caldaria* "a warm bath," from the word *calidus* "warm."]

cau·li·flow·er (kô′lə flou′ər, kol′ē flou′ər) *n.* **1.** the usually white head of dense undeveloped flowers of a plant related to the cabbage, eaten as a vegetable either raw or cooked. **2.** the low-growing plant bearing this head.

caulk (kôk) *also,* **calk.** *v.t.* to fill up (a seam, crack, or joint) with tar, oakum, or other substance so that it will not leak; make watertight or airtight. —*n.* a substance used for caulking.

caulk·er (kô′kər) *also,* **calk·er.** *n.* **1.** a person who caulks. **2.** a tool used for caulking.

caulk·ing (kô′king) *n.* a substance used for filling up a seam, crack, or joint, as tar or oakum, so that it won't leak.

caus·al (kô′zəl) *adj.* of, indicating, or acting as a cause: *There is often a causal relationship between poor study habits and poor grades.* —**caus′al·ly,** *adv.*

cau·sal·i·ty (kô zal′i tē) *n.*, *pl.* **cau·sal·i·ties.** the principle that every effect requires a cause; the relationship between cause and effect.

cause (kôz) *n.* **1.** a person or thing that makes something

C

happen or produces an effect: *The hurricane was the cause of great damage along the coast.* **2.** a basis, as for action; reason; motive: *There is no cause for alarm.* **3.** something that is of concern or interest to an individual or group, and to which they give their support: *Helping the poor is a worthy cause.* —*v.t.*, **caused, caus·ing.** to make happen or result in; bring about: *The traffic jam caused us to be late. Careless driving causes many accidents.* —**cause′less,** *adj.*

cause·way (kôz′wā′) *n.* a raised road or path, as across a body of water.

caus·tic (kôs′tik) *adj.* **1.** capable of corroding or destroying animal tissue; corrosive: *a caustic chemical.* **2.** sarcastic; cutting; biting: *Caustic remarks may hurt feelings.* —*n.* a substance that destroys or corrodes animal tissue.

caus·ti·cal·ly (kôs′ti kə lē, kôs′ti klē) *adv.* in a caustic manner; sarcastically.

caustic soda, another term for **sodium hydroxide.**

cau·ter·ize (kô′tə rīz′) *v.t.*, **cau·ter·ized, cau·ter·iz·ing.** to sear with a hot instrument or a caustic substance, especially in order to destroy dead tissue or prevent infection. —**cau′ter·i·za′tion,** *n.*

cau·tion (kô′shən) *n.* **1.** care with regard to danger or risk; prudence; wariness: *The scientist used caution in working with chemicals.* **2.** a warning. —*v.t.* to urge (someone) to be careful; warn: *The counselor cautioned us to watch out for poison ivy.*

cau·tious (kô′shəs) *adj.* showing, exercising, or characterized by caution; careful: *An inexperienced skier must be cautious when trying new slopes.* —**cau′tious·ly,** *adv.* —**cau′tious·ness,** *n.*

cav·al·cade (kav′əl kād′) *n.* **1.** a procession, especially of people on horseback or in vehicles. **2.** a large and impressive group or gathering: *A cavalcade of movie stars attended the award ceremony.* **3.** a series of events: *a cavalcade of circus acts.*

cav·a·lier (kav′ə lîr′) *n.* **1.** a horseman, especially one who is armed; knight. **2.** a gallant or courteous gentleman, especially one serving as a lady's escort. **3. Cavalier.** a supporter of Charles I of England in his struggle with Parliament from 1641 to 1649. —*adj.* free and easy, sometimes in a haughty or disdainful manner: *a cavalier attitude.* —**cav′a·lier′ly,** *adv.*

cav·al·ry (kav′əl rē) *n.*, *pl.* **cav·al·ries. 1.** a military unit trained to fight on horseback. **2.** in some countries, a military unit made up of armored vehicles, such as tanks. [From the Italian word *cavalleria* meaning both "cavalry" and "knighthood," from the word *cavaliere* "knight," going back to the Late Latin word *caballus* "inferior horse, nag."]

cav·al·ry·man (kav′əl rē mən) *n.*, *pl.* **cav·al·ry·men** (kav′əl rē mən). a member of a cavalry.

cave (kāv) *n.* a natural hollow chamber or hole beneath the earth's surface or in the side of a mountain. —*v.t.*, **caved, cav·ing.** to hollow out.
 ·to cave in. to fall or cause to fall in or down; collapse: *The walls of the old tunnel caved in.*

ca·ve·at emp·tor (kā′vē at′ emp′tôr) *Latin.* let the buyer beware.

cave dweller 1. a person who lives in a cave. **2.** another term for **cave man.**

cave–in (kāv′in′) *n.* **1.** a caving in or collapse, as of a mine or tunnel. **2.** the site of such a collapse.

cave man, a human being of the Stone Age who lived in caves.

cav·ern (kav′ərn) *n.* an underground cave, especially one of very great size.

cav·ern·ous (kav′ər nəs) *adj.* **1.** full of or containing caverns. **2.** like a cavern; hollow and deep.

cav·i·ar (kav′ē är′) *also,* **cav·i·are.** *n.* the salted eggs of sturgeon or certain other large fish, eaten as a food.

cav·il (kav′əl) *v.i.*, **cav·iled, cav·il·ing;** *also, British,*

cav·illed, cav·il·ling. to find fault unnecessarily; make petty objections; quibble. —*n.* trivial criticism.

cav·i·ty (kav′i tē) *n.*, *pl.* **cav·i·ties. 1.** a hollow place; hole. **2.** a hollow space in a tooth caused by decay. **3.** a space within the body. The stomach, intestines, liver, and kidneys are located in the abdominal cavity.

ca·vort (kə vôrt′) *v.i. Informal.* to run and jump around playfully; frisk: *The puppies cavorted in the grass.*

ca·vy (kā′vē) *n.*, *pl.* **ca·vies.** any of several rodents of South America, having a rounded body, short legs, and small ears. The best-known cavy is the guinea pig.

caw (kô) *n.* a harsh cry or call of a crow, raven, or similar bird. —*v.i.* to make this cry or call.

cay (kā, kē) *n.* a low mound or island of sand and, often, coral fragments; key.

cay·enne (kī en′, kā en′) *n.* a hot spice made from the ground seeds and pods of any of several hot red peppers.

cay·man (kā′mən) another spelling of **caiman.**

Ca·yu·ga (kā ū′gə, kī ū′gə) *n.*, *pl.* **Ca·yu·ga** or **Ca·yu·gas.** a member of a tribe of Iroquois Indians formerly living in what is now New York State.

cay·use (kī üs′, kī′üs) *n.* an Indian pony of the western United States.

CB, Citizens Band. [Short for C(*itizens*) B(*and*).]

Cb, the symbol for columbium.

cc., cubic centimeter; cubic centimeters.

C clef, a movable clef indicating that the line of the staff on which it is placed represents middle C. See **clef** for illustration.

Cd, the symbol for cadmium.

CD, compact disc.

CDC, Centers for Disease Control.

Ce, the symbol for cerium.

cease (sēs) *v.*, **ceased, ceas·ing.** —*v.i.* to come to an end; stop: *The rain had ceased by four o'clock.* —*v.t.* to put an end to; discontinue: *That factory will cease production.*

cease–fire (sēs′tīr′) *n.* **1.** a temporary halt of fighting by mutual agreement of opposing sides; armistice. **2.** an order to troops to stop firing.

cease·less (sēs′lis) *adj.* never stopping; endless; continual. —**cease′less·ly,** *adv.* —**cease′less·ness,** *n.*

ce·cro·pi·a moth (si krō′pē ə) a large silkworm moth native to the eastern United States, having colorful markings.

ce·cum (sē′kəm) *also,* **cae·cum.** *n.*, *pl.* **ce·ca** (sē′kə). the pouch at the beginning of the large intestine, to which the appendix is attached.

ce·dar (sē′dər) *n.* **1.** any of several evergreen trees of the pine family, having rough, dark gray bark and numerous branches that bear needle-shaped leaves. **2.** the durable, fragrant wood of these trees, used for making chests and cabinets.

cedar waxwing, a crested bird native to North America, having brownish gray feathers with yellow, black, and red markings.

cede (sēd) *v.t.*, **ced·ed, ced·ing.** to give up possession of; surrender; yield: *Spain ceded the territory to France.*

ce·dil·la (si dil′ə) *n.* a mark (¸) placed under certain letters to indicate pronunciation. In English it is used especially under *c* in some words borrowed from French, such as *façade,* to indicate the sound of *s.*

ceil·ing (sē′ling) *n.* **1.** the interior, overhead covering or surface of a room. **2.** the maximum height at which an

---

at; āpe; fär; câre; end; mē; it; īce; pîerce; hot; ōld;
sông, fôrk; oil; out; up; ūse; rüle; pull; tûrn; chin;
sing; shop; thin; <u>th</u>is; hw in white; zh in treasure.
The symbol ə stands for the unstressed vowel sound
heard in about, taken, pencil, lemon, and circus.

airplane can fly under standard air conditions. **3.** vertical visibility measured from sea level to the bottom of the lowest clouds. **4.** the highest or upper limit set on anything: *The government set a ceiling on prices.*
·**to hit the ceiling.** *Informal.* to lose one's temper; become very angry.

cel·an·dine (sel′ən dīn′, sel′ən dēn′) *n.* a plant of the poppy family that is sometimes grown as a garden plant because of its yellow flowers.

cel·e·brant (sel′ə brənt) *n.* **1.** a person who participates in a celebration. **2.** a priest who officiates at a Mass or other religious service.

cel·e·brate (sel′ə brāt′) *v.,* **cel·e·brat·ed, cel·e·brat·ing.** —*v.t.* **1.** to observe or commemorate (an event) with ceremonies or festivities: *We celebrated their anniversary with a party.* **2.** to perform publicly with the proper ceremonies: *The priest celebrated Mass.* **3.** to honor or praise publicly; extol: *The skater's victory was celebrated in all the newspapers.* —*v.i.* **1.** to observe or commemorate an event with ceremonies or festivities. **2.** *Informal.* to have a merry time.

cel·e·brat·ed (sel′ə brā′tid) *adj.* admired by many; famous.

cel·e·bra·tion (sel′ə brā′shən) *n.* **1.** the act of celebrating. **2.** the ceremonies or festivities carried on to celebrate something: *All the members of the team were at the victory celebration.*

ce·leb·ri·ty (sə leb′ri tē) *n., pl.* **ce·leb·ri·ties. 1.** a person who is well-known or much publicized: *The best-selling book made the author a celebrity.* **2.** the condition of being well-known or much publicized.

ce·ler·i·ty (sə ler′i tē) *n.* swiftness; speed.

cel·er·y (sel′ə rē) *n.* **1.** the crisp, green or creamy white leafstalks of a plant of the parsley family, eaten either raw or cooked. **2.** the plant bearing these leafstalks.

ce·les·ta (sə les′tə) *n.* a keyboard musical instrument resembling a small piano and having steel plates that are struck by hammers to produce bell-like tones.

ce·les·tial (sə les′chəl) *adj.* **1.** of or relating to the sky or heavens: *The planets are celestial bodies.* **2.** of heaven; heavenly; divine: *the celestial beauty of an angel.* —**ce·les′tial·ly,** *adv.*

celestial equator, the great circle formed by the intersection of the plane of the earth's equator and the celestial sphere.

celestial pole, either of the two intersections of the earth's axis with the celestial sphere.

celestial sphere, an imaginary sphere surrounding the earth and representing the entire sky. The stars, planets, and other heavenly bodies appear to be located on the surface of the celestial sphere.

cel·i·ba·cy (sel′ə bə sē) *n.* the state of being celibate.

cel·i·bate (sel′ə bit) *n.* a person who remains unmarried, especially in accordance with religious vows. —*adj.* unmarried: *The church required that its priests be celibate.*

cell (sel) *n.* **1.** a small, usually plain, room, as in a prison, convent, or monastery. **2.** the basic unit of all living organisms, consisting of a mass of protoplasm with a nucleus near the center, and surrounded by a cell membrane or wall. **3.** a device that changes chemical, solar, or light energy into electrical energy. **4.** a small cavity or compartment, such as one of the

six-sided compartments in a honeycomb. **5.** *Computers.* a place in the memory of a computer where a single unit of information, such as a character or a byte, is stored.

cel·lar (sel′ər) *n.* a room or group of rooms, either wholly or partly underground, usually under a building and often used as a storage place.

cell division, the process in which a cell divides into two new cells, each with the same number of chromosomes as the original.

cel·list (chel′ist) *also,* **'cel·list.** *n.* a person who plays the cello. Also, **violoncellist.**

cell membrane, the very thin membrane that covers the entire surface of a cell.

cel·lo (chel′ō) *also,* **'cel·lo.** *n., pl.* **cel·los.** an instrument of the violin family, between the viola and double bass in size and pitch. Also, **violoncello.**

cel·lo·phane (sel′ə fān′) *n.* a thin, flexible, usually transparent material made from cellulose, used especially for wrapping.

cel·lu·lar (sel′yə lər) *adj.* **1.** of, relating to, or resembling a cell or cells. **2.** consisting of cells.

cellular phone, a mobile telephone, usually used in motor vehicles, that operates within a network of radio transmitters that send and relay signals from one geographical area to another.

cello

cel·lu·loid (sel′yə loid′) *n.* a strong, transparent, flammable plastic made from nitrocellulose, alcohol, and camphor.

cel·lu·lose (sel′yə lōs′) *n.* a compound of carbon, hydrogen, and oxygen that is the major component of the walls of plant cells. It is used especially to make paper, rayon, and other products.

cellulose acetate, a substance made by treating cellulose with acetic acid and other compounds, used to make synthetic acetate fibers.

cellulose nitrate, another term for **nitrocellulose.**

cell wall, in plants, bacteria, and other monerans, the outer layer that covers the cell membrane.

Cel·si·us scale (sel′sē əs, sel′shəs) the official name of the **centigrade** scale. [From the Swedish astronomer Anders *Celsius* (1701–1744), who devised this scale.]

Celt (kelt, selt) *n.* **1.** a member of a Celtic-speaking people, including the Irish, Highland Scots, Welsh, Cornish, and Bretons. **2.** a member of an ancient people of central and western Europe, including the Gauls and Britons.

Cel·tic (kel′tik, sel′tik) *n.* a group of languages belonging to the Indo-European language family, including Irish, Scottish Gaelic, Welsh, and Cornish. —*adj.* of or relating to the Celts, their languages, or their culture.

Celtic cross, a Latin cross with a circle behind the intersection of the bars of the cross.

ce·ment (sə ment′) *n.* **1.** a material used in building,

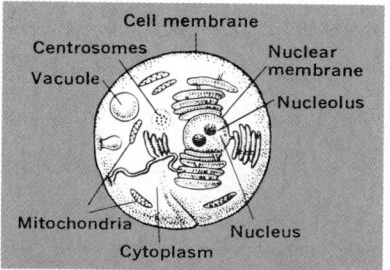

cell *(def. 2)*

Cell membrane

Centrosomes

Nuclear membrane

Vacuole

Nucleolus

Mitochondria

Nucleus

Cytoplasm

made by burning a mixture of limestone, clay or shale, silica, gypsum, and other substances to produce a powder that forms a slow-hardening paste when mixed with water. **2.** *Informal.* concrete. **3.** any soft substance, such as glue, that hardens to join things together. **4.** anything that joins together or unites; bond. —*v.t.* **1.** to fasten or join together with cement: *I cemented the wing to the model airplane.* **2.** to coat or cover with cement. **3.** to bind or unite: *This agreement cements their partnership.*

cem·e·ter·y (sem′i ter′ē) *n., pl.* **cem·e·ter·ies.** a place for burying the dead; graveyard. [From the Middle French word *cimitere* meaning "cemetery," from the Late Latin word *coemeterium,* from the Greek word *koimēterion* "sleeping place," from *koiman* "to put to sleep."]

Ce·no·zo·ic (sē′nə zō′ik, sen′ə zō′ik) *n.* the most recent geological era, including the Tertiary and Quaternary periods; age of mammals. —*adj.* of, relating to, or characteristic of this era. [Formed from the Greek words *kainos* meaning "new, recent" and *zōikos* meaning "of animals."]

cen·ser (sen′sər) *n.* a container in which incense is burned, used especially in religious ceremonies.

cen·sor (sen′sər) *n.* **1.** a person employed by a government or organization to examine material, such as books, plays, or motion pictures, for the purpose of removing or suppressing anything that is considered improper, undesirable, or harmful. **2.** an official, usually employed by a government during wartime, who examines letters, literature, and other materials in order to remove any information that is confidential or dangerous to national security. **3.** in ancient Rome, one of the two officials who were in charge of taking the census and supervising public morals. —*v.t.* to examine and deal with as a censor: *Many famous books have been censored.*

▲ **Censor** should not be confused with **censure**. To **censor** is to remove or suppress material that is considered dangerous, indecent, or offensive: *Certain scenes of the movie were censored for its showing on television.* To **censure** is to express disapproval of or blame: *Congress censured the senator for revealing important government secrets.*

cen·so·ri·ous (sen sôr′ē əs) *adj.* severely or harshly critical: *A censorious manner wins few friends.* —**cen·so′ri·ous·ly,** *adv.* —**cen·so′ri·ous·ness,** *n*

cen·sor·ship (sen′sər ship′) *n.* **1.** the act or system of censoring. **2.** the office or power held by a censor.

cen·sur·a·ble (sen′shər ə bəl) *adj.* worthy of being censured.

cen·sure (sen′shər) *v.t.,* **cen·sured, cen·sur·ing.** to express disapproval of or find fault with; blame; condemn: *Journalists censured the athlete for poor sportsmanship.* —*n.* an expression of disapproval or blame; condemnation. ▲ See **censor** for usage note. —**cen′sur·er,** *n.*

cen·sus (sen′səs) *n., pl.* **cen·sus·es.** an official count of the people of a country or district, made in order to obtain certain statistics, such as age, sex, occupation, or economic status.

cent (sent) *n.* a coin of the United States, Canada, and some other countries, equal to one hundredth of a dollar.

cent. 1. centered. **2.** centigrade. **3.** central. **4.** century.

cen·taur (sen′tôr) *n. Greek Mythology.* one of a race of creatures having the head, arms, and torso of a man, and the body and legs of a horse.

cen·ta·vo (sen tä′vō) *n., pl.* **cen·ta·vos.** one hundredth of

centaur

various monetary units, as of the peso in certain Latin-American countries.

cen·te·nar·i·an (sen′tə när′ē ən) *n.* a person who is one hundred years old or older.

cen·te·nar·y (sen′tə ner′ē, sen ten′ə rē) *n., pl.* **cen·te·nar·ies. 1.** another word for **centennial.** **2.** a period of one hundred years. —*adj.* of or relating to a period of one hundred years or to a hundredth anniversary; centennial.

cen·ten·ni·al (sen ten′ē əl) *n.* a hundredth anniversary or its celebration: *The town was settled in 1856 and had its centennial in 1956.* —*adj.* **1.** of or relating to a period of one hundred years. **2.** of or relating to a hundredth anniversary: *a centennial celebration.* —**cen·ten′ni·al·ly,** *adv.*

cen·ter (sen′tər) *also, British,* **cen·tre.** *n.* **1.** a point within a circle or sphere equally distant from all points of the circumference or surface. **2.** the middle point, part, or place of anything: *the center of a page, candies with chocolate centers, the center of a room.* **3.** a person, place, or thing around which interest, activity, or the like is concentrated: *to be the center of attention at a party. That city is a tourist center.* **4.** a point, line, or axis around which anything revolves, such as a wheel. **5.** *also,* **Center.** a group holding moderate political views. **6.** *Sports.* **a.** in football, the player who lines up in the middle of the offensive line and snaps the ball back. **b.** in basketball, the player whose position is in the center of the playing area. **c.** in hockey, the player whose position is in the center of the front line. —*v.t.* **1.** to place or fix in or at the center: *We centered the picture on the wall.* **2.** to draw toward or gather around one point; concentrate: *to center one's attention on a problem.* —*v.i.* to be centered or concentrated: *This story centers on the life of an astronaut.*

cen·ter·board (sen′tər bôrd′) *n.* a board or plate lowered through a slot in the bottom of a sailboat that does not have a fixed keel, to prevent drifting.

center field *Baseball.* **1.** the middle section of the outfield behind second base. **2.** the position of the player stationed in this area.

center of gravity, the point in a body around which its mass is equally distributed.

cen·ter·piece (sen′tər pēs′) *n.* an ornamental object, such as a vase of flowers or a bowl of fruit, placed in the center of a table.

Centers for Disease Control, an agency of the U.S. government concerned with health education, environmental and occupational health, and the spread and control of disease.

cen·tes·i·mal (sen tes′ə məl) *adj.* relating to or divided into hundredths. —**cen·tes′i·mal·ly,** *adv.*

centi- *combining form* a hundredth part of: *centigram, centimeter.*

cen·ti·grade (sen′ti grād′) *adj.* of, according to, or designating the temperature scale on which the freezing point is at 0 degrees and the boiling point is at 100 degrees under standard atmospheric pressure. A change of 5 degrees on the centigrade scale is equal to a change of 9 degrees on the Fahrenheit scale.

cen·ti·gram (sen′ti gram′) *also, British,* **cen·ti·gramme.** *n.* a unit of metric weight equal to 1/100 gram.

cen·ti·li·ter (sen′tə lē′tər) *also, British,* **cen·ti·li·tre.**

at; āpe; fär; câre; end; mē; it; īce; pîerce; hot; ōld; sông, fôrk; oil; out; up; ūse; rüle; půll; tûrn; chin; sing; shop; thin; this; hw in white; zh in treasure. The symbol ə stands for the unstressed vowel sound heard in about, taken, pencil, lemon, and circus.

C

157

n. a unit of capacity in the metric system equal to ¹/₁₀₀ liter, or 0.0034 fluid ounce.

cen·time (sän′tēm) *n.* one hundredth of any of certain monetary units, such as the franc.

cen·ti·me·ter (sen′tə mē′tər) *also, British,* **cen·ti·me·tre.** *n.* a unit of metric measure equal to ¹/₁₀₀ meter (0.3937 inch).

cen·ti·mo (sen′tə mō′) *n., pl.* **cen·ti·mos.** one hundredth of various monetary units.

cen·ti·pede (sen′tə pēd′) *n.* any of a group of small animals that resemble worms, having a flattened body made up of many segments, each bearing a pair of legs. The first pair of legs is modified into a pair of poisonous fangs. [Going back to the Latin words *centum* "one hundred" and *pes* "foot."]

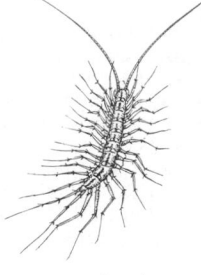

centipede

cen·tral (sen′trəl) *adj.* **1.** in, at, or near the center or middle: *The railroad station has a central location in town.* **2.** of or forming the center. **3.** being the thing from which other things come or upon which they depend: *the central character of a book.* **4.** having a controlling or directing influence: *a central agency of the government.* **5.** operating from a single location, usually one near the center of an area: *central heating, central air conditioning.* —*n.* the main telephone exchange of an area, such as a town or city. —**cen′tral·ly,** *adv.*

Central Intelligence Agency, an executive agency that is charged with coordinating the intelligence activities of all the departments of the United States Government.

cen·tral·ize (sen′trə līz′) *v.,* **cen·tral·ized, cen·tral·iz·ing.** —*v.t.* **1.** to bring together at a center; make central. **2.** to bring or organize under one control or a central authority: *to centralize a country's government.* —*v.i.* to come together at a center. —**cen′tral·i·za′tion,** *n.*

central nervous system, the part of the nervous system composed of the brain and the spinal cord in animals with backbones. It coordinates all the activities of the nervous system.

Central Powers, the countries that fought against the Allies in World War I: Germany, Austria-Hungary, Bulgaria, and Turkey.

central processing unit, the part of a computer that contains the main memory and hardware for controlling all functions.

Central Standard Time, the standard time used in much of the central United States and Canada. It is 6 hours earlier than Greenwich Time.

cen·tre (sen′tər) *British.* *n., v.,* **cen·tred, cen·tring.** another spelling of **center.**

cen·trif·u·gal (sen trif′yə gəl, sen trif′ə gəl) *adj.* moving or directed away from a center. —**cen·trif′u·gal·ly,** *adv.* [Going back to the Latin words *centrum* "the center of a circle" and *fugere* "to flee."]

centrifugal force, the force generated when a body is moving in a curved path, tending to move the body away from the center of the curve. If you whirl a ball on a string over your head, the outward pull you feel is centrifugal force.

cen·tri·fuge (sen′trə fūj′) *n.* **1.** a device using centrifugal force to separate substances of different densities, as cream from milk, by spinning them at high speeds. **2.** a large machine that simulates the effects of gravity, usually consisting of a capsule or chair spun in a circle at the end of a long support. It is used in training astronauts. —*v.t.,* **cen·tri·fuged, cen·tri·fug·ing.** to subject to the action of a centrifuge.

cen·tri·ole (sen′trē ōl′) *n.* a tiny cylindrical body in all animal cells and many plant cells. Centrioles duplicate

themselves just before mitosis and move to opposite ends of the cell during mitosis, where they form the poles of the spindle to which the chromosomes move.

cen·trip·e·tal (sen trip′i təl) *adj.* moving or directed toward a center. —**cen·trip′e·tal·ly,** *adv.*

centripetal force, the force generated when a body is moving in a curved path, tending to move the body toward the center of the curve. If you whirl a ball on a string over your head, the inward pull exerted by your hand is centripetal force. If you remove the centripetal force by letting go of the string, the ball will fly off in a straight line rather than continue to spin.

cen·tro·some (sen′trə sōm′) *n.* an area in the cytoplasm of a cell that contains the centrioles.

cen·tu·ri·on (sen tùr′ē ən, sen tyùr′ē ən) *n.* a commander of a century in the ancient Roman army.

cen·tu·ry (sen′chə rē) *n., pl.* **cen·tu·ries.** **1.** a period of 100 years. From 1650 to 1750 is a century. **2.** a period of 100 years reckoned forward or backward from some fixed date, especially from the birth of Jesus: *the twentieth century A.D.* **3.** a unit of the ancient Roman army, originally consisting of 100 men.

century plant, an agave found in deserts of Mexico and the southwestern United States, having thick, spiny-edged leaves and a flower stalk 20–40 feet (6–12 meters) tall. [From the former belief that this plant blooms once in a century.]

century plant

ce·phal·ic (sə fal′ik) *adj.* of or relating to the head.

ceph·a·lo·pod (sef′ə lə pod′) *n.* any of a group of sea animals including the octopus, squid, and cuttlefish, having a clearly defined head with large, well-developed eyes, a sharp beak, and muscular tentacles around the mouth that bear suckers.

ceph·a·lo·tho·rax (sef′ə lō thôr′aks) *n., pl.* **ceph·a·lo·tho·rax·es** or **ceph·a·lo·tho·ra·ces** (sef′ə lō thôr′ə sēz′). in such animals as spiders and lobsters, the part of the body that includes the head and thorax. It is separate from the abdomen.

ce·ram·ic (sə ram′ik) *adj.* of or relating to objects made of baked clay, such as pottery, earthenware, or porcelain. —*n.* an object made of baked clay.

ce·ram·ics (sə ram′iks) *n.* the art or technique of making objects by shaping clay and then baking it at a high temperature. ▲ used with a singular verb.

cer·a·mist (ser′ə mist′, sə ram′ist) *n.* an expert in ceramics or an artist who makes ceramic objects.

Cer·ber·us (sûr′bər əs) *n.* *Greek and Roman Mythology.* a three-headed dog guarding the entrance to Hades.

ce·re·al (sîr′ē əl) *n.* **1.** any grass, such as wheat, oats, rye, barley, or rice, that yields grain. **2.** the grain of such a grass. **3.** a food made from this grain, especially a breakfast food such as oatmeal. —*adj.* of or relating to edible grain or to the grass that produces it.

Cerberus

cer·e·bel·lum (ser′ə bel′əm) *n., pl.* **cer·e·bel·lums** or **cer·e·bel·la** (ser′ə bel′ə). the part of the brain that coordinates the activity of the muscles. It is located in the back of the skull.

ce·re·bral (sə rē′brəl, ser′ə brəl) *adj.* **1.** of or relating to the brain or to the cerebrum: *a cerebral hemorrhage.* **2.** relating to, involving, or appealing to the intellect rather than the emotions; intellectual.

cerebral cortex, the thick, folded outer layer of the cerebrum of the brain. The cerebral cortex is divided into areas responsible for voluntary movement, learning, memory, and interpretation of messages from the senses.

cerebral palsy, lack of control over the muscles, resulting from damage to the brain before or during birth.

ce·re·bro·spi·nal (sə rē'brō spī'nəl, ser'ə brō spī'nəl) *adj.* of, relating to, or affecting the brain and spinal cord.

ce·re·brum (sə rē'brəm, ser'ə brəm) *n.*, *pl.* **ce·re·brums** or **ce·re·bra** (sə rē'brə, ser'ə brə). the largest part of the human brain, occupying the entire upper portion of the skull. The cerebrum controls voluntary movements and conscious mental activities.

cere·ment (sîr'mənt) *n.* a cloth used to wrap a dead body; shroud.

cer·e·mo·ni·al (ser'ə mō'nē əl) *adj.* **1.** relating to or showing ceremony; formal: *a ceremonial dinner.* **2.** used in connection with a ceremony: *ceremonial robes.* —*n.* a set of rites or formalities observed on or for some particular occasion; ritual. —**cer'e·mo'ni·al·ly,** *adv.*

cer·e·mo·ni·ous (ser'ə mō'nē əs) *adj.* **1.** very careful about ceremony; very polite: *a ceremonious person, a ceremonious bow.* **2.** marked by or done with ceremony: *a ceremonious occasion.* —**cer'e·mo'ni·ous·ly,** *adv.* —**cer'e·mo'ni·ous·ness,** *n.*

cer·e·mo·ny (ser'ə mō'nē) *n.*, *pl.* **cer·e·mo·nies.** **1.** a formal act or set of acts done on a special or important occasion: *a wedding ceremony, a graduation ceremony, an inaugural ceremony.* **2.** very polite or formal conduct: *The guests got up and left without ceremony.*
·**to stand on ceremony.** to behave with or insist on strict formality: *You needn't stand on ceremony with us.*

Ce·res (sîr'ēz) *n. Roman Mythology.* the goddess of grain and agriculture. In Greek mythology she was called Demeter.

ce·rise (sə rēs') *n.* a bright red color resembling a ripe cherry —*adj* having the color cerise; bright red.

ce·ri·um (sîr'ē əm) *n.* a soft gray metallic element that is used in refining processes and in alloys. It is the most abundant element of the rare-earth group. Symbol: **Ce** [From the asteroid *Ceres,* discovered two years before the discovery of this element, from the Roman goddess *Ceres.*]

cer·tain (sûr'tən) *adj.* **1.** free from doubt, fully confident; positive; sure: *I am certain that I am correct.* **2.** beyond doubt or question; true: *The eruption shows it is certain that the volcano is still active.* **3.** bound to happen; inevitable: *Capture meant certain death to the spy.* **4.** agreed upon; settled; determined: *They plan to meet at a certain time.* **5.** that may be depended on; reliable; trustworthy: *a certain cure for a headache.* **6.** known, but not named or specified; particular: *Certain people don't approve of your plan.* **7.** some, but not much: *There has been a certain amount of improvement in the patient's health.*
·**for certain.** without doubt; surely: *The police never knew for certain who had committed the crime.*

cer·tain·ly (sûr'tən lē) *adv.* without a doubt; surely: *I will certainly be there.*

cer·tain·ty (sûr'tən tē) *n.*, *pl.* **cer·tain·ties.** **1.** the quality, state, or fact of being certain: *I can say with certainty that you will win the prize.* **2.** something certain; established fact: *It is a certainty that the earth revolves around the sun.*

cer·tif·i·cate (sər tif'i kit) *n.* an official document declaring the truth of certain facts: *a birth certificate, a marriage certificate, a death certificate.*

cer·ti·fi·ca·tion (sûr'tə fi kā'shən) *n.* **1.** the act of certifying or the state of being certified. **2.** a certified statement; certificate.

certified public accountant, an accountant who has received a certificate from a state stating that he or she has met the requirements of its laws.

cer·ti·fy (sûr'tə fī') *v.t.,* **cer·ti·fied, cer·ti·fy·ing.** **1.** to declare (something) to be true, accurate, or certain, especially by a signed statement or official document; testify to: *The document certifies the date of your birth.* **2.** to guarantee the quality or value of: *to certify milk, to certify a check.*

cer·ti·tude (sûr'ti tüd', sûr'ti tūd') *n.* a feeling of being certain.

ce·ru·le·an (sə rü'lē ən) *n.* a sky-blue color; azure. —*adj.* having the color cerulean; sky-blue.

cer·vi·cal (sûr'vi kəl) *adj.* of or relating to a cervix: *cervical bones.*

cer·vix (sûr'viks) *n.*, *pl.* **cer·vix·es** or **cer·vi·ces** (sûr'və sēz'). **1.** the neck. **2.** a neck-shaped part of the body, especially the outer end of the uterus.

ce·sar·e·an (si zâr'ē ən) *also,* **ce·sar·i·an.** *n.* see cesarean section.

cesarean section *also,* **caesarean section.** the delivery of a baby from its mother's uterus by a surgical incision made through the abdomen into the uterus. It is performed when normal delivery is impossible or dangerous. [From Julius *Caesar,* who supposedly was delivered in this way.]

ce·si·um (sē'zē əm) *also,* **cae·si·um.** *n.* a soft, silver-colored metallic element used in photoelectric cells. It is one of the rarest metals. Symbol: **Cs** [Formed from the Latin word *caesius* meaning "bluish gray." Cesium was discovered by its characteristic blue lines in a spectrum analysis.]

ces·sa·tion (se sā'shən) *n.* a ceasing or halting; stop: *a cessation of fighting.*

ces·sion (sesh'ən) *n.* the act of ceding; giving up or surrendering to another: *a cession of territory, a cession of rights.*

cess·pool (ses'pül') *n.* a pit, well, or other underground container for collecting sewage from the toilets and sinks of a house.

ce·ta·cean (si tā'shən) *adj.* of or relating to an order of mammals that resemble fish and live entirely in water, such as whales, dolphins, and porpoises. *n.* any one of these mammals.

Cf, the symbol for californium.

cf., compare [Short for the Latin word *confer* meaning "compare," from *conferre* meaning "to collect, bring together."]

cg., centigram; centigrams. Also, **cg, cgm.**

ch. **1.** chapter. **2.** church.

cha–cha (chä'chä') *n.* **1.** a ballroom dance of Latin-American origin, similar to the mambo. **2.** the music for this dance.

cha·conne (sha kôn') *n.* **1.** a very old dance, perhaps of Mexican origin. **2.** a musical form in slow triple time, characterized by continuous variations.

chafe (chāf) *v.,* **chafed, chaf·ing.** —*v.t.* **1.** to wear away or make sore by friction or rubbing: *The diaper chafed the baby's skin.* **2.** to make angry; irritate; annoy. **3.** to restore warmth to by rubbing: *We chafed each other's numb hands.* —*v.i.* **1.** to be worn away or made sore by friction or rubbing. **2.** to be irritated or annoyed: *Most people chafe when they are constantly and needlessly criticized.*

---

at; āpe; fär; câre; end; mē; it; īce; pîerce; hot; ōld; sông, fôrk; oil; out; up; ūse; rüle; pùll; tûrn; chin; sing; shop; thin; this; hw in white; zh in treasure. The symbol ə stands for the unstressed vowel sound heard in about, taken, pencil, lemon, and circus.

159

chaff¹ (chaf) *n.* **1.** the husks of wheat, oats, rye, and other grains, separated from the seed by threshing. **2.** finely cut hay or straw used as feed for livestock. **3.** any worthless matter; refuse. [From the Old English word *ceaf* meaning "seed husks."]

chaff² (chaf) *v.t.* to tease or make fun of in a good-natured way: *The other golfers chaffed me when I swung and missed the ball.* —*n.* good-natured teasing. [Perhaps a form of *chafe.*]

chaf·finch (chaf′inch) *n., pl.* **chaf·finch·es.** a European finch having a pleasant, short song. It is popular as a pet.

chaf·ing dish (chā′fing), a pan or dish with a heating device underneath it, used for cooking or for keeping food warm at the table.

cha·grin (shə grin′) *n.* a feeling of annoyance or distress because one has failed or been disappointed or embarrassed. —*v.t.* to annoy or distress by failure, disappointment, or embarrassment: *to be deeply chagrined by failure.*

chafing dish

chain (chān) *n.* **1.** a series of connected links or rings, usually of metal, used chiefly to bind, hold, or pull something, or as an ornament: *The chain of a bicycle transmits power from the pedals to the wheels. A chain of flowers hung from the statue.* **2.** a series of connected things: *a chain of mountains, the chain of events leading up to a war.* **3. chains.** anything that binds or restrains. **4.** a number of similar business establishments under the same ownership or management: *a chain of restaurants, a chain of movie theaters.* **5.** a measuring instrument consisting of 100 links of equal length, used by surveyors and engineers, and equal to either 66 feet (in surveying) or 100 feet (in engineering). —*v.t.* **1.** to fasten, secure, or connect with a chain: *I chained my bicycle to the post.* **2.** to restrain or confine; bind: *An unexpected amount of work chained them to their desks.*

chain gang, a group of convicts chained together, usually while at hard labor outdoors.

chain letter, a letter sent to a number of people, asking each to send a copy in turn to a specific number of other persons.

chain–link fence (chān′lingk′) a fence made from thick wire of galvanized steel, interlinked in a diamond-shaped pattern.

chain mail, flexible armor for the body, made of small metal rings or links joined together.

chain reaction 1. a series of atomic reactions that, once started, can sustain itself automatically. In a chain reaction, an atomic nucleus that has been split gives off neutrons, which strike other nuclei. This causes these nuclei to split and give off additional neutrons, which in turn collide with other nuclei, thus continuing the process. **2.** any series of events, each of which is caused by the preceding one and is the cause of the following one.

chain store, one of a group of retail stores owned or managed by the same company and selling similar goods.

chair (châr) *n.* **1.** a piece of furniture designed to seat one person, usually having a back and legs and sometimes arms. **2.** an office or position of authority or dignity: *a chair in French literature at a university.* **3.** a presiding officer; moderator: *The speaker rose to address the chair.* —*v.t.* to preside over; act as moderator of: *to chair the art department at the university, to chair a panel discussion.*

·**to take the chair.** to take the position of moderator; preside at or open a meeting.

chain mail

chair lift, a series of seats suspended from a moving cable, used to carry people, especially skiers, up and down a mountain slope.

chair·man (châr′mən) *n., pl.* **chair·men** (châr′mən). a person in charge of a meeting, committee, board, or organization.

chair·man·ship (châr′mən ship′) *n.* the position, duties, or term of office of a chairman.

chair·per·son (châr′pûr′sən) *n.* a chairman or chairwoman.

chairlift

chair·wom·an (châr′wùm′ən) *n., pl.* **chairwom·en** (châr′wim′ən). a woman in charge of a meeting, committee, board, or organization.

chaise (shāz) *n.* **1.** a light, usually two-wheeled carriage, often with a hood or folding top, usually seating one or two passengers. Also, **shay. 2.** see **chaise longue.**

chaise longue (shāz′lông′) a chair with a long, couch-like seat on which a person can sit with legs outstretched. Also, **chaise lounge.**

chal·ced·o·ny (kal sed′ə nē) *n., pl.* **chal·ced·o·nies.** a variety of quartz having a waxy luster and occurring in various colors. Agate is a kind of chalcedony.

cha·let (sha lā′) *n.* **1.** a house having a wide, sloping roof with overhanging eaves, commonly found in Switzerland and other nearby regions. **2.** any house built in this style. **3.** any herder's hut or cottage in the Alps.

chal·ice (chal′is) *n.* **1.** a drinking cup or goblet. **2.** a cup or vessel containing the wine used in the Holy Communion service. **3.** a cup-shaped flower.

chalk (chôk) *n.* **1.** a soft, powdery, white or gray form of limestone that is made up mostly of tiny seashells. Chalk is used especially to make lime and cement and sometimes as a fertilizer. **2.** a piece of this substance or a similar material, usually in the form of a crayon and often colored, used for writing and drawing on a blackboard. —*v.t.* **1.** to mark, write, or draw with chalk: *to chalk pictures on the sidewalk.* **2.** to rub or treat with chalk. —**chalk′like′,** *adj.* [From the Old English word *cealc* meaning "limestone, plaster," from the Latin word *calx* meaning "lime, limestone."]

·**to chalk up. a.** to score or earn: *Our center chalked up thirty points in the game.* **b.** to charge or credit: *You can chalk up that mistake to ignorance.*

chalk·board (chôk′bôrd′) *n.* another word for **blackboard.**

chalk·y (chô′kē) *adj.,* **chalk·i·er, chalk·i·est. 1.** resembling chalk: *a chalky powder.* **2.** of or containing chalk. —**chalk′i·ness,** *n.*

chal·lenge (chal′ənj) *v.t.,* **chal·lenged, chal·leng·ing. 1.** to invite or call to take part in a struggle or contest; dare to fight or compete: *I challenged my friends to a race around the block.* **2.** to call into question; doubt or dispute: *to challenge a person's opinions.* **3.** to make demands on the talents or energy of; arouse the interest of: *This novel challenges the imagination. The science project challenged the entire class.* **4.** to stop and demand identification from: *The sentry challenged anyone who approached the gate.* **5.** *Law.* to object or take exception to: *to challenge a prospective juror.* —*n.* **1.** an invitation or call to take part in a fight or contest: *Our team accepted their challenge.* **2.** a calling into question; doubting or disputing. **3.** something that demands the use of one's talents or energy: *I find chemistry a real challenge.* **4.** a demand for identification from a sentry. **5.** *Law.* a formal objection, especially to the qualifications of a juror.

chal·leng·er (chal′ən jər) *n.* **1.** a person or thing that challenges: *The explorers were hailed as courageous challengers of the jungle.* **2.** a boxer who seeks to fight a champion for the title.

chal·lis (shal′ē) *also,* **chal·lie.** *n.* a soft, lightweight woolen, cotton, or rayon fabric, usually having a printed design, used especially for scarves and neckties.

cham·ber (chām′bər) *n.* **1.** a room, especially a bedroom. **2.** *also,* **chambers.** a room where a judge conducts business when not holding a court session. **3.** a hall where a legislature or other body meets. **4.** a legislative or judicial body or assembly: *The Senate is the upper chamber of Congress.* **5.** the reception room of a person of authority or rank, such as in a palace. **6.** a cavity or enclosed space in the body of an animal or plant: *the four chambers of the heart.* **7.** the rear portion of the barrel of a firearm, into which the cartridge or shell is inserted. —*v.t.* to provide with a chamber.

cham·ber·lain (chām′bər lin) *n.* **1.** a person in charge of a royal or noble household; steward. **2.** a person who receives or keeps funds and revenues; treasurer.

cham·ber·maid (chām′bər mād′) *n.* a woman whose work is making beds and cleaning bedrooms, especially in a hotel, motel, or other place providing accommodation.

chamber music, music written for a small group of instruments and suitable for performance in a room or small hall.

chamber of commerce, an association organized to promote the interests of the businesses of a particular town, state, region, or country.

chamber pot, a portable container that is used as a toilet.

cham·bray (sham′brā) *n.* a cotton fabric woven with colored and white threads, used especially for dresses, shirts, and pajamas. [Another form of *Chambrai,* the city in France where this fabric was first produced.]

cha·me·leon (kə mēl′yən) *n.* **1.** any of various small, slow-moving lizards that can change the color of their skin to match their surroundings. **2.** a person whose mood or opinions change readily; changeable or fickle person.

cham·ois (sham′ē) *n., pl.* **cham·ois** (sham′ēz) **1.** a small, goatlike antelope of the mountains of Europe and western Asia. It has a long, reddish brown coat that turns dark brown in the winter. **2.** a soft, pliable leather, originally made from the skin of the chamois, now made from the skins of sheep, goats, and deer. **3.** a cotton cloth made to resemble this leather.

cham·o·mile (kam′ə mīl′, kam′ə mēl′) *also,* **cam·o·mile.** *n.* any of several strong-smelling plants found in temperate regions, having flowers that resemble the daisy. The flowers of certain species are dried and used to make tea.

champ[1] (champ) *v.t.* **1.** to bite and chew vigorously and noisily; munch: *to champ oats.* **2.** to bite upon restlessly or impatiently: *The horse was champing its bit.* —*v.i.* to make biting or chewing movements with the jaws and teeth. [Perhaps imitative of the sound of chewing.]

·**to champ at the bit.** to show signs of restlessness or impatience: *The players were champing at the bit as they waited for the game to start.*

champ[2] (champ) *n. Informal.* champion.

cham·pagne (sham pān′) *n.* a sparkling, bubbling white or light pink wine. [From *Champagne,* a region in northeastern France where this wine is produced.]

cham·paign (sham pān′) *n.* flat, open country; plain.

cham·pi·on (cham′pē ən) *n.* **1.** the winner of first place or first prize in a competition: *a boxing champion. Our school is the league champion in basketball.* **2.** a person who fights for or defends a person or cause: *a champion of conservation, a champion of freedom of speech.* —*adj.* having won first place or first prize; superior to all others: *a champion wrestler.* —*v.t.* to fight for or defend; support: *to champion the cause of civil rights.*

cham·pi·on·ship (cham′pē ən ship′) *n.* **1.** the position or honor of being a champion: *Who held the tennis championship last year?* **2.** a competition to determine a champion: *We watched the championship on television.* **3.** the act of championing; defense or support.

chance (chans) *n.* **1.** the unknown cause of the way things take place; happening of events by accident; fate; luck; fortune: *I met them entirely by chance. We left matters to chance.* **2.** the likelihood of something happening; probability or possibility: *There's a chance we made a mistake. That team has little chance of winning.* **3.** an opportunity: *The prisoner saw the chance to escape. I have a chance to visit Europe.* **4.** a risk, gamble: *Don't take chances when you are swimming alone.* **5.** a ticket in a lottery, raffle, or similar contest. —*v.,* **chanced, chanc·ing.** —*v.i.* to happen by chance: *Our paths chanced to cross in the park.* —*v.t.* to take the chance of; risk: *We chanced buying tickets at the last minute.* —*adj.* happening by chance; unplanned; accidental: *a chance meeting, a chance remark.*

·**to chance on** or **to chance upon.** to find or meet unexpectedly or accidentally: *I chanced on the lost key while looking for my pen.*

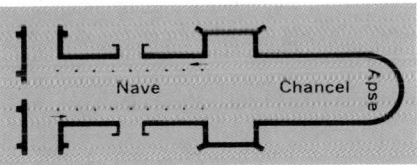

chancel

chan·cel (chan′səl) *n.* the space around the altar of a church, used by the clergy and the choir. It is often set off by a railing, lattice, or screen.

chan·cel·ler·y (chan′sə lə rē) *n., pl.* **chan·cel·ler·ies** **1.** the position or office of a chancellor. **2.** the office of an embassy, legation, or consulate.

chan·cel·lor (chan′sə lər) *n.* **1.** the prime minister in certain European countries, such as West Germany and Austria. **2.** the president of certain American universities. **3.** the judge of a court of equity in some states of the United States. **4.** an official who serves as the chief secretary of a sovereign or embassy.

Chancellor of the Exchequer *also,* **chancellor of the exchequer.** the cabinet minister in the British government who is in charge of financial affairs.

chan·cel·lor·ship (chan′sə lər ship′) *n.* the position or term of office of a chancellor.

chan·cer·y (chan′sə rē) *n., pl.* **chan·cer·ies.** **1.** a court of law that deals with matters for which there are no fair remedies under the common law or the civil law. **2.** see **chancellery** *(def. 2).*

at; āpe; fär; câre; end; mē; it; īce; pîerce; hot; ōld; sông, fôrk; oil; out; up; ūse; rūle; pull; tûrn; chin; sing; shop; thin; this; hw in white; zh in treasure. The symbol ə stands for the unstressed vowel sound heard in about, taken, pencil, lemon, and circus.

chan·cre (shang′kər) *n.* a sore or ulcer that develops on the skin as the first sign of certain infectious diseases.

chanc·y (chan′sē) *adj.* **chanc·i·er, chanc·i·est.** subject to chance; uncertain: *a chancy enterprise.*

chan·de·lier (shan′də lîr′) *n.* a lighting fixture designed to be hung from a ceiling, usually having several lights arranged on projecting arms or branches. [From the French word *chandelier* meaning "candlestick," going back to the Latin word *candelabrum* "a branched candlestick," from *candela* "candle."]

chan·dler (chand′lər) *n.* **1.** a person who makes or sells candles. **2.** a dealer or merchant, especially one who deals in groceries or ship's supplies.

change (chānj) *v.,* **changed, chang·ing.** —*v.t.* **1.** to make different: *We changed the arrangement of the furniture. I've changed my attitude toward work.* **2.** to replace (something) with another or others of the same or a similar kind: *to change one's shirt, to change one's job. The mechanic changed the oil in the engine.* **3.** to give and receive; exchange: *The two of us changed seats.* **4.** to give or receive the equivalent of (money) in smaller units: *Can you change a ten dollar bill for me?* —*v.i.* **1.** to become different: *The scenery changed as we drove south. The tennis player changed on becoming famous.* **2.** to put on other clothes: *The actors changed between scenes.* **3.** to transfer from one train, airplane, bus, or the like to another: *The passengers going to Des Moines had to change at Chicago.* —*n.* **1.** the act or fact of changing: *a change in plans, a change in the weather.* **2.** something that may be substituted for another: *a change of clothing.* **3.** something different from the usual: *For a change they took a vacation in the winter.* **4.** coins as distinguished from paper money: *I've got lots of change in my pocket.* **5.** the money returned when the amount paid is more than the amount owed: *I gave the cashier a dollar and got 40 cents in change.* **6.** money equal in value to a coin or bill of a higher denomination: *Could I have ten dimes as change for a dollar bill?* —**chang′er,** *n.*

change·a·ble (chān′jə bəl) *adj.* **1.** likely to change; variable: *a changeable personality, changeable weather.* **2.** that can be changed: *a changeable plan.* **3.** changing in color or appearance when looked at from different points of view: *changeable silk.* —**change′a·ble·ness,** *n.* —**change′a·bly,** *adv.*

change·ful (chānj′fəl) *adj.* full of changes; given to change; changeable; variable. —**change′ful·ly,** *adv.* —**change′ful·ness,** *n.*

change·less (chānj′lis) *adj.* that does not change; constant; enduring: *the changeless rhythm of the tides.* —**change′less·ly,** *adv.* —**change′less·ness,** *n.*

change·ling (chānj′ling) *n.* **1.** a child secretly substituted for another. **2.** in folklore, a child left by fairies in place of a child they have stolen.

change·o·ver (chānj′ō′vər) *n.* a change, shift, or transfer, as from one activity, method, or system to another: *a changeover from diesel to electric power.*

chan·nel (chan′əl) *n.* **1.** the deepest part of a river, harbor, or other waterway, often dredged and maintained as a passage for boats and ships. **2.** the bed of a stream, river, or other waterway. **3.** a body of water that connects two larger bodies of water. **4.** a groove or furrow: *a channel for run-off.* **5.** the means by which something is directed or carried: *a channel of communication.* **6.** channels. a proper or official route or means, especially of communication: *The request for new typewriters had to go through channels.* **7.a.** a frequency or band of frequencies assigned to a radio or television station for the transmission of electronic signals: *This old television set can only pick up one channel.* **b.** a frequency or band of frequencies used by certain telecommunications devices, such as CB radios or mobile telephones. —*v.t.,* **chan·neled, chan·nel·ing;** *also,* British, **chan·nelled, chan·nel·ling. 1.** to cut out as a channel: *The stream*

channeled its way down the mountain. **2.** to direct through a channel: *They channeled the stream onto the neighboring property.* **3.** to form a channel or groove in.

chant (chant) *n.* **1.** a singing or shouting of words over and over, usually with a strong rhythm: *The crowd broke into a chant when the candidate appeared.* **2.** a simple melody in which a number of syllables or words are sung on one note. **3.** a religious text sung in this manner. —*v.t.* **1.** to sing or shout over and over: *to chant a slogan.* **2.** to sing to a chant, as in a church service: *to chant a psalm.* **3.** to sing. —*v.i.* **1.** to recite or shout a chant: *The protesters chanted in the street below.* **2.** to sing a chant: *The choir chanted at the beginning of the service.* —**chant′er,** *n.*

chan·teuse (shan tüs′, shan tüz′) *n.* French. a female singer, especially one who sings in a nightclub or cabaret.

chan·tey (shan′tē, chan′tē) *also,* **chan·ty, shan·tey, shan·ty.** *n., pl.* **chan·teys.** a song sung by sailors in rhythm with their work.

chan·ti·cleer (chan′tə klîr′) *n.* a rooster. ▲ used chiefly as a proper name in fables and literature.

Chan·til·ly (shan til′ē) *n.* a delicate lace made of silk or other fibers, used chiefly for evening and bridal gowns. Also, **Chantilly lace.** [From *Chantilly,* the town in northern France where this lace was first made.]

chan·ty (shan′tē, chan′tē) *n., pl.* **chan·ties.** another spelling of **chantey.**

Cha·nu·kah (hä′nə kə) another spelling of **Hanukkah.**

cha·os (kā′os) *n.* **1.** a state of complete confusion and disorder: *The village was in chaos after the earthquake.* **2. Chaos.** *Greek Mythology.* the confused and formless state that existed before the creation of the universe. [From the Latin word *chaos* meaning "empty space," from the Greek word *chaos* "abyss, space."]

cha·ot·ic (kā ot′ik) *adj.* in complete confusion and disorder: *The candidate's headquarters was chaotic on the night of the election.* —**cha·ot′i·cal·ly,** *adv.*

chap[1] (chap) *v.,* **chapped, chap·ping.** —*v.t.* to split, crack, or make rough: *My hands are chapped from washing dishes.* —*v.i.* to become split, cracked, or roughened: *My lips always chap in the winter.* [From the Middle English word *chappen* meaning "to crack open."]

chap[2] (chap) *n. Informal.* a man or boy; fellow. [Short for the earlier word *chapman* meaning "peddler," from the Old English word *cēapman* "merchant," from the words *cēap* "trade" + *man* "person."]

chap., chapter.

chap·ar·ral (shap′ə ral′) *n.* a dense thicket of low or shrubby trees or thorny shrubs, usually found in dry, sunny regions.

cha·peau (sha pō′) *n., pl.* **cha·peaus** or **cha·peaux** (sha pō′, sha pōz′). a hat. [From the French word *chapeau,* going back to the Medieval Latin word *cappellus* meaning "head covering," from the Late Latin word *cappa* "head covering" or "cloak."]

chap·el (chap′əl) *n.* **1.** a place of worship that is smaller than a church. **2.** a room or space within a church, having its own altar and used for special or small services. **3.** a place of worship in a school, college, hospital, military post, or the like. **4.** a service or services in a chapel, especially at a school or college: *Students were required to attend chapel twice each week.*

chap·er·on (shap′ə rōn′) *n.* **1.** an older or married person who attends and supervises a social gathering of young unmarried people. **2.** an older or married woman who accompanies a young unmarried woman in public. —*v.t.* to act as chaperon for: *My mother and father chaperoned the dance.*

chap·er·one (shap′ə rōn′) *n., v.,* **chap·er·oned, chap·er·on·ing.** another spelling of **chaperon.**

chap·lain (chap′lin) *n.* a member of the clergy who performs religious functions for groups or organizations, such as a military unit, a prison, or a school.

chap·let (chap′lit) *n.* **1.** a wreath or garland worn on the head. **2.** a short rosary. **3.** any string of beads; necklace.

chaps (chaps, shaps) *pl. n.* strong leather leggings worn over trousers by cowhands to protect their legs while riding horseback. [Short for the Mexican Spanish word *chaparreras* meaning "chaps," from the Spanish word *chaparro* "chaparral." Chaps were worn as protection from the thorns of the chaparral.]

chaps

chap·ter (chap′tər) *n.* **1.** a main division of a book or other writing. **2.** a main division or part of anything: *The Civil War was a critical chapter in American history.* **3.** a local branch or division of an organization, such as a club, fraternity, or society.

char (chär) *v.*, **charred, char·ring.** —*v.t.* **1.** to burn slightly or partially; scorch. **2.** to reduce to charcoal by burning: *to char wood.* —*v.i.* to become charred.

char·ac·ter (kar′ik tər) *n.* **1.** all the qualities or features that are typical of or serve to distinguish a person, group, or thing; individual nature: *That author's stories have a gloomy character. The countryside has a different character as you travel west.* **2.** all the qualities of a person, good or bad, that make up his or her moral nature; moral quality: *a person with a fine, honest character.* **3.** moral strength or excellence; integrity: *a young person of character.* **4.** a person represented in a novel, play, motion picture, or the like: *Hamlet is one of the most famous characters in literature.* **5.** *Informal.* a person who is odd, eccentric, amusing, or very different. **6.** a position or function; capacity; status: *I signed the document in my character as president.* **7.** a mark or sign used as a symbol in writing or printing, such as a letter of the alphabet.

·**in character.** in keeping with a person's disposition or usual behavior.

·**out of character.** not in keeping with a person's disposition or usual behavior.

char·ac·ter·is·tic (kar′ik tə ris′tik) *n.* a quality or feature that is typical of or serves to distinguish a person, group, or thing from others: *Tact is my cousin's outstanding characteristic. The ability to fly is a characteristic of bats.* *adj.* relating to or indicating the character of a person or thing: *Lemons have a characteristic taste. Rudeness is not characteristic of these children.* —**char·ac·ter·is′ti·cal·ly,** *adv.*

char·ac·ter·ize (kar′ik tə rīz′) *v.t.*, **char·ac·ter·ized, char·ac·ter·iz·ing. 1.** to be a characteristic of; distinguish: *That disease is characterized by a high fever.* **2.** to describe the character or qualities of; portray: *The author characterizes the countryside as teeming with life.* —**char′ac·ter·i·za′tion,** *n.*

cha·rades (shə rādz′) *pl. n.* a game in which the players try to guess a word or phrase that another player acts out without speaking. To show the word *characterize,* a player might act out "car," "actor," and "eyes." ▲ used with a singular verb.

char·coal (chär′kōl′) *n.* a black, soft substance that is a form of carbon, made by partially burning wood or other plant or animal matter. It is used as fuel, in filters, and as a pencil for drawing.

chard (shärd) *n.* see **Swiss chard.**

charge (chärj) *v.*, **charged, charg·ing.** —*v.t.* **1.** to fix or ask as a price: *The shop charged ten dollars to repair the radio.* **2.** to require payment from: *The neighbor charged us for the broken window.* **3.** to put off payment for (something) until a later time: *I charged the gifts at the shop.* **4.** to rush violently upon or toward in an attack: *The bull charged the farmer. The troops charged the fortress.* **5.** to bring an accusation against or put blame upon; accuse: *The police charged two teenagers with the theft.* **6.** to give a task, duty, or responsibility to: *A baby-sitter is charged with the care of children while their parents are away.* **7.** to fill or load: *They charged the cannon with shot. The reply was charged with emotion.* **8.** to supply with a quantity of electricity or electrical energy: *to charge a storage battery.* **9.** to command or order: *The judge charged the jury to disregard the testimony.* —*v.i.* **1.** to rush violently or go quickly: *I charged up the stairs after the cat.* **2.** to fix or ask a price: *Does that store charge for delivery?* —*n.* **1.** the required payment; price asked or fixed: *The charge for admission was $1.50.* **2.** a purchase that is to be paid for at a later time. **3.** a violent or rushing attack: *The enemy's charge was turned back.* **4.** the signal or order for such an attack: *The bugler sounded the charge.* **5.** an accusation: *They were arrested on a charge of robbery.* **6.** care, custody, or management: *The ranger had charge of 2,000 acres of forest.* **7.** a person or thing under the care, custody, or management of another: *The orphans were made charges of their grandparents.* **8.** task, duty, or responsibility: *The orphans' education became the charge of their guardians.* **9.** the quantity that something is fitted to receive and hold, such as the amount of gunpowder in a cartridge or shell. **10.** the amount of electrical energy possessed by an object. **11.** a command, order, or instruction: *a judge's charge to a jury.* —**charge′a·ble,** *adj.*

·**in charge.** in the position of authority or responsibility; in command.

·**in charge of.** in control of; responsible for.

charge account, an arrangement by which a person may make purchases to be paid for at a later date.

charge card, a small card bearing a person's identification, used for making purchases on a charge account.

char·gé d'af·fairs (shär zhā′ də fâr′) *pl.* **char·gés d'af·fairs** (shär zhāz′də fâr′). a diplomatic official who serves as a temporary substitute for an ambassador or minister. [From the French phrase *chargé d'affaires* meaning "(one) charged with affairs."]

charg·er (chär′jər) *n.* **1.** a horse trained for use in battle. **2.** a person or thing that charges. **3.** a device used to give an electrical charge to storage batteries.

char·i·ot (char′ē ət) *n.* a two-wheeled vehicle drawn by two, three, or four horses and driven from a standing position, used in ancient times in warfare, processions, and races.

char·i·ot·eer (char′ē ə tîr′) *n.* the driver of a chariot.

cha·ris·ma (kə riz′mə) *n.* a rare personal quality that attracts the loyalty and devotion of a large following of people: *the charisma of a great leader.*

char·is·mat·ic (kar′iz mat′ik) *adj.* having or showing charisma: *a charismatic leader.*

char·i·ta·ble (char′i tə bəl) *adj.* **1.** of or for charity; giving help to the poor or needy: *a charitable organization.* **2.** merciful, or forgiving in judging others; kindly; tolerant: *It was charitable of you to overlook their bad manners.* **3.** generous in giving help to the poor or needy. —**char′i·ta·ble·ness,** *n.* —**char′i·ta·bly,** *adv.*

char·i·ty (char′i tē) *n., pl.* **char·i·ties. 1.** the giving of help to the poor or needy. **2.** money or other help given to the poor or needy: *The family refused to accept charity after the flood.* **3.** a fund, institution, or organization for helping the poor or needy: *Give generously to your favorite*

---

at; āpe; fär; câre; end; mē; it; īce; pîerce; hot; ōld; sông, fôrk; oil; out; up; ūse; rüle; pùll; tûrn; chin; sing; shop; thin; <u>th</u>is; hw in white; zh in treasure. The symbol ə stands for the unstressed vowel sound heard in about, taken, pencil, lemon, and circus.

charity. **4.** mercy or forgiveness in judging others; kindness; tolerance: *The soldiers treated their former enemies with charity.* **5.** love of one's fellow human beings: *faith, hope, and charity.* [From the Old French word *charité* meaning "goodwill" and "charity," from the Late Latin word *caritas* "Christian love," from the Latin word *caritas* "dearness," from the word *carus* "dear, beloved."]

char·la·tan (shär′lə tən) *n.* a person who pretends or claims to have knowledge or skill that he or she does not actually possess; quack; impostor. [From the French word *charlatan,* from the Italian word *ciarlatano* meaning "a quack" and "an inhabitant of *Cerreto,*" an Italian town. Cerreto had a reputation as the home of dishonest people.]

Charles·ton (chärl′stən) *n.* a lively dance in 4/4 time, popular especially in the 1920s. [From *Charleston,* South Carolina.]

char·ley horse (chär′lē) a painful cramp in a muscle, especially in the leg.

charm (chärm) *n.* **1.** the power to fascinate, attract, or delight greatly: *a performer of great charm. That resort holds much charm for vacationers.* **2.** any fascinating, attractive, or delightful quality or feature: *A small pond is the property's greatest charm.* **3.** a small ornament or trinket, often worn on a chain bracelet. **4.** something worn to ward off evil or bring good luck; amulet: *I carry a rabbit's foot as a charm.* **5.** any action or formula that is supposed to have magic power. —*v.t.* **1.** to fascinate, attract, or delight greatly; captivate: *Your story charmed everyone at the party.* **2.** to affect as if by magic; bewitch: *The playing of the flute charmed the cobra.* **3.** to endow with or protect by or as if by magic power: *to lead a charmed life.* —**charm′er,** *n.*

charm·ing (chär′ming) *adj.* full of charm; fascinating, attractive, or delightful: *a charming person, a charming little house.* —**charm′ing·ly,** *adv.*

char·nel house (chär′nəl) a place in which the bones or bodies of the dead are placed.

Char·on (kâr′ən, kar′ən) *n. Greek Mythology.* the boatman who ferried the souls of the dead across the river Styx to the entrance of Hades.

chart (chärt) *n.* **1.** a sheet showing information in the form of lists, diagrams, tables, graphs, or the like: *a weather chart, a population chart.* **2.** a map, especially one with information for sailors, such as the depth of water or the location of rocks, channels, harbors, and the like. —*v.t.* **1.** to make a map or chart of: *to chart a coastline.* **2.** to plan or map out: *to chart a course of action.*

char·ter (chär′tər) *n.* **1.** a formal document issued by a government or a ruler to a person, group, or corporation, granting the right to organize for carrying on some activity and imposing certain duties and obligations. **2.** a document setting forth the aims and principles of a body or organization, such as a group of nations. **3.** written permission from a society or organization to establish a new local chapter or branch. **4.** a leasing or renting of an aircraft, bus, or the like: *Those planes are available for charter.* —*v.t.* **1.** to lease or hire by charter: *Our school chartered three buses for the trip.* **2.** to grant a charter to; establish by charter: *The state chartered a bank.*

char·treuse (shär trüz′, shär trüs′) *n.* **1.** a pale yellowish green color. **2.** a green, yellow, or white liqueur. —*adj.* having the color chartreuse; pale yellowish green.

char·wom·an (chär′wüm′ən) *n., pl.* **char·wom·en** (chär′wim′ən). a woman hired to do cleaning and scrubbing in homes, offices, or public buildings.

char·y (châr′ē) *adj.,* **char·i·er, char·i·est. 1.** hesitant about danger or risks; careful; cautious; wary: *The fox was chary of hunters.* **2.** reluctant in granting or giving; not lavish; sparing. —**char′i·ly,** *adv.* —**char′i·ness,** *n.*

Cha·ryb·dis (kə rib′dis) *n. Greek Mythology.* a hideous monster having the form of a raging whirlpool, dwelling in the Strait of Messina opposite the cave of the monster Scylla. Sailors who were not devoured by Scylla were drowned by Charybdis.

chase (chās) *v.,* **chased, chas·ing.** —*v.t.* **1.** to go after and try to catch; pursue: *The cat chased the birds. The police chased the thief down the alley.* **2.** to cause to leave quickly or flee; drive: *I chased the deer out of my yard.* —*v.i.* **1.** to follow in pursuit: *The children chased after the ball that rolled toward the street.* **2.** *Informal.* to rush about; hurry: *They chased all over town looking for a caterer.* —*n.* **1.** the act of chasing; pursuit: *to join in a chase. They caught the puppy after a long chase.* **2. the chase.** the sport of hunting. **3.** something chased or hunted; quarry. ·**to give chase.** to run or go after; chase; pursue.

chas·er (chā′sər) *n.* **1.** a person or thing that chases. **2.** *Informal.* a drink, as of water or beer, taken after a drink of hard liquor.

chasm (kaz′əm) *n.* **1.** a deep, yawning crack or gap in the earth's surface; gorge. **2.** a great difference of feelings, beliefs, opinions, or the like: *a chasm between two rival political parties.*

Chas·sid (has′id) *n., pl.* **Chas·si·dim** (has′i dim, hä-sē′dim). another spelling of **Hasid.** —**Chas·sid·ic** (ha-sid′ik) *adj.*

Chas·si·dism (has′i diz′əm) *n.* another spelling of **Hasidism.**

chas·sis (chas′ē, shas′ē) *n., pl.* **chas·sis** (chas′ēz, shas′ēz). **1.** the part of a motor vehicle that supports the body, including the frame, wheels, engine, steering mechanism, and other mechanical parts. **2.** the frame that supports the body of an aircraft. **3.** the framework on which the parts of a radio or television set are mounted.

chaste (chāst) *adj.* **1.** pure in thought and action; moral, virtuous, or decent: *a chaste person.* **2.** simple in style; not ornate or extreme. —**chaste′ly,** *adv.* —**chaste′ness,** *n.*

chas·ten (chā′sən) *v.t.* **1.** to punish in order to correct or improve: *to chasten a puppy.* **2.** to restrain; subdue: *The firm speech chastened the crowd.* —**chas′ten·er,** *n.*

chas·tise (chas tīz′) *v.t.,* **chas·tised, chas·tis·ing.** to punish, reprimand, or discipline severely. —**chas·tise′ment,** *n.* —**chas·tis′er,** *n.*

chas·ti·ty (chas′ti tē) *n.* the state or quality of being chaste or pure.

chas·u·ble (chaz′ə bəl, chaz′yə bəl) *n.* a sleeveless outer garment worn by a priest officiating at Mass.

chat (chat) *v.i.,* **chat·ted, chat·ting.** to talk in a light, familiar, or informal manner: *The two friends chatted about the weather.* —*n.* **1.** informal, friendly talk. **2.** any of several songbirds having a chattering cry.

cha·teau (sha tō′) *also,* **châ·teau.** *n., pl.* **cha·teaus** or **cha·teaux** (sha tōz′). **1.** a French castle. **2.** a large and elaborate country house, especially one in France.

chat·e·laine (shat′ə lān′) *n.* **1.** the mistress or lady of a castle, chateau, or fashionable household. **2.** an ornamental chain or clasp, usually worn at a woman's waist, to which keys, a purse, or other articles may be attached.

chat·tel (chat′əl) *n.* any article of personal property that can be moved, such as furniture, clothing, livestock, or an automobile.

chat·ter (chat′ər) *v.i.* **1.** to talk rapidly and foolishly, usually about matters of little importance; jabber: *They chattered on and on about their clothes.* **2.** to click together quickly or uncontrollably: *My teeth chattered from the cold.* **3.** to make quick, short sounds: *The magpies chattered in the trees.* —*v.t.* to say rapidly or foolishly: *to chatter nonsense.* —*n.* **1.** rapid, foolish talk. **2.** the act or sound of chattering: *the chatter of starlings.* —**chat′ter·er,** *n.*

chat·ter·box (chat′ər boks′) *n., pl.* **chat·ter·box·es.** a person who talks too much.

chat·ty (chat′ē) *adj.,* **chat·ti·er, chat·ti·est. 1.** given to chatting; talkative. **2.** full of chat; light, familiar, and informal: *a chatty letter.* —**chat′ti·ly,** *adv.* —**chat′ti·ness,** *n.*

chauf·feur (shō′fər, shō fûr′) *n.* a person whose work is driving an automobile. —*v.t.* to act or work as a chauffeur for: *Could you chauffeur us to the airport?*

chau·tau·qua (shə tô′kwə) *also,* **Chau·tau·qua.** *n.* **1.** an educational movement begun in 1874 at Chautauqua, a city in New York State, that established summer programs of instruction in education, religion, and the arts. **2.** any of various similar programs.

chau·vin·ism (shō′və niz′əm) *n.* **1.** greatly exaggerated and boastful devotion to one's country or its military glory; fanatical patriotism. **2.** greatly exaggerated pride in one's own group, race, or sex. [From the French word *chauvinisme* meaning "chauvinism," from Nicholas *Chauvin,* a character in a play who was known for his blind patriotism and devotion to Napoleon.]

chau·vin·ist (shō′və nist) *n.* **1.** a person who has a greatly exaggerated and boastful devotion to his or her country. **2.** a person who has a greatly exaggerated pride in his or her own group, race, or sex. —**chau′vin·ist′ic,** *adj.*

cheap (chēp) *adj.* **1.** low in price, especially as compared with its value: *Milk is cheap in that store. It was a good dinner and very cheap, too.* **2.** charging low prices: *a cheap dress shop.* **3.** of little value or worth; inferior in quality: *a cheap toy, a novel printed on cheap paper.* **4.** not willing to spend money; stingy: *to be too cheap to buy a new coat.* **5.** not worthy of respect; vulgar, common, or immoral: *That gaudy outfit makes you look cheap.* **6.** costing little effort or trouble: *Talk is cheap.* —*adv.* at a low price: *I bought this car cheap.* —**cheap′ly,** *adv.* —**cheap′ness,** *n.*

cheap·en (chē′pən) *v.t., v.i.* to make or become cheap or cheaper.

cheap·skate (chēp′skāt′) *n. Informal.* a stingy person.

cheat (chēt) *v.t.* **1.** to treat in a dishonest manner; swindle or trick: *They cheated us out of our share of the money.* **2.** to escape from by cleverness or good luck: *to cheat death.* —*v.i.* to act in a dishonest manner: *to cheat at card games. They were accused of cheating on the test.* —*n.* **1.** a person who cheats. **2.** the act of cheating; fraud; deception. —**cheat′er,** *n.*

check (chĕk) *n.* **1.** a sudden stop: *Our lack of money put a check to our vacation plans.* **2.** a person or thing that stops, controls, or limits: *The leash was a check on the dog. Bad weather was a check on our enthusiasm.* **3.** a test or other means to see if something is as it should be; examination, inspection, or investigation: *The supervisor made a check on the workers. A quick check of the facts showed that the story was true.* **4.** a mark (√) used to indicate that something has been approved, noted, or otherwise examined: *The teacher put a check next to the name of each pupil who was present.* **5.** *also,* **cheque.** a written order directing a bank to pay a stated amount of money from the account of the person who signs it: *I gave the store a check to pay for the new lamp.* **6.** a slip of paper listing an amount owed, especially in payment for a meal in a restaurant. **7.** a ticket, tag, or token that makes it possible for a person to reclaim something that has been left for temporary safekeeping: *Do you have the checks for our suitcases?* **8.** a pattern of squares like that of a checkerboard. **9.** one of these squares. **10.** *Chess.* the position of a king when it is under direct attack from one of the opposing pieces and is threatened with being captured on the next move. —*v.t.* **1.** to bring to a sudden stop: *The army checked the enemy's advance.* **2.** to hold in control; restrain; curb: *to check one's temper. I checked my impulse to laugh at the mistake.* **3.** to compare for accuracy or agreement: *Check your answers with the ones in the back of the book.* **4.** to test (something) to see if it is as it should be; examine, inspect, or investigate: *The*

mechanic checked the engine to be sure it was running properly.* **5.** to mark with a check: *Please check the correct answer to each question.* **6.** to leave for temporary safekeeping, as in a checkroom: *to check one's coat, to check a package.* **7.** to mark with a pattern of small squares. **8.** *Chess.* to place (an opponent's king) in check. —*v.i.* to correspond accurately; agree: *My totals check with yours.*

· **in check.** under control or restraint: *to keep one's anger in check.*

· **to check in.** to register as a guest at a hotel or motel.

· **to check on** or **to check up on.** to make an examination, inspection, or investigation: *The doctor checked on the bandage on my leg.*

· **to check out.** **a.** to pay one's bill and depart from a hotel or motel. **b.** to prove to be true or correct: *The suspect's alibi checked out, and the police dropped the charges.* **c.** to add up prices for payment, especially in a supermarket.

check·book (chĕk′bŭk′) *n.* a book of blank checks issued by a bank.

checked (chĕkt) *adj.* marked with squares; checkered: *a checked tablecloth.*

check·er[1] (chĕk′ər) *n.* **1.** a person who checks. **2.** a cashier, especially in a supermarket. [*Check* + -*er*[1].]

check·er[2] (chĕk′ər) *n.* **1.** one of the flat, circular, usually red or black pieces used in the game of checkers. **2.** a pattern of squares of alternating colors. **3.** one of these squares. —*v.t.* to mark with squares of alternating colors. [From the Old French word *eschequier* meaning "chessboard," from the word *eschec* "to put the king in check (in chess)," going back to the Arabic word *shāh* with the same meaning, from the Persian word *shāh* "king."]

check·er·board (chĕk′ər bôrd′) *n.* a square board marked off into sixty-four alternately colored squares, used in playing checkers and chess; chessboard.

check·ered (chĕk′ərd) *adj.* **1.** marked with squares of alternating colors: *a checkered scarf.* **2.** filled with changes of fortune: *a checkered career.*

check·ers (chĕk′ərz) *n.* a game for two people played on a checkerboard, each player having twelve pieces. The game is over when one of the players cannot make a move because all his or her pieces have been captured or blocked. ▲ used with a singular verb. Also, *British,* **draughts.**

checking account, a bank account against which checks may be drawn by the depositor.

check·list (chĕk′list′) *n.* a list of items, such as names, tasks, or purchases, used as a source of reference: *I have a checklist of things to pack for camping trips.*

check·mate (chĕk′māt′) *v.t.,* **check·mat·ed, check·mat·ing.** **1.** *Chess.* to put (the opponent's king) in check from which no escape is possible, thus winning the game. **2.** to defeat or thwart completely. —*n.* **1.** *Chess.* a move that checkmates the opponent's king, or the position of a king when it has been checkmated. **2.** a complete defeat. [From the Old French exclamation *eschec mat!* announcing a checkmate, going back to the Persian phrase *shāh māt* meaning "the king is dead."]

check·out (chĕk′out′) *n.* **1.** a checking out, as in a supermarket. **2.** a place for checking out.

check·point (chĕk′point′) *n.* a place where vehicles or travelers are stopped for inspection.

check·rein (chĕk′rān′) *n.* a short rein connecting a bit to a harness, used to keep a horse from lowering its head.

---

at; āpe; fär; câre; end; mē; it; īce; pîerce; hot; ōld; sông, fôrk; oil; out; up; ūse; rüle; pull; tûrn; chin; sing; shop; thin; this; hw in white; zh in treasure. The symbol ə stands for the unstressed vowel sound heard in about, taken, pencil, lemon, and circus.

check·room (chek′rüm′, chek′rŭm′) *n.* a room in which personal property, such as hats, coats, or packages, may be left temporarily for safekeeping.

checks and balances, procedures that limit the power of one branch of a government by giving some power to another branch. A system of checks and balances is built into the constitution of the United States, limiting the power of the executive, legislative, and judicial branches.

check·up (chek′up′) *n.* **1.** a complete physical examination. **2.** any thorough examination or inspection.

Ched·dar (ched′ər) *also,* **ched·dar.** *n.* any of several types of hard, smooth cheese, ranging in color from white to orange and in taste from strong and sharp to mild. [From *Cheddar,* the village in England where this cheese was first made.]

cheek (chēk) *n.* **1.** either side of the face below the eye. **2.** something resembling this part of the face in shape or position. **3.** *Informal.* saucy or disrespectful boldness; insolence; impudence.

cheek·bone (chēk′bōn′) *n.* either of two bones at the upper part of the cheek, just below the eye.

cheek·y (chē′kē) *adj.,* **cheek·i·er, cheek·i·est.** *Informal.* saucy; insolent; impudent: *a cheeky youngster.* —**cheek′i·ly,** *adv.* —**cheek′i·ness,** *n.*

cheep (chēp) *v.i.* to make a faint, shrill, chirping sound, as a young bird, mouse, or bat; peep. —*n.* such a sound.

cheer (chîr) *n.* **1.** a lively shout of approval, praise, encouragement, or joy: *A cheer arose from the crowd when the astronauts appeared.* **2.** a set of words or sounds used by spectators to encourage or show enthusiasm for a contestant or athletic team: *a school cheer.* **3.** gladness, joy, or gaiety: *There is a general feeling of cheer as the holiday season nears.* **4.** something that gives joy or gladness; comfort; encouragement: *The doctor spoke words of cheer to the sick child.* **5.** a state of mind or spirits; mood: *to be of good cheer.* —*v.t.* **1.** to salute or acclaim with cheers: *The crowd cheered the rescuers of the children.* **2.** to make hopeful or glad: *The mourners were cheered by the kind words. The good news cheered us.* —*v.i.* **1.** to utter cheers: *We cheered as the runner neared the finish line.* **2.** to become hopeful or glad (usually with *up*): *I cheered up when the rain stopped.*

cheer·ful (chîr′fəl) *adj.* **1.** showing or feeling cheer; full of good spirits; happy; joyous: *a cheerful person, a cheerful smile.* **2.** bringing cheer: *a cheerful fire, a cheerful room.* **3.** ready to help; willing: *a cheerful worker.* —**cheer′ful·ly,** *adv.* —**cheer′ful·ness,** *n.*

cheer·lead·er (chîr′lē′dər) *n.* a person who leads organized cheering, especially at a sports event.

cheer·less (chîr′lis) *adj.* without cheer; joyless; gloomy. —**cheer′less·ly,** *adv.* —**cheer′less·ness,** *n.*

cheer·y (chîr′ē) *adj.,* **cheer·i·er, cheer·i·est.** bringing or full of cheerfulness; gay: *a cheery greeting, a cheery person.* —**cheer′i·ly,** *adv.* —**cheer′i·ness,** *n.*

cheese (chēz) *n.* a food made from the curds of milk pressed into a solid mass or cake.

cheese·burg·er (chēz′bûr′gər) *n.* a hamburger with cheese melted on top of the meat.

cheese·cake (chēz′kāk′) *n.* a rich, creamy cake made of cream cheese or cottage cheese, eggs, sugar, milk, and various flavorings.

cheese·cloth (chēz′klôth′) *n.* a thin, loosely woven cotton cloth, first used for wrapping cheese.

chees·y (chē′zē) *adj.,* **chees·i·er, chees·i·est.** **1.** of or like cheese. **2.** *Slang.* of inferior quality; poorly made; cheap.

chee·tah (chē′tə) *n.* an animal of the cat family that resembles a leopard and is found in Africa and southern

cheetah

Asia. It can run at speeds up to 70 miles per hour (112 kilometers per hour) for short distances and is sometimes tamed and trained to hunt.

chef (shef) *n.* **1.** the head cook, as of a restaurant, hotel, or large household. **2.** any person who cooks.

chef-d'oeu·vre (shā dü′vrə) *n., pl.* **chefs-d'oeu·vre** (shā dü′vrə) a masterpiece, especially one in art, literature, or music.

chef's salad, a salad consisting of greens, strips of cheese, cold meats, often hard-boiled eggs, and garnishes. It is often served as the main dish of a meal.

che·la (kē′lə) *n., pl.* **che·lae** (kē′lē). a claw of a lobster, crab, or scorpion.

chem. **1.** chemical. **2.** chemist. **3.** chemistry.

chem·i·cal (kem′i kəl) *adj.* of, relating to, or produced by chemistry. —*n.* a substance obtained by or used in a chemical process. —**chem′i·cal·ly,** *adv.*

Lobster chela

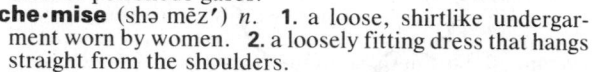
chela

chemical engineer, a specialist in chemical engineering.

chemical engineering, the science or profession of applying chemical knowledge and principles to industrial processes.

chemical warfare, the use in war of chemicals or chemical products, such as poisonous gases.

che·mise (shə mēz′) *n.* **1.** a loose, shirtlike undergarment worn by women. **2.** a loosely fitting dress that hangs straight from the shoulders.

chem·ist (kem′ist) *n.* **1.** a person who is a student of or expert in chemistry. **2.** *British.* another word for **druggist.**

chem·is·try (kem′ə strē) *n., pl.* **chem·is·tries.** **1.** the science that deals with the composition and properties of substances and the changes that take place when they react with other substances. **2.** chemical composition, property, or process: *the chemistry of carbon.* [From the Old French word *alchemie* meaning "alchemy," going back to the Arabic word *al-kimīyā* "the alchemy," from the Late Greek word *chēmiā* meaning "chemistry, transmutation of metals."]

che·mo·ther·a·py (kē′mō ther′ə pē, kem′ō ther′ə pē) *n.* the use of chemical substances to treat diseases. Chemotherapy is used in cancer treatment to poison the diseased cells.

chem·ur·gy (kem′ər jē) *n.* the branch of chemistry that deals with the development of new industrial uses for plant and animal products.

che·nille (shə nēl′) *n.* **1.** a yarn, often made of cotton, silk, or rayon, with a velvety, fuzzy pile, used for embroidery, tassels, and fringes. **2.** a fabric woven from this yarn, used for such items as rugs and bedspreads.

cheque (chek) *n.* *British.* another spelling of **check** *(def. 5).*

cher·ish (cher′ish) *v.t.* **1.** to treat with affection; care for tenderly; hold dear. **2.** to hold or entertain in the mind; cling to: *to cherish a memory.*

Cher·o·kee (cher′ə kē) *n., pl.* **Cher·o·kee** or **Cher·o·kees.** **1.** a member of a tribe of North American Indians, formerly the largest tribe in the southeastern United States, now living mostly in Oklahoma. **2.** the language of this tribe.

che·root (shə rüt′) *n.* a cigar cut square at both ends.

cher·ry (cher′ē) *n., pl.* **cher·ries.** **1.** a small, round or heart-shaped fruit of any of several trees or shrubs, grown in temperate regions of the world, having a smooth skin and a fleshy pulp enclosing a pit. **2.** the tree or shrub bearing this fruit, having clusters of white or pink flowers. **3.** the wood of this tree or shrub. **4.** a bright red color. —*adj.* having the color cherry; bright red.

cher·ub (cher′əb) *n., pl. (defs. 1, 2)* **cher·u·bim** cher′ə bim′) or *(def. 3)* **cher·ubs.** **1.** an angel of high rank. **2.** a representation of a cherub in art, usually as a chubby, winged child. **3.** a beautiful, innocent, or sweet child.

che·ru·bic (chə rü′bik) *adj.* of or resembling a cherub.

cher·vil (chûr′vəl) *n.* **1.** a plant related to parsley, whose leaves are used in salads and soups. **2.** a similar plant having a root that is eaten as a vegetable, either raw or cooked.

Chesh·ire cat (chesh′ər, chesh′îr) in Lewis Carroll's *Alice's Adventures in Wonderland,* a grinning cat that gradually faded away until only its grin remained.

chess (ches) *n.* a game for two played on a chessboard, each player having sixteen pieces. The players take turns moving their pieces, the object of the game being to checkmate the opponent's king.

a game of **chess**

chess·board (ches′bôrd′) *n.* a square board marked off into sixty-four alternately colored squares, used in playing chess or checkers; checkerboard.

chess·man (ches′man′, ches′mən) *n., pl.* **chess·men** (ches′men′, ches′mən). any of the pieces used in playing chess.

chest (chest) *n.* **1.** the front part of the body in humans and other mammals, extending from the neck to the abdomen. **2.** the area inside the body from the neck to the abdomen, enclosed by the ribs, breastbone, and spinal column, and containing the heart and lungs. **3.** a large, strong box with a lid, that is used for storing or shipping things: *a tool chest, a toy chest.* **4.** see **chest of drawers.**

ches·ter·field (ches′tər fēld′) *n.* **1.** a single-breasted topcoat having concealed buttons and a velvet collar. **2.** a davenport or sofa, usually having upright, upholstered arms. [From the Earl of *Chesterfield.*]

chest·nut (ches′nut′) *n.* **1.** the smooth-shelled, sweet nut of a tree belonging to the beech family, having a reddish brown color and growing inside a large, prickly bur. **2.** the tree producing this nut, having leathery, oblong leaves and fragrant flowers. **3.** the wood of this tree. **4.** a reddish brown color. **5.** a reddish brown horse. —*adj.* having the color chestnut; reddish brown.

chest of drawers, a piece of furniture that consists of a frame containing a set of drawers, used for holding clothing, linens, or other articles.

chev·a·lier (shev′ə lîr′) *n.* **1.** a knight. **2.** a member of an order of merit.

Chev·i·ot (shev′ē ət, chev′ē ət) *n.* **1.** any of a small, hardy breed of sheep with thick, short wool. **2. cheviot.** **a.** a rough woolen fabric woven in raised diagonal lines, used for suits and coats, formerly made from the wool of Cheviots. **b.** a coarse cotton cloth resembling this. [From the *Cheviot* Hills, on the border of Scotland and England, where this breed originated.]

chev·ron (shev′rən) *n.* an emblem or insignia consisting of stripes meeting at an angle, worn on the sleeve of a military or police uniform to indicate rank, length of service, or some other distinction.

chevrons

chew (chü) *v.t.* **1.** to crush or grind with the teeth: *Chew your food thoroughly.* **2.** to make by chewing: *The puppy chewed a hole in the slipper.* —*v.i.* to crush or grind something with the teeth. —*n.* something that is chewed or is for chewing: *a chew of tobacco.*

chewing gum, a gummy preparation that is sweetened and flavored for chewing, usually made of chicle.

chew·y (chü′ē) *adj.,* **chew·i·er, chew·i·est.** soft or sticky and needing much chewing in order to be eaten: *chewy caramels.* —**chew′i·ness,** *n.*

Chey·enne (shī en′, shī an′) *n., pl.* **Chey·enne** or **Chey·ennes.** **1.** a member of a tribe of North American Indians formerly living on the Great Plains, now living mainly in Montana and Oklahoma. **2.** the language of this tribe.

chg., charge.

chi (kī) *n.* the twenty-second letter of the Greek alphabet (Χ, χ).

chic (shēk) *adj.* attractive, tasteful, and fashionable in style; stylish; smart: *a chic dress, a chic dancer.* —*n.* taste; elegance; style. [From the French word *chic* meaning "stylish, smart."]

Chi·ca·na (chi kä′nə) *n., pl.* **Chi·ca·nas.** a female American of Mexican birth or descent.

chi·can·er·y (shi kā′nə rē) *n., pl.* **chi·can·er·ies.** the use of unfair or deceitful methods; trickery.

Chi·ca·no (chi kä′nō) *n., pl.* **Chi·ca·nos.** an American of Mexican birth or descent. [From the Mexican Spanish word *chicano,* from the word *mejicano* meaning "an American of Mexican descent."]

chick (chik) *n.* **1.** a young chicken. **2.** the young of certain other birds. **3.** a child.

chick·a·dee (chik′ə dē′) *n.* a small North American bird, having gray or brown feathers with black, white, or brown markings and a black head.

Chick·a·saw (chik′ə sô′) *n., pl.* **Chick·a·saw** or **Chick·a·saws.** **1.** a member of a tribe of North American Indians formerly living in what is now Tennessee and northern Mississippi, now living in Oklahoma. **2.** The language of this tribe.

chick·en (chik′ən) *n.* **1.** a farm bird that is raised for its flesh and eggs; a hen or rooster. **2.** a young hen or rooster. **3.** the flesh of a chicken. **4.** any young bird. **5.** *Slang.* a cowardly person. —*adj. Slang.* cowardly.

chicken pox *also,* **chick·en·pox** (chik′ən poks′), a mild but highly contagious disease that is caused by a virus and usually occurs in children. It is characterized by a blotchy red rash that develops into blisters and, finally, scabs. Also, **varicella.**

chicken wire, a light wire netting used especially for enclosures for poultry.

chick–pea (chik′pē′) *n.* **1.** the large, round seed of a plant, eaten raw or cooked as a vegetable. **2.** the plant itself, bearing one or two seeds in a short pod. Also, **garbanzo.**

chick·weed (chik′wēd′) *n.* a common weed having a creeping root, oval leaves, and tiny white flowers.

at; āpe; fär; câre; end; mē; it; īce; pîerce; hot; ōld; sông, fôrk; oil; out; up; ūse; rüle; pùll; tûrn; chin; sing; shop; thin; this; hw in white; zh in treasure. The symbol ə stands for the unstressed vowel sound heard in about, taken, pencil, lemon, and circus.

C

chic·le (chik′əl) *n.* a gum obtained from the milky juice of several evergreen trees of tropical America, used chiefly for making chewing gum.

chic·o·ry (chik′ə rē) *n., pl.* **chic·o·ries. 1.** a plant that is related to lettuce, having blue flowers and lance-shaped leaves. **2.** the leaves of this plant, used as salad greens. **3.** the root of this plant, often roasted and ground to be mixed with coffee or used as a substitute for coffee.

chide (chīd) *v.t.,* **chid·ed** or **chid** (chid), **chid·ed** or **chid** or **chid·den** (chid′ən), **chid·ing.** to scold mildly.

chief (chēf) *n.* a person who is highest in rank or authority; head or leader of a group: *the chief of police, the chief of an Indian tribe.* —*adj.* **1.** highest in rank or authority: *the chief officer, the chief cook, the chief executive of a company.* **2.** most important; principal; main: *My chief reason for moving was to find a better job.*

·**in chief.** of the highest rank or authority; at the head: *the editor in chief of a newspaper.*

Chief Executive, the president of the United States.

chief justice 1. the presiding or head judge of a court having several judges. **2. Chief Justice.** the head of the U.S. Supreme Court.

chief·ly (chēf′lē) *adv.* **1.** mainly; mostly: *The dish consisted chiefly of meat.* **2.** above all; especially: *Some teenagers are chiefly interested in sports.*

chief of staff *pl.* **chiefs of staff. 1.** in the armed forces, a senior officer or head of a staff; the principal assistant to a commander. **2. Chief of Staff.** the highest-ranking officer of the U.S. Army or Air Force.

chief of state, the formal head of a nation, charged with ceremonial duties: *The king or queen of England is the chief of state of the United Kingdom.*

chief·tain (chēf′tən) *n.* a chief or leader, especially of a tribe or clan: *a bandit chieftain.*

chief·tain·cy (chēf′tən sē) *n., pl.* **chief·tain·cies.** the position or rank of a chieftain.

chif·fon (shi fon′) *n.* a sheer, lightweight fabric, usually of silk or rayon, used for such items as scarves and dresses. —*adj.* **1.** made of or resembling chiffon. **2.** made partially of beaten egg whites or gelatin, which give a light, airy consistency: *lemon chiffon pie.*

chif·fo·nier (shif′ə nîr′) *n.* a high bureau or chest of drawers, often having a mirror at the top.

chig·ger (chig′ər) *also,* **jig·ger.** *n.* **1.** the tiny, round, red larva of any of several kinds of mites. It pierces the skin of humans and other mammals, and sucks out blood, leaving red spots and causing severe itching. **2.** see **chigoe** *(def. 1).*

chi·gnon (shēn′yon) *n.* a twist or knot of hair worn usually at the nape of the neck by women.

chig·oe (chig′ō) *n.* **1.** a small sand flea that sucks blood, found in tropical America and Africa. The female burrows under the skin of humans and other mammals, causing painful sores and itching. **2.** see **chigger** *(def. 1).*

Chi·hua·hua (chi wä′wə) *also,* **chi·hua·hua.** *n.* a dog of a breed originally native to Mexico, having large, pointed ears and a smooth or wavy coat that is usually tan. It is the smallest breed of dog. [From *Chihuahua,* the state in northern Mexico where this breed originated.]

chil·blain (chil′blān′) *n.* a painful, itchy swelling or reddening of the skin, especially the hands and feet, caused by exposure to cold.

child (chīld) *n., pl.* **chil·dren. 1.** an offspring of a human being; son or daughter: *an only child, several children.* **2.** a boy or girl between birth and adolescence; young boy or girl: *a program intended for children.* **3.** a baby; infant. **4.** a descendant: *the children of Israel.* **5.** a person who is a product of a certain condition, place, or time: *a child of poverty.* —**child′less,** *adj.*

·**with child.** pregnant.

child abuse, physical or psychological injury, neglect, or mistreatment of a child, as by an adult.

child·birth (chīld′bûrth′) *n.* the act of giving birth to a child or children.

child·hood (chīld′hụd′) *n.* the period from birth to adolescence; time of being a child.

child·ish (chīl′dish) *adj.* **1.** of, like, or suitable for a child: *a childish dress.* **2.** immature; silly: *childish fears.* —**child′ish·ly,** *adv.* —**child′ish·ness,** *n.*

child·like (chīld′līk′) *adj.* relating to or suitable for a child; like a child; innocent; simple; trusting: *to have a childlike affection for stray animals.*

chil·dren (chil′drən) the plural of **child.**

Children's Crusade, an unsuccessful crusade to recover the Holy Land from the Muslims, undertaken by thousands of French and German children in 1212.

child's play, anything that is easily done.

chil·i (chil′ē) *also,* **chil·e, chil·li.** *n., pl.* **chil·ies. 1.** the dried pod of a kind of red pepper used to make a hot spice. **2.** the plant that this pod grows on, found in tropical America. **3.** see **chili con carne.**

chili con car·ne (kon kär′nē) *also,* **chile con car·ne.** a highly seasoned dish made of meat, red peppers, tomato sauce, and, usually, beans.

chili sauce, a highly spiced sauce used as a seasoning, made of red peppers, tomatoes, vinegar, sugar, and onions.

chill (chil) *n.* **1.** coldness, especially a mild but unpleasant coldness: *There was a chill in the air this morning.* **2.** a feeling of coldness in the body, usually accompanied by shivering: *I got a chill from sleeping without blankets.* **3.** a depressing or discouraging influence or effect; lack of warmth or friendliness: *The argument cast a chill over the party.* **4.** a feeling of fear or anxiety: *The horrible sight sent a chill through us.* —*v.t.* **1.** to make cold: *to chill wine.* **2.** to cause a sensation of cold in: *The night air chilled me.* **3.** to harden the surface of (a metal) by sudden cooling. —*v.i.* to become cold. —*adj.* chilly: *a chill wind.* —**chill′er,** *n.*

chil·li (chil′ē) *n., pl.* **chil·lies.** another spelling of **chili.**

chill·y (chil′ē) *adj.,* **chill·i·er, chill·i·est. 1.** cold: *chilly night air.* **2.** affected by, sensitive to, or feeling cold: *I felt chilly without my sweater.* **3.** not friendly; lacking warmth: *a chilly welcome.* —**chill′i·ness,** *n.*

Chi·mae·ra (ki mîr′ə, kī mîr′ə) *n., pl.* **Chi·mae·ras.** another spelling of **Chimera.**

chime (chīm) *n.* **1. chimes.** a set of large bells, tuned to a musical scale, that produce tones when swung or struck. **2. chimes.** a musical instrument made of a set of metal tubes that sound when struck with a mallet. **3.** a single bell, as in a clock. **4.** *also,* **chimes.** a sound or series of musical sounds made by a chime. —*v.,* **chimed, chim·ing.** —*v.t.* **1.** to produce a musical sound by striking; ring: *to chime bells.* **2.** to give or announce by ringing: *The clock chimed the hour.* —*v.i.* to ring.

·**to chime in.** to join in or interrupt a conversation: *Bystanders chimed in with ideas on what to do.*

Chi·me·ra (ki mîr′ə, kī mîr′ə) *also,* **Chi·mae·ra.** *n., pl.* **Chi·me·ras. 1.** *Greek Mythology.* a monster that breathed fire, with a lion's head, a goat's body, and a serpent's tail. **2. chimera. a.** any imaginary monster. **b.** a wild, ridiculous, or fantastic idea; silly fancy.

chi·mer·i·cal (ki mîr′i kəl) *adj.* **1.** not real; imaginary. **2.** filled with wild ideas; whimsical; fanciful.

chim·ney (chim′nē) *n., pl.* **chim·neys. 1.** an upright structure used to carry smoke or vapor from a fireplace or furnace. **2.** the part of such a structure rising above a roof. **3.** a smokestack. **4.** a tube, usually of glass, surrounding the flame of a lamp.

chimney piece, see **mantel** *(def. 2).*

chimney sweep, a person whose work is cleaning out soot from chimneys.

chimney swift, a North American bird resembling a swallow and having narrow, crescent-shaped wings and dull feathers. It often builds its nest in unused chimneys.

chimp (chimp) *n. Informal.* see **chimpanzee.**

chim·pan·zee (chim′pan zē′, chim pan′zē) *n.* an ape native to western and central Africa, having brownish black hair. Chimpanzees are highly intelligent and smaller than gorillas.

chin (chin) *n.* the part of the face below the mouth and above the neck. —*v.t.*, **chinned**, **chin·ning.** to lift (oneself) up to an overhead horizontal bar by pulling with the arms until the chin is level with or above the bar.

chi·na (chī′nə) *n.* **1.** a fine pottery composed chiefly of clay, feldspar, and flint, believed to have originated in China. China differs from porcelain in that it is baked twice. **2.** objects, especially dishes, that are made of this material. **3.** any pottery or dishes.

chimpanzee

Chi·na·man (chī′nə mən) *n., pl.* **Chi·na·men** (chī′nə mən). see **Chinese** (*def.* 2). ▲ **Chinaman** is now generally considered to be offensive; **Chinese** is preferred.

Chi·na·town (chī′nə toun′) *n.* a Chinese section of any city outside China, as in San Francisco or New York.

chi·na·ware (chī′nə wâr′) *n.* **1.** see **china** (*def.* 2). **2.** dishes of any kind.

chinch (chinch) *n., pl.* **chinch·es. 1.** see **chinch bug. 2.** any bedbug.

chinch bug, a small, black-and-white insect of North and Central America that is very destructive to wheat, corn, and other cereal grasses, especially in dry weather.

chin·chil·la (chin chil′ə) *n.* **1.** a small, squirrellike rodent of the Andes, having large, dark eyes and broad ears rounded at the tip. **2.** the valuable, very fine, silver or bluish gray fur of this animal, used to make coats and jackets, and to trim other apparel. **3.** a heavy fabric with a tufted finish, usually made partially or entirely of wool, that is used for such items as coats and suits.

chine (chīn) *n.* **1.** the backbone; spine. **2.** a cut of meat including all or part of an animal's backbone.

Chi·nese (chī nēz′, chī nēs′) *n., pl.* **Chi·nese. 1.** a person who was born in or is a citizen of China. **2.** a person of Chinese descent. **3.** the language of China, consisting of many dialects. Mandarin, the dialect spoken in Beijing, is the standard form of Chinese. —*adj.* of or relating to China, its people, their language, or culture.

Words From Other Languages

Many English words borrowed from Chinese are for foods and customs that Chinese immigrants introduced.

chop suey	a Chinese-American dish of chopped vegetables and meat or fish
chow	a slang word for food
chow mein	a Chinese-American dish of meat, vegetables, and rice or noodles
gung ho	very eager and enthusiastic
kowtow	to kneel or bow showing respect
kung fu	a Chinese martial art
pidgin	a language formed by mixing words from two or more languages
shantung	a soft, textured fabric, often silk
tea	a drink made by soaking dry leaves
wonton	a food made by wrapping noodle dough around a filling

Chinese checkers, a game for two to six players, using marbles on a board shaped like a six-pointed star and containing holes in each triangle of the star. The object is to move the marbles that fill one triangle to the opposite triangle.

Chinese Empire, China from the time of the first emperor until it became a republic in 1912.

Chinese gooseberry, another term for **kiwi** (*def.* 2).

Chinese lantern, a lantern of thin, usually decorated, paper that can be collapsed and folded flat. Also, **Japanese lantern.**

Chinese puzzle 1. a puzzle that is complicated or hard to solve. **2.** anything complicated and hard to solve.

Chinese Wall, see **Great Wall of China.**

chink¹ (chingk) *n.* a small, narrow opening; crack: *The chinks in the wall admitted light.* —*v.t.* to fill in the chinks of; plug: *to chink a wall with mud.* [Probably originally from the Old English word *cine* meaning "a crack, fissure."]

chink² (chingk) *n.* a short, sharp sound, as of metal or glass striking together. —*v.t.* to cause to make a short, sharp sound. —*v.i.* to make a short, sharp sound: *The ice cubes chinked in the glass.* [Representation of this sound.]

chi·no (chē′nō) *n., pl.* **chi·nos. 1.** a strong twill fabric, often made of cotton, used for durable clothing. **2. chinos.** pants made from this fabric.

Chi·nook (shi nŭk′) *n., pl.* **Chi·nook** or **Chi·nooks. 1.** a member of a tribe of North American Indians who formerly lived near the mouth of the Columbia River in what is now the state of Washington. **2.** the language spoken by these people. **3. chinook. a.** a warm, moist southwest wind that blows from the sea along the coasts of Washington and Oregon. **b.** a warm, dry wind that blows down from the Rocky Mountains to the neighboring plains.

Chinook Jargon, a pidgin made up of elements of Chinook, other American Indian languages, English, and French. It was formerly used among American Indians and traders in the northwestern United States and Canada.

chintz (chints) *n.* a cotton fabric, usually having a glossy finish and printed with a colorful pattern.

chintz·y (chint′sē) *adj.*, **chintz·i·er, chintz·i·est.** *Informal.* cheap; tawdry.

chin-up (chin′up′) *n.* an act of chinning oneself.

chip (chip) *n.* **1.** a small, usually thin, piece that has been

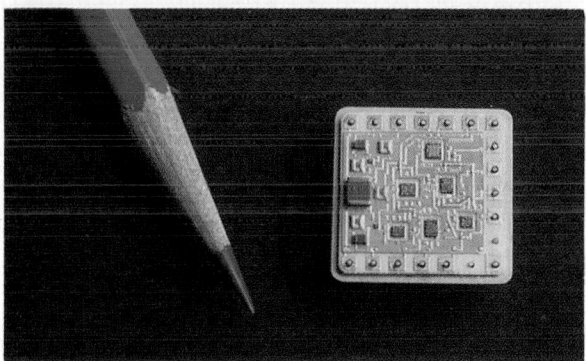

chip (*def.* 6)

at; āpe; fär; câre; end; mē; it; īce; pîerce; hot; ōld; sông, fôrk; oil; out; up; ūse; rüle; půll; tûrn; chin; sing; shop; thin; <u>th</u>is; hw in white; zh in treasure. The symbol ə stands for the unstressed vowel sound heard in about, taken, pencil, lemon, and circus.

169

cut or broken off: *a chip of wood.* **2.** a place where such a piece has been cut or broken off: *a chip on the edge of a glass.* **3.** a small, usually thin, slice of food, such as a potato chip. **4.** *British.* a French fried potato: *fish and chips.* **5.** a disk or counter used in place of money in certain games, such as poker. **6.** a very small piece of semiconductor material that holds an integrated circuit. Also *(def. 6),* **microchip.** —*v.,* **chipped, chip·ping.** —*v.t.* **1.** to cut or break off a piece or pieces from: *to chip a bone, to chip a cup.* **2.** to shape or produce by cutting off small pieces. —*v.i.* to break off in small pieces: *The paint on the wall chipped.*

·**a chip off the old block.** *Informal.* a person who is very much like one of his or her parents.

·**a chip on one's shoulder.** *Informal.* an aggressive or hostile attitude or manner.

·**to chip in.** *Informal.* to give one's share; contribute: *Every student chipped in to buy a gift for the teacher who was leaving.*

Chip·e·wy·an (chip′ə wī′ən) *n., pl.* **Chip·e·wy·an** or **Chip·e·wy·ans.** **1.** a member of an American Indian tribe living in northwestern Canada. **2.** the Athapascan language spoken by this tribe.

chip·munk (chip′mungk) *n.* a small North American rodent related to the squirrel, having brown or gray fur with stripes on the back and tail, large cheek pouches, and a slender, flattened tail.

chipmunk

chipped beef, beef that is sliced thinly and smoked or dried, sometimes served with a cream sauce.

chip·per (chip′ər) *adj. Informal.* lively or happy.

Chip·pe·wa (chip′ə wä′, chip′ə-wā′) *n., pl.* **Chip·pe·wa** or **Chip-pe·was.** another word for **Ojibwa.**

chipping sparrow, a sparrow of eastern and central North America that is reddish brown on the top of the head.

Chi·ron (kī′ron) *n. Greek Mythology.* a wise centaur, skilled in the arts, medicine, and prophecy. He was the teacher of many Greek heroes, including Jason, Achilles, and Hercules.

chi·rop·o·dist (kə rop′ə dist) *n.* another word for **podiatrist.**

chi·rop·o·dy (kə rop′ə dē) *n.* another word for **podiatry.**

chi·ro·prac·tic (kī′rə prak′tik) *n.* a system of treating disease by massaging and manipulating the joints by hand, especially those of the spinal column. —*adj.* of, relating to, or involving chiropractic: *a chiropractic school, chiropractic treatment.*

chi·ro·prac·tor (kī′rə prak′tər) *n.* a person who practices chiropractic.

chirp (chûrp) *n.* a short, sharp sound, such as that made by small birds and certain insects. —*v.i.* to make such a sound.

chir·rup (chîr əp, chûr′əp) *n.* a lively series of chirps. —*v.i.* to chirp continuously.

chis·el (chiz′əl) *n.* a metal tool with a sharp edge at the end of a blade, used to cut or shape stone, wood, or metal. —*v.t.,* **chis-eled, chis·el·ing;** *also, British,* **chis·elled, chis·el·ling.** **1.** to cut or shape with a chisel. **2.** *Slang.* to cheat; swindle: *The dishonest cashier chiseled them out of ten dollars.* —**chis′el·er;** *also, British,* **chis′el·ler,** *n.*

chit·chat (chit′chat′) *n.* **1.** light, informal conversation. **2.** small talk; gossip. —*v.i.,* **chit·chat·ted, chit·chat·ting.** to talk informally: *The two friends chitchatted about the coming vacation.*

chisel

chi·tin (kī′tin) *n.* a horny substance forming the hard outer covering in insects and certain other animals —**chi′tin·ous,** *adj.*

chit·ter·lings (chit′linz) *also,* **chit·lings, chit·lins.** *pl. n.* the small intestines of pigs, prepared as food.

chiv·al·rous (shiv′əl rəs) *adj.* **1.** having or showing the qualities characteristic of chivalry, such as gallantry, honor, and courtesy. **2.** of or relating to chivalry. —**chiv′al·rous·ly,** *adv.* —**chiv′al·rous·ness,** *n.*

chiv·al·ry (shiv′əl rē) *n.* **1.** the qualities of an ideal knight, such as gallantry, honor, courtesy, generosity, respect for women, protection of the weak, and skill in battle. **2.** the way of life of knights during the Middle Ages. **3.** a group of knights. [From the Old French word *chevalerie* meaning "knighthood," from the word *chevalier* "mounted warrior, knight," going back to the Late Latin word *caballus* "inferior horse, nag."]

chive (chīv) *n.* **1.** the long, slender leaves of a plant related to the onion, used as a garnish or seasoning. **2.** the plant bearing these leaves.

chlo·ral (klôr′əl) *n.* a colorless, oily liquid having a strong odor, used especially in the manufacture of DDT.

chloral hydrate, a white crystalline compound prepared from chlorine, ethyl alcohol, and water. It is used to produce sleep.

chlo·ride (klôr′īd) *n.* a compound of chlorine with another element or radical, especially a salt of hydrochloric acid.

chloride of lime, a white powder used for bleaching and disinfecting, prepared by treating slaked lime with chlorine. Also **bleaching powder.**

chlo·rin·ate (klôr′ə nāt′) *v.t.,* **chlo·rin·at·ed, chlo·rin·at·ing.** to combine or treat with chlorine, especially in order to kill bacteria: *to chlorinate the water in a swimming pool.* —**chlo′rin·a′tion,** *n.*

chlo·rine (klôr′ēn) *n.* an element of the halogen group that occurs as a heavy, poisonous, greenish yellow gas with a strong odor. Chlorine and its compounds are used in bleaching and disinfecting. Symbol: **Cl** [Formed from the Greek word *chlōros* meaning "greenish yellow."]

chlo·ro·form (klôr′ə fôrm′) *n.* a compound of carbon, hydrogen, and chlorine in the form of a colorless non-burning liquid with a sweetish smell. Formerly used as an anesthetic, it is now used especially as a solvent to dissolve rubber, fats, and other substances. —*v.t.* to make unconscious or kill by means of chloroform.

Chlo·ro·my·ce·tin (klôr′ə mī sē′tin) *n. Trademark.* an antibiotic drug that is very effective in the treatment of certain diseases, especially typhoid fever.

chlo·ro·phyll (klôr′ə fil′) *also,* **chlo·ro·phyl.** *n.* an organic compound of carbon, hydrogen, nitrogen, oxygen, and magnesium. It is the green coloring matter of plants and is needed by them for making food materials by changing carbon dioxide and water into sugar.

chlo·ro·plast (klôr′ə plast′) *n.* any of the small bodies in a plant cell that contain chlorophyll. Photosynthesis is carried out in chloroplasts.

chm., chairman. Also, **chmn.**

chock (chok) *n.* a block or wedge put under, in front of, or behind something to keep it from moving, as in front of the wheels of an airplane on the ground. —*v.t.* to furnish or keep in position with a chock or chocks.

chock·a·block (chok′ə blok′) *adj.* very crowded: *The museum's walls were chockablock with paintings.*

chock–full (chok′fŭl′) *also,* **chuck–full.** *adj.* as full as can be; crammed: *The trunk was chock-full of old clothes.*

choc·o·late (chô′kə lit, chok′ə lit) *n.* **1.** a food product made from ground and roasted cacao beans. **2.** a drink made by dissolving chocolate or cocoa in milk or water. **3.** a candy made of or coated with chocolate: *a box of chocolates.* **4.** a dark brown color. —*adj.* **1.** made of or flavored with chocolate: *a cake with chocolate icing.* **2.** having the color chocolate.

Choc·taw (chok′tô) n., pl. **Choc·taw** or **Choc·taws**. **1.** a member of a tribe of North American Indians formerly living in parts of what are now Mississippi, Alabama, and Louisiana, now living in Oklahoma. **2.** the language of this tribe.

choice (chois) n. **1.** the act or instance of choosing: *It took me ten minutes to make a choice between the two books.* **2.** the power or opportunity to choose: *We were given a choice between the two movies.* **3.** a person or thing that is chosen: *Who is your choice for mayor?* **4.** a variety from which to choose: *a menu with a wide choice of dishes.* **5.** an alternative: *Our only choice was to go home.* —adj., **choic·er, choic·est. 1.** worthy of being chosen; select; excellent: *We searched through the forest until we found a choice spot for a picnic.* **2.** carefully selected: *The artist showed us a few choice works.* **3.** indicating a U.S. government grade of meat that is less tender than prime. —**choice′ly,** adv.

choir (kwīr) n. **1.** an organized group of singers, especially one used in a religious service. **2.** the part of a church set apart for the use of such singers.

choir·boy (kwīr′boi′) n. a boy who sings in a choir.

choir·girl (kwīr′gûrl′) n. a girl who sings in a choir.

choir·mas·ter (kwīr′mas′tər) n. a director of a choir.

choke (chōk) v., **choked, chok·ing.** —v.t. **1.** to prevent or hinder the breathing of: *The dense smoke choked us as we entered the burning building.* **2.** to stop up; block; clog: *Dirt choked the drain.* **3.** to fill completely: *The closet was choked with camping gear.* **4.** to stop the growth, progress, or action of: *to choke a fire with water.* **5.** to regulate the amount of air that enters (a gasoline engine) in order to enrich the fuel mixture. —v.i. **1.** to be prevented or hindered from breathing: *to choke on a bone.* —n. **1.** the act or sound of choking. **2.** a valve that regulates the amount of air that enters the carburetor of a gasoline engine.
· **to choke back.** to hold back or repress; stifle: *to choke back anger.*
· **to choke off.** to put an end to or block; stop: *to choke off debate, to choke off the supply of fuel.*
· **to choke up. a.** to become speechless, as from sorrow or anger. **b.** *Informal.* to give a poor performance because of tension or nervousness: *The young actor choked up on opening night.*

choke·cher·ry (chōk′cher′ē) n., pl. **choke·cher·ries. 1.** the bitter cherrylike fruit of a shrub of the rose family, used to make jams and jellies. **2.** the shrub bearing this fruit.

chok·er (chō′kər) n. **1.** a person or thing that chokes. **2.** a necklace that fits tightly around the throat.

chol·er (kol′ər) n. irritability or anger.

chol·er·a (kol′ər ə) n. an infectious disease of the intestines, characterized by severe vomiting and diarrhea. It is usually caused by drinking water or eating food that is contaminated by certain bacteria.

chol·er·ic (kol′ər ik) adj. easily irritated or angered. [From the Old French word *coleric* meaning "bad-humored" or "having a surplus of choler," from the word *colere* "choler," going back to the Greek word *cholē* "bile" or "gall." *Choler* was once thought to be one of the four humors of the body and to cause bad temper if present in great amounts.]

cho·les·ter·ol (kə les′tə rôl′, kə les′tə rōl′) n. a fatty material that is present in all animal tissues, needed for the digestion of fats, the production of certain hormones, and the manufacture of vitamin D. It is believed that large amounts of this substance in the blood increase the possibility of heart disease.

choose (chüz) v., **chose, cho·sen, choos·ing.** —v.t. **1.** to select from all that are available: *Choose the apples you want from the basket.* **2.** to prefer and decide (to do something): *We chose to leave the party early.* —v.i. **1.** to make a selection. **2.** to think fit. —**choos′er,** n.

choos·y (chü′zē) also, **choos·ey.** adj., **choos·i·er, choos·i·est.** *Informal.* very careful in making a choice; fussy; particular: *to be choosy about clothes.*

chop[1] (chop) v., **chopped, chop·ping.** —v.t. **1.** to cut by a quick blow or series of blows with a sharp instrument: *to chop a tree down with an ax.* **2.** to make or form in this way: *The firefighter chopped a hole in the wall.* **3.** to cut into pieces: *to chop onions.* **4.** to make shorter in length or duration: *The reporter chopped the story by eliminating three paragraphs.* **5.** to hit (a ball) with a short, quick, downward stroke, as in tennis. —v.i. to make cutting strokes. —n. **1.** a short, quick, downward cutting stroke or blow. **2.** a small cut of meat, as of lamb, pork, or veal, that usually includes a piece of the rib. [Probably from the Middle English word *chappen* meaning "to crack open."]

chop[2] (chop) v.i., **chopped, chop·ping.** to change or shift suddenly. [From the Old English word *cēapian* meaning "to bargain, trade," from the word *cēap* meaning "trade, business."]

chop·per (chop′ər) n. **1.** a person or thing that chops. **2.** *Informal.* a helicopter.

chop·py[1] (chop′ē) adj., **chop·pi·er, chop·pi·est. 1.** rough with short, broken waves: *a choppy sea.* **2.** marked by short, jerky movements or sounds. [*Chop*[1] + -y[1].] —**chop′pi·ness,** n.

chop·py[2] (chop′ē) adj., **chop·pi·er, chop·pi·est.** changing or shifting suddenly: *a choppy wind.* [*Chop*[2] + -y[1].]

chops (chops) pl. n. **1.** the jaw or cheek. **2.** the mouth. [From the earlier form *chap*, of uncertain origin.]

chop·sticks (chop′stiks′) pl. n. a pair of long, slender sticks, usually wood, plastic, or ivory, that are held between the thumb and fingers and are used for eating. Chopsticks were first developed in China.

eating with **chopsticks**

chop su·ey (chop′ sü′ē) a dish of Chinese-American origin, consisting of vegetables such as mushrooms, onions, bean sprouts, and bamboo shoots, cooked with small pieces of meat, fish, or chicken, and usually served with rice. [From the Cantonese phrase *shap sui* meaning "odds and ends."]

cho·ral (adj., kôr′əl; n., kə ral′, kôr′əl) adj. **1.** of or relating to a choir or chorus. **2.** performed by or written

at; āpe; fär; câre; end; mē; it; īce; pîerce; hot; ōld; sông, fôrk; oil; out; up; ūse; rüle; pull; tûrn; chin; sing; shop; thin; <u>th</u>is; hw in white; zh in treasure. The symbol ə stands for the unstressed vowel sound heard in about, taken, pencil, lemon, and circus.

C

for a choir or chorus: *choral music.* —*n.* another spelling of **chorale.**

cho·rale (kə ral′) *also,* **cho·ral.** *n.* **1.** a hymn having a plain melody and stately rhythm, usually sung in unison. **2.** a group of people singing such music; chorus.

chord[1] (kôrd) *n.* a combination of three or more musical tones or notes sounded at the same time to produce a harmony. [From the Middle English word *cord,* short for *accord* meaning "harmony, agreement."]

chord[2] (kôrd) *n.* **1.** a straight line segment joining any two points on the circumference of a circle. **2.** a feeling or emotion: *Seeing someone in trouble strikes a sympathetic chord in me.* [From the Latin word *chorda* meaning "catgut, string," from the Greek word *chordē* "string."]

chor·date (kôr′dāt) *n.* any animal of the group that includes all animals with either backbones or notochords.

chore (chôr) *n.* **1.** a small or minor job: *I have daily chores to do on the farm.* **2.** a hard or unpleasant task: *It's a real chore to mow this lawn.*

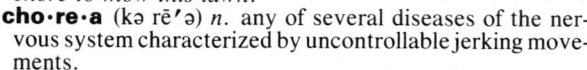

chord[2] *(def. 1)*
AB and CD
are **chords**

cho·re·a (kə rē′ə) *n.* any of several diseases of the nervous system characterized by uncontrollable jerking movements.

cho·re·o·graph (kôr′ē ə graf′) *v.t.* to create, arrange, or direct (dance movement), as for ballet.

cho·re·og·ra·pher (kôr′ē og′rə fər) *n.* a person who creates, arranges, or directs dance movements, as for ballet.

cho·re·og·ra·phy (kôr′ē og′rə fē) *n.* **1.** the art of creating, arranging, or directing dance movement. **2.** dancing or dance movement, as in a ballet.

chor·is·ter (kôr′ə stər) *n.* **1.** a person who sings in a choir. **2.** a person who leads a choir.

cho·roid (kôr′oid) *n.* the membrane forming the middle coat of the eyeball and lying between the sclera and the retina. The choroid, in the front of the eye, forms the iris. Also, **choroid coat.**

chor·tle (chôr′təl) *v.i.,* **chor·tled, chor·tling.** to laugh with a snorting chuckle. —*n.* such a laugh.

cho·rus (kôr′əs) *n., pl.* **cho·rus·es. 1.** a large, organized group of people who sing together. **2.** a group of people who sing, dance, and often play minor parts, as in a musical comedy. **3.** a musical composition to be sung by a large group, usually written for four or more parts. **4.** a part of a song that is repeated after each stanza; refrain. **5.** a group of people who recite or speak at the same time: *the chorus in an ancient Greek drama.* **6.** the saying or uttering of something by a group of people all at the same time: *The joke produced a chorus of laughter.* —*vt.,* **cho·rused, cho·rus·ing.** to utter at the same time.

·**in chorus.** all together: *The dogs howled in chorus.*

chose (chōz) the past tense of **choose.**

cho·sen (chō′zən) *v.* the past participle of **choose.** —*adj.* selected by preference; select.

chow[1] (chou) *n. Slang.* food. [Perhaps originally from the Pekingese word *chiao* meaning "meat-filled dumpling."]

chow[2] (chou) *n.* a dog of a breed originally developed in China, having a large head, a thick, usually brown or black coat, and a bluish black tongue. Also, **chow chow.** [From the Chinese dialect word *kaú* meaning "dog."]

chow·der (chow′dər) *n.* a thick soup usually made of fish or shellfish, especially clams, with vegetables and sometimes milk.

chow mein (chou′ mān′, shou′ mān′) a dish of Chinese-American

chow[2]

origin, made of shredded fish or meat and vegetables such as celery, onions, and bean sprouts. It is usually served with rice and fried noodles. [From the Pekingese phrase *ch'ao mien* meaning "fried dough."]

Christ (krīst) *n.* the title given Jesus of Nazareth by his followers.

chris·ten (kris′ən) *v.t.* **1.** to receive into a Christian church by baptism; baptize. **2.** to give a name to at baptism: *What did the young parents christen their child?* **3.** to give a name to: *to christen a ship.*

Chris·ten·dom (kris′ən dəm) *n.* **1.** the countries of the world in which Christianity is the main religion, considered as a group. **2.** Christians as a group.

chris·ten·ing (kris′ə ning) *n.* the act or ceremony of baptizing and naming a baby; baptism.

Chris·tian (kris′chən) *n.* a person who believes in and follows the teachings of Jesus; a member of the religion based on these teachings. —*adj.* **1.** of or relating to Jesus or his teachings. **2.** believing in Jesus and following his teachings; belonging to the religion based on these teachings: *Easter is celebrated by all the Christian people of the world.* **3.** of or relating to Christians or Christianity.

Chris·ti·an·i·ty (kris′chē an′i tē) *n.* **1.** the religion based on the teachings of Jesus; the Christian religion. **2.** Christians as a group; Christendom.

Chris·tian·ize (kris′chə nīz′) *v.t.,* **Chris·tian·ized, Chris·tian·iz·ing.** to convert someone to Christianity.

Christian name, the name given to a person born of Christian parents at birth or baptism, as distinguished from the family name.

Christian Science, a religion founded by Mary Baker Eddy in 1866. It stresses healing by spiritual means.

Christian Scientist, a person who believes in Christian Science.

Christ·like (krīst′līk′) *adj.* having or showing the spirit of Jesus; like Jesus.

Christ·mas (kris′məs) *n.* the yearly celebration of the birth of Jesus. It falls on December 25.

Christmas Eve, the evening before Christmas.

Christ·mas·tide (kris′məs tīd′) *n.* the season of Christmas.

Christmas tree, an evergreen or artificial tree decorated with lights and ornaments at Christmas time.

chro·mat·ic (krō mat′ik) *adj.* **1.** of, relating to, or containing a color or colors. **2.** relating to the chromatic scale. —**chro·mat′i·cal·ly,** *adv.*

chromatic scale, a musical scale progressing entirely by half tones.

chro·ma·tin (krō′mə tin) *n.* the material in the cell nucleus that makes up the chromosomes during cell division.

chro·ma·tog·ra·phy (krō′mə tog′rə fē) *n.* the process for separating and analyzing the chemical compounds in a mixture by absorption.

chrome (krōm) *n.* **1.** another word for **chromium. 2.** something plated with chromium or an alloy of chromium.

chro·mic (krō′mik) *adj.* relating to or containing chromium.

chro·mi·um (krō′mē əm) *n.* a hard, brittle, silver-white metallic element. It is used to plate metals and in alloys to provide strength and resistance to corrosion. Symbol: **Cr** [From the French word *chrome* meaning "chromium," from the Greek word *chrōma* "color." Chromium compounds have many colors.]

chro·mo·some (krō′mə sōm′) *n.* a tiny structure in the nuclei of living cells, composed chiefly of proteins and DNA. Chromosomes carry the genes that determine sex, size, color, and many other characteristics.

chro·mo·sphere (krō′mə sfîr′) *n.* **1.** a gaseous layer several thousand miles thick that surrounds the sun and is visible as a red ring during a total solar eclipse. It is made up mostly of hydrogen, helium, and calcium. **2.** a similar gaseous layer around a star.

chron. **1.** chronological. **2.** chronology.

Chron., Chronicles.

chron·ic (kron′ik) *adj.* **1.** (of an illness) lasting a long time or coming back again and again: *chronic asthma.* **2.** done or doing by habit; habitual; constant: *a chronic complainer.* [Going back to the Greek word *chronikos* meaning "of time," from *chronos* "time."] —**chron·i·cal·ly,** *adv.*

chron·i·cle (kron′i kəl) *n.* a detailed record of events in the order in which they happened; history. —*v.t.,* **chron·i·cled, chron·i·cling.** to record in a chronicle. —**chron′i·cler,** *n.*

Chron·i·cles (kron′i kəlz) *n.* either of two books, I Chronicles and II Chronicles, of the Old Testament. ▲ used with a singular verb.

chron·o·log·i·cal (kron′ə loj′i kəl) *adj.* arranged according to the order in which events happened. —**chron·o·log′i·cal·ly,** *adv.*

chro·nol·o·gy (krə nol′ə jē) *n., pl.* **chro·nol·o·gies.** **1.** the arrangement of events in the order in which they happened. **2.** a table or list arranged in this way. **3.** the science of arranging and recording the dates of events and the order in which they happened.

chro·nom·e·ter (krə nom′i tər) *n.* a clock that is specially designed for keeping time very accurately, used for scientific purposes.

chrys·a·lid (kris′ə lid) *n.* another word for **chrysalis.** —*adj.* of or relating to a chrysalis.

chrys·a·lis (kris′ə lis) *n., pl.* **chry·sal·i·des** (kri sal′i dēz′) or **chrys·a·lis·es.** **1.** a moth or butterfly in the stage of metamorphosis during which it is enclosed in a cocoon and is undergoing changes in structure before emerging as a winged adult. **2.** a cocoon. Also, **chrysalid.**

chry·san·the·mum (krə san′thə məm) *n.* **1.** the round, showy flower of any of a large group of plants growing in many different colors. **2.** the leafy plant bearing this flower, widely cultivated as a garden plant. [From the Latin word *chrysanthemum* meaning "marigold," from the Greek word *chrysanthemon* "golden flower, marigold," from the words *chrysos* "gold" + *anthemon* "flower."]

chub (chub) *n., pl.* **chubs** or **chub.** any of several freshwater and saltwater fish, such as the minnow.

chub·by (chub′ē) *adj.,* **chub·bi·er, chub·bi·est.** round and plump. —**chub′bi·ness,** *n.*

chuck¹ (chuk) *n.* **1.** a gentle or playful pat or tap, especially under the chin. **2.** *Informal.* a toss. —*v.t.* **1.** to pat or tap gently or playfully, especially under the chin. **2.** *Informal.* to throw or toss. [Possibly from the Old French word *choquer* meaning "to knock, strike."]

chuck² (chuk) *n.* **1.** a device for holding a piece of work or a tool in a machine, such as a lathe or drill. **2.** a cut of beef including parts from the neck and the shoulder blade to the first three ribs. [A form of *chock*.]

chuck–full (chuk′fûl′) *adj.* another word for **chock-full.**

chuck·le (chuk′əl) *v.i.,* **chuck·led, chuck·ling.** to laugh in a soft manner, especially to oneself: *I chuckled as I read the letter.* —*n.* a soft laugh.

chuck wagon, a wagon that carries cooking equipment and food, as for cowhands.

chuck·wal·la (chuk′wä′lə) *n.* a lizard related to the iguana, found in the southwestern United States and northwestern Mexico.

chug (chug) *n.* a short, dull, explosive sound, such as that made by the exhaust of an engine. —*v.i.,* **chugged, chug·ging.** to move with or make such sounds: *The old car chugged along the highway.*

chum (chum) *n.* a close friend. —*v.i.,* **chummed, chum·ming.** to be close friends.

chuck²
chuck of
a drill

Chu·mash (chü′mash) *n., pl.* **Chu·mash** or **Chu·mash·es.** a member of one of several American Indian tribes formerly living along the coast of southern California.

chum·my (chum′ē) *adj.,* **chum·mi·er, chum·mi·est.** *Informal.* very friendly; intimate.

chump (chump) *n.* *Informal.* a person who is easily fooled or taken advantage of.

chunk (chungk) *n.* *Informal.* **1.** a thick piece or lump: *a chunk of wood, a chunk of ice.* **2.** an amount; quantity: *a large chunk of time.*

chunk·y (chung′kē) *adj.,* **chunk·i·er, chunk·i·est.** **1.** short and compact; stocky: *a chunky baby.* **2.** like a chunk; thick.

church (chûrch) *n.* **1.** a building for public worship, especially one for Christian worship. **2.** Christian worship; religious services: *to go to church on Sunday.* **3.** Christians as a group. **4. Church.** a particular group of Christians having similar beliefs; denomination: *the Presbyterian Church, the Roman Catholic Church.* **5.** the profession of a member of the clergy.

church·go·er (chûrch′gō′ər) *n.* a person who goes to church regularly.

Church Latin, the form of Latin used by the Roman Catholic Church.

church·man (chûrch′mən) *n., pl.* **church·men** (chûrch′mən). **1.** a clergyman. **2.** a member of a church.

Church of Christ, Scientist, the official name of the Christian Science Church.

Church of England, the national church of England, headed by the British monarch. It was established by Henry VIII in the sixteenth century.

Church of Jesus Christ of Latter-day Saints, the official name of the Mormon Church.

church·war·den (chûrch′wôr′dən) *n.* in the Church of England and the Protestant Episcopal Church, an elected lay official whose duty is the management of church property, finances, and business affairs.

church·wom·an (chûrch′wŭm′ən) *n., pl.* **church·wom·en** (chûrch′wim′ən). a woman who is a member of a church.

church·yard (chûrch′yärd′) *n.* the ground around or adjoining a church, often used as a cemetery.

churl (chûrl) *n.* a surly, ill-bred person.

churl·ish (chûr′lish) *adj.* surly; ill-bred; rude. —**churl′ish·ly,** *adv.* —**churl′ish·ness,** *n.*

churn (chûrn) *n.* a vessel in which cream or milk is shaken or beaten to separate the fat in order to make butter. —*v.t.* **1.** to shake or beat (cream or milk) in a churn. **2.** to make (butter) in a churn. **3.** to stir or cause to move with violent motion: *The plow churned up the soil.* —*v.i.* **1.** to work or operate a churn. **2.** to move violently: *The water churned in the rapids. My stomach churned before I gave my speech.*

chute (shüt) *n.* **1.** an inclined or vertical trough or passage down or through which various things may be passed or carried: *a mail chute, a coal chute.* **2.** a waterfall or rapids in a river. **3.** a steep or curving slope, as for toboggans. **4.** *Informal.* see **parachute.**

chut·ney (chut′nē) *n., pl.* **chut·neys.** a sauce or relish made of fruits, herbs, spices, and vinegar.

chutz·pah (hut′spə) *n.* *Informal.* shameless impudence; nerve; gall. [From the Yiddish word *chutzpah* meaning "arrogance, nerve," from the Hebrew word *ḥuṣpāh* "nerve."]

C

at; āpe; fär; câre; end; mē; it; īce; pîerce; hot; ōld; sông; fôrk; oil; out; up; ūse; rüle; pull; tûrn; chin; sing; shop; thin; this; hw in white; zh in treasure. The symbol ə stands for the unstressed vowel sound heard in about, taken, pencil, lemon, and circus.

173

chyme (kīm) *n.* the thick, pulpy mass of partly digested food that passes from the stomach into the small intestine.

CIA, Central Intelligence Agency.

ci·ca·da (si kā′də) *n., pl.* **ci·ca·das** or **ci·ca·dae** (si-kā′dē). a large insect with two pairs of transparent wings. The male makes a loud, shrill sound by means of two vibrating plates on its abdomen.

cicada

–cide *combining form* **1.** the act of killing: *genocide.* **2.** the killer of: *insecticide.* [From the Latin suffix *-cidium* meaning "a killing," from the word *caedere* meaning "to cut," "to strike," or "to kill."]

ci·der (sī′dər) *n.* the juice pressed from apples, used as a drink and in making certain products, such as vinegar.

ci·gar (si gär′) *n.* a roll of tobacco leaves prepared for smoking.

cig·a·rette (sig′ə ret′, sig′ə ret′) *also,* **cig·a·ret.** *n.* a small roll of finely shredded tobacco leaves, wrapped in thin paper, used for smoking.

cil·i·a (sil′ē ə) *pl. n., sing.* **cil·i·um.** **1.** the eyelashes. **2.** the very small hairlike structures that line the two main branches of the windpipe and their smaller branching tubes. Cilia are constantly in motion and filter the air entering and leaving the lungs. **3.** similar hairlike structures on certain cells, such as paramecia, that move to and fro allowing the cell to move.

cil·i·ar·y (sil′ē er′ē) *adj.* **1.** relating to or like cilia; hairlike. **2.** of or relating to the ciliary body.

ciliary body, a portion of the membrane of the eye whose ligaments and muscles support and adjust the shape of the lens of the eyeball.

cil·i·um (sil′ē əm) the singular of **cilia.**

cinch (sinch) *n., pl.* **cinch·es.** **1.** a strap for fastening a saddle or pack on a horse. **2.** *Slang.* something sure or easy: *If you study hard, passing the test will be a cinch.* —*v.t.* **1.** to fasten a cinch around; bind firmly. **2.** *Slang.* to make sure of: *The new evidence cinched the case.*

cin·cho·na (sin kō′nə) *n.* **1.** any of a group of trees or shrubs having smooth oblong leaves and pink or cream-colored flowers, found in South America, Asia, and Jamaica. **2.** the bark of this tree, which yields quinine and other similar drugs. Also *(def. 2),* **Peruvian bark.**

cinc·ture (singk′chər) *n.* a belt or girdle.

cin·der (sin′dər) *n.* **1.** a substance, especially coal, that is burning but is no longer flaming. **2.** a substance, such as wood or coal, that has burned but has not been reduced to ashes. **3. cinders.** the ashes from a fire. **4.** a speck, as of dirt or ash: *The wind was blowing and I got a cinder in my eye.*

cinder block, a building brick that is partially hollow, made from concrete that contains cinders.

Cin·der·el·la (sin′də rel′ə) *n.* a girl in a fairy tale who was forced by her stepmother and stepsisters to work very hard. With the help of her fairy godmother she later married a prince.

cin·e·ma (sin′ə mə) *n.* **1.** a motion-picture theater. **2.** motion pictures as a form of art. **3.** the business of making motion pictures. —**cin′e·mat′ic,** *adj.*

cin·e·ma·tog·ra·phy (sin′ə mə tog′rə fē) *n.* the art or process of photographing motion pictures.

cin·na·bar (sin′ə bär′) *n.* a red or brownish red mineral that is the chief source of mercury.

cin·na·mon (sin′ə mən) *n.* **1.** a reddish brown spice made from the dried bark of a tree grown in tropical regions. **2.** the bark itself, either ground or rolled into sheets. **3.** the tree yielding this bark. **4.** a light, reddish brown color. —*adj.* having the color cinnamon; light reddish brown.

ci·on (sī′ən) another spelling of **scion** *(def. 1).*

ci·pher (sī′fər) *also,* **cy·pher.** *n.* **1.** the number zero.

2. the numeral representing this; 0. **3.** a person or thing that is of no value or importance. **4.** a system of secret writing that cannot be understood by those who do not have the key or pattern; code. —*v.t.* **1.** to write (a message) in cipher. —*v.i.* to do arithmetic.

cir·ca (sûr′kə) *prep.* around; about. ▲ used especially to show an approximate date: *The volcano erupted circa A.D. 500.*

cir·ca·di·an (sûr kā′dē ən, sûr kad′ē ən, sûr′kə dī′ən) *adj.* having a natural rhythm or cycle of approximately 24 hours: *Human beings have a circadian sleep pattern.* [Formed from the Latin words *circa* meaning "about, around" + *dies* "day" + the English suffix *-an.*]

Cir·ce (sûr′sē) *n. Greek Mythology.* a beautiful enchantress who lived on an island and who changed half of Odysseus's men into swine.

cir·cle (sûr′kəl) *n.* **1.** a continuous, closed curved line, every point of which is equally distant from the center. **2.** a plane figure enclosed by such a line; the area within a circle. **3.** something shaped like a circle, such as a halo, crown, or ring. **4.** a group of people sharing common interests: *a large circle of friends.* —*v.,* **cir·cled, cir·cling.** —*v.t.* **1.** to form a circle around; surround: *The enemy circled the camp.* **2.** to move around (someone or something) in a circle: *The airplane circled the airport.* —*v.i.* to move around in a circle: *The outfielder circled under the high fly ball.*

cir·clet (sûr′klit) *n.* **1.** a small circle. **2.** an ornamental ring or band worn about the head, neck, arm, or finger.

cir·cuit (sûr′kit) *n.* **1.** the act of going around; a circular course; revolution: *The earth completes its circuit around the sun in a year.* **2.** a regular journey from one place to another, as by a judge or preacher. **3.** the district traveled through in such a journey, especially the district assigned to a judge for holding court. **4.** a system or part of a system of electronic parts through which an electric current flows; the path of an electric circuit. **5.** a group of theaters under one management, presenting movies or plays at the same time or in turn.

circuit board, a flat piece of material, usually fiberglass, on which integrated circuits are mounted.

circuit breaker, a safety switch that automatically interrupts the flow of current through an electric circuit when the current becomes dangerously strong.

circuit court, formerly, a court that sat at intervals in various places within the territory over which it had jurisdiction.

cir·cu·i·tous (sər kū′i təs) *adj.* not direct; roundabout: *We took a circuitous route to avoid the traffic jam.* —**cir·cu′i·tous·ly,** *adv.* —**cir·cu′i·tous·ness,** *n.*

circuit rider, formerly, a minister who traveled over a circuit to preach.

cir·cu·lar (sûr′kyə lər) *adj.* **1.** having the form of a circle; round: *a circular driveway, a necktie with a circular pattern.* **2.** moving in or forming a circle: *The skater moved in a circular path around the ice.* —*n.* printed material, such as a letter or advertisement, for general circulation: *The store distributed circulars advertising its spring sale.* —**cir′cu·lar·ly,** *adv.*

cir·cu·lar·i·ty (sûr′kyə lar′i tē) *n.* the state or quality of being circular.

cir·cu·lar·ize (sûr′kyə lə rīz′) *v.t.,* **cir·cu·lar·ized, cir·cu·lar·iz·ing.** to send circulars to.

circular saw, a power saw having a thin, metal disk with a toothed edge mounted in a framework. The disk is rotated at a high speed.

cir·cu·late (sûr′kyə lāt′) *v.,* **cir·cu·lat·ed, cir·cu·lat·ing.** —*v.i.* **1.** to move in a circular course back to the starting point: *Blood circulates in the body.* **2.** to move or pass from place

circular saw

to place or person to person; move freely: *Air circulates in a room.* —*v.t.* to cause to circulate: *The teacher circulated the picture around the room.*

circulating library, a library from which books may be borrowed or rented. Also, **lending library.**

cir·cu·la·tion (sûr′kyə lā′shən) *n.* **1.** movement from place to place or person to person: *Gold coins are no longer in circulation in this country.* **2.** the movement of the blood to and from the heart through the blood vessels of the body. **3.** the number of copies of a newspaper or magazine that are distributed and sold: *The circulation of the newspaper is over 30,000.*

cir·cu·la·to·ry (sûr′kyə lə tôr′ē) *adj.* of or relating to circulation, especially of the blood.

circulatory system, the system in the body made up of the heart, the blood vessels, blood, and the lymph system. The circulatory system transports nutrients, gases, and other materials throughout the body.

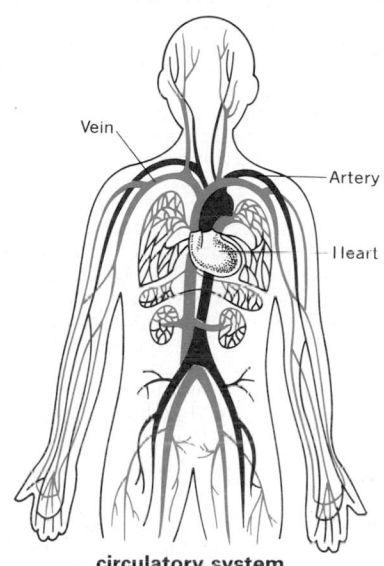

Vein

Artery

Heart

circulatory system

circum– *prefix* around; about: *circumnavigate.*

cir·cum·cise (sûr′kəm sīz′) *v.t.,* **cir·cum·cised, cir·cum·cis·ing.** to remove the foreskin of.

cir·cum·ci·sion (sûr′kəm sizh′ən) *n.* **1.** the act or rite of circumcising. **2. Circumcision.** a feast day commemorating the circumcision of the infant Jesus. It falls on January 1.

cir·cum·fer·ence (sər kum′fər əns) *n.* **1.** a line bounding any rounded plane figure, especially a circle. **2.** the measurement of this line; the distance around something: *the circumference of the earth.*

cir·cum·flex (sûr′kəm fleks′) *n., pl.* **cir·cum·flex·es.** a mark placed over a letter to show something about its pronunciation. In this dictionary, the mark (ˆ) over a letter *o* shows that it is pronounced as in the word *fork.* Also, **circumflex accent.** —*adj.* pronounced or marked with a circumflex.

cir·cum·lo·cu·tion (sûr′kəm lō kū′shən) *n.* **1.** a roundabout or indirect way of speaking; use of too many words. **2.** an instance of this; roundabout expression: *"The bicycle that belongs to me" is a circumlocution for "my bicycle."*

cir·cum·nav·i·gate (sûr′kəm nav′i gāt′) *v.t.,* **cir·cum·nav·i·gat·ed, cir·cum·nav·i·gat·ing.** to sail completely around: *to circumnavigate the earth.* —**cir′cum·nav·i·ga′tion,** *n.*

cir·cum·scribe (sûr′kəm skrib′) *v.t.,* **cir·cum·scribed, cir·cum·scrib·ing.** **1.** to draw a line around; form the boundaries of; encircle. **2.** to put restrictions on; limit:

The doctor circumscribed the amount of work the patient could do after leaving the hospital. **3.a.** to draw (a geometric figure) around another geometric figure so that the outer figure touches the inner at as many points as possible: *to circumscribe a circle around a pentagon.* **b.** to enclose (a geometric figure) in this way. [From the Latin word *circumscribere* meaning "to draw around, limit," from the words *circum* "circle" + *scribere* "to draw, write."]

cir·cum·spect (sûr′kəm spekt′) *adj.* considering or examining carefully all sides of a problem before acting or making a decision; cautious. —**cir′cum·spect′ly,** *adv.*

cir·cum·spec·tion (sûr′kəm spek′shən) *n.* circumspect action or behavior; caution; prudence.

cir·cum·stance (sûr′kəm stans′) *n.* **1.** a condition, act, or event that is connected to and often affects another condition, act, or event: *Good weather was one circumstance that helped to make our picnic a success.* **2.** *also,* **circumstances.** the state of affairs surrounding and affecting a person or action: *Due to circumstances, the game was canceled.* **3.** a fact or event: *Getting the job was a happy circumstance.* **4. circumstances.** financial condition: *They worked to escape the poor circumstances of their youth.* **5.** a formal or splendid ceremony or display: *The crowning of the new queen was accompanied by great pomp and circumstance.* **6.** detail, especially full detail: *The scientist explained the discovery with great circumstance.*

•**under no circumstances.** under no conditions; never.

•**under the circumstances.** things being as they are: *Under the circumstances, we have no choice but to leave immediately.*

cir·cum·stan·tial (sûr′kəm stan′shəl) *adj.* **1.** relating to, affected by, or depending on circumstances: *The fact that they were seen leaving the victim's house the night of the murder is circumstantial.* **2.** not essential; incidental; secondary: *The author included many circumstantial details in the story.* **3.** full of details; particular: *a circumstantial account of the accident.* —**cir′cum·stan′tial·ly,** *adv.*

circumstantial evidence, evidence describing the circumstances surrounding an event rather than the event itself.

cir·cum·vent (sûr′kəm vent′) *v.t.* **1.** to go around: *We took the long way home in order to circumvent the traffic.* **2.** to avoid or evade, as through trickery or cleverness: *to circumvent the rules.* —**cir′cum·ven′tion,** *n.*

cir·cus (sûr′kəs) *n., pl.* **cir·cus·es.** **1.** a traveling show, usually featuring acrobats, clowns, and both trained and wild animals. **2.** all the persons, animals, and equipment associated with such a show. **3.** a performance given by such a show. **4.** in ancient Rome, a long, open arena with rows of seats, used especially for horse and chariot races. [From the Latin word *circus* meaning "ring, circle."]

cir·rho·sis (si rō′sis) *n.* a disease of the liver marked by the growth of scar tissue and the destruction of normal liver cells. It causes the liver to gradually shrink and become hard.

cir·ro·cu·mu·lus (sir′ō kū′myə ləs) *n., pl.* **cir·ro·cu·mu·lus** or **cir·ro·cu·mu·li** (sir′ō kū′myə lī′). a high-level cloud similar to, but smaller than, an altocumulus. See **cloud** *(def. 1).*

cir·ro·stra·tus (sir′ō strā′təs, sir′ō strat′əs) *n., pl.* **cir-**

at; āpe; fär; câre; end; mē; it; īce; pîerce; hot; ōld; sông, fôrk; oil; out; up; ūse; rüle; pŭll; tûrn; chin; sing; shop; thin; this; hw in white; zh in treasure. The symbol ə stands for the unstressed vowel sound heard in about, taken, pencil, lemon, and circus.

C

ro·stra·tus or **cir·ro·stra·ti** (sir′ō strā′tī, sir′ō strat′ī). a high-level cloud consisting of ice crystals that form a thin sheet. See **cloud** (def. 1).

cir·rus (sir′əs) n., pl. **cir·rus** or **cir·ri** (sir′ī). a thin, white, wispy, high-level cloud composed of ice crystals in small patches or bands. See **cloud** (def. 1).

cis·tern (sis′tərn) n. a natural or artificial reservoir or tank for storing liquids, especially rainwater.

cit·a·del (sit′ə dəl) n. 1. a fortress built so as to overlook or dominate a city. 2. any refuge or fortified place.

ci·ta·tion (sī tā′shən) n. 1. the act of citing or quoting. 2. the passage or words quoted; quotation: *The lecture included a number of citations from ancient records.* 3. a public commendation or award for bravery or outstanding achievement. 4. a summons to appear before a court of law; ticket.

cite (sīt) v.t., **cit·ed, cit·ing.** 1. to quote (a passage or author), especially as an authority: *I cited an article in the encyclopedia to support my statement.* 2. to mention or refer to as support, proof, or confirmation: *The lawyer cited several previous decisions that had a bearing on the case.* 3. to give a public commendation or award to for bravery or outstanding achievement. 4. to summon to appear before a court of law.

citizen (def. 1)
a group of new American **citizens**

cit·i·zen (sit′ə zən) n. 1. a person who is born in a country or who chooses to become a member of a country by law, and who owes allegiance to and has rights and privileges recognized by its government. 2. a permanent resident, especially of a city or town: *the citizens of Los Angeles.*

cit·i·zen·ry (sit′ə zən rē) n., pl. **cit·i·zen·ries.** citizens as a group.

citizens band, in the United States, a set of radio frequencies designated by the federal government for private two-way radio communications over relatively short distances.

cit·i·zen·ship (sit′ə zən ship′) n. the status of being a citizen, including its rights, duties, and privileges.

cit·rate (sit′rāt) n. a salt or ester of citric acid.

cit·ric (sit′rik) adj. of or obtained from citrus fruits.

citric acid, a sour-tasting acid composed of carbon, hydrogen, and oxygen, found in almost all plants but especially in lemons, limes, and other citrus fruits. It is used chiefly as a flavoring and in medicines.

cit·ron (sit′rən) n. 1. a large fruit resembling a lemon, valued mainly for its thick, yellow-green rind, which is used in desserts and in making liqueurs and perfumes. 2. the shrub or tree bearing this fruit. 3. the preserved or candied rind of this fruit, used especially in fruit cakes.

cit·ron·el·la (sit′rə nel′ə) n. 1. a pale yellow oil obtained from the leaves of a plant of the grass family, having a lemon fragrance and used to make insect repellent and to scent soaps and cosmetics. 2. the plant from which this oil is obtained.

cit·rus (sit′rəs) n. 1. any of a group of shrubs and small trees valued for their fruit, grown in warm regions throughout the world. 2. see **citrus fruit**. —adj. of or relating to such trees or their fruit.

citrus fruit, a fleshy, juicy fruit of any of a group of shrubs and small trees, such as the orange, lemon, lime, or grapefruit.

cit·y (sit′ē) n., pl. **cit·ies.** 1. an area where many people live and work, especially one that has its own local government; a large and important town. 2. in the United States, an area of local government that is chartered by the state in which it is located and that usually has a mayor or a city manager. 3. the people who live in a city. 4. employees or representatives of a city government: *The city keeps the streets clear of snow.* —adj. of or relating to a city. [From the Old French word *cité* meaning "large town" and "body of citizens," from the Latin word *civitas* "community, state" and "citizenship," from *civis* "citizen."]

city hall 1. a building serving as the administrative headquarters of a city government. 2. the governing body of a city: *City hall issued a statement on the problem of crime.*

city manager, an official appointed by a city council to manage the city's government.

cit·y–state (sit′ē stāt′) n. a self-governing political unit consisting of a city and sometimes the surrounding territory that it controls. Ancient Athens was a city-state.

civ·et (siv′it) n. 1. an animal related to the mongoose, native to the warmer regions of Africa, Europe, and Asia, having a narrow head, a pointed muzzle, and a slender body. Also, **civet cat.** 2. the fur of this animal. 3. a thick, yellowish substance secreted by the civet, having a strong musky odor. It is used in perfumes.

civet (def. 1)

civ·ic (siv′ik) adj. 1. of or relating to a city: *Keeping our city clean is a matter of civic pride.* 2. of or relating to a citizen or citizenship: *It is a person's civic duty to vote.*

civ·ics (siv′iks) n. the study of the function, services, and purpose of a government and of the duties, rights, and privileges of citizenship. ▲ used with a singular verb.

civ·il (siv′əl) adj. 1. of or relating to a citizen or citizens. 2. of or relating to the relations between a government and its citizens: *civil affairs.* 3. taking place within the boundaries of a nation or among its citizens; domestic; internal: *civil strife.* 4. not connected with the church or the military: *a civil wedding ceremony.* 5. coolly polite; courteous. ▲ **Civil** and **polite** both mean having good manners. **Civil** merely indicates a lack of rudeness: *I gave a civil answer even though I was angry.* **Polite** implies good manners and thoughtfulness: *The nurse was always polite to patients' relatives.*

civil defense, organized plans for defense and protection to be carried out by civilians in case of enemy attack.

civil disobedience, a refusal to obey a law or laws as a means of protest against something regarded as being morally wrong.

civil engineer, a person whose profession is civil engineering.

civil engineering, the profession of designing and directing the construction of roads, bridges, and other public works.

ci·vil·ian (si vil′yən) *n.* **1.** a person who is not a member of the armed forces. **2.** a person who does not belong to a police force, firefighting unit, or similar organization. —*adj.* of or relating to civilians.

ci·vil·i·ty (si vil′i tē) *n., pl.* **ci·vil·i·ties. 1.** cool politeness. **2.** an act or expression of politeness or courtesy.

civ·i·li·za·tion (siv′ə lə zā′shən) *n.* **1.** a stage of human society marked by a high level of social, cultural, political, and intellectual development. **2.** the countries and peoples that have reached such a stage of development. **3.** the way of life of a particular people, place, or time: *medieval civilization, ancient Greek civilization.* **4.** the act or process of civilizing or of becoming civilized.

civ·i·lize (siv′ə līz′) *v.t.,* **civ·i·lized, civ·i·liz·ing.** to bring out of a primitive or savage state or condition; educate in the arts, science, government, or the like.

civil law, the body of law of a state or country that controls and regulates the rights of citizens.

civil liberty also, **civil liberties.** the freedom of a person to enjoy the individual rights guaranteed by the laws or constitution, such as freedom of speech, without undue interference by the government.

civ·il·ly (siv′ə lē) *adv.* in a coolly polite way.

civil marriage, a marriage performed by a government official instead of by a member of the clergy.

civil rights, the individual rights of a citizen, such as the right to vote, freedom of speech, and equal protection under the law.

civil servant, a person who is employed in the civil service.

civil service, the branch of governmental service that is not concerned with military, judicial, or legislative matters. Members of the civil service are appointed or are hired on the basis of merit after passing certain examinations.

civil war 1. a war between two sections or groups within a country. **2. Civil War.** in the United States, the war between the North and the South from 1861 to 1865.

Cl, the symbol for chlorine.

cl. 1. centiliter; centiliters. **2.** claim. **3.** class. **4.** clause. **5.** clearance.

clab·ber (klab′ər) *n.* milk that has curdled in the process of souring. —*v.i.* to curdle while souring.

clack (klak) *v.i.* to make a short, sharp sound: *The typewriter clacked noisily.* —*v.t.* to cause to make a short, sharp sound. —*n.* a short, sharp sound.

clad (klad) a past tense and past participle of **clothe.**

claim (klām) *v.t.* **1.** to ask for or demand as one's own; assert one's right to: *The squatter claimed the land. None of the passengers claimed the suitcase.* **2.** to declare as a fact or as true; maintain; contend: *Several people claimed to have seen the accident.* **3.** to call for; require: *Work on the new book claimed the better part of the author's day.* —*n.* **1.** the right to something: *My claim to the inheritance was questioned.* **2.** a declaration of something as a fact or as true; contention: *The police could not disprove the suspect's claims of innocence.* **3.** a demand for something due: *After the fire, the store's owner filed a claim with the insurance company.* **4.** something that is claimed, such as a piece of land.

　·**to lay claim to.** to assert one's right to: *The old prospector laid claim to the abandoned mine.*

claim·ant (klā′mənt) *n.* a person who makes a claim.

clair·voy·ance (klâr voi′əns) *n.* the supposed ability to see or know about objects or events that are not in sight or that cannot be seen.

clair·voy·ant (klâr voi′ənt) *adj.* of, relating to, or having clairvoyance. —*n.* a person who is clairvoyant.

clam (klam) *n.* a soft-bodied animal without a backbone, having a hinged double shell. Clams are mollusks, and are found in both salt and fresh water. Many clams are highly valued as food. —*v.i.,* **clammed, clam·ming.** to dig for clams.

　·**to clam up.** *Slang.* to become or remain silent; stop talking.

clam·bake (klam′bāk′) *n.* an outdoor party at which clams and other kinds of seafood are served.

clam·ber (klam′bər) *v.i.* to climb by using both the hands and feet: *The explorers clambered up the steep mountainside.* —*n.* the act of clambering.

clam·my (klam′ē) *adj.,* **clam·mi·er, clam·mi·est.** cold and damp: *a clammy old basement.* —**clam′mi·ness,** *n.*

clam·or (klam′ər) *n.* **1.** a loud, noisy outcry or protest; uproar: *A clamor went up when the audience was told that the show was canceled.* **2.** any loud and continuous noise: *the clamor of trumpets.* —*v.i.* to make loud, continuous cries or demands: *The crowd clamored for the box office to open.*

clam·or·ous (klam′ər əs) *adj.* **1.** loud and noisy: *a clamorous protest against new taxes.* **2.** making loud, noisy outcries or protests: *a clamorous audience.* —**clam′or·ous·ly,** *adv.* —**clam′or·ous·ness,** *n.*

clamp (klamp) *n.* a device used to hold things firmly together, especially one with jaws that close or can be closed tightly. —*v.t.* to fasten with or place in a clamp or clamps.

　·**to clamp down on.** *Informal.* to become more strict with.

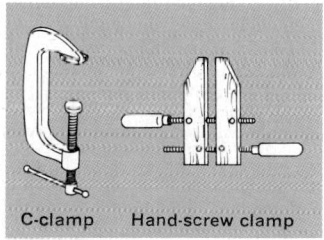

C-clamp　　Hand-screw clamp

clamps

clan (klan) *n.* **1.** a group of families in a community who claim descent from the same ancestor, as in the Scottish Highlands. **2.** a group of people closely united by a common interest; clique. **3.** *Informal.* a family: *The whole clan met twice a year.*

clan·des·tine (klan des′tin) *adj.* secret, especially for an evil or illegal purpose: *The detectives uncovered a clandestine still.* —**clan·des′tine·ly,** *adv.*

clang (klang) *n.* a loud, harsh, ringing sound: *the clang of a fire alarm.* —*v.t.* to cause to make such a sound. —*v.i.* to make such a sound.

clan·gor (klang′gər, klang′ər) *n.* **1.** a series of clangs: *The clangor of bells could be heard all over town.* **2.** a clang. —**clan′gor·ous,** *adj.*

clank (klangk) *n.* a loud, sharp, metallic sound: *the clank of chains.* —*v.t.* to cause to make such a sound. —*v.i.* to make such a sound: *The anchor clanked against the side of the ship.*

clan·nish (klan′ish) *adj.* **1.** relating to or characteristic of a clan. **2.** tending to stick closely together in a group;

---

at; āpe; fär; câre; end; mē; it; īce; pîerce; hot; ōld; sông, fôrk; oil; out; up; ūse; rüle; pùll; tûrn; chin; sing; shop; thin; this; hw in white; zh in treasure. The symbol ə stands for the unstressed vowel sound heard in about, taken, pencil, lemon, and circus.

C

cliquish: *The people in this neighborhood are clannish.*

clans·man (klanz′mən) *n., pl.* **clans·men** (klanz′mən). a member of a clan.

clap (klap) *n.* **1.** a short, sharp sound: *a clap of thunder, a clap of the hands.* **2.** a friendly slap: *a clap on the back.* —*v.,* **clapped, clap·ping.** —*v.t.* **1.** to strike (one's hands) together. **2.** to strike with a clap: *The child clapped the blocks together.* **3.** to strike in a friendly way with the palm of the hand. **4.** to put or place, especially with a sudden or forceful motion: *I clapped my hands over my ears. The guard clapped the prisoner into a cell.* —*v.i.* **1.** to strike one's hands together, especially as an expression of approval or enjoyment; applaud: *The audience clapped at the end of the speech.* **2.** to make a short, sharp sound: *The shutters clapped in the strong wind.*

clap·board (klab′ərd, klap′bôrd′) *n.* a long, thin, narrow board, having one edge thicker than the other, used as siding on wooden buildings. —*v.t.* to cover with clapboards.

clap·per (klap′ər) *n.* **1.** the tongue of a bell. **2.** a person or thing that claps.

clap·trap (klap′trap′) *n.* nonsense; foolishness.

claque (klak) *n.* **1.** a person or organized group hired to applaud a performance, as in a theater. **2.** a group of people who fawn and flatter.

clar·et (klar′it) *n.* **1.** a dry red wine. **2.** a deep purplish red color. —*adj.* having the color claret; deep purplish red.

clar·i·fi·ca·tion (klar′ə fi kā′shən) *n.* **1.** the act of clarifying. **2.** something clarified.

clar·i·fy (klar′ə fī′) *v.,* **clar·i·fied, clar·i·fy·ing.** —*v.t.* **1.** to make more understandable; explain: *The candidates were asked to clarify their stands on the issue of prison reform.* **2.** to make pure and clear: *to clarify butter.* —*v.i.* **1.** to become more understandable. **2.** to become pure and clear.

clar·i·net (klar′ə net′) *n.* a musical instrument of the woodwind family, having a single-reed mouthpiece and played by means of finger holes and keys. —**clar′i·net′ist,** *n.*

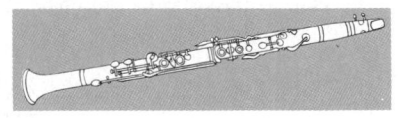

clarinet

clar·i·on (klar′ē ən) *adj.* loud and clear: *the clarion sound of a bugle.* —*n.* a trumpet having a clear, shrill tone, popular in the seventeenth and eighteenth centuries.

clar·i·ty (klar′i tē) *n.* the quality of being clear; clearness: *clarity of expression.*

clash (klash) *n., pl.* **clash·es.** **1.** a loud, harsh noise: *the clash of swords.* **2.** a strong disagreement or conflict: *There was a clash between the Republicans and the Democrats over the bill.* —*v.i.* **1.** to come together with a clash: *The pots clashed to the floor.* **2.** to be in conflict: *The green rug and the purple chairs clash.* —*v.t.* to cause to strike together with a clash: *to clash cymbals.*

clasp (klasp) *n.* **1.** a fastening, such as a hook, used to hold two objects or parts together. **2.** a close or tight grasp or embrace. —*v.t.* **1.** to fasten together with a clasp. **2.** to hold or grasp closely or tightly: *to clasp a baby to oneself, to clasp someone's hand.*

class (klas) *n., pl.* **class·es.** **1.** a number of persons or things that are grouped together because they are alike in some way: *a class of sailboats.* **2.** a group of students taught or studying together: *The biology class took a field trip to the zoo.* **3.** a meeting of such a group: *I have a history class at nine o'clock.* **4.** a group of students in school or college who are ranked together or graduate in the same year: *the junior class, the class of 1972.* **5.** a rank or division of society having similar economic, educational, or social characteristics: *the working class,* the upper class. **6.** a level, grade, or quality: *third class mail, reservations in the lowest class on a boat.* **7.** a group of related animals or plants forming a category that ranks below a phylum or division and above an order: *Dogs belong to the class that comprises mammals.* **8.** *Slang.* excellence or elegance, especially of style: *Your clothes have a lot of class.* —*v.t.* to place or group in a class; classify: *I would class them among the nicest people I have ever met.*

clas·sic (klas′ik) *adj.* **1.** serving or used as a standard, model, or guide because of its high quality: *That cathedral is a classic example of Gothic architecture.* **2.** simple, regular, and refined, as in style or lines: *This suit has a classic design.* **3.** typical or traditional: *the classic symptoms of a disease.* **4.** relating to ancient Greece or Rome; classical. —*n.* **1.** a work of art or literature considered to be of such high quality or excellence that it serves as a standard or model: *Many of the plays of Shakespeare are classics.* **2.** an author or artist similarly considered. **3. the classics.** the literature of ancient Greece and Rome. **4.** any event that is considered typical or traditional: *The World Series is the classic of baseball.*

clas·si·cal (klas′i kəl) *adj.* **1.** relating to or characteristic of ancient Greece or Rome and their art, literature, or culture: *a classical scholar.* **2.** *Music.* of or relating to music that conforms to certain, chiefly European standards of form and style and is regarded as being of long-lasting interest and high value. Classical music is generally distinguished from popular or folk music. **3.** considered to be standard and authoritative: *The course covers classical economic theories.* **4.** classic. —**clas′si·cal·ly,** *adv.*

clas·si·cism (klas′ə siz′əm) *n.* **1.** the principles of perfect order, harmony, and clarity found in the literature and art of ancient Greece and Rome, and present as ideals in all ages. **2.** adherence to these principles.

clas·si·cist (klas′ə sist) *n.* **1.** a person who follows the principles of classicism. **2.** a student of or an expert in the classics.

clas·si·fi·ca·tion (klas′ə fi kā′shən) *n.* **1.** the act of classifying. **2.** a specific, systematic arrangement of things into categories. *The Dewey decimal system is used in the classification of books. Taxonomy is the classification of living things.*

clas·si·fied (klas′ə fīd′) *adj.* **1.** arranged in groups or classes. **2.** secret, especially for reasons of national security: *The government has much classified information.* **3.** containing classified ads: *I looked in the classified section of the newspaper for a job.*

classified ad, a small advertisement, usually in a special section of a newspaper or magazine, as for help wanted or for a house or other item offered for sale. Also, **classified advertisement, want ad.**

clas·si·fy (klas′ə fī′) *v.t.,* **clas·si·fied, clas·si·fy·ing.** **1.** to arrange or group in classes according to a system: *Library books are classified according to subject matter.* **2.** to keep secret: *Governments classify many documents for reasons of national security.* —**clas′si·fi′a·ble,** *adj.* —**clas′si·fi′er,** *n.*

class·mate (klas′māt′) *n.* a member of the same class in school or college: *My parents met when they were classmates in high school.*

class·room (klas′rüm′, klas′rùm′) *n.* a room in which classes are held.

clat·ter (klat′ər) *n.* **1.** a loud rattling noise: *The clatter of dishes from the kitchen disturbed the customers in the restaurant.* **2.** noisy disorder; commotion: *the clatter of traffic in the streets.* **3.** noisy talk; chatter: *the clatter at a large party.* —*v.i.* **1.** to make a loud, rattling noise: *The pots and pans clattered as they fell.* **2.** to move with such a noise: *The wagon clattered over the wooden bridge.* **3.** to talk noisily; chatter. —*v.t.* to cause to clatter.

clause (klôz) *n.* **1.** a group of words containing a subject and predicate and forming part of a sentence. The two kinds of clauses are the independent clause and the dependent clause. **2.** a part of a formal or legal document, such as a contract or lease: *A clause in our lease forbids us to have pets in the apartment.*

claus·tro·pho·bi·a (klôs′trə fō′bē ə) *n.* an abnormal fear of being in any small, crowded, or enclosed place.

clav·i·chord (klav′i kôrd′) *n.* a stringed musical instrument with a keyboard, whose tones are produced by the striking of brass wedges against metal strings. It was a forerunner of the piano.

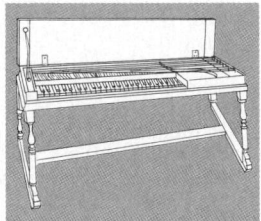
clavichord

clav·i·cle (klav′i kəl) *n.* either of the two long slender bones connecting the breastbone and the shoulder blade; collarbone.

cla·vier (klə vîr′) *n.* **1.** any stringed musical instrument with a keyboard, such as the clavichord, harpsichord, or piano. **2.** the keyboard of a musical instrument, especially of a stringed instrument, such as a piano.

claw (klô) *n.* **1.a.** a sharp, usually curved nail on the foot of a bird or animal. **b.** a foot with such a nail or nails. **2.** one of the pincers of a shellfish, such as a lobster or crab. **3.** anything like a claw, such as the forked end of the head of a hammer. —*v.t.* to scratch or tear with claws: *The puppy was clawing the door.* —**claw′like′**, *adj.*

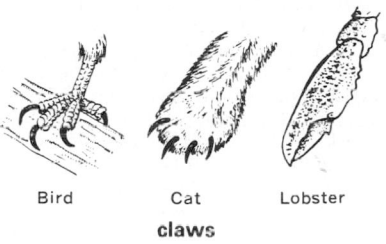
Bird   Cat   Lobster
claws

clay (klā) *n.* a fine-grained earth that can be molded when wet, but hardens permanently when it is dried or baked. Clay is used in the making of pottery and bricks. —**clay′like′**, *adj.*

clay·ey (klā′ē) *adj.*, **clay·i·er, clay·i·est. 1.** of, like, or containing clay. **2.** covered with clay.

clay pigeon, a clay disk tossed into the air as a target in trapshooting.

clean (klēn) *adj.* **1.** free from dirt or filth; unsoiled; unstained: *After playing football, I changed into clean clothes.* **2.** free from impure matter; pure: *clean water, clean air.* **3.** characterized by or having high moral standards; honorable: *to live a clean life.* **4.** fair or within the rules: *a clean player, a clean game.* **5.** smooth or even: *a clean cut. The sculpture has clean lines.* **6.** complete or thorough: *to make a clean break with a troubled past.* —*adv.* **1.** all the way; completely or thoroughly; entirely: *The arrow passed clean through the target.* **2.** in a clean manner. —*v.t.* **1.** to make free of dirt or impure matter: *to clean a car, to clean clothes by washing.* **2.** to remove or get rid of by cleaning: *to clean dishes off a table, to clean grease from a shirt.* **3.** to prepare (chicken, fish, or other food) for cooking. —*v.i.* to do or undergo cleaning. —**clean′ness**, *n.*

·**to clean out. a.** to remove dirt, trash, or other matter from; make neat or clean. **b.** to make empty or use up: *We cleaned out our food supply this weekend.* **c.** *Informal.* to take away all the money of: *That last business deal cleaned us out.*

·**to clean up. a.** to clear of dirt, trash, or other matter; make neat or clean. **b.** *Informal.* to make a lot of money: *I cleaned up in the card game.* **c.** to eliminate corruption from: *to clean up government.*

clean–cut (klēn′kut′) *adj.* **1.** clearly defined, as in outline or meaning; clear; definite: *The witness gave a clean-cut statement of the facts.* **2.** having a wholesome or pleasing appearance or personality: *a clean-cut youth.*

clean·er (klē′nər) *n.* **1.** a person whose work or business is cleaning, especially dry cleaning. **2.** something that cleans, as a machine or chemical substance.

clean·li·ness (klen′lē nis) *n.* **1.** the state of being clean. **2.** the habit of always being clean.

clean·ly¹ (klen′lē) *adj.*, **clean·li·er, clean·li·est.** habitually clean or kept clean: *a cleanly person.* [From the Old English word *clænlīc* meaning "pure, cleanly."]

clean·ly² (klēn′lē) *adv.* in a clean manner: *The bow of the motorboat cut the water cleanly.* [From the Old English word *clænlīce* meaning "purely, entirely."]

cleanse (klenz) *v.t.*, **cleansed, cleans·ing. 1.** to free from dirt, filth, or other matter: *to cleanse a wound.* **2.** to free from guilt or evil; make pure: *to cleanse one's soul.*

cleans·er (klen′zər) *n.* a substance that is used for cleaning, such as soap or detergent.

clean–up (klēn′up′) *n.* a thorough removal of dirt, disorder, or other unwanted conditions: *The mayor promised a cleanup of crime in the city.*

clear (klir) *adj.* **1.** free from anything that darkens, dims, or clouds; bright: *a clear morning, a clear sky.* **2.** easily seen through; not murky: *clear water, clear glass.* **3.** not having blemishes or flaws: *clear skin.* **4.** not blocked; open: *The road into town is now clear.* **5.** easily seen, heard, or understood; distinct: *a clear view, a clear voice. Your directions were not very clear.* **6.** not to be doubted; obvious: *It was clear that we could proceed no further.* **7.** free from confusion, uncertainty, or doubt: *clear thinking, a clear head.* **8.** not troubled or disturbed; free from guilt or blame: *a clear conscience.* **9.** with no further charges or expenses to be deducted; net: *We made a clear profit on the sale.* —*adv.* **1.** in a clear manner; plainly; distinctly: *to shout loud and clear.* **2.** all the way; completely; entirely: *I climbed clear to the top of the tree.* —*v.t.* **1.** to free from anything that occupies, obstructs, or blocks: *Please clear the aisles. The police cleared the street of traffic.* **2.** to remove (something) that occupies, obstructs, or blocks: *We cleared the snow from the driveway. Please clear the dishes off the table.* **3.** to pass by, over, or through without touching: *The plane barely cleared the trees.* **4.** to free from guilt, blame, or responsibility: *The new testimony cleared them of wrongdoing.* **5.** to go through or pass, especially without difficulty: *The bill cleared the Senate.* **6.** to gain or receive as profit after all charges and expenses have been deducted: *We clear $50,000 a year after taxes.* —*v.i.* **1.** to become clear: *The sky cleared.* **2.** to pass away or disappear: *When the smoke cleared, we could see the burning building.* —**clear′ly**, *adv.* —**clear′ness**, *n.*

·**in the clear.** *Informal.* free of guilt, blame, or responsibility.

·**to clear out.** *Informal.* to go away; leave: *We cleared out of the gym so the team could practice.*

·**to clear up.** to make or become clear: *It rained all morning, but it cleared up in the afternoon. The detective cleared up the mystery of the missing jewels.*

clear·ance (klîr′əns) *n.* **1.** the act of clearing: *a ship's narrow clearance of a reef, the clearance of a school during a fire drill.* **2.** approval or authorization: *The*

at; āpe; fär; câre; end; mē; it; īce; pîerce; hot; ōld; sông, fôrk; oil; out; up; ūse; rüle; pull; tûrn; chin; sing; shop; thin; **this**; hw in white; zh in treasure. The symbol ə stands for the unstressed vowel sound heard in about, taken, pencil, lemon, and circus.

C

scientist was given clearance to examine the secret plans. The ship received clearance to enter the port. **3.** the sale of merchandise at reduced prices. Also, **clearance sale.** **4.** the space between two things, such as an overpass and the road underneath it: *This tunnel has a clearance of fifteen feet. The truck had three feet of clearance in the tunnel.*

clear–cut (*adj.* klîr′kut′; *v.* klîr′kut′) *adj.* **1.** having a distinct outline: *a clear-cut profile.* **2.** completely evident or clear; obvious: *It was a clear-cut case of mistaken identity.* —*v.t.,* **clear-cut, clear-cut·ting.** to remove all the trees from (an area) by cutting: *This land was clear-cut in the 1930s.*

clear·head·ed (klîr′hed′id) *adj.* not mentally confused; alert: *Although everyone else panicked because of the fire, the teenager remained clearheaded.*

clear·ing (klîr′ing) *n.* a piece of land, especially within a thickly wooded area, that is free of trees or brush.

clear·ing·house (klîr′ing hous′) *also,* **clearing house.** *n., pl.* **clear·ing·hous·es** (klîr′ing hou′ziz). **1.** a place where accounts and claims, as between banks or brokers, are settled by means of a central computer or by exchange of checks or stocks. **2.** any central headquarters for collection and distribution, as of funds or information.

cleat (klēt) *n.* **1.** a piece of rubber, leather, or metal attached to the sole of a shoe to prevent slipping. Shoes with cleats are used in football. **2.** a piece of metal or wood with projections at both ends, used for controlling or fastening ropes, especially on a dock

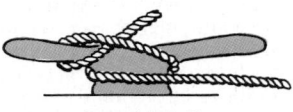

cleat (def. 2)

or boat. **3.** a piece or strip of wood or iron fastened across a surface to give support or to prevent slipping, as on a ramp.

cleav·age (klē′vij) *n.* **1.** the state or process of being cleft; split; division: *the cleavage of a trunk into branches.* **2.** *Biology.* a series of cell divisions by which a fertilized egg splits into a number of smaller cells without increasing in overall size. This process changes the egg into an embryo. **3.** a tendency of certain crystals and rocks to split in a way that produces smooth plane surfaces.

cleave[1] (klēv) *v.,* **cleaved** or **cleft** or **clove, cleaved** or **cleft** or **clo·ven, cleav·ing.** —*v.t.* **1.** to split or part by force; divide: *to cleave a log with an ax.* **2.** to pass through; pierce: *The ship's prow cleaved the waters.* **3.** to form by cutting: *The hikers cleaved a trail through the forest.* —*v.i.* **1.** to come apart; split: *The piece of wood cleaved in two.* **2.** to pass or go: *The ship cleaved through the waves.* [From the Old English word *clēofan* meaning "to split."]

cleave[2] (klēv) *v.i.,* **cleaved, cleav·ing.** **1.** to stick fast; adhere: *Mud cleaved to my shoes.* **2.** to remain attached, devoted, or faithful: *to cleave to one's religious beliefs.* [From the Old English word *clīfian* meaning "to stick, adhere."]

cleav·er (klē′vər) *n.* a short-handled tool with a broad blade, used for chopping, especially by butchers.

clef (klef) *n. Music.* a symbol placed on a staff to indicate the name and pitch of the notes on the various lines and spaces.

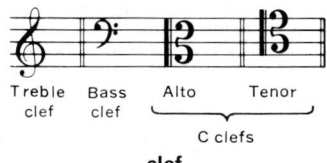

Treble clef Bass clef Alto Tenor

C clefs

clef

cleft (kleft) *v.* a past tense and past participle of **cleave**[1]. —*n.* a space or opening made by splitting; crack: *a cleft in a rock.* —*adj.* partly or completely divided or split: *a person with a cleft chin.*

cleft palate, a split in the palate of the roof of the mouth, sometimes extending to the upper lip. A cleft palate is a birth defect.

clem·a·tis (klem′ə tis, kli mat′is) *n.* any of a group of mostly climbing plants with showy white, red, blue, pink, or purple flowers.

clem·en·cy (klem′ən sē) *n.* **1.** mercy in punishing or judging; leniency: *The judge showed clemency by giving probation to the young thief.* **2.** mildness, as of weather or climate.

clem·ent (klem′ənt) *adj.* **1.** forgiving, merciful, or understanding; lenient: *a clement judge.* **2.** mild; temperate: *clement weather.* —**clem′ent·ly,** *adv.*

clench (klench) *v.t.* **1.** to close or press together tightly: *to clench one's fists, to clench one's teeth.* **2.** to grasp or grip firmly; clutch: *They clenched each other's hands as they entered the doctor's office.* **3.** another word for **clinch** (*v.t.* defs. 2, 3). —*n., pl.* **clench·es.** the act of clenching; firm grasp or grip.

cler·gy (klûr′jē) *n., pl.* **cler·gies.** persons ordained for religious service, such as ministers, priests, or rabbis.

cler·gy·man (klûr′jē mən) *n., pl.* **cler·gy·men** (klûr′jē-mən), a person ordained as a minister, priest, rabbi, or the like; member of the clergy.

cler·gy·wom·an (klûr′jē wum′ən) *n., pl.* **cler·gy·wom·en** (klûr′jē wim′ən). a woman ordained as a minister, priest, rabbi, or the like.

cler·ic (kler′ik) *n.* a member of the clergy.

cler·i·cal (kler′i kəl) *adj.* **1.** of or relating to clerks or office workers or their work: *Typing is a clerical job.* **2.** of or characteristic of a member of the clergy or the clergy: *a clerical collar.* —**cler′i·cal·ly,** *adv.*

clerk (klûrk) *n.* **1.** a person employed in an office to keep records, accounts, or files, and do other general office work, such as typing. **2.** a person employed in a store to sell goods; salesclerk. **3.** an official who keeps records and does routine business, as in a court of law or legislature: *a county clerk, a town clerk.* —*v.i.* to work or act as a clerk: *Last summer I clerked in a sporting goods store.* [From the Old French word *clerc* meaning both "clerk" and "cleric," from the Church Latin word *clericus* "priest," from the Greek word *klērikos* "priest." In the Middle Ages, the few people who could read and write were mostly priests and monks.]

clev·er (klev′ər) *adj.* **1.** mentally sharp and alert; having a keen mind; quick-witted: *The clever child was able to solve the difficult problem.* **2.** showing mental sharpness and quickness: *The captain of the football team came up with a clever play. The lecturer made a clever remark.* **3.** having or showing skill in doing something, especially with the hands: *The students were clever at making things out of wood.* —**clev′er·ly,** *adv.* —**clev′er·ness,** *n.*

clew (klü) *n. British.* another spelling of **clue.**

cli·ché (klē shā′) *n.* an expression, phrase, or idea that has lost its originality or effect because it has been used too much. *As pretty as a picture is a cliché.*

click (klik) *n.* a light, sharp, often metallic sound: *We heard the click of the key in the lock.* —*v.t.* to cause to make a click or clicks: *The soldiers clicked their heels together and saluted.* —*v.i.* **1.** to move with a click; produce a click or clicks: *Their heels clicked on the sidewalk.* **2.** *Informal.* to become understandable; make sense: *Everything suddenly clicked in the mystery when I read the next chapter.* **3.** *Informal.* to be a success: *The author's new play clicked.*

cli·ent (klī′ənt) *n.* **1.** a person, group, or company that uses the professional services of another: *a lawyer's clients.* **2.** a customer of any business.

cli·en·tele (klī′ən tel′) *n.* clients or customers as a group: *That restaurant caters to a wealthy clientele.*

cliff (klif) *n.* a high, steep face of rock or earth.

cliff dweller *also,* **Cliff Dweller.** a member of a group of prehistoric people who built their houses in caves or on ledges along the walls of cliffs. They were the ancestors of the Pueblo Indians of the southwestern United States.

cliff dwelling, a dwelling built in a cave or on a ledge of a cliff wall. Ruins of cliff dwellings are found in Arizona, New Mexico, Utah, and Colorado.

cliff dwelling

cliff·hang·er (klif′hang′ər) *also,* **cliff·hang·er.** *n.* **1.** an exciting adventure serial whose parts or installments always end at a point full of suspense. **2.** any contest or situation having an outcome that is not known or settled until the very end: *The close election was a real cliff-hanger.*

cliff swallow, a swallow that lives in colonies in mud nests under the eaves of buildings or against cliffs.

cli·mac·tic (klī mak′tik) *adj.* of, relating to, or forming a climax: *The third scene was the climactic one.*

cli·mate (klī′mit) *n.* **1.** the typical weather conditions of a particular place or region, usually considered in terms of average temperature, humidity, rainfall, and wind conditions. **2.** any place or region considered in terms of its typical weather conditions: *I want to live in a mild climate.* **3.** the outlook, mood, or trend among a group of people; atmosphere: *The climate was one of excitement before the game.*

cli·mat·ic (klī mat′ik) *adj.* of or relating to climate. —**cli·mat′i·cal·ly,** *adv.*

cli·ma·tol·o·gy (klī′mə tol′ə jē) *n.* the science dealing with the study of climate.

cli·max (klī′maks) *n., pl.* **cli·max·es.** **1.** the highest point, as of development, interest, or excitement: *The summer's climax was our big party in August.* **2.** the turning point or point of highest interest or excitement in the action or theme of a play, book, or similar work: *The climax in the film came when the detective discovered who the murderer was.* **3.** the final stage in the ecological development of a given community of plants, animals, and other organisms, in which species are stable and perpetuate themselves as long as the same ecological conditions persist. Also, **climax community.** —*v.t.* to bring to a climax: *The evening was climaxed by the presentation of the awards.* —*v.i.* to reach a climax.

climb (klīm) *v.i.* **1.** to move upward or toward the top of something by using the hands or feet: *I climbed to the top of the tree.* **2.** to move or go by using the hands or feet: *to climb through a window, to climb into bed.* **3.** to go upward or move higher; rise: *The plane climbed to an altitude of 12,000 feet. Prices climbed last year. The road climbs for a mile.* **4.** to grow in an upward direction by twining around or clinging to another object for support: *The vines climbed up the side of the cottage.* —*v.t.* to move toward the top of (something) by using the hands or feet: *The worker climbed the ladder.* —*n.* **1.** the act or process of climbing: *Their climb up the hill took an hour.* **2.** the distance to be climbed: *It's only a short climb to the top from here.* **3.** a place or thing to be climbed: *That cliff is a dangerous climb.*

climb·er (klī′mər) *n.* **1.** a person or thing that climbs. **2.** any climbing plant, such as ivy.

clime (klīm) *n. Archaic.* country; region.

clinch (klinch) *v.t.* **1.** to make final and definite; settle conclusively: *to clinch a business deal.* **2.** to fasten firmly, as a driven nail or bolt, by bending over or flattening the point that sticks out. **3.** to fasten (objects) together by using nails, bolts, or similar fastenings. Also (*defs. 2, 3*), **clench.** —*v.i.* to grasp or hold an opponent's or each other's arms or body, especially in boxing. —*n., pl.* **clinch·es.** **1.** the act of clinching: *The boxers went into a clinch.* **2.** a kind of knot in which the loose end is lashed back through a loop.

clinch
(n., def. 2)

clinch·er (klin′chər) *n.* **1.** a person or thing that clinches, especially a nail made for clinching. **2.** *Informal.* a final or deciding point, as in an argument: *Of all the reasons for not moving there, the high rent is the clincher.*

cling (kling) *v.i.,* **clung, cling·ing.** **1.** to stick closely, as if glued: *The wet shirt clung to my back.* **2.** to hold tightly, as by grasping or embracing: *The shivering children clung to each other in fear.* **3.** to be or stay near, as if attached: *The car clung to the road as it rounded the curve.* **4.** to remain attached: *to cling to a routine, to cling to a belief.* —*n.* see **clingstone.**

cling·stone (kling′stōn′) *n.* a fruit, especially a peach, in which the flesh or pulp is not easily separated from the pit or stone.

clin·ic (klin′ik) *n.* **1.** a place connected with a hospital or medical school, where patients come for treatment, often at a low cost or without charge. **2.** a place where specialists treat or study certain types of patients or certain diseases: *a maternity clinic, a cancer clinic.* **3.** a place or organization offering advice or instruction in some field: *a reading clinic.* **4.** instruction or a class offered at such a place or by such an organization: *A driving clinic will be held at the high school.* **5.** instruction given by doctors to medical students, in which a patient is examined and treated in the presence of the students.

clin·i·cal (klin′i kəl) *adj.* **1.** of or relating to a clinic. **2.** based on or dealing with the direct observation and treatment of patients rather than laboratory experimentation: *clinical psychology.* **3.** scientific and unemotional: *The novel contained a clinical description of the effects of war.* —**clin′i·cal·ly,** *adv.*

clink (klingk) *v.t.* to cause to make a light, sharp, ringing sound: *They clinked their glasses together in a toast.* —*v.i.* to make a light, sharp, ringing sound: *The coins clinked in my pocket as I walked.* —*n.* a light, sharp, ringing sound.

clink·er (kling′kər) *n.* **1.** a stony mass consisting of impurities that remain after coal is burned. **2.** *Slang.* a mistake; error.

clip¹ (klip) *v.,* **clipped, clip·ping.** —*v.t.* **1.** to cut, with shears or scissors; remove or detach by cutting: *Clip off the loose strands of thread when you finish sewing. I clipped the article out of the newspaper.* **2.** to make shorter by cutting; trim: *to clip one's nails, to clip a hedge.* **3.** to trim or cut the hair or fleece of: *to clip a poodle, to clip sheep.* **4.** to make shorter: *The last scene*

at; āpe; fär; câre; end; mē; it; īce; pîerce; hot; ōld; sông, fôrk; oil; out; up; ūse; rūle; pull; tûrn; chin; sing; shop; thin; this; hw in white; zh in treasure. The symbol ə stands for the unstressed vowel sound heard in about, taken, pencil, lemon, and circus.

181

was clipped because the play was too long. **5.** *Informal.* to hit with a quick, sharp blow: *to clip someone on the chin.* —*v.i.* **1.** to cut or trim. **2.** *Informal.* to move quickly: *We clipped along toward the next town.* —*n.* **1.** the act of clipping. **2.** the amount of wool obtained from sheep at one shearing or during one season. **3.** *Informal.* a rate or pace: *The bus moved along at a rapid clip.* **4.** *Informal.* a quick, sharp blow or punch. [From the Old Norse word *klippa* meaning "to cut off, cut short."]

clip² (klip) *n.* **1.** a device that grips or holds articles together: *a paper clip, a money clip.* **2.** a piece of jewelry that fastens with a clip or clasp: *a tie clip.* **3.** a holder for ammunition for certain firearms that fits into the magazine. —*v.t.,* **clipped, clip·ping.** to fasten with a clip: *to clip papers together.* [From the Old English word *clyppan* meaning "to surround," "embrace," "grip."]

clip·board (klip'bôrd') *n.* a board with a clip at one end for holding paper or a pad, used as a portable writing surface.

clip·per (klip'ər) *n.* **1.** *also,* **clippers.** a tool or instrument for clipping, cutting, or shearing: *a barber's clippers.* **2.** a fast-sailing cargo ship developed in the United States in the nineteenth century, having a narrow beam and usually, three square-rigged masts. **3.** a person who clips.

clipper *(def. 2)*

clip·ping (klip'ing) *n.* **1.** a piece that is cut off or out, especially an item that is cut from a newspaper or magazine. **2.** the act of cutting or trimming.

clique (klēk, klik) *n.* a small group of people friendly with each other, who stick together and are often unfriendly to outsiders.

cli·quish (klē'kish, klik'ish) *adj.* **1.** likely to form and stay within cliques: *The club members are all very cliquish.* **2.** having the characteristics of a clique: *a cliquish group.* —**cli'quish·ly,** *adv.* —**cli'quish·ness,** *n.*

clit·or·is (klit'ər is, kli tôr'is) *n., pl.* **clit·or·is·es** or **clit·or·i·des** (kli tôr'i dēz'). a small organ at the end of the vulva.

clo·a·ca (klō ā'kə) *n., pl.* **clo·a·cae** (klō ā'sē). a chamber found in birds, fish, reptiles, amphibians, and some mammals, into which the intestinal, urinary, and genital canals open.

cloak (klōk) *n.* **1.** a loose outer garment, with or without sleeves. **2.** something that covers or hides: *The robbery took place under the cloak of darkness.* —*v.t.* **1.** to cover with or as if with a cloak: *The designer cloaked the model in black.* **2.** to cover; hide; disguise: *to cloak a meeting with the pretense of a social gathering.*

cloak·room (klōk'rüm', klōk'rum') *n.* a room in a restaurant, theater, or other place, where coats, hats, umbrellas, and the like may be left temporarily; coatroom.

clob·ber (klob'ər) *v.t. Slang.* **1.** to hit with great force. **2.** to defeat severely.

clock¹ (klok) *n.* a device for measuring and showing time, usually with hands that pass over a dial marked to show hours or minutes or with a digital display. A clock is not meant to be worn or carried about by a person as a watch is. —*v.t.* to find out or record the performance or speed of, as with a stopwatch; time: *to clock a race, to clock a runner.* [From either the Old French word *cloke* or the Middle Dutch word *clocke,* both meaning "bell" or "clock" and going back to the Medieval Latin word *clocca* "bell."]

clock² (klok) *n.* an ornamental design woven or embroidered on the side of a sock or stocking. [Probably from *clock¹.* This design was originally shaped like a bell.]

clock radio, an appliance consisting of a radio receiver with a built-in timer that can be set to turn on the radio at a designated time, especially as an alarm to awaken a sleeper.

clock·wise (klok'wīz') *adv., adj.* in the direction in which the hands of a clock move.

clock·work (klok'wûrk') *n.* a mechanism made up of gears, wheels, and springs, such as that which runs a clock or other mechanical device.

·like clockwork. with great regularity, precision, and smoothness: *We rehearsed so carefully that the performance went like clockwork.*

clod (klod) *n.* **1.** a lump or mass, especially of earth or clay. **2.** a dull, awkward, or stupid person.

clod·hop·per (klod'hop'ər) *n.* **1.** a clumsy, awkward boor. **2.** **clodhoppers.** large, heavy shoes or boots.

clog (klog) *v.,* **clogged, clog·ging.** —*v.t.* **1.** to block or stop up: *Dirt clogged the pipes. Heavy traffic clogged the roads.* **2.** to hinder the progress or action of: *The snow clogged traffic.* —*v.i.* to become blocked or stopped up. —*n.* **1.** a shoe or sandal with a thick sole of wood or cork. **2.** anything that hinders or blocks progress or action.

clois·ter (kloi'stər) *n.* **1.** a place of religious seclusion, such as a monastery. **2.** a covered walk along the wall or walls of a building, having a row of columns on one side. **3.** any quiet, solitary place. —*v.t.* to shut away in a quiet place.

cloister *(def. 2)*

clone (klōn) *n.* **1.** any of a group of genetically identical organisms reproduced asexually from a single ancestor. **2.** a person or thing that is, seems to be, or functions as a duplicate of another. —*v.,* **cloned, clon·ing.** —*v.t.* **1.** to cause to grow as a clone. **2.** to make a duplicate, copy, or imitation of: *to clone a computer.* —*v.i.* to grow as a clone. [From the Greek word *klōn* meaning "slip²" or "twig."]

close (*v., n. def. 1,* klōz; *adj., adv., n. def. 2,* klōs) *v.,* **closed, clos·ing.** —*v.t.* **1.** to move (something) so as to block or cover up an entrance, passage, or opening; shut: *to close a window, to close one's mouth.* **2.** to bring together the parts of so as to leave no opening or to form a whole: *to close a book. The troops closed ranks.* **3.** to fill or block; stop up: *The landslide closed the mountain pass.* **4.** to keep or stop from operating: *The principal closed the school because of the blizzard.* **5.** to bring to an end; finish: *The speaker closed the lecture with a joke.* —*v.i.* **1.** to become shut: *The door closed with a bang.* **2.** to stop operation: *Banks close on legal holidays.* **3.** to come to an end; finish: *This story closes happily.* **4.** to come together, as parts of a whole: *The wound closed after a week.* —*adj.,* **clos·er, clos·est.** **1.** with little space or time between; near: *Our house is close to the school. This cloth has a close weave. Spring vacation is close.* **2.** not distant in relation, degree, or condition: *close relatives. The Spanish language is close to Portuguese.* **3.** attached or marked by strong affection or loyalty: *a close friend.* **4.** very much like another: *a close copy, a close resemblance.* **5.** careful and strict; exact; thorough: *Pay close attention to what I say. The police carried out a close investigation of the crime.* **6.** decided by a narrow margin: *a close race.* **7.** fitting tightly: *a close fit, close quarters.* **8.** lacking fresh or freely blowing air; stifling; stuffy: *It's close in this room.* **9.** carefully guarded: *a close secret.* **10.** stingy: *to be close with money.* —*adv.* in a close position or manner:

I held the child close in my arms. You're not parked close enough to the curb. —*n.* **1.** end; finish: *We returned to our homes at the close of day.* **2.** an enclosed place, especially enclosed land beside a cathedral or other building. —**close·ly** (klōs′lē), *adv.* —**close·ness** (klōs′- nis), *n.*

 ·**to close in** or **to close in on.** to come near and surround: *Government frigates closed in on the pirate ship.*

 ·**to close out.** to sell (merchandise), usually at much lower prices, to eliminate from inventory: *The store closed out its summer clothes.*

close call (klōs) *Informal.* a narrow escape, as from danger or harm. Also, **close shave.**

closed–cap·tioned (klōzd′kap′shənd) *adj.* (of a television program) broadcast with captions for the convenience of viewers with hearing impairments. The captions can be viewed only with the aid of a decoding device attached to a television receiver.

closed circuit **1.** an electric circuit through which current can flow without interruption. **2.** a television system in which signals are sent out, usually by a cable, to a limited and selected number of receivers. Also (*def. 2*), **closed- circuit television.** —**closed′-cir′cuit,** *adj.*

closed–cir·cuit television (klōzd′sûr′kit) a system for sending television signals by cable to a limited number of receivers, especially within a school, office, or other building.

closed shop, a factory or place of business in which only union members are employed.

close–fist·ed (klōs′fis′tid) *adj.* stingy; miserly: *The close- fisted millionaire wouldn't give a dime to charity.*

close–grained (klōs′grānd′) *adj.* having fine and closely arranged fibers, crystals, or particles: *close-grained wood.*

close–knit (klōs′nit′) *adj.* closely united, as by kinship, friendship, or common purpose: *a close-knit family.*

close·mouthed (klōs′mouthd′, klōs′moutht′) *adj.* not talking much; reserved; secretive: *Don't be so close- mouthed about your opinion.*

close·out (klōz′out′) *also,* **close-out.** *n.* a sale in which merchandise is sold at much lower prices: *The furniture store is having a closeout on rugs.*

close shave (klōs) *Informal.* another term for **close call.**

clos·et (kloz′it) *n.* **1.** a small room or recess, usually with a door, for storing clothing. **2.** a cabinet, enclosed space, or small room for storing household utensils, food, or other articles: *a broom closet, a china closet.* **3.** a small, private room, especially one used for prayer or study. —*v.t.* to shut up in a room, as if for a conference or private talk: *The general was closeted with the staff, making plans for the attack.*

close–up (klōs′up′) *also,* **close·up.** *n.* **1.** a photograph taken at close range or with a telescopic lens: *The tooth- paste advertisement showed a close-up of two smiling people.* **2.** a close or detailed view or look: *a close-up of a problem.*

clo·sure (klō′zhər) *n.* **1.** the act of closing or the state of being closed. **2.** something that closes or shuts. **3.** another word for **cloture.**

clot (klot) *n.* a mass or lump formed by the thickening of a liquid: *a clot of blood.* —*v.,* **clot·ted, clot·ting.** —*v.i.* to form into clots: *The blood from the wound clotted.* —*v.t.* to cause to form into clots.

cloth (klôth) *n., pl.* **cloths** (klôthz, klôths). **1.** material made by weaving, knitting, braiding, or pressing textile fibers; fabric: *a bolt of cloth.* **2.** a piece of such fabric, used for a particular purpose: *Put a cloth on the table before you set it.* **3. the cloth.** the clergy.

clothe (klōth) *v.t.,* **clothed** or **clad, cloth·ing. 1.** to put clothes on; dress: *The baby was warmly clothed in a snowsuit.* **2.** to provide with clothes: *It takes a good deal of money to clothe a large family.* **3.** to cover as if with clothing: *Snow clothed the field. The judge was clothed with dignity.*

clothes (klōz, klōthz) *pl. n.* **1.** articles of clothing. **2.** see **bedclothes.**

clothes·horse (klōz′hôrs′, klōthz′hôrs′) *n.* **1.** a frame on which clothes are hung to dry or air. **2.** *Informal.* a person who takes great pleasure in owning and wearing fashionable clothes.

clothes·line (klōz′līn′, klōthz′līn′) *n.* a rope or wire on which clothes and other laundry are hung to dry on air.

clothes moth, any of a group of small moths whose larvae feed on wool, fur, and other materials.

clothes·pin (klōz′pin′, klōthz′pin′) *n.* a clamp or forked piece of wood or plastic used to fasten clothes on a line.

clothes tree, an upright pole with hooks or pegs near the top on which to hang clothes.

cloth·ier (klōth′yər) *n.* a person who sells or makes cloth or clothing.

cloth·ing (klō′thing) *n.* **1.** articles worn to protect, cover, or adorn the body; clothes; garments. **2.** any covering.

clo·ture (klō′chər) *n.* a method of ending debate in a legislative body in order to bring a question to a vote. Also, **closure.**

cloud (kloud) *n.* **1.** a mass of water vapor or ice particles floating in the air high above the earth. Low-level clouds, such as cumulus, occur at altitudes up to 8,000 feet (2,400 meters). Middle-level clouds, such as altocumulus, occur at altitudes of 8,000–20,000 feet (2,400–6,000 meters). High-level clouds, such as cirrus, occur at altitudes of 20,000–40,000 feet (6,000–12,200 meters). **2.** any similar mass, as of smoke or steam: *A cloud rose from the tall smokestack. The cavalry rode off in a cloud of dust.* **3.** a great number or mass of persons or things in motion: *A cloud of migrating birds filled the sky.* **4.** something that darkens, threatens, troubles, disgraces, or the like: *A cloud of gloom settled over the team when it lost the championship.* —*v.t.* **1.** to cover with a cloud or clouds: *Mists clouded the sun. Smoke from the burning house clouded the street.* **2.** to darken or make dim or confused: *My judgment was clouded by the jealousy I felt.* **3.** to make gloomy or troubled: *Anger clouded their faces.* **4.** to put under suspicion; sully: *The rumors could cloud your reputation.* —*v.i.* to become cloudy: *The sky clouded suddenly. Their faces clouded with worry.* **cloud′like′** *adj.*

cloud·burst (kloud′bûrst′) *n.* a sudden, heavy rainfall.

cloud chamber, a device used to make the paths of subatomic particles visible by means of a gas supersatu rated with water vapor. The vapor condenses as the particles move through it, forming a cloudlike trail. Cloud chambers are used in the study of nuclear physics.

cloud·less (kloud′lis) *adj.* without clouds; clear; bright: *The sun shone brightly in the cloudless sky.* —**cloud′- less·ly,** *adv.* —**cloud′less·ness,** *n.*

cloud nine *Informal.* a state of great happiness: *I was on cloud nine when I won a free trip to England.*

cloud seeding, any of various methods for producing rain artificially by scattering particles, usually of dry ice or a chemical, into clouds.

cloud·y (klou′dē) *adj.,* **cloud·i·er, cloud·i·est. 1.** cov ered with or hidden by clouds; overcast: *a cloudy sky.* **2.** having little sunshine: *a cloudy day.* **3.** not clear: *a cloudy pond, cloudy ideas.* **4.** gloomy: *to put on a cloudy face.* —**cloud′i·ly,** *adv.* —**cloud′i·ness,** *n.*

clout (klout) *n.* **1.** a heavy blow, as with the hand: *During*

---

at; āpe; fär; câre; end; mē; it; īce; pîerce; hot; ōld; sông, fôrk; oil; out; up; ūse; rüle; pull; tûrn; chin; sing; shop; thin; this; hw in white; zh in treasure. The symbol ə stands for the unstressed vowel sound heard in about, taken, pencil, lemon, and circus.

the scuffle, the victim received a clout on the side of the head. **2.** *Informal.* influence or power: *political clout.* —*v.t.* to hit, as with the hand.

clove¹ (klōv) *n.* **1.** the dried, unopened flower bud of a tropical evergreen tree, used as a spice. **2.** the tree bearing this bud, having oval, oblong leaves. [From the Old French phrase *clou (de girofle)* meaning "nail (of a clove tree)." This bud resembles a nail.]

clove² (klōv) *n.* one of the smaller sections of certain large plant bulbs: *a clove of garlic.* [From the Old English word *clufu* with the same meaning.]

clove³ (klōv) *n.* a past tense of **cleave¹**.

clove hitch, a knot used to tie a rope around something, such as a spar or pole.

clo·ven (klō′vən) *v.* a part participle of **cleave¹**. —*adj.* split; divided: *the cloven hoof of a cow.*

clo·ver (klō′vər) *n.* any of a group of plants bearing leaves usually composed of three leaflets, and rounded heads or spikes of small, fragrant red, white, yellow, or purple flowers, widely grown as food for cattle.

·**in clover.** living in wealth and luxury: *After the success of the book the author was in clover.*

clo·ver·leaf (klō′vər lēf′) *n.*, *pl.* **clo·ver·leaves** (klō′vər lēvz′). a highway intersection that consists of a series of curving ramps, usually shaped in part like a four-leaf clover, connecting highways crossing each other on different levels.

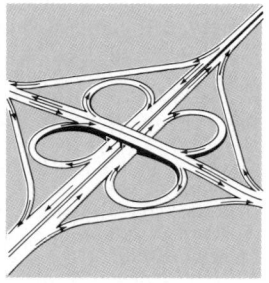

cloverleaf

clown (kloun) *n.* **1.** a person in a circus, carnival, or similar show, who amuses the audience by playing tricks or jokes and is usually dressed in a ridiculous costume with funny makeup. **2.** any person who plays tricks or jokes. —*v.i.* to act like a clown.

clown·ish (kloun′nish) *adj.* of or resembling a clown: *clownish behavior.* —**clown′ish·ly**, *adv.* —**clown′ish·ness**, *n.*

cloy (kloi) *v.t.* to make weary with too much of something that is usually pleasant: *All those fancy meals cloyed my appetite.* —*v.i.* to become unpleasant through too much of something that is usually pleasant: *The excitement of constant travel cloyed after a month.*

club (klub) *n.* **1.** a heavy stick, thicker at one end, used especially as a weapon. **2.** any of various sticks or bats used to hit a ball in certain games, such as golf. **3.** a group of people who meet together for pleasure or for some special purpose: *a social club, an athletic club.* **4.** a place, building, or room where the members of such a group meet. **5.** a nightclub. **6. a.** a playing card marked with one or more black figures shaped like this: ♣ **b. clubs.** the suit of such cards. —*v.*, **clubbed, clubbing.** —*v.t.* to beat or strike with a club. —*v.i.* to unite for a common purpose.

club car, a railroad passenger car equipped with chairs for lounging, card tables, and usually a bar or buffet.

club·foot (klub′fut′) *n.*, *pl.* **club·feet. 1.** a condition in which the foot is deformed or twisted out of position, caused by abnormal development before birth. **2.** a deformed or twisted foot. —**club′foot′ed**, *adj.*

club·house (klub′hous′) *n.*, *pl.* **club·hous·es** (klub′hou′ziz). a building used by a club.

club moss, a small evergreen plant that grows along the ground and bears small, upright branches covered with tiny, dark green leaves that look like pine needles.

club sandwich, a sandwich made with three slices of bread, usually toasted, and a filling of meat, lettuce, tomato, and a dressing.

club soda, another term for **soda water.**

cluck (kluk) *n.* **1.** a low sound made by a hen when sitting on eggs or calling her chicks. **2.** any similar sound. —*v.i.* **1.** to make the low sound of a hen. **2.** to make a similar sound. —*v.t.* to call or express by clucking.

clue (klü) *n.* *also, British,* **clew.** a guide or key that aids in finding the solution to a problem or mystery: *The case stumped the police, who had few clues to follow.*

clump (klump) *n.* **1.** a small group of things of the same kind, gathered or lying close together: *The rabbit hopped out of a clump of bushes.* **2.** a thick mass or lump: *Clumps of earth clung to the roots of the plant.* **3.** a heavy, dull, thumping sound. —*v.t.* to gather or form into a clump. —*v.i.* to walk heavily and clumsily. —**clump′y**, *adj.*

clum·sy (klum′zē) *adj.*, **clum·si·er**, **clum·si·est. 1.** lacking grace or skill; awkward: *a clumsy dancer.* **2.** unskillfully or awkwardly shaped, done, or made: *clumsy boots.* —**clum′si·ly**, *adv.* —**clum′si·ness**, *n.*

clung (klung) the past tense and past participle of **cling.**

clus·ter (klus′tər) *n.* **1.** a group of things of the same kind growing or situated together: *Grapes grow in a cluster. The ring had a cluster of pearls.* **2.** any group of similar persons or things: *There were clusters of people waiting for the parade to come.* —*v.i.* to group or form into a cluster or clusters: *The campers clustered around the fire.*

clutch¹ (kluch) *v.t.* to grasp or hold tightly or firmly: *I clutched the money in my hand on the way to the grocery store.* —*v.i.* to try to grasp or seize (with *at*): *the kitten clutched at my leg.* —*n.*, *pl.* **clutch·es. 1.** a strong hold; grip: *I felt a clutch on my arm.* **2.** a claw, paw, or hand that clutches: *The bird could not escape from the clutches of the hawk.* **3. clutches.** control; power: *The messenger fell into the clutches of the enemy.* **4.** a device in a machine, such as an automobile, that connects or disconnects a motor and a drive shaft. **5.** the lever or pedal that operates such a device. **6.** *Informal.* a serious or crucial situation: *to be at one's best in the clutch.* [From the Old English word *clyccan* meaning "to grasp or grip tightly."]

clutch² (kluch) *n.*, *pl.* **clutch·es. 1.** the number of eggs laid or incubated at one time. **2.** a brood of chickens. [Probably from the Middle English word *clekken* meaning "to give birth to, create," from the Old Norse word *klekja* "to hatch."]

clut·ter (klut′ər) *n.* a confused or disorderly state or collection of things: *a clutter of papers on a street.* —*v.t.* to crowd or litter with a confused or disorderly collection of things: *The porch was cluttered with old newspapers.*

Cly·tem·nes·tra (klī′təm nes′trə) *n.* *Greek Legend.* the wife of Agamemnon, who killed him on his return from Troy and who was later killed by her son, Orestes.

Cm, the symbol for curium.

cm, cm., centimeter; centimeters.

Co, the symbol for cobalt.

co– *prefix* **1.** with; together: *coexist.* **2.** fellow; joint: *copilot.* **3.** equally: *coextend.*

co., Co. 1. company; Company. **2.** County.

c.o., in care of. Also, **c/o.**

CO 1. postal abbreviation for Colorado. **2.** Commanding Officer. **3.** conscientious objector.

coach (kōch) *n.*, *pl.* **coach·es. 1.** a large, four-wheeled closed carriage drawn by horses, with seats inside for passengers and a raised seat outside for the driver. **2.** a railroad passenger car. **3.** a bus. **4.** a class of passenger accommodations offering the low-

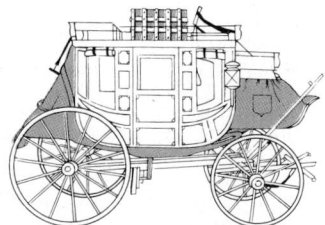

coach *(def. 1)*

est rates for traveling, as on trains or airplanes. **5.** a teacher or trainer, as of an athlete or athletic team, singer, actor, or dancer: *a football coach.* —*v.t.* to act as a coach to; train or teach: *to coach a swimming team.* —*v.i.* to act as a coach.

coach·man (kōch′mən) *n., pl.* **coach·men** (kōch′mən) a person who drives a coach or carriage.

co·ad·ju·tor (kō aj′ə tər) *n.* **1.** an assistant; helper. **2.** a bishop appointed to assist another bishop.

co·ag·u·lant (kō ag′yə lənt) *n.* a substance that causes a liquid to coagulate.

co·ag·u·late (kō ag′yə lāt′) *v.,* **co·ag·u·lat·ed, co·ag·u·lat·ing.** —*v.t.* to change (something) from a liquid into a thickened mass; clot. —*v.i.* to become changed from a liquid into a thickened mass. [From the Latin word *coagulatus,* past participle of *coagulare* meaning "to curdle," going back to the Latin prefix *co-* "with, together" + *agere* "to drive, do, make."] —**co·ag′u·la′tion,** *n.*

coal (kōl) *n.* **1.** a black or dark brown substance that burns easily and is widely used as a fuel. It has a high carbon content and is formed mostly of plant matter that has been buried deep in the earth for centuries and has undergone physical and chemical change because of great heat and pressure. **2.** a piece of this substance. **3.** any piece of fuel, such as wood or coal, that is glowing or burned. —*v.t.* to provide with coal: *to coal a ship.* —*v.i.* to take on a supply of coal.

coal·er (kō′lər) *n.* **1.** a ship, freight car, railroad, or the like that carries coal. **2.** a person who sells or supplies coal.

co·a·lesce (kō′ə les′) *v.i.,* **co·a·lesced, co·a·lesc·ing. 1.** to grow together so as to form one body; fuse: *The two parts of the broken bone coalesced.* **2.** to unite, as into one unit or organization; combine: *The opposing factions coalesced to form a new political party.* —**co′a·les′cence,** *n.*

coal gas 1. a mixture of gases, made up chiefly of hydrogen and methane, produced by heating bituminous coal without air. It is used especially in open-hearth furnaces and as a source of such compounds as ammonia and benzene. **2.** the gas given off by burning coal.

co·a·li·tion (kō′ə lish′ən) *n.* an alliance of political leaders, parties, or nations for some special purpose: *a liberal coalition.*

coal oil, another term for **kerosene.**

coal scuttle, a pail or other container, often with a wide projecting lip, for carrying or holding coal.

coal tar, a black, sticky substance left after heating bituminous coal without air, used in many synthetic products, such as dyes, nylon, aspirin, and plastics.

co–an·chor (kō ang′kər) *n.* a person who serves jointly with another person as anchor of a news broadcast. —*v.t.* to serve as anchor of (a news broadcast) jointly with another person.

coarse (kôrs) *adj.,* **coars·er, coars·est. 1.** made of large parts or particles: *coarse sand.* **2.** lacking fineness of texture; thick or rough: *coarse cloth, coarse skin.* **3.** lacking refinement or delicacy; vulgar: *coarse behavior, coarse language.* **4.** of inferior or poor quality or worth. —**coarse′ly,** *adv.* —**coarse′ness,** *n.*

coars·en (kôr′sən) *v.t.* to make coarse: *Years of hard work coarsened the miner's hands.* —*v.i.* to become coarse.

coast (kōst) *n.* **1. a.** the land next to the sea: *We hiked along the coast looking for sea birds.* **b.** the sea next to a large body of land: *We sailed the Maine coast last summer.* **2. the Coast.** a region of the United States bordering the Pacific Ocean. **3.** a slide down a hill or similar incline, as on a sled. —*v.i.* **1.** to ride or slide along an incline by the force of gravity: *to coast down a hill on a sled.* **2.** to continue to move after power has been shut off: *The car coasted after we turned off the*

engine. **3.** to advance or move long without making any effort: *I couldn't coast through high school.* **4.** to sail along or near a coast. —*v.t.* to sail along or near the coast of.

coast·al (kōs′təl) *adj.* of, at, near, or along a coast.

coas·ter (kōs′tər) *n.* **1.** a small mat or tray placed under a glass or bottle to protect the surface beneath. **2.** a ship that engages in trade along a coast. **3.** a sled or toboggan.

Coast Guard 1. a military service responsible for preserving safety and order along the coasts and inland waterways of the United States. **2. coast guard.** any similar military service.

coast·line (kōst′līn′) *n.* the outline or contour of a coast.

coast·ward (kōst′wərd) *adj.* directed toward the coast: *a coastward course.* —*adv.* also, **coast·wards.** toward the coast: *to drift coastward.*

coast·wise (kōst′wīz′) *adj.* following or carried on along the coast: *coastwise trade.* —*adv.* by way of or along the coast.

coat (kōt) *n.* **1.** an outer garment with sleeves, usually designed to be worn outdoors over other clothing. **2.** a natural, external covering, such as the hair or fur of an animal: *A healthy dog usually has a glossy coat.* **3.** any layer that covers a surface: *a coat of paint.* —*v.t.* to cover with a layer: *The stove was coated with grease.*

co·a·ti (kō ä′tē) *n., pl.* **co·a·tis.** an animal resembling a raccoon and having a long body, yellowish brown, gray, or red fur, a long, striped tail, and a flexible snout. It is found in Central and South America. Also, **co·a·ti·mun·di** (kō ä′tē-mun′dē).

coat·ing (kō′ting) *n.* a layer covering a surface: *A thin coating of dust covered the furniture.*

coat of arms *pl.* **coats of arms. 1.** a group of designs and figures arranged on a shield or other surface, serving as the emblem of some person, family, or institution. **2.** a shield, or a drawing of a shield, marked with such an emblem.

coati

coat of mail *pl.* **coats of mail.** a shirt or coat made of chain mail, formerly worn as armor.

coat·room (kōt′rüm′, kōt′rŏŏm′) *n.* another word for **cloakroom.**

coat·tails (kōt′tālz′) *pl. n.* the back part of a formal coat or jacket, such as a cutaway or swallow-tailed coat. **·on (someone's) coattails.** benefiting from being associated with someone else, especially someone in politics who is in power or enjoys popularity: *to ride the president's coattails into office.*

co·au·thor (kō ô′thər) *n.* an author who writes with another author. —*v.t.* to write with another author: *They coauthored a series of articles about colonial history.*

coax (kōks) *v.t.* **1.** to persuade or try to persuade, as by flattery, pleasant manner, or soft, gentle speech: *to coax a person to do something.* **2.** to get by coaxing: *I coaxed extra money from my parents.* —**coax′er,** *n.*

co·ax·i·al cable (kō ak′sē əl) high-frequency telephone, telegraph, and television cable for sending out thousands of electronic signals at the same time, consisting

at; āpe; fär; câre; end; mē; it; īce; pîerce; hot; ōld; sông, fôrk; oil; out; up; ūse; rüle; pùll; tûrn; chin; sing; shop; thin; <u>th</u>is; hw in white; zh in treasure. The symbol ə stands for the unstressed vowel sound heard in about, taken, pencil, lemon, and circus.

of one or more thin metal tubes, each of which has a single wire running through it.

cob (kob) *n.* **1.** see **corncob** *(def. 1).* **2.** a thickset horse with short legs. **3.** a male swan.

co·balt (kō′bôlt) *n.* a hard, silver-white metallic element, used to make alloys that withstand high temperatures and that are highly magnetic. Cobalt is also used to color glass and ceramics. Symbol: **Co** [From the German word *Kobalt* meaning this element, from the Middle High German word *kobolt* "goblin, fairy." People formerly believed that by magic cobalt destroyed the silver ore where it was found.]

cobalt blue 1. a deep blue pigment made from cobalt. **2.** deep blue color.

cobalt 60, a radioactive isotope of cobalt, used in radiology.

cob·ble¹ (kob′əl) *v.t.,* **cob·bled, cob·bling.** to mend or make (shoes or boots). [From the Middle English word *cobelere* meaning "a cobbler."]

cob·ble² (kob′əl) *n.* a cobblestone. —*v.t.,* **cob·bled, cob·bling.** to pave with cobblestones. [Short for *cobblestone,* from the English dialect word *cob* meaning "lump," of uncertain origin.]

cob·bler (kob′lər) *n.* **1.** a person whose work is mending or making shoes. **2.** a fruit pie baked in a deep dish, having no bottom crust and a thick top crust.

cob·ble·stone (kob′əl stōn′) *n.* a naturally rounded stone, formerly used in paving streets.

co·bel·lig·er·ent (kō′bi lij′ər′ənt) *n.* a nation that aids or cooperates with another in waging war, but is not bound by a formal alliance.

COBOL (kō′bôl′) *n.* a computer coding system designed for business use. [Short for *CO(mmon) B(usiness)-O(riented) L(anguage).*]

co·bra (kō′brə) *n.* a large, poisonous snake found in Africa and Asia. When excited it raises its head and flattens its neck so that it takes on the appearance of a hood.

cob·web (kob′web′) *n.* **1.** a web spun by a spider. **2.** anything like a spider's web.

co·caine (kō kān′, kō′kān) *also,* **co·cain.** *n.* a habit-forming drug obtained from the leaves of a South American shrub, used in medicine as a local anesthetic.

coc·cus (kok′əs) *n., pl.* **coc·ci** (kok′sī). a bacterium that has a spherical or oval shape. See **bacteria** for illustration.

coc·cyx (kok′siks) *n., pl.* **coc·cy·ges** (kok′si jēz′). a small triangular bone at the base of the spinal column.

coch·i·neal (koch′ə nēl′) *n.* a dark red dye made from the dried bodies of certain insects of Latin America, used chiefly as a coloring in foods, inks, and cosmetics.

coch·le·a (kok′lē ə) *n., pl.* **coch·le·ae** (kok′lē ē′). the tube of the inner ear, shaped somewhat like a snail shell, containing the sensory ends of the auditory nerve.

cock¹ (kok) *n.* **1.** a male chicken; rooster. **2.** the male of various other birds. **3.** the hammer of a firearm. **4.** the position into which the hammer of a firearm is brought when pulled back for firing. **5.** a device, as a faucet or valve, used to control the flow of a liquid or gas. **6.** an upward turn or tilt to one side: *the cock of a hat.* —*v.t.* **1.** to pull back the hammer of (a firearm) to a firing position: *to cock a pistol.* **2.** to turn up or upward or tilt to one side, especially in a jaunty or lively way: *The dog cocked its ears when I whistled.* [From the Old English word *cocc* meaning "male bird."]

cock² (kok) *n.* a small, conical haystack. —*v.t.* to arrange in small, conical haystacks. [Probably of Scandinavian origin.]

cock·ade (ko kād′) *n.* a knot of ribbon or similar ornament worn as a badge or sign of rank, especially on a hat.

cock·a·too (kok′ə tü′) *n., pl.* **cock·a·toos.** any of various crested parrots of Australia, the East Indies, and southwestern Asia, having white feathers.

cock·a·trice (kok′ə tris′) *n.* a legendary serpent, supposedly hatched from a cock's egg, whose glance was said to cause death.

cock·crow (kok′krō′) *n.* the time when roosters begin to crow; dawn.

cocked hat, a hat with the brim turned up so as to form two or more points.

cock·er (kok′ər) *n.* a person who breeds fighting cocks.

cock·er·el (kok′ər əl) *n.* a young rooster.

cocker spaniel, a small spaniel having a short body, long, silky hair, and drooping ears, kept as a bird dog or house pet.

cock·eyed (kok′īd) *adj.* **1.** cross-eyed. **2.** *Slang.* tilted to one side; off-center: *Your cap is cockeyed.* **3.** *Slang.* absurd; foolish: *a cockeyed idea.*

cock·fight (kok′fīt′) *n.* a fight between gamecocks that are often fitted with spurs.

cock·horse (kok′hôrs′) *n.* another word for **rocking horse.**

cock·le¹ (kok′əl) *n.* **1.** a shellfish related to the clam whose flesh is used for food. It is enclosed in two heart-shaped shells. **2.** see **cockleshell. 3.** a wrinkle; pucker. —*v.t.,* **cock·led, cock·ling.** to wrinkle; pucker. [From the Old French word *coquille* meaning "shell," going back to the Latin word *conchylium* "shellfish," from the Greek word *konchylion* "little mollusk," from the word *konchē* "conch."]

 ·**to warm the cockles of one's heart.** to make one very happy or pleased.

cock·le² (kok′əl) *n.* any of several weeds that grow in grain fields. [From the Old English word *coccel* meaning these weeds.]

cock·le·bur (kok′əl bûr′) *n.* any of a group of weeds found widely in North America and bearing spiny burs.

cock·le·shell (kok′əl shel′) *n.* **1.** the shell of a cockle. **2.** a small, light, shallow boat.

cock·ney (kok′nē) *also,* **Cock·ney.** *n., pl.* **cock·neys. 1.** a person who was born or lives in the old eastern district of London, England. **2.** the dialect spoken by cockneys. —*adj.* relating to cockneys or their dialect.

cock·pit (kok′pit′) *n.* **1.** the compartment in an airplane where the pilot and copilot sit. **2.** a pit or enclosed area for cockfights. **3.** an open space in a sailboat or other small boat where pilot and passengers sit.

cockpit *(def. 1)*

cock·roach (kok′rōch′) *n.* any of a group of brown or black insects, with oval, flattened bodies, bristly legs, and long antennae. Some species are common household pests.

cocks·comb (koks′kōm′) *n.* **1.** the comb or fleshy red crest on the head of a rooster. **2.** *also,* **coxcomb.** a jester's cap resembling this in shape. **3.** any of a group of plants having showy red, purple, yellow, or white flower spikes that resemble a rooster's comb.

cock·sure (kok′shûr′) *adj.* too confident or sure of oneself. —**cock′sure′ly**, *adv.* —**cock′sure′ness**, *n.*

cock·swain (kok′sən, kok′swān′) another spelling of **coxswain.**

cock·tail (kok′tāl′) *n.* **1.** an iced, alcoholic drink made by mixing liquor with flavorings, such as fruit juices. **2.** any of various appetizers or juices served at the beginning of a meal: *a shrimp cocktail, a tomato cocktail.*

cock·y (kok′ē) *adj.,* **cock·i·er, cock·i·est.** *Informal.* too confident or sure of oneself; self-confident in a swaggering way: *a cocky bully.* —**cock′i·ly**, *adv.* —**cock′i·ness**, *n.*

co·co (kō′kō) *n., pl.* **co·cos.** **1.** see **coconut.** **2.** see **coconut palm.**

co·coa (kō′kō) *n.* **1.** a brown powder made by drying, roasting, and grinding cacao seeds and removing the fat. It is used especially in making chocolate drinks. **2.** a chocolate drink made by mixing this powder with hot milk or water and sugar. **3.** a light, dull brown color. —*adj.* having the color cocoa; light dull brown.

cocoa butter, a yellowish white fat obtained from cacao seeds, used in making chocolate, soap, and cosmetics.

co·co·nut (kō′kə nut′) *also,* **co·coa·nut.** *n.* **1.** the large, oval fruit of the coconut palm, having a smooth outer rind, a reddish brown husk, and a hard inner shell lined with edible white meat and containing a milky fluid. **2.** the white meat of this fruit, often shredded for use in puddings, pies, and cakes. **3.** see **coconut palm.**

coconut oil, an oil obtained from the dried fruit of coconuts, used in making soap, shampoo, and many other products.

coconut palm, a tall palm tree with huge feathery leaves that bears coconuts.

co·coon (kə kün′) *n.* **1.** protective case made of silk, leaves, or other materials that encloses the pupa of certain insects, such as the silkworm, while it is developing into an adult. **2.** any similar protective covering.

cod (kod) *n., pl.* **cod** or **cods.** **1.** an important food fish found in colder northern ocean waters, especially of the Atlantic Ocean. **2.** any of various related fishes of northern Atlantic and Pacific waters. Also, **codfish.**

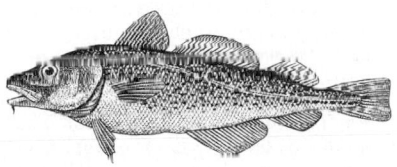

cod *(def. 1)*

c.o.d., C.O.D. **1.** cash on delivery. **2.** collect on delivery.

co·da (kō′də) *n.* the passage at the end of a musical composition or movement that brings it to a formal close.

cod·dle (kod′əl) *v.t.,* **cod·dled, cod·dling.** **1.** to treat tenderly or too indulgently; pamper: *The couple tried not to coddle their only child.* **2.** to cook gently in a liquid at or just below the boiling point; simmer: *to coddle eggs.*

code (kōd) *n.* **1.** a system of writing used to keep messages secret or brief, in which letters, words, numbers, or other symbols stand for the letters and words of the message: *During the war, many government communications were sent in code.* **2.** a system of sending messages, in which sounds, light flashes, flags, or other signals stand for numbers, letters, or words: *In order to operate a telegraph, you must learn the code.* **3.** a collection of laws arranged in a systematic way: *the penal code.* **4.** any system or collection of principles and rules of conduct: *a moral code, a code of honor.* **5.** any system using binary numbers to represent letters, numbers, or other characters. —*v.t.,* **cod·ed, cod·ing.** to put into the form of a code: *to code a message.*

co·deine (kō′dēn) *also,* **co·dein.** *n.* a habit-forming drug obtained from opium, used to relieve pain and coughing and to produce sleep.

cod·fish (kod′fish′) *n., pl.* **cod·fish** or **cod·fish·es.** another word for **cod.**

codg·er (koj′ər) *n. Informal.* an odd or grumpy person, especially one who is old.

cod·i·cil (kod′ə sil) *n.* a part added to a will to add to, change, or explain something in it.

cod·i·fy (kod′ə fī′, kō′də fī′) *v.t.,* **cod·i·fied, cod·i·fy·ing.** to arrange in a systematic way; put into a code: *The general codified the army's regulations.* —**cod′i·fi′er**, *n.*

cod·ling moth (kod′ling) a moth whose larvae feed on apples, pears, and other fruits.

cod–liv·er oil (kod′liv′ər) an oil obtained from the livers of cod and certain other fish, used as a source of vitamins A and D.

co·ed (kō′ed′) *also,* **co·ed.** *Informal.* *n.* a female student, especially at a college. —*adj.* having both male and female students.

co·ed·u·ca·tion (kō′ej ə kā′shən) *n.* the education of male and female students in classes together at a school or college.

co·ed·u·ca·tion·al (kō′ej ə kā′shə nəl) *adj.* educating male and female students in classes together at a school or college. —**co′ed·u·ca′tion·al·ly**, *adv.*

co·ef·fi·cient (kō′i fish′ənt) *n.* a number or algebraic expression put before and multiplying an algebraic expression. In $3x^2y$, 3 is the numerical coefficient of x^2y; in $3x^2(y + z)$, $3x^2$ is the coefficient of $(y + z)$.

coe·la·canth (sē′lə kanth′) *n.* a large, primitive fish having fleshy flippers shaped like paddles, found off the eastern coast of Africa. It is thought to be an important link in the evolution from sea to land animals.

coe·len·ter·ate (si len′tə rāt′) *n.* any of a group of animals having no backbone, including corals, jellyfish, and hydras, usually found in salt water. They have a body resembling a sac, with tentacles around a single mouth opening. —*adj.* belonging to or characteristic of this group.

co·erce (kō ûrs′) *v.t.,* **co·erced, co·erc·ing.** to force by violence or threats: *The pirates coerced their captives into serving them as slaves.* —**co·erc′er**, *n.*

co·er·cion (kō ûr′shən) *n.* the use of force to compel or control: *The prisoner stated that the confession was obtained by coercion.*

co·er·cive (kō ûr′siv) *adj.* tending or serving to coerce. —**co·er′cive·ly**, *adv.* —**co·er′cive·ness**, *n.*

co·e·val (kō ē′vəl) *adj.* of, belonging to, or living in the same age or time; contemporary.

co·ex·ist (kō′eg zist′) *v.i.* **1.** to exist in or at the same place or time as another: *Many species of animals coexisted in the jungle.* **2.** to live together peacefully, in spite of differences in policy or principle: *The two nations learned to coexist.* —**co′ex·ist′ence**, *n.* —**co′ex·ist′ent**, *adj.*

cof·fee (kô′fē) *n.* **1.** a dark brown beverage made from ground and roasted coffee beans and hot or boiling water. **2.** the coffee beans themselves, either whole or ground. **3.** any of a group of tropical evergreen shrubs and small trees that bear coffee beans. **4.** a rich, dark brown color. —*adj.* having the color coffee. [From the Italian word *caffe*, from the Turkish word *kahve*, from the Arabic word *qaḥwa*, all meaning "coffee."]

---

at; āpe; fär; câre; end; mē; it; īce; pîerce; hot; ōld; sông, fôrk; oil; out; up; ūse; rüle; pùll; tûrn; chin; sing; shop; thin; **this**; hw in white; zh in treasure. The symbol ə stands for the unstressed vowel sound heard in about, taken, pencil, lemon, and circus.

coffee bean, the seed of the coffee plant.

coffee cake, a rich, sweet cake made with spices and often nuts and fruits.

cof·fee·house (kô′fē hous′) *n., pl.* **cof·fee·hous·es** (kô′fē hou′ziz). a place where coffee and other refreshments are served.

cof·fee·pot (kô′fē pot′) *n.* a container, usually with a cover, for making or serving coffee.

coffee shop, a restaurant, often having a counter, where coffee and food are served.

coffee table, a low table, usually placed in front of a sofa.

cof·fer (kô′fər) *n.* **1.** a box or chest, especially one used for holding money or other valuables. **2. coffers.** treasury; funds: *Years of war had emptied the coffers of the nation.*

cof·fer·dam (kô′fər dam′) *n.* a temporary watertight enclosure built in water and pumped dry so that foundations, bridge piers, or similar structures may be built.

cof·fin (kô′fin) *n.* a box or case into which a dead person is placed for burial.

cog (kog) *n.* **1.** one of a series of teeth on the rim of a wheel that transmits or receives motion by locking into similar teeth on another wheel or on a track. **2.** see **cogwheel.**

co·gen·cy (kō′jən sē) *n.* the state or quality of being cogent.

co·gent (kō′jənt) *adj.* having the power to be convincing: *a cogent argument.* —**co′gent·ly,** *adv.*

cog·i·tate (koj′i tāt′) *v.i.,* **cog·i·tat·ed, cog·i·tat·ing.** to think or consider carefully; meditate; ponder: *I cogitated a long time on the problem.* —**cog′i·ta′tion,** *n.*

co·gnac (kōn′yak) *n.* a brandy that is amber in color and has a mellow flavor. [From *Cognac,* the town in southwestern France where it was originally made.]

cog·nate (kog′nāt) *adj.* **1.** related by having the same origin; coming from the same source: *cognate words, cognate languages.* **2.** related by having the same ancestor or parentage: *cognate families.* —*n.* a person or thing that is cognate: *The English word "church" and the Scottish word "kirk" are cognates.*

cog·ni·tion (kog nish′ən) *n,* the act or power of knowing or perceiving.

cog·ni·zance (kog′nə zəns) *n.* **1.** knowledge or perception: *That theory is beyond the cognizance of a child.* **2.** notice: *We took cognizance of those facts in making our decision.*

cog·ni·zant (kog′nə zənt) *adj.* having cognizance; aware: *After the accident, the victim was barely cognizant of what had happened.*

cog·no·men (kog nō′mən) *adj.* **1.** a family name; surname. **2.** any name, especially a nickname.

cog·wheel (kog′hwēl′, kog′wēl′) *n.* a wheel with teeth on its rim, for transmitting or receiving motion.

co·here (kō hîr′) *v.i.,* **co·hered, co·hering. 1.** to stick or hold together: *A mass of mud coheres.* **2.** to be logically connected or related.

co·her·ence (kō hîr′əns) *n.* **1.** logical connection: *There was no coherence to what the frightened child tried to say.* **2.** the act of sticking or holding together. Also, **co·her·en·cy** (kō hîr′ən sē).

co·her·ent (kō hîr′ənt) *adj.* **1.** logically connected: *The terrified clerk could not give a coherent account of the robbery.* **2.** sticking or holding together. **3.** able to make sense or be understood; intelligible: *The sedative was so strong that the patient was no longer coherent.* —**co·her′ent·ly,** *adv.*

co·he·sion (kō hē′zhən) *n.* **1.** the act or state of co-

hering: *cohesion between bricks and mortar. The sentences in your essay lack cohesion.* **2.** the attraction between molecules of a substance, as a drop of water, that holds the substance together.

co·he·sive (kō hē′siv) *adj.* capable of, having, or causing cohesion. —**co·he′sive·ly,** *adv.* —**co·he′sive·ness,** *n.*

co·hort (kō′hôrt) *n.* **1.** a companion, associate, or follower: *the bandits and their cohorts.* **2.** any one of ten divisions that made up a legion in the ancient Roman army. **3.** any band, company, or group.

coif (koif) *n.* **1.** a cap that fits closely on the head. Some nuns wear coifs under their veils. Knights wore leather coifs under their helmets. **2.** see **coiffure.** —*v.t.* **1.** to cover with a coif. **2.** to dress or arrange (the hair).

coif·fure (kwä fyur′) *n.* a way in which one's hair is worn or arranged: *The elaborate coiffure was in keeping with the elegant suit.*

coil (koil) *n.* **1.** anything made up of a series of spirals or rings: *a coil of rope.* **2.** one of the spirals or rings of such a series. **3.** a pipe or a series of connected pipes arranged in rows, used to conduct heat or liquids, as in a radiator. **4.** a spiral wire for conducting electricity. —*v.i.* **1.** to form coils: *As the dog ran in circles, its leash coiled around the tree.* **2.** to move in a winding course: *The road coiled around the mountain.* —*v.t.* to wind in coils: *Coil the hose loosely.*

coin (koin) *n.* **1.** a piece of metal stamped with official government markings and of fixed weight and value, used as money. **2.** metal money. —*v.t.* **1.** to make (money) by stamping metal: *The government coins money at the mint.* **2.** to make (metal) into coins. **3.** to make up; invent: *to coin a new word.* —**coin′er,** *n.*

coin·age (koi′nij) *n.* **1.** the act, process, or right of making coins. **2.** something that is coined; metal money. **3.** the act or process of making up or inventing: *"Skyjack" is a word of recent coinage.* **4.** something that is made up or invented.

cogwheels

Language Note

In language, **coinage** is the process of making up a word. The word that has been created is also called a coinage. The process of coinage is used when we need a word to represent a new idea, object, or process for which there has not previously been a name. Such a new word can be created in various ways. Some coinages are created by combining foreign words, such as our word *telephone,* which was made by combining the Greek words for "far" and "sound." Existing English words can also be combined, as in the word *railroad,* which is an eighteenth-century coinage, and *motel,* which is a modern coinage made by blending the words *motor* and *hotel.* Words are also coined from proper names, such as the electrical unit *watt,* which is a coinage from the name of the Scottish inventor James Watt. People also coin words in order to get a humorous or special effect in speaking or writing. Very often these words disappear from the language. Other such coinages, such as the words *discombobulate* and *chortle,* have become part of our language.

co·in·cide (kō′in sīd′) *v.t.,* **co·in·cid·ed, co·in·cid·ing. 1.** to occur at the same time: *The team's practice coincided with my appointment with the dentist.* **2.** to occupy the same area or place in space: *The two roads coincide for fifty miles.* **3.** to agree exactly; correspond: *Their views coincided.*

co·in·ci·dence (kō in′si dəns) *n.* **1.** a remarkable occurrence of events or circumstances at the same time and apparently by mere chance: *By coincidence I met my next-door neighbor in Canada last summer.* **2.** the fact or condition of coinciding: *The coincidence of two triangles.*

co·in·ci·dent (kō in′si dənt) *adj.* **1.** occurring at the same time: *My birthday is coincident with their wedding anniversary.* **2.** occupying the same area or place in space: *coincident circles.* **3.** in exact agreement; corresponding: *You gave a description that was coincident with the facts.* —**co·in′ci·dent·ly,** *adv.*

co·in·ci·den·tal (kō in′si den′təl) *adj.* characterized by, resulting from, or involving coincidence: *The police did not believe it was coincidental that the suspect was seen at the scene of the crime.* —**co·in′ci·den′tal·ly,** *adv.*

coke (kōk) *n.* a gray-black solid fuel that is obtained by heating bituminous coal in the absence of oxygen. It burns with much heat and little smoke or ash and is used especially in blast furnaces.

col–, a form of the prefix **com-** before *l,* as in *collateral.*

col. 1. colony. **2.** color; colored. **3.** column.

Col., Colonel.

col·an·der (kul′ən dər, kol′ən dər) *n.* a metal or plastic container with holes in the bottom and sides, used to rinse or drain liquid from food.

colander

cold (kōld) *adj.* **1. a.** having a low temperature; lacking warmth or heat: *Alaska has a cold climate.* **b.** having less heat than is usual or expected: *The ocean is cold today. My dinner is cold.* **2.** feeling a lack of warmth or heat; chilly: *The children were cold after playing outside.* **3.** not friendly or kind: *a cold person. Our rivals greeted us with a cold smile.* **4.** not fresh; stale or weak: *The bloodhounds could not follow the cold scent.* **5.** *Informal.* unconscious: *I was knocked cold when I fell down the stairs.* —*n.* **1.** a lack of warmth or heat: *Many plants do not thrive in the cold.* **2.** the feeling caused by a lack of warmth or heat: *Cold always makes my teeth chatter.* **3.** a common illness marked by sneezing, coughing, and a running or stuffed nose. Also, **common cold.** —*adv. Informal.* **1.** thoroughly; completely: *After studying for a week, I know this lesson cold.* **2.** without any knowledge or preparation ahead of time: *We had to go into the contest cold.* —**cold′ly,** *adv.* —**cold′ness,** *n.*

  ·**cold feet.** the lack or loss of courage: *They got cold feet at the last moment and fled.*

  ·**out in the cold.** ignored or neglected: *I felt left out in the cold when I wasn't invited to the party.*

  ·**to catch cold** or **to take cold.** to become ill with a cold.

  ·**to throw cold water on.** to discourage: *They threw cold water on our vacation plans.*

cold–blood·ed (kōld′blud′id) *adj.* **1.** having blood that varies in temperature with the temperature of the surrounding air or water. Fish, snakes, and turtles are cold-blooded animals. **2.** lacking feeling or sympathy; cruel: *a cold-blooded criminal.* —**cold′-blood′ed·ly,** *adv.* —**cold′-blood′ed·ness,** *n.*

cold cream, a creamy substance used for cleansing and soothing the skin.

cold cuts, cooked meat that has been sliced and is served cold, such as roast beef, turkey, or ham.

cold front, the forward edge of a mass of cold air moving into an area of warmer air.

cold–heart·ed (kōld′här′tid) *adj.* without feeling or sympathy; unkind. —**cold′-heart′ed·ly,** *adv.* —**cold′-heart′ed·ness,** *n.*

cold shoulder *Informal.* a deliberate show of unfriendliness; snub; slight: *to get the cold shoulder.*

cold sore, a blister in or near the mouth, often accompanying a cold or fever. Also, **fever sore, fever blister.**

cold storage, the storage of perishable objects in an artificially cooled chamber.

cold war 1. *also,* **Cold War.** the state of hostility and rivalry after World War II, between the United States and its allies on one side and the Soviet Union and its allies on the other, generally stopping short of military conflict. **2.** any state of intense political or economic rivalry between nations, stopping short of actual warfare.

cold wave, a period of sudden, unusually cold weather.

cole (kōl) *n.* any of various plants belonging to the same family as the cabbage, such as kale. Also, **cole·wort** (kōl′wûrt′).

cole·slaw (kōl′slô′) *n.* a salad made of sliced, shredded, or grated raw cabbage, mixed with a dressing. Also, **slaw.** [From the Dutch word *koolsla* meaning "coleslaw," from the words *kool* meaning "cabbage" + *sla* meaning "salad."]

co·le·us (kō′lē əs) *n., pl.* **co·le·us·es.** any of a group of tropical plants sometimes grown as houseplants because of their showy, patterned leaves of orange, purple, red, or yellow. [Formed from the Greek word *koleos* meaning "sheath." Coleus stamens are joined to form a sheath.]

col·ic (kol′ik) *n.* a sudden attack of severe pain in the stomach or intestines, especially in infants. —**col′ick·y,** *adj.*

col·i·se·um (kol′ə sē′əm) *n.* **1.** a large, usually oval building or stadium in which athletic contests and other entertainments are presented. Also, **colosseum. 2. Coliseum.** another spelling of **Colosseum.**

co·li·tis (kə lī′tis) *n.* inflammation of the colon.

coll. 1. colleague. **2.** college. **3.** colloquial.

collaborate
students **collaborating** on a project

col·lab·o·rate (kə lab′ə rāt′) *v.i.,* **col·lab·o·rat·ed, col·lab·o·rat·ing. 1.** to work with another or others: *Marie and Pierre Curie collaborated in doing scientific research.* **2.** to aid or cooperate with the enemy, especially with an enemy that is occupying one's country. —**col·lab′o·ra′tion,** *n.* —**col·lab′o·ra′tor,** *n.*

col·lage (kə läzh′) *n.* **1.** a work of art made by pasting paper, cloth, metal, and other materials or objects together on a surface. **2.** the art or technique of producing such works.

at; āpe; fär; câre; end; mē; it; īce; pîerce; hot; ōld; sông, fôrk; oil; out; up; ūse; rüle; pùll; tûrn; chin; sing; shop; thin; <u>th</u>is; hw in white; zh in treasure. The symbol ə stands for the unstressed vowel sound heard in about, taken, pencil, lemon, and circus.

col·lapse (kə laps′) v., **col·lapsed**, **col·laps·ing**. —v.i. **1.** to fall in; cave in: *The walls collapsed from the force of the explosion.* **2.** to fold together: *This cot collapses for easy storage.* **3.** to fail or break down completely or suddenly: *Our plans collapsed. The messenger collapsed after finally reaching headquarters.* —v.t. to cause to collapse: *to collapse a folding table and put it away.* —n. **1.** the act of falling in; a cave-in: *Hundreds of miners were injured in the collapse of the shaft.* **2.** any complete or sudden failure or breakdown: *The collapse of the negotiations led to a strike.*

col·laps·i·ble (kə lap′sə bəl) also, **col·laps·a·ble**. adj. capable of being folded together: *a collapsible life raft.*

col·lar (kol′ər) n. **1.** the part of a garment at the neckline, usually sewed on as a separate piece. **2.** a separate band of jewels, cloth, fur, or other material worn to decorate the neckline. **3.** a band of leather or metal placed around the neck of an animal, such as a dog. **4.** a cushioned band that fits over a horse's neck to bear the strain of the load it pulls. **5.** any of various devices that prevent or limit sideward motion, such as a ring on a rod or shaft. —v.t. **1.** to put a collar on: *to collar a dog.* **2. a.** to seize by the collar. **b.** *Informal.* to lay hold of; seize: *The police collared the thief a week after the robbery.*

col·lar·bone (kol′ər bōn) n. either of two bones connecting the breastbone and the shoulder blade; clavicle.

col·lard (kol′ərd) n. **1.** a variety of kale grown in the southern United States. **2. collards.** the dark green leaves of this plant eaten as a vegetable. Also *(def. 2)*, **collard greens.**

col·late (kə lāt′, kol′āt, kō′lāt) v.t., **col·lat·ed**, **col·lat·ing**. **1.** to arrange in proper order: *to collate pages of a report.* **2.** to compare critically and carefully.

col·lat·er·al (kə lat′ər əl) n. property given to a lender of money as security that the loan will be repaid. —adj. **1.** situated or placed side by side; parallel: *collateral railways.* **2.** connected with something, but secondary in importance: *My main interest is history, and my collateral interests include geography and economics.* **3.** guaranteed or backed by collateral: *a collateral loan.* **4.** descended from common ancestors, but in a different line: *Children of cousins are collateral relatives.* —**col·lat′er·al·ly**, adv.

col·la·tion (kə lā′shən) n. **1.** the act of collating. **2.** a light, informal, usually cold meal.

col·league (kol′ēg) n. a fellow member of a profession or other group; fellow worker or associate.

col·lect (kə lekt′) v.t. **1.** to gather (something) together; assemble: *We collected old clothes for the rummage sale.* **2.** to make a collection of as a hobby or for study: *My cousin collects stamps.* **3.** to ask for and receive (payments or contributions): *The state collects tolls on this highway.* **4.** to call for and remove: *The city collects the garbage on Mondays.* **5.** to regain control of or summon up: *to collect one's thoughts.* —v.i. **1.** to gather together; assemble: *A large crowd collected to hear the speaker.* **2.** to pile up; accumulate: *Dust often collects under a bed.* **3.** to ask for and receive payments or contributions: *Our club collects for charity.* —adj. paid for at the time or place of delivery or by the receiver: *a collect telephone call.* —adv. so as to be paid for at the time or place of delivery or by the receiver: *to telephone someone collect.* —**col·lect′a·ble**; also, **col·lect′i·ble**, adj.

col·lect·ed (kə lek′tid) adj. **1.** gathered together; assembled: *the collected works of an author.* **2.** in control of oneself; composed: *to remain calm and collected during a crisis.* —**col·lect′ed·ly**, adv.

col·lec·tion (kə lek′shən) n. **1.** the act or process of collecting: *The collection of trash is carried out by the sanitation department.* **2.** something gathered together, especially as a hobby or for study: *a coin collection.* **3.** a payment or contribution collected: *We took up a collection to buy a gift for the teacher.* **4.** something that has accumulated: *a collection of leaves on a lawn.*

col·lec·tive (kə lek′tiv) adj. **1.** of, relating to, or done by a group of persons or things; common; united: *A collective effort helped the team win the championship.* **2.** representing a whole or collection: *the collective needs of a community.* **3.** owned or managed by a group: *a collective business.* —n. **1.** see **collective noun.** **2.** an organization or undertaking owned and managed by a group or marked by collectivism: *The members of the collective voted to reduce prices.* —**col·lec′tive·ly**, adv.

collective bargaining, a negotiation between workers or their union representatives and employers about wages, hours, working conditions, or the like.

collective farm, a farm operated and managed jointly by a group of farmers, often under the direction of the government.

collective noun, a singular noun referring to a group of persons or things. It takes a singular verb if the group acts as a single unit: *The jury was unable to agree on a verdict.* It takes a plural verb if the group acts as individuals: *The jury were divided in their opinions.*

col·lec·tiv·ism (kə lek′tə viz′əm) n. **1.** an economic and political system in which the means of production and distribution are owned and controlled by the government, by the people as a group, or by the people who work in a particular industry as a group. **2.** an economic and political theory that advocates such a system.

col·lec·tor (kə lek′tər) n. **1.** a person who collects objects of interest or value: *a rare-book collector, a coin collector.* **2.** a person who is employed to collect money due: *a tax collector, a toll collector.* **3.** any thing that collects.

col·leen (kol′ēn, ko lēn′) n. a girl, especially an Irish girl.

col·lege (kol′ij) n. **1.** a school of higher education entered after high school that grants degrees upon completion of courses of study. **2.** a major division in a university that offers a four-year course of study leading to a bachelor's degree. **3.** a school for training and instruction in a particular field: *a barber college.* **4.** a group of persons having common duties and powers: *a college of surgeons.*

col·le·gian (kə lē′jən) n. a college student.

col·le·giate (kə lē′jit) adj. of or relating to college or college students: *collegiate clothing styles.*

col·lide (kə līd′) v.i., **col·lid·ed**, **col·lid·ing**. **1.** to come together with force; crash: *The car and the truck collided at the intersection.* **2.** to come into conflict; clash.

col·lie (kol′ē) n. a dog originally bred for tending sheep, having a long, narrow head, a slender body, and usually, a long-haired coat of white and tan or white, tan, and black.

col·lier (kol′yər) n. *British.* **1.** a coal miner. **2.** a ship for carrying coal.

col·lier·y (kol′yə rē) n., pl. **col·lier·ies.** a coal mine with its buildings and equipment.

col·li·sion (kə lizh′ən) n. **1.** the act of coming together with force; act of colliding: *The bus driver suffered a broken leg in the collision.* **2.** a conflict; clash.

collie

col·loid (kol′oid) n. a substance evenly scattered through another substance in particles that are larger than ordinary molecules but that are too small to be visible to the naked eye. Both the particles and the medium in which they are scattered may be a gas, liquid, or solid. —**col·loi·dal** (kə loi′dəl), adj. —**col·loi′dal·ly**, adv.

col·lo·qui·al (kə lō′kwē əl) adj. (of language) used in ordinary or familiar conversation, rather than formal speech or writing: *"Big wheel" is a colloquial term for "an important person."* —**col·lo′qui·al·ly**, adv. —**col·lo′qui·al·ness**, n.

col·lo·qui·al·ism (kə lō′kwē ə liz′əm) *n.* **1.** a colloquial word or phrase: *"Hit the sack" is a colloquialism meaning "go to bed."* **2.** the use of colloquial words or phrases.

col·lo·quy (kol′ə kwē) *n., pl.* **col·lo·quies.** a conversation, discussion, or conference, especially a formal one.

col·lu·sion (kə lü′zhən) *n.* a secret agreement or cooperation between two or more people for an illegal or deceitful purpose.

Colo., Colorado.

co·logne (kə lōn′) *n.* a fragrant liquid made from alcohol and scented oils and used as perfume. [From *Cologne*, the German city where it was first produced.]

co·lon[1] (kō′lən) *n.* a mark of punctuation (:), used chiefly to introduce, set apart, or direct attention to something that follows, such as a list or series, a quotation, or an explanation. [Originally from the Greek word *kōlon* meaning "a limb" and later "a clause." This mark is used to separate clauses.]

co·lon[2] (kō′lən) *n., pl.* **co·lons** or **co·la** (kō′lə). the main part of the large intestine, connecting the cecum and the rectum. It absorbs water, minerals, and vitamins from the digested food that passes through it. [From the Latin word *colon* meaning "large intestine," from the Greek word *kolon* with the same meaning.]

colo·nel (kûr′nəl) *n.* a military officer usually ranking above a lieutenant colonel and below a brigadier general.

co·lo·ni·al (kə lō′nē əl) *adj.* **1.** of or relating to a colony or colonies: *colonial government, a colonial empire.* **2.** *also,* **Colonial. a.** of or relating to the thirteen British colonies that became the United States of America. **b.** characteristic of this period in American history: *colonial architecture, colonial furniture.* —*n.* a person who was born or is living in a colony. —**co·lo·ni·al·ly,** *adv.*

co·lo·ni·al·ism (kə lō′nē ə liz′əm) *n.* the policy of a nation seeking to acquire or keep control over other peoples or territories.

col·o·nist (kol′ə nist) *n.* **1.** a person who was born or is living in a colony. **2.** a person who helps to found or settle a colony.

col·o·nize (kol′ə nīz′) *v.,* **col·o·nized, col·o·niz·ing.** —*v.t.* **1.** to establish a colony or colonies in; send colonists to: *Spain colonized much of South America.* **2.** to travel to and settle in; occupy as a colony. *English settlers colonized Plymouth.* —*v.i.* to establish a colony or colonies. —**col·o·ni·za·tion,** *n.* —**col·o·niz′er,** *n.*

col·on·nade (kol′ə nād′) *n.* a series of columns, placed at regular intervals, usually supporting a roof or other structure.

colonnade

col·o·ny (kol′ə nē) *n., pl.* **col·o·nies. 1.** any territory that is under the control of another, usually distant, country. **2.** a body of settlers living in an area apart from,

but under the control of, the country from which they came: *A colony of English Puritans settled in Massachusetts.* **3.** the area or land itself: *California was a Spanish colony.* **4. the Colonies.** the thirteen British colonies that became the first states of the United States: New Hampshire, Massachusetts, Rhode Island, Connecticut, New York, New Jersey, Pennsylvania, Delaware, Maryland, Virginia, North Carolina, South Carolina, and Georgia. **5.** a group of people living or drawn together in an area because of common nationality, religion, or interests: *an American colony in Paris.* **6.** a group of animals or plants of the same kind, living or growing together in the same place: *a colony of bees.*

col·or (kul′ər) *also, British,* **col·our.** *n.* **1.** a quality of something resulting from the way it transmits or reflects light. Different colors, such as red, blue, or yellow, are caused when light of different wavelengths, reflected by an object, strikes the retina of the eye. **2.** one of the parts of the spectrum; a particular hue, tint, or shade: *Orange is my favorite color.* **3.** something used for coloring, such as a paint, dye, or pigment. **4.** the coloring of the skin, especially of the face; complexion: *to have a healthy color.* **5.** a skin pigmentation or complexion, especially when thought of as a racial feature: *That company hires workers without regard to race or color.* **6.** a vivid, lively, or interesting quality: *The professor's stories added color to the lecture. That baseball player has a lot of color.* **7. colors. a.** any color or pattern of colors, as of a badge or uniform: *My school's colors are red and black.* **b.** a flag or banner, especially the national flag: *The general saluted the colors as the parade passed by.* —*v.t.* **1.** to give or apply color to, as by painting, dyeing, or staining: *The child colored the pictures with a yellow crayon.* **2.** to cause to appear different from reality: *The witnesses colored their testimony to protect their friend.* **3.** to change in character or nature; affect; influence: *Your judgment is being colored by your emotions.* —*v.i.* to become red in the face; blush; flush. —**col′or·er,** *n.*

·to show one's true colors. to reveal one's true self or nature.

col·or·a·tion (kul′ə rā′shən) *n.* an arrangement of colors; coloring.

col·or·a·tu·ra (kul′ər ə tùr′ə, kul′ər ə tyùr′ə) *n.* **1.** ornamental passages in vocal music, such as trills or runs. **2.** music characterized by such ornamentation. **3.** a high soprano voice having a wide range, trained for singing such music. **4.** a singer with such a voice. *adj.* **1.** characterized by coloratura. **2.** able to sing coloratura.

col·or·bear·er (kul′ər bâr′ər) *n.* a person who carries the colors or flag, as in a ceremony or parade.

col·or–blind (kul′ər blīnd′) *adj.* affected by color blindness.

color blindness, a lack of ability to see colors. It is usually a difficulty in distinguishing between certain colors, such as red and green, but sometimes it is an inability to distinguish any colors except black, white, and gray.

col·ored (kul′ərd) *adj.* **1.** having color, especially other than solid black or white: *This book has colored illustrations.* **2.** of a race other than the Caucasian race, especially of the Negro race. ▲ formerly used as a term without offense; now usually considered offensive. **3.** influenced, as by prejudice or emotion; distorted; slanted: *The defendant's parents gave a highly colored account of what had occurred.*

---

at; āpe; fär; câre; end; mē; it; īce; pîerce; hot; ōld; sông, fôrk; oil; out; up; ūse; rüle; pùll; tûrn; chin; sing; shop; thin; this; hw in white; zh in treasure. The symbol ə stands for the unstressed vowel sound heard in about, taken, pencil, lemon, and circus.

C

col·or·fast (kul′ər fast′) *adj.* (of fabrics) having color that will not fade or run.

col·or·ful (kul′ər fəl) *adj.* **1.** full of bright color: *a colorful tie.* **2.** vivid, lively, or interesting: *a colorful speaker, a colorful tale of life as a cowhand.* —**col′or·ful·ly,** *adv.* —**col′or·ful·ness,** *n.*

col·or·ing (kul′ər ing) *n.* **1.** the way in which anything is colored: *the coloring of the autumn landscape, the coloring of spring flowers.* **2.** something used to give color: *food coloring.* **3.** the act or technique of applying color. **4.** a false appearance or show: *lies with the coloring of truth.*

coloring book, a book of outline drawings for coloring with crayons or other materials.

col·or·ize (kul′ə rīz′) *v.t.,* **col·or·ized, col·or·iz·ing.** to add computer-generated colors to, as to a motion picture originally produced in black and white. —**col′or·i·za′·tion,** *n.* Trademark: **Colorization.**

col·or·less (kul′ər lis) *adj.* **1.** not vivid, lively, or interesting; dull: *a colorless personality.* **2.** without color: *a colorless liquid.* **3.** dull in color; pale: *The sick child's face was colorless.* —**col′or·less·ly,** *adv.* —**col′or·less·ness,** *n.*

co·los·sal (kə los′əl) *adj.* extremely large; gigantic; immense: *The pyramids of ancient Egypt are colossal structures.* —**col·los′sal·ly,** *adv.*

Col·os·se·um (kol′ə sē′əm) *n.* **1.** an oval-shaped amphitheater in Rome that was the site of games and fights between gladiators in ancient times. Part of it is still standing. Also, **Coliseum. 2. colosseum.** another spelling of **coliseum.**

Co·los·sians (kə lō′shəns) *n.* a book of the New Testament, consisting of a letter written by Saint Paul to a Christian community in Asia Minor. ▲ used with a singular verb.

co·los·sus (kə los′əs) *n., pl.* **co·los·si** (kə los′ī) or **co·los·sus·es. 1.** a gigantic statue. **2.** a person or thing of gigantic size or great power.

Colossus of Rhodes, a bronze statue of the sun god Helios that stood at the entrance to the harbor of Rhodes. It was built about 280 B.C., with a height of more than 100 feet (30 meters).

col·our (kul′ər) *British.* another spelling of **color.**

colt (kōlt) *n.* **1.** a young horse, especially a male. **2.** the young of any similar animal, especially a male.

col·ter (kōl′tər) *also,* **coul·ter.** *n.* a sharp blade or disk attached to a plow to cut the earth in front of the plowshare.

Co·lum·bi·a (kə-lum′bē ə) *n.* the United States of America. ▲ used in songs and poems.

col·um·bine (kol′əm bīn′) *n.* **1.** a showy, usually drooping flower of any of a group of plants related to the buttercup. It grows in many colors and has five projecting petals that resemble tubes. **2.** the plant bearing this flower.

Col·um·bine (kol′əm bīn′) *n.* a female character in pantomime and comedy, the sweetheart of Harlequin.

columbine *(def. 1)*

Co·lum·bus Day (kə lum′bəs) a legal holiday celebrated annually to commemorate the discovery of America by Christopher Columbus on October 12, 1492. This holiday is now celebrated on the second Monday in October.

col·umn (kol′əm) *n.* **1.** a written or printed group of items arranged one above the others: *a column of numbers.* **2.** a narrow, vertical section of printed or written words on a sheet or page, separated by lines or by blank spaces: *This page has two columns.* **3.** an article that appears regularly in a newspaper or magazine, usually written by one person and dealing with a particular subject: *a sports column, a fashion column.* **4.** a slender, upright structure serving as a support or ornament for part of a building, or standing alone as a monument. **5.** something resembling such a structure: *A column of smoke appeared above the hill.* **6.** a military formation in which soldiers, vehicles, ships, or the like are arranged one behind the other in one or more rows.

Capital

Shaft

Base

column
(def. 4)

co·lum·nar (kə lum′nər) *adj.* **1.** relating to or resembling a column. **2.** made of or with columns: *columnar temples.*

col·um·nist (kol′əm nist, kol′ə mist) *n.* a person who writes a column in a newspaper or magazine.

com– *prefix* in association with; together: *combine, committee, companion.*

com. 1. comedy. **2.** commerce. **3.** common; commonly.

Com. 1. Commissioner. **2.** Commission; Committee.

co·ma[1] (kō′mə) *n., pl.* **co·mas.** a state of deep unconsciousness from which a person cannot be aroused. It may be caused by disease, injury, or poison and may last for a short time, or in rare cases, for years. [Originally from the Greek word *kōma* meaning "a deep sleep."]

co·ma[2] (kō′mə) *n., pl.* **co·mae** (kō′mē). a mass of gases that resembles a cloud, found around the nucleus of a comet. [From the Latin word *coma* meaning "hair," from the Greek word *komē* "hair."]

Co·man·che (kə man′chē) *n., pl.* **Co·man·che** or **Co·man·ches. 1.** a member of a tribe of North American Indians formerly living in the southern Great Plains, now living in Oklahoma. **2.** the language of this tribe.

co·ma·tose (kō′mə tōs′, kom′ə tōs′) *adj.* **1.** being in a coma: *a comatose patient.* **2.** of or resembling a coma: *The patient was in a comatose state.*

comb (kōm) *n.* **1.** a piece of plastic, bone, metal, or other sturdy material, having teeth and used for smoothing, arranging, or fastening the hair. **2.** something resembling a comb in shape or use, such as a card for cleaning and separating fibers. **3.** a thick, usually reddish, fleshy growth on the head of roosters and other fowl. **4.** see **honeycomb. 5.** see **currycomb.** —*v.t.* **1.** to smooth or arrange (the hair) with a comb. **2.** to remove with a comb: *I combed the knots from my hair.* **3.** to search (something) thoroughly and with care; look everywhere in: *The police combed the woods looking for the lost child.*

comb *(def. 3)*

com·bat (*n.,* kom′bat; *v.,* kəm bat′, kom′bat) *n.* **1.** fighting between enemy military forces: *The soldier was wounded in combat.* **2.** a fight, contest, or struggle: *The investors engaged in combat to control the corporation.* —*v.t.,* **com·bat·ed, com·bat·ing;** *also, British,* **com·bat·ted, com·bat·ting. 1.** to fight with; oppose in battle: *The troops combated the enemy.* **2.** to take measures or struggle against; oppose vigorously: *to combat household pests.* —**com·bat′er**, *n.*

com·bat·ant (kəm bat′ənt, kom′bə tənt) *n.* a person or group of persons fighting or ready to fight. —*adj.* ready or eager to fight.

com·bat·ive (kəm bat′iv) *adj.* ready or eager to fight. —**com·bat′ive·ly**, *adv.* —**com·bat′ive·ness**, *n.*

comb·er (kō′mər) *n.* 1. a long, rolling wave that curls over or breaks at the crest. 2. a person or thing that combs.

com·bi·na·tion (kom′bə nā′shən) *n.* 1. something that is formed by combining; mixture; union: *The color pink is a combination of red and white.* 2. a series of numbers or letters dialed in a certain sequence to open a combination lock: *Only the guard knows the combination to the safe.* 3. the act of combining or the state of being combined. 4. an alliance or association of persons or groups to further some common purpose. 5. *Mathematics.* any of the possible arrangements of a certain number or of all the elements of a set. Some possible combinations of *x, y,* and *z* are *xyz, zxy,* and *yzx.*

combination lock, a lock opened by turning one or more dials to a series of numbers or letters in a certain sequence or pattern.

com·bine (*v.,* kəm bīn′; *n.,* kom′bīn) *v.,* **com·bined, com·bin·ing.** —*v.t.* 1. to bring into close relationship; join together; unite: *The friends combined their efforts to get the work done faster.* 2. to cause to mix together; mingle; blend: *Combine eggs, flour, and milk to make the batter.* 3. to possess or show at the same time: *The book combines a call for reform and a sense of humor.* —*v.i.* 1. to join together; unite: *The thirteen colonies combined to form the United States.* 2. to unite to form a chemical compound: *One atom of carbon combines with two atoms of oxygen to form a molecule of carbon dioxide.* —*n.* 1. an alliance of persons or groups for a common purpose. 2. a farm machine that combines the functions of a harvester and a thresher by cutting, threshing, and cleaning grains and other field crops.

combining form, a word or a stem of a word, often of Greek or Latin origin, that is used only to form compound words and derivatives, such as *psycho-* in the word *psychoanalysis.*

com·bo (kom′bō) *n., pl.* **com·bos.** 1. a small group of musicians who perform together: *a jazz combo.* 2. *Informal.* a combination.

com·bus·ti·ble (kəm bus′tə bəl) *adj.* capable of catching fire and burning. *Paper and dry leaves are highly combustible.* —*n.* a substance that can catch fire and burn. —**com·bus′ti·bil′i·ty**, *n.* —**com·bus′ti·bly**, *adv.*

com·bus·tion (kəm bus′chən) *n.* 1. the act or process of burning. 2.a. the rapid oxidation of a substance accompanied by the release of heat and sometimes light: *the combustion of gasoline in an engine.* b. the slow oxidation of a substance accompanied by little heat and no light: *the combustion of food in the body.*

Comdr., Commander.

come (kum) *v.i.,* **came, come, com·ing.** 1. to move to or toward the person speaking; draw near; approach: *Will you please come here? The parade is coming down the street now.* 2. to reach a place; arrive: *The horse came to the first barrier and jumped.* 3. to reach a particular state or condition: *The water came to a boil. The problem has already come to my attention.* 4. to exist or occur at a particular place or position: *Five comes before six. Spring came late this year.* 5. to reach; extend: *My hair comes to my waist.* 6. to be born; descend: *The governor comes from a well-known family.* 7. to happen: *How did you come to meet them?* 8. to exist or happen as a result: *No good will come of lying.* 9. to be offered, sold, or made: *This dress comes in several colors.* 10. to prove or turn out to be: *The prediction came true.* 11. to become: *The rope came untied.*

•**to come about. a.** to take place; happen; occur. **b.** *Sailing.* to change direction and reset the sails.

•**to come across.** to find or meet by chance: *I came across these old pictures while I was cleaning out the attic.*

•**to come around. a.** to become conscious again. **b.** to change one's opinion or position so as to agree with another's.

•**to come by. a.** to obtain; get: *Where did you come by that loud tie?* **b.** to pay a visit; stop by.

•**to come down. a.** to be passed down through tradition: *The custom of Thanksgiving has come down to us from the Pilgrims.* **b.** to lose position or standing.

•**to come down with.** to become ill with: *to come down with the flu.*

•**to come forward.** to offer or present oneself for work or duty: *Two volunteers came forward. A surprise witness came forward with new testimony.*

•**to come in for.** to receive or be subjected to; get: *The coach came in for a share of the blame.*

•**to come into.** to inherit: *I came into the property when my grandparents died.*

•**to come off.** *Informal.* to take place; happen: *The party came off successfully.*

•**to come out. a.** to become known: *The truth has come out at last.* **b.** to declare oneself publicly: *The candidate came out for local control of public schools.* **c.** to be presented to the public: *That movie came out last year.* **d.** to turn out; end; result: *Everything will come out all right.* **e.** to make a formal social debut.

•**to come through. a.** to endure or finish successfully: *Only three out of ten applicants came through the training program.* **b.** *Informal.* to perform or do what is expected: *You always come through when we need you.*

•**to come to. a.** to become conscious again. **b.** to be equal to; amount to: *The bill comes to five dollars.*

•**to come up.** to arise: *The question came up during our discussion.*

•**to come upon.** to find or meet with by chance.

•**to come up with.** *Informal.* to think of or produce.

come·back (kum′bak′) *n.* 1. a return to a former favorable condition or position: *The ex-champion made a remarkable comeback and won the title.* 2. a clever retort.

co·me·di·an (kə mē′dē ən) *n.* 1. an entertainer who tells jokes or performs funny stunts or routines to make an audience laugh, as on stage or on a television program. 2. an actor who plays comic roles. 3. *Informal.* a person who tries to make others laugh.

co·me·di·enne (kə mē′dē en′) *n.* a woman who tells jokes or performs funny stunts or routines to entertain an audience.

come·down (kum′doun′) *n.* a change for the worse in position or status.

com·e·dy (kom′i dē) *n., pl.* **com·e·dies.** 1. a play, skit, or other dramatic presentation that is funny. 2. a play that has a happy ending. 3. the branch of drama composed of such plays. 4. any humorous situation or action. —**co·med′ic**, *adj.*

come·ly (kum′lē) *adj.,* **come·li·er, come·li·est.** pleasing in appearance; good-looking: *a comely youth.* —**come′li·ness**, *n.*

come-on (kum′ôn′, kum′on′) *n. Informal.* something used to attract or tempt, especially deceptively; lure: *The*

at; āpe; fär; câre; end; mē; it; īce; pîerce; hot; ōld; sông, fôrk; oil; out; up; ūse; rüle; pull; tûrn; chin; sing; shop; thin; this; hw in white; zh in treasure. The symbol ə stands for the unstressed vowel sound heard in about, taken, pencil, lemon, and circus.

193

advertisement was just a come-on, because the bike wasn't as fancy as it looked in the picture.

com·er (kum′ər) *n.* **1.** a person who comes or arrives: *The champion was willing to take on all comers.* **2.** *Informal.* a person or thing that shows great promise: *The sportswriters are saying that our new pitcher is a real comer.*

com·et (kom′it) *n.* a bright heavenly body made up of ice, frozen gases, and dust particles, and having a long, visible tail that points away from the sun. A comet travels around the sun in an elliptical orbit. [From the Old English word *cométa* meaning "comet," from the Latin word *cometa* "comet," from the Greek phrase *komētēs* (*astēr*) "long-haired (star)." A comet's tail resembles strands of hair.]

come·up·pance (kum′up′əns) *also,* **come·up·ance.** *n. Informal.* a setback or punishment that one deserves.

com·fit (kum′fit, kom′fit) *n.* a piece of candy or candied fruit.

com·fort (kum′fərt) *n.* **1.** a state of ease or well-being with freedom from pain, distress, or want: *to live in comfort.* **2.** relief from the distress caused by pain or sorrow: *Your cheerful letter brought comfort to me when I was in the hospital.* **3.** a person or thing that provides relief, ease, or well-being: *Our neighbors were a comfort to us after the fire.* **4.** the ability to give ease and well-being: *These soft pillows add to the comfort of the chair.* —*v.t.* to ease the grief or sorrow of; console: *We tried to comfort the crying child.*

com·fort·a·ble (kumf′tə bəl, kum′fər tə bəl) *adj.* **1.** giving ease or comfort: *a comfortable bed, a comfortable dress.* **2.** free from distress; at ease: *I never feel comfortable talking in front of a large group.* **3.** more than adequate: *a comfortable income. Our football team had a comfortable lead.* —**com′fort·a·ble·ness,** *n.* —**com′fort·a·bly,** *adv.*

com·fort·er (kum′fər tər) *n.* **1.** a person or thing that comforts. **2.** a quilted blanket or covering for a bed.

com·fort·ing (kum′fər ting) *adj.* offering or giving relief from sorrow or worry; consoling: *comforting words from a friend.* —**com′fort·ing·ly,** *adv.*

com·ic (kom′ik) *adj.* **1.** of or relating to comedy: *a comic actor.* **2.** causing laughter or mirth; amusing; funny: *a comic situation.* —*n.* **1.** a comedian. **2.** **comics.** comic strips. **3.** see **comic book.**

com·i·cal (kom′i kəl) *adj.* causing laughter or mirth; amusing; funny: *The children laughed at the clown's comical antics.* —**com′i·cal·ly,** *adv.*

comic book, a booklet of comic strips, sometimes comprising one long strip.

comic opera, a humorous opera or operetta, usually having a happy ending and some spoken dialogue.

comic strip, a series of cartoon drawings relating a story or incident, often printed regularly in a newspaper.

com·ing (kum′ing) *adj.* **1.** approaching; arriving: *Vacation starts this coming Monday.* **2.** *Informal.* on the way to being important or popular: *Space travel is the coming thing.* —*n.* approach; arrival: *the coming of spring, the coming of nightfall.*

com·ing–out (kum′ing out′) *n. Informal.* a formal social debut.

com·i·ty (kom′i tē) *n., pl.* **com·i·ties.** mutual respect or courtesy; politeness: *comity between nations.*

com·ma (kom′ə) *n.* a punctuation mark (,) used to separate ideas or items in a series, and to set off certain grammatical constructions, such as main clauses.

com·mand (kə mand′) *v.t.* **1.** to give an order to; direct with authority: *The general commanded the troops to advance.* **2.** to have authority or power over; rule: *Great Britain once commanded the seas.* **3.** to deserve and get: *The teacher commanded our respect and admiration.* **4.** to be able to get: *The doctor commanded high fees.* **5.** to control the position or location of: *The tower com-*

manded the small town. —*v.i.* to be in a position of authority or power; be in control: *born to command.* —*n.* **1.** the act of commanding: *At the sergeant's command, the troops halted.* **2.** something that is commanded; order: *My dog obeyed my command to sit.* **3.** the possession of authority; power to command: *to assume complete command of a project.* **4.** control or mastery: *a good command of Italian.* **5.** the people, things, or area under a commander: *The two platoons belonged to different commands.*

com·man·dant (kom′ən dant′, kom′ən dänt′) *n.* an officer in charge of a military installation or district.

com·man·deer (kom′ən dir′) *v.t.* to seize (private property), especially for military use: *The army commandeered the hotel for use as a barracks.*

com·mand·er (kə man′dər) *n.* **1.** an officer in command of a military unit. **2.** in the U.S. Navy or Coast Guard, an officer ranking above a lieutenant commander and below a captain. **3.** a person who is officially in command; leader: *The sheriff was the commander of the search party.*

commander in chief, *also,* **Commander in Chief.** *pl.* **commanders in chief.** the supreme commander of the armed forces of a country. In the United States, the president is the commander in chief.

com·mand·ing (kə man′ding) *adj.* **1.** demanding attention or respect: *The senators had a commanding air about them.* **2.** in charge: *a commanding officer.*

com·mand·ment (kə mand′mənt) *n.* **1.** *also,* **Commandment.** a law, especially one of the Ten Commandments. **2.** a command or order.

com·man·do (kə man′dō) *n., pl.* **com·man·dos** or **com·man·does.** a soldier specially trained for scouting and quick raids.

com·mem·o·rate (kə mem′ə rāt′) *v.t.,* **com·mem·o·rat·ed, com·mem·o·rat·ing.** **1.** to serve as a memorial to: *The statue in the park commemorates the soldiers of the Civil War.* **2.** to honor the memory of; celebrate: *Our class put on a pageant to commemorate the Pilgrims.* —**com·mem·o·ra′tion,** *n.*

com·mem·o·ra·tive (kə mem′ə rā′tiv, kə mem′ər ə tiv) *adj.* serving to commemorate: *commemorative postage stamps.*

com·mence (kə mens′) *v.,* **com·menced, com·menc·ing.** —*v.i.* to begin; start: *The program will commence at eight o'clock.* —*v.t.* to begin or start (something).

com·mence·ment (kə mens′mənt) *n.* **1.** a beginning; start. **2.** a ceremony in which a college or school gives degrees and diplomas to graduating students.

commencement *(def. 2)*

com·mend (kə mend′) *v.t.* **1.** to speak of with approval; praise: *My boss commended me for my work.* **2.** to give over to someone's care; entrust: *Our neighbors commended their plants to us while they were away.* **3.** to recommend: *I commend this book to you.*

com·mend·a·ble (kə men′də bəl) *adj.* worthy of praise: *a commendable piece of work.*

com·men·da·tion (kom′ən dā′shən) *n.* **1.** the act of commending; praise. **2.** something that expresses approval or praise; citation: *The firefighters received commendations for bravery.* —**com·men·da·to·ry** (kə men′də tôr′ē), *adj.*

com·men·sal (kə men′səl) *adj.* of or relating to commensalism. —*n.* a plant or animal living in commensalism.

com·men·sal·ism (kə men′sə liz′əm) *n.* a relationship between two organisms of different kinds in which one is benefited and the other is neither benefited nor harmed. Such a relationship exists between cowbirds and the grazing cattle that cowbirds follow in order to eat the insects and grubs that grazing uncovers.

com·men·su·rate (kə mən′sər it, kə men′shər it) *adj.* **1.** in proper proportion; equal to: *The reward for capturing the criminal was not commensurate with the risk involved.* **2.** having the same measure; of equal size: *Our gains were commensurate with our losses.* —**com·men′su·rate·ly,** *adv.*

com·ment (kom′ent) *n.* **1.** a brief statement or remark that explains, describes, or criticizes: *Our teacher's comments on the book made it sound interesting. Your sarcastic comments are beginning to bother me.* **2.** gossip; discussion: *The children's rude behavior was the subject of much comment.* —*v.i.* to make a comment or comments: *The coach took time to comment on last week's game.*

com·men·tar·y (kom′ən ter′ē) *n., pl.* **com·men·tar·ies. 1.** a series of notes or remarks that explain, describe, or criticize: *a commentary on Shakespeare's plays. We watched the news commentary on television.* **2.** anything that points out or serves as an example: *This sloppy report is a sad commentary on the student's lack of effort.*

com·men·ta·tor (kom′ən tā′tər) *n.* a person who comments on something, especially one who comments on the news on radio or television.

com·merce (kom′ərs) *n.* the buying and selling of goods or services, especially on a large scale; business; trade.

com·mer·cial (kə mûr′shəl) *adj.* **1.** of or relating to business or trade: *a commercial venture. I'm taking accounting and other commercial subjects at school.* **2.** made for or concerned with financial profit: *commercial products. The book got bad reviews from the critics, but it was a commercial success.* **3.** supported by revenues from advertisers: *a commercial television station.* —*n.* an advertising message on radio or television: *The show was interrupted every few minutes by a commercial.* —**com·mer′cial·ly,** *adv.*

commercial bank, a bank that offers most or all banking services, including checking and savings accounts and the granting of loans.

com·mer·cial·ism (kə mûr′shə liz′əm) *n.* **1.** the placing of too much emphasis on financial profit. **2.** the methods and principles of commerce.

com·mer·cial·ize (kə mûr′shə līz′) *v.t.,* **com·mer·cial·ized, com·mer·cial·iz·ing. 1.** to make commercial or businesslike. **2.** to exploit for profit: *The new stores and hotels commercialized the scenic town.* —**com·mer′cial·i·za′tion,** *n.*

com·min·gle (kə ming′gəl) *v.t., v.i.,* **com·min·gled, com·min·gling.** to mix together; mingle.

com·mis·er·ate (kə miz′ə rāt′) *v.,* **com·mis·er·at·ed, com·mis·er·at·ing.** —*v.i.* to feel or express sympathy: *We commiserated with them over the loss of their dog.* —*v.t.* to feel or express sympathy for; pity. —**com·mis′er·a′tion,** *n.*

com·mis·sar (kom′ə sär′) *n.* **1.** an official of a Communist Party whose duties are political indoctrination, the enforcement of party loyalty, and the like. **2.** formerly, a head of a government department in the Soviet Union.

com·mis·sar·y (kom′ə ser′ē) *n., pl.* **com·mis·sar·ies. 1.** a store that sells food and supplies, as in a military camp. **2.** a place to eat, such as a cafeteria. **3.** a person who is acting for another; deputy; representative.

com·mis·sion (kə mish′ən) *n.* **1.** a group of persons appointed or elected to perform certain duties: *The president set up a commission to investigate the causes of crime.* **2.** a fee for services or work done, usually a percentage of the total price: *The salesclerk received a commission of fifty dollars on the sale.* **3.** the act of committing: *the commission of a crime.* **4.** a position of military rank and authority: *The officers received their commissions after completing training.* **5. a.** the act of giving a person the authority to perform a task or duty. **b.** a document giving such authority: *The inspector's commission was displayed in the office.* **6.** the task or duty for which authority is given. **7.** an assignment to create a work of art: *The artist received a commission to paint the mural.* —*v.t.* **1.** to give military rank and authority to: *to commission an officer.* **2.** to give authority to; empower: *The company commissioned a private detective to investigate the theft.* **3.** to order a work of art: *The city commissioned a mural for the new library.* **4.** to put (a warship) into service.

·in commission. in service or use; in working order.

·out of commission. not in service or use; not in working order: *The bombing put three ships out of commission.*

commissioned officer, in the United States, an officer of the armed forces who receives a commission from the president.

com·mis·sion·er (kə mish′ə nər) *n.* **1.** a member of a commission. **2.** an official in charge of a government department: *a parks commissioner, a highway commissioner.* **3.** an official who is the head of a professional sports league: *a baseball commissioner.*

com·mit (kə mit′) *v.t.,* **com·mit·ted, com·mit·ting. 1.** to do or perform (something wrong): *to commit a crime, to commit a mistake. The shortstop committed three errors.* **2.** to put into the charge or keeping of another; entrust: *The doctor committed the patient to the nurses' care.* **3.** to put into official custody, as of a prison or mental institution: *The judge committed the convicted criminal for five years.* **4.** to devote or pledge; bind: *to commit oneself fully to a plan.* —**com·mit′ta·ble,** *adj.*

·to commit to memory. to learn by heart; memorize.

com·mit·ment (kə mit′mənt) *n.* **1.** the act of committing or the state of being committed. **2.** an obligation; pledge: *Previous commitments will keep me from attending the picnic.* Also, **com·mit·tal** (kə mit′əl).

com·mit·tee (kə mit′ē) *n.* a group of persons appointed or elected to perform certain duties: *The dance was planned by the social committee.*

com·mit·tee·man (kə mit′ē mən) *n., pl.* **com·mit·tee·men** (kə mit′ē mən). a member of a committee.

com·mit·tee·wom·an (kə mit′ē wùm′ən) *n., pl.* **com·mit·tee·wom·en** (kə mit′ē wim′ən). a woman who is on a committee.

com·mode (kə mōd′) *n.* **1.** a chest of drawers. **2.** a small piece of furniture containing a chamber pot or a washstand. **3.** see **toilet** (def. 2).

com·mo·di·ous (kə mō′dē əs) *adj.* having plenty of room; roomy; spacious: *a commodious apartment.* —**com·mo′di·ous·ly,** *adv.* —**com·mo′di·ous·ness,** *n.*

com·mod·i·ty (kə mod′i tē) *n., pl.* **com·mod·i·ties.**

at; āpe; fär; câre; end; mē; it; īce; pîerce; hot; ōld; sông, fôrk; oil; out; up; ūse; rüle; pùll; tûrn; chin; sing; shop; thin; this; hw in white; zh in treasure. The symbol ə stands for the unstressed vowel sound heard in about, taken, pencil, lemon, and circus.

something that can be bought and sold; article of trade: *wheat, corn, and other agricultural commodities.*

com·mo·dore (kom′ə dôr′) *n.* **1.** in the U.S. Navy, an officer ranking above a captain and below a rear admiral. This rank has not been used since World War II. **2.** the president or head of a yacht club.

com·mon (kom′ən) *adj.* **1.** happening or appearing often; usual: *It is a common mistake to dial a wrong number. Blond hair is common among people from northern Europe.* **2.** general; widespread: *Their quarrel is now a matter of common knowledge.* **3.** belonging equally to two or more; shared by all alike: *The club is made up of people with a common interest in music.* **4.** relating to the community as a whole; public: *the common good, to provide for the common defense.* **5.** not distinguished by special or outstanding characteristics; average; standard: *the common people, the common housefly. Replying to an invitation is a matter of common courtesy.* **6.** of coarse, poor quality; unrefined, or vulgar: *common manners.* —*n. also,* **commons.** a plot of land, such as a pasture or park, that is owned or used by the public. —**com′mon·ness,** *n.*

•**in common.** used or possessed by more than one; shared equally: *friends with many interests in common.*

com·mon·al·ty (kom′ən əl tē) *n., pl.* **com·mon·al·ties.** the common people, as opposed to royalty or the nobility.

common carrier, a railroad, steamship line, or other company that transports goods or people for a fee.

common cold, see **cold** *(n., def. 3).*

common denominator, a number that can be divided evenly by each of the denominators of a given group of fractions. The number 18 is a common denominator of $\frac{1}{3}$, $\frac{5}{6}$, and $\frac{2}{9}$, since $\frac{1}{3} = \frac{6}{18}$, $\frac{5}{6} = \frac{15}{18}$, and $\frac{2}{9} = \frac{4}{18}$.

common divisor, a number or algebraic expression that can divide two or more other numbers or algebraic expressions without leaving a remainder. The number 3 is a common divisor of 6, 9, 15, and 21. Also, **common factor.**

com·mon·er (kom′ə nər) *n.* a member of the common people, especially a person who is not of noble rank.

common fraction, a fraction whose numerator and denominator are whole numbers, such as $\frac{1}{4}$ or $\frac{3}{5}$.

common law, a system of law based on custom and usage as interpreted in court decisions, rather than on laws that have been enacted.

common logarithm, a logarithm having a base of 10.

com·mon·ly (kom′ən lē) *adv.* **1.** usually; generally; ordinarily: *I commonly arrive at work at 9:00.* **2.** in a common manner.

Common Market, an economic association formed in 1958 by France, West Germany, Italy, Belgium, the Netherlands, and Luxembourg to eliminate barriers to trade among its members. Denmark, Great Britain, Greece, Ireland, Portugal, and Spain are also now members. Also, **European Economic Community** or **EEC.**

common multiple, a number or algebraic expression that can be divided by two or more other numbers or algebraic expressions without leaving a remainder. The number 20 is a common multiple of 2, 4, 5, and 10.

common noun, a noun that names any one or all of the members of a class, rather than any one particular person, place, or thing. Common nouns can be used immediately after the word *the. Dog, dogs, street, and streets* are common nouns; *Abraham Lincoln, Joan of Arc,* and *Delaware* are not.

com·mon·place (kom′ən plās′) *adj.* not original, remarkable, or interesting; ordinary: *Snow is a commonplace occurrence in Maine, but not in Florida.* —*n.* **1.** an ordinary or obvious remark. **2.** anything ordinary or uninteresting; everyday thing. —**com′mon·place′ness,** *n.*

com·mons (kom′ənz) *n.* **1.** a hall or building for dining, especially at a college or university. ▲ used with a singular verb. **2. Commons.** see **House of Commons.** ▲ used with a singular or plural verb. **3.** see **common.** ▲ used with a singular verb.

common sense, good sense and wisdom based on experience rather than special knowledge; sound practical judgment.

common stock, the stock of a corporation that gives the owner voting rights and the possibility of receiving dividends after the dividends due to preferred stock have been paid.

com·mon·weal (kom′ən wēl′) *n.* **1.** the general or public welfare; common good. **2.** *Archaic.* another word for **commonwealth.**

com·mon·wealth (kom′ən welth′) *n.* **1.** the people of a nation or state. **2.** a nation or state that is governed by the people; republic or democracy. **3.** any of certain states of the United States. Kentucky, Massachusetts, Pennsylvania, and Virginia use *commonwealth* rather than *state* as an official name. **4. the Commonwealth.** see **Commonwealth of Nations.**

Commonwealth of Nations, a worldwide association made up of Great Britain and most of the nations and territories that once were a part of the British Empire. Also, **the Commonwealth, British Commonwealth of Nations.**

com·mo·tion (kə mō′shən) *n.* a noisy disturbance or disorder; confusion: *There was a commotion when the bat flew into the dining room.*

com·mu·nal (kə mū′nəl) *adj.* **1.** of, relating to, or like a commune or community. **2.** belonging to the people of a community; public —**com·mu′nal·ly,** *adv.*

com·mune[1] (kə mūn′) *v.i.,* **com·muned, com·mun·ing.** **1.** to talk or be with closely: *to commune with nature.* **2.** to receive Holy Communion. [From the Old French word *comuner* meaning "to share" or "have in common," from the word *comun* "common," from the Latin word *communis* "common" or "general."]

com·mune[2] (kom′ūn) *n.* **1.** a community in which property is owned in common and work and living quarters are shared. **2.** the smallest unit of local government in certain European countries, such as France, Italy, and Belgium. **3. the Commune. a.** a revolutionary committee in Paris that governed France from 1792 to 1794. **b.** the revolutionary government of Paris from March 18 to May 28, 1871. [From the French word *commune* meaning "township," from the Medieval Latin *communia* "group sharing a common life," from the Latin word *communis* "common" or "general."]

com·mu·ni·ca·ble (kə mū′ni kə bəl) *adj.* capable of being carried or passed along from one person to another: *Polio is a communicable disease.*

com·mu·ni·cant (kə mū′ni kənt) *n.* **1.** a person who receives Holy Communion. **2.** a person who communicates.

com·mu·ni·cate (kə mū′ni kāt′) *v.,* **com·mu·ni·cat·ed, com·mu·ni·cat·ing.** —*v.t.* **1.** to make known or understood; give knowledge or information of: *You communicated your ideas very well in the essay.* **2.** to carry or pass along: *to communicate a disease.* —*v.i.* **1.** to exchange or share feelings, thoughts, or information: *I've been communicating with them by mail.* **2.** to be connected or form a connecting passage: *This passageway communicates with the tunnel leading to the mine.* —**com·mu′ni·ca′tor,** *n.*

com·mu·ni·ca·tion (kə mū′ni kā′shən) *n.* **1.** the transfer of information, such as facts, wishes, or emotions: *Some Indians used smoke signals as a means of communication.* **2.** something communicated: *The reporter's communications were sent by telegram.* **3.** the act or process of communicating. **4. communications.** a system for communicating, especially one involving telephone, telegraph, radio, or television: *Communications in the flooded area are still not working.*

Communication is the conveying of any kind of information from one person or place to another. The information can be facts, thoughts, orders, or anything else that can be known or felt. A crying baby, a smile, a handshake, a locked door, and a growling dog can all communicate information to us if we know how to interpret them as signs. We receive some kind of information from each of them, even though the precise meaning may not be altogether clear. Facial expressions, gestures, and physical actions such as a nod of the head, a wave of the hand, or a shrug of the shoulders are all examples of the type of general communication known as body language. Human language, however, provides a means of conveying more precise information.

Language, which was first spoken and only later written, is probably the most important human achievement. Unlike gestures or other means of communication, human language can express our most complex thoughts and knowledge. In its written form, language has made it possible for us to store vast amounts of information that can be communicated to anyone who is able to read. Anything written is timeless. It can be passed from one generation to another.

communications satellite, an artificial satellite that relays radio, television, telephone, or other signals between ground stations on earth.

com·mu·ni·ca·tive (kə mū′ni kā′tiv, kə mū′ni kə tiv) *adj.* ready to communicate or disclose information; talkative. —**com·mu′ni·ca′tive·ly,** *adv.* —**com·mu′ni·ca′tive·ness,** *n.*

com·mun·ion (kə mūn′yən) *n.* **1.** a sharing of feelings or thoughts; fellowship: *There was a close communion between the two friends.* **2.** a group of churches having common religious beliefs. **3. Communion. a.** see **Holy Communion. b.** the part of a church service during which Holy Communion is received.

com·mu·ni·qué (kə mū′ni kā′) *n.* an official communication or announcement: *A communiqué from the commanding general announced the enemy's surrender.* [From the French word *communiqué* meaning "official bulletin," from the word *communiquer* "to communicate," from the Latin word *communicare* "to share, impart."]

com·mu·nism (kom′yə niz′əm) *n.* **1.** a social and economic system based on the theories of Karl Marx and Friedrich Engels and later modified by Vladimir Lenin and others. Under this system, all property and goods are owned by the government or state and the products of labor are shared by all. **2.** *also,* **Communism. a.** a political movement working to promote this system. **b.** a system of government based on this, as in the Soviet Union. **3.** any social system in which goods and services are shared by all.

com·mu·nist (kom′yə nist) *also,* **Com·mu·nist.** *n.* **1.** a member of a Communist Party. **2.** a person who advocates or supports communism. —*adj.* relating to communism, communists, or a Communist Party. —**com′mu·nis′tic,** *adj.*

Communist Party, a political party that supports or advocates communism.

com·mu·ni·ty (kə mū′ni tē) *n., pl.* **com·mu·ni·ties.** **1.** a group of people living in the same area and under the same government; the people of a district or town: *Our community voted to build a new library.* **2.** the district or town itself. **3.** a number of people joined together by common interests: *the academic community, the business community.* **4.** society in general; the public: *We must consider the welfare of the community as a whole.*

5. similarity; agreement. **6.** all the animals, plants, and other organisms that live in a certain area and interact with each other, considered as a group. **7.** common ownership: *community of resources.*

community center, a meeting place that is used by a community for recreational, social, and cultural activities.

community chest, a fund of voluntary contributions made by the people of a community for local charities and welfare activities.

community college, a junior college, especially one partially supported by the community it serves.

community property, in some states of the United States, property acquired during a marriage, by either partner, which is considered to be owned equally by both partners.

com·mu·ta·tion (kom′yə tā′shən) *n.* **1.** regular travel to and from work, especially over a long distance. **2.** a reduction or change, as of a prison sentence or penalty. **3.** a substitution, as of one type of payment for another.

commutation ticket, a discount ticket for a railroad or other form of transportation to be used for a specified number of rides or over a particular period of time.

com·mu·ta·tive (kom′yə tā′tiv, kə mū′tə tiv) *adj. Mathematics.* relating to or designating a law stating that the sum or product of two or more quantities will be the same regardless of their order. For example: $2 + 5$ is the same as $5 + 2$, and $a \times b$ is the same as $b \times a$.

com·mu·ta·tor (kom′yə tā′tər) *n.* a device in an electric generator or motor that causes a change in direction of the current.

com·mute (kə mūt′) *v.,* **com·mut·ed, com·mut·ing.** —*v.i.* to travel regularly to and from work, especially between a suburb and a city: *I can commute by train or by bus.* —*v.t.* to reduce or change: *to commute a prison sentence.*

com·mut·er (kə mū′tər) *n.* a person who regularly travels a relatively long distance to and from work, as from a suburb to a city. —*adj.* used by or designed for commuters: *a commuter railroad that runs between the suburbs and the city, a commuter airline.*

comp. 1. comparative. **2.** compare. **3.** compound.

com·pact[1] (*adj.,* kəm pakt′, kom′pakt; *v.,* kəm pakt′; *n.,* kom′pakt) *adj.* **1.** tightly packed together; dense: *Compact snow is good for making snowballs.* **2.** taking up a relatively small space or area: *A compact suitcase is convenient for traveling on an airplane.* **3.** solidly built but not tall: *compact hockey players.* **4.** said or written in few words; concise: *a compact article.* —*v.t.* to pack together closely and firmly; pack: *The gardener compacted the soil around the roots of the plants.* —*n.* **1.** a small case containing face powder and a mirror, designed to be carried in a purse. **2.** an automobile that is smaller than a standard model. [From the Latin word *compactus,* past participle of *compingere* "to join or put together," from the prefix *com-* "with, together" + *pangere* "to fix, set."] —**com·pact′ly,** *adv.*

com·pact[2] (kom′pakt) *n.* an agreement or contract: *The Mayflower Compact was an agreement among the Pilgrims as to how their new colony would be governed.* [From the Latin word *compactum* meaning "an agreement," going back to the word *compacisci* "to make an agreement."]

at; āpe; fär; câre; end; mē; it; īce; pîerce; hot; ōld; sông, fôrk; oil; out; up; ūse; rüle; pùll; tûrn; chin; sing; shop; thin; <u>th</u>is; hw in white; zh in treasure. The symbol ə stands for the unstressed vowel sound heard in about, taken, pencil, lemon, and circus.

197

compact disc (kom′pakt) *also,* **compact disk.** an optical disk about 4¾ inches (12 centimeters) in diameter, carrying a digital sound recording that can be read and played by means of a laser beam. Trademark: **Compact Disc.**

com·pac·tor (kəm-pak′tər, kom′pak-tər) *also,* **com·pac·ter.** *n.* a device that presses garbage into a small compact mass for easy disposal.

com·pan·ion (kəm-pan′yən) *n.* **1.** a person who often goes

compact disc

along or associates with another; friend; comrade: *We two were constant companions last summer.* **2.** any person who accompanies another. **3.** a person employed to stay with or assist another: *to be hired as a companion for an invalid.* **4.** something that matches something else; one of a pair: *I lost the companion to this glove.* [From the Old French word *compaignon* meaning "comrade," from the Late Latin word *companio* "comrade," from the Latin prefix *com-* "with, together" + *panis* "bread." A companion is someone who shares your bread.]

com·pan·ion·a·ble (kəm pan′yə nə bəl) *adj.* capable of being a good companion; easy to be with; sociable. —**com·pan′ion·a·bil′i·ty,** *n.* —**com·pan′ion·a·bly,** *adv.*

com·pan·ion·ship (kəm pan′yən ship′) *n.* the state of being companions; friendship; fellowship.

com·pan·ion·way (kəm pan′yən wā′) *n.* **1.** a stairway leading from the deck of a ship to the cabin or deck below. **2.** the space where such a stairway is located.

com·pa·ny (kum′pə nē) *n., pl.* **com·pa·nies.** **1.** a guest or guests: *We had company for dinner.* **2.** a business firm or establishment: *My cousin has been with the oil company for twelve years.* **3.** companionship; fellowship: *to be lonesome for the company of others.* **4.** a companion or companions: *Do you judge people by the company they keep?* **5.** a group of people gathered together: *The guide led the company of tourists through the museum.* **6.** a group of performers; troupe: *a theatrical company.* **7.** a military unit made up of two or more platoons, forming part of a battalion. **8.** a ship's crew, including the officers.

·**to keep company. a.** to date; court: *My parents kept company for a long time before they were married.* **b.** to be with: *I kept them company for an hour.*

·**to part company. a.** to separate and go in different directions. **b.** to end an association or friendship: *The partners finally parted company after a long dispute.*

compar., comparative.

com·pa·ra·ble (kom′pər ə bəl) *adj.* **1.** capable of being compared: *We bought gifts of comparable value for the twins.* **2.** worthy of comparison: *Our school orchestra is not comparable to a professional one.* —**com′pa·ra·bly,** *adv.*

com·par·a·tive (kəm par′ə tiv) *adj.* **1.** involving, based on, or pertaining to comparison: *a comparative study of frogs and toads.* **2.** judged by comparison; not absolute; relative: *They are comparative strangers to me; I have met them only once.* **3.** *Grammar.* relating to or designating the comparative degree of an adjective or adverb. "Faster" is the comparative form of "fast." —*n. Grammar.* **1.** the degree of an adjective or adverb that indicates an increase in quantity, quality, or relation. **2.** a word or group of words expressing this degree. "Colder," "darker," and "more complicated" are comparatives. —**com·par′a·tive·ly,** *adv.*

Language Note

The **comparative** of an adjective or adverb in English is usually formed by adding *-er* to the root word, as in *deep/deeper*, *green/greener*, and *rich/richer*. Sometimes the last letter of the root word is doubled, as in *sad/sadder*. If the final letter of the root word is a vowel, it is often dropped or changed, as in *wide/wider* and *funny/funnier*. A few words have a comparative form that is completely different from the basic word, such as *good/better* and *bad/worse*.

If a word has two or more syllables, another comparative can usually be formed by placing the word *more* in front of it. The comparative of *beautiful* is *more beautiful*.

The comparative form is used to compare the quality or quantity that the adjective describes. One building may be *tall*, but comparison with another may show that the second building is *taller* than the first.

com·pare (kəm pâr′) *v.,* **com·pared, com·par·ing.** —*v.t.* **1.** to study in order to find likenesses and differences: *The police compared the fingerprints on the gun with those on the door.* **2.** to consider or speak of as similar or alike; liken: *The human brain has been compared to a computer.* **3.** *Grammar.* to form the positive, comparative, and superlative degrees of (an adjective or adverb). —*v.i.* to be worthy of being compared; be considered alike or similar: *The new building can't compare with the old one.* ▲ To **compare** is to show the likenesses and the differences between persons or things. To **contrast** is to show only the differences between persons or things.

·**beyond compare.** without equal: *a view beyond compare.*

com·par·i·son (kəm par′ə sən) *n.* **1.** the act of comparing or the state of being compared: *A comparison of the teams seems to show that Saturday's game will be close.* **2.** a likeness; similarity: *There is no comparison between these two radios.* **3.** *Grammar.* a change in the form of an adjective or adverb to indicate the positive, comparative, or superlative degrees.

com·par·i·son–shop (kəm par′ə sən shop′) *v.i.,* **com·par·i·son-shopped, com·par·i·son-shop·ping.** **1.** to compare the prices of different brands of the same item or of the same item in different stores. **2.** to act or serve as a comparison shopper.

comparison shopper, an employee of a store whose job is to shop in competing stores to check on their prices and quality and selection of merchandise.

com·part·ment (kəm pärt′mənt) *n.* a division or section of an enclosed space: *This wallet has a separate compartment for coins.*

com·part·men·tal·ize (kəm pärt′men′tə līz′) *v.t.,* **com·part·men·tal·ized, com·part·men·tal·iz·ing.** to divide into separate compartments or categories.

com·pass (kum′pəs, kom′pəs) *n., pl.* **com·pass·es.** **1.** a device for showing directions, made up of a magnetized needle that is free to point to the north magnetic pole. **2.** the outer limits or boundary of an enclosed area: *The children were told to stay within the compass of the school grounds.* **3.** range within limits; scope: *That job is not within the compass of a beginner's abilities.* **4.** *also,* **compasses.** a device for drawing circles and measuring distances, made up of two straight and equal legs connected at one end. **5.** the range of tones of a voice or musical instrument. —*v.t.* **1.** to make a circuit of; go around: *Their voyage compassed the globe.* **2.** to circle around; surround; encompass: *The mountains compassed the valley.*

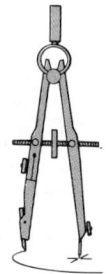

compass *(def. 4)*

3. to grasp mentally; understand: *The child could not compass such a difficult idea.* **4.** to accomplish or gain; achieve.

com·pas·sion (kəm pash′ən) *n.* sympathy for another's suffering or misfortune, combined with a desire to help.

com·pas·sion·ate (kəm pash′ə nit) *adj.* feeling or showing compassion; sympathetic. —**com·pas′sion·ate·ly**, *adv.*

compass rose, a circle divided into thirty-two points of the compass, especially one printed on a map for use in air or sea navigation: *North by northwest and east by southeast are two points on a compass rose.*

com·pat·i·ble (kəm pat′ə bəl) *adj.* capable of existing well together; in harmony: *The two roommates were no longer compatible.* —**com·pat′i·bil′i·ty**, *n.* —**com·pat′i·bly**, *adv.*

com·pa·tri·ot (kəm pā′trē ət) *n.* a person from one's own country; fellow citizen.

com·peer (kəm pîr′) *n.* **1.** a person of equal rank; equal; peer. **2.** a comrade; companion.

com·pel (kəm pel′) *v.t.,* **com·pelled, com·pel·ling. 1.** to drive, urge, or cause with force or as if with force; oblige: *The rain compelled us to cancel our picnic.* **2.** to obtain or bring about by force: *The army compelled obedience to the dictator's rule.*

com·pen·di·ous (kəm pen′dē əs) *adj.* forming a summary; short but complete; concise: *a compendious handbook on camping.*

com·pen·di·um (kəm pen′dē əm) *n., pl.* **com·pen·di·ums** or **com·pen·di·a** (kəm pen′dē ə). a brief summary covering a subject completely.

com·pen·sate (kom′pən sāt′) *v.,* **com·pen·sat·ed, com·pen·sat·ing.** —*v.t.* to make payment to (a person or persons) for work done, or for an injury or loss: *The company compensated us for extra hours worked. The insurance money could never fully compensate them for the loss of their house.* —*v.i.* to be a balance; make up: *The rain on Friday compensated for the dry week.* —**com′pen·sa′tive, com·pen·sa·to·ry** (kəm pen′sə tôr′ē), *adj.*

com·pen·sa·tion (kom′pən sā′shən) *n.* **1.** the act of compensating. **2.** something that makes payment for work done, or for an injury or loss: *We received compensation from the state for the land taken for the new road.* **3.** salary or wages; pay.

com·pete (kəm pēt′) *v.i.,* **com·pet·ed, com·pet·ing.** to strive against another or others, as in a contest; vie: *The students competed for the mathematics prize.*

com·pe·tence (kom′pi təns) *n.* **1.** the state of being competent; ability; fitness: *You must prove your competence as a pilot before you will be licensed to fly alone.* **2.** enough money to provide a comfortable living. Also, **com·pe·ten·cy** (kom′pi tən sē).

com·pe·tent (kom′pi tənt) *adj.* having or showing enough ability or knowledge; capable: *Only competent swimmers should use the deep end of the pool. Although inexperienced, the mechanic did a competent job.* —**com′pe·tent·ly**, *adv.*

com·pe·ti·tion (kom′pi tish′ən) *n.* **1.** the act of competing; rivalry: *The competition for scholarships was keen.* **2.** something that tests or proves skill or ability; contest: *a skating competition.*

com·pet·i·tive (kəm pet′i tiv) *adj.* of, involving, or using competition: *a competitive sport, a highly competitive business.* —**com·pet′i·tive·ly**, *adv.* —**com·pet′i·tive·ness**, *n.*

com·pet·i·tor (kəm pet′i tər) *n.* a person or thing that competes: *There were ten competitors for the job.*

com·pi·la·tion (kom′pə lā′shən) *n.* **1.** the act of compiling. **2.** something that has been compiled, as a list or report.

com·pile (kəm pīl′) *v.t.,* **com·piled, com·pil·ing. 1.** to collect and put together in a list or report: *to compile*

statistics. **2.** to make or form by collecting material from various sources: *to compile an anthology of poems.* —**com·pil′er**, *n.*

com·pla·cen·cy (kəm plā′sən sē) *n.* a feeling of self-satisfaction. Also, **com·pla·cence** (kəm plā′səns).

com·pla·cent (kəm plā′sənt) *adj.* pleased with oneself or one's position; self-satisfied: *The complacent champion did not bother to train for the match with the challenger.* —**com·pla′cent·ly**, *adv.*

com·plain (kəm plān′) *v.i.* **1.** to find fault; express dissatisfaction: *They complained that the exam was too hard.* **2.** to talk about one's pains or ills. **3.** to make an accusation or charge: *We complained to the police about our noisy neighbors.* —**com·plain′er**, *n.*

com·plain·ant (kəm plā′nənt) *n.* a person who files a formal complaint in a lawsuit.

com·plaint (kəm plānt′) *n.* **1.** an expression of dissatisfaction: *We took our complaints to the store manager.* **2.** a cause for complaining: *I have no complaint with the food in this restaurant.* **3.** an illness; ailment: *Chicken pox is a common complaint of children.* **4.** a formal charge or accusation in a lawsuit.

com·plai·sance (kəm plā′səns, kəm plā′zəns) *n.* a willingness to please others; agreeableness.

com·plai·sant (kəm plā′sənt, kəm plā′zənt) *adj.* willing to please others; obliging; agreeable. —**com·plai′sant·ly**, *adv.*

com·ple·ment (*n.,* kom′plə mənt; *v.,* kom′plə ment′) *n.* **1.** something that makes complete: *The new table is just the right complement for the room.* **2.** the required number or amount: *The football team now has its full complement of players.* **3.** *Grammar.* a word or phrase that completes a sentence or predicate. In the sentence *The sky is blue, blue* is a complement. —*v.t.* to make complete: *The background music nicely complements the action in the movie.* ▲ See **compliment** for usage note.

com·ple·men·ta·ry (kom′plə men′tə rē, kom′plə men′-trē) *adj.* making whole; completing: *The rubber boots were complementary to the rain outfit.*

complementary angle, either of two angles whose sum is 90 degrees.

complementary colors, two colors of the spectrum that produce white or gray light when combined. Red and green are complementary colors.

com·plete (kəm plēt′) *adj.* **1.** having all its parts or elements; whole; entire: *a complete deck of cards.* **2.** ended; finished: *The report is now complete.* **3.** total; thorough: *The show was a complete success.* —*v.t.,* **com·plet·ed, com·plet·ing. 1.** to make whole: *to complete a set.* **2.** to make perfect; make entirely satisfactory: *The delicious dinner completed a wonderful day.* **3.** to bring to an end; finish: *Let's complete this book before we start another.* —**com·plete′ly**, *adv.* —**com·plete′ness**, *n.*

com·ple·tion (kəm plē′shən) *n.* the act of completing or the state of being completed.

com·plex (*adj.,* kəm pleks′, kom′pleks; *n.,* kom′pleks) *adj.* **1.** hard to understand or do: *a complex problem.* **2.** made up of many related parts: *complex machinery.* —*n., pl.* **com·plex·es. 1.** a whole made up of a combination of related parts: *The new housing complex will have a hotel as well as several apartment buildings.* **2.** a group of related ideas or feelings that can influence a person's behavior to an abnormal degree, although he or

C

she is not aware of having them: *to have a complex about being neat.* —**com·plex′ly,** *adv.*

complex fraction, a fraction having a common fraction, mixed number, or algebraic expression in the numerator, denominator, or both. The fraction ½ / 2¼ is a complex fraction. Also, **compound fraction.**

com·plex·ion (kəm plek′shən) *n.* **1.** the color and general appearance of the skin, especially of the face. **2.** the general appearance or character of anything: *The addition of the new players changed the complexion of the team.*

com·plex·i·ty (kəm plek′si tē) *n., pl.* **com·plex·i·ties. 1.** the state or quality of being complex: *The complexity of the problem baffled us all.* **2.** something complex.

complex sentence, a sentence that has one independent clause and one or more dependent clauses. For example: *After playing tennis for an hour, they decided to go for a swim.*

com·pli·ance (kəm plī′əns) *n.* **1.** the act of complying or giving in. **2.** readiness or tendency to give in to others. Also, **com·pli·an·cy** (kəm plī′ən sē).
·**in compliance with.** in agreement with; according to: *They acted in compliance with our request.*

com·pli·ant (kəm plī′ənt) *adj.* complying or ready to comply; giving in; yielding. —**com·pli′ant·ly,** *adv.*

com·pli·cate (kom′pli kāt′) *v.t.,* **com·pli·cat·ed, com·pli·cat·ing.** to make hard to understand or do; make complex or difficult: *My friend's clumsy help only complicated my job.* [From the Latin word *complicatus,* past participle of *complicare* meaning "to fold together," from the prefix *com-* "with, together" + *plicare* "to fold."]

com·pli·cat·ed (kom′pli kā′tid) *adj.* hard to understand or do; complex: *The directions were too complicated to follow.*

com·pli·ca·tion (kom′pli kā′shən) *n.* **1.** the act of complicating. **2.** a complicated state or condition: *Train delays caused a complication of the plans for our departure.* **3.** something that complicates or causes difficulty: *Poor health and other complications kept me out of school for almost a month.*

com·plic·i·ty (kəm plis′i tē) *n.* the state of being an accomplice, especially in wrongdoing: *complicity in a crime.*

com·pli·ment (*n.,* kom′plə mənt; *v.,* kom′plə ment′) *n.* **1.** an expression of admiration or praise; flattering comment: *to receive compliments on one's cooking.* **2.** a courtesy: *Pay me the compliment of returning this call.* **3. compliments.** an expression of regard, greeting, or good wishes: *Extend my compliments to your family.* —*v.t.* to pay a compliment to; praise; congratulate: *We complimented them on their work.* ▲ **Compliment** and **complement** are often confused. To **compliment** is to admire or praise a person: *We complimented the musicians on their performance.* To **complement** is to complete something: *These new shoes complement my suit.*

com·pli·men·ta·ry (kom′plə men′tə rē, kom′plə men′trē) *adj.* **1.** containing or expressing a compliment. **2.** without charge; free: *complimentary tickets to a game.*

com·ply (kəm plī′) *v.i.,* **com·plied, com·ply·ing.** to act in agreement, as with a request or rule: *I will comply with your wishes.*

com·po·nent (kəm pō′nənt) *n.* **1.** an essential part or ingredient: *One component of hiking gear is a good pair of shoes.* **2.** one of the devices, as an amplifier or speaker, that makes up a hi-fi or video system. —*adj.* being an essential part or ingredient: *the component parts of a machine.*

com·port (kəm pôrt′) *v.t.* to behave or conduct (oneself): *You comport yourself well in the classroom.* —*v.i.* to suit or agree: *A joking attitude does not comport with the role of a judge.*

com·port·ment (kəm pôrt′mənt) *n.* behavior; conduct.

com·pose (kəm pōz′) *v.,* **com·posed, com·pos·ing.** —*v.t.* **1.** to be the elements or parts of; make up: *Six or*

twelve persons compose a jury. The fabric was composed of synthetic fibers. **2.** to make or form from parts or elements; fashion: *I composed my paper from different sources.* **3.** to create (an artistic work). **4.** to make quiet or calm: *They tried to compose themselves after hearing the shocking news.* **5.** *Printing.* **a.** to set (type). **b.** to set the type for: *The printer composed the first page of the book.* —*v.i.* to create a musical work.

com·posed (kəm pōzd′) *adj.* having or showing self-control; calm. —**com·pos·ed·ly** (kəm pō′zid lē), *adv.*

com·pos·er (kəm pō′zər) *n.* a person who composes something, especially one who composes music.

com·pos·ite (kəm poz′it) *adj.* **1.** made up of various parts or elements: *a composite picture made up of parts of old snapshots.* **2.** belonging to a family of plants having florets clustered together in dense flower heads that look like single flowers. Chrysanthemums and daisies are composite flowers. —*n.* something that is composed of various parts or elements.

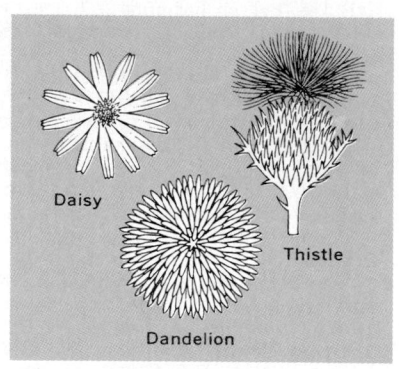

composite flowers

composite number, a number that can be divided without a remainder by one or more numbers as well as by itself and 1. The numbers 4, 6, 8, 9, and 10 are composite numbers.

com·po·si·tion (kom′pə zish′ən) *n.* **1.** the act of forming parts into a whole; the act of composing, as a work of writing, art, or music: *The musician spent several years in the composition of the opera.* **2.** the parts that make up a whole: *The chemist analyzed the moon rock to determine its composition.* **3.** something composed, especially a work of writing, art, or music: *a composition about colonial America.* **4.** the way in which something is composed: *The winning photograph has a balanced composition.* **5.** a mixture of substances: *The crew used a composition containing gravel and asphalt to pave the road.* **6.** *Printing.* the setting of type.

com·pos·i·tor (kəm poz′i tər) *n.* see **typesetter** *(def. 1).*

com·post (kom′pōst) *n.* a mixture of decayed plants, manure, and the like, used to fertilize soil.

com·po·sure (kəm pō′zhər) *n.* self-control; calmness: *Your composure during the fire had a calming influence on everyone around you.*

com·pote (kom′pōt) *n.* **1.** fruit that is stewed in syrup. **2.** a shallow bowl or dish having a stem, usually used for fruit or candy.

com·pound[1] (*adj.,* kom′pound; *v.,* kəm pound′; *n.,* kom′pound) *adj.* composed of two or more parts. —*v.t.* **1.** to mix (parts) to form something: *The Indians compounded water, sand, and clay to form bricks.* **2.** to make (something) by combining various parts or ingredients: *The druggist compounded medicine for the patient.* **3.** to add to: *I compounded my troubles at school by failing two subjects.* —*n.* **1.** a combination of two or more parts; mixture. **2.** a substance formed by the chemical combination of two or more elements: *A carbohydrate is a compound of carbon, hydrogen, and oxygen.* **3.** a word composed of two or more words that are written together or joined with a hyphen. The words *blueberry* and *fair-haired* are compounds. A combination of two words that has its own special meaning, such as *common sense,* may also be called a compound. [From the Middle French word *compondre* meaning "to put together, arrange," from the Latin word *componere* "to put together," from the prefix *com-* "with, together" + *ponere* "to put."] —**com·pound'a·ble,** *adj.* —**com·pound'er,** *n.*

com·pound² (kom'pound) *n.* an enclosed area containing a house or other building: *a prison compound.* [From the Malay word *kampung* meaning "gathering" or "enclosure."]

compound eye, an eye having many units, each with its own lens. Insects have compound eyes.

compound fraction, another term for **complex fraction.**

compound fracture, a fracture in which the broken bone sticks out through the skin.

compound interest, the interest paid or to be paid on both the original sum of money and the interest already accumulated.

compound leaf, a leaf having two or more leaflets on a common leafstalk.

compound sentence, a sentence that consists of two or more independent clauses, usually connected by a conjunction or conjunctions. For example: *I went to the store, and later we went to the movies.*

com·pre·hend (kom'pri hend') *v.t.* **1.** to grasp with the mind; understand: *I was not able to comprehend the explanation of the mathematics problem.* **2.** to take in or contain; include: *The file comprehends the title of every book in the library.*

com·pre·hen·si·ble (kom'pri hen'sə bəl) *adj.* capable of being understood; understandable: *The wounded soldier's words were not comprehensible.* —**com'pre·hen'si·bil'i·ty,** *n.* —**com'pre·hen'si·bly,** *adv.*

com·pre·hen·sion (kom'pri hen'shən) *n.* the act or power of grasping something with the mind; understanding: *The theory of relativity is beyond my comprehension.*

com·pre·hen·sive (kom'pri hen'siv) *adj.* **1.** covering a great deal; including much: *a comprehensive study of the Civil War.* **2.** capable of understanding many things: *a comprehensive mind.* —**com'pre·hen'sive·ly,** *adv.* —**com'pre·hen'sive·ness,** *n.*

com·press (*v.,* kəm pres'; *n.,* kom'pres) *v.t.* to press or squeeze together; force into a smaller space: *The machine compressed cotton into bales.* —*n., pl.* **com·press·es.** a pad or cloth used to apply pressure, heat, cold, or medicine to some part of the body. —**com·press'i·bil'i·ty,** *n.* —**com·press'i·ble,** *adj.*

compressed air, air that has been reduced in volume by compression. Its pressure when released is used to operate machinery, such as paint sprayers, pneumatic drills, and brakes.

com·pres·sion (kəm presh'ən) *n.* **1.** the act or process of compressing. **2.** the state of being compressed.

com·pres·sive (kəm pres'iv) *adj.* compressing or tending to compress.

com·pres·sor (kəm pres'ər) *n.* a person or thing that compresses, especially a machine that compresses gases: *an air compressor.*

com·prise (kəm prīz') *v.t.,* **com·prised, com·pris·ing.** to be composed of; consist of.

com·pro·mise (kom'prə mīz') *n.* **1.** the settlement of an argument or disagreement by having each side agree to give up some part of its claims or demands. **2.** the result of such a settlement. —*v.,* **com·pro·mised, com·pro·mis·ing.** —*v.i.* to make a compromise: *Neither candidate could win the nomination, so the party compromised and picked a third person to run.* —*v.t.* to expose to suspicion or danger: *to compromise one's reputation.* —**com'pro·mis'er,** *n.*

comp·trol·ler (kən trō'lər) *n.* see **controller** *(def. 2).*

com·pul·sion (kəm pul'shən) *n.* **1.** the act of compelling or the state of being compelled. **2.** a strong impulse to do something: *a compulsion to eat peanuts.*

com·pul·sive (kəm pul'siv) *adj.* of, relating to, or caused

by compulsion: *a compulsive liar, compulsive acts.* —**com·pul'sive·ly,** *adv.* —**com·pul'sive·ness,** *n.*

com·pul·so·ry (kəm pul'sə rē) *adj.* **1.** imposed as a requirement or duty; required: *In that company, retirement at age seventy is compulsory. Attendance at the lecture was compulsory for all students.* **2.** involving or using force.

com·punc·tion (kəm pungk'shən) *n.* an uneasiness caused by feelings of guilt; twinge of conscience: *to have no compunction about borrowing things without asking.*

com·pu·ta·tion (kom'pyə tā'shən) *n.* **1.** the act, process, or method of computing. **2.** the result of computing.

com·pute (kəm pūt') *v.t.,* **com·put·ed, com·put·ing.** to find out or calculate by using mathematics: *The builder computed the cost of the garage.* [From the Latin word *computare* meaning "to determine" and "to count," from the prefix *com-* "with, together" + *putare* "to consider, think."]

com·put·er (kəm pū'tər) *n.* **1.** an electronic device that performs complex mathematical calculations rapidly, using information and instructions it receives and stores. **2.** any device or person that computes.

computer *(def. 1)*

com·put·er-aid·ed design (kəm pū'tər ā'did) the process of designing vehicles, buildings, road, and other things with the help of computers.

computer-aided instruction (kəm pū'tər ā'did) the use of computers as a teaching tool.

computer-aided manufacture (kəm pū'tər ā'did) the process of manufacturing with machinery that has been programmed to operate by computer.

computer graphics, pictures, charts, diagrams, and other graphic material produced and processed by a computer, as opposed to letters and numerals.

com·put·er·ize (kəm pū'tə rīz') *v.t.,* **com·put·er·ized, com·put·er·iz·ing.** **1.** to control by or store in an electronic computer: *to computerize data.* **2.** to equip with electronic computers: *to computerize an office, to computerize a printing plant.*

computer language, a set of symbols, such as letters, numerals, and punctuation marks, together with rules for using them, used to communicate instructions to a computer.

computer literacy, understanding of the basic principles

at; āpe; fär; câre; end; mē; it; īce; pîerce; hot; ōld; sông, fôrk; oil; out; up; ūse; rüle; pŭll; tûrn; chin; sing; shop; thin; **this**; hw in white; zh in treasure. The symbol ə stands for the unstressed vowel sound heard in about, taken, pencil, lemon, and circus.

C

201

of computer hardware and software, together with the ability to use them for practical purposes.

computer science, the study of the theory, design, and application of computer hardware and software.

com·rade (kom′rad) *n.* **1.** a close friend or companion. **2.** a person who works with or shares the same interests as another or others.

com·rade·ship (kom′rad ship′) *n.* the condition of being a comrade or comrades; fellowship; companionship.

con[1] (kon) *adv.* against: *We debated the problem pro and con.* —*n.* a reason, argument, or person against something: *Let's discuss the pros and cons of buying the car.* [Short for the Latin word *contra* meaning "against."]

con[2] (kon) *v.t.,* **conned, con·ning.** to study carefully; learn very well. [Originally from the Old English word *cunnian* meaning "to try (to know)" or "to test."]

con[3] (kon) *v.t.,* **conned, con·ning.** *Slang.* **1.** to cheat, swindle, or defraud: *The crook conned us out of all our money.* **2.** to trick or dupe: *My pals conned me into paying for everyone's ticket.* —*n.* a swindle. [Short for *confidence.* Such a swindle requires misplaced confidence in the swindler.]

con[4] (kon) *n.* *Slang.* a convict. [Short for *convict.*]

con–, the form of the prefix **com–** before all consonants except *b, h, l, m, p, r,* and *w,* as in *concentrate, congenial.*

con·cave (*adj.,* kon kāv′, kon′kāv; *n.,* kon′kāv) *adj.* curving inward, as the inside of a bowl. —*n.* a concave surface. —**con·cave′ly,** *adv.* —**con·cave′ness,** *n.*

con·cav·i·ty (kon kav′i tē) *n., pl.* **con·cav·i·ties.** **1.** the state of being concave. **2.** a concave surface.

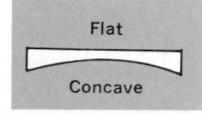

concave lens

con·ceal (kən sēl′) *v.t.* **1.** to put or keep out of sight; hide: *I concealed the key under the dashboard.* **2.** to keep secret: *to conceal anger by smiling.* —**con·ceal′a·ble,** *adj.* —**con·ceal′er,** *n.*

con·ceal·ment (kən sēl′mənt) *n.* **1.** the act of concealing or the state of being concealed. **2.** a means or place for concealing.

con·cede (kən sēd′) *v.,* **con·ced·ed, con·ced·ing.** —*v.t.* **1.** to admit as true: *The candidate conceded defeat in the election.* **2.** to grant or yield: *The small country had to concede land to the invader.* —*v.i.* to make a concession; yield: *The candidate would not concede until all the votes were counted.*

con·ceit (kən sēt′) *n.* **1.** a very high opinion of oneself or of one's achievements; vanity: *Fame and success went to their heads and filled them with conceit.* **2.** a witty or fanciful thought or expression.

con·ceit·ed (kən sē′tid) *adj.* having a very high opinion of oneself or of one's achievements; vain. —**con·ceit′ed·ly,** *adv.* —**con·ceit′ed·ness,** *n.*

con·ceiv·a·ble (kən sē′və bəl) *adj.* capable of being thought of, imagined, or believed; imaginable. —**con·ceiv′a·bil′i·ty,** *n.* —**con·ceiv′a·bly,** *adv.*

con·ceive (kən sēv′) *v.,* **con·ceived, con·ceiv·ing.** —*v.t.* **1.** to form or develop (something) in the mind; devise: *The engineers conceived a design for a new spacecraft.* **2.** to picture (something) in the mind; think of or imagine: *We could not conceive such a thing.* **3. a.** to become pregnant with (a child). **b.** to bring into being in the womb. ▲ used only in the passive: *to be conceived.* —*v.i.* **1.** to form an idea; think: *The team could not conceive of losing.* **2.** to become pregnant. —**con·ceiv′er,** *n.*

con·cen·trate (kon′sən trāt′) *v.,* **con·cen·trat·ed, con·cen·trat·ing.** —*v.t.* **1.** to bring or direct closely to one place, point, or goal; focus or fix on: *The team concentrated their efforts on winning the game.* **2.** to make stronger or thicker: *Boil down the sauce to concentrate its flavor.* —*v.i.* **1.** to direct all of one's efforts or attention: *I could not concentrate on studying because the room was noisy.* **2.** to come closely together in one

place: *The protesters concentrated outside city hall for the rally.* —*n.* something that has been concentrated: *a concentrate of orange juice.* —**con′cen·tra′tor,** *n.*

con·cen·tra·tion (kon′sən trā′shən) *n.* **1.** the act of concentrating or the state of being concentrated. **2.** close attention: *A ringing telephone disturbed my concentration on the problem.* **3.** something concentrated: *There is a concentration of houses along the shore.* **4.** the strength of something, such as a solution.

concentration camp, a camp that is fenced and guarded, used by a government or military ruler to confine prisoners of war or other persons deemed threatening or undesirable.

con·cen·tric (kən sen′trik) *adj.* having a common center: *concentric circles.* Also, **con·cen·tri·cal** (kən sen′tri kəl). —**con·cen′tri·cal·ly,** *adv.*

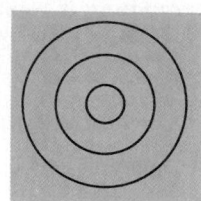

concentric circles

con·cept (kon′sept) *n.* a general idea, especially one based on a person's knowledge or experience: *From observation we arrived at a concept of how the machine worked.*

con·cep·tion (kən sep′shən) *n.* **1.** the act of forming concepts. **2.** a general idea; concept: *It appears that my conception of good manners is different from yours.* **3.** the act of becoming pregnant or of being conceived.

con·cep·tu·al (kən sep′chü əl) *adj.* of or relating to conceptions or concepts: *This drawing is purely conceptual.* —**con·cep′tu·al·ly,** *adv.*

con·cep·tu·al·ize (kən sep′chü ə līz′) *v.,* **con·cep·tu·al·ized, con·cep·tu·al·iz·ing.** —*v.t.* to form a conception or concept of: *I find it difficult to conceptualize what life on Mars would be like.* —*v.i.* to form a conception or concept.

con·cern (kən sûrn′) *v.t.* **1.** to be of interest or importance to; have to do with: *What the president says and does concerns us all.* **2.** to cause to worry; trouble: *Your illness concerns me very much.* —*n.* **1.** something that is of interest or importance to: *What I read is my concern, not yours.* **2.** worried interest: *The students showed much concern for their sick classmate.* **3.** a business establishment; company: *a large clothing concern.*

con·cerned (kən sûrnd′) *adj.* **1.** interested; involved: *to be concerned with politics.* **2.** having or showing worried interest: *to be concerned about poor grades.*

con·cern·ing (kən sûr′ning) *prep.* having to do with; relating to; regarding: *We watched a special program on television concerning skin diving.*

con·cert (kon′sərt) *n.* a public performance of music: *a jazz concert.* —*adj.* of or relating to concerts: *a concert pianist, a concert hall.*

·in concert. toward the same end; together: *We worked in concert to finish the job.*

con·cert·ed (kən sûr′tid) *adj.* planned or carried out by mutual agreement: *The band members made a concerted effort to improve their playing.*

con·cer·ti·na (kon′sər tē′nə) *n.* a musical instrument resembling a small accordion.

con·cer·to (kən cher′tō) *n., pl.* **con·cer·tos** or **con·cer·ti** (kən cher′tē). a musical composition for one or more solo instruments accompanied by an orchestra.

con·ces·sion (kən sesh′ən) *n.* **1.** the act of granting or conceding: *My parents made a concession and allowed me to use the car on weekends.* **2.** something granted or conceded: *The labor union demanded a number of concessions from the factory owner.* **3.** a privilege or right granted by a government or other authority to operate a business at a certain place. **4.** the business itself: *an ice-cream concession.*

con·ces·sion·aire (kən sesh′ə nâr′) *n.* a person who has been granted a concession, as at an athletic stadium or fairground.

conch (kongk, konch) n., pl. **conchs** (kongks) or **conch-es** (kon′chiz). **1.** a saltwater snail having a large spiral shell. **2.** the shell of this snail.

con·cil·i·ate (kən sil′ē āt′) v.t., **con·cil·i·at·ed**, **con·cil·i·at·ing**. **1.** to overcome the hostility or mistrust of; win over; placate: *The shopkeeper tried to conciliate the angry customer by giving a refund.* **2.** to make compatible; reconcile. —**con·cil′i·a′tion**, n. —**con·cil′i·a′tor**, n.

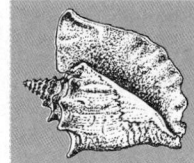

conch *(def. 2)*

con·cil·i·a·to·ry (kən sil′ē ə tôr′ē) adj. meant to or tending to conciliate: *a conciliatory manner.*

con·cise (kən sīs′) adj. expressing what is meant in few words; terse: *The instructions for using the machine were clear and concise.* [From the Latin word *concisus* meaning "divided, short," past participle of *concidere* meaning "to cut to pieces," from the prefix *com-* "with, together" + *caedere* "to cut, strike."] —**con·cise′ly**, adv. —**con·cise′ness**, n.

con·clave (kon′klāv) n. **1.** a private meeting. **2.** a meeting of the cardinals of the Roman Catholic Church to elect a pope.

con·clude (kən klüd′) v., **con·clud·ed**, **con·clud·ing**. —v.t. **1.** to bring to an end; finish: *The lecturer concluded the talk with a joke.* **2.** to arrange or settle finally: *The two countries concluded a treaty.* **3.** to come to an opinion about: *What do you conclude from these facts?* —v.i. to come to an end; close: *The church service concluded with the singing of a hymn.* —**con·clud′er**, n.

con·clu·sion (kən klü′zhən) n. **1.** the final part of something; end: *The conclusion of the movie was very sad.* **2.** a final result or arrangement; settlement: *The conclusion of the deal took place in the lawyer's office.* **3.** a final opinion reached by reasoning: *The judge's conclusion was that the evidence was true.*

con·clu·sive (kən klü′siv) adj. ending argument or doubt; final: *The arrowheads were conclusive evidence that Indians once lived in the area.* —**con·clu′sive·ly**, adv. —**con·clu′sive·ness**, n.

con·coct (kon kokt′, kən kokt′) v.t. **1.** to prepare by mixing several ingredients: *to concoct a stew with beef, potatoes, and carrots.* **2.** to put together; devise: *to concoct a plan.* —**con·coc′tion**, n.

con·com·i·tant (kon kom′i tənt, kən kom′i tənt) adj. accompanying: *a concomitant event.* —n. something that happens with or accompanies something else. —**con·com′i·tant·ly**, adv.

con·cord (kon′kôrd, kong′kôrd) n. **1.** peace and harmony between persons, countries, or things; accord. **2.** a treaty establishing peace and harmony between countries.

con·cord·ance (kon kôr′dəns) n. **1.** agreement; harmony. **2.** an alphabetical index of the important words of a book, such as the Bible, that gives the passages in which the words occur.

con·cord·ant (kon kôr′dənt) adj. agreeing; harmonious: *concordant political views.* —**con·cord′ant·ly**, adv.

con·cor·dat (kon kôr′dat) n. **1.** a formal agreement. **2.** a treaty between the Vatican and a country about church affairs.

con·course (kon′kôrs) n. **1.** a large gathering; crowd. **2.** a large, open place where crowds gather, as in a bus or train station. **3.** a moving or coming together: *a concourse of ideas.*

con·crete (kon′krēt, kon krēt′) n. a mixture of crushed stone or gravel, sand, cement, and water that becomes hard when it dries. —adj. **1.** made of concrete: *a concrete driveway.* **2.** of or relating to things or events that can be seen, felt, or experienced, rather than merely thought about: *A chair is a concrete object.* **3.** of or relating to specific persons, things, or events: *The teacher asked for*

concrete facts about the fall of the Roman Empire. —**con·crete′ly**, adv. —**con·crete′ness**, n.

con·cu·bine (kong′kyə bīn′) n. a woman who lives with a man without marrying him.

con·cur (kən kûr′) v.i., **con·curred**, **con·cur·ring**. **1.** to have the same opinion; agree: *We concur in our interest in sports.* **2.** to act or work together: *Their hard work and intelligence concurred to make them a success.* **3.** to happen at the same time.

con·cur·rence (kən kûr′əns, kən kur′əns) n. **1.** a sharing of the same opinion; agreement. **2.** an acting or working together. **3.** a happening at the same time.

con·cur·rent (kən kûr′ənt, kən kur′ənt) adj. **1.** existing or happening at the same time: *The early development of human society was concurrent with the Ice Age.* **2.** acting together. **3.** in agreement: *concurrent ideas.* —**con·cur′rent·ly**, adv.

con·cus·sion (kən kush′ən) n. **1.** a violent shaking or jarring; shock: *The building shook from the concussion of the explosion.* **2.** an injury caused by a fall or blow, especially to the brain or spine.

con·demn (kən dem′) v.t. **1.** to disapprove of strongly: *They condemned the politician's dishonesty.* **2.** to show or declare the guilt of; convict: *The thief was condemned by the jury.* **3.** to set the punishment of; sentence: *The judge condemned the criminal to ten years in jail.* **4.** to declare to be unfit for further use: *The slum building was condemned and torn down.* **5.** to take (private property) for public use: *to condemn land for a state highway.*

con·dem·na·tion (kon′dem nā′shən, kon′dəm nā′shən) n. **1.** the act of condemning or the state of being condemned. **2.** strong disapproval.

con·den·sate (kon′den sāt′) n. material formed when a substance condenses, as when a gas changes to a liquid.

con·den·sa·tion (kon′den sā′shən, kon′dən sā′shən) n. **1.** the act of condensing or the state of being condensed. **2.** something that results from condensing: *a condensation of a novel.* **3.** the changing of a gas to a liquid or solid form: *the condensation of steam into water.*

con·dense (kən dens′) v., **con·densed**, **con·dens·ing**. —v.t. **1.** to make thicker or more compact; reduce the volume of: *to condense a sauce by boiling it.* **2.** to make shorter and more concise; abridge: *to condense a novel to the length of a short story.* **3.** to change (a gas) into a liquid or solid form. —v.i. to become condensed. —**con·den′sa·ble**, adj.

condensed milk, cow's milk that has been thickened by boiling away part of the water content and sweetened with sugar, used especially in cooking.

con·dens·er (kən den′sər) n. **1.** a person or thing that condenses. **2.** a device that receives and stores an electric charge; capacitor. **3.** an apparatus for changing a gas into a liquid.

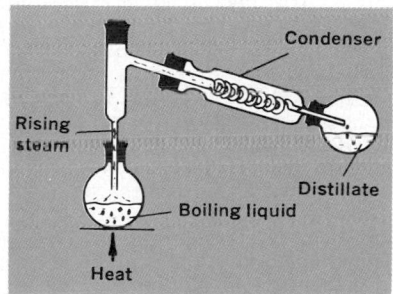

condenser *(def. 3)*

Labels in figure: Condenser; Distillate; Boiling liquid; Rising steam; Heat

at; āpe; fär; câre; end; mē; it; īce; pîerce; hot; ōld; sông, fôrk; oil; out; up; ūse; rüle; pull; tûrn; chin; sing; shop; thin; this; hw in white; zh in treasure. The symbol ə stands for the unstressed vowel sound heard in about, taken, pencil, lemon, and circus.

C

con·de·scend (kon'di send') *v.i.* **1.** to come down willingly to a humbler or lower level: *The scientist condescended and gave a talk to the children.* **2.** to do or say something in a snobbish or superior way.

con·de·scend·ing (kon'di sen'ding) *adj.* characterized by a snobbish or superior manner. —**con·de·scend'ing·ly,** *adv.*

con·de·scen·sion (kon'di sen'shən) *n.* **1.** a coming down to a humbler or lower level. **2.** a snobbish or superior attitude or manner.

con·di·ment (kon'də mənt) *n.* something used to make food more flavorful, such as a seasoning, spice, or sauce.

con·di·tion (kən dish'ən) *n.* **1.** the way that a person or thing is or exists: *The tramp's clothes were in shabby condition. The patient's condition was serious.* **2.** a state of physical fitness: *An athlete must keep in condition.* **3.** social position; rank: *a person of humble condition.* **4.** something needed before something else can take place or exist; something on which another thing depends: *Hard work is usually a condition for getting good grades.* **5.** something that limits or restricts: *My parents set up several conditions for using the car.* **6.** a disease or ailment; illness: *a heart condition.* **7. conditions.** circumstances that affect one's way of life or activities: *poor living conditions, working conditions.* —*v.t.* **1.** to put in a healthy or fit condition: *Regular exercise conditions the body.* **2.** to limit or restrict: *Laziness often conditions a person's success.* **3.** to accustom to: *Living in Alaska soon conditioned us to cold weather.* **4.** to cause to respond in a certain way by repeatedly pairing two stimuli, as a sound and food: *The scientist conditioned the dog to salivate when a bell rang.*

·**on condition that.** provided that; if: *You may go on condition that you come home early.*

con·di·tion·al (kən dish'ə nəl) *adj.* **1.** depending on a condition or conditions. **2.** *Grammar.* expressing a condition. In the sentence *If you go, I will go too, If you go* is a conditional clause. —**con·di'tion·al·ly,** *adv.*

con·di·tioned (kən dish'ənd) *adj.* **1.** having or subject to a condition or conditions. **2.** in good physical condition; fit. **3.** *Psychology.* of or relating to a conditioned response; learned.

con·di·tion·er (kən dish'ə nər) *n.* a substance added or applied to something to maintain or improve its condition: *a shampoo with a hair conditioner.*

con·do (kon'dō) *n., pl.* **con·dos.** *Informal.* a condominium.

con·dole (kən dōl') *v.i.,* **con·doled, con·dol·ing.** to express sympathy; *to condole with a widow.*

con·do·lence (kən dō'ləns) *n.* an expression of sympathy: *We sent our condolences to the family.*

con·dom (kon'dəm) *n.* a sheath used to cover the penis during sexual intercourse to help prevent the spread of sexually transmitted diseases and sometimes as a method of birth control.

con·do·min·i·um (kon'də min'ē əm) *n., pl.* **con·do·min·i·ums. 1.** an apartment house, town house, or the like, or a group of such structures, in which the living units are owned by the individual tenants. **2.** an individual living unit within such a structure or group. [From the Latin prefix *com-* meaning "with, together" + *dominium* meaning "lordship, rule."]

con·done (kən dōn') *v.t.,* **con·doned, con·don·ing.** to excuse or forgive; overlook: *I can't condone bad behavior.* ▲ See **excuse** for usage note.

con·dor (kon'dər, kon'dôr) *n.*

condor

either of two very large vultures having black-and-white feathers and a bare, dark gray head and neck. One species is found in the mountains of South America; the other was formerly found in the mountains of California.

con·duce (kən düs', kən dūs') *v.i.,* **con·duced, con·duc·ing.** to help bring about (with *to* or *toward*): *Getting enough sleep conduces to good health.*

con·du·cive (kən dü'siv, kən dū'siv) *adj.* helping to bring about; leading (with *to*): *A brisk walk is conducive to a good appetite.* —**con·du'cive·ness,** *n.*

con·duct (*n.,* kon'dukt; *v.* kən dukt') *n.* **1.** the way that a person behaves or acts: *The child's conduct was usually very good.* **2.** guidance or control; management: *Successful conduct of the business has made them rich.* —*v.t.* **1.** to take charge of; control; manage: *The copilot conducted the landing very successfully.* **2.** to direct or lead, such as an orchestra, chorus, or other musical group: *Who will conduct the orchestra next season?* **3.** to behave (oneself): *Try to conduct yourself well in front of the guests.* **4.** to act as a guide: *My cousin conducted us safely to the station.* **5.** to transmit or carry: *Cast iron conducts heat evenly. The gutter conducts rainwater from the roof.* —**con·duct'i·bil'i·ty,** *n.* —**con·duct'i·ble,** *adj.*

con·duct·ance (kən duk'təns) *n.* the characteristic of a material that allows it to conduct electric current.

con·duc·tion (kən duk'shən) *n.* **1.** the flow of heat, electricity, or sound by the transmission of energy from one particle to another. **2.** a carrying or conveying: *the conduction of water by pipes.*

con·duc·tive (kən duk'tiv) *adj.* able to conduct heat, electricity, or sound.

con·duc·tiv·i·ty (kon'duk tiv'i tē) *n.* the ability of a material or body to conduct heat, electricity, or sound: *The electrical conductivity of rubber is low. The thermal conductivity of aluminum is high.*

con·duc·tor (kən duk'tər) *n.* **1.** a person who conducts; director; guide; leader. **2.** the director of an orchestra, chorus, or other musical group. **3.** a person on a train, streetcar, or bus who collects the tickets or fares and announces stops. **4.** a material or body that conducts heat, electricity, or sound.

conductor directing an orchestra

con·duit (kon'dü it, kon'dwit, kon'dit) *n.* **1.** a channel, pipe, or tube used to carry liquids. **2.** a tube or pipe that protects electric wires or cables.

cone (kōn) *n.* **1.** a solid that narrows to a point from a circular base. **2.** an object shaped like a cone: *an ice-cream cone.* **3.** a cone-shaped, rounded, or tubular structure with scales that bear seeds, growing on pines and other evergreen trees, and on a few deciduous trees, such as the larch. **4.** a cell in the retina of the eye that is sensitive to color and bright light.

Con·es·to·ga wagon (kon′ə stō′gə) a wagon with an arched canvas top, used by pioneers to cross the American prairies.

co·ney (kō′nē) *n., pl.* **coneys.** another spelling of **cony.**

con·fec·tion (kən fek′shən) *n.* any sweet food or mixture, such as a piece of candy, a preserve, or a pastry.

con·fec·tion·er (kən fek′shə nər) *n.* a person

Conestoga wagon

who makes or sells confections, such as candy or pastry.

con·fec·tion·er·y (kən fek′shə ner′ē) *n., pl.* **con·fec·tion·er·ies.** 1. a place where confections are made or sold. 2. candies or sweets; confections.

con·fed·er·a·cy (kən fed′ər ə sē) *n., pl.* **con·fed·er·a·cies.** 1. a union of countries, states, or persons joined together for a common purpose; league; alliance. 2. **the Confederacy.** the Confederate States of America.

con·fed·er·ate (*n., adj.,* kən fed′ər it; *v.,* kən fed′ə rāt′) *n.* 1. a person or group joined with another for a common purpose; ally. 2. **Confederate.** a person who was a citizen of or fought for the Confederate States of America. —*v.t., v.i.,* **con·fed·er·at·ed, con·fed·er·at·ing.** to unite in a confederacy. —*adj.* 1. united in a confederacy. 2. **Confederate.** of or relating to the Confederate States of America.

Confederate States of America, the union of the eleven southern states that seceded from the United States in 1860 and 1861. They were Alabama, Arkansas, Florida, Georgia, Louisiana, Mississippi, North Carolina, South Carolina, Tennessee, Texas, and Virginia.

con·fed·er·a·tion (kən fed′ə rā′shən) *n.* 1. the act of confederating or the state of being confederated. 2. an alliance of countries or states for a common purpose.

con·fer (kən fûr′) *v.,* **con·ferred, con·fer·ring.** —*v.i.* to meet and talk together; have a discussion: *The bankers conferred before agreeing on the loan.* —*v.t.* to give as a gift or honor: *The general conferred a medal on the soldier.*

con·fer·ence (kon′fər əns) *n.* 1. a meeting for the purpose of talking about something of common interest. 2. an association of schools, churches, athletic teams, or similar groups.

con·fess (kən fes′) *v.t.* 1. to make known or admit: *to confess oneself wrong on a question. The thief confessed guilt.* 2. to make known to a priest: *to confess one's sins.* 3. to hear the confession of: *The priest confessed the parishioners.* —*v.i.* 1. to make known or admit one's guilt: *The prisoner finally confessed.* 2. to confess one's sins to a priest.

con·fess·ed·ly (kən fes′id lē) *adv.* by one's confession or admission; admittedly.

con·fes·sion (kən fesh′ən) *n.* 1. the act of confessing. 2. something that is confessed: *The court accepted the prisoner's confession.*

con·fes·sion·al (kən fesh′ə nəl) *n.* a small enclosed area in a church where a priest hears confessions. —*adj.* of or relating to confession.

con·fes·sor (kən fes′ər) *n.* 1. a priest who hears confessions. 2. a person who confesses.

con·fet·ti (kən fet′ē) *n.* small bits of paper thrown about as a sign of celebration, as at a parade. [From the Italian word *confetti,* plural of *confetto* meaning "confection, candy," going back to the Latin word *conficere* "to prepare," from the prefix *com-* "with, together" + *facere* "to do." At Carnival time, small candies used to be tossed about in celebration. Later, the same word was applied to bits of colored paper tossed in the same way.]

con·fi·dant (kon′fi dant′, kon′fi dänt′, kon′fi dant′,

kon′fi dänt′) *n.* a person to whom one confides secrets or personal matters.

con·fide (kən fīd′) *v.,* **con·fid·ed, con·fid·ing.** —*v.t.* 1. to tell as a secret; entrust (a personal matter): *to confide one's fears to a friend.* 2. to give into another's care; entrust: *They confided their baby into the nurse's care.* —*v.i.* 1. to tell secrets or personal matters: *I confided in my good friend.* 2. to put trust or have faith: *They confide in your good judgment.* —**con·fid′er,** *n.*

con·fi·dence (kon′fi dəns) *n.* 1. firm trust or faith; reliance: *to have confidence in a friend's honesty.* 2. faith in oneself; self-assurance. 3. something told in trust; secret: *My friend entrusted me with several confidences.* ·**in confidence.** privately and as a secret: *I tell you this in confidence.*

con·fi·dent (kon′fi dənt) *adj.* 1. firmly trusting; certain; sure: *I'm confident that our team will win.* 2. having faith in oneself; self-assured. —**con′fi·dent·ly,** *adv.*

con·fi·den·tial (kon′fi den′shəl) *adj.* 1. told or kept in secrecy or privacy: *This letter is confidential.* 2. suggesting confidence: *a confidential manner.* 3. entrusted with secret or private matters: *The executive has a confidential secretary.* —**con′fi·den′tial·ly,** *adv.*

con·fid·ing (kən fī′ding) *adj.* tending to confide; trusting. —**con·fid′ing·ly,** *adv.*

con·fig·u·ra·tion (kən fig′yə rā′shən) *n.* form or shape resulting from the arrangement of parts.

con·fine (*v.,* kən fīn′; *n.,* kon′fin) *v.t.,* **con·fined, con·fin·ing.** 1. to keep within limits; restrict: *Confine your essay to a single page.* 2. to restrict to a particular place; keep or shut in: *The sheriff confined the prisoner in a cell. Illness confined me to bed.* —*n. usually,* **confines.** a limit; boundary; border: *The dog was not permitted within the confines of the house.*

con·fine·ment (kən fīn′mənt) *n.* 1. the act of confining or the state of being confined. 2. the state of being confined because of childbirth.

con·firm (kən fûrm′) *v.t.* 1. to prove to be true or without mistakes; verify: *The senator confirmed the report that the bill would soon come to a vote.* 2. to consent to officially; approve; ratify: *The Senate confirmed the judge's nomination to the Supreme Court.* 3. to make firm or firmer; strengthen: *The flood that followed the fire only confirmed the town's desire to rebuild.* 4. to admit to full membership in a church or synagogue.

con·fir·ma·tion (kon′fər mā′shən) *n.* 1. the act of confirming. 2. something that confirms; proof: *The newspaper waited for confirmation before printing the story.* 3. the rite or ceremony for admitting someone to full membership in a church or synagogue.

con·firmed (kən fûrmd′) *adj.* 1. firmly established; proved. 2. resulting or acting from habit; habitual: *a confirmed bird watcher.* —**con·firm′ed·ly** (kən fur′mid lē), *adv.*

con·fis·cate (kon′fis kāt′) *v.t.,* **con·fis·cat·ed, con·fis·cat·ing.** to seize by authority, as for the public treasury: *The property was confiscated to pay overdue taxes. Customs agents confiscated the smuggled goods.* —**con′fis·ca′tion,** *n.*

con·fla·gra·tion (kon′flə grā′shən) *n.* a very large fire that causes much damage.

con·flict (*n.,* kon′flikt; *v.,* kən flikt′) *n.* 1. a fight, especially one that is drawn out: *A conflict broke out between the two countries.* 2. a struggle between opposing

at; āpe; fär; câre; end; mē; it; īce; pîerce; hot; ōld; sông, fôrk; oil; out; up; ūse; rüle; pull; tûrn; chin; sing; shop; thin; **this**; hw in white; zh in treasure. The symbol ə stands for the unstressed vowel sound heard in about, taken, pencil, lemon, and circus.

C

views or ideas; disagreement: *The reports in the newspapers are in conflict.* —*v.i.* to be opposed; disagree: *The two accounts of the robbery conflict.*

con·flu·ence (kon'flü əns) *n.* **1.** a flowing together: *A confluence of streams forms the river.* **2.** a crowding or coming together of people or things.

con·flu·ent (kon'flü ənt) *adj.* flowing together: *confluent rivers.*

con·form (kən fôrm') *v.i.* **1.** to behave or think in agreement with a rule or standard: *The soldiers conformed to local customs while stationed in the foreign country.* **2.** to be the same or similar; correspond: *The house conformed to the architect's plans.* —*v.t.* to bring into agreement; make the same: *I don't conform my taste in music to that of my friends.* —**con·form'er,** *n.*

confluence at Pittsburgh, Pa.

con·form·a·ble (kən fôr'mə bəl) *adj.* **1.** corresponding; similar. **2.** obedient: *to be conformable to authority.* —**con·form'a·bly,** *adv.*

con·form·ance (kən fôr'məns) *n.* conformity.

con·for·ma·tion (kon'fôr mā'shən) *n.* **1.** the way in which the parts of something are arranged; shape or structure: *the conformation of a mountain.* **2.** the act of conforming or the state of being conformed.

con·form·ist (kən fôr'mist) *n.* a person who conforms to standard or popular beliefs or practices.

con·form·i·ty (kən fôr'mi tē) *n., pl.* **con·form·i·ties.** **1.** agreement or similarity: *The school insisted on conformity in dress.* **2.** behavior or thought in agreement with a rule or standard.

con·found (kon found', kən found') *v.t.* **1.** to put in a state of confusion; bewilder: *The arithmetic problem confounded the student.* **2.** to mistake one thing for another; confuse: *to confound a dream for reality.* —**con·found'ed·ly,** *adv.*

con·front (kən frunt') *v.t.* **1.** to come or bring face to face with: *A difficult decision confronted us.* **2.** to face boldly or with defiance: *to confront the enemy.* —**con'fron·ta'tion,** *n.*

Con·fu·cian·ism (kən fū'shə niz'əm) *n.* a social and ethical system based on the teachings of Confucius and his followers, emphasizing the maintenance of peace and justice and devotion to one's family and ancestors.

con·fuse (kən fūz') *v.t.,* **con·fused, con·fus·ing.** **1.** to fill with doubt or uncertainty; bewilder; perplex: *Confused by the street signs, I took the wrong turn.* **2.** to take (one person or thing) for another; mistake; mix up: *People are always confusing me with my cousin.* **3.** to throw into disorder: *to confuse items that had been sorted.* **4.** to embarrass. —**con·fus·ed·ly** (kən fū'zid lē), **con·fus'ing·ly,** *adv.*

con·fu·sion (kən fū'zhən) *n.* **1.** the state of being confused; bewilderment or disorder: *My confusion prevented me from answering the question correctly. The noise and confusion in the room made studying difficult.* **2.** a mistaking or mixing up of one person or thing for another. **3.** embarrassment.

con·fute (kən fūt') *v.t.,* **con·fut·ed, con·fut·ing.** to prove false or wrong; disprove: *The facts confute the argument. The two debaters confuted their opponents.* —**con·fut'a·ble,** *adj.* —**con·fu·ta·tion** (kon'fyü tā'shən) *n.* —**con·fut'er,** *n.*

Cong. **1.** Congregational. **2.** Congressional.

con·ga (kong'gə) *n.* **1.** a dance of Cuban origin in which

dancers form a single line and follow each other across the dance floor. **2.** the fast music for this dance.

con·geal (kən jēl') *v.i.* **1.** to change from a liquid to a solid by cooling or freezing: *Oil congeals in cold weather.* **2.** to thicken or coagulate. —*v.t.* to change (something) from a liquid to a solid. —**con·geal'a·ble,** *adj.* —**con·geal'er,** *n.* —**con·geal'ment,** *n.*

con·gen·ial (kən jēn'yəl) *adj.* **1.** having similar tastes and interests: *congenial friends.* **2.** to a person's liking; agreeable; pleasant: *a congenial job, a congenial atmosphere.* —**con·ge·ni·al·i·ty** (kən jē'nē al'i tē), *n.* —**con·gen'ial·ly,** *adv.*

con·gen·i·tal (kən jen'i təl) *adj.* existing before or from the time of birth: *a congenital heart defect.* —**con·gen'i·tal·ly,** *adv.*

con·ger (kong'gər) *n.* any of a group of large eels found in warm salt waters, valued as food. Also, **conger eel.**

con·gest (kən jest') *v.t.* **1.** to fill so full as to overcrowd: *On weekends, automobiles congest the highways near the city.* **2.** to fill (an organ or other part of the body) with too great an amount of blood, mucus, or other matter. —*v.i.* to become congested.

con·ges·tion (kən jes'chən) *n.* **1.** an overcrowded condition: *There was congestion in the skies around the airport.* **2.** too great an amount of blood, mucus, or other matter in an organ or part of the body: *I had a sore throat and congestion in my nasal passages.*

con·glom·er·ate (*v.,* kən glom'ə rāt'; *adj., n.,* kən glom'ər it) *v.,* **con·glom·er·at·ed, con·glom·er·at·ing.** —*v.t.* to collect together into a mass or heap. —*v.i.* to be collected together into a mass or heap. —*adj.* **1.** massed together. **2.** clustered into or forming a mass: *conglomerate rock.* —*n.*

conglomerate (*n.,* def. 2)

1. a mass formed of different parts. **2.** sedimentary rock formed of pebbles or gravel cemented together by some material, such as clay. **3.** a corporation formed of many different companies.

con·glom·er·a·tion (kən glom'ə rā'shən) *n.* **1.** a mass formed of different parts. **2.** the act of conglomerating.

Con·go·lese (kong'gə lēz', kong'gə lēs') *n., pl.* **Con·go·lese.** **1.** a person who was born in or is a citizen of the Congo. **2.** a person who was a citizen of the Republic of the Congo, now called Zaire. —*adj.* of or relating to either the Congo or the former Democratic Republic of the Congo, their people, or their culture.

con·go snake (kong'gō) a salamander resembling an eel and having two pairs of small, weak legs. The congo snake is found in swampy regions of the southern United States. Also, **congo eel.**

con·grat·u·late (kən grach'ə lāt') *v.t.,* **con·grat·u·lat·ed, con·grat·u·lat·ing.** to express one's happiness or pleasure at the success or good fortune of: *We congratulated the newlyweds.*

congo snake

con·grat·u·la·tion (kən grach'ə lā'shən) *n.* **1.** the act of congratulating. **2. congratulations.** an expression of happiness or pleasure at another's success or good fortune.

con·grat·u·la·to·ry (kən grach'ə lə tôr'ē) *adj.* expressing congratulation: *a congratulatory telegram.*

con·gre·gate (kong'gri gāt') *v.i.,* **con·gre·gat·ed, con·gre·gat·ing.** to come together in a crowd or mass; assemble: *The fans congregated around the movie star.*

[From the Latin word *congregatus*, past participle of *congregare* meaning "to assemble," going back to the prefix *com-* "with, together" and *grex* "flock."]

con·gre·ga·tion (kong′gri gā′shən) *n.* **1.** the act of coming together in a crowd or mass. **2.** a gathering of people, especially for a religious service. **3.** a collection of things.

con·gre·ga·tion·al (kong′gri gā′shə nəl) *adj.* **1.** of or relating to a congregation. **2. Congregational.** of or relating to a Protestant denomination holding that each church is independent and responsible only to Jesus.

Con·gre·ga·tion·al·ist (kong′gri gā′shə nə list) *n.* a member of a Congregational church.

con·gress (kong′gris) *n., pl.* **con·gress·es.** **1.** the lawmaking body of any of various countries, especially of a republic. **2. Congress.** a branch of the U.S. government that makes laws, made up of the Senate and the House of Representatives. **3.** a formal meeting, as of representatives, to discuss a matter of common interest: *a medical congress.*

con·gres·sion·al (kən gresh′ə nəl) *adj.* **1.** of or relating to a congress. **2. Congressional.** of or relating to Congress.

con·gress·man (kong′gris mən) *n., pl.* **con·gress·men** (kong′gris mən). a member of Congress, especially of the House of Representatives.

con·gress·wom·an (kong′gris wùm′ən) *n., pl.* **con·gress·wom·en** (kong′gris wim′ən). a woman who is a member of Congress, especially of the House of Representatives.

con·gru·ence (kong′grü əns, kən grü′əns) *n.* the state of being congruent; agreement. Also, **con·gru·en·cy** (kong′grü ən sē, kən grü′ən sē).

con·gru·ent (kong′grü ənt, kən grü′ənt) *adj.* **1.** agreeing in every way; harmonious: *congruent beliefs.* **2.** *Geometry.* exactly alike in shape and size. Two triangles are congruent if the sides and angles of one are equal to the sides and angles of the other. **—con·gru′ent·ly,** *adv.*

con·gru·i·ty (kən grü′i tē) *n.* the state of being congruous; agreement; harmony.

con·gru·ous (kong′grü əs) *adj.* harmoniously related; suitable; fitting. **—con′gru·ous·ness,** *n.*

con·i·cal (kon′i kəl) *adj.* **1.** shaped like a cone. **2.** of or relating to a cone. Also, **con·ic** (kon′ik). **—con′i·cal·ly,** *adv.*

co·ni·fer (kon′ə fər, kō′nə fər) *n.* any of a large group of trees and shrubs that bear cones. Most conifers, such as the firs, spruces, and pines, are evergreen and bear needle-shaped leaves.

co·nif·er·ous (kō nif′ər əs) *adj.* **1.** bearing cones. **2.** of or relating to the conifers.

conj. **1.** conjugation. **2.** conjunction.

con·jec·tur·al (kən jek′chər əl) *adj.* based on or involving conjecture: *a conjectural solution to a problem.* **—con·jec′tur·al·ly,** *adv.*

con·jec·ture (kən jek′chər) *n.* **1.** the act of forming an opinion not based on proof. **2.** an opinion or conclusion so formed; guess: *Our conclusions about life elsewhere in the universe are all conjecture.* **—v., con·jec·tured, con·jec·tur·ing.** **—v.i.** to form an opinion not based on proof; guess: *The scientist conjectured about how the world began.* **—v.t.** to form an opinion about (something) without proof.

con·join (kən join′) *v.t.* to join together; unite. **—v.i.** to join together; unite: *The two countries conjoined to form an alliance.* **—con·join′er,** *n.*

con·joint (kən joint′) *adj.* joined together; united. **—con·joint′ly,** *adv.*

con·ju·gal (kon′jə gəl) *adj.* relating to marriage: *conjugal happiness.* **—con′ju·gal·ly,** *adv.*

con·ju·gate (*v.,* kon′jə gāt′; *adj.,* kon′jə git) *v.,* **con·ju·gat·ed, con·ju·gat·ing.** **—v.t.** to give the different forms of (a verb) in a certain order. The present tense of the verb "to be" is conjugated: *I am, you are, he, she,* or *it is, we are, you are, they are.* **—v.i.** *Biology.* to join together in conjugation. **—adj.** joined together, especially in pairs; coupled. [From the Latin word *conjugatus,* past participle of *conjugare* meaning "to join together" and "to marry," from the prefix *com-* "with, together" + *jugare* "to join."]

con·ju·ga·tion (kon′jə gā′shən) *n.* **1.** the act of conjugating or the state of being conjugated. **2.** the different forms of a verb, indicating tense, person, number, and mood. **3.** *Biology.* the temporary joining together of two similar cells with an accompanying transfer of hereditary material.

con·junc·tion (kən jungk′shən) *n.* **1.** the act of joining together or the state of being joined together. **2.** a word used to connect words, phrases, clauses, or sentences. *And, but,* and *if* are conjunctions. **3.** *Astronomy.* the apparent meeting of two or more planets or other heavenly bodies at the same celestial longitude.

con·junc·ti·va (kon′jungk tī′və) *n., pl.* **con·junc·ti·vas** or **con·junc·ti·vae** (kon′jungk tī′vē). the membrane that covers the front of the eyeball and lines the inner surface of the eyelids.

con·junc·tive (kən jungk′tiv) *adj.* joining together; connecting; uniting. **—con·junc′tive·ly,** *adv.*

con·junc·ti·vi·tis (kən jungk′tə vī′tis) *n.* an inflammation of the conjunctiva; pinkeye.

con·ju·ra·tion (kon′jə rā′shən, kun′jə rā′shən) *n.* **1.** a set form of words used in conjuring; incantation; spell. **2.** the practice or performance of magic. **3.** a summoning of supernatural beings by using a sacred name.

con·jure (kon′jər, kun′jər) *v.,* **con·jured, con·jur·ing.** **—v.t.** to summon or cause (something) to appear by using magic words: *The sorcerer conjured spirits.* **—v.i.** **1.** to summon demons or spirits by means of spells; practice sorcery. **2.** to perform magic tricks.
·to conjure up. to cause to appear or to bring about by or as if by magic: *The chef conjured up a delicious meal.*

con·jur·er (kon′jər ər, kun′jər ər) *also,* **con·ju·ror.** *n.* **1.** a wizard; sorcerer. **2.** a person who does magic tricks; magician.

Conn., Connecticut.

con·nect (kə nekt′) *v.t.* **1.** to join or fasten together; unite; link: *The workers connected the boxcar to the freight train. A highway connects the two towns.* **2.** to think of as having a close relationship: *We often connect clowns with circuses.* **3.** to have as an associated part or feature: *a dinner connected with a political campaign. Poor business at the resort was connected with bad weather.* **—v.i.** **1.** to be or become joined; meet: *This wire connects with the television antenna. The two rooms connect.* **2.** (of buses, trains, or airplanes) to be scheduled so that passengers can change from one route to another. **—con·nect′er;** *also,* **con·nec·tor,** *n.* **—con·nect′i·ble,** *adj.*

con·nec·tion (kə nek′shən) *n.* **1.** the act of connecting; linking up: *The connection of the pipes under the sink was difficult work.* **2.** the state of being connected; relationship or association: *The teacher's connection with the school lasted many years. They studied the connection between conditions in the slums and disease.* **3.** something that connects; connecting part; link: *a faulty connection in wiring.* **4.** a related person; distant relative: *a connec-*

at; āpe; fär; câre; end; mē; it; īce; pîerce; hot; ōld; sông, fôrk; oil; out; up; ūse; rüle; pùll; tûrn; chin; sing; shop; thin; this; hw in white; zh in treasure. The symbol ə stands for the unstressed vowel sound heard in about, taken, pencil, lemon, and circus.

tion by marriage. **5.** a person with whom one has a useful relationship: *I got the job through a business connection.* **6.** a scheduling of buses, trains, or airplanes that allows the passenger to change from one route to another: *After my train arrives in New Orleans, I have to make a plane connection to Chicago.*

con·nec·tive (kə nek′tiv) *adj.* tending or serving to connect. —*n.* **1.** something that connects. **2.** a word used to connect words, phrases, and clauses. Conjunctions and relative pronouns are connectives.

connective tissue, tissue, such as cartilage or bone, that serves to connect and support other tissues and organs.

con·ning tower (kon′ing) **1.** a structure on the deck of a submarine, used as an entrance and for observation. **2.** the armored pilothouse on the deck of a warship.

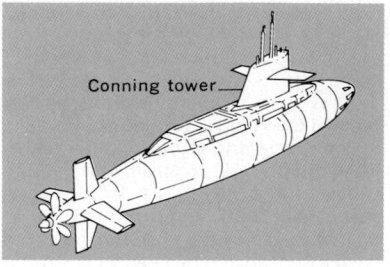

Conning tower

conning tower *(def. 1)*

con·niv·ance (kə nī′vəns) *n.* the act of conniving.

con·nive (kə nīv′) *v.i.,* **con·nived, con·niv·ing. 1.** to permit or encourage wrongdoing by overlooking or pretending not to know about it: *The city official connived at health code violations.* **2.** to cooperate secretly; conspire. —**con·niv′er,** *n.*

con·nois·seur (kon′ə sûr′) *n.* a person who is able to judge something, such as the fine arts, because of good taste and expert knowledge. [From the obsolete French word *connoisseur* meaning "one who knows," from the Old French word *connoistre* "to know," from the Latin word *cognoscere* "to know, understand."]

con·no·ta·tion (kon′ə tā′shən) *n.* a meaning that a word or phrase suggests in addition to its literal meaning. The word *summer,* for example, may have the connotation of hot weather, vacation, and picnics.

con·note (kə nōt′) *v.t.,* **con·not·ed, con·not·ing.** to suggest a meaning in addition to the literal meaning: *The word "red" is the name of a color but it can also connote danger.* ▲ See **denote** for usage note. —**con′no·ta·tive,** *adj.*

con·nu·bi·al (kə nü′bē əl, kə nū′bē əl) *adj.* relating to or characteristic of marriage.

con·quer (kong′kər) *v.t.* **1.** to get possession of by force: *to conquer a country.* **2.** to overcome by force; defeat; vanquish: *to conquer an enemy.* **3.** to overcome by one's own effort: *I finally conquered my shyness.* —*v.i.* to be victorious. —**con′quer·a·ble,** *adj.*

con·quer·or (kong′kər ər) *n.* a person who conquers.

con·quest (kon′kwest, kong′kwest) *n.* **1.** the act of conquering or the fact of having conquered. **2.** something conquered: *Mexico was once a conquest of Spain.*

con·quis·ta·dor (kon kēs′tə dôr′, kon kwis′tə dôr′) *n., pl.* **con·quis·ta·dors** or **con·quis·ta·do·res** (kon-kēs′tə dôr′ās, kon kēs′tə dôr′ēz). a Spanish conqueror in Mexico and Peru during the sixteenth century. [From the Spanish word *conquistador,* from *conquistar* meaning "to conquer," going back to the Latin word *conquirere* "to seek for, collect," from the prefix *com-* "with, together" + *quaerere* "to ask, seek."]

con·san·guin·i·ty (kon′sang gwin′i tē) *n.* kinship by descent from the same ancestor; relationship by blood.

con·science (kon′shəns) *n.* a sense or understanding of what is right and what is wrong that prompts a person to do right.

con·sci·en·tious (kon′shē en′shəs) *adj.* **1.** guided by one's conscience: *to be conscientious in one's dealings*

with people. **2.** capable of or showing much thought and care; painstaking: *a conscientious student, to do conscientious work.* —**con′sci·en′tious·ly,** *adv.* —**con′sci·en′tious·ness,** *n.*

conscientious objector, a person whose religious beliefs or conscience will not allow fighting in a war.

con·scious (kon′shəs) *adj.* **1.** knowing or realizing; aware: *I was conscious of a cat brushing against my leg.* **2.** awake and able to sense things: *Despite the blow on the head, the miner remained conscious.* **3.** felt by or known to oneself: *conscious anger.* **4.** done on purpose; deliberate: *I made a conscious effort to remain calm.* —**con′scious·ly,** *adv.*

con·scious·ness (kon′shəs nis) *n.* **1.** the state of being conscious; awareness: *I lost consciousness after I fell down the stairs.* **2.** all of a person's feelings and thoughts.

con·script (*v.,* kən skript′; *adj., n.,* kon′skript) *v.t.* to force (someone) by law to serve in the armed forces; draft. —*adj.* drafted. —*n.* a person who is forced by law to serve in the armed forces; draftee.

con·scrip·tion (kən skrip′shən) *n.* forced enrollment in a country's armed forces by law; draft: *to raise an army by conscription.*

con·se·crate (kon′si krāt) *v.t.,* **con·se·crat·ed, con·se·crat·ing. 1.** to make or declare holy: *to consecrate a shrine.* **2.** to dedicate or devote to a particular purpose: *to consecrate one's life to helping the poor.* —**con′se·cra′tion,** *n.* —**con′se·cra′tor,** *n.*

con·sec·u·tive (kən sek′yə tiv) *adj.* following one after another without a break: *1, 2, 3, and 4 are consecutive whole numbers. Our team won ten consecutive games.* —**con·sec′u·tive·ly,** *adv.* —**con·sec′u·tive·ness,** *n.*

con·sen·sus (kən sen′səs) *n.* a general agreement or opinion: *The consensus of the townspeople favored the new highway.* ▲ It is repetitious to say "consensus of opinion" because **consensus** means the general opinion.

con·sent (kən sent′) *v.i.* to give one's permission; agree to: *My parents would not consent to my request to use the car.* —*n.* an allowing or agreement: *You have my consent to sign the contract.*

con·se·quence (kon′si kwens′) *n.* **1.** something that results from an earlier action or happening; outcome: *You must suffer the consequences of your bad behavior.* **2.** importance: *Their opinion is of little consequence to me.*

con·se·quent (kon′si kwent′, kon′si kwənt) *adj.* following as a result or effect: *a heavy rainfall and consequent flood.*

con·se·quen·tial (kon′si kwen′shəl) *adj.* **1.** following as a result or effect. **2.** of consequence; important: *Your opinion is more consequential to me than what the others say.* **3.** self-important. —**con′se·quen′tial·ly,** *adv.*

con·se·quent·ly (kon′si kwent′lē, kon′si kwənt lē) *adv.* as a result; therefore: *I didn't study, and consequently I failed.*

con·ser·va·tion (kon′sər vā′shən) *n.* a preserving or protecting from loss, harm, or waste, especially the preserving or protecting of natural resources, such as forests, rivers, and wildlife.

con·ser·va·tion·ist (kon′sər vā′shə nist) *n.* a person who supports the preserving or protecting of natural resources.

conservation of energy, a principle of physics stating that energy can be neither created nor destroyed, but can only be changed from one form to another.

conservation of mass, a principle of physics stating that mass can be neither created nor destroyed, and that the total mass of a system remains constant regardless of the interaction of its parts.

conservation of mass and energy, a principle of physics stating that the total amount of mass and energy in a system remains constant, although mass may be converted into energy and energy converted into mass within the system.

con·serv·a·tism (kən sûr′və tiz′əm) *n.* a preference for things as they are or have been; opposition to change.

con·serv·a·tive (kən sûr′və tiv) *adj.* **1.** preferring things as they are or have been; opposing change. **2.** *also,* **Conservative.** of or belonging to a political party that is generally opposed to major change and favors the preservation of existing, or restoration of former, institutions, traditions, and practices. **3.** cautious; moderate: *a conservative investor, a conservative estimate.* **4.** showing traditional taste: *conservative clothes.* **5. Conservative.** of, relating to, or practicing Conservative Judaism. —*n.* **1.** a person who is conservative, especially in politics or religion. **2.** *also,* **Conservative.** a member of a conservative political party. —**con·serv′a·tive·ly,** *adv.* —**con·serv′a·tive·ness,** *n.*

Conservative Judaism, the branch of Judaism that preserves most traditional Jewish religious practices but adopts change when necessary to accommodate modern circumstances.

con·serv·a·to·ry (kən sûr′və tôr′ē) *n., pl.* **con·serv·a·to·ries.** **1.** a school of music or other arts. **2.** a greenhouse for growing and displaying plants.

con·serve (*v.,* kən sûrv′; *n.,* kon′sûrv′, kən sûrv′) *v.t.* **con·served, con·serv·ing.** **1.** to preserve or protect from loss, harm, or waste; keep safe: *Conserve your strength for the game.* **2.** to preserve with sugar: *to conserve fruit.* —*n. also,* **conserves.** preserves, especially a mixture of two or more fruits stewed in sugar, often with raisins and nuts.

con·sid·er (kən sid′ər) *v.t.* **1.** to think seriously or carefully about: *The coach asked me to consider playing on the team.* **2.** to think to be; regard as; believe: *This is considered the finest view of the valley.* **3.** to take into account; keep in mind: *This car is in good shape, when you consider its age.* **4.** to think of; have regard for (others and their feelings): *You think only of yourself and never consider anyone else.* —*v.i.* to think carefully.

con·sid·er·a·ble (kən sid′ər ə bəl) *adj.* **1.** highly thought of; important: *a considerable figure in the community.* **2.** great in amount or extent: *That pianist has considerable talent.* —**con·sid′er·a·bly,** *adv.*

con·sid·er·ate (kən sid′ər it) *adj.* having or showing regard for others and their feelings; thoughtful: *It was considerate of you to drive us to the airport.* —**con·sid′er·ate·ly,** *adv.* —**con·sid′er·ate·ness,** *n.*

con·sid·er·a·tion (kən sid′ə rā′shən) *n.* **1.** the act of thinking seriously or carefully about something; careful thought: *After long consideration, I decided to sell the car.* **2.** something that should be considered; reason: *The car's low price and good condition were two considerations for buying it.* **3.** regard for others and their feelings; thoughtfulness; respect: *You can show consideration for others by listening to what they have to say.* **4.** something given in payment; fee: *The carpenter refuses to do any extra work except for a consideration.*

·**in consideration of. a.** because of; in view of. **b.** in return for: *I received a gold watch in consideration of my many years with the company.*

·**to take into consideration.** to make allowances for; take into account: *In passing sentence, the judge took into consideration the fact that it was the youth's first offense.*

·**under consideration.** being considered: *Several people were under consideration for the job.*

con·sid·ered (kən sid′ərd) *adj.* carefully thought out: *a considered reply.*

con·sid·er·ing (kən sid′ər ing) *prep.* taking into account; in view of: *Considering that it has been snowing all day, the roads aren't in bad shape.*

con·sign (kən sīn′) *v.t.* **1.** to hand over formally; transfer or deliver: *They consigned the property to their children.* **2.** to send or deliver (merchandise): *The dealer consigned the toys to the storekeeper.* —**con·sign′a·ble,** *adj.*

con·sign·ment (kən sīn′mənt) *n.* **1.** the act of consigning or the state of being consigned. **2.** something sent or delivered: *A consignment of radios arrived at the warehouse.*

con·sist (kən sist′) *v.i.* **1.** to be made up or composed: *Bricks consist mostly of clay.* **2.** to be contained or exist: *Good health consists partly in eating properly.*

con·sist·en·cy (kən sis′tən sē) *n., pl.* **con·sist·en·cies.** **1.** the degree of firmness, thickness, or stiffness: *That paint has a consistency like glue.* **2.** a keeping to a particular way of thinking or acting: *Their life had little consistency, as they were continually moving around.* **3.** agreement or harmony: *There is a consistency between the old and new parts of the building.* Also, **con·sist·ence** (kən sis′təns).

con·sist·ent (kən sis′tənt) *adj.* **1.** keeping to a particular way of thinking or acting: *They were consistent in going to the movies every weekend.* **2.** in agreement or harmony: *The story they told the police was not consistent with the facts brought out in the trial.* —**con·sist′ent·ly,** *adv.*

con·sis·to·ry (kən sis′tə rē) *n., pl.* **con·sis·to·ries.** a council or court of a church, especially a meeting of cardinals of the Roman Catholic Church for taking care of church business.

con·so·la·tion (kon sə lā′shən) *n.* **1.** the act of consoling. **2.** someone or something that consoles.

consolation prize, an award given to a person who competes in a contest but does not win.

con·sole¹ (kən sōl′) *v.t.,* **con·soled, con·sol·ing.** to comfort or cheer (someone) in grief or sorrow; solace: *I tried to console the weeping child.* [From the French word *consoler* meaning "to console," from the Latin word *consolari* with the same meaning.]

con·sole² (kon′sōl) *n.* **1.** the cabinet of a radio, television set, or phonograph that rests on the floor. **2.** the desklike case of an organ, containing the keyboard, stops, and pedals. **3.** a table supported against a wall by brackets or by legs resembling brackets. [From the French word *console* meaning "bracket" and "console table."]

con·sol·i·date (kən sol′i dāt′) *v.t.* **con·sol·i·dat·ed, con·sol·i·dat·ing.** **1.** to join together; unite; combine: *We consolidated our savings and bought a baseball bat.* **2.** to make secure or strong: *The army consolidated its position by building fortifications.*

con·sol·i·da·tion (kən sol′i dā′shən) *n.* the act of consolidating or the state of being consolidated.

con·som·mé (kon′sə mā′) *n.* a clear soup made from the stock of meat, poultry, or vegetables.

con·so·nance (kon′sə nəns) *n.* **1.** harmony; agreement. **2.** a harmony of sounds, especially of tones in music.

con·so·nant (kon′sə nənt) *n.* **1.** a speech sound made by blocking the passage of air through the mouth with the lips, teeth, or tongue. **2.** any letter of the alphabet representing such a sound, such as *d, f,* or *p.* —*adj.* **1.** in agreement or harmony. **2.** consonantal. —**con′so·nant·ly,** *adv.*

con·so·nan·tal (kon′sə nan′təl) *adj.* relating to or having one or more consonants.

con·sort (*n.,* kon′sôrt; *v.,* kən sôrt′) *n.* **1.** a husband or wife; spouse. **2.** a ship that accompanies another. —*v.i.* to keep company; associate: *I don't consort with liars.*

con·spic·u·ous (kən spik′ū əs) *adj.* **1.** easily seen: *a conspicuous stain on the rug.* **2.** attracting attention; striking: *Your bright red jacket is very conspicuous in the*

---

at; āpe; fär; câre; end; mē; it; īce; pîerce; hot; ōld; sông, fôrk; oil; out; up; ūse; rūle; pùll; tûrn; chin; sing; shop; thin; this; hw in white; zh in treasure. The symbol ə stands for the unstressed vowel sound heard in about, taken, pencil, lemon, and circus.

C

crowd.   The party was a conspicuous success.   **—con·spic′u·ous·ly,** *adv.*   **—con·spic′u·ous·ness,** *n.*

con·spir·a·cy (kən spir′ə sē) *n., pl.* **con·spir·a·cies.** **1.** the act of secretly planning together to perform some evil or illegal act. **2.** a plan that has been made; plot. **3.** a group making such a plan.

con·spir·a·tor (kən spir′ə tər) *n.*   a person who conspires; plotter.

con·spire (kən spīr′) *v.i.,* **con·spired, con·spir·ing.** **1.** to plan a conspiracy; plot: *The rebels conspired to overthrow the government.* **2.** to work or act together: *All things conspired to make it a perfect day for the hike.* **—con·spir′er,** *n.*

con·sta·ble (kon′stə bəl, kun′stə bəl) *n.* **1.** a public officer, usually in a small town or rural area, with somewhat less power than a sheriff. **2.** *British.* a police officer.

con·stab·u·lar·y (kən stab′yə ler′ē) *n., pl.* **con·stab·u·lar·ies.** **1.** all the constables of a district. **2.** a police force organized on military lines, but not part of the regular army.

con·stan·cy (kon′stən sē) *n.* **1.** the condition of remaining unchanged: *The constancy of the good weather made our vacation enjoyable.* **2.** unchanging devotion or loyalty; steadfastness; faithfulness: *to show constancy in friendships.*

con·stant (kon′stənt) *adj.* **1.** not subject to change; remaining the same; unchanging: *The weather has been constant this week.* **2.** continuing without a break; happening over and over again; continual: *constant chatter.* **3.** loyal; steadfast; faithful: *a constant friend.* **—***n.* something that does not change: *The value of pi, or* π, *is a mathematical constant.* **—con′stant·ly,** *adv.*

con·stel·la·tion (kon′stə lā′shən) *n.* **1.** a group of stars forming a pattern that suggests an object, animal, or mythological character: *Ursa Major is a constellation.* **2.** *Astrology.* a grouping of the planets and stars that are said to influence a person's character and fate. **3.** a brilliant or distinguished group of people. [From the Middle French word *constellation,* going back to the Latin prefix *com-* ''with, together'' + *stella* ''star.'']

con·ster·na·tion (kon′stər nā′shən) *n.* a feeling of alarm or amazement leading to confusion or fear: *We discovered to our consternation that the house was on fire.*

con·sti·pate (kon′stə pāt′) *v.t.,* **con·sti·pat·ed, con·sti·pat·ing.** to cause constipation in.

con·sti·pa·tion (kon′stə pā′shən) *n.* a condition marked by difficult or irregular bowel movements.

con·stit·u·en·cy (kən stich′ü ən sē) *n., pl.* **con·stit·u·en·cies.** **1.** all the voters in a district who elect a legislator to represent them. **2.** the district represented.

con·stit·u·ent (kən stich′ü ənt) *adj.* **1.** needed as a part; serving to form a whole; component: *Hydrogen and oxygen are the constituent parts of water.* **2.** having the authority to establish a government, or to create or amend a constitution: *a constituent assembly.* **—***n.* **1.** a part that is needed to form a whole; component: *Wood pulp is an important constituent of paper.* **2.** a person who elects another as a representative; voter: *The senator's constituents were in favor of lower taxes.*

con·sti·tute (kon′sti tüt′, kon′sti tūt′) *v.t.,* **con·sti·tut·ed, con·sti·tut·ing.** **1.** to make up; compose; form: *Four quarts constitute a gallon.* **2.** to appoint: *We constituted a committee to plan the dance.* **3.** to set up; establish: *The city council constituted new traffic regulations.*

con·sti·tu·tion (kon′sti tü′shən, kon′sti tū′shən) *n.* **1.** the way in which something is made up; physical make-up or composition: *The athlete has a strong constitution.* **2.** the fundamental principles by which a country, state, or other organized group is governed. **3. the Constitution.** the document containing the supreme law and plan of government of the United States. **4.** the act of constituting; establishment.

con·sti·tu·tion·al (kon′sti tü′shə nəl, kon′sti tū′shə nəl) *adj.* **1.** of or relating to the constitution of a person or thing: *to have a constitutional weakness in one's lungs.* **2.** of, coming from, in agreement with, or controlled by a constitution: *constitutional amendments, constitutional rights.   The United States has a constitutional form of government.* **—***n.* a walk taken for one's health. **—con′sti·tu′tion·al·ly,** *adv.*

con·sti·tu·tion·al·i·ty (kon′sti tü′shə nal′i tē, kon′sti tū′shə nal′i tē) *n.* agreement with a constitution of a country, state, or other organized group: *The constitutionality of the new law was questioned.*

con·strain (kən strān′) *v.t.* **1.** to make (someone) do something; force or obligate: *Conscience constrained me to do the right thing.* **2.** to hold back; restrain: *to constrain one's anger.   The prisoner was constrained by handcuffs.* **—con·strain′ed·ly** (kən strā′nid lē), *adv.* **—con·strain′er,** *n.*

con·straint (kən strānt′) *n.* **1.** a holding back of natural feelings; restraint: *The children showed respectful constraint during the ceremony.* **2.** force or obligation: *The horse slowed under constraint from the reins.*

con·strict (kən strikt′) *v.t.* to make smaller or narrower by or as by pressing together; squeeze; compress: *to constrict a blood vessel with a tourniquet.* **—con·stric′tive,** *adj.*

con·stric·tion (kən strik′shən) *n.* **1.** the act of constricting or the state of being constricted. **2.** something that constricts or is constricted. **—con·stric′tive,** *adj.*

con·stric·tor (kən strik′tər) *n.* **1.** something that constricts. **2.** any of various snakes, such as the python, boa, and anaconda, that kill by squeezing their prey and suffocating it. **3.** a muscle that tightens or compresses a part of the body.

con·struct (kən strukt′) *v.t.* to put together; build: *The builders constructed a shed in the backyard.* **—con·struc′tor,** *n.*

con·struc·tion (kən struk′shən) *n.* **1.** the act or process of constructing: *The construction of the skyscraper was started a year ago.* **2.** the way in which something is constructed: *The old house is of good construction.* **3.** something constructed; structure. **4.** the way in which something is understood; interpretation; explanation: *to put the wrong construction on someone's comments.* **5.** *Grammar.* the arrangement of words to form a sentence, clause, or phrase. **—con·struc′tion·al,** *adj.* **—con·struc′tion·al·ly,** *adv.*

a new house under **construction**

con·struc·tive (kən struk′tiv) *adj.* **1.** serving to improve or help; useful: *The teacher tries to give constructive criticism.* **2.** of or relating to construction; structural. **—con·struc′tive·ly,** *adv.* **—con·struc′tive·ness,** *n.*

con·strue (kən strü′) *v.t.,* **con·strued, con·stru·ing.** **1.** to explain the meaning of; interpret: *I construed your words as a compliment.* **2.** to analyze (a sentence, clause, or phrase) in order to show how the words are used or arranged.

con·sul (kon′səl) *n.* **1.** an official appointed by a nation to live in a foreign city in order to protect that nation's citizens and commercial interests there. **2.** either of the two most important elected officials in the ancient Roman republic.

con·su·lar (kon′sə lar) *adj.* of or relating to a consul or consulate.

con·su·late (kon′sə lit) *n.* **1.** the official home or head-quarters of a consul. **2.** the term of office of a consul.

con·sult (kən sult′) *v.t.* **1.** to look to or seek for information or advice: *I consulted an encyclopedia to find the answer. If you feel ill, consult a doctor.* **2.** to have regard for; think of; consider: *I wish you had consulted me before inviting more people to the party.* —*v.i.* to meet in order to ask advice or share ideas or opinions: *The young doctor consulted with the specialist before treating the patient.*

con·sult·ant (kən sul′tənt) *n.* **1.** a person who gives professional advice. **2.** a person who seeks information or advice.

con·sul·ta·tion (kon′səl tā′shən) *n.* **1.** the act of consulting. **2.** a meeting to ask advice or share ideas or opinions: *The lawyers held a consultation to decide on the best strategy in the lawsuit.*

con·sume (kən süm′) *v.t.,* **con·sumed, con·sum·ing.** **1.** to use up: *An automobile consumes gasoline.* **2.** to eat or drink up: *We consumed a large meal.* **3.** to destroy, especially by fire: *Fire consumed the building.* **4.** to occupy all the attention of: *to be consumed with curiosity.* —**con·sum′a·ble,** *adj.*

con·sum·er (kən sü′mər) *n.* **1.** a person or thing that consumes. **2.** someone who buys and uses things offered for sale, such as food, services, or clothing. **3.** an organism, usually an animal, that feeds on another organism.

consumer goods, products made to meet basic human needs, not to produce other goods. Food and clothing are consumer goods.

con·sum·er·ism (kən sü′mə riz′əm) *n.* the policy or practice of protecting consumers from unsafe or defective goods and services and false advertising.

con·sum·mate (*v.,* kon′sə māt′; *adj.,* kən sum′it, kon′sə mit) *v.t.,* **con·sum·mat·ed, con·sum·mat·ing.** to complete or make perfect; finish or fulfill: *The architect consummated a life's work by designing the skyscraper.* —*adj.* reaching the highest degree, complete or perfect: *an artist of consummate skill.* —**con·sum′mate·ly,** *adv.* —**con′sum·ma′tion,** *n.*

con·sump·tion (kən sump′shən) *n.* **1.** the act of consuming or the state of being consumed. **2.** the amount consumed: *increased consumption of gasoline.* **3.** a wasting disease, especially tuberculosis of the lungs.

con·sump·tive (kən sump′tiv) *adj.* **1.** of, relating to, or having consumption, especially tuberculosis of the lungs. **2.** tending to consume; destructive; wasteful. —*n.* a person having consumption. —**con·sump′tive·ly,** *adv.* —**con·sump′tive·ness,** *n.*

cont., continued. Also, **contd.**

con·tact (kon′takt) *n.* **1.** a touching or meeting: *The lamp is in contact with the table. The two cars stopped at the moment of contact.* **2.** the state of being in communication: *We lost contact with them until they wrote us a letter. The teacher comes in contact with many students.* **3.** a useful association: *a business contact.* **4.** see **contact lens.** **5.** the point of connection between two conductors that permits an electrical current to flow, as in a switch. **6.** a device for opening or closing such a connection. —*v.t.* **1.** to bring into contact; touch. **2.** *Informal.* to communicate with: *Contact me tomorrow by telephone.*

contact lens, a thin plastic lens worn directly on the eye to help a person see better. Also, **contact.**

con·ta·gion (kən tā′jən) *n.* **1.** the spreading of disease by direct or indirect contact. **2.** a disease spread in this manner. **3.** the spreading of an idea or emotion: *A contagion of laughter spread through the crowd.*

con·ta·gious (kən tā′jəs) *adj.* **1.** spread by direct or indirect contact: *We all caught the contagious disease within a week.* **2.** readily spread: *Fear can be contagious.* —**con·ta′gious·ly,** *adv.* —**con·ta′gious·ness,** *n.*

con·tain (kən tān′) *v.t.* **1.** to have in it; hold inside itself: *The jar contains coffee.* **2.** to be made up of or include as a part: *A quart contains two pints. This salad dressing contains oil and vinegar.* **3.** to keep under control; hold back: *to contain one's anger at an insult.* —**con·tain′a·ble,** *adj.*

con·tain·er (kən tā′nər) *n.* a box, can, jar, or the like that contains or holds something; receptacle.

con·tain·ment (kən tān′mənt) *n.* **1.** the policy of preventing something, as a hostile country, from becoming too powerful or dangerous. **2.** the act or process of containing something or the state of being contained: *Containment of the forest fire was our first aim.*

con·tam·i·nant (kən tam′ə nənt) *n.* something that contaminates or makes impure: *The beaches were closed when contaminants were found in the water.*

con·tam·i·nate (kən tam′ə nāt′) *v.t.,* **con·tam·i·nat·ed, con·tam·i·nat·ing.** to make unclean or impure by contact; pollute: *Garbage contaminated the water.* —**con·tam′i·na′tor,** *n.*

con·tam·i·na·tion (kən tam′ə nā′shən) *n.* **1.** the act or process of contaminating or the state of being contaminated; pollution: *Food should be kept covered to prevent contamination.* **2.** something that contaminates; impurity.

contd., continued.

con·temn (kən tem′) *v.t.* to treat with contempt; despise; scorn.

con·tem·plate (kon′təm plāt′) *v.,* **con·tem·plat·ed, con·tem·plat·ing.** —*v.t.* **1.** to give a great deal of attention to; look at or think about long and carefully: *The young graduates contemplated the future.* **2.** to have in mind; intend: *I'm contemplating going for a ride.* —*v.i.* to meditate; ponder: *In the park you see people sitting and contemplating.*

con·tem·pla·tion (kon′təm plā′shən) *n.* **1.** the act of looking at or thinking about something long and carefully: *I spent a long time in contemplation of the painting.* **2.** meditation, especially religious meditation. **3.** expectation or intention: *We bought a guidebook in contemplation of our trip.*

con·tem·pla·tive (kon′təm plā′tiv, kən tem′plə tiv) *adj.* of, relating to, or characterized by contemplation: *a contemplative person, a contemplative afternoon.* —**con′tem·pla′tive·ly,** *adv.* —**con′tem·pla′tive·ness,** *n.*

con·tem·po·ra·ne·ous (kən tem′pə rā′nē əs) *adj.* belonging to or happening during the same period of time: *The Civil War and the rise of the Republican Party were contemporaneous.* —**con·tem′po·ra′ne·ous·ly,** *adv.* —**con·tem′po·ra′ne·ous·ness,** *n.*

con·tem·po·rar·y (kən tem′pə rer′ē) *adj.* **1.** belonging to or living at the same time: *Queen Victoria and President Lincoln were contemporary figures.* **2.** belonging to the present time; current; modern: *contemporary art.* —*n., pl.* **con·tem·po·rar·ies.** a person who belongs to or lives at the same time as another or others: *We are contemporaries of the first men to walk on the moon.*

---

at; āpe; fär; câre; end; mē; it; īce; pîerce; hot; ōld; sông, fôrk; oil; out; up; ūse; rüle; pùll; tûrn; chin; sing; shop; thin; this; hw in white; zh in treasure. The symbol ə stands for the unstressed vowel sound heard in about, taken, pencil, lemon, and circus.

C

con·tempt (kən tempt′) *n.* **1.** a feeling that a person or thing is low, mean, or worthless; scorn; disdain: *I have contempt for someone who would throw trash out a car window.* **2.** the state of being scorned or despised; disgrace: *to be held in contempt by everyone for dishonesty.* **3.** disrespect for or disobedience of a law court or lawmaking body: *They were fined for contempt of court.*

con·tempt·i·ble (kən temp′tə bəl) *adj.* deserving of or held in contempt or scorn. —**con·tempt′i·ble·ness,** *n.* —**con·tempt′i·bly,** *adv.*

con·temp·tu·ous (kən temp′chü əs) *adj.* showing contempt; scornful: *a contemptuous remark.* —**con·temp′tu·ous·ly,** *adv.* —**con·temp′tu·ous·ness,** *n.*

con·tend (kən tend′) *v.i.* to compete against another in or as in a contest: *The two runners contended for first place.* —*v.t.* to argue: *They contended that their plan would work.* —**con·tend′er,** *n.*
·**to contend with.** to deal or struggle with: *The Eskimo have to contend with harsh weather.*

con·tent¹ (kon′tent) *n.* **1.** *usually,* **contents.** all that is contained inside: *The contents spilled out when the suitcase came open.* **2.** facts or topics discussed; subject matter: *What was the content of the letter? This book doesn't have a table of contents.* **3.** amount of something held or able to be held: *the water content of an apple.* [From the Latin word *contentum* meaning "that which is contained," from *contentus,* past participle of *continēre* "to hold together, contain," from the prefix *com-* "with, together" + *tenēre* "to hold."]

con·tent² (kən tent′) *adj.* wanting nothing else; free of desire for more; satisfied: *I'm content to eat only two meals a day.* —*v.t.* to make content; satisfy: *A word of praise will content me.* —*n.* contentment; satisfaction: *After eating, the baby went to sleep in complete content.* [From the Middle French word *content* meaning "satisfied," from the Latin word *contentus* "restrained, satisfied," going back to the word *continēre* "to hold together, contain."]

con·tent·ed (kən ten′tid) *adj.* enjoying contentment; satisfied. —**con·tent′ed·ly,** *adv.* —**con·tent′ed·ness,** *n.*

con·ten·tion (kən ten′shən) *n.* **1.** a disagreement or dispute; argument; quarrel. **2.** a point that a person supports or argues for: *It is my cousin's contention that dogs are smarter than cats.*

con·ten·tious (kən ten′shəs) *adj.* fond of arguing; argumentative; quarrelsome. —**con·ten′tious·ly,** *adv.* —**con·ten′tious·ness,** *n.*

con·tent·ment (kən tent′mənt) *n.* the state of being happy and content; satisfaction.

con·test (*n.,* kon′test; *v.,* kən test′) *n.* **1.** something that tests or proves skill or ability, such as a game or race; competition for a prize, honor, or position: *Who won the pie-eating contest? The senator entered the contest for governor.* **2.** a struggle or conflict: *a contest between nations.* —*v.t.* **1.** to struggle in order to win (something); fight for: *The soldiers contested every bit of ground.* **2.** to challenge or dispute: *The pitcher contested the decision of the umpire.* —**con·test′a·ble,** *adj.*

con·test·ant (kən tes′tənt) *n.* a person who takes part in a contest.

con·text (kon′tekst) *n.* the words, phrases, or sentences that surround a word, sentence, or passage and influence or make clear its meaning: *It was difficult to understand what the senator's statement meant because it was quoted out of context. You can often understand the meaning of an unfamiliar word from the context in which it is used.*

con·tex·tu·al (kən teks′chü əl) *adj.* relating to or depending on the context. —**con·tex′tu·al·ly,** *adv.*

con·ti·gu·i·ty (kon′ti gū′i tē) *n., pl.* **con·ti·gu·i·ties.** **1.** the state of being in actual contact. **2.** nearness.

con·tig·u·ous (kən tig′ū əs) *adj.* **1.** in actual contact; touching: *Michigan, Indiana, and Ohio are contiguous states.* **2.** close; near: *The two houses are contiguous,* separated only by a low hedge. —**con·tig′u·ous·ly,** *adv.* —**con·tig′u·ous·ness,** *n.*

con·ti·nence (kon′tə nəns) *n.* self-restraint or moderation. Also, **con·ti·nen·cy** (kon′tə nən sē).

con·ti·nent¹ (kon′tə nənt) *n.* **1.** one of the seven great land areas on the earth. The continents are Asia, Africa, North America, South America, Antarctica, Europe, and Australia. **2. the Continent.** the mainland of Europe. [From the Latin phrase *(terra) continens* meaning "(land) holding together," "mainland," from *continens,* present participle of *continēre* "to hold together, contain," from the prefix *com-* "with, together" + *tenēre* "to hold."]

continent¹
The **continents** of Asia, Africa, Antarctica, Europe, and Australia can be seen here.

con·ti·nent² (kon′tə nənt) *adj.* practicing self-restraint or moderation. [From the Latin word *continens* with the same meaning, from the present participle of *continēre* "to hold together, contain."]

con·ti·nen·tal (kon′tə nen′təl) *adj.* **1.** *also,* **Continental.** on or characteristic of the mainland of Europe; European: *I learned about continental cooking in Paris.* **2. Continental.** of or relating to the American colonies during and just after the American Revolution: *the Continental army.* **3.** of or resembling a continent: *a continental landmass.* —*n.* **1.** *also,* **Continental.** a person who lives on the mainland of Europe; European. **2. Continental.** a soldier in the American army established by the Continental Congress.

Continental Congress, the assembly of delegates from the American colonies that met from 1774 to 1781.

continental divide **1.** an elevation of land that separates river systems flowing toward one side of a continent from those flowing toward the other side. **2. Continental Divide.** such an elevation in western North America formed by the various peaks of the Rocky Mountains, separating rivers flowing eastward from those flowing westward. Also *(def. 2),* **Great Divide.**

continental drift, the theory that for millions of years the continents have been slowly moving across the earth's surface and changing their positions.

continental shelf, the broad edge of a continent that forms a shelf extending underwater from the shore to a depth of approximately 600 feet (200 meters).

con·tin·gen·cy (kən tin′jən sē) *n., pl.* **con·tin·gen·cies.** **1.** an event that can possibly take place; chance happening: *A mountain climber tries to prepare for every contingency.* **2.** the quality or state of being conditional or uncertain.

con·tin·gent (kən tin′jənt) *adj.* **1.** depending on an uncertain condition or event; conditional: *Our trip to Europe is contingent upon our making enough money this summer.* **2.** likely to happen, but not certain; possible: *A contingent result of our trip to the city is that we may see my grandparents.* **3.** happening by chance; accidental. —*n.* a group sent by another, larger group as a share or quota: *a contingent of firefighters.* —**con·tin′gent·ly,** *adv.*

con·tin·u·al (kən tin′ū əl) *adj.* **1.** continuing without a break; continuous: *the continual rumble of traffic in the city.* **2.** happening over and over again; repeated: *The continual noise of a dog barking kept us awake.* —**con·tin′u·al·ly,** *adv.*

con·tin·u·ance (kən tin′ū əns) *n.* **1.** the act of continuing or the state of being continued. **2.** *Law.* a postponement of a court action to a future date.

con·tin·u·a·tion (kən tin'ū ā'shən) *n.* **1.** a continuing or remaining without a break: *Many citizens were against a continuation of the war.* **2.** a continuing after a break; resumption: *the continuation of school after the spring holiday.* **3.** something that continues anything already started; added part: *This television program is a continuation of last week's program.*

con·tin·ue (kən tin'ū) *v.,* **con·tin·ued, con·tin·u·ing.** —*v.i.* **1.** to not stop in an action: *The snowfall continued for two days.* **2.** to remain in a place, position, or condition: *to continue as principal. The weather continued to be cold.* **3.** to start again after a break; resume: *The meeting will continue after lunch.* —*v.t.* **1.** to not stop with; not bring to an end: *to continue work despite an illness.* **2.** to start again with after a break; resume: *The professor will continue the lecture tomorrow.* **3.** to cause to remain in a place or position; retain. **4.** *Law.* to postpone (a court action) to a future date. —**con·tin'u·a·ble,** *adj.*

con·ti·nu·i·ty (kon'tə nū'i tē, kon'tə nū'i tē) *n., pl.* **con·ti·nu·i·ties.** **1.** the state or quality of being continuous. **2.** a logical connection, as of ideas; coherence: *The story was hard to understand because it lacked continuity.*

con·tin·u·ous (kən tin'ū əs) *adj.* continuing without a break; unbroken. —**con·tin'u·ous·ly,** *adv.* —**con·tin'u·ous·ness,** *n.*

con·tort (kən tôrt') *v.t.* to change the usual form or appearance of by twisting or bending out of shape; distort: *The patient's face was contorted with pain.*

con·tor·tion (kən tôr'shən) *n.* **1.** the act of contorting or the state of being contorted. **2.** a twisted or bent shape: *The acrobat's body could take on some amazing contortions.*

con·tor·tion·ist (kən tôr'shə nist) *n.* a person who contorts, especially a performer who twists and bends the body into unusual positions.

con·tour (kon'tùr) *n.* the shape of an object, figure, or body, or the line representing this: *The contour of the earth can be seen from an orbiting spacecraft.* —*adj.* **1.** following the contours of hilly land when plowing or planting in order to prevent soil erosion: *contour farming.* **2.** made to fit the shape of something: *contour sheets for a bed.*

contour line, a line on a map connecting points of equal elevation.

contour map, a map that shows the relative elevations of a surface by means of contour lines.

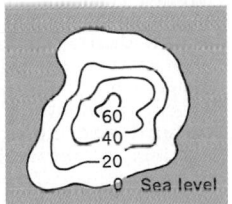

contour map
of an island

contra- *prefix* against; opposite: *contradiction.*

con·tra·band (kon'trə band') *n.* **1.** goods forbidden by law from being imported or exported; smuggled goods: *The weapons were seized as contraband.* **2.** unlawful trade in such goods; smuggling: *The government tried to prevent contraband in drugs.* —*adj.* forbidden by law from being imported or exported: *The contraband goods were confiscated.*

con·tra·bass (kon'trə bās') *n., pl.* **con·tra·bass·es.** a musical instrument having a range below the bass, such as the double bass.

con·tra·cep·tion (kon'trə sep'shən) *n.* the prevention of conception; birth control.

con·tra·cep·tive (kon'trə sep'tiv) *adj.* relating to or used for contraception: *a contraceptive device.* —*n.* a substance or device for preventing conception.

con·tract (*v.,* kən trakt', *also* kon'trakt *for v.t. def. 3 and v.i. def. 2; n.,* kon'trakt) *v.t.* **1.** to draw together (the parts of a thing); make shorter or make smaller. **2.** to get or acquire: *to contract pneumonia, to contract a debt.* **3.** to establish by agreement: *The two businesses* contracted a merger. **4.** to shorten (a word, syllable, or phrase) by omitting or combining sounds or letters. *Are not* can be contracted to *aren't.* —*v.i.* **1.** to draw together; become shorter or smaller: *The leather strap contracted as it dried.* **2.** to make or enter into an agreement: *The farmer contracted to lease the land.* —*n.* **1.** an agreement between two or more parties to do or not to do something, especially an agreement that the law will enforce: *The strike finally ended when the union voted to accept the contract.* **2.** a document containing the terms of such an agreement.

con·trac·tile (kən trak'təl) *adj.* having the ability to contract or cause contraction: *the contractile force of cold.*

contractile vacuole, a small cavity found in many one-celled organisms that pumps excess water and waste from the organism. See *ameba* for illustration.

con·trac·tion (kən trak'shən) *n.* **1.** the act or process of contracting or the state of being contracted: *the contraction of a muscle, the contraction of a disease.* **2.** a shortened form of a word, syllable, or phrase. *Wouldn't* is a contraction of *would not.*

con·trac·tor (kon'trak tər, kən trak'tər) *n.* a person who agrees to supply goods or do a job for a fixed price: *a building contractor.*

con·trac·tu·al (kən trak'chü əl) *adj.* of, relating to, or having the force of a contract: *contractual duties.*

con·tra·dict (kon'trə dikt') *v.t.* **1.** to say the opposite of or deny (a statement); declare to be untrue: *The witness contradicted earlier testimony.* **2.** to assert the opposite of or deny what is stated by (someone): *They contradicted each other.* **3.** to be opposed to; disagree with: *Your words contradict your behavior.* [From the Latin word *contradictus,* past participle of *contradicere* meaning "to speak against," from the words *contra* "against, opposite" + *dicere* "to say, speak."]

con·tra·dic·tion (kon'trə dik'shən) *n.* **1.** a statement that contradicts another: *That speech contains many contradictions.* **2.** the act of contradicting. **3.** opposition or disagreement; inconsistency. *There seems to be a contradiction between the two newspapers about the facts.*

con·tra·dic·to·ry (kon'trə dik'tə rē) *adj.* **1.** contradicting; opposing; inconsistent: *contradictory accounts of an accident.* **2.** tending to contradict: *a contradictory person.* —**con'tra·dic'tor·i·ly,** *adv.* —**con'tra·dic'tor·i·ness,** *n.*

con·tra·dis·tinc·tion (kon'trə dis tingk'shən) *n.* a distinction by contrast or opposition.

con·trail (kon'trāl') *n.* a stream of condensed water vapor that forms from the exhaust gases or exterior surfaces of an aircraft or rocket flying at a high altitude.

con·tral·to (kən tral'tō) *n., pl.* **con·tral·tos.** **1.** the lowest female voice. **2.** a singer who has such a voice. **3.** a musical part for such a voice. —*adj.* **1.** able to sing contralto. **2.** for the contralto.

con·trap·tion (kən trap'shən) *n.* *Informal.* a mechanical device; gadget; contrivance.

con·trar·i·wise (kon'trer ē wīz', kən trâr'ē wīz') *adv.* **1.** in the opposite direction or the opposite order. **2.** on the

con·trar·y (kon'trer ē, *also* kən trâr'ē *for adj. def. 2*) *adj.* **1.** entirely different; opposite: *People from different parts of the world often have contrary ideas.* **2.** tending to oppose or contradict: *A contrary person enjoys dis-*

at; āpe; fär; câre; end; mē; it; īce; pîerce; hot; ōld;
sông, fôrk; oil; out; up; ūse; rüle; pùll; tûrn; chin;
sing; shop; thin; this; hw in white; zh in treasure.
The symbol ə stands for the unstressed vowel sound
heard in about, taken, pencil, lemon, and circus.

agreement. **3.** unfavorable; adverse: *Contrary winds put the ship off its course.* —*n., pl.* **con·trar·ies.** the opposite: *I believe that the contrary of what they say is actually the truth.* —**con′trar·i·ly,** *adv.* —**con′trar·i·ness,** *n.*

· **on the contrary.** just the opposite: *On the contrary, we are not going to the party.*

con·trast (*v.,* kən trast′; *n.,* kon′trast) *v.t.* to compare in order to show differences: *The lecturer contrasted two ancient civilizations.* —*v.i.* to show differences when compared: *The white hat contrasted sharply with the black dress.* —*n.* **1.** the act of contrasting or the state of being contrasted: *The rich and poor sections of that city are in sharp contrast with each other.* **2.** a difference, as one shown by contrasting: *the contrast between darkness and light.* **3.** a person or thing showing differences: *This car is quite a contrast to the one you used to own.* ▲ See **compare** for usage note.

con·trib·ute (kən trib′ūt, kən trib′yùt) *v.,* **con·trib·ut·ed, con·trib·ut·ing.** —*v.t.* **1.** to give along with others: *to contribute money to a hospital fund.* **2.** to write (an article, story, or the like) for a newspaper or magazine. —*v.i.* **1.** to give money, time, effort, or the like along with others: *to contribute to charity, to contribute to a discussion.* **2.** to write an article, story, or the like for a newspaper or magazine: *That professor often contributes to educational magazines.* **3.** to help bring about: *Good weather contributed to the success of the fair.*

con·tri·bu·tion (kon′trə bū′shən) *n.* **1.** the act of contributing: *A political campaign depends largely on the contribution of money or time by supporters.* **2.** something that is contributed: *I wrote a check for a contribution to charity.*

con·trib·u·tor (kən trib′yə tər) *n.* a person who contributes: *a contributor to a museum's building fund.*

con·trib·u·to·ry (kən trib′yə tôr′ē) *adj.* helping to bring about a result; contributing: *Adequate rain was a contributory factor in the large harvest.*

con·trite (kən trīt′, kon′trīt) *adj.* **1.** deeply sorry for one's faults or wrongdoing; remorseful; penitent: *I felt contrite about my rude behavior.* **2.** showing deep sorrow or regret: *a contrite apology.* —**con·trite′ly,** *adv.* —**con·trite′ness,** *n.*

con·tri·tion (kən trish′ən) *n.* deep sorrow or regret for one's faults or wrongdoing; penitence.

con·triv·ance (kən trī′vəns) *n.* **1.** something contrived, such as a plan, scheme, or mechanical device. **2.** the act of contriving.

con·trive (kən trīv′) *v.t.,* **con·trived, con·triv·ing. 1.** to plan in a clever or ingenious way; scheme; plot: *The gang contrived a bank robbery.* **2.** to bring about or manage, especially with difficulty: *They contrived to keep their plans secret.* **3.** to create or invent; design: *to contrive a new lock.* —**con·triv′er,** *n.*

con·trol (kən trōl′) *n.* **1.** the ability to make someone or something do what one wants; authority: *The dictator had absolute control over the country. The rudder gives you control over the boat.* **2.** a holding in check; restraint: *to have trouble keeping control of one's temper.* **3.** a method or means of restraint; check: *The president proposed new controls over wages and prices.* **4.** also, **controls.** a device or system for operating, regulating, or guiding a machine, such as an airplane or spacecraft. **5.** a standard of comparison used to measure or check the results of a scientific experiment. —*v.t.,* **con·trolled, con·trol·ling. 1.** to have power to make someone or something do what one wants; have authority over: *The federal government controls interstate commerce. I controlled the flow of water by turning the faucet on and off.* **2.** to hold in check; curb; restrain: *Please make a greater effort to control your temper.* —**con·trol′la·ble,** *adj.*

con·trol·ler (kən trō′lər) *n.* **1.** a person who controls.

2. also, **comptroller.** a person in charge of spending and finances, as in a bank or company.

control rod, a rod made of a material, such as boron or cadmium, that absorbs neutrons. It is inserted into a nuclear reactor to control the rate of radioactive fission.

control tower, a tower on an airfield from which air traffic is directed, especially by radio.

control tower

con·tro·ver·sial (kon′trə vûr′shəl) *adj.* causing or characterized by controversy: *a controversial person, a controversial subject.* —**con′tro·ver′sial·ly,** *adv.*

con·tro·ver·sy (kon′trə vûr′sē) *n., pl.* **con·tro·ver·sies.** a dispute, especially one that leads to much debate: *The new tax caused widespread controversy.*

con·tro·vert (kon′trə vûrt′) *v.t.* to oppose or deny; contradict: *The facts controvert the testimony of the witness.* —**con′tro·vert′i·ble,** *adj.*

con·tu·ma·cious (kon′tə mā′shəs, kon′tyə mā′shəs) *adj.* stubbornly and willfully disobedient; rebellious.

con·tu·ma·cy (kon′tù mə sē, kon′tyù mə sē) *n., pl.* **con·tu·ma·cies.** a stubborn and willful disobedience of authority.

con·tu·me·ly (kon′tù mə lē, kon′tyù mə lē) *n., pl.* **con·tu·me·lies. 1.** rudeness in actions or speech; scornful insolence: *to treat a person with contumely.* **2.** an instance of such insolence; humiliating insult.

con·tu·sion (kən tü′zhən, kən tū′zhən) *n.* an injury in which the skin is not broken; bruise.

co·nun·drum (kə nun′drəm) *n.* **1.** a riddle whose answer involves a pun. For example: *What would an elephant bring on a trip? Its trunk.* **2.** any puzzling or difficult problem.

con·va·lesce (kon′və les′) *v.i.,* **con·va·lesced, con·va·lesc·ing.** to regain health and strength gradually after illness; recover: *I convalesced at home for two weeks after my operation.*

con·va·les·cence (kon′və les′əns) *n.* **1.** a gradual recovery of health and strength after illness. **2.** the period of this recovery.

con·va·les·cent (kon′və les′ənt) *adj.* **1.** recovering from illness: *a convalescent patient.* **2.** for or relating to convalescence or a convalescent person or persons: *a convalescent home.* —*n.* a person who is convalescing.

con·vec·tion (kən vek′shən) *n.* **1.** the transfer of heat from one part of a gas or liquid to another by heated currents of the gas or liquid. Convection occurs because of differences in density. **2.** the act of conveying.

con·vene (kən vēn′) *v.,* **con·vened, con·ven·ing.** —*v.i.* to come together, especially for a meeting; assemble: *The legislature convened.* —*v.t.* to cause to assemble: *The club president convened the members.*

con·ven·ience (kən vēn′yəns) *n.* **1.** the quality of being convenient: *the convenience of frozen foods.* **2.** ease;

comfort: *An information service is provided for the convenience of tourists.* **3.** something that gives ease or comfort: *A washing machine is one of many modern conveniences.*

  •**at one's convenience.** at a time or place, or under conditions, suited to one's needs or wishes.

con·ven·ient (kən vēn′yənt) *adj.* **1.** suited to one's needs or purposes; giving ease or comfort: *It is convenient to have a dishwasher if you have a large family.* **2.** within easy reach; near: *My parents are looking for a home that is convenient to transportation.* **3.** easy to do; not requiring effort or causing difficulty: *Is it convenient to meet at noon?* —**con·ven′ient·ly,** *adv.*

con·vent (kon′vent) *n.* **1.** a group of nuns living together under strict religious discipline. **2.** the building or buildings occupied by such a group; nunnery.

con·ven·tion (kən ven′shən) *n.* **1.** a formal meeting for a particular purpose: *a political convention.* **2.** the persons present at such a meeting. **3.** the generally accepted practices or standards of a society: *They ignored convention and lived exactly as they wanted.* **4.** a generally accepted rule or custom: *Saying "How are you?" when you meet someone is a convention.* **5.** an agreement between countries or persons.

con·ven·tion·al (kən ven′shə nəl) *adj.* **1.** following generally accepted practices or standards: *It was a conventional approach to solving a problem.* **2.** following accepted custom or usage; customary: *conventional manners.* **3.** showing little imagination: *a conventional person, a conventional work of art.* —**con·ven′tion·al·ly,** *adv.*

con·ven·tion·al·i·ty (kən ven′shə nal′i tē) *n., pl.* **con·ven·tion·al·i·ties.** **1.** the quality or character of being conventional: *The conventionality of their opinions often becomes boring.* **2.** a conventional custom, practice, or rule.

con·verge (kən vûrj′) *v.,* **con·verged, con·verg·ing.** —*v.i.* to come together or tend to come together at a place or point: *Three major roads converged at the intersection. Seagulls converged on the fishing fleet.* —*v.t.* to cause to converge.

con·ver·gence (kən vûr′jəns) *n.* **1.** the act or process of converging. **2.** the point of converging: *the convergence of two roads.*

con·ver·gent (kən vûr′jənt) *adj.* coming to a point; converging.

converging lens, a lens that is thicker in the middle than at the edges, causing light rays to converge and focus on a point. See **lens** for illustration.

con·ver·sant (kən vûr′sənt) *adj.* familiar or acquainted: *to be conversant with American history.*

con·ver·sa·tion (kon′vər sā′shən) *n.* informal or friendly talk between people.

con·ver·sa·tion·al (kon′vər sā′shə nəl) *adj.* **1.** of or characteristic of conversation: *a conversational tone.* **2.** fond of or good at conversation. —**con′ver·sa′tion·al·ly,** *adv.*

con·ver·sa·tion·al·ist (kon′vər sā′shə nə list) *n.* a person who is fond of or good at conversation.

con·verse¹ (kən vûrs′) *v.i.,* **con·versed, con·vers·ing.** to talk together in an informal and friendly way. [From the Old French word *converser* meaning "to associate with," from the Latin word *conversari* "to live with" or "keep company with."]

con·verse² (*adj.,* kən vûrs′; *n.,* kon′vûrs) *adj.* opposite in order, direction, or action; reversed; contrary. —*n.* **1.** something that is the opposite or contrary of something else: *Day is the converse of night.* **2.** a proposition in logic that is derived from another by interchanging the subject and predicate terms. The statement *Some Mondays are holidays* is the converse of the statement *Some holidays are Mondays.* [From the Latin word *conversus,* past participle of *convertere* meaning "to turn about,"

from the prefix *com-* "with, together" + *vertere* "to turn, turn around."]

con·ver·sion (kən vûr′zhən) *n.* **1.** the act or process of converting; change in character, condition, or use: *the conversion of water into ice, the conversion of an attic into a bedroom.* **2.** a change in a person's belief, opinion, or course of action: *a religious conversion.*

con·vert (*v.,* kən vûrt′; *n.,* kon′vûrt) *v.t.* **1.** to change in character, condition, or use: *to convert matter into energy, to convert a couch into a bed.* **2.** to cause (someone) to change a belief, opinion, or course of action: *We will soon convert you to our way of thinking. Missionaries tried to convert the tribe to Christianity.* **3.** to exchange for an equivalent: *We converted Swiss francs into dollars.* —*v.i.* to change one's beliefs, course of action, or religion. —*n.* a person who has converted or been converted, as from one religious belief to another.

con·vert·er (kən vûr′tər) *n.* **1.** a person or thing that converts. **2.** a machine for changing alternating electric current to direct current, or direct current to alternating current.

con·vert·i·ble (kən vûr′tə bəl) *adj.* **1.** capable of being converted: *This convertible sofa also serves as a bed.* **2.** (of an automobile) having a roof that can be folded back. —*n.* something convertible, as an automobile having a roof that can be folded back. —**con·vert′i·bil′i·ty,** *n.* —**con·vert′i·bly,** *adv.*

con·vex (kon veks′, kon′veks) *adj.* curved outward, as the outside of a circle or sphere: *a convex lens.* —**con·vex′ly,** *adv.* —**con·vex′ness,** *n.*

con·vex·i·ty (kon vek′si tē) *n., pl.* **con·vex·i·ties.** **1.** the quality or condition of being convex. **2.** a convex surface or thing.

Convex   Concave

convex and concave surfaces

con·vey (kən vā′) *v.t.* **1.** to take or carry from one place to another; transport: *The train conveyed the goods from the factory to the warehouse.* **2.** to serve as the medium for; transmit; conduct: *These pipes convey water from the reservoir to the city.* **3.** to express; communicate: *We conveyed our sympathy in a letter.* **4.** to transfer the ownership of, as property, from one person to another.

con·vey·ance (kən vā′əns) *n.* **1.** the act of conveying. **2.** something that transports or carries, especially a vehicle: *Buses and trains are public conveyances.* **3.** the transfer of the ownership of property from one person to another. **4.** the document by which such a transfer is made.

con·vey·or (kən vā′ər) *also,* **con·vey·er.** *n.* **1.** a person or thing that conveys. **2.** see **conveyor belt.**

conveyor belt *also,* **conveyer belt.** a mechanical device for transporting objects over relatively short distances, usually designed as a moving, continuous belt or a series of rollers.

con·vict (*v.,* kən vikt′; *n.,* kon′vikt) *v.t.* to find or prove (someone) guilty of a criminal charge: *The jury convicted the defendant of robbery.* —*n.* a person serving a prison sentence.

con·vic·tion (kən vik′shən) *n.* **1.** the act of finding or proving (someone) guilty of a criminal charge. **2.** the state of being found or proved guilty. **3.** a firm belief or opinion: *the conviction that all people are equal.*

con·vince (kən vins′) *v.t.,* **con·vinced, con·vinc·ing.** to

at; āpe; fär; câre; end; mē; it; īce; pîerce; hot; ōld; sông, fôrk; oil; out; up; ūse; rüle; pull; tûrn; chin; sing; shop; thin; this; hw in white; zh in treasure. The symbol ə stands for the unstressed vowel sound heard in about, taken, pencil, lemon, and circus.

215

cause (someone) to believe or feel certain; persuade: *I convinced them that I was right. I was convinced of the sincerity of your apology.*

con·vinc·ing (kən vin′sing) *adj.* having power to convince; persuasive: *The actor gave a convincing portrayal of a ghost.* —**con·vinc′ing·ly,** *adv.*

con·viv·i·al (kən viv′ē əl) *adj.* **1.** fond of parties and good times with friends; sociable. **2.** festive: *a convivial atmosphere.* —**con·viv·i·al·i·ty** (kən viv′ē al′i tē), *n.* —**con·viv′i·al·ly,** *adv.*

con·vo·ca·tion (kon′və kā′shən) *n.* **1.** a group of persons called together; assembly: *a convocation of students before graduation.* **2.** a calling together of such a group; summons to assemble.

con·voke (kən vōk′) *v.t.,* **con·voked, con·vok·ing.** to call together; summon to meet or assemble: *to convoke a legislature.*

con·vo·lut·ed (kon′və lü′tid) *adj.* **1.** turned in or wound up on itself; intricately twisted or coiled: *Inside the old radio was a puzzling mass of convoluted wires.* **2.** very intricate; complicated: *The novel tells a convoluted tale of spies and intrigue that is difficult to follow.*

con·vo·lu·tion (kon′və lü′shən) *n.* a coiling, twisting, or winding together: *the convolutions of a snake.*

con·voy (*n.,* kon′voi; *v.* kon′voi, kən voi′) *n.* **1.** a group of ships or vehicles traveling with a protective escort: *a convoy of tankers.* **2.** a group, as of warships, troops, or aircraft, that acts as a protective escort: *a convoy of destroyers escorted the aircraft carrier.* **3.** any group of persons or vehicles traveling together: *A convoy of trucks passed us on the highway.* —*v.t.* to accompany or escort in order to provide protection.

con·vulse (kən vuls′) *v.t.,* **con·vulsed, con·vuls·ing.** **1.** to shake or disturb violently: *An earthquake convulsed the city. A revolution convulsed the nation.* **2.** to cause to shake with strong emotion or fits of laughter: *to be convulsed with anger. The clown's antics convulsed the children.* **3.** to cause violent, involuntary contractions of the muscles. —*v.i.* to experience violent, involuntary contractions of the muscles.

con·vul·sion (kən vul′shən) *n.* **1.** a violent, involuntary contraction or series of contractions of the muscles. **2.** a fit of laughter. **3.** a violent shaking or disturbance; upheaval.

con·vul·sive (kən vul′siv) *adj.* **1.** of, like, or causing a convulsion or convulsions. **2.** having convulsions. —**con·vul′sive·ly,** *adv.*

co·ny (kō′nē) also **co·ney.** *n., pl.* **co·nies. 1.** rabbit fur. **2.** a rabbit, especially the European rabbit.

coo (kü) *n.* a soft, murmuring sound, such as that made by a pigeon or dove. —*v.i.,* **cooed, coo·ing. 1.** to make such a sound. **2.** to speak softly and lovingly.

cook (kük) *v.t.* to prepare (food) for eating by using heat, as by roasting, boiling, baking, or frying. —*v.i.* **1.** (of food) to be cooked; undergo cooking. **2.** to prepare food for eating; act as a cook: *Not everyone cooks well.* —*n.* a person who prepares food for eating.

·**to cook up.** *Informal.* to think of or invent, as a plan, excuse, or story.

cook·book (kük′bük′) *n.* a book containing recipes and other information about food and its preparation.

cook·er (kük′ər) *n.* an apparatus or utensil for cooking food: *a steam cooker.*

cook·er·y (kük′ə rē) *n., pl.* **cook·er·ies.** the art or practice of preparing and cooking food.

cook·ie (kük′ē) also **cook·y.** *n.* a small, usually flat cake baked from sweetened dough.

cook·out (kük′out′) *n.* an outdoor gathering at which food is cooked and eaten.

cook·y (kük′ē) *n., pl.* **cook·ies.** another spelling of **cookie.**

cool (kül) *adj.* **1.** lacking warmth but not very cold: *a cool breeze.* **2.** giving protection or relief from heat: *a*

cool summer dress. **3.** not excited; calm; composed: *to remain cool in the face of danger.* **4.** lacking enthusiasm or warmth; not cordial: *The movie got a cool reception from the critics.* **5.** *Slang.* excellent; great. **6.** *Informal.* without exaggeration; actual: *a cool million dollars.* —*n.* **1.** something cool, as a time or place: *We took a walk in the cool of early morning.* **2.** *Slang.* calmness: *to keep one's cool.* —*v.t.* to make cool: *to cool soup by letting it stand.* —*v.i.* to become cool: *The air cooled overnight. My anger cooled as time passed.* —**cool′ly,** *adv.* —**cool′ness,** *n.*

cool·ant (kü′lənt) *n.* a substance used to cool machinery, as the liquid in an automobile engine.

cool·er (kü′lər) *n.* **1.** a container or apparatus for keeping or making something cool: *a cooler for vegetables.* **2.** something that cools, such as an iced drink.

cool·head·ed (kül′hed′id) *adj.* not easily excited or disturbed; calm.

coo·lie (kü′lē) *n.* an unskilled Asian laborer, especially one working for low wages.

cooling tower, a large structure built next to a nuclear power plant to remove heat from the water used to cool the nuclear reactor. The water is then reused.

coon (kün) *n.* see **raccoon.**

coop (küp, kůp) *n.* a cage, pen, or enclosure for fowl or small animals: *a rabbit coop.* —*v.t.* to confine in a coop or any small space: *They cooped the dog up in the kitchen until the guests had gone.*

co–op (kō′op′) *n.* see **cooperative.**

coop·er (kü′pər, kůp′ər) *n.* a person who makes or repairs barrels, casks, and similar containers.

co·op·er·ate (kō op′ə rāt′) also, **co-op·er·ate.** *v.i.,* **co-op·er·at·ed, co-op·er·at·ing.** to work or act with another or others for a common purpose; unite in action: *The three classes cooperated in planning a party.*

co·op·er·a·tion (kō op′ə rā′shən) also, **co-op·er·a·tion.** *n.* the act or process of cooperating; working with another or others for a common purpose.

co·op·er·a·tive (kō op′ər ə tiv, kō op′ə rā′tiv) also, **co-op·er·a·tive.** *adj.* **1.** willing to work together with another or others: *a very cooperative coworker.* **2.** of or characterized by cooperation: *The family made painting the house a cooperative effort.* **3.** of, relating to, or referring to a cooperative. —*n.* **1.** a business enterprise, such as a food store or farm produce distributor, that is owned and operated by its members, who share its profits or benefits. **2.** a place where such an enterprise is located. **3.** an apartment building or complex in which each resident owns a share of the whole building or complex, occupies an apartment, and pays a share of the total costs. **4.** an apartment in such a building or complex. Also, **co-op.** —**co·op′er·a·tive·ly,** *adv.* —**co·op′er·a·tive·ness,** *n.*

co·or·di·nate (*v.,* kō ôr′də nāt′; *adj., n.,* kō ôr′də nit) also, **co-or·di·nate.** *v.,* **co·or·di·nat·ed, co·or·di·nat·ing.** —*v.t.* to cause to work well together; bring into proper working order; harmonize: *to coordinate the work of several agencies.* —*v.i.* to work well together; act in harmony. —*adj.* of equal rank or importance: *coordinate clauses.* —*n.* **1.** a person or thing that is equal in rank or importance to another. **2.** *Mathematics.* one of a set of numbers that give the position of a point in a line, in a plane, or in three-dimensional space. —**co·or′di·nate·ly,** *adv.* —**co·or′di·na′tor,** *n.*

coordinating conjunction, a conjunction used to join two or more words or groups of words of the same type, such as nouns or independent clauses. In the sentence *Bill and Mary like to ski, but Jane and Mike prefer to swim or jog,* the conjunctions *and, but,* and *or* are coordinating conjunctions.

co·or·di·na·tion (kō ôr′də nā′shən) also, **co-or·di·na·tion.** *n.* **1.** the act of coordinating or the state of being coordinated. **2.** a working well together, as of parts of the body: *Swimming requires muscular coordination.*

coot (küt) *n., pl.* **coots,** *also (def. 1)* **coot.** **1.** a water bird having short wings and usually black or gray feathers. **2.** *Informal.* a foolish person, especially a foolish old man.

cop (kop) *n. Informal.* a police officer.

cope[1] (kōp) *v.i.,* **coped, cop·ing.** to struggle or deal successfully: *I had trouble coping with the extra homework.* [From the Old French word *colper* meaning "to strike," form the word *colp* "a blow," going back to the Latin word *colaphus* "a blow," from the Greek word *kolaphos* "a blow."]

coot *(def. 1)*

cope[2] (kōp) *n.* a long cape worn by bishops, priests, and other clergy during processions and certain religious services. [Originally from the Late Latin word *cappa* meaning "hood" or "cape[1]."]

co·pe·pod (kō'pə pod') *n.* any of a large group of tiny crustaceans found in salt water or fresh water, having six pairs of limbs and without compound eyes or a shell. Some copepods are parasites of fish, and others live in plankton.

Co·per·ni·can (kə pûr'ni kən) *adj.* of or relating to Copernicus or to his theory that the earth revolves around the sun and that the apparent movement of the stars is due to the earth's rotation on its axis.

cop·i·er (kop'ē ər) *n.* **1.** a person or thing that makes copies, especially an office machine that makes copies of letters, documents, or other materials. **2.** a person who imitates.

co·pi·lot (kō'pī'lət) *n.* the assistant pilot in an aircraft, who assists and relieves the head pilot.

cop·ing (kō'ping) *n.* a layer of brick or stone on the top of a masonry wall, usually sloped for shedding water.

coping saw, a narrow-bladed saw in a U-shaped frame, used for very fine work, such as cutting sharp angles or curves in wood.

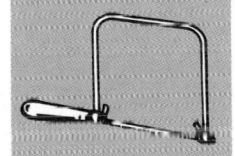

coping saw

co·pi·ous (kō'pē əs) *adj.* large in quantity; plentiful; abundant: *The lost child shed copious tears. We had a copious supply of food for the long hike.* **—co'pi·ous·ly,** *adv.* **—co'pi·ous·ness,** *n.*

cop·per (kop'ər) *n.* **1.** a reddish metallic element that is ductile and malleable, and is an excellent conductor of heat and electricity. Brass and bronze are among the alloys of copper. Symbol: **Cu** **2.** a reddish brown color. **3.** a coin made of copper or bronze, as a penny. *—adj.* **1.** made of copper: *a copper pan.* **2.** having the color copper; reddish brown. *—v.t.* to cover or coat with copper. [From the Old English word *coper* meaning this metal, going back to the Latin phrase *(aes) Cyprium* "(ore) of Cyprus." Cyprus was one of the main sources of copper in ancient times.] **—cop'per·y,** *adj.*

cop·per·as (kop'ər əs) *n.* a greenish crystalline compound of iron and sulfur, used in medicine, in photography, and in making inks and dyes.

cop·per·head (kop'ər hed') *n.* **1.** a poisonous snake of the eastern United States, having a copper-colored head and a light brown body with dark brown markings. **2. Copperhead.** a Northerner who sympathized or was thought to sympathize with the Confederacy during the Civil War.

cop·per·plate (kop'ər plāt') *n.* **1.** a thin piece of copper etched or engraved with a picture, design, or writing. **2.** a print made from such a plate. **3.** a printing process using such plates.

cop·per·smith (kop'ər smith') *n.* a person who works with copper, especially one who makes objects from copper.

cop·pice (kop'is) *n.* another word for **copse.**

cop·ra (kop'rə) *n.* the dried meat of the coconut. It is the source of coconut oil.

copse (kops) *n.* a thicket or grove of small trees or bushes. Also, **coppice.**

Copt (kopt) *n.* **1.** an Egyptian who is descended from the ancient Egyptians. **2.** a member of the Coptic Church.

cop·ter (kop'tər) *n. Informal.* see **helicopter.**

Cop·tic (kop'tik) *adj.* of or relating to the Copts, their language, or their culture. *—n.* a language descended from ancient Egyptian, formerly spoken by the Copts. It is now used only in the services of the Coptic Church.

Coptic Church, the Christian church of Egypt and formerly of Ethiopia.

cop·u·la (kop'yə lə) *n.* another word for **linking verb.**

cop·u·late (kop'yə lāt') *v.i.,* **cop·u·lat·ed, cop·u·lat·ing.** to have sexual intercourse. **—cop·u·la'tion,** *n.*

cop·u·la·tive verb (kop'yə lə tiv, kop'yə lā'tiv) another term for **linking verb.**

cop·y (kop'ē) *n., pl.* **cop·ies. 1.** a reproduction of an original; duplicate; imitation: *a copy of a picture, a copy of a piece of furniture, a copy of a letter.* **2.** one of a number of books, magazines, newspapers, or the like: *I bought two copies of the book.* **3.** material to be set in print for a newspaper, book, or the like. **4.** the words for an advertisement, news story, or the like, as distinguished from the illustrations: *I spent six months turning out copy for a fashion magazine.* *—v.,* **cop·ied, cop·y·ing.** *—v.t.* **1.** to make a copy of (something): *to copy a letter, to copy a dress.* **2.** to make or do something in imitation of: *The young painter copied the great artist's methods.* *—v.i.* to make a copy or copies.

cop·y·book (kop'ē bùk') *n.* a book containing examples of handwriting for students to copy.

cop·y·cat (kop'ē kat') *n. Informal.* a person who imitates another or others.

cop·y·ist (kop'ē ist) *n.* a person who makes written copies, especially of documents or manuscripts.

cop·y·right (kop'ē rīt') *n.* the sole right to produce, publish, or sell a literary, musical, or artistic work, granted by law for a certain number of years. *—v.t.* to get a copyright for: *to copyright a song.* *—adj.* relating to or protected by copyright.

cop·y·writ·er (kop'ē rī'tər) *n.* a person who writes copy, especially for advertisements.

co·quet·ry (kō'ki trē, kō ket'rē) *n., pl.* **co·quet·ries.** the behavior or actions of a coquette; flirtation.

co·quette (kō ket') *n.* a woman who flirts with men. **—co·quet'tish,** *adj.* **—co·quet'tish·ly,** *adv.* **—co·quet'tish·ness,** *n.*

co·qui·na (kō kē'nə) *n.* a soft, whitish limestone made up of fragments of seashells and corals, used for building.

cor·a·cle (kôr'ə kəl) *n.* a small, light boat made by stretching animal skins or other waterproof material over a frame.

cor·al (kôr'əl) *n.* **1.** a hard substance resembling limestone, usually found in tropical waters. It is secreted by certain tiny sea animals, called polyps. **2.** any of the polyps that secrete this substance. **3.** a mass or structure formed by the skeletons of these animals, such as a reef. **4.** a pinkish red color. *—adj.* **1.** made of coral: *a coral reef.* **2.** having the color coral.

at; āpe; fär; câre; end; mē; it; īce; pîerce; hot; ōld; sông, fôrk; oil; out; up; ūse; rüle; pùll; tûrn; chin; sing; shop; thin; <u>th</u>is; hw in white; zh in treasure. The symbol ə stands for the unstressed vowel sound heard in about, taken, pencil, lemon, and circus.

coral reef

coral reef, a formation of limestone built up from the skeletons of certain species of coral. Coral reefs are found in shallow tropical seas.

coral snake, a narrow-headed, poisonous American snake having red, black, and yellow bands.

cord (kôrd) *n.* **1.** a string or thin rope made of several strands twisted or woven together: *I tied the package with cord.* **2.** an insulated electric cable used to connect an appliance to an outlet or to make other electrical connections: *the cord of a lamp.* **3.** a structure in the body resembling a cord, such as the spinal cord. **4. a.** a rib or ridge on the surface of a fabric. **b.** a fabric containing such ridges, as corduroy. **5.** a quantity of cut wood, usually equaling 128 cubic feet (3.6 cubic meters) arranged in a pile 4 feet wide, 4 feet high, and 8 feet long. —*v.t.* **1.** to bind or fasten with cord; furnish with a cord. **2.** to pile (wood) in cords. —**cord'like'**, *adj.*

cord·age (kôr'dij) *n.* **1.** cords or ropes, especially those in a ship's rigging. **2.** a quantity of cut wood measured in cords.

cord·ed (kôr'did) *adj.* **1.** fastened with cord. **2.** having ribs or ridges or twills; ribbed.

cor·dial (kôr'jəl) *adj.* warm and friendly; hearty. —*n.* a sweet alcoholic drink; liqueur. —**cor'dial·ly**, *adv.*

cor·di·al·i·ty (kôr'jē al'i tē) *n., pl.* **cor·di·al·i·ties.** warmth or friendliness; heartiness: *They welcomed us with cordiality.*

cor·dil·le·ra (kôr'dəl yâr'ə, kôr'də lâr'ə, kôr dil'ər ə) *n.* a long series of mountain ranges, usually making up the main mountain chain of a large land area.

cor·don (kôr'dən) *n.* **1.** a line of troops, police, or barricades set up to guard or close off an area. **2.** a cord or ribbon worn diagonally across the chest as a badge of honor or rank. —*v.t.* to form or place a cordon around: *The police cordoned the burning building.*

cor·do·van (kôr'də vən) *n.* **1.** a soft, fine-grained leather. **2.** a shoe made of this leather. **3.** a dark grayish brown. **4.** a dark grayish red. —*adj.* **1.** having the color cordovan. [From the Spanish word *cordobán* meaning this kind of leather, from *Córdoba*, Spain.]

cor·du·roy (kôr'də roi') *n.* **1.** a fabric, usually made of cotton, with a velvety, ribbed surface, used for clothing and upholstery. **2. corduroys.** slacks made of corduroy. —*adj.* made of corduroy.

corduroy road, a road constructed of logs laid side by side with the length across the roadbed.

cord·wood (kôrd'wùd') *n.* wood sold by the cord or cut for piling in cords.

core (kôr) *n.* **1.** the hard or papery central part of certain fruits, such as apples and pears, that contains the seeds. **2.** the central, essential, or innermost part of anything: *the core of the earth, an argument built around a core of fact.* —*v.t.,* **cored, cor·ing.** to remove the core of: *to core an apple.* —**cor'er**, *n.*

co·ri·an·der (kôr'ē an'dər) *n.* **1.** the aromatic, seedlike fruit of a plant of the parsley family, used in cooking and medicines. **2.** the plant bearing these seeds. [From the Old French word *coriandre* meaning this herb, from the Latin word *coriandrum*, from the Greek word *koriandon* meaning this herb.]

Co·rin·thi·an (kə rin'thē ən) *adj.* **1.** of or relating to Corinth, its people, or their culture. **2.** of or relating to the most elaborate of the three orders of classical Greek architecture, characterized by columns having bell-shaped capitals decorated with acanthus leaves. —*n.* **1.** an inhabitant of Corinth. **2. Corinthians.** either of the two books of the New Testament written by the Apostle Paul to the Christians of Corinth.

Corinthian capital

cork (kôrk) *n.* **1.** the light, thick, porous outer bark of the cork oak, used especially as insulating material and for floats. **2.** something made of cork, especially a stopper for a bottle or other container. **3.** the tissue forming the outer bark of woody plants, acting as a protective covering. —*v.t.* to stop or provide with cork or a cork: *to cork a wine bottle.*

cork·er (kôr'kər) *n. Slang.* an outstanding or remarkable person or thing.

cork oak, an oak tree native to the Mediterranean region, from whose bark cork is obtained.

cork·screw (kôrk'skrü') *n.* a device for removing corks from bottles, usually having a pointed, metal spiral that is driven into the cork. —*adj.* shaped like a corkscrew; spiral; winding: *a corkscrew mountain road.*

cork·y (kôr'kē) *adj.,* **cork·i·er, cork·i·est.** of, relating to, or like cork.

corm (kôrm) *n.* a thick, fleshy, bulblike underground stem of certain plants, such as the crocus or gladiolus.

cor·mo·rant (kôr'mər ənt) *n.* a large sea bird with dark feathers, having webbed feet, a hooked bill, and a pouch under the beak for holding fish.

corn¹ (kôrn) *n.* **1.** a grain that grows in rows on the large ears of a tall, coarse grass, used for food. **2.** the plant bearing this grain, having a jointed stalk and broad leaves. Also (*defs. 1, 2*), **maize, Indian corn. 3.** an ear of this plant. **4.** *British.* any food grain or the plant it grows on. **5.** *Informal.* something considered old-fashioned, trite, or too sentimental.

cormorant

—*v.t.* to preserve or season (meat) in strong brine or with coarse, dry salt. [From the Old English word *corn* meaning "seed, grain."]

corn² (kôrn) *n.* a small hardening and thickening of the skin caused by friction or pressure, occurring especially on a toe. [From the Middle French word *corn* meaning ''horn'' or ''hornlike swelling,'' from the Latin word *cornu* ''horn.'']

corn bread, bread made with cornmeal.

corn·cob (kôrn′kob) *n.* **1.** the almost woody core of an ear of corn, on which the kernels grow in rows. **2.** a tobacco pipe with a bowl that is made from a hollowed, dried corncob.

corn·crib (kôrn′krib′) *n.* a bin or small building for storing cobs of corn, built with slats that are spaced for ventilation.

cor·ne·a (kôr′nē ə) *n.* the transparent outer covering or wall of the front of the eyeball, lying over the iris and the pupil.

corned (kôrnd) *adj.* (of meat) preserved or seasoned in strong brine or with coarse, dry salt: *corned beef.*

cor·ner (kôr′nər) *n.* **1.** the point or place where two lines or surfaces meet; angle: *the sharp corners of a table, the corner of a room.* **2.** the place where two streets meet. **3.** a place that is hidden, secret, or private: *The children played in their own little corner of the attic.* **4.** a region or part, especially one far away: *The politician campaigned in every corner of the state.* **5.** a place or position that is awkward or threatening, especially one from which escape is almost impossible: *The police had driven the robber into a corner.* **6.** the purchase or control of enough of a particular stock or commodity to raise the price: *to have a corner on grain.* —*adj.* **1.** at or near a corner: *the corner drugstore.* **2.** designed for or used in a corner: *a corner cabinet.* —*v.t.* **1.** to force or drive into an awkward or threatening place or position, especially one from which escape is almost impossible: *We cornered the escaped chicken in the shed.* **2.** to form or get a corner on (a stock or commodity).

　·**to cut corners.** to reduce time, effort, or expenses in doing something; economize: *The construction workers cut corners by using inexpensive materials to build the house.*

　·**to turn the corner** or **to turn a corner.** to pass the point, as in an illness, where the worst is behind.

cor·ner·stone (kôr′nər stōn′) *n.* **1.** a stone that lies at the corner of a building. **2.** such a stone laid at a ceremony to mark the starting point in building. **3.** a fundamental principle or part; foundation; basis: *Freedom is the cornerstone of democracy.*

cor·net (kôr net′) *n.* a brass musical instrument that is similar to the trumpet but has a mellower sound.

cor·net·ist (kôr net′ist) *also,* **cor·net·tist.** *n.* a person who plays a cornet.

corn·field (kôrn′fēld) *n.* a field in which corn is grown.

corn·flakes (kôrn′flāks′) *pl. n.* small, crisp flakes made from corn, eaten as a breakfast cereal.

corn·flow·er (kôrn′flou′ər) *n.* **1.** the blue, purple, pink, or white flower of a plant widely grown in North America. **2.** the plant bearing this flower.

corn·husk (kôrn′husk′) *n.* the coarse leaves or husk enclosing an ear of corn.

cor·nice (kôr′nis) *n.* **1.** a projecting ornamental molding along the top of a pillar, wall, or building. **2.** a molding along the walls of a room just below the ceiling.

Cor·nish (kôr′nish) *adj.* of or relating to Cornwall, its people, their language, or culture. —*n.* a Celtic language that was formerly spoken in Cornwall. It became extinct in about 1800.

corn·meal (kôrn′mēl′) *also,* **corn meal.** *n.* meal made from coarsely ground corn.

corn pone, a simple corn bread that is baked or fried, usually made without milk or eggs.

corn·stalk (kôrn′stôk) *n.* a stalk of corn.

corn·starch (kôrn′stärch′) *n.* a white, powdery starch made from corn, used in cooking as a thickening agent.

corn syrup, a thick, sweet liquid made from cornstarch and used in cooking.

cor·nu·co·pi·a (kôr′nə kō′pē ə, kôr′nyə kō′pē ə) *n.* **1.** a curved, twisted horn overflowing with fruit, grain, and vegetables. It is a symbol of abundance and prosperity. Also, **horn of plenty.** **2.** any container or ornament shaped like a horn or cone.

corn·y (kôr′nē) *adj.,* **corn·i·er, corn·i·est.** *Informal.* old-fashioned, trite, or too sentimental: *a corny joke, a corny movie.*

co·rol·la (kə rol′ə) *n.* the petals of a flower.

cor·ol·lar·y (kôr′ə ler′ē, kor′ə ler′ē) *n., pl.* **cor·ol·lar·ies.** **1.** a statement that follows naturally from a statement already proved and therefore requires no separate proof. **2.** anything that follows naturally; natural result.

**cornucopia
(def. 1)**

co·ro·na (kə rō′nə) *n.* **1.** the ring of light seen around the sun, moon, or other heavenly body, caused by mist or clouds in the earth's atmosphere. **2.** the outer atmosphere of the sun. **3.** a crownlike part in some flowers, as in the center of a daffodil.

cor·o·nar·y (kôr′ə ner′ē, kor′ə ner′ē) *adj.* of or relating to either of two arteries that branch from the aorta and supply blood to the muscular tissue of the heart. *n., pl.* **cor·o·nar·ies.** see **coronary thrombosis.**

coronary artery disease, disease of the blood vessels that supply blood to the muscle of the heart. It often occurs when fatty substances clog the inside of the arteries, making it difficult for blood to pass through them.

coronary thrombosis, a blockage in either of the coronary arteries caused by formation of a blood clot.

cor·o·na·tion (kôr′ə nā′shən, kor′ə nā′shən) *n.* the act or ceremony of crowning, as a king or queen.

cor·o·ner (kôr′ə nər, kor′ə nər) *n.* a local official whose chief duty is to investigate any death that is not clearly due to natural causes.

cor·o·net (kôr′ə net′, kor′ə net′) *n.* **1.** a small crown worn by a noble. **2.** a head ornament somewhat like a crown, especially one that is made with precious metals, jewels, or flowers.

Corp. **1.** Corporal. **2.** Corporation.

cor·po·ral¹ (kôr′pər əl) *adj.* of or relating to the human body; physical; *corporal punishment.* [From the Old French word *corporal,* from the Latin word *corporalis* ''of the body,'' from the word *corpus* ''body.''] —**cor′po·ral·ly,** *adv.*

cor·po·ral² (kôr′pər əl, kôr′prəl) *n.* the lowest noncommissioned officer in the U.S. Army or Marine Corps, ranking below a sergeant. [From the obsolete French word *corporal* meaning this officer, from the Italian word *caporale* with the same meaning, from the word *capo* meaning ''head'' or ''chief,'' from the Latin word *caput* meaning ''head.'']

cor·po·rate (kôr′pər it, kôr′prit) *adj.* **1.** of, relating to, or forming a corporation: *a corporate policy, a corporate meeting.* **2.** of or relating to a united group; joint; collective: *The corporate action of consumers led to lower food prices.* —**cor′po·rate·ly,** *adv.*

cor·po·ra·tion (kôr′pə rā′shən) *n.* an organization made up of a group of people who have been given the legal

at; āpe; fär; câre; end; mē; it; īce; pîerce; hot; ōld; sông, fôrk; oil; out; up; ūse; rüle; pull; tûrn; chin; sing; shop; thin; <u>th</u>is; hw in white; zh in treasure. The symbol ə stands for the unstressed vowel sound heard in about, taken, pencil, lemon, and circus.

power to act as one person. A corporation is created by a government charter and usually has the right to buy and sell property and to enter into contracts.

cor·po·re·al (kôr pôr′ē əl) *adj.* **1.** of the body; not spiritual. **2.** having substance; material; tangible. —**cor·po′re·al·ly,** *adv.*

corps (kôr) *n., pl.* **corps** (kôrz). **1.** a military unit with a special function: *a medical corps.* **2.** a military unit consisting of a headquarters, two or more divisions, and additional support units, and forming part of an army. **3.** a group of persons acting or working together: *a corps of volunteers, the diplomatic corps.*

corps de bal·let (kôr′də ba lā′, kôr′də bal′ā) the dancers in a ballet company who generally perform as a group rather than as soloists.

corpse (kôrps) *n.* a dead body, especially of a human being.

cor·pu·lent (kôr′pyə lənt) *adj.* fat or stout; obese. —**cor′pu·lence,** *n.*

cor·pus·cle (kôr′pus′əl) *n.* **1.** a particle in the blood or lymph, especially a red or white blood cell. **2.** any minute particle.

cor·ral (kə ral′) *n.* **1.** a fenced enclosure for cattle, horses, or other livestock. **2.** a circular area formed by wagons for defense against attack. —*v.t.,* **cor·ralled, cor·ral·ling. 1.** to drive into or enclose in a corral: *to corral a herd of horses.* **2.** to capture by surrounding or gathering together: *Police corralled the entire gang.* **3.** to form (wagons) into a corral.

cor·rect (kə rekt′) *adj.* **1.** agreeing with fact or truth; free from error; accurate: *the correct answer to a problem.* **2.** according to the accepted or approved standard; proper: *A jacket and tie is the correct dress for the party.* —*v.t.* **1.** to change (something wrong or false) to what is right or true: *to correct a mistaken idea.* **2.** to bring into agreement with fact or truth; make free from error: *to correct a theory to account for new data.* **3.** to note or mark the errors in: *to correct a spelling test.* **4.** to punish or scold in order to improve: *to correct a child for behaving badly.* **5.** to adjust to or make agree with a standard: *to correct poor eyesight with glasses.* —**cor·rect′ly,** *adv.* —**cor·rect′ness,** *n.*

cor·rec·tion (kə rek′shən) *n.* **1.** the act of correcting or the state of being corrected: *Correction of the problem in the car's engine took several hours.* **2.** a change made to correct an error: *Keep a list of the corrections you make.* **3.** the act of punishing or scolding in order to improve.

cor·rec·tive (kə rek′tiv) *adj.* tending or meant to correct or improve: *corrective lenses, corrective criticism.* —*n.* something that corrects or tends to correct an error. —**cor·rec′tive·ly,** *adv.*

cor·re·late (kôr′ə lāt′, kor′ə lāt′) *v.,* **cor·re·lat·ed, cor·re·lat·ing.** —*v.t.* to place in a meaningful relation; show a connection between: *The police tried to correlate the two accounts of the accident.* —*v.i.* to be meaningfully related: *These facts seem to correlate.*

cor·re·la·tion (kôr′ə lā′shən, kor′ə lā′shən) *n.* **1.** a meaningful relation; connection: *a close correlation between poor sanitation and disease.* **2.** the act of correlating.

cor·rel·a·tive (kə rel′ə tiv) *adj.* **1.** having or involving a mutual relation: *to have correlative interests in nature and in conservation.* **2.** *Grammar.* complementing one another and commonly used together. In the sentence *I'll let you know either Tuesday or Wednesday, either* and *or* are correlative conjunctions. —*n.* **1.** either of two correlative things. **2.** *Grammar.* a correlative word. —**cor·rel′a·tive·ly,** *adv.*

cor·re·spond (kôr′ə spond′, kor′ə spond′) *v.i.* **1.** to be in agreement or harmony; match: *Our tastes in music do not correspond.* **2.** to be similar or equivalent, as in character or function: *The gills of a fish correspond to*

the lungs of a mammal. **3.** to communicate by exchanging letters: *The two friends corresponded for many years.*

cor·re·spon·dence (kôr′ə spon′dəns, kor′ə spon′dəns) *n.* **1.** agreement or similarity: *The detectives found a close correspondence between the stories of the two witnesses.* **2.** communication by exchange of letters. **3.** letters written or exchanged: *The company keeps copies of all its correspondence.*

cor·re·spon·dent (kôr′ə spon′dənt, kor′ə spon′dənt) *n.* **1.** a person who communicates with another by letter. **2.** a person employed, as by a newspaper or magazine, to send news and commentary from a particular place or area: *the Moscow correspondent for a newspaper.* —*adj.* corresponding.

cor·re·spond·ing (kôr′ə spon′ding, kor′ə spon′ding) *adj.* **1.** matching or identical: *The two chairs have a corresponding design.* **2.** having a similar function, position, form, or the like: *corresponding ranks in the army and navy.* —**cor·re·spond′ing·ly,** *adv.*

cor·ri·dor (kôr′i dər, kor′i dər) *n.* a long hallway or passageway in a building: *a hotel corridor.* [From the French word *corridor* meaning "passage," from the Italian word *corridore* "long passageway" and "runner," going back to the Latin word *currere* meaning "to run."]

cor·rob·o·rate (kə rob′ə rāt′) *v.t.,* **cor·rob·o·rat·ed, cor·rob·o·rat·ing.** to strengthen or support, as by giving additional proof; confirm: *The evidence of the witnesses corroborated the defendant's story.* —**cor·rob′o·ra′tion,** *n.* —**cor·rob′o·ra′tive,** *adj.*

cor·rode (kə rōd′) *v.,* **cor·rod·ed, cor·rod·ing.** —*v.t.* to eat or wear away gradually, especially by chemical action: *This acid corrodes metal.* —*v.i.* to become corroded: *Some metals corrode easily.*

cor·ro·sion (kə rō′zhən) *n.* **1.** the act or process of corroding. **2.** the result of corroding.

cor·ro·sive (kə rō′siv) *adj.* tending to corrode; capable of producing corrosion: *a corrosive acid.* —*n.* a substance that corrodes. —**cor·ro′sive·ly,** *adv.* —**cor·ro′sive·ness,** *n.*

cor·ru·gate (kôr′i gāt′, kor′i gāt′) *v.,* **cor·ru·gat·ed, cor·ru·gat·ing.** —*v.t.* to shape into parallel ridges or folds; wrinkle. —*v.i.* to become shaped in this way.

corrugated paper, heavy paper or cardboard shaped into parallel ridges, used for packaging.

cor·ru·ga·tion (kôr′i gā′shən, kor′i gā′shən) *n.* **1.** the act of corrugating or the state of being corrugated. **2.** one of a series of parallel ridges or folds; wrinkle.

cor·rupt (kə rupt′) *adj.* **1.** influenced by bribery; dishonest; crooked: *corrupt officials.* **2.** wicked or immoral; depraved: *a corrupt life.* **3.** changed from the original or correct form or version, as by additions or errors: *a corrupt translation of a book.* **4.** rotten; decayed. —*v.t.* **1.** to cause to act dishonestly, as by bribery: *The lure of money corrupted the mayor.* **2.** to make morally wicked. **3.** to change from the original or correct form or version: *to corrupt the text of a manuscript.* **4.** to make rotten; decay. —*v.i.* to become corrupt. —**cor·rupt′er,** *n.* —**cor·rupt′ly,** *adv.* —**cor·rupt′ness,** *n.*

cor·rupt·i·ble (kə rup′tə bəl) *adj.* capable of being corrupted. —**cor·rupt′ly,** *adv.* —**cor·rupt′ness,** *n.*

cor·rup·tion (kə rup′shən) *n.* **1.** the act of corrupting or the state of being corrupted. **2.** dishonest behavior. **3.** the state of being morally bad; wickedness; depravity. **4.** a corrupted form or version, as of a text or language. **5.** rot; decay.

cor·rup·tive (kə rup′tiv) *adj.* tending to corrupt; causing corruption: *Dishonest friends may have a corruptive influence on you.*

cor·sage (kôr säzh′) *n.* a flower arrangement worn by a woman, usually on the shoulder, waist, or wrist.

cor·sair (kôr′sâr) *n.* **1.** a privateer or pirate, especially of the Barbary Coast. **2.** a privateering or pirate ship.

cor·se·let (*def. 1* kôr′sə let′; *def. 2* kôrs′lit) *n.* **1.** an undergarment similar to a cor-set. **2.** *also,* **cors·let.** a plate of armor for the upper part of the body.

cor·set (kôr′sit) *n.* a close-fitting undergarment worn to shape and support the waist and hips.

cor·tege (kôr tezh′) *also,* **cor·tège.** *n.* **1.** a ceremonial procession, especially a funeral procession. **2.** a group of fol-lowers or attendants; retinue.

cor·tex (kôr′teks) *n., pl.* **cor·ti·ces** (kôr′tə sēz′). **1.** the outer part of an internal organ. **2.** the wrinkled gray matter covering most of the brain. **3.** the bark of a tree.

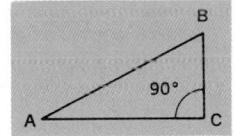

corselet *(def. 2)*

cor·ti·cal (kôr′ti kəl) *adj.* of, relating to, or consisting of a cortex. —**cor′ti·cal·ly,** *adv.*

cor·ti·sone (kôr′tə zōn′, kôr′tə sōn′) *n.* a hormone produced by the cortex of the adrenal gland or made synthetically, used to treat arthritis and some allergies.

co·run·dum (kə run′dəm) *n.* a mineral made up of aluminum oxide, second only to diamonds in hardness. The dark-colored variety is used for polishing and grinding; transparent varieties include such gems as sapphires and rubies.

cor·vette (kôr vet′) *also,* **cor·vet.** *n.* **1.** a fast armed ship, smaller than a destroyer, used especially to escort other ships. **2.** a former warship smaller than a frigate.

cor·ymb (kôr′imb, kôr′im, kor′imb, kor′im) *n.* a type of floral growth in which individual small stemmed flowers grow from different levels on a main stem, but reach approximately the same height and form a flat-topped cluster, as in cherry blossoms.

cos., cosine.

co·se·cant (ko se′kənt, kō sē′kant) *n.* (of an acute angle in a right triangle) the ratio of the hy-potenuse to the side opposite the angle.

co·sign (kō′sīn′, kō sīn′) *v.t.* **1.** to sign (a document) jointly with another or others: *Three countries cosigned the treaty.* **2.** to add one's

cosecant of
angle *A* = *AB/BC*

signature to (a contract) and accept responsibility to fulfill the terms if the other signer fails to do so. —*v.i.* to act as a co-signer. —**co′sign′er,** *n.*

co·sine (kō′sīn) *n.* (of an acute angle in a right triangle) the ratio of the angle's adjacent side to the hypotenuse.

cos·met·ic (koz met′ik) *n.* a preparation, such as lipstick, pow-der, or rouge, used to beautify the body, especially the face or hair. —*adj.* used or done to improve the appearance of something, as of the body.

cosine of
angle *A* = *AC/AB*

cos·mic (koz′mik) *adj.* **1.** of or relating to the universe as a whole: *cosmic law.* **2.** of great extent; vast; endless: *cosmic implications.* **3.** of or from outer space. —**cos′mi·cal·ly,** *adv.*

cosmic rays, high-frequency rays of great penetrating force, consisting mainly of positively charged particles that come to the earth from outer space.

cos·mol·o·gy (koz mol′ə jē) *n.* the branch of astron-omy that studies the structure and development of the entire physical universe, including galaxies, stars, and other bodies.

cos·mo·naut (koz′mə nôt′) *n.* an astronaut, especially one from the Soviet Union. [Probably from the Russian word *kosmonavt* meaning "cosmonaut," which was formed from the Greek words *kosmos* "world, cosmos" + *nautēs* "sailor."]

cos·mo·pol·i·tan (koz′mə pol′i tən) *adj.* **1.** composed of or having characteristics or people from many different countries: *a cosmopolitan city.* **2.** not narrow in attitude, viewpoint, or interest; at home in all parts of the world: *a cosmopolitan person, a cosmopolitan style.* —*n.* a person who is cosmopolitan in attitude or viewpoint.

cos·mos (koz′məs, koz′mōs) *n., pl.* **cos·mos·es.** **1.** the universe considered as an ordered and harmonious system. **2.** any ordered and harmonious system. **3.** a tall plant with showy flowers and delicate leaves, commonly grown in gardens.

Cos·sack (kos′ak) *n.* in Russian history, a member of a people living mainly in southeastern Russia and noted for their horsemen and cavalrymen.

cost (kôst) *n.* **1.** an amount of money paid or charged for something; price; expense: *The cost of this used car is only $500.* **2.** a loss or sacrifice: *The war was won at a great cost of lives.* **3. costs.** the expenses of a lawsuit. —*v.t.,* **cost, cost·ing. 1.** to be obtained at the price of: *This book cost ten dollars.* **2.** to cause the loss or sacrifice of: *The accident cost two lives. The injury cost the team the services of its best player.*

•**at all costs** or **at any cost.** regardless of the cost.

cos·tal (kos′təl) *adj.* of, relating to, or near a rib.

cost–ef·fec·tive (kôst′i fek′tiv) *adj.* effective in pro-ducing the best results in relation to the money spent: *The city sought cost-effective measures to reduce pollution.*

cos·ter·mon·ger (kôs′tər mung′gər, kôs′tər mong′gər) *n. British.* a person who sells food, such as fruit, vegetables, or fish, in the street.

cost·ly (kôst′lē) *adj.,* **cost·li·er, cost·li·est.** costing much: *costly jewelry, a costly mistake.* —**cost′li·ness,** *n.*

cost of living, the average cost of goods and services considered necessary, as for a person or family, during a given period of time.

cos·tume (*n.,* kos′tüm, kos′tūm; *v.,* kos tüm′, kos-tūm′) *n.* **1.** an outfit worn in order to portray someone else: *a Halloween costume, costumes for a play.* **2.** a style of dress, including accessories and hair style, be-longing to a particular time, place, or people: *a peasant costume.* **3.** special clothing worn for a particular occasion or activity: *a riding costume.* —*v.t.,* **cos·tumed, cos·tum·ing.** to provide with a costume.

costume jewelry, jewelry made with glass or other inexpensive materials rather than with precious stones.

cos·tum·er (kos tü′mər, kos tū′mər, kos′tü mər, kos′tū mər) *n.* a person who makes, sells, or rents cos-tumes.

co·sy (kō′zē) *adj.,* **co·si·er, co·si·est,** *n., pl.* **co·sies.** another spelling of **cozy.** —**co′si·ly,** *adv.* —**co′si·ness,** *n.*

cot¹ (kot) *n.* a narrow bed, especially one made of canvas stretched on a folding frame. [From the Hindi word *khāt* meaning "bed, couch."]

cot² (kot) *n.* **1.** a small house; cottage. **2.** a small structure for shelter or protection, especially one for animals. [From the Old English word *cot* meaning "cottage, dwell-ing."]

at; āpe; fär; câre; end; mē; it; īce; pîerce; hot; ōld; sông, fôrk; oil; out; up; ūse; rüle; pull; tûrn; chin; sing; shop; thin; <u>th</u>is; hw in white; zh in treasure. The symbol ə stands for the unstressed vowel sound heard in about, taken, pencil, lemon, and circus.

C

co·tan·gent (kō tan′jənt, kō′tan′jənt) *n.* (of an acute angle in a right triangle) the ratio of the angle's adjacent side to the side opposite.

cote (kōt) *n.* a small shelter for animals or birds.

co·te·rie (kō′tə rē) *n.* a small group of people who share a particular interest and often meet socially.

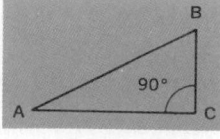

cotangent of
angle *A = AC/BC*

co·til·lion (kə til′yən) *n.* **1.** an elaborate ballroom dance popular in the nineteenth century, usually led by one couple. **2.** the music for such a dance. **3.** a formal ball.

cot·tage (kot′ij) *n.* a small house, usually in the country or in a summer resort.

cottage cheese, an unripened, soft, white cheese made of strained and seasoned curds of sour skim milk.

cot·tag·er (kot′i jər) *n.* a person who lives or vacations in a cottage.

cot·ter (kot′ər) *also,* **cot·tar.** *n.* a Scottish tenant farmer.

cotter pin, a split pin whose ends are spread after it has been inserted in a hole or slot so that it will stay in place, holding parts of a machine or device together.

cot·ton (kot′ən) *n.* **1.** soft white, gray, or brown fibers that grow in a fluffy mass in large seed pods of certain plants, used in making textiles and other products. **2.** the woody, branching shrub bearing these fibers. **3.** thread made of cotton fibers. **4.** any fabric woven of cotton. —*adj.* having to do with or made of cotton.

cotton *(defs. 1 and 2)*

cotton candy, a light, fluffy candy consisting of thin fibers of melted sugar spun or wound around a cone or stick.

cotton gin, see **gin[2]**.

cot·ton·mouth (kot′ən mouth′) *n, pl.* **cot·ton·mouths** (kot′ən mou<u>th</u>z′). another word for **water moccasin.**

cot·ton·seed (kot′ən sēd′) *n., pl.* **cot·ton·seeds** or **cot·ton·seed.** the seed of the cotton plant, from which cottonseed oil is extracted.

cottonseed oil, an oil extracted from cottonseed, used for cooking and in making soap and paints.

cot·ton·tail (kot′ən tāl′) *n.* a North American rabbit that has brown or grayish fur and a short, fluffy white tail.

cot·ton·wood (kot′ən wùd′) *n.* **1.** any of several North American poplars, having leathery, triangular leaves with toothed edges and tiny brown seeds covered with silky white hairs. **2.** the light, soft wood of this tree.

cot·ton·y (kot′ə nē) *adj.* like cotton; soft, downy, and white.

cot·y·le·don (kot′ə lē′dən) *n.* the undeveloped leaf that forms part of a plant embryo. In many plants the cotyledon develops into the first leaf or one of the first pair of leaves to grow above the ground.

couch (kouch) *n., pl.* **couch·es. 1.** a piece of furniture, usually upholstered, for several people to sit on; sofa. **2.** any place for sleeping or resting. —*v.t.* to put into words; express: *I couched my argument carefully.*

cou·gar (kü′gər) *n.* a tawny or grayish brown wildcat of North, Central, and South America, having a small, round head, long limbs, and a slender, muscular body. Also, **puma, mountain lion, panther.**

cough (kôf) *v.i.* to force air from the lungs with a sudden sharp sound. —*v.t.* to expel by coughing: *to cough blood.* —*n.* **1.** the act or sound of coughing. **2.** an illness or condition that causes frequent coughing.

cough drop, a small medicated lozenge, usually flavored and sweetened, for relieving coughs.

cough syrup, a liquid, often containing a medicine, used to suppress the urge to cough or loosen phlegm or mucus from the respiratory tract.

could (kùd) *auxiliary verb* **1.** a past tense of **can[1]. 2.** used to express possibility: *What you say could be true, but I'm not sure.* **3.** used to express ability: *Many countries could do more to reduce pollution.* **4.** used to make polite requests: *Could you help us move this desk, please?* **5.** used to ask permission: *Could I use your dictionary for a day or two?* **6.** used to offer a suggestion: *You could always start over and do it a different way.*

could·n't (kùd′ənt) *contr.* could not.

couldst (kùdst) *Archaic.* the second person singular past tense of **can[1]. ▲** used with **thou.**

cou·lee (kü′lē) *n.* **1.** in the western United States, a deep gulch or ravine, often dry in summer, that has been formed by running water. **2.** a stream of lava.

cou·lomb (kü′lom, kü′lōm) *n.* a unit used as a measure of the quantity of electric charge. It is the amount of charge that in 1 second passes a given point in a wire carrying a current of 1 ampere.

coul·ter (kōl′tər) *n.* another spelling of **colter.**

coun·cil (koun′səl) *n.* **1.** a group of people called together to give advice, discuss a problem, or make a decision. **2.** a body of persons elected or appointed to govern or make laws in a city or town.

coun·cil·man (koun′səl mən) *n., pl.* **coun·cil·men** (koun′səl mən). a member of a council, especially of the council of a city or town.

coun·ci·lor (koun′sə lər) *also, British,* **coun·cil·lor.** *n.* a member of a council; councilman or councilwoman.

coun·cil·wom·an (koun′səl wùm′ən) *n., pl.* **coun·cil·wom·en** (koun′səl wim′ən). a woman who is a member of a council, especially of a city or town.

coun·sel (koun′səl) *n.* **1.** an exchange of ideas, opinions, or advice; consultation; deliberation: *The leaders of the government met for counsel.* **2.** advice: *I failed to listen to the wise counsel of my friend.* **3.** a lawyer or group of lawyers giving legal advice: *the counsel for the defendant.* —*v.t.* **1.** to give advice to; advise: *to counsel a friend.* **2.** to recommend: *to counsel caution.*

·to take counsel. to seek or exchange ideas, opinions, or advice; consult: *to take counsel with friends.*

coun·sel·ing (koun′sə ling) *n.* professional advice in solving educational, career, emotional, or medical problems: *marriage counseling; genetic counseling.*

coun·se·lor (koun′sə lər) *also, British,* **coun·sel·lor.** *n.* **1.** a person who gives counsel or advice; adviser: *a career counselor.* **2.** a person who gives legal advice; lawyer. **3.** a person who supervises children at a camp.

count[1] (kount) *v.t.* **1.** to find out the total number of; add up: *to count the eggs in a carton.* **2.** to list or say numbers in order up to (a certain number): *to count ten.* **3.** to take into account; include in counting: *There were forty people in the bus, counting the driver.* **4.** to believe to be; consider: *I count them as friends.* —*v.i.* **1.** to list or say numbers in order: *to count up to five.* **2.** to be of value; have importance; matter: *Try to make every minute count.* **3.** to be taken into account; be included in counting. —*n.* **1.** the act of counting; numbering: *to make a count*

of the people at a meeting. **2.** a number obtained by counting; total. **3.** *Law.* each distinct charge in an accusation: *The defendant pleaded not guilty to the first two counts.* [From the Old French word *conter* meaning "to reckon" or "tell," from the Latin word *computare* "to reckon, calculate," from the prefix *com-* "with, together" + *putare* "to think, consider."]
· **to count for.** to be equal to; be worth: *to count for much in the long run.*
· **to count in.** to include: *If you're having a party, count me in.*
· **to count off.** to divide into equal groups by counting: *The coach told the students to count off by fours.*
· **to count on** or **to count upon.** to rely or depend on: *Can I count on you if I need help?*
· **to count out.** **a.** to exclude; omit: *We'll have to count our dog out if we're going on a camping trip.* **b.** to declare (a fallen boxer) the loser if the boxer cannot rise before a count of ten seconds is completed.

count² (kount) *n.* a European nobleman having a rank corresponding to that of a British earl. [From the Old French word *conte* meaning this nobleman, from the Late Latin word *comes* "member of the emperor's court," from the Latin word *comes* "companion," especially "companion of a prince"]

count·down (kount′doun′) *n.* **1.** the act or process of counting backward from a given time to zero to indicate the time remaining before the launching of a rocket, the explosion of a bomb, or the like. **2.** the preparations carried out during this counting. **3.** the time during which this counting is done: *Technicians made final adjustments during the countdown.*

coun·te·nance (koun′tə nəns) *n.* **1.** the face; features: *a handsome countenance.* **2.** an expression of the face; look: *an unhappy countenance.* **3.** approval or support; encouragement: *We will give no countenance to cheating.* —*v.t.,* **coun·te·nanced, coun·te·nanc·ing.** to give approval to; support; encourage: *The boss does not countenance laziness.*

count·er¹ (koun′tər) *n.* **1.** a long table, as in a store, restaurant, or bank, where sales are made, business is conducted, or food or drinks are served. **2.** any long shelf or flat working area, as in a kitchen. **3.** a thing used in counting, especially a small disk used for keeping score in certain games. **4.** an imitation coin; token. [From the Anglo-Norman word *counteour* meaning "counting table" or "counting house," from the Medieval Latin word *computatorium* "place for counting," from the Latin word *computare* "to reckon, calculate."]

count·er² (koun′tər) *n.* a person or thing that counts, especially a mechanical device for counting. [From the Middle French word *conteor* meaning "one who counts," probably from the Latin word *computator* with the same meaning, from the word *computare* meaning "to reckon, calculate."]

coun·ter³ (koun′tər) *adv.* in an opposite direction or way; opposite; contrary: *to act counter to the rules.* —*adj.* opposite; contrary: *Their plan is counter to mine.* —*v.t.* **1.** to go or act counter to; oppose: *They countered our proposal.* **2.** to deal a blow in boxing in return for (an opponent's blow). —*v.i.* **1.** to make an opposing move: *The debater countered with another argument.* **2.** to deal a blow in boxing in return for an opponent's blow: *The champion countered with a left to the head.* —*n.* **1.** something that is opposite or contrary. **2.** a boxing blow in return for an opponent's blow. **3.** a stiff piece on the inside of the heel of a shoe. [From the Old French word *contre* meaning "against," from the Latin word *contra* "against, opposite."]

counter– *combining form* **1.** in opposition to; against: *counteract.* **2.** in return: *counterattack.* **3.** corresponding: *counterpart.*

coun·ter·act (koun′tər akt′) *v.t.* to act against the effect or force of; neutralize; check: *The medicine could not counteract the disease.*

coun·ter·at·tack (koun′tər ə tak′) *n.* an attack made to counter another attack: *to launch a counterattack against an invading force.* —*v.i.* to make a counterattack. —*v.t.* to make a counterattack against.

coun·ter·bal·ance (*n.,* koun′tər bal′əns; *v.,* koun′tər bal′əns) *n.* **1.** a weight used to balance another weight. **2.** any power or influence that balances or offsets an opposing power or influence: *The job's high pay is a counterbalance to its dangerousness.* —*v.t.,* **coun·ter·bal·anced, coun·ter·bal·anc·ing.** to act as a counterbalance to; offset.

coun·ter·check (koun′tər chek′) *n.* **1.** something that stops or opposes something else. **2.** a check made to confirm an earlier check. —*v.t.* to confirm by a second check; double-check.

coun·ter·claim (koun′tər klām′) *n.* an opposing claim, especially an action by the defendant against the plaintiff in a lawsuit.

coun·ter·clock·wise (koun′tər klok′wīz′) *adv., adj.* in the direction opposite to the movement of a clock's hands.

coun·ter·cul·ture (koun′tər kul′chər) *n.* a culture, especially of young people, that is opposed to the standards and traditions of established society.

coun·ter·es·pi·o·nage (koun′tər es′pē ə näzh′, koun′tər es′pē ə nij) *n.* the use of espionage by a country to prevent and counteract espionage by another country.

coun·ter·feit (koun′tər fit′) *v.t.* **1.** to make a copy of in order to deceive or defraud: *It is a crime to counterfeit money.* **2.** to make a pretense of; pretend; feign: *to counterfeit sympathy.* —*v.i.* to make counterfeits. —*n.* a copy or imitation made in order to deceive or defraud; forgery. —*adj.* **1.** made in imitation of an original in order to deceive or defraud; not genuine: *a counterfeit $100 bill.* **2.** pretended; feigned: *counterfeit kindness.* —**coun·ter·feit·er,** *n.*

coun·ter·in·sur·gen·cy (koun′tər in sûr′jən sē) *n., pl.* **coun·ter·in·sur·gen·cies.** military action taken against guerrillas or other insurgents.

coun·ter·in·tel·li·gence (koun′tər in tel′i jəns) *n.* actions carried on by a government to counteract espionage and sabotage activities of an enemy.

coun·ter·man (koun′tər man′) *n., pl.* **coun·ter·men** (koun′tər men′). a person who waits on customers at a counter, especially in a cafeteria or restaurant.

coun·ter·mand (*v.,* koun′tər mand′, koun′tər mand′; *n.,* koun′tər mand′) *v.t.* to cancel or reverse (an order or command). —*n.* an order or command cancelling or reversing an earlier order or command.

coun·ter·march (koun′tər märch′) *n., pl.* **coun·ter·march·es.** a march back or in the opposite direction. —*v.i.* to perform a countermarch.

coun·ter·meas·ure (koun′tər mezh′ər) *n.* an action taken to counteract another action.

coun·ter·of·fen·sive (koun′tər ə fen′siv) *n.* an attack launched by a military force to turn back an enemy attack.

coun·ter·pane (koun′tər pān′) *n.* a quilt or cover for a bed; bedspread.

coun·ter·part (koun′tər pärt′) *n.* **1.** a person or thing corresponding to or closely resembling another: *The U.S. Congress is the counterpart of the British Parliament.* **2.** a person or thing that completes or complements

at; āpe; fär; câre; end; mē; it; īce; pîerce; hot; ōld; sông, fôrk; oil; out; up; ūse; rüle; pùll; tûrn; chin; sing; shop; thin; **th**is; hw in white; zh in treasure. The symbol ə stands for the unstressed vowel sound heard in about, taken, pencil, lemon, and circus.

another: *I found my left shoe, but I can't find its counterpart.*

coun·ter·point (koun'tər point') *n.* **1.** the art or technique of composing music in which one or more melodies are played or sung at the same time in harmony with a main melody. **2.** one or more melodies added to a main melody in this way.

coun·ter·poise (koun'tər poiz') *n.* **1.** a weight that balances another weight; counterbalance. **2.** any influence or power that balances or offsets an opposing influence or power. **3.** the state of being in balance. —*v.t.*, **coun·ter·poised, coun·ter·pois·ing.** to act as a counterpoise to; counterbalance.

coun·ter·pro·duc·tive (koun'tər prə duk'tiv) *adj.* tending to defeat one's purpose, as by producing a result opposite to what is intended: *Too much training in sports can be counterproductive.*

coun·ter·rev·o·lu·tion (koun'tər rev'ə lü'shən) *n.* a revolution opposed to an earlier revolution and seeking to reverse its effects: *The general led a counterrevolution against the rebels who had established a new government.*

coun·ter·rev·o·lu·tion·ar·y (koun'tər rev'ə lü'shə ner'ē) *adj.* relating to a counterrevolution —*n.*, *pl.* **coun·ter·rev·o·lu·tion·ar·ies.** a person who takes part in or supports a counterrevolution.

coun·ter·sign (*n.* koun'tər sīn'; *v.* koun'tər sīn', koun'tər sīn') *n.* **1.** a secret sign or signal given in answer to another, especially a military password given in answer to the challenge of a guard or sentry. **2.** a signature added to a previously signed check or other document to confirm it or to show that it is authentic. —*v.t.* to sign (a document already signed by another) in order to confirm or authenticate it: *The treasurer of the company countersigned the checks.*

coun·ter·sink (koun'tər singk') *v.t.*, **coun·ter·sunk, coun·ter·sink·ing. 1.** to enlarge the upper part of (a hole or cavity) to make room for the head of a screw, bolt, or the like. **2.** to set (a screw, bolt, or the like) in a hole enlarged in this way. —*n.* **1.** a hole made in this way. **2.** a tool for making such a hole.

coun·ter·spy (koun'tər spī') *n.*, *pl.* **coun·ter·spies.** a spy who is employed to detect and counteract the activities of enemy spies.

coun·ter·ten·or (koun'tər ten'ər) *n.* **1.** the highest adult male voice. **2.** a singer who has such a voice. **3.** a musical part for such a voice.

coun·ter·weight (koun'tər wāt') *n.* a weight balancing another weight; counterbalance; counterpoise.

count·ess (koun'tis) *n.*, *pl.* **count·ess·es. 1.** the wife or widow of a count or, in Great Britain, of an earl. **2.** a woman holding in her own right a rank equal to that of a count or an earl.

counting house, a building, office, or room used for such purposes as bookkeeping, correspondence, or business transactions.

counting number, a number used in counting the numbers of a set; any whole number except 0. One, 2, 3, 64, and 179 are counting numbers; ⅔ and −5 are not.

count·less (kount'lis) *adj.* too many to be counted; innumerable: *There are countless stars in the sky.*

count noun, a noun that names something that can be counted. *Cat, chair,* and *sandwich* are count nouns. *Thunder* and *butter* are not, since we do not say "three thunders" or "two butters."

coun·tri·fied (kun'trə fīd') *adj.* **1.** looking or acting like someone from the country. **2.** like or appropriate for the country or country life; rural; rustic.

coun·try (kun'trē) *n.*, *pl.* **coun·tries. 1.** an area of land; region, district, or territory: *farm country, mountain country.* **2.** an area of land that has definite boundaries and a common form of government; nation: *Brazil, Chile, and Argentina are countries in South America.* **3.** the land of a nation: *Much of the country of Egypt is desert.* **4.** the

people of a nation: *The whole country feared the dictator.* **5.** the land where a person was born or of which he or she is a citizen. **6.** the region outside of cities and towns; rural area: *On Sunday we went for a drive in the country.* —*adj.* of or relating to the country; rural: *a country road, country property.*

country and western, a kind of popular music that originated in the southern and western United States, played mostly on stringed instruments such as the guitar, banjo, and fiddle. Also, **country music.**

country club, a private club, usually located in a suburb, equipped with facilities for recreation, such as a golf course, a swimming pool, or tennis courts.

coun·try·folk (kun'trē fōk') *n.*, *pl.* **coun·try·folk** or **coun·try·folks.** people who live in rural areas.

coun·try·man (kun'trē mən) *n.*, *pl.* **coun·try·men** (kun'trē mən). **1.** a person who was born in or is a citizen of one's own country; compatriot. **2.** a person who lives in the country.

country music, another term for **country and western.**

coun·try·seat (kun'trē sēt') *n.* a mansion or estate in the country.

coun·try·side (kun'trē sīd') *n.* **1.** a rural region or district; country. **2.** the people living in the country: *The whole countryside was at the county fair.*

coun·try·wom·an (kun'trē wùm'ən) *n.*, *pl.* **coun·try·wom·en** (kun'trē wim'ən). **1.** a woman who was born in or is a citizen of one's own country. **2.** a woman who lives in the country.

coun·ty (koun'tē) *n.*, *pl.* **coun·ties. 1.** one of the sections into which most states of the United States are divided, usually having its own government. **2.** one of the districts into which certain countries are divided, such as Great Britain and Ireland. **3.** the people of a county. [From the Old French word *conté* meaning "territory ruled by a count," from the Late Latin word *comitatus* "office or position of a count," from the word *comes* "a count²" or "member of the emperor's court."]

county seat, a town or city that is the center of government for a county.

coup (kü) *n.*, *pl.* **coups** (küz). **1.** a sudden, brilliant action; unexpected, clever maneuver; master stroke: *Getting the leader of the opposition to support your plan was quite a coup.* **2.** see **coup d'etat.**

coup d'e·tat (kü'dā tä') *pl.* **coups d'e·tat** (kü'dā tä'). a sudden overthrow of a government. [From the French phrase *coup d'état* meaning "a blow to the state."]

coupe (küp, kü pā') *also,* **cou·pé** (kü pā'). *n.* **1.** a two-door automobile that is smaller than a sedan, seating two to six people. **2.** a short, four-wheeled, closed carriage with seats inside for two people and a seat outside for the driver.

cou·ple (kup'əl) *n.* **1.** two things of the same kind joined together or thought of together; pair. **2.** two people who are married or engaged or are partners in a dance, game, or other activity. ▲ used with a singular or plural verb. **3.** *Informal.* a small number; several; few: *We walked a couple of miles.* —*v.*, **cou·pled, cou·pling.** —*v.t.* to join or unite in a pair or pairs: *to couple two railroad cars.* —*v.i.* to join or unite in a pair or pairs.

cou·pler (kup'lər) *n.* **1.** a person or thing that couples. **2.** an interlocking device used to connect two railroad cars. Also, **coupling.**

cou·plet (kup'lit) *n.* two successive lines of verse, usually rhyming and in the same meter, that form a unit. For example: *Earth, receive an honored guest;/William Yeats is laid to rest* (W. H. Auden).

cou·pling (kup'ling) *n.* **1.** the act of joining together. **2.** any of various devices for joining parts of machinery. **3.** another word for **coupler** (def. 2).

cou·pon (kü'pon, kū'pon) *n.* **1.** a part of a ticket, certificate, or printed advertisement that can be detached, giving the person holding it some right: *You will be* admitted at half price if you present this coupon. **2.** a printed statement of the interest due on a bond, that can be detached and presented for payment at a specified time. [From the French word *coupon* meaning "a piece cut off" or "coupon," from the word *couper* "to cut," from the Latin word *colpus* "a slap," from the Greek word *kolaphos* "a slap."]

cour·age (kûr′ij, kur′ij) *n.* a quality that makes it possible for a person to face danger or difficulties without giving in to fear; bravery; boldness: *It took courage to speak out against the dictator.*

cou·ra·geous (kə rā′jəs) *adj.* having or showing courage; brave; fearless: *a courageous person, a courageous act.* —**cou·ra′geous·ly,** *adv.* —**cou·ra′geous·ness,** *n.*

cour·i·er (kûr′ē ər, kûr′ē ər) *n.* a messenger, especially one carrying an important or urgent message: *a diplomatic courier.*

course (kôrs) *n.* **1.** a moving from one point to the next; onward movement; progress; advance: *in the course of human events. I grew four inches during the course of a year.* **2.** a line or path in which something moves; direction or route taken: *The ship sailed on a westward course. The course of the river curved to the north.* **3.** a natural or regular order or development: *The disease has run its course.* **4.** a way of acting or proceeding: *Your wisest course would be to make no comment on what happened.* **5.** an area used for certain sports or games: *a race course.* **6.** a series or group of similar things: *a course of medical treatments.* **7.** a series of studies in a school, college, or university: *a secretarial course, a liberal arts course.* **8.** one of the classes or subjects in such a series of studies: *a course in typing, a history course.* **9.** a part of a meal served at one time: *The main course was chicken.* —*v.i.,* **coursed, cours·ing.** to move swiftly; run; flow: *Tears coursed down their cheeks.*

·**of course.** as is or was to be expected; naturally; certainly: *Of course I'll help you. Of course, there will be an inquiry into the matter.*

cours·er (kôr′sər) *n.* a swift or spirited horse.

course·ware (kôrs′wâr′) *n.* computer programs designed to help students learn specific subjects, especially for use in a classroom.

court (kôrt) *n.* **1.** an open space that is partly or entirely enclosed by walls or buildings; courtyard. **2.** a short street. **3.** a level, sometimes walled space or area marked off for certain games: *a basketball court, a squash court.* **4.** the residence of a king, queen, or other royal ruler; royal palace. **5.** the family, friends, and advisers of a king, queen, or other royal ruler. **6.** a royal ruler together with officials and advisers, considered as a ruling power. **7.** a formal assembly held by a royal ruler: *The king and queen held court at the summer palace.* **8.** a place where justice is carried out or trials are held; courtroom or courthouse. **9.** one or more persons appointed to hear legal cases and administer justice; judge or judges. **10.** an assembly of such persons to administer justice: *Court is held five days a week.* **11.** attention given to win favor: *to pay court to someone.* —*v.t.* **1.** to seek the love or affection of; woo. **2.** to pay flattering attention to (a person) to win favor: *The movie producer courted the famous star.* **3.** to try to get or gain; seek: *to court flattery, to court a person's favor.* **4.** to act so as to invite: *to court danger, to court defeat.* —*v.i.* to carry on a courtship: *The young couple has courted for a year.*

cour·te·ous (kûr′tē əs) *adj.* having or showing good manners; considerate of others; polite; gracious: *a courteous person, a courteous reply.* —**cour′te·ous·ly,** *adv.* —**cour′te·ous·ness,** *n.*

cour·te·san (kôr′tə zən, kûr′tə zən) *n.* a prostitute, especially one who associates with clients of wealth and high rank.

cour·te·sy (kûr′tə sē) *n., pl.* **cour·te·sies. 1.** courteous behavior; politeness. **2.** a courteous act; favor.

court·house (kôrt′hous′) *n., pl.* **court·hous·es** (kôrt′-hou′ziz). **1.** a building in which courts of law are held. **2.** a building housing the main offices of a county government.

cour·ti·er (kôr′tē ər) *n.* **1.** a person who attends the court of a king, queen, or other royal ruler. **2.** a person who tries to win favor by flattery.

court·ly (kôrt′lē) *adj.,* **court·li·er, court·li·est.** suitable for a royal court; refined; elegant; polished: *courtly manners.* —**court′li·ness,** *n.*

court–mar·tial (kôrt′mär′shəl) *n., pl.* **courts-mar·tial** or **court-mar·tials. 1.** a military court that tries members of the armed forces for offenses against military law. **2.** a trial by such a court. —*v.t.,* **court-mar·tialed, court-mar·tial·ing;** *also, British,* **court-mar·tialled, court-mar·tial·ling.** to try by court-martial: *The soldier was court-martialed for striking an officer.*

Court of St. James's, the royal court of Great Britain.

court·room (kôrt′rüm′, kôrt′rum′) *n.* a room in which a court of law is held.

courtroom

court·ship (kôrt′ship′) *n.* a courting; wooing.

court tennis, a form of tennis played on an indoor court having high walls off which the ball may be hit.

court·yard (kôrt′yärd′) *n.* an open area surrounded by walls or buildings, in or next to a large building.

cou·sin (kuz′in) *n.* **1.** a son or daughter of one's uncle or aunt. **2.** any relative with whom one shares a common ancestor. ▲ First cousins have the same pair of grandparents; second cousins have great-grandparents in common.

cou·ture (kü tür′) *n.* the designing, making, and selling of fashionable clothes for women.

co·va·lent bond (kō vā′lənt) a chemical bond formed when two neighboring atoms share a pair of electrons.

cove (kōv) *n.* **1.** a small, sheltered inlet or bay in a shoreline. **2.** a sheltered hollow, as in hills or a wood.

cov·en (kuv′ən) *n.* a gathering or assembly of witches.

cov·e·nant (kuv′ə nənt) *n.* an agreement between two or more persons or groups, especially a solemn and formal one: *A general association of nations must be formed under specific covenants* (Woodrow Wilson). —*v.i.* to enter into a covenant.

Cov·en·try (kuv′ən trē, kov′ən trē) *n.* a state of being completely ignored by one's associates; banishment or exclusion from society. ▲ used especially in the phrase *to*

at; āpe; fär; câre; end; mē; it; īce; pîerce; hot; ōld; sông, fôrk; oil; out; up; ūse; rüle; pull; tûrn; chin; sing; shop; thin; this; hw in white; zh in treasure. The symbol ə stands for the unstressed vowel sound heard in about, taken, pencil, lemon, and circus.

225

send to Coventry. [From *Coventry*, the city in England where Royalists were sent to be imprisoned during the English Civil War.]

cov·er (kuv′ər) *v.t.* **1.** to put something over or upon: *I covered the table with a tablecloth. The workers covered the furniture before painting.* **2.** to be over the surface of; spread or extend over: *Snow covered the ground. The dog was covered with mud.* **3.** to hide from view or knowledge; conceal: *to cover a mistake with a lie. Darkness covered the thief's flight.* **4.** to protect against loss or harm: *This health insurance plan covers all the employees of the company.* **5.** to travel or pass over: *The bus covered the distance in fifteen minutes.* **6.** to deal with; treat; include: *This book covers the subject of the American Revolution. The rules cover every possible situation.* **7. a.** to aim a firearm or other weapon at: *The police officer covered the thief with a pistol.* **b.** to protect by shooting or being ready to shoot at an enemy: *The artillery covered the brigade while it crossed the river.* **8.** to get the details of; report: *This newspaper covers sports thoroughly.* **9.** to be enough: *Will $20 cover dinner?* **10.** *Sports.* **a.** to guard or defend against (an opposing player): *to cover a receiver in football.* **b.** to be responsible for defending (an area or position): *to cover a base in baseball.* —*n.* **1.** something that covers: *the cover of a book.* **2.** protection or shelter: *The hikers took cover in a barn when the storm broke.* **3.** something that hides or disguises: *The thief escaped under the cover of darkness.* **4.** a place setting for one person at a table, including silverware, dishes, and linens.

·**under cover.** secret or secretly.

cov·er·age (kuv′ər ij, kuv′rij) *n.* **1.** the extent or degree to which something is covered. **2.** all the risks covered by the terms of an insurance policy. **3.** the act, manner, or extent of gathering and reporting news: *The television networks provided coverage of the election.*

cov·er·all (kuv′ər ôl′) *also,* **cov·er·alls.** *n.* a loose-fitting one-piece garment worn by workers to protect their clothes.

cover crop, a crop planted in a field or orchard to protect the soil from erosion or to enrich the soil between plantings of other crops. Clover and rye are often planted as cover crops.

covered wagon, a large wagon with a canvas cover spread on hoops or other supports, used especially by pioneers traveling westward in the United States.

cov·er·ing (kuv′ər ing) *n.* anything that covers.

cov·er·let (kuv′ər lit) *n.* an outer covering for a bed.

cov·ert (kuv′ərt, kō′vərt) *adj.* kept out of sight; secret; concealed; hidden: *a covert glance. They made a covert attempt to communicate with the prisoner.* —*n.* **1.** a hiding place; shelter. **2.** a thicket that gives shelter to wild animals or game. —**cov′ert·ly,** *adv.* —**cov′ert·ness,** *n.*

cov·er·up (kuv′ər up′) *n.* an attempt to conceal something, especially something dishonest or illegal.

cov·et (kuv′it) *v.t.* to have an eager desire for (something that belongs to another person): *I coveted my best friend's new baseball glove.*

cov·et·ous (kuv′i təs) *adj.* eagerly desiring something belonging to another person: *Don't be so covetous of your friends' possessions.* —**cov′et·ous·ly,** *adv.* —**cov′et·ous·ness,** *n.*

cov·ey (kuv′ē) *n., pl.* **cov·eys.** **1.** a small flock of partridges, quail, grouse, or similar birds. **2.** any small group: *a covey of students.*

cow[1] (kou) *n.* **1.** the full-grown female of domestic cattle, raised especially to provide milk. **2.** the female of certain other large animals, such as the moose, elephant, or whale. [From the Old English word *cū* meaning "a cow."]

cow[2] (kou) *v.t.* to frighten with threats; make afraid; intimidate: *The bully cowed the whole class.* [From the

Old Norse word *kūga* meaning "to frighten, oppress."]

cow·ard (kou′ərd) *n.* a person who lacks courage; person who is very easily frightened, or who runs away from any form of danger or trouble.

cow·ard·ice (kou′ər dis) *n.* lack of courage; shameful fear of danger, difficulty, or pain.

cow·ard·ly (kou′ərd lē) *adj.* **1.** lacking courage; easily made afraid: *a cowardly person.* **2.** suitable for a coward; showing a lack of courage: *a cowardly act.* —*adv.* like a coward: *Don't act so cowardly.* —**cow′ard·li·ness,** *n.*

cow·bell (kou′bel′) *n.* a small bell hung around a cow's neck to indicate where it is.

cow·bird (kou′bûrd′) *n.* a small blackbird of North and South America that is often found living near cattle. Cowbirds frequently lay their eggs in the nests of other birds.

cow·boy (kou′boi′) *n.* a person who herds and tends cattle on a ranch, usually riding on horseback to perform the work.

cow·catch·er (kou′kach′ər) *n.* a metal frame on the front of a locomotive or streetcar for clearing the tracks of obstructions.

cow·er (kou′ər) *v.i.* to crouch or cringe, as in fear or shame: *The dog cowered in the corner during the thunderstorm.*

cow·girl (kou′gûrl′) *n.* a woman who herds or tends cattle on a ranch, usually riding on horseback to perform the work.

cow·hand (kou′hand′) *n.* a person who works on a cattle ranch; cowboy or cowgirl.

cow·herd (kou′hûrd′) *n.* a person who herds or tends cattle.

cow·hide (kou′hīd′) *n.* **1.** the hide of a cow. **2.** leather made from it. **3.** a strong, flexible whip made of braided leather or rawhide.

cowl (koul) *n.* **1.** a hood attached to a monk's robe. **2.** a monk's robe with a hood. **3.** the top front part of an automobile body to which the windshield and dashboard are attached. **4.** see **cowling.**

cow·lick (kou′lik′) *n.* a tuft of hair that grows in a different direction from the rest of the hair and will not lie flat.

cowl·ing (kou′ling) *n.* a streamlined, metal covering for a section of an airplane, especially one designed to cover an engine. Also, **cowl.**

co·work·er (kō′wûr′kər) *n.* a person with whom one works; fellow worker.

cow·pea (kou′pē′) *n.* **1.** a bushy or trailing vine related to the bean, widely planted as a forage or cover crop. It bears long pods containing kidney-shaped seeds that are eaten as a vegetable. **2.** the seed of this plant.

cow·poke (kou′pōk′) *n. Informal.* a cowhand.

cow·pox (kou′poks′) *n.* a mild but very contagious disease of cows caused by the same kind of virus that causes smallpox in humans. Smallpox vaccine is prepared from the cowpox virus.

cow·punch·er (kou′pun′chər) *n. Informal.* a cowhand.

cow·rie (kou′rē) *also,* **cow·ry.** *n., pl.* **cow·ries.** **1.** a small, glossy, brightly colored shell of any of various sea snails commonly found in warm, shallow waters of the Pacific and Indian Oceans. **2.** one of these snails.

cow·slip (kou′slip′) *n.* **1.** a wild plant related to the primrose, having fragrant yellow flowers. **2.** the flower of this plant. **3.** another word for **marsh marigold.**

cox·comb (koks′kōm′) *n.* **1.** a vain and pretentious person; conceited dandy. **2.** see **cockscomb** (*def. 2*).

cox·swain (kok′sən, kok′swān′) *also,* **cock·swain.** *n.* a person who steers a boat, especially the one who steers and gives directions to rowers in a racing shell.

coy (koi) *adj.* **1.** shy or modest; bashful. **2.** pretending to be shy or modest. —**coy′ly,** *adv.* —**coy′ness,** *n.*

coy·o·te (kī ō′tē, kī′ōt) *n., pl.* **coy·o·tes** or **coy·o·te.** a wolf of the prairies of central and western North America known for its howling at night. Also, **prairie wolf.**

coy·pu (koi′pü) *n., pl.* **coy·pus** or **coy·pu.** another word for **nutria.**

coz·en (kuz′ən) *v.t.* to cheat; deceive. —**coz′en·er,** *n.*

coz·en·age (kuz′ə nij) *n.* the act or practice of cozening; fraud.

co·zy (kō′zē) also, **co·sy.** *adj.,* **co·zi·er, co·zi·est.** warm and comfortable; snug: *The kitten found a cozy spot by the fire.* —*n., pl.* **co·zies.** a padded cloth or knitted cover for keeping the contents of a teapot warm. —**co′zi·ly,** *adv.* —**co′zi·ness,** *n.*

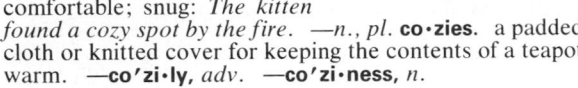

coyote

cp., compare.

c.p., candlepower.

C.P., Communist Party.

C.P.A., Certified Public Accountant.

cpd., compound.

Cpl., Corporal.

CPR, a sequence of emergency procedures aimed at restoring normal breathing and circulation of the blood when a person's heart has stopped beating. It includes mouth-to-mouth resuscitation and massage of the heart by applying rhythmic pressure on the breastbone. [An abbreviation of *c*(ardio) *p*(ulmonary) *r*(esuscitation).]

cps **1.** characters per second. **2.** cycles per second.

CPU, central processing unit.

Cr, the symbol for **chromium.**

crab[1] (krab) *n.* **1.** any of a group of animals having a hard shell and no backbone and living in water, especially salt water. Crabs have a broad, flat body, four pairs of jointed legs, and a pair of pincer claws. Many kinds of crabs are highly valued as food. **2.** any of various similar animals, such as the horseshoe crab. **3.** a machine or apparatus for hoisting or hauling heavy weights. **4.** a cross, ill-tempered person. —*v.i.,* **crabbed, crab·bing. 1.** to fish for or catch crabs. **2.** *Informal.* to find fault; complain. [From the Old English word *crabba* meaning "saltwater crab."] **crab′ber,** *n.* —**crab′like′,** *adj.*

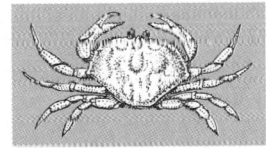

crab[1] *(def. 1)*

crab[2] (krab) *n.* see **crab apple.** [Of uncertain origin.]

crab apple **1.** any of various small, hard, sour apples, used for making jelly. **2.** the tree bearing this apple.

crab·bed (krab′id) *adj.* **1.** easily irritated; ill-tempered; crabby. **2.** (of handwriting) hard to read or make out; cramped. —**crab′bed·ly,** *adv.* —**crab′bed·ness,** *n.*

crab·by (krab′ē) *adj.,* **crab·bi·er, crab·bi·est.** easily irritated; ill-tempered; crabbed. —**crab′bi·ly,** *adv.* —**crab′bi·ness,** *n.*

crab grass, a coarse, hardy grass that spreads rapidly and is a common weed in lawns and gardens.

crack (krak) *n.* **1.** a break in something that does not cause its parts to separate completely: *a crack in a dish, a crack in the ice on a pond.* **2.** a sound like that made by something breaking; sudden, sharp noise: *the crack of a whip, the crack of a bat hitting a baseball.* **3.** *Informal.* a sharp, heavy blow: *The falling branch gave me a crack on the head.* **4.** a narrow opening: *There are cracks between the boards. Leave the window open a crack.* **5.** an instant; moment: *the crack of dawn.* **6.** *Informal.* a try; attempt: *Let me have a crack at opening that jar.* **7.** *Slang.* a witty or clever remark; joke; wisecrack:

You're always making cracks about my cooking. **8.** *Slang.* a form of the highly addictive drug cocaine. —*v.i.* **1.** to break without completely separating into parts; become split: *The cup cracked when it hit the floor.* **2.** to make a sudden, sharp noise, as in breaking: *The dry twig cracked underfoot.* **3.** to be harsh, shrill, or uneven; change suddenly in tone: *The announcer's voice cracked.* **4.** *Informal.* to break down; fail: *The soldier cracked under the pressure of combat.* —*v.t.* **1.** to cause to break without completely separating into parts: *The boiling water cracked the glass.* **2.** to cause to make a sudden, sharp sound: *The magician cracked the whip.* **3.** *Informal.* to hit or strike with a sharp blow: *I cracked my head against the shelf.* **4.** *Informal.* to break into; force open: *A thief cracked the safe.* **5.** to find the solution to; learn the meaning of: *to crack a secret code.* **6.** to subject (petroleum) to the process of cracking. —*adj. Informal.* excellent; first-rate: *a crack football player.*

·**cracked up to be.** *Informal.* claimed or believed to be: *This new soap is not all it's cracked up to be.*

·**to crack a joke.** to make a witty or clever remark; tell a joke.

·**to crack down on.** to take strict measures against; become strict with: *to crack down on crime.*

·**to crack up.** *Informal.* **a.** to crash: *to crack up a car.* **b.** to suffer a mental breakdown.

crack·down (krak′doun′) *n.* a sudden, strict enforcement of laws or rules: *a crackdown on illegal gambling.*

cracked (krakt) *adj.* **1.** having a crack or cracks; broken without a complete separation of parts: *a cracked dish.* **2.** broken into small pieces; crushed: *cracked wheat.* **3.** (of the voice) harsh, shrill, or uneven; changing in tone. **4.** *Informal.* crazy; insane.

crack·er (krak′ər) *n.* a thin, crisp biscuit.

crack·er·jack (krak′ər jak′) *Slang. n.* a person or thing of exceptional ability or quality. —*adj.* of exceptional ability or quality: *a crackerjack tennis player.*

crack·ing (krak′ing) *n.* the process of breaking down complex molecules of petroleum into simpler molecules by means of heat and pressure. Greater amounts of gasoline are obtained by cracking.

crack·le (krak′əl) *v.i.,* **crack·led, crack·ling.** to make a series of slight, sharp sounds: *The dry leaves crackled when we walked on them.* —*n.* **1.** a series or one of a series of slight, sharp sounds: *the crackle of burning twigs.* **2.** a pattern of very small, irregular cracks in the surface of certain kinds of china or glassware.

crack·ling (krak′ling) *n.* **1.** a series of slight, sharp sounds. **2.** the crisp, browned skin of roasted pork. **3. cracklings.** the crisp part remaining after lard or fat has been removed from pork or chicken by frying.

crack·ly (krak′lē) *adj.* making a crackling sound: *crackly wrapping paper.*

crack·pot (krak′pot′) *Informal. n.* a very eccentric or crazy person. —*adj.* eccentric; crazy; foolish: *a crackpot scheme for making money.*

crack–up (krak′up′) *n.* **1.** a crash or collision, as of a car or airplane. **2.** *Informal.* a mental or physical breakdown.

cra·dle (krā′dəl) *n.* **1.** a small bed for a baby, usually on rockers. **2.** a place or region where something starts or begins to develop: *Greece has been called the cradle of democracy.* **3.** a framework supporting something large,

at; āpe; fär; câre; end; mē; it; īce; pîerce; hot; ōld; sông, fôrk; oil; out; up; ūse; rüle; pùll; tûrn; chin; sing; shop; thin; **th**is; hw in white; zh in treasure. The symbol ə stands for the unstressed vowel sound heard in about, taken, pencil, lemon, and circus.

C

as a ship, while it is being built or repaired. **4.** the part of a telephone that holds the receiver. **5.** a box on rockers used to wash gold from earth. **6.** a frame with several long curved prongs, attached to a scythe, to collect stalks of grain as they are cut. —*v.t.*, **cra·dled, cra·dling. 1.** to put, rock, or hold in or as if in a cradle: *to cradle a child in one's arms.* **2.** to support in or on a cradle, as a ship. **3.** to wash (earth containing gold) in a cradle. **4.** to cut (grain) using a cradle.

craft (kraft) *n.* **1.** special skill or ability: *The cabinetmaker worked with precision and craft.* **2.** skill in deceiving; deceit; guile; cunning. **3.** a trade or occupation requiring special skill or ability: *the craft of carpentry.* **4.** all the members of a trade collectively. **5.** a boat, ship, or aircraft: *a pirate craft.* **6.** boats, ships, or aircraft: *All small craft remained in the harbor until the storm had passed.*

crafts·man (krafts′mən) *n., pl.* **crafts·men** (krafts′-mən). a person who has skill in a craft; skilled worker; artisan.

crafts·man·ship (krafts′mən ship′) *n.* the skill or work of a craftsman or craftswoman: *The beautifully made desk shows superb craftsmanship.*

crafts·per·son (krafts′pûr′sən) *n., pl.* **crafts·per·sons.** a person who has skill in a craft; skilled worker; craftsman; artisan.

crafts·wom·an (krafts′wŭm′ən) *n., pl.* **crafts·wom·en** (krafts′wim′ən). a woman who has skill in a craft; female artisan.

craft union, a labor union whose members work in a single craft or occupation.

craft·y (kraf′tē) *adj.*, **craft·i·er, craft·i·est.** skillful or showing skill in deceiving; sly; wily; cunning: *a crafty swindler, a crafty scheme.* —**craft′i·ly,** *adv.* —**craft·i·ness,** *n.*

crag (krag) *n.* a steep, rugged rock or cliff.

crag·gy (krag′ē) *adj.*, **crag·gi·er, crag·gi·est. 1.** having many crags; steep and rugged: *Northern Scotland is a craggy region.* **2.** rough and uneven: *a face with craggy features.* —**crag′gi·ness,** *n.*

cram (kram) *v.*, **crammed, cram·ming.** —*v.t.* **1.** to fill (something) completely or with more than it normally or easily holds: *I crammed my suitcase with clothes.* **2.** to force or crowd (something) into a tight or crowded space: *We crammed more than a hundred books into the small bookcase.* —*v.i. Informal.* to study hastily and intensely for an examination or the like: *They're cramming for tomorrow's test.*

cramp¹ (kramp) *n.* **1.** a sharp, painful tightening that occurs suddenly in a muscle or group of muscles: *The runner suffered a leg cramp and was forced to drop out of the race.* **2.** a spasm that develops in a muscle that has tired from being used too much: *to get a cramp in a hand from writing too long.* **3. cramps.** sharp pains in the abdomen. —*v.t.* to cause to have a cramp or cramps. —*v.i.* to suffer a cramp. [From the Middle French word *crampe* meaning "painful contraction."]

cramp² (kramp) *n.* **1.** a metal bar bent at the ends, used for holding together pieces of stone, timber, or the like. **2.** anything that confines or hinders. —*v.t.* **1.** to fasten or hold with a cramp. **2.** to confine or limit; restrict; hamper: *Our vacation plans were cramped by a lack of money.* [From the Middle Dutch word *crampe* meaning "a hook."]

cram·pon (kram′pən) *n.* **1.** one of a hinged pair of iron bars bent in the form of hooks, used to lift heavy objects. **2. crampons.** spiked iron plates attached to the soles of shoes or boots to help in climbing mountains or walking on ice.

cran·ber·ry (kran′ber′ē, kran′bə rē) *n., pl.* **cran·ber·ries. 1.** the sour, red berry of a low, creeping shrub, used for sauce, juice, and jelly. **2.** the shrub bearing this fruit, growing in bogs and swamps.

crane (krān) *n.* **1.** a large wading bird that lives in swamps and marshes, having very long, thin legs and a long neck and bill. **2.** a large machine for lifting and moving heavy weights by means of cables attached to a long, movable arm. **3.** any of various devices in which a movable arm is used to support something. —*v.*, **craned, cran·ing.** —*v.t.* to stretch out (the neck) in order to see better. —*v.i.* to stretch out the neck: *The people in the back row had to crane to see the stage.*

cra·ni·al (krā′nē əl) *adj.* of or relating to the skull: *The blow injured a cranial nerve.*

cra·ni·um (krā′nē əm) *n., pl.* **cra·ni·ums** or **cra·ni·a** (krā′nē-ə). **1.** the skull. **2.** the part of the skull that encloses the brain.

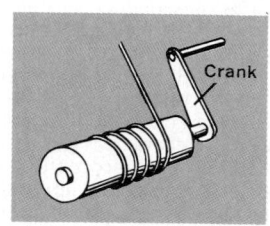
crane *(def. 1)*

crank (krangk) *n.* **1.** a device that transmits motion from one part of a machine to another by turning. A crank has an arm or handle attached at right angles to the end of a shaft. **2.** *Informal.* a person who has odd ideas or behaves oddly; eccentric or unbalanced person: *Police said that the odd telephone calls were the work of a crank.* **3.** *Informal.* a grouchy, ill-tempered person. —*v.t.* to start or operate with a crank: *It was necessary to crank the engine of some old automobiles by hand.* —*adj.* of, relating to, or from a person who is a crank: *a crank telephone call.*

crank *(def. 1)*

crank·case (krangk′kās′) *n.* a metal case enclosing the crankshaft of an engine, as in an automobile.

crank·shaft (krangk′shaft′) *n.* a shaft driven by or driving a crank. The crankshaft of an automobile engine serves to change the up-and-down motion of the pistons into the rotary motion of the shaft that drives the wheels.

crank·y (krang′kē) *adj.*, **crank·i·er, crank·i·est.** cross or ill-tempered; irritable; grouchy. —**crank′i·ly,** *adv.* —**crank′i·ness,** *n.*

cran·ny (kran′ē) *n., pl.* **cran·nies.** a small, narrow opening; crack; crevice; chink.

crape (krāp) another spelling of **crepe.**

crap·pie (krap′ē) *n.* a North American freshwater fish related to the sunfish, used for food.

craps (kraps) *n.* a gambling game played with two dice.

crash¹ (krash) *n., pl.* **crash·es. 1.** a sudden, loud noise, as of something shattering or breaking: *There was a crash when the ball went through the window.* **2.** a heavy fall or breaking with force: *the crash of a tree through the roof.* **3.** a violent, destructive collision or fall, as of a car or airplane: *There have been several crashes at that intersection.* **4.** a sudden failure or breakdown in a computer operation. **5.** a sudden ruin or collapse, as of a business: *Many people lost money in the stock market crash.* —*v.i.* **1. a.** to make a sudden, loud noise: *The thunder crashed overhead.* **b.** to move with much noise: *We heard them crashing through the bushes.* **2.** to fall or break with force and a loud noise: *The cups crashed to the floor.* **3.** to collide violently or destructively: *The car crashed into a tree.* **4.** to land or fall so as to be damaged or destroyed: *The plane crashed during the storm.* **5.** (of a computer operation) to fail or stop suddenly. **6.** to suffer sudden collapse or ruin: *The business crashed last year.* —*v.t.* **1.** to cause to break noisily and violently; smash; shatter: *They crashed their* *glasses against the table.* **2.** to cause (an aircraft, automobile, or the like) to be in a crash: *The pilot crashed the plane into a forest.* **3.** *Informal.* to enter (a dance, theater, stadium, or the like) without being invited or without having a ticket: *Some teenagers from out of town tried to crash the party.* —*adj.* carried out with all possible speed, effort, and resources: *a crash program to build new housing.* [From the Middle English word *crashen* meaning "to smash" or "to be shattered," probably from the Old French word *crasir* "to shatter, crush."]

crash² (krash) *n.* a cotton or linen cloth made from uneven and irregular yarns, used for towels, tablecloths, curtains, and the like. [Short for the Russian word *krashenina* meaning "colored linen," from the word *krashenie* "coloring."]

crash–dive (krash′dīv′) *v.,* **crash-dived, crash-div·ing.** —*v.i.* to make a crash dive. —*v.t.* to cause to make a crash dive: *to crash-dive a submarine.*

crash dive, a sudden rapid dive made by a submarine, especially to avoid attack by an enemy aircraft or ship.

crash helmet, a padded helmet for protection against head injury, worn especially by motorcyclists, automobile racers, and pilots.

crash–land (krash′land′) *v.i., v.t.* to make or cause to make a crash landing: *to crash-land a plane in a field.*

crash landing, the landing of an aircraft under emergency conditions that make a normal landing impossible, especially in a way that causes some damage to the aircraft.

crass (kras) *adj.* stupid and vulgar; coarse: *crass behavior, a crass disregard for the feelings of others.* —**crass′ly,** *adv.* —**crass′ness,** *n.*

crate (krāt) *n.* a box, case, or framework, usually of wooden slats, used for protecting things during shipping or storage: *an orange crate, a furniture crate.* —*v.t.,* **crat·ed, crat·ing.** to pack in a crate or crates: *The farmer crated the lettuce to be sent to the market.*

cra·ter (krā′tər) *n.* **1.** a bowl-shaped hollow area at the mouth of a volcano. **2.** any hole in the ground resembling this, such as one caused by the explosion of a bomb or by the impact of a meteorite. **3.** any of numerous circular depressions in the surface of the moon, usually surrounded by a high ridge and believed to be caused either by the impact of meteorites or by volcanic action.

crater (def. 3)

cra·vat (krə vat′) *n.* a necktie or a scarf worn as a necktie.

crave (krāv) *v.t.,* **craved, crav·ing. 1.** to long or yearn for; desire eagerly: *The artist craved fame.* **2.** to need greatly; require: *The wound craved a doctor's attention.* **3.** to ask for earnestly; beg: *The knight craved a favor of the court.*

cra·ven (krā′vən) *adj.* extremely cowardly. —*n.* a complete coward —**cra′ven·ly,** *adv.* —**cra′ven·ness,** *n.*

crav·ing (krā′ving) *n.* an eager desire; longing; yearning: *The exhausted travelers had a craving for sleep.*

craw (krô) *n.* **1.** the crop of a bird or insect. **2.** the stomach of any animal.

craw·fish (krô′fish′) *n., pl.* **craw·fish** or **craw·fish·es.** another word for **crayfish.**

crawl (krôl) *v.i.* **1.** to move slowly by dragging the body

along the ground, as an earthworm does. **2.** to move slowly on hands and knees: *The baby crawled across the room.* **3.** to move slowly: *Traffic crawled through the city.* **4.** to swarm or be alive with crawling things: *The picnic table was crawling with ants.* **5.** to feel as if covered with crawling things: *The ghost story made my skin crawl.* —*n.* **1.** the act of crawling; slow crawling motion: *Traffic was slowed to a crawl during the snowstorm.* **2.** a rapid swimming stroke performed with the face down, in which the arms are lifted over the head one after the other and the feet kick continuously.

crawl space, a narrow space under a roof or floor, usually one that gives access to wiring or plumbing.

cray·fish (krā′fish′) *n., pl.* **cray·fish** or **cray·fish·es.** any of various small shellfish that closely resemble the lobster, found in fresh water in most parts of the world and frequently used as food. Also, **crawfish.**

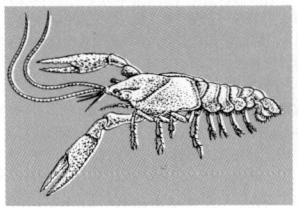

crayfish

cray·on (krā′on, krā′ən) *n.* **1.** a colored stick or pencil of wax material, chalk, charcoal, or another substance, used for drawing and writing. **2.** a drawing made with a crayon or crayons. —*v.t.* to draw, color, or mark with a crayon or crayons: *The children crayoned the poster for the fair. Don't crayon that wall!*

craze (krāz) *n.* something that is very popular for a short time; fad: *Long skirts were a craze last year.* —*v.t.,* **crazed, craz·ing. 1.** to make insane: *The sudden tragedy almost crazed the family.* **2.** to make very small cracks in the surface of (a piece of china or glassware): *to craze a vase.*

cra·zy (krā′zē) *adj.,* **cra·zi·er, cra·zi·est. 1.** not having a sound or normal mind; mentally ill; insane; mad: *The prisoner nearly became crazy from years of confinement.* **2.** caused by or showing mental illness. **3.** not practical or sensible; foolish; silly: *That is the craziest idea that I have ever heard of.* **4.** *Informal.* very fond or enthusiastic: *They are crazy about cars.* —**cra′zi·ly,** *adv.* —**cra′zi·ness,** *n.*

crazy bone, another term for **funny bone.**

crazy quilt, a quilt made of pieces of cloth of different materials, shapes, colors, and designs, that are sewed together without any regular pattern.

creak (krēk) *v.i.* to make a sharp grating or squeaking sound: *The old rocking chair creaks.* —*n.* a sharp grating or squeaking sound: *The rusty old gate swung open with a creak. I heard the creak of branches in the wind.*

creak·y (krē′kē) *adj.,* **creak·i·er, creak·i·est.** making creaks or likely to creak: *an old staircase with creaky steps.* —**creak′i·ly,** *adv.* —**creak′i·ness,** *n.*

cream (krēm) *n.* **1.** the fatty, yellowish part of milk, that contains butterfat and rises to the top of milk that is not homogenized. **2.** a food made from or resembling this substance in some way: *chocolate creams, cream of tomato soup.* **3.** a soft preparation used to cleanse or protect the skin: *hand cream, shaving cream.* **4.** the best or choicest part of anything: *the cream of the crop, the cream of society.* **5.** the color of cream; yellowish white. —*v.t.* **1.** to remove the cream from; skim: *to cream milk.* **2.** to cook with cream, milk, or a cream sauce: *to cream*

at; āpe; fär; câre; end; mē; it; īce; pîerce; hot; ōld; sông, fôrk; oil; out; up; ūse; rüle; pùll; tûrn; chin; sing; shop; thin; this; hw in white; zh in treasure. The symbol ə stands for the unstressed vowel sound heard in about, taken, pencil, lemon, and circus.

229

onions. **3.** to blend into a soft, creamy mass: *to cream butter and sugar.* *—v.i.* to form cream or a creamy substance on the top. *—adj.* having the color of cream; yellowish white: *a dress of cream velvet.*

cream cheese, a soft, smooth, white cheese made from a mixture of milk and cream.

cream·er (krē′mər) *n.* **1.** a small pitcher used for serving cream. **2.** a powder or liquid used like cream in coffee or tea but containing no dairy products.

cream·er·y (krē′mə rē) *n., pl.* **cream·er·ies. 1.** a place where butter, cheese, and other dairy products are made. **2.** a place where milk, cream, and dairy products are sold.

cream of tar·tar (tär′tər) a white, powdery compound containing potassium, hydrogen, carbon, and oxygen, used especially in baking powder, and also in medicine.

cream·puff (krēm′puf′) *n.* a very light pastry shell filled with custard or whipped cream.

cream sauce, a sauce made of cream or milk cooked with flour and butter.

cream·y (krē′mē) *adj.,* **cream·i·er, cream·i·est. 1.** containing cream; having much cream: *a rich, creamy dessert.* **2.** resembling cream, as in appearance or color: *a creamy scum on a pond.* **—cream′i·ness,** *n.*

crease (krēs) *n.* **1.** a line or mark made by folding, wrinkling, or pressing cloth, paper, or the like; fold; ridge: *the crease in a pair of trousers.* **2.** any similar line or mark. *—v.,* **creased, creas·ing.** *—v.t.* **1.** to make a crease or creases on or in: *Years of exposure to the sun and wind had creased the sailor's face.* **2.** to graze with a bullet. *—v.i.* to become creased: *Our clothes creased when we crammed them into the trunk.*

cre·ate (krē āt′) *v.t.,* **cre·at·ed, cre·at·ing. 1.** to bring into being; cause to exist: *The constitutional convention created a new government.* **2.** to give rise to; bring about; cause: *Your rude attitude created ill will.* **3.** to produce by one's own thought or imagination: *That author has created many famous characters.*

cre·a·tion (krē ā′shən) *n.* **1.** the act of creating: *The creation of the motion picture took many months.* **2.** anything that has been created, especially something that is produced by human intelligence or imagination: *These paintings are brilliant creations.* **3.** the world and all things in and around it; universe. **4. the Creation.** in the Bible, God's act of creating the universe.

cre·a·tion·ism (krē ā′shə niz′em) *n.* **1.** the belief that the universe, and everything in it, was created by God in its present form and did not slowly evolve or develop. **2.** the doctrine that the universe was created by God in the exact way described in the book of Genesis.

cre·a·tive (krē ā′tiv) *adj.* **1.** having the power to create: *A poet must have a creative imagination.* **2.** showing originality: *creative thinking.* **—cre·a′tive·ly,** *adv.* **—cre·a′tive·ness,** *n.*

cre·a·tiv·i·ty (krē′ā tiv′i tē) *n.* the quality of being creative; ability to create.

cre·a·tor (krē ā′tər) *n.* **1.** a person or thing that creates. **2. the Creator.** God.

crea·ture (krē′chər) *n.* **1.** any living being, especially an animal as distinct from a human being: *a sea creature, the creatures of the forest.* **2.** a human being. **3.** a person who is completely dependent upon or under the influence of someone or something; tool: *to be a creature of habit.*

crèche (kresh, krāsh) *n.* a model of the scene at the birth of Jesus, often displayed at Christmas.

cre·dence (krē′dəns) *n.* belief: *Don't give any credence to those rumors.*

cre·den·tials (kri den′shəlz) *pl. n.* letters or documents that prove a person's identity or authority: *The ambassadors presented their credentials to the court.*

cred·i·ble (kred′ə bəl) *adj.* capable of being believed; believable; reliable: *a credible witness; a credible account.* **—cred′i·bil′i·ty,** *n.* **—cred′i·bly,** *adv.*

cred·it (kred′it) *n.* **1.** belief in the truth of something; faith; trust: *Do you give credit to that story?* **2.** a good reputation: *a person with great credit in our town.* **3.** praise for some action or quality: *You deserve great credit for working so hard to improve your marks.* **4.** a person or thing that brings honor, approval, or praise: *That student is a credit to the school.* **5. credits.** acknowledgments for work done or help given, as in a motion picture: *The director's name appeared in the credits.* **6.** trust or confidence in a person's ability and intention to pay debts: *Several stores have extended them credit.* **7.** a reputation in financial matters: *Your credit is no longer good at the store, because you did not pay your bills.* **8.** *Bookkeeping.* **a.** an entry of an amount in an account as payment of an existing or future debt: *Carry that payment as a credit against next month's billing.* **b.** the right-hand side of an account where such entries are made. **9.** a balance in one's favor, as in a bank account: *I have a credit of fifty dollars in my account.* **10.** the time allowed for payment of a debt: *to have six months' credit.* **11.** an official entry on a student's record showing satisfactory completion of a course of study: *I received credit for the history course.* **12.** a unit of such study: *to take three credits of math.* *—v.t.* **1.** to believe; trust: *Do you expect me to credit that silly story?* **2.** to give financial credit to: *The bank credited the checks to my account.* **3.** to attribute to: *History credits the Chinese with inventing gunpowder.*
·on credit. with the understanding that one will pay at a future time.

cred·it·a·ble (kred′i tə bəl) *adj.* bringing or deserving honor or credit; praiseworthy: *a creditable effort to solve a difficult problem.* **—cred′it·a·ble·ness,** *n.* **—cred′it·a·bly,** *adv.*

credit card, a card entitling its holder to buy things or obtain services on credit.

cred·i·tor (kred′i tər) *n.* a person to whom a debt is owed.

credit union, a cooperative association that pools the savings of its members and draws from the savings to lend money to its members at low interest rates.

cred·it·wor·thy (kred′it wûr′thē) *adj.* qualified to receive financial credit: *The bank considered the small company creditworthy because it had repaid all its previous loans.*

cre·do (krē′dō, krā′dō) *n., pl.* **cre·dos.** a statement of belief; creed.

cre·du·li·ty (kri dü′li tē, kri dū′li tē) *n.* a readiness to believe, trust, or accept without proof; gullibility.

cred·u·lous (krej′ə ləs) *adj.* ready to believe, trust, or accept without proof; gullible. **—cred′u·lous·ly,** *adv.* **—cred′u·lous·ness,** *n.*

Cree (krē) *n., pl.* **Cree** or **Crees. 1.** a member of a tribe of North American Indians, formerly living in eastern and central Canada, now living mainly in Manitoba. **2.** the language of this tribe.

creed (krēd) *n.* **1.** a formal statement of religious belief. **2.** any formal statement of belief, principles, or opinions.

creek (krēk, krik) *n.* a small stream, usually larger than a brook and smaller than a river.

Creek (krēk) *n., pl.* **Creek** or **Creeks. 1.** a member of a confederacy of North American Indian tribes, formerly living in Alabama, Georgia, and northern Florida, now living in Oklahoma. **2.** the language of these tribes.

creel (krēl) *n.* **1.** an angler's basket for holding fish. **2.** a wicker trap for catching fish, crabs, or lobsters.

creep (krēp) *v.i.,* **crept, creep·ing. 1.** to move with the body close to a surface, especially on hands and knees along the ground; crawl: *The baby crept across the room. A spider crept across the window.* **2.** to move slowly, timidly, or stealthily: *Traffic crept along the highway. The burglar crept toward the open window.* **3.** to move or behave in a humble manner: *The child who had been scolded crept from the room.* **4.** to feel as if things were crawling over the skin: *The sound in the dark made my flesh creep.* **5.** (of a plant) to grow along a surface by sending out small tendrils or roots along the length of the stem: *Vines crept up the wall.* —*n.* **1.** the act of creeping; slow movement. **2. the creeps.** *Informal.* a feeling as if things were crawling over the skin, caused by fear or horror: *That horror movie gave me the creeps.*

creep·er (krē′pər) *n.* **1.** a person or thing that creeps. **2.** any plant that grows along a surface by sending out small tendrils or roots along the length of the stem, such as ivy. **3.** a small bird that creeps up and down tree trunks to find insects to feed on.

creep·y (krē′pē) *adj.*, **creep·i·er, creep·i·est.** having or causing a feeling of things crawling over the skin, as from fear or horror. —**creep′i·ly,** *adv.* —**creep′i·ness,** *n.*

cre·mate (krē′māt, kri māt′) *v.t.*, **cre·mat·ed, cre·mat·ing. 1.** to burn (a dead body) to ashes. **2.** to consume by fire; burn up. —**cre·ma′tion,** *n.*

cre·ma·to·ri·um (krē′mə tôr′ē əm, krem′ə tôr′ē əm) *n.*, *pl.* **cre·ma·to·ri·ums** or **cre·ma·to·ri·a** (krē′mə tôr′ē-ə, krem′ə tôr′ē ə). a furnace or place for cremation. Also, **cre′ma·tor′y.**

Cre·ole (krē′ōl) *n.* **1.** a direct descendant of the first French and Spanish settlers of the Gulf Coast, especially Louisiana. **2.** a Spanish or French person born in the West Indies or Latin America. **3. a.** the dialect of French spoken by Creoles in Louisiana. **b.** see **Haitian Creole. 4.** a person who has both black and Creole ancestors. —*adj.* **1.** of or relating to Creoles. **2. creole.** (of food) prepared with sweet peppers, tomatoes, and onions and highly seasoned.

cre·o·sol (krē′ə sôl′) *n.* a colorless, oily, aromatic liquid used as an antiseptic.

cre·o·sote (krē′ə sōt′) *n.* **1.** a colorless or yellowish oily liquid obtained by distilling wood tar and used in medicines and antiseptics. **2.** a similar liquid obtained from coal tar and used as a wood preservative. —*v.t.*, **cre·o·sot·ed, cre·o·sot·ing.** to treat with creosote.

crepe (krāp) *n.* *also,* **crêpe, crape. 1.** any of various fabrics made of silk, cotton, rayon, and wool, and having a crinkled surface. **2.** a band of black crepe worn or hung as a sign of mourning. **3.** a thin pancake, usually folded to hold a filling: *a strawberry crepe.* [From the French word *crêpe* meaning this fabric, from the Old French word *crespe* "curly," from the Latin word *crispus* "curled, crinkled."]

crepe paper, a thin paper with a crinkled surface.

crepe rubber, rubber with a crinkled surface, used especially for the soles of shoes.

crept (krept) the past tense and past participle of **creep.**

cre·scen·do (kri shen′dō) *adj.*, *adv.* with a gradual increase in loudness or force. —*n.*, *pl.* **cre·scen·dos. 1.** a gradual increase in loudness or force. **2.** *Music.* a crescendo passage.

cres·cent (kres′ənt) *n.* **1.** the shape of the visible part of the moon in its first or last quarter. **2.** anything with this shape: *The row of houses was built in a crescent.* —*adj.* **1.** increasing; growing. **2.** shaped like the moon in its first or last quarter.

cress (kres) *n.*, *pl.* **cress·es. 1.** the pungent leaves of any of several plants, especially watercress, used as a garnish or in salads. **2.** any of these plants.

cres·set (kres′it) *n.* a metal container mounted on a pole or suspended from above, containing burning pitch-covered rope, oil, grease, wood, or other fuel to give light.

crest (krest) *n.* **1.** a tuft, ridge, or other natural growth on the head, neck, or back of a bird or other animal, as the comb of the rooster. **2.** a plume or similar ornament on the top of a helmet. **3.** a decoration above a coat of arms. **4.** the highest point or stage of anything: *the crest of a wave. The musicians reached the crest of their popularity with their second album.* —*v.i.* to reach the highest point or stage: *The flood crested late Sunday night.*

crest·ed (kres′tid) *adj.* having a crest.

crest·fall·en (krest′fô′lən) *adj.* having had one's feelings or pride hurt; dejected; disheartened: *to be crestfallen because one wasn't invited to a party.*

Cre·ta·ceous (kri tā′shəs) *n.* the last geological period of the Mesozoic era, during which sandstone, limestone, and chalk deposits were formed. —*adj.* of, relating to, or characteristic of this period. [From the Latin word *cretaceus* meaning "chalklike," from the word *creta* "chalk."]

Cre·tan (krē′tən) *adj.* of or relating to Crete or its people. —*n.* a person who was born in or is a citizen of Crete.

cre·tin (krē′tən) *n.* a person having cretinism.

cre·tin·ism (krē′tə niz′əm) *n.* a condition present at birth or developing in infancy, characterized by stunted physical and mental development. It is caused by a severe lack of thyroid secretion.

cre·tonne (krē′ton, kri ton′) *n.* a strong, medium-weight cotton fabric in bold print patterns, used for curtains, draperies, and slipcovers.

cre·vasse (kri vas′) *n.* **1.** a deep crack or crevice, especially in a glacier. **2.** a break in a dike, levee, or dam.

crev·ice (krev′is) *n.* a narrow crack into or through something: *The wind blew in through the crevices in the walls of the cabin.*

crew[1] (krü) *n.* **1.** all the persons who have a job on a ship, aircraft, or spacecraft. **2.** all of these persons except the officers. **3.** a group of people assigned to or working together on a job: *a road crew, a wrecking crew.* **4.** any group of people; crowd; company. **5.** the members of a rowing team. [From the Old French word *creue* meaning "an increase" or "reinforcement," from the word *creistre* "to grow," from the Latin word *crescere* "to grow."]

crew[2] (krü) a past tense of **crow[1].**

crew cut, a style of haircut in which the hair is closely cropped.

crew·el (krü′əl) *n.* a loosely twisted worsted yarn, used for embroidery.

crew·el·work (krü′əl wûrk′) *n.* embroidery done with wool yarn on linen or other fabric.

crib (krib) *n.* **1.** a baby's small bed with high sides, usually barred. **2.** a manger or rack used to hold food for cattle. **3.** a small building or bin used to store corn, grain, salt, or the like. **4.** a framework of wood or metal used to strengthen or support, as in a mine shaft. **5.** *Informal.* notes or other aids used dishonestly by students, especially during examinations. —*v.*, **cribbed, crib·bing.** —*v.t.* **1.** to close in a crib; confine. **2.** *Informal.* to use dishonestly (another's words or ideas). —*v.i.* *Informal.* to use notes or other aids dishonestly: *Two students cribbed on the history examination.*

crib·bage (krib′ij) *n.* a card game, usually for two, three, or four players. The score is kept on a small board into which pegs fit.

crick (krik) *n.* a painful stiffness or cramp of the muscles, especially of the neck or back.

crick·et[1] (krik′it) *n.* a hopping insect, related to the grasshopper, having strong hind legs and long, slender antennae. The male of the species makes a chirping noise by rubbing the bases or edges of the forewings together. [From the

cricket[1]

Old French word *criquet* meaning this insect, from the word *criquer* "to rattle, crackle."]

crick·et² (krik'it) *n.* **1.** a game played in Great Britain and other countries on an oval grass field with a ball, bats, and wickets by two teams of eleven players each. **2.** *Informal.* fair play; good sportsmanship. [From the Middle French word *criquet* meaning "a wicket, stick," from the Middle Dutch word *cricke* "a crutch, stick."] —**crick'et·er,** *n.*

cried (krīd) the past tense and past participle of **cry.**

cri·er (krī'ər) *n.* **1.** a person who cries. **2.** an official who makes public announcements.

crime (krīm) *n.* **1.** an act that is forbidden by the law and for which a person can be punished. Murder, robbery, and blackmail are crimes. **2.** criminal activity: *There is much crime in that neighborhood.*

crim·i·nal (krim'ə nəl) *n.* a person who has committed a crime: *The criminal was sentenced to prison for robbery.* —*adj.* **1.** relating to crime or its punishment: *a criminal court.* **2.** guilty of crime. **3.** of or like crime. —**crim'i·nal·ly,** *adv.*

criminal law, a body of law defining crimes against the community, state, or nation and establishing punishments for the guilty.

crim·i·nol·o·gy (krim'ə nol'ə jē) *n.* the scientific study of crime and criminals. —**crim'i·nol'o·gist,** *n.*

crimp (krimp) *v.t.* to press into small, regular ridges, folds, or pleats: *to crimp paper.* —*n.* something that has been crimped; ridge; fold.

·to put a crimp in. *Informal.* to make difficult or complicated; hinder: *The rain put a crimp in their plans for a picnic.*

crimp·y (crim'pē) *adj.,* **crimp·i·er, crimp·i·est.** having small regular ridges, folds, or pleats.

crim·son (krim'zən, krim'sən) *n.* a deep red color. —*adj.* having the color crimson.

cringe (krinj) *v.i.,* **cringed, cring·ing.** **1.** to shrink, flinch, or crouch, as in fear, pain, or horror: *The mouse cringed when it saw the snake.* **2.** to behave in a humble manner; fawn. —**cring'er,** *n.*

crin·kle (kring'kəl) *v.,* **crin·kled, crin·kling.** —*v.i.* **1.** to form wrinkles or ripples; wrinkle: *Your nose crinkles when you laugh.* **2.** to make a rustling or crackling sound; crackle: *The fallen leaves crinkled when we walked on them.* —*v.t.* **1.** to cause to form wrinkles or ripples; crumple: *I crinkled the paper when I sat on it.* **2.** to cause to rustle or crackle. —*n.* **1.** a wrinkle; ripple. **2.** a rustle; crackle. —**crin'kly,** *adj.*

cri·noid (krī'noid) *n.* any of a group of colorful, flower-shaped saltwater animals, having branched arms around a single mouth opening. Crinoids are usually found in deep tropical waters.

crin·o·line (krin'ə lin) *n.* **1.** a stiff petticoat worn to give fullness to a skirt or dress. **2.** a stiff fabric used as a lining for skirts, hats, or the like.

crip·ple (krip'əl) *n.* a person or animal that cannot move normally because of injury, defect, or the loss of a part of the body. —*v.t.,* **crip·pled, crip·pling.** **1.** to make a cripple of: *The injuries from the accident crippled the skier.* **2.** to keep from working properly; disable: *The snowstorm crippled airline service.* —**crip'pler,** *n.*

cri·sis (krī'sis) *n., pl.* **cri·ses** (krī'sēz). **1.** an important and decisive turning point or event: *The battle of Stalingrad was a crisis in World War II.* **2.** a condition or period of difficulty or danger: *The war caused a crisis*

crinoid

in the nation's economic affairs. **3.** a turning point in an acute disease, toward either recovery or death.

crisis center, an organization or service that assists people in an emergency, such as the aftermath of an earthquake, or provides information and counseling to those in need of immediate assistance for emotional problems, for example, runaways or individuals suffering from severe depression.

crisp (krisp) *adj.* **1.** easily crumbled or crushed; brittle: *crisp potato chips.* **2.** firm and fresh: *crisp lettuce.* **3.** keen and bracing; brisk; invigorating: *a cold, crisp autumn day.* **4.** clear and short: *The general's orders were crisp and forceful.* **5.** (of hair) curly, wavy, or wiry. —*v.t.* to make crisp. —**crisp'ly,** *adv.* —**crisp'ness,** *n.*

crisp·y (kris'pē) *adj.,* **crisp·i·er, crisp·i·est.** brittle; crisp. —**crisp'i·ness,** *n.*

criss·cross (kris'krôs') *adj.* arranged in or marked with crossed lines; crossed; crossing. —*adv.* crosswise. —*n., pl.* **criss·cross·es.** a mark or pattern made by crossing lines. —*v.t.* **1.** to mark with crossing lines. **2.** to cross repeatedly: *We crisscrossed the neighborhood looking for our dog.* —*v.i.* to form a crisscross: *The paths of the hikers crisscrossed in the snow.*

cri·te·ri·on (krī tîr'ē ən) *n., pl.* **cri·te·ri·a** (krī tîr'ē ə) or **cri·te·ri·ons.** a rule, standard, or test by which something or someone can be judged or measured: *Location and price are two criteria to consider when buying a house.*

cri·tic (krit'ik) *n.* **1.** a person who judges the merits or faults of books, plays, motion pictures, music, paintings, or the like, especially as a profession: *What do the critics say about the new play?* **2.** a person who judges severely or unfavorably; faultfinder.

crit·i·cal (krit'i kəl) *adj.* **1.** inclined to find fault or judge severely or unfavorably: *The committee was critical of every plan that we suggested.* **2.** of or relating to critics or criticism: *a critical review of a new book.* **3.** of or relating to a crisis: *Winning the scholarship was a critical event in my life. The patient's condition is now critical.* —**crit'i·cal·ly,** *adv.*

crit·i·cism (krit'ə siz'əm) *n.* **1.** the act of criticizing. **2.** disapproval; faultfinding. **3.** the art or profession of judging the merits or faults of something. **4.** a critical comment, article, or review: *The new play had favorable criticisms in the newspaper.*

crit·i·cize (krit'ə sīz') *v.,* **crit·i·cized, crit·i·ciz·ing.** —*v.i.* to judge harshly or unfavorably; find fault: *Don't be so quick to criticize.* —*v.t.* **1.** to find fault with: *They criticized my behavior.* **2.** to discuss, judge, or examine the merits of: *to criticize a poem, to criticize a motion picture.* —**crit'i·ciz'er,** *n.*

cri·tique (kri tēk') *n.* a critical comment, article, or review.

crit·ter (krit'ər) *n. Informal.* a creature; animal.

croak (krōk) *n.* a deep, hoarse sound like that made by a frog or raven. —*v.i.* **1.** to make a deep, hoarse sound. **2.** to speak in a deep, hoarse voice. —*v.i.* to say with a croak.

Cro·at (krō'at) *n.* **1.** a person who was born in or is a citizen of Croatia. **2.** Serbo-Croatian as it is spoken and written in Croatia; Croatian.

Cro·a·tian (krō ā'shən) *adj.* of or relating to Croatia, its people, their language, or culture. —*n.* **1.** a Croat. **2.** the language of Croatia; Croat.

cro·chet (krō shā') *v.,* **cro·cheted** (krō shād'), **cro·chet·ing** (krō shā'ing). —*v.i.* to make interlocking loops or stitches using a single needle with a hook at one end. —*v.t.* to make by crocheting. —*n.* needlework done or made by crocheting.

crock (krok) *n.* an earthenware pot or jar.

crock·er·y (krok'ə rē) *n.* pots, dishes, and the like made of earthenware.

croc·o·dile (krok′ə dīl′) *n.* a large, lizardlike reptile having a thick skin and a long, narrow snout. Crocodiles are found in both fresh water and salt water in swampy areas of tropical and subtropical Asia, Africa, and America, especially along the Nile. They have strong jaws with long rows of teeth. See **alligator** for illustration.

crocodile tears, pretended or insincere tears. [From an old saying that crocodiles moaned to attract victims and wept while eating them.]

cro·cus (krō′kəs) *n., pl.* **cro·cus·es.** **1.** a cup-shaped flower of any of a group of plants, grown as a garden flower of various colors. Most crocuses bloom in early spring. **2.** the plant bearing this flower, having a single flower stalk and grasslike leaves, growing directly from an underground bulblike stem.

Croe·sus (krē′səs) *n.* any very rich man. [From *Croesus* (d. 546? B.C.), king of Lydia, known for his great wealth.]

croft (krôft) *n. British.* **1.** a small field for farming, especially one next to a house. **2.** a small rented farm.

crois·sant (krə sänt′) *n.* a rich, flaky roll in the shape of a crescent. [From the French word *croissant* meaning "crescent," used as the name for this roll.]

Croix de Guerre (krwä′də gâr′) a French military decoration awarded for distinguished service in war. [From the French phrase *croix de guerre* meaning "(the) cross of war."]

Cro-Mag·non (krō mag′non) *n.* a member of a prehistoric group of humans living in Europe and distinguished by a well-developed brain, tall, erect stature, and the use of stone and bone implements. [From *Cro-Magnon,* a cave in southern France where remains of this form of human were found.]

crone (krōn) *n.* a withered old woman.

Cro·nus (krō′nəs) *n. Greek Mythology.* the youngest of the Titans, who overthrew his father, Uranus, to become ruler of the universe and was in turn overthrown by his son, Zeus. In Roman Mythology he was called Saturn.

cro·ny (krō′nē) *n., pl.* **cro·nies.** a close friend; pal.

crook (kruk) *n.* **1.** a bent, curved, or hooked thing or part: *the crook of the arm.* **2.** any bend, curve or turn: *The pilot knew the crooks of the river by heart.* **3.** a shepherd's staff with a curve at one end. **4.** *Informal.* a person not to be trusted; thief; swindler. —*v.t.* to bend into a curved or hooked form: *to crook one's finger.* —*v.i.* to be or become crooked; bend; curve.

crook·ed (kruk′id) *adj.* **1.** not straight; bent; twisted: *a crooked path.* **2.** dishonest: *a crooked person, a crooked plan.* —**crook′ed·ly,** *adv.* —**crook′ed·ness,** *n.*

croon (krün) *v.i.* **1.** to sing or hum in a soft, low tone: *I crooned to the baby.* **2.** to sing in a soft and sentimental manner. —*v.t.* **1.** to sing or hum (a song or melody) in a soft, low tone. **2.** to sing (a popular song) in a soft and sentimental manner. —*n.* a soft, low singing or humming. —**croon′er,** *n.*

crop (krop) *n.* **1.** any plant or plant product growing or gathered for use, such as wheat, corn, or cotton. **2.** the entire amount of any plant product gathered in one place or season: *The wheat crop was not large this year.* **3.** a group or collection of anything appearing or produced together: *a crop of new students, a crop of lies.* **4.** the act or result of cropping. **5.** a short haircut. **6.** a pouch between the mouth and the stomach in some birds, in which food is

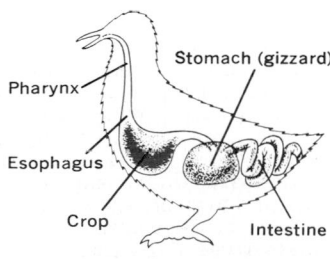

Pharynx
Stomach (gizzard)
Esophagus
Crop
Intestine

crop *(n., def. 6)*

prepared for digestion; craw. **7.** a short whip with a leather loop in place of a lash. —*v.t.,* **cropped, crop·ping.** **1.** to bite off or cut the top end of: *Sheep crop grass very short. The gardener cropped the hedges.* **2.** to cut short; trim; clip: *The barber cropped my hair.* **3.** to cause to bear a crop; raise crops on: *They cropped several acres with barley.*

·to crop up. to come up or appear unexpectedly: *Something cropped up and we had to change our plans at the last minute.*

crop-dust·ing (krop′dus′ting) *n.* the spraying of pesticides on crops, as from an airplane.

crop-dusting

crop·per (krop′ər) *n. Informal.* **1.** a heavy fall, as from a horse. **2.** *Informal.* a failure in an undertaking; collapse.

·to come a cropper. to fail miserably; collapse.

crop rotation, a method of farming in which crops grown in the same ground are changed, or rotated, in an orderly sequence. Crop rotation helps to replace soil nutrients used up by some crops and to control diseases and pests.

cro·quet (krō kā′) *n.* an outdoor game in which each player uses a mallet to drive a ball through small, arched wickets that are arranged in a particular order to form a course.

cro·quette (krō ket′) *n.* a small rounded or cone-shaped mass of chopped meat, fish, or vegetables, mixed with beaten egg and bread crumbs and fried in deep fat.

cro·sier (krō′zhər) *n.* an ornamental staff in the shape of a crook, carried as a symbol of office by or before bishops during religious ceremonies.

at; āpe; fär; câre; end; mē; it; īce; pîerce; hot; ōld; sông, fôrk; oil; out; up; ūse; rüle; pùll; tûrn; chin; sing; shop; thin; this; hw in white; zh in treasure. The symbol ə stands for the unstressed vowel sound heard in about, taken, pencil, lemon, and circus.

C

cross (krôs) *n., pl.* **cross·es.** **1.** an upright stake with a horizontal bar across it. The ancient Romans used it as an instrument of torture and execution. **2. the Cross.** the cross on which Jesus was crucified. **3.** a representation of the cross upon which Jesus died, thought of as the symbol of Christianity. **4.** this representation mounted with the figure of Jesus; crucifix. **5.** any object, figure, or mark formed by the crossing of two lines. **6.** any trouble, misfortune, or suffering. **7.** someone or something that combines the characteristics of two or more persons or things: *A motorcycle is a cross between a bicycle and an automobile.* **8.** an instance of crossbreeding. **9.** the result of crossbreeding; hybrid: *A mule is a cross between a horse and a donkey.* —*v.t.* **1.** to move or pass from one to the other side of; go across: *The ship crossed the ocean in seven days.* **2.** to place or lay one thing or part over another: *to cross one's legs.* **3.** to pass (each other) so as to intersect: *That street crosses the railroad tracks.* **4.** to draw a line or lines through or across: *Cross all your "t's" neatly.* **5.** to cancel by drawing a line or lines across: *Cross my name off the list.* **6.** to extend across; span: *The bridge crosses the river.* **7.** to pass while going in different directions: *Your letter must have crossed mine in the mail.* **8.** to interfere with; oppose: *Cross them and they will be angry.* **9.** to make a hand signal representing the Cross upon or over. **10.** to crossbreed (animals or plants). —*v.i.* **1.** to move, pass, or extend across: *The trail crosses through the woods.* **2.** to pass so as to intersect; lie or be crosswise: *The friends met where the two roads crossed.* —*adj.* **1.** bad-tempered; peevish: *a cross word.* **2.** lying or passing across or crosswise: *cross ventilation, cross streets.* —**cross'ly,** *adv.* —**cross'ness,** *n.*

·**to cross one's fingers.** to hope for good luck or success, as by placing one's middle finger over the index finger.
·**to cross one's mind.** to come into one's mind; occur to one: *The thought never crossed my mind.*

cross·bar (krôs'bär') *n.* **1.** a bar fixed across a structure: *the crossbar on a bicycle.* **2.** a line going across: *the crossbar on the letter "H."*

cross·beam (krôs'bēm') *n.* any large beam that crosses another or crosses from wall to wall.

cross·bill (krôs'bil') *n.* a songbird having a sharply curved bill with overlapping tips.

cross·bones (krôs'bōnz') *pl. n.* see **skull and crossbones.**

cross·bow (krôs'bō') *n.* a weapon widely used in the Middle Ages, consisting of a bow mounted crosswise at the front of a grooved stock along which arrows, stones, or other missiles are guided before being released.

cross·breed (krôs'brēd') *v.t.,* **cross·bred** (krôs'bred'), **cross·breed·ing.** to breed (plants or animals) with those of different kinds in order to produce hybrids. —*n.* an individual or type that is produced by crossbreeding; a hybrid plant or animal; cross.

cross·coun·try (krôs'kun'trē) *adj.* **1.** across open country or fields instead of following roads: *a cross-country race.* **2.** from one end of a country to the other: *a cross-country flight.* —*adv.* in a cross-country course.

cross·cut (krôs'kut') *adj.* made or used for cutting across: *a crosscut blade.* —*n.* a course or path across. —*v.t.,* **cross·cut, cross·cut·ting.** to cut across.

crosscut saw, a saw having beveled teeth shaped like knives, used for cutting wood across the grain.

cross–ex·am·ine (krôs'eg zam'in) *v.t.,* **cross·ex·am·ined, cross·ex·am·in·ing.** **1.** to question (a witness who has already testified for the opposing side) to check the reliability of testimony or character. **2.** to question closely

crosses
(n., def. 3)

Latin · Papal · Maltese · Celtic

to check the reliability of previous answers: *The reporters cross-examined the officials on important policy questions.* —**cross'·ex·am'i·na'tion,** *n.* —**cross'·ex·am'·in·er,** *n.*

cross–eyed (krôs'īd') *adj.* having one or both eyes turned inward toward the nose.

cross–fer·ti·li·za·tion (krôs'fûr'tə lə zā'shən) *n.* fertilization in which a reproductive cell from a female individual unites with a reproductive cell from a separate male individual.

cross–fire (krôs'fīr') *n.* **1.** gunfire from two or more positions crossing each other: *A bystander was caught in crossfire between the bank robbers and the police.* **2.** a rapid and lively exchange of words: *a crossfire of argument in a debate.*

cross–grained (krôs'grānd') *adj.* **1.** having the grain running crosswise, diagonally, or irregularly: *cross-grained wood.* **2.** stubborn; contrary.

cross–hatch (krôs'hach') *v.t.* to mark or shade with parallel lines that cross each other: *A section of the map was crosshatched to represent water.*

cross·ing (krô'sing) *n.* **1.** the act of going across: *The ship made an Atlantic crossing.* **2.** a place or point of intersection, as of roads. **3.** a place where something, as a street or river, may be crossed. **4.** the act of crossbreeding.

cross–leg·ged (krôs'leg'id, krôs'legd') *adv.* with the ankles crossed and the knees out: *The children sat cross-legged on the floor.*

cross–patch (krôs'pach') *n. Informal.* a bad-tempered person; grouch.

cross–piece (krôs'pēs') *n.* a piece of any material placed or lying across something else.

cross–pol·li·na·tion (krôs'pol'ə nā'shən) *n.* the transfer of pollen from the anther of one flower to the stigma of another by wind, water, insects, or birds.

cross–pur·pose (krôs'pûr'pəs) *n.* an opposing or conflicting purpose.

·**at cross-purposes.** opposing or hindering each other's efforts through misunderstanding.

cross–ques·tion (krôs'kwes'chən) *v.t.* to question closely or repeatedly, as in cross-examining.

cross–ref·er·ence (krôs'ref'ər əns) *n.* a reference from one part of a book or index to another part, pointing out where additional information can be found. In this dictionary, the phrase "see **skull and crossbones**" under the entry **crossbones** is a cross-reference.

cross–road (krôs'rōd') *n.* **1.** a road crossing another or a road leading from one main road to another. **2. crossroads. a.** a place where roads cross. **b.** a point where an important decision must be made. ▲ used with either a singular or plural verb in definition 2.

cross section **1.** a plane section produced by cutting across an object, especially at right angles to its length. **2.** a piece cut in this manner. **3.** a sampling of people or things considered representative or typical of the whole: *A cross section of opinion in the state showed that the senator would be reelected.*

cross–stitch (krôs'stitch') *n., pl.* **cross·stitch·es.** **1.** a stitch made by crossing over another, forming an X. **2.** needlework made with this stitch. —*v.t.* to sew with a cross-stitch.

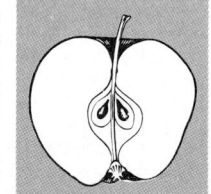

cross section
of an apple

cross–town (krôs'toun') *adj.* going across a town or city: *a crosstown bus, crosstown traffic.* —*adv.* across a town or city: *to drive crosstown.*

cross–trees (krôs'trēz') *pl. n.* two horizontal bars attached near the top of a mast on a sailing ship to spread the rigging or support a work platform.

cross·walk (krôs'wôk') *n.* a lane marked off for use by pedestrians in crossing a street.

cross·way (krôs′wā′) *n.* another word for **crossroad**.

cross·wise (krôs′wīz′) *also,* **cross·ways.** *adv.* **1.** so as to cross; across: *The bridge was built crosswise over the stream.* **2.** in the form of a cross: *The logs were laid crosswise in the fireplace.*

cross·word puzzle (krôs′wûrd′) a puzzle in which words or phrases are filled in on a pattern of numbered squares in answer to a list of clues having corresponding numbers. The words usually intersect each other in such a way that they read both across and down.

crotch (kroch) *n., pl.* **crotch·es. 1.** the place where the human body divides into the two legs. **2.** a place where limbs or branches divide: *the crotch of a tree.*

crotch·et (kroch′it) *n.* **1.** an odd notion; whim. **2.** a small hook or hooked instrument.

crotch·et·y (kroch′i tē) *adj.* full of odd notions or whims: *a crotchety hermit.* —**crotch′et·i·ness,** *n.*

crouch (krouch) *v.i.* **1.** to stoop or bend low, especially with the knees bent, as an animal does when about to spring or when trying to hide: *The tiger crouched in the bushes waiting for its prey.* **2.** to cringe or cower: *The frightened puppy crouched at the feet of its owner.* —*n., pl.* **crouch·es. 1.** the act or manner of crouching. **2.** a crouching position.

croup¹ (krüp) *n.* an inflammation of the throat and windpipe, especially in children, characterized by a high-pitched, barking cough and difficult breathing. It is caused by infection or allergy. [From the obsolete word *croup* meaning "to make a hoarse cough."] —**croup′y,** *adj.*

croup² (krüp) *n.* the highest part of the rump of a horse or other animal. [From the Old French word *crope* meaning "rump."]

crou·ton (krü′ton, krü ton′) *n.* a small cube of toasted or fried bread, often served in soup or salads.

crow¹ (krō) *v.i.* **crowed** or *(def. 1)* **crew, crowed, crow·ing. 1.** to utter the shrill cry of a rooster. **2.** to utter a delighted, happy cry. **3.** to boast in triumph; exult: *The runner crowed over winning the race.* —*n.* **1.** the cry of a rooster. **2.** a delighted, happy cry. [From the Old English word *crāwan* meaning "to make the cry of a rooster."]

crow² (krō) *n.* **1.** a bird having glossy black feathers and a harsh, croaking cry or caw. **2.** any of various similar birds, such as the raven, magpie, or jay. [From the Old English word *crāwe* meaning this bird.]

crow² (def. 1)

•**as the crow flies.** in a straight line: *That town is only 20 miles away as the crow flies, but 40 miles over the mountain roads.*

•**to eat crow.** *Informal.* to be forced to humble oneself: *When my mistake was pointed out I had to eat crow.*

Crow (krō) *n., pl.* **Crow** or **Crows. 1.** a member of a tribe of North American Indians formerly living along the Missouri River in the Great Plains. **2.** the language of the Crow, a member of the Siouan language family.

crow·bar (krō′bär′) *n.* a bar of iron or steel with a wedge-shaped end that is sometimes slightly bent and forked, used as a lever or pry.

crowd (kroud) *n.* **1.** a large number of people gathered together; throng: *We tried to make our way through the crowd at the fair.* **2.** *Informal.* a particular group of people; set; clique: *That crowd is too young for me.* **3.** people in general; the masses. —*v.t.* **1.** to push or shove aside, to make room for oneself: *Please don't crowd me.* **2.** to fill too full: *Fans crowded the entrance to the stadium.* **3.** to press or force (into a close space); cram: *I crowded everything into a small suitcase.* —*v.i.* **1.** to gather closely or in large numbers: *We crowded around the table to get our food.* **2.** to press forward; advance by pushing: *The passengers crowded into the bus.*

crown (kroun) *n.* **1.** an ornamental covering for the head worn by a monarch or member of royalty, often of jewels and precious metal. **2.** a wreath, band, or other circular ornament for the head: *a crown of flowers.* **3.** the power or authority of a monarch. **4.** *also,* **the Crown.** a sovereign ruler; monarch. **5.** the highest part of anything; top: *They climbed to the crown of the hill.* **6.** the head. **7.** the upper part of a hat or other head covering. **8.** an honor; reward: *the middleweight boxing crown.* **9.** the part of a tooth visible outside the gum. **10.** an artificial substitute for this part, usually made of gold, porcelain, or plastic. **11.** a former British silver coin, worth five shillings. —*v.t.* **1.** to make a monarch; enthrone: *They crowned the emperor and empress in the cathedral.* **2.** to be the top part of: *Whipped cream crowned the dessert.* **3.** to add the finishing touch to; complete: *The prize crowned the artist's career.* **4.** to recognize officially as: *to crown a team national champion.* **5.** to put an artificial crown on (a tooth).

crown colony, a colony that is under the authority of the British Crown and is administered by the British government.

crown prince, a man or boy who is the heir to a throne.

crown princess 1. the wife of a crown prince. **2.** a woman or girl who is the heir to a throne.

crow's-feet (krōz′fēt′) *n., pl.* wrinkles near the outer corners of the eyes.

crow's-nest (krōz′nest′) *n.* a small enclosed platform or other structure near the top of a ship's mast, used as a lookout.

CRT, cathode-ray tube.

cru·cial (krü′shəl) *adj.* likely to decide or help decide a contest or conflict or be a turning point; critical: *a crucial battle, a crucial game. The candidate's opposition to new taxes proved to be a crucial issue in the election.* **cru′cial·ly,** *adv.*

cru·ci·ble (krü′sə bəl) *n.* **1.** a container that can resist very great heat, used for melting chemicals, metals, and ores. **2.** a severe test or trial.

cru·ci·fix (krü′sə fiks′) *n., pl.* **cru·ci·fix·es. 1.** a cross with the crucified figure of Jesus upon it. **2.** a cross considered as a Christian symbol.

cru·ci·fix·ion (krü′sə fik′shən) *n.* **1.** the act of crucifying or the state of being crucified. **2. Crucifixion. a.** the execution of Jesus on the Cross. **b.** a picture, statue, or other representation of this.

cru·ci·fy (krü′sə fī′) *v.t.,* **cru·ci·fied, cru·ci·fy·ing. 1.** to put to death by nailing or binding the hands and feet to an upright cross. **2.** to treat cruelly; persecute; torment. —**cru′ci·fi′er,** *n.*

crude (krüd) *adj.,* **crud·er, crud·est. 1.** in a natural or raw state; unrefined: *crude rubber.* **2.** done or made without skill; rough: *The hunters built a crude shack in the woods.* **3.** lacking tact, taste, or refinement; rude: *crude behavior, a crude joke.* —**crude′ly,** *adv.* —**crude′ness,** *n.*

crude oil, oil as it comes from the ground in its natural state, before refining.

cru·di·ty (krü′di tē) *n., pl.* **cru·di·ties. 1.** the quality or state of being crude. **2.** something crude, such as a remark or act.

cru·el (krü′əl) *adj.* **1.** willing or ready to cause suffering or pain to others: *The cruel owner beat the tired horse.* **2.** willing to watch others suffer; callous. **3.** causing

at; āpe; fär; câre; end; mē; it; īce; pîerce; hot; ōld; sông, fôrk; oil; out; up; ūse; rüle; pùll; tûrn; chin; sing; shop; thin; this; hw in white; zh in treasure. The symbol ə stands for the unstressed vowel sound heard in about, taken, pencil, lemon, and circus.

suffering or pain: *The cold was cruel this winter.* —**cru′-el·ly**, *adv.* —**cru′el·ness**, *n.*

cru·el·ty (krü′əl tē) *n., pl.* **cru·el·ties. 1.** the quality or state of being cruel: *Their cruelty toward their animals was unforgivable.* **2.** a cruel act or acts.

cru·et (krü′it) *n.* a small glass bottle for holding vinegar, oil, or other dressings.

cruise (krüz) *v.,* **cruised, cruis·ing.** —*v.i.* **1.** to sail from place to place without any special destination, as for pleasure or business: *The yacht cruised about the islands.* **2.** to move or ride from place to place: *The police car cruised through the area.* **3.** to move at the speed of maximum efficiency, as an aircraft or automobile. —*v.t.* to cruise over or around in: *The liner cruised the Mediterranean.* —*n.* a voyage, especially one taken for pleasure.

cruet

cruis·er (krü′zər) *n.* **1.** a warship that is less heavily armed than a battleship and designed for speed. **2.** a motorboat having a cabin equipped for living on board, used for short cruises. **3.** a police car used to patrol. **4.** a person or thing that cruises.

cruising speed, the speed at which an aircraft, powered boat, or automobile operates with maximum efficiency.

crul·ler (krul′ər) *n.* a small cake made of sweetened dough cut into strips that are twisted together and fried in deep fat. [From the Dutch word *krulle* meaning "a twisted cake," from the word *krul* "curly."]

crumb (krum) *n.* **1.** a tiny piece, as of bread, cake, or similar food. **2.** a small bit of something; scrap: *We got only crumbs of information about their trip.* **3.** the soft inner part of bread. —*v.t.* **1.** to break into crumbs. **2.** to prepare for cooking by covering or dressing with crumbs.

crum·ble (krum′bəl) *v.,* **crum·bled, crum·bling.** —*v.t.* to break into small pieces: *I crumbled the bread and fed it to the pigeons.* —*v.i.* **1.** to fall into small pieces: *The pages of the old letter crumbled when I touched them.* **2.** to fall apart or be destroyed: *Our hopes for winning crumbled when our best player was injured.*

crum·bly (krum′blē) *adj.,* **crum·bli·er, crum·bli·est.** likely to crumble; easily crumbled: *crumbly bread.* —**crum′bli·ness**, *n.*

crum·pet (krum′pit) *n.* a soft, unsweetened batter cake that is baked on a griddle, then usually toasted and buttered.

crum·ple (krum′pəl) *v.,* **crum·pled, crum·pling.** —*v.t.* to press or crush (something) into wrinkles or folds: *to crumple paper.* —*v.i.* **1.** to become wrinkled or creased: *The hat crumpled when I sat on it.* **2.** to give way or fall down as though being folded; collapse: *The wounded soldier crumpled to the ground.* —*n.* a wrinkle or fold.

crunch (krunch) *v.t.* **1.** to chew or bite with a crushing or crackling sound: *to crunch carrots.* **2.** to crush or grind noisily: *The car wheels crunched the gravel.* —*v.i.* **1.** to chew noisily: *to crunch on some celery.* **2.** to give out a crushing or crackling sound: *The dry mud crunched under our feet.* **3.** to move with a crushing or crackling sound. —*n., pl.* **crunch·es. 1.** the act or sound of crunching. **2.** a time or situation of great pressure; crisis: *Farmers faced a crunch after months of drought.*

crunch·y (krun′chē) *adj.,* **crunch·i·er, crunch·i·est.** making a crackling sound: *crunchy potato chips.*

crup·per (krup′ər) *n.* **1.** a leather strap attached to the back of a saddle and passing over the horse's back and around its tail to prevent the saddle from sliding forward. **2.** the rump of a horse; croup.

cru·sade (krü sād′) *n.* **1.** *also,* **Crusade.** any of the military expeditions undertaken by European Christians between 1096 and 1270 to capture the Holy Land from the Muslims. **2.** any vigorous campaign for the advancement of a cause or against something seen as evil: *The*

new mayor promised a crusade against crime. —*v.i.,* **cru·sad·ed, cru·sad·ing.** to take part in a crusade. [From the Middle French word *croisade* and the Spanish word *cruzada*, both of which mean "crusade," and both of which go back to the Latin word *crux* meaning "cross." The crusaders wore the sign of the cross.] —**cru·sad′er**, *n.*

cruse (krüz) *n. Archaic.* an earthenware jug, pot, or bottle.

crush (krush) *v.t.* **1.** to press or squeeze forcefully so as to break, put out of shape, or damage: *The shock of the crash crushed the bicycle.* **2.** to break into small pieces by pressing, grinding, or pounding: *a machine that crushes rock.* **3.** to put down; subdue: *The dictator crushed the uprising by force. Their spirits were crushed when they failed the examination.* **4.** to crowd or press: *I was crushed against the door of the bus by the mob of passengers.* —*v.i.* to become wrinkled or broken; be put out of shape by pressure. —*n., pl.* **crush·es. 1.** the act of crushing or the state of being crushed. **2.** a closely packed crowd of people: *I was caught in the crush at the parade.* **3.** *Informal.* a strong, often brief, and sometimes foolish love or liking for a person: *to have a crush on someone.* —**crush′er**, *n.*

Cru·soe, Robinson (krü′sō) see **Robinson Crusoe.**

crust (krust) *n.* **1.** the outside, often hard or crisp, part of bread. **2.** a piece of this. **3.** any dry, hard piece of bread. **4.** the outer coating or layer of certain foods: *This fried chicken has a thick crust on it.* **5.** any hard or brittle outer coating: *The lake was covered with a thin crust of ice.* **6.** the hard outer layer of the earth. —*v.t.* **1.** to cover with a crust: *Ice crusted the highway.* **2.** to form into a crust: *to crust pie dough.* —*v.i.* to become covered with a crust.

crus·ta·cean (kru stā′shən) *n.* any of a group of animals without backbones that have hard shells and jointed bodies, that usually live in water and breathe through gills. Lobsters, crabs, shrimp, and barnacles are crustaceans. The wood louse is a land-dwelling crustacean. —*adj.* of or relating to crustaceans.

crust·y (krus′tē) *adj.,* **crust·i·er, crust·i·est. 1.** having or resembling a crust: *crusty rolls.* **2.** bad-tempered and harsh in manner or speech. —**crust′i·ly**, *adv.* —**crust′-i·ness**, *n.*

crutch (kruch) *n., pl.* **crutch·es. 1.** a staff or support used to help a lame person in walking, especially one having a grip for the hand and either a crosspiece that fits into the armpit or a curved piece that fits around the forearm. **2.** anything that gives support: *Our neighbors were a welcome crutch after the fire damaged our house.*

crux (kruks) *n., pl.* **crux·es. 1.** the most important, fundamental, or decisive point: *the crux of an argument.* **2.** a difficult or perplexing problem.

cry (krī) *v.,* **cried, cry·ing.** —*v.i.* **1.** to shed tears; weep: *The baby cried when it was hungry.* **2.** to call loudly; shout: *The people on the sinking ship cried for help.* **3.** (of an animal) to make its characteristic call: *The seagulls cried as they glided above the beach.* —*v.t.* **1.** to call loudly; shout: *Someone cried, "Fire!"* **2.** to announce or advertise publicly as being for sale: *The sidewalk vendors cried their wares.* —*n., pl.* **cries. 1.** a loud call or shout: *The children gave a cry of joy when they saw the puppy.* **2.** a fit of weeping: *to have a good cry over a sad movie.* **3.** a call for help: *The lifeguard heard the cry and rescued the swimmer from the undertow.* **4.** a public outcry; clamor: *a cry for justice.* **5.** a rallying call or slogan. **6.** the characteristic call of an animal or bird: *the cry of a coyote, the cry of a seagull.*

•**a far cry.** a long distance; long way: *The money we collected is a far cry from what we need.*

•**in full cry.** in full pursuit, as a pack of hounds.

•**to cry for.** to be in great need of; demand: *The problem of slums cries for attention.*

cry·ba·by (krī′bā′bē) *n.*, *pl.* **cry·ba·bies.** a person who cries or complains often.

cry·ing (krī′ing) *adj.* demanding immediate attention or remedy: *a crying need for more doctors.*

cry·o·gen·ics (krī′ə jen′iks) *n.* the branch of physics dealing with the structure and properties of materials at very low temperatures. ▲ used with a singular verb.

crypt (kript) *n.* an underground chamber or vault, especially one beneath the main floor of a church, used chiefly as a burial place.

cryp·tic (krip′tik) *adj.* having a puzzling or hidden meaning: *a cryptic remark.* —**cryp′ti·cal·ly,** *adv.*

cryp·to·gram (krip′tə gram′) *n.* a message written in a secret code or cipher.

cryp·to·graph (krip′tə graf′) *n.* **1.** another word for **cryptogram.** **2.** a system of secret writing; cipher.

cryp·tog·ra·pher (krip tog′rə fər) *n.* a person who specializes in cryptography.

cryp·tog·ra·phy (krip tog′rə fē) *n.* the science of writing and reading cryptograms.

crys·tal (kris′təl) *n.* **1.** a solid body bounded by flat surfaces, whose atoms, molecules, or ions are arranged in an orderly and repeated pattern: *crystals of salt.* **2.** a clear, colorless variety of quartz; rock crystal. **3.** very transparent and brilliant glass. **4.** drinking glasses, bowls, vases, or other objects made of this glass. **5.** the transparent covering over the face of a watch. —*adj.* **1.** made of crystal: *a crystal goblet.* **2.** resembling crystal; clear; transparent: *crystal waters.*

crystal ball, a ball of transparent glass, crystal, or similar material, believed to reveal future events when looked into.

crys·tal·line (kris′tə lin) *adj.* **1.** made of crystal or crystals. **2.** having the structure of a crystal. **3.** resembling crystal; clear: *a crystalline lake.*

crystalline lens, another term for **lens** (*def. 3*).

crys·tal·lize (kris′tə līz′) *v.*, **crys·tal·lized, crys·tal·liz·ing.** —*v.t.* **1.** to cause to form crystals or become crystalline: *The student crystallized salt as part of a chemistry experiment.* **2.** to give a definite or fixed form to: *I crystallized my ideas before I began writing the story.* —*v.i.* **1.** to form into crystals; become crystalline. **2.** to assume a definite or fixed form: *My impressions of life in the woods crystallized during our camping trip.* —**crys′tal·li·za′tion,** *n.*

crys·tal·log·ra·phy (kris′tə log′rə fē) *n.* the branch of science that deals with the form, structure, and physical and chemical properties of crystals.

Cs, the symbol for cesium.

CS 1. Christian Science. **2.** Civil Service.

CST, Central Standard Time.

ct., cent.

Ct., Connecticut.

CT, postal abbreviation for Connecticut.

cts., cents.

Cu, the symbol for copper. [From the Late Latin word *cuprum* meaning "copper," from the Latin phrase (*aes*) *Cyprium* "(metal) of Cyprus." Cyprus was one of the main sources of copper in ancient times.]

cu., cubic.

cub (kub) *n.* **1.** the young of certain animals, such as bears, wolves, lions, and tigers. **2.** a beginner or apprentice, especially in the newspaper business. **3.** see **cub scout.**

cub·by·hole (kub′ē hōl′) *n.* a small, enclosed or partly enclosed space.

cube (kūb) *n.* **1.** a solid figure with six equal, square sides. **2.** something resembling this figure in shape: *a cube of sugar, an ice cube.* **3.** the product of a number or quantity that is multiplied by itself twice; the third power of a number. The cube of 2 is 8, that is, $2^3 = 2 \times 2 \times 2 = 8$. —*v.t.*, **cubed, cub·ing. 1.** to cut or form into cubes: *to cube potatoes.* **2.** to raise (a number or quantity) to the third power.

cube root, a number or quantity that produces a given number or quantity when multiplied by itself twice. The cube root of 8 is 2.

cub·ic (kū′bik) *adj.* **1.** of or having length, breadth, and thickness. **2.** relating to or involving the cube of a number; of the third power. **3.** shaped like a cube; cubical.

cu·bi·cal (kū′bi kəl) *adj.* shaped like a cube.

cubic centimeter, a unit of volume in the metric system equal to the volume of a rectangular solid 1 centimeter long, 1 centimeter wide, and 1 centimeter deep; 0.06 cubic inch.

cubic foot, a unit of volume equal to the volume of a rectangular solid 1 foot long, 1 foot wide, and 1 foot deep; 0.03 cubic meter.

cubic inch, a unit of volume equal to the volume of a rectangular solid 1 inch long, 1 inch wide, and 1 inch deep; 16 cubic centimeters.

cu·bi·cle (kū′bi kəl) *n.* a small room, compartment, or partitioned area.

cubic measure, a unit or system of units for measuring volume.

cubic meter, a unit of volume in the metric system equal to the volume of a rectangular solid 1 meter long, 1 meter wide, and 1 meter deep; 35 cubic feet.

cub·ism (kū′biz əm) *n.* a movement in art, especially painting, begun in the early twentieth century. Cubism used basic geometric forms to represent objects.

cubism represented in
Pablo Picasso's painting "The Three Musicians"

cu·bit (kū′bit) *n.* an ancient unit of measure based on the length of the forearm from the elbow to the fingertips. Its value usually ranged between 18 inches and 22 inches (45–60 centimeters).

cu·boi·dal (kū boi′dəl) *adj.* shaped like a cube.

cub scout, a member of the Cub Scouts.

Cub Scouts, the junior division of the Boy Scouts, for boys from eight to ten years of age.

---

at; āpe; fär; câre; end; mē; it; īce; pîerce; hot; ōld; sông, fôrk; oil; out; up; ūse; rüle; pùll; tûrn; chin; sing; shop; thin; <u>th</u>is; hw in white; zh in treasure. The symbol ə stands for the unstressed vowel sound heard in about, taken, pencil, lemon, and circus.

cuck·oo (kü′kü, kŭk′ü) *n., pl.* **cuck·oos. 1.** any of a group of slender, long-tailed birds having a two-note call, found in tropical and temperate regions throughout the world. The European cuckoo lays its eggs in the nests of other birds. **2.** the call of the cuckoo, or an imitation of it. —*adj. Informal.* crazy; silly: *That was really a cuckoo idea.*

cuckoo *(def. 1)*

cuckoo clock, a clock with a toy cuckoo that pops out, usually on the hour, and announces the time by making a sound similar to a cuckoo's call.

cu. cm., cubic centimeter; cubic centimeters.

cu·cum·ber (kü′kum bər) *n.* **1.** a fleshy, green vegetable, usually eaten in salads or pickled. **2.** the vine bearing this vegetable.

cud (kud) *n.* partially digested, barely chewed food that cattle and certain other animals bring back into the mouth from the first stomach for a thorough second chewing.

cud·dle (kud′əl) *v.* **cud·dled, cud·dling.** —*v.i.* to lie close and snug; nestle; snuggle: *The two kittens cuddled together in the basket.* —*v.t.* to hold (someone or something) closely in one's arms, especially to make warm and snug: *The child cuddled the puppy.* —*n.* a warm or fond embrace.

cudg·el (kuj′əl) *n.* a short, thick stick used as a weapon; club. —*v.t.,* **cudg·eled, cudg·el·ing;** *also, British,* **cudg·elled, cudg·el·ling.** to beat with a cudgel.
　·to cudgel one's brains. to think hard: *We cudgeled our brains trying to remember their last name.*

cue¹ (kü) *n.* **1.** a signal, before or during a stage performance, for an actor to speak or begin some action: *The slamming of a door was my cue to scream.* **2.** any similar signal to begin or do something: *The candidate's arrival was the band's cue to begin to play.* **3.** a guiding suggestion or hint as to what to do or how to behave: *Take a cue from me and applaud when I do.* —*v.t.,* **cued, cu·ing.** to give a cue to: *Stand backstage and cue the actors.* [From the earlier *q.,* short for the Latin word *quando* meaning "when," used in scripts to direct actors when to enter onto the stage.]

cue² (kü) *n.* **1.** a long, tapering stick used to hit the ball in billiards and pool. **2.** see **queue** *(def. 2).* [From the French word *queue* meaning "cue²" and "tail," going back to the Latin word *cauda* "tail."]

cue ball, in billiards and pool, the ball intended to be hit by the cue and then in turn to strike and move one or more of the other balls.

cuff¹ (kuf) *n.* **1.** a band, fold, or similar piece at the bottom of a sleeve, usually at the wrist. **2.** a turned-up fold on the bottom of a trouser leg. **3.** see **handcuff.** [From the Middle English word *cuffe* meaning "glove," perhaps from the Medieval Latin word *cuphia* "headdress."]
　·off the cuff. *Informal.* with little or no preparation: *Since I hadn't read the book, I had to give an answer off the cuff.*
　·on the cuff. *Informal.* on credit: *to pay for something on the cuff.*

cuff² (kuf) *v.t.* to strike with the hand. —*n.* a blow, especially with the hand. [Perhaps of Scandinavian origin.]

cuff link, one of a pair of linked fastenings for the cuffs of a shirt.

cu. ft., cubic foot; cubic feet.

cu. in., cubic inch; cubic inches.

cui·rass (kwi ras′) *n., pl.* **cui·rass·es.** a piece of armor consisting of a breastplate and a back plate.

cui·sine (kwi zēn′) *n.* **1.** the manner or style of cooking or preparing food: *the cuisine of Spain.* **2.** the food prepared, especially at a restaurant: *The cuisine at the hotel is excellent.*

cul–de–sac (kul′də sak′) *n., pl.* **cul-de-sacs** or **culs-de-sac.** a street or passage closed at one end; dead end.

cu·li·nar·y (kü′le ner′ē) *adj.* of, relating to, or used in cooking or the kitchen: *culinary herbs, culinary skills.*

cull (kul) *v.t.* **1.** to pick out from a group; select: *We culled the oldest books from the library shelves.* **2.** to look over carefully and make a selection; pick over: *The storekeeper culled the basket of peaches.* —*n.* something selected, especially to be put aside as inferior.

culm¹ (kulm) *n.* the stem of certain grasses, usually hollow except at the nodes. [From the Latin word *culmus* meaning "a stalk, stem."]

culm² (kulm) *n.* coal dust or refuse. [From the Middle English word *colme* with the same meaning.]

cul·mi·nate (kul′mə nāt′) *v.,* **cul·mi·nat·ed, cul·mi·nat·ing.** —*v.i.* to reach the highest or final point; come to a climax: *The border clashes between the two countries culminated in war.* —*v.t.* to bring to a close or to the highest point; complete; climax: *The charity culminated its drive for funds with an auction.*

cul·mi·na·tion (kul′mə nā′shən) *n.* the point at which something culminates; highest point; climax.

cu·lotte (kü′lot, kü′lot) *also,* **cu·lottes** *n.* women's wide trousers that may be short or long, designed to look like a skirt.

cul·pa·ble (kul′pə bəl) *adj.* deserving blame: *Littering is a culpable act.* —**cul′pa·bil′i·ty,** *n.* —**cul′pa·bly,** *adv.*

cul·prit (kul′prit) *n.* **1.** a person guilty of some offense or crime: *The police caught the culprit in the bank robbery.* **2.** a person who has been charged with a crime, as in a court of law.

cult (kult) *n.* **1.** a particular form or system of religious worship: *Ancient civilizations had many cults of the sun.* **2.** the enthusiastic devotion of a group to a particular person, thing, or idea: *A cult grew around the singer.* **3.** the followers or members of a cult.

cul·ti·vate (kul′tə vāt′) *v.t.,* **cul·ti·vat·ed, cul·ti·vat·ing. 1.** to prepare and use (land) for raising crops; till. **2.** to plant and improve the growth of by labor and care: *to cultivate roses, to cultivate corn.* **3.** to loosen the soil around (growing plants) in order to uproot the weeds and reduce water loss. **4.** to improve or develop by education or training: *to cultivate good eating habits, to cultivate one's mind.* **5.** to seek the friendship of: *The ambitious decorator cultivated people with large houses.*

cul·ti·vat·ed (kul′tə vā′tid) *adj.* **1.** (of soil) prepared and used for growing crops. **2.** produced or improved by cultivation; not wild: *cultivated flowers.* **3.** improved by education or training. **4.** cultured; refined.

cul·ti·va·tion (kul′tə vā′shən) *n.* **1.** the act of cultivating or state of being cultivated. **2.** the improvement or development of something by education or training: *the cultivation of manners.* **3.** culture; refinement.

cul·ti·va·tor (kul′tə vā′tər) *n.* **1.** a person who cultivates. **2.** a tool or machine for uprooting weeds and loosening the ground around growing plants.

cul·tur·al (kul′chər əl) *adj.* of, relating to, or tending to develop culture: *cultural activities.* —**cul′tur·al·ly,** *adv.*

cul·ture (kul′chər) *n.* **1.** the way of life of a group of people at a particular time, including their customs, beliefs, and arts: *the culture of the ancient Greeks.* **2.** a knowledge of intellectual and artistic accomplishments and of what is considered to be fine in taste and manners: *They are people of culture.* **3.** the improvement

cultivators *(def. 2)*

or development of the mind or body, as by education or training: *physical culture.* **4.** the cultivation of the soil. **5.** the care and raising of plants or animals, especially with an interest in improving them: *the culture of silkworms.* **6.** the result of this: *a silkworm culture.* **7.** the growth of living cells or organisms, as viruses or bacteria, in a special preparation for scientific study. *—v.t.,* **cultured, cul·tur·ing.** to grow (living cells or organisms) in a special preparation for scientific study: *to culture bacteria.*

cul·tured (kul′chərd) *adj.* **1.** having or showing culture; educated; refined: *a cultured person, cultured speech.* **2.** produced or raised under controlled, artificial conditions: *a cultured pearl.*

cul·vert (kul′vərt) *n.* a drain for water under roads, sidewalks, and railroads.

cum·ber (kum′bər) *v.t.* to hinder; encumber.

cum·ber·some (kum′bər-səm) *adj.* not easily managed or carried; clumsy; unwieldy: *a cumbersome package.* **—cum′ber·some·ly,** *adv.* **—cum′ber·some·ness,** *n.*

culvert

cum·brous (kum′brəs) *adj.* unwieldy; cumbersome. **—cum′brous·ly,** *adv.* **—cum′brous·ness,** *n.*

cum·in (kum′ən, kŭm′ən, kū′mən) *n.* **1.** the aromatic, hot-tasting, seedlike fruit of an herb of the parsley family, used in curry powder and as a flavoring in such foods as cheese, meat, and pickles. **2.** the small delicate herb itself, widely grown in southern Europe and India.

cum lau·de (kŭm lou′dē, kum lô′də) with honors or praise: *to graduate from college cum laude.* [From the Latin phrase *cum laude* meaning "with honor."]

cum·mer·bund (kum′ər bund′) *n.* a broad sash worn around the waist, especially with a tuxedo.

cum·quat (kum′kwot) another spelling of **kumquat.**

cu·mu·la·tive (kū′myə lə tiv) *adj.* increasing in size, strength, or value by constant additions: *The cumulative evidence from experiments finally led to acceptance of the theory.* **—cu′mu·la·tive·ly,** *adv.* **—cu′mu·la·tive·ness,** *n.*

cu·mu·lo·nim·bus (kū′myə lo nim′bəs) *n., pl.* **cu·mu·lo·nim·bus.** a cloud that develops from a cumulus cloud or clouds into a large, dark, vertical structure that extends upward 2–5 miles (3.2–8 kilometers). Taller formations cause thunderstorms. See **cloud** (*def.* 1).

cu·mu·lus (kū′myə ləs) *n., pl.* **cu·mu·lus** or **cu·mu·li** (kū′myə lī′). a dense, low-level cloud made up of rounded mounds billowing upward from a flat base. In the sunlight they appear brilliant white. See **cloud** (*def.* 1).

cu·ne·i·form (kū nē′ə fôrm′) *n.* a system of writing distinguished by wedge-shaped characters, used in ancient times by the Sumerians, Babylonians, Assyrians, and Persians. *—adj.* wedge-shaped.

cun·ning (kun′ing) *adj.* **1.** clever or skilled in deceiving; tricky; sly: *a cunning thief.* **2.** *Informal.* cute or appealing; charming: *a cunning baby.* *—n.* **1.** cleverness or skill in deception; craftiness; slyness: *The swindler's plan showed a good deal of cunning.* **2.** skill in workmanship; expertness. **—cun′ning·ly,** *adv.* **—cun′ning·ness,** *n.*

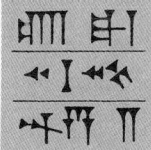

cuneiform

cup (kup) *n.* **1.** a small, open container, usually bowl-shaped and having a handle, used chiefly for drinking. **2.** the amount contained in a cup; cupful: *a cup of soup.* **3.** a unit of measure equal to eight fluid ounces or half a pint. **4.** an ornamental cup or cup-shaped vase given as a prize, especially in sports. **5.** anything resembling a cup in shape. **6. a.** a metal container in a hole on a golf course.

b. the hole itself. *—v.t.,* **cupped, cup·ping.** **1.** to shape like a cup: *to cup one's hands.* **2.** to place in or as if in a cup: *I cupped my chin in my hand.*

cup·bear·er (kup′bâr′ər) *n.* formerly, a person who filled and served cups of wine.

cup·board (kub′ərd) *n.* **1.** a closet or cabinet with shelves, especially for dishes or food. **2.** any small closet or cabinet.

cup·cake (kup′kāk′) *n.* a small cake baked in a cup-shaped pan or mold.

cup·ful (kup′fŭl′) *n., pl.* **cup·fuls.** the amount that a cup holds.

Cu·pid (kū′pid) *n.* **1.** *Roman Mythology.* the god of love and son of Venus, usually pictured as a winged boy with a bow and arrows. In Greek mythology he was called Eros. **2.** *also,* **cupid.** any picture or other representation of a naked winged boy, especially with a bow and arrows, considered as a symbol of love.

cu·pid·i·ty (kū pid′i tē) *n.* an eager desire for possession, especially of wealth; greed.

cu·po·la (kū′pə lə) *n.* **1.** a structure like a small dome or tower rising above a roof. **2.** a rounded roof or ceiling; dome.

cur (kûr) *n.* **1.** a mongrel dog, especially a worthless or bad-tempered one. **2.** a nasty, worthless person.

cur·a·ble (kyŭr′ə bəl) *adj.* capable of being cured: *a curable disease.* **—cur′a·bil′i·ty,** *n.*

cu·rate (kyŭr′it) *n.* a member of the clergy who assists the pastor, rector, or vicar of a parish.

cur·a·tive (kyŭr′ə tiv) *adj.* having the tendency or power to cure or remedy; relating to or used in

cupola (def. 1)

the cure of disease: *curative medicine, curative treatment.* *—n.* something that cures; remedy.

cu·ra·tor (kyŭ rā′tər, kyŭr′ā tər) *n.* a person in charge of all or part of the collection or exhibit at a museum, art gallery, zoo, or the like.

curb (kûrb) *n.* **1.** a border of concrete, stone, or other material along the edge of a street or sidewalk; outer edge of a sidewalk. **2.** something that restrains or controls; check: *The candidate called for a curb on spending.* **3.** a chain or strap fastened to a horse's bit and passing under its lower jaw, used to hold back or control the horse when the reins are pulled. *—v.t.* to hold back or control; check: *to curb one's anger, to curb inflation.*

curb·ing (kûr′bing) *n.* the material forming or used for making a curb along a street or sidewalk.

curb·stone (kûrb′stōn′) *n.* a stone or row of stones along the edge of a street or sidewalk.

curd (kûrd) *also,* **curds.** *n.* the thick, clotted portion of milk that separates from the watery part when milk sours, used in making cheese.

cur·dle (kûr′dəl) *v.,* **cur·dled, cur·dling.** *—v.i.* to form into curd: *The milk curdled.* *—v.t.* to cause to form into curd: *You'll curdle the cream sauce if you get it too hot.* **·to make (one's) blood curdle.** to fill (someone) with horror or fear; terrify.

cure (kyŭr) *n.* **1.** a return to a healthy or sound condition; recovery: *The patient's cure was hastened by plenty of rest.* **2.** something, such as a medicine or method of

at; āpe; fär; câre; end; mē; it; īce; pîerce; hot; ōld; sông, fôrk; oil; out; up; ūse; rüle; pŭll; tûrn; chin; sing; shop; thin; this; hw in white; zh in treasure. The symbol ə stands for the unstressed vowel sound heard in about, taken, pencil, lemon, and circus.

treatment, that restores health; remedy: *There is no known cure for that disease.* **3.** anything that corrects an unwanted or harmful condition or situation: *Taking a trip may be the cure for your boredom.* —*v.*, **cured, cur·ing.** —*v.t.* **1.** to restore to a healthy or sound condition; make well: *The treatment cured the patient.* **2.** to get rid of: *This medicine might cure your sore throat.* **3.** to preserve or prepare for use, as by drying, smoking, or chemically treating: *to cure fish, to cure tobacco.* —*v.i.* to be or become preserved or processed by curing: *The meat was hung in the smokehouse to cure.*

cu·ré (kyù rā′) *n. French.* a parish priest.

cure–all (kyùr′ôl′) *n.* something that is thought to cure all diseases or evils.

cur·few (kûr′fū) *n.* **1.** an order or rule requiring certain persons to be indoors or at home before a fixed time, especially at night. **2.** the hour at which such an order or rule becomes effective. **3.** the sounding of a bell at evening time as a signal. In medieval European towns, a curfew was a signal to the people to put out lights and fires and go to bed. [From the Anglo-Norman word *coeverfu* meaning "cover fire," from the Old French words *covrir* "to cover" + *feu* "fire."]

cu·rie (kyùr′ē, kyù rē′) *n.* a unit of measurement of radioactivity. [From the Polish chemist and physicist Marie *Curie* (1867–1934).]

cu·ri·o (kyùr′ē ō′) *n., pl.* **cu·ri·os.** an object valued as a curiosity: *I collect old china figurines and other such curios.*

cu·ri·os·i·ty (kyùr′ē os′i tē) *n., pl.* **cu·ri·os·i·ties.** **1.** the desire for knowledge, especially of something new, strange, or unknown. **2.** an object that arouses interest because it is strange, rare, or unusual.

cu·ri·ous (kyùr′ē əs) *adj.* **1.** eager to know or learn: *Most young children are very curious.* **2.** strange, rare, or unusual: *There were curious markings on the wall of the cave.* —**cu′ri·ous·ly,** *adv.* —**cu′ri·ous·ness,** *n.*

cu·ri·um (kyùr′ē əm) *n.* a radioactive element produced artificially from plutonium. Symbol: **Cm** [From the chemists and physicists Marie *Curie* (1867–1934) and Pierre *Curie* (1859–1906).]

curl (kûrl) *v.t.* **1.** to twist or form into coils or ringlets: *to curl one's hair.* **2.** to bend or form into a curved or spiral shape: *to curl a ribbon around one's finger.* —*v.i.* **1.** to take the form of coils or ringlets: *My hair curls when it gets wet.* **2.** to move in a curved or spiral shape: *The smoke curled up from the chimney.* —*n.* **1.** a coiled or curved lock of hair; ringlet. **2.** something having a curved or spiral shape: *We decorated the cake with chocolate curls.*

·**to curl up.** to sit or lie down in a comfortable position, as with the back curved and the legs drawn up.

curl·er (kûr′lər) *n.* a device on which hair is wound to make it curl.

cur·lew (kûr′lü) *n.* a wading bird of arctic and temperate regions, having long legs, a long, slender, curved bill, and usually, brown feathers.

curl·i·cue (kûr′li kū′) *n.* a fancy curve, twist, or flourish, as in handwriting.

curl·ing (kûr′ling) *n.* a game played on ice, in which large, rounded stones are slid toward a circular target, the object being to come as close as possible to the target.

curlew

curl·y (kûr′lē) *adj.*, **curl·i·er, curl·i·est.** **1.** curling or tending to curl: *curly hair.* **2.** having curls: *a curly head.* —**curl′i·ness,** *n.*

cur·rant (kûr′ənt, kur′ənt) *n.* **1.** a small, sour berry of any of several shrubs, used especially for making jelly, syrup, and wine. **2.** the shrub on which this berry grows.

3. a small, seedless raisin used especially in cakes, pies, and buns.

cur·ren·cy (kûr′ən sē, kur′ən sē) *n., pl.* **cur·ren·cies.** **1.** the money that is used in a country. **2.** general use or acceptance: *That custom has little currency in this country.* **3.** a passing from person to person; circulation: *The rumor gained wide currency.*

cur·rent (kûr′ənt, kur′ənt) *adj.* **1.** of or belonging to the present time; in progress: *the current year. My current address is on the envelope.* **2.** commonly used or accepted; prevalent: *a current belief.* **3.** passing from person to person; in wide circulation. —*n.* **1.** a portion of a body of water or of air continuously flowing in approximately the same path: *The current swept the bottle downstream. A cold current of air came into the room when I opened the door.* **2.** the flow of electricity in an electric circuit or through any conducting body or medium. **3.** a general course, movement, or tendency; trend: *the current of political thought.*

cur·rent·ly (kûr′ənt lē, kur′ənt lē) *adv.* at the present time: *They are currently away on a trip.*

cur·ric·u·lar (kə rik′yə lər) *adj.* of or relating to a curriculum.

cur·ric·u·lum (kə rik′yə ləm) *n., pl.* **cur·ric·u·la** (kə rik′yə lə) or **cur·ric·u·lums.** all the courses of study offered at a school, college, or university.

cur·ry¹ (kûr′ē, kur′ē) *v.t.*, **cur·ried, cur·ry·ing.** to rub down and clean (a horse or other animal) with a brush or currycomb. [From the Anglo-Norman word *curreier* meaning "to prepare, arrange" and "to curry a horse," from the Old French word *correier* with the same meanings, of Germanic origin.]

·**to curry favor.** to try to win favor, as by flattery: *The neighborhood politician curried favor with the mayor, hoping to be appointed to a city job.*

cur·ry² (kûr′ē, kur′ē) *n., pl.* **cur·ries.** **1.** a powder made from various dried, ground spices. Also, **curry powder.** **2.** a spicy sauce made from this. **3.** food seasoned with this powder or sauce. —*v.t.*, **cur·ried, cur·ry·ing.** to flavor or prepare (food) with curry. [From the word *kari* meaning "sauce" in a language of southern India.]

cur·ry·comb (kûr′ē kōm′, kur′ē kōm′) *n.* a brush with rows of teeth rather than bristles, usually of metal or rubber, for currying a horse or similar animal. —*v.t.* to rub down or groom with a currycomb.

curse (kûrs) *n.* **1.** a wish that evil or harm may come to someone or something. **2.** the evil or harm that has been wished for. **3.** a word or words used in swearing; profane language. **4.** something that brings or causes evil or harm. —*v.*, **cursed** or **curst, curs·ing.** —*v.t.* **1.** to call down evil or harm upon; damn. **2.** to use profane language against; swear at. **3.** to cause evil, harm, or suffering to: *Corruption cursed the city's government.* —*v.i.* to utter a curse or curses; swear.

curs·ed (kûr′sid, kûrst) *v.* a past tense and past participle of **curse.** —*adj. also,* **curst. 1.** deserving a curse; evil; hateful. **2.** under a curse; damned.

cur·sive (kûr′siv) *adj.* written or printed with the letters joined together: *Script is cursive handwriting.* —**cur′sive·ly,** *adv.*

cur·sor (kûr′sər) *n.* the movable square, bar, or other symbol on a computer screen that indicates where the operator is working or where the next keyboarded character will appear. —*v.i.* to move the cursor across a computer screen: *Cursor over to the right margin.*

cur·so·ry (kûr′sə rē) *adj.* not thorough; rapid; hasty: *I gave the letter a cursory reading.* —**cur′so·ri·ly,** *adv.*

curst (kûrst) *v.* a past tense and past participle of **curse.** —*adj.* another spelling of **cursed.**

curt (kûrt) *adj.* rudely brief or abrupt: *A curt nod was the only response to my greeting.* —**curt′ly,** *adv.* —**curt′ness,** *n.*

cur·tail (kər tāl′) *v.t.* to cut short or cut down; lessen; reduce: *to curtail a program, to curtail expenses.* —**cur·tail′ment,** *n.*

cur·tain (kûr′tin) *n.* **1.** a piece or pieces of cloth or other material hung at a window or door as a decoration or screen. **2.** the hanging screen or drapery used to conceal the stage of a theater from the view of the audience. **3.** the lowering or closing of the curtain in a theater to indicate the end of a performance, act, or scene. **4.** anything that screens or covers like a curtain: *A curtain of fog hid the tops of the buildings.* —*v.t.* to provide, shut off, or cover with a curtain.

curtain call, the reappearance of a performer or performers on stage to acknowledge the applause of the audience, usually at the end of a performance.

curt·sey (kûrt′sē) *n., pl.* **curt·seys.** another spelling of **curtsy.**

curt·sy (kûrt′sē) *n. also,* **curt·sey.** *pl.* **curt·sies.** a gesture of respect or greeting by women and girls, made by bending the knees and lowering the body slightly. —*v.i.,* **curt·sied, curt·sy·ing.** to make a curtsy.

cur·va·ture (kûr′və chər) *n.* **1.** the quality or condition of being curved: *The curvature of the earth could be seen in the satellite photograph.* **2.** something curved. **3.** an abnormal curving, as of the spine.

curvature of the earth

curve (kûrv) *n.* **1.** a continuously bent line having no straight parts or angles, such as an arc of a circle. **2.** something having the shape of a curve: *a curve in a road.* **3.** a baseball or softball pitched so that it spins away from a straight path as it passes the batter. **4.** *Mathematics.* any set of points that satisfy a certain mathematical condition. —*v.,* **curved, curv·ing.** —*v.i.* **1.** to have or take the form of a curve: *The driveway curves as it nears the house.* **2.** to move in a curve: *The ball curved to the left.* —*v.t.* to cause to curve.

cush·ion (kùsh′ən) *n.* **1.** a pillow or soft pad, used to sit, rest, or lie on. **2.** something like a cushion in shape or use: *We sat on a cushion of leaves.* **3.** anything that absorbs shock or protects against harm: *The savings account will be a cushion until I find another job.* —*v.t.* **1.** to absorb or lessen the shock or effect of: *The snow cushioned my fall.* **2.** to place or seat on a cushion; support: *to cushion someone's head.* **3.** to provide with a cushion or cushions. —**cush′ion·like′,** *adj.*

cusp (kusp) *n.* **1.** a point or pointed end: *A crescent moon has two cusps.* **2.** a point or pointed end on the grinding surface or crown of a tooth.

cus·pid (kus′pid) *n.* another word for **canine tooth.**

cus·pi·dor (kus′pi dôr′) *n.* another word for **spittoon.**

cuss (kus) *Informal. v.t.* to swear at: *The angry cabby cussed the driver of the car that bumped into the taxi.* —*v.i.* to swear; curse. —*n., pl.* **cuss·es. 1.** an odd person or animal. **2.** a curse.

cus·tard (kus′tərd) *n.* a sweet dessert made from eggs, sugar, milk, and flavoring, either baked or boiled.

cus·to·di·an (kə stō′dē ən) *n.* **1.** a person who has care or custody of a person or thing; guardian; keeper. **2.** a person responsible for the care of a building; janitor.

cus·to·dy (kus′tə dē) *n., pl.* **cus·to·dies. 1.** keeping; care; guardianship: *The grandparents took custody of the children after their parents died.* **2.** the state of being in the charge of the police; imprisonment: *The police took the suspect into custody immediately after the robbery.*

cus·tom (kus′təm) *n.* **1.** an accepted social habit or pattern of behavior of a group. Customs are learned and passed from one generation to another. Having a turkey for dinner on Thanksgiving is a custom in the United States. **2.** the usual way of acting or doing things; habit: *It is our custom to visit the museum every Saturday.* **3.** the regular business given to a store or other business establishment: *We give our custom to the grocer on the corner.* **4. customs. a.** taxes or duties imposed by a government on goods imported from foreign countries. **b.** the government agency that inspects imported goods and collects the taxes or duties on them. —*adj.* **1.** making things the way someone requested or needs: *a custom tailor.* **2.** custom-made: *a custom suit.*

cus·tom·ar·y (kus′tə mer′ē) *adj.* according to or based on custom; usual; habitual: *It is customary in our family to have Thanksgiving dinner at midday.* —**cus′tom·ar′i·ly,** *adv.*

cus·tom·er (kus′tə mər) *n.* **1.** a person who shops or buys, especially a person who deals regularly at a particular store. **2.** *Informal.* anyone with whom a person has to deal: *a tough customer.*

cus·tom·house (kus′təm hous′) *n., pl.* **cus·tom·hous·es** (kus′təm hou′ziz). a government office or building where customs on imported goods are collected and where ships or their cargoes are formally admitted to the country.

cus·tom·ize (kus′tə mīz′) *v.t.,* **cus·tom·ized, cus·tom·iz·ing.** to build or alter according to individual requirements: *to customize a car.*

cus·tom–made (kus′təm mād′) *adj.* made especially for a particular person: *a custom-made suit.*

cut (kut) *v,* **cut, cut·ting.** —*v.t.* **1.** to separate or divide into parts with a sharp-edged instrument: *to cut a rope, to cut a pie into slices.* **2.** to pierce, slit, or wound with a sharp instrument; make an opening in: *I cut my foot on the jagged rock.* **3.** to remove or take away with a sharp-edged instrument: *I cut dead branches from the tree.* **4.** to make shorter by removing a part or parts: *to cut hair, to cut grass, to cut a speech.* **5.** to make or shape by cutting: *to cut a pattern for a dress, to cut a hole in a fence.* **6.** to make smaller or less; reduce: *We have to cut expenses this year. The store cut its prices during the sale.* **7.** to leave out or remove: *The director cut two scenes from the play.* **8.** to put an end to or stop: *The driver cut the motor and removed the key.* **9.** to go across or through: *A road cuts the field near one corner.* **10.** to hurt the feelings of: *Your rudeness cut me deeply.* **11.** to have (a tooth or teeth) grow through the gum. **12.** *Informal.* to be absent from, especially without permission: *to cut classes.* **13.** *Informal.* to pretend not to recognize or know; snub: *They cut me in the street without a word.* —*v.i.* **1.** to act or do the work of a sharp-edged instrument: *This saw cuts well.* **2.** to be cut:

at; āpe; fär; câre; end; mē; it; īce; pîerce; hot; ōld; sông, fôrk; oil; out; up; ūse; rüle; pùll; tûrn; chin; sing; shop; thin; **th**is; hw in white; zh in treasure. The symbol ə stands for the unstressed vowel sound heard in about, taken, pencil, lemon, and circus.

Silk cuts easily. **3.** to go or move by the shortest or most direct route: *We cut through the park on the way home.* **4.** to cross or pass: *The road cuts through the swamp.* **5.** to change direction suddenly or sharply; swerve: *The driver cut to the right to avoid hitting the dog.* **6.** to go through or pierce like a sharp-edged instrument: *The cold wind cut through our clothes.* —*n.* **1.** an opening or wound made with a sharp instrument or edge: *I got a cut on my hand from the broken glass.* **2.** a slice, stroke, or blow with a sharp-edged instrument: *to sever a rope with one cut of a knife.* **3.** a piece or part, cut or cut off: *a good cut of beef.* **4.** a reduction, as in price; decrease: *a cut in salary, a cut in prices.* **5.** the way or shape in which a thing is cut; style: *The cut of that coat makes you look slimmer.* **6.** a remark or action that hurts the feelings. **7.** a passage or channel made by cutting, digging, or blasting. **8.** a stroke or swing at a ball, as in baseball. **9.** **a.** an engraved block or plate from which a picture is printed. **b.** a picture made from such a block or plate. **10.** *Informal.* a share or part, as of profits: *the salespeople get a seven percent cut on all sales.* **11.** a shortcut: *We took a cut through the woods to save time.* —*adj.* having been cut: *a cut foot, cut flowers.*

   ·**cut and dried.** **a.** arranged or settled beforehand. **b.** not interesting; dull; boring: *a cut and dried speech.*
   ·**cut out.** suited or fit by nature: *I'm not cut out for that kind of work.*
   ·**to cut back.** to reduce, as prices.
   ·**to cut down.** **a.** to cause to fall by cutting: *to cut down a tree.* **b.** to reduce in size or amount.
   ·**to cut in.** **a.** to break or move into suddenly or out of turn: *Don't cut in at the head of the line.* **b.** to interrupt, as a conversation. **c.** to interrupt a dancing couple in order to take the place of one partner.
   ·**to cut up.** *Informal.* to behave in a mischievous, boisterous way.

cu·ta·ne·ous (kū tā′nē əs) *adj.* of, relating to, or affecting the skin: *a cutaneous infection.*

cut·a·way (kut′ə wā′) *n.* a man's formal coat for daytime wear, cut so as to slope back from the waistline in front to the tails in back.

cut·back (kut′bak′) *n.* a reduction: *a cutback in government spending.*

cute (kūt) *adj.*, **cut·er**, **cut·est.** **1.** charmingly pretty or attractive; adorable; appealing: *a cute baby.* **2.** clever; shrewd: *a cute trick.* —**cute′ly**, *adv.* —**cute′ness**, *n.*

cu·ti·cle (kū′ti kəl) *n.* **1.** the tough skin surrounding the base and sides of a fingernail or toenail. **2.** a protective outer layer of a plant or animal, such as the epidermis of the skin of a human being.

cut·lass (kut′ləs) *n., pl.* **cut·lass·es.** a short sword with a wide, flat, slightly curved blade.

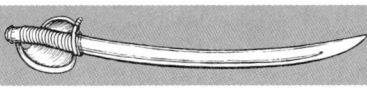
cutlass

cut·ler·y (kut′lə rē) *n.* **1.** cutting instruments, such as knives and scissors. **2.** knives, forks, and other utensils used in eating or serving food.

cut·let (kut′lit) *n.* **1.** a thin slice of meat, usually of veal, that is cut from the leg or ribs and is broiled or fried. **2.** a flat cake made of chopped meat, fish, or other food: *veal cutlets.*

cut·off (kut′ôf′) *n.* **1.** a stopping or cutting off of something, especially the flow of steam or other fluid into the cylinder of an engine. **2.** the point at which this is done. **3.** a device for cutting off the flow of something, as steam or other fluid. **4.** a shorter road or route cutting across or through something; shortcut. **5.** **cutoffs.** shorts made by cutting short the legs of trousers, especially jeans. —*adj.* at or during which something ends or expires: *The cutoff date for contest entries is May 6.*

cut·out (kut′out′) *n.* **1.** something cut out or designed to be cut out: *The book has paper cutouts of animals.* **2.** a device for letting the exhaust gases from an automobile engine pass directly into the air rather than through the muffler.

cut·rate (kut′rāt′) *adj.* **1.** offering goods or services at reduced or cheap prices: *a cut-rate drugstore.* **2.** sold or selling at reduced or cheap prices: *cut-rate clothing.*

cut·ter (kut′ər) *n.* **1.** a person who cuts, especially a person whose job is cutting: *a diamond cutter, a dress cutter.* **2.** a device or machine for cutting. **3.** a single-masted sailboat. **4.** a small, fast ship used by the Coast Guard. **5.** a small boat carried on a ship, used to take people to and from the ship. **6.** a small, light sleigh, usually made to be drawn by one horse.

cut·throat (kut′thrōt′) *n.* a murderer or murderous thug. —*adj.* ruthless; merciless: *cutthroat thieves, cutthroat business methods.*

cut·ting (kut′ing) *adj.* **1.** able to cut; sharp: *the cutting edge of a knife, a cutting wind.* **2.** hurting the feelings; sarcastic: *a cutting remark.* —*n.* **1.** the act of a person or thing that cuts. **2.** a small shoot or other part cut from a plant and used to grow a new plant. **3.** a newspaper or magazine clipping.

cut·tle·bone (kut′əl bōn′) *n.* the hard inner shell or plate of cuttlefish, used for making polishing powder. It is often placed in bird cages to provide the birds with minerals.

cut·tle·fish (kut′əl fish′) *n., pl.* **cut·tle·fish** or **cut·tle·fish·es.** a saltwater animal related to the octopus, found in warm, shallow waters of the Atlantic and Indian Oceans. It has arms with suckers and a hard inner shell. When in danger, it may release an inky fluid.

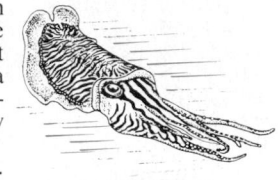
cuttlefish

cut·up (kut′up′) *n. Informal.* a person who clowns, plays tricks, or behaves in a mischievous or boisterous way, especially to attract attention.

cut·worm (kut′wûrm′) *n.* the larva or caterpillar of any of several moths. The cutworm feeds at night on the leaves and stems of cultivated crops and garden plants.

cwt., hundredweight.

–cy *suffix* (used to form nouns) **1.** the quality, state, condition, or fact of being: *bankruptcy.* **2.** the office, position, or rank of: *captaincy.*

cy·a·nide (sī′ə nīd′, sī′ə nid) *n.* any of several very poisonous compounds, used especially as pesticides and in the extraction of metal from ore.

cy·ber·net·ics (sī′bər net′iks) *n.* the science dealing with communication and control processes in humans and other animals and in electronic machines, especially computers. ▲ used with a singular verb.

cy·cad (sī′kad) *n.* any of a group of primitive evergreen plants that grow in warm climates. The plants resemble palms and have cones that bear seeds.

cyc·la·men (sī′klə mən, sik′lə mən) *n.* **1.** the showy flower of any of a group of plants, having pink, purple, rose, or white petals. **2.** the plant bearing this flower, having heart-shaped leaves.

cy·cle (sī′kəl) *n.* **1.** a complete course or series of events or phenomena that occur over and over again in a definite order: *the cycle of the seasons.* **2.** a period of time during which such a course or series occurs and completes itself. **3.** a unicycle, bicycle, tricycle, or motorcycle. **4.** a group of stories, poems, or plays about a particular figure, event, or theme: *This cycle of myths deals with the origins of the earth and human beings.* **5.** *Physics.* a complete round or series of changes in a quantity that varies periodically, as alternating current. —*v.i.,* **cy·cled, cy·cling.** to ride a cycle, especially a bicycle.

cy·clic (sī′klik, sik′lik) *adj.* **1.** moving or coming in cycles: *the cyclic changing of the seasons.* **2.** of or relating to a cycle. **3.** of, relating to, or characterized by an arrangement of atoms in a ring or closed chain. Also, **cy·cli·cal** (sī′kli kəl, sik′li kəl). —**cy′cli·cal·ly,** *adv.*

cy·clist (sī′klist) *n.* a person who rides a unicycle, bicycle, tricycle, or motorcycle.

cy·clone (sī′klōn) *n.* **1.** a disturbance in the atmosphere in which winds rotate around a moving center of low air pressure. Cyclone winds circle clockwise in the Northern Hemisphere and counterclockwise in the Southern Hemisphere. **2.** any violent windstorm, such as a hurricane or tornado.

cy·clon·ic (sī klon′ik) *adj.* **1.** of or relating to a cyclone: *cyclonic winds.* **2.** like a cyclone; destructive.

cy·clo·pe·di·a (sī′klə pē′dē ə) *also,* **cy·clo·pae·di·a.** *n.* another word for **encyclopedia.**

cy·clo·pe·dic (sī′klə pē′dik) *also,* **cy·clo·pae·dic.** *adj.* another word for **encyclopedic.**

Cy·clops (sī′klops) *n., pl.* **Cy·clo·pes** (sī klō′pēz). *Greek Mythology.* one of a race of giants having only one eye, located in the center of the forehead.

cy·clo·tron (sī′klə tron′) *n.* a device that accelerates charged atomic particles to very high speeds.

cyg·net (sig′nit) *n.* a young swan.

cyl., cylinder.

cyl·in·der (sil′ən dər) *n.* **1.** a solid geometric figure bounded by two equal, parallel circles and a curved surface that is formed by a straight line moving parallel to itself with its ends always on the circumferences of the circles. **2.** something resembling a cylinder in shape, such as a can. **3.** the rotating part of a revolver that contains chambers for cartridges. **4.** a chamber in which the piston of an engine or pump moves.

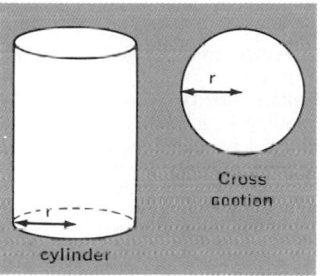

cylinder *(def. 1)*

cy·lin·dri·cal (sə lin′dri kəl) *adj.* having the form of a cylinder; shaped like a cylinder: *a cylindrical can.* —**cy·lin′dri·cal·ly,** *adv.*

cym·bal (sim′bəl) *n.* a musical instrument consisting of a circular, slightly concave metal plate that produces a ringing sound when clashed against another cymbal or struck, as with a drumstick.

cyn·ic (sin′ik) *n.* a person who tends to doubt the sincerity, goodness, or unselfishness of human motives and actions. —*adj.* cynical.

cyn·i·cal (sin′i kəl) *adj.* having or showing disbelief in or doubt about the sincerity, goodness, or unselfishness of human motives and actions: *a cynical politician, a cynical attitude, a cynical smile.* —**cyn′i·cal·ly,** *adv.*

cyn·i·cism (sin′ə siz′əm) *n.* **1.** a cynical disposition, character, or quality. **2.** a cynical remark, act, or opinion.

cy·no·sure (sī′nə shŭr′, sin′ə shŭr′) *n.* a person or thing that attracts attention; center or object of attraction, interest, or admiration: *The movie star was the cynosure of all present.*

cy·pher (sī′fər) another spelling of **cipher.**

cy·press (sī′prəs) *n.* **1.** any of a group of evergreen trees or shrubs found in southern Europe, Asia, and North America, having closely overlapping, scalelike leaves and woody cones. **2.** the wood of these trees.

Cyp·ri·an (sip′rē ən) *n.* another word for **Cypriot.**

Cyp·ri·ot (sip′rē ət) *also,* **Cyp·ri·ote** (sip′rē ōt′, sip′rē ət). *n.* **1.** a person who was born in or is a citizen of Cyprus. **2.** the ancient or modern Greek dialect of Cyprus. —*adj.* of or relating to Cyprus, its people, their languages, or their culture.

Cy·ril·lic alphabet (sə ril′ik) the alphabet used in writing and printing Russian, Ukrainian, Bulgarian, and certain other Slavic languages.

cyst (sist) *n.* **1.** an abnormal sac in the body, usually containing a liquid substance. **2.** a protective outer covering formed around an organism, such as a protozoan, during reproduction or in an inactive stage.

cyst·ic (sis′tik) *adj.* **1.** of, relating to, or resembling a cyst. **2.** having or containing a cyst or cysts. **3.** of or relating to the gall bladder or to the urinary bladder.

cystic fibrosis, an inherited disease, usually appearing during childhood, that affects the ducts of certain glands. It is often characterized by inadequate functioning of the pancreas and lungs.

cys·ti·tis (si stī′tis) *n.* inflammation of the bladder, usually caused by an infection.

cy·tol·o·gist (sī tol′ə jist) *n.* an expert in cytology.

cy·tol·o·gy (sī tol′ə jē) *n.* the branch of biology that deals with the study of cells, including their formation, structure, and function.

cy·to·plasm (sī′tə plaz′əm) *n.* all the protoplasm of a cell outside the nucleus.

CZ, postal abbreviation for the Canal Zone.

C.Z., Canal Zone.

czar (zär) *also,* **tsar, tzar.** *n.* **1.** any of the emperors of Russia before the revolution of 1917. **2.** a person having great or absolute power or authority: *a czar of the motion picture industry.* [From the Russian title *tsar,* applied to the Russian emperor, going back to the Latin title *Caesar,* applied to the Roman emperors since Augustus, from Gaius Julius *Caesar* (100?–44 B.C.), Roman statesman and general.]

cza·ri·na (zä rē′nə) *also,* **tsa·ri·na, tza·ri·na.** *n.* **1.** the wife of a Russian czar. **2.** an empress of Russia.

Czech (chek) *n.* **1.** a member of a branch of the Slavic people, including the Bohemians and Moravians. **2.** see **Czechoslovak. 3.** a language of Czechoslovakia. —*adj.* of or relating to Czechoslovakia, its people, or their languages.

Czech·o·slo·vak (chek′ə slō′vak, chek′ə slō′väk) *n.* a person who was born in or is a citizen of Czechoslovakia. *adj.* of or relating to Czechoslovakia, its people, or their languages. Also, **Czechoslovakian.**

---

at; āpe; fär; câre; end; mē; it; īce; pîerce; hot; ōld; sông, fôrk; oil; out; up; ūse; rüle; pull; tûrn; chin; sing; shop; thin; this; hw in white; zh in treasure. The symbol ə stands for the unstressed vowel sound heard in about, taken, pencil, lemon, and circus.

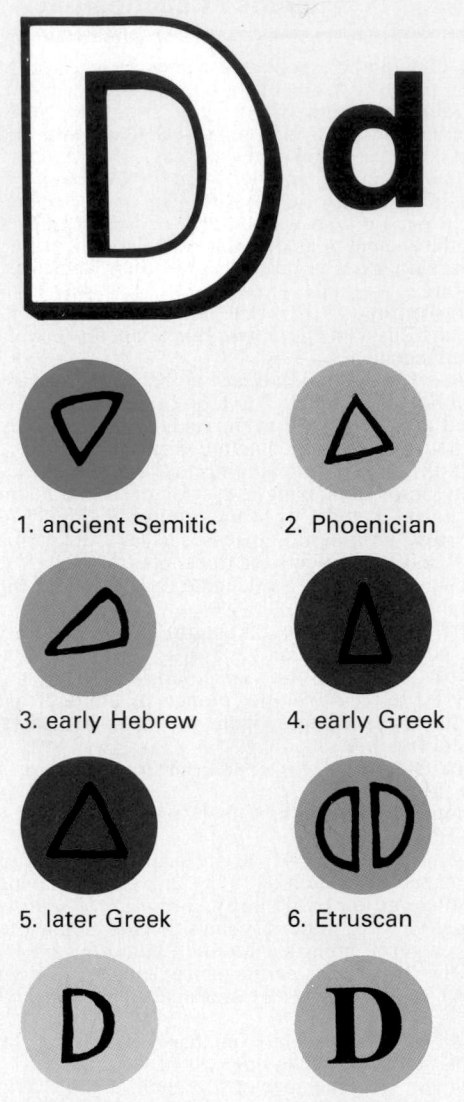

1. ancient Semitic
2. Phoenician
3. early Hebrew
4. early Greek
5. later Greek
6. Etruscan
7. Latin
8. English

D is the fourth letter of the English alphabet. The ancient Semitic letter *daleth* (1), meaning "door," is the earliest letter that corresponds to our modern letter **D**. The early alphabets that developed from the ancient Semitic, including Phoenician (2) and early Hebrew (3), all used some form of triangle as the basic shape of this letter. The Greeks borrowed *daleth*, making only slight changes in its shape, and called it *delta* (4). In later centuries, *delta* was written in the form of an equilateral triangle (5). The Etruscans (6) changed the shape of *delta* by rounding two of the triangle's sides. This form was used, with only slight changes, in the Latin alphabet (7). By about the fourth century B.C., the Romans were writing this letter almost exactly as we write the capital letter **D** today (8).

d, D (dē) *n., pl.* **d's, D's. 1.** the fourth letter of the English alphabet. **2.** the fourth item in a series or group. **3.** the Roman numeral for 500. **4.** *Music.* the second note of the scale of C major.

D 1. the symbol for deuterium. **2.** *Physics.* density.

d. 1. date. **2.** day; days. **3.** dead. **4.** degree. **5.** diameter. **6.** died. **7.** dime. **8.** dollar. **9.** penny; pence: *6d.* [For *def. 9*, from the Latin word *denarius*, a small coin.]

D. 1. December. **2.** Democrat. **3.** department. **4.** Doctor. **5.** Dutch.

D.A., district attorney.

dab (dab) *v.,* **dabbed, dab·bing.** —*v.t.* **1.** to pat or stroke gently with something soft or moist: *The nurse dabbed the wound with cotton.* **2.** to apply with a light, quick touch: *The artist dabbed green paint on the canvas.* —*v.i.* to pat or stroke gently, as with something soft or moist: *I dabbed at the mud on the rug with a wet cloth.* —*n.* **1.** a small, moist mass of something: *a dab of clay, a dab of paint.* **2.** a little bit: *a dab of mashed potatoes.* **3.** a light, quick pat or stroke.

dab·ble (dab'əl) *v.,* **dab·bled, dab·bling.** —*v.i.* **1.** to do something occasionally or in a casual manner: *to dabble in politics, to dabble at painting.* **2.** to splash or play gently, as in water. —*v.t.* to splash or dip (something) gently, as in water. —**dab'bler,** *n.*

da ca·po (dä kä'pō) *Music.* from the beginning (used as a direction to repeat a passage).

dace (dās) *n., pl.* **dace** or **dac·es.** any of various minnows commonly found in small streams of North America and Europe.

da·cha (dä'chə) *n.* a country house, especially one in Russia.

dachs·hund (däks'hùnt', däks'hùnd') *n.* a small dog having a long body, very short legs, drooping ears, and a red, tan, or black-and-tan coat. [From the German word *Dachshund* meaning this dog, from the words *Dachs* "badger" + *Hund* "dog." This dog was bred to hunt badgers.]

dachshund

Da·cron (dā'kron, dak'ron) *n. Trademark.* **1.** a strong synthetic textile fiber that does not wrinkle or stretch, used especially for clothing. **2.** a yarn or fabric made of this fiber.

dac·tyl (dak'təl) *n.* **1.** in modern English verse, a metrical foot consisting of one accented syllable followed by two unaccented syllables. The line *Think of her mournfully, gently and humanly* (Thomas Hood) contains four dactyls. **2.** a line of verse made up of such feet. **3.** a toe or a finger; digit. —**dac·tyl·ic** (dak til'ik), *adj.*

dad (dad) *n.* Informal. father.

dad·dy (dad'ē) *n., pl.* **dad·dies.** *Informal.* father.

dad·dy–long·legs (dad'ē lông'legz') *n., pl.* **dad·dy-long·legs.** an animal related to the spider and having long, slender legs. It does not spin a web.

Daed·a·lus (ded'ə ləs) *n. Greek Legend.* a skillful craftsman and inventor who designed the Labyrinth in Crete and was later imprisoned in it with his son, Icarus. Daedalus then fashioned artificial wings of feathers and wax, with which he and his son escaped. Icarus flew too near to the sun, which melted the wax holding his wings, causing him to fall into the sea.

daf·fo·dil (daf'ə dil') *n.* **1.** the flower of any of several plants, having yellow or white petals that surround the base of a trumpet-shaped center. **2.** the plant bearing this flower, having tall, stiff, slender leaves and growing from a bulb.

daff·y (daf'ē) *adj.,* **daff·i·er, daff·i·est.** *Informal.* **1.** silly; foolish. **2.** crazy; insane.

daft (daft) *adj.* **1.** crazy; insane. **2.** silly; foolish. —**daft'ly,** *adv.* —**daft'ness,** *n.*

dag·ger (dag'ər) *n.* **1.** a small weapon having a pointed blade, used for stabbing. **2.** a mark (†) used in printing to indicate a reference to a footnote or other note.

da·guerre·o·type (də gâr'ə tīp') *n.* **1.** an early method of taking photographs by using silver-coated copper plates that are sensitive to light. **2.** a picture made in this way. [From the French word *daguerréotype,* from the French painter Louis *Daguerre* (1789–1851), who invented this method.]

dahl·ia (dal'yə, däl'yə) *n.* **1.** a showy flower growing in various bright colors. **2.** the leafy plant bearing this flower. [From the Swedish botanist Anders *Dahl* (d. 1789).]

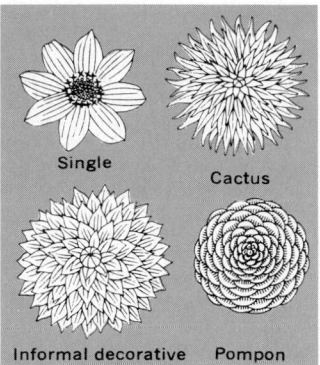
Single   Cactus
Informal decorative   Pompon
dahlias *(def. 1)*

dai·ly (dā'lē) *adj.* appearing, done, or happening every day or every weekday: *a daily newspaper, a daily routine, daily pay.* —*n., pl.* **dai·lies.** a newspaper published every day or every weekday. —*adv.* day after day; every day: *That newspaper column is published daily.*

dain·ty (dān'tē) *adj.,* **dain·ti·er, dain·ti·est. 1.** delicately beautiful or graceful: *a dainty vase.* **2.** having delicate tastes or fussy habits; picky: *a dainty eater.* **3.** pleasing to the taste; delicious: *dainty cakes.* —*n., pl.* **dain·ties.** a delicious bit of food, delicacy. —**dain'ti·ly,** *adv.* —**dain'ti·ness,** *n.*

dair·y (dâr'ē) *n., pl.* **dair·ies. 1.** a room or building where milk and milk products are made and stored. **2.** a store or company that sells milk and milk products. **3.** see **dairy farm.**

dairy cattle, cows bred and raised especially for milk production.

dairy farm, a farm where dairy cattle are raised, often having special facilities for producing large amounts of fresh milk for market. Also, **dairy.**

dair·y·ing (dâr'ē ing) *n.* the business of a dairy farm.

dair·y·maid (dâr'ē mād') *n.* a girl or woman who works in a dairy; milkmaid.

da·is (dā'is, dās) *n., pl.* **da·is·es** (dā'ə sēz'). a slightly raised platform, as for a throne, speaker's desk, or seats for guests of honor.

dai·sy (dā'zē) *n., pl.* **dai·sies. 1.** a flower usually having pink, yellow, or white petallike florets surrounding a yellow center. **2.** the plant bearing this flower.

Da·ko·ta (də kō'tə) *n.* **1.** a member of a tribe of North American Indians formerly living on the Great Plains. Also, **Sioux. 2.** the Siouan language spoken by this tribe. —**Da·ko'tan,** *adj., n.*

Da·lai La·ma (dä lī' lä'mə) formerly, the political leader and a spiritual leader of the Buddhists of Tibet.

dale (dāl) *n.* a small valley.

dal·li·ance (dal'ē əns) *n.* **1.** the act of wasting time; delaying. **2.** a flirtation or trifling.

dal·ly (dal'ē) *v.,* **dal·lied, dal·ly·ing.** —*v.i.* **1.** to waste time; linger; delay: *If you dally any longer, you will miss the bus.* **2.** to flirt or play; trifle: *to dally with danger.* —*v.t.* to waste (time): *Don't dally away the entire morning just talking.*

Dal·ma·tian (dal mā'shən) *n.* **1.** a large dog of a breed believed to have been developed in Dalmatia, having a short-haired white coat speckled with small black or brown spots. **2.** a person who was born or lives in Dalmatia. —*adj.* of or relating to Dalmatia or its people.

dam¹ (dam) *n.* **1.** a structure made of concrete, earth, or other material, built across a stream or river to hold back flowing water. **2.** the body of water held back by a dam. —*v.t.,* **dammed, damming. 1.** to hold back by a dam; furnish with a dam: *to dam a river.* **2.** to hold or keep back; restrain: *I couldn't dam up my feelings.* [Probably from the Middle Low German word *dam* with the same meaning.]

dam² (dam) *n.* the female parent of a four-footed animal, such as a horse or cow. [From the Old French word *dame* meaning "lady," from the Latin word *domina* "lady," feminine form of *dominus* "lord."]

dam¹ *(n., def. 1)*

dam·age (dam'ij) *n.* **1.** harm or injury that causes loss: *The tornado caused great damage to the town.* **2. damages.** *Law.* the money claimed or allowed as payment to make up for injury or loss. —*v.t.,* **dam·aged, dam·ag·ing.** to cause damage to; harm or injure: *to damage a car, to damage a person's reputation.*

Da·mas·cus steel (də mas'kəs) a tough steel whose surface is decorated with a wavy pattern, originally made at Damascus. Damascus steel was used for sword blades during the Middle Ages.

dam·ask (dam'əsk) *n.* **1.** a reversible cloth made of various fibers woven with elaborate patterns or designs, used especially for tablecloths and napkins. **2.** another word for **Damascus steel. 3.** a deep pink or rose color. —*adj.* **1.** made of or resembling damask. **2.** having the color damask.

dame (dām) *n.* **1.** *British.* **a.** a woman having an honorary rank corresponding to that of a knight. **b.** the wife or widow of a knight or baronet. **2.** formerly, a woman of rank, position, or authority; lady. **3.** an elderly woman. **4.** *Slang.* a woman or girl.

damn (dam) *v.t.* **1.** to declare (something) to be bad, worthless, or a failure: *The critics damned the play.* **2.** to curse or swear at. **3.** to condemn to eternal punishment in hell. —*n.* the saying of "damn" as an expression of anger, annoyance, or disappointment. —*adv. Informal.* very. —*interj.* an expression of anger, annoyance, or disappointment.

at; āpe; fär; câre; end; mē; it; īce; pîerce; hot; ōld; sông, fôrk; oil; out; up; ūse; rüle; půll; tûrn; chin; sing; shop; thin; this; hw in white; zh in treasure. The symbol ə stands for the unstressed vowel sound heard in about, taken, pencil, lemon, and circus.

dam·na·ble (dam′nə bəl) *adj.* deserving to be damned; outrageous; detestable. —**dam′na·bly,** *adv.*

dam·na·tion (dam nā′shən) *n.* **1.** the act of damning or the state of being damned. **2.** condemnation to eternal punishment in hell. —*interj.* damn.

damned (damd) *adj.* **1.** condemned as bad, worthless, or a failure. **2.** condemned to eternal punishment in hell. —*adv. Informal.* very.

Dam·o·cles (dam′ə klēz′) *n. Greek Legend.* a courtier of the king of Syracuse who praised the happiness of kings. The king showed Damocles the dangers of wealth and power by inviting him to a magnificent feast at which Damocles sat with a sword suspended above his head by a single hair.

Da·mon (dā′mən) *n. Roman Legend.* a Greek youth who pledged his life for his friend Pythias, who had been condemned to death.

damp (damp) *adj.* slightly wet; moist: *a damp cloth, a damp cellar, damp weather.* —*n.* **1.** moisture; humidity: *The damp made the paint on the walls peel.* **2.** something that checks, discourages, or saddens; damper. **3.** a harmful gas found especially in mines. —*v.t.* **1.** to make damp; dampen. **2.** to lessen in force or strength; check: *to damp a fire, to damp one's spirits.* —**damp′ly,** *adv.* —**damp′ness,** *n.*

damp·en (dam′pən) *v.t.* **1.** to make damp; moisten. **2.** to lessen the force or strength of; check; depress: *The rain dampened our enthusiasm for a picnic.* —*v.i.* to become damp. —**damp′en·er,** *n.*

damp·er (dam′pər) *n.* **1.** a person or thing that checks, discourages, or saddens: *Lack of money put a damper on our vacation plans.* **2.** a movable plate used to control the draft in a fireplace, stove, or furnace. **3.** a device for deadening vibration, especially of piano strings.

dam·sel (dam′zəl) *n.* a young girl; maiden.

dam·sel·fly (dam′zəl flī′) *n.* a slender, brightly colored insect that closely resembles the dragonfly but has four wings that are folded over its back when at rest.

dam·son (dam′zən, dam′sən) *n.* **1.** the small, round, dark purple fruit of a plum tree, having a tart flavor and used mainly in preserves. **2.** the tree bearing this fruit.

dance (dans) *v.,* **danced, danc·ing.** —*v.i.* **1.** to move the body or feet rhythmically, usually in time to music. **2.** to move about in a lively or excited way; leap about: *The presents made the child dance with joy.* **3.** to move or bob up and down: *The sunlight danced on the water's surface.* —*v.t.* **1.** to perform or take part in (a dance): *to dance the polka.* **2.** to cause to dance: *The bride's father danced her around the room.* —*n.* **1.** a prescribed series of rhythmical steps or movements, usually done to music: *The waltz is a well-known dance.* **2.** the act or instance of dancing. **3.** *also,* **the dance.** the art of dancing: *an appreciation of the dance, to study dance.* **4.** a social gathering for dancing: *There will be a dance Friday night at the high school.* **5.** one round of dancing: *Who was your partner for the last dance?* **6.** a piece of music written for dancing.

danc·er (dan′sər) *n.* a person who dances, especially a person whose profession is dancing.

dan·de·li·on (dan′də lī′ən) *n.* **1.** a yellow flower of any of a group of plants. **2.** the plant bearing this flower, having a cluster of long, jagged leaves around the base of a hollow stalk. The leaves may be eaten in salads or cooked as a vegetable. [From the Middle French phrase *dent de lion* meaning "tooth of the lion," used as the name of this plant because its jagged leaves reminded people of teeth.]

dan·der (dan′dər) *n.* loose flakes or scales that shed from the skin: *It seems that I am allergic to my cat's dander.*

·**to get one's dander up.** to make or become angry.

dan·dle (dan′dəl) *v.t.,* **dan·dled, dan·dling. 1.** to move

(someone) up and down on one's knees or in one's arms: *I dandled the baby on my knee.* **2.** to fondle; pamper; pet. —**dan′dler,** *n.*

dan·druff (dan′drəf) *n.* small white or grayish scales of dead skin shed from the scalp.

dan·dy (dan′dē) *n., pl.* **dan·dies. 1.** a man who is fussy or concerned about the elegance of his clothes and appearance; fop. **2.** *Informal.* something very good. —*adj.,* **dan·di·er, dan·di·est.** *Informal.* very good; excellent.

Dane (dān) *n.* a person who was born in or is a citizen of Denmark.

dan·ger (dān′jər) *n.* **1.** the chance or risk of harm, injury, evil, or loss; peril: *The children knew the danger of skating on thin ice.* **2.** an instance or cause of harm, risk, or peril: *Narrow, winding roads can be a danger to drivers.*

dan·ger·ous (dān′jər əs) *adj.* **1.** full of danger; risky; hazardous: *Driving too fast is dangerous.* **2.** likely to cause harm: *A tiger can be a dangerous animal.* —**dan′ger·ous·ly,** *adv.* —**dan′ger·ous·ness,** *n.*

dan·gle (dang′gəl) *v.,* **dan·gled, dan·gling.** —*v.i.* **1.** to hang or swing loosely: *The broken branch dangled from the tree.* **2.** to follow longingly or closely: *A crowd of fans dangled after the movie star step for step.* —*v.t.* to make (something) hang or swing loosely: *They dangled their feet over the side of the dock.* —**dan′gler,** *n.*

dangling participle, a participle that does not clearly relate to the word it is supposed to modify. In the sentence *Arriving at the seashore, the sight of waving palm trees delighted the travelers,* the participle *arriving* is a dangling participle because it seems to modify *sight,* but it is intended to modify *travelers.*

Dan·iel (dan′yəl) *n.* a book of the Old Testament containing the story of the Hebrew prophet Daniel and his prophecies.

Dan·ish (dā′nish) *adj.* of or relating to Denmark, its people, their language, or culture. —*n.* the language of Denmark.

Danish pastry, a sweet, rich pastry made with raised dough.

dank (dangk) *adj.* disagreeably damp; moist and cold: *a dank basement.* —**dank′ly,** *adv.* —**dank′ness,** *n.*

Daph·ne (daf′nē) *n. Greek Mythology.* a nymph who escaped from her pursuer, the god Apollo, by being changed into a laurel tree.

dap·per (dap′ər) *adj.* fashionable and attractive in dress or appearance; neat; trim.

dap·ple (dap′əl) *adj.* having spots; spotted: *a dapple horse.* Also, **dap·pled** (dap′əld). —*n.* **1.** a spot or dot, as on an animal's skin or coat. **2.** an animal having a spotted coat. —*v.,* **dap·pled, dap·pling.** —*v.t.* to mark with spots: *Sunlight through the leaves dappled the lawn.* —*v.i.* to become marked with spots.

dare (dâr) *v.,* **dared** or *(archaic)* **durst, dar·ing.** —*v.t.* **1.** to challenge (someone) to do something, especially as proof of courage or ability: *They dared me to dive from the high board.* **2.** to be courageous or impudent enough to try: *to dare to climb a mountain. Don't you dare talk to me that way!* **3.** to meet boldly and defiantly: *The sailor dared the storm by sailing through it.* ▲ **Dare,** when used with the pronouns *he, she,* or *it* in the present tense, sometimes is used in the form *dare* instead of *dares: Dare she do such a thing? He dare not speak.* —*v.i.* to have enough courage or impudence to try or do something: *Several people were skating on the thin ice, but I didn't dare.* —*n.* a challenge: *Take the dare and see if you can ride the horse bareback.* —**dar·er,** *n.*

dare·dev·il (dâr′dev′əl) *n.* a daring person. —*adj.* **1.** daring, fearless: *The acrobats performed daredevil stunts.* **2.** reckless; rash.

dare·say (dâr′sā′) *also,* **dare say.** *v.t., v.i.* to think or suppose: *I daresay the mayor's speech will cause contro-*

versy. ▲ **Daresay** is used only in the present tense and only with the pronoun *I*.

dar·ing (dâr′ing) *n.* adventurous courage; boldness. —*adj.* courageous and adventurous; fearless: *The soldiers received medals for their daring raid of the enemy's camp.* —**dar′ing·ly,** *adv.*

dark (därk) *adj.* **1.** having little or no light: *a dark night, a dark room.* **2.** not light-colored: *a dark complexion, dark hair, a dark blue.* **3.** gloomy; cheerless; dismal: *Don't always look on the dark side of things.* **4.** hidden from view or knowledge; secret; mysterious: *The rebels kept their plot dark.* **5.** evil; wicked; heinous: *dark deeds.* —*n.* **1.** a partial or total absence of light: *The child was afraid of the dark.* **2.** night; nightfall: *The thieves crept away after dark.* **3.** a dark color or shade: *There are many lights and darks in that painting.* —**dark′ly,** *adv.* —**dark′ness,** *n.*

·**in the dark.** **a.** hidden or secret: *The general kept the military plans in the dark.* **b.** in a state of ignorance; uninformed: *We were in the dark about their schemes.*

Dark Ages also, **dark ages.** the period in European history from about A.D. 476 to about A.D. 1000, between the fall of the Western Roman Empire and the rise of the Middle Ages. It has been traditionally thought of as a time when learning and culture were neglected and civilization did not advance.

dark·en (där′kən) *v.t.* to make or become dark or darker: *Storm clouds darkened the sky.* —**dark′en·er,** *n.*

dark horse **1.** an unexpected winner in a horse race, about whom little is known and whose chances of winning had been considered small. **2.** a person who unexpectedly receives a nomination for political office.

dark·ish (där′kish) *adj.* somewhat dark.

dark·ling (därk′ling) *adv.* in the dark. —*adj.* dark; dim; obscure: *And we are here as on a darkling plain* (Matthew Arnold, "Dover Beach"). ▲ used in literature.

dark·room (därk′rüm′, därk′rum′) *n.* a room in which photographic work is done, designed so that all outside light is kept out.

dar·ling (där′ling) *n.* **1.** a person who is very dear or much loved. **2.** a favorite: *That writer was once the darling of novel readers.* —*adj.* **1.** dearly loved; cherished. **2.** *Informal.* charmingly attractive; cute: *What a darling outfit!*

darn¹ (därn) *v.t.* to mend by weaving stitches across a hole: *to darn the toe of a sock.* —*n.* a place mended by darning. [Probably from the French dialect word *darner* meaning "to mend."]

darn² (därn) *Informal.* another word for **damn.** [Euphemism for *damn*.]

darning needle **1.** a long needle with a large eye, used for darning. **2.** another term for **dragonfly.**

dart (därt) *n.* **1.** a long, slender, pointed object resembling an arrow, used in playing certain games. **2. darts.** a game in which these objects are thrown at a target. **3.** a slender, pointed weapon to be

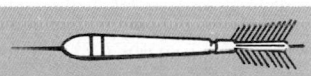

dart *(n., def. 1)*

thrown by hand or shot from a blowgun. **4.** a sudden, swift movement. **5.** a tapered tuck sewn in a garment to give it a better fit. —*v.i.* to spring or move suddenly and swiftly: *The rabbit darted from the bushes.* —*v.t.* **1.** to throw or move suddenly and rapidly: *The lizard darted its tongue at the insect.* **2.** to send suddenly: *I darted an angry look at my friend.*

dash (dash) *v.i.* **1.** to move with speed; rush: *The dog dashed after the rabbit.* **2.** to strike or hit with violence; smash: *Waves dashed against the ship.* —*v.t.* **1.** to strike violently against: *The waves dashed the shore.* **2.** to shatter or break with force or violence; smash: *The storm dashed the ship against the rocks.* **3.** to splash; spatter:

The children dashed each other with water. **4.** to ruin or destroy: *The bad news dashed our hopes.* —*n.*, *pl.*

dash·es. **1.** a sudden rush or movement: *The hikers made a dash for cover when the rain started.* **2.** a small amount added or mixed in: *Add another dash of salt to the stew.* **3.** a short race at top speed: *the 50-yard dash.* **4.** spirited energy and style: *That young actor has dash.* **5.** a short horizontal line (—) used in writing or printing, as for showing a pause or break in a sentence or indicating that something has been left out. **6.** *Telegraphy.* a long signal used with a shorter one to represent numbers or letters, as in Morse code. **7.** see **dashboard.**

·**to dash off.** **a.** to hurry away; leave quickly. **b.** to make, write, or complete quickly or hastily: *Dash off a letter to your family before we leave.*

dash·board (dash′bôrd′) *n.* a panel equipped with gauges and controls, located in front of the driver in an automobile or similar vehicle. Also, **dash.**

dash·ing (dash′ing) *adj.* **1.** courageous and spirited: *the dashing young star of a movie.* **2.** showy; stylish: *dashing costumes.* **dash′ing·ly,** *adv.*

das·tard (das′tərd) *n.* a mean, base coward. —*adj.* see **dastardly.**

das·tard·ly (das′tərd lē) *adj.* mean and cowardly; sneaking. —**das′tard·li·ness,** *n.*

da·ta (dā′tə, dat′ə) *pl. n.*, *sing.* **da·tum.** **1.** information from which conclusions can be drawn; facts and figures. **2.** *Computers.* information processed by a computer. ▲ used with either a singular or plural verb: *Scientific data indicate that our theory is wrong.* *Accurate data is sometimes difficult to find.*

da·ta·base (dā′tə bās′, dat′ə bās′) *n.* a collection of data that is organized by categories so that information can be retrieved logically and easily, as by a computer.

data processing, the organization and analysis of large amounts of information by computers or other machines.

date¹ (dāt) *n.* **1.** a day of the month or year: *Today's date is January 21.* **2.** a specific point or period of time when something happened or is to happen: *The date of my birth is April 3, 1945.* *The date for the party is June 12.* **3.** an inscription stating when something was written or made: *The cornerstone of the building bears the date 1954.* **4.** *Informal.* an appointment or social engagement for a specified time or place: *The friends made a date for next Tuesday.* **5.** *Informal.* a person with whom such an appointment or engagement is made: *You can pick up your date for the party at seven o'clock.* —*v.*, **dat·ed, dat·ing.** —*v.t.* **1.** to furnish or mark with a date: *The secretary dated the letter.* **2.** to determine or fix the time of; give a date to: *Archaeologists dated the statue after much study.* **3.** *Informal.* to go out on dates with (someone): *They have been dating each other for about four months.* —*v.i.* **1.** to belong to, or come from, a particular time or era: *This custom dates from the seventeenth century.* **2.** to meet socially with someone. [From the Middle French word *date* with the same meaning, going back to the Latin phrase *data (Romae)* meaning "given (at Rome)," used to date documents, from *data, datus,* past participle of *dare* "to give."]

·**out of date.** no longer in fashion or use; unfashionable: *The old suit was out of date.*

·**to date.** up to and including the present time.

·**up to date.** **a.** according to the latest style or thought;

---

at; āpe; fär; câre; end; mē; it; īce; pîerce; hot; ōld; sông, fôrk; oil; out; up; ūse; rüle; pùll; tûrn; chin; sing; shop; thin; this; hw in white; zh in treasure. The symbol ə stands for the unstressed vowel sound heard in about, taken, pencil, lemon, and circus.

modern. **b.** including the newest facts or information: *I keep my diary up to date by writing in it each night.*

date² (dāt) *n.* **1.** the oval fruit of the date palm, having thick, sweet flesh that can be eaten. **2.** see **date palm.** [From the Old French word *date* meaning this fruit, going back to the Latin word *dactylus* "date²," from the Greek word *daktylos* "a finger," used as the name of this fruit.]

dat·ed (dā′tid) *adj.* **1.** marked with a date: *dated telephone bills.* **2.** old-fashioned: *The clothes in that old movie are dated.*

date·less (dāt′lis) *adj.* **1.** without a date; bearing no date: *The letter was dateless.* **2.** having no limit or end.

date·line (dāt′līn′) *n.* a line in a piece of printed material, such as an article or newspaper, that gives its date and place of origin.

date line, see **International Date Line.**

date palm, a tall, tropical tree related to the palm, having a straight, shaggy trunk topped with divided leaves and bearing thick clusters of fruit. Also, **date².**

da·tive (dā′tiv) *n.* **1.** the grammatical case in Latin, Russian, and certain other languages that indicates the indirect object of a verb or the object of certain prepositions. **2.** a word in this case. —*adj.* of or belonging to the dative.

da·tum (dā′təm, dat′əm) *n., pl.* **da·ta.** A single piece of information; a single fact.

daub (dôb) *v.t.*

date palm

1. to coat, cover, or smear with a soft substance, such as grease or clay: *to daub the cracks in a wall with plaster.* **2.** to spread (a soft adhesive substance) on or over a surface: *to daub paint on a canvas.* **3.** to paint (something) crudely or poorly. —*v.i.* to paint coarsely or poorly. —*n.* **1.** a smear or smudge; spot: *daubs of dirt on the rug.* **2.** a substance used for daubing, such as plaster or clay. **3.** a crudely painted picture.

daugh·ter (dô′tər) *n.* **1.** a female child, considered in relation to one or both of her parents. **2.** any female descendant. **3.** a female considered in relation to her origin as a child is related to a parent: *She is a daughter of Scotland.*

daughter cell *Biology.* a cell that results from division or replication.

daugh·ter-in-law (dô′tər in lô′) *n., pl.* **daugh·ters-in-law.** the wife of one's son.

daugh·ter·ly (dô′tər lē) *adj.* of, relating to, or proper for a daughter: *daughterly affection.*

daunt (dônt) *v.t.* to frighten or dishearten: *The astronaut was not daunted by the dangers of space travel.*

daunt·less (dônt′lis) *adj.* having no fear; courageous; daring. —**daunt′less·ly,** *adv.* —**daunt′less·ness,** *n.*

dau·phin (dô′fin) *n.* the oldest son of the king of France. ▲ used as a title from 1349 to 1830.

dav·en·port (dav′ən pôrt′) *n.* **1.** a large, upholstered sofa, especially one that converts into a bed. **2.** a writing desk or table, often with drawers.

dav·it (dav′it, dā′vit) *n.* **1.** one of a pair of movable or curved arms that can project over the stern or side of a boat or ship, used especially for raising or lowering a small boat. **2.** a similar device used for raising or lowering the anchor of a ship.

Da·vy Jones (dā′vē jōnz′) the spirit of the sea.

Davy Jones's locker, the bottom of the ocean, especially as the grave of those who drown at sea.

daw (dô) *n.* see **jackdaw.**

daw·dle (dô′dəl) *v.,* **daw·dled, daw·dling.** —*v.i.* to waste time; linger: *to dawdle over breakfast.* —*v.t.* to waste (time); idle: *to dawdle the afternoon away.* —**daw′dler,** *n.*

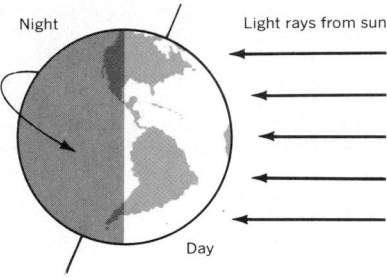

davits *(def. 1)*

dawn (dôn) *n.* **1.** the first appearance of light in the morning; daybreak. **2.** the beginning or first appearance: *the dawn of a new era, the dawn of civilization.* —*v.i.* **1.** to begin to grow light in the morning; to become day. **2.** to begin to be clear, understood, or perceived: *It suddenly dawned on us that we were being tricked.* **3.** to begin to appear, develop, or open: *The space age dawned in the twentieth century.*

day (dā) *n.* **1.** the period of light between the rising and setting of the sun; daytime. *In the Northern Hemisphere, June 21 is the longest day of the year.* **2.** the light of day; daylight. **3.** the length of time required for the earth to complete one rotation on its axis, approximately 24 hours. **4.** the length of time required by any heavenly body to complete one rotation on its axis. **5.** the part of a day passed in a particular way or place: *a school day.* **6.** the hours of a day devoted to work. **7.** a specific period of 24 hours set aside for a particular purpose: *Tomorrow is their wedding day.* **8.** a period of existence, success, or influence: *Knighthood has had its day.* **9.** *also,* **days.** a particular time or period; era: *This house wasn't even built in the days when I was a child.*

day·break (dā′brāk′) *n.* the time each morning when daylight first appears; dawn.

day care, daytime care, including supervision, medical services, and the providing of meals, for preschool children or elderly people. —**day-care,** *adj.*

day-care center (dā′ kâr′) a nursery for the care of small children during the day, especially while their parents work. Also, **day nursery.**

day·dream (dā′drēm′) *n.* a fanciful, dreamy imagining: *I had a daydream of being a movie star.* —*v.i.* to have daydreams. —**day′dream′er,** *n.*

day·light (dā′līt′) *n.* **1.** the light of day: *During the morning the room was filled with daylight.* **2.** the daytime. **3.** the dawn; daybreak: *We do many farm chores before daylight.* **4.** public view: *The reporter brought the matter out into the daylight.* **5.** **daylights.** *Informal.* wits; sense: *That horror movie scared the daylights out of me.*

daylight saving time, a system of time in which clocks are set one or more hours ahead of standard time. It is used especially during summer months to provide more hours of daylight at the end of the working day.

day nursery, another term for **day-care center.**

Day of Atonement, another term for **Yom Kippur.**

day school 1. a school that holds classes only during the day. 2. a private school whose students live at home.

day·time (dā′tīm′) *n.* the period of time between the rising and setting of the sun.

day–to–day (dā′tə dā′) *adj.* 1. of, relating to, or happening every day; daily: *Brushing your teeth is an important part of a day-to-day routine.* 2. dealing with things one day at a time, with little thought for the future: *to run a business on a day-to-day basis.*

daze (dāz) *v.t.,* **dazed, daz·ing.** to stun or confuse, as by a blow; bewilder: *The punch dazed the boxer.* —*n.* a dazed state or condition: *The auto accident left the driver in a daze.* —**daz·ed·ly** (dā′zid lē), *adv.*

daz·zle (daz′əl) *v.t.,* **daz·zled, daz·zling.** 1. to dim the vision of or make almost blind with too much light: *The bright morning sun dazzled us.* 2. to overpower or impress, as by brilliance, splendor, or the like: *The quarterback's outstanding play dazzled the fans.* —*n.* the act of dazzling or the state of being dazzled: *overwhelmed by the dazzle of the city's sights.* —**daz′zler,** *n.* —**daz′zling·ly,** *adv.*

dB, decibel.

DC 1. direct current. 2. postal abbreviation for the District of Columbia.

D.C. 1. direct current. 2. District of Columbia.

d.c., direct current.

D.D., Doctor of Divinity.

D.D.S., Doctor of Dental Surgery.

DDT, a powdery compound that is very poisonous to humans and animals. It was formerly much used as an insecticide.

DE, postal abbreviation for Delaware.

de– *prefix* 1. **a.** to remove (something) from: *defrost.* **b.** to remove from (something): *dethrone.* 2. to lower: *devalue.* 3. to do the opposite of, reverse, or undo: *decode.*

dea·con (dē′kən) *n.* 1. in certain Christian churches, a member of the clergy or a layperson who assists the priest or minister. 2. a member of the clergy ranking next below a priest.

dea·con·ess (dē′kə nis) *n., pl.* **dea·con·ess·es.** a woman who is a church assistant.

dead (ded) *adj.* 1. no longer living; having died; lifeless: *A dead plant cannot bloom.* 2. like death; still: *a dead sleep.* 3. not having life; inanimate: *dead stones.* 4. lacking power, force, usefulness, or interest: *a dead law, a dead tennis ball.* 5. no longer active, working, or in use: *a dead volcano, a dead language. The telephone is dead.* 6. complete; absolute: *a dead silence.* 7. without error; sure; certain: *a dead shot.* 8. exact; direct: *The arrow hit the target at dead center.* 9. *Informal.* very tired; exhausted. —*adv.* 1. completely; absolutely; entirely: *The hikers were dead tired. You are dead right.* 2. directly; straight: *The exit from the highway is dead ahead.* —*n.* 1. dead persons as a group: *We here highly resolve that these dead shall not have died in vain* (Abraham Lincoln). Also, **the dead.** 2. the time of greatest intensity, as of coldness, darkness, or quiet: *the dead of night, the dead of winter.* —**dead′ness,** *n.*

dead·beat (ded′bēt′) *n. Slang.* 1. a person who avoids paying bills. 2. an idle person; loafer.

dead·en (ded′ən) *v.t.* 1. to make less active, forceful, or intense; weaken: *to deaden sound, to deaden pain.* 2. to make less sensitive; numb; dull: *The dentist used a drug to deaden the nerve of the tooth.*

dead–end (ded′end′) *adj.* having or being a dead end: *a dead-end street.*

dead end 1. a street, alley, or passage closed at one end. 2. a situation or point from which no progress can be made: *The negotiations had reached a dead end.*

dead heat, a race in which two or more competitors tie.

dead letter, a letter that is unclaimed or cannot be delivered, especially because of a wrong address.

dead·line (ded′līn′) *n.* a set time by which something must be completed; time limit: *The deadline for the first edition of the newspaper was five o'clock in the morning.*

dead·lock (ded′lok′) *n.* a stopping of progress that results when two opposing sides are unable to reach an agreement; standstill. —*v.t., v.i.* to bring or come to a deadlock.

dead·ly (ded′lē) *adj.,* **dead·li·er, dead·li·est.** 1. causing or tending to cause death; fatal: *a deadly blow, a deadly poison.* 2. aiming or intending to kill or destroy; mortal: *They are deadly enemies.* 3. extremely effective or dangerous: *The soldier took deadly aim.* 4. like death: *The victim's skin had a deadly pallor.* 5. very great; extreme: *a deadly silence.* —*adv.* 1. in a manner resembling death: *deadly pale from fear.* 2. *Informal.* very; extremely: *deadly serious.* —**dead′li·ness,** *n.*

deadly nightshade, see **belladonna** (*def.* 1).

dead·pan (ded′pan′) *adj. Informal.* showing or expressing no emotion: *a deadpan expression.*

dead reckoning, the calculation of the position of a boat, ship, or aircraft by using the records of its speed and last known position and the compass readings of the course steered.

Dead Sea Scrolls, ancient manuscripts, dating from about 100 B.C. to A.D. 100, found in caves near the western shore of the Dead Sea. The Dead Sea Scrolls contain some of the oldest known copies of several books of the Old Testament.

dead weight 1. a heavy, oppressive weight, as of a lifeless body or thing. 2. a heavy or oppressive burden: *The company struggled under the dead weight of debt.* 3. the weight of a ship, truck, or other means of transportation when not loaded.

dead·wood (ded′wŭd′) *n.* 1. the dead portion of a woody plant. 2. a person or thing that has little or no use or value.

deaf (def) *adj.* 1. wholly or partly unable to hear. 2. unwilling to hear or listen; heedless: *Don't be deaf to their pleas for help.* —*n.* **the deaf.** deaf persons as a group. —**deaf′ly,** *adv.* —**deaf′ness,** *n.*

deaf·en (def′ən) *v.t.* 1. to make deaf. 2. to stun or overwhelm with noise: *The noise in the factory deafened us.*

deaf–mute (def′mūt′) *n.* a person who cannot hear or speak.

deal (dēl) *v.,* **dealt, deal·ing.** —*v.i.* 1. to be engaged or concerned; have to do: *This book deals with dogs.* 2. to act or behave: *The police dealt roughly with the rioters.* 3. to take action; consider: *I will deal with the problem right away.* ▲ usually followed by *with* for definitions 1, 2, and 3. 4. to do business; trade: *That store deals in antiques.* ▲ usually followed by *in.* 5. to give out cards to the players of a card game: *It's your turn to deal.* —*v.t.* 1. to give out (cards) to the players of a card game: *Deal seven cards to each player.* 2. to give to a person as a share; distribute: *I dealt out apples to the children.* 3. to give or deliver: *The fighter dealt his opponent a heavy blow.* —*n.* 1. *Informal.* a transaction or arrangement, especially in business: *My cousins made a deal to sell their house.* 2. a bargain: *Did you get a good deal on that used car?* 3. *Informal.* treatment: *to get a fair deal.* 4. the act of giving out cards to the players of a card game.

•**a great deal** or **a good deal. a.** a large amount or

at; āpe; fär; câre; end; mē; it; īce; pîerce; hot; ōld; sông, fôrk; oil; out; up; ūse; rüle; pùll; tûrn; chin; sing; shop; thin; <u>th</u>is; hw in white; zh in treasure. The symbol ə stands for the unstressed vowel sound heard in about, taken, pencil, lemon, and circus.

quantity: *I spent a good deal of time writing that poem.* **b.** to a great extent or degree; very much: *They travel a great deal.*

deal·er (dē′lər) *n.* **1.** a person or a business that buys or sells something: *an antique dealer.* **2.** a person who gives out the cards in a card game. —**deal′er·ship′,** *n.*

deal·ing (dē′ling) *n.* **1.** a way of acting. **2. dealings.** relations, transactions, or communications with others, especially in business: *The store owners were always honest in their dealings.*

dealt (delt) the past tense and past participle of **deal.**

dean (dēn) *n.* **1.** a person at a college or university who is in charge of the discipline, activities, studies, and guidance of the students: *the academic dean, the dean of students.* **2.** the head of a faculty or division of a school, college, or university: *the dean of a law school.* **3.** the chief official of a cathedral. **4.** a person who has been a member the longest, as of an association or group: *Who is the dean of American sportswriters?*

dear (dîr) *adj.* **1.** greatly loved; beloved: *a dear friend.* **2.** highly esteemed. ▲ used as a form of address in letters: *Dear Sir, Dear Madam.* **3.** high-priced; costly; expensive: *Would you buy that suit if it weren't so dear?* —*n.* a beloved person; darling. —*adv.* **1.** affectionately; fondly: *I held them very dear.* **2.** at a high price. —*interj.* an exclamation of emotion, as surprise or distress. —**dear′ly,** *adv.* —**dear′ness,** *n.*

dearth (dûrth) *n.* a scant supply; scarcity; lack: *a dearth of food, a dearth of information.*

dear·y (dîr′ē) *also,* **dear·ie.** *n., pl.* **dear·ies.** *Informal.* dear one; darling.

death (deth) *n.* **1.** the permanent stop of all vital functions in a plant or animal; the end of life. **2.** the state or condition of being dead. **3.** the ending or destruction of anything; extinction: *the death of the Roman Empire, the death of silent movies.* **4.** the cause of dying: *Fast driving will be the death of them.*
·**at death's door.** close to death; dying.
·**to put to death.** to kill or execute.
·**to death.** to the extreme; excessively: *The sudden clap of thunder scared me to death.*

death·bed (deth′bed′) *n.* **1.** the bed on which a person dies. **2. on one's deathbed.** in the last hours of life.

death·blow (deth′blō′) *n.* **1.** a blow that causes death. **2.** something that causes the end or destruction of something: *The earthquake was the deathblow to the town.*

death·less (deth′lis) *adj.* never dying; immortal; eternal: *the deathless writings of ancient Greece.* —**death′less·ness,** *n.*

death·like (deth′līk′) *adj.* characteristic of or like death.

death·ly (deth′lē) *adj.* **1.** characteristic of or like death: *a deathly pale complexion.* **2.** causing death; deadly: *a deathly blow.* —*adv.* **1.** in a deathlike manner. **2.** extremely; very: *The child was deathly afraid of snakes.*

death rate, the proportion of the number of deaths to the total number of people in a given area, usually stated in terms of the number of deaths per thousand people per year.

death's–head (deths′hed′) *n.* the human skull, or a figure representing it, used to symbolize death.

de·ba·cle (di bä′kəl, di bak′əl) *n.* a sudden and complete downfall or collapse; rout; ruin: *The last battle was a great debacle and the army was forced to surrender.*

de·bar (di bär′) *v.t.,* **de·barred, de·bar·ring.** to shut out; exclude; prohibit; bar: *A person who is not a citizen is debarred from voting.* —**de·bar′ment,** *n.*

de·bark (di bärk′) *v.i.* to land; disembark: *The passengers debarked in New York.* —*v.t.* to unload from a ship or airplane: *to debark cargo.* —**de·bar·ka·tion** (dē′bär·kā′shən), *n.*

de·base (di bās′) *v.t.,* **de·based, de·bas·ing.** to lower in quality, value, or character: *to debase coinage, to debase oneself by lying.* —**de·base′ment,** *n.*

de·bat·a·ble (di bā′tə bəl) *adj.* open to discussion or dispute; able to be debated: *The merits of this plan are debatable.*

de·bate (di bāt′) *n.* **1.** a discussion or argument; dispute: *There was much debate about the new tax law.* **2.** a formal discussion of the arguments for and against a question or issue, especially a public contest in which two people or teams argue opposite sides of a given topic. —*v.,* **de·bat·ed, de·bat·ing.** —*v.t.* **1.** to argue about or discuss, as at a public meeting: *The two candidates debated the issue of controlling crime.* **2.** to think about; consider: *They debated whether or not they would go to the movies.* —*v.i.* **1.** to discuss or argue a matter. **2.** to consider: *to debate about buying a car.* —**de·bat′er,** *n.*

de·bauch (di bôch′) *v.t.* to lead away from moral behavior; corrupt; deprave. —*v.i.* to indulge in too much eating, drinking, or revelry; dissipate. —*n.* **1.** another word for **debauchery. 2.** an instance of debauching: *The party turned into a drunken debauch.* —**de·bauch′er,** *n.*

de·bauch·er·y (di bô′chə rē) *n., pl.* **de·bauch·er·ies.** too much indulgence in eating, drinking, or revelry.

de·bil·i·tate (di bil′i tāt′) *v.t.,* **de·bil·i·tat·ed, de·bil·i·tat·ing.** to lessen the strength or vitality of; weaken: *The disease debilitated the patient.* —**de·bil′i·ta′tion,** *n.*

de·bil·i·ty (di bil′i tē) *n., pl.* **de·bil·i·ties.** lack of strength or vigor; feebleness.

deb·it (deb′it) *n.* **1.** the entry of a debt in an account. **2.** an item entered in an account as a debt. **3.** the left-hand side or column of an account where such entries are recorded. —*v.t.* **1.** to enter (a debt) in an account. **2.** to charge with a debt: *to debit an account with $300.*

deb·o·nair (deb′ə nâr′) *also,* **de·bo·naire.** *adj.* gaily courteous, charming, and pleasant: *a debonair movie star.* —**deb′o·nair′ly,** *adv.* —**deb′o·nair′ness,** *n.*

de·brief (dē brēf′) *v.t.* to question or instruct a person, as a pilot or diplomat, at the end of a mission or term of service.

de·bris (də brē′, dā′brē) *also,* **dé·bris.** *n.* remains of something broken or destroyed; rubbish: *The earthquake left the streets filled with debris.*

debt (det) *n.* **1.** something that is owed to another: *a debt of $100.* **2.** the obligation to pay or give something to another. **3.** the condition of owing or being obligated: *to be in debt, to get out of debt.*

debt·or (det′ər) *n.* a person who owes something to another.

de·bug (dē bug′) *v.t.,* **de·bugged, de·bug·ging.** to find and correct errors in (a computer program or system).

de·bunk (di bungk′) *v.t.* to expose or ridicule as false, pretentious, or exaggerated: *to debunk the claims made in an advertisement.*

de·but (dā bū′, dā′bū) *also,* **dé·but.** *n.* **1.** a first public appearance, as of a performer on stage. **2.** a formal introduction of a young woman into society. **3.** a beginning, as of a career or course of action. —*v.i., v.t.,* **de·but·ed** (dā būd′, dā′būd), **de·but·ing** (dā bū′ing, dā′bū ing). to appear or present for the first time: *The orchestra debuted last week. The company debuts its new product tomorrow.*

deb·u·tante (deb′yü tänt′) *also,* **dé·bu·tante.** *n.* a young woman who is making her formal entrance into society.

Dec., December.

deca– *combining form* ten: *decahedron.*

dec·ade (dek′ād) *n.* a period of ten years.

dec·a·dence (dek′ə dəns) *n.* **1.** the process of decay; decline; deterioration: *the gradual decadence of an empire.* **2.** a period or condition of decline, as in morals, art, or literature.

dec·a·dent (dek′ə dənt) *adj.* characterized by or undergoing decay or deterioration, as in morals, art, or literature: *a decadent society.* —*n.* a person who is decadent. —**dec′a·dent·ly,** *adv.*

de·caf·fein·at·ed (dē kaf′ə nā′tid) *adj.* having had the caffeine or most of the caffeine removed: *decaffeinated coffee.*

dec·a·gon (dek′ə gon′) *n.* a plane figure having ten sides and ten angles.

dec·a·he·dron (dek′ə hē′drən) *n., pl.* **dec·a·he·drons** or **dec·a·he·dra** (dek′ə-hē′drə). a solid figure having ten plane surfaces.

de·cal (dē′kal, di kal′) *n.* a design or picture that is made to be transferred from specially treated paper to glass, wood, or other surfaces. Also, **decalcomania.**

de·cal·co·ma·ni·a (di kal′kə mā′nē ə) *n.* **1.** the art or process of transferring designs or pictures from specially treated paper to glass, wood, and other surfaces. **2.** another word for decal.

dec·a·li·ter (dek′ə lē′tər) *also,* **dec·a·li·tre.** *n.* a metric measure of volume, equal to 10 liters (2.64 gallons).

Regular decagon

Concave decagon

decagons

Dec·a·logue (dek′ə lôg′, dek′ə log′) *also,* **Dec·a·log.** *n.* in the Bible, the Ten Commandments.

de·camp (di kamp′) *v.i.* **1.** to leave a camp; break camp. **2.** to depart quickly or secretly; run away: *The thieves decamped under the cover of night.* —**de·camp′ment,** *n.*

de·cant (di kant′) *v.t.* **1.** to pour off (a liquid) gently without disturbing the sediment: *to decant wine.* **2.** to pour from one container to another.

de·cant·er (di kan′tər) *n.* a decorative glass bottle with a stopper, usually used for wine or liquor.

de·cap·i·tate (di kap′i tāt′) *v.t.,* **de·cap·i·tat·ed, de·cap·i·tat·ing.** to cut off the head of; behead. —**de·cap′i·ta′tion,** *n.*

de·cath·lon (di kath′lon) *n.* an athletic contest consisting of ten different track and field events. The contestant scoring the highest total points for all events is the winner.

de·cay (di kā′) *n.* **1.** a rotting; decomposition, as of vegetable or animal matter: *tooth decay.* **2.** a gradual decline, as in strength or quality: *a decay in health, the decay of an empire.* **3.** *Physics.* the changing of an atomic nucleus of a radioactive element into another isotope of the same element or into a nucleus of a different element. —*v.i.* **1.** to rot; decompose: *The potatoes had decayed in the storage bin.* **2.** to decline gradually, as in quality or strength. **3.** *Physics.* to undergo decay.

de·cease (di sēs′) *n.* the act of dying; death. —*v.i.,* **de·ceased, de·ceas·ing.** to die.

de·ceased (di sēst′) *adj.* dead. —*n.* **the deceased.** dead person or persons: *Friends and relatives of the deceased went to the funeral.*

de·ce·dent (di sē′dənt) *n.* *Law.* a dead person: *The decedent left money to charity.*

de·ceit (di sēt′) *n.* **1.** the act or practice of deceiving; deception; lying: *Their deceit was discovered and punished.* **2.** something that is meant to deceive; trick. **3.** the quality of being deceitful; deceitfulness: *full of deceit.*

de·ceit·ful (di sēt′fəl) *adj.* **1.** given to deceiving; lying: *a deceitful person.* **2.** meant to deceive; false: *a deceitful answer.* —**de·ceit′ful·ly,** *adv.* —**de·ceit′ful·ness,** *n.*

de·ceive (di sēv′) *v.,* **de·ceived, de·ceiv·ing.** —*v.t.* to make (someone) believe something that is false; mislead: *The thief deceived us by pretending to be our friend.* —*v.i.* to use deceit; lie. —**de·ceiv′er,** *n.*

de·cel·er·ate (dē sel′ə rāt′) *v.,* **de·cel·er·at·ed, de·cel·er·at·ing.** —*v.t.* to decrease the speed or rate of: *steps to decelerate the inflation in the economy.* —*v.i.* to decrease speed; slow down. —**de·cel′er·a′tion,** *n.* —**de·cel′er·a′tor,** *n.*

De·cem·ber (di sem′bər) *n.* the twelfth and last month

of the year, having thirty-one days. [From the Old French word *Decembre* meaning this month, from the Latin word *December,* the tenth month of the Roman calendar, from the word *decem* "ten."]

de·cen·cy (dē′sən sē) *n., pl.* **de·cen·cies. 1.** proper behavior, as in speech, actions, or dress: *the decency to admit one's error.* **2. decencies.** the things that are needed for a respectable or comfortable manner of living.

de·cent (dē′sənt) *adj.* **1.** in accordance with the standards of society, as in morality or social conduct; respectable: *a decent family.* **2.** in accordance with the standards of good taste; proper: *It is not decent to pry into other people's business.* **3.** kind; generous: *It was very decent of you to help us.* **4.** fairly good; passable; satisfactory: *She makes a decent salary. He gets decent grades.* —**de′cent·ly,** *adv.* —**de′cent·ness,** *n.*

de·cen·tral·ize (dē sen′trə līz′) *v.t.,* **de·cen·tral·ized, de·cen·tral·iz·ing.** to redistribute most of the centralized power, authority, or production of (a government, industry, or other body) by giving it to smaller groups or units: *to decentralize a school system.* —**de·cen′tral·i·za′tion,** *n.*

de·cep·tion (di sep′shən) *n.* **1.** the act of deceiving or the state of being deceived. **2.** something that deceives or is meant to deceive; trick: *victims of a crafty deception.*

de·cep·tive (di sep′tiv) *adj.* characterized by deception; meant to deceive: *You can't hide your anger with a deceptive smile.* —**de·cep′tive·ly,** *adv.* —**de·cep′tive·ness,** *n.*

deci– *combining form* one tenth of: *deciliter, decimeter.*

dec·i·bel (des′ə bel′) *n.* a unit for measuring the loudness of sounds: *A vacuum cleaner generates a sound level of about 70 decibels.* [*Deci-* "one tenth" + *bel* a unit of loudness, from the American inventor Alexander Graham Bell (1847–1922).]

de·cide (di sīd′) *v.,* **de·cid·ed, de·cid·ing.** —*v.i.* **1.** to make up one's mind; resolve: *They decided to go home by bus.* **2.** to make a judgment; come to a conclusion: *The judge decided in favor of the defendant.* —*v.t.* **1.** to determine or settle, as a dispute or question: *The umpire decided the question in our team's favor.* **2.** to determine the result of: *The last touchdown decided the game.* **3.** to cause (someone) to come to a decision: *The high price decided me against buying that coat.*

de·cid·ed (di sī′did) *adj.* **1.** definite; unquestionable: *The taller basketball player had a decided edge over the others.* **2.** determined; sure: *to speak in a decided tone of voice.* —**de·cid′ed·ly,** *adv.* —**de·cid′ed·ness,** *n.*

de·cid·u·ous (di sij′ū əs) *adj.* **1.** (of a tree, shrub, or other plant) shedding its leaves each year: *A maple is a deciduous tree.* **2.** falling off or shed at a particular season or stage of growth: *deciduous leaves, deciduous antlers.*

dec·i·gram (des′i gram′) *n.* a metric unit of weight, equal to ⅒ gram (.0035 ounce).

dec·i·li·ter (des′ə lē′tər) *also,* **dec·i·li·tre.** *n.* a metric measure of volume, equal to ⅒ liter (3.38 ounces).

dec·i·mal (des′ə məl) *adj.* relating to or based on the number 10; proceeding by tens. —*n.* **1.** a number based on multiples of tens, such as 10×10, 10×100, $10 \times 1,000$. **2.** a number containing a decimal point; decimal fraction.

decimal fraction, a fraction whose denominator is equal to ten or a multiple of ten. The fractions ⁵⁄₁₀ and ⁷⁵⁄₁₀₀ expressed as decimal fractions are .5 and .75.

at; āpe; fär; câre; end; mē; it; īce; pîerce; hot; ōld; sông, fôrk; oil; out; up; ūse; rüle; pùll; tûrn; chin; sing; shop; thin; this; hw in white; zh in treasure. The symbol ə stands for the unstressed vowel sound heard in about, taken, pencil, lemon, and circus.

decimal point, a period placed before a decimal fraction.

decimal system, a system of computation having the number 10 as its base.

dec·i·mate (des′ə māt′) *v.t.*, **dec·i·mat·ed, dec·i·mat·ing.** to destroy or kill a large number or proportion of: *The fire decimated the trees in the forest.* —**dec′i·ma′tion,** *n.*

de·ci·pher (di sī′fər) *v.t.* **1.** to make out the meaning of (something illegible or difficult to understand): *to decipher messy handwriting, to decipher a riddle.* **2.** to interpret or translate (something written in code) by using a key; decode: *The expert deciphered the enemy's message.* —**de·ci′pher·a·ble,** *adj.*

de·ci·sion (di sizh′ən) *n.* **1.** the act of making up one's mind: *I hesitated because of the difficulty of the decision.* **2.** the act of reaching a conclusion or making a judgment about something, as a controversy or question: *The decision will be left to the jury.* **3.** a judgment or conclusion reached or given: *The umpire's decision was final.* **4.** the quality of being decided; firmness; determination: *A person of decision rarely alters an opinion.*

de·ci·sive (di sī′siv) *adj.* **1.** settling something finally and completely; conclusive: *a decisive victory.* **2.** characterized by decision; resolute: *a decisive tone of voice.* —**de·ci′sive·ly,** *adv.* —**de·ci′sive·ness,** *n.*

deck (dek) *n.* **1.** a platform or other flat surface serving as a floor or level in a boat or ship. **2.** any similar platform or flat surface. **3.** a set of playing cards. **4.** a component in an audio or video system in which the tape is recorded or played: *a cassette deck.* —*v.t.* **1.** to dress or adorn; ornament: *They decked the room with paper streamers.* **2.** to provide with a deck. **3.** *Slang.* to knock down: *The boxer decked the referee by accident.*

   ·on deck. *Informal.* **a.** on hand and ready for use or action. **b.** ready and waiting for one's turn: *The next batter was on deck.*

deck hand, a sailor who performs manual tasks.

de·claim (di klām′) *v.i.* **1.** to speak or recite publicly; give an oration. **2.** to speak in a loud, showy way: *The speaker declaimed against the new law.* —*v.t.* to say or recite (something) in a loud, showy way: *The actor declaimed a monologue from the play.* —**de·claim′er,** *n.*

dec·la·ma·tion (dek′lə mā′shən) *n.* **1.** the act of declaiming. **2.** the art of speaking or reciting publicly; public speaking. **3.** a formal, prepared public speech or recitation.

de·clam·a·to·ry (di klam′ə tôr′ē) *adj.* **1.** of or relating to declamation. **2.** loud and showy: *a declamatory speech against an opponent.*

dec·la·ra·tion (dek′lə rā′shən) *n.* **1.** the act of declaring. **2.** something that is declared; announcement. **3.** a formal statement: *Congress issued a declaration of war.* **4.** a statement of goods that may be taxed.

Declaration of Independence, the document declaring the thirteen American colonies independent of Great Britain, written mainly by Thomas Jefferson and adopted on July 4, 1776, by the Second Continental Congress.

de·clar·a·tive (di klar′ə tiv) *adj.* making a statement or affirmation: *"I like oranges" is a declarative sentence.*

de·clare (di klâr′) *v.*, **de·clared, de·clar·ing.** —*v.t.* **1.** to make known publicly or formally; announce; proclaim: *The legislature declared a new state holiday.* **2.** to state positively or strongly; assert: *They declared that they were ready to fight for their rights.* **3.** to make a full statement or account of (goods that may be taxed). —*v.i.* to announce an opinion or choice: *The newspaper declared for the incumbent candidate.*

de·clen·sion (di klen′shən) *n.* **1.** the changing of the forms or endings of nouns, pronouns, and adjectives to show case, gender, and number. **2.** a group of such words whose grammatical forms follow the same pattern, as in Latin, Greek, and certain other languages.

dec·li·na·tion (dek′lə nā′shən) *n.* **1.** a leaning, bending, or sloping downward; inclination. **2.** an angular difference between the direction in which a magnetic compass points and the direction of the true North Pole. **3.** a polite refusal.

de·cline (di klīn′) *v.*, **de·clined, de·clin·ing.** —*v.t.* **1.** to refuse (something) politely: *to decline an invitation.* **2.** to give the grammatical forms of (a noun, pronoun, or adjective). —*v.i.* **1.** to refuse politely. **2.** to fall into an inferior or poor condition; weaken: *The patient's health was declining.* **3.** to fall or become less: *Stock prices declined.* **4.** to bend or slope downward. —*n.* **1.** a decrease, as in influence, strength, or amount: *a decline in population.* **2.** a downward bend or slope. **3.** a period during which something is drawing to a close or weakening: *Decades of decline preceded the empire's fall.*

de·cliv·i·ty (di kliv′i tē) *n., pl.* **de·cliv·i·ties.** a downward slope.

de·code (dē kōd′) *v.t.*, **de·cod·ed, de·cod·ing.** to interpret or translate from code into ordinary language by using a key: *to decode a secret message.*

de·com·pose (dē′kəm pōz′) *v.*, **de·com·posed, de·com·pos·ing.** —*v.i.* **1.** to decay; rot: *The old tree stump was decomposing.* **2.** to separate into basic parts or elements. —*v.t.* **1.** to cause to decay or rot. **2.** to separate (something) into its basic parts or elements: *to decompose a chemical compound.* —**de·com·po·si·tion** (dē′kom pə zish′ən),** *n.*

de·com·pos·er (dē′kəm pō′zər) *n.* an organism, such as a bacterium, that breaks down dead plant and animal matter into simpler substances that can be used by other organisms.

de·com·press (dē′kəm pres′) *v.t.* to cause to undergo decompression.

de·com·pres·sion (dē′kəm presh′ən) *n.* the reduction or removal of pressure, especially of high atmospheric pressure on the human body. Deep-sea divers must undergo gradual decompression as they surface.

de·con·ges·tant (dē′kən jes′tənt) *n.* a medicine that relieves congestion in the nose or nasal sinuses. —*adj.* of or relating to a medication that relieves congestion in the nose or nasal sinuses.

de·con·tam·i·nate (dē′kən tam′ə nāt′) *v.t.*, **de·con·tam·i·nat·ed, de·con·tam·i·nat·ing.** to make (a contaminated area or object) safe by removing harmful materials, such as poison gas, bacteria, or radioactive wastes. —**de′con·tam′i·na′tion,** *n.*

de·con·trol (dē′kən trōl′) *v.t.*, **de·con·trolled, de·con·trol·ling.** to remove controls from, especially government controls: *to decontrol rents.* —*n.* the removal of controls.

dé·cor (dā kôr′, dā′kôr) also, **de·cor.** *n.* **1.** a decorative plan and style, as of a room: *furnished in modern décor.* **2.** scenery, as in a theatrical or television presentation.

dec·o·rate (dek′ə rāt′) *v.t.*, **dec·o·rat·ed, dec·o·rat·ing.** **1.** to make more beautiful; ornament; adorn: *They decorated the town for the Fourth of July.* **2.** to plan and execute the style and design of (a room or rooms), as by selecting and arranging furniture, choosing fabrics, paint, or wallpaper, or adding ornamentation. **3.** to honor, as with a medal: *The army decorated the soldier for bravery.*

dec·o·ra·tion (dek′ə rā′shən) *n.* **1.** the act or process of decorating. **2.** something used to decorate; ornament; adornment. **3.** a mark of honor, as a medal or ribbon.

Decoration Day, another term for **Memorial Day.**

dec·o·ra·tive (dek′ər ə tiv) *adj.* serving to decorate; ornamental: *The gift shop sold many decorative objects.* —**dec′o·ra·tive·ly,** *adv.* —**dec′o·ra·tive·ness,** *n.*

dec·o·ra·tor (dek′ə rā′tər) *n.* a person who decorates, especially an interior decorator.

dec·o·rous (dek′ər əs) *adj.* characterized by decorum; in good taste; proper; suitable. —**dec′o·rous·ly,** *adv.* —**dec′o·rous·ness,** *n.*

de·co·rum (di kôr′əm) *n.* propriety or good taste, as in behavior or speech: *act with decorum.*

de·coy (*n.*, dē′koi, di koi′; *v.*, di koi′) *n.* **1.** an artificial bird used to lure birds into a trap or within gunshot range. **2.** a person or thing that lures, as into danger: *The fancy car was a decoy to trap the thief.* **3.** a trick; deception. —*v.t.* **1.** to lure (birds or other animals) into a trap or within gunshot range. **2.** to lure into danger by a decoy.

decoy
a person painting a **decoy**

de·crease (*v.*, di krēs′; *n.*, dē′krēs, di krēs′) *v.*, **de·creased, de·creas·ing.** —*v.i.* to become less; diminish; abate: *The number of traffic accidents decreased last year.* —*v.t.* to cause to become less; reduce: *to decrease the speed of an automobile, to decrease prices.* —*n.* **1.** the act or process of decreasing; lessening: *A decrease in sales reduced the store's profits.* **2.** the amount by which something decreases or is decreased: *a decrease of 10 degrees in the temperature outside.*

de·cree (di krē′) *n.* **1.** *Law.* a decision or order issued by a court: *a divorce decree.* **2.** any official decision or order; edict: *The official decree raised taxes.* —*v.t.*, **de·creed, de·cree·ing.** to order, decide, or appoint by decree: *The president decreed a national holiday.*

dec·re·ment (dek′rə mənt) *n. Mathematics.* the amount by which the value of a variable quantity decreases.

de·crep·it (di krep′it) *adj.* broken down or feeble because of old age or overuse: *a decrepit old house.* —**de·crep′it·ly,** *adv.*

de·crep·i·tude (di krep′i tüd′, di krep′i tūd′) *n.* the condition of being decrepit.

de·cre·scen·do (dē′krə shen′dō) *n.*, *pl.* **de·cre·scen·dos.** *Music.* **1.** a gradual decrease in loudness or force. **2.** a passage in which this occurs. —*adj.* gradually decreasing in loudness or force. —*adv.* with a gradual decrease in loudness or force.

de·cry (di krī′) *v.t.*, **de·cried, de·cry·ing. 1.** to express strong disapproval of; speak out against; condemn: *The teacher decried cheating on exams.* **2.** to try to lower the value of; belittle: *to decry a college education.*

ded·i·cate (ded′i kāt′) *v.t.*, **ded·i·cat·ed, ded·i·cat·ing. 1.** to set apart for or devote to a special purpose or use: *The new company will be dedicated to computer research. The temple was dedicated to the Olympian gods.* **2.** to give or devote totally or very earnestly: *The doctors dedicated themselves to finding a cure for cancer.* **3.** to inscribe (a book or other artistic composition) to a friend or patron in order to show respect, gratitude, or affection.

ded·i·ca·tion (ded′i kā′shən) *n.* **1.** the act of dedicating or the state of being dedicated. **2.** an inscription in a book or other artistic work, dedicating it to a friend or patron.

ded·i·ca·to·ry (ded′i kə tôr′ē) *adj.* of or serving as a dedication.

de·duce (di düs′, di dūs′) *v.t.*, **de·duced, de·duc·ing.** to reach or draw (a conclusion) from something known or assumed; infer: *I deduced that you were unhappy from your frown.* —**de·duc′i·ble,** *adj.*

de·duct (di dukt′) *v.t.* to take away or subtract from a total: *The company deducts income taxes from your salary.* —**de·duct′i·ble,** *adj.*

de·duc·tion (di duk′shən) *n.* **1.** the act of deducting; subtraction. **2.** something that is deducted: *a deduction taken from pay.* **3.** the act or method of reaching a conclusion by reasoning from a general principle to particular cases or facts. **4.** something that is deduced; conclusion; inference.

de·duc·tive (di duk′tiv) *adj.* of, using, or based on deduction: *deductive thinking.* —**de·duc′tive·ly,** *adv.*

deed (dēd) *n.* **1.** something done; act; action: *Helping the neighbors clean their garage was a good deed.* **2.** a legal document showing or proving ownership of real estate. —*v.t.* to transfer (real estate) by deed: *They deeded their house to their children.*

dee·jay (dē′jā′) *n. Informal.* a disc jockey.

deem (dēm) *v.t.* to think; believe; judge: *Do you deem it wise to accept that job?*

deep (dēp) *adj.* **1.** going or reaching far downward from the surface or top: *a deep well, deep water, a deep hole, a deep cut.* **2.** great in degree; intense; extreme: *a deep sleep, deep insight.* **3.** going or reaching far inward or backward from the front or outer edge: *a deep closet, deep woods.* **4.** difficult to understand; obscure: *That book is too deep for me.* **5.** completely occupied; absorbed; engrossed: *We didn't hear your knock because we were deep in conversation.* **6.** strongly felt; profound: *deep sorrow.* **7.** dark and rich in color: *a deep brown.* **8.** low in pitch: *a deep voice, the deep tones of an organ.* **9.** having a specified dimension downward, inward, or backward: *a pool 12 feet deep.* —*adv.* **1.** in, at, to, or with a great depth; deeply: *The explorers went deep into the jungle.* **2.** far on in time; late: *The meeting continued deep into the night.* —*n.* **1.** the part or time of greatest intensity, as of coldness, darkness, or quiet: *the deep of winter, the deep of night.* **2. the deep.** the sea. —**deep′ly,** *adv.* —**deep′ness,** *n.*

deep·en (dē′pən) *v.t.*, *v.i.* to make or become deep or deeper: *The workers deepened the hole by digging.*

deep-fry (dēp′frī′) *v.t.*, **deep-fried, deep-fry·ing.** to fry by completely covering with hot oil or fat.

deep-root·ed (dēp′rü′tid, dēp′rut′id) *adj.* firmly fixed; deep-seated: *a deep-rooted friendship that was never shaken by a quarrel.*

deep-sea (dēp′sē′) *adj.* of, in, or relating to the deeper parts of the ocean: *deep-sea fishing, a deep-sea diver.*

deep-seat·ed (dēp′sē′tid) *adj.* firmly fixed; deeply rooted: *a deep-seated fear of high places.*

deep-set (dēp′set′) *adj.* placed or fixed deeply: *deep-set eyes.*

deer (dîr) *n.*, *pl.* **deer.** any of various swift, cud-chew-

deer

at; āpe; fär; câre; end; mē; it; īce; pîerce; hot; ōld; sông, fôrk; oil; out; up; ūse; rüle; pull; tûrn; chin; sing; shop; thin; this; hw in white; zh in treasure. The symbol ə stands for the unstressed vowel sound heard in about, taken, pencil, lemon, and circus.

D

ing animals, as the moose, the elk, and the reindeer. All male deer and some female deer have antlers that are shed each year.

deer mouse, a mouse of North and Central America, having tan or brown fur with white markings on the underside.

deer·skin (dîr′skin′) *n.* **1.** the hide of a deer. **2.** leather made from this hide.

def. **1.** definition. **2.** defense.

de·face (di fās′) *v.t.,* **de·faced, de·fac·ing.** to spoil or mar the surface or appearance of: *to deface a monument with graffiti.* —**de·face′ment,** *n.*

de fac·to (dē fak′tō) existing in reality, with or without legal right; actual: *de facto racial segregation. While the president was ill, the firm's vice president was the de facto leader of the company.* [From the Latin phrase *de facto* meaning "from the fact."]

def·a·ma·tion (def′ə mā′shən) *n.* the act of defaming; slander or libel: *sued for defamation of character.*

de·fam·a·to·ry (di fam′ə tôr ē) *adj.* damaging to the reputation; slanderous or libelous.

de·fame (di fām′) *v.t.,* **de·famed, de·fam·ing.** to attack or ruin the good name or reputation of; slander or libel. —**de·fam′er,** *n.*

de·fault (di fôlt′) *n.* a failure to do something required, especially failure to take part in or complete a scheduled game or contest: *If they don't show up for the game, their team will lose by default.* —*v.i.* to fail or neglect to do something required: *Don't default in your payment of the debt.* —**de·fault′er,** *n.*

de·feat (di fēt′) *v.t.* **1.** to overcome in a contest or conflict of any kind; win a victory over: *to defeat an opponent in tennis, to defeat the enemy in battle.* **2.** to prevent the success of; frustrate; thwart: *to defeat a purpose, to defeat a person's hopes.* —*n.* the act of overcoming or the state of being overcome in a contest or conflict: *to suffer bitter defeat.*

de·feat·ism (di fē′tiz əm) *n.* the state of mind or behavior characteristic of a defeatist.

de·feat·ist (di fē′tist) *n.* a person who expects defeat or who accepts it too readily or too soon. —*adj.* characteristic of a defeatist: *a defeatist attitude.*

def·e·cate (def′i kāt′) *v.i.,* **def·e·cat·ed, def·e·cat·ing.** to excrete waste from the bowels. —**def′e·ca′tion,** *n.*

de·fect (*n.,* dē′fekt, di fekt′; *v.,* di fekt′) *n.* **1.** an imperfection, flaw, or weakness; fault; blemish: *The only defect in this glass bowl is a small chip.* **2.** the lack of something necessary for completeness or perfection; deficiency: *a speech defect.* —*v.i.* to desert a group, country, or cause, especially to go to another that is opposed to it: *The spy defected to the enemy.* —**de·fec′tor,** *n.*

de·fec·tion (di fek′shən) *n.* the act of deserting a group, country, or cause, especially to go to another that is opposed to it.

de·fec·tive (di fek′tiv) *adj.* **1.** having a defect or defects; imperfect; incomplete: *Defective wiring can cause fires.* **2.** having less than normal mental or physical ability. —*n.* a person who has less than normal mental or physical ability. —**de·fec′tive·ly,** *adv.* —**de·fec′tive·ness,** *n.*

de·fence (di fens′) *British.* another spelling of **defense.**

de·fend (di fend′) *v.t.* **1.** to guard against attack, injury, or danger; protect: *The troops defended the city.* **2.** to support, justify, or argue for by word or deed: *to defend one's rights.* **3.** *Law.* to plead the case or cause of (an accused person): *The lawyer defended the prisoner in court.* —**de·fend′er,** *n.*

de·fend·ant (di fen′dənt) *n.* a person against whom a civil or criminal action is brought in a court of law.

de·fense (di fens′) *also, British,* **de·fence.** *n.* **1.** the act of guarding against attack, injury, or danger; protection: *The army prepared for the defense of the city against enemy attack.* **2.** a person or thing that protects; means

of protection: *The dike was the town's only defense against floods.* **3.** support or justification by word or deed: *The governor spoke in defense of the new law.* **4.** an argument, speech, or writing that supports or justifies: *The scientist's defense of the theory lacked definite proof.* **5.** the defending team, players, or side in a game. **6. a.** the arguments presented in court by a defendant or his or her lawyer. **b.** a defendant and his or her lawyer or lawyers.

de·fense·less (di fens′lis) *adj.* having no defense; helpless; unprotected: *The wolves guarded their defenseless cubs.* —**de·fense′less·ly,** *adv.* —**de·fense′less·ness,** *n.*

de·fen·si·ble (di fen′sə bəl) *adj.* **1.** that can be defended; justifiable: *a defensible action.* **2.** that can be defended against attack, injury, or danger: *a defensible coastline.* —**de·fen′si·bil′i·ty,** *n.* —**de·fen′si·bly,** *adv.*

de·fen·sive (di fen′siv) *adj.* **1.** serving to defend; protective: *defensive armor.* **2.** having or using defenses: *a defensive attitude, a defensive person.* —*n.* a position or attitude of defense. —**de·fen′sive·ly,** *adv.* —**de·fen′sive·ness,** *n.*

·**on the defensive.** assuming a protective attitude: *They were on the defensive because they'd been criticized.*

de·fer¹ (di fûr′) *v.t.,* **de·ferred, de·fer·ring.** to put off to a future time; postpone: *The court will defer judgment until all the facts are known.* [From the Old French word *differer* meaning "to postpone," from the Latin word *differre* meaning both "to disperse" and "to postpone."] —**de·fer′ra·ble,** *adj.*

de·fer² (di fûr′) *v.i.,* **de·ferred, de·fer·ring.** to yield in judgment or opinion; give in respectfully: *I deferred to my parents' wishes.* [From the Old French word *deferer* meaning "to yield," from the Late Latin word *deferre* "to yield" or "pay respect to," from the Latin word *deferre* "to bear away" and "grant, allow," from the words *de-* "away" + *ferre* "to bear, bring."]

def·er·ence (def′ər əns) *n.* a courteous respect or regard: *to have deference for one's elders.*

·**in deference to.** out of respect for: *Flags were lowered in deference to the dead leader.*

def·er·en·tial (def′ə ren′shəl) *adj.* characterized by or showing deference; respectful: *a deferential attitude.* —**def′er·en′tial·ly,** *adv.*

de·fer·ment (di fûr′mənt) *n.* the act of putting off or delaying; postponement: *deferment from military service.* Also, **de·fer·ral** (di fûr′əl).

de·fi·ance (di fī′əns) *n.* bold or open resistance to authority, an opponent, or an opposing force; contempt of opposition or authority: *The rioters showed their defiance by deliberately breaking the law.*

de·fi·ant (di fī′ənt) *adj.* characterized by or showing defiance; boldly or openly resisting: *a defiant act.* —**de·fi′ant·ly,** *adv.* [From the French word *défiant,* past participle of *défier* meaning "to defy."]

de·fi·cien·cy (di fish′ən sē) *n., pl.* **de·fi·cien·cies.** **1.** the condition of being deficient; lack of something necessary: *a mental deficiency, a vitamin deficiency.* **2.** the amount by which something is lacking; deficit: *a deficiency of ten dollars.*

deficiency disease, a disease, as scurvy or rickets, caused by the lack of some necessary vitamin or other element in the diet.

de·fi·cient (di fish′ənt) *adj.* **1.** not adequate in quantity or supply; insufficient: *a diet deficient in vitamins.* **2.** lacking something necessary; incomplete; imperfect: *The student who was deficient in biology credits took extra courses to compensate.* [From the Latin word *deficiens,* present participle of *deficere* meaning "to lack something necessary," "to fail."] —**de·fi′cient·ly,** *adv.*

def·i·cit (def′ə sit) *n.* the amount by which something, especially a sum of money, falls short of what is due, required, or expected; shortage: *There was a ten dollar deficit in our food budget, because we budgeted fifty dollars and owed the grocer sixty dollars.*

de·file¹ (di fīl′) *v.t.*, **de·filed, de·fil·ing.** **1.** to spoil the purity of; taint: *to defile a sacred temple.* **2.** to make filthy, dirty, or impure; pollute: *to defile a stream with garbage.* [From the Middle English word *defoulen* meaning "to trample on, defile," from the Old French word *defouler* "to trample on."] **—de·file′ment,** *n.*

de·file² (di fīl′) *v.i.*, **de·filed, de·fil·ing.** to march in a narrow column or single line. **—n.** a narrow passage in a mountain region, especially one that permits travel only in a narrow column or single line. [From the French word *défiler* meaning "to march in a column," from the words *dé-* "from, away" and *fil* "a thread, line," from the Latin word *filum* "a thread."] **—de·file′ment,** *n.*

de·fine (di fīn′) *v.t.*, **de·fined, de·fin·ing.** **1.** to state the meaning or meanings of (a word or phrase): *Can you define the word "rebuff"?* **2.** to describe, fix, or set forth exactly or authoritatively: *The Constitution of the United States defines the powers of the president.* **3.** to determine or fix the limits or extent of: *The river defined the boundary between the two countries.* **4.** to make clear or distinct in outline or form: *The bright sky boldly defined the mountain.* **—de·fin′a·ble,** *adj.* **—de·fin′er,** *n.*

def·i·nite (def′ə nit) *adj.* **1.** clearly defined; precise; exact: *He has definite ideas on the subject of education.* **2.** positive; certain; sure: *It is definite that the school will get a new principal.* **3.** having fixed limits: *a definite boundary.* **—def′i·nite·ly,** *adv.* **—def′i·nite·ness,** *n.*

definite article, the article *the.*

def·i·ni·tion (def′ə nish′ən) *n.* **1.** a statement of the meaning of a word or phrase. **2.** a statement of the true nature or characteristics of a thing. **3.** sharpness of outline; distinctness; clearness: *This photograph lacks definition.*

In a dictionary, a **definition** is supposed to describe everything that a word means and nothing that it does not mean. A definition of the word *dog* should be general enough to cover anything that is a dog, and should be specific enough to exclude anything that is not a dog. It is easier to decide what a dog isn't and to leave that out of a definition. It is more difficult to decide what to include. If you try to say everything that a dog is, you will probably give more facts than most readers really need or want to know, and you may include facts that are true only of some dogs, but not all dogs.

Most early dictionaries gave very little information in their definitions. In one dictionary a dog was defined as a "well-known creature," and in another as a "well-known domestic quadruped." These definitions could also describe a cow, a horse, or a cat. In a good modern dictionary, a definition of the word *dog* includes enough information to help the reader understand what a dog is and distinguish it from other animals. Unlike an encyclopedia, a dictionary must leave out facts that are not necessary, even though they are correct and, perhaps, interesting.

The most difficult kind of word to define is an abstract word. Abstract words, such as *beauty, sorrow,* and *kindness,* do not name physical things that you can see, touch, hear, or smell. They name feelings or ideas or statements describing the quality of a thing. We cannot adequately define an abstract word by using "facts" alone. To help you understand what it means, we also show how such a word is used in a sentence.

de·fin·i·tive (di fin′i tiv) *adj.* **1.** most nearly correct and complete: *the definitive biography of the country's founder.* **2.** conclusive; final; decisive: *a definitive answer.* **—de·fin′i·tive·ly,** *adv.* **—de·fin′i·tive·ness,** *n.*

de·flate (di flāt′) *v.,* **de·flat·ed, de·flat·ing.** **—v.t.** **1.** to let out the air or gas of: *to deflate a tire, to deflate a balloon.* **2.** to reduce in importance: *to deflate a boastful person's ego.* **3.** to reduce the amount, size, or level of: *to deflate prices.* **—v.i.** to collapse or become smaller, as through loss of air or gas.

de·fla·tion (di flā′shən) *n.* **1.** the act of deflating or the state of being deflated. **2.** a decline in the general level of prices, resulting from a reduction in money supply or spending.

de·flect (di flekt′) *v.t.* to cause to turn aside or change direction; bend from a straight course: *The wind deflected the flight of the ball.* **—v.i.** to turn aside or change direction.

de·flec·tion (di flek′shən) *n.* **1.** the act of deflecting or the state of being deflected; deviation. **2.** the amount of such turning or deviation. **3.** the amount that an indicator on a measuring instrument moves or deviates from the zero reading on its scale.

de·fo·li·ant (dē fō′lē ənt) *n.* a chemical that defoliates plants, chiefly used in farming to remove unwanted leaves and in warfare to destroy crops or plants.

de·fo·li·ate (dē fō′lē āt′) *v.t.*, **de·fo·li·at·ed, de·fo·li·at·ing.** **1.** to strip of leaves: *to defoliate plants.* **2.** to destroy an area of vegetation, as a forest or jungle. **—de·fo′li·a′tion,** *n.*

de·for·est (dē fôr′ist, dē for′ist) *v.t.* to clear or strip of forests or trees. **—de·for′est·a′tion,** *n.*

de·form (di fôrm′) *v.t.* **1.** to spoil the form or shape of: *The plastic bottle was deformed by the heat of the fire.* **2.** to make ugly; mar the beauty of; disfigure.

de·for·ma·tion (def′ər mā′shən, dē′fôr mā′shən) *n.* **1.** the act of deforming or the state of being deformed. **2.** a result or condition of being deformed; deformity.

de·formed (di fôrmd′) *adj.* improperly formed; especially distorted: *The dog's deformed leg was caused by an accident.*

de·form·i·ty (di fôr′mi tē) *n., pl.* **de·form·i·ties.** **1.** an improperly formed or distorted part of the body. **2.** the condition of being deformed.

de·fraud (di frôd′) *v.t.* to take something away from (a person) by fraud; cheat; swindle: *The employee defrauded the bank of several thousand dollars.*

de·fray (di frā′) *v.t.* to pay (costs or expenses): *The college raised its tuition to help defray additional expenses.*

de·frost (di frôst′) *v.t.* **1.** to make free of frost or ice: *to defrost a refrigerator.* **2.** to thaw: *to defrost frozen meat.* **—v.i.** **1.** to become free of frost or ice: *The refrigerator will defrost overnight.* **2.** to become thawed.

de·frost·er (di frôs′tər) *n.* a device that removes or prevents the formation of ice or frost, as on an automobile windshield.

deft (deft) *adj.* skillful and nimble; adroit: *the deft fingers of a pianist. Your deft handling of the difficult situation prevented a crisis.* **—deft′ly,** *adv.* **—deft′ness,** *n.*

de·funct (di fungkt′) *adj.* no longer existing or active; dead; extinct: *a defunct business.*

de·fuse (dē fūz′) *v.t.*, **de·fused, de·fus·ing.** **1.** to remove the fuse from: *to defuse an unexploded bomb.* **2.** to lessen the danger or intensity of: *to defuse political tensions.*

de·fy (di fī′) *v.t.*, **de·fied, de·fy·ing.** **1.** to resist (opposition or authority) boldly or openly; oppose with contempt: *to defy the law.* **2.** to resist completely or successfully; withstand: *That problem defies solution.* **3.** to challenge; dare: *I defy you to match my record in swim-*

at; āpe; fär; câre; end; mē; it; īce; pîerce; hot; ōld; sông, fôrk; oil; out; up; ūse; rüle; pùll; tûrn; chin; sing; shop; thin; ᴛʜis; hw in white; zh in treasure. The symbol ə stands for the unstressed vowel sound heard in about, taken, pencil, lemon, and circus.

ming. [From the Old French word *defier* meaning "to defy," earlier "to renounce faith in God," going back to the Latin words *dis-* "against" and *fidere* "to trust."]

deg., degree; degrees.

de·gen·er·a·cy (di jen′ər ə sē) *n.* **1.** the state of being degenerate, especially in moral character. **2.** the process of degenerating; deterioration.

de·gen·er·ate (*v.*, di jen′ə rāt′; *adj.*, *n.*, di jen′ər it) *v.i.*, **de·gen·er·at·ed, de·gen·er·at·ing. 1.** to become worse or inferior in condition, character, or quality; deteriorate: *Your health will gradually degenerate if the disease isn't treated.* **2.** (of an organism) to regress to a less complex or less developed form. —*adj.* having become worse or inferior in condition, character, or quality; deteriorated; degraded: *a degenerate society.* —*n.* a person who is morally degraded. —**de·gen·er·ate·ly** (di jen′ər it lē), *adv.*

de·gen·er·a·tion (di jen′ə rā′ shən) *n.* **1.** the act or process of degenerating. **2.** the state of being degenerated.

de·gen·er·a·tive (di jen′ər ə tiv, di jen′ə rā′tiv) *adj.* relating to, characterized by, or causing degeneration: *a degenerative disease, a degenerative change in form.*

deg·ra·da·tion (deg′rə dā′shən) *n.* **1.** the act of degrading or the state of being degraded. **2.** a degraded condition.

de·grade (di grād′) *v.t.*, **de·grad·ed, de·grad·ing. 1.** to lower in character, quality, or estimation; debase: *Lying degrades a person.* **2.** to lower in rank or position, especially as a punishment.

de·gree (di grē′) *n.* **1.** one of a series of stages or steps in a process or course: *The child learned to walk by degrees.* **2.** intensity, amount, or extent: *a high degree of intelligence, helping to the greatest degree possible.* **3.** social rank or position: *a person of low degree.* **4.** a rank or title given by a school, college, or university to a student for completion of a course of study or to a person as an honor: *a degree in history.* **5.** a unit of measurement for temperature, varying according to the scale used. ▲ The symbol for degrees (°) is often used with figures: *70° Fahrenheit.* **6.** *Mathematics.* a unit of measurement for angles or arcs, equal to ¹⁄₃₆₀ of the circumference of a circle. **7.** *Algebra.* **a.** the rank of a monomial term as determined by the sum of the exponents of the variables. The terms x^4 and xy^3 are both of the fourth degree. **b.** the rank of a polynomial as determined by the sum of the exponents of the term of the highest degree. The equation $xy^4 + yz$ is of the fifth degree. **8.** *Grammar.* one of the three forms of comparison of adjectives or adverbs. For the adjective *good*, *good* is the positive degree, *better* is the comparative degree, and *best* is the superlative degree. **9.** *Law.* the relative seriousness of a particular crime: *murder in the first degree.*

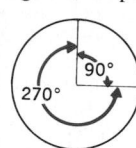

degree
(def. 6)

de·gree–day (di grē′dā′) *n.* a unit representing the amount of difference between the average temperature for a given day and a standard, usually 65 degrees Fahrenheit (18 degrees Celsius), used for estimating fuel and power requirements.

de·hu·mid·i·fy (dē′hū mid′ə fī′) *v.t.*, **de·hu·mid·i·fied, de·hu·mid·i·fy·ing.** to remove moisture from (air or other gases). —**de′hu·mid′i·fi·ca′tion,** *n.* —**de′hu·mid′i·fi′er,** *n.*

de·hy·drate (dē hī′drāt) *v.*, **de·hy·drat·ed, de·hy·drat·ing.** —*v.t.* to remove water or moisture from: *to dehydrate food.* —*v.i.* to lose water or moisture; become dry. —**de′hy·dra′tion,** *n.*

de·ice (dē īs′) *v.t.*, **de·iced, de·ic·ing.** to remove ice from or prevent ice from forming on: *to deice a windshield.*

de·i·fi·ca·tion (dē′ə fi kā′shən) *n.* the act of deifying or the state of being deified.

de·i·fy (dē′ə fī′) *v.t.*, **de·i·fied, de·i·fy·ing. 1.** to make

a god of: *The ancient Egyptians deified the sun.* **2.** to worship as a god; regard as an object of worship: *to deify a monarch, to deify wealth.*

deign (dān) *v.i.* to think worthy of oneself; condescend: *I would not deign to consider such an offer.* —*v.t.* to see fit to grant or give: *They deigned no reply.*

de·ism (dē′iz əm) *n.* the belief that the universe and its natural laws were created by God, but that natural laws, not the will of God, govern its operation.

de·ist (dē′ist) *n.* a person who believes in deism.

de·i·ty (dē′i tē) *n.*, *pl.* **de·i·ties. 1.** a god or goddess; divine being. **2.** divine nature or condition; divinity. **3. the Deity.** God.

dé·jà vu (dā′zhä vü′) the illusion that one has previously experienced something that is actually being experienced for the first time: *Although I had never been there before, as soon as I entered the museum I felt a strong sense of déjà vu.*

de·ject (di jekt′) *v.t.* to make low in spirits; dishearten; depress: *The defeat dejected the team.*

de·ject·ed (di jek′tid) *adj.* characterized by or showing low spirits; disheartened; depressed: *dejected over a loss, a dejected look.* —**de·ject′ed·ly,** *adv.* —**de·ject′ed·ness,** *n.*

de·jec·tion (di jek′shən) *n.* lowness of spirits; depression; sadness.

de ju·re (dē jùr′ē) by right; according to law: *a de jure ruler.* [From the Latin phrase *de jure* meaning "according to law."]

Del., Delaware.

Del·a·ware (del′ə wâr′) *n.*, *pl.* **Del·a·ware** or **Del·a·wares. 1.** a member of a North American Indian tribe formerly living in the Delaware River valley. **2.** the Algonquian language of this tribe.

de·lay (di lā′) *v.t.* **1.** to put off to a future time; postpone: *The umpire delayed the start of the baseball game because of the rain.* **2.** to make late; hinder the progress of; detain: *Heavy traffic delayed us.* —*v.i.* to put off or slow down action; linger: *You will miss the bus if you delay any longer.* —*n.* **1.** the act of delaying or the state of being delayed: *The train's delay was caused by a derailment.* **2.** the amount of time something is delayed: *There will be a brief delay before the show begins.*

de·lec·ta·ble (di lek′tə bəl) *adj.* highly pleasing or delightful, especially to the taste; delicious: *a delectable loaf of hot bread.*

del·e·gate (*n.*, del′i gāt′, del′i git; *v.*, del′i gāt′) *n.* a person given authority to represent or act for another or others; representative; deputy: *Every chapter sent delegates to the club's national convention.* —*v.t.*, **del·e·gat·ed, del·e·gat·ing. 1.** to give (power, authority, or responsibility) to another or others. **2.** to appoint or send as a delegate: *The club delegated me to head the fund-raising drive.*

del·e·ga·tion (del′i gā′shən) *n.* **1.** a group of delegates: *A delegation of war veterans marched in the parade.* **2.** the act of delegating or the state of being delegated.

de·lete (di lēt′) *v.t.*, **de·let·ed, de·let·ing.** to cross out or take out (something written or printed); omit; cancel: *I'll delete your name from the list of volunteers.*

del·e·te·ri·ous (del′i tîr′ē əs) *adj.* causing harm; injurious; hurtful: *Smoking is deleterious to your health.* —**del′e·te′ri·ous·ly,** *adv.* —**del′e·te′ri·ous·ness,** *n.*

de·le·tion (di lē′shən) *n.* **1.** the act of deleting or the state of being deleted. **2.** something that has been deleted.

delft (delft) *n.* glazed earthenware decorated in patterns inspired by Chinese porcelains.

delft plate

del·i (del′ē) *n. Informal.* see **delicatessen.**

de·lib·er·ate (*adj.,* di lib′ər it; *v.,* di lib′ə rāt′) *adj.*
1. carefully thought out or planned; intentional; studied:
We made a deliberate attempt to ignore their rude comments. **2.** careful and slow in deciding; not hasty or rash:
The executive was deliberate in all business dealings with others. **3.** unhurried in action or movement; slow: *The cat stalked the bird with deliberate steps.* —*v.,* **de·lib·er·at·ed, de·lib·er·at·ing.** —*v.i.* to think or consider carefully: *They deliberated whether or not they should go to the party.* —*v.t.* to think over or discuss carefully; debate: *The Senate has been deliberating the question for three days.* —**de·lib′er·ate·ly,** *adv.* —**de·lib′er·ate·ness,** *n.*

de·lib·er·a·tion (di lib′ə rā′shən) *n.* **1.** careful thought or consideration: *They decided to go only after much deliberation.* **2.** a discussion and consideration by a group of people of the reasons for and against something: *the deliberations of a jury.* **3.** slowness and care in decision or action: *to speak with deliberation.*

de·lib·er·a·tive (di lib′ə rā′tiv, di lib′ər ə tiv) *adj.* relating to deliberation: *The state legislature is a deliberative assembly.*

del·i·ca·cy (del′i kə sē) *n., pl.* **del·i·ca·cies.** **1.** fineness of structure, quality, texture, or form; daintiness; frailty: *the delicacy of lace.* **2.** a rare or choice food: *Caviar is a delicacy.* **3.** physical weakness: *The twins played sports despite their delicacy.* **4.** the quality of requiring tact, skill, or care in treatment or handling: *the delicacy of a situation, a matter of great delicacy.* **5.** fineness of taste, skill, or feeling. **6.** sensitivity to what is becoming, proper, or modest.

del·i·cate (del′i kit) *adj.* **1.** fine or dainty in structure, quality, texture, or form: *a delicate piece of lace, a face with delicate features.* **2.** pleasing to the senses in a soft, mild, or subtle way: *a delicate perfume, a delicate color, a delicate flavor.* **3.** easily damaged; fragile: *a delicate flower, a delicate crystal glass.* **4.** very susceptible to disease or injury: *a delicate child.* **5.** requiring tact, skill, or care in treatment or handling; difficult: *a delicate topic of conversation, a delicate brain operation.* **6.** finely skilled or sensitive: *a delicate touch, a delicate measuring instrument.* —**del′i·cate·ly,** *adv.* —**del′i·cate·ness,** *n.*

del·i·ca·tes·sen (del′i kə tes′ən) *n.* **1.** a store that sells prepared foods, such as cooked meats, salads, and cheeses. **2.** the foods sold in such a store. Also, **deli.**

de·li·cious (di lish′əs) *adj.* highly pleasing or delightful, especially to the taste or smell: *delicious fruit, a delicious meal.* —**de·li′cious·ly,** *adv.* —**de·li′cious·ness,** *n.*

de·light (di līt′) *n.* **1.** a high degree of pleasure; joy: *We could not conceal our delight at seeing them again.* **2.** something that gives great pleasure: *The dancer's performance was a delight to watch.* —*v.t.* to give great pleasure or joy to; please highly: *The puppet show delighted the children.* —*v.i.* to have or take great pleasure: *to delight in helping others.*

de·light·ed (di lī′tid) *adj.* highly pleased; gratified: *They said they would be delighted to come to the party.* —**de·light′ed·ly,** *adv.*

de·light·ful (di līt′fəl) *adj.* highly pleasing; giving delight: *a delightful story, a delightful person.* —**de·light′ful·ly,** *adv.* —**de·light′ful·ness,** *n.*

de·lin·e·ate (di lin′ē āt′) *v.t.,* **de·lin·e·at·ed, de·lin·e·at·ing.** **1.** to draw or show the outline of; sketch: *The map delineated the boundaries between the two countries.* **2.** to describe in words; portray: *The author of the novel delineated the characters clearly.*

de·lin·e·a·tion (di lin′ē ā′shən) *n.* **1.** the act or process of delineating. **2.** something that delineates, such as a drawing or description.

de·lin·quen·cy (di ling′kwən sē) *n., pl.* **de·lin·quen·cies.** **1.** failure or neglect of duty or obligation. **2.** a fault; offense; misdeed. **3.** see **juvenile delinquency.**

de·lin·quent (di ling′kwənt) *adj.* **1.** failing in or neglectful of a duty or obligation: *delinquent in paying one's bills.* **2.** guilty of a fault, offense, or misdeed. **3.** due and unpaid: *delinquent taxes.* —*n.* a person who is delinquent. —**de·lin′quent·ly,** *adv.*

de·lir·i·ous (di lir′ē əs) *adj.* **1.** temporarily out of one's mind; raving: *The fever made the patient delirious.* **2.** wildly excited: *I was delirious with joy when I won the award.* —**de·lir′i·ous·ly,** *adv.* —**de·lir′i·ous·ness,** *n.*

de·lir·i·um (di lir′ē əm) *n.* **1.** a temporary disturbance of the mind, occurring during high fevers or intoxication. Delirium is characterized by confusion, restlessness, and hallucinations. **2.** wild excitement or emotion.

de·liv·er (di liv′ər) *v.t.* **1.** to carry or take to a particular place or person: *to deliver mail, to deliver groceries.* **2.** to give forth in words or sound; utter; pronounce: *to deliver a speech.* **3.** to strike: *to deliver a blow.* **4.** to throw; pitch: *The pitcher delivered a curve ball.* **5.** to surrender or hand over: *The spy delivered the secrets to the enemy.* **6.** to help in the birth of: *The doctor delivered the twins.* **7.** to set free; rescue; save: *to deliver slaves from bondage.* —*v.i.* to make deliveries: *Does that supermarket deliver?* —**de·liv′er·er,** *n.*

de·liv·er·ance (di liv′ər əns) *n.* **1.** the act of setting free; release. **2.** a judgment or opinion expressed formally or publicly.

de·liv·er·y (di liv′ə rē) *n., pl.* **de·liv·er·ies.** **1.** the act of carrying or taking something to a particular place or person: *That laundry makes deliveries to its customers.* **2.** something carried or brought: *The eggs were missing from the grocery delivery.* **3.** a manner of speaking or singing: *The singer's delivery was too weak.* **4.** the act or manner of sending forth, discharging, or striking: *The pitcher had an awkward delivery.* **5.** the act of giving birth. **6.** the act of giving up; handing over; surrender. **7.** the act of setting free or saving; release.

dell (del) *n.* a small, usually wooded glen or valley.

Del·phic (del′fik) *adj.* **1.** relating to the ancient Greek city of Delphi, the oracle of Apollo at Delphi, or Apollo himself. **2.** *also,* **delphic.** having more than one meaning; ambiguous.

Delphic oracle, the oracle or the prophetess of Apollo at Delphi, famed for giving advice or prophecies having more than one meaning.

del·phin·i·um (del fin′ē əm) *n., pl.* **del·phin·i·ums.** a plant that

delphinium flowers

at; āpe; fär; câre; end; mē; it; īce; pîerce; hot; ōld;
sông; fôrk; oil; out; up; ūse; rüle; pull; tûrn; chin;
sing; shop; thin; this; hw in white; zh in treasure.
The symbol ə stands for the unstressed vowel sound
heard in about, taken, pencil, lemon, and circus.

D

has dense spikes of flowers, usually blue or purple. Also, **larkspur.**

del·ta (del'tə) **1.** the fourth letter of the Greek alphabet (Δ, δ), corresponding to English *D, d*. **2.** something having the triangular shape of this letter. **3.** an area of land that is formed by deposits of silt, sand, and pebbles at the mouth of a river.

delta wing, a broadly triangular aircraft wing.

de·lude (di lüd') *v.t.,* **de·lud·ed, de·lud·ing.** to mislead the mind or judgment of; deceive: *The dishonest politician deluded the voters by promising impossible reforms.*

del·uge (del'ūj, del'ūzh) *n.* **1.** a great flood. **2.** a heavy rain; downpour: *They were drenched by the deluge before they could reach shelter.* **3.** anything that overwhelms or rushes like a flood: *That resort has a deluge of tourists during the holiday season.* **4. the Deluge.** in the Old Testament, the great flood in the time of Noah. —*v.t.,* **del·uged, del·ug·ing. 1.** to flood with water: *The heavy rain deluged the valley.* **2.** to overwhelm by any great rush: *The store was deluged with complaints.*

de·lu·sion (di lü'zhən) *n.* **1.** a false idea or belief: *the delusion that money can buy happiness.* **2.** the act of deluding or the state of being deluded.

de·lu·sive (di lü'siv) *adj.* tending to mislead the mind or judgment. —**de·lu'sive·ly,** *adv.* —**de·lu'sive·ness,** *n.*

de·luxe (di luks') *adj.* exceptionally fine in quality or elegance: *A deluxe room at the hotel is luxurious but expensive.*

delve (delv) *v.i.,* **delved, delv·ing. 1.** to make a careful investigation or search for information: *The detectives delved into the facts of the crime.* **2.** *Archaic.* to dig.

Dem., Democrat; Democratic.

de·mag·net·ize (dē mag'ni tīz') *v.t.,* **de·mag·net·ized, de·mag·net·iz·ing.** to remove the magnetic charge from.

dem·a·gog·ic (dem'ə goj'ik) *adj.* of, relating to, or characteristic of a demagogue.

dem·a·gogue (dem'ə gog', dem'ə gôg') *also,* **dem·a·gog.** *n.* a public leader or politician who appeals to the emotions and prejudices of people to gain or keep power.

dem·a·gogu·er·y (dem'ə gog'ə rē, dem'ə gô'gə rē) *n.* the actions, practices, or principles of a demagogue.

de·mand (di mand') *v.t.* **1.** to ask for insistently: *The angry customer demanded a refund.* **2.** to ask for with authority; claim as a right: *The judge demanded silence in the courtroom.* **3.** to require as necessary or useful; call for; need: *This job demands careful attention.* —*n.* **1.** the act of demanding: *Your demand for a raise in salary was turned down.* **2.** something demanded: *This job makes many demands on my time.* **3.** the desire for a product together with the ability to buy it: *The demand for the book led the publisher to print more copies.* —**de·mand'er,** *n.*

 ·**in demand.** sought after; wanted: *The singer's new recording was much in demand.*

de·mand·ing (di man'ding) *adj.* needing or insisting on much care, attention, time, or effort: *a demanding person, a demanding task.*

de·mar·cate (di mär 'kāt, dē'mär kāt') *v.t.* **de·mar·cat·ed, de·mar·cat·ing. 1.** to fix or mark the limits or boundaries of: *We put up signs to demarcate our property in the woods behind our house.* **2.** to separate or distinguish.

de·mar·ca·tion (dē'mär kā'shən) *n.* **1.** the marking or fixing of limits or boundaries: *the demarcation of parcels of land.* **2.** separation; distinction: *the demarcation between youth and old age, a line of demarcation between two archaeological levels.*

de·mean¹ (di mēn') *v.t.* to lower the dignity or status of; degrade; debase: *I would not demean myself by asking for charity.* [*De-* + *mean².*]

de·mean² (di mēn') *v.t.* to behave or conduct (oneself): *The children demeaned themselves well at their new*

school. [From the Old French word *demener* with the same meaning.]

de·mean·or (di mē'nər) *n.* the way a person behaves or conducts himself or herself; manner: *I maintained a calm demeanor.*

de·ment·ed (di men'tid) *adj.* having a severe mental illness; insane. —**de·ment'ed·ly,** *adv.*

de·mer·it (dē mer'it) *n.* **1.** a mark against a person for bad work or behavior: *The teacher gave the student a demerit for misbehaving in class.* **2.** something that deserves blame; fault.

de·mesne (di mān', di mēn') *n.* **1.** the manor house and land belonging to a feudal lord. **2.** domain; realm.

De·me·ter (di mē'tər) *n. Greek Mythology.* the goddess of agriculture and the fertility and fruits of the earth. In Roman mythology she was called Ceres.

dem·i·god (dem'ē god') *n.* **1.** an inferior or lesser god. **2.** the child of a god or goddess and a mortal.

dem·i·john (dem'ē jon') *n.* a narrow-necked bottle of glass or earthenware, usually enclosed in wicker and holding from one to ten gallons.

de·mil·i·tar·ize (dē mil'i tə rīz') *v.t.,* **de·mil·i·tar·ized, de·mil·i·tar·iz·ing.** to remove military installations or troops from (an area or zone): *The two warring nations agreed to demilitarize a four-mile zone between their countries.* —**de·mil'i·ta·ri·za'tion,** *n.*

de·mise (di mīz') *n.* **1.** death: *The president's demise saddened the nation.* **2.** end: *the demise of slavery.*

dem·i·tasse (dem'ē tas') *n.* **1.** a small cup of black, usually strong, coffee. **2.** a small cup in which such coffee is commonly served.

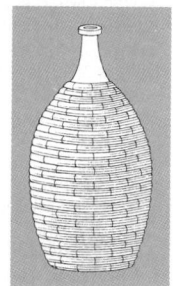
demijohn

de·mo·bi·lize (dē mō'bə līz') *v.t.,* **de·mo·bi·lized, de·mo·bi·liz·ing. 1.** to disband or dismiss from military service: *The government demobilized the troops when the war ended.* **2.** to change from a state of readiness for war; put on a peacetime basis: *The country demobilized its industries after the war.* —**de·mo'bi·li·za'tion,** *n.*

de·moc·ra·cy (di mok'rə sē) *n., pl.* **de·moc·ra·cies. 1.** a government that is run by the people, who rule either directly or through elected representatives. **2.** a nation or state having such a government. **3.** the belief that all people are equal socially and politically. [Originally from the Greek word *dēmokratia* meaning "rule by the people," from the words *dēmos* "people" and *kratos* "power, strength."]

▲ **Democracy** and **republic** do not always mean the same thing. In a **democracy** the people may rule directly, as by town meetings, or they may have indirect control through elected representatives, as in the federal government of the United States. In a **republic** power is always held by elected representatives, rather than by the people themselves.

Word Family

Democracy is one of several English words derived from the Greek word *demos*, meaning "people." **Democracy,** or government by the people, is based on **democratic** principles. Supporters of **democracy** are called **democrats** (with a lower-case "d"). In an **undemocratic** land some people may work to **democratize** the government. A **demagogue** is someone who leads by using tactics of **demagoguery,** appealing to people's prejudices and fears. If a disease is **endemic,** it affects a certain group of people, whereas a disease that infects many people may become an **epidemic.**

dem·o·crat (dem′ə krat′) *n.* **1.** a person who believes in or supports democracy as a principle of government. **2.** a person who believes that all people are equal socially and politically. **3. Democrat.** a member of the Democratic Party of the United States.

dem·o·crat·ic (dem′ə krat′ik) *adj.* **1.** of, relating to, or supporting democracy. **2.** believing all people are equal socially and politically. **3. Democratic.** of, relating to, or characteristic of the Democratic Party of the United States. **—dem′o·crat′i·cal·ly,** *adv.*

Democratic Party, one of the two major political parties in the United States.

de·moc·ra·tize (di mok′rə tīz′) *v.t., v.i.,* **de·moc·ra·tized, de·moc·ra·tiz·ing.** to give to or acquire the characteristics, or more of the characteristics, of democracy.

dem·o·graph·ic (dem′ə graf′ik) *adj.* of or relating to demography.

dem·o·graph·ics (dem′ə graf′iks) *pl. n.* statistics and other information that describe the social characteristics of a given group of people, such as their age, sex, and income: *Many advertisers study demographics to help them locate potential customers.*

de·mog·ra·phy (di mog′rə fē) *n.* the science of describing human populations with the help of statistics, such as average age, income levels, and birth rates. [From the French word *démographie* with the same meaning, from the Greek word *dēmos* meaning ''people'' and the French suffix *-graphie* ''-graphy.'']

de·mol·ish (di mol′ish) *v.t.* **1.** to tear down or apart; destroy the structure of: *The wreckers demolished the old building.* **2.** to destroy or ruin completely: *New evidence demolished the lawyer's case.* **—de·mol′ish·ment,** *n.*

dem·o·li·tion (dem′ə lish′ən) *n.* the act of demolishing or the state of being demolished.

de·mon (dē′mən) *n.* **1.** an evil spirit, devil. **2.** a very wicked or cruel person. **3.** a person who shows great skill or energy in some activity: *a demon on ice skates, a demon for work.*

de·mo·ni·ac (di mō′nē ak′, dē′mə nī′ək) *adj.* **1.** of or like a demon or evil spirit; devilish. **2.** caused by a demon or evil spirit. Also, **de·mo·ni·a·cal** (dē′mə nī′ə kəl). **—n.** a person supposedly possessed by a demon. **—de·mo·ni·a·cal·ly** (dē′mə nī′ə klē), *adv.*

de·mon·stra·ble (di mon′strə bəl) *adj.* able to be proved, shown, or made clear: *a demonstrable theory.* **—de·mon′stra·bil′i·ty,** *n.* **—de·mon′stra·bly,** *adv.*

dem·on·strate (dem′ən strāt′) *v.,* **dem·on·strat·ed, dem·on·strat·ing. —v.t. 1.** to prove or make clear: *The recent election demonstrated the voters' support of the mayor's policies.* **2.** to describe, explain, or show by use of experiments or examples: *The teacher demonstrated the principle of static electricity.* **3.** to make a show of; express openly: *The crowd demonstrated its support of the senator with loud cheers.* **4.** to show the uses or merits of (a product): *The salesclerk demonstrated the camera in the department store.* **—v.i.** to hold or take part in a public meeting or parade to show feelings toward a particular issue or person: *A group of citizens demonstrated against pollution.*

dem·on·stra·tion (dem′ən strā′shən) *n.* **1.** something that proves clearly: *Your rescue of the child from the burning house was a demonstration of true bravery.* **2.** an explaining or showing by the use of experiments or examples: *The science teacher gave a demonstration of the law of gravity.* **3.** an open show or expression of feeling or emotion: *The prisoner reacted to the judge's sentence with a demonstration of anger.* **4.** a public meeting or parade to show feeling toward a particular issue or person: *The workers held a demonstration to demand a raise in wages.* **5.** the act of showing the uses or merits of a product: *a demonstration of a sewing machine.*

de·mon·stra·tive (di mon′strə tiv) *adj.* **1.** showing one's feelings or emotions openly, especially affectionate ones: *The demonstrative parents hugged and kissed their child.* **2.** showing or explaining clearly: *a demonstrative experiment on the properties of magnetism.* **3.** *Grammar.* pointing out a particular person or thing. In the sentence *This book is mine and that one is yours, this* and *that* are demonstrative adjectives. **—n.** a demonstrative adjective or pronoun. In the sentence *I need these,* the pronoun *these* is a demonstrative. **—de·mon′stra·tive·ly,** *adv.* **—de·mon′stra·tive·ness,** *n.*

dem·on·stra·tor (dem′ən strā′tər) *n.* **1.** a person who demonstrates, especially a person who takes part in a demonstration of public feeling. **2.** something used for demonstration, such as a sample product used in demonstrations to customers.

de·mor·al·ize (di môr′ə līz′, di mor′ə līz′) *v.t.,* **de·mor·al·ized, de·mor·al·iz·ing. 1.** to lower or destroy the morale of; deprive of courage, confidence, or hope; dishearten: *A series of defeats demoralized the team.* **2.** to lower the morals of; corrupt. **—de·mor′al·iz·a′tion,** *n.*

de·mote (di mōt′) *v.t.,* **de·mot·ed, de·mot·ing.** to reduce to a lower grade or rank: *to demote a soldier from corporal to private.* **—de·mo′tion** (di mō′shən) *n.*

de·mur (di mûr′) *v.i.,* **de·murred, de·mur·ring.** to make an objection; show disapproval: *The child demurred when told to do extra homework.* **—n.** the act of demurring; an objection raised.

de·mure (di myŭr′) *adj.,* **de·mur·er, de·mur·est. 1.** quiet and modest; shy; reserved: *behavior that is demure and polite.* **2.** pretending to be shy or modest; coy. **—de·mure′ly,** *adv.* **—de·mure′ness,** *n.*

den (den) *n.* **1.** a place where a wild animal lives; lair: *a bear's den.* **2.** a private room, usually small and cozy, for relaxation or study. **3.** a hideout or secret place, especially one in which criminals have their headquarters. **4.** a group of about eight cub scouts.

de·na·ture (dē nā′chər) *v.t.,* **de·na·tured, de·na·tur·ing. 1.** to make (a substance) unfit for drinking or eating without destroying its other useful properties: *to denature alcohol.* **2.** to change the nature of. **—de·na′tur·a′tion,** *n.*

den·drite (den′drīt) *n.* a small branched fiber in a nerve cell that conducts impulses to the cell body.

de·ni·al (di nī′əl) *n.* **1.** the act of saying that something is untrue: *The judge listened to the defendant's denial of the charges.* **2.** the act of refusing something asked for or desired: *Their denial of my request for a contribution was disappointing.* **3.** a refusal to acknowledge a connection with or responsibility for. **4.** a refusal to accept or believe in something: *a scientist's denial of a superstition.*

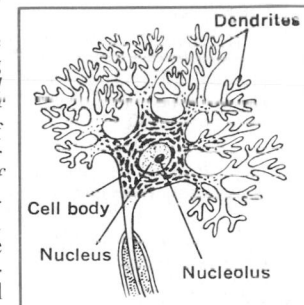

Dendrites
Cell body
Nucleus
Nucleolus

dendrite

den·i·grate (den′i grāt′) *v.t.,* **den·i·grat·ed, den·i·grat·ing.** to blacken the reputation of; slander. **—den′i·gra′tion,** *n.*

at; āpe; fär; câre; end; mē; it; īce; pîerce; hot; ōld; sông, fôrk; oil; out; up; ūse; rüle; pùll; tûrn; chin; sing; shop; thin; <u>th</u>is; hw in white; zh in treasure. The symbol ə stands for the unstressed vowel sound heard in about, taken, pencil, lemon, and circus.

D

259

den·im (den′im) *n.* **1.** a heavy, twilled cotton fabric used for such items as jeans and sportswear. **2. denims.** overalls or trousers made of this fabric. [Short for the French phrase *(serge) de Nîmes* meaning "(serge cloth) from *Nîmes*," a city in southern France where this cloth was first made.]

den·i·zen (den′ə zən) *n.* a person or animal that lives in a particular place; inhabitant; dweller: *Wolves are denizens of the forest.*

de·nom·i·nate (di nom′ə nāt′) *v.t.,* **de·nom·i·nat·ed, de·nom·i·nat·ing.** to give a name to; name; designate.

de·nom·i·nate number (di nom′ə nit) a number that specifies a quantity by limiting a unit of measurement. In the expression *5 pounds,* 5 is a denominate number.

de·nom·i·na·tion (di nom′ə nā′shən) *n.* **1.** a religious group or sect: *a Protestant denomination.* **2.** a unit in a particular system of numbers, measures, or values: *A dime and a nickel are coins of different denominations.* **3.** a name for a group or class of things; designation.

de·nom·i·na·tion·al (di nom′ə nā′shə nəl) *adj.* relating to or controlled by a religious denomination or sect: *to attend a denominational school.* —**de·nom′i·na′tion·al·ly,** *adv.*

de·nom·i·na·tor (di nom′ə nā′tər) *n.* a number below or to the right of the line in a fraction, indicating the number of equal parts into which the whole is divided; divisor. In the fraction ½, 2 is the denominator.

de·no·ta·tion (dē′nō tā′shən) *n.* **1.** the exact and literal meaning of a word or phrase, as distinct from what it suggests. **2.** the act of denoting or the state of being denoted.

de·note (di nōt′) *v.t.,* **de·not·ed, de·not·ing. 1.** to be a sign of; indicate: *A rapidly falling barometer denotes an approaching storm.* **2.** to be a name for; mean: *The word "dentist" denotes a doctor whose work is the care of teeth.* **3.** to be a mark or symbol for: *The sign ° denotes degrees.* ▲ **Denote** and **connote** both refer to the meaning of a word. To **denote** is to convey the literal meaning of a word. To **connote** is to suggest an associated meaning in addition to the literal meaning. The word "lion" *denotes* a large animal of the cat family, but it *connotes* strength and courage.

de·noue·ment (dā′ nü män′) *also,* **dé·noue·ment.** *n.* the final outcome or solution of the plot in a play or story, or of a complex or difficult situation.

de·nounce (di nouns′) *v.t.,* **de·nounced, de·nounc·ing. 1.** to attack or speak against publicly or openly: *The senator denounced the rise in food prices.* **2.** to inform against; accuse: *They denounced the forger to the police.* **3.** to announce formally the end of (a treaty, armistice, or other agreement). —**de·nounce′ment,** *n.* —**de·nounc′er,** *n.*

dense (dens) *adj.,* **dens·er, dens·est. 1.** having parts closely packed together; thick; compact: *a dense forest, a dense crowd.* **2.** *Informal.* stupid or dull. —**dense′ly,** *adv.* —**dense′ness,** *n.*

den·si·ty (den′si tē) *n., pl.* **den·si·ties. 1.** the quality or condition of being closely packed together; thickness; compactness: *The density of the tall grass made walking difficult.* **2.** *Physics.* the ratio of the mass of a substance to its volume: *Iron has a greater density than wood.* **3.** quantity per unit of area, volume, length, or time: *The density of population in that country is very high.* **4.** *Informal.* stupidity.

dent (dent) *n.* **1.** a hollow or depression in a surface made by a blow or pressure: *a dent in an automobile fender.* **2.** headway; progress: *We worked all night, but barely made a dent in the work.* —*v.t.* to make a hollow or depression in. —*v.i.* to become dented: *This metal dents easily.*

den·tal (den′təl) *adj.* **1.** of, for, or relating to the teeth. **2.** of, relating to, or used in dentistry: *dental equipment.*

dental floss, a strong thread used to clean between the teeth.

dental hygienist, a person trained and licensed to clean and examine teeth.

den·ti·frice (den′tə fris) *n.* a paste, powder, or liquid used for cleaning the teeth.

den·tin (den′tin) *also,* **den·tine** (den′tēn, den tēn′). *n.* the hard, bony material forming the major part of a tooth, covered by the enamel.

den·tist (den′tist) *n.* a doctor who specializes in the health, care, and treatment of the teeth, gums, and mouth.

den·tist·ry (den′tis trē) *n.* **1.** the branch of medical science dealing with the health, care, and treatment of the teeth and gums. **2.** the work done by a dentist.

den·ti·tion (den tish′ən) *n.* **1.** the number, shape, and arrangement of teeth: *The dentition of a horse is different from that of a dog.* **2.** the natural development and emergence of teeth; teething.

den·ture (den′chər) *n.* an artificial replacement tooth or set of teeth.

de·nude (di nüd′, di nūd′) *v.t.,* **de·nud·ed, de·nud·ing.** to strip of all covering; make bare: *The heavy bombing denuded the land of all plants.*

de·nun·ci·a·tion (di nun′sē ā′shən) *n.* **1.** a public expression of disapproval; open condemnation. **2.** the act of informing against; accusation.

de·ny (di nī′) *v.t.,* **de·nied, de·ny·ing. 1.** to declare (something) to be untrue: *They denied that they had committed the crime.* **2.** to refuse to believe or accept as being true or valid; reject: *to deny a superstition.* **3.** to refuse to give or grant: *My boss denied my request for a raise.* **4.** to refuse to acknowledge; disavow: *to deny one's family.* —**de·ni′er,** *n.*

·**to deny onself.** to manage without (things that one wants): *I denied myself new clothes in order to save money.*

de·o·dor·ant (dē ō′dər ənt) *n.* something that removes or covers up unpleasant odors, especially a product designed to control body odors. —*adj.* able to remove or cover up unpleasant odors: *a deodorant soap.*

de·o·dor·ize (dē ō′də rīz′) *v.t.,* **de·o·dor·ized, de·o·dor·iz·ing.** to destroy or cover up the unpleasant odor of. —**de·o′dor·i·za′tion,** *n.* —**de·o′dor·iz′er,** *n.*

de·ox·i·dize (dē ok′si dīz′) *v.t.,* **de·ox·i·dized, de·ox·i·diz·ing.** to remove oxygen from, especially by means of a chemical reaction. —**de·ox′i·di·za′tion,** *n.* —**de·ox′i·diz′er,** *n.*

de·ox·y·ri·bo·nu·cle·ic acid (dē ok′sē rī′bō nü klē′ik, dē ok′sē rī′bō nū klē′ik) see **DNA.**

de·part (di pärt′) *v.i.* **1.** to go away; leave: *The plane departs at nine o'clock. We departed in a hurry.* **2.** to differ or change: *They departed from their usual habit of arriving at school early and were an hour late.*

de·part·ed (di pär′tid) *adj.* past; gone: *departed fame.* —*n.* **the departed.** a person or persons who have died.

de·part·ment (di pärt′mənt) *n.* **1.** a separate part or division of an organization or government: *the police department of a city, the sales department of a company, the English department of a school.* **2.** an administrative district of government, especially in France.

de·part·men·tal (dē′pärt men′təl) *adj.* of or relating to a department: *a departmental meeting.*

department store, a large retail store selling a variety of merchandise organized in separate departments.

de·par·ture (di pär′chər) *n.* **1.** the act of departing: *The departure of the plane was on time.* **2.** a change, as from a standard or usual course of action; deviation: *a departure from habit.* **3.** the act of setting out, as on a course of action: *This law marks a new departure in civil rights legislation.* **4.** *Archaic.* death.

de·pend (di pend′) *v.i.* **1.** to place confidence; rely: *You can always depend on me to help.* **2.** to rely for what is needed or wanted: *While he was a student he depended on his parents for support.* **3.** to be influenced or determined: *Whether she takes the job depends on what the salary is.* ▲ usually followed by *on.*

de·pen·da·ble (di pen′də bəl) *adj.* able to be depended on; reliable: *a dependable worker who is always on time.* —**de·pen·da·bil′i·ty**, *n.* —**de·pen′da·bly**, *adv.*

de·pen·dence (di pen′dəns) *n.* **1.** the state of relying on another for what is needed or wanted: *the dependence of a baby on its parents.* **2.** the state of being influenced or determined by something else: *the dependence of crops on rain.* **3.** trust; reliance. **4.** a physical or psychological need for a drug not taken for medicinal purposes, resulting from prolonged use of the drug. Also, **dependency.**

de·pen·den·cy (di pen′dən sē) *n.,* *pl.* **de·pen·den·cies.** **1.** a country or territory that is governed by another country but is not part of the governing country: *Puerto Rico is a dependency of the United States.* **2.** another word for **dependence.**

de·pen·dent (di pen′dənt) *adj.* **1.** relying on another for what is needed or wanted: *I am dependent on you for help with this project.* **2.** influenced or determined by something: *Our plans for the picnic are dependent on the weather.* —*n.* a person who depends on another for support or help. —**de·pen′dent·ly,** *adv.*

dependent clause, a clause that functions as a noun, adjective, or adverb within a sentence and cannot stand alone. In the sentence *After we had played tennis for an hour, we decided to go for a swim,* the clause *After we had played tennis for an hour* is a dependent clause. Also, **subordinate clause.**

de·pict (di pikt′) *v.t.* **1.** to represent by drawing or painting; picture; portray: *The artist depicted the ocean.* **2.** to represent in words; describe: *The poet depicted the sound of the waves.* —**de·pic′tion,** *n.*

de·pil·a·to·ry (di pil′ə tôr′ē) *n.,* *pl.* **de·pil·a·to·ries.** a substance for removing hair. —*adj.* capable of removing hair: *a depilatory cream.*

de·plane (dē plan′) *v.t.,* **de·planed, de·plan·ing.** to get off an airplane after landing.

de·plete (di plēt′) *v.t.,* **de·plet·ed, de·plet·ing.** to reduce in amount; use up: *The campers depleted their food supply after three days. My strength was depleted by the long hike.* —**de·ple′tion,** *n.*

de·plor·a·ble (di plôr′ə bəl) *adj.* **1.** deserving to be deplored. *Your behavior in the classroom was deplorable.* **2.** wretched; miserable: *There were deplorable living conditions in the city's slums.* —**de·plor′a·bly,** *adv.*

de·plore (di plôr′) *v.t.,* **de·plored, de·plor·ing.** **1.** to disapprove of strongly: *The speaker deplored the use of violence to bring about changes in society.* **2.** to be very sorry about; regret deeply; lament: *We deplored the death of our dear friend.*

de·ploy (di ploi′) *v.t.* **1.** to spread out (troops or ships) in a long line of battle. **2.** to spread out according to a plan: *The newspaper deployed reporters all over the country to cover the election.* —**de·ploy′ment,** *n.*

de·pop·u·late (dē pop′yə lāt′) *v.t.,* **de·pop·u·lat·ed, de·pop·u·lat·ing.** to reduce the population of, as by massacre or expulsion: *Heavy bombing depopulated the city.* —**de·pop′u·la′tion,** *n.*

de·port (di pôrt′) *v.t.* **1.** to force to leave a country; expel: *The authorities deported the criminal as an undesirable alien.* **2.** to behave or conduct (oneself) in a specified way: *The candidates deported themselves poorly in their noisy debate.*

de·por·ta·tion (dē′pôr tā′shən) *n.* expulsion from a country.

de·port·ment (di pôrt′mənt) *n.* the way in which a person acts or behaves; conduct; bearing: *the orderly deportment of a soldier.*

de·pose (di pōz′) *v.t.,* **de·posed, de·pos·ing.** **1.** to remove

from a throne or other high office: *The rebels deposed the monarch.* **2.** *Law.* to declare under oath, especially in a written statement.

de·pos·it (di poz′it) *v.t.* **1.** to put (money or valuables) in a bank or other place for safekeeping: *She deposited five dollars in her savings account.* **2.** to set or lay down; place: *He deposited the groceries on the table. The river deposited silt at its mouth.* **3.** to put in; insert: *Deposit a coin in the slot.* —*n.* **1.** something put in a place for safekeeping, especially money in a bank. **2.** something given as part payment or security: *They put a deposit of $150 on a new car.* **3.** something that has settled: *a deposit of dust on the window sill.* **4.** a natural layer, as of a mineral: *a large deposit of iron ore.*

dep·o·si·tion (dep′ə zish′ən) *n.* **1.** removal from a throne or other high office. **2.** a sworn statement given by a witness out of court, intended to be used as testimony in court. **3.** the act or process of laying down: *The delta at the mouth of the river was formed by the deposition of silt.* **4.** something deposited; deposit.

de·pos·i·tor (di poz′i tər) *n.* a person who makes a deposit, especially a person who deposits money in a bank.

de·pos·i·to·ry (di poz′i tôr′ē) *n.,* *pl.* **de·pos·i·to·ries.** a place where something is deposited for safekeeping.

de·pot (*def. 1* dē′pō; *def. 2* dep′ō; *def. 3* dep′ō, dē′pō) *n.* **1.** a railroad station or bus terminal. **2.** a place where military supplies and equipment are stored. **3.** a storage place; storehouse; warehouse.

de·prave (di prāv′) *v.t.,* **de·praved, de·prav·ing.** to make morally bad; corrupt.

de·praved (di prāvd′) *adj.* morally bad; corrupt; perverted.

de·prav·i·ty (di prav′i tē) *n.,* *pl.* **de·prav·i·ties.** **1.** the state of being depraved; corruption. **2.** a depraved act or practice.

dep·re·cate (dep′ri kāt′) *v.t.,* **dep·re·cat·ed, dep·re·cat·ing.** to express disapproval of; disparage; belittle: *The critic deprecated the author's latest novel.* —**dep′re·ca′tion,** *n.*

dep·re·ca·to·ry (dep′ri kə tôr′ē) *adj.* expressing disapproval: *deprecatory remarks.*

de·pre·ci·ate (di prē′shē āt′) *v.,* **de·pre·ci·at·ed, de·pre·ci·at·ing.** —*v.t.* **1.** to lower the price or value of. **2.** to represent as of little value; belittle: *Your petty comments depreciated our efforts to help.* —*v.i.* to fall in price or value: *The value of the dollar sometimes depreciates.* —**de·pre′ci·a′tor,** *n.* —**de·pre′ci·a·to′ry,** *adj.*

de·pre·ci·a·tion (di prē′shē ā′shən) *n.* a decrease in value as a result of wear, age, or use: *the depreciation of a car over the years.*

dep·re·da·tion (dep′ri dā′shən) *n.* the act of plundering or destroying; ravaging.

de·press (di pres′) *v.t.* **1.** to lower in spirits; make gloomy; sadden: *The death of the dog depressed the child.* **2.** to lessen in force, vigor, or activity; weaken: *The medicine depressed the patient's pulse rate.* **3.** to press or push down: *to depress the accelerator in an automobile.*

de·pres·sant (di pres′ənt) *n.* **1.** a drug or other substance that reduces or slows down nervous, muscular, or other body activities. Sedatives are depressants. **2.** anything that depresses.

---

at; āpe; fär; câre; end; mē; it; īce; pîerce; hot; ōld; sông, fôrk; oil; out; up; ūse; rüle; pùll; tûrn; chin; sing; shop; thin; <u>th</u>is; hw in white; zh in treasure. The symbol ə stands for the unstressed vowel sound heard in about, taken, pencil, lemon, and circus.

D

de·pressed (di prest′) *adj.* **1.** low in spirits; sad. **2.** decreased in activity, force, value, or price. **3.** having a weak economy, as with high unemployment and a low standard of living: *a depressed area of a country.* **4.** pressed down: *a depressed key on a typewriter.*

de·pres·sion (di presh′ən) *n.* **1.** a sunken place or surface; hollow: *The car bumped over the depression in the road.* **2.** lowness of spirits; sadness; dejection: *The win erased the team's depression.* **3.** an emotional state, characterized by persistent lowness of spirits and feelings of dejection and despair, that often interferes with a person's ability to function normally. **4.** a period marked by a severe reduction in business activity, a rise in unemployment, and falling wages and prices. **5.** the act of pressing down.

dep·ri·va·tion (dep′rə vā′shən) *n.* the act of depriving or the state of being deprived.

de·prive (di prīv′) *v.t.*, **de·prived, de·priv·ing. 1.** to take way from (used with *of*): *The proposed highway will deprive the children of their playground.* **2.** to keep from having or enjoying: *to deprive a citizen of the right to vote.*

dept., department.

depth (depth) *n.* **1.** the distance downward, inward, or from front to back: *The depth of the pool was five feet. The depth of the building lot was 250 feet.* **2.** the quality of being deep; deepness: *It took great depth of understanding to solve that problem.* **3.** deepness of feeling or thought: *That movie is amusing, but it has no depth.* **4.** *also,* **depths. a.** the deepest, lowest, or furthest part: *The treasure lay buried in the depths of the ocean.* **b.** the most intense or extreme state or stage: *the depths of sorrow.*

depth charge, an explosive charge designed to be dropped in the water and go off at a certain depth, used especially against submarines. Also, **depth bomb.**

dep·u·ta·tion (dep′yə tā′shən) *n.* **1.** a person or persons authorized to represent another or others; delegation: *A deputation from the striking miners demanded higher wages.* **2.** the act of appointing or serving as a substitute or representative.

de·pute (di pūt′) *v.t.*, **de·put·ed, de·put·ing. 1.** to appoint as one's substitute, delegate, or agent. **2.** to transfer, as work or authority, to another.

dep·u·tize (dep′yə tīz′) *v.t.*, **dep·u·tized, dep·u·tiz·ing.** to appoint as deputy.

dep·u·ty (dep′yə tē) *n., pl.* **dep·u·ties.** a person appointed or authorized to act for or take the place of another or others: *The sheriff appointed deputies to help in the capture of the criminal.*

de·rail (dē rāl′) *v.t.* to cause to run off the rails: *The damaged tracks derailed the train.* —*v.i.* to run off the rails. —**de·rail′ment,** *n.*

derail
a **derailed** train

de·rail·leur (di rā′lər) *n.* a device on a bicycle that shifts the drive chain from one sprocket to another to change gears. [From the French word *dérailleur*, from the word *dérailler* meaning "to throw off track."]

de·range (di rānj′) *v.t.*, **de·ranged, de·rang·ing. 1.** to disturb the order or arrangement of. **2.** to make insane.

de·range·ment (di rānj′mənt) *n.* **1.** mental illness; insanity. **2.** disturbance of order or arrangement; disorder.

der·by (dûr′bē; *esp. for def. 2a,* där′bē) *n., pl.* **der·bies. 1.** a hard, round hat with a narrow rolled brim. **2. Derby. a.** a race for three-year-old horses, held annually near London, England. **b.** any similar horse race: *the Kentucky Derby.* **3.** any large race or contest.

de·reg·u·late (dē reg′yə lāt′) *v.t.*, **de·reg·u·lat·ed, de·reg·u·lat·ing.** to free from government regulations or controls: *to deregulate the banking industry.*

der·e·lict (der′ə likt′) *n.* **1.** a homeless, wandering person; vagrant; tramp. **2.** property abandoned by the owner or guardian, especially a ship abandoned at sea. —*adj.* **1.** neglectful of one's duty; negligent: *The sentry was derelict in failing to notice the approach of the enemy.* **2.** abandoned by the owner: *a derelict ship.*

der·e·lic·tion (der′ə lik′shən) *n.* **1.** neglect of one's duty: *The guard's dereliction allowed the prisoners to escape.* **2.** the act of abandoning or the state of being abandoned; desertion.

de·ride (di rīd′) *v.t.*, **de·rid·ed, de·rid·ing.** to treat with contempt or scorn; laugh at; ridicule: *Some people deride traditional customs as being old-fashioned.*

de·ri·sion (di rizh′ən) *n.* scornful contempt; mockery; ridicule.

de·ri·sive (di rī′siv) *adj.* showing or characterized by derision; mocking; ridiculing: *derisive laughter.* —**de·ri′sive·ly,** *adv.* —**de·ri′sive·ness,** *n.*

der·i·va·tion (der′ə vā′shən) *n.* **1.** the act of deriving or the state of being derived. **2.** a source or origin: *This legend is of Irish derivation.* **3.** something derived; derivative: *This custom is a derivation from an earlier English one.* **4.** the process of tracing the origin and development of a word. **5.** a statement of the history of a word; etymology. **6.** the formation of a new word from an existing word, root, or stem, especially by the addition of a prefix or suffix, such as *kindness* from *kind.*

Language Note

In language, **derivation** usually refers to the formation of a word by the addition of a prefix or a suffix to an existing word. Because of derivation, there is almost no limit to the number of words that can exist in our language. Not all the derivations that are possible are used in our language or recorded in a dictionary, but these derivations could exist and would be easily understood by someone reading or hearing them. If you take *friend* as a root word, you can make the common words *friendly, friendliness, friendless, friendship, befriend, unfriendly,* and *unfriendliness* and the uncommon or nonexistent words *nonfriend, antifriend, semifriend,* and *friendhood.*

de·riv·a·tive (di riv′ə tiv) *adj.* not original; derived: *a derivative theory.* —*n.* **1.** something derived. **2.** a word formed from another by derivation.

de·rive (di rīv′) *v.*, **de·rived, de·riv·ing.** —*v.t.* **1.** to obtain from a source or origin: *to derive pleasure from reading.* **2.** to trace the origin of (something) from or to its source: *to derive a word.* —*v.i.* to come from a source; originate: *The word "democracy" derives from Greek.*

der·ma (dûr′mə) *n.* another word for **dermis.**

derm·a·bra·sion (dûr′mə brā′zhən) *n.* surgical removal or reduction of acne scars or other blemishes by gentle abrasion of the skin.

der·mal (dûr′məl) *adj.* of or relating to the skin.

der·ma·ti·tis (dûr′mə tī′tis) *n.* inflammation of the skin.

der·ma·tol·o·gist (dûr′mə tol′ə jist) *n.* a doctor who specializes in dermatology.

der·ma·tol·o·gy (dûr′mə tol′ə jē) *n.* the branch of medical science dealing with the skin and its diseases.

der·mis (dûr′mis) *n.* the layer of skin beneath the epidermis. Also, **derma**.

der·o·gate (der′ə gāt′) *v.t.,* **der·o·gat·ed, der·o·gat·ing.** to lessen the importance or merit of; belittle: *The writer derogated the works of other authors.* —**der′o·ga′tion,** *n.*

der·rog·a·to·ry (di rog′ə tôr′ē) *adj.* tending to lessen in importance or estimation; disparaging; belittling: *Derogatory comments usually make people angry.*

der·rick (der′ik) *n.* **1.** a mechanism for lifting and moving heavy objects, consisting of a vertical support to which a slanted boom with hoisting tackle is attached. **2.** the framework over an oil well or other drill hole that supports the drilling machinery. [*Derrick* originally meant "a gallows," from a famous seventeenth-century English hangman named *Derrick*.]

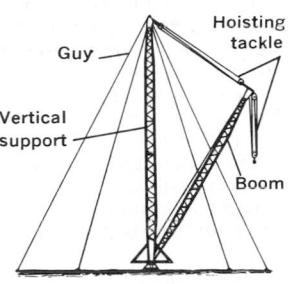

derrick *(def. 1)*

der·ring–do (der′ing dü′) *n.* courageous behavior or deeds; daring: *The pirate tale was full of derring-do.*

der·rin·ger (der′in jər) *n.* an early type of pistol, small enough to be easily concealed. [From the American gunsmith Henry *Deringer* (d. 1869), who invented this pistol.]

der·vish (dûr′vish) *n., pl.* **der·vish·es.** a member of any of various Muslim religious orders that practice chastity and poverty. Certain dervishes are known for using howling and whirling in their worship.

de·sal·i·nate (dē sal′ə nāt′) *v.t.,* **de·sal·i·nat·ed, de·sal·i·nat·ing.** to remove salt from: *to desalinate sea water.*

des·cant (*n.,* des′kant; *v.,* des kant′) *n. Music.* a melody that is sung or played above another melody, usually by several soprano voices or instruments. —*v.i.* to speak at length.

de·scend (di send′) *v.i.* **1.** to move or pass from a higher place to a lower one; come or go downward: *They rode up the hill on horseback, but descended on foot.* **2.** to slope or extend downward: *The hikers walked along a mountain path that descended to a lake.* **3.** to be handed down by inheritance: *The property descended from the parents to their children.* **4.** to come down from an earlier source or ancestor: *Our family descends from the first French colonists.* **5.** to attack suddenly and violently: *The soldiers descended on the helpless village.* **6.** to lower oneself morally or intellectually; stoop: *They were so hungry that they descended to stealing in order to get food.* —*v.t.* to come or go downward on or along: *to descend a mountain trail.*

de·scen·dant (di sen′dənt) *n.* a person who is descended from a particular ancestor or group of ancestors: *I am a descendant of early Spanish settlers.* —*adj.* coming or going downward.

de·scent (di sent′) *n.* **1.** movement from a higher place to a lower one: *the descent of an elevator.* **2.** downward slope or inclination: *a hill with a steep descent.* **3.** ancestry or birth: *That family is of Russian descent.* **4.** a sudden attack.

de·scribe (di skrīb′) *v.t.,* **de·scribed, de·scrib·ing.** **1.** to give a picture in words; tell or write about: *This essay describes our trip to Michigan. Describe the person you saw at the window.* **2.** To designate in a particular way; label: *to describe someone as an expert.* **3.** to draw or trace the outline of: *to describe a circle with a compass.* —**de·scrib′a·ble,** *adj.*

de·scrip·tion (di skrip′shən) *n.* **1.** the act of giving a picture of in words: *The bank teller's description of the robber was very detailed.* **2.** a statement or account that describes. **3.** kind; sort; variety: *There were cats of every description at the show.* **4.** the act of tracing in outline.

de·scrip·tive (di skrip′tiv) *adj.* giving a picture in words: *The tourists were given descriptive pamphlets about places to visit in England.* —**de·scrip′tive·ly,** *adv.* —**de·scrip′tive·ness,** *n.*

de·scry (di skrī′) *v.t.,* **de·scried, de·scry·ing.** to catch sight of; make out from afar: *The sailor descried land in the distance.*

des·e·crate (des′i krāt′) *v.t.,* **des·e·crat·ed, des·e·crat·ing.** to destroy the sacredness of; treat with irreverence; profane: *to desecrate a tomb.* —**des′e·crat′er,** *n.* —**des′e·cra′tion,** *n.*

de·seg·re·gate (dē seg′ri gāt′) *v.t.,* **de·seg·re·gat·ed, de·seg·re·gat·ing.** to eliminate racial segregation in: *to desegregate a school system.* —**de·seg′re·ga′tion,** *n.*

des·ert[1] (dez′ərt) *n.* **1.** a sandy or rocky region with very little rainfall, having little or no vegetation. **2.** any area of land with little or no plant or animal life. —*adj.* **1.** relating to or living in a desert: *desert cactuses.* **2.** not lived in or on; uninhabited; desolate: *a desert island.* [From the Old French word *desert* meaning "a desert," going back to the Latin word *desertus,* past participle of *deserere* meaning "to desert, abandon."]

de·sert[2] (di zûrt′) *v.t.* to go away from (someone or something), especially one that should not be left; abandon; forsake: *The soldier deserted the army. Please don't desert us in our time of need.* —*v.i.* to go away from one's duty, post, or cause: *The sentry deserted to the enemy.* [From the French word *déserter* meaning "to abandon," going back to the Latin word *desertus,* past participle of *deserere* meaning "to abandon."] —**de·sert′er,** *n.*

de·sert[3] (di zûrt′) *n. also,* **de·serts.** a deserved reward or punishment: *to get one's just deserts.* [From the Old French word *deserte,* past participle of *deservir* meaning "to deserve," from the Latin word *deservire* "to serve well," from the words *de-* "away, from" + *servire* "to serve."]

de·ser·tion (di zûr′shən) *n.* the act of deserting or the state of being deserted: *desertion from the army.*

de·serve (di zûrv′) *v.t.,* **de·served, de·serv·ing.** to have a claim to; be worthy of; merit: *Rude behavior deserves punishment. You deserve praise for your good grades.*

de·serv·ed·ly (di zûr′vid lē) *adv.* according to merit; justly; rightfully: *They were deservedly praised for their achievements.*

de·serv·ing (di zûr′ving) *adj.* **1.** worthy; meriting: *deserving of one's attention.* **2.** worthy of or qualified to receive help, especially financial help: *The scholarship was given to a deserving student.*

---

at; āpe; fär; câre; end; mē; it; īce; pîerce; hot; ōld; sông, fôrk; oil; out; up; ūse; rüle; pull; tûrn; chin; sing; shop; thin; **this**; hw in white; zh in treasure. The symbol ə stands for the unstressed vowel sound heard in about, taken, pencil, lemon, and circus.

des·ic·cate (des′i kāt′) *v.t.*, **des·ic·cat·ed, des·ic·cat·ing.** to dry up completely: *The brook was desiccated by the long drought.*

des·ic·cat·or (des′i kā′tər) *n.* a device for drying foods.

de·sign (di zīn′) *n.* **1.** a plan, sketch, or outline made to serve as a guide or pattern: *an architect's design for a house.* **2.** an arrangement or combination of parts, details, or colors; pattern: *a blue and red design in a carpet, a floral design.* **3.** the art of making designs: *a school of design.* **4.** a plan, scheme, or project to be carried out: *My design for success is hard work.* **5.** *also,* **designs.** a secret or evil plot or scheme: *The greedy guard had designs on the jewels.* —*v.t.* **1.** to make a first plan, sketch, or outline of; make a pattern for: *to design a spacecraft, to design an automobile.* **2.** to plan and make with artistic skill; arrange the parts, details, or colors of: *to design a dress.* **3.** to form in the mind; plan; conceive: *to design a plot for a novel.* **4.** to have as an aim or purpose; intend: *a book designed for younger readers, clothes designed for casual wear.*

des·ig·nate (dez′ig nāt′) *v.t.*, **des·ig·nat·ed, des·ig·nat·ing.** **1.** to point out or indicate by a distinctive mark, sign, or name; specify; signify: *The boundaries of the state are designated on the map.* **2.** to call by a particular name or title: *The head of the government of the United States is designated "President."* **3.** to select for a particular purpose, duty, or office; appoint: *Who was designated chairman of the school board?*

designated hitter *Baseball.* a player who is in the lineup but without a fielding position, and who bats in place of the pitcher.

des·ig·na·tion (dez′ig nā′shən) *n.* **1.** the act of pointing out or indicating something: *the designation of a place to meet.* **2.** a distinguishing name, title, or mark: *the designation "Your Majesty."* **3.** selection for a particular purpose, duty, or office; appointment: *The president of the company is responsible for the designation of department heads.*

de·sign·ed·ly (di zī′nid lē) *adv.* on purpose.

de·sign·er (di zī′nər) *n.* a person who designs, especially a person who devises patterns or styles for manufacture or construction: *a dress designer, an automobile designer.*

de·sign·ing (di zī′ning) *adj.* **1.** having low motives; scheming: *a crafty, designing person.* **2.** showing planning or forethought. —*n.* the practice or art of making designs or patterns.

de·sir·a·ble (di zīr′ə bəl) *adj.* worth having or wishing for; sought after: *That busy corner is a desirable location for a drugstore.* —**de·sir′a·bil′i·ty,** *n.* —**de·sir′a·bly,** *adv.*

de·sire (di zīr′) *v.t.*, **de·sired, de·sir·ing.** **1.** to have a strong wish for; long for; crave: *to desire success.* **2.** to express a wish for; request: *We desire information about vacationing in the mountains.* —*n.* **1.** a longing; wish: *a desire for wealth.* **2.** an expressed wish; request. **3.** something desired: *My main desire is the successful completion of the course.*

de·sir·ous (di zīr′əs) *adj.* having desire; desiring: *The young novelist was desirous of fame.*

de·sist (di zist′, di sist′) *v.i.* to cease some action; stop: *The two armies desisted from fighting and signed a truce.*

desk (desk) *n.* **1.** a piece of furniture having a broad, flat surface and usually drawers or compartments, used especially for reading or writing. **2.** a table or counter at which certain duties or services are performed, such as the place in a hotel where guests register. **3.** a division or department of an organization or office: *the city desk of a newspaper.*

desk·top (desk′top′) *n.* the top or working surface of a desk. —*adj.* designating equipment that can fit on a desktop: *a desktop computer.*

des·o·late (*adj.*, des′ə lit; *v.*, des′ə lāt′) *adj.* **1.** lacking inhabitants; deserted: *a desolate ghost town, a desolate*

a **desolate** landscape

beach. **2.** left alone; without companionship; lonely: *We felt desolate after our neighbors moved away.* **3.** laid waste; devastated: *The forest was left desolate by the fire.* **4.** miserable; cheerless; dreary: *Living conditions for the early pioneers were desolate.* —*v.t.*, **des·o·lat·ed, des·o·lat·ing.** **1.** to lay waste; devastate: *The tornado desolated the area.* **2.** to make miserable, wretched, or forlorn: *The news of your illness has desolated us.*

des·o·la·tion (des′ə lā′shən) *n.* **1.** the act of making desolate; devastation. **2.** loneliness; sadness: *Their desolation grew as days passed and their lost dog was not found.* **3.** a ruined or deserted condition: *We found the old house in complete desolation.* **4.** a desolate place or region.

de·spair (di spâr′) *n.* **1.** a complete loss of hope: *I felt the despair of being lost and alone.* **2.** a person or thing that causes loss of hope: *The muscle strain was the despair of the runner.* —*v.i.* to lose hope; be without hope: *After three days, we despaired of ever finding the lost puppy.* —**de·spair′ing,** *adj.* —**de·spair′ing·ly,** *adv.*

des·patch (di spach′) another spelling of **dispatch.**

des·patch·er (di spach′ər) another spelling of **dispatcher.**

des·per·a·do (des′pə rä′dō) *n., pl.* **des·per·a·does** or **des·per·a·dos.** a bold, desperate, or reckless outlaw.

des·per·ate (des′pər it) *adj.* **1.** reckless because of urgency or loss of hope; ready or willing to take any risk; rash: *We made a desperate dash to get out of the path of the storm.* **2.** done without regard to what happens afterward; irresponsible: *a desperate act.* **3.** having an urgent desire: *desperate for attention.* **4.** having little or no hope of improvement or recovery; extremely bad; hopeless: *a desperate illness.* **5.** deep; extreme: *desperate concern.* —**des′per·ate·ly,** *adv.* —**des′per·ate·ness,** *n.*

des·per·a·tion (des′pə rä′shən) *n.* **1.** recklessness arising from loss of hope: *A rock crumbled and, in desperation, the mountaineer grasped a tree root from the ledge above.* **2.** the act of despairing; despair.

des·pi·ca·ble (des′pi kə bəl, di spik′ə bəl) *adj.* deserving scorn; hateful; contemptible: *Cruelty to animals is despicable.* —**des′pi·ca·ble·ness,** *n.* —**des′pi·ca·bly,** *adv.*

de·spise (di spīz′) *v.t.*, **de·spised, de·spis·ing.** to look down on as hateful; scorn: *I always tell the truth and despise dishonesty in any form.*

de·spite (di spīt′) *prep.* in spite of; notwithstanding: *We had a picnic despite the rain.*

de·spoil (di spoil′) *v.t.* to take away all the possessions of by force; rob; pillage; plunder: *The soldiers despoiled the enemy town.* —**de·spoil′er,** *n.* —**de·spo·li·a·tion** (di spō′lē ā′shən) *n.*

de·spond (di spond′) *v.i.* to lose heart or hope; be depressed: *Although you failed the test, do not despond.* —*n.* despondency: *in a state of despond.*

de·spon·den·cy (di spon′dən sē) *n.* loss of heart or hope; depression; dejection. Also, **de·spon·dence** (di spon′dəns).

de·spon·dent (di spon′dənt) *adj.* having lost heart or hope; depressed; dejected: *I was despondent when my friend became ill.* —**de·spon′dent·ly,** *adv.*

des·pot (des′pət) *n.* **1.** a ruler who governs with unlimited authority; absolute ruler; autocrat. **2.** any person who rules with unlimited authority; tyrant; oppressor.

des·pot·ic (des pot′ik) *adj.* of or like a despot or despotism; tyrannical. —**des·pot′i·cal·ly,** *adv.*

des·pot·ism (des′pə tiz′əm) *n.* **1.** the rule of a despot. **2.** a government or state ruled by a despot.

des·sert (di zûrt′) *n.* a course served at the end of a meal, usually a sweet food, such as cake, pie, fruit, or ice cream.

des·ti·na·tion (des′tə nā′shən) *n.* a place to which a person is going or a thing is sent: *The airplane's destination is Paris.*

des·tine (des′tin) *v.t.,* **des·tined, des·tin·ing. 1.** to set apart for a particular purpose or use; intend: *That land is destined for the new hospital.* **2.** to fix beforehand; predetermine: *The young doctor seemed destined for greatness in medicine.*

des·ti·ny (des′tə nē) *n., pl.* **des·ti·nies. 1.** what happens to a person or thing; lot; fortune: *It was their destiny to become great writers.* **2.** what is fated to happen; course of events determined beforehand: *It seemed to be our destiny to lose every game.*

des·ti·tute (des′ti tüt′, des′tə tūt′) *adj.* **1.** lacking the things necessary for life; in great need: *The villagers were left destitute by the flood.* **2.** entirely lacking; wanting: *The barren plain was destitute of trees.*

des·ti·tu·tion (des′ti tü′shən, des′ti tū′shən) *n.* **1.** extreme poverty; great need. **2.** a deprivation; absence; lack.

de·stroy (di stroi′) *v.t.* **1.** to break into pieces; ruin completely; wreck: *The earthquake destroyed the city. Locusts destroyed the crops.* **2.** to put an end to; do away with: *My failure at the basketball tryouts destroyed my hopes of joining the team.* **3.** to kill: *The horse had to be destroyed because its broken leg could not be healed.*

de·stroy·er (di stroi′ər) *n.* **1.** a person or thing that destroys. **2.** a small, fast warship, armed with guns, depth charges, torpedoes, and sometimes guided missiles.

de·struct (di strukt′) *n.* the intentional destruction of a rocket or other missile that fails to function properly after it has been launched. —*adj.* designed to destroy such a rocket or missile: *a destruct mechanism.* —*v.t.* to be destroyed automatically. —*v.t.* to destroy.

de·struc·ti·ble (di struk′tə bəl) *adj.* able to be destroyed. —**de·struc′ti·bil′i·ty,** *n.*

de·struc·tion (di struk′shən) *n.* **1.** the act of destroying: *The police charged them with the destruction of public property.* **2.** the condition or state of being destroyed; ruin: *The total destruction of the city was a result of the earthquake.* **3.** a cause or means of destroying.

de·struc·tive (di struk′tiv) *adj.* **1.** causing destruction: *Termites are destructive to wooden buildings.* **2.** tending to tear down or discredit: *destructive criticism.* —**de·struc′tive·ly,** *adv.* —**de·struc′tive·ness,** *n.*

des·ul·to·ry (des′əl tôr′ē) *adj.* shifting or jumping from one thing to another; without plan or method; irregular; disconnected: *They had a desultory conversation about many things.* —**des′ul·to·ri·ly,** *adv.* —**des′ul·to·ri·ness,** *n.*

de·tach (di tach′) *v.t.* **1.** to unfasten and separate; disconnect: *The engineer detached three cars from the train. The salesclerk detached the price tag from the gift.* **2.** to send away on a special mission: *The commanding officer detached a patrol to search the area for enemy soldiers.*

de·tach·a·ble (di tach′ə bəl) *adj.* able to be detached: *a shirt with a detachable collar.* —**de·tach′a·bil′i·ty,** *n.* —**de·tach′a·bly,** *adv.*

de·tached (di tacht′) *adj.* **1.** not connected; unattached: *The detached garage was twenty feet behind the house.* **2.** not interested; indifferent; aloof; unconcerned: *A detached attitude toward homework won't help to improve your grades.* **3.** lacking prejudice; impartial: *The reporter was a detached observer at the trial.*

de·tach·ment (di tach′mənt) *n.* **1.** the act of detaching or the state of being detached; separation. **2.** a group of soldiers or ships assigned to special duty: *A detachment of ten soldiers remained behind to guard the prisoners.* **3.** a standing apart; indifference; aloofness. **4.** the lack of prejudice or bias; impartiality: *The judge had to consider the case with detachment.*

de·tail (di tāl′, dē′tāl) *n.* **1.** a small or secondary part of a whole; item; particular: *Modern scholars know few details of the life of that author.* **2.** treatment of matters item by item; attention to particulars: *The detail in the portrait was painted with great care.* **3.** a small group assigned to some special duty: *A detail of police officers patrolled the troubled area.* —*v.t.* **1.** to tell or describe item by item: *I detailed my camping experiences to the class.* **2.** to assign to or send on special duty: *Troops were detailed to guard the frontier.*

·in detail. part by part; minutely: *The newspaper described the day's events in detail.*

de·tailed (di tāld′, dē′tāld) *adj.* **1.** having many details: *The witness gave a detailed description of the accident.* **2.** showing careful attention to detail: *The detective made a detailed examination of the room.*

de·tain (di tān′) *v.t.* **1.** to keep from going; hold back; delay: *A flat tire detained us during our trip.* **2.** to keep in custody; confine: *The police detained the robbery suspect.* —**de·tain′ment,** *n.*

de·tect (di tekt′) *v.t.* to find out; discover: *to detect smoke, to detect a secret plot.* —**de·tect′a·ble;** also, **de·tect′i·ble,** *adj.*

de·tec·tion (di tek′shən) *n.* the act of finding out or the state of being found out; discovery.

de·tec·tive (di tek′tiv) *n.* a police officer or other person who makes investigations to get evidence and information, especially in order to solve crimes. —*adj.* **1.** relating to detectives and their work: *a detective story.* **2.** used for the purpose of detection: *The detective methods helped to solve the crime.*

de·tec·tor (di tek′tər) *n.* **1.** any device that indicates the presence of smoke, radioactivity, an electric current, or the like. **2.** a device, as in a radio receiver, that helps convert radio waves into sound waves. **3.** a person or thing that detects.

dé·tente (dā tänt′) also, **de·tente.** *n.* a lessening of political tension between unfriendly nations. [From the French word *détente* meaning "a loosening, easing," from the word *détendre* "to relax, slacken," going back to the Latin words *dis-* "apart" and *tendere* "to stretch."]

de·ten·tion (di ten′shən) *n.* **1.** the act of detaining or holding back. **2.** the state of being detained; delay. **3.** a keeping in custody; confinement: *The suspect is in detention in the city jail.*

de·ter (di tûr′) *v.t.,* **de·terred, de·ter·ring.** to discourage from acting or going ahead, especially by arousing fear or doubt: *The huge waves deterred us from going swimming.* —**de·ter′ment,** *n.*

at; āpe; fär; câre; end; mē; it; īce; pîerce; hot; ōld; sông, fôrk; oil; out; up; ūse; rüle; pull; tûrn; chin; sing; shop; thin; this; hw in white; zh in treasure. The symbol ə stands for the unstressed vowel sound heard in about, taken, pencil, lemon, and circus.

265

de·ter·gent (di tûr′jənt) *n.* a synthetic cleaning agent that resembles soap in its cleansing action but not in its manufacture or chemical composition. —**de·ter′gent,** *adj.*

de·te·ri·o·rate (di tîr′ē ə rāt′) *v.,* **de·te·ri·o·rat·ed, de·te·ri·o·rat·ing.** —*v.i.* to lessen in character, quality, condition, or value; become worse: *The car deteriorated with age.* —*v.t.* to make worse: *The damp climate deteriorated the shingles of the house.* —**de·te′ri·o·ra′tion,** *n.*

de·ter·mi·na·ble (di tûr′mə nə bəl) *adj.* able to be determined.

de·ter·mi·nant (di tûr′mə nənt) *n.* something that determines; a determining factor: *The low cost of the house was the determinant that made us decide to buy it.* —*adj.* determining.

de·ter·mi·nate (di tûr′mə nit) *adj.* having defined limits; fixed; definite: *a determinate quantity in mathematics.* —**de·ter′mi·nate·ly,** *adv.* —**de·ter′mi·nate·ness,** *n.*

de·ter·mi·na·tion (di tûr′mə nā′shən) *n.* **1.** a fixed and firm purpose: *Our determination to succeed was not affected by the obstacles we met.* **2.** the act of reaching a decision; deciding or settling: *The judge reached a determination in the case.* **3.** the act of finding out something by observation, calculation, or investigation: *the determination of the amount of uranium in an ore.*

de·ter·mine (di tûr′min) *v.t.,* **de·ter·mined, de·ter·min·ing.** **1.** to decide or settle definitely or beforehand: *The members of the committee determined the date for the next meeting.* **2.** to find out by observation, calculation, or investigation: *The botanist determined the species of the plant.* **3.** to decide firmly; resolve: *I determined that I would be a success as an author.* **4.** to be the cause or deciding factor of: *The number of votes each candidate receives will determine the result of the election.*

de·ter·mined (di tûr′mind) *adj.* having or showing determination or fixed purpose; resolute: *The basketball team made a determined effort to win.* —**de·ter′mined·ly,** *adv.* —**de·ter′mined·ness,** *n.*

de·ter·min·er (di tûr′mə nər) *n.* **1.** a person or thing that determines. **2.** *Grammar.* a word belonging to a class of noun modifiers that includes articles, demonstratives, possessive adjectives, and other words. Determiners always precede the noun they modify, occupying either the first position in a noun phrase or the second position after another determiner. *Our* in the phrase *our house* and *the* in the phrase *the blue car* are determiners.

de·ter·rence (di tûr′əns) *n.* the act of deterring.

de·ter·rent (di tûr′ənt) *adj.* discouraging; deterring; restraining: *This insect repellent has a deterrent effect on mosquitoes.* —*n.* a person or thing that deters: *The cold, barren landscape was a deterrent to possible settlers.*

de·test (di test′) *v.t.* to dislike very much; hate; loathe: *I detest any sort of cruelty to animals.*

de·test·a·ble (di tes′tə bəl) *adj.* deserving to be detested; hateful; abominable: *Hijacking is a detestable crime.* —**de·test′a·ble·ness,** *n.* —**de·test′a·bly,** *adv.*

de·tes·ta·tion (dē′tes tā′shən) *n.* **1.** a very great hatred or dislike. **2.** a person or thing that is detested.

de·throne (dē thrōn′) *v.t.,* **de·throned, de·thron·ing.** **1.** to remove from a throne; depose: *The police uncovered a plot to dethrone the king and queen.* **2.** to remove from any high position: *The young boxer dethroned the champion by winning the bout.* —**de·throne′ment,** *n.*

det·o·nate (det′ə nāt′) *v.,* **det·o·nat·ed, det·o·nat·ing.** —*v.t.* to cause to explode suddenly and with a loud noise: *to detonate dynamite.* —*v.i.* to explode suddenly and with a loud noise: *The dynamite detonated.* —**det′o·na′tion,** *n.*

det·o·na·tor (det′ə nā′tər) *n.* a device or small explosive used to detonate a large quantity of explosive material.

de·tour (dē′tūr) *n.* **1.** a road used temporarily while another road cannot be traveled. **2.** a roundabout or indirect way. —*v.i.* to make a detour: *The driver detoured around the construction on the highway.* —*v.t.* to cause to make a detour: *The police detoured the traffic because of the accident ahead.*

de·tox·i·fi·ca·tion (dē tok′sə fi kā′shən) *n.* **1.** medical treatment and counseling to help a person overcome addiction to drugs or alcohol. **2.** any of the processes by which the body changes toxins into less toxic substances.

de·tract (di trakt′) *v.i.* to lessen in value, quality, importance, or reputation: *The shabby rug detracted from the appearance of the otherwise nicely decorated room.* —**de·trac′tion,** *n.* —**de·trac′tor,** *n.*

det·ri·ment (det′rə mənt) *n.* **1.** damage, injury, or harm: *How do you pursue all your hobbies without detriment to your studies?* **2.** something that causes damage, injury, or harm: *Lack of political experience is a detriment to your candidacy for mayor.*

det·ri·men·tal (det′rə men′təl) *adj.* causing damage; injurious; harmful: *Poor eating habits can be detrimental to health.* **det′ri·men′tal·ly,** *adv.*

de·tri·tus (di trī′təs) *n.* **1.** fragments of rock, as gravel or sand, torn away from a larger mass by such forces as erosion or glacial ice. **2.** disintegrated material; debris.

deuce¹ (düs, dūs) *n.* **1.** a playing card having two symbols of the suit it represents. **2.** the face of a die having two spots. **3.** a throw of the dice that totals two. **4.** *Tennis.* a tie score of forty points or more each in a game. [From the Old French word *deus* meaning "two," going back to the Latin word *duo* "two."]

deuce² (düs, dūs) *interj. Informal.* bad luck; the devil. ▲ used as a mild oath or exclamation: *What the deuce was that?* [Probably from the Low German word *duus* meaning "deuce¹, lowest throw in dice," going back to the Latin word *duo* "two."]

Deut., Deuteronomy.

deu·te·ri·um (dü tîr′ē əm, dū tîr′ē əm) *n.* an isotope of hydrogen having one neutron and one proton in the nucleus and about twice the atomic weight of ordinary hydrogen. Symbol: D Also, **heavy hydrogen.**

Deu·ter·on·o·my (dü′tə ron′ə mē, dū′tə ron′ə mē) *n.* the fifth book of the Old Testament.

deutsche mark (doich) the basic unit of currency in West Germany.

de·val·u·ate (dē val′ū āt′) *v.t.,* **de·val·u·at·ed, de·val·u·at·ing.** **1.** to lower the official value of (a currency): *to devaluate the dollar.* **2.** to lessen the value of. —**de·val′u·a′tion,** *n.*

de·val·ue (dē val′ū) *v.t.,* **de·val·ued, de·val·u·ing.** another word for **devaluate.**

dev·as·tate (dev′ə stāt′) *v.t.,* **dev·as·tat·ed, dev·as·tat·ing.** **1.** to lay waste; make desolate; destroy; ravage: *Locusts devastated the crops.* **2.** to overwhelm, as with surprise: *They were devastated by the news of the disaster.* —**dev′as·tat′ing,** *adj.* —**dev′as·tat′ing·ly,** *adv.* —**dev′as·ta′tor,** *n.*

dev·as·ta·tion (dev′ə stā′shən) *n.* the act of devastating or the state of being devastated; destruction.

de·vel·op (di vel′əp) *v.t.* **1.** to bring into being or activity: *to develop an interest in sports at an early age.* **2.** to change (someone or something) gradually: *The demand for speed and comfort has developed air travel greatly over the past forty years.* **3.** to cause to grow or expand: *You develop your muscles by exercise. Developing the skills of a carpenter takes years of work.* **4.** to put to use: *to develop the natural resources of a country.* **5.** to build houses or other buildings on (land). **6.** to work out in detail: *The rest of the book developed the ideas of the first chapter.* **7.** to make known; reveal; disclose. **8.** *Photography.* to treat (an exposed film, plate, or print) with a chemical solution to make the image appear. —*v.i.* **1.** to come into being or activity: *A rash developed on his skin after he ate the fruit.* **2.** to change gradually: *The small river port developed into one of the country's* largest cities. **3.** to grow: *The young ruler developed into a strong leader.* **4.** to become known: *Several new facts developed after the case had already been decided.*

de·vel·op·er (di vel′ə pər) *n.* **1.** a person or thing that develops. **2.** *Photography.* the chemical solution that makes visible the image on a film, plate, or print.

de·vel·op·ing (di vel′ə ping) *adj.* (of a country or region) not yet having achieved a high level of economic or industrial development: *developing nations.*

de·vel·op·ment (di vel′əp mənt) *n.* **1.** the act or process of developing: *The development of this spacecraft took many years.* **2.** the state of having been developed: *I exercised to improve my muscular development.* **3.** an event or occurrence: *political developments.* **4.** a group of houses or other buildings, often of similar design and construction. —**de·vel′op·men′tal,** *adj.*

de·vi·ant (dē′vē ənt) *adj.* deviating from a standard or norm, as from accepted standards of social behavior. —*n.* a person whose behavior deviates from what is considered standard or normal by a group or society.

de·vi·ate (dē′vē āt′) *v.i.,* **de·vi·at·ed, de·vi·at·ing.** to turn aside from a course of action, line of thought, or the like: *The story was funny, but it deviated from the truth.*

de·vi·a·tion (dē′vē ā′shən) *n.* **1.** the act of deviating: *Getting up at five o'clock is a deviation from my usual routine.* **2.** the amount of deviating.

de·vice (di vīs′) *n.* **1.** something made or invented for a particular purpose; mechanism: *a device to open a can.* **2.** a plan or scheme; trick. **3.** an ornamental figure or design, especially on a coat of arms.
·**to leave (someone) to his** or **her own devices.** to permit (someone) to handle as he or she thinks best.

dev·il (dev′əl) *n.* **1.** *also,* **Devil, the Devil.** a supernatural being considered to be the supreme ruler of hell, the chief spirit of evil, and the opponent of God, often represented as a creature having horns, a tail, and cloven hooves; Lucifer; Satan. **2.** any evil spirit; demon. **3.** a wicked, cruel, or ill-natured person. **4.** a person of great cleverness, mischievousness, impudence, or recklessness. **5.** a wretched or pitiful person: *The poor devil hasn't any decent clothing to wear.* **6.** an apprentice or person who runs errands in a printing shop. *Also,* **printer's devil.** —*v.t.,* **dev·iled, dev·il·ing;** *also, British,* **dev·illed, dev·il·ling. 1.** to tease; torment: *The pain in my back has been deviling me.* **2.** to prepare (food) by using hot seasonings, especially mustard or pepper: *to devil eggs.*

dev·il·fish (dev′əl fish′) *n., pl.* **dev·il·fish** or **dev·il·fish·es. 1.** another word for **manta. 2.** a large octopus.

dev·il·ish (dev′ə lish) *adj.* **1.** relating to or like the devil or a devil; evil; cruel. **2.** full of mischief; mischievous. —**dev′il·ish·ly,** *adv.* —**dev′il·ish·ness,** *n.*

dev·il–may–care (dev′əl mā kâr′) *adj.* carefree or reckless: *a devil-may-care attitude toward work.*

dev·il·ment (dev′əl ment) *n.* a devilish activity; mischief.

dev·il·ry (dev′əl rē) *n., pl.* **dev·il·ries.** another word for **deviltry.**

devil's advocate 1. a person who supports an unpopular, questionable, or opposing position or cause, especially for the sake of argument: *I agree with you, but let me play devil's advocate and offer some objections.* **2.** in the Roman Catholic Church, an official who is named to give evidence and arguments opposed to the beatification or canonization of a candidate.

devil's food cake, a rich, dark chocolate cake.

dev·il·try (dev′əl trē) *n., pl.* **dev·il·tries. 1.** evilness; wickedness. **2.** mischievous behavior.·

de·vi·ous (dē′vē əs) *adj.* **1.** turning aside from the direct way; roundabout; wandering: *to take a devious route to avoid heavy traffic.* **2.** attempting to deceive; not straightforward, frank, or direct: *a devious scheme to gain wealth.* —**de′vi·ous·ly,** *adv.* —**de′vi·ous·ness,** *n.*

de·vise (di vīz′) *v.t.,* **de·vised, de·vis·ing. 1.** to think

out; invent; plan: *to devise a secret code.* **2.** to give or leave (property) by a will. —**de·vis′er,** *n.*

de·void (di void′) *adj.* entirely without; lacking (used with *of*): *The project was devoid of leadership.*

de·volve (di volv′) *v.,* **de·volved, de·volv·ing.** —*v.t.* to transfer (work or responsibility) to another: *Congress has devolved some of its authority to certain government agencies.* —*v.i.* to be passed on to another: *When I retired, the business devolved on my children.*

De·vo·ni·an (də vō′nē ən) *n.* the fourth period of the Paleozoic era, characterized by an abundance of primitive fish and the appearance of amphibians. —*adj.* of, relating to, or characteristic of this period.

de·vote (di vōt′) *v.t.,* **de·vot·ed, de·vot·ing. 1.** to give or apply earnestly, as oneself or one's time, effort, or attention, to some person or purpose: *I devoted much energy to building the garage. They devoted themselves to study.* **2.** to set apart for a particular use or purpose: *They devoted a room in the house to recreation.*

de·vot·ed (di vō′tid) *adj.* **1.** loyal; faithful: *a devoted friend.* **2.** dedicated to some purpose. —**de·vot′ed·ly,** *adv.* —**de·vot′ed·ness,** *n.*

dev·o·tee (dev′ə tē′) *n.* a person devoted to anything; enthusiast: *a devotee of baseball.*

de·vo·tion (di vō′shən) *n.* **1.** a strong attachment to or affection for someone; loyalty; faithfulness: *parents' devotion to their children.* **2.** the act of devoting or the state of being devoted. **3.** religious piety; devoutness. **4. devotions.** religious worship; prayers.

de·vo·tion·al (di vō′shə nəl) *adj.* relating to religious devotion; used in worship. —**de·vo′tion·al·ly,** *adv.*

de·vour (di vour′) *v.t.* **1.** to eat up with great greed or vigor: *The hungry lion devoured its prey. Since we hadn't eaten all day, we devoured our dinner.* **2.** to consume destructively: *Fire devoured the house.* **3.** to take in greedily or eagerly with the ears, eyes, or mind: *to devour a book.* **4.** to absorb or engross completely: *to be devoured by grief.* —**de·vour′ing·ly,** *adv.*

de·vout (di vout′) *adj.* **1.** devoted to worship and prayer; religious; pious: *a devout member of a church.* **2.** showing devotion or piety: *devout prayer.* **3.** earnest; sincere: *devout wishes for success.* —**de·vout′ly,** *adv.* —**de·vout′ness,** *n.*

dew (dü, dū) *n.* **1.** moisture from the air that condenses during the night in small drops on cool surfaces. **2.** any light moisture in small drops, such as tears or perspiration. **3.** anything fresh, pure, or refreshing like dew: *the dew of youth.* —*v.t.* to moisten with or as if with dew.

dew·ber·ry (dü′ber′ē, dü′ber′e) *n., pl.* **dew·ber·ries. 1.** the sweet, black berry of any of several trailing or climbing shrubs of the rose family, similar to the blackberry. **2.** the shrub bearing this berry.

dew·claw (dü′klô′, dü′klô′) *n.* **1.** the small inner toe on the foot of certain dogs that has no function. **2.** the false hoof above the true hoof in deer, cattle, hogs, and other animals.

dew·drop (dü′drop′, dü′drop′) *n.* a drop of dew.

Dew·ey decimal system (dü′ē, dü′ē) the system used in some libraries for classifying books and other publications according to subject matter. It uses the num-

dewclaw (def. 1)

bers 000 to 999 to designate major categories and decimal numbers to indicate special subdivisions of these fields. [From the American educator and librarian Melvil L. *Dewey* (1851–1931), who devised it.]

dew·lap (dü′lap′, dū′lap′) *n.* the loose fold of skin under the throat of cattle and certain other animals.

DEW line (dü, dū) a chain of radar stations across North America above the Arctic Circle, maintained to provide advance warning of the approach of hostile aircraft or missiles. [Short for *D(istant) E(arly) W(arning)*.]

dew point, the temperature at which dew forms or vapor condenses into liquid.

Dewlap

dew·y (dü′ē, dū′ē) *adj.*, **dew·i·er, dew·i·est. 1.** moist with dew: *dewy grass.* **2.** resembling or suggesting dew. —**dew′i·ly,** *adv.* —**dew′i·ness,** *n.*

dex·ter (dek′stər) *adj.* of or on the right-hand side.

dex·ter·i·ty (dek ster′i tē) *n.* skill in using the hands, body, or mind: *The gymnast's performance showed great physical dexterity. The diplomat handled the matter with dexterity.*

dex·ter·ous (dek′stər əs, dek′strəs) *adj.* having or showing skill in using the hands, body, or mind: *Magicians and acrobats are dexterous.* Also, **dextrous.** [From the Latin word *dexter* meaning "on the right hand" or "dexterous, skillful."] —**dex′ter·ous·ly,** *adv.* —**dex′ter·ous·ness,** *n.*

dex·trin (dek′strin) *also,* **dex·trine** (dek′strēn, dek′strin). *n.* a gummy substance obtained from the partial chemical breakdown of starch, used especially as an adhesive.

dex·trose (dek′strōs) *n.* a colorless, crystalline sugar found in many plants and in blood. Also, **grape sugar.**

dex·trous (dek′strəs) *n.* another spelling of **dexterous.**

DH, designated hitter.

di- *prefix* twofold; twice; double: *dioxide, digraph.*

dia- *prefix* across; through: *diagonal, diagram.*

di·a·be·tes (dī′ə bē′tis, dī′ə bē′tēz) *n.* a disease in which too little insulin is made or used in the body, resulting in excess sugar in the blood, damage to the blood vessels, and, sometimes, death.

di·a·bet·ic (dī′ə bet′ik) *adj.* of, relating to, or having diabetes. —*n.* a person having diabetes.

di·a·bol·i·cal (dī′ə bol′i kəl) *adj.* **1.** having the qualities of the devil; very cruel or wicked; fiendish: *The detectives uncovered a diabolical plot to blow up the airplane.* **2.** relating to the devil or devils. Also, **di·a·bol·ic** (dī′ə bol′ik). —**di·a·bol′i·cal·ly,** *adv.* —**di·a·bol′i·cal·ness,** *n.*

di·a·crit·ic (dī′ə krit′ik) *n.* see **diacritical mark.** —*adj.* another word for **diacritical.**

di·a·crit·i·cal (dī′ə krit′i kəl) *adj.* serving to distinguish, as the sounds of letters.

diacritical mark, a mark or sign (such as ¨, ^, ¯, ´, or `) placed over, under, or across a letter to indicate pronunciation or as part of the spelling.

di·a·dem (dī′ə dem′) *n.* **1.** a crown. **2.** a cloth headband, often set with jewels and precious metals, formerly worn as a crown by Oriental rulers.

di·aer·e·sis (dī er′ə sis) *n.* another spelling of **dieresis.**

di·ag·nose (dī′əg nōs′) *v.*, **di·ag·nosed, di·ag·nos·ing.** —*v.t.* to make a diagnosis of: *The doctor diagnosed the patient's illness as pneumonia.* —*v.i.* to make a diagnosis.

di·ag·no·sis (dī′əg nō′sis) *n., pl.* **di·ag·no·ses** (dī′əg nō′sēz). **1.** the act or process of finding out the nature of a disease or other harmful condition by careful examination and study of symptoms: *The doctor's diagnosis revealed that I had the measles.* **2.** an investigation and study of facts to find out the basic characteristics of something: *They made a complete diagnosis of the housing problem.* **3.** the conclusion reached by careful examination of symptoms or study of facts: *The mechanic's diagnosis was that the stalled car's battery was dead.*

di·ag·nos·tic (dī′əg nos′tik) *adj.* relating to, helpful in, or used in diagnosis: *diagnostic procedures, diagnostic equipment.* —*n.* a computer program that tests hardware or software and alerts the user to any problems.

di·ag·nos·ti·cian (dī′əg nos tish′ən) *n.* a person who makes diagnoses, especially one who specializes in medical diagnoses.

di·ag·o·nal (dī ag′ə nəl) *adj.* **1.** *Geometry.* **a.** connecting two nonadjacent angles of a figure. **b.** connecting two nonadjacent edges of a solid figure. **2.** having a slanting direction: *The fabric has a diagonal pattern.* —*n.* **1.** a diagonal straight line or plane. **2.** anything slanting. —**di·ag′o·nal·ly,** *adv.*

di·a·gram (dī′ə gram′) *n.* a figure, plan, or drawing giving the outline or general scheme of something, used to show how it is put together or how it works, or to show a process or the results of an action: *a diagram of the floors of a building, a diagram of a machine part, a diagram of troop movements during a battle.* —*v.t.*, **di·a·gramed, di·a·gram·ing;** also, British, **di·a·grammed, di·a·gram·ming.** to show by a diagram; make a diagram of: *If you first diagram the problem, you may be able to solve it.*

di·a·gram·mat·ic (dī′ə grə mat′ik) *adj.* **1.** in the form of a diagram: *a diagrammatic sketch of an engine.* **2.** in outline; sketchy. Also, **di·a·gram·mat·i·cal** (dī′ə grə mat′i kəl). —**di′a·gram·mat′i·cal·ly,** *adv.*

di·al (dī′əl, dīl) *n.* **1.** a surface on which the amount or degree of something is displayed by using a pointer, numbers, letters, or other marks. The faces of clocks, compasses, and meters are dials. **2.** the movable disk or other device on a radio or television for tuning in to a station or channel. **3.** the disk on the front of certain telephones that is rotated to signal the numbers of the telephone being called. **4.** see **sundial.** —*v.t.*, **di·aled, di·al·ing;** also, British, **di·alled, di·al·ling 1.** to call by means of a telephone dial: *to dial a wrong number.* **2.** to tune in, as on a radio: *Dial the station that has the news broadcast.* **3.** to select or operate by means of a dial: *to dial the combination of a safe.* —*v.i.* to operate or use a dial, as in telephoning: *If you get a bad connection, hang up and dial again.*

di·a·lect (dī′ə lekt′) *n.* a form of a language that is spoken in a particular area or by a particular group and differs from other forms of the same language in some of its grammar, pronunciation, vocabulary, or idioms.

Language Note

The term **dialect** refers to a special way that language is used and spoken by a group of people. Some people believe that a dialect is an inferior variety of a language, but, in fact, everyone speaks a dialect. To a student of language, no one dialect is better than any other.

For the most part, dialects are regional, representing the patterns of speech used by people in a given geographic area. Such patterns often enable a listener to identify the region of the country from which a speaker comes. In the United States, for example, people who live in the South, the New England states, and the Midwest, to name just three dialect areas, speak differently from one another. New Englanders often do not pronounce the *r* in *park* or *car*, and some Midwesterners' pronunciation of *wash* may sound like "worsh" to someone from another part of the country.

Dialects also contain distinctive expressions and idioms. In some parts of the country, for example, people use the expression *kitty-corner* to mean what people in other regions mean by using *catty-corner.* If the time is 9:45, in some dialects it is said to be *a quarter of ten,* in others *a quarter to ten,* and in still others *a quarter till ten.* Each different expression is part of its own dialect, and, like the dialects themselves, none can be said to be more correct than the others.

di·a·lec·tal (dī'ə lek'təl) *adj.* relating to or characteristic of a dialect.

di·a·logue (dī'ə lôg', dī'ə log') *also,* **di·a·log.** *n.* **1.** the parts that are conversation in a play, novel, or similar work: *a comedy with witty dialogue.* **2.** a conversation between two or more persons: *The two friends who had not seen each other for a long time carried on a lengthy dialogue.* **3.** a literary work written in the form of a conversation between two or more persons: *Plato wrote many dialogues.* **4.** an exchange of ideas: *There was a dialogue between different groups in the community before the election.*

a **dialogue**
between friends

dial tone, the steady humming sound of a telephone, indicating to the user that a call may be dialed.

di·al·y·sis (dī al'ə sis) *n.* a method of removing from the blood wastes that are usually removed by the kidneys. As a medical treatment it is administered to patients whose kidneys are not working properly. In dialysis, blood is filtered through a machine, and the cleaned blood is returned to the body.

diam., diameter.

di·am·e·ter (dī am'ı tər) *n.* **1.** a straight line passing through the center of a circle or sphere, from one side to the other. **2.** the length of such a line; the width or thickness of something: *The diameter of the earth is about 8,000 miles.*

diameter

di·a·met·ri·cal (dī'ə met'ri kəl) *adj.* **1.** of or along a diameter: *The surveyor took a diametrical measurement of the tree.* **2.** directly opposite; completely contrary: *The two candidates have diametrical views on that issue.* Also, **di·a·met·ric** (dī'ə met'rik).

di·a·met·ri·cal·ly (dī'ə met'ri klē) *adv.* **1.** along a diameter; straight through: *The apple was cut diametrically.* **2.** directly; completely: *The two politicians were diametrically opposed on many issues.*

di·a·mond (dī'mənd, dī'ə mənd) *n.* **1.** a mineral that is usually colorless, consisting of pure carbon in a crystalline form. It is the hardest natural substance known. Diamonds are used as precious gems when cut and polished and in industry for cutting and grinding. **2.** a gemstone cut from this mineral, especially when cut and polished for use in jewelry. **3.** *Geometry.* a plane figure with four equal sides, forming two acute and two obtuse angles. **4. a.** a playing card marked with one or more red figures in the shape of a diamond (♦). **b. diamonds.** the suit of such cards. **5.** *Baseball.* **a.** the infield. **b.** the entire field. —*adj.* **1.** resembling, made of, or set with a diamond or

diamonds: *a diamond necklace.* **2.** of or being the sixtieth or seventy-fifth anniversary of an event: *a diamond wedding anniversary.*

dia·mond·back (dī'mənd bak', dī'ə mənd bak') *n.* **1.** a large rattlesnake having diamond-shaped markings on its back, found in the southeastern United States. **2.** *also,* **diamondback terrapin.** a turtle with diamond-shaped markings on its shell, found in Atlantic coastal waters.

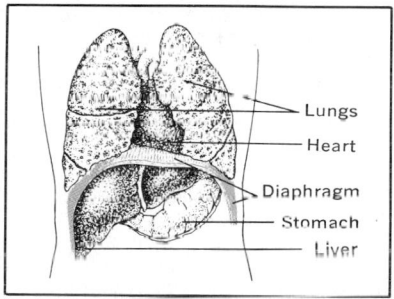

diamondback *(def. 2)*

Di·an·a (dī an'ə) *n.* *Roman Mythology.* the goddess of the moon, the woods, and hunting. In Greek mythology she was called Artemis.

di·a·pa·son (dī'ə pā'zən) *n.* **1.** either of two principal stops in a pipe organ that extend through the entire range of the organ. **2.** the entire range of a voice or instrument. **3.** a fixed standard of musical pitch. **4.** another word for **tuning fork. 5.** an outpouring of harmonious sound.

dia·per (dī'pər, dī'ə pər) *n.* **1.** a baby's undergarment consisting of a soft, absorbent material, drawn up between the legs and fastened at the waist. **2.** a pattern made up of small, constantly repeated, geometric figures. **3.** white cotton or linen cloth woven with such a pattern. —*v.t.* to put a diaper on (a baby).

di·aph·a·nous (dī af'ə nəs) *adj.* sheer enough to be seen through or to let light through: *diaphanous cloth.*

di·a·phragm (dī'ə fram') *n.* **1.** a membrane of muscle and connective tissue between the chest cavity and abdominal cavity, used in inhaling and exhaling. **2.** any membrane or partition that serves to separate. **3.** a disk used in converting sound to electrical impulses or electrical impulses to sound, as in a telephone or micro-

	Lungs
	Heart
	Diaphragm
	Stomach
	Liver

diaphragm *(def. 1)*

phone. **4.** a mechanism that can be adjusted to control the amount of light entering the lens of a camera, microscope, or similar instrument.

di·a·rist (dī'ə rist) *n.* a person who keeps a diary.

di·ar·rhe·a (dī'ə rē'ə) *also,* **di·ar·rhoe·a.** *n.* a condition marked by frequent and loose bowel movements.

di·a·ry (dī'ə rē) *n., pl.* **di·a·ries. 1.** a daily record of events, especially of the writer's personal experiences, observations, and thoughts. **2.** a book in which such a record is kept.

di·as·to·le (dī as'tə lē') *n.* the period of expansion or relaxation of the heart during which the heart chambers are filled with blood. These periods alternate rhythmically with systoles, or periods of contraction.

di·a·stol·ic (dī'ə stol'ik) *adj.* relating to, involving, or taken during the diastole: *diastolic blood pressure.*

---

at; āpe; fär; câre; end; mē; it; īce; pîerce; hot; ōld; sông, fôrk; oil; out; up; ūse; rüle; pùll; tûrn; chin; sing; shop; thin; this; hw in white; zh in treasure. The symbol ə stands for the unstressed vowel sound heard in about, taken, pencil, lemon, and circus.

di·a·tom (dī′ə tom′) *n.* any of a large group of microscopic, one-celled algae that live in fresh and salt water and have cell walls made up mostly of silica.

di·a·ton·ic (dī′ə ton′ik) *adj. Music.* of or relating to the standard major or minor scale that has eight tones.

di·a·tribe (dī′ə trīb′) *n.* a bitter, violent, often lengthy criticism: *The mayor's speech was a diatribe against the governor.*

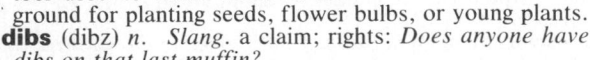

diatoms

dib·ble (dib′əl) *n.* a pointed hand tool used to make holes in the ground for planting seeds, flower bulbs, or young plants.

dibs (dibz) *n. Slang.* a claim; rights: *Does anyone have dibs on that last muffin?*

dice (dīs) *pl. n., sing.* **die. 1.** small cubes of wood, plastic, or other material, marked on each side with from one to six spots, used in games of chance, usually in a pair. **2.** a gambling game played with dice. —*v.t.,* **diced, dic·ing.** to cut into small cubes: *to dice potatoes.*

di·chot·o·my (dī kot′ə mē) *n., pl.* **dichotomies.** division into two parts or categories, especially categories that are very different from or opposed to one another: *to emphasize the dichotomy between peace and war.*

dick·ens (dik′inz) *interj. Informal.* devil; deuce. ▲ used as a mild oath or exclamation: *Where the dickens is my coat?*

Dick·en·si·an (di ken′zē ən) *adj.* of, relating to, or similar to Charles Dickens or his writings.

dick·er (dik′ər) *v.i.* to trade by bargaining or haggling in a petty way: *The customer and the seller spent a long time dickering over the price of the car.* —*n.* **1.** petty bargaining. **2.** a petty bargain.

dick·ey (dik′ē) *also,* **dick·y.** *n., pl.* **dick·eys. 1.** an article of clothing, usually having a collar covering the neck and part of the chest, designed to be worn under a shirt, jacket, sweater, or other garment. **2.** a false shirt front. **3.** any small bird.

dick·y (dik′ē) *n., pl.* **dick·ies.** another spelling of **dickey.**

di·cot·y·le·don (dī kot′ə lē′dən) *n.* a plant that has two cotyledons, or seed leaves, in the embryo. Dicotyledons make up one of the two classes of flowering plants. Also, **di·cot** (dī′kot). —**di·cot′y·le′don·ous,** *adj.*

dic·ta (dik′tə) a plural of **dictum.**

Dic·ta·phone (dik′tə fōn′) *n. Trademark.* an instrument to record and reproduce speech, used especially for the recording or dictating of business letters that are to be typed at a later time.

dic·tate (*v.,* dik′tāt, dik tāt′; *n.,* dik′tāt) *v.,* **dic·tat·ed, dic·tat·ing.** —*v.t.* **1.** to say or read (something) aloud to be written down or recorded by another: *I dictated the letter to my secretary.* **2.** to order or give as a command, with or as if with authority: *The victorious nation dictated the conditions of peace.* —*v.i.* **1.** to say or read aloud something to be written down or recorded by another: *The teacher dictated in French to the class.* **2.** to give orders or exercise authority. —*n.* a principle, rule, or command that must be followed: *Everyone is subject to the dictates of the law.*

dic·ta·tion (dik tā′shən) *n.* **1.** the act of dictating something to be written down or recorded by another: *The students listened carefully to the teacher's dictation.* **2.** material that is dictated or recorded: *Part of the French exam was a dictation.* **3.** the act of giving orders with authority.

dic·ta·tor (dik′tā tər, dik tā′tər) *n.* **1.** a ruler who has absolute power and authority, especially one who is cruel, unjust, or tyrannical. **2.** a person who has great authority in some field or about some subject: *a dictator of fashion.* **3.** a person who dictates something to be written down or recorded.

dic·ta·to·ri·al (dik′tə tôr′ē əl) *adj.* **1.** relating to or characteristic of a dictator: *dictatorial powers.* **2.** tending to give orders or be tyrannical; overbearing: *a dictatorial football coach.* —**dic′ta·to′ri·al·ly,** *adv.*

dic·ta·tor·ship (dik tā′tər ship′, dik′tā tər ship′) *n.* **1.** the period of time during which a dictator rules; office of a dictator: *During the general's dictatorship, freedom of the press was abolished.* **2.** a state or government ruled by a dictator: *That country was a dictatorship until civil war broke out.* **3.** a form of government in which absolute power is held by a dictator.

dic·tion (dik′shən) *n.* **1.** the way in which ideas are expressed in words; choice and arrangement of words in speaking or writing: *The diction of poetry is often different from ordinary conversation.* **2.** the manner and quality of saying or pronouncing words; enunciation: *An actor must have clear diction.*

dic·tion·ar·y (dik′shə ner′ē) *n., pl.* **dic·tion·ar·ies. 1.** a book containing words of a language, usually arranged in alphabetical order, together with information about them, such as what they mean, how they are pronounced, how they are used, and where they came from. **2.** a book containing words of one language arranged in alphabetical order, and giving their meanings in another language: *an Italian-English dictionary.* **3.** a book containing and defining words used in a special area of interest or knowledge, usually arranged in alphabetical order: *a sports dictionary.*

Language Note

In relation to the long history of written language, the **dictionary** is a new invention. The earliest ancestors of modern dictionaries were probably glossaries made by Romans who were reading the works of Greek authors. These ancient glossaries, like most early dictionaries, contained only foreign or difficult words and did not attempt to record all the words of a language. These glossaries differed from a modern dictionary in that they usually gave only synonyms, rather than definitions, for the words that were listed.

Before the invention of printing, it was almost impossible to produce a book of the length of a dictionary. One of the first large-scale English glossaries was a book finished in 1440 that translated 10,000 English words into Latin. In 1552 there appeared the first dictionary containing not only the Latin equivalents of English words, but the English definitions as well.

In 1755, the first great dictionary of the English language was published. This book, written by Samuel Johnson, is called *A Dictionary of the English Language.* The first great American dictionary was *An American Dictionary of the English Language,* written by Noah Webster and published in 1828. Webster's purpose in writing the dictionary was to show and record the differences that had developed between American and British English.

Because our language is always changing and people's needs for a dictionary vary greatly, new dictionaries are constantly being written. Among the specialized dictionaries published are technical dictionaries that record and define the language of a particular science or profession, slang dictionaries, and student dictionaries. Unlike a standard dictionary, a student dictionary omits certain technical and archaic words, many more illustrations are used to aid the reader in understanding definitions, and extra information on usage is given in order to help the student use language in the clearest, most effective way.

dic·tum (dik′təm) *n., pl.* **dic·ta** or **dic·tums. 1.** a formal authoritative statement or opinion: *The dictums of the Roman emperors were regarded as law.* **2.** a popular saying: *"A penny saved is a penny earned" is a dictum.*

did (did) the past tense of **do**[1].

di·dac·tic (dī dak′tik) *adj.* **1.** intended to instruct or to guide moral behavior: *a didactic story whose moral is that "Crime does not pay."* **2.** often tending to moralize or to instruct or lecture others: *Your didactic manner sometimes offends people.* —**di·dac′ti·cal·ly,** *adv.*

did·n't (did′ənt) *contr.* did not.

Di·do (dī′dō) *n. Greek and Roman Legend.* a queen of Carthage who fell in love with Aeneas and killed herself when he left her.

didst (didst) *Archaic.* the second person singular, past tense, of **do**[1].

die[1] (dī) *v.i.,* **died, dy·ing. 1.** to stop living; become dead: *Millions of people died in World War II.* **2.** to pass out of existence; come to an end (often with *out*): *The pony express died with the coming of the telegraph. The feudal system died out centuries ago.* **3.** to lose force or strength; stop being active: *The wind suddenly died as the sailboat neared shore.* **4.** to stop functioning or operating: *The engine died just before the car reached the finish line.* **5.** to end, pass, or fade gradually (often with *away, out,* or *down*): *The music died away in the distance.* **6.** *Informal.* to suffer terribly: *I was dying of boredom while I stayed home with the flu.* **7.** *Informal.* to want very much; desire strongly: *We are dying to see you again.* [From the Old Norse word *deyja* meaning "to die."]

·**to die off.** to die one by one until all are gone: *The small herd died off during the drought.*

die[2] (dī) *n. pl. (def. 1)* **dice** or *(def. 2)* **dies. 1.** one of a pair of dice. **2.** any of various machines or devices used to shape, stamp, or cut out an object, especially a metal block or plate used to stamp designs on coins. [From the Old French word *dé* with the same meaning.]

·**the die is cast.** the decision is made and cannot be avoided or changed.

die-hard (dī′härd′) *also,* **die·hard.** *adj.* resisting stubbornly to the very end; refusing to change or give in: *a die-hard bigot.* —*n.* a person who refuses to give in or change his or her views.

di·er·e·sis (dī er′ə sis) *also,* **di·aer·e·sis.** *n., pl.* **di·er·e·ses** (dī er′ə sēz′). the diacritical mark consisting of two dots (¨) placed over a vowel to show that it is pronounced in a separate syllable, as in *naive.*

die·sel (dē′zəl) *also,* **Die·sel.** *n.* **1.** see **diesel engine. 2.** a vehicle powered by a diesel engine. —*adj.* of or for a diesel engine: *diesel fuel.*

diesel engine *also,* **Diesel engine.** an internal-combustion engine in which heat produced by the compression of air in the engine's cylinders ignites the fuel oil. Also, **diesel motor.** [From the German automotive engineer Rudolf *Diesel* (1858–1913), who designed it.]

Di·es I·rae (dē′äs ir′ā) a medieval Latin hymn that describes Judgment Day, traditionally sung at masses for the dead. [From the Medieval Latin phrase *Dies irae* meaning "Day of wrath," the opening words of this hymn.]

di·et[1] (dī′it) *n.* **1.** food and drink usually eaten by a person or animal: *My diet includes meat, vegetables, and fruit. A lion's diet consists of meat.* **2.** a regulated selection of food and drink chosen for reasons of health or weight control: *People with high blood pressure are sometimes put on low-salt diets.* —*v.i.* to eat according to a particular diet, especially in order to lose weight: *She dieted for several weeks and lost 12 pounds.* [From the Old French word *diete* meaning "a person's food and drink," from the Latin word *diaeta* "prescribed diet," from the Greek word *diaita* "way of living."] —**di′et·er,** *n.*

di·et[2] (dī′it) *n.* **1.** a formal assembly or meeting for discussion: *A diet of church officials met to consider changes in the service.* **2.** a lawmaking body or council, such as the national legislature of Japan. [From the Medieval Latin word *dieta* meaning "day appointed for a meeting" or "assembly," going back to the Latin word *dies* "day."]

di·e·tar·y (dī′i ter′ē) *adj.* relating to diet: *Certain dietary rules must be observed for good health.*

di·e·tet·ic (dī′i tet′ik) *adj.* **1.** relating to diet or to regulation of the use of food. **2.** prepared for use in special diets, especially diets intended to produce a loss in weight: *Dietetic sweets are made without sugar.* —**di′e·tet′i·cal·ly,** *adv.*

di·e·tet·ics (dī′i tet′iks) *n.* the branch of science dealing with diet and nutrition, meal planning, and the preparation and serving of food. ▲ used with a singular verb.

di·e·ti·tian (dī′i tish′ən) *also,* **di·e·ti·cian.** *n.* a person trained in dietetics, usually employed by a hospital, school, or similar institution.

dif·fer (dif′ər) *v.i.* **1.** to be not the same; be unlike: *Although they are twins, they differ greatly in looks.* **2.** to have a difference of opinion; disagree: *The candidate differs with the other members of the party on that issue.*

dif·fer·ence (dif′ər əns, dif′rəns) *n.* **1.** the state or quality of being unlike or different: *Was there a difference between the two answers?* **2.** an instance of this: *I noticed a difference in your attitude after I apologized.* **3.** a distinguishing characteristic: *The only difference between the two cars is the price.* **4.** the amount by which one quantity is greater or less than another; remainder left after subtracting one quantity from another: *The difference between 16 and 12 is 4.* **5.** a disagreement in opinion: *They managed to settle their differences without a fight.* **6.** an instance of disagreement; dispute: *A difference arose between the neighbors over the exact boundary line between their property.*

·**to make a difference.** to have an effect on or change a situation; matter: *Getting enough sleep makes a difference in how one feels and looks.*

dif·fer·ent (dif′ər ənt, dif′rənt) *adj.* **1.** not alike or similar: *She and her husband have very different taste in furniture.* **2.** not the same; separate; distinct: *It rained two different times this afternoon.* **3.** not like most others; not ordinary; unusual: *Your new design is quite different from others I've seen.* —**dif′fer·ent·ly,** *adv.*

▲ The word *from* is usually used after **different,** especially in careful writing: *My handwriting is very different from yours.* "Different *than*" is also widely used, but many people prefer not to use it in formal writing or speech. In British English, the phrase "different *to*" is often used.

dif·fer·en·tial (dif′ə ren′shəl) *adj.* relating to, involving, or based on a difference or differences: *differential rates on freight charges.* —*n.* **1.** a differential amount, factor, wage, or rate: *a pressure differential.* **2.** *also,* **differential gear.** a system of gears that enables driving wheels on the same axle of a motor vehicle to turn at different speeds when the vehicle rounds a curve. —**dif′fer·en′tial·ly,** *adv.*

dif·fer·en·ti·ate (dif′ə ren′shē āt′) *v.,* **dif·fer·en·ti·at·ed, dif·fer·en·ti·at·ing.** —*v.t.* **1.** to form or make up the difference in; serve to distinguish between: *Coloring differentiates the male from the female in some species of birds.* **2.** to see or tell the differences in (something); distinguish between: *Not many people could differentiate this counterfeit bill from real money.* —*v.i.* **1.** to become different or specialized. **2.** to see or tell a difference: *Only their parents can differentiate between the twins.* —**dif′fer·en·ti·a′tion,** *n.*

---

at; āpe; fär; câre; end; mē; it; īce; pîerce; hot; ōld; sông, fôrk; oil; out; up; ūse; rüle; pull; tûrn; chin; sing; shop; thin; this; hw in white; zh in treasure. The symbol ə stands for the unstressed vowel sound heard in about, taken, pencil, lemon, and circus.

dif·fi·cult (dif′i kult′, dif′i kəlt) *adj.* **1.** hard to do or perform; demanding effort; not easy: *Crossing the river during the flood was a difficult task.* **2.** hard to solve or understand: *a difficult problem, a difficult poem.* **3.** hard to deal with, get along with, or please: *a difficult customer who never seemed satisfied with a product.*

dif·fi·cul·ty (dif′i kul′tē, dif′i kəl tē) *n., pl.* **dif·fi·cul·ties. 1.** the fact or condition of being difficult: *the difficulty of learning to drive a car. Walking on your hands is a trick of great difficulty.* **2.** something that is difficult to do, understand, or deal with; obstacle: *The hikers encountered many difficulties during the trip.* **3.** considerable effort; struggle: *I speak French with difficulty. They had difficulty fitting everything into their suitcases.* **4.** an embarrassing or troublesome state of affairs, especially a financial dilemma. **5.** a disagreement; conflict; trouble: *There was always some diplomatic difficulty between the two countries.*

dif·fi·dence (dif′i dəns) *n.* a lack of confidence in oneself; shyness.

dif·fi·dent (dif′i dənt) *adj.* lacking confidence in oneself; shy. **—dif′fi·dent·ly,** *adv.*

dif·fract (di frakt′) *v.t.* **1.** to bend or break up. **2.** to cause to undergo diffraction.

dif·frac·tion (di frak′shən) *n.* **1.** the bending of the path of a ray of light as it passes close to the edge of an object or through a narrow slit. The light wave bent in this way will spread out to form a series of light and dark bands or the colored bands of the spectrum. **2.** the similar bending of other kinds of waves, such as sound, electricity, or X rays.

dif·fuse (*adj.,* di fūs′; *v.,* di fūz′) *adj.* **1.** widely spread out; scattered: *diffuse light.* **2.** using many words; wordy: *a diffuse writer.* **—***v.,* **dif·fused, dif·fus·ing. —***v.t.* **1.** to scatter in all directions; spread widely: *The colors of the sunset were diffused across the sky. If you diffuse your talents, you may not become a success in anything.* **2.** to cause (gases or liquids) to mix together by diffusion. **—***v.i.* **1.** to be or become scattered; spread out: *The warmth from the fire diffused throughout the room.* **2.** to mix together by diffusion: *Every gas diffuses at a certain rate.* **—dif·fuse·ly** (di fūs′lē), *adv.* **—dif·fuse·ness** (di fūs′nis), *n.*

dif·fu·sion (di fū′zhən) *n.* **1.** the act of diffusing or the state of being diffused; spreading; dispersion: *The diffusion of information was greatly aided by the coming of radio and television.* **2.** wordiness in speech or writing. **3.** a gradual mixing together of the molecules of gases or of liquids. Diffusion is due to the movement of the molecules from an area where there are many of them to an area where there are few.

dig (dig) *v.,* **dug, dig·ging. —***v.t.* **1.** to break up or turn over and remove (earth), as with a shovel, the hands, or claws. **2.** to make or form by digging; hollow out: *to dig a hole, to dig a tunnel.* **3.** to obtain or remove by digging: *to dig potatoes.* **4.** to discover or obtain by search or investigation: *It took the reporter weeks to dig up the information for the article.* **5.** to poke; prod: *The rider dug the horse with the spurs.* **6.** to thrust or plunge: *The bronco dug its hooves into the ground and bucked.* **7.** *Slang.* **a.** to understand. **b.** to like or appreciate. **—***v.i.* **1.** to break up or turn over and remove the earth, as with a shovel, the hands, or claws: *The dog was digging in the yard for bones.* **2.** to make a way by or as if by digging: *The workers dug through the mountain to complete the highway.* **—***n.* **1.** a thrust or poke: *a dig in the ribs.* **2.** *Informal.* a sarcastic remark; cutting statement: *I don't appreciate your digs about my haircut.* **3.** the site of an archaeological excavation.

·to dig in. a. to dig trenches or holes for military defense. **b.** to begin to eat.

di·gest (*v.,* di jest′, dī jest′; *n.,* dī′jest) *v.t.* **1.** to break down (food materials) by the process of digestion. **2.** to think over for a time or fully understand: *It took them a while to digest the surprising news of their child's engagement.* **—***v.i.* to go through digestion: *Protein digests slowly.* **—***n.* a collection or summary of literary, historical, legal, or scientific material.

di·gest·i·ble (di jes′tə bəl, dī jes′tə bəl) *adj.* capable of being digested; easily digested. **—di·gest′i·bil′i·ty,** *n.*

di·ges·tion (di jes′chən, dī jes′chən) *n.* **1.** the process by which food materials are broken down into simple compounds that can be used as nutrients by the body. **2.** the ability to digest food: *The patient's digestion is good.*

di·ges·tive (di jes′tiv, dī jes′tiv) *adj.* relating to, for, or aiding digestion: *the digestive tract.*

digestive system, the system that breaks food down so that it can be used by the body. In mammals, the digestive system includes the mouth and teeth, pharynx, esophagus, stomach, intestines, and enzymes and other chemicals that the body produces to break down the food.

digestive system

dig·ger (dig′ər) *n.* **1.** a person who digs. **2.** a tool or machine for digging.

dig·gings (dig′ingz) *pl. n.* **1.** a place where digging is done, such as a mine. **2.** materials dug out. **3.** *Informal.* living quarters.

dig·it (dij′it) *n.* **1.** a finger or toe. **2.** any of the ten Arabic numerals from 0 through 9.

dig·i·tal (dij′i təl) *adj.* **1.** relating to or resembling a digit or digits. **2.** having digits. **3.** having a numerical display: *a digital watch.* **4.** operating on the principle of the binary digits 0 and 1, used to represent all values. **—***n.* a key on a keyboard instrument played with the finger.

digital computer, a computer that operates with numbers, particularly with the digits 0 and 1 used to represent all values.

dig·i·tal·is (dij′i tal′is) *n.* **1.** a drug used for stimulating the heart, prepared from the dried leaves of the foxglove. **2.** the plant from which this drug is made; foxglove.

an archaeological **dig**

dig·ni·fied (dig′nə fīd′) *adj.* marked by or showing dignity of manner or style; noble; stately.

dig·ni·fy (dig′nə fī′) *v.t.*, **dig·ni·fied, dig·ni·fy·ing.** **1.** to give dignity to; make noble; honor: *The governor dignified the ceremony by attending.* **2.** to give undeserved distinction or attention to: *Don't dignify the rumor by repeating it.*

dig·ni·tar·y (dig′ni ter′ē) *n., pl.* **dig·ni·tar·ies.** a person who has a high position or office, as in government or the church: *Several foreign dignitaries were entertained by the president.*

dig·ni·ty (dig′ni tē) *n., pl.* **dig·ni·ties.** **1.** nobility of character or manner; stateliness, serenity, or self-respect: *Throughout great hardship and poverty they always kept their dignity.* **2.** the state or quality of being worthy, honorable, or noble: *Real dignity lies in what you are, not in what you own.* **3.** level of excellence or importance: *The judge swore to uphold the dignity of the court.* **4.** a high office, rank, or title.

Word Family

English has derived a number of words from the Latin word *dignus,* meaning ''worthy, worthwhile.'' To have **dignity** is to be a worthy person, and to make someone worthy is to **dignify** that person. A government official is often called a **dignitary.** An arrogant person might become **disdainful** of some others, but might **deign** to be with people of equal status. People not treated with **dignity** may suffer **indignities,** which may cause them to feel **indignant** or filled with **indignation.**

di·graph (dī′graf) *n.* two letters used to represent one sound, such as *oa* in *boat* or *sh* in *ship.*

di·gress (di gres′, dī gres′) *v.i.* to depart or wander from the main subject in speaking or writing: *The professor digressed during the lecture to tell an interesting story.*

di·gres·sion (di gresh′ən, dī gresh′ən) *n.* **1.** the act of digressing: *The speaker's frequent digressions began to bore the audience.* **2.** something that digresses: *The next chapter is a long digression on the author's view of politics.*

di·gres·sive (di gres′iv, dī gres′iv) *adj.* tending to digress; marked by digression. —**di·gres′sive·ly,** *adv.* —**di·gres′sive·ness,** *n.*

dike (dīk) *n.* a high bank, wall, or other structure built to prevent flooding by holding back the waters of a sea or river. —*v.t.,* **diked, dik·ing.** to provide, protect, or surround with a dike or dikes.

di·lap·i·dat·ed (di lap′i dā′tid) *adj.* fallen into ruin or decay; broken down: *a dilapidated old tool shed.*

di·lap·i·da·tion (di lap′i dā′shən) *n.* a condition of ruin or decay: *They found several of the old houses in complete dilapidation.*

di·late (dī lāt′, dī′ lāt′) *v.,* **di·lat·ed, di·lat·ing.** —*v.t.* to make larger or wider; cause to expand: *Taking a deep breath will dilate your chest.* —*v.i.* **1.** to become larger or wider; expand: *The kitten's eyes dilated with fear when it was startled.* **2.** to speak or write at length: *The returning explorers dilated upon their adventures for over an hour.* —**di·la′tion,** *n.*

dil·a·to·ry (dil′ə tôr′ē) *adj.* **1.** tending to delay or be negligent: *Don't be dilatory in paying your bills.* **2.** tending to cause delay, either to gain time or to postpone action: *The senator used dilatory tactics to prevent passage of the bill.* —**dil′a·to′ri·ly,** *adv.* —**dil′a·to′ri·ness,** *n.*

di·lem·ma (di lem′ə) *n.* a situation requiring a difficult choice between two or more things, often between things that are equally unpleasant or unsatisfactory: *the dilemma of enduring a toothache or having the tooth pulled.*

dil·et·tante (dil′i tänt′, dil′i tänt′) *n., pl.,* **dil·et·tantes** or **dil·et·tan·ti** (dil′ə tän′tē). a person who pursues an art or science in a superficial way or merely for amusement.

dil·i·gence (dil′i jəns) *n.* serious, constant attention and effort: *Check every detail with diligence.*

dil·i·gent (dil′i jənt) *adj.* **1.** careful and hard-working in whatever is done: *a diligent student who really deserved good grades.* **2.** showing or carried out with painstaking care and effort: *Many hours were spent in a diligent search.* —**dil′i·gent·ly,** *adv.*

dill (dil) *n.* **1.** the dried seedlike fruit and fresh or dried leaves of a plant related to parsley, used chiefly as a spice to flavor pickles and other foods. **2.** the plant bearing this fruit.

dill pickle, a pickled cucumber flavored with dill.

dil·ly·dal·ly (dil′ē dal′ē) *v.i.,* **dil·ly·dal·lied, dil·ly·dal·ly·ing.** to waste time: *They dillydallied all day and never finished the work.*

di·lute (di lüt′, dī lüt′) *v.t.,* **di·lut·ed, di·lut·ing.** **1.** to thin or weaken by adding a liquid: *to dilute fruit juice with water, to dilute paint with turpentine.* **2.** to weaken or reduce the strength or purity of by adding something else: *The addition of new teams to the league spread out the talent and diluted the quality of play.* —*adj.* diluted; weak: *a dilute acid.*

di·lu·tion (di lü′shən, dī lü′shən) *n.* **1.** the act of diluting or the state of being diluted. **2.** something that is or has been diluted.

dim (dim) *adj.,* **dim·mer, dim·mest.** **1.** having or giving little light; not bright: *a dim light bulb, a dim corner of a basement.* **2.** not clear to the senses; indistinct; faint: *I saw the dim outline of a figure in the distance.* **3.** not clear to the mind; vague; confused: *She had only a dim recollection of the accident.* **4.** not seeing, hearing, or understanding clearly: *eyes that were dim with tears.* **5.** not favorable; discouraging: *Why do you take such a dim view of our idea?* —*v.,* **dimmed, dim·ming.** —*v.t.* to make dim: *Dim the car's headlights.* —*v.i.* to grow or become dim. —**dim′ly,** *adv.* —**dim′ness,** *n.*

dime (dīm) *n.* a coin of the United States equal to ten cents or one tenth of a dollar.

di·men·sion (di men′shən) *n.* **1.** any extent that can be measured, such as length, breadth, thickness, or height. **2. dimensions.** the measurements of a specific geometrical shape, such as a square, rectangle, or triangle: *The room's dimensions are 20 feet by 12 feet by 10 feet. Space travel is measured in four dimensions, including time.* **3.** size, scope, or importance: *The dimensions of this problem have not yet been fully realized by the public.*

di·men·sion·al (di men′shə nəl) *adj.* relating to or having a dimension or dimensions.

dime store, a store offering a wide variety of inexpensive merchandise. Also, **five-and-ten, five-and-dime.**

di·min·ish (di min′ish) *v.t.* to make smaller or less, as in size, amount, importance, or degree: *The decision to raise taxes diminished the governor's popularity.* —*v.i.* to become smaller or less: *The campers' food supply gradually diminished as the days wore on.* —**di·min′ish·ing,** *adj.*

di·min·u·en·do (di min′ū en′dō) *Music. adj.* with gradually decreasing loudness or force. —*adv.* with gradually decreasing loudness or force. —*n., pl.* **di·min·u·en·dos.** **1.** a gradual decrease in loudness or force. **2.** a passage played with a gradual decrease in loudness or force.

---

at; āpe; fär; câre; end; mē; it; īce; pîerce; hot; ōld; sông, fôrk; oil; out; up; ūse; rüle; pùll; tûrn; chin; sing; shop; thin; this; hw in white; zh in treasure. The symbol ə stands for the unstressed vowel sound heard in about, taken, pencil, lemon, and circus.

dim·i·nu·tion (dim'ə nü'shən, dim'ə nü'shən) *n.* the act of diminishing or the state of being diminished; reduction; decrease.

di·min·u·tive (di min'yə tiv) *adj.* **1.** small in size; tiny: *the diminutive hands of a baby.* **2.** *Grammar.* expressing smallness, familiarity, or affection. For example, *-let* in *droplet* and *-ie* in *Annie* are diminutive suffixes. —*n.* **1.** a small kind or variety of something. **2.** a word formed from another either by change in structure or by the addition of a suffix, expressing smallness, familiarity, or affection. *Piglet* is a diminutive of *pig.* The nickname *Joe* is a diminutive of *Joseph.*

dim·i·ty (dim'i tē) *n., pl.* **dim·i·ties.** a sheer, crisp cotton fabric, usually woven with heavy, raised threads forming a striped or checkered arrangement, used for such items as blouses, dresses, or curtains.

dim·mer (dim'ər) *n.* **1.** a device that dims an electric light. **2.** A device that switches automobile headlights between high beam and low beam.

dim·ple (dim'pəl) *n.* a small, slight hollow in the surface of the skin, especially as formed in the chin, or in the cheek in the act of smiling. —*v.,* **dim·pled, dim·pling.** —*v.t.* to mark with dimples: *A smile dimpled his cheeks.* —*v.i.* to form dimples: *Her face dimpled when she smiled.*

dim sum (dim' sum') **1.** in Chinese cooking, a dish consisting usually of steamed or fried dumplings stuffed with meats, fish, or vegetables. **2.** an assortment of such delicacies served as a meal. [From the Cantonese phrase *dím sàm* meaning "small heart" or "small center" used as the name of this food.]

din (din) *n.* loud, continuous noise or clatter: *the din of machines in a factory, the din of a New Year's Eve party.* —*v.,* **dinned, din·ning.** —*v.t.* to say over and over in a persistent way: *Why are you dinning your complaints into my ear?* —*v.i.* to make a din.

di·nar (di när') *n.* **1.** a unit of money in various countries, such as Yugoslavia, Iraq, Iran, Algeria, and Tunisia. **2.** an ancient gold coin used in Arab countries.

dine (dīn) *v.,* **dined, din·ing.** —*v.i.* **1.** to eat dinner: *The family always dines at six o'clock. Mom and Dad dined out to celebrate their anniversary.* **2.** to eat (with *on* or *upon*): *to dine on roast beef.* —*v.t.* to provide with dinner; give a dinner for: *to dine an important guest.*

din·er (dī'nər) *n.* **1.** a person who dines. **2.** another word for **dining car. 3.** a small, informal restaurant, sometimes designed to resemble a dining car.

di·nette (dī net') *n.* an alcove or small room used for dining.

ding (ding) *n.* **1.** a sound made by a bell. **2.** any similar sound. —*v.i.* to make a ringing sound. —*v.t.* to cause (something) to make a ringing sound.

ding–dong (ding'dông', ding'dong') *n.* **1.** the sound of a bell when it is struck repeatedly. **2.** any similar sound.

din·ghy (ding'ē) *n., pl.* **din·ghies.** a small, open boat, propelled either by oars or by an outboard motor or fitted with a small mast for sailing. Dinghies are often used as tenders for larger boats.

din·gle (ding'gəl) *n.* a small, wooded valley; dell.

din·go (ding'gō) *n., pl.* **din·goes.** a wild dog of Australia resembling a wolf, having pointed ears, reddish brown fur, and a long, bushy tail with a white tip.

din·gy (din'jē) *adj.,* **din·gi·er, din·gi·est.** having a dirty, dull, or dreary appearance; not bright and fresh: *The sheets looked dingy even after they were washed. The miser lived in a dingy one-room apartment.* —**din'gi·ly,** *adv.* —**din'gi·ness,** *n.*

dining car, a railroad car in

dingo

which meals are served to the passengers. Also, **diner.**

dining room, a room in which meals are served and eaten, as in a home or hotel.

dink·y (ding'kē) *adj.,* **dink·i·er, dink·i·est.** *Informal.* of little value, size, or importance; small or insignificant.

din·ner (din'ər) *n.* **1.** the principal meal of the day: *We eat dinner at our grandparents' house on Thanksgiving.* **2.** a formal meal in honor of some person or occasion; banquet: *There was a dinner after the wedding ceremony.*

din·ner·ware (din'ər wâr') *n.* the dishes, glasses, and utensils used to eat a meal.

din·o·flag·el·late (din'ə flaj'ə lāt') *n.* any of a large group of plankton found mostly in the ocean and having two whiplike flagella that help them move.

din·o·saur (dī'nə sôr') *n.* a member of a large group of extinct reptiles that lived millions of years ago. Dinosaurs were of various sizes, and some were the largest land animals that ever lived, growing to 87 feet (26.5 meters) long and weighing up to 50 tons (45 metric tons). Their existence is known from fossil remains of their bones.

dint (dint) *n.* **1.** force; power. ▲ now used chiefly in the phrase *by dint of: by dint of argument, by dint of effort.* **2.** another word for **dent.** —*v.t.* to make a dent in.

di·oc·e·san (dī os'ə sən) *adj.* of or relating to a diocese. —*n.* the bishop of a diocese.

di·o·cese (dī'ə sis, dī'ə sēz') *n., pl.* **di·o·ces·es** (dī'ə-sēz', dī'ə sis'iz). the church district under a bishop's authority.

di·ode (dī'ōd) *n.* an electronic component with two terminals, through which current can pass in only one direction.

Di·o·ny·sus (dī'ə nī'səs) *also,* **Di·o·ny·sos.** *n. Greek Mythology.* the god of fertility and wine. In Roman mythology he was called Bacchus.

di·o·ram·a (dī'ə ram'ə, dī'ə rä'mə) *n.* **1.** a picture viewed from a distance through a small opening, in which various realistic effects are produced by means of lighting and other devices. **2.** an exhibit consisting of sculptured figures, stuffed animals, or other lifelike models, placed in a realistic setting against a curved, painted background.

di·ox·ide (dī ok'sīd) *n.* an oxide containing two atoms of oxygen in each molecule.

dip (dip) *v.,* **dipped** or **dipt, dip·ping.** —*v.t.* **1.** to put or let down into something, especially a liquid, for a moment: *She dipped the brush into the paint. He dipped his hand into the bowl to pick the winning ticket.* **2.** to obtain or lift up and out by scooping: *to dip water from a pool.* **3.** to lower and raise again quickly: *to dip a flag in a salute.* **4.** to immerse (sheep or other animals) in a disinfectant or insecticide solution. **5.** to dye by immersing in a liquid. **6.** to make (a candle) by plunging a wick into melted tallow or wax over and over again. —*v.i.* **1.** to plunge into and then emerge from water or other liquid, especially quickly. **2.** to sink or go down: *The sun dipped below the horizon. Prices on the stock market dipped at the end of the week.* **3.** to slope downward: *The land dips as it meets the sea.* **4.** to reach into, especially in order to take something out: *I dipped into my pocket for some change.* —*n.* **1.** the act of dipping, especially a brief immersion in water: *They took a dip in the ocean.* **2.** a liquid preparation into which something is dipped, as for dyeing or disinfecting. **3.** a sudden drop or decline. **4.** a downward slope: *a dip in a road.* **5.** a creamy mixture intended to be scooped up on crackers or similar food. **6.** the quantity of something taken out or up by dipping; scoop: *a dip of ice cream.*

diph·the·ri·a (dif thîr'ē ə, dip thîr'ē ə) *n.* a serious bacterial disease that is highly contagious, characterized by fever and difficulty in breathing.

diph·thong (dif'thông, dip'thông) *n.* a blend of two vowel sounds in one syllable that is pronounced as one speech sound. The *ou* in *mouse* and the *oy* in *boy* are diphthongs.

di·plo·ma (di plō′mə) *n.* a certificate given by a school or college to a graduating student, showing that a program of study has been completed or that a degree has been granted.

di·plo·ma·cy (di plō′mə sē) *n.* **1.** the art or practice of managing political relations between nations and carrying on negotiations between governments. **2.** skill or tact in dealing with other people or with situations, especially so as to avoid anything that would be awkward or unpleasant: *You showed diplomacy in not pointing out my mistake in front of other people.*

dip·lo·mat (dip′lə mat′) *n.* **1.** a person who is employed or skilled in managing relations between nations, especially an official representing a government to a foreign country or international assembly. **2.** any person skilled in dealing with others; tactful person. Also, **diplomatist.**

dip·lo·mat·ic (dip′lə mat′ik) *adj.* **1.** of, relating to, or connected with relations between nations: *diplomatic affairs.* **2.** having or showing skill or tact in dealing with other people. —**dip′lo·mat′i·cal·ly,** *adv.*

diplomatic immunity, the freedom from taxes, duties, and legal proceedings that is granted to diplomats stationed in a foreign country.

di·plo·ma·tist (di plō′mə tist) *n.* another word for **diplomat.**

dip·per (dip′ər) *n.* **1.** a person or thing that dips. **2.** a cup-shaped container having a long, straight handle, used for scooping up liquids; ladle. **3. Dipper.** the Big Dipper or the Little Dipper.

dip·stick (dip′stik′) *n.* a graduated rod used to measure the amount of liquid in a space or container, as of oil in the crankcase of an automobile.

dipt (dipt) a past tense and past participle of **dip.**

dip·ter·ous (dip′tər əs) *adj.* of or belonging to an order of insects that have only one full pair of wings, including the gnat, mosquito, and housefly. The second set of wings appears as small appendages.

dip·tych (dip′tik) *n.* a double painting or carving consisting of two panels hinged together, especially one depicting a religious subject.

dire (dīr) *adj.,* **dir·er, dir·est.** **1.** causing great fear or suffering; dreadful; horrible: *a dire calamity, dire poverty.* **2.** extremely urgent; desperate: *The wounded soldier was in dire need of medical attention.* —**dire′ly,** *adv.* —**dire′ness,** *n.*

diptych

di·rect (di rekt′, dī rekt′) *v.t.* **1.** to manage or control the course or affairs of: *to direct traffic, to direct the affairs of a country.* **2.** to give instructions to; order; command: *The general directed the troops to attack.* **3.** to tell or show (someone) the way: *Can you direct me to the nearest police station?* **4.** to cause to move in a particular direction; turn; aim: *He directed his gaze to where she was pointing.* **5.** to intend (words) to be heard by someone; address: *The teacher directed the remarks to the entire class.* **6.** to lead, guide, or supervise the production or performance of: *to direct a film.* —*adj.* **1.** going in a straight line or by the shortest course: *a direct route.* **2.** with nothing or no one between; immediate: *direct contact.* **3.** straightforward; plain; honest: *a direct question.* **4.** in an unbroken line of descent: *a direct ancestor.* **5.** exact; absolute; complete: *the direct opposite.* **6.** in the exact words of the speaker or author: *a direct quotation.* **7.** of or by the action of the people or electorate without the work of representatives: *the direct election of senators.* —*adv.* directly: *This plane will fly direct to New York.* —**di·rect′ness,** *n.*

direct address *Grammar.* when speaking to someone, the use of the person's name or of a word identifying the person, as in the sentences *Kim, come here* and *Professor, I enjoyed your lecture.*

direct current, an electric current in which the flow of electrons is in one direction only.

di·rec·tion (di rek′shən, dī rek′shən) *n.* **1.** management or control; guidance: *The recruits are under the direction of a sergeant.* **2.** a line or course along which something moves, faces, or lies: *The direction of the airplane changed from north to northeast. They were walking in the direction of the park.* **3.** also, **directions.** an order or instruction about how to proceed or act: *Follow the doctor's directions. The directions on the package say to put the vegetables in boiling water.* **4.** a tendency or line of development: *That senator has made efforts in the direction of reform.* **5.** the supervision and organization of the parts and presentation of a play, film, or other performance.

di·rec·tion·al (di rek′shə nəl, dī rek′shə nəl) *adj.* **1.** of, relating to, or showing direction: *the directional signals of an automobile.* **2.** *Electronics.* able to send or receive signals in one direction only: *a directional antenna.*

direction finder, a radio receiving device that determines the direction of incoming radio signals, usually by means of a rotating antenna in the form of a loop or rectangle.

di·rec·tive (di rek′tiv, dī rek′tiv) *n.* an order, regulation, or instruction, especially one issued by a higher authority: *On the day of the maneuvers, all officers received directives from headquarters.*

di·rect·ly (di rekt′lē, dī rekt′lē) *adv.* **1.** in a direct line or manner; straight: *The car headed directly toward them.* **2.** without anything or anyone between: *The new clerk was directly responsible for the confusion.* **3.** without delay; at once: *to return directly.* **4.** exactly; absolutely: *His political views are directly opposed to hers.*

direct object, a word or words indicating the person or thing that receives the action expressed by a transitive verb. In the sentence *I hit the ball,* the direct object is *the ball.*

di·rec·tor (di rek′tər, dī rek′tər) *n.* **1.** a person or thing that manages or controls: *a camp director, a funeral director.* **2.** a person who supervises and guides the performers and technicians in the production of a film, play, television program, or other show or performance. **3.** one of a group of board members chosen to control or govern the affairs of a company or institution.

di·rec·tor·ate (di rek′tər it, dī rek′tər it) *n.* **1.** the office or position of director. **2.** a group of directors.

di·rec·to·ri·al (di rek tôr′ē əl, dī′rek tôr′ē əl) *adj.* **1.** of or relating to a director or directorate: *directorial duties.* **2.** that directs; directive: *a directorial memo.*

di·rec·to·ry (di rek′tə rē, dī rek′tə rē) *n.* **1.** an alphabetical or classified list, as of the names, addresses, or occupations of a group of people: *a company directory.* **2.** *Computers.* a listing of all the files stored in memory or on a disk.

direct primary, an election held to select a party candidate to run for office in a general election. The direct primary is an election by popular vote.

direct proportion, the mathematical relationship of two variables when one equals the other multiplied by a constant. For example, if $a = bc$, and c is a constant, then a and b are in direct proportion.

at; āpe; fär; câre; end; mē; it; īce; pîerce; hot; ōld; sông, fôrk; oil; out; up; ūse; rüle; pull; tûrn; chin; sing; shop; thin; this; hw in white; zh in treasure. The symbol ə stands for the unstressed vowel sound heard in about, taken, pencil, lemon, and circus.

di·rec·trix (di rek′triks, dī rek′triks) n., pl. **di·rec·trix·es.** *Geometry.* a fixed line that guides the motion of another line as it generates a surface or guides the motion of a point as it generates a curve.

direct tax, a tax levied directly on the persons who must pay it, such as an income tax.

dire·ful (dīr′fəl) adj. dire; dreadful; terrible. —**dire′ful·ly,** adv. —**dire′ful·ness,** n.

dirge (dûrj) n. a song, hymn, or tune of grief or mourning, especially one performed at a funeral.

dir·i·gi·ble (dir′i jə bəl, də rij′ə bəl) n. a lighter-than-air craft that is driven by motors and can be steered.

dirk (dûrk) n. another word for **dagger.**

dirn·dl (dûrn′dəl) n. **1.** a woman's dress with a fitted bodice and a full skirt gathered at the waist. **2.** a full skirt gathered at the waist.

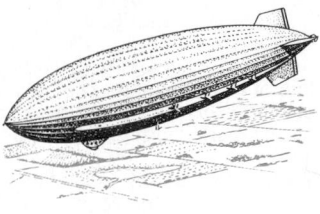
dirigible

dirt (dûrt) n. **1.** mud, dust, or other material that soils or makes something unclean: *We washed the dirt off the car.* **2.** earth or soil, especially when loose: *The gardener filled all the flowerpots with dirt.* **3.** something despised or worthless: *Your friends might treat you like dirt if you were convicted of a crime.* **4.** indecent writing, pictures, or speech. **5.** *Informal.* gossip, especially of a nasty or shocking nature.

dirt bike, a lightweight motorcycle specially designed for riding on dirt roads, trails, and the like.

dirt–cheap (dûrt′ chēp′) adj. very inexpensive: *That bookcase was dirt-cheap.* —adv. at a very low price: *We bought a used car dirt-cheap.*

dirt·y (dûr′tē) adj., **dirt·i·er, dirt·i·est. 1.** soiled with dirt; not clean; filthy: *a dirty towel.* **2.** tending to soil or make unclean: *Digging the hole was a hard and dirty job.* **3.** low or nasty; despicable: *a dirty trick.* **4.** not decent; vulgar; obscene: *a dirty joke.* **5.** not sportsmanlike; unfair: *a dirty fighter.* **6.** *Informal.* full of spite; resentful; insulting: *I gave them a dirty look when they laughed at my idea.* **7.** (of weather) stormy; unsettled. —v.t., v.i., **dirt·ied, dirt·y·ing.** to make or become dirty: *White shoes dirty easily.* —**dirt′i·ness,** n.

dis– prefix **1.** opposite or lack of; not: *disobedience.* **2.** undoing of; reverse of: *disconnect.* **3.** deprivation of; removal from: *dispossession.*

dis·a·bil·i·ty (dis′ə bil′i tē) n., pl. **dis·a·bil·i·ties. 1.** the loss or lack of ability; disabled condition: *The insurance policy covers disability arising from injury.* **2.** something that disables; handicap: *Not having a high school diploma can be a disability when looking for a job.*

dis·a·ble (dis ā′bəl) v.t., **dis·a·bled, dis·a·bling.** to take ability or power away from; make unable to move, work, or act as usual: *A broken leg disabled the athlete for months.* —**dis·a′ble·ment,** n.

dis·a·bled (dis ā′bəld) adj. **1.** having a disability; crippled: *These funds will finance a training program for disabled veterans.* **2.** broken or temporarily out of order: *a disabled vehicle.* —n. **the disabled.** people with a disability or disabilities, taken as a group.

dis·a·buse (dis′ə būz′) v.t., **dis·a·bused, dis·a·bus·ing.** to free from false or mistaken ideas: *I must disabuse you of that idea, because it is absolutely wrong.*

dis·ad·van·tage (dis′ad van′tij) n. **1.** something that interferes with or prevents success; drawback; handicap: *Being short is a disadvantage to a basketball player.* **2.** a loss; injury; harm: *It will be to your disadvantage if you turn down such a generous offer.*

dis·ad·van·taged (dis′ad van′tijd) adj. lacking a decent standard of living: *Many disadvantaged families live in slums.* —n. **the disadvantaged.** disadvantaged people, taken as a group.

dis·ad·van·ta·geous (dis ad′vən tā′jəs) adj. causing disadvantage; unfavorable. —**dis·ad′van·ta′geous·ly,** adv. —**dis·ad′van·ta′geous·ness,** n.

dis·af·fect (dis′ə fekt′) v.t. to destroy the affection or loyalty of; make unfriendly: *The brutal tactics of the new government disaffected many who had supported it.* —**dis′af·fec′tion,** n.

dis·a·gree (dis′ə grē′) v.i., **dis·a·greed, dis·a·gree·ing. 1.** to differ in opinion: *The teacher disagreed with my statement.* **2.** to quarrel; argue: *They disagreed violently, but they've since made up.* **3.** to fail to agree or harmonize: *The various newspaper accounts of the robbery disagreed.* **4.** to cause physical discomfort or ill effects (followed by with): *Hot weather disagrees with me. Spicy foods disagree with my stomach.*

dis·a·gree·a·ble (dis′ə grē′ə bəl) adj. **1.** not to one's taste or liking; unpleasant: *a disagreeable odor, a disagreeable task.* **2.** having a bad temper; nasty; quarrelsome: *You're often disagreeable in the morning.* —**dis′a·gree′a·ble·ness,** n. —**dis′a·gree′a·bly,** adv.

dis·a·gree·ment (dis′ə grē′mənt) n. **1.** a difference of opinion. **2.** a quarrel; argument. **3.** a failure to agree; difference: *The disagreement between the suspects' stories aroused the suspicion of the police.*

dis·al·low (dis′ə lou′) v.i. **1.** to deny the truth or validity of: *to disallow a claim.* **2.** to refuse to allow; prohibit: *to disallow gambling.*

dis·ap·pear (dis′ə pîr′) v.i. **1.** to pass from sight; vanish: *The sun disappeared below the horizon.* **2.** to cease to exist or be known: *The dinosaurs disappeared centuries ago.*

dis·ap·pear·ance (dis′ə pîr′əns) n. the act or fact of disappearing.

dis·ap·point (dis′ə point′) v.t. **1.** to fail to fulfill the hope, desire, or expectation of: *The team's poor showing in the game disappointed the coach.* **2.** to prevent the realization or fulfillment of (something); thwart; frustrate: *to disappoint a person's hopes.* —**dis′ap·point′ed,** adj.

dis·ap·point·ment (dis′ə point′mənt) n. **1.** the state or feeling of being disappointed: *We couldn't hide our disappointment when the experiment failed.* **2.** a person or thing that disappoints: *The failed experiment was a disappointment to the class.* **3.** the act or fact of disappointing.

dis·ap·pro·ba·tion (dis ap′rə bā′shən) n. disapproval.

dis·ap·prov·al (dis′ə prü′vəl) n. **1.** the act of disapproving. **2.** an unfavorable opinion or feeling; dislike: *I showed my disapproval by frowning.*

dis·ap·prove (dis′ə prüv′) v., **dis·ap·proved, dis·ap·prov·ing.** —v.t. **1.** to have or express an unfavorable opinion of (something); condemn: *My parents disapproved our rude behavior.* **2.** to refuse to approve; reject: *The boss disapproved your request for a vacation.* —v.i. to have or express an unfavorable opinion: *I disapprove of practical jokes that hurt people's feelings.* —**dis′ap·prov′ing·ly,** adv.

dis·arm (dis ärm′) v.t. **1.** to take a weapon or weapons from: *The sheriff disarmed the prisoners.* **2.** to relieve of anger, hostility, or suspicion: *The stranger's charming manner disarmed the frightened family.* **3.** to make harmless by removing the means to injure or attack: *to disarm a bomb.* —v.i. **1.** to lay down arms: *The rebels agreed to disarm.* **2.** to reduce, limit, or do away with military weapons or forces.

dis·ar·ma·ment (dis är′mə mənt) n. the act of disarming, especially the reduction, limitation, or elimination of military weapons or forces.

dis·arm·ing (dis är′ming) adj. tending to do away with anger, hostility, or suspicion: *a disarming smile.* —**dis·arm′ing·ly,** adv.

dis·ar·range (dis′ə rānj′) v.t., **dis·ar·ranged, dis·ar·rang-**

ing. to disturb the order or arrangement of; create disorder in: *I disarranged everything in the closet looking for the missing boot.* —**dis'ar·range'ment,** *n.*

dis·ar·ray (dis'ə rā') *n.* **1.** a condition of disorder or confusion; lack of orderly arrangement: *The burglars left the apartment in complete disarray.* **2.** a condition of disorder or incompleteness of dress: *When the fire broke out in the dormitory, the students ran from their rooms in disarray.* —*v.t.* to throw into disorder or confusion.

dis·as·sem·ble (dis'ə sem'bəl) *v.t.,* **dis·as·sem·bled, dis·as·sem·bling.** to take apart: *to disassemble an engine.*

dis·as·so·ci·ate (dis'ə sō'shē āt', dis'ə sō'sē āt') *v.t.,* **dis·as·so·ci·at·ed, dis·as·so·ci·at·ing.** to cut off association or connection with; separate from: *Both candidates disassociated themselves from their party's stand on that issue.* —**dis'as·so'ci·a'tion,** *n.*

dis·as·ter (di zas'tər) *n.* any event causing much suffering, distress, or loss; sudden or great misfortune. [From the French word *désastre* meaning "calamity," going back to the Latin words *dis-* "against" and *astrum* "star." The ancients believed that the stars controlled human fortunes and sometimes worked to bring about destruction.]

dis·as·trous (di zas'trəs) *adj.* causing or accompanied by disaster: *a disastrous flood, a disastrous mistake.* —**dis·as'trous·ly,** *adv.*

dis·a·vow (dis'ə vou') *v.t.* to deny knowledge of or responsibility for: *The suspect disavowed the confession even though the police had recorded it.*

dis·a·vow·al (dis'ə vou'əl) *n.* the act of disavowing.

dis·band (dis band') *v.t.* to break up, as a group or organization: *to disband a regiment.* —*v.i.* to stop functioning as an organized body; break up: *The club disbanded after three meetings.* —**dis·band'ment,** *n.*

dis·bar (dis bär') *v.t.,* **dis·barred, dis·bar·ring.** to expel (a lawyer) officially from the legal profession. —**dis·bar'ment,** *n.*

dis·be·lief (dis'bi lēf') *n.* lack of belief; refusal to believe: *Your face showed disbelief when you were told the news.*

dis·be·lieve (dis'bi lēv') *v.,* **dis·be·lieved, dis·be·liev·ing.** —*v.t.* to have no belief in (someone or something): *The police disbelieved the suspect's alibi.* —*v.i.* to refuse to believe in someone or something: *to disbelieve in the existence of ghosts.* —**dis'be·liev'er,** *n.*

dis·bur·den (dis bûr'dən) *v.t.* **1.** to rid of a burden or load: *to disburden a ship, to disburden an animal.* **2.** to relieve of something burdensome or oppressive: *to disburden one's conscience by telling the truth.*

dis·burse (dis bûrs') *v.t.,* **dis·bursed, dis·burs·ing.** to pay out (funds). —**dis·burs'er,** *n.*

dis·burse·ment (dis bûrs'mənt) *n.* **1.** the act of disbursing or paying out. **2.** the money paid out.

disc (disk) *n.* **1.** a phonograph record. **2.** another spelling of **disk.**

dis·card (*v.,* dis kärd'; *n.,* dis'kärd) *v.t.* **1.** to reject or give up as useless, worthless, or unwanted; cast aside: *The scientists discarded the old theory when the new one proved correct. I discarded my overcoat as soon as I entered the heated room.* **2.** *Card Games.* **a.** to throw away or put aside (an unwanted card or cards). **b.** to play (a card other than a trump or the suit led). —*n.* **1.** the act of discarding or the state of being discarded. **2.** a person or thing that is discarded. **3.** a card or cards discarded.

disc brake, a brake that operates by the friction of pads that press against both sides of a disk that rotates with a wheel.

dis·cern (di sûrn', di zûrn') *v.t.* **1.** to recognize as different and distinct; to separate or distinguish mentally: *to discern good from evil.* **2.** to make out or recognize: *We could barely discern the ship in the fog.* —*v.i.* to

see a difference; distinguish: *to discern between truth and falsehood.* —**dis·cern'er,** *n.*

dis·cern·i·ble (di sûr'nə bəl, di zûr'nə bəl) *adj.* able to be discerned. —**dis·cern'i·bly,** *adv.*

dis·cern·ing (di sûr'ning, di zûr'ning) *adj.* having or showing keen perception, judgment, or understanding: *a discerning judge of character, discerning taste in art.* —**dis·cern'ing·ly,** *adv.*

dis·cern·ment (di sûrn'mənt, di zûrn'mənt) *n.* **1.** the act of discerning. **2.** keenness of perception, judgment, or understanding; insight.

dis·charge (*v.,* dis chärj'; *n.,* dis'chärj) *v.,* **dis·charged, dis·charg·ing.** —*v.t.* **1.** to release from service, office, or employment; dismiss: *to discharge a worker, to discharge a soldier from the army.* **2.** to release from care or custody; grant liberty: *to discharge a prisoner, to discharge a patient from the hospital.* **3.** to let go or clear out; remove or unload: *The boat discharged its passengers at the pier.* **4.** to fulfill the requirements of; carry out: *to discharge an errand, to discharge a duty.* **5.** to fire; shoot: *to discharge a bow, to discharge a gun.* **6.** to send forth: *The river discharged its water into the bay.* **7.** to relieve of responsibility, duty, or obligation: *to discharge a jury.* **8.** to pay off; settle: *to discharge a debt.* **9.** to rid of an electric charge; withdraw electricity from: *to discharge a battery.* —*v.i.* **1.** to send forth contents: *The smaller pipes discharged into the main one.* **2.** to go off, as a firearm; fire. **3.** to lose an electrical charge. —*n.* **1.** a dismissal, as from service, office, or employment. **2.** release from care or custody: *the discharge of a prisoner.* **3.** something that dismisses or releases, such as a certificate discharging a person from military service. **4.** the act of firing or going off, as a weapon. **5.** the act of carrying out; performance: *to be faithful in the discharge of one's duties.* **6.** the act of flowing or letting out: *the discharge of rainwater from a sewer pipe.* **7.** something that is discharged or sent forth: *a watery discharge from an open sore.* **8.** the act of paying off or settling: *the discharge of a debt.* **9.** the act of removing contents or a burden; unloading: *the discharge of cargo.* **10.** the transference of electricity between two charged bodies.

dis·ci·ple (di sī'pəl) *n.* **1.** a follower of a particular teacher or doctrine: *Plato was a disciple of Socrates.* **2.** any of the early followers of Jesus, especially one of the Apostles.

dis·ci·pli·nar·i·an (dis'ə plə nâr'ē ən) *n.* a person who enforces or is in favor of strict discipline: *The captain was a stern disciplinarian who was feared by all the sailors.*

dis·ci·pli·nar·y (dis'ə plə ner'ē) *adj.* of, relating to, or used in discipline: *disciplinary measures.*

dis·ci·pline (dis'ə plin) *n.* **1.** training that molds, corrects, or perfects something, such as the mind or moral character. **2.** orderly, obedient, or restrained conduct; self-control: *The students showed excellent discipline during the fire drill.* **3.** punishment given to train or correct: *The child's rude behavior demanded severe discipline.* **4.** a branch of instruction or knowledge; field of study: *Mathematics and physics are related disciplines.* **5.** a set or system of rules for conduct: *Cadets at the academy must observe strict discipline.* —*v.t.,* **dis·ci·plined, dis·ci·plin·ing.** **1.** to train to be obedient; keep in order or under control: *to discipline troops.* **2.** to develop or train, as by instruction or exercise: *to discipline one's mind.* **3.** to punish.

---

at; āpe; fär; câre; end; mē; it; īce; pîerce; hot; ōld; sông, fôrk; oil; out; up; ūse; rūle; pùll; tûrn; chin; sing; shop; thin; <u>th</u>is; hw in white; zh in treasure. The symbol ə stands for the unstressed vowel sound heard in about, taken, pencil, lemon, and circus.

disc jockey

disc jockey *also,* **disk jockey.** an announcer or master of ceremonies on a radio program of recorded music.

dis·claim (dis klām′) *v.t.* **1.** to deny any claim to, responsibility for, or connection with; refuse to accept as one's own: *The driver disclaimed any responsibility for the accident.* **2.** to give up a legal right or claim to: *We disclaimed a share in our cousin's estate.*

dis·claim·er (dis klā′mər) *n.* something, such as a statement or written notice: that disclaims: *The mayor issued a disclaimer denying any knowledge of the scandal.*

dis·close (dis klōz′) *v.t.,* **dis·closed, dis·clos·ing. 1.** to make known; reveal: *to disclose a secret, to disclose one's intentions.* **2.** to expose to view; lay bare; uncover: *The excavation disclosed the ruins of an ancient city.*

dis·clo·sure (dis klō′zhər) *n.* **1.** the act of disclosing: *The disclosure of such information is against company rules.* **2.** something that is disclosed: *The news of the president's illness was a startling disclosure.*

dis·co (dis′kō) *n., pl.* **dis·cos. 1.** a form of popular music for dancing, often using electronically synthesized sounds, and characterized by a strong bass beat. **2.** see **disco·theque.** *—adj.* of or relating to disco or a discotheque: *disco songs.* *—v.i.* **dis·coed, dis·co·ing.** to dance to disco.

dis·col·or (dis kul′ər) *v.t.* to change or spoil the color of; stain: *Heat and smoke had discolored the kitchen wallpaper.* *—v.i.* to become changed or spoiled in color: *This fabric will discolor if washed in hot water.* **dis·col′ored,** *adj.*

dis·col·or·a·tion (dis kul′ə rā′shən) *n.* **1.** the act of discoloring or the state of being discolored. **2.** a discolored spot or mark; stain.

dis·com·bob·u·late (dis′kəm bob′yə lāt′) *v.t.,* **dis·com·bob·u·lat·ed, dis·com·bob·u·lat·ing.** *Informal.* to confuse; upset: *The roar of the crowd discombobulated the tennis player.*

dis·com·fit (dis kum′fit) *v.t.* **1.** to throw into confusion; embarrass: *The reporter's pointed question discomfited the mayor.* **2.** to defeat the plans or expectations of; frustrate: *The arrival of the police discomfited the thieves.* **3.** to defeat or overthrow in battle; rout.

dis·com·fi·ture (dis kum′fi chər) *n.* the act of discomfiting or the state of being discomfited.

dis·com·fort (dis kum′fərt) *n.* **1.** lack of comfort; uneasiness: *The question caused me discomfort because I did not know the answer.* **2.** something that causes discomfort: *Sleeping on the couch for one night shouldn't be a discomfort for you.* *—v.t.* to make uncomfortable or uneasy.

dis·com·mode (dis′kə mōd′) *v.t.,* **dis·com·mod·ed, dis·com·mod·ing.** to cause inconvenience to; disturb; trouble.

dis·com·pose (dis′kəm pōz′) *v.t.,* **dis·com·posed, dis·com·pos·ing.** to disturb the calm or composure of; make

nervous or uneasy: *The jeers of the crowd did not discompose the speaker.*

dis·com·po·sure (dis′kəm pō′zhər) *n.* the state of being discomposed: *The more they laughed at my mistake, the more my discomposure increased.*

dis·con·cert (dis′kən sûrt′) *v.t.* **1.** to disturb the self-possession or composure of; embarrass; confuse: *Their rude laughter disconcerted us.* **2.** to throw into disorder; upset or frustrate. *—dis′con·cert′ing·ly,* *adv.*

dis·con·nect (dis′kə nekt′) *v.t.* to break the connection of or between: *The technician disconnected the television set before fixing it. The workers disconnected the locomotive from the train.* *—dis′con·nec′tion,* *n.*

dis·con·nect·ed (dis′kə nek′tid) *adj.* **1.** lacking order or logic: *a disconnected speech, disconnected thoughts.* **2.** physically or electronically separated, broken, or ended: *a disconnected telephone.* *—dis′con·nect′ed·ly,* *adv.* *—dis′con·nect′ed·ness,* *n.*

dis·con·so·late (dis kon′sə lit) *adj.* so sad as to be without cheer, hope, or comfort: *The children were disconsolate after their pet ran away.* *—dis·con′so·late·ly,* *adv.* *—dis·con′so·late·ness,* *n.*

dis·con·tent (dis′kən tent′) *n.* lack of contentment; dissatisfaction; restlessness: *Overcrowding in the jails caused much discontent among the prisoners.* Also, **discontentment.** *—v.t.* to make discontented. *—adj.* discontented: *The player was discontent with the way the manager ran the team.*

dis·con·tent·ed (dis′kən ten′tid) *adj.* uneasy in mind; not contented; dissatisfied; restless. *—dis′con·tent′ed·ly,* *adv.* *—dis′con·tent′ed·ness,* *n.*

dis·con·tent·ment (dis′kən tent′mənt) *n.* another word for **discontent.**

dis·con·tin·u·a·tion (dis′kən tin′ū ā′shən) *n.* the act of discontinuing or the state of being discontinued. Also, **dis·con·tin·u·ance** (dis′kən tin′ū əns).

dis·con·tin·ue (dis′kən tin′ū) *v.,* **dis·con·tin·ued, dis·con·tin·u·ing.** *—v.t.* to put an end or halt to; stop: *I discontinued my subscription to the magazine.* *—v.i.* to come to an end: *Publication of the newspaper discontinued.*

dis·con·ti·nu·i·ty (dis′kon tə nü′i tē, dis′kon tə nū′i tē) *n., pl.* **dis·con·ti·nu·i·ties. 1.** a lack of continuity. **2.** a gap or break.

dis·con·tin·u·ous (dis′kən tin′ū əs) *adj.* not continuous; interrupted; broken. *—dis′con·tin′u·ous·ly,* *adv.*

dis·cord (dis′kôrd) *n.* **1.** a lack of agreement or harmony; disagreement; conflict: *There was constant discord among the members of the committee.* **2.** harsh, clashing, or unpleasant sounds. **3.** *Music.* lack of harmony in notes sounded at the same time; dissonance.

dis·cord·ant (dis kôr′dənt) *adj.* **1.** not in agreement or harmony; disagreeing; conflicting: *discordant opinions.* **2.** harsh, clashing, or unpleasant in sound: *discordant noises.* *—dis·cor′dance,* *n.* *—dis·cord′ant·ly,* *adv.*

dis·co·theque (dis′kō tek′) *n.* a nightclub or other place for dancing, especially to recorded music.

dis·count (*n.,* dis′kount′; *v.,* dis′kount′, dis kount′) *n.* a deduction of a specified amount or percentage, as from a price or other amount: *to sell a radio at a 25% discount.* *—v.t.* **1.** to offer for sale at a reduced rate: *That store discounts its merchandise.* **2.** to take off or deduct (a specified amount or percentage) from the total amount charged or owed: *The seller discounted 15% from the price.* **3.** to view as exaggerated or not entirely true: *Discount most of the stories about that athlete's ability.*

dis·coun·te·nance (dis koun′tə nəns) *v.t.,* **dis·coun·te·nanced, dis·coun·te·nanc·ing. 1.** to look upon with disfavor or disapproval; discourage: *The school discountenanced the students' plans for raising money.* **2.** to make ashamed or embarrassed: *The discovery of the error discountenanced us.*

dis·cour·age (dis kûr′ij, dis kur′ij) *v.t.,* **dis·cour·aged,**

dis·cour·ag·ing. 1. to lessen the courage, hope, or confidence of; dishearten: *I won the race because my slow start did not discourage me.* **2.** to try to prevent by expressing disapproval of; frown upon: *The principal discouraged unexcused absences.* **3.** to prevent, interfere with, or hinder: *Bad weather discouraged them from going on a picnic. Strict laws were passed in an attempt to discourage crime.*

dis·cour·age·ment (dis kûr′ij mənt, dis kur′ij mənt) *n.* **1.** the act of discouraging. **2.** the state or feeling of being discouraged: *The team was filled with discouragement by the defeat.* **3.** something that discourages: *Failure to pass an examination can be a discouragement.*

dis·course (*n.,* dis′kôrs; *v.,* dis kôrs′) *n.* **1.** a formal speech or writing, as a lecture or sermon: *The guest speaker gave a discourse on prehistoric people.* **2.** conversation; talk. —*v.i.,* **dis·coursed, dis·cours·ing.** to speak or write formally and at length on a subject: *The police chief discoursed on the need for more public cooperation in fighting crime.*

dis·cour·te·ous (dis kûr′tē əs) *adj.* not courteous; rude; impolite: *a discourteous reply.* —**dis·cour·te·ous·ly,** *adv.* —**dis·cour·te·ous·ness,** *n.*

dis·cour·te·sy (dis kûr′tə sē) *n., pl.* **dis·cour·te·sies. 1.** lack of courtesy; rudeness; impoliteness: *I was offended by your discourtesy in not introducing me.* **2.** a discourteous act: *It would be a discourtesy to leave the party without thanking our hosts.*

dis·cov·er (dis kuv′ər) *v.t.* **1.** to come upon or see (something) for the first time: *De Soto discovered the Mississippi River.* **2.** to learn of; come to know of: *We discovered the mistake too late.* —**dis·cov·er·er,** *n.*

dis·cov·er·y (dis kuv′ə rē) *n., pl.* **dis·cov·er·ies. 1.** the act of discovering: *The discovery of the error was too late.* **2.** something discovered: *The dollar in my pocket was a pleasant discovery.*

dis·cred·it (dis kred′it) *v.t.* **1.** to cause to be doubted or disbelieved; destroy belief, confidence, or trust in: *New facts discredited the old theory.* **2.** to damage the credit or reputation of; disgrace: *The unsportsmanlike conduct of the football team discredited the entire school.* **3.** to refuse to believe or give credit to: *I discredit all rumors.* —*n.* **1.** lack or loss of credit or reputation: *conduct that brings discredit on an entire family.* **2.** lack or loss of belief, confidence, or trust; doubt: *If you get into the habit of lying, you will bring everything you say into discredit.* **3.** something that discredits: *That one dishonest deal is a discredit to the good name of the firm.*

dis·cred·it·a·ble (dis kred′i tə bəl) *adj.* bringing discredit; disgraceful: *Lying is a discreditable act.* —**dis·cred′it·a·bly,** *adv.*

dis·creet (di skrēt′) *adj.* having or showing tact and careful judgment in speech and action; prudent: *Be discreet enough not to reveal the secret.* —**dis·creet′ly,** *adv.* —**dis·creet′ness,** *n.*

▲ **Discreet** and **discrete** are pronounced alike, but they have different meanings. **Discreet** means prudent or careful: *The diplomat had to be discreet in discussing the country's foreign policy.* **Discrete** means separate or distinct: *The patient was given discrete injections of two different drugs.*

dis·crep·an·cy (dis skrep′ən sē) *n., pl.* **dis·crep·an·cies.** lack of agreement or consistency; difference; variation: *a discrepancy in the testimony of the witnesses.*

dis·crep·ant (di skrep′ənt) *adj.* lacking agreement or consistency; conflicting or inconsistent: *discrepant descriptions of an accident by two witnesses.*

dis·crete (di skrēt′) *adj.* detached from others; separate; distinct: *The word ''heart'' has several discrete meanings.* ▲ See **discreet** for usage note. —**dis·crete′ly,** *adv.* —**dis·crete′ness,** *n.*

dis·cre·tion (di skresh′ən) *n.* **1.** the quality of being discreet; good judgment; caution; prudence: *You showed much discretion in not revealing who told you the story.* **2.** the freedom or power to act according to one's own judgment: *The students left the choice of how much to spend on the teacher's gift to my discretion.*

dis·cre·tion·ar·y (di skresh′ə ner′ē) *adj.* left to or determined by one's own judgment or discretion: *The delegate to the conference was given discretionary powers.*

dis·crim·i·nate (di skrim′ə nāt′) *v.i.,* **dis·crim·i·nat·ed, dis·crim·i·nat·ing. 1.** to act or treat differently without a sound reason; show prejudice: *It is against the law to discriminate against people because of their race or religion.* **2.** to notice a difference; make a distinction: *to discriminate between good and bad poetry.* —**dis·crim′i·na′tor,** *n.*

dis·crim·i·nat·ing (di skrim′ə nā′ting) *adj.* **1.** noticing and making distinctions with accuracy; keen: *a discriminating judge of character.* **2.** noticing or paying attention to small details; particular: *to be discriminating in one's choice of clothes.* **3.** making or forming a difference: *The color of their eyes is a discriminating feature between the twins.* **4.** showing prejudice. —**dis·crim′i·nat′ing·ly,** *adv.*

dis·crim·i·na·tion (di skrim′ə nā′shən) *n.* **1.** the act of discriminating. **2.** unfair difference in treatment; prejudice: *The applicants were judged without discrimination as to race, color, or creed.* **3.** the ability to make distinctions with accuracy; keen judgment: *They showed taste and discrimination in furnishing their home.*

dis·crim·i·na·to·ry (di skrim′ə nə tôr′ē) *adj.* showing or marked by prejudice, especially racial prejudice: *Discriminatory practices in hiring people for jobs are against the law.* —**dis·crim′i·na·to′ri·ly,** *adv.*

dis·cur·sive (dis kûr′siv) *adj.* wandering from one subject to another: *The professor's discursive lecture soon confused most of the students.*

dis·cus (dis′kəs) *n.* a heavy, circular plate that is thrown for distance in athletic contests to test skill and strength.

dis·cuss (di skus′) *v.t.* to exchange or present ideas or opinions about; consider in conversation or writing: *The council discussed plans for a new city hall. This article discusses the American Revolution.*

dis·cus·sion (di skush′ən) *n.* **1.** the act of discussing: *The student's question at the end of the speech started a discussion.* **2.** an instance of discussing: *The book's discussion of the Middle Ages was thirty pages long.*

dis·dain (dis dān′) *n.* a feeling of contempt and dislike for something or someone thought of as unworthy or beneath one; scorn: *Don't treat the younger children with disdain.* —*v.t.* to consider unworthy or beneath oneself; look down on; scorn: *Despite their poverty the old couple disdained charity.*

dis·dain·ful (dis dān′fəl) *adj.* feeling or showing disdain; scornful. —**dis·dain·ful·ly,** *adv.*

dis·ease (di zēz′) *n.* **1.** a disturbance in the function of an organ or an organism resulting from a specific cause or causes, such as infection, and characterized by particular symptoms: *Mumps is usually a childhood disease. Many elm trees have died from a disease spread by insects.* **2.** any harmful condition: *Poverty is a disease of society.*

dis·eased (di zēzd′) *adj.* affected with or suffering from disease: *a diseased tree.*

dis·em·bark (dis′em bärk′) *v.i.* to get off a ship or airplane: *The tourists from Europe disembarked at New*

---

at; āpe; fär; câre; end; mē; it; īce; pîerce; hot; ōld; sông, fôrk; oil; out; up; ūse; rüle; pùll; tûrn; chin; sing; shop; thin; this; hw in white; zh in treasure. The symbol ə stands for the unstressed vowel sound heard in about, taken, pencil, lemon, and circus.

York. —*v.t.* to put or let off a ship or airplane: *to disembark passengers at a port.* —**dis·em·bar·ka·tion** (dis em'bär kā'shən), *n.*

dis·em·bod·ied (dis'em bod'ēd) *adj.* separated from the body: *disembodied spirits.*

dis·em·bow·el (dis'em bou'əl) *v.t.* to take out the bowels or entrails of. —**dis'em·bow'el·ment,** *n.*

dis·en·chant (dis'en chant') *v.t.* to free from enchantment or pleasant illusion; disillusion: *They had thought the area was scenic, but they were disenchanted when they visited it.* —**dis'en·chant'ment,** *n.*

dis·en·cum·ber (dis'en kum'bər) *v.t.* to relieve or free from something that burdens or troubles: *The tired shoppers disencumbered themselves of their packages.*

dis·en·fran·chise (dis'en fran'chīz) *v.t.,* **dis·en·fran·chised, dis·en·fran·chis·ing.** to take away a right or privilege from, especially the right to vote. Also, **disfranchise.** —**dis'en·fran'chise·ment,** *n.*

dis·en·gage (dis'en gāj') *v.,* **dis·en·gaged, dis·en·gag·ing.** —*v.t.* **1.** to release or loosen from something that holds, connects, or entangles: *to disengage the arrow from the target.* **2.** to free, as from an engagement, promise, or obligation: *We disengaged ourselves from the business deal as soon as we realized it was a fraud.* —*v.i.* to release, detach, or free oneself: *The two wrestlers disengaged.* —**dis'en·gage'ment,** *n.*

dis·en·tan·gle (dis'en tang'gəl) *v.,* **dis·en·tan·gled, dis·en·tan·gling.** —*v.t.* to free from tangles or confusion: *The child disentangled the kite string. The detective tried to disentangle the witness's story.* —*v.i.* to become free from tangles or confusion. —**dis'en·tan'gle·ment,** *n.*

dis·es·teem (dis'e stēm') *v.t.* to have a low opinion of. —*n.* lack of esteem; disfavor: *That theory is held in disesteem by most scientists.*

dis·fa·vor (dis fā'vər) *n.* **1.** displeasure or lack of favor; dislike; disapproval: *The students looked with disfavor on the plan to shorten the spring vacation.* **2.** the state of being regarded unfavorably: *The student who cheated fell into disfavor with the class.* **3.** an unkind, unfair, or damaging act: *I did you a disfavor by not sticking up for you.* —*v.t.* to dislike; disapprove.

dis·fig·ure (dis fig'yər) *v.t.,* **dis·fig·ured, dis·fig·ur·ing.** to spoil or destroy the beauty or appearance of: *Scars from the accident disfigured the patient's face. Billboards disfigured the view from the highway.* —**dis·fig'ure·ment,** *n.*

dis·fran·chise (dis fran'chīz) *v.t.,* **dis·fran·chised, dis·fran·chis·ing.** another word for **disenfranchise.** —**dis·fran'chise·ment,** *n.*

dis·gorge (dis gôrj') *v.t.,* **dis·gorged, dis·gorg·ing.** **1.** to throw up (something swallowed); vomit. **2.** to throw or pour (something) forth, especially with force: *The volcano disgorged lava and smoke. The crowded bus disgorged its passengers at the station.*

dis·grace (dis grās') *n.* **1.** loss of honor, respect, or favor; shame: *to bring disgrace upon one's good name.* **2.** the state of being dishonored or out of favor: *The president of the company resigned in disgrace when the fraud was discovered.* **3.** a person or thing that brings about shame, dishonor, or reproach: *These slum conditions are a disgrace to the city.* —*v.t.,* **dis·graced, dis·grac·ing.** **1.** to bring shame, dishonor, or reproach to or upon: *to disgrace one's family.* **2.** to dismiss from favor or grace; treat with disfavor: *The monarch disgraced the disloyal adviser in front of the entire court.*

dis·grace·ful (dis grās'fəl) *adj.* characterized by, deserving, or causing disgrace; shameful: *disgraceful behavior.* —**dis·grace'ful·ly,** *adv.* —**dis·grace'ful·ness,** *n.*

dis·grun·tle (dis grun'təl) *v.t.,* **dis·grun·tled, dis·grun·tling.** to put in a bad humor; make dissatisfied, displeased, or cross: *Annoying tasks always disgruntle me.* —**dis·grun'tled,** *adj.* —**dis·grun'tle·ment,** *n.*

dis·guise (dis gīz') *v.t.,* **dis·guised, dis·guis·ing. 1.** to change the appearance or dress to hide the identity of: *The children disguised themselves as ghosts on Halloween.* **2.** to hide; conceal: *Disguise the taste of the cough medicine by mixing it with orange juice. He disguised his sadness with a happy smile.* —*n.* **1.** something that disguises: *A wig was part of her clever disguise.* **2.** the act of disguising: *The spy was a master of disguise.* **3.** the state of being disguised: *a blessing in disguise.*

dis·gust (dis gust') *n.* a feeling of extreme dislike or distaste: *They were filled with disgust by such obvious lies.* —*v.t.* to cause strong distaste or loathing in; sicken: *The piles of garbage during the sanitation strike disgusted many people.*

dis·gust·ed (dis gus'tid) *adj.* filled with or showing disgust: *a disgusted look, a disgusted person.* —**dis·gust'ed·ly,** *adv.*

dis·gust·ing (dis gus'ting) *adj.* causing disgust; offensive. —**dis·gust'ing·ly,** *adv.*

dish (dish) *n., pl.* **dish·es. 1.** a plate, shallow bowl, or other similar container used for holding or serving food. **2.** a single serving of food on or in a dish; dishful: *to have a dish of ice cream for dessert.* **3.** food prepared in a particular way: *Spaghetti is my favorite dish.* **4.** a radio, radar, or television antenna with a reflector shaped like a bowl. —*v.t.* to put or serve in a dish (usually with *up* or *out*): *The cook dished up dinner as soon as everyone sat down.*

dish *(def. 4)*

dish·cloth (dish'klôth') *n.* a cloth used for washing dishes. Also, **dishrag.**

dis·heart·en (dis här'tən) *v.t.* to cause to lose hope or courage; discourage; depress: *Losing the game disheartened the team.* —**dis·heart'en·ing·ly,** *adv.*

di·shev·eled (di shev'əld) also, **di·shev·elled.** *adj.* not neat or in order; rumpled; tousled; untidy: *disheveled hair, a disheveled appearance.*

dish·ful (dish'fŭl') *n., pl.* **dish·fuls.** the amount that a dish can hold.

dis·hon·est (dis on'ist) *adj.* **1.** given to lying, stealing, or cheating; not honest: *a dishonest person.* **2.** characterized by or showing a lack of honesty: *The salesperson used dishonest methods to sell the product.* —**dis·hon'est·ly,** *adv.*

dis·hon·es·ty (dis on'ə stē) *n., pl.* **dis·hon·es·ties. 1.** lack of honesty. **2.** a dishonest act or statement.

dis·hon·or (dis on'ər) *n.* **1.** lack or loss of honor or reputation; shame; disgrace: *to prefer death to dishonor.* **2.** a person or thing that causes shame or disgrace: *It is no dishonor to admit you are wrong if you make a mistake.* —*v.t.* to bring shame or disgrace to: *The traitor dishonored the army.*

dis·hon·or·a·ble (dis on'ər ə bəl) *adj.* **1.** characterized by or causing dishonor; shameful; disgraceful: *dishonorable conduct.* **2.** lacking honor; without honor: *a dishon-*

orable person. —dis·hon′or·a·ble·ness, n. —dis·hon′or·a·bly, adv.

dish·rag (dish′rag′) n. another word for **dishcloth**.

dish·tow·el (dish′tou′əl) n. a towel for drying dishes.

dish·wash·er (dish′wô′shər, dish′wosh′ər) n. 1. a machine for washing dishes and cooking utensils. 2. a person who washes dishes and cooking utensils, especially in a restaurant or similar establishment.

dish·wa·ter (dish′wô′tər) n. water in which dishes are washed or have been washed.

dis·il·lu·sion (dis′i lü′zhən) v.t. to free from an illusion or false idea, especially a false idea about the truth or goodness of someone or something: *The scandals in the city government disillusioned the mayor's admirers.* —n. freedom from illusion; disillusionment.

dis·il·lu·sion·ment (dis′i lü′zhən mənt) n. the act of disillusioning or the state of being disillusioned.

dis·in·cli·na·tion (dis in′klə nā′shən) n. a slight distaste or unwillingness: *The lazy child had a disinclination to do hard work.*

dis·in·cline (dis′in klīn′) v.t., **dis·in·clined, dis·in·clin·ing.** to make unwilling: *The low salary disinclined me to take the job.* —dis′in·clined′, adj.

dis·in·fect (dis′in fekt′) v.t. to destroy disease-causing microorganisms in: *to disinfect a hospital room.* —dis′in·fec′tion, n.

dis·in·fect·ant (dis′in fek′tənt) n. a substance used to destroy disease-causing microorganisms. —adj. serving to disinfect: *a disinfectant soap.*

dis·in·her·it (dis′in her′it) v.t. to exclude (an heir) from an inheritance or from the right to inherit: *Their parents threatened to disinherit them if they married at such a young age.* —dis′in·her′it·ance, n.

dis·in·te·grate (dis in′ti grāt′) v., **dis·in·te·grat·ed, dis·in·te·grat·ing.** —v.i. 1. to break up into particles, fragments, or parts: *This type of rock disintegrates under pressure.* 2. to fall apart or be destroyed by breaking into parts: *The empire disintegrated after it lost the war.* 3. *Physics.* to undergo a nuclear change as a result of radioactive decay. —v.t. to cause to disintegrate: *The floodwaters disintegrated the foundations of the house.* —dis·in′te·gra′tion, n.

dis·in·ter (dis′in tûr′) v.t., **dis·in·terred, dis·in·ter·ring.** 1. to remove from a grave or tomb; dig up: *to disinter a body.* 2. to bring to light; reveal: *The reporter disinterred unknown facts about the author's early life.* —dis′in·ter′ment, n.

dis·in·ter·est·ed (dis in′trə stid, dis in′tə res′tid) adj. not having a personal interest in a matter; not influenced by selfish motives; impartial: *A judge should take a disinterested view of the cases that come before the court.* ▲ See **uninterested** for usage note. —dis·in′ter·est·ed·ly, adv. —dis·in′ter·est·ed·ness, n.

dis·joint (dis joint′) v.t. 1. to take apart or separate at the joints: *to disjoint a turkey.* 2. to put out of joint; dislocate: *I fell and disjointed my shoulder during track practice.* 3. to disturb or destroy the order, connection, or unity of: *Racial or religious conflict disjoints a society.* —adj. *Mathematics.* (of sets) having no members in common. The sets [A, B, C], [1, 2, 3], and [½, ¼, ⅛] are disjoint.

dis·joint·ed (dis join′tid) adj. 1. lacking order, connection, or unity; disconnected; incoherent: *The dazed driver gave only a disjointed description of the accident.* 2. taken apart or separated at the joints: *a disjointed chicken.* —dis·joint′ed·ly, adv. —dis·joint′ed·ness, n.

disk (disk) *also,* **disc.** n. 1. a flat, thin, circular object, such as a coin, plate, or phonograph record.

disk of a sunflower

2. something that resembles a disk in appearance, such as the round, flat shape that a heavenly body seems to have when viewed from the earth: *the disk of the sun.* 3. *Computers.* a flat, circular piece of plastic or metal covered with a magnetic film on which information is stored. 4. a flat, circular part of a plant or animal, such as the center of a daisy and certain other flowers, or the rings of elastic tissue between the bones of the spinal column. —disk′like′, adj.

disk drive, a device in a computer that allows a user to store data on or retrieve it from a hard disk, floppy disk, or the like.

disk·ette (di sket′) n. a magnetic disk that is enclosed in a protective envelope, used to store computer data; floppy disk.

disk harrow, a farm tool that is used to break up and cultivate the soil, consisting of a series of sharp disks that are set on a rotating shaft.

disk jockey, another spelling of **disc jockey.**

dis·like (dis līk′) n. a feeling of not liking or being opposed to something; attitude of disapproval or displeasure; distaste: *I have a strong dislike for hot weather.* —v.t., **dis·liked, dis·lik·ing.** to have a feeling against; consider disagreeable; not like: *Do you dislike doing housework?*

dis·lo·cate (dis′lō kāt′, dis lō′kāt) v.t., **dis·lo·cat·ed, dis·lo·cat·ing.** 1. to upset the order of; throw into confusion; disrupt: *The nation's economy was dislocated by war.* 2. to put out of proper place or order; displace: *to dislocate a book on a library shelf.* 3. to put (a limb) out of joint: *The skater fell on the ice and dislocated an arm.* —dis′lo·ca′tion, n.

dis·lodge (dis loj′) v.t., **dis·lodged, dis·lodg·ing.** to move or force out of a place or position: *The avalanche dislodged large rocks from the cliff. The hounds managed to dislodge the fox from its hiding place.*

dis·loy·al (dis loi′əl) adj. going against one's allegiance; not loyal; unfaithful: *It was disloyal of them to hope that their own team would lose the game.* —dis·loy′al·ly, adv.

dis·loy·al·ty (dis loi′əl tē) n., pl. **dis·loy·al·ties.** 1. lack of loyalty; unfaithfulness: *We were greatly saddened by the disloyalty of our friends during our time of need.* 2. a disloyal act.

dis·mal (diz′məl) adj. 1. causing gloom or depression; dreary; miserable: *It was a damp and dismal winter day. The forest was a dismal sight after the fire.* 2. feeling gloom; depressed: *I was dismal because I had failed the test.* 3. very bad; dreadful; terrible: *The project was a dismal failure.* [Anglo-Norman *dis mal* evil days; originally referring to certain days being marked as unlucky on calendars of the Middle Ages.] —dis′mal·ly, adv. —dis′mal·ness, n.

dis·man·tle (dis man′təl) v.t., **dis·mantled, dis·man·tling.** 1. to pull down or take apart; disassemble: *to dismantle a machine for shipment.* 2. to strip of covering, furniture, or equipment: *Dismantle the room before you start painting.* —dis·man′tle·ment, n.

dis·may (dis mā′) *v.t.* **1.** to fill with fear or alarm; take away the courage of; make afraid: *The sight of the enemy forces dismayed the soldier.* **2.** to trouble or discourage greatly; depress; dishearten: *The audience's lack of interest dismayed the speaker.* —*n.* a feeling of alarm or uneasiness; frightened amazement: *We were filled with dismay when we heard the bad news.*

dis·mem·ber (dis mem′bər) *v.t.* **1.** to cut or tear off the limbs of; tear limb from limb: *The lion dismembered the dead antelope.* **2.** to divide into parts or sections: *The conquering nations dismembered the defeated country.* —**dis·mem′ber·ment,** *n.*

dis·miss (dis mis′) *v.t.* **1.** to send away or allow to leave: *The teacher dismissed the class.* **2.** to discharge, as from a position or job; fire: *to dismiss an employee for stealing.* **3.** to put aside from attention or serious consideration; reject: *to dismiss a story as a rumor.* **4.** *Law.* to dispense with (an action or suit) without further hearing: *The judge dismissed the case because of lack of evidence.*

dis·miss·al (dis mis′əl) *n.* **1.** the act of dismissing or the state of being dismissed. **2.** a written or spoken order dismissing someone, as from a job: *Those employees will be given their dismissal at the end of the week.*

dis·mount (dis mount′) *v.i.* to get off or down, as from a horse; alight: *The rider dismounted from the bicycle.* —*v.t.* **1.** to remove (something) from its setting, support, or mounting: *to dismount a cannon.* **2.** to knock off or bring down, as from a horse; unseat: *The blow from an enemy's lance dismounted the knight.* **3.** to take apart; disassemble; dismantle: *to dismount a machine.*

dis·o·be·di·ence (dis′ə bē′dē əns) *n.* refusal or failure to obey an order or rule: *The child was punished for disobedience.*

dis·o·be·di·ent (dis′ə bē′dē ənt) *adj.* refusing or failing to obey; not obedient: *The disobedient child ignored the teacher's instruction to be quiet.* —**dis′o·be′di·ent·ly,** *adv.*

dis·o·bey (dis′ə bā′) *v.t.* to refuse or fail to obey (someone or something): *The soldier disobeyed the lieutenant's orders.* —*v.i.* to refuse or fail to obey: *That dog always disobeys.*

dis·o·blige (dis′ə blīj′) *v.t.,* **dis·o·bliged, dis·o·blig·ing.** to act contrary to the wishes of; refuse to oblige: *I don't like to disoblige you, but I won't be able to attend your party.*

dis·or·der (dis ôr′dər) *n.* **1.** lack of order or regular arrangement; confusion: *The room was in disorder after the police searched it for the missing jewels.* **2.** a breach of peace or public order, such as a riot; public disturbance: *The police tried to quiet the disorders in the streets.* **3.** a physical or mental sickness; ailment: *a disorder of the stomach, a nervous disorder.* —*v.t.* **1.** to disturb the order or regular arrangement of; throw into confusion: *Noisy demonstrations disordered the political convention.* **2.** to make physically or mentally sick.

dis·or·der·ly (dis ôr′dər lē) *adj.* **1.** lacking order or regular arrangement; messy; untidy: *The papers lay in a disorderly pile.* **2.** causing a public disturbance; uncontrolled; unruly: *a disorderly crowd.* **3.** guilty of disorderly conduct: *arrested for being drunk and disorderly.* —**dis·or′der·li·ness,** *n.*

disorderly conduct, any behavior that is considered to be a minor violation of public peace, order, or decency.

dis·or·gan·ize (dis ôr′gə nīz′) *v.t.,* **dis·or·gan·ized, dis·or·gan·iz·ing.** to upset or destroy the organization, arrangement, or order of; throw into confusion and disorder: *Heavy shelling by the enemy disorganized the army's retreat.* —**dis·or′gan·i·za′tion,** *n.*

dis·or·gan·ized (dis ôr′gə nīzd′) *adj.* lacking organization, arrangement, or order: *a disorganized project, a novel with a badly disorganized plot.*

dis·o·ri·ent (dis ôr′ē ent′) *v.t.* to disturb the sense of direction or position of; cause to lose one's bearings; mix up; confuse: *Wandering through the narrow, winding streets of the old city disoriented me. Revolution had disoriented the country's social order.* —**dis·o′ri·en·ta′tion,** *n.*

dis·own (dis ōn′) *v.t.* to refuse to recognize as one's own; deny responsibility for or connection with; reject: *The couple disowned their children and left their fortune to charity.*

dis·par·age (di spar′ij) *v.t.,* **dis·par·aged, dis·par·ag·ing.** **1.** to speak critically or slightingly of; belittle: *The candidate for mayor disparaged the achievements of the incumbent.* **2.** to bring discredit upon; lower in reputation. —**dis·par′age·ment,** *n.*

dis·par·ag·ing (di spar′i jing) *adj.* that disparages; belittling; slighting: *They made disparaging remarks about the strange statue.* —**dis·par′ag·ing·ly,** *adv.*

dis·par·ate (di spar′it, dis′pər it) *adj.* widely separated; unlike; dissimilar: *The two political parties have disparate points of view on that issue.* —**dis·par′ate·ly,** *adv.*

dis·par·i·ty (di spar′i tē) *n., pl.* **dis·par·i·ties.** lack of agreement or similarity; inequality or difference: *There is a great disparity between the report and what happened.*

dis·pas·sion·ate (dis pash′ə nit) *adj.* free from prejudice or strong feeling; unbiased; impartial: *an honest, dispassionate judge.* —**dis·pas′sion·ate·ly,** *adv.* —**dis·pas′sion·ate·ness,** *n.*

dis·patch (di spach′) *also,* **des·patch.** *v.t.* **1.** to send off quickly to a certain place or for a certain purpose: *to dispatch a telegram, to dispatch an official messenger.* **2.** to finish or dispose of quickly or promptly: *to dispatch a business deal.* **3.** to put to death; kill —*n., pl.* **dis·patch·es.** **1.** the act of dispatching: *the dispatch of a messenger.* **2.** prompt or quick action; quickness; speed: *The urgency of the situation called for great dispatch.* **3.** a written message sent off quickly or promptly, especially an official government or military communication. **4.** a news story or report, as from a special reporter or a news service: *The newspaper received a dispatch from its correspondent in London.*

dis·patch·er (di spach′ər) *also,* **des·patch·er.** *n.* **1.** a person who dispatches. **2.** a person who directs the arrivals and departures of trains, buses, taxicabs, or other scheduled modes of transport.

dis·pel (di spel′) *v.t.,* **dis·pelled, dis·pel·ling.** to drive away or cause to disappear; disperse: *The wind dispelled the smoke. Your reassuring words dispelled our doubts.*

dis·pen·sa·ble (di spen′sə bəl) *adj.* that can be done without; not essential; unimportant: *Because my suitcase was too heavy, I removed all the dispensable items.* —**dis·pen′sa·bil′i·ty,** *n.*

dis·pen·sa·ry (di spen′sə rē) *n., pl.* **dis·pen·sa·ries.** **1.** a room in which medicines and medical supplies are given out or dispensed: *a hospital dispensary.* **2.** a place where medicines and medical treatment are given without charge or for a small fee.

dis·pen·sa·tion (dis′pən sā′shən) *n.* **1.** the act of dispensing; giving out; distribution: *The dispensation of supplies in the disaster area was delayed.* **2.** something that is dispensed or distributed: *The victims received a financial dispensation from the government.* **3.** a system of administration; management; rule: *the dispensation of justice.* **4.** official permission to disregard a law, especially a church law: *a papal dispensation.*

dis·pense (di spens′) *v.t.,* **dis·pensed, dis·pens·ing.** **1.** to give or deal out in portions; distribute: *Various charities dispense clothing to the needy. This machine dispenses gum.* **2.** to prepare and give out (medicine), especially by a doctor's prescription. **3.** to carry out or apply; administer: *to dispense justice.*
·to dispense with. a. to get along without: *You can dispense with a coat now that the weather is warm.* **b.** to do away with; make unnecessary: *The speaker dispensed with formalities and started the discussion.*

dis·pens·er (di spen′sər) *n.* **1.** a person or thing that dispenses. **2.** a container or mechanical device that dispenses something in convenient units or portions: *a liquid soap dispenser was mounted above the sink.*

dis·per·sal (di spûr′səl) *n.* the act of dispersing or the state of being dispersed; breaking up; scattering.

dis·perse (di spûrs′) *v.*, **dis·persed, dis·pers·ing.** —*v.t.* **1.** to break up and send off in different directions; scatter: *The police dispersed the crowd.* **2.** to drive away or cause to vanish; dispel: *The winds dispersed the smoke.* **3.** *Physics.* to separate (radiation) into its component parts according to frequency or wavelength. A beam of white light can be dispersed into a spectrum of colors by being passed through a prism. —*v.i.* to break up and go in different directions; scatter; dissipate: *The congregation dispersed when the service ended.*

dis·per·sion (di spûr′zhən, di spûr′shən) *n.* **1.** the act of dispersing or the state of being dispersed. **2.** *Physics.* the separation of radiation into its component parts according to frequency or wavelength.

dis·pir·it (di spir′it) *v.t.* to depress or lower the spirits of; discourage: *The failure of the experiments greatly dispirited the scientist.*

dis·pir·it·ed (di spir′i tid) *adj.* depressed; dejected; discouraged: *The dispirited team could no longer stop their opponents from scoring.* —**dis·pir′it·ed·ly,** *adv.* —**dis·pir′it·ed·ness,** *n.*

dis·place (dis plās′) *v.t.*, **dis·placed, dis·plac·ing. 1.** to take the place of; replace: *Television displaced motion pictures as America's most popular form of entertainment.* **2.** to move or shift from the usual or proper place or position. **3.** to force (someone) to leave home or country: *The apartment fire displaced five families.* **4.** to remove from a position or office: *to displace an officer of the government.* **5.** *Physics.* to take or occupy the space of (a certain weight or volume of fluid): *A floating object displaces an amount of water equal to its own weight.*

displaced person, a person driven or taken from his or her own country or region, usually as a result of war.

dis·place·ment (dis plās′mənt) *n.* **1.** the act of displacing or the state of being displaced. **2.** the distance that something has moved from its original place or position. **3.** *Physics.* the weight or volume of fluid displaced by a body floating or immersed in it. The weight of the fluid displaced by a floating body equals the weight of the body itself.

dis·play (di splā′) *v.t.* **1.** to expose to view; cause to be seen; exhibit; show: *to display a poster, to display a flag, to display data on a computer terminal.* **2.** to make obvious; reveal: *to display fear, to display one's ignorance.* **3.** to make a show of; show off; flaunt: *The couple proudly displayed their wealth.* —*n.* **1.** the act of displaying: *a display of anger.* **2.** an exhibition or show: *The museum had a display of early American furniture.* **3.** something that is displayed or exhibited: *The display of flowers at the show was beautifully arranged.* **4.** a showing off: *Their neighbors were offended by their display of wealth.* **5.** *Electronics.* a device that provides a visual representation of information, as on a computer, digital watch, or calculator: *an LED display.*

dis·please (dis plēz′) *v.*, **dis·pleased, dis·pleas·ing.** —*v.t.* to fail to please; cause annoyance to; offend; irritate. —*v.i.* to cause displeasure or annoyance.

dis·pleas·ure (dis plezh′ər) *n.* the state or feeling of being displeased; annoyance; disapproval: *Her frown showed her displeasure with his behavior.*

dis·port (di spôrt′) *v.t.* to amuse or divert (oneself): *The puppies disported themselves in the yard.* —*v.i.* to play; frolic.

dis·pos·a·ble (di spō′zə bəl) *adj.* **1.** made to be thrown away after being used: *disposable paper napkins, disposable diapers.* **2.** free to be used; at hand; available: *disposable income.*

dis·pos·al (di spō′zəl) *n.* **1.** the act of getting rid of something; throwing away: *the disposal of garbage.* **2.** the act of dealing with or settling something: *the disposal of certain business matters.* **3.** a transferring of something to another, as by gift or sale: *the disposal of money in a will, the disposal of merchandise.*

·at one's disposal. available for use as one pleases: *The family car will be at your disposal this week.*

dis·pose (di spōz′) *v.t.* **dis·posed, dis·pos·ing. 1.** to make inclined or willing: *Favoritism disposed you to decide the contest in their favor.* **2.** to make susceptible or subject: *Frailness disposed the child to frequent illness.* **3.** to place in a particular order or position; arrange: *The farmer disposed the plants in rows.* —**dis·pos′er,** *n.*

·to dispose of. a. to get rid of; throw away: *to dispose of garbage.* **b.** to attend to or finish with; settle: *He quickly disposed of his work.* **c.** to part with, as by gift or sale; transfer to another: *She disposed of her country property.* **d.** to consume (food or drink).

dis·posed (di spōzd′) *adj.* having a tendency; willing or inclined: *That lazy student is not disposed to work hard.*

dis·po·si·tion (dis′pə zish′ən) *n.* **1.** a person's general or usual way of acting, thinking, or feeling; temperament; nature: *an irritable disposition, a pleasant disposition.* **2.** a tendency or inclination: *a disposition to accept the ideas of others too readily.* **3.** a placing or being placed in a particular order; arrangement: *the orderly disposition of trees in an orchard.* **4.** management or settlement: *the disposition of business affairs.* **5.** a transferring of something to another, as by gift or sale: *the disposition of property outlined in a will.*

dis·pos·sess (dis′pə zes′) *v.t.* to put out of possession of something, especially by legal action: *The landlord dispossessed the tenants for not paying their rent.* —**dis′pos·ses′sion,** *n.*

dis·proof (dis prüf′) *n.* **1.** the act of disproving; refutation: *There has been no disproof of this evidence as yet.* **2.** something that disproves.

dis·pro·por·tion (dis′prə pôr′shən) *n.* lack of proper proportion or symmetry; disparity: *There is a disproportion between the price of that house and its true value.*

dis·pro·por·tion·ate (dis′prə pôr′shə nit) *adj.* out of proportion in size, amount, or degree; lacking proportion: *The two arms of the statue are disproportionate to the body. Their salaries are disproportionate to the amount of work they do.* —**dis′pro·por′tion·ate·ly,** *adv.* —**dis′pro·por′tion·ate·ness,** *n.*

dis·prove (dis prüv′) *v.t.*, **dis·proved, dis·prov·ing.** to prove to be false or incorrect; refute: *The photograph disproves your claim that you have never met the defendant.*

dis·put·a·ble (di spü′tə bəl, dis′pyə tə bəl) *adj.* that can be disputed or called into question; debatable: *Whether or not the suspect is really guilty is disputable.*

dis·pu·tant (di spü′tənt) *n.* a person who takes part in a dispute, debate, or argument.

dis·pu·ta·tion (dis′pyü tā′shən) *n.* **1.** the act of disputing. **2.** a debate or argument.

dis·pute (di spüt′) *v.*, **dis·put·ed, dis·put·ing.** —*v.t.* **1.** to debate or quarrel about; discuss; argue: *The issue was disputed at the council meeting.* **2.** to deny or question the validity, accuracy, or existence of; express doubt or opposition to: *to dispute someone's authority, to dispute a statement.* **3.** to fight or compete for the possession of;

at; āpe; fär; câre; end; mē; it; īce; pîerce; hot; ōld; sông, fôrk; oil; out; up; ūse; rüle; pull; tûrn; chin; sing; shop; thin; this; hw in white; zh in treasure. The symbol ə stands for the unstressed vowel sound heard in about, taken, pencil, lemon, and circus.

strive or contend for: *The two countries disputed the territory located at their common border.* —*v.i.* to take part in argument, discussion, or debate: *The politicians disputed with each other on various issues.* —*n.* **1.** a difference of opinion; argument or debate: *A judge had to settle the dispute over the ownership of the house.* **2.** a quarrel: *a bitter dispute between two neighbors.*

dis·qual·i·fi·ca·tion (dis kwol′ə fi kā′shən) *n.* **1.** the act of disqualifying or the state of being disqualified. **2.** something that disqualifies: *A criminal conviction is a disqualification from police service.*

dis·qual·i·fy (dis kwol′ə fī′) *v.t.*, **dis·qual·i·fied, dis·qual·i·fy·ing. 1.** to make or declare unfit, unqualified, or unsuitable: *Poor eyesight disqualifies many from pilot training. Your age disqualifies you from voting.* **2.** to bar from competition or from winning a prize or contest: *The officials disqualified the runner from the race for leaving the racecourse.*

dis·qui·et (dis kwī′it) *v.t.* to make uneasy, anxious, or restless; disturb; alarm: *The bad news disquieted us.* —*n.* lack of calm or peacefulness; uneasiness; unrest: *There was a feeling of disquiet among the ship's passengers as the storm approached.*

dis·qui·e·tude (dis kwī′i tüd′, dis kwī′i tūd′) *n.* a state of uneasiness or unrest; anxiety; disquiet.

dis·qui·si·tion (dis′kwə zish′ən) *n.* a formal discussion or essay; dissertation.

dis·re·gard (dis′ri gärd′) *v.t.* to pay no attention to; treat without regard or respect; ignore: *I disregard all gossip and rumors. Don't disregard others' feelings on this matter.* —*n.* lack of attention or regard; neglect: *Your actions show a disregard for the school's regulations.*

dis·re·pair (dis′ri pâr′) *n.* the state of being in need of repairs; a poor, run-down condition: *The old house had fallen into disrepair.*

a house in **disrepair**

dis·rep·u·ta·ble (dis rep′yə tə bəl) *adj.* **1.** not having a good reputation; not reputable, respectable, or decent: *a disreputable company, a disreputable part of town.* **2.** not respectable in appearance; shabby: *a disreputable old jacket.* —**dis·rep′u·ta·ble·ness,** *n.* —**dis·rep′u·ta·bly,** *adv.*

dis·re·pute (dis′ri pūt′) *n.* lack or loss of reputation or regard; ill repute; discredit; disfavor: *That scientific theory is now in disrepute.*

dis·re·spect (dis′ri spekt′) *n.* lack of respect, reverence, or courtesy: *The child's rude and selfish actions showed disrespect for the rights of others.*

dis·re·spect·ful (dis′ri spekt′fəl) *adj.* having or show-ing disrespect; rude; impolite: *It was disrespectful of you to make such critical remarks about your guests.* —**dis′re·spect′ful·ly,** *adv.* —**dis′re·spect′ful·ness,** *n.*

dis·robe (dis rōb′) *v.*, **dis·robed, dis·rob·ing.** to undress or cause to be undressed: *to disrobe before bathing. The doctor disrobed the unconscious victim.*

dis·rupt (dis rupt′) *v.t.* to throw into disorder or confusion; break up or apart; upset: *A nearby police siren disrupted the class.* —**dis·rupt′er,** *n.*

dis·rup·tion (dis rup′shən) *n.* **1.** the act of disrupting or the state of being disrupted. **2.** a break; interruption.

dis·rup·tive (dis rup′tiv) *adj.* causing disruption: *a disruptive influence.* —**dis·rup′tive·ly,** *adv.* —**dis·rup′tive·ness,** *n.*

dis·sat·is·fac·tion (dis′sat is fak′shən, dis sat′is-fak′shən) *n.* a condition or feeling of being dissatisfied; discontent: *The mayor lost the election because of popular dissatisfaction.*

dis·sat·is·fac·to·ry (dis′sat is fak′tə rē, dis sat′is fak′-tə rē) *adj.* another word for **unsatisfactory.**

dis·sat·is·fied (dis sat′is fīd′) *adj.* **1.** not satisfied; displeased: *The dissatisfied workers struck for higher wages.* **2.** showing discontent or displeasure: *a dissatis-fied look.*

dis·sat·is·fy (dis sat′is fī′) *v.t.*, **dis·sat·is·fied, dis·sat·is·fy·ing.** to fail to satisfy; cause discontent to; disappoint; displease: *The actor's poor performance dissatisfied the film's director.*

dis·sect (di sekt′, dī sekt′) *v.t.* **1.** to cut apart or divide into parts for the purpose of study or scientific examination: *The biology student dissected a frog.* **2.** to examine carefully and critically; analyze in great detail: *The teacher dissected the poem and explained it to the class.*

dis·sec·tion (di sek′shən, dī sek′shən) *n.* **1.** the act of dissecting: *the dissection of an earthworm to study its parts.* **2.** something that has been dissected, as an animal being studied. **3.** a detailed analysis or criticism.

dis·sem·ble (di sem′bəl) *v.*, **dis·sem·bled, dis·sem·bling.** —*v.t.* **1.** to disguise or conceal the true nature of (one's character, feelings, or intentions): *to dissemble one's excitement by acting bored.* **2.** to put on a false appearance of; pretend; feign: *The corrupt official dissembled honesty.* —*v.i.* to disguise or conceal one's true character, feelings, or intentions by pretense. —**dis·sem′bler,** *n.*

dis·sem·i·nate (di sem′ə nāt′) *v.t.*, **dis·sem·i·nat·ed, dis·sem·i·nat·ing.** to scatter widely; spread abroad; diffuse: *to disseminate information, to disseminate leaf-lets.* —**dis·sem′i·na′tion,** *n.*

dis·sen·sion (di sen′shən) *n.* a strong difference of opinion or feeling; disagreement; conflict: *There was dissension among the president's advisors.*

dis·sent (di sent′) *v.i.* **1.** to differ in opinion or feeling; withhold approval; disagree: *Many people dissented from the policy of the government.* **2.** to refuse to conform to the rules, doctrines, or beliefs of an established church. —*n.* **1.** strong difference of opinion or feeling; disagreement; opposition: *A dictatorship does not permit dissent in political matters.* **2.** refusal to conform to the rules, doctrines, or beliefs of an established church.

dis·sent·er (di sen′tər) *n.* **1.** a person who dissents. **2.** *also,* **Dissenter.** a person who refuses to conform to the rules, doctrines, or beliefs of an established church, especially the Church of England.

dis·ser·ta·tion (dis′ər tā′shən) *n.* a long, formal essay or discussion on a particular subject, especially one written to obtain the degree of doctor from a university.

dis·serv·ice (dis sûr′vis) *n.* harm; injury: *Those politi-cians did their party a great disservice by their dishonest actions.*

dis·sev·er (di sev′ər) *v.t.* to cut or divide into parts; sever; separate.

dis·si·dence (dis′i dəns) *n.* dissent; disagreement.

dis·si·dent (dis′i dənt) *adj.* not agreeing; dissenting: *dissident views on an issue.* —*n.* a person who disagrees; dissenter.

dis·sim·i·lar (di sim′ə lər) *adj.* not similar or alike; different: *A deer and a bear are dissimilar animals. He and his sister have dissimilar interests.* —**dis·sim′i·lar·ly,** *adv.*

dis·sim·i·lar·i·ty (di sim′ə lar′i tē) *n., pl.* **dis·sim·i·lar·i·ties.** lack of similarity; difference: *There is great dissimilarity between the clothes of today and those worn in colonial times.*

dis·sim·u·late (di sim′yə lāt′) *v.t., v.i.,* **dis·sim·u·lat·ed, dis·sim·u·lat·ing.** to disguise or conceal (feelings or intentions) by pretense; dissemble. —**dis·sim′u·la′tion,** *n.*

dis·si·pate (dis′ə pāt′) *v.,* **dis·si·pat·ed, dis·si·pat·ing.** —*v.t.* **1.** to disperse or drive away; scatter; dispel: *The winds dissipated the haze.* **2.** to spend wastefully or foolishly; squander: *In three years the heirs dissipated the family fortune.* —*v.i.* **1.** to become dispersed or scattered; be dispelled: *By noon the mist had dissipated.* **2.** to indulge in foolish or extravagant pleasures, especially so as to harm oneself.

dis·si·pat·ed (dis′ə pā′tid) *adj.* given to indulging in harmful or foolish pleasures.

dis·si·pa·tion (dis′ə pā′shən) *n* **1.** the act of scattering or dispersing. **2.** indulgence in harmful or foolish pleasures.

dis·so·ci·ate (di sō′she at′, di sō′se at′) *v.t.,* **dis·so·ci·at·ed, dis·so·ci·at·ing.** to break the association or connection of; separate: *I dissociated myself from that club.* —*v.i.* Chemistry. to undergo dissociation.

dis·so·ci·a·tion (di sō′shē ā′shən, di sō′sē ā′shən) *n.* **1.** the act of dissociating or the state of being dissociated. **2.** *Chemistry.* the breakup of a substance into its components, as under heat or pressure.

dis·sol·u·ble (di sol′yə bəl) *adj.* able to be dissolved.

dis·so·lute (dis′ə lüt′) *adj.* wicked in conduct; immoral; corrupt: *a dissolute youth, a dissolute life.* —**dis′so·lute·ly,** *adv.* —**dis′so·lute′ness,** *n.*

dis·so·lu·tion (dis′ə lü′shən) *n.* **1.** a breaking up; ending: *the dissolution of a business.* **2.** the act or process of changing from a solid or liquid to a gas. **3.** separation into parts; disintegration.

dis·solve (di zolv′) *v.,* **dis·solved, dis·solv·ing.** —*v.t.* **1.** to cause (a substance) to change from a solid or gas into a liquid; cause to pass into solution with a liquid: *The chef dissolved the sugar in the boiling water.* **2.** to separate into parts; disintegrate. **3.** to put an end to; terminate: *to dissolve a partnership.* —*v.i.* **1.** to pass into solution; become liquid: *The ice cubes in the drink dissolved.* **2.** to dwindle or disappear gradually; fade away: *Our prospects for winning the election were dissolving rapidly.* **3.** to break up; disperse: *The fog dissolved.* **4.** in motion pictures and television, to change scenes by having one image gradually fade out of view as the next image gradually appears. —**dis·solv′a·ble,** *adj.*

dis·so·nance (dis′ə nəns) *n.* **1.** a harsh or unpleasant sound or combination of sounds; discord. **2.** lack of harmony or agreement; disagreement.

dis·so·nant (dis′ə nənt) *adj.* **1.** harsh or unpleasant in sound; not harmonious. **2.** lacking harmony or agreement; at variance; disagreeing: *dissonant views on a subject.* —**dis′so·nant·ly,** *adv.*

dis·suade (di swād′) *v.t.,* **dis·suad·ed, dis·suad·ing.** to keep (someone) from doing something by persuasion or advice: *She dissuaded him from resigning his job.*

dis·sua·sion (di swā′zhən) *n.* the act of dissuading.

dis·sua·sive (di swā′siv) *adj.* tending or meant to dissuade. —**dis·sua′sive·ly,** *adv.* —**dis·sua′sive·ness,** *n.*

dist. **1.** distance. **2.** district.

dis·taff (dis′taf) *n.* a stick on which wool, flax, cotton, or other fibers are held for use in spinning, either by hand or with a spinning wheel.

distaff side, the mother's side of a family.

Distaff
Spindle
distaff

dis·tance (dis′təns) *n.* **1.** the amount of space between two things, objects, or points: *The distance from the hospital to the school is ten blocks.* Astronomers can measure the distance of the moon from the earth. **2.** a far-off point or place; distant region or position: *The driver saw another car in the distance.* **3.** the fact or quality of being distant. —*v.t.,* **dis·tanced, dis·tanc·ing.** to leave far behind, as in a race; outdistance.
·**to keep one's distance.** to remain aloof or reserved.

dis·tant (dis′tənt) *adj.* **1.** far off or away in space; not near: *Pluto is a distant planet. The ranch is distant from the nearest town.* **2.** separated (from); removed (from): *The highway is eight miles distant from the house.* **3.** far away in time: *Dinosaurs lived in the distant past.* **4.** to or from a distance: *a distant rumble of thunder.* **5.** far apart or remote in relationship, connection, or degree: *distant cousins.* **6.** not friendly or familiar; cool in manner: aloof; reserved: *They've been very distant toward me since our argument.* —**dis′tant·ly,** *adv.*

dis·taste (dis tāst′) *n.* lack of taste or liking for something; dislike: *to have a distaste for spinach, to have a distaste for hard work.*

dis·taste·ful (dis tāst′fəl) *adj.* causing dislike; unpleasant; disagreeable; offensive: *Arguing or shouting in public is distasteful behavior.* —**dis·taste′ful·ly,** *adv.* —**dis·taste′ful·ness,** *n.*

dis·tem·per (dis tem′pər) *n.* any one of several highly contagious diseases of dogs, cats, and certain other animals, caused by a virus. Distemper often causes death, especially among puppies and cats. [From the Late Latin word *distemperare* meaning "to put out of order," "mix badly," from the Latin prefix *dis-* meaning "apart" + *temperare* meaning "to mix in proper proportion."]

dis·tend (di stend′) *v.t.* to enlarge by pressure from within; stretch out; swell; expand: *Water pressure had distended the weak spot in the hose.* —*v.i.* to become distended; swell: *My stomach distended because of my illness.*

dis·til (di stil′) *v.,* **dis·tilled, dis·til·ling.** *British.* another spelling of **distill.**

dis·till (di stil′) *also, British,* **dis·til.** *v.t.* **1.** to heat (a liquid or other substance) until evaporation takes place and then condense the vapor given off: *to distill water in order to purify it.* **2.** to produce by distilling: *to distill whiskey, to distill alcohol from grain.* **3.** to obtain as if by distilling; extract the essence of: *to distill wisdom from experience, to distill a moral from a story.* —*v.i.* **1.** to undergo distillation. **2.** to fall in drops; trickle.

dis·til·late (dis′tə lit, dis′tə lāt′) *n.* **1.** a product obtained by distillation. **2.** any central or essential part; essence.

at; āpe; fär; câre; end; mē; it; īce; pîerce; hot; ōld; sông, fôrk; oil; out; up; ūse; rüle; pùll; tûrn; chin; sing; shop; thin; *this;* hw in white; zh in treasure. The symbol ə stands for the unstressed vowel sound heard in about, taken, pencil, lemon, and circus.

dis·til·la·tion (dis'tə lā'shən) *n.* **1.** the act or process of separating the parts of a liquid or other substance that boil at a lower temperature from those that boil at a higher temperature, by heating until evaporation takes place and then condensing the vapor given off. **2.** something that is distilled; extract: *a distillation of a long speech.* **3.** the state of being distilled.

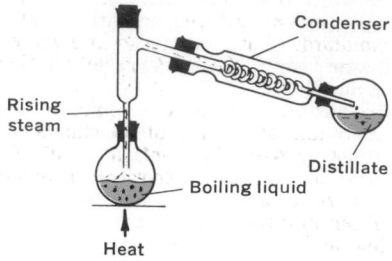

distillation *(def. 1)*

dis·till·er (di stil'ər) *n.* **1.** a person or thing that distills. **2.** a person or company that makes distilled liquors, such as rye, bourbon, or vodka.

dis·till·er·y (di stil'ə rē) *n., pl.* **dis·till·er·ies.** a place where distilling is performed, especially an industrial plant where distilled liquors are made.

dis·tinct (di stingkt') *adj.* **1.** not the same; not identical; separate: *The twins had distinct personalities.* **2.** different in quality or kind: *The Spanish language is distinct from Japanese.* **3.** clearly seen, heard, or understood; clear; plain: *The sound of the drums was distinct even from a distance.* **4.** unquestionable; definite; unmistakable: *There has been a distinct improvement in your work.* **—dis·tinct'ly,** *adv.* **—dis·tinct'ness,** *n.*

dis·tinc·tion (di stingk'shən) *n.* **1.** the act of making or noting a difference: *to make a distinction between truth and fiction.* **2.** the condition or quality of being distinct; difference: *The distinction between a dog and a cat is clear.* **3.** a distinguishing mark or characteristic: *That student has the distinction of being the fastest runner in the school.* **4.** a quality that makes a person worthy of special recognition or honor; excellence; superiority: *to receive an award for distinction in art.* **5.** a mark or symbol of special recognition or honor.

dis·tinc·tive (di stingk'tiv) *adj.* serving to distinguish or having a distinguishing quality; characteristic: *the distinctive scent of roses.* **—dis·tinc'tive·ly,** *adv.* **—dis·tinc'tive·ness,** *n.*

dis·tin·guish (di sting'gwish) *v.t.* **1.** to recognize or indicate as different: *to distinguish gold from brass, to distinguish a counterfeit bill from a genuine one.* **2.** to be a distinctive characteristic or quality of; characterize: *Brilliant red plumage distinguishes the male cardinal from the female.* **3.** to see or hear clearly; discern; perceive: *They could see three people walking toward them but could not distinguish their faces in the fog.* **4.** to make famous or worthy of special notice: *Those senators have distinguished themselves as advocates of civil rights.* *—v.i.* to recognize or show a difference: *to distinguish between a poisonous snake and a harmless one.* **—dis·tin'guish·a·ble,** *adj.*

dis·tin·guished (di sting'gwisht) *adj.* **1.** famous for significant achievement or excellent qualities; eminent; celebrated: *a distinguished diplomat, a distinguished scientist.* **2.** having the look of a famous or important person; dignified: *Their uniforms made them look quite distinguished.*

dis·tort (di stôrt') *v.t.* **1.** to twist or bend out of shape; change the natural or usual form of: *The curved mirror distorted my image.* **2.** to change so as to give a false impression; misrepresent: *The newspaper distorted my meaning by misquoting me.*

dis·tor·tion (di stôr'shən) *n.* **1.** the act of distorting. **2.** the state of being distorted. **3.** something that is distorted: *That account of the trial is filled with distortions.*

dis·tract (di strakt') *v.t.* **1.** to turn away the mind or attention of; divert: *Noise distracted me from my homework.* **2.** to confuse or perplex; unsettle; disturb: *A series of questions from customers distracted the new salesclerk.* **3.** to disturb or agitate the mind of: *Worry about their missing child distracted the parents.*

dis·trac·tion (di strak'shən) *n.* **1.** the act of turning away the mind or attention. **2.** something that draws away the mind or attention: *The parade outside was a distraction to the students in the classroom.* **3.** great confusion or agitation of the mind: *Your constant yelling nearly drove us to distraction.* **4.** something that relieves or relaxes the mind; amusement; diversion: *Building model airplanes is a pleasant distraction for me.*

dis·traught (di strôt') *adj.* **1.** mentally confused or bewildered; very upset; distracted: *The passengers were distraught with fear as the storm approached.* **2.** crazed; mad.

dis·tress (di stres') *n.* **1.** great suffering of body or mind; pain or sorrow; misery: *The famine brought distress to the people.* **2.** something that causes pain or suffering: *His sister's illness was a great distress to him.* **3.** a condition or situation of danger, trouble, or great need. *—v.t.* to cause pain, suffering, or sorrow to: *The bad news from home distressed them.* **—dis·tress'ing·ly,** *adv.*

dis·tress·ful (di stres'fəl) *adj.* causing or bringing distress; painful. **—dis·tress'ful·ly,** *adv.*

dis·trib·ute (di strib'ūt) *v.t.,* **dis·trib·ut·ed, dis·trib·ut·ing.** **1.** to divide and give out in shares; deal out: *The teacher distributed books to the students.* **2.** to scatter or spread out over an area or surface: *The farmer distributed seed over the plowed land.* **3.** to divide or arrange into groups or categories; classify: *The scientists distributed the plants they had found according to their species.*

dis·tri·bu·tion (dis'trə bū'shən) *n.* **1.** the act of distributing: *the distribution of clothes and food to flood victims.* **2.** the way in which something is distributed: *an uneven distribution of work.* **3.** something that is distributed: *water distribution to farmland.* **4.** the process or system by which goods are sent from those who produce them to those who use them.

dis·trib·u·tive (di strib'yə tiv) *adj.* **1.** of or relating to distribution. **2.** *Grammar.* referring to each member of a group considered individually. *Each* and *every* are distributive words. **3.** *Mathematics.* relating to a law or principle stating that the product of multiplication is the same when the operation is performed on a whole set as when it is performed on the individual members of the set. For example: $4 \times (2 + 5) = 4 \times 2 + 4 \times 5$ and $a \times (b + c) = (a \times b) + (a \times c)$. *—n. Grammar.* a distributive word or expression. **—dis·trib'u·tive·ly,** *adv.*

dis·trib·u·tor (di strib'yə tər) *n.* **1.** a person or thing that distributes. **2.** a person or company that sells goods to retailers or consumers. **3.** a device that distributes electric current to the spark plugs of a gasoline engine so that they fire in proper sequence.

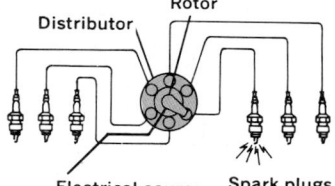

distributor *(def. 3)*

dis·trict (dis'trikt) *n.* **1.** a division of a country, state, city, or other area, marked off for a special purpose: *a school district, an election district.* **2.** any region or locality having a particular characteristic: *the theater district of a city.* *—v.t.* to divide or organize into districts. [From the French word *district,* from the Medieval Latin word *districtus* meaning "jurisdiction," from the Latin word *districtus,* past participle of *distringere* "to stretch out."]

district attorney, a lawyer who acts as an attorney for the government in a certain district, such as a county. A district attorney prosecutes persons accused of crime.

dis·trust (dis trust') *v.t.* to have no trust or confidence in; be suspicious of; doubt: *I distrust that television commercial.* —*n.* lack of trust or confidence; suspicion.

dis·trust·ful (dis trust'fəl) *adj.* having or showing distrust; suspicious; doubtful: *distrustful of fast-talking salespeople.* —**dis·trust'ful·ly**, *adv.* —**dis·trust'ful·ness**, *n.*

dis·turb (di stûrb') *v.t.* **1.** to make uneasy or anxious: *The news of the accident disturbed him.* **2.** to break in upon; interrupt; bother: *Don't disturb her while she's working.* **3.** to interfere with the peace or quiet of: *The noisy trucks disturbed the neighborhood.* **4.** to upset the order or arrangement of: *The child disturbed the toys on the shelf.* —**dis·turb'er**, *n.*

dis·turb·ance (di stûr'bəns) *n.* **1.** the act of disturbing or the state of being disturbed. **2.** something that disturbs: *Their noisy laughter was a disturbance to the others in the room.* **3.** noise and confusion; uproar: *The police officer went to see what the disturbance was about.*

di·sul·fide (dī sul'fīd) *n.* a compound in which two atoms of sulfur are combined with another atom or radical.

dis·un·ion (dis ūn'yən) *n.* **1.** a breaking into parts; separation. **2.** lack of agreement or unity; disagreement.

dis·u·nite (dis'ū nīt') *v.,* **dis·u·nit·ed, dis·u·nit·ing.** —*v.t.* **1.** to break into parts; separate. **2.** to cause to disagree. —*v.i.* to come apart; become separate.

dis·u·ni·ty (dis ū'ni tē) *n.* lack of unity; disunion.

dis·use (dis ūs') *n.* lack of use: *The books have collected dust from disuse.*

ditch (dich) *n., pl.* **ditch·es.** a long, narrow hole dug in the ground; trench. —*v.t.* **1.** to land (a disabled airplane) on water. **2.** to throw into a ditch. **3.** to dig a ditch in or around. **4.** *Slang.* to get rid of; get away from: *The bank robbers ditched the stolen car.* —*v.i.* to land a disabled airplane on water.

dith·er (dith'ər) *n.* the condition of being stirred up, excited, and confused: *I was in a dither when I heard I had won the grand prize.*

dit·to (dit'ō) *n., pl.* **dit·tos. 1.** the same as appeared or was mentioned before. **2.** see **ditto mark. 3.** a copy; duplicate.

ditto mark, one of a pair of small marks (″) placed under something written or printed to show that it is to be repeated.

dit·ty (dit'ē) *n., pl.* **dit·ties.** a short, simple song.

di·ur·nal (dī ûr'nəl) *adj.* **1.** occurring every day; daily: *the diurnal ebb and flow of the tides.* **2.** of, occurring, or active during the daytime: *An animal that hunts during the day is diurnal.* **3.** (of a flower) opening during the day and closing at night. —**di·ur'nal·ly**, *adv.*

di·va (dē'və) *n., pl.* **di·vas.** a famous female opera singer; prima donna.

di·van (di van', dī'van) *n.* a long, low couch or sofa, usually having no back or arms.

dive (dīv) *v.,* **dived** or **dove, dived, div·ing.** —*v.i.* **1.** to plunge headfirst, as into water: *He dived into the pool.* **2.** to plunge downward rapidly at a steep angle: *The submarine dived. The bomber dove toward its target.* **3.** to go, dash, or drop suddenly and quickly: *The frightened children dived under the covers when they heard the thunder.* **4.** to enter deeply into something: *She dove into her studies.* —*v.t.* to send (an aircraft) into a dive. —*n.* **1.** a headfirst or downward plunge, as into water. **2.** a steep, rapid plunge, as of an aircraft. **3.** *Informal.* a cheap, low nightclub, tavern, or bar.

dive bomber, a plane that dives down steeply toward the target as its bombs are released.

div·er (dī'vər) *n.* **1.** a person or thing that dives. **2.** a person who works or explores underwater. **3.** any of various diving birds, such as the loon.

di·verge (di vûrj', dī vûrj') *v.,* **di·verged, di·verg·ing.** —*v.i.* **1.** to move in different directions from a common point or from each other; draw apart; branch out: *The two*

roads ran side by side for several miles, and then diverged. **2.** to differ, as in opinion: *The two friends' tastes in music diverge.* **3.** to turn aside or deviate, as from a rule or standard. —*v.t.* to cause to diverge.

di·ver·gence (di vûr'jəns, dī vûr'jəns) *n.* **1.** the act of moving out in different directions from a common point. **2.** a difference, as of opinion. **3.** a turning aside or deviation, as from a rule or standard.

di·ver·gen·cy (di vûr'jən sē, dī vûr'jən sē) *n., pl.* **di·ver·gen·cies.** another word for **divergence.**

di·ver·gent (di vûr'jənt, dī vûr'jənt) *adj.* **1.** moving in different directions; diverging: *divergent paths.* **2.** differing, as in opinion. **3.** turning aside or deviating, as from a rule or standard. —**di·ver'gent·ly**, *adv.*

diverging lens, a lens that is thinner in the middle than at the edges. A diverging lens bends light waves away from its center.

diverging lenses

di·vers (dī'vərz) *adj.* various; several: *There are divers ways of doing the job.*

di·verse (di vûrs', dī vûrs', dī'vûrs) *adj.* **1.** different; unlike: *diverse opinions. The students in the class come from diverse backgrounds.* **2.** of different kinds; varied; diversified: *a diverse collection of shells, diverse interests.* —**di·verse'ly**, *adv.* —**di·verse'ness**, *n.*

di·ver·si·fi·ca·tion (di vûr'sə fi kā'shən, dī vûr'sə fi kā'shən) *n.* the act of diversifying or the state of being diversified.

di·ver·si·fy (di vûr'sə fī', dī vûr'sə fī') *v.,* **di·ver·si·fied, di·ver·si·fy·ing.** —*v.t.* to make diverse; give variety to; vary: *The hotel diversified its menu with Japanese, French, and Greek food.* —*v.i.* to deal in different products: *The company diversified, and began manufacturing toys as well as radios.*

di·ver·sion (di vûr'zhən, dī vûr'zhən) *n.* **1.** the act of diverting or the state of being diverted. **2.** something that distracts the attention: *Create a diversion while we sneak up on them from behind.* **3.** amusement; entertainment; pastime: *My favorite diversion is playing golf.*

di·ver·si·ty (di vûr'si tē, dī vûr'si tē) *n., pl.* **di·ver·si·ties. 1.** the condition of being diverse: *the diversity of a group of people.* **2.** variety: *a diversity of opinion.*

di·vert (di vûrt', dī vûrt') *v.t.* **1.** to change the direction or course of; turn aside: *The police diverted traffic from the scene of the accident.* **2.** to distract the attention of. **3.** to amuse; entertain: *The children were diverted by the clown's antics.*

di·vest (di vest', dī vest') *v.t.* **1.** to deprive (someone or oneself), as of a right. **2.** to strip, as of clothing or ornament. **3.** to rid of; renounce: *I divest myself of all claims to the property.* **4.** to sell off (an investment): *The company divested its holdings in the stock market.*

di·vide (di vīd') *v.,* **di·vid·ed, di·vid·ing.** —*v.t.* **1.** to separate into parts or pieces; split up: *The child divided the orange into four parts.* **2.** to separate into parts or pieces and give out; distribute; share: *We divided the profits among ourselves.* **3.** to cause to be separated into parts: *The fence divides our land from theirs.* **4.** to separate or arrange into groups: *The teacher divided the children in the class according to their reading level.* **5.** to separate into opposing sides or opinions; disunite:

---

at; āpe; fär; câre; end; mē; it; īce; pîerce; hot; ōld; sông, fôrk; oil; out; up; ūse; rüle; pùll; tûrn; chin; sing; shop; thin; <u>th</u>is; hw in white; zh in treasure. The symbol ə stands for the unstressed vowel sound heard in about, taken, pencil, lemon, and circus.

The argument divided the friends. **6.** *Mathematics.* to show how many times (one number) contains another number. For example, when you divide 8 by 2, you get 4 ($8 \div 2 = 4$), showing that 8 contains the number 2 four times. —*v.i.* **1.** to become separated into parts. **2.** to become separated into opposing sides: *The Senate divided on that issue.* —*n.* a ridge or other raised area of land separating two regions drained by different rivers and their tributaries; watershed. —**di·vid′ed,** *adj.*

div·i·dend (div′i dend′) *n.* **1.** the number or quantity that is to be divided by another number or quantity. When you divide 15 by 3, the dividend is 15. **2.** the money earned by a corporation for a particular period of time, divided among the stockholders as their share of the profits of the business. **3.** a share of such money given to a stockholder. **4.** a bonus or benefit.

di·vid·er (di vī′dər) *n.* **1.** a person or thing that divides. **2. dividers.** an instrument for measuring and marking distances.

div·i·na·tion (div′ə nā′shən) *n.* **1.** the art or practice of foretelling the future or the unknown by interpreting signs or omens or by magic. **2.** the act of divining. **3.** something that is divined; prophecy.

di·vine (di vīn′) *adj.* **1.** of or relating to God or a god: *divine will.* **2.** given by or coming from God or a god: *divine forgiveness.* **3.** directed toward or devoted to God or a god; sacred; religious: *divine worship.* **4.** having the nature or characteristics of God or a god; heavenly: *divine beauty.* **5.** excellent or extremely talented: *a divine poet.* **6.** *Informal.* extremely delightful: *The party was divine.* —*v.t.,* **di·vined, di·vin·ing. 1.** to foretell (the future or the unknown) by interpreting signs or omens or by magic. **2.** to guess: *You never divined that we had planned a surprise party for you.* —*n.* a clergyman; priest. —**di·vine′ly,** *adv.* —**di·vine′ness,** *n.* —**di·vin′er,** *n.*

diving bell, a large, hollow, watertight container open at the bottom and supplied with air, used for work underwater.

diving board, a springy board fastened at one end and extending out over water, especially over a swimming pool. An athlete jumps from the end of the board to begin a dive into the water. Also, **springboard.**

diving suit, a heavy, waterproof suit with a helmet, used for working under water. Air is supplied through tubes from the surface or from portable tanks worn by the diver.

divining rod, a forked branch or stick held by the ends and thought to be able to show where underground water or minerals can be found by bending downward at such a point.

di·vin·i·ty (di vin′i tē) *n., pl.* **di·vin·i·ties. 1.** the state or quality of being God or a god. **2.** a divine being; deity; god. **3.** the study of God and religion; theology: *a school of divinity in a university.* **4. the Divinity.** God.

di·vis·i·ble (di viz′ə bəl) *adj.* **1.** capable of being divided: *a divisible quantity.* **2.** capable of being divided without a remainder: *The number 8 is divisible by 2 and 4.* —**di·vis′i·bil′i·ty,** *n.*

di·vi·sion (di vizh′ən) *n.* **1.** the act of dividing or the state of being divided. **2.** one of the parts into which something is divided: *Poetry and grammar are two divisions of this English course.* **3.** something that divides: *The fence acted as a division between the two yards.* **4.** lack of agreement: *The divisions among the members caused the club to disband.* **5.** in modern armies, a unit that is part of a corps and is composed of different regiments. **6.** *Mathematics.* the process of dividing two numbers to show how many times one number contains the other number.

di·vi·sion·al (di vizh′ə nəl) *adj.* of or relating to a division.

division of labor, a system of working in which parts of the work are done by specific groups or individuals.

di·vi·sive (di vī′siv) *adj.* causing or tending to cause

disagreement or discord: *divisive political issues.* —**di·vi′sive·ly,** *adv.* —**di·vi′sive·ness,** *n.*

di·vi·sor (di vī′zər) *n.* **1.** the number or quantity by which another number or quantity is to be divided. When you divide 15 by 3, the divisor is 3. **2.** a number that divides another without leaving a remainder.

di·vorce (di vôrs′) *n.* **1.** the legal ending of a marriage. **2.** any complete separation. —*v.t.* **di·vorced, di·vorc·ing. 1.** to free oneself from (one's spouse) by divorce. **2.** to legally dissolve the marriage of: *The judge divorced the couple.* **3.** to separate; sever: *We divorced ourselves from the quarrel.* —*v.i.* to obtain a divorce.

di·vor·cé (di vôr sā′) *n.* a divorced man.

di·vor·cée (di vôr sā′, di vôr sē′) *n.* a divorced woman.

div·ot (div′ət) *n.* a piece of sod torn up by a golf club in making a stroke.

di·vulge (di vulj′, dī vulj′) *v.t.* **di·vulged, di·vulg·ing.** to make known; disclose: *to divulge a secret.*

div·vy (div′ē) *v.t.,* **div·vied, div·vy·ing.** *Informal.* to divide; allot; distribute (often used with *up*): *We divvied up the food left over and each took some home.*

Dix·ie (dik′sē) *n.* the South, especially the part of the South that was in the Confederate States of America. Also, **Dixieland.**

Dix·ie·land (dik′sē land′) *n.* **1.** a style of jazz developed in New Orleans. **2.** another name for **Dixie.**

diz·zy (diz′ē) *adj.,* **diz·zi·er, diz·zi·est. 1.** having the feeling of whirling and falling; giddy: *The children twirled until they were dizzy.* **2.** causing or tending to cause giddiness: *a dizzy height.* **3.** having a feeling of confusion or bewilderment. —*v.t.* to make dizzy. —**diz′zi·ly,** *adv.* —**diz′zi·ness,** *n.*

DMZ, demilitarized zone.

DNA, a nucleic acid found in the chromosomes of all living cells, consisting of a ladder-shaped strand made up of alternating units of sugar and phosphate connected by a nitrogen base. It carries hereditary information from parent to child and determines the exact structure of all the protein produced by the cells. [Short for *d*(eoxyribo)*n*(ucleic) *a*(cid).]

do¹ (dü) *v.,* **did** or (*archaic*) **didst, done, do·ing.** Present tense: *sing.,* first person **do;** second, **do** or (*archaic*) **do·est** or **dost;** third, **does** or (*archaic*) **do·eth** or **doth;** *pl.,* **do.** —*v.t.* **1.** to carry out or perform: *He always does his duty. The nurses did everything they could to make the patient comfortable.* **2.** to produce or create; make: *The artist did a sketch. She did her report on the causes of the American Revolution.* **3.** to bring to an end; complete; finish: *I have done the work I promised to do.* **4.** to deal with or take care of; attend to: *to do one's hair, to do the dishes.* **5.** to work out; solve: *The students couldn't do the algebra problem.* **6.** to bring about or be the cause of: *It'll do you good to take a vacation.* **7.** to give or grant: *He did his friend a good turn.* **8.** to work at, especially as a job: *What is she planning to do for a living when she graduates from college?* **9.** to satisfy the needs of; serve; suffice: *The extra money from home will do them for a while.* **10.** to travel at a speed of: *The car was doing 75 miles an hour.* —*v.i.* **1.** to behave or act in a certain way: *Please do as you are told.* **2.** to fare or manage; get along: *The patient is doing well.* **3.** to serve the purpose; be satisfactory: *That light jacket won't do for skiing.* **4.** used as a substitute for a verb already used, to avoid repetition: *You speak French as well as I do.* —*auxiliary verb.* **1.** used **a.** to ask a question: *Does she need a new coat?* **b.** to form an expression with *not: He does not want any. I did not find the book.* **2.** used to give emphasis: *Do be quiet! They do enjoy your company.* [From the Old English word *dōn* meaning "to do, make."]

·**to do away with. a.** to kill. **b.** to put an end to: *to do away with slavery.*

·**to do in.** *Informal.* **a.** to kill. **b.** to tire out: *All that walking really did us in.*

·**to do over. a.** to do again: *I made several typing mistakes on the first page, so I did it over.* **b.** to redecorate: *They did over the room with fresh paint and a new carpet.*

·**to do up.** *Informal.* **a.** to tie or wrap up: *The salesclerk did up the package.* **b.** to put in order; arrange: *I did up my hair.*

·**to make do.** to get along or manage: *They can make do without the extra money.*

do² (dō) *n.* *Music.* **1.** the first and last note of the major scale. **2.** the note C. [From the Italian word *do,* as the name of this note.]

do., ditto.

dob·bin (dob'in) *n.* a horse, especially a gentle, plodding one that does farm work.

Do·ber·man pin·scher (dō'bər mən pin'shər) a dog belonging to a breed originally developed in Germany, having a long head, slender legs, and usually a sleek, black or brown coat. [From the German phrase *Dobermann pinscher,* from the German dog breeder Ludwig *Dobermann* (1834–1894) + the word *pinscher,* a breed of hunting dog.]

Doberman pinscher

doc·ile (dos'əl) *adj.* easily managed, trained, or taught: *a docile pet, a docile child.* —**doc'ile·ly,** *adv.*

do·cil·i·ty (do sil'i tē) *n.* the state or quality of being docile.

dock¹ (dok) *n.* **1.** a structure built along the shore or out from the shore, used as a landing place where boats and ships can be tied up and passengers and cargo loaded and unloaded; wharf; pier. **2.** an area of water between two piers where boats and ships can be moored; slip. **3.** an area for loading or unloading goods, as from delivery trucks. **4.** see **dry dock.** —*v.t.* **1.** to bring (a boat or ship) to a dock. **2.** to bring together (two or more orbiting objects, such as spacecraft) in space. —*v.i.* **1.** to come into a dock: *The ship docked last night.* **2.** (of orbiting objects) to come together in space. [From the Middle Dutch word *docke* with the same meaning.]

dock² (dok) *n.* **1.** the solid, fleshy part of an animal's tail. **2.** the stump of a tail left after clipping or cropping. —*v.t.* **1.** to cut the end off or shorten: *to dock a horse's tail.* **2.** to deduct from: *The company docked my wages for missing a day of work.* [Probably from the Old English suffix *-docca,* as found in words such as *fingerdocca* meaning "finger muscle."]

dock³ (dok) *n.* the place in a criminal court where the defendant stands or sits during a trial. [From the Flemish word *dok* meaning "a cage."]

dock⁴ (dok) *n.* any of a group of plants related to buckwheat, usually having large, wavy-edged leaves. [From the Old English word *docce* meaning these plants.]

dock·age (dok'ij) *n.* **1.** the amount charged for using a dock. **2.** the facilities for docking a boat or ship.

dock·et (dok'it) *n.* **1.** a list of cases that are to be tried by a court of law. **2.** a list of legal judgments given in a particular court. **3.** any list or calendar of things to be done; agenda. **4.** a label or tag attached to something, such as a package or document, and listing its contents. —*v.t.* **1.** to enter in a docket. **2.** to put a label or tag on (something, such as a package or document).

dock·yard (dok'yärd') *n.* a place containing docks, workshops, and warehouses where boats and ships can be built, equipped, and repaired.

doc·tor (dok'tər) *n.* **1.** a person who is licensed to practice any of various branches of medicine, such as pediatrics or psychiatry; physician or surgeon. **2.** a person who is licensed to practice any of various related sciences, such as dentistry, osteopathy, or veterinary medicine. **3.** a person who has been awarded a doctorate. —*v.t.* **1.** to treat with medicine; try to cure. **2.** to tamper with: *The clerk doctored the records by changing the dates.*

Word Family

The meanings of words often change over time. This is evident from the meanings of most of the English words derived from the Latin word *docere,* meaning "to teach." People with considerable instruction and training may receive **doctorates.** They may be referred to as **doctors,** and some of them do teach, especially in universities. Today, the word **doctor** most often refers to a person trained in medicine, someone who may not teach at all. Tools for teaching include **documents,** which contain important facts, and the **documentary,** which offers facts on film. The collection of accepted facts about a subject may become **doctrine.** Sometimes words take on shades of meaning. **Docile,** for example, means more than "able to be taught," and **indoctrination** describes a very negative type of teaching.

doc·tor·al (dok'tər əl) *adj.* of, relating to, or studying for a doctorate: *a doctoral thesis, a doctoral student.*

doc·tor·ate (dok'tə rit) *n.* **1.** the highest graduate degree given by a university. **2.** such a degree awarded as an honor.

doc·tri·nal (dok'trə nəl) *adj.* of, relating to, or based on doctrine: *a doctrinal controversy.*

doc·trine (dok'trin) *n.* **1.** a belief or set of beliefs held by a particular group, such as a church or political party: *the doctrines of a religion.* **2.** something that is taught; teachings: *political doctrine.*

doc·u·dra·ma (dok'yə drä'mə, dok'yə dram'ə) *n.* a television or motion-picture drama based on real events but with some or many fictional elements.

doc·u·ment (*n.,* dok'yə mənt; *v.,* dok'yə ment') *n.* something written or printed that gives information, support, or proof about a particular object or matter. Deeds, maps, and official records are documents. —*v.t.* to support or prove with facts, evidence, or examples.

doc·u·men·ta·ry (dok'yə men'tə re) *adj.* **1.** relating to, supported by, or consisting of documents: *Do you have documentary evidence for that statement?* **2.** dealing with or giving facts: *a documentary program about wolves.* —*n.,* *pl.* **doc·u·men·ta·ries.** a documentary motion picture, television program, or radio program.

doc·u·men·ta·tion (dok'yə mən tā'shən) *n.* **1.** the preparation of documents. **2.** documentary proof: *There was no documentation for the statement* **3.** *Computers.* manuals, diagrams, or other information that describe the design or operation of hardware and software.

dod·der (dod'ər) *v.i.* **1.** to move feebly and shakily; totter: *The old dog doddered down the street.* **2.** to tremble or shake, as from age. —**dod'der·ing,** *adj.*

dodge (doj) *v.,* **dodged, dodg·ing.** —*v.t.* **1.** to keep away from or avoid by moving aside quickly or suddenly: *to dodge a blow.* **2.** to get out of or evade by trickery or cunning: *The senator dodged the reporter's question about campaign finances.* —*v.i.* to move quickly or suddenly:

at; āpe; fär; câre; end; mē; it; īce; pîerce; hot; ōld; sông, fôrk; oil; out; up; ūse; rüle; pŭll; tûrn; chin; sing; shop; thin; <u>th</u>is; hw in white; zh in treasure. The symbol ə stands for the unstressed vowel sound heard in about, taken, pencil, lemon, and circus.

The fleeing thief dodged in and out of the crowd. —*n.*
1. the act of dodging. **2.** a trick used to cheat or deceive. **3.** a clever scheme.

dodg·er (doj′ər) *n.* **1.** a person who dodges, especially one who uses trickery or cunning: *a tax dodger.* **2.** a type of bread or cake made of cornmeal and baked or fried. **3.** a small handbill.

do·do (dō′dō) *n., pl.* **do·dos** or **do·does.** **1.** a species of flightless bird, now extinct. The dodo had a large head, a heavy hooked bill, and a short tail of curly feathers. **2.** *Slang.* a stupid person. [From the Portuguese word *doudo* meaning "stupid."]

doe (dō) *n.* the female of the deer, antelope, and certain other animals.

do·er (dü′ər) *n.* a person who does something, especially a person of action: *a doer of brave deeds.*

does (duz) the present indicative, third person singular, of **do¹.**

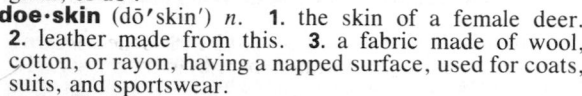

dodo *(def. 1)*

doe·skin (dō′skin′) *n.* **1.** the skin of a female deer. **2.** leather made from this. **3.** a fabric made of wool, cotton, or rayon, having a napped surface, used for coats, suits, and sportswear.

does·n't (duz′ənt) *contr.* does not.

do·est (dü′ist) *Archaic.* the present indicative, second person singular, of **do¹.**

do·eth (dü′ith) *Archaic.* the present indicative, third person singular, of **do¹.**

doff (dof, dôf) *v.t.* to remove (an article of clothing): *I doffed my jacket and hung it in the closet.*

dog (dôg) *n.* **1.** a four-footed, meat-eating animal of which there are more than 200 distinct breeds, which vary greatly in appearance. Dogs are commonly kept as pets or for protection. **2.** any of a group of animals related to the dog, such as the wolf or fox. **3.** the male of any of these animals. **4.** any of various mechanical devices used to fasten, hold, or grip. **5.** *Informal.* a man or boy: *You're a sly dog.* **6.** *Informal.* a person or thing that is considered ugly, undesirable, or of poor quality: *That rusty old car is a real dog.* —*v.t.,* **dogged, dog·ging.** to follow closely or pursue; hound.

dog·bane (dôg′bān′) *n.* any of a group of plants having clusters of small, white or pink bell-shaped flowers.

dog·cart (dôg′kärt′) *n.* **1.** a light, open, one-horse carriage, usually two-wheeled, having two seats set back to back. **2.** a small cart drawn by one or more dogs.

dog·catch·er (dôg′kach′ər) *n.* a person employed to pick up stray or unlicensed dogs.

dog days, the sultry days of July and August. [A translation of the Latin phrase *dies canicularis* meaning "days of the dog star," because the Romans believed that Sirius, called the *Dog Star,* was so positioned in the sky as to cause excessive heat during this time.]

doge (dōj) *n.* the chief magistrate in the former republics of Genoa and Venice.

dog–ear (dôg′îr′) *n.* the turned-down corner of a page of a book or magazine. —*v.t.* to turn down the corner of (a page). —**dog′-eared′,** *adj.*

dog·fight (dôg′fīt′) *n.* **1.** a fight between dogs, or a fight resembling this; rough, violent dispute or brawl. **2.** combat between fighter planes.

dog·fish (dôg′fish′) *n., pl.* **dog·fish** or **dog·fish·es.** a small shark having a long, slender, grayish green body, a pointed snout, and a large, forked tail.

dog·ged (dô′gid) *adj.* not yielding; stubborn; persevering: *dogged courage.* —**dog′ged·ly,** *adv.* —**dog′ged·ness,** *n.*

dog·ger·el (dô′gər əl) *n.* poetry having little or no artistic worth, often comical. —*adj.* resembling or composed of such poetry.

dog·gy (dô′gē) *also,* **dog·gie.** *n., pl.* **dog·gies.** a dog, especially a little dog.

doggy bag, *also,* **doggie bag.** a bag or other container provided by a restaurant in which a person can carry home food left over from a meal eaten at the restaurant.

dog·house (dôg′hous′) *n., pl.* **dog·hous·es** (dôg′hou′ziz). a shelter built for a dog.
·**in the doghouse.** *Informal.* in disfavor.

do·gie (dō′gē) *also,* **dogy.** *n.* in the western United States, a stray calf on the range.

dog·ma (dôg′mə) *n., pl.* **dog·mas** or **dog·ma·ta** (dôg′mə-tə). **1.** a doctrine accepted as true and as having the authority of a church. **2.** any doctrine accepted as true and having authority: *a political dogma.*

dog·mat·ic (dôg mat′ik) *adj.* **1.** stating opinions or beliefs in a positive and haughty manner: *The dogmatic lecturer disregarded our objections.* **2.** of or relating to dogma; doctrinal. Also, **dog·mat·i·cal** (dôg mat′i kəl). —**dog·mat′i·cal·ly,** *adv.*

dog·ma·tism (dôg′mə tiz′əm) *n.* a positive and haughty statement of opinions or beliefs.

dog·ma·tist (dôg′mə tist) *n.* a person who expresses dogmas or who is dogmatic.

do–good·er (dü′gŏŏd′ər) *n.* *Informal.* a person who is idealistic and eager to change things for the better.

dog–pad·dle (dôg′pad′əl) *v.i.,* **dog-pad·dled, dog-pad·dling.** to use the dog paddle in swimming.

dog paddle, a simple stroke in swimming with the body in an almost upright position, the hands paddling at the surface, and the legs kicking.

dog·sled (dôg′sled′) *n.* a sled that is pulled by one or more dogs.

Dog Star, another name for **Sirius.**

dog·trot (dôg′trot′) *n.* a gentle, easy trot.

dog·wood (dôg′wŏŏd′) *n.* **1.** a tree or shrub bearing greenish yellow flowers surrounded by pink or white leaves that look like petals. **2.** the hard, heavy wood of this tree.

dogy (dō′gē) another spelling of **dogie.**

doi·ly (doi′lē) *n., pl.* **doi·lies.** a small piece of linen, lace, paper or other material, placed on furniture as a kind of decoration or to protect the top surface of a table.

dogwood flowers and fruit

do·ings (dü′ingz) *pl. n.* **1.** activities, deeds, or events: *social doings.* **2.** behavior; conduct.

do–it–your·self (dü′it yər self′) *adj.* designed to be built or used by someone who is not an expert: *a do-it-yourself kit for building a bookcase.*

Dol·by (dōl′bē) *n.* *Trademark.* a circuit in many tape recorders and other high-fidelity devices that reduces the amount of background noise heard when a recording is played back.

dol·drums (dōl′drəmz, dol′drəmz) *n., pl.* **1.** dull or depressed mood; low spirits. **2.** certain regions of the ocean near the equator that are calm, with light winds and frequent tropical showers.

dole (dōl) *n.* **1.** something given out as charity, such as money, food, or clothing. **2.** anything given in little amounts; small portion. —*v.t.,* **doled, dol·ing.** **1.** to give out as charity. **2.** to give in little amounts: *They doled out the apples to the children one by one.*

dole·ful (dōl′fəl) *adj.* full of or expressing grief or sorrow; sad: *a doleful cry, a doleful look.* —**dole′ful·ly,** *adv.* —**dole′ful·ness,** *n.*

doll (dol) *n.* **1.** a child's toy made to look like a human being, especially a baby or child.   **2.** *Informal.* an attractive or delightful person.   —*v.t.* *Informal.* to dress smartly (with *up*): *They dolled themselves up for the party.*

dol·lar (dol′ər) *n.*   **1.** the standard unit of money in the United States, equal to one hundred cents.   **2.** the standard unit of money in certain other countries, such as Canada, New Zealand, and Australia.   **3.** a piece of paper currency or silver or gold coin equal to one dollar.

dol·lop (dol′əp) *n.*   **1.** a lump, blob, or portion: *a dollop of paint, a dollop of mashed potatoes.*   **2.** a small amount: *a dull speech without even a dollop of humor.*

doll·y (dol′ē) *n., pl.* **doll·ies.**   **1.** a child's word for a doll.   **2.** any of several kinds of low frames or platforms with wheels, used for moving heavy loads.

dol·men (dōl′mən, dol′mən) *n.*   a prehistoric structure consisting of a large stone slab resting on two or more stones placed up-right.

dolmen

do·lo·mite (dō′lə mīt′, dol′ə mīt′) *n.*   **1.** a mineral whose crystals are usually pink or white in color.   **2.** a rock resembling limestone and consisting mainly of dolomite.

do·lor (dō′lər) *n.*   sorrow; grief.

do·lor·ous (dō′lər əs, dol′ər əs) *adj.*   causing or expressing sorrow or grief: *a dolorous cry.*   —**do′lor·ous·ly,** *adv.*   —**do′lor·ous·ness,** *n.*

dol·phin (dol′fin) *n.*   **1.** any of a group of mammals related to the whale, found in all seas and in some rivers. Dolphins have scaleless black, brown, or gray skin, two flippers, and usually a snout shaped like a beak.   **2.** a saltwater fish found in warm waters, used as food.

dolphins

dolt (dōlt) *n.*   a dull, stupid person.   —**dolt′ish,** *adj.*   —**dolt′ish·ly,** *adv.*   —**dolt′ish·ness,** *n.*

–dom *suffix* (used to form nouns)   **1.** office, rank, or realm of: *earldom, kingdom.*   **2.** the state of being: *freedom, wisdom.*   **3.** all of those who are: *officialdom.*

do·main (dō mān′) *n.*   **1.** the land controlled or governed by a ruler or government; realm.   **2.** a field of knowledge or interest: *the domain of science.*   **3.** the land owned by one person or family; estate.

dome (dōm) *n.*   **1.** a round roof resembling a hemisphere, built on a circular or multisided base.   **2.** something like this in shape: *the dome of a mountain.*   —*v.t.,* **domed, dom·ing.**   to cover with a dome.

do·mes·tic (də mes′tik) *adj.*   **1.** of or relating to the home, household, or family: *domestic life, domestic problems.*   **2.** devoted to or fond of things having to do with the home and family: *a domestic person.*   **3.** living with or near people and cared for by them; domesticated; tame:

The cat is a domestic animal.   **4.** of or made in one's own country: *domestic wine.*   —*n.*   a household servant.   —**do·mes′ti·cal·ly,** *adv.*

do·mes·ti·cate (də mes′ti kāt′) *v.t.,* **do·mes·ti·cat·ed, do·mes·ti·cat·ing.**   **1.** to adapt, tame, or develop for human use.   **2.** to make fond of or used to a home, household affairs, and family life.   —**do·mes′ti·ca′tion,** *n.*

do·mes·tic·i·ty (dō′mes tis′i tē) *n., pl.* **do·mes·tic·i·ties.**   **1.** home and family life.   **2.** devotion to one's home and family.   **3.** domesticities. household affairs.

domestic science, another term for **home economics.**

dom·i·cile (dom′ə sīl′, dō′mə sīl′) *n.*   **1.** a place where one lives; home; dwelling.   **2.** an official or legal residence.   —*v.t.,* **dom·i·ciled, dom·i·cil·ing.**   to establish in a domicile.

dom·i·nance (dom′ə nəns) *n.*   the state or fact of being dominant.

dom·i·nant (dom′ə nənt) *adj.*   **1.** having the main influence, authority, or control; most important: *Great Britain was once the dominant country in the world.*   **2.** most prominent or striking: *Blue is the dominant color in this room.*   **3.** *Music.* of, based upon, or relating to the fifth tone of a scale.   **4.** relating to or indicating one of a pair of hereditary characteristics appearing in an organism, that hides or dominates the other when both are present.   —*n.*   **1.** *Music.* the fifth tone of a scale.   G is the dominant in the key of C.   **2.** a dominant hereditary characteristic.   —**dom′i·nant·ly,** *adv.*

dom·i·nate (dom′ə nāt′) *v.,* **dom·i·nat·ed, dom·i·nat·ing.**   —*v.t.*   **1.** to have the main influence, authority, or control over: *A person with a forceful personality can dominate people.*   **2.** to have a commanding or towering position over; tower over: *Skyscrapers dominate New York's skyline.*   —*v.i.*   **1.** to have the main influence, authority, or control: *France dominated in Europe during the time of Napoleon.*   **2.** to have a commanding or towering position.   —**dom′i·na′tor,** *n.*

dom·i·na·tion (dom′ə nā′shən) *n.*   **1.** the act of dominating or the state of being dominated.   **2.** influence, authority, or control; rule; sway: *The defeated country was under the domination of a foreign army.*

dom·i·neer (dom′ə nîr′) *v.i.*   to control or rule in an arrogant or harsh way; be overbearing or like a tyrant: *The bully domineered over the other children.*   —*v.t.*   to control or rule (others) in an arrogant or harsh way; tyrannize.

dom·i·neer·ing (dom′ə nîr′ing) *adj.*   tending to domineer; overbearing; tyrannical.   —**dom′i·neer′ing·ly,** *adv.*

Do·min·i·can (də min′i kən) *adj.*   **1.** of or relating to Saint Dominic or to the religious order founded by him.   **2.** of, relating to, or characteristic of the Dominican Republic.   —*n.*   **1.** a member of the Roman Catholic order founded by Saint Dominic in 1215.   **2.** a person who was born in or is a citizen of the Dominican Republic.

dom·i·nie (dom′ə ne) *n.*   *Scottish.* a schoolmaster.

do·min·ion (də min′yən) *n.*   **1.** the power or right to rule; supreme authority: *The monarch had dominion over all the land.*   **2.** a territory or country controlled or governed by a particular ruler or government.   **3.** Dominion. formerly, any of a group of self-governing states belonging to the British Commonwealth, such as Canada or Australia.

Dominion Day, see **Canada Day.**

---

at; āpe; fär; câre; end; mē; it; īce; pîerce; hot; ōld; sông, fôrk; oil; out; up; ūse; rüle; pull; tûrn; chin; sing; shop; thin; <u>th</u>is; hw in white; zh in treasure. The symbol ə stands for the unstressed vowel sound heard in about, taken, pencil, lemon, and circus.

dom·i·no (dom′ə nō′) *n.*, *pl.* **dom·i·noes.** **1.** a small black tile divided into halves, each half either being blank or having from one to six white dots, used in playing certain games. **2. dominoes.** a game played with these tiles.

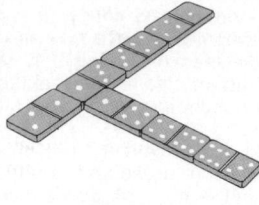

dominoes

don¹ (don) *n.* **1. Don.** Sir. ▲ Spanish form of respectful or polite address for a man, usually used before the first name only: *Don José.* **2.** a Spanish nobleman or gentleman. **3.** a head or tutor of a college at certain British universities. [From the Spanish title *don* meaning ''lord,'' from the Latin word *dominus* ''master, lord.'']

don² (don) *v.t.,* **donned, don·ning.** to put on: *to don one's coat.* [A contraction of the phrase *do on.*]

do·ña (dōn′yə) *n.* **1. Doña.** Lady; Madam. ▲ Spanish form of respectful or polite address for a married woman, usually used before the first name only: *Doña María.* **2.** a Spanish noblewoman or lady. [From the Spanish title *doña* meaning ''lady,'' from the Latin word *domina* ''mistress, lady,'' feminine form of *dominus* ''master, lord.'']

do·nate (dō′nāt) *v.t.,* **do·nat·ed, do·nat·ing.** to give to; contribute: *to donate a painting to a museum.*

do·na·tion (dō nā′shən) *n.* **1.** the act of giving; contributing: *Many students took part in the yearly donation of clothing to the poor.* **2.** a gift; contribution: *They gave a large donation to charity.*

done (dun) *v.* the past participle of **do.** —*adj.* **1.** completed; finished: *The work is done.* **2.** cooked.

don·jon (dun′jən, don′jən) *n.* the strong inner tower of a castle; keep.

Don Juan (don wän′, don hwän′) a legendary Spanish nobleman, famous for his many love affairs.

don·key (dong′kē, dung′kē) *n.*, *pl.* **don·keys.** **1.** a domestic animal that resembles a small horse but has longer ears and a shorter mane; ass. The donkey is often used as a beast of burden. **2.** a stupid or stubborn person.

don·na (don′ə, dō′nə) *n.* **1. Donna.** lady; madam. ▲ Italian form of respectful or polite address for a married woman, usually used before the first name only. **2.** an Italian noblewoman or lady. [From the Italian title *donna* meaning ''lady,'' from the Latin word *domina* ''mistress, lady,'' feminine form of *dominus* ''master, lord.'']

donkey *(def. 1)*

don·nish (don′ish) *adj.* bookish or pedantic.

don·ny·brook (don′ē brŭk′) *n.* a rough, noisy brawl; free-for-all. [From the name *Donnybrook,* a town in Ireland where a fair was held, at which such brawls were said to be common.]

do·nor (dō′nər) *n.* a person who donates: *a blood donor.*

do-noth·ing (dü′nuth′ing) *adj.* not active, especially in regard to making changes or improvement: *a do-nothing city council.*

Don Qui·xo·te (don′ kē hō′tē, don kwik′sət) the hero of a novel of the same name by the Spanish writer Miguel de Cervantes. In the novel, Don Quixote is an idealistic, impractical old man who believes he is a knight and who tries to fight evil and injustice.

don't (dōnt) *contr.* do not.

doo·dad (dü′dad′) *n. Informal.* a small, decorative object.

doo·dle (dü′dəl) *v.,* **doo·dled, doo·dling.** —*v.i.* to draw or scribble idly or aimlessly: *He doodled all over the paper while talking on the telephone.* —*v.t.* to draw or scribble (something) in an idle or aimless manner: *She doodled a face in the margin of her paper.* —*n.* a design or drawing made by doodling. —**doo′dler,** *n.*

doo·dle·bug (dü′dəl bug′) *n.* the larva of the ant lion.

doom (düm) *n.* **1.** something that cannot be escaped, especially something bringing pain, ruin, or death. **2.** a harsh sentence or judgment: *The judge pronounced the murderer's doom.* —*v.t.* **1.** to pronounce a harsh judgment against; condemn. **2.** to destine, especially to a bad or tragic end: *Without good leadership, the program is doomed to fail.*

Dooms·day (dümz′dā′) *also,* **dooms·day.** *n.* **1.** another name for **Judgment Day.** **2.** any day of final judgment.

door (dôr) *n.* **1.** a structure, usually made of wood, glass, or metal, that serves to open or close an entrance or opening in something, such as a building or automobile. **2.** doorway: *He's standing in the door.* **3.** a room or building with a door: *Her room is four doors away. They live two doors down the street.* **4.** any means of entrance or exit: *Many people think of college as the door to business success.*

door·bell (dôr′bel′) *n.* a bell or buzzer on or near a door that is used by someone wanting to come in.

door·jamb (dôr′jam′) *n.* the vertical piece forming the side of a doorway.

door·knob (dôr′nob′) *n.* the handle on a door, used to open it.

door·man (dôr′man′, dôr′mən) *n.*, *pl.* **door·men** (dôr′mən). an attendant at the door of a building, such as a hotel, department store, or apartment house, who helps people entering and leaving.

door·mat (dôr′mat′) *n.* a mat placed before a doorway, used by people coming in for wiping their shoes.

door·nail (dôr′nāl′) *n.* a nail having a large head, used to strengthen or decorate doors.

  ·**dead as a doornail.** dead beyond a doubt.

door·plate (dôr′plāt′) *n.* a plate, usually of metal, placed on or near a door of an apartment, office, or house, bearing the occupant's name, address, and the like.

door·sill (dôr′sil′) *n.* the base or threshold at a doorway.

door·step (dôr′step′) *n.* a step or steps leading from an outside door to the ground or sidewalk.

door·stop (dôr′stop′) *n.* **1.** a device, as a wedge or spring, used to hold a door open or to prevent it from slamming shut. **2.** a device, usually with a rubber tip, attached to a door or wall to prevent the opening door from hitting and damaging the wall.

door-to-door (dôr′tə dôr′) *adj.* making or involving a call at every residence in an area: *a door-to-door salesperson, a door-to-door survey.* —*adv.* with a call at every residence in an area: *to solicit magazine subscriptions door-to-door.*

door·yard (dôr′yärd′) *n.* the yard around a house, especially near the door.

do·pa·mine (dō′pə mēn′) *n.* a chemical substance found in the central nervous system that transmits nerve impulses. Dopamine helps control movement and emotions.

dope (dōp) *n.* **1.** *Informal.* a stupid, dull-witted person. **2.** *Informal.* a drug or narcotic. **3.** *Slang.* secret information. **4.** a thick liquid or pasty substance used as a surface coating or preparation. —*v.t.,* **doped, dop·ing.** *Slang.* to give dope to; drug.

do·pey (dō′pē) *adj.,* **do·pi·er, do·pi·est.** *Informal.* mentally slow; stupid.

Dop·pler effect (dop′lər) *Physics.* the apparent change in the frequency of a sound, light, or other wave as the distance between the moving source of the wave and the observer changes. The frequency becomes lower as the distance between the source and the observer becomes greater, and higher as the distance between the source and the observer becomes less. [From the Austrian physicist Christian J. *Doppler* (1803–1853), who first investigated this phenomenon.]

Dor·ic (dôr′ik, dor′ik) *adj.* of or relating to the first and simplest of the three orders, or styles, of classical Greek architecture, characterized by columns having no base and very plain capitals.

dorm (dôrm) *n. Informal.* see **dormitory.**

dor·man·cy (dôr′mən sē) *n.* the state of being dormant: *Plants do not grow during dormancy.*

Doric capital

dor·mant (dôr′mənt) *adj.* **1.** temporarily quiet or inactive: *a dormant volcano.* **2.** in a sleeping or inactive condition.

dor·mer (dôr′mər) *n.* **1.** a window that is mounted vertically on a sloping roof. Also, **dormer window. 2.** a roofed projection containing such a window.

dor·mi·to·ry (dôr′mi tôr′ē) *n., pl.* **dor·mi·to·ries. 1.** a building designed as a common residence, as for students at a college to live and sleep in. **2.** a room containing a number of beds, as in a school.

dor·mouse (dôr′mous′) *n., pl.* **dor·mice** (dôr′mīs′). a rodent found in Europe, Africa, and Asia, resembling a squirrel and usually having brown or gray fur. Dormice hibernate for up to six months of the year.

dor·sal (dôr′səl) *adj.* of, on, or near the back of the body: *a dorsal fin.*

do·ry (dôr′ē) *n., pl.* **do·ries.** a deep, flat-bottomed rowboat having high sides sloping upward and outward, used for fishing.

dormouse

dos·age (dō′sij) *n.* **1.** the amount of a medicine or other medical treatment in a single dose. **2.** the giving of such a dose.

dose (dōs) *n.* **1.** the amount of a medicine or other medical treatment prescribed to be given or taken at one time. **2.** an amount, especially of something painful or harmful: *That dose of freezing weather nearly killed the crops.* —*v.t.,* **dosed, dos·ing.** to give (medicine) to: *to dose a person with antibiotics.*

dos·si·er (dos′ē ā′, dô′sē ā′) *n.* a collection of detailed documents or papers relating to some subject or person.

dost (dust) *Archaic.* the present indicative, second person singular, of **do**¹.

dot (dot) *n.* **1.** a small, usually round, mark; speck or very small spot: *Make a dot on the paper with the tip of your pencil.* **2.** *Telegraphy.* the shorter of the two signals used to represent numbers or letters, as in Morse code. —*v.t.,* **dot·ted, dot·ting. 1.** to mark with a dot or dots: *The artist dotted the canvas with yellow and blue.* **2.** to be scattered over or about: *Houses dotted the hillside.*

　·**on the dot.** at exactly the specified time: *The train left the station at seven o'clock on the dot.*

dot·age (dō′tij) *n.* the state of being feeble-minded, especially because of old age; senility.

dot·ard (dō′tərd) *n.* a person whose mind is feeble, especially from old age.

dote (dōt) *v.i.,* **dot·ed, dot·ing. 1.** to lavish extreme or excessive affection: *The grandparents doted on the child.* **2.** to be feeble-minded, especially because of old age.

doth (duth) *Archaic.* the present indicative, third person singular, of **do**¹.

Dou·ay Bible (dü′ā) an English translation, done by Roman Catholic scholars, of the Latin Vulgate Bible of St. Jerome. Also, **Douay Version.** [From *Douai,* the city in northern France where the Old Testament of this translation of the Bible was first published.]

dou·ble (dub′əl) *adj.* **1.** twice as great, as many, or as much, as in size, amount, or strength: *You pay double*

fare for a first-class ticket. **2.** having or forming two like or identical parts; paired: *People formed a double line in front of the theater. The room has double doors that open out onto the garden.* **3.** having or combining two parts, intentions, uses, or the like: *This statement has a double meaning. The secret agent led a double life.* **4.** *Botany.* having more than one set of petals or sepals. —*adv.* in pairs or twos; doubly: *to see double.* —*n.* **1.** something that is twice as much: *Ten is the double of five.* **2.** a person or thing that closely resembles or looks exactly like another: *Your cousin is your double.* **3.** *Baseball.* a hit that enables the batter to reach second base safely. **4. doubles.** a game, as of tennis, having two players on each side. —*v.,* **dou·bled, dou·bling.** —*v.t.* **1.** to make twice as great, as much, or as many, as in size or amount: *Increased efficiency doubled the company's profits in five years.* **2.** to fold or bend, as to make two layers: *to double a sheet of paper, to double a blanket.* **3.** to be or contain twice the number or amount of. **4.** to clench (the fist): *to double one's fist in rage.* **5.** (of a ship) to sail or go around: *to double a cape.* —*v.i.* **1.** to become twice as great, as much, or as many: *The price of this product has doubled over the last three years.* **2.** to serve two purposes or functions: *This sofa doubles as a bed.* **3.** to turn, especially sharply or suddenly, and trace the same or similar course (usually followed by *back*): *We knew we were lost, so we turned around and doubled back.* **4.** to fold or bend: *to double up with pain, to double over with laughter.* **5.** to be a substitute: *to double for the star in a play.* **6.** *Baseball.* to hit a double: *The batter doubled to left field.*

　·**on the double.** *Informal.* quickly: *Deliver this message and get back here on the double.*

　·**to double up.** *Informal.* to share living quarters with another: *If there's only one room left, you and I will have to double up.*

double bar *Music.* see **bar** (*def. 10c*).

double bass (bās) the largest and deepest-toned instrument of the violin family, usually having four strings, and played in an upright position. Also, **bass viol, contrabass.**

double bassoon, a large bassoon, the largest and deepest-toned instrument of the oboe family, pitched an octave lower than the ordinary bassoon.

double bed, a bed large enough for two adults, having a standard width of 54 inches (137 centimeters).

double boiler, a cooking utensil consisting of a pair of pots, one fitting into the other. The upper pot contains the food, which is cooked gently by the heat from boiling water in the lower pot.

dou·ble–breast·ed (dub′əl bres′tid) *adj.* (of garments such as coats or jackets) overlapping enough to make two thicknesses across the breast and having two rows of buttons.

dou·ble–check (dub′əl chek′) *v.t., v.i.* to check again, especially for accuracy: *Double-check your spelling before handing in your paper.*

double chin, a fold of fatty flesh under the chin.

dou·ble–cross (dub′əl krôs′) *v.t. Informal.* to deceive or betray (someone) by failing to act as one has promised; be false to. —**dou′ble-cross′er,** *n.*

double cross *Informal.* an act of betrayal; treachery.

dou·ble–date (dub′əl dāt′) *v.i.,* **dou·ble-dat·ed, dou·ble-dat·ing.** to go on a double date: *My cousin and I often double-date.*

at; āpe; fär; câre; end; mē; it; īce; pîerce; hot; ōld; sông, fôrk; oil; out; up; ūse; rüle; pùll; tûrn; chin; sing; shop; thin; <u>th</u>is; hw in white; zh in treasure. The symbol ə stands for the unstressed vowel sound heard in about, taken, pencil, lemon, and circus.

double date, a social occasion or event shared by two couples.

dou·ble–deal·er (dub′əl dē′lər) *n.* a person who acts in a deceitful, dishonest, or treacherous way.

dou·ble–deal·ing (dub′əl dē′ling) *n.* deceitful, dishonest, or treacherous behavior or action. —*adj.* given to or characterized by such behavior or action.

double-decker *(def. 1)*

dou·ble–deck·er (dub′əl dek′ər) *n.* **1.** a vehicle, as a bus, having two decks or levels. **2.** a sandwich consisting of three slices of bread and two layers of filling.

dou·ble–dig·it (dub′əl dij′it) *adj.* of or amounting to a number or percentage between 10 and 99: *double-digit inflation.*

double eagle, a former gold coin of the United States, worth twenty dollars when in use as currency.

dou·ble–edged (dub′əl ejd′) *adj.* **1.** having two sharp edges: *a double-edged sword.* **2.** capable of being understood in two ways or of having two, opposite effects: *a confusing speech containing several double-edged statements.*

dou·ble en·ten·dre (dub′əl än tän′drə) a word or expression having two meanings, one of which is usually indecent or suggestive. [From the obsolete French phrase *double entendre* meaning ''double meaning.'']

dou·ble–head·er (dub′əl hed′ər) *n.* two games played on the same day in close succession, as in baseball.

double jeopardy, the condition of being tried again for the same offense for which one has already been tried and judged (prohibited by the U.S. Constitution).

dou·ble–joint·ed (dub′əl join′tid) *adj.* having extremely flexible joints that permit movement of the body into unusual angles or positions.

dou·ble–knit (dub′əl nit′) *n.* a fabric made from two layers of knitted material interwoven closely together.

double negative, the use in the same statement of two negative words or phrases, especially to express one negative idea.

▲ At one time, the use of a **double negative** was common in English. Famous writers often used double, and even triple, negatives, such as *Thou hast spoken no word this while, nor understood none neither* (Shakespeare, *Love's Labour's Lost*). Today, however, a double negative is not generally considered to be good English, and is used only in special contexts, such as *I am not unaware of his problems.*

dou·ble–park (dub′əl pärk′) *v.t., v.i.* to park (a motor vehicle) next to one that is already parked parallel to the curb.

double play, a baseball play in which two base runners are put out.

double pneumonia, pneumonia affecting both lungs.

dou·ble–quick (dub′əl kwik′) *adj.* very quick; hurried; rapid. —*n.* see **double time** *(def. 1).*

double standard, a standard that is applied more strictly to one group than to another, especially a code of moral behavior permitting women less freedom than men.

double star, two stars that appear very close to one another. Most double stars can be distinguished as separate stars only when viewed through a telescope.

dou·blet (dub′lit) *n.* **1.** a close-fitting waist-length jacket, with or without sleeves, worn especially by men in Western Europe from about 1400 to 1650. **2.** one of two or more words derived from the same original source, but in different ways. The words *custom* and *costume* are doublets.

doublet *(def. 1)*

double take, a delayed reaction, as to a joke or surprising situation.

dou·ble–talk (dub′əl tôk′) *n.* deliberately deceptive or meaningless talk, often mixing actual words with meaningless syllables.

dou·ble–time (dub′əl tīm′) *v.,* **double-timed, dou·ble–tim·ing.** —*v.i.* to move in double time. —*v.t.* to cause to move in double time.

double time 1. *Military.* a rapid marching rate of 180 3-foot (91-centimeter) steps per minute. **2.** a rate of pay that is twice one's normal pay rate.

dou·bloon (du blün′) *n.* a former Spanish gold coin.

dou·bly (dub′lē) *adv.* in a twofold manner or degree; twice as: *We rechecked our calculations to make doubly sure there was no error.*

doubt (dout) *v.t.* to be unconvinced, uncertain, or distrustful about; hesitate to believe or accept; question: *She doubted the truth of his story.* —*v.i.* to be unconvinced or undecided in opinion or belief; be unconvinced, uncertain, or distrustful. —*n.* **1.** a feeling of disbelief, uncertainty, or distrust: *He had doubts about her sincerity.* **2.** the state or condition of being unconvinced, uncertain, or distrustful: *The outcome of the election was in doubt.* —**doubt′er,** *n.*

·**no doubt. a.** without question; certainly **b.** most likely; probably.

·**without doubt.** without question; certainly: *That was without doubt the best book I've ever read.*

doubt·ful (dout′fəl) *adj.* **1.** having, showing, or experiencing doubt: *Her doubtful look showed that she lacked confidence. His friends were doubtful about his chances of success.* **2.** subject to or causing doubt; not clear or sure; uncertain: *The outcome of the war was doubtful. It's doubtful whether they'll go to the party.* **3.** of questionable character: *a doubtful reputation.* —**doubt′ful·ly,** *adv.* —**doubt′ful·ness,** *n.*

doubting Thomas, a person who is habitually doubtful and refuses to believe anything without proof; skeptic. [From *Thomas,* the Apostle who doubted that Jesus had been raised from the dead.]

doubt·less (dout′lis) *adv.* **1.** unquestionably; certainly. *Your excellent work will doubtless impress the judges.* **2.** probably. Also, **doubt·less·ly** (dout′lis lē) —*adj.* free from doubt or uncertainty.

douche (düsh) *n.* **1.** a jet of water or other liquid directed into or onto a body part, organ, or cavity for cleansing or medicinal purposes. **2.** a device, as a spray or syringe, for administering a douche.

dough (dō) *n.* **1.** a soft, thick mass worked or kneaded from a mixture of flour or meal, liquid, and other ingredients, then baked. **2.** any soft, thick, pasty mass. **3.** *Slang.* money.

dough·nut (dō′nut′) *n.* a small, usually ring-shaped, cake made of dough, usually leavened and sweetened, cooked by frying in deep fat.

dough·ty (dou′tē) *adj.,* **dough·ti·er, dough·ti·est.** steadfast and courageous; valiant: *The knight was a doughty warrior.* —**dough′ti·ly,** *adv.* —**dough′ti·ness,** *n.*

dough·y (dō'ē) *adj.*, **dough·i·er, dough·i·est**. of or like dough, as in appearance; pasty: *a doughy complexion.*

Doug·las fir (dug'ləs) **1.** an evergreen timber tree of the pine family, found in western North America, having reddish brown ridged bark and bearing oval cones. It may grow to a height of 300 feet (70 meters). **2.** the hard, strong wood of this tree, used chiefly in construction.

dour (dùr, dour) *adj.* **1.** sullenly gloomy; grim; forbidding: *a dour look.* **2.** unyielding; stern. **—dour'ly**, *adv.* **—dour'ness**, *n.*

douse (dous) *v.t.*, **doused, dous·ing**. **1.** to plunge into water or other liquid: *Douse the burning rag in a bucket of water.* **2.** to throw water or other liquid over; drench: *The children doused each other with the hose.* **3.** *Informal.* to put out; extinguish: *Douse the lights.*

dove¹ (duv) *n.* **1.** any of various small or medium-sized birds related to the pigeon, including the mourning dove and turtledove. A dove is often used as a symbol of peace. **2.** a person who favors or supports resolving international conflicts by peaceful means, as through negotiation. [From the Middle English word *douve* with the same meaning, perhaps from Old English.]

dove² (dōv) a past tense of **dive.**

dove·cote (duv'kōt') *also,* **dove·cot** (duv'kot'). *n.* a small house or shelter for doves or pigeons, usually having compartments and placed on a pole or other structure.

dove·tail (duv'tāl') *n.* **1.** a wedge-shaped projection designed to interlock with a mortise or corresponding opening, as in a piece of wood, to form a strong joint. **2.** a joint formed by the interlocking of such pieces. **—v.t.** to fit together or join, as two boards, by means of dovetails. **—v.i.** to fit together precisely, compactly, or harmoniously: *Their schedules dovetailed, so they decided to travel together.*

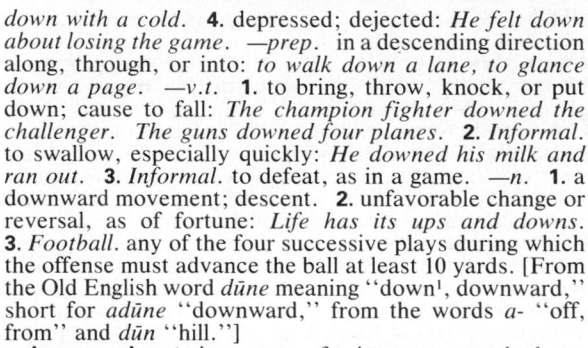

dovetails

dow·a·ger (dou'ə jər) *n.* **1.** a widow who holds property or a title from her deceased husband. **2.** a dignified, elderly lady.

dow·dy (dou'dē) *adj.*, **dow·di·er, dow·di·est**. not stylish or smart in appearance or dress; unfashionable or shabby: *I tried on a dowdy old dress from the closet.* **—n.,** *pl.* **dow·dies**. a dowdy woman. **—dow'di·ly**, *adv.* **dow'di·ness**, *n.*

dow·el (dou'əl) *n.* a peg or pin designed to fit into corresponding holes in two adjacent pieces to hold them together. **—v.t.,** **dow·eled, dow·el·ing**; *also, British,* **dow·elled, dow·el·ling**. to fasten or furnish with dowels.

dow·er (dou'ər) *n.* **1.** the part of a deceased man's property that is given by law to his widow. **2.** another word for **dowry**. **—v.t.** to provide with a dower.

down¹ (doun) *adv.* **1.** from a higher to a lower place, level, or position; in a descending direction; toward the ground: *He stepped down from the ladder. We looked down upon the valley.* **2.** to or on the ground, floor, or bottom: *The boxer knocked the former champion down.* **3.** to, toward, or in a lower place, position, direction, or condition: *She pulled the shades down.* **4.** to, toward, or in a more southern direction or location: *They drove down from New York to Florida.* **5.** to or in a calmer or less active or intense state: *The crowd quieted down.* **6.** with seriousness; earnestly: *to get down to work.* **7.** from an earlier time or individual: *The dress was handed down to her younger sister.* **8.** at the time of purchase: *He paid thirty dollars down and the rest in installments.* **9.** in writing; on paper: *She took down their names.* **—adj.** **1.** going or directed downward; descending: *a down staircase.* **2.** in a lower place, level, or position: *The shades are down.* **3.** sick; ill; ailing: *She's*

dowels

down with a cold. **4.** depressed; dejected: *He felt down about losing the game.* **—prep.** in a descending direction along, through, or into: *to walk down a lane, to glance down a page.* **—v.t.** **1.** to bring, throw, knock, or put down; cause to fall: *The champion fighter downed the challenger. The guns downed four planes.* **2.** *Informal.* to swallow, especially quickly: *He downed his milk and ran out.* **3.** *Informal.* to defeat, as in a game. **—n.** **1.** a downward movement; descent. **2.** unfavorable change or reversal, as of fortune: *Life has its ups and downs.* **3.** *Football.* any of the four successive plays during which the offense must advance the ball at least 10 yards. [From the Old English word *dūne* meaning "down¹, downward," short for *adūne* "downward," from the words *a-* "off, from" and *dūn* "hill."]

  ·down and out. in a state of misery or wretchedness because of a complete lack of money or friends.

  ·down on. *Informal.* angry at, annoyed with, or hostile to: *We were down on you for playing that joke on us.*

  ·down with. do away with; eliminate: *Down with tyranny!*

down² (doun) *n.* **1.** fine, soft feathers, as on young birds or under the outside feathers of certain adult birds. **2.** any fine, soft hair or fuzz. [From the Old Norse word *dūnn* with the same meaning.]

down·beat (doun'bēt') *n. Music.* **1.** a downward gesture made by a conductor to indicate the first accented beat in a measure. **2.** the first beat or the first accented beat in a measure.

down·cast (doun'kast') *adj.* **1.** low or dejected in spirits; sad. **2.** directed downward: *downcast eyes.*

down·fall (doun'fôl') *n.* **1.** a descent to a lower position or standing; fall, as from power or prosperity; ruin: *The downfall of the government was caused by the corruption of its officials.* **2.** a person or thing causing this. **3.** a fall of rain or snow, especially when sudden or heavy.

down·grade (doun'grād') *n.* a downward or descending slope, as of a hill or road. **—v.t.,** **down·grad·ed, down·grad·ing**. **1.** to lower in rank, position, or salary; demote. **2.** to lessen the importance or worth of; belittle: *to downgrade a person's achievements.*

  ·on the downgrade. becoming worse; declining: *Their reputation as a team is on the downgrade.*

down·heart·ed (doun'här'tid) *adj.* depressed or discouraged in spirit; sad; dejected. **—down'heart'ed·ly**, *adv.* **—down'heart'ed·ness**, *n.*

down·hill (doun'hil') *adv.* **1.** in a descending or downward direction; toward the bottom of a hill: *The wagon rolled downhill.* **2.** into or toward a lower or worse level or condition: *The patient's physical condition has been going downhill.* **—adj.** sloping or going downward on or as if on a hill: *a downhill road, a downhill race.*

down–home (doun'hōm') *adj.* of, relating to, or having characteristics traditionally associated with rural areas or rural people, especially of the southern United States: *the informality and earthiness of down-home folk.*

Down·ing Street (dou'ning) the British prime minister or cabinet. [From the address *10 Downing Street,* London, residence of the British prime minister.]

down·load (doun'lōd') *v.t.* **1.** to transfer (data) from a larger to a smaller computer. **2.** to transfer (data) from one computer to another by means of a modem or other telecommunications device.

down payment, a partial payment made when a person

at; āpe; fär; câre; end; mē; it; īce; pîerce; hot; ōld; sông, fôrk; oil; out; up; ūse; rüle; pùll; tûrn; chin; sing; shop; thin; <u>th</u>is; hw in white; zh in treasure. The symbol ə stands for the unstressed vowel sound heard in about, taken, pencil, lemon, and circus.

D

purchases something. The balance is to be paid later, sometimes in installments.

down·play (doun'plā') *v.t.* to treat as having little or no importance; understate the importance of; play down: *to downplay a serious error.*

down·pour (doun'pôr') *n.* a heavy fall of rain.

down·right (doun'rīt') *adj.* **1.** thorough; absolute; utter: *This article is downright nonsense. They're downright liars.* **2.** frankly direct; straightforward; forthright: *a downright reply.* —*adv.* thoroughly; utterly.

downs (dounz) *pl. n.* open, rolling, grassy land, especially in southern and southeastern England. [Old English *dūn.*]

down·stairs (doun'stârz') *adv.* **1.** down the stairs. **2.** on or to a lower floor or level. —*adj.* situated on a lower or main floor: *a downstairs neighbor.*

down·stream (doun'strēm') *adv., adj.* in the direction of the current or flow of a stream: *The canoe drifted slowly downstream.*

Down syndrome (doun) a genetic disorder characterized by mental retardation and eyes that appear slanted. It is caused by the presence of one extra chromosome. Also, **Down's syndrome.** [From the British physician John L. H. *Down* (1828–1896), who discovered it.]

down–to–earth (doun'tü ûrth') *adj.* realistic, practical: *a mature, down-to-earth young person.*

down·town (doun'toun') *adv.* to, toward, or in the business center or geographically lower part of a town or city: *I work downtown.* —*adj.* of or relating to the business center or geographically lower part of a town or city: *a downtown office, a downtown branch of a bank.*

down·trod·den (doun'trod'ən) *adj.* abused or oppressed, as by those in power: *the downtrodden serfs of the feudal period.*

down under *Informal.* a nickname for **Australia** or **New Zealand.** —*adv.* in or to Australia or New Zealand.

down·ward (doun'wərd) *adv.* **1.** from a higher to a lower place, level, or condition. **2.** from an earlier time or individual: *This custom has been passed downward through many generations.* Also, **down·wards** (doun'wərdz). —*adj.* moving from a higher to a lower place, level, or condition.

down·wind (doun'wind') *adj.* in the direction to which the wind is blowing.

down·y (dou'nē) *adj.,* **down·i·er, down·i·est. 1.** of or covered with down. **2.** like down; soft; fluffy. —**down'-i·ness,** *n.*

dow·ry (dou'rē) *n., pl.* **dow·ries.** in some societies, the money or property that a woman brings to her husband at the time of her marriage.

dowse (dous) *v.i.,* **dowsed, dows·ing.** to use a divining rod to search for underground water or minerals.

dox·ol·o·gy (dok sol'ə jē) *n., pl.* **dox·ol·o·gies.** a hymn praising God.

doz., dozen; dozens.

doze (dōz) *v.i.,* **dozed, doz·ing. 1.** to sleep lightly or for a short while; be half asleep; nap: *She's dozing on the couch.* **2.** to fall into a light, brief sleep: *He dozed off while reading.* —*n.* a light or brief sleep.

doz·en (duz'ən) *n., pl.* **doz·ens** or **doz·en.** a group of twelve.

doz·enth (duz'ənth) *adj.* another word for **twelfth.**

DP, displaced person.

dpt., department.

Dr. 1. Doctor. **2.** Drive.

drab (drab) *n.* **1.** a dull, yellowish brown or gray color. **2.** a thick, strong woolen or cotton cloth of this color, often woven with a twill. —*adj.,* **drab·ber, drab·best. 1.** lacking brightness; dull or cheerless: *to live a drab, miserable life.* **2.** having the color drab. —**drab'ly,** *adv.* —**drab'ness,** *n.*

drach·ma (drak'mə) *n., pl.* **drach·mas** or **drach·mae** (drak'mē). **1.** the basic unit of money in Greece. **2.** a

silver coin of ancient Greece. **3.** a unit of weight of ancient Greece. **4.** any of several modern weights, especially a dram.

draft (draft) *also,* **draught.** *n.* **1.** a current of air in an enclosed space or area: *She felt a draft on her back from the open window.* **2.** a device for regulating the flow of air, as in a fireplace. **3.** the first or rough version of something written: *a draft of a proposed law, a draft of an essay.* **4.** a sketch, plan, or design of something to be made, such as a building. **5.** the act or process of selecting an individual or individuals for some special purpose: *The senator accepted the party's draft and outlined the campaign plans.* **6.** the act or process of selecting persons, as for compulsory military service: *The government instituted a draft to increase the size of the army.* **7.** individuals selected by a draft: *The team acquired two new players in last year's draft.* **8.** a written order directing the payment of a specified amount of money, as from one person or bank to another. **9.** the act of drawing or pulling something, such as a loaded wagon. **10.** the act of drinking. **11.** the amount taken in one drink. **12.** the act of drawing in a fishnet. **13.** the amount of fish taken in a net at one time. **14.** *Nautical.* the depth of water that a ship displaces when loaded. —*v.t.* **1.** to prepare a first or rough sketch or version of; make an outline or plan of: *to draft a speech.* **2.** to select for some special purpose, especially for compulsory military service: *He was drafted into the army after he graduated from college.* —*adj.* **1.** used for pulling loads: *a draft animal.* **2.** drawn or ready to be drawn from a tap; not bottled; *draft beer.*

draft·ee (draf tē') *n.* a person who is drafted, as for military service.

drafts·man (drafts'mən) *also, British,* **draughts·man.** *n., pl.* **drafts·men** (drafts'mən). a person who draws or designs plans for machinery, buildings, and other structures and facilities.

drafts·man·ship (drafts'mən ship') *n. also, British,* **draughtsmanship.** the work or skill of a draftsman.

draft·y (draf'tē) *also, British,* **draught·y.** *adj.,* **draft·i·er, draft·i·est.** exposed to or admitting drafts of air: *a drafty hallway.* —**draft'i·ly,** *adv.* —**draft'i·ness,** *n.*

drag (drag) *v.,* **dragged, drag·ging.** —*v.t.* **1.** to pull or draw heavily, slowly, or with great effort; haul: *He dragged the heavy suitcase along the ground.* **2.** to search the bottom of, as with a net or hook; dredge: *to drag a lake for a sunken boat.* **3.** to continue for a painfully long period of time: *to drag out a story.* —*v.i.* **1.** to be pulled or drawn along: *The prisoners' chains dragged behind them.* **2.** to move heavily, slowly, or with great effort: *Her feet dragged as she walked along wearily.* **3.** to pass or move slowly or painfully: *The sad days dragged on, one by one.* —*n.* **1.** a person or thing that hinders or slows down: *My lack of ambition proved to be a drag on my career.* **2.** something that is used in searching the bottom of a body of water, such as a net, hook, or dredge. **3.** something that is pulled or hauled along a surface. **4.** *Slang.* a person or thing that is dull or boring.

drag·gle (drag'əl) *v.,* **drag·gled, drag·gling.** —*v.t.* to make wet or dirty, as by dragging through mud. —*v.i.* to become wet or dirty, as by being dragged through mud.

drag·net (drag'net') *n.* **1.** a net, usually bag-shaped, to be towed over the bottom of a body of water for catching fish or the like. **2.** a system or operation for locating, gathering in, or catching something or someone, such as a wanted criminal.

drag·on (drag'ən) *n.* an imaginary monster somewhat like a huge lizard, usually depicted with claws and wings, and often represented as breathing fire and smoke.

drag·on·fly (drag'ən flī') *n., pl.* **drag·on·flies.** any of a large group

dragonfly

D

of slender-bodied insects found near fresh water and feeding on mosquitoes and other insects. Dragonflies have broad heads, compound eyes, and two pairs of thin, veined wings. Also, **darning needle.**

dra·goon (drə gün′) *n.* **1.** a heavily armed member of a cavalry. **2.** formerly, a mounted member of an infantry armed with a musket. —*v.t.* to force or pressure into doing something: *Colleagues dragooned the senator into voting for the tax bill.*

drag race, a race on a short, straight course between automobiles beginning from a dead stop, the winner being the car that passes a certain point first.

drain (drān) *v.t.* **1.** to draw water or other liquid from; empty or dry by drawing off liquid: *to drain a pool, to drain a bathtub.* **2.** to draw off (a liquid) gradually or completely: *to drain water from a pool.* **3.** to use up; exhaust: *All feeling had been drained out of him in the fight* (Ernest Hemingway). *The long hike drained my strength.* **4.** to drink all the liquid from; empty by drinking: *She drained her glass.* —*v.i.* **1.** to become dry or empty by the flowing off or away of liquid: *The dishes drained on the counter.* **2.** to flow off or away gradually: *The water drained out of the hole in the pail.* **3.** to release or discharge waters: *The river drains into the sea.* —*n.* **1.** an opening, channel, pipe, or similar device for drawing off water or other liquid: *The bathtub drain is clogged.* **2.** a thing that uses up or exhausts: *The project was a drain on the institute's funds.*

drain·age (drā′nij) *n.* **1.** the act or process of draining. **2.** a system of natural or artificial drains. **3.** something that is drained off.

drain·pipe (drān′pīp′) *n.* a pipe for draining water or other liquid.

drake (drāk) *n.* a male duck.

dram (dram) *n.* **1.** an apothecaries' weight equal to 60 grains, or ⅛ ounce (3.9 grams). **2.** an avoirdupois weight equal to 27.343 grams. **3.** see **fluid dram. 4.** a small drink, especially of alcoholic liquor.

dra·ma (drä′mə, dram′ə) *n.* **1.** a literary work telling a story and written to be performed; play. **2.** the branch of literature made up of such works. **3.** the art or profession of writing, acting in, or producing plays. **4.** a situation or series of events having dramatic qualities: *The history of space exploration is an exciting drama.* **5.** a dramatic state, quality, or effect. *The witness's revealing testimony was filled with drama.*

dra·mat·ic (drə mat′ik) *adj.* **1.** of, relating to, or characteristic of drama or plays. **2.** like a drama, as in emotional impact; exciting; striking: *a dramatic appeal for mercy, the dramatic events leading to the revolution.* —**dra·mat′i·cal·ly,** *adv.*

dra·mat·ics (drə mat′iks) *n.* **1.** the art or activity of producing or performing plays. ▲ used with a singular verb. **2.** exaggerated or theatrical behavior. ▲ used with a plural verb: *Your dramatics are beginning to annoy your friends.*

dram·a·tist (dram′ə tist, drä′mə tist) *n.* a person who writes dramas; playwright.

dram·a·ti·za·tion (dram′ə tə zā′shən, drä′mə tə zā′shən) *n.* **1.** the act of dramatizing. **2.** something that is dramatized; dramatized version or representation: *a dramatization of the signing of the Constitution.*

dram·a·tize (dram′ə tīz′, drä′mə tīz′) *v.t.*, **dram·a·tized, dram·a·tiz·ing. 1.** to put into the form of a play; adapt for dramatic performance: *to dramatize a novel.* **2.** to express in an exaggerated or theatrical way; cause to seem exciting or spectacular: *Don't dramatize all your problems.*

drank (drangk) a past tense of **drink.**

drape (drāp) *v.*, **draped, drap·ing.** —*v.t.* **1.** to cover or decorate with cloth hanging loosely: *Drape a sheet over the chair to keep it clean.* **2.** to place or arrange, as cloth or clothing, in loose, graceful folds. **3.** to arrange, spread,

or let fall casually or carelessly: *She draped her feet over the chair.* —*v.i.* to hang or fall in loose folds. —*n.* **1.** *usually,* **drapes.** drapery: *He pulled the drapes back.* **2.** the way in which cloth hangs.

drap·er (drā′pər) *n.* a dealer in cloth or dry goods.

dra·per·y (drā′pə rē) *n., pl.* **dra·per·ies. 1.** cloth hung or arranged in loose, graceful folds, especially when used as a window curtain. **2.** the draping or arranging of cloth.

dras·tic (dras′tik) *adj.* having a forceful or severe effect; rigorous; extreme: *The president resorted to drastic measures to curb inflation.* —**dras′ti·cal·ly,** *adv.*

draught (draft) *n. British.* another spelling of **draft.**

draughts (drafts, dräfts) *n. British.* the game of checkers. ▲ used with a singular verb.

draughts·man (drafts′mən) *n., pl.* **draughts·men** (drafts′mən). *British.* **1.** another spelling of **draftsman. 2.** a piece in the game of checkers.

draught·y (draf′tē) *adj.*, **draught·i·er, draught·i·est.** *British.* another spelling of **drafty.**

draw (drô) *v.*, **drew, drawn, draw·ing.** —*v.t.* **1.** to cause to move in a particular direction or to a particular position by pulling: *She drew the blankets over her head.* **2.** to cause to follow behind by the use of force or effort; drag; haul: *Two oxen drew the wagon.* **3.** to remove or bring out, as by pulling from a holder; take out: *The policeman drew his revolver. Draw the cork from the bottle.* **4.** to create a picture or likeness of with pen, pencil, or the like: *The artist drew a cat.* **5.** to describe or represent in words: *The speaker drew a grim picture of conditions in the slums.* **6.** to mark or trace: *to draw lines on paper.* **7.** to stretch, extend, or pull tight: *She drew the bowstring and fired the arrow.* **8.** to cause to come; bring; attract: *This band always draws a large audience. I drew his attention to the mistake.* **9.** to bring forth or result in; evoke: *His actions drew criticism from his superiors.* **10.** to close; shut: *Please draw the drapes.* **11.** to write out or draft formally or in proper form: *to draw a contract, to draw up a will.* **12.** to take in, as by inhaling or sucking: *to draw a deep breath.* **13.** to take out (funds); withdraw: *to draw thirty dollars from a bank account.* **14.** (of a ship) to displace (a certain depth of water) when loaded. —*v.i.* **1.** to create a picture or likeness: *This artist draws beautifully.* **2.** to approach; come; move: *The train drew near the station. He drew back in terror.* **3.** to shrink; become contracted: *Her eyebrows drew together in a frown.* **4.** to cause or allow a current of air to pass: *The chimney is not drawing well.* **5.** to tie, as in a game. —*n.* **1.** the act of drawing. **2.** something that is drawn. **3.** a game or contest in which there is no winner; tie. **4.** a gully or ravine into or through which water drains.
 ·**to draw away.** to move ahead, as in a race.
 ·**to draw out. a.** to extend or lengthen; prolong: *You draw out your stories until they become boring.* **b.** to cause or persuade to talk freely: *to draw out a shy person.*
 ·**to draw up. a.** to come or bring to a stop: *The car drew up in front of the bank.* **b.** to arrange; align: *The general drew up the troops in battle order.*

draw·back (drô′bak′) *n.* an unpleasant or objectionable feature or characteristic; shortcoming; disadvantage: *The main drawback of that house is that it needs a new furnace.*

---

at; āpe; fär; câre; end; mē; it; īce; pîerce; hot; ōld; sông, fôrk; oil; out; up; ūse; rüle; pull; tûrn; chin; sing; shop; thin; this; hw in white; zh in treasure. The symbol ə stands for the unstressed vowel sound heard in about, taken, pencil, lemon, and circus.

297

drawbridge

draw·bridge (drô′brij′) *n.* a bridge that can be wholly or partly raised, lowered, or drawn aside so as to permit or prevent passage.

drawer (*def. 1* drôr; *def. 2* drô′ər) *n.* **1.** a compartment, open at the top, usually with a handle, that slides into a piece of furniture, such as a bureau, and is drawn out to be opened and pushed in to be closed. **2.** a person who draws.

drawers (drôrz) *pl. n.* another word for **underpants**.

draw·ing (drô′ing) *n.* **1.** the act of a person or thing that draws. **2.** a picture, sketch, or design, usually made by the use of pencil, pen, crayon, or similar material: *an ink drawing of a bird.* **3.** the art or technique of making such a picture, sketch, or design: *Your drawing has improved.* **4.** the selection of the winning chance or chances in a lottery or raffle: *The drawing will be held next Saturday.*

drawing board, a board on which paper or other material is placed or mounted for making drawings.

drawing room, a room for receiving or entertaining guests, such as a parlor or formal reception room.

drawl (drôl) *v.i.* to speak slowly, especially with a drawing out of the vowel sounds. —*v.t.* to pronounce in a drawling manner. —*n.* the act or manner of speech of a person who drawls.

drawn (drôn) the past participle of **draw**.

drawn butter, melted butter, often thickened and seasoned, used as a sauce for food.

draw·string (drô′string′) *n.* a string, cord, or tape run through a hem, as around the mouth of a bag, which, when pulled, draws together or closes an opening.

dray (drā) *n.* a low, strong cart with detachable sides, used for carrying heavy loads. —*v.t.* to carry or transport by dray.

dray·man (drā′mən) *n., pl.* **dray·men** (drā′mən). a person whose work is driving a dray.

dread (dred) *v.t.* **1.** to look forward to with fear or anxiety; fear greatly: *Don't dread going to the dentist.* **2.** to look forward to with misgiving or distaste: *He dreaded telling her the bad news.* —*n.* a fear or uneasiness, as over something that will or may happen. —*adj.* causing fear, terror, or awe: *a dread disease.*

dread·ful (dred′fəl) *adj.* **1.** causing fear or awe; terrible: *a dreadful monster.* **2.** very bad; awful: *a dreadful headache, a dreadful movie.* —**dread′ful·ly,** *adv.* —**dread′ful·ness,** *n.*

dread·nought (dred′nôt′) *also,* **dread·naught.** *n.* a battleship with heavy armor and very large guns.

dream (drēm) *n.* **1.** a series of thoughts, images, and sensations seen or experienced during sleep: *I had a frightening dream last night.* **2.** a fanciful thought entertained while awake, especially a wild or vain fancy; daydream. **3.** a strong or earnest hope or desire; cherished goal: *My one great dream is to become an astronaut.* **4.** something having great beauty or charm. —*v.,* **dreamed** or **dreamt, dream·ing.** —*v.i.* **1.** to have a dream or dreams: *I dreamt about a new bike last night.* **2.** to have daydreams or fantasies: *She dreams of going to Europe.* **3.** to think of as at all possible: *We wouldn't dream of going to that party.* —*v.t.* **1.** to see or imagine in a dream: *He dreamt he was a millionaire.* **2.** to believe possible; suppose; imagine: *They never dreamed the movie would be so long.* —*adj.* *Informal.* exactly as wished for; ideal: *That's their dream house.*

•**to dream up.** *Informal.* to create or devise in one's imagination; concoct: *to dream up an excuse for being late.*

dream·er (drē′mər) *n.* **1.** a person who dreams. **2.** a person who seems to live in a world of fantasy.

dream·land (drēm′land′) *n.* **1.** the place where a person is said to be while sleeping; realm of dreams. **2.** a delightful or ideal place existing only in the imagination.

dreamt (dremt) a past tense and past participle of **dream**.

dream·y (drē′mē) *adj.,* **dream·i·er, dream·i·est.** **1.** like a dream; vague; indistinct: *a dreamy recollection.* **2.** given to dreaming or daydreaming: *a dreamy young person.* **3.** soothing; relaxing: *dreamy music.* **4.** of, relating to, or full of dreams. —**dream′i·ly,** *adv.* —**dream′i·ness,** *n.*

drear (drir) *adj.* *Archaic.* another word for **dreary**.

drear·y (drir′ē) *adj.,* **drear·i·er, drear·i·est.** **1.** causing or characterized by sadness or gloom; dismal; depressing: *a dark and dreary room, the dreary prospects of a lonely life.* **2.** dull or uninteresting; monotonous: *I think that Monday is the dreariest day of the week.* —**drear′i·ly,** *adv.* —**drear′i·ness,** *n.*

dredge[1] (drej) *n.* **1.** a machine equipped for scooping up or removing mud, sand, and other substances from the bottom of a body of water. **2.** an apparatus equipped with a net for gathering shellfish and other objects from the bottom of a harbor, bay, or other body of water. —*v.,* **dredged, dredg·ing.** —*v.t.* **1.** to clear out, deepen, or enlarge with a dredge: *to dredge a harbor.* **2.** to gather or remove with or as if with a dredge (often with *up*): *to dredge mud, to dredge up facts.* —*v.i.* to use a dredge. [Perhaps from a form of Old English *dragan* "to draw, drag, pull."]

dredge[2] (drej) *v.t.,* **dredged, dredg·ing.** to sprinkle or coat with a powdered substance, especially sugar or flour: *Dredge the chicken with flour before frying.* [From the obsolete word *dredge* "a sweetmeat."]

dredg·er[1] (drej′ər) *n.* **1.** a person or thing that dredges. **2.** a boat used in dredging. [*Dredge*[1] + *-er*[1].]

dredg·er[2] (drej′ər) *n.* a container with holes in its lid, used for sprinkling powdered substances, as sugar or flour, on food. [*Dredge*[2] + *-er*[1].]

dregs (dregz) *pl. n.* **1.** small pieces of matter that settle at the bottom of a liquid, especially a beverage: *the dregs of coffee.* **2.** the most worthless or undesirable part: *the dregs of society.*

drench (drench) *v.t.* to wet (someone or something) thoroughly; soak: *The sudden rainfall drenched us on the way home from school.*

Dres·den (drez′dən) *n.* a fine porcelain decorated with elaborate, brightly colored designs, made near Dresden, Germany.

dress (dres) *v.,* **dressed** or **drest, dress·ing.** —*v.t.* **1.** to put clothes on; clothe: *The nurse dressed the baby.* **2.** to decorate; adorn; trim: *to dress a store window.* **3.** to clean or prepare meat for cooking or sale: *to dress a chicken.* **4.** to put medication or a dressing on (a wound or sore): *to dress a burn.* **5.** to comb and arrange (hair). **6.** to groom or curry (an animal). **7.** to arrange in a straight line, as a line of soldiers. —*v.i.* **1.** to put on clothes: *I dress very slowly in the morning.* **2.** to select and wear clothes: *You dress well.* **3.** to put on or wear formal clothes. —*n., pl.* **dress·es.** **1.** a garment for a woman or girl, cut to appear as one piece and usually extending from the neck to the legs. **2.** clothing; apparel; attire: *soldiers in battle dress.* **3.** a style or choice of clothing; manner of wearing clothes: *Have you always been so conservative in your dress?* —*adj.* **1.** of or for a dress: *dress material, a dress pattern.* **2.** relating to or suitable for a formal or ceremonial occasion: *a dress suit, a dress uniform.*

   •**to dress down.** *Informal.* to scold severely.

   •**to dress up.** to put on clothing more elaborate or fancy than that usually worn.

dress·er¹ (dres′ər) *n.* **1.** a person who dresses something: *a window dresser.* **2.** a person who assists another in dressing, as for the stage. **3.** a person who dresses in a particular way: *a fancy dresser.* [*Dress* + *-er¹.*]

dress·er² (dres′ər) *n.* **1.** a chest of drawers, often with a mirror; bureau. **2.** a sideboard or set of shelves for holding dishes and kitchen utensils. [From the Old French word *dreceor* meaning "a sideboard," from the word *drecier* "to prepare."]

dress·ing (dres′ing) *n.* **1.** the act of a person or thing that dresses. **2.** a sauce, especially for salads. **3.** a medication or bandage applied to a wound or sore. **4.** a mixture of bread or cracker crumbs and other ingredients, usually seasoned, used to stuff poultry, fish, or roasts; stuffing.

dress·ing–down (dres′ing doun′) *n.* *Informal.* a severe scolding: *I got a dressing-down from my parents for coming in late.*

dressing gown, a robe, especially a long, loose one, usually worn before or while dressing or for lounging.

dressing room, a room for changing clothes, as in a theater.

dressing table, a table, often with drawers, having a mirror for use while grooming and dressing oneself.

dress·mak·er (dres′mā′kər) *n.* a person whose work is making and altering dresses or other articles of clothing for women.

dress·mak·ing (dres′mā′king) *n.* the work or skill of a dressmaker.

dress rehearsal, a full rehearsal in costume of a theatrical presentation or similar performance, especially the final rehearsal.

dress·y (dres′ē) *adj.,* **dress·i·er, dress·i·est. 1.** suitable for formal occasions; elegant; elaborate: *That outfit is much too dressy to wear to a picnic.* **2.** stylish; fashionable: *a dressy social affair.* —**dress′i·ness,** *n.*

drest (drest) a past tense and past participle of **dress.**

drew (drü) the past tense of **draw.**

drib·ble (drib′əl) *v.,* **drib·bled, drib·bling.** —*v.i.* **1.** to fall or flow in drops or small quantities; trickle: *Rain dribbled through the cracks in the roof.* **2.** to let saliva run from the mouth; drivel; drool. **3.** to come little by little or in small amounts: *Contributions dribbled in day by day.* **4.** to move a ball by a succession of bounces or kicks, as in basketball or soccer. —*v.t.* **1.** to let fall or flow in drops or small quantities: *The faucet is dribbling cold water.* **2.** to move (a ball) by a succession of bounces or kicks, as in basketball or soccer. —*n.* **1.** a small quantity of a liquid falling in drops or flowing in a thin stream. **2.** the act of dribbling a ball. —**drib′bler,** *n.*

drib·let (drib′lit) *also,* **drib·blet.** *n.* a small amount or part; bit.

dried (drīd) the past tense and past participle of **dry.**

dri·er (drī′ər) *adj.* the comparative of **dry.** —*n.* **1.** a person or thing that dries. **2.** another spelling of **dryer.**

dri·est (drī′ist) *adj.* the superlative of **dry.**

drift (drift) *v.i.* **1.** to be moved, driven, or carried along by currents of water or air: *The boat drifted downstream. Columns of smoke drifted toward the sky.* **2.** to move or seem to move aimlessly and without any particular goal or purpose: *The tramp drifted from town to town. Some people drift through life.* **3.** to gather or accumulate in heaps by the force of wind or water: *The snow drifted*

against the garage. —*v.t.* to cause to drift: *The wind drifted the snow.* —*n.* **1.** an act or instance of being driven along by currents of water or air. **2.** the direction of movement or drifting, especially of a current of water. **3.** something driven along or heaped up by air or water currents. **4.** a general course of movement; tendency; trend: *The drift of the discussion changed from history to politics.* **5.** a meaning or intent: *I did not quite understand the drift of your remark.* **6.** material, such as sand, gravel, or rocks, that has been moved from one place and deposited in another by a glacier or by the melted water from a glacier. **7.** the movement off course of a ship, aircraft, or missile, due especially to water or air currents.

drift·er (drif′tər) *n.* a person or thing that drifts, especially a person who moves aimlessly from one job or place to another.

drift·wood (drift′wůd′) *n.* wood drifting on open water or washed ashore by the water.

drill¹ (dril) *n.* **1.** a tool with cutting edges or a pointed end, used for boring holes in wood, plaster, concrete, or other hard substances. **2.** the machine operating such a tool. **3.** strict training or instruction by repeated exercises and practice: *military drill. The class got a lot of drill in algebra.* —*v.t.* **1.** to pierce or bore a hole in (something) with a drill. **2.** to make (a hole) by boring: *I drilled three holes in the wall for the brackets of the shelf.* **3.** to train or instruct by repeated exercises and practice: *to drill soldiers in marching. The teacher drilled the class in math all morning.* —*v.i.* **1.** to bore or make a hole with a drill: *to drill for oil.* **2.** to go through or perform drills: *The band drills for two hours every day after school.* [From the Middle Dutch word *drillen* meaning "to drill."] —**drill′er,** *n.*

drill¹
electric **drill**

drill² (dril) *n.* **1.** a machine that plants seeds by making a hole or furrow, dropping in the seed and sometimes fertilizer or other soil preparation, and then covering it with soil. **2.** a small furrow in which seeds are planted. —*v.t.* to sow (seed) in rows. [Of uncertain origin.]

drill press, a machine tool consisting of one or more drills mounted on an upright stand and having an adjustable horizontal table on which the material that is to be drilled is placed.

dri·ly (drī′lē) another spelling of **dryly.**

drink (dringk) *v.,* **drank, drunk, drink·ing.** *v.t.* **1.** to take into the mouth and swallow: *He drinks milk with his meals.* **2.** to take in or soak up; absorb: *The sponge drank up the water. The plants drank in the rain.* **3.** to swallow the contents of: *She quickly drank a cup of coffee and ran out.* **4.** to take in through the senses or the mind: *We drank in the beauty of the woodland scene.* **5.** to give or join in (a toast): *The guests drank a toast to the bride and groom.* —*v.i.* **1.** to take liquid into the mouth and swallow it. **2.** to drink alcoholic beverages. **3.** to make or join in a toast: *We drank to their success.* —*n.* **1.** a liquid for drinking; beverage: *Lemonade is a favorite cold drink.* **2.** a portion of liquid swallowed: *a drink of water.* **3.** a portion of alcoholic beverage. **4.** alcoholic beverages: *Drink was the artist's downfall.* —**drink′er,** *n.*

drink·a·ble (dring′kə bəl) *adj.* suitable or safe for drink-

at; āpe; fär; câre; end; mē; it; īce; pîerce; hot; ōld; sông, fôrk; oil; out; up; ūse; rüle; půll; tûrn; chin; sing; shop; thin; this; hw in white; zh in treasure. The symbol ə stands for the unstressed vowel sound heard in about, taken, pencil, lemon, and circus.

ing: *That stream is polluted, so its water is no longer drinkable.*

drip (drip) *v.,* **dripped, drip·ping.** —*v.i.* **1.** to fall in drops: *The rain came through the roof and dripped from the ceiling.* **2.** to have moisture or liquid falling in drops: *The leaky bucket dripped all over the floor.* —*v.t.* to let (something) fall in drops: *He accidentally dripped paint from the brush.* —*n.* **1.** a falling of liquid in drops. **2.** a liquid falling in drops. **3.** the sound made by a liquid falling in drops: *She could hear the drip of rain outdoors.*

drip–dry (drip′drī′) *adj.* of or referring to a fabric or garment that dries quickly when hung dripping wet and requires little or no ironing: *a drip-dry shirt.*

drip·pings (drip′ingz) *pl. n.* the melted fat and juices that drip from meat, fowl, or fish while cooking.

drive (drīv) *v.,* **drove, driv·en, driv·ing.** —*v.t.* **1.** to cause to move by physical force: *The waves drove the ship onto the rocks. They drove their attackers off.* **2.** to force into some act or condition: *He complained that the noise was driving him crazy.* **3.** to put in motion and direct the movement of; steer: *to drive a car.* **4.** to carry in a car or other vehicle: *He drove the children to the party.* **5.** to cause to penetrate by force: *to drive a nail into wood.* **6.** to force to work hard; overwork: *She's been driving herself lately and needs a vacation badly.* **7.** to carry on or bring about with force or vigor: *She certainly drives a hard bargain.* **8.** to cause to go rapidly, as by hitting or throwing with force: *The batter drove the baseball over the fence.* **9.** *Golf.* to strike (the ball) forcefully, especially from a tee. **10.** to set or keep in motion or operation; supply the power for: *Electricity drives this machine.* **11.** to form or produce by making an opening: *to drive a tunnel through a mountain.* —*v.i.* **1.** to operate and steer a car or other vehicle: *He drives too fast.* **2.** to go or be carried in a car or other vehicle: *They drove through the park.* **3.** to rush, dash, or move forcefully or violently: *The hurricane winds drove against the house.* —*n.* **1.** a trip in a car or other vehicle: *They took a drive in the country.* **2.** a driveway or a public road on which to drive: *The winding drive to the house was covered with gravel.* **3.** the act of driving, especially a gathering together and moving forward: *a cattle drive.* **4.** an organized group effort for some specific purpose; campaign: *a drive to collect clothing for flood victims.* **5.** forceful energy; vigor: *Her drive and enthusiasm helped make the project a success.* **6.** a strong, motivating force that moves an animal or person to action: *the hunger drive.* **7.** the act or instance of driving a ball or other object; forceful blow or stroke: *The batter hit a drive to left field.* **8.** the way in which power is transmitted to the wheels in a motor vehicle: *rear-wheel drive.*

·**to drive at.** to mean or intend to say; suggest: *What were you driving at when you made that remark?*

drive–in (drīv′in′) *n.* **1.** an outdoor motion-picture theater where patrons remain in their parked cars while viewing a movie projected on a large screen. **2.** any place of business, such as a bank or restaurant, designed to serve customers while they remain in their cars. —*adj.* designed to give service to customers while they remain in their cars: *a drive-in bank.*

driv·el (driv′əl) *v.i.,* **driv·eled, driv·el·ing;** *also, British,* **driv·elled, driv·el·ling.** **1.** to let saliva run from the mouth; dribble; slobber. **2.** to talk in a childish or foolish way; talk nonsense. —*n.* **1.** childish, foolish, or ridiculous talk; nonsense. **2.** saliva flowing from the mouth.

driv·en (driv′ən) the past participle of **drive.**

driv·er (drī′vər) *n.* **1.** a person or thing that drives, especially a person who drives a car or other vehicle. **2.** a golf club with a blocklike head and a slightly sloped face, designed to drive balls long distances from the tee. **3.** any machine part that transmits motion or power.

drive shaft, a shaft that transmits power from a source to wheels or to other parts to be driven.

drive·way (drīv′wā′) *n.* a private road leading to a house, garage, or other building from a road or street.

driz·zle (driz′əl) *v.i.,* **driz·zled, driz·zling.** to rain steadily in fine, misty drops. —*n.* a fine, misty rain. —**driz′zly,** *adj.*

droll (drōl) *adj.* amusingly odd or quaint: *a droll fellow.* —**droll′ly,** *adv.* —**droll′ness,** *n.*

droll·er·y (drō′lə rē) *n., pl.* **droll·er·ies. 1.** the quality of being droll; quaint humor. **2.** something droll, as a story. **3.** the behavior or antics of a droll person; jesting.

drom·e·dar·y (drom′ə der′ē) *n., pl.* **drom·e·dar·ies.** a single-humped camel native to Arabia and North Africa.

drone[1] (drōn) *n.* **1.** a male bee, especially a honeybee, that develops from an unfertilized egg, does no work, and cannot sting. The drone mates once with the queen bee and then dies. **2.** a person who lives on the work of others; idler; loafer. **3.** a pilotless aircraft directed by remote control. [From the Old English word *drān* meaning "male bee."]

dromedary

drone[2] (drōn) *v.,* **droned, dron·ing.** —*v.i.* **1.** to make a continuous, low, humming sound: *The planes droned overhead.* **2.** to talk in a dull, monotonous tone: *The speaker droned on and on.* —*v.t.* to say (something) in a dull, monotonous tone. —*n.* a dull, continuous buzzing or humming sound: *The drone of countless mosquitoes kept us awake.* [Possibly from *drone*[1], in imitation of the sound made by a bee.]

drool (drül) *v.i.* **1.** to let saliva run from the mouth; drivel: *The baby drooled all over the bib.* **2.** to water at the mouth, as in anticipation of food: *I drooled at the thought of a steak dinner.* **3.** *Informal.* to show great delight or enthusiasm: *We drooled over the new car.*

droop (drüp) *v.i.* **1.** to hang or sink down: *The dead flowers drooped over the side of the vase.* **2.** to become weak; lose energy or vigor: *His spirits drooped at the thought of losing the game.* **3.** to become discouraged or depressed: —*v.t.* to let hang or sink down: *The sleepy child drooped her head.* —*n.* the act or fact of drooping; drooping position.

droop·y (drü′pē) *adj.,* **droop·i·er, droop·i·est. 1.** drooping or tending to droop. **2.** gloomy; discouraged: *a droopy face.* —**droop′i·ly,** *adv.* —**droop′i·ness,** *n.*

drop (drop) *v.,* **dropped** or **dropt, drop·ping.** —*v.i.* **1.** to fall in small amounts, as a liquid: *Beads of perspiration dropped from his forehead as he worked.* **2.** to fall or go down, especially rapidly or suddenly: *The wet dish dropped from my hand. The runners dropped to their knees after the race.* **3.** to fall or decline in amount or degree; become less: *Business at the summer resort dropped during the winter.* **4.** to fall or move to a position that is lower, inferior, or further back: *I dropped behind the other runners.* **5.** to cease to be of concern; come to an end: *She suggested that they let the matter drop.* **6.** to pay a casual or unexpected visit: *They said they would drop by this evening.* **7.** to fall or pass into a particular state, condition, or activity: *After two hours of tossing and turning, I finally dropped off to sleep.* —*v.t.* **1.** to let fall by letting go of: *You dropped your keys on the floor.* **2.** to cause to move or go down; lower: *When he realized he was being stared at, the shy boy dropped his eyes.* **3.** to let fall in small amounts: *The leaky pail dropped water all over the floor.* **4.** to stop pursuing or dealing with: *to drop a course in school, to drop a subject of discussion.* **5.** to write and send: *She dropped her parents a postcard when she arrived at camp.* **6.** to say or refer to in a casual or incidental way: *to drop a hint.* **7.** to let

out or leave after transporting: *The bus dropped the children in front of the school.* **8.** (of animals) to give birth to. **9.** to cause to fall, as by striking or shooting: *The hunter dropped the deer with one shot.* **10.** to leave out; omit: *to drop a stitch in knitting.* **11.** to break off an association or connection with: *The company dropped ten employees.* **12.** *Slang.* to lose: *to drop money at the racetrack.* —*n.* **1.** a small quantity of liquid that is shaped like a tiny ball or pear: *a drop of water, a drop of blood.* **2.** any very small amount of liquid: *There was only a drop of soda left in the bottle.* **3.** a very small amount: *We didn't have a drop of strength left after the long hike.* **4.** something resembling a drop of liquid in shape or size, such as a piece of candy. **5.** an act or instance of dropping; descent; fall. **6.** a sudden decline or decrease: *a drop in prices, a drop in temperature.* **7. drops.** a liquid medicine to be administered in drops: *eye drops.* **8.** the distance between a higher and a lower level; distance or depth to which anything drops: *There was a 40-foot drop from the third floor to the street.* **9.** a slit or other opening, as in a mailbox, into which something is inserted or dropped.
·**to drop out.** to withdraw; quit: *to drop out of school.*
drop cloth, a large sheet, as of cloth or plastic, used especially by painters to protect furniture and floors from dripping or spilled paint.
drop·let (drop′lit) *n.* a tiny drop.
drop·out (drop′out′) *also,* **drop-out.** *n.* **1.** a student who withdraws from school, especially high school, before graduating. **2.** a person who drops out or withdraws: *a dropout from society.*
drop·per (drop′ər) *n.* **1.** a glass tube with a rubber bulb at one end and a small opening at the other end, used for measuring, transferring, or applying liquids in drops. **2.** a person or thing that drops.
drop·pings (drop′ingz) *pl. n.* the dung of animals.
drop·sy (drop′sē) *n.* another word for **edema.**
dropt (dropt) a past tense and past participle of **drop.**
dro·soph·i·la (dro sof′ə lə, drə sof′ə lə) *n., pl.* **dro·soph·i·las** or **dro·soph·i·lae** (drō sof′ə lē′, drə sof′ə lē′). a type of fruit fly often studied in controlled genetics experiments.
dross (drôs) *n.* **1.** the waste or impure matter that rises to the surface of molten metals. **2.** any worthless matter; refuse; waste.
drought (drout) *also,* **drouth** (drouth). *n.* a long period of dry weather; prolonged lack of rainfall.
drove[1] (drōv) the past tense of **drive.**
drove[2] (drōv) *n.* **1.** a group of animals moving or driven along together: *a drove of cattle, a drove of sheep.* **2.** a group of human beings moving or acting together; crowd: *On a hot, muggy day people head for the beaches in droves.* [Old English *drāf* herd.]
dro·ver (drō′vər) *n.* **1.** a person who takes a drove of cattle, sheep, or other animals to market. **2.** a sheep or cattle dealer.
drown (droun) *v.i.* to die by suffocation in water or other liquid. —*v.t.* **1.** to kill by suffocation in water or other liquid. **2.** to cover with a flood; drench: *The dam broke and its waters drowned the entire valley. Don't drown your pancakes in syrup.* **3.** to lessen or smother the sound of by greater loudness; muffle: *The roar of the train drowned out her words.* **4.** to get rid of: *He tried to drown his sorrow by working day and night.*
drowse (drouz) *v.i.,* **drowsed, drows·ing.** to be half asleep; doze: *You were drowsing during class.* —*n.* the state of being half asleep.
drow·sy (drou′zē) *adj.,* **drow·si·er, drow·si·est. 1.** sleepy or inclined to sleep; half asleep: *Everyone felt drowsy after the large dinner.* **2.** characterized by quiet peacefulness: *a drowsy little village.* **3.** causing sleepiness. —**drow′si·ly,** *adv.* —**drow′si·ness,** *n.*
drub (drub) *v.t.,* **drubbed, drub·bing. 1.** to beat severely, as with a stick; thrash. **2.** to defeat decisively; rout.

drudge (druj) *n.* a person who works hard at wearying, boring, or menial tasks. —*v.i.,* **drudged, drudg·ing.** to work hard at wearying, boring, or menial tasks.
drudg·er·y (druj′ə rē) *n., pl.* **drudg·er·ies.** wearying, boring, or menial labor.
drug (drug) *n.* **1.** any chemical agent that affects living cells, especially one used to treat disease or discomfort in human beings and animals. **2.** a substance to which a person may become addicted; narcotic. —*v.t.,* **drugged, drug·ging. 1.** to give drugs to, especially narcotic drugs: *to drug a patient before an operation.* **2.** to add a drug or drugs to (food or drink), especially a narcotic or poisonous drug. **3.** to affect or overcome as if with a drug.
drug abuse, the use of a drug for other than medicinal purposes, usually a cause or result of drug addiction.
drug addict, a person who is addicted to a drug, such as heroin or cocaine.
drug·gist (drug′ist) *n.* **1.** a person licensed to fill prescriptions; pharmacist. **2.** a person who owns or operates a drugstore.
drug·store (drug′stôr′) *n.* a store where medicines, drugs, medical supplies, and various other items are sold.
dru·id (drü′id) *also,* **Dru·id.** *n.* a member of a pre-Christian religious order among the Celts.
drum (drum) *n.* **1.** a percussion instrument usually consisting of a hollow cylinder or frame with a membrane stretched tightly over one or both ends, played by beating on the membrane with sticks or the hands. **2.** a sound produced when a drum is beaten. **3.** any similar sound: *The drum of your fingers on the table made me nervous.* **4.** something resembling a drum in shape. **5.** a cylindrical metal container, as for oil. **6.** a metal cylinder around which something, as cable, is wound. **7.** see **eardrum.** —*v.,* **drummed, drum·ming.** —*v.i.* **1.** to beat or play a drum. **2.** to beat or tap rhythmically or repeatedly: *He drummed on the desk with his fingers.* **3.** to sound like a drum; pound; resound: *The noise drummed in her ears.* —*v.t.* to perform or play on or as if on a drum.
·**to drum up.** to raise or create through much effort: *The senator tried to drum up support for the proposed law.*

drum (n., def. 1)

drum·beat (drum′bēt′) *n.* the sound of a stroke on a drum.
drum·lin (drum′lin) *n.* an oval mound formed from glacial deposits.

at; āpe; fär; câre; end; mē; it; īce; pîerce; hot; ōld; sông, fôrk; oil; out; up; ūse; rüle; pull; tûrn; chin; sing; shop; thin; this; hw in white; zh in treasure. The symbol ə stands for the unstressed vowel sound heard in about, taken, pencil, lemon, and circus.

drum major, a person who leads or directs a marching band.

drum majorette, a girl who twirls a baton while marching with a band in a parade.

drum·mer (drum′ər) *n.* **1.** a person who plays a drum. **2.** *Informal.* a traveling sales representative.

drum·stick (drum′stik′) *n.* **1.** a stick for beating a drum. **2.** the lower part of the leg of a fowl, especially when cooked.

drunk (drungk) *v.* the past participle of **drink.** —*adj.* **1.** exhibiting lack of control of one's faculties because of too much drinking of alcoholic liquor; intoxicated. **2.** powerfully affected; overwhelmed: *drunk with success, drunk with joy.* —*n. Informal.* **1.** a person who is drunk, especially one who habitually drinks too much alcoholic liquor. **2.** a drinking spree.

drunk·ard (drung′kərd) *n.* a person who habitually drinks too much alcoholic liquor; person who is often drunk.

drunk·en (drung′kən) *adj.* **1.** drunk; intoxicated. **2.** caused by being drunk: *a drunken rage, a drunken stupor.* —**drunk′en·ly,** *adv.* —**drunk′en·ness,** *n.*

drunk·o·me·ter (drung kom′ə tər) *n.* a device that chemically analyzes a person's breath to determine the alcoholic content of the blood.

dry (drī) *adj.,* **dri·er, dri·est. 1.** not wet or damp; free from moisture: *After a few hours in the sun, the bathing suits were dry.* **2.** empty of water or other liquid: *The well has been dry for a month.* **3.** not under or in water: *They stepped from the boat onto dry land.* **4.** having or characterized by little or no rainfall: *It was the driest summer in years.* **5.** free from tears: *dry eyes.* **6.** thirsty: *I was dry after the long hike.* **7.** without butter or other spreads: *dry toast.* **8.** not giving milk: *a dry cow.* **9.** witty in an ironic, matter-of-fact way: *a dry sense of humor.* **10.** not interesting; dull; boring: *a dry book.* **11.** not liquid; lacking moisture: *dry cereal.* **12.** not sweet or fruity: *dry wine.* **13.** *Informal.* prohibiting the manufacture, sale, or use of alcoholic beverages: *a dry state.* —*v.,* **dried, dry·ing.** —*v.t.* to make dry; remove moisture from: *We dried the dishes. The sun dried up the puddles.* —*v.i.* to become dry; lose moisture: *My wet hair dried in the sun. The creek dried up last summer.* —**dry′ness,** *n.*

dry·ad (drī′əd) *also,* **Dry·ad.** *n. Greek Mythology.* a nymph living in trees; wood nymph.

dry cell, an electric cell in which the electrolyte is in a form that does not spill, such as a paste or jelly.

dry–clean (drī′klēn′) *v.t.* to clean (clothes or other cloth articles) with chemical solvents instead of in water.

dry cleaner 1. a person or business that does dry cleaning. **2.** a substance used in dry cleaning.

dry cleaning, the act or process of cleaning clothes or other cloth articles with chemical solvents instead of in water.

dry dock, any of various watertight structures in which a ship can be docked to allow for repairs or maintenance of the hull.

dry·er (drī′ər) *also,* **dri·er.** *n.* **1.** a device or appliance for drying: *a hair dryer, a clothes dryer.* **2.** a substance added to paints, varnishes, and other materials to make them dry more quickly.

dry farming, the growing of crops in an area that is semiarid or on land that is not irrigated, using methods that conserve soil moisture, such as contour farming.

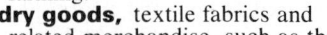
a ship in **dry dock**

dry goods, textile fabrics and related merchandise, such as thread, ribbon, and lace.

dry ice, an extremely cold solid, made by compressing and then cooling carbon dioxide. Dry ice is widely used as a refrigerant because it changes from a solid back to a gas without becoming liquid.

dry·ly (drī′lē) *also,* **dri·ly.** *adv.* in a dry manner.

dry measure, a system of units for measuring the volume of dry commodities, as grain, vegetables, or fruit.

dry rot, decay of seasoned timber resulting in its crumbling to a dry powder, caused by any of various fungi.

dry run, a practice session; trial; rehearsal.

dry–shod (drī′shod′) *adj.* having or keeping one's shoes or feet dry; without getting the feet wet.

DST, daylight saving time.

du·al (dü′əl, dū′əl) *adj.* **1.** composed or consisting of two; twofold; double: *dual controls.* **2.** referring or relating to two.

du·al·i·ty (dü al′i tē, dū al′i tē) *n., pl.* **du·al·i·ties.** the state or quality of being composed or consisting of two items or parts: *the duality of light and shadow in a painting.*

dub¹ (dub) *v.t.,* **dubbed, dub·bing. 1.** to confer knighthood upon by tapping on the shoulder with a sword; make a knight: *The queen dubbed the famous explorer ''Sir Edmund.''* **2.** to give a title or nickname to; name: *Her friends dubbed her ''Freckles.''* **3.** to speak of or refer to as: *He was dubbed a fool merely because he spoke so seldom.* [From either the Old English word *dubbian* or the Old French word *adober,* both meaning ''to create a knight''; of uncertain origin.]

dub² (dub) *v.t.,* **dubbed, dub·bing. 1.** to provide (a film or other recording) with a new soundtrack, especially one in which the dialogue is in another language: *The French movie was dubbed into English.* **2.** to insert or substitute (music, dialogue, or other sounds) in the soundtrack of a film or other recording. [Short for *double.*]

du·bi·ous (dü′bē əs, dū′bē əs) *adj.* **1.** feeling or showing doubt or uncertainty; hesitant; skeptical: *Your friends were dubious about your chances of winning.* **2.** of questionable character; suspect: *a person of dubious reputation.* **3.** causing doubt; not clear: *a dubious reply.* —**du′bi·ous·ly,** *adv.* —**du′bi·ous·ness,** *n.*

du·cal (dü′kəl, dū′kəl) *adj.* of or relating to a duke or duchy.

duc·at (duk′ət) *n.* any of several gold or silver coins formerly used in certain European countries.

duch·ess (duch′is) *n., pl.* **duch·ess·es. 1.** the wife or widow of a duke. **2.** a woman holding in her own right a rank equal to a duke's, especially the female sovereign of a duchy.

duch·y (duch′ē) *n., pl.* **duch·ies.** the territory under the rule of a duke or duchess; dukedom.

duck¹ (duk) *n.* **1.** any of various wild or domestic waterfowl having a relatively short neck and legs, webbed feet, and usually a broad, flat bill. **2.** a female duck, as distinguished from the male, or drake. **3.** the flesh of a duck used as food. [From the Old English word *duce* meaning this bird.]

duck² (duk) *v.t.* **1.** to plunge or thrust under water quickly or suddenly: *The children ducked the swimming instructor in the lake.* **2.** to lower or bend (the head or body) suddenly and quickly: *I ducked my head to avoid being hit by the ball.* **3.** to avoid or evade: *to duck a punch, to duck a question.* —*v.i.* **1.** to lower the head or body quickly or suddenly, as to avoid being hit: *Everyone ducked when they heard the gunshots.* **2.** to move quickly; dart: *The thieves ducked around the corner when they saw the police coming.* —*n.* the act of ducking. [From the Middle English word *douken* ''to plunge or dive,'' from Old English.]

duck³ (duk) *n.* **1.** a very strong cotton fabric similar to, but lighter in weight than, canvas, used for making small sails, tents, and clothes. **2. ducks.** trousers made of this fabric. [From the Dutch word *doek* meaning "linen cloth, canvas."]

duck⁴ (duk) *n.* a military truck that can travel on land and water, used especially during World War II. [From its military code designation, *DUKW.*]

duck·bill (duk′bil′) *n.* another word for **platypus.** Also, **duck-billed platypus.**

duck–billed (duk′bild′) *adj.* having a bill like a duck's.

ducking stool, a device for punishment formerly used in England and colonial America, consisting of a long plank with a chair at the end in which offenders were tied to be plunged into water.

duck·ling (duk′ling) *n.* a young duck.

duck·pin (duk′pin′) *n.* **1. duckpins.** a bowling game played with pins smaller than those used in tenpins, and a smaller ball. ▲ used with a singular verb. **2.** a pin used in this game.

duck·weed (duk′wēd′) *n.* any of various very small, stemless green plants that float on still water, often forming a coating on the surface.

duct (dukt) *n.* **1.** a tube, pipe, or channel that carries something, such as a liquid or gas. **2.** a tube or channel for carrying a body fluid, especially a fluid secreted by a gland. **3.** a pipe or channel for electric wires or cables. —**duct′less,** *adj.*

duc·tile (duk′təl) *adj.* **1.** able to be hammered out thin or drawn out into wire without breaking; malleable: *ductile metals.* **2.** easily molded or shaped; pliable: *Modeling clay is ductile.* **3.** easily controlled or influenced; tractable: *a ductile person.* —**duc·til·i·ty** (duk til′i tē), *n.*

duct·less gland (dukt′lis) any of various glands without ducts that secrete hormones directly into the blood or lymph; endocrine gland.

dud (dud) *n.* **1.** a bomb or shell that fails to explode. **2. duds.** *Informal.* another word for **clothing. 3.** *Slang.* a person or thing that is a failure.

dude (dūd, dōōd) *n.* **1.** a man who is very concerned with his clothes. **2.** *Informal.* a city-bred person, especially someone from the eastern U.S. visiting a ranch.

dude ranch, a ranch operated as a resort for tourists.

dudg·eon (duj′ən) *n.* a feeling of anger, resentment, or offense. ▲ used chiefly in the phrase *in high dudgeon: After the argument, they stalked out of the room in high dudgeon.*

due (dū, dōō) *adj.* **1.** owed or owing, as a debt; owed and expected to be paid; payable: *The rent will be due on the first of the month. The final payment on the loan is due.* **2.** owed or owing, as by right or custom; appropriate; proper: *The lawyer addressed the judge with all due respect.* **3.** as much as is necessary; adequate; sufficient: *The children were cautioned to use due care when crossing the street.* **4.** required or expected to arrive, be present, or be ready: *The train is due at 5:30.* —*n.* **1.** something that is due or owed. **2. dues.** a fee or charge, especially one paid to a group or organization for the rights of membership. —*adv.* straight; directly; exactly: *The ship sailed due north.*

·due to. a. caused by: *The delay was due to heavy traffic.* **b.** because of: *The project was abandoned due to lack of support.* ▲ Some people still object to the use of **due to** to mean "because of" or "on account of," but this use is widely accepted as standard English.

du·el (dū′əl, dōō′əl) *n.* **1.** a formal fight between two people with swords or pistols. Duels are arranged to settle an argument or decide a point of honor and are fought according to certain established rules. **2.** any contest or struggle between two opponents: *a duel of wits.* —*v.*, **du·eled, du·el·ing;** *also, British,* **du·elled, du·el·ling.** —*v.i.* to fight a duel. —*v.t.* to fight a duel with (someone). —**du′el·er;** *also, British,* **du′el·ler,** *n.*

du·el·ist (dū′ə list, dōō′ə list) *also, British,* **du·el·list.** *n.* a person who fights a duel.

du·en·na (dū en′ə, dōō en′ə) *n.* **1.** an elderly woman who serves as the chaperon or escort of a young unmarried girl in a Spanish or Portuguese family. **2.** any chaperon.

due process of law, the carrying out of the law according to established legal principles and in such a way that the rights of the individual are protected. Also, **due process.**

du·et (dū et′, dōō et′) *n.* **1.** a musical composition for two voices or instruments. **2.** two musical performers.

duf·fel (duf′əl) *n.* **1.** a coarse woolen cloth with a thick nap. **2.** equipment or supplies, especially for camping.

duffel bag, a cylindrical bag, usually of canvas, used for carrying clothes, equipment, or other belongings.

dug (dug) the past tense and past participle of **dig.**

du·gong (dū′gông′, dū′gong′) *n.* a plant-eating sea mammal having a blunt snout, a short, flat tail, and a pair of front flippers.

dugong

dug·out (dug′out′) *n.* **1.** a rough shelter or dwelling formed by digging a hole in the ground or in a hillside or other slope, often covered by sod, logs, or other material. **2.** *Baseball.* an area enclosed on three sides but open to the playing field, often below field level, in which players sit when not at bat or in the field. **3.** a canoe or boat made by hollowing out a large log.

duke (dük, dōōk) *n.* **1.** a British nobleman of the highest rank outside the royal family. **2.** a nobleman of certain other European countries having a similar rank. **3.** a prince who rules an independent duchy. **4. dukes.** *Slang.* fists: *Put up your dukes.*

duke·dom (dük′dəm, dōōk′dəm) *n.* **1.** the territory ruled by a duke; duchy. **2.** the title or rank of a duke.

dul·cet (dul′sit) *adj.* soothing or agreeable, especially to the ear; sweet; pleasant: *the dulcet tones of a fine voice.*

dul·ci·mer (dul′sə mər) *n.* **1.** a musical instrument having metal strings and played by striking the strings with two leather-covered hammers. **2.** a musical instrument with three or more strings stretched over a long, oval board having frets. The strings are plucked with a quill or the fingers.

dull (dul) *adj.* **1.** not sharp or pointed; blunt: *a dull blade, a pencil with a dull point.* **2.** not interesting; boring; tedious: *a dull speech, a dull subject.* **3.** lacking in intelligence or mental quickness; slow to learn or understand: *a dull student.* **4.** not keenly felt; not intense: *a dull ache.* **5.** not bright, clear, or vivid: *a dull red, a dull finish on a floor.* **6.** not distinct or ringing in sound; muffled: *a dull thud.* —*v.t.* to make dull: *to dull a blade.* —*v.i.* to become dull: *The razor will dull if you use it to cut wood.* —**dull′ness,** *n.* —**dul′ly,** *adv.*

dull·ard (dul′ərd) *n.* a person who is stupid or slow-witted; dolt.

du·ly (dū′lē, dōō′lē) *adv.* **1.** in a fitting or proper manner; suitably; rightly: *The sheriff's deputies were duly sworn in.* **2.** to the extent or degree that is due; adequately; sufficiently: *These proposals should be duly considered.* **3.** when due; at the proper time: *The bill was duly paid.*

dumb (dum) *adj.* **1.** lacking the power of speech; mute: *a person who is deaf and dumb.* **2.** temporarily speechless: *We were struck dumb when we heard the story.* **3.** not speaking; silent; taciturn: *The prisoner remained dumb.*

---

at; āpe; fär; câre; end; mē; it; īce; pîerce; hot; ōld; sông, fôrk; oil; out; up; ūse; rüle; pull; tûrn; chin; sing; shop; thin; this; hw in white; zh in treasure. The symbol ə stands for the unstressed vowel sound heard in about, taken, pencil, lemon, and circus.

refusing to answer any questions. **4.** *Informal.* stupid: *What a dumb thing to do!* —**dumb′ly,** *adv.* —**dumb′ness,** *n.*

dumb·bell (dum′bel′) *n.* **1.** a bar with heavy, usually metal, balls or disks at either end, used for exercising. **2.** *Slang.* a stupid person.

dumb·found (dum found′, dum′found′) *also,* **dumfound.** *v.t.* to strike dumb, as with amazement; astonish: *Why were you dumbfounded to find out that you had passed the test?*

dumb show, gestures without speech; pantomime.

dumb·wait·er (dum′wā′tər) *n.* **1.** a small elevator used to carry dishes, food, rubbish, or other articles from one floor to another. **2.** a movable serving table or stand.

dum·dum (dum′dum′) *n.* a bullet made to expand on impact, causing a large wound. Also, **dumdum bullet.** [From *Dum Dum,* a town near Calcutta, India, where these bullets were formerly made.]

dum·found (dum found′, dum′found′) another spelling of **dumbfound.**

dum·my (dum′ē) *n., pl.* **dum·mies.** **1.** a figure of the human body used to represent or serve as a real person: *department store dummies, a ventriloquist's dummy.* **2.** something made to resemble the real thing: *The actor's gun was a dummy.* **3.** a person seeming to act independently or for his or her own interests but really controlled by another. **4.** a player, as in bridge, whose cards are laid face up on the table and played by his or her partner. **5.** a sample, as of a book or magazine, usually consisting of blank pages, arranged to show the size and appearance of the final version. **6.** *Informal.* a stupid person; dolt. —*adj.* **1.** imitation; sham: *a dummy rifle.* **2.** seeming to act independently but really serving or controlled by another: *a dummy president of a corporation.*

dump (dump) *v.t.* **1.** to throw down or let fall in a heap or mass; fling down or drop heavily or suddenly: *The truck dumped the gravel in the driveway. He dumped his books on the bed.* **2.** to unload or empty the contents of (a container), as by overturning: *She dumped out her briefcase on the table.* **3.** *Informal.* to get rid of or throw away: *to dump the garbage, to dump a failing politician.* —*n.* **1.** a place where rubbish or garbage is deposited. **2.** a pile or heap of rubbish or other discarded materials. **3.** a place for temporary storage of military supplies: *an ammunition dump.* **4.** *Slang.* a messy, shabby, or unattractive place: *The hotel was a real dump.* **5.** *Computers.* the display or printing out of the entire contents in a file or in memory.

dump·ling (dump′ling) *n.* **1.** a ball of dough that is boiled or steamed and usually served with meat. **2.** a dessert made by enclosing fruit in a piece of dough and baking or steaming it.

dumps (dumps) *pl. n.* a gloomy or depressed state of mind; low spirits: *to be down in the dumps.*

Dump·ster (dump′stər) *also,* **dump·ster.** *n. Trademark.* a very large container for holding trash, designed to be lifted and emptied into a special truck.

dump truck, a truck having a rear bed that can be tilted so that its contents can slide off through an open tailgate.

dump·y (dump′pē) *adj.,* **dump·i·er, dump·i·est.** short and stout; squat. —**dump′i·ness,** *n.*

dun¹ (dun) *v.t.,* **dunned, dun·ning.** to make repeated demands upon (someone) for payment of a debt: *The department store kept dunning them for their past due bills.* —*n.* **1.** the repeated demand for payment of a debt. **2.** a person who duns. [Of uncertain origin.]

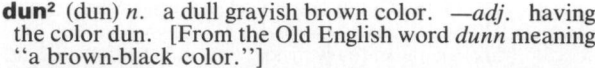

dumbbells
(def. 1)

dun² (dun) *n.* a dull grayish brown color. —*adj.* having the color dun. [From the Old English word *dunn* meaning "a brown-black color."]

dunce (duns) *n.* a person who is slow at learning; dull-witted or ignorant person. [From the word *Dunsmen,* a term of ridicule applied to the followers of the Scottish theologian and scholar John *Duns* Scotus (1266?–1308).]

dune (dün, dūn) *n.* a mound, hill, or ridge of sand that is heaped up by the wind.

dune buggy, a motor vehicle with oversize tires, used for driving on beaches and sand dunes. Also, **beach buggy.**

dung (dung) *n.* solid waste matter that is eliminated by animals; manure.

dun·ga·ree (dung′gə rē′) *n.* **1.** a denim fabric used for such items as work clothes, sportswear, and sails. **2. dungarees.** trousers or work clothes made of this fabric. [From the Hindi word *dungrī* meaning a kind of coarse cloth.]

dun·geon (dun′jən) *n.* a dark cell or prison, especially one underground: *the dungeon of a castle.*

dung·hill (dung′hil′) *n.* a heap of dung.

dunk (dungk) *v.t.* **1.** to dip (something to eat) into a liquid: *to dunk doughnuts into coffee.* **2.** to push or plunge (someone) underwater briefly; duck.

du·o (dü′ō, dū′ō) *n., pl.* **du·os.** **1.** another word for duet. **2.** a pair; couple.

du·o·dec·i·mal (dü′ə des′ə məl, dū′ə des′ə məl) *adj.* relating to or based on twelfths or the number twelve; proceeding by twelves: *duodecimal multiplication.* —*n.* a number in a duodecimal system.

duodecimal system, a system of numbers in which the base is twelve, rather than ten, as in the decimal system.

du·o·de·nal (dü′ə dē′nəl, dū′ə dē′nəl, dü od′ə nəl, dū od′ə nəl) *adj.* of or relating to the duodenum: *a duodenal ulcer.*

du·o·de·num (dü′ə dē′nəm, dū′ə dē′nəm, dü od′ə nəm, dū od′ə nəm) *n., pl.* **du·o·de·na** (dü′ə dē′nə, dü′ə dē′nə, dü od′ə nə, dū od′ə nə) or **du·o·de·nums.** the first section of the small intestine, extending from the stomach to the jejunum.

dupe (düp, dūp) *n.* a person who is easily tricked or deceived, or who unknowingly is used by another: *She was a dupe of the racketeers.* —*v.t.,* **duped, dup·ing.** to make a dupe of; trick or deceive: *He was duped into helping the prisoners make their escape.*

du·ple (dü′pəl, dū′pəl) *adj.* **1.** double; twofold. **2.** *Music.* having two, or a multiple of two, beats to the measure: *duple time, duple meter.*

du·plex (dü′pleks, dū′pleks) *adj.* having two parts; double; twofold. —*n.* a duplex house or apartment.

duplex apartment, an apartment having rooms on two floors.

duplex house, a house having two separate single-family units.

du·pli·cate (*adj., n.,* dü′pli kit, dū′pli kit; *v.,* dü′pli kāt′, dū′pli kāt′) *adj.* **1.** exactly like something else; being an exact copy of an original: *a duplicate list, a duplicate key.* **2.** having or consisting of two corresponding or identical parts; double; twofold. —*n.* **1.** a copy exactly like an original; exact copy: *The secretary kept a duplicate of the business letter.* **2.** something corresponding in every way to something else; counterpart; double: *This jacket is a duplicate of yours.* —*v.t.,* **du·pli·cat·ed, du·pli·cat·ing.** **1.** to make an exact copy of; reproduce: *to duplicate a letter.* **2.** to do again; repeat: *The tennis champion tried hard to duplicate past victories.*

·in duplicate. in two identical copies: *Type this letter in duplicate.*

du·pli·ca·tion (dü′pli kā′shən, dū′pli kā′shən) *n.* **1.** the act of duplicating or the state of being duplicated. **2.** a copy or counterpart; duplicate.

du·pli·ca·tor (dü′pli kā′tər, dū′pli kā′tər) *n.* a machine for making copies, especially of pages of written or typed material.

du·plic·i·ty (dü plis′i tē, dū plis′i tē) *n., pl.* **du·plic·i·ties.** acting in a way that is opposite to one's true feelings or beliefs in order to deceive; deceitfulness: *the duplicity of a spy.*

du·ra·bil·i·ty (dùr′ə bil′i tē, dyùr′ə bil′i tē) *n.* the quality of being durable; ability to resist wear, decay, or change.

du·ra·ble (dùr′ə bəl, dyùr′ə bəl) *adj.* **1.** able to resist wear or decay: *a durable floor covering, durable shoes.* **2.** able to resist change or stress; stable; enduring: *a durable friendship.* —**du′ra·ble·ness,** *n.* —**du′ra·bly,** *adv.*

du·rance (dùr′əns, dyùr′əns) *n.* forced confinement or imprisonment. ▲ used chiefly in the phrase *in durance vile.*

du·ra·tion (dù rā′shən, dyù rā′shən) *n.* the length of time during which anything continues or exists: *They fought in Europe for the duration of the war. The peace between the two countries was of short duration.*

du·ress (dù res′, dyù res′) *n.* **1.** the condition of being compelled to do something by force or threat: *The prisoner signed the confession under duress.* **2.** unlawful confinement or imprisonment.

dur·ing (dùr′ing, dyùr′ing) *prep.* **1.** throughout the time or duration of: *They live in the country during the summer.* **2.** at some point in the course of: *We arrived at the theater during the second act.*

durst (dûrst) *Archaic.* a past tense of **dare.**

du·rum (dùr′əm, dyùr′əm) *n.* a type of wheat having hard, amber-colored kernels used in producing a high-quality flour from which macaroni, spaghetti, and similar products are made. Also, **durum wheat.**

dusk (dusk) *n.* **1.** the time of day just before nightfall; twilight. **2.** shade or gloom; darkness: *in the dusk of the forest.* —*adj.* dark or gloomy.

dusk·y (dus′kē) *adj.,* **dusk·i·er, dusk·i·est. 1.** dark in color: *The dress was a dusky brown.* **2.** without light; shadowy; dim: *a dusky day, a dusky room.* —**dusk′i·ly,** *adv.* —**dusk′i·ness,** *n.*

dust (dust) *n.* **1.** fine, dry particles of earth or other matter: *The passing car raised a cloud of dust.* **2.** ground, especially as the burial place of the dead; earth. **3.** what remains of something, as a dead body, after decay or destruction. —*v.t.* **1.** to remove dust from, as by brushing or wiping: *to dust a table.* **2.** to cover or sprinkle: *to dust a cake with powdered sugar, to dust crops with insecticide.* —*v.i.* to remove dust, especially from furniture.
·**to bite the dust.** to die, especially in battle.

dust bowl *also,* **Dust Bowl.** an area of dry, dusty land having irregular rainfall and frequent dust storms, especially such an area that developed in the western plains of the United States in the 1930s.

dust·er (dus′tər) *n.* **1.** a person or thing that dusts. **2.** a cloth, brush, or other device for removing dust from objects. **3.** a loose-fitting, knee-length housecoat. **4.** a long, lightweight coat formerly worn in open automobiles to protect clothing from dust.

dust jacket 1. a removable, usually illustrated paper cover for a book. **2.** a casing for a phonograph record.

dust·pan (dust′pan′) *n.* a broad, short-handled utensil resembling a shovel, used for collecting dust swept from a floor.

dust storm, a strong wind that carries clouds of dust across dry plains or desert regions.

dust·y (dus′tē) *adj.,* **dust·i·er, dust·i·est. 1.** full of or covered with dust: *a dusty old trunk.* **2.** like dust; powdery: *a dusty snow.* **3.** having the color of dust; grayish: *dusty hair.* —**dust′i·ness,** *n.*

Dutch (duch) *adj.* of or relating to the Netherlands, its people, or their language. —*n.* **1. the Dutch,** the people of the Netherlands. **2.** the language of the Netherlands.
·**in Dutch.** *Informal.* in trouble or disfavor: *I'm in Dutch with my parents for coming home late.*
·**to go Dutch.** *Informal.* to have each person pay for himself or herself, as on a date.

Words From Other Languages

Although the Netherlands is a small country, its travelers and explorers spread the Dutch language to many other countries. Because the Dutch were noted sailors, many Dutch words borrowed into English are sailing terms.

boom	the arm of a derrick or support for a sail
coleslaw	a salad of shredded cabbage and dressing
drill	a pointed tool used for boring holes
easel	a stand for an artist's canvas
etch	to use acid to engrave on metal
Santa Claus	the legendary jolly old man who brings Christmas presents
skipper	the captain of a ship
sloop	a sailboat with one mast
splint	a firm support for a broken bone
stoop	a short flight of front steps
yacht	a small ship for racing or pleasure

Dutch door, a door that is divided horizontally into two parts, allowing either the top or bottom part to be open or closed separately.

Dutch·man (duch′mən) *n., pl.* **Dutch·men** (duch′mən), a person who was born in or is a citizen of the Netherlands.

Dutch oven. 1. a heavy metal or ceramic pot with a tight-fitting cover, used chiefly for cooking meats and stews. **2.** a metal box having one side that opens, placed before a fire for cooking by reflected heat.

Dutch treat *Informal.* a meal, entertainment, or outing at which each person pays for all of his or her own expenses by agreement.

Dutch door

at; āpe; fär; câre; end; mē; it; īce; pîerce; hot; ōld; sông, fôrk; oil; out; up; ūse; rüle; pùll; tûrn; chin; sing; shop; thin; this; hw in white; zh in treasure. The symbol ə stands for the unstressed vowel sound heard in about, taken, pencil, lemon, and circus.

du·te·ous (dü′tēəs, dū′tē əs) *adj.* dutiful; obedient. —**du′te·ous·ly**, *adv.* —**du′te·ous·ness**, *n.*

du·ti·a·ble (dü′tē ə bəl, dū′tē ə bəl) *adj.* subject to the payment of customs duty or taxes: *a shipment of dutiable imports.*

du·ti·ful (dü′tə fəl, dū′tə fəl) *adj.* **1.** doing one's duty or duties; obedient; respectful: *a dutiful child, a dutiful citizen who always votes.* **2.** showing or resulting from a sense of duty: *The store manager displayed a dutiful interest in the customers' complaints.* —**du′ti·ful·ly**, *adv.* —**du′ti·ful·ness**, *n.*

du·ty (dü′tē, dū′tē) *n., pl.* **du·ties. 1.** something that a person is bound to do; obligation: *It is the duty of parents to care for their children properly.* **2.** a sense of what is right: *I was motivated by duty, and not by any hope of reward, when I returned the wallet I found.* **3.** an act or action that is required by or is a part of a person's work or position: *One of the duties of a teacher is grading papers.* **4.** a tax imposed on certain goods that are brought into or taken out of a country.

dwarf (dwôrf) *n., pl.* **dwarfs** or **dwarves** (dwôrvz). **1.** a fully grown, abnormally proportioned person, animal, or plant of less than normal size for its kind. **2.** in folklore, a little man, often represented as ugly and deformed, having unusual or magical powers or skills. **3.** see **dwarf star.** —*v.t.* **1.** to cause to seem small, as by contrast or comparison: *Most professional basketball players dwarf other people.* **2.** to keep from growing to the normal size; stunt: *to dwarf a tree.* —*adj.* of unusually small size; diminutive: *dwarf trees.*

dwarf·ish (dwôr′fish) *adj.* like a dwarf; unusually small. —**dwarf′ish·ly**, *adv.* —**dwarf′ish·ness**, *n.*

dwarf star, a star that emits an average amount of light and is of average or less than average size and mass. The sun is a dwarf star. Also, **dwarf.**

dwell (dwel) *v.i.,* **dwelt** or **dwelled, dwell·ing. 1.** to make one's home; live; reside: *to dwell in the suburbs, to dwell in a cottage by the sea.* **2.** to exist or be present: *The memory of those childhood years dwells in our hearts.* —**dwell′er**, *n.*

  ·**to dwell on** or **to dwell upon.** to think, write, or speak about for a long time: *The speaker dwelt at length upon the final point. Don't dwell too much on painful memories.*

dwell·ing (dwel′ing) *n.* a place where a person lives; house; abode.

dwelt (dwelt) a past tense and past participle of **dwell.**

DWI, driving while intoxicated.

dwin·dle (dwin′dəl) *v.i.,* **dwin·dled, dwin·dling.** to become gradually smaller or less; shrink; diminish: *After the parade was over, the crowd began to dwindle. Hopes for their safety dwindled.*

Dy, the symbol for dysprosium.

dye (dī) *n.* **1.** a coloring matter used to give a particular hue to cloth, hair, food, or other materials. Dye is either obtained from natural substances in plants, animals, and minerals, or produced synthetically. **2.** a color or hue, especially as produced by dyeing. —*v.,* **dyed, dye·ing.** —*v.t.* to give a particular color to, especially by soaking in a liquid dye: *Let's dye these curtains green.* —*v.i.* to take on color in dyeing. —**dy′er**, *n.*

dyed–in–the–wool (dīd′in thə wûl′) *adj.* thoroughgoing; through and through; complete: *a dyed-in-the-wool political conservative.*

dye·ing (dī′ing) *n.* the act, process, or trade of coloring cloth, hair, or other materials with dye.

dye·stuff (dī′stuf′) *n.* a substance used as a dye or as a source of dye.

dy·ing (dī′ing) *v.* the present participle of **die¹.** —*adj.* **1.** approaching death; about to die: *the confession of a dying person.* **2.** of or associated with death or dying; at death: *dying words.* **3.** coming to an end; fading: *a dying flame.*

dyke (dīk) *n., v.,* **dyked, dyk·ing.** another spelling of **dike.**

dy·nam·ic (dī nam′ik) *adj.* **1.** characterized by or full of energy and vigor; forceful: *a dynamic personality, a dynamic leader.* **2.** characterized by change or activity: *a dynamic new government.* **3.** of or relating to energy or force in motion. **4.** of or relating to dynamics. —**dy·nam′i·cal·ly**, *adv.*

dy·nam·ics (dī nam′iks) *n.* **1.** the branch of physics dealing with bodies in motion. ▲ used with a singular verb. **2.** the motivating or governing forces operating in any field or activity: *the dynamics of human behavior.* ▲ used with a plural verb.

dy·na·mism (dī′nə miz′əm) *n.* the state or quality of being dynamic; energy; vigor; forcefulness: *a dance group known for its dynamism.*

dy·na·mite (dī′nə mīt′) *n.* **1.** an explosive consisting of an absorbent material saturated with nitroglycerin, usually packed in cylindrical sticks. **2.** *Informal.* a person or thing that has a spectacular effect. —*v.t.,* **dy·na·mit·ed, dy·na·mit·ing.** to blow up or destroy with dynamite. —**dy′na·mit′er**, *n.*

dy·na·mo (dī′nə mō′) *n., pl.* **dy·na·mos. 1.** an electric generator or motor, especially one that produces direct current. **2.** *Informal.* an energetic, forceful person.

dy·nas·tic (dī nas′tik) *adj.* of or relating to a dynasty.

dy·nas·ty (dī′nə stē) *n., pl.* **dy·nas·ties. 1.** a line of rulers who belong to the same family. **2.** a series of related people or organizations that are noted for success: *After three straight championships, the team was considered a dynasty.* **3.** the period of time during which a dynasty rules.

dyne (dīn) *n. Physics.* a unit of force equal to the amount of force that must be applied to a mass of one gram to produce an acceleration of one centimeter per second for each second that the force is applied.

dys·en·ter·y (dis′ən ter′ē) *n.* any of several diseases of the intestines, characterized by severe diarrhea, often accompanied by discharges of blood or mucus, pain, and cramps. Dysentery is caused by various organisms, such as bacteria, parasites, or viruses.

dys·func·tion (dis fungk′shən) *n.* abnormal or weakened functioning, as of an organ of the body: *The kidneys are so vital to good health that any dysfunction is a very serious matter.*

dys·gen·ic (dis jen′ik) *adj.* harmful to hereditary traits: *Radioactive fallout may have a dysgenic effect on future generations.*

dys·lex·i·a (dis lek′sē ə) *n.* a disorder that makes learning to read and write very difficult. A common form of dyslexia involves reading letters in the wrong order, such as reading "b" for "d" or "was" for "saw." [From the scientific Latin word *dyslexia,* formed from the Greek words *dys-* meaning "bad" + *lexis* meaning "speech, word."]

dys·lex·ic (dis lek′sik) *adj.* of, relating to, or having dyslexia. —*n.* a person having dyslexia.

dys·pep·si·a (dis pep′sē ə, dis pep′shə) *n.* poor digestion; indigestion.

dys·pep·tic (dis pep′tik) *adj.* **1.** of, relating to, or suffering from dyspepsia. **2.** gloomy or irritable. —*n.* a person who has dyspepsia.

dys·pro·si·um (dis prō′sē əm) *n.* a metallic element of the rare-earth group. It is more magnetic than any other known substance and is superconductive. It is used in nuclear reactors. Symbol: **Dy** [Formed from the Greek word *dysprositos* meaning "hard to get at." This element was discovered only after great difficulty.]

dz., dozen; dozens.

1. ancient Semitic
2. Phoenician
3. early Hebrew
4. Greek
5. Etruscan
6. Latin
7. English

E is the fifth letter of the English alphabet. Its earliest ancestor was the letter *he,* representing an *h* sound in the ancient Semitic alphabets (1). *He* was used, with only slight changes in its shape, in the Phoenician (2) and early Hebrew (3) alphabets. When the early Greeks borrowed *he,* they called it *epsilon* (4), at first using it for both the consonant sound *h* and the vowel sound *e.* Since the Greeks had another letter, *eta,* for the *h* sound, *epsilon* eventually was used only for the vowel sound *e.* This later form was adopted by the Etruscans (5), who eventually reversed it and gave it its modern shape. Both the form and pronunciation of this letter were used in the Latin alphabet (6). By about 2,400 years ago, the Latin **E** was being written almost exactly as we write the capital letter **E** today (7).

e, E (ē) *n., pl.* **e's, E's. 1.** the fifth letter of the English alphabet. **2.** the fifth item in a series or group. **3.** *Music.* the third note of the scale of C major.

E *Physics.* energy.

E. 1. East. **2.** Eastern. **3.** English.

ea., each.

each (ēch) *adj.* every one of two or more persons or things considered separately or singly: *Each house on the street has a small yard. Each player on the team wore a uniform.* —*pron.* every individual person or thing, as in a group or whole: *Each of my friends is going to camp for the summer. We each have our own bedroom.* —*adv.* for each; apiece: *These cookies are a quarter each.*

 ·**each other.** Each of two or more in an action or relationship that is shared by the other or others; one another: *They have known each other for twenty years.*

ea·ger (ē′gər) *adj.* **1.** filled with desire; wanting very much: *The child was eager to start school.* **2.** characterized by or showing much interest or enthusiasm: *The hockey fans had eager looks on their faces.* —**ea′ger·ly,** *adv.* —**ea′ger·ness,** *n.*

ea·gle (ē′gəl) *n.* **1.** any of a group of birds of prey related to the hawk, having very sharp eyesight, a sharply hooked bill, and strong claws. **2.** a representation of an eagle, often used as a symbol or emblem. **3.** a former gold coin of the United States. It was worth ten dollars.

ea·gle–eyed (ē′gəl īd′) *adj.* able to see clearly; sharp-sighted.

ea·glet (ē′glit) *n.* a young eagle.

ear[1] (îr) *n.* **1.** the organ of the body by which people and animals hear. In mammals, the ear has three parts: the external ear, the middle ear, and the inner ear. **2.** in humans and other mammals, the outer, visible part of this organ of hearing: *The dog pricked up its ears at the noise.* **3.** the sense of hearing: *I have a keen ear. That music is pleasing to the ear.* **4.** the ability to hear and understand the differences in sounds, especially musical sounds: *to have no ear for music.* **5.** attention: *to have someone's ear.* **6.** something resembling the outer part of the ear in shape or position, such as the handle of a pitcher. [From the Old English word *ēare* meaning this organ.]

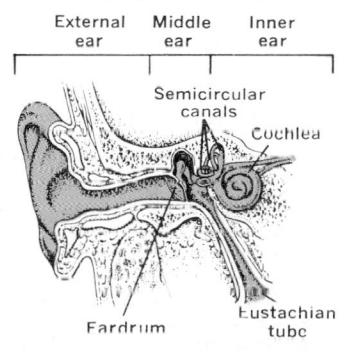

human **ear**

 ·**to be all ears.** to listen eagerly: *We were all ears when we heard the scout leader mention a camping trip.*

 ·**to go in one ear and out the other.** to leave no impression; be heard but not remembered.

 ·**to play by ear.** to play (a musical instrument) without following written music.

ear[2] (îr) *n.* the part of a cereal plant, such as corn or wheat, on which the grains or seeds grow. [From the Old English word *ēar* meaning "a spike of corn."]

ear·ache (îr′āk′) *n.* a pain in the middle or inner ear.

ear·drum (îr′drum′) *n.* a thin membrane that separates the external ear from the middle ear and vibrates when sound waves strike it; tympanic membrane.

ear·ful (îr′fúl′) *n., pl.* **ear·fuls. 1.** a flow of interesting or surprising news or gossip: *My friend gave me an earful about what happened while I was away.* **2.** a scolding or sharp reprimand: *to get an earful from the boss for being late.*

earl (ûrl) *n.* a British nobleman ranking below a marquis and above a viscount.

earl·dom (ûrl′dəm) *n.* the rank, title, or lands of an earl.

ear·lobe (îr′lōb′) *n.* the lower, fleshy part of the outer ear.

ear·ly (ûr′lē) *adj.,* **ear·li·er, ear·li·est.** **1.** happening in or near the beginning; relating to the first part: *I watered the plants in the early morning.* **2.** happening or doing something before the customary or expected time: *The farmer is an early riser.* **3.** happening soon: ~~We would~~ *like to hold the meeting at an early date.* —*adv.* **1.** in or near the beginning: *It's still too early to know who will win the World Series.* **2.** before the customary or expected time: *to arrive at work early.* —**ear′li·ness,** *n.*

early bird *Informal.* a person who does something earlier than others, especially a person who gets up early.

ear·mark (îr′märk′) *n.* **1.** a mark of identification, usually a cut, made on the ear of an animal. **2.** a distinguishing mark or feature; characteristic; sign: *This book has all the earmarks of a great novel.* —*v.t.* **1.** to make an earmark on. **2.** to set aside for a specific purpose: *My parents earmarked that money for our summer vacation.*

ear·muffs (îr′mufs′) *pl. n.* a pair of coverings worn to protect the ears against the cold.

earn (ûrn) *v.t.* **1.** to receive (something as payment) in return for work done: *to earn twenty-five dollars a week mowing lawns.* **2.** to get as a result of doing something; be worthy of: *to earn high grades by working hard.* **3.** to produce as income; yield: *My savings account earns seven percent interest a year.* —**earn′er,** *n.*

ear·nest¹ (ûr′nist) *adj.* **1.** sincere or serious in purpose or feeling: *to be an earnest student.* **2.** showing or characterized by sincere feeling: *to offer an earnest apology for a rude remark.* [From the Old English word *eornoste* meaning "serious."] —**ear′nest·ly,** *adv.* —**ear′nest·ness,** *n.*

ear·nest² (ûr′nist) *n.* something given as an indication or pledge of something to come, such as a deposit of money. [From the earlier form *erles* meaning "money given as a pledge," from the Old French word *erres* with the same meaning, going back to the Hebrew word *′ērābhōn* "a pledge."]

earn·ings (ûr′ningz) *pl. n.* money earned, such as wages or profits.

ear·phone (îr′fōn′) *n.* a receiver, as for a radio or television set, held at or worn over or in the ear.

ear·plug (îr′plug′) *n.* a plug made of pliable material and placed in the ear to keep out water or noise.

ear·ring (îr′ring′) *n.* an ornament worn on or hung from the earlobe.

ear·shot (îr′shot′) *n.* the distance within which a sound, especially the human voice, can be heard: *Please stay within earshot in case I need you.*

ear·split·ting (îr′split′ing) *adj.* extremely loud; deafening: *an earsplitting crash.*

earth (ûrth) *n.* **1.** *also,* **Earth.** the planet on which humans live, the fifth largest planet of the solar system and third in order of distance from the sun. **2.** the ground; dry land: *After the long sea voyage, the sailors were glad to feel the earth under their feet again.* **3.** soil; dirt: *The gardener loosened the earth around the plants.* **4.** the people who live on the planet earth: *World peace would make the earth rejoice.*

·down to earth. simple, practical, and straightforward.

earth·en (ûr′thən) *adj.* **1.** made of earth. **2.** made of baked clay: *The earthen jug has a reddish brown color.*

earth·en·ware (ûr′thən wâr′) *n.* pottery made of clay baked at a low temperature.

earth·ling (ûrth′ling) *n.* an inhabitant of the earth; human being.

earth·ly (ûrth′lē) *adj.,* **earth·li·er, earth·li·est.** **1.** of or relating to the earth rather than to heaven; worldly: *I lost all my earthly possessions in a fire.* **2.** possible: *These worn-out shoes are of no earthly use.* —**earth′li·ness,** *n.*

earth·quake (ûrth′kwāk′) *n.* a movement of a part of the earth's surface, caused by the sudden shifting of rock along a fault or by volcanic or other disturbances.

earth science, any one of the sciences dealing with the structure, features, and history of the interior or surface of the earth. Geology, oceanography, and meteorology are earth sciences.

earth·shak·ing (ûrth′shā′king) *adj.* of fundamental or profound significance: *The invention of the microscope was an earthshaking event in science.*

earth·ward (ûrth′wərd) *adj.* moving toward the earth: *an earthward motion.* —*adv. also,* **earthwards** (ûrth′wərdz). toward the earth: *The plane plunged earthward.*

earth·work (ûrth′wûrk′) *n.* a fortification made of earth.

earth·worm (ûrth′wûrm′) *n.* a worm that has a long, segmented body and lives in the soil. Also, **angleworm.**

earth·y (ûr′thē) *adj.,* **earth·i·er, earth·i·est.** **1.** of, containing, or like soil: *an earthy smell, an earthy color.* **2.** natural and hearty: *earthy people.* **3.** unrefined; coarse: *earthy language.* —**earth′i·ness,** *n.*

ear·wig (îr′wig′) *n.* an insect having a hard, slender body and a pair of movable pincers at the end of its abdomen.

ease (ēz) *n.* **1.** freedom from pain, discomfort, toil, or worry; comfort: *The family lived a life of ease at the resort.* **2.** freedom from great effort or difficulty: *to swim with ease.* **3.** freedom from stiffness, nervousness, or embarrassment: *an ease of manner that showed self-confidence.* —*v.,* **eased, eas·ing.** —*v.t.* **1.** to free from pain, discomfort, or worry; comfort or relieve: *The boat's safe arrival eased the minds of those on shore.* **2.** to make less; lighten: *The medicine eased the ache in my back.* **3.** to lessen the pressure or strain of (something); loosen: *to ease a tight waistband, to ease a rope.* **4.** to move or place (something) slowly and carefully: *to ease a car onto the ramp of a ferry boat.* —*v.i.* to move slowly and carefully.

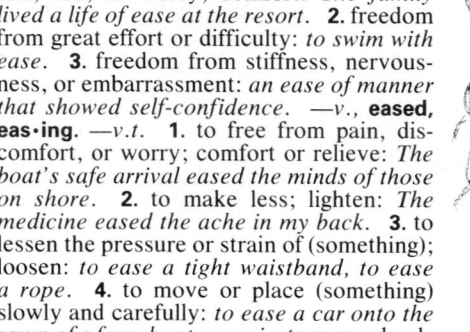
earwig

·at ease. **a.** free from stiffness or nervousness: *The hosts' friendly manner helped their guests feel at ease.* **b.** *Military.* in a relaxed standing position with the feet apart and the hands behind the back. ▲ often used as a command.

ea·sel (ē′zəl) *n.* an upright frame or tripod, used especially to hold an artist's canvas.

ease·ment (ēz′mənt) *n.* **1.** a right to use a piece of land in a particular way, held by someone who does not own the land: *The electric company held an easement to string transmission wires across my property.* **2.** the piece of land for which such a right is held.

eas·i·ly (ē′zə lē) *adv.* **1.** without difficulty, discomfort, or great effort: *A strong person can move those boxes easily.* **2.** without a doubt; certainly: *My best friend is easily the best player on the team.*

eas·i·ness (ē′zē nis) *n.* the quality or state of being easy.

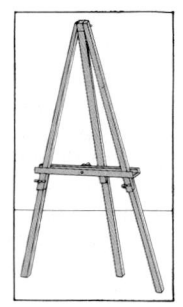
easel

east (ēst) *n.* **1.** the direction a person faces when watching the sun rise. East is one of the four main points of the compass, located directly opposite west. **2.** *also,* **East.** any region or place lying in this direction. **3. the East. a.** a region in the United States along the Atlantic coast, especially the area east of the Allegheny Mountains and north of Maryland. **b.** Asia and the islands close to it. —*adj.* **1.** toward or in the east. **2.** from the east: *an east wind.* —*adv.* toward the east: *to drive east.*

east·bound (ēst′bound′) *adj.* going east: *an eastbound freight train.*

East·er (ēs′tər) *n.* **1.** the holy day on which Christians celebrate the resurrection of Jesus. In the Western Church, Easter occurs on the Sunday after the first full moon on or following March 21st. **2.** the Sunday on which this holy day is celebrated.

east·er·ly (ēs′tər lē) *adj., adv.* **1.** toward the east: *an easterly direction.* **2.** from the east: *an easterly wind.*

east·ern (ēs′tərn) *adj.* **1.** toward or in the east: *the eastern part of the state.* **2.** *also,* **Eastern.** of, relating to, or characteristic of the east or East. **3.** coming from the east: *an eastern breeze.* **4. Eastern.** Oriental: *Eastern philosophy.*

Eastern Church 1. another term for **Orthodox Church.** **2.** any of various Christian churches, such as the Coptic Church in Africa, deriving from the church of the Byzantine Empire.

east·ern·er (ēs′tər nər) *n.* **1.** a person who was born or is living in the east. **2.** *usually,* **Easterner.** a person who was born or is living in the eastern part of the United States.

Eastern Hemisphere, the half of the earth that includes Europe, Asia, Africa, and Australia.

east·ern·most (ēs′tərn mōst′) *adj.* farthest east.

Eastern Orthodox Church, another term for **Orthodox Church.**

Eastern Roman Empire, another term for **Byzantine Empire.**

Eastern Standard Time, the local time used in much of the eastern United States and Canada. It is 5 hours earlier than Greenwich Time.

east·ward (ēst′wərd) *adv.* toward the east. Also, **east·wards** (ēst′wərdz). —*adj.* toward or in the east. —*n.* an eastward direction, point, or place.

eas·y (ē′zē) *adj.,* **eas·i·er, eas·i·est.** **1.** needing little effort; not hard to do: *an easy job.* **2.** free from discomfort, trouble, or worry: *an easy life.* **3.** not demanding, harsh, or strict; lenient: *an easy teacher.* **4.** comfortable or restful: *This car has an easy ride.* **5.** not stiff, formal, or awkward: *an easy manner.* **6.** not hurried: *We hiked along at an easy pace.* —*adv. Informal.* easily.

·**to take it easy.** *Informal.* **a.** to avoid too much effort or activity; relax. **b.** to stay calm.

easy chair, a comfortable chair, especially a padded armchair.

eas·y·go·ing (ē′zē gō′ing) *adj.* tending to be calm and unhurried; good-natured; relaxed.

eat (ēt) *v.,* **ate, eat·en, eat·ing.** —*v.t.* **1.** to take in through the mouth and swallow, especially to chew and swallow: *to eat a slice of pizza.* **2.** to destroy or wear away gradually: *Rust has eaten away the surface of the metal lawn furniture.* **3.** to use up or waste: *Hospital bills quickly ate up their savings.* **4.** to make as if by eating: *The acid ate holes in the material. The termites ate their way through the log.* —*v.i.* **1.** to take or eat food; have a meal: *Our family eats at six o'clock.* **2.** to destroy or wear away gradually, as by gnawing or corroding: *The acid ate into the copper plate.* **3.** to chew or bore: *The termites ate through the floor.* —**eat′er,** *n.*

eat·a·ble (ē′tə bəl) *adj.* fit to be eaten; edible. —*n. also,* **eatables.** something fit to be eaten; food.

eaves (ēvz) *pl. n.* the overhanging edge or edges of a sloping roof.

Eaves

eaves·drop (ēvz′drop′) *v.i.,* **eaves·dropped, eaves·drop·ping.** to listen to the private conversation of others without their knowing it. —**eaves′drop′per,** *n.*

ebb (eb) *n.* **1.** the flowing out of the tide from shore. **2.** a point or condition of decline or decay: *The actor's fame was at a low ebb.* —*v.i.* **1.** to flow out. **2.** to become less or weaker: *Hope of finding the lost child began to ebb.* [From the Old English word *ebba* meaning ''the flowing out of the tide.'']

ebb tide, the tide that flows out from shore.

eb·on·ite (eb′ə nīt′) *n.* a hard, black rubber treated with sulfur, used for plumbing, electrical equipment, and bowling balls.

eb·on·y (eb′ə nē) *n., pl.* **eb·on·ies.** **1.** a hard, black wood, used especially for piano keys, knife handles, and cabinets. **2.** the tree yielding this wood, found in Africa, Sri Lanka, and the East Indies. —*adj.* **1.** made of ebony. **2.** like ebony, especially in color.

e·bul·lient (i bul′yənt) *adj.* overflowing or bubbling over with excitement or enthusiasm: *The winner of the contest was ebullient.* [From the Latin word *ebulliens,* present participle of *ebullire* meaning ''to bubble or boil over.''] —**e·bul′lience, e·bul′lien·cy,** *n.* —**e·bul′lient·ly,** *adv.*

ec·cen·tric (ek sen′trik) *adj.* **1.** not conforming to normal or usual practices or behavior; peculiar; odd: *The eccentric millionaire always wore old clothes and carried a broken umbrella.* **2.** *Mathematics.* not having the same center: *eccentric circles.* **3.** having its axis set off center: *an eccentric wheel, an eccentric gear.* —*n.* **1.** a person who is eccentric: *After living alone for so many years, my next-door neighbor had turned into a real eccentric.* **2.** a wheel that is set off center on a revolving shaft, used to change circular motion into back-and-forth motion. [From the Middle Latin word *eccentricus* meaning ''out of the center,'' from the Greek word *ekkentros* with the same meaning.] —**ec·cen′tri·cal·ly,** *adv.*

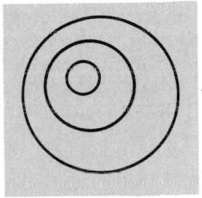

eccentric
circles

ec·cen·tric·i·ty (ek′sen tris′i tē) *n., pl.* **ec·cen·tric·i·ties.** **1.** the state or quality of being eccentric: *the eccentricity of an axis.* **2.** an act or trait that is unusual or odd; peculiarity. **3.** the amount or degree by which something is eccentric.

Ec·cle·si·as·tes (i klē′zē as′tēz) *n.* a book of the Old Testament, traditionally held to have been written by King Solomon.

ec·cle·si·as·tic (i klē′zē as′tik) *n.* a member of the clergy. —*adj.* another word for **ecclesiastical.**

ec·cle·si·as·ti·cal (i klē′zē as′ti kəl) *adj.* of or relating to the church or the clergy: *ecclesiastical books, ecclesiastical garments.* —**ec·cle′si·as′ti·cal·ly,** *adv.*

ech·e·lon (esh′ə lon′) *n.* **1.** a formation of soldiers, ships, or airplanes in a steplike arrangement. **2.** a particular level of command, authority, or responsibility: *The generals and admirals are in the highest echelon of the military organization. The clerical workers are in the lower echelons of the bureaucracy.* [From the French word *échelon* meaning ''rung of a ladder,'' from the word *échelle* ''ladder,'' going back to the Latin word *scala* ''ladder.'']

at; āpe; fär; câre; end; mē; it; īce; pîerce; hot; ōld; sông, fôrk; oil; out; up; ūse; rüle; pull; tûrn; chin; sing; shop; thin; this; hw in white; zh in treasure. The symbol ə stands for the unstressed vowel sound heard in about, taken, pencil, lemon, and circus.

E

e·chid·na (i kid′nə) *n.*, *pl.* **e·chid·nas**. either of two egg-laying mammals native to Australia, Tasmania, and New Guinea, having thick, grayish brown fur, spines, and a long snout. Also, **spiny anteater**.

e·chi·no·derm (i kī′nə dûrm′) *n.* any of a group of saltwater animals, such as the starfish and sea urchin, having a spiny skin and a body made up of equal parts that radiate from a central point.

echidna

Ech·o (ek′ō) *n. Greek Mythology.* a mountain nymph who was deprived by the goddess Hera of her power of speech, except to repeat the final words of others.

ech·o (ek′ō) *n.*, *pl.* **ech·oes**. **1.** the repetition of a sound made by sending back sound waves from a surface that blocks them. **2.** any repetition or close imitation of something, such as the ideas or opinions of another. —*v.t.* **1.** to send back the sound of: *The cavern walls echoed our cries.* **2.** to repeat or closely imitate: *The students echoed the thoughts of their teacher.* —*v.i.* **1.** to send back an echo: *The corridor of the school echoed with voices and footsteps.* **2.** to be repeated by an echo: *Joyous laughter echoed through the house.* [From either the Old French word *echo* or the Latin word *echo*, both going back to the Greek word *ēchō* "echo."]

é·clair (ā klâr′) *n.* an oblong pastry shell filled with whipped cream or custard and usually topped with chocolate icing.

é·clat (ā klä′) *n.* **1.** a brilliant or striking effect or success: *The guitarist performed with great éclat.* **2.** great applause or praise; acclaim: *The new play was received with éclat.*

ec·lec·tic (e klek′tik) *adj.* taking what seems best from different sources: *an eclectic painter, an eclectic musical program.* —*n.* a person who uses an eclectic method or approach. —**ec·lec′ti·cal·ly,** *adv.*

ec·lec·ti·cism (e klek′tə siz′əm) *n.* an eclectic method, system, or philosophy.

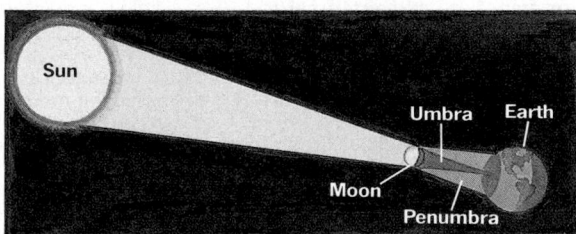

solar **eclipse**

lunar **eclipse**

e·clipse (i klips′) *n.* **1.** a partial or total darkening or hiding of the sun, the moon, or a planet. In a solar eclipse the moon passes between the sun and the earth, partly or totally blocking the sun's rays and darkening certain areas of the earth, and causing the sun to be partially or totally hidden from those areas of the earth. In a lunar eclipse the earth moves between the sun and the moon, blocking the sun's rays and partially or totally darkening the moon. **2.** any overshadowing or dimming, as of reputation or importance. —*v.t.*, **e·clipsed, e·clips·ing. 1.** to cause an eclipse of: *The moon eclipsed the sun.* **2.** to overshadow or dim; outshine; surpass: *The star's performance eclipsed those of the other actors.*

e·clip·tic (i klip′tik) *n.* the path that the sun appears to follow in a year around the celestial sphere. —*adj. also,* **e·clip·ti·cal** (i klip′ti kəl). of or relating to eclipses or to the ecliptic. —**e·clip′ti·cal·ly,** *adv.*

ec·o·log·i·cal (ek′ə loj′i kəl, ē′kə loj′i kəl) *adj.* of or relating to ecology. Also, **ec′o·log′ic. —ec′o·log′i·cal·ly,** *adv.*

e·col·o·gist (ē kol′ə jist) *n.* an expert in ecology.

e·col·o·gy (ē kol′ə jē) *n.* a branch of biology that deals with the relationships of living things to their surroundings and to each other.

ec·o·nom·ic (ek′ə nom′ik, ē′kə nom′ik) *adj.* **1.** of or relating to the science of economics: *economic theory.* **2.** of or relating to money matters or concerns; financial: *They sold the house because of economic considerations.* **3.** of or relating to the management of money, manufactured goods, or other resources: *the economic policies of a nation.*

ec·o·nom·i·cal (ek′ə nom′i kəl, ē′kə nom′i kəl) *adj.* not wasting money, goods, or other resources; frugal: *an economical shopper.* —**ec′o·nom′i·cal·ly,** *adv.*

ec·o·nom·ics (ek′ə nom′iks, ē′kə nom′iks) *n.* **1.** the science that deals with the production, distribution, and use of goods, money, natural resources, and services. ▲ used with a singular verb. **2.** financial aspects or factors: *the economics of building a bridge.* ▲ used with a plural verb.

e·con·o·mist (i kon′ə mist) *n.* a student of or an expert in economics.

e·con·o·mize (i kon′ə mīz′) *v.*, **e·con·o·mized, e·con·o·miz·ing.** —*v.i.* to be careful or cautious in the use of money, goods, or other resources; be frugal and thrifty: *We economized and managed to save money toward a trip to Europe.* —*v.t.* to use carefully and wisely: *to economize fuel.*

e·con·o·my (i kon′ə mē) *n.*, *pl.* **e·con·o·mies. 1.** a system, method, or result of managing the production, distribution, and use of money, goods, natural resources, and services: *That nation's economy is growing rapidly.* **2.** the careful or cautious use of money, goods, or other resources; thrift. —*adj.* money-saving: *an economy car.* [From the Latin word *oeconomia* meaning "management of a household," from the Greek word *oikonomia* with the same meaning, going back to the words *oikos* "house" and *nemein* "to manage."]

Word Family

The Greek word for "house," *oikos,* is the root for a wide range of English words. Originally, **economy** referred to the management of a household. Today, **economic** issues are national and international in scope and have professional **economists** studying them. As anyone concerned with **ecology** knows, **ecological** problems affect both nature and people. To take an interest in all these things is to have an **ecumenical** view and not a **parochial** one. A **parishioner** might support local **parish** schools throughout a **diocese**. In Louisiana, the word **parish** also means a division of the state similar to a county in other states.

ec·o·sys·tem (ek′ō sis′təm, ē′kō sis′təm) *n.* all the living things within a particular area and their relationship to each other and to their physical environment. For example, air, water, algae, insects, fish, frogs, soil, and rocks are some of the things that make up the ecosystem of a pond.

ec·ru (ek′rü) *n.* a pale yellowish brown color. —*adj.* having the color ecru.

ec·sta·sy (ek′stə sē) *n., pl.* **ec·sta·sies.** a feeling or state of overwhelming joy or delight; rapture: *The children were in ecstasy at the thought of going to the circus.*

ec·stat·ic (ek stat′ik) *adj.* **1.** overwhelmed with joy or delight; enraptured: *to be ecstatic about winning a contest.* **2.** of, resulting from, or causing ecstasy: *ecstatic applause from the audience.* —**ec·stat′i·cal·ly,** *adv.*

ecto– *prefix* outside: *ectoderm.*

ec·to·derm (ek′tə dûrm′) *n.* the outermost of the three cell layers of an embryo in an early stage of its development. The ectoderm develops into the outer layer of skin, the nervous sytem, and the sense organs.

–ectomy *suffix* (used to form nouns) removal of: *tonsillectomy.* [From the scientific Latin suffix *-ectomia* meaning "surgical removal," from the Greek word *ektemnein* "to cut out," from the words *ex-* "out" + *temnein* "to cut."]

ec·to·plasm (ek′tə plaz′əm) *n.* the outer layer of the cytoplasm of a cell.

ec·u·men·i·cal (ek′yə men′i kəl) *adj.* **1.** including the entire world; worldwide; universal. **2.** of or relating to all Christian churches: *an ecumenical council called by the pope.* **3.** promoting worldwide Christian unity.

ec·ze·ma (ek′sə mə, eg′zə mə, eg ze′mə) *n.* a skin disorder characterized by redness, itching, and scaly patches. It is often caused by an allergy.

–ed[1] *suffix* (used to form the past tense of regular verbs): *I walked to work last week.* [From the Old English suffix *-ede* used to form the past tense.]

–ed[2] *suffix* **1.** (used to form the past participle of regular verbs): *We have walked to work every day this month.* **2.** (used to form adjectives from nouns): **a.** characterized by or having: *a blue-eyed baby.* **b.** having the characteristics of; like: *a prejudiced person, a dogged pursuit.* [From the Old English suffix *-ed* used to form the past participle.]

ed. **1.** edited. **2.** edition. **3.** editor.

E·dam (ē′dəm, ē′dam) *n.* a mild, yellow cheese, usually sold in the form of a ball covered with red wax. [From *Edam,* the village in the Netherlands where it was first made.]

ed·dy (ed′ē) *n., pl.* **ed·dies.** a current of air or water moving against the main current, especially with a circular or whirling motion; small whirlwind or whirlpool. —*v.i.,* **ed·died, ed·dy·ing.** to move with a circular or whirling motion; whirl: *Smoke eddied from the chimney.*

e·del·weiss (ā′dəl vīs′) *n.* **1.** a flower having tiny yellow petals surrounded by white leaves. **2.** a small plant bearing this flower, found on high mountains in Europe and Asia.

e·de·ma (i dē′mə) *n., pl.* **e·de·ma·ta** (i dē′mə tə). an abnormal accumulation of a watery fluid in body tissues or cavities. Also, **dropsy.**

E·den (ē′dən) *n.* **1.** see **Garden of Eden. 2.** a place of extreme delight or happiness; paradise.

edge (ej) *n.* **1.** a line or place where an object or area begins or ends; extreme or outermost border: *I sat on the edge of my chair. We walked down to the edge of the lake.* **2.** a thin, cutting side of a blade, as of a knife or tool: *the sharp edge of a knife.* **3.** strength or intensity: *Eating the crackers took the edge off my appetite.* **4.** *Informal.* a better position; advantage: *Our candidate has a slight edge on the incumbent.* —*v.,* **edged, edging.** —*v.t.* **1.** to furnish with a border; form a border on: *The dressmaker edged the fabric with fringe.* **2.** to move

slowly or gradually: *The workers edged the large crate across the floor.* —*v.i.* to move slowly or gradually: *to edge toward the door.*

·on edge. very impatient, tense, or nervous: *The players were on edge as they waited for the game to begin.*

edge·wise (ej′wīz′) *adv.* **1.** with the edge forward. **2.** on or toward the edge. Also, **edge·ways** (ej′wāz′).

·to get a word in edgewise. to succeed in saying something in a conversation dominated by a talkative person: *I disagreed with the idea, but I couldn't get a word in edgewise.*

edg·ing (ej′ing) *n.* something that forms an edge or is joined to an edge; trimming.

edg·y (ej′ē) *adj.,* **edg·i·er, edg·i·est.** very impatient, tense, or nervous; on edge. —**edg′i·ness,** *n.*

ed·i·ble (ed′ə bəl) *adj.* that can be eaten; fit to eat: *These mushrooms are edible.* —*n.* something fit to eat; food. —**ed′i·ble·ness,** *n.*

e·dict (ē′dikt) *n.* an official command or order from a ruler or other person having authority.

ed·i·fi·ca·tion (ed′ə fi kā′shən) *n.* moral instruction or improvement: *Sermons are for the edification of the congregation.*

ed·i·fice (ed′ə fis) *n.* a building, especially a large and impressive one.

ed·i·fy (ed′ə fī′) *v.t.,* **ed·i·fied, ed·i·fy·ing.** to instruct or improve, especially morally or spiritually: *That fable edifies all who read it.*

ed·it (ed′it) *v.t.* **1.** to correct, improve, and otherwise prepare for publication: *to edit the manuscript of a textbook.* **2.** to review, cut, and arrange for presentation: *to edit a film before showing it to the class.* **3.** to be in charge of preparing for publication: *My neighbor edits the town newspaper.*

e·di·tion (i dish′ən) *n.* **1.** the form in which a book or other written work is published: *That dictionary is now published in a two-volume edition.* **2.** the total number of copies of a publication printed from the same plates or type: *the first edition of a book.* **3.** a single copy of such a publication: *the morning edition of a newspaper.*

ed·i·tor (ed′i tər) *n.* **1.** a person who edits written material. **2.** a person in charge of a newspaper or magazine or one of its sections.

ed·i·to·ri·al (ed′i tôr′ē əl) *n.* an article in a newspaper or magazine, or a statement on television or radio, expressing the opinion or viewpoint of the editor, publisher, or owner on a particular topic. —*adj.* of or relating to an editor or an editor's statements: *editorial freedom, editorial responsibility.* —**ed′i·to′ri·al·ly,** *adv.*

ed·i·to·ri·al·ize (ed′i tôr′ē ə līz′) *v.i.,* **ed·i·to·ri·al·ized, ed·i·to·ri·al·iz·ing.** **1.** to express opinions in or as if in an editorial. **2.** to introduce personal opinions or comments into a report that is supposed to be objective: *Stick to the facts; don't editorialize!*

ed·i·tor·ship (ed′i tər ship′) *n.* the position, functions, or authority of an editor.

EDP, electronic data processing.

ed·u·ca·ble (ej′ə kə bəl) *adj.* able to be educated.

ed·u·cate (ej′ə kāt′) *v.t.,* **ed·u·cat·ed, ed·u·cat·ing.** **1.** to give knowledge or skill to; teach or train. **2.** to provide schooling for; send to school: *The cost of educating children is very high.*

ed·u·cat·ed (ej′ə kā′tid) *adj.* **1.** having an education,

E

at; āpe; fär; câre; end; mē; it; īce; pîerce; hot; ōld; sông, fôrk; oil; out; up; ūse; rüle; pull; tûrn; chin; sing; shop; thin; this; hw in white; zh in treasure. The symbol ə stands for the unstressed vowel sound heard in about, taken, pencil, lemon, and circus.

especially a good one. **2.** developed by education or training: *the educated speech of a radio announcer.* **3.** based on information or experience: *to make an educated guess.*

ed·u·ca·tion (ej′ə kā′shən) *n.* **1.** the act or process of educating: *A person's education at college usually takes four years.* **2.** the knowledge or skill that a person gains by being educated: *a scholar of great education.* **3.** study of the problems and methods of teaching and learning: *to major in education at college.*

ed·u·ca·tion·al (ej′ə kā′shə nəl) *adj.* **1.** of or relating to education: *an educational institution, a person's educational background.* **2.** giving knowledge or skill; instructive: *an educational television program.* —**ed′u·ca′tion·al·ly,** *adv.*

educational television 1. television programs of educational or instructional material, as for students. **2.** another term for **public television.**

ed·u·ca·tive (ej′ə kā′tiv) *adj.* **1.** tending to educate; educational. **2.** of or relating to education: *the educative process.*

ed·u·ca·tor (ej′ə kā′tər) *n.* **1.** a person whose profession is to educate others. **2.** a person who is an expert or authority in the field of education.

e·duce (i düs′, i dūs′) *v.t.,* **e·duced, e·duc·ing.** to bring out; draw forth: *The supervisor educed good work from the employees.* —**e·duc′i·ble,** *adj.*

Ed·ward·i·an (ed wär′dē ən, ed wôr′dē ən) *adj.* relating to or characteristic of the reign of Edward VII: *Edwardian architecture, Edwardian fashions.*

–ee *suffix* (used to form nouns from verbs) **1.** a person to whom something is done or given: *inductee, payee.* **2.** a person who performs some action or is in some condition: *standee.*

EEG 1. electroencephalogram. **2.** electroencephalograph.

eel (ēl) *n., pl.* **eels** or **eel.** any of a group of fish having a long body with a smooth skin not covered by scales.

eel·grass (ēl′-gras′) *n.* a grass that grows in shallow water and has branching stems with long, ribbon-like leaves.

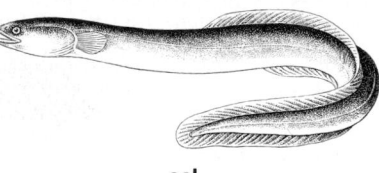

eel

e'en (ēn) *adv. Archaic.* another word for **even.**

e'er (âr) *adv. Archaic.* another word for **ever.**

–eer *suffix* **1.** (used to form nouns) **a.** a person who makes: *pamphleteer, profiteer.* **b.** a person who has to do with: *auctioneer.* **2.** (used to form verbs) to have to do with: *electioneer.*

ee·rie (ir′ē) *also,* **ee·ry.** *adj.,* **ee·ri·er, ee·ri·est. 1.** strange and frightening; weird; uncanny: *The Halloween decorations gave an eerie look to the room.* **2.** nervously uneasy; fearful: *Walking down the deserted street gave us an eerie feeling.* —**ee′ri·ly,** *adv.* —**ee′ri·ness,** *n.*

ef·face (i fās′) *v.t.,* **ef·faced, ef·fac·ing. 1.** to destroy by or as if by rubbing out; erase: *The name on the old sign has been effaced by the wind and rain. I tried to efface the bad memory.* **2.** to keep (oneself) from attracting attention. —**ef·face′ment,** *n.* —**ef·fac′er,** *n.*

ef·fect (i fekt′) *n.* **1.** something brought about by a cause or agent; result: *The child's blindness was one of the effects of the accident.* **2.** the power or ability to influence or bring about a result: *The bad news had no effect on them.* **3.** the state or fact of being in force: *The club members wanted to put their plan into effect.* **4.** an impression made on the mind or senses: *Some painters achieve dramatic effects by their use of color.* **5.** something used to make such an impression: *The play used excellent lighting effects.* **6. effects.** property; possessions: *We quickly packed our personal effects and left the*

hotel. ▲ *See* **affect** for usage note. —*v.t.* to bring about; produce as a result; cause: *Congress effected a program to provide health care for elderly people.*

·for effect. in order to make an impression; for show.

·in effect. in actual fact; in reality: *There are, in effect, only two good players on the team.*

·to take effect. to begin to do or accomplish something; start to have results: *The pill should take effect in an hour.*

ef·fec·tive (i fek′tiv) *adj.* **1.** bringing about or able to bring about a desired effect: *an effective discussion that brought everyone into agreement.* **2.** in force or operation: *The new sales tax will not be effective until later this summer.* **3.** making a striking impression; impressive: *to be an effective speaker.* —**ef·fec′tive·ly,** *adv.* —**ef·fec′tive·ness,** *n.*

ef·fec·tu·al (i fek′chü əl) *adj.* bringing about or able to bring about a desired effect. —**ef·fec′tu·al·ly,** *adv.*

ef·fec·tu·ate (i fek′chü āt′) *v.t.,* **ef·fec·tu·at·ed, ef·fec·tu·at·ing.** to bring about or cause; accomplish.

ef·fem·i·na·cy (i fem′ə nə sē) *n.* the state or quality of being effeminate.

ef·fem·i·nate (i fem′ə nit) *adj.* (of a man or boy) having the appearance, behavior, or traits suitable to or usual in a woman; womanish; unmanly. —**ef·fem′i·nate·ly,** *adv.* —**ef·fem′i·nate·ness,** *n.*

ef·fer·ent (ef′ər ənt) *adj.* carrying away from a central organ or point: *efferent nerve fibers.*

ef·fer·vesce (ef′ər ves′) *v.i.,* **ef·fer·vesced, ef·fer·vesc·ing. 1.** to give off bubbles of gas, as carbonated water does. **2.** to be lively, bright, and full of spirit. —**ef·fer·ves·cence** (ef′ər ves′əns), *n.*

ef·fer·ves·cent (ef′ər ves′ənt) *adj.* **1.** giving off bubbles of gas; bubbling. **2.** full of spirit; bright and lively: *The twins were very effervescent at the party.*

ef·fete (e fēt′) *adj.* without strength or vigor; worn out; decadent: *an effete civilization.* —**ef·fete′ness,** *n.*

ef·fi·ca·cious (ef′i kā′shəs) *adj.* bringing about or able to bring about a desired effect; effective. —**ef′fi·ca′cious·ly,** *adv.*

ef·fi·ca·cy (ef′i kə sē) *n., pl.* **ef·fi·ca·cies.** the power to bring about a desired effect; effectiveness.

ef·fi·cien·cy (i fish′ən sē) *n., pl.* **ef·fi·cien·cies. 1.** the quality of being efficient. **2.** the ratio of the useful work done by a machine to the energy that is supplied to it.

ef·fi·cient (i fish′ənt) *adj.* bringing about or able to bring about a desired effect with as little effort or waste as possible; effective or competent: *a highly efficient machine, a capable and efficient worker.* —**ef·fi′cient·ly,** *adv.*

ef·fi·gy (ef′i jē) *n., pl.* **ef·fi·gies. 1.** a representation or likeness of a person, especially a sculptured image: *a bronze effigy of a popular leader.* **2.** a crude representation of a disliked or hated person.

·to burn in effigy or **to hang in effigy.** to burn or hang publicly a crude representation of someone as an expression of public contempt: *The angry citizens burned the governor in effigy.*

ef·flo·res·cence (ef′lə res′əns) *n.* **1.** the act, state, or period of flowering. **2.** *Chemistry.* the act or process of changing from crystals to a powder by loss of water of crystallization when exposed to air. **3.** any eruption or rash on the skin. —**ef·flo·res′cent,** *adj.*

ef·fort (ef′ərt) *n.* **1.** the use of the strength of the body or the power of the mind to do something: *Climbing the stairs took much effort for the old couple.* **2.** an attempt, especially a strong attempt: *to make an effort to get to school on time.* **3.** the product or result of hard work: *This painting is the artist's first effort.*

ef·fort·less (ef′ərt lis) *adj.* showing or needing little or no effort; easy: *an effortless task.* —**ef′fort·less·ly,** *adv.* —**ef′fort·less·ness,** *n.*

ef·fron·ter·y (i frun′tə rē) *n.* shameless boldness or

rudeness; insolence: *They had the effrontery to ask me for a favor after they had insulted me.*

ef·ful·gence (i ful′jəns) *n.* great brightness; radiance or splendor.

ef·ful·gent (i ful′jənt) *adj.* bright; radiant.

ef·fu·sion (i fū′zhən) *n.* **1.** the act of pouring out: *The doctor stopped the effusion of blood from the cut.* **2.** something that pours out. **3.** an unrestrained pouring forth of ideas, feelings, or words.

ef·fu·sive (i fū′siv) *adj.* showing more feeling than is called for or desired; gushing: *An effusive expression of thanks can seem insincere.* —**ef·fu′sive·ly,** *adv.* —**ef·fu′sive·ness,** *n.*

eft (eft) *n.* a young newt that lives on land until it matures.

e.g., for example. [Abbreviation of Latin *exemplī grātiā.*]

egg¹ (eg) *n.* **1.** an oval or round reproductive body produced in the female sex organs of certain animals such as reptiles, birds, and some mammals, from which a young animal hatches: *The butterfly laid its eggs on the leaf.* **2.** a hard-shelled oval body produced by a bird, especially a hen, used as food: *a dozen eggs.* **3.** the contents of this: *a fried egg.* **4.** the reproductive cell produced in the female sex organs of most animals; ovum. Also, **egg cell.** **5.** *Slang.* a person; fellow: *My roommate is a good egg.* [From the Old Norse word *egg* meaning "bird's egg."]

egg² (eg) *v.t.* to encourage to do some action; urge; incite: *My friends egged me on to play the trick.* [From the Old Norse word *eggja* meaning "to incite, urge."]

egg·beat·er (eg′bē′tər) *n.* a kitchen utensil with rotating blades, used for beating eggs, whipping cream, and mixing cooking ingredients.

egg cell, see **egg¹** *(def. 4).*

egg cream, a cold drink made of milk and carbonated water, flavored with a syrup.

egg·head (eg′hed′) *n. Slang.* an intellectual person. ▲ often used to show disapproval.

egg·nog (eg′nog′) *n.* a drink made of raw eggs mixed with milk or cream, sugar, and spices, and often containing an alcoholic beverage such as rum.

egg·plant (eg′plant′) *n.* **1.** the oval-shaped fruit of a bushy plant, usually blackish purple in color, cooked and eaten as a vegetable. **2.** the plant bearing this fruit.

egg roll, a thin, tubular piece of dough that is filled with a mixture of ingredients, such as minced vegetables, meat, and shrimp, and fried.

egg·shell (eg′shel′) *n.* **1.** the hard, thin shell of a bird's egg. **2.** a pale yellow, tan, or ivory color. —*adj.* **1.** having the color eggshell; pale yellow, tan, or ivory. **2.** thin and fragile: *an eggshell porcelain cup.*

e·gis (ē′jis) another spelling of **aegis.**

eg·lan·tine (eg′lən tīn′, eg′lən tēn′) *n.* another word for **sweetbrier.**

e·go (ē′gō) *n., pl.* **e·gos. 1.** a person's awareness of his or her needs and desires, and of everything else that makes him or her different and separate from others; a person's own distinct self. **2.** self-centeredness or conceit. **3.** confidence in oneself; self-esteem: *Getting good grades in school boosted my ego.*

e·go·cen·tric (ē′gō sen′trik) *adj.* believing oneself to be the center of everything; self-centered. —*n.* an egocentric person.

e·go·ism (ē′gō iz′əm) *n.* **1.** too much concern with one's own welfare and interests; selfishness or self-centeredness. **2.** conceit; egotism.

e·go·ist (ē′gō ist) *n.* **1.** a selfish or self-centered person. **2.** a conceited person; egotist.

e·go·is·tic (ē′gō is′tik) *adj.* relating to or characterized by egoism. Also, **egoistical.** —**e′go·is′ti·cal·ly,** *adv.*

eggplant *(def. 1)*

e·go·ma·ni·a (ē′gō mā′nē ə) *n.* extreme or abnormal egotism.

e·go·ma·ni·ac (ē′gō mā′nē ak′) *n.* an extremely egotistic person.

e·go·tism (ē′gə tiz′əm) *n.* **1.** a very high opinion of oneself; conceit. **2.** a great tendency to talk or write about oneself, especially in a bragging or boastful manner. **3.** selfishness; egoism.

e·go·tist (ē′gə tist) *n.* **1.** a conceited, boastful person. **2.** a selfish or self-centered person; egoist.

e·go·tis·tic (ē′gə tis′tik) *adj.* relating to or characterized by egotism. Also, **egotistical.** —**e′go·tis′ti·cal·ly,** *adv.*

ego trip *Informal.* something done mainly out of vanity or selfishness: *Did you run for class president because you wanted to serve the class, or was it just an ego trip?*

e·gre·gious (i grē′jəs) *adj.* openly or outrageously bad; flagrant: *to make an egregious error by lying to a judge in court.* —**e·gre′gious·ly,** *adv.* —**e·gre′gious·ness,** *n.*

e·gress (ē′gres) *n.* **1.** the act of going out. **2.** a place or means of going out; way out; exit.

e·gret (ē′grit) *n.* **1.** any of several herons with long legs and long necks, usually having white tufts of long, lacy feathers. **2.** a feather from such a bird.

E·gyp·tian (i jip′shən) *n.* **1.** a person who was born in or is a citizen of Egypt. **2.** a person who lived in ancient Egypt. **3.** the language of the ancient Egyptians. —*adj.* of or relating to Egypt, its people, or their culture.

Egyptian cotton, a fine, silky cotton with long fibers, grown chiefly in Egypt.

eh (ā) *interj.* **1.** used to express surprise, doubt, or failure to hear what was said: *Eh, speak up please; I can't hear you.* **2.** used at the end of a sentence as if to ask for agreement or confirmation of being understood: *These are pretty big pineapples, eh?*

egret *(def. 1)*

ei·der (ī′dər) *n.* **1.** any of a group of saltwater ducks living in the northern parts of the Pacific and Atlantic oceans. Also, **eider duck. 2.** see **eiderdown.**

ei·der·down (ī′dər doun′) *n.* **1.** the small, soft feathers from the breast of the female eider, used to stuff pillows and quilts. **2.** a quilt filled with eiderdown.

eight (āt) *n.* **1.** the cardinal number that is one more than seven. **2.** a symbol representing this number, such as 8

at; āpe; fär; câre; end; mē; it; īce; pîerce; hot; ōld; sông, fôrk; oil; out; up; ūse; rūle; pull; tûrn; chin; sing; shop; thin; *this*; hw in white; zh in treasure. The symbol ə stands for the unstressed vowel sound heard in about, taken, pencil, lemon, and circus.

or VIII. **3.** something having this many units or things, such as a playing card. —*adj.* numbering one more than seven.

eight·een (ā'tēn') *n.* **1.** the cardinal number that is eight more than ten. **2.** a symbol representing this number, such as 18 or XVIII. **3.** something having this many units or things. —*adj.* numbering eight more than ten.

eight·eenth (ā'tēnth') *adj.* **1.** (the ordinal of eighteen) next after the seventeenth. **2.** being one of eighteen equal parts. —*n.* **1.** something that is next after the seventeenth. **2.** one of eighteen equal parts; ¹/₁₈.

eight·fold (āt'fōld') *adj.* **1.** eight times as great or numerous. **2.** having or consisting of eight parts. —*adv.* so as to be eight times greater or more numerous.

eighth (ātth) *adj.* **1.** (the ordinal of eight) next after the seventh. **2.** being one of eight equal parts. —*n.* **1.** something that is next after the seventh. **2.** one of eight equal parts; ¹/₈. **3.** *Music.* see **octave** (*defs. 1a, b, c*). —*adv.* in the eighth place.

eighth note *Music.* a note that is sounded for one eighth as long as a whole note.

eight·i·eth (ā'tē ith) *adj.* **1.** (the ordinal of eighty) next after the seventy-ninth. **2.** being one of eighty equal parts. —*n.* **1.** something that is next after the seventy-ninth. **2.** one of eighty equal parts; ¹/₈₀.

eight·y (ā'tē) *n., pl.* **eight·ies. 1.** the cardinal number that is eight times ten. **2.** a symbol representing this number, such as 80 or LXXX. —*adj.* numbering eight times ten.

ein·stein·i·um (īn stī'nē əm) *n.* an artificially produced radioactive element used in nuclear physics research. It was discovered in the debris of a nuclear explosion. Symbol: **Es** [From the German physicist Albert *Einstein* (1879–1955).]

ei·ther (ē'thər, ī'thər) *adj.* **1.** one or the other: *They didn't like either plan.* **2.** one and the other; each of two: *There were no houses on either side of the road.* —*pron.* one or the other: *Either is fine with me.* —*conj.* one or the other. ▲ used with *or* before the first of two possibilities: *Either be quiet or leave. You may telephone either tonight or tomorrow.* —*adv.* any more so; also. ▲ used for emphasis after a negative: *I can't do this kind of work, and they can't either.*

e·jac·u·late (i jak'yə lāt') *v.t.,* **e·jac·u·lat·ed, e·jac·u·lat·ing. 1.** to utter suddenly and briefly; blurt out; exclaim. **2.** to discharge semen. —**e·jac·u·la'tion,** *n.*

e·ject (i jekt') *v.t.* to give off, force out, or throw out: *The rifle ejects empty cartridges automatically. The manager ejected the noisy customer from the store.* —**e·jec'tor,** *n.*

e·jec·tion (i jek'shən) *n.* **1.** the act of ejecting or the state of being ejected. **2.** something ejected, such as lava from a volcano.

eke (ēk) *v.t.,* **eked, ek·ing. to eke out. 1.** to barely manage to make (a living): *to eke out a living by selling used clothing.* **2.** to add to in order to make barely enough: *to eke out a meal by adding rice to leftovers.*

EKG 1. electrocardiogram. **2.** electrocardiograph.

e·lab·o·rate (*adj.,* i lab'ər it; *v.,* i lab'ə rāt') *adj.* **1.** worked out with great care and in great detail: *The scientist developed an elaborate theory concerning the origin of life.* **2.** highly detailed or ornamented; ornate: *fancy and elaborate furniture.* —*v.,* **e·lab·o·rat·ed, e·lab·o·rat·ing.** —*v.i.* to give greater detail or fuller treatment to something spoken or written: *The teacher asked me to elaborate on my suggestion.* —*v.t.* to work out carefully and in greater detail: *to elaborate a plan to raise money.* —**e·lab·o·rate·ly** (i lab'ər it lē), *adv.* —**e·lab'o·rate·ness,** *n.*

e·lab·o·ra·tion (i lab'ə rā'shən) *n.* **1.** the act of elaborating or the state of being elaborated. **2.** something added, as a detail: *The design is good, but it has too many elaborations.*

é·lan (ā län', ā lan') *n.* enthusiasm, vivacity, and dash: *an entertainer who performs with great élan.* [From the French word *élan,* from the Middle French word *(s')eslancer* meaning "to rush," going back to the Latin words *ex* "out of" and *lancea* "lance."]

e·land (ē'lənd) *n., pl.* **e·land** or **e·lands.** a large antelope found in southern Africa, having humped shoulders and long, twisted horns.

e·lapse (i laps') *v.i.,* **e·lapsed, e·laps·ing.** (of time) to slip by; pass: *Three years elapsed before their return.*

e·las·tic (i las'tik) *adj.* **1.** capable of returning to its original size or shape after being stretched, twisted, or squeezed: *A rubber band is elastic.* **2.** capable of changing to fit new conditions; flexible; accommodating: *an elastic set of rules.*

eland

3. having a bouncing quality: *an elastic walk.* —*n.* **1.** a fabric made stretchable by having rubber threads or strands running through it. **2.** a rubber band. —**e·las'ti·cal·ly,** *adv.*

e·las·tic·i·ty (i las tis'i tē, ē'las tis'i tē) *n.* the state or quality of being elastic.

e·late (i lāt') *v.t.,* **e·lat·ed, e·lat·ing.** to put in high spirits; make joyful or proud: *The good news elated us.*

e·lat·ed (i lā'tid) *adj.* in high spirits; filled with joy or pride. —**e·lat'ed·ly,** *adv.*

e·la·tion (i lā'shən) *n.* a feeling of joy or pride: *We were filled with elation at our good fortune.*

el·bow (el'bō) *n.* **1.** the joint between the lower arm and the upper arm. **2.** something having a bend like the elbow, such as a curved pipe. —*v.t.* **1.** to push with or as if with the elbows; shove aside: *to elbow someone in order to pass.* **2.** to make or force (one's way) by pushing with or as if with the elbows: *to elbow one's way along a crowded corridor.* —*v.i.* to go forward by pushing with or as if with the elbows: *to elbow through a crowd.*

elbow grease *Informal.* much energy or effort; hard work.

el·bow·room (el'bō rüm', el'bō rum') *n.* enough room, especially to move or work in.

eld·er¹ (el'dər) *adj.* born earlier; older: *an elder sister.* —*n.* **1.** a person who is older. **2.** an older, influential member, as of a family or community: *The tribe's elders met to decide on important matters.* **3.** an officer in any of various churches. [From the Old English word *eldra* meaning "older," from the word *eald* meaning "old."]

el·der² (el'dər) *n.* any of a group of shrubs and small trees bearing red

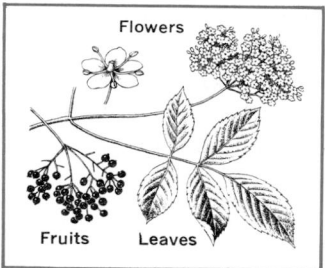

elder²

or purplish black berries that are often eaten. Also, **elderberry.** [From the Old English word *ellærn* meaning "elder tree."]

el·der·ber·ry (el'dər ber'ē, el'dər bə rē) *n., pl.* **el·der·ber·ries. 1.** the berry of the elder, used especially for making wines, jellies, and pies. **2.** see **elder².**

eld·er·ly (el'dər lē) *adj.* past middle age; rather old. —*pl. n.* **the elderly.** people who are old.

elder statesman, a retired statesman who advises government leaders.

eld·est (el'dist) *adj.* born first; oldest: *I am the eldest of three children.*

El Do·ra·do (el də rä'dō) *also,* **El·do·ra·do.** *n.* **1.** a legendary place in South America, sought by sixteenth-century Spanish explorers because they believed that it was full of gold and jewels. **2.** any place of great wealth.

e·lect (i lekt') *v.t.* **1.** to choose by voting: *The towns-people elected a new mayor.* **2.** to select or decide; choose: *to elect biology as a major in college.* —*adj.* elected to an office but not yet formally installed. ▲ used in combination after a noun: *senator-elect.* —*pl. n.* **the elect. 1.** people who belong to a favored, specially chosen group. **2.** people chosen by God for salvation.

e·lec·tion (i lek'shən) *n.* **1.** the act of electing or the state of being elected. **2.** the process of choosing a person or persons, especially for an office, by voting: *Did your parents vote in the election last year?*

e·lec·tion·eer (i lek'shə nîr') *v.i.* to work or campaign for the election of a candidate or political party.

e·lec·tive (i lek'tiv) *adj.* **1.** chosen or filled by vote: *The presidency is an elective office.* **2.** open to choice; not required: *an elective course in school.* **3.** having the power or right to choose by vote: *an elective assembly.* —*n.* a subject or course that is not required and may be chosen by a student in high school or college: *to choose an art course as an elective.*

e·lec·tor (i lek'tər) *n.* **1.** a person who has the right to vote in an election. **2.** a member of the U.S. electoral college. Before an election, a body of electors is selected by each political party in each state and pledged to the party's candidate. Voters on election day cast their ballots for one of the presidential candidates, and thus for one of the groups of electors pledged to that candidate.

e·lec·tor·al (i lek'tər əl) *adj.* of or relating to an election or electors: *the electoral process.*

electoral college, a group of representatives, called electors, chosen by vote in an election, who formally elect the president and vice president of the United States.

e·lec·tor·ate (i lek'tər it) *n.* all the persons who have the right to vote in an election.

e·lec·tric (i lek'trik) *adj.* **1.** of or relating to electricity. **2.** carrying or operated by electricity: *electric wires, an electric iron.* **3.** caused by electricity. *an electric shock,* **4.** producing electricity: *an electric generator.* **5.** exciting; thrilling: *an electric sensation.*

e·lec·tri·cal (i lek'tri kəl) *adj.* **1.** another word for **electric** (*defs. 1–4*). **2.** dealing with electricity: *electrical engineering.* —**e·lec'tri·cal·ly,** *adv.*

electric chair 1. a chair used to execute a criminal sentenced to death by electrocution. **2.** the penalty of death by electrocution: *The prisoner was sentenced to the electric chair.*

electric eel, a long freshwater fish found in South America that resembles an eel and is able to give off strong electric shocks to protect itself and to catch its prey.

electric eye, a photoelectric cell used to open a door, to ring a bell, or to do similar tasks.

e·lec·tri·cian (i lek trish'ən) *n.* a person who designs, installs, or repairs electric wiring or equipment.

e·lec·tric·i·ty (i lek tris'i tē) *n.* **1.** energy carried especially by electrons and protons, usually through wires, and capable of driving motors and of producing light and heat. **2.** an electric current. **3.** a strong feeling of excitement.

e·lec·tri·fi·ca·tion (i lek'trə fi kā'shən) *n.* the act of electrifying or the state of being electrified.

e·lec·tri·fy (i lek'trə fī') *v.t.,* **e·lec·tri·fied, e·lec·tri·fy·ing. 1.** to charge with electricity: *The farmer electrified the fence around the cow pasture.* **2.** to equip for the use of electricity. **3.** to excite; thrill; startle: *The acrobat's daring feat electrified the crowd.*

electro– *combining form* of, relating to, or by means of electricity: *electromagnet, electrocute.*

e·lec·tro·car·di·o·gram (i lek'trō kär'dē ə gram') *n.* a graph recording the electrical activity of the heart as it contracts and relaxes, made on an electrocardiograph. Also, **cardiogram.**

e·lec·tro·car·di·o·graph (i lek'trō kär'dē ə graf') *n.* an instrument that receives and records electrical impulses sent out by the heart as it contracts and relaxes, used especially to detect heart disorders. Also, **cardiograph.**

e·lec·tro·cute (i lek'trə kūt') *v.t.,* **e·lec·tro·cut·ed, e·lec·tro·cut·ing.** to execute or kill by electricity. —**e·lec'tro·cu'tion,** *n.*

e·lec·trode (i lek'trōd) *n.* part of an electric circuit through which electrons enter or leave a gas or liquid solution.

e·lec·tro·en·ceph·a·lo·gram (i lek'trō en sef'ə lə gram') *n.* a graph produced by an electroencephalograph that shows the electrical activity of the brain.

e·lec·tro·en·ceph·a·lo·graph (i lek'trō en sef'ə lə graf') *n.* an instrument that records the electrical activity of the brain, used to determine a patient's level of consciousness and to diagnose abnormalities of the brain.

e·lec·trol·y·sis (i lek trol'ə sis) *n.* **1.** the breaking down of a liquified or dissolved substance into its component parts by passage of an electric current through the substance. **2.** the permanent removal of unwanted body hair by destroying the root cells with an electrified needle.

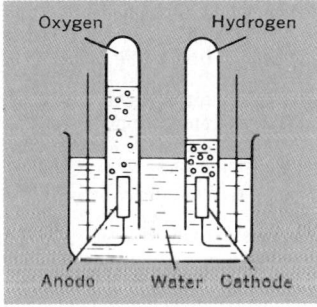
electrolysis of water

e·lec·tro·lyte (i lek'trə līt') *n.* **1.** any nonmetallic substance that will conduct an electric current, especially a liquid solution. **2.** a chemical compound that, when liquified or in solution, will separate into ions and conduct an electric current.

e·lec·tro·lyze (i lek'trə līz') *v.t.,* **e·lec·tro·lyzed, e·lec·tro·lyz·ing.** to break down by electrolysis.

e·lec·tro·mag·net (i lek'trō mag'nit) *n.* a piece of iron with insulated wire wound around it, that becomes a magnet when an electric current is passed through the wire.

e·lec·tro·mag·net·ic (i lek'trō mag net'ik) *adj.* **1.** of or produced by an electromagnet. **2.** of or relating to electromagnetism.

electromagnetic wave, a wave of energy that is made up of electric and magnetic fields and that can travel through empty space at around 186,000 miles per second (300,000 kilometers per second). Radio waves, light rays, and X rays are electromagnetic waves.

e·lec·tro·mag·net·ism (i lek'trō mag'ni tiz'əm) *n.* **1.** magnetism produced by a current of electricity. **2.** a branch of physics that studies the relation between magnetism and electricity.

e·lec·tro·mo·tive (i lek'trə mō'tiv) *adj.* **1.** producing a flow of electricity. **2.** of or relating to electromotive force.

at; āpe; fär; câre; end; mē; it; īce; pîerce; hot; ōld; sông, fôrk; oil; out; up; ūse; rüle; pull; tûrn; chin; sing; shop; thin; this; hw in white; zh in treasure. The symbol ə stands for the unstressed vowel sound heard in about, taken, pencil, lemon, and circus.

E

315

electromotive force 1. a force that causes an electric current to flow in a circuit. **2.** the amount of energy derived from an electric source.

e·lec·tron (i lek′tron) *n.* a subatomic particle that carries the smallest negative electric charge.

electron gun, a device that sends out and focuses a beam of electrons. An electron gun at one end of a television picture tube sends out a beam of electrons to the picture screen.

e·lec·tron·ic (i lek tron′ik) *adj.* of or relating to electrons or electronics. —**e·lec′tron′i·cal·ly,** *adv.*

electronic banking, a system of conducting banking transactions in which accounts are credited and debited with transfers of funds by means of computer systems that record the transactions.

electronic bulletin board, a group of messages created and edited on a computer system and made accessible to subscribers at remote terminals by means of a telecommunications link.

electronic mail 1. a system of sending messages by means of computer terminals linked together. **2.** messages sent or received in this way.

e·lec·tron·ics (i lek tron′iks) *n.* a branch of physics dealing with the motion of electrons and other charged particles in a vacuum and in gases. The study of electronics has led to the development of the radio, television, and many other inventions. ▲ used with a singular verb.

electron microscope, a device that makes extremely small things visible by means of a beam of electrons rather than a beam of light. It has much higher power than an ordinary microscope.

electron tube, a sealed container of glass or metal in which electrons move through a vacuum or gas. An electron tube produces, amplifies, or regulates electrical signals.

electron volt, the amount of energy gained by an electron when it is accelerated to a position with an electrical potential that is 1 volt greater.

e·lec·tro·plate (i lek′trə plāt′) *v.t.,* **e·lec·tro·plat·ed, e·lec·tro·plat·ing.** to apply a metal coating to the surface of (an object) by means of electrolysis.

e·lec·tro·scope (i lek′trə skōp′) *n.* an instrument used to discover and measure electric charges.

e·lec·tro·ther·a·py (i lek′trō ther′ə pē) *n.* the use of electricity in the treatment of various diseases.

e·lec·tro·type (i lek′trə tīp′) *n.* **1.** a metal plate used in printing, made by the electroplating process, which duplicates the original plate. **2.** a print made from such a plate. —*v.t.,* **e·lec·tro·typed, e·lec·tro·typ·ing.** to make such a plate or plates of.

el·e·gance (el′i gəns) *n.* the state or quality of being elegant.

el·e·gant (el′i gənt) *adj.* **1.** showing richness and good taste: *an elegant coat.* **2.** showing grace, dignity, and refinement: *elegant manners.* —**el′e·gant·ly,** *adv.*

el·e·gi·ac (el′i jī′ak, i lē′jē ak) *adj.* of, relating to, or suitable for an elegy.

el·e·gize (el′i jīz′) *v.,* **el·e·gized, el·e·giz·ing.** —*v.t.* to mourn in an elegy. —*v.i.* to write an elegy.

el·e·gy (el′i jē) *n., pl.* **el·e·gies.** a mournful or sad poem or musical work, especially one written to mourn someone who has died.

el·e·ment (el′ə mənt) *n.* **1.** a substance, such as iron, carbon, oxygen, or hydrogen, that cannot be changed into a simpler substance by ordinary chemical means. Elements consist entirely of atoms having the same atomic number. **2.** a basic part from which something is made or formed: *Architects must study the elements of good design.* **3.** the natural or most comfortable environment for a person or living thing: *The ocean is the whale's element.* **4.** *Mathematics.* a member of a set. **5. the elements.** the forces of the atmosphere, such as rain, wind, or snow.

element 104, see **rutherfordium.**
element 105, see **hahnium.**
element 106, see **unnilhexium.**
element 107, see **unnilseptium.**

el·e·men·tal (el′ə men′təl) *adj.* **1.** of or relating to a force of nature: *The elemental power of the hurricane caused much destruction.* **2.** like a force of nature; natural, primitive, or unrestrained: *elemental passions.* **3.** being a basic part of anything: *an elemental substance.*

el·e·men·ta·ry (el′ə men′tə rē, el′ə men′trē) *adj.* of, relating to, or dealing with the simple basic parts or beginnings of something: *an elementary knowledge of science, a course in elementary French.*

elementary particle, see **subatomic particle.**

elementary school, a school that includes the first six or eight grades, and sometimes kindergarten. Also, **grade school, grammar school.**

el·e·phant (el′ə fənt) *n., pl.* **el·e·phants** or **el·e·phant.** the largest and most powerful land animal, native to the tropical regions of Africa and Asia, having a massive head and body, thick skin, a long, muscular trunk, and a pair of ivory tusks.

African elephant   Indian elephant

el·e·phan·tine (el′ə-fan′tin, el′ə fan′tīn) *adj.* **1.** like an elephant in size, strength, or movement. **2.** of or relating to an elephant.

el·e·vate (el′ə vāt′) *v.t.,* **el·e·vat·ed, el·e·vat·ing. 1.** to lift up; raise: *to elevate a car so that the brakes can be repaired.* **2.** to raise or improve the mental or moral level of: *The inspiring sermon elevated the congregation.* **3.** to raise in rank or position: *to be elevated from clerk to manager.*

el·e·va·tion (el′ə vā′shən) *n.* **1.** the act of elevating or the state of being elevated. **2.** something elevated, such as a raised place or surface. **3.** height above the earth's surface or above sea level.

el·e·va·tor (el′ə vā′tər) *n.* **1.** a car, platform, or cage and the machinery for raising or lowering it, used for carrying people or things from one level to another, especially from one floor to another in a building. **2.** a building used for handling and storing grain or other crops. **3.** one of two movable, flat pieces attached to the tail of an airplane. When the elevators are lowered, the tail of the plane rises and the nose drops.

e·lev·en (i lev′ən) *n.* **1.** the cardinal number that is one more than ten. **2.** a symbol representing this number, such as 11 or XI. **3.** something having this many units or things, such as a football or soccer team. —*adj.* numbering one more than ten.

e·lev·enth (i lev′ənth) *adj.* **1.** (the ordinal of eleven) next after the tenth. **2.** being one of eleven equal parts. —*n.* **1.** something that is next after the tenth. **2.** one of eleven equal parts; $\frac{1}{11}$.

eleventh hour, the last possible moment, just before it is too late: *The strike was prevented by a settlement at the eleventh hour.*

elf (elf) *n., pl.* **elves.** a small, often mischievous, fairy or sprite having magical powers.

elf·in (el′fin) *adj.* of or like an elf; impish; mischievous: *an elfin grin.*

elf·ish (el′fish) *adj.* of or like an elf; elfin. —**elf′ish·ly,** *adv.* —**elf′ish·ness,** *n.*

e·lic·it (i lis′it) *v.t.* to bring out or draw forth: *to elicit a response to a question.*

▲ **Elicit** and **illicit** are pronounced alike, but they have different meanings. **Elicit** is a verb that means to bring out: *My greeting elicited no reply from the stranger.* **Illicit** is an adjective that means illegal: *A smuggler brings goods into a country by illicit means.*

el·i·gi·bil·i·ty (el′i jə bil′i tē) *n.* the state or quality of being eligible.

el·i·gi·ble (el′i jə bəl) *adj.* **1.** qualified or meeting the requirements for something: *A person under 35 is not eligible to run for the Senate.* **2.** desirable or suitable, especially for marriage: *an eligible bachelor.* —**el′i·gi·bly**, *adv.*

e·lim·i·nate (i lim′ə nāt′) *v.t.*, **e·lim·i·nat·ed, e·lim·i·nat·ing. 1.** to get rid of; remove: *The president promised to eliminate hunger in the nation.* **2.** to leave out of consideration; disregard: *In their search for a new home, they eliminated all houses without a backyard.* **3.** to expel (waste matter) from the body; excrete.

e·lim·i·na·tion (i lim′ə nā′shən) *n.* the act of eliminating or the state of being eliminated.

e·li·sion (i lizh′ən) *n.* the leaving out or slurring over of a vowel or a syllable in pronunciation, such as the leaving out of the *ha* sound of *have* in *They've already gone home.*

e·lite (i lēt′, ā lēt′) *also,* **é·lite.** *n.* **1.** the best or finest members, as of a society or social group. **2.** a size of type for typewriters, providing twelve characters to the inch.

e·lit·ist (i lē′tist, ā lē′tist) *n.* **1.** a person who is a member of an elite. **2.** a person who regards himself or herself as a member of an elite.

e·lix·ir (i lik′sər) *n.* **1.** a substance that alchemists in former times believed could extend life forever and change base metals, such as iron and lead, into gold. **2.** a sweetened alcoholic solution containing medicine. **3.** a universal remedy; cure-all.

E·liz·a·be·than (i liz′ə bē′thən, i liz′ə beth′ən) *adj.* of or relating to Queen Elizabeth I or the time in which she lived. —*n.* an English person of this time.

elk (elk) *n., pl.* **elk** or **elks. 1.** a large deer of the mountain regions of western North America, having a coat that is mainly fawn colored. The male has antlers measuring more than 5 feet across. Also, **wapiti. 2.** a European moose related to the American moose.

ell¹ (el) *n.* **1.** the letter L. **2.** something shaped like an L, such as an addition to the main part of a building.

ell² (el) *n.* an old measure of length ranging from 27 inches (68.5 centimeters) to 45 inches (114 centimeters), used especially for measuring cloth. [From the Old English word *eln* "a cubit" or "length of the forearm."]

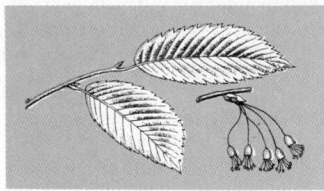

elk *(def. 1)*

el·lipse (i lips′) *n.* a closed curve resembling an oval, but having both ends alike. It consists of a set of points whose distances from two fixed points add up to a fixed sum.

el·lip·sis (i lip′sis) *n., pl.* **el·lip·ses** (i lip′sēz). **1.** the leaving out of a word or words strictly required by grammatical rules to complete the construction of a sentence, but not necessary for the understanding of its meaning. For example, *They arrived sooner than expected* instead of *They arrived sooner than they had been expected to arrive* is an ellipsis. **2.** a mark or marks (. . ., * * *, or —) used to show that something has been left out in writing or printing.

el·lip·ti·cal (i lip′ti kəl) *adj.* **1.** of or shaped like an ellipse. **2.** of or relating to ellipsis; with a word or words left out. Also, **el·lip·tic** (i lip′tik). —**el·lip′ti·cal·ly**, *adv.*

elm (elm) *n.* **1.** a tall, hardy tree, often grown for ornament or shade. **2.** the hard, heavy wood of this tree.

El Ni·ño (el nēn′yō) a warm current of water that forms during the months of December and January in the Pacific Ocean off the coasts of Ecuador and Peru. [From the Spanish phrase *el Niño* meaning "the (Christ) Child." This current appears around the time of Christmas.]

elm leaves and flowers

el·o·cu·tion (el′ə kū′shən) *n.* **1.** the art of public speaking or reading. **2.** manner of speaking or reading in public.

e·lon·gate (i lông′gāt) *v.*, **e·lon·gat·ed, e·lon·gat·ing.** —*v.t.* to make longer; stretch; lengthen. —*v.i.* to become longer or stretched out. —*adj.* long and thin; lengthened. —**e′lon·ga′tion**, *n.*

e·lope (i lōp′) *v.i.*, **e·loped, e·lop·ing.** to run away secretly to get married. —**e·lope′ment**, *n.*

el·o·quence (el′ə kwəns) *n.* **1.** language that is expressive and effective: *Her speech was full of eloquence and wit.* **2.** the ability to use language effectively: *Winston Churchill's eloquence was well-known.* **3.** the quality of being expressive and effective: *The eloquence of the lawyer's plea aroused the jury's sympathy.*

el·o·quent (el′ə kwənt) *adj.* having or showing eloquence: *an eloquent orator, an eloquent speech.* —**el′o·quent·ly**, *adv.*

else (els) *adj.* **1.** other; different: *I mistook you for someone else.* **2.** additional; more; further: *If anyone else comes, we won't have enough chairs.* —*adv.* **1.** in another time, place, or manner; instead: *Where else did you go?* **2.** under other circumstances; if not; otherwise: *Dress warmly, or else you'll catch cold.*

else·where (els′hwâr′, els′wâr′) *adv.* in, at, or to another place; somewhere else: *You'll have to look elsewhere for that information.*

e·lu·ci·date (i lü′si dāt) *v.t.*, **e·lu·ci·dat·ed, e·lu·ci·dat·ing.** to make clear; explain: *The debater elucidated a point by giving several examples.* —**e·lu′ci·da′tion**, *n.*

e·lude (i lüd′) *v.t.*, **e·lud·ed, e·lud·ing. 1.** to avoid or escape, as by cleverness or trickery; evade: *The bandit eluded the police.* **2.** to be beyond the memory or understanding of: *The answer to the riddle eluded us.*

e·lu·sion (i lü′zhən) *n.* the act of eluding; evasion.

e·lu·sive (i lü′siv) *adj.* **1.** hard to explain, understand, or perceive: *an elusive idea, an elusive scent.* **2.** hard to catch or follow: *an elusive criminal.* Also, **e·lu·so·ry** (i lü′sə rē) —**e·lu′sive·ly**, *adv.* —**e·lu′sive·ness**, *n.*

el·ver (el′vər) *n.* a young eel, especially one that is migrating upstream from the ocean.

elves (elvz) the plural of **elf.**

E·ly·sian (i lizh′ən, i lē′zhən, i liz′ē ən) *adj.* **1.** of or relating to Elysium. **2.** blissful; happy.

E·ly·sium (i lizh′əm, i lē′zhəm, i liz′ē əm) *n.* **1.** *Greek Mythology.* a happy land where heroes and good people lived after death. Also, **Elysian Fields. 2.** any place of perfect happiness; paradise.

'em (əm) *pron. Informal.* another word for **them.**

em-, the form of the prefix **en-** used before *b, p,* and sometimes *m,* as in *embroider, empower.*

---

at; āpe; fär; câre; end; mē; it; īce; pîerce; hot; ōld; sông, fôrk; oil; out; up; ūse; rüle; pull; tûrn; chin; sing; shop; thin; <u>th</u>is; hw in white; zh in treasure. The symbol ə stands for the unstressed vowel sound heard in about, taken, pencil, lemon, and circus.

e·ma·ci·ate (i mā′shē āt′) *v.t.*, **e·ma·ci·at·ed, e·ma·ci·at·ing.** to cause to become abnormally thin; cause to lose much weight or flesh: *A long illness had emaciated the patient.* —**e·ma′ci·a′tion,** *n.*

em·a·nate (em′ə nāt′) *v.i.*, **em·a·nat·ed, em·a·nat·ing.** to come forth; arise; originate: *The smoke emanated from the chimney.* —**em′a·na′tion,** *n.*

e·man·ci·pate (i man′sə pāt′) *v.t.*, **e·man·ci·pat·ed, e·man·ci·pat·ing.** to free from control or restraint; liberate: *to emancipate a slave.* [From the Latin word *emancipatus,* past participle of *emancipare* meaning "to set free," from the words *ex-* meaning "away, out of" + *mancipium* "ownership," from the words *manus* "hand" and *capere* "to take."] —**e·man′ci·pa′tion,** *n.* —**e·man′ci·pa′tor,** *n.*

Emancipation Proclamation, a proclamation by President Abraham Lincoln on January 1, 1863, that freed all slaves in the territory still at war with the Union.

e·mas·cu·late (*v.,* i mas′kyə lāt′; *adj.,* i mas′kyə lit, i mas′kyə lāt′) *v.t.*, **e·mas·cu·lat·ed, e·mas·cu·lat·ing. 1.** to remove the sex glands of (a male); castrate. **2.** to deprive of strength, force, or vigor; weaken. —*adj.* deprived of strength, force, or vigor. —**e·mas′cu·la′tion,** *n.*

em·balm (em bäm′) *v.t.* to treat (a dead body) with certain chemicals to temporarily keep it from decaying. —**em·balm′er,** *n.*

em·bank (em bangk′) *v.t.* to protect or enclose with an embankment, dike, or similar structure.

em·bank·ment (em bangk′mənt) *n.* **1.** a bank of earth, stones, or other materials, used to support a roadbed or to hold back water. **2.** the act of embanking.

em·bar·go (em bär′gō) *n.,* *pl.* **em·bar·goes. 1.** an order by a government preventing merchant ships from entering or leaving its ports. **2.** a restriction put on trade by law, especially upon the import, export, or sale of certain goods: *an embargo on the sale of arms to warring countries.* **3.** any restriction or prohibition. —*v.t.,* **em·bar·goed, em·bar·go·ing.** to put an embargo on.

embankment *(def. 1)*

em·bark (em bärk′) *v.i.* **1.** to go aboard a ship for a trip: *The passengers embarked at San Francisco.* **2.** to begin or set out, as on an adventure: *The explorers embarked on a dangerous expedition.* —*v.t.* to put or take on board a ship. —**em′bar·ka′tion,** *n.*

em·bar·rass (em bar′əs) *v.t.* **1.** to cause to feel uncomfortable or ashamed: *My foolish mistake embarrassed me.* **2.** to make difficult; hinder; impede.

em·bar·rass·ing (em bar′ə sing) *adj.* causing embarrassment: *an embarrassing situation.* —**em·bar′rass·ing·ly,** *adv.*

em·bar·rass·ment (em bar′əs mənt) *n.* **1.** the act of embarrassing or the state of being embarrassed. **2.** something that embarrasses.

em·bas·sy (em′bə sē) *n.,* *pl.* **em·bas·sies. 1.** the official home and office of an ambassador in a foreign country. **2.** an ambassador and his or her staff: *The embassy gave a party for the visiting dignitaries.* **3.** the position or duties of an ambassador.

em·bat·tled (em bat′əld) *adj.* **1.** armed and ready for battle: *The embattled troops awaited the outbreak of war.* **2.** fortified against attack: *an embattled fortress.* **3.** involved in conflict or controversy: *an embattled politician.*

em·bed (em bed′) *also,* **im·bed.** *v.t.,* **em·bed·ded, em·bed·ding. 1.** to set or enclose in surrounding matter: *The*

workers embedded the pole in cement. *The arrow was embedded in the tree.* **2.** to place or plant firmly, as in the mind: *The event is embedded in my memory.*

em·bel·lish (em bel′ish) *v.t.* **1.** to make beautiful by adding ornament; decorate; adorn: *The jeweler embellished the case with pearls and rubies.* **2.** to make (a story) more interesting by adding interesting or fanciful details. —**em·bel′lish·ment,** *n.*

em·ber (em′bər) *n.* **1.** a piece of wood or coal glowing in the ashes of a fire. **2. embers.** the glowing remains of a fire.

em·bez·zle (em bez′əl) *v.t.,* **em·bez·zled, em·bez·zling.** to steal (money entrusted to one's care): *The bank official embezzled thousands of dollars.* —**em·bez′zle·ment,** *n.* —**em·bez′zler,** *n.*

em·bit·ter (em bit′ər) *v.t.* to make bitter; cause to feel resentful: *The couple's repeated business failures embittered them.*

em·bla·zon (em blā′zən) *v.t.* **1.** to adorn or decorate, as with bright colors or the symbols of heraldry: *to emblazon a shield with a coat of arms.* **2.** to praise; celebrate: *The army's deeds were emblazoned by the country's poets.*

em·blem (em′bləm) *n.* an object or figure that identifies or represents something: *The hats of the band members bore the emblem of their school. The crown is an emblem of monarchy.*

em·blem·at·ic (em′blə mat′ik) *adj.* of, relating to, or being an emblem; symbolic: *A gold medal is emblematic of first place in the Olympic games.* Also, **em·blem·at·i·cal** (em′blə mat′i kəl)

em·bod·i·ment (em bod′ē mənt) *n.* **1.** the act of embodying or the state of being embodied. **2.** a person or thing that embodies something: *That famous professor is the embodiment of good scholarship.*

em·bod·y (em bod′ē) *v.t.,* **em·bod·ied, em·bod·y·ing. 1.** to give concrete or visible form to: *The statue embodies the sculptor's idea of beauty.* **2.** to collect into or make part of an organized whole; incorporate: *The report embodied the findings of ten scientists.*

em·bold·en (em bōl′dən) *v.t.* to make bold or bolder; encourage.

em·bo·lism (em′bə liz′əm) *n.* the blockage of a blood vessel by material carried in the blood, such as a blood clot or a mass of fat.

em·bo·lus (em′bə ləs) *n.,* *pl.* **em·bo·li** (em′bə lī′). a blood clot, mass of fat, gas bubble, or other material that causes a blockage of a blood vessel.

em·boss (em bôs′) *v.t.* **1.** to decorate or cover (a surface) with a design that is raised: *My stationery is embossed with my initials.* **2.** to raise (a design) on a surface: *The printer embossed my return address on the envelopes.*

em·bow·er (em bou′ər) *v.t.* to shelter in a bower.

em·brace (em brās′) *v.,* **em·braced, em·brac·ing.** —*v.t.* **1.** to take or hold in the arms as a sign of love or affection; hug: *to embrace a friend at the railroad station.* **2.** to take up as one's own; adopt: *to embrace medicine as a career.* **3.** to take willingly: *to embrace an opportunity.* **4.** to include; contain: *Botany embraces the study of all plant life.* **5.** to surround; enclose: *A fence embraced the old house.* —*v.i.* to hug one another: *The children embraced before they parted.* —*n.* the act of holding in the arms; hug: *to welcome an embrace.*

em·bra·sure (em brā′zhər) *n.* an opening in a wall through which a gun may be fired. The sides usually spread outward to permit the gun to be swung from side to side.

em·broi·der (em broi′dər) *v.t.* **1.** to decorate with a design in needlework: *I embroidered the napkins with a floral design.* **2.** to make (a design) in needlework: *to embroider your initials on the new towels.* **3.** to make (a story) more interesting by adding false or exaggerated details. —*v.i.* to do embroidery.

em·broi·der·y (em broi′də rē) *n., pl.* **em·broi·der·ies.**
1. the act or art of decorating with designs done in needle-work. **2.** an embroidered design or work: *The embroidery on that dress is beautiful.*

em·broil (em broil′) *v.t.*
1. to involve in conflict or difficulty: *to become embroiled in a quarrel.* **2.** to throw into confusion or disorder: *The bus strike embroiled the whole city.*

em·bry·o (em′brē ō′) *n., pl.* **em·bry·os.** **1.** an organism in the early stages of its development, after fertilization and before hatching or birth. The human embryo is called a fetus after the first two months of development.

embroidery *(def. 2)*

2. an undeveloped plant within a seed. **3.** the beginning stage or form of anything: *The idea was still in embryo.* —*adj.* another word for **embryonic.**

em·bry·ol·o·gist (em′brē ol′ə jist) *n.* a person who specializes in embryology.

em·bry·ol·o·gy (em′brē ol′ə jē) *n.* the branch of biology dealing with the formation and development of embryos.

em·bry·on·ic (em′brē on′ik) *adj.* of, relating to, or like an embryo: *embryonic development, the embryonic stages of a program.*

em·cee (em′sē′) *Informal. n.* a master of ceremonies. —*v.t., v.i.* to act as master of ceremonies (of).

e·mend (i mend′) *v.t.* to remove errors from or make changes in; correct. *The editors emended the text before it was published.*

e·men·da·tion (ē′mən dā′shən) *n.* **1.** the act of emending. **2.** an alteration or correction.

em·er·ald (em′ər əld) *n.* **1.** a bright green precious stone. **2.** a bright green color. —*adj.* having the color emerald; bright green.

Emerald Isle, a name for Ireland in song and literature.

e·merge (i mûrj′) *v.i.* **e·merged, e·merg·ing.** **1.** to come into view: *Ten people emerged from the elevator.* **2.** to come into being or notice: *New facts emerged from the investigation.* **3.** to rise or come out, as from a difficult situation: *to emerge from an accident unharmed.*

e·mer·gence (i mûr′jəns) *n.* the act or process of emerging: *This season saw the emergence of a new Broadway star.*

e·mer·gen·cy (i mûr′jən sē) *n., pl.* **e·mer·gen·cies.** a situation or happening that requires immediate action: *The police acted quickly in the traffic emergency.* —*adj.* for use in an emergency: *an emergency exit, emergency funds.*

e·mer·gent (i mûr′jənt) *adj.* coming into view or being: *emergent political reforms.*

e·mer·i·tus (i mer′i təs) *adj.* retired from service, usually because of age, while keeping rank and title: *a professor emeritus.* —*n., pl.* **e·mer·i·ti** (i mer′i tī′). a person who is emeritus.

em·er·y (em′ə rē) *n.* a hard black or brown mixture of minerals, used chiefly in powdered form for grinding and polishing.

emery board, a piece of cardboard coated with powdered emery, used in filing the fingernails.

e·met·ic (i met′ik) *n.* a medicine that causes vomiting. —*adj.* causing vomiting: *an emetic drug.*

em·i·grant (em′i grənt) *n.* a person who leaves one place or country to live in another: *My ancestors were emigrants from Scotland.* —*adj.* leaving one place or country to live in another.

▲ **Emigrant** and **immigrant** are sometimes confused. An **emigrant** is a person who leaves his or her country to live in another country. An **immigrant** is a person who enters a new country to live there.

em·i·grate (em′i grāt) *v.i.,* **em·i·grat·ed, em·i·grat·ing.** to leave one place or country to live in another: *to emigrate from Europe to the United States.*

em·i·gra·tion (em′i grā′shən) *n.* **1.** the act or process of emigrating: *The population of Ireland has decreased because of emigration.* **2.** emigrants as a group.

em·i·gré (em′i grā′) *also,* **é·mi·gré.** *n.* a person who leaves one country or place to live in another, usually for political reasons. [From the French word *émigré* meaning "an emigrant," from the word *émigrer* "to emigrate," from the Latin word *emigrare* "to move away from," from the words *ex-* meaning "away, out of" + *migrare* "to migrate."]

em·i·nence (em′ə nəns) *n.* **1.** high rank or standing; position above all others: *The scientist achieved eminence in the field of physics.* **2.** a high place on the earth's surface: *The architect built the house on an eminence to take advantage of the view.* **3. Eminence.** a title or form of address used in referring or speaking to a cardinal of the Roman Catholic Church. ▲ usually preceded by *His* or *Your.*

em·i·nent (em′ə nənt) *adj.* above all others, as in rank, power, or achievement; distinguished: *an eminent writer, an eminent accomplishment.* —**em′i·nent·ly,** *adv.*

eminent domain, the power or right of a government to take privately owned land for public use and to pay the owner.

e·mir (ə mîr′) *n.* **1.** a chief, prince, or military leader in certain Arab or Muslim countries. **2.** a descendant of Muhammad. **3.** formerly, any of certain high Turkish officials.

e·mir·ate (em′ər it, ə mîr′it) *n.* **1.** the office, rank, or authority of an emir. **2.** the territory ruled by an emir.

em·is·sar·y (em′ə ser′ē) *n., pl.* **em·is·sar·ies.** an agent, as of a government, sent on a mission: *Emissaries of many nations met at the international conference.*

e·mis·sion (i mish′ən) *n.* **1.** the act or process of emitting. **2.** something that is emitted: *light, heat, and other emissions from the sun.*

e·mis·sive (i mis′iv) *adj.* able to emit; emitting.

e·mit (i mit′) *v.t.,* **e·mit·ted, e·mit·ting.** **1.** to send forth or give off; discharge: *Boiling water emits steam. Fireflies emit light but not heat.* **2.** to utter: *The patient emitted a cry of pain.*

Em·man·u·el (i man′u əl) another spelling of **Immanuel.**

e·mol·lient (i mol′yənt) *adj.* soothing and softening, especially to the skin. —*n.* a substance that softens and soothes: *Lanolin is an emollient for the skin.*

e·mote (i mōt′) *v.i.,* **e·mot·ed, e·mot·ing.** to show emotion, especially in an exaggerated or affected way.

e·mo·tion (i mō′shən) *n.* **1.** strong feeling: *to read a poem with emotion.* **2.** a particular feeling, as love, hate, happiness, or sorrow: *The actors portrayed a wide range of emotions.*

e·mo·tion·al (i mō′shə nəl) *adj.* **1.** of, relating to, or showing emotion: *an emotional quarrel, an emotional outburst.* **2.** easily influenced by emotion: *an emotional person.* **3.** appealing to or arousing emotion: *The lawyer made an emotional plea to the jury.* —**e·mo′tion·al·ly,** *adv.*

---

at; āpe; fär; câre; end; mē; it; īce; pîerce; hot; ōld;
sông, fôrk; oil; out; up; ūse; rüle; pull; tûrn; chin;
sing; shop; thin; <u>th</u>is; hw in white; zh in treasure.
The symbol ə stands for the unstressed vowel sound
heard in about, taken, pencil, lemon, and circus.

e·mo·tion·al·ism (i mō′shə nə liz′əm) *n.* **1.** a tendency to show or be affected by emotion too easily. **2.** an appeal to the emotions: *The speech was full of emotionalism.*

e·mo·tive (i mō′tiv) *adj.* **1.** showing, causing, or appealing to emotion. **2.** of or relating to emotion.

em·pa·na·da (em′pə nä′də) *n.* a Mexican turnover with a savory or sweet filling, as of ground meat, vegetables, or fruit. [From the Spanish word *empanada* meaning ''breaded,'' used as the name of this food, from the word *empanar* ''to bread,'' going back to the Latin words *en-* ''in, into'' and *panis* ''bread.'']

em·pan·el (em pan′əl) another word for **impanel.**

em·pa·thize (em′pə thīz′) *v.i.,* **em·pa·thized, em·pa·thiz·ing.** to experience empathy: *The newspaper reporter was able to empathize with the farm workers.*

em·pa·thy (em′pə thē) *n.* a sharing of another's feelings or state of mind without actually going through the same experiences.

em·per·or (em′pər ər) *n.* the male ruler of an empire.

em·pha·sis (em′fə sis) *n., pl.* **em·pha·ses** (em′fə sēz′). **1.** special importance given to something: *Too little emphasis was placed on the safety regulations.* **2.** something that is given special importance: *Faith was the emphasis of the sermon.* **3.** vocal stress or force given to a particular syllable, word, or phrase.

em·pha·size (em′fə sīz′) *v.t.,* **em·pha·sized, em·pha·siz·ing.** to give emphasis to; stress: *a speech emphasizing the need for conservation of wildlife.*

em·phat·ic (em fat′ik) *adj.* **1.** spoken or done with emphasis: *The senator issued an emphatic denial of the newspaper story.* **2.** forceful; insistent: *to remain emphatic on a point.* **3.** striking; definite: *The mayor suffered an emphatic defeat in the election.* **—em·phat′i·cal·ly,** *adv.*

em·phy·se·ma (em′fə sē′mə) *n.* a disease that hinders breathing, characterized by enlargement of and damage to the air sacs in the lungs.

em·pire (em′pīr) *n.* **1.** a group of countries or territories ruled or controlled by the government of one country. **2.** a country or group of countries or territories ruled by an emperor or empress. **3.** absolute power or authority. **4.** a large territory or business controlled by one person or a group of people: *The millionaire had built up a vast real estate empire.*

em·pir·ic (em pir′ik) *n.* a person whose knowledge is based entirely on practical experience, experiments, or what can actually be seen. *—adj.* another word for **empirical.**

em·pir·i·cal (em pir′i kəl) *adj.* based on practical experience, experiments, or what can actually be seen: *The results of the experiments were empirical proof of the scientist's theories.* **—em·pir′i·cal·ly,** *adv.*

em·pir·i·cism (em pir′ə siz′əm) *n.* **1.** a method or practice based on practical experience, experiments, or what can actually be seen. **2.** a theory in philosophy that all knowledge is based on experience gained through the senses.

em·pir·i·cist (em pir′ə sist) *n.* a person who practices or supports empiricism.

em·place·ment (em plās′mənt) *n.* a place or position prepared for heavy guns.

em·ploy (em ploi′) *v.t.* **1.** to give work to (someone) for pay; hire: *The store employed extra workers during the holiday season.* **2.** to make use of: *The gardener employed a shovel, a hoe, and other tools.* **3.** to take up or fill; occupy: *My hobbies employ much of my time.* *—n.* the state or condition of being employed: *The agent was in the employ of a foreign country.* **—em·ploy′a·ble,** *adj.*

em·ploy·ee (em ploi′ē, em′ploi ē′) *also,* **em·ploy·e.** *n.* a person who works for a person or business for pay.

em·ploy·er (em ploi′ər) *n.* a person or business that employs a person or a group of people for pay.

em·ploy·ment (em ploi′mənt) *n.* **1.** the act of employ-

ing or the state of being employed. **2.** work that a person does; job: *Most of the students found employment this summer.*

em·po·ri·um (em pôr′ē əm) *n., pl.* **em·po·ri·ums** or **em·po·ri·a** (em pôr′ē ə). **1.** a large store selling many different kinds of things. **2.** a principal center of trade or commerce.

em·pow·er (em pou′ər) *v.t.* **1.** to give power or authority to; authorize: *The ambassador was empowered to sign the treaty.* **2.** to make possible; enable; permit: *Scientific advances have empowered us to explore space.*

em·press (em′pris) *n., pl.* **em·press·es.** **1.** the wife or widow of an emperor. **2.** a woman who rules an empire.

emp·ty (emp′tē) *adj.,* **emp·ti·er, emp·ti·est.** **1.** having nothing or no one in it; lacking what is usually inside: *an empty glass, an empty room.* **2.** lacking force or meaning; hollow: *an empty promise, an empty threat.* *—v.,* **emp·tied, emp·ty·ing.** *—v.t.* **1.** to take out the contents of; make empty: *to empty a wastebasket.* **2.** to take out (the contents of something): *Empty the water out of the bathtub.* *—v.i.* **1.** to become empty: *The theater emptied when the movie ended.* **2.** to pour or flow out; discharge: *That river empties into the sea.* *—n., pl.* **emp·ties.** *Informal.* something that is empty, such as a container or bottle. **—emp′ti·ly,** *adv.* **—emp′ti·ness,** *n.*

emp·ty–hand·ed (emp′tē han′did) *adj.* **1.** with nothing in the hands. **2.** with nothing gotten or gained: *They came away from the negotiations empty-handed.*

emp·ty–head·ed (emp′tē hed′id) *n.* lacking good sense or intelligence; foolish or stupid.

empty set *Mathematics.* a set that has no members; null set. The set of even numbers between 8 and 10 is an empty set.

em·pyr·e·al (em pir′ē əl, em′pə rē′əl) *adj.* of or relating to the empyrean; celestial.

em·py·re·an (em′pə rē′ən) *n.* **1.** the highest heaven in ancient and medieval astronomy. **2.** the visible heavens; sky. *—adj.* another word for **empyreal.**

e·mu (ē′mū) *n.* a large bird of Australia, related to the ostrich. The emu cannot fly, but it can run as fast as 40 miles per hour.

em·u·late (em′yə lāt′) *v.t.,* **em·u·lat·ed, em·u·lat·ing.** to try to equal or go beyond, especially by imitating: *to emulate an older brother or sister.*

em·u·la·tion (em′yə lā′shən) *n.* the effort or desire to equal or go beyond someone.

em·u·lous (em′yə ləs) *adj.* eager to equal or go beyond; competitive. **—em′u·lous·ly,** *adv.* **—em′u·lous·ness,** *n.*

emu

e·mul·si·fy (i mul′sə fī′) *v.t.,* **e·mul·si·fied, e·mul·si·fy·ing.** to make into an emulsion. **—e·mul′si·fi·ca′tion,** *n.* **—e·mul′si·fi′er,** *n.*

e·mul·sion (i mul′shən) *n.* **1.** a mixture made up of very small droplets of one liquid suspended, rather than dissolved, in another liquid. **2.** a coating on photographic film, plates, or paper that is sensitive to light.

en– *prefix* **1.** (used to form verbs from nouns) **a.** to put in, into, or on: *encase, enthrone.* **b.** to cover or surround with: *encircle, enshroud.* **2.** (used to form verbs from adjectives and nouns) to cause to be or be like; make: *enable, enslave.*

–en¹ *suffix* **1.** (used to form verbs from adjectives) to cause to be or become: *sharpen, madden, harden.* **2.** (used to form verbs from nouns) to cause or come to have: *heighten, strengthen, lengthen.* [From the Old English verb suffix *-nian.*]

-en² *suffix* (used to form adjectives from nouns) made of or resembling: *silken, wooden, golden.* [From the Old English suffix *-en* meaning "made of."]

-en³ *suffix* used in the past participles of certain irregular verbs: *risen, written.* [From the Old English suffix *-en* used to form past participles of verbs.]

-en⁴ *suffix* used in the plural of some nouns: *children, brethren, oxen.* [From the Old English suffix *-an* used to form plurals of certain nouns.]

en·a·ble (e nā′bəl, i nā′bəl) *v.t.*, **en·a·bled, en·a·bling.** to give enough power, ability, or opportunity to; make able: *A scholarship enabled the talented athlete to go to college.*

en·act (e nakt′, i nakt′) *v.t.* **1.** to make into law: *Congress enacted a bill on education this year.* **2.** to act out on stage; perform: *Two talented students enacted the parts of the queen and king in this year's class play.*

en·act·ment (e nakt′mənt, i nakt′mənt) *n.* **1.** a making into law: *the enactment of a bill in Congress.* **2.** something that is enacted.

e·nam·el (i nam′əl) *n.* **1.** a hard, glossy substance used to decorate or protect a surface, such as metal or pottery, to which it is fused. **2.** paint that dries to form a hard, glossy coating. **3.** the hard, glossy substance that is the outer covering of a tooth. —*v.t.*, **e·nam·eled, e·nam·el·ing;** *also,* British, **e·nam·elled, e·nam·el·ling.** to cover with enamel or any hard, glossy coating.

e·nam·el·ware (i nam′əl wâr′) *n.* objects coated with enamel, such as kitchenware or dinnerware.

en·am·ored (i nam′ərd) *adj.* taken by love; charmed; captivated: *The enamored couple couldn't take their eyes off each other.*

·**to be enamored of.** to be in love with: *The young fan was foolishly enamored of the movie star.*

en·camp (en kamp′) *v.i.* to settle in a camp; make a camp: *The scouts encamped in the valley.* —*v.t.* to place in a camp: *to encamp the soldiers near the river.*

en·camp·ment (en kamp′mənt) *n.* **1.** a place occupied by a camp; camp. **2.** the people in a camp. **3.** the act of encamping or the state of being encamped.

en·cap·su·late (en kap′sə lāt′) *v.t.* **en·cap·su·lat·ed, en·cap·su·lat·ing.** **1.** to put in or as if in a capsule. **2.** to put into a brief form; condense; summarize: *The book's author encapsulates events of the last century in the second chapter.*

en·case (en kās′) *v.t.*, **en·cased, en·cas·ing.** to enclose in or as if in a case: *jewels encased in a glass box, a broken leg encased in a plaster cast.* Also, **incase.**

-ence *suffix* (used in nouns) the action, quality, state, or condition of being: *independence, coherence, reference.*

en·ceph·a·li·tis (en sef′ə lī′tis) *n.* inflammation of the brain.

en·chain (en chān′) *v.t.* to bind with or as if with chains.

en·chant (en chant′) *v.t.* **1.** to cast a spell on; bewitch: *The witch had enchanted the entire castle.* **2.** to charm or delight greatly: *Everyone was enchanted by the child's performance in the play.* —**en·chant′er,** *n.*

en·chant·ing (en chan′ting) *adj.* very charming or delightful: *The children's ballet was enchanting.* —**en·chant′ing·ly,** *adv.*

en·chant·ment (en chant′mənt) *n.* **1.** the act of enchanting or the state of being enchanted. **2.** something that enchants.

en·chan·tress (en chan′tris) *n., pl.* **en·chan·tress·es.** **1.** a woman who casts spells; witch; sorceress. **2.** any charming or fascinating woman.

en·chase (en chās′) *v.t.*, **en·chased, en·chas·ing.** **1.** to decorate (a surface), as with engraved work. **2.** to engrave or carve (a design) on a surface: *The jeweler enchased the family crest on the silver box.* **3.** to place in a setting: *to enchase a jewel.*

en·chi·la·da (en′chə lä′də) *n.* a tortilla filled with meat or cheese, served with a spicy tomato or chili sauce.

[From the Spanish word *enchilada*, from the word *enchilar* meaning "to season with chili," from the words *en-* (from the Latin prefix *in-*) "in, into" + *chile* "red pepper," from the Nahuatl word *chilli* "red pepper."]

en·cir·cle (en sûr′kəl) *v.t.*, **en·cir·cled, en·cir·cling.** **1.** to form a circle around; surround: *The campers encircled the bonfire.* **2.** to move in a circle around: *Many satellites encircle the earth today.* —**en·cir′cle·ment,** *n.*

en·clave (en′klāv) *n.* **1.** a territory surrounded by the territory of another country: *Vatican City is an enclave.* **2.** a district inhabited by a minority group: *a Chinese enclave in an American city.*

en·close (en klōz′) *v.t.*, **en·closed, en·clos·ing.** **1.** to close in on all sides; surround: *The field was enclosed by trees.* **2.** to include with a letter or parcel: *to enclose a picture with a letter.* **3.** to contain: *The letter enclosed a check.* Also, **inclose.**

en·clo·sure (en klō′zhər) *also,* **in·clo·sure.** *n.* **1.** the act of enclosing or the state of being enclosed. **2.** something that is enclosed. **3.** something that encloses, such as a fence or wall.

en·code (en kōd′) *v.t.*, **en·cod·ed, en·cod·ing.** to put into code: *to encode a message before sending it.* —**en·cod′er,** *n.*

en·co·mi·um (en kō′mē əm) *n., pl.* **en·co·mi·ums** or **en·co·mi·a** (en kō′mē ə). high praise expressed in a formal way; eulogy.

en·com·pass (en kum′pəs, en kom′pəs) *v.t.* **1.** to form a circle around; encircle; surround: *A moat encompassed the castle.* **2.** to contain or include: *The autobiography encompasses every aspect of the writer's life.*

en·core (äng′kôr, än′kôr) *interj.* again. ▲ used as a call to a performer or performers to perform again. —*n.* **1.** a call made by an audience to a performer or performers to perform again. **2.** something that is performed in response to such a call: *The pianist played three encores.* —*v.t.*, **en·cored, en·cor·ing.** to call for an encore from.

en·coun·ter (en koun′tər) *v.t.* **1.** to meet unexpectedly; come upon: *to encounter an old friend in a strange city.* **2.** to meet in conflict; confront in battle: *The soldiers encountered the enemy and defeated them.* **3.** to be faced with; experience: *to encounter little resistance to a plan.* —*n.* **1.** an unexpected or casual meeting: *The story was about an encounter with creatures from outer space.* **2.** a meeting of enemies in conflict; skirmish: *Repeated encounters with the enemy had tired the troops.*

en·cour·age (en kûr′ij, en kur′ij) *v.t.*, **en·cour·aged, en·cour·ag·ing.** **1.** to inspire with courage, hope, or confidence; hearten: *The good weather encouraged us to continue our hike.* **2.** to give support to; help; promote: *The bank lowered its interest rate on loans to encourage borrowing.*

en·cour·age·ment (en kûr′ij mənt, en kur′ij mənt) *n.* **1.** the act of encouraging or the state of being encouraged. **2.** something that encourages: *The cheers were an encouragement to the runner.*

en·cour·ag·ing (en kûr′i jing, en kur′i jing) *adj.* giving courage, hope, or confidence: *encouraging news, an encouraging smile.* —**en·cour′ag·ing·ly,** *adv.*

en·croach (en krōch′) *v.i.* **1.** to intrude on the property or rights of another; trespass: *They felt that their neighbors encroached on their privacy.* **2.** to go beyond usual or natural limits: *Every spring the river encroached farther on the land.* —**en·croach′ment,** *n.*

at; āpe; fär; câre; end; mē; it; īce; pîerce; hot; ōld; sông, fôrk; oil; out; up; ūse; rüle; pùll; tûrn; chin; sing; shop; thin; <u>th</u>is; hw in white; zh in treasure. The symbol ə stands for the unstressed vowel sound heard in about, taken, pencil, lemon, and circus.

en·crust (en krust′) *v.t.* **1.** to cover with a crust or hard coating: *Dried mud encrusted our shoes.* **2.** to cover or decorate, as with jewels: *The sword handle was encrusted with diamonds.* Also, **incrust.**

en·crus·ta·tion (en′krus tā′shən) *n.* **1.** the act of encrusting or the state of being encrusted. **2.** something that encrusts: *An encrustation of gold and jewels covered the jewelry box.* Also, **incrustation.**

encrust
a crown **encrusted** with jewels

en·cryp·tion (en-krip′shən) *n.* the act of putting a message or signal into a form of secret writing or code.

en·cum·ber (en kum′bər) *v.t.* **1.** to hinder the motion or action of, as with a burden: *Bulky packages encumbered the holiday travelers.* **2.** to weigh down or burden, as with cares or duties: *Financial worries encumbered the elderly couple.* **3.** to block or obstruct, as with obstacles: *Old furniture encumbered the hallway.*

en·cum·brance (en kum′brəns) *n.* something that hinders; burden. Also, **incumbrance.**

–ency *suffix* (used in nouns) the act, fact, quality, or state of being: *dependency, consistency.*

en·cyc·li·cal (en sik′li kəl) *n.* a letter written by a pope to his bishops about important matters relating to the Church.

en·cy·clo·pe·di·a (en sī′klə pē′dē ə) *also,* **en·cy·clo·pae·di·a.** *n.* a reference work in one or more volumes, containing information on all branches of knowledge or on a special subject, usually in articles arranged alphabetically.

en·cy·clo·pe·dic (en sī′klə pē′dik) *also,* **en·cy·clo·pae·dic.** *adj.* covering a broad range of subjects or information: *to have an encyclopedic knowledge of history.*

end (end) *n.* **1.** the point or part at which something that has length starts or stops: *They each held an end of the rope.* **2.** the part that concludes; final part: *The end of the book was better than the beginning.* **3.** the point at which something is over or no longer exists: *The end of the war is in sight.* **4.** the outermost limit; boundary: *They lived at the end of town.* **5.** the result of an action; purpose; goal: *The end does not always justify the means.* **6.** death or destruction. **7.** *also,* **ends.** a part left over; remnant; fragment: *The store has put its carpet ends on sale.* **8.** *Football.* either of the two players or positions on the left or right end of the line. —*v.t.* **1.** to bring to an end; conclude; finish: *to end a meeting.* **2.** to be or form the end of: *The clown act ended each circus performance.* —*v.i.* **1.** to come to an end: *The play ended at ten o'clock.* **2.** to reach a final state or condition: *to end as the winner of the race.*

•**at loose ends.** in an unsettled or confused state.

•**on end. a.** in an upright position. **b.** without stopping; in succession: *to work for days on end.*

•**to end up.** to be in a final position or state; become: *You will end up wealthy someday.*

•**to make ends meet.** to manage to spend no more than one earns.

en·dan·ger (en dān′jər) *v.t.* to put in danger; imperil:
The fire endangered several of the adjacent buildings.

en·dan·gered (en dān′jərd) *adj.* (of a plant or animal species) in danger of becoming extinct: *The whooping crane is an endangered species.*

en·dear (en dîr′) *v.t.* to make dear or beloved: *The puppy endeared itself to the children.* —**en·dear′ing·ly,** *adv.*

en·dear·ment (en dîr′mənt) *n.* **1.** the act of endearing or the state of being endeared. **2.** an action or word that expresses love or affection: *a valentine full of endearments.*

en·deav·or (en dev′ər) *also, British,* **en·deav·our.** *v.i.* to make an effort; strive; try: *The neighbors endeavored to get the cat out of the tree.* —*n.* a serious attempt to do or accomplish something; effort.

en·dem·ic (en dem′ik) *adj.* occurring in or restricted to a particular place or group of people: *Malaria is endemic to tropical and subtropical regions.* —*n.* an endemic disease.

end·ing (en′ding) *n.* a final part; conclusion: *The story has a sad ending.*

en·dive (en′dīv) *n.* **1.** creamy white or curly green leaves of a plant related to chicory, usually eaten raw in salads. **2.** the plant bearing these leaves.

end·less (end′lis) *adj.* **1.** having no limit or end; boundless: *endless space.* **2.** never stopping; constant; incessant: *endless repetition, endless interruptions.* **3.** having the ends joined so as to form a circle or loop; continuous: *an endless chain.* —**end′less·ly,** *adv.* —**end′less·ness,** *n.*

end·most (end′mōst′) *adj.* at or nearest to the end; farthest: *We sat in the endmost seats in the row.*

endo– *prefix* inside: *endoderm, endoskeleton.*

en·do·car·di·um (en′dō kär′dē əm) *n., pl.* **en·do·car·di·a** (en′dō kär′dē ə). a thin membrane lining the heart.

en·do·crine (en′də krin, en′də krīn′) *adj.* **1.** producing secretions that pass directly into the bloodstream or lymph. **2.** of or relating to an endocrine gland or its secretion. —*n.* **1.** see **endocrine gland.** **2.** a secretion of an endocrine gland; hormone.

endive
leaves and root

endocrine gland, any of various glands without ducts, such as the thyroid and pituitary, that secrete hormones directly into the bloodstream or lymph; ductless glands.

endocrine system, the body system composed of all the endocrine glands.

en·do·cri·nol·o·gy (en′də kri nol′ə jē, en′də krī nol′ə-jē) *n.* a branch of medicine dealing with the endocrine glands and their secretions.

en·do·derm (en′də dûrm′) *n.* the innermost of the three cell layers of an embryo in an early stage of its development. The endoderm develops into the lining of the stomach, intestines, and lungs, and into certain internal organs, such as the liver and pancreas.

en·do·plasm (en′də plaz′əm) *n.* the inner portion of the cytoplasm of a cell, containing the nucleus.

en·dor·phin (en dôr′fin) *n.* any of a group of chemicals in the brain and pituitary gland that are believed to help the body relieve pain. [Formed from the Greek word *end(on)* meaning ''within'' and the word *(m)orphin(e).*]

en·dorse (en dôrs′) *v.t.,* **en·dorsed, en·dors·ing. 1.** to sign one's name on the back of (a check, note, or similar document): *You must endorse that check before cashing it.* **2.** to give support to; approve: *The senator enthusiastically endorsed the president's statement.* Also, **indorse.** —**en·dors′er,** *n.*

en·dorse·ment (en dôrs′mənt) *also,* **in·dorse·ment.** *n.* **1.** the act of endorsing. **2.** writing, as a signature or comments, that is placed on the back of a check, note, or similar document. **3.** approval or support; sanction.

en·do·scope (en′də skōp′) *n.* any of several medical instruments used to look inside hollow organs and tubes of the body.

en·do·skel·e·ton (en′dō skel′i tən) *n.* the inner skeleton that supports the body of certain animals. Fish, dogs, humans, and other animals with backbones all have endoskeletons.

en·do·sperm (en′də spûrm′) *n.* food material in many plant seeds that surrounds and gives nourishment to the embryo.

en·dow (en dou′) *v.t.* **1.** to give money or property to as a source of income: *Several wealthy families endowed the new library.* **2.** to provide with an ability, talent, or quality: *a dancer endowed with natural grace.*

en·dow·ment (en dou′mənt) *n.* **1.** money or property given to provide a source of income, as for a church or college: *That college has a large endowment.* **2.** talent, ability, or quality: *to have a keen mind, a sharp wit, and other natural endowments.* **3.** the act of endowing.

end table, a small table placed at the end of a sofa or beside a chair.

en·dur·a·ble (en dûr′ə bəl, en dyûr′ə bəl) *adj.* that can be endured; bearable: *The pain was constant, but endurable.* **—en·dur′a·bly,** *adv.*

en·dur·ance (en dûr′əns, en dyûr′əns) *n.* **1.** the power of bearing up under hardships or difficulties, such as pain, stress, or fatigue: *A long-distance runner must have a great amount of endurance.* **2.** the power of lasting; continued existence: *the endurance of a custom through the ages.*

en·dure (en dûr′, en dyûr′) *v.,* **en·dured, en·dur·ing.** —*v.t.* **1.** to undergo without yielding; stand; bear: *The hikers endured the rain and wind without complaint.* **2.** to put up with; tolerate: *I won't endure such rudeness.* —*v.i.* **1.** to continue to be; last: *Though they were apart, their friendship endured.* **2.** to suffer without yielding; hold out: *The family endured throughout all its financial troubles.*

en·dur·ing (en dûr′ing, en dyûr′ing) *adj.* lasting; permanent: *an enduring memory.*

end·ways (end′wāz′) *adv.* **1.** with the end forward. **2.** on end; upright. **3.** lengthwise. **4.** end to end. Also, **endwise** (end′wīz′).

end zone, the area at either end of a football field between the goal line and the final boundary of the field. It is ten yards deep.

en·e·ma (en′ə mə) *n.* **1.** the forcing of liquid through the anus into the rectum, usually to help cause a bowel movement. **2.** the liquid used for this.

en·e·my (en′ə mē) *n., pl.* **en·e·mies. 1.** a person who has hatred for, or wishes to cause harm to, another: *The corrupt politician had many enemies.* **2.** a hostile nation or military force: *The enemy attacked at dawn.* **3.** a person belonging to such a nation or force. **4.** something dangerous or harmful: *Disease is an enemy of living things.* —*adj.* of or relating to a hostile nation or military force: *enemy troops, an enemy camp.*

en·er·get·ic (en′ər jet′ik) *adj.* having, using, or showing energy; vigorous; forceful: *an energetic worker, an energetic mind.* **—en′er·get′i·cal·ly,** *adv.*

en·er·gize (en′ər jīz′) *v.t.,* **en·er·gized, en·er·giz·ing.** to give energy or power to. **—en′er·giz′er,** *n.*

en·er·gy (en′ər jē) *n., pl.* **en·er·gies. 1.** the ability or tendency to act with force: *Children often have more energy than their parents.* **2.** also, **energies.** power used in action or work: *It took a lot of energy to move the furniture. We put all our energies into solving the problem.* **3.** *Physics.* the capacity for doing work. Energy takes various different forms, such as radiant energy, electrical energy, chemical energy, and mechanical energy. **4.** a source or supply of power for making electricity or doing mechanical work: *wind energy.*

Word Family

A variety of English words are derived from *ergon*, the Greek word meaning "work" or "effort." Work is done with **energy** by **energetic** people and, when done, work can be measured in **ergs.** When two things **energize** each other and in the process of working together produce what neither could create alone, there is **synergism.** **Argon,** an inert chemical element, means "not-work." The science of **metallurgy** works with metals, and the word **surgery** comes from the Greek word meaning "handwork." An **allergy** indicates that the body is working in a "different kind of way," as when it responds adversely to medicine and causes an **allergic** reaction. Some efforts are religious rather than scientific, as with **liturgy,** which is "the work of the people" during a religious service.

en·er·vate (en′ər vāt′) *v.t.,* **en·er·vat·ed, en·er·vat·ing.** to lessen the strength or vitality of; weaken: *Frequent wars enervated the country.* **—en′er·va′tion,** *n.*

en·fee·ble (en fē′bəl) *v.t.,* **en·fee·bled, en·fee·bling.** to make feeble; weaken: *The long illness enfeebled the elderly patient.* **—en·fee′ble·ment,** *n.*

en·fold (en fōld′) *v.t.* **1.** to wrap in folds; envelop: *to enfold fragile glassware in tissue paper.* **2.** to embrace; clasp: *I enfolded the puppy in my arms.* Also, **infold.**

en·force (en fôrs′) *v.t.,* **en·forced, en·forc·ing. 1.** to make certain that (a law or rule) is observed; force obedience to: *The police in that town enforce the laws strictly.* **2.** to obtain by force: *Monitors in the halls enforce silence.* **3.** to give force to; strengthen: *The lawyers enforced their case with new evidence.* **—en·force′a·ble,** *adj.*

en·force·ment (en fôrs′mənt) *n.* the act or process of enforcing: *The club president believed in strict enforcement of the rules.*

en·fran·chise (en fran′chīz) *v.t.,* **en·fran·chised, en·fran·chis·ing. 1.** to give the right to vote to: *Women were not enfranchised in the United States until the twentieth century.* **2.** to set free; liberate: *to enfranchise slaves.* **—en·fran′chise·ment,** *n.*

eng. 1. engine. **2.** engineer; engineering.

Eng. 1. England. **2.** English.

en·gage (en gāj′) *v.,* **en·gaged, en·gag·ing.** —*v.t.* **1.** to hire (a person) or secure (services): *The company engaged two new employees. The builder engaged the professional skills of an electrician.* **2.** to obtain the use of; reserve: *to engage a hotel room.* **3.** to attract and hold (one's attention or interest); involve: *The story engaged the children's interest.* **4.** to keep busy; occupy: *Planning the dance engaged much of our time.* **5.** to bind or pledge (oneself): *The scientists engaged themselves to find a cure for the disease.* **6.** to pledge to marry; betroth: *The couple were engaged in January and married in June.* **7.** to meet in combat; encounter and fight: *The soldiers engaged the enemy forces at dawn.* **8.** *Mechanics.* to interlock with; mesh. —*v.i.* **1.** to occupy or involve oneself; take part: *to engage in the serious study of mathematics.* **2.** to pledge oneself; promise: *to engage to pay the costs of a project.* **3.** to enter into combat. **4.** *Mechanics.* to interlock; mesh: *The gears engaged.*

at; āpe; fär; câre; end; mē; it; īce; pîerce; hot; ōld; sông, fôrk; oil; out; up; ūse; rüle; pùll; tûrn; chin; sing; shop; thin; *this;* hw in white; zh in treasure. The symbol ə stands for the unstressed vowel sound heard in about, taken, pencil, lemon, and circus.

E

en·gage·ment (en gāj′mənt) *n.* **1.** the act of engaging or the state of being engaged. **2.** a promise to marry; betrothal. **3.** a meeting or a promise to meet with someone at a certain time; appointment: *to have an engagement for dinner.* **4.** employment or period of employment: *The singer signed a contract for a two-week engagement at the nightclub.* **5.** a meeting of enemy forces; battle. **6.** a pledge or agreement: *The bankrupt company failed to fulfill all its engagements.*

en·gag·ing (en gā′jing) *adj.* pleasingly attractive; winning; charming: *an engaging smile.* —**en·gag′ing·ly,** *adv.*

en·gen·der (en jen′dər) *v.t.* to bring into being; cause; produce: *A hostile attitude engenders much ill will.*

en·gine (en′jin) *n.* **1.** a machine that converts energy into mechanical work. **2.** a railroad locomotive. **3.** any mechanical device: *Cannons are engines of war.*

en·gi·neer (en′jə nîr′) *n.* **1.** a person who is skilled in one of the branches of engineering: *an electrical engineer, an aeronautical engineer.* **2.** a person who drives or manages an engine, especially a railroad locomotive. **3.** any skillful manager; shrewd leader: *The general was the chief engineer of the victory.* —*v.t.* **1.** to plan, construct, or manage as an engineer: *to engineer the building of a bridge.* **2.** to manage or lead skillfully or shrewdly: *The politician engineered a successful campaign.*

en·gi·neer·ing (en′jə nîr′ing) *n.* the science or profession of putting matter and energy to practical use.

Eng·lish (ing′glish) *n.* **1.** a language spoken in the United Kingdom, the United States, Canada, Australia, New Zealand, and in various other parts of the world. **2. the English.** the people of England. **3.** *also,* **english.** a spin given to a ball by striking it off-center or by throwing or bowling it with a twist of the wrist. —*adj.* **1.** of or relating to England or its people. **2.** of, relating to, or expressed in the English language. See **Old English** for further information.

English horn, a woodwind instrument similar to the oboe, but having a lower pitch.

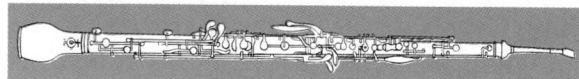

English horn

Eng·lish·man (ing′glish mən) *n., pl.* **Eng·lish·men** (ing′glish mən). a person who was born in or is a citizen of England.

English muffin, a round, flat, unsweetened muffin, usually eaten toasted.

English sparrow, another term for **house sparrow.**

English system, the system of measurement in which the foot is the fundamental unit of length, the pound is the fundamental unit of weight or mass, and the second is the fundamental unit of time. The system has been officially replaced in Great Britain by the metric system, but it is still used in the United States.

Eng·lish·wom·an (ing′glish wùm′ən) *n., pl.* **Eng·lish·wom·en** (ing′glish wim′ən). a woman who was born in or is a citizen of England.

en·gorge (en gôrj′) *v.t.* **en·gorged, en·gorg·ing. 1.** to fill with blood; congest. **2.** to eat greedily; gorge. —**en·gorge′ment,** *n.*

en·graft (en graft′) *v.t.* **1.** to graft (a shoot from one tree or plant) into or onto another. **2.** to set firmly; implant. Also, **ingraft.**

en·grave (en grāv′) *v.t.,* **en·graved, en·grav·ing. 1.** to cut or carve letters, figures, or the like into: *to engrave a tombstone.* **2.** to cut or carve (letters, figures, or the like) into an object or surface: *to engrave initials on a ring.*

3. to cut (letters, figures, or the like) into a metal plate or other material for printing. **4.** to print (something) from a metal plate or other material cut in this way: *to engrave an invitation.* **5.** to impress deeply; fix permanently: *The coach's words were engraved in my mind.* —**en·grav′er,** *n.*

en·grav·ing (en grā′ving) *n.* **1.** the art or process of creating a design, inscription, or picture by cutting letters or lines into a metal plate, stone, wood, or other material. **2.** the design, inscription, or picture created in this way. **3.** an engraved printing plate. **4.** a printed impression made from such a plate.

en·gross (en grōs′) *v.t.* **1.** to occupy all the attention of; absorb: *to be engrossed in a good book, to be completely engrossed by an actor's performance.* **2.** to write or copy out (a document or the like) in large letters or in a formal manner.

en·gulf (en gulf′) *v.t.* to swallow up or completely surround; overwhelm: *The avalanche engulfed the small cabin. Civil war engulfed the country.*

en·hance (en hans′) *v.t.,* **en·hanced, en·hanc·ing.** to make greater, as in quality or value; heighten: *The right seasonings will enhance the flavor of this stew.* —**en·hance′ment,** *n.*

e·nig·ma (i nig′mə) *n.* a person or thing that is puzzling or hard to understand; riddle; mystery: *The origin of the universe remains an enigma. That person is a total enigma to me.*

en·ig·mat·ic (en′ig mat′ik) *adj.* of or like an enigma; mysterious; puzzling: *an enigmatic smile.* Also, **en·ig·mat·i·cal** (en′ig mat′i kəl).

en·join (en join′) *v.t.* **1.** to order, direct, or urge: *The doctor enjoined me to take better care of my health.* **2.** to order (a person or group) to do or to keep from doing some act, as by a court order: *The court enjoined the union from striking for a period of thirty days.*

en·joy (en joi′) *v.t.* **1.** to experience joy, pleasure, or satisfaction in: *The class enjoyed the party.* **2.** to have the use or benefit of: *to enjoy good health.*

·to enjoy oneself. to have a good time.

en·joy·a·ble (en joi′ə bəl) *adj.* giving or capable of giving enjoyment: *The family spent a very enjoyable day in the country.* —**en·joy′a·ble·ness,** *n.* —**en·joy′a·bly,** *adv.*

en·joy·ment (en joi′mənt) *n.* **1.** the act of enjoying: *the enjoyment of prosperity.* **2.** something that gives joy, pleasure, or satisfaction: *My work is my greatest enjoyment.* **3.** joy, pleasure, or satisfaction.

en·kin·dle (en kin′dəl) *v.t.,* **en·kin·dled, en·kin·dling.** another word for **kindle.**

en·lace (en lās′) *v.t.,* **en·laced, en·lac·ing. 1.** to bind with or as if with laces; encircle; enfold. **2.** to intertwine; entangle.

en·large (en lärj′) *v.,* **en·larged, en·larg·ing.** —*v.t.* to increase the size or amount of; make larger: *to enlarge a house, to enlarge a photograph.* —*v.i.* to become larger: *Bus service increased as the town enlarged.*

·to enlarge on or **to enlarge upon.** to write or speak about in more detail: *The speaker was asked to enlarge upon an earlier comment.*

en·large·ment (en lärj′mənt) *n.* **1.** the act of enlarging or the state of being enlarged. **2.** a thing that enlarges by being added; addition. **3.** an enlarged form of something else, such as a photograph that is larger than the original.

en·larg·er (en lär′jər) *n.* a device for making photographic prints larger than the original negatives.

en·light·en (en lī′tən) *v.t.* to give knowledge or wisdom to; free from prejudice, ignorance, or superstition.

en·light·en·ment (en lī′tən mənt) *n.* **1.** the act of enlightening or the state of being enlightened. **2. Enlightenment.** an eighteenth-century European philosophical movement based on the use of reason and on skepticism toward traditional beliefs. Enlightenment thinkers stressed the use of experiments in science.

en·list (en list′) *v.i.* **1.** to join the armed forces voluntarily: *My best friend enlisted in the army after graduation.* **2.** to join in some cause: *The entire class enlisted in the charity drive.* —*v.t.* **1.** to enroll (someone) for military service; induct. **2.** to get for some project or cause: *I enlisted the help of my friends when I moved to my new apartment.*

en·list·ed (en lis′tid) *adj.* of or relating to the part of a military or naval force below commissioned or warrant officers.

en·list·ment (en list′mənt) *n.* **1.** the act of enlisting or the state of being enlisted. **2.** a period of time for which a person enlists.

en·liv·en (en lī′vən) *v.t.* to make lively or cheerful; animate: *Many witty comments enlivened the discussion.*

en masse (än mas′, en mas′) in a group; all together: *The club's officers resigned en masse.* [From the French phrase *en masse,* going back to the Latin words *in* meaning "in" and *massa* meaning "a lump, mass."]

en·mesh (en mesh′) *v.t.* to catch or entangle, as in a net: *A struggle for power enmeshed the leaders of the opposing parties.*

en·mi·ty (en′mi tē) *n., pl.* **en·mi·ties.** a bitter feeling, as between enemies; ill will; hatred: *The enmity between the two countries is giving way to harmony.*

en·no·ble (en nō′bəl) *v.t.,* **en·no·bled, en·no·bling.** **1.** to raise in nature, quality, or reputation: *The soldiers' brave deeds ennobled them in the eyes of their comrades.* **2.** to give a title of nobility to: *The monarch ennobled the famous warrior.* —**en·no′ble·ment,** *n.*

en·nui (än wē′) *n.* a feeling of listlessness and unhappiness resulting from a lack of interesting things to think about or do; boredom. [From the French word *ennui,* going back to the Latin phrase *in odio* meaning "in hatred."]

e·nor·mi·ty (i nôr′mi tē) *n., pl.* **e·nor·mi·ties.** **1.** extreme wickedness: *The enormity of the crime shocked the townspeople.* **2.** something extremely wicked or outrageous; atrocity.

e·nor·mous (i nôr′məs) *adj.* much greater than the usual size, amount, or degree; extremely large: *Some dinosaurs were enormous. The war caused an enormous amount of suffering.* —**e·nor′mous·ly,** *adv.* —**e·nor′-mous·ness,** *n.*

e·nough (i nuf′) *adj.* as much or as many as needed or desired: *enough room in the car, enough players for a baseball game.* —*n.* a quantity or amount that satisfies a need or desire: *There is enough here to feed the whole family.* —*adv.* **1.** in an amount or degree that satisfies a need or desire: *The steak is not cooked enough. Are you feeling well enough to travel?* **2.** quite; very: *The path up the mountain is certainly steep enough.* **3.** fairly; moderately: *The children behaved well enough.* —*interj.* that's enough; stop.

en·quire (en kwīr′) another word for **inquire.**

en·quir·y (en kwīr′ē, en′kwə rē) *n., pl.* **en·quir·ies.** another word for **inquiry.**

en·rage (en rāj′) *v.t.,* **en·raged, en·rag·ing.** to put into a rage; make very angry: *Drivers who ignore the speed limit enrage the community.*

en·rapt (en rapt′) *adj.* charmed; enraptured.

en·rap·ture (en rap′chər) *v.t.,* **en·rap·tured, en·rap-tur·ing.** to bring into a state of rapture; delight greatly: *The circus enraptured adults as well as children.*

en·rich (en rich′) *v.t.* **1.** to make rich or richer: *Money from the school fair enriched the scholarship fund. The guide's comments enriched our appreciation of the old castle.* **2.** to improve, as by adding desirable elements or ingredients: *to enrich flour with vitamins and minerals lost in processing.* —**en·rich′ment,** *n.*

en·roll (en rōl′) *also,* **en·rol.** *v.,* **en·rolled, en·roll·ing.** —*v.t.* **1.** to make a member: *The teacher enrolled seven new students in the class.* **2.** to put or record (a name) on a list. —*v.i.* **1.** to become a member of; join: *to enroll at a university.* **2.** to have or put one's name on a list: *to enroll as voters.*

en·roll·ment (en rōl′mənt) *also,* **en·rol·ment.** *n.* **1.** the act of enrolling or the state of being enrolled. **2.** the number of persons enrolled: *Enrollment in that college declined this year.*

en route (än rüt′) on the way: *They will stop for lunch en route to the museum.* [From the French phrase *en route,* from the words *en* meaning "in, on" + *route* meaning "road."]

en·sconce (en skons′) *v.t.,* **en·sconced, en·sconc·ing.** **1.** to settle comfortably and securely: *I ensconced myself in a chair by the fire.* **2.** to hide or shelter: *The children were ensconced in the garden shed during the entire rainstorm.*

en·sem·ble (än säm′bəl) *n.* **1.** all the parts of something considered as a whole; total effect: *The furniture made an attractive ensemble.* **2.** a set of matching clothes; costume: *Her ensemble consisted of a dress, shoes, a hat, and a coat.* **3.** a small group of musicians performing together: *The string ensemble gave three concerts during the week.* **4.** a group of musicians or other performers in a production; supporting cast: *The whole ensemble joined the star for a curtain call.*

en·shrine (en shrīn′) *v.t.,* **en·shrined, en·shrin·ing.** **1.** to enclose in or as if in a shrine. **2.** to hold sacred; cherish: *Their words are enshrined in my memory.* —**en·shrine′ment,** *n.*

en·shroud (en shroud′) *v.t.* to hide from view; conceal: *Darkness enshrouded the house.*

en·sign (en′sən; *defs. 1, 3 also* en′sīn) *n.* **1.** a flag or banner, especially a national or a naval flag. **2.** in the U.S. Navy or Coast Guard, the lowest-ranking commissioned officer, ranking below a lieutenant junior grade. **3.** an emblem of rank or office.

en·si·lage (en′sə lij) *n.* another word for **silage.**

en·slave (en slāv′) *v.t.,* **en·slaved, en·slav·ing.** to make a slave of; reduce to slavery: *The harsh conquerors tried to enslave the entire population. Large debts enslaved the struggling family.* —**en·slave′ment,** *n.*

en·snare (en snâr′) *v.t.,* **en·snared, en·snar·ing.** to catch in a snare; trap: *The trapper ensnared a weasel and several rabbits.* Also, **insnare.**

en·sue (en sü′) *v.i.,* **en·sued, en·su·ing.** **1.** to come or happen afterward; follow: *The first chapters were better than those that ensued.* **2.** to happen as a result: *The two rival gangs met, and a brief fight ensued.*

en·sure (en shŏŏr′) *v.t.,* **en·sured, en·sur·ing.** **1.** to make sure or certain; guarantee: *Careful planning helped to ensure the success of the project.* **2.** to make safe or secure; protect: *Vaccinations ensure people against diseases.* Also, **insure.** ▲ **Ensure** and **insure** are both used in the two senses given here. **Insure** is also used in an additional sense, meaning to protect against loss by means of financial insurance.

–ent *suffix* **1.** (used to form adjectives) being or acting in a particular state or manner: *independent.* **2.** (used in nouns) a person or thing that performs a particular action: *president.*

---

at; āpe; fär; câre; end; mē; it; īce; pîerce; hot; ōld; sông, fôrk; oil; out; up; ūse; rüle; pull; tûrn; chin; sing; shop; thin; this; hw in white; zh in treasure. The symbol ə stands for the unstressed vowel sound heard in about, taken, pencil, lemon, and circus.

en·tab·la·ture (en tab′lə chər) *n.* a horizontal structure used in Greek and Roman architecture, supported on columns and composed of an architrave, frieze, and cornice.

en·tail (en tāl′) *v.t.* to impose or require; involve: *a job that entails much traveling.* —**en·tail′ment,** *n.*

en·tan·gle (en tang′gəl) *v.t.,* **en·tan·gled, en·tan·gling. 1.** to catch in a tangle or net; ensnare: *The swimmer's legs were entangled in seaweed.* **2.** to involve, as in difficulties: *An innocent bystander became entangled in the argument.* **3.** to cause to become knotted or tangled; snarl: *The kitten entangled the yarn.* **4.** to confuse or complicate: *to entangle an explanation with unnecessary facts.*

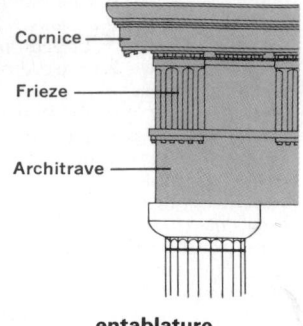

Cornice

Frieze

Architrave

entablature

en·tan·gle·ment (en tang′gəl mənt) *n.* **1.** the act of entangling or the state of being entangled. **2.** something that entangles.

en·tente (än tänt′) *n.* **1.** an understanding or agreement between countries. An entente is less binding than a formal alliance. **2.** countries having such an understanding or agreement.

en·ter (en′tər) *v.t.* **1.** to go or come into: *They entered the building. A sudden idea entered my mind.* **2.** to pass through the surface of; penetrate; pierce: *The bullet entered the police officer's arm.* **3.** to become a member or participant in; join: *to enter a university.* **4.** to cause to be admitted or accepted; enroll: *to enter a dog in competition.* **5.** to set down in writing; make a record of; register: *I entered my name in the guest book.* **6.** to take the first steps in; begin; start: *The cadets entered a new phase of their training.* —*v.i.* **1.** to go or come in: *Everyone applauded when the actor entered.* **2.** to pierce; penetrate: *The bullet entered above the shoulder.*

· **to enter into. a.** to begin to take part in; engage in: *The candidate entered into politics at a young age.* **b.** to form a part of: *Many factors entered into their decision not to go.*

· **to enter on** or **to enter upon.** to set out on; begin; start: *The travelers entered upon the voyage eagerly.*

en·ter·i·tis (en′tə rī′tis) *n.* inflammation of the lining of the intestines.

en·ter·prise (en′tər prīz′) *n.* **1.** a project or undertaking, especially one that is difficult or important: *an oil company's overseas enterprises.* **2.** readiness to take part in such undertakings; energy; initiative: *The assignment called for a person of enterprise and tact.*

en·ter·pris·ing (en′tər prī′zing) *adj.* showing energy and initiative; venturesome: *The enterprising youngsters sold cold drinks at the beach.*

en·ter·tain (en′tər tān′) *v.t.* **1.** to hold the attention of pleasantly; divert, interest, or amuse: *The clown entertained the children.* **2.** to have or receive as a guest; give hospitality to: *Every summer they entertain the neighbors at a party.* **3.** to bear in mind; consider: *We entertained the idea of moving to another city.* —*v.i.* to have or receive guests: *That family entertains often.*

en·ter·tain·er (en′tər tā′nər) *n.* a person who entertains, especially a professional performer.

en·ter·tain·ing (en′tər tā′ning) *adj.* serving to entertain; engaging; amusing: *The play was long, but entertaining.* —**en′ter·tain′ing·ly,** *adv.*

en·ter·tain·ment (en′tər tān′mənt) *n.* **1.** the act of entertaining. **2.** something that entertains, especially a performance: *A magician provided the entertainment.* **3.** the receiving of guests; hospitality.

en·thrall (en thrôl′) *also,* **en·thral.** *v.t.,* **en·thralled, en·thrall·ing. 1.** to hold spellbound; captivate; charm: *Everyone in the audience was enthralled by the skill of the gymnasts.* **2.** to make a slave of; enslave. —**en·thrall′ment,** *n.*

en·throne (en thrōn′) *v.t.,* **en·throned, en·thron·ing. 1.** to place on a throne in a ceremony: *to enthrone a monarch.* **2.** to place in a position of authority or reverence. —**en·throne′ment,** *n.*

en·thuse (en thüz′) *v.,* **en·thused, en·thus·ing.** *Informal.* —*v.i.* to show enthusiasm. —*v.t.* to make enthusiastic. ▲ avoided in careful writing and speech.

en·thu·si·asm (en thü′zē az′əm) *n.* eager and lively interest; zeal: *to show enthusiasm for a plan.*

en·thu·si·ast (en thü′zē ast′) *n.* a person who is filled with enthusiasm; zealous supporter or follower: *a golf enthusiast.*

en·thu·si·as·tic (en thü′zē as′tik) *adj.* full of enthusiasm; zealous: *A crowd of enthusiastic admirers surrounded the singer.* —**en·thu′si·as′ti·cal·ly,** *adv.*

en·tice (en tīs′) *v.t.,* **en·ticed, en·tic·ing.** to attract by offering pleasure or reward; tempt. —**en·tice′ment,** *n.*

en·tire (en tīr′) *adj.* **1.** having all the parts or elements; total; complete; whole: *The entire team was present at the ceremony. I donated the entire sum to charity.* **2.** not broken; in one piece; intact: *Only one house remained entire after the flood.*

en·tire·ly (en tīr′lē) *adv.* **1.** without exception; completely: *I agree with you entirely.* **2.** solely; only: *The decision is entirely up to you.*

en·tire·ty (en tīr′tē) *n., pl.* **en·tire·ties. 1.** the state of being whole or complete: *The opera was too long to be performed in its entirety.* **2.** something that is entire;′ whole: *I spent the entirety of my day cleaning the yard.*

en·ti·tle (en tī′təl) *v.t.,* **en·ti·tled, en·ti·tling. 1.** to give a title or name to; call: *to entitle a new book.* **2.** to give a claim or right to; qualify: *The winner was entitled to a free trip to Chicago. What entitles you to criticize me?*

en·ti·ty (en′ti tē) *n., pl.* **en·ti·ties.** something with real existence; a distinct thing: *The house and the property were sold as separate entities.*

en·tomb (en tüm′) *v.t.* **1.** to place in a tomb; bury. **2.** to serve as a tomb for: *The snow from the avalanche entombed the mountain climbers.* —**en·tomb′ment,** *n.* Also, **intomb.**

en·to·mo·log·i·cal (en′tə mə loj′i kəl) *adj.* of or relating to entomology. Also, **en·to·mo·log·ic** (en′tə mə·loj′ik).

en·to·mol·o·gist (en′tə mol′ə jist) *n.* an expert in entomology.

en·to·mol·o·gy (en′tə mol′ə jē) *n.* the branch of zoology dealing with insects.

en·tou·rage (än′tü räzh′) *n.* a group of attendants, followers, or companions, especially one accompanying a person of high rank: *The king and queen never traveled without their entourage.*

en·trails (en′trālz, en′trəlz) *pl. n.* the inner parts of a human being or animal, especially the intestines.

en·train (en trān′) *v.i.* to go aboard a train. —*v.t.* to put aboard a train.

en·trance¹ (en′trəns) *n.* **1.** the act of entering: *Everyone rose at the judge's entrance. The campaign marked the candidate's entrance into politics.* **2.** a place or means for entering: *an entrance to a building.* **3.** the right or power of entering; admittance: *to be given free entrance to a concert.* [From the Old French word *entrance* meaning "a passage for entering," "a going in," or "a beginning," from the word *entrer* "to go into, begin," from the Latin word *intrare* "to enter, go into."]

en·trance² (en trans′) *v.t.,* **en·tranced, en·tranc·ing. 1.** to put into a trance. **2.** to fill with delight or wonder; charm: *The jugglers entranced the audience.* [En- + trance.]

en·trant (en'trənt) *n.* **1.** a person who enters a contest; contestant: *All the entrants were judged by a panel of experts.* **2.** a person who enters anything.

en·trap (en trap') *v.t.*, **en·trapped, en·trap·ping. 1.** to catch in a trap. **2.** to use illegal enticement that lures a person into committing a crime that the person might not otherwise have committed.

en·trap·ment (en trap'mənt) *n.* **1.** the act of entrapping, especially illegal actions by a police officer that lure a person into committing a crime that the person might not otherwise have committed. **2.** the state of being entrapped.

en·treat (en trēt') *v.t.* to ask earnestly; beg; beseech: *The prisoner entreated the court for mercy.*

en·treat·y (en trē'tē) *n., pl.* **en·treat·ies.** an earnest request; plea.

en·tre·chat (än'tre shä') *n.* in ballet, a leap during which a dancer crosses his or her feet a number of times, sometimes beating them together.

en·tree (än'trā) *also*, **en·trée.** *n.* **1.** a main dish or course at a meal. **2.** the freedom or right to enter; access; admission: *The reporters finally gained entree into the senator's office.*

en·trench (en trench') *v.t.* **1.** to place in a trench; surround with trenches: *The troops entrenched themselves well beyond the range of enemy fire.* **2.** to establish firmly or securely: *The idea became entrenched in my mind.* Also, **intrench.**

en·trench·ment (en trench'mənt) *n.* **1.** the act of entrenching. **2.** a trench or a series of trenches, usually with a bank of earth built along the side facing the enemy. Also, **intrenchment.**

en·tre·pre·neur (än'trə prə nûr', än'trə prə nûr') *n.* a person who organizes and controls a business or other financial undertaking.

en·trust (en trust') *v.t.* **1.** to put something in the trust of; charge with a responsibility: *I entrusted a friend with the care of my pet for the weekend.* **2.** to give over the care of; assign responsibility for: *to entrust the completion of a job to an assistant.* Also, **intrust.**

en·try (en'trē) *n., pl.* **en·tries. 1.** the act or instance of entering: *My unexpected entry into the race surprised my family.* **2.** a place for entering; entrance: *Barricades blocked the entry to the building.* **3.** a written item included in a book, diary, list, or other record: *an entry in a ship's log.* **4.** something that is entered in a contest or race: *All entries must be submitted before May 1.* **5.** a word or phrase that is defined or otherwise explained in a dictionary, usually printed in heavy, dark type.

en·try–lev·el (en'trē lev'əl) *adj.* of, relating to, or being a job at a level low enough to enable a new employee to fill it while acquiring skill and experience: *high school graduates looking for entry-level jobs.*

en·twine (en twīn') *v.t.*, **en·twined, en·twin·ing.** to twine together; twist or twine around: *The children entwined their arms around each other. Flowers were entwined in the wreath.*

e·nu·mer·ate (i nü'mə rāt', i nü'mə rāt') *v.t.*, **e·nu·mer·at·ed, e·nu·mer·at·ing. 1.** to name one by one; list: *to enumerate the reasons for a decision.* **2.** to find the number of; count. —**e·nu'mer·a'tor,** *n.*

e·nu·mer·a·tion (i nü'mə rā'shən, i nü'mə rā'shən) *n.* **1.** the act of enumerating. **2.** a list or catalog.

e·nun·ci·ate (i nun'sē āt') *v.*, **e·nun·ci·at·ed, e·nun·ci·at·ing.** —*v.t.* **1.** to pronounce (words or speech sounds), especially in a particular manner; articulate: *The speech teacher taught us to enunciate every word clearly.* **2.** to state definitely; announce. —*v.i.* to pronounce words or speech sounds, especially in a particular manner: *That actor enunciates beautifully.* —**e·nun'ci·a'tor,** *n.*

e·nun·ci·a·tion (i nun'sē ā'shən) *n.* **1.** a way of pronouncing: *poor enunciation.* **2.** a statement; declaration: *an enunciation of rules.*

en·vel·op (en vel'əp) *v.t.* to wrap up or cover completely: *Clouds enveloped the mountain peak.*

envelop
fog **enveloping** a bridge

en·ve·lope (en'və lōp', än'və lōp') *n.* **1.** a flat wrapper or container made of paper, used especially for mailing letters. **2.** something that envelops; covering; wrapper. **3.** the outer covering of a balloon or airship.

en·vel·op·ment (en vel'əp mənt) *n.* **1.** the act of enveloping or the state of being enveloped. **2.** something that envelops; covering; wrapping.

en·ven·om (en ven'əm) *v.t.* **1.** to fill with venom; make poisonous. **2.** to fill with hate or vindictiveness; embitter.

en·vi·a·ble (en'vē ə bəl) *adj.* worthy of envy; desirable: *to have an enviable record in school.*

en·vi·ous (en'vē əs) *adj.* having, feeling, or showing envy: *to be envious of a friend's popularity.* —**en'vi·ous·ly,** *adv.* —**en'vi·ous·ness,** *n.*

en·vi·ron·ment (en vī'rən mənt, en vī'ərn mənt) *n.* **1.** all of the objects, influences, and conditions that surround and affect the development of a living thing: *In order to survive, an animal must be able to adapt to changes in its environment.* **2.** surroundings or conditions in which people live or work: *That school has a pleasant environment.* **3. the environment.** the surroundings or conditions in which all inhabitants of the earth live; the air, land, and water.

en·vi·ron·men·tal (en vī'rən men'təl, en vī'ərn men'təl) *adj.* of or relating to environment or the environment. —**en·vi'ron·men'tal·ly,** *adv.*

en·vi·ron·men·tal·ist (en vī'rən men'tə list, en vī'ərn men'tə list) *n.* a person who is concerned about the quality of the environment, especially about the effects of pollution of the earth's air, land, and water and the exhaustion of the earth's natural resources.

en·vi·rons (en vī'rənz, en'vər ənz) the surrounding districts of a town or city; outskirts.

en·vis·age (en viz'ij) *v.t.*, **en·vis·aged, en·vis·ag·ing.** to form a mental picture of: *to envisage how a room will look with new furniture.*

en·vi·sion (en vizh'ən) *v.t.* to form an idea of; imagine: *Can you envision what life will be like in a hundred years?*

en·voy (en'voi, än'voi) *n.* **1.** a representative sent by one country to another, ranking next below an ambassador. **2.** anyone sent as messenger or representative of another.

---

at; āpe; fär; câre; end; mē; it; īce; pîerce; hot; ōld; sông, fôrk; oil; out; up; ūse; rüle; pûll; tûrn; chin; sing; shop; thin; <u>th</u>is; hw in white; zh in treasure. The symbol ə stands for the unstressed vowel sound heard in about, taken, pencil, lemon, and circus.

en·vy (en′vē) *n., pl.* **en·vies.** **1.** a feeling of resentment, jealousy, or desire brought on by another person's abilities, possessions, or good fortune. **2.** the object of this feeling: *My new bicycle made me the envy of my friends.* —*v.t.,* **en·vied, en·vy·ing.** **1.** to feel envy toward (someone); regard with envy. **2.** to feel envy because of: *My friends envy my good grades.* —**en′vi·er,** *n.*

en·wrap (en rap′) *v.t.,* **en·wrapped, en·wrap·ping.** to enfold; envelop.

en·zyme (en′zīm) *n.* a chemical substance produced in the living cells of all bacteria, plants, and animals. Some enzymes control activities within the cells that provide energy and materials for rebuilding and repair. Others control such activities outside the cell as digestion and blood clotting.

E·o·cene (ē′ə sēn′) *n.* the second geological epoch of the Tertiary period of the Cenozoic era, when such animals as the horse, the elephant, and the camel first appeared. —*adj.* of, relating to, or characteristic of this epoch.

e·o·hip·pus (ē′ō hip′əs) *n.* a small, early ancestor of the horse, found as a fossil in Eocene deposits in North America and Europe.

e·on (ē′ən, ē′on) *also,* **ae·on.** *n.* **1.** a very long, indefinite period of time. **2.** the largest division of geological time, including at least two eras.

ep·au·let (ep′ə let′) *also,* **ep·au·lette.** *n.* an ornament worn on the shoulder of a uniform, such as a military uniform, and in some other styles of dress.

e·phed·rine (i fed′rin) *n.* a drug used to relieve hay fever and asthma.

e·phem·er·al (i fem′ər əl) *adj.* **1.** lasting for a very short time; short-lived; fleeting: *the ephemeral beauty of a rainbow.* **2.** *Biology.* lasting for a day.

e·phem·er·on (i fem′ə ron′) *n., pl.* **e·phem·er·a** (i fem′ər ə) or **e·phem·er·ons.** a person or thing that is short-lived.

E·phe·sians (i fē′zhənz) *n.* a book of the New Testament, written as a letter by the Apostle Paul to the Christians in Ephesus. ▲ used with a singular verb.

epi– *prefix* on; over; above; after; attached to: *epidermis, epilogue.*

ep·ic (ep′ik) *n.* **1.** a long, narrative poem that tells of the adventures and achievements of heroes in legend or history: *The Greek poet Homer wrote an epic entitled* The Odyssey. **2.** any written work or play having similar characteristics: *The novel* Moby Dick *by Herman Melville is an epic of the sea.* —*adj. also,* **ep·i·cal** (ep′i kəl). **1.** of, relating to, or like an epic: *an epic poem.* **2.** suitable for an epic; heroic: *the epic events of pioneer life in the United States.* —**ep′i·cal·ly,** *adv.*

ep·i·cen·ter (ep′i sen′tər) *n.* the point on the surface of the earth directly above the center of an earthquake.

ep·i·cure (ep′i kyur′) *n.* a person who has developed a refined taste for good food and drink: *That epicure often dines in fancy and expensive restaurants.*

ep·i·cu·re·an (ep′i kyu rē′ən, ep′i kyur′ē ən) *adj.* **1.** having refined tastes or habits, especially in eating and drinking. **2.** fit or suitable for an epicure: *an epicurean meal.* —*n.* another word for **epicure.**

ep·i·dem·ic (ep′i dem′ik) *n.* **1.** the rapid spread or sudden, widespread appearance of a disease among many people at the same time: *an epidemic of measles.* **2.** the rapid spread or sudden, widespread appearance of anything: *an epidemic of burglaries.* —*adj.* spreading among and affecting many people at the same time; widespread: *an epidemic disease.*

ep·i·der·mis (ep′i dur′mis) *n.* **1.** a protective outer layer of the skin of animals with backbones. The epidermis does not contain blood vessels or nerves. **2.** a protective outer layer of cells of seed plants and ferns. —**ep′i·der′mal,** *adj.*

ep·i·glot·tis (ep′i glot′is) *n.* a thin, triangular flap of cartilage that blocks the entrance to the windpipe during swallowing, preventing foreign matter from entering the lungs.

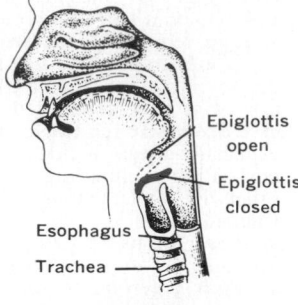

epiglottis

ep·i·gram (ep′i gram′) *n.* **1.** a brief, pointed statement expressing a thought in a witty manner, for example: *There is only one thing in the world worse than being talked about, and that is not being talked about* (Oscar Wilde). **2.** a short poem with a witty, clever ending.

ep·i·gram·mat·ic (ep′i grə mat′ik) *adj.* **1.** of, relating to, or using epigrams. **2.** like or suitable to an epigram; witty, pointed, and brief.

ep·i·graph (ep′i graf′) *n.* **1.** an inscription, as on a building, tombstone, or monument. **2.** a quotation, as at the beginning of a book or a chapter of a book, suggesting the theme of the contents. [From the Greek word *epigraphē* meaning "inscription," from the word *epigraphein* "to write upon," from the words *epi–* "upon" + *graphein* "to write."]

ep·i·lep·sy (ep′ə lep′sē) *n.* a disorder of the brain, characterized by seizures that may take the form of convulsions or loss of consciousness.

ep·i·lep·tic (ep′ə lep′tik) *adj.* of, relating to, or having epilepsy: *an epileptic seizure.* —*n.* a person who has epilepsy.

ep·i·logue (ep′ə lôg′, ep′ə log′) *also,* **ep·i·log.** *n.* **1.** a passage or section added to the end of a story, poem, or other written work as an explanation, summary, or conclusion. **2.** a speech or short poem addressed to the audience by one of the actors at the end of a play.

ep·i·neph·rine (ep′ə nef′rin, ep′ə nef′rēn) *n.* another word for **adrenaline.**

E·piph·a·ny (i pif′ə nē) *n.* a Christian holy day that falls on January 6. In the Western Church, it celebrates the visit of the Three Wise Men to the infant Jesus. In the Eastern Church, it celebrates the baptism of Jesus.

ep·i·phyte (ep′ə fīt′) *n.* any of various plants that grow on other plants for support, but usually do not harm the plant on which they live. Also, **air plant.** —**ep·i·phyt·ic** (ep′ə fit′ik), *adj.*

Epis. **1.** Episcopal. **2.** Episcopalian. **3.** Epistle.

e·pis·co·pa·cy (i pis′kə pə sē) *n., pl.* **e·pis·co·pa·cies.** **1.** a system of church government by bishops. **2.** another word for **episcopate.**

e·pis·co·pal (i pis′kə pəl) *adj.* **1.** of or relating to bishops. **2.** governed by bishops. **3. Episcopal.** of or relating to the Church of England or the Episcopal Church.

Episcopal Church, a church in the United States that agrees with the Church of England in doctrine, beliefs, and most practices.

E·pis·co·pa·lian (i pis′kə pāl′yən) *n.* a member of an Episcopal church, such as the Episcopal Church. —*adj.* another word for **Episcopal.**

e·pis·co·pate (i pis′kə pit, i pis′kə pāt′) *n.* **1.** the position, rank, or term of office of a bishop. **2.** the district under the authority of a bishop; diocese. **3.** bishops as a group. Also, **episcopacy.**

ep·i·sode (ep′ə sōd′) *n.* **1.** an incident or event that stands out in a series of events. **2.** an incident or event that is separate from the main plot or subject of a novel or other written work. **3.** an installment of a play, story, or the like that is presented in serial form, as on television: *an episode of a soap opera.*

e·pis·tle (i pis′əl) *n.* **1.** a long, formal letter. **2. Epistle.** any one of the letters written by an Apostle and contained in the New Testament. **3.** a selection from one of these, read as part of a Christian service.

ep·i·taph (ep′i taf′) *n.* a brief statement in memory of a dead person, usually inscribed on a tombstone or monument.

ep·i·the·li·um (ep′ə thē′lē əm) *n., pl.* **ep·i·the·li·ums** or **ep·i·the·li·a** (ep′ə thē′lē ə). a thin sheet of body tissue that consists of one or more layers of cells, covering the entire surface of the body and lining the body cavities. —**ep′i·the′li·al,** *adj.*

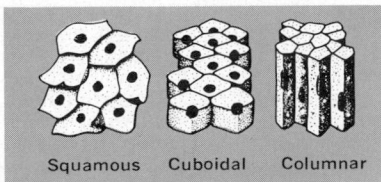

epithelium cells

ep·i·thet (ep′ə thet′) *n.* a descriptive word or phrase used with or in place of a name to indicate some characteristic or quality, as "the Lion-Hearted" in "Richard the Lion-Hearted."

e·pit·o·me (i pit′ə mē) *n.* **1.** a person or thing that has or represents all the qualities or characteristics of something: *The elegant room was the epitome of good taste.* **2.** a short account or summary of a speech, book, or other written work; abridgment.

e·pit·o·mize (i pit′ə mīz′) *v.t.,* **e·pit·o·mized, e·pit·o·miz·ing. 1.** to be the epitome of: *The king and queen epitomized wise rulers.* **2.** to make a short account or summary of (a written work).

e plu·ri·bus u·num (ē′ plŭr′ə bəs ū′nəm) *Latin.* out of many, one. It is the motto on the official seal of the United States.

ep·och (ep′ək) *n.* **1.** a period of time marked by some extraordinary characteristic, development, or course of events: *an epoch of social and political change.* **2.** a division of geological time smaller than a period: *In the Pleistocene epoch glaciers advanced and receded.*

ep·ox·y (e pok′sē) *n., pl.* **ep·ox·ies.** any of various strong chemical adhesives made from a synthetic resin. —*v.t.,* **ep·ox·ied, ep·ox·y·ing.** to glue or bond together with epoxy.

ep·si·lon (ep′sə lon′) *n.* the fifth letter of the Greek alphabet (E, ε).

Ep·som salts (ep′səm) *also,* **Epsom salt.** a bitter compound consisting of colorless crystals. It is used especially as a laxative and in baths for sore muscles or minor infections. [From *Epsom,* the town in England where the compound was originally obtained from the water of a mineral spring.]

eq. 1. equal. **2.** equation. **3.** equator. **4.** equivalent.

eq·ua·ble (ek′wə bəl) *adj.* **1.** not easily disturbed or upset; tranquil: *an equable state of mind.* **2.** not changing; unvarying; steady: *an equable temperature.* —**eq′ua·bly,** *adv.*

e·qual (ē′kwəl) *adj.* **1.** the same, as in amount, number, rank, or size: *Four quarts are equal to one gallon.* **2.** having the same rights, privileges, and responsibilities: *All people are equal under the law.* **3.** evenly matched or balanced; even: *Their chances to win are equal.* **4.** *Mathematics.* (of sets) having exactly the same members. The sets [12, 23, 59, 74] and [59, 12, 74, 23] are equal. —*n.* a person or thing that is equal: *You are my equal as a tennis player.* —*v.t.,* **e·qualed, e·qual·ing;** *also, British,* **e·qualled, e·qual·ling. 1.** to be equal to: *Two plus two equals four.* **2.** to make or do something equal to: *No one has equaled that doctor's service to the community. The athlete equaled the world record in the 100-yard dash.* —**e′qual·ly,** *adv.*

·**equal to.** having the strength or ability necessary for: *We had few resources and were not equal to the job.*

e·qual·i·ty (i kwol′i tē) *n.* the state or quality of being equal, especially the state of having the same rights, privileges, and responsibilities.

e·qual·ize (ē′kwə līz′) *v.t.,* **e·qual·ized, e·qual·iz·ing.** to make equal: *to equalize the water pressure in two tanks.* —**e′qual·i·za′tion,** *n.* —**e′qual·i′zer,** *n.*

equal opportunity employer, an employer that agrees not to practice discrimination in employment because of race, color, sex, religion, national origin, age, or handicap.

equal sign, a mathematical symbol (=) used to show that two quantities or expressions are equal, as in $1 + 6 = 7$.

e·qua·nim·i·ty (ē′kwə nim′i tē, ek′wə nim′i tē) *n.* evenness of mind or temper; calmness: *The candidate accepted defeat with equanimity.*

e·quate (i kwāt′) *v.t.,* **e·quat·ed, e·quat·ing. 1.** to consider, treat, or represent as equal or comparable: *to equate good manners with real concern for others.* **2.** to consider or represent as related: *Some people equate wealth and happiness.* **3.** *Mathematics.* to state the equality of; put in the form of an equation.

e·qua·tion (i kwā′zhən) *n.* **1.** *Mathematics.* a mathematical statement that one quantity or expression is equal to another quantity or expression, especially a statement using an equal sign. $9 + 6 = 15$ and $3x - y = 0$ are equations. **2.** *Chemistry.* an expression representing a chemical reaction indicated by the symbol (=) or (→), as in $FeS + 2HCl = FeCl_2 + H_2S$.

e·qua·tor (i kwā′tər) *n.* an imaginary line encircling the earth halfway between the North and South Poles. The equator is the line from which degrees of latitude are measured.

e·qua·to·ri·al (ē′kwə tôr′ē əl, ek′wə tôr′ē əl) *adj.* **1.** of, at, or near the equator: *an equatorial country.* **2.** characteristic of the equator: *equatorial heat.*

eq·uer·ry (ek′wə rē) *n., pl.* **eq·uer·ries. 1.** formerly, an officer of a royal or noble household in charge of its horses. **2.** a personal attendant to any of the members of the British royal family.

e·ques·tri·an (i kwes′trē ən) *adj.* **1.** of or relating to horsemen or horsewomen, horsemanship, or horseback riding. **2.** mounted on horseback: *an equestrian performer in a circus.* **3.** showing a person mounted on horseback: *an equestrian statue.* —*n.* a rider, especially a performer on horseback in a circus or other show.

e·ques·tri·enne (i kwes′trē en′) *n.* a woman who is an equestrian.

equi– *combining form* **1.** equal: *equilibrium.* **2.** equally: *equidistant.*

e·qui·dis·tant (ē′kwi dis′tənt) *adj.* being the same distance from a given point, line, or plane; equally distant: *The two houses are equidistant from the road.*

e·qui·lat·er·al (ē′kwə lat′ər əl) *adj.* having all sides equal in length: *an equilateral triangle.*

e·qui·lib·ri·um (ēk′kwə lib′rē əm) *n.* **1.** a state of balance, especially between forces acting on or within a body or system: *A scale having equal weights on each side is in equilibrium.* **2.** mental and emotional balance: *I usually maintain my equilibrium under stress.*

e·quine (ē′kwīn, ek′wīn) *adj.* of, relating to, or like a horse.

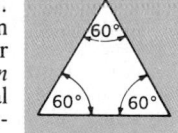

equilateral triangle

at; āpe; fär; câre; end; mē; it; īce; pîerce; hot; ōld; sông, fôrk; oil; out; up; ūse; rüle; pùll; tûrn; chin; sing; shop; thin; this; hw in white; zh in treasure. The symbol ə stands for the unstressed vowel sound heard in about, taken, pencil, lemon, and circus.

E

e·qui·noc·tial (ē′kwə nok′shəl) *adj.* **1.** of or relating to an equinox. **2.** happening at or near the time of an equinox: *an equinoctial storm.*

e·qui·nox (ē′kwə noks′) *n., pl.* **e·qui·nox·es.** either of the two times of the year when day and night are of equal length all over the earth. During these two times the sun is directly above the equator. In the Northern Hemisphere, the vernal equinox takes place about March 21, and marks the beginning of spring. The autumnal equinox takes place about September 23, and marks the beginning of autumn.

e·quip (i kwip′) *v.t.,* **e·quipped, e·quip·ping.** to provide or outfit with whatever is necessary for a particular purpose or use: *to equip a boat for a long cruise.*

eq·ui·page (ek′wə pij) *n.* **1.** equipment, as for an army or camp; gear. **2.** a carriage, especially when fully outfitted with horses, driver, and attendants.

e·quip·ment (i kwip′mənt) *n.* **1.** anything that is necessary or provided for a particular purpose or use; supplies; gear: *camping equipment, sports equipment.* **2.** the act of equipping or the state of being equipped.

e·qui·poise (ē′kwə poiz′, ek′wə poiz′) *n.* **1.** a state of balance or equilibrium. **2.** a weight or force that balances another; counterbalance.

eq·ui·ta·ble (ek′wi tə bəl) *adj.* fair or just: *an equitable law.* —**eq′ui·ta·bly,** *adv.*

eq·ui·ty (ek′wi tē) *n., pl.* **eq·ui·ties. 1.** the quality of being fair and just: *the equity of a law.* **2.** something that is fair and just. **3. a.** a set of rules and principles dealing with legal matters not covered under the common law. **b.** the legal system dealing with such matters: *a case in equity.* **4.** the value of property remaining after debts are subtracted.

e·quiv·a·lence (i kwiv′ə ləns) *n.* the state or condition of being equivalent.

e·quiv·a·lent (i kwiv′ə lənt) *adj.* **1.** equal, as in value, force, effect, or meaning; corresponding: *A quarter is equivalent to five nickels. Shaking one's head is equivalent to saying no.* **2.** *Mathematics.* (of sets) having the same number of members. The sets [1,2,3,4] and [2,4,6,8] are equivalent. —*n.* something that is equivalent: *Ten dimes are the equivalent of one dollar.*

e·quiv·o·cal (i kwiv′ə kəl) *adj.* **1.** capable of being understood in more than one way; having more than one possible meaning; ambiguous: *an equivocal answer.* **2.** undecided or uncertain; doubtful: *The evidence gathered by the detective was of equivocal value.* **3.** of a suspicious nature; questionable: *equivocal behavior.* —**e·quiv′o·cal·ly,** *adv.*

e·quiv·o·cate (i kwiv′ə kāt′) *v.i.,* **e·quiv·o·cat·ed, e·quiv·o·cat·ing.** to express oneself in language having more than one possible meaning, especially in order to mislead others or to avoid committing oneself: *The senator has equivocated on that issue for many years.* —**e·quiv′o·ca′tor,** *n.*

e·quiv·o·ca·tion (i kwiv′ə kā′shən) *n.* **1.** the act of equivocating. **2.** an equivocal statement.

Er, the symbol for erbium.

–er¹ *suffix* **1.** (used to form nouns from verbs) a person or thing that carries out the action of the verb: *driver, grater.* **2.** (used to form nouns) **a.** a person who was born or is living in: *northerner, New Yorker.* **b.** a person who makes or is concerned with: *hatter, biographer.* **c.** a person or thing that is or is characterized by: *foreigner.* [From both the Old English suffix *-ere* and the Old French suffix *-ier* (from the Latin suffix *-arius*), both meaning "one that does."]

–er² *suffix* used to form the comparative degree of adjectives and adverbs: *colder, sooner.* [From the Old English suffix *-ra* with the same meaning.]

e·ra (îr′ə, er′ə) *n.* **1.** a period of time marked by certain events, conditions, ideas, persons, or things: *The reign of Queen Victoria is called the Victorian era.* **2.** a period of time measured from or beginning with a particular event: *The Christian era begins at the date of Jesus' birth.* **3.** one of the major divisions of geological time, including several epochs.

e·rad·i·cate (i rad′i kāt′) *v.t.,* **e·rad·i·cat·ed, e·rad·i·cat·ing.** to root out; remove or destroy completely; eliminate; abolish: *to eradicate weeds, to eradicate a disease.* —**e·rad′i·ca′tion,** *n.* —**e·rad′i·ca′tor,** *n.*

e·rase (i rās′) *v.,* **e·rased, e·ras·ing.** —*v.t.* **1.** to rub, scrape, or scratch out; wipe off: *I erased the notes written in the margin.* **2.** to remove marks, writing, or recorded information from: *Will you erase the blackboard?* **3.** to remove or destroy completely as if by rubbing or blotting out: *Time had not erased their memories of the war.* —*v.i.* **1.** to be capable of being erased: *Make light pencil lines so that they will erase easily.* **2.** to remove marks, writing, or recorded information: *The tape recorder erases if it is operated in reverse.* —**e·ras′a·ble,** *adj.*

e·ras·er (i rā′sər) *n.* a device for erasing, such as a piece of rubber for removing marks made with a pencil.

e·ra·sure (i rā′shər) *n.* **1.** the act of erasing. **2.** something that has been erased, such as a word or letter. **3.** the place or mark left where something has been erased.

er·bi·um (ûr′bē əm) *n.* a silver-gray metallic element of the rare-earth group. It is used to color glass. Symbol: **Er** [From the letters *-erb-* in the name *Ytterby,* the Swedish town where it was first discovered.]

ere (âr) *Archaic. prep.* before in time. —*conj.* **1.** before. **2.** rather than.

e·rect (i rekt′) *adj.* in a vertical or upright position; raised: *The dog was trained to stand with its ears and tail erect.* —*v.t.* **1.** to build; construct: *to erect an apartment house.* **2.** to raise or put in a vertical or upright position: *It takes only a few minutes to erect this tent.* **3.** to create or set up: *The Aztecs erected an advanced civilization.* —**e·rect′ly,** *adv.* —**e·rect′ness,** *n.*

e·rec·tion (i rek′shən) *n.* **1.** the act of erecting or the state of being erected. **2.** something that is erected, such as a building or other structure. **3.** a stiffening of a part of the body.

erg (ûrg) *n.* *Physics.* a unit of work equal to the work done by a force of 1 dyne acting through a distance of 1 centimeter.

er·go (ûr′gō) *adv., conj.* *Latin.* therefore.

er·go·nom·ics (ûr′gə nom′iks) *n.* the science of designing objects in such a way that human beings can use them more efficiently and comfortably: *A knowledge of ergonomics made it possible to design a chair that helped reduce back pain.* ▲ used with a singular verb. [From the Greek word *ergon* meaning "work" and the word *(ec)onomic(s).*]

er·mine (ûr′min) *n., pl.* **er·mines** or **er·mine. 1.** a weasel having a brown coat that usually changes to white in winter. **2.** the white winter fur of this animal, used especially for women's coats and for trimming on royal or judges' robes in some European countries.

ermine (def. 1)

e·rode (i rōd′) *v.,* **e·rod·ed, e·rod·ing.** —*v.t.* **1.** to wear or wash away gradually by rubbing or friction: *The heavy rains eroded the topsoil on the hills.* **2.** to eat into or away; corrode: *Salt water collected in the bottom of the boat and eroded the metal parts.* **3.** to form (a channel or the like) by a gradual eating or wearing away: *The glacier had eroded a valley in the side of the mountain.* **4.** to cause to decay or disappear gradually: *Arguments eroded our friendship.* —*v.i.* to become eroded; undergo erosion.

E·ros (îr'os, er'os) *n. Greek Mythology.* the god of love and son of Aphrodite. In Roman mythology he was called Cupid.

e·ro·sion (i rō'zhən) *n.* a gradual wearing, washing, or eating away, especially of the soil and rock of the earth's surface by glaciers, running water, waves, or wind: *Sand dunes help prevent the erosion of the shore by the ocean waves.*

erosion
rock formation shaped by **erosion**

e·ro·sive (i rō'siv) *adj.* causing erosion; eroding.

e·rot·ic (i rot'ik) *adj.* having to do with, causing, or influenced by sexual love or passion.

err (ûr, er) *v.i.* **1.** to do something wrong; make a mistake; be in error: *I erred in making my decision before I knew all the facts.* **2.** to do something that is morally wrong.

er·rand (er'ənd) *n.* **1.** a short trip to do something, sometimes for someone else. **2.** the purpose or object of such a trip.

er·rant (er'ənt) *adj.* **1.** traveling or roaming in search of adventure; wandering; roving: *the errant knights of the Middle Ages.* **2.** straying from the proper place or correct behavior; erring: *an errant child, errant conduct.*

er·rat·ic (i rat'ik) *adj.* **1.** acting or moving in an irregular or confused way: *the erratic path of a tornado.* **2.** straying from the accepted or usual standard; not regular or predictable: *erratic weather, erratic behavior.* —**er·rat'i·cal·ly,** *adv.*

er·ro·ne·ous (i rō'nē əs) *adj.* marked by or containing error; mistaken; incorrect: *an erroneous conclusion.* —**er·ro'ne·ous·ly,** *adv.* —**er·ro'ne·ous·ness,** *n.*

er·ror (er'ər) *n.* **1.** something incorrectly done, believed, or stated; mistake: *spelling errors.* **2.** the state or condition of being mistaken or incorrect: *They are in error if they think I will give up that easily.* **3.** the amount by which something is wrong: *How large was the error in your calculations?* **4.** *Baseball.* a misplay by a fielder that allows a base runner to reach a base safely or a batter to remain at bat when, if the play had been made properly, the runner or batter would have been put out.

error message, a sentence or code number appearing on the screen of a computer or on a printout that indicates an error in the program or data.

er·satz (er'zäts) *adj.* serving as a substitute; artificial; synthetic: *ersatz coffee, ersatz leather.* [From the German word *Ersatz* meaning "replacement," from the word *ersetzen* "to replace."]

erst·while (ûrst'hwīl', ûrst'wīl') *adj.* former: *an erstwhile friend.* —*adv. Archaic.* formerly.

er·u·dite (er'yů dīt', er'ů dīt') *adj.* having or showing much knowledge or learning; scholarly; learned: *an erudite speaker.* —**er'u·dite'ly,** *adv.* —**er'u·dite'ness,** *n.*

er·u·di·tion (er'yů dish'ən, er'ů dish'ən) *n.* much knowledge or learning; scholarship.

e·rupt (i rupt') *v.i.* **1.** to throw forth something suddenly and violently: *The geyser erupts every few hours.* **2.** to burst or be thrown forth: *Enough lava had erupted from the volcano to bury the entire village.* **3.** to break out suddenly and violently: *A fight erupted during the game between the opposing teams.* **4.** to break out, as in a rash: *Many teenagers erupt with acne.* —*v.t.* to throw forth (something, such as steam, water, or lava) suddenly and violently.

e·rup·tion (i rup'shən) *n.* **1.** the act of erupting: *The last eruption of that volcano was in 1900.* **2.** a slight inflammation of the skin; rash.

e·rup·tive (i rup'tiv) *adj.* **1.** bursting forth; tending to erupt: *an eruptive geyser.* **2.** causing or characterized by a rash, such as certain diseases. **3.** of or relating to volcanic eruptions; formed by a volcano.

-ery *suffix* (used to form nouns) **1.** a place of business or place where something is made, stored, or sold: *bakery, brewery.* **2.** a place or home for: *nunnery.* **3.** the art, practice, or profession of: *thievery, cookery.* **4.** the state or condition of: *slavery.* **5.** the characteristics, practices, or principles of: *knavery, trickery.* **6.** a collection or group of: *greenery, crockery.*

e·ryth·ro·cyte (i rith'rə sīt') *n.* another word for **red blood cell.**

e·ryth·ro·my·cin (i rith'rə mī'sin) *n.* an antibiotic used to treat a wide range of infections caused by bacteria. [Formed from the Greek words *erythros* meaning "red" and *mykes* meaning "fungus."]

Es, the symbol for einsteinium.

es·ca·late (es'kə lāt') *v.,* **es·ca·lat·ed, es·ca·lat·ing.** —*v.t.* to increase or enlarge by stages: *to escalate a war.* —*v.i.* to be increased or enlarged by stages: *The quarrel between the two friends escalated into a fight.* —**es'ca·la'tion,** *n.*

es·ca·la·tor (es'kə lā'tər) *n.* a moving stairway made up of a series of steps attached to a continuous chain, used for carrying passengers from one floor or level to another.

es·cal·lop (e skol'əp, e skal'əp) *n.* another word for **scallop.**

es·ca·pade (es'kə pād') *n.* action or behavior that is wild, reckless, or full of adventure.

es·cape (e skāp') *v.,* **es·caped, es·cap·ing.** —*v.i.* **1.** to get away or free; gain or regain liberty: *The bird escaped from the cage.* **2.** to avoid or remain free from capture, punishment, harm, or danger: *The guards chased the bank robbers, but they escaped in the crowd.* **3.** to leak or flow out from a container or enclosure: *Gas escaped from the pipe.* —*v.t.* **1.** to get away or free from; elude: *to escape the traffic by taking a side street.* **2.** to avoid or remain free from: *The driver of the car narrowly escaped death.* **3.** to fail to be noticed or remembered by; slip by or away from: *Their name escapes me at the moment.* **4.** to slip out from unintentionally: *A sigh escaped my lips.* —*n.* **1.** the act of escaping: *Their escape was by way of the sea.* **2.** the fact or state of having escaped. **3.** a way of escaping: *A rope ladder served as an escape from the burning house.* **4.** a way of temporarily avoiding or forgetting problems, worries, or the like: *Reading detective stories is my escape.*

at; āpe; fär; câre; end; mē; it; īce; pîerce; hot; ōld; sông, fôrk; oil; out; up; ūse; rüle; pull; tûrn; chin; sing; shop; thin; this; hw in white; zh in treasure. The symbol **ə** stands for the unstressed vowel sound heard in about, taken, pencil, lemon, and circus.

es·cape·ment (e skāp′mənt) *n.* **1.** a device in a clock or watch made up of a small toothed wheel and a catch. The back-and-forth movement of the catch allows one tooth of the wheel to escape at each swing, thus controlling the regular movement of a system of gears that moves the hands. **2.** a mechanism that regulates the movement of a typewriter carriage during use.

escapement
(def. 1)

escape velocity, the minimum speed that something, such as a rocket or other space vehicle, must reach to escape the gravitational pull of the earth or another celestial body. Escape velocity from earth is approximately 7 miles per second (11.2 kilometers per second).

es·cap·ism (e skă′piz əm) *n.* the tendency to escape the dull routine and responsibilities of daily life by daydreaming or by reading, watching television, or the like.

es·ca·role (es′kə rōl′) *n.* a plant bearing curly green leaves, used especially in salads. It is a kind of endive.

es·carp·ment (e skärp′mənt) *n.* a steep slope or cliff. **2.** a fortification consisting of a steep slope.

es·chew (es chü′) *v.t.* to keep away from; avoid; shun: *to eschew wickedness.*

es·cort (*n.,* es′kôrt; *v.,* e skôrt′, es′kôrt) *n.* **1.** a person or persons who accompany another or others as a courtesy, honor, or protection: *The visiting monarch had an escort of armed guards.* **2.** a man or boy who accompanies a woman or girl to a party, dance, or the like. **3.** one or more ships or airplanes accompanying or protecting another. —*v.t.* to accompany as a courtesy, honor, or protection; act as an escort to: *My date escorted me to the party. The police escorted the senator to a limousine after the rally.*

es·crow (es′krō) *Law. n.* a deed or bond, or money or other property, held by a third person until certain conditions are fulfilled.

  ·**in escrow.** held by a third person until certain conditions are fulfilled: *to place rent in escrow.*

es·cutch·eon (e skuch′ən) *n.* a shield or shield-shaped surface carrying a coat of arms.

–ese *suffix* **1.** (used to form nouns) **a.** a person who was born in or is a citizen of: *Burmese.* **b.** the language of: *Japanese.* **2.** (used to form adjectives) of, relating to, or coming from: *Chinese.*

Es·ki·mo (es′kə mō′) *n., pl.* **Es·ki·mo** or **Es·ki·mos.** **1.** a member of a Mongoloid race of people living in Alaska, northern Canada, Greenland, and northeastern Siberia. **2.** either of the two languages spoken by these people. —*adj.* of or relating to the Eskimos, their language, or their culture.

escutcheon

Eskimo dog, a dog of a breed native to Greenland and northern Canada, having a thick, shaggy coat, broad chest, and curved bushy tail, used by the Eskimos to draw heavy sleds. The name is often also applied to other dogs used by the Eskimos, such as the Alaskan malamute, Siberian husky, and Samoyed.

e·soph·a·gus (i sof′ə gəs) *n., pl.* **e·soph·a·gi** (i sof′ə-jī′). a passageway or tube through which food passes from the mouth to the stomach; gullet. See **digestive system** for illustration.

es·o·ter·ic (es′ə ter′ik) *adj.* **1.** understood by or intended for a small and select group of people; of or for a chosen few: *esoteric rites, an esoteric doctrine.* **2.** hard to understand: *an esoteric discussion on the meaning of life.* **3.** kept secret; private; confidential. —**es′o·ter′i·cal·ly,** *adv.*

esp., especially.

ESP, extrasensory perception.

es·pa·drille (es′pə dril′) *n.* a casual shoe usually having a canvas upper part and a flexible sole made of rope.

es·pal·ier (e spal′yər, e spal′yā) *n.* **1.** a tree or shrub trained to grow in a flattened, horizontal position against a framework or a wall. **2.** a framework on which such a plant is trained to grow. —*v.t.* to train on or provide with an espalier: *to espalier a fruit tree.*

es·pe·cial (e spesh′əl) *adj.* special; particular: *The smallest kitten was an especial favorite of the children.*

es·pe·cial·ly (e spesh′ə lē) *adv.* particularly; principally; exceptionally: *The sea is rough here, especially in the winter. I called especially to speak to my cousin.*

Es·pe·ran·to (es′pə rän′tō, es′pə ran′tō) *n.* an artificial language based on the major European languages, having a simplified system of grammar.

es·pi·o·nage (es′pē ə näzh′, es′pē ə nij) *n.* the practice of spying, especially the use of spies by one country to discover the military or political secrets of other countries.

es·pla·nade (es′plə näd′, es′plə näd′) *n.* an open, level space, especially along a shore, used as a public walkway or roadway; promenade.

es·pous·al (e spou′zəl) *n.* **1.** the act of espousing; adoption; advocacy: *the espousal of a political doctrine.* **2.** *also,* **espousals.** a ceremony of engagement or marriage.

es·pouse (e spouz′) *v.t.,* **es·poused, es·pous·ing. 1.** to take up or adopt; advocate or embrace: *to espouse a religious belief.* **2.** to marry; wed. **3.** to promise or give in marriage.

es·pres·so (e spres′ō) *n., pl.* **es·pres·sos.** a strong coffee made by forcing steam through finely ground, darkly roasted coffee beans. [From the Italian phrase *(caffè) espresso* meaning "pressed out (coffee)," from the word *esprimere* "to press out, express," going back to the Latin words *ex-* "out, out of" and *premere* "to press."]

es·prit (e sprē′) *n.* a lively wit; spirit; vivacity.

es·prit de corps (e sprē′ de kôr′) a feeling of pride, loyalty, and devotion found in a group and among its members. [From the French phrase *esprit de corps* meaning "spirit of a body of people," going back to the Latin words *spiritus* "spirit, breath," *de* "of," and *corpus* "body."]

es·py (e spī′) *v.t.,* **es·pied, es·py·ing.** to catch sight of (something hidden or at a distance); see: *We espied the children in the bushes.*

Esq., Esquire.

es·quire (es′kwīr) *n.* **1.** a young attendant to a medieval knight; squire. **2.** a man belonging to the English gentry, ranking next below a knight. **3. Esquire.** a form of respectful or polite address used in writing. ▲ in Britain, placed after any man's last name and a comma. In the United States, often placed after the name of a lawyer of either sex. In both countries it is usually abbreviated as *Esq.*

–ess *suffix* used to form feminine nouns: *actress, waitress.*

es·say (*n.,* es′ā, *def. 2 also* e sā′; *v.,* e sā′) *n.* **1.** a short written composition on a particular subject. **2.** an effort or attempt to do something; endeavor. —*v.t.* to try; attempt.

es·say·ist (es′ā ist) *n.* a writer of essays.

es·sence (es′əns) *n.* **1.** something that makes a thing what it is; necessary and basic part: *The essence of poetry is invention* (Samuel Johnson). **2.** a substance containing, in concentrated form, the basic parts of the thing from which it is taken; extract: *essence of peppermint.* **3.** a perfume.

es·sen·tial (i sen′shəl) *adj.* **1.** very important or necessary: *It is essential that we arrive early for the surprise party.* **2.** forming or being the basis of something; fundamental: *Having a good sense of balance is essential to riding a bike.* **3.** necessary to health and growth and that cannot be made by the body but must be ingested in food:

an essential amino acid. —*n.* a necessary or basic part: *to outline the essentials of a plan.* —**es·sen′tial·ly,** *adv.*

essential oil, any of various oils that give a plant its characteristic flavor or fragrance. Essential oils are extracted from plant tissues and used to make perfumes and flavorings.

–est[1] *suffix* **1.** (used to form the superlative degree of adjectives) most: *coldest.* **2.** (used to form the superlative degree of adverbs) most: *soonest.* [From the Old English superlative suffix *-est.*]

–est[2] *suffix* used to form the archaic second person singular of verbs: *doest.* [From the Old English verb suffix *-est.*]

est. 1. established. **2.** estate. **3.** estimated.

EST, Eastern Standard Time.

es·tab·lish (e stab′lish) *v.t.* **1.** to set up permanently; found: *to establish a colony in a new land, to establish a university.* **2.** to settle securely or permanently, as in a place, position, or occupation: *I established myself in the clothing business.* **3.** to introduce and win permanent acceptance for; gain recognition of: *to establish a theory, to establish one's reputation.* **4.** to show or prove to be true: *to establish a motive, to establish a fact.*

established church, a church recognized as the official church of a particular nation.

es·tab·lish·ment (e stab′lish mənt) *n.* **1.** the act of establishing or the state of being established. **2.** something established, such as a household, business, or institution: *Stores and restaurants are private establishments; the police and fire departments are public establishments.* **3. the Establishment.** the group of people or institutions that have the most influence or control in a nation or society.

es·tate (e stāt′) *n.* **1.** a large piece of land with a large house; landed property: *The wealthy family spent their summers at a country estate.* **2. a.** all the property or possessions of a person, especially at his or her death. **b.** the type and extent of interest a person has in property, especially land: *A tenant's estate is much more limited than an owner's.* **3.** a condition or stage in life.

es·teem (e stēm′) *v.t.* to consider good or important; have high regard or respect for; value highly: *to esteem someone's opinion.* —*n.* **1.** high regard or respect: *Their acts of charity won them much esteem in the community.* **2.** Archaic. judgment; consideration.

es·ter (es′tər) *n.* an organic compound formed by the reaction of an alcohol with an acid, occurring naturally as animal or vegetable fat, oil, or wax.

Es·ther (es′tər) *n.* a book of the Old Testament that tells the story of a Jewish queen of Persia who saved her people from being slaughtered.

es·thete (es′thēt) another spelling of **aesthete.**

es·thet·ic (es thet′ik) another spelling of **aesthetic.**

es·thet·ics (es thet′iks) another spelling of **aesthetics.**

es·ti·ma·ble (es′tə mə bəl) *adj.* worthy of or deserving high regard or respect: *The senator has an estimable reputation for honesty.* —**es′ti·ma·bly,** *adv.*

es·ti·mate (*n.,* es′tə mit; *v.,* es′tə māt′) *n.* **1.** a judgment or opinion, as of the value, quality, extent, size, or cost of something: *an estimate of the height of a mountain, an estimate of the age of an antique.* **2.** a written statement of this: *The mechanic gave us an estimate on repairing the car.* —*v.t.,* **es·ti·mat·ed, es·ti·mat·ing.** to form a judgment or opinion of; calculate: *We estimated that the trip would take three hours.*

es·ti·ma·tion (es′tə mā′shən) *n.* **1.** a judgment or opinion: *The plan was a good one in their estimation.* **2.** the act of estimating. **3.** a favorable opinion; regard or respect; esteem: *a leader held in the highest estimation by everyone.*

es·ti·vate (es′tə vāt′) *v.i.,* **es·ti·vat·ed, es·ti·vat·ing.** to spend the summer in a dormant or inactive state, as some animals do.

Es·to·ni·an (es tō′nē ən) *adj.* of or relating to Estonia or its people. —*n.* **1.** a person who was born in or is a citizen of Estonia. **2.** the language of Estonia.

es·trange (e strānj′) *v.t.,* **es·tranged, es·trang·ing. 1.** to turn (someone) from kind or friendly feelings to unkind or unfriendly feelings; alienate: *I estranged my friends by arguing with them constantly.* **2.** to keep apart: *The twins estranged themselves from the rest of the class.* —**es·trange′ment,** *n.*

es·tro·gen (es′trə jən) *n.* any of a group of hormones secreted by the ovaries. Estrogen causes the body to produce the female characteristics that develop during puberty.

es·trous (es′trəs) *adj.* relating to or involving estrus.

estrous cycle, a series of changes in the sexual organs and behavior of female mammals that is associated with the estrus and that prepares the females for mating and bearing young.

es·trus (es′trəs) *n.* the period during which a female mammal is able to mate and conceive; heat.

es·tu·ar·y (es′chü er′ē) *n., pl.* **es·tu·ar·ies. 1.** the mouth or lower course of a river where the current meets the sea and is affected by the tides. **2.** an arm or inlet of the sea.

–et *suffix* (used to form nouns) small: *leaflet, ringlet.*

e·ta (ā′tə, ē′tə) *n.* the seventh letter of the Greek alphabet (H, η).

é·ta·gère (ā′tə zhâr′) *n.* a piece of furniture having open shelves for the display of small decorative objects. [From the French word *étagère,* going back to the Old French word *estage* "floor, station, stage."]

et al (et al′, et äl′, et ôl′) and others. [From the Latin phrase *et alia* meaning "and others."]

etc., et cetera: *At the zoo we saw many kinds of animals: lions, tigers, monkeys, bears, etc.*

et cet·er·a (et set′ər ə) and so forth; and the rest; and others. [From the Latin phrase *et cetera* meaning "and the rest."]

etch (ech) *v.t.* **1.** to engrave (a picture or design) on a surface by means of acid. **2.** to make a picture or design on (a surface) by this method. —*v.i.* to engage in the art of etching.

etch·ing (ech′ing) *n.* **1.** the art or process of engraving a picture or design on a surface, usually of metal, by means of acid. After the surface of the plate is waxed, the design is scratched into the wax. The plate is then dipped into an acid solution, which eats away the exposed parts. **2.** an etched figure, design, or plate. **3.** an impression or print made by covering an etched plate with ink and running it through a printing press, thus transferring the design to a piece of paper.

e·ter·nal (i tûr′nəl) *adj.* **1.** without beginning or end; lasting forever. **2.** forever the same; never changing: *the eternal laws of nature.* **3.** seeming to last or continue forever; perpetual: *We complained about the eternal noise of the construction next door.* —*n.* **the Eternal.** God. —**e·ter′nal·ly,** *adv.*

e·ter·ni·ty (i tûr′ni tē) *n., pl.* **e·ter·ni·ties. 1.** time without beginning or end; infinite time. **2.** all future time, especially the time after death. **3.** a seemingly endless length of time: *I waited an eternity in the dentist's office.*

–eth *suffix* used to form the archaic third person singular of verbs: *doeth.*

eth·a·nol (eth′ə nôl′) another word for **alcohol** (*def. 1*).

at; āpe; fär; câre; end; mē; it; īce; pîerce; hot; ōld; sông, fôrk; oil; out; up; ūse; rüle; pùll; tûrn; chin; sing; shop; thin; **th**is; hw in white; zh in treasure. The symbol ə stands for the unstressed vowel sound heard in about, taken, pencil, lemon, and circus.

e·ther (ē′thər) *n.* a colorless, flammable liquid with a strong, sweetish odor, used especially as an anesthetic and as a solvent.

e·the·re·al (i thîr′ē əl) *adj.* **1.** very light and delicate; airy: *ethereal music.* **2.** of or relating to heaven or the heavens; heavenly. —**e·the′re·al·ly,** *adv.*

eth·i·cal (eth′i kəl) *adj.* **1.** of or relating to ethics or standards of right and wrong. **2.** according to accepted standards of conduct, especially the standards or code of a profession: *It is not ethical for a lawyer to reveal information about a client's case.* —**eth′i·cal·ly,** *adv.*

eth·ics (eth′iks) *pl. n.* **1.** a branch of philosophy that deals with human conduct, the meaning of moral codes, and the standards for judging right and wrong. ▲ used with a singular verb. **2.** standards of conduct, as of a profession: *the ethics of the medical profession.* ▲ used with a plural verb.

E·thi·o·pi·an (ē′thē ō′pē ən) *adj.* of or relating to Ethiopia, its people, or their culture. —*n.* a person who was born in or is a citizen of Ethiopia.

eth·nic (eth′nik) *adj.* of or relating to a group of people having certain characteristics in common, such as language, culture, history, race, or national origin.

eth·no·log·i·cal (eth′nə loj′i kəl) *adj.* of or relating to ethnology. —**eth′no·log′i·cal·ly,** *adv.*

eth·nol·o·gy (eth nol′ə jē) *n.* **1.** the study and comparison of the cultures of living peoples. **2.** the study of the various racial and ethnic groups of the world, and of their origin, characteristics, customs, cultures, and distribution.

e·thol·o·gy (ē thol′ə jē) *n.* the study of the behavior of animals in their natural environment.

eth·yl (eth′əl) *n.* a chemical radical present in many compounds, such as ether and ethyl alcohol.

ethyl alcohol, see **alcohol** (def. 1).

eth·yl·ene (eth′ə lēn′) *n.* a colorless, flammable gas that is usually obtained from petroleum and natural gas. It is used to improve the color of citrus fruits.

ethylene gly·col (glī′kôl) a liquid chemical used as an antifreeze for automobile engines.

et·i·quette (et′i kit, et′i ket′) *n.* **1.** forms of proper or polite behavior in society; good manners. **2.** rules for proper or formal conduct in a specific area, such as a profession or official ceremony: *the etiquette of diplomacy.*

E·trus·can (i trus′kən) *adj.* of, like, or relating to Etruria. —*n.* **1.** a person who lived in Etruria. **2.** the language of Etruria.

–ette *suffix* (used to form nouns) **1.** small: *kitchenette.* **2.** female: *majorette.* **3.** a substitute for or imitation of: *Leatherette.*

é·tude (ā′tüd, ā′tūd) *n.* a musical composition for a solo instrument, intended mainly for practice. [From the French word *étude* meaning "a study," from the Latin word *studium* "zeal, application."]

et·y·mo·log·i·cal (et′ə mə loj′i kəl) *adj.* of or relating to etymology. —**et′y·mo·log′i·cal·ly,** *adv.*

et·y·mol·o·gist (et′ə mol′ə jist) *n.* a student of or an expert in etymology.

et·y·mol·o·gy (et′ə mol′ə jē) *n., pl.* **et·y·mol·o·gies.** **1.** the history of a word, tracing it from its origin to its present form, including the changes in spelling and meaning that have taken place. **2.** the study of the history of words.

Language Note

An **etymology** traces the history of a word from its earliest roots to its modern form in our language. People used to feel that the purpose of tracing the history of a word was to learn its "true" meaning and "proper" usage. However, the belief that the original meaning of a word is its correct meaning was rejected in the nineteenth century. At that time, etymologies were studied by scholars who were interested in discovering the origin of words, not in establishing how the words should be used. Modern scholars go even further in their study of etymologies. They study a word not only with respect to its own history, but also with respect to the history, culture, and language of the people who have created and used the word.

If the origin and history of a word are known, the word will be recognized as a native word or as a borrowing from another language. Native words can be traced back to Old English and can be shown to be related to similar words in other Germanic languages. Most of the words in a dictionary of English are not native, but are borrowings from other languages. Borrowings arise from various kinds of contact between English and another language. For example, when the Normans invaded England, they gave the English language many French words. When the explorers and colonists appeared in America, they often borrowed American Indian words to name the new things they encountered in the New World.

The etymologies of older words are, in fact, often more easily discovered than those of modern words. Today, with increased travel and such modern forms of mass communication as radio and television, words come into our language at a faster rate than at any other time in history. Tracing the origins of these new words is often difficult and sometimes impossible. The precise origin of the new word *reggae*, used for a style of music, is not known, even though scholars believe that it must come from some language spoken in the Caribbean.

Although some words have interesting etymologies, such as *boycott, tantalize,* and *candidate,* most words can be traced back to simple origins that are of interest mainly to linguists. Because of this, the dictionary omits many etymologies that would not be of special interest to the reader. It does include those etymologies that provide an interesting or surprising story about the history of a word or that provide a good example of some type of linguistic process or principle.

Eu, the symbol for europium.

eu·ca·lyp·tus (ū′kə lip′təs) *n., pl.* **eu·ca·lyp·tus·es** or **eu·ca·lyp·ti** (ū′kə lip′tī). any of a large group of evergreen trees or shrubs widely grown in warm climates for their hard, durable wood, resins, and oils.

Eu·cha·rist (ū′kə rist) *n.* another term for **Holy Communion.**

Eu·cha·ris·tic (ū′kə ris′tik) *adj.* of or relating to the Eucharist.

eu·gen·ic (ū jen′ik) *adj.* **1.** relating to the improvement of the human race according to the principles of eugenics. **2.** of or relating to eugenics. —**eu·gen′i·cal·ly,** *adv.*

eu·gen·ics (ū jen′iks) *n.* the study of the improvement of the human race by controlling heredity, as by a careful selection of parents. ▲ used with a singular verb.

eu·gle·na (ū glē′nə) *n.* a microscopic, green, one-celled organism that lives in water.

eu·lo·gist (ū′lə jist) *n.* a person who eulogizes.

eu·lo·gis·tic (ū′lə jis′tik) *adj.* of or relating to eulogy; praising.

eu·lo·gize (ū′lə jīz′) *v.t.,* **eu·lo·gized, eu·lo·giz·ing.** to praise highly in speech or writing; deliver a eulogy about.

eu·lo·gy (ū′lə jē) *n., pl.* **eu·lo·gies.** a speech or writing in praise of a person or thing, especially a person who has just died: *to deliver a eulogy at a funeral.*

eu·nuch (ū′nək) *n.* **1.** a castrated man. **2.** a castrated man in the service of an Oriental ruler as a court official or harem guard.

eu·phe·mism (ū′fə miz′əm) *n.* **1.** the use of a mild word or expression in place of a blunt or harsh one. **2.** a word or expression used in this way.

Language Note

A **euphemism** is a mild, vague, or polite word or phrase that is used in place of one that is more precise, blunt, or realistic. Every society judges some actions, things, or concepts to be too disagreeable, offensive, or shocking to be referred to directly. When something is thought of in this way, so are the words that refer to it. Euphemisms are created to replace these unacceptable or forbidden words.

For example, it was once acceptable to refer to a country that was not as economically, educationally, and politically advanced as our own as *primitive* or *backward*. These words were rejected as sounding too arrogant and disdainful and were replaced by the milder term *under-developed*. This word was also in turn rejected, and the more positive term *emerging* is now being used in its place. Obviously, the condition being described has not changed. What has changed is the way that people feel about the words that describe the condition.

In the nineteenth century, many words that referred to the body and to sex were considered taboo. For example, the word *leg* was replaced by the euphemism *limb*. This prudishness was sometimes carried to ridiculous lengths. An English novelist visiting America in 1837 wrote with surprise of having heard the legs of a piano being called its limbs.

The most difficult and frightening things for most people to talk about are aging and death, and a great many of our modern euphemisms refer to them. We say that people *depart, pass on, pass away,* or *are no longer with us* because these words sound less harsh and final than the word *die*. A person who is over sixty-five years old is less likely to be described as *old* and more likely to be called a *senior citizen*. Poverty is another subject that we, in a land of great wealth, try to treat euphemistically. So we often refer to the poor as being *underprivileged, economically deprived,* or *members of a low-income group,* rather than simply as being *poor*. A *slum* is often called a *depressed area* or even *the inner city*.

The purpose of language is to communicate, but the use of euphemisms is often, at best, an attempt not to communicate and, at worst, it can be an attempt to deceive.

---

eu·phe·mis·tic (ū′fə mis′tik) *adj.* of or using euphemisms; serving as a euphemism. —**eu′phe·mis′ti·cal·ly,** *adv.*

eu·pho·ni·ous (ū fō′nē əs) *adj.* pleasant and agreeable in sound; pleasant to hear: *The call of a nightingale is more euphonious than the call of a crow.* —**eu·pho′ni·ous·ly,** *adv.*

eu·pho·ni·um (ū fō′nē əm) *n.* a brass musical instrument shaped like a tuba but having a more mellow tone. Some euphoniums have two bells.

eu·pho·ny (ū′fə nē) *n., pl.* **eu·pho·nies.** the quality of having a pleasant sound.

eu·pho·ri·a (ū fôr′ē ə) *n.* a feeling of well-being and great happiness.

Eur. 1. Europe. 2. European.

Eur·a·sian (yù rā′zhən) *adj.* 1. of or relating to Eurasia. 2. of mixed European and Asian descent. —*n.* a person who is of mixed European and Asian descent.

eu·re·ka (yù rē′kə) *interj.* used as an exclamation of triumph upon the sudden discovery of something or the solving of a problem. [From the Greek exclamation *heurēka* meaning "I have found (it)!" Archimedes supposedly said this when he discovered the test for determining the purity of gold.]

Eu·ro·pe·an (yùr′ə pē′ən) *adj.* of or relating to Europe or its people. —*n.* 1. a person who was born in Europe or is a citizen of a European country. 2. a person of European descent.

European Economic Community, the official name of the **Common Market.**

eu·ro·pi·um (yù rō′pē əm) *n.* a metallic element of the rare-earth group, used in nuclear reactors and in color-television tubes. Symbol: **Eu** [From *Europa,* Latin form of the word *Europe.*]

Eu·sta·chi·an tube (ū stā′shən, ū stā′kē ən) a canal or passage extending from the pharynx to the middle ear. The Eustachian tube equalizes the air pressure on the inside of the eardrum with the atmospheric pressure on the outside. [From the Italian anatomist Bartolommeo *Eustachio* (1524?–1574), who discovered it.]

eu·tha·na·sia (ū′thə nā′zhə) *n.* the painless killing of a person suffering from a painful and incurable disease. Also, **mercy killing.**

eu·troph·i·ca·tion (ū trof′i kā′shən) *n.* a process affecting lakes and other bodies of water, in which an increase in the nutrients in the water causes algae to increase abnormally. The amount of oxygen in the water decreases, and plants and fish die as a result.

EVA, extravehicular activity.

e·vac·u·ate (i vak′ū āt′) *v.t.,* **e·vac·u·at·ed, e·vac·u·at·ing.** 1. to leave or make empty; vacate: *The troops evacuated their position. Police evacuated the theater.* 2. to cause to leave; remove: *Firefighters evacuated the tenants from the burning building.* 3. to discharge waste matter from: *to evacuate the bowels.* 4. to discharge (waste matter): *to evacuate feces.*

e·vac·u·a·tion (i vak′ū ā′shən) *n.* 1. the act of evacuating or the state of being evacuated. 2. the discharge of waste matter from the body, especially from the bladder or bowels.

e·vac·u·ee (i vak′ū ē′, i vak′ū ē′) *n.* a person removed from an area of danger or disaster: *The evacuees from the flooded area were housed in the school.*

e·vade (i vād′) *v.t.,* **e·vad·ed, e·vad·ing.** 1. to avoid, as by trickery or cunning; elude: *The fox evaded the hounds and hunters.* 2. to escape or avoid the responsibility of: *to evade taxes.* 3. to avoid answering: *to evade a question.*

e·val·u·ate (i val′ū āt′) *v.t.,* **e·val·u·at·ed, e·val·u·at·ing.** 1. to establish the value or amount of; appraise: *to evaluate a stamp collection.* 2. to determine the meaning or importance of; assess: *The diplomat was asked to evaluate the peace talks.*

e·val·u·a·tion (i val′ū ā′shən) *n.* 1. the act or process of evaluating. 2. the result of evaluating; appraisal or judgment.

ev·a·nes·cence (ev′ə nes′əns) *n.* a gradual passing or fading away: *the evanescence of a rainbow.*

ev·a·nes·cent (ev′ə nes′ənt) *adj.* tending to pass or fade away gradually; fleeting.

e·van·gel·i·cal (ē′van jel′i kəl) *adj.* 1. of, in, or according to the four Gospels or the New Testament. 2. teaching that salvation of the soul is achieved through a personal conversion to religious faith in Jesus, and that the Bible is the only religious authority: *an evangelical church.* —*n.* a person who belongs to an evangelical church. —**e′van·gel′i·cal·ly,** *adv.*

e·van·gel·ism (i van′jə liz′əm) *n.* enthusiastic preaching or spreading of the Gospel, as by traveling preachers or at revival meetings; work of evangelists.

---

at; āpe; fär; câre; end; mē; it; īce; pîerce; hot; ōld; sông, fôrk; oil; out; up; ūse; rüle; pull; tûrn; chin; sing; shop; thin; this; hw in white; zh in treasure. The symbol ə stands for the unstressed vowel sound heard in about, taken, pencil, lemon, and circus.

e·van·gel·ist (i van′jə list) *n.* **1.** a preacher of the Gospel, especially one who travels from place to place and holds religious meetings. **2. Evangelist.** one of the four authors of the Gospels: Matthew, Mark, Luke, or John.

e·van·gel·is·tic (i van′jə lis′tik) *adj.* **1.** of or relating to the Evangelists. **2.** of or relating to evangelists or evangelism.

e·vap·o·rate (i vap′ə rāt′) *v.,* **e·vap·o·rat·ed, e·vap·o·rat·ing.** —*v.i.* **1.** to be changed from a liquid or solid into a vapor: *Water evaporates when boiled.* **2.** to fade away or disappear; vanish: *Their fears evaporated when the lost child reappeared.* —*v.t.* **1.** to cause (a liquid or solid) to change into a vapor: *The sun soon evaporated the morning dew.* **2.** to remove moisture from, as by heating: *to evaporate milk.*

evaporated milk, unsweetened canned milk, made by removing some of the water from whole milk.

e·vap·o·ra·tion (i vap′ə rā′shən) *n.* **1.** a change from a liquid or solid state into a vapor; vaporization. **2.** the removal of moisture or liquid.

e·vap·o·ra·tor (i vap′ə rā′tər) *n.* an apparatus for removing moisture or liquid.

e·va·sion (i vā′zhən) *n.* **1.** the act of evading something, such as a duty or question: *to be charged with income tax evasion.* **2.** the means of evading something: *Changing the subject in response to a question is an evasion.*

e·va·sive (i vā′siv) *adj.* that evades or tends to evade; characterized by evasion: *evasive answers, an evasive person.* —**e·va′sive·ly,** *adv.* —**e·va′sive·ness,** *n.*

eve (ēv) *n.* **1.** also, **Eve.** the evening or day just before a holiday or other important day. **2.** the period just before an important happening: *the eve of an election, the eve of an invasion.* **3.** evening. ▲ used in literature.

e·ven¹ (ē′vən) *adj.* **1.** without slope or hills; completely flat; level: *an even piece of ground, even countryside.* **2.** at the same level; of uniform height: *The two mountain peaks looked even in the distance.* **3.** the same throughout; equally distributed: *an even coat of paint.* **4.** free from variations or sudden changes; regular; constant: *an even rhythm, an even heartbeat.* **5.** not easily excited; calm: *an even disposition.* **6.** the same or equal, as in amount, size, or quantity: *The score in the game was even.* **7.** that can be divided exactly by two: *Four is an even number.* **8.** exact: *I ran an even mile.* **9.** on equal terms: *Pay me back the quarter and we'll be even.* —*adv.* **1.** at the very same moment; while; just: *They came ashore even as the sun was setting.* **2.** as a matter of fact; actually; indeed: *to be happy, even joyous.* **3.** though it may seem unlikely: *They were generous even to strangers.* **4.** in comparison; still; yet: *Today's weather is even better than yesterday's.* —*v.t.* to make even: *The steamroller evened the road surface. The last touchdown evened the score of the game.* [From the Old English word *efen* meaning "level, equal."] —**e′ven·ly,** *adv.* —**e′ven·ness,** *n.*

·**to get even with.** to get revenge upon: *I'll get even with them for trying to cheat me.*

e·ven² (ē′vən) *n.* evening. ▲ used in literature. [From the Old English word *æfen* meaning "evening."]

e·ven·hand·ed (ē′vən han′did) *adj.* not biased; impartial; fair; just: *an evenhanded decision, an evenhanded referee.*

eve·ning (ēv′ning) *n.* **1.** the period following the afternoon and continuing through early nighttime; period from twilight to bedtime. **2.** the last part or closing period, as of a life. —*adj.* of, relating to, or occurring in the evening: *evening classes, the evening meal.*

evening star, the first planet, most often Venus or rarely Mercury, to appear after sunset in the western sky.

e·ven·song (ē′vən sông′) *n.* **1.** in the Anglican Church, a prayer service said or sung in the evening. **2.** in the Roman Catholic Church, vespers.

e·vent (i vent′) *n.* **1.** anything that happens, especially a happening of some importance. **2.** any of the contests in a program or series of sports: *The mile run was the main event in the track meet.* **3.** the outcome of anything; result; conclusion.

·**in any event.** in any case; at any rate; whatever happens.

·**in the event of.** if (something) should occur; in case of: *In the event of rain, the game will be played tomorrow.*

e·ven–tem·pered (ē′vən tem′pərd) *adj.* not easily disturbed, excited, or angered; calm.

e·vent·ful (i vent′fəl) *adj.* **1.** marked by important or interesting happenings: *an eventful year.* **2.** having important results; momentous: *an eventful meeting.*

e·ven·tide (ē′vən tīd′) *n.* evening. ▲ used in literature.

e·ven·tu·al (i ven′chü əl) *adj.* **1.** happening at some time in the future; bound to occur: *The eventual death of the dictator will bring chaos.* **2.** resulting from events that go before; final; ultimate: *The eventual outcome of the project will depend on how much money is raised.*

e·ven·tu·al·i·ty (i ven′chü al′i tē) *n., pl.* **e·ven·tu·al·i·ties.** a possible event or condition; possibility.

e·ven·tu·al·ly (i ven′chü ə lē) *adv.* in the end; ultimately; finally.

ev·er (ev′ər) *adv.* **1.** at any time: *Did you ever go to Ireland?* **2.** at all times; always: *to be ever willing to help a friend.* **3.** throughout all time: *They lived happily ever after.* **4.** in any possible way: *How can we ever repay you?*

·**ever so.** *Informal.* very; exceedingly; extremely: *The salesclerk was ever so helpful.*

▲ In informal speech *ever* is used to give emphasis to a question or exclamation: *What ever do you mean? Was it ever hot at the beach today!*

ev·er·glade (ev′ər glād′) *n.* a large region of low, marshy land partly covered with tall grass.

everglade

ev·er·green (ev′ər grēn′) *adj.* (of shrubs, trees, or other plants) having green leaves or needles throughout the year. —*n.* an evergreen shrub, tree, or other plant.

ev·er·last·ing (ev′ər las′ting) *adj.* **1.** existing, continuing, or lasting forever; eternal. **2.** lasting for a long time: *everlasting joy.*

ev·er·more (ev′ər môr′) *adv.* for and at all times; forever; eternally.

eve·ry (ev′rē) *adj.* **1.** each of the persons or things that make up a group or whole; each without excepting any: *Every student in the class was present today.* **2.** all possible; the utmost: *I have every confidence in your ability.* **3.** at a regular interval of: *The pills should be taken every four hours.*

•**every bit.** in every way; entirely; quite: *You're every bit as smart as they are.*

•**every now and then** or **every now and again.** from time to time; occasionally: *They come to visit us every now and then.*

•**every other.** each alternate; each second: *That program is broadcast every other week.*

•**every so often.** from time to time; occasionally.

eve·ry·bod·y (ev′rē bod′ē, ev′rē bud′ē) *pron.* every person. ▲ **Everybody** and **everyone** are both singular. In formal usage, they are used with a singular pronoun: *Everyone should do his or her share of the work.* In informal usage, they are sometimes used with a plural pronoun: *Everybody raised their hands to answer the question.*

eve·ry·day (ev′rē dā′) *adj.* **1.** of or relating to every day; daily: *everyday chores.* **2.** suitable for ordinary days: *everyday clothes.* **3.** not unusual; commonplace; ordinary: *an everyday occurrence.*

eve·ry·one (ev′rē wun′) *pron.* every person; everybody: *Everyone agreed that it was a good movie.* ▲ See **everybody** for usage note.

eve·ry·thing (ev′rē thing′) *pron.* **1.** all things; all: *We took everything we needed for the trip.* **2.** what is important, highly valued, or very much wanted: *Their grandchildren meant everything to them.*

eve·ry·where (ev′rē hwâr′, ev′rē wâr′) *adv.* in every place; in all places: *They traveled everywhere in England during their long trip.*

e·vict (i vikt′) *v.t.* to throw out or remove (a tenant) from a building or other property; dispossess: *The tenant was evicted for not paying the rent for several months.* —**e·vic′tion,** *n.*

ev·i·dence (ev′i dəns) *n.* **1.** something that serves to prove or disprove a belief or conclusion; proof: *The scientists produced much research as evidence for their theory.* **2.** the statements of witnesses or other material used to prove something in a court of law. **3.** an indication or sign: *Their silence was evidence of their anger.* —*v.t.,* **ev·i·denced, ev·i·denc·ing.** to give proof of; show clearly; demonstrate: *Lines of people waiting to buy tickets evidenced the play's success.*

•**in evidence.** plainly seen; easily noticed: *The effects of the war were very much in evidence.*

ev·i·dent (ev′i dənt) *adj.* easily seen or understood; clear; apparent: *It was evident that no one understood the lecturer.*

ev·i·dent·ly (ev′i dənt lē) *adv.* clearly; apparently; obviously: *It is cloudy and windy outside, so evidently a storm is approaching.*

e·vil (ē′vəl) *adj.* **1.** morally bad; wicked; sinful: *an evil person, evil thoughts.* **2.** causing trouble or injury; harmful: *an evil custom, evil laws.* **3.** characterized by or threatening misfortune or suffering; disastrous; unlucky: *an evil omen, evil times.* —*n.* **1.** the state or condition of being morally bad; wickedness; sin: *The dictator's rule was a reign of evil. The sermon was about good and evil.* **2.** something that causes trouble or injury; something harmful: *War is a great evil.* —**e′vil·ly,** *adv.* —**e′vil·ness,** *n.*

e·vince (i vins′) *v.t.,* **e·vinced, e·vinc·ing.** to make evident; show clearly: *I evinced my anger by banging my fist on the table.*

e·vis·cer·ate (i vis′ə rāt′) *v.t.,* **e·vis·cer·at·ed, e·vis·cer·at·ing.** **1.** to remove the internal organs, especially the intestines, from; disembowel. **2.** to take away the force or meaning of: *The bill was eviscerated before being passed by the legislature.* —**e·vis′cer·a′tion,** *n.*

ev·o·ca·tion (ē′vō kā′shən, ev′ə kā′shən) *n.* the act of evoking.

e·voc·a·tive (i vok′ə tiv) *adj.* tending, serving, or having the power to evoke, especially memories, emotions, or the like: *a peaceful afternoon evocative of childhood summers in the country.*

e·voke (i vōk′) *v.t.,* **e·voked, e·vok·ing.** to call forth or bring out; elicit: *The reporter's question evoked an angry response. The song evoked happy memories.*

ev·o·lu·tion (ev′ə lü′shən) *n.* **1.** a gradual process of development, growth, or change through a series of stages: *the evolution of music, the evolution of a society.* **2.** *Biology.* **a.** gradual change in groups of plants, animals, or other living things, resulting from tiny changes in the genes that are passed from one generation to the next over many years. **b.** the theory that all living plants and animals arose from earlier and simpler forms of life over millions of generations. **3.** *Mathematics.* the process of extracting the root of a number.

ev·o·lu·tion·ary (ev′ə lü′shə ner′ē) *adj.* **1.** of, relating to, or resulting from gradual development or growth. **2.** of, relating to, or agreeing with the theory of evolution.

ev·o·lu·tion·ist (ev′ə lü′shə nist) *n.* a person who believes in or supports the theory of evolution.

e·volve (i volv′) *v.,* **e·volved, e·volv·ing.** —*v.t.* to develop gradually; work out: *to evolve a new scientific theory.* —*v.i.* **1.** to undergo gradual development or growth. **2.** *Biology.* to undergo evolution.

ewe (ū) *n.* an adult female sheep.

ew·er (ū′ər) *n.* a wide-mouthed pitcher, used especially for holding or pouring water.

ex– *prefix* **1.** out of or from: *exhale, exit, export.* **2.** thoroughly; completely: *exasperate.* **3.** former; previous. **3.** followed by a hyphen and another word to form a compound: *ex-president, ex-employee.*

ewer

ex. **1.** examined. **2.** example.

Ex., Exodus.

ex·ac·er·bate (eg zas′ər bāt′) *v.t.,* **ex·ac·er·bat·ed, ex·ac·er·bat·ing.** to make more intense, severe, or bitter, as pain or feelings: *If you say anything more to them, it will only exacerbate the bad feelings between you.*

ex·act (eg zakt′) *adj.* **1.** very accurate; precise; correct: *The clock gives the exact time. I gave the clerk a check for the exact amount.* **2.** being the same in every way: *an exact copy.* **3.** characterized by or showing accuracy: *an exact thinker.* —*v.t.* to demand and get by force or authority: *to exact the payment of a debt on time, to exact obedience to a command.* —**exact′ness,** *n.*

ex·act·ing (eg zak′ting) *adj.* **1.** very demanding; strict; severe: *an exacting teacher.* **2.** requiring great skill, accuracy, care, or attention: *an exacting task.*

ex·ac·tion (eg zak′shən) *n.* **1.** the act of exacting. **2.** something that is exacted, such as taxes, duties, or tribute.

ex·act·i·tude (eg zak′ti tüd′, eg zak′ti tūd′) *n.* the quality of being exact; accuracy; precision.

ex·act·ly (eg zakt′lē) *adv.* **1.** in an exact manner; accurately; precisely: *to follow instructions exactly.* **2.** entirely or quite: *The accident happened exactly as the witness described it.*

ex·ag·ger·ate (eg zaj′ə rāt′) *v.,* **ex·ag·ger·at·ed, ex-**

---

at; āpe; fär; câre; end; mē; it; īce; pîerce; hot; ōld; sông, fôrk; oil; out; up; ūse; rüle; pull; tûrn; chin; sing; shop; thin; this; hw in white; zh in treasure. The symbol ə stands for the unstressed vowel sound heard in about, taken, pencil, lemon, and circus.

ag·ger·at·ing. —v.t. **1.** to make (something) seem more, larger, or greater than it is; overstate: *to exaggerate the seriousness of a problem, to exaggerate a person's faults.* **2.** to make more noticeable or more important than usual: *The mimes exaggerated their gestures and facial expressions.* —v.i. to make something seem more, larger, or greater than it is; overstate: *I exaggerated when describing the fish I had caught.*

ex·ag·ger·a·tion (eg zaj′ə rā′shən) n. **1.** the act of exaggerating or the state of being exaggerated. **2.** an instance of exaggerating; overstatement: *Their description of their travel adventures was an exaggeration.*

ex·alt (eg zôlt′) v.t. **1.** to praise; glorify; extol: *to exalt honesty above all other virtues.* **2.** to raise, as in rank, position, character, or esteem.

ex·al·ta·tion (eg′zôl tā′shən, ek′sôl tā′shən) n. **1.** the act of exalting or the state of being exalted. **2.** a feeling of great joy, delight, or pride; elation.

ex·alt·ed (eg zôl′tid) adj. **1.** high, as in rank, position, or character: *an exalted member of the medical profession.* **2.** noble, lofty, elevated, or sublime: *exalted prose.*

ex·am (eg zam′) n. see **examination**.

ex·am·i·na·tion (eg zam′ə nā′shən) n. **1.** the act or process of examining: *The examination of the office files lasted one hour.* **2.** a test, especially of knowledge, skill, or qualifications: *I had an examination in chemistry.* **3.** a checking and testing of the body or a part of the body, as by a dentist or physician. **4.** a questioning of a witness in a court of law.

ex·am·ine (eg zam′in) v.t., **ex·am·ined, ex·am·in·ing.** **1.** to look at closely and carefully; investigate; inspect: *to examine merchandise before buying it.* **2.** to test, especially in order to check or learn the knowledge or skill of: *to examine applicants for a job.* **3.** to subject (a person or body part) to checking and testing, as by a physician or a dentist. **4.** to question (a witness) in a court of law. —**ex·am·in·er,** n.

ex·am·ple (eg zam′pəl) n. **1.** one particular thing belonging to a group of things, that serves to show what the others are like; sample; illustration: *The art teacher hung several examples of the painter's work on the wall.* **2.** a person or thing that is worthy of imitation; model: *That student's study habits are a good example for others to follow.* **3.** a problem or exercise used to illustrate a rule, method, or process, as in arithmetic. **4.** something used to serve as a warning to others: *The judge made an example of the criminals by giving them harsher sentences than expected.*

·**for example.** by way of illustration; for instance.

·**to set an example.** to serve as a model for others: *The older children were asked to set an example for the younger ones.*

ex·as·per·ate (eg zas′pə rāt′) v.t., **ex·as·per·at·ed, ex·as·per·at·ing.** to irritate greatly; provoke to anger; infuriate: *The child's constant crying exasperated the babysitter.*

ex·as·per·a·tion (eg zas′pə rā′shən) n. the act of exasperating or the state of being exasperated.

Ex·cal·i·bur (eks kal′ə bər) n. the legendary sword of King Arthur.

ex·ca·vate (eks′kə vāt′) v.t., **ex·ca·vat·ed, ex·ca·vat·ing.** **1.** to remove by digging: *The workers excavated the dirt at the housing site with a steam shovel.* **2.** to uncover by digging; unearth: *The archaeologists excavated the ruins of an ancient city.* **3.** to make by hollowing out; dig: *The miners excavated a tunnel in the side of the mountain.* **4.** to make a hole in; hollow out: *They excavated the mountainside for a tunnel.*

ex·ca·va·tion (eks′kə vā′shən) n. **1.** the act or process of excavating. **2.** a hole made by excavating: *A new building will go up on the site of the excavation.* **3.** something uncovered by excavating, such as ruins.

ex·ca·va·tor (eks′kə vā′tər) n. a person or thing that excavates, especially a machine used for digging, such as a steam shovel.

ex·ceed (ek sēd′) v.t. **1.** to go beyond the limit of: *The driver exceeded the speed limit. The contributions exceeded $10,000.* **2.** to be greater than or superior to; surpass: *Your knowledge of history exceeds mine.*

ex·ceed·ing (ek sē′ding) adj. unusually great; surpassing. —adv. Archaic. another word for **exceedingly.**

ex·ceed·ing·ly (ek sē′ding lē) adv. unusually; extremely.

excavator

ex·cel (ek sel′) v., **ex·celled, ex·cel·ling.** —v.t. to be better or greater than, as in ability or quality; surpass; outdo. —v.i. to be better or greater than others; surpass others: *to excel in music and art.*

ex·cel·lence (ek′sə ləns) n. the fact or state of excelling; superiority, as in ability or quality.

ex·cel·len·cy (ek′sə lən sē) n., pl. **ex·cel·len·cies. 1.** another word for **excellence. 2. Excellency.** a title of honor or form of address used in referring or speaking to governors, ambassadors, or other high officials. ▲ often preceded by *His, Her,* or *Your.*

ex·cel·lent (ek′sə lənt) adj. remarkably good; superior; exceptional. —**ex′cel·lent·ly,** adv.

ex·cel·si·or (ek sel′sē ər) n. fine shavings, as of wood or paper, used as a packing material or stuffing.

ex·cept (ek sept′) prep. with the exception of; excluding; but: *Everyone went to the party except me.* —conj. only; but: *I would go with you, except that I have to work.* —v.t. to leave out; exclude or omit: *to except certain students from the final examination.*

ex·cept·ing (ek sep′ting) prep. with the exception of; except: *a store open every day excepting Sundays.*

ex·cep·tion (ek sep′shən) n. **1.** the act of excepting or the state of being excepted. **2.** a person or thing that is left out or is different from others.

·**to take exception.** to object; protest: *to take exception to an insulting remark.*

ex·cep·tion·a·ble (ek sep′shə nə bəl) adj. tending to cause objection; objectionable: *an insulting, exceptionable comment.* —**ex·cep′tion·a·bly,** adv.

ex·cep·tion·al (ek sep′shə nəl) adj. out of the ordinary; unusual; extraordinary: *exceptional talent, an exceptional student.* —**ex·cep′tion·al·ly,** adv.

ex·cerpt (n., ek′sûrpt; v., ek sûrpt′) n. a passage or scene selected from a larger work: *to read excerpts from a book, to see excerpts from a new film.* —v.t. to take out a passage or scene from; extract; quote: *to excerpt a novel.*

ex·cess (ek′ses, ek ses′) n., pl. **ex·cess·es. 1.** an amount greater than what is usual, needed, or desired; more than enough: *An excess of water in the river caused a flood.* **2.** an amount or degree by which one thing is greater than another: *I spent an excess of ten dollars over my budget.* **3.** a doing of any action to a harmful degree: *to avoid excess in eating candy.* —adj. being greater than what is usual, needed, or desired; extra: *excess baggage on an airplane.*

·**in excess of.** greater or more than: *Their bank balance was in excess of $500.*

·**to excess.** too much: *to eat to excess.*

ex·ces·sive (ek ses′iv) *adj.* beyond what is necessary, usual, or proper; immoderate: *to spend an excessive amount of money on clothes.* —**ex·ces′sive·ly,** *adv.* —**ex·ces′sive·ness,** *n.*

ex·change (eks chānj′) *v.t.,* **ex·changed, ex·chang·ing.** **1.** to give and receive (similar things): *The friends exchanged gifts.* **2.** to give (one thing) in return for something similar: *I exchanged American dollars for British pounds when I arrived in London.* **3.** to give up for something in return: *By going to prison, the thief exchanged a life of ease for one of hard labor.* **4.** to return (a purchase) for something else: *to exchange a sweater for a shirt.* —*n.* **1.** the act of giving and receiving: *an exchange of prisoners of war.* **2.** the act of giving one thing in return for another: *the exchange of a purchase.* **3.** something that is given or received in return for something else: *a poor exchange.* **4.** a place where things, such as commodities or securities, are bought, sold, or traded: *a jewelry exchange.* **5.** a central office where telephone lines are connected for a town or part of a large city.

ex·change·a·ble (eks chān′jə bəl) *adj.* that can be exchanged: *Merchandise bought on sale is not exchangeable.* —**ex·change′a·bil′i·ty,** *n.*

ex·cheq·uer (eks chek′ər) *n.* **1.** a royal or national treasury. **2.** any treasury, as of an organization. **3. Exchequer.** the department of the British government that manages the national finances, including the collection and spending of the public revenue.

ex·cise[1] (ek′sīz) *n.* an indirect tax on the manufacture, sale, or use of certain things, such as liquor, tobacco, or gasoline. Also, **excise tax.** [From the Middle Dutch word *excijs* with the same meaning, from the Old French word *acceis* "tax," going back to the Latin words *ad* meaning "to, toward" and *census* "register of citizens," "tax."]

ex·cise[2] (ek sīz′) *v.t.,* **ex·cised, ex·cis·ing.** to remove by cutting: *to excise a tumor, to excise a paragraph from an essay.* [From the Latin word *excisus,* past participle of *excidere* meaning "to cut out," from the words *ex-* meaning "out, out of" + *caedere* "to cut."] —**ex·ci·sion** (ek sizh′ən), *n.*

ex·cit·a·ble (ek sī′tə bəl) *adj.* easily excited: *an excitable child.* —**ex·cit′a·bil′i·ty, ex·cit′a·ble·ness,** *n.* —**ex·cit′a·bly,** *adv.*

ex·cite (ek sīt′) *v.t.,* **ex·cit·ed, ex·cit·ing.** **1.** to stir up the mind or feelings of: *The idea of a picnic excited the children. The candidate's speech excited the crowd.* **2.** to call forth: *to excite fear, to excite curiosity.* **3.** to increase the activity of (an organ or organism); stimulate.

ex·cit·ed (ek sī′tid) *adj.* stirred up; aroused; agitated. —**ex·cit′ed·ly,** *adv.*

ex·cite·ment (ek sīt′mənt) *n.* **1.** the act of exciting or the state of being excited. **2.** something that excites.

ex·cit·ing (ek sī′ting) *adj.* causing excitement; stirring; thrilling: *exciting stories about a trip to Africa.*

ex·claim (ek sklām′) *v.t.* to speak or cry out suddenly, as in anger or surprise: *"You took my baseball but without asking me!" exclaimed my friend.*

ex·cla·ma·tion (ek′sklə mā′shən) *n.* **1.** the act of exclaiming. **2.** something exclaimed.

exclamation point, a punctuation mark (!) used after a word, phrase, or sentence to indicate an exclamation, as of anger or surprise. Also, **exclamation mark.**

ex·clam·a·to·ry (ek sklam′ə tôr′ē) *adj.* using, containing, or expressing exclamation.

ex·clude (ek sklüd′) *v.t.,* **ex·clud·ed, ex·clud·ing.** **1.** to keep from entering; shut out: *All those under sixteen were excluded from seeing the movie.* **2.** to leave out; omit: *The publisher excluded certain passages from the original book in the new edition.*

ex·clu·sion (ek sklü′zhən) *n.* the act of excluding or the state of being excluded.

ex·clu·sive (ek sklü′siv) *adj.* **1.** belonging to a single individual or group; not divided or shared: *The couple have exclusive ownership of the hotel.* **2.** open to or admitting only a certain select group: *to belong to an exclusive club.* **3.** complete; entire: *The matter will be given our exclusive attention.* **4.** being the only one of its kind; single; unique: *to give an exclusive interview.* —**ex·clu′sive·ly,** *adv.* —**ex·clu′sive·ness,** *n.*

·exclusive of. leaving out; excluding: *The price is fifty dollars, exclusive of the sales tax.*

ex·com·mu·ni·cate (eks′kə mū′ni kāt′) *v.t.,* **ex·com·mu·ni·cat·ed, ex·com·mu·ni·cat·ing.** to expel (a person) from membership in a church. —**ex′com·mu′ni·ca′tion,** *n.*

ex·co·ri·ate (ek skôr′ē āt′) *v.t.,* **ex·co·ri·at·ed, ex·co·ri·at·ing.** **1.** to strip off or scrape the skin of. **2.** to scold harshly. —**ex·co′ri·a′tion,** *n.*

ex·cre·ment (ek′skrə mənt) *n.* waste matter discharged from the body, especially from the bowels.

ex·cres·cence (ek skres′əns) *n.* any abnormal growth or addition, such as a wart or mole.

ex·crete (ek skrēt′) *v.t.,* **ex·cret·ed, ex·cret·ing.** to discharge (waste matter) from the body.

ex·cre·tion (ek skrē′shən) *n.* **1.** the act of excreting. **2.** matter excreted, such as sweat or urine.

ex·cre·to·ry (ek′skri tôr′ē) *adj.* of, relating to, or for excretion: *an excretory organ.*

ex·cru·ci·at·ing (ek skrü′shē ā′ting) *adj.* causing extreme pain or suffering; agonizing; torturous. —**ex·cru′ci·at′ing·ly,** *adv.*

ex·cul·pate (ek′skul pāt′, ek skul′pāt) *v.t.,* **ex·cul·pat·ed, ex·cul·pat·ing.** to declare free from blame or a charge of guilt; exonerate. —**ex′cul·pa′tion,** *n.*

ex·cur·sion (ek skûr′zhən, ek skûr′shən) *n.* **1.** a short trip made for a special purpose or for pleasure: *an excursion to a museum.* **2.** a round trip on a train, ship, or other public conveyance at a reduced rate: *a weekend train excursion to the seashore.*

ex·cus·a·ble (ek skū′zə bəl) *adj.* that can be forgiven; pardonable: *an excusable error.* —**ex·cus′a·bly,** *adv.*

ex·cuse (*v.,* ek skūz′; *n.,* ek skūs′) *v.t.,* **ex·cused, ex·cus·ing.** **1.** to give pardon or forgiveness to: *Please excuse us for bothering you.* **2.** to release from duty, obligation, or attendance: *The judge excused the jury. I was excused from class to go to the doctor.* **3.** to accept as understandable; disregard; overlook: *We excused the dog's barking because it was a puppy.* **4.** to serve as a reason or explanation for; justify. —*n.* **1.** a reason given in explanation; justification: *Oversleeping is not a good excuse for being late.* **2.** the act of excusing. **3.** *Informal.* example; sample: *That's a poor excuse for a sailboat.*

·to excuse oneself. a. to make an apology for oneself. **b.** to ask to be released, as from attendance or duty.

ex·e·cra·ble (ek′si krə bəl) *adj.* **1.** that deserves disgust or hatred; abominable; detestable. **2.** of poor quality; very bad. —**ex′e·cra·ble·ness,** *n.* —**ex′e·cra·bly,** *adv.*

ex·e·crate (ek′si krāt′) *v.t.,* **ex·e·crat·ed, ex·e·crat·ing.** **1.** to condemn severely; curse. **2.** to have disgust or hatred for; abominate; detest.

ex·e·cra·tion (ek′si krā′shən) *n.* **1.** the act of execrating. **2.** a curse. **3.** a person or thing that is execrated.

ex·e·cute (ek′si kūt′) *v.t.,* **ex·e·cut·ed, ex·e·cut·ing.** **1.** to carry out; fulfill: *to execute an order.* **2.** to put into effect; administer; enforce: *to execute a law.* **3.** to put to

---

at; āpe; fär; câre; end; mē; it; īce; pîerce; hot; ōld; sông, fôrk; oil; out; up; ūse; rüle; pull; tûrn; chin; sing; shop; thin; **this;** hw in white; zh in treasure. The symbol ə stands for the unstressed vowel sound heard in about, taken, pencil, lemon, and circus.

death, especially according to a legal sentence: *to execute a convicted murderer.* **4.** to produce, especially according to a plan or design: *A well-known artist executed that painting.* **5.** to carry out or make valid by doing whatever is legally required: *The lawyer executed the will.*

ex·e·cu·tion (ek'si kū'shən) *n.* **1.** the act of carrying out or putting into effect: *the execution of a plan.* **2.** the act of putting a person to death, especially by a legal sentence. **3.** the manner of producing or performing something, such as a work of art or piece of music. **4.** a carrying out or making valid by doing whatever is legally required: *the execution of a will, execution of a contract.*

ex·e·cu·tion·er (ek'si kū'shə nər) *n.* a person who puts someone to death.

ex·ec·u·tive (eg zek'yə tiv) *adj.* **1.** of, relating to, or suitable for the management of affairs in business or industry: *to hold an executive position as vice president of a company.* **2.** concerned with the administration of government or the enforcement of laws. —*n.* **1.** a person who directs or manages affairs, as of a corporation: *A meeting of the company's executives was called.* **2.** the branch of government responsible for administering laws and for managing the affairs of a nation. **3.** a person or persons that make up this branch of government.

ex·ec·u·tor (eg zek'yə tər; *def. 2 also* ek'si kū'tər) *n.* **1.** a person named in a will to carry out its terms. **2.** a person who carries out something or puts something into effect.

ex·ec·u·trix (eg zek'yə triks) *n., pl.* **ex·ec·u·trix·es.** a woman named in a will to carry out its terms.

ex·em·pla·ry (eg zem'plə rē) *adj.* **1.** serving as a model or example; worthy of imitation: *exemplary behavior.* **2.** serving as a warning: *exemplary punishment.*

ex·em·pli·fi·ca·tion (eg zem'plə fi kā'shən) *n.* **1.** the act of exemplifying. **2.** something that exemplifies; model or example.

ex·em·pli·fy (eg zem'plə fī') *v.t.,* **ex·em·pli·fied, ex·em·pli·fy·ing.** to serve as a model or example of; show by example.

ex·empt (eg zempt') *v.t.* to free from a duty or requirement; excuse: *to be exempted from a final examination because of good grades.* —*adj.* freed from a duty or requirement; excused: *Church property is exempt from real estate taxes.*

ex·emp·tion (eg zemp'shən) *n.* **1.** the act of exempting or the state of being exempted. **2.** a deduction from taxable income allowed for oneself and for each of one's dependents.

ex·er·cise (ek'sər sīz') *n.* **1.** physical activity that trains or improves the body: *Walking is good exercise.* **2.** an activity or lesson designed or done for practice: *The book has arithmetic exercises at the end of each chapter.* **3.** active use or performance: *the exercise of patience, the exercise of power.* **4.** *also,* **exercises.** a ceremony, program, or proceedings: *The graduation exercises included speeches and the presentation of awards.* —*v.,* **ex·er·cised, ex·er·cis·ing.** —*v.t.* **1.** to train or improve by means of exercise: *Riding a bicycle exercises the legs.* **2.** to make active use of; employ: *I exercised my right as a citizen by voting.* **3.** to perform or fulfill: *to exercise the duties of governor.* —*v.i.* to perform exercises: *to exercise in a gymnasium.*

ex·ert (eg zûrt') *v.t.* to make active use of: *I exerted my influence in getting free tickets to the concert.*
  ·to exert oneself. to make a great effort; try hard: *I exerted myself to make my guests feel welcome.*

ex·er·tion (eg zûr'shən) *n.* **1.** great effort: *Climbing a mountain involves much physical exertion.* **2.** the act or process of putting forth or into action: *Solving the problem demanded the exertion of much thought.*

ex·ha·la·tion (eks'hə lā'shən) *n.* **1.** the act or process of exhaling. **2.** something that is exhaled, such as air or an odor.

ex·hale (eks hāl') *v.,* **ex·haled, ex·hal·ing.** —*v.t.* **1.** to breathe out (air) from the lungs. **2.** to give off (vapor or an odor): *to exhale carbon dioxide.* —*v.i.* to breathe out air from the lungs: *We inhale and exhale in breathing.*

ex·haust (eg zôst') *v.t.* **1.** to make very weak or tired: *The long, hot hike exhausted the children.* **2.** to use up completely: *The campers exhausted their supply of water. The child's bad behavior exhausted my patience.* **3.** to study, develop, or treat thoroughly: *I exhausted that subject in my essay.* **4.** to draw out: *to exhaust a gas from a container.* —*n.* **1.** the escape or discharge of used steam or gases from an engine. **2.** waste products, such as steam or gases, that escape or are discharged. **3.** a pipe or other means of passage by which such waste products escape or are discharged. —**ex·haust'ed·ly,** *adv.* —**ex·haust'i·bil'i·ty,** *n.* —**ex·haust'i·ble,** *adj.*

ex·haus·tion (eg zôs'chən) *n.* **1.** the act of exhausting or the state of being exhausted. **2.** a lack of strength or energy; extreme fatigue.

ex·haus·tive (eg zôs'tiv) *adj.* overlooking or omitting nothing; thorough: *an exhaustive survey.* —**ex·haus'tive·ly,** *adv.* —**ex·haus'tive·ness,** *n.*

ex·hib·it (eg zib'it) *v.t.* **1.** to put on public display; show publicly: *The gallery exhibited the artist's paintings.* **2.** to make known; show; reveal: *to exhibit great talent in playing the piano.* —*n.* **1.** a public display; show: *We went to see the exhibit of sculpture.* **2.** a thing or things displayed publicly: *My science exhibit won first prize.* **3.** a document or thing used as evidence in a court of law: *The bank robber's gun was marked as an exhibit and shown to the jury.* —**ex·hib'it·er,** *n.*

ex·hi·bi·tion (ek'sə bish'ən) *n.* **1.** the act of exhibiting: *an exhibition of bravery.* **2.** a public display: *a skiing exhibition, an automobile exhibition.*

ex·hi·bi·tion·ism (ek'sə bish'ə niz'əm) *n.* the act of attracting attention to oneself.

ex·hi·bi·tion·ist (ek'sə bish'ə nist) *n.* a person who intentionally attracts attention to himself or herself; show-off.

ex·hib·i·tor (eg zib'i tər) *n.* a person or thing that exhibits or presents an exhibition.

ex·hil·a·rate (eg zil'ə rāt') *v.t.,* **ex·hil·a·rat·ed, ex·hil·a·rat·ing.** to make cheerful, lively, or excited; stimulate: *Their trip to the amusement park exhilarated them all.* —**ex·hil'a·rat'ing·ly,** *adv.*

ex·hil·a·ra·tion (eg zil'ə rā'shən) *n.* **1.** an exhilarated feeling or condition. **2.** the act of exhilarating.

ex·hort (eg zôrt') *v.t.* to try to persuade by appeal, argument, or warning; urge strongly: *to exhort the crew of a ship to mutiny.*

ex·hor·ta·tion (eg'zôr tā'shən, ek'sôr tā'shən) *n.* **1.** the act of exhorting. **2.** something that exhorts or is intended to exhort, such as a sermon.

ex·hor·ta·tive (eg zôr'tə tiv) *adj.* serving or intended to exhort.

ex·hu·ma·tion (eks'hū mā'shən) *n.* the act of exhuming: *the exhumation of a corpse.*

ex·hume (eks hūm') *v.t.,* **ex·humed, ex·hum·ing.** **1.** to remove (something buried, especially a corpse) from the earth; dig up. **2.** to bring to light; disclose; reveal: *The detective exhumed hidden facts about the crime.*

ex·i·gen·cy (ek'sə jən sē) *n., pl.* **ex·i·gen·cies.** **1.** a situation requiring prompt action, assistance, or attention; emergency: *I met the exigency by calling an ambulance for the injured people.* **2.** *also,* **exigencies.** urgent needs: *the exigencies of survival.*

ex·i·gent (ek'sə jənt) *adj.* requiring prompt action, assistance, or attention; urgent; pressing: *exigent needs.*

ex·ile (eg'zīl, ek'sīl) *v.t.,* **ex·iled, ex·il·ing.** to send away (a person) from his or her country or home by law or decree: *The government exiled them because of their political activities.* —*n.* **1.** the state of being exiled: *Exile was the fate of many aristocrats after the French Revo-*

lution. **2.** a person who is sent away from his or her country or home.

ex·ist (eg zist') *v.i.* **1.** to be real; have reality: *Do you believe that ghosts exist?* **2.** to continue to have being or life: *The prisoners could not exist on bread and water.* **3.** to be present or found; occur: *Outside of zoos, koalas exist only in Australia.*

ex·ist·ence (eg zis'təns) *n.* **1.** the state or fact of existing. **2.** a condition or way of existing; living; life: *The early colonists in America had a hard struggle for existence.* **3.** all that exists.

ex·ist·ent (eg zis'tənt) *adj.* **1.** now existing; present. **2.** having existence; living: *Dinosaurs are no longer existent.*

ex·it (eg'zit, ek'sit) *n.* **1.** the way out: *We left the theater by the rear exit.* **2.** the act of leaving; departure. **3.** the departure of a performer from the stage: *The actor made an exit amid much applause.* —*v.i.* to leave; go out; depart: *They exited by the back door.*

exo– *prefix* outside: *exosphere, exoskeleton.*

ex·o·bi·ol·o·gist (ek'sō bī ol'ə jist) *n.* an expert in exobiology.

ex·o·bi·ol·o·gy (ek'sō bī ol'ə jē) *n.* the branch of biology concerned with the search for and study of life in outer space.

ex·o·crine gland (ek'sə krin, ek'sə krīn') any of various glands, such as the salivary glands, that secrete through a duct rather than directly into the bloodstream or lymph.

Exod., Exodus.

ex·o·dus (ek'sə dəs) *n.* **1.** a departure, especially of a great many people: *an exodus from the cities to the suburbs.* **2. the Exodus.** the departure of the Israelites from Egypt under the leadership of Moses. **3. Exodus.** the second book of the Old Testament, containing an account of this departure.

ex of·fi·ci·o (cks' ə fish'ē ō') by virtue of or because of one's office or position: *A governor of a state is ex officio in command of the state's militia and police force.*

ex·on·er·ate (eg zon'ə rāt') *v.t.,* **ex·on·er·at·ed, ex·on·er·at·ing.** to free from blame or guilt; prove or declare innocent: *The new evidence fully exonerated the accused prisoner.* —**ex·on·er·a'tion,** *n.*

ex·or·bi·tance (eg zôr'bi təns) *n.* a going beyond proper, reasonable, or usual limits: *to be angered by the exorbitance of food prices.*

ex·or·bi·tant (eg zôr'bi tənt) *adj.* going beyond proper, reasonable, or usual limits; excessive: *exorbitant prices, exorbitant demands.* —**ex·or'bi·tant·ly,** *adv.*

ex·or·cise (ek'sôr sīz') *also,* **ex·or·cize.** *v.t.,* **ex·or·cised, ex·or·cis·ing.** **1.** to drive out (an evil spirit), as by prayer or magic. **2.** to free (a person or place) from an evil spirit. —**ex'or·cis·er,** *n.*

ex·or·cism (ek'sôr siz'əm) *n.* **1.** the act or fact of exorcising. **2.** prayers or incantations used in exorcising.

ex·or·cist (ek'sôr sist) *n.* a person who exorcises.

ex·or·cize (ek'sôr sīz') *v.t.,* **ex·or·cized, ex·or·ciz·ing.** another spelling of **exorcise.**

ex·o·skel·e·ton (ek'sō skel'ə tən) *n.* an external hard covering, such as the shell of a lobster or the scales and plates of a fish.

ex·o·sphere (ek'sō sfir') *n.* the outermost layer of the earth's atmosphere, lying above the ionosphere and gradually merging with outer space.

ex·o·spher·ic (ek'sō sfer'ik) *adj.* of or relating to the exosphere.

ex·ot·ic (eg zot'ik) *adj.* **1.** of or belonging to another part of the world; not native; foreign: *exotic flowers, exotic birds.* **2.** strangely beautiful or fascinating; strikingly unusual: *an exotic painting.* —*n.* something exotic, such as a plant. —**ex·ot'i·cal·ly,** *adv.*

ex·pand (ek spand') *v.t.* **1.** to make larger, as in size; enlarge: *Heat expands metal.* **2.** to stretch or spread

(something) out; unfold. **3.** to develop or express (something) in fuller form or greater detail: *to expand an idea.* **4.** to develop a number or algebraic expression to its completed or fullest form according to given rules. The algebraic expression $(a + b)^3$, when expanded, is $a^3 + 3a^2b + 3ab^2 + b^3$. —*v.i.* **1.** to grow larger in size, extent, or scope: *Metal expands when heated. The baseball league expanded by adding four new teams.* **2.** to stretch or spread out; unfold. —**ex·pand'a·ble,** *adj.*

·**to expand on.** to discuss in greater detail: *The teacher expanded on the causes of the American Revolution.*

ex·panse (ek spans') *n.* a wide, unbroken stretch or area: *a vast expanse of desert.*

ex·pan·si·ble (ek span'sə bəl) *adj.* capable of being expanded. —**ex·pan'si·bil'i·ty,** *n.*

ex·pan·sion (ek span'shən) *n.* **1.** the act of expanding or the state of being expanded. **2.** the amount or degree of enlargement or increase: *An eagle has a wing expansion of up to six feet.* **3.** something expanded: *This television play is an expansion of a short story.* **4.** a number or algebraic expression in its expanded form. The expansion of $(x + y)^2$ is $x^2 + 2xy + y^2$; the expansion of *125* is $(1 \times 10 \times 10) + (2 \times 10) + (5 \times 1)$. **5.** the process of economic growth.

ex·pan·sion·ism (ek span'shə niz'əm) *n.* the policy or practice of expanding the territory of a nation, especially at the expense of other nations. —**ex·pan'sion·ist,** *n., adj.*

ex·pan·sive (ek span'siv) *adj.* **1.** able to expand. **2.** extending widely; broad; extensive. **3.** generous and outgoing; demonstrative; open: *an expansive host.* —**ex·pan'sive·ly,** *adv.* —**ex·pan'sive·ness,** *n.*

ex·pa·ti·ate (ek spā'shē āt') *v.i.,* **ex·pa·ti·ated, ex·pa·ti·at·ing.** to write or speak at length or in detail: *The explorer expatiated for hours on life in the Arctic.*

ex·pa·tri·ate (*v.,* eks pā'trē āt'; *n.,* eks pā'trē it, eks-pā'trē āt') *v.t.,* **ex·pa·tri·at·ed, ex·pa·tri·at·ing.** **1.** to force (a person) out of his or her native country. **2.** to voluntarily withdraw (oneself) from one's native country: *Many American writers expatriated themselves to Europe after World War I.* —*n.* a person who is expatriated.

ex·pect (ek spekt') *v.t.* **1.** to look forward to as certain or likely: *They had expected a larger group at the party.* **2.** to look for as just, necessary, or right: *The teacher expected an explanation for the student's lateness.* **3.** *Informal.* to think; suppose: *I expect they're not home.*

·**to be expecting** *Informal.* to be awaiting the birth of one's child.

ex·pect·an·cy (ek spek'tən sē) *n., pl.* **ex·pect·an·cies. 1.** the state of expecting. **2.** something that is expected.

ex·pect·ant (ek spek'tənt) *adj.* **1.** having or showing expectation: *an expectant look.* **2.** waiting in expectation: *to be expectant of a promotion.* **3.** awaiting the birth of one's child: *classes for expectant parents.* —**ex·pect'ant·ly,** *adv.*

ex·pec·ta·tion (ek'spek tā'shən) *n.* **1.** the act of expecting. **2.** the state of expecting; expectancy. **3.** *also,* **expectations.** a reason or ground for expecting; hope, as of future good or success: *to have expectations of getting a good job after graduating from college.*

ex·pec·to·rant (ek spek'tər ənt) *n.* a medicine that helps the body discharge phlegm or mucus from the respiratory tract. —*adj.* aiding the discharge of phlegm or mucus from the respiratory tract.

---

at; āpe; fär; câre; end; mē; it; īce; pierce; hot; ōld; sông, fôrk; oil; out; up; ūse; rüle; pùll; tûrn; chin; sing; shop; thin; **th**is; hw in white; zh in treasure. The symbol ə stands for the unstressed vowel sound heard in about, taken, pencil, lemon, and circus.

E

ex·pec·to·rate (ek spek′tə rāt′) *v.t.*, *v.i.*, **ex·pec·to·rat·ed**, **ex·pec·to·rat·ing.** to cough up and spit out something from the throat or lungs. —**ex·pec′to·ra′tion,** *n.*

ex·pe·di·en·cy (ek spē′dē ən sē) *n.*, *pl.* **ex·pe·di·en·cies.** **1.** the state or quality of being expedient. **2.** a concern for personal gain or advantage rather than for what is right or just: *The politician's campaign was influenced more by the expediency of winning the election than by the needs of the people.* **3.** something that is expedient. Also, **ex·pe·di·ence** (ek spē′dē əns).

ex·pe·di·ent (ek spē′dē ənt) *adj.* **1.** based on personal gain or advantage rather than on what is right or just. **2.** suitable or useful for a given situation or purpose; appropriate. —*n.* something used to bring about a desired result. —**ex·pe′di·ent·ly,** *adv.*

ex·pe·dite (ek′spi dīt′) *v.t.*, **ex·pe·dit·ed**, **ex·pe·dit·ing.** **1.** to speed up the process or progress of: *to expedite a shipment.* **2.** to do quickly and efficiently: *to expedite a task.* —**ex′pe·dit′er,** *n.*

ex·pe·di·tion (ek′spi dish′ən) *n.* **1.** a journey made for a specific purpose: *The explorers made an expedition to the North Pole.* **2.** the people, ships, or equipment involved in such a journey. **3.** prompt and efficient action; promptness; dispatch: *to perform a task with expedition.*

arctic **expedition**

ex·pe·di·tion·ar·y (ek′spi dish′ə ner′ē) *adj.* of, relating to, or making up an expedition: *an expeditionary force.*

ex·pe·di·tious (ek′spi dish′əs) *adj.* quick and efficient: *to use expeditious means to finish a job on time.* —**ex′pe·di′tious·ly,** *adv.* —**ex′pe·di′tious·ness,** *n.*

ex·pel (ek spel′) *v.t.*, **ex·pelled**, **ex·pel·ling.** **1.** to force to leave: *to expel a student from school.* **2.** to drive out or discharge by force; force out: *to expel one's breath.*

ex·pend (ek spend′) *v.t.* **1.** to pay out; spend: *A great deal of money was expended for the new hospital.* **2.** to use up; consume: *to expend much energy.*

ex·pend·a·ble (ek spen′də bəl) *adj.* **1.** capable of being expended. **2.** that may be sacrificed, often in order to gain a larger advantage: *The general regarded some of the troops as expendable, and sent them on a dangerous mission.*

ex·pend·i·ture (ek spen′di chər) *n.* **1.** the act of expending. **2.** something that is expended, such as money, time, or effort.

ex·pense (ek spens′) *n.* **1.** the spending of money; expenditure: *Remodeling the house involved great expense.* **2.** the cause of spending money: *The rent on my apartment is my biggest monthly expense.* **3.** money spent in order to buy or do something; cost: *We cannot afford the expense of a new car.* **4.** loss, injury, or sacrifice: *The war was won at great expense to both countries.*

5. expenses. money spent in doing something, especially an assigned job or task: *The company provides traveling expenses for its sales staff.*

ex·pen·sive (ek spen′siv) *adj.* high in price; very costly: *an expensive fur coat, an expensive car.* —**ex·pen′sive·ly,** *adv.* —**ex·pen′sive·ness,** *n.*

ex·pe·ri·ence (ek spir′ē əns) *n.* **1.** something that a person has seen, done, or taken part in: *The refugees told us of their experiences in the war.* **2.** knowledge, skill, or wisdom gained through seeing, doing, or taking part in something, often over a period of time: *The job requires three years' experience as an accountant. The babysitter didn't have any experience in dealing with children.* —*v.t.*, **ex·pe·ri·enced**, **ex·pe·ri·enc·ing.** to have happen to one; undergo: *We experienced real fear when the plane developed engine trouble.*

ex·pe·ri·enced (ek spir′ē ənst) *adj.* made skillful, knowledgeable, or wise through experience: *an experienced politician, an experienced carpenter.*

ex·per·i·ment (*n.*, ek sper′ə mənt; *v.*, ek sper′ə ment′) *n.* a test or trial to discover or illustrate something, especially of a scientific nature: *Benjamin Franklin's experiments showed that lightning is an electrical discharge.* —*v.i.* to make an experiment or experiments: *The teacher had us experiment with chemical solutions.* —**ex·per′i·ment′er,** *n.*

ex·per·i·men·tal (ek sper′ə men′təl) *adj.* **1.** relating to, derived from, or based on experiments: *experimental evidence in chemistry.* **2.** used for experimentation: *an experimental drug.* **3.** of or like an experiment; tentative: *to take an experimental dip in a cold stream.* —**ex·per′i·men′tal·ly,** *adv.*

ex·per·i·men·ta·tion (ek sper′ə mən tā′shən) *n.* the act or process of experimenting.

ex·pert (ek′spûrt; *for adj., also,* ek spûrt′) *n.* a person having special skill or knowledge in something; specialist; authority: *an expert in mathematics, an expert on foreign affairs.* —*adj.* **1.** highly skilled or knowledgeable: *an expert skier.* **2.** characteristic of or from an expert; authoritative: *expert advice.* —**ex·pert′ly,** *adv.* —**ex·pert′ness,** *n.*

ex·pert·ise (ek′spər tēz′) *n.* special skill or knowledge.

expert system, a computer program that follows steps or decision-making procedures used by experts in a specific field of study, such as those in medical diagnosis or engineering design and analysis.

ex·pi·ate (ek′spē āt′) *v.t.*, **ex·pi·at·ed**, **ex·pi·at·ing.** to make amends for; atone for: *to expiate a sin by confessing.*

ex·pi·a·tion (ek′spē ā′shən) *n.* **1.** the act of expiating. **2.** something that expiates; means of atonement.

ex·pi·ra·tion (ek′spə rā′shən) *n.* **1.** a closing or ending; termination: *The expiration of the union contract is at the end of the month.* **2.** the act of breathing out air; exhalation.

ex·pire (ek spīr′) *v.i.*, **ex·pired**, **ex·pir·ing.** **1.** to come to an end; terminate: *The lease on our apartment expires on May 1. Our magazine subscription expires with the March issue.* **2.** to force out air from the lungs; exhale. **3.** to die.

ex·plain (ek splān′) *v.t.* **1.** to make clear or understandable: *The pilot explained that the plane's departure would be delayed by the storm.* **2.** to tell the meaning of; interpret: *to explain the plot of a novel.* **3.** to give the reason or reasons for; account for: *Can you explain your absence from school?*

ex·pla·na·tion (ek′splə nā′shən) *n.* **1.** the act or process of explaining: *a teacher's explanation of an arithmetic problem.* **2.** something that makes a thing clear or understandable.

ex·plan·a·tory (ek splan′ə tôr′ē) *adj.* that explains or makes clear: *The explanatory notes at the end of each chapter are very helpful.*

ex·ple·tive (ek′spli tiv) *n.* an exclamation or oath. *"Darn!"* is a mild expletive.

ex·plic·a·ble (ek splik′ə bəl, ek′spli kə bəl) *adj.* capable of being explained: *an explicable error.*

ex·pli·cate (ek′spli kāt′) *v.t.*, **ex·pli·cat·ed, ex·pli·cat·ing.** to explain clearly and in detail.

ex·pli·ca·tion (ek′spli kā′shən) *n.* 1. the act or process of explicating. 2. an explanation, as of a passage in a text; interpretation. 3. a detailed account or description.

ex·plic·it (ek splis′it) *adj.* clearly stated or expressed: *to give explicit instructions not to be disturbed.* —**ex·plic′it·ly,** *adv.* —**ex·plic′it·ness,** *n.*

ex·plode (ek splōd′) *v.*, **ex·plod·ed, ex·plod·ing.** —*v.i.* 1. to burst suddenly and violently with a loud noise; blow up: *The sealed bottle exploded in the fire. The firecracker exploded on the sidewalk.* 2. to expand suddenly and violently, giving off light, heat, and noise: *The nitroglycerin exploded on impact.* 3. to break forth violently or noisily: *to explode with rage.* 4. to increase rapidly: *That country's population has exploded in the last few years.* —*v.t.* 1. to cause (something) to burst suddenly and violently with a loud noise. 2. to cause to expand suddenly and violently, giving off light, heat, and noise. 3. to prove wrong: *The theory that the earth was flat was exploded long ago.*

ex·ploit (*n.*, ek′sploit; *v.*, ek sploit′) *n.* a heroic deed or act; bold feat: *The general's exploits in the war are well-known.* —*v.t.* 1. to use unjustly or unfairly for selfish profit or advantage: *to exploit workers by underpaying them.* 2. to make practical use of; use or develop profitably: *to exploit the natural resources of a region.* —**ex·ploit′a·ble,** *adj.* —**ex·ploit′er,** *n.*

ex·ploi·ta·tion (ek′sploi tā′shən) *n.* 1. use or development: *the exploitation of water as a source of power.* 2. unjust or unfair use for selfish reasons: *the exploitation of migrant workers.*

ex·plo·ra·tion (ek′splə rā′shən) *n.* the act of exploring or an instance of exploring, especially for the purpose of discovering or investigating unknown or unfamiliar regions.

ex·plor·a·to·ry (ek splôr′ə tôr′ē) *adj.* of, relating to, or for exploration: *an exploratory voyage.*

ex·plore (ek splôr′) *v.t.*, **ex·plored, ex·plor·ing.** 1. to travel over or in (unknown or unfamiliar regions) in order to discover or investigate: *to explore the surface of the moon.* 2. to examine or look through or into closely; scrutinize: *The historian explored the causes of the Civil War.*

ex·plor·er (ek splôr′ər) *n.* a person who explores.

ex·plo·sion (ek splō′zhən) *n.* 1. the act of bursting or expanding suddenly and violently: *an atomic explosion.* 2. a loud noise caused by exploding: *The explosion of the dynamite was deafening.* 3. a sudden, violent outburst of emotion: *an explosion of rage.* 4. a large, rapid increase: *a population explosion.*

ex·plo·sive (ek splō′siv) *adj.* 1. of, relating to, or like an explosion. 2. tending or liable to explode or cause an explosion: *A bomb is an explosive device. The boss has an explosive temper.* —*n.* a substance that can explode: *Dynamite is an explosive.* —**ex·plo′sive·ly,** *adv.* —**ex·plo′sive·ness,** *n.*

ex·po·nent (ek spō′nənt) *n.* 1. a person who explains or interprets something: *an exponent of Einstein's theories.* 2. a person or thing that represents or symbolizes something, such as an idea, principle, or cause: *Patrick Henry was a fierce exponent of liberty.* 3. *Mathematics.* a numeral or symbol placed at the upper right side of another numeral or symbol to indicate the number of times it is to be multiplied by itself. In 4^3 the exponent is 3, indicating $4 \times 4 \times 4$; in A^2 the exponent is 2, indicating $A \times A$; in 5^x the exponent is x, indicating 5 multiplied by itself x times.

ex·port (*v.*, ek spôrt′, ek′spôrt; *n.*, eks′pôrt) *v.t.* to carry or send (goods or products) to other countries for sale or trade: *Colombia exports coffee to the United States.* —*n.* 1. something that is exported: *Wool is an important Australian export.* 2. the act or process of exporting. —**ex·port′er,** *n.*

ex·por·ta·tion (ek′spôr tā′shən) *n.* 1. the act of exporting: *the exportation of wheat.* 2. something that is exported.

ex·pose (ek spōz′) *v.t.*, **ex·posed, ex·pos·ing.** 1. to place in contact with or leave open to the action or influence of: *to be exposed to new ideas, to be exposed to the mumps.* 2. to leave (oneself) open, as to danger, ridicule, or criticism: *The soldiers exposed themselves to a surprise attack by the enemy.* 3. to make known; disclose; reveal: *to expose a conspiracy, to expose a crime.* 4. to cause to be seen; display: *A short skirt exposes the knees.* 5. to allow light to reach (a photographic film or plate). —**ex·pos′er,** *n.*

ex·po·sé (ek′spō zā′) *n.* 1. a public disclosure of something secret or shameful, such as a scandal or crime. 2. a book or article making such a disclosure.

ex·po·si·tion (ek′spə zish′ən) *n.* 1. a large public show or display, as of industrial products. 2. the act or process of setting forth or explaining facts or ideas. 3. a detailed statement or explanation of facts or ideas, especially in writing. 4. the first section in certain musical forms in which the theme of the movement or composition is introduced.

ex·pos·i·tor (ek spoz′i tər) *n.* a person who explains something.

ex·pos·i·to·ry (ek spoz′i tôr′ē) *adj.* relating to, like, or containing an explanation; explanatory.

ex post fac·to (eks′pōst′fak′tō) created or put into effect after something has happened, but applying to it nevertheless: *A law passed in 1985 to prosecute someone for something done in 1984 would be ex post facto.*

ex·pos·tu·late (ek spos′chə lāt′) *v.i.*, **ex·pos·tu·lat·ed, ex·pos·tu·lat·ing.** to present reasons against something one opposes: *The senator expostulated with a colleague concerning the proposed bill.* —**ex·pos′tu·la′tion,** *n.* —**ex·pos·tu·la·to·ry** (ek spos′chə lə tôr′ē), *adj.*

ex·po·sure (ek spō′zhər) *n.* 1. the act of exposing or the state of being exposed. 2. a lack of protection from the elements resulting in harm, especially serious harm: *One of the stranded mountain climbers died of exposure to the extreme cold.* 3. a position in relation to a point of the compass: *a room with a southern exposure.* 4. the act or process of exposing a photographic film or plate to light. 5. the length of time needed for this. 6. a section of film that is exposed to light.

exposure meter, another term for **light meter.**

ex·pound (ek spound′) *v.t.* 1. to set forth in detail: *to expound a theory.* 2. to make clear the meaning of; explain; interpret. —**ex·pound′er,** *n.*

ex·press (ek spres′) *v.t.* 1. to put into words: *to express an opinion.* 2. to show or reveal outwardly; indicate: *to express happiness by smiling.* 3. to make known; communicate: *Those paintings express the artist's love of nature.* 4. to represent, as by a figure, symbol, or formula; indicate: *The sign ÷ expresses division.* 5. to send (something) by a system of rapid transportation or delivery: *to express a package.* 6. to press out; squeeze out: *to*

---

at; āpe; fär; câre; end; mē; it; īce; pîerce; hot; ōld; sông, fôrk; oil; out; up; ūse; rüle; pull; tûrn; chin; sing; shop; thin; **th**is; hw in white; zh in treasure. The symbol ə stands for the unstressed vowel sound heard in about, taken, pencil, lemon, and circus.

E

express the juice from grapes in order to make wine. —*adj.* **1.** particular or sole; special: *to call a friend for the express purpose of borrowing money.* **2.** clear and unmistakable: *to give express orders.* **3.** of or relating to a system of rapid transportation or delivery: *an express bus, an express company.* —*adv.* by a system of rapid transportation or delivery: *to send a package express.* —*n., pl.* **ex·press·es. 1.** a system for the rapid and direct transportation or delivery of goods or money. **2.** a company engaged in such transportation or delivery. **3.** a train, bus, or elevator that is quick and direct and makes few or no stops. —**ex·press′i·ble,** *adj.*

·**to express oneself.** to put one's thoughts or opinions into words: *I like to express myself by writing poetry.*

ex·pres·sion (ek spresh′ən) *n.* **1.** the act of expressing or putting something into words, such as thoughts, opinions, or ideas. **2.** an outward show; indication: *Crying is an expression of grief.* **3.** a particular look or tone of voice that expresses a thought or feeling: *The coach's face wore an expression of disapproval.* **4.** an effective manner of communicating feeling or meaning: *The student read the poem with expression.* **5.** a particular word or phrase: *"Look before you leap" is a familiar expression.* **6.** a symbol or combination of symbols used to indicate a mathematical quantity or operation.

ex·pres·sion·less (ek spresh′ən lis) *adj.* showing little or no thought or feeling: *an expressionless face.*

ex·pres·sive (ek spres′iv) *adj.* **1.** that expresses; expressing: *I spoke in a manner expressive of my anger.* **2.** full of feeling or meaning: *an expressive tone of voice, an expressive look.* **3.** of, relating to, or concerned with expression. —**ex·pres′sive·ly,** *adv.* —**ex·pres′sive·ness,** *n.*

ex·press·ly (ek spres′lē) *adv.* **1.** particularly or solely; specially: *to go to a party expressly to see a friend.* **2.** in clear terms; plainly: *The children were expressly warned against feeding the bears.*

ex·press·man (ek spres′mən) *n., pl.* **ex·press·men** (ek-spres′mən). a person who works for an express company.

ex·press·way (ek spres′wā′) *n.* a wide, usually divided highway built for rapid and direct traveling.

ex·pro·pri·ate (eks prō′prē āt′) *v.t.,* **ex·pro·pri·at·ed, ex·pro·pri·at·ing.** to take (private property) from a person or business by official authority, especially for public use. —**ex·pro′pri·a′tion,** *n.*

ex·pul·sion (ek spul′shən) *n.* the act of expelling or the state of being expelled.

ex·punge (ek spunj′) *v.t.,* **ex·punged, ex·pung·ing.** to delete or erase: *to expunge passages from a manuscript.* —**ex·pung′er,** *n.*

ex·pur·gate (ek′spər gāt′) *v.t.,* **ex·pur·gat·ed, ex·pur·gat·ing.** to remove objectionable passages or words from: *to expurgate a book.* —**ex′pur·ga′tion,** *n.*

ex·qui·site (ek skwiz′it, ek′skwi zit) *adj.* **1.** of great beauty, charm, or perfection: *an exquisite face.* **2.** of great excellence or high quality: *a vase of exquisite workmanship, exquisite taste in clothes.* **3.** intensely sharp; keen: *exquisite delight.* —**ex·qui′site·ly,** *adv.* —**ex·qui′site·ness,** *n.*

ex·tant (ek′stənt, ek stant′) *adj.* not lost, destroyed, or extinct; still existing: *The only extant copy of the book is in a private collection.*

ex·tem·po·ra·ne·ous (ek stem′pə rā′nē əs) *adj.* spoken, made, or done with little or no preparation; impromptu: *The winner of the scholarship made a few extemporaneous remarks.* —**ex·tem′po·ra′ne·ous·ly,** *adv.* —**ex·tem′po·ra′ne·ous·ness,** *n.*

ex·tem·po·re (ek stem′pə rē) *adv.* with little or no preparation; offhand; extemporaneously: *The politician spoke extempore.* —*adj.* spoken, made, or done with little or no preparation; extemporaneous; impromptu.

ex·tem·po·rize (ek stem′pə rīz′) *v.t.,* **ex·tem·po·rized, ex·tem·po·riz·ing.** to speak, make, or do (something) with little or no preparation; improvise: *The mayor extemporized a welcoming speech.* —**ex·tem′po·ri·za′tion,** *n.*

ex·tend (ek stend′) *v.t.* **1.** to make longer; lengthen: *The builders extended the road for three more miles. We extended our visit.* **2.** to stretch out: *The bird extended its wings. Extend your right leg.* **3.** to offer or give: *The store extended credit to them.* **4.** to increase, as in size or scope: *The ancient Romans extended their empire into Asia and Africa.* —*v.i.* to continue in distance or time; stretch out: *The driveway extends from the house to the main road.* —**ex·tend′i·ble,** *adj.*

extended family, a family that includes parents, children, and other near relatives, such as grandparents, usually all being in one household.

ex·tend·er (ek sten′dər) *n.* something that extends, especially a substance or ingredient added to another to increase its bulk or to modify it in some way.

ex·ten·sion (ek sten′shən) *n.* **1.** the act of extending or the state of being extended. **2.** something that extends. **3.** an additional telephone connected to the same line as the main one.

ex·ten·sive (ek sten′siv) *adj.* **1.** covering or extending over a large area; great in extent; vast: *an extensive ranch.* **2.** broad, as in scope, effect, or range: *a politician's extensive influence, a scholar's extensive research.* **3.** large in amount, degree, or number: *an extensive fortune.* —**ex·ten′sive·ly,** *adv.* —**ex·ten′sive·ness,** *n.*

ex·ten·sor (ek sten′sôr) *n.* any muscle that straightens or stretches out a part of the body, especially an arm or leg.

ex·tent (ek stent′) *n.* the space, amount, degree, or limit to which something extends or is extended: *What is the extent of your duties? I agree with you to a certain extent.*

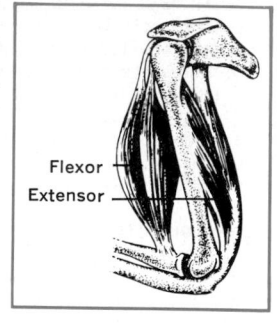

Flexor
Extensor

extensor in the arm

ex·ten·u·ate (ek sten′ū āt′) *v.t.,* **ex·ten·u·at·ed, ex·ten·u·at·ing.** to lessen the seriousness of (something, such as a fault or offense), by serving as an excuse or explanation: *The criminal's youth does not extenuate the crime.* —**ex·ten′u·a′tion,** *n.*

ex·ten·u·at·ing (ek sten′ū ā′ting) *adj.* serving to make a fault or offense less serious: *The criminal's temporary insanity was regarded as an extenuating circumstance.*

ex·te·ri·or (ek stîr′ē ər) *n.* **1.** the outer surface or part; outside: *The exterior of the building is made of marble.* **2.** an outward look or manner: *to have a calm exterior.* —*adj.* **1.** of, relating to, or on the outside; outer; external: *The exterior paint of the house was white.* **2.** coming or acting from the outside: *exterior help, exterior causes.*

ex·ter·mi·nate (ek stûr′mə nāt′) *v.t.,* **ex·ter·mi·nat·ed, ex·ter·mi·nat·ing.** to wipe out; destroy: *to exterminate household pests.* —**ex·ter′mi·na′tion,** *n.*

ex·ter·mi·na·tor (ek stûr′mə nā′tər) *n.* a person or thing that exterminates, especially a person whose business is exterminating cockroaches, termites, rats, and the like.

ex·ter·nal (ek stûr′nəl) *adj.* **1.** of, relating to, or on the outside; outer: *an external coat of paint on a house.* **2.** from without: *an external force, external causes.* **3.** relating to outward appearance: *an external calm, an external beauty.* **4.** on or to be used on the outside of the body: *Rubbing alcohol is for external use only.* —*n., pl.* **externals.** outward form, appearance, feature, or circumstance: *to put too much emphasis on externals in judging people.* —**ex·ter′nal·ly,** *adv.*

external ear, the outer, visible part of the ear and the passage leading to the eardrum; outer ear.

ex·tinct (ek stingkt′) *adj.* **1.** no longer in existence: *The dodo is extinct.* **2.** no longer active; inactive; extinguished: *an extinct volcano.*

ex·tinc·tion (ek stingk′shən) *n.* **1.** the state or condition of being or becoming extinct: *Efforts have been made to prevent the extinction of the buffalo.* **2.** the act of extinguishing or the state of being extinguished.

ex·tin·guish (ek sting′gwish) *v.t.* **1.** to put out: *to extinguish a fire, to extinguish all the lights in a house.* **2.** to put an end to; destroy: *Rain did not extinguish the high spirits of the picnickers.* —**ex·tin′guish·a·ble,** *adj.*

ex·tin·guish·er (ek sting′gwi shər) *n.* **1.** a person or thing that extinguishes. **2.** see **fire extinguisher.**

ex·tir·pate (ek′stər pāt′, ek stûr′pāt) *v.t.,* **ex·tir·pat·ed, ex·tir·pat·ing. 1.** to remove or destroy completely: *The government tried to extirpate bad living conditions in the slums by providing new housing.* **2.** to tear up by the roots; uproot.

ex·tol (ek stōl′) *also,* **ex·toll.** *v.t.,* **ex·tolled, ex·tol·ling.** to praise highly; laud: *The teacher extolled the famous poet's sonnets.*

ex·tort (ek stôrt′) *v.t.* to obtain (something) by threats or force: *to extort money by blackmail, to extort a confession.* —**ex·tort′er,** *n.*

ex·tor·tion (ek stôr′shən) *n.* **1.** an obtaining of money or another valuable thing by threats or force. **2.** something that is extorted.

ex·tor·tion·ate (ek stôr′shə nit) *adj.* very excessive; exorbitant: *We can't afford such extortionate prices.*

ex·tor·tion·ist (ek stôr′shə nist) *n.* a person who is guilty of or practices extortion. Also, **ex·tor·tion·er** (ek stôr′shə nər).

ex·tra (ek′strə) *adj.* more than what is usual, expected, or needed; additional: *to work extra hours, to receive extra pay.* —*n.* **1.** something in addition to what is usual, expected, or needed. **2.** a special edition of a newspaper that carries an account of an unusually important news event: *The paper published an extra to announce the outbreak of war.* **3.** a person hired to play a minor, usually nonspeaking, part in a motion picture or other production. —*adv.* unusually: *an extra large size, extra dry wine.*

extra– *prefix.* outside; beyond; besides: *extraterritorial, extracurricular.*

ex·tract (*v.,* ek strakt′; *n.,* ek′strakt) *v.t.* **1.** to draw or pull out by effort or force: *to extract a tooth.* **2.** to obtain (a substance) by pressing, cooking, distilling, or some other means: *to extract salt from sea water, to extract wine from grapes.* **3.** to obtain by force, threats, or similar oppression: *to extract information from a suspected thief.* **4.** to derive (something) from a particular source: *to extract great pleasure from winning an award.* **5.** to take out or select: *to extract a passage from a book.* —*n.* **1.** something that is extracted: *an extract from a book.* **2.** a concentrated form of a food: *I used vanilla extract to flavor the pudding.*

ex·trac·tion (ek strak′shən) *n.* **1.** the act of extracting or the state of being extracted. **2.** ancestry or birth; descent; lineage: *to be of Swedish extraction.*

ex·trac·tor (ek strak′tər) *n.* a person or thing that extracts.

ex·tra·cur·ric·u·lar (ek′strə kə rik′yə lər) *adj.* not part of the regular course of study: *Working on the school paper and playing on the football team are extracurricular activities.*

ex·tra·dite (ek′strə dīt′) *v.t.,* **ex·tra·dit·ed, ex·tra·dit·ing. 1.** to surrender or turn over (a person accused of a crime) to the authorities of another nation or state where the crime was committed. **2.** to obtain the surrender of (a person accused of a crime) from another nation or state.

ex·tra·di·tion (ek′strə dish′ən) *n.* the act of extraditing.

ex·tra·mu·ral (ek′strə myŏŏr′əl) *adj.* involving participants from more than one school or organization.

ex·tra·ne·ous (ek strā′nē əs) *adj.* **1.** that has little or nothing to do with the subject; not pertinent; irrelevant: *That statement is extraneous to this discussion.* **2.** coming from the outside; not belonging; foreign: *I have some extraneous matter in my eye.*

ex·traor·di·nar·y (ek strôr′də ner′ē,   ek′strə ôr′də·ner′ē) *adj.* beyond or above the usual or ordinary; very unusual or remarkable; exceptional: *an athlete who has extraordinary strength and stamina, a person of extraordinary intelligence.* —**ex·traor′di·nar′i·ly,** *adv.*

ex·tra·sen·sor·y (ek′strə sen′sə rē) *adj.* beyond the range of normal perception by any of the senses: *Extrasensory phenomena include clairvoyance and telepathy.*

extrasensory perception, the ability to perceive external objects, thoughts, or events without the aid of the senses.

ex·tra·ter·res·tri·al (ek′strə tə res′trē əl) *adj.* found or originating in regions outside the earth and its atmosphere: *A meteor is an extraterrestrial body.* —*n.* a being found or coming from outside the earth: *an extraterrestrial from another planet.*

ex·tra·ter·ri·to·ri·al (ek′strə ter′i tôr′ē əl)   *adj.* **1.** outside the legal jurisdiction of the country in which it is located: *The embassy is extraterritorial.* **2.** outside the territory of a country: *extraterritorial waters.*

ex·trav·a·gance (ek strav′ə gəns) *n.* **1.** lavish or wasteful spending of money: *They lived very simply and avoided any extravagance.* **2.** going beyond reasonable limits, as in speech or behavior: *Extravagance of praise may mask insincerity.* **3.** an instance of excess or wastefulness: *Buying all that jewelry was an extravagance I regretted later.*

ex·trav·a·gant (ek strav′ə gənt) *adj.* **1.** lavish or wasteful in the spending of money: *The extravagant family soon used up all their savings.* **2.** beyond reasonable limits; unrestrained: *extravagant demands.* —**ex·trav′a·gant·ly,** *adv.*

extravaganza of fireworks

ex·trav·a·gan·za (ek strav′ə gan′zə) *n.* a lavish, elaborate show or production, as in a theater; spectacle.

at; āpe; fär; câre; end; mē; it; īce; pîerce; hot; ōld; sông, fôrk; oil; out; up; ūse; rūle; pŭll; tûrn; chin; sing; shop; thin; <u>th</u>is; hw in white; zh in treasure. The symbol ə stands for the unstressed vowel sound heard in about, taken, pencil, lemon, and circus.

E

345

ex·tra·ve·hic·u·lar activity (ek'strə vē hik'yə lər) any of various maneuvers or experiments performed by an astronaut outside a vehicle in outer space.

ex·treme (ek strēm') *adj.,* **ex·trem·er, ex·trem·est.** **1.** of the greatest or highest degree; very great or severe: *The wounded solider was in extreme pain. The mountain climbers were in extreme danger because of a possible avalanche.* **2.** going beyond what is usual, reasonable, or average: *The mayor took extreme measures to halt crime in the streets.* **3.** farthest: *Their house was at the extreme end of the block.* —*n.* **1.** the greatest or highest degree: *enthusiastic to the extreme.* **2.** the farthest point: *The lighthouse was at one extreme of the island.* **3. extremes.** complete opposites: *joy and grief are extremes.* **4.** *Mathematics.* the first or last term of a proportion. In the proportion *a:b::c:d, a* and *d* are the extremes. —**ex·treme'ly,** *adv.* —**ex·treme'ness,** *n.*

 ·**to go to extremes.** to use extreme measures; do something drastic.

extremely high frequency, a radio freqency between 30,000 and 300,000 megahertz.

ex·trem·ist (ek strē'mist) *n.* a person who supports extreme measures or holds extreme views, especially in politics. —*adj.* of or relating to extremists.

ex·trem·i·ty (ek strem'i tē) *n., pl.* **ex·trem·i·ties. 1.** the farthest or last part or point; very end: *The Cape of Good Hope is near the southern extremity of Africa.* **2. extremities.** the hands and feet. **3.** greatest or highest degree: *the extremity of grief.* **4.** an extreme action or measure: *The people of the town were forced to the extremity of fleeing their homes when the floodwaters rose.* **5.** a condition of extreme danger or distress.

ex·tri·ca·ble (ek'stri kə bəl) *adj.* capable of being extricated.

ex·tri·cate (ek'stri kāt') *v.t.,* **ex·tri·cat·ed, ex·tri·cat·ing.** to set free or remove, as from entanglement or difficulty: *The hunter extricated the rabbit from the trap. I extricated myself from debt by taking a second job.* —**ex'tri·ca'tion,** *n.*

ex·trin·sic (ek strin'sik) *adj.* **1.** not essential to the nature of a thing; extraneous: *That statement is extrinsic to the discussion.* **2.** coming or acting from without; external: *an extrinsic force.* —**ex·trin'si·cal·ly,** *adv.*

ex·tro·vert (ek'strə vûrt') *n.* an outgoing person who is more interested in other people and events than in his or her own thoughts or feelings.

▲ An **extrovert** is the opposite of an **introvert.** An introvert is a person concerned mainly with himself or herself rather than with other people and events.

ex·tro·vert·ed (ek'strə vûr'tid) *adj.* tending to be more interested in other people and what goes on around one than in one's own thoughts or feelings.

ex·trude (ek strüd') *v.,* **ex·trud·ed, ex·trud·ing.** —*v.t.* **1.** to force or push out, as by squeezing: *The volcano extruded lava.* **2.** to shape (plastic or metal) by forcing through a die or mold. —*v.i.* to stick out.

ex·tru·sion (ek strü'zhən) *n.* the act or process of extruding.

ex·u·ber·ance (eg zü'bər əns) *n.* the state or quality of being exuberant.

ex·u·ber·ant (eg zü'bər ənt) *adj.* **1.** overflowing with high spirits; enthusiasm, or vigor; elated: *I was exuberant when I heard the good news.* **2.** abundant or lavish: *exuberant praise.* **3.** luxuriant in growth: *exuberant tropical foliage.* —**ex·u'ber·ant·ly,** *adv.*

ex·u·da·tion (eks'yü dā'shən) *n.* **1.** the act of exuding. **2.** something that is exuded, such as sweat.

ex·ude (eg züd', ek süd') *v.,* **ex·ud·ed, ex·ud·ing.** —*v.t.* **1.** to discharge (a substance) gradually; ooze forth: *The hard work made them exude sweat.* **2.** to give forth: *to exude warmth, to exude charm.* —*v.i.* to come out gradually; ooze out: *Sap exuded from the pine tree.*

ex·ult (eg zult') *v.i.* to rejoice greatly; be joyful: *The basketball players exulted in their victory.* —**ex·ult'ing·ly,** *adv.*

ex·ult·ant (eg zul'tənt) *adj.* triumphantly joyful; jubilant; elated. —**ex·ult'ant·ly,** *adv.*

ex·ul·ta·tion (eg'zul tā'shən, ek'sul tā'shən) *n.* triumphant joy; jubilation; elation: *There was great exultation when the home team won.*

eye (ī) *n.* **1.** the organ of the body by which people and animals see. **2.** the colored part of this organ; iris: *to have blue eyes.* **3.** the area surrounding the eye, including the eyelids: *a swollen eye.* **4.** also, **eyes.** eyesight; vision: *My eyes are not as good as they used to be.* **5.** a look; glance; gaze: *to cast an envious eye at a friend's new bicycle.* **6.** a careful or close watch: *Please keep an eye on the road when you drive.* **7.** the ability to judge with the eye: *to have an eye for beauty.* **8.** *also,* **eyes.** a point of view; opinion; judgment: *In the eyes of your fellow citizens, you are an honest person.* **9.** something resembling the eye in shape, position, or use, such as the bud of a potato or the hole at the end of a needle through which the thread passes. **10.** the small, cloudless center of a hurricane, having very light winds and low pressure. —*v.t.,* **eyed, ey·ing** or **eye·ing.** to watch carefully or closely: *The detective eyed the suspect's every movement.*

 ·**an eye for an eye.** punishment or revenge similar or equal to the injury or damage suffered.

 ·**in the public eye.** often noticed by the public; widely known.

 ·**to catch (someone's) eye.** to attract (someone's) attention: *I tried to catch your eye by waving.*

 ·**to see eye to eye.** to agree completely: *They didn't see eye to eye on the strategy for the game.*

 ·**to set eyes on** or **to lay eyes on.** to catch sight of; see: *I hadn't set eyes on my old school friend in years.*

 ·**with an eye to** or **with an eye toward.** with a view to; with the purpose of: *We are saving money with an eye to buying a new movie camera.*

eye·ball (ī'bôl') *n.* the ball-shaped portion of the eye, enclosed by the eyelids and the eye socket.

eye·brow (ī'brou') *n.* **1.** the bony ridge over the eye. **2.** the fringe of hair growing on this.

eye·catch·ing (ī'kach'ing) *adj.* attracting one's attention; very appealing; striking: *an eye-catching advertisement.*

eye·cup (ī'kup') *n.* a small cup with a rim shaped to fit closely over the eye, used in washing the eyes or applying medicine to them.

eye·drop·per (ī'drop'ər) *n.* a dropper for applying medicine to the eye.

eye·ful (ī'fūl') *n., pl.* **eye·fuls. 1.** an amount of something blown, thrown, or squirted into the eye: *an eyeful of sand.* **2.** a full or satisfying view; good look: *The final dance number gave the audience an eyeful of dazzling footwork and splendid costumes.* **3.** *Informal.* a person who is very attractive.

eye·glass (ī'glas') *n., pl.* **eye·glass·es. 1.** a lens to improve a person's eyesight. **2. eyeglasses.** a pair of glass lenses mounted in frames, used to improve a person's eyesight. **3.** an eyepiece.

eye·lash (ī'lash') *n., pl.* **eye·lash·es. 1.** one of the stiff hairs growing on the edge of the eyelid. **2.** *also,* **eyelashes.** a fringe of these hairs.

eye·less (ī'lis) *adj.* without eyes or blind.

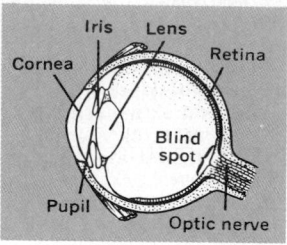

human **eye**

eye·let (ī′lit) *n.* **1.** a small hole in a material, such as leather or cloth, for a cord or lace to go through: *Shoelaces are passed through eyelets.* **2.** a metal or plastic ring lining such a hole to strengthen it. **3.** a small hole edged with stitches, used to make a pattern or edging in embroidery. **4.** any of various fabrics, especially cotton, decorated with this pattern.

eye·lid (ī′lid′) *n.* a movable, protective fold of skin that can close over the eyeball.

eye·lin·er (ī′lī′nər) *n.* a cosmetic used to outline the eyes to emphasize their shape.

eye–o·pen·er (ī′ō′pə nər) *n.* *Informal.* something surprising or revealing, as a piece of news or an experience: *Our team's victory over the league champions was an eye-opener to many people.*

eye·piece (ī′pēs′) *n.* the lens or combination of lenses nearest to the eye of the user in an optical instrument, especially a telescope or microscope.

eye shadow, a tinted cosmetic cream, powder, or liquid applied to the eyelids.

eye·sight (ī′sīt′) *n.* **1.** the power or ability to see; sight; vision: *A hawk has very keen eyesight.* **2.** the distance that the eye can see: *The ocean was within eyesight of the house.*

eye socket, the bony cavity in which the eyelid is located; orbit.

eye·sore (ī′sôr′) *n.* something ugly or unpleasant to look at: *That old shack is an eyesore.*

eye·spot (ī′spot′) *n.* a simple organ of sight in many lower animals, such as flatworms.

eye·stalk (ī′stôk′) *n.* a jointed, movable stalk with a compound eye on its tip, as in lobsters and shrimp.

eye·strain (ī′strān′) *n.* fatigue of the eyes.

eye·tooth (ī′tüth′) *n., pl.* **eye·teeth** (ī′tēth′). either one of the two canine teeth in the upper jaw between the incisors and the bicuspids.

eye·wash (ī′wôsh′, ī′wosh′) *n.* **1.** a liquid used to rinse or medicate the eyes. **2.** *Slang.* nonsense; hogwash.

eye·wit·ness (ī′wit′nis) *n., pl.* **eye·wit·ness·es.** a person who has actually seen something happen and therefore can testify about it: *an eyewitness to a robbery.*

ey·rie (âr′ē, îr′ē, īr′ē) *also,* **ey·ry.** *n., pl.* **ey·ries.** another spelling of **aerie.**

E·ze·ki·el (i zē′kē əl) *n.* a book of the Old Testament containing the writings of the prophet Ezekiel.

Ez·ra (ez′rə) *n.* a book of the Old Testament that is believed to have been written by the scribe Ezra.

E

at; āpe; fär; câre; end; mē; it; īce; pîerce; hot; ōld; sông, fôrk; oil; out; up; ūse; rüle; pùll; tûrn; chin; sing; shop; thin; this; hw in white; zh in treasure. The symbol ə stands for the unstressed vowel sound heard in about, taken, pencil, lemon, and circus.

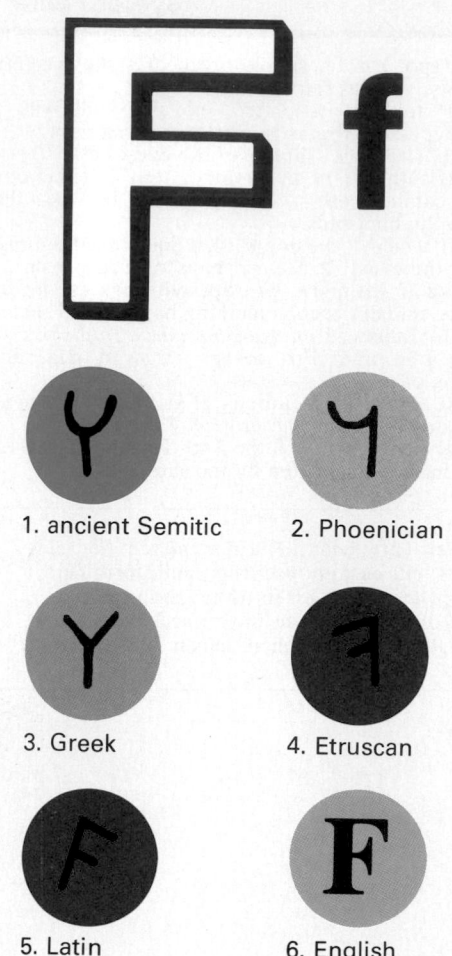

F f

1. ancient Semitic
2. Phoenician
3. Greek
4. Etruscan
5. Latin
6. English

F is the sixth letter of the English alphabet. Although the *f* sound, as the *f* in *fish*, was not represented in early alphabets, the shape of the letter **F**, like the letters, **U**, **V**, **W**, and **Y**, developed from the ancient Semitic letter *waw* (1), which depicted a hook and stood for the *w* sound as the *w* in water. When the Phoenicians (2) borrowed *waw*, they used it to represent both the consonant sound *w* and the vowel sound *ü*, as heard in the English word *rude*. The Greeks adopted *waw* and called it *upsilon* (3), writing it as the capital letter **Y** is written today. *Upsilon* was used to represent only the vowel sound *ü*; the *w* sound was represented by a letter called *digamma,* which looked something like a modern capital letter **F**. The Etruscans (4) borrowed a modified form of *digamma* and used it to stand for the *f* sound. The Etruscan form of *digamma* was adopted to represent the *f* sound in the Latin alphabet (5). By about 2,400 years ago, the Roman letter **F** was written almost exactly as we write it today (6).

f, F (ef) *n., pl.* **f's, F's.** 1. the sixth letter of the English alphabet. 2. the sixth item in a series or group. 3. *Music.* the fourth note of the scale of C major.
f. 1. female. 2. feminine. 3. forte. 4. franc.
F 1. Fahrenheit. 2. the symbol for fluorine.
F. 1. February. 2. French. 3. Friday.
fa (fä) *n. Music.* 1. the fourth note of the major scale. 2. the note F.
fa·ble (fā′bəl) *n.* 1. a short story meant to teach a moral or lesson, especially one using animals as characters. 2. legend; myth. 3. a story or statement that is not true; falsehood.
fa·bled (fā′bəld) *adj.* 1. told about or described in fables; mythical; legendary: *a fabled hero.* 2. not real; fictitious; made up. 3. famous.
fab·ric (fab′rik) *n.* 1. a material that is woven, knitted, or produced in some way from natural or synthetic fibers; cloth. Tweed, flannel, jersey, and felt are fabrics. 2. a system of connected or related parts; framework; structure: *the fabric of society.*
fab·ri·cate (fab′ri kāt′) *v.t.,* **fab·ri·cat·ed, fab·ri·cat·ing.** 1. to make up; invent: *to fabricate an excuse.* 2. to make, manufacture, or build by putting parts together: *to fabricate a boat.* —**fab′ri·ca′tion,** *n.*
fab·u·list (fab′yə list) *n.* a person who makes up or writes fables.
fab·u·lous (fab′yə ləs) *adj.* 1. amazing; incredible: *to spend fabulous sums of money on clothes.* 2. *Informal.* exceptionally good; wonderful: *We had a fabulous time at the party.* 3. of or like a fable; imaginary; legendary: *a winged dragon and other fabulous monsters.* —**fab′u·lous·ly,** *adv.* —**fab′u·lous·ness,** *n.*
fa·cade (fə säd′) *also,* **fa·çade.** *n.* 1. the front of a building. 2. a false front or outward appearance; illusion; pretense: *to maintain a facade of prosperity.*
face (fās) *n.* 1. the front of the head. The eyes, nose, and mouth are parts of the face. 2. a look or expression; countenance: *The winners all had happy faces.* 3. a queer or twisted look or expression; grimace: *to make faces in the mirror.* 4. *Informal.* boldness; impudence: *I can't believe you had the face to say that in front of everybody at the party.* 5. dignity; self-respect: *to lose face, to save face.* 6. the front, main, or outward surface of something: *the face of a cliff, the face of a clock.* 7. appearance; look: *On its face it was a quiet town.* 8. *Geometry.* one of the surfaces or sides of a solid: *the six faces of a cube.* 9. *Printing.* a. the surface of a piece of type, on which the letter or character to be printed is cut. b. the style or design of this surface. —*v.,* **faced, fac·ing.** —*v.t.* 1. to have or turn the face toward: *Please face the camera. The house faces the park.* 2. to cause to turn in a particular direction: *Face the plant toward the light.* 3. to meet openly; confront: *to face a problem.* 4. to realize and admit; accept: *to face the facts.* 5. to cover or line (a surface): *to face the collar of a coat with fur, to face the walls of a room with paneling.* —*v.i.* to be turned or placed with the face in a particular direction: *The house faced west.*
•**face to face.** facing each other.
•**face to face with.** exposing oneself to; risking: *to come face to face with danger.*
•**in the face of.** a. in the presence of: *to run in the face of danger.* b. in spite of: *The prisoner claimed innocence in the face of evidence proving guilt.*
•**on the face of it.** from its outward appearance; seemingly: *On the face of it, the experiment was a success, but further research was needed.*
•**to face up to.** a. to meet or oppose boldly: *to face up to danger.* b. to admit and accept: *to face up to a mistake.*
•**to one's face.** directly and boldly in one's presence: *Would you say that to your friend's face?*

Word Family

The Latin word *facies*, meaning "face," is the root of a number of English words. When you **face** someone for the first time you often see only a **facade**, that is, the **superficial** features of the person, such as **facial** beauty. True friendship gets beneath such **surfaces** and reveals the many **facets** of a person's personality. Over time, friends share many memories that are not easily **effaced**.

face card, a jack, queen, or king in a deck of playing cards.

face–lift (fās'lift') *n.* **1.** an operation to tighten sagging or wrinkled skin on the face. **2.** a change to repair, alter, or renovate something, especially a superficial change. *The old city hall is being painted to give it a face-lift.*

fac·et (fas'it) *n.* **1.** any of the small, polished plane surfaces of a cut gem. **2.** any of various sides or aspects: *the many facets of a problem, the facets of someone's personality.* **3.** any of the segments of the external surface of the compound eye of insects and certain animals.

facet
gem with nine
facets showing

fa·ce·tious (fə sē'shəs) *adj.* showing or given to light humor; not serious; frivolously amusing: *a facetious speaker, a facetious comment.* **—fa·ce'tious·ly,** *adv.* **—fa·ce'tious·ness,** *n.*

face value **1.** the value appearing on currency, stamps, bonds, banknotes, and the like. **2.** apparent value: *We accepted the announcement at face value.*

fa·cial (fā'shəl) *adj.* of, for, or relating to the face. *n.* a massage or other treatment for the face. **—fa'cial·ly,** *adv.*

fac·ile (fas'əl) *adj.* **1.** acting or working with skill and ease: *a facile writer, a facile mind.* **2.** requiring little effort; easily done: *a facile task, a facile conclusion.* **3.** having a mild disposition; easygoing: *a facile nature.* **—fac'ile·ly,** *adv.* **—fac'ile·ness,** *n.*

fa·cil·i·tate (fə sil'i tāt') *v.t.,* **fa·cil·i·tat·ed, fa·cil·i·tat·ing.** to make easier; aid in the operation of; assist: *Zip codes facilitate mail service.*

fa·cil·i·ty (fə sil'i te) *n., pl.* **fa·cil·i·ties.** **1.** ease of doing; freedom from difficulty: *This new car can be driven with facility.* **2.** skill or ability; aptitude: *That carpenter has great facility.* **3.** often, **facilities.** something, as a building or piece of equipment, that provides a convenience or serves a particular purpose: *cooking facilities.*

fac·ing (fā'sing) *n.* **1. a.** a piece of fabric sewn inside or outside along an edge of a garment to strengthen or trim it. **b.** the fabric used for this. **2.** a covering in front for ornamentation, protection, or other purposes: *a house with marble facing.*

fac·sim·i·le (fak sim'ə lē) *n.* an exact copy or reproduction: *a facsimile of the Declaration of Independence.*

fact (fakt) *n.* **1.** something known to be true or real, or to have actually happened: *to support an argument with facts. The police investigated the facts of the crime.* **2.** the quality or state of being actual; reality; truth: *to distinguish fact from fiction.* **3.** a thing done, especially a criminal or evil act: *to feel shame after the fact.*

　•**as a matter of fact.** in real truth or fact; really: *As a matter of fact, the job was much easier than I thought it would be.*

　•**in fact.** in real truth or fact; really.

fac·tion (fak'shən) *n.* **1.** a group of people within a larger group or organization that acts against other such groups to promote its own ends. **2.** strife or disagreement within an organization.

fac·tion·al (fak'shə nəl) *adj.* of or characteristic of a faction or factions; between or among factions: *factional strife.*

fac·tious (fak'shəs) *adj.* **1.** tending to cause disagreement: *a factious political leader.* **2.** of, relating to, or characterized by faction: *factious disputes.* **—fac'tious·ly,** *adv.* **—fac'tious·ness,** *n.*

fac·ti·tious (fak tish'əs) *adj.* not natural or real; artificial: *a factitious show of friendship.* **—fac·ti'tious·ly,** *adv.* **—fac·ti'tious·ness,** *n.*

fac·tor (fak'tər) *n.* **1.** one of several elements that brings about a result or is part of the formation of a thing or circumstance: *Sunny weather and good food were factors in the picnic's success.* **2.** any of the numbers or algebraic expressions that, when multiplied together, form a product. The factors of $14xy$ are 2, 7, x, and y. **—v.t.** to separate (a mathematical product) into its factors.

fac·to·ri·al (fak tôr'ē əl) *n.* the product of an integer and all lower positive integers. The factorial of 3, written as 3!, is $3 \times 2 \times 1 = 6$.

fac·to·ry (fak'tə rē) *n., pl.* **fac·to·ries.** a building or group of buildings where goods are manufactured.

fac·to·tum (fak tō'təm) *n.* a person employed to do all kinds of work, particularly odd jobs.

fac·tu·al (fak'chü əl) *adj.* **1.** of or relating to facts. **2.** consisting of or based on facts: *a factual account of an accident.* **—fac'tu·al·ly,** *adv.*

fac·ul·ty (fak'əl tē) *n., pl.* **fac·ul·ties.** **1.** one of the natural powers of the mind or body: *the faculty of speech, to be in full possession of one's faculties.* **2.** a special skill or aptitude; talent: *a faculty for putting people at their ease.* **3.** the teaching staff of a school, college, or university. **4.** a department of learning at a college or university: *the faculty of law.*

fad (fad) *n.* a popular practice, interest, or fashion followed enthusiastically for a short time.

fade (fād) *v.,* **fad·ed, fad·ing.** **—v.i. 1.** to lose color, brightness, or distinctness: *Some fabrics fade in the wash.* **2.** to lose freshness, vigor, or strength; wither: *The appeal of the city faded after we had been there some months.* **3.** to disappear gradually; die down: *The sound of the footsteps faded away.* **—v.t.** to cause to fade: *Sunlight faded my curtains.*

　•**to fade in.** to become or make gradually clearer or louder, as an image or sound.

　•**to fade out.** to become or make gradually less clear or loud.

fade–in (fād'in') *n.* in motion pictures, television, radio, or recording, the gradual appearance of an image or sound.

fade–out (fād'out') *n.* in motion pictures, television, radio, or recording, the gradual disappearance of an image or sound: *The movie ended with a fade-out of the setting sun.*

faer·ie (fâr'ē), *also,* **faer·y.** *n. Archaic.* another spelling of **fairy.**

fag (fag) *v.t.,* **fagged, fag·ging.** to tire by hard work; exhaust: *After the race, I was completely fagged.*

fag end **1.** a frayed or unfinished end, as of a piece of cloth or rope. **2.** the last and worst part of anything; remnant: *the fag end of a tiring day.*

fag·ot (fag'ət) *also,* **fag·got.** *n.* a bundle of sticks, twigs, or branches, used especially for fuel.

Fahr·en·heit (far'ən hīt') *adj.* of, according to, or des-

at; āpe; fär; câre; end; mē; it; īce; pîerce; hot; ōld;
sông, fôrk; oil; out; up; ūse; rūle; pùll; tûrn; chin;
sing; shop; thin; this; hw in white; zh in treasure.
The symbol ə stands for the unstressed vowel sound
heard in about, taken, pencil, lemon, and circus.

ignating the temperature scale on which the freezing point of water is at 32 degrees and the boiling point is at 212 degrees under standard atmospheric pressure. [From the German physicist Gabriel Daniel *Fahrenheit* (1686–1736), who devised this scale.]

fail (fāl) *v.i.* **1.** to be unsuccessful in doing or achieving something attempted, desired, or expected: *The plan failed when it was tested.* **2.** to be unsuccessful in passing an examination or subject. **3.** to become weaker, as in health or strength: *The old dog's eyesight failed.* **4.** to stop working; die out: *The plane crashed because the engines failed.* **5.** to be insufficient; fall short; run out: *The water supply failed.* **6.** to go bankrupt. —*v.t.* **1.** to neglect or not do: *You failed to get to school on time.* **2.** to prove to be of no use or help to; disappoint: *Real friends won't fail you when you need them.* **3.** to abandon; desert: *My courage failed me.* **4.** to receive a grade of failure in (an examination or subject). **5.** to give a grade of failure to (a student).
 • **without fail.** despite whatever happens; definitely: *We will be there without fail.*

fail·ing (fā'ling) *n.* shortcoming; fault: *My cousin's chief failing is rudeness.* —*prep.* in the absence of; without: *Failing a reply, we will cancel your subscription.*

faille (fīl) *n.* a ribbed fabric, usually made with silk or rayon yarn, used for clothing.

fail–safe (fāl'sāf') *adj.* **1.** designed to stop or alter an operation automatically in case of a malfunction: *a fail-safe device in a nuclear reactor.* **2.** guaranteed not to fail; safe from failure; foolproof: *a fail-safe plan.*

fail·ure (fāl'yər) *n.* **1.** being unable to achieve something attempted, desired, or expected: *Failure to win their first game discouraged the team.* **2.** a person or thing that is unsuccessful: *The book was a failure because very few copies were sold.* **3.** omission or neglect (of something required): *failure to pay one's bills.* **4.** a failing to pass an examination or subject. **5.** a grade or mark indicating this. **6.** a ceasing to work; dying out: *a power failure.* **7.** a falling short; insufficiency: *a crop failure.* **8.** bankruptcy.

fain (fān) *Archaic. adv.* with pleasure; gladly. —*adj.* glad; willing.

faint (fānt) *adj.* **1.** dim; indistinct: *a faint light, a faint cry.* **2.** without enthusiasm or strength; feeble: *faint praise, a faint attempt to be friendly.* **3.** weak and dizzy; likely to faint: *The workers were faint with hunger.* **4.** with little courage: *a faint heart.* —*n.* a brief loss of consciousness caused by a temporary decrease in the amount of blood that flows to the brain. —*v.i.* to lose consciousness briefly. —**faint'ly,** *adv.* —**faint'ness,** *n.*

faint·heart·ed (fānt'här'tid) *adj.* lacking courage; timid. —**faint'heart'ed·ly,** *adv.* —**faint'heart'edness,** *n.*

fair¹ (fâr) *adj.* **1.** free from prejudice; just; impartial: *The judge made a fair decision.* **2.** according to accepted rules or standards: *fair play.* **3.** moderately good or acceptable; average: *a fair chance of winning.* **4.** light in coloring: *a fair complexion.* **5.** not cloudy; clear; bright; sunny: *fair weather.* **6.** pleasing in appearance; attractive; beautiful. **7.** *Baseball.* staying inside the foul lines. **8.** legitimately open to attack or pursuit: *Deer are fair game in the hunting season.* —*adv.* in a fair manner; according to the rules: *A good sport plays fair.* [From the Old English word *fæger* meaning "beautiful, pleasing."] —**fair'ness,** *n.*
 • **to bid fair.** to seem likely or favorable: *It bids fair to rain.*

fair² (fâr) *n.* **1.** an exhibition, as of livestock and farming products or of cultural and industrial displays of different nations. Fairs often have shows, competitions, and other entertainment. **2.** the exhibition and sale of articles for some charitable cause; bazaar: *a church fair.* **3.** a gathering of people to exhibit and sell goods: *a book fair.* [From the Old French word *feire* meaning "market," from the Medieval Latin word *feria* "market" or "holiday," from the Latin word *feriae* "holidays." It was the custom to hold a fair on religious holidays.]

fair ball *Baseball.* a batted ball that stays inside the foul lines.

fair game **1.** animals, birds, or fish that can be lawfully hunted. **2.** any person or thing considered fit for pursuit, attack, or acquisition: *Refreshments left over after the party were fair game for anyone who stopped by.*

fair·ground (fâr'ground') *n.* often, **fairgrounds.** an outdoor place where fairs are held.

fair–haired (fâr'hârd') *adj.* having light-colored hair.

fair·ish (fâr'ish) *adj.* moderately good, well, or large.

fair·ly (fâr'lē) *adv.* **1.** in a fair manner; justly; impartially; honestly: *The fans did not think that the umpire had ruled fairly.* **2.** somewhat; moderately: *a fairly large amount of money.* **3.** actually; completely: *The audience fairly roared its approval.*

fair–mind·ed (fâr'mīn'did) *adj.* not prejudiced or biased; impartial; just: *a fair-minded judge.* —**fair'mind'ed·ness,** *n.*

fair trade, trade under an agreement that forbids a seller to sell certain products for less than a minimum price set by the manufacturer or distributor.

fair·way (fâr'wā') *n.* the mowed area on a golf course between the tee and putting green.

fair·y (fâr'ē) *n.,* pl. **fair·ies.** a tiny imaginary creature supposed to possess magic powers. —*adj.* **1.** of or relating to fairies. **2.** like a fairy, as in delicateness or grace. **3.** having the magic powers of or being a fairy.

fair·y·land (fâr'ē land') *n.* **1.** the imaginary land of the fairies. **2.** any enchanting, beautiful place.

fairy tale **1.** a story, usually for children, about fairies. **2.** an unbelievable or highly imaginative story or lie.

fairy tale
an illustration from the **fairy tale**
Little Red Riding Hood

fait ac·com·pli (fet'ə kôm plē', fā'tä kom plē') *pl.* **faits ac·com·plis** (fet'ə kôm plē', fā'tä kom plēz'). something done that no longer can be changed or reversed. [From the French phrase *fait accompli* meaning "accomplished fact," going back to the Latin words *factum* "deed," *ad* "to," and *complēre* "to fulfill."]

faith (fāth) *n.* **1.** a belief not based on proof: *My friends accepted my excuse on faith.* **2.** reliance or trust: *to have faith in one's doctor.* **3.** a belief in God or the doctrines of a religion. **4.** a system of religious belief: *the Protestant faith.* ▲ **Faith** and **belief** both mean the acceptance of something as true or real. *Faith* is based on an acceptance of something that cannot be proved. *Belief* is often used to mean *faith;* but *belief* may be based on thought and reason also.

• **in bad faith.** dishonestly; without sincerity.
• **in good faith.** honestly; sincerely: *to bargain in good faith.*
• **to break faith.** to break a promise; fail to be faithful to someone or something.
• **to keep faith.** to keep a promise; remain faithful or loyal.

faith·ful (fāth′fəl) *adj.* **1.** steadfast in loyalty and devotion; trustworthy: *a faithful friend.* **2.** accurate; true; exact: *a faithful copy of a document.* —*n.* **the faithful. a.** the followers or supporters of a religion. **b.** the loyal followers or supporters of any cause or group. —**faith′ful·ly,** *adv.* —**faith′ful·ness,** *n.*

faith·less (fāth′lis) *adj.* **1.** not loyal; not keeping one's word; untrustworthy: *a faithless friend.* **2.** without faith or belief, especially religious belief. —**faith′less·ly,** *adv.* —**faith′less·ness,** *n.*

fake (fāk) *n.* a person or thing that is not genuine; fraud; sham: *It's not a genuine antique; it's a fake.* —*v.t.,* **faked, fak·ing. 1.** to pretend; feign: *The opossum faked death until the predator went away.* **2.** to make (something) seem genuine in order to deceive; counterfeit: *The accounts were faked to show a profit that didn't exist.* —*adj.* not genuine; false: *a fake fireplace, a fake mustache.* —**fak′er,** *n.*

fak·er·y (fā′kə rē) *n., pl.* **fak·er·ies. 1.** the act of faking. **2.** something that is faked: *That forged document is a good fakery.*

fa·kir (tə kir′, tə′kər) *n.* a Muslim or Hindu religious man who takes a vow of poverty and supports himself by begging.

fal·con (fôl′kən, fal′kən, fô′kən) *n.* **1.** any of various swift-flying birds of prey that resemble hawks, having pointed wings and a short, hooked bill. **2.** a hawk that has been trained to hunt birds and small game.

fal·con·er (fôl′kə nər, fal′kə nər, fô′kə nər) *n.* **1.** a person who hunts with falcons. **2.** a breeder or trainer of falcons.

fal·con·ry (fôl′kən rē, fal′kən rē, fô′kən rē) *n.* **1.** the sport of hunting with falcons; hawking. **2.** the art of training falcons to hunt birds and small game.

fal·de·ral (fal′də ral′) *also,* **fal·de·rol** (fal′də rol′). *n.* another spelling of **folderol.**

fall (fôl) *v.i.,* **fell, fall·en, fall·ing. 1.** to come down from a higher place by the force of gravity; drop: *The book fell off the shelf. Snow fell during the night.* **2.** to come down suddenly or involuntarily from an upright position: *to fall on an icy sidewalk.* **3.** to break into ruins and come down: *The bridge fell into the river.* **4.** to become lower or less, as in quantity, quality, or strength: *The noise fell to a whisper. Production at the factory fell sharply.* **5.** to strike or land: *The arrow fell wide of the target.* **6.** to take place; happen; occur: *Christmas falls on December 25th.* **7.** to come as if by dropping from a higher place: *Night fell.* **8.** to pass into a particular condition; become: *to fall ill, to fall in love.* **9.** to be defeated, captured, or overthrown: *The city fell after a long siege.* **10.** to be wounded or killed, as in battle. **11.** to give in to temptation; sin: *In the Bible, Adam and Eve fell when they ate the apple.* **12.** to be classified or divided: *His book falls into three parts.* **13.** to show sadness or disappointment: *The child's face fell.* **14.** to hang down: *The dress fell in soft folds.* **15.** to pass by inheritance or right: *The estate falls to the eldest child.* **16.** to be said:

Angry words fell from the dictator's lips. **17.** to slope downward: *The land falls from the house to the lake.* —*n.* **1.** the act of coming down from a higher place by the force of gravity: *the fall of a meteor.* **2.** the amount of anything that comes down: *a six-inch fall of rain.* **3.** the distance through which anything falls: *It's a short fall from the branch to the ground.* **4.** a sudden or involuntary drop from an upright position: *The skater took a hard fall.* **5.** capture, destruction, or defeat; overthrow: *the fall of the Roman Empire.* **6.** a decline in reputation, rank, or dignity: *a fall from favor.* **7.a.** the act of yielding to temptation; sin. **b. the Fall.** the sin of disobedience to God in the Bible by Adam and Eve, who ate the forbidden fruit. **8.** a decrease, as in value, quality, or quantity: *a fall in prices.* **9.** season between summer and winter, when leaves fall; autumn. **10.** *usually,* **falls.** waterfall; cascade. ▲ used with a singular or plural verb. **11.** a woman's hairpiece, usually worn to add length or fullness. **12.** in wrestling, the act of throwing one's opponent on the back so that both shoulders touch the mat at the same time. —*adj.* of, relating to, or suitable for the autumn: *fall clothing.*

• **to fall back.** to retreat; withdraw: *The troops fell back.*
• **to fall back on. a.** to rely on for help. **b.** to retreat or go back to.
• **to fall behind.** to fail to keep up: *to fall behind in one's work.*
• **to fall for.** *Informal.* to be deceived or tricked by: *They fell for the swindler's plan.*
• **to fall in. a.** to take a place in line. **b.** to cave in.
• **to fall in with. a.** to meet and join company with: *I fell in with some amusing people on my trip.* **b.** to agree with; be favorable to.
• **to fall off.** to become less; diminish; drop: *the demand for the product fell off.*
• **to fall on** or **to fall upon. a.** to attack vigorously; assault. **b.** to come upon; discover; find: *I fell upon an interesting book in the library.*
• **to fall out. a.** to have a quarrel; argue: *They fell out over whose job it was to cook.* **b.** to leave a place in line.
• **to fall short.** to fail to meet a certain standard, goal, or requirement (with *of*).
• **to fall through.** to come to nothing; fail: *Their plans fell through.*
• **to fall to. a.** to set about; begin: *We fell to work.* **b.** to begin to attack. **c.** to start eating.
• **to fall under. a.** to be classified as; be included in: *That book falls under the heading of fiction.* **b.** to be or come under the influence of: *to fall under a spell.*

fal·la·cious (fə lā′shəs) *adj.* **1.** based on or containing a fallacy; not logical. **2.** deceptive; misleading: *fallacious appeals.* —**fal·la′cious·ly,** *adv.* —**fal·la′cious·ness,** *n.*

fal·la·cy (fal′ə sē) *n., pl.* **fal·la·cies. 1.** a false or mistaken belief; misconception: *the fallacy that the world is flat.* **2.** false reasoning; unsound argument.

fall·en (fô′lən) *v.* the past participle of **fall.** —*adj.* **1.** having come down from a higher place; dropped: *fallen snow.* **2.** degraded or disgraced: *a fallen idol.* **3.** captured, overthrown, or defeated: *a fallen castle.* **4.** having died, especially in battle: *a fallen hero.*

fal·li·ble (fal′ə bəl) *adj.* liable to be deceived or mistaken: *Even the best judge is sometimes fallible.* —**fal′li·bil′i·ty,** *n.* —**fal′li·bly,** *adv.*

at; āpe; fär; câre; end; mē; it; īce; pîerce; hot; ōld; sông, fôrk; oil; out; up; ūse; rüle; pùll; tûrn; chin; sing; shop; thin; <u>th</u>is; hw in white; zh in treasure. The symbol ə stands for the unstressed vowel sound heard in about, taken, pencil, lemon, and circus.

fall·ing–out (fô′ling out′) *n., pl.* **fall·ings-out** or **fall-ing-outs.** a disagreement or quarrel: *The two friends had a brief falling-out over who should be team captain.*

falling star, another term for **meteor.**

fall line, the boundary between a plateau and a lower land mass, marked by waterfalls and rapids.

fal·lo·pi·an tube (fə lō′pē ən) *also,* **Fal·lo·pi·an tube.** either of a pair of long, thin tubes in female mammals through which eggs pass from the ovaries to the uterus.

fall·out (fôl′out′) *n.* particles that fall to the earth from the atmosphere, such as radioactive dust from a nuclear explosion or ash from a volcanic eruption or forest fire.

fal·low (fal′ō) *adj.* (of land) tilled and left without being planted for one or more growing seasons. —*n.* fallow land.

fallow deer, a small European deer that usually has a yellowish coat with white spots.

false (fôls) *adj.,* **fals·er, fals-est. 1.** not true; incorrect: *a false statement, a false accusation.* **2.** not genuine or natural; artificial: *false modesty.* **3.** misleading; deceptive: *false advertising.* **4.** disloyal; unfaithful: *a false friend.* **5.** untruthful; dishonest: *a false witness.* —**false′ly,** *adv.* —**false′ness,** *n.*

false·hood (fôls′hŭd′) *n.* **1.** a false statement; lie. **2.** the quality of being false; absence of truth: *to distinguish between falsehood and truthfulness.* **3.** something that is false, as a theory or idea.

fallow deer

false teeth, a complete or partial set of artificial teeth used in place of real teeth; denture.

fal·set·to (fôl set′ō) *n., pl.* **fal·set·tos. 1.** an unnaturally high-pitched voice used by a singer, especially a tenor. **2.** a singer who has such a voice. —*adj.* of or for such a voice. —*adv.* in falsetto: *to sing falsetto.*

fal·si·fy (fôl′sə fī′) *v.,* **fal·si·fied, fal·si·fy·ing.** —*v.t.* **1.** to change in order to deceive; make false: *to falsify the date of one's birth, to falsify an accident report.* **2.** to give a false account of; misrepresent: *This book falsifies the events of the Civil War.* —*v.i.* to tell falsehoods; lie. —**fal′si·fi·ca′tion,** *n.* —**fal′si·fi′er,** *n.*

fal·si·ty (fôl′si tē) *n., pl.* **fal·si·ties. 1.** the state or quality of being false; untruthfulness. **2.** something that is false; falsehood.

Fal·staff, Sir John (fôl′staf) the fat, boastful, swaggering old knight, given to drinking, jesting, and good-natured lying, in Shakespeare's *Henry IV* and *The Merry Wives of Windsor.*

Fal·staff·i·an (fôl staf′ē ən) *adj.* of, characteristic of, or like Falstaff: *Falstaffian bragging.*

fal·ter (fôl′tər) *v.i.* **1.** to act with hesitation or uncertainty; waver: *to falter in one's resolve.* **2.** to move unsteadily: *The baby faltered as it tried to take a step.* **3.** to speak with hesitation; stammer: *The witness faltered while describing the accident.* —**fal′ter·er,** *n.* —**fal′ter·ing·ly,** *adv.*

fame (fām) *n.* a widespread reputation, especially for great achievement: *The singer's fame spread quickly.*

famed (fāmd) *adj.* well-known; famous.

fa·mil·ial (fə mil′yəl, fə mil′ē əl) *adj.* **1.** of, related to, or like a family: *familial bonds of love.* **2.** passed on genetically; hereditary: *a familial disease.*

fa·mil·iar (fə mil′yər) *adj.* **1.** commonly seen, heard, or experienced; well-known: *a familiar tune. Smog is a familiar sight in some cities.* **2.** aware of or knowing facts or details of something or someone: *I am familiar with the book.* **3.** close; intimate: *to be on familiar terms with one's neighbors.* **4.** informal; friendly: *an easy and familiar manner.* **5.** too friendly or intimate; presumptuous; forward. —*n.* **1.** a close friend or associate. **2.** *Folklore.* a spirit or demon supposed to help someone: *The witch's familiar took the form of a cat.* —**fa-mil′iar·ly,** *adv.*

fa·mil·i·ar·i·ty (fə mil′ē ar′i tē) *n., pl.* **fa·mil·i·ar·i·ties. 1.** a close acquaintance with something: *to have familiarity with a subject.* **2.** friendliness or intimacy: *to be on terms of familiarity.* **3.** friendliness that is too bold; forwardness. **4.** an action suitable only for a person of close acquaintance: *to resent the familiarities of a stranger.*

fa·mil·iar·ize (fə mil′yə rīz′) *v.t.,* **fa·mil·iar·ized, fa·mil·iar·iz·ing. 1.** to make (oneself or someone else) accustomed or well-acquainted: *to familiarize oneself with the duties of a new job.* **2.** to make (something) well known: *Advertising familiarized the new soft drink.* —**fa·mil′iar·i·za′tion,** *n.*

fam·i·ly (fam′ə lē, fam′lē) *n., pl.* **fam·i·lies. 1.** a group of people forming a household, such as a parent or parents and children: *Twenty families live on our street.* **2.** the children of the same parents: *The couple raised a large family.* **3.** a group of people connected by blood or marriage; relatives. **4.** a group of people descended from a common ancestor; house, line, or clan. **5.** a group of things related by common or similar characteristics: *a family of musical instruments.* **6.** *Biology.* a group of related animals, plants, or other organisms, ranking in taxonomic classification below an order and above a genus. *Zebras, asses, and horses belong to the horse family.* **7.** a group of related languages descended from a common language. *The English language belongs to the Indo-European family.* —*adj.* of, relating to, or suitable for a family: *a family gathering.*

family name, a last name; surname.

family room, a room in a home used for casual relaxation, as for playing games or watching television.

family therapy, a form of psychotherapy that seeks to improve relationships within a family. Family therapy concentrates on problems that affect the family as a whole, rather than on those that affect only a single individual.

family tree, a chart or diagram showing the ancestry, relationships, and descent of the members of a family.

fam·ine (fam′in) *n.* **1.** a very great and widespread lack or scarcity of food: *Many people died during the famine.* **2.** a great scarcity of anything; dearth: *a fuel famine.*

fam·ished (fam′isht) *adj.* very hungry; starving.

fa·mous (fā′məs) *adj.* having great fame; very well-known; renowned: *a famous author, a famous play.*

fa·mous·ly (fā′məs lē) *adv.* very well; splendidly: *We got along famously.*

fan[1] (fan) *n.* **1.** a device, usually shaped like part of a circle, that is waved by hand to make a small current of air. Fans are often collapsible and are made of various materials, such as paper, ivory, or feathers. **2.** anything resembling an open fan, such as the tail of a peacock. **3.** a mechanical device having blades that are rotated by a motor. Fans are used for producing a current of air to cool, heat, or ventilate. —*v.,* **fanned, fan·ning.** —*v.t.* **1.** to move (air) with or as with a fan: *The bird's wings fanned the air.* **2.** to direct a current of air upon or toward with a fan: *to fan the flames of a fire.* **3.** to blow gently or refreshingly upon: *The cool breeze fanned my face.* **4.** to stir up; excite: *The touchdown fanned the crowd's enthusiasm.* **5.** to spread out like a fan: *to fan a deck of cards.* **6.** *Baseball.* to cause (a batter) to strike out. —*v.i.* **1.** to spread out like a fan. **2.** *Baseball.* to strike out. [From the Old English word *fann* meaning "a device for separating grain from chaff."] —**fan′like,** *adj.*

fan[2] (fan) *n. Informal.* an enthusiastic devotee or admirer, as of a sport or performer. [Short for *fanatic.*]

fa·nat·ic (fə nat′ik) *n.* a person whose devotion to a cause or belief is unreasonably strong or enthusiastic: *a religious fanatic.* —*adj.* another word for **fanatical.**

fa·nat·i·cal (fə nat′i kəl) *adj.* unreasonably enthusiastic or devoted. Also, **fanatic.** —**fa·nat′i·cal·ly,** *adv.*

fa·nat·i·cism (fə nat′ə siz′əm) *n.* unreasonable enthusiasm or zeal.

fan·cied (fan′sēd) *adj.* imagined; imaginary: *To the little child the dark room was filled with fancied dangers.*

fan·ci·er (fan′sē ər) *n.* a person who has a special liking for or interest in something: *a cat fancier.*

fan·ci·ful (fan′sə fəl) *adj.* **1.** suggested by fancy; imaginary; unreal: *a fanciful story about dragons.* **2.** showing imagination: *a fanciful costume.* **3.** influenced by fancy; imaginative; whimsical: *a fanciful mind.* —**fan′ci·ful·ly,** *adv.* —**fan′ci·ful·ness,** *n.*

fan·cy (fan′sē) *n., pl.* **fan·cies. 1.** the imagination, especially of a whimsical kind: *The unicorn is a creature of fancy.* **2.** something that is imagined by the fancy. **3.** an idea or opinion based on few or no facts; notion; supposition: *a mere fancy.* **4.** a preference or inclination; fondness; liking: *a fancy for cowboy movies, a sudden fancy to visit the zoo.* —*adj.,* **fan·ci·er, fan·ci·est. 1.** made to please the fancy; highly decorated; ornamental; elaborate: *fancy embroidery.* **2.** of highest quality; superior; choice: *fancy fruits and vegetables.* **3.** *Informal.* very high; extravagant: *That store charges fancy prices.* **4.** showing or requiring great skill or grace; intricate: *fancy diving.* —*v.t.,* **fan·cied, fan·cy·ing. 1.** to picture in the mind; imagine: *to fancy oneself a hero.* **2.** to have a fondness for; like: *Which dress do you fancy the most?* **3.** to think without being certain: *I fancy I saw the wolf here.* —**fan′ci·ly,** *adv.* —**fan′ci·ness,** *n.*

fan·cy·work (fan′sē wûrk′) *n.* ornamental needlework, as embroidery or tatting.

fan·dan·go (fan dang′gō) *n., pl.* **fan·dan·gos. 1.** a lively Spanish dance usually performed with castanets. **2.** the music for this dance.

fan·fare (fan′fâr′) *n.* **1.** a short tune sounded by bugles, trumpets, or other brass instruments, used especially for military and ceremonial occasions. **2.** a great noise, fuss, excitement, or activity, as in celebration of something: *The victory was greeted with fanfare.*

fang (fang) *n.* **1.** a long, pointed tooth with which an animal slashes or holds its prey. **2.** one of the two sharp, hollow or grooved teeth with which a poisonous snake injects venom. **3.** any pointed, tapered projection.

fan·light (fan′līt′) *n.* a semicircular window over a door or window.

fan·tail (fan′tāl′) *n.* **1.** a tail, end, or part resembling an open fan. **2.** a domestic pigeon having a fantail.

fanlight

fan·tas·tic (fan tas′tik) *adj.* **1.** very unusual or strange; odd; grotesque: *driftwood in fantastic shapes.* **2.** existing in the mind only; imaginary: *the fantastic fears of children.* **3.** *Informal.* particularly good; splendid: *a fantastic view from a mountain top.* **4.** extraordinary; remarkable; amaz-

ing: *to eat a fantastic amount.* Also, **fan·tas·ti·cal** (fan-tas′ti kəl). —**fan·tas′ti·cal·ly,** *adv.*

fan·ta·sy (fan′tə sē) *also,* **phan·ta·sy.** *n., pl.* **fan·ta·sies. 1.** imagination or fancy. **2.** an unreal or grotesque fancy: *fantasies brought on by a high fever, to have fantasies in one's daydreams.* **3.** a fanciful or imaginative creation or invention: *The novel is a fantasy about life on Mars.*

far (fär) *adv.,* **far·ther** or **fur·ther, far·thest** or **fur·thest. 1.** at or to a great distance in space: *to travel far from home.* **2.** at or to a distant time, degree, or extent: *We worked far into the night. The job is far from finished.* **3.** to or at a certain distance, time, or degree: *Your practical jokes always go too far.* **4.** to a great degree; very much: *It would be far better if you came back tomorrow.* —*adj.,* **far·ther** or **fur·ther, far·thest** or **fur·thest. 1.** distant in time or space: *the far future, the far north.* **2.** more distant; farther: *the far side of the moon.* **3.** going or reaching over a long distance or time: *a far journey.*

•**as far as.** to the distance, degree, or extent that: *Read as far as you can in ten minutes.*

•**by far.** very much: *That is by far the best choice.*

•**far and away.** without a doubt; very much: *This is far and away the best restaurant in town.*

•**in so far as.** to the degree or extent that: *In so far as I know, they are coming next week.*

•**so far. a.** up to now: *I've saved five dollars so far.* **b.** up to a certain point or extent: *You can go just so far in being frank.*

•**so far as.** to the degree or extent that.

far·ad (far′əd) *n.* a unit of electrical capacitance. An object that stores one coulomb of charge when raised to a potential of one volt has a capacitance of one farad.

far·a·day (far′ə dā′) *n.* in electrolysis, the quantity of electricity necessary to deposit or dissolve an amount of a substance equivalent to one gram. One faraday is equal to about 96,500 coulombs. [From the English physicist Michael *Faraday* (1791–1867)]

far·a·way (fär′ə wä′) *adj.* **1.** at a great distance; remote: *to travel to faraway places.* **2.** dreamy; pensive: *a faraway look in one's eyes.*

farce (färs) *n.* **1.** a humorous play in which the situation and characters are greatly exaggerated. **2.** an absurd pretense; mockery: *The meeting turned out to be a farce.*

far·ci·cal (fär′si kəl) *adj.* of, relating to, characteristic of, or like a farce; absurd; ludicrous. **far·ci·cal·i·ty** (fär′si kal′i tē), *n.* —**far′ci·cal·ly,** *adv.*

far cry, a great distance; long way: *The official statement was a far cry from the truth.*

fare (fâr) *n.* **1.** the cost of a ride on a bus, train, airplane, or other conveyance. **2.** a passenger who pays a fare: *How many fares can that bus carry?* **3.** food and drink: *The restaurant served English fare.* —*v.i.,* **fared, far·ing. 1.** to get along; do: *to fare well at school.* **2.** to turn out; result; happen: *Things fared badly with us on our trip.*

fare·well (fâr′wel′) *interj.* good-bye and good luck. —*n.* **1.** parting word; good-bye: *The guests said their farewells and left.* **2.** the act of parting; departure; leave-taking. —*adj.* of or relating to a farewell; last: *a farewell dinner, a farewell speech.*

far-fetched (fär′fecht′) *adj.* not natural or reasonable; forced; strained: *The defendant's alibi was so far-fetched that the jury did not believe it.*

far-flung (fär′flung′) *adj.* covering a great distance or area; widespread: *a far-flung empire.*

at; āpe; fär; câre; end; mē; it; īce; pîerce; hot; ōld; sông, fôrk; oil; out; up; ūse; rüle; pull; tûrn; chin; sing; shop; thin; *this;* hw in white; zh in treasure. The symbol ə stands for the unstressed vowel sound heard in about, taken, pencil, lemon, and circus.

F

fa·ri·na (fə rē′nə) *n.* a flour or meal made from cereal grains, nuts, or starchy roots, used as a breakfast cereal or in puddings.

farm (färm) *n.* **1.** an area of land used to raise crops, livestock, or poultry. **2.** a tract of water used for the cultivation of fish or other forms of marine life: *an oyster farm.* —*v.t.* to cultivate (land). —*v.i.* to grow crops or raise livestock or poultry: *My neighbors farm for a living.*

farm·er (fär′mər) *n.* a person who lives on or runs a farm.

farmers′ market, a market to which farmers can bring vegetables and other farm products for sale directly to consumers.

farm·hand (färm′hand′) *n.* a person who works on a farm, especially a hired laborer.

farm·house (färm′hous′) *n., pl.* **farm·hous·es** (färm′hou′ziz). a house on a farm, especially one in which the owner or manager lives.

farm·ing (fär′ming) *n.* the business of raising crops, livestock, or poultry; agriculture.

farm·land (färm′land′) *n.* land that is being farmed or that is suitable for farming.

farm·stead (färm′sted′) *n.* a farm and its buildings.

farm team, a minor-league team owned by or associated with a major-league club.

farm·yard (färm′yärd′) *n.* a yard enclosed by or surrounding farm buildings.

far-off (fär′ôf′) *adj.* distant; remote: *to visit far-off lands.*

far-out (fär′out′) *adj.* *Slang.* unconventional; extreme: *far-out taste in clothing.*

far-reach·ing (fär′rē′ching) *adj.* having wide influence, effect, or range: *far-reaching changes.*

far·ri·er (far′ē ər) *n.* *British.* a blacksmith who shoes horses.

far·row (far′ō) *n.* a litter of pigs. —*v.i.* to give birth to a litter of pigs.

far·see·ing (fär′sē′ing) *adj.* **1.** able to see distant objects. **2.** having or showing foresight and careful planning; farsighted: *a farseeing executive, a farseeing program to improve public education.*

far·sight·ed (fär′sī′tid) *adj.* **1.** able to see distant objects more clearly than those nearby. **2.** having or showing foresight and careful planning; prudent: *a farsighted leader.* —**far′sight′ed·ly,** *adv.* —**far′sight′ed·ness,** *n.*

far·ther (fär′thər) a comparative of **far.** —*adv.* **1.** at or to a more distant point in space: *The raft drifted farther from the dock.* **2.** to a greater degree or extent; more completely. —*adj.* **1.** more distant: *They live at the farther side of town.* **2.** more; additional; further.

▲ **Farther** or **further** can be used interchangeably. **Farther** is somewhat more common when distance is referred to: *You jumped two feet farther than I did.* **Further** is used more often than *farther* in the sense of "additional": *The district attorney called for further investigation of the incident.*

far·ther·most (fär′thər mōst′) *adj.* most distant or remote; farthest.

far·thest (fär′thist) a superlative of **far.** —*adv.* **1.** at or to the most distant point in space: *Is Pluto the planet farthest from the Sun?* **2.** to the greatest degree or extent; most completely. —*adj.* most distant: *the farthest hill.*

far·thing (fär′thing) *n.* **1.** a former British coin, equal to one-fourth of a penny. **2.** something of very little value; the smallest amount.

far·thin·gale (fär′thing gāl′) *n.* a framework for holding out a skirt, worn in the sixteenth and seventeenth centuries.

fas·ci·nate (fas′ə nāt′) *v.t.,* **fas·ci·nat·ed, fas·ci·nat·ing.** **1.** to attract and hold the close interest of by some special quality or charm; captivate: *The magician's tricks fascinated the audience.* **2.** to hold motionless or paralyze,

as by terror or awe: *The snake fascinated its prey.* —**fas′ci·na′tor,** *n.*

fas·ci·nat·ing (fas′ə nā′ting) *adj.* very interesting or captivating: *a fascinating speaker, a fascinating story.* —**fas′ci·nat′ing·ly,** *adv.*

fas·ci·na·tion (fas′ə nā′shən) *n.* **1.** the act of fascinating or the state of being fascinated. **2.** very strong attraction; charm; enchantment.

fas·cism (fash′iz əm) *n.* **1.** Fascism. a political movement that controlled Italy from 1922 to 1943 under the dictatorship of Benito Mussolini. Fascism established strict economic controls and attempted to organize most phases of Italian life. **2.** any similar movement, such as Naziism, that advocates a nationalist dictatorship, private ownership of property but state control of the economy, and suppression of opposing political movements. **3.** the doctrines or methods of any such movement.

fas·cist (fash′ist) *n.* **1.** Fascist. a member of the ruling political party in Italy under the dictatorship of Benito Mussolini. **2.** a member of any similar political party. **3.** a person who believes in and supports fascism. —*adj. also,* Fascist. of, relating to, or supporting fascism or fascists.

fash·ion (fash′ən) *n.* **1.** clothing; apparel: *The store was showing spring fashions.* **2.** the current custom or style, as in dress, speech, or behavior: *the latest fashion, a game that is no longer in fashion.* **3.** manner; way: *to act in a carefree fashion.* —*v.t.* to give form to; shape; mold: *The cobbler fashioned a boot out of leather.*

•**after a fashion** or **in a fashion.** to some extent, but not completely or too well: *They washed the car after a fashion.*

fash·ion·a·ble (fash′ə nə bəl) *adj.* **1.** following current styles or practices; in fashion; stylish: *a fashionable hair style.* **2.** of, relating to, or used by people who set or follow styles: *a fashionable restaurant.* —**fash′ion·a·bly,** *adv.*

fast¹ (fast) *adj.* **1.a.** acting, moving, or done with speed; quick; rapid: *a fast train, a fast thinker, a fast game.* **b.** designed for or enabling speedy movement: *the fast lane of a highway.* **2.** (of a clock or watch) ahead of the correct time. **3.** wild and dissipated: *a fast life, a fast group of people.* **4.** firmly attached; secure; tight: *a fast knot, to have a fast grip on a rope.* **5.** loyal; faithful; steadfast: *fast friends.* **6.** (of colors) not easily faded. —*adv.* **1.** in a firm manner; securely; tightly: *The tent was held fast by stakes. This stamp will not stick fast.* **2.** soundly; deeply: *fast asleep.* **3.** with speed; quickly; rapidly: *The horse ran fast.* **4.** in a wild, dissipated manner. [From the Old English word *fæst* meaning "firm, fixed."]

fast² (fast) *v.i.* to eat little or no food or only certain kinds of food, especially as a religious observance. —*n.* **1.** the act of fasting. **2.** a day or period of fasting. [From the Old English word *fæsten* meaning "a fast, fasting," from the word *fæstan* "to abstain from food."]

fast·back (fast′back′) *n.* an automobile with a roof that slopes down to the rear in an unbroken curve.

fas·ten (fas′ən) *v.t.* **1.** to attach firmly; connect; join: *to fasten a pin to a dress. The team fastened the blame for their defeat on poor pitching.* **2.** to make fast; close tightly; secure: *to fasten a door, to fasten a seat belt.* **3.** to direct steadily or fix: *I fastened my attention on the book.* —*v.i.* **1.** to become attached or firmly joined: *This snap won't fasten.* **2.** to take a firm hold; concentrate: *to fasten on a plan.*

fas·ten·er (fas′ə nər) *n.* **1.** something that fastens; fastening. **2.** someone who fastens.

fas·ten·ing (fas′ə ning) *n.* **1.** something that fastens, as a hook, bolt, or button. **2.** the act of making fast.

fast–food (fast′füd′) *adj.* of or serving fast foods: *a fast-food restaurant.*

fast food, a food that can be cooked with little preparation and then sold to be eaten in a restaurant or taken out. Fast foods often have been prepared beforehand, frozen, and then reheated.

fas·tid·i·ous (fas tid′ē əs) *adj.* difficult to please or satisfy, particularly in matters of taste: *to be fastidious about clothing, a fastidious eater.* —**fas·tid′i·ous·ly,** *adv.* —**fas·tid′i·ous·ness,** *n.*

fast·ness (fast′nis) *n., pl.* **fast·ness·es.** **1.** the quality or state of being securely fixed. **2.** swiftness; rapidity: *We prefer sureness to fastness.* **3.** stronghold: *The fort was an impenetrable fastness.*

fat (fat) *n.* **1.** any of a group of oily or greasy substances that are white or yellow in color, found especially in deposits in certain tissues of animals and some plants, for which they serve as reserve sources of energy. Fats are compounds of carbon, hydrogen, and oxygen. **2.** animal tissue consisting mainly of such a substance. **3.** a fat or oil used in cooking: *to fry potatoes in fat.* **4.** too much weight; obesity. —*adj.,* **fat·ter, fat·test.** **1.** having much flesh or fat; obese or plump: *a fat child, a fat dog.* **2.** containing much fat, oil, or grease; fatty: *fat hamburger, fat gravy.* **3.** containing much; full; abundant: *a fat wallet.* **4.** profitable. —*v.t.,* **fat·ted, fat·ting.** to fatten. —**fat′ness,** *n.*

fa·tal (fā′təl) *adj.* **1.** causing death: *a fatal injury, a fatal accident.* **2.** causing destruction or ruin; disastrous: *a fatal mistake.* **3.** very important or decisive; fateful: *Finally, the fatal day of the exam arrived.*

fa·tal·ism (fā′tə liz′əm) *n.* **1.** the belief that all events are determined beforehand by fate and cannot be changed by people. **2.** the acceptance of what happens, without struggling against it, on the basis of this belief.

fa·tal·ist (fā′tə list) *n.* a person who believes in, or bases his or her conduct on, fatalism.

fa·tal·is·tic (fā′tə lis′tik) *adj.* relating to, believing in, or basing one's conduct on fatalism. —**fa·tal′is·ti·cal·ly,** *adv.*

fa·tal·i·ty (fā tal′i tē) *n., pl.* **fa·tal·i·ties.** **1.** a death resulting from a disaster; fatal accident: *highway fatalities.* **2.** the ability to cause death; deadly influence or effect: *the fatality of a disease.*

fa·tal·ly (fā′tə lē) *adv.* so as to cause death or disaster; mortally: *to be fatally ill.*

fat·back (fat′bak′) *n.* a fatty strip of meat from the back of a hog, usually salted and dried.

fate (fāt) *n.* **1.** the power that is believed to determine events before they happen and over which humans have no control. **2.** something that is believed to be caused by fate; unavoidable lot or fortune; destiny: *It was their fate to die young.* **3.** the final state; outcome: *The fate of the project is undetermined.*

fat·ed (fā′tid) *adj.* **1.** determined in advance by fate; destined: *Our team was fated to win.* **2.** destined to disaster; doomed.

fate·ful (fāt′fəl) *adj.* **1.** determining what will happen; decisive; critical: *a fateful battle, a fateful decision.* **2.** showing or telling what will happen; prophetic: *fateful words.* **3.** causing death or disaster; deadly. —**fate′ful·ly,** *adv.* —**fate′ful·ness,** *n.*

Fates (fāts) *pl. n. Greek and Roman Mythology.* the three goddesses who controlled human life and destiny.

fa·ther (fä′thər) *n.* **1.** a male parent. **2.** a man who acts or is thought of as a male parent; guardian or provider. **3.** a man who originates, invents, or founds something: *Gutenberg was the father of printing.* **4.** a man who is an important leader: *the town fathers.* **5.** *also,* **Father.** a title of respect used to address a priest or another clergyman. **6. Father.** God. **7.** a male ancestor; forefather. —*v.t.* **1.** to be the father of: *to father two sons and a daughter.* **2.** to act as a father toward: *to father an orphan.* **3.** to originate, invent, or found: *The revolutionists fathered a new form of government.*

fa·ther·hood (fä′thər hùd′) *n.* the state of being a father.

fa·ther-in-law (fä′thər in lô′) *n., pl.* **fa·thers-in-law.** the father of one's husband or wife.

fa·ther·land (fä′thər land′) *n.* the country in which a person or his or her ancestors were born.

fa·ther·less (fä′thər lis) *adj.* **1.** having no living father. **2.** having no known father.

fa·ther·ly (fä′thər lē) *adj.* **1.** of, relating to, or characteristic of a father: *fatherly advice.* **2.** like a father: *a fatherly teacher.* —**fa′ther·li·ness,** *n.*

Father's Day, a day set aside in honor of fathers, celebrated each year on the third Sunday in June.

fath·om (fath′əm) *n., pl.* **fath·oms** or **fath·om.** a unit of measure equal to 6 feet (1.83 meters), used especially in nautical measurements, as for the depth of water. —*v.t.* **1.** to measure the depth of (water); sound. **2.** to understand fully: *to fathom the meaning of a poem.* —**fath′om·a·ble,** *adj.*

fath·om·less (fath′əm lis) *adj.* **1.** too deep to be measured. **2.** difficult or impossible to understand; incomprehensible.

fa·tigue (fə tēg′) *n.* **1.** a loss of strength that is caused by hard work or mental effort; weariness; exhaustion. **2.** the cause of such weariness; toil; exertion. **3.** manual labor done by military personnel. Also, **fatigue duty.** **4. fatigues.** a work uniform worn by military personnel. —*v.t.,* **fa·tigued, fa·ti·guing.** to cause weariness in; tire out: *The hard work fatigued me.*

fat·ten (fat′ən) *v.t.* to make fat or plump; fill out: *to fatten turkeys for market.* —*v.i.* to grow or become fat: *to fatten on rich desserts.*

fat·ty (fat′ē) *adj.,* **fat·ti·er, fat·ti·est.** **1.** made of or containing fat, especially in large amounts. **2.** like fat; greasy; oily. —**fat′ti·ness,** *n.*

fatty acid, any of several organic compounds that make up a large part of animal and plant fat and other biological substances.

fa·tu·i·ty (fə tü′i tē, fə tu′i te) *n., pl.* **fa·tu·i·ties.** **1.** smug stupidity or foolishness. **2.** something that is fatuous, as an action or statement.

fat·u·ous (fach′ü əs) *adj.* smugly stupid or foolish; inane: *a fatuous remark.* —**fat′u·ous·ly,** *adv.* —**fat′u·ous·ness,** *n.*

fau·cet (fô′sit) *n.* a device that controls the flow of water or another liquid from a pipe or container by means of a valve; tap.

fault (fôlt) *n.* **1.** something that spoils character, appearance, or structure; flaw: *The roof collapsed because of a fault in the beams. A bad temper is a serious fault.* **2.** the responsibility for a mistake or wrongdoing: *The accident was no one's fault.* **3.** mistake; error: *faults in arithmetic.* **4.** *Geology.* a break in a rock mass. The mass on one side of the break is displaced with respect to the mass on the other side. One cause of earthquakes is movement along a fault. **5.** a failure to serve the ball into the correct area of the court in tennis, squash, and similar games. —*v.t.* **1.** to find fault with; blame. **2.** *Geology.* to cause or produce a fault in. —*v.i. Geology.* to develop a fault.

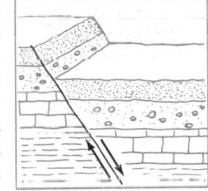

fault (n., def. 4)

·**at fault.** deserving blame; wrong: *They are not at fault in this case.*

---

at; āpe; fär; câre; end; mē; it; īce; pîerce; hot; ōld; sông, fôrk; oil; out; up; ūse; rüle; pùll; tûrn; chin; sing; shop; thin; <u>th</u>is; hw in white; zh in treasure. The symbol ə stands for the unstressed vowel sound heard in about, taken, pencil, lemon, and circus.

•**to a fault.** excessively; extremely: *generous to a fault.*

•**to find fault.** to look for and point out a fault; complain: *the kind of person who tends to find fault rather than to praise.*

•**to find fault with.** to criticize: *You seem to find fault with everything.*

fault·find·er (fôlt′fīn′dər) *n.* a person who looks for and points out faults; person who criticizes too much.

fault·find·ing (fôlt′fīn′ding) *n.* the act or habit of criticizing or pointing out faults. —*adj.* tending to point out faults; critical.

fault·less (fôlt′lis) *adj.* without a fault; perfect. —**fault′less·ly,** *adv.* —**fault′less·ness,** *n.*

fault·y (fôl′tē) *adj.,* **fault·i·er, fault·i·est.** having faults or defects: *faulty reasoning.* —**fault′i·ly,** *adv.* —**fault′i·ness,** *n.*

faun (fôn) *n. Roman Mythology.* a minor god of the woods and fields, having the body of a man and the ears, horns, legs, and tail of a goat. In Greek mythology it was called a satyr.

fau·na (fô′nə) *n., pl.* **fau·nas** or **fau·nae** (fô′nē) the animals characteristic of a particular region, time, or environment: *the fauna of the African plains.*

Faust (foust) *n. German Legend.* a magician and philosopher who sold his soul to the devil in return for knowledge and power.

faux pas (fō′ pä′) *pl.* **faux pas** (fō′ päz′, fō′ pä′). an embarrassing mistake, especially a social one: *Forgetting my host's name was a faux pas.* [From the French phrase *faux pas* meaning "a false step," going back to the Latin words *falsus* "deceptive, false" and *passus* "step."]

fa·vor (fā′vər) *n.* **1.** an act of kindness or good will: *Do me the favor of lending me that book.* **2.** friendly regard; approval; liking: *The teacher looked on us with favor.* **3.** special consideration or kindness; partiality: *Judges must not show favor to their friends.* **4.** the condition of being liked, highly regarded, or approved: *That politician is in favor with the people.* **5.** something given, as a souvenir at a party; gift. —*v.t.* **1.** to show favor to; oblige: *Please favor us with a reply.* **2.** to approve of; like: *to favor long hair.* **3.** to show special consideration for; be partial to: *to favor one child over another, a law that favors rural areas.* **4.** to want or expect to win or be successful: *Which runner do you favor in this race?* **5.** to prove advantageous to; make easy; assist: *Crowded conditions favor the spread of disease.* **6.** to treat with gentleness; spare: *to favor a sprained ankle.* **7.** to look like; resemble: *She favors her father.*

•**in favor of.** **a.** in support of; supporting: *The students were in favor of longer vacations.* **b.** to the advantage of: *The jury decided in favor of the defendant.*

•**in one's favor.** to one's advantage or interest: *The score was 35 to 13 in our favor.*

fa·vor·a·ble (fā′vər ə bəl) *adj.* **1.** approving; complimentary: *a favorable review.* **2.** in one's favor; advantageous: *favorable conditions for sailing. The speaker made a favorable impression.* **3.** granting something desired or requested: *I hope that my application for a job will receive a favorable reply.* —**fa′vor·a·ble·ness,** *n.* —**fa′vor·a·bly,** *adv.*

fa·vor·ite (fā′vər it) *adj.* looked upon with special liking or favor; liked best: *Spring is my favorite time of the year.* —*n.* **1.** a person or thing that is liked best: *Mystery stories are my favorites. Of all my records, that is my favorite.* **2.** in a contest, the competitor that is most likely to win: *That horse is the favorite in the next race.*

favorite son, a political leader nominated as a presidential candidate by the delegates of his state at a national nominating convention, usually principally as an honor.

fa·vor·it·ism (fā′vər i tiz′əm) *n.* the unfair favoring of one or more persons over others; partiality: *The coach tried not to show favoritism in selecting team members.*

fawn¹ *(def. 1)*

fawn¹ (fôn) *n.* **1.** a deer less than one year old. **2.** a light yellowish-brown color. —*adj.* having the color fawn. [From the Old French word *faon* meaning "young of an animal" or "young deer," from the Latin word *fetus* "offspring."]

fawn² (fôn) *v.i.* **1.** to seek favor by acting in a slavish manner: *They fawned on the powerful leader.* **2.** (of dogs) to show affection, as by wagging the tail. [From the Middle English word *faunen* with the same meanings, from the Old English word *fagnian* "to rejoice," from the word *fægan* "glad."]

fax (faks) *n., pl.* **fax·es.** **1.** a method of electronically transmitting pictures or texts, as by telephone lines or radio. **2.** an image or document transmitted by fax. —*v.t.* to transmit by fax.

faze (fāz) *v.t.,* **fazed, faz·ing.** *Informal.* to upset; disconcert: *All the noise didn't faze me a bit.*

FBI, Federal Bureau of Investigation.

F clef *Music.* another term for **bass clef.**

Fe, the symbol for iron. [Short for the Latin word *ferrum* meaning "iron."]

fe·al·ty (fē′əl tē) *n., pl.* **fe·al·ties.** **1.** the loyalty and duty owed by a vassal or feudal tenant to a lord. **2.** loyalty; faithfulness.

fear (fîr) *n.* **1.** a strong feeling caused by the awareness or threat of danger, pain, or evil; dread: *They trembled with fear in the storm.* **2.** the state of feeling fear: *to live in fear.* **3.** a feeling of concern or anxiety: *We had a fear that our sick dog would not get well.* **4.** a cause for fear or alarm; danger: *There was no fear of failing the exam.* —*v.t.* **1.** to be afraid of: *Many children fear the dark.* **2.** to feel concerned or anxious about: *We feared we would miss the bus.* —*v.i.* to feel fear; be afraid.

•**to fear for.** to be concerned about: *to fear for one's safety.*

fear·ful (fîr′fəl) *adj.* **1.** feeling fear; afraid: *to be fearful of a barking dog.* **2.** causing fear; dreadful; frightening: *The blizzard was fearful.* **3.** showing fear: *a fearful look.* **4.** *Informal.* very bad; offensive: *fearful table manners.* —**fear′ful·ly,** *adv.* —**fear′ful·ness,** *n.*

fear·less (fîr′lis) *adj.* showing or feeling no fear. —**fear′less·ly,** *adv.* —**fear′less·ness,** *n.*

fear·some (fîr′səm) *adj.* **1.** causing fear; frightening. **2.** feeling fear; frightened. —**fear′some·ly,** *adv.* —**fear′some·ness,** *n.*

fea·si·ble (fē′zə bəl) *adj.* **1.** capable of being done or carried out; practicable: *a feasible design for a bridge.* **2.** capable of being used successfully; suitable: *a feasible site for a dam.* **3.** likely; probable: *a feasible explanation for being absent.* —**fea′si·bil′i·ty,** *n.* —**fea′si·bly,** *adv.*

feast (fēst) *n.* **1.** an elaborate, plentiful, and rich meal, especially one prepared for many guests on a special occasion: *a wedding feast.* **2.** a religious celebration or festival: *the feast of the Annunciation.* **3.** something that gives great pleasure; treat: *The snow-capped mountains*

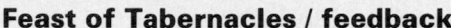

were a feast for our eyes. —*v.t.* **1.** to give great pleasure to: *Feast your eyes on this beautiful painting.* **2.** to provide a feast for; entertain richly. —*v.i.* to have or partake of a feast; eat richly: *We feasted and relaxed the whole week.*

Feast of Tabernacles, another term for **Sukkoth.**

Feast of Weeks, another term for **Shavuoth.**

feat (fēt) *n.* an act or deed, especially one showing great skill, strength, or courage.

feath·er (feth′ər) *n.* **1.** one of the light outgrowths that cover a bird's skin. A feather consists of a horny, hollow shaft with soft, flexible barbs on either side. **2.** something like a feather in appearance or lightness, as a fringe of hair on the leg of a dog. —*v.t.* **1.** to provide with feathers: *to feather a dart.* **2.** to turn (the blade of an oar) parallel to the water's surface after a stroke. —**feath′er·like′,** *adv.*

·**feather in one's cap.** an act to be proud of: *Winning the lead role was a feather in the young actor's cap.*

feather bed, a soft, warm quilt or mattress filled with feathers.

feath·er·bed·ding (feth′ər bed′ing) *n.* the requiring of an employer to hire or continue to employ more people than are needed to do a job, especially as practiced by some labor unions to preserve jobs.

Shaft

Barbs

Quill

feather
(n., def. 1)

feath·er·weight (feth′ər wāt′) *n.* **1.** a boxer competing in the second from the lowest weight class, weighing not more than 126 pounds. **2.** a wrestler or weightlifter in a similar class. **3.** a person or thing that is very small or unimportant.

feath·er·y (feth′ə rē) *adj.* **1.** covered with or having feathers. **2.** like a feather; light and soft.

fea·ture (fē′chər) *n.* **1.** an important or distinctive part or characteristic of something: *Great speed is a feature of this car.* **2.** a part of the face, as the eyes, nose, mouth, or chin. **3.** a full-length motion picture, especially one shown as a main attraction. **4.** anything presented as a main or special attraction: *Tonight's feature will be a trapeze act.* **5.** a story, article, or column of special interest, appearing in a newspaper or magazine. —*v.,* **fea·tured, fea·tur·ing.** —*v.t.* to give an important place to: *The concert features a guitarist.* —*v.i.* to play an important part: *School issues featured prominently in the campaign.*

Feb., February.

Feb·ru·ar·y (feb′rū er′ē, feb′ū er′ē) *n., pl.* **Feb·ru·ar·ies.** the second month of the year, having twenty-eight days in regular years and twenty-nine days in leap years.

fe·cal (fē′kəl) *adj.* of or relating to feces.

fe·ces (fē′sēz) *pl. n.* the solid waste matter discharged from the bowels; excrement.

feck·less (fek′lis) *adj.* **1.** weak; feeble. **2.** irresponsible; careless: *a feckless youth.*

fe·cund (fē′kənd, fek′ənd) *adj.* producing or able to produce much; fertile: *fecund earth, a fecund mind.*

fe·cun·di·ty (fi kun′di tē) *n.* the quality of being fecund; fertility; fruitfulness; productiveness.

fed (fed) the past tense and past participle of **feed.**

·**fed up.** *Informal.* disgusted, annoyed, or bored: *After waiting for an hour, we got fed up and left.*

fed·er·al (fed′ər əl, fed′rəl) *adj.* **1.** of, relating to, or formed by an agreement between states or other groups establishing a central government to control matters of common concern, with each of the states or groups keeping control over its own affairs. **2.** of or relating to a central government formed in this way. **3.** *also,* **Federal.** of or relating to the central government of the United States, as distinguished from the governments of the individual states. **4. Federal.** of, relating to, or supporting the Union

during the Civil War. —*n.* **Federal.** a person who supported the Union during the Civil War, especially a Union soldier.

Federal Bureau of Investigation, an agency of the U.S. government, responsible for investigating violations of federal law and subversive activities against the United States.

fed·er·al·ism (fed′ər ə liz′əm, fed′rə liz′əm) *n.* **1.** the principle or system of federal government. **2.** belief in or support of such a system of government. **3. Federalism.** the principles of the Federalist Party.

fed·er·al·ist (fed′ər ə list, fed′rə list) *n.* **1.** a person who believes in or supports a federal system of government. **2. Federalist.** a member or supporter of the Federalist Party.

Federalist Party, a political party in the United States, active from 1788 to at least 1824, that supported the adoption of the Constitution and advocated a strong central government. Its principal leader was Alexander Hamilton.

fed·er·al·ize (fed′ər ə līz, fed′rə līz′) *v.t.,* **fed·er·al·ized, fed·er·al·iz·ing. 1.** to unite in a federal union. **2.** to place under the control of a federal government.

fed·er·ate (*v.,* fed′ə rāt′; *adj.,* fed′ər it) *v.,* **fed·er·at·ed, fed·er·at·ing.** —*v.t.* to unite in a federal union. —*v.i.* to form a federal union: *The states federated to form one nation.* —*adj.* united in a federation.

fed·er·a·tion (fed′ə rā′shən) *n.* **1.** the act of forming a federal union by agreement between states, nations, or other groups. **2.** a union formed in this way, especially as a form of government: *a federation of nations to promote peace, a federation of labor unions.*

fe·do·ra (fi dôr′ə) *n.* a soft felt hat with a curved brim and a lengthwise crease in the top.

fee (fē) *n.* **1.** a charge or payment for a service or privilege: *a license fee, a registration fee.* **2.** an estate in land held from a feudal lord; fief. **3.** see **fee simple.**

fee·ble (fē′bəl) *adj.,* **fee·bler, fee·blest. 1.** lacking physical strength; weak: *The feeble patient needed to rest in bed.* **2.** lacking force, strength, or effectiveness: *a feeble cry, a feeble try.* —**fee′ble·ness,** *n.* —**fee′bly,** *adv.*

fee·ble·mind·ed (fē′bəl mīn′did) *adj.* having less than normal intelligence. —**fee′ble·mind′ed·ly,** *adv.* —**fee′ble·mind′ed·ness,** *n.*

fedora

feed (fēd) *v.,* **fed, feed·ing.** —*v.t.* **1.** to give food or nourishment to: *to feed a baby.* **2.** to provide as food or nourishment: *to feed grain to cattle.* **3.** to provide with something that is used for growth or maintaining existence: *Melting snow from the mountains feeds the rivers each spring.* **4.** to supply (material to be used or consumed): *to feed data into a computer, to feed fuel into an engine.* **5.** to supply material to be used or consumed by: *to feed a fire.* —*v.i.* (of animals) to eat: *Cows are feeding in that pasture.* —*n.* **1.** food for animals; fodder. **2.** *Informal.* a meal; food.

feed·back (fēd′bak′) *n.* **1.** *Electronics.* the return of a part of the output of a machine, system, or process to the input, especially in order to correct, control, or modify the output. **2.** *Biology.* a process by which living things regulate or correct their own voluntary and involuntary

at; āpe; fär; câre; end; mē; it; īce; pîerce; hot; ōld; sông, fôrk; oil; out; up; ūse; rüle; pull; tûrn; chin; sing; shop; thin; this; hw in white; zh in treasure. The symbol ə stands for the unstressed vowel sound heard in about, taken, pencil, lemon, and circus.

F

activities. The body uses feedback when it perspires to cool itself in response to a high temperature.

feed·er (fē′dər) n. **1.** a person or thing that feeds. **2.** anything that supplies or leads into a main line, such as a tributary of a river, a branch of a railroad, or a side road leading into a highway.

feel (fēl) v., **felt, feel·ing.** —v.t. **1.** to sense or examine by touching or handling; touch: *The doctor felt the patient's pulse.* **2.** to be aware of by touch: *to feel the cold, to feel the rain on one's face.* **3.** to be affected by: *to feel pity.* **4.** to hold as an opinion; believe: *They felt that the rule was unfair.* **5.** to try to find (one's way) by touching; grope: *In the dark I felt my way up the stairs.* —v.i. **1.** to be aware of being: *to feel happy, to feel hot.* **2.** to produce the sensation or feeling of being; seem: *The water feels warm. Today feels like spring.* **3.** to search or explore by touch; grope: *I felt in my pocket for my wallet. The doctor felt for broken bones.* **4.** to have sympathy or compassion: *to feel deeply for a sick friend.* —n. a quality that is sensed or learned by touching: *the cold feel of snow.*
  ·to feel like. to have an interest in or desire for: *Do you feel like playing today?*
  ·to feel out. to try to discover in a cautious way: *to feel out one's boss for a raise.*
  ·to feel up to. to feel able to or ready for: *The swimmer had a cold and did not feel up to racing.*

feel·er (fē′lər) n. **1.** an organ of touch in an animal's body, especially the antenna of an insect, or the tentacles of an invertebrate, such as an octopus. **2.** an act, remark, or plan used to feel out a person or group: *A peace feeler was sent to the enemy.*

feel·ing (fē′ling) n. **1.** the ability to feel by touching; sense of touch: *I rubbed my numb foot to bring back the feeling.* **2.** a sensation: *a feeling of dampness, a feeling of hunger.* **3.** an emotion, as joy, fear, or anger. **4.** an awareness; impression: *a feeling of security.* **5. feelings.** the sensitive part of one's character or nature: *Criticism can hurt one's feelings.* **6.** tender emotion, especially sympathy or pity: *to have great feeling for a suffering child.* **7.** opinion; belief; sentiment: *It is my feeling that you are right.* —adj. having or showing sympathy: *Your feeling remark helped to lift my spirits.* —**feel′ing·ly,** adv.

fee simple, an estate in land, over which the owner has complete rights.

feet (fēt) the plural of **foot.**

feign (fān) v.t. to put on a false appearance of; pretend: *to feign sickness, to feign friendliness.* —v.i. to make believe; pretend.

feint (fānt) n. **1.** a blow or movement meant to deceive, especially one used in boxing, fencing, or warfare to take away attention from the real point of attack. **2.** a false appearance or show; pretense: *They made a feint of listening to our concerns.* —v.i. to make a feint: *The boxer feinted with the left hand.*

feist·y (fī′stē) *Informal.* adj., **feist·i·er, feist·iest. 1.** excitable; touchy; quick-tempered: *a feisty terrier eager for a fight.* **2.** spirited; lively; frisky.

feld·spar (feld′spär′) n. any of a group of crystalline minerals made up of aluminum silicates with sodium, potassium, and calcium. Feldspars are found in igneous rock and are used commercially in making glass.

fe·lic·i·tate (fi lis′i tāt′) v.t., **fe·lic·i·tat·ed, fe·lic·i·tat·ing.** to salute at a happy time; congratulate.

fe·lic·i·ta·tion (fi lis′i tā′shən) n. an expression of pleasure over another's happiness or good fortune; congratulation.

fe·lic·i·tous (fi lis′i təs) adj. **1.** suitable to the occasion; appropriate; apt: *a felicitous choice of words.* **2.** showing skill at appropriate expression: *a felicitous speaker.* —**fe·lic′i·tous·ly,** adv. —**fe·lic′i·tous·ness,** n.

fe·lic·i·ty (fi lis′i tē) n., pl. **fe·lic·i·ties. 1.** great hap-

piness; bliss. **2.** a source of happiness; blessing. **3.** skill at appropriate expression: *to write with felicity.* **4.** a suitable or appropriate expression.

fe·line (fē′līn) adj. **1.** of or relating to cats or the cat family. **2.** like a cat: *The dancer moved with feline grace.* —n. an animal belonging to the cat family, such as a lion, tiger, or domestic cat.

fell¹ (fel) the past tense of **fall.**

fell² (fel) v.t. **1.** to strike and knock down; cause to fall: *The hunter felled the deer. The blow felled the tiring boxer.* **2.** to cut down (a tree or trees). **3.** in sewing, to finish (a seam) by joining the edges, turning them under, and stitching them to the fabric. [From the Old English word *fellan* meaning ''to cause to fall.'']

fell³ (fel) adj. **1.** cruel; savage; dreadful: *a fell pirate.* **2.** destructive; deadly: *a fell disease.* [From the Old French word *fel* meaning ''cruel, fierce.'']

fell⁴ (fel) n. the skin or hide of an animal; pelt. [From the Old English word *fel* meaning ''pelt².'']

fel·lah (fel′ə) n., pl. **fel·lahs** or **fel·la·hin** (fel′ə hēn′) or **fel·la·heen** (fel′ə hēn′). a peasant or laborer in Arabic-speaking countries.

fel·loe (fel′ō) n. another word for **felly.**

fel·low (fel′ō) n. **1.** a man or boy: *What a clever fellow he is.* **2.** a person in general; individual; anyone: *Give a fellow a chance!* **3.** companion; comrade; associate: *I was happy with my fellows.* **4.** a member of a learned society. **5.** a graduate student who holds a fellowship at a university or college. **6.** one of a pair, as of shoes or gloves; mate; match. —adj. belonging to the same class, group, or condition: *fellow workers, fellow Americans.*

fel·low·ship (fel′ō ship′) n. **1.** companionship, friendliness: *the warm fellowship between schoolmates.* **2.** a group of people joined by common interests, beliefs, or goals; brotherhood or sisterhood; society. **3.** a position or sum of money given to a graduate student in a university or college to allow him or her to continue studying.

fel·ly (fel′ē) n., pl. **fel·lies.** the rim or a section of the rim of a wheel, into which the outer ends of the spokes fit. Also, **felloe.**

fel·on (fel′ən) n. a person who has committed a felony.

fe·lo·ni·ous (fə lō′nē əs) adj. of, relating to, or classified as a felony: *a felonious assault.* —**fe·lo′ni·ous·ly,** adv. —**fe·lo′ni·ous·ness,** n.

fel·o·ny (fel′ə nē) n., pl. **fel·o·nies.** any of various crimes, as murder or rape, designated by law to be more serious than a misdemeanor.

felt¹ (felt) the past tense and past participle of **feel.**

felt² (felt) n. a fabric, usually composed of wool, hair, or fur, made by pressing together layers of fibers, rather than by weaving or knitting them. —adj. made of felt: *a felt hat.* [From the Old English word *felt* meaning ''felt cloth.'']

felt–tip pen (felt′tip′) *also,* **felt-tip.** a pen holding ink that flows through a tip made of felt.

fem., female; feminine.

fe·male (fē′māl) adj. **1.** of or relating to the sex that bears young or produces eggs. **2.** of or characteristic of the female sex; feminine. **3.** of or relating to a plant that bears flowers that have only pistils. **4.** (of an object or device) having a hollowed part into which a corresponding part fits, as an electric socket. —n. a female person, animal, or plant.

fem·i·nine (fem′ə nin) adj. **1.** of, characteristic of, or relating to a woman: *feminine taste, feminine interests.* **2.** having qualities or characteristics traditionally regarded as womanly, such as gentleness and delicateness. **3.** (of a man) effeminate; womanish. **4.** of or relating to the female sex. **5.** *Grammar.* of the gender that includes words applying to females or things classified as female.

fem·i·nin·i·ty (fem′ə nin′i tē) n. **1.** the quality or state of being feminine. **2.** effeminacy; womanishness.

fem·i·nism (fem′ə niz′əm) n. **1.** the principle that women are entitled to the same social, economic, and political rights as men. **2.** a movement to obtain such rights for women.

fem·i·nist (fem′ə nist) *n.* a person who believes in or supports feminism. —**fem′i·nis′tic,** *adj.*

fe·mur (fē′mər) *n., pl.* **fe·murs** or **fem·o·ra** (fem′ər ə). the long bone of the upper leg, extending from the pelvis to the knee; thighbone.

fen (fen) *n.* a marshy lowland; swamp; bog.

fence (fens) *n.* **1.** a structure, often made of wire or wood, used to bound, surround, or protect an area: *a fence around a yard, a fence around a construction site.* **2.** a person who receives and sells stolen goods. —*v.,* **fenced, fenc·ing.** —*v.t.* to surround or separate with a fence or other enclosure: *to fence in cattle.* —*v.i.* to practice the sport of fencing.
  ·**on the fence.** undecided about something.

fenc·er (fen′sər) *n.* a person who fights with a foil or sword.

fenc·ing (fen′sing) *n.* **1.** the art or sport of fighting with a foil or sword. **2.** the material used in making fences. **3.** a fence or fences.

fend (fend) *v.* **to fend for oneself.** to provide for or take care of oneself.
  ·**to fend off.** to ward off; defend against: *to fend off a blow to the head.*

fencing *(def. 1)*

fend·er (fen′dər) *n.* **1.** a metal covering projecting over the wheel of an automobile, bicycle, or other vehicle to protect against splashed water or mud. **2.** a metal frame or screen placed in front of a fireplace to protect against escaping coals or sparks. **3.** a metal frame projecting from the front of a locomotive or streetcar, used to push obstacles from the tracks. **4.** a pad or similar device hung between the side of a boat and a dock or the like, to protect against damage from the boat's movement.

fen·nel (fen′əl) *n.* **1.** the fragrant seeds of a plant that taste like licorice and are used as a flavoring in certain foods and liqueurs. **2.** the plant itself, bearing bright green feathery leaves and clusters of yellow flowers.

fe·ral (fîr′əl, fer′əl) *adj.* **1.** not domesticated; wild: *Feral cats lived on the abandoned farm.* **2.** like a wild beast; savage.

fer-de-lance (fer′də lans′) *n.* a very poisonous tropical American snake related to the rattlesnake.

fer·ment (*v.,* fər ment′; *n.,* fûr′ment) *v.i.* **1.** to undergo chemical fermentation. **2.** to be excited or agitated; seethe. —*v.t.* **1.** to cause chemical fermentation in. **2.** to excite or agitate; stir up: *to ferment ill will.* —*n.* **1.** a substance or agent causing chemical fermentation, as the enzymes secreted by yeast or certain bacteria. **2.** a state of excitement, agitation, or unrest: *political ferment.*

fer·men·ta·tion (fûr′men tā′shən) *n.* **1.** a chemical reaction or series of chemical reactions in carbohydrates caused by enzymes, resulting in the formation of bubbles of gas. Fermentation causes milk to turn sour and the juice of grapes to turn into wine. **2.** the process of undergoing this reaction. **3.** excitement; agitation; unrest.

fer·mi·um (fûr′mē əm) *n.* a radioactive element produced artificially. It was discovered in the debris of a nuclear explosion. Symbol: **Fm** [From the Italian physicist Enrico *Fermi* (1901–1954).]

fern (fûrn) *n.* any of a large group of plants that lack flowers, often have large, feathery leaves, and reproduce by spores instead of seeds.

fe·ro·cious (fə rō′shəs) *adj.* **1.** wild and dangerous; fierce: *ferocious beasts, ferocious warriors.* **2.** *Informal.* very intense: *a ferocious headache.* —**fe·ro′cious·ly,** *adv.* —**fe·ro′cious·ness,** *n.*

fe·roc·i·ty (fə ros′i tē) *n., pl.* **fe·roc·i·ties.** the state or quality of being ferocious; fierceness: *the ferocity of a wild animal.*

fer·ret (fer′it) *n.* an animal resembling a weasel, usually having yellowish white fur and pink eyes. It is sometimes trained to hunt rats, mice, and rabbits. —*v.t.* **1.** to hunt (game) with ferrets: *to ferret rabbits.* **2.** to bring to light; search; hunt: *to ferret out the facts.* —*v.i.* **1.** to hunt with ferrets: *to ferret for rabbits.* **2.** to search: *They ferreted through old shops to find rare books.*

fer·ric (fer′ik) *adj.* of or containing iron.

Fer·ris wheel (fer′is) a large, upright, revolving wheel with seats hung within its rim, used as an amusement ride. [From the American engineer George W. G. *Ferris* (1859–1896), who invented it.]

ferret

fer·rous (fer′əs) *adj.* of or containing iron.

fer·rule (fer′əl, fer′ül) *also,* **fer·ule.** *n.* a metal ring or cap put around the end of a cane, tool handle, or umbrella, to give added strength or protect against splitting.

fer·ry (fer′ē) *n., pl.* **fer·ries.** **1.** a boat or other craft used to carry people, vehicles, and goods across a river or other narrow body of water. **2.** a docking or crossing place for a ferry. —*v.,* **fer·ried, fer·ry·ing.** —*v.t.* **1.** to carry across a narrow body of water by a boat or other craft: *They ferried the storm victims to the mainland.* **2.** to cross (a body of water) in a ferryboat: *to ferry the Mississippi.* **3.** to deliver (an airplane) by flying it to a

ferry

particular destination. —*v.i.* to cross a body of water in a ferryboat.

fer·ry·boat (fer′ē bōt′) *n.* a boat used as a ferry.

fer·ry·man (fer′ē′mən) *n., pl.* **fer·ry·men** (fer′ē mən). a person who owns, operates, or works on a ferry.

fer·tile (fûr′təl) *adj.* **1.** producing or able to produce crops or vegetation abundantly: *fertile soil.* **2.** able to produce young, eggs, seeds, pollen, or the like: *a fertile animal.* **3.** able to develop into a new individual: *a fertile egg.* **4.** mentally productive; inventive: *a fertile imagination.*

fer·til·i·ty (fər til′i tē) *n.* **1.** the state or quality of being fertile; productiveness. **2.** the number of offspring produced by a population; birthrate.

fer·ti·li·za·tion (fûr′tə lə zā′shən) *n.* **1.** the act of fertilizing or the state of being fertilized. **2.** *Biology.* the uniting of a sperm cell with an egg cell to form a cell that will develop into a new individual.

fer·ti·lize (fûr′tə līz′) *v.t.*, **fer·ti·lized, fer·ti·liz·ing.** **1.** to make fertile or productive. **2.** to put fertilizer on: *to fertilize a field.* **3.** *Biology.* to make (an egg cell) capable of reproducing a new individual.

fer·ti·liz·er (fûr′tə lī′zər) *n.* a substance, such as manure or certain chemicals, added to the soil to make it more productive.

fer·ule[1] (fer′əl, fer′ül) *n.* a flat stick, as a ruler, used to punish schoolchildren by striking them, especially on the hand. —*v.t.*, **fer·uled, fer·ul·ing.** to punish with a ferule. [Late Latin *ferula.*]

fer·ule[2] (fer′əl, fer′ül) another spelling of **ferrule.**

fer·ven·cy (fûr′vən sē) *n.* great warmth or intensity of feeling; ardor; fervor.

fer·vent (fûr′vənt) *adj.* having or showing great warmth or intensity of feeling; ardent: *fervent prayers, a fervent appeal for justice.* —**fer′vent·ly,** *adv.*

fer·vid (fûr′vid) *adj.* very intense in feeling; impassioned; fervent: *fervid devotion to a cause.* —**fer′vid·ly,** *adv.* —**fer′vid·ness,** *n.*

fer·vor (fûr′vər) *n.* great warmth or intensity of feeling; ardor: *patriotic fervor.*

fes·tal (fes′təl) *adj.* of or suitable for a feast or holiday.

fes·ter (fes′tər) *v.i.* **1.** to form pus, as a wound. **2.** to become increasingly strong, as a feeling of resentment or anger: *Jealousy festered in the losing contestant's mind.* —*n.* a small sore that forms pus.

fes·ti·val (fes′tə vəl) *n.* **1.** a feast, holiday, or celebration, especially one that takes place every year: *a harvest festival, a religious festival.* **2.** a period or program of activities or cultural events: *a film festival.*

fes·tive (fes′tiv) *adj.* relating to or suitable for a festival; festal; gay: *On Thanksgiving, the house had a festive appearance.* —**fes′tive·ly,** *adv.*

fes·tiv·i·ty (fes tiv′i tē) *n., pl.* **fes·tiv·i·ties.** **1.** the rejoicing and gaiety typical of a celebration or other joyous occasion. **2. festivities.** festive activities; merrymaking: *wedding festivities.*

fes·toon (fes tün′) *n.* **1.** an ornamental string or chain, as of flowers, leaves, or ribbons, hanging in a curve between two points. **2.** a carved, molded, or painted ornament resembling this. —*v.t.* **1.** to decorate with festoons: *The walls were festooned with crepe paper.* **2.** to arrange in festoons.

fe·ta (fet′ə) *n.* a soft, white cheese made from sheep's or goat's milk and preserved in brine.

fe·tal (fē′təl) *adj.* of, relating to, like, or characteristic of a fetus.

fetch (fech) *v.t.* **1.** to go after and bring back; come and take back; get: *to fetch a chair from another room.* **2.** to cause to come; succeed in bringing; draw forth: *to fetch an answer.* **3.** to be sold for; bring in: *The car should fetch at least $2,000.* —*v.i.* to go after or get something and bring it back: *to teach a dog to fetch.*

fetch·ing (fech′ing) *adj.* attractive; charming. —**fetch′ing·ly,** *adv.*

fete (fāt, fet) *also,* **fête.** *n.* a festival or large celebration. —*v.t.,* **fet·ed, fet·ing.** to entertain or honor with a fete.

fet·id (fet′id, fē′tid) *adj.* having a bad smell; stinking: *a fetid swamp.* —**fet′id·ly,** *adv.* —**fet′id·ness,** *n.*

fet·ish (fet′ish, fē′tish) *n., pl.* **fet·ish·es.** **1.** an object believed to have magical or supernatural powers. **2.** anything to which unreasonable devotion, concern, or reverence is given: *to make a fetish of neatness.* **3.** an unreasonable or abnormal attachment to or concern about something, especially an object.

fet·ish·ism (fet′i shiz′əm, fē′ti shiz′əm) *n.* **1.** a belief in or devotion to fetishes. **2.** an unreasonable concern with or devotion to something. —**fet′ish·ist,** *n.*

fet·lock (fet′lok′) *n.* **1.** a tuft of hair on the back part of the leg of a horse or similar animal, just above the hoof. **2.** the part of the leg where this tuft grows.

fet·ter (fet′ər) *n.* **1.** a chain or shackle placed on the feet to restrain movement. **2.** anything that confines or restrains: *The students rebelled against the fetters of the school's strict rules.* —*v.t.* **1.** to bind with fetters; shackle: *The jailers fettered the prisoner.* **2.** to bind; confine; restrain: *to fetter a people with harsh laws.*

fet·tle (fet′əl) *n.* a condition or state of the body or mind: *After a month's vacation, we were in fine fettle.*

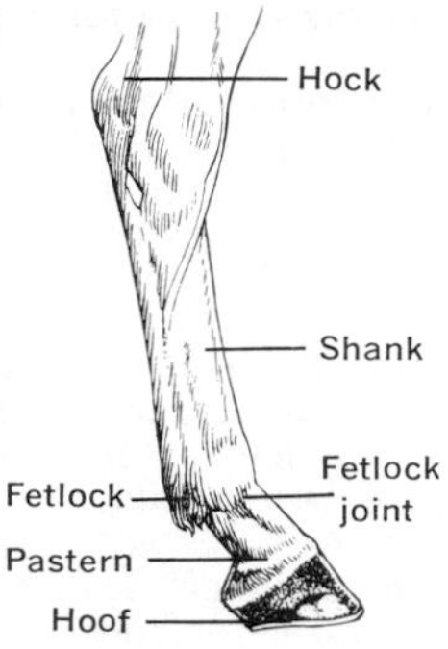

fet·tuc·ci·ne (fet′ə chē′nē) *also,* **fet·tu·ci·ni.** pasta in the form of long, narrow strips. ▲ used with a singular or plural verb. [From the Italian word *fettuccine* meaning "little ribbons," used as the name of this food, from the word *fetta* "slice" or "ribbon."]

fetlock and other parts of a horse's leg

(labels: Hock, Shank, Fetlock joint, Fetlock, Pastern, Hoof)

fe·tus (fē′təs) *also,* **foe·tus.** *n., pl.* **fe·tus·es.** an animal embryo in its later stages of development in the womb or egg, especially a human embryo from the beginning of the third month of pregnancy until birth.

feud (fūd) *n.* **1.** a bitter quarrel between families, tribes, or clans, usually lasting for many years and marked by violent and deadly clashes. **2.** bitter and lasting hatred or conflict between individuals or groups: *a feud between two candidates for political office.* —*v.i.* to carry on a feud. [From the Old French word *faide* meaning "lasting hostility," of Germanic origin.]

feu·dal (fū′dəl) *adj.* **1.** relating to or characteristic of feudalism: *feudal law.* **2.** of or relating to a fief: *feudal rights.*

feu·dal·ism (fū′də liz′əm) *n.* a political, economic, and social system in western Europe during the Middle Ages. It was based upon the relation between a lord who provided land and protection and a vassal who in return pledged military and certain other services to the lord.

feu·dal·is·tic (fū′də lis′tik) *adj.* of or relating to feudalism.

feudal system, another term for **feudalism.**

feu·da·to·ry (fū′də tôr′ē) *adj.* owing feudal allegiance to a lord: *a feudatory noble.* —*n., pl.* **feu·da·to·ries.** a person holding land by feudal law; vassal.

fe·ver (fē′vər) *n.* **1.** a body temperature higher than normal. **2.** any of various diseases marked by higher than normal body temperature, such as yellow fever. **3.** a state of great excitement, anxiety, or restlessness: *The children were in a fever of anticipation before the party.*

fever blister, another term for **cold sore.**

fe·vered (fē′vərd) *adj.* having or affected by fever.

fe·ver·ish (fē′vər ish) *adj.* **1.** having a fever, especially a slight degree of fever: *a feverish patient.* **2.** showing, characteristic of, or caused by fever: *feverish symptoms, feverish dreams.* **3.** causing fever. **4.** excited or restless, as if from fever: *There was feverish activity in the dormitory as the weekend approached.* —**fe′ver·ish·ly,** *adv.* —**fe′ver·ish·ness,** *n.*

fever pitch, a state of great excitement; activity, excitement, or commotion: *to work at fever pitch.*

fever sore, another term for **cold sore.**

few (fū) *adj.* not many: *Few people attended the meeting.* —*n.* **1.** not many persons or things; a small number: *Many were invited, but few actually came. I sold only a few of the papers.* **2. the few.** the minority: *one of the few who have been to the moon.* ▲ See **less** for usage note.
· **quite a few.** *Informal.* a large number; good many: *Quite a few of my friends have bicycles.*

fez (fez) *n., pl.* **fez·zes.** a brimless felt cap, usually red, having a flat crown and ornamented with a tassel, worn especially by Middle Eastern men.

ff., and the following (pages, lines, sections, or the like).

fi·an·cé (fē′än sā′, fē än′sā) *n.* a man to whom a woman is engaged to be married.

fi·an·cée (fē′än sā′, fē än′sā) *n.* a woman to whom a man is engaged to be married.

fez

fi·as·co (fē as′kō) *n., pl.* **fi·as·coes** or **fi·as·cos.** a complete or humiliating failure: *Rain turned the hike into a fiasco.*

fi·at (fē′ät, fī′ət, fī′at) *n.* an official order or decree.

fib (fib) *n.* a lie about something unimportant; trivial lie. —*v.i.,* **fibbed, fib·bing.** to tell a fib. —**fib′ber,** *n.*

fi·ber (fī′bər) also, *British,* **fibre.** *n.* **1.** any fine, threadlike part of a substance: *cotton fibers, a nerve fiber.* **2.** a substance composed of such parts: *rope made of hemp fiber.* **3.** the composition or structure of such a substance; texture: *cloth of coarse fiber.* **4.** the fine, threadlike material in plant foods such as fruits, vegetables, and whole grains, that cannot be digested by the body. Fiber stimulates the movement of food waste through the intestines. **5.** essential character, nature, or strength: *moral fiber.*

fi·ber·board (fī′bər bôrd′) *n.* a material made of fibers, especially of wood, compressed into sheets and used for panels, partitions, or the like.

fi·ber·glass (fī′bər glas′) *n.* a durable, nonflammable material made of fine threads of glass, used for insulation, textiles, boat bodies, and many other purposes. Trademark: **Fiberglas.**

fiber optics, the technology of transmitting information by means of very thin, transparent fibers of glass or plastic. This technology is used in modern communications to send telephone and computer messages over long distances. ▲ used with a singular verb.

fi·bre (fī′bər) *British.* another spelling of **fiber.**

fi·bril·la·tion (fib′rə lā′shən) *n.* rapid, uncontrolled beating of the heart muscle. The heart cannot pump blood efficiently during fibrillation.

fi·brin (fī′brin) *n.* a fibrous, insoluble substance formed during the clotting of blood.

fi·brin·o·gen (fī brin′ə jən) *n.* a soluble protein in the blood plasma from which fibrin is formed.

fi·broid (fī′broid) *adj.* made up of or resembling fibers or fibrous tissue: *a fibroid tumor.*

fi·brous (fī′brəs) *adj.* made up of, having, or resembling fibers.

fib·u·la (fib′yə lə) *n., pl.* **fib·u·lae** (fib′yə lē′) or **fib·u·las.** the outer and more slender of the two bones of the human lower leg, extending from the knee to the ankle.

-fic *suffix* (used to form adjectives) making; causing: *terrific.*

-fication *suffix* (used to form nouns) the act of making: *purification.*

fick·le (fik′əl) *adj.* that cannot be relied upon or predicted; changeable; capricious: *a fickle friend, fickle fate.* —**fick′le·ness,** *n.*

fic·tion (fik′shən) *n.* **1.** prose works, such as novels and short stories, that tell about wholly or partly imaginary characters and events. **2.** something made up or imagined, as a story, explanation, or statement: *A newspaper reporter must be able to distinguish fact from fiction.*

fic·tion·al (fik′shə nəl) *adj.* relating to, appearing in, or like fiction: *a fictional character in a movie.* —**fic′tion·al·ly,** *adv.*

fic·tion·al·ize (fik′shə nə līz′) *v.t.,* **fic·tion·al·ized, fic·tion·al·iz·ing.** to make into fiction; give a fictional account of: *to fictionalize one's life in a novel.* —**fic′tion·al·i·za′tion,** *n.*

fic·ti·tious (fik tish′əs) *adj.* not real or true; made-up: *a fictitious identity.* —**fic·ti′tious·ly,** *adv.* —**fic·ti′tious·ness,** *n.*

fid·dle (fid′əl) *n. Informal.* a violin or other instrument of the violin family. —*v.,* **fid·dled, fid·dling.** —*v.i. Informal.* **1.** to play a fiddle. **2.** to make aimless or nervous movements, as with the fingers or hand; fidget: *to fiddle nervously while talking.* —*v.t. Informal.* to play (a tune) on a fiddle. —**fid′dler,** *n.*
· **to fiddle away.** to waste (time) in an idle or trifling way: *to fiddle away the afternoon.*
· **to fiddle with.** to touch or tinker; manipulate: *Fiddle with the dial to improve the radio reception.*

fiddler crab, any of a group of burrowing crabs, the male of which has one claw much larger than the other.

fid·dle·sticks (fid′əl stiks′) *interj.* nonsense.

fi·del·i·ty (fi del′i tē, fī del′i tē) *n., pl.* **fi·del·i·ties.** **1.** faithfulness to duties, obligations, or vows, steadfast loyalty. **2.** accuracy, as in writing or copying something: *The novel was written with fidelity to history.* **3.** the degree of accuracy with which electronic devices, such as record players, reproduce original sound.

fiddler crab

fidg·et (fij′it) *v.i.* to make restless movements; be nervous or uneasy: *The audience fidgeted in their seats.* —*n.* **1.** a person who fidgets. **2. the fidgets.** a condition of restlessness or uneasiness, often characterized by nervous movements: *I had the fidgets all morning before the test.*

fidg·et·y (fij′i tē) *adj.* restless; uneasy.

fi·du·ci·ar·y (fi dü′shē er′ē) *adj.* of or relating to the management of money or property by one person or institution on behalf of another: *A trust fund is a fiduciary arrangement.* —*n., pl.* **fi·du·ci·ar·ies.** a person or institution that is responsible for managing money or property on behalf of another; trustee.

fie (fī) *interj.* for shame: *Fie on you!*

fief (fēf) *n.* an estate in land held by a vassal in return for military and certain other services given to the feudal lord, and the land involved. Also, **fee.**

field (fēld) *n.* **1.** a piece of land having few or no trees. **2.** a piece of cleared land, usually bounded, used or

at; āpe; fär; câre; end; mē; it; īce; pierce; hot; ōld; sông, fôrk; oil; out; up; ūse; rüle; pull; tûrn; chin; sing; shop; thin; this; hw in white; zh in treasure. The symbol ə stands for the unstressed vowel sound heard in about, taken, pencil, lemon, and circus.

suitable for cultivation or pasture: *a wheat field.* **3.** a region or area containing and yielding some natural resource: *an oil field.* **4.** a broad, level expanse: *a field of snow.* **5.** a place of battle. **6.** a battle: *The field was won after four hours.* **7.** an area or region of active military operations: *In the spring, the army took to the field.* **8.** *Sports.* **a.** an enclosed piece of ground, or one with defined boundaries, on which games are played or events are held: *a football field.* **b.** a portion or division of such an area, usually surrounded by or next to a track, where such contests as the pole vault, long jump, and discus throw are held. **9.** all those who take part in a particular event or contest: *the field of candidates for governor. The winner finished five yards ahead of the field.* **10.** the surface on which something is shown: *white figures against a field of black.* **11.** a range or area of interest; sphere of activity: *the field of medicine.* **12.** *Physics.* the area or space within which a particular effect or property, as electricity, magnetism, or gravity, may be measured at every point. **13.** the space or range within which objects are visible: *in one's field of vision.* **14.** an area or setting without controlled conditions or away from an office, laboratory, or the like: *This procedure works in experiments, but will it work in the field?* —*v.t.* **1.** to catch, stop, or pick up (a ball in play), especially in baseball. **2.** to put or send (a team or player) into a position in the field. —*v.i.* **1.** to act as a fielder, especially in baseball. —*adj.* of, relating to, or growing in a field: *field flowers.*

field day **1.** a day set aside for athletic contests, games, and races. **2.** a day or time of unusual opportunity, as for fun: *The children had a field day while their parents were away.*

field·er (fēl′dər) *n.* **1.** *Baseball.* any of the players in the field attempting to put out the team at bat. **2.** any player with such defensive duties in softball, cricket, or similar ball games.

field glasses, binoculars. Also, **field glass.**

field goal **1.** *Football.* a play in which the ball is kicked over the crossbar and between the posts of the opponent's goal. It scores three points. **2.** *Basketball.* a goal made while the ball is in play. It scores two or three points, depending on how far the player shooting the ball is from the basket.

field guide, a book used to identify plants, animals, rocks, or other things found in nature: *a field guide to mushrooms.*

field hockey, a game played on a field by two teams of eleven players each. Wooden sticks with curved ends are used to hit the ball along the ground, the object being to drive the ball into the opponent's goal.

field hospital, a temporary military hospital close to a combat area.

field house, a building near an athletic field, having dressing rooms, showers, and the like for the athletes, room for storing sports equipment, and sometimes indoor tracks or fields.

field magnet, a magnet used to produce and maintain a magnetic field, especially in an electric motor or generator.

field marshal, an officer of the next to highest rank in the armies of Great Britain and certain other nations.

field mouse, any of various short-tailed mice living in fields and meadows.

field–test (fēld′test′) *v.t.* to subject (something) to a field test: *These new binoculars seem good, but I want to field-test them in the mountains this weekend.*

field test, a test of the performance, durability, or effectiveness of something under normal conditions of use rather than under controlled conditions, as in a laboratory.

field trip, a trip away from the classroom for firsthand observation and study, as to a museum, factory, or farm.

fiend (fēnd) *n.* **1.** an evil spirit; devil; demon. **2. the Fiend.** the Devil; Satan. **3.** a very wicked or cruel person. **4.** *Informal.* a person who is very devoted to a particular field, interest, or activity: *a chess fiend.* **5.** *Informal.* a person who is addicted to a practice or habit, especially one that is harmful: *a drug fiend.*

fiend·ish (fēn′dish) *adj.* **1.** very wicked or cruel; devilish. **2.** very difficult, as if designed by a fiend: *a fiendish task.* —**fiend′ish·ly,** *adv.* —**fiend′ish·ness,** *n.*

fierce (fîrs) *adj.,* **fierc·er, fierc·est.** **1.** cruel or violent in nature or behavior; savage: *a fierce enemy.* **2.** violent or intense in force or activity; raging: *a fierce storm, fierce fighting.* —**fierce′ly,** *adv.* —**fierce′ness,** *n.*

fier·y (fîr′ē, fī′ə rē) *adj.,* **fier·i·er, fier·i·est.** **1.** containing or made up of fire; aflame; flaming: *a fiery furnace.* **2.** hot as fire; burning: *the fiery sands of the desert.* **3.** like fire; flashing; glowing: *a fiery red, a fiery sunset, fiery eyes.* **4.** full of feeling; ardent; passionate: *a fiery speech.* **5.** excitable; irritable: *a fiery temper.* —**fier′i·ly,** *adv.* —**fier′i·ness,** *n.*

fi·es·ta (fē es′tə) *n.* **1.** a religious festival, especially a saint's day as celebrated in Spain or Latin America. **2.** any festive celebration; holiday.

fife (fīf) *n.* a shrill-toned musical instrument of the flute family, often used with drums in marching bands. —*v.,* **fifed, fifing.** —*v.t.* to play (a tune) on a fife. —*v.i.* to play a fife. —**fif′er,** *n.*

fif·teen (fif′tēn′) *n.* **1.** the cardinal number that is five more than ten. **2.** the symbol representing this number, as 15 or XV. **3.** something having this many units or things. —*adj.* numbering five more than ten.

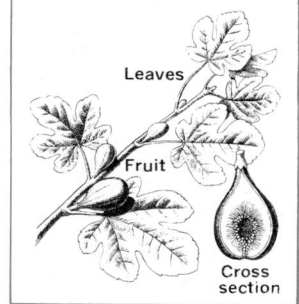
fife

fif·teenth (fif′tēnth′) *adj.* **1.** (the ordinal of fifteen) next after the fourteenth. **2.** being one of fifteen equal parts. —*n.* **1.** something that is next after the fourteenth. **2.** one of fifteen equal parts; $1/15$.

fifth (fifth) *adj.* **1.** (the ordinal of five) next after the fourth. **2.** being one of five equal parts. —*n.* **1.** something that is next after the fourth. **2.** one of five equal parts; $1/5$. **3.** $1/5$ of a gallon (0.757 liters), used as a measure of liquor. **4.** *Music.* **a.** a note that is a total of three whole steps and one half step above a given note. G is the fifth of C. **b.** an interval of three whole steps and one half step. **c.** a combination of two notes that are separated by this interval. —*adv.* in the fifth place.

fifth column, a group of persons within a country who secretly aid its enemies. [From a remark by a rebel general during the Spanish Civil War, who supposedly said he had four columns of troops marching on Madrid and a *fifth column* of sympathizers within the city.]

fifth columnist, a member of a fifth column.

fif·ti·eth (fif′tē ith) *adj.* **1.** (the ordinal of fifty) next after the forty-ninth. **2.** being one of fifty equal parts. —*n.* **1.** something that is next after the forty-ninth. **2.** one of fifty equal parts; $1/50$.

fif·ty (fif′tē) *n., pl.* **fif·ties.** **1.** the cardinal number that is five times ten. **2.** the symbol representing this number, as 50 or L. —*adj.* numbering five times ten.

fif·ty-fif·ty (fif′tē fif′tē) *Informal. adj.* **1.** sharing equally; equal: *a fifty-fifty division of profits.* **2.** as likely to turn out one way as another; even: *a fifty-fifty chance of winning.* —*adv.* equally: *to share expenses fifty-fifty.*

fig (fig) *n.* **1.** a small, sweet fruit having many tiny seeds.

Leaves

Fruit

Cross section

fig

2. the shrub or small tree bearing this fruit, grown mainly in the Mediterranean region and California. **3.** the smallest amount; least bit: *I don't care a fig for your idea.*

fig., figure.

fight (fīt) *n.* **1.** a physical struggle between two opposing individuals or groups; battle; conflict: *a fight between two gangs.* **2.** a contest between two boxers; boxing match. **3.** dispute; quarrel; argument: *to have a fight over who should wash the dishes.* **4.** any struggle, especially one to gain some objective or goal: *a fight for control of a government.* **5.** the power or will to carry on a struggle: *The dazed boxer had no fight left.* —*v.,* **fought, fighting.** —*v.t.* **1.** to take part in a physical struggle or combat with: *The British fought the Americans in 1776.* **2.** to oppose in a boxing match: *The champion fought three opponents last year.* **3.** to struggle against: *We fought the blaze for hours.* **4.** to carry on or wage (a battle, contest, or struggle): *The battle was fought on a plain.* **5.** to gain or make (one's way) by struggle: *to fight one's way through a crowd.* —*v.i.* **1.** to take part in a physical struggle or combat: *The two armies fought for days.* **2.** to struggle, as to reach a goal or to preserve something: *to fight for equal rights, to fight for one's life.*

  •**to fight off. a.** to drive away or defend against by fighting: *The militia fought off the invading army.* **b.** to struggle to get rid of or avoid: *to fight off a cold.*

fight·er (fī′tər) *n.* **1.** a person who fights. **2.** a professional boxer. **3.** a fast, maneuverable airplane designed for use against enemy airplanes or ground forces, usually having a crew of one or two.

fig·ment (fig′mənt) *n.* something imagined or made up; fiction: *The dragon was a figment of the child's imagination.*

fig·ur·a·tive (fig′yər ə tiv) *adj.* **1.** using, based on, or characteristic of a figure of speech; not literal; metaphorical. *To throw caution to the wind* is a figurative expression. **2.** containing or using many figures of speech; flowery: *figurative poetry.* **3.** representing by a symbol or by a figure or likeness: *a figurative ceremony.* —**fig′ur·a·tive·ly,** *adv.* —**fig′ur·a·tive·ness,** *n.*

fig·ure (fig′yər) *n.* **1.** a symbol representing a number, such as 0, 1, 2, 3. **2. figures.** the use of such symbols in calculating; arithmetic: *Are you good at figures?* **3.** an amount or value as expressed in figures; price; sum: *The figure asked for the house was too high.* **4.** a visible form or appearance of anything; shape; outline: *The figure of a child was silhouetted in the window.* **5.** a human body or form: *a slender figure.* **6.** a person as he or she appears or looks to others: *Your strange clothes made you seem a comical figure.* **7.** a person, especially one of importance; character: *a figure of strength. The mayor is a public figure.* **8.** a picture, likeness, or representation, as of a human form: *The figure of a head appears on this coin.* **9.** a diagram; illustration; drawing: *This figure shows an automobile engine.* **10.** a design; pattern: *The cloth had bold figures woven into it.* **11.** *Geometry.* a bounded surface or space; series of lines, solids, or surfaces having a definite shape: *The circle is a plane figure. The sphere is a solid figure.* **12.** a set or series of movements, as in dancing or skating. **13.** see **figure of speech.** —*v.,* **figured, fig·ur·ing.** —*v.t.* **1.** to solve or find out by using numbers; calculate; compute: *to figure the cost of a trip, to figure the solution to an arithmetic problem.* **2.** to ornament or cover with a design or pattern: *The wallpaper was figured with roses.* **3.** *Informal.* to think or believe: *They figured the worst of the storm was over.* —*v.i.* to appear or be prominent: *Several well-known politicians figured in the news.*

  •**to figure on.** *Informal.* **a.** to depend on; plan on: *They figured on us to help. They figured on getting a loan so they could buy the car.* **b.** to take into consideration: *We had not figured on the possibility of rain.*

  •**to figure out.** to arrive at the explanation of; under-

stand: *I figured out who the murderer was before the end of the book.*

fig·ure·head (fig′yər hed′) *n.* **1.** a person having a position of authority but no real power or responsibility. **2.** a carved, ornamental figure, usually of wood, on the bow of a ship.

figure of speech, a form of expression in which words are used out of their literal sense to produce a vivid, forceful, or poetic effect. Similes and metaphors are figures of speech.

In language, a **figure of speech** is a word or phrase that is used to give a special effect. The meaning of the words in a figure of speech is usually not the literal meaning. Figures of speech are often used in poetry and other creative writing to express feelings and experiences in a fresh, vivid, or artistic way. You probably use figures of speech in your everyday speaking and writing without realizing it. We often use simile, which is a very common type of figure of speech: *as big as a house. You eat like a pig.* Metaphor is also a frequently used figure of speech: *Their holiday in Europe was heaven.* Another kind of figure of speech is called hyperbole: *It took forever for the mail to arrive.*

Figures of speech are tools for using language creatively, but when they are used excessively they can become trite. A figure of speech that has been overused is called a cliché. Examples of clichés are *white as snow, fit as a fiddle, to swim like a fish,* and *the tip of the iceberg.* When figures of speech are misused, the result can be confusing or illogical: *The politician threw in the sponge when the storm of protest broke.*

fig·ur·ine (fig′yə rēn′) *n.* a small carved or molded figure; statuette.

fil·a·ment (fil′ə mənt) *n.* **1.** a very fine thread or a part like a thread; fiber: *a filament of a spider's web.* **2.** a fine wire in an electric bulb, usually of tungsten, that gives off light when an electric current passes through it. **3.** the wire in a vacuum tube that sends out electrons when heated by the passage of an electric current and that often acts as a cathode. **4.** the tiny stalklike part that supports the anther in the stamen of a flower.

fil·bert (fil′bərt) *n.* **1.** a thick-shelled nut. Also, **hazelnut. 2.** the shrub bearing this nut.

filch (filch) *v.t.* to steal, especially something of little value; pilfer. —**filch′er,** *n.*

filament
(def. 2)

file¹ (fīl) *n.* **1.** any device, as a folder, drawer, or cabinet, in which papers, cards, records, or documents are arranged in order for easy reference. **2.** a set of such items arranged in order. **3.** *Computers.* a collection of data created on a computer and stored as a unit on disk or in memory. —*v.,* **filed, fil·ing.** —*v.t.* **1.** to keep (papers or similar items) arranged in order. **2.** to place in a file: *The clerk filed the letter in the top drawer.* **3.** to hand in legally or

at; āpe; fär; câre; end; mē; it; īce; pîerce; hot; ōld; sông; fôrk; oil; out; up; ūse; rūle; pull; tûrn; chin; sing; shop; thin; <u>this</u>; hw in white; zh in treasure. The symbol ə stands for the unstressed vowel sound heard in about, taken, pencil, lemon, and circus.

officially; enter on a record: *to file a report, to file one's tax return.* —*v.i.* to make an application: *to file for a hunting permit.* [From the Middle French word *filer* meaning "to string documents on a wire," from the Old French word *filer* "to spin thread," going back to the Latin word *filum* "a thread."] —**fil′er,** *n.*

file² (fīl) *n.* **1.** a line of persons, animals, or things placed one behind another: *a file of soldiers.* **2.** any row of squares on a chessboard running from one player toward the other. —*v.i.,* **filed, fil·ing.** to march or move in a file: *The soldiers filed out of the barracks.* [From the French word *file* meaning "a file of soldiers," going back to the Latin word *filum* "a thread."]

file³ (fīl) *n.* a steel tool having one or more closely ridged surfaces, used to cut, smooth, or grind down hard substances. —*v.t.,* **filed, fil·ing.** to cut, smooth, or grind down with a file. [From the Old English word *fēol,* meaning this tool.]

fi·let (fi lā′, fil′ā) *n.* **1.** net or lace with a square mesh. **2.** see **fillet** *(def. 3).*

fi·let mi·gnon (fi lā′ min yon′) *pl.* **fi·lets mignons.** a small, thick steak from the tip of the tenderloin, noted for its tenderness. [From the French phrase *filet mignon* meaning "dainty filet."]

fil·i·al (fil′ē əl) *adj.* relating or suitable to a son or daughter: *filial love.* —**fil′i·al·ly,** *adv.*

fil·i·bus·ter (fil′ə bus′tər) *n.* a method of delaying or stopping action on a legislative issue by the use of lengthy speeches, prolonged debate, or other delaying tactics. —*v.i., v.t.* to hinder or block legislative action by use of a filibuster, as by prolonged speeches. —**fil′i·bus·ter·er,** *n.*

fil·i·gree (fil′i grē′) *n.* **1.** delicate ornamental work of intertwined gold or silver wire. **2.** anything ornamental, delicate, or fanciful, such as a pattern or design: *The sun shining through the leaves made a green and gold filigree.* —*adj.* like, made of, or ornamented with filigree: *filigree earrings.* —*v.t.,* **fil·i·greed, fil·i·gree·ing.** to adorn with filigree.

fil·ings (fī′lingz) *pl. n.* particles removed by a file.

Fil·i·pi·no (fil′ə pē′nō) *n., pl.* **Fil·i·pi·nos.** a person who was born in or is a citizen of the Philippines. —*adj.* another word for **Philippine.**

fill (fil) *v.t.* **1.** to supply with as much as can be held or contained; make full, as a container or space: *to fill a bucket with water.* **2.** to take up or occupy the whole capacity or space of: *The crowd filled the auditorium.* **3.** to spread over or throughout: *Smoke filled the room. Angry shouts filled the air.* **4.** to fulfill; satisfy; meet: *to fill the requirements of a job.* **5.** to supply or make up whatever is required or asked for: *to fill a grocery order, to fill a prescription.* **6.** to stop up or close by putting something in; plug: *to fill a hole in a wall with plaster.* **7.** to put a filling in (a tooth). **8.** to hold or occupy, as a position or office: *to fill the office of treasurer.* **9.** to put or place a person into: *to fill a vacancy on the Supreme Court.* —*v.i.* to become full: *The room filled with smoke.* —*n.* **1.** a quantity that is enough to fill or satisfy a desire or need: *Eat your fill.* **2.** something used to fill: *Stone and gravel were used as fill for the hole.*

•**to fill in. a.** to fill completely with something: *The workers filled in the hole with sand.* **b.** to complete by inserting something: *to fill in a questionnaire.* **c.** to insert to make something complete: *Don't forget to fill in your name on the form.* **d.** to act as a substitute: *I filled in for the regular cook tonight.*

•**to fill out. a.** to complete by inserting something: *to fill out a form.* **b.** to become larger, fuller, or more rounded: *The thin child filled out during the summer.*

•**to fill up.** to make or become completely full: *I filled up the gas tank. The bathtub filled up in a few minutes.*

•**to have one's fill.** to have enough or too much: *We've had our fill of rainy weather.*

fill·er (fil′ər) *n.* **1.** a person or thing that fills. **2.** a material used to fill something. **3.** an item, especially a brief paragraph, used to fill space in a newspaper or magazine: *The local newspaper had a filler about the birthplaces of several famous people.* **4.** paper for a loose-leaf notebook.

fil·let (fil′it; *n., def. 3, v., def. 2* fi lā′) *n.* **1.** a narrow band or ribbon for binding or adorning the hair. **2.** a narrow band or strip of any material. **3.** *also,* **fi·let.** a lean, boneless piece or slice of fish or meat. —*v.t.* **1.** to bind or adorn with a fillet. **2.** to cut (fish or meat) into fillets.

fill·ing (fil′ing) *n.* **1.** a substance used to fill something: *pie filling.* **2.** a substance used to fill a cavity in a tooth. **3.** the act of filling.

filling station, another term for **gas station.**

fil·lip (fil′ip) *n.* **1.** a light blow from the nail of a finger that has been pressed against the thumb and suddenly released. **2.** something that arouses, excites, or enlivens; stimulus: *That good news was a fillip to my spirits.* —*v.t.* **1.** to tap or strike with a fillip. **2.** to move by a fillip.

fil·ly (fil′ē) *n., pl.* **fil·lies.** a young female horse.

film (film) *n.* **1.** a thin layer, sheet, or covering: *The windows were covered with a film of dirt.* **2.** a thin, flexible roll or strip of material coated with a substance sensitive to light, used in making photographs. **3.** such a roll or strip containing pictures to be projected on a screen. **4.** a motion picture: *We saw a good foreign film.* **5.** a thin veil or haze that blurs: *a film of tears.* —*v.t.* **1.** to cover with a thin layer or haze. **2.** to photograph with a motion-picture camera: *I filmed the football game.* **3.** to make a motion picture of: *to film a popular novel.* —*v.i.* **1.** to become covered or blurred by a thin layer or haze: *The windows filmed with dust from the road.* **2.** to be suitable for filming: *Some plays do not film well.*

film·strip (film′strip′) *n.* a length of film containing pictures that are projected one at a time on a screen, often used as a teaching aid.

film·y (fil′mē) *adj.,* **film·i·er, film·i·est. 1.** composed of or resembling a thin layer; gauzy: *The curtains were made of a filmy material.* **2.** covered with a thin layer of something; hazy: *a filmy mirror.* —**film′i·ness,** *n.*

fil·ter (fil′tər) *n.* **1.** a device for straining solids or impurities from a liquid or gas. **2.** porous material used in such a device, such as sand, charcoal, or paper. **3.** a device that allows waves of certain frequencies to pass and stops the passage of others: *a lens filter for a camera.* —*v.t.* **1.** to pass (a liquid or gas) through a filter; strain: *The water was filtered through charcoal.* **2.** to act as a filter for. **3.** to separate or remove by a filter: *The solid particles were filtered from the solution.* —*v.i.* to pass slowly: *Sunlight filtered through the leaves.*

fil·ter·a·ble (fil′tər ə bəl) *also,* **fil·tra·ble** (fil′trə bəl). *adj.* **1.** capable of being filtered. **2.** capable of passing through a filter that stops bacteria: *a filterable virus.*

filth (filth) *n.* **1.** disgusting dirt or refuse: *Industrial filth pollutes the air and water.* **2.** a dirty or foul condition: *I would never allow a pet of mine to live in filth.* **3.** something offensive or indecent; obscenity. **4.** obscene language.

filth·y (fil′thē) *adj.,* **filth·i·er, filth·i·est. 1.** covered with or containing filth; dirty; foul: *filthy streets.* **2.** offensive; obscene. **3.** highly unpleasant or objectionable; contemptible: *a filthy lie.* —**filth′i·ly,** *adv.* —**filth′i·ness,** *n.*

fil·trate (fil′trāt) *n.* liquid that has been passed through a filter. —*v.t.,* **fil·trat·ed, fil·trat·ing.** to pass through a filter. —**fil·tra′tion,** *n.*

file³

fin (fin) *n.* **1.** one of the movable winglike parts extending from the body of a fish. A fish uses its fins to propel, guide, and balance itself in the water. **2.** a similar structure of other water animals, such as whales and some porpoises. **3.** something resembling a fin in shape or use. **4.** a vertical surface attached to an aircraft or rocket to provide stability in flight.

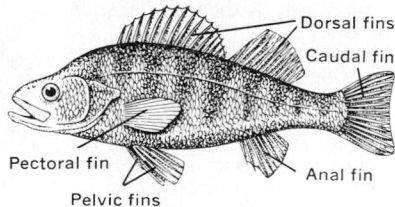

Dorsal fins
Caudal fin
Pectoral fin
Anal fin
Pelvic fins

fin *(def. 1)*

fi·na·gle (fi nā′gəl) *v.*, **fi·na·gled, fi·na·gling.** *Informal.* —*v.t.* **1.** to get or manage (something) by trickery or deceit; wangle: *I finagled a free ticket to the game.* **2.** to cheat or trick (someone): *The swindler finagled them out of their money.* —*v.i.* to use trickery or deceit; cheat.

fi·nal (fī′nəl) *adj.* **1.** coming at the end; last: *the final chapter of a novel, the final days of the year.* **2.** allowing no further action, discussion, or change; deciding completely; conclusive: *The decision of the judges is final.* —*n.* **1.** the last examination of a school or college course: *a history final.* **2.** also, **finals.** the last and decisive game, match, or event in a series of athletic contests: *Our team reached the finals of the tournament.*

fi·na·le (fi nä′lē) *n.* **1.** the last part or conclusion. **2.** the concluding part of a piece of music or a play.

fi·nal·ist (fī′nə list) *n.* a person who takes part in the final match or event of a series of games or contests.

fi·nal·i·ty (fī nal′i tē) *n.*, *pl.* **fi·nal·i·ties.** **1.** the state or quality of being final, settled, or complete; conclusiveness: *to state a position with finality.* **2.** something final.

fi·nal·ize (fī′nə līz′) *v.t.*, **fi·nal·ized, fi·nal·iz·ing.** to put into final or finished form; bring to completion: *We must finalize our plans.* —**fi′nal·i·za′tion,** *n.*

fi·nal·ly (fī′nə lē) *adv.* **1.** at the end; at last; in conclusion: *We finally reached our destination. Finally, they thanked us and left.* **2.** decisively; conclusively: *We must deal with this problem effectively and finally.*

fi·nance (fi nans′, fī′nans) *n.* **1.** the management of money affairs of individuals, businesses, or governments. **2. finances.** the money affairs or resources of a government, organization, or individual; funds; revenue; income. —*v.t.*, **fi·nanced, fi·nanc·ing.** to provide money for: *My parents financed my college education.*

fi·nan·cial (fi nan′shəl, fī nan′shəl) *adj.* relating to money matters or finance: *a financial crisis, the financial section of a newspaper.* —**fi·nan′cial·ly,** *adv.*

fin·an·cier (fin′an sîr′, fī′nan sîr′) *n.* **1.** a person skilled in financial matters, such as a banker. **2.** a person active in financial operations on a large scale.

finch (finch) *n.*, *pl.* **finch·es.** any of several groups of small songbirds that have a cone-shaped bill and stout body, as the goldfinch and canary.

find (fīnd) *v.t.*, **found, find·ing.** **1.** to come upon accidentally; meet with by chance; happen on: *I found a wallet on the sidewalk.* **2.** to get or learn by calculation; obtain (the solution to a problem): *to find the sum of several numbers.* **3.** to discover or learn: *to find a place to live, to find a cure for a disease. I found I couldn't study well without a good night's sleep.* **4.** to look for and recover (something lost): *I found your missing necklace. Please find my coat.* **5.** to get by arrangement or management: *I haven't found time to read that book.* **6.** to arrive at; reach: *The arrow found its*

finch

target. **7.** to determine and declare: *The jury found the defendant guilty.* **8.** to feel or think to be; consider; regard: *Many people find the climate here too humid.* —*n.* something that is found, especially something of value: *The ancient sculpture was a priceless find.*

·**to find oneself.** to discover one's abilities or talents and the best way to use them: *After changing jobs many times, I finally found myself.*

·**to find out.** to learn; discover: *We found out that prices were much higher in the city.*

find·er (fīn′dər) *n.* **1.** a person or thing that finds. **2.** a small, extra lens or other device built in or attached to a camera for sighting the object or area to be photographed. Also, **viewfinder.** **3.** a small telescope attached to a larger one to help sight the objects to be viewed.

find·ing (fīn′ding) *n.* **1.** the act of a person or thing that finds; discovery. **2.** something found. **3.** also, **findings.** the result or conclusions of an investigation or inquiry: *The researchers will publish their findings next week.*

fine¹ (fīn) *adj.*, **fin·er, fin·est.** **1.** of high grade or quality; very good; excellent: *a fine speech, a fine musician, fine foods.* **2.** very satisfactory; enjoyable: *We had a fine time at the party.* **3.** refined; elegant; polished: *fine manners.* **4.** delicate, as in structure, texture, or detail: *fine facial features, fine linen, fine embroidery.* **5.** subtle: *to make a fine distinction in an argument.* **6.** very thin; slender: *a fine thread.* **7.** very small: *fine sand. That book has fine print.* **8.** sharp; keen: *the fine edge of a razor.* **9.** free from clouds or rain; clear; bright: *fine weather.* **10.** free from impurities or foreign matter; pure; refined: *fine gold.* —*adv.* *Informal.* very well: *I'm doing fine in school.* [From the Old French word *fin* meaning "perfect, exact," going back to the Latin word *finis* "end, limit."] —**fine′ness,** *n.*

fine² (fīn) *n.* a sum of money to be paid as punishment for an offense: *a fine of fifty dollars for littering.* —*v.t.*, **fined, fin·ing.** to punish by a fine: *to fine a motorist for speeding.* [From the Old French word *fin* meaning "end" or "settlement," from the Medieval Latin word *finis* "final payment," going back to the Latin word *finis* "end, conclusion."]

fine arts, those arts concerned mainly with the creation of beauty, including painting, drawing, and sculpture, and sometimes architecture, literature, music, drama, and the dance.

fin·er·y (fī′nə rē) *n.*, *pl.* **fin·er·ies.** fine or showy clothes or ornaments.

fi·nesse (fi nes′) *n.* **1.** refinement or skill in doing something: *The violinist played with remarkable finesse.* **2.** the smooth or skillful handling of a difficult or awkward situation: *The mediator showed great finesse in settling the dispute.*

fine–tune (fīn′tün′, fīn′tün′) *v.t.*, **fine-tuned, fine-tuning.** to make fine adjustments in to achieve the best possible results: *to fine-tune an engine, to fine-tune a speech.*

fin·ger (fing′gər) *n.* **1.** one of the five separate parts at the end of the hand, especially the four other than the thumb; digit. **2.** the part of a glove that is made to cover a finger. **3.** anything like a finger in shape or use: *fingers of sunlight.* **4.** the width of a finger or an amount, as of liquid in a glass, about equal to this width. —*v.t.* **1.** to touch, feel, or handle with the fingers; toy with: *I fingered the silk gently.* **2.** *Music.* to play with the fingers: *to*

at; āpe; fär; câre; end; mē; it; īce; pîerce; hot; ōld; sông; fôrk; oil; out; up; ūse; rüle; pull; tûrn; chin; sing; shop; thin; this; hw in white; zh in treasure. The symbol ə stands for the unstressed vowel sound heard in about, taken, pencil, lemon, and circus.

finger a guitar, to finger a chord. **3.** *Slang.* to inform on; identify (as a cause or culprit): *Two friends fingered the defendant as the forger.*

•**to put one's finger on.** to indicate or point out precisely or correctly: *I can't put my finger on the cause of the problem.*

fin·ger·board (fing′gər bôrd′) *n.* a strip of wood on the neck of a violin, guitar, or similar instrument, against which the strings are pressed by the fingers.

finger bowl, a small bowl containing water for rinsing the fingers during or after a meal.

fin·ger·ing (fing′gər ing) *n.* **1.** the act of touching or handling with the fingers. **2.** *Music.* **a.** the action or method of using the fingers in playing a musical instrument: *a difficult fingering on the guitar.* **b.** numerals or other notations on a piece of music indicating which fingers are to be used in playing its notes.

fin·ger·nail (fing′gər nāl′) *n.* a horny substance that forms a hard layer on the upper surface of the end of a finger.

finger painting 1. a method of painting by spreading paint on dampened paper with the fingers or palms. **2.** a painting made in this way.

fin·ger·print (fing′gər print′) *n.* an impression of the markings on the inner surface of the tip of a finger, especially such an impression made with ink and used for identification. —*v.t.* to take the fingerprints of.

fin·i·cal (fin′i kəl) *adj.* another word for **finicky.** —**fin′i·cal·ly,** *adv.*

fin·ick·y (fin′i kē) *adj.* too particular; fussy: *a finicky eater.*

fi·nis (fin′is, fī′nis) *n.* end; conclusion. [From the Latin word *finis.*]

fin·ish (fin′ish) *v.t.* **1.** to bring to an end; come to the end of; complete; end: *to finish speaking, to finish a job.* **2.** to use up or consume completely: *to finish a jar of jam.* **3.** to treat the surface of: *We used clear varnish to finish the cabinet.* —*v.i.* to reach or come to an end: *I finished before the time was up.* —*n., pl.* **fin·ish·es. 1.** the last stage of anything; conclusion; end: *the finish of a race, a fight to the finish.* **2.** the surface or texture of something: *The table has a shiny finish.* **3.** a material used to coat or finish a surface, such as varnish. —**fin′ish·er,** *n.*

•**to finish off. a.** to complete; end: *to finish off a school year with a party.* **b.** to defeat, destroy, or kill.

•**to finish up.** to complete; end: *Finish up what you are working on as soon as possible.*

fin·ished (fin′isht) *adj.* **1.** ended; completed: *The finished report contained several mistakes.* **2.** polished; perfected: *a finished work of art.* **3.** highly skilled or accomplished: *a finished dancer.*

finishing school, a private school that emphasizes social and cultural attainments in order to prepare young women for entrance into society.

finish line, a line that marks the end of a course or race.

fi·nite (fī′nīt) *adj.* **1.** having a beginning and an end; having limits or bounds: *The lifetime of a human being is finite.* **2.** *Mathematics.* **a.** that can be completed by counting: *a finite number, a finite set.* **b.** not infinite or infinitesimal: *a finite width.* **3.** *Grammar.* (of a verb) limited by person, number, tense, or mood. In the sentence *We attend school, attend* is a finite verb. —**fi′nite·ly,** *adv.*

Finn (fin) *n.* a person who was born in or is a citizen of Finland.

fin·nan had·die (fin′ən had′ē) smoked haddock.

Finn·ish (fin′ish) *n.* the language spoken principally in Finland. —*adj.* of or relating to Finland, its people, their language, or their culture.

fin·ny (fin′ē) *adj.* **1.** having fins. **2.** like a fin. **3.** relating to or abounding in fish: *finny waters.*

fiord (fyôrd) another spelling of **fjord.**

fir (fûr) *n.* **1.** any of a group of evergreen trees of the same family as the pine, bearing cones. **2.** the wood of such a tree.

fire (fīr) *n.* **1.** the flame, heat, and light given off in burning. **2.** something burning, as wood, coal, or other fuel: *Add another log to the fire.* **3.** destructive burning: *A bolt of lightning started the forest fire.* **4.** an intense emotion, feeling, or spirit; fervor; passion: *the fire of enthusiasm, eyes full of fire.* **5.** the discharge of firearms; shooting: *the crackle of rifle fire.* **6.** a rapid or very strong series of outbursts: *The proposal faced a fire of objections.* —*v.,* **fired, firing.** —*v.t.* **1.** to supply with fuel; tend the fire of: *to fire a furnace.* **2.** to set on fire: *to fire a heap of dead leaves.* **3.** to treat by the use of heat; bake: *to fire pottery.* **4.** to shoot: *to fire a shotgun, to fire an arrow.* **5.** to arouse the feelings or passions of; inflame; excite: *to fire one's anger. Stories about pirates fired my imagination.* **6.** to direct or throw suddenly or with force: *The shortstop fired the ball to home plate. The lawyer fired questions at the witness.* **7.** to dismiss from a job; discharge: *The firm fired seven employees.* —*v.i.* to discharge firearms or other weapons; shoot: *The police fired into the air.*

fir twig with cone

•**on fire. a.** burning; ignited. **b.** full of intense emotion, feeling, or spirit; passionate.

•**to catch fire.** to begin to burn.

•**to fire up.** to start a fire, as in an engine, furnace, or boiler.

•**to hang fire. a.** to fail to discharge immediately: *The cannon hung fire.* **b.** to fail to act or decide quickly: *The legislature hung fire on the tax question.*

•**to open fire.** to begin to shoot.

•**under fire. a.** exposed to the enemy's shooting or attack. **b.** exposed to criticism or blame.

fire alarm 1. a signal calling attention to a fire. **2.** a device for giving such a signal.

fire ant, any of various ants whose sting feels like a burn, especially a species originally from South America that is a major pest in the southeastern United States.

fire·arm (fīr′ärm′) *n.* a weapon from which a shot is discharged by an explosive charge, especially one that can be carried and fired by one person, as a rifle, pistol, or shotgun.

fire·ball (fīr′bôl′) *n.* **1.** something resembling a ball of fire, as the sun. **2.** a brilliant meteor; shooting star. **3.** a luminous cloud of hot gases produced by a nuclear explosion.

fire·boat (fīr′bōt′) *n.* a boat equipped with apparatus for fighting fires.

fireboat

fire·brand (fīr′brand′) n. **1.** a piece of burning wood. **2.** a person who arouses unrest or anger; agitator.

fire·break (fīr′brāk′) n. a strip of land that is plowed or cleared so that it will stop the spread of a fire.

fire·bug (fīr′bug′) n. Informal. a person who purposely sets destructive fires; arsonist.

fire·crack·er (fīr′krak′ər) n. a paper cylinder containing an explosive and an attached fuse, exploded as a noise-maker.

fire·damp (fīr′damp′) n. a gas formed in coal mines that is dangerously explosive when mixed with certain pro-portions of air.

fire·dog (fīr′dôg′) n. another word for **andiron**.

fire drill, a practice drill, especially in school or aboard ship, involving the procedures to be followed in case of fire.

fire engine, a truck designed to carry equipment with which to fight fire, especially one that has a pumping apparatus to spray water or chemicals on a fire.

fire escape, a metal stairway or ladder attached to the out-side of a building for use as a means of escape in case of fire.

fire extinguisher, an apparatus containing chemicals that can be sprayed on a fire to put it out.

fire·fight·er (fīr′fī′tər) n. a person who is paid or volunteers to put out and prevent fires.

fire·fight·ing (fīr′fī′ting) n. the work of a firefighter. —adj. of, relating to, or used in the work of a firefighter: *firefighting equipment.*

fire·fly (fīr′flī′) n., pl. **fire·flies.** any of a number of small beetles that give off flashes of phosphorescent light as a mating signal. Also, **lightning bug.**

fire·house (fīr′hous′) n., pl. **fire·hous·es** (fīr′hou′ziz). a building housing firefighters and equipment for putting out fires. Also, **fire station.**

fire hydrant, see **hydrant.**

fire·light (fīr′līt′) n. the light from a fire, especially an open fire.

fire·man (fīr′mən) n., pl. **fire·men** (fīr′mən). **1.** a person who is paid, as by a city, or volunteers to put out and prevent fires. Also, **firefighter. 2.** a person who tends the fire in a furnace or steam engine, especially on a locomotive; stoker. **3.** an enlisted person in the navy who tends engineering machinery.

fire·place (fīr′plās′) n. **1.** an opening in a room at the base of a chimney, in which fires are built. **2.** a structure outdoors in which a fire is built.

fire·plug (fīr′plug′) n. a hydrant.

fire·proof (fīr′pro̅o̅f′) adj. resistant to fire; that will not burn: *a fireproof building.* —v.t. to make fireproof.

fire screen, a metal screen placed in front of a fireplace to prevent sparks from flying into the room.

fire·side (fīr′sīd′) n. **1.** the space around a fireplace; hearth. **2.** home or home life. —adj. of, in, or near the hearth or home.

fire station, another term for **firehouse.**

fire tower, a tower, usually overlooking a forest, where a lookout is posted to watch for and report fires.

fire·trap (fīr′trap′) n. a building that is likely to catch on fire easily or that would be hard to escape in a fire.

fire truck, another term for **fire engine.**

fire wall, a wall of fireproof material designed to prevent the spread of fire from one room or section of a building to another.

fire·wood (fīr′wu̇d′) n. wood used for fuel.

fire·works (fīr′wûrks′) pl. n. **1.** devices that are de-signed to be burned or exploded to produce a brilliant display of light or loud noises, as during an outdoor celebration. **2.** a show or display in which such devices are set off.

firing pin, the part of a firearm that strikes the primer to explode the charge.

firm¹ (fûrm) adj. **1.** not yielding to pressure; solid: *firm ground.* **2.** not easily moved; securely fixed: *a firm foundation.* **3.** fixed or settled; not changing: *It is my firm belief that all people are equal. The price of wheat is firm this year.* **4.** steadfast and constant; unwavering: *a firm friend.* **5.** steady or determined: *a firm voice, a firm hand.* —adv. firmly: *The strikers stood firm in their demands.* —v.t. to make firm: *Exercise will firm your muscles.* —v.i. to become firm: *The plaster of Paris firmed in the mold. The price of my stock firmed after weeks of fluctuation.* [From the Old French word *ferme* meaning ''strong, fixed,'' from the Latin word *firmus* ''steadfast, strong.''] —**firm′ly,** adv. —**firm′ness,** n.

firm² (fûrm) n. a company or partnership of two or more persons for carrying on a business; business establishment: *a law firm.* [From the Italian word *firma* meaning both ''signature'' and ''name of a business partnership,'' from the word *firmare* ''to confirm in writing,'' going back to the Latin word *firmus* ''steadfast, strong.'']

fir·ma·ment (fûr′mə mənt) n. the heavens; sky.

firm·ware (fûrm′wâr′) n. computer programs or data stored permanently in ROM. Firmware cannot be changed by normal keyboard operations.

first (fûrst) adj. **1.** (the ordinal of one) before all others in an order or series: *Our team finished in first place.* **2.** before all others in time; earliest: *George Washington was the first president of the United States.* **3.** before all others in importance or excellence; superior; highest; best: *first among writers of the period.* **4.** Music. (of a performer or instrument) playing or singing the part of highest pitch or principal melodic importance: *first violin, first tenor.* —adv. **1.** before all other persons or things, as in order or importance: *I placed first in the skiing competition.* **2.** before any other action, time, or event: *Come to see us first.* **3.** for the first time: *I first heard the news yesterday.* **4.** rather; sooner: *Eat raw oysters? I would starve first!* —n. **1.** a person or thing that is first, as in importance, order, time, or place: *This invention is the first of its kind.* **2.** the first day of a month: *Our rent is due on the first.* **3.** beginning: *There was trouble from the first.* **4.** the lowest forward gear, as of an automobile.

first–aid (fûrst′ād′) adj. of or for first aid: *a first-aid kit.*

first aid, emergency treatment given to an ill or injured person before full medical care can be obtained.

first·born (fûrst′bôrn′) adj. born first; eldest. —n. the first-born child.

first–class (fûrst′klas′) adj. **1.** of the highest rank or best quality: *a first-class performance.* **2.** of or relating to a class of mail consisting primarily of letters, parcels, and other written or sealed matter. **3.** of or relating to the best-equipped or most luxurious accommodations on a ship, airplane, or train. —adv. by first-class mail or travel accommodations: *to send a package first-class.*

first class 1. first-class travel accommodations. **2.** first-class mail.

first–de·gree burn (fûrst′di grē′) a burn of the outer layer of the skin; a burn that causes redness.

first·hand (fûrst′hand′) adj. direct from the original source: *firsthand knowledge of an event.* —adv. from the original source: *to learn of something firsthand.*

first lady 1. the wife of the president of the United States, of the leader of another country, or of a state

at; āpe; fär; câre; end; mē; it; īce; pîerce; hot; ōld; sông, fôrk; oil; out; up; ūse; ru̅le; pu̇ll; tûrn; chin; sing; shop; thin; this; hw in white; zh in treasure. The symbol ə stands for the unstressed vowel sound heard in about, taken, pencil, lemon, and circus.

F

governor. **2.** a leading or outstanding woman in a particular field or profession: *the first lady of the theater*.

first lieutenant, an officer in the U.S. Army, Air Force, or Marine Corps, ranking above a second lieutenant and below a captain.

first·ly (fûrst′lē) *adv.* in the first place; first.

first person, a verb, pronoun, or inflected form that indicates the speaker. *I* and *we* are pronouns of the first person.

first–rate (fûrst′rāt′) *adj.* **1.** of the highest class, quality, or importance: *a first-rate military power*. **2.** excellent; very good: *a first-rate tennis player*. —*adv. Informal.* excellently.

firth (fûrth) *n.* a long, narrow arm of the sea.

fis·cal (fis′kəl) *adj.* **1.** relating to the treasury, finances, or revenues of a government: *fiscal policy*. **2.** relating to money matters; financial. —**fis′cal·ly**, *adv.*

fiscal year, any twelve-month period used as a basis for settling financial accounts in a business or government.

fish (fish) *n., pl.* **fish** or **fish·es**. **1.** a cold-blooded water animal having a backbone, gills for breathing, fins for, and, usually, a scaly outer covering for protection. **2.** the flesh of fish used as food. —*v.i.* **1.** to catch or try to catch fish: *to fish for trout*. **2.** to get or try to get something by cunning or indirect means: *They fished for an invitation to the party*. **3.** to search: *I fished in my pocket for a nickel.* —*v.t.* **1.** to catch or try to catch fish in: *to fish a stream.* **2.** to catch or try to catch (fish): *to fish minnows.* **3.** to find and bring out: *I fished my keys out of my purse.*

fish·er (fish′ər) *n.* **1.** a person who fishes; fisherman. **2.** any animal that catches fish for food. **3.** a meat-eating North American mammal related to the marten, having a long body, short legs, and a pointed face. **4.** the dark brown fur of this animal.

fish·er·man (fish′ər mən). *n., pl.* **fish·er·men** (fish′ər mən). a person who fishes as an occupation or for sport.

fish·er·y (fish′ə rē) *n., pl.* **fisher·ies**. **1.** the occupation or business of catching fish. **2.** a place for catching fish. **3.** fish hatchery.

fisher *(def. 3)*

fish farm, a place where fish are raised, usually in large pools, to be sold as food.

fish hatchery, a place where fish are bred under controlled conditions.

fish hawk, another term for **osprey**.

fish·hook (fish′hŏk′) *n.* a hook, usually barbed, for catching fish.

fish·ing (fish′ing) *n.* the occupation or sport of catching fish.

fishing rod, a long pole, usually made of wood, metal, fiberglass, or some other material, with a line, a hook, and usually a reel attached to it, used to catch fish.

fishing tackle, the equipment used in fishing, such as rods, lines, hooks, and nets.

fish·mon·ger (fish′mung′gər, fish′mong′gər) *n.* a person who deals in fish.

fish·pond (fish′pond′) *n.* a pond containing fish, especially a pond stocked with fish for sport or food.

fish·wife (fish′wīf′) *n., pl.* **fish·wives** (fish′wīvz′). **1.** a woman who sells fish. **2.** a coarse, abusive woman.

fish·y (fish′ē) *adj.,* **fish·i·er, fish·i·est.** **1.** like a fish, as in odor or taste. **2.** consisting of fish. **3.** full of fish. **4.** *Informal.* unlikely or suspicious: *There was something fishy about their excuse*. **5.** without expression; dull: *a fishy stare*. —**fish′i·ness**, *n.*

fis·sion (fish′ən) *n.* **1.** the act of splitting or breaking apart. **2.** *Physics.* the splitting of an atomic nucleus into two parts, occurring when the nucleus is bombarded by and absorbs a neutron. Fission is accompanied by the release of large amounts of energy. **3.** *Biology.* a method of reproduction in which the parent cell divides to form two or more new cells. Many single-celled plants and animals reproduce by means of fission.

fis·sion·a·ble (fish′ə nə bəl) *adj.* capable of undergoing nuclear fission. Uranium and plutonium are fissionable materials.

fis·sure (fish′ər) *n.* a long, narrow opening; crack: *a fissure in a rock.*

fist (fist) *n.* a hand tightly closed with fingers doubled into the palm.

fist·ful (fist′fŭl′) *n., pl.* **fist·fuls.** another word for **handful**.

fist·i·cuffs (fis′ti kufs′) *pl. n.* **1.** a fight with the fists. **2.** the art of boxing.

fis·tu·la (fis′chə lə) *n., pl.* **fis·tu·las** or **fis·tu·lae** (fis′chə lē′). a passage that connects body cavities or organs that are normally not connected. A fistula can be present from birth or be the result of the improper healing of a wound or abscess.

fit¹ (fit) *adj.,* **fit·ter, fit·test.** **1.** adapted to or qualified for an end, object, or purpose; suited: *This water is not fit to drink.* **2.** right or proper: *behavior not fit for a public official.* **3.** having the necessary qualifications; competent: *to be fit for a job.* **4.** ready: *The fruit will be fit to eat in three days.* **5.** in good physical or mental condition; healthy: *Exercise to keep fit.* —*v.,* **fit·ted** or **fit, fit·ting.** —*v.t.* **1.** to be suitable or proper for; be adapted to: *Let the punishment fit the crime.* **2.** to be of the proper or correct size or shape for: *The coat fits me well.* **3.** to make fit or suitable; alter; adjust: *to fit a speech to the occasion.* **4.** to supply with what is necessary or suitable; equip: *The beds were fitted with bright new covers.* **5.** to measure for something: *The tailor fitted me for a suit.* ▲ past tense and past participle, only **fitted**. **6.** to adjust, join, or insert: *to fit the pieces of a puzzle together.* —*v.i.* **1.** to be suitable or proper. **2.** to be of the proper size or shape: *The shirt fits perfectly.* **3.** to be in harmony: *The abstract painting did not fit with the other pictures in the room.* —*n.* **1.** the way in which something fits: *The jacket had a loose fit.* **2.** a thing that fits or is fitted: *The dress is a perfect fit.* [Probably of Scandinavian origin.] —**fit′ly,** *adv.* —**fit′ness,** *n.*

fit² (fit) *n.* **1.** a sudden, acute seizure or attack of illness: *an epileptic fit, a coughing fit.* **2.** a sudden outburst of emotion or activity: *a fit of anger, a fit of laughter, a fit of hard work.* [From the Old English word *fitt* meaning "conflict."]

·**by fits and starts** or **in fits and starts.** in an irregular way: *to work by fits and starts.*

·**to have a fit** or **to throw a fit.** *Informal.* to show extreme anger; become very upset: *Don't throw a fit just because we can't go to the movies this weekend.*

fitch (fich) *n., pl.* **fitch·es.** **1.** the European polecat. **2.** its fur, used to make coats and jackets.

fit·ful (fit′fəl) *adj.* not regular; restless: *fitful sleep, a fitful breeze.* —**fit′ful·ly,** *adv.* —**fit′ful·ness,** *n.*

fit·ter (fit′ər) *n.* **1.** a person who fits or alters garments. **2.** a person who supplies, installs, and fixes parts, machinery, or fittings: *a pipe fitter.*

fit·ting (fit′ing) *adj.* suitable; proper; appropriate: *fitting praise, a fitting end to a story.* —*n.* **1.** the act of a person who fits. **2.** the trying on of an article of clothing so that it can be marked for alterations. **3.** an accessory part or attachment used to adjust something: *a pipe fitting.* —**fit′ting·ly,** *adv.* —**fit′ting·ness,** *n.*

five (fīv) *n.* **1.** the cardinal number that is one more than four. **2.** a symbol representing this number, such as 5 or V. **3.** something having this many units or things, as a playing card. —*adj.* numbering one more than four.

five–and–ten (fīv′ən ten′) *n.* a store selling a variety of low-priced merchandise. Also, **dime store, five-and-dime** (fīv′ən dīm′).

five·fold (fīv′fōld′) *adj.* **1.** five times as great or numerous. **2.** having or consisting of five parts. —*adv.* so as to be five times greater or more numerous.

Five Nations, see **Iroquois.**

fix (fiks) *v.t.* **1.** to mend; repair: *to fix a broken chair.* **2.** to prepare (food or a meal): *to fix dinner.* **3.** to make firm, stable, or secure; fasten tightly: *The campers fixed the stakes for the tent in the ground.* **4.** to settle or arrange definitely; establish; set: *to fix a price, to fix a date for the wedding.* **5.** to direct or hold steadily: *They fixed their attention on me.* **6.** to place or put: *Police fixed responsibility for the accident on the driver.* **7.** to treat so as to make permanent or lasting: *to fix colors in a fabric.* **8.** *Photography.* to treat (a photograph) with a chemical solution so that it will not fade. **9.** *Informal.* to put in order; get ready; arrange: *Fix this room for our guests.* **10.** *Informal.* to influence the result of (a contest) to one's advantage, as by a bribe: *to fix a boxing match.* **11.** *Informal.* to get revenge upon; get even with; punish: *I'll fix them for what they did.* —*n., pl.* **fix·es. 1.** *Informal.* a position from which it is difficult to escape; difficulty; predicament: *to get oneself into a fix.* **2.** *Slang.* a dosage of a narcotic. **3.** the position of a ship or aircraft, as determined by observations or from radio signals: *The Coast Guard sought to get a fix on the sinking ship.* —**fix′a·ble,** *adj.* —**fix′er,** *n.*

·**to fix on** or **to fix upon.** to decide on; choose; select: *to fix on a plan.*

·**to fix up.** *Informal.* **a.** to mend; repair: *Our neighbor fixed up our broken lawn mower.* **b.** to provide what is needed for: *We fixed them up with a place to spend the night.*

fix·a·tion (fik sā′shən) *n.* **1.** the act of fixing or the state of being fixed. **2.** a treatment to make a dye or color permanent, as in photographic film. **3.** a strong and persistent attachment to a person, thing, or idea.

fix·a·tive (fik′sə tiv) *n.* something that fixes or makes permanent, especially a substance sprayed on a charcoal or crayon drawing to preserve it. —*adj.* fixing or making permanent.

fixed (fikst) *adj.* **1.** made firm in position; securely placed or fastened; not movable: *fixed seats in a theater.* **2.** steadily directed; not moving: *a fixed stare.* **3.** not changing; settled: *a fixed rate of interest.* **4.** definite; resolute: *a fixed purpose.* **5.** *Informal.* prearranged dishonestly as to result or decision: *a fixed race.* —**fix·ed·ly** (fik′sid lē), *adv.* —**fix′ed·ness,** *n.*

fixed star, a star that appears to remain in the same position in relation to other stars, because of its great distance from the earth.

fix·ings (fik′singz) *pl. n. Informal.* garnishes; accessories; trimmings: *The family ate a turkey dinner with all the fixings.*

fix·ture (fiks′chər) *n.* **1.** anything fixed or securely fastened into place, especially a permanently attached part or accessory of a house: *bathroom fixtures, a light fixture.* **2.** a person or thing permanently associated with a particular place or job: *That old professor is a fixture at the college.*

fizz (fiz) *v.i.* to make a hissing or sputtering sound. —*n., pl.* **fizz·es. 1.** a hissing sound. **2.** an effervescent or bubbling beverage, such as champagne, certain mineral waters, or soda water.

fiz·zle (fiz′əl) *v.i.,* **fiz·zled, fiz·zling. 1.** to make a hissing or sputtering sound: *The wet wood fizzled in the fireplace.* **2.** *Informal.* to fail or end feebly, especially after a good start: *All our plans fizzled.* —*n.* **1.** a hissing or sputtering sound. **2.** *Informal.* a person or thing that does not succeed; failure.

fizz·y (fiz′ē) *adj.,* **fizz·i·er, fizz·i·est.** fizzing; bubbling.

fjord

fjord (fyôrd) *also,* **fiord.** —*n.* a deep, narrow inlet of the sea between high, steep banks or cliffs, especially one along the coast of Norway.

Fl, the symbol for fluorine.

fl., flourished. ▲ This abbreviation is used before the date or dates when a person was successful or is generally accepted as having been alive.

FL, postal abbreviation for Florida.

Fla., Florida.

flab·ber·gast (flab′ər gast′) *v.t. Informal.* to overwhelm with surprise or amazement; astonish: *The news that I had won the contest flabbergasted me.*

flab·by (flab′ē) *adj.,* **flab·bi·er, flab·bi·est.** lacking firmness or force; soft: *flabby muscles, a flabby mind.* —**flab′bi·ly,** *adv.* —**flab′bi·ness,** *n.*

flac·cid (flak′sid) *adj.* lacking firmness; limp; weak: *flaccid muscles.* —**flac·cid′i·ty,** *n.* —**flac′cid·ly,** *adv.*

fla·con (flak′ən, fla kon′) *n.* a small bottle or flask that is closed with a stopper: *a flacon of perfume.*

flag[1] (flag) *n.* a piece of cloth having various colors and designs on it that is used as a symbol of a country or organization, or as a signal. —*v.t.,* **flagged, flag·ging. 1.** to put a flag or flags on; decorate with flags. **2.** to stop or signal: *to flag a taxicab.* **3.** to signal with a flag or a similar method: *to flag messages.* [Of uncertain origin.]

flag[2] (flag) *n.* **1.** any of various irises having sword-shaped leaves and blue, yellow, purple, or white flowers. **2.** a flower of any of these plants. [From the Middle English word *flagge* meaning "a reed or rush."]

flag[3] (flag) *v.i.,* **flagged, flag·ging.** to grow weak or tired; lose vigor: *The audience's interest flagged.* [Possibly of Scandinavian origin.]

flag[4] (flag) *n.* see **flagstone.** —*v.t.,* **flagged, flag·ging.** to pave with flagstones. [From the Middle English word *flagge* meaning "a flagstone" or "block of peat," from the Old Norse word *flaga* "a slab."]

Flag Day, the anniversary of the day in 1777 when the Stars and Stripes was made the official flag of the United States. It falls on June 14.

flag·el·late (*adj.,* flaj′ə lit, flaj′ə lāt′; *v.,* flaj′ə lāt′) *adj.* **1.** having a flagellum or flagella. **2.** shaped like a flagellum. —*v.t.,* **flag·el·lat·ed, flag·el·lat·ing.** to whip; scourge. —**flag′el·la′tion,** *n.*

at; āpe; fär; câre; end; mē; it; īce; pîerce; hot; ōld; sông, fôrk; oil; out; up; ūse; rüle; pùll; tûrn; chin; sing; shop; thin; this; hw in white; zh in treasure. The symbol ə stands for the unstressed vowel sound heard in about, taken, pencil, lemon, and circus.

369

fla·gel·lum (flə jel′əm) *n., pl.* **fla·gel·la** (flə jel′ə) or **fla·gel·lums. 1.** a long whiplike tail or part that enables certain cells, bacteria, and protozoa to move. **2.** a whip.

flag·eo·let (flaj′ə let′) *n.* a wind instrument like a flute, having six finger holes, four on the top and two below.

flag·man (flag′mən) *n., pl.* **flagmen** (flag′mən). a person who signals with a flag or lantern, as at a highway construction site.

flag officer, a naval officer above the rank of captain, entitled to display a flag showing his or her rank.

flag·on (flag′ən) *n.* **1.** a large container for liquids, having a handle, a spout, and usually a cover. **2.** a large bottle for wine, ale, or the like. **3.** the contents of a flagon: *We drank a flagon among us.*

flag·pole (flag′pōl′) *n.* a pole on which a flag is raised and flown. Also, **flagstaff.**

fla·grant (flā′grənt) *adj.* openly bad or wrong; scandalous: *flagrant violations of the law, a flagrant display of cowardice.* —**fla′gran·cy,** *n.* —**fla′grant·ly,** *adv.*

flag·ship (flag′ship′) *n.* a ship carrying, and flying the flag of, the commanding officer of a fleet.

flag·staff (flag′staf′) *n.* another word for **flagpole.**

flag·stone (flag′stōn′) *n.* a large, flat stone, used for paving.

flail (flāl) *n.* a device used for threshing grain by hand. It is made of a wooden staff at the end of which a wide, short stick is hung so as to swing freely. —*v.t.* **1.** to strike with a flail; thresh. **2.** to wave or swing, especially violently or quickly: *I flailed my arms at the bees swarming around me.*

flair (flâr) *n.* **1.** an ability to choose what is good; discernment: *The room had been decorated with flair.* **2.** a natural talent: *a flair for acting.*

flak (flak) *n.* **1.** antiaircraft fire. **2.** fragments from exploding shells fired at enemy aircraft. **3.** *Slang.* criticism or abuse: *The proposal met with much flak.*

flake (flāk) *n.* a small, thin, flat piece: *a flake of snow, flakes of paint peeling off a wall.* —*v.,* **flaked, flak·ing.** —*v.t.* to chip or peel off in flakes: *to flake paint from a wall.* —*v.i.* to peel off in flakes: *The plaster cracked and flaked.*

flak·y (flā′kē) *adj.,* **flak·i·er, flak·i·est. 1.** consisting of flakes: *Mica is a flaky mineral.* **2.** separating easily into flakes: *The pie crust was flaky and light.* **3.** *Slang.* eccentric; odd. —**flak′i·ly,** *adv.* —**flak′i·ness,** *n.*

flam·boy·ance (flam boi′əns) *n.* the quality of being flamboyant.

flam·boy·ant (flam boi′ənt) *adj.* **1.** overly decorated; showy; florid: *a flamboyant writing style, flamboyant fashions.* **2.** brilliant; colorful: *a flamboyant sunset.* **3.** having wavy or flamelike lines or curves, as some Gothic architecture. **4.** showy or without restraint: *flamboyant behavior.* —**flam·boy′ant·ly,** *adv.*

flame (flām) *n.* **1.** one of the tongues of light given off by a fire: *Flames shot out of the burning house.* **2.** ignited gas or vapor that gives off light and heat: *Lower the flame under the frying pan.* **3.** the condition or state of burning: *to burst into flame.* **4.** something like a flame: *The sun was a flame on the horizon.* **5.** strong emotional feeling; passion; ardor: *the flame of love.* —*v.i.,* **flamed, flaming. 1.** to burn with flames; burst into flame; blaze: *The fire flamed intensely.* **2.** to light up or glow as if with flames: *My face flamed with embarrassment.* **3.** to break out with violence or passion: *to flame with anger.* —**flame′like,** *adj.*

fla·men·co (flə meng′kō) *n.* **1.** a Spanish Gypsy style of dancing, characterized by stamping of the feet, clapping of the hands, and the use of castanets. **2.** the music accompanying this dance.

flagellum
of a
protozoan

flame·thrower (flām′thrō′ər) *n.* a weapon or instrument that throws a stream of burning fuel.

flam·ing (flā′ming) *adj.* **1.** in flames; blazing; fiery. **2.** brilliant: *flaming colors.* **3.** ardent; passionate: *a flaming speech.* —**flam′ing·ly,** *adv.*

fla·min·go (flə ming′gō) *n., pl.* **fla·min·gos** or **fla·min·goes.** any of various wading birds of tropical and subtropical regions, having a long, thin neck and legs, webbed feet, and pinkish white to crimson feathers.

flam·ma·ble (flam′ə bəl) *adj.* able to be set on fire easily; combustible. —*n.* something that is flammable. —**flam′ma·bil′i·ty,** *n.*

flange (flanj) *n.* a projecting rim or collar on an object, designed to keep it in place, to attach it to another object, or to strengthen it. The wheels of a railroad car have flanges to keep them on the tracks.

flank (flangk) *n.* **1.** the part between the ribs and the hip on either side of a human being or animal. **2.** a cut of meat, especially beef, from this part of an animal. **3.** the right or left side of a military unit, formation, position, or fortification. **4.** the side of anything: *the flank of a building.* —*v.t.* **1.** to be located at the side of: *Two statues flanked the entrance of the library.* **2.** to attack or move around the flank of: *to flank an enemy fleet.*

flank·er (flang′kər) *n.* **1.** a person or thing that flanks. **2.** *Football.* an offensive back who lines up in a position on a flank.

flan·nel (flan′əl) *n.* **1.** a soft cotton fabric, having a nap on one or both sides, used for such items as nightgowns, infants' wear, and shirts. Also, **flannelette. 2.** a soft woolen fabric having a slight nap. **3. flannels.** clothes made of flannel.

flan·nel·ette (flan′ə let′) *n.* see **flannel** *(def. 1).*

flap (flap) *v.,* **flapped, flap·ping.** —*v.t.* to move up and down, especially with a muffled, slapping sound: *The birds flapped their wings.* —*v.i.* **1.** to move the wings or arms up and down, especially with a muffled, slapping sound. **2.** to sway or wave loosely, especially with noise: *The curtains flapped in the breeze.* —*n.* **1.** a flapping motion. **2.** the muffled slapping sound made when something flaps. **3.** the part of an envelope folded down in closing or sealing it. **4.** a piece of material attached at only one edge so that it may move, especially one covering the opening of a pocket. **5.** a hinged section on the back edge of an airplane wing that is used to increase lift during a takeoff or a landing. **6.** *Slang.* a dispute, commotion, or scandal.

flap·jack (flap′jak′) *n.* another word for **pancake.**

flap·per (flap′ər) *n.* **1.** a person or thing that flaps. **2.** *Informal.* a young woman of the 1920s who was unconventional in dress and behavior.

flare (flâr) *v.i.,* **flared, flar·ing. 1.** to burn with a sudden, very bright light, especially for only a short time: *The match flared in the darkness and then went out.* **2.** to break out in sudden or violent emotion: *Tempers flared.* **3.** to open or spread outward: *This skirt flares from the waist.* —*n.* **1.** a sudden, bright light, usually lasting only a short time. **2.** a device that produces a fire or blaze of light, used to signal or provide light. **3.** a sudden outburst, as of emotion or activity: *a flare of anger.* **4.** a widening or spreading outward: *the flare of a skirt.*

·**to flare up.** to become suddenly angry, excited, or inflamed: *They flared up at the suggestion. The fever flared up again overnight.*

flare-up (flâr′up′) *n.* **1.** a sudden outburst of flame or light. **2.** *Informal.* a sudden or violent burst of activity or emotion: *a flare-up of violence, a flare-up of a rash.*

flash (flash) *n., pl.* **flash·es. 1.** a sudden, brief burst, as of light or flame: *a flash of lightning.* **2.** a very brief period of time; instant; moment: *I'll be there in a flash.* **3.** a sudden outburst or brief display: *a flash of merriment, a flash of inspiration.* **4.** a brief bulletin or report of very recent or urgent news. —*v.i.* **1.** to burst forth in sudden, brief light or fire: *Lightning flashed in the sky.* **2.** to reflect or burst forth with light; shine; gleam: *eyes flashing with anger.* **3.** to burst suddenly into view or perception: *An idea flashed into my mind.* **4.** to come or move suddenly or quickly: *The car flashed by.* —*v.t.* **1.** to cause to flash: *They flashed the light in our eyes.* **2.** to communicate by flashes, as by telegraph or radio: *The news was flashed all over the country.* —*adj.* happening or done very quickly; lasting for a short time: *a flash fire.* —**flash′er,** *n.*

·**flash in the pan.** a person or something that at first seems promising or successful, but in the end is a failure.

flash·back (flash′bak′) *n.* **1.** a break in the normal time sequence of a motion picture, radio script, novel, or play, during which a scene describing earlier events is introduced. **2.** a scene or episode introduced in this way.

flash·bulb (flash′bulb′) *n.* an electric bulb that gives off a very bright flash, used for taking photographs.

flash·card (flash′kärd′) *n.* any of a set of cards having words, numbers, or other information on them, used in classroom drills or in private study.

flash flood, a sudden, violent flood usually caused by heavy rainfall.

flash·gun (flash′gun′) *n.* a device used to hold and set off a flashbulb.

flash·light (flash′līt′) *n.* a portable electric light powered by batteries.

flash·y (flash′ē) *adj.,* **flash·i·er, flash·i·est. 1.** brilliant for a short time; sparkling; flashing. **2.** showy; gaudy: *a flashy car.* —**flash′i·ly,** *adv.* —**flash′i·ness,** *n.*

flask (flask) *n.* **1.** a small, flattened bottle, as for holding liquor, made to be carried in the pocket. **2.** a rounded glass container with a long neck, used in laboratory work.

flat¹ (flat) *adj.,* **flat·ter, flat·test. 1.** smooth or even: *a flat field. It is easy to bicycle on a flat road.* **2.** lying or stretched at full length; spread out: *to lie flat on one's back.* **3.** having little depth or thickness; shallow: *a flat sheet of metal.* **4.** plain; positive; absolute: *a flat denial, a flat refusal.* **5.** fixed; unchangeable: *a flat rate.* **6.** lacking in interest or vigor; lifeless; dull: *a flat performance.* **7.** not shiny or glossy: *flat paint.* **8.** containing little or no air; deflated: *a flat tire.* **9.** *Music.* **a.** below the true, regular, or intended pitch. **b.** one half note lower than natural pitch. **c.** having a flat in the signature. **10.** having an even surface, without projections or depressions: *The south wall has windows and balconies, but the north wall is flat.* —*n.* **1.** a flat part or surface: *the flat of a sword, the flat of the hand.* **2.** a tract of low-lying, level land. **3. flats.** women's shoes having low heels. **4.** a tire from which air is escaping or has escaped. **5.** *Music.* **a.** a tone or note lowered one half note below its natural pitch. **b.** a symbol (♭) that indicates such a tone or note. **6.** a shallow box, as for holding young plants until they are put in the soil. —*adv.* **1.** in a flat manner; flatly: *The cat lay flat on the ground.* **2.** exactly; precisely: *I got home in four minutes flat.* **3.** *Music.* below the true pitch: *to sing flat.* —*v.,* **flatted, flatting.** —*v.t.* **1.** to make flat. **2.** *Music.* to sing or play flat. —*v.i.* to become flat. [From the Old Norse word *flatr* meaning "level."] —**flat′ly,** *adv.* —**flat′ness,** *n.*

flat² (flat) *n.* an apartment or suite of rooms on one floor of a building. [From the Old English word *flet* meaning "floor, dwelling."]

flat·bed (flat′bed′) *n.* a motor vehicle with a truck bed or trailer that has no top or sides.

flat·boat (flat′bōt′) *n.* a large boat with a flat bottom, used for carrying freight on rivers or canals.

flat·car (flat′kär′) *n.* a railroad car consisting of a platform without a roof or sides, used for carrying freight.

flat·fish (flat′fish′) *n.,* *pl.* **flat·fish** or **flat·fish·es.** any of a group of fish that have flattened bodies. In the adult both eyes are on the upper side of the body. Halibut, flounder, and sole are flatfish.

flat·foot (flat′fut′) *n.,* *pl.* **flat·feet. 1.** a condition in which the arch of the foot is abnormally low and most or all of the sole touches the ground. **2.** a foot with an abnormally low arch. **3.** *Slang.* a police officer, especially one who patrols on foot.

flat·foot·ed (flat′fut′id) *adj.* **1.** having flat feet. **2.** *Informal.* off one's guard; not ready; unprepared: *to be caught flatfooted.* **3.** firm; not to be changed or compromised: *a flatfooted refusal.* —**flat′foot′ed·ly,** *adv.* —**flat′foot′ed·ness,** *n.*

flat·i·ron (flat′ī′ərn) *n.* a heavy iron for pressing clothes, especially one that must be heated in an oven or fireplace before it can be used.

flat·land (flat′land′) *n.* land that is almost or completely flat, with no hills or valleys.

flat·ten (flat′ən) *v.t.* **1.** to make flat or flatter. **2.** to knock down: *The big wind flattened the corn.* —*v.i.* **1.** to become flat or flatter. **2.** to fall or lie flat. —**flat′ten·er,** *n.*

flat·ter (flat′ər) *v.t.* **1.** to praise too much or insincerely. **2.** to try to please or gain the favor of by praising too much or insincerely. **3.** to cause to be pleased; compliment: *I was flattered by the invitation.* **4.** to show favorably, especially to show as more attractive than is actually the case: *The photograph flatters the building.* —**flat′ter·er,** *n.* —**flat′ter·ing·ly,** *adv.*

flat·ter·y (flat′ə rē) *n.,* *pl.* **flat·ter·ies. 1.** the act of flattering. **2.** a flattering remark or speech.

flat·tish (flat′ish) *adj.* somewhat flat.

flat·top (flat′top′) *n.* *Informal.* **1.** an aircraft carrier. **2.** hair cut short and flat across the top of the head.

flat·u·lent (flach′ə lənt) *adj.* having or producing gas in the stomach or intestines. —**flat′u·lence,** *n.*

flat·ware (flat′wâr′) *n.* **1.** table utensils, such as knives, forks, and spoons. **2.** dishes that are more or less flat, such as plates, platters, or saucers.

flat·worm (flat′wurm′) *n.* any of a large group of soft, flat bodied worms, including the tapeworm.

flaunt (flônt) *v.i.* **1.** to show off in order to impress others; make a gaudy display. **2.** to wave or flutter freely: *Banners were flaunting at the stadium entrance.* —*v.t.* to show or display boldly or boastfully: *to flaunt one's achievements.* —*n.* the act of flaunting. —**flaunt′ing·ly,** *adv.*

▲ **Flaunt** and **flout** are spelled and pronounced in a similar way, but they have different meanings. **Flaunt** means to show off in a boastful way in order to impress others: *They flaunt their wealth by buying an expensive new car every year.* **Flout** means to defy or treat with contempt: *They flouted the law by refusing to pay taxes.*

flau·tist (flô′tist, flou′tist) *n.* another word for **flutist.**

fla·vor (flā′vər) *also, British,* **fla·vour.** *n.* **1.** a particular or characteristic taste: *Pepper will give the stew a spicy flavor.* **2.** flavoring; seasoning: *Ice cream is made with chocolate, vanilla, and other flavors.* **3.** characteristic, distinctive, or main quality; aura: *That story has a quaint flavor.* —*v.t.* to give flavor to: *to flavor apple pie with cinnamon.* —**fla′vor·ful,** *adj.* —**fla′vor·some,** *adj.*

fla·vor·ing (flā′vər ing) *n.* something added to food or drink to give or heighten flavor: *lemon flavoring.*

flaw (flô) *n.* something that takes away from or spoils completeness, soundness, or perfection: *Quick temper is a flaw in your character. The glass had a flaw in it.* —*v.t.* to make defective.

at; āpe; fär; câre; end; mē; it; īce; pîerce; hot; ōld; sông, fôrk; oil; out; up; ūse; rūle; pŭll; tûrn; chin; sing; shop; thin; this; hw in white; zh in treasure. The symbol ə stands for the unstressed vowel sound heard in about, taken, pencil, lemon, and circus.

flaw·less (flô′lis) *adj.* having no flaw; perfect: *a flaw-less emerald, a flawless complexion, a flawless perform-ance.* —**flaw′less·ly,** *adv.* —**flaw′less·ness,** *n.*

flax (flaks) *n.* **1.** a fiber that is obtained from the stem of a plant and prepared to be spun into thread. Flax is used to make linen and such products as rope and rugs. **2.** the plant itself.

flax·en (flak′sən) *adj.* **1.** made of flax: *flaxen thread.* **2.** having a pale yellow color like that of flax fiber: *flaxen hair.*

flax·seed (flaks′sēd′) *n.* the seed of flax, used to make linseed oil; linseed.

flay (flā) *v.t.* **1.** to strip off the skin or outer covering of, as by lashing. **2.** to criticize or scold severely or harshly.

flea (flē) any of a large group of wingless insects that feed on the blood of mammals and birds. They have strong legs for leaping and sharp mouth parts for piercing the skin and sucking blood. Fleas may transmit certain dis-eases, such as bubonic plague.

flea collar, a collar for dogs, cats, or other pets that contains a chem-ical for killing fleas.

flea

fleck (flek) *n.* **1.** a small patch or streak of light or color; spot: *flecks of sunlight, black marble with flecks of white in it.* **2.** a small particle; flake; speck: *flecks of dust.* —*v.t.* to mark with flecks; spot: *to fleck a wall with paint.*

fled (fled) the past tense and past participle of **flee.**

fledge (flej) *v.,* **fledged, fledg·ing.** —*v.t.* **1.** to provide (an arrow) with feathers. **2.** to rear (a young bird) until it is able to fly. —*v.i.* (of a young bird) to grow the feathers needed for flight.

fledg·ling (flej′ling) *also,* **fledge·ling.** *n.* **1.** a young bird just fledged. **2.** a young or inexperienced person.

flee (flē) *v.,* **fled, flee·ing.** —*v.i.* **1.** to run away, as from danger or pursuit; take flight: *The robbers fled down the alley.* **2.** to move or pass away swiftly: *Color fled from the sky.* —*v.t.* to run away or try to escape from: *The family fled the burning house.* —**fle′er,** *n.*

fleece (flēs) *n.* **1.** a coat of wool covering a sheep or similar animal. **2.** the quantity of wool sheared from a sheep or similar animal at any one time. **3.** something resembling fleece: *a fleece of snow.* **4.** a fabric with a thick nap or pile resembling the wool of a sheep, used for lining clothes. —*v.t.,* **fleeced, fleec·ing.** **1.** to shear the fleece from. **2.** to deprive of money or property by deception; cheat; swindle. —**fleec′er,** *n.*

fleec·y (flē′sē) *adj.,* **fleec·i·er, fleec·i·est.** **1.** made of or covered with fleece. **2.** like fleece: *fleecy clouds.* —**fleec′i·ness,** *n.*

fleet¹ (flēt) *n.* **1.** a group of warships under one command. **2.** a group of boats or vehicles working together or under one management: *a fleet of taxis, a fishing fleet.* [From the Old English word *flēot* meaning "ship," from the word *flēotan* "to float, swim."]

fleet² (flēt) *adj.* swift; fast: *The deer is a fleet animal.* —*v.i.* to move or pass swiftly. [From the Middle English word *flēten* meaning "to flow, glide," from the Old English word *flēotan* "to float, swim."] —**fleet′ly,** *adv.* —**fleet′ness,** *n.*

fleet admiral, an officer of the highest rank in the U.S. Navy.

fleet·ing (flē′ting) *adj.* passing quickly; very brief: *a fleeting glimpse, a fleeting moment.* —**fleet′ing·ly,** *adv.* —**fleet′ing·ness,** *n.*

Flem·ing (flem′ing) *n.* **1.** a Belgian whose native lan-guage is Flemish. **2.** one of the people of the region of Flanders.

Flem·ish (flem′ish) *n.* **1. the Flemish.** the people of Flanders. **2.** a Germanic language resembling Dutch and spoken chiefly in northern Belgium and northeastern France. —*adj.* of or relating to Flanders, its people, or their language.

flesh (flesh) *n.* **1.** the soft part of the body of a human being or animal that covers the bones, consisting mainly of muscle and fat. **2.** the parts of an animal used as food; meat. **3.** the soft, pulpy part of fruits or vegetables used as food: *the flesh of a peach.* **4.** the body as distinguished from the soul or spirit: *The spirit indeed is willing, but the flesh is weak* (Matthew XXV:41).

·**flesh and blood.** family or other close relatives.

·**in the flesh.** present before one's eyes; in person: *You're taller in the flesh than you look in pictures.*

flesh·ly (flesh′lē) *adj.,* **flesh·li·er, flesh·li·est.** **1.** sen-sual; carnal: *fleshly desires.* **2.** of or relating to the flesh or body; bodily; physical. —**flesh′li·ness,** *n.*

flesh·y (flesh′ē) *adj.,* **flesh·i·er, flesh·i·est.** **1.** having much flesh; plump; fat. **2.** of or like flesh. **3.** firm and pulpy: *a fleshy fruit, fleshy leaves.* —**flesh′i·ness,** *n.*

fleur–de–lis (flûr′də lē′) *n., pl.* **fleurs-de-lis** (flûr′də lēz′). **1.** a heraldic design representing an iris, used as an emblem by the former royal family of France. **2.** see **iris** *(defs. 2, 3).*

flew (flü) a past tense of **fly².**

flex (fleks) *v.t.* **1.** to bend: *to flex one's arm. The ar-chers flexed their bows.* **2.** to tight-en or contract; tense: *to flex one's leg muscles before beginning physical exercises.*

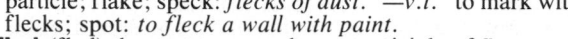

fleur-de-lis *(def. 1)*

flex·i·ble (flek′sə bəl) *adj.* **1.** able to bend without breaking: *Rubber is flexible.* **2.** able to adjust easily to change; adaptable: *a flexible schedule, flexible rules.* —**flex′i·bil′i·ty, flex′i·ble·ness,** *n.* —**flex′i·bly,** *adv.*

Word Family

Flexible is one of several English words that come from *flectere,* a Latin word that means "to bend, curve, turn around." The muscles that bend, or **flex,** our arms are called **flexors,** and they react with a **reflex** in response to a stimulus. Muscular **flexibility** lets you **deflect** an object heading your way, although an **inflexible** person might stand there and get hit. When light hits a **reflector,** it is bent back to its source; if the **reflector** is a mirror, it sends back an image called a **reflection.** Verbs are **inflected** to **reflect** changes in tense, the way **inflections** in your tone of voice show changes in your mood. Changes in the pronunciation of a vowel can be shown by a mark called a **circumflex.**

flex·ion (flek′shən) *n.* the act of bending a limb or contracting a flexor muscle.

flex·or (flek′sər) *n.* any muscle that bends a limb or other part of the body. See **extensor** for illustration.

flick (flik) *n.* **1.** a light, quick, snapping movement or stroke: *a flick of the wrist, a flick with a whip.* **2.** a sound made by such a movement or stroke. —*v.t.* **1.** to hit or remove (something) with a light, quick, snapping move-ment or stroke: *to flick crumbs from one's lap, to flick a horse's rump with a whip.* **2.** to make a quick, snapping movement with: *to flick a towel at someone.*

flick·er¹ (flik′ər) *v.i.* **1.** to shine or burn with an unsteady or wavering light: *The match flickered in the breeze.* **2.** to move back and forth with a quick, fluttering move-ment; quiver; tremble: *Shadows flickered on the wall.*

—*n.* **1.** an unsteady or wavering light: *I saw the flicker of a candle in the window.* **2.** a slight indication; brief appearance: *a flicker of hope, a flicker of interest.* **3.** a quick fluttering or quivering movement: *the flicker of an eyelid.* [From the Old English word *flicerian* meaning "to flutter, hover."]

flick·er² (flik′ər) *n.* a North American woodpecker having yellow or red markings on its wings and tail. [Possibly from *flick* + -er¹.]

flied (flīd) a past tense and past participle of **fly²** (*v.i.* def. 7).

fli·er (flī′ər) *also,* **fly·er.** *n.* **1.** a person or thing that flies: *That sea gull is a graceful flier.* **2.** an aviator. **3.** a thing that moves swiftly, such as an express train. **4.** a small handbill or leaflet, especially one used in advertising.

flies (flīz) *n.* the plural of **fly¹** and **fly².** —*v.* the third person singular, present tense of **fly².**

flight¹ (flīt) *n.* **1.** the act, manner, or power of flying: *the graceful flight of the butterfly.* **2.** the distance or course traveled by something flying, as an airplane or bird. **3.** a group of things flying or passing through the air together: *a flight of swallows.* **4.** a trip made by or in an aircraft: *the ten o'clock flight to Washington.* **5.** a passing above or beyond the ordinary: *a flight of fancy.* **6.** a series of stairs or steps between floors or landings. [From the Old English word *flyht* meaning "the act of flying," from the word *flēogan* "to fly²."]

flicker²

flight² (flīt) *n.* the act of fleeing. [From the Middle English word *fliht* with the same meaning, probably from Old English.]

·**to put to flight.** to cause to flee; rout: *to put enemy troops to flight.*

flight attendant, a person who serves passengers on an airplane.

flight bag, a small bag of cloth, plastic, or other material, used for carrying clothes and personal effects on board an airplane.

flight·less (flīt′lis) *adj.* (of birds) not able to fly: *The ostrich is flightless.*

flight recorder, an electronic device that records information about an aircraft in operation, such as instrument readings or conversations in the cockpit, and that can be retrieved and analyzed after an accident to help determine the cause. Also, **black box.**

flight·y (flī′tē) *adj.,* **flight·i·er, flight·i·est.** given to sudden whims or impulses; frivolous; giddy. —**flight′i·ness,** *n.*

flim·sy (flim′zē) *adj.,* **flim·si·er, flim·si·est. 1.** lacking strength or substance; thin; frail: *a blouse made of a flimsy material.* **2.** not convincing or adequate; weak: *a flimsy excuse, a flimsy argument.* —**flim′si·ly,** *adv.*

flinch (flinch) *v.i.* to draw back or away, as from something painful, dangerous, or unpleasant; shrink; wince: *I always flinch at loud noises.* —*n.* the act or an instance of flinching.

fling (fling) *v.,* **flung, fling·ing.** —*v.t.* **1.** to throw with force or violence; hurl: *They flung stones at the old barn.* **2.** to send or put suddenly or violently; thrust: *to fling one's hands up in disgust.* —*v.i.* to move suddenly or violently; rush headlong. —*n.* **1.** the act of flinging. **2.** a period of freely indulging oneself, as in pleasures: *to have a fling before settling down.* **3.** a lively or spirited dance, especially the Highland fling.

·**to have a fling at** or **to take a fling at.** to have a try at; make an attempt at: *Would you like to take a fling at playing this game?*

flint (flint) *n.* **1.** a hard variety of quartz, usually dull gray in color, that produces sparks when struck against steel. **2.** a piece of this used for kindling a fire.

flint·lock (flint′lok′) *n.* **1.** a gunlock in which a flint is struck against steel to produce sparks and ignite gunpowder. **2.** an old-fashioned firearm with such a gunlock.

flint·y (flin′tē) *adj.,* **flint·i·er, flint·i·est. 1.** consisting of or containing flint. **2.** hard; unyielding; cruel: *a flinty heart, a flinty look.* —**flint′i·ly,** *adj.* —**flint′i·ness,** *n.*

flip (flip) *v.,* **flipped, flip·ping.** —*v.t.* **1.** to toss with a quick, jerking movement, especially so as to cause to turn over in the air: *to flip a coin.* **2.** to turn over, especially with a quick, jerking movement: *I flipped the pages of the book.* **3.** to move with a quick, jerking movement: *to flip a switch.* —*v.i.* to move or turn with a jerk: *The fish flipped onto its back.* —*n.* **1.** a quick turning or jerking movement: *to turn a switch on with a flip of one's finger.* **2.** a turning over, as in a dive or somersault. —*adj.,* **flip·per, flip·pest.** *Informal.* impertinent; saucy; flippant: *a flip remark.*

flip·pant (flip′ənt) *adj.* lacking proper respect or seriousness: *a flippant answer, a flippant attitude.* —**flip′pan·cy,** *n.* —**flip′pant·ly,** *adv.*

flip·per (flip′ər) *n.* **1.** a broad, flat limb, as of a seal, dolphin, penguin, or turtle, that is adapted for swimming. **2.** one of a pair of broad, paddle-shaped rubber shoes, worn as an aid to swimming or skin diving.

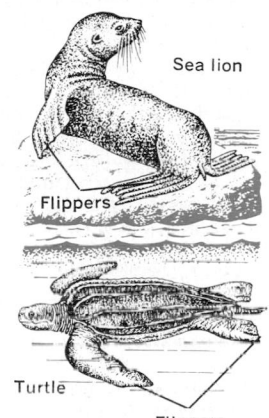

Sea lion

Flippers

Turtle

Flippers

flipper *(def. 1)*

flip side *Informal.* **1.** the reverse and usually less popular side of a phonograph record. **2.** the reverse; the other or opposite side or aspect: *The mayor's new safety program seemed an effective measure, but the flip side was the high cost of the project.*

flirt (flûrt) *v.i.* **1.** to act romantic in a coy or playful way: *to flirt with someone at a party.* **2.** to trifle or toy: *to flirt with danger, to flirt with an idea.* —*v.t.* to move quickly; flick: *The squirrel flirted its tail.* —*n.* **1.** a person who flirts. **2.** a quick movement: *With a flirt of its tail the bird was gone.*

flir·ta·tion (flûr tā′shən) *n.* **1.** the act of flirting. **2.** a brief or casual romance.

flir·ta·tious (flûr tā′shəs) *adj.* **1.** inclined to flirt. **2.** characteristic of a flirt: *flirtatious behavior.* —**flir·ta′tious·ly,** *adv.* —**flir·ta′tious·ness,** *n.*

flit (flit) *v.i.,* **flit·ted, flit·ting. 1.** to move or fly lightly and swiftly; dart: *Butterflies flitted among the flowers.* **2.** to pass lightly and swiftly: *Thoughts flitted through my mind.*

flitch (flich) *n., pl.* **flitch·es.** the salted and cured side of a hog.

float (flōt) *v.i.* **1.** to rest on or at the surface of a liquid: *Sailboats floated on the lake. I floated on my back in the pool.* **2.** to drift or be carried along in the air: *The clouds floated across the sky. Leaves floated down from the trees.* **3.** to hover or move as if carried along in this

at; āpe; fär; câre; end; mē; it; īce; pîerce; hot; ōld; sông; fôrk; oil; out; up; ūse; rüle; pùll; tûrn; chin; sing; shop; thin; this; hw in white; zh in treasure. The symbol ə stands for the unstressed vowel sound heard in about, taken, pencil, lemon, and circus.

manner: *Rumors were floating around town.* —*v.t.*
1. to cause to float: *to float lumber down a river.* **2.** to offer for sale, as stocks or bonds; put on the market: *to float an issue of stock.* —*n.* **1.** a thing that floats or helps something else to float, such as a raft. **2.** an exhibit carried on a vehicle or wheeled platform in parades or pageants. **3.** a hollow metal ball or other device that floats on the surface of a body of liquid and regulates the level, supply, or outflow of the liquid, as in a boiler or the tank of a toilet. —**float'er,** *n.*

floating rib, a rib attached to the backbone but not to the breastbone. In human beings the bottom two pairs of ribs are floating ribs.

flock (flok) *n.* **1.** a group of animals of one kind gathered or herded together: *a flock of crows, a shepherd's flock.* **2.** a large number or group: *a flock of reporters.* **3.** the members of a church; congregation. —*v.i.* to move or gather in crowds: *People flocked to the beaches during the hot weather.*

floe (flō) *n.* a mass or sheet of floating ice. Also, **ice floe.**

flog (flog) *v.t.,* **flogged, flog·ging.** to beat or whip severely, especially as punishment.

flood (flud) *n.* **1.** a great flow or overflowing of water, especially over normally dry land. **2.** a great outpouring of anything: *a flood of tears, a flood of words.* **3.** *also,* **the Flood.** in the Bible, the great flood that occurred in the time of Noah. —*v.t.* **1.** to cover or cause to be covered with a flood; inundate: *The valley was flooded when the dam broke.* **2.** to fill or overwhelm, as with a flood: *The box office was flooded with requests for tickets.* —*v.i.* to rise in a flood; overflow.

flood·gate (flud'gāt') *n.* a gate in a waterway designed to control the flow of water.

flood·light (flud'līt') *n.* **1.** a lamp that provides a broad beam of bright light. **2.** a broad beam of light projected by such a lamp. —*v.t.,* **flood·light·ed** or **flood·lit, flood·light·ing.** to light with a floodlight.

flood·plain (flud'plān') *n.* a plain along a river, made by deposits of earth from floodwaters.

flood tide, the tide that is flowing in toward the shore.

flood·wa·ter (flud'wô'tər, flud'wot'ər) *n.* water flooding normally dry land.

floor (flôr) *n.* **1.** the lower surface of a room on which one stands or walks. **2.** any surface like a floor in position or use; bottom surface: *the ocean floor, the forest floor.* **3.** a story of a building: *My office is on the second floor.* **4.** a part of a room or building, as in a legislative house, where members sit, speak, and carry on business: *The bill was debated on the floor of the Senate.* **5.** the right or privilege to speak to an assembly: *The chair gave me the floor.* —*v.t.* **1.** to cover or furnish with a floor: *to floor a porch.* **2.** to knock down: *The boxer was floored twice.* **3.** *Informal.* to bewilder or surprise completely; dumbfound: *I was floored by the news that the job was mine.*

floor·ing (flôr'ing) *n.* **1.** material for making floors. **2.** a floor or floors: *The church had stone flooring.*

floor show, entertainment presented in a nightclub, usually consisting of singing, dancing, and/or comedy acts.

floor·walk·er (flôr'wô'kər) *n.* a person employed in a store to supervise sales and services.

flop (flop) *v.,* **flopped, flop·ping.** —*v.i.* **1.** to drop or fall loosely, clumsily, or heavily: *to flop into a chair, to flop into bed.* **2.** to move, swing, or flap about loosely or clumsily: *The spaniel's ears flopped about its face.* **3.** *Informal.* to be completely unsuccessful; fail: *The play flopped.* —*v.t.* to throw or drop heavily: *I flopped my books onto the table.* —*n.* **1.** the act of flopping: *a flop on the ice.* **2.** *Informal.* a failure.

flop·py (flop'ē) *adj.,* **flop·pi·er, flop·pi·est.** that flops or tends to flop: *a large hat with a floppy brim.* —*n., pl.* **flop·pies.** see **floppy disk.** —**flop'pi·ly,** *adv.* —**flop'pi·ness,** *n.*

floppy disk *Computers.* a plastic disk coated with a magnetic substance and housed inside a protective envelope. It is used to store computer data. Also, **diskette.**

floppy disk

flo·ra (flôr'ə) *n., pl.* **flo·ras** or **flo·rae** (flôr'ē). the plants or plant life characteristic of a particular region or period.

flo·ral (flôr'əl) *adj.* of, relating to, depicting, or like flowers: *a floral arrangement, floral wallpaper, a floral scent.*

Flor·en·tine (flôr'ən tēn', flôr'ən tīn') *n.* a person who was born in or is living in Florence, Italy. —*adj.* of or relating to Florence, its people, or their culture.

flo·ret (flôr'it) *n.* **1.** a small flower. **2.** *Botany.* one of the small flowers that make up the head of a composite plant, such as the dandelion, daisy, or sunflower.

flor·id (flôr'id, flor'id) *adj.* **1.** flushed with redness; ruddy: *a florid complexion.* **2.** too elaborate; ornate; flowery: *The author has a florid style.* —**flor'id·ly,** *adv.* —**flor'id·ness,** *n.*

flor·in (flôr'in, flor'in) *n.* any of various European coins, such as a former British coin worth two shillings.

flo·rist (flôr'ist, flor'ist) *n.* a person who raises or sells flowers and ornamental plants.

floss (flôs', flos') *n.* **1.** short silk fibers. **2.** a soft, loosely twisted thread used for embroidery. **3.** the soft, silky fibers of fluff found in cotton, corn, milkweed, and other plants. —*v.t.* to clean with dental floss: *Floss your teeth after every meal.* —*v.i.* to clean the teeth with dental floss: *I always floss after lunch.*

floss·y (flô'sē, flos'ē) *adj.,* **floss·i·er, floss·i·est.** of, relating to, or like floss.

flo·til·la (flō til'ə) *n.* **1.** a fleet of small vessels: *a flotilla of sailboats.* **2.** a small fleet. **3.** in the U.S. Navy, a group of small ships, as destroyers.

flot·sam (flot'səm) *n.* the wreckage of a ship or its cargo, found floating on the sea.

flounce¹ (flouns) *v.t.,* **flounced, flounc·ing.** to go or move with an abrupt or impatient motion of the body: *The child flounced out of the room in anger.* —*n.* an abrupt or impatient motion of the body: *to sit down with a flounce.* [Possibly of Scandinavian origin.]

flounce² (flouns) *n.* a wide strip of cloth, gathered along one edge and attached as a trimming, as on the hem of a skirt. —*v.t.,* **flounced, flounc·ing.** to trim or furnish with a flounce or flounces. [From the Middle English word *frounce* meaning "a wrinkle, crease," from the Old French word *froncir* "to wrinkle, fold."]

floun·der¹ (floun'dər) *v.i.* **1.** to move or struggle with stumbling or plunging motions: *to flounder about in the mud.* **2.** to struggle in an embarrassed, awkward, or confused way: *The beginner floundered through the first lesson.* [Probably a form of *founder¹.*]

floun·der² (floun'dər) *n., pl.* **floun·der** or **floun·ders.** any of a number of salt-water flatfishes used for food. [From the Middle English word *flounder,* probably of Germanic origin.]

flour (flour, flou'ər) *n.* a fine, powdery meal made by grinding and

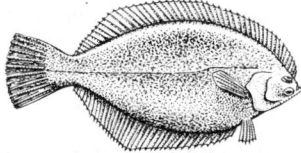
flounder²

sifting grain, especially wheat. Flour is used to make baked goods. —*v.t.* to cover or sprinkle with flour.

flour·ish (flûr′ish) *v.i.* **1.** to grow or develop strongly or prosperously; thrive: *Crops flourish in rich soil. Business is flourishing.* **2.** to reach or be at the highest point of development or achievement: *The Aztec civilization flourished centuries ago.* —*v.t.* to wave about with bold or sweeping gestures; brandish: *to flourish a flag.* —*n., pl.* **flour·ish·es. 1.** a fancy or showy action or display. **2.** a decorative stroke in writing. **3.** a passage or series of notes added to a musical work.

flout (flout) *v.t.* to treat with contempt; show no respect for; scoff at; defy: *to flout the law, to flout tradition.* —**flout′er,** *n.* ▲ See **flaunt** for usage note.

flow (flō) *v.i.* **1.** to move or pass along steadily in a stream: *The river flows northward. The electricity flowed through the wire.* **2.** to move along smoothly or continuously: *Conversation at the party flowed freely. Crowds flowed toward the stadium.* **3.** to be full or plentiful; overflow: *My heart was flowing with happiness.* **4.** to hang, fall, or ripple loosely: *The horse's mane flowed down its neck.* **5.** to rise, as the tide: *The waters ebb and flow.* —*n.* **1.** the act or way of flowing: *to stop the flow of blood.* **2.** any continuous movement; outpouring; stream: *the flow of traffic.* **3.** something that flows.

flow·chart (flō′chärt′) *also,* **flow chart.** *n.* **1.** a diagram that shows how an operation is carried out step by step from start to finish. **2.** a diagram that shows the structural levels of an organization, project, or the like.

flow·er (flou′ər) *n.* **1.** the part of certain plants that is composed of the reproductive organs and their surrounding, usually brightly colored petals; blossom; bloom. **2.** a plant grown for the beauty of its blossoms: *We planted tulips and other flowers along the path.* **3.** the condition or time of blossoming: *an apple orchard in flower.* **4.** the finest or choicest part or example: *the flower of a country's youth.* **5.** the finest or most active period: *in the flower of youth, the days when knighthood was in flower.* —*v.i.* **1.** to produce flowers; bloom: *Cherry trees flower in the early spring.* **2.** to be at or reach fullest development or growth: *Musical ability may flower early.* —**flow′er·like′,** *adj.*

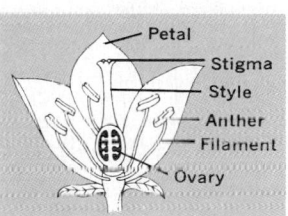

Petal
Stigma
Style
Anther
Filament
Ovary

parts of a **flower**

flow·ered (flou′ərd) *adj.* having flowers or decorated with a design of flowers: *a flowered hillside.*

flow·er·et (flou′ər it) *n.* a small flower.

flower girl, a young girl who carries flowers and precedes the bride in a wedding procession.

flowering plant, any of a large group of plants including trees and shrubs whose seeds are enclosed in an ovary. Flowering plants make up the largest division of the plant kingdom, including more than half of all known plants. Also, **angiosperm.**

flow·er·pot (flou′ər pot′) *n.* a pot, made of clay or other material, in which to grow plants.

flow·er·y (flou′ə rē) *adj.,* **flow·er·i·er, flow·er·i·est. 1.** covered with or like flowers. **2.** using or containing fancy, elegant, or ornate language: *a flowery letter.* —**flow′er·i·ness,** *n.*

flown (flōn) a past participle of **fly².**

fl. oz., fluid ounce; fluid ounces.

flu (flü) *n.* see **influenza.**

flub (flub) *Informal. v.t.,* **flubbed, flub·bing.** to spoil or ruin; botch; bungle: *The actors flubbed their lines during rehearsal. The fielder flubbed an easy catch.* —*n.* an error; blunder.

fluc·tu·ate (fluk′chü āt′) *v.i.,* **fluc·tu·at·ed, fluc·tu·at·ing.** to rise and fall; change; waver: *The water level*

fluctuated. *Prices on the stock market fluctuate.* —**fluc′tu·a′tion,** *n.*

flue (flü) *n.* a passage through which smoke, hot air, or waste gases pass, as in a chimney.

flu·en·cy (flü′ən sē) *n.* ease or smoothness in speaking or writing.

flu·ent (flü′ənt) *adj.* **1.** spoken or written smoothly and easily: *fluent poetry, fluent English.* **2.** capable of speaking or writing smoothly and effortlessly: *I am fluent in Spanish.* —**flu′ent·ly,** *adv.*

fluff (fluf) *n.* **1.** a soft, light, downy material. **2.** a soft, downy mass: *A fluff of hair lay on the barber's floor.* **3.** *Informal.* an error or blunder, especially one made by a performer: *the pianist's embarrassing fluff.* —*v.t.* **1.** to shake, pat, or puff out into a soft mass: *to fluff up a pillow. The bird fluffed its feathers.* **2.** *Informal.* to make an error or blunder in: *The actor fluffed the speech.*

fluff·y (fluf′ē) *adj.,* **fluff·i·er, fluff·i·est.** consisting of, covered with, or resembling fluff: *a fluffy sweater.* —**fluff′i·ly,** *adv.* —**fluff′i·ness,** *n.*

flu·id (flü′id) *n.,* **1.** a substance, as a liquid or gas, that is capable of flowing, has no definite shape, and adapts itself to the shape of any container that confines it. **2.** any liquid: *The doctor told me to drink plenty of fluids.* —*adj.* **1.** capable of flowing; not solid; liquid or gaseous. **2.** of, relating to, or consisting of fluids: *a fluid diet.* **3.** changing readily; not fixed, firm, or stable: *Our plans are fluid.* —**flu′id·ly,** *adv.* —**flu′id·ness,** *n.*

Word Family

The Latin word *fluere,* meaning "to flow," has given us many English words. A **fluid,** such as water, is a substance that flows, and a **confluence** is the place where the waters of two rivers flow together. Where a river flows into the ocean, its waters merge with the ceaseless **flux** of the tides. The level of wealth, as well as that of the ocean, can **fluctuate,** and a sudden **influx** of money would make a person quite **affluent,** even **influential.** Someone who regards great **affluence** as **superfluous** might choose instead to become **fluent** in foreign languages, travel abroad, and gain international **influence.** It was once thought that a force flowed from the stars and **influenced** people's actions. The word **influenza,** or **flu,** was derived from an Italian word for this same imaginary force.

fluid dram, a liquid measure of capacity equal to ⅛ of a fluid ounce (3.7 milliliters).

flu·id·i·ty (flü id′i tē) *n.* the condition or quality of being fluid.

fluid ounce, a liquid measure of capacity equal to ¹⁄₁₆ of a pint (29.57 milliliters).

fluke¹ (flük) *n.* **1.** either of the two flat, triangular pieces on an anchor that catch in the ground underwater. **2.** a barb or barbed head, as of an arrow, harpoon, or spear. **3.** either of the two horizontal fins of a whale's tail. [Perhaps from *fluke³.*]

fluke² (flük) *n.* an unexpected or accidental stroke or turn, especially of good luck; chance happening: *We met by a fluke.* [Of uncertain origin.]

at; āpe; fär; câre; end; mē; it; īce; pîerce; hot; ōld; sông, fôrk; oil; out; up; ūse; rüle; pùll; tûrn; chin; sing; shop; thin; this; hw in white; zh in treasure. The symbol ə stands for the unstressed vowel sound heard in about, taken, pencil, lemon, and circus.

F

fluke³ (flük) *n.* **1.** any of various flatfish, especially a flounder. **2.** any of a group of parasitic flatworms that live in many kinds of animals; trematode. [From the Old English word *flōc* meaning "flatfish."]

flume (flüm) *n.* **1.** a deep, narrow passage or ravine through which a stream runs. **2.** an artificial chute or trough that carries water, as for moving logs or furnishing water power.

flum·mox (flum'əks) *v.t. Informal.* to confuse; bewilder; perplex: *I was completely flummoxed by the difficult math problem.*

flung (flung) the past tense and past participle of **fling**.

flunk (flungk) *Informal. v.t.* **1.** to fail to pass; fail: *to flunk a test.* **2.** to give a failing grade or mark to: *The teacher flunked five students.* —*v.i.* to fail, as in an examination.
  •**to flunk out.** to be dismissed, as from a school, because of failing grades.

flunk·ey (flung'kē) *n., pl.* **flunk·eys.** another spelling of **flunky**.

flunk·y (flung'kē) *n., pl.* **flunk·ies. 1.** a person who fawns on or does menial tasks for another. **2.** formerly, a footman or other male servant.

fluo·resce (flù res', flô res') *v.i.,* **fluo·resced, fluo·resc·ing.** to produce or show fluorescence.

fluo·res·cence (flù res'əns, flô res'əns) *n.* **1.** a giving off of light from a substance that is absorbing radiant energy, such as X rays or ultraviolet rays. Fluorescence continues only as long as the substance is exposed to the source of energy. **2.** a light given off in this way.

fluo·res·cent (flù res'ənt, flô res'ənt) *adj.* producing, resulting from, or showing fluorescence.

fluorescent lamp, an electric lamp that produces ultraviolet light and converts it into visible light.

fluor·i·date (flùr'i dāt', flôr'i dāt') *v.t.,* **fluor·i·dat·ed, fluor·i·dat·ing.** to add a fluoride to (drinking water), especially in order to reduce tooth decay. —**fluor·i·da'tion,** *n.*

fluo·ride (flùr'īd, flôr'īd) *n.* a compound consisting of fluorine and another element or radical.

fluo·rine (flùr'ēn, flôr'ēn) *n.* a greenish yellow, poisonous, gaseous element of the halogen group. It is the most reactive nonmetallic element and is used to fluoridate water. Symbol: **F** [From the French word *fluorine,* going back to the Latin word *fluor* meaning "a flow," from the word *fluere* "to flow." Minerals containing fluorine were used to help metals melt more easily during refining.]

fluor·o·scope (flùr'ə skōp', flôr'ə skōp') *n.* an instrument used to examine internal structures or parts, as of the body. It consists of an X-ray machine and a fluorescent screen that shows patterns of light and shadow cast by the different amounts of X rays allowed to pass through the internal structures or parts. —*v.t.,* **fluor·o·scoped, fluor·o·scop·ing.** to examine with a fluoroscope.

flur·ry (flûr'ē, flur'ē) *n., pl.* **flur·ries. 1.** a sudden commotion; stir: *a flurry of activity, a flurry of excitement.* **2.** a light, scattered snowfall or rainfall, usually accompanied by gusts of wind. **3.** a brief, sudden gust: *a flurry of wind.* —*v.t.,* **flur·ried, flur·ry·ing.** to agitate.

flush¹ (flush) *v.i.* **1.** to turn red; blush; glow: *The western sky flushed as the sun sank. I flushed when everyone shouted "Surprise!"* **2.** to flow or rush suddenly: *Water flushed through the pipes.* —*v.t.* **1.** to cause to redden: *Fever flushed the child's face.* **2.** to clean, empty, or wash with a sudden, rapid rush or flow, as of water: *to flush a toilet.* **3.** to make proud or excited: *They were flushed with success.* —*n., pl.* **flush·es. 1.** a reddish color or glow. **2.** a rush or surge of pride, excitement, or other emotion. **3.** a flowing vigor or freshness: *the first flush of spring.* **4.** a rapid, sudden rush or flow, as of water. [Of uncertain origin.]

flush² (flush) *adj.* **1.** having direct contact; touching: *The table was flush against the wall.* **2.** even or level, as with a surface: *The top of the wall is flush with the roof.* **3.** well supplied, especially with money. —*adv.* **1.** in immediate or direct contact: *I set the bureau flush against the wall.* **2.** in an even or level manner: *They placed the second picture flush with the first.* **3.** directly; squarely: *to hit someone flush on the chin.* [Perhaps from *flush¹.*]

flush³ (flush) *v.t.* to drive from cover or from a hiding place: *to flush birds from a hedge.* [From the Middle English word *flusshen* meaning "to rush, spring" and "to flush³."]

flush⁴ (flush) *n., pl.* **flush·es.** in poker, a hand in which all of the cards are of the same suit. [From the Middle French word *flus* with the same meaning, from the Latin word *fluxus* "a flow, flux," from the word *fluere* "to flow."]

flus·ter (flus'tər) *v.t.* to cause to be embarrassed or nervous; agitate and confuse: *The laughter flustered the speaker.* —*n.* a state of agitated or nervous confusion.

flute (flüt) *n.* **1.** a musical instrument of the woodwind family, consisting of a hollow wood or metal tube with keys along its length and played by blowing across a mouth hole near one end. **2.** a shallow, rounded groove on the shaft of a column. **3.** any similar groove, especially a decorative one. —*v.,* **flut·ed, flut·ing.** —*v.i.* **1.** to play on a flute. **2.** to make a sound like that of a flute: *Birds fluted in the trees.* —*v.t.* **1.** to utter with a sound like that of a flute. **2.** to make flutes in: *to flute the edges of a pie crust.*

flute *(n., def. 1)*

flut·ing (flü'ting) *n.* **1.** a decoration with flutes or grooves. **2.** a groove or a series of grooves.

flut·ist (flü'tist) also, **flau·tist.** *n.* a person who plays the flute.

flut·ter (flut'ər) *v.i.* **1.** to wave or flap quickly and lightly: *The flag fluttered in the breeze.* **2.** to fly, hover, or flap the wings lightly and quickly: *Butterflies fluttered among the flowers.* **3.** to fall or move with light, irregular motion: *Leaves fluttered to the ground.* **4.** to move about lightly, quickly, or in a nervous, excited way. **5.** to beat quickly and irregularly, as the heart. —*v.t.* to cause to flutter: *to flutter one's eyelashes.* —*n.* **1.** a quick, light movement: *the flutter of a bird's wings.* **2.** a condition of nervous excitement: *to be in a flutter.* —**flut'ter·er,** *n.*

flux (fluks) *n., pl.* **flux·es. 1.** constant change or movement: *Our plans are in a state of flux.* **2.** a flowing or flow. **3.** a substance, such as lime, that makes metals melt more easily, used chiefly in metal refining. **4.** a substance, such as rosin, used in soldering to help the fusion of metals by preventing oxidation. **5.** *Physics.* **a.** the rate of flow of fluids, particles, or energy, such as light or other radiant energy, through a given area. **b.** see **magnetic flux.**

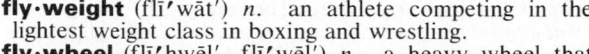

fly¹ (flī) *n., pl.* **flies. 1.** any of a large group of insects, including houseflies, mosquitoes, and gnats, that have sucking mouth parts and one pair of transparent wings. **2.** any of various other flying insects. **3.** a fishhook that is decorated with feathers or other material, so that it looks like an insect. [From the Old English word *flēoge* meaning "a winged insect."]

fly² (flī) *v., (v.i. defs. 1–6, v.t.)* **flew, flown, fly·ing** or *(v.i. def. 7)* **flied, fly·ing.** —*v.i.* **1.** to move through the air by using wings, as a bird does. **2.** to operate, move, or travel in an aircraft or spacecraft: *The pilot flew to Chicago. They flew to Los Angeles last night.* **3.** to pass, move, or be propelled through the air by the wind or other force: *The ocean spray flew into our faces.* **4.** to wave or flutter in the air: *A flag flew from the ship's mast.* **5.** to move or pass swiftly; speed: *They flew up the stairs to help the child.* **6.** to change rapidly and suddenly from one state, condition, or position to another: *to fly into a rage.* **7.** *Baseball.* to hit a fly ball: *The batter flied to left field.* —*v.t.* **1.** to cause to move through the air: *I flew my kite in the park.* **2.** to operate (an aircraft or spacecraft): *They flew their plane to the frozen lake.* **3.** to travel or pass over, as in an aircraft: *They flew the Atlantic Ocean in five hours.* **4.** to carry or transport by air: *They flew supplies to the flooded town.* **5.** to flee: *They had to fly the country.* —*n., pl.* **flies. 1.** a flap of material covering a zipper or row of buttons on a piece of clothing, especially on the front of a pair of trousers. **2.** a piece of canvas put up in front of or over a tent to provide extra protection. **3.** *Baseball.* see **fly ball.** [From the Old English word *flēogan* meaning "to fly."]

·**on the fly.** while still in flight; before touching the ground: *to catch a ball on the fly.*

·**to let fly.** to throw or shoot: *to let fly a stone.*

fly ball *Baseball.* a ball hit high into the air.

fly·by (flī′bī′) *n., pl.* **fly·bys.** the flight of a spacecraft close to a celestial body to collect scientific data.

fly·catch·er (flī′kach′ər) *n.* any of various birds that feed on insects that they catch while flying.

fly·er (flī′ər) another spelling of **flier.**

flying boat, a seaplane having a body shaped at the bottom like the hull of a boat, on which it floats.

flying buttress, an arched support between a pier or other structure and the wall of a building, used to help the wall bear the outward pressure caused by the weight of the roof.

flying fish, any of a group of saltwater fish that are found in warm waters and have one or two pairs of large, stiff winglike fins that enable them to leap into the air and glide for some distance.

flying jib, a small, triangular sail set out in front of the jib.

flying saucer, any of various unidentified flying objects that are said to be shaped like a saucer and thought by some people to be from outer space.

flying squirrel, any of various squirrels having winglike membranes between the front and hind legs that enable them to make long, gliding leaps through the air.

fly·leaf (flī′lēf′) *n., pl.* **fly·leaves** (flī′-lēvz′). a blank sheet of paper at the beginning or end of a book.

fly·pa·per (flī′pā′pər) *n.* paper covered with a sticky or poisonous substance, used to catch or kill flies.

fly·speck (flī′spek′) *n.* **1.** a tiny spot of dirt left by a fly. **2.** any tiny spot. —*v.t.* to make flyspecks on.

fly swatter, a device for killing flies or other insects, usually a square piece of mesh attached to a long handle.

fly·way (flī′wā′) *n.* a particular air route along which birds regularly migrate.

flying buttresses

fly·weight (flī′wāt′) *n.* an athlete competing in the lightest weight class in boxing and wrestling.

fly·wheel (flī′hwēl′, flī′wēl′) *n.* a heavy wheel that regulates the speed of an engine.

Fm, the symbol for fermium.

FM 1. a method of radio broadcasting by which a signal is transmitted over radio carrier waves by altering the frequency of the waves. **2.** a broadcasting system using this method. **3.** of, relating to, or using an FM broadcasting system: *an FM radio, an FM station.* [Short for *F(requency) M(odulation).*]

f-number, in photography, a number obtained by dividing the focal length of a lens by its diameter. The f-number expresses the size to which the lens opening in a camera is adjusted and indicates the amount of light let in by the lens at that setting. The lower the f-number the wider the lens opening.

foal (fōl) *n.* a young horse, donkey, zebra, or other member of the horse family, especially one less than one year of age. —*v.i.* to give birth to a foal: *The mare foaled in the spring.*

foam (fōm) *n.* a frothy mass of bubbles, as that formed on the surface of a liquid: *the foam formed by breaking waves.* —*v.i.* **1.** to form or produce foam: *The water foamed when I added the soap.* **2.** to flow in a foam: *The water foamed through the opening.*

foam rubber, a spongy rubber used for mattresses, upholstery, and insulation.

foam·y (fō′mē) *adj.,* **foam·i·er, foam·i·est.** covered with, consisting of, or like foam. —**foam′i·ness,** *n.*

fob¹ (fob) *n.* **1.** a short chain or ribbon attached to a watch, often worn hanging from a watch pocket. **2.** an ornament worn at the end of such a chain or ribbon. **3.** a small pocket for holding a watch, as in the front of a vest or just below the waist in trousers. [Probably of Germanic origin.]

fob² (fob) *v.t.,* **fobbed, fob·bing.** *Archaic.* to trick; cheat. [From the Middle English word *fobben* meaning "to deceive."]

·**to fob off. a.** to get rid of (something worthless) by trickery or deception: *to fob off counterfeit money.* **b.** to put (someone) off by trickery or deception.

f.o.b. or **F.O.B.,** free on board.

fo·cal (fō′kəl) *adj.* of, at, or relating to a focus: *at the focal point.* —**fo′cal·ly,** *adv.*

focal length, the distance from the center of a lens or mirror to the focus. Also, **focal distance, focus.**

fo′·c·sle (fōk′səl) *n.* see **forecastle.**

fo·cus (fō′kəs) *n., pl.* **fo·cus·es** or **fo·ci** (fō′sī) **1.** the point at which converging rays, especially light rays, meet after being refracted by a lens or reflected by a mirror. **2.** the point from which diverging rays, especially light rays, appear to originate, after having undergone such refraction or reflection. **3.** another word for **focal length. 4.** an

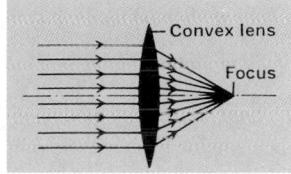

focus *(n., def. 1)*

adjustment, as of a lens or the eye, necessary to produce a clear image: *These binoculars are not in focus.* **5.** the condition of being clear or understandable: *Your talk brought things into focus for us.* **6.** a central point or center, as of activity, interest, or importance: *The speaker was the focus of attention.* **7.** *Geometry.* a fixed point or one of two fixed points used in determining an ellipse, parabola, or hyperbola. **8.** the center or point of origin of an earthquake. —*v.,* **fo·cused, fo·cus·ing;** *also, British,* **fo·cussed, fo·cus·sing.** —*v.t.* **1.** to bring to a focus or into focus: *Wait while I focus the camera.* **2.** to fix; concentrate: *The audience focused its attention on the stage.* —*v.i.* to become focused. [From the Latin word *focus* meaning "hearth." The hearth was the central point, or focus, of the home.]

fod·der (fod′ər) *n.* food for livestock, made from various grasses, alfalfa, or the stalks and leaves of corn.

foe (fō) *n.* enemy; adversary: *Are you friend or foe? In wartime, soldiers train to defeat the foe.*

foe·tus (fē′təs) *n., pl.* **foe·tus·es.** another spelling of **fetus.**

fog (fôg, fog) *n.* **1.** a cloud of very small water droplets in the air, at or close to the earth's surface. **2.** any hazy condition: *a fog of dust, a fog of smoke.* **3.** a condition of confusion or bewilderment; daze: *I was really in a fog after the exam.* *v.,* **fogged, fog·ging.** —*v.t.* **1.** to cover or obscure with or as if with fog: *The windows were fogged.* **2.** to confuse; bewilder: *The heat fogged my brain.* —*v.i.* to become covered or obscured with fog.

fog·gy (fô′gē, fog′ē) *adj.,* **fog·gi·er, fog·gi·est. 1.** full of or obscured by fog: *a foggy day.* **2.** confused or unclear; vague: *foggy thinking.* —**fog′gi·ly,** *adv.* —**fog′gi·ness,** *n.*

fog·horn (fôg′hôrn′, fog′hôrn′) *n.* a horn or similar device that is used for sounding warning signals during a fog, as to boats.

fo·gy (fō′gē) *also,* **fo·gey.** *n., pl.* **fo·gies.** a person who has old-fashioned ideas, habits, or ways.

foi·ble (foi′bəl) *n.* a minor weakness of character; shortcoming: *I'll overlook your foibles.*

foil¹ (foil) *v.t.* to interfere with or stop from being successful: *The police foiled the robbery.* [From the Middle English word *foilen* meaning "to trample upon," from the Old French word *fouler* "to trample on, hurt" and "to prepare woolen cloth," going back to the Latin word *fullo* "one who prepares woolen cloth."]

foil² (foil) *n.* **1.** metal hammered or rolled into a very thin, flexible sheet: *aluminum foil.* **2.** a person or thing that sets off another by comparison or contrast: *A black sweater is a good foil for blond hair.* [From the Old French word *foil* meaning "leaf," from the Latin word *folium* "leaf."]

foil³ (foil) *n.* a long, flexible fencing sword that tapers from the hilt to the point. The point of a foil is blunted or padded to prevent injury. [Probably from *foil¹.*]

foist (foist) *v.t.* to pass off or offer (something false or worthless) as genuine or valuable: *Don't try to foist a ridiculous story on us.*

fold¹ (fōld) *v.t.* **1.** to bend or double over: *Fold the paper in half.* **2.** to close, collapse, or make more compact by bending or bringing the part together: *Fold the chairs and put them in the corner.* **3.** to bring together and interlock or intertwine: *to fold one's hands in one's lap.* **4.** to bring close to the body: *The bird folded its wings.* **5.** to put the arms around; embrace; clasp: *I folded the crying child in my arms.* **6.** *Cooking.* To add or blend (an ingredient) into a mixture by repeatedly turning one part over another gently: *Next fold the egg whites into the batter.* **7.** to wrap (something) up: *Fold your lunch in wax paper.* —*v.i.* **1.** to be or become folded: *Paper folds more easily than cardboard.* **2.** *Informal.* to end or close, especially as a result of financial failure: *The business folded. The play folded within a week.* —*n.* **1.** a part that is folded; pleat: *The dress hung in graceful folds.* **2.** a mark or crease made by folding: *Cut the paper along the fold.* [From the Old English word *fealdan* meaning "to wrap, bend, double together."]

fold² (fōld) *n.* **1.** a pen or other enclosure for livestock, especially for sheep. **2.** a group, such as the congregation of a church or a political party, under the guidance of a leader or having common beliefs, aims, or values. [From the Old English word *falod* meaning "enclosure, pen²."]

–fold *suffix* **1.** (a specified number of) times as much or as great: *a twofold increase.* **2.** having (a specified number of) parts: *a twofold problem.*

fold·a·way (fōld′ə wā′) *adj.* designed to be folded up and put out of the way when not in use: *a foldaway bed.*

fold·er (fōl′dər) *n.* **1.** a holder or container for loose papers, usually a folded sheet of light cardboard. **2.** a sheet of printed material, as a circular, timetable, or map, folded into a number of pages: *The travel folder showed pictures of London.* **3.** a person or thing that folds.

fol·de·rol (fol′də rol′) *also,* **fal·de·ral.** *n.* foolish talk.

fo·li·age (fō′lē ij) *n.* leaves on a tree or other plant.

fo·li·a·tion (fō′lē ā′shən) *n.* the act or process of putting forth leaves.

fo·lic acid (fō′lik) a vitamin of the vitamin B complex. A deficiency of folic acid can cause certain forms of anemia.

fo·li·o (fō′lē ō′) *n., pl.* **fo·li·os. 1.** a sheet of paper folded once to form two leaves, or four pages, of a book. **2.** a book usually more than eleven inches in height, made up of sheets folded in this way. **3.** a page number of a book. —*adj.* of or having the size or form of a folio.

folk (fōk) *n., pl.* **folk** or **folks. 1.** *also,* **folks.** people: *city folk, old folks.* **2. folks.** *Informal.* one's family or relatives, especially one's parents. **3.** a nation or race; people. —*adj.* of or coming from the common people: *a folk custom, folk art.*

folk dance 1. a dance originating among the common people of a region or country and handed down from generation to generation. **2.** the music for such a dance.

a **folk dance**

folk etymology 1. a change in the form of a word because of an incorrect assumption about its origin. **2.** a popular but incorrect belief about the origin of a word.

Language Note

In language, a **folk etymology** is a wrong idea about the origin or meaning of a word. A folk etymology often seems to be common sense and may be widely accepted, but it has no historical truth. In certain cases, a folk etymology can become so generally accepted that changes take place in the spelling or meaning of a word as a result. For example, the article of furniture called a *chaise longue* takes its name from the French phrase meaning "long chair." But because this chair is used for lounging, many people now call it a *chaise lounge*. People tend to change unfamiliar words to connect them with words that are familiar. The word *lounge* is well known, while *longue* is not.

Sometimes folk etymology arises in an attempt to explain what is not understood. People who did not know Spanish heard the word *cucaracha* as the name of an insect. By folk etymology they changed the Spanish word to the more English-sounding word *cockroach*. Some people have also changed *asparagus* by folk etymology to *sparrow-grass*.

An area in which folk etymology is quite common is the creation of fanciful acronyms. Acronyms, which are words made by combining the first letter or letters of a series of words, are a relatively new feature of our language. Despite this, many people believe that some of the old and common words of our language developed this way. For example, the informal word *cop*, meaning "a policeman," is often explained as being an acronym formed from *Constable of Police*, the words that supposedly used to be written on a policeman's hat. Actually, *cop* is a much older word, going back to the Latin word *capere*, meaning "to take."

folk·lore (fōk′lôr′) *n.* the tales, beliefs, customs, or other traditions of a people or region, handed down from generation to generation.

folk music, the traditional music of the common people of a region or country.

folk rock, a form of popular music that combines elements of folk music and rock 'n' roll.

folk singer, a singer who performs folk songs.

folk song 1. a traditional song, usually originating among the common people and handed down from generation to generation. Folk songs often have a simple tune and appear in different versions. 2. a modern song written in the style of a traditional folk song.

folk·sy (fōk′sē) *adj.,* **folk·si·er, folk·si·est.** *Informal.* friendly, informal, or simple. —**folk′si·ly,** *adv.* —**folk′·si·ness,** *n.*

folk·tale (fōk′tāl′) *n.* a story that is part of the folklore of a people and often appears in different versions.

folk·way (fōk′wā′) *n.* a tradition or custom of a people or group.

fol·li·cle (fol′i kəl) *n.* 1. a small cavity, sac, or gland in the body. Hair grows from follicles. 2. a dry fruit that splits open along one seam when it is ripe and releases its seeds.

fol·low (fol′ō) *v.t* 1. to go or come after: *The dog followed me obediently. Spring follows winter.* 2. to go along: *Follow the river to the fork.* 3. to act according to; obey: *to follow orders. Follow directions.* 4. to watch or observe closely: *The police followed the suspect's movements from across the street. Fans followed the movie star's career.* 5. to understand: *I don't follow your reasoning.* 6. to use as a guide or model; imitate: *Follow your cousin's example.* 7. to make a living from: *to follow the legal profession.* 8. to result from: *Disaster followed the flood.* 9. to try to overtake or capture; pursue: *The detective followed the suspect for three days.* —*v.i.* to go, come, or happen after some person or thing: *Spring quickly passed and summer followed.*

·**to follow through. a.** to continue with to an end; complete: *to follow through an assignment.* **b.** to continue the motion of a stroke after hitting the ball, as in tennis or golf.

·**to follow up.** to add to the effect of by doing something more: *The enemy followed up the bombardment with a massive attack.*

·**to follow up on.** to pursue to an end: *The reporter followed up on the story.*

fol·low·er (fol′ō ər) *n.* 1. a person or thing that follows.

2. a person who follows the beliefs or ideas of another, as a supporter, disciple, or admirer: *a follower of a presidential candidate.*

fol·low·ing (fol′ō ing) *adj.* coming after or next in order or time: *the following morning.* —*n.* 1. a body of followers: *That author has a large following.* 2. **the following.** those about to be mentioned: *the following will be in the play.*

fol·low-up (fol′lō up′) *n.* 1. the act of following up. 2. something used or done to make an original action or thing effective, such as a letter sent to remind someone of an obligation or a medical examination of a patient after recovery from surgery. —*adj.* of or relating to a follow-up: *follow-up care for a patient released from a hospital.*

fol·ly (fol′ē) *n., pl.* **fol·lies.** 1. a lack of good sense or understanding; foolishness. 2. something foolish.

fo·ment (fō ment′) *v.t.* to stir up; incite: *to foment rebellion, to foment trouble.* —**fo·ment′er,** *n.*

fond (fond) *adj.* 1. liking or loving: *fond of animals, a fond smile.* 2. too loving or indulgent; doting: *a fond grandparent.* 3. deeply felt; cherished: *a fond wish.* —**fond′ly,** *adv.* —**fond′ness,** *n.*

fon·dant (fon′dənt) *n.* a smooth, creamy mixture made of sugar, used as a filling or icing or eaten as candy.

fon·dle (fon′dəl) *v.t.,* **fon·dled, fon·dling.** to stroke or touch lovingly or tenderly; caress: *I fondled the dog's ears.* —**fon′dler,** *n.*

fon·due (fon dü′, fon dū′) *n.* 1. melted cheese, seasonings, and often white wine brandy, served as a hot dip for cubes of bread. 2. a similar dish made of melted cheese, eggs, butter, milk, and seasonings, usually baked as a casserole. 3. pieces of food that are cooked, usually at the table, by being dipped briefly into hot oil or other liquid: *beef fondue.* [From the French word *fondue* meaning "dish of melted cheese and eggs," from the word *fondre* "to melt, cast metal," going back to the Latin word *fundere* "to melt, cast (metal), pour out."]

font¹ (font) *n.* 1. a basin or other receptacle, often made of stone, used to hold the water for baptism. 2. a basin or other receptacle for holy water. 3. a fountain; source: *a font of wisdom.* [From the Old English word *font* meaning "baptismal font," going back to the Latin word *fons* "spring, fountain."]

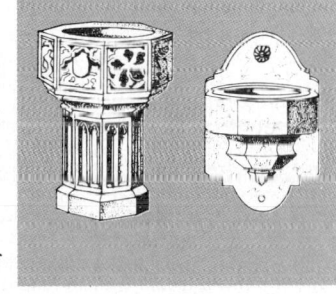

fonts¹

font² (font) *n.* *Printing.* a complete assortment of type of one size and style. [From the French word *fonte* meaning "a casting (of metals)," from the word *fondre* "to melt, cast metal," going back to the Latin word *fundere* "to melt, cast (metal), pour out."]

food (füd) *n.* 1. something that is eaten or taken in by a plant or animal to sustain life, provide energy, and aid in growth and repair of tissues; nourishment. 2. nourishment that is eaten rather than drunk: *food and drink.* 3. something that stimulates or aids an activity: *The book was food for thought.*

food chain, a sequence of the living things of a commu-

at; āpe; fär; câre; end; mē; it; īce; pîerce; hot; ōld; sông, fôrk; oil; out; up; ūse; rüle; pull; tûrn; chin; sing; shop; thin; this; hw in white; zh in treasure. The symbol ə stands for the unstressed vowel sound heard in about, taken, pencil, lemon, and circus.

F

nity, in which each plant, animal, or other organism in the sequence feeds upon the one below it. An example of a food chain is plant—plant louse—ladybug—spider—small bird—hawk. Each dash in the food chain means "is eaten by."

food poisoning, a sickness caused by eating foods that have been contaminated by harmful bacteria or toxins.

food processor, an electric appliance consisting of a container in which rapidly rotating blades chop, slice, mince, or otherwise process food.

food stamp, a coupon issued by the federal government that can be exchanged for food.

food web, a network of interrelated food chains in an ecological community.

food·stuff (füd′stuf′) *n.* a substance used as food.

fool (fül) *n.* **1.** a person who lacks judgment or good sense; unwise or silly person. **2.** a clown formerly kept by royalty or the nobility to entertain the household; jester. —*v.t.* to deceive; trick: *My disguise did not fool the children.* —*v.i.* **1.** to act like a fool; be silly: *Stop fooling and get to work.* **2.** to act or speak in a jesting or playful manner; tease; joke: *Don't be angry; I was only fooling.* —*adj. Informal.* foolish; silly: *a fool notion.*
  ·**to fool around.** *Informal.* to spend time idly or aimlessly: *The team was fooling around and not really practicing.*
  ·**to fool with.** to play or meddle aimlessly or thoughtlessly with: *Do not fool with that machine.*

fool·er·y (fü′lə rē) *n., pl.* **fool·er·ies.** foolish behavior.

fool·har·dy (fül′här′dē) *adj.,* **fool·har·di·er, fool·har·di·est.** bold or daring in a foolish way; rash; reckless: *a foolhardy youth, a foolhardy thing to do.* —**fool′har′di·ly,** *adv.* —**fool′har′di·ness,** *n.*

fool·ish (fü′lish) *adj.* **1.** showing a lack of understanding or good sense; unwise; silly: *Buying that old car was foolish.* **2.** like or relating to a fool; ridiculous; absurd: *You look foolish in that hat.* —**fool′ish·ly,** *adv.* —**fool′ish·ness,** *n.*

fool·proof (fül′prüf′) *adj.* so simple or safe as to make error, misuse, or failure impossible: *a foolproof plan.*

fools·cap (fülz′kap′) *n.* **1.** writing paper varying in size from about 12 by 15 inches (30 by 38 centimeters) to 13½ by 17 inches (34 by 43 centimeters). **2.** another spelling of **fool's cap.**

fool's cap, a jester's cap or hood, usually having several drooping peaks from which bells are hung.

fool's gold, any of various minerals that look like gold, such as pyrite.

foot (füt) *n., pl.* **feet. 1.** the end part of the leg, on which humans and certain other animals stand or walk. **2.** any similar part or organ in other animals and plants. **3.** something like a foot in shape, position, or use. **4.** the lowest or supporting part: *the foot of a mountain, the foot of a ladder.* **5.** the part far from or opposite the head: *the foot of a bed.* **6.** a part that covers the foot: *the foot of a stocking.* **7.** a measure of length equal to 12 inches (approximately 30.5 centimeters). **8.** a basic unit of rhythm in poetry, consisting of a group of accented and unaccented syllables. The line *The time/you won/your town/the race* has four feet. —*v.t. Informal.* to pay, as a bill: *We footed the cost of the party.*
  ·**on foot.** walking or running: *I came on foot.*
  ·**to foot it.** *Informal.* to walk.
  ·**to put one's foot down.** to make up one's mind and act firmly: *I put my foot down and refused to go.*
  ·**under foot.** in the way: *The kittens were under foot.*

foot·age (füt′ij) **1. a.** the amount of motion-picture film used, as for an individual scene. **b.** the content of motion-picture footage: *an adventure film with good footage shot in the Amazon jungle.*

foot·ball (füt′bôl) *n.* **1.** a game played between two teams of eleven players each on a field one hundred yards long with goals at each end. Points are made by getting the ball across the opponent's goal line. **2.** the oval ball used in this game, usually having an inflatable rubber bladder inside a leather covering. **3.** any of several other games that involve kicking a ball. ▲ Outside of the United States and Canada, *football* most often refers to soccer. **4.** a ball used in any of these games.

foot·board (füt′bôrd′) *n.* **1.** a board or small platform used to support or rest the feet. **2.** an upright board at the foot of a bed.

foot·bridge (füt′brij′) *n.* a bridge for pedestrians only.

foot–candle (füt′kan′dəl) *also,* **foot·can·dle.** *n.* a unit for measuring illumination, equal to the amount of light produced by one candle on a surface at a distance of 1 foot.

foot·ed (füt′id) *adj.* **1.** having a foot or feet: *a footed goblet.* **2.** having a specified kind or number of feet. ▲ used in combination in definition 2: *flatfooted, a four-footed animal.*

foot·fall (füt′fôl′) *n.* a footstep or its sound.

foot·hill (füt′hill′) *n.* a low hill at the foot of a mountain or mountain range.

foot·hold (füt′hōld′) *n.* **1.** a place where one may stand or walk securely; hold or support for the feet: *The climber used cracks in the cliff as footholds.* **2.** a firm or secure position from which it is possible to go forward: *Once the disease gained a foothold, it spread rapidly.*

foot·ing (füt′ing) *n.* **1.** the secure or firm placing of the feet: *to lose one's footing.* **2.** a hold or support for the feet: *The icy ledge provided no footing.* **3.** a secure position or condition: *to put a business on a sound footing.* **4.** position with regard to each other; relationship: *We are on a friendly footing with our neighbors.*

foot·less (füt′lis) *adj.* **1.** lacking a foot or feet. **2.** having no basis; insubstantial: *footless daydreams.*

foot·lights (füt′līts′) *pl. n.* lights in one or more rows along the front of a stage, at the actors' feet.

foot·loose (füt′lüs′) *adj.* free to travel about or live as one pleases; free from responsibilities.

foot·man (füt′mən) *n., pl.* **foot·men** (füt′mən). a male servant in uniform, as one who assists a butler with various jobs.

foot·note (füt′nōt′) *n.* a note, comment, or explanation, usually at the bottom of a page and indicated in the text by a number or symbol referring to it.

foot·path (füt′path′) *n., pl.* **foot·paths** (füt′pathz′, füt′paths). a path for pedestrians.

foot–pound (füt′pound′) *n.* a unit of work or energy, equal to the amount of energy required to raise 1 pound a distance of 1 foot.

foot·print (füt′print′) *n.* a mark or impression made by a foot: *footprints in the sand. The children made dirty footprints all over the kitchen floor.*

foot·race (füt′rās′) *n.* a race run on foot.

foot·rest (füt′rest′) *n.* something, as a small stool or platform, on which the feet may be rested.

foot soldier, a soldier trained or equipped to fight on foot; infantryman.

foot·sore (füt′sôr′) *adj.* having sore or tired feet, as from much walking.

foot·step (füt′step′) *n.* **1.** a step or tread of the foot: *a baby's first awkward footsteps.* **2.** the sound made by this: *I heard footsteps in the hall.* **3.** the distance covered in a step.
  ·**to follow in someone's footsteps.** to imitate or follow the same course as someone: *I followed in my parents' footsteps and became a teacher.*

foot·stool (füt′stül′) *n.* a low stool on which to place the feet when sitting.

foot·wear (füt′wâr′) *n.* coverings to be worn on the feet, such as shoes or slippers.

foot·work (füt′würk′) *n.* the use of the feet, as in boxing or dancing.

fop (fop) *n.* a man or boy who is too vain about his

appearance and has affected manners; dandy. **—fop′pish,** *adj.* **—fop′pish·ness,** *n.* **—fop′pish·ly,** *adv.*

fop·per·y (fop′ə rē) *n., pl.* **fop·per·ies.** the behavior, clothing, or manner of a fop.

for (fôr; *unstressed* fər) *prep.* **1.** as long as: *We worked for an hour.* **2.** as far as: *They hiked for five miles.* **3.** used with or made for: *That closet is for canned goods.* **4.** as a result of; because of: *They were praised for their good works.* **5.** in support or defense of: *to be willing to fight for what one believes in.* **6.** to or in the amount of: *a check for fifty dollars.* **7.** at the cost or price of: *I got it for five dollars.* **8.** in order to become or do: *The senator is running for president.* **9.** in order to go toward or reach: *They've already left for school.* **10.** in order to obtain: *to fish for trout.* **11.** sent to; given to; belonging to: *This letter is for you.* **12.** in place of; instead of: *to use a cardboard carton for a table.* **13.** on behalf of: *The lawyer spoke for her client.* **14.** Considering the usual nature or characteristics of: *It is cool for August.* **15.** with the purpose of; with an eye to: *I'm saving for my college education.* **16.** serving as: *We had eggs for breakfast.* **17.** because of the effect on: *Exercise can be good for your health.* **18.** in spite of: *For all you've said, I'm not convinced.* **19.** in honor of: *These buildings were named for a governor.* **—conj.** seeing that; because: *We should go, for it is late.*

for·age (fôr′ij, for′ij) *n.* **1.** hay, grain, and other food for cows, horses, and similar animals. **2.** a search for food or supplies. **—v., for·aged, for·ag·ing.** **—v.i.** **1.** to hunt or search for food or supplies: *The birds foraged in the snow.* **2.** to make a search. **—v.t.** **1.** to get by hunting or searching: *to forage a meal.* **2.** to get food or supplies from, especially by force; plunder: *The troops foraged the countryside.* **—for′ag·er,** *n.*

for·ay (fôr′ā, for′ā) *n.* an attack or raid, especially for plunder. **—v.i.** to raid; plunder: *The soldiers forayed in the enemy's lands.*

for·bad (fər bad′) a past tense of **forbid.**

for·bade (fər bad′, fər bād′) a past tense of **forbid.**

for·bear[1] (fôr bâr′) *v.,* **for·bore, for·borne, for·bear·ing.** **—v.i.** **1.** to keep oneself from doing something; hold back; refrain: *to forbear from arguing with a friend.* **2.** to control oneself or be patient: *When your friends are exasperating, try to forbear, if you can.* **—v.t.** to keep oneself from (doing something); refrain from: *I could not forbear smiling at my embarrassed friend.* [From the Old English word *forberan* ''to forbear.'']

for·bear[2] (fôr′bâr′) another spelling of **forebear.**

for·bear·ance (fôr bâr′əns) *n.* **1.** the act of forbearing. **2.** self-control or patience: *You showed great forbearance during your illness.*

for·bid (fər bid′) *v.t.,* **for·bade** or **for·bad, for·bid·den** or (*archaic*) **for·bid, for·bid·ding.** to order not to do something; refuse to allow; prohibit: *I forbid you to go out. The school forbids eating in the classrooms.*

for·bid·ding (fər bid′ing) *adj.* looking unfriendly or dangerous; frightening; grim: *The old house was dark and forbidding.* **—for·bid′ding·ly,** *adv.*

for·bore (fôr bôr′) the past tense of **forbear**[1].

for·borne (fôr bôrn′) the past participle of **forbear**[1].

force (fôrs) *n.* **1.** power, strength, or energy: *The storm struck with great force. The force of the explosion broke windows in nearby buildings.* **2.** the use of such power, strength, or energy; violence: *The sheriff dragged the outlaw off by force.* **3.** the power to convince, influence, or control: *The force of the argument won us over.* **4.** a group of people organized or available for some purpose or activity: *a police force.* **5. forces.** armed forces: *That country's forces won the war in six weeks. My cousin joined the forces.* **6.** *Physics.* something that causes a body to move or to change or stop its motion: *the force of gravity.* **—v.t., forced, forc·ing.** **1.** to make (someone) do something: *Your question forced me to solve the*

problem. *The city council forced the mayor to resign.* **2.** to get by force: *My friend's arguments forced a change in my ideas.* **3.** to bring forth by an effort: *The loser forced a smile.* **4.** to cause to open or give way by using force; break open: *to force a lock.* **5.** to make by force: *to force one's way through a crowd.* **6.** *Baseball.* to cause (a base runner) to be put out by hitting the ball so that the base runner is forced to run toward the next base. **7.** to make grow faster by applying artificial light or the like: *to force flowers.* **—forc′er,** *n.*

·in force. in operation or effect: *The rule against smoking is still in force.*

forced (fôrst) *adj.* **1.** done because of the use of force: *The road was built by forced labor.* **2.** affected; strained: *a forced smile.* **3.** done because of an emergency: *The plane made a forced landing.*

force·ful (fôrs′fəl) *adj.* full of or having much force; powerful; vigorous; effective: *a forceful shove, a forceful personality.* **—force′ful·ly,** *adv.* **—force′ful·ness,** *n.*

for·ceps (fôr′seps) *n., pl.* **for·ceps.** an instrument used for holding or pulling, especially by dentists or surgeons.

for·ci·ble (fôr′sə bəl) *adj.* **1.** done by force; resulting from force: *The police made a forcible entry into the apartment.* **2.** having force; powerful; effective: *a forcible argument.* **—for′ci·bly,** *adv.*

ford (fôrd) *n.* a shallow place where a river, stream, or other body of water may be crossed. **—v.t.** to cross (a body of water) at a shallow place. **—ford′able,** *adj.*

fore[1] (fôr) *adj.* at or toward the front; forward: *the fore part of a plane.* **—n.** the bow of a boat or ship. **—adv.** at or toward the bow of a boat or ship. [From the Old English word *fore* meaning ''for, before.'']

·to the fore. into view or a prominent position: *My friend came to the fore as the best athlete in school.*

fore[2] (fôr) *interj.* a word shouted as a warning on a golf course to persons ahead just before a ball is hit. [Probably short for *before*.]

fore– *prefix* **1.** in front: *foremast, forelock.* **2.** coming beforehand: *forenamed, foretell.*

fore–and–aft (fôr′ən aft′) *adj.* set lengthwise on a ship: *a fore-and-aft sail.*

fore and aft **1.** from bow to stern of a ship. **2.** in, at, or toward both the bow and the stern of a ship.

fore·arm[1] (fôr′ärm′) *n.* the part of the arm between the elbow and wrist. [From *fore-* + *arm*[1].]

fore·arm[2] (fôr ärm′) *v.t.* to prepare beforehand for something, especially for trouble. [From *fore-* + *arm*[2].]

fore·bear (fôr′bâr′) *also,* **for·bear.** *n.* an ancestor.

fore·bode (fôr bōd′) *v.t.,* **fore·bod·ed, fore·bod·ing.** **1.** to be a warning of: *Many ancient Romans believed that certain omens foreboded disaster.* **2.** to have a feeling of (something evil or bad to come). **—fore·bod′er,** *n.*

fore·bod·ing (fôr bō′ding) *n.* a feeling that something evil or bad is going to happen.

fore·cast (fôr′kast′) *v.t.,* **fore·cast** or **fore·cast·ed, fore·cast·ing.** to tell what may or will happen; make known ahead of time; predict: *to forecast the weather.* **—n.** a prediction: *a weather forecast.* **—fore′cast′er,** *n.*

fore·cas·tle (fōk′səl, fôr′kas′əl) *n.* **1.** the part of the upper deck of a ship that is in front of the foremast. **2.** sailors' quarters located in the forward section of a ship. Also, **fo′c'sle.**

fore·close (fôr klōz′) *v.,* **fore·closed, fore·clos·ing.** **—v.t.** **1.** to take away the right to pay off (a mortgage).

---

at; āpe; fär; câre; end; mē; it; īce; pîerce; hot; ōld; sông, fôrk; oil; out; up; ūse; rüle; pull; tûrn; chin; sing; shop; thin; **th**is; hw in white; zh in treasure. The symbol ə stands for the unstressed vowel sound heard in about, taken, pencil, lemon, and circus.

2. to prevent; stop: *The speaker foreclosed all discussion by refusing to answer questions.* —*v.i.* to foreclose a mortgage: *The bank foreclosed, and the farmer lost the property.*

fore·clo·sure (fôr klō′zhər) *n.* a legal proceeding that takes away a person's right to pay off a mortgage and to keep possession of mortgaged property, because the conditions of the mortgage have not been met.

fore·deck (fôr′dek′) *n.* the forward part of a ship's main deck.

fore·doom (fôr düm′) *v.t.* to doom ahead of time.

fore·fa·ther (fôr′fä′thər) *n.* a male ancestor.

fore·fin·ger (fôr′fing′gər) *n.* the finger next to the thumb; index finger.

fore·foot (fôr′fût′) *n., pl.* **fore·feet.** one of the front feet of an insect or a four-legged animal.

fore·front (fôr′frunt′) *n.* a place in the front; first or most important position: *the forefront of a battle, the forefront of a reform movement.*

fore·gath·er (fôr gath′ər) another spelling of **forgather.**

fore·go (fôr gō′) *v.t.,* **fore·went, fore·gone, fore·go·ing.** another spelling of **forgo.**

fore·go·ing (fôr gō′ing) *adj.* going before; preceding: *the foregoing example.*

fore·gone (fôr′gôn′, fôr′gon′) *adj.* having gone before or gone by; previous; past: *in a foregone era.*

fore·ground (fôr′ground′) *n.* **1.** the part of a picture or view nearest to a person's eye. **2.** the most important position; forefront.

fore·hand (fôr′hand′) *adj.* made with the arm held outward from the body and the palm of the hand toward the front: *a forehand stroke in tennis.* Also, **fore·hand·ed** (fôr′han′did). —*n.* a forehand stroke, as in tennis.

fore·head (fôr′id, fôr′hed′) *n.* the part of the face above the eyes.

for·eign (fôr′ən, for′ən) *adj.* **1.** of or from another country; not native: *a foreign accent.* **2.** outside a person's own country: *Have you visited foreign lands?* **3.** with or related to other countries: *foreign policy, foreign trade.* **4.** not belonging or characteristic: *Selfishness is foreign to my friend's nature.* —**for′eign·ness,** *n.*

One of the most important characteristics of the English language is its ability to absorb **foreign words.** A word that is considered to be "native to" or originally English is one that can be found in Old English. Such words can be shown to be of Germanic origin by their relationship to words in other Germanic languages. Only about one fifth of our modern English vocabulary is derived from Old English. All other words have been borrowed from foreign languages.

This borrowing began even in the Old English period, when Roman missionaries brought Christianity to England in the sixth century. The missionaries introduced some Latin words since Latin was the language of the Church at that time. These included such common words as *angel, candle,* and *priest.* Between the ninth and eleventh centuries, the Vikings raided and later settled along the eastern shores of England. They brought Scandinavian words such as *knife, sky,* and the pronouns *they* and *them* into the language.

The single most important event in the history of the development of our language was the Norman invasion of England in 1066. The Normans brought a dialect of French to England. As the rulers of England for about 200 years, they used French to discuss everything of any importance. Thus, most of our words for law, government, and cooking (to name just a few areas) come from French. Latin, which had become the language of education and philosophy as well as religion, also contributed

new words to English during the Norman period. It is estimated that half the words in Modern English have their roots in Latin. In the sixteenth century, with the revived interest in classical learning, many Greek words also entered English. Latin and Greek have continued to be the source of technical and scientific words in English.

In the following centuries, words continued to be borrowed as international trade brought English into contact with many other languages. The spread of the British Empire, the growth of American commerce, and the immigration of large numbers of people to America enriched the English language with many new borrowed words. Among these borrowed words are *tycoon* from Japanese, *tea* from Chinese, *khaki* from Hindi, *boomerang* from a native Australian language, *sarong* from Malay, *taboo* from Polynesian, *quinine* from the South American Indian language Quechua, *igloo* from the Eskimo language, and the Arabic word *safari,* which was borrowed through Swahili.

foreign aid, assistance given by one country to another country, especially to a less developed country in order to help it develop its economy and military forces and to strengthen the ties between the two countries.

for·eign·er (fôr′ə nər, for′ə nər) *n.* a person born in another country; citizen of another country.

foreign minister, in certain countries, the minister in charge of diplomatic relations and other dealings with foreign countries.

foreign policy, the official political positions and actions of a country in its relations with other countries.

fore·know (fôr nō′) *v.t.,* **fore·knew** (fôr nü′, fôr nū′), **fore·known, fore·know·ing.** to know (something) ahead of time.

fore·knowl·edge (fôr′nol′ij, fôr nol′ij) *n.* knowledge of something before it happens or exists.

fore·leg (fôr′leg′) *n.* one of the front legs of an insect or a four-legged animal.

fore·limb (fôr′lim′) *n.* a front limb of an animal.

fore·lock (fôr′lok′) *n.* a lock or tuft of hair growing above the forehead.

fore·man (fôr′mən) *n., pl.* **fore·men** (fôr′mən). **1.** a worker who supervises a group of workers, as in a factory or plant. **2.** a person who chairs and speaks for a jury.

fore·mast (fôr′mast′, fôr′məst) *n.* the mast nearest the bow of a ship.

fore·most (fôr′mōst′) *adj.* first in position, rank, or importance: *the foremost novelist of a period.* —*adv.* before anything else.

fore·noon (fôr′nün′) *n.* the period of time between sunrise and noon; morning.

fo·ren·sic (fə ren′sik) *adj.* of, relating to, or used in courts of law or public discussion and debate: *forensic arguments.* —**fo·ren′si·cal·ly,** *adv.*

fore·or·dain (fôr′ôr dān′) *v.t.* to fix or decide ahead of time; predestine. —**fore·or·dain′ment,** *n.*

fore·part (fôr′pärt′) *n.* the first, front, or early part.

fore·paw (fôr′pô′) *n.* a front paw.

fore·quar·ter (fôr′kwôr′tər) *n.* **1.** the front section of a side of beef or other meat, including the leg and shoulder. **2. forequarters.** the forelegs, shoulders, and nearby parts of a living animal.

fore·run·ner (fôr′run′ər) *n.* **1.** a person or thing that comes before another; predecessor; ancestor: *The bicycle was the forerunner of the motorcycle.* **2.** a sign of something to come: *A brisk wind is often the forerunner of rain.* **3.** a person who is sent to announce the approach of something or someone; herald.

fore·sail (fôr′sāl′, fôr′səl) *n.* **1.** the lowest sail on the foremast of a square-rigged ship. **2.** the principal sail on the foremast of a schooner.

fore·see (fôr sē′) *v.t.*, **fore·saw** (fôr sô′), **fore·seen**, **fore·see·ing**. to know or see ahead of time: *We foresaw the difficulty of climbing the mountain but made the climb anyway.* —**fore·see′a·ble**, *adj.* —**fore·se′er**, *n.*

fore·shad·ow (fôr shad′ō) *v.t.* to suggest or indicate beforehand.

fore·short·en (fôr shôr′tən) *v.t.* to shorten (lines or objects) in a drawing or painting to create an impression of depth and distance to the eye. —**fore·short′ened**, *adj.* —**fore·short′en·ing**, *n.*

fore·sight (fôr′sīt′) *n.* **1.** care or thought for the future: *They showed foresight in bringing enough food and water for the long hike.* **2.** the ability to know or see ahead of time what is likely to happen.

fore·sight·ed (fôr′sī′tid, fôr sī′tid) *adj.* having or showing foresight. —**fore′sight′ed·ly**, *adv.* —**fore′sight′ed·ness**, *n.*

fore·skin (fôr′skin′) *n.* a fold of skin that covers the end of the penis; prepuce. It is removed in circumcision.

for·est (fôr′ist, for′ist) *n.* a heavy growth of trees and other plants, usually covering a large area of land. —*v.t.* to plant or cover with trees; make into a forest.

fore·stall (fôr stôl′) *v.t.* to hinder, prevent, or get ahead of by taking action in advance: *Careful planning forestalled failure. The company forestalled its competitors by advertising quickly.* —**fore·stall′er**, *n.*

for·est·a·tion (fôr′ə stā′shən, for′ə stā′shən) *n.* the planting or care of forests.

for·est·er (fôr′ə stər, for′ə stər) *n.* a person whose work is managing, developing, and protecting forests.

forest ranger, an officer in charge of the protection of a forest, especially a public forest.

for·est·ry (fôr′ə strē, for′ə strē) *n.* the science that deals with the management, development, and protection of forests.

fore·taste (fôr′tāst′) *n.* a brief taste or sample of something to come: *The cold fall day was a foretaste of winter.*

fore·tell (fôr tel′) *v.t.*, **fore·told**, **fore·tell·ing**. to tell of ahead of time; give a prophecy of: *The prophet foretold war.*

fore·thought (fôr′thôt′) *n.* care or thought for the future; planning in advance; foresight.

fore·top (fôr′top′, fôr′təp) *n.* a platform at the top of the lower section of a foremast.

for·ev·er (fôr ev′ər, fər ev′ər) *adv.* **1.** throughout all time; without ever coming to an end; eternally. **2.** without letting up; always; constantly: *to be forever complaining.*

for·ev·er·more (fôr ev′ər môr′, fər ev′ər môr′) *adv.* for always; forever.

fore·warn (fôr wôrn′) *v.t.* to warn ahead of time.

fore·went (fôr went′) the past tense of **forego**.

fore·wing (fôr′wing′) *n.* either of the two front wings of a four-winged insect.

fore·wom·an (fôr′wum′ən) *n.*, *pl.* **fore·wom·en** (fôr′wim′ən). **1.** a woman who supervises a group of workers, as in a factory. **2.** a woman who chairs and speaks for a jury.

fore·word (fôr′wûrd′, fôr′wərd) *n.* a short statement found at the opening of a book; preface.

for·feit (fôr′fit) *v.t.* to lose as a penalty for some fault, mistake, or misdeed: *The team forfeited the game because it did not show up to play.* —*n.* something lost as a penalty for some fault, mistake, or misdeed.

for·fei·ture (fôr′fi chər) *n.* **1.** the act of forfeiting. **2.** something that is forfeited.

for·gath·er (fôr gath′ər) *also*, **fore·gath·er**. *v.i.* to meet or gather together; assemble.

for·gave (fôr gāv′) the past tense of **forgive**.

forge¹ (fôrj) *n.* **1.** a furnace or hearth in which metal is heated and softened so that it can be hammered into shape. **2.** a workshop in which metals are heated in such a furnace or hearth and then hammered into shape; smithy. —*v.*, **forged**, **forg·ing**. —*v.t.* **1.** to heat (metal) in a forge

and then hammer into shape. **2.** to make or form; fashion: *to forge an agreement.* **3.** to make or copy (something) with the intention of deceiving or cheating someone; counterfeit; falsify: *to forge a document, to forge a signature.* —*v.i.* **1.** to commit forgery. **2.** to work at a forge. [From the Old French word *forge* meaning "works where one melts iron," going back to the Latin word *fabrica* "workshop," from the word *faber* "worker, artisan."]

forge² (fôrj) *v.i.*, **forged**, **forg·ing**. to move forward slowly but steadily: *The ferry forged through the choppy water. We forged ahead on the project.* [Of uncertain origin.]

for·ger·y (fôr′jə rē) *n.*, *pl.* **for·ger·ies**. **1.** the crime of making or copying something, such as a document or signature, with the intention of deceiving or cheating someone. **2.** something that is forged: *The contract was a forgery.*

for·get (fər get′) *v.t.*, **for·got**, **for·got·ten** or **for·got**, **for·get·ting**. **1.** to be unable to remember; fail to recall: *I forgot your telephone number.* **2.** to fail to think of or do, especially through carelessness or thoughtlessness; neglect; overlook: *I forgot to close the door.* —**for·get′ta·ble**, *adj.* —**for·get′ter**, *n.*

for·get·ful (fər get′fəl) *adj.* **1.** likely to forget; having a poor memory: *My forgetful cousin always has to ask my address.* **2.** failing to think of or do something; neglectful; careless. —**for·get′ful·ly**, *adv.* —**for·get′ful·ness**, *n.*

for·get–me–not (fər get′mē not′) *n.* **1.** a small blue, pink, or white flower growing singly or in clusters. **2.** the small plant that bears these flowers, widely cultivated in gardens.

for·give (fər giv′) *v.*, **for·gave**, **for·giv·en**, **for·giv·ing**. —*v.t.* **1.** to cease to blame or feel resentment toward (someone): *They forgave me for breaking the window.* **2.** to pardon; excuse: *to forgive an insult.* —*v.i.* to grant pardon. —**for·giv′a·ble**, *adj.* —**for·giv′er**, *n.* ▲ See **excuse** for usage note.

forget-me-not

for·give·ness (fər giv′nis) *n.* **1.** the act of forgiving or the state of being forgiven. **2.** a willingness to forgive.

for·giv·ing (fər giv′ing) *adj.* having or showing forgiveness: *a forgiving nature.* —**for·giv′ing·ly**, *adv.* —**for·giv′ing·ness**, *n.*

for·go (fôr gō′) *also*, **fore·go**. *v.t.*, **for·went**, **for·gone**, **for·go·ing**. to keep oneself from; give up; do without: *to forgo lunch.* —**for·go′er**, *n.*

for·got (fər got′) the past tense and a past participle of **forget**.

for·got·ten (fər got′ən) a past participle of **forget**.

fork (fôrk) *n.* **1.** a utensil having a handle at one end and two or more prongs at the other, used especially for lifting or handling food. **2.** something resembling a fork in shape, such as a tool used for digging or lifting. **3.** a branching or dividing into branches: *a fork of a river, a fork of a tree where the branches begin.* **4.** one of the branches into which a thing divides: *Follow the left fork of the road.* —*v.t.* to lift, spear, or pitch with a fork: *We forked the*

---

at; āpe; fär; câre; end; mē; it; īce; pîerce; hot; ōld; sông, fôrk; oil; out; up; ūse; rüle; pull; tûrn; chin; sing; shop; thin; <u>th</u>is; hw in white; zh in treasure. The symbol ə stands for the unstressed vowel sound heard in about, taken, pencil, lemon, and circus.

hay into the wagon. —*v.i.* to divide into branches: *The road forks just ahead.* —**fork′like′**, *adj.*
·**to fork over, to fork out,** or **to fork up.** *Informal.* to hand over: *The thief forked over the stolen jewelry.*
forked (fôrkt) *adj.* shaped like a fork; divided into forks: *The snake had a forked tongue.*
fork·lift (fôrk′lift′) a motor-driven vehicle with a me-

forklift

chanical lifting device on the front to which steel prongs are attached. The prongs can be inserted under heavy loads to move them from one place to another.
for·lorn (fôr lôrn′) *adj.* **1.** unhappy or wretched, as from being lost and lonely: *The child with the ragged clothes looks forlorn.* **2.** abandoned; forsaken; deserted: *The old farm had a forlorn look.* —**for·lorn′ly**, *adv.* —**for·lorn′ness**, *n.*
form (fôrm) *n.* **1.** the outline of something; shape: *the faint form of a skyscraper in the fog.* **2.** a body or figure: *The ox has a powerful form.* **3.** the outward appearance of something: *In the tale, the spirit took a human form.* **4.** the particular state something is in: *a medicine in liquid form.* **5.** kind; type; variety: *The tree is a form of plant.* **6.** a way of doing something: *Practice will improve your form in diving.* **7.** fitness of mind or body; condition: *The athlete is in top form.* **8.** a document having blank spaces for filling in required information: *The student got used to filling out forms.* **9.** a way of behaving or conducting oneself: *It was bad form to act rudely. We were silent as a matter of form.* **10.** a traditional practice or ritual: *a form followed in a church service.* **11.** a grade or class in a secondary school. **12.** *Grammar.* any of the ways in which a word may appear, usually as a result of a change in the spelling or pronunciation. *Men is the plural form of man; went is a form of the verb go.* **13.** a way something is arranged or organized: *music in sonata form. Here is a form to follow in writing letters.* **14.** a frame or mold in which liquid substances such as cement are put to harden. —*v.t.* **1.** to give form to; make or produce; fashion: *The artist formed a figure out of clay.* **2.** to make up: *Students formed the majority of the crowd.* **3.** to think of; conceive: *to form a plan.* **4.** to develop: *to form a habit.* **5.** to organize; arrange: *to form a committee.* **6.** *Grammar.* to make, as by changing spelling or pronunciation: *to form the past tense of a verb by adding "-ed."* —*v.i.* **1.** to take shape: *Clouds formed in the sky.* **2.** to come into being; be produced: *Mold formed on the stale bread.*
·**to form into.** to take the form of: *Below 32 degrees, water forms into ice.*
for·mal (fôr′məl) *adj.* **1.** stiff, proper, or polite in behavior: *formal people.* **2.** requiring strict form or ceremony,

or elaborate dress: *a formal banquet.* **3.** suitable for a formal event: *formal dress.* **4.** done or made with or to satisfy authority; official: *a formal statement, a formal requirement.* **5.** relating to form rather than content; for the sake of form. —*n.* something that is formal, such as a dance or an evening gown. —**for′mal·ly**, *adv.*
form·al·de·hyde (fôr mal′də hīd′) *n.* a colorless, poisonous gas, used especially in solution to preserve and disinfect.
for·mal·ism (fôr′mə liz′əm) *n.* the strict observance of or attention to conventional or traditional forms.
for·mal·i·ty (fôr mal′i tē) *n., pl.* **for·mal·i·ties. 1.** the state or quality of being formal. **2.** proper or very polite behavior: *The secretary treated all of us with formality.* **3.** a correct or official procedure: *All the legal formalities were followed.* **4.** something that is a matter of form only: *I was certain of getting the job, and the test was a mere formality.*
for·mal·ize (fôr′mə līz′) *v.t.,* **for·mal·ized, for·mal·iz·ing. 1.** to make formal. **2.** to give a definite or official form to: *to formalize an agreement.* —**for′mal·i·za′tion,** *n.* —**for′mal·iz′er,** *n.*
for·mat (fôr′mat) *n.* **1.** the way a book, magazine, or other publication is formed, including arrangement of parts, size, and kind of type used. **2.** the way in which something is organized or planned. —*v.t.,* **for·mat·ted, for·mat·ting. 1.** to arrange in a format. **2.** *Computers.* to prepare (a computer disk) to accept data for storage.
for·ma·tion (fôr mā′shən) *n.* **1.** the act or process of forming: *the formation of ice from water.* **2.** something formed: *a rock formation.* **3.** the way in which something is formed: *The troops lined up in parade formation.*
form·a·tive (fôr′mə tiv) *adj.* **1.** giving or capable of giving form: *a formative industrial process.* **2.** of or relating to growth or development: *the formative years of childhood.*
for·mer (fôr′mər) *adj.* **1.** the first of two mentioned. ▲ used with **latter,** which refers to the second of two mentioned: *Although Guinea and Guyana sound alike, the former nation (Guinea) is in Africa and the latter nation (Guyana) in South America.* **2.** belonging to or happening in the past; previous: *a former governor, in former times.*
for·mer·ly (fôr′mər lē) *adv.* in time past; once; previously: *Muskets were formerly used by many armies.*
For·mi·ca (fôr mī′kə) *n. Trademark.* a plastic covering made in thin layers, used especially to cover counters and other surfaces in kitchens and bathrooms.
for·mi·da·ble (fôr′mi də bəl) *adj.* **1.** causing fear, dread, or awe: *a formidable opponent.* **2.** difficult to deal with or do: *painting the house was a formidable job.* —**for′mi·da·bil′i·ty,** *n.* —**for′mi·da·bly,** *adv.*
form·less (fôrm′lis) *adj.* without a definite or regular shape; shapeless. —**form′less·ly,** *adv.* —**form′less·ness,** *n.*
for·mu·la (fôr′myə lə) *n., pl.* **for·mu·las** or **for·mu·lae** (fôr′myə lē′). **1.** a set method for doing something; fixed rule or recipe: *There is no formula for making friends.* **2.** a set order or form of words, used in conventional expressions: *"Yours truly" is a formula for closing a letter.* **3.** an expression using symbols and numbers for a chemical compound: *The formula for carbon dioxide is CO_2.* **4.** an expression of a relationship, fact, or rule in mathematical symbols: *The formula for the circumference of a circle is $c = \pi d$.* **5.** something made according to a recipe: *formula for a baby.*
for·mu·late (fôr′myə lāt′) *v.t.,* **for·mu·lat·ed, for·mu·lat·ing. 1.** to develop or state in a clear, exact, or systematic way: *The general formulated a plan of attack.* **2.** to express in a formula. —**for′mu·la′tion,** *n.* —**for′mu·la′tor,** *n.*

for·sake (fôr sāk′) *v.t.*, **for·sook** (fôr sŏok′), **for·sak·en**, **for·sak·ing. 1.** to give up completely: *to forsake one's old beliefs.* **2.** to leave or desert: *My friends have forsaken me.* —**for·sak′er**, *n.*

for·sooth (fôr sōoth′) *adv. Archaic.* in truth; indeed.

for·swear (fôr swâr′) *v.*, **for·swore** (fôr swôr′), **for·sworn, for·swear·ing.** —*v.t.* to swear to give up: *When did you forswear smoking?* —*v.i.* to swear falsely.

for·syth·i·a (fôr sith′ē ə) *n.* any of a group of shrubs having bell-shaped yellow flowers that grow in clusters along the stems. [From the English botanist William *Forsyth* (1737–1804), who introduced it from China.]

fort (fôrt) *n.* a fortified building or area that can be defended against an enemy; fortification.

forte[1] (fôrt) *n.* something a person does especially well; strong point: *Mathematics was the scientist's forte.* [From the French word *fort* meaning "strength," from the adjective *fort* "strong," from the Latin word *fortis* "strong."]

for·te[2] (fôr′tā) *Music. adj.* loud and forceful. —*adv.* loudly and forcefully. [From the Italian word *forte* meaning "strong, loud," from the Latin word *fortis* "strong."]

forth (fôrth) *adv.* **1.** forward in time or place; onward: *from this day forth.* **2.** out into view: *The tree put forth leaves.*

forth·com·ing (fôrth′kum′ing) *adj.* **1.** about to happen or appear: *Anyone could win in the forthcoming election.* **2.** ready when needed or expected: *Relief will be forthcoming for those left homeless by the flood.*

forth·right (fôrth′rīt′) *adj.* going straight to the point; straightforward; frank. —**forth′right′ly**, *adv.* —**forth′right′ness**, *n.*

forth·with (fôrth′with′, fôrth′with′) *adv.* without delay; at once; immediately: *The doctor came forthwith.*

for·ti·eth (fôr′tē ith) *adj.* **1.** (the ordinal of forty) next after the thirty-ninth. **2.** being one of forty equal parts. —*n.* **1.** something that is next after the thirty-ninth. **2.** one of forty equal parts; ¹⁄₄₀.

for·ti·fi·ca·tion (fôr′tə fi kā′shən) *n.* **1.** the act of fortifying. **2.** something that fortifies, such as a wall or ditch. **3.** a fortified place or building.

for·ti·fy (fôr′tə fī′) *v.t.*, **for·ti·fied, for·ti·fy·ing. 1.** to protect with a wall, ditch, or other fortification. **2.** to strengthen the structure of; make strong or stronger: *The townspeople fortified the levee against the flood. These facts will fortify my argument.*

tor·tis·si·mo (tôr tis′ə mo′) *Music. adj.* very loud. —*adv.* very loudly.

for·ti·tude (fôr′ti tūd′, fôr′ti tōod′) *n.* courage or strength in the face of pain, danger, or misfortune.

fort·night (fôrt′nīt′) *n.* two weeks.

fort·night·ly (fôrt′nīt′lē) *adv.* once every two weeks. —*adj.* happening or appearing every two weeks. —*n.*, *pl.* **fort·night·lies.** something published every two weeks, such as a magazine.

FORTRAN (fôr′tran) a computer language used principally for solving problems in science and engineering. [Short for *for(mula) tran(slation)*.]

for·tress (fôr′tris) *n.*, *pl.* **for·tress·es. 1.** a fortified place; stronghold; fort. **2.** a person or thing that protects or gives security: *These investments are a fortress against poverty.*

for·tu·i·tous (fôr tū′i təs, fôr tōo′i təs) *adj.* **1.** happening by chance; accidental: *a fortuitous meeting in a crowd.* **2.** fortunate; lucky: *a fortuitous happening.* —**for·tu′i·tous·ly**, *adv.* —**for·tu′i·tous·ness**, *n.*

for·tu·nate (fôr′chə nit) *adj.* **1.** having good fortune; lucky: *You are fortunate to have won the scholarship.* **2.** bringing good fortune; favorable: *We started our trip under fortunate circumstances.* —**for′tu·nate·ly**, *adv.*

for·tune (fôr′chən) *n.* **1.** something that happens or is going to happen to a person, whether good or bad; fate: *The gypsy claimed to tell fortunes by looking into a crystal ball.* **2.** luck, especially when good: *It was our good fortune to meet you when we did.* **3.** great wealth; riches: *a fortune in stocks and bonds.*

fortune cookie, a thin, folded cookie containing a piece of paper on which is printed a fortune, saying, or humorous message.

for·tune·tell·er (fôr′chən tel′ər) *n.* a person who claims to be able to tell another person's fortune.

for·ty (fôr′tē) *n.*, *pl.* **for·ties. 1.** the cardinal number that is four times ten. **2.** a symbol representing this number, such as 40 or XL. —*adj.* numbering four times ten.

for·ty-nin·er (fôr′tē nī′nər) *n.* a person who went to California seeking gold in the gold rush of 1849.

fo·rum (fôr′əm) *n.* **1.** the public square or marketplace of an ancient Roman city, where important political and business activities took place. **2.** an assembly or meeting for the discussion of issues or questions of public interest: *A forum was held to discuss the new law.* **3.** a court of law.

for·ward (fôr′wərd) *adv.* **1.** *also,* **forwards.** toward what is ahead or in front; onward: *Step forward to accept your trophy.* **2.** toward the future: *We are looking forward to the trip.* **3.** into view; forth: *I brought forward an opinion.* —*adj.* **1.** in, at, near, or toward the front: *a ship's forward cabin.* **2.** moving or directed toward a point in front: *a forward pass.* **3.** advanced or progressive: *forward ideas.* **4.** bold or rude: *They are very forward children.* —*v.t.* **1.** to send onward or ahead, especially to a new address: *Forward my mail to my new address.* **2.** to help along; promote; advance: *to forward the cause of peace.* —*n.* a player whose position is at or near the front line in certain games, such as basketball or hockey.

for·ward·ly (fôr′wərd lē) *adv.* boldly or rudely.

for·ward·ness (fôr′wərd nis) *n.* **1.** boldness or rudeness. **2.** the condition of being advanced or progressive. **3.** the state of being ready or eager.

for·went (fôr went′) the past tense of **forgo.**

fos·sil (fos′əl) *n.* **1.** a part of the remains or a trace of an animal or plant that lived long ago: *fossils of prehistoric sea animals found in some rocks.* **2.** *Informal.* a person or thing that is old-fashioned, outmoded, or belonging to the past. —*adj.* of, relating to, or forming a fossil.

fossil fuel, any fuel developed from the fossilized remains of prehistoric plants and animals. Fossil fuels include coal, petroleum, and natural gas.

fossil *(def. 1)*

fos·sil·ize (fos′ə līz′) *v.*, **fos·sil·ized, fos·sil·iz·ing.** *v.t.* to change into a fossil. —*v.i.* to become a fossil: *The bones of the dinosaur fossilized.* —**fos′sil·i·za′tion**, *n.*

fos·ter (fôs′tər) *v.t.* **1.** to help the growth or development of: *The teacher fostered our interest in science.* **2.** to bring up; rear: *to foster a child.* —*adj.* **1.** providing shelter, food, and supervision temporarily for one or more persons who are not related by birth or adoption. Such care is often arranged and paid for by a social service agency: *foster care, foster parents, a foster home.* **2.** receiving temporary parental care from an adult who is not related by birth or adoption: *a foster child.*

fought (fôt) the past tense and past participle of **fight.**

foul (foul) *adj.* **1.** very unpleasant or disgusting: *a foul odor.* **2.** containing dirt or filth: *foul air, foul water.* **3.** cloudy, rainy, or stormy: *foul weather.* **4.** very bad; evil; vile: *a foul deed.* **5.** breaking the rules; unfair: *a foul blow in boxing.* **6.** offending decency: *foul language.* **7.** *Baseball.* outside the foul line: *The ball was foul.* —*n.* **1.** a breaking of rules: *The athlete committed a foul.* **2.** see **foul ball.** —*v.t.* **1.** to make dirty; soil: *They fouled the water by throwing in garbage.* **2.** to tangle: *I fouled my fishing line.* **3.** *Sports.* to commit a foul against: *The boxers fouled each other by hitting below the belt.* **4.** *Baseball.* to hit (a ball) into foul territory. **5.** to stop up; clog: *Hair fouled the drain.* —*v.i.* **1.** to be or become dirty. **2.** to become tangled: *The rope fouled when we tried to coil it.* **3.** *Sports.* to break a rule of a game. **4.** *Baseball.* to hit a foul ball. —*adv.* afoul: *to run foul of the law.* —**foul′ly,** *adv.* —**foul′ness,** *n.*

·to foul up. to confuse or bungle: *The flat tire fouled up our schedule.*

fou·lard (fü lärd′) *n.* a soft, lightweight fabric made of silk, rayon, cotton, or other similar fibers, used especially for neckties, scarves, and dresses.

foul ball *Baseball.* a batted ball that goes outside the foul lines. If caught in the air it is an out, but a base runner may advance after the catch.

foul line *Baseball.* either of the lines that extend from home plate through first or third base to the limits of the playing field.

foul play, dishonest or treacherous action, especially when violent.

foul-up (foul′up′) *n. Informal.* **1.** a state of confusion or breakdown; mix-up or mess: *a series of bad mistakes that produced a real foul-up in our plans.* **2.** a mechanical problem: *a foul-up in a car's transmission.*

found¹ (found) the past tense and past participle of **find.**

found² (found) *v.t.* **1.** to bring into being; start or set up: *The students founded a science club.* **2.** to set firmly; base; ground: *My argument is founded on fact.* [From the Old French word *fonder* meaning "to establish," from the Latin word *fundare* "to lay the foundation of" or "establish," from the word *fundus* "bottom, base."]

found³ (found) *v.t.* **1.** to melt and pour (metal) into a mold. **2.** to form or make by pouring molten metal into a mold; cast. [From the Middle French word *fondre* meaning "to melt, cast (metal)," from the Latin word *fundere* "to melt, cast (metal), pour out."]

foun·da·tion (foun dā′shən) *n.* **1.** the act of founding or the state of being founded; establishment. **2.** something serving as a base or support; basis: *the foundation of a building, the foundations of society.* **3.** an organization that has been endowed especially to support worthwhile causes, such as scientific, artistic, or scholarly work. **4.** the fund endowed for such an organization; endowment.

foun·der¹ (foun′dər) *v.i.* **1.** to fill with water and sink: *The boat foundered in the storm.* **2.** to fall down: *Several buildings foundered in the earthquake.* **3.** to fail completely: *The business foundered.* **4.** to stumble and become lame or disabled: *The horse foundered on the rocky path.* —*v.t.* to cause to founder. [From the Old French word *fondrer* meaning "to sink," from the word *fond* "bottom," from the Latin word *fundus* "bottom, base."]

found·er² (foun′dər) *n.* a person who founds, starts, or sets up something: *the founder of a business.* [*Found²* + *-er¹*.]

found·er³ (foun′dər) *n.* a person who melts and casts metal. [*Found³* + *-er¹*.]

Founding Father **1.** any of the colonial statesmen of the period of the American Revolution, especially those who helped to write the Constitution of the United States. **2. founding father.** a person who originates or establishes something, such as an institution or movement; founder.

found·ling (found′ling) *n.* a deserted infant whose parents are not known.

found·ry (foun′drē) *n., pl.* **found·ries. 1.** a place where metal is melted and cast. **2.** the act or process of founding metal.

fount (fount) *n.* **1.** source: *That book is a fount of knowledge.* **2.** fountain; spring.

foun·tain (foun′tən) *n.* **1.** a stream of water made to rise or shoot up in order to provide water for drinking or to serve as a decoration. **2.** a structure designed for such a stream: *a marble fountain in a park.* **3.** a spring of water coming out of the earth. **4.** the source of anything: *The coach is a fountain of facts about baseball.* **5.** see **soda fountain.**

foun·tain·head (foun′tən hed′) *n.* **1.** a spring from which a stream flows; source of a stream. **2.** the primary source or origin of anything.

fountain pen, a pen having a reservoir that holds and feeds ink to the writing point.

four (fôr) *n.* **1.** the cardinal number that is one more than three. **2.** a symbol representing this number, such as 4 or IV. **3.** something having this many units or things, such as a playing card. —*adj.* numbering one more than three.

·on all fours. a. on all four feet: *The cat landed on all fours.* **b.** on hands and knees: *We were on all fours looking for the lost contact lens.*

four·fold (fôr′fōld′) *adj.* **1.** four times as great or numerous. **2.** having or consisting of four parts. —*adv.* so as to be four times greater or more numerous.

Four-H clubs (fôr′āch′) also, **4-H clubs.** an organization for youth, sponsored by the U.S. government, to teach skills in agriculture and home economics. [From its *four*fold purpose of improving the *h*ead, *h*eart, *h*ands, and *h*ealth of its members.]

four-leaf clover (fôr′lēf′) a clover with four leaflets, considered to bring good luck to a person who finds it.

four–post·er (fôr′pōs′tər) *n.* a bedstead with four tall corner posts for supporting a canopy or curtains.

four·score (fôr′skôr′) *adj., n.* four times twenty; eighty.

four·some (fôr′səm) *n.* **1.** a group of four persons. **2.** something played or done by four persons, such as a round of golf.

four·square (fôr′skwâr′) *adj.* **1.** square. **2.** frank; forthright. **3.** firm. —*adv.* squarely; firmly.

four·teen (fôr′tēn′) *n.* **1.** the cardinal number that is four more than ten. **2.** a symbol representing this number, such as 14 or XIV. **3.** something having this many units or things. —*adj.* numbering four more than ten.

four·teenth (fôr′tēnth′) *adj.* **1.** (the ordinal of fourteen) next after the thirteenth. **2.** being one of fourteen equal parts. —*n.* **1.** something that is next after the thirteenth. **2.** one of fourteen equal parts; $\frac{1}{14}$.

fourth (fôrth) *adj.* **1.** (the ordinal of four) next after the third. **2.** being one of four equal parts. —*n.* **1.** something that is next after the third. **2.** one of four equal parts; $\frac{1}{4}$. **3.** *Music.* **a.** a note that is a total of two whole steps and one half step above a given note. F is the fourth of C. **b.** an interval of two whole steps and one half step. **c.** a combination of two notes that are separated by this interval. **4.** the fourth forward gear, as of an automobile. —*adv.* in the fourth place.

fourth dimension, in the theory of relativity, the concept of time, considered with the three spatial dimensions of length, width, and depth.

fourth estate, the press; journalists or journalism.

Fourth of July, another term for **Independence Day.**

fowl (foul) *n., pl.* **fowl** or **fowls. 1.** a hen or rooster;

chicken. **2.** any other domestic bird raised for its meat, such as a turkey, pheasant, or duck. **3.** the flesh of a fowl used as food. **4.** any bird.

fox (foks) *n., pl.* **fox·es. 1.** any of a group of wild animals belonging to the dog family, having a pointed nose, large erect ears, a bushy tail, and a thick coat. **2.** the fur of a fox. **3.** a sly, crafty person. —*v.t. Informal.* to trick or deceive; outwit: *The escaped prisoner foxed the posse by hiding until it had passed by.* —**fox'like'**, *adj.*

fox *(n., def. 1)*

Fox (foks) *n., pl.* **Fox** or **Foxes. 1.** a member of a North American Indian tribe formerly living in the Great Lakes region and now living in Iowa. **2.** the Algonquian language spoken by this tribe.

fox·glove (foks'gluv') *n.* a plant bearing white, yellow, or purple thimble-shaped flowers on long spikes. The dried leaves of the foxglove are used in making the drug digitalis.

fox·hole (foks'hōl') *n.* a hole dug in the ground by soldiers to give themselves shelter from enemy fire.

fox·hound (foks'hound') *n.* a medium-sized hound with a keen sense of smell, usually having a tan, black, and white coat, trained especially to hunt foxes.

fox·tail (foks'tāl') *n.* **1.** the tail of a fox. **2.** any of various grasses bearing flower spikes that resemble the tail of foxes.

fox terrier, a small terrier having a long head, short tail, and a smooth or wiry white coat with tan or black and tan markings. Fox terriers were once used to drive foxes from their burrows.

foxglove

fox·trot (foks'trot) *v.i.,* **fox·trot·ted, fox·trot·ting.** to dance the fox trot.

fox trot 1. a dance that combines slow steps and short, quick steps. **2.** the music for this dance.

fox·y (fok'sē) *adj.,* **fox·i·er, fox·i·est.** like a fox; sly; crafty. —**fox'i·ly,** *adv.* —**fox'i·ness,** *n.*

foy·er (foi'ər) *n.* **1.** the lobby of a theater, hotel, or other public building. **2.** the entrance hall in a house or apartment.

Fr, the symbol for francium.

fr. 1. fragment. **2.** franc. **3.** from.

Fr. 1. Father. **2.** France. **3.** French. **4.** Friday.

fra·cas (frā'kəs) *n., pl.* **fra·cas·es.** a loud quarrel or fight; brawl.

frac·tion (frak'shən) *n.* **1.** a part of a whole; small part: *Only a fraction of the crowd attending the game left before the game was over.* **2.** *Mathematics.* a quantity expressing the division of one number by a second number, written as two numerals separated by a line, such as $\frac{2}{3}$, $\frac{3}{4}$, or $\frac{12}{16}$.

frac·tion·al (frak'shə nəl) *adj.* **1.** of, relating to, or forming a fraction or fractions: *Four inches is a fractional part of a foot.* **2.** small or unimportant: *You've made only a fractional improvement in your work.*

frac·tious (frak'shəs) *adj.* **1.** difficult to control; unruly. **2.** bad-tempered or quarrelsome; cranky. —**frac'tious·ly,** *adv.* —**frac'tious·ness,** *n.*

frac·ture (frak'chər) *v.,* **frac·tured, frac·tur·ing.** —*v.t.* to crack, split, or break (something): *to fracture an ankle.*

—*v.i.* to crack, split, or break: *My arm fractured in the accident.* —*n.* **1.** the act of breaking or the state of being broken. **2.** a crack, split, or break, as in a bone.

frag·ile (fraj'əl) *adj.* tending to break easily: *That porcelain cup is fragile.* —**frag'ile·ly,** *adv.* —**fra·gil·i·ty** (frə jil'i tē), *n.*

frag·ment (*n.,* frag'mənt; *v.,* frag'ment, frag ment') *n.* **1.** a part broken off; small piece: *The archaeologists found fragments of pottery.* **2.** a part of something left incomplete or unfinished: *a fragment of a novel, fragments of conversation.* —*v.t.* to break (something) into fragments: *I fragmented the glass pitcher when I dropped it.* —*v.i.* to break into fragments.

frag·men·tar·y (frag'mən ter'ē) *adj.* made up of fragments; broken; incomplete: *the fragmentary remains of a jar. The police had only a fragmentary report of the crime.*

frag·men·ta·tion (frag'mən tā'shən) *n.* the act or process of breaking into fragments.

fra·grance (frā'grəns) *n.* a sweet or pleasing smell: *The flowers have a pleasant fragrance.*

fra·grant (frā'grənt) *adj.* having a sweet or pleasing smell: *a fragrant garden.* —**fra'grant·ly,** *adv.*

frail (frāl) *adj.* **1.** lacking in strength; weak: *The child was too frail to take part in sports.* **2.** easily broken or torn; delicate; fragile: *frail, old lace.* **3.** weak in morals or character. —**frail'ness,** *n.*

frail·ty (frāl'tē) *n., pl.* **frail·ties. 1.** the state or quality of being frail; weakness. **2.** a fault resulting from moral weakness: *Gambling can be a costly frailty.*

frame (frām) *n.* **1.** a structure that holds or borders something: *a window frame, a picture frame, frames for eyeglasses.* **2.** a structure that gives shape or supports something; framework: *the metal frame of a bed, the wooden frame of a house.* **3.** the way in which one's body is formed; build: *to have a thin frame.* **4.** one of the pictures on a roll of motion-picture film. **5.** one of the ten divisions of a game of bowling. —*v.t.,* **framed, fram·ing. 1.** to set in a border: *The artist framed the painting.* **2.** to form, draw up, or make: *The lawyer framed questions clearly.* **3.** *Informal.* to cause (an innocent person) to appear guilty by using false evidence. —**fram'er,** *n.*

frame house, a house constructed on a wooden framework, usually covered with siding or shingles.

frame of mind, the state of a person's mind or feeling; mood: *Losing my job put me in a low frame of mind.*

frame–up (frām'up') *n. Informal.* a scheme to make an innocent person appear guilty through the use of false evidence.

frame·work (frām'wûrk') *n.* a structure that gives shape or support to something: *the framework of a building, the framework of a novel.*

franc (frangk) *n.* a monetary unit and coin of France, Belgium, Switzerland, Luxembourg, and many other countries.

fran·chise (fran'chīz) *n.* **1.** the right to vote; suffrage: *The United States Constitution gives the franchise to persons who are eighteen years old.* **2.** the right to have or do something, given to an individual or group, especially by a government or business firm: *a franchise to operate a bus service, a franchise to sell food at the park.* **3.** the geographical area for which such a privilege is given.

---

at; āpe; fär; câre; end; mē; it; īce; pîerce; hot; ōld; sông, fôrk; oil; out; up; ūse; rüle; pull; tûrn; chin; sing; shop; thin; this; hw in white; zh in treasure. The symbol ə stands for the unstressed vowel sound heard in about, taken, pencil, lemon, and circus.

F

Fran·cis·can (fran sis′kən) *adj.* **1.** of or relating to Saint Francis of Assisi or to the religious order that he founded. **2.** belonging to this order: *a Franciscan monk.* —*n.* a member of this order.

fran·ci·um (fran′sē əm) *n.* a rare, radioactive metallic element. Symbol: **Fr** [From *France,* the homeland of its discoverer, Marguerite Perey.]

frank[1] (frangk) *adj.* honest and open in expressing one's thoughts and feelings; outspoken; candid: *Let me be frank and tell you what I really think.* —*v.t.* **1.** to mark (a letter, package, or other mail) for delivery without charge. **2.** to send (mail) without charge. —*n.* **1.** the right or privilege to send mail without charge: *Members of Congress are given the frank.* **2.** a mark indicating this right or privilege. —**frank′ly,** *adv.* —**frank′ness,** *n.*

frank[2] (frangk) *n. Informal.* see **frankfurter.**

Frank (frangk) *n.* a member of a Germanic people who conquered Gaul in the late fifth century A.D., and who gave their name to present-day France.

Frank·en·stein (frang′kən stīn′) *n.* **1.** the young scientist in Mary Shelley's novel *Frankenstein,* who creates a monster that eventually destroys him. **2.** the monster. **3.** anything that threatens or destroys its creator.

frank·furt·er (frangk′fər tər) *n.* **1.** a reddish sausage made of beef, beef mixed with pork, or poultry and shaped like a cylinder. **2.** such a sausage served hot in a long, soft roll, often with mustard, relish, or sauerkraut. Also, **hot dog.** [From the German word *Frankfurter* meaning "of *Frankfurt,* Germany."]

frank·in·cense (frang′kin sens′) *n.* a resin from certain Asian and African trees, burned as an incense.

Frank·ish (frang′kish) *adj.* of or relating to the Franks. —*n.* the language of the Franks.

fran·tic (fran′tik) *adj.* wildly excited by worry, grief, fear, or anger; frenzied: *They were frantic when their child became lost.* —**fran′ti·cal·ly;** *also,* **fran′tic·ly,** *adv.* —**fran′tic·ness,** *n.*

frap·pé (*adj., n., def. 1* fra pā′; *n., def. 2* frap) *adj.* iced; chilled. —*n.* **1.** a beverage that is partly frozen or served over shaved ice. **2. frappe.** a beverage made with ice cream, such as a milkshake.

fra·ter·nal (frə tûr′nəl) *adj.* **1.** of or relating to a brother or brothers; brotherly. **2.** of or relating to an association of people who join together for fellowship or because of common interests. —**fra·ter′nal·ly,** *adv.*

fraternal twins, twins of the same or opposite sex that develop from two separate fertilized egg cells and therefore do not necessarily look alike. Fraternal twins are different from identical twins, which develop from the same fertilized egg cell and therefore look alike.

fra·ter·ni·ty (frə tûr′ni tē) *n., pl.* **fra·ter·ni·ties. 1.** a social organization of men or boys, often having student chapters in colleges. **2.** the state or quality of being brotherly; brotherhood. **3.** a group of people sharing the same interests or profession: *the medical fraternity.*

frat·er·nize (frat′ər nīz′) *v.i.,* **frat·er·nized, frat·er·niz·ing.** to associate closely with someone in a friendly or brotherly way: *The players were told not to fraternize with the other team before the game.* —**frat′er·ni·za′tion,** *n.*

frat·ri·cide (frat′rə sīd′) *n.* the act of killing one's brother or sister. [Originally from the Latin word *fratricidium* with the same meaning, from the word *frater* "brother" + the suffix *-cidium* "-cide."]

Frau (frou) *n., pl.* **Frau·en** (frou′ən) or **Fraus.** a married woman; wife. ▲ German form of respectful or polite address for a married woman.

fraud (frôd) *n.* **1.** deceit or trickery, especially the tricking of another person in order to cheat him or her of rights or property. **2.** a person or thing that deceives; impostor or sham.

fraud·u·lent (frô′jə lənt) *adj.* **1.** given to or using fraud; deceitful; dishonest: *The fraudulent merchant cheated the customers.* **2.** characterized by or done by fraud: *a fraudulent sale.* —**fraud′u·lence, fraud′u·len·cy,** *n.* —**fraud′u·lent·ly,** *adv.*

fraught (frôt) *adj.* filled: *a mission fraught with danger.*

Fräu·lein (froi′līn) *n., pl.* **Fräu·lein** or **Fräu·leins.** an unmarried woman; young lady. ▲ German form of respectful or polite address for an unmarried woman.

fray[1] (frā) *n.* a noisy quarrel or fight: *I joined the fray and got a bloody nose.* [A form of *affray.*]

fray[2] (frā) *v.t.* **1.** to cause (something, such as cloth or rope) to separate into loose threads, especially along the edges: *Hard wear had frayed my coat cuffs.* **2.** to strain or irritate: *nerves frayed from excitement.* —*v.i.* to become frayed; ravel. [From the French word *frayer* meaning "to rub against."]

fraz·zle (fraz′əl) *v.t.,* **fraz·zled, fraz·zling. 1.** to wear to shreds; fray. **2.** to tire out; exhaust: *The long, demanding job left us frazzled.* —*v.i.* to become frazzled. —*n.* the state of being frazzled: *worn to a frazzle.*

freak (frēk) *n.* **1.** a person, animal, or plant that has not developed normally; monstrosity. **2.** anything odd or unusual. **3.** *Slang.* a person greatly or excessively devoted to or fascinated by something: *an exercise freak.* —*adj.* not normal; odd or unusual; bizarre: *a freak accident.*

freak·ish (frē′kish) *adj.* **1.** of or relating to a freak; abnormal. **2.** odd or unusual: *a freakish turn of events.* —**freak′ish·ly,** *adv.* —**freak′ish·ness,** *n.*

freck·le (frek′əl) *n.* a small brownish spot on the skin, often caused or darkened by exposure to the sun. —*v.,* **freck·led, freck·ling.** —*v.t.* to mark (something) with freckles. —*v.i.* to become marked with freckles.

free (frē) *adj.,* **fre·er, fre·est. 1.** having one's liberty; not under the control or domination of another; not a slave. **2. a.** having political liberty to vote, express opinions, organize to pursue goals, and the like. **b.** having a government that allows such liberty: *a free country.* **3.** not held back, restrained, or confined: *the dancer's free, graceful movements. You are free to come and go. They are free with their money.* **4.** relieved of something that causes worry, pain, or effort: *free from care.* **5.** without cost or payment: *We received free tickets to the show.* **6.** not busy; available: *free time.* **7.** not following regular rules, patterns, or words: *a free translation.* **8.** not swayed or influenced: *a free choice.* **9.** not blocked or occupied: *a free passageway, a free seat.* **10.** not subject to custom duties or other taxes: *free trade.* **11.** *Chemistry.* not part of a compound; not combined: *free oxygen.* —*adv.* **1.** without cost or payment: *Children were admitted free.* **2.** in a free manner; easily: *The colts ran free across the meadow.* —*v.t.,* **freed, free·ing. 1.** to make free; set loose: *The child freed the trapped animal.* **2.** to save from or relieve of something: *The prize money helped free them from debt.* —**free′ly,** *adv.* —**free′ness,** *n.*

free·bie (frē′bē) *also,* **free·bee.** *n. Slang.* something obtained or received free of charge.

free·board (frē′bôrd′) *n.* the part of the side of a ship that is out of the water.

free·boot·er (frē′bū′tər) *n.* a person who plunders; pirate.

free·born (frē′bôrn′) *adj.* not born in slavery; born free.

freed·man (frēd′mən) *n., pl.* **freed·men** (frēd′mən). a person who has been freed from slavery.

free·dom (frē′dəm) *n.* **1.** the condition of being free: *The colonists struggled for their freedom.* **2.** a setting free, as from slavery or prison. **3.** ease of movement or action. **4.** openness or frankness in manner or speech. **5.** full use: *We gave our guests the freedom of our home.*

freed·wom·an (frēd′wum′ən) *n., pl.* **freed·wom·en** (frēd′wim′ən). a woman who has been freed from slavery.

free enterprise, an economic system in which people are able to own and operate businesses for profit with little control by the government. Also, **private enterprise.**

free fall **1.** the fall of a body through air without any artificial restraint, as without an open parachute. **2.** the part of a parachute jump before the parachute is opened.

free fall
a group of parachutists in free fall

free–for–all (frē′fər ôl′) *n.* a noisy fight or quarrel.

free·hand (frē′hand′) *adj.* drawn or sketched by hand without measuring or using a drawing instrument, such as a ruler. —*adv.* by hand without measuring or using a drawing instrument.

free·hold (frē′hōld′) *n.* **1.** a piece of land held for life with the right to give it to one's heirs. **2.** the holding of land in this way. —**free′hold′er,** *n.*

free–lance (frē′lans′) *also,* **free·lance.** *adj.* of, relating to, or working as a free lance. —*v.i.,* **free-lanced, free-lanc·ing.** to work as a free lance.

free lance *also,* **free·lance.** a trained person, especially a writer or artist, who sells his or her work to anyone who will buy it. Also, **free′-lanc′er.**

free·man (frē′mən) *n., pl.* **free·men** (frē′mən). **1.** a person who is free from bondage or slavery; a free man or woman. **2.** a person who is a citizen.

Free·ma·son (frē′mā′sən) *n.* a member of a secret organization that teaches brotherly love and mutual aid. Also, **Mason.**

Free·ma·son·ry (frē′mā′sən rē) *n.* **1.** the beliefs and practices of the Freemasons. **2.** Freemasons as a group. Also, **Masonry.**

free on board, delivered onto a ship, train, or the like by the seller without charge to the buyer.

Free Soil Party, a U.S. political party formed in 1848 that was against bringing slavery into the western territories and admitting new slave states into the Union.

free–spo·ken (frē′spō′kən) *adj.* given to speaking frankly; outspoken.

free·stand·ing (frē′stan′ding) *adj.* standing alone or independently; not supported by any framework or attachment: *a freestanding wall, a freestanding sculpture.*

Free State, a U.S. state in which slavery was not allowed during the period before the Civil War.

free·stone (frē′stōn′) *adj.* having a pit that separates easily from the flesh of the fruit: *a freestone peach.* —*n.* **1.** any fine-grained stone, such as limestone or sandstone, that can be cut easily in any direction without splitting. **2.** a freestone fruit, such as a plum.

free·style (frē′stīl′) *adj.* in swimming, using or allowing any stroke the swimmer chooses. —*n.* a freestyle swimming race or event.

free·think·er (frē′thing′kər) *n.* a person whose opinions, as on religion, are based on his or her own thinking or judgment instead of on tradition or the opinions of others.

free verse, poetry that does not have a regular meter or rhyme scheme.

free·way (frē′wā′) *n.* a highway with no toll charges, usually divided for fast and direct driving.

free·wheel·ing (frē′hwē′ling, frē′wē′ling) *adj. Informal.* **1.** acting freely or casually: *a freewheeling news commentator.* **2.** not bound by rules or restraints: *a freewheeling discussion.*

free·will (frē′wil′) *adj.* given or done freely; voluntary: *a freewill offering.*

free will **1.** the power of choosing freely what one is going to do without being directed or influenced by others; free choice: *I did it of my own free will.* **2.** the doctrine that people have free choice and are responsible for what they do.

freeze (frēz) *v.,* **froze, fro·zen, freez·ing.** —*v.i.* **1.** to change into a solid state or form by cold. When water freezes, it becomes ice. **2.** to become covered or blocked with ice: *The lake froze last night. The water pipes froze.* **3.** to be or become very cold: *We froze waiting for the bus in the snowstorm.* **4.** to become fixed because of cold: *The windshield wiper froze and wouldn't work.* **5.** to be unable to move because of fear or shock: *I froze when I saw the bear.* **6.** to stop moving or become fixed: *"Freeze!" cried the police officer to the criminals.* **7.** to be damaged, destroyed, or killed by frost or extreme cold: *The orange crop froze this winter.* **8.** to become unfriendly, formal, or aloof: *The child froze around strangers.* —*v.t.* **1.** to cause to change to a solid state or form by cold; cause to become ice: *to freeze water.* **2.** to cover or block (something) with ice: *The cold weather froze the lake.* **3.** to preserve (food) by quickly lowering its temperature: *to freeze a steak.* **4.** to damage, destroy, or kill by frost or extreme cold. **5.** to fix or set at a particular amount or level: *The government froze food prices.* —*n.* **1.** the act of freezing or the state of being frozen. **2.** a period of extremely cold weather.

freeze–dry (frēz′drī′) *v.t.,* **freeze-dried, freeze-dry·ing.** to dry while frozen under high vacuum for preservation: *to freeze dry coffee.*

freeze frame, in motion pictures and television, a single frame of film that is repeated many times to give the effect of action or movement that has been frozen.

freez·er (frē′zər) *n.* **1.** a refrigerator or section in a refrigerator that freezes food rapidly and keeps it from spoiling for long periods of time. **2.** a machine for freezing ice cream.

freezer burn, a condition in which frozen foods acquire a dull grayish color or unpleasant appearance and lose moisture and flavor as a result of improper packaging or storage.

freezing point, the temperature at which a liquid freezes. The freezing point of water at sea level is 32 degrees Fahrenheit or 0 degrees Celsius.

freight (frāt) *n.* **1.** the transportation of goods by means of land, air, or water. **2.** the goods transported by such means; cargo. **3.** the charge for the transportation of goods by such means. **4.** see **freight train.** —*v.t.* **1.** to load with goods for transportation. **2.** to send by freight.

freight car, a railroad car for carrying freight.

freight·er (frā′tər) *n.* **1.** a ship used mainly for transporting cargo. **2.** a person who receives and transports freight.

freight train, a railroad train composed of freight cars.

French (french) *n.* **1.** the French. the people of France. **2.** the language of France. It is also spoken in parts of

F

Belgium, Switzerland, and Canada, and in Haiti and many African nations. —*adj.* of or relating to France, its people, their language, or culture.

The most important single event in the shaping of the English language was the introduction of **French** to England by the Norman invaders in 1066. As conquerors, the Normans established French as the language of the court, the military, the law, and the upper classes. English continued to be spoken by the native population, but the role of the English language in society lost much of its importance. For a time, English fell out of use among literate, educated people.

However, the speakers of English greatly outnumbered the Normans, and English was later restored as the common language of the land. The Normans remained very powerful and important in society, but they were nevertheless the minority, and they gradually came to think of England as their home. By the fourteenth century the Normans were fighting the French on the Continent. Partly as a patriotic act and partly because of the increasing power of the general English-speaking population, English became the official language of Parliament in 1362. But the form of English, which we now call Middle English, differed from the English spoken before the Norman Conquest, in large part because the vast number of words it borrowed from French were treated just as any other English word. (Probably about 60 percent of the words in any standard dictionary today come from French.)

The impact of the Normans and the French they spoke is still clear in Modern English. Most of our legal, military, and political terms, many words associated with religion and education, and nearly all of the words associated with culture, the arts, and even cooking come from French. Although the English words *king* and *queen* remained in the language, most other words that indicated noble rank, such as *prince, duke, baron,* and *countess,* came from the Normans.

This blending of two languages is the main reason why English is so rich in synonyms. When one of a pair of synonyms derives from Old English and the other from Norman French, the simpler, more concrete word will usually derive from Old English, while the more difficult, more formal, or abstract word will come from French. Examples of such pairs are the native English words *room, hide, feed,* and *begin,* and their French-derived synonyms *chamber, conceal, nourish,* and *commence.* Perhaps nowhere is the relative social status of Old English and Norman French more evident than in the terms for animals and the meats they yield. Since English was the language of the peasants during the Norman period, the word for an animal that had to be raised or hunted, such as *calf, ox, pig,* and *deer,* usually came from English. When these animals were served as food, they were referred to by their French names: *veal, beef, pork,* and *venison.*

French and Indian War, a war in North America in which the French and their Indian allies fought against the British and their Indian allies, from 1754 to 1763.

French cuff, the cuff of a sleeve that is folded back and fastened with a cuff link.

French doors, a pair of doors with glass panes. The doors open in the middle.

French dressing, a salad dressing made of oil, vinegar, and spices.

french fries also, **French fries.** *sing.* **french fry.** potatoes cut into thin strips and fried in deep fat until brown and crisp.

french-fry (french′frī′) also, **French-fry.** *v.t.,* **french-fried, french-fry·ing.** to fry by covering with hot fat, as potato strips or onion rings.

French horn, a brass musical instrument that has a long, coiled tube ending in a flared bell, and makes a rich, mellow tone.

French·man (french′mən) *n., pl.* **French·men** (french′mən). a person who was born in or is a citizen of France.

French Revolution, a revolution in France from 1789 to 1799 that overthrew the monarchy and aristocracy and resulted in the establishment of a republic.

French toast, bread dipped in a mixture of egg and milk and then fried.

French windows, a pair of doorlike windows hinged at opposite sides and opening in the middle.

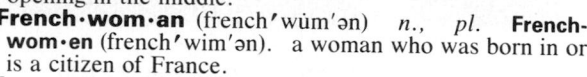

French horn

French·wom·an (french′wùm′ən) *n., pl.* **French·wom·en** (french′wim′ən). a woman who was born in or is a citizen of France.

fre·net·ic (frə net′ik) *adj.* frenzied; frantic: *frenetic activity.* —**fre·net′i·cal·ly,** *adv.*

fren·zied (fren′zēd) *adj.* marked by frenzy; frantic.

fren·zy (fren′zē) *n., pl.* **fren·zies.** an outburst of great emotion, wild excitement, or frantic activity: *a frenzy of grief, a frenzy of preparation for a party.*

fre·quen·cy (frē′kwən sē) *n., pl.* **fre·quen·cies. 1.** the state of happening or taking place again and again. **2.** the number of times something happens or takes place during a period of time; rate of occurrence: *The frequency of the heartbeat in a grown person is between sixty and ninety beats a minute.* **3.** *Mathematics.* the ratio of the number of times an event occurs to the total number of possible occurrences. **4.** the number of cycles per second of an alternating current, electromagnetic radiation, or sound.

In language, **frequency** refers to the number of times that a letter or word appears. The frequency of a letter or word is determined by examining how many times it occurs in books, magazines, and other writing, or how often it is used in conversation. In one study of reading matter, particularly that used in schools, the ten words that appeared most often were *the, of, and, a, to, in, is, you, that,* and *it.* These words are among the first that we learn when we begin to read, and they are basic building blocks of our language.

The letter of the alphabet with the highest frequency in our language is the letter *e.* The most frequent *initial letter* is *s.* This means that more words in our language begin with *s* than with any other letter. The second most common initial letter is *c.* More than 20 percent of the words in this dictionary begin with either *c* or *s.* The least commonly used initial letters are *q, x, y,* and *z.* Less than 2 percent of the words in this dictionary begin with *q, x, y,* or *z.*

frequency modulation, see FM.

fre·quent (*adj.,* frē′kwənt; *v.,* fri kwent′, frē′kwənt) *adj.* **1.** taking place again and again; happening often: *There are frequent thunderstorms here.* **2.** appearing often; regular; habitual: *a frequent visitor.* —*v.t.* to go to often; be at or in regularly: *I frequented the theater when I was in New York.* —**fre′quent·er,** *n.* —**fre′quent·ly,** *adv.*

fres·co (fres′kō) *n., pl.* **fres·coes** or **fres·cos. 1.** the art or method of painting on a surface of wet plaster. **2.** a picture or design painted using this method. —*v.t.*, **frescoed, fres·co·ing.** to paint by using this method.

fresh (fresh) *adj.* **1.** newly done, made, gathered, or obtained: *a fresh coat of paint, a fresh wound.* **2.** not known, seen, or used before; new: *a fresh day, fresh news.* **3.** clean: *fresh air, a fresh shirt.* **4.** different; additional; another: *a fresh start.* **5.** not faded; vivid: *The words remained fresh in my mind.* **6.** not stale, spoiled, or wilted: *fresh bread, fresh flowers.* **7.** not preserved, canned, frozen, pickled, or the like: *fresh fruit.* **8.** looking healthy or youthful: *a fresh complexion.* **9.** cool and pleasant; refreshing: *a fresh breeze.* **10.** (of water) not salty. **11.** not tired; rested: *I felt fresh after sleeping for an hour.* **12.** *Informal.* showing rudeness or boldness; impudent. —**fresh′ly,** *adv.* —**fresh′ness,** *n.*

fresh·en (fresh′ən) *v.t.* to make fresh: *The rain freshened the air.* —*v.i.* to become fresh.
 ·**to freshen up.** to make fresh, as by cleaning, washing, or changing clothes: *They freshened up the room for our visit. We freshened up before dinner.*

fresh·et (fresh′it) *n.* **1.** the sudden rise or overflow of a stream, caused by heavy rains or melted snow. **2.** a stream of fresh water flowing into the sea.

fresh·man (fresh′mən) *n., pl.* **fresh·men** (fresh′mən). a student in the first year of high school or college.

fresh·wa·ter (fresh′wô′tər) *adj.* of, relating to, or living in fresh water: *a freshwater fish.*

fret¹ (fret) *v.,* **fret·ted, fret·ting.** —*v.i.* to be upset, unhappy, or worried: *Don't fret about what happened.* —*v.t.* **1.** to make upset, unhappy, or worried. **2.** to wear away: *The acid fretted the metal.* —*n.* the condition of being upset or worried. [From the Old English word *fretan* meaning "to eat up, consume."]

fret² (fret) *n.* a decorative pattern, usually having short, straight lines within a band or border. —*v.t.,* **fret·ted, fret·ting.** to decorate with a fret. [From the Old French word *frete* meaning "interlaced work."]

fret³ (fret) *n.* one of a series of bars or ridges of wood, metal, or other material across the neck of such instruments as the guitar or banjo, used to help the player place the fingers correctly. [Of uncertain origin.]

fret·ful (fret′fəl) *adj.* tending to fret; irritable. —**fret′ful·ly,** *adv.* —**fret′fulness,** *n.*

fret·work (fret′wûrk′) *n.* decorative openwork made of frets.

Freud·i·an (froi′dē ən) *adj.* of, relating to, or following the theories, methods, or teachings of Sigmund Freud. —*n.* a follower of the theories, methods, or teachings of Sigmund Freud.

Fri., Friday.

fri·a·ble (frī′ə bəl) *adj.* easily crumbled or crushed into powder: *friable rock.* —**fri′a·bil′i·ty, fri′a·ble·ness,** *n.*

fri·ar (frī′ər) *n.* a man who is a member of any of the monastic orders of the Roman Catholic Church, such as the Franciscans or Dominicans.

fri·ar·y (frī′ə rē) *n., pl.* **fri·ar·ies. 1.** a building or group of buildings where friars live. **2.** a brotherhood of friars.

fric·as·see (frik′ə sē′) *n.* a dish made up of meat, especially chicken, that is stewed, and served in a sauce made with its own gravy. —*v.t.,* **fric·as·seed, fric·as·see·ing.** to make (meat) into a fricassee.

fric·tion (frik′shən) *n.* **1.** the rubbing of one object against another: *the friction of a rope on one's hand.* **2.** *Physics.* a force that resists movement between two surfaces that are touching one another: *The friction between the parts of a machine can be reduced by oiling.* **3.** anger or ill will caused by conflict or disagreement.

fric·tion·al (frik′shə nəl) *adj.* of, relating to, or brought about by friction. —**fric′tion·al·ly,** *adv.*

friction tape, a moisture-resistant adhesive tape, used especially to protect and insulate exposed electric wires.

Fri·day (frī′dē, frī′dā) *n.* the sixth day of the week. [From the Old English word *Frīgedæg* meaning "Friday, day devoted to the goddess Frig," from the words *Frīg,* queen of the gods in Germanic mythology + *dæg* "day."]

fried (frīd) the past tense and past participle of **fry¹.**

friend (frend) *n.* **1.** a person who is known well and regarded with affection by another; person one knows well and likes. **2.** a person who supports: *the friends of the museum.* **3.** a person on the same side: *Are you friend or foe?* **4. Friend.** a member of the Society of Friends. Also, *(def. 4),* **Quaker.**
 ·**to make friends with.** to become a friend of.

friend·less (frend′lis) *adj.* having no friends. —**friend′less·ness,** *n.*

friend·ly (frend′lē) *adj.,* **friend·li·er, friend·li·est. 1.** of, relating to, or characteristic of a friend: *friendly advice, a friendly letter.* **2.** showing friendship, kindness, or warmth of feeling: *a friendly person, a friendly gesture.* **3.** not hostile: *friendly relations between nations.* **4.** helpful or favorable: *a friendly breeze.* —**friend′li·ness,** *n.*

friend·ship (frend′ship′) *n.* **1.** the state or fact of being friends. **2.** a mutual liking or attachment between friends.

frieze (frēz) *n.* **1.** a horizontal band, often decorated with sculpture or other ornamentation, between the cornice and architrave of a building. **2.** any decorative horizontal band, as around the top of a wall or building.

frig·ate (frig′it) *n.* **1.** formerly, a three-masted, square-rigged sailing warship. **2.** a warship used for escort and patrol duties.

frigate bird, any of various tropical sea birds having long, pointed wings, dark feathers, and a thin, hooked bill.

frigate

fright (frīt) *n.* **1.** sudden, violent alarm or terror: *The people in the burning building were seized with fright.* **2.** *Informal.* a person or thing that is ugly, shocking, or ridiculous in appearance: *I was a fright after three months of camping.*

fright·en (frī′tən) *v.t.* **1.** to make suddenly alarmed or afraid; terrify or scare: *The explosion frightened them.* **2.** to drive or scare by terrifying or scaring: *The dog frightened squirrels from the yard.* —*v.i.* to become suddenly alarmed or afraid: *Wild deer frighten easily.*

fright·en·ing (frī′tə ning) *adj.* causing fright; alarming; terrifying. —**fright′en·ing·ly,** *adv.*

fright·ful (frīt′fəl) *adj.* **1.** causing fright: *a frightful enemy.* **2.** disgusting, shocking, or revolting: *Living conditions in the slums were frightful.* **3.** *Informal.* very unpleasant or disagreeable: *a frightful headache.* **4.** *Informal.* extreme; great: *I'm in a frightful rush to catch the bus.* —**fright′ful·ly,** *adv.* —**fright′ful·ness,** *n.*

frig·id (frij′id) *adj.* **1.** very cold: *a frigid winter.* **2.** lacking warmth of feeling or enthusiasm; unfriendly or indifferent: *a frigid welcome.* —**fri·gid′i·ty, frig′id·ness,** *n.* —**frig′id·ly,** *adv.*

Frigid Zone, either of two extremely cold regions of the

frets²

at; āpe; fär; câre; end; mē; it; īce; pîerce; hot; ōld;
sông, fôrk; oil; out; up; ūse; rüle; pùll; tûrn; chin;
sing; shop; thin; <u>th</u>is; hw in white; zh in treasure.
The symbol ə stands for the unstressed vowel sound
heard in about, taken, pencil, lemon, and circus.

earth, one lying north of the Arctic Circle and the other south of the Antarctic Circle.

fri·jol (frē′hōl) *also*, **fri·jo·le** (frē hō′lē). *n., pl.* **fri·joles** (frē′hōlz, frē hō′lēz). any of various beans used for food, especially in the southwestern United States, Mexico, and Central and South American countries. [From the Spanish word *frijol* meaning ''kidney bean,'' going back to the Greek word *phasēlos,* a kind of bean.]

frill (fril) *n.* **1.** an ornamental trimming consisting of a strip of material, such as lace, gathered and attached along one edge and left free along the other; ruffle. **2.** *also*, **frills.** anything showy or unnecessary: *a plain meal with no frills.* —**frill′y,** *adj.*

fringe (frinj) *n.* **1.** a border or trimming consisting of hanging threads, cords, tassels, or the like. **2.** anything like such a border or trimming: *A fringe of bushes lined the driveway.* **3.** an outer edge; border; margin: *the fringe of a city.* —*v.t.,* **fringed, fring·ing. 1.** to provide with a fringe. **2.** to serve as a fringe for: *Flowers fringed the path to the house.*

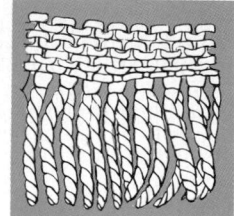

fringe (n., def. 1)

fringe benefit, any benefit received by an employee in addition to wages or salary, such as pensions, health insurance, sick leave, or paid vacations.

frip·per·y (frip′ə rē) *n., pl.* **frip·per·ies. 1.** cheap, showy clothes or ornaments. **2.** showiness or pretense.

Fris·bee (friz′bē) *n. Trademark.* a plastic disk that is designed to be tossed back and forth through the air.

Fri·sian (frizh′ən, frē′zhən) *adj.* of or relating to Friesland, its people, their language, or their culture. —*n.* **1.** a person who was born in or is a citizen of Friesland. **2.** the Germanic language of Friesland.

frisk (frisk) *v.i.* to leap, skip, or move about playfully: *The kittens frisked in the yard.* —*v.t. Informal.* to search (someone), especially for concealed weapons, by running the hand quickly over the pockets and clothing.

frisk·y (fris′kē) *adj.,* **frisk·i·er, frisk·i·est.** playful; lively. —**frisk′i·ly,** *adv.* —**frisk′i·ness,** *n.*

frit·ter¹ (frit′ər) *v.t.* to waste little by little: *to fritter away money, to fritter away time doing nothing.* [Perhaps from the obsolete word *fitters* meaning ''small pieces, rags.''] —**frit′ter·er,** *n.*

frit·ter² (frit′ər) *n.* a small cake made of fried batter, often containing fruit, vegetables, meat, or fish: *an apple fritter, a corn fritter.* [From the Old French word *friture* with the same meaning, going back to the Latin word *frigere* ''to roast, fry.'']

fri·vol·i·ty (fri vol′i tē) *n., pl.* **fri·vol·i·ties. 1.** the quality or condition of being frivolous. **2.** a frivolous act or thing.

friv·o·lous (friv′ə ləs) *adj.* **1.** lacking seriousness or sense; silly. **2.** of little importance; trivial: *The researcher was too busy to pay attention to frivolous matters.* —**friv′o·lous·ly,** *adv.* —**friv′o·lous·ness,** *n.*

frizz (friz) *also*, **friz.** *v.,* **frizzed, friz·zing.** —*v.t.* to form into small, tight curls: *to frizz one's hair.* —*v.i.* to become frizzed: *My hair frizzes when it gets wet.* —*n., pl.* **frizz·es.** something frizzed, especially hair.

friz·zle¹ (friz′əl) *v.,* **friz·zled, friz·zling.** —*v.t.* to form into small, tight curls; frizz. —*v.i.* to become frizzled. —*n.* something frizzed, especially hair. [Of uncertain origin.]

friz·zle² (friz′əl) *v.,* **friz·zled, friz·zling.** —*v.t.* to fry (food) until crisp: *to frizzle bacon.* —*v.i.* to fry or cook with a sizzling noise. [Probably from *fry¹.*]

friz·zly (friz′lē) *adj.,* **friz·zli·er, friz·zli·est.** another word for **frizzy.**

friz·zy (friz′ē) *adj.,* **friz·zi·er, friz·zi·est.** having small, tight curls. —**friz′zi·ly,** *adv.* —**friz′zi·ness,** *n.*

fro (frō) *adv.* **to and fro.** in different directions; back and forth: *The children ran to and fro across the yard.*

frock (frok) *n.* **1.** a woman's or girl's dress. **2.** a long, loose robe, especially one worn by monks and friars.

frock coat, a man's double-breasted coat reaching to the knees, popular in the late nineteenth century.

frog (frôg, frog) *n.* **1.** any of a group of web-footed, tailless amphibians that usually live in or near water and have strong hind legs adapted for leaping. **2.** a triangular horny pad on the sole of a horse's foot. **3.** a device that permits the wheels of a railroad car to pass over the junction at intersecting tracks without difficulty. **4.** *Informal.* a slight irritation of the throat causing hoarseness. **5.** an ornamental fastening for clothing, usually made of braid that forms a loop on one side and a button on the other side. [From the Old English word *frogga* meaning this amphibian.]

frog (def. 1)

frog kick, in swimming, a kick in which both legs are drawn up with the knees pointed outward, then thrust out together to the rear and closed. It is used in the breaststroke.

frog·man (frôg′man′, frog′man′) *n., pl.* **frog·men** (frôg′men′, frog′men′). a swimmer who is specially equipped and trained for underwater work, especially for military purposes.

frol·ic (frol′ik) *v.i.,* **frol·icked, frol·ick·ing.** to move about or play with spirit or gaiety; make merry. —*n.* **1.** gay or spirited activity; romp. **2.** merriment; gaiety.

frol·ic·some (frol′ik səm) *adj.* gay and spirited; merry.

from (from, frum; *unstressed* frəm) *prep.* **1.** starting at; beginning with: *We flew from New York to Chicago. I worked from nine o'clock to five.* **2.** with a particular person, place, or thing as the source or origin: *a letter from home, light from the sun.* **3.** out of: *I took the money from my pocket.* **4.** out of the control, keeping, or possession of: *The rabbit escaped from the trap.* **5.** out of the whole of: *to subtract two from five, to cut a slice from a pizza.* **6.** at a distance of; out of contact with: *ten miles from my house.* **7.** by reason of; because of: *to act from a sense of duty, to shiver from the cold.*

frond (frond) *n.* **1.** the leaf of a fern or palm. **2.** a leaflike part of certain other plants such as seaweed.

front (frunt) *n.* **1.** the part that faces forward: *The jacket had a zipper in the front.* **2.** the first or foremost part: *The introduction is in the front of the book.* **3.** a place or position ahead of or before: *Sit in front of me.* **4.** a person's attitude or manner when facing anything: *a bold front.* **5.** a large movement uniting various groups for the achievement of a common goal: *the labor front.* **6.** land facing or lying along a street, river, or the like; frontage: *We rented a cabin on the lake front.* **7.** the line or area of fighting between two enemy forces. **8.** *Informal.* **a.** an outward appearance: *to maintain a front of wealth.* **b.** an apparently respectable person or thing used to hide unlawful dealings or activities: *The drugstore was a front for gambling activities.* **9.** the boundary between two air masses of different origin and temperatures: *a warm front.* —*adj.* at, on, or near the front: *the front door of a house, the front page of a newspaper.* —*v.t.* **1.** to face toward: *The cottage fronts the lake.* **2.** to provide with a front: *They fronted the building with red brick.* **3.** to meet face to face; defy; oppose: *to front an enemy.* —*v.i.* to have the front (toward or on a certain location); face: *The house fronts on the street.*

front·age (frun′tij) *n.* **1.** the front of a building or lot. **2.** the length of this. **3.** land between a building and a street. **4.** land facing or lying along a street, river, or the like: *ocean frontage.*

fron·tal (frun′təl) *adj.* **1.** of, on, in, or at the front: *a* *frontal attack.* **2.** of or relating to the forehead. —*n.* the bone of the front of the skull, forming the forehead. —**fron′tal·ly,** *adv.*

fron·tier (frun tîr′) *n.* **1.** the settled region of a country lying along the border of unsettled or undeveloped territory. **2.** that part of a country lying along the border of another country; border: *On my trip I crossed Canada's frontier with the United States.* **3.** also, **frontiers.** any new or unexplored area: *the frontiers of medicine.* —*adj.* of, at, or on the frontier: *a frontier town.*

fron·tiers·man (frun tîrz′mən) *n., pl.* **fron·tiers·men** (frun tîrz′mən). a person who lives on the frontier.

fron·tis·piece (frun′tis pēs′) *n.* an illustration facing the title page of a book or division of a book.

front·let (frunt′lit) *n.* **1.** a band or ornament worn on the forehead, especially a decorative headband of the Middle Ages. **2.** the forehead of an animal or bird when it is a different color from the rest of the body.

front-page (frunt′pāj′) *adj.* printed on, or important enough to be printed on, the front page of a newspaper: *a front-page story, a front-page scandal.*

front·run·ner (frunt′run′ər) *n.* the leading contestant in any competition: *the frontrunner in the race for mayor.*

frost (frôst) *n.* **1.** a deposit of minute ice crystals formed by the freezing of dew or water vapor on the surface of an exposed object or on the ground. **2.** a freezing condition of the atmosphere; severe cold: *Frost damaged the orange crop.* **3.** the act of freezing. —*v.t.* **1.** to cover with frost. **2.** to damage or destroy by frost. **3.** to cover with something like frost: *to frost glass.* **4.** to cover with frosting: *to frost a cake.*

frost·bite (frôst′bīt′) *n.* a frozen or partly frozen condition of some part of the body as a result of too much exposure to extreme cold. —*v.t.,* **frost·bit** (frost′bit′), **frost·bit·ten, frost·bit·ing.** to damage or destroy by freezing: *The mountain climber's fingers and toes were frostbitten by the cold.*

frost·ed (frôs′tid) *adj.* **1.** covered with frost: *frosted blades of grass.* **2.** covered with frosting; iced: *a frosted cake.* **3.** having a dull surface like frost: *frosted glass.*

frost·ing (frôs′ting) *n.* **1.** a mixture of sugar, a liquid, butter, flavoring, and sometimes egg whites, used to cover baked goods; icing. **2.** a dull finish like frost on glass or metal.

frost·y (frôs′tē) *adj.,* **frost·i·er, frost·i·est. 1.** producing frost; freezing: *frosty weather.* **2.** covered with frost: *frosty windows.* **3.** cold in manner or feeling: *a frosty welcome.* —**frost′i·ly,** *adv.* —**frost′i·ness,** *n.*

froth (frôth) *n.* **1.** a mass of bubbles formed in or on a liquid; foam: *the froth on a glass of soda.* **2.** something light, trivial, or worthless, as ideas or conversation. —*v.i.* to give out or form froth; foam: *The rabid dog frothed at the mouth.* —*v.t.* to cause to foam.

froth·y (frô′thē) *adj.,* **froth·i·er, froth·i·est. 1.** covered with or full of froth; foamy. **2.** light, trivial, or worthless: *a frothy speech, a frothy newspaper column.* —**froth′i·ly,** *adv.* —**froth′i·ness,** *n.*

fro·ward (frō′wərd) *adj.* not easily managed; stubborn or disobedient: *a froward child.* —**fro′ward·ly,** *adv.* —**fro′ward·ness** *n.*

frown (froun) *n.* **1.** a wrinkling of the brow, as in anger, thought, or disapproval. **2.** any expression of anger or disapproval: *The idea met with the frown of the entire committee.* —*v.i.* **1.** to wrinkle the brow, as in anger, thought, or disapproval: *The teacher frowned at me.* **2.** to look with anger or disapproval: *My parents frowned on my staying out late.* —*v.t.* to show by wrinkling the brow: *to frown annoyance.*

frowz·y (frou′zē) *adj.,* **frowz·i·er, frowz·i·est. 1.** having a dirty or messy look; unkempt: *frowzy hair.* **2.** having an unpleasant smell; musty. —**frowz′i·ly,** *adv.* —**frowz′i·ness,** *n.*

froze (frōz) the past tense of **freeze.**

fro·zen (frō′zən) *v.* the past participle of **freeze.** —*adj.* **1.** changed into ice; made hard by cold. **2.** covered or clogged with ice: *a frozen lake, frozen water pipes.* **3.** unable to move: *frozen with fear.* **4.** preserved by freezing quickly: *a frozen turkey.* **5.** damaged or destroyed by frost or extreme cold: *frozen crops.* **6.** very cold; frigid: *a frozen climate.* **7.** fixed or set at a particular amount or level: *frozen wages.* **8.** cold and unfeeling: *a frozen stare.*

fruc·tose (fruk′tōs, fruk′tōs) *n.* a simple sugar occurring naturally in fruits and honey. Also, **fruit sugar.**

fru·gal (frü′gəl) *adj.* **1.** not wasteful; economical; saving: *a frugal housekeeper.* **2.** of little cost or amount; meager; spare: *a frugal meal.* —**fru·gal·i·ty** (frü gal′i tē), *n.* —**fru′gal·ly,** *adv.*

fruit (früt) *n., pl.* **fruit** or **fruits. 1.** the part of a plant that contains the seeds. Acorns, melons, and pea pods are fruits. **2.** any plant product that can be eaten, such as an orange, apple, or pear. **3.** any useful plant product: *the fruits of the fields.* **4.** the result of an action: *Our success was the fruit of hard work.* —*v.i.* to have or bear fruit.

fruit·age (frü′tij) *n.* **1.** the state or process of producing fruit. **2.** a crop of fruit. **3.** the result of any action.

fruit·cake (früt′kāk′) *n.* a rich cake containing preserved or dried fruit, nuts, and spices, and sometimes wine or brandy.

fruit fly, a small fly, such as the drosophila, whose larvae feed chiefly on decaying fruit.

fruit·ful (früt′fəl) *adj.* **1.** producing good results; profitable: *a fruitful discussion.* **2.** bearing much fruit or many offspring: *a fruitful tree.* —**fruit′ful·ly,** *adv.* —**fruit′ful·ness,** *n.*

fru·i·tion (frü ish′ən) *n.* **1.** the accomplishment of one's efforts; fulfillment: *to bring one's ideas to fruition.* **2.** the bearing of fruit.

fruit·less (früt′lis) *adj.* **1.** having no effect or result; useless: *a fruitless effort.* **2.** bearing no fruit or offspring; barren: *a fruitless tree.* —**fruit′less·ly,** *adv.* —**fruit′less·ness,** *n.*

fruit sugar, another term for **fructose.**

fruit·y (frü′tē) *adj.,* **fruit·i·er, fruit·i·est.** of, relating to, or like fruit, as in taste or smell. —**fruit′i·ness,** *n.*

frump (frump) *n.* a dowdy, often old-fashioned person. —**frump′ish, frump′y,** *adj.*

frus·trate (frus′trāt) *v.t.,* **frus·trat·ed, frus·trat·ing. 1.** to keep from doing or achieving something; disappoint or thwart: *to be frustrated by not finding a job.* **2.** to prevent (something) from being fulfilled; defeat: *Rainy weather frustrated our plans.*

frus·tra·tion (frus trā′shən) *n.* **1.** the act of frustrating or the state of being frustrated. **2.** something that frustrates. **3.** a feeling of being frustrated.

fry¹ (frī) *v.,* **fried, fry·ing.** —*v.t.* to cook (something) in hot fat, usually over direct heat: *to fry potatoes.* —*v.i.* to cook in hot fat: *The fish fried quickly.* —*n., pl.* **fries.** a social gathering, usually outdoors, at which food is fried and eaten: *a fish fry.* [From the Old French word *frire* meaning "to cook in a frying pan with fat," from the Latin word *frigere* "to roast, fry."]

fry² (frī) *n., pl.* **fry.** a newly hatched fish. [Probably from the Anglo-Norman word *frie* meaning "spawn," from the Old French word *freier* "to rub" or "to spawn," from the Latin word *fricare* "to rub."]

---

at; āpe; fär; câre; end; mē; it; īce; pîerce; hot; ōld; sông, fôrk; oil; out; up; ūse; rüle; pull; tûrn; chin; sing; shop; thin; this; hw in white; zh in treasure. The symbol ə stands for the unstressed vowel sound heard in about, taken, pencil, lemon, and circus.

fry·er (frī′ər) *n.* **1.** a young chicken suitable for frying. **2.** a deep pan for frying food. **3.** a person or thing that fries.

frying pan, a shallow pan, used for frying food.

ft. **1.** feet; foot. **2.** fort. **3.** fortification.

fuch·sia (fū′shə) *n.* **1.** any of a large group of tropical American shrubs or small trees, bearing pink, red, or purple clusters of funnel-shaped, drooping flowers. **2.** a bright purplish pink color. —*adj.* having the color fuchsia. [From the German botanist Leonhard *Fuchs* (1501–1566).]

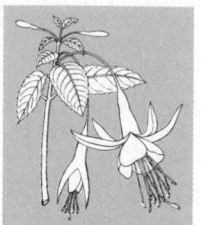
fuchsia
(n., def. 1)

fud·dle (fud′əl) *v.t.,* **fud·dled, fud·dling.** to muddle or confuse, as with liquor; befuddle.

fud·dy-dud·dy (fud′ē dud′ē) *n., pl.* **fud·dy-dud·dies.** *Informal.* **1.** a person who is old-fashioned or stuffy. **2.** a person who is fussy or overly critical about trifles.

fudge (fuj) *n.* **1.** a soft candy made of sugar, milk, butter, chocolate or other flavoring, and sometimes nuts. **2.** empty talk; nonsense; foolishness.

Fueh·rer (fyūr′ər) another spelling of **Führer.**

fu·el (fū′əl) *n.* **1.** a substance burned as a source of heat and power, such as coal, wood, or oil. **2.** something that keeps alive or increases an emotion: *Their rude words added fuel to my anger.* —*v.,* **fu·eled, fu·el·ing;** also, British, **fu·elled, fu·el·ling.** —*v.t.* to supply with fuel: *to fuel an airplane.* —*v.i.* to take in fuel.

fuel cell, a device that produces electricity by a direct chemical reaction between a fuel and an oxidizer.

fuel injection **1.** the spraying of gasoline into the intake manifold or combustion chamber of an automobile engine. **2.** the system that provides for this process. It is fitted to some motor-vehicle engines in place of a carburetor or carburetors.

fuel oil, a petroleum product burned as fuel, as to heat a building.

fu·gi·tive (fū′ji tiv) *n.* a person who flees or has fled, as from danger or pursuit: *a fugitive from the law.* —*adj.* **1.** fleeing or having fled. **2.** not lasting; fleeting: *fugitive thoughts.*

fugue (fūg) *n.* a musical composition based on one or more short themes or subjects that are repeated by different voices or instruments and developed according to the rules of counterpoint.

Füh·rer (fyūr′ər) also, **Fueh·rer.** *n. German.* **1.** a leader. **2. der Führer.** the title of Adolf Hitler as head of Nazi Germany.

–ful *suffix* **1.** full of or characterized by: *graceful, peaceful.* **2.** tending or able to: *forgetful, helpful.* **3.** having the qualities of: *manful.* **4.** the number or amount that fills or will fill: *spoonful, glassful.*

ful·crum (fùl′krəm) *n., pl.* **ful·crums** or **ful·cra** (fùl′krə). the support or point of support upon which a lever rests, or about which it turns when in use.

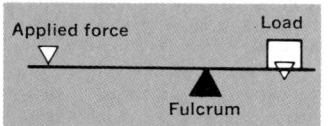
Applied force   Load
Fulcrum
fulcrum

ful·fill (fùl fil′) also, **ful·fil.** *v.t.,* **ful·filled, ful·fill·ing.** **1.** to carry out or bring to completion; cause to happen: *to fulfill a dream, to fulfill a promise.* **2.** to meet or satisfy: *to fulfill the requirements for a job.* **3.** to bring to an end (a period of time or a task); finish: *to fulfill.* **4.** to do or perform (a duty or request).

ful·fill·ment (fùl fil′mənt) also, **ful·fil·ment.** *n.* **1.** the act or process of being fulfilled. **2.** something that fulfills.

full (fùl) *adj.* **1.** containing as much or as many as possible; with no empty space: *a full glass of water.* **2.** having or containing a large number, quantity, or amount: *a house full of people. The report was full of errors.* **3.** complete, as in extent, quantity, or number; entire: *a full dozen, a full day, a full set of dishes.* **4.** having reached the greatest possible size, degree, or amount: *full strength, full speed.* **5.** filled with enough food or drink: *I am full.* **6.** having a rounded outline; well filled out; plump: *full hips, a full face.* **7.** strong, clear, and rich: *full tones, a full voice.* **8.** having loose, wide folds or much cloth: *a full skirt.* —*adv.* **1.** straight; directly: *to look someone full in the face.* **2.** to the greatest possible degree or extent; completely; entirely: *Fill the bag full.* **3.** very; exceedingly: *You know full well that I am right.* —**full′ness,** *n.*

·**in full.** **a.** to or for the entire amount: *Pay the bill in full.* **b.** without shortening or cutting: *They reprinted the document in full.*

·**to the full.** completely; entirely: *My grandparents enjoy life to the full.*

full·back (fùl′bak′) *n. Football.* a player on the offensive team who usually lines up farthest behind the front line.

full blast, with full power or resources; at maximum capacity, power, or speed: *a factory operating at full blast, a stereo playing full blast.*

full-blood·ed (fùl′blud′id) *adj.* **1.** of unmixed race, breed, or ancestry. **2.** full of energy or vigor; hearty.

full-blown (fùl′blōn′) *adj.* **1.** (of flowers) in full bloom: *a full-blown rose.* **2.** fully developed or perfected.

full dress, formal attire, as worn for ceremonial occasions.

full-fledged (fùl′flejd′) *adj.* **1.** having full rank or status: *a full-fledged citizen.* **2.** fully developed or mature: *a full-fledged bird.*

full gainer, a dive in which the diver jumps from the diving board while facing forward, does a full backward somersault, and lands in the water feet first and facing away from the board.

full-grown (fùl′grōn′) *adj.* having reached full size or maturity; fully grown: *a full-grown horse.*

full-length (fùl′lengkth′, fùl′length′) *adj.* **1.** showing or covering the whole length of an object or figure: *a full-length mirror, a full-length dress.* **2.** not shortened or cut: *a full-length film.*

full moon **1.** the moon when the whole of its face is seen illuminated. **2.** the time of month when this occurs.

full-rigged (fùl′rigd′) *adj.* (of a ship) having complete rigging for three or more masts and a full set of sails.

full-scale (fùl′skāl′) *adj.* **1.** of the same size as the original; of actual size: *a full-scale drawing.* **2.** not limited; complete: *a full-scale war.*

full-serv·ice (fùl′sûr′vis) *adj.* providing a variety of services: *a full-service bank, a full-service gas station.*

full-time (fùl′tīm′) *adj.* for or during the normal or usual hours of working time: *a full-time employee, a full-time schedule.* —*adv.* on a full-time basis: *to work full-time as a typist.*

ful·ly (fùl′ē) *adv.* **1.** to the fullest extent or degree; completely; entirely: *to be fully aware of the facts.* **2.** at least; not less than: *You are fully two hours late.*

ful·mi·nate (fùl′mə nāt′) *v.,* **ful·mi·nat·ed, ful·mi·nat·ing.** —*v.i.* **1.** to make loud and violent threats, protests, or denunciations: *The speaker fulminated against the increase in crime.* **2.** to explode with sudden violence. —*v.t.* **1.** to shout or issue with loud threats, protests, or denunciations. **2.** to cause (something) to explode with sudden violence. —*n.* any of several explosive substances used as detonators. —**ful′mi·na′tion,** *n.*

ful·some (fùl′səm) *adj.* so much as to be offensive to good taste: *fulsome praise.* —**ful′some·ly,** *adv.* —**ful′some·ness,** *n.*

fum·ble (fum′bəl) *v.,* **fum·bled, fum·bling.** —*v.i.* **1.** to search or grope about clumsily: *to fumble in the dark looking for the door.* **2.** to make an awkward or clumsy attempt: *I fumbled at opening the lock.* **3.** to handle or finger something clumsily or aimlessly: *to fumble nervously with a ring.* **4.** in sports, to lose hold of a ball. —*v.t.* **1.** to handle or deal with awkwardly: *to fumble one's chance.* **2.** in sports, to lose hold of (a ball). —*n.* **1.** the act of fumbling. **2.** a ball that is fumbled. —**fum′bler,** *n.*

fume (fūm) *n.* **1.** *also,* **fumes.** a smoke, gas, or vapor, especially when irritating or offensive: *the fumes of a car's exhaust.* **2.** a strongly penetrating odor: *fumes from the dump.* —*v.,* **fumed, fum·ing.** —*v.i.* **1.** to give off fumes. **2.** to be filled with or express anger or irritation: *I fumed as I waited in the heavy traffic.* —*v.t.* to expose to or treat with fumes.

fu·mi·gant (fū′mi gənt) *n.* a substance used in fumigating.

fu·mi·gate (fū′mi gāt′) *v.t.,* **fu·mi·gat·ed, fu·mi·gat·ing.** to expose to fumes, especially so as to disinfect: *They fumigated the room to kill the cockroaches.* —**fu′mi·ga′tion,** *n.* —**fu′mi·ga′tor,** *n.*

fun (fun) *n.* **1.** amusement or enjoyment; diversion; recreation: *The children had fun riding their sleds.* **2.** playfulness or gaiety: *full of fun.*
  •**for fun** or **in fun.** not seriously; in jest; playfully.
  •**to make fun of** or **to poke fun at.** to laugh at; ridicule.

func·tion (fungk′shən) *n.* **1.** the proper or natural action or use of anything; purpose: *The function of the kidneys is to filter wastes from the body.* **2.** a special duty or action required of a person: *What is your function on the committee?* **3.** a formal social gathering or official ceremony. **4.** *Mathematics.* **a.** a quantity whose value depends on the value of another quantity. **b.** the relationship between two sets in which at least one element of the second set is paired with one element of the first set. —*v.i.* **1.** to work; act: *The motor functions best when it is kept well oiled.* **2.** to perform the role of something else; serve: *The box functioned as a table.*

func·tion·al (fungk′shə nəl) *adj.* **1.** of or relating to a function or functions: *functional problems, a functional disorder of the stomach.* **2.** having a function: *Is this part functional or merely decorative?* **3.** designed, made, or adapted so that the use is easy: *a functional kitchen.* **4.** *Mathematics.* relating to or designating a function. —**func′tion·al·ly,** *adv.*

func·tion·ar·y (fungk′shə ner′ē) *n., pl.* **func·tion·ar·ies.** a public official: *The mayor is an important functionary.*

function word, a word used to express grammatical relationship in a sentence or phrase, such as a conjunction, preposition, or auxiliary verb.

You can divide all the words of our language into two basic types: **function words** and **content words.** The primary importance of content words lies in their meaning. These include nouns, such as *dog, chair,* and *friendship;* verbs, such as *run, sleep,* and *seem;* adjectives, such as *strong, happy,* and *cold;* and adverbs, such as *busily, very,* and *away.* Content words often change their form: nouns are marked with an *-s* in the plural, verbs are marked with *-ed* in the past tense, and most adjectives are marked with *-er* in their comparative form.

The importance of function words, on the other hand, does not lie in their meaning as vocabulary, but in their use or function in a phrase or sentence. For this reason, you might find it difficult to define function words, although you can easily observe how they affect the meaning of the content words they are used with. Func-

tion words include the articles *the, a,* and *an;* prepositions, such as *of, by, with,* and *for;* and conjunctions, such as *and, but, or, since, after,* and *until.* Some adverbs are also function words, such as *then, nevertheless,* and *therefore.* Unlike content words, which represent things, ideas, or actions, function words have little or no meaning in themselves. Instead, they indicate relationships between content words in phrases or sentences.

The number of function words in English is relatively small, and they do not change their form as content words do. While there are hundreds of thousands of content words in English, with more being added all the time, there has been almost no change in the group of function words for hundreds of years. Nevertheless, as the building blocks of our language, function words are the most commonly used words in English.

func·tor (fungk′tər) *n.* another term for **function word.**

fund (fund) *n.* **1.** a sum of money set aside for a specific purpose: *a fund for a political campaign.* **2.** a stock or supply: *This book has a fund of information on railroads.* **3. funds.** money that is readily available: *What funds do you have to finance the business?* —*v.t.* to provide a fund or money for: *to fund an organization.*

fun·da·men·tal (fun′də men′təl) *adj.* relating to or serving as a foundation; basic; essential: *Rules are fundamental to any game.* —*n.* **1.** anything that forms or serves as the basis of a system, principle, rule, or law: *the fundamentals of arithmetic.* **2.** *Physics.* the component of a wave that has the lowest frequency. —**fun′da·men′tal·ly,** *adv.*

fun·da·men·tal·ism (fun′də men′tə liz′əm) *also,* **Fun·da·men·tal·ism.** *n.* **1.** a movement in American Protestantism characterized by a belief in the historical accuracy of the Bible. **2.** the beliefs of people in this movement. —**tun′da·men′tal·ist,** *n., adj.*

fund·rais·ing (fund′rā′zing) *n.* the act of raising money to support an organization or activity, such as a charity or political campaign.

fu·ner·al (fū′nər əl) *n.* **1.** the burial or cremation of the body of a dead person, together with religious services or other accompanying ceremonies. **2.** the procession accompanying the body of a dead person to the place of burial or cremation. —*adj.* of or suitable for a funeral: *a funeral oration.*

funeral home, a business establishment with rooms for preparing the dead for burial or cremation and often a chapel for funeral services. Also, **funeral parlor.**

fu·ne·re·al (fū nîr′ē əl) *adj.* **1.** of, relating to, or suitable for a funeral. **2.** sad; gloomy; dismal: *a funereal atmosphere.* —**fu·ne′re·al·ly,** *adv.*

fun·gal (fung′gəl) *adj.* of, relating to, or caused by fungus: *a fungal disease.* Also, **fungous.**

fun·gi (fun′jī) a plural of **fungus.**

fun·gi·cide (fun′jə sīd′) *n.* any substance that kills fungi.

fun·gous (fung′gəs) *adj.* another word for **fungal.**

fun·gus (fung′gəs) *n., pl.* **fun·gi** or **fun·gus·es.** **1.** any of a kingdom of living things that lack flowers, leaves, or chlorophyll and live on plant or animal matter. Mildews, mushrooms, and molds are fungi. **2.** a diseased, spongy growth on the body.

at; āpe; fär; câre; end; mē; it; īce; pîerce; hot; ōld; sông, fôrk; oil; out; up; ūse; rüle; pùll; tûrn; chin; sing; shop; thin; this; hw in white; zh in treasure. The symbol ə stands for the unstressed vowel sound heard in about, taken, pencil, lemon, and circus.

fu·nic·u·lar (fū nik′yə lər) *n.* a railway system in which two cars attached to both ends of a cable move alternately up and down a steep slope by counterbalancing and pulling each other.

funk (fungk) *n. Informal.* **1.** a state of fear or panic. **2.** a state of depression or moodiness.

funk·y¹ (fung′kē) *adj.,* **funk·i·er, funk·i·est.** *Informal.* in a state of funk; fearful; panicky. [Probably of Low German origin.]

funk·y² (fung′kē) *adj.,* **funk·i·er, funk·i·est. 1.** having the deeply felt, emotional quality of the blues: *funky music.* **2.** *Slang.* unconventional, offbeat, or odd: *funky clothes.* [Of uncertain origin.]

fun·nel (fun′əl) *n.* **1.** a utensil with a tube at one end and a wide, cone-shaped mouth at the other, used for pouring a substance into a container with a small opening. **2.** a round chimney or smokestack, as on a steamship or locomotive. **3.** something shaped like a funnel: *the funnel of a tornado.* —*v.,* **fun·neled, fun·nel·ing;** *also, British,* **fun·nelled, fun·nel·ling.** —*v.t.* to cause (something) to pass through a funnel: *to funnel water into a jar.* —*v.i.* to pass through or as through a funnel: *The water funneled down the drainpipe.*

funnel
(n., def. 1)

fun·nies (fun′ēz) *pl. n.* **1.** comic strips. **2.** the section of a newspaper containing them.

fun·ny (fun′ē) *adj.,* **fun·ni·er, fun·ni·est. 1.** causing laughter or amusement; comical: *a funny joke.* **2.** *Informal.* strange or suspicious; odd: *You gave me a funny look. There's something funny going on.* —**fun′ni·ly,** *adv.* —**fun′ni·ness,** *n.*

funny bone, a part of the elbow where a nerve passes very close to the skin. When it is struck, a sharp, tingling sensation is felt in the arm and hand. Also, **crazy bone.**

funny papers, another term for **funnies.**

fur (fûr) *n.* **1.** the soft, thick, hairy coat of certain animals. **2.** a piece of animal skin with such a coat, prepared for use in clothing, rugs, and other items. **3.** an article of clothing, as a coat, made of such skin. **4.** a coating of fuzzy foul matter, as on the tongue of a sick person. —*v.,* **furred, fur·ring.** —*v.t.* **1.** to cover, trim, or line with fur. **2.** to coat with a fuzzy deposit of foul matter. —*v.i.* to become coated with a fuzzy deposit of foul matter. —**fur′less,** *adj.* —**fur′like′,** *adj.*

fur·be·low (fûr′bə lō′) *n.* **1.** a frill, ruffle, or similar trimming on clothing. **2.** *also,* **furbelows.** any showy or useless trimming. —*v.t.* to furnish or trim with furbelows.

fur·bish (fûr′bish) *v.t.* **1.** to make bright by rubbing; polish; burnish: *We furbished the silver mug.* **2.** to restore to a fresh or usable condition; renovate: *to furbish an old chair.* —**fur′bish·er,** *n.* —**fur′bish·ment,** *n.*

Fu·ries (fyŏŏr′ēz) *n. Greek and Roman Mythology.* three hideous female spirits who punished wrongdoers.

fu·ri·ous (fyŏŏr′ē əs) *adj.* **1.** extremely angry; full of rage: *to be furious at an insulting remark.* **2.** extremely violent or intense: *furious thunderstorms.* **3.** very great, as of activity, speed, or energy: *The car raced at a furious speed.* —**fu′ri·ous·ly,** *adv.* —**fu′ri·ous·ness,** *n.*

furl (fûrl) *v.t.* to roll up and fasten, as to a staff or mast: *to furl a sail.* —*v.i.* to become furled. —*n.* **1.** the act of furling or the state of being furled. **2.** a rolled-up section, as of a flag.

fur·long (fûr′lông) *n.* a measure of distance equal to one eighth of a mile, or 220 yards (201.2 meters).

fur·lough (fûr′lō) *n.* an official leave of absence from duty, especially in the armed services. —*v.t.* to give a furlough to.

fur·nace (fûr′nis) *n.* a structure or apparatus containing an enclosed chamber in which intense heat is produced, as for heating buildings or melting metals.

fur·nish (fûr′nish) *v.t.* **1.** to equip with furniture, fix-

tures, or appliances: *The family furnished their new home.* **2.** to supply with whatever is necessary or wanted; provide: *to furnish with facts.* —**fur′nish·er,** *n.*

fur·nish·ings (fûr′ni shingz) *pl. n.* **1.** furniture, fixtures, or appliances, as for a house or office. **2.** articles of clothing and accessories.

fur·ni·ture (fûr′ni chər) *n.* movable articles, such as tables, chairs, or beds, used to equip a room for use.

fu·ror (fyŏŏr′ôr) *n.* **1.** a great outburst of enthusiasm or excitement; commotion: *There was a furor at the bank when the theft was discovered.* **2.** frenzy or rage.

fur·ri·er (fûr′ē ər) *n.* a person who deals in or works with furs.

fur·row (fûr′ō, fur′ō) *n.* **1.** a long, narrow groove or channel made in the ground by a plow. **2.** any long, narrow groove or channel, as a rut: *furrows in a dirt road.* **3.** something like a groove or channel: *furrows in one's forehead.* —*v.t.* **1.** to make a furrow or furrows in, as with a plow. **2.** to make deep wrinkles in: *Age had furrowed their faces.*

fur·ry (fûr′ē) *adj.,* **fur·ri·er, fur·ri·est. 1.** made of or like fur: *a furry rug.* **2.** covered with fur. —**fur′ri·ness,** *n.*

fur·ther (fûr′thər) *adj.* a comparative of **far. 1.** additional; more: *without further delay, further discussion.* **2.** more distant in time, space, or degree; farther. —*adv.* a comparative of **far. 1.** at or to a more distant point in time or space; farther. **2.** to a greater degree or extent; more: *to inquire further into a problem.* **3.** in addition; moreover. —*v.t.* to help forward; promote or support: *to further the cause of peace.* ▲ See **farther** for usage note.

fur·ther·ance (fûr′thər əns) *n.* the act of furthering; advancement; promotion.

fur·ther·more (fûr′thər môr′) *adv.* in addition; moreover; besides.

fur·ther·most (fûr′thər mōst′) *adj.* most distant; furthest.

fur·thest (fûr′thist) *adv.* a superlative of **far. 1.** at or to the most distant point in time or space: *My throw went furthest of all.* **2.** to the greatest degree or extent; most. —*adj.* a superlative of **far.** most distant in time, space, or degree.

fur·tive (fûr′tiv) *adj.* **1.** done by stealth; secret: *a furtive glance.* **2.** shifty; sly: *furtive eyes, a furtive thief.* —**fur′tive·ly,** *adv.* —**fur′tive·ness,** *n.*

fu·ry (fyŏŏr′ē) *n., pl.* **fu·ries. 1.** violent, uncontrollable anger. **2.** a fit of such anger: *to be in a fury because of an insult.* **3.** violence; fierceness: *the fury of a storm.* **4.** a person having a violent or uncontrollable temper. **5. Fury.** one of the Furies.

furze (fûrz) *n.* another word for **gorse.**

fuse¹ (fūz) *also,* **fuze.** *n.* **1.** a strip of metal inserted in an electric circuit. It melts and breaks the circuit if the current becomes too strong. **2.** a length of cord or tubing filled or soaked with material that will burn, used to set off an explosive charge: *the fuse on a stick of dynamite.* **3.** see **fuze.** [From the Italian word *fuso* meaning "spindle, shaft," from the Latin word *fusus* "spindle."]

fuse² (fūz) *v.,* **fused, fus·ing.** —*v.t.* **1.** to melt (something), especially by heating. **2.** to blend or unite by melting together: *to fuse metals.* —*v.i.* **1.** to melt, especially by heating. **2.** to be or become united by melting together: *The two committees fused into one.* [From the Latin word *fusus,* past participle of *fundere* meaning "to melt, cast (metal); pour out."]

fu·see (fū zē′) *n.* **1.** a match with a large head that will burn in a wind. **2.** a red or green flare used as a railroad signal.

fu·se·lage (fū′sə läzh′, fū′sə lij) *n.* the main body of an airplane, carrying the passengers, cargo, and crew.

fu·si·ble (fū′zə bəl) *adj.* capable of being fused or melted: *a fusible metal.* —**fu′si·bil′i·ty,** *n.*

fu·sil·ier (fū′zə lîr′) *also,* **fu·sil·eer.** *n.* **1.** a soldier of any of several historic regiments of the British army. **2.** formerly, a soldier armed with a light flintlock musket.

fu·sil·lade (fū′sə lād′) *n.*   **1.** the discharge or firing of firearms at the same time or continuously.   **2.** anything like this: *a fusillade of criticism.*

fu·sion (fū′zhən) *n.*   **1.** the act or process of fusing; melting together: *the fusion of metals.*   **2.** the state of being fused: *metals in fusion.*   **3.** the union or blending together of different things, as of political parties.   **4.** something formed by fusing; fused mass.   **5.** a popular music that combines two or more styles, especially a combination of jazz and another style.   **6.** *Physics.* the combining of two light nuclei to form a heavier nucleus. Fusion occurs when the light nuclei are heated to extremely high temperatures, releasing huge amounts of energy, as in the explosion of a hydrogen bomb.

fusion bomb, another term for **hydrogen bomb.**

fuss (fus) *n., pl.* **fuss·es.**   **1.** unnecessary stir or bother over small or unimportant things: *There was a great fuss when the schedule was changed.*   **2.** a slight quarrel or dispute; spat: *The children had a fuss over the game's rules.*   **3.** a protest or complaint: *The passengers will make a fuss if the train is late.* —*v.i.*   **1.** to make an unnecessary stir: *You are fussing over unimportant details.*   **2.** to have a slight quarrel or dispute.   —**fuss′er,** *n.*

fuss·y (fus′ē) *adj.,* **fuss·i·er, fuss·i·est.**   **1.** hard to please; finicky: *They are fussy about food.*   **2.** requiring much attention to details: *I had a fussy job to do.*   **3.** elaborately made or trimmed: *a fussy dress.*   —**fuss′i·ly,** *adv.* —**fuss′i·ness,** *n.*

fust·y (fus′tē) *adj.,* **fust·i·er, fust·i·est.**   **1.** having a stale smell; musty; moldy: *a fusty old trunk.*   **2.** old-fashioned in appearance or behavior; not up-to-date.   —**fust′i·ly,** *adv.* —**fust′i·ness,** *n.*

fu·tile (fū′təl) *adj.*   **1.** useless or hopeless; ineffective; vain: *The workers and the owners of the factory made futile efforts to settle the strike.*   **2.** not important; trivial.   —**fu′tile·ly,** *adv.*

fu·til·i·ty (fū til′i tē) *n., pl.* **fu·til·i·ties.**   **1.** the quality of being futile.   **2.** something that is futile.

fu·ton (fū′ton) *n.*   a Japanese bed quilt or mattress, traditionally placed on the floor for sleeping. It can also be used on a wooden frame. [From the Japanese word *futon.*]

fu·ture (fū′chər) *adj.*   **1.** that is to be or happen in time to come: *I hope your future work will be better.*   **2.** *Grammar.* indicating a state or action in time to come. —*n.*   **1.** time that is to come: *In the future, please call if you are going to be late.*   **2.** something that will be or happen in time to come: *No one can predict the future with certainty.*   **3.** the opportunity of success or prosperity in time to come: *You have a good future in business.*   **4.** *Grammar.* the future tense or a verb in this tense.

future perfect   **1.** a verb tense expressing an action or state of being that is completed before a specified time in the future. It is formed in English with "will have" or "shall have." In the sentence *I will have finished the job by tomorrow, will have finished* is in the future perfect tense.   **2.** a verb form in this tense.

future tense   **1.** a verb tense expressing an action or state happening or existing in time to come. In the sentence *They will come tomorrow, will come* is in the future tense.   **2.** a verb form in this tense.

fu·tur·is·tic (fū′chə ris′tik) *adj.*   of or relating to the future; predicted for the future: *futuristic devices; futuristic writings.*   —**fu′tur·is′ti·cal·ly,** *adv.*

fu·tu·ri·ty (fū tûr′i tē, fū tyûr′i tē) *n., pl.* **fu·tu·ri·ties.**   **1.** the future.   **2.** the state or quality of being future.   **3.** a future event.

fuze (fūz) *also,* **fuse.** *n.*   **1.** a device used to detonate a bomb or torpedo.   **2.** see **fuse**[1].

fuzz (fuz) *n.*   fine particles, hairs, or fibers: *peach fuzz.*

fuzz·y (fuz′ē) *adj.,* **fuzz·i·er, fuzz·i·est.**   **1.** having or covered with fuzz.   **2.** resembling fuzz.   **3.** not clear; indistinct; blurred: *fuzzy thinking.*   —**fuzz′i·ly,** *adv.* —**fuzz′i·ness,** *n.*

-fy *suffix* (used to form verbs)   **1.** to cause to be or become; make: *simplify, pacify.*   **2.** to become: *solidify.*   **3.** to make similar to: *countrify.*

---

at; āpe; fär; câre; end; mē; it; īce; pîerce; hot; ōld; sông, fôrk; oil; out; up; ūse; rüle; pull; tûrn; chin; sing; shop; thin; **th**is; hw in white; zh in treasure. The symbol ə stands for the unstressed vowel sound heard in about, taken, pencil, lemon, and circus.

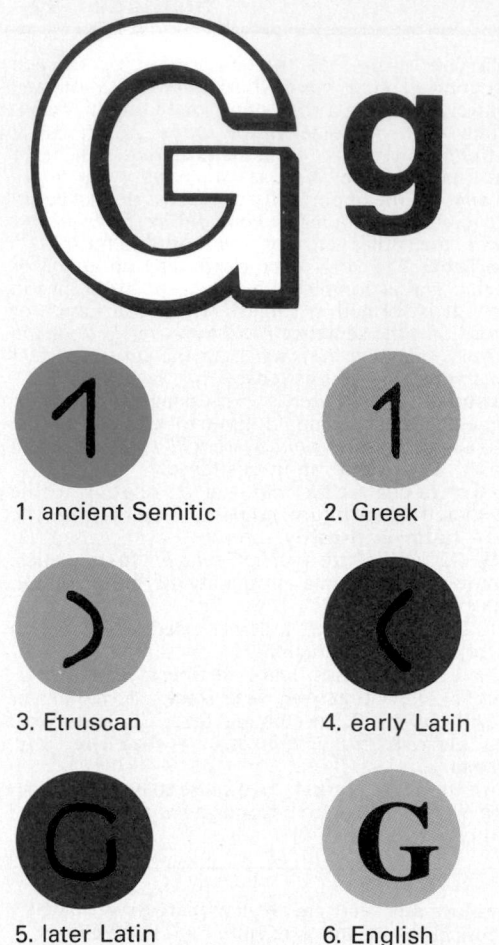

1. ancient Semitic
2. Greek
3. Etruscan
4. early Latin
5. later Latin
6. English

G is the seventh letter of the English alphabet. Although the modern letter **G** was developed from the Latin letter **C**, it has its roots in the earliest alphabets. The oldest form of **G** was *gimel* (1), the third letter of the ancient Semitic alphabets. *Gimel* was passed down, with only slight changes, through various alphabets and adopted by the Greeks, who called it *gamma* (2). Both *gimel* and *gamma* represented a hard *g* sound, as the *g* in the English word *game*. The Etruscans (3) borrowed *gamma* and, because they made no distinction between a hard *g* and a *k*, used it to represent both sounds. When the Romans adopted the Etruscan alphabet for their own language, Latin, they also used a form of *gamma* to stand for both the hard *g* and *k* sounds. Since in Latin the *k* sound was more common than the hard *g* sound, the Latin letter **C** (4) eventually came to be used only for the *k* sound. About 2,300 years ago, the Romans devised a new letter (5) to represent the hard *g* sound. This letter, which was made by adding a short line to the letter **C**, was written almost exactly as we write a capital **G** today (6).

g, G (jē) *n.*, *pl.* **g's, G's.** **1.** the seventh letter of the English alphabet. **2.** *Music.* the fifth note of the scale of C major. **3.** the unit of measurement of the force acting on bodies undergoing acceleration. It is equal to the force of gravity at sea level.

g. 1. gauge. **2.** gram; grams.

G. 1. Gulf. **2.** specific gravity.

Ga, the symbol for gallium.

Ga., Georgia.

GA, postal abbreviation for Georgia.

G.A., General Assembly.

gab (gab) *v.i.*, **gabbed, gab·bing.** *Informal.* to talk idly or too much; chatter: *I gabbed on the phone for hours.* —*n.* idle or excessive talk; chatter. —**gab'ber,** *n.*

gab·ar·dine (gab'ər dēn') *n.* **1.** a strong, closely woven fabric having diagonal ribs on its surface. It is used for coats, slacks, and other garments. **2.** another spelling of **gaberdine** *(def. 1).*

gab·ble (gab'əl) *v.*, **gab·bled, gab·bling.** —*v.i.* to talk rapidly or foolishly without making sense; jabber. —*v.t.* to say (something) rapidly or foolishly without making sense: *Embarrassed, I gabbled an excuse for arriving late.* —*n.* rapid, foolish, or meaningless talk. —**gab'bler,** *n.*

gab·by (gab'ē) *adj.*, **gab·bi·er, gab·bi·est.** *Informal.* very talkative.

gab·er·dine (gab'ər dēn') *n.* **1.** a loose cloak or smock worn by men in the Middle Ages. **2.** another spelling of **gabardine** *(def. 1).*

ga·ble (gā'bəl) *n.* **1.** the section of an outside wall surface, usually triangular, between the sides of a sloped roof. **2.** any architectural feature having the form of a gable, as over a door or window.

ga·bled (gā'bəld) *adj.* having or built with a gable or gables.

gable roof, a ridged roof that forms a gable at each end.

Ga·bri·el (gā'brē əl) *n.* in the Bible, the archangel chosen by God as a messenger.

gad (gad) *v.t.*, **gad·ded, gad·ding.** to move about restlessly or

gables

aimlessly, as in search of fun or excitement; roam.

gad·a·bout (gad'ə bout') *n.* *Informal.* a person who moves about restlessly or aimlessly, especially in search of fun or excitement.

gad·fly (gad'flī') *n.*, *pl.* **gad·flies. 1.** a large blood-sucking fly that bites animals, especially horses and cattle. **2.** a person who constantly annoys, irritates, or stirs up others.

gad·get (gaj'it) *n.* *Informal.* a small mechanical device.

gad·o·lin·i·um (gad'ə lin'ē əm) *n.* a metallic element of the rare-earth group. It is used in nuclear reactors. Symbol: **Gd** [From the Finnish chemist Johann *Gadolin* (1760–1852).]

Gae·a (jē'ə) *also,* **Gai·a.** *n.* *Greek Mythology.* the earth goddess who was the mother and wife of Uranus and mother of the Cyclopes and Titans.

Gael (gāl) *n.* **1.** see **Highlander** *(def. 2a).* **2.** a Celt of Scotland, Ireland, or the Isle of Man.

Gael·ic (gā'lik) *adj.* of or relating to the Gaels or their languages. —*n.* any of the Celtic languages of the Gaels, especially those traditionally spoken in Ireland and Scotland.

gaff (gaf) *n.* **1.** a large, sharp hook at the end of a pole, used to help pull large fish out of the water. **2.** a spar for extending the upper edge of a fore-and-aft sail. —*v.t.* to hook or land (a fish) with a gaff.

gaf·fer (gaf′ər) *n.* **1.** an old man. **2.** an electrician who is responsible for the lighting of a motion-picture or television set.

gag (gag) *n.* **1.** something stuffed into or put over the mouth to prevent a person from talking or crying out. **2.** anything used to restrain or suppress freedom of speech. **3.** *Slang.* an amusing act or remark; joke. —*v.,* **gagged, gag·ging.** —*v.t.* **1.** to prevent from speaking or crying out by means of a gag: *The kidnapers gagged their captives.* **2.** to restrain or suppress freedom of speech; silence: *The government gagged the revolutionary newspaper.* **3.** to cause to choke, retch, or vomit. —*v.i.* to choke, retch, or vomit: *I gagged when I swallowed the medicine.*

gage¹ (gāj) *n.* something given as security that an obligation or promise will be fulfilled; pledge. [From the Old French word *gage* meaning "a pledge," of Germanic origin.]

gage² (gāj) another spelling of **gauge.**

gag·gle (gag′əl) *n.* **1.** a flock of geese. **2.** a group; cluster: *A gaggle of photographers waited for the rock stars to arrive.*

Gai·a (jē′ə) another spelling of **Gaea.**

gai·e·ty (gā′i tē) *also,* **gay·e·ty.** *n., pl.* **gai·e·ties. 1.** the state or quality of being gay; cheerfulness. **2.** merrymaking; festivity: *the gaieties of the holiday season.* **3.** brightness or showiness, as of appearance or dress.

gai·ly (gā′lē) *also,* **gay·ly.** *adv.* in a gay manner.

gain (gān) *v.t.* **1.** to get by effort; obtain; secure: *to gain the advantage in an argument.* **2.** to get or develop as an increase, addition, advantage, or profit: *to gain weight, to gain strength.* **3.** to get in competition or combat; win: *to gain a battle, to gain a victory.* **4.** to get to; arrive at; reach: *to gain port before a storm.* —*v.i.* **1.** to improve, progress, or advance: *to gain in health.* **2.** to advance nearer, as to an opponent in a race; come closer: *The black horse is gaining on the brown one.* —*n.* **1.** something that is gained: *The halfback made a gain of ten yards on that last play.* **2. gains.** something acquired as profits, earnings, or winnings. **3.** the act of gaining; acquisition.

gain·er (gā′nər) *n.* **1.** a person or thing that gains. **2.** see **full gainer.**

gain·ful (gān′fəl) *adj.* bringing or producing gain; profitable. —**gain′ful·ly,** *adv.*

gain·say (gān′sā′) *v.t.,* **gain·said** (gān′sād′, gān′sed′), **gain·say·ing.** to deny, contradict, or oppose: *Do not gainsay the facts.*

gainst (genst) *also,* **'gainst.** *prep. Archaic.* against.

gait (gāt) *n.* **1.** a particular manner of moving on foot: *to walk with a slow gait.* **2.** any of the particular ways in which a horse steps or runs, as a trot or a gallop.

gai·ter (gā′tər) *n.* **1.** a covering made of cloth or leather for the ankle, and sometimes the lower leg, worn over the top of a shoe. **2.** a shoe with elastic inserts on the sides. **3.** an overshoe with a cloth top.

gal (gal) *n. Informal.* a girl or woman.

gal., gallon; gallons.

ga·la (gā′lə, gal′ə) *adj.* of, relating to, or suitable for a festive occasion; festive: *a birthday marked with a gala celebration.* —*n.* a festive occasion or celebration.

ga·lac·tic (gə lak′tik) *adj.* of or relating to a galaxy or galaxies, especially the Milky Way.

Gal·a·had (gal′ə had′) in the legends of King Arthur, the purest and most virtuous knight of the Round Table. According to one story, he was the only knight to find the Holy Grail.

Gal·a·te·a (gal′ə tē′ə) *n. Greek Legend.* the statue of a maiden sculpted by Pygmalion, who then fell in love with it. Aphrodite brought the statue to life in answer to Pygmalion's prayers.

Ga·la·tians (gə lā′shənz) *n.* a book of the New Testament, an epistle written by the Apostle Paul.

gal·ax·y (gal′ək sē) *n., pl.* **gal·ax·ies. 1.** any of the vast groupings of stars, dust, and gases scattered throughout the universe. **2.** *also,* **Galaxy.** the Milky Way. **3.** a brilliant or splendid group: *a galaxy of celebrities.*

gale (gāl) *n.* **1.** a very strong wind, especially one having a velocity of from 32 to 63 miles per hour (51–101 kilometers per hour). **2.** a noisy outburst, as of laughter.

ga·le·na (gə lē′nə) *n.* a gray metallic ore. It is the principal source of lead and an important source of silver.

Gal·i·le·an (gal′ə lē′ən) *adj.* of or relating to Galilee or its people. —*n.* **1.** a person who was born in or is living in Galilee. **2. the Galilean.** another name for **Jesus.**

gall¹ (gôl) *n.* **1.** see **bile** *(def. 1).* **2.** something bitter or unpleasant: *the gall of disappointment.* **3.** bitterness of feeling; hatred. **4.** *Informal.* impudence; nerve: *They had the gall to talk back to their grandparents.* [From the Old English word *gealla* meaning "bile, gall.¹"]

gall² (gôl) *v.t.* **1.** to make sore by rubbing or chafing. **2.** to annoy or irritate: *It galled me to hear my friend insulted.* —*v.i.* to become sore or chafed. —*n.* a sore spot on the skin caused by rubbing or chafing. [From the Old English word *gealla* meaning "a sore spot caused by irritation," probably from the Latin word *galla* "gallnut."]

gall³ (gôl) *n.* an abnormal growth or swelling on a plant, usually caused by insects, fungi, or bacteria. [From the Old French word *galle* with the same meaning, from the Latin word *galla* "gallnut."]

gal·lant (*adj., def. 1* gal′ənt; *adj., def. 2, n.,* gə lant′, gal′ənt) *adj.* **1.** brave or noble in spirit or conduct; heroic: *a gallant soldier.* **2.** polite and attentive to women; courtly. —*n.* **1.** a brave or noble man. **2.** a fashionable or dashing young man. **3.** a man who is particularly polite and attentive to women. —**gal′lant·ly,** *adv.*

gal·lant·ry (gal′ən trē) *n., pl.* **gal·lant·ries. 1.** bravery or nobleness of spirit or conduct; heroism: *a medal for gallantry in combat.* **2.** courtly politeness and attentiveness to women. **3.** courtly or polite action or speech: *The members of the royal court exchanged gallantries.*

gall·blad·der (gôl′blad′ər) *n.* a small, muscular sac that is attached to the liver and in which bile is stored.

gal·le·on (gal′ē ən) *n.* a large sailing ship, usually having four masts with square sails, a square stern, and three or four decks. It was used from the fifteenth to the seventeenth centuries.

gal·ler·y (gal′ə rē) *n., pl.* **gal·ler·ies. 1.** a room or building where works of art are shown or sold. **2.** a narrow platform or passage, usually roofed and open on one side, projecting from the wall of a building; balcony. **3.** a platform or floor projecting over the rear part of the main floor of a building, especially the highest of a series of such floors in a theater, usually containing the cheapest seats. **4.** the part of the audience occupying the highest gallery of a theater. **5.** a group of spectators, as at a sports event: *The gallery applauded the golfer's difficult putt.* **6.** a long, narrow corridor or passage, often open or having windows on one side. **7.** a room or building used for a particular activity, such as target shooting.

---

at; āpe; fär; câre; end; mē; it; īce; pîerce; hot; ōld;
sông, fôrk; oil; out; up; ūse; rūle; pūll; tûrn; chin;
sing; shop; thin; this; hw in white; zh in treasure.
The symbol ə stands for the unstressed vowel sound
heard in about, taken, pencil, lemon, and circus.

G

gal·ley (gal′ē) *n., pl.* **gal·leys.** **1.** a long, low ship of ancient and medieval times, propelled by sails and by a row of oars on either side or sometimes by several rows, one above the other. **2.** the kitchen of a ship or airplane. **3.** *Printing.* **a.** see **galley proof.** **b.** a long, shallow metal tray for holding type that has been set.

galley (def. 1)

galley proof *Printing.* a proof printed from type set in a galley, used especially for making corrections in the printed matter before it is made up into pages.

gall·fly (gôl′flī′) *n., pl.* **gall·flies.** any of various insects that deposit their eggs in plant tissue, causing galls to form.

Gal·lic (gal′ik) *adj.* **1.** of or relating to Gaul or its people. **2.** of or relating to France or its people; French.

gall·ing (gô′ling) *adj.* extremely annoying; irritating; exasperating: *a galling defeat.*

gal·li·um (gal′ē əm) *n.* a rare, bluish white metallic element that has a very low melting point. It is used as a semiconductor. Symbol: **Ga** [Formed from the Latin word *gallus* meaning "rooster, cock[1]," from the humorous translation into Latin of the first name of the French physicist *Lecoq* de Boisbaudran, which is French for "the rooster."]

gal·li·vant (gal′ə vant′) *v.i.* to wander about or travel in search of fun or excitement; gad.

gall·nut (gôl′nut′) *n.* a nut-shaped growth or swelling, especially on oak trees.

gal·lon (gal′ən) *n.* a unit of liquid measure. In the United States it is equal to 4 quarts, or 231 cubic inches (3.785 liters).

gal·lop (gal′əp) *n.* **1.** the fastest gait of a horse or other four-footed animal, in which all four feet are off the ground at the same time during each leaping stride. **2.** a ride or run at a gallop. —*v.i.* **1.** to ride or move at a gallop. **2.** to go or act very fast; hurry; race. —*v.t.* to cause to gallop: *to gallop a horse around a corral.* —**gal′lop·er,** *n.*

gal·lows (gal′ōz) *n., pl.* **gal·lows** or **gal·lows·es.** **1.** a framework usually consisting of upright beams supporting a crossbar from which a noose is suspended, used for hanging criminals. **2.** the punishment of death by hanging: *to be sentenced to the gallows.*

gall·stone (gôl′stōn′) *n.* a small, hard mass that sometimes forms in the gallbladder or its ducts.

ga·lore (gə lôr′) *adj.* in large or plentiful amounts: *There was entertainment galore at the circus.* ▲ The words *galore* and *aplenty* function as adjectives and appear after the noun they modify.

ga·losh (gə losh′) *n., pl.* **ga·losh·es.** a rubber overshoe reaching above the ankles, usually worn in wet or snowy weather.

gals., gallons.

gal·van·ic (gal van′ik) *adj.* of or relating to direct electric current, especially when produced by chemical action.

gal·va·nism (gal′və niz′əm) *n.* **1.** direct current electricity, especially when produced by chemical action. **2.** the use of such electricity in medicine. [From the Italian physiologist Luigi *Galvani* (1737–1798), who experimented with electricity and animals.]

gal·va·nize (gal′və nīz′) *v.t.,* **gal·va·nized, gal·va·niz·ing.** **1.** to cover (metal, especially iron or steel) with a protective coating of zinc to prevent rusting. **2.** to rouse suddenly; startle; excite: *The unexpected news galvanized us into action.* **3.** to stimulate by the application of electric current. —**gal′va·ni·za′tion,** *n.*

gal·va·nom·e·ter (gal′və nom′i tər) *n.* an instrument for detecting and measuring electric current and determining the direction of its flow.

gam·bit (gam′bit) *n.* **1.** in chess, an opening move in which a pawn or other piece is risked or sacrificed to gain some advantage. **2.** any move or maneuver designed to gain an advantage or achieve a desired result.

gam·ble (gam′bəl) *v.,* **gam·bled, gam·bling.** —*v.i.* **1.** to play games of chance, especially for money. **2.** to take a risk: *The coach gambled by using an inexperienced pitcher.* —*v.t.* **1.** to bet or wager (something of value): *I gambled a dollar at the bingo game.* **2.** to lose or squander by gambling: *to gamble away a fortune.* —*n.* **1.** any risk or uncertain undertaking. **2.** the playing of a game of chance, especially for money. —**gam′bler,** *n.*

gam·bol (gam′bəl) *v.i.,* **gam·boled, gam·bol·ing;** *also, British,* **gam·bolled, gam·bol·ling.** to run, skip, or leap about in play; frolic: *to gambol in the woods.* —*n.* running, skipping, or leaping about in play; frolic.

gam·brel roof (gam′brəl) a ridged roof having two slopes on each side, the lower slope being steeper than the upper.

game¹ (gām) *n.* **1.** a form of playing; pastime; amusement: *Hide-and-seek is a children's game.* **2.** a contest or other competitive play in which the players must follow specific rules: *the game of baseball, the game of poker.* **3.** a single match between two opposing players or teams: *Our school won yesterday's football game.* **4.** one of several parts in a fixed series or number of contests: *the first game of a set of tennis.* **5.** the score at any given point in a competition: *In the third inning the game was tied.* **6.** the materials or equipment used in playing certain games: *I bought toys and games for the birthday party.* **7.** a plan, scheme, or trick: *Some people's game is pretending to be what they aren't.* **8.** wild animals, birds, or fish, hunted or caught for sport or for food. **9.** the flesh of such animals used for food: *The chef's specialty is barbecued game.* **10.** *Informal.* a profession, activity, or undertaking: *The senator has been in the political game for twenty years.* —*adj.,* **gam·er, gam·est.** **1.** plucky and resolute: *a game football team.* **2.** *Informal.* having enough spirit or will; ready: *Are you game for a swim in the cold water?* **3.** of or relating to game: *game laws.* —*v.i.,* **gamed, gam·ing.** to play games of chance, especially for money; gamble. [From the Old English word *gamen* meaning "fun, amusement."] —**game′ly,** *adv.*

game² (gām) *adj.* lame or injured: *a game leg.* [Of uncertain origin.]

game·cock (gām′kok′) *n.* a rooster bred and trained for fighting.

game·keep·er (gām′kē′pər) *n.* a person employed to breed, protect, and care for game in a government preserve or on private lands.

game show, a television program featuring a game in which guest players compete for prizes.

game·ster (gām′stər) *n.* a person who gambles; gambler.

gam·ete (gam′ēt, gə mēt′) *n.* *Biology.* either of two mature reproductive cells such as the sperm or ovum of an animal or the pollen or ovule of a plant, capable of uniting to form a new organism.

ga·me·to·phyte (gə mē′tə fīt′) *n.* *Botany.* in the life cycle of plants, a plant or generation of plants in which sex cells, or gametes, are produced.

game warden, a public official who enforces the hunting and fishing laws in a given district.

gam·in (gam′in) *n.* a neglected or homeless child left to roam the streets; urchin.

gam·ing (gā′ming) *n.* the act or practice of playing games of chance, especially for money; gambling.

gam·ma (gam′ə) *n.* the third letter of the Greek alphabet (Γ, γ), corresponding to the English letter G, g.

gamma globulin, any of a group of proteins in blood

plasma. Most gamma globulins are antibodies that protect the body against a recurrence of certain diseases, such as measles or polio. An injection of gamma globulins is sometimes given to protect a person from such diseases as hepatitis.

gamma ray, electromagnetic radiation similar to X rays but of shorter wavelength and greater penetrating power, given off by the nuclei of radioactive atoms.

gam·ut (gam′ət) *n.* **1.** the entire range, scope, or extent of anything: *the gamut of emotions from ecstasy to despair.* **2.** the entire series of recognized notes or tones in modern music.

gam·y (gā′mē) *adj.,* **gam·i·er, gam·i·est. 1.** having the taste or smell of game, especially game that has been kept uncooked until slightly spoiled. **2.** brave; plucky; courageous. —**gam′i·ly,** *adv.* —**gam′i·ness,** *n.*

gan·der (gan′dər) *n.* **1.** an adult male goose. **2.** *Slang.* a look, especially a long look: *Take a gander at these plans.*

gang (gang) *n.* **1.** a group of people who work together for illegal or criminal purposes: *a gang of thieves.* **2.** a group of laborers working together under one foreman; crew. **3.** *Informal.* a group of people who are friends: *Our gang went to a party after the movie.* **4.** a group of youths from one neighborhood who band together, especially to fight other such groups. —*v.i. Informal.* to form a group or gang.

·**to gang up on.** *Informal.* to attack or oppose together or as a group: *We ganged up on the intruder.*

gan·gling (gang′gling) *adj.* awkwardly tall and thin.

gan·gli·on (gang′glē ən) *n., pl.* **gan·gli·a** (gang′glē ə) or **gan·gli·ons.** a group of nerve cell bodies outside the brain or spinal cord.

gang·plank (gang′plangk′) *n.* a movable bridge between a ship and a wharf, used for boarding or leaving the ship.

gan·grene (gang′grēn) *n.* the death and decay of body tissue occurring when the blood supply is cut off as a result of disease or injury. —*v.,* **gan·grened, gan·gren·ing.** —*v.t.* to cause gangrene in. —*v.i.* to become affected with gangrene. —**gan′gre·nous,** *adj.*

gang·ster (gang′stər) *n.* a member of a gang of criminals.

gang·way (*n.,* gang′wā′; *interj.,* gang′wā′) *n.* **1.** a passageway. **2.** a passageway on either side of the upper deck of a ship. **3.** an opening in the side of a ship for boarding passengers or loading freight. **4.** a gangplank. —*interj.* get out of the way; make room.

gan·net (gan′it) *n.* any of various web-footed seabirds of coastal islands and waters of most temperate regions. Gannets have long, pointed bills and mainly white feathers, and are able to fly long distances.

gant·let[1] (gônt′lit) another spelling of **gauntlet**[1].
gant·let[2] (gônt′lit) another spelling of **gauntlet**[2].

gan·try (gan′trē) *n., pl.* **gan·tries. 1.** a framework consisting of a horizontal bridge set on upright supports that may be stationary or mounted on wheels. Gantries are used especially to support movable cranes and railroad signals. **2.** see **gantry scaffold.**

gantry crane, a crane mounted on a gantry.

gantry scaffold, a movable scaffold, used to assemble and service a space rocket on its launching pad.

Gan·y·mede (gan′ə mēd′) *n. Greek Mythology.* a beautiful youth who was the favorite of Zeus and cupbearer to the Olympian gods.

gaol (jāl) *n. British.* another spelling of **jail.** —**gaol′er,** *n.*

gap (gap) *n.* **1.** a break, crack, or opening, as in a wall. **2.** a deep ravine or pass through a mountain ridge. **3.** an unfilled part or space; break in conti-

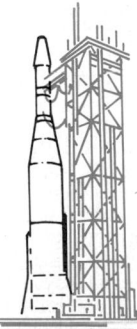

**gantry
scaffold**

nuity: *a gap of a week in the diary.* **4.** a wide difference or divergence, as of opinion, character, or ideas: *a gap between what they say and what they do.* —*v.t., v.i.,* **gapped, gap·ping.** to make or form a gap.

gape (gāp) *v.i.,* **gaped, gap·ing. 1.** to stare with the mouth open, as in wonder or surprise: *to gape at the lift-off of a spacecraft.* **2.** to open the mouth wide, as when yawning. **3.** to open or be opened wide, as a gap or hole. —*n.* **1.** the act of gaping. **2.** a large opening or space. [From the Old Norse word *gapa* meaning "to open the mouth."] —**gap′er,** *n.*

gar (gär) *n., pl.* **gars** or **gar.** any of a group of predatory freshwater fish of North and Central America that have long jaws with sharp teeth and a long, narrow body covered with bony scales.

ga·rage (gə razh′, gə räj′; *British* gar′äzh, gar′ij) *n.* a private or commercial building where motor vehicles are kept, repaired, or serviced. —*v.t.,* **ga·raged, ga·rag·ing.** to put or keep in a garage.

garage sale, a sale of used, unwanted personal or household items, usually held in a garage or yard. Also, **yard sale.**

garb (gärb) *n.* clothing or attire, especially a particular or distinctive form of dress: *military garb.* —*v.t.* to clothe; dress: *actors garbed as French courtiers.*

gar·bage (gär′bij) *n.* **1.** waste material, especially animal or vegetable matter that has been thrown away as food scraps from a kitchen. **2.** anything worthless or offensive: *The book I'm reading is garbage.*

garbage disposal, a machine that is attached to a sink and disposes of garbage by grinding it up to be carried away with the waste water.

gar·ban·zo (gär bän′zō) *n., pl.* **gar·ban·zos.** another word for **chickpea.** [From the Spanish word *garbanzo.*]

gar·ble (gär′bəl) *v.t.,* **gar·bled, gar·bling. 1.** to confuse or mix up unintentionally: *to garble a telephone message.* **2.** to make unfair or misleading selections from (facts or a text) in order to give a false impression or to distort: *The partisan newspaper garbled the candidate's speeches.* —*n.* the act of garbling. —**gar′bler,** *n.*

gar·çon (gär sôn′) *n., pl.* **gar·çons** (gär sôn′). *French.* **1.** a waiter. **2.** a young man; boy.

gar·den (gär′dən) *n.* **1.** a plot of ground where flowers, vegetables, herbs, or other plants are grown. **2.** *also,* **gar·dens.** a park or other piece of ground used by the public for recreation or amusement: *The class went to the public gardens.* —*adj.* relating to or grown in a garden: *Petunias are common garden flowers.* —*v.i.* to work in a garden: *I garden on weekends.* —*v.t.* to cultivate as a garden: *We gardened the lot behind their house.*

garden apartment 1. a ground-floor apartment rented with an adjoining garden. **2.** an apartment building, usually having landscaped grounds and only a few stories of apartments.

gar·den·er (gärd′nər) *n.* a person who cultivates or tends a garden as a job or hobby.

gar·de·nia (gär dēn′yə) *n.* **1.** a fragrant yellow or white

**gardenia
(cape jasmine)**

G

at; āpe; fär; câre; end; mē; it; īce; pîerce; hot; ōld; sông, fôrk; oil; out; up; ūse; rüle; pùll; tûrn; chin; sing; shop; thin; this; hw in white; zh in treasure. The symbol ə stands for the unstressed vowel sound heard in about, taken, pencil, lemon, and circus.

flower having waxy, dish-shaped petals. **2.** the shrub or tree bearing this flower. [From the Scottish naturalist Alexander *Garden* (1730–1791).]

Garden of Eden, in the Bible, the original home of Adam and Eve.

gar·gan·tu·an (gär gan′chü ən) *adj.* of enormous size; gigantic; huge: *a gargantuan redwood tree.* [From *Gargantua,* a giant in the satire *Gargantua and Pantagruel* by François Rabelais.]

gar·gle (gär′gəl) *v.,* **gar·gled, gar·gling.** —*v.i.* to wash or rinse the throat or mouth with a liquid kept in motion by an exhalation of the breath. —*v.t.* to use (a liquid) for gargling: *to gargle salt water.* —*n.* a liquid used for gargling.

gar·goyle (gär′goil) *n.* a waterspout, usually in the form of a grotesque human or animal figure, projecting from the gutter of a building to carry off rainwater, or as an ornament.

gargoyle

gar·ish (gâr′ish, gar′ish) *adj.* too bright or ornate; flashy; gaudy. —**gar′ish·ly,** *adv.* —**gar′ish·ness,** *n.*

gar·land (gär′lənd) *n.* a wreath of flowers, leaves, vines, or similar materials, usually worn on the head for decoration, especially as a token of honor. —*v.t.* to decorate with a garland or garlands.

gar·lic (gär′lik) *n.* **1.** the strong-tasting bulb of a plant that is widely cultivated in most parts of the world, used to season food. The bulb is composed of separate sections called cloves. **2.** the plant bearing this bulb, having long, flat, ridged leaves and bearing clusters of small pink or purple flowers.

gar·ment (gär′mənt) *n.* an article of clothing.

garment bag, a bag, usually of plastic, cloth, or leather, fitted with a hanger, used for storing clothes or for holding and protecting them during travel.

gar·ner (gär′nər) *v.t.* **1.** to earn, accumulate, or collect: *The business garnered large profits.* **2.** to gather and store in or as if in a granary: *to garner grain during a harvest.* —*n.* **1.** a store of anything: *a garner of knowledge.* **2.** a place for storing grain; granary.

gar·net (gär′nit) *n.* **1.** any of a group of hard minerals found in various colors. The deep red variety is most commonly used as a gem. **2.** a deep red color. —*adj.* having the color garnet; deep red.

gar·nish (gär′nish) *v.t.* **1.** to decorate or trim: *robes garnished with gems and fur.* **2.** to decorate (food) with something that improves its appearance or flavor: *to garnish fish with lemon slices.* **3.** to garnishee. —*n., pl.* **gar·nish·es. 1.** something placed on or around food to improve its appearance or flavor. **2.** a decoration or trimming.

gar·nish·ee (gär′ni shē′) *v.t.,* **gar·nish·eed, gar·nish·ee·ing.** to hold or seize (a person's money or property) by legal authority in payment of a debt. Also, **garnish.**

gar·ret (gar′it) *n.* the uppermost floor or room of a house, directly below the roof; attic.

gar·ri·son (gar′ə sən) *n.* **1.** a military post. **2.** the soldiers stationed in a town or post. —*v.t.* **1.** to station soldiers in (a town or post): *to garrison a village to protect it from the enemy.* **2.** to station (soldiers) in a garrison.

gar·ru·li·ty (gə rü′li tē) *n.* the quality of being garrulous; talkativeness.

gar·ru·lous (gar′ə ləs) *adj.* given to too much talking, especially about unimportant matters; talkative. —**gar′-ru·lous·ly,** *adv.* —**gar′ru·lous·ness,** *n.*

gar·ter (gär′tər) *n.* **1.** a band or strap, usually elastic, worn to hold up a stocking or sock. **2. Garter. a.** see **Order of the Garter. b.** the badge of this order. —*v.t.* to fasten or support with a garter.

garter snake, any of a group of harmless brownish or greenish snakes found in North and Central America, usually having yellow stripes along the body.

gas (gas) *n., pl.* **gas·es. 1.** the form of matter that is neither solid nor liquid, characterized by the ability of its atoms or molecules to move about easily and independently. It has no definite shape or volume and expands to fill its container. **2.** any gas or gaseous mixture other than air. **3.** any gas or gaseous mixture that will burn, used for heating or lighting, such as natural gas. **4.** any gas or gaseous mixture used as an anesthetic. **5.** a chemical substance, such as mustard gas or tear gas, that is intentionally released in the air to irritate, stun, or kill. **6.** see **gasoline.** —*v.t.,* **gassed, gas·sing. 1.** to irritate, stun, or kill with gas, as in chemical warfare. **2.** to supply with gas or gasoline: *to gas a car up before a long drive.*

gas chamber, a sealed room in which one or more persons are executed by poisonous gas.

gas·e·ous (gas′ē əs, gash′əs) *adj.* relating to or in the form of gas: *a gaseous state, a gaseous substance.*

gas–guz·zler (gas′guz′lər) *n. Informal.* an automobile that uses an excessive amount of gasoline.

gash (gash) *n., pl.* **gash·es.** a long, deep cut or wound: *The doctor closed the gash with ten stitches.* —*v.t.* to make a gash in: *to gash a finger while cutting bread.*

gas·ket (gas′kit) *n.* a ring, disk, or other piece of packing used to seal a joint or closure, as in a pipe or piston.

gas·light (gas′līt′) *n.* **1.** the light produced by the burning of gas. **2.** something that burns gas, such as a lamp.

gas mask, a mask having a filter, worn over the mouth, nose, and eyes to protect the wearer from breathing in harmful substances.

gas·o·hol (gas′ə hôl′) *n.* a fuel used in motor vehicles, made from gasoline and alcohol.

gas·o·line (gas′ə lēn′, gas′ə lēn′) *n.* a fuel for internal-combustion engines in automobiles, etc. It is obtained from petroleum or natural gas.

gasp (gasp) *v.i.* to draw in the breath suddenly, sharply, or with difficulty, as in fear or surprise, or when one is out of breath. —*v.t.* to utter while gasping: *The excited child gasped the news to us.* —*n.* the act or an instance of gasping.

gas station, an establishment that sells gasoline, oil, and other things necessary to keep motor vehicles operating, often having repair facilities as well. Also, **filling station, service station.**

gas·sy (gas′ē) *adj.,* **gas·si·er, gas·si·est.** full of, containing, or like gas: *a gassy mixture.*

gas·tric (gas′trik) *adj.* of, relating to, or near the stomach.

gastric juice, a digestive fluid secreted by glands in the stomach lining, containing hydrochloric acid and certain enzymes, such as pepsin and rennin.

gas·tro·nom·ic (gas′trə nom′ik) *adj.* of or relating to gastronomy. Also, **gas·tro·nom·i·cal** (gas′trə nom′i kəl).

gas·tron·o·my (gas tron′ə mē) *n.* the art or science of good eating.

gas·tro·pod (gas′trə pod′) *n.* any of a group of mollusks, including the snail, slug, and whelk, that move by means of a muscular foot on the underside of the body. Most gastropods have a single-chambered, usually spiral shell. —*adj.* of or relating to gastropods.

gas·tru·la (gas′trü lə) *n., pl.* **gas·tru·lae** (gas′trü lē′) an early stage in the development of an embryo, following the blastula stage, during which the ectoderm, endoderm, and mesoderm are formed.

gat (gat) *Archaic.* a past tense of **get.**

gate (gāt) *n.* **1.** a movable barrier, usually swinging on hinges, used to close off a passage, as in a wall or fence. **2.** an opening in a wall or fence for entering or leaving, especially such an opening equipped with a gate. **3.** a device used to control the flow of a fluid, especially water, as through a pipe, dam, or lock. **4.** the number of people who pay to see a sports event, play, or other contest or performance. **5.** the total amount of money received from these people: *a gate of $2,000.*

gate crasher, a person who gains admittance to a party or other private gathering without being invited, or to a performance or sporting event without having a ticket.

gate·house (gāt′hous′) *n., pl.* **gate·hous·es** (gāt′-hou′ziz). a house or other structure built next to or over a gate, used especially as the gatekeeper's quarters.

gate·keep·er (gāt′kē′pər) *n.* a person in charge of a gate.

gate·post (gāt′pōst′) *n.* a post on which a gate is hinged or to which a gate is fastened when closed.

gate·way (gāt′wā′) *n.* **1.** an opening in a wall or fence that may be closed with a gate, used for entering or leaving. **2.** the means of entering someplace or achieving something: *the gateway to the West, the gateway to happiness.*

gath·er (gath′ər) *v.t.* **1.** to bring together in one place or group: *to gather one's clothes for a trip.* **2.** to get or collect from various places or sources; accumulate: *The bird gathered twigs for its nest.* **3.** to pick and harvest (fruit or crops): *to gather corn.* **4.** to increase little by little; gain gradually: *The ball gathered speed as it rolled down the hill.* **5.** to learn or realize by observation or reasoning; conclude: *I gather from your remarks that you didn't like the movie.* **6.** to take and hold; enfold: *to gather a child in one's arms.* **7.** to draw (cloth) into pleats, folds, or puckers along a line of stitching: *to gather a skirt at the waist.* —*v.i.* **1.** to come together or assemble: *Students gathered in the auditorium.* **2.** to increase or collect gradually: *Sweat gathered on my brow.* —*n.* a pleat, fold, or pucker made by gathering. —**gath′er·er,** *n.*

gath·er·ing (gath′ər ing) *n.* **1.** the act of a person or thing that gathers. **2.** a meeting, assembly, or crowd.

Gat·ling gun (gat′ling) an early type of machine gun, having a cluster of barrels that were rotated around a central axis by a hand crank, each barrel being fired in turn. [From the American inventor Richard J. *Gatling* (1818–1903).]

gauche (gōsh) *adj.* lacking social grace; awkward or tactless: *a gauche remark.* [From the French word *gauche* meaning "warped, awkward" and "left, left-handed."]

gau·cho (gou′cho) *n., pl.* **gau·chos.** a cowhand of the pampas of South America, especially such a person who is of mixed Spanish and Indian descent.

gaud·y (gô′dē) *adj.,* **gaud·i·er, gaud·i·est.** tastelessly bright or ornate; showy or cheap: *gaudy jewelry.* —**gaud′i·ly,** *adv.* —**gaud′i·ness,** *n.*

gauge (gāj) *also,* **gage.** *n.* **1.** a standard measure or scale of measurements. **2.** an instrument or device used for measuring or indicating measurements: *a pressure gauge.* **3.** a means of estimating or judging; standard:

gaucho

The students' performance on this test is a gauge of their reading ability. **4.** the distance between two rails on a railroad. The standard U.S. gauge is 56.5 inches (143.5 centimeters). **5.** the diameter of the bore of a gun, especially a shotgun. **6.** thickness or diameter, as of a sheet of metal or a wire. —*v.t.,* **gauged, gaug·ing.** **1.** to determine accurately the dimensions, amount, force, or capacity of, especially with a gauge; measure: *to gauge the speed of the wind.* **2.** to estimate or judge; appraise: *The jeweler gauged the value of the diamond.* —**gauge′a·ble,** *adj.* —**gaug′er,** *n.*

Gaul (gôl) *n.* **1.** a Celtic inhabitant of ancient Gaul. **2.** a Frenchman.

gaunt (gônt) *adj.* **1.** extremely thin and with sunken eyes, as from hunger or illness; haggard. **2.** bare and gloomy; grim; bleak: *a gaunt stretch of desert.* —**gaunt′ly,** *adv.* —**gaunt′ness,** *n.*

gaunt·let[1] (gônt′lit) *also,* **gant·let.** *n.* **1.** a heavy glove, usually made of leather covered with armor plate or mail, used in medieval times to protect the hand. **2.** a glove having a long, flaring cuff extending above the wrist. [From the Old French word *gantelet* meaning "mitten," from the word *gant* "glove," of Germanic origin.]

  ·**to take up the gauntlet.** to accept a challenge.

  ·**to throw down the gauntlet.** to challenge, as to combat.

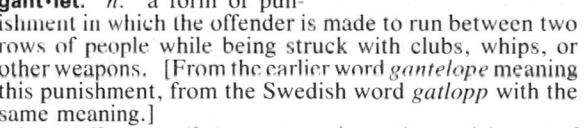

(def. 1)   (def. 2)

gauntlet[1]

gaunt·let[2] (gônt′lit) *also,* **gant·let.** *n.* a form of punishment in which the offender is made to run between two rows of people while being struck with clubs, whips, or other weapons. [From the earlier word *gantelope* meaning this punishment, from the Swedish word *gatlopp* with the same meaning.]

  ·**to run the gauntlet.** **a.** to undergo the punishment of the gauntlet. **b.** to be subjected to a series of difficulties or severe opposition or criticism.

gauze (gôz) *n.* a very thin, lightweight cloth woven from any of various fibers, used for such items as bandages, surgical dressings, and curtains.

gauz·y (gô′zē) *adj.,* **gauz·i·er, gauz·i·est.** resembling gauze; thin; transparent. —**gauz′i·ness,** *n.*

gave (gāv) the past tense of **give.**

gav·el (gav′əl) *n.* a small mallet used by the person in charge of a trial, meeting, or other gathering to call for attention or order.

ga·votte (gə vot′) *n.* **1.** a dance of French origin, resembling the minuet, but much faster and livelier. **2.** the music for this dance.

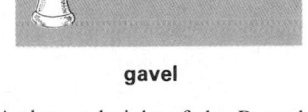

gavel

Ga·wain (gä′win, gə wān′) *n.* in the legends of King Arthur, a knight of the Round Table and the nephew of King Arthur.

gawk (gôk) *v.i. Informal.* to stare stupidly; gape.

gawk·y (gô′kē) *adj.,* **gawk·i·er, gawk·i·est.** awkward; clumsy. —**gawk′i·ly,** *adv.* —**gawk′i·ness,** *n.*

G

at; āpe; fär; câre; end; mē; it; īce; pîerce; hot; ōld; sông; fôrk; oil; out; up; ūse; rüle; pùll; tûrn; chin; sing; shop; thin; this; hw in white; zh in treasure. The symbol ə stands for the unstressed vowel sound heard in about, taken, pencil, lemon, and circus.

gay (gā) *adj.*, **gay·er**, **gay·est**. **1.** full of joy and fun; merry; happy. **2.** brightly colored or showy: *a gay design.* **3.** homosexual. —*n.* a homosexual person. —**gay′ness**, *n.*

gay·e·ty (gā′i tē) another spelling of **gaiety**.

gay·ly (gā′lē) another spelling of **gaily**.

gaze (gāz) *v.i.*, **gazed**, **gaz·ing**. to look long and steadily, as in admiration or wonder. —*n.* a long, steady look.

ga·ze·bo (gə zē′bō) *n.*, *pl.* **ga·ze·bos**. a small, open-air or screened-in structure, usually with a view of pleasant surroundings, used as a retreat or resting spot, as in a garden or park. [Of uncertain origin.]

ga·zelle (gə zel′) *n.*, *pl.* **ga·zelles** or **ga·zelle**. any of various small, graceful antelopes found in hot, dry regions of Africa and Asia. Gazelles have curving horns and some can run as fast as 60 miles per hour (95 kilometers per hour).

ga·zette (gə zet′) *n.* **1.** a newspaper or similar periodical. **2.** an official publication, as of a government or institution. —*v.t.*, **ga·zet·ted**, **ga·zet·ting**. to publish, list, or announce in a gazette.

gaz·et·teer (gaz′ə tîr′) *n.* a book or list of geographical names.

gaz·pa·cho (gə spä′chō) *n.* a cold soup made of chopped tomatoes and other raw vegetables, often combined with olive oil, vinegar, and spices. [From the Spanish word *gazpacho*.]

G.B., Great Britain.

G clef, another term for **treble clef.**

Gd, the symbol for gadolinium.

Ge, the symbol for germanium.

gear (gîr) *n.* **1.** a wheel having a toothed edge designed to mesh with or fit into the teeth of another similar wheel. **2.** a mechanical arrangement or assembly of such wheels, used for transmitting or changing motion, as in an automobile: *first gear, low gear.* **3.** a mechanism or part of a mechanism within a machine, performing a specific function: *steering gear.* **4.** any equipment used for a specific purpose: *fishing gear, camping gear.* —*v.t.* **1.** to furnish or equip with gears. **2.** to adapt, change, or regulate (something) in order to make it conform to or suit something else: *to gear a campaign to capture the middle-class vote.* —*v.i.* to come into or be in gear; mesh: *The teeth of the wheels gear into each other.*

·**in gear.** connected or engaged, as one gear with another or with a motor.

·**out of gear.** not connected or engaged, as one gear with another or with a motor.

gear·ing (gîr′ing) *n.* a system of gears for transmitting motion or power.

gear·shift (gîr′shift′) *n.* a device for connecting or disconnecting any of several sets of gears in a transmission system, as in an automobile.

gear·wheel (gîr′hwēl′, gîr′wēl′) *n.* a wheel having a toothed edge; cogwheel; gear.

geck·o (gek′ō) *n.*, *pl.* **geck·os** or **geck·oes**. a tropical lizard having pads on the bottom of the toes covered with thousands of very tiny hooks that enable it to walk on smooth surfaces, such as walls and ceilings.

gee[1] (jē) *interj.* **1.** to the right. **2.** Forward; faster. ▲ used to direct horses, mules, and certain other animals. —*v.i.*, *v.t.*, **geed**, **gee·ing.** to turn or cause to turn to the right.

gee[2] (jē) *interj.* used to express enthusiasm or surprise.

geese (gēs) the plural of **goose.**

Gei·ger counter (gī′gər) an electronic device that is used to detect and measure the intensity of ionizing radiation. This radiation may be in the form of X rays, gamma rays, or cosmic rays. [From the German physicist Hans *Geiger* (1882–1945), one of its inventors.]

gei·sha (gā′shə, gē′shə) *n.*, *pl.* **gei·sha** or **gei·shas.** a Japanese girl who has been trained to provide entertainment in a teahouse, as by singing, dancing, and making amusing conversation.

gel (jel) *n.* a form of material whose consistency is halfway between that of a liquid and a solid, like jelly. In a gel, tiny particles of one material are evenly distributed throughout another material. A gel is a type of colloid. —*v.i.*, **gelled**, **gel·ling.** to take on the form of a gel: *The egg whites will gel when they are cooked.*

gel·a·tin (jel′ə tən) *also,* **gel·a·tine.** *n.* **1.** a colorless, tasteless protein substance obtained from skin, bones, and other animal tissues. Gelatin dissolves in hot water and forms a jellylike mass when it cools. It is used in jellies, desserts, and other foods, and in the manufacture of drugs and photographic film. **2.** a preparation or product made with or resembling gelatin.

gel·a·tine (jel′ə tən, jel′ə tēn′) another spelling of **gelatin.**

ge·lat·i·nous (jə lat′ə nəs) *adj.* **1.** of or like gelatin. **2.** containing gelatin.

ge·la·to (jə lä′tō) *n.* a type of Italian ice cream with an especially smooth and creamy texture. [From the Italian word *gelato* meaning "something frozen" or "ice cream," from the word *gelare* "to freeze," going back to the Latin word *gelu* "icy coldness, frost."]

geld (geld) *v.t.*, **geld·ed** or **gelt**, **geld·ing.** to castrate (a horse or similar animal).

geld·ing (gel′ding) *n.* a gelded animal, especially a gelded horse.

gelt (gelt) a past tense and past participle of **geld.**

gem (jem) *n.* **1.** a cut and polished precious or semiprecious stone; jewel. **2.** a person or thing that is considered perfect, extremely beautiful, or precious: *This novel is a gem.* —*v.t.*, **gemmed**, **gem·ming.** to set or adorn with or as if with gems: *Tiny blossoms gemmed the branches of the cherry trees.*

Gem·i·ni (jem′ə nī′) *n.* **1.** a constellation in the northern sky, thought to resemble the twin brothers Castor and Pollux. **2.** the third sign of the zodiac. ▲ used with a singular verb in both definitions.

gems·bok (gemz′bok′) *n.*, *pl.* **gems·bok** or **gems·boks.** a large southern African antelope having very long, straight horns, a long, tufted tail, and a sandy gray coat with dark markings on the side and face.

gem·stone (jem′stōn′) *n.* a mineral or petrified material that can be used in jewelry.

gen. **1.** gender. **2.** general. **3.** genitive. **4.** genus.

Gen., General.

gemsbok

gen·darme (zhän′därm) *n.*, *pl.* **gen·darmes** (zhän′därmz). **1.** an armed policeman in France and French-speaking parts of certain other European countries. **2.** *Informal.*any policeman.

gen·der (jen′dər) *n.* **1.** *Grammar.* One of the classes, such as masculine, feminine, and neuter, into which certain kinds of words are divided. In English, words like *father*, *he*, and *rooster* are of the masculine gender; *mother*, *she*, and *her* are of the feminine gender; *building* and *it* are of the neuter gender. **2.** sex: *There should be no job discrimination because of gender.*

gene (jēn) *n.* a small section of a chromosome that determines the characteristics of an individual and the traits passed from an individual to its offspring. Genes are made up of DNA.

ge·ne·a·log·i·cal (jē′nē ə loj′i kəl) *adj.* of or relating to genealogy: *a genealogical trait.* —**ge′ne·a·log′i·cal·ly**, *adv.*

ge·ne·al·o·gist (jē′nē ol′ə jist, jē′ne al′ə jist) *n.* a person who traces or studies genealogies.

ge·ne·al·o·gy (jē′nē ol′ə jē, jē′nē al′ə jē) *n., pl.* **ge·ne·al·o·gies. 1.** the study of the descent of persons or families from an ancestor or ancestors. **2.** an account or chart of such a descent for a particular person or family. **3.** a direct descent from an ancestor or ancestors; pedigree; lineage: *Our genealogy goes back to the American Revolution.*

Word Family

Many English words can be traced back to the Greek word *genos,* meaning "race" or "family," and the related suffix *-genes,* meaning "born of." **Genealogy** is the study of a family extending as far back toward its **genesis** as possible. Family characteristics are passed on by **genes. Genetic** engineering may one day prevent or cure many **genetic** diseases, but there are concerns that this science, like the earlier **eugenics,** could be used to bring about **genocide.** Although certain segments of American society are relatively **homogeneous,** the United States as a whole has earned the designation "melting pot" because of its **heterogeneous** makeup.

gen·er·a (jen′ər ə) the plural of **genus.**

gen·er·al (jen′ər əl) *adj.* **1.** concerned with or affecting everyone or the whole: *a general election, to work for the general welfare of the people.* **2.** common or occurring among many or most; widespread; prevalent: *a word in general use.* **3.** not limited to a particular group, use, or area: *a general rule.* **4.** not concerned with details or specifics: *to speak in a general way.* —*n.* **1.** the commander of a large army; military officer of the highest rank. **2.** in the U.S. Army and Air Force, an officer ranking above lieutenant general and below general of the army or general of the air force. **3.** in the U.S. Marine Corps, an officer of the highest rank. **4.** any officer ranking above a colonel.
·**in general.** for the most part; commonly.

General Assembly 1. the main deliberative body of the United Nations, in which every member nation is represented. **2.** the legislature in certain states of the United States.

general delivery 1. the department of the post office that handles mail picked up at a post office window by the person to whom it is addressed. **2.** the mail handled by this department.

general election, an election in which voters make their final choice among the official candidates for public office.

gen·er·al·is·si·mo (jen′ər ə lis′ə mō′) *n., pl.* **gen·er·al·is·si·mos.** in certain countries, the commander in chief of all the military forces of the country, or of several armies in the field.

gen·er·al·ist (jen′ər ə list) *n.* a person whose interest or expertise covers a wide range of fields or activities rather than being specialized.

gen·er·al·i·ty (jen′ə ral′i tē) *n., pl.* **gen·er·al·i·ties. 1.** a statement, phrase, or idea that is not concerned with details or specifics, especially one that is too broad or vague to be meaningful: *to speak in generalities.* **2.** the greater part or number; main body; majority. **3.** the quality or condition of being general.

gen·er·al·i·za·tion (jen′ər ə lə zā′shən) *n.* **1.** the act of generalizing. **2.** a generalizing statement, idea, or rule: *To say that all firefighters are brave is a generalization.*

gen·er·al·ize (jen′ər ə līz′) *v.,* **gen·er·al·ized, gen·er·al·iz·ing.** —*v.i.* **1.** to treat a subject without going into details or specifics; speak in or use generalities. **2.** to form a general rule or principle from particular facts or

instances. —*v.t.* to give a more general form to; state in general terms.

gen·er·al·ly (jen′ər ə lē) *adv.* **1.** in most cases; as a rule; usually: *I generally walk to school.* **2.** for the most part; commonly: *That theory is generally accepted by scientists.* **3.** without regard to specific details: *Generally, the book was good.*

general of the air force, in the U.S. Air Force, an officer of the highest rank.

general of the army, in the U.S. Army, an officer of the highest rank.

general practitioner, a doctor whose practice is not limited to a specific branch of medicine.

gen·er·al–pur·pose (jen′ər əl pûr′pəs) *adj.* suitable for more than one purpose: *a general-purpose cleanser.*

gen·er·al·ship (jen′ər əl ship′) *n.* **1.** the military skill of a general. **2.** skill in management of any sort; leadership. **3.** the rank, office, or term of office of a general.

general store, a store, usually in a rural or small community, that carries a large variety of items but is not divided into departments.

gen·er·ate (jen′ə rāt′) *v.t.,* **gen·er·at·ed, gen·er·at·ing.** to produce or cause to be; bring into existence: *to generate electricity, to generate excitement.*

gen·er·a·tion (jen′ə rā′shən) *n.* **1.** a group of individuals born at about the same time: *the postwar generation.* **2.** one step or degree in the line of natural descent, as of people, animals, or plants. Children, their parents, and their grandparents make up three generations. **3.** the period of time, usually about thirty years, between the birth of one generation and the next. **4.** a group of objects produced at approximately the same time and possessing similar characteristics: *the next generation of computers.* **5.** the act or process of causing to be or bringing into existence; production.

generation gap, the difference in values, attitudes, and outlook between one generation and the next, especially between parents and adolescents.

gen·er·a·tive (jen′ər ə tiv, jen′ə rā′tiv) *adj.* **1.** of or relating to production of offspring. **2.** having the ability or power to produce or bring into existence.

gen·er·a·tor (jen′ə rā′tər) *n.* **1.** a device that changes mechanical energy into electrical energy. **2.** an apparatus for the production of gas or steam. **3.** a person or thing that generates.

ge·ner·ic (jə ner′ik) *adj.* **1.** of, relating to, or applied to a whole kind, class, or group; general: *"Fruit" is a generic term.* **2.** of, relating to, or characteristic of a genus of plants, animals, or other organisms. **3.** not under trademark registration: *generic drugs, generic canned goods.* —**ge·ner′i·cal·ly,** *adv.*

gen·er·os·i·ty (jen′ə ros′i tē) *n., pl.* **gen·er·os·i·ties. 1.** willingness to give or share freely; quality of being unselfish. **2.** the quality of being noble-minded and free from meanness; graciousness. **3.** a generous act.

gen·er·ous (jen′ər əs) *adj.* **1.** having or showing a willingness to give or share freely; unselfish: *a generous gift, a generous person.* **2.** noble-minded and gracious; free from meanness: *a generous nature.* **3.** large or plentiful; abundant: *a generous helping of food.* —**gen′er·ous·ly,** *adv.*

gen·e·sis (jen′ə sis) *n., pl.* **gen·e·ses** (jen′ə sēz′). the coming into being of anything; beginning; origin.

at; āpe; fär; câre; end; mē; it; īce; pîerce; hot; ōld; sông, fôrk; oil; out; up; ūse; rüle; pu̇ll; tûrn; chin; sing; shop; thin; <u>th</u>is; hw in white; zh in treasure. The symbol ə stands for the unstressed vowel sound heard in about, taken, pencil, lemon, and circus.

G

Gen·e·sis (jen′ə sis) *n.* the first book of the Old Testament, giving an account of the origin of the world.

gene–splic·ing (jēn′splī′sing) *n.* any of various methods for joining a fragment of DNA from one organism to the genetic material of another organism to produce recombinant DNA.

ge·net·ic (jə net′ik) *adj.* **1.** of or relating to genetics. **2.** of, relating to, or produced by a gene or genes: *a genetic trait.* **3.** of or relating to the origin and development of anything. —**ge·net′i·cal·ly,** *adv.*

genetic code, the arrangement of the sections of DNA in a chromosome that determines the characteristics of an organism.

genetic engineering, the altering of the genetic material of a cell or an organism by means of techniques such as gene-splicing. Genetic engineering can be used to develop vaccines and create new and useful organisms, such as bacteria that produce human insulin.

ge·net·i·cist (jə net′ə sist) *n.* an expert in genetics.

ge·net·ics (jə net′iks) *n.* the branch of biology that deals with the principles of heredity and the inherited similarities and differences found in organisms. ▲ used with a singular verb.

Ge·ne·va Convention (jə nē′və) an international agreement regulating the wartime treatment of sick and wounded soldiers and prisoners of war. It was first adopted in 1864 at Geneva, Switzerland.

gen·ial (jēn′yəl) *adj.* **1.** pleasant and cheerful; friendly; cordial: *a genial host.* **2.** favorable to life or growth; pleasantly warm and comfortable: *a genial climate.* —**gen′ial·ly,** *adv.*

ge·ni·al·i·ty (jē′nē al′i tē) *n.* the quality or condition of being genial.

ge·nie (jē′nē) *n., pl.* **ge·nies** or *(def. 2)* **ge·ni·i.** **1.** a spirit who will fulfill wishes and follow commands. **2.** another spelling of **jinni.**

ge·ni·i (jē′nē ī′) **1.** the plural of **genius** *(def. 7).* **2.** a plural of **genie.**

gen·i·tal (jen′i təl) *adj.* of or relating to the sex organs.

gen·i·ta·li·a (jen′i tā′lē ə, jen′i tāl′yə) *pl. n.* another word for **genitals.**

gen·i·tals (jen′i təlz) *pl. n.* the reproductive organs, especially the external sex organs.

gen·i·tive (jen′i tiv) *n.* **1.** the grammatical case in certain languages that indicates possession, source, or origin. It corresponds to the possessive case in English. **2.** a word or construction in this case. —*adj.* of, relating to, or indicating this case.

gen·ius (jēn′yəs) *n., pl.* **gen·ius·es** or *(def. 7)* **ge·ni·i.** **1.** extraordinary mental power, especially as shown by creativity or inventiveness in science or the arts: *Marie and Pierre Curie were people of genius.* **2.** a person who has such power. **3.** a person having a very high intelligence quotient. **4.** a great natural ability or talent for a particular thing: *a genius for drawing.* **5.** a person who has such an ability or talent: *a genius at diplomatic negotiations.* **6.** a person who has a powerful influence over another or others: *an evil genius.* **7.** a guardian spirit, as of a person or place.

gen·o·cide (jen′ə sīd′) *n.* the extermination or destruction of an entire national, cultural, or racial group.

Gen·o·ese (jen′ō ēz′, jen′ō ēs′) *n., pl.* **Gen·o·ese.** a person who was born in or is a citizen of Genoa. —*adj.* of or relating to Genoa or its people.

gen·o·type (jē′nə tīp′, jen′ə tīp′) *n.* the genetic makeup of an organism, especially as distinguished from its phenotype. [From the Greek word *genos* meaning "origin" or "race, kind" + the English word *type*.]

gen·re (zhän′rə) *n.* a particular kind, class, or style, especially of work in literature or art: *a master of the genre of the short story.*

genre painting, a style of painting that shows scenes and events from everyday life.

gen·teel (jen tēl′) *adj.* **1.** polite in manner or behavior; well-bred or refined: *a genteel person.* **2.** of, relating to, or suitable for those who are well-bred or refined: *genteel manners.* **3.** artificially or excessively refined or polite. —**gen·teel′ness,** *n.*

gen·tian (jen′shən) *n.* a plant found in temperate and mountainous regions, bearing blue flowers and usually leaves without stalks.

gen·tile (jen′tīl) *also,* **Gen·tile.** *n.* **1.** a person who is not a Jew, especially a Christian. **2.** among Mormons, a person who is not a Mormon. —*adj.* of or relating to a gentile or gentiles.

gen·til·i·ty (jen til′i tē) *n., pl.* **gen·til·i·ties.** **1.** the refinement or good manners characteristic of a person who is well-bred. **2.** the condition of belonging to the upper class. **3.** members of the upper class.

gen·tle (jen′təl) *adj.,* **gen·tler, gen·tlest.** **1.** mild and kindly in manner, nature, or tone: *to be gentle with a baby.* **2.** not severe, rough, or loud; soft; moderate: *the gentle tapping of rain on the roof.* **3.** easily handled; tame: *a gentle horse.* **4.** not extreme or abrupt; gradual: *a gentle slope.* **5.** of good family or birth; wellborn. **6.** characteristic of or like one of good family; polite or refined. —**gen′tle·ness,** *n.* —**gen′tly,** *adv.*

gen·tle·folk (jen′təl fōk′) *pl. n.* people of good family and breeding.

gen·tle·man (jen′təl mən) *n., pl.* **gen·tle·men** (jen′təl-mən). **1.** a man who is honorable, courteous, and considerate. **2.** a man of good family and high social standing. **3.** any man: *There is a gentleman at the door.* **4. gentlemen.** a form of respectful or polite address, used especially in speaking or writing to a group of men.

gen·tle·man·ly (jen′təl mən lē) *adj.* having the character, behavior, or appearance of a gentleman; courteous; well-bred. —**gen′tle·man·li·ness,** *n.*

gentleman's agreement, an unwritten agreement guaranteed only by the honor of the people involved, and not legally binding. Also, **gentlemen's agreement.**

gen·tle·wom·an (jen′təl wùm′ən) *n., pl.* **gen·tle·wom·en** (jen′təl wim′ən). **1.** a woman of good family and high social standing. **2.** a well-mannered, refined woman; lady. **3.** formerly, a woman attending a lady of rank.

gen·tri·fi·ca·tion (jen′trə fi kā′shən) *n.* the conversion of a run-down urban area, especially a poor or working-class neighborhood, into one that is more expensive or exclusive, resulting in an increase in property values and displacement of the original residents and businesses.

gen·tri·fy (jen′trə fī′) *v.t.,* **gen·tri·fied, gen·tri·fy·ing.** to change (a neighborhood, block, or the like) by gentrification.

gen·try (jen′trē) *n.* **1.** people of good family or high social standing. **2.** the social class ranking below the nobility. **3.** the people of any particular class or group.

gen·u·flect (jen′yù flekt′) *v.i.* to bend the knee while standing or touch the knee to the ground, as in worship or respect.

gen·u·flec·tion (jen′yù flek′shən) *n.* the act of genuflecting.

gen·u·ine (jen′ū in) *adj.* **1.** actually being what it seems or is claimed to be; real; true: *a genuine antique.* **2.** free from pretense or dishonesty; sincere: *a genuine expression of sympathy, a genuine person.* —**gen′u·ine·ly,** *adv.* —**gen′u·ine·ness,** *n.*

ge·nus (jē′nəs) *n., pl.* **gen·er·a.** **1.** the category of biological classification ranking next below a family and next above a species. **2.** any group of related things; kind; sort; class.

geo– *combining form* relating to the earth: *geophysics.*

ge·o·cen·tric (jē′ō sen′trik) *adj.* **1.** as measured or viewed from the earth's center. **2.** based on the idea that the earth is the center of the universe: *a geocentric system of astronomy.*

ge·o·chem·is·try (jē′ō kem′ə strē) *n.* the branch of chemistry dealing with the chemical composition of the earth's crust and the chemical changes that take place there.

ge·ode (jē′ōd) *n.* **1.** a hollow stone whose inner surface is lined with crystals. **2.** the inner cavity itself. [From the Latin word *geodes* meaning "precious stone," from the Greek word *geōdēs* "earthlike," from the word *gē* "earth."]

ge·o·des·ic (jē′ə des′ik, jē′ə dē′sik) *n.* the shortest line segment that joins two points lying on a surface, especially a curved surface. —*adj.* **1.** of or relating to geodesy. **2.** of or relating to geodesic lines.

geodesic dome, a light, strong, dome-shaped structure, usually made of a framework of triangular or polygonal shapes and covered with plastic sheeting.

ge·od·e·sy (jē od′ə sē) *n.* the science concerned with determining the shape and measurements of the earth and with the mapping of large areas of its surface.

geog., geographer; geographical; geography.

ge·og·ra·pher (jē og′rə fər) *n.* an expert in geography.

ge·o·graph·i·cal (jē′ə graf′i kəl) *adj.* of or relating to geography. Also, **ge·o·graph·ic** (jē′ə graf′ik). —**ge·o·graph′i·cal·ly,** *adv.*

geographical mile, a measure of length equal to ⅟₆₀ of a degree of the earth's equator, approximately 6,080 feet (1,850 meters).

ge·og·ra·phy (jē og′rə fē) *n., pl.* **ge·og·ra·phies.** **1.** the study of the characteristics of and differences between particular places on the surface of the earth, and of all the physical and cultural factors affecting these characteristics. Geography includes the study of the earth's natural surface, its climate, the distribution of plant, animal, and human life, and human use of and relationship to the environment. **2.** the surface or natural features of a particular place or region: *the rugged geography of Siberia.*

geol., geological; geologist; geology.

ge·o·log·i·cal (jē′ə loj′i kəl) *adj.* of or relating to geology. Also, **ge·o·log·ic** (jē′ə loj′ik). —**ge·o·log′i·cal·ly,** *adv.*

ge·ol·o·gist (jē ol′ə jist) *n.* an expert in geology.

ge·ol·o·gy (jē ol′ə jē) *n., pl.* **ge·ol·o·gies.** **1.** the science that deals with the earth's structure, composition, and history, including the changes that have taken place on the earth's surface and the processes, such as erosion, by which such changes have occurred. **2.** the structure and composition of the earth in a particular area.

geom., geometric; geometrician; geometry.

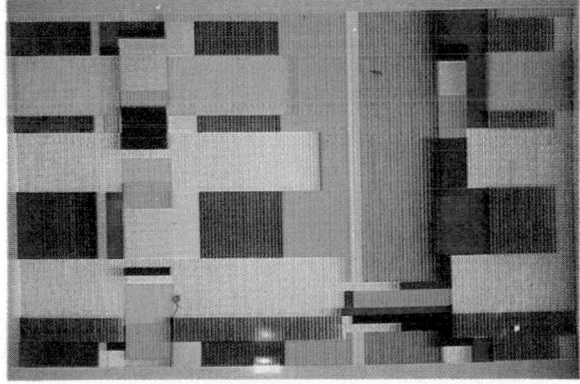

a **geometric** design

ge·o·met·ric (jē′ə met′rik) *adj.* **1.** of or relating to geometry. **2.** made up of or decorated with straight lines, angles, circles, triangles, or similar forms: *a geometric design.* Also, **ge·o·met·ri·cal** (jē′ə met′ri kəl). —**ge·o·met′ri·cal·ly,** *adv.*

ge·om·e·tri·cian (jē om′i trish′ən) *n.* a student of or an expert in geometry.

geometric progression *Mathematics.* a series in which each number is multiplied by a given factor in order to obtain the next number. 1½, 3, 6, 12, 24 is a geometric progression in which the given factor is 2.

ge·om·e·try (jē om′i trē) *n., pl.* **ge·om·e·tries.** **1.** the branch of mathematics that deals with the properties, measurements, and relations of points, lines, angles, plane figures, and solids. **2.** shape or design: *the geometry of a building.*

ge·o·mor·phol·o·gy (jē′ō môr fol′ə jē) *n.* the science that deals with the physical features of the surface of the earth and the geological processes by which they are produced.

ge·o·phys·i·cal (jē′ō fiz′i kəl) *adj.* of or relating to geophysics.

ge·o·phys·i·cist (jē′ō fiz′ə sist) *n.* a student of or an expert in geophysics.

ge·o·phys·ics (jē′ō fiz′iks) *n.* the earth science that deals with the physical nature, motions, atmosphere, and oceans of the earth. ▲ used with a singular verb.

Geor·gian (jôr′jən) *adj.* **1.** of or relating to the reigns of the first four kings of England named George, who ruled from 1714 to 1830: *The house was designed in the style of the Georgian period.* **2.** of or relating to the state of Georgia. **3.** of or relating to the republic of Georgia or its people. —*n.* **1.** a person who was born in or is a citizen of the state of Georgia. **2.** a person who was born in or is a citizen of the republic of Georgia. **3.** the language of the republic of Georgia.

ge·o·ther·mal (jē′ō thûr′məl) *adj.* **1.** of or relating to the heat that occurs naturally under the earth's surface, as in hot springs. **2.** of or relating to the use of this heat to produce power or provide heat for buildings.

ge·ot·ro·pism (jē ot′rə piz′əm) *n.* the movement or growth of plants and certain other organisms in response to the force of gravity.

Ger., German; Germany.

ge·ra·ni·um (jə rā′nē əm) *n.* **1.** any of a group of plants, widely grown for their showy clusters of usually red, pink, or white flowers. **2.** any of various related plants, having lobed leaves and small, usually white or purple flowers. **3.** the flower of any of these plants.

geranium

ger·bil (jûr′bil) *n.* a rodent that lives in burrows, native to desert regions of southern Africa and Asia. It has a slender, tufted tail and a short, soft coat that is usually gray, brown, or reddish. Gerbils are sometimes kept as pets.

ger·fal·con (jûr′fôl′kən, jûr′fal′kən, jûr′fô′kən) another spelling of **gyrfalcon.**

ger·i·at·rics (jer′e at′riks) *n.* the branch of medicine that deals with diseases of old age and the care and treatment of old people. ▲ used with a singular verb.

germ (jûrm) *n.* **1.** any tiny living organism, especially one that causes disease. Germs can be seen only with the aid of a microscope. **2.** the earliest form or stage in the development of an organism. **3.** the earliest form or stage of anything: *the germ of a plan.*

G

Ger·man (jûr′mən) n. **1.** a person who was born in or is a citizen of Germany. **2.** the Germanic language spoken mainly in Germany, Austria, and parts of Switzerland. —*adj.* of or relating to Germany, its people, their language, or their culture.

Words From Other Languages

English belongs to the same family of languages as German, and the two languages share many related words inherited from a common parent language. There are also many German words that entered the English language after the two languages had separated.

dachshund	a breed of dog with a long, low body
delicatessen	a shop that sells prepared foods
frankfurter	a type of sausage, often on a roll
hamburger	a cooked patty of ground beef
liverwurst	a kind of sausage made of liver
nickel	a type of hard metal, or a 5-cent coin
noodle	a narrow strip of dough
pretzel	a food of rolled baked dough that is often twisted and salted
quartz	a kind of hard, nonmetallic mineral
sauerkraut	shredded, fermented cabbage
waltz	a kind of dance in ¾ time
yodel	a style of singing in a high, wavering voice

ger·mane (jər mān′) *adj.* directly or closely related; pertinent; relevant: *Your comments are in no way germane to the discussion.*

Ger·man·ic (jər man′ik) n. the branch of related languages that includes English, German, Dutch, Flemish, Norwegian, Swedish, Danish, and Icelandic. Also, **Teutonic.** —*adj.* **1.** of or relating to this family of languages. **2.** another word for **German.** **3.** another word for **Teutonic.**

ger·ma·ni·um (jər mā′nē əm) n. a hard, brittle, grayish white metalloid element, used in the manufacture of transistors. Symbol: **Ge** [Formed from the Medieval Latin word *Germania* meaning ''Germany,'' from the homeland of its discoverer, Clemens Winkler.]

German measles, another term for **rubella.**

German shepherd, a large dog of a breed developed in Germany, having a thick coat of black, brown, or gray fur. It is often trained for use as a watchdog, guard dog, or guide dog for the blind. Also, **police dog, Alsatian.**

German shepherd

German silver, any of a group of silver-colored alloys of copper, nickel, and zinc that have good resistance to corrosion. Also, **nickel silver.**

germ cell, a male or female reproductive cell; sperm or egg.

ger·mi·cid·al (jûr′mə sī′dəl) *adj.* capable of killing germs: *a germicidal liquid.*

ger·mi·cide (jûr′mə sīd′) n. a chemical substance that kills germs, especially germs that cause disease.

ger·mi·nate (jûr′mə nāt′) *v.,* **ger·mi·nat·ed, ger·mi·nat·ing.** —*v.i.* to start to grow or develop, as from a seed; sprout. —*v.t.* to cause to grow or develop: *Warmth and moisture germinate seeds.* —**ger′mi·na′tion,** n.

germ plasm, a substance in germ cells that contains the material of heredity.

germ warfare, another term for **biological warfare.**

ger·ry·man·der (jer′ē man′dər, ger′ē man′dər) n. **1.** the division of a state or other political unit into voting districts that give one political party an unfair advantage. **2.** a voting district formed by such a division. —*v.t.* to divide (a state or other political unit) into voting districts that give one political party an unfair advantage. [From the name of the governor of Massachusetts, Elbridge *Gerry* (1744–1814), + (sala)*mander*. While Gerry was in office, the state's voting districts were rearranged to give his party an advantage. One of the new districts had the shape of a salamander.]

ger·und (jer′ənd) n. a verb form that ends with -*ing* and is used as a noun. In the sentence *Swimming is good exercise,* the word *swimming* is a gerund.

Ge·sta·po (gə stä′pō) n. the secret police force of Nazi Germany.

ges·ta·tion (jes tā′shən) n. **1.** the period from conception to birth, during which the unborn young develop in the uterus; pregnancy. **2.** the conceiving or developing of something, such as a project, plan, or idea.

ges·tic·u·late (jes tik′yə lāt′) *v.i.,* **ges·tic·u·lat·ed, ges·tic·u·lat·ing.** to make or use gestures to express a thought or feeling or to emphasize something, as in speaking.

ges·tic·u·la·tion (jes tik′yə lā′shən) n. **1.** an emphatic or expressive gesture. **2.** the act of gesticulating.

ges·ture (jes′chər) n. **1.** a movement of the head, body, or limbs, used to express a thought or feeling, or to emphasize what is said: *I used hand gestures to indicate the size of the fish I had caught.* **2.** something said or done for effect or as a symbol: *to shake hands as a gesture of friendship.* —*v.i.,* **ges·tured, ges·tur·ing.** to make or use gestures: *The police officer gestured to us to stop.*

Ge·sund·heit (gə zünt′hīt′) *interj.* German. used to wish good health to someone who has just sneezed.

get (get) *v.,* **got, got** or **got·ten, get·ting.** —*v.t.* **1.** to obtain possession of; receive or acquire: *to get a new coat, to get an idea.* **2.** to earn; gain: *The team got three touchdowns.* **3.** to go for and return with; fetch: *Please get me a glass of water.* **4.** to cause to be done or become: *to get a haircut, to get a fire under control.* **5.** to become ill with; suffer from; catch: *to get the mumps.* **6.** to make ready; prepare: *to get lunch.* **7.** to possess; have: *I've got curly hair.* **8.** to be obliged: *You've got to clean up your room.* **9.** *Informal.* to understand; comprehend: *I get the idea.* —*v.i.* **1.** to come to or reach: *to get to shore safely, to get to work on time.* **2.** to move, come, or go: *to get into an elevator, to get down from a ladder.* **3.** to be or become: *to get lost, to get ready to leave.*

·to get along. a. to be on good terms; be compatible: *to get along with one's boss.* **b.** to manage: *to get along on little money.* **c.** to go away or move on. **d.** to advance or progress, especially in age or time: *My grandparents are getting along in years.*

·to get around. a. to move or go from place to place. **b.** to be circulated; become known: *The rumor got around quickly.* **c.** to avoid; evade.

·to get at. a. to arrive; reach. **b.** to attempt to express; mean: *I don't see what you're getting at.*

·to get away. a. to leave; depart. **b.** to escape.

·to get away with. *Informal.* to do (something) without being noticed, caught, or punished: *to get away with a mistake.*

·to get back. a. to return: *to get back from a trip.* **b.** to recover: *to get back one's strength.*

·to get back at. *Slang.* to take revenge on.

·to get by. a. to manage; survive: *If we're frugal, we can get by on ten dollars a week.* **b.** to pass without being stopped or noticed: *The soldiers waited until dark so that they could get by the enemy sentries.*

·to get in. a. to go in; enter. **b.** to come in; arrive: *The* train got in at noon. **c.** to put in; insert: *They talk so much that I can never get in a word.*

·to get off. a. to move down from or out of. **b.** to start; depart. **c.** to be released or escape: *The students got off with only a mild reprimand.*

·to get on. a. to move up on or into: *to get on a horse.* **b.** to advance or progress, especially in age or time: *It's getting on toward midnight.* **c.** to proceed: *Let's get on with these chores.*

·to get out. a. to go away; depart. **b.** to get away; escape. **c.** to become known: *No one knew how the secret got out.* **d.** to publish; issue: *to get out a daily newspaper.*

·to get out of. to escape: *to get out of an embarrassing situation.*

·to get over. to recover from: *to get over a cold.*

·to get together. a. to come together, especially informally. **b.** to come to an agreement.

·to get up. a. to rise from bed or sleep. **b.** to sit or stand up.

get·a·way (get′ə wā′) *n. Informal.* **1.** the act of escaping: *Let's make a fast getaway after this boring speech is over.* **2.** the start of a race.

get-to·geth·er (get′tə geth′ər) *n. Informal.* an informal meeting, gathering, or party.

get-up (get′up′) *n. Informal.* **1.** a dress or costume, especially an unusual one; outfit. **2.** the style or way in which something is made or arranged; arrangement.

get-up-and-go (get′up′ən gō′) *n. Informal.* vigor; energy.

gew·gaw (gū′gô′) *n.* a gaudy, worthless plaything or ornament; showy trifle; bauble. *—adj.* showy but without value; gaudy.

gey·ser (gī′zər) *n.* a natural hot spring from which steam and hot water shoot into the air after being heated below the surface by surrounding masses of hot rock.

ghast·ly (gast′lē) *adj.,* **ghast-li·er, ghast·li·est. 1.** horrible; dreadful: *the ghastly sights of war.* **2.** deathly pale; like a ghost: *The accident victim's face bore a ghastly look.* **3.** *Informal.* extremely bad or unpleasant: *a ghastly mistake.* *—adv.* in a ghastly manner; dreadfully. *—ghast′li·ness, n.*

gher·kin (gûr′kin) *n.* a small, prickly, many-seeded cucumber used for making pickles.

ghet·to (get′ō) *n., pl.* **ghettos** or **ghet·toes. 1.** a section of a city, especially a slum area, in which members of a minority group live because of social discrimination or economic pressure. **2.** the section of a European city where Jews were formerly required to live.

ghost (gōst) *n.* **1.** the spirit of a dead person, thought of as making its presence known to the living in a visible form or in some other way; specter. **2.** a shadowy outline or likeness: *a ghost of a smile.* **3.** slightest bit: *The visiting team doesn't have a ghost of a chance of winning the game.*

·to give up the ghost. to die.

ghost·ly (gōst′lē) *adj.,* **ghost·li·er, ghost·li·est.** relating to or like a ghost: *The scarecrow took on a ghostly shape in the dim light.* *—ghost′li·ness, n.*

ghost town, a town that has been deserted, especially a mining town in the western United States abandoned after the nearby mines closed.

ghost·writ·er (gōst′rī′tər) *also,* **ghost-writ·er.** *n.* a person who writes a speech, article, book, or other work for another person who gets credit for the work.

geyser

ghoul (gül) *n.* **1.** *Muslim Legend.* a horrible demon believed to rob graves and feed on human corpses. **2.** anyone who robs graves. **3.** a person who enjoys revolting acts or horrible things. *—ghoul′ish, adj.* *—ghoul′ish·ly, adv.* *—ghoul′ish·ness, n.*

GHz, gigahertz.

GI (jē′ī′) *n., pl.* **GI's, GIs.** *Informal.* an enlisted man in the U.S. military service, especially the Army. *—adj.* **1.** of, relating to, or characteristic of GI's: *a GI haircut.* **2.** issued by the U.S. government for use by the armed forces: *GI boots.* [Originally short for *g*(alvanized) *i*(ron), written by U.S. Army clerks listing items made of this metal. It was later misunderstood to mean *g*(overnment) *i*(ssue) or *g*(eneral) *i*(ssue) and in this sense was applied to enlisted men.]

gi·ant (jī′ənt) *n.* **1.** in folklore and legend, a huge and powerful creature having human form. **2.** a person or thing that is extraordinary, as in strength, importance, size, or ability: *an intellectual giant, an industrial giant.* *—adj.* extremely large or great; huge: *a giant telescope.*

giant panda, see panda (def. 1).

giant star, any of a group of very bright, large stars.

gib·ber (jib′ər) *v.i.* to speak rapidly and senselessly; jabber. *—n.* gibberish.

gib·ber·ish (jib′ər ish) *n.* **1.** meaningless or unintelligible speech or writing. **2.** speech or writing that is pretentious, obscure, or needlessly technical.

gib·bet (jib′it) *n.* **1.** a gallows. **2.** an upright post with a projecting part from which the bodies of executed criminals were hung. *—v.t.,* **gib·bet·ed, gib·bet·ing. 1.** to hang (a corpse) on a gibbet. **2.** to put (a person) to death by hanging.

gib·bon (gib′ən) *n.* any of various small, tree-dwelling apes of southeastern Asia and the East Indies, having long, slender limbs and no tail.

gib·bous (gib′əs) *adj.* **1.** curved out; rounded; convex. **2.** of or relating to that phase of the moon or a planet in which it appears more than half full but less than full.

gibe (jīb) *also,* **jibe.** *n.* a mocking remark; jeer; taunt. *—v., gibed, gib·ing. —v.i.* to utter gibes; jeer. *—v.t.* to utter gibes at.

gib·let (jib′lit) *n. usually,* **gib·lets.** the heart, liver, and gizzard of a fowl, parts that are usually cooked separately and often used in gravies.

gibbon

gid·dy (gid′ē) *adj.,* **gid·di·er, gid·di·est. 1.** having a spinning sensation in one's head; dizzy. **2.** causing or tending to cause dizziness. **3.** lacking seriousness; frivolous; flighty. *—gid′di·ly, adv. —gid′di·ness, n.*

gift (gift) *n.* **1.** something given; present; donation: *a wedding gift.* **2.** natural ability; talent: *a gift for writing.* **3.** the act or power of giving.

gift·ed (gif′tid) *adj.* having natural ability; talented: *a gifted artist.*

gig¹ (gig) *n.* **1.** a light, open, two-wheeled carriage drawn by a single horse. **2.** a long, light ship's boat propelled by oars, sails, or a motor. [Probably of Scandinavian origin.]

at; āpe; fär; câre; end; mē; it; īce; pîerce; hot; ōld; sông, fôrk; oil; out; up; ūse; rüle; pùll; tûrn; chin; sing; shop; thin; this; hw in white; zh in treasure. The symbol ə stands for the unstressed vowel sound heard in about, taken, pencil, lemon, and circus.

G

gig² (gig) *n.* **1.** a fishing spear. **2.** a device made of hooks fastened back to back, used to catch fish by their bodies. —*v.i.*, **gigged**, **gig·ging.** to catch (fish) with a gig. [Of uncertain origin.]

gi·ga·hertz (jig′ə hûrts′, gig′ə hûrts′) *n.*, *pl.* **gi·ga·hertz.** a unit equal to 1 billion hertz, used in measuring the frequency of electromagnetic waves.

gi·gan·tic (jī gan′tik) *adj.* like or resembling a giant, especially in size; huge; enormous: *A gigantic wave washed over the boat.*

gig·gle (gig′əl) *v.i.*, **gig·gled**, **gig·gling.** to laugh in a silly, high-pitched, or nervous way. —*n.* a silly, high-pitched, or nervous laugh. —**gig′gler**, *n.*

Gi·la monster (hē′lə) a large, poisonous lizard found in desert regions of northern Mexico and the southwestern United States. It has a black or brown scaly body with orange or yellow blotches. [From the *Gila* River in Arizona.]

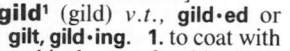

Gila monster

gild¹ (gild) *v.t.*, **gild·ed** or **gilt**, **gild·ing.** **1.** to coat with a thin layer of gold. **2.** to make attractive; brighten or adorn. **3.** to make (something) seem better than it is. [From the Old English word *gyldan* with the same meaning.]

gild² (gild) another spelling of **guild.**

gill¹ (gil) *n.* **1.** the organ of breathing for fish and most other water animals, consisting of a thin layer of tissue well supplied with blood. It is capable of absorbing oxygen from the water and releasing carbon dioxide from the blood. **2.** one of the thin, bladelike structures on the underside of the cap of many types of mushrooms. [Of Scandinavian origin.]

gill² (jil) *n.* a liquid measure equal to ¼ of a pint (118.3 milliliters). [From the Old French word *gille* meaning this measure.]

gilt (gilt) *v.* a past tense and past participle of **gild¹.** —*adj.* covered with gold or having a golden color; gilded. —*n.* gold or similar material used in gilding.

gim·crack (jim′krak′) *n.* a showy object of little use and value; gewgaw. —*adj.* showy but of little use and value.

gim·let (gim′lit) *n.* a small tool with a screw point and a cross handle, used for boring holes.

gim·mick (gim′ik) *n. Slang.* **1.** a clever feature or idea, especially one that is used to attract attention. **2.** a small device or gadget.

gin¹ (jin) *n.* a strong alcoholic liquor that is distilled from grains and flavored with juniper berries. [From the earlier word *geneva* meaning this drink, from the obsolete Dutch word *genevr* "juniper," going back to the Latin word *juniperus* "juniper."]

gin² (jin) *n.* a machine for separating cotton from its seeds. Also, **cotton gin.** —*v.t.*, **ginned**, **gin·ning.** to separate (cotton) from its seeds with a gin. [From the Old French word *engin* meaning "a machine, engine," going back to the Latin word *ingenium* "natural temper" or "genius, talent."]

gin³ (jin) *n.* see **gin rummy.**

gin·ger (jin′jər) *n.* **1.** any of a group of plants grown in tropical and subtropical regions for their roots, which can be eaten. **2.** a spice that is ground from these roots, used in cooking and in medicine. **3.** the root itself, often candied or preserved in syrup. **4.** *Informal.* liveliness; high spirits; pep.

ginger ale, a carbonated soft drink that is flavored with ginger.

ginger beer, a drink similar to ginger ale but with a stronger ginger flavor.

gin·ger·bread (jin′jər bred′) *n.* **1.** a dark, sweet cake

gimlet

or cookie flavored with ginger and molasses. **2.** gaudy ornamentation, as on furniture or buildings. —*adj.* cheap and showy; gaudy.

gin·ger·ly (jin′jər lē) *adv.* with extreme caution; carefully; timidly: *to walk gingerly on thin ice.* —*adj.* extremely cautious or wary: *gingerly steps.*

gin·ger·snap (jin′jər snap′) *n.* a thin, crisp cookie flavored with ginger and molasses.

ging·ham (ging′əm) *n.* a strong, medium-weight cotton fabric made with dyed yarn, usually woven in checks, stripes, or plaids.

gin·gi·vi·tis (jin′jə vī′təs) *n.* inflammation of the gums, often causing the gums to become swollen and to bleed easily.

gink·go (ging′kō) *n.*, *pl.* **gink·goes.** also, **ging·ko.** a large tree with fan-shaped leaves, native to China. Ginkgoes are often planted as an ornamental or shade tree.

gin rummy, a variation of the card game rummy, in which two players form matched sets of cards until one of the players has matched all his or her cards or has ten points or fewer of unmatched cards.

gin·seng (jin′seng) *n.* **1.** either of two low plants grown in North America and Asia, having a thick, branched root and bearing toothed leaves and small, pale green flowers. **2.** the root of this plant, traditionally used in medicine by the Chinese.

Gip·sy (jip′sē) another spelling of **Gypsy.**

gipsy moth, another spelling of **gypsy moth.**

gi·raffe (jə raf′) *n.* the tallest living animal, native to Africa. The giraffe has a very long neck, long and slender legs, two or four small bony horns, and a coat with brown patches outlined with white.

gird (gûrd) *v.t.*, **girt** or **gird·ed**, **gird·ing.** **1.** to surround or encircle with a belt or girdle: *to gird one's waist with a gold chain.* **2.** to encircle as if with a belt; hem in; enclose. **3.** to prepare (oneself): *to gird oneself for a test.*

gird·er (gûr′dər) *n.* a large horizontal beam, as of steel or wood, usually used as a support, as for a floor or the framework of a bridge or building.

giraffe

gir·dle (gûr′dəl) *n.* **1.** a flexible undergarment worn to support or shape the waist, abdomen, or hips; corset. **2.** a belt or band worn around the waist. **3.** anything that encircles in the manner of a belt. —*v.t.*, **gir·dled**, **gir·dling.** **1.** to encircle with a belt or girdle. **2.** to encircle as if with a belt; surround: *Trees girdled the lake.*

girl (gûrl) *n.* **1.** a female child from birth to the time she is a young woman. **2.** a young unmarried woman. **3.** a female servant. **4.** *Informal.* a female sweetheart. **5.** *Informal.* any woman.

girl·friend (gûrl′frend′) *n. Informal.* a female friend, especially a sweetheart.

girl·hood (gûrl′hùd′) *n.* the time or state of being a girl.

girl·ish (gûr′lish) *adj.* of, relating to, or fit for girls or girlhood. —**girl′ish·ly**, *adv.* —**girl′ish·ness**, *n.*

girl scout, a member of the Girl Scouts.

Girl Scouts, an organization for young girls, founded to develop character and physical fitness and encourage helpfulness to others.

girt (gûrt) a past tense and past participle of **gird.**

girth (gûrth) *n.* **1.** the distance around something; circumference: *the girth of a column.* **2.** a strap or band that is passed under the belly of a horse or other animal to keep a saddle or pack in place. —*v.t.* **1.** to fasten or fit with a girth. **2.** to surround; encircle; gird.

gist (jist) *n.* a main idea; central point: *the gist of a speech.*

give (giv) *v.*, **gave, giv·en, giv·ing.** —*v.t.* **1.** to hand over to another as a present: *I gave my parents records for their anniversary.* **2.** to transfer ownership of (something) in exchange for something else, especially to sell for payment: *The dealer gave us the car for $2,000.* **3.** to hand over or deliver: *Give me the letter. Give these games to the twins.* **4.** to confer as an honor: *to give first prize to the winner of a contest.* **5.** to grant: *to give permission.* **6.** to communicate to another; transmit; send: *Please give my regards to your cousin.* **7.** to assign or allot: *The teacher gave me the job of handing out the papers.* **8.** to administer: *to give medicine to a baby.* **9.** to provide; supply: *to give food to the hungry, to give evidence in court.* **10.** to issue forth in words, sound, or motion: *to give a shout, to give the signal to start.* **11.** to arrange and carry out: *to give a party.* **12.** to sacrifice; surrender: *to give one's life in war.* —*v.i.* **1.** to make a donation; contribute: *to give to charity.* **2.** to move or bend under pressure; yield: *The dam gave under the heavy rainfall.* —*n.* the quality of being elastic; flexibility: *This fabric has a lot of give.* —**giv′er,** *n.*

· **to give and take. a.** to compromise: *The two cousins learned to give and take in order to keep from arguing.* **b.** to talk in a good-natured way.

· **to give away. a.** to give as a gift; donate: *to give away books one has already read.* **b.** to present (the bride) to the bridegroom in a marriage ceremony. **c.** to reveal; expose: *You gave away your hiding place when you sneezed.*

· **to give back.** to return: *I gave back the money I borrowed.*

· **to give in.** to stop opposing; yield: *My parents gave in and let me drive the car.*

· **to give off.** to put forth; emit: *The flowers gave off a sweet fragrance.*

· **to give out. a.** to distribute or issue: *to give out free samples.* **b.** to make public; announce: *to give out information.* **c.** to become exhausted, broken down, or used up: *The swimmer gave out after ten laps.*

· **to give up. a.** to yield; surrender. **b.** to stop; cease: *to give up smoking.* **c.** to acknowledge that one has failed and stop trying. **d.** to abandon as hopeless or useless: *to give up the search for a lost dog.* **e.** to devote completely: *to give up one's life to medical research.*

· **to give way.** to yield under pressure; break down.

give–and–take (giv′ ən tāk′) *n.* **1.** a mutual yielding or concession; compromise. **2.** a good-natured exchange of talk; banter.

give·a·way (giv′ ə wā′) *n. Informal.* **1.** the revealing of something, such as a secret, accidentally; exposure. **2.** something given away or sold at a very low price, as to promote sales.

giv·en (giv′ ən) *v.* the past participle of **give.** —*adj.* **1.** inclined; disposed; prone: *a person given to spreading gossip.* **2.** stated; specified: *to do something at a given time.*

given name, the name given to a person at birth or baptism; first name.

giz·mo (giz′ mō) *n., pl.* **giz·mos.** *Slang.* a gadget or object, especially one whose name is not known or remembered: *We really need one of those gizmos for punching holes in paper.*

giz·zard (giz′ ərd) *n.* the muscular second part of the stomach of a bird, in which partially digested food from the first part of the stomach is finely ground.

gla·cial (glā′ shəl) *adj.* **1.** of, relating to, or produced by ice or glaciers. **2.** of or relating to a period of time when glaciers covered large areas of the earth, especially the Pleistocene epoch. **3.** cold; icy: *a glacial manner.* —**gla′cial·ly,** *adv.*

glacial epoch, see **ice age** (*def. 1*).

glacier

gla·cier (glā′ shər) *n.* a large mass of ice moving slowly over some land surface or down a valley. A glacier is formed over a long period of time from the accumulation of snow in areas where the amount of snow that falls is greater than the amount that melts.

glad (glad) *adj.*, **glad·der, glad·dest.** **1.** feeling or expressing joy, pleasure, or satisfaction; happy: *We were glad to hear of your success.* **2.** causing joy or pleasure; pleasing: *glad tidings.* **3.** very willing: *They will be glad to go with us.* —**glad′ly,** *adv.* —**glad′ness,** *n.*

glad·den (glad′ ən) *v.t.* to make glad.

glade (glād) *n.* an open space in a wood or forest.

glad·i·a·tor (glad′ ē ā′tər) *n.* **1.** a slave, captive, or paid professional who took part in public combat in the arenas of ancient Rome. **2.** a person who takes part in a fight, dispute, or controversy.

glad·i·o·lus (glad′ ē ō′ləs) *n., pl.* **glad·i·o·li** (glad′ ē ō′lī) or **glad·i·o·lus·es.** **1.** a funnel-shaped, showy flower that grows in long clusters. **2.** the leafy plant bearing this flower, having stiff, sword-shaped leaves. Also, **glad·i·o·la** (glad′ ē ō′lə). [From the Latin word *gladiolus* meaning "a small sword," used as the name of this flower, from the word *gladius* "sword."]

gladiolus

glad·some (glad′ səm) *adj.* causing joy or pleasure.

glam·or·ize (glam′ ə rīz′) *v.i.*, **glam·or·ized, glam·or·iz·ing.** to make glamorous: *The movie was criticized because it glamorized crime.*

glam·or·ous (glam′ ər əs) *adj.* full of glamour; fascinatingly attractive; alluring: *a glamorous film star.* —**glam′or·ous·ly,** *adv.* —**glam′or·ous·ness,** *n.*

glam·our (glam′ ər) *also,* **glam·or.** *n.* alluring excitement or charm; fascinating attraction: *the glamour of the movie industry.*

glance (glans) *n.* a brief or hurried look: *to give someone an angry glance.* —*v.i.*, **glanced, glanc·ing.** **1.** to take a brief or hurried look: *I glanced at the magazines in the dentist's office.* **2.** to strike a surface and move off at a slant: *The bullet glanced off the rock.*

gland (gland) *n.* an organ, tissue, or cell that produces

---

at; āpe; fär; câre; end; mē; it; īce; pîerce; hot; ōld; sông, fôrk; oil; out; up; ūse; rüle; pull; tûrn; chin; sing; shop; thin; this; hw in white; zh in treasure. The symbol ə stands for the unstressed vowel sound heard in about, taken, pencil, lemon, and circus.

G

and discharges one or more substances that are used by or discharged from the body. Important glands include the thyroid and pituitary glands and the liver, kidneys, and pancreas.

glan·du·lar (glan′jə lər) *adj.* **1.** of, relating to, or affecting a gland: *a glandular disease.* **2.** consisting of or containing a gland or glands: *glandular tissue.*

glare (glâr) *n.* **1.** a strong, usually unpleasant light, as from sunlight reflected on a shiny surface. **2.** a piercing, hostile look or stare. —*v.,* **glared, glar·ing.** —*v.i.* **1.** to shine with a strong, harsh light. **2.** to look or stare piercingly and with hostility: *The angry fighters glared at each other.* —*v.t.* to express with a glare: *The defendant glared defiance at the jury.*

glar·ing (glâr′ing) *adj.* **1.** giving off or reflecting a harsh light; unpleasantly bright. **2.** extremely conspicuous; flagrant: *a glaring mistake.* **3.** staring piercingly and with hostility. —**glar′ing·ly,** *adv.*

glar·y (glâr′ē) *adj.,* **glar·i·er, glar·i·est.** dazzling; glaring.

glas·nost (glas′nōst, gläz′nəst) *n.* in the Soviet Union, an official policy of open and public discussion of problems and issues.

glass (glas) *n., pl.* **glass·es. 1.** a hard, brittle, usually transparent material made by melting a mixture of sand, soda, and lime. **2.** an open container, especially of glass and usually without a handle, used chiefly for drinking. **3.** a glassful: *to drink a glass of water.* **4.** something partly or entirely made of glass, such as a window, a mirror, or a telescope. **5. glasses.** see **eyeglasses.** —*adj.* made of glass: *a glass bottle.* —*v.t.* to enclose or protect with glass: *They glassed in the open porch.*

glass·blow·er (glas′blō′ər) *n.* a person whose work is glassblowing.

glass·blow·ing (glas′blō′ing) *n.* the art or process of shaping a mass of molten glass by blowing a controlled stream of air through a tube into the mass.

glass·ful (glas′fül′) *n., pl.* **glass·fuls.** the amount that a drinking glass can hold.

glass·ine (gla sēn′) *n.* a thin, glazed translucent paper, used especially for book jackets and envelope windows.

glass snake, a lizard with no legs that resembles a snake, having a tail that breaks off easily into small pieces. The glass snake is able to grow a new tail.

glass·ware (glas′wâr′) *n.* objects made of glass, especially drinking glasses.

glass·y (glas′ē) *adj.,* **glass·i·er, glass·i·est. 1.** resembling glass; smooth and shiny: *the glassy surface of a lake.* **2.** fixed, expressionless, or lifeless: *a glassy stare.* —**glass′i·ly,** *adv.* —**glass′i·ness,** *n.*

glau·co·ma (glô kō′mə, glou kō′mə) *n.* a serious eye disease characterized by increased pressure in the eyeball. It may lead to damage of the retina and gradual loss of sight.

glaze (glāz) *v.,* **glazed, glaz·ing.** —*v.t.* **1.** to furnish or fit with glass: *to glaze a window.* **2.** to cover with a smooth, glossy coating: *to glaze doughnuts with sugar. The pottery was glazed to make it shiny.* —*v.i.* to become glassy or glazed: *His eyes glazed with pain.* —*n.* **1.** a smooth, glossy covering or coating. **2.** any substance used to produce such a covering or coating.

gla·zier (glā′zhər) *n.* a person who installs panes of glass, as in windows and doors.

gleam (glēm) *n.* **1.** a flash or beam of bright light: *the gleam of a flashlight in the distance.* **2.** reflected brightness, as from a polished surface: *the gleam of a new car.* **3.** a faint or brief appearance or sign: *a gleam of hope.* —*v.i.* to shine or reflect light: *The knight's armor gleamed in the sunlight.*

glean (glēn) *v.t.* **1.** to gather (grain) left on a field after reaping. **2.** to collect slowly and with great effort: *to glean information.* —**glean′er,** *n.*

glean·ings (glē′ningz) *pl. n.* things obtained by gleaning.

glee (glē) *n.* **1.** joy or delight; merriment: *to laugh with glee.* **2.** a song for three or more male voices, without accompaniment, popular in the eighteenth century.

glee club, a group organized for singing choral music.

glee·ful (glē′fəl) *adj.* full of glee; merry; joyous. —**glee′ful·ly,** *adv.* —**glee′ful·ness,** *n.*

glen (glen) *n.* a small, narrow, usually secluded valley.

glen·gar·ry (glen gar′ē) *also,* **Glengarry.** *n., pl.* **glen·gar·ries.** a Scottish cap made of wool, having straight sides, a crease lengthwise across the top, and, often, short ribbon streamers at the back.

glib (glib) *adj.,* **glib·ber, glib·best.** speaking or spoken with little thought or sincerity: *The used car dealer was a glib talker. She always has a glib excuse for being late.* —**glib′ly,** *adv.* —**glib′ness,** *n.*

glide (glīd) *v.i.,* **glid·ed, glid·ing. 1.** to move smoothly, continuously, and effortlessly: *Skaters glided over the ice.* **2.** to pass gradually and unnoticed: *The time glided by.* **3.** to maintain flight or descend slowly without the use of power. —*n.* **1.** the act of moving smoothly and effortlessly. **2.** the act of gliding.

glid·er (glī′dər) *n.* **1.** an aircraft made of light materials and designed to fly without the aid of an engine, relying on rising air currents to remain aloft. **2.** a piece of furniture with a seat suspended from a frame so that it can swing backward and forward.

glim·mer (glim′ər) *n.* **1.** a dim, unsteady light. **2.** a faint hint or sign; inkling: *a glimmer of hope.* —*v.i.* to shine with dim, unsteady light; flicker.

glimpse (glimps) *n.* a brief look; passing glance: *I had a glimpse of the driver's face as the car sped by.* —*v.,* **glimpsed, glimps·ing.** —*v.t.* to get a brief look at; see for a moment. —*v.i.* to look quickly; glance: *to glimpse at a road sign.*

glint (glint) *n.* a bright, quick flash; gleam; sparkle. —*v.i.* to shine; gleam.

glis·san·do (gli sän′dō) *n., pl.* **glis·san·di** (gli sän′dē). *Music.* **1.** a gliding effect performed in various ways, as by rapidly running one finger over the white keys of a piano or sliding one finger along the string of a harp. **2.** a passage performed with such an effect. —*adj.* performed with such an effect.

glis·ten (glis′ən) *v.i.* to shine or sparkle with reflected light: *The snow glistened in the sun.* —*n.* a gleam or sparkle.

glitch (glich) *n. Slang.* a minor breakdown or malfunction, especially in a mechanism or computer program.

glit·ter (glit′ər) *v.i.* **1.** to shine with a bright light; sparkle: *The jewels glittered.* **2.** to be attractive or showy. —*n.* **1.** sparkling brightness or light: *the glitter of polished crystal.* **2.** showiness; splendor: *the glitter of a fancy costume ball.* **3.** small bits of sparkling material, used for ornamentation. —**glit′ter·y,** *adj.*

glitz (glits) *n. Slang.* glitter; flashy display; showiness: *The remodeled restaurant was all glitz, with its mirrored walls and shiny brass fixtures.* [Probably from the German word *glitzern* meaning "to glitter."]

glitz·y (glit′sē) *adj.* **glitz·i·er, glitz·i·est.** glittery; flashy; showy: *a glitzy hotel lobby, glitzy costumes.*

gloat (glōt) *v.i.* to observe or think about with great satisfaction and often malicious delight: *to gloat over an opponent's loss in an election.*

glob (glob) *n.* a rounded mass, lump, or drop: *a glob of paint.*

glob·al (glō′bəl) *adj.* **1.** of or relating to the entire world; worldwide: *global warfare.* **2.** shaped like a globe; spherical. —**glob′al·ly,** *adv.*

globe (glōb) *n.* **1.** the earth; world. **2.** a sphere on which a map of the earth or of the heavens is drawn. **3.** a spherical body; sphere. **4.** anything resembling a sphere in shape, such as a glass covering for a light bulb.

globe·trot·ter (glōb′trot′ər) *n.* a person who travels widely, often to places all over the world.

glo·bose (glō′bōs) *adj.* having the shape of a globe.

glob·u·lar (glob′yə lər) *adj.* **1.** having the shape of a globe; spherical. **2.** made up of globules.

glob·ule (glob′ūl) *n.* a small ball or drop: *a globule of oil.*

glob·u·lin (glob′yə lin) *n.* any of a group of proteins found in many plant and animal cells. Globulins are not soluble in water but can be dissolved in dilute salt solutions. They occur in seed, milk, egg yolks, and blood plasma.

glock·en·spiel (glok′ən spēl′, glok′ən shpēl′) *n.* a musical instrument consisting of a series of metal bars mounted in a frame, played by being struck with two small hammers.

gloom (glüm) *n.* **1.** complete or partial darkness; dimness: *The car's headlights pierced the gloom.* **2.** sadness or dejection; low spirits: *We were filled with gloom over the loss of our pet dog.* —*v.i.* **1.** to be or look sad, depressed, or displeased. **2.** to be or become dark or dismal.

glockenspiel

gloom·y (glü′mē) *adj.,* **gloom·i·er, gloom·i·est. 1.** dark; dim: *a gloomy hallway.* **2.** low in spirits; melancholy; depressed; dejected: *I was gloomy after I lost the race.* **3.** causing gloom; sad or depressing: *gloomy predictions about the economy.* —**gloom′i·ly,** *adv.* —**gloom′i·ness,** *n.*

Glo·ri·a (glôr′ē ə) *n.* **1.** any of several hymns of praise to God that begin with the Latin word *Gloria.* **2.** a musical setting for any of these.

glo·ri·fi·ca·tion (glôr′ə fi kā′shən) *n.* the act of glorifying or the state of being glorified.

glo·ri·fy (glôr′ə fī′) *v.t.,* **glo·ri·fied, glo·ri·fy·ing. 1.** to exalt; praise; honor: *The Romans glorified Julius Caesar.* **2.** to give glory to; worship; adore: *hymns that glorify God. The achievements of the three children glorified their family name.* **3.** to cause to appear more glorious or splendid than it actually is: *a novel that glorifies war.* —**glo′ri·fi′er,** *n.*

glo·ri·ous (glôr′ē əs) *adj.* **1.** having or deserving glory; famous: *The Declaration of Independence is a glorious document.* **2.** bringing glory: *a glorious deed.* **3.** magnificent; splendid: *a glorious day, a glorious sunset.* **4.** *Informal.* extremely enjoyable or delightful: *We had a glorious time at the birthday party.* —**glo′ri·ous·ly,** *adv.*

glo·ry (glôr′ē) *n., pl.* **glo·ries. 1.** great praise, honor, or distinction; fame; renown: *The glory accorded a Nobel prize winner.* **2.** a person or thing that brings praise, honor, distinction, or renown; source of pride: *The glory of the tropical island was its climate.* **3.** great beauty or splendor; magnificence: *The sun shone in all its glory.* **4.** the state or condition of greatest magnificence or prosperity: *That country was in its glory during the years just before the war.* **5.** the highest degree of self-satisfaction or pleasure: *The actors were in their glory in front of the television cameras.* **6.** praise and honor offered in worship or adoration: *Give glory to God.* —*v.i.,* **glo·ried, glo·ry·ing.** to rejoice proudly or triumphantly; exult: *to glory in an election victory.*

gloss¹ (glôs) *n., pl.* **gloss·es. 1.** the surface shine of something; luster: *the gloss of a waxed floor.* **2.** a deceptive appearance: *After their gloss of politeness wore off, we found them rather rude.* —*v.t.* **1.** to put a shine or luster on. **2.** to minimize or attempt to hide: *to gloss over a mistake.* [Of Scandinavian origin.]

gloss² (glôs) *n., pl.* **gloss·es. 1.** an explanation or interpretation, as of a text; commentary. **2.** a glossary. **3.** a translation of a foreign word or phrase, as in an etymology in a dictionary. —*v.t.* to provide a gloss for; explain or comment on. [From the Latin word *glossa* meaning "difficult word requiring explanation," from the Greek word *glōssa* meaning "tongue, language."]

glos·sa·ry (glos′ə rē) *n., pl.* **glos·sa·ries.** a list of the difficult words found in a text or a list of technical terms in a particular subject area, each with an accompanying gloss or definition.

gloss·y (glôs′ē) *adj.,* **gloss·i·er, gloss·i·est.** having a shiny surface; lustrous. —*n., pl.* **gloss·ies.** a photograph printed on smooth, glossy paper. —**gloss′i·ly,** *adv.* —**gloss′i·ness,** *n.*

glot·tis (glot′is) *n., pl.* **glot·tis·es** or **glot·ti·dies** (glot′i-dēz′) **1.** the narrow opening in the larynx between the vocal cords. **2.** the part of the larynx containing the vocal cords.

glove (gluv) *n.* **1.** a covering for the hand usually made of fabric or leather with separate sections for each finger. **2.** any of several coverings for the hand used in various sports, such as baseball or golf. **3.** see **boxing glove.** —*v.t.,* **gloved, glov·ing. 1.** to cover or provide with a glove or gloves. **2.** to catch in a glove: *The shortstop gloved the ball and threw it to first base.*

glove compartment, a small storage space in the dashboard of an automobile.

glow (glō) *n.* **1.** the light or shine from a heated substance. **2.** a similar light or shine without heat: *the glow given off by a firefly.* **3.** brightness or warmth of color: *Her face had the glow of good health.* **4.** a warm, ardent feeling or appearance: *a glow of pleasure.* —*v.i.* **1.** to shine from intense heat: *The candle glowed brightly.* **2.** to shine without heat: *The hands on my watch glow in the dark.* **3.** to show a bright or warm color: *My cheeks glowed from the cold.* **4.** to show or be filled with enthusiasm or emotion: *The children's eyes glowed with excitement when they watched the aerialists.*

glow·er (glou′ər) *v.i.* to look at angrily or threateningly; scowl: *The bicyclers glowered at the driver who had nearly hit them.* —*n.* An angry or threatening stare. —**glow′-er·ing·ly,** *adv.*

glow·ing (glō′ing) *adj.* **1.** emitting light and intense heat: *glowing coals in the fireplace.* **2.** shining or reflecting bright light: *a chandelier or glowing crystal.* **3.** having the reddish facial color of good health or excitement: *glowing cheeks.* **4.** enthusiastic and favorable: *a glowing review of a new novel.* —**glow′ing·ly,** *adv.*

glow·worm (glō′wûrm′) *n.* any of various insect larvae that give off light, such as the larva of the firefly.

glu·cose (glü′kōs) *n.* **1.** a simple sugar occurring in plants and animals. It is an important source of energy for the body. **2.** a thick, yellowish syrup made from starch, used in foods, in intravenous feedings, in the curing of tobacco, and in the tanning industry.

glue (glü) *n.* **1.** a substance used to join or stick things together, made by boiling animal hooves, bones, and skins. **2.** any sticky substance used for the same purpose. —*v.t.,* **glued, glu·ing. 1.** to attach or fasten with glue: *to glue broken pieces of pottery together.* **2.** to attach or fasten firmly: *The horror movie had my eyes glued to the screen.*

glue·y (glü′ē) *adj.,* **glu·i·er, glu·i·est. 1.** like or resembling glue; sticky. **2.** full or smeared with glue: *a gluey surface.*

glum (glum) *adj.,* **glum·mer, glum·mest.** gloomy; sullen. —**glum′ly,** *adv.* —**glum′ness,** *n.*

glut (glut) *v.t.,* **glut·ted, glut·ting. 1.** to satisfy completely or to excess: *We glutted ourselves at dinner.* **2.** to supply

at; āpe; fär; câre; end; mē; it; īce; pîerce; hot; ōld; sông; fôrk; oil; out; up; ūse; rüle; pull; tûrn; chin; sing; shop; thin; this; hw in white; zh in treasure. The symbol ə stands for the unstressed vowel sound heard in about, taken, pencil, lemon, and circus.

G

413

(a market) with goods to excess; oversupply. —*n.* a supply that is greater than needed.

glu·ten (glü′tən) *n.* a tough, sticky protein substance in flour made from wheat, rye, and other grains.

glu·ti·nous (glü′tə nəs) *adj.* like glue; sticky.

glut·ton (glut′ən) *n.* **1.** a person who eats too much. **2.** a person who has great fondness or capacity for something: *a glutton for work.*

glut·ton·ous (glut′ə nəs) *adj.* given to overeating. —**glut′ton·ous·ly,** *adv.* —**glut′ton·ous·ness,** *n.*

glut·ton·y (glut′ə nē) *n., pl.* **glut·ton·ies.** excess in eating.

glyc·er·in (glis′ər in) *also,* **glyc·er·ine.** *n.* a colorless, syrupy, sweet liquid obtained from fats or produced synthetically, used especially in making nitroglycerin, medicines, soaps, and certain plastics.

glyc·er·ol (glis′ə rôl′) *n.* another word for **glycerin.**

gly·co·gen (glī′kə jən) *n.* a substance that is one of the forms in which sugar is stored in the bodies of animals and in some algae and fungi. When needed for use by the body, it is changed into glucose.

gm., gram; grams.

G-man (jē′man′) *n., pl.* **G-men** (jē′men′). *Informal.* an agent of the Federal Bureau of Investigation. [Short for *G*(overnment) man.]

gnarl (närl) *n.* a knot or lump, as on a tree. —*v.* to make knotted, twisted, or deformed.

gnarled (närld) *adj.* **1.** having many rough, twisted knots, as a tree trunk or branches. **2.** rough or rugged in appearance: *a farmer's gnarled hands.*

gnash (nash) *v.t.* to strike, grate, or grind (the teeth) together, as in anger or pain.

gnat (nat) *n.* any of various small, winged insects that have sharp, piercing mouth parts. Some gnats suck blood, while others feed on plants.

gnaw (nô) *v.,* **gnawed, gnawed** or **gnawn, gnaw·ing.** —*v.t.* **1.** to bite (something) repeatedly with the teeth: *The dog gnawed the bone.* **2.** to make by gnawing: *The puppy gnawed a hole through the box.* **3.** to cause constant discomfort, pain, or trouble to. —*v.i.* **1.** to bite repeatedly: *The lion gnawed on the bars of its cage.* **2.** to torment or trouble: *Mean behavior can gnaw at one's conscience.*

gneiss (nīs) *n., pl.* **gneiss·es.** a rock composed of layers of light-colored feldspar and quartz, alternating with darker layers of other minerals.

gnome (nōm) *n.* in folklore, a dwarf who lives in the earth and guards treasures of precious metals and stones.

GNP, gross national product.

gnu (nü, nū) *n., pl.* **gnus** or **gnu.** any of several swift antelopes of Africa having a head like that of an ox, short horns that curve sharply upward, and a long tail. Also, **wilde-beest.**

gnu

go (gō) *v.,* **went, gone, going.** —*v.i.* **1.** to move or pass along; travel: *The car is going too fast.* **2.** to move away; depart; leave: *I have to go now.* **3.** to advance or move toward someone or something, or in a particular direction: *The movie sounds like a good one; let's go.* **4.** to be in action; operate: *The machines are kept going day and night.* **5.** to be given or awarded: *The money went to their children when they died.* **6.** to be or continue in a particular state or condition: *Your goodness will not go unrewarded.* **7.** to pass or enter into a particular state or condition; become: *to go insane, to go into hiding.* **8.** to be spent, used, or applied: *Most of the money went for food.* **9.** to proceed or be guided: *We have to go by the*

rules. **10.** to extend, reach, or lead: *The road goes east from here.* **11.** to be suitable; harmonize; match: *These shoes go with that dress.* **12.** to pass; elapse: *When you are busy, time goes quickly.* **13.** to be sold: *The sofa went for fifty dollars at the auction.* **14.** to proceed or end in a specified manner: *Things went well at the meeting today.* **15.** to fail, break down, or give way: *One's eyesight sometimes goes when one grows older.* **16.** to be expressed or phrased: *Do you remember how that song goes?* **17.** to have a usual or proper place; belong: *These sheets go in the linen closet.* **18.** to be able to be contained; fit: *Will all these books go into that box?* **19.** to be capable of being divided: *Eight goes into forty five times.* —*v.t.* to move, travel, or proceed along: *Are you going my way?* —*n., pl.* **goes.** *Informal.* **1.** spirit; energy; vigor: *You are always full of go.* **2.** a try; attempt: *I'll have a go at fixing the radio.* **3.** a success: *They are determined to make a go of the business.*

•**no go.** *Informal.* not to be done; useless; hopeless.

•**on the go.** *Informal.* constantly active or in motion: *We were on the go all day long.*

•**to go.** remaining; left: *There are only six days to go before the holidays.*

•**to go about. a.** to be occupied with or busy at: *to go about one's business.* **b.** to change direction.

•**to go along.** to agree or cooperate: *We go along with your idea.*

•**to go around.** to be enough: *Is there enough food to go around?*

•**to go back on.** *Informal.* to fail to keep or be loyal to: *Never go back on your word.*

•**to go by.** to pass unnoticed or be disregarded: *We'll let the error go by this time.*

•**to go down.** to be recorded or remembered: *The scientist's discovery will go down in history.*

•**to go for.** *Informal.* **a.** to try to get or obtain. **b.** to favor or support. **c.** to be strongly attracted by or interested in.

•**to go in for.** *Informal.* to like or engage in: *to go in for sports.*

•**to go into. a.** to examine or discuss: *We can't go into that problem now.* **b.** to enter or take up, as a profession or study: *My cousin went into medicine.*

•**to go off. a.** to explode or be discharged: *The gun went off accidentally.* **b.** to ring: *My alarm went off at 6 A.M.* **c.** *Informal.*to take place; happen; occur.

•**to go on. a.** to continue or proceed: *The meeting went on until midnight.* **b.** to take place; happen; occur: *What's going on here?* **c.** to approach; near: *It's going on two years since we last saw them.*

•**to go out. a.** to be extinguished: *The fire went out.* **b.** to take part in social affairs or date: *I go out with my friends every Saturday night.* **c.** to be a candidate; try: *Are you going out for the soccer team?*

•**to go over. a.** to examine carefully: *The accountant went over the company's books.* **b.** to read, rehearse, or review: *I went over my notes before the exam.*

•**to go through. a.** to undergo; experience: *They went through one hardship after another.* **b.** to search or examine thoroughly: *The thief went through all the drawers.* **c.** to be accepted or approved: *My application went through and I was hired.* **d.** to spend or wear out completely.

•**to go through with.** to carry out to the end; complete.

•**to go together.** to harmonize; match: *The blouse and the skirt go together.*

•**to go to pieces.** to become extremely upset.

•**to go under.** to fail: *Their business went under.*

•**to go with.** to date one person for a long period of time.

•**to let go. a.** to release or set free. **b.** to allow to pass by without taking action or notice.

·**to let oneself go. a.** to give way to one's feelings or desires. **b.** to fail to take care of oneself properly.

goad (gōd) *n.* **1.** a sharp-pointed stick used for driving cattle or oxen. **2.** anything that drives or urges. —*v.t.* to drive or urge with a goad.

go·a·head (gō′ə hed′) *n. Informal.* a signal, order, or permission to proceed: *Our teacher gave us the go-ahead for the class picnic.*

goal (gōl) *n.* **1.** an end to which effort is directed; aim: *My goal in life is to become a successful writer.* **2.** the terminal point of a race or journey. **3.** an area or object into or through which players in certain games try to get a ball or puck in order to score. **4.** the act of getting a ball or puck into or through such an area or object. **5.** the point or points made by such an act.

goal·ie (gō′lē) *n.* another word for **goalkeeper.**

goalkeeper

goal·keep·er (gōl′kē′pər) *n.* the player who defends the goal in certain games, such as ice hockey, lacrosse, and soccer. Also, **goalie, goaltender.**

goal line, either of two lines marking the goals in a game.

goal·post (gōl′pōst′) *n.* a structure consisting of a pair of posts and a crossbar, used as the goal in football and certain other games.

goal·tend·er (gōl′ten′dər) *n.* another word for **goalkeeper.**

goat (gōt) *n.* **1.** any of various cud-chewing animals related to the sheep, having hollow horns and frequently a tuft of hair under the chin. **2.** *Informal.* **a.** a person who is made to take the blame or punishment for others; scapegoat. **b.** a person who is the butt of a joke. —**goat′like′,** *adj.*

goat·ee (gō tē′) *n.* a small pointed beard.

goat·herd (gōt′hûrd′) *n.* a person who tends goats.

goat·skin (gōt′skin′) *n.* **1.** the skin of a goat. **2.** the leather made from this skin. **3.** a container made from this leather, used especially for wine.

gob¹ (gob) *n. Informal.* **1.** a mass or lump. **2. gobs.** a large quantity; a lot: *We prepared gobs of food for the picnic.* [From the Old French word *gobe* meaning "lump of food, chunk."]

gob² (gob) *n. Slang.* a sailor in the U.S. Navy. [Of uncertain origin.]

gob·ble¹ (gob′əl) *v.t.,* **gob·bled, gob·bling. 1.** to eat (food) rapidly and greedily. **2.** *Informal.* to seize eagerly or greedily. [From the Middle English word *gobben* meaning "to drink greedily."]

gob·ble² (gob′əl) *v.i.,* **gob·bled, gob·bling.** to make the throaty sound characteristic of a male turkey. —*n.* such a sound. [Representation of this sound.]

gob·ble·dy·gook (gob′əl dē gŭk′) *also,* **gob·ble·de·gook** *n. Informal.* speech or writing that is wordy, complicated, and hard to understand.

gob·bler (gob′lər) *n.* a male turkey.

go·be·tween (gō′bi twēn′) *n.* a person who goes back and forth between persons or groups to make arrangements, conduct business, or settle disputes.

gob·let (gob′lit) *n.* a drinking glass with a base and stem.

gob·lin (gob′lin) *n.* an ugly, mischievous sprite or elf, especially one that is evil or wicked.

God (god) *n.* **1.** The Supreme Being in monotheistic religions considered as the eternal, all-powerful creator and ruler of the universe. **2. god. a.** any of various deities, especially a male deity, as in Greek and Roman mythology, believed to have special powers over the lives and affairs of humans. **b.** an image of a god that is an object of worship; idol. **3.** a person or thing that is made an object of worship, devotion, or admiration.

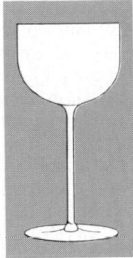
goblet

god·child (god′chīld′) *n., pl.* **god·chil·dren** (god′-chil′drən).** a person for whom another person acts as sponsor, as at baptism.

god·daugh·ter (god′dô′tər) *n.* a female godchild.

god·dess (god′is) *n., pl.* **god·dess·es. 1.** a female deity, as in Greek and Roman mythology, believed to have special powers over the lives and affairs of humans. **2.** an extremely beautiful woman.

god·fa·ther (god′fä′thər) *n.* a man who acts as a sponsor for a child, as at baptism.

God·head (god′hed′) *n.* **1.** God. **2.** *also,* **godhead.** divine nature; divinity.

god·less (god′lis) *adj.* **1.** not believing in God or a god. **2.** wicked. —**god′less·ness,** *n.*

god·like (god′līk′) *adj.* suitable to or like God or a god.

god·ly (god′lē) *adj.,* **god·li·er, god·li·est.** faithful to God and obeying God's laws; pious. —**god′li·ness,** *n.*

god·moth·er (god′muth′ər) *n.* a woman who acts as a sponsor for a child, as at baptism.

god·par·ent (god′pâr′ənt) *n.* a godfather or godmother.

God's acre, a cemetery, especially in a churchyard.

god·send (god′send′) *n.* something that is needed or desired and arrives or happens unexpectedly: *The inheritance was a godsend to the poor couple.*

god·son (god′sun′) *n.* a male godchild.

God·speed (god′spēd′) *n.* a success; good luck.

go·fer (gō′fər) *n. Slang.* an employee whose duties include running errands for a work crew or office staff. [From the phrase *go for* meaning "to fetch."]

go-get·ter (gō′get′ər) *n. Informal.* a person who is full of energy and ambition.

gog·gle (gog′əl) *v.i.,* **gog·gled, gog·gling.** to roll one's eyes or stare with bulging eyes.

gog·gles (gog′əlz) *pl. n.* large, close-fitting eyeglasses used to protect the eyes, as from wind, dust, or sparks. Skiers and welders often wear goggles.

gog·gle-eyed (gog′əl īd′) *adj.* having rolling, bulging, or staring eyes.

G

at; āpe; fär; câre; end; mē; it; īce; pîerce; hot; ōld; sông, fôrk; oil; out; up; ūse; rüle; pùll; tûrn; chin; sing; shop; thin; <u>th</u>is; hw in white; zh in treasure. The symbol ə stands for the unstressed vowel sound heard in about, taken, pencil, lemon, and circus.

go·ing (gō′ing) *n.* **1.** the act of moving away or departing: *Their going was unexpected.* **2.** the condition of a surface or the environment, as for walking, driving, or flying: *The going was muddy because of heavy rain.* —*adj.* **1.** working or moving: *My watch is in going condition.* **2.** operating successfully: *The shop is a going business.* **3.** current; prevailing: *What is the going price for that type of car?* **4.** *Informal.* in existence; around: *I think that is the funniest joke going.*

goings on, actions, behavior, or incidents, especially when disapproved of: *Police investigated the strange goings on at the old house.*

goi·ter (goi′tər) *also,* **goi·tre.** *n.* an enlargement of the thyroid gland causing a swelling in the neck. It is often caused by improper functioning of the thyroid or a deficiency of iodine in the diet.

gold (gōld) *n.* **1.** a heavy, soft, yellow metallic element that is extremely ductile, malleable, and resistant to corrosion. It has long been used as a standard for currency. Gold is also used in making jewelry, coins, and electronic devices. Symbol: **Au** **2.** coins made of this metal. **3.** wealth; riches. **4.** a bright yellow color. **5.** anything resembling or compared to gold, as in worth or beauty: *a heart of gold.* —*adj.* **1.** relating to, containing, or made of gold: *a gold bracelet, a gold tooth.* **2.** having the color gold; bright yellow. [From the Old English word *gold.*]

gold·brick (gōld′brik′) *v.i.* *Slang.* to get out of or avoid work or duty, as by pretending to be ill. —*n.* a person, especially in the armed forces, who gets out of or avoids work or duty. —**gold′brick·er,** *n.*

gold·en (gōl′dən) *adj.* **1.** made of or containing gold: *a golden locket.* **2.** having the color or luster of gold: *the golden sun.* **3.** excellent or very valuable: *a golden opportunity.* **4.** very happy and prosperous; flourishing: *the golden age of a country's history.* **5.** of or marking the fiftieth year or event in a series: *My grandparents recently celebrated their golden wedding anniversary.*

golden age, a period during which the highest level of achievement, progress, or prosperity is reached: *the golden age of Greece, the golden age of exploration.*

golden eagle, a large eagle of the Northern Hemisphere, having dark brown feathers with golden tints on the head and back of the neck.

Golden Fleece *Greek Legend.* the sheepskin from a golden ram, kept in a grove guarded by a dragon. It was stolen by Jason and the Argonauts.

golden mean, a course or way that avoids extremes; moderation.

gold·en·rod (gōl′dən rod′) *n.* a plant having clusters of small, usually yellow flowers on tall, branching stalks.

golden rule, the rule of conduct that one should treat others as one wishes to be treated.

gold–filled (gōld′fild′) *adj.* made of or containing metal covered with a layer of gold.

gold·finch (gōld′finch′) *n., pl.* **gold·finch·es.** **1.** an American finch, the male of which is bright yellow with black markings in the summer. **2.** a European songbird having a red face and yellow markings on its wings.

gold·fish (gōld′fish′) *n., pl.* **gold·fish** or **gold·fish·es.** a freshwater fish related to the carp and native to southeastern Asia, ranging in color from gold to black. Many varieties are raised in home aquariums and outdoor ponds.

gold leaf, gold beaten into extremely thin sheets, used in gilding.

gold mine **1.** a mine from which gold ore is obtained. **2.** a rich source of something valuable or desired: *This book is a gold mine of information.*

gold rush, a sudden rush of people to an area where gold has been discovered, as to California in 1849.

gold·smith (gōld′smith′) *n.* a person who makes or deals in objects of gold, such as jewelry.

gold standard, a monetary system by which the value of a nation's currency is based on the gold that the nation possesses.

golf (golf) *n.* a game played on a golf course with a small, hard ball and a set of golf clubs. The object of the game is to hit the ball into a series of holes with as few strokes as possible. —*v.i.* to play the game of golf. —**golf′er,** *n.*

golf club **1.** any of various clubs with long, thin shafts and wooden or iron heads, used to hit the ball in golf. **2.** A club made up of golfers. **3.** The clubhouse and land belonging to such a club.

golf course, an area of land for playing golf, usually having eighteen holes. Also, **golf links.**

gol·ly (gol′ē) *interj.* *Informal.* a word used to express surprise or wonder.

go·nad (gō′nad) *n.* a male or female sex organ in which reproductive cells develop and in which sex hormones are produced. The ovaries are the female gonads, and the testes are the male gonads.

gon·do·la (gon′də lə) *n.* **1.** a long, narrow, flat-bottomed boat with high peaks at the ends, propelled at the stern by one person with an oar or pole. It is used to carry passengers on the canals of Venice. **2.** see **gondola car.** **3.** a car suspended under a dirigible or balloon.

gondola car, a railroad freight car with low sides and no top.

gon·do·lier (gon′də lîr′) *n.* a person who rows or poles a gondola.

gondola (def. 1)

gone (gôn, gon) *v.* the past participle of **go.** —*adj.* **1.** moved away; left; departed: *They are gone for the summer.* **2.** used up or spent: *The casserole is all gone, but there's still plenty of turkey left.* **3.** dead. **4.** beyond hope or recovery; lost; ruined. **5.** characterized by weakness or faintness: *a gone feeling.*

gon·er (gô′nər, gon′ər) *n.* *Informal.* a person or thing that is dying, ruined, lost, or beyond help or recovery.

gong (gông, gong) *n.* **1.** a large metal disk that makes a loud, resonant tone when struck. **2.** a saucer-shaped bell sounded by a mechanical hammer.

gon·or·rhe·a (gon′ə rē′ə) *also,* **gon·or·rhoe·a.** *n.* a contagious bacterial disease that causes inflammation of the genital and urinary organs. If left untreated, it can lead to serious complications.

goo (gü) *n.* *Informal.* any sticky substance, such as glue.

goo·ber (gü′bər) *n.* *Informal.* a peanut.

good (gůd) *adj.,* **bet·ter, best.** **1.** above average in quality; not bad or poor: *a good movie.* **2.** agreeable; pleasant: *good news.* **3.** kind or helpful; considerate: *My parents are very good to me.* **4.** skillful; talented: *a good dancer.* **5.** honorable: *a good reputation.* **6.** sound or reliable: *a good investment, good advice.* **7.** genuine or valid: *a good excuse.* **8.** beneficial; advantageous: *The new trade agreement was good for the country's economy.* **9.** representative; typical: *That is a good example of Greek architecture*. **10.** not impaired; sound: *good health*. **11.** fairly great, as in amount or extent; considerable: *a good number of people at the party*. **12.** well-behaved; obedient: *a good child*. **13.** thorough: *a good scolding*. **14.** not spoiled; fresh: *Is the meat still good?* —*n*. **1.** benefit; advantage: *I am telling you this for your own good*. **2.** moral goodness; virtue. —*adv*. *Informal*. well.

·**as good as**. almost; practically: *The game is as good as over*.

·**for good**. finally; permanently: *Our teacher is leaving for good*.

·**good and**. *Informal*. completely or extremely; thoroughly: *Their comments made me good and angry*.

·**good for**. **a**. able to last or remain valid or functioning for: *The offer is good for another month*. **b**. able or willing to pay or give.

·**no good**. worthless or useless.

·**to make good**. **a**. to keep or fulfill: *I made good my promise to pay the money back*. **b**. to make up for; repay or replace: *to make good the damage done in a car collision*. **c**. to be successful.

·**to the good**. as a profit or advantage.

Good Book, the Bible.

good-bye (gùd'bī') *also,* **good-by**. *interj*. farewell. —*n., pl.* **good-byes**. farewell: *After the necessary good-byes, we left the house*. [From the earlier salutation *God be with you!*]

good day, an expression of greeting or farewell used in the daytime.

good evening, an expression of greeting or farewell used in the evening.

good-for-noth·ing (gùd'fər nuth'ing) *adj*. useless or worthless. —*n*. a person who is idle, worthless, or useless.

Good Friday, the Friday before Easter, commemorating the crucifixion of Jesus.

good-heart·ed (gùd'här'tid) *adj*. kind or generous. —**good'-heart'ed·ly,** *adv*. —**good'-heart'ed·ness,** *n*.

good-hu·mored (gùd'hū'mərd) *adj*. having or showing a cheerful, pleasant, or friendly mood or feeling. —**good'-hu'mored·ly,** *adv*.

good-look·ing (gùd'lùk'ing) *adj*. pleasing or attractive in appearance; beautiful or handsome.

good·ly (gùd'lē) *adj.,* **good·li·er, good·li·est**. fairly large, as in amount or degree: *Their trip cost a goodly sum of money*. —**good'li·ness,** *n*.

good·man (gùd'mən) *n., pl.* **good·men** (gùd'mən). *Archaic*. **1.** the master or male head of a household. **2.** a title of respect for a man below the rank of gentleman; mister.

good morning, an expression of greeting or farewell used in the morning.

good-na·tured (gùd'nā'chərd) *adj*. having or showing a pleasant or kindly disposition; agreeable. —**good'-na'tured·ly,** *adv*. —**good'-na'tured·ness,** *n*.

good·ness (gùd'nis) *n*. **1.** the state or quality of being good. **2.** the best or most valuable part of something. —*interj*. used to express surprise.

goods (gùdz) *pl. n*. **1.** things that are sold; merchandise; wares. **2.** personal property; belongings: *They lost all their worldly goods in the fire*. **3.** fabric; cloth.

Good Samaritan **1.** in the New Testament, a traveler who aided a fellow traveler who had been beaten and robbed. **2.** any person who is compassionate and helpful toward others.

good·wife (gùd'wīf') *n., pl.* **good·wives** (gùd'wīvz'). *Archaic*. **1.** the mistress of a household. **2.** a title of respect for a woman below the rank of lady.

good·will (gud'wil') *also,* **good will**. *n*. **1.** kindness or friendliness: *a feeling of goodwill toward others*. **2.** cheerful consent; willingness: *They accepted the task*

with goodwill. **3.** an intangible asset of a business, resulting from the good relations it has established with the public.

good·y (gùd'ē) *n., pl.* **good·ies**. *Informal*. something that is good to eat or that is otherwise pleasurable or desirable. *interj*. used to express delight or pleasure.

goo·ey (gü'ē) *adj.,* **goo·i·er, goo·i·est**. *Informal*. soft and sticky.

goof (güf) *Informal. n*. **1.** a stupid or clumsy mistake; blunder. **2.** a stupid, silly, or blundering person. —*v.i*. to make a stupid or clumsy mistake; blunder. —*v.t*. to make a mess of: *I really goofed up that assignment*.

·**to goof off**. to avoid work or duty or do nothing: *The banker spent most of the day goofing off*.

goof·y (gü'fē) *adj.,* **goof·i·er, goof·i·est**. *Slang*. stupid, silly, or ridiculous. —**goof'i·ness,** *n*.

goon (gün) *n*. *Slang*. **1.** a hoodlum or thug. **2.** a stupid, rough, or clumsy person.

goose (güs) *n., pl.* **geese**. **1.** any of various wild or tame web-footed water birds, found throughout most of the world, resembling, but larger than, a duck and usually having a longer neck. **2.** a female goose. A male goose is called a gander. **3.** the flesh of a goose, used as food. **4.** *Informal*. a foolish, silly person.

·**to cook one's goose**. *Informal*. to ruin one's chances.

goose *(def. 1)*

goose·ber·ry (güs'ber'ē, güz'bə rē) *n., pl.* **goose·ber·ries**. **1.** a tart berry of any of a group of usually thorny shrubs widely grown in many parts of Europe and North America. **2.** the shrub bearing this berry.

goose flesh, a temporary, rough condition of the skin making it look like the skin of a goose, caused by the contraction of tiny muscles at the base of each hair. It usually results from cold or fear. Also, **goose bumps, goose pimples**.

goose·neck (güs'nek') *n*. something long and curved like a goose's neck, such as a flexible support for a desk lamp.

goose·step (güs'step') *v.i.,* **goose-stepped, goose-step·ping**. to march in a goose step.

goose step, a marching step in which the legs are held straight and kicked high with the knees unbent.

G.O.P., Grand Old Party; the Republican Party.

go·pher (go'fər) *n*. **1.** any of various burrowing rodents found throughout North and Central America, having large cheek pouches. **2.** a ground squirrel.

Gor·di·an knot (gôr'dē ən) *Greek Legend*. an intricate knot that could be untied only by the person who should rule Asia. Alexander the Great, instead of trying to untie the knot, cut through it with his sword.

gopher

·**to cut the Gordian knot**. to find and use quick or bold means to solve a problem or difficulty.

gore¹ (gôr) *n*. blood that has been shed, especially when thick or clotted. [From the Old English word *gor* meaning "dung, dirt."]

gore² (gôr) *v.t.,* **gored, gor·ing**. (of an animal) to pierce

at; āpe; fär; câre; end; mē; it; īce; pîerce; hot; ōld; sông, fôrk; oil; out; up; ūse; rüle; pùll; tûrn; chin; sing; shop; thin; <u>th</u>is; hw in white; zh in treasure. The symbol ə stands for the unstressed vowel sound heard in about, taken, pencil, lemon, and circus.

with a horn or tusk: *The bull gored the unlucky matador.* [From the Middle English word *goren* meaning "to pierce, stab."]

gore³ (gôr) *n.* a triangular piece of fabric, used to add fullness, as in umbrellas, sails, or certain skirts. —*v.t.*, **gored, gor·ing.** to make or furnish with a gore or gores. [From the Old English word *gāra* meaning "triangular piece of land."]

gorge (gôrj) *n.* **1.** a deep, narrow opening or passage between steep and rocky sides of walls or mountains. **2.** a mass that stops up or clogs a passage: *an ice gorge.* **3.** *Archaic.* the throat; gullet. —*v.*, **gorged, gorg·ing.** —*v.t.* **1.** to stuff with food: *to gorge oneself at dinner.* **2.** to swallow or eat greedily: *Don't gorge your food!* —*v.i.* to stuff oneself with food. —**gorg'er,** *n.* **·to make one's gorge rise.** to cause to feel anger or disgust.

gor·geous (gôr'jəs) *adj.* **1.** dazzling or magnificent, as in beauty or brilliance: *gorgeous autumn leaves.* **2.** *Informal.* delightful or enjoyable; wonderful: *We had a gorgeous time at your party.* —**gor'geous·ly,** *adv.* —**gor'geous·ness,** *n.*

Gor·gon (gôr'gən) *n.* *Greek Legend.* any of three sisters who had snakes for hair and whose faces were so horrible that anyone who looked at them was turned to stone.

go·ril·la (gə ril'ə) *n.* an ape of Africa, having a large, heavy body, short legs, long arms, and a gray or black coat. It is the largest and most powerful ape. [Formed from the Greek word *Gorillai,* the name of a tribe of supposedly hairy women.]

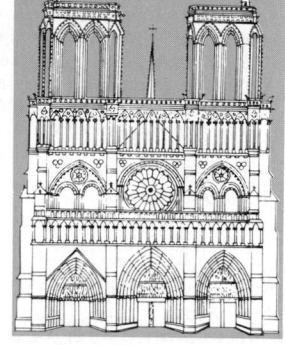

gor·mand·ize (gôr'mən dīz') *v.i.*, **gor·mand·ized, gor·mand·iz·ing.** to eat like a glutton; gorge. —**gor'mand·iz'er,** *n.*

gorp (gôrp) *n.* a high-energy snack consisting of a mixture of foods such as nuts, seeds, dried fruit, or chocolate.

gorse (gôrs) *n.* any of a group of spiny shrubs found in Europe, Asia,

gorilla

and parts of North America, bearing yellow flowers. Also, **furze.**

gor·y (gôr'ē) *adj.*, **gor·i·er, gor·i·est.** **1.** covered with gore; bloody. **2.** characterized by bloodshed: *a gory clash of two armies.* **3.** like gore; disgusting; horrible: *They spared us the gory details of the accident.* —**gor'i·ly,** *adv.* —**gor'i·ness,** *n.*

gosh (gosh) *interj.* used to express pleasure or surprise.

gos·hawk (gos'hôk') *n.* a powerful, short-winged hawk of northern North America, Europe, and Asia.

Go·shen (gō'shən) *n.* a land of plenty and peace. [From *Goshen,* the fertile region of northern Egypt where the Israelites lived before the Exodus.]

gos·ling (goz'ling) *n.* a young goose.

gos·pel (gos'pəl) *n.* **1.** the teachings of Jesus and the Apostles. **2.** Gospel. **a.** any one of the first four books of the New Testament, believed to have been written by Matthew, Mark, Luke, and John. **b.** a part of one of these books read in a religious service. **3.** something accepted as absolutely true or serving as a guide for action: *The rebels preached the gospel of revolution.* **4.** see **gospel music.** —*adj.* of, relating to, or according to the gospel.

gospel music, a kind of religious vocal music developed by Southern blacks that combines the rhythms and intensity of spirituals with the melodies and harmonies of folk music. Also, **gospel.**

gos·sa·mer (gos'ə mər) *n.* **1.** a fine, filmy cobweb, seen especially in autumn floating in the air or suspended from bushes or grass. **2.** any light or filmy substance. **3.** a

light, delicate, gauzelike fabric. —*adj.* of or like gossamer; light, filmy, or delicate.

gos·sip (gos'ip) *n.* **1.** idle talk or rumors, often unfriendly, especially about the personal affairs of other people. **2.** a person who is fond of repeating gossip. —*v.*, **gos·siped, gos·sip·ing.** —*v.i.* to repeat gossip: *to gossip about one's friends.* —**gos'sip·er,** *n.*

gos·sip·y (gos'ə pē) *adj.* **1.** fond of gossip: *a gossipy person.* **2.** full of gossip: *a gossipy newspaper column.*

got (got) the past tense and a past participle of **get.**

Goth (goth) *n.* a member of a Germanic people that invaded the Roman Empire in the third, fourth, and fifth centuries A.D.

Goth·ic (goth'ik) *adj.* **1.** of or relating to a style of architecture developed in Europe between the twelfth and sixteenth centuries, characterized by pointed arches, rib vaulting, and flying buttresses. **2.** of or relating to the Goths, their language, or their culture. **3.** *also,* **gothic.** of, relating to, or characteristic of a literary style emphasizing the grotesque, horrible, violent, and mysterious. —*n.* **1.** the language of the Goths. **2.** Gothic architecture.

got·ten (got'ən) a past participle of **get.**

gouge (gouj) *n.* **1.** a tool like a chisel but having a curved, hollow blade, used for cutting rounded grooves or holes in wood. **2.** a groove or hole made by gouging. **3.** *Slang.* the act of cheating or defrauding. —*v.t.*, **gouged, goug·ing.** **1.** to cut or scoop out with or as with a gouge. **2.** to dig, tear, or poke (usually with *out*): *to gouge out an eye.* **3.** *Slang.* to cheat or defraud.

Gothic cathedral

gou·lash (gü'läsh) *n.*, *pl.* **gou·lash·es.** a stew made of beef or veal and vegetables, usually seasoned with paprika.

gourd (gôrd) *n.* **1.** the hard-shelled fruit of any of a group of trailing or climbing vines. **2.** the vine bearing this fruit. **3.** the dried shell of a gourd, used as a dipper, cup, or bowl.

gour·mand (gùr'mənd, gùr-mänd') *n.* **1.** a person who loves fine food and drink. **2.** a glutton.

gour·met (gùr mā', gùr'mā) *n.* a person who is expert in choosing and judging fine food and drink.

gout (gout) *n.* **1.** a disease characterized by painful swelling of the joints, especially the big toe. **2.** a drop or clot: *a gout of blood.*

gourd *(def. 1)*

gout·y (gou'tē) *adj.*, **gout·i·er, gout·i·est.** **1.** of, relating to, or like gout. **2.** caused by or causing gout. —**gout'i·ly,** *adv.* —**gout'i·ness,** *n.*

gov., Gov. 1. government. **2.** governor.

gov·ern (guv'ərn) *v.t.* **1.** to rule, control, or direct by right of authority: *In the United States, Congress and the president govern the nation.* **2.** to direct or influence; guide: *Concern for their own welfare governed their actions.* **3.** to hold in check; restrain; curb: *Govern your temper.* —**gov'ern·a·ble,** *adj.*

gov·ern·ess (guv'ər nis) *n.*, *pl.* **gov·ern·ess·es.** a woman employed to teach and train children in their home.

gov·ern·ment (guv'ərn mənt, guv'ər mənt) *n.* **1.** an organization or body that rules, controls, or directs a city, state, nation, or other political unit: *to work for the federal government.* **2.** a system or form of ruling by which a given political unit is governed: *parliamentary government, democratic government.* **3.** control or authority; rule: *My cousin took part in the government of our student society.* —**gov′ern·men′tal,** *adj.* —**gov′ern·men′tal·ly,** *adv.*

gov·er·nor (guv′ər nər) *n.* **1.** the chief executive of a state of the United States. **2.** an official appointed to govern a province, colony, or territory. **3.** a person who manages or directs a social organization or financial institution: *the board of governors of a club.* **4.** an automatic device for regulating the speed of an engine by controlling the rate at which fuel or steam is supplied to the engine.

gov·er·nor·ship (guv′ər nər ship′) *n.* the duties, position, or term of office of a governor.

govt., Govt., government.

gown (goun) *n.* **1.** a woman's dress, especially a formal dress. **2.** a long, loose outer garment worn to show the wearer's office, profession, or status; robe. **3.** a nightgown or dressing gown. —*v.t.* to dress in a gown.

GP, general practitioner.

gr. 1. grade. **2.** grain. **3.** gram; grams. **4.** gross.

Gr. 1. Grecian. **2.** Greece. **3.** Greek.

grab (grab) *v.,* **grabbed, grab·bing.** —*v.t.* **1.** to grasp or snatch suddenly: *The dog grabbed the bone from the table.* **2.** to obtain by force or in an unscrupulous or illegal way: *an army grabbing the land of a conquered people.* **3.** to take, get, or have: *to grab a sandwich for lunch.* —*v.i.* to make a grasping or snatching motion: *The drowning child grabbed for the life preserver.* —*n.* the act of grabbing: *The baseball player made a grab at the ball.* —**grab′ber,** *n.*

grab bag, a bag filled with wrapped articles, from which a person takes one without knowing what it is.

grace (grās) *n.* **1.** beauty or harmony of form, movement, or manner: *The ballet dancers performed with grace.* **2.** a short prayer or blessing before or after a meal. **3.** good manners; consideration: *They had the grace to apologize for leaving the party early.* **4.** the favor and love of God. **5.** an attractive or charming quality or accomplishment: *Playing the piano is a social grace.* **6.** see **grace period. 7. Grace.** worship; eminence. A used to address or speak of royalty, nobility, or clergy: *Your Grace.* **8. Graces.** *Greek Mythology.* three young and beautiful sister goddesses who gave beauty, happiness, and charm. —*v.t.,* **graced, grac·ing. 1.** to add grace or beauty to; adorn: *The lovely park graced the city.* **2.** to favor or honor: *The queen and king graced the ball with their presence.*

·**in the bad graces of.** disliked or disapproved by; in disfavor with.

·**in the good graces of.** liked or approved by; in favor with.

grace·ful (grās′fəl) *adj.* having beauty or harmony of form, movement, or manner: *a graceful acrobat.* —**grace′ful·ly,** *adv.* —**grace′ful·ness,** *n.*

grace·less (grās′lis) *adj.* **1.** without beauty or harmony of form, movement, or manner. **2.** without a sense of what is right or proper. —**grace′less·ly,** *adv.* —**grace′less·ness,** *n.*

grace note *Music.* a note added to ornament the melody or harmony.

grace period, an allowance of extra time: *That company allows a three-week grace period to pay a bill after it is due.*

gra·cious (grā′shəs) *adj.* **1.** having or showing kindness and courtesy: *a gracious host.* **2.** elegant, leisurely, and comfortable: *gracious living.* **3.** merciful; kindly. —*interj.* used to express surprise. —**gra′cious·ly,** *adv.* —**gra′cious·ness,** *n.*

grack·le (grak′əl) *n.* any of several North American blackbirds having a long, wedge-shaped tail and shiny black feathers.

gra·da·tion (grā dā′shən) *n.* **1.** a gradual change by a series of steps, stages, or degrees: *a control to produce gradations of volume from loud to soft.* **2.** a step, stage, or degree in such a series: *the gradations of colors in a rainbow.*

grade (grād) *n.* **1.** any one of the divisions of study in an elementary or high school, usually one year's work: *I am in the sixth grade.* **2.** a number or letter showing how well a student has done in work at school: *a grade of eighty on a geography paper.* **3.** a degree or step in quality, value, rank, or order: *a grade of beef, the grade of sergeant.* **4.** a class or group of people or things that are the same or equal, as in quality, value, or rank: *These are the best grade of eggs that we carry.* **5.** the slope of a road or railroad track: *a steep grade on a mountain road.* —*v.,* **grad·ed, grad·ing.** —*v.t.* **1.** to arrange or sort in grades; classify: *The farmer graded the eggs by size and color.* **2.** to give a grade to: *The teacher was grading term papers.* **3.** to make (ground) more level; lessen the slope of: *The bulldozer graded the new road.* —*v.i.* to pass through a series of stages or degrees; change gradually: *The colors graded from dark red to bright pink.*

Word Family

The Latin word *gradus,* meaning "a step, grade, approach," has become a common part of many English words. The "steps" by which we proceed through school are called **grades.** Although the progress may seem very **gradual,** with study and hard work students eventually **graduate.** At **graduation,** a person is awarded a **degree** (a word also taken from this root). The **gradation** markings on a measuring cup indicate how much of something it contains. The slope of a hill is called its **gradient.**

From the verb form of this same Latin word *gradus* we derive numerous words containing the form -*gress.* Movement forward is called **progress,** and a person who makes such a **progression** from one stage to another may well be called **progressive.** The opposite is to move backward, or to **regress.** An attacking move may be considered **aggressive.** To "go off" the path of an idea is to **digress.** Officials "come together" to make laws in a **congress,** as do the members of the U.S. **Congress.**

grade crossing, a place where a railroad track crosses a road or another railroad track at the same level.

grad·er (grā′dər) *n.* **1.** a person or thing that grades. **2.** a pupil in a certain grade in school: *a twelfth grader.*

grade school, another term for **elementary school.**

gra·di·ent (grā′dē ənt) *n.* **1.** the amount or degree of slope, as of a road or railroad track. **2.** a sloping surface. **3.** *Physics.* the rate at which a variable quantity, such as temperature or pressure, changes.

grad·u·al (graj′ü əl) *adj.* **1.** moving, changing, or happening slowly or by degrees: *a gradual change in the*

at; āpe; fär; câre; end; mē; it; īce; pîerce; hot; ōld; sông, fôrk; oil; out; up; ūse; rüle; pùll; tûrn; chin; sing; shop; thin; <u>th</u>is; hw in white; zh in treasure. The symbol ə stands for the unstressed vowel sound heard in about, taken, pencil, lemon, and circus.

G

weather. **2.** not steep or abrupt: *a gradual rise in a road.* —**grad′u·al·ly,** *adv.* —**grad′u·al·ness,** *n.*

grad·u·ate (*v.,* graj′ü āt′; *n., adj.,* graj′ü it) *v.,* **grad·u·at·ed, grad·u·at·ing.** —*v.i.* to receive a diploma or degree after the completion of a course of study. —*v.t.* **1.** to give an academic diploma or degree to (someone) for the completion of a course of study. **2.** to mark with or divide into degrees, units, or similar divisions. —*n.* a person who has been given a diploma or degree for completion of a course of study. —*adj.* of, relating to, or taking postgraduate courses: *a graduate student, graduate seminars.*

grad·u·a·tion (graj′ü ā′shən) *n.* **1.** the act of graduating or the state of being graduated. **2.** the ceremony of giving diplomas or degrees, as at a school or university. **3.** a mark or series of marks showing degrees or quantity, used for measuring: *graduations on a thermometer.*

graf·fi·ti (grə fē′tē) *pl. n.,* *sing.* **graf·fi·to** (grə fē′tō). words or drawings on walls, fences, sidewalks, etc.

graft¹ (graft) *v.t.* **1.** to put a shoot, bud, or branch from one plant, especially a tree, into a cut or slit in another so that the two pieces will grow together and eventually form one plant. **2.** to transplant (skin or bone) from one part of the body to another or from one person to another: *to graft new skin onto a burned arm.* —*n.* **1.** a shoot, bud, or branch that has been grafted. **2.** a piece of skin or bone surgically transplanted from one part of the body to another, or from one person to another. **3.** the act or process of grafting. [From the Old French word *grafe* meaning "stylus" or "slender shoot of a plant," from the Latin word *graphium* "stylus," from the Greek word *grapheion* "pencil, stylus."]

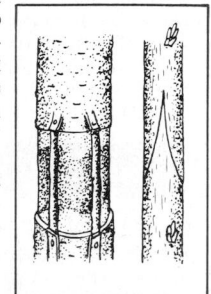

graft¹ *(n., def. 1)*

graft² (graft) *n.* **1.** the gaining of money or advantages by dishonest means, especially through one's political influence or position. **2.** something gained by such means. —*v.i.* to gain money or advantages by dishonest means. [Of uncertain origin.] —**graft′er,** *n.*

gra·ham (grā′əm) *adj.* made from or consisting of unsifted whole-wheat flour: *graham crackers.*

Grail (grāl) *n.* see **Holy Grail.**

grain (grān) *n.* **1.** the seed of various cereal grasses, such as rye, wheat, oats, or corn. **2.** the plants bearing such seeds. **3.** a tiny, hard particle: *a grain of sand, a grain of sugar.* **4.** the markings or patterns in wood, stone, cloth or other materials caused by the arrangement of fibers or layers. **5.** a very small unit of weight, equal to 64.8 milligrams. **6.** the smallest possible amount; tiny bit: *There isn't a grain of truth in what they said.*

grain alcohol, see **alcohol** *(def. 1).*

grain elevator, a building for the storage of grain.

grain·y (grā′nē) *adj.,* **grain·i·er, grain·i·est.** **1.** of or like grains; granular. **2.** having a grain: *grainy wood.* —**grain′i·ness,** *n.*

gram (gram) *also, British,* **gramme.** *n.* a unit of mass or weight in the metric system, equal to ¹⁄₂₈ of an ounce.

-gram¹ *combining form* something written or drawn: *telegram, diagram.* [Originally from the Greek word *gramma* meaning "letter" or "something written," from the word *graphein* "to write."]

-gram² *combining form* of a gram; grams: *centigram, kilogram.* [From the word *gram.*]

gram atom, the quantity of a chemical element having a weight in grams numerically equal to the atomic weight of the element. One gram atom of aluminum, which has an atomic weight of 27, weighs 27 grams.

gram·mar (gram′ər) *n.* **1.** the study of the structure and forms of words in a language and of the way the words are used by people to communicate. **2.** the rules governing the way words in a language are arranged to form phrases, clauses, and sentences. **3.** a book about grammar. **4.** grammar as part of a course of study in school: *I was never very interested in grammar.* **5.** the use of words according to accepted or standard principles; usage: *Many people are concerned with proper grammar.*

Language Note

Grammar is the system of arranging words so that the meaning of what is said or written is clearly communicated. This system is based on a series of rules, most of which come naturally to us as we use our language and hear it used. The five words in the sentence *Give me your red pencil* can be arranged 120 different ways, yet we instinctively know in what order the words should go. Young children learn to speak long before they have any conscious idea of the rules of grammar. They hear language and quickly learn how to make themselves understood. In early times, English grammar existed in only this way; there was little interest in setting down rules.

The first real interest in the organized study of English grammar began in the fifteenth and sixteenth centuries, when there was a great revival of interest in the Greek and Latin languages. The study of Latin grammar, in particular, deeply influenced later attitudes and theories about English grammar, even though Latin grammar is unrelated to English grammar. In the late seventeenth century, English scholars became very interested in "purifying" the language, and they began devising new rules and refinements of grammar. For example, you may still hear about a very precise rule about when to use the words *shall* and *will,* a "rule" first set down by an English grammarian in 1653. An eighteenth-century rule condemned the use of a double negative, stating that two negatives would cancel each other out rather than add further negative emphasis. The fact that many great writers, including Shakespeare, had used the double negative did not change the new feeling that its use was incorrect.

In the nineteenth century, linguists began to reject such ideas. They studied grammar by tracing the natural, historical development of English in its own terms, rather than in relation to Latin or to artificial rules. They realized that the true basis for grammar is found in what is actually said, rather than what artificial rules demand should be said.

Modern grammar focuses mainly on communication. For this reason, there has been a trend toward eliminating those rules that make using language difficult and complicated, and emphasizing those rules or concepts that make communication through language simple, natural, and effective.

gram·mar·i·an (grə mâr′ē ən) *n.* a student of or an expert in grammar.

grammar school **1.** another term for **elementary school.** **2.** a secondary school, especially in England, in which college preparatory subjects are emphasized.

gram·mat·i·cal (grə mat′i kəl) *adj.* **1.** of or relating to grammar. **2.** following the rules of grammar: *The sentence "I bought a shirt white" is not grammatical.* —**grammat′i·cal·ly,** *adv.* —**gram·mat′i·cal·ness,** *n.*

gramme (gram) another spelling of **gram.**

gram·o·phone (gram′ə fōn′) *n.* a phonograph.

gram·pus (gram′pəs) *n., pl.* **gram·pus·es.** a large dolphin found in all seas except those in polar regions.

gra·na·ry (grā′nə rē, gran′ə rē) *n., pl.* **gra·na·ries.** a storehouse for grain.

grand (grand) *adj.* **1.** large and impressive; magnificent: *a grand palace.* **2.** noble or dignified: *The judge was a grand person.* **3.** including everything; complete: *The grand total of their winnings was $3,000.* **4.** most important; main; principal: *The dance was held in the grand ballroom.* **5.** *Informal.* very good or excellent: *We had a grand time at the party.* —*n.* **1.** see **grand piano.** **2.** *Slang.* $1,000. —**grand′ly,** *adv.* —**grand′ness,** *n.*

grand·aunt (grand′ant′, grand′änt′) *n.* an aunt of one's father or mother. Also, **great-aunt.**

grand·child (grand′chīld′) *n., pl.* **grand·chil·dren** (grand′chil′drən). a child of one's son or daughter.

Grand Cou·lee (kü′lē) a large dam on the Columbia River, in east-central Washington.

grand·daugh·ter (gran′dô′tər) *n.* a daughter of one's son or daughter.

grand duchess 1. the wife or widow of a grand duke. **2.** a woman ruling a grand duchy. **3.** in czarist Russia, a princess of the royal family.

grand duchy, a territory under the rule of a grand duke or grand duchess.

grand duke 1. the ruler of a grand duchy. **2.** in czarist Russia, a prince of the royal family.

gran·dee (gran dē′) *n.* **1.** a Spanish or Portuguese nobleman of the highest rank. **2.** any person of high rank or great importance.

gran·deur (gran′jər) *n.* the state or quality of being majestic or imposing; magnificence; splendor.

grand·fa·ther (grand′fä′thər) *n.* **1.** the father of one's father or mother. **2.** a forefather; ancestor.

grandfather clock *also,* **grandfather's clock.** a clock having a pendulum and enclosed in a tall, usually wooden cabinet that stands on the floor.

grand·fa·ther·ly (grand′fä′thər lē) *adj.* having or showing qualities thought of as typical of a grandfather; kindly; benevolent.

gran·dil·o·quence (gran dil′ə kwəns) *n.* the quality of being grandiloquent.

gran·dil·o·quent (gran dil′ə kwənt) *adj.* using or characterized by a pompous or pretentious style. —**gran·dil′o·quent·ly,** *adv.*

gran·di·ose (gran′dē ōs′) *adj.* **1.** imposing or impressive; magnificent. **2.** trying to seem grand; pompous or pretentious: *a grandiose style of writing.* —**gran′di·ose′ly,** *adv.*

grandfather clock

grand jury, a jury chosen to hear accusations in criminal cases and bring indictments if there is enough evidence for a trial in a court of law.

grand larceny, larceny in which the value of the property taken is greater than a certain amount established by local law.

grand·ma (grand′mä′, gram′ə) *n.* *Informal.* grandmother.

grand·moth·er (grand′muth′ər) *n.* **1.** the mother of one's father or mother. **2.** a female ancestor.

grand·moth·er·ly (grand′muth′ər lē) *adj.* having or showing qualities thought of as typical of a grandmother; kindly; benevolent.

grand·neph·ew (grand′nef′ū) *n.* a son of one's nephew or niece. Also, **great-nephew.**

grand·niece (grand′nēs′) *n.* a daughter of one's nephew or niece. Also, **great-niece.**

Grand Old Party, the Republican Party of the United States.

grand opera, an opera in which the entire text is sung.

grand·pa (grand′pä′, gram′pə) *n.* *Informal.* grandfather.

grand·par·ent (grand′pâr′ənt) *n.* a grandfather or grandmother.

grand piano, a piano having horizontally arranged strings in a harp-shaped case.

grand·sire (grand′sīr′) *n.* *Archaic.* **1.** a grandfather. **2.** a male ancestor. **3.** an old man.

grand slam 1. *Bridge.* the winning of all thirteen tricks in a hand. **2.** *Baseball.* a home run hit with the bases loaded.

grand·son (grand′sun′) *n.* a son of one's son or daughter.

grand·stand (grand′stand′) *n.* **1.** a seating area for spectators, as at an outdoor sports event or parade. **2.** the spectators seated in such an area: *Loud cheers came from the grandstand.* —*v.i.,* **grand·stand·ed, grand·stand·ing.** to act in a way that is unnecessarily showy in order to impress those who are watching.

grand·un·cle (grand′ung′kəl) *n.* an uncle of one's father or mother. Also, **great-uncle.**

grange (grānj) *n.* **1.** *British.* a farm and the buildings on it. **2. Grange.** an organization founded in 1867 to promote the interests and welfare of farm families and rural communities in the United States.

gran·ite (gran′it) *n.* a hard, durable igneous rock that is composed of feldspar and quartz with specks of darker minerals, often used for buildings and monuments.

gran·ny (gran′ē) *also,* **gran·nie.** *n., pl.* **gran·nies.** *Informal.* **1.** a grandmother. **2.** an old woman.

granny knot, a knot like a square knot but with the ends crossing the opposite way, causing it to jam easily.

gra·no·la (grə nō′lə) *n.* a mixture of rolled oats, dried fruit, nuts, and honey or brown sugar, used as a breakfast cereal or health food.

granny knot

grant (grant) *v.t.* **1.** to give (what is asked for); allow; confer: *The teacher granted us permission to go home early.* **2.** to admit to be true; concede: *I'll grant that your argument is correct.* **3.** to give or confer, especially by a formal act: *to grant a charter to colonists.* —*n.* **1.** the act of granting. **2.** something that is granted, such as property or a right or privilege. —**grant′a·ble,** *adj.* —**grant′er,** *n.*

·to take for granted. a. to assume to be true. **b.** to accept, possess, or regard without thought, considera-

---

at; āpe; fär; câre; end; mē; it; īce; pîerce; hot; ōld; sông, fôrk; oil; out; up; ūse; rüle; pùll; tûrn; chin; sing; shop; thin; this; hw in white; zh in treasure. The symbol ə stands for the unstressed vowel sound heard in about, taken, pencil, lemon, and circus.

G

tion, or acknowledgment: *They took my help for granted and weren't really grateful for it.*

grant·ee (gran tē′) *n.* a person to whom a grant is made.

grant·or (gran′tər, gran tôr′) *n.* a person who makes a grant.

gran·u·lar (gran′yə lər) *adj.* **1.** consisting of, containing, or like grains or granules: *Sugar is granular.* **2.** having a granulated surface.

gran·u·late (gran′yə lāt′) *v.t.,* **gran·u·lat·ed, gran·u·lat·ing.** **1.** to form into grains or granules. **2.** to roughen the surface of. —**gran′u·la′tion,** *n.*

gran·ule (gran′ūl) *n.* a very small particle; grain.

grape (grāp) *n.* **1.** a smooth, thin-skinned fruit of any of a group of climbing woody vines. Grapes usually grow in large clusters and are usually green or purple in color. They are used to make wine and are eaten dried as raisins or raw as a fruit. **2.** the vine bearing this fruit.

grape·fruit (grāp′früt′) *n., pl.* **grape·fruit** or **grape·fruits.** **1.** a large, round citrus fruit of an evergreen tree. It has a thick skin that ranges in color from pale yellow to reddish brown and a tart, pink or white, juicy pulp. **2.** the tree that bears this fruit.

grape·shot (grāp′shot′) *n.* a cluster of small iron balls used as a charge for cannon.

grape sugar, another term for **dextrose.**

grape·vine (grāp′vīn′) *n.* **1.** a vine bearing grapes. **2.** *Informal.* a secret or informal way of spreading news or information: *The thieves learned that the police were after them through the underworld grapevine.*

graph (graf) *n.* **1.** a diagram showing the changes of and the relationship between two or more things by a series of dots, bars, or lines. **2.** *Mathematics.* a representation of a function or equation plotted on coordinate axes. —*v.t.* to show or represent by a graph.

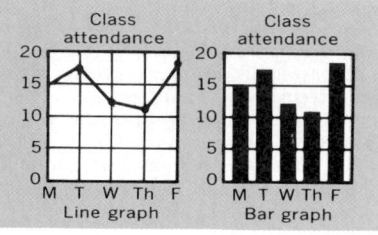

graph *(n., def. 1)*

–graph *combining form* **1.** a machine or other apparatus that writes or records: *telegraph, seismograph.* **2.** something that is written or recorded: *autograph.*

graph·ic (graf′ik) *adj.* **1.** vividly described; lifelike: *a graphic description of a battle.* **2.** of, relating to, or represented by a graph. **3.** of or relating to graphics or the graphic arts. **4.** of or relating to writing: *Letters of the alphabet are graphic symbols.* —**graph′i·cal·ly,** *adv.*

graphic arts, painting, photography, and other arts in which forms are represented visually on a flat surface, especially those arts in which impressions are made from blocks, plates, and the like, such as etching or lithography.

graph·ics (graf′iks) *pl. n.* **1.** pictorial material such as drawings or photographs, as used in books, newspapers, or other printed matter. **2.** paintings, lithographs, posters, and the like, as produced in the graphic arts. **3.** see **computer graphics.**

graph·ite (graf′īt) *n.* a soft, black crystalline form of carbon, commonly used as a lubricant when mixed with oil and as lead for pencils when mixed with clay.

graph·ol·o·gy (gra fol′ə jē) *n.* the study of handwriting, especially when used to try to analyze a person's character or personality traits.

graph paper, paper ruled in small squares, oblongs, or other divisions, on which graphs, charts, and diagrams can be drawn.

–graphy *combining form* **1.** writing or other forms of representing done in a specified way: *photography.* **2.** a descriptive science: *oceanography.*

grap·nel (grap′nəl) *n.* **1.** another word for **grappling iron.** **2.** a small anchor with three to six hooks.

grap·ple (grap′əl) *v.,* **grap·pled, grap·pling.** —*v.t.* to seize or hold with a grappling iron. —*v.i.* to struggle: *a prizefighter grappling with an opponent. I grappled with the problem of how to start my term paper.* —*n.* **1.** the act of grappling. **2.** see **grappling iron.**

grappling iron, any of various devices having one or more hooks or clamps, used especially for seizing or holding something.

grapnel *(def. 2)*

grasp (grasp) *v.t.* **1.** to take hold of firmly with the hand: *The batter grasped the baseball bat.* **2.** to understand; comprehend: *Geometry is sometimes hard for students to grasp.* —*n.* **1.** the act or instance of grasping. **2.** the power or ability to grasp: *Happiness was within their grasp.* **3.** understanding: *You have a good grasp of algebra.* **4.** firm control; possession: *The patriots freed the country from the grasp of the enemy.*

grasp·ing (gras′ping) *adj.* **1.** greedy. **2.** that grasps. —**grasp′ing·ly,** *adv.* —**grasp′ing·ness,** *n.*

grass (gras) *n., pl.* **grass·es.** **1.** any of a large group of plants having jointed, usually hollow stems and narrow leaves called blades, and often bearing spikes of small flowers. Wheat, rye, oats, corn, sugarcane, rice, and bamboo are grasses. **2.** any of a number of such plants covering lawns, pastures, or fields. **3.** the land on which grass grows, such as a lawn or pasture. —**grass′like′,** *n.*

grass·hop·per (gras′hop′ər) *n.* any of a group of plant-eating, chirping, winged insects having long, powerful hind legs used for jumping.

grass·land (gras′land′) *n.* land on which grass grows, used for pasture.

grass–roots (gras′rüts′, gras′ruts′) *adj.* of, relating to, or coming from the common

grasshopper

people, especially in rural areas: *a candidate with grass-roots support.*

grass·y (gras′ē) *adj.,* **grass·i·er, grass·i·est.** **1.** covered with or having much grass. **2.** consisting of or containing grass. **3.** like grass, especially in color. —**grass′i·ness,** *n.*

grate[1] (grāt) *n.* **1.** a framework of crossed bars set in or over an opening, as in a window, door, or drain; grating. **2.** a framework or basket of iron bars to hold burning fuel, as in a fireplace or furnace. **3.** a fireplace. —*v.t.,* **grat·ed, grat·ing.** to fit or furnish with a grate or grating. [From the Medieval Latin word *grata* meaning "hurdle" or "wicker frame," from the Latin word *cratis* with the same meanings.]

grate[2] (grāt) *v.,* **grat·ed, grat·ing.** —*v.t.* **1.** to make into small pieces or shreds by rubbing against a rough surface: *to grate carrots.* **2.** to rub together in a way that produces a harsh, scraping sound; grind: *to grate one's teeth.* —*v.i.* **1.** to make a harsh, scraping sound by rubbing: *The old iron gate grated on its rusty hinges.* **2.** to have an annoying or irritating effect: *Their selfish attitude grates on my nerves.* [From the Middle French word *grater* meaning "to scratch," of Germanic origin.]

grate·ful (grāt′fəl) *adj.* **1.** thankful; appreciative: *a grateful child.* **2.** showing gratitude: *a grateful look.* **3.** pleasing; welcome: *a grateful shower of rain.* —**grate′ful·ly,** *adv.* —**grate′ful·ness,** *n.*

grat·er (grā′tər) *n.* **1.** a kitchen utensil having a rough surface of sharp, raised edges used to grate vegetables, cheese, spices, and other foods. **2.** a person or thing that grates.

grat·i·fi·ca·tion (grat′ə fi kā′shən) *n.* **1.** the act of gratifying or the condition of being gratified. **2.** something that causes pleasure or satisfaction.

grat·i·fy (grat′ə fī′) v.t., **grat·i·fied**, **grat·i·fy·ing**. **1.** to give pleasure or satisfaction to; please: *I was gratified by the news that my friend had recovered from the flu.* **2.** to satisfy, indulge, or humor, as a feeling, need, or desire: *to gratify a child's whim.* —**grat′i·fi′er**, n.

grat·i·fy·ing (grat′ə fī′ing) adj. that gratifies; pleasing or satisfying. —**grat′i·fy′ing·ly**, adv.

grat·ing[1] (grā′ting) n. a framework of parallel or crossed bars set in or over an opening, such as a window or sewer, and serving as a cover, guard, or screen. [*Grate*[1] + *-ing*[1].]

grat·ing[2] (grā′ting) adj. **1.** making a harsh or irritating sound: *a grating door hinge.* **2.** annoying; irritating: *a grating habit.* [*Grate*[2] + *-ing*[2].]

grat·is (grat′is, grā′tis) adv. without charge; free: *I got two tickets to the ball game gratis.* —adj. given or provided without charge; free.

grat·i·tude (grat′i tüd′, grat′i tūd′) n. the quality or condition of being grateful, as for a kindness or favor.

gra·tu·i·tous (grə tü′i təs, grə tū′i təs) adj. **1.** given without payment or return; free. **2.** without good reason or cause; unjustifiable: *a gratuitous insult.* —**gra·tu′i·tous·ly**, adv. —**gra·tu′i·tous·ness**, n.

gra·tu·i·ty (grə tü′i tē, grə tū′i tē) n., pl. **gra·tu·i·ties**. a gift, especially of money, given in return for services; tip.

grave[1] (grāv) n. **1.** a hole dug in the earth for the burial of a body. **2.** any place of burial: *The ship split and went to a watery grave.* **3. the grave.** death. [From the Old English word *græf* with the same meaning.]

grave[2] (grāv; *def. 4 also* gräv) adj., **grav·er**, **grav·est**. **1.** of great importance; weighty: *a grave decision.* **2.** of a threatening nature; dangerous; critical: *a grave illness.* **3.** earnest and dignified; sober; sedate: *a grave, humorless person.* **4.** marked or pronounced with a grave accent. [From the French word *grave*, from the Latin word *gravis* meaning "heavy, weighty."] —**grave′ly**, adv. —**grave′ness**, n.

grave[3] (grāv) v.t., **graved**, **graved** or **grav·en**, **grav·ing**. to form or shape by carving; sculpt; engrave. [From the Old English word *grafan* meaning "to carve" or "to dig out."]

grave accent (grāv′, grāv′) a mark ( ) placed over a vowel in certain languages to show correct pronunciation, as in French *père*. In English it is used to show that the *e* in the ending syllable *-ed* is to be pronounced, as in *preparèd*.

grav·el (grav′əl) n. pebbles and small pieces of rock, often mixed with sand, used especially for roads and walks. —v.t., **grav·eled**, **grav·el·ing**; *also, British,* **grav·elled**, **grav·el·ling**. to cover or lay with gravel: *to gravel a driveway.*

grav·el·ly (grav′ə lē) adj. **1.** of or like gravel. **2.** (of the voice) harsh; grating.

grav·en (grā′vən) a past participle of **grave**[3].

grave·stone (grāv′stōn′) n. a stone marking a grave.

grave·yard (grāv′yärd′) n. a cemetery.

grav·i·tate (grav′i tāt′) v.i., **grav·i·tat·ed**, **grav·i·tat·ing**. **1.** to move or tend to move by the force of gravity. **2.** to move or be attracted by a strong influence: *The two new students in the class gravitated toward each other.* **3.** to sink or fall: *The sediment in the liquid gravitated to the bottom of the container.*

grav·i·ta·tion (grav′i tā′shən) n. **1.** the force of attraction that exists between any two objects in the universe. Gravitation keeps the stars on their courses and the planets in their orbits. It also keeps people and objects on the surface of the earth. **2.** the act or process of gravitating. **3.** a movement toward or attraction to someone or something as the result of a strong influence. —**grav′i·ta′tion·al**, adj. —**grav′i·ta′tion·al·ly**, adv.

grav·i·ty (grav′i tē) n., pl. **grav·i·ties**. **1.** the force that

pulls things toward the center of the earth. It is gravity that causes objects to fall when they are dropped and pulls them back to earth when they are thrown upward. The pull of gravity on a body is called the weight of the body. **2.** another word for **gravitation**. **3.** weight; heaviness: *an object's center of gravity.* **4.** serious or solemn nature: *the gravity of the president's speech.*

gra·vy (grā′vē) n., pl. **gra·vies**. **1.** the juice that comes out from meat during and after cooking. **2.** a thickened sauce made by mixing this juice with other ingredients, such as flour and seasonings.

gray (grā) *also,* **grey**. n. a color made by mixing black and white. —adj. **1.** having the color gray. **2.** dark, gloomy, or dismal: *a gray day.* **3.** having gray hair. —v.t., v.i. to make or become gray: *hair that is graying.* —**gray′ly**, adv. —**gray′ness**, n.

gray·beard (grā′bîrd′) n. an old man.

gray·ish (grā′ish) adj. somewhat gray: *a grayish sky.*

gray·lag (grā′lag′) n. a species of wild goose found in Europe and Asia.

gray·ling (grā′ling) n. a silver-blue or purple fish related to the trout, found in cold, running streams, and valued as both a food and a game fish.

gray matter **1.** grayish tissue in the brain and spinal cord containing some cell fibers and nerve cells. **2.** *Informal.* intelligence; brains.

graze[1] (grāz) v., **grazed**, **graz·ing**. —v.i. to feed on growing grass: *Cattle and sheep grazed in the meadow.* —v.t. **1.** to put (livestock) to feed on growing grass: *They grazed the herd in the north pasture.* **2.** to feed on (growing grass). [From the Old English word *grasian* with the same meaning, from the word *græs* "grass."]

graze[2] (grāz) v., **grazed**, **graz·ing**. —v.t. **1.** to scrape the skin from slightly: *The bullet grazed the soldier's arm.* **2.** to touch or rub against lightly in passing. —v.i. to move so as to touch, rub, or scrape something lightly. —n. **1.** the act or instance of grazing. **2.** a scratch, scrape, or slight wound caused by grazing. [Perhaps from *graze*[1].]

graz·ing (grā′zing) n. pasture land; pasturage.

grease (n., grēs; v., grēs, grēz) n. **1.** soft animal fat, especially when it has been melted: *bacon grease.* **2.** a thick, oily substance, used especially as a lubricant. —v.t., **greased**, **greas·ing**. to smear or lubricate with grease: *to grease the wheels of an automobile.* —**greas′er**, n.

grease paint, a thick makeup having a heavy oil or wax base, used by actors and actresses.

greas·y (grē′sē, grē′zē) adj., **greas·i·er**, **greas·i·est**. **1.** smeared or soiled with grease: *greasy overalls.* **2.** containing much grease or fat. **3.** like grease. —**greas′i·ly**, adv. —**greas′i·ness**, n.

great (grāt) adj. **1.** very large, as in size, number, or extent: *a great crowd.* **2.** unusual in ability or achievement: *a great writer.* **3.** important; remarkable: *a great scientific discovery.* **4.** more than usual; extreme: *great suffering.* **5.** *Informal.* very good; excellent: *a great vacation.* —**great′ness**, n.

great–aunt (grāt′ant′, grāt′änt′) n. another word for **grandaunt**.

great circle, any circle on a sphere formed by a plane intersecting the surface of the sphere and passing through the center of the sphere.

great·coat (grāt′kōt′) n. a heavy overcoat.

G

at; āpe; fär; câre; end; mē; it; īce; pîerce; hot; ōld; sông, fôrk; oil; out; up; ūse; rüle; pùll; tûrn; chin; sing; shop; thin; this; hw in white; zh in treasure. The symbol ə stands for the unstressed vowel sound heard in about, taken, pencil, lemon, and circus.

Great Dane, a dog of a breed noted for its large size and strength, having a square muzzle and a smooth, short-haired coat.

Great Dane

Great Divide, another term for **Continental Divide.**

great·er (grā′tər) *adj.* **1.** the comparative of **great.** **2.** designating an area, as a city, and the area adjacent to it: *the greater metropolitan area.*

great–grand·child (grāt′gran′chĭld′) *n., pl.* **great–grand·chil·dren** (grāt′grand′chil′drən). a child of one's grandchild.

great–grand·daugh·ter (grāt′gran′dô′tər) *n.* a daughter of one's grandchild.

great–grand·fa·ther (grāt′grand′fä′thər) *n.* the father of one's grandmother or grandfather.

great–grand·moth·er (grāt′grand′muth′ər) *n.* the mother of one's grandmother or grandfather.

great–grand·par·ent (grāt′grand′pâr′ənt) *n.* the mother or father of one's grandmother or grandfather.

great–grand·son (grāt′grand′sun′) *n.* a son of one's grandchild.

great·heart·ed (grāt′här′tid) *adj.* **1.** having a generous and forgiving nature; noble. **2.** brave.

great horned owl, a large, dark brown owl with prominent ear tufts found throughout North and South America.

great·ly (grāt′lē) *adv.* **1.** in or to a great degree; very much: *to be greatly impressed.* **2.** in a great manner.

great–neph·ew (grāt′nef′ū) *n.* another word for **grandnephew.**

great–niece (grāt′nēs′) *n.* another word for **grandniece.**

Great Spirit, the chief god of the religion of certain North American Indian tribes.

great–un·cle (grāt′ung′kəl) *n.* another word for **granduncle.**

Great Wall of China, a wall extending about 1,500 miles (2,400 kilometers) along the boundary between north and northwest China and Mongolia. It dates from the third century B.C. and was originally built as a defense against invaders. Also, **Great Wall, Chinese Wall.**

great white shark, a large shark found in tropical and warm seas. It is gray or brown above and white below and can reach a length of 20 feet (6 meters).

greave (grēv) *n.* armor for the leg below the knee.

grebe (grēb) *n.* any of various diving water birds having feet set well back on the body and lobed toes.

Gre·cian (grē′shən) *adj., n.* another word for **Greek.**

grebe

Gre·co–Ro·man (grē′kō rō′mən, grek′ō rō′mən) *adj.* of or characteristic of ancient Greece and Rome: *Greco-Roman art.*

greed (grēd) *n.* a very great, usually selfish, desire to have or get something: *greed for power, greed for wealth.*

greed·y (grē′dē) *adj.,* **greed·i·er, greed·i·est.** **1.** eager to have or get something; wanting more than one's share: *to be greedy for money.* **2.** wanting to eat or drink too much or too quickly; gluttonous. —**greed′i·ly,** *adv.* —**greed′i·ness,** *n.*

Greek (grēk) *adj.* of or relating to Greece, its people, their language, or their culture. Also, **Grecian.** —*n.* **1.** a person who was born in or is a citizen of Greece. **2.** a person who lived in ancient Greece. **3.** the language of Greece.

Language Note

Greek is one of several languages that have played a large part in the shaping of our modern English vocabulary. Although it has not contributed as much to our common vocabulary as Old English, French, or Latin, the Greek language is the source of about half of the vocabulary of the modern sciences. Some Greek words came into English indirectly, through languages that had themselves borrowed from Greek vocabulary. Early examples are words like *priest* and *monk,* which were Greek words borrowed first by Latin and then from Latin into Old English. The earliest large-scale adoption of Greek into English came in the fifteenth and sixteenth centuries. At that time, there was a great revival of interest in classical culture and in the liberal arts, science, and religion. Among the Greek words that came into our language during this time are *epic, drama, tragedy, comedy, history, biography,* and *music* in the liberal arts; *physics, energy, atom,* and *diagnosis* in science; and *theology* and *dogma* in religion.

Greek cross, a cross having four arms of equal length.

Greek Orthodox Church, the established church of Greece, a self-governing member of the Orthodox Church.

green (grēn) *n.* **1.** the color of growing grass and of leaves in spring and summer. It is between yellow and blue in the spectrum. **2.** a grassy, usually level, piece of land used for a particular purpose: *a village green.* **3.** *Golf.* the area around a cup, having very thick, closely cut grass. Also, **putting green. 4. greens. a.** the green leaves or stems of certain plants, such as turnips, lettuce, spinach, or dandelions, used for food: *salad greens.* **b.** freshly cut leaves or branches used for decoration: *The mantelpiece was decorated with greens for the holiday.* —*adj.* **1.** having the color green: *a green coat.* **2.** covered with growing plants, grass, or green leaves: *green pastures.* **3.** not fully grown or mature; not ripe: *green tomatoes.* **4.** consisting of edible green leaves or other plant parts: *a green salad.* **5.** having little or no training or experience; immature: *a green recruit in the marines.* **6.** having a pale, sickly color, as from illness or fear: *The children's faces were green when they came off the roller coaster.* **7.** not dried, cured, or otherwise ready for use: *green lumber.* —**green′ness,** *n.*

green·back (grēn′bak′) *n.* a U.S. paper currency with the back printed in green.

Greenback Party, a U.S. political party organized in 1874 and active through the 1880s. It favored the use of paper currency that could not be converted into gold and silver.

green card, an official identity card issued to a foreign citizen who has the right to live and work in the United States.

green bean, another term for **string bean.**

green·er·y (grē′nə rē) *n.* green plants or leaves.

green–eyed (grēn′īd′) *adj.* **1.** having green eyes. **2.** jealous.

green·gage (grēn′gāj′) *n.* a sweet plum having a greenish yellow skin and pulp. [From Sir William *Gage,* a botanist who brought this fruit to England from France in about 1725.]

green·gro·cer (grēn′grō′sər) *n. British.* a person who sells fresh vegetables and fruit.

green·horn (grēn′hôrn′) *n. Informal.* **1.** an inexperienced person; person without training. **2.** a person who is easily fooled. [*green* "immature" + *horn,* earlier referring to a young animal whose horns are not yet fully formed.]

greenhouse

green·house (grēn′hous′) *n., pl.* **green·hous·es** (grēn′hou′ziz). a building made chiefly of glass in which temperature and humidity can be controlled and in which plants can be cultivated all year; hothouse.

greenhouse effect, the process in which heat from the sun is trapped in the earth's atmosphere by carbon dioxide, resulting in higher temperatures and a warming of the surface of the earth. It is believed that an increase in the amount of carbon dioxide caused by industrial pollution can hasten this process.

green·ing (grē′ning) *n.* any of several apples having a greenish yellow skin when ripe and a tart flavor, used especially for cooking.

green·ish (grē′nish) *adj.* somewhat green.

green light 1. a green traffic light that gives permission to go ahead. **2.** *Informal.* the permission to go ahead with a particular project or activity: *Our parents gave us the green light to go on the camping trip.*

green onion, see **scallion.**

green pepper, an unripe sweet pepper.

green soap, a soft soap used especially in treating skin disorders.

green·sward (grēn′swôrd′) *n.* ground that is green with growing grass; turf.

green thumb, a special talent for making plants grow.

Green·wich Time (gren′ich) *also,* **Greenwich Mean Time.** the time at the prime meridian in Greenwich, England, used as the standard time by which time zones of the world are established.

green·wood (grēn′wud′) *n.* a forest when the leaves are green, as in the summer.

greet (grēt) *v.t.* **1.** to speak to or welcome in a friendly or polite way: *to greet guests at the door.* **2.** to meet or receive: *The famous pianist was greeted with applause.* **3.** to appear to welcome: *The sun greeted us with its warming rays.* —**greet′er,** *n.*

greet·ing (grē′ting) *n.* **1.** the act or words of a person who greets another or others. **2. greetings.** friendly wishes, especially from someone absent: *My friends sent greetings on my birthday.* —*interj.* **greetings.** hello.

greeting card, see **card**[1] *(def. 4).*

gre·gar·i·ous (gri gâr′ē əs) *adj.* **1.** enjoying and happy to be with others; sociable; outgoing. **2.** living in flocks, herds, or groups: *Sheep are gregarious.* —**gre·gar′i·ous·ly,** *adv.* —**gre·gar′i·ous·ness,** *n.*

Word Family

Although the various English words that are derived from the Latin word *grex* meaning "herd" or "flock" seem to be very different in their meanings, a closer look will reveal how they are related. Someone who is always found with a "herd" or group of friends is called **gregarious.** When people **congregate,** a group forms. The resulting **congregation** is made up of the **aggregate** number of participants. If something differs from the group in an undesirable way, it is considered to be **egregious.** To **segregate** is to separate someone or some group from the larger "flock."

Gre·go·ri·an (gri gôr′ē ən) *adj.* of, relating to, or introduced by one of several popes named Gregory, especially Pope Gregory I or Pope Gregory XIII.

Gregorian calendar, a calendar now in use in most countries of the world. Introduced as a reform of the Julian calendar by Pope Gregory XIII in 1582, it provides for an ordinary year of 365 days and a leap year of 366.

Gregorian chant, a type of music traditionally used in the liturgy of the Roman Catholic and certain other churches, introduced by Pope Gregory I; plainsong.

grem·lin (grem′lin) *n.* a small, mischievous spirit blamed for sudden or unaccountable troubles, especially in airplane engines.

gre·nade (gri nād′) *n.* **1.** a small bomb that can be thrown by hand or fired by a rifle. **2.** a glass container filled with chemicals that are released when the container is thrown and smashed.

gren·a·dier (gren′ə dir′) *n.* **1.** a member of the first regiment of infantry in the British Army, attached to the royal household. **2.** formerly, a soldier who threw hand grenades.

grew (grü) the past tense of **grow.**

grey (grā) another spelling of **gray.**

grey·hound (grā′hound′) *n.* a tall, slender, swift dog, having a blue-gray, black, white, brown, or red short-haired coat, raised especially for racing or hunting.

grid (grid) *n.* **1.** an arrangement of parallel or intersecting bars or wires with openings between them; grating: *The hot air came through grids in the floor.* **2.** a pattern of intersecting lines that divides a map or chart into small squares. **3.** a metal plate used as an electrode in a storage battery. **4.** an electrode in a vacuum tube, used to control the flow of electrons.

greyhound

G

---

at; āpe; fär; câre; end; mē; it; īce; pîerce; hot; ōld; sông, fôrk; oil; out; up; ūse; rüle; pull; tûrn; chin; sing; shop; thin; **th**is; hw in white; zh in treasure. The symbol ə stands for the unstressed vowel sound heard in about, taken, pencil, lemon, and circus.

grid·dle (grid′əl) *n.* a heavy, flat metal pan used especially for cooking pancakes. —*v.t.*, **grid·dled, grid·dling.** to cook on a griddle.

grid·dle·cake (grid′əl kāk′) *n.* a pancake.

grid·i·ron (grid′ī′ərn) *n.* **1.** a football field. **2.** see **grill** (*def. 1*).

grief (grēf) *n.* **1.** very great sadness or deep sorrow: *a parent's grief at the death of a child.* **2.** the cause of such sadness or sorrow: *The loss of my dog was a great grief.*
  ·**to come to grief.** to meet with disaster; fail: *The expedition came to grief when two mountain climbers were hurt.*

grief–strick·en (grēf′strik′ən) *adj.* overcome by grief; deeply anguished: *We were grief-stricken by the news of the accident.*

griev·ance (grē′vəns) *n.* a real or imagined wrong that causes anger, resentment, or distress: *the strikers' grievances about working conditions.*

grieve (grēv) *v.*, **grieved, griev·ing.** —*v.t.* to feel grief; mourn: *to grieve for the victims of an earthquake.* —*v.t.* to cause to feel grief; sadden deeply.

griev·ous (grē′vəs) *adj.* **1.** causing grief, deep sorrow, or great pain: *a grievous illness.* **2.** of a very serious nature; grave; outrageous: *a grievous crime.* **3.** showing or full of grief; sorrowful; mournful: *a grievous cry of pain.* —**griev′ous·ly,** *adv.* —**griev′ous·ness,** *n.*

grif·fin (grif′ən) *also,* **grif·fon.** *n.* a mythical creature with the head and wings of an eagle and the body and legs of a lion.

grill (gril) *n.* **1.** a cooking utensil having a framework of parallel metal bars or wires on which food is placed to be broiled over an open fire. Also, **gridiron. 2.** food, especially meat, that has been broiled on a grill. **3.** a restaurant that specializes in grilled foods. —*v.t.* **1.** to broil on a grill: *The campers grilled hamburgers for supper.* **2.** to question closely and relentlessly: *The police grilled the suspected bank robber for eight hours.*

grille (gril) *n.* a grating, often of ornamental metalwork, used to cover or enclose a space as a screen or gate.

grill·work (gril′wûrk′) *n.* a grille or a pattern of grilles: *the grillwork of an automobile.*

grille

grilse (grils) *n.*, *pl.* **grilse.** a young Atlantic salmon on its first return from the sea to fresh water.

grim (grim) *adj.*, **grim·mer, grim·mest. 1.** having a stern or forbidding quality or look: *The old house was grim and dirty.* **2.** not yielding; resolute: *The team played with grim determination.* **3.** without mercy; fierce: *a grim battle.* **4.** horrifying; ghastly: *The soldier told grim stories about the war.* —**grim′ly,** *adv.* —**grim′ness,** *n.*

gri·mace (grim′əs, gri mās′) *n.* a twisting of the face showing pain, disgust, or displeasure: *I made a grimace when I tasted the bitter medicine.* —*v.i.*, **gri·maced, gri·mac·ing.** to twist the face in such a way; make a grimace.

grime (grīm) *n.* dirt covering or rubbed into a surface. —*v.t.*, **grimed, grim·ing.** to cover with grime; soil: *The walls were grimed by the smoke and grease in the air.*

grim·y (grī′mē) *adj.*, **grim·i·er, grim·i·est.** full of or covered with grime; filthy: *grimy windows.* —**grim′i·ness,** *n.*

grin (grin) *v.i.*, **grinned, grin·ning. 1.** to smile broadly: *to grin at a joke.* **2.** to draw back the lips and show the teeth, as in scorn or anger: *The cat spat and grinned when I tried to get it down from the roof.* —*n.* a broad smile.

grind (grīnd) *v.*, **ground, grind·ing.** —*v.t.*, **1.** to crush or chop into small pieces or powder: *to grind corn into meal.*

2. to make or produce by crushing: *to grind pepper from peppercorns.* **3.** to wear down, smooth, or sharpen by rubbing against something rough: *to grind a mirror for a telescope.* **4.** to rub together, press down, or move in a harsh or noisy way: *to grind one's teeth in anger.* **5.** to work by turning a crank: *to grind a coffee mill.* **6.** to oppress harshly: *laborers ground down by cruel overseers.* —*v.i.* *Informal.* to work or study hard or for a long time: *to grind away for a math exam.* —*n.* **1.** the size of the pieces of a material that has been crushed: *There are several different grinds of coffee.* **2.** the act of grinding. **3.** hard, long work or study: *the grind of working a 12-hour day.* **4.** *Informal.* a person who is thought to spend too much time and effort at studying or working.
  ·**to grind out.** to produce mechanically without imagination or special effort: *to grind out trite poems for greeting cards.*

grind·er (grīn′dər) *n.* **1.** a person or thing that grinds: *a coffee grinder.* **2.** any one of the back teeth; molar.

grind·stone (grīnd′stōn′) *n.* a stone disk that can be turned on an axle to sharpen tools, as knives or axes, or to polish or smooth things.
  ·**to keep one's nose to the grindstone.** to work steadily or very hard at one's job.

grip (grip) *n.* **1.** a firm hold; tight grasp: *to keep a good grip on a dog's leash.* **2.** the ability to hold firmly. **3.** a way of holding or taking hold of something, such as a golf club, tennis racket, or other piece of sports equipment. **4.** a special manner of shaking or clasping hands, especially one used by members of a secret or fraternal organization. **5.** firm control;

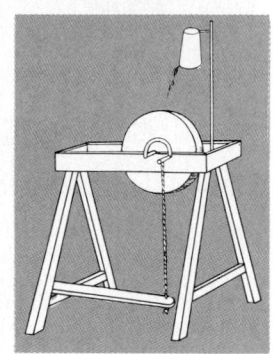

grindstone

power: *a country in the grip of a dictator.* **6.** a mental grasp; knowledge: *a grip on algebra.* **7.** the part of certain pieces of sports equipment by which they are intended to be held. **8.** a small suitcase. —*v.t.*, **gripped, grip·ping. 1.** to take hold of firmly and tightly: *to grip a baseball bat.* **2.** to attract and keep the interest of: *The movie really gripped me.* —**grip′per,** *n.*
  ·**to come to grips with.** to face and deal with in a firm, decisive manner: *to come to grips with a difficult problem.*

gripe (grīp) *v.*, **griped, grip·ing.** —*v.i.* **1.** *Informal.* to complain; grumble: *to gripe about extra homework.* **2.** to have spasmodic pain in the bowels. —*v.t.* **1.** *Informal.* to irritate; annoy: *The umpire's decision griped the team.* **2.** to cause spasmodic pain in the bowels: *Raw vegetables sometimes gripe me.* —*n.* **1.** *Informal.* a complaint: *to have gripes about a new job.* **2.** *usually* **gripes.** spasmodic pain in the bowels.

grippe (grip) *n.* a disease resembling influenza.

gris·ly (griz′lē) *adj.*, **gris·li·er, gris·li·est.** causing horror, revulsion, or fear; gruesome: *a grisly sight.* —**gris′li·ness,** *n.*

grist (grist) *n.* grain that is to be ground.

gris·tle (gris′əl) *n.* a tough tissue found in meat; cartilage.

gris·tly (gris′lē) *adj.*, **gris·tli·er, gris·tli·est.** consisting of, containing, or like gristle.

grist·mill (grist′mil′) *n.* a mill for grinding grain.

grit (grit) *n.* **1.** very small, hard particles of sand or stone. **2.** strength of mind and spirit; courage. **3.** a coarse sandstone. —*v.t.*, **grit·ted, grit·ting.** to grind or tightly clamp together (the teeth).

grits (grits) *pl. n.* **1.** coarsely ground hominy, used as a cereal and in bread and puddings. Also, **hominy grits. 2.** coarsely ground, hulled grain.

grit·ty (grit′ē) *adj.*, **grit·ti·er, grit·ti·est.** **1.** of, containing, or like grit. **2.** covered or soiled with grit. **3.** having or showing strength of mind and spirit; courageous. —**grit′ti·ness,** *n.*

griz·zled (griz′əld) *adj.* **1.** gray or mixed with gray: *a grizzled beard.* **2.** gray-haired.

griz·zly (griz′lē) *n., pl.* **griz·zlies.** a grizzly bear. —*adj.,* **griz·zli·er, griz·zli·est.** grayish; grizzled.

grizzly bear, a long-clawed bear of western North America, having a large head and body and usually brown or gray fur.

grizzly bear

groan (grōn) *n.* a deep, sad sound, as of grief, pain, or disapproval; moan. —*v.i.* **1.** to make such a sound: *to groan from the pain of an injured leg.* **2.** to make a sound like this: *The roof creaked and groaned under the weight of the snow.* **3.** to be overburdened or strained: *The shelves groaned with books.* —*v.t.* to express or say with a groan: *The fans groaned their disappointment when their team lost.* —**groan′er,** *n.*

groat (grōt) *n.* an English silver coin worth four pennies, used from the fourteenth century through the seventeenth century.

gro·cer (grō′sər) *n.* a person who owns or manages a grocery.

gro·cer·y (grō′sə rē) *n., pl.* **gro·cer·ies.** **1.** a store that sells food and household supplies. **2. groceries.** goods, especially food, sold by such a store.

grog (grog) *n.* **1.** a drink made by mixing rum or whiskey with water. **2.** any alcoholic beverage. [From "Old Grog," nickname of the English admiral Edward Vernon (1684–1757), who ordered that the rum given to sailors be diluted with water.]

grog·gy (grog′ē) *adj.*, **grog·gi·er, grog·gi·est.** not fully alert or awake; in a dazed or unsteady condition: *to be groggy from lack of sleep.* —**grog′gi·ly,** *adv.* —**grog′gi·ness,** *n.*

groin (groin) *n.* **1.** a hollow on either side of the front of the body where the thigh joins the abdomen. **2.** a curved edge formed by the intersection of two vaults on a ceiling. —*v.t.* to build with groins.

grom·met (grom′it) *n.* **1.** a ring, as of metal or plastic, that reinforces a hole in material. **2.** a ring of rope or metal to hold oars in place or to fasten the edges of sails to spars.

groom (grüm, grùm) *n.* **1.** see **bridegroom. 2.** a person who washes, curries, and otherwise takes care of horses. —*v.t.* **1.** to wash, curry, and otherwise take care of (horses). **2.** to make neat, tidy, and attractive in appearance: *to groom one's hair and fingernails.* **3.** to train or prepare (someone) for some purpose, such as political office.

grooms·man (grümz′mən, grùmz′mən) *n., pl.* **grooms·men** (grümz′mən, grùmz′mən). a man who attends the bridegroom at a wedding.

groove (grüv) *n.* **1.** a long, narrow channel or depression in a surface: *The car wheels made grooves on the dirt road. A phonograph record has grooves.* **2.** a narrow, limited way of doing things; routine; rut: *He has been too thoroughly trained to progress along a certain groove ever to question it* (Eugene O'Neill). —*v.t.,* **grooved, grooving.** to make a groove or grooves in.

grope (grōp) *v.,* **groped, grop·ing.** —*v.i.* **1.** to feel about with the hands: *to grope for a door handle in the dark.* **2.** to search blindly and uncertainly: *to grope for a solution to a problem.* —*v.t.* to find (one's way) by groping. —**grop′ing·ly,** *adv.*

gros·beak (grōs′bēk′) *n.* any of various songbirds having a large, cone-shaped bill.

gros·grain (grō′grān′) *n.* a closely woven, ribbed fabric, often of silk or rayon, used chiefly for ribbons.

gross (grōs) *adj.* **1.** with nothing taken away; total; entire: *a net income of $650 from gross earnings of $1,000.* **2.** very obvious; glaring; flagrant: *a gross mistake, a gross injustice.* **3.** not refined; coarse; vulgar: *gross behavior, a gross joke.* **4.** very fat. —*n., pl.* **gross·es** (*def. 1*); **gross** (*def. 2*). **1.** the total amount, as of income, before deductions: *a gross of 5 million dollars.* **2.** twelve dozen. —*v.t.* to earn a total of before deductions: *That motion picture grossed more than 10 million dollars.* —**gross′ly,** *adv.* —**gross′ness,** *n.*

gross national product, the total value of all the goods and services produced by a country during a certain period of time.

gro·tesque (grō tesk′) *adj.* **1.** distorted, deformed, unnatural, or ugly in shape or appearance: *The human figures in the strange painting were all grotesque.* **2.** amusingly absurd; ludicrous: *a slapstick comedy with lots of grotesque characters and situations.* —**gro·tesque′ly,** *adv.* —**gro·tesque′ness,** *n.*

grot·to (grot′ō) *n., pl.* **grot·toes** or **grot·tos.** **1.** a cave. **2.** a structure made to resemble a cave, as for a shrine.

grouch (grouch) *n., pl.* **grouch·es.** **1.** a person who is very irritable, sulky, or ill-tempered. **2.** a sulky or grumbling mood. —*v.i.* to grumble or sulk: *I grouched for hours because I had to clean up the mess in my room.*

grouch·y (grou′chē) *adj.*, **grouch·i·er, grouch·i·est.** in a bad mood; irritable; sulky. —**grouch′i·ly,** *adv.* —**grouch′i·ness,** *n.*

ground¹ (ground) *n.* **1.** the solid surface of the earth; soil; land: *The ground was covered with snow.* **2. grounds.** the land surrounding a house, institution, or other building: *The school grounds were beautifully planted with trees and flowers.* **3.** *also,* **grounds.** an area or piece of land put aside for a particular use: *a parade ground, picnic grounds.* **4.** *also,* **grounds.** a reason; basis; foundation: *grounds for suspicion.* **5.** an underlying surface or background: *The wallpaper is printed with a red floral design on a green ground.* **6. grounds.** the particles or bits that settle at the bottom of a liquid or are left over in the container that held it; dregs: *Throw out the coffee grounds.* **7.** a connection between an electric conductor and the earth. —*v.t.* **1.** to place or set on the ground; cause to touch the ground. **2.** to provide a firm foundation or basis for; base: *Their fears were grounded on superstition.* **3.** to instruct in the first or basic principles or elements of a subject: *to ground oneself in mathematics.* **4.** to forbid (a person or aircraft) to fly; keep on the ground: *The plane was grounded for three hours because of bad weather.* **5.** to connect (an electric wire or other conductor) with the earth. **6.** to cause (a boat or ship) to run aground: *to ground a ship on a shoal.* —*v.i.* **1.** to fall to or strike the ground. **2.** (of a boat or ship) to run aground. **3.** *Baseball.* to hit a ground ball: *The batter grounded to the shortstop.* —*adj.* **1.** of, on, at, or near the surface of the earth: *a ground attack by enemy troops.* **2.** operating, living, or growing on or near the surface of the earth: *an overwhelming superiority in ground forces.* [From the Old English word *grund* meaning "bottom" or "ground¹."]

·**to break ground.** to begin building something.

---

at; āpe; fär; câre; end; mē; it; īce; pîerce; hot; ōld; sông; fôrk; oil; out; up; ūse; rüle; pùll; tûrn; chin; sing; shop; thin; this; hw in white; zh in treasure. The symbol ə stands for the unstressed vowel sound heard in about, taken, pencil, lemon, and circus.

G

·**to gain ground.** to make progress: *The railroad gained ground in its effort to end the engineers' strike.*
·**to give ground.** to withdraw from attack; retreat; yield: *The army had to give ground after the enemy's attack.*
·**to ground out.** in baseball, to hit a ground ball that puts one out at first base.
·**to hold one's ground.** to maintain one's position; not retreat, yield, or withdraw.
·**to lose ground.** to move farther away from a goal; go backwards.

ground² (ground) the past tense and past participle of **grind.**

ground ball *Baseball.* a batted ball that strikes the ground in the infield and then rolls or moves along in low bounces. Also, **grounder.**

ground crew, personnel responsible for the servicing and maintenance of aircraft.

ground·er (groun′dər) *n.* another word for **ground ball.**

ground floor, the floor in a building that is level or nearly level with the ground.

ground·hog (ground′hôg′, ground′hog′) *n.* another word for **woodchuck.**

Groundhog Day, February 2, the day when the groundhog, according to popular belief, comes out of hibernation. If the groundhog sees its shadow, it is said to return underground while winter weather continues for another six weeks.

ground crew

ground·less (ground′lis) *adj.* having no good reason, cause, or justification: *a groundless fear of the dark.* —**ground′less·ly,** *adv.* —**ground′less·ness,** *n.*

ground·nut (ground′nut′) *n.* **1.** any of several plants of the pea family having underground parts used for food, especially the peanut. **2.** the underground parts of such a plant.

ground pine, any of several club mosses.

ground rule, a basic rule of procedure that governs a particular situation or activity: *My parents laid down a few ground rules for the party I planned to give.*

ground·speed (ground′spēd′) *n.* the speed of an aircraft relative to the ground over which it is traveling.

ground squirrel **1.** any of various rodents that live in burrows in the ground, usually having gray or light brown fur, often with striped or spotted markings. Also, **gopher.** **2.** a chipmunk. **3.** a prairie dog.

ground swell **1.** broad, deep waves or a rolling sea, caused by a distant storm or earthquake. **2.** a sudden, rapid increase or surge: *a ground swell of support for a candidate.*

ground water, water that has flowed or seeped

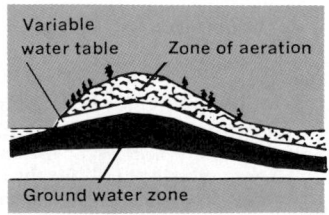

ground water

beneath the surface of the earth and saturated the soil and other porous material below. It is the source of water for wells and underground springs.

ground·work (ground′wûrk′) *n.* the first work or material on which something is built or based; foundation: *I completed the groundwork for my term paper in the public library.*

group (grüp) *n.* **1.** a number of persons or things found together or thought of as forming a unit. **2.** a number of persons or things classed together because of similarities: *The Italians and the Irish are two of the ethnic groups that emigrated to this country in large numbers.* **3.** a number of chemical elements having similar characteristics and arranged in a column on the periodic table. **4.** an arrangement of atoms attached to different molecules, giving similar characteristics to a family of compounds. —*v.t.* to arrange or place in a group: *The counselor grouped the younger children together.* —*v.i.* to form or belong to a group: *The skiers grouped around the fire.*

group·er (grü′pər) *n., pl.* **group·ers** or **group·er.** any of a number of saltwater fish having huge mouths and sharp teeth. Many are food fish and some may weigh as much as 1,000 pounds (450 kilograms).

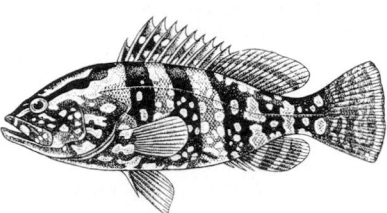

grouper

group·ie (grü′pē) *n. Slang.* **1.** a fan of rock music who follows a particular performer or group around on tours. **2.** a fan or follower of any celebrity or activity.

group·ing (grü′ping) *n.* **1.** the act of placing in a group. **2.** a set of things arranged in a group: *There was an attractive grouping of paintings on one wall.*

group therapy, a form of psychological therapy in which a group of patients, usually with the help of a therapist, try to understand and deal with their emotional problems by openly discussing them.

grouse (grous) *n., pl.* **grouse** or **grous·es.** any of a group of game birds, including the ruffed grouse and prairie chicken, having brown, black, or gray feathers, often with white markings, and feathered legs.

grove (grōv) *n.* **1.** a small group of trees without underbrush. **2.** a group of fruit trees, especially citrus trees: *an orange grove.*

grov·el (gruv′əl, grov′əl) *v.i.,* **grov·eled, grov·el·ing;** *also, British,* **grov·elled, grov·el·ling. 1.** to act in a cringing or humble way, as through fear or the desire to please or flatter: *to grovel in the presence of an elderly relative in hopes of getting an inheritance.* **2.** to lie or crawl face downward, as in fear or humility: *The subjects groveled before their monarch.* —**grov′el·er;** *also, British,* **grov′el·ler,** *n.*

grow (grō) *v.,* **grew, grown, grow·ing.** —*v.i.* **1.** to mature or become larger by a natural process of development: *I grew two inches this year.* **2.** to expand or increase, as in size, amount, or degree: *My savings account began to grow rapidly.* **3.** to be produced and develop; thrive; flourish: *Orchids grow wild in the jungles of South America.* **4.** to come into existence; arise: *Bitter feelings grew from the argument.* **5.** to come to be by degrees; become: *They grew rich as their business expanded.* —*v.t.* **1.** to cause to grow; raise; cultivate: *That farmer grows tomatoes.* **2.** to allow to grow: *to grow a mustache.* **3.** to cover with a growth: *The lawn was grown with weeds.*

·**to grow out of. a.** to outgrow: *The children have grown out of their baby clothes.* **b.** to develop or arise from: *Arguments often grow out of misunderstandings.*

·to grow up. to become an adult: *I want to be a firefighter when I grow up.*

grow·er (grō′ər) *n.* **1.** a person who grows something: *the largest wheat grower in the state.* **2.** a plant that grows in a certain way: *a rapid grower.*

growing season, the period suitable for growth and reproduction of a plant in a particular climate.

growl (groul) *v.i.* **1.** to make a deep, harsh, rumbling sound in the throat: *The bear growled as we approached its cage.* **2.** to speak or make an angry sound or sounds like this. —*v.t.* to express or say with a deep, harsh, rumbling sound. —*n.* **1.** a deep, harsh, rumbling sound made by a dog or other animal. **2.** any sound resembling this.

grown (grōn) *v.* the past participle of **grow.** —*adj.* having reached full growth or maturity; adult: *no way for a grown person to behave.*

grown–up (*adj.*, grōn′up′; *n.*, grōn′up′) *adj.* **1.** adult; mature: *We tried to act grown-up when visiting the museum.* **2.** characteristic of or suitable for adults: *grown-up behavior.* —*n.* an adult: *The grown-ups watched as the children swam in the pool.*

growth (grōth) *n.* **1.** the process of growing; development: *We studied human growth in biology class.* **2.** increase, as in size, importance, or power: *the growth of a company.* **3.** something that grows or has grown: *a growth of weeds.* **4.** a mass of new tissue that results from an abnormal increase in cells and serves no useful function for the body; tumor.

grub (grub) *n.* **1.** a thick, soft larva, especially of a beetle, that resembles a worm. **2.** *Informal.* food. —*v.*, **grubbed, grub·bing.** —*v.i.* **1.** to dig in the ground; root: *Pigs grub for food with their hooves and snouts.* **2.** to work very hard, especially doing menial or dreary work. —*v.t.* to dig up by the roots: *to grub out the weeds in a lawn.* —**grub′ber,** *n.*

grub·by (grub′ē) *adj.*, **grub·bi·er, grub·bi·est.** dirty; grimy; filthy. —**grub′bi·ness,** *n.*

grub·stake (grub′stāk′) *n.* money or supplies advanced to a prospector in return for a share of future profits. —*v.t.*, **grub·staked, grub·stak·ing.** to supply with a grubstake.

grudge (gruj) *n.* a strong feeling of ill will, anger, or resentment. —*v.t.*, **grudged, grudg·ing.** to give or allow unwillingly; begrudge. —**grudg′ing·ly,** *adv.*

gru·el (grü′əl) *n.* a thin porridge made by boiling meal, especially oatmeal, in water or milk.

gru·el·ing (grü′ə ling) *also*, **gru·el·ling.** *adj.* very difficult or punishing; exhausting: *The marathon is a grueling race.*

grue·some (grü′səm) *adj.* causing horror, disgust, or fear; frightful; repulsive. —**grue′some·ly,** *adv.* —**grue′some·ness,** *n.*

gruff (gruf) *adj.* **1.** (of the voice) deep and rough. **2.** abrupt, stern, or rude: *a person with a gruff manner but a kind heart.* —**gruff′ly,** *adv.* —**gruff′ness,** *n.*

grum·ble (grum′bəl) *v.*, **grum·bled, grum·bling.** —*v.i.* **1.** to mutter in discontent; complain in a grouchy manner. **2.** to rumble. —*v.t.* to express or say by grumbling. —*n.* **1.** a mutter of discontent or complaint. **2.** a rumble. —**grum′bler,** *n.*

grump (grump) *n.* an ill-tempered, complaining person.

grump·y (grum′pē) *adj.*, **grump·i·er, grump·i·est.** ill-tempered and complaining: *I try not to be grumpy when I get up in the morning.* —**grump′i·ly,** *adv.* —**grump′i·ness,** *n.*

grunt (grunt) *n.* **1.** a short, deep, hoarse sound, such as that made by a hog. **2.** any of a group of tropical saltwater fish that make a similar sound by rubbing their teeth together. —*v.i.* **1.** to make the short, deep, hoarse sound of a hog. **2.** to make a similar sound: *We all grunted as we pushed the stalled car along.* —*v.t.* to say or express with a grunt: *to grunt one's refusal of a request.*

Gt. Br. *also*, **Gt. Brit.** Great Britain.

GU, postal abbreviation for Guam.

gua·na·co (gwä nä′kō) *n., pl.* **gua·na·cos.** a wild, long-legged animal of South America, related to the llama, having a long, slender neck and large, pointed ears.

gua·nine (gwä′nēn) *n.* a purine base that is an essential constituent of DNA and RNA.

gua·no (gwä′nō) *n., pl.* **gua·nos. 1.** the waste matter of seabirds, widely used as fertilizer, found in large deposits on islands off the coast of Peru. **2.** any similar fertilizer, such as the excrement of bats.

guar·an·tee (gar′ən tē′) *n.* **1.** a pledge given by a seller to a buyer to repair, replace, or refund the purchase price of the seller's product if it is not what it is claimed to be or if anything goes wrong with it within a certain period of time; warranty. **2.** anything that assures a certain outcome or condition: *Beauty is no guarantee of happiness.* **3.** a guarantor. **4.** see **guaranty** (*defs. 1,2*). —*v.t.*, **guar·an·teed, guar·an·tee·ing. 1.** to give a guarantee for: *to guarantee a watch for one year.* **2.** to agree to be responsible for the debts or obligations of another; make a guaranty. **3.** to make sure or certain: *That band will guarantee the success of the dance.* **4.** to state or affirm (something); promise: *I guarantee that the work will be finished on time.*

guar·an·tor (gar′ən tôr′) *n.* a person who makes or gives a guarantee.

guar·an·ty (gar′ən tē′) *n., pl.* **guar·an·ties. 1.** an agreement or promise to be responsible for the debts or obligations of another person if that person should fail to take care of them. **2.** something given or taken as security for a debt or obligation. **3.** a guarantee; warranty.

guard (gärd) *v.t.* **1.** to watch over or tend carefully to keep safe from harm; defend; protect: *Secret Service agents guard the president.* **2.** to maintain close watch or supervision over, as to prevent escape or to control activity: *Police guarded the prisoners.* **3.** in certain sports, to attempt to prevent (an opponent) from scoring. **4.** to provide a cover, shield, or other protective device for: *Using this lotion will guard your skin against the sun.* —*v.i.* to take precautions or care: *to guard against illness.* —*n.* **1.** a person or group that guards: *a museum guard.* **2.** a cover, attachment, or other device that protects against loss, injury, or damage. **3.** careful or restraining watch or supervision: *A sentry kept guard at the door.* **4.** something that guards or protects; defense; safeguard: *Brushing your teeth after each meal is a good guard against tooth decay.* **5.** *Football.* one of two players positioned at the right and the left of the center. **6.** *Basketball.* one of two players whose usual position is toward the rear of the court.

·off (one's) guard. not alert; unprepared: *The troops were caught off guard by the enemy.*

·on (one's) guard. prepared or watchful; alert.

·to stand guard. a. to serve as a sentry. **b.** to keep a protective watch.

guard cell *Botany.* one of a pair of bean-shaped cells found next to a pore on the outer surface of a leaf. Their reactions to heat and light control the movement of gases into and out of the leaf through the pores.

guard·ed (gär′did) *adj.* **1.** cautious; prudent: *a guarded reply to a provocative question.* **2.** closely watched, defended, or restrained. —**guard′ed·ly,** *adv.*

---

at; āpe; fär; câre; end; mē; it; īce; pîerce; hot; ōld; sông, fôrk; oil; out; up; ūse; rüle; pu̇ll; tûrn; chin; sing; shop; thin; this; hw in white; zh in treasure. The symbol ə stands for the unstressed vowel sound heard in about, taken, pencil, lemon, and circus.

G

guard·house (gärd′hous′) *n.*, *pl.* **guard·hous·es** (gärd′hou′ziz). **1.** a building used as a jail for military prisoners. **2.** a building used to house people on military guard duty.

guard·i·an (gär′dē ən) *n.* **1.** a person or thing that guards or watches over; protector: *A judge is a guardian of justice.* **2.** a person who is entrusted by law to take care of the person, property, or rights of another: *The court appointed a guardian for the children after their parents died.* —*adj.* protecting: *a guardian angel.* —**guard′i·an·ship′**, *n.*

guard·rail (gärd′rāl′) *n.* a railing for support or protection, as on a staircase or a highway.

guard·room (gärd′rüm′, gärd′rum′) *n.* a room used by people on military guard duty.

guards·man (gärdz′mən) *n.*, *pl.* **guards·men** (gärdz′mən). **1.** a guard. **2.** a soldier in the National Guard. **3.** a soldier in a unit of the British army that is attached to the royal household.

gua·va (gwä′və) *n.* **1.** a round or pear-shaped fruit, having a sweet, firm flesh, that is used for making jellies and other sweets. **2.** the tree or shrub bearing this fruit, grown in tropical America, having large, oval leaves and white flowers.

gu·ber·na·to·ri·al (gü′bər nə tôr′ē əl) *adj.* of or relating to a governor or the office of governor: *a gubernatorial election.*

gudg·eon (guj′ən) *n.* **1.** a freshwater fish of Europe, easily caught and often used for bait. **2.** any of various similar fish, as the minnow.

Guern·sey (gûrn′zē) *n.*, *pl.* **Guern·seys. 1.** any of a breed of dairy cattle originally developed on Guernsey in the Channel Islands, typically having a reddish or tan coat with white markings.

guer·ril·la (gə ril′ə) *also*, **gue·ril·la.** *n.* a member of a band of fighters, usually not part of a regular army, who combat the enemy with such acts as sabotage, ambushes, and sudden raids. —*adj.* of, relating to, or involving guerrillas: *guerrilla warfare.*

guess (ges) *v.t.* **1.** to form an opinion or estimate of (something) without complete or certain knowledge or evidence: *Without a clock I could only guess what time it was.* **2.** to judge (something) correctly by doing this: *to guess the answer to a teacher's question.* **3.** to think; believe; suppose: *I guess they forgot about the meeting.* —*v.i.* to make a guess: *Are you sure of your answer, or are you just guessing?* —*n.*, *pl.* **guess·es.** an opinion, estimate, or conclusion formed by guessing: *My guess is that the mayor will be reelected.* —**guess′er**, *n.*

guess·work (ges′wûrk′) *n.* the process or result of guessing: *to arrive at an answer by guesswork.*

guest (gest) *n.* **1.** a person who is received and entertained by another, as for a party, meal, or visit. **2.** a person who pays for lodgings, food, and other services, as at a hotel, boarding house, or restaurant.

guf·faw (gu fô′) *n.* a loud, hearty burst of laughter. —*v.i.* to laugh loudly and heartily: *Everyone guffawed when I fell into the swimming pool.*

guid·ance (gīd′dəns) *n.* **1.** the act or process of guiding; leadership; direction: *to write a term paper under a teacher's guidance.* **2.** something that guides. **3.** counseling and advice dealing with educational and career plans and personal problems, especially that given to pupils by school services. **4.** the process by which a missile can be guided while in flight.

guide (gīd) *n.* **1.** a person who shows the way or directs, as someone employed to lead or conduct a tour or hunting trip. **2.** a person or thing that directs conduct or a course of action: *Let your conscience be your guide.* **3.** see **guidebook. 4.** a book explaining or outlining the basic elements of some subject: *a guide to medieval literature.* **5.** a part of a machine serving to steady or direct motion or action. —*v.t.*, **guid·ed, guid·ing. 1.** to show the way

to; lead; conduct: *The scout guided the hunters through the forest.* **2.** to direct the course or motion of: *The driver guided the truck around the curves in the road.* **3.** to lead or direct the actions, affairs, or motives of; regulate: *Let your common sense guide you.*

guide·book (gīd′bük′) *n.* a book of directions and information for travelers and tourists.

guided missile, a missile that is guided during its flight by electronic signals or other means.

guide dog, a dog specially trained to act as a guide for a blind person. Also, **Seeing Eye dog.**

guide dogs

guide·line (gīd′līn′) *n.* a direction or procedure to be followed in determining some course of action: *The city council laid down guidelines for establishing new programs to help the homeless.*

guide·post (gīd′pōst′) *n.* a post at a roadside or intersection bearing a sign giving directions for travelers.

guide word, one of the two or more words appearing at the top of a page or set of pages in a dictionary or other reference book, used to show what the first and last entries on a page are.

guild (gild) *also*, **gild.** *n.* **1.** in the Middle Ages, a group of merchants or artisans in one trade or craft, organized to maintain standards of work and to protect the interests of members. **2.** any organization of persons with similar interests or aims: *an actors' guild.*

guil·der (gil′dər) *n.* **1.** the monetary unit in the Netherlands. **2.** any of several coins formerly used in the Netherlands, Germany, and Austria. Also, **gulden.**

guild·hall (gild′hôl′) *n.* a hall in which a guild meets.

guile (gīl) *n.* cunning; deceit; slyness.

guile·ful (gīl′fəl) *adj.* full of guile; cunning; deceitful.

guile·less (gīl′lis) *adj.* without guile; sincere; honest.

guil·lo·tine (gil′ə tēn′, gē′ə tēn′) *n.* a machine consisting of a heavy blade that falls between two grooved posts, used for beheading people. It was widely used to execute people in France during the French Revolution. —*v.t.*, **guil·lo·tined, guil·lo·tin·ing.** to behead by the guillotine. [From the French word *guillotine*, from the French physician Joseph *Guillotin* (1738–1814), who urged its use as a relatively painless method of execution.]

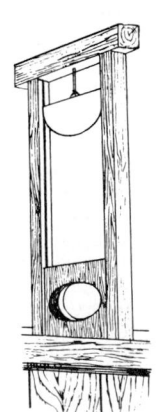

guillotine

guilt (gilt) *n.* **1.** the state or fact of having done wrong, especially of having committed a crime: *The new evidence definitely proved the defendant's guilt.* **2.** a wrongful action; guilty behavior; wrongdoing. **3.** a feeling of regret, shame, or of being to blame for having done wrong: *The children felt guilt because they had cheated to win the game.* —**guilt′less,** *adj.*

guilt·y (gil′tē) *adj.,* **guilt·i·er, guilt·i·est. 1.** having done wrong; deserving of blame or punishment: *We are all guilty of losing our temper sometimes.* **2.** convicted of a crime: *The prisoners were guilty of arson.* **3.** feeling or showing guilt or a sense of guilt: *a guilty conscience, a guilty look.* —**guilt′i·ly,** *adv.*

guin·ea (gin′ē) *n.* **1.** an English gold coin last minted in 1813, fixed in value at twenty-one shillings. **2.** in England, a sum of money equal to twenty-one shillings.

guinea fowl, a fowl similar to the pheasant and native to Africa, having dark gray feathers speckled with white. They are widely domesticated and raised for food.

guinea hen 1. a female guinea fowl. **2.** a guinea fowl.

guinea pig 1. a small, plump rodent having a large head, small rounded ears, and a long or short coat that may be solid or spotted or streaked with different colors. It is widely used in experiments for biological

guinea fowl

and medical research and is often kept as a pet. **2.** any person or thing used in experimentation: *When my cousin cooks a new dish, I have to act as a guinea pig and taste it.*

Guin·e·vere (gwin′ə vîr′) *n.* in legend, the beautiful wife of King Arthur. She was loved by Lancelot, a knight of the Round Table.

guise (gīz) *n.* **1.** an outward appearance; semblance: *The mayor presented an old approach to the problem of unemployment in a*

guinea pig *(def. 1)*

new guise. **2.** an assumed or false appearance, pretense: *Under the guise of friendship, they betrayed all the people who had trusted them.* **3.** *Archaic.* a style or manner of dress.

gui·tar (gi tär′) *n.* a musical instrument having a long neck, usually six strings, and a body shaped somewhat like a violin. It is played by plucking or strumming the strings with the fingers or a plectrum.

gulch (gulch) *n., pl.* **gulch·es.** a deep, narrow valley with steep sides, especially one marking the course of a stream or torrent; ravine.

gul·den (gül′dən, gúl′dən) *n., pl.* **gul·dens** or **gul·den.** another word for **guilder.**

gulf (gulf) *n.* **1.** a body of water forming an indentation in the shoreline of an ocean or sea, usually larger and deeper than a bay. **2.** a deep hollow in the earth; chasm. **3.** any wide separation: *There is a great gulf between the rich and the poor in that country.*

gull¹ (gul) *n.* any of several long-winged birds found on most seacoasts and near large bodies of water, having webbed feet, a thick, slightly hooked beak, and usually gray and white feathers. Also, **sea gull.** [Of Celtic origin.]

gull² (gul) *v.t.* to trick; cheat; dupe: *Swindlers gulled us into giving them money.* —*n.* a person who is easily tricked or cheated; dupe. [Perhaps from the earlier word *gull* meaning "to swallow," from the Old French word *gole* "throat," from the Latin word *gula* "throat."]

gul·let (gul′it) *n.* **1.** the tube or passage through which food passes from the mouth to the stomach; esophagus. **2.** the throat.

gul·li·ble (gul′ə bəl) *adj.* believing or trusting in almost

anything; easily tricked, cheated, or duped: *You would have to be very gullible to believe such a silly story.* —**gul′li·bil′i·ty,** *n.* —**gul′li·bly,** *adv.*

gul·ly (gul′ē) *n., pl.* **gul·lies.** a ditch or channel cut in the earth by running water; small ravine.

gulp (gulp) *v.t.* **1.** to swallow hastily, greedily, or in large amounts (often with *down*): *to gulp down a sandwich.* **2.** to choke back or stifle as if by swallowing: *to gulp down one's anger.* —*v.i.* to draw in or swallow air, as in surprise or fear. —*n.* **1.** the act of gulping: *to drink a small glass of milk in three gulps.* **2.** the amount swallowed at one time; mouthful.

gum¹ (gum) *n.* **1.** a thick, sticky juice produced by various plants and trees, that dissolves or softens in cold water and hardens when exposed to air or heat. **2.** any similar plant or tree substance, such as resin. **3.** a preparation made from such substances, used in manufacturing textiles, adhesives, dyes, and paints. **4.** see **chewing gum. 5.** a glue or other substance used to make paper stick to something else: *There is no gum on the back of this stamp.* **6.** see **gum tree.** —*v.t.* **gummed, gum·ming.** —*v.t.* to coat, clog, stiffen, or glue with gum or a gummy substance: *The machine gummed the back of the stamps.* —*v.i.* to become coated, clogged, stiffened, or glued with gum or as if with gum. [From the Old French word *gomme* meaning "resin, gum¹," going back to the Egyptian word *kemai* with the same meaning.]

gum² (gum) *also,* **gums.** *n.* the tough fleshy tissue surrounding the teeth. [From the Old English word *gōma* meaning "roof of the mouth."]

gum arabic, a gum obtained from any of several trees, used chiefly in the manufacture of candies, adhesives, inks, textiles, and medicines. Also, **acacia.**

gum·bo (gum′bō) *n., pl.* **gum·bos. 1.** the okra plant and its pods. **2.** a soup thickened with okra pods and usually containing other vegetables and meat or fish. **3.** a fine soil that becomes very sticky when wet.

gum·drop (gum′drop′) *n.* a small, jellylike piece of candy made of gum arabic or gelatin that is sweetened and usually coated with sugar.

gum·my (gum′ē) *adj.,* **gum·mi·er, gum·mi·est. 1.** of, containing, or resembling gum; sticky. **2.** covered or clogged with gum or something sticky. —**gum′mi·ness,** *n.*

gump·tion (gump′shən) *n. Informal.* determined courage and energy; initiative; nerve: *It took a lot of gumption to stand up to that bully.*

gum resin, a mixture of gum and resin, usually obtained by cutting the outer covering of certain plants.

gum tree, any tree that produces gum, such as certain eucalyptus trees.

gun (gun) *n.* **1.** any of various weapons, such as a pistol, rifle, or cannon, made up of a metal tube through which a bullet or other projectile is shot by the force of an explosive. **2.** any device resembling a gun in shape or use: *a dart gun, a spray gun.* **3.** the firing of a gun as a signal or salute. —*v.,* **gunned, gun·ning.** —*v.t.* **1.** *Informal.* to shoot (a person or animal) with a gun (often with *down*). **2.** *Informal.* to open the throttle of so as to increase the speed: *The driver gunned the engine.* —*v.i.* to shoot or hunt with a gun.

• **to stick to one's guns.** to be firm in spite of opposition; refuse to retreat or yield.

at; āpe; fär; câre; end; mē; it; īce; pîerce; hot; ōld; sông; fôrk; oil; out; up; ūse; rüle; púll; tûrn; chin; sing; shop; thin; this; hw in white; zh in treasure. The symbol ə stands for the unstressed vowel sound heard in about, taken, pencil, lemon, and circus.

G

gun·boat (gun′bōt′) *n.* a small, armed ship used for patrolling rivers and coastal waters.

gun·cot·ton (gun′kot′ən) *n.* an explosive made by treating cotton or other cellulose fibers with a mixture of concentrated nitric and sulfuric acids.

gun·fire (gun′fīr′) *n.* the shooting of a gun or guns.

gung ho (gung′hō′) *Slang.* very enthusiastic; eager.

gun·lock (gun′lok′) *n.* the part of the mechanism in certain guns by which the charge is exploded.

gun·man (gun′mən) *n., pl.* **gun·men** (gun′mən). a person armed with a gun, especially a criminal: *Three gunmen robbed the bank.*

gun·met·al (gun′met′əl) *n.* **1.** any of various metallic alloys with a grayish color, used for making such items as chains, buckles, and other trinkets. **2.** a kind of bronze formerly used for making guns. **3.** a dark gray color with a bluish tinge. —*adj.* of or like gunmetal.

gun·nel (gun′əl) another spelling of **gunwale**.

gun·ner (gun′ər) *n.* **1.** a soldier or other member of the armed forces who operates or helps to operate guns or artillery. **2.** a naval warrant officer in charge of guns or artillery. **3.** a person who hunts with a gun.

gun·ner·y (gun′ə rē) *n.* the use and firing of guns.

gun·ny (gun′ē) *n., pl.* **gun·nies.** a strong, coarse fabric made of jute or hemp, used especially for making sacks or bags.

gun·ny·sack (gun′ē sak′) *n.* a sack or bag made of gunny or other coarse material.

gun·point (gun′point′) *n.* the end of a gun barrel.
·**at gunpoint.** under threat of being shot: *to be held up at gunpoint.*

gun·pow·der (gun′pou′dər) *n.* an explosive made up of charcoal, sulfur, and potassium nitrate, used especially in cartridges, artillery shells, fireworks, and blasting.

gun·shot (gun′shot′) *n.* **1.** a bullet or other shot fired from a gun. **2.** the distance within which a gun will shoot accurately; range of a gun: *The troops fired when the enemy came within gunshot.* **3.** the firing of a gun: *We could hear gunshots in the distance.*

gun·smith (gun′smith′) *n.* a person who makes or repairs firearms.

gun·stock (gun′stok′) *n.* a wooden support or handle to which the barrel of a gun is attached.

gun·wale (gun′əl) *also,* **gun·nel.** *n.* the upper edge of the side of a ship or boat.

gup·py (gup′ē) *n., pl.* **gup·pies.** a small, slender fish native to tropical fresh waters of Trinidad and northern South America, the male of which is brightly colored. It is widely raised in home aquariums. [From the natu-

guppy

ralist from Trinidad, R. J. L. *Guppy* (d. 1916), who gave specimens of this fish to the British Museum.]

gur·gle (gûr′gəl) *v.,* **gur·gled, gur·gling.** —*v.i.* **1.** to flow or run in an irregular current and with a bubbling sound: *The stream gurgled around the rocks.* **2.** to make a similar sound: *The baby cooed and gurgled with delight.* —*v.t.* to utter with a gurgling sound. —*n.* the act or sound of gurgling.

gu·ru (gü′rü, gü rü′) *n.* **1.** a holy man and religious and spiritual teacher, especially in the Hindu religion. **2.** *Informal.* a respected leader or teacher.

gush (gush) *v.i.* **1.** to flow or rush out suddenly and abundantly: *Water gushed from the broken pipe.* **2.** *Informal.* to speak or write with too much feeling or enthusiasm in a foolish way: *The young poet gushed with sentimentality.* —*v.t.* to give forth in a sudden and

abundant flow: *The cut gushed blood.* —*n., pl.* **gush·es.** a sudden rush or outflow: *a gush of water.*

gush·er (gush′ər) *n.* an oil well that gives forth oil abundantly without being pumped.

gush·y (gush′ē) *adj.,* **gush·i·er, gush·i·est.** showing too much feeling or enthusiasm in a foolish way: *a gushy greeting, a gushy person.* —**gush′i·ness,** *n.*

gus·set (gus′it) *n.* **1.** a triangular piece of material inserted into a garment or other article to strengthen or expand some part of it. **2.** a triangular metal brace or bracket that is used to strengthen a corner or angle of a structure.

gust (gust) *n.* **1.** a sudden, strong rush of wind or air. **2.** any sudden burst or outflow, as of rain or fire. **3.** an outburst of emotion, as anger or enthusiasm.

gus·ta·to·ry (gus′tə tôr′ē) *adj.* of or relating to the sense of taste.

gus·to (gus′tō) *n.* great enthusiasm or enjoyment: *We ate with gusto after returning from our hike.*

gust·y (gus′tē) *adj.,* **gust·i·er, gust·i·est.** characterized by or coming in gusts; windy; blustery: *the gusty weather of March.* —**gust′i·ly,** *adv.* —**gust′i·ness,** *n.*

gut (gut) *n.* **1.** the digestive tract or any part of it, especially the stomach or intestine. **2. guts. a.** *Slang.* courage; pluck: *It took guts to play when you were injured.* **b.** entrails; bowels. **3.** see **catgut.** —*v.t.,* **gut·ted, gut·ting.** **1.** to remove the entrails of. **2.** to destroy the inside of: *Fire gutted the house.* —*adj.* *Slang.* **1.** felt deeply or instinctively; spontaneous; visceral: *a gut feeling, a gut reaction.* **2.** basic or vital; fundamental: *gut issues in politics.*

gut·ta-per·cha (gut′ə pûr′chə) *n.* a pliable, pale gray material obtained from the milky juice of several species of evergreen trees found in Malaya and the East Indies. It is used especially in electrical insulation, in dentistry, and as waterproofing.

gut·ter (gut′ər) *n.* **1.** a narrow channel, ditch, or low area along the side of a street or road to carry off surface water. **2.** a trough fixed under or along the eaves of a roof to carry off rainwater. **3.** any channel or groove, as at the side of a bowling alley. —*v.t.* to form gutters in or furnish with gutters. —*v.i.* **1.** to flow in streams. **2.** (of a candle) to melt rapidly so that the wax or tallow runs down the sides in channels.

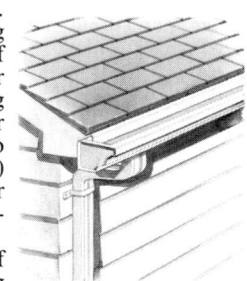

gutter *(n., def. 2)*

gut·tur·al (gut′ər əl) *adj.* **1.** of or relating to the throat. **2.** having a harsh, rasping quality, as a sound produced in the throat: *a fierce, guttural growl.* **3.** pronounced with the back of the tongue raised toward the soft palate. The *g* in *go* is a guttural sound. —*n.* a guttural sound. —**gut′tur·al·ly,** *adv.*

guy¹ (gī) *n.* a rope, chain, wire, or rod used to steady or secure something. —*v.t.,* **guyed, guy·ing.** to steady or secure with a guy. [Probably from the Dutch word *gei* meaning "a rope used to raise a sail."]

guy² (gī) *Informal. n.* **1.** a man; fellow. **2. guys.** *Informal.* persons of either sex: *I'm going to the movies with my sister and the rest of the guys.* —*v.t.,* **guyed, guy·ing.** to make fun of; tease. [From the Englishman *Guy* Fawkes (1570–1606), leader of a plot to blow up the English Houses of Parliament in 1605. The word originally referred to the effigy of Guy Fawkes that is burned on the anniversary of the plot, November 5.]

guz·zle (guz′əl) *v.t., v.i.,* **guz·zled, guz·zling.** to drink (something) greedily or excessively. —**guz′zler,** *n.*

gym (jim) *n.* **1.** see **gymnasium. 2.** a course in physical education in a school or college.

gym·na·si·um (jim nā′zē əm) *n., pl.* **gym·na·si·ums** or **gym·na·si·a** (jim nā′zē ə). **1.** a room or building having equipment for physical exercise or training and for indoor sports. **2. Gymnasium.** a secondary school in some European countries, equivalent to a high school.

gym·nast (jim′nast, jim′nəst) *n.* a person skilled in gymnastics.

gym·nas·tic (jim nas′tik) *adj.* of or relating to gymnastics.

gym·nas·tics (jim nas′tiks) *pl. n.* **1.** physical exercises designed to develop strength, agility, coordination, and balance. **2.** the art, practice, or sport of such exercises. ▲ used with a singular verb in definition 2.

gymnastics

gym·no·sperm (jim′nə spûrm′) *n.* any of a large group of plants whose seeds are not enclosed in ovaries and are generally borne in cones. Gymnosperms include pines, spruces, firs, larches, hemlocks, cedars, junipers, and the redwood.

gy·ne·col·o·gist (gī′ni kol′ə jist, jin′i kol′ə jist) *n.* a doctor who specializes in gynecology.

gy·ne·col·o·gy (gī′ni kol′ə jē, jin′i kol′ə jē) *n.* the branch of medicine dealing with the functions and disorders of the female reproductive system.

gyp (jip) *Slang. v.t.,* **gypped, gyp·ping.** to cheat or swindle. —*n.* **1.** a fraud; swindle. **2.** a cheat; swindler.

gyp·sum (jip′səm) *n.* a common mineral used especially in cements, in plaster of Paris, and as a fertilizer.

Gyp·sy (jip′sē) *also,* **Gip·sy.** *n., pl.* **Gyp·sies. 1.** *also* **gypsy.** a member of a wandering Caucasian people having dark skin and black hair, who left northwestern India and appeared in Europe around the fourteenth century. They now live mainly in Europe and the United States. **2.** the language spoken by Gypsies; Romany

gypsy moth *also,* **gipsy moth.** a moth native to Europe and Japan, and now found in the northeastern United States, whose larvae eat the leaves of trees.

gy·rate (jī′rāt) *v.i.,* **gy·rat·ed, gy·rat·ing.** to move in a circle or spiral or around an axis or fixed point; whirl; rotate: *The dancing couple gyrated around the room.*

gy·ra·tion (jī rā′shən) *n.* the act of gyrating; circular or spiral motion.

gyr·fal·con (jûr′fôl′kən, jûr′fal′kən, jûr′fô′kən) *also,* **ger·fal·con.** *n.* a powerful falcon living mainly in the Arctic, having white or gray plumage. It is the largest of the falcons.

gy·ro[1] (jī′rō) *n., pl.* **gy·ros. 1.** see **gyrocompass. 2.** see **gyroscope.** [Short for *gyrocompass,* from the Greek word *gyros* meaning "round, rounded" + the English word *compass.*]

gy·ro[2] (jîr′ō, jī′rō, zhîr′ō) *n., pl.* **gy·ros.** a sandwich of pita filled with grilled lamb or beef and usually tomatoes and onion. [From the Modern Greek word *gyros* "a turning," used as the name of this food. The meat is roasted on a turning spit.]

gy·ro·com·pass (jī′rō kum′pəs, jī′rō kom′pəs) *n., pl.* **gy·ro·com·pass·es.** a compass that uses a spinning gyroscope to indicate true north rather than magnetic north.

gy·ro·scope (jī′rə skōp′) *n.* a wheel mounted so that the axis on which it spins can point in any direction. When the wheel is spinning, the axis sets itself in a fixed direction and resists changes from that direction. Gyroscopes are used in ships and airplanes as stabilizers, compasses, and automatic pilots.

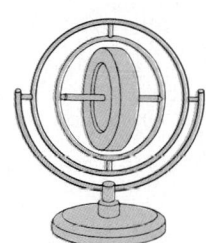
gyroscope

gyve (jīv) *Archaic. n.* a fetter or shackle, especially for the leg. —*v.t.,* **gyved, gyv·ing.** to bind with or as if with fetters; shackle.

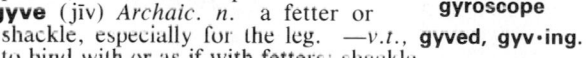

at; āpe; fär; câre; end; mē; it; īce; pierce; hot; ōld; sông, fôrk; oil; out; up; ūse; rüle; pull; tûrn; chin; sing; shop; thin; this; hw in white; zh in treasure. The symbol ə stands for the unstressed vowel sound heard in about, taken, pencil, lemon, and circus.

G

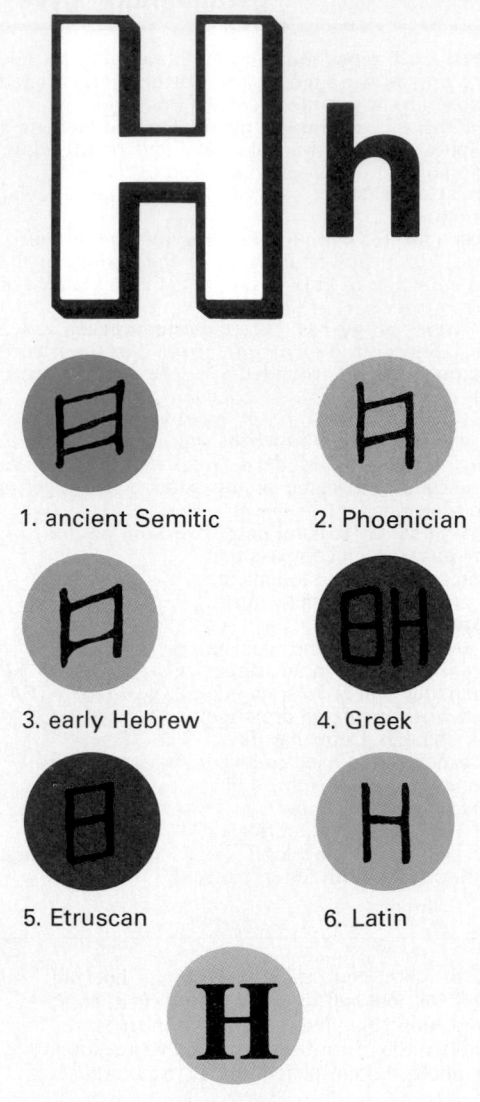

1. ancient Semitic
2. Phoenician
3. early Hebrew
4. Greek
5. Etruscan
6. Latin
7. English

H is the eighth letter of the English alphabet. The earliest form of the letter **H** was probably the letter *cheth*, or *het,* in the ancient Semitic (1), Phoenician (2), and early Hebrew (3) alphabets. *Cheth*, which may have meant "fence," represented an *h* sound made at the back of the throat. When the ancient Greeks borrowed *cheth*, they called it *eta* (4). The early form of *eta* looked very much like a square modern capital letter **B**. Later, the Greeks gave it the modern form of two tall lines connected by a short bar. The Etruscans (5) borrowed the earlier form of *eta*. Although most of the Latin letters came from the Etruscan alphabet, the Latin letter **H** (6) came directly from the later form of the Greek *eta*. By about 2,400 years ago, this letter was being written almost exactly the way we write the capital letter **H** today (7).

h, H (āch) *n., pl.* **h's, H's.** the eighth letter of the English alphabet.

h., H. 1. height. **2.** hour; hours. **3.** hundred.

H, the symbol for hydrogen.

ha (hä) *interj.* **1.** *also,* **hah.** used to express a sudden feeling, as of surprise, joy, triumph, or scorn. **2.** used to express laughter.

ha·be·as cor·pus (hā′bē əs kôr′pəs) a writ or order to bring a prisoner before a court or judge to determine if he or she is being held lawfully. [From the Medieval Latin phrase *habeas corpus* meaning "you shall have the body," from the opening words of this document.]

hab·er·dash·er (hab′ər dash′ər) *n.* a person who sells clothing and accessories for men.

hab·er·dash·er·y (hab′ər dash′ə rē) *n., pl.* **hab·er·dash·er·ies. 1.** the goods sold by a haberdasher. **2.** a haberdasher's shop.

ha·bil·i·ment (hə bil′ə mənt) *n.* clothing; dress.

hab·it (hab′it) *n.* **1.** an action done so often or for so long a time that one does not think about it and usually cannot stop or control it: *Biting one's nails is a bad habit.* **2.** a customary or usual way of acting: *Is it your habit to read the paper before dinner? The book deals with the eating habits of animals.* **3.** an addiction: *a drug habit.* **4.** a characteristic type of dress: *a nun's habit, a riding habit.* —*v.t.* to dress or clothe (oneself): *The jockeys habited themselves in blue and gold.*

hab·it·a·ble (hab′i tə bəl) *adj.* suitable for living in; able to be lived in or on: *Clean up your room and make it habitable. The planet Jupiter is not habitable by humans.*

hab·i·tant (hab′i tənt) *n.* an inhabitant; dweller.

hab·i·tat (hab′i tat′) *n.* **1.** the area or region in which an animal or plant naturally lives or grows: *The desert is the habitat of the cactus.* **2.** a place where a person or thing is most frequently found.

hab·i·ta·tion (hab′i tā′shən) *n.* **1.** the place where one lives; living quarters. **2.** the act of inhabiting; occupancy: *These slums are not fit for human habitation.*

hab·it–form·ing (hab′it fôr′ming) *adj.* causing or tending to cause a habit or addiction, especially a physical addiction: *habit-forming drugs.*

ha·bit·u·al (hə bich′ü əl) *adj.* **1.** done by or resulting from habit: *habitual optimism.* **2.** being or acting in a certain way by habit: *a habitual smoker, a habitual latecomer.* **3.** commonly occurring or used; usual; regular: *a habitual diet.* —**ha·bit′u·al·ly,** *adv.*

ha·bit·u·ate (hə bich′ü āt′) *v.t.,* **ha·bit·u·at·ed, ha·bit·u·at·ing.** to make used to something; accustom: *Living near a highway habituated them to noise.* —**ha·bit′u·a′tion,** *n.*

ha·bit·u·é (hə bich′ü ā′) *n.* a person who goes regularly or frequently to a particular place.

ha·ci·en·da (hä′sē en′də) *n.* **1.** a landed estate, ranch, or plantation. **2.** in the southwestern United States and Spanish America, a low, sprawling ranch house with wide porches. [From the Spanish word *hacienda* meaning both "landed estate" and "domestic work," going back to the Latin word *facienda* "things to be done," from the word *facere* "to do."]

hack¹ (hak) *v.t.* to cut or chop unevenly or crudely with heavy blows, as with a hatchet or cleaver: *I hacked the dead limbs off the tree.* —*v.i.* **1.** to make uneven or crude cuts or chops; deal cutting blows: *The gardener hacked at the branches.* **2.** to give short, harsh, repeated coughs. —*n.* **1.** an uneven or crude cut or chop made with a heavy blow. **2.** a short, harsh, repeated cough. [From the Old English root *-haccian* meaning "to cut, chop."]

hack² (hak) *n.* **1.** a person who does dull or routine work solely for money. **2.** a carriage for hire; hackney. **3.** an old, worn-out horse. **4.** *Informal.* a taxicab. **5.** a horse kept for hire or for general work. —*v.i. Informal.* to drive a taxicab. —*adj.* **1.** working or done solely for money: *a hack writer, a hack job.* **2.** typical of such a hack work; dull or routine: *hack writing.* [Short for *hackney.*]

hack·ber·ry (hak′ber′ē, hak′bə rē) *n., pl.* **hack·ber·ries. 1.** any of a large group of shrubs and trees related to the elm, having gray bark and tiny flowers. **2.** the fruit of this tree.

hack·er (hak′ər) *n.* a person who devotes much time to using computers, especially someone who is skillful in gaining access to other computer systems without proper authorization.

hack·le (hak′əl) *n.* **1.** any of the long, slender feathers on the neck of certain birds, especially the rooster. **2.** an artificial fishing fly made with such feathers. **3. hackles.** the hairs along the neck and back of a dog or other animal that stand up when it is angry or frightened.

hack·ney (hak′nē) *n., pl.* **hack·neys. 1.** a horse used for ordinary or everyday riding or driving. **2.** a carriage for hire. —*adj.* let out, employed, or done for hire. [From the Middle English word *hakenei* meaning "a hackney horse," probably from the name *Hackney,* a borough northeast of London.]

hack·neyed (hak′nēd) *adj.* made dull or ordinary by being used too often; trite: *"As busy as a bee" is a hackneyed phrase.* [From *hackney,* a horse used for everyday riding, because such a horse was often worn out from being overused.]

hack·saw (hak′sô′) *n.* a saw having a narrow, fine-toothed blade held firm in a frame, used especially for cutting metal.

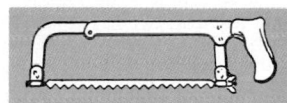
hacksaw

had (had; *unstressed* həd, əd) the past tense and past participle of **have.** ▲ often used to show what is preferred or necessary. *Had rather* means "would prefer to": *I had rather leave now. Had better* means "ought to": *You had better study if you want to pass the test.*

had·dock (had′ək) *n., pl.* **had·dock** or **had·docks.** a food fish of the northern Atlantic related to the cod, having five fins and a black line running along each side of the body from the gills to the tail.

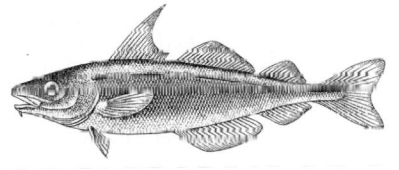
haddock

Ha·des (hā′dēz) *n.* **1.** *Greek Mythology.* a place where the spirits of the dead dwell; underworld. **2.** the god who rules the underworld; Pluto. **3. hades.** hell.

had·n't (had′ənt) *contr.* had not.

hadst (hadst) *Archaic.* the second person singular, past tense of **have.**

haf·ni·um (haf′nē əm) *n.* a gray metallic element found in combination with zirconium. Hafnium is used to control the consumption of nuclear fuel in atomic submarines and nuclear power plants. Symbol: **Hf** [From *Hafnia,* the Latin form of *Copenhagen,* the city in Denmark where it was discovered.]

haft (haft) *n.* the handle of a knife, sword, or other tool or weapon.

hag (hag) *n.* **1.** an ugly, often evil or vicious old woman. **2.** a witch. **3.** see **hagfish.**

hag·fish (hag′fish′) *n., pl.* **hag·fish** or **hag·fish·es.** any of a group of saltwater fishes that resemble eels, having a round, sucking mouth surrounded by tentacles. Some attach themselves by mouth to other fish, bore into their bodies, and feed on their organs, often leaving only skin and bones.

Hag·ga·dah (hə gä′də) *also,* **Hag·ga·da.** *n., pl.* **Hag-**

ga·doth (hə gä′dōt, hä gä dōt′) or **Hag·ga·dot.** a book of services for the celebration of the Jewish festival of Passover, including prayers, the story of the Exodus, legends, and songs.

Hag·ga·i (hag′ē ī′) *n.* the book of the Old Testament containing the prophecies of Haggai.

hag·gard (hag′ərd) *adj.* having a worn look, as from fatigue, anxiety, hunger, or suffering. —**hag′gard·ly,** *adv.* —**hag′gard·ness,** *n.*

hag·gle (hag′əl) *v.i.,* **hag·gled, hag·gling.** to bargain or argue in a petty way: *haggling with the grocer about prices. The children haggled over who was going to ride the bicycle first.* —*n.* the act of haggling. —**hag′gler,** *n.*

hah (hä) another spelling of **ha.**

ha-ha (hä′hä′) *interj.* used to express amusement or scorn.

hahn·i·um (hä′nē əm) *n.* a proposed name for the artificially produced radioactive element with atomic number 105. Also, **element 105, nielsbohrium, unnilpentium.** Proposed symbol: **Ha**

Hai·da (hī′də) *n., pl.* **Hai·da** or **Hai·das.** a member of a North American Indian tribe living along the coast of British Columbia.

hai·ku (hī′kü) *n., pl.* **hai·ku.** a form of Japanese poetry containing seventeen syllables in three lines, usually on a subject from nature.

hail¹ (hāl) *v.t.* **1.** to greet by calling or shouting: *I hailed them across the street.* **2.** to attract the attention of through motions or calls: *to hail a taxi.* **3.** to acknowledge with acclaim; salute: *Many people hailed the astronauts.* —*n.* **1.** a greeting. **2.** a motion or call intended to attract attention. —*interj.* used as an expression of acclaim, welcome, or salutation: *Hail to the victor!* [From the Middle English greeting *heil!,* going back to the Old Norse word *heill* meaning "whole, sound, well," from its use in a greeting meaning "Good luck!" or "Be well!"] —**hail′er,** *n.*

·**to hail from.** to come from: *They hail from Detroit.*

hail² (hāl) *n.* **1.** small, usually round pieces of ice that fall in a shower, especially during thunderstorms. **2.** a heavy shower of anything: *They escaped in a hail of bullets.* —*v.i.* to pour down hail: *It hailed for an hour.* —*v.t.* to pour down or shower heavily: *They hailed presents on us.* [From the Old English word *hægl* meaning "hail²."]

Hail Mary, a Roman Catholic prayer to the Virgin Mary. Also, **Ave Maria.**

hail·stone (hāl′stōn′) *n.* a pellet of hail.

hail·storm (hāl′stôrm′) *n.* a storm in which hail falls.

hair (hâr) *n.* **1.** a fine, threadlike growth on the skin of humans and other mammals. **2.** a mass of such growths, as on the head of humans or the bodies of animals. **3.** a similar growth on the body of insects. **4.** a fine, threadlike growth on the outer layer of plants. **5.** an extremely

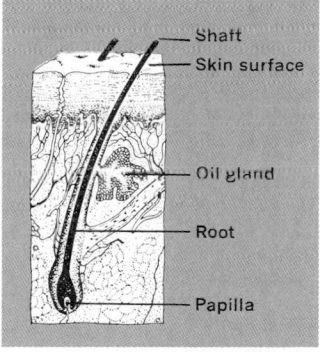

root of a **hair**

H

small amount or distance; least degree: *missing the bull's-eye by a hair.* —*adj.* **1.** of or containing hair: *a hair mattress.* **2.** for the hair: *a hair dryer.* —**hair′less,** *adj.* —**hair′like′,** *adj.*

·**to let one's hair down.** to relax completely: *I can really let my hair down with my friends.*

·**to split hairs.** to make very fine or petty distinctions.

hair·breadth (hâr′bredth′) *also,* **hairsbreadth, hair′s-breadth.** *adj.* very narrow or close: *a hairbreadth escape.* —*n.* another spelling of **hairsbreadth.**

hair·brush (hâr′brush′) *n., pl.* **hair·brush·es.** a brush used for grooming the hair.

hair·cloth (hâr′klôth′) *n.* a stiff, coarse cloth made of horsehair or camel's hair, used chiefly for upholstering furniture and for stiffening clothing.

hair·cut (hâr′kut′) *n.* the act or service of cutting hair, or the style in which it is cut.

hair·do (hâr′dü′) *n., pl.* **hair·dos.** the style in which the hair is arranged.

hair·dress·er (hâr′dres′ər) *n.* a person whose job is to style, cut, and arrange hair.

hair·line (hâr′līn′) *n.* **1.** the line where hair growth ends on the head, especially around the forehead. **2.** a very thin or fine line.

hair·piece (hâr′pēs′) *n.* a quantity of real or artificial hair made into a removable wig, toupee, or fall and worn to cover baldness or as part of a hair style.

hair·pin (hâr′pin′) *n.* a small, U-shaped pin, usually made of wire, shell, or plastic, used to keep hair or a hairpiece in place. —*adj.* shaped like a hairpin; U-shaped: *a hairpin curve in the road.*

hair·rais·ing (hâr′rā′zing) *adj. Informal.* causing great fear; terrifying.

hairs·breadth (hârz′bredth′) *also,* **hair′s-breadth, hair·breadth.** *n.* an extremely small space or margin: *to lose by a hairsbreadth.* —*adj.* another spelling of **hairbreadth.**

hair spray, a liquid cosmetic that is sprayed on the hair to hold it in place.

hair·spring (hâr′spring′) *n.* a fine, coiled spring in a watch or clock that regulates the movement of the balance wheel.

hair trigger, a trigger that can set off a firearm with very slight pressure.

hair·y (hâr′ē) *adj.,* **hair·i·er, hair·i·est.** **1.** covered with hair; having much hair. **2.** of or resembling hair. **3.** *Slang.* hair-raising: *Taming lions is a hairy job.* —**hair′i·ness,** *n.*

Hai·tian (hā′shən, hā′tē ən) *n.* **1.** a person who was born in or is a citizen of Haiti. **2.** see **Haitian Creole.** —*adj.* of or relating to Haiti, its people, their dialect, or their culture.

Haitian Creole, the language of the Haitians. It is a dialect of French. Also, **Creole, Haitian.**

hake (hāk) *n., pl.* **hake** or **hakes.** a valuable food fish related to the cod, found in cold and temperate seas.

hal·berd (hal′bərd) *also,* **hal·bert** (hal′bərt) *n.* a weapon in the form of a long spear with a hook-shaped blade at the top, used especially in fifteenth- and sixteenth-century Europe.

hal·cy·on (hal′sē ən) *adj.* peaceful and happy: *the halcyon days of youth.* —*n.* a mythical bird identified with the kingfisher, that supposedly could calm the winds and sea and build its nest in the water. [From the Latin word *halcyon* meaning "kingfisher," from the Greek word *alkyōn,* the name of a mythical bird.]

hale¹ (hāl) *adj.,* **hal·er, hal·est.** in good physical condition; healthy; robust. ▲ used chiefly in the phrase *hale and hearty.* [From the Old English word *hāl* meaning "whole, healthy."]

hale² (hāl) *v.t.,* **haled, hal·ing.** **1.** to force (someone) to go: *to hale a thief into court.* **2.** to drag or pull, especially by force. [From the Old French word *haler* meaning "to drag, pull," of Germanic origin.]

half (haf) *n., pl.* **halves. 1.** either of two equal parts into which anything is or may be divided: *A pint is half of a quart.* **2.** *Sports.* **a.** either of two time periods into which certain games are divided. **b.** an intermission between these two periods, such as in football or basketball. **c.** one of the two divisions of an inning in baseball. **d.** see **halfback.** —*adj.* **1.** being one of two equal parts; forming a half: *a half gallon of ice cream.* **2.** lacking in some part; incomplete; partial: *a half truth.* —*adv.* **1.** to the extent of a half: *half full.* **2.** not completely; partially: *half understood, half believed.*

·**in half.** into two equal parts.

half·back (haf′bak′) *n.* **1.** in football, an offensive player whose position is behind the line of scrimmage and who runs with the ball, catches or throws passes, or blocks. **2.** in some other sports, such as soccer, a player who is positioned behind the forward line and in front of the back line.

half·baked (haf′bākt′) *adj.* **1.** not completely cooked or baked. **2.** *Informal.* showing a lack of planning, intelligence, or common sense: *a half-baked plan.*

half·breed (haf′brēd′) *n.* a person whose parents are of different races, especially the child of one Caucasian and one American Indian parent. ▲ considered offensive.

half brother, a brother related through one parent only.

half·caste (haf′kast′) *n.* a person whose parents are of different races, especially the child of one European and one Asian parent. ▲ considered offensive.

half dollar, a coin of the United States and Canada, equal to fifty cents.

half gainer, a dive in which the diver jumps off the diving board while facing the water, does a backward half somersault, and lands in the water headfirst, facing the board.

half·heart·ed (haf′här′tid) *adj.* lacking interest or enthusiasm: *a halfhearted attempt.* —**half′heart′ed·ly,** *adv.* —**half′heart′ed·ness,** *n.*

half hitch, a knot made by passing the end of a rope around an object, then through the loop thus formed, and finally drawing the end tight.

half·hour (haf′our′) *n.* **1.** a half of an hour; thirty minutes. **2.** a point thirty minutes past a given hour: *The bus runs on the half-hour.* —*adj.* of, lasting for, or occurring at a half-hour: *a half-hour ride.*

half·life (haf′līf′) *n.* the time it takes for any given amount of a radioactive isotope to decay to half that amount. Different radioactive materials decay at different rates.

half·mast (haf′mast′) *n.* the position of a flag about halfway down from the top of a mast, staff, or pole, used especially as a sign of mourning or as a distress signal. Also, **half-staff.**

half·moon (haf′mün′) *n.* **1.** the moon when only half of its disk appears bright. **2.** anything in the shape of a half-moon.

half note *Music.* a note that is sounded for one half as long as a whole note.

half·pen·ny (hā′pə nē, hāp′nē) *n., pl.* **half·pence** (hā′pəns) or **half·pen·nies.** a former coin of Great Britain equal to half a penny.

half sister, a sister related through one parent only.

half·staff (haf′staf′) *n.* another word for **half-mast.**

half step *Music.* the difference in pitch between any two keys next to each other on a keyboard instrument. Also, **half tone, semitone.**

half·tone (haf′tōn′) *n.* in art or photography, any tone between a highlight and a deep shadow.

half tone, another term for **half step.**

half·track (haf′trak′) *also,* **half·track.** *n.* an armored military vehicle having wheels in front and tracks or treads like those on a tank in the rear.

half·truth (haf′trüth′) *n.* a statement that contains only part of the truth, especially one that is intended to deceive: *half-truths and false rumors about an opponent.*

half·way (haf′wā′) *adv.* **1.** at or to the midway point; half the distance: *to climb halfway up a mountain.* **2.** not completely; partially: *The movie is halfway over.* —*adj.* **1.** midway between two points: *The racers reached the halfway mark.* **2.** incomplete; partial: *Halfway measures will not solve the problem.*

half–wit (haf′wit′) *n.* **1.** a feeble-minded person. **2.** a foolish or stupid person. —**half′wit′ted,** *adj.*

hal·i·but (hal′ə bət) *n., pl.* **hal·i·but** or **hal·i·buts.** a large flatfish found in northern waters of the Atlantic and Pacific oceans and highly valued as a source of food and vitamin oil. Some species weigh up to several hundred pounds.

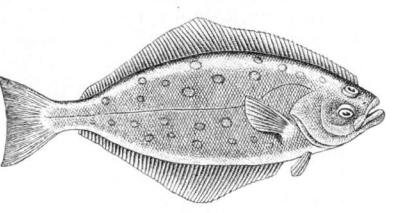

halibut

hal·ite (hal′īt, hā′līt) *n.* another word for **rock salt.**

hal·i·to·sis (hal′i tō′sis) *n.* a condition in which the breath has a bad odor; bad breath.

hall (hôl) *n.* **1.** a passageway onto which rooms open in a house or building; corridor. **2.** a passageway or room at the entrance to a building; vestibule or lobby. **3.** a room or building in which public meetings, entertainment, or lectures are held: *a concert hall.* **4.** a room or building in a school, college, or university set aside for a particular purpose: *a dining hall.*

hal·le·lu·jah (hal′ə lü′yə) *also,* **hal·le·lu·iah.** *interj.* praise ye the Lord. Also, **alleluia.** ▲ used to express praise or joy, as in prayers and hymns.

Hal·ley's comet (hal′ēz) a comet that can be seen from the earth every seventy-six years. It was last seen in 1986. [From the English astronomer Edmund *Halley* (1656–1742), who calculated its orbit and predicted its return.]

hall·mark (hôl′märk′) *n.* **1.** an official symbol stamped on gold and silver items to guarantee their high quality or purity. **2.** any mark that indicates high quality, purity, or genuineness. **3.** a distinguishing quality or characteristic: *Suspense is a hallmark of a good mystery.* —*v.t.* to stamp with a hallmark. [From Goldsmiths' *Hall* in London, where gold and silver articles were assayed and stamped.]

hall of fame, a room or building containing tablets, busts, or other items honoring famous or outstanding people: *a sports hall of fame.*

hal·loo (hə lü′) *interj.* used to attract attention or to urge on hounds in fox hunting. —*n., pl.* **hal·loos.** a call or cry of *halloo.* —*v.i.,* **hal·looed, hal·loo·ing. 1.** to call or shout, especially to attract attention. **2.** to urge on hounds with cries of *halloo.*

hal·low (hal′ō) *v.t.* to make sacred or holy; sanctify: *The church officials hallowed the ground for burial.*

hal·lowed (hal′ōd) *adj.* **1.** made holy; sanctified. **2.** regarded as sacred or holy. —**hal′lowed·ness,** *n.*

Hal·low·een (hal′ə wēn′, hol′ə wēn′) *also,* **Hal·low·e'en.** *n.* the eve of All Saints' Day, now celebrated especially by children in costumes and masks. It falls on October 31. [Short for *all hallow even,* the eve of All Saints' Day in the Christian Church, from the words *all* + obsolete English *hallow* meaning "saint" + *even²*.]

Hal·low·mas (hal′ō məs) *n.* another word for **All Saints' Day.**

hal·lu·ci·nate (hə lü′sə nāt′) *v.i.,* **hal·lu·ci·nat·ed, hal·lu·ci·nat·ing.** to have hallucinations.

hal·lu·ci·na·tion (hə lü′sə nā′shən) *n.* **1.** the experience of seeing or hearing something that is not really there. **2.** something seen or heard in such an experience: *The voices I heard were only hallucinations.*

hal·lu·ci·na·to·ry (hə lü′sə nə tôr′ē) *adj.* of, relating to, or causing hallucinations; hallucinogenic.

hal·lu·cin·o·gen (hə lü′sə nə jen′) *n.* any of several drugs that cause hallucinations, such as LSD.

hal·lu·cin·o·gen·ic (hə lü′sə nə jen′ik) *adj.* of, relating to, or causing hallucinations: *a hallucinogenic drug.*

hall·way (hôl′wā′) *n.* **1.** a passageway in a house or building; corridor. **2.** an entrance hall; foyer.

ha·lo (hā′lō) *n., pl.* **ha·los** or **ha·loes. 1.** in art, a ring or disk of light surrounding the head of a saint, angel, or other sacred figure. **2.** a circle of light that appears to surround the sun, the moon, or another heavenly body, caused by the reflection and refraction of light by ice crystals in the earth's upper atmosphere.

hal·o·gen (hal′ə jən) *n.* any of the five very active elements that combine readily with metals to form salts. They are fluorine, chlorine, iodine, bromine, and astatine.

halt¹ (hôlt) *n.* a temporary stop in movement or activity: *Production at the factory came to a halt.* —*v.t.* to cause to stop: *The crew halted the train.* —*v.i.* to come to a stop: *The parade halted in front of the reviewing stand.* [From the German command *halt!,* from the word *halten* meaning "to stop, hold still."]

halt² (hôlt) *v.i.* **1.** to hesitate or be in doubt; waver; falter: *The child's voice halted in apprehension.* **2.** *Archaic.* to be lame; limp. —*adj. Archaic.* unable to walk without limping; lame. [From the Old English word *healt* meaning "lame, limping."] —**halt′ing,** *adj.* —**halt′ing·ly,** *adv.*

hal·ter (hôl′tər) *n.* **1.** a rope or strap used for leading or tying an animal, usually designed to fit around the animal's nose and over or behind its ears. **2.** a garment resembling a blouse, worn by women and girls, that usually fastens behind the neck, leaving the arms and most of the back bare. —*v.t.* to put a halter on or tie with a halter: *to halter a horse.*

hal·vah (hül vä′) *also,* **hal·va.** *n.* a dense, flaky confection consisting mainly of ground sesame seeds and honey. [From the Yiddish word *halva,* going back to the Arabic word *halwā* meaning "sweetmeat."]

halve (hav) *v.t.,* **halved, halv·ing. 1.** to divide into two equal parts: *to halve an apple.* **2.** to share equally: *We halved our food during the hike.* **3.** to lessen by half: *For only two people, halve the recipe.*

halves (havz) the plural of **half.**

hal·yard (hal′yərd) *n. Nautical.* a rope or tackle used for hoisting or lowering something, such as a sail, yard, or flag.

ham (ham) *n.* **1.** the meat from the hind leg or shoulder of a hog, usually cured and smoked. **2.** the hind leg of an animal, especially a hog. **3. hams.** the back part of the thighs and buttock. **4.** *Informal.* an actor who performs in a showy or exaggerated way. **5.** *Informal.* an amateur radio operator. —*v.i.,* **hammed, ham·ming.** *Informal.* (of an actor) to act in a showy or exaggerated way.

ham·burg·er (ham′bûr′gər) *n.* **1.** ground beef: *half a pound of hamburger.* **2.** a round patty of such meat, broiled or fried and often served on a bun or roll. Also, **ham·burg** (ham′bûrg′). [Short for *Hamburger steak,* from *Hamburg,* a city in Germany.]

ham·let (ham′lit) *n.* a cluster of houses in the country; small village.

Ham·let (ham′lit) *n.* the central character in William

H

Shakespeare's play *Hamlet*, a prince of Denmark who seeks to avenge his father's murder.

ham·mer (ham′ər) *n.* **1.** a tool with a solid head of metal or other material set crosswise on a handle, usually used for driving nails and beating or shaping metal. **2.** anything resembling such a tool in shape or function, such as the lever that strikes a bell in a clock or a small gavel used by an auctioneer. **3.** the part of a gun that strikes the firing pin, causing the gun to go off. **4.** another word for **malleus**. **5.** a metal ball attached to a wire, thrown for distance in athletic contests. —*v.t.* **1.** to strike again and again with or as if with a hammer; drive; pound: *to hammer nails into a board, to hammer a wall with one's fist.* **2.** to pound into shape or form with a hammer: *to hammer a bowl out of metal.* **3.** to force by repetition: *It's no use trying to hammer sense into a fool.* —*v.i.* to strike blows again and again with or as if with a hammer: *to hammer at a door with one's fists.* —**ham′mer·er,** *n.*

ham·mer·head (ham′ərhed′) *n.* a shark whose head extends on each side in a broad, flat lobe, resembling a double-headed hammer.

hammerhead

ham·mer·lock (ham′ər lok′) *n.* a wrestling hold in which an opponent's arm is twisted and held up tightly in a right-angle position behind the back.

ham·mock (ham′ək) *n.* a swinging bed made from a long piece of canvas, leather, or netting hung between two supports, such as trees or poles.

hammock

ham·per¹ (ham′pər) *v.t.* to interfere with the action or progress of: *Stalled cars hampered efforts to remove the snow.* [From the Middle English word *hamperen* meaning both ''to surround, enclose'' and ''to harass.'']

ham·per² (ham′pər) *n.* a large basket or other container, usually with a cover: *a picnic hamper, a hamper for laundry.* [From the Old French word *hanepier* meaning ''basket, receptacle for storing goblets,'' from the word *hanap* ''goblet, cup,'' of Germanic origin.]

ham·ster (ham′stər) *n.* a rodent that resembles a mouse, having a stout body, stumpy tail, and large cheek pouches.

ham·string (ham′string′) *n.* **1.** in humans and other primates, the tendon at the back of the knee. **2.** in animals with four legs, the great tendon at the back of the hock. —*v.t.,* **ham·strung** (ham′strung′), **ham·string·ing. 1.** to cripple (a person or animal) by cutting the hamstring. **2.** to destroy the efficiency or power of; make ineffective: *The project was hamstrung by a lack of funds.*

hand (hand) *n.* **1.** the end part of the arm from the wrist down, consisting of the palms, fingers, and thumb. **2.** anything resembling a hand in shape or function, such as the pointers on a clock. **3.** *also,* **hands.** personal possession or control: *to take the law into one's own hands.* **4.** a direction in relation to one of the hands; side: *at my left hand.* **5.** a worker who does manual labor; laborer: *a harvest hand.* **6.** a member of a group or crew: *All hands were ordered on deck.* **7.** a way of doing something: *a deft hand at juggling.* **8.** an active part or influence in something; share; role: *Each club member had a hand in the decision.* **9.** help; assistance: *Give me a hand moving the piano.* **10.** a round of applause; clapping: *The audience gave the singer a big hand.* **11.a.** a single round of a card game: *Let's play another hand.* **b.** the cards held by a player during a round. **c.** the players in a card game: *We need one more hand to play.* **12.** handwriting style; penmanship. **13.** a promise or pledge of marriage. **14.** a unit of measure equal to 4 inches (10.2 centimeters), used in expressing the height of a horse: *That horse stands sixteen hands at the shoulder.* —*v.t.* **1.** to give or pass with the hand: *Hand this to the cashier.* **2.** to lead or help with the hand. —*adj.* **1.** of, relating to, or for the hand or hands: *hand lotion.* **2.** done or operated by hand: *a hand tool.* **3.** suited to be held in the hand: *a hand mirror.*

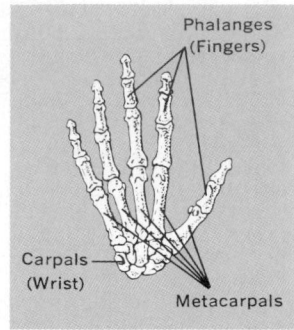

bones of the **hand**

•**at hand. a.** nearby or ready for use. **b.** near in time; close.
•**at the hand of** or **at the hands of.** by the action of: *The captives suffered at the hands of the enemy.*
•**by hand.** with the hands, rather than with machinery: *to wash clothes by hand.*
•**from hand to hand.** from one person to another.
•**from hand to mouth.** without considering or providing for the future.
•**hand and foot. a.** with both hands and feet tied or confined. **b.** totally: *to wait on someone hand and foot.*
•**hand in hand. a.** holding each other's hand: *to walk hand in hand.* **b.** in close association; together: *Good study habits and good grades usually go hand in hand.*
•**hand over fist.** rapidly and in great quantity: *to make money hand over fist.*
•**hands down.** with great ease; without effort: *to win hands down.*
•**in hand. a.** in one's possession. **b.** under one's control: *The police had the mob well in hand.*
•**off one's hands.** out of one's control or responsibility.
•**on hand. a.** readily available for use: *to have cash on hand.* **b.** present: *A large crowd was on hand.*
•**on one hand** or **on the one hand.** from one side or viewpoint.
•**on one's hands.** in one's possession or control.
•**on the other hand.** from another side or viewpoint.
•**out of hand.** out of control: *Things got out of hand at the bar when a fight broke out.*
•**the upper hand.** superior position; advantage.
•**to change hands.** to pass from one person or group to another.
•**to force one's hand.** to make one act before one has intended to act.
•**to hand down. a.** to pass along, as from one generation to another. **b.** to make and announce (a decision): *The Supreme Court handed down a decision.*

·to hand in. to give, as to someone in authority; deliver: *to hand in one's resignation.*

·to hand on. to pass along; hand down.

·to hand out. to give out to people; distribute.

·to hand over. to yield or give up to another.

·to have one's hands full. to be busy with as much as or more than one can do: *I have my hands full with five children.*

·to lay one's hand on. a. to get possession of; seize. **b.** to injure or harm; attack.

·to tie one's hands. to hinder one's efforts; prevent one from acting.

·to try one's hand at. to make an attempt at (doing something): *Try your hand at learning some new songs.*

·to turn one's hand to. to begin to work at: *They turned their hand to running a family store.*

·to wash one's hands of. to refuse to associate with or be responsible for any longer.

hand·bag (hand′bag′) *n.* **1.** a bag or case for carrying small articles, such as cosmetics and a wallet; pocketbook. **2.** a small suitcase.

hand·ball (hand′bôl′) *n.* **1.** a game in which the players hit a small, hard ball against a wall with the hand. **2.** the ball used in this game.

hand·bar·row (hand′bar′ō) *n.* a flat, rectangular frame having handles at each end, used for lifting and carrying loads.

hand·bill (hand′bil′) *n.* a printed announcement or advertisement, intended to be given out to people by hand.

hand·book (hand′bŭk′) *n.* a book containing basic information or instructions on a particular subject.

hand·cart (hand′kärt′) *n.* a small cart moved by hand.

hand·cuff (hand′kuf′) *n.* either of a pair of metal rings joined by a short chain and locked around the wrist of a person to be restrained, such as a prisoner. —*v.t.* to put handcuffs on: *The police officer handcuffed the thief.*

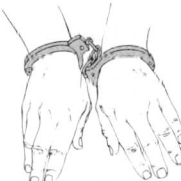

handcuffs

hand·ed (han′did) *adj.* **1.** characterized by, done with, or designed for (a specified) hand. ▲ used in combination: *a left-handed jump shot.* **2.** characterized by or done with (a specified number of) hands or people. ▲ used in combination: *a game of two-handed bridge.*

hand·ful (hand′fŭl′) *n., pl.* **hand·fuls. 1.** the amount the hand can hold at one time: *a handful of peanuts.* **2.** a small number or quantity: *a handful of people.* **3.** as much as one can manage: *My little cousin is a handful to take care of.*

hand grenade, a small explosive device designed to be thrown by hand, set off by a fuze.

hand·gun (hand′gun′) *n.* a firearm that can be held and fired with one hand; pistol.

hand·i·cap (han′dē kap′) *n.* **1.** a race, contest, or game in which some contestants are given certain advantages or disadvantages so that all have an equal chance of winning. **2.** an advantage or disadvantage given in such a race, contest, or game. **3.** anything that places a person at a disadvantage and hampers achievement: *Being short can be a handicap in playing basketball.* —*v.t.,* **hand·i·capped, hand·i·cap·ping. 1.** to place at a disadvantage; hamper: *Poor eyesight handicapped me in my work.* **2.** (in a contest) to give one or more handicaps to: *to handicap an opponent.* —**hand′i·cap′per,** *n.*

hand·i·capped (han′dē kapt′) *adj.* having a handicap; disabled: *a handicapped person.* —*n.* handicapped persons considered as a group: *the handicapped.*

hand·i·craft (han′dē kraft′) *n.* **1.** a trade, occupation, or art in which great skill with the hands is required, such as weaving or pottery. **2.** skill in working with the hands. **3.** an object made or work done by a skilled hand.

hand·i·work (han′dē wûrk′) *n.* **1.** work done by hand: *embroidered handiwork.* **2.** the product of one's work or action: *Hurt feelings are the handiwork of thoughtless remarks.*

hand·ker·chief (hang′kər chif, hang′kər chēf′) *n.* **1.** a soft piece of cloth, usually square, used especially to wipe the nose or brow or worn as an ornament. **2.** a larger piece of cloth worn around the head or neck; kerchief.

han·dle (han′dəl) *n.* the part of an object that is made to be grasped by the hand: *to carry a suitcase by the handle.* —*v.,* **han·dled, han·dling.** —*v.t.* **1.** to touch or hold with the hand or hands: *Please do not handle the glassware.* **2.** to work at with the hands: *to handle clay.* **3.** to manage, control, or train: *to handle dogs.* **4.** to act on or toward; deal or cope with: *to handle a problem.* **5.** to deal in; trade in: *Does this store handle radios?* —*v.i.* to act in a certain way or respond to being handled: *This car handles nicely.* —**han′dler,** *n.*

·to fly off the handle. to become very angry suddenly.

han·dle·bar (han′dəl bär′) *also,* **han·dle·bars.** *n.* a usually curved steering bar connected with the front wheel of a bicycle, motorcycle, or similar vehicle, having right and left ends, often with a grip for the rider to hold.

han·dle·bar mustache (han′dəl bär′) a thick mustache extending in a prominent curve to either side.

hand·made (hand′mād′) *adj.* made by hand rather than by machine: *a handmade sweater.*

hand·maid (hand′mād′) *n.* a female servant or personal attendant. Also, **hand·maid·en** (hand′mā′dən).

hand–me–down (hand′mē doun′) *n.* something, especially a piece of clothing, that has been owned or used by one person and then given to another person for additional use. —*adj.* secondhand; used.

hand organ, a portable musical instrument combining features of an organ and a music box, played by means of a hand crank. Also, **barrel organ.**

hand·out (hand′out′) *n.* **1.** food, clothing, or money given out to a beggar. **2.** a prepared news story or statement released to the press for free publicity. **3.** anything handed out without charge, such as a pamphlet or leaflet.

hand·rail (hand′rāl′) *n.* a railing that may be grasped by the hand, used especially as a guard on stairs or at the edge of a balcony.

hand·saw (hand′sô′) *n.* a saw used with one hand.

hand·shake (hand′shāk′) *n.* the act of clasping and shaking a person's hand as a sign of greeting, friendliness, or agreement: *They concluded the deal with a handshake.*

hand·some (han′səm) *adj.,* **hand·som·er, hand·som·est. 1.** having a pleasing, often masculine or dignified appearance; good-looking: *a handsome actor, a handsome desk.* **2.** considerable in size or quantity; fairly large: *The lawyer was paid a handsome fee.* **3.** characterized by generosity; gracious. —**hand′some·ly,** *adv.* —**hand′some·ness,** *n.*

hands–on (handz′ôn′, handz′on′) *adj.* involving direct, personal experience or participation, as in the operation of equipment: *For our computer course we read the textbook at home and get hands-on training in class.*

hand·spike (hand′spīk′) *n.* a bar used as a lever.

hand·spring (hand′spring′) *n.* a kind of somersault in which a person springs onto both hands and then returns to a standing position.

H

hand·stand (hand′stand′) *n.* the act of balancing the body on the hands with the legs extended upward.

hand–to–hand (hand′tə hand′) *adj.* in direct contact; at close quarters: *hand-to-hand combat.*

hand–to–mouth (hand′tə mouth′) *adj.* without considering or providing for the future, especially because of a lack of money: *a hand-to-mouth existence.*

hand·work (hand′wûrk′) *n.* work done by hand; handiwork.

hand·writ·ing (hand′rī′ting) *n.* **1.** writing done by hand; writing that is not typewritten or printed. **2.** the style or manner of writing; penmanship: *Your handwriting is hard to read.*

hand·writ·ten (hand′rit′ən) *adj.* written by hand: *handwritten invitations.*

hand·y (han′dē) *adj.,* **hand·i·er, hand·i·est. 1.** within reach; at hand; nearby: *Keep your pen and paper handy.* **2.** able to use the hands skillfully: *handy with tools.* **3.** convenient or easy to use or handle: *a handy carrying case.* —**hand′i·ly,** *adv.* —**hand′i·ness,** *n.*
·**to come in handy.** to be helpful: *An ability to speak French will come in handy in Europe.*

hand·y·man (han′dē man′) *n., pl.* **hand·y·men** (han′dē men′). a person who is skilled in doing or working at various small jobs.

hang (hang) *v.,* **hung** or *(v.t. def. 3)* **hanged, hanging.** —*v.t.* **1.** to fasten or attach (an object) from above only, without any support from below: *to hang towels to dry.* **2.** to attach (an object) with a hinge, so as to swing or move freely: *to hang a garden gate.* **3.** to kill by suspending by the neck, as from a gallows. **4.** to bend forward or downward; droop: *to hang one's head in shame.* **5.** to furnish, cover, or decorate with anything that is suspended or attached: *to hang a room with tapestries.* **6.** to attach or suspend for decoration or display: *to hang wallpaper, to hang pictures.* —*v.i.* **1.** to be attached to or suspended from something above; dangle: *A wire hung from the ceiling.* **2.** to be fastened so as to swing or move freely. **3.** to die by hanging. **4.** to cling, especially for support; hold fast: *They hung onto the capsized boat.* **5.** to depend: *The defendant's fate hung on the jury's decision.* **6.** to bend forward or downward; droop: *The tree hangs over the pond.* **7.** to float or be suspended: *Polluted air hung over the city.* —*n.* **1.** the way in which something hangs or falls: *the hang of a dress.* **2.** a particular way of doing something; knack: *to get the hang of riding a bicycle.* **3.** a general meaning: *to get the hang of a conversation.*
·**to hang back.** to be reluctant to move forward; hesitate: *Don't hang back in the doorway.*
·**to hang out. a.** to lean out of: *The dog hung out the car window.* **b.** *Slang.* to spend time: *They usually hang out in the park.*
·**to hang together. a.** to keep together; be united: *Those who were opposed to the proposal hung together.* **b.** to be related in a logical or understandable way.
·**to hang up. a.** to suspend from a hanger or peg: *Hang up the coats in the hall.* **b.** to end a telephone conversation by replacing the receiver in its cradle. **c.** to hinder the progress of; delay.

han·gar (hang′ər, hang′gər) *n.* a building for sheltering and servicing aircraft.

hang·dog (hang′dôg′) *adj.* having an ashamed, defeated, or cringing manner or appearance: *a hangdog look.*

hang·er (hang′ər) *n.* **1.** a frame or device on which something is hung, especially one that fits under the shoulders of a coat or other garment. **2.** a loop or ring for hanging something, as at the back of the neck of a coat. **3.** a person who hangs something: *a wallpaper hanger.*

hang·er–on (hang′ər ôn′, hang′ər on′) *n., pl.* **hang·ers–on.** someone who clings to a person or group, especially for personal gain, favors, or prestige.

hang glider 1. a large sail shaped like a kite, beneath which a person hangs face down in a harness, used for hang gliding. **2.** a person who engages in hang gliding.

hang gliding

hang gliding, the sport of gliding and soaring in the air with a hang glider, launched from a hill or cliff.

hang·ing (hang′ing) *n.* **1.** an execution in which a person is hanged, as from a gallows. **2.** *also,* **hangings.** a drape or other fabric that hangs as a decoration, as from a wall or window. —*adj.* **1.** attached to something above: *a hanging lamp.* **2.** leaning over; overhanging: *a hanging balcony.* **3.** placed on a steep slope: *hanging gardens.*

hang·man (hang′mən) *n., pl.* **hang·men** (hang′mən). a person who hangs criminals condemned to death.

hang·nail (hang′nāl′) *n.* a piece of skin partially torn away and hanging loose at the side or base of a fingernail.

hang·out (hang′out′) *n. Informal.* a place where a person or group spends much time.

hang·o·ver (hang′ō′vər) *n.* **1.** a feeling of being sick that can follow drinking alcohol, marked by nausea or a headache. **2.** something remaining from a past time or condition.

hang–up (hang′up′) *n. Informal.* **1.** an emotional problem or confusion that seemingly cannot be cleared up or removed. **2.** anything that hampers or delays progress.

hank (hangk) *n.* **1.** a loop or coil, as of hair. **2.** a length of yarn, thread, or similar material, especially one of yarn containing a specific number of yards. A hank of cotton or silk yarn contains 840 yards (768 meters); a hank of worsted yarn contains 560 yards (512 meters).

han·ker (hang′kər) *v.i.* to desire strongly; yearn or crave.

han·ker·ing (hang′kər ing) *n.* a strong desire; yearning.

Han·o·ve·ri·an (han′ō vir′ē ən) *n.* **1.** a person who was born in or is a citizen of Hanover. **2.** a member or supporter of the English royal family of Hanover. —*adj.* **1.** of, like, or relating to Hanover. **2.** of or relating to the English royal family of Hanover: *George I was a Hanoverian king.*

Han·sen's disease (han′sənz) another term for **leprosy.** [From the Norwegian physician Gerhard A. H. Hansen (1841–1912), who discovered the bacterium that causes leprosy.]

han·som (han′səm) *n.* a low, two-wheeled, covered carriage for two

hansom

passengers, drawn by one horse and having the driver's seat raised behind the cab. [From the English architect Joseph A. *Hansom* (1803–1882), who designed it.]

Ha·nuk·kah (hä′nə kə) *also*, **Cha·nu·kah.** *n.* a Jewish holiday commemorating the rededication of the Temple of Jerusalem after the victory of Judas Maccabeus over the king of ancient Syria in 165 B.C. It is celebrated by lighting candles on eight successive nights. [From the Hebrew word *hanukkāh* meaning ''dedication.'']

hap (hap) *Archaic. n.* chance; luck. —*v.i.,* **happed, hap·ping.** to occur by chance; happen.

hap·haz·ard (hap haz′ərd) *adj.* characterized by a lack of order, direction, or planning: *clothes scattered in a haphazard manner.* —**hap·haz′ard·ly,** *adv.* —**hap·haz′ard·ness,** *n.*

hap·less (hap′lis) *adj.* unlucky; unfortunate. —**hap′·less·ly,** *adv.* —**hap′less·ness,** *n.*

hap·ly (hap′lē) *adv. Archaic.* by chance; perhaps.

hap·pen (hap′ən) *v.i.* **1.** to take place; occur: *The accident happened last week.* **2.** to take place without plan or reason; occur by chance: *Your birthday happens to be the same day as mine.* **3.** to come or go by chance: *I happened along just after the accident.*
  ·**to happen on** or **to happen upon.** to meet or find accidentally: *The scientist happened on the discovery.*
  ·**to happen to. a.** to be done to; befall: *Something happened to the phone, and it doesn't work.* **b.** to become of: *What ever happened to your cousins?*

hap·pen·ing (hap′ə ning) *n.* something that happens; event; occurrence.

hap·pi·ly (hap′ə lē) *adv.* **1.** with pleasure, joy, or contentment: *They lived happily on their farm.* **2.** luckily; fortunately: *Happily, no one was hurt.*

hap·pi·ness (hap′ē nis) *n.* **1.** the quality or state of being joyous, glad, or contented. **2.** good fortune; luck.

hap·py (hap′ē) *adj.,* **hap·pi·er, hap·pi·est. 1.** having, showing, or bringing pleasure, joy, or contentment: *a happy child, a happy home.* **2.** lucky; fortunate: *a happy discovery.* **3.** well-suited; apt: *a happy choice of words.*

hap·py-go-luck·y (hap′ē gō luk′ē) *adj.* free from care or worry; carefree; lighthearted.

har·a-kir·i (har′ə kîr′ē) *n.* suicide by cutting open the abdomen with a knife. It is a form of ritual suicide in Japan. Also, **hari-kiri, seppuku.** [From the Japanese phrase *hara kiri* meaning ''suicide by disembowelment,'' from the words *hara* ''belly'' + *kiri* ''to cut.'']

ha·rangue (hə rang′) *n.* a long, noisy, often pompous speech, delivered with anger or strong feeling. —*v.,* **ha·rangued, ha·rangu·ing.** —*v.t.* to address with a harangue: *The counselor harangued us about our practical jokes.* —*v.i.* to deliver a harangue. —**ha·rangu′er,** *n.*

har·ass (har′əs, hə ras′) *v.t.* **1.** to bother or annoy repeatedly; torment: *The visiting team complained that they had been harassed by the crowd.* **2.** to trouble (an enemy) by repeated raids or attacks. —**har′ass·ment,** *n.*

har·bin·ger (här′bin jər) *n.* a person or thing that goes before to announce or indicate what is coming: *A robin is a harbinger of spring.* —*v.t.* to act as a harbinger of.

har·bor (här′bər) *n.* **1.** a protected place on the coastline of a sea, lake, or river, used as a shelter for ships and boats. **2.** any place of shelter. —*v.t.* **1.** to give shelter or protection to; conceal: *to harbor a criminal.* **2.** to keep or foster in the mind: *to harbor a grudge.* —*v.i.* to take shelter in a harbor.

har·bor·age (här′bər ij) *n.* **1.** a shelter for ships and boats. **2.** any shelter.

hard (härd) *adj.* **1.** not easily pierced, dented, or crushed; solid and firm to the touch: *the hard surface of a concrete floor.* **2.** requiring or involving much physical or mental effort to do, make, or deal with: *a hard task, a hard decision, a hard person to get along with.* **3.** not easy

to understand, master, or explain: *a hard problem.* **4.** causing sorrow, pain, or discomfort; severe; harsh: *a hard life.* **5.** without sympathy or sensitivity; stern; strict: *a hard heart.* **6.** showing or carried on with great energy or vigor: *a hard day's work.* **7.** having great force or strength: *a hard blow.* **8.** containing much alcohol: *hard liquor.* **9.** (of water) containing minerals that interfere with the foaming and cleansing action of soap. **10.** (of currency) easily converted into gold or other currencies. **11.** *Phonetics.* (of *c* or *g*) pronounced with the sound of *k* in *cat* or *g* in *good.* —*adv.* **1.** with effort or energy; strenuously; persistently: *to work hard.* **2.** with force or strength: *It rained hard.* **3.** with difficulty: *breathing hard after the race.* **4.** with a deep emotional reaction: *to take tragic news hard.* —**hard′ness,** *n.*
  ·**hard and fast.** that cannot be changed or put aside; fixed; strict: *a hard and fast rule.*
  ·**hard of hearing.** partially deaf.
  ·**hard up.** *Informal.* in need of (something): *hard up for a job.*
  ·**to be hard put.** to have much difficulty or trouble: *I was hard put to find an excuse for my lateness.*

hard·ball (härd′bôl′) *n.* **1.** the game of baseball, as opposed to softball. **2.** *Informal.* to use tough, aggressive, even ruthless methods: *to play hardball in business to eliminate competition.* —*adj.* tough, aggressive, even ruthless: *hardball tactics in politics.*

hard-bit·ten (härd′bit′ən) *adj.* not easily moved by the emotions; tough: *a hard-bitten newspaper reporter.*

hard-boiled (härd′boild′) *adj.* **1.** (of eggs) boiled until the yolk and white are solid. **2.** *Informal.* not sympathetic or sensitive; tough: *a hard-boiled detective.*

hard coal, another term for **anthracite.**

hard copy, printed information from a computer file, as opposed to information displayed on a monitor or stored on disk.

hard-core (härd′kôr′) *adj.* **1.** relating or belonging to the most central part of something: *the hard-core workers in a political campaign.* **2.** not likely to yield to change or to persuasion to change: *hard-core poverty.*

hard disk, a permanently installed computer disk that stores more data than a removable diskette can.

hard·en (här′dən) *v.i.* **1.** to become solid and firm to the touch: *The clay hardened in the sun.* **2.** to become strong, tough, or rigid: *The recruits hardened during basic training.* **3.** to become less sympathetic or sensitive. —*v.t.* **1.** to make solid and firm to the touch. **2.** to make less sympathetic or sensitive: *hardened by years of loneliness.* **3.** to make strong, tough, or rigid.

hard hat *also*, **hard-hat** (härd′hat′). **1.** a protective hat made of a hard material, worn especially by construction workers. **2.** *Informal.* a construction worker.

hard·head·ed (härd′hed′id) *adj.* **1.** not easily tricked or moved by the emotions; practical; shrewd: *a hardheaded trader.* **2.** stubborn; willful: *to be hardheaded and not admit a mistake.* —**hard′head′ed·ly,** *adv.* —**hard′head′ed·ness,** *n.*

hard·heart·ed (härd′här′tid) *adj.* without sympathy or sensitivity; lacking pity; cruel; unfeeling. —**hard′heart′ed·ly,** *adv.* —**hard′heart′ed·ness,** *n.*

har·di·hood (här′dē hud′) *n.* boldness, daring, and firmness of character: *The hardihood of the settlers was put to the test during their first winter.*

H

at; āpe; fär; câre; end; mē; it; īce; pîerce; hot; ōld; sông, fôrk; oil; out; up; ūse; rüle; pùll; tûrn; chin; sing; shop; thin; <u>th</u>is; hw in white; zh in treasure. The symbol ə stands for the unstressed vowel sound heard in about, taken, pencil, lemon, and circus.

441

har·di·ness (här′dē nis) *n.* **1.** the state of being hardy; physical endurance; strength. **2.** boldness; daring.

hard landing, the landing of a spacecraft on the earth, the moon, or another body in outer space at so high a speed that the vehicle or its equipment is damaged.

hard line, a firmly held opinion or point of view: *to take a hard line regarding the need to reduce taxes.* —**hard′-line,** *adj.* —**hard′-lin′er,** *n.*

hard·ly (härd′lē) *adv.* **1.** only just; barely: *We could hardly see in the dim light.* **2.** not quite; not likely. **3.** in a hard or severe way: *They treated the prisoners hardly.*

hard palate, the bony part of the palate at the front of the roof of the mouth, separating the mouth from the nasal cavity.

hard·pan (härd′pan′) *n.* **1.** a layer of hard earth underneath soft soil, through which roots cannot penetrate. **2.** hard, unbroken ground. **3.** a firm foundation.

hard sauce, an uncooked, creamy mixture of butter, sugar, and flavoring, used as a topping for dishes.

hard·ship (härd′ship′) *n.* a cause or condition of difficulty, pain, or suffering, such as poverty or illness: *The lack of rain caused the farmers great hardship.*

hard·tack (härd′tak′) *n.* a hard, dry biscuit, traditionally eaten by sailors. Also, **sea biscuit, ship biscuit.**

hard·top (härd′top′) *n.* an automobile having the general design of a convertible, but with a rigid top that does not fold back.

hard·ware (härd′wâr′) *n.* **1.** metal articles or parts, such as tools, nails and screws, or cutlery. **2.** weapons, especially heavy equipment. **3.** the physical equipment of a computer as distinguished from its programs, data, or the like.

hard·wood (härd′wud′) *n.* **1.** any of a large group of trees usually having broad leaves that are shed every year, such as the oak, beech, or maple. **2.** the wood of such a tree, usually denser, heavier, and harder than softwood, used to make such items as furniture, flooring, and athletic equipment. **3.** any hard, compact, heavy wood.

har·dy (här′dē) *adj.,* **har·di·er, har·di·est. 1.** able to endure hardship or harsh physical conditions; strong; robust. **2.** (of plants) able to endure the cold of winter without protection.

hare (hâr) *n., pl.* **hares** or **hare.** an animal similar to but usually larger than a rabbit, having very long ears, powerful hind legs and feet, and a short tail.

hare·bell (hâr′bel′) *n.* a plant having a slender stem with bright blue flowers shaped like bells.

hare·brained (hâr′brānd′) *adj.* showing a lack of common sense and careful thought; foolish; reckless: *a harebrained scheme.*

hare·lip (hâr′lip′) *n.* a birth defect in which the upper lip is split, often impairing speech. —**hare′-lipped′,** *adj.*

hare

har·em (hâr′əm, har′əm) *n.* **1.** the part of a Muslim house where the women live. **2.** the women of a Muslim household. [From the Arabic word *harīm* meaning "sacred place" or "forbidden place." Men are forbidden to enter harems.]

har·i–kar·i (har′ē kar′ē) *n.* another word for **hara-kiri.**

hark (härk) *v.i.* to listen. ▲ used chiefly as a command.
·**to hark back.** to go back, as to a previous time in one's memory: *The custom harks back to the last century.*

hark·en (här′kən) another spelling of **hearken.**

har·le·quin (här′lə kwin, här′lə kin) *n.* **1. Harlequin.** a stock character in pantomime and comedy, traditionally appearing in a costume of many bright colors, and wearing a mask. **2.** a clown; buffoon. —*adj.* having a brightly colored pattern; parti-colored.

har·lot (här′lət) *n.* a prostitute or woman of loose or immoral behavior.

har·lot·ry (här′lə trē) *n.* the state or quality of being a harlot; behavior of a harlot.

harm (härm) *n.* **1.** the cause of damage, pain, or loss; injury; hurt: *No harm will come to you.* **2.** a moral injury or offense; evil; wrong: *They saw no harm in lying to their friends.* —*v.t.* to do damage to; hurt: *The leader said that they wouldn't harm the hostages.*

harm·ful (härm′fəl) *adj.* causing or capable of causing harm; injurious or damaging: *Stress is harmful to your health.* —**harm′ful·ly,** *adv.* —**harm′ful·ness,** *n.*

harm·less (härm′lis) *adj.* not capable of causing harm; not injurious or damaging: *a harmless snake, a harmless prank.* —**harm′less·ly,** *adv.* —**harm′less·ness,** *n.*

har·mon·ic (här mon′ik) *adj.* **1.** of, relating to, or characterized by musical harmony. **2.** of or relating to a higher tone or tones produced with the main tone or tones when a musical note is played. —*n. Music.* see **overtone.**

har·mon·i·ca (här mon′i kə) *n.* a musical wind instrument consisting of a small slotted case that contains a series of metal reeds. It is played by inhaling and exhaling through the slots. Also, **mouth organ.**

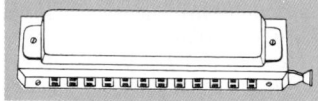

harmonica

har·mo·ni·ous (här mō′nē əs) *adj.* **1.** characterized by agreement in feelings, thoughts, or actions; in accord; friendly: *a harmonious relationship.* **2.** having elements that combine agreeably or pleasingly: *a harmonious mixture of colors.* **3.** agreeable or pleasing to the ear; sweet-sounding. —**har·mo′ni·ous·ly,** *adv.*

har·mo·ni·um (här mō′nē əm) *n., pl.* **har·mo·ni·ums.** a keyboard musical instrument whose tones are produced by currents of air causing small metal reeds to vibrate. Also, **reed organ.**

har·mo·nize (här′mə nīz′) *v.,* **har·mo·nized, har·mo·niz·ing.** —*v.i.* **1.** to arrange, sing, or play in harmony: *The voices harmonized in song.* **2.** to be in agreement; combine agreeably or pleasingly: *The color scheme harmonizes with the one in the dining room.* —*v.t.* **1.** to bring into agreement; make harmonious. **2.** to add notes, usually of lower pitch (to a melody), so as to form chords; add harmony to. —**har′mo·ni·zer,** *n.*

har·mo·ny (här′mə nē) *n., pl.* **har·mo·nies. 1.** a combination of musical notes sounded together so as to form chords. **2.** the science or study of this. **3.** any sweet or pleasant sound. **4.** an agreement of feeling, thoughts, or actions; good relations: *to live in harmony.* **5.** an agreeable or pleasing combination of elements: *a harmony of colors.*

har·ness (här′nis) *n., pl.* **har·ness·es. 1.** the gear of a draft animal, including a combination of straps and bands by which the animal is attached to the load it is pulling, and the headgear by which the animal is controlled and guided. **2.** any combination of straps and bands resembling this: *a dog's harness.* **3.** *Archaic.* the armor for a knight, soldier, or horse. —*v.t.* **1.** to put a harness on. **2.** to control and make use of: *to harness water power.*

harp (härp) *n.* a musical instrument consisting of a series of strings set in a frame, played by plucking the strings with the fingers. —*v.i.* to play on a harp.
·**to harp on.** to refer to over and over again; talk about too much: *You're always harping on how much tax you pay.*

harp·ist (här′pist) *n.* a person who plays the harp.

harp

har·poon (här pün′) *n.* a barbed weapon resembling a spear with a rope attached, used to kill or capture whales and other sea animals. It is thrown by hand or shot from a gun. —*v.t.* to strike, catch, or kill with a harpoon: *They harpooned the whale.* —**har·poon′-er**, *n.*

harp·si·chord (härp′-si kôrd′) *n.* a stringed

harpoon

musical instrument with a keyboard, that was widely used in the sixteenth through eighteenth centuries. It resembles a grand piano, but has wire strings plucked by leather or quill points, and produces a tone more like that of a guitar.

Har·py (här′pē) *n., pl.* **Har·pies.** 1. *Greek Mythology.* one of several foul-smelling, ugly monsters having an old woman's head and the body, wings, and claws of a bird. 2. **harpy.** a greedy, cruel, or shrewish person.

har·que·bus (här′kwə bəs) *also,* **ar·que·bus.** *n., pl.* **har·que·bus·es.** an early portable firearm, used in the fifteenth and sixteenth centuries, later replaced by the musket.

har·ri·dan (har′i dən) *n.* a mean, old woman.

har·ri·er[1] (har′ē ər) *n.* 1. a medium-sized hound dog of a breed developed in England, originally raised for hunting hares. 2. a runner in a cross-country race. [*Hare* + *-ier*.]

har·ri·er[2] (har′ē ər) *n.* 1. a person or thing that harries. 2. any of various hawks that prey on rodents, frogs, and other small animals. [*Harry* + *-er*[1].]

har·row (har′ō) *n.* a heavy frame with upright disks or teeth, drawn by a horse or tractor to break up and level plowed land. —*v.t.* 1. to draw a harrow over (land). 2. to cause (someone) much pain, fright, or distress. —**har′row·er**, *n.*

har·ry (har′ē) *v.t.,* **har·ried, har·ry·ing.** 1. to trouble constantly; torment; vex: *The attorney harried the witness with difficult questions.* 2. to rob or pillage, as in a raid or attack.

harsh (härsh) *adj.* 1. rough or unpleasant to any of the physical senses: *The sergeant has a loud, harsh voice. The towel felt harsh against my sunburned skin.* 2. very cruel; severe: *The prisoners received harsh treatment.* —**harsh′ly**, *adv.* —**harsh′ness**, *n.*

hart (härt) *n., pl.* **harts** or **hart.** a stag, especially a male red deer after its fifth year.

har·te·beest (här′tə bēst′) *n., pl.* **har·te·beests** or **har·te·beest.** a large, reddish brown African antelope having a long, narrow head and ringed, U-shaped horns that bend backward at the tips.

har·um-scar·um (har′əm skar′əm) *adj.* reckless or rash. —*adv.* in a reckless or rash manner: *They raced harum-scarum down the block.*

har·vest (här′vist) *n.* 1. the act of gathering a crop when it is ripe: *Today we finished the wheat harvest.* 2. the crop that is gathered; season's yield of a crop: *a large harvest of corn.* 3. the time of year when ripened crops are gathered. 4. the result of any action, effort, or labor: *a harvest of good will.* —*v.t.* 1. to gather, as a crop: *to harvest corn.* 2. to gather the crop from: *to harvest the wheat fields.* 3. to get as a result of: *to harvest the benefits of a long, productive life.* —*v.i.* to gather a crop.

har·vest·er (här′və stər) *n.* 1. any of various machines for harvesting field crops, especially a reaper. 2. a person who harvests.

harvest moon, the full moon occurring nearest the autumnal equinox.

has (haz) the third person singular, present indicative of **have.**

has-been (haz′bin′) *n. Informal.* a person who is no longer popular, powerful, or effective: *A movie star is now a has-been.*

hash (hash) *n., pl.* **hash·es.** 1. a mixture of cooked potatoes, and often onions or other vegetables, chopped fine and fried. 2. a mess; jumble; muddle: *The new typist made a hash of the letter.* —*v.t.* 1. to chop into small pieces. 2. to discuss; review: *We hashed over our plans for the trip.*

hash·ish (hash′ēsh, ha shēsh′) *also,* **hash·eesh.** *n.* the more potent parts of a marijuana plant, smoked or ingested as a narcotic drug.

Has·id (has′id) *n., pl.* **Ha·sid·im** (has′i dim, hä sē′dim). a follower of Hasidism. Also, **Chassid.** [From the Hebrew word *ḥāsīdh* meaning "pious."] —**Ha·sid·ic** (hə-sid′ik) *adj.*

Has·i·dism (has′i diz′əm) *n.* a Jewish sect and movement that stresses mysticism, strict ritual observance, and intense religious feeling, usually centered on a venerated spiritual leader or leaders. Also, **Chassidism.**

has·n't (haz′ənt) *contr.* has not.

hasp (hasp) *n.* any of various types of clasps or fastenings, especially a hinged metal clasp that fits over a staple and is fastened by a pin or padlock, used to keep a door, window, or box closed.

has·sle (has′əl) *Informal. n.* 1. a heated argument; squabble. 2. a bother; irritation; struggle: *Getting home during the rainstorm was a hassle.* —*v.,* **has·sled, has·sling.** —*v.i.* to squabble; fight. —*v.t.* to bother or irritate.

hasp

has·sock (has′ək) *n.* 1. a low, cushioned stool or other piece of furniture used to rest the feet on, or to sit or kneel on. 2. a tuft of coarse grass.

hast (hast) *Archaic.* the second person singular, present indicative of **have.** ▲ used with *thou.*

haste (hāst) *n.* quickness or speed in moving or acting; hurry: *In our haste we forgot the keys.*
   ·**to make haste.** to move quickly; hurry.

has·ten (hā′sən) *v.t.* to cause to move or act quickly; speed up: *Outrage at the government's cruelty hastened its downfall.* —*v.i.* to move or act quickly; hurry.

hast·y (hās′tē) *adj.,* **hast·i·er, hast·i·est.** 1. swift in motion or action; hurried; quick: *a hasty meal.* 2. characterized by careless hurry; rash: *Some hasty remarks are later regretted.* —**hast′i·ly**, *adv.* —**hast′i·ness**, *n.*

hasty pudding, a mush made of flour, cornmeal, or oatmeal boiled with water or milk.

hat (hat) *n.* a covering for the head, usually having a brim and crown. —*v.t.,* **hat·ted, hat·ting.** to furnish or cover with a hat.
   ·**to pass the hat.** to take up a collection; ask for contributions.
   ·**to take off one's hat to.** to praise or congratulate.
   ·**to talk through one's hat.** to speak ignorantly; talk nonsense.
   ·**to toss one's hat into the ring.** to enter into a contest, especially as a candidate for office.
   ·**under one's hat.** as a secret; in confidence.

hat·band (hat′band′) *n.* a cloth band around the crown of a hat, just above the brim.

hat·box (hat′boks′) *n., pl.* **hat·box·es.** a box or piece of luggage for holding a hat.

---

at; āpe; fär; câre; end; mē; it; īce; pîerce; hot; ōld; sông, fôrk; oil; out; up; ūse; rüle; pull; tûrn; chin; sing; shop; thin; <u>th</u>is; hw in white; zh in treasure. The symbol ə stands for the unstressed vowel sound heard in about, taken, pencil, lemon, and circus.

H

hatch¹
a turtle hatching from its egg

hatch¹ (hach) *v.t.* **1.** to cause young to be brought forth from (an egg): *to hatch eggs in an incubator.* **2.** to bring forth (young) from the egg: *The hen hatched the chicks.* **3.** to devise or bring forth, as a plan or plot. —*v.i.* **1.** to come forth from the egg: *The chicks hatched by pecking through their shells.* **2.** (of eggs) to produce young: *All the eggs hatched today.* —*n., pl.* **hatch·es.** **1.** the act of hatching. **2.** a brood of young that have been hatched. [From the Middle English word *hacchen* "to incubate eggs," from Old English.]

hatch² (hach) *n., pl.* **hatch·es.** **1.** an opening in the deck of a ship leading to lower decks or to the hold. Also, **hatchway.** **2.** a cover or trap door for such an opening. **3.** the lower half of a door or gate with two movable parts. [From the Old English word *hæc* "a gate, small door."]

hatch·back (hach′bak′) *n.* an automobile with a sloping back section and rear window that open to give access to a storage area.

hatch·er·y (hach′ə rē) *n., pl.* **hatch·er·ies.** a place where eggs are hatched, especially fish or poultry eggs.

hatch·et (hach′it) *n.* **1.** a small ax with a short handle, designed to be used with one hand. **2.** a tomahawk.
  ·to bury the hatchet. to stop fighting; make peace.

hatch·way (hach′wā′) *n.* see **hatch²** *(def. 1).*

hate (hāt) *v.,* **hat·ed, hat·ing.** —*v.t.* **1.** to have very strong feelings against; have an intense dislike for: *I hate cruelty toward animals.* **2.** to think of as unpleasant or distasteful; dislike: *I hate to sew.* —*v.i.* to feel intense dislike. —*n.* **1.** an intense dislike or bitterness: *Their hate for prison life grew as time went on.* **2.** a person or thing that is hated. —**hat′er,** *n.*

hate·ful (hāt′fəl) *adj.* **1.** deserving or causing hatred; detestable: *a hateful practice.* **2.** feeling or showing hate; full of hate: *a hateful remark, a hateful stare.* —**hate′-ful·ly,** *adv.* —**hate′ful·ness,** *n.*

hath (hath) *Archaic.* the third person singular, present indicative of **have.**

hat·pin (hat′pin′) *n.* a long, sometimes ornamental pin for fastening a hat to one's hair.

hat·rack (hat′rak′) *n.* a rack or pole with hooks, used to hold hats or other garments.

ha·tred (hā′trid) *n.* a strong feeling against someone or something; great dislike or bitterness.

hat·ter (hat′ər) *n.* a person who makes, sells, or repairs hats.

hau·berk (hô′bûrk′) *n.* a long coat of chain mail or scale armor worn in medieval Europe.

haugh·ty (hô′tē) *adj.,* **haugh·ti·er, haugh·ti·est.** having or showing much pride in oneself and disdain for others. —**haugh′ti·ly,** *adv.* —**haugh′ti·ness,** *n.*

haul (hôl) *v.t.* **1.** to pull or draw with force; drag; tug: *We hauled the cart up the hill.* **2.** to transport, as in a truck or car: *Railroads haul freight.* —*v.i.* to pull; tug. —*n.* **1.** the act of hauling: *It was an easy haul by truck.* **2.** something that is gotten or taken, as by catching or winning: *a big haul of fish.* **3.** the distance over which a load is hauled: *From here to the warehouse is a long haul.* —**haul′er,** *n.*

haunch (hônch) *n., pl.* **haunch·es.** **1.** the part of the body including the hip, buttock, and upper thigh in humans and other primates and four-footed animals. **2.** the leg and loin of an animal, such as a deer or sheep, that is used for food.

haunt (hônt) *v.t.* **1.** (of ghosts or spirits) to visit or inhabit: *A ghost haunts that house.* **2.** to come often to the mind of so as to trouble or bother: *Memories of the shipwreck haunted the old sailor.* **3.** to visit often; frequent: *to haunt antique shops.* —*n.* **1.** a place often visited; hangout: *The barn was our haunt during rainy days.* **2.** *Informal.* a ghost.

haunt·ed (hôn′tid) *adj.* visited or inhabited by ghosts: *a haunted house.*

haunt·ing (hôn′ting) *adj.* appearing or coming to the mind often; hard to forget: *a haunting melody.* —**haunt′ing·ly,** *adv.*

haut·boy (hō′boi′) *n.* another word for **oboe.**

hau·teur (hō tûr′) *n.* a haughty or arrogant manner; arrogance: *With much hauteur, the guard told me to leave.*

Ha·va·su·pai (hä′və sü′pī) *n., pl.* **Ha·va·su·pai** or **Ha·va·su·pais.** a member of a North American Indian tribe living in the area of the Grand Canyon.

have (hav) *v.,* **had, hav·ing.** Present tense: *sing.,* first person, **have;** second, **have** or *(archaic)* **hast;** third, **has** or *(archaic)* **hath;** *pl.,* **have.** —*v.t.* **1.** to own or be in possession of: *They have a house in the country.* **2.** to contain or be characterized by: *The year has twelve months.* **3.** to hold or keep in the mind: *Do you have any doubts?* **4.** to engage in; carry on or out: *The family had a discussion about vacation plans.* **5.** to experience; undergo: *We had a good time at the party. Did you have the mumps when you were young?* **6.** to give birth to: *Our dog had puppies.* **7.** to be obligated: *I have to go to the grocery store.* **8.** to receive, take, or obtain: *I had a long telephone call last night.* —*auxiliary verb* used with past participles to form the perfect tenses, expressing completed action: *We have done the work. We had done the work. We shall have done the work.* —*n.* a person or country that is rich or has ample resources.
  ·to have done. to get through; stop: *Let's pay all the bills now and have done with them.*
  ·to have it in for. *Informal.* to have or hold a grudge against.
  ·to have it out. to settle a matter once and for all, as by discussion.
  ·to have on. to be wearing: *That's a fine suit you have on.*
  ·to have to do with. to be connected or associated with; relate to.

ha·ven (hā′vən) *n.* **1.** a sheltered harbor; port. **2.** a place of safety or shelter; refuge: *The quiet park was a welcome haven from the noise of the city.*

have–not (hav′not′) *n.* a person or country that has little or no property, wealth, or resources.

have·n't (hav′ənt) *contr.* have not: *We haven't been introduced.*

hav·er·sack (hav′ər sak′) *n.* a bag worn over the shoulders or suspended at one's side by a strap, used to carry food and other supplies, as by a soldier or hiker.

hav·oc (hav′ək) *n.* great destruction; devastation; ruin: *The flood caused havoc in the town.*

haw¹ (hô) *n.* **1.** the fruit of a hawthorn. **2.** another word for **hawthorn**. **3.** a kind of viburnum. [From the Old English word *haga* meaning "hedge, hawthorn."]

haw² (hô) *v.i.* to hesitate in speaking; grope for words. ▲ usually used in the phrase *to hem and haw.* —*n.* a stammering sound made by a speaker when hesitating between words. [Representation of this sound.]

haw³ (hô) *interj.* to the left. ▲ used to direct horses, mules, and certain other animals. —*v.t.* to cause to turn to the left. —*v.i.* to turn to the left. [Of uncertain origin.]

Ha·wai·i–A·leu·tian Standard Time (hə wī′ē ə lü′- shən) the local time used in Hawaii and the western Aleutian Islands. It is 10 hours earlier than Greenwich Time.

Ha·wai·ian (hə wī′ən) *n.* **1.** a person who was born in or is a citizen of Hawaii. **2.** a Polynesian language spoken chiefly in Hawaii. —*adj.* of or relating to Hawaii, its people, their language, or their culture.

hawk¹ (hôk) *n.* **1.** a bird of prey having a sharp, hooked beak, strong talons, and short, rounded wings. **2.** any of various other birds of prey, such as the eagle or kite. **3.** a person who favors or supports the use of military force to resolve international conflicts. —*v.i.* to hunt game with trained hawks. [From the Old English word *hafoc* meaning this bird.] —**hawk′ish**, *adj.*

hawk¹ *(def. 1)*

hawk² (hôk) *v.t.* to offer (goods) for sale by calling out in public: *to hawk goods in the marketplace.* [From the word *hawker².*]

hawk³ (hôk) *v.i.* to clear the throat noisily by coughing. —*v.t.* to bring up (phlegm) by coughing. —*n.* a noisy effort to clear the throat. [Representation of this sound.]

hawk·er¹ (hô′kər) *n.* a person who uses trained hawks in hunting; falconer. [From the Old English word *hafocere* with the same meaning, from the word *hafoc* "hawk¹."]

hawk·er² (hô′kər) *n.* a person who offers goods for sale by calling out in public. [From the Low German word *höker* with the same meaning, from the Middle Low German word *hoken* "to peddle."]

hawk–eyed (hôk′īd′) *adj.* having keen vision or being especially observant: *The hawk-eyed sailor high on the mast spotted land several miles away.*

hawse (hôz) *n.* the part of a ship's bow having holes through which hawsers or cables may go.

haw·ser (hô′zər) *n.* a heavy rope or cable used especially for mooring and towing ships.

haw·thorn (hô′thôrn′) *n.* any of a large group of thorny shrubs or trees related to the rose, bearing small red, yellow, or black berries. Also, **haw**.

hay (hā) *n.* any of various plants, such as grass, alfalfa, or clover, cut and dried for use as feed for livestock. —*v.i.* to mow, dry, and store hay. —*v.t.* to feed with hay.

  ·**to hit the hay.** *Slang.* to go to bed: *We didn't hit the hay until after midnight.*

  ·**to make hay while the sun shines.** to take full advantage of an opportunity.

hay·cock (hā′kok′) *n.* a small, cone-shaped pile of hay.

hay fever, an allergy to pollens inhaled from the air, characterized by a stopping up of the nostrils, itching of the eyes, and sneezing.

hay·fork (hā′fôrk′) *n.* **1.** a pitchfork. **2.** a mechanical device for moving or loading hay.

Hawser

hawse

hay·loft (hā′lôft′) *n.* a loft or upper section in a stable or barn, used for storing hay.

hay·mow (hā′mou′) *n.* **1.** another word for **hayloft**. **2.** a pile of hay stored in a barn.

hay·rack (hā′rak′) *n.* **1.** a rack or frame for holding hay on which livestock may feed. **2.** a framework mounted on a wagon, used for holding hay or other bulky material.

hay·rick (hā′rik′) *n.* another word for **haystack**.

hay·ride (hā′rīd′) *n.* a pleasure ride in a wagon partly filled with hay, taken by a group as an outing.

hay·seed (hā′sēd′) *n.* **1.** the seed of any of various grasses. **2.** clinging bits of straw, chaff, and seed that fall from hay when it is moved. **3.** *Slang.* a person from the country; bumpkin; hick.

hay·stack (hā′stak′) *n.* a pile of hay stacked outdoors. Also, **hayrick**.

hay·wire (hā′wīr′) *n.* wire used for baling hay. —*adj. Informal.* **1.** out of order; broken down. **2.** crazy or upset.

haz·ard (haz′ərd) *n.* **1.** a chance of danger, harm, or loss; risk; peril: *the hazards of mountain climbing.* **2.** a source of danger or harm: *Icy roads are a hazard to motorists.* **3.** any obstruction on a golf course, such as sand or water. —*v.t.* **1.** to dare to put forth; to venture: *I'll hazard a guess.* **2.** to expose to danger, harm, or loss; risk: *to hazard one's life.* [From the Old French word *hasard* meaning "risk, accident," also the name of a game played with dice, going back to the Arabic word *az-zahr* "the die."]

haz·ard·ous (haz′ər dəs) *adj.* involving danger, harm, or loss; risky: *a hazardous journey.* —**haz′ard·ous·ly**, *adv.* —**haz′ard·ous·ness**, *n.*

hazardous waste, any waste material or industrial by-products that may endanger health or pollute the environment if not managed or disposed of properly.

haze¹ (hāz) *n.* **1.** mist, smoke, dust, or the like in the air: *an early morning haze.* **2.** vagueness of mind; mental confusion. [From *hazy.*]

haze² (hāz) *v.t.,* **hazed, haz·ing.** to humiliate and play pranks on, especially as part of initiation in a college or a college fraternity. [Of uncertain origin.]

ha·zel (hā′zəl) *n.* **1.** any of a group of shrubs or trees of North America and Europe, bearing nuts that can be eaten, and having oval, tooth-edged leaves and clusters of small flowers. **2.** a light brown color, like that of the hazelnut. —*adj.* **1.** of or relating to the hazel. **2.** having the color hazel; light brown: *hazel eyes.*

ha·zel·nut (hā′zəl nut′) *n.* the light brown, round or oval, edible nut of a hazel. Also, **filbert.**

ha·zy (hā′zē) *adj.,* **ha·zl·er, ha·zl·est.** **1.** full of or blurred by haze: *a hazy day, a hazy view.* **2.** not clear; vague; confused: *My knowledge of physics is hazy.* —**ha′zi·ly**, *adv.* —**ha′zi·ness**, *n.*

H–bomb (āch′bom′) *n.* another term for **hydrogen bomb**.

hazelnut

he (hē) *pron.* **1.** a male person or animal that has been mentioned or spoken about before: *Russell promised that he would be on time.* **2.** a person; anyone: *He who hesitates is lost.* —*n., pl.* **hes.** a male person or animal: *Is the kitten a he or a she?*

He, the symbol for helium.

at; āpe; fär; câre; end; mē; it; īce; pîerce; hot; ōld; sông, fôrk; oil; out; up; ūse; rüle; pùll; tûrn; chin; sing; shop; thin; *th*is; hw in white; zh in treasure. The symbol ə stands for the unstressed vowel sound heard in about, taken, pencil, lemon, and circus.

H

445

head (hed) *n., pl.* **heads** or *(def. 9)* **head.** **1.** in humans and other animals having a backbone, the upper part of the body that contains the brain and the eyes, ears, nose, and mouth. **2.** a similar part of any other animal or organism. **3.** the top or uppermost part of anything: *the head of the stairs.* **4.** the foremost part of anything; front: *the head of a line.* **5.** the leading or commanding part, position, or rank: *the head of the table. The young officer was put at the head of the company.* **6. a.** a part of a tool, weapon, or machine that cuts, strikes, or engraves: *the head of a hammer.* **b.** a part resembling a head in position or shape: *the head of a pin.* **7.** a person above others in rank; chief; leader: *the head of the tribe.* **8.** mental ability; aptitude: *to have a good head for figures.* **9.** a single person or animal, especially when considered as one of a number: *fifty head of cattle.* **10. heads.** the side of a coin bearing the main design; often stamped with an image of a person's head. **11.** foam or froth on the surface of certain liquids, especially beer. **12.** a firm cluster of leaves, as of cabbage or lettuce, or leafstalks, flowers, or any other plant part, usually growing from the top of a main stem. **13.** the tip or point, as of a boil or pimple. **14.** pressure, as of a fluid: *a head of steam.* **15.** a tightly stretched membrane covering the end or ends of a drum, tambourine, or similar instrument. **16.** a title or topic; heading: *The report is divided under five main heads.* **17.** *Nautical.* **a.** the forward part of a ship; bow. **b.** the upper corner or top of a sail. **c.** a toilet. **18.** the magnetic device on a tape deck or computer disk drive that records, reads, or erases electronic signals on the tape or disk. —*adj.* **1.** chief; principal; commanding: *the head lifeguard.* **2.** situated at the top or front. —*v.t.* **1.** to be or go at the top or front of: *The bishop headed the procession. Your name heads the list.* **2.** to be the chief or leader of; be in charge of; direct. **3.** to turn or direct the course of: *I headed the ship northward.* **4.** to fit or furnish with a head or heading. —*v.i.* to move in a certain direction or toward a specified point: *The ship headed for the open sea.*

• **head and shoulders above.** greatly superior to: *Our team was head and shoulders above the others.*
• **head over heels. a.** in a somersault: *I tumbled head over heels down the stairs.* **b.** completely; thoroughly: *head over heels in love.*
• **one's head off.** *Informal.* too much; excessively: *talking my head off.*
• **on one's head.** as one's responsibility.
• **out of one's head** or **off one's head.** *Informal.* crazy; insane.
• **over one's head.** beyond one's power or ability to understand, handle, or manage: *Mathematics has always been way over my head.*
• **to go over someone's head.** to bypass (someone) and go to a higher authority: *They went over the teacher's head and complained to the principal.*
• **to go to one's head. a.** to make one dizzy or intoxicated: *The wine went to my head.* **b.** to make one conceited: *All those compliments will go to your head.*
• **to head off.** to get in front of and turn back or aside: *The posse tried to head off the robbers.*
• **to keep one's head above water.** to manage to avoid disaster, loss, or failure.
• **to make head or tail of.** to understand: *I wasn't able to make head or tail of the book.*
• **to turn one's head.** to make one conceited: *All the attention you got at the dance turned your head.*

head·ache (hed'āk') *n.* **1.** a pain in the head. **2.** *Informal.* a source or cause of annoyance, trouble, or worry: *The flat tire was an added headache on the long drive.*

head·band (hed'band') *n.* a narrow band, usually of cloth, worn around the head to hold the hair in place or as an ornament.

head·board (hed'bôrd') *n.* a board at the head of a bed.

head·dress (hed'dres') *n., pl.* **head·dress·es.** a covering or decoration for the head.

headdress

head·ed (hed'id) *adj.* **1.** having a head or heading. **2.** grown or formed into a head, such as cabbage. **3.** having a specified kind of head. ▲ used in combination: *red-headed.* **4.** having a specified number of heads. ▲ used in combination: *a two-headed giant.*

head·er (hed'ər) *n.* **1.** a person or thing that removes heads, especially a machine that removes the heads from grain. **2.** a person or thing that puts on or makes heads, as for rivets or nails.
• **to take a header.** to fall or plunge headfirst.

head·first (hed'fûrst') *adv.* **1.** with the head going in front: *I dove headfirst into the pool.* Also, **head·fore·most** (hed'fôr'mōst'). **2.** hastily and without thinking; rashly: *to jump headfirst into a difficult situation.*

head·gear (hed'gîr') *n.* a covering for the head, especially one worn for protection: *football headgear.*

head·hunt·er (hed'hun'tər) *n.* a member of certain primitive peoples who practice the custom of cutting off the head of an enemy and preserving it as a trophy.

head·ing (hed'ing) *n.* **1.** a title or subtitle that describes or sets apart a section of a written work. **2.** a part serving as or forming the top or front of anything. **3.** a direction or course, as of a ship or aircraft.

head·land (hed'lənd) *n.* a point of land jutting out into the water; cape.

head·less (hed'lis) *adj.* **1.** having no head; beheaded. **2.** having no leader or chief.

head·light (hed'līt') *n.* a bright light on the front of an automobile, motorcycle, or other vehicle.

head·line (hed'līn') *n.* one or more lines printed in large or heavy type at the top of an article, as in a newspaper, that tells what the article is about. —*v.t.*, **head·lined**, **head·lin·ing.** **1.** to provide with a headline. **2.** to be the main attraction of (a theatrical presentation): *A magic act headlined the show.*

head·lock (hed'lok') *n.* a wrestling hold in which the arm or arms encircle the opponent's head.

head·long (hed'lông') *adv.* **1.** with the head foremost; headfirst. **2.** with great speed: *Events raced headlong to a crisis.* **3.** without giving much thought; rashly; recklessly: *to rush headlong into a business deal.* —*adj.* **1.** made or moving with the head foremost: *a headlong dive.* **2.** very speedy. **3.** rash; reckless.

head·man (hed'man') *n., pl.* **head·men** (hed'men'). a chief; leader.

head·mas·ter (hed'mas'tər) *n.* a man who is the principal or head of a school, especially a private elementary or secondary school.

head·mis·tress (hed'mis'trəs) *n., pl.* **head·mis·tress·es.** a woman who is the principal or head of a school, especially a private elementary or secondary school.

head of state, the official of highest rank in a national government, such as a president or monarch.

head–on (hed′ôn′, hed′on′) *adj., adv.* with the head or front end foremost: *a head-on collision, to collide head-on.*

head·phone (hed′fōn′) *n.* a radio or telephone receiver held against or worn over the ear by means of a band that fits over the head.

head·piece (hed′pēs′) *n.* **1.** a covering for the head, such as a hat, cap, or helmet. **2.** a pair of headphones.

head·quar·ters (hed′kwôr′tərz) *n.* **1.** the center of operations from which a commanding officer, chief, or other leader issues orders. **2.** any center of operations, as of a business; main office: *The firm's headquarters are in New York.* **3.** the entire staff of a center of operations. ▲ used with a singular or plural verb.

head·rest (hed′rest′) *n.* a support for the head.

head·room (hed′rüm′, hed′rùm′) *n.* clear space overhead; room above the head; headway: *a small car with very little headroom.*

head·set (hed′set′) *n.* **1.** a pair of headphones. **2.** a device combining an earphone or earphones and a microphone.

heads·man (hedz′mən) *n., pl.* **heads·men** (hedz′mən). a person who beheads condemned criminals; public executioner.

head·stand (hed′stand′) *n.* the balancing of the body on the head in an upside-down vertical position, usually with the help of the hands.

head start **1.** the advantage of starting a race ahead of others. **2.** a similar advantage in any competition.

head·stone (hed′stōn′) *n.* **1.** a stone set at the head of a grave; tombstone. **2.** the principal stone in a structure, such as a cornerstone or keystone.

head·strong (hed′strông′) *adj.* **1.** determined to have one's own way or do as one pleases; willful. **2.** characterized by or resulting from stubbornness; rash: *Headstrong decisions may lead to trouble.*

head·wait·er (hed′wā′tər) *n.* a person who is in charge of the waiters in a restaurant and sometimes is responsible for taking reservations and seating customers.

head·wa·ters (hed′wô′tərz) *pl. n.* small streams at the source of a river that join to form the main channel.

head·way (hed′wā′) *n.* **1.** forward motion or progress: *The ship made little headway in the storm.* **2.** clear space overhead, as under a bridge.

head·wind (hed′wind′) *n.* a wind blowing from the direction in which something, such as a ship, is moving.

head·y (hed′ē) *adj.*, **head·i·er, head·i·est** **1.** tending to make one dizzy or giddy; intoxicating: *a heady wine.* **2.** headstrong; willful. —**head′i·ness,** *n.*

heal (hēl) *v.i.* to become whole or sound; get well: *The wound healed without leaving a scar. My arm healed quickly.* —*v.t.* **1.** to return to health or soundness; make well; cure: *The doctor healed the sick child.* **2.** to remedy, repair, or remove: *Nothing could heal the rift between the two friends.* —**heal′er,** *n.*

health (helth) *n.* **1.** soundness of body and mind; freedom from defect or disease. **2.** the condition of body or mind: *The doctor said I was in very good health.*

health club, a club with facilities and equipment for physical exercise and indoor sports.

health food, any food thought to be especially good for one's health, especially food without preservatives or other chemical additives, or food grown without the use of chemical fertilizers or pesticides.

health·ful (helth′fəl) *adj.* **1.** promoting or good for the health; wholesome: *a healthful diet.* **2.** having good health; healthy. —**health′ful·ly,** *adv.* —**health′ful·ness,** *n.*

health·y (hel′thē) *adj.*, **health·i·er, health·i·est** **1.** having good health; well: *a healthy child.* **2.** characteristic of or showing good health or sound condition: *a healthy appearance, a healthy outlook on life.* **3.** promoting or

good for the health; healthful. **4.** *Informal.* considerable or great: *I kept a healthy distance from the dog.* —**health′i·ly,** *adv.* —**health′i·ness,** *n.*

heap (hēp) *n.* **1.** a collection of things piled together; mass: *a heap of clothes on the floor.* **2.** *also,* **heaps.** *Informal.* a large number or quantity; a lot: *heaps of coins.* —*v.t.* **1.** to make into a heap; pile: *I heaped the dirty clothes on the bed.* **2.** to fill (something) full or more than full: *The cook heaped the dish with potatoes.* **3.** to give or cast in large amounts: *The director heaped compliments on the actors after their performance.*

hear (hîr) *v.*, **heard** (hûrd), **hear·ing.** —*v.t.* **1.** to receive or be able to receive (sound) by means of the ear: *I heard someone call my name. Did you hear a noise?* **2.** to pay attention to; listen to: *Hear all sides of the argument before you decide.* **3.** to be informed of; become aware of: *We heard the news from a neighbor.* **4.** to give a formal, official, or legal hearing to: *The judge heard the testimony.* —*v.i.* **1.** to receive or be able to receive sound by means of the ear: *I can't hear well, so you will have to speak louder.* **2.** to receive information or be told: *I haven't heard yet.* —**hear′er,** *n.*

· **to hear of.** to allow, consider, or agree to: *They would not hear of our leaving so early.*

· **to hear out.** to listen to until the end: *I promised to hear them out before deciding.*

hear·ing (hîr′ing) *n.* **1.** the faculty or sense by which sound is perceived; ability to hear: *You have very good hearing.* **2.** the act or process of perceiving sound. **3.** the opportunity to be heard; audience: *We were granted a hearing to tell our story.* **4.** a formal, official, or legal investigation or trial. **5.** the distance within which sound may be heard; earshot.

hearing aid, a small electronic device that makes sounds louder, worn to improve poor hearing.

heark·en (här′kən) *also,* **hark·en** —*v.i.* to pay close attention; listen carefully: *to hearken to a plea.*

hear·say (hîr′sā′) *n.* information received from others instead of by personal knowledge; gossip; rumor.

hearse (hûrs) *n.* a vehicle for carrying a dead person from one place to another before or after a funeral service.

heart (härt) *n.* **1.** in humans and other animals having a backbone, the hollow, muscular organ that pumps the blood through the body by beating regularly. **2.** a similar part in any other animal or organism. **3.** the region of the body containing the heart; bosom. **4.** the heart considered as the center of a person's innermost feelings, thoughts, or emotions: *I spoke from the heart when I thanked them.* **5.** love and affection: *The little puppy won our hearts.* **6.** disposition; nature: *a kind heart.* **7.** mental

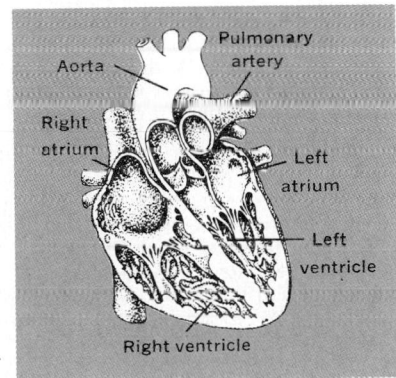

human **heart**

at; āpe; fär; câre; end; mē; it; īce; pîerce; hot; ōld; sông, fôrk; oil; out; up; ūse; rüle; pùll; tûrn; chin; sing; shop; thin; <u>th</u>is; hw in white; zh in treasure. The symbol ə stands for the unstressed vowel sound heard in about, taken, pencil, lemon, and circus.

447

H

state; mood: *They spoke of the accident with a heavy heart.* **8.** firmness of will; spirit; courage: *The team lost heart after their defeat.* **9.** the center or innermost part of anything: *The tranquil waterway seemed to lead into the heart of an immense darkness* (Joseph Conrad). **10.** the main, vital, or most important part: *the heart of the matter.* **11.** anything shaped like the heart: *The children cut out paper hearts.* **12. a.** a playing card marked with one or more red figures (♥) in the shape of a heart. **b. hearts.** the suit of such playing cards. **13. hearts.** a card game in which the players try to win either none or all of the cards of this suit.

·**after one's own heart.** corresponding or conforming perfectly to one's own ideas, tastes, or desires.
·**at heart.** in one's innermost thoughts or feelings: *a good person at heart.*
·**by heart.** by or from memory: *to know a poem by heart.*
·**to break one's heart.** to cause one to feel great sorrow, disappointment, or grief.
·**to set one's heart on.** to desire strongly; long for.
·**to take to heart. a.** to consider seriously or carefully. **b.** to be deeply affected or worried by.
·**with all one's heart. a.** with great sincerity or earnestness. **b.** very willingly; gladly.

heart·ache (härt′āk′) *n.* great sorrow or grief.

heart attack, a sudden, serious disruption in the function of the heart, usually resulting from blockage of an artery supplying blood to the heart.

heart·beat (härt′bēt′) *n.* a beat of the heart, consisting of one complete contraction and relaxation.

heart·break (härt′brāk′) *n.* overwhelming sorrow or grief.

heart·break·ing (härt′brā′king) *adj.* causing overwhelming sorrow or grief: *heartbreaking news.*

heart·bro·ken (härt′brō′kən) *adj.* overwhelmed with sorrow or grief. —**heart′bro′ken·ly,** *adv.*

heart·burn (härt′bûrn′) *n.* a burning sensation under the breastbone, usually caused by too much acid in the stomach or irritation of the lower part of the esophagus.

heart·ed (här′tid) *adj.* having or marked by a (specified kind of) disposition. ▲ used in combination: *heavy-hearted, goodhearted.*

heart·en (här′tən) *v.t.* to give heart to; encourage; cheer.

heart·felt (härt′felt′) *adj.* deeply and earnestly felt; sincere; genuine: *heartfelt thanks.*

hearth (härth) *n.* **1.** the floor of a fireplace, often extending out into the room. **2.** home; fireside. **3.** the lowest part of a blast furnace, in which molten metal and slag collect.

hearth·stone (härth′stōn′) *n.* **1.** the stone forming a hearth. **2.** the family circle; home; fireside.

heart·i·ly (här′tə lē) *adv.* **1.** with genuine sincerity or friendliness; earnestly: *to welcome guests heartily.* **2.** with enthusiasm or vigor; eagerly; vigorously: *to laugh heartily.* **3.** with a good appetite: *After the day's labors, the farmer ate heartily.* **4.** completely; thoroughly; exceedingly: *We heartily support their plan.*

heart·land (härt′land′) *n.* a central geographical area, especially one whose control is considered economically, politically, or militarily essential.

heart·less (härt′lis) *adj.* without kindness, sympathy, or pity; unfeeling; cruel: *a heartless remark, a heartless ruler.* —**heart′less·ly,** *adv.* —**heart′less·ness,** *n.*

heart–rend·ing (härt′ren′ding) *adj.* causing much sorrow or anguish: *a heart-rending story.*

hearts·ease (härts′ēz′) *also,* **heart's-ease.** *n.* peace of mind; tranquillity.

heart·sick (härt′sik′) *adj.* deeply depressed or unhappy.

heart·strings (härt′stringz′) *pl. n.* strongest or deepest feelings or affections: *The sad story touched their heartstrings.*

heart–to–heart (härt′tə härt′) *adj.* frank; sincere: *a heart-to-heart talk.*

heart·warm·ing (härt′wôr′ming) *adj.* causing warm, tender, pleasant feelings: *a heartwarming reunion of childhood friends.*

heart·wood (härt′wŭd′) *n.* the hard, central portion of the wood of a tree.

heart·y (här′tē) *adj.,* **heart·i·er, heart·i·est.** **1.** full of affection, warmth, or kindness; cordial; friendly: *a hearty welcome.* **2.** very enthusiastic; vigorous, unrestrained: *a hearty laugh.* **3.** of sound health; strong and well. **4.** satisfying to the appetite; full; nourishing: *a hearty meal.* **5.** needing or using much food: *a hearty appetite.* —*n., pl.* **heart·ies.** a bold, good fellow or comrade. —**heart′i·ness,** *n.*

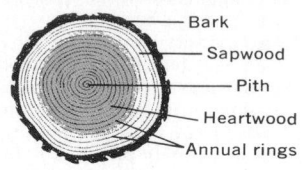

heartwood

heat (hēt) *n.* **1.** the state or quality of being hot. **2.** degree of hotness; temperature. **3.** great warmth; high temperature: *The heat in the room is unbearable.* **4.** mechanism that provides warmth for a house or other building: *We turned on the heat as soon as we got home.* **5.** the most intense or violent stage; point of greatest excitement or activity: *in the heat of battle.* **6.** *Physics.* a form of energy represented by the random motion of molecules, atoms, or smaller particles of a body. It is transferred from body to body by contact or by radiation. **7.** a single trial or effort in a contest, as a race, used to determine which contestants will compete in the finals. **8.** the period during which female animals are able to become pregnant. —*v.t., v.i.* to make or become hot or warm: *to heat milk. The milk heated quickly.*

heat·ed (hē′tid) *adj.* very angry or excited: *a heated argument.* —**heat′ed·ly,** *adv.*

heat·er (hē′tər) *n.* an apparatus, such as a stove, furnace, or radiator, that produces or gives heat or warmth.

heat exhaustion, a condition in which the body loses excessive amounts of fluids due to long exposure to high temperatures. It is characterized by low blood pressure, clammy skin, a low body temperature, and faintness or unconsciousness.

heath (hēth) *n.* **1.** a flat, open wasteland overgrown with heather or low bushes. **2.** any plant or shrub growing on such land, especially heather. **3.** any of a large group of shrubs or small trees bearing needle-shaped leaves and tiny green, white, pink, purple, or red flowers.

hea·then (hē′thən) *n., pl.* **hea·thens** or **hea·then.** **1.** a person who does not believe in the God of the Christians, Jews, or Muslims. **2.** an uncivilized or uncultured person. —*adj.* **1.** of or relating to heathens; pagan: *heathen gods.* **2.** uncivilized or uncultured.

hea·then·dom (hē′thən dəm) *n.* **1.** heathen practices or beliefs; paganism. **2.** heathen countries or people.

hea·then·ish (hē′thə nish) *adj.* **1.** of or relating to heathens. **2.** characteristic of heathens; uncivilized.

heath·er (heth′ər) *n.* **1.** a low evergreen shrub bearing small, usually purple or pink bell-shaped flowers in dense clusters. It grows wild and is found especially in Scotland. **2.** the flower of this shrub.

heat pump, a device that heats a building by transferring heat from one location to another by means of a pressurized refrigerant. The heat used may be extracted from the ground, a pond of water, or some other outside source.

heat shield, the covering on a spacecraft designed to protect it against the intense heat caused by friction during reentry into the earth's atmosphere.

heat·stroke (hēt′strōk′) *n.* a serious condition in which the body temperature reaches dangerously high levels as a result of overexposure to high temperatures. It is characterized by fever, rapid pulse, hot and usually dry skin, and sometimes unconsciousness.

heat wave, a period of extremely hot weather.

heave (hēv) *v.*, **heaved** or (*Nautical*) **hove, heav·ing.**
—*v.t.* **1.** to lift or raise with force or effort: *to heave bales of hay onto a truck.* **2.** to throw, especially with great effort: *Who heaved that rock through the window?* **3.** to utter or give out with much effort: *to heave a sigh of relief.* —*v.i.* **1.** to rise and fall continuously in a rhythmic manner. **2.** to rise and swell; bulge. **3.** to retch; vomit. —*n.* **1.** the act or effort of heaving. **2. heaves.** a chronic respiratory disease of horses. ▲ used with a singular verb.
·**to heave in sight** or **to heave into sight.** to come into view over the horizon, as a ship.
·**to heave to.** to bring a ship to a standstill.

heav·en (hev′ən) *n.* **1.** in the Christian religion, the dwelling place of God, the angels, and those who are saved. **2. Heaven.** the Supreme Being; God. **3.** *also,* **heavens.** the space above and around the earth; sky. **4.** any place or condition of happiness or beauty.

heav·en·ly (hev′ən lē) *adj.* **1.** of, belonging to, or in heaven; divine; holy. **2.** of, relating to, or in the sky: *The sun and moon are heavenly bodies.* **3.** fit for or characteristic of heaven; happy, pleasing, or beautiful: *This is a heavenly spot for a picnic.* —**heav′en·li·ness,** *n.*

heav·en·ward (hev′ən wərd) *adv. also,* **heav·en·wards.** toward heaven. —*adj.* directed toward heaven.

Heav·i·side layer (hev′ē sīd′) the second layer of the atmosphere, existing at 55 to 75 miles (90–120 kilometers) above the earth. Certain radio waves can be transmitted by repeated bouncing between the earth and this layer. [From the English physicist Oliver *Heaviside* (1850–1925), who suggested its existence.]

heav·y (hev′ē) *adj.*, **heav·i·er, heav·i·est. 1.** hard to lift or move; of great weight: *heavy furniture.* **2.** having more than the usual weight or density: *heavy paper, heavy cloth, heavy cream.* **3.** of an unusually large amount, size, volume, or quantity: *a heavy snow, heavy traffic, a heavy eater.* **4.** difficult to do, accomplish, or deal with: *a heavy responsibility.* **5.** showing or feeling grief; sorrowful; sad: *a heavy heart.* **6.** considerable or pronounced: *to speak English with a heavy accent.* **7.** acting or moving slowly, clumsily, or with difficulty: *We heard heavy steps on the stairs.* **8.** overcast; gloomy: *heavy skies.* **9.** loud and deep; resounding: *a heavy bass voice.* **10.** hard to travel over or through: *heavy underbrush.* **11.** producing or processing basic materials like oil or steel: *heavy industry.* **12.** serious in effect: *a heavy fall.* —*n.*, *pl.* **heav·ies.** a villain or villainous character: *a heavy in the movies.* —*adv.*, **heav·i·er, heav·i·est.** in a heavy manner; heavily: *Troubles weighed heavy upon us.* —**heav′i·ly,** *adv.* —**heav′i·ness,** *n.*
·**to hang heavy.** to pass slowly, as time.

heav·y–du·ty (hev′ē dü′tē, hev′ē dū′tē) *adj.* designed, made, or constructed for sturdiness and long wear.

heav·y–hand·ed (hev′ē han′did) *adj.* **1.** clumsy; awkward: *Delicacy is required in this situation, not an unsubtle, heavy-handed approach.* **2.** oppressive; harsh; cruel: *the tyrant's heavy-handed reign.*

heav·y–heart·ed (hev′ē här′tid) *adj.* full of or showing sadness; depressed. —**heav′y-heart′ed·ness,** *n.*

heavy hydrogen, another term for **deuterium.**

heavy metal, a type of rock music with a heavy beat and highly amplified instruments, especially electric guitars.

heav·y·set (hev′ē set′) *adj.* having a solid, sturdy, and compact build.

heavy water, water composed of deuterium and ordinary oxygen.

heav·y·weight (hev′ē wāt′) *n.* **1.** a person or animal of much more than average weight. **2.** an athlete who competes in a high weight class in boxing, wrestling, or weightlifting. **3.** someone very important.

He·be (hē′bē) *n. Greek Mythology.* the goddess of youth.

He·bra·ic (hi brā′ik) *adj.* of or relating to the Hebrews, their language, or their culture.

He·brew (hē′brü) *n.* **1.** a member of one of the Jewish tribes of ancient times; Israelite. **2.** a Semitic language originally spoken by the ancient Jews. It is the religious language of Judaism. A modern form of Hebrew is the official language of Israel. —*adj.* another word for **Hebraic.**

Words From Other Languages

Many Hebrew words in English come from the Bible.

amen	"may it be so," said after prayers
camel	a desert animal with one or two humps
hallelujah	"praise the Lord," sung in hymns
messiah	a savior or deliverer
Sabbath	a day for rest and religious worship

He·brews (hē′brüz) *n.* a book of the New Testament, thought to have been written by Paul.

Hec·a·te (hek′ə tē) *n. Greek Mythology.* the goddess who had power over the moon, the earth, and the realm of the dead. She was also associated with witchcraft and magic.

hec·a·tomb (hek′ə tōm′) *n.* **1.** in ancient Greece and Rome, a public sacrifice of 100 oxen or other animals at one time. **2.** any great slaughter or sacrifice.

heck·le (hek′əl) *v.t.*, **heck·led, heck·ling.** to harass (a speaker) with questions, taunts, and noises. —**heck′ler,** *n.*

hec·tare (hek′târ) *n.* a unit of area in the metric system, equal to 10,000 square meters, or about 2½ acres.

hec·tic (hek′tik) *adj.* **1.** characterized by great excitement, agitation, haste, and activity: *a hectic day.* **2.** flushed and feverish, as from illness.

hec·tor (hek′tər) *v.t.* to threaten or bully. —*n.* a brawling, swaggering fellow; bully.

Hec·tor (hek′tər) *n. Greek Legend.* the eldest son of King Priam of Troy, killed by Achilles.

he'd (hēd) *contr.* **1.** he had. **2.** he would.

hedge (hej) *n.* **1.** a row of shrubs or small trees growing close together, forming a fence or barrier. **2.** any barrier or boundary. **3.** the act or means of protecting oneself against loss or risk: *I saved money as a hedge against unexpected expenses.* —*v.*, **hedged, hedg·ing.** —*v.t.* **1.** to surround, enclose, or separate with a hedge. **2.** to protect oneself from losing money on (a bet or investment) by making another bet or investment that would make up for any possible loss on the first. **3.** to surround with a barrier to prevent or obstruct free movement. —*v.i.* to avoid giving a direct answer or committing oneself: *The politician hedged when asked about the proposed tax.*

hedge·hog (hej′hôg′, hej′hog′) *n.* an insect-eating animal having a pointed snout and a thick mass of sharp, hard spines on its back and sides. When frightened or attacked, it rolls up into a tight ball with only its spines exposed.

hedge·row (hej′rō′) *n.* a row of shrubs or small trees close together; hedge.

hedgehog

H

heed (hēd) *v.t.* to pay careful attention to; mind: *Heed my advice.* —*v.i.* to pay careful attention; listen. —*n.* careful attention; notice: *The children paid no heed.*

heed·ful (hēd′fəl) *adj.* giving or taking heed; attentive; mindful. —**heed′ful·ly**, *adv.* —**heed′ful·ness**, *n.*

heed·less (hēd′lis) *adj.* not paying careful attention; unmindful. —**heed′less·ly**, *adv.* —**heed′less·ness**, *n.*

hee·haw (hē′hô′) *n.* **1.** the braying sound made by a donkey. **2.** a loud, rude laugh. —*v.i.* **1.** to make the braying sound of a donkey. **2.** to laugh in a loud, rude manner.

heel[1] (hēl) *n.* **1.** the rounded, projecting rear part of the human foot, below the ankle. **2.** the fleshy, rounded part of the palm of the hand, near the wrist. **3.** that part of a stocking, shoe, or other piece of footwear that covers the heel. **4.** the part of a shoe or boot that is under or raises the heel: *Certain shoe styles have low heels.* **5.** anything resembling the heel of the human foot in shape, use, or position. **6.** *Informal.* a low or hateful person. —*v.t.* **1.** to furnish with a heel or heels: *to heel a shoe.* **2.** to follow close behind. —*v.i.* to follow closely: *The dog was taught to heel.* [From the Old English word *hēla* with the same meaning.]
   ·**down at the heel** or **down at the heels.** poor or shabby.
   ·**on the heels of.** close behind or immediately after.
   ·**to take to one's heels.** to run away; flee.

heel[2] (hēl) *v.i.* to lean to one side: *The ship heeled in the rough seas.* —*v.t.* to cause to lean to one side. —*n.* the act of heeling; list. [From the Middle English word *heelden* meaning "to pour out" and "to incline, lean[1]," from the Old English word *hildan* "to incline."]

heft (heft) *Informal. v.t.* **1.** to lift up; heave: *The movers hefted the sofa onto the truck.* **2.** to test the weight of by lifting: *to heft a grapefruit.* —*n.* **1.** weight; heaviness. **2.** the greater part; bulk.

heft·y (hef′tē) *adj.,* **heft·i·er, heft·i·est.** *Informal.* **1.** big and strong; muscular. **2.** heavy; weighty.

He·gi·ra (hi jī′rə, hej′ər ə) *n.* **1.** the flight of Muhammad from Mecca to Medina in A.D. 622, marking the establishment of Islam. **2. hegira.** a sudden departure or flight, especially from a dangerous or oppressive situation.

heif·er (hef′ər) *n.* a young cow that has not given birth to a calf.

heigh–ho (hī′hō′) *interj. Archaic.* used to express surprise, happiness, sadness, or weariness.

height (hīt) *n.* **1.** the distance or measurement from bottom to top: *The height of the statue is eleven feet.* **2.** the state or condition of being relatively tall or high: *Height is an advantage in basketball.* **3.** the distance above a given level, such as the sea or horizon. **4.** *also,* **heights.** a high point or place: *to be afraid of heights.* **5.** greatest degree; culmination: *the height of fashion.* **6.** the highest point or part of something; summit: *at the height of one's career.*

height·en (hī′tən) *v.t.* **1.** to make high or higher; increase the height of. **2.** to increase (something) in amount, degree, or intensity: *The disappearance of the witness heightened the suspense of the trial.* —*v.i.* **1.** to become high or higher. **2.** to increase, as in amount, degree, or intensity.

Heim·lich maneuver (hīm′lik) a first-aid procedure for dislodging food or some object from the windpipe of someone who is choking. The rescuer stands behind the victim, places a fist on the upper abdomen just below the ribs, and applies sudden pressure. This forces air up the windpipe and propels the object out of the throat. [From the American surgeon H. J. *Heimlich* (b. 1920), who devised the procedure.]

hei·nous (hā′nəs) *adj.* extremely wicked; hateful; atrocious: *The dictator was guilty of heinous crimes.* —**hei′-nous·ly**, *adv.* —**hei′nous·ness**, *n.*

heir (âr) *n.* a person who inherits or is entitled to inherit money, property, or the like after the death of the owner.

heir apparent *pl.* **heirs apparent.** a person who will become heir to a throne, title, or inheritance when an owner or ancestor dies.

heir·ess (âr′is) *n., pl.* **heir·ess·es.** a woman who inherits or is entitled to inherit money, property, or the like: *The young heiress has a fortune of ten million dollars.*

heir·loom (âr′lüm′) *n.* a personal possession handed down in a family from generation to generation.

heir presumptive *pl.* **heirs presumptive.** a person who will become heir to a throne, title, or inheritance if an heir more closely related to the ancestor is not born: *The queen's oldest cousin is the heir presumptive.*

held (held) the past tense and past participle of **hold**[1].

Hel·en of Troy (hel′ən) *Greek Legend.* the queen of King Menelaus of Sparta, known for her beauty. When she was carried off by the Trojan prince Paris, the Greeks, in revenge, waged war against Troy.

hel·i·cal (hel′i kəl) *adj.* of, relating to, or having the form of a helix. —**hel′i·cal·ly**, *adv.*

hel·i·ces (hel′ə sēz′) a plural of **helix**.

hel·i·con (hel′i kon′) *n.* a very large tuba that is carried over the shoulder, used especially in marching bands.

hel·i·cop·ter (hel′i kop′tər) *n.* an aircraft supported in

helicopter

the air by one or more motor-driven rotors that rotate horizontally above the craft. [From the French word *hélicoptère*, meaning this aircraft, formed from the Greek words *helix* "spiral" and *pteron* "wing."]

he·li·o·cen·tric (hē′lē ō sen′trik) *adj.* having or regarding the sun as the center of the planetary system or universe.

he·li·o·graph (hē′lē ə graf′) *n.* an instrument for signaling by means of mirrors that reflect light from the sun. The signal may be interrupted by a shutter to form a code. —*v.t.* to signal by means of a heliograph.

He·li·os (hē′lē os′) *n. Greek Mythology.* the god of the sun. In Roman mythology he was called Sol.

he·li·o·trope (hē′lē ə trōp′) *n.* **1.** any of a group of plants and shrubs growing wild in warm regions of the world, bearing clusters of fragrant, tube-shaped blue, pink, white, or purple flowers. **2.** a reddish purple color. —*adj.* having the color heliotrope; reddish purple.

he·li·ot·ro·pism (hē′lē ot′rə piz′əm) *n.* a response of plants and certain other organisms that causes them to move or turn toward the sunlight.

hel·i·port (hel′ə pôrt′) *n.* a place, as on the top of a building, for helicopters to take off and land.

he·li·um (hē′lē əm) *n.* an extremely light, colorless,

odorless inert gaseous element. It is used in a certain kind of welding and to inflate balloons, blimps, and dirigibles. Helium has the lowest boiling point and is the second most abundant element in the universe, after hydrogen. Symbol: **He** [Formed from the Greek word *hēlios* meaning "the sun." Helium was first discovered in the spectrum of the sun's light.]

he·lix (hē′liks) *n., pl.* **he·lix·es** or **hel·i·ces**. **1.** anything having a spiral shape, such as the thread of a screw. **2.** a curve lying along the surface of a cylinder or cone at a fixed angle.

hell (hel) *n.* **1.** Also, **Hell.** in the Christian religion, the dwelling place of Satan and the fallen angels, where the wicked will be punished after death. **2.** in various religions, the dwelling place of the dead; Hades. **3.** any place or condition of great evil, torment, or misery: *The prison was a hell on earth.*

he'll (hēl) *contr.* **1.** he will. **2.** he shall.

hell·bend·er (hel′ben′dər) *n.* a large salamander that lives in the rivers and streams of the eastern and southern United States, having a flat body and a wide head.

hel·le·bore (hel′ə bôr′) *n.* **1.** any of a group of thick-rooted plants often cultivated for their large, attractive flowers that grow at the ends of long stalks. **2.** a tall, poisonous plant related to the lily.

Hel·lene (hel′ēn) *n.* a Greek.

Hel·len·ic (he len′ik) *adj.* of or relating to Greece, especially ancient Greece before the time of Alexander the Great. —*n.* a branch of the Indo-European language family, to which Greek and its dialects, both ancient and modern, belong.

Hel·le·nis·tic (hel′ə nis′tik) *adj.* of or relating to the period in Greek history after the death of Alexander the Great in 323 B.C. until the first century B.C.

hell·ish (hel′ish) *adj.* like, relating to, or fit for hell; horrible; fiendish: *a hellish crime.* —**hell′ish·ly,** *adv.* —**hell′ish·ness,** *n.*

hel·lo (he lō′) *interj.* used to express greeting, attract attention, or show surprise. —*n., pl.* **hel·los.** the saying of *hello: They gave us a loud hello when we arrived.* —*v.t., v.i.* **hel·loed, hel·lo·ing.** to say, call, or shout hello.

helm¹ (helm) *n.* **1.** the tiller, wheel, or entire steering apparatus of a ship. **2.** a place or position of control or authority; head: *I will take over the helm of the business when my boss retires.* [From the Old English word *helma* meaning "tiller".]

helm² (helm) *n. Archaic.* another word for **helmet.** [From the Old English word *helm* meaning "helmet."]

hel·met (hel′mit) *n.* any of various protective coverings for the head, such as those worn by soldiers or by players in certain sports, such as football or hockey.

helms·man (helmz′mən) *n., pl.* **helms·men** (helmz′-mən). a person who steers a ship; steersman.

hel·ot (hel′ət) *n.* **1.** *also,* **Helot.** one of a class of serfs in ancient Sparta, who had no rights or privileges of their own. **2.** any serf.

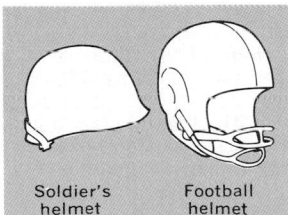

Soldier's helmet   Football helmet

helmets

help (help) *v.t.* **1.** to provide with support or aid, as in doing a task; be of service to: *We helped them paint the room. The child helped me up the stairs.* **2.** to assist (someone or something) in accomplishing a goal or achieving a desired result: *Your advice helped the team to win.* **3.** to make better or cure: *Nothing really helped my cold.* **4.** to prevent or put an end to: *I can't help the bad weather.* **5.** to keep from; avoid: *I couldn't help smiling when I heard the story.* —*v.i.* to provide support or aid, as in doing a task; be of service. —*n.* **1.** the act of providing support, aid, or service: *Do you need help?* **2.** a source of support, aid, or service: *You were a great help to me when I was in trouble.* **3.** a person or group of persons hired to work for another or others: *How much do they pay the help at the store?* **4.** the means of improving, remedying, or preventing: *There is no help for this condition.*

·**cannot help but.** cannot but: *I cannot help but admire your courage.*

·**to help oneself to.** to take, especially without permission: *The children helped themselves to all the cookies.*

·**to help out.** to provide support, aid, or service: *I helped out when they got behind in the work.*

help·er (hel′pər) *n.* a person or thing that provides support, aid, or service, as in doing a task.

help·ful (help′fəl) *adj.* giving or providing support, aid, or service. —**help′ful·ly,** *adv.* —**help′ful·ness,** *n.*

help·ing (hel′ping) *n.* an individual portion of food.

helping verb, another term for **auxiliary verb.**

help·less (help′lis) *adj.* **1.** unable to take care of oneself; dependent: *The victim was made helpless by the accident.* **2.** without power or strength: *The doctor felt helpless to save the dying dog.* **3.** without a source or means of relief, protection, or support. **4.** showing confusion or bewilderment: *With a helpless look, the firefighter walked away.* —**help′less·ly,** *adv.* —**help′less·ness,** *n.*

help·mate (help′māt′) *n.* a companion and helper, especially a wife or husband. Also, **help·meet** (help′mēt′).

hel·ter-skel·ter (hel′tər skel′tər) *adj.* hurried, confused, and disorderly. —*adv.* in a helter-skelter manner: *Don't throw your papers helter-skelter on the table.*

helve (helv) *n.* a handle, as of an ax, hatchet, or hammer.

hem¹ (hem) *n.* **1.** that part of a garment or piece of cloth made by turning the unfinished edge back and fastening it down, usually by sewing. **2.** the edge formed by this: *The hem is uneven.* —*v.t.,* **hemmed, hem·ming.** to turn back the unfinished edge of (a garment or piece of cloth) and fasten it down, usually by sewing: *to hem a dress.* [From the Old English word *hem.*]

·**to hem in** or **to hem about** or **to hem around.** to enclose in; encircle; surround: *The valley was hemmed in by steep cliffs.*

hem² (hem) *n., interj.* a sound resembling the clearing of the throat, made to attract attention or to show hesitation, doubt, or embarrassment. —*v.i.,* **hemmed, hem·ming.** to make this sound. [Representation of this sound.]

·**to hem and haw.** to hesitate in speaking, especially in order to avoid making a definite or clear statement.

hem·a·tite (hem′ə tīt′) *n.* a hard mineral that ranges in color from reddish brown to black, and is the principal ore of iron.

hemi- *prefix* half: *hemisphere.*

hem·i·sphere (hem′i sfīr′) *n.* **1.** one half of the earth, as divided by the equator or the Greenwich meridian. The equator divides the earth into the Northern and Southern hemispheres; the Greenwich meridian divides the earth into the Eastern and Western hemispheres. **2.** one half of a sphere.

hem·i·spher·ic (hem′i sfer′ik) *adj.* of, relating to, or shaped like a hemisphere. Also, **hem·is·pher·i·cal** (hem′i sfer′i kəl).

hem·line (hem′līn′) *n.* the bottom edge of a skirt or dress.

at; āpe; fär; câre; end; mē; it; īce; pîerce; hot; ōld; sông, fôrk; oil; out; up; ūse; rüle; pũll; tûrn; chin; sing; shop; thin; **th**is; hw in white; zh in treasure. The symbol ə stands for the unstressed vowel sound heard in about, taken, pencil, lemon, and circus.

H

hem·lock (hem′lok′) *n.* **1.** a tall evergreen tree related to the pine, having reddish bark and flat, blunt needles. **2.** the soft, coarse-grained wood of this tree. **3.** a poisonous plant related to parsley, having speckled, hollow stems with many branches and finely divided leaves, and bearing clusters of white flowers. **4.** the poison prepared from this plant.

he·mo·glo·bin (hē′mə glō′bin, hem′ə glō′bin) *n.* the iron-bearing protein matter in the red blood cells, carrying oxygen from the lungs to the tissues and carbon dioxide from the tissues to the lungs.

he·mo·phil·i·a (hē′mə fil′ē ə) *n.* a hereditary disease in which the blood clots very slowly, so that a small injury may result in excessive bleeding.

he·mo·phil·i·ac (hē′mə fil′ē ak′) *n.* a person who has hemophilia.

hem·or·rhage (hem′ər ij, hem′rij) *n.* a discharge of blood, especially one that is severe. —*v.i.,* **hem·or·rhaged, hem·or·rhag·ing.** to lose a large amount of blood. [From the Latin word *haemorrhagia* meaning "severe bleeding," from the Greek word *haimorrhagia* "severe bleeding," from the words *haima* "blood" and *rhein* "to flow."]

hem·or·rhoids (hem′ə roidz′, hem′roidz) *pl. n.* enlarged veins on or within the lower part of the rectum; piles.

hemp (hemp) *n.* **1.** a strong, tough fiber obtained from the stem of a tall plant, used chiefly to make rope and twine. **2.** the plant from which this fiber is obtained, having a hollow, thin stem and large leaves. Also, **marijuana. 3.** any of various drugs obtained from this plant, such as hashish or marijuana.

hemp·en (hem′pən) *adj.* made of or resembling hemp.

hem·stitch (hem′stich′) *v.t.* to stitch across an area of cloth from which cross threads have been removed, gathering the remaining threads into small bundles. —*n., pl.* **hem·stitch·es. 1.** ornamental needlework that has been hemstitched, often used to decorate borders and hems. Also, **hem·stitch·ing** (hem′stich′ing). **2.** a single stitch made by hemstitching.

hen (hen) *n.* **1.** the mature female of the domestic fowl. **2.** the female of various other birds.

hemstitch

hence (hens) *adv.* **1.** as a consequence or result; therefore: *I studied for several years in France, and hence learned to speak French fluently.* **2.** from this time: *The committee will meet again three weeks hence.* **3.** away from this place; from here.

hence·forth (hens′fôrth′) *adv.* from this time on; from now on. Also, **hence·for·ward** (hens′fôr′wərd).

hench·man (hench′mən) *n., pl.* **hench·men** (hench′mən). **1.** a willing partner in crime: *The burglar was helped by two henchmen.* **2.** a trusted follower.

hen·e·quen (hen′ə kin) *n.* **1.** a strong fiber obtained from a Mexican plant, used for making twine or rope. **2.** the plant that yields this fiber.

hen·house (hen′hous′) *n., pl.* **hen·hous·es** (hen′hou′ziz). a house, coop, or shelter for poultry.

hen·na (hen′ə) *n.* **1.** a reddish brown dye obtained from the dried leaves of a shrub of Australia, Asia, and Africa, used to color hair. **2.** the tall, slender shrub from whose leaves this dye is obtained. **3.** a reddish brown or copper color. —*v.t.,* **hen·naed, hen·na·ing.** to color or tint with henna: *to henna one's hair.* —*adj.* having the color henna; reddish brown.

hen·peck (hen′pek′) *v.t.* to dominate (one's husband) by constant nagging.

hen·ry (hen′rē) *n., pl.* **hen·rys** or **hen·ries.** *Physics.* a unit of inductance in an electric circuit. One henry is the amount of inductance that produces a force of one volt when the current changes at the rate of one ampere per second. [From Joseph *Henry,* 1797–1878, an American physicist.]

he·pat·i·ca (hi pat′i kə) *n.* a low-growing plant bearing three- to five-lobed leaves and small purple, pink, blue, or white flowers.

hep·a·ti·tis (hep′ə tī′tis) *n.* an inflammation of the liver that is usually caused by a virus. Hepatitis produces such symptoms as fever, weakness, and often jaundice.

hepta- *combining form* seven: *heptagon.*

hep·ta·gon (hep′tə gon′) *n.* a plane figure having seven sides and seven angles.

her (hûr) *pron.* the form of **she** used as the object of a verb or preposition: *I gave the book to her. We called her and offered her a ride.* —*adj.* of or belonging to her: *her blouse, her piano, her accomplishments.*

He·ra (hîr′ə) *n. Greek Mythology.* the goddess of marriage and the protector of married women, who was the sister and wife of Zeus. In Roman mythology she was called Juno.

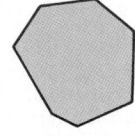

irregular
heptagon

Her·a·cles (her′ə klēz′) *also,* **Her·a·kles.** *n.* another name for **Hercules.**

her·ald (her′əld) *v.t.* to proclaim, be a sign of, or announce; usher in: *Trumpets heralded the hero's arrival.* —*n.* **1.** formerly, an officer who carried messages between princes or rulers. **2.** a person who proclaims or announces; messenger. **3.** a person or thing that announces or is a sign of someone or something to come: *The robin is the herald of spring.*

he·ral·dic (he ral′dik) *adj.* of or relating to heraldry or heralds.

her·ald·ry (her′əl drē) *n., pl.* **her·ald·ries. 1.** the science or art of describing and designing coats of arms or of tracing family descent. **2.** a coat of arms.

herb (ûrb, hûrb) *n.* **1.** any plant or plant part that is used for flavor in cooking, or in making medicines or perfumes and cosmetics. **2.** any flowering plant that does not form a woody stem, but instead dies down to the ground at the end of each growing season.

her·ba·ceous (hûr bā′shəs) *adj.* of, relating to, or having the characteristics of a plant that does not develop woody tissue.

herb·age (ûr′bij, hûr′bij) *n.* **1.** grass and other herbaceous plants, especially when used for grazing. **2.** the green leaves and stems of herbaceous plants.

herb·al (hûr′bəl, ûr′bəl) *adj.* of, relating to, made of, or containing herbs: *a herbal tea.* —*n.* a book about herbs or plants and their uses.

herb·al·ist (hûr′bə list, ûr′bə list) *n.* a person who grows, gathers, or studies herbs, especially one who studies the effect of herbs on the body.

her·bar·i·um (hûr bâr′ē əm) *n., pl.* **her·bar·i·ums** or **her·bar·i·a** (hûr bâr′ē ə). **1.** a collection of dried plant specimens. **2.** a place in which such a collection is kept.

her·bi·cide (hûr′bə sīd′) *n.* a chemical compound or other substance used to kill plants.

her·bi·vore (hûr′bə vôr′) *n.* any animal that feeds chiefly on plants, such as a cow or a kangaroo.

her·biv·o·rous (hûr biv′ər əs) *adj.* feeding chiefly on plants: *A cow is a herbivorous animal.*

her·cu·le·an (hûr′kyə lē′ən, hər kū′lē ən) *adj.* **1.** requiring great strength or effort: *Moving the boulder was a herculean task.* **2.** *also,* **Herculean.** like Hercules, especially in strength or courage. **3. Herculean.** of or relating to Hercules.

Her·cu·les (hûr′kyə lēz′) *n. Greek and Roman Legend.* a mortal son of Zeus, a hero celebrated for his exceptional strength and courage. Also, **Heracles, Herakles.**

herd[1] (hûrd) *n.* **1.** a group of animals, especially large animals, such as cattle, sheep, reindeer, or elephants, feeding, traveling, or being kept together. **2.** a large

number of people; crowd: *A herd of autograph seekers.*
—*v.t.* **1.** to group (persons or animals) in a herd: *They
herded the cattle and drove them to market.* **2.** to lead
or drive in a herd: *The guide herded us into the bus.*
—*v.i.* to group or join in a herd: *The cows herded together.*
[From the Old English word *heord* meaning "a flock,
herd¹."]

herd² (hûrd) *n.* see **herdsman.** —*v.t.* to take care of;
tend: *They herd goats in the mountains.* [From the Middle
English word *herden* meaning "to herd livestock" or "to
protect," from the word *herde* "a herdsman, shepherd,"
from the Old English word *hird* "shepherd" or "guardian."]

herds·man (hûrdz′mən) *n., pl.* **herds·men** (hûrdz′-
mən). a person who owns, tends, or drives a herd. Also,
herd·er (hûr′dər).

here (hîr) *adv.* **1.** at or in this place: *We come here every
year.* **2.** to or toward this place: *Bring the book here.*
3. at this point, as in time or place: *I suggest we stop here
and read the rest tomorrow.* **4.** now to be presented; as
follows: *Here is my answer.* **5.** in the present life. —*n.*
1. this place: *How can I get to town from here?* **2.** this
life: *the here and now.* —*interj.* used as an exclamation,
as in answering a roll call, calling an animal, or attracting
attention.
·**here and there.** in various places: *The balloons were
hung here and there for the party.*
·**neither here nor there.** not related to the matter being
discussed; not relevant or important.

here·a·bout (hîr′ə bout′) *also,* **here·a·bouts.** *adv.* about
or near this place; in this vicinity.

here·af·ter (hîr af′tər) *adv.* **1.** from now on; after this:
When you see them hereafter, be polite. **2.** after the
present life. —*n.* **the hereafter.** the life after the present
life; future life.

here·by (hîr′bī′) *adv.* by means of this: *I hereby resign.*

he·red·i·tar·y (hə red′i ter′ē) *adj.* **1.** passed on or capable of being passed on genetically from an animal or
plant to its offspring: *a hereditary disease.* **2.** taken or
coming from persons or groups of earlier times; inherited:
a hereditary custom, a hereditary right. **3.** passed or
capable of being passed from an ancestor to an heir
according to rules of descent: *a hereditary title.*

he·red·i·ty (hə red′i tē) *n., pl.* **he·red·i·ties.** **1.** the
process by which characteristics are passed on genetically
from an animal or plant to its offspring. **2.** all the
characteristics passed on in this way.

Here·ford (hûr′fərd) *n.* any of a breed of beef cattle
having a thick, curly red coat, a white face, and white
body markings.

here·in (hîr′in′) *adv.* in this place, matter, or circumstance; in this: *Herein lies your mistake.*

here·of (hîr′uv′, hîr′ov′) *adv.* of or concerning this.

here·on (hîr′ôn′, hîr′on′) *adv.* on this or immediately
after this; hereupon.

her·e·sy (her′ə sē) *n., pl.* **her·e·sies.** **1.** a religious belief
or doctrine that is contrary to the accepted belief or
doctrine of a church. **2.** the holding of such a belief or
doctrine. [From the Old French word *heresie* meaning
"heretical religious belief," going back to the Latin word
haeresis "sect, heretical doctrine," from the Greek word
hairesis "choice, sect."]

her·e·tic (her′i tik) *n.* a person who holds a religious
belief or doctrine that is contrary to accepted church
doctrine.

he·ret·i·cal (hə ret′i kəl) *adj.* of, relating to, or characterized by heresy: *heretical beliefs, a heretical movement.* —**he·ret′i·cal·ly,** *adv.*

here·to (hîr′tü′) *adv.* to this matter, subject, point, or
place.

here·to·fore (hîr′tə fôr′) *adv.* before now; until this
time.

here·un·to (hîr′un tü′) *adv.* to this matter, subject,
point, or place; hereto.

here·up·on (hîr′ə pôn′, hîr′ə pon′) *adv.* upon this or
immediately following this.

here·with (hîr with′, hîr with′) *adv.* **1.** along or together
with this. **2.** by means of this; hereby.

her·it·a·ble (her′i tə bəl) *adj.* that can be inherited.
—**her′it·a·bil′i·ty,** *n.*

her·it·age (her′i tij) *n.* **1.** something that is handed down
from previous generations or from the past; tradition: *The
right to vote is part of the American heritage.* **2.** all the
property that has been or may be inherited by someone,
including possessions or land.

her·maph·ro·dite (hûr maf′rə dīt′) *n.* an animal or
plant that has both male and female reproductive organs.
Many species of worms are hermaphrodites.

Her·mes (hûr′mēz) *n. Greek Mythology.* the god of
science and invention, who was the swift messenger of
the gods, usually pictured with winged sandals and helmet.
In Roman mythology he was called Mercury.

her·met·ic (hûr met′ik) *adj.* not allowing air or gas to
get in or out; airtight: *a hermetic seal.* Also, **her·met·i·
cal** (hûr met′i kəl).

her·met·i·cal·ly (hûr met′i kə lē, hûr met′i klē) *adv.*
so as to be airtight: *a hermetically sealed container.*

her·mit (hûr′mit) *n.* a person who lives alone, away
from other people, often for religious reasons.

her·mit·age (hûr′mi tij) *n.* **1.** a place where a hermit
lives. **2.** any dwelling place that is solitary or secluded.

hermit crab, any of a group of soft-bodied, mostly ocean-
dwelling crabs that occupy the empty shells of snails and
similar animals for protection.

hermit thrush, a North American
thrush having a brown body, white-
and-brown spotted breast, and reddish tail, noted for its melodious song.

Snail shell

Hermit crab

her·ni·a (hûr′nē ə) *n., pl.* **her·ni·as**
or **her·ni·ae** (hûr′nē ē′). a condition
in which a part of an organ bulges
out through the wall of its body cavity; rupture.

he·ro (hîr′ō) *n., pl.* **he·roes.** **1.** a person who is looked
up to and admired for bravery and other noble qualities.
2. a man or boy who performs a difficult or courageous
act. **3.** the chief male character in a story, play, or poem.
4. a sandwich made of a small loaf of bread filled with
meat, cheese, and vegetables.

he·ro·ic (hi rō′ik) *adj.* **1.** of, like, or suitable to a hero;
courageous: *The firefighter made a heroic attempt to save
the child's life.* **2.** relating to or describing the deeds of
heroes and heroines from myth and legend: *a heroic poem.*
Also, **he·ro·i·cal** (hi rō′i kəl). *n.* **heroics.** words or
actions that are overly dramatic, noble, or grand and are
done for effect. —**he·ro′i·cal·ly,** *adv.*

her·o·in (her′ō in) *n.* a white, crystalline narcotic drug
made from morphine. It is often addictive and, if too
much is taken, may be fatal.

her·o·ine (her′ō in) *n.* **1.** a woman admired and looked
up to for her bravery or noble qualities. **2.** a woman or
girl who performs a difficult or courageous act. **3.** the
chief female character in a story, play, or poem.

her·o·ism (her′ō iz′əm) *n.* **1.** the qualities of a hero or
heroine; bravery; fortitude. **2.** brave conduct that saves
or protects someone.

at; āpe; fär; câre; end; mē; it; īce; pîerce; hot; ōld;
sông, fôrk; oil; out; up; ūse; rüle; püll; tûrn; chin;
sing; shop; thin; this; hw in white; zh in treasure.
The symbol ə stands for the unstressed vowel sound
heard in about, taken, pencil, lemon, and circus.

453

her·on (her′ən) *n.* any of various wading birds usually having a long, slender neck, a long, pointed bill, and long, thin legs.

he·ron·ry (her′ən rē) *n., pl.* **he·ron·ries.** a place where herons congregate during the breeding season.

heron

her·pes (hûr′pēz) *n.* a disease that causes inflammation of the skin with clusters of blisters. It is caused by any one of several types of related viruses.

her·pe·tol·o·gy (hûr′pi tol′ə jē) *n.* the branch of zoology that deals with reptiles and amphibians. —**her′pe·tol′o·gist,** *n.*

Herr (her) *n., pl.* **Her·ren** (her′ən). mister; sir. ▲ German form of respectful or polite address for a man.

her·ring (her′ing) *n., pl.* **her·ring** or **her·rings.** a bony saltwater fish highly valued as food.

her·ring·bone (her′ing bōn′) *n.* a pattern of short lines slanting back from a central line to form a zigzag design resembling the spine of a herring. —*adj.* having or making this pattern: *a herringbone suit.*

hers (hûrz) *pron.* the one or ones that belong or relate to her: *My room was neat; hers was messy.* —*adj.* of or belonging to her.

her·self (hûr self′) *pron.* **1.** the form of **she** or **her** used to give emphasis to the word it goes with: *She herself was opposed to the idea.* **2.** the form of **she** or **her** used to show that the subject of a verb is the same as the direct object, indirect object, or object of a preposition: *She blamed herself for the accident. She bought herself a book. She kept the secret to herself.* **3.** her usual or normal self: *She has not been herself lately.*

hertz (hûrts) *n., pl.* **hertz.** a unit for measuring the frequency of vibrations and waves, equal to one cycle per second. [From the German physicist Heinrich R. *Hertz* (1857–1894), who was the first to broadcast radio waves.]

Hertz·i·an wave (hûrt′sē ən) an electromagnetic wave, such as a radio wave, produced by the speeding up or vibration of an electric charge.

he's (hēz) *contr.* **1.** he is. **2.** he has.

hes·i·tan·cy (hez′i tən sē) *n., pl.* **hes·i·tan·cies.** the quality or condition of being hesitant. Also, **hes·i·tance** (hez′i təns).

hes·i·tant (hez′i tənt) *adj.* lacking certainty or willingness; doubtful; reluctant. —**hes′i·tant·ly,** *adv.*

hes·i·tate (hez′i tāt′) *v.i.,* **hes·i·tat·ed, hes·i·tat·ing. 1.** to wait or stop a moment; pause briefly: *We hesitated and then rang the doorbell again.* **2.** to be unwilling: *I hesitate to ask because I know you will refuse.* **3.** to fail to take action or to delay an action because of fear, uncertainty, or doubt. —**hes′i·tat′ing·ly,** *adv.*

hes·i·ta·tion (hez′i tā′shən) *n.* **1.** a delay due to fear, uncertainty, or doubt: *to accept without hesitation.* **2.** the act or instance of stopping; pause: *In this dance there is a hesitation after each step.*

Hes·per·i·des (hes per′i dēz′) *pl. n. Greek Mythology.* the daughters of Atlas who guarded the golden apples given to Hera when she married Zeus.

Hes·per·us (hes′pər əs) *n.* the evening star.

Hes·sian (hesh′ən) *n.* **1.** a person who was born in or is a citizen of Hesse. **2.** a soldier from Hesse who was hired to fight for the British during the American Revolution. **3.** any hired soldier. —*adj.* of or relating to Hesse or its people.

hetero– *combining form* not the same: *heterodox.*

het·er·o·dox (het′ər ə doks′) *adj.* **1.** not the same as accepted beliefs or doctrines; unorthodox. **2.** holding opinions that are not the same as accepted beliefs or doctrines.

het·er·o·dox·y (het′ər ə dok′sē) *n., pl.* **het·er·o·dox·ies. 1.** the state or quality of being heterodox. **2.** a heterodox belief or doctrine.

het·er·o·ge·ne·ous (het′ər ə jē′nē əs) *adj.* **1.** made up of unlike or unrelated parts or elements; not homogeneous: *a heterogeneous nation.* **2.** differing in kind or nature; dissimilar: *a heterogeneous group of people.* —**het′er·o·ge′ne·ous·ly,** *adv.* —**het′er·o·ge′ne·ous·ness,** *n.*

het·er·o·sex·u·al (het′ər ə sek′shü əl) *adj.* of, relating to, or characterized by heterosexuality. —*n.* a heterosexual person.

het·er·o·sex·u·al·i·ty (het′ər ə sek′shü al′i tē) *n.* sexuality that is directed toward members of the opposite sex.

het·er·o·zy·gous (het′ər ə zī′gəs) *adj.* having two unlike forms of a gene for a particular hereditary trait.

hew (hū) *v.,* **hewed, hewed** or **hewn** (hūn), **hew·ing.** —*v.t.* **1.** to make or shape with cutting blows, as from an ax: *The farmer hewed fence posts from logs.* **2.** to strike or cut, as with an ax or sword; chop; hack: *I hewed off the dead branches.* —*v.i.* to conform or adhere: *to hew to accepted standards of behavior.* —**hew′er,** *n.*

hex (heks) *v.t.* to put an evil spell on; bewitch. —*n., pl.* **hex·es. 1.** an evil spell. **2.** a witch.

hexa– *combining form* six: *hexagon.*

hex·a·dec·i·mal (hek′sə des′ə məl) *adj.* of or relating to a system of numbers that has a base of 16. Hexadecimal numbers are often used in computer programs.

hex·a·gon (hek′sə gon′) *n.* a plane figure having six sides and six angles.

hex·ag·o·nal (hek sag′ə nəl) *adj.* of, relating to, or having the shape of a hexagon.

hex·a·he·dron (hek′sə hē′drən) *n., pl.* **hex·a·he·drons** or **hex·a·he·dra** (hek′sə hē′drə). a solid figure having six faces. A regular hexahedron is a cube.

hexagon

hex·am·e·ter (hek sam′i tər) *n.* a line of verse consisting of six metrical feet. For example: *Ghosts' of the / fear' some O' / Fla' hertys / ride' through the / val' leys of / Gal' way.*

hey (hā) *interj.* used to attract attention or to express a sudden feeling, as of surprise, pleasure, or annoyance.

hey·day (hā′dā′) *n.* a period of greatest strength, popularity, or prosperity: *They were unbeatable in their heyday.*

Hf, the symbol for hafnium.

hf. 1. half. **2.** high frequency.

HF, high frequency.

Hg, the symbol for mercury. [From the Latin word *hydrargyrus* meaning "mercury, quicksilver."]

H.H. 1. Her Highness. **2.** His Highness. **3.** His Holiness.

hi (hī) *interj. Informal.* hello.

HI, postal abbreviation for Hawaii.

H.I., Hawaiian Islands.

hi·a·tus (hī ā′təs) *n., pl.* **hi·a·tus·es** or **hi·a·tus.** a break, gap, or empty space, as in time: *After a brief hiatus, the argument flared up again.*

Hi·a·wath·a (hī′ə woth′ə, hī′ə wô′thə) *n.* an Indian brave who is the hero of a poem by Henry Wadsworth Longfellow.

hi·ba·chi (hi bä′chē) *n.* a utensil for cooking, consisting of a grill covering a deep container in which charcoal is burned. [From the Japanese word *hibachi,* from the words *hi* meaning "fire" + *bachi* meaning "bowl."]

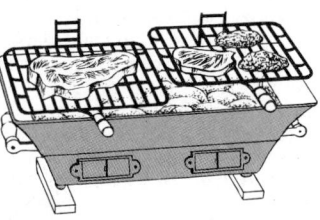
hibachi

hi·ber·nate (hī′bər nāt′) *v.i.,* **hi·ber·nat·ed, hi·ber·nat·ing.** to spend the winter in a dormant or inactive state, as do many animals, such as bears, squirrels, snakes, most amphibians, a few fish and birds, and certain insects. —**hi'ber·na'tion**, *n.*

hi·bis·cus (hī bis'kəs, hi bis'kəs) *n., pl.* **hi·bis·cus·es.** any of a large group of plants, shrubs, or trees bearing large, bell-shaped flowers of various colors.

hibiscus flowers

hic·cup (hik'up) *also,* **hic·cough** (hik'up). *n.* **1.** a spasm of involuntary inhaling of the breath that is stopped suddenly by a closing of the vocal cords. **2.** the sharp sound caused by this spasm. **3. hiccups.** the condition of being affected by such spasms: *to have the hiccups.* —*v.i.,* **hic·cupped, hic·cup·ping.** to inhale with a spasm, with a sharp sound like a catch in the voice.

hick (hik) *Informal. n.* a person who is awkward or naive, especially one from a rural area. — *adj.* of, characteristic of, or suited to a hick or hicks: *a hick town.*

hick·o·ry (hik'ə rē) *n., pl.* **hick·o·ries.** **1.** any of a group of tall trees found in North America, having gray bark and hard nuts. **2.** the hard, strong wood of this tree, used especially for tool handles. **3.** the round or oblong nut of this tree, which can be eaten.

hid·den (hid'ən) *v.* a past participle of **hide¹.** —*adj.* not easily seen, found, or known; concealed or secret.

hide¹ (hīd) *v.,* **hid** (hid), **hid·den** or **hid, hid·ing.** —*v.t.* **1.** to put or keep out of sight: *We hid the presents for your birthday.* **2.** to keep from the knowledge of others; keep secret: *Sometimes it is difficult to hide your feelings.* **3.** to prevent from being seen; cover up: *Heavy snow hid the tracks.* —*v.i.* to keep oneself out of sight; conceal oneself: *The rabbit hid in the high grass.* [From the Old English word *hȳdan* meaning "to conceal, hide¹."]

hide² (hīd) *n.* **1.** the skin of an animal, either raw or tanned. **2.** *Informal.* the human skin. —*v.t.,* **hid·ed, hid·ing.** *Informal.* to give a severe beating; thrash. [From the Old English word *hȳd* with the same meaning.]
  •**neither hide nor hair.** absolutely nothing: *They could find neither hide nor hair of the cat.*

hide–and–seek (hīd'ən sēk') *n.* a game in which one of the players has to find all of the others after they have hidden themselves.

hide·a·way (hīd'ə wā') *n.* a secret or secluded place where one may hide or be alone.

hide·bound (hīd'bound') *adj.* stubbornly narrow-minded.

hid·e·ous (hid'ē əs) *adj.* very ugly; horrible; detestable: *a hideous creature, hideous crimes.* —**hid'e·ous·ly,** *adv.* —**hid'e·ous·ness,** *n.*

hide·out (hīd'out') *n.* a place where one can hide, especially where a criminal can hide from the police.

hid·ing¹ (hīd'ding) *n.* **1.** a state or place of concealment. **2.** the act of concealing. [*Hide¹* + *-ing¹.*]

hid·ing² (hīd'ding) *n. Informal.* a severe beating or thrashing. [From the earlier *hide* meaning "to beat, flog," from *hide².*]

hie (hī) *v.,* **hied, hie·ing** or **hy·ing.** *Archaic.* —*v.t.* to hurry; hasten: *to hie oneself home.* —*v.i.* to go quickly; hurry.

hi·er·ar·chi·cal (hī'ə rär'ki kəl) *adj.* of, relating to, or consisting of a hierarchy.

hi·er·ar·chy (hī'ə rär'kē) *n., pl.* **hi·er·ar·chies.** **1.** an organization of persons or things by rank: *the governmental hierarchy.* **2.** a body of clergy organized in this manner. **3.** church government by such a body of clergy.

hi·er·o·glyph (hī'ər ə glif') *n.* see **hieroglyphic.**

hi·er·o·glyph·ic (hī'ər ə glif'ik) *n.* **1.** a picture or symbol representing an object, word, syllable, or sound, used

hieroglyphics

in writing by certain ancient peoples, especially the Egyptians. **2.** a system of writing that uses hieroglyphics. **3.** any writing that is difficult to read. —*adj.* **1.** of, relating to, or resembling hieroglyphics. **2.** written in hieroglyphics. [From the French word *hieroglyphique* meaning "hieroglyphic," going back to the Greek word *hieroglyphikos* "relating to ancient Egyptian writing," from the words *hieros* "sacred" + *glyphē* "carving."] —**hi'er·o·glyph'i·cal·ly,** *adv.*

hi–fi (hī'fī') *n.* **1.** see **high fidelity.** **2.** equipment for reproducing sound with high fidelity. —*adj.* of or relating to high fidelity.

hig·gle·dy–pig·gle·dy (hig'əl dē pig'əl dē) *adv.* in jumbled confusion or disorder. *adj.* jumbled; confused.

high (hī) *adj.* **1.** reaching upward a great distance; tall: *The walls around the fort were high. The high mountains blocked the sun.* **2.** being or elevated some distance above the ground or other surface: *The bridge is high above the water.* **3.** having a specified height: *forty stories high.* **4.** reaching to or made from a great height: *a high dive, a high jump.* **5.** great or above average, as in force, amount, or degree: *high winds, high speed, high hopes.* **6.** above or more important than others, as in rank or position: *a high church official.* **7.** of a noble or lofty nature: *high ideals.* **8.** very good or favorable: *They have a high opinion of you.* **9.** very happy; joyful: *in high spirits.* **10.** raised above the middle range in pitch; shrill: *The soprano sang a high note.* **11.** *Slang.* feeling the effect of alcohol or a drug. —*adv.* at or to a high position, point, or degree: *We climbed high up the mountain.* —*n.* **1.** a high position, point, or degree: *The temperature reached a new high.* **2.** an arrangement of gears that produces the greatest speed, as in an automobile engine.
  •**high and dry. a.** completely up out of water: *The ship was stranded high and dry on the rocks.* **b.** without aid or assistance; alone; abandoned: *They left us high and dry.*
  •**high and low.** in every place; everywhere: *We looked high and low for the missing book.*

at; āpe; fär; câre; end; mē; it; īce; pîerce; hot; ōld; sông, fôrk; oil; out; up; ūse; rüle; pull; tûrn; chin; sing; shop; thin; **this**; hw in white; zh in treasure. The symbol ə stands for the unstressed vowel sound heard in about, taken, pencil, lemon, and circus.

H

·on high. a. in or at a high place or position; above: *The flag waved on high.* **b.** in heaven.

high beam, a beam of a headlight aimed to illuminate objects in the distance.

high blood pressure, blood pressure in the arteries that is consistently higher than normal. It often has no apparent cause, but it may sometimes be a symptom of disease in another part of the body. Also, **hypertension.**

high·born (hī′bôrn′) *adj.* of noble birth.

high·boy (hī′boi′) *n.* a tall chest of drawers supported on legs.

high·brow (hī′brou′) *Informal. n.* a person who has or seems to have cultivated tastes or interests. —*adj.* of, relating to, or suitable for a highbrow: *highbrow music.*

high·chair (hī′châr′) *n.* a chair for feeding a young child, having high legs and a tray placed across the arms.

higher education, education beyond the high school level, especially education at a college or university.

high·er-up (hī′ər up′) *n. Informal.* a person having a high rank or position.

high·fa·lu·tin (hī′fə lü′tən) *adj. Informal.* pompous or overly refined, as in speech or manner.

high fidelity, the reproduction of sound, as on a phonograph, so that it is as close to the original as possible. —**high′-fi·del′i·ty,** *adj.*

high-flown (hī′flōn′) *adj.* lofty or extravagant, as in ambitions, ideas, or language.

high frequency, a radio frequency between 3 and 30 megahertz. —**high′-fre′quen·cy,** *adj.*

High German, the literary and official form of the German language.

high-grade (hī′grād′) *adj.* of the highest quality.

high-hand·ed (hī′han′did) *adj.* acting or done in a haughty way without consideration for others; arrogant and ruthless: *high-handed business methods.* —**high′-hand′ed·ly,** *adv.* —**high′-hand′ed·ness,** *n.*

high-hat (hī′hat′) *Informal. v.t.,* **high-hat·ted, high-hat·ting.** to treat snobbishly; snub. —*adj.* snobbish.

High Holidays, the two most sacred Jewish holidays, Rosh Hashanah and Yom Kippur. Also, **High Holy Days.**

high jinks (jingks) lively, good-natured pranks or fun.

high jump 1. a field event in which the contestant jumps over a crossbar set between two uprights. **2.** such a jump.

high·land (hī′lənd) *n.* **1.** *also,* **highlands.** a hilly or mountainous region of a country. **2.** a portion of land, such as a hill or plateau, rising above the land around it. —*adj.* **1.** of, relating to, or characteristic of such a region or portion of land. **2. Highland.** of or relating to the Highlands of Scotland.

high·land·er (hī′lən dər) *n.* **1.** a person living in a highland. **2. Highlander. a.** a member of the Gaelic people who live in the Highlands of Scotland. **b.** a soldier of a regiment recruited from the Highlands of Scotland.

Highland fling, a lively Scottish folk dance that originated in the Highlands.

high·light (hī′līt′) *n.* **1.** a point or area in a painting or picture that is represented as brightly lighted. **2.** the most important, interesting, or memorable part of something: *The turkey was the highlight of the holiday meal.* —*v.t.,* **high·light·ed, high·light·ing. 1.** to give a highlight or highlights to. **2.** to give emphasis or importance to.

high·light·er (hī′lī′tər) *n.* **1.** a pen with a broad felt tip and bright ink, used to mark passages in a text for emphasis without obscuring the text. **2.** a cosmetic used to emphasize the eyes, cheeks, or other part of the face.

high·ly (hī′lē) *adv.* **1.** in or to a high degree; very much: *a highly ambitious person.* **2.** with much approval or praise; very favorably: *The teacher thinks highly of your work.* **3.** at a high price: *The actor is highly paid.*

High Mass, a Mass in which certain parts of the liturgy are sung or chanted.

high-mind·ed (hī′mīn′did) *adj.* having or characterized by noble ideals or feelings. —**high′-mind′ed·ness,** *n.*

high·ness (hī′nis) *n.* **1.** the state or quality of being high; loftiness. **2. Highness.** a form of address used in speaking of or to a member of a royal family, preceded by *His, Her,* or *Your.*

high noon 1. exactly twelve o'clock in the daytime. **2.** the highest point or pinnacle; acme: *the high noon of a ballplayer's career.*

high-pitched (hī′picht′) *adj.* **1.** having a high pitch; shrill. **2.** (of a roof) having a steep slope.

high-pres·sure (hī′presh′ər) *adj.* **1.** having, using, or able to withstand pressure higher than normal. **2.** having high atmospheric pressure. **3.** *Informal.* using aggressive methods of persuasion: *a high-pressure sales approach.* —*v.t.,* **high-pres·sured, high-pres·sur·ing.** to use aggressive methods of persuasion on: *They tried to high-pressure us into buying the car.*

high-rise (hī′rīz′) *n.* a building with many stories. —*adj.* having many stories: *a highrise apartment house.*

high·road (hī′rōd′) *n.* a main road; highway.

high school, a school attended after elementary school, usually comprising grades nine through twelve or ten through twelve, or sometimes seven through twelve.

high seas, those portions of the seas and oceans that are not within the territorial boundaries of any country.

high-sound·ing (hī′soun′ding) *adj.* having an important or pretentious sound: *a high-sounding name.*

high-spir·it·ed (hī′spir′i tid) *adj.* having a proud, courageous, or fiery spirit.

high-strung (hī′strung′) *adj.* very tense or nervous; excitable.

high-tech (hī′tek′) *adj.* **1.** relating to, characteristic of, or decorated in the style of high tech. **2.** of or relating to high technology.

high tech (tek) a style of interior decoration for homes and offices that uses utilitarian, unadorned equipment and materials for furnishings, such as those found in factories and warehouses.

high technology, any technology that involves highly advanced, specialized, or sophisticated scientific procedures or equipment, such as those used in electronics, computer design, or genetic engineering. —**high′-tech·nol′o·gy,** *adj.*

high-ten·sion (hī′ten′shən) *adj.* having or using a high voltage: *a high-tension wire.*

high tide 1. the tide at its highest level. **2.** the time when this level is reached.

high time, later than the proper time but not too late: *It is high time you start thinking about your future.*

high treason, treason against one's own government or monarch.

high·way (hī′wā′) *n.* a public road, especially one that is extensive and a major route of travel.

high·way·man (hī′wā′mən) *n., pl.* **high·way·men** (hī′wā′mən). a robber who holds up travelers on a public road.

high wire, a tightly stretched wire placed high above the ground, on which acrobats perform.

hi·jack (hī′jak′) *v.t.* **1.** to seize or take (a vehicle in transit) by force: *Two terrorists hijacked the airplane.* **2.** to steal (cargo) from a vehicle in transit: *The thieves hijacked a truckload of tires.* —**hi′jack′er,** *n.*

hike (hīk) *v.,* **hiked, hik·ing.** —*v.i.* to walk a long distance, especially for pleasure or exercise. —*v.t.* **1.** to raise or pull up, especially with a sharp movement: *to hike up one's pants.* **2.** to increase sharply: *The bus company hiked its fare.* —*n.* **1.** a long walk or march. **2.** an increase: *a hike in rent.* —**hik′er,** *n.*

hi·la (hī′lə) the plural of **hilum.**

hi·lar·i·ous (hi lâr′ē əs, hi lar′ē əs) *adj.* **1.** extremely funny; very amusing: *hilarious stories.* **2.** noisily gay or cheerful: *a hilarious party.* —**hi·lar′i·ous·ly,** *adv.* —**hi·lar′i·ous·ness,** *n.*

hi·lar·i·ty (hi lar′i tē, hi lâr′i tē) *n.* **1.** great merriment or laughter; boisterous gaiety. **2.** an extremely humorous quality or aspect; funniness.

hill (hil) *n.* **1.** a part of the earth's surface that is usually rounded and raised above the surrounding land, but is not as high as a mountain. **2.** a small heap or mound: *a hill made by ants.* **3.** a small mound or pile of earth in which seed is planted: *a hill of beans.*

hill·bil·ly (hil′bil′ē) *n., pl.* **hill·bil·lies.** *Informal.* a person who lives in or comes from the backwoods or mountain country, especially from such an area in the southern United States. —*adj.* of or relating to hillbillies or to their culture: *hillbilly music.*

hill·ock (hil′ək) *n.* a small hill or mound.

hill·side (hil′sīd′) *n.* the side or slope of a hill.

hill·top (hil′top) *n.* the top of a hill.

hill·y (hil′ē) *adj.,* **hill·i·er, hill·i·est. 1.** having many hills: *hilly country, a hilly road.* **2.** like a hill; steep. —**hill′i·ness,** *n.*

hilt (hilt) *n.* the handle of a sword, dagger, or similar weapon.

·**to the hilt.** thoroughly; completely: *I'm involved in this project to the hilt.*

hi·lum (hī′ləm) *n., pl.* **hi·la.** a mark or scar formed on a seed at the point where it was attached to the cone or flower.

him (him; *unstressed* im) *pron.* the form of **he** used as the object of a verb or preposition: *We saw him last night at the theater. I lent the book to him.*

him·self (him self′) *pron.* **1.** the form of **he** or **him** used to give emphasis to the word it goes with: *The repairman himself was unable to solve the problem.* **2.** the form of **he** or **him** used to show that the subject of a verb is the same as the direct object, indirect object, or object of a preposition: *He corrected himself and continued speaking. He told himself it was the right thing to do. He has the habit of talking to himself.* **3.** his usual or normal self: *He just wasn't himself last night.*

hind¹ (hīnd) *adj.,* **hind·er, hind·most** or **hind·er·most.** at the back; rear: *The dog hurt one of its hind legs.* [From the Middle English word *hinde* meaning "rear, back," from the word *bihinde* "behind."]

hind² (hīnd) *n., pl.* **hinds** or **hind.** a doe, especially a female red deer in and after its third year. [From the Old English word *hind.*]

hin·der¹ (hin′dər) *v.t.* to delay or make difficult the movement or progress of; hold back: *The storm hindered the search for the missing child. Stubbornness hinders one in making friends.* [From the Old English word *hindrian* meaning "to obstruct, keep back."]

hin·der² (hīn′dər) *adj.* at the back or rear. [From the Old English word *hinder* meaning "back, behind, on the further side."]

hind·er·most (hīn′dər mōst′) *adj.* another word for **hindmost.**

Hin·di (hin′dē) *n.* a language of the Indo-European family of languages, spoken in northern India. It is one of the official languages of India.

hind·most (hīnd′mōst′) *adj.* farthest back; nearest the rear. Also, **hindermost.**

hind·quar·ter (hīnd′kwôr′tər) *n.* **1.** the back half of a side of beef, lamb, veal, or other meat, including the leg and loin. **2. hindquarters.** the rear part of an animal.

hin·drance (hin′drəns) *n.* **1.** a person or thing that hinders; obstacle: *Lack of education will be a hindrance to you.* **2.** the act of hindering.

hilts

hind·sight (hīnd′sīt′) *n.* the understanding of an event after it is over, especially of what should have been done.

Hin·du (hin′dü) *n.* **1.** a person who believes in the teachings, beliefs, or practices of Hinduism. **2.** a member of one of the peoples of India that speak an Indo-European language. —*adj.* of, relating to, or characteristic of Hindus or Hinduism.

Hin·du·ism (hin′dü iz′əm) *n.* the chief religious, philosophical, and social system of India. The goal of Hinduism is salvation through communion with the Supreme Being, or Brahman, who appears in the form of the three major gods: Brahma, the creator; Vishnu, the sustainer; and Shiva, the destroyer.

Hin·du·sta·ni (hin′dü stä′nē, hin′dü stan′ē) *adj.* of or relating to India, its people, their languages, or their culture. —*n.* a language, including elements of Hindi and Urdu, that is spoken throughout most parts of India.

hinge (hinj) *n.* **1.** a movable joint, usually consisting of two metal plates attached to one another by a pin, on which a door, gate, or the like can swing, turn, or otherwise move. **2.** a similar joint in the body of man or an animal, such as the elbow or knee, or that between the halves of a clam shell. —*v.,* **hinged, hing·ing.** —*v.t.* to furnish with or attach by a hinge or hinges. —*v.i.* to depend: *The prisoner's fate hinges upon the jury's decision.*

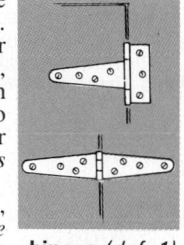

hinges *(def. 1)*

hint (hint) *n.* a slight sign, indication, or suggestion: *a hint of spring in the morning air.* —*v.t.* to give a slight sign, indication, or suggestion of: *They hinted to me that they knew about the party.* —*v.i.* to make a hint. —**hint′er,** *n.*

hin·ter·land (hin′tər land′) *n.* **1.** a region or district lying inland from the coast. **2.** a region that is far from cities and towns; back country.

hip¹ (hip) *n.* **1.** the projecting part of each side of the human body, where the top of the thighbone joins the side of the pelvis. **2.** the corresponding part of the body of animals. **3.** the joint between the thighbone and the pelvic bone. [From the Old English word *hype* meaning this body part.]

hip² (hip) *n.* the ripe fruit of a rosebush. [From the Old English word *heope* with the same meaning.]

hip³ (hip) *adj.,* **hip·per, hip·pest.** *Slang.* familiar with or informed about what is happening or what is new: *hip to the latest dance steps.* [Of uncertain origin.]

hip·bone (hip′bōn′) *n.* either of two large, irregularly shaped bones forming the two sides of the pelvic cavity; ilium.

hip·pie (hip′ē) *n.* any of a number of young people who, especially in the 1960s, turned away from many of the traditional values and practices of conventional society, and developed their own style of behavior and dress.

hip·po (hip′ō) *n. Informal.* see **hippopotamus.**

Hip·po·crat·ic oath (hip′ə krat′ik) a vow taken by most beginning physicians that sets forth an ethical code for medical practice.

hip·po·drome (hip′ə drōm′) *n.* **1.** in ancient Greece and Rome, an outdoor arena for horse races and chariot races. **2.** an arena or similar structure for circuses, horse shows, or other spectacles.

---

at; āpe; fär; câre; end; mē; it; īce; pierce; hot; ōld; sông, fôrk; oil; out; up; ūse; rüle; pùll; tûrn; chin; sing; shop; thin; <u>th</u>is; hw in white; zh in treasure. The symbol ə stands for the unstressed vowel sound heard in about, taken, pencil, lemon, and circus.

hip·po·pot·a·mus (hip′ə pot′ə məs) *n.,* *pl.* **hip·po·pot·a·mus·es** or **hip·po·pot·a·mi** (hip′ə pot′ə mī′). a very large plant-eating animal, native to central and southern Africa, living in and near rivers and lakes, and having a massive, thick-skinned, hairless body, short legs, and the largest mouth of any land animal. [From

hippopotamus

the Latin word *hippopotamus,* from the Greek word *hippopotamos* meaning this animal, from the words *hippos* ''horse'' + *potamos* ''river.'']

hire (hīr) *v.t.,* **hired, hir·ing. 1.** to engage the services of (a person) for pay: *The school hired two new science teachers.* **2.** to pay for the use of (a thing): *They hired a car for the trip.* **3.** to give the use of (a thing) or the services of (a person) in return for payment: *We hired out our boat for the summer.* —*n.* **1.** payment for the use of an object, services rendered, or labor performed. **2.** the act of hiring.
·**for hire.** available for use or work in return for payment.

hire·ling (hīr′ling) *n.* a person who works only for the sake of money, especially a person who can be hired to do something unpleasant or dishonest. —*adj.* of or like a hireling; mercenary.

hir·sute (hûr′süt) *adj.* having much hair; hairy. —**hir′sute·ness,** *n.*

his (hiz) *pron.* the one or ones that belong or relate to him: *We went to the movies with my sisters and his.* —*adj.* of or belonging to him: *His dog is his constant companion.*

His·pan·ic (hi span′ik) *adj.* of or relating to Spain or to Spanish America: *Hispanic culture.* —*n.* a person of Spanish or Latin American descent in the United States: *They were the first Hispanics to attend the school.*

hiss (his) *v.i.* **1.** to make a sound like a prolonged *s: The startled snake hissed.* **2.** to make such a sound to show disapproval or dislike: *The angry crowd hissed when the politician spoke.* —*v.t.* **1.** to show disapproval of by hissing: *The fans hissed the umpire.* **2.** to say or express by hissing. —*n., pl.* **hiss·es.** a sound like a prolonged *s.*

hist. 1. historian. **2.** historical. **3.** history.

his·ta·mine (his′tə mēn′) *n.* a chemical compound found in certain plant and animal cells. When released, histamine has certain effects on the body, such as lowering the blood pressure. Histamine is also released by the body in allergic reactions and causes tissues to swell.

his·tol·o·gy (hi stol′ə jē) *n.* the study of plant and animal tissues through a microscope.

his·to·ri·an (hi stôr′ē ən) *n.* **1.** a person who writes history. **2.** a student of or an expert in history.

his·tor·ic (hi stôr′ik) *adj.* **1.** famous or important in history: *a historic old fort.* **2.** another word for **historical.**

his·tor·i·cal (hi stôr′i kəl) *adj.* **1.** of or relating to history: *historical events.* **2.** based on the facts or events of history: *a historical novel.* —**his·tor′i·cal·ly,** *adv.*

his·to·ry (his′tə rē) *n., pl.* **his·to·ries. 1.** the story or record of what has happened in the past, especially of a country, people, or person: *the history of the United States, the history of the American Indians.* **2.** all past events in general: *human history.* **3.** the branch of knowledge or study dealing with past events: *a class in history.* **4.** the recorded or known past of something: *That old house has an interesting history.*

his·tri·on·ic (his′trē on′ik) *adj.* **1.** overly emotional or theatrical in behavior or speech. **2.** of or relating to actors or acting.

his·tri·on·ics (his′trē on′iks) *pl. n.* overly emotional or theatrical behavior or speech.

hit (hit) *v.,* **hit, hit·ting.** —*v.t.* **1.** to give a blow to; strike: *I hit the ball over the fence. The boxers hit each other* repeatedly. **2.** to come against or strike (someone or something) with force: *The car hit the tree. The bullet hit the target.* **3.** to cause (something) to come against or strike someone or something with force: *I hit my fist against the wall.* **4.** to come to; reach: *The car can hit 55 miles per hour in less than 10 seconds.* **5.** to have a painful or bad effect on: *The lack of jobs hit the town hard.* **6.** to become suddenly plain or clear to: *The truth hit me at the last moment.* **7.** *Baseball.* to make (a base hit): *to hit a home run.* —*v.i.* **1.** to give a blow. **2.** to come against someone or something with force; collide: *The cars hit with a loud crash.* **3.** to arrive or appear: *The tornado hit without warning.* **4.** to discover or arrive at: *We hit upon the solution to the problem.* —*n.* **1.** a blow or strike: *The bomb made a direct hit on the town.* **2.** a person or thing that is successful: *The guitarist was the hit of the party. That song was a hit.* **3.** see **base hit.** —**hit′ter,** *n.*
·**to hit it off.** to like or get along well with one another.

hit-and-run (hit′ən run′) *adj.* of or relating to an accident in which a driver hits someone or something and then drives away from the scene of the accident.

hitch (hich) *v.t.* **1.** to attach, as with a hook, rope, or strap; fasten; tie: *The farmer hitched the horse to the wagon.* **2.** to raise with a quick, jerky movement: *to hitch up one's suspenders.* **3.** *Informal.* to get by hitchhiking: *I hitched a ride to the station.* —*v.i.* **1.** to become fastened or caught: *The zipper hitched halfway up.* **2.** *Informal.* to hitchhike. —*n., pl.* **hitches. 1.** something used to connect two things together; fastening; catch: *The hitch between the car and the trailer broke.* **2.** an unexpected delay or obstacle: *The class play went without a hitch.* **3.** a quick, jerky movement: *I gave my trousers a hitch.* **4.** any of various knots used for temporary fastenings. **5.** *Informal.* time spent in military service: *a three-year hitch in the navy.*

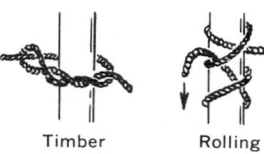

Clove   Timber   Rolling

types of **hitch** knots

hitch·hike (hich′hīk′) *v.i.,* **hitch·hiked, hitch·hik·ing.** *Informal.* to travel by getting free rides from passing cars or trucks. —**hitch′hik′er,** *n.*

hitching post, a railing or pole to which animals, especially horses, may be tied.

hith·er (hith′ər) *adv.* to or toward this place: *Come hither.* —*adj.* on or toward this side; nearer.

hith·er·to (hith′ər tü′) *adv.* up to this time; until now: *A hitherto unknown singer became the star of the show.*

hith·er·ward (hith′ər wərd) *adv.* to or toward this place; hither.

hit-or-miss (hit′ər mis′) *adj.* done without care or planning; haphazard; random: *a hit-or-miss approach.*

Hit·tite (hit′īt) *n.* **1.** a member of a people whose civilization dominated Asia Minor and part of Syria between 2000 and 1200 B.C. **2.** an ancient language of the Hittites, belonging to the Indo-European family of languages. —*adj.* of or relating to the Hittites, their language, or their culture.

HIV, any of several retroviruses, at least one of which causes AIDS by invading the body's immune system and destroying certain cells that help fight disease. [Short for *h*(uman) *i*(mmunodeficiency) *v*(irus).]

hive (hīv) *n.* **1.** a box or house for bees, especially honeybees, to build a nest in. **2.** a colony of bees living in a hive. **3.** a place swarming with busy people: *The airport was a hive of activity.* —*v.t.,* **hived, hiv·ing.** to put (bees) into a hive.

hives (hīvz) *pl. n.* an itching skin rash, usually caused by an allergy. ▲ used with a singular or plural verb.

H.M.S., His (or Her) Majesty's Ship.

ho (hō) *interj.* **1.** used to express pleasure, laughter, surprise, or doubt. **2.** used to attract attention or call attention to: *Land ho!*

Ho, the symbol for holmium.

hoar (hôr) *adj.* another word for **hoary.** —*n.* another word for **hoarfrost.**

hoard (hôrd) *v.t.* to save and store or hide away: *That squirrel is hoarding nuts for the winter.* —*n.* a thing or things saved and stored or hidden away, especially for future use: *a hoard of canned goods in the cupboard.* —**hoard′er,** *n.*

hoar·frost (hôr′frôst′) *n.* frost, especially when it forms a white coating on a surface.

hoar·hound (hôr′hound′) another spelling of **horehound.**

hoarse (hôrs) *adj.,* **hoars·er, hoars·est. 1.** sounding deep and harsh or grating: *After a cold, you may have a hoarse voice.* **2.** having a harsh or grating voice. —**hoarse′ly,** *adv.* —**hoarse′ness,** *n.*

hoar·y (hôr′ē) *adj.,* **hoar·i·er, hoar·i·est. 1.** white or gray: *a hoary beard, leaves hoary with frost.* **2.** old; ancient. —**hoar′i·ness,** *n.*

hoax (hōks) *n., pl.* **hoax·es.** a trick or deception, meant as a practical joke or to fool others: *The report that a serpent had been sighted in the lake was a hoax.* —*v.t.* to trick or deceive by a hoax. —**hoax′er,** *n.*

hob[1] (hob) *n.* a shelf or ledge at the back or side of the inside of a fireplace, used for keeping food warm. [Of uncertain origin.]

hob[2] (hob) *n.* hobgoblin; elf. [From the Middle English word *hobbe* meaning "hobgoblin," from *Hobbe,* a form of the name *Robert.*]

 ·**to play hob with** or **to raise hob with.** *Informal.* to make trouble for; do mischief to: *My cousin's slowness played hob with our plan to leave early.*

hob·ble (hob′əl) *v.,* **hob·bled, hob·bling.** —*v.i.* to move or walk awkwardly with a limp: *hobbling around in a cast.* —*v.t.* **1.** to tie the front legs or hind legs of (a horse or other animal) together to prevent it from moving far. **2.** to hinder or hamper: *Lack of time hobbled the project.* —*n.* **1.** a rope or strap used to hobble an animal. **2.** an awkward walk or movement; limp.

hob·ble·de·hoy (hob′əl dē hoi′) *n.* a young boy, especially one who is awkward or gawky.

hob·by (hob′ē) *n., pl.* **hob·bies** an activity or interest that is pursued for pleasure in one's spare time.

hob·by·horse (hob′ē hôrs′) *n.* **1.** a toy consisting of a horse's head that is attached to a pole that a child can straddle and pretend to ride. **2.** another word for **rocking horse.**

hob·gob·lin (hob′gob′lin) *n.* **1.** a mischievous goblin or elf. **2.** an imaginary thing that causes fear; bogy.

hob·nail (hob′nāl′) *n.* a nail with a large head, used to protect the soles of heavy boots or shoes.

hob·nob (hob′nob′) *v.i.,* **hob·nobbed, hob·nob·bing.** to be on close or familiar terms; be friendly: *They hobnob with the most important people in the city.*

ho·bo (hō′bō) *n., pl.* **ho·boes** or **ho·bos.** a person who wanders from place to place and usually begs or does odd jobs for a living; tramp.

hock[1] (hok) *n.* the joint in the hind leg of a horse or cow or similar animal that is above the fetlock joint. It corresponds to the human ankle. [From the Old English word *hōh* meaning "heel."]

hock[2] (hok) *v.t. Informal.* to pawn. [From the Dutch word *hok* meaning "an enclosure, pen" or "prison."]

 ·**in hock.** *Informal.* **a.** in the possession of a pawnbroker. **b.** in debt.

hock·ey (hok′ē) *n.* **1.** a game played on ice by two teams of six players wearing skates. The players hit a rubber disk, called a puck, with hockey sticks, the object being to get the puck into the opponent's goal. Also, **ice hockey. 2.** see **field hockey.**

hockey stick, a long stick with a flat, thin blade, used to hit the puck in ice hockey.

ho·cus–po·cus (hō′kəs pō′kəs) *n.* **1.** meaningless words used in performing magic tricks. **2.** any bit of trickery or nonsense.

hod (hod) *n.* **1.** a long-handled tool that consists of a V-shaped container that is closed at one end, used for carrying bricks, mortar, and similar materials on the shoulder. **2.** a coal scuttle.

hodge·podge (hoj′poj′) *n.* a confused mixture; mess; jumble: *The attic was filled with a hodgepodge of old clothes, furniture, and toys.*

hoe (hō) *n.* a tool with a wide, thin blade set at an angle to a long handle, used especially for weeding and loosening soil. —*v.,* **hoed, hoe·ing.** —*v.t.* to dig or cultivate with a hoe: *I was hoeing my vegetable garden.* —*v.i.* to use a hoe. —**ho′er,** *n.*

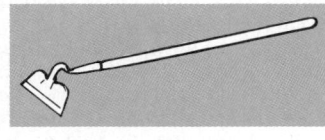

hoe

hoe·cake (hō′kāk′) *n.* a coarse bread made of cornmeal.

hoe·down (hō′doun′) *n.* **1.** a square dance, especially a lively or noisy one. **2.** a party or similar social gathering at which hoedowns are danced.

hog (hôg, hog) *n.* **1.** a full-grown pig, raised for its meat. **2.** *Informal.* a greedy or filthy person. —*v.t.,* **hogged, hog·ging.** *Informal.* to take more than one's share of: *Don't hog the cookies! The truck hogged the road.*

hogan

ho·gan (hō′gän) *n.* a dwelling used by the Navaho Indians, usually made of timber and branches and covered with earth.

hog·gish (hô′gish, hog′ish) *adj.* greedy or filthy. —**hog′gish·ly,** *adv.* —**hog′gish·ness,** *n.*

hog·nose snake (hôg′nōz′, hog′nōz′) any of several thick-nosed, harmless North American snakes.

hogs·head (hôgz′hed′, hogz′hed′) *n.* **1.** a large cask or barrel, especially one that can hold from 63 to 140 gallons (238–530 liters). **2.** a liquid measure, especially one equal to 63 gallons (238 liters).

hog–tie (hôg′tī′, hog′tī′) *v.t.,* **hog-tied, hog-ty·ing. 1.** to

at; āpe; fär; câre; end; mē; it; īce; pîerce; hot; ōld; sông, fôrk; oil; out; up; ūse; rüle; pull; tûrn; chin; sing; shop; thin; <u>th</u>is; hw in white; zh in treasure. The symbol ə stands for the unstressed vowel sound heard in about, taken, pencil, lemon, and circus.

H

tie up by binding the four feet together: *to hog-tie a calf before branding it.* **2.** to confine or restrain; hamper; hinder: *a new social program hog-tied by lack of funds.*

hog·wash (hôg′wôsh′, hŏg′wôsh′, hôg′wŏsh′, hŏg′wŏsh′) *n.* **1.** worthless or nonsensical talk or writing. **2.** refuse fed to hogs; swill.

hoi pol·loi (hoi′pə loi′) the common people; the masses.

hoist (hoist) *v.t.* to lift or pull up, especially by means of ropes and pulleys or a crane: *The sailors hoisted the cargo on board.* —*n.* **1.** an apparatus used for hoisting, such as a block and tackle. **2.** the act of hoisting.

hold[1] (hōld) *v.*, **held, hold·ing.** *v.t.* **1.** to take and keep in the hands or arms; clasp; grip: *Hold the packages while I unlock the door.* **2.** to support or bear: *Will that chair hold your weight?* **3.** to keep in a certain position; maintain: *to hold a pose.* **4.** to have control or influence over: *The play held the audience's attention.* **5.** to keep under control; check: *The dam held the flooding river.* **6.** to be able to contain: *A sponge holds water. This bus can hold fifty people.* **7.** to keep or have in the mind: *to hold an opinion, to hold a grudge.* **8.** to keep by force against an enemy; defend: *The troops held the fort.* **9.** to carry on or engage in: *to hold a conversation, to hold a meeting.* **10.** to believe to be; think; consider: *They hold us responsible for the accident.* **11.** to have and keep possession of; occupy: *I held the position of class treasurer last year.* —*v.i.* **1.** to remain fast: *The anchor held even in the rough seas.* **2.** to keep one's clasp or grip: *Hold tightly to the railing as you come down the steps.* **3.** to stay faithful or attached; adhere: *to hold to a promise.* **4.** to remain or continue in a state, position, or condition. —*n.* **1.** the act of holding; grasp; grip: *a tight hold on a rope.* **2.** a controlling force; strong influence: *The dictator kept a tight hold on the people.* **3.** something that can be grasped, as for support: *I found enough holds to climb the cliff.* **4.** *Music.* a sign or symbol indicating a pause. [From the Old English word *healdan* meaning "to keep, support, defend."]

·**to hold down. a.** to keep under control: *The police held down the crowd.* **b.** to have and work at: *to hold down a job.*

·**to hold forth. a.** to talk at great length: *to hold forth on a subject.* **b.** to offer; propose.

·**to hold in. a.** to keep in check; curb; restrain. **b.** to control or hide (one's feelings).

·**to hold off.** to keep away or at a distance.

·**to hold on. a.** to keep one's hold or grasp on something. **b.** to continue; last. **c.** to stop; wait: *Hold on!*

·**to hold one's own.** to keep one's condition, advantage, or position; stand one's ground.

·**to hold out. a.** to last; continue: *The food supply held out for a week.* **b.** to continue to resist: *The troops in the fort held out for two weeks.*

·**to hold over. a.** to keep for future action or consideration; postpone: *The proposal was held over for the next meeting.* **b.** to stay or keep beyond the regular time: *The movie was held over for another week.*

·**to hold up. a.** *Informal.* to rob. **b.** to bring or point attention to: *The book was held up as an example of good writing.* **c.** to stop or delay.

·**to hold with.** to approve of: *I don't hold with their plan.*

hold[2] (hōld) *n.* an area or space where cargo is stowed in a ship or airplane. *A ship's hold is below the main deck.* [Probably a form of *hole*.]

hold·er (hōl′dər) *n.* **1.** a person who holds something, especially an owner of property or a title. **2.** something to hold something else with: *Use a holder to take the pan from the oven.*

hold·ing (hōl′ding) *n.* **1.** *also,* **holdings.** property owned, especially land, stocks, or bonds. **2.** *Sports.* the act of illegally hindering the movement of an opposing player with the hands or arms, as in football or basketball.

holding company, a company that exists for the primary purpose of holding ownership of other companies, usually by owning portions of stock. A holding company is generally not involved in the other companies' day-to-day operations.

holding pattern 1. a path flown by an aircraft as it waits for permission to land. **2.** any period or condition during which there is no change or progress; a static situation.

hold·up (hōld′up′) *n.* **1.** a robbery by someone who is armed. **2.** a stoppage or delay: *a traffic holdup.*

hole (hōl) *n.* **1.** a hollow place or cavity in something solid; pit: *The workers filled in a hole in the street.* **2.** an opening in or through something: *holes in the elbows of a sweater.* **3.** a small, dingy, filthy place. **4.** a flaw; defect; fault: *There were many holes in the prisoner's alibi.* **5.** *Informal.* an awkward or embarrassing position: *Can you help me out of this hole by lending me money?* **6.** *Golf.* **a.** a small cup sunk into a green, into which the ball is hit. **b.** one of the divisions of a golf course. —*v.t.*, **holed, hol·ing. 1.** to make a hole or holes in: *The ground was holed along the road for telephone posts.* **2.** to hit or drive (a golf ball) into a hole.

·**to hole up. a.** to hibernate: *The bear holed up for the winter.* **b.** to hide oneself: *The fugitive holed up in an abandoned house.*

hol·i·day (hŏl′i dā′) *n.* **1.** a day on which most people do not work, especially a day that is fixed by custom or law to celebrate a special event: *The Fourth of July is an American holiday.* **2.** *also,* **holidays.** a period of rest or freedom from work; vacation: *I'm going away for the holidays.* **3.** a holy day. —*adj.* relating or suited to a holiday: *holiday shopping.*

ho·li·ness (hō′lē nis) *n.* **1.** the state or quality of being holy. **2. Holiness.** the title for the pope. ▲ used with **Your** when speaking to the pope and with **His** when speaking of him.

ho·lis·tic (hō lis′tik) *adj.* emphasizing understanding of the whole person and the interaction of physical, mental, and social factors: *holistic medicine.*

Hol·land·er (hŏl′ən dər) *n.* see **Dutchman.**

hol·ler (hŏl′ər) *Informal. v.t.* to shout loudly. —*v.i.* to cry out loudly. —*n.* a loud shout.

hol·low (hŏl′ō) *adj.* **1.** having a hole or space inside; not solid: *A water pipe is hollow. The squirrel lived in a hollow tree trunk.* **2.** having a shape like a cup or bowl; scooped out: *The car bounced over a hollow place in the road.* **3.** deeply set; sunken: *hollow cheeks.* **4.** deep and muffled: *Their footsteps made a hollow sound in the cave.* **5.** without sincerity or truth; false: *The defeated team's praise of the winners was hollow.* —*n.* **1.** a hollow or empty space; hole: *I tripped over the hollow in the path.* **2.** a valley: *The farm was set in a hollow surrounded by rolling hills.* —*v.t.* **1.** to form by making hollow: *They hollowed out a tunnel in the hill.* **2.** to make hollow: *The tree trunk was hollowed out by disease.* —**hol·low·ly,** *adv.* —**hol′low·ness,** *n.*

hol·ly (hŏl′ē) *n., pl.* **hol·lies. 1.** any of a group of trees or woody shrubs with glossy, spiny-toothed leaves and bright red berries. **2.** the leaves and berries that grow on this tree, widely used as Christmas decorations.

hol·ly·hock (hŏl′ē hok′) *n.* **1.** a stalk of large, showy flowers of various colors, growing on a tall plant that has wrinkled leaves and a strong, hairy stem. **2.** the plant bearing these flowers.

holm (hōm) *n.* see **holm oak.**

Holmes. see **Sherlock Holmes.**

hol·mi·um (hōl′mē əm) *n.* a lustrous metallic element of the rare-earth group. Symbol: **Ho** [From *Holmia,* the Latin form of *Stockholm,* the capital of Sweden, home of the scientist who discovered it.]

hollyhock *(def. 1)*

holm oak, an evergreen oak grown in warm regions of the world, and having broad, leathery leaves.

hol·o·caust (hol′ə kôst′, hō′lə kôst′) *n.* **1.** a great or complete destruction, especially by fire. **2.** a sacrifice that is entirely consumed by fire. **3. the Holocaust.** the systematic persecution and murder of millions of European Jews by the Nazis during World War II. [From the Old French word *holocauste* meaning "whole burnt offering or sacrifice," going back to the Greek word *holokauston,* from the words *holos* "whole" + *kaustos* "burnt."]

Hol·o·cene (hol′ə sēn′) *n.* the Recent geological epoch. —*adj.* of, relating to, or characteristic of this epoch.

hol·o·gram (hol′ə gram′, hō′lə gram′) *n.* a type of photograph made by exposing film to certain kinds of light, such as laser beams. When properly lit, the hologram produces a three-dimensional picture.

hol·o·graph (hol′ə graf′, hō′lə graf′) *adj.* written entirely in the handwriting of the person who signed it: *a holograph document.* —*n.* any document written in this way.

ho·log·ra·phy (hə log′rə fē) *n.* the process or technology of making holograms. [Formed from the Greek word *holos* meaning "whole, complete" + the English suffix *-graphy.*] —**ho·lo·graph·ic** (hō′lə graf′ik, hol′ə graf′ik) *adj.*

Hol·stein (hōl′stīn′, hōl′stēn′) *n.* any of a breed of black-and-white dairy cattle. It is the largest dairy breed.

hol·ster (hōl′stər) *n.* a leather case for a firearm, especially one attached to a belt at the waist or shoulder for a pistol.

ho·ly (hō′lē) *adj.,* **ho·li·er, ho·li·est.** **1.** belonging to, dedicated to, or coming from God; sacred: *a holy altar.* **2.** free from sin; pious; saintly: *The church leader was regarded by many as a holy person.* **3.** worthy of or inspiring reverence.

holster

holy city, a city considered sacred by the followers of a particular religion.

Holy Communion 1. a church service in which bread and wine are consecrated and distributed to the congregation to commemorate the Last Supper. **2.** the bread and wine used in this service.

holy day, a day set apart for religious observance.

Holy Father, a title and form of address used in speaking or referring to the pope.

Holy Ghost, another term for **Holy Spirit.**

Holy Grail *Medieval Legend.* the sacred cup or dish used by Jesus at the Last Supper, and by one of his followers to catch drops of his blood at the Crucifixion. King Arthur's Knights of the Round Table searched for the Holy Grail.

holy of holies, the innermost chamber of the Temple in ancient Jerusalem. It housed the Ark of the Covenant and could be entered only by the high priest on the Day of Atonement.

Holy Roman Empire, an empire in western and central Europe that was founded by Charlemagne in 800 and that lapsed into anarchy late in the ninth century. It was revived by Otto I of Germany in 962 and lasted until 1806.

Holy Scripture, see **Bible** (*def. 1*).

Holy See, the office, authority, or jurisdiction of the pope.

Holy Spirit, the third person of the Trinity.

ho·ly·stone (hō′lē stōn′) *n.* a flat piece of soft sandstone, used for scouring the wooden decks of ships. —*v.t.,* **ho·ly·stoned, ho·ly·ston·ing.** to scrub with a holystone.

Holy Thursday, the Thursday before Easter, commemorating the Last Supper.

holy water, water blessed by a priest, used in religious services.

Holy Week, the week before Easter, beginning with Palm Sunday.

Holy Writ, see **Bible** (*def. 1*).

hom·age (hom′ij, om′ij) *n.* **1.** honor, respect, or reverence: *The university paid homage to the professor at commencement.* **2.** the formal acknowledgment of allegiance and obligation by a feudal vassal to his lord.

hom·bre (ôm′brā, ōm′brē) *n.* *Informal.* man; fellow.

home (hōm) *n.* **1.** the place in which a person lives; residence: *My home is in that apartment house.* **2.** the home thought of as a family unit; family; household: *a happy home, a broken home.* **3.** a country, region, town, or locality where one was born or raised or where one lives: *New York has been my home for five years now.* **4.** a place or region where something is commonly found: *Australia is the home of the koala.* **5.** an institution or establishment for the shelter and care of certain people: *a home for orphans, a home for the aged.* **6.** a goal or place of safety in certain sports and games. **7.** see **home plate.** —*adv.* **1.** at, to, or toward home: *Write home every week.* **2.** to the place or mark aimed at: *The bullet struck home.* **3.** to the very heart or center: *The criticism hit home.* —*v.,* **homed, hom·ing.** —*v.i.* **1.** to go or return home. **2.** to have a home. —*v.t.* to cause to go toward a particular point or target: *to home an airplane by radar.* —**home′like′,** *adj.*

·**at home.** **a.** at one's ease; comfortable: *I always felt at home in their house.* **b.** ready to receive visitors.

home base, another term for **home plate.**

home·bod·y (hōm′bod′ē) *n., pl.* **home·bod·ies.** a person who likes to stay at home or whose interests center on the home.

home·com·ing (hōm′kum′ing) *n.* **1.** a return to one's home, especially after an extended absence. **2.** an annual celebration for alumni in many colleges and universities.

home computer, a microcomputer used in the home for games or simple tasks, such as word processing.

home economics, the science, art, and study of managing a household, including such subjects as cooking, budgeting household money, and child care.

home·grown (hōm′grōn′) *adj.* **1.** grown or produced at home or locally: *homegrown fruits and vegetables.* **2.** native to, developed in, or characteristic of a particular locality: *a local art show featuring homegrown talent.*

home·land (hōm′land′) *n.* a country that a person was born in or considers home.

home·less (hōm′lis) *adj.* having no home. —*n.* homeless persons considered as a group: *the homeless.*

home·ly (hōm′lē) *adj.,* **home·li·er, home·li·est.** **1.** having plain features; not good-looking; unattractive. **2.** of a familiar or everyday nature; simple: *homely manners, homely food.* —**home′li·ness,** *n.*

home·made (hōm′mād′) *adj.* **1.** made at home: *homemade cookies.* **2.** crudely or simply done.

home·mak·er (hōm′mā′kər) *n.* a person who stays at home and manages a household.

ho·me·o·sta·sis (hō′mē ō stā′sis) *n.* the tendency of a living organism to maintain stable internal conditions essential to its normal functioning when external conditions threaten to alter such stability. An example of homeostasis is the regulation of body temperature.

home·own·er (hōm′ō′nər) *n.* a person who owns a home.

home plate *Baseball.* a slab beside which a baseball player stands to hit a pitched ball, and which must be touched after rounding the bases in order to score a run.

at; āpe; fär; câre; end; mē; it; īce; pîerce; hot; ōld; sông, fôrk; oil; out; up; ūse; rüle; pull; tûrn; chin; sing; shop; thin; this; hw in white; zh in treasure. The symbol ə stands for the unstressed vowel sound heard in about, taken, pencil, lemon, and circus.

461

hom·er (hō′mər) *n.* *Informal.* another term for home run.

Ho·mer·ic (hō mer′ik) *adj.* of, relating to, or characteristic of Homer, his poetry, or the period of Greek history about which he wrote.

home·room (hōm′rüm′, hōm′rùm′) *n.* **1.** a classroom to which the students of a class report to have their attendance checked and to hear school announcements. **2.** the time during which such a class meets.

home rule, a system under which one political unit within a larger one, as a city within a state, is granted power to manage its own affairs.

home run **1.** a hit made by a baseball player who is then able to round the bases and score a run. **2.** a score made in such a way.

home·sick (hōm′sik′) *adj.* sad or ill because one is away from one's home or family; longing for home. —**home′-sick′ness,** *n.*

home·spun (hōm′spun′) *adj.* **1.** spun or made at home. **2.** simple and plain in character: *homespun jokes.* —*n.* **1.** a fabric woven of yarn spun at home or by hand. **2.** any of various coarse fabrics woven to resemble this.

home·stead (hōm′sted′) *n.* **1.** a house with its buildings and the land they are on. **2.** a parcel of 160 acres (64.8 hectares) of public land granted by the United States government to a settler for farming. —*v.t.* to settle on and claim (land). —*v.i.* to settle and claim a homestead. —**home′stead·er,** *n.*

home·stretch (hōm′strech′) *n., pl.* **home·stretch·es. 1.** the straight part of a track between the last turn and the finish line. **2.** the last part of any trip or effort.

home·town (hōm′toun′) *n.* the town or city where a person was born or raised or where a person has lived a long time.

home·ward (hōm′wərd) *adv.* also, **homewards.** toward home: *The hikers turned homeward.* —*adj.* directed toward home: *a homeward trip.*

home·work (hōm′wûrk′) *n.* **1.** a school lesson to be studied or prepared outside the classroom, usually at home. **2.** any work done at home.

home·y (hō′mē) *adj.,* **hom·i·er, hom·i·est.** *Informal.* informal and friendly; cozy; comfortable.

hom·i·cid·al (hom′ə sī′dəl, hō′mə sī′dəl) *adj.* **1.** of or relating to homicide; murderous: *a homicidal maniac, a homicidal rage.* **2.** tending to homicide.

hom·i·cide (hom′ə sīd′, hō′mə sīd′) *n.* the killing of one person by another. [From the Old French word *homicide,* from the Latin word *homicida* meaning "a killer," going back to the words *homo* "man, person" and *caedere* "to cut, kill."]

hom·i·ly (hom′ə lē) *n., pl.* **hom·i·lies. 1.** a sermon, especially one based on some portion of the Bible. **2.** a solemn and usually long talk, especially about morals. **3.** a short saying with a moral or inspirational point.

homing pigeon, a pigeon trained to fly home, often used to carry messages. Also, **carrier pigeon.**

hom·i·nid (hom′ə nid) *n.* any member of the family of primates that includes humans: *Humans are the only hominids living today.* —*adj.* of or relating to a hominid or hominids: *hominid fossils.*

hom·i·ny (hom′ə nē) *n.* kernels of white corn that have been dried and hulled, prepared for eating by being mixed with water and boiled.

hominy grits, see grits *(def. 1).*

homo– *combining form* same: *homograph, homogenize.*

ho·mo·ge·ne·i·ty (hō′mə jə nē′i tē) *n.* the state or quality of being homogeneous.

ho·mo·ge·ne·ous (hō′mə jē′nē əs) *adj.* **1.** of the same kind; similar or identical: *two homogeneous parts.* **2.** having a similar character or similar parts throughout: *a homogeneous mixture.* —**ho′mo·ge′ne·ous·ly,** *adv.* —**ho′mo·ge′ne·ous·ness,** *n.*

ho·mog·e·nize (hə moj′ə nīz′) *v.t.,* **ho·mog·e·nized, ho·mog·e·niz·ing.** to make homogeneous.

homogenized milk, milk in which the fat particles are distributed evenly throughout and do not separate and rise to the top as cream.

hom·o·graph (hom′ə graf′) *n.* a word with the same spelling as another, but with a different origin, meaning, and, sometimes, pronunciation. *Bear* meaning "to hold up or carry" and *bear* meaning "a large, heavy animal" are homographs, as are *bow* meaning "to bend forward at the waist" and *bow* meaning "a weapon for shooting arrows."

ho·mol·o·gous (hə mol′ə gəs) *adj.* corresponding, as in position, proportion, function, or structure. The human arm, the wing of a bird, and the foreleg of a horse are homologous.

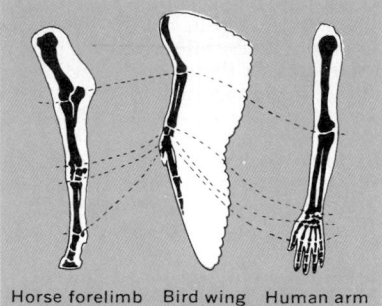

Horse forelimb   Bird wing   Human arm

homologous structures

hom·o·nym (hom′ə nim′) *n.* a word with the same pronunciation as another, but with a different meaning and, often, a different spelling. *Lean* meaning "to bend" and *lean* meaning "thin" are homonyms, as are *boar* and *bore.*

hom·o·phone (hom′ə fōn′) *n.* **1.** a word with the same pronunciation as another, but with a different meaning and spelling. *Know* and *no* are homophones. **2.** any word with the same pronunciation as another; homonym. **3.** a letter or group of letters having the same sound as another. The letters *ks* and *x* are homophones.

ho·mop·ter·ous (hə mop′tər əs) *adj.* of or belonging to a group of insects including aphids and cicadas, characterized by sucking mouth parts and membranous wings.

Ho·mo sa·pi·ens (hō′mō sā′pē ənz) the human being viewed as the only living species of the genus *Homo.* [From a scientific Latin phrase meaning "wise human being."]

ho·mo·sex·u·al (hō′mə sek′shü əl) *adj.* of, relating to, or characterized by homosexuality. —*n.* a homosexual person.

ho·mo·sex·u·al·i·ty (hō′mə sek′shü al′i tē) *n.* sexuality that is directed toward members of one's own sex.

ho·mo·zy·gous (hō′mə zī′gəs) *adj.* having two like forms of a gene for a particular hereditary trait.

Hon. 1. Honorable. **2.** Honorary.

hon·cho (hon′chō) *n., pl.* **hon·chos.** *Slang.* a person who is in charge or is very important; a boss or head of an organization, establishment, department, or division. [From the Japanese word *hanchō* meaning "squad leader," from the words *han* "squad, group" + *chō* "chief."]

hone (hōn) *n.* a whetstone with a fine grain, used to sharpen the cutting edges of tools, as razors or scissors. —*v.t.,* **honed, hon·ing.** to sharpen on or as on a hone.

hon·est (on′ist) *adj.* **1.** truthful, fair, or trustworthy, as in character or actions: *an honest person, an honest effort.* **2.** earned or gotten fairly and without deceit: *to make an honest living.* **3.** sincere; frank; open: *an honest face.* —**hon′est·ly,** *adv.* —**hon′est·ness,** *n.*

hon·es·ty (on′ə stē) *n.* **1.** the state or quality of being honest: *The honesty of the witness is not in question.* **2.** truthfulness; sincerity; fairness: *I could not, in all honesty, agree to their terms.*

hon·ey (hun′ē) *n., pl.* **hon·eys. 1.** a thick, sweet liquid, made by bees from the nectar they collect from flowers, used for food and as a sweetening agent. **2.** a sweet quality; sweetness. **3.** sweet one; darling; dear. —*adj.* of, like, or containing honey; sweet. —*v.t.,* **hon·eyed** or **hon·ied, hon·ey·ing. 1.** to sweeten with honey. **2.** to talk to in a sweet or flattering manner.

hon·ey·bee (hun′ē bē′) *n.* any bee that makes and stores honey.

honeycomb *(def. 1)*

hon·ey·comb (hun′ē kōm′) *n.* **1.** a wax structure formed by bees, consisting of six-sided cells arranged back to back, used for storing honey, pollen, eggs, and larvae. **2.** anything resembling this in appearance or structure. —*adj.* like a honeycomb: *Termites chew wood in a honeycomb pattern.* —*v.t.* to make full of holes or cavities like a honeycomb: *Secret passages honeycombed the castle.*

hon·ey·dew (hun′ē dü′, hun′ē dū′) *n.* **1.** see **honeydew melon. 2.** a sweet substance secreted on leaves and stems by aphids and certain other plant-sucking insects. **3.** a sweet substance that oozes from the leaves of certain plants in hot weather.

honeydew melon, a melon having a smooth, creamy yellow rind and sweet, light green or white flesh.

hon·ey·moon (hun′ē mün′) *n.* a vacation taken by a newly married couple, usually immediately after the wedding. —*v.i.* to go or be on a honeymoon. —**hon′ey·moon′er,** *n.*

hon·ey·suck·le (hun′ē suk′əl) *n.* any of a group of erect or climbing shrubs, often bearing fragrant, bell-shaped flowers.

hon·ied (hun′ēd) a past tense and past participle of **honey.**

honk (hongk) *n.* **1.** the cry of a goose. **2.** any similar sound, especially that made by the horn of an automobile. —*v.i.* to utter or make such a sound. —*v.t.* to cause (something) to make such a sound: *Stop honking the horn!* —**honk′er,** *n.*

hon·or (on′ər) *also, British,* **hon·our.** *n.* **1.** a sense of what is right or moral; integrity: *A person of honor would not lie.* **2.** a good name or reputation; position of being respected; credit: *The leader's honor was at stake.* **3.** a source or cause of respect, esteem, or pride: *It was a great honor to receive the award.* **4.** glory; renown; fame: *They shared in the honor.* **5. Honor.** a title of respect used in speaking or referring to certain officials, such as a judge or mayor, preceded by *His, Her,* or *Your.* **6. honors.** something done or given as a sign of respect, esteem, or distinction: *The hero was buried with full military honors.* **7. honors.** special recognition given to a student by a school or college for outstanding academic achievement: *to graduate with honors.* —*v.t.* **1.** to regard with great respect or esteem: *Honor thy father and thy mother.* **2.** to give honor to; favor. **3.** to accept as valid for payment or credit: *to honor a credit card.*

·**in honor of.** to give honor to; to celebrate or show respect for: *The college was named in honor of its chief benefactor.*

hon·or·a·ble (on′ər ə bəl) *adj.* **1.** characterized by or having a sense of what is right or moral: *an honorable trader.* **2.** bringing honor or distinction; creditable: *an honorable achievement.* **3.** worthy of honor and respect: *an honorable profession.* **4.** having high rank or position; noble; illustrious: *descended from an honorable family.* **5.** done with honor or respect: *The soldier received an honorable discharge.* **6. Honorable.** a title of respect used in speaking of certain government officials, such as members of Congress and cabinet officers, or certain members of the nobility. —**hon′or·a·ble·ness,** *n.* —**hon′or·a·bly,** *adv.*

hon·o·rar·i·um (on′ə rār′ē əm) *n., pl.* **hon·o·rar·i·ums** or **hon·o·rar·i·a** (on′ə rār′ē ə). a fee for services given, especially by a professional person: *The visiting lecturer received an honorarium of $300.*

hon·or·ar·y (on′ə rer′ē) *adj.* **1.** given as an honor: *an honorary degree from a university.* **2.** holding a title or position as an honor without the usual duties or a salary.

honor roll 1. a list of students who have achieved high grades. **2.** a list of local citizens who have served in the armed forces, usually displayed in a public place.

honor system, a system under which a person is trusted to obey rules and carry out responsibilities without being closely watched or directly supervised, used especially in schools and colleges and in certain prisons.

hon·our (on′ər) *British.* another spelling of **honor.**

hood[1] (hůd) *n.* **1.** a covering for the head and back of the neck, often attached to the neckline of a coat, jacket, or other garment. **2.** anything resembling a hood in shape or use, such as the loose skin on the neck of a cobra. **3.** a movable metal covering over the engine of an automobile. **4.** a fold of cloth worn over the back of an academic gown. —*v.t.* to cover or furnish with a hood. [From the Old English word *hōd* meaning "a head-covering, hood[1]."]

hood[2] (hůd) *n. Slang.* hoodlum.

-hood *suffix* **1.** the state, quality, or condition of being: *childhood, motherhood.* **2.** the entire group, class, or body of: *priesthood.*

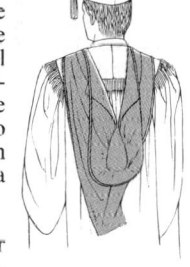

hood[1] *(def. 4)*

hood·ed (hůd′id) *adj.* **1.** having, wearing, or covered with a hood. **2.** shaped like a hood.

hood·lum (hüd′ləm, hůd′ləm) *n. Informal.* **1.** a young ruffian or rowdy. **2.** a gangster; thug.

hood·wink (hůd′wingk′) *v.t.* to trick or deceive.

hoof (hůf, hüf) *n., pl.* **hooves** or **hoofs. 1.** a hard, horny covering on the feet of certain animals, as horses, cattle, pigs, or deer. **2.** the whole foot of such an animal.

·**on the hoof.** (of cattle or other farm animals) not butchered; alive.

hoof·beat (hůf′bēt′, hüf′bēt′) *n.* the sound made by a hoofed animal when it walks, trots, or runs.

hoofed (hůft, hüft) *adj.* having hooves.

hook (hůk) *n.* **1.** a sharply bent piece of

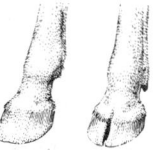

Single-toe hoof / Cloven hoof

---

at; āpe; fär; câre; end; mē; it; īce; pîerce; hot; ōld; sông, fôrk; oil; out; up; ūse; rüle; pull; tûrn; chin; sing; shop; thin; *this*; hw in white; zh in treasure. The symbol ə stands for the unstressed vowel sound heard in about, taken, pencil, lemon, and circus.

metal, wood, or other firm material, having one or more free ends used for catching, hanging, fastening, or holding something: *a coat hook.* **2.** a curved piece of wire with a barb at one end, used for catching fish; fishhook. **3. a.** something like a hook in shape or use. **b.** something designed to attract attention or interest. **4.** a sharp bend or angle in the length or course of something, as in a river. **5.** a projecting point or spit of land. **6.** *Golf.* a stroke in which the ball curves to the left if the golfer is right-handed, to the right if left-handed. **7.** *Boxing.* a short, swinging blow made with the arm bent. **8.** *Baseball.* a pitch that curves. —*v.t.* **1.** to attach, fasten, or hang with a hook or hooks: *The sailor hooked the line to a cleat.* **2.** to catch or take hold of with a hook: *My cousin hooked three trout in the stream.* **3.** to make into the shape of a hook; bend; crook: *I hooked my leg over the arm of the chair.* **4.** to make, as a rug or mat, by pulling yarn or strips of cloth through a piece of fabric by means of a hook. **5.** *Golf.* to hit (a ball) so that it hooks. —*v.i.* **1.** to have the form of a hook; curve. **2.** to be attached, fastened, or hung with a hook or hooks: *The skirt hooks on the side.* —**hook′like′,** *adj.*

·**by hook or by crook.** by any means, fair or foul; in any way possible: *The dishonest politician was determined to win the election by hook or by crook.*

·**on one's own hook.** *Informal.* by oneself; independently: *I got the job on my own hook, without any help from my parents.*

·**to hook up.** to assemble (a mechanical or electrical device) and connect to a source of power: *The electrician hooked up the doorbell.*

hook·ah (húk′ə) *n.* a smoking pipe of Oriental origin, having a long tube attached to a container of water through which the smoke is drawn and cooled.

hook and eye, a clothing fastener consisting of a metallic or plastic hook and a loop or bar to which the hook may be attached.

hooked (húkt) *adj.* **1.** curved or bent like a hook. **2.** having a hook or hooks. **3.** *Informal.* Addicted or devoted to, or fascinated by, something: *hooked on television.*

hooked rug, a rug made by looping yarn or strips of cloth through a piece of fabric, as canvas or burlap.

hook·up (húk′up′) *n.* **1.** the arrangement and connection of electric or electronic parts or circuits, such as a network of television stations. **2.** any arrangement, relationship, or connection of separate or related parts.

hook·worm (húk′wûrm′) *n.* **1.** any of several small, threadlike, parasitic worms that live in the intestines of humans and other animals. They bite into blood vessels and feed on the blood. **2.** a disease that is caused by hookworms. It is characterized by anemia and weakness.

hook·y (húk′ē) *n. Informal.* **to play hooky.** to stay out of school without permission or a good excuse.

hoo·li·gan (hü′li gən) *n.* a ruffian or hoodlum.

hoop (hüp, húp) *n.* **1.** a circular band or ring, as of wood or metal, for holding together the staves of a barrel. **2.** a child's toy consisting of a large circular band of wood, metal, or plastic that can be rolled along the ground or spun around the body. **3.** a flexible, circular band of whalebone or metal, formerly used to make a woman's skirt stand out from her body. —*v.t.* to bind or fasten with a hoop or hoops.

hoop skirt, a woman's skirt worn over a framework of flexible hoops connected by tapes to make the skirt stand out.

hoo·ray (hù rā′) another spelling of **hurrah.**

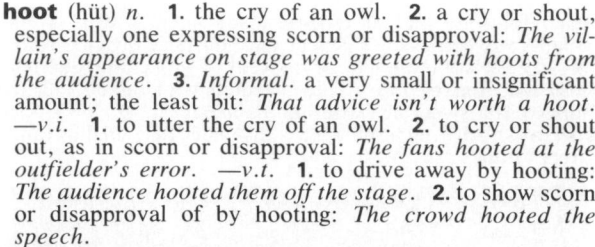

hookah

hoot (hüt) *n.* **1.** the cry of an owl. **2.** a cry or shout, especially one expressing scorn or disapproval: *The villain's appearance on stage was greeted with hoots from the audience.* **3.** *Informal.* a very small or insignificant amount; the least bit: *That advice isn't worth a hoot.* —*v.i.* **1.** to utter the cry of an owl. **2.** to cry or shout out, as in scorn or disapproval: *The fans hooted at the outfielder's error.* —*v.t.* **1.** to drive away by hooting: *The audience hooted them off the stage.* **2.** to show scorn or disapproval of by hooting: *The crowd hooted the speech.*

hoot·en·an·ny (hü′tə nan′ē, hüt′nan′ē) *n., pl.* **hoot·en·an·nies.** a gathering at which folk singers perform, often with the audience participating.

Hoo·ver Dam (hü′vər) a large dam on the Colorado River between Nevada and Arizona, formerly known as **Boulder Dam.**

hooves (hùvz, hüvz) a plural of **hoof.**

hop¹ (hop) *v.,* **hopped, hop·ping.** —*v.i.* **1.** to make a short leap or series of leaps on one foot. **2.** to move in short leaps on both or all feet at once: *The frog hopped along the edge of the pond.* —*v.t.* **1.** to jump over: *The rabbit hopped the fence.* **2.** *Informal.* to board and ride in (a vehicle), especially without paying: *The hobo hopped a freight train going west.* —*n.* **1.** the act of hopping. **2.** *Informal.* a trip, especially in an airplane. **3.** *Informal.* a dance or dancing party. **4.** *Informal.* a bounce or rebound. [From the Old English word *hoppian* meaning "to hop, leap."]

hop² (hop) *n.* **1. hops.** the cone-shaped, greenish yellow flower clusters of any of a group of plants related to hemp, containing bitter-tasting oils and used in the brewing of beer and other malt beverages. **2.** a long-stemmed, climbing plant bearing this fruit. —*v.t.,* **hopped, hop·ping.** to flavor or treat with hops. [From the Middle Dutch word *hoppe* meaning this plant.]

hope (hōp) *v.,* **hoped, hop·ing.** —*v.t.* **1.** to desire with expectation of fulfillment: *We hope your book will be published.* **2.** to wish, believe, or trust: *I hope you will enjoy your vacation.* —*v.i.* to have expectation or desire: *The politician hoped for the support of all the people in the state.* —*n.* **1.** a desire accompanied by expectation of fulfillment: *All the children have hopes of going to college.* **2.** something that is hoped for: *The hope of good weather kept us looking to the sky.* **3.** a person or thing on which hopes are placed or centered.

hope·ful (hōp′fəl) *adj.* **1.** full of or showing hope. **2.** inspiring hope; promising fulfillment: *a hopeful sign.* —*n.* a person who is considered likely to succeed or who desires success: *Many young hopefuls tried out for the play.* —**hope′ful·ly,** *adv.* —**hope′ful·ness,** *n.*

hope·less (hōp′lis) *adj.* **1.** having or feeling no hope: *After losing their jobs they felt hopeless.* **2.** inspiring no hope: *The patient's condition is hopeless.* —**hope′-less·ly,** *adv.* —**hope′less·ness,** *n.*

Ho·pi (hō′pē) *n., pl.* **Ho·pi** or **Ho·pis.** **1.** a member of a tribe of Pueblo Indians living in northeastern Arizona. **2.** the language spoken by the Hopi.

hop·per (hop′ər) *n.* **1.** a person or thing that hops, such as a grasshopper. **2.** a container with a narrow opening at the bottom, used to hold grain, coal, or other material, and to empty it into another container or part.

hop·scotch (hop′skoch′) *n.* a children's game played on a course usually consisting of a pattern of numbered squares drawn on the pavement or ground. The players hop into the squares in sequence and try to pick up a stone or other object that has been tossed into one of the squares.

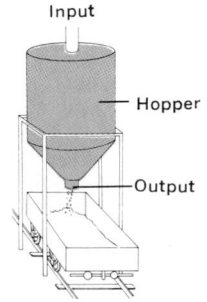

hopper *(def. 2)*

hor. **1.** horizon. **2.** horizontal.

ho·ra (hôr′ə) *also,* **ho·rah.** *n.* a traditional Romanian and Israeli folk dance performed by dancers moving in a circle.

horde (hôrd) *n.* **1.** a large group; swarm; multitude: *A horde of people poured out of the stadium.* **2.** a group of wandering people; nomadic tribe or clan.

hore·hound (hôr′hound′) *also,* **hoar·hound.** *n.* **1.** an aromatic plant related to the mint, having whitish, woolly leaves and stems and bearing clusters of small flowers. **2.** a candy or cough medicine flavored with a bitter extract obtained from the leaves of this plant.

ho·ri·zon (hə rī′zən) *n.* **1.** the line where the sky and the earth or sea seem to meet: *Two ships were barely visible on the horizon.* **2.** the limit or range of knowledge, interest, or experience: *Meeting new people widened my horizons.*

hor·i·zon·tal (hôr′ə zon′təl, hor′ə zon′təl) *adj.* **1.** parallel to level ground; level. **2.** of, relating to, or near the horizon. —*n.* something horizontal, such as a line, plane, or direction. —**hor′i·zon′tal·ly,** *adv.*

hor·mo·nal (hôr mō′nəl) *adj.* of, relating to, or caused by a hormone or hormones: *a hormonal imbalance in the body.*

hor·mone (hôr′mōn) *n.* any of numerous chemical substances formed in the endocrine glands that enter the bloodstream directly and affect the activity of other organs. Hormones regulate body growth, control sexual activity and development, and maintain the body's chemical balance. [From the Greek word *hormōn,* present participle of *horman* meaning "to set in motion, stir up," from the word *hormē* meaning "impulse, assault."]

horn (hôrn) *n.* **1.** a hard, permanent, hollow growth on the head of various hoofed animals, including cattle, sheep, antelope, and rhinoceroses. **2.** one of the antlers of a deer. **3.** a hornlike projection on the head of various other animals, such as the tuft of feathers on a horned owl. **4.** the substance or material of which horn is composed. **5.** a container formed from or shaped like a horn. **6.** *Music.* **a.** any of various brass instruments usually consisting of a coiled metal tube that gradually widens into a flaring bell, especially the French horn. **b.** *Informal.* any wind instrument, especially a trumpet. **c.** any wind instrument resembling or originally made from the horn of an animal. **7.** a device used to sound a warning signal: *The bus driver honked the horn at the children.* **8.** something shaped like a horn, such as a cape or peninsula. **9.** either of the pointed ends of a crescent, as of the moon. —**horn′less,** *adj.* —**horn′like′,** *adj.*

 ·**to horn in.** *Slang.* to enter without being invited; butt in; intrude: *to horn in on a conversation.*

horn·bill (hôrn′bil′) *n.* any of various birds living in forests of Africa, Asia, and the East Indies, usually having a large, colorful bill with a horny growth on top. Hornbills range from 2 to 5 feet (60–150 centimeters) in length.

horn·blende (hôrn′blend′) *n.* a mineral, usually dark green or black, found in granite and various igneous and metamorphic rocks.

horn·book (hôrn′bůk′) *n.* **1.** a primer consisting of a page with the alphabet and a prayer or numerals on it, covered with a sheet of transparent horn and fastened in a frame with a handle. It was formerly used in teaching children to read. **2.** a beginning treatise.

horned (hôrnd) *adj.* having a horn, horns, or hornlike growths: *a horned moon, a horned snail.*

hornbill

horned owl, any of various large owls having hornlike tufts of feathers on the top of the head.

horned toad, an insect-eating lizard common in dry areas of the western United States, having short, spiny horns on the head and fringed scales along the sides of the body. Also, **horned lizard.**

horned toad

hor·net (hôr′nit) *n.* any of various large wasps that live in colonies and are often reddish brown or black with dull markings. Female hornets have stingers and can give a painful sting.

horn of plenty, another term for **cornucopia.**

horn·pipe (hôrn′pīp′) *n.* **1.** a lively British folk dance, usually done by one person, formerly popular among sailors. **2.** the music for such a dance.

horn·y (hôr′nē) *adj.,* **horn·i·er, horn·i·est. 1.** made of horn or of something like it. **2.** having a horn, horns, or hornlike growths. **3.** hard like horn; calloused.

hor·o·scope (hôr′ə skōp′, hor′ə skōp′) *n.* **1.** a prediction about one's personal future, often containing advice, especially for a particular day. It is based on an interpretation of the positions of the planets at a given time. **2.** the relative positions of the planets at any particular moment, especially at the time of a person's birth. **3.** a diagram of the twelve signs of the zodiac with relation to the positions of the planets, used to predict the future.

hor·ren·dous (hô ren′dəs, ho ren′dəs) *adj.* horrible; dreadful; frightful. —**hor·ren′dous·ly,** *adv.*

hor·ri·ble (hôr′ə bəl, hor′ə bəl) *adj.* **1.** causing or tending to cause horror; terrible; dreadful: *The scene of the accident was horrible.* **2.** *Informal.* extremely unpleasant, disagreeable, shocking, or ugly: *a horrible temper.* —**hor′ri·ble·ness,** *n.* —**hor′ri·bly,** *adv.*

hor·rid (hôr′id, hor′id) *adj.* **1.** causing horror; dreadful. **2.** *Informal.* extremely unpleasant, disagreeable, or shocking. —**hor′rid·ly,** *adv.* —**hor′rid·ness,** *n.*

hor·ri·fy (hôr′ə fī′, hor′ə fī′) *v.t.,* **hor·ri·fied, hor·ri·fying. 1.** to cause to feel horror: *The news of the war horrified us.* **2.** *Informal.* to shock greatly and unpleasantly.

hor·ror (hôr′ər, hor′ər) *n.* **1.** a feeling of great fear and dread; terror. **2.** a great dislike; loathing: *to have a horror of snakes.* **3.** the quality of causing horror: *the horror of war.* **4.** a person or thing that causes horror. **5.** *Informal.* something that is very disagreeable, shocking, or ugly: *That blue suit is a horror.*

hors d'oeuvre (ôr dûrv′) *pl.* **hors d'oeuvres** (ôr dûrvz′). a hot or cold appetizer, such as olives, celery, or cheese, that is served before the main courses of a meal. [From the French phrase *hors d'œuvre* meaning "outside of the work," used as the name of this side dish.]

horse (hôrs) *n., pl.* **hors·es. 1.** a four-

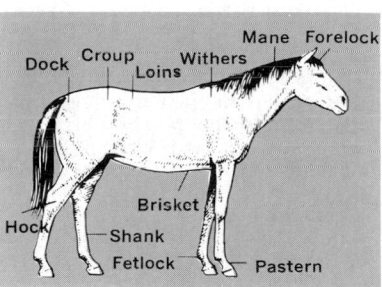
horse *(def. 1)*

Labels: Dock, Croup, Loins, Withers, Mane, Forelock, Brisket, Hock, Shank, Fetlock, Pastern

legged, hoofed animal having a long, flowing mane and tail. Horses are used for pulling and carrying loads and for riding. **2.** a full-grown male horse. **3.** a gymnastic apparatus consisting of a leather-covered block mounted on four legs, used for vaulting and other exercises. **4.** a frame or structure, usually having four legs, used for holding or supporting something. **5.** mounted troops; cavalry. —*v.t.*, **horsed, hors·ing.** to furnish with a horse or horses.

·**to horse around.** *Slang.* to play roughly.

horse·back (hôrs′bak′) *n.* the back of a horse. —*adv.* on a horse: *to ride horseback.*

horse chestnut 1. a large tree widely grown in Europe and the United States, bearing clusters of white flowers. **2.** the nut of this tree, containing one or two large, shiny, brown, poisonous seeds.

horse·flesh (hôrs′flesh′) *n.* **1.** horses as a group: *That trainer is a good judge of horseflesh.* **2.** the flesh of a horse.

horse·fly (hôrs′flī′) *n., pl.* **horse·flies.** a large fly having a stout, hairy, usually black or brown body. The female attacks various animals, including humans, and gives a painful bite.

horse·hair (hôrs′hâr′) *n.* **1.** the hair of a horse, especially from the mane or tail. **2.** a stiff fabric made with this hair, usually in combination with other fibers, used especially for upholstery. —*adj.* made of, covered, or stuffed with horsehair.

horse·hide (hôrs′hīd′) *n.* **1.** the hide of a horse. **2.** the leather made from this hide.

horse latitudes, two regions of high atmospheric pressure and mainly calm, dry weather, extending over the oceans at about 30 degrees north and south of the equator.

horse·laugh (hôrs′laf′) *n.* a loud, coarse, or boisterous laugh.

horse·man (hôrs′mən) *n., pl.* **horse·men** (hôrs′mən). **1.** a man who rides on horseback. **2.** a man skilled in riding or handling horses.

horse·man·ship (hôrs′mən ship′) *n.* the art of riding or handling horses.

horse·play (hôrs′plā′) *n.* rough, boisterous play or fun.

horse·pow·er (hôrs′pou′ər) *n.* a unit for measuring power, or rate of work, as of an engine. One horsepower is equal to 550 foot-pounds per second, or 746 watts.

horse·rad·ish (hôrs′rad′ish) *n.* **1.** an herb in the mustard family, having long leaves, white flowers, and a large white root. **2.** a pungent sauce made from the root of the horseradish.

horse sense *Informal.* plain, practical common sense.

horse·shoe (hôrs′shü′) *n.* **1.** a U-shaped piece of metal curved to fit the shape of a horse's hoof, attached by means of nails driven into the hard, horny outer shell of the hoof. **2.** something shaped like a horseshoe. **3. horseshoes.** a game for two or more players in which the object is to pitch a U-shaped piece so that it encircles a stake, normally placed 40 feet (12.2 meters) away from the pitcher, or lands closest to the stake. ▲ used with a singular verb. —*v.t.* **horse·shoed, horse·shoe·ing.** to provide with horseshoes.

horseshoe crab, a saltwater animal having a horseshoe-shaped shell and a stiff spine.

horse trade *Informal.* a deal or transaction arranged by shrewd bargaining. —**horse′trad′er,** *n.*

horse·whip (hôrs′hwip′, hôrs′wip′) *n.* a whip used for driving or controlling horses. —*v.t.*, **horse·whipped, horse·whip·ping.** to beat with or as if with a horsewhip.

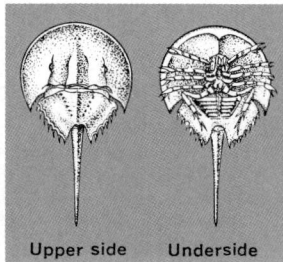

Upper side   **Underside**

horseshoe crab

horse·wom·an (hôrs′wùm′ən) *n., pl.* **horse·wom·en** (hôrs′wim′ən). **1.** a woman who rides on horseback. **2.** a woman who is skilled in the art of riding or handling horses.

hors·y (hôr′sē) *adj.,* **hors·i·er, hors·i·est.** *also,* **hors·ey. 1.** relating to or suggestive of a horse or horses: *a horsy smell.* **2.** interested in or fond of horses or sports involving horses. —**hors′i·ly,** *adv.* —**hors′i·ness,** *n.*

hor·ta·to·ry (hôr′tə tôr′ē) *adj.* serving to urge or encourage.

hor·ti·cul·tur·al (hôr′ti kul′chər əl) *adj.* of or relating to horticulture.

hor·ti·cul·ture (hôr′ti kul′chər) *n.* **1.** the art and science of growing flowers, fruits, vegetables, and ornamental plants. **2.** the growing of a garden.

hor·ti·cul·tur·ist (hôr′ti kul′chər ist) *n.* a specialist in horticulture.

ho·san·na (hō zan′ə) *interj.* praise to God. —*n.* a cry of *hosanna.*

hose (hōz) *n., pl.* **hose** or *(def. 1)* **hos·es. 1.** a flexible tube of rubber, canvas, or other material, used for carrying water or other liquids to a desired point. **2.** stockings or socks. **3.** close-fitting trousers resembling tights, formerly worn by men. —*v.t.*, **hosed, hos·ing.** to spray, wash, or water with a hose.

Ho·se·a (hō zē′ə) *n.* a book of the Old Testament believed to have been written by the Hebrew prophet Hosea.

ho·sier·y (hō′zhə rē) *n.* stockings and socks.

hos·pice (hos′pis) *n.* **1.** a place of lodging for pilgrims or other travelers, especially one maintained by a religious order. **2.** an organization or facility that provides medical care and emotional support to people who are dying and to their families. [From the French word *hospice* meaning "place of lodging for travelers," from the Latin word *hospitium* "lodging, hospitality," from the word *hospes* "host" or "guest."]

hos·pi·ta·ble (hos′pi tə bəl, ho spit′ə bəl) *adj.* **1.** characterized by or giving a friendly and generous welcome to guests or to strangers: *The hotel staff was very hospitable. The hospitable families opened their homes to visiting foreign students.* **2.** receptive or open in mind or outlook: *The committee members were hospitable to my plan.* —**hos′pi·ta·bly,** *adv.*

hos·pi·tal (hos′pi təl) *n.* a place giving medical, surgical, or psychiatric treatment to the sick or injured.

hos·pi·tal·i·ty (hos′pi tal′i tē) *n., pl.* **hos·pi·tal·i·ties.** the act, practice, or quality of being hospitable.

hos·pi·tal·i·za·tion (hos′pi tə lə zā′shən) *n.* **1.** the act of hospitalizing or the state of being hospitalized: *The doctor insisted on the immediate hospitalization of the sick patient.* **2.** the period of time during which a person is hospitalized. **3.** a form of insurance providing part or total payment of a patient's hospital expenses.

hos·pi·tal·ize (hos′pi tə līz′) *v.t.,* **hos·pi·tal·ized, hos·pi·tal·iz·ing.** to put in a hospital as a patient: *The skier was hospitalized with a broken leg.*

host¹ (hōst) *n.* **1.** someone who receives or entertains others, usually as guests in the home. **2.** the keeper of an inn or hotel. **3.** a living plant or animal in or upon which a parasite lives and gets nourishment. —*v.t.* to be or serve as host for: *to host a birthday party for a friend.* [From the Old French word *hoste* meaning "one giving hospitality," from the Latin word *hospes* meaning both "host¹" and "guest."]

host² (hōst) *n.* a large number; multitude: *On a clear night you can see a host of stars.* [From the Old French word *hoste* meaning "army, assembly," from the Late Latin word *hostis* "army," from the Latin word *hostis* "outsider, enemy."]

host³ (hōst) *also,* **Host.** *n.* a wafer of unleavened bread used for Holy Communion in the Roman Catholic Church and certain other churches. [From the Middle English word *hoste* meaning "a sacrificial offering" and "communion wafer,'' from the Latin word *hostia* ''sacrificial offering.'']

hos·tage (hos′tij) *n.* a person held or given as security that certain promises or conditions will be fulfilled: *The general was held as a hostage by the enemy until the peace treaty was signed.*

hos·tel (hos′təl) *n.* a lodging place, especially a supervised lodging place for young people on hiking or bicycling trips.

hos·tel·ry (hos′təl rē) *n., pl.* **hos·tel·ries.** an inn or hotel.

host·ess (hōs′tis) *n., pl.* **host·ess·es. 1.** a woman who receives or entertains others, usually as guests in her own home. **2.** a woman employed, as by a restaurant or nightclub, to greet and assist customers. **3.** a stewardess. **4.** a woman who keeps an inn or hotel.

hos·tile (hos′təl) *adj.* **1.** feeling or showing hatred or dislike: *The speaker was shouted down by the hostile crowd.* **2.** of or belonging to an enemy: *The battalion encountered hostile forces.* —**hos′tile·ly,** *adv.*

hos·til·i·ty (ho stil′i tē) *n., pl.* **hos·til·i·ties. 1.** the state of being hostile; antagonism. **2.** a hostile act. **3. hostilities.** acts of war; warfare; war: *The hostilities ended when the truce was signed.*

hos·tler (hos′lər, os′lər) *also,* **os·tler.** *n.* a person who takes care of horses at an inn or stable.

hot (hot) *adj.,* **hot·ter, hot·test. 1.** having a high temperature; having much warmth or heat: *It was surprisingly hot for an autumn day.* **2.** feeling warmth or heat: *I was hot after playing basketball.* **3.** having a burning or spicy taste; pungent; sharp: *Some Mexican food is very hot.* **4.** having or carrying an electrical current or charge, especially one of high voltage: *a hot wire.* **5.** characterized by or showing anger; angry: *The candidates exchanged hot words over the issue.* **6.** very active; violent; raging: *a hot battle.* **7.** following very closely; close behind: *The police were hot on the heels of the robber.* **8.** in hunting, strong or fresh: *The trail of the fox was hot.* **9.** *Informal.* in demand; popular: *Skis are a hot item during the winter.* **10.** *Slang.* recently stolen or illegally gotten: *The thief tried to sell the hot jewelry.* **11.** radioactive: *Some of the wreckage was still hot many years after the nuclear explosion.* —*adv.* in a hot manner. —**hot′ly,** *adv.* —**hot′ness,** *n.*

hot air *Slang.* empty or boastful talk or writing.

hot·bed (hot′bed′) *n.* **1.** a bed of earth protected by a frame of glass, used for growing plants. The soil is heated by decaying manure or by electricity, steam, or hot water pipes. **2.** a place where anything grows or develops rapidly, especially something bad: *The investigation of the police department exposed a hotbed of crime.*

hot–blood·ed (hot′blud′id) *adj.* very excitable; passionate; impulsive; rash.

hot cake, a pancake; griddlecake.
  ·**to go like hot cakes** or **to sell like hot cakes.** *Informal.* to be sold quickly and in great quantity.

hot cross bun, a sweet bun containing small bits of dried fruit, such as raisins, and marked with a cross made of icing, traditionally eaten during Lent.

hot dog *Informal.* another term for **frankfurter.**

ho·tel (hō tel′) *n.* a place that rents rooms to travelers and usually provides a restaurant and other services.

hot·foot (hot′fŭt′) *v.i.* to go very quickly; hurry. —*adv.* in great haste.

hot·head (hot′hed′) *n.* a hotheaded person.

hot·head·ed (hot′hed′id) *adj.* **1.** easily angered. **2.** reckless; rash: *a hotheaded decision.* —**hot′head·ed·ly,** *adv.* —**hot′head·ed·ness,** *n.*

hot·house (hot′hous′) *n., pl.* **hot·hous·es** (hot′hou′ziz). a heated building, made mainly of glass, where plants are grown; greenhouse. —*adj.* grown in a hothouse: *hothouse flowers.*

hot line *also,* **hot·line** (hot′līn′). **1.** a direct telephone link kept ready for use in a crisis or emergency, as by the heads of two governments. **2.** a telephone service established to provide callers with immediate and confidential counseling or assistance for a particular problem: *a drug abuse hot line, a hot line for runaways.*

hot plate, a small electrical device usually consisting of one or two burners, used for cooking or heating food.

hot rod *Slang.* an automobile, especially an older car rebuilt for high speeds.

hot seat *Informal.* an uncomfortable or unpleasant position or situation: *I was in the hot seat when asked to read my book report aloud, because I hadn't finished it yet.*

hot shot (hot′shot′) *n. Slang.* a person who is skilled and successful in something, often one who shows conceit about it: *The playground was filled with hot shots showing off on their skateboards.*

hot spring, a natural spring that produces hot water, especially one whose water temperature is greater than 98 degrees Fahrenheit (37 degrees Celsius).

hot-tem·pered (hot′tem′pərd) *adj.* easily angered; hotheaded; short-tempered.

Hot·ten·tot (hot′ən tot′) *n., pl.* **Hot·ten·tot** or **Hot·ten·tots. 1.** a member of a southern African people. **2.** the language of the Hottentots. —*adj.* of or relating to the Hottentot or their language.

hot water *Informal.* a state of difficulty; trouble.

hound (hound) *n.* **1.** any of various dogs that were originally bred and trained to hunt, such as the beagle and bloodhound. **2.** any dog. —*v.t.* **1.** to chase or pursue without stopping: *The police hounded the thief.* **2.** *Informal.* to urge persistently; nag; pester: *Don't hound me about borrowing my bicycle.*

hour (our) *n.* **1.** a unit of time equal to ¹⁄₂₄ of a day; sixty minutes. **2.** one of the twelve points on a clock or watch indicating such a unit of time. **3.** a definite time of day as indicated by a clock or watch: *At what hour should we leave?* **4.** a particular time for some activity: *the dinner hour.* **5.** an indefinite period of time: *You helped us in our hour of need.* **6. hours.** a fixed time devoted to one's work or other regular activity: *The doctor has office hours four days a week.* **7. a.** the amount of distance that can be traveled in an hour: *We were an hour from home.* **b.** the amount of work that can be done in an hour: *We were an hour from finishing the job.* **8.** in colleges and universities, a unit of academic credit, one of which is usually given for each class hour per week.

hour·glass (our′glas′) *n., pl.* **hour·glass·es.** a device for measuring time, consisting of a glass container with a narrow passage in the middle through which a quantity of sand or mercury runs from the upper to the lower part in exactly one hour.

hour hand, the short hand on a clock or watch, indicating the hour.

hour·ly (our′lē) *adj.* **1.** done, occurring, or counted every hour: *hourly airplane departures.* **2.** done in the course of or computed on the basis of an hour: *hourly wages.* —*adv.* every hour: *The nurse looked in on me hourly.*

hourglass

house (*n.,* hous; *v.,* houz) *n., pl.* **hous·es** (hou′ziz). **1.** a building or part of a building in which people live. **2.** people, especially a

H

467

family, living in a house; household. **3.** a building used for a particular purpose: *a movie house.* **4.** an audience, as in a theater. **5.** *also,* **House.** a legislative or deliberative body: *Both houses of Congress passed the bill.* **6.** *also,* **House.** a royal or noble family: *Queen Elizabeth II of England is a member of the House of Windsor.* **7.** a place occupied by a business, or the business itself: *a publishing house.* —*v.t.,* **housed, hous·ing. 1.** to provide with a house; shelter; lodge: *to house refugees in tents.* **2.** to store or keep in a house or building: *The art collection was housed in the museum.*
  ·**on the house.** at the expense of the owner; free.
  ·**to clean house. a.** to clean a house or put it in order. **b.** to remove people or things that are undesirable.
  ·**to keep house.** to manage and take care of a house.
house·boat (hous′bōt′) *n.* a boat or barge that is fitted out as a place to live.

houseboats

house·break (hous′brāk′) *v.t.,* **house·broke, house·bro·ken, house·break·ing.** to make (a pet) housebroken.
house·break·ing (hous′brā′king) *n.* the act of breaking into and entering a house with intent to steal or commit some other crime. —**house′break′er,** *n.*
house·bro·ken (hous′brō′kən) *adj.* (of a pet) trained not to excrete indoors.
house·coat (hous′kōt′) *n.*—a robe or similar garment worn at home.
house·fly (hous′flī′) *n., pl.* **house·flies.** a fly that lives in and around houses, feeding on food and garbage. It is found in almost all parts of the world. It may carry many disease-producing germs.
house·hold (hous′hōld′) *n.* **1.** all the people who live in a house. **2.** the members of a royal or noble family and their attendants. —*adj.* **1.** of or relating to a household; domestic: *household chores.* **2.** familiar; common: *The actor's name became a household word.*
house·hold·er (hous′hōl′dər) *n.* **1.** a person who owns or lives in a house. **2.** the head of a family.
house·keep·er (hous′kē′pər) *n.* a person hired to manage the affairs of a household.
house·keep·ing (hous′kē′ping) *n.* the maintenance of a household and the managing of its affairs.
house·maid (hous′mād′) *n.* a woman hired to do housework.
house·moth·er (hous′muth′ər) *n.* a woman who supervises a group of young people living together, as in a dormitory.
House of Burgesses, the popularly elected lower house of the legislature in colonial Virginia or Maryland.
House of Commons, the lower, elective house of either the British or Canadian Parliament. Also, **Commons.**
house of correction, a place for the confinement and rehabilitation of persons convicted of minor offenses.

House of Lords, the upper house of the British Parliament, composed of the nobility and high-ranking clergy.
House of Representatives, the lower house of the U.S. Congress and of many state legislatures, in which representation is based on population.
house·plant (hous′plant′) *n.* any plant grown indoors.
house sparrow, a songbird found throughout warm and temperate regions of the world, having dull gray-and-brown feathers with black-and-white markings. Also, **English sparrow.**
house·top (hous′top′) *n.* the roof or top of a house.
house·warm·ing (hous′wôr′ming) *n.* a party given when people move into a house.
house·wife (hous′wīf′) *n., pl.* **house·wives** (hous′-wīvz′). a woman, especially a married woman, who manages a home and its affairs.
house·work (hous′wûrk′) *n.* work done in housekeeping, such as washing, ironing, cleaning, and cooking.
hous·ing (hou′zing) *n.* **1.** houses as a group: *The city built new housing for poor families.* **2.** the act of sheltering or of providing houses. **3.** any shelter or covering. **4.** a frame, plate, or casing that supports, secures, or contains a machine or part of a machine. [From the Middle English word *housinge* meaning "buildings, property" and "shelter," from *housen* "to house," going back to the Old English word *hūs* "a house."]
hove (hōv) a past tense and past participle of **heave.**
hov·el (huv′əl, hov′əl) *n.* **1.** a small, very poor house or shack; hut. **2.** an open shed, as for sheltering cattle or tools.
hov·er (huv′ər, hov′ər) *v.i.* **1.** to remain suspended in the air over or around a particular spot: *The bird hovered over its nest.* **2.** to linger or remain nearby: *to hover over a sick child.* **3.** to continue in an indeterminate state; waver: *to hover between tears and laughter.*
hov·er·craft (huv′ər kraft′, hov′ər kraft′) *n.* a vehicle that can travel over land or water on a thin cushion of high-pressure air created beneath the craft by means of fans or rotors. Trademark: **Hovercraft.**
how (hou) *adv.* **1.** in what manner or way; by what means: *How do you plan to get home?* **2.** to what degree, amount, or extent: *How hot is it today? How did you like the movie?* **3.** in what state or condition: *How are you today?* **4.** for what reason or purpose; why: *How did they happen to be there?* **5.** with what meaning; to what effect: *How did you interpret that last statement?*
  ·**how about.** what do you think of; would you like: *How about coming to the party with us?*
  ·**how come.** *Informal.* how does it happen that: *How come you weren't in school yesterday?*
how·be·it (hou bē′it) *adv.* however it may be; nevertheless. ▲ used in literature.
how·dah (hou′də) *n.* a seat, usually with a railing and canopy, used for riding on the back of an elephant or camel.
how·dy (hou′dē) *interj.; n., pl.* **how·dies.** *Informal.* hello.
how·ev·er (hou ev′ər) *conj.* nevertheless; yet; notwithstanding: *We both passed the test; however, some other students failed.* —*adv.* **1.** in whatever way; by whatever means: *You may do the job however you like.* **2.** to whatever degree or extent: *However far our dog wanders, it always comes home.*
how·itz·er (hou′it sər) *n.* a cannon of medium length, used to fire shells at high angles of elevation.

howdah

howl (houl) *v.i.* **1.** to make a loud, wailing cry as that of a dog or wolf: *The dog howled at night. The wind howled.* **2.** to utter a similar loud cry: *I howled when I stubbed*

my toe. The joke made us howl with laughter. —v.t.
1. to utter or express with howling. **2.** to force or drive by howling: *The audience howled the actor off the stage.* —*n.* **1.** a loud, wailing cry, as that of a dog or wolf. **2.** any howling sound.

how·so·ev·er (hou′sō ev′ər) *adv.* **1.** in whatever way; by whatever means. **2.** to whatever degree or extent.

hoy·den (hoi′dən) *n.* a boisterous, ill-mannered, or saucy girl or woman. —**hoy′den·ish,** *adj.*

hp, horsepower.

HQ, hq, headquarters.

hr., hour.

H.R., House of Representatives.

H.R.H., His (or Her) Royal Highness.

H.S., High School.

ht., height.

hub (hub) *n.* **1.** the central part of a wheel, into which the axle is inserted. **2.** a central point of interest, importance, or activity.

hub·bub (hub′ub) *n.* a loud, confused noise, as of many voices or sounds; uproar.

hub·cap (hub′kap′) *n.* a removable metal disk covering the hub of a wheel.

huck·le·ber·ry (huk′əl ber′ē) *n., pl.* **huck·le·ber·ries.**
1. a small, shiny, blue or black berry resembling the blueberry but darker in color and having hard seeds. **2.** the low shrub bearing this fruit, growing wild in North and South America and bearing drooping clusters of tiny reddish flowers.

huck·ster (huk′stər) *n.* **1.** a person who sells small articles, especially a peddler. **2.** a person who does business in a mean, petty, or unscrupulous way.

hud·dle (hud′əl) *v.,* **hud·dled, hud·dling.** —*v.i.* **1.** to crowd or nestle, as from cold or fear: *The children huddled together around the campfire.* **2.** to draw oneself together; hunch: *The cold wind made me huddle inside my coat.* **3.** *Football.* to gather behind the line of scrimmage before a play in order to receive signals. **4.** *Informal.* to meet privately in order to consult or confer: *The judges huddled before announcing the winner.* —*v.t.* to drive or crowd together closely. —*n.* **1.** a group of persons or things crowded or clustered together. **2.** *Football.* a gathering of players behind the line of scrimmage before a play in order to receive signals. **3.** *Informal.* a small, private meeting or conference: *The mayor's advisers went into a huddle.*

hue¹ (hū) *n.* one part of the spectrum; a color or shade. [From the Old English word *hiw* meaning "shape, form, kind."]

hue² (hū) *n.* **hue and cry.** a public stir or outcry, as of alarm or opposition: *The newspaper raised a great hue and cry when the scandal was disclosed.* [From the Old French word *heu* meaning "the sound of a trumpet" or "an outcry," probably a representation of the sound of this cry.]

huff (huf) *n.* a sudden, temporary feeling of anger or indignation: *Don't walk off in a huff just because of a joke.* —*v.i.* to puff; blow: *I huffed and puffed and blew out the candles.* —*v.t.* to make angry; offend.

huff·y (huf′ē) *adj.,* **huff·i·er, huff·i·est.** **1.** easily offended; touchy. **2.** offended; sulking. —**huff′i·ly,** *adv.* —**huff′i·ness,** *n.*

hug (hug) *v.t.,* **hugged, hug·ging.** **1.** to clasp the arms around and hold close, especially in affection; embrace closely. **2.** to grasp and squeeze tightly with the arms, as a bear does. **3.** to keep close to: *The bicyclist hugged the curb.* —*n.* a strong clasp with the arms, especially as a sign of affection; embrace.

huge (hūj) *adj.,* **hug·er, hug·est.** of great size, extent, or degree; extremely large. —**huge′ly,** *adv.* —**huge′ness,** *n.*

Hu·gue·not (hū′gə not′) *n.* a French Protestant of the sixteenth or seventeenth century.

huh (hu) *interj.* used to express surprise, contempt, doubt, or lack of understanding.

hu·la (hü′lə) *n.* a traditional Hawaiian dance in which movements of the dancers' arms and hands are used to relate a story. Also, **hu·la-hu·la** (hü′lə hü′lə).

hulk (hulk) *n.* **1.** a large, clumsy person or thing. **2.** the body of an old, wrecked or dismantled ship. **3.** the shell of something that has been abandoned, wrecked, or gutted: *Only the hulk of the building remained after the explosion.* **4.** a ship used for a prison, storehouse, or similar purpose other than sailing.

hulk·ing (hul′king) *adj.* huge and clumsy; bulky.

hull (hul) *n.* **1.** the outer covering of a seed, as of a nut or grain of rice. **2.** the small leaves at the base of the stem of certain fruits, such as strawberries or raspberries. **3.** any outer covering. **4.** the frame or body of a ship, not including the masts, sails, yards, and rigging. —*v.t.* to remove the hull of: *to hull peanuts.* —**hull′er,** *n.*

hul·la·ba·loo (hul′ə bə lü′) *n., pl.* **hul·la·ba·loos.** a great noise, excitement, or confusion; uproar.

hum (hum) *v.,* **hummed, hum·ming.** —*v.i.* **1.** to make a low, continuous, murmuring sound: *Bumblebees hummed in the garden.* **2.** to sing with closed lips, without saying words. **3.** *Informal.* to be in a condition of busy activity: *Things were really humming on election night.* —*v.t.* to sing (something) with closed lips, without saying words: *to hum a tune.* —*n.* **1.** a low, continuous, murmuring sound: *the hum of machinery.* **2.** a singing with closed lips, without saying words.

hu·man (hū′mən, ū′mən) *adj.* **1.** of or relating to human beings or humanity: *the human body, human life.* **2.** having or showing the qualities characteristic of human beings: *human nature, human weaknesses.* **3.** consisting of human beings: *The police formed a human wall around the building.* —*n.* see **human being.** —**hu′man·ness,** *n.*

human being, a member of the human race; person; man, woman, or child.

hu·mane (hū mān′, ū mān′) *adj.* having or showing sympathy and compassion; kind; merciful: *the fight for humane treatment of the mentally retarded.* —**hu·mane′ly,** *adv.* —**hu·mane′ness,** *n.*

hu·man·ism (hū′mə niz′əm, ū′mə niz′əm) *n.* any system of thought or action concerned with human interests, needs, values, and ideals.

hu·man·ist (hū′mə nist, ū′mə nist) *n.* **1.** a follower or student of any philosophy concerned primarily with human interests, needs, values, and ideals. **2.** a student of the humanities, especially a classical scholar.

hu·man·i·tar·i·an (hū man′i târ′ē ən, ū man′i târ′ē ən) *adj.* concerned with or promoting the general welfare of humanity. —*n.* a person who devotes himself or herself to the welfare of humanity.

hu·man·i·tar·i·an·ism (hū man′i târ′ē ə niz′əm, ū man′i târ′ē ə niz′əm) *n.* humane or humanitarian principles or action.

hu·man·i·ty (hū man′i tē, ū man′i tē) *n., pl.* **hu·man·i·ties.** **1.** human beings as a group; the human race; mankind. **2.** the quality or condition of being human; human character or nature. **3.** the quality of being humane; kindness; benevolence. **4. the humanities.** the branch of learning concerned with human culture, including languages, literature, philosophy, and art.

---

at; āpe; fär; câre; end; mē; it; īce; pîerce; hot; ōld; sông, fôrk; oil; out; up; ūse; rüle; pull; tûrn; chin; sing; shop; thin; this; hw in white; zh in treasure. The symbol ə stands for the unstressed vowel sound heard in about, taken, pencil, lemon, and circus.

H

hu·man·ize (hū′mə nīz′, ū′mə nīz′) *v.t.*, **hu·man·ized, hu·man·iz·ing.** **1.** to give or attribute a human character to; make human. **2.** to cause to be kind, merciful, or benevolent; make humane. —**hu′man·i·za′tion,** *n.*

hu·man·kind (hū′mən kīnd′, ū′mən kīnd′) *n.* the human race; humanity; mankind.

hu·man·ly (hū′mən lē, ū′mən lē) *adv.* **1.** within human ability or power; by human means: *It isn't humanly possible to run that far in two minutes.* **2.** in accordance with human nature; in a human manner: *to act humanly.*

hu·man·oid (hū′mə noid′, ū′mə noid′) *adj.* having human form or character; looking or behaving like a human. —*n.* a humanoid being: *The cover of the science fiction magazine pictured humanoids from other galaxies.*

hum·ble (hum′bəl) *adj.,* **hum·bler, hum·blest.** **1.** having or showing a modest estimate or opinion of one's importance or worth; not proud. **2.** low in position, station, or condition; not pretentious: *a humble house.* —*v.t.,* **hum·bled, hum·bling.** **1.** to make humble in spirit; humiliate. **2.** to make lower in position, station, or condition. —**hum′ble·ness,** *n.* —**hum′bly,** *adv.*

hum·bug (hum′bug′) *n.* **1.** foolish or empty talk; nonsense. **2.** something intended to deceive or trick; hoax; sham. **3.** a person who tries to deceive or trick others; impostor; fraud. —*v.t.,* **hum·bugged, hum·bug·ging.** to deceive or trick; cheat.

hum·drum (hum′drum′) *adj.* lacking variety or excitement; monotonous; dull: *humdrum routine.*

hu·mer·us (hū′mər əs) *n., pl.* **hu·mer·i** (hū′mə rī′). the long bone in the upper arm or forelimb, extending from the shoulder to the elbow.

hu·mid (hū′mid, ū′mid) *adj.* containing or characterized by the presence of much water vapor; moist; damp: *a hot and humid summer day.*

hu·mid·i·fy (hū mid′ə fī′, ū mid′ə fī′) *v.t.,* **hu·mid·i·fied, hu·mid·i·fy·ing.** to make more humid or moist, as the air in a room. —**hu·mid′i·fi′er,** *n.*

hu·mid·i·ty (hū mid′i tē, ū mid′i tē) *n.* **1.** moistness or dampness, especially of the atmosphere. **2.** *Meteorology.* the ratio, expressed as a percentage, of the amount of water vapor present in the air to the maximum amount the air could hold at the same temperature; relative humidity.

hu·mi·dor (hū′mi dôr′, ū′mi dôr′) *n.* a container or storage room for cigars or other tobacco products, containing a device that keeps the air and tobacco moist.

hu·mil·i·ate (hū mil′ē āt′, ū mil′ē āt′) *v.t.,* **hu·mil·i·at·ed, hu·mil·i·at·ing.** to lower the pride or dignity of; cause to seem foolish or worthless: *humiliated by failure.*

hu·mil·i·a·tion (hū mil′ē ā′shən, ū mil′ē ā′shən) *n.* **1.** a feeling of shame or extreme embarrassment. **2.** the act of humiliating or the state of being humiliated.

hu·mil·i·ty (hū mil′i tē, ū mil′i tē) *n.* the quality of being humble; lack of pride or arrogance.

hum·ming·bird (hum′ing bûrd′) *n.* any of various small, brightly colored American birds having a slender, pointed bill and narrow wings that beat very rapidly. It is capable of flying sideways and backwards. [From the *humming* sound made by this bird's rapidly moving wings.]

hum·mock (hum′ək) *n.* **1.** a low mound of earth or rock; knoll. **2.** a bump or ridge on an ice field. —**hum′mock·y,** *adj.*

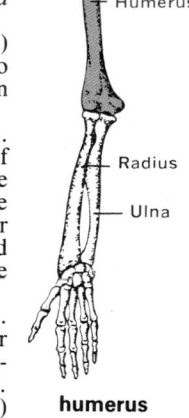

humerus

hummingbird

hu·mong·ous (hū mong′gəs, ū mong′gəs) *adj. Slang.* extremely large; enormous; gigantic; huge.

hu·mor (hū′mər, ū′mər) *also, British,* **hu·mour.** *n.* **1.** the quality of something that makes it amusing or funny. **2. sense of humor.** the ability to appreciate or express what is amusing or funny. **3.** speech, writing, or action that is amusing or funny: *a writer well known for humor.* **4.** a temporary state of mind; mood: *The thought of a vacation put me in a good humor.* —*v.t.* to give in to the moods, wishes, or whims of (someone); indulge: *to humor someone by listening to a story again.* [From the Old French word *humor* meaning ''one of the fluids that determine a person's health and temperament,'' from the Latin word *umor* ''liquid, fluid.'' In former times, the body was thought to consist of four *humors,* whose mixture would determine a person's health and character.]

hu·mor·ist (hū′mər ist, ū′mər ist) *n.* **1.** a professional writer or performer of humorous material. **2.** a person with a good sense of humor.

hu·mor·less (hū′mər lis, ū′mər lis) *adj.* without a sense of humor or humorous qualities. —**hu′mor·less·ness,** *n.*

hu·mor·ous (hū′mər əs, ū′mər əs) *adj.* characterized by or full of humor; funny; comical: *a humorous writer, a humorous situation.* —**hu′mor·ous·ly,** *adv.* —**hu′mor·ous·ness,** *n.*

hump (hump) *n.* **1.** a rounded lump, as on the back of a camel. **2.** a hillock; mound. —*v.t.* to bend or arch so as to form a hump.

hump·back (hump′bak′) *n.* a hunchback. —**hump′-backed′,** *adj.*

humph (humf) *interj.* a word used to express contempt, dissatisfaction, or doubt.

hu·mus (hū′məs, ū′məs) *n.* a dark substance in the soil, consisting of decayed animal or vegetable matter and containing nitrogen and other plant nutrients.

Hun (hun) *n.* **1.** a member of a wandering Asian people who invaded Europe in the fourth and fifth centuries A.D., and helped to destroy the Roman Empire. **2.** a barbarous, willfully destructive person.

hunch (hunch) *v.t.* to draw up, raise, or bend: *The cold air made me hunch my shoulders.* —*vi.* to assume a bent, stooped, or crouched posture. —*n., pl.* **hunch·es.** **1.** *Informal.* a guess or feeling. **2.** a rounded lump; hump.

hunch·back (hunch′bak′) *n.* **1.** a person who has a hump on the back caused by a curving of the spine. **2.** a back having such a hump. —**hunch′backed′,** *adj.*

hun·dred (hun′drid) *n., pl.* **hun·dreds** or **hun·dred.** **1.** the cardinal number that is ten times ten. **2.** a symbol representing this number, such as 100 or C. —*adj.* numbering ten times ten.

hun·dredth (hun′dridth) *adj.* **1.** (the ordinal of hundred) next after the ninety-ninth. **2.** being one of a hundred equal parts. —*n.* **1.** something that is next after the ninety-ninth. **2.** one of a hundred equal parts; 1/100.

hun·dred·weight (hun′drid wāt′) *n., pl.* **hun·dred·weight** or **hun·dred·weights.** a unit of weight equal to 100 pounds avoirdupois (45.36 kilograms) in the United States.

hung (hung) a past tense and past participle of **hang.**

Hun·gar·i·an (hung gâr′ē ən) *n.* **1.** a person who was born in or is a citizen of Hungary. **2.** the language of the Hungarians. Also (*def. 2*), **Magyar.** —*adj.* of or relating to Hungary, its people, their language, or culture.

hun·ger (hung′gər) *n.* **1.** discomfort, pain, or weakness caused by lack of food. **2.** a desire or craving for food: *The banana satisfied my hunger for fruit.* **3.** any strong desire or craving: *a hunger for praise.* —*v.i.* to have or feel a need or desire for food. **2.** to have a strong desire or craving: *That child hungers for affection.*

hunger strike, a refusal to eat, as by a prisoner or political leader, in order to protest something or to attain certain goals.

470

hung jury, a jury so divided in opinion that it is unlikely ever to agree on a verdict and is therefore dismissed by the judge.

hun·gry (hung′grē) *adj.,* **hun·gri·er, hun·gri·est. 1.** desiring or needing food. **2.** caused by or suggestive of a lack of or desire for food: *The dog has a hungry look.* **3.** having a strong desire or craving; eager; longing: *hungry for companionship.* —**hun′gri·ly,** *adv.* —**hun′gri·ness,** *n.*

hunk (hungk) *n. Informal.* a large lump or piece; chunk: *The keeper fed the lion a hunk of meat.*

hunt (hunt) *v.t.* **1.** to chase (game) for the purpose of killing or catching. **2.** to try to get or find; search for: *to hunt for a book in the library.* **3.** to search (a place) carefully and thoroughly: *to hunt the prairie for buffalo, to hunt the woods for an escaped prisoner.* —*v.i.* **1.** to chase game for the purpose of killing or catching. **2.** to look for; seek: *to hunt for buried treasure.* **3.** to search thoroughly or carefully: *I hunted through my pockets for some change.* —*n.* **1.** the act or instance of hunting game. **2.** a group of persons hunting game together. **3.** the act or instance of looking for something; search.

hunt·er (hun′tər) *n.* **1.** a person who hunts game. **2.** a person who searches for something. **3.** a horse or dog used in hunting.

hunt·ing (hun′ting) *n.* the act or sport of chasing game for the purpose of killing or catching.

hunt·ress (hun′tris) *n., pl.* **hunt·ress·es.** a female hunter.

hunts·man (hunts′mən) *n., pl.* **hunts·men** (hunts′-mən). **1.** a person who hunts game; hunter. **2.** a person who manages a hunt, especially a fox hunt.

hur·dle (hûr′dəl) *n.* **1.** an obstacle over which a runner

hurdle *(n., def. 1)*

must leap in certain track events. **2. hurdles.** a race in which the contestants must leap over hurdles while running. **3.** an obstacle, difficulty, or problem: *Getting a college education was a hurdle.* **4.** a movable frame made of sticks or narrow boards, used as a temporary fence or pen. —*v.t.,* **hur·dled, hur·dling. 1.** to jump over (a hurdle or similar obstacle) in a race. **2.** to overcome or surmount (an obstacle or difficulty). —**hur′dler,** *n.*

hur·dy–gur·dy (hûr′dē gûr′dē) *n., pl.* **hur·dy-gur·dies.** any of various mechanical musical instruments played by turning a handle or crank.

hurl (hûrl) *v.t.* **1.** to throw with violence or force; fling: *to hurl a rock through the window.* **2.** to utter or emit with vehemence: *The crowd hurled insults at the speaker.* —*n.* the action of throwing forcefully or violently. —**hurl′er,** *n.*

hurl·y–burl·y (hûr′lē bûr′lē) *n., pl.* **hurl·y-burl·ies.** noisy disorder; tumult; turmoil.

Hu·ron (hyùr′ən) *n.* **1.** *pl.* **Huron** or **Hurons.** a member of a tribe of North American Indians, formerly living east of Lake Huron, now living in Oklahoma and Quebec. **2.** the language of this tribe.

hur·rah (hə rä′) *interj.* used to express joy, triumph, praise, or encouragement. —*n.* a shout of joy, triumph, praise, or encouragement. —*v.i.* to shout hurrah; cheer. Also, **hoo·ray** (hə rä′), **huzzah.**

hur·ri·cane (hûr′i kān′, hur′i kān′) *n.* **1.** a storm of tropical origin with violent winds of 75 miles per hour (120 kilometers per hour) or more. The winds spin around a calm center and are accompanied by heavy rain, high tides, and flooding in coastal regions. **2.** something resembling a hurricane in force or speed; violent outburst: *a hurricane of emotion.*

hur·ried (hûr′ēd, hur′ēd) *adj.* done, made, or carried on quickly or too quickly: *a hurried glance, a hurried letter full of spelling mistakes.* —**hur′ried·ly,** *adv.* —**hur′ried·ness,** *n.*

hur·ry (hûr′ē, hur′ē) *v.,* **hur·ried, hur·ry·ing.** —*v.i.* to move or act with speed; go faster than is easy or natural: *Because we were late we had to hurry. If we don't hurry, we'll miss the train.* —*v.t.* **1.** to cause or urge to act, move, or go with greater speed: *We hurried the children along.* **2.** to cause or urge to act, move, or go too quickly; rush: *The judge would not be hurried into making a decision.* —*n.* **1.** the act of hurrying. **2.** the state or condition of wanting or needing to act, move, or go with greater speed: *I was in a hurry.*

hurt (hûrt) *v.,* **hurt, hurt·ing.** —*v.t.* **1.** to cause physical pain or injury to: *I slipped and hurt my back.* **2.** to do harm to; damage: *The scandal hurt the mayor's reputation.* **3.** to cause mental pain or suffering to; injure the feelings of: *The insult hurt them deeply.* —*v.i.* **1.** to be painful: *This knee hurts.* **2.** to cause or inflict pain or injury: *The injection didn't hurt much.* —*n.* any pain or suffering: *The medication will ease the hurt in your arm.*

hurt·ful (hûrt′fəl) *adj.* causing hurt; painful; injurious. *The child was upset by the hurtful remark.* —**hurt′-ful·ly,** *adv.* —**hurt′ful·ness,** *n.*

hur·tle (hûr′təl) *v.i.,* **hur·tled, hur·tling. 1.** to strike, especially violently or noisily: *The car went out of control and hurtled against the fence.* **2.** to move rapidly, especially with much force or noise: *Arrows hurtled through the air.*

hus·band (huz′bənd) *n.* the man in a married couple; married man. —*v.t.* to manage carefully, use or spend economically: *to husband one's time and energy.*

hus·band·ry (huz′bən drē) *n.* **1.** the cultivation of the soil and the breeding and raising of livestock; agriculture; farming. **2.** careful management; thrift.

hush (hush) *n., pl.* **hush·es.** a silence or stillness, especially after noise or commotion has ceased: *A hush fell over the audience.* —*v.t.* **1.** to quiet, silence, or calm: *The teacher hushed the noisy children.* **2.** to keep knowledge or discussion of (something) from spreading: *The principal hushed the news about our teacher's leaving.* —*interj.* be quiet; be calm.

husk (husk) *n.* **1.** the outer covering, especially when dry, of certain seeds or fruits, such as an ear of corn. **2.** the outer shell or covering of something, especially when it is useless or worthless. —*v.t.* to remove the husk of: *to husk corn.* —**husk′er,** *n.*

at; āpe; fär; câre; end; mē; it; īce; pîerce; hot; ōld; sông, fôrk; oil; out; up; ūse; rüle; pùll; tûrn; chin; sing; shop; thin; *this;* hw in white; zh in treasure. The symbol ə stands for the unstressed vowel sound heard in about, taken, pencil, lemon, and circus.

H

husk·y¹ (hus′kē) *adj.*, **husk·i·er, husk·i·est. 1.** big and strong: *a husky child.* **2.** hoarse and deep in tone: *a husky voice.* —*n., pl.* **husk·ies.** *Informal.* a big, strong person. [*Husk* + -y¹.] —**husk′i·ly,** *adv.* —**husk′i·ness,** *n.*

husk·y² (hus′kē) *also,* **Husk·y.** *n., pl.* **husk·ies.** see **Siberian husky.** [Probably a form of *Eskimo.*]

hus·sar (hə zär′) *n.* a member of a light cavalry regiment in any of several European armies.

hus·sy (huz′ē, hus′ē) *n., pl.* **hus·sies. 1.** a woman of improper behavior or low character. **2.** a saucy, mischievous girl.

hus·tle (hus′əl) *v.*, **hus·tled, hus·tling.** —*v.i.* **1.** to move or work quickly or energetically: *I had to hustle to finish on time.* **2.** *Slang.* to make money by clever or dishonest means. —*v.t.* to hasten along by force; move hurriedly: *The nurse hustled patients in and out of the office.* —*n.* *Informal.* energy and enthusiasm; drive: *The new salesperson has lots of hustle.*

hus·tler (hus′lər) *n.* *Informal.* **1.** a person who works hard or energetically. **2.** a person who earns a living by scheming, begging, or cheating.

hut (hut) *n.* a small, roughly or simply built house or shelter.

hutch (huch) *n., pl.* **hutch·es. 1.** a covered pen or box for keeping rabbits or other small animals. **2.** a cupboard with open shelves. **3.** a chest or bin that is used for storing things, such as china or linen.

hwy., highway.

huz·zah (hə zä′) *interj., n.* another word for **hurrah.**

hy·a·cinth (hī′ə sinth′) *n.* **1.** a fragrant flower of any of a group of plants related to the lily. It is shaped like a funnel and grows in long clusters. **2.** the plant bearing this flower.

hy·brid (hī′brid) *n.* **1.** the offspring of two animals or plants of different varieties, lines, or breeds, that combines the differing qualities of the parents. **2.** anything derived from different sources or made up of unlike elements. —*adj.* of, relating to, or of the nature of a hybrid: *a hybrid flower.*

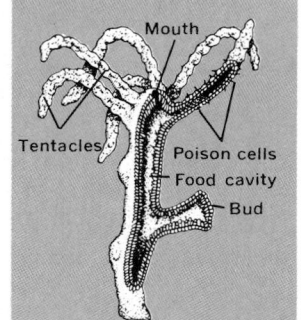
hyacinth

hy·brid·ism (hī′bri diz′əm) *n.* **1.** the condition, quality, or fact of being hybrid. **2.** the production of hybrids.

hy·brid·ize (hī′bri dīz′) *v.t.*, **hy·brid·ized, hy·brid·iz·ing.** to cause to produce hybrids. —**hy′brid·i·za′tion,** *n.*

hy·dra (hī′drə) *n., pl.* **hy·dras** or **hy·drae** (hī′drē). **1. Hydra.** *Classical Mythology.* a deadly monster that resembled a snake and had nine heads and the power to grow two more whenever one was cut off. **2.** a small freshwater animal related to the jellyfish, having a tube-shaped body with a single mouth opening. The mouth is surrounded by thin tentacles having stinging cells that carry poison. If a hydra is cut into pieces, each piece will develop into a new animal.

hydra *(def. 2)*
Mouth
Tentacles
Poison cells
Food cavity
Bud

hy·dran·gea (hī drān′jə) *n.* **1.** a large, showy flower that grows in clusters of usually white, blue, or pink blossoms. **2.** the shrub or vine bearing this flower.

hy·drant (hī′drənt) *n.* a street fixture for drawing water directly from a water main, consisting of an upright pipe with spouts to which hoses may be attached. Also, **fire hydrant.**

hy·drate (hī′drāt) *n.* any crystalline substance formed by the union of a chemical compound with molecules of water in a definite ratio. —*v.t.*, **hy·drat·ed, hy·drat·ing.** to combine (a chemical compound) with water to form a hydrate. —**hy·dra′tion,** *n.*

hy·drau·lic (hī drô′lik) *adj.* **1.** operated by water or some other fluid: *hydraulic brakes.* **2.** of or relating to the forces exerted by fluids in motion and at rest, or to the science of hydraulics. **3.** hardening under water: *hydraulic cement.* —**hy·drau′li·cal·ly,** *adv.*

hydraulic ram, a pump that uses the energy of moving water to pump part of the water to a higher level.

hy·drau·lics (hī drô′liks) *n.* the branch of science that deals with fluids in motion and at rest, and their use to perform work. ▲ used with a singular verb.

hy·dra·zine (hī′drə zēn′) *n.* a colorless, poisonous liquid that has an odor like ammonia. It is a compound of nitrogen and hydrogen and is used especially as a rocket fuel.

hy·dride (hī′drīd) *also,* **hy·drid** (hī′drid) *n.* a compound of hydrogen with an element or radical.

hydro- *combining form* **1.** of or relating to water: *hydrodynamics, hydroplane.* **2.** *Chemistry.* combined with or made up of hydrogen: *hydrocarbon.*

hy·dro·car·bon (hī′drə kär′bən, hī′drə kär′bən) *n.* any of a large group of organic compounds composed solely of the chemical elements hydrogen and carbon.

hy·dro·chlo·ric acid (hī′drə klôr′ik) a poisonous, highly corrosive solution of hydrogen chloride in water. Its fumes cause severe irritation of the eyes and nose.

hy·dro·cy·an·ic acid (hī′drō sī an′ik) a weak, colorless, poisonous acid having an odor like bitter almonds. It is a solution of a compound of hydrogen, carbon, and nitrogen in water and is used to make plastics and pesticides. Also, **prussic acid.**

hy·dro·dy·nam·ic (hī′drō dī nam′ik) *adj.* of or relating to the forces exerted by fluids in motion or to the science of hydrodynamics. —**hy′dro·dy·nam′i·cal·ly,** *adv.*

hy·dro·dy·nam·ics (hī′drō dī nam′iks) *n.* the branch of science that deals with the forces exerted by fluids in motion. ▲ used with a singular verb.

hy·dro·e·lec·tric (hī′drō i lek′trik) *adj.* of or relating to electricity generated by water power.

hy·dro·foil (hī′drə foil′) *n.* **1.** a blade or wing-shaped structure under a motor-powered boat. The hydrofoil raises the hull of the boat out of the water when the boat reaches a certain speed, eliminating the resistance of the water against the hull and increasing the speed of the boat. **2.** a boat fitted with hydrofoils.

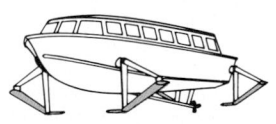
hydrofoils

hy·dro·gen (hī′drə jən) *n.* the simplest, lightest, and most abundant element in the universe. It is a colorless, tasteless, and odorless nonmetallic element that is a highly flammable gas at normal temperatures. Symbol: **H** [From the French word *hydrogène* meaning this gas, formed from the Greek words *hydōr* "water" + *gennan* "to produce." When hydrogen burns, it produces water.]

hy·dro·gen·ate (hī′drə je nāt′, hī droj′ə nāt′) *v.t.*, **hy·dro·gen·at·ed, hy·dro·gen·at·ing.** to combine or treat with hydrogen: *Oils are hydrogenated to produce margarine.* —**hy′dro·gen·a′tion,** *n.*

hydrogen bomb, a bomb whose enormous destructive power is caused by the fusion of hydrogen atoms to form helium atoms. Its destructive force is similar to, but much greater than, that of an atomic bomb. Also, **H-bomb, fusion bomb.**

hydrogen peroxide, a colorless, unstable liquid that is an active oxidizing agent, diluted for use as a bleach and antiseptic. It is highly explosive in concentrated form.

hy·drog·ra·phy (hī drog′rə fē) *n.* the scientific measurement, charting, and description of oceans, lakes, rivers, and other surface waters, especially to determine their use for navigation. —**hy·dro·graph·ic** (hī'drə-graf'ik), *adj.*

hy·drol·y·sis (hī drol'ə sis) *n., pl.* **hy·drol·y·ses** (hī-drol'ə sēz'). a chemical reaction involving one or more substances and water. Starch undergoes hydrolysis to form glucose.

hy·drom·e·ter (hī drom'i tər) *n.* an instrument for measuring the specific gravity of liquids.

hy·dro·pho·bi·a (hī'drə fō'bē ə) *n.* **1.** see **rabies. 2.** an excessive, abnormal fear of water.

hy·dro·plane (hī'drə plān') *n.* **1.** a motorboat whose hull is designed to skim over the surface of the water rather than push through it. Hydroplanes are used especially in racing. **2.** another word for **seaplane.**

hy·dro·pon·ics (hī'drə pon'iks) *n.* the science or practice of cultivating plants in a liquid nutrient solution rather than in soil. ▲ used with a singular verb.

hy·dro·sphere (hī'drə sfīr') *n.* **1.** all the water on the surface of the earth. **2.** all the moisture in the atmosphere surrounding the earth.

hy·dro·stat·ic (hī'drə stat'ik) *adj.* of or relating to the science of hydrostatics.

hy·dro·stat·ics (hī'drə stat'iks) *n.* the branch of physics dealing with the forces exerted by fluids at rest. ▲ used with a singular verb.

hy·dro·ther·a·py (hī'drō ther'ə pē) *n.* the scientific treatment of disease by means of water.

hy·drot·ro·pism (hī drot'rə piz'əm) *n.* the tendency of a plant to grow toward moisture.

hy·drous (hī'drəs) *adj.* (of a chemical compound) containing water, especially in chemical combination.

hy·drox·ide (hī drok'sīd) *n.* any chemical compound containing one or more hydroxyl radicals.

hy·drox·yl (hī drok'səl) *n.* a chemical ion or group consisting of one atom of oxygen and one of hydrogen.

hy·dro·zo·an (hī'drə zō'ən) *n.* any of various saltwater and freshwater animals, including hydras and corals, generally existing in two different forms, that of a free-swimming jellyfish and that of a stationary polyp. —*adj.* of or relating to hydrozoans.

hy·e·na (hī ē'nə) *n.* a wolflike animal native to Africa and Asia, having strong jaws and front legs that are longer than the back ones. A hyena feeds chiefly on decaying carcasses by day and is known for its laughing cry.

hy·giene (hī'jēn) *n.* **1.** practices or conditions that aid good health. **2.** the science that deals with the maintenance of good health and the prevention of infection and disease.

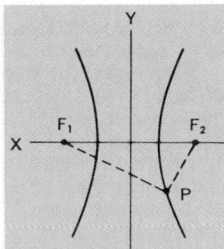

hyena

hy·gi·en·ic (hī'jē en'ik, hī jen'ik) *adj.* **1.** free from anything dangerous to good health; sanitary. **2.** of or relating to health or hygiene. —**hy'gi·en'i·cal·ly,** *adv.*

hy·gien·ist (hī jē'nist, hī'jē en'ist) *n.* a person who is trained or expert in the principles of hygiene.

hy·grom·e·ter (hī grom'i tər) *n.* an instrument for determining the humidity of the atmosphere.

hy·gro·met·ric (hī'grə met'rik) *adj.* of or relating to hygrometry or a hygrometer.

hy·grom·e·try (hī grom'i trē) *n.* the study of the moisture of the atmosphere.

hy·gro·scope (hī'grə skōp') *n.* an instrument that records variations in the humidity of the atmosphere.

hy·gro·scop·ic (hī'grə skop'ik) *adj.* readily attracting or absorbing moisture from the atmosphere.

hy·ing (hī'ing) a present participle of **hie.**

hy·men (hī'mən) *n.* a fold of membrane partially covering the opening of the vagina.

Hy·men (hī'mən) *n. Greek Mythology.* the god of marriage.

hymn (him) *n.* **1.** a song of praise to God or a god. **2.** any song or ode of praise or joy.

hym·nal (him'nəl) *n.* a book or collection of hymns for use in a religious service. Also, **hymn·book** (him'bùk').

hype (hīp) *n. Slang.* advertising or publicity with exaggerated, often misleading claims: *There was a lot of hype surrounding the introduction of the new computer.* —*v.t.,* **hyped, hyp·ing.** to advertise or publicize with exaggerated, often misleading claims.

hy·per (hī'pər) *adj. Slang.* easily agitated or excited.

hyper- *prefix* excessive or excessively: *hypercritical.*

hy·per·a·cid·i·ty (hī'pər ə sid'i tē) *n.* excessive acidity, especially of gastric juice.

hy·per·ac·tive (hī'pər ak'tiv) *adj.* overly or abnormally active: *a hyperactive child, a hyperactive gland.* —**hy·per·ac·tiv·i·ty** (hī'pər ak tiv'i tē), *n.*

hy·per·bo·la (hī pûr'bə lə) *n.* an open curve with two branches consisting of a set of points in a plane whose distances from two fixed points, or foci, differ by a constant value.

hy·per·bo·le (hī pûr'bə lē) *n.* a figure of speech consisting of an extreme exaggeration not meant to be taken literally. For example: *I shopped in a million stores today.*

hyperbola

P = any point on hyperbola; F_1 and F_2 = foci; PF_1 − PF_2 = a constant.

Language Note

In language, **hyperbole** is a figure of speech that is used to give special emphasis to a statement by exaggerating it. Hyperbole is often used in everyday speaking and writing. The difference between hyperbole and simple exaggeration is that the exaggeration of hyperbole is so great that no one would take it literally or believe it to be true. For example, if you say "I'm so hungry I could eat a horse," people will understand that you are just using a colorful expression to convey the idea that you are very hungry. If you simply exaggerate and say "I'm so hungry I could eat four sandwiches," then it is not clear whether what you are saying is to be accepted as truth or exaggeration.

---

hy·per·bol·ic (hī'pər bol'ik) *adj.* **1.** of, relating to, or using hyperbole; exaggerated or exaggerating. **2.** of, relating to, or having the form of a hyperbola.

hy·per·crit·i·cal (hī'pər krit'i kəl) *adj.* too critical. —**hy'per·crit'i·cal·ly,** *adv.*

hy·per·sen·si·tive (hī'pər sen'si tiv) *adj.* overly or abnormally sensitive: *hypersensitive skin, to be hypersensitive to criticism.* —**hy'per·sen'si·tive·ness,** *n.* —**hy'per·sen'si·tiv'i·ty,** *n.*

hy·per·son·ic (hī'pər son'ik) *adj.* of or relating to an object that is moving at a rate of at least five times the speed of sound, or to its speed.

---

at; āpe; fär; câre; end; mē; it; īce; pîerce; hot; ōld; sông, fôrk; oil; out; up; ūse; rüle; pùll; tûrn; chin; sing; shop; thin; <u>th</u>is; hw in white; zh in treasure. The symbol ə stands for the unstressed vowel sound heard in about, taken, pencil, lemon, and circus.

H

hy·per·ten·sion (hī′pər ten′shən) *n.* another term for high blood pressure.

hy·per·tro·phy (hī pûr′trə fē) *n.* excessive growth of a body organ or tissue.

hy·per·ven·ti·late (hī′pər ven′tə lāt′) *v.i.,* **hy·per·ven·ti·lat·ed, hy·per·ven·ti·lat·ing.** to breathe too rapidly or deeply, as under emotional stress, causing a drop in the level of carbon dioxide in the blood and consequent dizziness or fainting. —**hy′per·ven·ti·la′tion,** *n.*

hy·phae (hī′fē) *pl. n., sing.* **hy·pha** (hī′fə). the thin, threadlike fibers that form the mycelium of a fungus.

hy·phen (hī′fən) *n.* a punctuation mark (-) used to connect two or more elements or words to form a compound word, or to join the syllables of a word that have been separated, as at the end of a line.

hy·phen·ate (hī′fə nāt′) *v.t.,* **hy·phen·at·ed, hy·phen·at·ing.** to separate, connect, or write with a hyphen: *to hyphenate a word.* —**hy′phen·a′tion,** *n.*

hyp·no·sis (hip nō′sis) *n., pl.* **hyp·no·ses** (hip nō′sēz). 1. a trance resembling sleep, induced by deep relaxation and concentration, characterized by extreme responsiveness to suggestion. It is sometimes used to produce anesthesia or overcome unwanted habits. 2. another word for **hypnotism** (*def. 1*).

hyp·not·ic (hip not′ik) *adj.* 1. of or relating to hypnosis or hypnotism: *a hypnotic trance.* 2. tending to produce sleep or a trance that is like sleep: *The speaker had a droning, hypnotic voice. The long, straight highway had a hypnotic effect on drivers.* —*n.* 1. something, as a drug, that produces sleep. 2. a person who is or can be easily hypnotized. —**hyp·not′i·cal·ly,** *adv.*

hyp·no·tism (hip′nə tiz′əm) *n.* 1. the science, practice, or act of inducing hypnosis. 2. another word for **hypnosis** (*def. 1*).

hyp·no·tist (hip′nə tist) *n.* a person who induces hypnosis.

hyp·no·tize (hip′nə tīz′) *v.t.,* **hy·no·tized, hyp·no·tiz·ing.** 1. to put (someone) in a hypnotic trance; induce hypnosis in: *The doctor hypnotized the patient.* 2. to fascinate; enthrall: *I was hypnotized by the bird's beauty.* —**hyp′no·tiz′er,** *n.*

hy·po (hī′pō) *n., pl.* **hy·pos.** *Informal.* a hypodermic syringe or injection.

hy·po·chon·dri·a (hī′pə kon′drē ə) *n.* a neurotic disorder that is characterized by excessive worry over one's health and imagined diseases and symptoms.

hy·po·chon·dri·ac (hī′pə kon′drē ak′) *n.* a person who suffers from hypochondria. —*adj.* of, relating to, or suffering from hypochondria.

hy·poc·ri·sy (hi pok′rə sē) *n., pl.* **hy·poc·ri·sies.** 1. the act or practice of presenting one's character, feelings, or beliefs as being other than they really are, especially by pretending to be good or pious. 2. an act of hypocrisy: *Feigning a love of children is one of their hypocrisies.*

hyp·o·crite (hip′ə krit′) *n.* a person who is given to or practices hypocrisy. —**hyp′o·crit′i·cal,** *adj.* —**hyp′o·crit′i·cal·ly,** *adj.*

hy·po·der·mic (hī′pə dûr′mik) *adj.* 1. lying beneath the skin. 2. injected under the skin. —*n.* 1. see **hypodermic syringe.** 2. an injection given with a needle or syringe. [Formed from the Greek words *hypo* meaning "under" + *derma* meaning "skin."]

hypodermic syringe, a syringe with a hollow needle that is inserted underneath the skin in order to inject or remove fluids. Also, **hypodermic needle.**

hy·po·gly·ce·mi·a (hī′pō glī sē′mē ə) *n.* an abnormally low amount of the sugar glucose in the blood. It most commonly occurs when a person with diabetes takes too much insulin. [Formed from the Greek words *hypo* meaning "under," *glykys* "sweet," and *haima* "blood."]

hy·po·sul·fite (hī′pə sul′fīt) *n.* another word for **sodium thiosulfate.**

hy·pot·e·nuse (hī pot′ə nūs′, hī pot′ə nūs′) *n.* the side of a right triangle opposite the right angle.

hy·po·thal·a·mus (hī′pə thal′ə-məs) *n., pl.* **hy·po·thal·a·mi** (hī pə-thal′ə mī′). the part of the brain that controls various body functions, such as the heartbeat and body temperature.

hy·po·ther·mi·a (hī pə thûr′mē ə) *n.* a low body temperature, usually caused by long exposure to a cold environment.

hy·poth·e·sis (hī poth′ə sis) *n., pl.* **hy·poth·e·ses** (hī-poth′ə sēz′). an unproved, temporary explanation or supposition that is based on known facts and can be used as a basis for further experimentation or investigation; theory.

hy·poth·e·size (hī poth′ə sīz′) *v.i.,* **hy·poth·e·sized, hy·poth·e·siz·ing.** to make a hypothesis.

hy·po·thet·i·cal (hī′pə thet′i kəl) *adj.* of the nature of, involving, or based on a hypothesis or theory; theoretical: *a hypothetical example.* Also, **hy·po·thet·ic** (hī′-pə thet′ik). —**hy′po·thet′i·cal·ly,** *adv.*

hy·rax (hī′raks) *n., pl.* **hy·rax·es** or **hy·ra·ces** (hī′rə-sēz′). any of various animals of Africa and the Middle East that closely resemble rabbits and have claws that are like hooves, sharp canine teeth, and a coarse black, brownish gray, or tan coat.

hys·sop (his′əp) *n.* 1. a stiff plant related to the mint, having leaves with a pungent odor that were formerly used for flavoring food and for medicinal purposes. 2. in the Old Testament, a plant whose twigs were used for sprinkling water in purification ceremonies.

hys·te·ri·a (hi ster′ē ə, hi stîr′ē ə) *n.* 1. excessive, uncontrollable terror, panic, or other strong emotion; frenzy: *an outbreak of mob hysteria.* 2. any of several psychiatric disorders, usually characterized by physical symptoms, as paralysis or amnesia, that have no physical cause. [Formed from the Greek word *hystera* meaning "womb." This disorder was formerly believed to affect only women, as a result of disturbances of the womb.]

hys·ter·ic (hi ster′ik) *n.* a person who suffers from hysteria. —*adj.* another word for **hysterical.**

hys·ter·i·cal (hi ster′i kəl) *adj.* 1. resembling or caused by hysteria; uncontrollably emotional; frenzied: *a hysterical outburst, a fit of hysterical sobbing.* 2. of, characteristic of, or occurring as a symptom of hysteria: *hysterical blindness.* 3. suffering from or prone to hysteria. 4. *Informal.* extremely funny: *The joke was hysterical.* —**hys·ter′i·cal·ly,** *adv.*

hys·ter·ics (hi ster′iks) *pl. n.* a fit of uncontrollable emotion, especially of laughing and crying at the same time.

Hz, hertz.

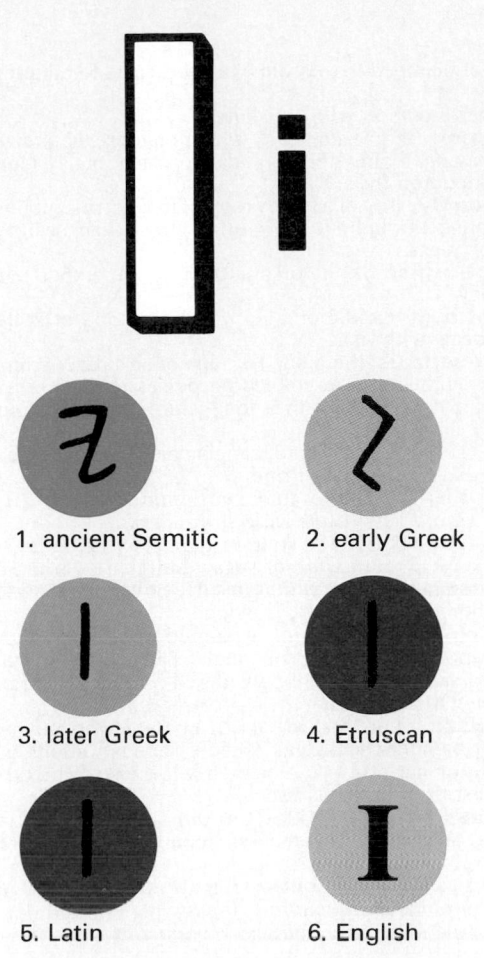

1. ancient Semitic   **2.** early Greek

3. later Greek   **4.** Etruscan

5. Latin   **6.** English

I is the ninth letter of the English alphabet. The earliest form of the letter I was in the ancient Semitic alphabets, where this symbol was called *yod* (1), meaning "hand." The early Greeks (2) adopted *yod* and simplified it by making it a tall vertical line with a short horizontal stroke at the top and bottom. They called this letter *iota*. The Greek *iota* was equivalent to the short vowel *i*. By about the fifth century B.C., the Greeks were writing *iota* as a single vertical line (3). The Etruscans (4) and the Romans (5) adopted this form of *iota*. In Latin, this letter sometimes represented the vowel *i* and sometimes the consonant *j*. Our modern capital letter **I** (6) is usually written with a short horizontal stroke at the top and bottom of the vertical line.

The dot that we write over the small letter *i* was not used until about 1,000 years ago. In the style of writing used at that time, the small letters *m* and *n* were made up of strokes that each looked like a small letter *i*. Because of this, a word containing a combination of these letters, such as the Latin *minimus,* was very hard to read. The addition of a dot over the small letter *i* helped the reader to distinguish the letters.

i, I (ī) *n., pl.* **i's, I's. 1.** the ninth letter of the English alphabet. **2.** something having the shape of this letter. **3.** the Roman numeral for 1.

I (ī) *pron.* the person who is speaking or writing: *I telephoned my friend.*

I, the symbol for iodine.

i., intransitive.

I. 1. Island; Islands. **2.** Isle; Isles.

Ia., Iowa.

IA, postal abbreviation for Iowa.

–ial, a form of the suffix **-al¹,** as in *bestial.*

i·amb (ī'amb) *n.* **1.** in poetry, a metrical foot in verse consisting of an unaccented or short syllable followed by an accented or long syllable. The line *And we/are here/as on/a dark/ling plain* (Matthew Arnold, "Dover Beach") contains five iambs. **2.** a line of verse that is made up of such feet.

i·am·bic (ī am'bik) *adj.* of, relating to, or containing iambs. —*n.* **1.** an iamb. **2.** *usually,* **iambics.** poetry written in iambs.

–ian, a form of the suffix **-an,** as in *Australian.*

ib., ibid.

i·bex (ī'beks) *n., pl.* **i·bex** or **i·bex·es.** a wild goat that lives in the mountains of Europe, Asia, and northern Africa, having ridged, curving horns which in the male may grow to as much as 5 feet in length.

ibid., in the work previously mentioned or cited. [Short for the Latin word *ibidem* meaning "in the same place."]

–ibility, a form of the suffix **-ability,** as in *sensibility, flexibility.*

ibex

i·bis (ī'bis) *n., pl.* **i·bis·es** or **i·bis.** a large, long-legged wading bird related to the stork and heron and having a long, downward-curving bill.

–ible, a form of the suffix **-able,** as in *convertible.*

–ic *suffix* **1.** (used to form adjectives from nouns) **a.** of or relating to: *dramatic, Celtic.* **b.** having the qualities of; being or like: *athletic, angelic.* **c.** made of or containing: *alcoholic, iambic.* **d.** produced or caused by: *volcanic.* ▲ Many words ending in *-ic* have more than one of the above meanings. **2.** *Chemistry.* having a higher valence than a related compound or ion whose name ends in *-ous: ferric.*

IC, integrated circuit.

–ical *suffix* **1.** (used to form adjectives from nouns) of, relating to, characterized by, or caused by: *economical, philosophical.* **2.** (used to form adjectives) of, relating to, or characterized by: *ethical.*

Ic·a·rus (ik'ər əs) *n.* see **Daedalus.**

ICBM, a ballistic missile with a range of over 3,000 miles (4,800 kilometers). [Short for *i*(nter)*c*(ontinental) *b*(allistic) *m*(issile).]

ice (īs) *n.* **1.** the solid state of water, normally produced at or below 32 degrees Fahrenheit (0 degrees Celsius). **2.** the frozen surface of a body of water, such as a lake: *We cut a hole in the ice to fish.* **3.** something that looks or feels like ice. **4.** a frozen dessert made of sweetened water and fruit flavoring or fruit juice. —*v.,* **iced, ic·ing.** —*v.i.* to become blocked or covered with ice: *The lake iced over. The door lock iced up.* —*v.t.* **1.** to cause ice to form on; cover with ice. **2.** to chill or keep cold, especially with ice: *to ice lemonade.* **3.** to cover or decorate with icing; frost. **4.** to change into ice.

·on thin ice. in a dangerous or risky situation.

ice age 1. any period of time when glaciers covered much of the surface of the earth. **2. Ice Age.** another term for **Pleistocene.**

ice·berg (īs′bûrg′) *n.* a large mass of floating ice that has broken off from a glacier or polar icecap.

ice·boat (īs′bōt′) *n.* **1.** a light, often triangular, frame equipped with runners and sails for sailing on ice. **2.** another word for **icebreaker.**

ice·bound (īs′bound′) *adj.* **1.** obstructed by ice: *an icebound coast.* **2.** held fast or surrounded by ice: *an icebound ship.*

ice·box (īs′boks′) *n., pl.* **ice·box·es. 1.** a box or chest cooled by blocks of ice, used for storing food and drinks. **2.** a refrigerator.

ice·break·er (īs′brā′kər) *n.* a ship

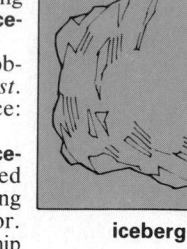

iceberg

with a strong prow, used in harbors, rivers, and other waterways to break or open a channel through ice. Also, **iceboat.**

ice·cap (īs′kap′) *n.* a cone-shaped or dome-shaped glacier covering a land area and moving out from the center in all directions.

ice–cold (īs′kōld′) *adj.* very cold: *I would like a glass of ice-cold milk.*

ice cream, a frozen dessert made chiefly of milk or cream, sweeteners, and flavoring. **—ice-cream,** *adj.* **1.** made of ice cream: *an ice-cream cake.* **2.** used with ice cream: *an ice-cream cone.*

ice field, a large mass of floating ice, found especially in polar regions.

ice floe, see **floe.**

ice hockey, see **hockey** (*def. 1*).

ice·house (īs′hous′) *n., pl.* **ice·hous·es** (īs′hou′ziz). a building for storing ice.

Ice·lan·dic (īs lan′dik) *adj.* of or relating to Iceland, its people, their language, or culture. —*n.* the Germanic language spoken in Iceland.

ice·man (īs′man′) *n., pl.* **ice·men** (īs′men′). a person whose job or business is selling or delivering ice.

ice pack 1. a bag or folded cloth filled with ice and applied to parts of the body to relieve pain or lessen swelling. **2.** another term for **pack ice.**

ice pick, a pointed tool used to break or chip ice.

ice sheet, a thick layer of ice covering a large area of land for a long period of time.

a couple **ice-skating**

ice–skate (īs′skāt′) *v.i.,* **ice-skat·ed, ice-skat·ing.** to skate on ice.

ice skate 1. a shoe, usually covering the ankle, with a metal runner permanently attached to it, used for skating on ice. **2.** a runner, mounted in a frame, that can be strapped or clamped to the sole of a shoe, used for skating on ice.

ice skater, a person who ice-skates.

ich·neu·mon (ik nü′mən) *n.* **1.** a mongoose native to Africa, having a gray body and brownish black feet. **2.** see **ichneumon fly.**

ichneumon fly, any of a large group of insects resembling wasps, found throughout the world. Its larvae destroy many crop pests.

ich·thy·ol·o·gist (ik′thē ol′ə jist) *n.* an expert in ichthyology.

ich·thy·ol·o·gy (ik′thē ol′ə jē) *n.* the branch of zoology that deals with fish.

ich·thy·o·saur (ik′thē ə sôr′) *n.* any of an extinct group of marine reptiles that resembled porpoises. The ichthyosaur had a large head with a long, thin snout and four paddlelike flippers.

i·ci·cle (ī′si kəl) *n.* a pointed, hanging piece of ice formed by water that freezes as it drips.

i·ci·ly (ī′sə lē) *adv.* in a cold, unfriendly manner: *The customer stared icily at the rude store clerk.*

i·ci·ness (ī′sē nis) *n.* the state or quality of being icy.

ic·ing (ī′sing) *n.* a mixture of sugar, butter, flavoring, a liquid, and sometimes egg whites, used to cover or decorate cakes or other baked goods; frosting.

i·con (ī′kon) *also,* **i·kon.** *n.* a painted picture or other representation of a holy person, such as Jesus, the Virgin Mary, or a saint. Icons are considered sacred by Christians in the Orthodox Church.

i·con·o·clast (ī kon′ə klast′) *n.* **1.** a person who attacks traditional or cherished ideas, beliefs, or institutions as being false or harmful. **2.** a person who destroys icons or is against their religious use.

i·con·o·clas·tic (ī kon′ə klas′tik) *adj.* **1.** acting as an iconoclast or characteristic of an iconoclast. **2.** of or relating to iconoclasts.

–ics *suffix* (used to form nouns) **1.** an art, science, or field of study: *physics, mathematics, linguistics.* **2.** methods, systems, practices, or activities: *gymnastics, statistics, acrobatics.*

i·cy (ī′sē) *adj.,* **i·ci·er, i·ci·est. 1.** made of, containing, or covered with ice: *an icy sidewalk.* **2.** very cold: *icy winds, icy hands.* **3.** without warmth of feeling; cold and unfriendly: *an icy welcome.*

I'd (īd) *contr.* **1.** I had. **2.** I should. **3.** I would.

ID 1. postal abbreviation for Idaho. **2.** identification.

Ida., Idaho.

i·de·a (ī dē′ə) *n.* **1.** something formed by or in the mind; thought: *The author had an idea for a new novel.* **2.** a belief or opinion: *to have strong ideas about religion.* **3.** a plan of action or intention: *to have an idea of becoming an artist.* **4.** the aim or purpose of something: *The idea of the game of golf is to hit the ball into the hole.*

i·de·al (ī dē′əl) *n.* **1.** an idea or standard of perfection or excellence: *The Declaration of Independence contains many of the ideals of the founders of our nation.* **2.** a person or thing regarded as being without fault and worthy of imitation or admiration: *The astronaut was the ideal of many children.* **3.** the best or most satisfactory situation; aim or goal. —*adj.* **1.** being exactly what one would hope for; most desirable or suitable: *The breeze makes it an ideal day for sailing.* **2.** existing only in the mind.

i·de·al·ism (ī dē′ə liz′əm) *n.* **1.** acting or striving to act in accordance with ideals or standards of perfection or excellence. **2.** a theory in philosophy that reality is essentially mental or spiritual rather than physical. Idealists believe either that nothing is real except what exists in a person's mind, or that reality exists in ideal forms that are outside of a person's mind.

i·de·al·ist (ī dē′ə list) *n.* **1.** a person who thinks or acts according to personal ideals. **2.** a person who thinks that things are better than they are. **3.** a person who follows idealism in philosophy. —i'**de·al·is'tic,** *adj.* —i'**de·al·is'ti·cal·ly,** *adv.*

i·de·al·ize (ī dē'ə līz') *v.t.,* **i·de·al·ized, i·de·al·iz·ing.** to think of or represent as without fault: *Some people idealize the way things were in the past. The artist idealized the wealthy banker in the painted portrait.* —i·de'·al·i·za'tion, *n.*

i·de·al·ly (ī dē'ə lē) *adv.* **1.** in the best possible manner; perfectly or very well: *The new school suits us ideally.* **2.** under the best or most desirable conditions; in theory: *Ideally, each child should receive three shots of the vaccine.*

i·den·ti·cal (ī den'ti kəl) *adj.* **1.** one and the same; the very same: *We saw the identical car somewhere else an hour later.* **2.** exactly alike: *identical uniforms, identical answers.* —i·**den'ti·cal·ly,** *adv.*

identical twins, twins of the same sex that develop from a single fertilized egg cell and therefore look precisely alike.

i·den·ti·fi·ca·tion (ī den'tə fi kā'shən) *n.* **1.** the act of identifying or the state of being identified. **2.** something used to prove or to establish one's identity: *We carried our passports as identification.*

i·den·ti·fy (ī den'tə fī') *v.,* **i·den·ti·fied, i·den·ti·fy·ing.** —*v.t.* **1.** to prove that (someone or something) is a particular person or thing: *The burglary victims identified the jewels as their own. How many species of birds can you identify?* **2.** to regard or treat as identical; assume to be one and the same: *The Roman goddess Venus is identified with the Greek goddess Aphrodite.* **3.** to connect closely; associate: *to identify money with success.* —*v.i.* to become as one with another or others: *to identify with a character in a movie or novel.* —i·**den'ti·fi'a·ble,** *adj.*

i·den·ti·ty (ī den'ti tē) *n., pl.* **i·den·ti·ties. 1.** a person's sense of being different from other persons; individuality. **2.** the fact or condition of being a certain person or thing: *to establish your identity by showing your driver's license.* **3.** the state or condition of being identical: *the identity of two accounts of an accident.* **4.** *Mathematics.* a statement of equality that is true for all values of a variable. The equation $3x + 2x = 5x$ is true for all values of x and is therefore an identity.

identity element, an element in a set that, when added to or multiplied by another element, yields that element. For addition, 0 is the identity element, since $7 + 0 = 7$. For multiplication, 1 is the identity element, since $7 \times 1 = 7$.

id·e·o·gram (id'ē ə gram') *n.* another word for **ideograph.**

id·e·o·graph (id'ē ə graf') *n.* a written symbol that stands for an object or idea rather than for a word, used in certain languages, such as Chinese.

i·de·o·log·i·cal (ī'de ə loj'i kəl, id'ē ə loj'i kəl) *adj.* of or based on ideologies or an ideology.

i·de·ol·o·gy (ī'dē ol'ə jē, id'ē ol'ə jē) *n., pl.* **i·de·ol·o·gies.** the beliefs, attitudes, ideas, and doctrines that are held by the members of a group, such as a political party.

ides (īdz) *pl. n.* in the ancient Roman calendar, the fifteenth day of March, May, July, or October, and the thirteenth day of the other months.

id·i·o·cy (id'ē ə sē) *n., pl.* **id·i·o·cies. 1.** severe mental retardation. ▲ now considered obsolete. **2.** great silliness or stupidity. **3.** a silly or stupid action.

id·i·om (id'ē əm) *n.* **1.** an expression whose meaning cannot be understood from the meanings of the individual words composing it. **2.** the language or dialect of a particular people or a specific region: *the idiom of the American Southwest.* **3.** the characteristic way in which words are used in a particular language.

id·i·o·mat·ic (id'ē ə mat'ik) *adj.* **1.** having the nature of or containing an idiom or idioms: *an idiomatic expression.* **2.** following the characteristic pattern of a particular language: *idiomatic English.* —**id'i·o·mat'i·cal·ly,** *adv.*

id·i·o·syn·cra·sy (id'ē ō sing'krə sē) *n., pl.* **id·i·o·syn·cra·sies.** an unusual or distinguishing characteristic of an individual, such as a habit or mannerism; peculiarity. [From the Greek word *idiosynkrasia* meaning "peculiar temperament," going back to the word *idios* "one's own," the prefix *syn-* "with," and the word *krasis* "mixture."] —**id·i·o·syn·crat·ic** (id'ē ō sin krat'ik), *adj.*

id·i·ot (id'ē ət) *n.* **1.** a person who is mentally retarded and cannot develop beyond a mental age of four years. ▲ now considered obsolete. **2.** a very silly or stupid person; fool. [From the Old French word *idiote* meaning "a simple or mentally deficient person," going back to the Greek word *idiotēs* "private person" or "ignorant person," from the word *idios* "one's own, private."]

id·i·ot·ic (id'ē ot'ik) *adj.* very silly or stupid; foolish. —**id'i·ot'i·cal·ly,** *adv.*

i·dle (ī'dəl) *adj.,* **i·dler, i·dlest. 1.** not working, in use, or busy: *an idle machine.* **2.** not willing to work; lazy. **3.** having little worth, usefulness, or importance: *an idle pastime, idle chatter.* —*v.i.,* **i·dled, i·dling. 1.** to spend time doing nothing: *Our guest idled around the house all morning.* **2.** (of machines) to run slowly, out of gear, or without transmitting power: *The car motor idled.* —i'**dle·ness,** *n.* —i'**dly,** *adv.*

·**to idle away.** to spend (time) doing nothing; waste: *to idle away an afternoon.*

i·dler (īd'lər) *n.* a person who is lazy; loafer.

i·dol (ī'dəl) *n.* **1.** an image or representation of a god, used as an object of worship. **2.** a person who is greatly loved or admired: *The athlete was the idol of many fans.*

i·dol·a·ter (ī dol'ə tər) *n.* a person who worships an idol or idols.

i·dol·a·trous (ī dol'ə trəs) *adj.* **1.** of, relating to, or characteristic of idolatry. **2.** given to worshiping an idol

I

at; āpe; fär; câre; end; mē; it; īce; pîerce; hot; ōld; sông, fôrk; oil; out; up; ūse; rüle; pu̇ll; tûrn; chin; sing; shop; thin; this; hw in white; zh in treasure. The symbol ə stands for the unstressed vowel sound heard in about, taken, pencil, lemon, and circus.

or idols. **3.** admiring and loving very much. —**i·dol′a·trous·ly,** *adv.*

i·dol·a·try (ī dol′ə trē) *n., pl.* **i·dol·a·tries. 1.** the worship of idols. **2.** very great admiration or love.

i·dol·ize (ī′də līz′) *v.t.,* **i·dol·ized, i·dol·iz·ing. 1.** to have very great admiration or love for: *The teenagers idolized the singer.* **2.** to worship as an idol. —**i′dol·i·za′tion,** *n.*

i·dyll (ī′dəl) *also,* **i·dyl.** *n.* **1.** a short poem or work of prose that describes peaceful, simple events or scenes of country life. **2.** an event or scene suitable for such a work.

i·dyl·lic (ī dil′ik) *adj.* **1.** of, relating to, or having the nature of an idyll. **2.** peaceful, simple, and charming: *an idyllic spot for a picnic.*

i.e., that is. [An abbreviation of Latin *id est.*]

–ier *suffix* (used to form nouns) a person who does or has to do with something: *cashier, financier, bombardier, carrier.*

if (if) *conj.* **1.** in case that; supposing that: *If I hurt your feelings, I'm sorry. Even if it rains, the game will be played.* **2.** on condition that: *I will sing, if you will accompany me.* **3.** whether: *I don't know if they'll be there.* **4.** even though; although: *It was a nice, if humid, day.* **5.** used to express a wish, surprise, or annoyance: *If we had only known.*

if·fy (if′ē) *adj.,* **if·fi·er, if·fi·est.** *Informal.* not certain or definite; questionable: *The outcome of the election is still iffy.*

ig·loo (ig′lü) *n., pl.* **ig·loos.** a dome-shaped hut used by Eskimos, usually built of blocks of hardened snow.

building an **igloo**

ig·ne·ous (ig′nē əs) *adj.* **1.** produced by great heat or volcanic action: *an igneous rock.* **2.** relating to or characteristic of fire.

ig·nite (ig nīt′) *v.,* **ig·nit·ed, ig·nit·ing.** —*v.t.* to burn or set on fire; kindle: *We ignited the pile of dead leaves with a match.* —*v.i.* to begin to burn; catch fire: *Oily rags will ignite easily.*

ig·ni·tion (ig nish′ən) *n.* **1.** the act of igniting or the state of being ignited. **2.** the system for igniting the fuel and air mixture within the cylinders of an internal-combustion engine.

ig·no·ble (ig nō′bəl) *adj.* **1.** without honor or worth; mean; base: *Cheating on an exam is an ignoble act.* **2.** of low birth or position. —**ig·no′ble·ness,** *n.* —**ig·no′bly,** *adv.*

ig·no·min·i·ous (ig′nə min′ē əs) *adj.* **1.** marked by or involving dishonor or disgrace; shameful: *ignominious punishment, an ignominious defeat.* **2.** deserving shame

or contempt: *ignominious behavior.* —**ig′no·min′i·ous·ly,** *adv.* —**ig′no·min′i·ous·ness,** *n.*

ig·no·min·y (ig′nə min′ē) *n., pl.* **ig·no·min·ies. 1.** disgrace or dishonor. **2.** something that causes or deserves disgrace or dishonor.

ig·no·ra·mus (ig′nə rā′məs, ig′nə ram′əs) *n., pl.* **ig·no·ra·mus·es.** an ignorant person. [From the character *Ignoramus,* a lawyer (whose name in Latin means "we do not know") in a satirical play *Ignoramus* written in 1615 by George Ruggle.]

ig·no·rance (ig′nər əns) *n.* the state or quality of being ignorant.

ig·no·rant (ig′nər ənt) *adj.* **1.** lacking in knowledge or education. **2.** not informed or aware: *to be ignorant of plans for a trip.* **3.** showing lack of knowledge or education: *an ignorant statement.* —**ig′no·rant·ly,** *adv.*

ig·nore (ig nôr′) *v.t.,* **ig·nored, ig·nor·ing.** to refuse to take notice of or recognize; pay no attention to: *Why did you ignore me when I spoke to you?*

i·gua·na (i gwä′nə) *n.* a large, greenish brown lizard, found in tropical America. The iguana usually lives in trees and has a large fold of skin hanging from its throat and a ridge of scales down the center of the back.

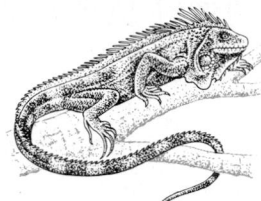

iguana

i·kon (ī′kon) another spelling of **icon.**

il–, the form of the prefix **in-¹** used before *l,* as in *illegitimate.*

IL, postal abbreviation for Illinois.

il·e·um (il′ē əm) *n., pl.* **il·e·a** (il′ē ə). the last section of the small intestine.

Il·i·ad (il′ē əd) *n.* an ancient Greek epic poem describing some of the events of the Trojan War. It is believed to have been composed by Homer.

il·i·um (il′ē əm) *n., pl.* **il·i·a** (il′ē ə). the broad upper portion of the hipbone.

ilk (ilk) *n.* kind; sort; class: *They do not associate with liars and others of that ilk.*

ill (il) *adj.,* **worse, worst. 1.** not healthy or well; sick: *to feel ill after eating too much.* **2.** not satisfactory; poor: *ill health, ill fortune.* **3.** hostile, cruel, or unfriendly: *ill feeling.* **4.** causing or caused by harm, destruction, or evil: *an ill wind. The war had many ill consequences.* —*adv.* **1.** in a harmful or unkind manner; badly: *Do not speak ill of them.* **2.** scarcely; hardly: *We can ill afford the time wasted.* —*n.* **1.** *usually,* **ills.** trouble, evil, or misfortune: *the ills of mankind.* **2.** a sickness or ailment: *Arthritis is a common ill.*

·**ill at ease.** nervous and uncomfortable: *Shy people often feel ill at ease with strangers.*

I'll (īl) *contr.* **1.** I shall. **2.** I will.

ill. 1. illustrated. **2.** illustration.

Ill., Illinois.

ill·ad·vised (il′əd vīzd′) *adj.* acting or done without sound advice or enough thought or consideration; unwise: *an ill-advised plan.*

ill·bred (il′bred′) *adj.* badly brought up or trained; unmannerly; rude.

il·le·gal (i lē′gəl) *adj.* **1.** not legal; unlawful: *Stealing is an illegal act.* **2.** against the official rules, as in sports. —**il·le′gal·ly,** *adv.*

il·le·gal·i·ty (il′ē gal′i tē) *n., pl.* **il·le·gal·i·ties. 1.** the state or quality of being illegal; unlawfulness. **2.** an illegal act.

il·leg·i·ble (i lej′ə bəl) *adj.* difficult or impossible to read; not legible: *The tiny handwriting on the envelope was completely illegible.* —**il·leg′i·bil′i·ty,** *n.* —**il·leg′i·bly,** *adv.*

il·le·git·i·ma·cy (il'i jit'ə mə sē) n., pl. **il·le·git·i·ma·cies.** the state or quality of being illegitimate.

il·le·git·i·mate (il'i jit'ə mit) adj. **1.** not authorized; not lawful: *an illegitimate ruler.* **2.** born to parents who are not married to each other: *an illegitimate child.* —**il'le·git'i·mate·ly,** adv.

ill–fat·ed (il'fā'tid) adj. **1.** having or doomed to have a bad fate or end; doomed from the start: *The ill-fated play closed after the second performance.* **2.** characterized by or causing misfortune; unlucky: *an ill-fated day.*

ill–fa·vored (il'fā'vərd) adj. unpleasant in appearance; ugly.

ill–got·ten (il'got'ən) adj. gotten by evil or dishonest means: *ill-gotten money.*

ill–hu·mored (il'hū'mərd, il'ū'mərd) adj. having or showing a bad temper or humor; irritable; cross.

il·lib·er·al (i lib'ər əl) adj. **1.** narrow-minded; bigoted; intolerant. **2.** not generous in giving; stingy.

il·lic·it (i lis'it) adj. forbidden by law; not allowed. —**il·lic'it·ly,** adv. —**il·lic'it·ness,** n. ▲ See **elicit** for usage note.

il·lim·it·a·ble (i lim'i tə bəl) adj. not capable of being limited or measured; limitless: *illimitable space.* —**il·lim'it·a·bly,** adv.

il·lit·er·a·cy (i lit'ər ə sē) n., pl. **il·lit·er·a·cies.** **1.** a lack of the ability to read or write. **2.** a lack of education or knowledge: *historical illiteracy.*

il·lit·er·ate (i lit'ər it) adj. **1.** unable to read or write. **2.** lacking or showing a lack of education or knowledge: *an illiterate opinion.* —n. a person who is illiterate. —**il·lit'er·ate·ly,** adv.

ill–man·nered (il'man'ərd) adj. having or showing bad manners; rude.

ill–na·tured (il'nā'chərd) adj. having or showing a disagreeable disposition. —**ill'–na'tured·ly,** adv.

ill·ness (il'nis) n., pl. **ill·ness·es. 1.** a condition or period of being ill: *to stay home from school during an illness.* **2.** a sickness; disease.

il·log·i·cal (i loj'i kəl) adj. **1.** not logical: *an illogical conclusion.* **2.** showing a lack of good sense or reasoning. —**il·log'i·cal·ly,** adv.

ill–starred (il'stärd') adj. ill-fated or unlucky.

ill–suit·ed (il'sü'tid) adj. not fitting; inappropriate: *Silly behavior is ill-suited to the seriousness of this occasion.*

ill–tem·pered (il'tem'pərd) adj. irritable; cross.

ill–timed (il'tīmd') adj. coming at the wrong or a bad time.

ill–treat (il'trēt') v.t. to treat badly or cruelly; abuse. —**ill'–treat'ment,** n.

il·lu·mi·nate (i lü'mə nāt') v.t., **il·lu·mi·nat·ed, il·lu·mi·nat·ing. 1.** to give light to; light up: *The sun illuminates the sky.* **2.** to decorate with lights: *to illuminate a fountain at night.* **3.** to make clear; explain: *The teacher's descriptions illuminate history more than any book.* **4.** to decorate (a scroll, manuscript, or page) with ornamental designs and pictures in gold, silver, and brilliant colors.

il·lu·mi·na·tion (i lü'mə nā'shən) n. **1.** the act of illuminating or the state of being illuminated. **2.** an amount or supply of light: *This lamp gives poor illumination.* **3.** decoration with lights. **4.** the decoration of a scroll, manuscript, or page of a book with ornamental designs and illustrations in gold, silver, and brilliant colors.

il·lu·mine (i lü'min) v.t., **il·lu·mined, il·lu·min·ing.** to illuminate.

illus. 1. illustrated. **2.** illustrator.

ill–use (v., il'ūz'; n., il'ūs') v.t., **ill–used, ill–us·ing.** to treat badly, cruelly, or unfairly; abuse. —n. bad, cruel, or unfair treatment.

il·lu·sion (i lü'zhən) n. **1.** a false or misleading idea or belief; misconception: *to have illusions about what life in*

a foreign country is like. **2.** an impression of the nature or appearance of something that is contrary to fact or reality: *The building gives the illusion of being taller than it really is.*

il·lu·sive (i lü'siv) adj. false or misleading; illusory. —**il·lu'sive·ly,** adv. —**il·lu'sive·ness,** n.

il·lu·so·ry (i lü'sə rē) adj. caused by or causing an illusion; false or misleading.

illust. 1. illustrated. **2.** illustration.

il·lus·trate (il'ə strāt', i lus'trāt') v.t., **il·lus·trat·ed, il·lus·trat·ing. 1.** to make clear or explain, as by the use of examples or comparisons: *The teacher illustrated how the human eye works by comparing it to a camera.* **2.** to provide with pictures, drawings, or diagrams that explain or decorate: *The publishers hired a famous artist to illustrate a book.* **3.** to be or serve as an example, explanation, or instance of: *These paintings illustrate the artist's early work.*

il·lus·tra·tion (il'ə strā'shən) n. **1.** something used to make clear or explain, such as an example or comparison. **2.** a picture, diagram, or drawing used to explain or decorate written or printed matter. **3.** the act or art of illustrating.

il·lus·tra·tive (i lus'trə tiv, il'ə strā'tiv) adj. used or serving to illustrate: *This book contains much illustrative material.* —**il·lus'tra·tive·ly,** adv.

il·lus·tra·tor (il'ə strā'tər) n. an artist who makes illustrations, as for books or magazines.

il·lus·tri·ous (i lus'trē əs) adj. **1.** distinguished or famous: *an illustrious diplomat.* **2.** marked by or giving greatness, distinction, or glory: *illustrious acts.* —**il·lus'tri·ous·ly,** adv. —**il·lus'tri·ous·ness,** n.

ill will, unfriendly feeling.

I'm (īm) contr. I am.

im–¹, the form of the prefix **in-¹** used before *b, m, p,* as in *immoral.*

im–², the form of the prefix **in-²** used before *b, m, p,* as in *imbibe.*

im·age (im'ij) n. **1.** a picture, statue, or other likeness of a person or thing: *The ancient coin had an image of the emperor on one side.* **2.** a picture or idea held in the mind of a person or thing that is not actually present: *I had formed an image of you before we met.* **3.** a person or thing that closely resembles another: *You are the image of your cousin.* **4.** a typical example; picture: *The gymnast is the image of good health.* **5.** a description or figure of speech, especially a metaphor or simile. **6.** an impression created by a person, group, or organization in the mind of the public: *The corporation wanted to change its public image.* **7.** a picture of an object produced when light rays from the object are focused on a surface, as by a lens or mirror. —v.t., **im·aged, im·ag·ing.** to make or form an image of.

im·age·ry (im'ij rē) n., pl. **im·age·ries. 1.** images formed in the mind, as by memory or imagination. **2.** the use of descriptions or figures of speech in writing or speech.

i·mag·i·na·ble (i maj'ə nə bəl) adj. that can be imagined: *to try every way imaginable to solve a puzzle.* —**i·mag'i·na·bly,** adv.

i·mag·i·nar·y (i maj'ə ner'ē) adj. **1.** existing only in the imagination; unreal. **2.** of or relating to imaginary numbers.

at; āpe; fär; câre; end; mē; it; īce; pîerce; hot; ōld; sông, fôrk; oil; out; up; ūse; rüle; pŭll; tûrn; chin; sing; shop; thin; **th**is; hw in white; zh in treasure. The symbol ə stands for the unstressed vowel sound heard in about, taken, pencil, lemon, and circus.

I

imaginary number, a number whose square is negative.

i·mag·i·na·tion (i maj′ə nā′shən) *n.* **1.** the power or process of forming images in the mind of things that are not actually present: *to relive a summer vacation in one's imagination.* **2.** the mental power or ability to create new images or ideas of things never experienced or to use or combine past images and ideas to form new ones: *It took great imagination to write that poem.*

i·mag·i·na·tive (i maj′ə nə tiv) *adj.* **1.** having or showing creative ability or a good imagination: *an imaginative child.* **2.** produced or characterized by creativity or imagination: *an imaginative story.* —**i·mag′i·na·tive·ly,** *adv.* —**i·mag′i·na·tive·ness,** *n.*

i·mag·ine (i maj′in) *v.,* **i·mag·ined, i·mag·in·ing.** —*v.t.* **1.** to picture (someone or something) in the mind; form a mental picture of: *to imagine life on another planet.* **2.** to suppose; guess: *I don't imagine they will come.* —*v.i.* to picture in the mind; think.

i·ma·go (i mā′gō) *n., pl.* **i·ma·goes** or **i·mag·i·nes** (i maj′ə nēz′). an insect in the adult stage.

i·mam (i mäm′) *n.* **1.** the prayer leader in a mosque. **2. Imam.** a Muslim religious leader considered by Shiites to be a successor of Muhammad. **3.** any of various Muslim religious and secular leaders who claim descent from Muhammad.

im·bal·ance (im bal′əns) *n.* a lack of balance.

im·be·cile (im′bə sil) *n.* **1.** a person who is mentally retarded and cannot develop beyond a mental age of eight years. ▲ now considered obsolete. **2.** a stupid or foolish person. —*adj.* another word for **imbecilic.**

im·be·cil·ic (im′bə sil′ik) *adj.* stupid or foolish: *imbecilic behavior.*

im·be·cil·i·ty (im′bə sil′i tē) *n., pl.* **im·be·cil·i·ties.** **1.** the condition of being an imbecile. **2.** stupidity or foolishness. **3.** an imbecilic thought, statement, or act.

im·bed (im bed′) *v.t.,* **im·bed·ded, im·bed·ding.** another spelling of **embed.**

im·bibe (im bīb′) *v.,* **im·bibed, im·bib·ing.** —*v.t.* **1.** to take into the mouth and swallow (liquid); drink. **2.** to take in as if by drinking; absorb: *The dry soil imbibed the water.* **3.** to take into the mind and keep: *to imbibe knowledge.* —*v.i.* to drink something, especially liquor.

im·bro·glio (im brōl′yō) *n., pl.* **im·bro·glios.** **1.** a complicated argument or disagreement: *The two neighbors got into an imbroglio over the boundaries of their property.* **2.** a confused or complicated situation.

im·bue (im bū′) *v.t.,* **im·bued, im·bu·ing.** **1.** to fill or inspire, as with emotions, ideals, or opinions: *The young lawyer was imbued with the spirit of justice.* **2.** to fill completely, as with color; saturate.

im·i·ta·ble (im′i tə bəl) *adj.* capable of being imitated.

im·i·tate (im′i tāt′) *v.t.,* **im·i·tat·ed, im·i·tat·ing.** **1.** to follow or try to follow the example of: *to imitate an older sister or brother.* **2.** to copy the behavior or mannerisms of; mimic: *to imitate a famous singer.* **3.** to make a copy or duplicate of: *The forger imitated the handwriting on the check.* **4.** to have the appearance of; look like; resemble: *The floors were carefully painted to imitate marble.*

im·i·ta·tion (im′i tā′shən) *n.* **1.** the act of imitating: *Imitation of a bird's call may attract other birds.* **2.** a copy, especially one that is of poor quality: *That is not a genuine antique clock, but only an imitation.* —*adj.* made to look like something genuine or superior; not real: *imitation mink.*

im·i·ta·tive (im′i tā′tiv) *adj.* **1.** imitating or tending to imitate: *Children are imitative of their elders.* **2.** characterized by or showing imitation: *The word "chirp" is imitative of the sound made by a bird.* —**im′i·ta′tive·ly,** *adv.* —**im′i·ta′tive·ness,** *n.*

im·i·ta·tor (im′i tā′tər) *n.* a person or thing that imitates.

im·mac·u·late (i mak′yə lit) *adj.* **1.** free from dust, grime, or clutter; very clean or neat: *My cousin's house is always immaculate.* **2.** free from fault or blemish; flawless: *an immaculate copy of the original, a person with an immaculate complexion.* **3.** free from sin; pure. —**im·mac′u·late·ly,** *adv.* —**im·mac′u·late·ness,** *n.*

Immaculate Conception, the Roman Catholic doctrine that the Virgin Mary was conceived free from original sin.

Im·man·u·el (i man′ū əl) *also,* **Em·man·u·el.** *n.* another name for the **Messiah.**

im·ma·te·ri·al (im′ə tîr′ē əl) *adj.* **1.** of little or no importance or value; unimportant: *It is immaterial to me whether they come or not.* **2.** not consisting of matter; spiritual. —**im′ma·te′ri·al·ly,** *adv.* —**im′ma·te′ri·al·ness,** *n.*

im·ma·ture (im′ə chùr′, im′ə tùr′, im′ə tyùr′) *adj.* **1.** not having reached full growth or development; not mature: *an immature plant.* **2.** foolish or childish: *immature behavior.* —**im′ma·ture′ly,** *adv.*

im·ma·tu·ri·ty (im′ə chùr′i tē, im′ə tùr′i tē, im′ə tyùr′i tē) *n.* the state or quality of being immature.

im·meas·ur·a·ble (i mezh′ər ə bəl) *adj.* that cannot be measured: *a treasure of immeasurable value.* —**im·meas′ur·a·bly,** *adv.*

im·me·di·a·cy (i mē′dē ə sē) *n.* the state or quality of being immediate.

im·me·di·ate (i mē′dē it) *adj.* **1.** done or happening without delay; instant: *an immediate answer.* **2.** of or relating to the present time: *I have no immediate plans.* **3.** close in time or space; near: *We do not plan on moving in the immediate future.* **4.** nearest in relationship: *They only invited the immediate family to the wedding.* **5.** with nothing coming between; direct: *The evidence had no immediate bearing on the case. Our wall is in immediate contact with theirs.* —**im·me′di·ate·ly,** *adv.* —**im·me′di·ate·ness,** *n.*

im·me·mo·ri·al (im′ə môr′ē əl) *adj.* going back beyond memory or record; ancient. —**im′me·mo′ri·al·ly,** *adv.*

im·mense (i mens′) *adj.* of great size, extent, or degree; very large; huge: *An immense building is under construction. The book was an immense success.* —**im·mense′ly,** *adv.* —**im·mense′ness,** *n.*

im·men·si·ty (i men′si tē) *n.* the state or quality of being immense; hugeness; vastness: *the immensity of the ocean.*

im·merse (i mûrs′) *v.t.,* **im·mersed, im·mers·ing.** **1.** to plunge or dip into water or other liquid so as to cover completely. **2.** to baptize by immersion. **3.** to involve deeply; absorb: *The audience was immersed in the play.*

im·mer·sion (i mûr′zhən) *n.* **1.** the act of immersing or the state of being immersed. **2.** a method of baptism in which all or part of the body is placed under water.

im·mi·grant (im′i grənt) *n.* a person who immigrates. ▲ See **emigrant** for usage note.

im·mi·grate (im′i grāt′) *v.i.,* **im·mi·grat·ed, im·mi·grat·ing.** to enter a country or region in which one was not born in order to make a permanent home there. —**im′mi·gra′tion,** *n.*

im·mi·nent (im′ə nənt) *adj.* about to happen; impending: *The darkening sky showed that a thunderstorm was imminent.* —**im′mi·nence,** *n.* —**im′mi·nent·ly,** *adv.*

im·mo·bile (i mō′bil) *adj.* **1.** not able to move or be moved; fixed: *an immobile park bench cemented into place.* **2.** not moving; motionless: *to stand immobile, like a statue.* —**im′mo·bil′i·ty,** *n.*

immobilize
broken leg immobilized in a cast

im·mo·bi·lize (i mō′bə līz′) *v.t.*, **im·mo·bi·lized, im·mo·bi·liz·ing.** to make immobile; fix in place. —**im·mo′bi·li·za′tion,** *n.*

im·mod·er·ate (i mod′ər it) *adj.* going beyond usual or proper limits; not moderate: *immoderate demands.* —**im·mod′er·ate·ly,** *adv.*

im·mod·est (i mod′ist) *adj.* **1.** lacking or showing a lack of modesty. **2.** tending to praise oneself too much; boastful. **3.** improper; indecent: *immodest clothing.* —**im·mod′est·ly,** *adv.*

im·mod·es·ty (i mod′ə stē) *n.* the state or quality of being immodest.

im·mo·late (im′ə lāt′) *v.t.*, **im·mo·lat·ed, im·mo·lat·ing.** to kill as a sacrifice. —**im′mo·la′tion,** *n.*

im·mor·al (i môr′əl, i mor′əl) *adj.* **1.** characterized by or showing wickedness; not moral: *immoral actions, an immoral person.* **2.** indecent or lewd. —**im·mor′al·ly,** *adv.*

im·mo·ral·i·ty (im′ə ral′i tē) *n.*, *pl.* **im·mo·ral·i·ties.** **1.** immoral character or quality. **2.** an immoral act.

im·mor·tal (i môr′təl) *adj.* **1.** never dying; living forever. **2.** remembered or famous through future time: *the immortal works of Shakespeare.* —*n.* **1.** an immortal being. **2.** a person remembered or famous through future time. —**im·mor′tal·ly,** *adv.*

im·mor·tal·i·ty (im′ôr tal′i tē) *n.* **1.** the supposed power of living on after death. **2.** the fact of being remembered or famous through future time; everlasting fame.

im·mor·tal·ize (i môr′tə līz′) *v.t.*, **im·mor·tal·ized, im·mor·tal·iz·ing.** to make remembered or famous through future time: *Many poets wrote verse that immortalized those they loved.*

im·mov·a·ble (i mü′və bəl) *adj.* **1.** not able to move or be moved; stationary. **2.** not easily changed or shaken; steadfast; unyielding: *to be immovable in one's opinions.* —*n.* **immovables.** property that cannot be moved from place to place, such as land. —**im·mov′a·bil′i·ty,** *n.* —**im·mov′a·bly,** *adv.*

im·mune (i mūn′) *adj.* **1.** protected from a disease or infection naturally, by inoculation, or by vaccination: *immune to measles.* **2.** of or relating to the production of antibodies, usually in response to a foreign substance in the body: *an immune response to a virus.* **3.** not affected by something, especially something disagreeable or harmful: *immune to threats.*

immune system, the system that protects the body from disease. White blood cells and antibodies are parts of the immune system.

im·mu·ni·ty (i mū′ni tē) *n.*, *pl.* **im·mu·ni·ties.** **1.** resistance to a disease or infection, especially as a result of vaccination or inoculation: *immunity to smallpox.* **2.** freedom or protection from anything disagreeable or harmful: *immunity from attack.* **3.** a special exemption, as from laws or taxes: *Foreign diplomats are often granted immunity from some of the laws of a country.*

im·mu·nize (im′yə nīz′) *v.t.*, **im·mu·nized, im·mu·niz·ing.** to make immune, as by vaccination against a disease. —**im′mu·ni·za′tion,** *n.*

im·mu·nol·o·gy (im′yə nol′ə jē) *n.* the branch of medicine dealing with immunity to disease, especially infections.

im·mure (i myur′) *v.t.*, **im·mured, im·mur·ing.** to enclose within walls, as in a prison. —**im·mure′ment,** *n.*

im·mu·ta·ble (i mū′tə bəl) *adj.* that cannot be changed; unchanging: *an immutable law of nature.* —**im·mu′ta·bil′i·ty, im·mu′ta·ble·ness,** *n.* —**im·mu′ta·bly,** *adv.*

imp (imp) *n.* **1.** a young or small demon; mischievous spirit. **2.** a mischievous child.

imp. 1. imperative. **2.** imperfect. **3.** imported; importer.

im·pact (im′pakt) *n.* **1.** the force or action of one object striking against another: *The glass shattered upon impact with the floor.* **2.** a strong effect or influence: *Computers have had a great impact on modern life.*

im·pact·ed (im pak′tid) *adj.* **1.** (of a tooth) pressed between the jawbone and another tooth so that it cannot grow out. **2.** closely packed together or wedged in.

im·pair (im pâr′) *v.t.* to lessen the quality, strength, or value of; damage; weaken: *The accident impaired my vision.* —**im·pair′ment,** *n.*

im·pal·a (im pal′ə) *n.* a small, slender African antelope having a reddish or golden brown coat. The impala is known for its ability to leap great distances.

im·pale (im pāl′) *v.t.*, **im·paled, im·pal·ing.** **1.** to fix on a stake or other pointed object by piercing. **2.** to torture or put to death by pushing onto a stake. —**im·pale′ment,** *n.*

Impala

im·pal·pa·ble (im pal′pə bəl) *adj.* **1.** that cannot be felt by the sense of touch: *impalpable shadows.* **2.** not easily understood or grasped by the mind; incomprehensible: *impalpable distinctions.* —**im·pal′pa·bil′i·ty,** *n.* —**im·pal′pa·bly,** *adv.*

im·pan·el (im pan′əl) *also*, **em·pan·el.** *v.t.*, **im·pan·eled, im·pan·el·ing;** *also, British*, **im·pan·elled, im·pan·el·ling.** **1.** to place (someone) on a panel or list, as for jury duty. **2.** to select (a jury) from such a list. —**im·pan′el·ment,** *n.*

im·part (im pärt′) *v.t.* **1.** to make known; tell; disclose: *to impart information.* **2.** to give; bestow: *The judge's presence imparted a sense of dignity to the committee.*

im·par·tial (im pär′shəl) *adj.* not favoring one more than another; without prejudice; unbiased: *Judges should be impartial.* —**im·par′tial·ly,** *adv.*

im·par·ti·al·i·ty (im pär′shē al′i tē) *n.* freedom from bias; fairness.

---

at; āpe; fär; câre; end; mē; it; īce; pierce; hot; ōld; sông, fôrk; oil; out; up; ūse; rüle; pull; tûrn; chin; sing; shop; thin; **this;** hw in white; zh in treasure. The symbol ə stands for the unstressed vowel sound heard in about, taken, pencil, lemon, and circus.

I

481

im·pass·a·ble (im pas'ə bəl) *adj.* that cannot be passed or traveled over, across, or through: *The road was impassable after the snowstorm.* —**im·pass'a·bil'i·ty,** *n.* —**im·pass'a·bly,** *adv.*

im·passe (im'pas') *n.* a position or situation from which it is impossible to advance or go on; deadlock: *The workers and the company reached an impasse in their negotiations.*

im·pas·sioned (im pash'ənd) *adj.* filled with passion or strong feeling; fiery; ardent: *The speaker made an impassioned plea for justice.*

im·pas·sive (im pas'iv) *adj.* not feeling or showing emotion; unmoved: *The defendant remained impassive throughout the trial.* —**im·pas'sive·ly,** *adv.* —**im·pas'sive·ness,** *n.*

im·pa·tience (im pā'shəns) *n.* **1.** irritation or annoyance because of delay or opposition; lack of patience. **2.** restless eagerness, as for change or activity.

im·pa·tiens (im pā'shənz) *n., pl.* **im·pa·tiens.** any of numerous plants with fleshy stems and flowers bearing five petals, grown in gardens or as houseplants for their colorful flowers.

im·pa·tient (im pā'shənt) *adj.* **1.** irritated or annoyed by delay or opposition: *The commuters were impatient because the train was late.* **2.** showing lack of patience: *an impatient answer.* **3.** restlessly eager: *The children were impatient for the weekend to come.* —**im·pa'tient·ly,** *adv.*

im·peach (im pēch') *v.t.* **1.** to bring formal charges against (a public official) for crime or misconduct in office. **2.** to question, challenge, or cast doubt on: *The defense attorney impeached the honesty of the witness.* —**im·peach'ment,** *n.*

im·pec·ca·ble (im pek'ə bəl) *adj.* free from error or defect; without fault; flawless: *impeccable manners, impeccable judgment.* —**im·pec'ca·bil'i·ty,** *n.* —**im·pec'ca·bly,** *adv.*

im·pe·cu·ni·ous (im'pi kū'nē əs) *adj.* having little or no money; poor; penniless. —**im'pe·cu'ni·ous·ly,** *adv.*

im·pede (im pēd') *v.t.,* **im·ped·ed, im·ped·ing.** to obstruct, hinder, or delay: *The rough seas impeded the ship's progress.* [From the Latin word *impedire* meaning "to shackle, hamper," going back to the prefix *in-* "not" and *pes* "foot."]

im·ped·i·ment (im ped'ə mənt) *n.* **1.** something that impedes; obstruction; obstacle. **2.** a physical defect: *a speech impediment.*

im·pel (im pel') *v.t.,* **im·pelled, im·pel·ling. 1.** to drive or urge to some action: *War impelled them to leave the country.* **2.** to propel or cause to move forward: *The boat was impelled by a strong wind.*

im·pend (im pend') *v.i.* to be about to happen; threaten: *A storm impends.*

im·pend·ing (im pen'ding) *adj.* about to happen; threatening: *an impending crisis.*

im·pen·e·tra·ble (im pen'i trə bəl) *adj.* **1.** that cannot be pierced, entered, or passed through: *an impenetrable forest.* **2.** that cannot be understood: *an impenetrable mystery.* —**im·pen'e·tra·bil'i·ty,** *n.* —**im·pen'e·tra·bly,** *adv.*

im·pen·i·tent (im pen'i tənt) *adj.* not penitent or sorry for having done wrong. —**im·pen'i·tent·ly,** *adv.*

imper., imperative.

im·per·a·tive (im per'ə tiv) *adj.* **1.** not to be avoided; absolutely necessary; urgent: *It is imperative that we leave at once.* **2.** of the nature of or expressing a command; commanding; authoritative: *an imperative tone of voice.* **3.** *Grammar.* of, relating to, or indicating the mood of a verb used to express commands, requests, or pleas. In the sentence *Go to your room,* the verb *go* is in the imperative mood. —*n.* **1.** something that is imperative, as a command or obligation. **2.** *Grammar.* **a.** the imperative mood. **b.** a verb or verb form in this mood. —**im·per'a·tive·ly,** *adv.* —**im·per'a·tive·ness,** *n.*

im·per·cep·ti·ble (im'pər sep'tə bəl) *adj.* too slight or gradual to be seen or noticed: *an imperceptible change.* —**im'per·cep'ti·bil'i·ty,** *n.* —**im'per·cep'ti·bly,** *adv.*

imperf., imperfect.

im·per·fect (im pûr'fikt) *adj.* **1.** having a fault or flaw; not perfect; faulty: *an imperfect diamond.* **2.** not fully developed, formed, or done; incomplete: *I have an imperfect understanding of French.* **3.** in certain languages, relating to or indicating the tense of a verb that expresses continuous or incomplete action in the past. —*n.* the imperfect tense. —**im·per'fect·ly,** *adv.* —**im·per'fect·ness,** *n.*

im·per·fec·tion (im'pər fek'shən) *n.* **1.** the state or quality of being imperfect. **2.** a fault; flaw: *There was an imperfection in the cloth.*

im·pe·ri·al (im pîr'ē əl) *adj.* **1.** of or relating to an empire or to an emperor or empress. **2.** of or relating to a country's military, political, or economic power or control over other countries or colonies. **3.** of great size or superior quality. —*n.* a small, pointed beard growing below the lower lip. —**im·pe'ri·al·ly,** *adv.*

im·pe·ri·al·ism (im pîr'ē ə liz'əm) *n.* **1.** the policy of extending a country's power or control over other countries or colonies by military, political, or economic means. **2.** an imperial system of government; rule of an emperor.

im·pe·ri·al·ist (im pîr'ē ə list) *n.* a person who favors or supports imperialism. —*adj.* of, relating to, or favoring imperialism: *imperialist policies.* —**im·pe'ri·al·is'tic,** *adj.* —**im·pe'ri·al·is'ti·cal·ly,** *adv.*

im·per·il (im per'əl) *v.t.,* **im·per·iled, im·per·il·ing;** *also, British,* **im·per·illed, im·per·il·ling.** to put in danger; expose to peril: *The driver's foolish actions imperiled the lives of the passengers.*

im·pe·ri·ous (im pîr'ē əs) *adj.* **1.** haughty or arrogant; domineering; overbearing: *an imperious way of speaking.* **2.** imperative; urgent: *an imperious need.* —**im·pe'ri·ous·ly,** *adv.* —**im·pe'ri·ous·ness,** *n.*

im·per·ish·a·ble (im per'i shə bəl) *adj.* not subject to destruction or decay; not perishable; enduring: *imperishable achievements.* —**im·per'ish·a·bil'i·ty,** *n.* —**im·per'ish·a·bly,** *adv.*

im·per·ma·nent (im pûr'mə nənt) *adj.* subject to change; not permanent; temporary. —**im·per'ma·nence,** *n.* —**im·per'ma·nent·ly,** *adv.*

im·per·me·a·ble (im pûr'mē ə bəl) *adj.* that cannot be penetrated, as by a fluid; impenetrable.

im·per·son·al (im pûr'sə nəl) *adj.* **1.** not concerned with or referring to a particular person or persons; not personal: *impersonal criticism.* **2.** without emotion or feeling. **3.** not existing as a person. **4.** *Grammar.* **a.** (of a verb) denoting an action by an unspecified subject, used in the third person singular. In the sentence *It snowed today, snowed* is an impersonal verb. **b.** (of a pronoun) referring to an indefinite subject. —**im·per'son·al·ly,** *adv.*

im·per·son·ate (im pûr'sə nāt') *v.t.,* **im·per·son·at·ed, im·per·son·at·ing. 1.** to take on or copy the appearance, behavior, or mannerisms of in order to amuse or deceive: *to impersonate a police officer.* **2.** to act the part or character of, as in a play. —**im·per'son·a'tion,** *n.* —**im·per'son·a'tor,** *n.*

im·per·ti·nence (im pûr'tə nəns) *n.* **1.** boldness and rudeness; insolence. **2.** an impertinent act or remark. **3.** lack of relevance or appropriateness.

im·per·ti·nent (im pûr'tə nənt) *adj.* **1.** offensively bold and rude; insolent: *an impertinent child.* **2.** not relevant or appropriate. —**im·per'ti·nent·ly,** *adv.*

im·per·turb·a·ble (im'pər tûr'bə bəl) *adj.* not easily excited or disturbed; calm. —**im'per·turb'a·bil'i·ty,** *n.* —**im'per·turb'a·bly,** *adv.*

im·per·vi·ous (im pûr′vē əs) *adj.* **1.** not easily affected, influenced, or disturbed: *to be impervious to criticism.* **2.** not allowing passage; impenetrable: *impervious to water.* —**im·per′vi·ous·ly,** *adv.* —**im·per′vi·ous·ness,** *n.*

im·pe·ti·go (im′pi tī′gō) *n.* a contagious bacterial skin disease characterized by blisters that break open and release pus.

im·pet·u·os·i·ty (im pech′ü os′i tē) *n., pl.* **im·pet·u·os·i·ties. 1.** the state or quality of being impetuous. **2.** an impetuous act.

im·pet·u·ous (im pech′ü əs) *adj.* **1.** rushing headlong into things; impulsive and energetic: *an impetuous person.* **2.** made or done impulsively and suddenly; rash: *an impetuous choice.* **3.** moving with great force or violence; rapid; furious: *the impetuous winds of a gale.* —**im·pet′u·ous·ly,** *adv.* —**im·pet′u·ous·ness,** *n.*

im·pe·tus (im′pi təs) *n., pl.* **im·pe·tus·es. 1.** the momentum of a moving body. **2.** the force that puts a body in motion. **3.** energy, strength, or other moving force; stimulus: *The rise in crime gave impetus to demands for more police.*

im·pi·e·ty (im pī′i tē) *n., pl.* **im·pi·e·ties. 1.** a lack of reverence or respect. **2.** an impious act.

im·pinge (im pinj′) *v.i.,* **im·pinged, im·ping·ing. 1.** to interfere with; encroach; infringe: *That proposed law impinges on freedom of speech.* **2.** to strike or hit: *The light from the movie projector impinged on the screen.* —**im·pinge′ment,** *n.*

im·pi·ous (im′pē əs, im pī′əs) *adj.* lacking reverence or respect. —**im′pi·ous·ly,** *adv.* —**im′pi·ous·ness,** *n.*

imp·ish (im′pish) *adj.* of or like an imp; mischievous: *an impish grin.* —**imp′ish·ly,** *adv.* —**imp′ish·ness,** *n.*

im·plac·a·ble (im plak′ə bəl, im plā′kə bəl) *adj.* that cannot be calmed or pacified: *implacable anger.* —**im·plac′a·bil′i·ty,** *n.* —**im·plac′a·bly,** *adv.*

im·plant (*v.,* im plant′; *n.,* im′plant) *v.t.* **1.** to fix firmly and deeply; instill: *They implanted a love of nature in their children.* **2.** to plant or root firmly: *The bulbs were implanted in the ground.* **3.** to insert (living tissue or a device) in the body by surgery, as in grafting. —*n.* living tissue or a device inserted in the body by surgery. —**im′plan·ta′tion,** *n.*

im·plau·si·ble (im plô′zə bəl) *adj.* not believable; unlikely: *an implausible explanation.* —**im·plau′si·bil′i·ty,** *n.* —**im·plau′si·bly,** *adv.*

im·ple·ment (*n.,* im′plə mənt; *v.,* im′plə ment′) *n.* something used in performing a task or other work; tool; instrument: *kitchen implements.* —*v.t.* to put into effect; carry out: *to implement a law.* —**im′ple·men·ta′tion,** *n.*

im·pli·cate (im′pli kāt′) *v.t.,* **im·pli·cat·ed, im·pli·cat·ing.** to claim or show to be involved, as in a crime: *The suspects implicated two others as having helped in the crime.*

im·pli·ca·tion (im′pli kā′shən) *n.* **1.** something that is implied; indirect suggestion. **2.** the act of implicating or the state of being implicated, as in a crime. **3.** the act of implying or the state of being implied.

im·plic·it (im plis′it) *adj.* **1.** suggested or understood, though not directly expressed: *Disapproval was implicit in the minister's frown.* **2.** without reservation or doubt; unquestioning; absolute: *implicit faith in the loyalty of a friend.* —**im·plic′it·ly,** *adv.* —**im·plic′it·ness,** *n.*

im·plore (im plôr′) *v.t.,* **im·plored, im·plor·ing. 1.** to plead with; ask earnestly; beg: *They implored the whole school to contribute to the fund.* **2.** to beg or pray for earnestly: *to implore forgiveness.*

im·ply (im plī′) *v.t.,* **im·plied, im·ply·ing. 1.** to suggest or express indirectly: *Are you implying that I caused the trouble?* **2.** to involve as a necessary part, condition, or consequence: *Having a high school diploma implies knowing how to read.* ▲ See **infer** for usage note.

im·po·lite (im′pə līt′) *adj.* not having or showing good manners; not courteous; rude. —**im′po·lite′ly,** *adv.* —**im′po·lite′ness,** *n.*

im·pol·i·tic (im pol′i tik) *adj.* not conforming to good judgment or policy; not politic; unwise.

im·pon·der·a·ble (im pon′dər ə bəl) *adj.* that cannot be weighed or evaluated with certainty. —*n.* an imponderable thing or factor: *There are too many imponderables for us to make a decision.* —**im·pon′der·a·ble·ness,** *n.* —**im·pon′der·a·bly,** *adv.*

im·port (*v.,* im pôrt′; *n.,* im′pôrt′) *v.t.* **1.** to bring in (goods) from a foreign country for sale or use: *to import tea from India.* **2.** to have as a meaning: *What do these words import?* —*n.* **1.** something that is imported for sale or use. **2.** the act of importing goods; importation. **3.** meaning; significance: *What is the import of your remark?* **4.** consequence; importance: *That is a matter of great import.*

im·por·tance (im pôr′təns) *n.* the state or quality of being important.

im·por·tant (im pôr′tənt) *adj.* **1.** having special value, consequence, or meaning: *Your friendship is very important to me.* **2.** having special authority, social position, or influence: *They are important members of the city council.* **3.** acting important; giving the impression of being important: *The diplomats had an important air about them.* —**im·por′tant·ly,** *adv.*

im·por·ta·tion (im′pôr tā′shən) *n.* **1.** the act of importing. **2.** something that is imported.

im·port·er (im pôr′tər, im′pôr′tər) *n.* a person or company in the business of importing goods.

im·por·tu·nate (im pôr′chə nit) *adj.* annoyingly or stubbornly persistent; insistent: *an importunate request.* —**im·por′tu·nate·ly,** *adv.* —**im·por′tu·nate·ness,** *n.*

im·por·tune (im′pôr tün′, im′pôr tūn′) *v.t.,* **im·por·tuned, im·por·tun·ing.** to trouble with constant requests or demands.

im·por·tu·ni·ty (im′pôr tü′ni tē, im′por tū′ni tē) *n., pl.* **im·por·tu·ni·ties.** the act of importuning or the state of being importunate.

im·pose (im pōz′) *v.,* **im·posed, im·pos·ing.** —*v.t.* **1.** to establish and apply by legal means as an obligation: *to impose taxes, to impose a penalty.* **2.** to inflict or force: *to impose one's will on others.* **3.** to force (one's presence): *They seem always to impose themselves on us when we're talking.* —*v.i.* **1.** to force oneself upon others; intrude. **2.** to take advantage of: *I wouldn't want to impose on our friendship by asking such a favor.* —**im·pos′er,** *n.*

im·pos·ing (im pō′zing) *adj.* causing awe or admiration because of great size or dignity; impressive: *an imposing building.* —**im·pos′ing·ly,** *adv.*

im·po·si·tion (im′pə zish′ən) *n.* **1.** the act of imposing. **2.** something that is imposed. **3.** a request or demand that takes advantage of someone's goodwill: *an imposition on a friendship.*

im·pos·si·bil·i·ty (im pos′ə bil′i tē) *n., pl.* **im·pos·si·bil·i·ties. 1.** the state or quality of being impossible. **2.** something that is impossible.

im·pos·si·ble (im pos′ə bəl) *adj.* **1.** not capable of being or happening; not possible: *It is impossible to live forever.* **2.** not capable of being realized or done: *That is an impossible scheme.* **3.** not capable of being endured; very

I

at; āpe; fär; câre; end; mē; it; īce; pîerce; hot; ōld; sông, fôrk; oil; out; up; ūse; rüle; pùll; tûrn; chin; sing; shop; thin; this; hw in white; zh in treasure. The symbol ə stands for the unstressed vowel sound heard in about, taken, pencil, lemon, and circus.

objectionable: *They are impossible people to work with. This is an impossible situation.* **4.** not acceptable as truth: *an impossible explanation.* —**im·pos'si·bly,** *adv.*

im·post (im'pōst') *n.* a tax or duty, especially on imported goods.

im·pos·tor (im pos'tər) *n.* a person who deceives by taking on the name or character of someone else: *It was soon discovered that they were not the real king and queen, only impostors.*

im·pos·ture (im pos'chər) *n.* a deception, especially by taking on the name or character of someone else.

im·po·tent (im'pə tənt) *adj.* lacking force or effectiveness; helpless: *Without ammunition the troops were impotent against enemy attack.* —**im'po·tence,** *n.* —**im'po·tent·ly,** *adv.*

im·pound (im pound') *v.t.* **1.** to shut up in a pound: *to impound a stray dog.* **2.** to seize and put in the custody of a court of law: *The court ordered that the company's papers and records be impounded until after the investigation.* **3.** to collect (water), as in a reservoir. —**im·pound'er,** *n.* —**im·pound'ment,** *n.*

im·pov·er·ish (im pov'ər ish) *v.t.* **1.** to make very poor: *Loss of crops by drought impoverished the farmers.* **2.** to take away the strength, richness, or resources of: *Poor farming methods impoverished the land.* —**im·pov'er·ish·ment,** *n.*

im·prac·ti·ca·ble (im prak'ti kə bəl) *adj.* not capable of being accomplished, carried out, or put into practice: *an impracticable plan.* —**im·prac'ti·ca·bil'i·ty,** *n.* —**im·prac'ti·ca·bly,** *adv.*

im·prac·ti·cal (im prak'ti kəl) *adj.* lacking good sense or usefulness; not practical: *It's impractical to take so many extra clothes on a short hike.*

im·prac·ti·cal·i·ty (im prak'ti kal'i tē) *n., pl.* **im·prac·ti·cal·i·ties.** **1.** the state or quality of being impractical. **2.** something impractical.

im·pre·ca·tion (im'pri kā'shən) *n.* **1.** the act of calling down a curse or other evil on someone. **2.** a curse.

im·pre·cise (im'prə sīs') *adj.* not precise; inexact; vague. —**im'pre·cise'ly,** *adv.*

im·preg·na·ble (im preg'nə bəl) *adj.* **1.** not capable of being taken by force; able to resist attack: *an impregnable fortress.* **2.** not capable of being moved, shaken, or overcome; firm: *an impregnable argument.* —**im·preg'na·bil'i·ty,** *n.* —**im·preg'na·bly,** *adv.*

im·preg·nate (im preg'nāt) *v.t.,* **im·preg·nat·ed, im·preg·nat·ing.** **1.** to make pregnant; cause to conceive. **2.** to make fertile; fertilize. **3.** to cause to be saturated with; permeate: *to impregnate wood with furniture polish.* —**im'preg·na'tion,** *n.*

im·pre·sa·ri·o (im'prə sär'ē ō', im'prə sar'ē ō') *n., pl.* **im·pre·sa·ri·os.** a person who organizes or manages entertainment events, especially ballets, operas, or concerts.

im·press¹ (*v.,* im pres'; *n.,* im'pres') *v.t.* **1.** to influence or produce a strong effect on the mind or feelings of: *The speaker's honesty impressed us.* **2.** to fix firmly in the mind: *I tried hard to impress your phone number on my memory.* **3.** to form or make a mark or design on (something) by pressing or stamping: *to impress wax with a seal.* **4.** to form or make by pressing or stamping: *to impress figures on coins.* —*n., pl.* **im·press·es.** **1.** the act of forming or making a mark or design on something by pressing or stamping. **2.** a mark or design made in this way. [From the Latin word *impressus,* past participle of *imprimere* meaning both "to press upon, stamp" and "to impress¹," from the prefix *in-* "in, into" + *premere* "to press."]

im·press² (im pres') *v.t.* **1.** to force to enter military service, especially the navy. **2.** to take (property) by force for public use. [*Im-²* + *press².*] —**im·press'ment,** *n.*

im·pres·sion (im presh'ən) *n.* **1.** an effect or influence produced on the mind, senses, or feelings: *The experience of flying for the first time left a lasting impression on me.* **2.** a feeling or judgment about someone or something: *My first impression of them proved to be correct.* **3.** a notion or belief: *I was under the impression that they were related to each other.* **4.** a mark or design produced by pressing or stamping: *We made impressions of our hands in the wet concrete.* **5.** an impersonation; imitation: *The child gave an impression of a monkey.* **6.** the act or process of impressing.

im·pres·sion·a·ble (im presh'ə nə bəl) *adj.* easily impressed or influenced: *an impressionable teenager.*

im·pres·sion·ism (im presh'ə niz'əm) *n.* **1.** a method or school of painting developed in the late nineteenth century by French painters. It is characterized by the direct observation of the effects of light on a subject at a given moment. **2.** a method and style of musical composition of the late nineteenth and early twentieth centuries in which rich harmonies are used to create mood and atmosphere.

impressionism
a painting by Claude Monet

im·pres·sion·ist (im presh'ə nist) *n.* a person who practices impressionism, especially in painting.

im·pres·sion·is·tic (im presh'ə nis'tik) *adj.* of, relating to, or characteristic of impressionism.

im·pres·sive (im pres'iv) *adj.* producing or tending to produce a strong impression on the mind; exciting attention, emotion, or admiration: *an impressive victory.* —**im·pres'sive·ly,** *adv.* —**im·pres'sive·ness,** *n.*

im·pri·ma·tur (im'prə mä'tər, im'prə mā'tər) *n.* **1.** an authorization to print or publish something, as a book or article, granted by an official of the Roman Catholic Church. **2.** authorization or approval: *The committee's plan has the imprimatur of the mayor.*

im·print (*n.,* im'print'; *v.,* im print') *n.* **1.** a mark or depression produced by pressing or stamping. **2.** an effect or mark: *Years of poverty left an imprint on the family.* **3.** a publisher's or printer's name, the place and date of publication, and sometimes a trademark, printed on the title page of a book. —*v.t.* **1.** to make or produce (a mark or design) by pressing or stamping. **2.** to produce a mark or design on by pressing or stamping; print. **3.** to fix firmly in the mind or memory.

im·pris·on (im priz'ən) *v.t.* **1.** to put or keep in prison. **2.** to confine or restrain in any way. —**im·pris'on·ment,** *n.*

im·prob·a·bil·i·ty (im prob'ə bil'i tē, im'prob ə bil'i tē) *n., pl.* **im·prob·a·bil·i·ties.** **1.** the quality of being improbable; unlikelihood. **2.** something improbable.

im·prob·a·ble (im prob′ə bəl) *adj.* not probable; unlikely: *an improbable story.* —**im·prob′a·bly,** *adv.*

im·promp·tu (im promp′tü, im promp′tü) *adj.* made or done without preparation or previous thought; offhand: *impromptu remarks.* —*n.* anything made or done on the spur of the moment. —*adv.* without preparation or previous thought: *to speak impromptu.* [From the French word *impromptu*, from the Latin phrase *in promptu* meaning "ready, at hand," from the words *in* "in, into" + *promptus* "ready."]

im·prop·er (im prop′ər) *adj.* 1. not according to fact, truth, or established usage; not correct. 2. not according to accepted standards of decency or good taste: *improper behavior.* —**im·prop′er·ly,** *adv.*

improper fraction, a fraction whose numerator is greater than, or equal to, its denominator, such as ⁸/₅ or ⁶/₆.

improper subset, any subset that is not a proper subset.

im·pro·pri·e·ty (im′prə prī′i tē) *n., pl.* **im·pro·pri·e·ties.** 1. the quality of being improper. 2. an improper act or behavior.

im·prove (im prüv′) *v.,* **im·proved, im·prov·ing.** —*v.t.* to make better: *I am taking lessons to improve my singing.* —*v.i.* to become better: *The weather has improved greatly since last week.* —**im·prov′a·ble,** *adj.*

·**to improve on** or **to improve upon.** to do or make something better than.

im·prove·ment (im prüv′mənt) *n.* 1. the act of improving or the state of being improved. 2. a change or addition that improves something, as in quality or value: *The new curtains are an improvement to the room.* 3. a person or thing that is better than another: *The team's new manager is an improvement over the past one.*

im·prov·i·dent (im prov′i dənt) *adj.* not cautious in providing for future needs; lacking foresight: *to be improvident in spending.* —**im·prov′i·dence,** *n.* —**im·prov′i·dent·ly,** *adv.*

im·prov·i·sa·tion (im prov′ə zā′shən) *n.* 1. the act or art of improvising. 2. something that is improvised.

im·pro·vise (im′prə vīz′) *v.t.,* **im·pro·vised, im·pro·vis·ing.** 1. to make up and perform without preparation or previous thought: *The children improvised a skit for their parents.* 2. to make from whatever materials are on hand: *to improvise a bookcase out of wooden crates.* —**im′pro·vis′er,** *n.*

im·pru·dent (im prü′dənt) *adj.* lacking prudence; unwise; rash. —**im·pru′dence,** *n.* —**im·pru′dent·ly,** *adv.*

im·pu·dence (im′pyə dəns) *n.* 1. the quality of being impudent; rudeness; insolence. 2. impudent speech or behavior.

im·pu·dent (im′pyə dənt) *adj.* rudely bold or forward; insolent: *an impudent child.* —**im′pu·dent·ly,** *adv.*

im·pugn (im pün′) *v.t.* to suggest there is something bad about; call into question: *They impugned my reasons for giving the gift.*

im·pulse (im′puls′) *n.* 1. a force or feeling that makes a person act without planning or thinking: *A sudden impulse led me to give away my favorite jacket.* 2. a sudden force that causes motion; thrust; push: *The impulse of falling water turns the mill wheel.* 3. the motion caused by the sudden application of force. 4. a brief surge or pulsation of power or energy: *an electrical impulse.* 5. a signal produced and carried by nerve cells to or from the central nervous system, serving to control activity in the body.

im·pul·sion (im pul′shən) *n.* 1. the act of impelling. 2. a driving motion. 3. an impulse to act.

im·pul·sive (im pul′siv) *adj.* 1. tending to act on impulse: *an impulsive person.* 2. resulting from impulse: *You will regret your impulsive decision.* 3. having the power of producing motion; thrusting. —**im·pul′sive·ly,** *adv.* —**im·pul′sive·ness,** *n.*

im·pu·ni·ty (im pū′ni tē) *n.* freedom from punishment, penalty, injury, or loss: *You cannot expect to break the law with impunity.*

im·pure (im pyür′) *adj.* 1. dirty; unclean: *impure water.* 2. containing another substance that is foreign or inferior: *an impure blend of spices.* 3. bad; corrupt: *impure thoughts, impure actions.*

im·pu·ri·ty (im pyür′i tē) *n., pl.* **im·pu·ri·ties.** 1. the state or quality of being impure. 2. a substance that makes something impure: *There are many impurities in the air we breathe.*

im·pu·ta·tion (im′pyə tā′shən) *n.* 1. the act or instance of imputing. 2. something that is imputed: *an imputation of guilt.*

im·pute (im pūt′) *v.t.,* **im·put·ed, im·put·ing.** to charge or lay the blame for: *They imputed the team's defeat to lack of practice.*

in (in) *prep.* 1. within; inside: *The suitcase is in the closet. The bird is in the cage.* 2. through or into: *Go in the door on your left.* 3. while, during, or after: *The weather here is cold in the winter.* 4. covered by or wearing: *My cousin is the person in the brown coat.* 5. out of: *One in every four children had cavities.* 6. affected by or having: *They are in bad health.* 7. with the purpose or result of; for: *to act in self-defense.* 8. with respect to; as regards: *The two students differ in ability.* —*adv.* 1. to or toward a point or place inside: *to come in out of the cold.* 2. at a specific place, especially one's home or office: *I stayed in because I had a cold. Is the doctor in?* —*adj.* 1. having power or control: *the in political party.* 2. relating to or understood only by a particular group: *an in joke.* 3. leading or going in: *the in door.* 4. *Informal.* in style; fashionable or popular: *Hats are in this year.* —*n.* 1. *usually,* **ins.** the people in office or in power. 2. a means of influencing or approaching: *to have an in with the boss.*

·**ins and outs.** all the details: *My friend knows the ins and outs of the clothing business.*

·**in that.** because; since.

·**to be in for.** to be due or certain to have or receive: *We are in for some bad weather.*

·**to have it in for.** to hold a grudge against.

In, the symbol for indium.

in-¹ *prefix* without; not: *inactivity, inaccurate.* [From the Latin prefix *in-* meaning "not."]

in-² *prefix* in; into: *indent, intrust.* [From the Latin prefix *in* meaning "in, into, within, on, toward," from the preposition *in* with the same meanings.]

in-³ *prefix* in; within; into: *infield, input, instep.* [From *in* and the Old English prefix *in-* meaning "in, into."]

in., inch; inches.

IN, postal abbreviation for Indiana.

in·a·bil·i·ty (in′ə bil′i tē) *n.* lack of power, means, or ability: *an inability to walk.*

in·ac·ces·si·ble (in′ək ses′ə bəl) *adj.* difficult or impossible to reach or approach; not accessible. —**in′ac·ces′si·bil′i·ty,** *n.* —**in′ac·ces′si·bly,** *adv.*

in·ac·cu·ra·cy (in ak′yər ə sē) *n., pl.* **in·ac·cu·ra·cies.** 1. the quality or condition of being inaccurate. 2. an error; mistake.

in·ac·cu·rate (in ak′yər it) *adj.* not accurate; wrong. —**in·ac′cu·rate·ly,** *adv.*

in·ac·tion (in ak′shən) *n.* lack of action; idleness.

I

at; āpe; fär; câre; end; mē; it; īce; pîerce; hot; ōld; sông, fôrk; oil; out; up; ūse; rüle; pu̇ll; tûrn; chin; sing; shop; thin; <u>th</u>is; hw in white; zh in treasure. The symbol ə stands for the unstressed vowel sound heard in about, taken, pencil, lemon, and circus.

in·ac·tive (in ak′tiv) *adj.* not active; idle; inert: *an inactive volcano.* —**in·ac′tive·ly,** *adv.*

in·ac·tiv·i·ty (in′ak tiv′i tē) *n.* lack of activity; idleness.

in·ad·e·qua·cy (in ad′i kwə sē) *n., pl.* **in·ad·e·qua·cies.** **1.** the state or quality of being inadequate. **2.** a way in which something or someone is inadequate: *An inadequacy of the machine is that it lacks a safety switch.*

in·ad·e·quate (in ad′i kwit) *adj.* less than required; not adequate: *an inadequate water supply, an inadequate excuse for being late.* —**in·ad′e·quate·ly,** *adv.*

in·ad·mis·si·ble (in′əd mis′ə bəl) *adj.* not to be admitted, considered, or allowed; not admissible: *The judge ruled that the testimony of the witness was inadmissible as evidence.* —**in′ad·mis′si·bil′i·ty,** *n.*

in·ad·ver·tence (in′əd vûr′təns) *n.* **1.** the quality of being inadvertent. **2.** a result of being inadvertent; mistake.

in·ad·ver·tent (in′əd vûr′tənt) *adj.* not intended; accidental: *an inadvertent discovery.* —**in′ad·ver′tent·ly,** *adv.*

in·ad·vis·a·ble (in′əd vī′zə bəl) *adj.* not advisable; unwise. —**in′ad·vis′a·bil′i·ty,** *n.* —**in′ad·vis′a·bly,** *adv.*

in·al·ien·a·ble (in āl′yə nə bəl) *adj.* that cannot be given up, taken away, or transferred: *The pursuit of happiness is an inalienable right of every citizen.* —**in·al′ien·a·bil′i·ty,** *n.* —**in·al′ien·a·bly,** *adv.*

in·ane (i nān′) *adj.* lacking intelligence; empty of meaning; silly and senseless: *a speech full of inane remarks.* —**in·ane′ly,** *adv.*

in·an·i·mate (in an′ə mit) *adj.* **1.** not moving, growing, or feeling; not alive: *Rocks are inanimate objects.* **2.** lacking spirit; dull. —**in·an′i·mate·ly,** *adv.* —**in·an′i·mate·ness,** *n.*

in·an·i·ty (i nan′i tē) *n., pl.* **in·an·i·ties.** **1.** the state or quality of being inane. **2.** something inane, as a remark or act.

in·ap·pli·ca·ble (in ap′li kə bəl, in′ə plik′ə bəl) *adj.* not relevant or suitable; not applicable: *The rule is inapplicable in this case.* **in·ap′pli·ca·bil′i·ty,** *n.*

in·ap·pre·cia·ble (in′ə prē′shə bəl) *adj.* too small to be given attention; slight; unimportant. —**in′ap·pre′cia·bly,** *adv.*

in·ap·pro·pri·ate (in′ə prō′prē it) *adj.* not appropriate; unsuitable: *It was inappropriate to laugh at such a serious moment.* —**in′ap·pro′pri·ate·ly,** *adv.* —**in′ap·pro′pri·ate·ness,** *n.*

in·apt (in apt′) *adj.* not suitable; inappropriate: *an inapt remark.* —**in·apt′ly,** *adv.* —**in·apt′ness,** *n.*

in·ap·ti·tude (in ap′ti tüd′, in ap′ti tūd′) *n.* lack of aptitude or skill.

in·ar·tic·u·late (in′är tik′yə lit) *adj.* **1.** not clearly expressed or pronounced: *The patient's speech was inarticulate because of the bandages around the mouth.* **2.** not able to express oneself in a clear or meaningful way. **3.** not fully expressed; not made definite and clear: *inarticulate anger.* **4.** not capable of speech or expression; mute. **5.** *Biology.* not jointed. —**in′ar·tic′u·late·ly,** *adv.* —**in′ar·tic′u·late·ness,** *n.*

in·ar·tis·tic (in′är tis′tik) *adj.* not artistic; lacking taste. —**in′ar·tis′ti·cal·ly,** *adv.*

in·as·much as (in′əz much′) in view of the fact that; since: *Inasmuch as you are here, you may as well stay for dinner.*

in·at·ten·tion (in′ə ten′shən) *n.* lack of attention.

in·at·ten·tive (in′ə ten′tiv) *adj.* not attentive; neglectful: *to be inattentive to details.* —**in′at·ten′tive·ly,** *adv.* —**in′at·ten′tive·ness,** *n.*

in·au·di·ble (in ô′də bəl) *adj.* that cannot be heard. —**in·au′di·bly,** *adv.*

in·au·gur·al (in ô′gyər əl) *adj.* of, relating to, or for an inauguration: *an inaugural ball.* —*n.* a speech or address made by a person being inaugurated, especially one made by a president of the United States.

in·au·gu·rate (in ô′gyə rāt′) *v.t.,* **in·au·gu·rat·ed, in·au·gu·rat·ing.** **1.** to install in office with a formal ceremony: *to inaugurate a governor.* **2.** to begin formally: *to inaugurate a new policy.* **3.** to open for public use with a formal ceremony: *to inaugurate a new highway.*

in·au·gu·ra·tion (in ô′gyə rā′shən) *n., pl.* **in·au·gu·ra·tions.** **1.** a formal ceremony installing a person in office. **2.** the act or instance of beginning something: *the inauguration of telephone service.* **3.** a formal ceremony marking the opening or beginning of something: *the inauguration of the new science building.*

in·aus·pi·cious (in′ô spish′əs) *adj.* not favorable for success; unlucky: *an inauspicious beginning.* —**in′aus·pi′cious·ly,** *adv.*

in·board (in′bôrd′) *adj.* **1.** inside the hull of a ship: *an inboard motor.* **2.** on an aircraft, closer or closest to the fuselage: *the right inboard engine.* —*adv.* inside the hull or within the sides of a ship: *to stow cargo inboard.*

in·born (in′bôrn′) *adj.* born in a person; natural.

in·bound (in′bound′) *adj.* inward bound: *an inbound train.*

in·bred (in′bred′) *adj.* **1.** inborn; natural: *inbred curiosity.* **2.** resulting from inbreeding.

in·breed (in′brēd′, in brēd′) *v.t.,* **in·bred, in·breed·ing.** to breed (closely related animals): *to inbreed a strain of cows.*

in·breed·ing (in′brē′ding) *n.* the breeding of closely related animals, resulting in certain traits becoming more dominant.

inc., incorporated.

In·ca (ing′kə) *n.* **1.** a member of a highly civilized Indian people who ruled a large empire in Peru and other parts of South America. The Incas were conquered by the Spanish in the sixteenth century. **2.** a ruler or a member of the ruling family of this people. —**In′can,** *adj., n.*

in·cal·cu·la·ble (in kal′kyə lə bəl) *adj.* **1.** too much or too many to be calculated: *an incalculable number of stars.* **2.** impossible to calculate beforehand; not predictable: *incalculable consequences.* —**in·cal′cu·la·bly,** *adv.*

in·can·des·cent (in′kən des′ənt) *adj.* **1.** glowing with heat. **2.** brightly shining; brilliant; sparkling: *incandescent wit.* [Originally from the Latin word *incandescens,* present participle of *incandescere* meaning "to become hot, glow," going back to the prefix *in-* "in, into" and *candēre* "to glow."] —**in′can·des′cence,** *n.*

incandescent lamp, a bulb in which light is produced by passing an electric current through a thin wire or filament, causing it to glow; light bulb. Also, **lamp.**

in·can·ta·tion (in′kan tā′shən) *n.* **1.** a formula of words spoken or chanted in casting a spell or performing other magic. **2.** the use of such a formula.

in·ca·pa·ble (in kā′pə bəl) *adj.* not capable: *an incapable employee. A baby is incapable of reading.* —**in·ca′pa·bil′i·ty,** *n.*

incandescent lamp

in·ca·pac·i·tate (in′kə pas′i tāt′) *v.t.,* **in·ca·pac·i·tat·ed, in·ca·pac·i·tat·ing.** to take away or limit the power or ability of: *A broken ankle incapacitated the gymnast.*

in·ca·pac·i·ty (in′kə pas′i tē) *n., pl.* **in·ca·pac·i·ties.** lack of power or ability.

in·car·cer·ate (in kär′sə rāt′) *v.t.,* **in·car·cer·at·ed, in·car·cer·at·ing.** to put in prison. —**in·car′cer·a′tion,** *n.*

in·car·nate (*adj.,* in kär′nit, in kär′nāt; *v.,* in kär′nāt) *adj.* in human form; personified: *to think of oneself as wisdom incarnate.* —*v.t.,* **in·car·nat·ed, in·car·nat·ing.**

1. to embody in human form; personify: *The Roman god Mars incarnated war.* **2.** to be a real or true example of; typify.

in·car·na·tion (in'kär nā'shən) *n.* **1.** the taking on of human form by a supernatural being. **2.** a person or thing that is a real or true example of some quality or ideal: *The lighthouse keeper was the incarnation of loneliness.* **3. the Incarnation.** the taking on of human flesh and nature by the Son of God in the person of Jesus.

in·case (in kās') *v.t.,* **in·cased, in·cas·ing.** another word for **encase.**

in·cau·tious (in kô'shəs) *adj.* not cautious; heedless. —**in·cau'tious·ly,** *adv.* —**in·cau'tious·ness,** *n.*

in·cen·di·ar·y (in sen'dē er'ē) *adj.* **1.** causing or designed to cause a fire: *incendiary grenades.* **2.** tending to excite, inflame, or anger; inflammatory: *an incendiary speech.* **3.** of or relating to arson. —*n., pl.* **in·cen·di·ar·ies.** a bomb, shell, grenade, or other device designed to cause a fire.

in·cense[1] (in'sens) *n.* **1.** any of several substances that produce a fragrant aroma when burned. **2.** the aroma or smoke produced by the burning of such a substance. **3.** any pleasant aroma: *the incense of a meadow.* [From the Old French word *encens* meaning this substance, going back to the Latin word *incensus,* past participle of *incendere* ''to set on fire,'' from the prefix *in-* ''in, into'' + *cendere* ''to burn.'']

in·cense[2] (in sens') *v.t.,* **in·censed, in·cens·ing.** to make very angry; enrage: *It incensed me when I realized that they were lying.* [From the Middle French word *incenser* meaning ''to set on fire'' or ''to enrage,'' going back to the Latin word *incendere* ''to set on fire,'' from the prefix *in-* ''in, into'' + *cendere* ''to burn.'']

in·cen·tive (in sen'tiv) *n.* something that urges to action; stimulus: *The possibility of a raise was offered as an incentive to work harder.*

in·cep·tion (in sep'shən) *n.* the point of beginning or being begun; commencement: *That television program was popular from its inception.*

in·ces·sant (in ses'ənt) *adj.* continuing without interruption; continuous; unceasing: *We were bothered by the incessant buzz of flies.* —**in·ces'sant·ly,** *adv.*

in·cest (in'sest') *n.* sexual activity between two persons who are closely related and cannot legally marry, such as a parent and child or a brother and sister.

in·ces·tu·ous (in ses'chü əs) *adj.* **1.** involving incest. **2.** guilty of incest. —**in·ces'tu·ous·ly,** *adv.* —**in·ces'tu·ous·ness,** *n.*

inch (inch) *n., pl.* **inch·es.** **1.** a measure of length, equal to ¹⁄₁₂ of a foot, or 2.54 centimeters. **2.** the smallest distance, amount, or degree: *They wouldn't budge an inch to help us.* —*v.i.* to move very slowly: *The snake inched through the grass.*

  •**every inch.** in every way; totally: *to look every inch a sailor.*

  •**inch by inch.** little by little.

  •**within an inch of.** very close to: *The driver came within an inch of having an accident.*

inch·worm (inch'würm') *n.* a caterpillar that moves by drawing the rear of the body up toward the front, forming a loop, and then stretching the front end forward. Also, **measuring worm.**

in·ci·dence (in'si dəns) *n.* **1.** the rate, frequency, or range in which something happens: *Our town has a low incidence of crime.* **2.** the act or fact of happening; occurrence. **3.** the falling or striking of light or a projectile on a surface.

inchworm

in·ci·dent (in'si dənt) *n.* **1.** an event or act; happening: *a funny incident.* **2.** a minor disturbance or conflict: *The*

protest march proceeded without incident. —*adj.* naturally connected with; belonging to as a part.

in·ci·den·tal (in'si den'təl) *adj.* **1.** happening without being expected: *an incidental meeting of friends on the street.* **2.** belonging to as a part, especially as a minor part: *There are many problems incidental to traveling in space.* —*n. often,* **incidentals.** something that is incidental or unimportant: *Just bring the necessary supplies; we can buy the incidentals on the way.*

in·ci·den·tal·ly (*def. 1* in'si den'tə lē; *def. 2* in'si dent'lē) *adv.* **1.** in an incidental manner. **2.** by the way: *Incidentally, have you heard about my new job?*

in·cin·er·ate (in sin'ə rāt') *v.t.,* **in·cin·er·at·ed, in·cin·er·at·ing.** to burn to ashes. —**in·cin'er·a'tion,** *n.*

in·cin·er·a·tor (in sin'ə rā'tər) *n.* a piece of equipment, such as a furnace, used to dispose of garbage or other waste material by burning it to ashes.

in·cip·i·ent (in sip'ē ənt) *adj.* just beginning or appearing: *the incipient stage of a disease.* —**in·cip'i·ence,** *n.*

in·cise (in sīz') *v.t.,* **in·cised, in·cis·ing.** **1.** to cut into. **2.** to carve; engrave.

in·ci·sion (in sizh'ən) *n.* **1.** the act of incising. **2.** a cut, especially as made by a scalpel in surgery.

in·ci·sive (in sī'siv) *adj.* penetrating; sharp: *an incisive mind, an incisive comment.* —**in·ci'sive·ly,** *adv.* —**in·ci'sive·ness,** *n.*

in·ci·sor (in sī'zər) *n.* any of the front teeth of the upper or lower jaw having sharp, flattened edges, used for cutting food.

in·cite (in sīt') *v.t.,* **in·cit·ed, in·cit·ing.** **1.** to move or urge; rouse: *The sounding of the alarm incited us to action.* **2.** to cause by urging or arousing: *to incite a riot.* —**in·cit'er,** *n.*

in·cite·ment (in sīt'mənt) *n.* **1.** the act of inciting. **2.** something that incites.

in·ci·vil·i·ty (in'sə vil'i tē) *n., pl.* **in·ci·vil·i·ties.** **1.** lack of politeness and courtesy. **2.** an impolite act.

incl. **1.** inclosure. **2.** including. **3.** inclusive.

in·clem·ent (in klem'ənt) *adj.* **1.** harsh, cold, or stormy: *The inclement weather kept us in the house all weekend.* **2.** not having or showing leniency or compassion; unmerciful: *an inclement ruler.* —**in·clem'en·cy,** *n.* —**in·clem'ent·ly,** *adv.*

in·cli·na·tion (in'klə nā'shən) *n.* **1.** a natural tendency; bent: *an inclination to thinness.* **2.** a preference or liking: *My friend has an inclination for all sports.* **3.** the act of bending or slanting. **4.** a slope; slant.

in·cline (*v.,* in klīn'; *n.,* in'klīn') *v.,* **in·clined, in·clin·ing.** —*v.i.* **1.** to be or go at an angle; slope; slant: *The road inclines upward.* **2.** to bend or lean: *The old sailor inclined forward on the rail.* **3.** to have a preference or liking for something: *My cousin inclines toward becoming a mechanic.* —*v.t.* **1.** to cause to bend, lean, slope, or slant. **2.** to give (someone) a preference or liking for something: *The teenagers' artistic interests inclined them toward careers in design.* —*n.* a surface that is at an angle: *The wagon rolled down the incline.*

in·clined (in klīnd') *adj.* **1.** having an inclination or tendency. **2.** sloping or leaning.

---

at; āpe; fär; câre; end; mē; it; īce; pîerce; hot; ōld; sông, fôrk; oil; out; up; ūse; rüle; pùll; tûrn; chin; sing; shop; thin; this; hw in white; zh in treasure. The symbol ə stands for the unstressed vowel sound heard in about, taken, pencil, lemon, and circus.

Incisors

487

inclined plane, any plane surface, such as a ramp, set at an angle of less than ninety degrees to a horizontal surface. An inclined plane is a simple machine that allows an object to be raised by less force than is needed to raise it vertically.

in·close (in klōz') *v.t.,* **in·closed, in·clos·ing.** another word for **enclose.**

in·clo·sure (in klō'zhər) another word for **enclosure.**

in·clude (in klüd') *v.t.,* **in·clud·ed, in·clud·ing.** 1. to have as part of the whole; contain: *The book includes an index.* 2. to put in a group or total: *to include the whole class in a field trip.*

in·clu·sion (in klü'zhən) *n.* 1. the act of including or the state of being included. 2. something included.

in·clu·sive (in klü'siv) *adj.* 1. including the specified limits and everything in between: *We will be gone five days, Monday to Friday inclusive.* 2. including everything; comprehensive: *an inclusive list of schools in an area.* —**in·clu'sive·ly,** *adv.* —**in·clu'sive·ness,** *n.*

in·cog·ni·to (in'kog nē'tō, in kog'ni tō') *adv.* having one's identity hidden; in disguise. —*adj.* being in disguise. [From the Italian word *incognito* meaning "unknown" or "disguised," from the Latin word *incognitus* "unknown," from the prefix *in-* "not" + *cognitus,* past participle of *cognoscere* "to know, recognize."]

in·co·her·ent (in'kō hîr'ənt) *adj.* 1. characterized by confused speech or thought; not understandable: *The patient was incoherent when brought to the hospital.* 2. not sticking together; disconnected. —**in'co·her'ence,** *n.* —**in'co·her'ent·ly,** *adv.*

in·com·bus·ti·ble (in'kəm bus'tə bəl) *adj.* that cannot burn. —*n.* an incombustible substance. —**in'com·bus'ti·bil'i·ty,** *n.*

in·come (in'kum') *n.* 1. payment in money for services or labor, or money gained from property or investments. 2. the amount of such payment: *a low income.*

income tax, a tax on yearly income.

in·com·ing (in'kum'ing) *adj.* coming in: *the incoming tide, incoming telephone calls, the incoming senior class.*

in·com·men·su·rate (in'kə men'shər it) *adj.* 1. not in proportion; not of equal size: *wages incommensurate with one's expenses.* 2. not measurable. —**in'com·men·su·rate·ly,** *adv.*

in·com·mode (in'kə mōd') *v.t.,* **in·com·mod·ed, in·com·mod·ing.** to bother or annoy; inconvenience.

in·com·mu·ni·ca·ble (in'kə mū'ni kə bəl) *adj.* that cannot be told or communicated.

in·com·mu·ni·ca·do (in'kə mū'ni kä'dō) *adj., adv.* without the right or means of communicating with others: *The prisoner was held incommunicado.*

in·com·pa·ra·ble (in kom'pər ə bəl) *adj.* 1. having no equal; matchless: *That opera singer has an incomparable voice.* 2. that cannot be compared. —**in·com'pa·ra·bly,** *adv.*

in·com·pat·i·ble (in'kəm pat'ə bəl) *adj.* not able to exist, be mixed, or work together in harmony: *incompatible personalities. Reading a good book is incompatible with watching television.* —**in'com·pat'i·bil'i·ty,** *n.* —**in'com·pat'i·bly,** *adv.*

in·com·pe·tent (in kom'pi tənt) *adj.* 1. not having or showing enough ability; not capable: *an incompetent typist, an incompetent repair job.* 2. not legally qualified: *A baby is incompetent to sign a contract.* —*n.* 1. a person who lacks ability. 2. a person who is not legally able to act for himself or herself, because of insanity, severe illness, or age. —**in·com'pe·tence,** *n.* —**in·com'pe·tent·ly,** *adv.*

in·com·plete (in'kəm plēt') *adj.* not complete; unfinished. —**in'com·plete'ly,** *adv.* —**in'com·plete'ness,** *n.*

incomplete dominance, a hereditary pattern in which neither of a pair of genes is completely dominant or completely recessive, so that the traits of each are blended in the offspring: *The crossing of the red flowers with the white ones produced offspring that were pink because of incomplete dominance.*

in·com·pre·hen·si·ble (in'kom pri hen'sə bəl) *adj.* that cannot be understood: *Chinese writing is incomprehensible to me.* —**in'com·pre·hen·si·bil'i·ty,** *n.* —**in'com·pre·hen'si·bly,** *adv.*

in·com·pre·hen·sion (in'kom prə hen'shən) *n.* the fact of not understanding.

in·con·ceiv·a·ble (in'kən sē'və bəl) *adj.* hard or impossible to imagine or think of: *Travel to other galaxies is at present inconceivable.* —**in'con·ceiv'a·bil'i·ty,** *n.* —**in'con·ceiv'a·bly,** *adv.*

in·con·clu·sive (in'kən klü'siv) *adj.* that does not end argument or doubt; not conclusive. —**in'con·clu'sive·ly,** *adv.* —**in'con·clu'sive·ness,** *n.*

in·con·gru·i·ty (in'kən grü'i tē) *n., pl.* **in·con·gru·i·ties.** 1. the quality or condition of being incongruous. 2. something that is incongruous.

in·con·gru·ous (in kong'grü əs) *adj.* not harmoniously related or joined; not suitable: *A fur hat and a bathing suit look incongruous together.* —**in·con'gru·ous·ly,** *adv.*

in·con·se·quence (in kon'si kwens') *n.* the condition or quality of being inconsequential.

in·con·se·quen·tial (in kon'si kwen'chəl) *adj.* 1. not leading to anything important; trivial. 2. not following from anything; unrelated. —**in'con'se·quen'tial·ly,** *adv.*

in·con·sid·er·a·ble (in'kən sid'ər ə bəl) *adj.* small or not worth considering. —**in'con·sid'er·a·bly,** *adv.*

in·con·sid·er·ate (in'kən sid'ər it) *adj.* having or showing little thought for others: *It was very inconsiderate of you to hang up in the middle of our conversation.* —**in'con·sid'er·ate·ly,** *adv.* —**in'con·sid'er·ate·ness,** *n.*

in·con·sist·en·cy (in'kən sis'tən sē) *n., pl.* **in·con·sist·en·cies.** 1. the quality or condition of being inconsistent. 2. something that is inconsistent.

in·con·sist·ent (in'kən sis'tənt) *adj.* 1. not in agreement; contradictory: *Their practice of praising peace while waging war is inconsistent.* 2. not keeping to the same thoughts or course of action. —**in'con·sist'ent·ly,** *adv.*

in·con·sol·a·ble (in kən sō'lə bəl) *adj.* too sad to be consoled; grief-stricken: *The parents were inconsolable when their child died.* —**in'con·sol'a·bly,** *adv.*

in·con·spic·u·ous (in'kən spik'ū əs) *adj.* likely to escape notice; not easily seen. —**in'con·spic'u·ous·ly,** *adv.* —**in'con·spic'u·ous·ness,** *n.*

in·con·stan·cy (in kon'stən sē) *n.* the state or quality of being inconstant.

in·con·stant (in kon'stənt) *adj.* 1. not faithful or steadfast; fickle. 2. likely to change; changeable. —**in·con'stant·ly,** *adv.*

in·con·test·a·ble (in'kən tes'tə bəl) *adj.* that cannot be disputed or questioned: *incontestable evidence.* —**in'con·test'a·bly,** *adv.*

in·con·tro·vert·i·ble (in'kon trə vûr'tə bəl, in kon'trə-vûr'tə bəl) *adj.* that cannot be argued against or debated; certain: *incontrovertible proof.* —**in'con·tro·vert'i·bly,** *adv.*

in·con·ven·ience (in'kən vēn'yəns) *n.* 1. the state or quality of being inconvenient. 2. an inconvenient situation or thing: *Not having a telephone is an inconvenience.* —*v.t.,* **in·con·ven·ienced, in·con·ven·ienc·ing.** to cause (someone) to have difficulty or trouble: *We hope the delay will not inconvenience you.*

in·con·ven·ient (in'kən vēn'yənt) *adj.* not favorable

or suitable for one's needs or purposes; not convenient; troublesome. —**in'con·ven'ient·ly**, *adv.*

in·cor·po·rate (in kôr'pə rāt') *v.*, **in·cor·po·rat·ed**, **in·cor·po·rat·ing**. —*v.t.* **1.** to include (something) as a part: *The proposed law incorporates many changes.* **2.** to form into a corporation: *to incorporate a business.* —*v.i.* to become or form a corporation. —**in·cor'po·ra'tion**, *n.*

in·cor·po·rat·ed (in kôr'pə rā'tid) *adj.* formed into a corporation.

in·cor·po·re·al (in'kôr pôr'ē əl) *adj.* having no material body; spiritual. —**in'cor·po're·al·ly**, *adv.*

in·cor·rect (in'kə rekt') *adj.* **1.** not agreeing with fact or truth; not accurate: *an incorrect answer.* **2.** not conforming to an approved standard; not proper. —**in'cor·rect'ly**, *adv.* —**in'cor·rect'ness**, *n.*

in·cor·ri·gi·ble (in kôr'i jə bəl, in kor'i jə bəl) *adj.* that cannot be made better or reformed; bad beyond all hope of correction: *an incorrigible criminal.* —*n.* a person who is incorrigible. —**in·cor'ri·gi·bil'i·ty**, *n.* —**in·cor'ri·gi·bly**, *adv.*

in·cor·rupt·i·ble (in'kə rup'tə bəl) *adj.* **1.** that cannot be corrupted; morally strong: *an incorruptible public official.* **2.** that does not decay or become rotten: *an incorruptible substance.* —**in'cor·rupt'i·bil'i·ty**, *n.* —**in'cor·rupt'i·bly**, *adv.*

in·crease (*v.*, in krēs'; *n.*, in'krēs) *v.*, **in·creased**, **in·creas·ing**. —*v.t.* to make greater, as in number or size: *The library has increased its collection of books.* —*v.i.* to become greater, as in number or size: *The school's enrollment has increased.* —*n.* **1.** the act or process of increasing; becoming greater. **2.** the amount by which something is increased: *I got a salary increase of ten dollars per week.*
·**on the increase.** increasing.

Word Family

English contains a number of words that can be traced back to the Latin word *crescere*, meaning "to grow." Any **increase** involves some kind of growth. Most people like to watch money **accrue**, but don't like to see it **decrease**. Others prefer to watch the moon appearing to grow from a **crescent** to a full moon. Music that grows louder is a **crescendo**. As an idea grows, it can take shape in the mind and become a **concrete** plan, but it may be necessary to **recruit** others to help carry it out. The **crew** of a ship in port might provide some help.

in·creas·ing·ly (in krē'sing lē) *adv.* to a greater and greater extent; more and more.

in·cred·i·ble (in kred'ə bəl) *adj.* impossible to believe. —**in·cred'i·bil'i·ty**, *n.* —**in·cred'i·bly**, *adv.*

in·cre·du·li·ty (in'krə dü'li tē, in'krə dū'li tē) *n.* refusal to believe; doubt.

in·cred·u·lous (in krej'ə ləs) *adj.* **1.** not able to believe something; skeptical; unbelieving: *When the discovery was first announced, many people were incredulous.* **2.** showing disbelief: *an incredulous gasp.* —**in·cred'u·lous·ly**, *adv.*

in·cre·ment (ing'krə mənt) *n.* **1.** something that is added to something; increase. **2.** an amount that is added.

in·crim·i·nate (in krim'ə nāt') *v.t.*, **in·crim·i·nat·ed**, **in·crim·i·nat·ing**. **1.** to charge with a crime or fault. **2.** to suggest or show the guilt of: *Having run away seemed to incriminate the suspect.* —**in·crim'i·na'tion**, *n.* —**in·crim'i·na·to'ry**, *adj.*

in·crust (in krust') another word for **encrust**.

in·crus·ta·tion (in'krus tā'shən) another word for **encrustation**.

in·cu·bate (ing'kyə bāt') *v.t.*, **in·cu·bat·ed**, **in·cu·bat·ing**. **1.** to sit on and keep (eggs) warm for hatching. **2.** to hatch artificially using heat: *The farmer incubated the eggs in an incubator.* **3.** to form or develop gradually: *to incubate an idea.* —*v.i.* to develop in or as if in an incubator: *A plan was incubating in our minds.*

in·cu·ba·tion (ing'kyə bā'shən) *n.* **1.** the process of incubating or the state of being incubated. **2.** the stage of a disease from the time of infection to the first appearance of symptoms.

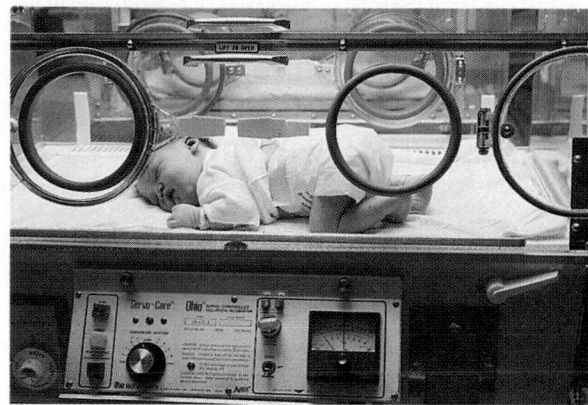

incubator *(def. 1)*

in·cu·ba·tor (ing'kyə bā'tər) *n.* **1.** a boxlike apparatus of glass or clear plastic that provides a steady, warm temperature for babies who are sick or born prematurely. **2.** a heated container used to hatch eggs or grow bacteria.

in·cu·des (ing ku'dez) the plural of **incus**.

in·cul·cate (in kul'kāt) *v.t.*, **in·cul·cat·ed**, **in·cul·cat·ing**. to fix firmly in the mind or memory by repeated teaching or example: *The parents inculcated a love of music in their children.* —**in·cul·ca'tion**, *n.*

in·cum·ben·cy (in kum'bən sē) *n.*, *pl.* **in·cum·ben·cies**. **1.** the act of holding an office and performing its duties. **2.** the term of office of an incumbent.

in·cum·bent (in kum'bənt) *adj.* **1.** imposed as a duty or obligation: *It is incumbent upon a witness to tell the truth.* **2.** holding an office: *an incumbent president.* **3.** lying, leaning, or resting upon something. —*n.* a person who holds an office.

in·cum·ber (in kum'bər) another word for **encumber**.

in·cum·brance (in kum'brəns) another word for **encumbrance**.

in·cur (in kûr') *v.t.*, **in·curred**, **in·cur·ring**. to bring (something) on oneself by one's own actions: *to incur expenses. The king incurred the wrath of the people.*

in·cur·a·ble (in kyùr'ə bəl) *adj.* that cannot be cured or healed: *an incurable disease.* —*n.* a person who has a disease that cannot be cured or healed. —**in·cur'a·bil'i·ty**, *n.* —**in·cur'a·bly**, *adv.*

in·cur·sion (in kûr'zhən) *n.* a sudden attack or raid: *an incursion of soldiers into the town.*

in·cus (ing'kəs) *n.*, *pl.* **in·cu·des**. one of the three small bones of the middle ear lying between the malleus and the stapes; anvil. See **stapes** for illustration.

I

at; āpe; fär; câre; end; mē; it; īce; pierce; hot; ōld; sông, fôrk; oil; out; up; ūse; rüle; pùll; tûrn; chin; sing; shop; thin; **th**is; hw in white; zh in treasure. The symbol ə stands for the unstressed vowel sound heard in about, taken, pencil, lemon, and circus.

Ind. 1. India. 2. Indian. 3. Indiana.

in·debt·ed (in det′id) *adj.* 1. owing gratitude, as for a kindness. 2. owing money; in debt.

in·debt·ed·ness (in det′id nis) *n., pl.* **in·debt·ed·ness·es.** 1. the state of being indebted. 2. an amount or the total amount owed.

in·de·cen·cy (in dē′sən sē) *n., pl.* **in·de·cen·cies.** 1. the quality or condition of being indecent. 2. something that is indecent.

in·de·cent (in dē′sənt) *adj.* 1. not modest or moral; obscene: *indecent language.* 2. not conforming to the standards of good taste; improper. —**in·de′cent·ly,** *adv.*

in·de·ci·sion (in′di sizh′ən) *n.* the inability to decide or to make up one's mind.

in·de·ci·sive (in′di sī′siv) *adj.* 1. not able to decide; hesitating: *an indecisive leader.* 2. not leading to a decision: *an indecisive contest.* —**in′de·ci′sive·ly,** *adv.* —**in′de·ci′sive·ness,** *n.*

in·dec·o·rous (in dek′ər əs) *adj.* not conforming to the standards of good taste; improper. —**in·dec′o·rous·ly,** *adv.* —**in·dec′o·rous·ness,** *n.*

in·deed (in dēd′) *adv.* really; truly: *I am indeed grateful to you.* —*interj.* used to express surprise, disbelief, or contempt: *Pigs with wings? Indeed!*

indef., indefinite.

in·de·fat·i·ga·ble (in′di fat′i gə bəl) *adj.* that does not become tired; tireless: *an indefatigable worker.* —**in′de·fat′i·ga·bil′i·ty,** *n.* —**in′de·fat′i·ga·bly,** *adv.*

in·de·fen·si·ble (in′di fen′sə bəl) *adj.* 1. that cannot be defended against attack: *The platoon's position became indefensible.* 2. that cannot be proved, justified, or excused: *an indefensible argument. Their acts are indefensible.* —**in′de·fen′si·bly,** *adv.*

in·de·fin·a·ble (in′di fī′nə bəl) *adj.* that cannot be defined. —**in′de·fin′a·bly,** *adv.*

in·def·i·nite (in def′ə nit) *adj.* 1. not clearly defined; not exact: *My plans for the summer are still indefinite.* 2. having no limits; unmeasured: *a line of indefinite length.* 3. *Grammar.* not specifying or determining the person, thing, place, time, or manner; not exact or precise. *Some, any,* and *other* are indefinite pronouns. —**in·def′i·nite·ly,** *adv.* —**in·def′i·nite·ness,** *n.*

indefinite article, the article *a* or *an.*

in·del·i·ble (in del′ə bəl) *adj.* 1. that cannot be removed or taken away: *indelible markings, indelible memories.* 2. that makes indelible writing or marks: *an indelible pen.* —**in·del′i·bil′i·ty,** *n.* —**in·del′i·bly,** *adv.*

in·del·i·ca·cy (in del′i kə sē) *n., pl.* **in·del·i·ca·cies.** 1. the quality of being indelicate. 2. something that is indelicate.

in·del·i·cate (in del′i kit) *adj.* 1. not tactful or considerate; coarse; crude: *indelicate behavior.* 2. not proper or modest; offensive: *indelicate language.* —**in·del′i·cate·ly,** *adv.* —**in·del′i·cate·ness,** *n.*

in·dem·ni·fy (in dem′nə fī′) *v.t.,* **in·dem·ni·fied, in·dem·ni·fy·ing.** 1. to compensate for damage, loss, expense, or injury: *The airline indemnified the passenger for the loss of a suitcase.* 2. to protect against future damage, loss, or expense; insure. —**in·dem′ni·fi·ca′tion,** *n.*

in·dem·ni·ty (in dem′ni tē) *n., pl.* **in·dem·ni·ties.** 1. a compensation given for damage, loss, expense, or injury. 2. protection against future damage, loss, or expense; insurance.

in·dent¹ (*v.,* in dent′; *n.,* in′dent) *v.t.* 1. to start (a line of writing, typing, or printing) farther in than the other lines, as at the beginning of a paragraph. 2. to cut or make toothlike notches in. —*n.* an indentation. [From the Old French word *endenter* meaning "to notch a document," from the prefix *en-* "in-²" + *dent* "tooth," from the Latin word *dens* "tooth."]

in·dent² (in dent′) *v.t.* to make a dent in. [*In-²* + *dent.*]

in·den·ta·tion (in′den tā′shən) *n.* 1. the act of indenting or the state of being indented. 2. a part that is set or pushed back from the rest; dent or recess.

in·den·tion (in den′shən) *n.* 1. the starting of a line of writing, typing, or printing farther in than the other lines: *to begin each paragraph with an indention.* 2. the empty or blank space left by this. 3. a dent or recess.

in·den·ture (in den′chər) *n.* a contract that binds a person, such as an apprentice, to work for another person for a stated period of time. —*v.t.,* **in·den·tured, in·den·tur·ing.** to bind (a person) by such a contract: *to be indentured as a servant.*

in·de·pend·ence (in′di pen′dəns) *n.* the state or quality of being independent: *The American colonies fought to win independence from England.*

Independence Day, a holiday observed on July 4, commemorating the adoption of the Declaration of Independence on July 4, 1776. Also, **Fourth of July.**

in·de·pend·ent (in′di pen′dənt) *adj.* 1. not influenced or controlled by another or others: *an independent mind, an independent person.* 2. not subject to the political control or rule of another or others: *an independent country.* 3. not connected with another; separate: *independent research, an independent grocery store.* 4. not connected with or supporting any political party: *an independent voter.* 5. having or providing enough to live on without working: *an independent income.* —*n.* 1. a person or thing that is independent. 2. someone who votes or is politically active without belonging to a party. —**in′de·pend′ent·ly,** *adv.*

independent clause, a clause in a sentence that can stand alone or as a complete sentence. In the sentence *After they had played tennis for an hour, they decided to go for a swim,* the clause *they decided to go for a swim* is an independent clause. Also, **main clause.**

in·de·scrib·a·ble (in′di skrī′bə bəl) *adj.* that cannot be described; beyond description: *a sunset of indescribable beauty.* —**in′de·scrib′a·bly,** *adv.*

in·de·struc·ti·ble (in′di struk′tə bəl) *adj.* that cannot be destroyed. —**in′de·struc′ti·bil′i·ty,** *n.* —**in′de·struc′ti·bly,** *adv.*

in·de·ter·mi·na·ble (in′di tûr′mə nə bəl) *adj.* that cannot be defined, decided, or determined: *a person of indeterminable age.* —**in′de·ter′mi·na·bly,** *adv.*

in·de·ter·mi·nate (in′di tûr′mə nit) *adj.* without defined limits; indefinite or vague: *We will be away for an indeterminate length of time.* —**in′de·ter′mi·nate·ly,** *adv.* —**in′de·ter′mi·nate·ness,** *n.*

in·dex (in′deks) *n., pl.* **in·dex·es** or **in·di·ces** (in′də sēz′). 1. an alphabetical list in a published work, such as a book or magazine, that gives the page where a reference to a particular subject or name can be found. 2. something that shows or indicates: *Their work is an index of their ability.* 3. a pointer or indicator, as the needle on the dial of a compass. —*v.t.* 1. to make an index for: *to index a book.* 2. to enter in an index: *to index a word.* —**in′dex·er,** *n.*

index card, a rectangular card used to record information, usually filed alphabetically in a box or drawer.

index finger, the finger next to the thumb; forefinger.

index of refraction, the ratio of the speed of light in a vacuum to its speed in a transparent medium, such as glass or water.

India ink, ink made from a black pigment, used for both writing and drawing.

In·di·an (in′dē ən) *n.* 1. see **American Indian** (*def. 1*). 2. any one of the languages of the American Indians. 3. a person who was born in or is a citizen of India, or is of Indian descent: *Many Indians live in Trinidad.* —*adj.* 1. of or relating to American Indians. 2. of or relating to

India or its people. [From *India;* Columbus believed that the New World land he had reached was India, so he called the native people *Indians*.]

Words From Other Languages

Words from the subcontinent of India entered the English language from Hindi and the many other major languages of India, Pakistan, and Bangladesh.

bandanna	a large, patterned or brightly colored handkerchief
bungalow	a small house or cottage
cheetah	a swift, spotted cat
dinghy	a small open boat, propelled by oars, motor, or sails
dungaree	a fabric used in jeans and sails
jungle	a dense, tropical forest
pajamas	clothing for sleeping, with a shirt and pants
sari	a woman's garment in the form of a cloth wrapped around the body
seersucker	a lightweight, crinkled fabric
shampoo	to wash hair with soap or detergent
veranda	an open porch, usually with a roof

Indian club, a bottle-shaped club used in arm exercises.
Indian corn, see **corn**[1] *(defs. 1, 2).*
Indian pipe, a waxy, white leafless plant with one bell-shaped flower.
Indian summer, a period of warm, mild weather occurring in autumn, usually after the first frost.
India paper, a thin, strong paper, used chiefly for Bibles.
India rubber *also,* **india rubber.** see **rubber** *(def. 1).*
in·di·cate (in′di kāt′) *v.t.* **in·di·cat·ed, in·di·cat·ing.** **1.** to be a sign of; show: *A high fever indicates the presence of a disease.* **2.** to direct attention to; point out: *The guide indicated the best trail for us to take.* **3.** to state or express briefly: *My friends indicated that they might go to camp this summer.*
in·di·ca·tion (in′di kā′shən) *n.* **1.** the act of indicating. **2.** something that indicates; sign: *There are many indications that you will do well in high school.*
in·dic·a·tive (in dik′ə tiv) *adj.* **1.** that points out, suggests, or expresses: *We gave them a gift indicative of our high regard.* **2.** *Grammar.* of or relating to the mood of a verb that expresses a fact or asks a question of fact. In the sentences *The water is hot* and *Did you buy something?* the verbs *is* and *buy* are in the indicative mood. —*n. Grammar.* **1.** the indicative mood. **2.** a verb in this mood. —**in·dic′a·tive·ly,** *adv.*
in·di·ca·tor (in′di kā′tər) *n.* **1.** a person or thing that indicates. **2.** any of various instruments that measure or record something, such as a dial in an airplane that indicates the plane's speed. **3.** a pointer on the dial of such an instrument. **4.** a substance, such as litmus, that indicates a chemical condition or change, especially by changing color.
in·di·ces (in′də sēz) a plural of **index.**
in·dict (in dīt′) *v.t.* **1.** (of a grand jury) to accuse formally of a crime. **2.** to accuse of an offense; criticize. —**in·dict′er;** *also,* **in·dict′or,** *n.*
in·dict·ment (in dīt′mənt) *n.* **1.** a formal, written accusation by a grand jury. **2.** any accusation or criticism.
in·dif·fer·ence (in dif′ər əns, in dif′rəns) *n.* **1.** lack of feeling, concern, or care: *They showed complete indifference to their neighbors' poverty.* **2.** lack of importance: *What they think is a matter of indifference to me.*
in·dif·fer·ent (in dif′ər ənt, in dif′rənt) *adj.* **1.** having

or showing a lack of feeling, concern, or care: *to be indifferent to other people's troubles.* **2.** not particularly good; routine; average: *The actor gave an indifferent performance.* —**in·dif′fer·ent·ly,** *adv.*
in·di·gence (in′di jəns) *n.* extreme need; poverty.
in·dig·e·nous (in dij′ə nəs) *adj.* originating, growing, or living naturally in a particular place; not brought in from outside; native: *Coyotes are indigenous to North America.* —**in·dig′e·nous·ly,** *adv.*
in·di·gent (in′di jənt) *adj.* not having enough to live on; poor; needy.
in·di·gest·i·ble (in′di jes′tə bəl, in′dī jes′tə bəl) *adj.* impossible or hard to digest. —**in′di·gest′i·bil′i·ty,** *n.*
in·di·ges·tion (in′di jes′chən, in′dī jes′chən) *n.* difficulty or discomfort in digesting food.
in·dig·nant (in dig′nənt) *adj.* filled with indignation: *I was indignant at my friend for telling a lie.* —**in·dig′nant·ly,** *adv.*
in·dig·na·tion (in′dig nā′shən) *n.* anger aroused by something unfair, cruel, or evil: *The community expressed its indignation at drunken drivers.*
in·dig·ni·ty (in dig′ni tē) *n., pl.* **in·dig·ni·ties.** an act or remark that humiliates, insults, or injures: *The child suffered the indignity of being called names by the bully.*
in·di·go (in′di gō′) *n., pl.* **in·di·gos** or **in·di·goes.** **1.** a very dark blue dye obtained from various plants or made artificially. **2.** any of the plants from which this dye is obtained. **3.** a deep violet-blue color. —*adj.* having the color indigo; violet-blue. [Originally from the Greek phrase *Indikon (pharmakon)* meaning "Indian (dye)," going back to the Persian word *Hind* "India."]
in·di·rect (in′di rekt′, in′dī rekt′) *adj.* **1.** not in a straight line; roundabout: *an indirect route.* **2.** having or depending on something that comes between; not immediate: *an indirect result.* **3.** not straightforward and open; devious: *The witness gave only an indirect answer.* —**in′di·rect′ly,** *adv.* —**in′di·rect′ness,** *n.*
indirect object, a person or thing indirectly affected by an action. In the sentence *I gave them a book, them* is the indirect object.
indirect tax, a tax on goods that is paid indirectly by the consumer because it is included in the price of the goods. The excise tax is an indirect tax.
in·dis·creet (in′di skrēt′) *adj.* lacking tact or careful judgment; not discreet: *Don't be indiscreet in discussing your personal affairs.* —**in′dis·creet′ly,** *adv.* —**in′dis·creet′ness,** *n.*
in·dis·cre·tion (in′di skresh′ən) *n.* **1.** the quality of being indiscreet. **2.** something that is indiscreet: *to commit an indiscretion.*
in·dis·crim·i·nate (in′di skrim′ə nit) *adj.* **1.** not noticing differences or making wise choices: *An indiscriminate television fan will watch any program.* **2.** random or confused. —**in′dis·crim′i·nate·ly,** *adv.*
in·dis·pen·sa·ble (in′di spen′sə bəl) *adj.* that cannot be done without; necessary or essential: *Good soil, water, and sunshine are indispensable to a successful garden.* —**in′dis·pen′sa·bil′i·ty,** *n.* —**in′dis·pen′sa·bly,** *adv.*
in·dis·posed (in′di spōzd′) *adj.* **1.** slightly ill. **2.** unwilling; disinclined: *to be indisposed to help someone.*
in·dis·po·si·tion (in dis′pə zish′ən, in′dis pə zish′ən) *n.* **1.** a slight illness. **2.** the condition of being unwilling; unwillingness.

I

at; āpe; fär; câre; end; mē; it; īce; pîerce; hot; ōld; sông, fôrk; oil; out; up; ūse; rūle; pull; tûrn; chin; sing; shop; thin; this; hw in white; zh in treasure. The symbol ə stands for the unstressed vowel sound heard in about, taken, pencil, lemon, and circus.

in·dis·put·a·ble (in′di spū′tə bəl) *adj.* that cannot be disputed; unquestionable: *These facts are indisputable.* —**in′dis·put′a·bil′i·ty,** *n.* —**in′dis·put′a·bly,** *adv.*

in·dis·sol·u·ble (in′di sol′yə bəl) *adj.* that cannot be dissolved or destroyed: *Our friendship is indissoluble.*

in·dis·tinct (in′di stingkt′) *adj.* not clear or sharp; not distinct. —**in′dis·tinct′ly,** *adv.* —**in′dis·tinct′ness,** *n.*

in·dis·tin·guish·a·ble (in′di sting′gwi shə bəl) *adj.*
1. that cannot be told apart: *The two houses are so similar that they are indistinguishable from one another.*
2. that cannot be seen or recognized: *an indistinguishable difference.*

in·di·um (in′dē əm) *n.* a rare, soft, silvery metallic element, used in alloys for jewelry and bearings, and to make semiconductors. Symbol: **In** [Formed from the Latin word *indicum* meaning "indigo." The element was discovered by the indigo lines in its spectrum.]

in·di·vid·u·al (in′də vij′ü əl) *adj.* **1.** single and distinct; separate: *Each individual house has its own yard.* **2.** for or by one only: *This play is an individual effort.* **3.** characteristic of one only: *to have an individual style of dressing.* —*n.* **1.** a person. **2.** a single person, being, or thing: *A herd of caribou may contain thousands of individuals.* —**in′di·vid′u·al·ly,** *adv.*

in·di·vid·u·al·ism (in′də vij′ü ə liz′əm) *n.* **1.** the theory and practice that emphasizes the worth, freedom, and well-being of the individual and one's right to think and live as one sees fit without the control or direction of others, especially of a government. **2.** action or thought by each person for his or her own ends without regard for others.

in·di·vid·u·al·ist (in′də vij′ü ə list) *n.* **1.** a person who thinks and acts in an independent manner. **2.** a person who practices or supports individualism.

in·di·vid·u·al·is·tic (in′də vij′ü ə lis′tik) *adj.* relating to individualism or individualists.

in·di·vid·u·al·i·ty (in′də vij′ü al′i tē) *n., pl.* **in·di·vid·u·al·i·ties. 1.** a quality that makes one person or thing different from others; individual character: *The artist's paintings show much individuality.* **2.** the condition of being an individual.

in·di·vid·u·al·ize (in′də vij′ü ə līz′) *v.t.,* **in·di·vid·u·al·ized, in·di·vid·u·al·iz·ing. 1.** to make individual; give a distinct character to: *The six houses on the block were nearly identical, individualized only by front doors painted in different colors.* **2.** to fit to an individual or to different individuals: *This school individualizes courses for students with special needs.*

in·di·vis·i·ble (in′də viz′ə bəl) *adj.* **1.** that cannot be divided. **2.** that cannot be divided without a remainder: *5 is indivisible by 2.* —**in′di·vis′i·bil′i·ty,** *n.* —**in′di·vis′i·bly,** *adv.*

in·doc·tri·nate (in dok′trə nāt′) *v.t.,* **in·doc·tri·nat·ed, in·doc·tri·nat·ing.** to teach (someone), especially a particular theory, belief, or principle. —**in·doc′tri·na′tion,** *n.*

In·do–Eu·ro·pe·an (in′dō yur′ə pē′ən) *n.* a family of languages that includes most languages spoken in Europe and the Americas and many of those spoken in Asia. English, Russian, Italian, Persian, and Hindi are Indo-European languages. —*adj.* of or relating to this family of languages.

Language Note

The **Indo-European** language family includes most, although not all, of the languages spoken from northern India to western Europe. Because of European colonial expansion, Indo-European languages are also spoken in North America, South America, Australia, Africa, and parts of Asia. Approximately one half of the world's population speaks an Indo-European language. These languages include English, German, French, Spanish, Italian, Russian, Greek, Irish, Persian, and Hindi.

If you have ever seen or heard any of these languages, you will probably find it hard to believe that they are related to English or to each other. But as early as the sixteenth century, language scholars had begun to notice that these languages had certain basic words in common. Among the words that were similarly pronounced or spelled in various Indo-European languages were the terms for family members and for the numerals one through ten. For example, the English word *brother* is similar to the German *bruder,* Irish *bráthair,* Latin *fräter,* Greek *phratēr,* Russian *brat,* Sanskrit *bhratā,* and Persian *biradar.* The English word *seven* is similar to the German *sieben,* Irish *seacht,* French *sept,* Latin *septem,* Greek *hepta,* and Russian *sem'.* Very basic words like these are usually not borrowed by one language from another; they exist in the earliest vocabulary of a language. Therefore, scholars reasoned that all Indo-European languages came from a single prehistoric language. The different Indo-European languages that exist today are believed to have been the result of waves of migration by groups of people who spoke the original Indo-European language. As they lost contact with each other, these groups developed different forms of their language. Over the centuries, these forms changed so greatly that they became separate languages. In the past 2,000 years we have seen this happen in Europe. The Romans took their language, Latin, with them throughout their empire. While Latin itself is only a written fossil today, the languages that developed from it are now spoken in various parts of the old Roman Empire: French, Spanish, Portuguese, and Italian.

Although no one has been able to establish precisely the original Indo-European homeland, scholars have done detective work that has produced some general ideas. The oldest recorded form of an Indo-European language dates from about 2,000 B.C. From this and from other early sources, it has been found that the ancient Indo-European language had many words relating to cold, northern regions, such as *snow, bear, wolf, salmon, birch,* and *beech.* Such words as *grape, olive, lion,* and *camel,* relating to warmer regions, appear to be later additions. The beech tree did not grow in Asia, and salmon existed mainly in the Baltic Sea. The early appearance of such words as *sheep, cow,* and *horse* suggests that the original Indo-European language developed in an area of grassy plains. From all this evidence, some scholars have suggested that the original Indo-European homeland was in eastern Europe, on the plains and uplands between the Baltic and Black Seas. Because there are no surviving written records to prove this theory, the location of the Indo-European language family will probably never be known with certainty.

in·do·lent (in′də lənt) *adj.* having or showing a dislike of work or effort; lazy; idle. —**in′do·lence,** *n.* —**in′do·lent·ly,** *adv.*

in·dom·i·ta·ble (in dom′i tə bəl) *adj.* that cannot be conquered: *an indomitable will.* —**in·dom′i·ta·bly,** *adv.*

In·do·ne·sian (in′də nē′zhən) *adj.* of or relating to Indonesia or its people. —*n.* **1.** a person who was born in or is a citizen of Indonesia. **2.** a form of Malay and the official language of Indonesia.

in·door (in′dôr′) *adj.* used or done within a building: *an indoor swimming pool, an indoor sport.*

in·doors (in′dôrz′) *adv.* in or into a house or building: *We moved the party indoors when it started to rain.*

in·dorse (in dôrs′) *v.t.,* **in·dorsed, in·dors·ing.** another word for **endorse.**

in·dorse·ment (in dôrs′mənt) another spelling of **endorsement.**

in·du·bi·ta·ble (in dü′bi tə bəl, in dū′bi tə bəl) *adj.* not to be doubted; certain. —**in·du′bi·ta·bly,** *adv.*

in·duce (in düs′, in dūs′) *v.t.,* **in·duced, in·duc·ing. 1.** to persuade to do something; influence: *They could not induce the visitor to stay.* **2.** to bring about; bring on; produce; cause: *The nurse gave me a drug to induce sleep.* **3.** to produce (electric current) by induction. **4.** to reason by induction.

in·duce·ment (in düs′mənt, in dūs′mənt) *n.* **1.** something attractive that leads someone to do something: *The extra money was an inducement to work harder.* **2.** the act of inducing or the state of being induced.

in·duct (in dukt′) *v.t.* **1.** to take into the armed forces: *to be inducted into the army.* **2.** to bring into a group; admit: *The club inducted four new members.* **3.** to install formally in an office: *to induct a new mayor.*

in·duc·tance (in duk′təns) *n.* the ability of an electric circuit to produce an electromotive force when the current in the circuit or in a neighboring circuit is changing.

in·duc·tee (in duk′tē′, in′duk tē′) *n.* a person who is being inducted, especially into the armed forces.

in·duc·tion (in duk′shən) *n.* **1.** the process by which a person is taken into the armed forces. **2.** the process or ceremony of being brought into a group or installed in an office: *We attended the induction of the new club president.* **3.** the act of inducing: *the induction of a hypnotized state.* **4.** *Electricity.* **a.** the process by which a body having electric or magnetic properties produces electric or magnetic properties in another body without touching it. **b.** the act or process of magnetizing an object by placing it in a magnetic field. **c.** the act or process of producing an electric current in a conductor by moving it through a magnetic field, or by moving the magnetic field itself. **5.** the act or method of reasoning from particular cases or facts to a general principle or conclusion.

induction coil, an electrical device that converts low-voltage direct current into high-voltage pulses.

in·duc·tive (in duk′tiv) *adj.* **1.** of or using induction: *a conclusion reached by inductive reasoning.* **2.** relating to, producing, or produced by electrical or magnetic induction. —**in·duc′tive·ly,** *adv.*

in·dulge (in dulj′) *v.,* **in·dulged, in·dulg·ing.** —*v.t.* **1.** to give way to; yield to: *I sometimes indulge my love for photography.* **2.** to yield to the whims or wishes of; give in to: *The grandparents indulge the child.* —*v.i.* to allow oneself to have, do, or enjoy something: *The students often indulge in television during study periods.*

in·dul·gence (in dul′jəns) *n.* **1.** the act of indulging. **2.** something that is indulged in: *Compact discs are a recent indulgence of mine.* **3.** something given by a person who is indulgent; favor. **4.** in the Roman Catholic Church, pardon from punishment for the sin that remains after the sin itself has been forgiven.

in·dul·gent (in dul′jənt) *adj.* characterized by indulgence: *an indulgent parent.* —**in·dul′gent·ly,** *adv.*

in·dus·tri·al (in dus′trē əl) *adj.* **1.** relating to, connected with, or produced by industry: *industrial workers, industrial wastes.* **2.** having highly developed industry: *an industrial society.* **3.** made for the use of industry: *industrial buildings, industrial equipment.* —**in·dus′tri·al·ly,** *adv.*

in·dus·tri·al·ist (in dus′trē ə list) *n.* a person who owns, manages, or has to do with industry.

in·dus·tri·al·ize (in dus′trē ə līz′) *v.t.,* **in·dus·tri·al·ized, in·dus·tri·al·iz·ing.** to set up or develop industry in: *to industrialize an area, to industrialize a country's economy.* —*v.i.* to become industrial: *Countries around the world are industrializing rapidly.* —**in·dus′tri·al·i·za′tion,** *n.*

industrial park, a section of land with factories, warehouses, or other industrial buildings, usually located in a suburban or rural area.

Industrial Revolution, changes in the way of life and the economy of Europe and the United States, beginning in the eighteenth century in England. It resulted from the development of factories with machines for manufacturing products, and the use of power from steam, oil, or electricity in place of human and animal power.

in·dus·tri·ous (in dus′trē əs) *adj.* working hard and steadily; diligent. —**in·dus′tri·ous·ly,** *adv.* —**in·dus′tri·ous·ness,** *n.*

in·dus·try (in′də strē) *n., pl.* **in·dus·tries. 1.** manufacturing plants and other businesses considered as a whole: *The townspeople are interested in attracting industry to their area.* **2.** a particular branch of business, trade, or manufacturing: *the tourist industry, the aircraft industry.* **3.** hard work; steady effort; diligence: *They showed much industry in performing the job.*

–ine *suffix* (used to form adjectives from nouns) of, like, or relating to: *Alpine, serpentine.*

in·e·bri·ate (*v.,* i nē′brē āt′; *n.,* i nē′brē it) *v.t.,* **in·e·bri·at·ed, in·e·bri·at·ing.** to make drunk. —*n.* a person who is drunk. —**in·e′bri·a′tion,** *n.*

in·ed·i·ble (in ed′ə bəl) *adj.* not fit as food; unsuitable for eating: *The burned meat was inedible.*

in·ef·fa·ble (in ef′ə bəl) *adj.* that cannot be described in words: *The view from here is one of ineffable beauty.* —**in·ef′fa·bil′i·ty,** *n.* —**in·ef′fa·bly,** *adv.*

in·ef·fec·tive (in′i fek′tiv) *adj.* **1.** not able to bring about a desired effect; not effective: *The method suggested for curing hiccups was ineffective.* **2.** not able or competent: *an ineffective person.* —**in′ef·fec′tive·ly,** *adv.* —**in′ef·fec′tive·ness,** *n.*

in·ef·fec·tu·al (in′i fek′chü əl) *adj.* that cannot or does not produce a desired effect: *ineffectual action, ineffectual advice.* —**in′ef·fec′tu·al·ly,** *adv.*

in·ef·fi·cien·cy (in′i fish′ən sē) *n., pl.* **in·ef·fi·cien·cies.** the state, quality, or fact of being inefficient.

in·ef·fi·cient (in′i fish′ənt) *adj.* **1.** involving, causing, or resulting in too much effort or waste; not efficient. **2.** not working or accomplishing something efficiently: *an inefficient typist.* —**in′ef·fi′cient·ly,** *adv.*

in·e·las·tic (in′i las′tik) *adj.* not elastic. —**in′e·las·tic′i·ty,** *n.*

in·el·e·gant (in el′i gənt) *adj.* not elegant. —**in·el′e·gance,** *n.* —**in·el′e·gant·ly,** *adv.*

in·el·i·gi·ble (in el′i jə bəl) *adj.* not qualified to be chosen: *I was ineligible for the team because of poor grades.* —*n.* a person who is ineligible. —**in·el′i·gi·bil′i·ty,** *n.* —**in·el′i·gi·bly,** *adv.*

in·ept (in ept′, i nept′) *adj.* **1.** awkward or clumsy: *to be inept at changing a tire.* **2.** out of place; not suitable: *an inept remark.* —**in·ept′ly,** *adv.* —**in·ept′ness,** *n.*

in·ept·i·tude (in ep′ti tüd′, in ep′ti tūd′, i nep′ti tüd′, i nep′ti tūd′) *n.* **1.** the quality of being inept. **2.** an inept act or remark.

in·e·qual·i·ty (in′i kwol′i tē) *n., pl.* **in·e·qual·i·ties. 1.** the fact or condition of not being equal: *inequality between rich and poor.* **2.** a mathematical statement showing that two numbers are not equal or that one number is greater or less than another number.

in·eq·ui·ta·ble (in ek′wi tə bəl) *adj.* not fair and just; not equitable: *an inequitable settlement of a dispute.* —**in·eq′ui·ta·bly,** *adv.*

in·eq·ui·ty (in ek′wi tē) *n., pl.* **in·eq·ui·ties. 1.** injustice; unfairness. **2.** something that is unfair and unjust.

at; āpe; fär; câre; end; mē; it; īce; pîerce; hot; ōld; sông, fôrk; oil; out; up; ūse; rüle; pùll; tûrn; chin; sing; shop; thin; this; hw in white; zh in treasure. The symbol ə stands for the unstressed vowel sound heard in about, taken, pencil, lemon, and circus.

I

in·e·rad·i·ca·ble (in′i rad′i kə bəl) *adj.* that cannot be rooted out or eradicated. —**in′e·rad′i·ca·bly,** *adv.*

in·ert (in ûrt′, i nûrt′) *adj.* **1.** without power to move or act; not moving. **2.** not reacting or combining readily with other substances; chemically inactive: *Helium is an inert gas.* **3.** not active; sluggish; slow.

in·er·tia (in ûr′shə, i nûr′shə) *n.* **1.** the tendency not to move or change: *My inertia kept me from turning off the television.* **2.** *Physics.* the property of all matter that causes it to remain in a state of rest if at rest, or, if moving, to continue moving in a straight line at a constant speed, unless acted upon by an outside force.

in·es·cap·a·ble (in′e skă′pə bəl) *adj.* that cannot be escaped or avoided; certain: *inescapable defeat.* —**in′-es·cap′a·bly,** *adv.*

in·es·ti·ma·ble (in es′tə mə bəl) *adj.* that cannot be estimated, measured, or valued; very great: *Your friendship is of inestimable worth to me.* —**in·es′ti·ma·bly,** *adv.*

in·ev·i·ta·ble (in ev′i tə bəl) *adj.* that cannot be avoided; obvious or certain: *an inevitable result.* —**in·ev′i·ta·bil′i·ty,** *n.* —**in·ev′i·ta·bly,** *adv.*

in·ex·act (in′eg zakt′) *adj.* not exact; not completely correct. —**in′ex·act′ly,** *adv.* —**in′ex·act′ness,** *n.*

in·ex·cus·a·ble (in′ek skū′zə bəl) *adj.* that cannot be excused or justified: *Cruelty to animals is inexcusable.* —**in′ex·cus′a·bly,** *adv.*

in·ex·haust·i·ble (in′eg zôs′tə bəl) *adj.* **1.** that cannot be used up easily: *The office seemed to have an inexhaustible supply of paper.* **2.** that does not become easily worn out or tired out; tireless: *The beaver is an inexhaustible swimmer.* —**in′ex·haust′i·bil′i·ty,** *n.* —**in′ex·haust′i·bly,** *adv.*

in·ex·o·ra·ble (in ek′sər ə bəl) *adj.* that does not change, stop, or yield, no matter what anyone says or does; unyielding: *Fate is inexorable.* —**in·ex′o·ra·bil′i·ty,** *n.* —**in·ex′o·ra·bly,** *adv.*

in·ex·pe·di·ent (in′ek spē′dē ənt) *adj.* not suitable or useful for a given purpose; not expedient. —**in′ex·pe′-di·en·cy,** *n.* —**in′ex·pe′di·ent·ly,** *adv.*

in·ex·pen·sive (in′ek spen′siv) *adj.* not costing much; cheap: *an inexpensive stereo.* —**in′ex·pen′sive·ly,** *adv.* —**in′ex·pen′sive·ness,** *n.*

in·ex·pe·ri·ence (in′ek spîr′ē əns) *n.* lack of experience, or of the knowledge or skill that comes with experience.

in·ex·pe·ri·enced (in′ek spir′ē ənst) *adj.* lacking experience, knowledge, or skill: *an inexperienced swimmer.*

in·ex·pert (in eks′pûrt, in′ek spûrt′) *adj.* not expert; unskilled. —**in·ex′pert·ly,** *adv.* —**in·ex′pert·ness,** *n.*

in·ex·plic·a·ble (in′ek splik′ə bəl, in ek′spli kə bəl) *adj.* that cannot be explained: *The cat's odd behavior is inexplicable.* —**in′ex·plic′a·bil′i·ty,** *n.* —**in′ex·plic′a·bly,** *adv.*

in·ex·press·i·ble (in′ek spres′ə bəl) *adj.* that cannot be expressed, especially by putting into words: *inexpressible feelings.* —**in′ex·press′i·bil′i·ty,** *n.* —**in′ex·press′i·bly,** *adv.*

in·ex·pres·sive (in′ek spres′iv) *adj.* having or showing little feeling or meaning; not expressive.

in·ex·tin·guish·a·ble (in′ek sting′gwi shə bəl) *adj.* that cannot be put out or destroyed: *an inextinguishable hope.* —**in′ex·tin′guish·a·bly,** *adv.*

in·ex·tri·ca·ble (in ek′stri kə bəl) *adj.* **1.** that cannot be cleared up or untangled: *an inextricable knot, inextricable confusion.* **2.** that cannot be escaped from: *We got into an inextricable situation.* —**in·ex′tri·ca·bly,** *adv.*

in·fal·li·ble (in fal′ə bəl) *adj.* **1.** not able to make a mistake: *No one is infallible.* **2.** reliable; unfailing; sure: *an infallible solution.* —**in·fal′li·bil′i·ty,** *n.* —**in·fal′li·bly,** *adv.*

in·fa·mous (in′fə məs) *adj.* **1.** widely known for wrong-doing: *an infamous criminal.* **2.** receiving or deserving condemnation; very bad: *infamous crimes.* —**in′-fa·mous·ly,** *adv.*

in·fa·my (in′fə mē) *n., pl.* **in·fa·mies.** **1.** the condition of being widely known for wrongdoing. **2.** the quality of being extremely bad: *the infamy of the crimes.* **3.** an infamous act: *the infamies of war.*

in·fan·cy (in′fən sē) *n., pl.* **in·fan·cies.** **1.** the condition or period of being an infant. **2.** the earliest period of development of anything: *When the computer was in its infancy, vacuum tubes were used to process data.*

in·fant (in′fənt) *n.* **1.** a child during the earliest period of life; baby. **2.** *Law.* a person who has not reached the age of legal responsibility; minor. —*adj.* **1.** of, relating to, or for an infant: *infant care, infant toys.* **2.** in the earliest period of development: *an infant industry.* [From the Old French word *enfaunt* meaning "young child," going back to the Latin word *infans* "mute, without speech."]

in·fan·ti·cide (in fan′tə sīd′) *n.* the killing of an infant. [From the Late Latin word *infanticidium* with the same meaning, from the Latin word elements *infans* "infant" + *-cidium* "a killing."]

in·fan·tile (in′fən tīl′) *adj.* **1.** too much like an infant; childish: *Infantile behavior by an older person is very unattractive.* **2.** of, relating to, or belonging to infancy.

infantile paralysis, another term for **poliomyelitis.**

in·fan·try (in′fən trē) *n., pl.* **in·fan·tries.** **1.** soldiers trained and equipped to fight on foot. **2.** the branch of an army made up of such soldiers. [From the French word *infanterie* meaning "foot soldiers," from the Italian word *infanteria*, from the word *infante* meaning "boy" or "foot soldier," from the Latin word *infans* "baby, minor."]

in·fan·try·man (in′fən trē mən) *n., pl.* **in·fan·try·men** (in′fən trē mən). a member of the infantry.

in·fat·u·ate (in fach′ü āt′) *v.t.,* **in·fat·u·at·ed, in·fat·u·at·ing.** to cause to have a foolish or childish attraction or passion: *My friend was infatuated with a rock singer.* —**in·fat′u·a′tion,** *n.*

in·fect (in fekt′) *v.t.* **1.** to cause disease in or contaminate by introducing harmful microorganisms or microscopic particles, such as bacteria or viruses. *The filthy bandage infected the wound.* **2.** to affect or influence: *Your happiness infected all of us.*

in·fec·tion (in fek′shən) *n.* **1.** the entering of part of the body by harmful microorganisms or microscopic particles, such as bacteria or viruses that cause disease. **2.** a disease or other harmful condition resulting from this. **3.** the state of being infected.

in·fec·tious (in fek′shəs) *adj.* **1.** (of a disease) that can be spread by infection. **2.** that can affect or influence others: *infectious laughter.* —**in·fec′tious·ly,** *adv.* —**in·fec′tious·ness,** *n.*

infectious mononucleosis, a contagious, but usually not serious, blood disease in which there are too many of a certain kind of white cell in the blood. It is characterized by fever, loss of appetite, and tiredness and is caused by a virus.

in·fe·lic·i·tous (in′fə lis′i təs) *adj.* **1.** not appropriate or suitable, unfitting: *an infelicitous comment.* **2.** unfortunate; unhappy: *an infelicitous turn of events.*

in·fe·lic·i·ty (in′fə lis′i tē) *n., pl.* **in·fe·lic·i·ties.** **1.** the state or quality of being infelicitous. **2.** something that is infelicitous.

in·fer (in fûr′) *v.t.,* **in·ferred, in·fer·ring.** to come to (an opinion) by reasoning from facts or observations: *I inferred from your accent that you were British.*

▲ **Infer** and **imply** have different meanings. To **infer** is to draw a conclusion from something that is known or hinted at: *I inferred from your frown that you were upset.* To **imply** is to suggest something without stating it directly: *Your smile implied satisfaction.*

in·fer·ence (in'fər əns) *n.* **1.** something that is inferred; conclusion. **2.** the act or process of inferring: *to reason by inference.*

in·fe·ri·or (in fîr'ē ər) *adj.* **1.** of poor quality, below average: *The food at that restaurant is inferior.* **2.** low or lower in quality, value, rank, or importance: *to feel inferior to other people.* —*n.* a person who is inferior to others, as in rank or importance.

in·fe·ri·or·i·ty (in fîr'ē ôr'i tē, in fîr'ē or'i tē) *n.* the quality or condition of being inferior.

inferiority complex, a general feeling that one is worth less than others or is of little worth or importance. At times a person with an inferiority complex tries to cover up such a feeling with arrogant, aggressive behavior.

in·fer·nal (in fûr'nəl) *adj.* **1.** of, relating to, or characteristic of hell. **2.** like or appropriate to hell; hellish: *infernal cruelty.* **3.** *Informal.* hateful: *an infernal nuisance.* —**in·fer'nal·ly,** *adv.*

in·fer·no (in fûr'nō) *n., pl.* **in·fer·nos. 1.** hell. **2.** any place resembling hell, especially in being hot or fiery: *The furnace room was an inferno.* **3.** a large, intense, or particularly destructive fire: *Firefighters eventually put out the inferno.* [From the Italian word *inferno* meaning "hell," going back to the Latin word *infernus* "lying beneath" or "of the underworld."]

in·fer·tile (in fûr'təl) *adj.* not fertile; barren. —**in'fer·til'i·ty,** *n.*

in·fest (in fest') *v.t.* to grow, spread, or exist in large numbers so as to cause trouble or harm: *Weeds infested the garden.* —**in'fes·ta'tion,** *n.*

in·fi·del (in'fi dəl, in'fi del') *n.* **1.** a person who does not believe in any religion. **2.** among Muslims, a person who does not accept Islam. **3.** among Christians, a person who does not accept Christianity. —*adj.* **1.** having no religious beliefs. **2.** not accepting a particular faith, such as Christianity or Islam.

in·fi·del·i·ty (in'fi del'i tē) *n., pl.* **in·fi·del·i·ties. 1.** lack of religious faith. **2.** unfaithfulness in marriage; adultery. **3.** an act of infidelity.

in·field (in'fēld') *n. Baseball.* **1.** the area bounded by the paths connecting the bases. **2.** the first, second, and third basemen and the shortstop.

in·field·er (in'fēl'dər) *n. Baseball.* a player who plays a position in the infield.

in·fil·trate (in fil'trāt, in'fil trāt') *v.*, **in·fil·trat·ed, in·fil·trat·ing.** —*v.t.* **1.** to move gradually and secretly into or through: *to infiltrate enemy lines. The police infiltrated the revolutionary organization.* **2.** to filter into or through; permeate. —*v.i.* to pass into or through a substance by filtering. —**in'fil·tra'tion,** *n.*

infin., infinitive.

in·fi·nite (in'fə nit) *adj.* **1.** having no limits or end; boundless: *Space seems to be infinite.* **2.** very great; immense: *to take infinite pains with one's work.* **3.** *Mathematics.* of or designating a quantity larger than any assigned number. —*n.* **1.** something that is infinite. **2.** *Mathematics.* an infinite quantity. **3. the Infinite.** God. —**in'fi·nite·ly,** *adv.* —**in'fi·nite·ness,** *n.*

in·fin·i·tes·i·mal (in'fi ni tes'ə məl) *adj.* so small as to be impossible or almost impossible to measure: *an infinitesimal speck of dust.* —**in'fi·ni·tes'i·mal·ly,** *adv.*

in·fin·i·tive (in fin'i tiv) *n.* a simple verb form that does not indicate person or number and is often preceded by *to.* In the sentences *My dog likes to run* and *We must leave,* the verb forms *to run* and *leave* are infinitives.

in·fin·i·tude (in fin'i tüd', in fin'i tūd') *n.* **1.** the quality of being infinite. **2.** an infinite quantity.

in·fin·i·ty (in fin'i tē) *n., pl.* **in·fin·i·ties. 1.** the state or quality of being infinite. **2.** something that is infinite, such as space or time. **3.** a very great amount or number: *an infinity of details.* **4.** *Mathematics.* a quantity of unlimited magnitude, larger than any assigned number, represented by the symbol ∞.

in·firm (in fûrm') *adj.* **1.** physically weak, as from old age: *My grandparents are both infirm.* **2.** lacking firmness of will, purpose, or character. —**in·firm'ly,** *adv.* —**in·firm'ness,** *n.*

in·fir·ma·ry (in fûr'mə rē) *n., pl.* **in·fir·ma·ries.** a place for the care or treatment of the sick or injured. Schools and factories often have infirmaries.

in·fir·mi·ty (in fûr'mi tē) *n., pl.* **in·fir·mi·ties. 1.** the state or quality of being infirm; physical weakness; feebleness. **2.** a physical defect or ailment.

in·flame (in flām') *v.t.*, **in·flamed, in·flam·ing. 1.** to excite to great emotion; stir up: *The speaker inflamed the audience.* **2.** to make hot, red, swollen, or painful: *The infection inflamed my finger.*

in·flam·ma·ble (in flam'ə bəl) *adj.* **1.** that can be set on fire easily: *an inflammable fluid.* **2.** easily excited or aroused: *an inflammable temper.* —*n.* something that can be set on fire easily. —**in·flam'ma·bil'i·ty,** *n.*

in·flam·ma·tion (in'flə mā'shən) *n.* **1.** a condition of a part of the body caused by a reaction to injury, infection, or irritation, and characterized by heat, redness, swelling, and pain. **2.** the act of inflaming or the state of being inflamed.

in·flam·ma·to·ry (in flam'ə tôr'ē) *adj.* **1.** tending to excite strong emotion or violent action: *an inflammatory speech.* **2.** relating to, causing, or characterized by inflammation.

in·flat·a·ble (in flā'tə bəl) *adj.* that can be inflated: *an inflatable rubber raft.*

inflatable rubber raft

in·flate (in flāt') *v.*, **in·flat·ed, in·flat·ing.** —*v.t.* **1.** to cause to swell by filling with air or gas: *to inflate a balloon.* **2.** to cause to puff up, especially with pride: *Fame can inflate one's ego.* **3.** to increase beyond usual levels: *to inflate prices.* —*v.i.* to become inflated. —**in·flat'er;** *also,* **in·fla'tor,** *n.*

in·fla·tion (in flā'shən) *n.* **1.** the act of inflating or the state of being inflated. **2.** a rise in the usual price level for goods and services.

in·fla·tion·ar·y (in flā'shə ner'ē) *adj.* of, relating to, or causing inflation.

in·flect (in flekt') *v.t.* **1.** to change or vary the tone or pitch of (the voice.) **2.** to vary the form of (a word) to

at; āpe; fär; câre; end; mē; it; īce; pîerce; hot; ōld; sông, fôrk; oil; out; up; ūse; rüle; pùll; tûrn; chin; sing; shop; thin; this; hw in white; zh in treasure. The symbol ə stands for the unstressed vowel sound heard in about, taken, pencil, lemon, and circus.

495

show tense, number, case, and the like.   **3.** to turn from a direct line or course; bend: *to inflect rays of light.*

in·flec·tion (in flek'shən) *also, British,* **in·flex·ion.** *n.* **1.** a change or variation in the tone or pitch of the voice: *A rising inflection is often used to ask a question.* **2.** *Language.* a process by which the form of a word is changed to show tense, number, case, and the like. **3.** the act of inflecting or the state of being inflected. **4.** a bend or angle.

Language Note

In language, **inflection** is the changing of the form of a word in order to show that there is a change in the use or meaning of the word in a sentence. In English, nouns, pronouns, verbs, adjectives and adverbs are inflected. The inflections of a noun are called its *declension.* The forms of a noun tell you whether the noun is singular or plural and whether or not it is possessive, such as *student, students, student's,* and *students'.* Pronouns are inflected to indicate the subject (*who*), the object (*whom*), and the possessive (*whose*).

The inflected forms of a verb are called its *conjugation.* The verb *dance* is conjugated *dance, dances* (for the third person singular), *danced,* and *dancing.* The inflected forms of an English adjective or adverb show comparison and are called the *comparative* and the *superlative* forms. The adjective *tall* has the comparative form *taller* and the superlative form *tallest.* Adverbs are inflected less often than adjectives. We usually use the words *more* or *most* before an adverb in order to produce the same effect that inflection has, as in *quickly, more quickly,* and *most quickly.* Some adverbs, such as *fast,* whose inflected forms are *faster* and *fastest,* are inflected in the same way that most adjectives are.

in·flec·tion·al (in flek'shə nəl) *also, British,* **in·flex·ion·al.** *adj.* of or showing grammatical inflection.

in·flex·i·ble (in flek'sə bəl) *adj.* **1.** that cannot be bent; stiff; rigid: *A fireplace poker is an inflexible metal rod.* **2.** unyielding in mind or purpose; adamant: *An inflexible person never admits being wrong.* **3.** that cannot be changed or altered. —**in·flex'i·bil'i·ty,** *n.* —**in·flex'i·bly,** *adv.*

in·flict (in flikt') *v.t.* **1.** to cause: *to inflict pain, to inflict a wound.* **2.** to impose (something unwelcome) on someone: *to inflict a burden, to inflict punishment.*

in·flic·tion (in flik'shən) *n.* **1.** the act of inflicting. **2.** something that is inflicted, such as punishment.

in·flo·res·cence (in'flô res'əns) *n.* a cluster of flowers on a stem or stems, or the arrangement of flowers in such a cluster.

in·flow (in'flō') *n.* **1.** the act of flowing in. **2.** something that flows in.

in·flu·ence (in'flü əns) *n.* **1.** the power or ability of a person or thing to produce an effect on others: *to have great influence over a friend.* **2.** an effect produced in this way: *That teacher had a great influence on my career.* **3.** a person or thing that has the power to affect others: *Those friends were a bad influence.* —*v.t.,* **in·flu·enced, in·flu·enc·ing.** **1.** to change or affect the

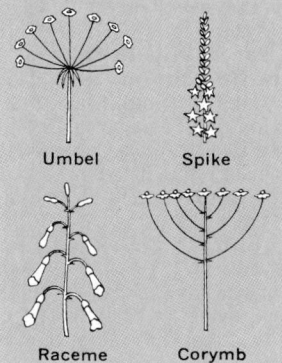

Umbel   Spike

Raceme   Corymb

inflorescence

thought or behavior of; persuade; sway: *My friend influenced me to stop smoking.* **2.** to have or produce an effect on; modify: *Their opinions influence my thinking. The computer has greatly influenced modern life.* [From the Old French word *influence* meaning "a power flowing from the stars," from the Medieval Latin word *influentia* with the same meaning, from the Latin word *influens,* present participle of *influere* meaning "to flow in," from the prefix *in-* "in, into" + *fluere* "to flow." It was formerly believed that forces flowing from the stars and planets influenced human life.]

in·flu·en·tial (in'flü en'shəl) *adj.* having or using influence: *The banker is a very influential person in that community.*

in·flu·en·za (in'flü en'zə) *n.* a highly contagious viral disease, characterized by fever, headache, coughing, exhaustion, and inflammation of the mucous membranes. Also, **flu.** [From the Italian word *influenza* meaning "influence (from the stars)" and used as the name of this disease, from the Medieval Latin word *influentia* "a fluid from the stars that affects human actions," from the former belief that such diseases were caused by the influence of the stars.]

in·flux (in'fluks') *n., pl.* **in·flux·es.** a flowing in: *the influx of goods into a country.*

in·fold (in fōld') another word for **enfold.**

in·form (in fôrm') *v.t.* to give information to; tell: *Please inform me when the train arrives.* —*v.i.* to reveal something secret or damaging: *The criminal informed on the other members of the gang.*

in·for·mal (in fôr'məl) *adj.* **1.** not marked by, needing, or following fixed rules or ceremonies; not formal; relaxed: *informal behavior, an informal wedding.* **2.** suitable for everyday or ordinary use or occasions: *informal clothes.* **3.** suitable for everyday speaking or writing. —**in·for'mal·ly,** *adv.*

Language Note

Informal language is language that is used in our everyday speech. It includes contractions and slang expressions that usually do not appear in official writing or public addresses. Although it is correct, informal language is not appropriate for all situations. If you were making a speech, writing a book report, or being introduced to the president, you would probably use some words that are different from those you use every day in conversations with your friends and family. This is not because such words are wrong, but rather because the situation is more formal.

Most people use different words in different situations without even being aware of it. For example, try to imagine when you would say *Hi,* rather than *How do you do; Thanks a lot,* rather than *I thank you very much;* or *It was lots of fun,* rather than *I had a very enjoyable time.* Although each of these examples is correct English, you can see that they might be used under different circumstances. Most of us use informal language as our normal way of speaking and writing. As in the case of most other problems of usage in our language, there are no real "rights" and "wrongs" in using informal language, but only a question of what kind of language is most appropriate to the situation.

in·for·mal·i·ty (in'fôr mal'i tē) *n., pl.* **in·for·mal·i·ties.** **1.** the state or quality of being informal. **2.** an informal act.

in·form·ant (in fôr'mənt) *n.* a person who gives information.

in·for·ma·tion (in′fər mā′shən) *n.* **1.** knowledge or facts about something: *We asked for information about the train schedule. The students got information on that subject from an encyclopedia.* **2.** the act of informing or the state of being informed. **3.** a person or service that answers questions and gives facts: *Information gave me your phone number.*

in·form·a·tive (in fôr′mə tiv) *adj.* giving information; instructive: *an informative book.*

in·formed (in fôrmd′) *adj.* having or based on information or knowledge: *The reporter got the story from an informed source inside the mayor's office.*

in·form·er (in fôr′mər) *n.* **1.** a person who informs on others, often for money: *an informer for the secret police.* **2.** any person who informs; informant.

infra– *prefix* below; beneath: *infrared.*

in·frac·tion (in frak′shən) *n.* the act of breaking a law or rule; violation: *They committed an infraction of the law by throwing litter in the street.*

in·fra·red (in′frə red′) *adj.* of or relating to electromagnetic radiation whose wavelengths are longer than those of visible light but shorter than those of radio waves. When a body absorbs infrared radiation, the body becomes heated.

in·fre·quent (in frē′kwənt) *adj.* not happening or appearing often; not frequent; rare: *to make infrequent visits.* —**in·fre′quen·cy,** *n.* —**in·fre′quent·ly,** *adv.*

in·fringe (in frinj′) *v.,* **in·fringed, in·fring·ing.** —*v.i.* to go or thrust in without a right; encroach; trespass: *to infringe on a neighbor's property, to infringe on the rights of others.* —*v.t.* to break or violate: *to infringe a law.* —**in·fringe′ment,** *n.* —**in·fring′er,** *n.*

in·fu·ri·ate (in fyùr′ē āt′) *v.t.,* **in·fu·ri·at·ed, in·fu·ri·at·ing.** to make furious; enrage: *The bully's taunts infuriated me.* —**in·fu′ri·a′tion,** *n.*

in·fuse (in fūz′) *v.t.,* **in·fused, in·fus·ing.** **1.** to put in gradually; instill: *The officer infused courage into the troops.* **2.** to inspire; imbue: *The parents infused the children with a sense of responsibility.* **3.** to steep or soak in a liquid: *The cook infused the tea leaves in the hot water.*

in·fu·sion (in fū′zhən) *n.* **1.** the act or process of infusing. **2.** a substance that is obtained by infusion: *a strong infusion of tea.*

–ing[1] *suffix* **1.** (used to form nouns from verbs) **a.** the act, art, process, or instance of performing the action of the root verb: *the fine points of sewing, their meeting, our skating.* **b.** the result of such action: *to make a drawing, to give a reading.* **2.** material used for a particular purpose: *lining, roofing, scaffolding.* **3.** something that does the action of the root verb: *bedding, covering.* [From the Old English suffix *-ung* with the same meaning.]

–ing[2] *suffix* **1.** used to form the present participle of verbs: *I am walking. We were talking.* **2.** used to form adjectives from the present participle of verbs: *a charming village, a leading citizen.* [From the Middle English suffix *-inge,* a form of the suffixes *-ind, -end,* from the Old English participial suffix *-ende.*]

in·gen·ious (in jēn′yəs) *adj.* **1.** made with or showing cleverness, originality, or imagination: *an ingenious plan, an ingenious mechanical toy.* **2.** having creative ability; imaginative; inventive: *an ingenious designer, an ingenious mystery writer.* —**in·gen′ious·ly,** *adv.* —**in·gen′ious·ness,** *n.*

in·gé·nue (än′jə nü′) *also,* **in·ge·nue.** *n., pl.* **in·gé·nues.** **1.** an innocent or naive girl or young woman. **2.** the role of such a person in a play. **3.** an actress who plays such a role. [From the French word *ingénue,* from the word *ingénu* meaning "ingenuous, direct," from the Latin word *ingenuus* "freeborn" or "frank, direct."]

in·ge·nu·i·ty (in′jə nü′i tē) *n.* the quality of being ingenious; cleverness or originality: *The teenager showed great ingenuity in building the radio from old parts.*

in·gen·u·ous (in jen′ū əs) *adj.* **1.** honest and frank; straightforward; candid: *The child was ingenuous with us, and told us exactly what happened.* **2.** innocent and simple; naive: *an ingenuous manner.* —**in·gen′u·ous·ly,** *adv.* —**in·gen′u·ous·ness,** *n.*

in·gest (in jest′) *v.t.* to take or put (food) into the body for digestion. —**in·ges′tion,** *n.*

in·gle·nook (ing′gəl nùk′) *n.* a corner beside a chimney or fireplace.

in·glo·ri·ous (in glôr′ē əs) *adj.* bringing no glory or honor; shameful; disgraceful: *an inglorious past.* —**in·glo′ri·ous·ly,** *adv.* —**in·glo′ri·ous·ness,** *n.*

in·got (ing′gət) *n.* a mass of metal cast into a shape, such as a bar or block.

in·graft (in graft′) another word for **engraft.**

in·grain (in grān′) *v.t.* to set or place deeply and lastingly; fix firmly.

in·grained (in grānd′) *adj.* deeply and lastingly fixed: *ingrained prejudice, an ingrained habit.*

in·grate (in′grāt′) *n.* an ungrateful person.

in·gra·ti·ate (in grā′shē āt′) *v.t.,* **in·gra·ti·at·ed, in·gra·ti·at·ing.** to bring (oneself) into another's favor: *The fans tried to ingratiate themselves with the rock star by running errands.* —**in·gra′ti·at·ing·ly,** *adv.*

in·grat·i·tude (in grat′i tüd′, in grat′i tūd′) *n.* lack of gratitude or appreciation.

in·gre·di·ent (in grē′dē ənt) *n.* **1.** any one of the parts of a mixture: *Flour, eggs, and sugar are ingredients of this cake.* **2.** a part of anything: *Working at a job that one enjoys is one ingredient of a happy life.*

in·gress (in′gres′) *n., pl.* **in·gress·es.** **1.** the act of going in; entrance. **2.** a place of entrance. **3.** the right to go in: *Everyone in town has ingress to the park.*

in·grown (in′grōn′) *adj.* grown into the flesh, as a hair or toenail.

In·hab·it (in hab′it) *v.t.* to live in or on: *Many birds inhabit the forest.*

in·hab·it·a·ble (in hab′i tə bəl) *adj.* that can be lived in or on: *an inhabitable planet.*

in·hab·it·ant (in hab′i tənt) *n.* a person or animal that lives permanently in a place; resident.

in·hal·ant (in hā′lənt) *n.* a medicine or other substance to be inhaled. —*adj.* used for inhaling.

in·ha·la·tion (in′hə lā′shən) *n.* **1.** the act of inhaling. **2.** an act of inhaling: *A gasp is an inhalation.*

in·ha·la·tor (in′hə lā′tər) *n.* a device used for inhaling medicine.

in·hale (in hal′) *v.,* **in·haled, in·hal·ing.** —*v.t.* to draw into the lungs: *We inhaled the fresh, clean mountain air.* —*v.i.* to draw something, such as air or tobacco smoke, into the lungs.

in·hal·er (in hā′lər) *n.* **1.** another word for **inhalator.** **2.** a device used to filter air that is breathed. **3.** a person who inhales something.

in·har·mo·ni·ous (in′här mō′nē əs) *adj.* not in harmony or agreement: *inharmonious sounds, an inharmonious family.* —**in′har·mo′ni·ous·ly,** *adv.* —**in′har·mo′ni·ous·ness,** *n.*

in·her·ent (in hîr′ənt, in her′ənt) *adj.* forming a per-

at; āpe; fär; câre; end; mē; it; īce; pîerce; hot; ōld; sông, fôrk; oil; out; up; ūse; rüle; pùll; tûrn; chin; sing; shop; thin; this; hw in white; zh in treasure. The symbol ə stands for the unstressed vowel sound heard in about, taken, pencil, lemon, and circus.

I

497

manent or basic part of a person or thing: *Their inherent good judgment kept them from making mistakes.* —**in·her′ent·ly,** *adv.*

in·her·it (in her′it) *v.t.* **1.** to receive from a former owner at his or her death: *to inherit property from a relative.* **2.** to receive from one's parent or parents: *The children inherited their parents' brown eyes.* **3.** to receive or come into possession of in any way: *We inherited the old furniture when we bought the house.*

in·her·it·ance (in her′i təns) *n.* **1.** something that is or may be inherited; legacy: *to receive a large inheritance from one's parents.* **2.** the act or fact of inheriting.

inheritance tax, a tax that is imposed on inherited property.

in·her·i·tor (in her′i tər) *n.* a person who inherits something; heir.

in·hib·it (in hib′it) *v.t.* to hold back; check; restrain: *Shyness often inhibits me around strangers.*

in·hi·bi·tion (in′hi bish′ən, in′i bish′ən) *n.* **1.** a restraint on some activity or on one's natural impulses: *The children showed few inhibitions when they misbehaved in public.* **2.** the act of inhibiting or the state of being inhibited: *to overcome inhibition.*

in·hos·pi·ta·ble (in hos′pi tə bəl, in′ho spit′ə bəl) *adj.* **1.** not offering hospitality to guests or visitors; not hospitable; unfriendly. **2.** not providing food, shelter, or other accommodation: *The arid land was inhospitable to settlers.* —**in·hos′pi·ta·bly,** *adv.*

in·hu·man (in hū′mən, in ū′mən) *adj.* **1.** lacking kindness, pity, or compassion; cruel; brutal: *inhuman punishment.* **2.** not like or characteristic of a human being: *an inhuman ability to stay underwater.* —**in·hu′man·ly,** *adv.*

in·hu·mane (in′hū mān′, in′ū mān′) *adj.* not feeling or showing kindness, pity, or compassion for other human beings or animals; not humane. —**in′hu·mane′ly,** *adv.*

in·hu·man·i·ty (in′hū man′i tē, in′ū man′i tē) *n., pl.* **in·hu·man·i·ties. 1.** the quality or condition of being inhuman or inhumane; lack of kindness, pity, or compassion. **2.** an instance of this.

in·im·i·cal (i nim′i kəl) *adj.* **1.** unfriendly; hostile: *They were inimical to my suggestion.* **2.** causing harm; injurious: *Lack of sleep is inimical to good health.* —**in·im′i·cal·ly,** *adv.*

in·im·i·ta·ble (i nim′i tə bəl) *adj.* that cannot be imitated; matchless: *the inimitable beauty of a sunset.* —**in·im′i·ta·bil′i·ty,** *n.* —**in·im′i·ta·bly,** *adv.*

in·iq·ui·tous (i nik′wi təs) *adj.* unjust or wicked: *an iniquitous act.* —**in·iq′ui·tous·ly,** *adv.* —**in·iq′ui·tous·ness,** *n.*

in·iq·ui·ty (i nik′wi tē) *n., pl.* **in·iq·ui·ties. 1.** great injustice or wickedness: *the iniquity of dictatorship.* **2.** a wicked or unjust act or deed.

i·ni·tial (i nish′əl) *adj.* of, relating to, or occurring at the beginning; first: *"R" is the initial letter of the word "rug."* —*n.* the first letter of a word or a name. —*v.t.,* **i·ni·tialed, i·ni·tial·ing;** *also, British,* **i·ni·tialled, i·ni·tial·ling.** to mark or sign with one's initial or initials: *The executive initialed the report after reading it.*

i·ni·tial·ly (i nish′ə lē) *adv.* at the beginning.

i·ni·ti·ate (*v.,* i nish′ē āt′; *n.,* i nish′ē it) *v.t.,* **i·ni·ti·at·ed, i·ni·ti·at·ing. 1.** to introduce or begin: *The librarian initiated a policy of lending books for a month.* **2.** to admit (a person) into an organization or group, especially with formal ceremonies: *to be initiated into a club.* **3.** to introduce to or instruct in some subject or practice: *The art teacher initiated the class in oil painting.* —*n.* a person who has been or is being initiated into an organization or group. —**i·ni′ti·a′tor,** *n.*

i·ni·ti·a·tion (i nish′ē ā′shən) *n.* **1.** the act of initiating

or the state of being initiated. **2.** the ceremonies by which one is admitted to an organization or group.

i·ni·tia·tive (i nish′ə tiv) *n.* **1.** the first step in doing or beginning something; lead: *Take the initiative and introduce yourself to them.* **2.** the ability to take a first step in beginning or doing something: *The lazy student did not have much initiative.* **3.** the right of citizens to introduce or enact a new law. **4.** the procedure by which this is done.

in·ject (in jekt′) *v.t.* **1.** to force (fluid) through the skin into a muscle, vein, or the like: *to inject serum into the bloodstream.* **2.** to force or drive (fluid) into something: *to inject fuel into an engine.* **3.** to throw in; introduce: *The lecturer tried to inject humor into a serious talk.* —**in·jec′tor,** *n.*

in·jec·tion (in jek′shən) *n.* **1.** the act or process of injecting. **2.** fluid that is injected.

in·ju·di·cious (in′jü′dish′əs) *adj.* showing lack of judgment; not judicious: *an injudicious decision.* —**in′ju·di′cious·ly,** *adv.* —**in′ju·di′cious·ness,** *n.*

in·junc·tion (in jungk′shən) *n.* **1.** a court order requiring or forbidding some act: *The mayor asked for an injunction against the strike.* **2.** a command; order.

in·jure (in′jər) *v.t.,* **in·jured, in·jur·ing. 1.** to do or cause damage to; harm: *Did you injure yourself when you fell off your bicycle?* **2.** to do wrong to: *They surely injured their neighbor's reputation by spreading such false rumors.*

in·ju·ri·ous (in jůr′ē əs) *adj.* causing harm or damage: *Pollution in rivers is injurious to fish.* —**in·ju′ri·ous·ly,** *adv.* —**in·ju′ri·ous·ness,** *n.*

in·ju·ry (in′jə rē) *n., pl.* **in·ju·ries.** damage or harm done to a person or thing: *The accident caused several slight injuries.*

in·jus·tice (in jus′tis) *n.* **1.** lack of justice; unfairness: *The defendant protested the injustice of the court's ruling.* **2.** an unjust act: *to do one's friend an injustice by gossiping.*

ink (ingk) *n.* **1.** a colored fluid or paste used for writing, drawing, or printing. **2.** a dark fluid ejected by cuttlefishes, squids, and other sea animals for protection when frightened. —*v.t.* to mark, cover, or color with ink.

ink·horn (ingk′hôrn′) *n.* a small container made of horn or similar material, formerly used to hold ink.

ink-jet printer (ingk′jet′) a high-speed printer that forms characters by spraying ink under pressure onto paper through a very fine nozzle.

ink·ling (ing′kling) *n.* **1.** a vague idea or notion: *I had no inkling of what they were talking about.* **2.** a slight suggestion; hint: *They gave us no inkling of their plans.*

ink·stand (ingk′stand′) *n.* **1.** a stand or rack for holding containers of ink and pens. **2.** another word for **inkwell.**

ink·well (ingk′wel′) *n.* a container for ink, especially on a desk.

ink·y (ing′kē) *adj.,* **ink·i·er, ink·i·est. 1.** dark or black in color: *An ominous, inky sky gave warning of the coming storm.* **2.** marked, covered, or stained with ink: *inky fingers from a leaking fountain pen.* —**ink′i·ness,** *n.*

in·laid (in′lād′, in′lād′) *v.* the past participle of **inlay.** —*adj.* **1.** set into a surface as a decoration: *The box had inlaid ivory on the lid.* **2.** decorated with a material, such as gold or ivory, set into the surface: *The table had an inlaid top.*

in·land (*adj.* in′lənd; *adv., n.* in′land′, in′lənd) *adj.* of, relating to, or located in the interior of a country or region; away from the coast or border: *an inland city, an inland waterway.* —*adv.* in or toward the interior of a country or region: *We drove inland from the coast for many miles.* —*n.* the interior part of a country or region.

in-law (in′lô′) *n. Informal.* a relative by marriage.

in·lay (*v.*, in lā′; *n.*, in′lā′) *v.t.*, **in·laid**, **in·lay·ing**.
1. to set into the surface of something so as to form a decorative design: *An artist had inlaid gold into the picture frame.* **2.** to decorate with a material set into the surface: *to inlay a cabinet with ivory.* —*n.* **1.** an inlaid design or material: *The jewel box is decorated with gold inlay.* **2.** a filling of gold, porcelain, or the like for a tooth.

inlay *(n., def. 1)*

in·let (in′let′) *n.* a narrow body of water between islands or leading inland from a larger body of water, as an estuary.

in·mate (in′māt′) *n.* a person confined in a prison, asylum, or similar place.

in me·mo·ri·am (in′mə môr′ē əm) as a memorial to; in memory of.

in·most (in′mōst′) *adj.* farthest in; innermost.

inn (in) *n.* **1.** a small hotel, especially for travelers. **2.** a restaurant or tavern.

in·nards (in′ərdz) *pl. n.* **1.** the internal organs of the body, especially those inside the chest and abdomen. **2.** the inner parts or workings of a machine, building, vehicle, or the like.

in·nate (i nāt′, in′āt) *adj.* **1.** that one has at birth; natural; inborn: *innate intelligence.* **2.** being or forming a basic characteristic: *the innate humor of a situation.* —**in·nate′ly**, *adv.* —**in·nate′ness**, *n.*

in·ner (in′ər) *adj.* **1.** located farther in: *The president's desk was in the inner office.* **2.** of or relating to the mind or soul: *one's inner life.* **3.** more private or intimate; personal: *one's inner feelings.*

inner city, an old, often central part of a city or metropolitan area, characterized by overcrowding and poverty.

inner ear, the innermost part of the ear, containing the cochlea, the semicircular canals, and the vestibule and functioning for both hearing and balance.

in·ner·most (in′ər mōst′) *adj.* **1.** farthest from the outside; most inward: *the innermost part of a building.* **2.** most private or intimate; deepest; *one's innermost feelings.*

inner tube, a rubber tube used inside a tire to hold air.

in·ning (in′ing) *n.* **1.** a division of a baseball game in which both teams bat, the visiting team first, until three players on each team are put out. **2. innings.** a chance for a team, party, or person to act: *After our opponents leave office, we'll get our innings.*

inn·keep·er (in′kē′pər) *n.* a person who owns or manages an inn.

in·no·cence (in′ə səns) *n.* the state or quality of being innocent.

in·no·cent (in′ə sənt) *adj.* **1.** free from guilt: *A defendant in a criminal case is innocent until proven guilty.* **2.** free from or knowing nothing of sin or evil; pure. **3.** not arising from or involving any bad motive; harmless: *an innocent prank, an innocent remark.* —*n.* a person, especially a child, who is free from or knows nothing of sin or evil. —**in′no·cent·ly**, *adv.*

in·noc·u·ous (i nok′ū əs) *adj.* harmless. —**in·noc′u·ous·ly**, *adv.*

in·no·vate (in′ə vāt′) *v.*, **in·no·vat·ed**, **in·no·vat·ing**. —*v.t.* to introduce (something new): *to innovate a method of doing a job.* —*v.i.* to introduce something new; make changes in something. —**in′no·va′tor**, *n.*

in·no·va·tion (in′ə vā′shən) *n.* **1.** something newly introduced; change: *Anesthesia was a great innovation in medicine.* **2.** the act of innovating.

in·no·va·tive (in′ə vā′tiv) *adj.* **1.** able or tending to innovate: *an innovative teacher.* **2.** characterized by innovation: *an innovative method of controlling pollution.* —**in′no·va′tive·ness**, *n.*

in·nu·en·do (in′ū en′dō) *n., pl.* **in·nu·en·does.** a hint or suggestion, especially one that is meant to cause harm or damage to a person's reputation: *The reports were filled with innuendoes about the senator's early life.*

in·nu·mer·a·ble (i nü′mər ə bəl, i nū′mər ə bəl) *adj.* too many to be counted: *There are innumerable stars in the sky.* —**in·nu′mer·a·ble·ness**, *n.* —**in·nu′mer·a·bly**, *adv.*

in·oc·u·late (i nok′yə lāt′) *v.t.*, **in·oc·u·lat·ed**, **in·oc·u·lat·ing**. **1.** to inject (into a person or animal) a biological substance, such as a serum or a vaccine, in order to produce immunity against a particular disease. [From the Latin word *inoculatus*, past participle of *inoculare* meaning "to engraft, implant," from the prefix *in-* "in, into" and *oculus* "eye, bud." Originally, the word *inoculate* referred to the grafting of a bud from one plant to another. The medical usage now common began in the eighteenth century with the first inoculations against smallpox.]

in·oc·u·la·tion (i nok′yə lā′shən) *n.* **1.** the act of inoculating. **2.** an injection given in order to produce immunity to a disease.

in·of·fen·sive (in′ə fen′siv) *adj.* not offensive; harmless: *an inoffensive person, inoffensive cartoons.* —**in′of·fen′sive·ly**, *adv.* —**in′of·fen′sive·ness**, *n.*

in·op·er·a·ble (in op′ər ə bəl) *adj.* not able to be cured or treated effectively by surgery.

in·op·er·a·tive (in op′ər ə tiv, in op′ə rā′tiv) *adj.* not working or producing an effect; not in force; not operative: *inoperative equipment, inoperative laws.*

in·op·por·tune (in op′ər tün′, in op′ər tūn′) *adj.* coming or happening at a bad time: *They chose an inopportune moment to visit us, just as we were leaving.* —**in·op′por·tune′ly**, *adv.* —**in·op′por·tune′ness**, *n.*

in·or·di·nate (in ôr′də nit) *adj.* beyond what is necessary or proper; too great; excessive: *inordinate demands.* —**in·or′di·nate·ly**, *adv.*

in·or·gan·ic (in′ôr gan′ik) *adj.* **1.** not related to, including, or made by animals or plants; not living: *Minerals are inorganic substances.* **2.** of or relating to matter that is not organic: *Inorganic compounds include water and salt. Inorganic chemistry is the study of elements and compounds that do not contain carbon.* —**in′or·gan′i·cal·ly**, *adv.*

in·pa·tient (in′pā′shənt) *n.* a patient who stays in a hospital, clinic, or similar institution while receiving care and treatment, as distinguished from an outpatient.

in·put (in′pùt′) *n.* **1.** anything put or taken in. **2.** the power or energy that is put into something, such as a machine. **3.** the information entered into a computer, as by a keyboard. —*v.t.* to enter information into a computer, as by a keyboard.

in·quest (in′kwest′) *n.* an inquiry made by a body

I

at; āpe; fär; câre; end; mē; it; īce; pîerce; hot; ōld; sông, fôrk; oil; out; up; ūse; rüle; pùll; tûrn; chin; sing; shop; thin; this; hw in white; zh in treasure. The symbol ə stands for the unstressed vowel sound heard in about, taken, pencil, lemon, and circus.

appointed by law, especially one made to find out the cause of a sudden or violent death.

in·quire (in kwīr′) *also,* **en·quire**. *v.,* **in·quired, in·quir·ing.** —*v.i.* **1.** to seek knowledge or information by asking a question or questions: *to inquire about someone's health.* **2.** to make an investigation, search, or examination: *The police inquired into the suspect's background.* —*v.t.* to seek knowledge or information about by asking a question or questions: *We stopped at a gas station to inquire the way.* —**in·quir′er,** *n.* —**in·quir′ing·ly,** *adv.*

in·quir·y (in kwīr′ē, in′kwə rē) *also,* **en·quir·y.** *n., pl.* **in·quir·ies.** **1.** the act of inquiring: *scientific inquiry.* **2.** an investigation, search, or examination: *an inquiry made by the police.* **3.** a question.

in·qui·si·tion (in′kwə zish′ən) *n.* **1.** strict or thorough inquiry or questioning. **2. the Inquisition.** the Roman Catholic court established in the thirteenth century to discover and punish heretics.

in·quis·i·tive (in kwiz′i tiv) *adj.* **1.** eager for knowledge; curious: *An inquisitive child.* **2.** too curious; nosy; prying: *to be inquisitive about other people's business.* —**in·quis′i·tive·ly,** *adv.* —**in·quis′i·tive·ness,** *n.*

in·quis·i·tor (in kwiz′i tər) *n.* **1.** a person who makes or conducts an inquisition or inquiry. **2. Inquisitor.** an official of the Inquisition.

in·road (in′rōd′) *n.* **1.** a sudden attack or raid. **2.** *also,* **inroads.** an advance that causes loss or injury to something or someone: *Paying the bills made inroads on our savings.*

in·rush (in′rush′) *n.* a sudden rushing or pouring in, as of water.

ins., inches.

in·sane (in sān′) *adj.* **1.** not having a sound or healthy mind; mentally ill; crazy. **2.** of or for insane people: *an insane asylum.* **3.** very foolish; senseless: *What an insane thing to do!* —**in·sane′ly,** *adv.*

in·san·i·tar·y (in san′i ter′ē) *adj.* bad for health; not sanitary; unclean.

in·san·i·ty (in san′i tē) *n., pl.* **in·san·i·ties.** **1.** the state of being insane; mental illness. **2.** extreme folly; senselessness: *It was insanity to try to drive in that blizzard last night.*

in·sa·tia·ble (in sā′shə bəl) *adj.* that cannot be satisfied: *an insatiable thirst.* —**in·sa′tia·bly,** *adv.*

in·scribe (in skrīb′) *v.t.,* **in·scribed, in·scrib·ing.** **1.** to write, carve, engrave, or mark (words or characters) on something: *The stonecutter inscribed the date on the tombstone.* **2.** to write, carve, engrave, or mark words or characters on: *The jeweler inscribed the locket with my friend's initials.* **3.** to write a message or note on (something, such as a book) in giving it to someone. **4.** to impress deeply, as though carving in. **5.** to draw (a geometric figure) within another figure so that the inner touches the outer at as many points as possible: *to inscribe a circle within a square.* —**in·scrib′er,** *n.*

in·scrip·tion (in skrip′shən) *n.* **1.** something inscribed: *an inscription on a ring, an inscription on a tombstone.* **2.** a message or note written on something, such as a book, in giving it to someone. **3.** the act of inscribing.

in·scru·ta·ble (inskrü′tə bəl) *adj.* that cannot be easily understood; mysterious: *inscrutable behavior.* —**in·scru′ta·bil′i·ty,** *n.* —**in·scru′ta·bly,** *adv.*

in·sect (in′sekt′) *n.* any of a group of small animals without a backbone, having a body divided into three parts. Insects have three pairs of legs and, in the adult, usually two pairs of wings. Flies, ants, grasshoppers, and beetles are insects.

in·sec·ti·cide (in sek′tə sīd′) *n.* a substance for killing insects and similar pests.

in·sec·ti·vore (in sek′tə vôr′) *n.* **1.** an animal, such as the hedgehog, mole, or shrew, that feeds chiefly on insects. **2.** a plant that feeds chiefly on insects.

in·sec·tiv·o·rous (in′sek tiv′ər əs) *adj.* feeding chiefly on insects.

in·se·cure (in′si kyùr′) *adj.* **1.** liable to give way or fail; unstable or unsafe: *The knot was very insecure.* **2.** not assured; uncertain: *an insecure position.* **3.** lacking in self-confidence: *an insecure person.* —**in′se·cure′ly,** *adv.*

in·se·cu·ri·ty (in′si kyùr′i tē) *n., pl.* **in·se·cu·ri·ties.** **1.** the state or quality of being insecure. **2.** a lack of self-confidence; self-doubt: *Rudeness is often caused by insecurity.*

in·sem·i·nate (in sem′ə nāt′) *v.t.,* **in·sem·i·nat·ed, in·sem·i·nat·ing.** to deposit semen in the reproductive organs of (a female); impregnate. —**in·sem·i·na′tion,** *n.*

in·sen·sate (in sen′sāt) *adj.* **1.** without life or sensation; inanimate: *insensate rocks.* **2.** lacking feeling or sensitivity: *to be insensate to beautiful music.* **3.** lacking sense or reason; stupid; foolish. —**in·sen′sate·ly,** *adv.*

in·sen·si·ble (in sen′sə bəl) *adj.* **1.** not able to feel or perceive: *insensible to pain, insensible to the suffering of others.* **2.** not aware: *They were insensible of the risks involved.* **3.** unconscious: *The miner was insensible for several minutes after being struck on the head.* **4.** too slight or gradual to be easily perceived; imperceptible: *insensible changes in temperature.* —**in·sen·si·bil′i·ty,** *n.* —**in·sen′si·bly,** *adv.*

in·sen·si·tive (in sen′si tiv) *adj.* **1.** not feeling or perceiving: *insensitive to beauty, insensitive to pain.* **2.** lacking feeling, sensitivity, or perception: *a cruel and insensitive person.* —**in·sen′si·tive·ly,** *adv.* —**in·sen′si·tive·ness, in·sen′si·tiv′i·ty,** *n.*

in·sep·a·ra·ble (in sep′ər ə bəl) *adj.* that cannot be separated: *inseparable friends.* —**in·sep′a·ra·bil′i·ty,** *n.* —**in·sep′a·ra·bly,** *adv.*

in·sert (*v.,* in sûrt′; *n.,* in′sûrt′) *v.t.* to put, set, or place in: *to insert a bookmark into a book, to insert a cork into a bottle.* —*n.* something inserted or to be inserted, such as an extra section in a newspaper or magazine.

in·ser·tion (in sûr′shən) *n.* **1.** the act of inserting. **2.** something inserted. **3.** a band of lace or embroidery to be sewed at each edge between parts of other material.

in·set (*v.,* in set′; *n.,* in′set′) *v.t.,* **in·set, in·set·ting.** to set, put, or place in; insert. —*n.* **1.** something inset or to be inset; insertion. **2.** a small map, diagram, or other illustration inserted within the borders of a larger one.

in·shore (in′shôr′) *adj.* **1.** near the shore. **2.** moving toward the shore. —*adv.* toward the shore.

in·side (in′sīd′, in sīd′, in′sīd′) *n.* **1.** the inner side, surface, or part; interior: *the inside of a car.* **2. insides.** *Informal.* the internal organs of the body. —*adj.* **1.** situated on or in the inside: *an inside seat on a boat.* **2.** known to only a few; confidential: *The reporter got the inside story.* —*adv.* **1.** on, in, or toward the inside; within: *I opened the door and stepped inside.* **2.** indoors: *The children played inside all day.* —*prep.* in or into the inside of; within: *I looked inside the closet.*

 •**inside of. a.** inside. **b.** within the space or limits of: *We'll finish this job inside of an hour.*

 •**inside out. a.** so that the inside is facing out: *to turn a jacket inside out.* **b.** thoroughly; totally: *I know this area of the city inside out.*

in·sid·er (in sī′dər) *n.* **1.** a person who is a member of a

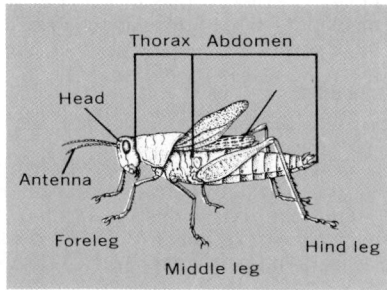

Thorax Abdomen

Head

Antenna

Foreleg

Middle leg

Hind leg

parts of an **insect**

certain group, society, or organization. **2.** a person who has or can obtain information that is known to only a few.

in·sid·i·ous (in sid′ē əs) *adj.* **1.** slyly treacherous or deceitful: *an insidious plot.* **2.** working in a hidden but harmful manner: *an insidious disease.* —**in·sid′i·ous·ly,** *adv.* —**in·sid′i·ous·ness,** *n.*

in·sight (in′sīt′) *n.* **1.** the ability to see into and understand the true character or nature of things: *The doctor had great insight into my problems.* **2.** an instance of such understanding.

in·sight·ful (in sīt′fəl) *adj.* having or showing insight; perceptive: *an insightful book reviewer, an insightful comment.*

in·sig·ni·a (in sig′nē ə) *n., pl.* **in·sig·ni·a** or **in·sig·ni·as.** an emblem, badge, medal, or other distinguishing mark of office, honor, or position: *The nurses wore a special insignia.*

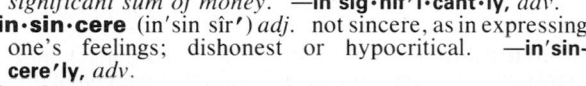

insignia

in·sig·nif·i·cance (in′sig nif′i kəns) *n.* the state or quality of being insignificant.

in·sig·nif·i·cant (in′sig nif′i kənt) *adj.* **1.** having little or no meaning or importance; not significant: *My problems seem insignificant compared to yours.* **2.** small in size or amount: *It's an insignificant sum of money.* —**in′sig·nif′i·cant·ly,** *adv.*

in·sin·cere (in′sin sir′) *adj.* not sincere, as in expressing one's feelings; dishonest or hypocritical. —**in′sin·cere′ly,** *adv.*

in·sin·cer·i·ty (in′sin ser′i tē) *n., pl.* **in·sin·cer·i·ties.** **1.** the quality of being insincere. **2.** an instance of being insincere.

in·sin·u·ate (in sin′ū āt′) *v.t.,* **in·sin·u·at·ed, in·sin·u·at·ing.** **1.** to suggest indirectly; imply; hint: *to insinuate that someone is lying.* **2.** to get in or introduce by an indirect or subtle way: *to insinuate oneself into the boss's favor.* —**in·sin′u·a′tion,** *n.*

in·sip·id (in sip′id) *adj.* **1.** lacking qualities that arouse interest or excite; dull; colorless: *an insipid person, an insipid novel.* **2.** without much taste or flavor; bland: *insipid food.* —**in·sip′id·ness,** *n.* —**in·sip′id·ly,** *adv.*

in·sist (in sist′) *v.t.* **1.** to demand (something) firmly and strongly: *The doctor insisted that the patient get plenty of rest.* **2.** to declare persistently and positively: *Your friend insisted that you were the best person for the job.*

·to insist on. a. to demand firmly and strongly: *They insisted on our coming to the party.* **b.** to continue in a course of action: *If you insist on shouting, I shall leave.*

in·sis·tence (in sis′təns) *n.* **1.** the act or instance of insisting. **2.** the quality of being insistent.

in·sis·tent (in sis′tənt) *adj.* **1.** firm or persistent, as in some demand: *Although we were having a good time, my cousin was insisting on going home.* **2.** demanding attention or notice: *The insistent ringing of the doorbell woke us.* —**in·sis′tent·ly,** *adv.*

in·snare (in snâr′) *v.t.,* **in·snared, in·snar·ing.** another word for **ensnare.**

in·so·far as (in′sō fär′) to such an exent as: *Insofar as we know, they are coming to the party.*

in·sole (in′sōl′) *n.* **1.** the inner sole of a shoe or boot. **2.** a layer of material laid on the sole inside a shoe or boot for warmth, waterproofing, or for a better fit.

in·so·lence (in′sə ləns) *n.* **1.** offensive rudeness or boldness. **2.** insolent speech or behavior.

in·so·lent (in′sə lənt) *adj.* offensively rude or bold: *The child made an insolent reply.* —**in′so·lent·ly,** *adv.*

in·sol·u·ble (in sol′yə bəl) *adj.* **1.** that cannot be dissolved: *an insoluble chemical.* **2.** that cannot be solved or explained: *an insoluble mystery.* —**in·sol′u·bil′i·ty,** *n.* —**in·sol′u·bly,** *adv.*

in·sol·vent (in sol′vənt) *adj.* not able to pay one's debts. —**in·sol′ven·cy,** *n.*

in·som·ni·a (in som′nē ə) *n.* the inability to sleep.

in·som·ni·ac (in som′nē ak′) *n.* a person who suffers from insomnia.

in·so·much (in′sō much′) *adv.* to such an extent or degree.

·insomuch as. inasmuch as; since.

in·spect (in spekt′) *v.t.* **1.** to look at closely and carefully, especially for errors, faults, or flaws: *The mechanic inspected the automobile for possible defects.* **2.** to examine formally or officially: *The general inspected the troops.*

in·spec·tion (in spek′shən) *n.* **1.** the act of inspecting, especially for errors, faults, or flaws. **2.** a formal or official examination.

in·spec·tor (in spek′tər) *n.* **1.** a person, especially an appointed official, who inspects. **2.** a police officer ranking next below a superintendent.

in·spi·ra·tion (in′spə rā′shən) *n.* **1.** the stimulation of the mind, feelings, or imagination: *The beauty of nature gave inspiration to the painter.* **2.** a person or thing that inspires: *The writer's friend was the inspiration for that character.* **3.** something inspired, such as an idea or action. **4.** the act of breathing in; inhalation.

in·spi·ra·tion·al (in′spə rā′shə nəl) *adj.* **1.** giving or tending to give inspiration; inspiring. **2.** resulting from inspiration; inspired.

in·spire (in spīr′) *v.,* **in·spired, in·spir·ing.** —*v.t.* **1.** to have a rousing effect or influence on; stimulate; stir: *The minister's words inspired the congregation.* **2.** to be the force or influence that results in (something specified): *The author's childhood experience inspired that novel.* **3.** to produce or arouse, as a thought or feeling: *The old poet inspired love and respect.* **4.** to cause to have a specified thought or feeling: *Success inspired hope for the future.* —*v.i.* to inhale. —**in·spir′er,** *n.*

In·sta·bil·i·ty (in′stə bil′i tē) *n.* lack of stability.

in·stall (in stôl′) *v.t.* **1.** to put in position for service or use: *to install an air conditioner.* **2.** to place (a person) in an office, rank, or position with ceremony: *We installed the new club president today.* **3.** to establish in a place or position; settle: *to install a guard at the gate.*

in·stal·la·tion (in′stə lā′shən) *n.* **1.** the act of installing or the state of being installed. **2.** a mechanical system or apparatus placed in position for use. **3.** a military base, including personnel, buildings, and equipment.

in·stall·ment[1] (in stôl′mənt) *also,* **in·stal·ment.** *n.* **1.** one of the portions of a sum of money owed to be paid at regular intervals: *to pay for a car in thirty installments.* **2.** any of several parts issued or presented at regular intervals: *The novel appeared in the magazine in weekly installments.* [From the obsolete word *estallment* meaning "payment by installment[1]," from the Old French word *staler* "to fix, set," from the word *estal* "fixed place, stall," of Germanic origin.]

in·stall·ment[2] (in stôl′mənt) *also,* **in·stal·ment.** *n.* the act of installing or the state of being installed; installation. [*Install* + *-ment.*]

installment plan, a system of paying for goods or services in specified amounts at regular intervals.

in·stance (in′stəns) *n.* an example or case: *an instance of great courage.*

---

at; āpe; fär; câre; end; mē; it; īce; pîerce; hot; ōld; sông, fôrk; oil; out; up; ūse; rüle; pull; tûrn; chin; sing; shop; thin; this; hw in white; zh in treasure. The symbol ə stands for the unstressed vowel sound heard in about, taken, pencil, lemon, and circus.

·**for instance.** by way of illustration; for example: *We enjoy team sports, for instance, baseball and basketball.*

in·stant (in′stənt) *n.* **1.** a very short period of time; moment: *We saw it for just an instant.* **2.** a particular moment or point in time: *I want to leave this instant.* —*adj.* **1.** without delay: *The computer gave us an instant reply.* **2.** pressing; urgent: *an instant need.* **3.** (of food products) prepared beforehand and packaged, often in powdered form, and requiring only the addition of a liquid, as water or milk, for final preparation: *instant oatmeal.*

in·stan·ta·ne·ous (in′stən tā′nē əs) *adj.* happening, done, or coming in an instant or without delay: *The lifeguard's reaction was instantaneous.* —**in′stan·ta·ne·ous·ly,** *adv.*

in·stant·ly (in′stənt lē) *adv.* without delay; at once.

instant re·play (rē′plā′) the playback, usually soon after the recording, of part of a videotape to show particular action, as in a televised sports event.

in·stead (in sted′) *adv.* in place of the person or thing mentioned; as a substitute or alternative: *The recipe called for butter, but we used margarine instead.*

·**instead of.** rather than; in place of: *We went for a walk instead of going straight home.*

in·step (in′step′) *n.* **1.** the arched upper surface of the human foot between the toes and the ankle. **2.** the part of a shoe, stocking, or other footwear that covers the instep.

in·sti·gate (in′sti gāt′) *v.t.,* **in·sti·gat·ed, in·sti·gat·ing. 1.** to cause by stirring up or urging; incite: *to instigate a riot.* **2.** to urge on to some action: *to instigate someone to commit a crime.* —**in′sti·ga′tion,** *n.* —**in′sti·ga′tor,** *n.*

in·still (in stil′) *also,* **in·stil.** *v.t.,* **in·stilled, in·stil·ling. 1.** to put in or introduce gradually or little by little: *The English teacher instilled a love of literature in us.* **2.** to pour in by drops.

in·stinct (in′stingkt′) *n.* **1.** a natural tendency to act in a certain way: *Birds build nests by instinct.* **2.** a natural aptitude; talent: *to have a definite instinct for painting.*

in·stinc·tive (in stingk′tiv) *adj.* **1.** arising from or done by instinct: *instinctive behavior.* **2.** of or relating to instinct. —**in·stinc′tive·ly,** *adv.*

in·sti·tute (in′sti tüt′, in′sti tūt′) *v.t.,* **in·sti·tut·ed, in·sti·tut·ing.** to set up or put into operation; establish; start: *to institute a new set of rules.* —*n.* **1.** an organization, school, or society set up to promote and carry on work in a particular field: *a music institute, a medical research institute.* **2.** the building or buildings housing such an organization.

in·sti·tu·tion (in′sti tü′shən, in′sti tū′shən) *n.* **1.** an organization, society, or similar establishment devoted to a particular purpose, especially one of a social, educational, or religious nature. **2.** the building or buildings housing such an establishment. **3.** the act of instituting; establishment. **4.** an established practice, custom, law, or system: *Public debate is an important institution in many countries.* —**in′sti·tu′tion·al,** *adj.*

in·sti·tu·tion·al·ize (in′sti tü′shə nə līz′, in′sti tū′shə-nə līz′) *v.t.* **1.** to make into or treat as an institution. **2.** to place in an institution, especially one for the care and treatment of an illness.

in·struct (in strukt′) *v.t.* **1.** to provide with knowledge, information, or skill; teach: *My parents instructed me in the correct use of tools.* **2.** to give directions or orders to: *The firefighters instructed us to move the parked car.*

in·struc·tion (in struk′shən) *n.* **1.** the act of teaching. **2. instructions.** explanations, directions, or orders: *If you follow my instructions, you won't get lost.* **3.** knowledge or information given. —**in·struc′tion·al,** *adj.*

in·struc·tive (in struk′tiv) *adj.* giving or providing knowledge or information; serving to instruct: *The lecture was interesting as well as instructive.* —**in·struc′tive·ly,** *adv.*

in·struc·tor (in struk′tər) *n.* **1.** a person who instructs; teacher. **2.** a teacher in a college or university who is of lower rank than a professor.

in·stru·ment (in′strə mənt) *n.* **1.** a tool, especially one designed or used for precise or careful work: *A scalpel is a surgical instrument.* **2.** a device for producing musical sounds: *The performer plays the guitar, the flute, and several other instruments.* **3.** a device for measuring, controlling, or a similar purpose: *navigational instruments.* **4.** the means by which something is done or brought about: *to be the instrument of someone else's plans.* **5.** a formal or legal document, such as a contract, deed, or will.

in·stru·men·tal (in′strə men′təl) *adj.* **1.** serving as a means; helpful: *My friend was instrumental in getting me the job.* **2.** relating to, composed for, or performed on musical instruments: *The troubadours composed both vocal and instrumental music.* —*n.* a composition for one or more musical instruments. —**in′stru·men′tal·ly,** *adv.*

in·stru·men·tal·ist (in′strə men′tə list) *n.* a person who plays a musical instrument.

in·stru·men·tal·i·ty (in′strə men tal′i tē) *n., pl.* **in·stru·men·tal·i·ties. 1.** the state or quality of being instrumental. **2.** something that serves or is used for some purpose; means.

in·stru·men·ta·tion (in′strə men tā′shən) *n.* **1.** an arrangement or composition of music for instruments, especially for an orchestra. **2.** the use of scientific, surgical, or other instruments. **3.** instruments used for a particular purpose: *the instrumentation on a car's dashboard.*

in·sub·or·di·nate (in′sə bôr′də nit) *adj.* not yielding to or obeying authority; disobedient. —**in′sub·or′di·nate·ly,** *adv.*

in·sub·or·di·na·tion (in′sə bôr′də nā′shən) *n.* the refusal to yield to or obey authority; disobedience: *The soldier who ignored the captain's orders was charged with insubordination.*

in·sub·stan·tial (in′səb stan′shəl) *adj.* **1.** not real; imaginary: *insubstantial hopes.* **2.** not strong, solid, or firm; flimsy: *insubstantial evidence.* —**in′sub·stan′tial·ly,** *adv.*

in·suf·fer·a·ble (in suf′ər ə bəl) *adj.* not to be endured; not tolerable; unbearable: *The speaker was an insufferable bore.* —**in′suf′fer·a·bly,** *adv.*

in·suf·fi·cien·cy (in′sə fish′ən sē) *n., pl.* **in·suf·fi·cien·cies.** a lack or deficiency, as in amount or quality.

in·suf·fi·cient (in′sə fish′ənt) *adj.* not enough; inadequate: *Profits were insufficient to keep the business going.* —**in′suf·fi′cient·ly,** *adv.*

in·su·lar (in′sə lər) *adj.* **1.** of, relating to, or characteristic of an island or its people. **2.** living or situated on an island. **3.** composing or forming an island. **4.** standing alone; isolated. **5.** narrow-minded; prejudiced: *an insular way of thinking.*

in·su·lar·i·ty (in′sə lar′i tē) *n.* **1.** the condition of being an island. **2.** the condition of living on an island or as if on an island: *the insularity of the pioneer's life.* **3.** narrow-mindedness; prejudice.

in·su·late (in′sə lāt′) *v.t.,* **in·su·lat·ed, in·su·lat·ing. 1.** to cover or surround with a material that does not conduct electricity, heat, or sound, such as rubber: *to insulate an electric wire.* **2.** to install a layer of material between the exterior and interior walls of (a building, refrigerator, or other structure) to reduce or prevent the passage of heat: *to insulate an attic.* **3.** to protect or isolate: *Parents often try to insulate their children from the harshness of life.*

in·su·la·tion (in′sə lā′shən) *n.* **1.** the material used in insulating: *We installed new insulation in our attic this fall.* **2.** the act of insulating or the condition of being insulated.

in·su·la·tor (in′sə lā′tər) *n.* something that insulates, especially a material or device that prevents the passage of electric current.

in·su·lin (in′sə lin) *n.* **1.** a hormone that is secreted by the pancreas and regulates the body's use and storage of sugar and other carbohydrates. **2.** a preparation containing this hormone, used in treating diabetes. It is obtained from the pancreas of cattle, sheep, or pigs or is produced artificially.

in·sult (*v.*, in sult′; *n.*, in′sult′) *v.t.* to speak to or treat in a rude, disrespectful, or scornful way. —*n.* an insulting remark or act. —**in·sult′ing·ly,** *adv.*

in·su·per·a·ble (in sü′pər ə bəl) *adj.* that cannot be overcome or surmounted: *insuperable obstacles.* —**in·su′per·a·bly,** *adv.*

in·sup·port·a·ble (in′sə pôr′tə bəl) *adj.* **1.** more than one can endure; unbearable; intolerable: *insupportable pain.* **2.** not supportable by evidence: *an insupportable charge of fraud.*

in·sur·a·ble (in shùr′ə bəl) *adj.* capable of being or fit to be insured.

in·sur·ance (in shùr′əns) *n.* **1.** protection against risk or loss by means of a contract between two parties whereby the insurer guarantees to pay a sum of money to the insured in case of death, accident, fire, theft, or the like in return for the regular payment of specified amounts by the insured. **2.** a contract guaranteeing such protection. **3.** the amount for which someone or something is insured. **4.** the amount paid for insurance; premium. **5.** the business of insuring persons or property. **6.** any protection against risk, harm, or loss.

in·sure (in shùr′) *v.t.*, **in·sured, in·sur·ing. 1.** to protect against risk or loss by means of insurance; cover with insurance: *to insure a car.* **2.** another word for **ensure.** ▲ See **ensure** for usage note.

in·sured (in shùrd′) *n.* a person who is protected or covered by insurance.

in·sur·er (in shùr′ər) *n.* a person or company that insures.

in·sur·gence (in sûr′jəns) *n.* the act of rebelling against established authority; revolt.

in·sur·gent (in sûr′jənt) *n.* **1.** a person who rebels against established authority. **2.** a member of a political party who rebels against the policies and decisions of the party. —*adj.* rising in revolt against authority; rebellious.

in·sur·mount·a·ble (in′sər moun′tə bəl) *adj.* that cannot be overcome: *insurmountable difficulties.* —**in′sur·mount′a·bly,** *adv.*

in·sur·rec·tion (in′sə rek′shən) *n.* a rebellion against established authority, especially against a government; revolt. —**in′sur·rec′tion·ist,** *n.*

in·tact (in takt′) *adj.* untouched or whole; not damaged or injured: *The tornado left few buildings intact.*

in·take (in′tāk′) *n.* **1.** the act of taking in. **2.** the amount taken in: *The doctors restricted my intake of solid food.* **3.** a place in a channel, pipe, or other narrow opening where fluid is taken in.

in·tan·gi·ble (in tan′jə bəl) *adj.* not capable of being perceived by the sense of touch: *Love and other emotions are intangible.* —*n.* something intangible. —**in·tan′gi·bil′i·ty,** *n.* —**in·tan′gi·bly,** *adv.*

in·te·ger (in′ti jər) *n.* any positive or negative whole number, or zero.

in·te·gral (in′ti grəl) *adj.* **1.** necessary to the completeness of a whole; essential: *Experimentation is integral to scientific research.* **2.** having no part or element missing; entire. **3.** relating to or being an integer.

in·te·grate (in′ti grāt′) *v.*, **in·te·grat·ed, in·te·grat·ing.** —*v.t.* **1.** to make available to all racial groups; desegregate: *to integrate a school.* **2.** to bring (parts) together into a whole: *The inventor integrated two existing devices to create the new machine.* **3.** to make whole by adding or bringing together all necessary parts. —*v.i.* to become available to all racial groups: *The old club integrated after several protests.*

integrated circuit, a tiny electronic circuit consisting of a group of electronic components, such as transistors and resistors, bonded together on a chip of silicon or other semiconductor material.

integrated circuit

in·te·gra·tion (in′ti grā′shən) *n.* **1.** the elimination of racial segregation, as in schools or housing. **2.** the act of integrating parts into a whole.

in·te·gra·tion·ist (in′ti grā′shə nist) *n.* a person who believes in or favors integration.

in·teg·ri·ty (in teg′ri tē) *n.* **1.** moral uprightness; honesty; sincerity: *The integrity of the candidate is an issue in the campaign.* **2.** the state of being complete.

in·teg·u·ment (in teg′yə mənt) *n.* the natural covering of an animal or plant, such as a skin, husk, shell, or rind.

in·tel·lect (in′tə lekt′) *n.* **1.** the power of the mind to know, understand, and reason. **2.** intelligence or mental ability, especially when highly developed. **3.** a person of great intelligence.

in·tel·lec·tu·al (in′tə lek′chü əl) *adj.* **1.** of or relating to the intellect: *someone of great intellectual ability.* **2.** appealing to, involving, or using the intellect: *Reading great literature is an intellectual pursuit.* **3.** possessing or showing intellect: *an intellectual writer.* —*n.* an intellectual person: *The café near the museum is popular with intellectuals.* —**in·tel·lec′tu·al·ly,** *adv.*

in·tel·li·gence (in tel′i jəns) *n.* **1.** the ability to learn, understand, and reason. **2.** secret information, especially about an enemy: *After receiving the intelligence, the commander ordered a retreat.* **3.** the agency engaged in collecting such information.

intelligence quotient, a number used to estimate a person's intelligence level. It is obtained by dividing a person's mental age, as shown by tests, by his or her real age, and multiplying by 100.

intelligence test, a test used to measure a person's mental development in relation to that of others.

---

at; āpe; fär; câre; end; mē; it; īce; pîerce; hot; ōld; sông, fôrk; oil; out; up; ūse; rüle; pùll; tûrn; chin; sing; shop; thin; this; hw in white; zh in treasure. The symbol ə stands for the unstressed vowel sound heard in about, taken, pencil, lemon, and circus.

I

in·tel·li·gent (in tel′i jənt) *adj.* having or showing intelligence; bright: *That was a very intelligent question to ask.* —**in·tel′li·gent·ly,** *adv.*

in·tel·li·gent·si·a (in tel′i jent′sē ə) *pl. n.* a well-educated group or class of persons within a society that is noted for its influence and activity in cultural and intellectual affairs. ▲ used with a singular or plural verb.

in·tel·li·gi·ble (in tel′i jə bəl) *adj.* capable of being understood; comprehensible: *The garbled statement was not intelligible.* —**in·tel′li·gi·bil′i·ty,** *n.* —**in·tel′li·gi·bly,** *adv.*

in·tem·per·ance (in tem′pər əns) *n.* a lack of moderation or restraint, as in the use of alcoholic beverages.

in·tem·per·ate (in tem′pər it, in tem′prit) *adj.* 1. lacking moderation, restraint, or self-control. 2. harsh; extreme: *intemperate weather.* —**in·tem′per·ate·ly,** *adv.*

in·tend (in tend′) *v.t.* 1. to have in mind as a purpose; plan: *We intend to start our vacation next week.* 2. to make or mean for a particular purpose, use, or person: *The resort is intended for local residents only.*

in·tend·ed (in tend′did) *adj.* 1. meant or planned; intentional: *an intended insult.* 2. that is to be; prospective: *her intended husband, his intended wife.* —*n.* an intended husband or wife.

in·tense (in tens′) *adj.* 1. of a very high degree; very great or strong: *intense heat.* 2. having or showing strong or earnest feeling: *an intense person, an intense look.* —**in·tense′ly,** *adv.*

in·ten·si·fi·er (in ten′sə fī′ər) *n. Grammar.* an intensive.

in·ten·si·fy (in ten′sə fī′) *v.,* **in·ten·si·fied, in·ten·si·fying.** —*v.t.* to make intense or more intense; increase: *The police intensified their search for the missing child.* —*v.i.* to become intense or more intense; grow in strength, amount, or degree: *The heat intensified as the fire began to spread.* —**in·ten′si·fi·ca′tion,** *n.*

in·ten·si·ty (in ten′si tē) *n., pl.* **in·ten·si·ties.** 1. the state or quality of being intense: *The light shone with great intensity.* 2. strength, amount, or degree: *The pain increased in intensity.* 3. the amount of strength of a form of energy, such as heat, light, or sound, per unit of area, volume, or mass.

in·ten·sive (in ten′siv) *adj.* 1. thorough or concentrated: *The patient needed intensive care.* 2. *Grammar.* giving force or emphasis. In the sentence *I myself did it, myself* is an intensive pronoun. —*n. Grammar.* an element, word, or phrase that gives emphasis without changing meaning; intensifier. The word *very* is an intensive in the sentence *I saw that very same movie two years ago.* —**in·ten′sive·ly,** *adv.*

in·tent¹ (in tent′) *n.* 1. an intention; aim: *My intent has always been to go to college.* 2. meaning; significance: *What was the intent of that remark?* [From the Old French word *entente* with the same meanings, from the Latin word *intentus* ''intent upon, waiting,'' from the word *intendo* ''to stretch forth'' or ''direct toward.'']

·**to all intents and purposes** or **for all intents and purposes.** in almost every way; practically; virtually.

in·tent² (in tent′) *adj.* 1. having the mind firmly fixed on something: *Are you intent on leaving? The student was intent on the book.* 2. firmly directed or fixed: *an intent look.* [From the Latin word *intentus* ''intent upon, waiting,'' from the word *intendo* ''to stretch forth'' or ''direct toward.''] —**in·tent′ly,** *adv.*

in·ten·tion (in ten′shən) *n.* something that is intended; purpose; plan: *I have no intention of going to the party. The governor had good intentions but was a weak administrator.*

in·ten·tion·al (in ten′shə nəl) *adj.* carefully thought out or planned; done on purpose: *My leaving that name off the guest list was intentional.* —**in·ten′tion·al·ly,** *adv.*

in·ter (in tûr′) *v.t.,* **in·terred, in·ter·ring.** to put (a dead body) into a grave or tomb; bury.

inter- *prefix* 1. one with the other; together: *interact.* 2. between or among: *intercollegiate, interchange.*

in·ter·act (in′tə rakt′) *v.i.* to act on or influence each other. —**in′ter·ac′tion,** *n.*

in·ter·ac·tive (in′tər ak′tiv) of or relating to a computer or other system that prompts the user to enter data and responds by giving information or by prompting the user to enter other data.

in·ter·breed (in′tər brēd′) *v.t.,* **in·ter·bred** (in′tər bred′), **in·ter·breed·ing.** to breed (animals or plants) with those of different varieties or lines; crossbreed.

in·ter·cede (in′tər sēd′) *v.i.,* **in·ter·ced·ed, in·ter·ced·ing.** 1. to plead on behalf of another or others: *The teacher interceded with the principal for the student who was in trouble.* 2. to come between opposing parties in an effort to settle a dispute.

in·ter·cel·lu·lar (in′tər sel′yə lər) *adj.* located among or found in the area between cells.

in·ter·cept (in′tər sept′) *v.t.* 1. to seize or stop on the way: *to intercept a pass, to intercept a note.* 2. to stop the course or progress of; check: *to intercept the flight of a missile.* 3. *Mathematics.* to mark off or bound some part of a line, plane, or surface. —**in′ter·cep′tion,** *n.*

in·ter·cep·tor (in′tər sep′tər) *n.* 1. a person or thing that intercepts. 2. a fast-climbing airplane designed to intercept attacking enemy aircraft.

in·ter·ces·sion (in′tər sesh′ən) *n.* 1. the act of interceding. 2. a prayer or plea that is made on behalf of another or others.

in·ter·ces·sor (in′tər ses′ər) *n.* a person who intercedes.

in·ter·change (*v.,* in′tər chānj′; *n.,* in′tər chānj′) *v.,* **inter·changed, in·ter·chang·ing.** —*v.t.* 1. to put each of (two things) in the place or position of the other: *The usher interchanged the two chairs.* 2. to give and receive mutually; exchange. —*v.i.* to change places one with the other. —*n.* 1. the act or instance of interchanging: *an interchange of ideas, an interchange of furniture.* 2. a place where a vehicle may move from one highway to another without interfering with the flow of traffic on either highway.

in·ter·change·a·ble (in′tər chān′jə bəl) *adj.* capable of being put or used in place of each other: *interchangeable machine parts.* —**in′ter·change′a·bly,** *adv.*

in·ter·col·le·giate (in′tər kə lē′jit) *adj.* carried on or occurring between colleges or universities: *intercollegiate baseball.*

in·ter·com (in′tər kom′) *n.* a radio or telephone system that provides communication within or between given areas, as between rooms of a building.

in·ter·com·mu·ni·cate (in′tər kə mū′ni kāt) *v.i.,* **in·ter·com·mu·ni·cat·ed, in·ter·com·mu·ni·cat·ing.** to communicate with each other or one another. —**in′ter·com·mu′ni·ca′tion,** *n.*

in·ter·con·nect (in′tər kə nekt′) *v.t.* to connect one with the other: *to interconnect wires.* —*v.i.* to be connected one with the other. —**in′ter·con·nec′tion,** *n.*

in·ter·con·ti·nen·tal (in′tər kon′tə nen′təl) *adj.* 1. traveling or capable of traveling from one continent to another: *an intercontinental missile.* 2. of, relating to, or involving more than one continent: *intercontinental trade.*

in·ter·course (in′tər kôrs′) *n.* 1. communication, relations, or dealings between individuals or groups; interchange, as of thoughts, ideas, or feelings: *cultural intercourse between nations.* 2. sexual intercourse.

in·ter·de·nom·i·na·tion·al (in′tər di nom′ə nā′shə nəl) *adj.* between, among, or involving different religious denominations: *an interdenominational service.*

in·ter·de·pen·dent (in′tər di pen′dənt) *adj.* dependent on each other or one another; mutually dependent.

—**in·ter·de·pen'dence,** *n.* —**in·ter·de·pend'ent·ly,** *adv.*

in·ter·dict (*v.,* in'tər dikt'; *n.,* in'tər dikt') *v.t.* **1.** to prohibit; forbid. **2.** in the Roman Catholic Church, to exclude from certain rites and sacraments. —*n.* **1.** an official prohibition. **2.** in the Roman Catholic Church, a punishment in which a person, district, or country is excluded from certain rites and sacraments. —**in'ter·dic'tion,** *n.*

in·ter·est (in'trist, in'tər ist) *n.* **1.** a feeling of concern, involvement, or curiosity: *to have a great interest in sports.* **2.** the cause or source of such feeling: *Painting is my main interest at the moment.* **3.** the power to arouse such feeling: *That book about sports cars had little interest for me.* **4.** *also,* **interests.** advantage; benefit; welfare: *Some people care only about their own interests.* **5.** money paid for the use or borrowing of money: *to pay interest on a loan.* **6.** a legal right, claim, or share: *to have a controlling interest in a business.* **7.** something in which a person has such a right, claim, or share. **8.** *usually,* **interests.** a group having a common concern, especially in a business or industry: *the mining interests.* —*v.t.* **1.** to arouse or hold the curiosity or attention of: *History interests me greatly.* **2.** to cause (a person) to take an interest in something: *My cousin tried to interest me in photography.*

in·ter·est·ed (in'tris tid, in'tə res'tid) *adj.* **1.** having or showing interest: *an interested listener.* **2.** having an interest or share. **3.** having a personal interest or prejudice: *an interested observer.* —**in'ter·est·ed·ly,** *adv.*

in·ter·est·ing (in'tris ting, in'tə res'ting) *adj.* arousing or holding interest or attention: *an interesting face, an interesting magazine.* —**in'ter·est·ing·ly,** *adv.*

interest rate **1.** the rate at which a borrower must pay interest on the amount of a loan that remains unpaid: *a car loan of $10,000 with an annual interest rate of 15 percent on the balance.* **2.** the rate at which an institution such as a savings bank pays interest on a deposit: *an interest rate of 5 percent on a savings account.*

in·ter·face (*v.* in'tər fās', in'tər fās'; *n.* in'tər fās') *v.i.,* **in·ter·faced, in·ter·fac·ing.** to function, act in coordination, or communicate (with a computer or other electronic device): *This computer is capable of interfacing with many different printers.* —*n.* **1.** the point at which computers or other electronic devices interact or exchange information. **2.** a device or program that allows such interaction or exchange of information.

in·ter·faith (in'tər fāth') *adj.* of, for, or involving people of different religions: *an interfaith place of worship, an interfaith conference.*

in·ter·fere (in'tər fîr') *v.i.,* **in·ter·fered, in·ter·fer·ing.** **1.** to concern oneself or intrude in the affairs of others without having been asked; meddle: *I wish you would stop interfering in my private life.* **2.** to cause an interruption or hindrance: *Your guitar playing interferes with my studying.*

in·ter·fer·ence (in'tər fîr'əns) *n.* **1.** the act of interfering. **2.** in radio and television, the disruption of a signal by other signals. **3.** *Football.* **a.** the blocking of opposing players in order to make way for the ball carrier. **b.** the player or players who provide such blocking. **4.** *Sports.* the illegal hindering of an opposing player, as in football or hockey.

in·ter·fer·on (in'tər fîr'on) *n.* any of several proteins produced by the cells of humans and other mammals in response to infection by a virus. Interferon inhibits reproduction of the virus and helps protect the cells from further infection.

in·ter·fuse (in'tər fūz') *v.t.,* **in·ter·fused, in·ter·fus·ing.** **1.** to mix together thoroughly; blend. **2.** to spread through; permeate. **3.** to cause to pass into or spread throughout. —**in'ter·fu'sion,** *n.*

in·ter·im (in'tər im) *n.* the time between; meantime.

—*adj.* for or happening during an interim; temporary: *an interim settlement of a dispute.*

in·te·ri·or (in tîr'ē ər) *n.* **1.** the inner side, surface, or part: *The interior of the cave was dark.* **2.** the part of a region or country that is away from the coast or border: *The interior of that country is mostly jungle.* **3.** the internal or domestic affairs of a country: *the Department of the Interior of the United States.* —*adj.* **1.** of, relating to, or on the inside. **2.** away from the coast or border; inland.

interior decoration, the art or business of planning, designing, and furnishing interiors, as of homes or offices, to provide beauty, comfort, and convenience.

interior decorator, a person whose business is interior decoration.

interj., interjection.

in·ter·ject (in'tər jekt') *v.t.* to put or throw in; insert abruptly: *to interject a comment in a discussion.*

in·ter·jec·tion (in'tər jek'shən) *n.* **1.** *Grammar.* a word or phrase that expresses emotion and is capable of standing alone. *Oh!* and *Wow!* are interjections. **2.** the act of interjecting. **3.** something interjected, as a remark or question.

in·ter·lace (in'tər lās') *v.,* **in·ter·laced, in·ter·lac·ing.** —*v.t.* to join by or as if by weaving together; intertwine: *to interlace garlands of flowers.* —*v.i.* to intertwine.

in·ter·lard (in'tər lärd') *v.t.* to give variety to by mixing in or inserting something different: *to interlard a speech with quotations from Shakespeare.*

in·ter·lock (in'tər lok') *v.i.* to lock or fit together closely: *The parts of this machine interlock.* —*v.t.* to cause to lock or fit together closely: *The bulls interlocked horns.*

in·ter·lop·er (in'tər lō'pər) *n.* a person who interferes in the affairs of others; meddler; intruder.

in·ter·lude (in'tər lüd') *n.* **1.** a period of time between events or the events that take place during such a period: *a brief interlude of rest in a busy day.* **2.** a short performance, as a pantomime, between the acts of a play. **3.** a short piece of music played between parts of a church service, acts of a play, or sections of a long musical composition.

in·ter·mar·riage (in'tər mar'ij) *n.* a marriage or the practice of marriage between persons of different religious faiths, races, or ethnic backgrounds.

in·ter·mar·ry (in'tər mar'ē) *v.i.,* **in·ter·mar·ried, in·ter·mar·ry·ing.** **1.** to marry outside one's religious, racial, or ethnic group. **2.** to become connected by marriage, as two families, tribes, or races. **3.** to marry within one's own family.

in·ter·me·di·ar·y (in'tər mē'dē er'ē) *n., pl.* **in·ter·me·di·ar·ies.** a person, group, or organization that comes between two or more opposing parties in order to bring about an agreement or compromise; mediator. —*adj.* **1.** acting as a mediator: *an intermediary agent.* **2.** being or coming between; intermediate: *an intermediary step in a process.*

in·ter·me·di·ate (in'tər mē'dē it) *adj.* being or coming in the middle or between: *an intermediate stage in a process.* —*n.* something that is intermediate.

in·ter·ment (in tûr'mənt) *n.* the act of interring; burial.

in·ter·mez·zo (in'tər met'sō, in'tər med'zō) *n., pl.* **in-**

I

at; āpe; fär; câre; end; mē; it; īce; pîerce; hot; ōld; sông, fôrk; oil; out; up; ūse; rüle; pull; tûrn; chin; sing; shop; thin; <u>th</u>is; hw in white; zh in treasure. The symbol ə stands for the unstressed vowel sound heard in about, taken, pencil, lemon, and circus.

ter·mez·zos or **in·ter·mez·zi** (in'tər met'sē, in'tər-med'zē). **1.** a short musical composition played between the acts of a play or opera. **2.** *Music.* **a.** a short, slow movement between the main parts of a long composition, as a symphony. **b.** a short, independent instrumental composition.

in·ter·mi·na·ble (in tûr'mə nə bəl) *adj.* endless or seeming to be endless: *The politician's speech was interminable.* —**in·ter'mi·na·bly,** *adv.*

in·ter·min·gle (in'tər ming'gəl) *v.t., v.i.,* **in·ter·min·gled, in·ter·min·gling.** to mix or mingle together.

in·ter·mis·sion (in'tər mish'ən) *n.* **1.** the interval or time between events or periods of activity: *There was a short intermission after the first act of the play.* **2.** an interruption; pause.

in·ter·mit·tent (in'tər mit'ənt) *adj.* alternately stopping and starting again; coming at intervals: *intermittent rain.* —**in'ter·mit'tent·ly,** *adv.*

in·ter·mix (in'tər miks') *v.t., v.i.* to mix together; intermingle.

in·tern¹ (in tûrn') *v.t.* to confine or restrict to a particular place, especially during a war. [From the French word *interner* meaning "to confine, restrict," from the word *interne* "internal," from the Latin word *internus* "internal, inward."]

in·tern² (in'tûrn) *n.* *also,* **in·terne.** **1.** a recently graduated doctor serving in a hospital or clinic under the supervision of experienced doctors. **2.** a student who is gaining practical experience by working under supervision in a professional position. —*v.i.* to be an intern. [From the French word *interne* meaning "resident medical student" or "boarder," from the adjective *interne* "internal," from the Latin word *internus* "internal, inward."]

in·ter·nal (in tûr'nəl) *adj.* **1.** of, relating to, or being on the inside; interior: *the stomach and other internal organs.* **2.** of or relating to the domestic matters or concerns of a country: *internal affairs.* **3.** to be taken internally: *internal medication.* —**in·ter'nal·ly,** *adv.*

in·ter·nal–com·bus·tion engine (in tûr'nəl kəm bus'-chən) an engine in which fuel is burned within the engine itself, usually in cylinders.

internal revenue, the income that a government receives from domestic taxes rather than from customs duties.

Internal Revenue Service, an agency of the U.S. government, in charge of collecting internal revenue, including personal income taxes.

in·ter·na·tion·al (in'tər nash'ə nəl) *adj.* of, relating to, or concerning two or more countries: *an international trade agreement.* —**in'ter·na'tion·al·ly,** *adv.*

International Date Line *also,* **international date line.** an imaginary line running approximately along the 180th meridian, in the middle of the Pacific Ocean, marking the time boundary between one day and the next. Also, **date line.**

in·ter·na·tion·al·ism (in'tər nash'ə nə liz'əm) *n.* the doctrine of mutual cooperation among countries and peoples for the benefit of humanity. —**in'ter·na'tion·al·ist,** *n.*

in·ter·na·tion·al·ize (in'tər nash'ə nə līz') *v.t.,* **in·ter·na·tion·al·ized, in·ter·na·tion·al·iz·ing.** to bring under international control; make international.

in·terne (in'tûrn) another spelling of **intern²** (*n.*).

in·ter·ne·cine (in'tər nes'ēn, in'tər nē'sīn, in tûr'nə-sēn') *adj.* **1.** relating to conflict among groups or among those within a larger group: *Internecine fighting between departments made it impossible to do business.* **2.** characterized by much bloodshed.

in·tern·ee (in'tûr nē') *n.* a person who is or has been interned, especially during a war.

in·tern·ist (in'tûr nist) *n.* a doctor who specializes in the diagnosis and nonsurgical treatment of diseases of adults.

in·tern·ment (in tûrn'mənt) *n.* the act of interning or the state of being interned, especially during a war.

in·tern·ship (in'tûrn ship') *n.* the period during which a person serves as an intern, as in a hospital or clinic.

in·ter·plan·e·tar·y (in'tər plan'i ter'ē) *adj.* between the planets: *interplanetary travel.*

in·ter·play (in'tər plā') *n.* action or influence on each other; interaction: *The story's suspense arises from the interplay of the two main characters.*

in·ter·po·late (in tûr'pə lāt') *v.t.,* **in·ter·po·lat·ed, in·ter·po·lat·ing.** **1.** to alter (a text) by putting in new material. **2.** to put (new material) into a text: *The actor interpolated several lines into the play.* **3.** *Mathematics.* to find the value of (a function, as a logarithm) between two known values. [From the Latin word *interpolatus,* past participle of *interpolare* meaning "to polish, change, give new form to," from the prefix *inter-* "between, among" and *polire* "to polish."] —**in·ter'po·la'tion,** *n.*

in·ter·pose (in'tər pōz') *v.,* **in·ter·posed, in·ter·pos·ing.** —*v.t.* **1.** to introduce into a conversation or speech: *to interpose an unnecessary remark.* **2.** to place between; insert. **3.** to put forth or assert in order to interfere or intervene: *to interpose an objection.* —*v.i.* to come between; intervene. —**in'ter·po·si'tion,** *n.*

in·ter·pret (in tûr'prit) *v.t.* **1.** to make clear or understandable; reveal the meaning of: *to interpret a dream.* **2.** to translate orally: *An assistant interpreted the foreign visitor's remarks for us.* **3.** to understand or regard: *The police officer interpreted the offer as a bribe.* **4.** to perform so as to bring out the meaning: *The pianist interpreted the concerto with great feeling.* —*v.i.* to act as an interpreter.

in·ter·pre·ta·tion (in tûr'pri tā'shən) *n.* **1.** the act of interpreting. **2.** the meaning that results from interpreting: *The student developed an imaginative interpretation of the poem.* **3.** a performance that brings out the meaning of something, as of a musical composition or dramatic role.

in·ter·pre·ta·tive (in tûr'pri tā'tiv) *adj.* another word for **interpretive.**

in·ter·pret·er (in tûr'pri tər) *n.* **1.** a person who interprets. **2.** a person who gives oral translations from one language to another.

in·ter·pre·tive (in tûr'pri tiv) *adj.* serving to interpret; explanatory. Also, **interpretative.**

in·ter·ra·cial (in'tər rā'shəl) *adj.* of, involving, or between members of different races: *an interracial marriage.*

in·ter·reg·num (in'tər reg'nəm) *n., pl.* **in·ter·reg·nums** or **in·ter·reg·na** (in'tər reg'nə). **1.** the time between the end of a ruler's reign and the beginning of the reign of a successor. **2.** any period of time without the usual ruling power or authority.

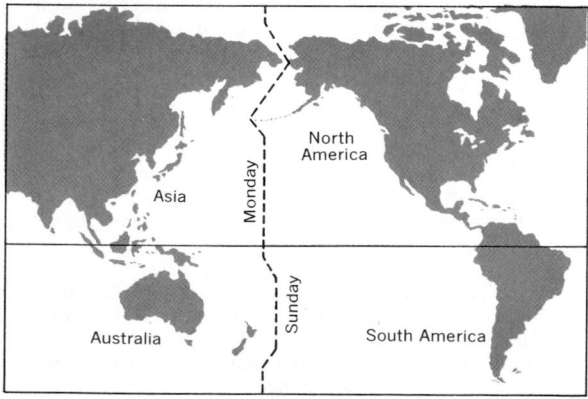

International Date Line

in·ter·re·late (in′tər ri lāt′) *v.t.*, *v.i.*, **in·ter·re·lat·ed**, **in·ter·re·lat·ing.** to bring or come into mutual or close relation. —**in′ter·re·la′tion, in′ter·re·la′tion·ship′**, *n.*

in·ter·re·lat·ed (in′tər ri lā′tid) *adj.* closely or mutually related to each other: *interrelated laws.*

in·ter·ro·gate (in ter′ə gāt′) *v.*, **in·ter·ro·gat·ed**, **in·ter·ro·gat·ing.** —*v.t.* to examine by questioning formally and methodically: *The police interrogated the prisoner.* —*v.i.* to ask questions. —**in·ter′ro·ga′tion**, *n.*

interrogation point, question mark. Also, **interrogation mark.**

in·ter·rog·a·tive (in′tə rog′ə tiv) *adj.* **1.** relating to or having the form of a question: *an interrogative sentence.* **2.** expressing or introducing a question. In the sentence *Who is it?* the word "who" is an interrogative pronoun. —*n.* a word or construction used in asking a question. —**in·ter·rog′a·tive·ly**, *adv.*

in·ter·ro·ga·tor (in ter′ə gā′tər) *n.* a person who interrogates; examiner; questioner.

in·ter·rog·a·to·ry (in′tə rog′ə tôr′ē) *adj.* expressing or asking a question; questioning.

in·ter·rupt (in′tə rupt′) *v.t.* **1.** to break in upon or stop (someone) in the course of an action or speech: *Please do not interrupt me when I am talking.* **2.** to stop or break off (activity or speech): *Don't interrupt your work to answer the phone.* **3.** to interfere with or make a break in: *The tall trees interrupted our view of the valley.* —*v.i.* to break in upon or stop an action or speech: *That child always interrupts when someone is speaking.*

Word Family

Many words in English are derived from the Latin word *rumpere*, meaning "to break." When a pipe breaks, the flow of water is broken, or **interrupted.** When a volcano **erupts**, it may do so **abruptly**, suddenly **disrupting** lives and **routing** people from their homes. Your daily **routine** involves **routes** of travel to and from school and work. When a company goes **bankrupt**, it causes a **rupture** in its employees' lives.

in·ter·rup·tion (in′tə rup′shən) *n.* **1.** the act of interrupting or the state of being interrupted. **2.** something that interrupts: *That question was an unnecessary interruption.*

in·ter·scho·las·tic (in′tər skə las′tik) *adj.* between or among schools: *interscholastic sports.*

in·ter·sect (in′tər sekt′) *v.t.* to divide by passing through or cutting across: *The river intersected the valley.* —*v.i.* to meet and cross each other: *Parallel lines never intersect.*

in·ter·sec·tion (in′tər sek′shən, in′tər sek′shən) *n.* **1.** a place of intersecting, especially where two or more roads or streets meet and cross. **2.** the act of intersecting or the state of being intersected. **3.** *Mathematics.* **a.** the points contained in common by two geometrical figures. **b.** the set of all the elements that are found in two or more given sets.

in·ter·sperse (in′tər spûrs′) *v.t.*, **in·ter·spersed**, **in·ter·spers·ing.** **1.** to scatter or insert (something) here and there among other things: *The author interspersed poems among the short stories in the book.* **2.** to vary by scattering or inserting something here and there: *to intersperse an article with literary quotations.* —**in·ter·sper·sion** (in′tər spur′shən), *n.*

in·ter·state (in′tər stāt′) *adj.* between or among two or more states, especially in the United States: *interstate highways.*

in·ter·stel·lar (in′tər stel′ər) *adj.* between or among the stars: *interstellar space.*

in·ter·stice (in tûr′stis) *n.*, *pl.* **in·ter·sti·ces** (in tûr′stə-

sēz′, in tûr′stə siz). a narrow space or opening between things or parts; crevice. —**in·ter·sti·tial** (in′tər stish′əl), *adj.*

in·ter·twine (in′tər twīn′) *v.t.*, *v.i.*, **in·ter·twined**, **in·ter·twin·ing.** to twine or twist together.

in·ter·val (in′tər vəl) *n.* **1.** time or space between: *An interval of a year passed before we were able to return.* **2.** *Music.* a difference in pitch between any two notes.
•**at intervals. a.** with spaces between; here and there: *Signs were placed at intervals along the road.* **b.** from time to time; now and then.

in·ter·vene (in′tər vēn′) *v.i.*, **in·ter·vened**, **in·ter·ven·ing.** **1.** to come between certain events or points in time: *Many years intervened before they met again.* **2.** to come between opposing parties; intercede: *Their friends intervened to help end their argument.* **3.** to come in or between so as to affect, change, or prevent: *I had made many plans, but my partner's sudden illness intervened.* **4.** to interfere in the affairs of another country. —**in·ter·ven·tion** (in′tər ven′shən), *n.*

in·ter·view (in′tər vū′) *n.* **1.** a meeting between a writer or reporter and a person from whom information is wanted. **2.** a broadcast or published report resulting from such a meeting. **3.** a meeting for a specific purpose, as to discuss employment: *The student put on a suit for the job interview.* —*v.t.* to conduct an interview with: *The reporter hopes to interview the famous artist.* —**in′ter·view′er**, *n.*

in·ter·weave (in′tər wēv′) *v.t.*, *v.i.*, **in·ter·wove** (in′tər wōv′) or **in·ter·weaved**, **in·ter·wo·ven** (in′tər wō′vən) or **in·ter·wove** or **in·ter·weaved**, **in·ter·weav·ing.** to weave, mix, or blend together.

in·tes·tate (in tes′tāt) *adj.* without having made a will: *to die intestate.*

in·tes·ti·nal (in tes′tə nəl) *adj.* of, relating to, or affecting the intestines. —**in·tes′ti·nal·ly**, *adv.*

in·tes·tine (in tes′tin) *n. usually,* **intestines.** that part of the alimentary canal extending from the stomach to the anus. The intestines are divided into the large intestine and the small intestine.

in·ti·ma·cy (in′tə mə-sē) *n.*, *pl.* **in·ti·ma·cies** **1.** the state of being intimate; closeness. **2.** an instance of such closeness.

in·ti·mate¹ (in′tə mit) *adj.* **1.** closely or personally associated; well-acquainted: *The two poets have been intimate friends for years.* **2.** of or resulting from great familiarity or closeness: *to have an intimate knowledge of a business.* **3.** personal or private: *A diary may contain one's most intimate thoughts.* —*n.* a very close friend or associate. [From the Latin word *intimus* meaning "inmost," "most profound," or "secret," from *inter* "between, in the midst of."] —**in′ti·mate·ly**, *adv.*

in·ti·mate² (in′tə māt′) *v.t.*, **in·ti·mat·ed**, **in·ti·mat·ing.**

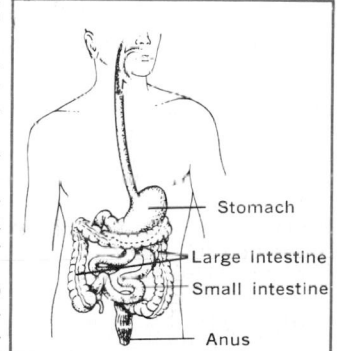

intestines

at; āpe; fär; câre; end; mē; it; īce; pîerce; hot; ōld; sông, fôrk; oil; out; up; ūse; rüle; pùll; tûrn; chin; sing; shop; thin; this; hw in white; zh in treasure. The symbol ə stands for the unstressed vowel sound heard in about, taken, pencil, lemon, and circus.

to make known indirectly; hint; imply: *The mayor intimated that the budget would be slashed.* [From the Late Latin word *intimatus,* past participle of *intimare* "to publish, make known," from the Latin word *intimus* "inmost," "most profound," or "secret," from *inter* "between, in the midst of."] —**in·ti·ma′tion,** *n.*

in·tim·i·date (in tim′i dāt′) *v.t.,* **in·tim·i·dat·ed, in·tim·i·dat·ing. 1.** to make fearful or timid: *The child was intimidated by the storm.* **2.** to influence or frighten by threats or violence: *The robbers intimidated the shopkeeper with a gun.* —**in·tim′i·da′tion,** *n.* —**in·tim′i·da′tor,** *n.*

in·to (in′tü, in′tə) *prep.* **1.** to or toward the inside of: *He bit into the apple. She came into the kitchen.* **2.** against so as to meet head on: *to bump into the door.* **3.** to the state or form of: *The water turned into ice. The dish broke into pieces.* **4.** dividing: *8 into 16 is 2.*

in·tol·er·a·ble (in tol′ər ə bəl) *adj.* not to be endured; unbearable: *The living conditions in the slums were intolerable.* —**in·tol′er·a·bly,** *adv.*

in·tol·er·ance (in tol′ər əns) *n.* **1.** an unwillingness to allow or accept differences of opinion or practice: *religious intolerance.* **2.** the inability to endure or tolerate something: *an intolerance to penicillin.*

in·tol·er·ant (in tol′ər ənt) *adj.* **1.** unwilling to allow or accept differences of opinion or practice; not tolerant: *Don't be intolerant of people who disagree with your beliefs.* **2.** unable to endure or tolerate: *My cat is intolerant of extreme heat.* —**in·tol′er·ant·ly,** *adv.*

in·to·na·tion (in′tō nā′shən) *n.* **1.** the act of intoning. **2.** the manner in which the voice rises and falls in pitch in speaking. **3.** *Music.* the production of tones that are accurate in pitch.

in·tone (in tōn′) *v.t., v.i.,* **in·toned, in·ton·ing.** to recite in a singing voice; chant.

in·tox·i·cant (in tok′si kənt) *n.* any substance that intoxicates, especially alcoholic liquor.

in·tox·i·cate (in tok′si kāt′) *v.t.,* **in·tox·i·cat·ed, in·tox·i·cat·ing. 1.** to make drunk. **2.** to excite greatly: *The sounds and smells of the country intoxicated me.* —**in·tox′i·ca′tion,** *n.*

intra– *prefix* inside of; within: *intrastate, intravenous.*

in·trac·ta·ble (in trak′tə bəl) *adj.* **1.** not easily managed; not tractable; stubborn: *an intractable child.* **2.** not easily treated, handled, used, or worked: *an intractable problem, an intractable subject.* —**in·trac′ta·bil′i·ty,** *n.* —**in·trac′ta·bly,** *adv.*

in·tra·mu·ral (in′trə myùr′əl) *adj.* consisting of or limited to participants within a school or organization: *intramural basketball.*

in·tran·si·gent (in tran′si jənt) *adj.* refusing to give in or compromise. —*n.* a person who is uncompromising. —**in·tran′si·gence,** *n.* —**in·tran′si·gent·ly,** *adv.*

in·tran·si·tive (in tran′si tiv) *adj. Grammar.* of or relating to an action that does not require a direct object. *The verbs die and rise are intransitive.* —**in·tran′si·tive·ly,** *adv.*

in·tra·state (in′trə stāt′) *adj.* existing or happening within a state, especially of the United States.

in·tra·ve·nous (in′trə vē′nəs) *adj.* within or into a vein: *an intravenous injection.* —**in′tra·ve′nous·ly,** *adv.*

in·trench (in trench′) another word for **entrench.**

in·trench·ment (in trench′mənt) another word for **entrenchment.**

in·trep·id (in trep′id) *adj.* having or showing no fear; courageous; fearless: *The intrepid explorers moved deeper into the jungle.* —**in·trep′id·ly,** *adv.* —**in·trep′id·ness,** *n.*

in·tri·ca·cy (in′tri kə sē) *n., pl.* **in·tri·ca·cies. 1.** the state or quality of being intricate: *The design was drawn with great intricacy.* **2.** something intricate: *the intricacies of a legal document.*

in·tri·cate (in′tri kit) *adj.* **1.** very involved or complicated: *an intricate machine.* **2.** difficult to understand: *an intricate problem.* —**in′tri·cate·ly,** *adv.*

in·trigue (*n.,* in′trēg, in·trēg′; *v.,* in trēg′) *n.* **1.** the use of underhanded and devious means: *There was much plotting and intrigue before the outbreak of war.* **2.** a secret scheme or plot: *a political intrigue.* **3.** a secret love affair. —*v.,* **in·trigued, in·trigu·ing.** —*v.t.* to arouse the curiosity or interest of; fascinate: *The story of the sailor's adventures intrigued us.* —*v.i.* to carry on an underhanded and devious scheme or plot: *The palace guards intrigued against the king.*

an **intricate** design

in·trin·sic (in trin′zik, in trin′sik) *adj.* belonging or basic to something by its very nature: *the intrinsic beauty of a rose.* —**in·trin′si·cal·ly,** *adv.*

intro– *prefix* into; inward; within: *introvert.*

in·tro·duce (in′trə düs′, in′trə dūs′) *v.t.,* **in·tro·duced, in·tro·duc·ing. 1.** to make acquainted formally: *Our host introduced us to the other guests.* **2.** to bring into use, knowledge, or notice: *The inventor introduced a new method of manufacturing the product.* **3.** to give first knowledge or experience to: *My friend introduced me to the ballet.* **4.** to bring forward for consideration; propose: *to introduce a motion to adjourn a meeting.* **5.** to bring or put in; insert: *The botanist introduced a new species of plant to the region.* **6.** to start; open; begin: *to introduce a lecture with a short poem.* —**in′tro·duc′er,** *n.*

in·tro·duc·tion (in′trə duk′shən) *n.* **1.** the act of introducing or the state of being introduced. **2.** something that serves to introduce, such as the preface of a book. **3.** something introduced: *The starling in North America was an introduction from England.*

in·tro·duc·to·ry (in′trə duk′tə rē) *adj.* serving to introduce; preliminary: *The senator began the speech with a few introductory remarks.*

in·tro·spec·tion (in′trə spek′shən) *n.* the examination of one's own thoughts or feelings.

in·tro·spec·tive (in′trə spek′tiv) *adj.* of, characterized by, or given to introspection. —**in′tro·spec′tive·ly,** *adv.*

in·tro·vert (in′trə vûrt′) *n.* a person who is chiefly concerned with his or her own thoughts and feelings rather than with other people or what goes on around him or her. ▲ See **extrovert** for usage note.

in·tro·vert·ed (in′trə vûr′tid) *adj.* tending to be more concerned with one's own thoughts and feelings rather than with other people and what goes on around one.

in·trude (in trüd′) *v.,* **in·trud·ed, in·trud·ing.** —*v.i.* to come in as a disturbing or unwelcome addition; enter without being asked or wanted: *We were trying to sleep when a noisy crowd intruded.* —*v.t.* to thrust or force: *to intrude one's opinion into someone else's conversation.* —**in·trud′er,** *n.*

in·tru·sion (in trü′zhən) *n.* **1.** the act of intruding. **2.** an instance of intruding.

in·tru·sive (in trü′siv) *adj.* intruding or tending to intrude: *intrusive questions.* —**in·tru′sive·ly,** *adv.*

in·trust (in trust′) another spelling of **entrust.**

in·tu·i·tion (in′tü ish′ən, in′tū ish′ən) *n.* **1.** a direct or immediate perception or understanding of truth without reasoning: *to know something by intuition.* **2.** the knowledge or insight resulting from such perception.

in·tu·i·tive (in tü′i tiv, in tū′i tiv) *adj.* **1.** of or relating to intuition: *intuitive ability.* **2.** coming from or characterized by intuition: *intuitive knowledge.* **3.** having intuition: *an intuitive person.* —**in·tu′i·tive·ly,** *adv.*

I·nu·it (in′ü it, in′ū it) *pl. n., sing.* **I·nuk** or **I·nu·it.**
1.a. the Eskimo people living in North America. **b.** the Eskimo people living in Greenland, Canada, and mainland Alaska, excluding the native people of the Aleutian Islands. **2.** the language spoken by the Inuit.

I·nuk (in′ük) *n.* a member of the Inuit. Also, **Inuit.**

in·un·date (in′ən dāt′) *v.t.,* **in·un·dat·ed, in·un·dat·ing. 1.** to cover with a flood: *The river overflowed its banks and inundated the valley.* **2.** to overwhelm: *The newspaper was inundated with responses to the ad.* —**in′un·da′tion,** *n.*

in·ure (in yùr′, i nùr′) *v.t.,* **in·ured, in·ur·ing.** to make tough or hardy by experience; accustom: *Living in an arctic climate will inure you to extreme cold.*

in·vade (in vād′) *v.,* **in·vad·ed, in·vad·ing.** —*v.t.* **1.** to enter and attack with an armed force, as for conquest: *Germany invaded France in 1940.* **2.** to enter and overrun as if to take possession: *Rabbits invaded the garden during the night.* **3.** to interfere with; infringe upon; violate: *to invade the privacy of others.* **4.** to penetrate and spread with harmful effects; infect: *Disease germs had invaded the patient's body.* —*v.i.* to make an invasion. —**in·vad′er,** *n.*

in·va·lid¹ (in′və lid) *n.* a person who is disabled by disease or injury. —*adj.* **1.** disabled by disease or injury. **2.** of, relating to, or for invalids. —*v.t.* to make an invalid of; disable. [From the French word *invalide* meaning "sick, disabled," from the Latin word *invalidus* "weak, infirm," from the prefix *in-* "not" + *validus* "strong, powerful."]

in·val·id² (in val′id) *adj.* without force, basis, or authority; not valid: *an invalid contract, an invalid excuse.* [From the Latin word *invalidus* "weak, infirm," from the prefix *in-* "not" + *validus* "strong, powerful."]

in·val·i·date (in val′i dāt′) *v.t.,* **in·val·i·dat·ed, in·val·i·dat·ing.** to make invalid: *This contract invalidates our previous agreement.* **in·val′i·da′tion,** *n.*

in·va·lid·i·ty (in′və lid′i tē) *n.* lack of validity.

in·val·u·a·ble (in val′ū ə bəl, in val′yə bəl) *adj.* of greater value or worth than can be measured; priceless. —**in·val′u·a·bly,** *adv.*

in·var·i·a·ble (in vâr′ē ə bəl, in var′ē ə bəl) *adj.* unchanging or unchangeable; not variable; constant; uniform: *the invariable heat of the tropics.* —**in·var′i·a·bil′i·ty,** *n.* —**in·var′i·a·bly,** *adv.*

in·va·sion (in vā′zhən) *n.* **1.** the entrance of an armed force, as into a country, in order to conquer or pillage. **2.** the act of invading or the state of being invaded. **3.** an intrusion or violation; infringement: *an invasion of one's rights.*

in·va·sive (in vā′siv) *adj.* **1.** tending to invade or spread: *An invasive disease may move from one organ to another.* **2.** involving invasion: *Surgery is an invasive form of treatment.* **3.** tending to intrude; intrusive: *Listening to telephone conversations is invasive of privacy.*

in·vec·tive (in vek′tiv) *n.* a violent accusation or verbal attack; harsh, abusive language: *The candidate directed much invective against the present mayor.*

in·veigh (in vā′) *v.i.* to utter a violent attack: *to inveigh against dictatorship.*

in·vei·gle (in vā′gəl, in vē′gəl) *v.t.,* **in·vei·gled, in·vei·gling.** to persuade or lure by deceit, coaxing, or flattery. —**in·vei′gler,** *n.*

in·vent (in vent′) *v.t.* **1.** to make or devise for the first time; create or originate: *to invent a new kind of engine.* **2.** to make up (something false or fictitious): *to invent rumors.*

in·ven·tion (in ven′chən) *n.* **1.** the act or process of inventing: *The invention of the computer had a great effect on industry.* **2.** something that is invented: *The phonograph was one of Edison's inventions.* **3.** a fictitious account; false statement: *That story is nothing but invention.* **4.** the ability to invent; inventiveness.

in·ven·tive (in ven′tiv) *adj.* **1.** skillful and resourceful; able to invent: *an inventive person.* **2.** of, relating to, or characterized by invention: *inventive ability.* —**in·ven′tive·ly,** *adv.* —**in·ven′tive·ness,** *n.*

in·ven·tor (in ven′tər) *n.* a person who invents, especially one who makes or devises a new device or process.

in·ven·to·ry (in′vən tôr′ē) *n., pl.* **in·ven·to·ries. 1.** a detailed list of articles in stock at a given time: *The inventory revealed that the store had too much merchandise on hand.* **2.** any detailed list of articles: *an inventory of books in a library.* **3.** the articles so listed. **4.** the act or process of making up such a list: *The store was closed for inventory.* —*v.t.,* **in·ven·to·ried, in·ven·to·ry·ing.** to make a detailed list of.

in·verse (in vûrs′, in′vûrs′) *adj.* opposite or reversed, as in order, position, direction, or effect. —*n.* **1.** the direct opposite; reverse. **2.** *Mathematics.* an element in a set that, when added to or multiplied by a given element, yields the identity element for addition or multiplication respectively. The **additive inverse** of 3 is −3; the **multiplicative inverse** of 3 is ⅓. Also *(def. 2),* **inverse element.** —**in·verse′ly,** *adv.*

in·ver·sion (in vûr′zhən) *n.* **1.** the act of inverting or the state of being inverted. **2.** something that is inverted.

in·vert (in vûrt′) *v.t.* **1.** to turn upside down: *The lens inverted the image.* **2.** to reverse the order, position, or relation of: *If you invert the letters of the word "star" you have "rats."* —**in·vert′i·ble,** *adj.*

in·ver·te·brate (in vûr′tə brit, in vûr′tə brāt′) *adj.* of or relating to an animal having no backbone. —*n.* an invertebrate animal, as a crab or a worm.

in·vest (in vest′) *v.t.* **1.** to put (money) to use for the purpose of obtaining profit or income: *to invest one's savings in stocks.* **2.** to give or devote (time, effort, or the like), especially for personal benefit or advantage: *The researchers invested much time and effort in the project.* **3.** to give power, authority, or privilege to: *The city charter invests the mayor with certain powers.* **4.** to formally put in an office, rank, or position: *to invest a new school principal.* **5.** to give a certain quality to: *The judge's manner of speaking invested every word with great dignity.* —*v.i.* to make an investment: *to invest in a new business.* —**in·ves′tor,** *n.*

in·ves·ti·gate (in ves′ti gāt′) *v.,* **in·ves·ti·gat·ed, in·ves·ti·gat·ing.** —*v.t.* to look into carefully in order to uncover facts or gain information; make a thorough examination of: *to investigate a crime.* —*v.i.* to make an investigation.

in·ves·ti·ga·tion (in ves′ti gā′shən) *n.* the act or process of investigating; careful, thorough examination or search: *Police continued their investigation of the vandalism.*

in·ves·ti·ga·tive (in ves′ti gā′tiv) *adj.* of, relating to, or engaged in investigating or an investigation: *an investigative reporter, investigative procedures.*

in·ves·ti·ga·tor (in ves′ti gā′tər) *n.* a person who investigates, such as a detective.

I

at; āpe; fär; câre; end; mē; it; īce; pîerce; hot; ōld; sông, fôrk; oil; out; up; ūse; rüle; pùll; tûrn; chin; sing; shop; thin; this; hw in white; zh in treasure. The symbol ə stands for the unstressed vowel sound heard in about, taken, pencil, lemon, and circus.

in·ves·ti·ture (in ves′ti chər) *n.* the act or ceremony of formally putting a person in an office, rank, or position.

in·vest·ment (in vest′mənt) *n.* **1.** the act of investing, especially the use of money to obtain profit or income. **2.** the amount of money that is invested. **3.** something in which money is invested, as stocks or bonds.

in·vet·er·ate (in vet′ər it) *adj.* **1.** confirmed in a habit or practice; habitual: *an inveterate gambler.* **2.** firmly established by tradition or custom; deep-rooted: *inveterate prejudices.* —**in·vet′er·ate·ly,** *adv.*

in·vid·i·ous (in vid′ē əs) *adj.* **1.** arousing or liable to arouse ill will or hatred; odious: *an invidious remark.* **2.** unfairly or offensively biased: *They made an invidious comparison between our work and theirs.* —**in·vid′i·ous·ly,** *adv.*

in·vig·o·rate (in vig′ə rāt′) *v.t.,* **in·vig·o·rat·ed, in·vig·o·rat·ing.** to fill with strength and energy; give vigor to: *The mountain air invigorated and refreshed us.* —**in·vig′o·rat′ing·ly,** *adv.* —**in·vig′o·ra′tion,** *n.*

in·vin·ci·ble (in vin′sə bəl) *adj.* not capable of being conquered or overcome; unconquerable: *an invincible army.* —**in·vin′ci·bil′i·ty,** *n.* —**in·vin′ci·bly,** *adv.*

in·vi·o·la·ble (in vī′ə lə bəl) *adj.* **1.** that must not be violated: *an inviolable oath.* **2.** that cannot be harmed or destroyed: *an inviolable fortress.* —**in·vi′o·la·bil′i·ty,** *n.* —**in·vi′o·la·bly,** *adv.*

in·vi·o·late (in vī′ə lit, in vī′ə lāt′) *adj.* not broken; not violated: *Their friendship remained strong and inviolate through the years.*

in·vis·i·ble (in viz′ə bəl) *adj.* that cannot be seen; not visible: *an invisible ghost.* —**in·vis′i·bil′i·ty,** *n.* —**in·vis′i·bly,** *adv.*

in·vi·ta·tion (in′vi tā′shən) *n.* **1.** the act of inviting. **2.** the written or spoken form by which a person is invited: *an invitation to a wedding.*

in·vite (in vīt′) *v.t.,* **in·vit·ed, in·vit·ing.** **1.** to make a courteous or formal request for the presence or participation of: *The newlyweds invited their friends to a party.* **2.** to ask for; request: *The editor invited comments from the readers of the magazine.* **3.** to tend to bring on; encourage or foster: *Such rude behavior can only invite trouble.* **4.** to attract; tempt: *The mountain view invited them to pause in their hike.* —**in·vit′er,** *n.*

in·vit·ing (in vī′ting) *adj.* tempting; attractive: *The water looked inviting on such a hot day.* —**in·vit′ing·ly,** *adv.*

in vi·tro (in vē′trō) (of a biological process) outside the living organism, as in a test tube: *The new drug shows good test results in vitro but has not yet been tried in animals or humans.*

in vi·vo (in vē′vō) (of a biological process) inside a living organism: *After proving that the new drug killed bacteria in test tubes, the doctors had to test it in vivo.*

in·vo·ca·tion (in′və kā′shən) *n.* **1.** the act of invoking, especially the calling upon in prayer for aid or protection; supplication. **2.** a prayer used in invoking, especially one spoken at the beginning of a public ceremony or formal religious service. **3.** an incantation used to summon a devil or spirit.

in·voice (in′vois′) *n.* an itemized list of goods sent to a buyer, indicating the quantities shipped, prices, and shipping charges. —*v.t.,* **in·voiced, in·voic·ing.** to make an invoice of: *to invoice a shipment of goods.*

in·voke (in vōk′) *v.t.,* **in·voked, in·vok·ing.** **1.** to call upon in prayer for aid or protection: *to invoke God.* **2.** to call or beg for earnestly: *to invoke a judge's mercy.* **3.** to call forth by charms or incantation; conjure: *to invoke the spirits of the dead.* **4.** to call into use for support: *to invoke a law.*

in·vol·un·tar·y (in vol′ən ter′ē) *adj.* **1.** not done willingly or by choice; not voluntary: *an involuntary act.* **2.** occurring without conscious control: *Breathing is an involuntary action.* —**in·vol′un·tar′i·ly,** *adv.*

in·volve (in volv′) *v.t.,* **in·volved, in·volv·ing.** **1.** to include as a necessary part, condition, or result: *Winning the race involves both skill and speed.* **2.** to draw or bring into an unfortunate or difficult situation: *Your unnecessary remark may involve you in the quarrel.* **3.** to occupy completely; absorb: *I was involved in reading the book all evening.* —**in·volve′ment,** *n.*

in·volved (in volvd′) *adj.* complicated; complex.

in·vul·ner·a·ble (in vul′nər ə bəl) *adj.* not capable of being harmed or injured; safe against attack: *an invulnerable defense.* —**in·vul′ner·a·bil′i·ty,** *n.* —**in·vul′ner·a·bly,** *adv.*

in·ward (in′wərd) *adv.* **1.** toward the inside, interior, or center: *The front door opens inward.* **2.** into or toward the mind or self: *When I am unhappy, my thoughts often turn inward.* Also, **in·wards.** —*adj.* **1.** toward the inside: *an inward push.* **2.** located within; inner; internal: *an inward pain.* **3.** in the mind or thought: *inward fears.*

in·ward·ly (in′wərd lē) *adv.* **1.** in, on, or toward the inside; within. **2.** in the mind or thought: *Although calm in appearance, the soldiers were inwardly terrified.*

i·o·dide (ī′ə dīd′) *n.* a chemical compound of iodine with another element or radical.

i·o·dine (ī′ə dīn′, ī′ə dēn′) *n.* **1.** an element of the halogen group that occurs as shiny, grayish black crystals that give off a violet-colored vapor when heated. Iodine is used in medicine and is essential to the thyroid gland. Symbol: I **2.** an antiseptic consisting of iodine dissolved in an alcohol solution. [From the French word *iode* meaning "iodine," from the Greek word *ioeidēs* "violet-colored," from the word *ion* "violet."]

i·o·dize (ī′ə dīz′) *v.t.,* **i·o·dized, i·o·diz·ing.** to treat with iodine or an iodide: *iodized salt.*

i·on (ī′ən, ī′on) *n.* an atom or group of atoms that has an electrical charge resulting from a loss or gain of one or more electrons. Positive ions are formed by a loss of electrons; negative ions are formed by a gain of electrons.

–ion *suffix* (used to form nouns from verbs) **1.** the act of: *discussion, completion.* **2.** the state of being: *depression, damnation.* **3.** the result of: *pollution, fusion.*

i·on·ic (ī on′ik) *adj.* of or relating to ions.

I·on·ic (ī on′ik) *adj.* **1.** of or relating to one of the three orders of classical Greek architecture, characterized by columns having scrolls on the capitals. **2.** of or relating to Ionia, its people, their language, or culture.

i·on·ize (ī′ə nīz′) *v.,* **i·on·ized, i·on·iz·ing.** —*v.t.* to produce ions in. —*v.i.* to be changed into ions. —**i′on·i·za′tion,** *n.*

i·on·o·sphere (ī on′ə sfīr′) *n.* a region of ionized gases in the earth's atmosphere, beginning approximately 50 miles (80 kilometers) above the earth's surface. The ionosphere reflects certain radio waves, making it possible to transmit radio communications over long distances on earth.

i·o·ta (ī ō′tə) *n.* **1.** the ninth letter of the Greek alphabet (I, ι), corresponding to the English letter I, i. **2.** a very small amount; bit: *without an iota of proof.*

IOU (ī′ō′ū′) *n., pl.* **IOU's.** an informal written promise to pay a debt. [From the phrase *I owe you.*]

ip·e·cac (ip′i kak′) *n.* a drug obtained from the dried root of a South American plant, used to induce vomiting in the treatment of poisoning.

IQ, see **intelligence quotient.**

Ir, the symbol for iridium.

ir-¹, a form of the prefix **in-¹** used before *r*, as in *irregular.*

ir-², a form of the prefix **in-²** used before *r*, as in *irruption.*

IRA (ī′är′ā′, ī′rə) *n., pl.* **IRA's.** a bank account, savings program, or other arrangement under which a person can set aside money that is not subject to taxes until after the person retires from work.

I·ra·ni·an (i rā′nē ən, i rä′nē ən) *n.* **1.** a person who was born in or is a citizen of Iran. **2.** the language of Iran. —*adj.* of or relating to Iran, its people, their language, or their culture.

i·ras·ci·ble (i ras′ə bəl) *adj.* easily irritated or made angry; irritable. —**i·ras′ci·bil′i·ty,** *n.* —**i·ras′ci·bly,** *adv.*

i·rate (ī rāt′, ī′rāt) *adj.* angry; enraged: *A group of irate citizens demanded to see the mayor.* —**i·rate′ly,** *adv.*

IRBM, a ballistic missile with a range of between 300 and 1,500 miles (500–2,500 kilometers). [Short for *i*(ntermediate)-*r*(ange) *b*(allistic) *m*(issile).]

ire (īr) *n.* anger; wrath.

ire·ful (īr′fəl) *adj.* full of ire; angry; wrathful: *an ireful glance.* —**ire′ful·ly,** *adv.*

ir·i·des·cent (ir′i des′ənt) *adj.* displaying shimmering and changing colors, like those reflected by soap bubbles. —**ir′i·des′cence,** *n.* —**ir′i·des′cent·ly,** *adv.*

i·rid·i·um (i rid′ē əm) *n.* an extremely hard, brittle, silver-white metallic element used in alloys of platinum and for electrical contacts and chemical apparatus. Symbol: **Ir** [From the Latin word *iris* meaning "rainbow." The element's compounds have a range of colors.]

i·ris (ī′ris) *n., pl.* **i·ris·es.** **1.** the circular, colored membrane between the cornea and the lens that controls the amount of light entering the eye. **2.** a showy flower of various colors, having three erect petals and three drooping petals. **3.** the plant bearing this flower, grown as a house and garden plant, usually having long, sword-shaped leaves.[Originally from the Greek word *iris* meaning "rainbow," "iris plant," and "iris of the eye."]

iris
(defs. 2 and 3)

I·rish (ī′rish) *n.* **1. the Irish.** the people of Ireland or their close descendants. **2.** the Celtic language traditionally spoken in Ireland. Also, **Gaelic.**

Words From Other Languages

Many Irish words became part of American English during the nineteenth and twentieth centuries. They were often words for Irish legends, customs, and objects.

balbriggan	a kind of knitted cotton cloth, used for hosiery and underwear
banshee	a female spirit who wails before a death
blarney	smooth, flattering talk
brogue	a kind of heavy, sturdy, laced shoe
donnybrook	a rough, noisy brawl or free-for-all
leprechaun	a mischievous Irish elf
shamrock	a three-leafed plant like a clover
shanty	a crude, flimsy hut or cabin
smithereens	tiny pieces or fragments
whiskey	a strong liquor made from grain

I·rish·man (ī′rish mən) *n., pl.* **I·rish·men** (ī′rish mən). a person who was born in Ireland or is a citizen of the Republic of Ireland or of Northern Ireland. **2.** a person of Irish descent living outside Ireland.

Irish potato, the common white potato.

Irish setter, a dog of a breed that originated in Ireland, having a coat of silky reddish hair.

Irish terrier, a short-haired dog having a reddish, wiry coat.

Irish wolfhound, a very large, tall dog having a rough, wiry, usually gray coat.

I·rish·wom·an (ī′rish wùm′ən) *n., pl.* **I·rish·wom·en** (ī′rish wim′ən). **1.** a woman who was born in Ireland or is a citizen of the Republic of Ireland or of Northern Ireland. **2.** a woman of Irish descent living outside Ireland.

Irish setter

irk (ûrk) *v.t.* to annoy; vex; bother: *It irks me to hear you talk about yourself all the time.*

irk·some (ûrk′səm) *adj.* annoying; tiresome: *an irksome job.* —**irk′some·ly,** *adv.* —**irk′some·ness,** *n.*

i·ron (ī′ərn) *n.* **1.** a grayish white metallic element that is very ductile, highly magnetic, and a good conductor of heat and electricity. Iron is the most important metal, and its alloys, such as steel, are the most widely used. Iron is an essential part of hemoglobin. Symbol: **Fe** **2.** anything that is hard, strong, or unyielding: *muscles of iron.* **3.** something made from iron or an alloy of iron. **4.** an appliance having a flat surface that is heated and used to press or smooth clothing and fabrics. **5.** a golf club with a metal head. **6. irons.** fetters or shackles: *The prisoner was in irons.* —*adj.* **1.** of or relating to iron: *The lion's cage had iron bars.* **2.** strong or unyielding: *an iron will.* —*v.t.* to smooth or press with a heated iron: *to iron a shirt.* —*v.i.* to iron fabric, especially clothing. [From the Old English word *īren* meaning this metal.]

·**to iron out.** to smooth out; settle: *We talked things over and ironed out our differences.*

Iron Age, the stage in the development of civilization following the Bronze Age, characterized by the widespread use of iron in tools and weapons.

i·ron·clad (*adj.* ī′ərn klad′; *n.* ī′ərn klad′) *adj.* **1.** covered or protected with iron or steel plates. **2.** difficult to change or break: *an ironclad regulation.* —*n.* a nineteenth-century warship covered wholly or partially with iron plates for protection.

Iron Curtain, an imaginary barrier of censorship and secrecy, regarded as separating the Soviet Union and other European Communist countries from the non-Communist world. [Originally referring to a curtain of iron used to prevent the spread of fire in a theater, later popularized by Winston Churchill in a speech made in 1946.]

i·ron·ic (ī ron′ik) *adj.* **1.** of, relating to, or characterized by irony: *an ironic situation, an ironic remark.* **2.** given to the use of irony: *an ironic writer.* Also, **i·ron·i·cal** (ī ron′i kəl). —**i·ron′i·cal·ly,** *adv.*

---

at; āpe; fär; câre; end; mē; it; īce; pîerce; hot; ōld; sông, fôrk; oil; out; up; ūse; rüle; pùll; tûrn; chin; sing; shop; thin; <u>th</u>is; hw in white; zh in treasure. The symbol ə stands for the unstressed vowel sound heard in about, taken, pencil, lemon, and circus.

I

ironing board, a padded board, usually on a folding frame, on which fabrics or clothing may be ironed.

iron lung, an apparatus used to maintain breathing when normal respiration is impaired, as when a person's chest muscles are paralyzed. An iron lung consists of a cylindrical tank that encloses the body, except the head, and air pumps that increase and decrease the air pressure in the tank.

i·ron·ware (ī′ərn wâr′) *n.* articles that are made of iron, such as pots and other utensils and tools.

i·ron·wood (ī′ərn wood′) *n.* **1.** any of a number of trees having hard, close-grained wood. **2.** the hard, durable wood of any of these trees, used especially for making tool handles and similar equipment.

i·ron·work (ī′ərn wûrk′) *n.* things made of iron.

i·ron·work·er (ī′ərn wûr′kər) *n.* **1.** a person whose work is smelting iron or manufacturing iron objects. **2.** a person who builds or repairs steel frameworks, as of bridges.

i·ron·works (ī′ərn wûrks′) *n.* a place where iron is smelted or where iron objects are manufactured. ▲ used with a singular or plural verb.

i·ro·ny (ī′rə nē, ī′ər nē) *n., pl.* **i·ro·nies.** **1.** a form of expression in which the intended meaning is the opposite of that expressed in words, as when a person says "Oh, wonderful!" upon hearing bad news. **2.** an event or outcome of events opposite to what was, or might naturally have been, expected. **3.** the oddness of such an unexpected event or outcome: *The irony of the situation lay in the fact that the weather forecasters' picnic was rained out.*

Ir·o·quois (ir′ə kwoi′) *n., pl.* **Ir·o·quois.** **1.** a member of a confederation of North American Indian tribes formerly living in what is now the state of New York. Originally called the Five Nations (the Seneca, Cayuga, Onondaga, Oneida, and Mohawk), the Iroquois became the Six Nations in 1722 when the Tuscaroras joined the confederation. **2.** a member of a tribe belonging to this confederation. **3.** any of the languages spoken by these Indians. —*adj.* of or relating to the Iroquois or their languages.

ir·ra·di·ate (i rā′dē āt′) *v.t.,* **ir·ra·di·at·ed, ir·ra·di·at·ing. 1.** to shed light upon; brighten; illuminate: *Brilliant flashes of lightning irradiated the night sky.* **2.** to expose to or treat with radiation. **3.** to send out in or as if in rays; radiate. —**ir·ra′di·a′tion,** *n.*

ir·ra·tion·al (i rash′ə nəl) *adj.* **1.** lacking reason; not rational: *The survivors of the crash wandered about in a confused and irrational state.* **2.** contrary to reason; illogical; absurd: *In anger we sometimes say things that are irrational.* —**ir·ra′tion·al·ly,** *adv.*

ir·ra·tion·al·i·ty (i rash′ə nal′i tē) *n.* the condition or quality of being irrational.

irrational number, a number that cannot be expressed as a quotient of integers or as an integer. $\sqrt{2}$ and π are irrational numbers.

ir·re·claim·a·ble (ir′i klā′mə bəl) *adj.* that cannot be reclaimed: *irreclaimable land.* —**ir′re·claim′a·bly,** *adv.*

ir·rec·on·cil·a·ble (i rek′ən sī′lə bəl) *adj.* **1.** that cannot be restored to friendly relations: *irreconcilable enemies.* **2.** that cannot be brought into agreement: *irreconcilable theories.* —**ir′rec′on·cil′a·bly,** *adv.*

ir·re·cov·er·a·ble (ir′i kuv′ər ə bəl) *adj.* that cannot be recovered or remedied: *an irrecoverable loss, irrecoverable damage.* —**ir′re·cov′er·a·bly,** *adv.*

ir·re·deem·a·ble (ir′i dē′mə bəl) *adj.* **1.** that cannot be bought back or paid off: *an irredeemable mortgage.* **2.** that cannot be converted into coin, such as certain kinds of paper money. **3.** that cannot be changed or remedied; hopeless: *an irredeemable criminal, an atmosphere of irredeemable gloom.* —**ir′re·deem′a·bly,** *adv.*

ir·re·duc·i·ble (ir′i dü′sə bəl, ir′i dū′sə bəl) *adj.* that cannot be reduced or simplified; not reducible. —**ir′re·duc′i·bly,** *adv.*

ir·ref·u·ta·ble (i ref′yə tə bəl, ir′i fū′tə bəl) *adj.* that cannot be refuted or disproved; indisputable: *irrefutable evidence.* —**ir·ref′u·ta·bly,** *adv.*

ir·reg·u·lar (i reg′yə lər) *adj.* **1.** not conforming to standards, custom, or usual practice; unusual: *irregular behavior.* **2.** not evenly or uniformly shaped, arranged, or spaced; uneven: *the irregular surface of the moon, an irregular knocking sound.* **3.** *Grammar.* not according to the usual or most common pattern of inflection. The verb *be* is irregular. —**ir·reg′u·lar·ly,** *adv.*

ir·reg·u·lar·i·ty (i reg′yə lar′i tē) *n., pl.* **ir·reg·u·lar·i·ties. 1.** the state or quality of being irregular. **2.** something that is irregular.

ir·rel·e·vance (i rel′ə vəns) *n.* **1.** the quality or fact of being irrelevant. **2.** something that is irrelevant. Also, **ir·rel·e·van·cy** (i rel′ə vən sē).

ir·rel·e·vant (i rel′ə vənt) *adj.* not bearing upon or connected with the matter at hand; not pertinent; inappropriate: *Many of your remarks were irrelevant to the conversation.* —**ir·rel′e·vant·ly,** *adv.*

ir·re·li·gious (ir′i lij′əs) *adj.* **1.** indifferent to or lacking religion; not religious. **2.** showing disrespect to religious principles; profane. —**ir′re·li′gious·ly,** *adv.*

ir·re·me·di·a·ble (ir′i mē′dē ə bəl) *adj.* that cannot be remedied or cured. —**ir′re·me′di·a·bly,** *adv.*

ir·rep·a·ra·ble (i rep′ər ə bəl) *adj.* (of damage, harm, or the like) that cannot be repaired, restored, or made right: *The hurricane did irreparable damage to the house.* —**ir·rep′a·ra·bly,** *adv.*

ir·re·place·a·ble (ir′i plā′sə bəl) *adj.* that cannot be replaced: *irreplaceable works of art.*

ir·re·press·i·ble (ir′i pres′ə bəl) *adj.* that cannot be repressed or restrained: *a cheerful teenager with irrepressible high spirits.* —**ir′re·press′i·bly,** *adv.*

ir·re·proach·a·ble (ir′i prō′chə bəl) *adj.* free from blame or criticism; above reproach; faultless: *irreproachable conduct, an irreproachable leader.* —**ir′re·proach′a·bly,** *adv.*

ir·re·sist·i·ble (ir′i zis′tə bəl) *adj.* that cannot be resisted or opposed: *The chocolate cake was an irresistible temptation to the dieter.* —**ir′re·sis′ti·bil′i·ty,** *n.* —**ir′re·sist′i·bly,** *adv.*

ir·res·o·lute (i rez′ə lüt′) *adj.* lacking decisiveness or certainty; hesitating: *The irresolute leader was never sure what to do.* —**ir·res′o·lute′ly,** *adv.* —**ir·res′o·lute′ness, ir·res′o·lu′tion,** *n.*

ir·re·spec·tive (ir′i spek′tiv) *adv.* regardless: *Anyone can apply for this job, irrespective of past experience.*

ir·re·spon·si·ble (ir′i spon′sə bəl) *adj.* **1.** not trustworthy or dependable; unreliable: *a careless and irresponsible worker.* **2.** not carefully considered: *an irresponsible decision, irresponsible behavior.* —**ir′re·spon′si·bil′i·ty,** *n.* —**ir′re·spon′si·bly,** *adv.*

ir·re·triev·a·ble (ir′i trē′və bəl) *adj.* that cannot be retrieved or recovered. —**ir′re·triev′a·bly,** *adv.*

ir·rev·er·ence (i rev′ər əns) *n.* **1.** lack of reverence or respect. **2.** an irreverent act or statement.

ir·rev·er·ent (i rev′ər ənt) *adj.* not feeling or showing reverence or respect; disrespectful: *an irreverent attitude toward one's elders.* —**ir·rev′er·ent·ly,** *adv.*

ir·re·vers·i·ble (ir′i vûr′sə bəl) *adj.* that cannot be reversed, changed, or undone; irrevocable: *an irreversible decision.* —**ir′re·vers′i·bly,** *adv.*

ir·rev·o·ca·ble (i rev′ə kə bəl) *adj.* that cannot be revoked or recalled; unalterable: *The decision was irrevocable.* —**ir·rev′o·ca·bly,** *adv.*

ir·ri·gate (ir′i gāt′) *v.t.,* **ir·ri·gat·ed, ir·ri·gat·ing. 1.** to supply with water, as by means of channels, streams, or pipes: *to irrigate a desert so that crops can be grown.* **2.** to cleanse (a wound or body cavity) with a flow of some liquid. —**ir'ri·ga'tion**, *n.*

ir·ri·ta·bil·i·ty (ir'i tə bil'i tē) *n., pl.* **ir·ri·ta·bil·i·ties.** **1.** the state or quality of being irritable: *The child's irritability was caused by weariness.* **2.** *Biology.* the ability to respond to a stimulus.

ir·ri·ta·ble (ir'i tə bəl) *adj.* **1.** easily excited to impatience or anger: *to be irritable when tired.* **2.** very sensitive: *I have irritable skin.* **3.** *Biology.* able to respond to stimuli. —**ir'ri·ta·ble·ness**, *n.* —**ir'ri·ta·bly**, *adv.*

ir·ri·tant (ir'i tənt) *n.* something that causes irritation. —*adj.* causing irritation.

ir·ri·tate (ir'i tāt') *v.t.,* **ir·ri·tat·ed, ir·ri·tat·ing.** **1.** to make impatient or angry; vex: *Their constant arguing irritates me.* **2.** to make sore or inflamed: *Smoke irritates the eyes.* —**ir'ri·tat'ing·ly**, *adv.* —**ir'ri·ta'tor**, *n.*

ir·ri·ta·tion (ir'i tā'shən) *n.* **1.** the act or process of irritating or the state of being irritated; vexation. **2.** an inflamed or painful condition: *a skin irritation.*

IRS, Internal Revenue Service.

is (iz) the third person singular, present indicative of **be.**

is., island.

I·sai·ah (ī zā'ə) *n.* a book of the Old Testament believed to have been written by the Hebrew prophet Isaiah.

is·chi·um (is'kē əm) *n., pl.* **is·chi·a** (is'kē ə). the lowest portion of the hipbone.

-ish *suffix* (used to form adjectives) **1.** of, belonging to, or relating to: *Jewish.* **2.** of the nature or character of; like: *childish, foolish.* **3.** somewhat: *bluish, youngish.*

Ish·ma·el (ish'mē əl, ish'mā əl) *n.* an outcast. [From *Ishmael,* the son of Abraham, who was cast out into the wilderness, according to the Book of Genesis.]

i·sin·glass (ī'zən glas', ī'zing glas') *n.* **1.** a white, odorless, very pure form of gelatin obtained from the air bladders of fish, especially sturgeon, used to make glue and clarify liquors. **2.** mica in thin sheets.

I·sis (ī'sis) *n.* the Egyptian goddess of fertility. She was the wife and sister of Osiris.

Is·lam (is'lam, is läm') *n.* **1.** the religion based on the teachings and writings of Muhammad as they appear in the Koran, asserting that there is only one god, Allah, and that Muhammad is Allah's prophet. **2.** the whole of the Muslim world, including Muslim civilization and the countries under Muslim rule.

Is·lam·ic (is lam'ik, is lä'mik) *adj.* of, relating to, or belonging to Islam; Muslim.

is·land (ī'lənd) *n.* **1.** a body of land entirely surrounded by water and smaller than a continent. **2.** anything resembling an island: *The park was an island of green in the middle of the city.* [From the Old English word *īgland* meaning ''island.'' The Modern English spelling *island* was influenced by the Old French word *isle* meaning ''isle, island.'']

is·land·er (ī'lən dər) *n.* a person who was born on, comes from, or is living on an island.

isle (īl) *n.* an island, especially a small island.

is·let (ī'lit) *n.* a little island.

islet of Lang·er·hans (läng'ər häns') any of the small masses of endocrine cells in the pancreas that secrete insulin. Also, **island of Langerhans.**

ism (iz'əm) *n.* a doctrine, theory, or system: *socialism, anarchism, and other isms.*

-ism *suffix* (used to form nouns) **1.** an action or practice: *criticism, baptism.* **2.** a state or condition: *parallelism, pessimism.* **3.** characteristic conduct or behavior: *patriotism, barbarism, heroism.* **4.** a distinguishing feature, aspect, or manner, as of language: *colloquialism.* **5.** a doctrine, system, or principle: *socialism, paganism.*

is·n't (iz'ənt) *contr.* is not.

i·so·bar (ī'sə bär') *n.* a line on a weather map connecting points having the same barometric pressure.

i·so·late (ī'sə lāt') *v.t.,* **i·so·lat·ed, i·so·lat·ing.** to place or set apart; separate from others: *Persons with contagious diseases were isolated from other patients.*

i·so·la·tion (ī'sə lā'shən) *n.* the act of isolating or the state of being isolated.

i·so·la·tion·ism (ī'sə lā'shə niz'əm) *n.* the policy of avoiding political, economic, or military involvements with foreign countries.

i·so·la·tion·ist (ī'sə lā'shə nist) *n.* a person who supports or is in favor of isolationism.

i·so·mer (ī'sə mər) *n.* any of two or more chemical compounds having the same molecular formula and thus the same composition, but differing in properties because their atoms are arranged differently.

i·so·met·ric (ī'sə met'rik) *adj.* of or relating to the contraction of a muscle in which there is increased tension rather than change in length: *isometric exercises.*

i·sos·ce·les (ī sos'ə lēz') *adj.* (of a triangle) having two sides whose lengths are equal.

i·so·therm (ī'sə thûrm') *n.* a line on a weather map connecting points having the same average temperature.

i·so·tope (ī'sə tōp') *n.* any of two or more kinds of atoms of the same element having the same atomic number but different mass numbers.

Is·ra·el (iz'rē əl, iz'rā əl) *n.* the people descended from the biblical patriarch Jacob, also called Israel; the Hebrew people.

Is·rae·li (iz rā'lē) *n., pl.* **Is·rae·lis.** a person who was born in or is a citizen of modern Israel. —*adj.* of or relating to modern Israel, its people, their language, or their culture.

Is·ra·el·ite (iz'rē ə līt', iz'rā ə līt') *n.* a descendant of the patriarch Jacob; Hebrew. —*adj.* of or relating to the Hebrews.

is·su·ance (ish'ü əns) *n.* the act of issuing.

is·sue (ish'ü) *n.* **1.** the act of sending or giving out: *an issue of licenses, an issue of supplies.* **2.** the act of going, passing, or flowing out: *an issue of blood from a wound.* **3.** something that is sent or given out, such as a certain quantity of magazines, newspapers, stamps, or books printed and distributed at one time. **4.** an individual copy of a magazine or other periodical. **5.** a subject under discussion or consideration. *The raising of taxes was the issue under debate.* **6.** offspring: *The money was willed to my cousins and their issue.* **7.** the outcome of an action or course of events; result; consequence. —*v.,* **is·sued, is·su·ing.** *v.t.* **1.** to send or give out: *to issue coins, to issue a statement.* **2.** to send forth; discharge; emit. **3.** to publish: *to issue a magazine.* —*v.i.* to go or come out; flow out; pour forth. —**is'su·er**, *n.*

•**at issue.** **a.** undecided; under consideration: *What is at issue here is whether to build a new gym or repair the old one.* **b.** not in agreement: *We were at issue over which movie to see.*

•**to take issue.** to disagree or argue: *I take issue with your statement that spiders are insects.*

-ist *suffix* (used to form nouns) **1.** a person who does or makes: *tourist, novelist.* **2.** a person who practices or has as a profession: *machinist, violinist.* **3.** a person who supports or is in favor of: *idealist, socialist.*

I

at; āpe; fär; câre; end; mē; it; īce; pîerce; hot; ōld; sông, fôrk; oil; out; up; ūse; rüle; pùll; tûrn; chin; sing; shop; thin; this; hw in white; zh in treasure. The symbol ə stands for the unstressed vowel sound heard in about, taken, pencil, lemon, and circus.

isth·mus (is′məs) *n., pl.* **isth·mus·es.** a narrow strip of land bordered by water and connecting two larger bodies of land.

it (it) *pron. sing.,* nominative, **it;** possessive, **its;** objective, **it;** *pl.,* nominative, **they;** possessive, **their, theirs;** objective, **them. 1.** a thing or animal previously mentioned: *Throw me the ball and I will catch it.* **2.** the subject of an impersonal verb: *It snowed last night.* **3.** the grammatical subject of a verb introducing a phrase or dependent clause that is the actual subject: *It is obvious that we have missed the train.* —*n.* in certain children's games, the person who has to do something special. In playing tag, the person who is *it* has to chase the other players.

ital., italic; italics.

Ital. 1. Italian. **2.** Italy.

I·tal·ian (i tal′yən) *n.* **1.** a person who was born in or is a citizen of Italy. **2.** a person of Italian descent. **3.** the language spoken in Italy and in parts of Switzerland. —*adj.* **1.** of, relating to, or characteristic of Italy, its people, their language, or culture. **2.** having its origin in Italy: *Italian wine.*

Words From Other Languages

Italian has contributed many words to the English language, especially in the fields of music, art, and cooking.

allegro	a fast, lively tempo in music
banister	a handrail along a staircase
cameo	a piece of stone or shell jewelry with a raised, carved design
cavalry	soldiers who fight on horseback
cello	a large stringed instrument
fresco	a picture painted on wet plaster
infantry	soldiers who fight on foot
miniature	very small or greatly reduced
piano	a musical term meaning "softly"
pizza	an open pie with tomato and cheese
umbrella	a device to protect people from rain
vendetta	a feud in which a family or group seeks revenge

i·tal·ic (i tal′ik, ī tal′ik) *adj.* of or relating to a style of type whose letters slant to the right: *This sentence is printed in italic type.* —*n. also,* **italics.** italic type.

i·tal·i·cize (i tal′ə sīz′, ī tal′ə sīz′) *v.t.,* **i·tal·i·cized, i·tal·i·ciz·ing.** to print in italic type.

itch (ich) *n., pl.* **itch·es. 1.** a tickling or stinging feeling in the skin that is relieved by scratching or rubbing. **2.** a restless, uneasy desire for something: *The young writer had an itch to travel across the country.* —*v.i.* **1.** to have or cause a tickling or stinging sensation in the skin: *The rash on my hand itches.* **2.** to have a restless, uneasy desire: *to be itching for a fight.*

itch·y (ich′ē) *adj.,* **itch·i·er, itch·i·est. 1.** characterized by, having, or causing an itch. **2.** restless; eager for something to happen. —**itch′i·ness,** *n.*

–ite *suffix* (used to form nouns) **1.** a person who was born or is living in: *New Jerseyite.* **2.** a supporter or follower of: *laborite.* **3.** a mineral or rock: *calcite, bauxite.*

i·tem (ī′təm) *n.* **1.** a unit or article included in a group, series, or list: *There are many valuable items in this stamp collection.* **2.** a bit of information, or a brief newspaper article or paragraph containing such information: *There was an item in the newspaper about the senator's speech.*

i·tem·ize (ī′tə mīz′) *v.t.,* **i·tem·ized, i·tem·iz·ing.** to give each item of; list by items: *We itemized our expenses for the month.*

it·er·ate (it′ə rāt′) *v.t.,* **it·er·at·ed, it·er·at·ing.** to say or do again; repeat. —**it′er·a′tion,** *n.*

i·tin·er·ant (ī tin′ər ənt) *adj.* traveling from place to place, especially for business or duty: *an itinerant worker.* —*n.* a person who travels from place to place, especially for business or duty. —**i·tin′er·ant·ly,** *adv.*

i·tin·er·ar·y (ī tin′ə rer′ē) *n., pl.* **i·tin·er·ar·ies. 1.** a planned course or route of travel, as for a journey: *Rome and Paris were included in our itinerary.* **2.** an account or record of travel. **3.** a guidebook for travelers.

–itis *suffix* (used to form nouns) inflammation of: *tonsillitis, bronchitis.*

it'll (it′əl) *contr.* **1.** it shall. **2.** it will.

its (its) *adj.* of or belonging to it: *The cat licked its paw.*

it's (its) *contr.* **1.** it has: *It's been nice to see you.* **2.** it is: *It's cold today.*

it·self (it self′) *pron.* **1.** the form of **it** used to give emphasis to the word it goes with: *The yard is overgrown with weeds, but the house itself is in good condition.* **2.** the form of **it** used to show that the subject is the same as the direct object, indirect object, or object of a preposition: *The cat washed itself. The child softly sang itself a song. The abandoned dog had to fend for itself.*

–ity *suffix* (used to form nouns) the state, condition, or quality of being: *formality, inferiority.*

I've (īv) *contr.* I have: *I've no money.*

–ive *suffix* (used to form adjectives) **1.** given to: *active, assertive, instructive.* **2.** of, relating to, or of the nature of: *massive, instinctive.*

i·vo·ry (ī′və rē) *n., pl.* **i·vo·ries. 1.** a smooth, hard, white substance that forms the tusks of elephants, walruses, and certain other animals. **2.** something made of this substance: *The museum has a fine collection of medieval ivories.* **3.** a creamy white color. **4. ivories.** *Slang.* the keys of a piano. —*adj.* **1.** of or resembling ivory. **2.** having the color ivory.

i·vy (ī′vē) *n., pl.* **i·vies. 1.** any of several climbing or creeping vines with shiny leaves, widely grown as decorative coverings for walls. **2.** any of various other climbing plants, such as poison ivy.

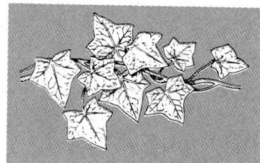

ivy (def. 1)

–ize *suffix* (used to form verbs) **1.** to act upon; make: *civilize, legalize.* **2.** to treat like: *idolize.* **3.** to treat or affect with: *oxidize.* **4.** to form into; become: *crystallize.* **5.** to be concerned with or engaged in: *economize.*

J j

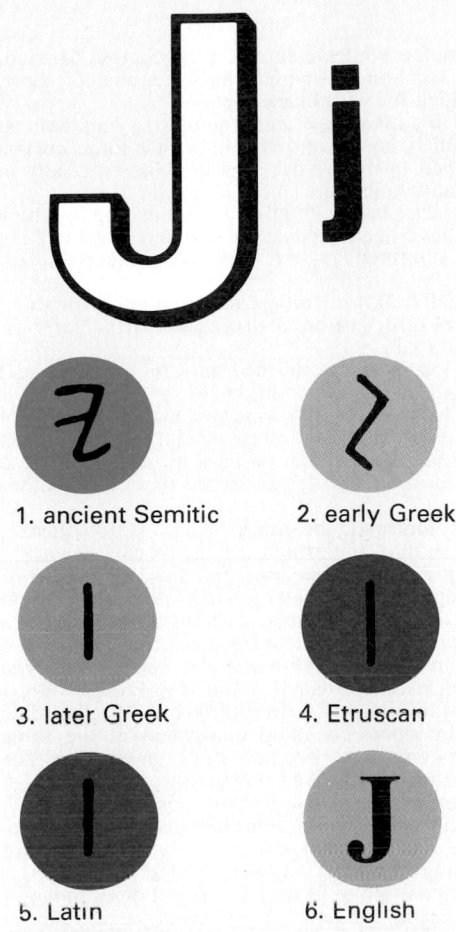

1. ancient Semitic
2. early Greek
3. later Greek
4. Etruscan
5. Latin
6. English

J is the tenth letter of the English alphabet. **J, U,** and **W** are the only letters that we use today that did not come from Latin or from an earlier alphabet. The letter **J** developed as a variation of the letter **I**. The earliest ancestor of **I** and **J** was the ancient Semitic symbol called *yod* (1), meaning "hand." The Greeks (2) simplified *yod* by making it a tall vertical line with a short horizontal stroke at the top and bottom. The Greek form of *yod* was called *iota* and was equivalent to the short vowel *i*. By about the fifth century B.C., the Greeks were writing *iota* as a single vertical line (3). This form of *iota* was adopted in the Etruscan (4) and the Latin (5) alphabets. In the Latin alphabet, the letter **I** stood for both a vowel sound and a consonant sound. In the Middle Ages, it became customary to lengthen the small letter *i* below the line when it appeared as the first letter of a word. This new form was written almost exactly as the letter **J** is written today (6). About 400 years ago, the letter **I** began to be used to represent only the vowel sound, and the letter **J**, used only for the consonant sound.

j, J (jā) *n., pl.* **j's, J's.** **1.** the tenth letter of the English alphabet. **2.** something having the shape of this letter.

jab (jab) *v.,* **jabbed, jab·bing.** —*v.t.* **1.** to poke or thrust at with something pointed: *I accidentally jabbed myself with a pin. I jabbed the sewing needle through the thick material.* **2.** to punch or strike at (something) with short, quick blows: *to jab a punching bag.* —*v.i.* **1.** to poke or thrust at sharply. **2.** to punch or strike with short, quick blows. —*n.* a sharp, quick thrust or blow.

jab·ber (jab'ər) *v.i.* to talk rapidly, indistinctly, or foolishly; chatter. —*n.* rapid, indistinct, or foolish talk; gibberish. —**jab'ber·er,** *n.*

ja·bot (zha bō') *n.* a ruffle or similar decoration of lace or other material, usually worn down the front of a dress or shirt.

jac·a·ran·da (jak'ə ran'də) *n.* any of a group of tropical American trees and shrubs bearing showy blue, violet, or white flowers.

jack (jak) *n.* **1.** any of various devices, usually portable, that are used for raising heavy objects a short distance. **2.** a playing card on which there is a picture of a young man. Also, **knave.** **3.a. jacks.** a game in which the object is to pick up a number of small, six-pointed metal pieces or similar objects while bouncing and catching a small rubber ball with the same hand. Also, **jackstones.** ▲ used with a singular verb. **b.** one of the playing pieces used in this game. Also, **jackstone.** **4.** a male donkey; jackass. **5.** a small flag flown by a ship, usually to show what country it is from. **6.** an electrical device into which a plug may be inserted to make a connection: *a telephone jack.* —*v.t.* **1.** to raise or move with a jack: *to jack up an automobile.* **2.** *Informal.* to increase: *The club jacked up its monthly dues.*

jack·al (jak'əl) *n.* any of various wild dogs of Africa, Asia, and southeastern Europe that have a pointed face, a bushy tail, and usually gray, buff, or reddish black fur. Jackals often feed on remains of another animal's prey.

jack·a·napes (jak'ə nāps') *n., pl.* **jackanapes.** a bold, rude, or conceited person; rascal.

jack·ass (jak'as') *n., pl.* **jack·ass·es.** **1.** a male donkey. **2.** a stupid or foolish person; blockhead.

jack·boot (jak'büt') *also,* **jack boot.** *n.* a sturdy military boot reaching above the knee.

jack·daw (jak'dô') *n.* a crow of Europe, Asia, and northern Africa, having glossy black feathers with a gray band around the throat and a gray underside. Also, **daw.**

jack·et (jak'it) *n.* **1.** a short coat that usually does not extend below the hips. **2.** an outer covering or casing, such as a removable paper cover for a book or a cardboard cover for a phonograph record. —*v.t.* to cover with a jacket; put a jacket on.

Jack Frost, frost or freezing weather thought of as a person.

jack·ham·mer (jak'ham'ər) *n.* a machine that is powered by compressed air, used to drill into rock, pavement, or similar hard materials.

jackhammer

jack–in–the–box (jak′in′thə boks′) *n., pl.* **jack–in–the–box·es**. a toy consisting of a box containing a doll, often in the form of a clown, that springs up when the lid of the box is opened.

jack–in–the–pul·pit (jak′in thə pŭl′pit, jak′in thə pul′pit) *n., pl.* **jack–in–the–pul·pits**. a plant of eastern North America, bearing tiny flowers that are enclosed within a leaf that is striped purple and green or white and is shaped like a hood.

jack·knife (jak′nīf′) *n., pl.* **jack·knives** (jak′nīvz). **1.** a large pocketknife. **2.** a dive in which the diver bends at the waist in midair and, keeping the legs straight, touches the feet with the hands before straightening out and entering the water. —*v.t., v.i.,* **jack·knifed, jack·knif·ing**. to double up or bend like a jackknife.

jack–of–all–trades (jak′əv ôl′trādz′) *n., pl.* **jacks–of–all–trades**. a person who can do many kinds of work.

jack–o′–lan·tern (jak′ə lan′tərn) *n., pl.* **jack–o′–lan·terns**. a pumpkin that has been hollowed out and carved so as to resemble a human face, used as a decoration or lantern at Halloween.

jack·pot (jak′pot′) *n.* the top prize in a game or contest: *That lottery has a $100,000 jackpot.*
·**to hit the jackpot. a.** to win a jackpot. **b.** to have great success or unexpected good fortune.

jack·rab·bit (jak′rab′it) *n.* any of several North American hares having very long ears and long, powerful hind legs.

jack·screw (jak′skrü′) *n.* a jack for raising objects, operated by means of a screw.

jack·stone (jak′stōn′) *n.* **1.** **jack·stones**. the game of jacks. **2.** one of the playing pieces used in this game; jack.

jack·straw (jak′strô′) *n.* **1.** **jack·straws**. a game in which a number of objects, usually thin sticks or light strips of wood or other material, are thrown into a pile and must be picked up one at a time without disturbing the rest of the pile. ▲ used with a singular verb. **2.** one of the sticks or other objects used in this game.

jackrabbit

jade¹ (jād) *n.* **1.** either of the two very hard minerals that are most commonly deep green to greenish white in color and are used for jewelry and carved ornaments. **2.** a deep green to greenish white color. —*adj.* having the color jade. [From the French word *jade*, from the obsolete Spanish phrase *(piedra de la) ijada* meaning ''(stone of the) loins.'' It was believed that jade could cure kidney stones.]

jade² (jād) *n.* an old, worthless, or ill-tempered horse. —*v.,* **jad·ed, jad·ing**. —*v.t.* to make dull, tired, or worn-out: *The large amount of candy I ate jaded my appetite.* —*v.i.* to become dull, tired, or worn-out. [From the Middle English word *jade*, perhaps from Anglo-Norman.]

jad·ed (jā′did) *adj.* **1.** tired or worn-out: *a jaded animal.* **2.** dulled, as from overindulgence; sated: *After watching television for a long time, they became jaded.* —**jad′ed·ly,** *adv.* —**jad′ed·ness,** *n.*

jag (jag) *n.* a sharp, projecting point. —*v.t.,* **jagged, jag·ging. 1.** to cut notches in. **2.** to make uneven or ragged by cutting or tearing.

jag·ged (jag′id) *adj.* having sharp, projecting points or uneven edges: *a piece of jagged rock, a jagged rip in cloth.* —**jag′ged·ly,** *adv.* —**jag′ged·ness,** *n.*

jag·uar (jag′wär) *n.* a large animal of the cat fam-

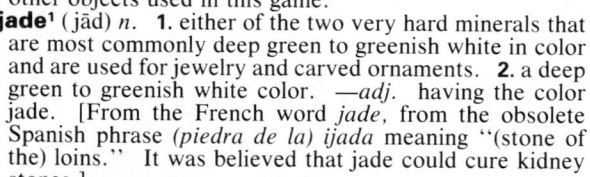
jaguar

ily, native to the southwestern United States, Mexico, and Central and South America, having a coat of short, tawny or golden fur with black spots.

jai a·lai (hī′ lī′, hī′ə lī′) a game similar to handball, in which the ball is hurled and caught with a long, curved basket strapped to the wrist. It is popular especially in Spain and Latin America.

jail (jāl) *also, British,* **gaol** (jāl). *n.* a building in which people who have been accused or convicted of breaking the law are confined. —*v.t.* to put or keep in jail; imprison.

jail·break (jāl′brāk′) *n.* an escape from jail or prison.

jail·er (jā′lər) *also,* **jail·or;** *British,* **gaol·er** (jā′lər). *n.* the keeper of a jail.

ja·lop·y (jə lop′ē) *n., pl.* **ja·lop·ies.** *Informal.* an old automobile that is in bad condition.

jal·ou·sie (jal′ə sē) *n.* **1.** a window made of a series of horizontal overlapping slats, often made of glass, that can be adjusted to regulate the passage of air and light. **2.** a blind or shade of similar design, made of wood or other materials.

jam¹ (jam) *v.,* **jammed, jam·ming.** —*v.t.* **1.** to squeeze, force, or press into or through a tight or close space: *I jammed all my clothes into one suitcase.* **2.** to fill or block up completely: *Shoppers jammed the stores.* **3.** to push, place, or thrust violently: *I jammed on the brakes to stop the car.* **4.** to cause to become stuck or wedged so as to be unworkable: *Rust and dirt had jammed the lock.* **5.** to bruise or crush: *I jammed my hand when I closed the drawer on it.* **6.** to interfere with (electronic signals), as by operating radio equipment at the same frequency. —*v.i.* **1.** to become stuck or wedged: *The key jammed in the lock.* **2.** to become unworkable through the sticking or wedging of some part: *The rifle jammed.* **3.** to force one's way into a confined space: *People jam into the subways during rush hour.* —*n.* **1.** a mass of people or things so tightly crowded together that it is difficult or impossible to move. **2.** the act of jamming or the state of being jammed. **3.** *Informal.* a difficult or troublesome situation; fix: *I was in a real jam for having missed the train.* [Of uncertain origin.]

jam² (jam) *n.* a food made by boiling fruit with sugar until it is thick, used as a spread on bread and other foods. [Probably from *jam¹.*]

jamb (jam) *also,* **jambe.** *n.* a post or surface forming the side of a doorway, window, or other opening.

jam·bo·ree (jam′bə rē′) *n.* **1.** a noisy or festive gathering or celebration. **2.** a large national or international assembly of Boy Scouts or Girl Scouts.

jam session, a gathering of jazz musicians in which they improvise freely.

Jan., January.

jan·gle (jang′gəl) *v.,* **jan·gled, jan·gling.** —*v.i.* to make a harsh or unpleasant sound: *The telephone jangled.* —*v.t.* **1.** to cause to make a harsh or unpleasant sound. **2.** to have an upsetting or irritating effect on: *The constant noise jangled my nerves.* —*n.* a harsh sound.

jan·i·tor (jan′i tər) *n.* a person employed to clean and service a building or establishment, such as an apartment house, school, or office.

Jan·u·ar·y (jan′ū er′ē) *n., pl.* **Jan·u·ar·ies.** the first month of the year, having thirty-one days. [Originally from the Latin *Januarius,* name of the first month of the Roman year, from the Roman god *Janus.*]

Ja·nus (jā′nəs) *n. Roman Mythology.* the god of gates and doors, usually represented as having two faces looking in opposite directions.

Jap. 1. Japan. **2.** Japanese.

ja·pan (jə pan′) *n.* **1.** any of various durable, glossy, black lacquers or varnishes, originally from Japan. **2.** a work varnished and decorated with this. —*adj.* relating to or varnished with japan. —*v.t.,* **ja·panned, ja·panning.** to varnish or lacquer with japan.

Jap·a·nese (jap′ə nēz′, jap′ə nēs′) *n.*, *pl.* **Jap·a·nese.**
1. a person who was born in or is a citizen of Japan.
2. the language of Japan. —*adj.* of or relating to Japan, its people, their language, or their culture.

Words From Other Languages

Many Japanese words in English are words for objects and ideas that Japanese immigrants brought with them or that American travelers to Japan adopted and borrowed.

bonsai	an artificially dwarfed tree
haiku	a type of seventeen-syllable poem
hara-kiri	a form of Japanese ritual suicide
honcho	a strong boss or leader
judo	a form of unarmed self-defense that uses leverage to defeat an opponent
karate	a form of unarmed self-defense that uses hands and legs as weapons
kimono	a loose robe with a sash
origami	the art of folding paper into shapes
sushi	a cold food of flavored rice with raw fish or vegetables
tofu	a cheese-like food made of soybeans
zori	a sandal with a single thong

Japanese beetle, a small, destructive beetle introduced into the United States from Japan. It has red wings and a green-and-brown oval body, and feeds on various plants.
Japanese lantern, another term for Chinese lantern.
jar¹ (jär) *n.* **1.** a cylindrical container that usually has a wide mouth, and is made of glass or earthenware. **2.** the amount contained in a jar; contents of a jar: *to use up a whole jar of jam.* [From the French word *jarre* meaning this container, going back to the Arabic word *jarrah* "earthen water vessel."]
jar² (jär) *v.*, **jarred, jar·ring.** —*v.t.* **1.** to cause to move suddenly by impact or shock; shake; vibrate: *The explosion jarred the building.* **2.** to have a harsh, disturbing, or unpleasant effect on: *The sudden clatter jarred our nerves.* —*v.i.* **1.** to have an irritating or upsetting effect: *Your loud laugh jars on my nerves.* **2.** to clash; conflict: *This verse . . . jars with the words which precede and follow* (Matthew Arnold). **3.** to make a harsh or discordant sound. —*n.* **1.** a shake or sudden movement; shock; jolt. **2.** a sudden, disturbing effect on the mind or senses. **3.** a harsh or discordant sound or combination of sounds. [Of uncertain origin.]
jar·gon (jär′gən) *n.* **1.** the technical or specialized language of a particular profession or other group. **2.** unclear or meaningless speech or writing; gibberish.
jas·mine (jaz′min) *n.* **1.** a fragrant bell-shaped flower growing in yellow, white, or pink clusters. **2.** a shrub bearing clusters of these flowers, widely grown throughout the world. Also, **jessamine.**
Ja·son (jā′sən) *n.* *Greek Legend.* the hero who led the Argonauts in search of the Golden Fleece.
jas·per (jas′pər) *n.* an opaque quartz that is usually red, brown, or yellow.
jaun·dice (jôn′dis) *n.* **1.** a yellow discoloration of the skin, the whites of the eyes, and the mucous membranes, caused by an excess of bile pigment in the blood. It is often a sign of liver malfunction. **2.** a state of mind or feeling, as envy, resentment, or some other negative emotion, that affects the point of view or distorts the judgment. —*v.t.*, **jaun·diced, jaun·dic·ing.** to affect the point of view or distort the judgment of; prejudice: *Fear of animals jaundiced their view of the forest.*

jaun·diced (jôn′dist) *adj.* **1.** affected with jaundice. **2.** affected by envy, jealousy, bitterness, or similar feeling; prejudiced.
jaunt (jônt) *n.* a short trip, especially one taken for pleasure. —*v.i.* to take such a trip.
jaun·ty (jôn′tē) *adj.*, **jaun·ti·er, jaun·ti·est. 1.** lively, carefree, or self-confident in air or manner; sprightly: *a jaunty tune.* **2.** smart; stylish: *a jaunty cap and jacket.* —**jaun′ti·ly**, *adv.* —**jaun′ti·ness**, *n.*
Ja·va (jä′və, jav′ə) *n.* **1.** the coffee grown on Java and other nearby islands. **2.** *also,* **java.** *Informal.* any coffee.
Java man, an extinct primitive human that resembled an ape but was able to walk erect. Its fossil remains, dating from the early Ice Age, were found in central Java. Also, **Pithecanthropus.**
Jav·a·nese (jav′ə nēz′, jav′ə nēs′) *n.*, *pl.* **Jav·a·nese. 1.** a person who was born in or is a citizen of Java. **2.** the language spoken in Java. —*adj.* of or relating to Java, its people, their language, or their culture.
jave·lin (jav′lin) *n.* **1.** a light spear, used chiefly as a weapon. **2.** a lightweight metal shaft that resembles a spear. It is thrown for distance in athletic contests. **3.** the contest in which it is thrown.
jaw (jô) *n.* **1.** either of the two bony structures forming the framework of the mouth and holding the teeth, especially the lower of these structures. **2.** *also,* **jaws.** the part of the face covering these structures; the mouth and its related parts. **3.** either of a pair of parts, as of a tool, that can be closed to grasp or hold something: *the jaws of a vise.* —*v.i.* *Slang.* to talk; chatter. —**jaw′like′**, *adj.*
jaw·bone (jô′bōn′) *n.* one of the bones of the jaw, especially the mandible.
jaw·break·er (jô′brā′kər) *n.* **1.** very hard candy or chewing gum. **2.** *Informal.* a word that is difficult to pronounce.
jay (jā) *n.* any of various noisy birds related to crows and magpies. Most jays have a crest and brightly colored feathers.
jay·walk (jā′wôk′) *v.i.* to cross a street without paying attention to traffic laws or signals. —**jay′walk′er**, *n.*
jazz (jaz) *n.* **1.** music of various styles originated by American blacks late in the nineteenth century. Jazz is characterized by improvisation and strong, swinging rhythm. **2.** *Slang.* exaggerated, insincere, or idle talk; nonsense. —*v.t.* to play or arrange (music) as jazz.
·**to jazz up,** to make more lively or exciting: *We jazzed up the room with brightly colored posters.*
jeal·ous (jel′əs) *adj.* **1.** fearful or suspicious of losing to someone else what one wishes to gain or keep, especially the love or affection of another person: *I was jealous when my friend went on vacation with someone I didn't know.* **2.** envious or resentful of a person or of a person's achievements or advantages: *jealous of a friend's success.* **3.** careful in guarding or keeping something: *The people were jealous of their precious freedoms.* —**jeal′ous·ly**, *adv.* —**jeal′ous·ness**, *n.*
jeal·ous·y (jel′ə sē) *n.*, *pl.* **jeal·ous·ies.** the state or quality of being jealous; jealous feeling or attitude.
jean (jēn) *n.* **1.** a strong cotton fabric, used chiefly for sportswear and work clothes. **2.** **jeans.** trousers or overalls made of this fabric or denim; dungarees.
jeep (jēp) *n.* a small, rugged motor vehicle for general use, developed originally for the U.S. armed forces.

J

at; āpe; fär; câre; end; mē; it; īce; pîerce; hot; ōld;
sông, fôrk; oil; out; up; ūse; rüle; pull; tûrn; chin;
sing; shop; thin; <u>th</u>is; hw in white; zh in treasure.
The symbol ə stands for the unstressed vowel sound
heard in about, taken, pencil, lemon, and circus.

jeer (jîr) *v.i.* to speak or shout in a scornful or mocking manner; scoff: *They jeered at me for boasting.* —*v.t.* to treat or speak to (someone) with scorn or mockery; taunt: *The fans jeered the player for dropping the ball.* —*n.* a scornful or mocking remark; taunt.

Jef·fer·so·ni·an (jef'ər sō'nē ən) *adj.* of or relating to Thomas Jefferson or his political principles.

Je·ho·vah (ji hō'və) *n.* in the Old Testament, God.

Jehovah's Witnesses, a Christian religious sect, founded in the United States in the late nineteenth century.

je·june (ji jün') *adj.* lacking interest, significance, or value; dull or empty: *a jejune speech.*

je·ju·num (ji jü'nəm) *n., pl.* **je·ju·na** (ji jü'nə). the middle section of the small intestine, extending from the duodenum to the ileum.

jell (jel) *v.i.* **1.** to change from a liquid to a solid resembling jelly. **2.** to assume definite form; become clear: *My ideas began to jell.*

jel·ly (jel'ē) *n., pl.* **jel·lies. 1.** any food preparation consisting mainly of gelatin or pectin and having a smooth, firm, elastic consistency, especially such a preparation made of boiled fruit juice and sugar: *grape jelly.* **2.** anything having the consistency of or resembling jelly. —*v.t.,* **jel·lied, jel·ly·ing. 1.** to make into jelly. **2.** to spread or prepare with jelly. —**jel'ly·like'**, *adj.*

jel·ly·bean (jel'ē bēn') *n.* a small, bean-shaped candy having a hard outer coating and a jellylike center.

jel·ly·fish (jel'ē fish') *n., pl.* **jel·ly·fish** or **jel·ly·fish·es.** any of a group of animals that are found chiefly in salt water and are shaped like an umbrella. A jellyfish has a soft, jellylike body with long, thin tentacles that have stinging cells.

jen·net (jen'it) *n.* a small Spanish horse.

jen·ny (jen'ē) *n., pl.* **jen·nies. 1.** see **spinning jenny. 2.** the female of certain animals, especially a donkey.

jeop·ard·ize (jep'ər dīz') *v.t.,* **jeop·ard·ized, jeop·ard·iz·ing.** to expose to loss or injury; endanger; imperil: *The fire jeopardized the business.*

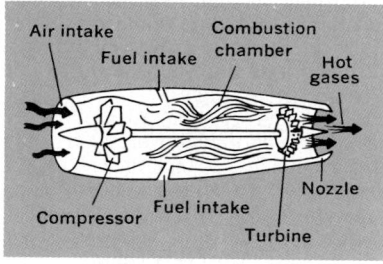

jellyfish

jeop·ard·y (jep'ər dē) *n.* the danger of loss, injury, or death; peril: *Firefighters sometimes put their lives in jeopardy.* [From the Anglo-Norman word *juparti* meaning "danger," from the Old French phrase *jeu parti* "divided game," the name of a game in which the chances are even.]

jer·bo·a (jər bō'ə) *n.* a small rodent native to desert regions of Asia and Africa. A jerboa has very long hind legs, a long tail with a tuft on the end, and a silky, buff-colored coat.

Jer·e·mi·ah (jer'ə mī'ə) *n.* a book of prophecies in the Old Testament, thought to have been written by the Hebrew prophet Jeremiah.

jerk¹ (jûrk) *n.* **1.** a sudden, sharp pull, twist, or push. **2.** a sudden contraction of a muscle, caused by reflex action. **3.** *Informal.* a stupid or foolish person. —*v.t.* to move or throw (something) with a sudden, sharp motion; give a sudden, sharp pull, twist, or push to: *I jerked my hand away from the hot stove.* —*v.i.* to move with a sudden, sharp motion or series of such motions: *The car jerked forward.* [Probably a form of the English dialect word *yerk* meaning "to pull tight."]

jerk² (jûrk) *v.t.* to cure (meat) by cutting it into strips and drying it, usually in the sun. [From the Spanish word *charqui* meaning "cured meat, jerky²," from a South American Indian language spoken in the Andes.]

jer·kin (jûr'kin) *n.* a short, tight jacket or waistcoat, usually sleeveless and often made of leather. It was worn chiefly in the sixteenth and seventeenth centuries.

jerk·y¹ (jûr'kē) *adj.,* **jerk·i·er, jerk·i·est. 1.** characterized by abrupt movements; moving with sudden starts and stops: *a jerky subway ride.* **2.** *Informal.* stupid or foolish. [*Jerk¹* + *-y¹*.] —**jerk'i·ly,** *adv.* —**jerk'i·ness,** *n.*

jerk·y² (jûr'kē) *n.* meat, especially beef, that has been cured and dried. [From *jerk².*]

jer·ry-built (jer'ē bilt') *adj.* built or put together carelessly, hastily, or with poor materials: *a jerry-built cottage.*

Jer·sey (jûr'zē) *n., pl.* **Jer·seys.** one of a breed of usually light brown dairy cattle originally developed on the island of Jersey.

jer·sey (jûr'zē) *n., pl.* **jer·seys. 1.** a machine-knitted fabric made of wool, cotton, silk, or synthetic fibers, used for clothing. **2.** a knitted sweater or shirt, usually a pullover, made of this or a similar fabric. [From the island of *Jersey* in the English Channel, where this fabric was first made.]

jes·sa·mine (jes'ə min) another spelling of **jasmine.**

jest (jest) *n.* **1.** something said or done to cause laughter; prank; joke. **2.** a playful mood or manner; playfulness; fun. **3.** an object of laughter or mockery. —*v.i.* to speak or act in a playful manner.

jest·er (jes'tər) *n.* a person who jests, especially a clown formerly kept in royal courts and noble households.

Jes·u·it (jezh'ü it, jez'ü it, jez'ū it) *n.* a member of the Society of Jesus, a Roman Catholic religious order for men.

jet¹ (jet) *n.* **1.** a stream of liquid, gas, or vapor, forcefully or suddenly shot forth from a nozzle, spout, or narrow opening. **2.** something shot forth in such a stream. **3.** the nozzle or spout from which such a stream comes: *the gas jets of a stove.* **4.** see **jet plane. 5.** see **jet engine.** —*v.,* **jet·ted, jet·ting.** —*v.i.* **1.** to be shot forth in a stream. **2.** to travel by jet plane. —*v.t.* **1.** to shoot (something) forth in a stream. **2.** to transport by jet plane. [From the Old French word *jeter* meaning "to throw," from the Latin word *jactare* "to throw."]

jet² (jet) *n.* **1.** a dense, black coal that can be highly polished, formerly used to make jewelry. **2.** any of several other materials, such as black quartz or glass, imitating this, used to make jewelry. **3.** a deep black color. —*adj.* **1.** made of or resembling jet. **2.** jet-black. [From the Old French word *jaiet* meaning this mineral, going back to the Greek word *gagatēs* "jet²," from *Gagas,* a town in Asia Minor where it is found.]

jet-black (jet'blak') *adj.* as black as jet; deep black.

je·té (zhə tā') *n.* in ballet, a leap in which the dancer pushes off the floor with one foot and lands on the other.

jet engine 1. an engine that produces power by burning a mixture of fuel and oxygen that is ejected out of the rear as hot exhaust gases. **2.** any engine that produces power by ejecting a stream of fluid.

Air intake — Combustion chamber — Fuel intake — Hot gases — Compressor — Fuel intake — Turbine — Nozzle

gas turbine **jet engine**

jet lag, disruption of a person's sleeping and eating habits, often accompanied by fatigue, experienced after traveling from one time zone to another.

jet plane, an airplane driven by jet propulsion.

jet-pro·pelled (jet'prə peld') *adj.* driven by jet propulsion: *a jet-propelled vehicle.*

jet propulsion 1. propulsion by means of a jet of fluid, such as hot gas. When the jet of fluid is ejected in one direction, it causes the body or vehicle from which it was ejected to move in the opposite direction. **2.** propulsion by means of one or more jet engines.

jet·sam (jet'səm) *n.* **1.** cargo or equipment thrown overboard in order to lighten a ship in distress. **2.** such

discarded cargo or equipment found washed ashore.
3. discarded, worthless, or miscellaneous things.

jet set, a social set composed of wealthy people who travel frequently to fashionable places around the world.

jet stream 1. a high-speed air current, usually found between 7 and 9 miles (11–14 kilometers) above the earth's surface. It moves generally west to east at speeds reaching over 200 miles per hour (320 kilometers per hour). **2.** a stream of gas or other fluid ejected from a jet engine.

jet·ti·son (jet′ə sən) *v.t.* **1.** to throw (cargo or equipment) overboard or off, especially in order to lighten a ship or aircraft in distress. **2.** to get rid of or discard (something unwanted, useless, or burdensome).

jet·ty (jet′ē) *n., pl.* **jet·ties. 1.** a structure of timber, concrete, steel, or a combination of these materials, built out into a body of water in order to affect the current or protect a harbor or coast. **2.** a wharf; pier.

Jew (jü) *n.* **1.** a member of a people descended from the group of Semitic tribes who lived in and around ancient Palestine, and among whom the beliefs and laws of Judaism were developed and followed. **2.** a person whose religion is Judaism.

jew·el (jü′əl) *n.* **1.** a precious stone; gem. **2.** any article of personal adornment, such as a ring, bracelet, or brooch, usually made of cut and polished gems in a setting of precious metal. **3.** a person or thing of great value or excellence. **4.** a gem or substitute for a gem used as a bearing in a watch.

jew·el·er (jü′ə lər) *also, British,* **jew·el·ler.** *n.* a person who makes, repairs, or deals in jewelry.

jew·el·ry (jü′əl rē) *also, British,* **jew·el·ler·y.** *n.* precious stones or other articles, as of gold, silver, or glass, for personal ornamentation; jewels as a group.

Jew·ish (jü′ish) *adj.* of, relating to, or characteristic of Jews or their culture.

Jew·ry (jü′rē) *n.* Jews as a group; the Jewish people.

Jew's harp, a small musical instrument that consists of a lyre-shaped metal frame and a flexible metal strip. It is held between the teeth when played and produces a twanging tone when the metal strip is plucked.

Jez·e·bel (jez′ə bel′) *also,* **jezebel.** *n.* a shameless or wicked woman.

jib (jib) *n.* a triangular sail set on a stay in front of the mast or foremast, usually smaller than the mainsail.

jibe¹ (jīb) *v.i.,* **jibed, jib·ing.** to shift a fore-and-aft sail or its boom from one side of a boat or ship to the other when sailing before the wind. —*v.t.* **1.** to shift (a sail or boom) in this manner. **2.** to change direction of (a boat or ship) so that a sail or boom shifts in this manner. [From the Dutch word *gijben* with the same meaning.]

jibe² (jīb) *n., v.,* **jibed, jib·ing.** another spelling of **gibe.**

jibe³ (jīb) *v.i.,* **jibed, jib·ing.** *Informal.* to be in harmony or accord; agree: *The stories told by the different witnesses simply don't jibe.* [Of uncertain origin.]

jif·fy (jif′ē) *n., pl.* **jif·fies.** *Informal.* a very short time; moment; instant.

jig (jig) *n.* **1.** a fast, lively dance, usually in triple time. **2.** the music for this dance. **3.** a device used for guiding a tool, such as a drill, or for holding in place material to be worked on with such a tool. **4.** a fishing lure designed to bob in the water, to attract fish. —*v.i.,* **jigged, jig·ging. 1.** to dance or play a jig. **2.** to move with a rapid jerking or bobbing motion.

jig·ger (jig′ər) *n.* **1.** small glass or cup used to measure liquor, holding about an ounce and a half. **2.** the amount contained in a jigger.

jib

jig·gle (jig′əl) *v.,* **jig·gled, jig·gling.** —*v.t.* to move (something) up and down or back and forth with quick, slight jerking motions. —*v.i.* to move up and down or back and forth with quick, slight jerking motions. —*n.* a jiggling motion.

jig·saw (jig′sô) *n.* a saw with a narrow blade set in a frame, used to cut curved or irregular lines.

jigsaw puzzle, a puzzle made up of a set of irregularly shaped cardboard or wooden pieces that can be fitted together to form a picture.

jilt (jilt) *v.t.* to cast off or desert (a lover or sweetheart). —**jilt′er,** *n.*

Jim Crow *also,* **jim crow.** *Informal.* segregation of or discrimination against blacks. [From the song *Jump, Jim Crow,* commonly performed in minstrel shows.]

jim·my (jim′ē) *n., pl.* **jim·mies.** a short crowbar used especially by burglars. —*v.t.,* **jim·mied, jim·my·ing.** to force or pry open with a jimmy.

jim·son·weed (jim′sən wēd′) *n.* a poisonous plant related to the nightshade, found in the tropics and many parts of North America. It has large, oval leaves and white or purple trumpet-shaped flowers.

jin·gle (jing′gəl) *v.,* **jin·gled, jin·gling.** —*v.i.* to make a light, metallic tinkling or ringing sound: *The coins jingled in my pocket.* —*v.t.* to cause to make a tinkling or ringing sound: *to jingle keys.* —*n.* **1.** a light, metallic tinkling or ringing sound: *the jingle of spurs.* **2.** a catchy or repeated series of words or sounds, especially a short, catchy song or verse: *musical jingles used in advertising.*

jin·go (jing′gō) *n., pl.* **jin·goes.** a person who supports or favors an aggressive, warlike foreign policy.

jin·go·ism (jing′gō iz′əm) *n.* extreme patriotism or chauvinism, tending to favor or support an aggressive foreign policy.

jin·ni (ji nē′, jin′ē) *n., pl.* **jinn.** in Arab folklore and literature, a spirit having magic powers and capable of taking on the form of a human or animal. Also, **genie.**

jin·rick·sha (jin rik′shô) *also,* **jin·rik·i·sha.** *n.* another word for **ricksha.** [From the Japanese word *jinrikisha* meaning "a vehicle drawn by a person's strength."]

jinx (jingks) *Informal. n., pl.* **jinx·es. 1.** a person or thing that is believed to bring bad luck; hex. **2.** a spell designed to cause bad luck; hex: *to put a jinx on someone.* —*v.t.* to bring or try to bring bad luck to; hex.

jit·ney (jit′nē) *n., pl.* **jit·neys.** *Informal.* a car or small bus that carries passengers for a fare, usually over a short regular route.

jit·ter (jit′ər) *Informal. v.i.* to be nervous or uneasy; fidget. —*n.* **jitters.** a fit of nervousness; extreme anxiety. —**jit′ter·y,** *adj.*

jit·ter·bug (jit′ər bug′) *Informal. n.* **1.** a lively, fast dance, popular especially during the 1940s. **2.** a person who does this dance. —*v.i.,* **jit·ter·bugged, jit·ter·bug·ging.** to dance the jitterbug.

jiu·jit·su (jü jit′sü) *n.* another spelling of **jujitsu.**

jive (jīv) *Slang. n.* **1.** jazz music, especially of the late 1930s and 1940s. **2.** the special terms or way of speaking used by jazz musicians and fans. **3.** deceptive, glib, or meaningless talk.

job (job) *n.* **1.** a position of work; employment: *I took a job in a store.* **2.** something that has to be done; task, duty, or responsibility: *It's your job to feed the dog.* **3.** a specific activity or piece of work: *The repair job will cost $300.*

at; āpe; fär; câre; end; mē; it; īce; pierce; hot; ōld; sông, fôrk; oil; out; up; ūse; rüle; pùll; tûrn; chin; sing; shop; thin; **this;** hw in white; zh in treasure. The symbol ə stands for the unstressed vowel sound heard in about, taken, pencil, lemon, and circus.

Job (jōb) *n.* the book of the Old Testament that tells the story of Job, a righteous man who patiently accepted the trials that God inflicted upon him to test his faith.

job action, any action, such as refusal to work, taken by a group of workers to press a demand or as a protest, as against unsatisfactory working conditions or pay.

job·ber (job'ər) *n.* a person who buys goods, as from a manufacturer, and sells them to retailers.

job·less (job'lis) *adj.* without a job; unemployed.

jock (jok) *n. Slang.* an athlete, especially an amateur male athlete.

jock·ey (jok'ē) *n., pl.* **jock·eys.** a person who rides horses in races, especially as a profession. —*v.,* **jockeyed, jock·ey·ing.** —*v.i.* **1.** to maneuver, especially in order to gain an advantage: *The sailboats jockeyed for position.* **2.** to ride a horse in a race. —*v.t.* **1.** to maneuver (someone or something): *to jockey a car into a parking space.* **2.** to ride (a horse) in a race.

jockeys racing thoroughbreds

jock·ey shorts, short, close-fitting underpants; briefs. Trademark: **Jockey.**

jock·strap (jok'strap') *n.* an elastic support for the male genitals, worn especially for athletics. Also, **athletic supporter.**

jo·cose (jō kōs') *adj.* given to or characterized by joking and jesting; merry; playful. —**jo·cose'ly,** *adv.* —**jo·cose'ness,** *n.*

jo·cos·i·ty (jō kos'i tē) *n., pl.* **jo·cos·i·ties. 1.** the state or quality of being jocose. **2.** a jocose act or remark; joke or jest.

joc·u·lar (jok'yə lər) *adj.* **1.** given to or characterized by joking and jesting; merry; playful. **2.** of the nature of or meant as a joke; humorous: *a jocular remark.* —**joc'u·lar·ly,** *adv.*

joc·u·lar·i·ty (jok'yə lar'i tē) *n., pl.* **joc·u·lar·i·ties. 1.** the state or quality of being jocular; merriment. **2.** a jocular act or remark; joke or jest.

joc·und (jok'ənd) *adj.* cheerful; merry; carefree.

jo·cun·di·ty (jō kun'di tē) *n., pl.* **jo·cun·di·ties. 1.** the state or quality of being jocund; cheerfulness. **2.** a jocund act or remark.

jodh·purs (jod'pərz) *pl. n.* trousers that are loose above the knee and close-fitting from knee to ankle, used for horseback riding.

Jo·el (jō'əl) *n.* a book of the Old Testament thought to have been written by the Hebrew prophet Joel.

jog (jog) *v.,* **jogged, jog·ging.** —*v.i.* to run or move at a slow, steady pace or trot: *The runners jogged lazily around the track.* —*v.t.* **1.** to cause to move by shaking or jerking; jolt. **2.** to give a slight shake or push to; nudge. **3.** to stir or stimulate: *to jog the memory.* —*n.* **1.** a shake, push, or nudge. **2.** a slow, steady, jolting pace or motion. —**jog'ger,** *n.*

jog·gle (jog'əl) *v.t., v.i.,* **jog·gled, jog·gling.** to shake slightly. —*n.* the act of joggling.

John (jon) *n.* the fourth book of the New Testament, thought to have been written by the Apostle John.

John Bull, a personification of England or the English.

John Doe 1. an unknown or fictitious person. ▲ used especially in legal documents to designate a fictitious person or a person whose real name is not known. **2.** the average man.

John Han·cock (han'kok) *Informal.* a person's signature or autograph. [From the president of the Continental Congress, *John Hancock* (1737–1793). His was the first and largest signature on the Declaration of Independence.]

john·ny·cake (jon'ē kāk') *n.* a flat, crisp bread made of cornmeal, water or milk, flour, and, sometimes, eggs.

join (join) *v.t.* **1.** to bring, put, or fasten together so as to become one: *I joined the ends of the rope in a knot. We joined hands and formed a circle.* **2.** to come into contact or union with: *This road joins the main highway.* **3.** to become a member or part of: *to join the army.* **4.** to come or enter into the company of: *Join us at our table for dinner.* —*v.i.* **1.** to take part with others; participate: *We joined in the celebration.* **2.** to become united or associated: *We joined to fight the epidemic.* **3.** to come into or be in contact or union: *At what point do the rivers join?* —*n.* a place or line of joining; seam.

join·er (joi'nər) *n.* **1.** *Informal.* a person who joins many clubs, committees, or other organized activities. **2.** a craftsperson or carpenter who makes woodwork and furniture. **3.** any person or thing that joins.

join·er·y (joi'nə rē) *n.* **1.** the skill of a joiner. **2.** woodwork, furniture, or other articles made by a joiner.

joint (joint) *n.* **1.** the place or part where two or more bones meet or join, usually in a way that allows the bones to move. **2.** any place or part at or by which two or more things are joined or fitted together. **3.** a part or section between such places or structures. **4.** one of the portions into which meat is cut by a butcher, especially one containing the bone. **5.** *Botany.* the point on a stem from which a leaf or branch grows. **6.** *Slang.* a cheap or disreputable bar, restaurant, or other gathering place. —*adj.* **1.** belonging to or used by two or more; held together or shared: *a joint bank account.* **2.** performed or produced by two or more working or acting together: *joint efforts, a joint attack.* **3.** sharing or acting with another or others: *joint owners.* **4.** of or involving both houses or branches of a legislature: *a joint session of Congress.* —*v.t.* **1.** to connect with a joint or joints. **2.** to divide or cut at the joints, as meat.

Joint Chiefs of Staff, the principal military advisers to the president of the United States. The group consists of a chairperson and the commanding officers of the army, the air force, the navy, and the marine corps.

joint custody, custody of a child shared equally by parents after a divorce or during a separation.

joint·ed (join'tid) *adj.* having a joint or joints.

joint·ly (joint'lē) *adv.* in conjunction; together: *The island is administered jointly by the two countries.*

joint–stock company, a company owned jointly by stockholders, each of whom has purchased transferable shares of the company. In a joint-stock company, it is the individual stockholders who are responsible for the debts of the company.

joist (joist) *n.* one of a series of parallel beams to which the boards of a floor or the laths of a ceiling are fastened.

joists

jo·jo·ba (hō hō'bə) *n.* a shrub native to southwestern North America, bearing a seed that contains an oil used in cosmetics.

joke (jōk) *n.* **1.** a story, usually ending with a funny line, intended to cause laughter or amusement. **2.** anything said or done to cause laughter or amusement, such as a funny remark or a prank: *They hid the keys as a joke.* **3.** a person or thing causing amusement or ridicule. —*v.i.,* **joked, jok·ing.** to tell or make jokes. —**jok′ing·ly,** *adv.*

jok·er (jō′kər) *n.* **1.** a person who jokes or is given to joking. **2.** either of two extra playing cards provided with a standard deck, often having a picture of a jester on it. Jokers are used in certain card games as wild cards or as trumps.

joke·ster (jōk′stər) *n.* a person who makes jokes or plays pranks.

jol·li·ty (jol′i tē) *n.* the state or quality of being jolly.

jol·ly (jol′ē) *adj.,* **jol·li·er, jol·li·est. 1.** full of fun, good humor, and high spirits: *a jolly old soul.* **2.** characterized by or causing mirth, gaiety, or good cheer: *a jolly song, jolly laughter.* —*v.t.,* **jol·lied, jol·ly·ing.** *Informal.* to amuse, humor, or flatter so as to put or keep in a good mood. —*adv. British. Informal.* extremely; very: *a jolly good book.* —**jol′li·ness,** *n.*

Jol·ly Rog·er (jol′ē roj′ər) a black flag with a white skull and crossbones on it, formerly flown by pirates.

jolt (jōlt) *v.t.* to cause to move with a rough, jerky motion; jar or shake up with a sudden bump or blow: *The impact jolted us out of our seats.* —*v.i.* to move with sudden bumpy jerks: *The carriage jolted along the dirt road.* —*n.* **1.** a rough, jerky motion: *The wagon stopped with a jolt.* **2.** an abrupt surprise or shock: *The news gave me a jolt.*

Jo·nah (jō′nə) *n.* the book of the Old Testament containing the story and prophecies of Jonah.

jon·quil (jong′kwəl) *n.* **1.** a fragrant yellow flower of a plant resembling the daffodil, having six petal-like segments surrounding a shallow, cup-shaped structure. **2.** the slender plant bearing this flower.

jonquil

josh (josh) *Informal. v.t.* to make fun of in a nice way; tease playfully. —*v.i.* to indulge in playful teasing.

Josh·u·a (josh′ü ə) *n.* the book of the Old Testament containing the history of the Israelites from the death of Moses to the settlement in Canaan.

jos·tle (jos′əl) *also,* **jus·tle.** *v.t.,* **jostled, jos·tling.** to bump, push, or shove (someone or something) roughly, as with the elbows: *They jostled me out of the way.* —*v.i.* to bump, push, or shove roughly. —*n.* a bump, push, or shove; a jostling. —**jos′tler,** *n.*

jot (jot) *n.* the least or smallest bit: *Your bragging doesn't impress me a jot.* —*v.t.,* **jot·ted, jot·ting.** to make a brief and hasty note of: *The witness jotted down the license number of the car.*

joule (jül, joul) *n. Physics.* a unit of work or energy in the meter-kilogram-second system of units, equal to the work done by a force of 1 newton acting through a distance of 1 meter. One joule is equivalent to 10^7 ergs. [From the English physicist James P. *Joule* (1818–1889).]

jounce (jouns) *v.t., v.i.,* **jounced, jounc·ing.** to move or shake up and down roughly: *The old wagon jounced along the road.* —*n.* a sudden, rough bump; bounce; jolt.

jour·nal (jûr′nəl) *n.* **1.** a record or account, especially one written every day, of events, experiences, or thoughts; diary. **2.** an official record, usually one written every day, of proceedings or transactions, such as the register of a legislative body. **3.** a magazine or periodical, especially one dealing with matters of current interest in a particular area: *The medical journal published the doctor's report.* **4.** a newspaper, especially one published every day. **5.** the part of a shaft or axle turning within a bearing.

jour·nal·ese (jûr′nə lēz′, jûr′nə lēs′) *n.* a clever, breezy style of writing that uses informal or colorful language, slang, fad expressions, and clichés, often superficial in its treatment of a topic: *The articles in this magazine are written in journalese.*

jour·nal·ism (jûr′nə liz′əm) *n.* the gathering and presentation of news, information, and opinions, especially in newspapers and magazines or over television and radio.

jour·nal·ist (jûr′nə list) *n.* a person whose occupation is journalism, especially a reporter or editor for a journal or for radio or television.

jour·nal·is·tic (jûr′nə lis′tik) *adj.* of, relating to, or characteristic of journalism or journalists.

jour·ney (jûr′nē) *n., pl.* **jour·neys. 1.** a trip, especially one over a long distance or taking a long time. **2.** the distance that is traveled, or that can be traveled, in a specified time: *four days' journey from here.* —*v.i.,* **jour·neyed, jour·ney·ing.** to make a trip; travel: *to journey through Europe.*

jour·ney·man (jûr′nē mən) *n., pl.* **jour·ney·men** (jûr′nē mən) **1.** a person who has completed an apprenticeship in a trade, craft, or skill, and works for another. **2.** an experienced and skilled worker.

joust (joust) *also,* **just.** *n.* a formal combat, often part of a tournament, between two knights on horseback or other persons armed with lances and other weapons. —*v.i.* to take part in a joust or jousts. —**joust′er,** *n.*

Jove (jōv) *n.* see **Jupiter** (def. 1).

jo·vi·al (jō′vē əl) *adj.* characterized by hearty good humor; merry; jolly. —**jo′vi·al·ly,** *adv.*

jo·vi·al·i·ty (jō′vē al′i tē) *n.* the state or quality of being jovial; jollity; merriment.

Jo·vi·an (jō′vē ən) *adj.* of, relating to, or like Jove.

jowl¹ (joul) *n.* **1.** flabby, sagging flesh hanging from or under the lower jaw. **2.** any similar fleshy part, such as the dewlap of a moose or the wattle of a fowl. [From the Old English word *ceole* meaning "throat."]

jowl² (joul) *n.* **1.** the jawbone or jaw, especially the lower jaw. **2.** the cheek. [From the Old English word *ceafl* meaning "jaw."]

joy (joi) *n.* **1.** a strong feeling of happiness or delight. **2.** someone or something that is the source or cause of such feeling: *The garden is a joy to the family.*

joy·ful (joi′fəl) *adj.* feeling, showing, or causing joy: *joyful children, a joyful look in one's eyes, a joyful sight.* —**joy′ful·ly,** *adv.* —**joy′ful·ness,** *n.*

joy·less (joi′lis) *adj.* feeling, showing, or causing no joy; sad: *a joyless smile, a joyless event.* —**joy′less·ly,** *adv.* —**joy′less·ness,** *n.*

joy·ous (joi′əs) *adj.* feeling, showing, or causing joy; marked by rejoicing: *Their marriage was a joyous occasion.* —**joy′ous·ly,** *adv.* —**joy′ous·ness,** *n.*

joy·ride (joi′rīd′) *n. Informal.* an automobile ride taken for fun, especially a reckless one or one in a stolen car. —*v.i.,* **joy·rode, joy·rid·den, joy·rid·ing.** to take a joyride.

joy·stick (joi′stik′) *n.* **1.** the flight control lever of an aircraft or other vehicle. **2.** a lever, usually connected to a computer or video game player, that can be moved in any direction to control the movement of a cursor in some programs or the movement of a character or playing piece in some games.

jr., junior.

ju·bi·lant (jü′bə lənt) *adj.* joyfully happy or triumphant;

J

at; āpe; fär; câre; end; mē; it; īce; pîerce; hot; ōld; sông, fôrk; oil; out; up; ūse; rüle; pull; tûrn; chin; sing; shop; thin; this; hw in white; zh in treasure. The symbol ə stands for the unstressed vowel sound heard in about, taken, pencil, lemon, and circus.

exultant: *After the game the victors were jubilant.*
—**ju'bi·lant·ly**, *adv.*

ju·bi·la·tion (jü'bə lā'shən) *n.* **1.** a feeling of joyful happiness or triumph. **2.** the act of rejoicing.

ju·bi·lee (jü'bə lē', jü'bə lē') *n.* **1.** a special anniversary, especially a twenty-fifth or fiftieth anniversary. **2.** a year, season, or occasion of joyful celebration and rejoicing.

Ju·da·ic (jü dā'ik) *adj.* of or relating to Jews or Judaism.

Ju·da·ism (jü'dē iz'əm, jü'dā iz'əm, jü'də iz'əm) *n.* the religion of the Jews, based chiefly on a belief in one God and the teachings of the Old Testament and the Talmud.

Ju·das (jü'dəs) also, **judas**. *n.* any betrayer or traitor. [From the Apostle *Judas*, who betrayed Jesus.]

Jude (jüd) *n.* a book of the New Testament thought to have been written by the Apostle Jude.

Ju·de·o–Chris·tian (jü dā'ō kris'chən) *adj.* based on or relating to both Judaism and Christianity: *Judeo-Christian traditions.*

judge (juj) *v.*, **judged, judg·ing.** —*v.t.* **1.** to hear and decide in a court of law and with legal authority the merits or guilt of: *to judge a case, to judge an accused person.* **2.** to settle or decide: *to judge a contest.* **3.** to form an opinion or evaluation: *Judge me by what I do, not by my appearance.* **4.** to criticize; condemn; censure: *to be too quick to judge other people.* **5.** to think; suppose; consider: *I judge them to be loyal.* —*v.i.* **1.** to form an opinion or evaluation: *I will listen to all sides and judge for myself.* **2.** to act or decide as a judge: *to judge among four contestants.* —*n.* **1.** an appointed or elected official who has authority to hear and decide cases in a court of law. **2.** a person appointed to decide the winner or victor in any contest, competition, or dispute: *judges at a dog show.* **3.** a person who is qualified to give an opinion about a particular subject: *a good judge of musical ability.* —**judg'er**, *n.*

Judg·es (juj'iz) *n.* the book of the Old Testament containing the history of the Israelites from the death of Joshua to the birth of Samuel.

judge·ship (juj'ship') *n.* the position, function, or term of office of a judge.

judg·ment (juj'mənt) also, **judge·ment.** *n.* **1.** the ability to judge wisely: *to show good judgment.* **2.** the act of judging. **3.** an opinion or conclusion reached through judging: *I will form my own judgment.* **4.** *Law.* a decree, verdict, order, or sentence given by a court of law.

Judgment Day also, **judgment day.** in certain religions, the day of God's final judgment of humanity, which is to occur on the day the world ends. Also, **Last Judgment, Doomsday.**

ju·di·cial (jü dish'əl) *adj.* **1.** of or relating to courts of law and the administration of justice: *the judicial branch of the government.* **2.** of, relating to, or appropriate to a judge: *judicial robes, judicial authority.* **3.** decreed or enforced by a judge or a court: *a judicial decision.* —**ju·di'cial·ly**, *adv.*

ju·di·ci·ar·y (jü dish'ē er'ē) *n.*, *pl.* **ju·di·ci·ar·ies.** **1.** the branch of government that has judicial power and that interprets and applies the law. **2.** the system of courts of a country. **3.** the judges of these courts as a group. —*adj.* of or relating to judges, courts of law, or the administration of justice.

ju·di·cious (jü dish'əs) *adj.* having or showing good judgment; wise: *a judicious commander of troops, a judicious plan.* —**ju·di'cious·ly**, *adv.* —**ju·di'cious·ness**, *n.*

ju·do (jü'dō) *n.* **1.** a method of unarmed combat and self-defense related to jujitsu and karate. It originated in Asia and developed from jujitsu. **2.** the sport of fighting by this method. [From the Japanese word *jūdō*, the name of this sport, from the words *jū* meaning "gentleness" + *dō* meaning "art, way."]

jug (jug) *n.* **1.** a rounded container of earthenware, glass, or other material, having a handle and a narrow neck that usually has a stopper or cap, used chiefly for holding liquids. **2.** a pitcher or similar container for liquids. **3.** the contents of a jug. —*v.t.*, **jugged, jug·ging.** to put or cook in a jug.

jug band, a small band that uses simple or improvised instruments, such as jugs, washboards, and kazoos, especially to play folk music or blues.

jug·ger·naut (jug'ər nôt') *n.* **1.** any overpowering force or object that advances relentlessly and destroys whatever is in its path. **2.** a custom, belief, or something similar to which people blindly devote or sacrifice themselves.

jug·gle (jug'əl) *v.*, **jug·gled, jug·gling.** —*v.t.* **1.** to keep (two or more balls or other objects) in continuous motion from the hands into the air by skillfully tossing and catching in rapid succession: *to juggle four oranges at once.* **2.** to change or manipulate in order to deceive or defraud: *The embezzler juggled the company's financial records.* —*v.i.* **1.** to perform or entertain as a juggler. **2.** to practice trickery with the intent of deceiving or defrauding. —*n.* **1.** the act of juggling. **2.** deception or fraud.

jug·gler (jug'lər) *n.* **1.** a person whose work or occupation is juggling: *a circus juggler.* **2.** a person who practices deception or fraud.

Ju·go·slav (ū'gō släv') *adj.* another spelling of **Yugo-slav.**

jug·u·lar (jug'yə lər) *adj.* **1.** of or relating to the neck or throat. **2.** of or relating to the jugular vein. —*n.* see **jugular vein.**

jugular vein, either of the two large blood vessels on opposite sides of the neck that return blood from the head and neck to the heart.

juice (jüs) *n.* **1.** the fluid contained in a plant or in plant tissues, especially the fluid that is pressed or squeezed from a fruit or vegetable for use as a drink. **2.** the fluid contained in animal flesh or tissues: *Let the roast cook in its own juice.* **3.** the fluid secreted in animal tissue: *gastric juices, intestinal juices.* **4.** *Slang.* electric current. —*v.t.*, **juiced, juic·ing.** to press or squeeze the juice from.

juic·er (jü'sər) *n.* an appliance used to extract juice from fruits and vegetables.

juic·y (jü'sē) *adj.*, **juic·i·er, juic·i·est.** **1.** having much juice: *a juicy orange.* **2.** *Informal.* of great interest; exciting curiosity: *juicy gossip.* —**juic'i·ly**, *adv.* —**juic'i·ness**, *n.*

ju·jit·su (jü jit'sü) also, **jiu·jit·su, ju·jut·su.** *n.* a method of unarmed self-defense or combat that originated in Japan, related to judo and karate. It uses the strength and weight of an opponent to one's own advantage.

juke·box (jük'boks') *n.*, *pl.* **juke·box·es.** an automatic phonograph enclosed in a cabinet and usually operated by inserting coins and pushing one or more buttons to select a record.

ju·lep (jü'ləp) *n.* a drink made of liquor, mint, sugar, and crushed ice.

Jul·ian calendar (jül'yən) the calendar established by Julius Caesar and modified by Augustus, providing for 365 days in a year, with every fourth year having 366 days. The number of days in each month and the order of months in the year correspond to the present-day Gregorian calender.

ju·li·enne (jü'lē en') *adj.* cut into thin strips: *julienne carrots.* —*n.* a clear soup containing vegetables cut in such a manner.

Ju·liet (jül'yət, jü'lē et') *n.* the heroine of Shakespeare's tragedy *Romeo and Juliet.*

Ju·ly (jü lī') *n.*, *pl.* **Ju·lies.** the seventh month of the year, having thirty-one days. [From the Old French word *Julie* meaning "July," from the Latin word *Julius* "July," from the Roman statesman and general Gaius *Julius* Caesar (100?–44 B.C.).]

jum·ble (jum'bəl) *v.t.*, **jum·bled, jum·bling.** to mix or throw into confusion and disorder: *The toys were jumbled together in a box.* —*n.* **1.** a confused or disordered mixture, collection, or mass.   **2.** a state of confusion or disorder.

jum·bo (jum′bō) *Informal. adj.* extremely large: *a jumbo bar of candy.* —*n., pl.* **jum·bos.** a person, animal, or thing that is unusually large. [From *Jumbo,* the name of a giant elephant shown in a circus by P. T. Barnum.]

jump (jump) *v.i.*   **1.** to spring into the air: *I jumped up to catch the ball.*
2. to move or go suddenly or abruptly: *They jumped to their feet when they heard the alarm.*
3. to move suddenly, as in surprise or fright: *Do you always jump when the phone rings?*   **4.** to increase or rise suddenly: *The temperature jumped sharply.*   **5.** to come or pass abruptly, as by leaving out the necessary steps: *We jumped to a conclusion before learning the facts.*
6. to accept or grab hastily and eagerly: *to jump at a chance, to jump at an offer.* —*v.t.*

jump *(n., def. 6)*

1. to cause to jump: *Jump your pony across the brook.*
2. to spring or pass over or by (something): *to jump a fence.*   **3.** *Informal.* to attack by surprise; pounce upon: *The thief jumped me as I opened the door.*   **4.** *Informal.* to board hastily or by jumping.   **5.** see **jump-start.** —*n.*
1. the act of jumping; spring; leap.   **2.** a place or thing to be jumped over or across: *There were five jumps in the race.*   **3.** the distance or space covered by a jump: *a jump of eight feet.*   **4.** a sudden start or jerk, as in surprise or fright.   **5.** a sudden increase or rise: *a jump in prices.*
6. any of a number of sports contests in jumping.   **7.** a leap by parachute from an airplane.   **8.** see **jump-start.**
· **to get the jump on** or **to have the jump on.** to get or have a head start or advantage over.
· **to jump the gun.** to start too quickly or too soon: *Two of the runners jumped the gun.*

jump ball, a basketball tossed by the referee between two opposing players who jump up and try to tap it to a teammate.

jump·er[1] (jum′pər) *n.*   **1.** a person or thing that jumps.
2. a cable, wire, or other conductor used, usually as a temporary measure, to complete or bypass a circuit. [*Jump* + *-er*[1].]

jump·er[2] (jum′pər) *n.*   **1.** a one-piece, sleeveless dress, usually worn over a blouse or sweater.   **2.** a loose shirt, smock, or jacket worn over other clothes to protect them, as by sailors or painters.   **3. jumpers.** a loose, one-piece garment worn by young children; rompers. [Probably from the English dialect word *jump* meaning a type of short coat.]

jumping bean, a seed of any of several plants native to Mexico.   It contains a small moth larva whose movements cause the seed to jump. Also, **Mexican jumping bean.**

jumping jack   **1.** a toy figure of a person or animal having jointed limbs that can be made to move by pulling attached strings or a lever.   **2.** an exercise that involves jumping from a standing position, spreading the legs and placing the hands together over the head, then jumping again and returning to the first position.

jump rope   **1.** a piece of rope, often with a handle at each end, used for skipping or jumping over as a game or exercise.   **2.** a game or exercise using such a rope.

jump shot, a basketball shot in which a player jumps and shoots the ball while in the air.

jump–start (jump′stärt′) *v.t.*   to start a motor vehicle by means of cables attached to the battery of another vehicle. —*n.* an act of jump-starting.

jump·suit (jump′süt′) *n.*   **1.** a one-piece garment, combining shirt and trousers, designed to be worn as coveralls by paratroopers.   **2.** any garment resembling this.

jump·y (jum′pē′) *adj.,* **jump·i·er, jump·i·est.**   **1.** nervous; jittery.   **2.** moving by jumps or sudden sharp movements. —**jump′i·ness,** *n.*

jun·co (jung′kō) *n., pl.* **jun·cos** or **jun·coes.** any of various North American songbirds, usually having gray and white feathers.

junc·tion (jungk′shən) *n.*   **1.** a place or station where railroad lines meet or cross.   **2.** any place or point where two or more things join or meet.   **3.** the act of joining or the state of being joined.

junc·ture (jungk′chər) *n.*   **1.** a point in time, especially one made important by a coming together of events or conditions: *At that juncture, the outbreak of war seemed inevitable.*   **2.** the place or point where two things are joined; joint: *a juncture of two highways.*   **3.** the act of joining or the state of being joined.

June (jün) *n.*   the sixth month of the year, having thirty days.   [From the Old French word *Juin* meaning "June," from the Latin word *Junius,* the name of a certain Roman clan.]

June bug, any of several brown beetles that emerge as adults in late spring or early summer, and are destructive to shrubs and trees. Their larvae feed on the roots of many crops.   Also, **June beetle.**

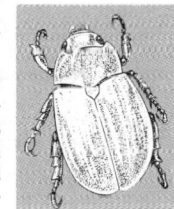

June bug

jun·gle (jung′gəl) *n.*   **1.** a dense and tangled mass of tropical vegetation, usually consisting of vines, ferns, and bushes as well as trees.   **2.** land overgrown with such a mass, usually inhabited by wild animals.   **3.** any wild, confused, or tangled growth or mass. *a jungle of highways and skyscrapers.*   **4.** a scene of ruthless competition or fierce struggle.

jungle gym, a structure of vertical and horizontal bars on which children can climb and play.

jun·ior (jün′yər) *adj.*   **1.** the younger of two. ▲ used after the name of a son whose father has the same name: *James Jones, Junior.*   **2.** of lower position, rank, or standing, or of more recent appointment or election: *a junior member of a law firm, the junior senator from New York.*   **3.** relating to, enrolled in, or designating the third year of a four-year high school or college program: *the junior class.*   **4.** of or for younger persons: *a junior library.*
—*n.*   **1.** a person who is younger than another: *to be someone's junior by three years.*   **2.** a person who is of lower position, rank, or standing or of more recent appointment.   **3.** a student in the third year of a four-year high school or college.

junior college, a school having a two-year course equivalent to the first two years of a four-year college.

---

at; āpe; fär; câre; end; mē; it; īce; pîerce; hot; ōld;
sông, fôrk; oil; out; up; ūse; rüle; pùll; tûrn; chin;
sing; shop; thin; this; hw in white; zh in treasure.
The symbol ə stands for the unstressed vowel sound
heard in about, taken, pencil, lemon, and circus.

J

junior high school, a school that usually includes grades seven and eight, and sometimes six or nine; any school between elementary school and senior high school.

ju·ni·per (jü′nə pər) *n.* any of a group of evergreen shrubs or trees related to the cypress. Junipers bear cones that look like berries, some of which yield an oil used to flavor gin.

junk¹ (jungk) *n.* **1.** old or discarded material, such as metal, wood, or rags. **2.** *Informal.* anything worthless or useless; rubbish; trash. **3.** *Slang.* a narcotic drug, especially heroin. —*v.t. Informal.* to throw away or discard as junk; scrap: *to junk an old car.* [From the Middle English word *jonk* meaning "old, disused cable."]

junk² (jungk) *n.* a flat-bottomed sailing vessel developed in China, having a square prow and lugsails. [From the Portuguese word *junco* meaning this vessel, from an Indonesian language.]

junk²

jun·ket (jung′kit) *n.* **1.** a trip or excursion, such as one made by a government official or business executive, often paid for by public funds and supposedly for the purpose of making an inspection or for other official business. **2.** a trip or tour, especially one made for pleasure. **3.** a food similar to custard, made of flavored and sweetened milk curdled by rennet. —*v.i.* to go on a junket.

junk food, food that is low in nutritional value but high in calories.

junk·ie (jung′kē) also, **junk·y.** *n., pl.* **junk·ies.** *Slang.* a narcotics addict, especially one who is addicted to heroin.

junk mail, unrequested mail, such as advertisements, circulars, and catalogs, sent to a large number of addresses.

junk·man (jungk′man′) *n., pl.* **junk·men** (jungk′men′). a person who buys or sells scrap material, such as metal, glass, paper, and rags.

junk·yard (jungk′yärd′) *n.* a place where junk is collected, stored, or resold.

Ju·no (jü′nō) *n. Roman Mythology.* the goddess who was the wife and sister of Jupiter and queen of the gods. She was also the protector of women and marriage. In Greek mythology she was called Hera.

jun·ta (hün′tə, jun′tə) *n.* **1.** a group that rules a country after the overthrow of a government. **2.** a legislative or administrative council or committee, especially in Latin America.

jun·to (jun′tō) *n., pl.* **jun·tos.** a small, usually secret group that gathers for some common purpose, especially for political intrigue.

Ju·pi·ter (jü′pi tər) *n.* **1.** *Roman Mythology.* the god who was the ruler of gods and humans, and was associated with the sky, and especially with lightning. In Greek mythology he was called Zeus. Also, **Jove. 2.** the largest planet of our solar system and fifth in order of distance from the sun. It has fourteen known moons.

Ju·ras·sic (jü ras′ik) *n.* the middle geological period of the Mesozoic era, during which the first known birds appeared. —*adj.* of, relating to, or characteristic of this period.

ju·ris·dic·tion (jùr′is dik′shən) *n.* **1.** the limits within which judicial or other authority may be exercised; range or extent of authority. **2.** the territory over which authority is exercised. **3.** the legal right to exercise authority, especially the authority to interpret or apply the law.

ju·ris·pru·dence (jùr′is prü′dəns) *n.* **1.** the science or philosophy of law. **2.** a body or system of laws. **3.** a branch or department of law: *medical jurisprudence.*

ju·rist (jùr′ist) *n.* a person who is expert in the law, such as a judge, lawyer, or legal scholar.

ju·ror (jùr′ər) *n.* a member of a jury.

ju·ry (jùr′ē) *n., pl.* **ju·ries. 1.** a group of persons selected to hear evidence on a matter submitted to them in a court of law and to make a decision according to the law and based on the evidence. **2.** a committee chosen to select the winners and award the prizes in a contest, exhibition, or other competition.

jury duty, service by a citizen as a juror in a court trial. Individual citizens are periodically called for jury duty.

just¹ (just) *adj.* **1.** that is fair and without prejudice: *a stern but just ruler, a legal system providing for just treatment of suspects.* **2.** rightly due or given; deserved; merited: *a just reward.* **3.** having a sound, reasonable, or adequate basis; well-founded: *just indignation.* **4.** legally valid; lawful; legitimate: *a just claim to the throne.* —*adv.* **1.** exactly; precisely: *It's just as I thought.* **2.** a very little while ago; very recently: *I just saw them.* **3.** by very little; by a narrow margin: *We arrived just in time.* **4.** only; merely: *It is just a cold.* **5.** *Informal.* simply; completely; positively: *That movie was just awful.* [From the Old French word *juste* meaning "fair, right," from the Latin word *justus* "upright, righteous, true," from the word *jus* "a right" or "law."] —**just′ly,** *adv.* —**just′ness,** *n.*

just² (just) another spelling of **joust.**

jus·tice (jus′tis) *n.* **1.** the state or quality of being just; fairness. **2.** the maintenance or administration of law: *a court of justice.* **3.** a judge of the Supreme Court of the United States or of a state supreme court.
·to do justice to. a. to treat or deal with (someone or something) in a just manner. **b.** to represent or show (someone or something) truly or well: *That picture doesn't do you justice.*

justice of the peace, a local public official who has the power to try minor cases, hold inquests and hearings, perform civil marriages, and carry out certain other duties.

jus·ti·fi·a·ble (jus′tə fī′ə bəl) *adj.* that can be justified.

jus·ti·fi·ca·tion (jus′tə fi kā′shən) *n.* **1.** the act of justifying or the state of being justified. **2.** something that justifies: *Your rudeness was justification for their anger.*

jus·ti·fy (jus′tə fī) *v.t.,* **jus·ti·fied, jus·ti·fy·ing. 1.** to show to be just or reasonable; vindicate: *Its great success justified our faith in the plan.* **2.** to declare or prove blameless; absolve. **3.** to set or type printed matter with an even margin along one or both sides.

jus·tle (jus′əl) another spelling of **jostle.**

jut (jut) *v.i.,* **jut·ted, jut·ting.** to stick out; project; protrude: *A piece of rock jutted from the face of the cliff.*

jute (jüt) *n.* **1.** a strong, flexible fiber, chiefly used to make burlap and twine. **2.** either of the two plants yielding this fiber, grown chiefly in India and Pakistan.

Jute (jüt) *n.* a member of a Germanic tribe, some of whom, along with the Angles and Saxons, invaded and settled in Britain during the fifth century A.D.

ju·ve·nile (jü′və nəl, jü′və nīl′) *adj.* **1.** of or suitable for children or young people: *a juvenile book, juvenile fashions.* **2.** childish; immature: *tantrums and other juvenile behavior.* **3.** young; youthful. —*n.* **1.** a young person; youth. **2.** an actor who plays youthful parts.

juvenile court, a court of law that handles cases involving persons under a certain age, usually eighteen.

juvenile delinquency, unlawful behavior by a person or persons usually under eighteen years of age.

juvenile delinquent, a person, usually under eighteen years of age, who is guilty of unlawful behavior but is too young to be held criminally responsible.

jux·ta·pose (juk′stə pōz′) *v.t.,* **jux·ta·posed, jux·ta·pos·ing.** to place (two or more things) side by side or close together, especially for contrast or comparison. —**jux′ta·po·si′tion,** *n.*

K k

1. ancient Semitic
2. Phoenician
3. early Hebrew
4. early Greek
5. later Greek
6. Latin
7. English

K is the eleventh letter of the English alphabet. The earliest form of **K** was the ancient Semitic letter *kaph* (1), meaning "hand" or "fist." When the Phoenicians (2) and early Hebrews (3) borrowed *kaph*, they made only slight changes in its shape. The ancient Greeks adopted *kaph* and called it *kappa* (4). In ancient times, the Greeks wrote either from right to left or in alternating rows of right to left and left to right. Later, when they began to write from left to right, the shape of certain letters, including *kappa*, was reversed (5). The Romans borrowed this new form of *kappa* for the Latin alphabet (6), and by about 2,400 years ago they were writing it almost exactly as we write the capital letter **K** today (7).

k, K (kā) *n., pl.* **k's, K's.** the eleventh letter of the English alphabet.

k. **1.** karat. **2.** kilogram. **3.** kopeck.

K **1.** the symbol for potassium. [From the scientific Latin word *kalium* meaning "potassium."] **2.** Kelvin. **3.** kilobyte; kilobytes.

Kaa·ba (kä′bə) *n.* a sacred Muslim shrine at Mecca. It is a small cubical structure containing a black stone, which is said to have been given to Abraham by the archangel Gabriel.

ka·bob (kə bob′) *also,* **ke·bab, ke·bob.** *n.* another word for **shish kebab.** [Originally from the Turkish word *kebap* meaning this food.]

Ka·bu·ki (kə bü′kē) *n.* a form of Japanese drama, originating in the late sixteenth century, characterized by elaborate costumes and stylized acting, singing, and dancing.

kai·ak (kī′ak) another spelling of **kayak.**

Kai·ser (kī′zər) *n.* **1.** any of the emperors of Germany from 1871 to 1918. **2.** any of the emperors of Austria from 1804 to 1918. **3.** any of the emperors of the Holy Roman Empire from 962 to 1806. [From the Old Norse word *keisari* meaning "emperor," going back to the Latin title *caesar,* applied to the Roman emperors since Augustus, from Gaius Julius *Caesar* (100?–44 B.C.), Roman statesman and general. In senses 1 and 2, English has directly borrowed the corresponding German term *Kaiser,* also going back to the Latin title *caesar.*]

kale (kāl) *n.* **1.** the broad, curly, bluish green leaves of a plant of the cabbage family, eaten cooked or raw as a vegetable. **2.** the plant itself.

ka·lei·do·scope (kə lī′də skōp′) *n.* **1.** a tube-shaped toy containing loose bits of colored glass or other small objects that are reflected by a set of mirrors as a series of continually changing patterns when the tube is held to the eye and turned. **2.** anything having continually changing patterns, or phases. [Formed from the Greek words *kalos* meaning "beautiful" + *eidos* meaning "form" + the English suffix *-scope.*] —**ka·lei·do·scop·ic** (kə - lī′də skop′ik), *adj.* —**ka·lei′do·scop′i·cal·ly,** *adv.*

ka·mi·ka·ze (kä′mi kä′zē) *n.* **1.** one of a group of Japanese pilots in World War II whose mission was to dive their planes onto a ship or other target in a suicidal attempt to destroy it. **2.** a plane flown by such a pilot. **3.** a person or thing whose actions resemble those of a kamikaze. —*adj.* of, like, or behaving like a kamikaze: *The wildly swerving automobile could only have been steered by a kamikaze driver.* [From the Japanese word *kamikaze* meaning "divine wind," referring to the typhoon which had destroyed a Mongol fleet in 1281 before it could invade Japan.]

Kam·pu·che·an (kam′pü chē′ən) *adj., n.* another word for **Cambodian.**

kan·ga·roo (kang′gə rü′) *n., pl.* **kan·ga·roos** or **kan·ga·roo.** an Australian mammal having small forelimbs, powerful hind legs adapted for leaping, and a long, muscular tail. The kangaroo is a marsupial. For about six months after birth, the baby kangaroo is carried in the mother's pouch.

kangaroo rat, any of various jumping rodents of Mexico and western North America.

Kans., Kansas.

ka·o·lin (kā′ə lin) *n.* a fine white clay used to make porcelain.

kangaroo

ka·pok (kā′pok) *n.* a light, fluffy fiber obtained from the seed pods of a tropical tree. It is used as a stuffing for life preservers, pillows, and mattresses and as an insulating material.

kap·pa (kap′ə) *n.* the tenth letter of the Greek alphabet (K, κ), corresponding to the English letter K, k.

kar·a·kul (kar′ə kəl) *n.* **1.** a sheep of a breed originally native to central Asia, having a narrow body and a broad tail. The young karakul has a coat of curled, gray or glossy black fur. **2.** another spelling of **caracul.** [From *Kara Kul,* a lake in Turkestan, where it was first raised.]

kar·at (kar′ət) *also,* **car·at.** *n.* a unit of measure used to express the degree of purity of gold. Fourteen-karat gold is 14 parts gold and 10 parts alloy.

children training in **karate**

ka·ra·te (kə rä′tē) *n.* a Japanese system of unarmed self-defense in which the hands, elbows, knees, and feet are used to strike an opponent at vulnerable points of the body. [From the Japanese word *karate* meaning "empty hand," used as the name of this form of self-defense because it uses no hand weapons.]

kar·ma (kär′mə) *n.* **1.** in Buddhism and Hinduism, the effect produced by all of the actions in a person's life, supposed to determine the person's destiny when he or she is reincarnated. **2.** fate; destiny.

Kashmir goat, a goat native to India, Tibet, and other regions in Asia, raised especially for its soft undercoat, which is used to make cashmere wool.

ka·ty·did (kā′tē did′) *n.* a large green grasshopper having long, threadlike antennae. The male makes a shrill, rasping noise by rubbing its wings together.

kay·ak (kī′ak) *also,* **kai·ak.** *n.* **1.** a type of canoe used in arctic regions. It is made of animal skins stretched over a light framework of wood or whalebone, having a small opening in the center for a paddler.

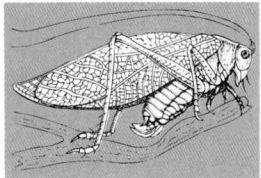

katydid

2. a light canoe resembling this, used in sports. —*v.i.* to travel in a kayak.

ka·zoo (kə zü′) *n., pl.* **ka·zoos.** a musical instrument consisting of a tube with a side hole covered with a thin membrane. It produces a buzzing sound when a player hums into the tube.

kc, kilocycle; kilocycles.

kcal, kilocalorie; kilocalories.

ke·a (kē′ə) *n.* a large green parrot of New Zealand, having a sharp, hooked bill.

ke·bab (kə bob′) *also,* **ke·bob, ka·bob.** *n.* another word for **shish kebab.**

keel (kēl) *n.* **1.** the main timber or steel piece extending lengthwise along the center of the bottom of a ship or boat and supporting the entire frame. **2.** the part in an aircraft resembling a ship's keel.

•**on an even keel.** steady; balanced: *My teacher's calm advice kept me on an even keel during the exam.*

•**to keel over. a.** to turn bottom up; capsize. **b.** to fall over suddenly; topple; collapse: *to keel over in a faint.*

keel·haul (kēl′hôl′) *v.t.* **1.** to drag (a person) under the keel of a ship from one side or end to the other as a punishment. **2.** to rebuke or punish severely.

keen[1] (kēn) *adj.* **1.** having a sharp cutting edge or point; able to cut or pierce easily: *a keen knife.* **2.** having or showing great mental sharpness; quick: *a keen mind.* **3.** very sensitive or acute: *That hound has a keen sense of smell.* **4.** very strong; intense: *to have a keen interest in sports.* **5.** piercing or cutting: *A keen wind whipped the snow.* **6.** full of enthusiasm; eager: *to be keen about traveling.* **7.** *Slang.* wonderful; excellent: *What a keen movie that was!* [From the Old English word *cēne* meaning "fierce, brave."] —**keen′ly,** *adv.* —**keen′ness,** *n.*

keen[2] (kēn) *n.* a wailing lament for the dead. —*v.i.* to wail loudly for the dead. [From the Irish word *caonim* meaning "I keen."]

keep (kēp) *v.,* **kept, keep·ing.** —*v.t.* **1.** to continue to have and hold: *We kept the kitten that followed us home.* **2.** to cause to continue in a certain condition, place, or relation: *I kept the sick child in bed. Put the meat in the refrigerator to keep it fresh.* **3.** to store, put, or hold: *Keep your toys in the closet.* **4.** to save: *to keep some food for late guests.* **5.** to have for one's use or service: *to keep a horse, to keep servants.* **6.** to make regular entries in: *to keep a diary.* **7.** to prevent; restrain: *The cold weather may keep the plants from budding.* **8.** to be faithful to; fulfill: *I kept my promise and mowed the lawn.* **9.** to celebrate or observe: *to keep Thanksgiving.* **10.** to look after the affairs of; manage: *to keep house.* **11.** to take care of; watch over: *The shepherd kept a flock of sheep.* —*v.i.* **1.** to stay or continue in a certain condition, place, or relation: *The teacher told us to keep quiet.* **2.** to restrain oneself; refrain: *I couldn't keep from crying at the sad movie.* **3.** to stay in good condition; last without spoiling: *Will this meat keep until tomorrow?* —*n.* **1.** things needed for a person to live, as food and shelter: *You can earn your keep by working.* **2.** The strongest part of a castle or fortress.

•**to keep to oneself. 1.** to stay away from the company of others. **2.** to keep (something) secret: *I kept the news to myself.*

•**to keep up. a.** to go at the same speed or rate: *The others ran off quickly, and I could not keep up.* **b.** to continue: *The noise of the machinery kept up all through the night.*

•**to keep up with. a.** to go at the same speed or rate as. **b.** to continue to be informed about: *I always keep up with current events.*

keep·er (kē′pər) *n.* a person who protects, takes care of, or is responsible for someone or something: *a keeper at a zoo, the keeper of an inn.* ▲often used in combination: *a shopkeeper, a gamekeeper.*

keep·ing (kē′ping) *n.* **1.** care, charge, or possession: *The jewels were placed in my keeping.* **2.** the celebration or observance: *the keeping of Thanksgiving.*

•**in keeping with.** in harmony with; appropriate: *Jokes are not in keeping with this solemn occasion.*

keep·sake (kēp′sāk′) *n.* something given or kept to remind one of the giver; memento.

keg (keg) *n.* **1.** a small barrel, usually holding 5 to 10 gallons (19–38 liters). **2.** a unit of weight for nails that is equal to 100 pounds (45 kilograms).

kelp (kelp) *n.* **1.** any of a large group of brown seaweeds growing along the coasts of the Atlantic and Pacific Oceans. **2.** the ashes of such seaweed, formerly a major source of potassium and iodine, now used mainly as a fertilizer.

Kel·vin (kel′vin) *adj.* of, according to, or designating the temperature scale on which a degree is equal in size to a centigrade degree and 0 degrees represents absolute zero (−273.15 degrees Celsius). [From the English physicist William Thomson, Lord *Kelvin* (1824–1907), who developed this scale.]

ken (ken) *n.* range of sight, knowledge, or understanding: *I'm afraid that calculus is beyond my ken.* —*v.i.,* **kenned, ken·ning.** *Scottish.* to know or understand.

ken·nel (ken′əl) *n.* **1.** a shelter for a dog or dogs. **2.** *also,* **kennels.** a place where dogs are bred, trained, or boarded. —*v.t.* to put or keep in a kennel.

kept (kept) the past tense and past participle of **keep.**

ker·a·tin (ker′ə tin) *n.* a tough, fibrous protein present in the skin tissue of all vertebrates. It forms the main part of horns, hoofs, hair, nails, bills, claws, and feathers.

ker·chief (kûr′chif) *n.* **1.** a piece of cloth, usually square, worn over the head or around the neck. **2.** see **handkerchief** (*def. 1*).

ker·nel (kûr′nəl) *n.* **1.** the grain or seed of various plants, such as wheat or corn. **2.** the softer, inner part of a seed or fruit. **3.** the central, most valuable, or most important part.

ker·o·sene (ker′ə sēn′) *also,* **ker·o·sine.** *n.* a colorless, highly volatile liquid distilled from petroleum, widely used as a fuel and cleaning solvent. It consists of a mixture of hydrocarbons.

kes·trel (kes′trəl) *n.* a small, reddish brown falcon native to North and South America. The male has blue-gray wings. Also, **sparrow hawk.**

ketch (kech) *n., pl.* **ketch·es.** a fore-and-aft-rigged sailing ship with two masts, similar to a yawl, but having the mizzenmast farther forward.

ketch·up (kech′əp) *also,* **cat·sup, catch·up.** *n.* a thick, seasoned sauce that is made of tomatoes, onions, salt, sugar, and spices and is used with many types of food.

ket·tle (ket′əl) *n.* **1.** any metal container used for boiling liquids or for cooking in liquid; pot. **2.** see **teakettle.**

ket·tle·drum (ket′əl drum′) *n.* a drum consisting of a hollow brass or copper hemisphere with a parchment top that can be tuned to a definite pitch.

key¹ (kē) *n., pl.* **keys. 1.** an instrument that opens or closes a lock by moving a bolt or tumblers. **2.** anything like this instrument in use or shape: *a roller skate key, a key that winds a clock, a key to open a can.* **3.** something that solves or explains: *The detectives found the key to the crime. A key to the pronunciations in this dictionary appears at the bottom of the page.* **4.** something that leads to or is a way of getting something: *Hard work is sometimes the key to success.* **5.** a place or position that gives control of entry or possession: *Gibraltar is the key to the Mediterranean Sea.* **6.** a person or thing that is thought of as the main or controlling force: *The quarterback was the key to the team.* **7.** a part pressed down in working a machine or instrument: *a piano key, a telegraph key, a typewriter key.* **8.** *Music.* a scale or system of notes in which all the notes bear a definite relationship to, and are based on and named for, a given note, which is the keynote: *a symphony in the key of F sharp.* **9.** a tone or pitch of the voice: *to speak in a high key.* **10.** general style or tone: *The letter was written in an angry key.* —*adj.* of great or chief importance; major; basic: *The manufacture of automobiles is a key industry in that state.* —*v.t.,* **keyed, key·ing. 1.** *Music.* to regulate the pitch or tone of: *to key an instrument to B flat.* **2.** to regulate or adjust (something) to suit a particular activity or occasion. [From the Old English word *cæg* meaning "a key¹."]

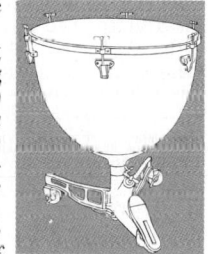
kettledrum

·to key up. to make nervous, tense, or excited: *I was keyed up thinking about the exam.*

key² (kē) *n., pl.* **keys.** a low, coastal island or reef, as along the southern tip of Florida. [From the Spanish word *cayo* with the same meaning, from a language of the West Indies.]

key·board (kē′bôrd′) *n.* an arrangement or set of keys, as in a piano, typewriter, or computer system. —*v.t.* to enter data into a computer by pressing keys on a keyboard connected to the computer.

key·hole (kē′hōl′) *n.* a hole through which a key is inserted into a lock.

key·note (kē′nōt′) *n.* **1.** *Music.* the note on which a scale or system of tones is based; tonic. **2.** the main or dominant idea, principle, theme, or mood: *Economic expansion was the keynote of the nation's foreign policy.* —*v.t.,* **key·not·ed, key·not·ing. 1.** to give or set the keynote of. **2.** to give the keynote speech at.

keynote speech, a speech, as at the convention of a political party, in which important issues and basic policy are presented. Also, **keynote address.**

key·pad (kē′pad′) *n.* **1.** a small keyboard. **2.** a section of a computer keyboard with keys for numbers and mathematical symbols, usually arranged like the keys of a calculator. **3.** a small panel with keys or buttons marked by letters or numbers.

key·punch (kē′punch′) *n., pl.* **key·punch·es.** a machine operated from a keyboard and used to record information by means of holes punched in cards.

key signature *Music.* the sharps or flats placed after the clef at the beginning of each staff, or at any point where there is a change of key, indicating the key of the music which follows.

key·stone (kē′stōn′) *n.* **1.** the central, topmost stone of an arch, which locks the remaining stones of the arch together. It is usually the last stone to be set in place. **2.** the main or basic element or part upon which related parts depend: *Singapore was the keystone of the power of the British Empire in the Far East.*

Keystone

kg., kilogram, kilograms.

khak·i (kak′ē, kä′kē) *n.* **1.** a dull, yellowish brown or tan color. **2.** a sturdy, twilled cotton cloth of this color. **3. khakis.** a garment made of this fabric, especially a military uniform. —*adj.* having a dull, yellowish brown color. [From the Hindi word *khākī* meaning "dusty," from the Persian word *khāk* "dust."]

khan (kän) *n.* **1.** a title formerly used by rulers of Mongol, Tatar, and Turkish tribes and by the Mongol emperors of China. **2.** a title of respect in Iran, Afghanistan, and central Asia.

khe·dive (kə dēv′) *n.* the title of the Turkish viceroys of Egypt from 1867 to 1914.

Khmer (kmâr′) *n.* **1.** a member of the ethnic group that makes up most of the people of Kampuchea. **2.** the language of Kampuchea. —**Khmer,** *adj.*

at; āpe; fär; câre; end; mē; it; īce; pîerce; hot; ōld; sông, fôrk; oil; out; up; ūse; rūle; pŭll; tûrn; chin; sing; shop; thin; this; hw in white; zh in treasure. The symbol ə stands for the unstressed vowel sound heard in about, taken, pencil, lemon, and circus.

K

kib·butz (ki bùts′) *n., pl.* **kib·but·zim** (ki bùt sēm′) a collective farm or settlement in modern Israel.

kib·itz (kib′its) *v.i. Informal.* to act as a kibitzer.

kib·itz·er (kib′it sər) *n. Informal.* **1.** a person who looks on at a card game and gives unwanted advice. **2.** anyone who gives unwanted advice or meddles in the affairs of others.

kick (kik) *v.t.* **1.** to strike with the foot or feet: *to kick a pebble on the beach.* **2.** to drive or move by striking with the foot or feet: *to kick a tin can into a sewer.* **3.** *Sports.* to score (a goal or point) by kicking the ball over the goal posts or into the goal, as in football or soccer. —*v.i.* **1.** to strike out with the foot or feet: *The swimmer tried to kick faster.* **2.** *Sports.* to put the ball in play or attempt to score or gain ground by kicking the ball, as in football or soccer. **3.** (of firearms) to recoil when fired. **4.** *Slang.* to complain; rebel: *I kicked at having to dry the dishes.* —*n.* **1.** the act or power of kicking the foot or feet: *The door can be shut with a kick.* **2.** the sudden springing back of a gun when fired. **3.** *Sports.* **a.** the act or instance of kicking a ball. **b.** a kicked ball: *to block a kick.* **c.** the distance a ball travels when kicked: *a fifty-yard kick.* **4.** *Slang.* a complaint; objection. **5.** *Slang.* a pleasing or exciting feeling; thrill. —**kick′er,** *n.*

·**to kick back.** *Slang.* to pay back (a portion of money received as a fee, commission, salary, or the like) as a kickback.

·**to kick off. 1.** *Football.* to make a kickoff. **2.** to begin; commence: *to kick off a stage show with a rousing song.*

·**to kick out.** *Informal.* to expel or eject forcefully or suddenly: *We heard that they had both been kicked out of school for cheating.*

Kick·a·poo (kik′ə pü′) *n., pl.* **Kick·a·poo** or **Kick·a·poos.** a member of a North American Indian tribe formerly living in the Great Lakes area, now living mostly in Kansas, Oklahoma, and Mexico.

kick·back (kik′bak′) *n.* an illegal or secret payment made by a seller of goods or services to the person who referred a buyer or client.

kick·off (kik′ôf′) *n.* **1.** a kick that puts the ball in play in football. **2.** the beginning; commencement: *The dance was the kickoff of the fund drive.*

kick·stand (kik′stand′) *n.* a movable metal bar attached to the underside of a bicycle or motorcycle that can be lowered into position with the foot to prop the vehicle upright when not in use.

kid (kid) *n.* **1.** a young goat. **2.** see **kidskin. 3.** *Informal.* a young person; child; youngster. —*adj.* **1.** *Informal.* (of a brother or sister) younger: *kid brothers and sisters.* **2.** made of kidskin: *kid gloves.* —*v.,* **kid·ded, kid·ding.** *Informal.* —*v.t.* **1.** to make fun of; tease: *They kidded me about my freckles.* **2.** to deceive (someone) as a joke; fool: *They tried to kid us into believing the story.* —*v.i.* to engage in good-humored fooling or teasing; joke. —**kid′der,** *n.*

kid·nap (kid′nap′) *v.t.,* **kid·napped** or **kid·naped, kid·nap·ping** or **kid·nap·ing.** to seize or hold (a person), especially for the purpose of getting a ransom. —**kid′nap′per;** *also,* **kid′nap′er,** *n.*

kid·ney (kid′nē) *n., p.* **kid·neys. 1.** either of a pair of organs located at the back of the abdominal cavity. The kidneys filter wastes out of the bloodstream, forming urine that is collected in the bladder. **2.** the kidney of certain animals, used as food.

kidney bean 1. the kidney-shaped seed of any of various varieties of a plant of the pea family, cooked and eaten as a vegetable. **2.** the plant bearing this seed.

kid·skin (kid′skin′) *n.* a leather made from the skin of young goats, used for such items as gloves and shoes.

kiel·ba·sa (kil bä′sə, kēl bä′sə) *n., pl.* **kiel·ba·sas** or **kiel·ba·sy** (kil bä′sē, kēl bä′sē). a smoked sausage fla-

vored with garlic and spices. [From the Polish word *kielbasa* meaning this sausage.]

kill[1] (kil) *v.t.* **1.** to take away the life of; cause the death of: *Automobile accidents kill thousands of Americans every year.* **2.** to put an end to; destroy: *Failing the examination killed my chances for the scholarship.* **3.** to defeat or veto: *to kill a proposed law.* **4.** *Informal.* to stop or turn off: *Kill the lights.* **5.** to cancel or stop the publication of: *The editor killed the story.* **6.** to pass (time) aimlessly or unproductively: *We killed an hour by wandering through the town.* **7.** *Informal.* to affect with severe pain, discomfort, or fatigue: *My back is killing me.* **8.** to overcome completely, as with laughter or embarrassment: *Your jokes are killing me.* —*v.i.* to cause death; be fatal: *An overdose of this drug can kill.* —*n.* **1.** the act or instance of killing, especially in hunting: *The hunters moved in for the kill.* **2.** the animal or animals killed: *The tiger dragged its kill into the jungle.* [From the Middle English word *killen* meaning "to kill[1]," probably from Old English.]

kill[2] (kil) *n.* a channel, creek, or stream. [From the Dutch word *kil* meaning "stream, channel."]

kill·deer (kil′dir′) *n., pl.* **kill·deers** or **kill·deer.** a North American wading bird having brownish feathers with two black bands across the breast.

kill·er (kil′ər) *n.* a person, animal, or thing that kills.

killer whale, a black-and-white sea mammal that preys on fish, penguins, seals, sea lions, and whales. It is closely related to the dolphins and porpoises.

killdeer

kill·ing (kil′ing) *n.* **1.** the act of killing. **2.** *Informal.* a sudden great profit or success: *to make a killing in the stock market.* —*adj.* causing or likely to cause death or destruction: *a killing blow, a killing frost.*

kill·joy (kil′joi′) *n.* a person who spoils or lessens the enjoyment or fun of others.

kiln (kil, kiln) *n.* a furnace or oven for burning, baking, or drying, used in making bricks, pottery, or charcoal.

ki·lo (kē′lō, kil′ō) *n., pl.* **ki·los.** see **kilogram.**

kilo- *prefix* one thousand: *kilocycle, kiloliter.*

kil·o·byte (kil′ə bīt′) *n. Computers.* 1,024 bytes.

kil·o·cal·o·rie (kil′ə kal′ə rē) *n.* another word for **calorie** (*def. 2*). Also, **large calorie.**

kil·o·cy·cle (kil′ə sī′kəl) *n.* **1.** a unit equal to 1,000 cycles. **2.** another word for **kilohertz.**

kil·o·gram (kil′ə gram′) *n.* a unit of mass and weight in the metric system equal to 1,000 grams, or 2.2046 pounds avoirdupois.

kil·o·gram–me·ter (kil′ə gram′mē′tər) *n.* a unit of work or energy, equal to about 7.2 foot-pounds. A kilogram-meter is the amount of energy required to raise a mass of 1 kilogram to a height of 1 meter.

kil·o·hertz (kil′ə hûrts′) *n., pl.* **kil·o·hertz.** a unit equal to 1,000 hertz, used in measuring the frequency of electromagnetic waves. Also, **kilocycle.**

kil·o·li·ter (kil′ə lē′tər) *n.* a unit of capacity in the metric system equal to 1,000 liters, or 1 cubic meter; 264.17 U.S. gallons or 1.308 cubic yards.

ki·lom·e·ter (ki lom′i tər, kil′ə mē′tər) *n.* a unit of length in the metric system equal to 1,000 meters, or 3,280.8 feet.

kil·o·ton (kil′ə tun′) *n.* **1.** a unit of weight equal to 1,000 tons. **2.** a unit of explosive force equivalent to that produced by the detonation of 1,000 tons of TNT.

kil·o·watt (kil′ə wot′) *n.* a unit of electrical power equal to 1,000 watts.

kil·o·watt–hour (kil′ə wot′our′) *n.* a unit of electrical energy equal to the energy consumed by a machine working at a constant rate of 1 kilowatt for 1 hour.

528

kilt (kilt) *n.* a pleated skirt usually made of tartan and reaching to the knees, especially one worn by men in the Scottish Highlands.

kil·ter (kil′tər) *n.* **out of kilter.** out of order; not in good condition: *The toaster is out of kilter.*

ki·mo·no (ki mō′nə) *n., pl.* **ki·mo·nos.** **1.** a loose robe or gown tied with a sash, worn by the Japanese. **2.** a loose dressing gown similar to this.

kin (kin) *n.* **1.** a person's whole family; relatives; kindred; kinsfolk. **2.** a kinsman; relative. —*adj.* related: *They are not kin to me.*
   •**next of kin.** a person or persons most closely related to one: *The police immediately notified the victim's next of kin.*

–kin *suffix* little; small: *lambkin.*

kind¹ (kīnd) *adj.* **1.** gentle, considerate, and friendly in nature or behavior; good-hearted: *kind to animals. It was kind of you to help me.* **2.** from or showing good-heartedness: *kind words, a kind act.* [From the Old English word *gecynde* meaning "natural, inborn."]

kind² (kīnd) *n.* a class, sort, or grouping; variety; type: *The whale is a kind of mammal. That store has many different kinds of sports equipment.* [From the Old English word *cynd* meaning "nature, kind²" or "sort."]
   •**in kind. a.** in goods or produce, rather than in money. **b.** with something of the same sort: *They insulted me, and I repaid them in kind.*
   •**kind of.** *Informal.* somewhat; rather: *I'm feeling kind of hungry.*

kin·der·gar·ten (kin′dər gär′tən) *n.* a class or division of school for children from four to six years old, coming before the first grade of elementary school. [From the German word *Kindergarten,* from the words *Kinder* meaning "children" + *Garten* meaning "garden."]

kind·heart·ed (kīnd′här′tid) *adj.* having or showing kindness or sympathy: *a kindhearted person, kindhearted actions.* —**kind′heart′ed·ly,** *adv.* —**kind′heart′ed·ness,** *n.*

kin·dle (kin′dəl) *v.,* **kin·dled, kin·dling.** —*v.t.* **1.** to set on fire; light: *The campers kindled the logs.* **2.** to arouse, stir up, or excite: *Rude behavior sometimes kindles anger.* **3.** to make bright or glowing: *The setting sun kindled the evening sky.* —*v.i.* **1.** to catch fire; begin to burn: *A dry forest is likely to kindle with the smallest spark.* **2.** to become aroused or stirred up. **3.** to become bright or glowing. Also, **enkindle.** —**kin′dler,** *n.*

kin·dling (kind′ling) *n.* material for starting a fire, especially small pieces of dry wood or twigs.

kind·ly (kīnd′lē) *adj.,* **kind·li·er, kind·li·est.** **1.** having or showing kindness; kind; benevolent: *a kindly face.* **2.** pleasant; agreeable: *a kindly breeze on a hot day.* —*adv.* **1.** in a kind or gentle manner: *Speak kindly to the lost child.* **2.** favorably; agreeably. **3.** as a favor; please: *Kindly mail this letter for me.* **4.** enthusiastically; cordially: *Thank you kindly.* —**kind′li·ness,** *n.*
   •**to take kindly to.** to like or accept: *You do not take kindly to criticism.*

kind·ness (kīnd′nis) *n., pl.* **kind·ness·es.** **1.** the quality or state of being kind: *I have always depended on the kindness of strangers* (Tennessee Williams). **2.** a kind treatment or act: *We thanked them for their many kindnesses.*

kin·dred (kin′drid) *n.* a person's whole family; relatives. —*adj.* **1.** like; similar: *a kindred spirit, kindred pursuits.* **2.** related by history or derivation; having common ancestors: *Spanish, French, and Italian are kindred languages.*

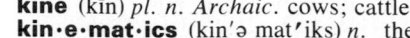

kine (kīn) *pl. n. Archaic.* cows; cattle.

kin·e·mat·ics (kin′ə mat′iks) *n.* the branch of mechanics dealing with the motion of moving bodies, without reference to the mass or force that is involved in the motion.

kin·e·scope (kin′ə skōp′) *n.* **1.** a motion-picture record of a television program. **2.** the picture tube of a television set. —*v.t.,* **kin·e·scoped, kin·e·scop·ing.** to make a kinescope of.

ki·net·ic (ki net′ik) *adj.* **1.** of or relating to motion. **2.** produced or caused by motion.

kinetic energy, the energy that an object has because of its motion.

ki·net·ics (ki net′iks) *n.* the branch of physics that deals with the effects of forces in causing or changing the motion of bodies. ▲ used with a singular verb.

kin·folk (kin′fōk′) *pl. n.* a person's relatives; family. Also, **kin·folks** (kin′fōks′).

king (king) *n.* **1.** a male ruler who holds limited or absolute power over a nation or state for life, usually by hereditary right. **2.** a person or thing that is supreme or is the best of its class: *The lion is often thought of as the king of the jungle. The owner of all those oil wells is known as an oil king.* **3.** a playing card bearing a picture of a king. **4.** a principal piece in the game of chess, capable of moving one square in any direction. The object in chess is to checkmate the opponent's king. **5.** a piece in the game of checkers that has moved across the board to the opponent's side and can now move both forward and backward. —**king′like′,** *adj.*

king
(def. 4)

king·bird (king′bûrd′) *n.* any of various songbirds that are classified as flycatchers, found throughout North America and South America.

king·bolt (king′bōlt′) *n.* a vertical bolt connecting the body of a wagon or other vehicle with the front axle. Also, **kingpin.**

king crab, a large crab having a small, triangular body and very long legs. It is valued as food and is found in the northern Pacific Ocean.

king·dom (king′dəm) *n.* **1.** a nation or state ruled by a king or queen. **2.** a realm, region, or sphere in which some condition or quality is supreme or prevails: *a cattle kingdom.* **3.** one of the five primary divisions of nature. Animals, plants, protists, monerans, and fungi each make up their own kingdom.

king·fish (king′fish′) *n., pl.* **king·fish** or **king·fish·es.** any of several saltwater food and game fish found along the Atlantic coast of the United States, having a dark gray body.

king·fish·er (king′fish′ər) *n.* any of various brightly colored birds having a large head and a long, pointed bill. It eats fish, insects, reptiles, and sometimes small animals or birds.

King James Version, an English translation of the Bible, authorized by King James I and first published in 1611.

king·ly (king′lē) *adj.,* **king·li·er, king·li·est.** characteristic of, like, or suitable for a king; royal; regal: *a kingly way of walking.* —*adv.* in a kingly manner; regally; royally. —**king′li·ness,** *n.*

king·pin (king′pin′) *n.* **1.** the pin that is positioned in

at; āpe; fär; câre; end; mē; it; īce; pîerce; hot; ōld; sông; fôrk; oil; out; up; ūse; rüle; pull; tûrn; chin; sing; shop; thin; <u>th</u>is; hw in white; zh in treasure. The symbol ə stands for the unstressed vowel sound heard in about, taken, pencil, lemon, and circus.

K

529

the center and in front of the other pins in bowling. **2.** another word for **kingbolt**. **3.** *Informal.* the chief person in a group or sphere.

Kings (kingz) *n.* **1.** in the Protestant Bible, either of two books (I Kings or II Kings) of the Old Testament, containing the history of the Jewish monarchy from the reign of Solomon to the fall of Jerusalem in 586 B.C. **2.** in the Douay Bible, one of four books of the Old Testament, equivalent to I and II Samuel and I and II Kings of the Protestant Bible.

king salmon, a large salmon found throughout the northern Pacific Ocean, important as a food fish.

King's English, standard, correct, or accepted usage of English in Great Britain. Also, **Queen's English.**

Language Note

The term **King's English,** or **Queen's English** as it is often called when a queen rules, is the form of English that is considered to be correct in Great Britain. The term refers to the way educated British people use the English language, and not necessarily to the way a king or queen actually speaks. Not all the rulers of Britain have spoken the King's English themselves (King George I was a German who could not speak English at all). Rather, this form of English got its name because of the idea that it had the official approval of the king or queen.

King's English is called a *prestige dialect,* which means that people consider it to be superior to other varieties, or dialects, of English. Linguists, who study language scientifically, do not believe that one dialect is actually better than another. You can quite effectively communicate with your family, neighbors, and classmates using the dialect that is the standard of English for those groups. But people are also judged by their ability to express themselves and to communicate according to other people's standards, not only those of their own group. In Great Britain, as in any other country, the way in which the most prominent, most successful, and best-educated people speak is treated as if it were the "correct" way. The King's English is not really more correct than other dialects, but social custom has established it as the acceptable standard for English in that society.

king·ship (king'ship') *n.* **1.** the position, office, or dignity of a king. **2.** government by a king; monarchy.

king–size (king'sīz') *adj.* larger or longer than is ordinary: *a king-size bed.* Also, **king–sized** (king'sīzd').

king snake, a nonpoisonous snake found from southern Canada to northern South America. It is a constrictor that feeds on other snakes and on rodents, lizards, frogs, and other small animals.

kink (kingk) *n.* **1.** a tight curl or sharp twist, as in a hair, wire, or rope. **2.** a painful muscle spasm or cramp; crick: *I got a kink in my back after lifting the sofa.* **3.** *Informal.* an imperfection or flaw, as in the plan or operation of something: *The engineer got the kinks out of the design of the car.* **4.** *Informal.* a mental quirk or whim. —*v.t.* to cause to form a kink or kinks. —*v.i.* to form a kink or kinks.

kin·ka·jou (king'kə jü') *n.* a small, slender, yellowish brown animal of Mexico and Central and South America that is related to the raccoon, having a long, prehensile tail and soft, woolly fur.

kink·y (king'kē) *adj.,* **kink·i·er, kink·i·est. 1.** full of kinks; tightly curled or twisted: *kinky*

kinkajou

hair. **2.** *Slang.* very strange or weird. —**kink'i·ness,** *n.*

kin·ship (kin'ship') *n.* **1.** a family relationship. **2.** any relationship or close connection.

kins·man (kinz'mən) *n., pl.* **kins·men** (kinz'mən). a male relative.

kins·wom·an (kinz'wùm'ən) *n., pl.* **kins·wom·en** (kinz'wim'ən). a female relative.

ki·osk (kē'osk, kē osk') *n.* a small structure with one or more open sides, used especially as a newsstand, bandstand, telephone booth, or subway entrance.

Ki·o·wa (kī'ə wə) *n., pl.* **Ki·o·wa** or **Ki·o·was.** a member of a North American Indian tribe living on the southern Great Plains.

kip·per (kip'ər) *v.t.* to cure (fish) by splitting, cleaning, and salting, and then drying, smoking, or preserving. —*n.* **1.** any of various kinds of fish,

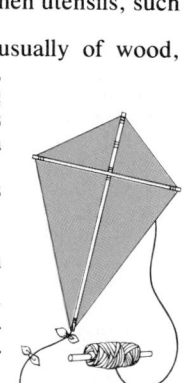

kiosk

especially herring, salmon, or sea trout, that have been kippered. **2.** a male salmon or sea trout during or shortly after spawning.

kirk (kûrk) *n. Scottish.* a church.

kis·met (kiz'met) *n.* fate; destiny.

kiss (kis) *v.t.* **1.** to touch with the lips as a sign of greeting, affection, desire, or respect. **2.** to touch lightly or softly: *When the sweet wind did gently kiss the trees* (Shakespeare, *The Merchant of Venice*). —*v.i.* to touch with the lips. —*n., pl.* **kiss·es. 1.** a touching with the lips as a sign of greeting, affection, desire, or respect. **2.** a light or gentle touch. **3.** a small candy, as one made of chocolate.

kit (kit) *n.* **1.** a set of tools, instruments, or equipment for a specific purpose: *a repair kit, a first-aid kit.* **2.** a collection of personal articles packed for traveling. **3.** a container for storing or carrying a kit: *a kit with spare parts in it.* **4.** a set of parts or materials to be assembled: *a chair kit.*

kitch·en (kich'ən) *n.* **1.** a room or place specially equipped or set apart for the preparation and cooking of food. **2.** the facilities, equipment, or staff of a kitchen: *The kitchen in that hotel operates 24 hours a day.*

kitch·en·ette (kich'ə net') *n.* a small kitchen.

kitchen police *Military.* **1.** the duty of helping the cook by performing kitchen chores. **2.** the enlisted persons assigned to such duty.

kitch·en·ware (kich'ən wâr') *n.* kitchen utensils, such as pots and pans.

kite (kīt) *n.* **1.** a lightweight frame, usually of wood, covered with paper, plastic, or cloth, flown into the air at the end of a long string for sport or recreation. **2.** any of various small hawks having a hooked bill, a forked tail, and long, narrow wings.

kith (kith) *n.* **kith and kin.** a person's friends, acquaintances, and relatives.

kit·ten (kit'ən) *n.* a young cat.

kit·ty¹ (kit'ē) *n., pl.* **kit·ties.** a kitten or cat. [*Kit(ten)* + -*y²*.]

kit·ty² (kit'ē) *n., pl.* **kit·ties.** money contributed by a group of people for some special purpose: *a kitty to pay for the party.* [*Kit* + -*y²*.]

kit·ty–cor·ner (kit'ē kôr'nər) *adv., adj.* other word for **catercorner.** Also, **kit·ty–cor·nered** (kit'ē kôr'nərd).

Kitty Litter *Trademark.* litter used for cats kept as household pets.

kite *(def. 1)*

kiwi *(def. 1)*

ki·wi (kē′wē) *n.*, *pl.* **ki·wis.** a bird of New Zealand that cannot fly, having a rounded body, a very long, slender bill, and brownish gray, furlike feathers. **2.** an oval, usually edible fruit having many seeds, green pulp, and a covering of reddish brown bristles when ripe. **3.** the climbing shrub that bears this fruit. Also *(defs. 2 and 3)*, **Chinese gooseberry.**

KKK, Ku Klux Klan.

klep·to·ma·ni·a (klep′tə mā′nē ə) *n.* a mental illness in which a person feels a very strong impulse to steal, especially items that are not needed.

klep·to·ma·ni·ac (klep′tə mā′nē ak′) *n.* a person who suffers from kleptomania.

klieg light (klēg) a bright arc lamp used especially in filming motion pictures.

klutz (kluts) *n.*, *pl.* **klutz·es.** *Slang.* an awkward or clumsy person. [From the Yiddish word *klotz* with the same meaning, from the German word *klotz* meaning "block of wood."]

km., kilometer; kilometers.

knack (nak) *n.* a special skill, ability, or method for doing something easily: *a knack for repairing things.*

knack·wurst (nok′wûrst′) *also,* **knock·wurst.** *n.* a short, thick, highly seasoned sausage.

knap·sack (nap′sak′) *n.* a bag for carrying clothes, equipment, or other supplies, strapped over the shoulders and carried on the back.

knave (nāv) *n.* **1.** a deceitful or dishonest, disloyal person; scoundrel. **2.** in card games, a jack. **3.** *Archaic.* **a.** a male servant. **b.** a man of humble birth.

knav·er·y (nā′və rē) *n.*, *pl.* **knav·er·ies.** behavior characteristic of a knave; deceitfulness; trickery.

knav·ish (nā′vish) *adj.* of, relating to, or characteristic of a knave; deceitful; dishonest. **—knav′ish·ly,** *adv.* **—knav′ish·ness,** *n.*

knapsack

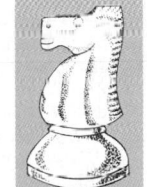

knead (nēd) *v.t.* to mix or work (a substance, such as dough or clay) into a uniform mass, especially by pressing and squeezing with the hands. **2.** to press and squeeze with the hands; massage: *The team's trainer kneaded the pitcher's sore arm.* **3.** to make or shape by kneading: *to knead a statue of clay.* **—knead′er,** *n.*

knee (nē) *n.* **1.** the joint of the human leg between the thigh and the lower leg. **2.** the region around this joint. **3.** any joint similar or corresponding to the human knee, such as the joint in the foreleg of hoofed mammals.

4. the part of a garment covering the knee. **—v.t.,** **kneed,** **knee·ing.** to strike or touch with the knee.

knee·cap (nē′kap′) *n.* a flat, triangular, movable bone at the front of the knee, protecting the joint from injury. Also, **patella.**

knee–deep (nē′dēp′) *adj.* **1.** so deep as to reach the knees: *The river is only knee-deep.* **2.** sunk to the knees: *The hikers were almost knee-deep in mud.* **3.** deeply involved or concerned: *knee-deep in the scandal.*

knee–high (nē′hī′) *adj.* so high or tall as to reach the knees. **—n.** a stocking that covers the leg up to the knee.

knee jerk, a reflex of the leg produced by a sharp tap to the tendon below the kneecap.

kneel (nēl) *v.i.,* **knelt** or **kneeled, kneel·ing.** to go or be down on a bent knee or knees. **—kneel′er,** *n.*

knee–pad (nē′pad′) *n.* a protective covering for the knee worn in certain sports, such as football or ice hockey.

knell (nel) *n.* **1.** the tolling of a bell, rung slowly and solemnly, as after a death or at a funeral. **2.** a warning of death or failure. **3.** any mournful sound. **—v.i.** (of a bell) to ring slowly and solemnly, as after a death or at a funeral; toll. **—v.t.** to summon or proclaim by or as if by a knell.

knelt (nelt) a past tense and past participle of **kneel.**

knew (nü, nū) the past tense of **know.**

Knick·er·bock·er (nik′ər bok′ər) *n.* **1.** a descendant of the early Dutch settlers of New York. **2.** a New Yorker. [From Diedrich *Knickerbocker,* the pen name under which Washington Irving wrote the book *History of New York* (1809).]

knick·ers (nik′ərz) *pl. n.* loose-fitting trousers ending just below the knee. Also, **knick·er·bock·ers** (nik′ər-bok′ərz).

knick·knack (nik′nak′) *also,* **nick·nack.** *n.* a small decorative object.

knife (nīf) *n.*, *pl.* **knives.** **1.** a tool for cutting, consisting of a sharp-edged blade attached to a handle. **2.** the cutting blade of a tool or machine. *v.,* **knifed, knif·ing. —v.t. 1.** to cut or stab with a knife. **2.** *Informal.* to slander, betray, or harm (someone) in an underhanded way. **—v.i.** to move or cut a way through something as if with a knife: *The boat knifed through the water.* **—knife′like′,** *adj.*

knight (nīt) *n.* **1.** in the Middle Ages, a mounted soldier who gave military service to a king or lord in return for the right to hold land, especially such a soldier who first served an apprenticeship as a page and squire. **2.** a man raised to honorary rank by a king or queen in recognition of personal merit or for services rendered to the crown or country. In Great Britain a knight is entitled to use *Sir* before his name. **3.** a piece in the game of chess shaped like a horse's head. **—v.t.** to raise to the rank of knight: *The king knighted the soldier for his courage.*

knight *(def. 3)*

knight–er·rant (nīt′er′ənt) *n.*, *pl.* **knights-er·rant.** a medieval knight who traveled in search of adventure to show his military skill, bravery, and chivalry.

knight·hood (nīt′hùd′) *n.* **1.** the rank or occupation of a knight. **2.** the behavior or qualities befitting a knight; chivalry. **3.** knights as a group.

---

at; āpe; fär; câre; end; mē; it; īce; pîerce; hot; ōld; sông, fôrk; oil; out; up; ūse; rüle; pùll; tûrn; chin; sing; shop; thin; this; hw in white; zh in treasure. The symbol ə stands for the unstressed vowel sound heard in about, taken, pencil, lemon, and circus.

K

knight·ly (nīt′lē) *adj.* of, relating to, or characteristic of a knight: *knightly deeds.* —**knight′li·ness**, *n.*

knish (knish) *n., pl.* **knish·es.** a baked or fried dumpling filled with potato, cheese, or meat.

knit (nit) *v.,* **knit·ted** or **knit, knit·ting.** —*v.t.* **1.** to make (a fabric or garment) by interlocking loops of yarn or thread, either by hand, by the use of knitting needles, or by machine. **2.** to join or fasten closely and securely: *Love knitted the family together.* **3.** to draw (the brows) together in wrinkles; furrow. —*v.i.* **1.** to make a cloth or garment by interlocking loops of yarn or thread. **2.** to come together closely: *The broken bone knitted well.* —*n.* a knitted fabric or garment. —**knit′ter**, *n.*

knit·ting (nit′ing) *n.* **1.** a knitted cloth or garment. **2.** the action of a person or thing that knits.

knitting needle, a long, slender rod, either straight or curved, having a blunt point at one or both ends, used in knitting.

knit·wear (nit′wâr′) *n.* clothing made of knitted cloth.

knives (nīvz) the plural of **knife.**

knob (nob) *n.* **1.** a rounded lump or part that sticks out: *I had a knob on my head where the ball hit me.* **2.** a rounded handle or dial, as for opening a door or drawer or for operating a radio or television. **3.** a rounded hill or mountain. —**knob′like′**, *adj.*

knob·by (nob′ē) *adj.,* **knob·bi·er, knob·bi·est.** **1.** covered with knobs or lumps. **2.** shaped like a knob: *knobby knees.*

knock (nok) *v.t.* **1.** to strike with a sharp, hard blow; hit: *The falling branch knocked me on the head.* **2.** to drive or force by hitting: *The batter knocked the ball out of the park.* **3.** to drive or bring (something) violently against something else; cause to collide: *Don't knock your leg against the table.* **4.** to hit or push so as to cause to fall: *to knock a glass to the floor.* **5.** to make by striking: *to knock a hole in the wall.* **6.** *Informal.* to find fault with: *The critics knocked the play.* —*v.i.* **1.** to strike a noisy blow or series of blows: *I knocked on the door.* **2.** to come into collision; bump: *Nervousness made my knees knock.* **3.** to make a pounding, clanking, or rattling sound: *The engine of the old car knocked.* —*n.* **1.** the act of knocking; a sharp, hard blow: *a knock on the head.* **2.** the sound made by a blow: *There was a knock on the door.* **3.** a pounding, clanking, or rattling sound, especially one in an automobile engine caused by faulty combustion. **4.** *Informal.* a misfortune; setback.

·**to knock about** or **knock around.** *Informal.* to wander from place to place.

·**to knock off. a.** *Informal.* to stop or discontinue: *to knock off work for lunch.* **b.** *Informal.* to complete; do: *The typist knocked off three letters in an hour.* **c.** *Informal.* to deduct (an amount or sum): *to knock off ten dollars from the price of an item.* **d.** *Slang.* to kill.

·**to knock out. a.** to make unconscious. **b.** *Informal.* to tire or exhaust completely: *The long hike really knocked me out.* **c.** *Informal.* to destroy: *The storm knocked out the electricity.*

knock·a·bout (nok′ə bout′) *n.* a small, one-masted sailboat, rigged with a mainsail and a jib. —*adj.* **1.** suitable for rough use or wear: *an old knockabout jacket.* **2.** rough; noisy; boisterous: *knockabout comedy.*

knock·down (nok′doun′) *adj.* **1.** powerful enough to knock down or overwhelm: *a knockdown punch.* **2.** made to be easily taken apart or put together: *a knockdown bookcase.* —*n.* the act of knocking down, as in a boxing match.

knock·er (nok′ər) *n.* **1.** a person or thing that knocks. **2.** a hinged knob, ring, or other device, usually made of metal, fastened to a door for use in knocking.

knock–kneed (nok′nēd′) *n.* having the legs curved inward so that the knees rub together in walking.

knock·out (nok′out′) *n.* **1.** a victory in boxing by means of a blow that leaves the opponent down and unable to rise and stand before the referee counts to ten. **2.** a blow that causes unconsciousness. —*adj.* causing a knockout: *a knockout punch.*

knock·wurst (nok′wûrst′) another spelling of **knack-wurst.**

knoll (nōl) *n.* a small, rounded hill or mound.

knot (not) *n.* **1.** a fastening made by intertwining rope, string, or the like, especially with one free end being passed through a loop and drawn tight. **2.** a lump or tangle made by the intertwining of thread, cord, or the like: *Let me comb the knots out of your hair.* **3.** a piece of material, such as ribbon, folded or tied into a knot and worn as an ornament or accessory. **4.** a small group or cluster of persons or things: *A knot of people waited for the train.* **5.** something intricate, involved, or difficult to solve: *It is too hard a knot for me* (Shakespeare, *Twelfth Night*).

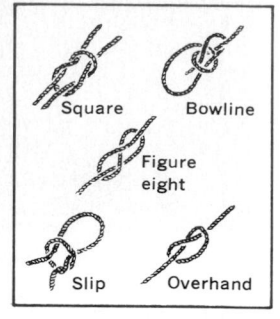

knots *(n., def. 1)*

6. something that forms or maintains a union; any tie or bond: *the marriage knot.* **7.** a hard, cross-grained lump of wood formed in a tree trunk at the point where a branch grows out from the tree. **8.** a cross section of such a lump, which shows as a roundish, cross-grained section in a board. **9.** a lump or swelling, as in a muscle or gland. **10.a.** a unit of speed of 1 nautical mile per hour, approximately equal to 6,076 feet per hour (1,852 meters per hour), or 1.15 statute miles. **b.** 1 nautical mile. —*v.,* **knot·ted, knot·ting.** —*v.t.* **1.** to tie in a knot; form a knot or knots in: *I knotted the string around the package.* **2.** to fasten with or by a knot. —*v.i.* to become tangled or snarled.

knot·hole (not′hōl′) *n.* a hole in a piece of cut wood where a knot has fallen out or been removed.

knot·ty (not′ē) *adj.,* **knot·ti·er, knot·ti·est.** **1.** having, covered with, or full of knots or bumps, as wood: *knotty pine.* **2.** hard to understand, solve, or explain; puzzling: *a knotty problem.* —**knot′ti·ness**, *n.*

know (nō) *v.t.,* **knew, known, know·ing.** **1.** to understand clearly; be certain of the facts or truth of: *Do you know the solution to this problem? I knew that it would rain when I saw the sky.* **2.** to be aware of: *I know exactly what I'm doing.* **3.** to be acquainted or familiar with: *I know them well, but I don't know their parents.* **4.** to have skill in or experience with: *to know how to type.* **5.** to have learned by memorizing; have in the mind: *to know the part perfectly.* **6.** to be able to tell the difference between; distinguish: *That critic knows good music from bad.* **7.** to meet with or experience: *They had known much sorrow and poverty in their life.* —*v.i.* **1.** to be aware: *They thought the party was a surprise, but we knew about it.* **2.** to have knowledge: *My cousin knows about car engines.* —**know′a·ble**, *adj.* —**know′er**, *n.*

·**in the know.** *Informal.* having special or secret information.

know·how (nō′hou′) *n. Informal.* the knowledge of how to do something; practical skill.

know·ing (nō′ing) *adj.* **1.** suggesting secret or private knowledge about something: *a knowing smile.* **2.** showing discernment or cunning; shrewd: *a knowing judge of human nature.* **3.** having knowledge; well-informed: *very knowing about horses.* —**know′ing·ly**, *adv.*

know–it–all (nō′it ôl′) *n. Informal.* a person who claims to know a great deal about everything and who rejects the opinions and advice of others.

knowl·edge (nol′ij) *n.* **1.** what is known from understanding, experience, study, or awareness: *My knowledge of physics is limited.* **2.** the fact of knowing: *The knowledge that the car might skid made me cautious.*

·**to one's knowledge** or **to the best of one's knowledge.** so far as one is aware: *I have never been to this town before, to the best of my knowledge.*

knowl·edge·a·ble (nol′i jə bəl) *adj.* having knowledge; well-informed: *knowledgeable about politics.* —**knowl′edge·a·bil′i·ty, knowl′edge·a·ble·ness,** *n.* —**knowl′edge·a·bly,** *adv.*

known (nōn) the past participle of **know.** —*adj.* generally, widely, or fully known: *a known fact.*

know–noth·ing (nō′nuth′ing) *n.* **1.** an ignorant person. **2. Know-Nothing.** a member of an American political party, prominent from 1853 to 1856, that opposed the political influence of immigrants.

knuck·le (nuk′əl) *n.* **1.** a joint of a finger, especially one connecting a finger to the hand. **2.** a cut of meat consisting of the hock or other joint of a four-legged animal. —*v.t.,* **knuck·led, knuck·ling.** to press, rub, or hit with the knuckles.

·**to knuckle under.** to give in; submit; yield: *The rebels would not knuckle under to the army.*

KO (kā′ō′) *Slang. n., pl.* **KO's.** a knockout in boxing. —*v.t.,* **KO'd, KO'ing.** to knock out in boxing: *to KO one's opponent.*

ko·a·la (kō ä′lə) *n.* an animal of Australia, having a chubby, tailless body covered with grayish blue fur, large, bushy ears, and a black nose. Koalas live mainly in trees, and the female carries her young in a pouch.

kohl·ra·bi (kōl rä′bē) *n., pl.* **kohl·ra·bies.** a plant of the cabbage family, having a white or purple, thick, round stem that looks like a turnip and is eaten as a vegetable.

koala

ko·la (kō′lə) *n.* **1.** a tropical evergreen tree having leathery oval leaves and bearing nuts and clusters of small, bell-shaped yellow flowers. **2.** its nuts, used chiefly to flavor soft drinks.

Ko·mo·do dragon (kə mō′dō) a lizard of Indonesia that is the largest in the world. It grows to a length of 12 feet (3.7 meters) and is able to kill large animals.

koo·doo (kü′dü′) *n., pl.* **koo·doos.** another spelling of **kudu.**

kook (kük) *n. Slang.* an odd or eccentric person: *People are staring at you because you're acting like a kook.* —**kook·y,** *adj.,* **kook·i·er, kook·i·est.**

kook·a·bur·ra (kŭk′ə bûr′ə, kŭk′ə bur′ə) *n.* a kingfisher of Australia that has a cry that sounds like loud, harsh laughter.

ko·peck (kō′pek) *also,* **ko·pek.** *n.* a copper or bronze coin of the Soviet Union, equal to ¹⁄₁₀₀ of a ruble.

Ko·ran (kô ran′, kô rän′) *n.* the sacred book of the Muslims, containing the religious and moral code of Islam. Muslims believe it contains the word of Allah, revealed by the archangel Gabriel to the prophet Muhammad.

Ko·re·an (kə rē′ən, kô rē′ən) *n.* **1.** a person who was born in or is a citizen of North Korea or South Korea. **2.** the language of Korea. —*adj.* of or relating to Korea, its people, or their language.

Korean War, the war between North Korea, aided by the People's Republic of China, and South Korea, aided by the United States and other United Nations members, which lasted from June 1950 until July 1953.

ko·sher (kō′shər) *adj.* **1.** conforming to Jewish ceremonial law, especially those laws relating to food and its preparation: *kosher meat.* **2.** serving or preparing food according to Jewish ceremonial law: *a kosher restaurant.*

3. *Slang.* right; proper: *Cheating isn't kosher.* —*v.t.* to prepare (food) according to Jewish ceremonial law. [From the Hebrew word *kāshēr* meaning ''fit, proper.'']

ko·to (kō′tō) *n., pl.* **ko·tos.** a Japanese musical instrument consisting of a sounding board over which are stretched strings that are plucked with plectrums.

kow·tow (kou′tou) *v.i.* **1.** to kneel and touch the forehead to the ground to show deep respect, submission, or worship. **2.** to show slavish respect: *I refused to kowtow to my boss.* —*n.* the act of kowtowing.

KP, kitchen police.

Kr, the symbol for krypton.

kraal (kräl) *n.* **1.** a village of South African blacks, usually surrounded by a fence or stockade. **2.** a pen for livestock, as cattle or sheep, in South Africa.

Krem·lin (krem′lin) *n.* **the Kremlin.** the government of the Soviet Union. [From the Russian word *kreml'* meaning ''citadel.'']

krill (kril) *n., pl.* **krill.** any of a group of small ocean crustaceans that resemble shrimp. Krill are eaten by various fish, seals, whales, and other animals.

Krish·na (krish′nə) *n.* a Hindu god worshiped as an incarnation of Vishnu.

Kriss Krin·gle (kris′ kring′gəl) another name for **Santa Claus.**

kryp·ton (krip′ton) *n.* a colorless, odorless, tasteless inert gaseous element, used in some electric light bulbs. Symbol: **Kr** [Formed from the Greek word *kryptos* meaning ''hidden,'' because the element is colorless, tasteless, and odorless.]

KS, postal abbreviation for Kansas.

ku·du (kü′dü) *also,* **koo·doo.** *n., pl.* **ku·dus.** a large African antelope having long, spirally twisted horns.

Ku Klux Klan (kü′ kluks′ klan′, kŭ′ kluks′ klan′) **1.** a secret society founded in the southern United States after the Civil War that used acts of terrorism against blacks and their supporters in an effort to reestablish the political and social dominance that white Southerners lost under Reconstruction. **2.** a secret society founded in 1915 and modeled on the original Ku Klux Klan but national in membership and directed against Roman Catholics, Jews, and immigrants as well as blacks.

kum·quat (kum′kwot) *also,* **cum·quat.** *n.* **1.** a small, oval orange or yellow fruit of any of a group of evergreen shrubs or trees, having a sweet rind and a sour pulp. **2.** a shrub or tree bearing this fruit.

kung fu (kung′fü′) a Chinese system of unarmed self-defense similar to karate. [From the Chinese word *gōngfu* meaning ''skill.'']

kur·cha·to·vi·um (kûr′chə tō′vē əm) *n.* see **rutherfordium.**

kW *also,* **kw.** kilowatt; kilowatts.

Kwa·ki·u·tl (kwä′kē ü′təl) *n., pl.* **Kwa·ki·u·tl** or **Kwa·ki·u·tls.** a member of a North American Indian tribe living on the northern coast of Vancouver Island and on the western coast of British Columbia.

kWh *also,* **kwh.** kilowatt-hour; kilowatt-hours.

Ky., Kentucky.

KY, postal abbreviation for Kentucky.

ky·mo·graph (kī′mə graf′) *n.* an instrument used for measuring and recording variations in fluid pressure, as in blood pressure or the pulse.

K

---

at; āpe; fär; câre; end; mē; it; īce; pîerce; hot; ōld; sông; fôrk; oil; out; up; ūse; rüle; pùll; tûrn; chin; sing; shop; thin; this; hw in white; zh in treasure. The symbol ə stands for the unstressed vowel sound heard in about, taken, pencil, lemon, and circus.

1. ancient Semitic
2. early Greek
3. later Greek
4. Etruscan
5. Latin
6. English

L is the twelfth letter of the English alphabet. The earliest form of **L** was the letter called *lamedh,* meaning "staff" or "rod," in the ancient Semitic alphabet (1). The ancient Greeks borrowed *lamedh* and, by reversing it and turning it upside-down, formed a new letter that they called *lambda* (2). By about the 5th century B.C., *lambda* was written as an upside-down letter V (3). This design was not adopted by the Etruscans, who wrote their letter **L** (4) very much as *lamedh* had been written. The Romans (5), who adopted the Etruscan alphabet, also based their letter **L** on *lamedh,* rather than *lambda.* By about 2,400 years ago, the Romans were writing this letter almost exactly the way we write the capital letter **L** today (6).

l, L (el) *n., pl.* **l's, L's. 1.** the twelfth letter of the English alphabet. **2.** something having the shape of this letter. **3. L.** the Roman numeral for 50.

l. 1. left. **2.** length. **3.** liter.

L., Latin.

la (lä) *n. Music.* **1.** the sixth note of the major scale. **2.** the note A.

La, the symbol for lanthanum.

La., Louisiana.

LA, postal abbreviation for Louisiana.

L.A., Los Angeles.

lab (lab) *n. Informal.* see **laboratory.**

la·bel (lā'bəl) *n.* **1.** a piece of cloth or paper that is fastened to something, such as a garment, package, or can, giving its name, manufacturer, contents, or other information. **2.** a word or short phrase used to describe, characterize, or classify a person, thing, or idea. —*v.t.,* **la·beled, la·bel·ing;** *also, British,* **la·belled, la·bel·ling. 1.** to put a label on. **2.** to describe or characterize by means of a label: *to label a chemical poisonous, to label a person a thief.* —**la'bel·er;** *also, British,* **la'bel·ler,** *n.*

la·bi·al (lā'bē əl) *adj.* **1.** of, relating to, or characteristic of the lips. **2.** *Phonetics.* made primarily by the lips in speaking. The sounds of the letters *m, p,* and *b* are labial sounds. —*n. Phonetics.* a vowel or consonant sound made by the lips.

la·bor (lā'bər) *also, British,* **la·bour.** *n.* **1.** physical or mental effort; work; toil. **2.** a specific task: *Hercules was given twelve labors to do.* **3.** persons who do manual work for a living, as a group. **4.** labor unions as a group. **5.** the effort of childbirth. —*v.i.* **1.** to do work; perform labor: *Workers labored daily in the coal mine.* **2.** to move slowly and with difficulty: *The old truck labored up the steep hill.* —*v.t.* to spend too much time on, or to work out in too much detail: *The speaker labored the point of the speech.*

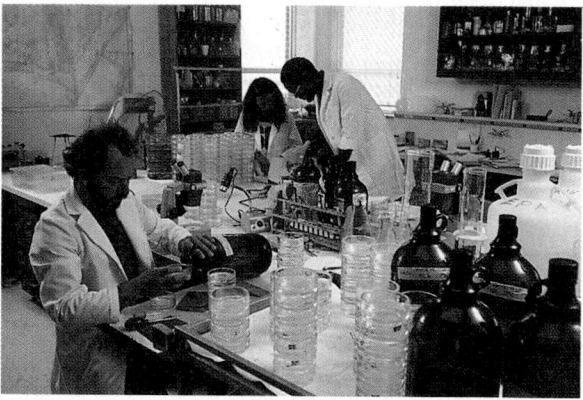

working in a **laboratory**

lab·o·ra·to·ry (lab'rə tôr'ē) *n., pl.* **lab·o·ra·to·ries.** a room, building, or workshop for teaching science or for making scientific experiments or tests.

Labor Day, a legal holiday in honor of working people, observed in the United States on the first Monday in September.

la·bored (lā'bərd) *adj.* done with effort; not easy; forced: *labored breathing, a labored style of writing.*

la·bor·er (lā'bər ər) *n.* a worker, especially one who does manual work for a living.

la·bo·ri·ous (lə bôr'ē əs) *adj.* **1.** needing much effort: *Checking all the names was a slow, laborious job.* **2.** hard-working; industrious: *a skilled, laborious carpenter.* —**la·bo'ri·ous·ly,** *adv.* —**la·bo'ri·ous·ness,** *n.*

la·bor·sav·ing (lā'bər sā'ving) *adj.* saving or designed to save work or effort: *a laborsaving appliance.*

labor union, an association of workers formed to protect and advance their interests, as by bargaining with employers for better wages and working conditions.

la·bour (lā′bər) *British.* another spelling of **labor.**

la·bur·num (lə bûr′nəm) *n.* any of a group of shrubs or small trees related to the pea, bearing hanging clusters of yellow flowers.

lab·y·rinth (lab′ə rinth′) *n.* **1.** a place with winding and connected passages or pathways in which it is easy to lose one's way; maze. **2.** any complicated or confusing arrangement, situation, or subject: *We got lost in the labyrinth of rooms in the museum.* **3. Labyrinth.** *Greek Mythology.* an underground maze in Crete designed by Daedalus to contain the Minotaur.

lab·y·rin·thine (lab′ə rin′thin) *adj.* of or like a labyrinth; intricate; complicated. Also, **lab·y·rin·thi·an** (lab′ə-rin′thē ən).

lac (lak) *n.* a reddish brown substance resembling resin that is left on trees in Asia by a female insect, used to make shellac and varnish.

lace (lās) *n.* **1.** a string, cord, or strip of leather passed or threaded through holes or eyelets to pull or hold together the edges or parts of something, such as a shoe. **2.** an ornamental, patterned fabric made by weaving together fine thread. —*v.*, **laced, lac·ing.** —*v.t.* **1.** to pull together or tighten with a lace or laces. **2.** to ornament or trim with lace. **3.** to fold together; interlace. —*v.i.* to fasten by means of a lace or laces. —*adj.* made of lace: *lace curtains.* [From the Old French word *lacier* meaning "to lace, fasten," from the Latin word *laqueare* "to ensnare," from the word *laqueus* "a noose, snare."]

lac·er·ate (las′ə rāt′) *v.t.*, **lac·er·at·ed, lac·er·at·ing.** **1.** to tear roughly or severely; mangle: *The sharp stones lacerated my arm when I fell.* **2.** to hurt or distress; wound: *Your harsh comment lacerated your friend's feelings.*

lac·er·a·tion (las′ə ra′shən) *n.* **1.** the act of lacerating. **2.** a rough, jagged tear or wound.

lace·wing (lās′wing′) *n.* any of a group of brown or green insects having four long wings veined in a lacy pattern.

lach·ry·mal (lak′rə məl) *also,* **lac·ri·mal.** *adj.* of or relating to tears or to the shedding of tears.

lach·ry·mose (lak′rə mōs′) *adj.* shedding tears or causing the shedding of tears; tearful or sad: *a lachrymose story.* —**lach′ry·mose′ly,** *adv.*

lack (lak) *v.t.* **1.** to be without or have too little of; need: *That poor family lacks food.* **2.** to be missing or short of: *My friend lacks an inch of being 6 feet tall.* —*v.i.* to be missing or needing: *What that athlete lacks in size is made up in speed.* —*n.* **1.** the state of being without or having too little: *The poor harvest was caused by a lack of rain.* **2.** something that is needed: *The most serious lack in your diet is vitamin A.*

lack·a·dai·si·cal (lak′ə dā′zi kəl) *adj.* lacking interest or energy; listless. —**lack′a·dai′si·cal·ly,** *adv.*

lack·ey (lak′ē) *n.*, *pl.* **lack·eys.** **1.** a person who follows or takes orders from another in a fawning, servile manner; flunky. **2.** a male servant, especially a footman.

lack·lus·ter (lak′lus′tər) *also,* British, **lack·lus·tre.** *adj.* lacking brightness, brilliance, or spirit; dull: *a lackluster performance.*

la·con·ic (lə kon′ik) *adj.* using few words to express much; terse; concise. [Originally from the Greek word *lakōnikos* meaning "Spartan," from *Lakōnikē* "Laconia," the region in Greece where Sparta is located. The Spartans were said to be terse.]

lac·quer (lak′ər) *n.* **1.** a fast-drying varnish containing manufactured and natural ingredients, used to protect and decorate objects of wood, metal, or other materials with a glossy coating. **2.** a varnish made from the sap of an Oriental sumac tree. **3.** wooden articles or decorative work covered with such varnish. —*v.t.* to coat with lacquer.

lac·ri·mal (lak′rə məl) another spelling of **lachrymal.**

la·crosse (lə krôs′) *n.* a game played with a ball by two teams having ten players each, using a special racket with a net on the end for catching, carrying, or throwing the ball. The object of the game is to get the ball into the opponent's goal.

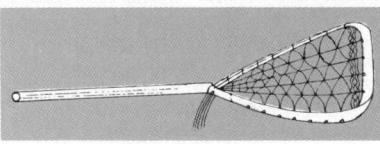

lacrosse racket

lac·tase (lak′tās) *n.* an enzyme found in yeast and in the digestive juices in the intestines of animals. Lactase aids in digestion by causing lactose to split into two simpler sugars.

lac·tate (lak′tāt) *v.i.*, **lac·tat·ed, lac·tat·ing.** to produce or give milk.

lac·ta·tion (lak tā′shən) *n.* **1.** the formation and secretion of milk by the mammary glands. **2.** the act or period of giving an infant or young animal milk from the breast or udder.

lac·tic (lak′tik) *adj.* of, relating to, or obtained from milk.

lactic acid, an acid formed in sour milk, in fermenting molasses, and in other foods. It is also produced in the muscles of the body during strenuous exercise.

lac·tose (lak′tōs) *n.* a white sugar present in milk. Also, **milk sugar.**

la·cu·na (lə kū′nə) *n.*, *pl.* **la·cu·nae** (lə kū′nē) or **la·cu·nas.** **1.** a space in which something has been left out; gap. **2.** a small cavity in bone or tissue.

lac·y (lā′sē) *adj.*, **lac·i·er, lac·i·est.** of or resembling lace. —**lac′i·ness,** *n.*

lad (lad) *n.* **1.** a young fellow; boy. **2.** *Informal.* a fellow; man.

lad·der (lad′ər) *n.* **1.** a structure made of two long side pieces joined by a series of crosspieces or rungs, used for climbing. **2.** any means of rising from one step or stage to another: *The employee started in the business at the bottom of the ladder as a clerk but later became the manager.*

lad·die (lad′ē) *n.* *Scottish.* a lad.

lade (lād) *v.*, **lad·ed, lad·ed** or **lad·en, lad·ing.** —*v.t.* **1.** to load (something, especially a ship with cargo): *The tanker was laden with petroleum.* **2.** to ladle. —*v.i.* **1.** to take on a load, as of cargo. **2.** to ladle liquid.

lad·en (lā′dən) *v.* a past participle of **lade.** —*adj.* **1.** loaded: *The ship was laden with riches.* **2.** weighed down; burdened: *The snow was falling from the laden branches of the pines* (Ernest Hemingway).

lad·ing (lā′ding) *n.* **1.** the act of loading. **2.** something that is loaded; freight; cargo.

la·dle (lā′dəl) *n.* a long-handled spoon with a cup-shaped bowl shaped like a cup, used for dipping liquids. —*v.t.*, **la·dled, la·dling.** to dip out with or carry in a ladle. —**la′dler,** *n.*

la·dy (lā′dē) *n.*, *pl.* **la·dies.** **1.** a polite term for a woman. **2.** the mistress of a household. **3.** a girl or woman of good family or breeding. **4.** a girl or woman who has good manners and good taste. **5. Lady.** In Great Britain, a woman of noble rank by birth, or the wife of a man holding

at; āpe; fär; câre; end; mē; it; īce; pîerce; hot; ōld; sông, fôrk; oil; out; up; ūse; rüle; půll; tûrn; chin; sing; shop; thin; this; hw in white; zh in treasure. The symbol ə stands for the unstressed vowel sound heard in about, taken, pencil, lemon, and circus.

L

the title of Lord. [From the Old English word *hlǣfdige* meaning "the mistress of a house."]

la·dy·bug (lā′dē bug′) *n.* any of a group of beetles having a round, humped body that is often bright red or orange with black spots. Most lady-bugs feed on aphids and other insect pests. Also, **la·dy·bird** (lā′dē bûrd′).

la·dy·fin·ger (lā′dē fing′gər) *n.* a small sponge cake like a finger in shape.

la·dy-in-wait·ing (lā′dē in wā′ting) *n., pl.* **la·dies-in-wait·ing.** a lady who is an attendant of a queen or princess.

la·dy·like (lā′dē līk′) *adj.* like or thought to be suitable for a lady.

la·dy·ship (lā′dē ship′) *n.* **1.** the rank, status, or position of a lady. **2. Ladyship.** the title or form of address used in speaking or referring to a Lady, usually preceded by *Her* or *Your.*

la·dy's-slip·per (lā′dēz slip′ər) *also,* **lady slipper.** *n.* an orchid of North America that bears flowers with a lower petal or lip resembling a shoe. Also, **moccasin flower.**

lag (lag) *v.i.,* **lagged, lag·ging. 1.** to fail to keep up or keep pace: *The little child lagged behind the rest of the family.* **2.** to drop or fall off; decline; slump: *My interest lagged after reading a few pages of the book.* —*n.* the act of lagging. —**lag′ger,** *n.*

la·ger (lä′gər) *n.* a light-bodied beer that is made by slow fermentation at low temperature and is aged for months before being used.

lag·gard (lag′ərd) *n.* a person or thing that lags. —*adj.* slow; backward.

la·goon (lə gün′) *n.* **1.** a shallow body of water partly or completely surrounded by a coral island or islands. **2.** a shallow body of sea water partly cut off from the sea by a narrow strip of land.

laid (lād) the past tense and past participle of **lay¹.**

laid-back *adj. Slang.* casual; relaxed; easygoing.

lain (lān) the past participle of **lie².**

lair (lâr) *n.* a home or resting place, especially of a wild animal.

laird (lârd) *n. Scottish.* an owner of a large estate; lord.

lais·sez faire (les′ā fâr′, lā′zä fâr′) the economic theory that commerce, business, and labor should be left alone or have as little interference or regulation by a government as possible. [From the French phrase *laissez faire* meaning "Allow (people) to do (as they wish)!" from the words *laisser* "to allow, let'" + *faire* "to do, make."] —**lais′sez-faire′,** *adj.*

la·i·ty (lā′i tē) *n., pl.* **la·i·ties. 1.** all persons who are members of a church but are not ordained for religious work. **2.** those who are not members of a certain profession or who are not trained in a certain field: *Lawyers use many legal words not familiar to the laity.*

lake (lāk) *n.* a large inland body of salt or fresh water, usually entirely surrounded by land.

lake dweller, a member of a prehistoric people who lived in lake dwellings.

lake dwelling, in prehistoric times, a hut built on a platform supported by piles over water or marshland.

lake trout, a large trout that is grayish green with pale spots, has a forked tail, and lives in lakes of North America.

la·ma (lä′mə) *n.* a priest or monk in Tibetan Buddhism.

lamb (lam) *n.* **1.** a young sheep. **2.** the meat from a lamb, used as food. **3.** the skin of a lamb. **4. the Lamb.** Jesus. **5.** a person who is gentle, weak, or innocent. —*v.i.* to give birth to a lamb.

lam·baste (lam bāst′, lam bast′) *also,* **lam·bast.** *v.t.,* **lam·bast·ed, lam·bast·ing.** *Informal.* **1.** to beat or thrash. **2.** to abuse with words.

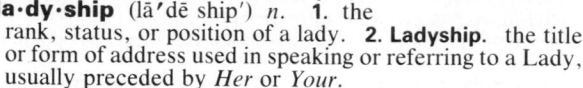
ladybug

lamb·da (lam′də) *n.* the eleventh letter (Λ, λ) of the Greek alphabet, corresponding to the English letter *L, l.*

lam·bent (lam′bənt) *adj.* **1.** shining with a soft glow: *lambent eyes, the lambent light of early morning.* **2.** (of a flame) flickering lightly over or on a surface. **3.** having lightness and brilliance: *a person with a lambent wit.*

lamb·kin (lam′kin) *n.* **1.** a little lamb. **2.** a person who is dearly loved, especially a young child.

lamb·skin (lam′skin′) *n.* **1.** the skin of a lamb, especially when prepared with the wool left on it and used for clothing. **2.** leather made from the skin of a lamb. **3.** parchment made from this leather.

lame (lām) *adj.,* **lam·er, lam·est. 1.** unable to walk easily or properly: *The old veteran is lame and has to walk with a cane.* **2.** stiff and painful: *a lame back.* **3.** poor or weak: *The employee offered a lame excuse for being late.* —*v.t.,* **lamed, lam·ing.** to make lame. —**lame′ly,** *adv.* —**lame′ness,** *n.*

la·mé (la mā′) *n.* a fabric woven with metallic threads.

lame duck 1. a public official who has not been reelected but continues to hold office. **2.** a person who is weak or useless.

la·ment (lə ment′) *v.t.* to feel or express sorrow, grief, or regret for or about: *to lament the loss of one's parents.* —*v.i.* to feel or express sorrow, grief, or regret. —*n.* **1.** an expression of sorrow, grief, or regret. **2.** a song or poem that expresses sorrow or grief.

lam·en·ta·ble (lam′ən tə bəl, lə men′tə bəl) *adj.* causing or likely to cause regret or sorrow: *a lamentable mistake.* —**lam′en·ta·bly,** *adv.*

lam·en·ta·tion (lam′ən tā′shən) *n.* **1.** the act of lamenting. **2.** mournful cries of sorrow or grief. **3. Lamentations.** the book of the Old Testament thought to have been written by Jeremiah.

lam·i·na (lam′ə nə) *n., pl.* **lam·i·nae** (lam′ə nē′) or **lam·i·nas. 1.** a thin plate, scale, or layer. **2.** *Botany.* the flat part of a leaf or petal.

lam·i·nate (*v.,* lam′ə nāt′; *n.,* lam′ə nit, lam′ə nāt′) *v.t.,* **lam·i·nat·ed, lam·i·nat·ing. 1.** to make by binding together different layers, as with glue or heat. **2.** to cover with thin sheets or layers. **3.** to beat or roll (metal) into thin plates. —*n.* something made by laminating, such as safety glass or plywood. —**lam′i·na′tor,** *n.*

lam·i·na·tion (lam′ə nā′shən) *n.* **1.** the process of laminating or the state of being laminated. **2.** a thin layer: *A lamination of plastic made the counter more durable.*

lamp (lamp) *n.* **1.** a device for making light, as by using an electric light bulb or by burning oil, kerosene, or gas. **2.** a light bulb. Also, **incandescent lamp. 3.** a device that gives off heat or other radiation, such as a sunlamp.

lamp·black (lamp′blak′) *n.* a black pigment consisting of almost pure carbon soot, made by burning oil or gas.

lamp·light (lamp′līt′) *n.* the light from a lamp or lamps.

lamp·light·er (lamp′lī′tər) *n.* formerly, a person whose job was to light gas or oil street lights at night.

lam·poon (lam pün′) *n.* a piece of writing that attacks and makes fun of someone or something. —*v.t.* to attack and make fun of in a lampoon. —**lam·poon′er,** *n.*

lamp·post (lamp′pōst′) *n.* a post supporting a lamp, as in a street or a park.

lam·prey (lam′prē) *n., pl.* **lam·preys.** any of a group of primitive saltwater and freshwater fish that look like eels. The lamprey has a round mouth with teeth for attaching itself to other fish in order to feed on their blood.

Lan·cas·tri·an (lang-kas′trē ən) *adj.* of or relating to the English house of Lancaster. —*n.* a member or supporter of the house of Lancaster.

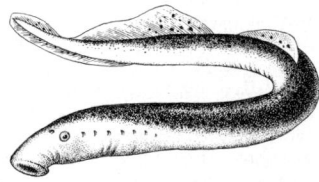
lamprey

lance (lans) *n.* **1.** a long spear, usually having a wooden shaft with a sharp metal head. **2.** any spearlike weapon or instrument. **3.** a soldier armed with a lance. —*v.t.*, **lanced, lanc·ing. 1.** to pierce with a lance. **2.** to open with a lancet: *The doctor lanced the boil.* [From the Old French word *lance* meaning this weapon, from the Latin word *lancea* "a lance."]

lance corporal, an enlisted person in the U.S. Marine Corps, ranking above a private first class and below a corporal.

Lan·ce·lot (lan'sə lot') *n.* in the legends of King Arthur, the bravest knight of the Round Table.

lanc·er (lan'sər) *n.* a cavalry soldier armed with a lance.

lanc·ers (lan'sərz) *n.* **1.** a dance that is a form of the quadrille. **2.** the music for such a dance. ▲ used with a singular verb.

lan·cet (lan'sit) *n.* a short surgical knife having two sharp edges.

lance·wood (lans'wŭd') *n.* **1.** a tough wood, used mainly for fishing rods and billiard cues. **2.** any of various tropical trees yielding this wood.

land (land) *n.* **1.** the part of the surface of the earth that is not under water: *The sailors sighted land after many days at sea.* **2.** ground or soil: *The land around the old house is low and swampy.* **3.** an area marked off by political, cultural, or other boundaries; country or region. **4.** the people who live in a country or region. **5.** real estate; property: *to invest in land.* —*v.i.* **1.** to come down from the air and alight on a surface: *The plane landed at the airport.* **2.** to come to land or shore: *The ship landed safely in the harbor.* **3.** to come ashore from a ship: *The troops landed.* **4.** to come to rest: *I threw my glove, and it landed on the table.* **5.** to end up: *The thief landed in jail.* —*v.t.* **1.** to bring down from the air onto a surface: *The pilot landed the plane carefully.* **2.** to set ashore from a ship or other vessel; unload onto land: *to land a cargo, to land passengers.* **3.** to cause to end up: *Fishing without a license will land you in trouble.* **4.** to bring (a fish) to land or into a boat. **5.** *Informal.* to win; get: *The teenager landed a good summer job.*

lan·dau (lan'dou, lan'dô) *n.* a carriage with four wheels, two seats, and a top that opens in the center and folds down in the back and front.

landau

land breeze, a breeze blowing toward the sea from the land.

land·ed (lan'did) *adj.* **1.** owning land: *landed gentry.* **2.** consisting of land: *landed property.*

land·fall (land'fôl') *n.* **1.** the act or instance of reaching or sighting land, as after a long voyage. **2.** the land so reached or sighted.

land·fill (land'fil') *n.* **1.** an area of land that has been filled in, usually by dumping refuse and mixing or covering it with soil: *These new houses were built on a landfill.* **2.** the refuse disposed of in this manner.

land·form (land'form') *n.* a feature on the surface of the earth, such as a valley or mountain range.

land grant, a gift of public land by the government for a public purpose, such as for the establishment of a college.

land·hold·er (land'hōl'dər) *n.* a person who owns land.

land·ing (lan'ding) *n.* **1.** the act or process of coming to the earth or land, or coming ashore. **2.** the space on a dock or pier for passengers coming ashore or for unloading a ship. **3.** a platform at the end of or between flights of stairs: *After climbing four flights, we rested on the landing before continuing to the top floor.*

landing field, an area of land for the takeoff and landing of aircraft.

landing gear, the wheels and other structures on which an aircraft lands.

landing stage, a floating platform for loading and unloading people and goods at a wharf or pier.

landing strip, a long, narrow area for the takeoff and landing of aircraft.

land·la·dy (land'lā'dē) *n., pl.* **land·la·dies. 1.** a woman who owns houses or apartments occupied by tenants. **2.** a woman who runs an inn, boarding house, or rooming house.

land·less (land'lis) *adj.* owning no land.

land·locked (land'lokt') *adj.* **1.** entirely or almost entirely surrounded by land: *a landlocked country.* **2.** living entirely in fresh water: *landlocked salmon.*

land·lord (land'lôrd') *n.* **1.** a person who owns houses or apartments occupied by tenants. **2.** a person who runs an inn, boarding house, or rooming house.

land·lub·ber (land'lub'ər) *n.* a person who has had little or no experience on board a ship.

land·mark (land'märk') *n.* **1.** an object in a landscape that is familiar or striking and serves as a guide. **2.** an important building or site: *The Civil War battlefield was declared a national landmark.* **3.** an important fact or event: *The development of the laser was a landmark of modern science.* **4.** an object that serves to mark a boundary line.

land·mass (land'mas') *n.* a large area of land.

land mine, an explosive device put underground and set to go off when people or vehicles pass over or near it.

land·own·er (land'ō'nər) *n.* a person who owns land. —**land'own'ing,** *adj.*

land·poor (land'pur') *adj.* owning much land, but not earning enough income from it to pay taxes or other expenses.

land·scape (land'skāp') *n.* **1.** a stretch or expanse of scenery that can be viewed from one point or place. **2.** a painting, photograph, or other picture showing such a stretch of scenery. —*v.,* **land·scaped, land·scap·ing.** —*v.t.* to beautify or improve (a piece of land) by planting trees and other plants and designing gardens. —*v.i.* to do landscape gardening.

landscape gardener, a person whose work is landscape gardening.

landscape gardening, the art or process of beautifying land, such as the grounds around a house, by planting trees and other plants and designing gardens.

land·slide (land'slīd') *n.* **1.** the sliding or falling down of a mass of soil or rock: *a landslide down a mountain slope.* **2.** a mass of soil or rock that slides down. **3.** an overwhelming victory in an election.

lands·man (landz'mən) *n., pl.* **lands·men** (landz'mən). a person who lives or works on land.

land·ward (land'wərd) *adj.* lying or going toward the land. —*adv.* also, **landwards.** toward the land.

lane (lān) *n.* **1.** a narrow way or road: *The child walked down the country lane.* **2.** a course or route bounded by definite lines: *a shipping lane, a traffic lane.* **3.** a narrow passage of wood along which bowling balls are rolled; bowling alley.

lan·guage (lang'gwij) *n.* **1.** an organized system of spoken sounds by which people communicate their thoughts and feelings to each other; human speech. **2.** a group of written symbols representing these spoken sounds. **3.** all the spoken sounds, and the written symbols representing

at; āpe; fär; câre; end; mē; it; īce; pîerce; hot; ōld; sông, fôrk; oil; out; up; ūse; rüle; pùll; tûrn; chin; sing; shop; thin; this; hw in white; zh in treasure. The symbol ə stands for the unstressed vowel sound heard in about, taken, pencil, lemon, and circus.

them, that make up a system by which the members of a nation, tribe, or other group communicate with each other: *the Spanish language, the languages of the American Indians.* **4.** any means of communication or expression, as by gestures, signs, or symbols: *Algebra is a language of mathematics.* **5.** the special words used by a particular profession: *military language, legal language.* **6.** words or wording: *We did not fully understand the language of the legal contract.* **7.** a means of communication used by animals: *Scientists hope someday to understand the language of dolphins.* **8.** the study of language; linguistics. **9.** see **computer language.**

Language Note

Only human beings have the ability to use **language.** They have been defined as "the language-using animals," and some scientists believe that the use of language is the only important characteristic that humans do not share with any other animal. It is language that helps make possible all forms of human thought and activity.

Until very recently, language scholars believed that children learned to use language by listening to their parents and other older people speak and then imitating them. Today, some *linguists,* or experts in the science of language, put forth the theory that people are born with a special ability to learn and use language. Children can make up thousands of new, understandable sentences that they have never heard before. These sentences consistently follow correct grammatical patterns, even though the children obviously have not yet learned anything about the rules of grammar. A child would not say "Want I ball the red" for "I want the red ball." Children's ability to form completely new sentences in a correct way is much too creative and sophisticated a skill to be considered as simply the result of an imitation of the speech of older people.

There are thousands of languages spoken by various peoples, and there does not seem to be any single feature that all of them share. Some linguists believe that certain principles of grammar govern all of them. It is known that any child will learn equally well whatever language he or she is first exposed to. If each child is born with a special ability to learn language, all languages must have something in common, or else the child could not use this special ability for different languages.

language arts, the courses, such as reading, spelling, grammar, composition, and literature, that are taught in elementary school, in middle or junior high school, and in high school to develop a student's skill in the use of language.

lan·guid (lang′gwid) *adj.* showing a lack of energy or force; weak; sluggish: *The languid youth spent the day in a hammock.* —**lan′guid·ly,** *adv.*

lan·guish (lang′gwish) *v.i.* **1.** to grow weak or feeble; lose health or vitality: *The farmer's crops languished from the long dry spell. The child languished from neglect.* **2.** to live under unpleasant conditions that cause a loss of health or vitality: *The people languished under the dictator's rule.* **3.** to suffer with desire or longing; pine: *The immigrant languished in the new country and missed the customs and language of the old.*

lan·guor (lang′gər) *n.* **1.** lack of vigor; weakness; fatigue: *Our languor was caused by the hot, humid weather.* **2.** tenderness or softness of mood or feeling: *The beautiful music brought on a feeling of languor.* —**lan′guor·ous,** *adj.*

lank (langk) *adj.* **1.** long and lean; slender: *The basketball player was tall and lank.* **2.** (of hair) limp and straight.

lank·y (lang′kē) *adj.,* **lank·i·er, lank·i·est.** ungracefully tall and thin; gangling. —**lank′i·ly,** *adv.* —**lank′i·ness,** *n.*

lan·o·lin (lan′ə lin) *also,* **lan·o·line** (lan′ə lin, lan′ə-lēn′). *n.* a fatty substance obtained from the wool of sheep, used in various ointments, cosmetics, and soaps.

lan·tern (lan′tərn) *n.* **1.** a casing or covering for a light, usually made to be carried: *a kerosene lantern.* **2.** the chamber at the top of a lighthouse in which the light is placed. **3.** a structure on the top of a roof or dome, with windows or openings to admit light and air.

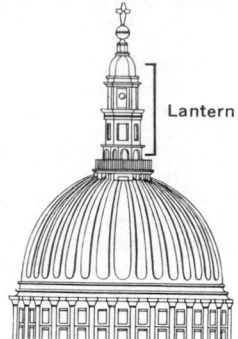

Lantern

lan·tha·num (lan′thə nəm) *n.* a soft, white metallic element of the rare-earth group, used in alloys. Symbol: **La** [Formed from the Greek word *lanthanein* meaning "to escape notice." The existence of the element was long undetected because it was mistaken for another element already identified.]

lan·yard (lan′yərd) *n.* **1.** a short

lantern *(def. 3)*

rope or cord used on ships to fasten or tighten things, such as the supports for the masts. **2.** a cord worn around the neck, used to hang a knife or whistle from. **3.** a cord with a small hook at one end, used in firing certain types of cannons.

La·oc·o·ön (lā ok′ō on′) *n. Greek Legend.* a Trojan priest who was killed with his sons by two sea serpents after he warned the Trojans against the Trojan Horse, the large wooden horse left by the Greeks supposedly as a gift.

La·o·tian (lā ō′shən) *n.* **1.** a person who was born in or is a citizen of Laos. **2.** the language of the Laotians. —*adj.* of or relating to Laos, its people, their language, or culture.

lap¹ (lap) *n.* **1.** the area in front between the waist and the knees of a seated person. **2.** the clothing that covers this area. **3.** responsibility or control: *to leave problems in someone's lap.* **4.** the place or condition in which someone is cared for: *to live in the lap of luxury.* [From the Old English word *læppa* meaning "the skirt of a garment."]

lap² (lap) *v.,* **lapped, lap·ping.** —*v.i.* **1.** to lie partly over or beside another; overlap: *The insect's wings lapped over one another.* **2.** to extend beyond something in space or time: *The morning meeting lapped over into the lunch hour.* **3.** to wind, wrap, or fold: *The long scarf lapped around my neck twice.* —*v.t.* **1.** to wind, wrap, or fold about: *The parent lapped the child in a blanket.* **2.** to lay (something) partly over or beside another: *to lap one shingle over another.* **3.** to get ahead of by one length or circuit of something, as a racetrack: *The runner lapped the other runners in the race.* —*n.* **1.** the act of lapping over. **2.** the part or amount of something that lies partly over another. **3.** one length or circuit of something, such as a racetrack: *At the finish line the winning car was a full lap ahead of the remaining cars in the race.* [From the Middle English word *lappen* meaning "to wrap around, envelop," from the Old English word *læppa* "the skirt of a garment."]

lap³ (lap) *v.,* **lapped, lap·ping.** —*v.t.* **1.** to drink (a liquid) by lifting it into the mouth with the tongue: *The cat lapped its milk.* **2.** to move or wash gently against with a splashing sound: *Waves lapped the dock.* —*v.i.* to move or wash something gently with a splashing sound: *The waves lapped against the rocks.* —*n.* **1.** the act of lapping. **2.** a gentle, splashing sound. [From the Old English word *lapian* meaning "to lick, lap³."]

lap dog, a pet dog that is small enough to be held easily on the lap.

la·pel (lə pel′) *n.* the part of the front of a coat or jacket that is folded back and forms a continuation of the collar.

lap·i·dar·y (lap′i der′ē) *n., pl.* **lap·i·dar·ies.** a person who engraves, cuts, or polishes precious stones. —*adj.* of or relating to the engraving, cutting, or polishing of precious stones.

lap·is laz·u·li (lap′is laz′ə lē, lap′is laz′yə le, lap′is lazh′ə lē) a semiprecious stone used for carvings or jewelry, usually deep blue or violet-blue.

Lap·land·er (lap′lan′dər) *n.* a person who was born or is living in Lapland.

Lapp (lap) *n.* **1.** a member of an ethnic group living in Lapland. **2.** the language of the Lapps.

lap robe, a fur robe or blanket used to protect the legs from the cold, as when a person is riding in an open carriage or sleigh.

lapse (laps) *n.* **1.** a mistake or error, especially a small or unimportant one: *a spelling lapse, a memory lapse.* **2.** a period or interval: *The wanderer returned after a lapse of ten years.* **3.** a slipping back, as from a moral standard: *a lapse into bad habits.* **4.** a gradual ending or falling into disuse: *a lapse of a conversation, a lapse of an insurance policy.* —*v.i.,* **lapsed, laps·ing. 1.** to slip back, as from a moral standard: *After dieting for a month, my friend lapsed into poor eating practices and gained weight.* **2.** to slip or fall: *The building lapsed into ruin.* **3.** to end or fall into disuse: *The contract lapsed.*

lap·wing (lap′wing′) *n.* a bird noted for its slow, irregular wing beat and a shrill, wailing cry.

lar·board (lär′bərd) *n., adj.* another word for **port²**.

lar·ce·ny (lär′sə nē) *n., pl.* **lar·ce·nies.** the crime of unlawfully taking away another person's property; theft. —**lar′ce·nous,** *adj.*

larch (lärch) *n., pl.* **larch·es. 1.** a tall tree related to the pine, bearing needle-shaped leaves that are shed each year. **2.** the hard, strong, durable wood of this tree.

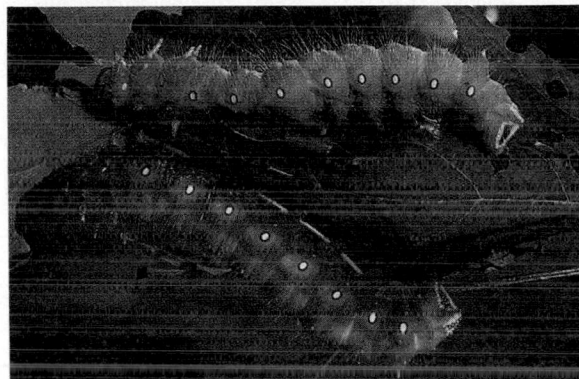
lapwing

lard (lärd) *n.* a soft, white fat made from the fatty tissue of a hog, used in cooking. —*v.t.* **1.** to add lard to or cover with lard. **2.** to stuff with pieces of fat before cooking. **3.** to add extra material to (speech or writing): *to lard a paragraph with quotations from Shakespeare.*

lar·der (lär′dər) *n.* **1.** a place where food is kept; pantry. **2.** a stock of food.

lar·es and pe·na·tes (lâr′ēz; pə nā′tēz, pə nä′tēz) **1.** the household gods of the ancient Romans. **2.** the treasured possessions of a family or household.

large (lärj) *adj.,* **larg·er, larg·est. 1.** of great size, amount, or number, especially in comparison with others of the same kind: *a large room, a large collection of stamps.* **2.** wide in range or capacity: *the large powers of a dictator.* —**large′ness,** *n.*
  •**at large. a.** at liberty; free: *The suspect is still at large.* **b.** of, relating to, or representing an entire area: *a council member at large.* **c.** as a whole; in general: *to talk about the world at large.*

large·heart·ed (lärj′här′tid) *adj.* generous; liberal; kindly. —**large′heart′ed·ness,** *n.*

large intestine, the lower part of the intestines, between the small intestine and the anus. As digested food passes through the large intestine, water is absorbed from it and feces are formed.

large·ly (lärj′lē) *adv.* to a great extent; mostly; mainly: *The newer buildings in the center of the town are largely made of brick.*

large–print (lärj′print′) *adj.* printed in large characters for more convenient use by persons with limited eyesight: *a large-print edition of a book or newspaper.*

large–scale (lärj′skāl′) *adj.* **1.** of a wide range; extensive: *a large-scale strike.* **2.** drawn or made to a large scale: *a large-scale model.*

lar·gess (lär jes′, lär′jis) *also,* **lar·gesse.** *n.* generous giving.

lar·go (lär′gō) *adj., adv. Music.* very slow and dignified; stately. —*n., pl.* **lar·gos.** a slow and dignified musical composition or passage.

lar·i·at (lar′ē ət) *n.* a long rope with a loop at one end, used for roping livestock; lasso. [From the phrase *la reata* meaning ''the lasso'' in the American variety of Spanish, from the article *la* ''the'' + the dialect word *reata* ''lasso,'' from the Spanish word *reatar* meaning ''to tie again.'']

lark¹ (lärk) *n.* **1.** any of a group of small, mostly Old World songbirds having a long, straight hind claw and, usually, gray-brown feathers. **2.** any of a group of similar but unrelated birds, such as the meadowlark. [From the Old English word *lāwerce* meaning ''an Old World lark¹.'']

lark² (lärk) *n.* something done just for fun; adventure or antic: *We jumped in the fountain for a lark.* —*v.i.* to do things just for fun. [Of uncertain origin.]

lark·spur (lärk′spûr′) *n.* another word for **delphinium**.

lar·va (lär′və) *n., pl.* **lar·vae** (lär′vē). **1.** an insect in the

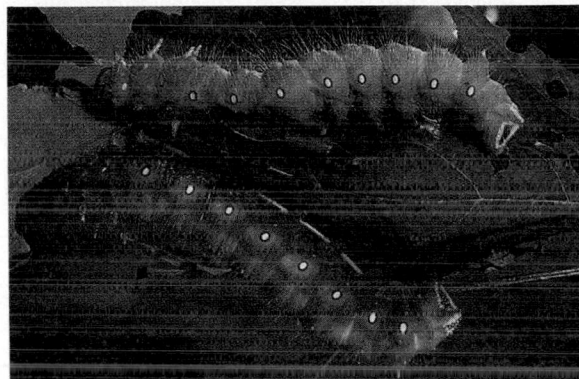
larva

early, usually wormlike, stage of metamorphosis after hatching from an egg, coming before the pupa stage. The caterpillar is the larva of butterflies and moths. **2.** the early form of an animal that undergoes metamorphosis. The tadpole is the larva of a frog.

lar·val (lär′vəl) *adj.* of, relating to, or in the shape of a larva: *The caterpillar is the larval stage of development in certain insects.*

lar·vi·cide (lär′və sīd′) *n.* a substance used to kill harmful insect larvae, such as some garden pests.

lar·yn·ge·al (lə rin′jē əl, lar′in jē′əl) *adj.* of, relating to, or affecting the larynx.

lar·yn·gi·tis (lar′ən jī′tis) *n.* inflammation of the larynx, often characterized by hoarseness, sometimes resulting in a temporary inability to speak normally.

---

at; āpe; fär; câre; end; mē; it; īce; pîerce; hot; ōld; sông, fôrk; oil; out; up; ūse; rüle; pull; tûrn; chin; sing; shop; thin; this; hw in white; zh in treasure. The symbol ə stands for the unstressed vowel sound heard in about, taken, pencil, lemon, and circus.

L

lar·ynx (lar′ingks) *n., pl.* **la·ryn·ges** (lə rin′jēz) or **lar·ynx·es.** the boxlike chamber at the upper end of the windpipe, containing the vocal cords and serving as the organ of speech; voice box.

la·sa·gna (lə zän′yə) *also,* **la·sa·gne.** *n.* **1.** a baked dish usually with layers of wide noodles, chopped meat, tomato sauce, and cheese. **2.** a broad, flat noodle.

las·civ·i·ous (lə siv′ē əs) *adj.* **1.** feeling, showing, or characterized by lust. **2.** tending to arouse lust. —**las·civ′i·ous·ly,** *adv.* —**las·civ′i·ous·ness,** *n.*

la·ser (lā′zər) *n.* a device that produces an extremely powerful beam of light consisting of light waves that are of the same wavelength and are in phase. The laser has many uses in industry, medicine, and communications. [Short for *l*(ight) *a*(mplification by) *s*(timulated) *e*(mission of) *r*(adiation).]

larynx

laser disc *also,* **laser disk.** another term for **optical disc.**

laser printer, a computer printer that uses a laser beam to form characters and graphics on paper.

lash¹ (lash) *n., pl.* **lash·es.** **1.** a stroke or blow with a whip: *The sailor was given ten lashes.* **2.** the flexible, often braided, part of a whip. **3.** see **eyelash.** **4.** a movement like that of a whip: *The lash of the cow's tail struck the farm worker in the face.* —*v.t.* **1.** to beat or strike with a whip: *The jockey lashed the racehorse.* **2.** to beat or strike forcefully or violently; dash against: *The hurricane winds lashed the boats in the harbor.* **3.** to wave or move to and fro like a whip; switch angrily: *The tiger lashed its tail.* **4.** to attack or scold sharply: *The newspaper article lashed the dishonest politician.* —*v.i.* **1.** to dash violently: *The waves lashed against the rocks.* **2.** to beat or strike with or as if with a whip. [From the Middle English word *lashen* meaning "to strike, beat."]

·**to lash out.** to make an attack with sudden violence or harsh, bitter words: *The writer lashed out against the critics.*

lash² (lash) *v.t.* to tie or fasten with a rope or cord: *The friends lashed logs together to make a raft.* [From the Old French word *lacier* meaning "to lace, fasten," from the Latin word *laqueare* "to ensnare," from the word *laqueus* "a noose, snare¹."]

lass (las) *n., pl.* **lass·es.** a young woman; girl.

las·sie (las′ē) *n.* a young girl.

las·si·tude (las′i tüd′, las′i tūd′) *n.* a tired feeling; weariness; exhaustion.

las·so (las′ō, la sü′) *n., pl.* **las·sos** or **las·soes.** a long rope with a loop, used for roping livestock. —*v.t.,* **las·soed, las·so·ing.** to rope with a lasso: *The cowboy lassoed the steer.*

last¹ (last) *adj.* **1.** following all others, as in order or time; final: *I was the last one in line. December is the last month of the year.* **2.** being the only one remaining: *That was the last apple.* **3.** next before the present; most recent; latest: *We saw a movie last night.* **4.** least expected or likely; most unlikely: *A palm tree is the last thing you would expect to see in Alaska.* —*adv.* **1.** after all the others; at the end: *Cake and coffee*

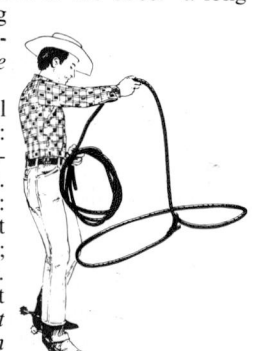

lasso

were served last.* **2.** at a time nearest the present; most recently: *When did you last write to your family?* **3.** in conclusion; finally. —*n.* **1.** a person or thing that is last: *The family was the last to learn of what happened.* **2.** the end; conclusion: *When will we hear the last of their troubles?* [From the Old English word *latost,* superlative of *læt* meaning "late, slow, sluggish."]

·**at last.** finally: *At last, the dog stopped barking.*

last² (last) *v.i.* **1.** to go on; continue: *The visit lasted for only fifteen minutes.* **2.** to stay in good condition: *These shoes will last longer if you take care of them.* **3.** to be enough: *The milk should last until morning.* [From the Old English word *læstan* meaning "to continue" and "to follow."]

last³ (last) *n.* a wood or metal form, shaped like a human foot, on which shoes are made or repaired. —*v.t.* to form (shoes) on a last. [From the Old English word *læste* meaning this object, from the word *last* "a covering for the foot."]

last–ditch (last′dich′) *adj.* made or done as a final effort, especially to prevent a crisis, failure, or disaster: *a last-ditch attempt to save an endangered species.*

last·ing (las′ting) *adj.* continuing or existing for a long time; permanent; enduring: *lasting fame.* —**last′ing·ly,** *adv.*

Last Judgment, another term for **Judgment Day.**

last·ly (last′lē) *adv.* in the last place; in conclusion: *Lastly, we will need people to help put up decorations for the party.*

last straw, the added factor that finally makes something impossible to bear or endure.

Last Supper, the final meal of Jesus and the Apostles on the night before the Crucifixion.

last word **1.** the final remark, as in an argument. **2.** the power to make a final decision or judgment; ultimate authority: *If there is a dispute among club members, the club president has the last word.* **3.** the final or definitive statement, treatment, or work: *This book is the last word on model airplanes.* **4.** *Informal.* the most recent style or development: *the last word in stereo equipment.*

lat., latitude.

Lat., Latin.

latch (lach) *n., pl.* **latch·es.** any device for keeping a door, window, or gate closed. A latch is usually made of a bar that falls or slides into a notch, hole, or groove. —*v.t.* to fasten the latch of (something). —*v.i.* to close with a latch: *Do the cabinet doors latch?*

·**to latch onto.** *Informal.* **a.** to attach oneself to; stick close to. **b.** to grasp or get.

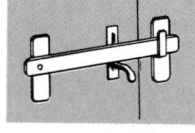

latch

latch·key (lach′kē′) *n., pl.* **latch·keys.** a key for opening the latch of a door or gate.

latch·string (lach′string′) *n.* a string passing through a hole in a door, used to open a latch.

late (lāt) *adj.* **lat·er, lat·est.** **1.** coming after the proper or expected time: *I was late for school this morning.* **2.** coming after the usual time: *We had a late lunch today.* **3.** being toward the end: *late summer.* **4.** beginning or taking place at an advanced time, especially at night: *a late telephone call, the late show on television.* **5.** of or relating to an advanced stage of history or development: *the late Middle Ages, the artist's late works.* **6.** recent: *a late scientific discovery.* **7.** recently dead: *My late uncle was a judge.* **8.** having recently held an office or position: *The late mayor denounced the new mayor's ideas.* —*adv.* **1.** after the proper, expected, or usual time: *to arrive late at a party.* **2.** at or until an advanced time, especially at night: *The young girl stayed up late.* [From the Old English word *læt* meaning "late, slow, sluggish."] —**late′ness,** *n.*

·of late. lately; recently: *Our neighbor has been acting rather strangely of late.*

late·com·er (lāt′kum′ər) *n.* **1.** a person who arrives late. **2.** a person or thing that has recently arrived.

la·teen (la tēn′) *adj.* relating to or having a sailing rig with a triangular sail hung from a long, slanting rod or yard, and extending both fore and aft of the mast.

Late Greek, a form of the Greek language used from about A.D. 300 to 600.

Late Latin, a form of the Latin language used from about A.D. 300 to 600.

late·ly (lāt′lē) *adv.* not long ago; recently: *Have you seen your cousin lately?*

la·tent (lā′tənt) *adj.* present but not active or seen; hidden: *the latent talents of a child.* **—la′ten·cy,** *n.*

lat·er (lā′tər) the comparative of **late.**

lat·er·al (lat′ər əl) *adj.* of, from, or toward the side: *a lateral doorway, a lateral shoot on the stem of a plant.* **—n.** in football, a pass thrown to the side or in a direction away from the opponent's goal. Also, **lateral pass.** **—v.i.** to throw a lateral. **—lat′er·al·ly,** *adv.*

lat·est (lā′tist) the superlative of **late.**

la·tex (lā′teks) *n., pl.* **lat·i·ces** or **la·tex·es.** **1.** a milky liquid that comes from a rubber tree and is made of small globules of pure rubber suspended in water. **2.** a similar milky liquid found in some other plants, such as milkweeds and poppies. **3.** a similar synthetic liquid, used as a base for certain paints.

lath (lath) *n.* any of the thin, narrow strips of wood or meshes of metal used to form a base for a coat of plaster or stucco or for tiles or slates, as on a roof. **—v.t.** to build or line with laths.

lathe (lāth) *n.* a machine that holds a long piece of wood, metal, or other material at both ends, and turns it for shaping by a cutting tool.

lath·er (lath′ər) *n.* **1.** foam, froth, or suds made especially from soap moistened with water. **2.** foam caused by sweating, as on a horse. **—v.i.** to form a lather. **—v.t.** to cover with lather: *to lather one's face before shaving.*

lat·i·ces (lat′ə sēz′) a plural of **latex.**

Lat·in (lat′in) *n.* **1.** the language of the ancient Romans. **2.** a member of any of the peoples, such as the Italians, Spanish, or Portuguese, whose languages are derived from Latin. **3.** a person who lived in ancient Rome. **—adj.** **1.** of, relating to, or written in Latin. **2.** of or relating to the people or countries that use languages derived from Latin. **3.** of or relating to ancient Rome or its people. **4.** of or relating to the alphabet used to write Latin and most European languages, including English.

Language Note

Latin has been a major influence on English because of its contribution of nearly half of English vocabulary and because of its impact on the form and style of our language. During the Middle Ages, Latin was the language of the Church, and therefore the language of all literate, educated people. Much of our vocabulary in the fields of religion, philosophy, and education comes from Latin. A knowledge of Latin (and later, of Greek) was required of anyone who wanted to be educated, and Latin remained the language of the universities until the nineteenth century. To this day, both traditional scientific vocabulary and many of the new scientific and technical terms come from Latin. The study of Latin, therefore, can be useful for understanding the origin and meaning of many English words.

Lat·in–A·mer·i·can (lat′in ə mer′i kən) *adj.* of or relating to Latin America.

Latin cross, a cross formed by one short horizontal bar that intersects a longer vertical bar near the top. It is used as a sacred symbol, especially by many Christian denominations.

La·ti·no (la tē′nō) *n., pl.* **La·ti·nos.** a person living in the United States who is of Latin-American origin or descent. [From the American Spanish word *Latino,* with the same meaning, from the Spanish word *latino* meaning "a Latin person."]

lat·i·tude (lat′i tüd′, lat′i tūd′) *n.* **1.** the distance north or south of the equator, expressed as degrees measured from the earth's center. All points of a given latitude form a circle running east and west and parallel to the equator. **2.** a place or region considered with respect to its latitude: *These plants thrive in warmer latitudes.* **3.** freedom from narrow restrictions: *The students were given great latitude in selecting topics for the essays they were to write.*

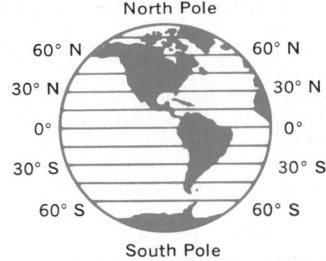

lines of **latitude**

lat·i·tu·di·nal (lat′i tü′də nəl, lat′i tū′də nəl) *adj.* of or relating to latitude.

la·trine (lə trēn′) *n.* a toilet for the use of a large number of people, especially in an army camp.

lat·ter (lat′ər) *adj.* **1.** the second of two mentioned: *If offered a choice between swimming and tennis, I would much prefer the latter sport.* ▲ See **former** for usage note. **2.** nearer to the end: *We spent the latter part of the evening at a party with friends on the other side of town.*

Lat·ter–day Saint (lat′ər dā′) a member of the Church of Jesus Christ of Latter-day Saints; Mormon.

lat·ter·ly (lat′ər lē) *adv.* at a recent time; recently; lately.

lat·tice (lat′is) *n.* **1.** a structure of crossed or interlaced strips, as of wood or metal, spaced to form a regular pattern of openings. **2.** something having this structure, such as a window. **—v.t.,** **lat·ticed, lat·tic·ing.** **1.** to form into or arrange like a lattice. **2.** to furnish with a lattice.

lat·tice·work (lat′is wûrk′) *n.* **1.** a lattice. **2.** lattices, or something made of lattices.

Lat·vi·an (lat′vē ən) *n.* **1.** a person who was born in or is a citizen of Latvia. **2.** the language of the Latvians. **—adj.** of or relating to Latvia, its people, their language, or culture.

lattice window

laud (lôd) *v.t.* to praise. **—n.** a hymn or song of praise.

laud·a·ble (lô′də bəl) *adj.* worthy of praise; commendable: *Everyone agrees that your work with the sick and aged is very laudable.* **—laud′a·bil′i·ty,** *n.* **—laud′a·bly,** *adv.*

lau·da·num (lô′də nəm) *n.* a medicinal solution of opium in alcohol.

---

at; āpe; fär; câre; end; mē; it; īce; pîerce; hot; ōld; sông, fôrk; oil; out; up; ūse; rüle; pùll; tûrn; chin; sing; shop; thin; this; hw in white; zh in treasure. The symbol ə stands for the unstressed vowel sound heard in about, taken, pencil, lemon, and circus.

L

laud·a·to·ry (lô′də tôr′ē) *adj.* containing or expressing praise.

laugh (laf) *v.i.* **1.** to make the sounds and the facial movements that show amusement, joy, scorn, or other emotions. **2.** to feel amusement or joy; be happy. —*v.t.* to produce an effect upon by laughing: *to laugh one's troubles away.* —*n.* the act, sound, or manner of laughing: *Your laugh is rather loud.* —**laugh′er,** *n.*
· **no laughing matter.** a serious matter.
· **to have the last laugh.** to win or have one's way at the end of a dispute, especially after apparently losing.
· **to laugh off.** to dismiss lightly; treat as not serious: *to laugh off an injury.*
· **to laugh up one's sleeve.** to laugh to oneself; to be secretly amused.

laugh·a·ble (laf′ə bəl) *adj.* causing or meriting laughter or scorn. —**laugh′a·ble·ness,** *n.* —**laugh′a·bly,** *adv.*

laugh·ing (laf′ing) *adj.* **1.** making or seeming to make the sounds of laughter: *a laughing brook.* **2.** laughable: *Your mistake is no laughing matter.* —*n.* laughter. —**laugh′ing·ly,** *adv.*

laughing gas, another term for **nitrous oxide.**

laugh·ing·stock (laf′ing stok′) *n.* an object of ridicule.

laugh·ter (laf′tər) *n.* the action or sound of laughing.

launch[1] (lônch) *v.t.* **1.** to put (a boat or ship) into the water. **2.** to push or propel by force into the air: *to launch a rocket.* **3.** to start (someone or something) on a course or career: *to launch a political career.* —*v.i.* **1.** to start something with enthusiasm. **2.** to move outward into the water or air. —*n., pl.* **launch·es.** the act of launching. [From the Norman French word *lancher* meaning "to throw, hurl," from the Late Latin word *lanceare* "to throw a lance," from the Latin word *lancea* "a lance."] —**launch′er,** *n.*

launch[2] (lônch) *n., pl.* **launch·es. 1.** an open motorboat. **2.** the largest boat carried by a warship. [From either the Spanish or Portuguese word *lancha* meaning a type of ship's boat.]

launch pad, an area or structure from which a rocket or missile is launched. Also, **launching pad.**

laun·der (lôn′dər) *v.t.* **1.** to wash or wash and iron (clothes or linens). **2.** to make (money obtained illegally) appear to be lawfully gained by directing it through another person or organization. —**laun′der·er,** *n.*

laun·dress (lôn′dris) *n., pl.* **laun·dress·es.** a woman who is employed to do laundering, or who works in a laundry.

Laun·dro·mat (lôn′drə mat′) *n. Trademark.* a self-service laundry with coin-operated washing machines and dryers.

laun·dry (lôn′drē) *n., pl.* **laun·dries. 1.** things that have been, are, or will be laundered. **2.** a place where laundering is done.

laun·dry·man (lôn′drē mən) *n., pl.* **laun·dry·men** (lôn′drē mən). **1.** a person who works in a laundry. **2.** a person who collects and delivers laundry.

laun·dry·wom·an (lôn′drē wùm′ən) *n., pl.* **laun·dry·wom·en** (lôn′drē wim′ən). a laundress.

lau·re·ate (lôr′ē it) *n.* **1.** a person given a special honor: *a Nobel laureate.* **2.** see **poet laureate.** [From the Latin word *laureatus* meaning "crowned with laurel," from *laurea* "laurel." It was the ancient Roman custom to honor poets, athletes, and other heroes by crowning them with a laurel wreath.]

lau·rel (lôr′əl) *n.* **1.** a medium-sized evergreen tree bearing spicy, lance-shaped leaves and clusters of tiny yellow flowers. **2.** any of a group of related trees or shrubs, such as the mountain laurel. **3. laurels.** an honor; distinction.
· **to rest on one's laurels.** to be satisfied with what one has already done.

la·va (lä′və, lav′ə) *n.* **1.** hot liquid rock from a volcano or an opening in the earth's surface. **2.** volcanic rock that has been formed by the cooling of such molten material.

lava *(def. 1)*

lav·a·to·ry (lav′ə tôr′ē) *n., pl.* **lav·a·to·ries. 1.** a room with sinks for washing the hands and face. **2.** a sink for washing. **3.** a toilet. [From the Late Latin word *lavatorium* meaning "place for washing," going back to the Latin word *lavare* "to wash."]

lave (lāv) *v.,* **laved, lav·ing.** —*v.t.* to wash or bathe (someone or something). —*v.i.* to wash or bathe.

lav·en·der (lav′ən dər) *n.* **1.** a pale reddish purple color. **2.** any of a group of plants and shrubs related to the mint, having narrow grayish leaves and spikes of fragrant pale purple flowers that yield an oil used in perfumes. **3.** the dried leaves and flowers of this plant, used mainly to give a pleasant fragrance to clothes or linen. —*adj.* **1.** having the color lavender; pale reddish purple. **2.** having the fragrance of lavender.

lav·ish (lav′ish) *adj.* **1.** giving or spending in great or wasteful amounts: *Our friends are much too lavish with their money.* **2.** given in great amounts; more than necessary: *The hosts served lavish amounts of whipped cream on the dessert.* —*v.t.* to give in great amounts: *The old couple lavished gifts on their grandchildren.* —**lav′ish·ly,** *adv.* —**lav′ish·ness,** *n.*

law (lô) *n.* **1.** a rule that allows or prohibits certain conduct or activities, fixed by custom or made by a group of people with authority, such as a legislature or court, and applied to an entire community, state, or country. **2.** a particular set of such rules: *international law, the law of the land.* **3.** the governing of people according to such rules: *respect for law and order.* **4.** an agent or agency, especially the police, that applies or enforces such rules: *The escaped convicts were eventually captured by the law.* **5.** a lawsuit: *to resort to law.* **6.** the study of such rules: *a student of law.* **7.** the profession of being a lawyer: *to practice law.* **8.** a rule or custom: *the laws of grammar.* **9.** a statement in science or mathematics about what always happens whenever certain events take place or certain conditions exist.
· **to lay down the law.** to command or order something with authority.

law–a·bid·ing (lô′ə bī′ding) *adj.* obedient to the law.

law·break·er (lô′brā′kər) *n.* a person who breaks the law.

law·ful (lô′fəl) *adj.* **1.** allowed by law: *lawful acts.* **2.** according to law: *a lawful marriage.* —**law′ful·ly,** *adv.* —**law′ful·ness,** *n.*

law·giv·er (lô′giv′ər) *n.* a person who makes a law or code of laws.

law·less (lô′lis) *adj.* **1.** not according to or obeying the law: *a lawless act, a lawless person.* **2.** not controlled by law: *a lawless frontier town.* —**law′less·ly,** *adv.* —**law′less·ness,** *n.*

law·mak·er (lô′mā′kər) *n.* a person who makes laws; legislator.

law·mak·ing (lô′mā′king) *n.* the making of laws. —*adj.* responsible for making laws: *a lawmaking body.*

lawn¹ (lôn) *n.* a grassy area that is kept closely mowed, especially around a house. [From the Old French word *lande* meaning "grassy area," of Celtic origin.]

lawn² (lôn) *n.* a lightweight, sheer cotton fabric, used for blouses and handkerchiefs. [From the French town *Laon,* known for the manufacture of linen.]

lawn bowling, another term for **bowls.**

lawn mower, any of various machines with revolving blades used for cutting grass.

lawn tennis, see **tennis** *(def. 1).*

law·ren·ci·um (lô ren′sē əm) *n.* a radioactive element produced artificially from californium. Symbol: **Lr** [From the American physicist Ernest O. *Lawrence* (1901–1958).]

law·suit (lô′süt′) *n.* a legal action begun in a court of law to settle a claim.

law·yer (lô′yər) *n.* a person whose profession is representing clients in lawsuits and advising them in legal matters; attorney.

lax (laks) *adj.* **1.** not careful or strict; not exact; negligent: *lax discipline.* **2.** not rigid or firm; slack: *a lax cord.* —**lax′ly,** *adv.* —**lax′ness,** *n.*

lax·a·tive (lak′sə tiv) *n.* a medicine that stimulates the emptying of the bowels.

lax·i·ty (lak′si tē) *n.* the state or quality of being lax.

lay¹ (lā) *v.,* **laid, lay·ing.** —*v.t.* **1.** to place or put down on something; cause to lie: *Please lay the plate on the table.* **2.** to make ready; prepare: *to lay plans for the coming holiday.* **3.** to put down and fasten in place: *The workers laid the carpet.* **4.** to make and deposit (an egg or eggs). **5.** to consider as caused by or resulting from something: *The farmer laid the poor crops to lack of rain.* **6.** to put: *The teacher laid much stress on good study habits.* **7.** to offer or present: *to lay claim to land.* **8.** to fix or set in a particular way or state: *to lay fears to rest.* **9.** to strike and cause to fall: *The punch laid the fighter low.* **10.** to bet: *The gambler laid twenty dollars on the winning team.* **11.** to place in a particular setting or location: *The novel is laid in colonial America.* —*v.i.* to lay an egg or eggs. —*n.* the way something lies or is arranged: *the lay of the land.* [From the Old English word *lecgan* meaning "to place, put."]

·**to lay aside** or **to lay away** or **to lay by.** to put away or save for future use; save; reserve: *to lay money aside for college.*

·**to lay bare.** to expose or make known: *All the facts are laid bare in the report.*

·**to lay down. a.** to assert or declare: *to lay down the law.* **b.** to give up; sacrifice: *to lay down one's life for one's country.*

·**to lay into.** *Informal.* to make a vigorous physical or verbal attack on.

·**to lay off. a.** to mark off; fix: *to lay off boundaries.* **b.** to dismiss from employment: *to lay off workers.* **c.** *Slang.* to stop: *to lay off teasing someone.*

·**to lay out. a.** to spread out and arrange: *to lay out one's clothes for packing.* **b.** to arrange according to a design or plan: *The general laid out the next day's attack.* **c.** to spend: *to lay out twenty dollars for a gift.* **d.** to prepare (a corpse) for burial.

·**to lay over.** to stop for a short time: *We laid over in Birmingham on our way to New Orleans.*

·**to lay to. a.** to engage in or do with vigor or enthusiasm. **b.** to bring a sailing vessel into the wind and keep it from moving.

·**to lay up. a.** to store or put aside for future use. **b.** to keep or be kept indoors because of illness or injury; confine: *My friend was laid up with the flu.*

lay² (lā) the past tense of **lie².**

lay³ (lā) *adj.* **1.** of or relating to those who are not members of the clergy. **2.** of or relating to those not in a certain profession, such as medicine or law. [From the Old French word *lai* meaning "secular" or "ignorant," going back to the Greek word *laos* "people."]

lay⁴ (lā) *n.* **1.** a short poem originally meant to be sung. **2.** a melody; song. [From the Old French word *lai* with the same meaning, of Celtic origin.]

lay·er (lā′ər) *n.* **1.** a single thickness laid on or over something: *There is a layer of ice on the street.* **2.** a chicken that lays eggs. —*v.t.* to make, arrange, or form in layers: *to layer a cake.* —**la′yer·ing,** *n.*

lay·ette (lā et′) *n.* a complete outfit for a newborn baby, including clothes, toilet articles, and bedding.

lay·man (lā′mən) *n., pl.* **lay·men** (lā′mən). **1.** a person who does not belong to a certain profession. **2.** a person who is not a member of the clergy.

lay·off (lā′ôf′) *n.* **1.** the act of firing or dismissing employees. **2.** a period of unemployment.

lay·out (lā′out′) *n.* **1.** the act or process of laying out. **2.** the way in which the various parts of something are located or arranged; design: *the layout of a building, the layout of a book.* **3.** a thing having or showing such a design.

lay·o·ver (lā′ō′vər) *n.* a stop in the course of a trip.

lay·per·son (lā′pûr′sən) *n.* **1.** a person who does not belong to a certain profession. **2.** a person who is not a member of the clergy.

laze (lāz) *v.i.,* **lazed, laz·ing.** to be lazy; loaf: *The tourists enjoyed lazing in the sun.*

la·zy (lā′zē) *adj.,* **la·zi·er, la·zi·est. 1.** not willing to work or make an effort to do anything. **2.** moving slowly; sluggish: *a lazy river.* **3.** causing the state or feeling of being lazy: *a lazy summer day* —**la′zi·ly,** *adv.* —**la′zi·ness,** *n.*

lb., pound; pounds. [Short for the Latin word *libra* meaning "a balance, scale" and "the Roman pound."]

lbs., pounds.

l.c., lower case.

l.c.d., L.C.D., least common denominator; lowest common denominator.

l.c.m., L.C.M., least common multiple; lowest common multiple.

lea (lē) *n.* a meadow; pasture.

leach (lēch) *v.t.* **1.** to drain or wash by filtering with water or other liquid. **2.** to dissolve or remove loose parts from (ashes, soils, ores, or other materials) by filtration with water or other liquid. —*n., pl.* **leach·es. 1.** a material or container used to leach. **2.** the act, instance, or result of leaching.

lead¹ (lēd) *v.,* **led, lead·ing.** —*v.t.* **1.** to show the way, especially by going first: *Our guide led us down the trail.* **2.** to conduct or guide, as by pulling or holding by the hand: *The dog led our blind neighbor across the street.* **3.** to be or show a route or way for: *This road will lead you into town.* **4.** to be ahead of or first in: *Our track team led their opponents in the race.* **5.** to be the head of; control or direct: *The officer led the troops.* **6.** to cause to arrive at a particular opinion or to do a particular

at; āpe; fär; câre; end; mē; it; īce; pierce; hot; ōld; sông, fôrk; oil; out; up; ūse; rüle; pull; tûrn; chin; sing; shop; thin; this; hw in white; zh in treasure. The symbol ə stands for the unstressed vowel sound heard in about, taken, pencil, lemon, and circus.

thing: *What led you to that conclusion? The doctor's advice led them to stop smoking.* **7.** to have or experience; live: *to lead a life of ease.* **8.** *Card Games.* to begin a round with (a card). —*v.i.* **1.** to go or be first; be ahead of all others: *The home team leads seven to three.* **2.** to show the way; be a guide. **3.** to be a route or way: *This hall leads to the bedrooms.* **4.** *Card Games.* to play the first card in a round. —*n.* **1.** the state or position of being ahead of all others: *Two runners shared the lead in the race.* **2.** the extent of being ahead: *a seven-yard lead.* **3.** an example or direction: *to follow someone's lead.* **4.** a piece of information that serves as a guide; clue: *The detective had several good leads on the crime.* **5.** the main role in a play, motion picture, or the like. **6.** a person who has such a role. **7.** an opening or introductory paragraph in a news story. **8.** *Baseball.* the position or distance of a base runner away from one base and toward the next. —*adj.* that is first; leading: *a lead article in a magazine, a lead runner in a race.* [From the Old English word *lǣdan* meaning "to lead¹."]

·**to lead off. a.** to begin; open: *The speaker led off the talk with jokes.* **b.** *Baseball.* to be the first person on a team to bat in an inning.

·**to lead on.** to draw or entice into foolish action or mistaken opinion: *It's unkind to lead people on.*

·**to lead up to.** to prepare the way for gradually: *The series of meetings and conferences led up to the trade agreement.*

lead² (led) *n.* **1.** a heavy, soft, bluish gray, poisonous metallic element that resists corrosion and conducts electricity poorly. It is used in car batteries and as a shield against radiation. Symbol: **Pb 2.** a thin stick of graphite mixed with clay in a pencil. **3.** a weight attached to a line used to determine the depth of water. **4.** bullets; shot. **5. leads.** frames made of metal, in which panes of glass are placed. —*v.t.* to cover, join, weight, or mix with lead. [From the Old English word *lēad* meaning this metal.]

lead·en (led′ən) *adj.* **1.** made of lead: *a leaden bucket.* **2.** dull gray like lead: *a leaden sky.* **3.** difficult to move; heavy: *tired, leaden legs.* **4.** gloomy; depressed: *the leaden feeling after a loss.*

lead·er (lē′dər) *n.* **1.** a person who leads: *the leader of a gang, the leader of a band.* **2.** a short length of material connecting the lure or hook to a fish line. —**lead′·er·less,** *adj.*

lead·er·ship (lē′dər ship′) *n.* **1.** the position or function of a leader. **2.** the ability to lead or guide others. **3.** direction or guidance: *This project lacks real leadership.* **4.** leaders as a group: *the union leadership.*

lead·ing (lē′ding) *adj.* **1.** chief or principal: *a leading cause of disease.* **2.** being or going first: *a leading horse in a race.* **3.** being or playing the lead: *the leading role in a play.*

leaf (lēf) *n., pl.* **leaves. 1.** the flat, usually green part of a plant, growing from a stem and serving to make food by means of photosynthesis. **2.** a sheet of paper in a book. **3.** a very thin sheet of metal, especially gold, used for decoration. **4.** an extra piece for making a table's surface larger. —*v.i.* **1.** to put forth leaves: *The trees leaf in the spring.* **2.** to turn and glance at the pages of something, as a book or magazine. [From the Old English word *lēaf* meaning the flat part of a plant.] —**leaf′like′,** *adj.*

·**to turn over a new leaf.** to

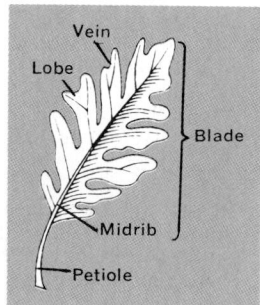

leaf (def. 1)

act in a different and better way: *The student vowed to turn over a new leaf and study two hours every evening.*

leaf·less (lēf′lis) *adj.* without leaves.

leaf·let (lēf′lit) *n.* **1.** a single sheet of printed matter, used to advertise or announce something; handbill; flyer. **2.** a small, unbound book; booklet: *This leaflet contains the instructions for operating the appliance.* **3.** a small or young leaf. **4.** *Botany.* one of the separate blades or divisions of a compound leaf.

leaf·stalk (lēf′stôk′) *n.* another word for **petiole.**

leaf·y (lē′fē) *adj.,* **leaf·i·er, leaf·i·est.** covered with leaves or resembling a leaf. —**leaf′i·ness,** *n.*

league¹ (lēg) *n.* **1.** an association of people or countries formed to promote their common interests. **2.** an association of athletic teams that compete regularly with each other: *a basketball league.* —*v.i.,* **leagued, lea·guing.** to band together into a league. [From the French word *ligue* with the same meaning, going back to the Latin word *ligare* "to bind, tie."]

·**in league.** associated together; working together.

league² (lēg) *n.* a measure of distance equal to 3 miles (4.8 kilometers). [From the Medieval Latin word *leuga* with the same meaning, of Celtic origin.]

League of Nations, an association of nations formed in 1920 to settle international disputes and to promote world peace. The League of Nations was disbanded in 1946 and replaced by the United Nations.

lea·guer (lē′gər) *n.* a member of a league.

leak (lēk) *n.* **1.** an accidental passage of something, such as water, air, or light, through a hole or other small opening: *The tire went flat because of a slow leak.* **2.** the hole itself: *Can you patch the leak in the rowboat?* **3.** the making known of secret information. —*v.i.* **1.** to have a leak: *The water pipes leak.* **2.** to pass through a hole or other small opening: *All the gasoline leaked out of the gas tank during the night.* **3.** to become known: *News of the plot leaked out.* —*v.t.* **1.** to pass or cause (something) to pass through a hole or other opening. **2.** to allow (secret information) to become known: *The lawyer leaked the testimony to the newspapers.*

leak·age (lē′kij) *n.* **1.** the act, process, or instance of leaking. **2.** the amount that leaks. **3.** something that is leaking or has leaked.

leak·y (lē′kē) *adj.,* **leak·i·er, leak·i·est.** having a leak or leaks. —**leak′i·ness,** *n.*

lean¹ (lēn) *v.,* **leaned** or **leant, lean·ing.** —*v.i.* **1.** to be at an angle from a straight, upright position: *The walls of the old shed lean outward.* **2.** to bend the body: *The customer leaned over the counter.* **3.** to rest on or against something for support: *Lean on my arm.* **4.** to depend on or use: *to lean on someone for encouragement.* **5.** to tend, as in opinion; be favorably inclined: *My taste in music leans toward jazz.* —*v.t.* **1.** to cause to bend: *to lean one's body over a railing.* **2.** to cause to be at an angle from a straight, upright position. —*n.* the act or state of leaning. [From the Old English word *hleonian* meaning "to lean¹, incline."]

lean² (lēn) *adj.* **1.** with little or no fat: *The star basketball player is tall and lean.* **2.** (of meat) containing little or no fat. **3.** not having or producing enough; meager; poor: *That was a lean year for farmers.* —*n.* a part of meat with little or no fat. [From the Old English word *hlǣne* with the same meaning.] —**lean′ness,** *n.*

lean·ing (lē′ning) *n.* a tendency to favor one thing over another; inclination.

leant (lent) a past tense and past participle of **lean¹.**

lean-to (lēn′tü′) *n., pl.*

lean-to (def. 2)

lean-tos. **1.** a shed or building having a roof that slopes in one direction, supported by the wall of a building against which it is built. **2.** a crude, usually open shelter, with a sloping roof formed of branches, twigs, and the like: *The hikers built a lean-to in the woods to protect their supplies from the rain.*

leap (lēp) *v.*, **leaped** or **leapt, leap·ing.** —*v.i.* **1.** to make a big jump: *The dancer leaped into the air.* **2.** to move eagerly or quickly: *The warriors leaped into battle.* —*v.t.* **1.** to make a big jump over: *The horse leaped a wall.* **2.** to cause to make a big jump: *The rider leaped the horse over the fence.* —*n.* **1.** a big jump: *The lion made a leap through a burning hoop.* **2.** the distance covered in a leap.

leap·frog (lēp'frôg', lēp'frog') *n.* a game in which players take turns jumping over the backs of the other players. —*v.t.* **leap·frogged, leap·frog·ging.** to leap over in a game of leapfrog.

leapt (lept, lēpt) a past tense and past participle of **leap.**

leap year, a year containing an extra day, February 29. Leap year occurs when the number of the year can be divided evenly by 4, except in the last year of a century, which must be divided evenly by 400.

Lear (lîr) *n.* a legendary king of Britain, the hero of Shakespeare's tragedy *King Lear.*

learn (lûrn) *v.*, **learned** or **learnt, learn·ing.** —*v.t.* **1.** to gain knowledge of or skill in (something) by study or experience: *The class is learning algebra.* **2.** to memorize: *That actor can't learn the lines in the play.* **3.** to find out about: *At last we've learned the truth!* —*v.i.* **1.** to gain knowledge or skill: *Different children learn at different rates.* **2.** to find out: *I was surprised to learn of their marriage.* —**learn'er,** *n.*

learn·ed (lûr'nid) *adj.* **1.** having or showing much knowledge: *a learned person.* **2.** produced by someone with much knowledge: *a learned study.* —**learn'ed·ly,** *adv.*

learn·ing (lûr'ning) *n.* **1.** the act of gaining knowledge or skill. **2.** knowledge gained by careful study: *a scholar of great learning.*

learnt (lûrnt) a past tense and past participle of the use of **learn.**

lease (lēs) *n.* **1.** a written agreement for the use of property for a specified period of time: *The newlyweds signed the lease for the apartment.* **2.** a period of time specified in such a contract: *The lease expires in two years.* —*v.t.*, **leased, leas·ing.** **1.** to take or hold a lease on: *to lease an automobile.* **2.** to allow to have or use with a lease: *The Smith family leased the property to them.*

leash (lēsh) *n.*, *pl.* **leash·es.** a strap, chain, or other line fastened to a dog or other animal to control or hold it. —*v.t.* to control or hold with or as with a leash: *Leash the dog to the post.*

least (lēst) *adj.* smallest in size, degree, amount, or importance: *That lazy worker did the least work of all.* —*n.* something that is least: *That is the least we can do.* —*adv.* in the smallest or lowest degree: *That neighbor is the least friendly person on the block.*
  ·at least. a. at the very minimum: *At least twenty people will come to the party.* **b.** at any rate; in any event: *They should at least let us know where they are.*
  ·in the least. at all: *I am not in the least interested.*

least common denominator, the smallest number that can be divided by each of the denominators of a given group of fractions without leaving a remainder. Also, **lowest common denominator.**

least common multiple, the smallest number that is an exact multiple of two or more given quantities. The least common multiple of 2, 3, and 4 is 12. Also, **lowest common multiple.**

least·wise (lēst'wīz') *adv.* *Informal.* at least; at any rate. Also, **least·ways** (lēst'wāz').

leath·er (leth'ər) *n.* material from an animal skin or hide, prepared for use by tanning. —*adj.* of or made of leather: *leather shoes.*

Leath·er·ette (leth'ə ret') *n.* *Trademark.* any of various plastics or fabrics that resemble leather in appearance.

leath·ern (leth'ərn) *adj.* **1.** made of leather. **2.** resembling leather.

leath·er·neck (leth'ər nek') *n.* *Slang.* a member of the U.S. Marines. [*Leather* + *neck;* from the *leather neck*(bands) that were formerly part of the U.S. Marine uniform.]

leath·er·y (leth'ə rē) *adj.* resembling leather: *leathery skin.* —**leath'er·i·ness,** *n.*

leave¹ (lēv) *v.*, **left, leav·ing.** —*v.i.* **1.** to go to another place; go away: *They left after a brief visit.* **2.** to depart or set out: *The plane leaves at 10:00.* —*v.t.* **1.** to go away from: *to leave the table after dinner.* **2.** to withdraw or depart from; quit: *to leave one's job for a better one.* **3.** to neglect to take along or remove; forget to bring: *to leave something behind.* **4.** to allow to be or remain in a particular state or condition: *to leave work unfinished.* **5.** to let remain; not use: *The food was left on the plate.* **6.** to entrust, refer, or commit: *to leave something in good hands.* **7.** to give by will; bequeath: *to leave property to one's heir.* **8.** to have remaining after subtraction: *10 minus 3 leaves 7.* [From the Old English word *læfan* with the same meaning.]
  ·to leave off. to stop: *Where did we leave off in our discussion?*
  ·to leave out. to omit or exclude.

leave² (lēv) *n.* **1.** permission to do something. **2.** permission to be absent, especially from military duty. Also, **leave of absence. 3.** the period that such permission lasts. [From the Old English word *lēaf* meaning "permission."]
  ·on leave. absent from duty with permission.
  ·to take leave of. to bid farewell to or leave behind.

leave³ (lēv) *v.i.*, **leaved, leav·ing.** to put forth leaves; leaf. [From the Middle English word *leven* meaning "to put forth leaves," from the word *leef* "leaf," from the Old English word *lēaf* "leaf."]

leav·en (lev'ən) *n.* **1.** a substance, such as yeast or baking powder, that causes dough to rise. **2.** an influence that changes something, as by making it lighter or more active: *Without the leaven of wit, the speech would have been dull.* —*v.t.* **1.** to cause (dough) to rise by adding a leaven. **2.** to spread through and change.

leav·en·ing (lev'ə ning) *n.* something that leavens.

leaves (lēvz) the plural of **leaf.**

leave–tak·ing (lēv'tā'king) *n.* the act of saying good-bye; bidding farewell.

leav·ings (lē'vingz) *pl. n.* something that remains unused: *The dogs ate the leavings from the table.*

lech·er·ous (lech'ər əs) *adj.* given to, characterized by, or showing lechery. —**lech'er·ous·ly,** *adv.* —**lech'er·ous·ness,** *n.*

lech·er·y (lech'ə rē) *n.* sexual desire or activity that is seen as excessive.

lec·i·thin (les'ə thin) *n.* **1.** any of a group of fatty compounds containing phosphorus, found in animal and plant tissues. **2.** a form of this substance obtained usually from soybeans, egg yolks, or corn, and used in making candy, ice cream, cosmetics, and other products.

L

---

at; ape; fär; câre; end; mē; it; īce; pîerce; hot; ōld; sông; fôrk; oil; out; up; ūse; rüle; pull; tûrn; chin; sing; shop; thin; this; hw in white; zh in treasure. The symbol ə stands for the unstressed vowel sound heard in about, taken, pencil, lemon, and circus.

lec·tern (lek′tərn) *n.* **1.** a stand with a sloping top for holding the written speech or other papers of a speaker. **2.** a reading desk in a church, especially one from which scripture lessons are read during services.

lec·ture (lek′chər) *n.* **1.** a prepared talk, given before an audience for the purpose of instruction: *a lecture on English literature.* **2.** a lengthy scolding: *to give someone a lecture for driving too fast.* —*v.,* **lec·tured, lec·tur·ing.** —*v.i.* to give a lecture or lectures: *to lecture at a university.* —*v.t.* **1.** to give a lecture to; instruct by means of a lecture. **2.** to scold.

lec·tur·er (lek′chər ər) *n.* a person who lectures.

led (led) the past tense and past participle of **lead¹.**

LED, an electronic device that emits light when a current is applied to its circuit. It is used to display numbers, letters, and symbols in watches, calculators, cameras, and other devices. [Short for *l*(ight) *e*(mitting) *d*(iode).]

Le·da (lē′də) *n.* *Greek Mythology.* the mother of two mortals, Castor and Clytemnestra, and of two immortals, Pollux and Helen of Troy.

ledge (lej) *n.* **1.** a narrow shelf or similar flat surface, such as one jutting out from the wall of a building. **2.** a narrow, flat surface jutting out from the side of a mountain or other natural formation.

ledg·er (lej′ər) *n.* an account book in which all the financial transactions of a business are recorded.

ledger line, a short line added above or below a musical staff for notes too high or too low to be put on the staff.

lee (lē) *n.* **1.** a shelter or protection. **2.** the side or part, especially of a ship, sheltered or turned away from the wind. —*adj.* sheltered from the wind: *the lee side of a ship.*

leech (lēch) *n., pl.* **leech·es. 1.** any of a group of worms found in salt water, fresh water, and damp soil, which suck the blood of animals. **2.** a person who clings to another or others for personal gain.

lectern *(def. 1)*

leech *(def. 1)*

leek (lēk) *n.* **1.** the leaves and stalk of a plant related to the lily, eaten as a vegetable. **2.** the plant itself, growing from a slender underground bulb.

leer (lîr) *n.* a sly look or sidelong glance expressing cunning, lust, or evil intent. —*v.i.* to look with a leer.

lee·ry (lîr′ē) *adj.* *Informal.* suspicious; wary: *I'm always somewhat leery of strangers.*

lees (lēz) *n.* sediment, especially of wine; dregs.

lee shore, the shore lying off the leeward side of a boat or ship, toward which the boat or ship may be driven by the wind.

lee·ward (lē′wərd, lü′ərd) *adj.* located on or moving toward the side toward which the wind is blowing. —*n.* the side or direction toward which the wind is blowing; lee. —*adv.* toward the lee.

lee·way (lē′wā′) *n.* **1.** extra time, space, or the like, making freedom of action or movement possible: *If we leave early, we will give ourselves plenty of leeway.* **2.** the sideways drift of a boat or ship to leeward, off its course.

left¹ (left) *adj.* **1.** of, on, or toward the side of the body that is to the west when one is facing north: *the left hand, the left side of the road.* **2.** also, **Left.** relating to or

having liberal or radical political views. —*n.* **1.** the left side or direction: *My cousin was seated on my left. The car skidded to the left.* **2.** also, **Left.** a party or group having liberal or radical political views. Also, **left wing.** **3.** a blow delivered with the left hand, as in boxing. —*adv.* to or toward the left: *Turn left at the next corner.* [From the Middle English word *lift* "left side," from the Old English word *lyft* meaning "weak."]

left² (left) the past tense and past participle of **leave¹.**

left field *Baseball.* **1.** the left section of the outfield when viewed from home plate. **2.** the position of the player stationed in this area. —**left fielder.**

left–hand (left′hand′) *adj.* **1.** on or toward the left: *a left-hand drawer of a desk.* **2.** of, for, relating to, or with the left hand: *a left-hand glove.*

left–hand·ed (left′han′did) *adj.* **1.** using the left hand naturally and more easily than the right: *a left-handed hitter in baseball.* **2.** done with the left hand. **3.** made to be held in or used by the left hand, as a tool. **4.** turning or moving from right to left; counterclockwise. **5.** doubtful, ironic, or insincere: *a left-handed compliment.* —*adv.* with the left hand.

left–hand·er (left′han′dər) *n.* a left-handed person, especially an athlete.

left·ist (lef′tist) *n.* a person who has liberal or radical political views. —*adj.* of, relating to, or characterized by liberal or radical political views.

left·o·ver (left′ō′vər) *n.* also, **leftovers.** something that remains unused, especially food remaining after a meal. —*adj.* unused or uneaten; remaining.

left–wing (left′wing′) *adj.* of, relating to, or belonging to the left wing.

left wing 1. see **left** (*n.,* def. 2). **2.** a portion of a political party or other group having a more liberal or radical outlook than the rest.

left·y (lef′tē) *n., pl.* **left·ies.** *Informal.* a left-handed person.

leg (leg) *n.* **1.** one of the limbs of human beings and animals used chiefly for supporting the body and for walking. **2.** something like a leg in shape, position, or function: *the leg of a chair.* **3.** the part of a garment, especially of trousers, that covers a leg. **4.** a distinct part or stage of a journey or course: *The first leg of the voyage took them to Australia.* **5.** *Mathematics.* a side of a triangle that is not the base or the hypotenuse.

·**on one's last legs.** *Informal.* close to death, collapse, or failure.

·**to leg it.** *Informal.* to walk quickly or run: *We legged it home when the rain started.*

·**to pull someone's leg.** *Informal.* to trick or tease; deceive.

leg·a·cy (leg′ə sē) *n., pl.* **leg·a·cies. 1.** money or property left to someone by a will. **2.** something handed down from previous generations or from the past; heritage.

le·gal (lē′gəl) *adj.* **1.** of, relating to, or concerned with law: *legal advice.* **2.** according to or permitted by law; lawful: *a person's legal rights, the legal owner of the property.* **3.** of, relating to, or characteristic of lawyers or the practice of law: *a legal mind, legal reasoning.* —**le′gal·ly,** *adv.*

legal age, the age at which a citizen achieves full adult legal rights and responsibilities, such as the right to make contracts.

le·gal·i·ty (li gal′i tē) *n., pl.* **le·gal·i·ties. 1.** the state or quality of being legal; lawfulness. **2.** a procedure required by law: *the legalities of buying a house.*

le·gal·ize (lē′gə līz′) *v.t.,* **le·gal·ized, le·gal·iz·ing.** to make legal or lawful. —**le′gal·i·za′tion,** *n.*

legal pad, a pad of writing paper, usually lined, measuring 8½ inches by 14 inches (21.6 centimeters by 35.6 centimeters).

legal tender, the coin or currency that, by law, must be accepted in payment of debts.

leg·ate (leg′it) *n.* an official representative, especially a person who represents the pope.

leg·a·tee (leg′ə tē′) *n.* a person to whom a legacy is left.

le·ga·tion (li gā′shən) *n.* **1.** a diplomatic representative below the rank of ambassador, and his or her staff. **2.** the official residence and offices of such a representative and staff in a foreign country.

le·ga·to (li gä′tō) *Music.* *adj.* smooth and even, with no breaks between tones. —*adv.* in a legato manner.

leg·end (lej′ənd) *n.* **1.** a story passed down through the years that is usually based on some facts and popularly thought of as true: *There are many legends about the adventures of Robin Hood.* **2.** such stories as a group, especially of a nation or culture: *Pocahontas is a character in American legend.* **3.** a legendary figure: *The general became a legend while still alive.* **4.** an inscription or motto, especially on a coin, medal, or coat of arms. **5.** an explanatory description accompanying a chart, map, or other illustration. [From the Old French word *legende* meaning "fable, myth" or "written account," going back to the Latin word *legenda* "things to be read," from the word *legere* "to gather, select" and "to read."]

leg·end·ar·y (lej′ən der′ē) *adj.* **1.** of, relating to, or characteristic of a legend or legends: *a legendary account of a battle.* **2.** celebrated or described in legend.

leg·er·de·main (lej′ər de mān′) *n.* **1.** skill in using the hands, especially in performing tricks; sleight of hand. **2.** artful trickery; deception.

leg·ged (leg′id, legd) *adj.* having a certain kind or number of legs. ▲ used in combination: *a four-legged animal.*

leg·gings (leg′ingz) *pl. n.* coverings of cloth or leather for the legs, usually reaching to the ankle.

leg·gy (leg′ē) *adj.,* **leg·gi·er, leg·gi·est. 1.** having awkwardly long legs. **2.** having attractive legs.

leg·horn (leg′hôrn′, *defs. 2 and 3 also* leg′ərn) *n.* **1. Leg·horn** any of a breed of small, hardy domestic fowl, raised chiefly for their white-shelled eggs. **2.** a fine, braided wheat straw used in the manufacture of hats. **3.** a hat made of this straw.

leg·i·ble (lej′ə bəl) *adj.* possible to read: *The faded letter was not legible.* —**leg·i·bil·i·ty,** *n.* —**leg·i·bly,** *adv.*

le·gion (lē′jən) *n.* **1.** a military unit in the army of ancient Rome, having from 3,000 to 6,000 foot soldiers and from 300 to 700 mounted soldiers. **2.** any large military unit; army. **3.** a vast number of persons or things; multitude: *a legion of stars in the sky.* **4.** any of various military or honorary organizations, such as the American Legion.

le·gion·ar·y (lē′jə ner′ē) *adj.* of or relating to a legion. —*n., pl.* **le·gion·ar·ies.** a soldier or member of a legion.

le·gion·naire (lē′jə nâr′) *n.* a member of a legion.

leg·is·late (lej′is lāt′) *v.,* **leg·is·lat·ed, leg·is·lat·ing.** —*v.i.* to make or pass a law or laws: *Parliament legislates for Canada.* —*v.t.* to cause, regulate, or bring about by passing laws: *Congress legislated increased benefits for veterans.*

leg·is·la·tion (lej′is lā′shən) *n.* **1.** the making or passing of laws. **2.** the laws made or passed: *to enact new legislation.*

leg·is·la·tive (lej′is lā′tiv) *adj.* **1.** of or relating to legislation: *legislative powers.* **2.** having the power to make or pass laws: *Congress is a legislative body.* **3.** of or relating to a legislature.

leg·is·la·tor (lej′is lā′tər) *n.* a member of a legislative body, especially a member of a state legislature or of Congress.

leg·is·la·ture (lej′is lā′chər) *n.* a government body made up of a group of persons having the power to make or pass laws for a state or country.

le·git·i·ma·cy (li jit′ə mə sē) *n.* the state or quality of being legitimate.

le·git·i·mate (li jit′ə mit) *adj.* **1.** according to law; lawful; rightful: *The judge ruled that the claim was legitimate.* **2.** logically correct or valid: *a legitimate argument.* **3.** genuine or reasonable: *a legitimate complaint.* **4.** born of parents who are legally married to each other: *a legitimate child.* —**le·git′i·mate·ly,** *adv.*

le·git·i·mize (li jit′ə mīz′) *v.t.,* **le·git·i·mized, le·git·i·miz·ing.** to make legitimate.

leg·ume (leg′ūm, li gūm′) *n.* **1.** any of a large group of plants that bear pods, including peas, beans, peanuts, and alfalfa. Legumes are grown as food crops, as fodder, and as natural fertilizers. **2.** a seed pod of such a plant, usually having the seeds in rows along the pod.

le·gu·mi·nous (li gū′mə nəs) *adj.* of or relating to legumes: *leguminous crops, leguminous vegetables.*

leg warmers

leg warmer, a covering for the lower portion of the leg, usually made from bulky knitted fabric. Leg warmers are worn especially for exercising or dance practice.

leg·work (leg′wûrk′) *n.* work that involves walking or traveling about, as in gathering information or running errands: *Being a newspaper reporter requires a lot of legwork.*

lei (lā) *n.* a wreath of flowers, leaves, or other material, often worn around the neck.

lei·sure (lē′zhər, lezh′ər) *n.* **1.** free or unoccupied time: *After retirement, my parents had the leisure to travel.* **2.** freedom from the demands of work or duty: *a life of leisure.* —*adj.* free or unoccupied: *leisure hours.*
·**at one's leisure.** when one has free time; at one's convenience: *Visit us at your leisure.*

lei·sure·ly (lē′zhər lē, lezh′ər lē) *adj.* characterized by leisure; unhurried; relaxed: *a leisurely walk.* —*adv.* in a relaxed or unhurried manner: *to stroll leisurely home.*

lem·ming (lem′ing) *n.* an arctic rodent having a stout body and long, chiefly yellowish brown fur.

lem·on (lem′ən) *n.* **1.** an oval fruit of a citrus tree, having a thick yellow rind and a juicy, sour pulp that can be eaten. **2.** the thorny evergreen tree bearing this fruit. **3.** a clear, bright yellow color. **4.** *Slang.* a person or thing that is unsatisfactory or worthless: *That car is a real*

L

at; āpe; fär; câre; end; mē; it; īce; pîerce; hot; ōld; sông, fôrk; oil; out; up; ūse; rüle; pull; tûrn; chin; sing; shop; thin; **this**; hw in white; zh in treasure. The symbol ə stands for the unstressed vowel sound heard in about, taken, pencil, lemon, and circus.

547

lemon. —*adj.* **1.** having the color lemon. **2.** made from or flavored with lemon: *lemon juice.*

lem·on·ade (lem′ə nād′) *n.* a drink made of lemon juice, water, and sugar.

le·mur (lē′mər) *n.* any of several small mammals that are distantly related to the monkey, found chiefly in Madagascar. Lemurs have large eyes that help them see in the dark, soft, woolly fur, and a long tail. [Formed from the Latin word *le-mures* meaning "ghosts." The name refers to the an- imals' appearance and noc- turnal habits.]

lemur

lend (lend) *v.,* **lent, lending.** —*v.t.* **1.** to grant the use of (something) with the understanding that it will be returned: *I'll lend you my records for the party.* **2.** to give the temporary use of (money) on condition of repayment and at a set rate of interest. **3.** to provide or give: *The darkness lent an air of mystery to the old house.* **4.** to make available for aid or support: *to lend assistance to someone in trouble.* —*v.i.* to make a loan or loans. —**lend′er,** *n.*

lending library, another term for **circulating library.**

length (lengkth, length, lenth) *n.* **1.** the extent of anything from end to end: *The length of the football field is 100 yards.* **2.** the extent from beginning to end: *the length of a vacation, the length of a book.* **3.** the state, quality, or fact of being long: *The length of the climb exhausted the climbers.* **4.** the measurement of anything considered as a unit: *We parked a car's length away from the sign.* **5.** a piece or portion of anything, usually of a certain or standard size: *a length of rope, a length of pipe.* ·**at length. a.** in full; in detail. **b.** after a time; finally.

length·en (lengk′thən, leng′thən, len′thən) *v.t., v.i.* to make or become longer.

length·wise (lengkth′wīz′, length′wīz′, lenth′wīz′) *adj., adv.* in the direction of the length: *a lengthwise rip in a coat, to saw a board lengthwise.* Also, **length·ways** (lengkth′wāz′, length′wāz′, lenth′wāz′).

length·y (lengk′thē, leng′thē, len′thē) *adj.,* **length- i·er, length·i·est.** much too long: *a lengthy speech.* —**length′i·ly,** *adv.* —**length′i·ness,** *n.*

len·i·en·cy (lē′nē ən sē, lēn′yən sē) *n.* the state or quality of being lenient. Also, **len·i·ence** (lē′nē əns, lēn′yəns).

le·ni·ent (lē′nē ənt, lēn′yənt) *adj.* not severe or harsh; merciful; tolerant: *a le- nient judge.* —**len′i- ent·ly,** *adv.*

lens (lenz) *n., pl.* **lens- es. 1.** a piece of glass or other transparent ma- terial, having one or both surfaces curved, which causes the light rays passing through them to either move apart or come together. Lenses are used in eyeglasses, cameras, microscopes, and other optical equip- ment. **2.** any combina- tion of such lenses. **3.** the colorless, trans- parent part of the eye in vertebrates and cephal- opods that focuses the image on the retina.

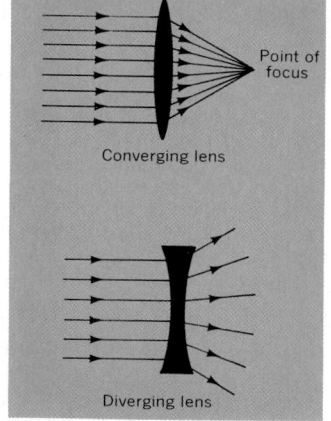
lenses *(def. 1)*

Point of focus

Converging lens

Diverging lens

lent (lent) the past tense and past participle of **lend.**

Lent (lent) *n.* the period of penitence and prayer observed in Christian churches during the forty days, excepting Sundays, from Ash Wednesday to Easter.

Lent·en (len′tən) *also.* **lent·en.** *adj.* of, relating to, or suitable for Lent: *a Lenten diet.*

len·til (len′təl) *n.* **1.** a seed of a plant related to the pea, cooked and eaten as a vegetable, especially in soups and stews. **2.** the plant itself, having broad pods containing one seed.

Le·o (lē′ō) *n.* **1.** a constellation in the northern sky, thought to resemble a lion in shape. **2.** the fifth sign of the zodiac.

le·o·nine (lē′ə nīn′) *adj.* relating to, characteristic of, or resembling a lion: *leonine courage.*

leop·ard (lep′ərd) *n.* a meat-eating animal of the cat family that is found in Africa, India, and east- ern Asia. It has either a brownish yellow coat marked with black spots or a solid black coat. [From the Old French word *leupart* meaning "leopard," going back to the Greek word *leo- pardos* "leopard," from the words *leōn* "lion" + *pardos* "leopard" or "panther."]

leopard

le·o·tard (lē′ə tärd′) *also,* **le·o·tards.** *n.* a close-fitting, one-piece garment extending from the neck or waist to the feet. [From the French aerialist Jules *Léotard* (1830– 1870), who popularized the use of this costume.]

lep·er (lep′ər) *n.* a person who has leprosy.

lep·re·chaun (lep′ri kon′, lep′ri kôn′) *n.* in Irish folk- lore, a mischievous elf resembling a little old man.

lep·ro·sy (lep′rə sē) *n.* an infectious disease caused by a bacterium and affecting the body tissues, especially the skin, nerves, and mucous membranes. Also, **Hansen's disease.**

lep·rous (lep′rəs) *adj.* **1.** having leprosy. **2.** of, relating to, or characteristic of leprosy.

les·bi·an (lez′bē ən) *n.* a female homosexual. —*adj.* of or relating to homosexuality between women. [From *Lesbos,* a Greek island that was home to the poet Sappho, who wrote love poems to her female friends.] —**les′- bi·an·ism,** *n.*

le·sion (lē′zhən) *n.* an injury; wound.

less (les) *adj.* a comparative of **little. 1.** not as much or as great in quantity, extent, or degree: *less food, less time, less money.* **2.** lower in rank or importance: *No less a person than the principal gave the order.* —*adv.* the comparative of **little:** *The movie was less funny than the book.* —*n.* a smaller amount or quantity: *I finished less of the work than I had planned.* —*prep.* with the subtraction of; minus: *Ten less seven is three.*
▲ **Less** and **fewer** both can mean "smaller in number." **Less** is used more often for things that cannot actually be counted: *The doctor advised the patient to eat less fatty food.* **Fewer** is used more often for things that can be counted: *The doctor advised the patient to eat fewer calories by skipping dessert.*

-less *suffix* **1.** (used to form adjectives from nouns) without; having no: *hopeless.* **2.** (used to form adjectives from verbs) that does not: *tireless.* **3.** (used to form adjectives from verbs) that cannot be: *countless.*

les·see (le sē′) *n.* a person to whom a lease is granted.

less·en (les′ən) *v.i.* to become less; decrease: *The pain lessened.* —*v.t.* to make less; reduce; diminish.

less·er (les′ər) *adj.* a comparative of **little:** *to choose the lesser of two evils.*

lesser panda, see **panda** *(def. 2).*

les·son (les′ən) *n.* **1.** a period of time given to the instruction of a particular subject or skill: *a French lesson, a skiing lesson.* **2.** something learned or studied, especially material assigned, presented, or learned at one time: *I didn't understand today's math lesson.* **3.** an event or experience serving to guide or warn: *This experience has taught me a lesson I'll never forget.* **4.** a selection from the Scriptures as part of a church service.

les·sor (les′ôr) *n.* a person who grants a lease.

lest (lest) *conj.* **1.** for fear that: *We came in through the back door lest someone should see us.* **2.** that. ▲ used after words expressing fear or worry: *I feared lest the children would lose their way in the forest.*

let¹ (let) *v.,* **let, let·ting.** —*v.t.* **1.** to give permission or opportunity to; permit; allow: *My parents let me use the boat.* **2.** to allow to pass, go, or come: *The child opened the cage door and let the bird out.* **3.** to cause; make: *I'll let you know my decision.* **4.** to rent or lease: *to let a cottage.* ▲ **Let** is also used as an auxiliary verb, usually in the imperative, to indicate: **a.** a suggestion, command, or warning: *Let's take a walk. Let's go!* **b.** something that is assumed or supposed: *Let x = 3.* —*v.i.* to be rented: *The apartment lets on a yearly basis.* [From the Old English word *lǣtan* meaning "to allow, permit."]

   ·**to let alone** or **let be.** to leave undisturbed; not interfere with or bother: *Let the dog be.*

   ·**to let down. a.** to allow to fall or descend; lower. **b.** to fail to fulfill the hopes or expectations of; disappoint: *When I needed help, you let me down.*

   ·**to let off. a.** to excuse from a duty or service. **b.** to give little or no punishment to; treat leniently: *The judge let the speeder off with a warning.*

   ·**to let on.** *Informal.* **a.** to allow to become known; reveal: *Did you let on that you knew the answer?* **b.** to claim falsely; pretend: *Let on that you understand; they won't know the difference.*

   ·**to let out. a.** to give forth; release: *to let out a scream.* **b.** to enlarge or extend (a garment or the like): *to let out a dress.*

   ·**to let up.** to stop or lessen in intensity: *We thought the storm would never let up.*

let² (let) *n.* in tennis, volleyball, and similar games, a stroke that must be repeated because of interference, especially a served ball that touches the net. [From the Old English word *lettan* meaning "to hinder, impede."]

-let *suffix* (used to form nouns) **1.** little: *booklet.* **2.** an article worn on or around (a part of the body): *anklet.*

let·down (let′doun′) *n.* **1.** a disappointment; disillusionment: *It was a real letdown when our plan failed.* **2.** a lessening or slowing up.

le·thal (lē′thəl) *adj.* causing or capable of causing death; deadly: *a lethal wound, a lethal poison.*

le·thar·gic (li thär′jik) *adj.* **1.** feeling or showing lethargy; sluggish. **2.** causing lethargy: *lethargic summer heat.* —**le·thar′gi·cal·ly,** *adv.*

leth·ar·gy (leth′ər jē) *n., pl.* **leth·ar·gies. 1.** the state or quality of being without strength, energy, or alertness; sluggishness. **2.** an abnormal condition characterized by excessive drowsiness or by prolonged deep sleep. [From the Late Latin word *lethargia* meaning "drowsiness," going back to the Greek word *lēthargos* "forgetful, lethargic."]

Le·the (lē′thē) *n.* **1.** *Greek and Roman Mythology.* a river in Hades whose water, when drunk, caused a person to forget the past. **2.** forgetfulness; oblivion.

let's (lets) *contr.* let us.

let·ter (let′ər) *n.* **1.** a mark or character, usually printed or written, that stands for one or more speech sounds; character of an alphabet: *There are four letters in the name "Mary."* **2.** a written or printed message sent by one person to another: *to mail a letter.* **3.** an official or legal document granting a specific right, authority, or privilege to a person: *a letter of credit.* **4.** the literal meaning or exact wording of something, as opposed to a more general meaning or interpretation: *the letter of the law.* **5. letters.** literary culture; literature: *a man of letters, a love of letters.* **6.** the initial of a school, college, or other institution given as an award: *The athlete was given a letter for being on the basketball team.* —*v.t.* **1.** to mark or write with letters: *to letter a sign.* **2.** to write (a word or words) in letters: *The word "exit" was lettered on the door.* —**let′ter·er,** *n.*

   ·**to the letter.** exactly as written or spoken; precisely: *He followed the instructions to the letter.*

letter carrier, another term for **mail carrier.**

let·ter·head (let′ər hed′) *n.* **1.** information printed at the top of a sheet of paper, usually the name and address of the sender. **2.** a sheet of paper with such a heading.

let·ter·ing (let′ər ing) *n.* **1.** the act or art of forming or drawing letters. **2.** letters so formed or drawn.

let·ter-per·fect (let′ər pûr′fikt) *adj.* correct in every detail; completely accurate.

let·ter-qual·i·ty (let′ər kwol′i tē) *adj.* **1.** (of a computer printer) capable of producing printouts of a quality equal to that of copy typed on a typewriter. **2.** (of a printout) equal in quality to that of copy typed on a typewriter.

Let·tish (let′ish) *n.* another word for **Latvian** (*def. 2*). —*adj.* another word for **Latvian.**

let·tuce (let′is) *n.* **1.** the large green or red leaves of any of several plants, forming a round, oval, or long head, eaten mainly as a raw vegetable in salads. **2.** a plant bearing these leaves.

let·up (let′up′) *n. Informal.* a lessening or slackening: *It snowed all day without any letup.*

leu·ke·mi·a (lü kē′mē ə) *n.* a cancerous disease characterized by the formation of abnormal numbers of white blood cells.

leu·ko·cyte (lü′kə sīt′) *also,* **leu·co·cyte.** *n.* another word for **white blood cell.**

Le·van·tine (lev′ən tīn′, lev′ən tēn′) *n.* a person who was born or is living in the Levant. —*adj.* of, relating to, or characteristic of the Levant.

lev·ee (lev′ē) *n.* **1.** a wall of earth and other materials built along the banks of a river to prevent flooding. **2.** a landing place, especially on a river; pier; quay.

lev·el (lev′əl) *adj.* **1.** having no part higher than another; flat; even: *The steamroller made the ground level.* **2.** parallel to the plane of the horizon; horizontal. **3.** being or placed at the same height or on the same plane as something else: *The two paintings were level with the window.* **4.** mentally well-balanced; sensible: *a level head.* —*n.* **1.** the relative position or degree of something in any scale or order: *a low level of economic development.* **2.** a horizontal surface, plane, or line from which the height of something is measured: *The building rises 200 feet above street level.* **3.** a relatively flat piece of land. **4.** height; depth; altitude: *The stream rose to a level of 3 feet.* **5.** a floor or story of a structure: *The car is parked on the lower level of the garage.* **6.** any of various devices used to determine whether a surface is horizontal, as in surveying or carpentry. —*v.,* **lev·eled, lev·el·ing;** *also, British,* **lev·elled, lev·el·ling.** —*v.t.* **1.** to make even, flat, or smooth: *The bulldozer leveled the mound of earth.* **2.** to bring to the level of the ground; destroy; raze: *Fire*

L

---

at; āpe; fär; câre; end; mē; it; īce; pîerce; hot; ōld; sông, fôrk; oil; out; up; ūse; rüle; pùll; tûrn; chin; sing; shop; thin; this; hw in white; zh in treasure. The symbol ə stands for the unstressed vowel sound heard in about, taken, pencil, lemon, and circus.

leveled the house. **3.** to bring to equality, as in degree, importance, or rank; equalize: *to level the classes of society.* **4.** to bring to a horizontal position and aim or point: *to level a gun at a target.* —*v.i. Informal.* to be frank and honest: *Good friends usually level with each other.* —**lev′el·er,** *n.* —**lev′el·ly,** *adv.* —**lev′el·ness,** *n.*

·**one's level best.** a person's very best.

·**on the level.** *Informal.* honest; upright or true.

lev·el·head·ed (lev′əl hed′id) *adj.* having or showing common sense and good judgment; sensible.

lev·er (lev′ər, lē′vər) *n.* **1.** a device made of a rigid rod or bar that transmits force or motion from one point to another as it rotates about a fixed point, or fulcrum. A lever is used to lift weights and pry things loose. **2.** anything that operates in this way, such as a crowbar. **3.** a projecting bar, handle, or piece that is moved to operate, control, or adjust a mechanism. —*v.t.* to move or pry with or as if with a lever.

lev·er·age (lev′ər ij, lē′vər ij) *n.* **1.** the action of a lever. **2.** the mechanical force or motion gained by use of a lever. **3.** an increased power to act or influence: *political leverage.*

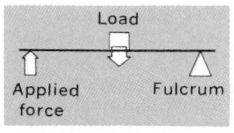

lever

le·vi·a·than (li vī′ə thən) *n.* **1.** in the Old Testament, a huge sea monster, thought to be either a whale or crocodile.

lev·i·tate (lev′i tāt′) *v.,* **lev·i·tat·ed, lev·i·tat·ing.** —*v.i.* **1.** to rise and float in the air, as by the force of magnetism. **2.** to appear to rise and float in the air, as if by magic or a supernatural power. —*v.t.* to cause to levitate. —**lev′i·ta′tion,** *n.*

Le·vite (lē′vīt) *n.* a member of the tribe descended from Levi. The Levites assisted the priests of the Jewish Temple.

Le·vit·i·cus (lə vit′i kəs) *n.* the third book of the Old Testament, containing the laws for the priests and Levites and the Jewish ceremonial laws.

lev·i·ty (lev′i tē) *n., pl.* **lev·i·ties.** a lack of seriousness in attitude or behavior.

lev·y (lev′ē) *v.t.,* **lev·ied, lev·y·ing.** **1.** to impose or collect by force or authority: *to levy taxes.* **2.** to draft or enlist (troops) for military service. **3.** to prepare for, start, or wage (war). —*n., pl.* **lev·ies.** **1.** anything collected by authority, such as troops or taxes. **2.** the act of levying.

lewd (lüd) *adj.* obscene; indecent; vulgar. [From the Middle English word *lewed* meaning "ignorant, uneducated" or "lay³, secular," from the Old English word *lǣwede* with the same meanings.]

lex·i·cog·ra·pher (lek′si kog′rə fər) *n.* a person whose profession is writing or compiling a dictionary.

lex·i·cog·ra·phy (lek′si kog′rə fē) *n.* the act or work of writing or compiling a dictionary.

Language Note

Lexicography is the making of dictionaries, and people who write dictionaries are called *lexicographers.* The first English dictionaries were produced in the sixteenth century, before scholars had begun to study language scientifically. Until the nineteenth century, dictionary makers often had to rely on guesswork rather than definite evidence about words. They wanted to standardize the use of English, so they gave their opinions as to the correct spelling, meaning, and use of words, directing people to speak and write according to these opinions.

But their examination of language was narrow, often limited to an analysis of the way they and their friends spoke and wrote, and perhaps a reading of the works of a few famous writers. So their dictionaries often did not reflect the way a great majority of people actually used language.

Today most lexicographers try not to make such fine personal judgments about words. They believe that their responsibility is to record the way language is really used, not to express opinions as to how it should be used. They base their work on a careful study of English as it is spoken and written at the present time. Lexicographers carefully examine a wide range of current books, magazines, newspapers, and other publications to determine what words are in use and how they are being used. They also listen carefully to the way people speak. From these observations, they decide what words to include in their dictionary and how to describe them.

lex·i·con (lek′si kən, lek′si kon′) *n.* **1.** a dictionary, especially of Greek, Hebrew, Latin, or another ancient language. **2.** a list of words belonging to a particular field, profession, activity, or the like.

Ley·den jar (lī′dən) a device for storing an electric charge, consisting of a glass jar that is coated almost to the top with metal foil inside and outside. The two coatings are equivalent to the two plates of a capacitor.

LF, low frequency.

Li, the symbol for lithium.

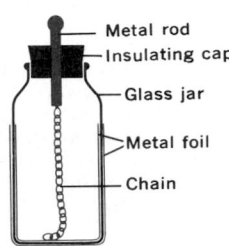

Leyden jar

li·a·bil·i·ty (lī′ə bil′i tē) *n., pl.* **li·a·bil·i·ties.** **1.** the state or condition of being liable. **2.** something for which one is liable, especially a financial obligation or debt. **3.** something that works to one's disadvantage; handicap: *Lack of a high school education is a liability.* **4. liabilities.** in accounting, all the debts or financial commitments of a business.

li·a·ble (lī′ə bəl) *adj.* **1.** legally responsible; obligated by law: *The owner of the car was liable for damages done to the other car.* **2.** subject or susceptible: *to be liable to heart trouble.* **3.** having or showing a possibility; apt; likely: *You are liable to fall on the icy sidewalk if you do not walk carefully.*

li·ai·son (lē′ə zon′, lē ā′zon) *n.* a line of communication between parts of an organization, such as military units, used to insure that actions are coordinated.

li·a·na (lē ä′nə, lē an′ə) *n.* a climbing vine, especially one that grows in a tropical rain forest.

li·ar (lī′ər) *n.* a person who tells lies.

li·ba·tion (lī bā′shən) *n.* **1.** the pouring out of wine or other liquid as an offering to a god. **2.** a liquid offered in this way.

li·bel (lī′bəl) *n.* **1.** the act or crime of damaging a person's reputation by printing, writing, or representing in a picture false or malicious information about him or her. **2.** any false or malicious statement or picture. —*v.t.,* **li·beled, li·bel·ing;** *also, British,* **li·belled, li·bel·ling.** to write or publish a libel about. —**li′bel·er;** *also, British,* **li′bel·ler,** *n.*

li·bel·ous (lī′bə ləs) *adj.* containing a libel: *a libelous accusation.*

lib·er·al (lib′ər əl) *adj.* **1.** characterized by or tending toward opinions favoring progress and reform, as in politics or religion. **2.** *also,* **Liberal.** of or belonging to a political party that favors progress and reform. **3.** free from prejudice; broad-minded; tolerant: *to be liberal in one's ideas.* **4.** characterized by generosity; generous; bountiful: *to be liberal with one's money.* **5.** plentiful; abundant: *a liberal supply.* **6.** not literal or strict: *a liberal interpretation of the law.* —*n.* **1.** a person who favors or supports progress and reform, as in politics. **2.** *also,* **Liberal.** a member of a liberal political party. —**lib′er·al·ly,** *adv.* —**lib′er·al·ness,** *n.*

liberal arts, subjects studied mainly for their cultural value rather than their immediate practical use, such as literature, languages, history, and philosophy.

lib·er·al·ism (lib′ər ə liz′əm) *n.* liberal principles and ideals; belief in progress and reform.

lib·er·al·i·ty (lib′ə ral′i tē) *n., pl.* **lib·er·al·i·ties.** **1.** generosity. **2.** a tolerant attitude or policy; broadmindedness. **3.** a generous gift.

lib·er·al·ize (lib′ər ə līz′) *v.t., v.i.,* **lib·er·al·ized, lib·er·al·iz·ing.** to make or become liberal or more liberal. —**lib′er·al·i·za′tion,** *n.*

lib·er·ate (lib′ə rāt′) *v.t.,* **lib·er·at·ed, lib·er·at·ing.** **1.** to set free; release: *to liberate slaves.* **2.** *Chemistry.* to free (a gas) from combination, as by heating. —**lib′er·a′tion,** *n.* —**lib′er·a′tor,** *n.*

lib·er·tar·i·an (lib′ər târ′ē ən) *n.* a person who advocates liberty, especially of thought or conduct. —**lib′er·tar′i·an·ism,** *n.*

lib·er·tine (lib′ər tēn′) *n.* a person who is lacking in moral restraint; dissolute person. —*adj.* dissolute; immoral.

lib·er·ty (lib′ər tē) *n., pl.* **lib·er·ties.** **1.** freedom from tyranny or foreign domination; political independence: *England was forced to grant the American colonies their liberty.* **2.** freedom from imprisonment, captivity, or other physical restraint: *The prisoners were finally given their liberty.* **3.** the ability to act as one pleases; freedom of choice: *You have the liberty to say what you want.* **4.** the freedom of thought and action possessed by the people of a state or nation: *Freedom of speech is an important liberty.* **5.** an action or speech that is too free or too familiar. **6.** freedom to move within certain limits: *The dog had the liberty of the entire house.* **7.** in the navy, time granted to a sailor to go ashore.

·**at liberty. a.** free. **b.** permitted; allowed: *I am not at liberty to tell you.* **c.** not busy or occupied.

the **Liberty Bell**
on display in Philadelphia

Liberty Bell, the bell rung on July 8, 1776, in Philadelphia to proclaim the signing of the Declaration of Independence by the Continental Congress.

Li·bra (lē′brə, lī′brə) *n.* **1.** a small, dim constellation in the southern sky just south of the celestial equator, thought to resemble a pair of scales. **2.** the seventh sign of the zodiac.

li·brar·i·an (lī brer′ē ən, lī brâr′ē ən) *n.* **1.** a person who is in charge of a library. **2.** a person who is trained for work in a library.

li·brar·y (lī′brer′ē, lī′brə rə) *n., pl.* **li·brar·ies.** **1.** a collection of books or other literary, artistic, or reference material. **2.** a room or building containing such a collection. **3.** a public or private institution that maintains and circulates such a collection. [From the Old French word *librairie* meaning "collection of books," going back to the Latin word *librarius* "relating to books," from the word *liber* "book."]

li·bret·tist (li bret′ist) *n.* a writer of a libretto.

li·bret·to (li bret′ō) *n., pl.* **li·bret·tos** or **li·bret·ti** (li bret′ē). **1.** the text or words of an opera or other long composition. **2.** a book or pamphlet containing such a text.

lice (līs) the plural of **louse.**

li·cense (lī′səns) *n.* **1.** a document, plate, tag, or other object that shows that the holder has official permission to do something, as to drive a car, or to own something, as a dog. **2.** permission given by law or authority to do something: *a license to handle classified documents.* **3.** too much or undisciplined freedom. **4.** the freedom to break or ignore certain rules or standards to achieve an effect: *I took the license of changing historical facts in my short story.* —*v.t.,* **li·censed, li·cens·ing.** to give a license to or for.

licensed practical nurse, a nurse who has completed certain training and educational requirements and is licensed by a state to provide care as a practical nurse under the supervision of a doctor or a registered nurse.

li·cen·see (lī′sən sē′) *also,* **li·cen·cee.** *n.* a person to whom a license has been granted.

license plate, a plate bearing the number of a license granted to the owner of a registered motor vehicle, attached to the rear, and often the front, of the vehicle.

li·cen·tious (li sen′shəs) *adj.* lacking moral restraint; immoral; lewd. —**li·cen′tious·ly,** *adv.* —**li·cen′tious·ness,** *n.*

li·chee (lē′chē) another spelling of **litchi.**

li·chen (lī′kən) *n.* any of a large group of plantlike organisms found in all parts of the world, usually growing on tree trunks, rocks, or the ground. Lichens consist of a fungus and an alga growing together.

lick (lik) *v.t.* **1.** to move the tongue over the surface of: *The kitten licked its paw.* **2.** to taste, eat, or remove by moving the tongue over: *to lick an ice-cream cone.* **3.** to move over or touch lightly or quickly: *Flames licked the logs in the fireplace.* **4.** *Informal.* to hit forcefully; thrash. **5.** *Informal.* to gain a victory over; defeat; overcome: *to lick an opponent, to lick a difficult problem.* —*n.* **1.** a stroke of the tongue over the surface of something: *to give a lollipop a lick.* **2.** a small quantity; bit: *They were too lazy to do a lick of work.* **3.** see **salt lick. 4.** *Informal.* a sharp blow.

lic·o·rice (lik′ər is, lik′ə rish) *n.* **1.** a sweet juice or extract obtained from the root of a plant, used as a flavoring in candy, medicine, and tobacco. **2.** the plant whose root yields this juice or extract. **3.** a candy flavored with licorice.

lid (lid) *n.* **1.** a hinged or removable cover placed over the opening of a container, box, pot, or other receptacle: *Put the lid on the garbage can.* **2.** see **eyelid.**

lie[1] (lī) *n.* a false statement made with the purpose of deceiving; falsehood. —*v.i.,* **lied, ly·ing. 1.** to make a false statement or statements with the purpose of deceiving: *to lie about one's age.* **2.** to give a false impression:

L

at; āpe; fär; câre; end; mē; it; īce; pîerce; hot; ōld; sông; fôrk; oil; out; up; ūse; rüle; pùll; tûrn; chin; sing; shop; thin; **th**is; hw in white; zh in treasure. The symbol ə stands for the unstressed vowel sound heard in about, taken, pencil, lemon, and circus.

Mirrors don't lie. [From the Old English word *lēogan* meaning "to tell a lie."]

lie² (lī) *v.i.*, **lay, lain, ly·ing. 1.** to be or place oneself in a flat or reclining position: *to lie in the grass, to lie on a couch.* **2.** to be or rest on a surface: *The blanket is lying on the bed.* **3.** to remain in a particular state or condition: *The treasure lay hidden in the forest.* **4.** to be located or placed: *Mexico lies south of Texas.* **5.** to continue in a specific direction: *A great future lies before us.* **6.** to be; be found; exist: *The defendant's fate lies in the hands of the jury.* **7.** to be buried, as in a grave or tomb. —*n.* the manner, direction, or position in which something lies: *the lie of the land.* [From the Old English word *licgan* with the same meaning.]

lie detector, an instrument that detects certain bodily changes that are assumed to occur when a person lies in answering questions. Also, **polygraph.**

lief (lēf) *adv.* **as lief.** as willingly; as gladly: *We would as lief go there as anywhere else.*

liege (lēj) *n.* **1.** a feudal lord or ruler having the right to the allegiance and service of vassals or subjects. **2.** a vassal or subject bound to give allegiance and service to a feudal lord or ruler. —*adj.* **1.** having the right to the allegiance and service of vassals or subjects. **2.** bound to give allegiance and service to a feudal lord or ruler.

liege·man (lēj′mən) *n., pl.* **liege·men** (lēj′mən). **1.** a vassal. **2.** a faithful follower or subject.

lien (lēn) *n.* a legal claim placed on the property of another for payment of a debt.

lieu (lü) *n.* **in lieu of.** in place of; instead of: *The salesclerk received commissions in lieu of salary.*

Lieut., Lieutenant.

lieu·ten·an·cy (lü ten′ən sē) *n., pl.* **lieu·ten·an·cies.** the rank, status, or commission of a lieutenant.

lieu·ten·ant (lü ten′ənt) *n.* **1.** in the U.S Army, Air Force, or Marine Corps, a first lieutenant or a second lieutenant. **2.** in the U.S. Navy or Coast Guard, an officer ranking next below a lieutenant commander and next above a lieutenant junior grade. **3.** a person who acts in the place of a superior; deputy. [From the Middle French word *lieutenant* meaning "an officer who takes the place of his superior," from the words *lieu* "place" (from the Latin word *locus* "place") + *tenant*, present participle of *tenir* "to hold" (going back to the Latin word *tenēre* "to hold").]

lieutenant colonel, in the U.S. Army, Air Force, and Marine Corps, an officer ranking next below a colonel and next above a major.

lieutenant commander, in the U.S. Navy or Coast Guard, an officer ranking next below a commander and next above a lieutenant.

lieutenant general, in the U.S. Army, Air Force, and Marine Corps, an officer ranking next below a general and next above a major general.

lieutenant governor, in most U.S. states, the second-ranking executive officer who takes over the governorship in case of the governor's death or absence.

lieutenant junior grade *pl.* **lieutenants junior grade.** in the U.S. Navy or Coast Guard, an officer ranking next below a lieutenant and next above an ensign.

life (līf) *n., pl.* **lives. 1.** the quality that distinguishes organisms that grow, reproduce, and adapt to their environment from all other matter. Animals, plants, and some other organisms have life. **2.** the state or fact of possessing this quality: *to lose one's life.* **3.** a spiritual existence coming after physical death: *Some people believe in life after death.* **4.** living organisms: *plant life. No life has been found on the moon.* **5.** a living being; person: *The firefighters helped to save many lives.* **6.** the period from birth to death: *to have a long and happy life.* **7.** the period during which something lasts or remains useful or effective: *Minor accidents can shorten the life of a car.* **8.** way of living: *military life, city life.* **9.** a written account

of a person's life; biography: *a life of a great general.* **10.** vitality; liveliness; spirit: *to be full of life.*

•**a matter of life and** (or **or**) **death.** something extremely important or urgent.

•**as big** (or **large**) **as life.** in person: *As we were talking about him, suddenly there he stood as big as life.*

•**for dear life.** to or as if to save one's life: *When the dog growled, she ran for dear life.*

•**for life.** for the rest of one's life.

•**to bring to life. a.** to cause to regain consciousness; revive. **b.** to make animated or lively. **c.** to make lifelike: *A great actor can bring a fictional character to life.*

•**to come to life. a.** to regain consciousness. **b.** to become animated or lively: *The city comes to life after dark.* **c.** to appear to be alive or real; become lifelike.

•**to take (someone's) life.** to kill (someone).

•**true to life.** faithfully representing real life: *a novel that is true to life.*

life-and-death (līf′ən deth′) *adj.* **1.** threatening to life: *a life-and-death medical crisis.* **2.** necessary for the maintenance of life: *a life-and-death operation.* **3.** of critical importance; crucial; decisive: *Success of the new product was a life-and-death matter for the failing company.* Also, **life-or-death** (līf′ər deth′).

life belt, a life preserver made like a belt.

life·blood (līf′blud′) *n.* **1.** the blood necessary to life. **2.** something that gives strength or energy: *Freedom of speech is the lifeblood of democracy.*

life·boat (līf′bōt′) *n.* a strong boat, usually carried on a larger ship, equipped for saving lives at sea or along the shore in case of shipwreck or other emergency.

life buoy, a life preserver, often ring-shaped, used to keep a person afloat.

life cycle *Biology.* the complete series of changes through which an organism passes from the beginning of its life to maturity, including reproduction.

life expectancy, the amount of time that a person or animal is likely to live or that an object is likely to exist or function.

life·guard (līf′gärd′) *n.* a person employed at a beach or a swimming pool to protect and aid swimmers.

life insurance 1. a contract between a person and an insurance company, under which the person regularly pays small sums of money over a specified period of time in return for a large sum of money that is paid to the person after a specified period of time or to the person's family or chosen beneficiary after the person dies. **2.** the sum of money specified in such a contract.

life jacket, a life preserver in the form of a jacket or vest.

life·less (līf′lis) *adj.* **1.** not having life. **2.** no longer alive; dead. **3.** not lively; dull. **4.** without living organisms: *a lifeless desert.* —**life′less·ly,** *adv.* —**life′less·ness,** *n.*

life·like (līf′līk′) *adj.* resembling or imitating real life: *The doll was amazingly lifelike.*

life·line (līf′līn′) *n.* **1.** a rope used for rescue, especially one attached to a life preserver and thrown to a person in the water. **2.** a line by which a diver is raised or lowered, and used by the diver for signaling. **3.** a route over which vital supplies are transported to a place.

life·long (līf′lông′) *adj.* lasting or continuing through a lifetime: *a lifelong struggle, lifelong friends.*

life preserver, a

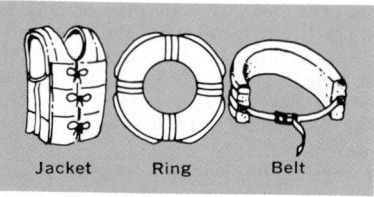

Jacket   Ring   Belt

life preservers

device used by a person to keep afloat, usually in the form of a belt, vest, or circular tube that is inflated with air or filled with cork or other buoyant material.

life raft, a wooden or inflatable rubber raft or boat, used by people forced to abandon a larger boat or airplane out on the water.

life·sav·er (līf′sā′vər) n. **1.** a person who saves another from death, as a lifeguard. **2.** *Informal.* a person or thing that provides help in a time of need or crisis. **3.** a life preserver in the form of a ring.

life·sav·ing (līf′sā′ving) *adj.* used in or designed for saving lives: *Ladders and ropes are used as lifesaving equipment.* —*n.* the skill and techniques used in saving a life or lives, especially from drowning: *The lifeguard won prizes for swimming and lifesaving.*

life-size (līf′sīz′) *adj.* of the same size as the thing portrayed: *a life-size portrait of a person.*

life span 1. the period or length of time that a person or animal lives or that an object exists or functions. **2.** the predicted length or average length of time that a person or animal will live or that an object will exist or function.

life·style (līf′stīl′) n. the various characteristics of the way a person or group lives, including work, recreational activities, interests, diet, style of dress, and the like.

life-sup·port system (līf′sə pôrt′) **1.** equipment that artificially performs an essential body function, such as breathing, used to maintain the life of a patient who would be unable to survive without it. **2.** the equipment that provides oxygen, regulates air temperature and pressure, and performs other functions to maintain an environment that can sustain life, as in a spacecraft or submarine: *The astronauts double-checked each mechanism in the life-support system.*

life·time (līf′tīm′) n. the period of time that a person, animal, or plant lives or a thing lasts: *a lifetime devoted to science, the lifetime of a car.* —*adj.* lasting for such a period: *a lifetime interest in collecting stamps.*

life·work (līf′wûrk′) n. the main or entire work of a lifetime: *The doctor's lifework was medical research.*

lift (lift) *v.t.* **1.** to raise to a higher position; pick up; elevate: *to lift a heavy suitcase.* **2.** to raise in rank, condition, or estimation; exalt: *The victory lifted the team's spirits.* **3.** to revoke or remove; cancel: *The ban on parking was lifted temporarily.* **4.** *Informal.* to steal: *The burglars lifted three radios.* **5.** *Informal.* to take and pass off as one's own (someone else's work or ideas); plagiarize: *to lift a paragraph from a textbook.* —*v.i.* **1.** to be or become raised. *This box is too heavy to lift.* **2.** to rise or seem to rise and disappear: *The fog lifted.* —*n.* **1.** the act of lifting. **2.** the distance or height to which a thing is lifted or raised. **3.** the amount that can be lifted at one time. **4.** a free ride given to a person: *The hitchhiker was given a lift into town.* **5.** an elevating influence or effect, especially a happy feeling: *The compliment gave me quite a lift.* **6.** *British.* see **elevator** *(def. 1).* **7.** one of the layers of leather, rubber, or plastic at the bottom of the heel of a shoe. —**lift′er,** *n.*

lift-off (lift′ôf′) also, **lift·off.** n. the action of a rocket or spacecraft as it rises from its launching pad.

lig·a·ment (lig′ə mənt) n. a band of strong tissue that connects two bones or cartilages or holds an organ of the body in place. [From the Latin word *ligamentum* meaning "band²," from the Latin word *ligare* "to bind, tie."]

lig·a·ture (lig′ə chûr′, lig′ə chər) n. **1.** something that is used to bind or tie. **2.** a thread, wire, or string used in surgery to tie off a blood vessel to stop bleeding. **3.** *Printing.* two or more letters joined together to form one character. The character æ is a ligature.

light¹ (līt) n. **1.** a form of radiation that can be detected by the human eye and that travels at a speed of about 186,000 miles per second (300,000 kilometers per second). **2.** a form of radiation similar to this but invisible to the human eye, especially ultraviolet or infrared radiation. **3.** the condition that makes seeing possible; illumination: *We walked slowly because there was almost no light in the tunnel.* **4.** a particular instance of such illumination: *a strong light, a bright light.* **5.** a source of illumination or brightness, such as a lamp or candle: *Turn off the lights when you leave.* **6.** the illumination that comes from the sun; daylight: *Plants grow rapidly when exposed to light.* **7.** dawn; daybreak. **8.** something, such as a flame or spark, used to set fire to a substance: *Give me a light for the candles.* **9.** knowledge or information; understanding: *The investigation shed new light on the mystery.* **10.** public knowledge: *That political scandal has recently come to light.* **11.** the way in which something is seen or judged: *Once I had graduated from college, my parents saw me in a new light.* **12.** an outstanding or well-known person: *a leading light in the field of medicine.* **13.** a bright color or shade: *lights and darks in a painting.* —*adj.* **1.** having light; bright; not dark: *The room was lighter in the morning than in the afternoon.* **2.** pale or whitish in color: *a light pink, a light complexion.* —*v.,* **light·ed** or **lit, light·ing.** —*v.t.* **1.** to cause to catch fire; kindle; ignite: *to light a candle.* **2.** to cause to give off light: *to light a lamp.* **3.** to give light to; illuminate: *One large bulb lighted the whole room.* **4.** to make bright or lively. **5.** to show the way to by means of a light or lights. —*v.i.* **1.** to take fire; become ignited: *Wet wood will not light easily.* **2.** to become bright or radiant: *The children's faces lighted up when they heard the good news.* [From the Old English word *lēoht* with the same meaning.]

·**in the light of.** because of: *In the light of this new evidence, the defendant must be found not guilty.*

·**to see the light.** to come to understand something: *The teacher explained the problem several times before I saw the light.*

light² (līt) *adj.* **1.** having little weight; not heavy: *a light suitcase.* **2.** having little weight in proportion to its size or bulk: *Foam rubber is light.* **3.** having less than the usual or standard weight: *a light summer jacket.* **4.** low in density, amount, force, or degree: *a light wind, a light rain.* **5.** easy to do or bear; not difficult: *light housework, light punishment.* **6.** moving easily; nimble; graceful; agile: *to be light on one's feet.* **7.** graceful in form or appearance; delicate: *The church had a small, light spire.* **8.** happy, cheerful; carefree: *a light heart.* **9.** meant to entertain; not serious: *light reading.* **10.** few or slight: *The army suffered light casualties.* **11.** not rich or fatty: *a diet of light foods.* **12.** having an airy or spongy consistency: *The cake is moist and light.* **13.** using fairly simple machinery, especially to produce consumer goods: *light industry.* **14.** having relatively light arms, equipment, or armor: *light cavalry, a light cruiser.* **15.** having fewer calories than is usual: *light beer.* —*adv.* lightly, especially without unnecessary equipment: *to travel light.* [From the Old English word *lēoht* meaning "not heavy."]

light³ (līt) *v.i.,* **light·ed** or **lit, light·ing.** **1.** to settle or come to rest, especially from flight: *A bee lighted on the flower.* **2.** to get down or descend; alight: *to light from a carriage.* **3.** to fall or strike suddenly: *The blow lighted on the boxer's chin.* [From the Old English word *līhtan* "to descend."]

·**to light into.** *Informal.* **a.** to attack. **b.** to scold.

·**to light on.** to find by chance: *After two hours of*

---

at; āpe; fär; câre; end; mē; it; īce; pîerce; hot; ōld; sông, fôrk; oil; out; up; ūse; rüle; pull; tûrn; chin; sing; shop; thin; this; hw in white; zh in treasure. The symbol ə stands for the unstressed vowel sound heard in about, taken, pencil, lemon, and circus.

L

thought, I finally lighted on a solution to the problem.
·**to light out.** *Informal.* to leave suddenly and hastily.
light bulb, a bulb in which light is produced by passing an electric current through a thin wire or filament, causing it to glow; incandescent lamp.

light·en¹ (līʹtən) *v.t.* to make lighter or brighter: *The painter lightened the color by adding white.* —*v.i.* **1.** to become light or bright: *The sky lightened after the storm.* **2.** to flash with lightning. [*Light*¹ + *-en*¹.]

light·en² (līʹtən) *v.t.* **1.** to reduce the weight or load of; make less heavy: *to lighten a burden.* **2.** to make less harsh or burdensome: *Machines lighten the work of laborers.* **3.** to make more cheerful; gladden; ease: *to lighten a person's spirits.* [*Light*² + *-en*¹.]

light·er¹ (līʹtər) *n.* a person or thing that causes something to ignite, especially a mechanical device used to light cigarettes, cigars, or the like. [*Light*¹ + *-er*¹.]

light·er² (līʹtər) *n.* a flat-bottomed barge usually used in a harbor for loading and unloading ships or for transporting goods short distances. —*v.t.* to transport (goods) in a lighter. [From the Middle English word *lightere* meaning this boat, probably from the word *lighten* "to lessen the burden."]

light·face (lītʹfās') *n. Printing.* a type whose characters have thin, light lines.

light–foot·ed (lītʹfut'id) *adj.* having a light and graceful step.

light·head·ed (lītʹhed'id) *adj.* **1.** somewhat faint or delirious; dizzy. **2.** not serious or sensible in attitude or behavior; flighty. —**light'head'ed·ly,** *adv.* —**light'-head'ed·ness,** *n.*

light·heart·ed (lītʹhär'tid) *adj.* free from care or anxiety; cheerful; gay. —**light'heart'ed·ly,** *adv.* —**light'-heart'ed·ness,** *n.*

lighthouse

light·house (lītʹhous') *n., pl.* **light·hous·es** (lītʹhou'ziz). a tower or similar structure equipped with a powerful light, usually built near a dangerous place as a warning and guide to ships.

light·ing (līʹting) *n.* **1.** the act of lighting or the state of being lighted; illumination. **2.** an arrangement or system of lights: *stage lighting.*

light·ly (lītʹlē) *adv.* **1.** with little weight or force; not heavily: *to stroke a cat lightly.* **2.** in a small degree or amount: *to season food lightly.* **3.** with a light or easy motion: *The leaf floated lightly down the stream.* **4.** in a light, quick manner; nimbly: *to step lightly.* **5.** in a carefree manner; cheerfully: *The team accepted its defeat lightly.* **6.** in a slighting manner: *to speak lightly of a person's accomplishments.*

light meter *Photography.* a device used to measure the intensity of light in a certain place and thus determine the correct exposure. Also, **exposure meter.**

light–mind·ed (lītʹmīn'did) *adj.* characterized by a lack of seriousness; frivolous.

light·ness¹ (lītʹnis) *n.* **1.** the quality or the state of being light; brightness. **2.** paleness of color. [From the Old English word *līhtness* with the same meaning.]

light·ness² (lītʹnis) *n.* **1.** the quality or the state of having relatively little weight, heaviness, force, or the like. **2.** the quality of being nimble or graceful; agility. **3.** freedom from sorrow or care; cheerfulness. **4.** lack of seriousness; frivolity. [*Light*² + *-ness*.]

light·ning (lītʹning) *n.* **1.** a flash of light in the sky, caused by an electrical discharge between clouds or between a cloud and the ground. **2.** the electrical discharge itself. —*adj.* having or moving with great speed or suddenness: *a lightning response to a question.*

lightning bug, another term for **firefly.**

lightning rod, a metal rod that is used to protect a building from damage by lightning by conducting electricity to the ground.

light pen, an electronic device resembling a pencil that is held in the hand and moved across a computer screen to enter commands or data.

light·ship (lītʹship') *n.* a ship having lights and signals, usually moored at a place that is dangerous to navigation as a warning and guide to ships.

light·weight (lītʹwāt') *n.* **1.** a person or thing of less than average weight. **2.** a boxer weighing less than a welterweight and more than a featherweight. **3.** *Informal.* a person of little importance, influence, skill, or intelligence: *With so little real power, our mayor is a political lightweight.* —*adj.* **1.** light in weight. **2.** of or relating to a lightweight. **3.** lacking a serious purpose: *a lightweight detective novel.*

light-year (lītʹyîr') *n.* an astronomical unit of distance equal to the distance that light travels through space in one year, or approximately 5.878 trillion miles (9.459 trillion kilometers).

lig·nite (ligʹnīt) *n.* a brownish black, low-quality coal in which the texture of the original wood can be seen.

lik·a·ble (līʹkə bəl) *also,* **like·a·ble.** *adj.* pleasing; agreeable: *a likable person.* —**lik'a·ble·ness,** *n.*

like¹ (līk) *prep.* **1.** having a close resemblance to; similar to: *to look like someone else.* **2.** in the same way as; similarly to: *You're acting like a baby!* **3.** characteristic or typical of: *It was just like them to forget your birthday.* **4.** such as: *to do well in subjects like math and science.* **5.** inclined to; desirous of: *Do you feel like going for a walk?* **6.** giving promise or indication of: *It looks like a long, cold winter.* —*adj.* **1.** having identical or similar form, appearance, or characteristics; similar: *The two friends had like hairstyles.* **2.** equal or equivalent: *to donate a like amount.* —*adv. Informal.* probably; likely: *They will arrive tomorrow, like as not.* —*n.* a person or thing that is considered equal, as in qualities or values, to another; match: *They found no one who was the champion's like.* —*conj. Informal.* **1.** in the way that; as: *This soup doesn't taste like it should.* **2.** as if; as though: *It looks like it will rain today.* [From the Old English word *gelīc* meaning "similar, alike."]

like² (līk) *v.,* **liked, lik·ing.** —*v.t.* **1.** to take pleasure in; enjoy: *to like baseball.* **2.** to feel affection, tenderness, or fondness for: *to like another person.* **3.** to wish or desire; prefer: *Would you like another bowl of soup?* —*v.i.* to have a desire or wish; choose; prefer: *Come whenever you like.* —*n. usually,* **likes.** preference; taste: *to have strange likes and dislikes.* [From the Old English word *lician* meaning "to please."]

-like *suffix* (used to form adjectives from nouns) **1.** resembling or similar to; having the characteristics of: *catlike,* *childlike*.   **2.** appropriate or fit for; suited to: *businesslike, ladylike*.

like·a·ble (lī′kə bəl) *adj*.   another spelling of **likable**. —**like′a·ble·ness**, *n*.

like·li·hood (līk′lē hůd′) *n*.   probability: *In all likelihood, I will leave tomorrow*.

like·ly (līk′lē) *adj.*, **like·li·er**, **like·li·est**.   **1.** apparently or probably true: *a likely cause*. **2.** having or showing a tendency or possibility: *It is likely to rain tomorrow*. **3.** having a good chance of occurring: *Although the rain stopped, a flood is still likely*. **4.** suitable, appropriate: *a likely spot to build a house*. **5.** promising: *a likely candidate*. —*adv*.   probably: *Those rapids are most likely very dangerous*.

lik·en (lī′kən) *v.t.*   to represent as like; compare: *to liken someone's eyes to stars*.

like·ness (līk′nis) *n., pl.* **like·ness·es**.   **1.** the state or quality of being alike; resemblance: *The two cousins' likeness was very noticeable*. **2.** a picture or other representation. **3.** appearance; form; guise: *In the story the elf took on the likeness of a bird*.

like·wise (līk′wīz′) *adv*.   **1.** in a like manner; similarly: *You became angry, and I reacted likewise*. **2.** in addition; also.

lik·ing (lī′king) *n*.   a preference or fondness: *to have a liking for pasta*.

li·lac (lī′lək) *n*.   **1.** a purple, pink, red, or white flower cluster made up of tiny, fragrant, tube-shaped flowers. **2.** the shrub or small tree that bears this flower. **3.** a pale, pinkish purple color. —*adj*.   having the color lilac.

lilt (lilt) *v.t., v.i.*   to sing or play (music) with a light, graceful rhythm. —*n*.   **1.** a lively song or tune with a light, graceful rhythm. **2.** a lively and rhythmic quality.

lilt·ing (lil′ting) *adj*.   having a lively, rhythmic quality: *a lilting tune, a lilting stride*.

lil·y (lil′ē) *n., pl.* **lil·ies**.   **1.** a showy, trumpet-shaped flower growing singly or in clusters. **2.** the plant bearing this flower, growing directly from an underground bulb. **3.** any of various other plants, such as the water lily. —*adj*.   like a lily, as in whiteness, delicacy, or beauty. —**lil′y·like′**, *adj*.

lily *(def. 1)*

lily of the valley *pl.* **lilies of the valley**.   **1.** a long cluster of small, fragrant, usually white, bell-shaped flowers that grow down one side of a stalk of a plant related to the lily. **2.** the plant bearing this flower, having long, oval leaves.

li·ma bean (lī′mə)   **1.** the pale green, kidney-shaped seed of a plant related to the pea, cooked and eaten as a vegetable. **2.** the plant bearing this seed.

limb (lim) *n*.   **1.** a part of the body of an animal or human other than the head and torso; an arm, leg, wing, or flipper. **2.** one of the large branches of a tree.

lim·ber (lim′bər) *adj*.   bending or moving easily; flexible: *to keep oneself limber by exercising*. —*v.t*. (usually with *up*) to make limber: *The athletes limbered up their bodies before the game*. —*v.i*. (usually with *up*) to become limber, especially by exercising. —**lim′ber·ness**, *n*.

lim·bo (lim′bō) *n., pl.* **lim·bos**.   **1.** *also*, **Limbo**. in Roman Catholic theology, the abode of souls not entitled to enter Heaven, but not condemned to the punishment of Hell, especially those of infants who died before being baptized. **2.** a place or condition of oblivion or neglect for unwanted, useless, or forgotten people or things: *The junkyard was a limbo of abandoned cars*.

Lim·burg·er (lim′bûr′gər) *n*.   a semisoft white cheese having a strong smell. [From the Flemish word *Limburger* meaning "of or from the Belgian province of *Limburg*," used as the name of this cheese.]

lime¹ (līm) *n*.   a white, powdery compound of calcium and oxygen, usually prepared by burning limestone. It is used in making cement and as a fertilizer. Also, **quicklime**. —*v.t.*, **limed**, **lim·ing**.   to treat with lime; apply lime to. [From the Old English word *līm* meaning "cement, lime¹."]

lime² (līm) *n*.   **1.** a small, yellowish green, oval or round citrus fruit having a thin rind and a juicy, tart pulp. **2.** the thorny evergreen tree bearing this fruit. [From the French word *lime*, going back to the Arabic word *līmah* meaning this fruit and tree.]

lime³ (līm) another word for **linden**.

lime·light (līm′līt′) *n*.   **1.** a strong light used in the theater to focus attention on a performer, part of the stage, or the like, originally produced by heating lime. **2.** a prominent position before the public; center of interest: *The election campaign put the candidate's family in the limelight*.

lim·er·ick (lim′ər ik) *n*.   a humorous verse form of five lines.   For example: *There was a strange couple of Reading/Who never knew where they were heading./They'd start to the east/On their way to a feast,/And end in the north at a wedding*. [From the refrain "Will you come up to *Limerick*?" used in some nonsense verse, from *Limerick*, a county in Ireland.]

lime·stone (līm′stōn′) *n*.   a rock consisting chiefly of calcium carbonate, used for building and for making lime.

lime·wa·ter (līm′wô′tər) *n*.   a solution of lime and water, used as an antacid and to test for the presence of carbon dioxide.

lim·it (lim′it) *n*.   **1.** the furthest range, extent, or boundary; point at which something ends or must end: *to reach the limit of one's patience*. **2.** *also*, **limits**. boundary: *Do not drive beyond the city limits*. **3.** the greatest amount or quantity allowed: *The hunter shot more than the limit of ducks*. —*v.t*.   to keep within a bound or bounds; restrict; confine: *to limit spending*.

lim·i·ta·tion (lim′i tā′shən) *n*.   **1.** something that limits; limiting condition or circumstance: *A lack of coordination is a serious limitation in sports*. **2.** the act of limiting or the state of being limited.

lim·it·ed (lim′i tid) *adj*.   **1.** kept within a limit or limits; restricted: *The offer is good for a limited time only*. **2.** lacking imagination, independence, or originality; narrow: *a limited person with few interests*. **3.** (of trains, buses, or other public conveyances) making only a small number of stops and carrying few passengers. **4.** restricting each stockholder's or partner's liability to the amount of money each has invested: *a limited company*. —*n*.   a limited train, bus, or other public conveyance.

lim·it·less (lim′it lis) *adj*.   having no limits; boundless.

limn (lim) *v.t*.   **1.** to paint or draw. **2.** to portray in words.

lim·o (lim′ō) *n., pl.* **lim·os**. *Informal*. see **limousine**.

lim·ou·sine (lim′ə zēn′, lim′ə zēn′) *n*.   **1.** a large sedan, often with a glass partition between the front and back seats, often driven by a chauffeur. **2.** a large automobile used as a commercial passenger vehicle: *an airport limousine*.

limp¹ (limp) *v.i*.   **1.** to walk lamely. **2.** to move or proceed slowly or with difficulty: *The old car limped along the dirt road*. —*n*.   a lame walk or movement. [Of uncertain origin, probably related to the Old English word *lemphalt* meaning "lame."]

at; āpe; fär; câre; end; mē; it; īce; pîerce; hot; ōld; sông, fôrk; oil; out; up; ūse; rüle; pull; tûrn; chin; sing; shop; thin; this; hw in white; zh in treasure. The symbol ə stands for the unstressed vowel sound heard in about, taken, pencil, lemon, and circus.

limp² (limp) *adj.* **1.** lacking stiffness or firmness; wilted: *After three days the flowers became limp.* **2.** without force or vigor; weak: *a limp argument.* [Of uncertain origin.] —**limp'ly,** *adv.* —**limp'ness,** *n.*

lim·pet (lim'pit) *n.* a brownish green saltwater shellfish that has a cone-shaped shell and clings to rocks, used chiefly for bait.

lim·pid (lim'pid) *adj.* clear or transparent: *a limpid pool of water.* —**lim·pid'i·ty,** *n.* —**lim'pid·ly,** *adv.*

lim·y (lī'mē) *adj.,* **lim·i·er, lim·i·est.** of, containing, or like lime.

linch·pin (linch'pin') *n.* **1.** a pin that passes through the end of an axle to keep the wheel in place. **2.** something that serves to hold different parts together in a complex arrangement or organization: *The secret police were the linchpin of the dictatorship.*

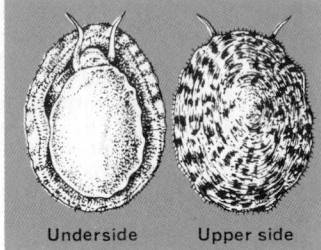

Underside   Upper side

limpet

Lin·coln's Birthday (ling'kənz) the anniversary of the birthday of Abraham Lincoln, observed as a legal holiday on February 12 or on the third Monday in February in some states of the United States.

lin·den (lin'dən) *n.* any of a large group of tall trees bearing broad, usually heart-shaped leaves and drooping clusters of small, fragrant pale yellow or white flowers. Also, **lime.**

line¹ (līn) *n.* **1.** a long, narrow mark or stroke, as that made by a pen, pencil, or tool: *White lines divided the lanes of the highway.* **2.** anything resembling such a mark: *a brow creased with lines of worry.* **3.** an outline, contour, or profile: *the sleek lines of a sports car.* **4.** a limit or boundary, as between two areas; border: *The town is two miles from the state line.* **5.** a division or separation between contrasting ideas, qualities, conditions, or the like: *the line between fantasy and reality.* **6.** a number of persons or things arranged in one continuous series; row: *We waited in a long line outside the movie theater.* **7.** a continuous series of persons or things following one another in time: *The Tudors were a line of English kings and queens.* **8.** a row of words or letters printed or written between the margins of a page or column. **9.** a short letter; note: *My friend dropped me a line thanking me for the gift.* **10.** a row of words forming a single unit of poetry: *There are six lines in each stanza of the poem.* **11. lines.** the spoken words of a theatrical presentation, especially those for a single performer: *The actor forgot the lines.* **12.** a course or direction of progress or movement: *An innocent bystander was caught in the line of fire.* **13.** a course of action, conduct, or thought; method: *I had trouble understanding the author's line of reasoning.* **14.** *also,* **lines.** a general plan, as of construction, action, or procedure: *The house was designed along very simple lines.* **15.** an area or range of interest, activity, or ability: *Cooking is my line.* **16.** a particular business or activity: *What is your line of work?* **17.** a kind of goods or merchandise: *The store is selling a new line of bicycles.* **18.** a wire or series of wires connecting points or stations in a telegraph or telephone system. **19.** a connection or contact made between two points in such a system: *Their line is busy.* **20.** a system of transportation: *a bus line.* **21.** one branch of such a system of transportation. **22.** a track of a railroad: *The workers laid down a new line over the mountains.* **23.** a cord, rope, wire, cable, or the like designed or used for a specific purpose: *a fishing line, to hang wet clothes on a line.* **24.** a channel, wire, or pipe that carries gas, water, or electricity, or the like, from one point to another. **25.** *Mathematics.* the path traced by a moving point thought of as having length but no thickness. A line may be straight or curved. **26.** *Football.* **a.** see **line of scrimmage. b.** the row of players arranged along the line of scrimmage at the beginning of a play. **27.** *also,* **lines.** the troops or the position in closest contact with opposing troops: *The soldier was captured behind enemy lines.* **28.** *Informal.* glib, often insincere talk: *The crook gave the police a line about being away the day of the theft.* —*v.,* **lined, lin·ing.** —*v.t.* **1.** to mark or cover with lines: *to line paper.* **2.** to arrange or form a line along: *Trees lined the edge of the road.* **3.** *Baseball.* to hit (a ball) so that it travels through the air in an almost level path: *The batter lined the first pitch to right field.* —*v.i.* *Baseball.* to hit a ball so that it travels through the air in an almost level path: *The batter lined to center field.* [From the Old English word *līne* meaning "a thread, cord, line¹" and the Old French word *ligne* with the same meanings, both from the Latin word *linea* "string, (linen) thread," from the word *linum* "flax" or "linen."]

•**all along the line.** at every point; in every way.

•**in line.** **a.** in a line or row. **b.** in agreement: *Most of the speaker's ideas were in line with my own.*

•**in line for.** due for or deserving of: *in line for a promotion.*

•**on a line.** even; level.

•**out of line.** **a.** not in a line or row. **b.** not in agreement. **c.** not proper or suitable; inappropriate: *Their behavior was out of line.*

•**to draw the line.** to set the limit.

•**to hold the line.** to maintain a firm position: *The government tried to hold the line against inflation.*

•**to line up. a.** to arrange in a line: *The teacher lined up the children according to height.* **b.** to form a line: *People lined up in front of the theater.* **c.** to gather, get, or arrange for: *to line up support for a proposed law.* **d.** to get into a formation: *The drummers lined up behind the trombonists. The team lined up for the next play.*

•**to read between the lines.** to understand a hidden meaning.

line² (līn) *v.t.,* **lined, lin·ing. 1.** to cover the inner surface of: *The tailor lined the jacket with silk.* **2.** to supply or fill: *The shelves were lined with books.* **3.** to be used as a lining or covering for: *Portraits lined the walls.* [From the Middle English word *linen* "to cover the inner surface," from the word *lin* "flax, linen."]

lin·e·age (lin'ē ij) *n.* **1.** a line of direct descent from an ancestor. **2.** those descended from a common ancestor; family.

lin·e·al (lin'ē əl) *adj.* **1.** in the direct line of descent: *The king's grandchild is a lineal heir to the throne.* **2.** of or based upon direct descent; hereditary: *a lineal right to a title.* **3.** of or like a line; linear. —**lin'e·al·ly,** *adv.*

lin·e·a·ment (lin'ē ə mənt) *n.* a feature, detail, or outline of a body or figure, especially of the face.

lin·e·ar (lin'ē ər) *adj.* **1.** of or relating to a line or lines. **2.** consisting of or making use of lines: *a linear drawing.* **3.** along a line or lines: *linear motion.* **4.** relating to length: *the linear dimensions of a room.* **5.** like a line; long and narrow: *a linear leaf.* —**lin'e·ar·ly,** *adv.*

linear accelerator, a particle accelerator in which charged subatomic particles are propelled in a straight line by an electric field that accelerates the particles to increasingly higher energies.

linear equation *Mathematics.* an algebraic equation whose graph is a straight line.

linear measure 1. measurement by length. **2.** a unit or system of units for measuring length.

line·back·er (līn'bak'ər) *n.* *Football.* a defensive player whose position is directly behind the linemen.

line drive *Baseball.* a strongly hit ball that travels relatively parallel to the ground in a nearly straight line.

line·man (līn′mən) *n., pl.* **line·men** (līn′mən). **1.** a person who installs or repairs telegraph, telephone, or electric wires. **2.** a person who inspects railroad tracks. **3.** *Football.* any of the players in the line.

lin·en (lin′ən) *n.* **1.** a strong cloth woven from flax fibers, used for dresses, suits, and tablecloths. **2.** *also,* **linens.** household articles, such as sheets, tablecloths, towels, and napkins, made of linen or similar cloth. —*adj.* made of linen: *linen napkins.*

line of force *Physics.* an imaginary line in a field of electric or magnetic force, showing the direction of force of the field.

line of scrimmage, an imaginary line running across a football field parallel to the goal lines, on which the ball is placed by the referee. A new line is established wherever the ball is ruled dead at the end of a play.

lin·er¹ (lī′nər) *n.* **1.** a ship or airplane operated by a transportation line. **2.** a person or thing that makes lines. **3.** *Baseball.* a line drive. [*Line¹* + *-er¹.*]

lin·er² (lī′nər) *n.* **1.** something serving as a lining: *a trash can liner.* **2.** a person who lines or fits a lining to something. [*Line²* + *-er¹.*]

line segment **1.** the part of a line between two given points on the line. **2.** a line with a definite point at each end.

lines·man (līnz′mən) *n., pl.* **lines·men** (līnz′mən). an official who assists the referee in football, tennis, hockey, and other sports.

line·up (līn′up′) *also,* **line-up.** *n.* **1.** an arrangement of persons or things in a line, row, or sequence. **2.** a number of people lined up by the police so that a criminal suspect can be identified by a victim or witness. **3.a.** the players on a team actually participating in play at any given time during a game. **b.** a list of such players.

-ling *suffix* (used to form nouns) **1.** little or unimportant: *duckling.* **2.** a person or thing that is related to, characterized by, or concerned with: *earthling.*

lin·ger (ling′gər) *v.i.* **1.** to stay on as if reluctant to leave; delay leaving: *The fans lingered outside the locker room after the game was over.* **2.** to go or act at a slow pace; dawdle: *Don't linger on the way home.*

lin·ge·rie (lan′zhə rā′, lan′zhə rē′) *n.* women's underwear, nightgowns, robes, and similar garments. [From the French word *lingerie* meaning both "underclothing" and "linen garments," from the Old French word *linge* "linen," going back to the Latin word *linum* "flax, linen."]

lin·go (ling′gō) *n., pl.* **lin·goes.** language or speech that is strange or hard to understand to a person who is unfamiliar with it: *sports lingo.*

lin·gua fran·ca (ling′gwə frang′kə) *n., pl.* **lin·gua fran·cas** or **lin·guae fran·cae** (ling′gwē fran′sē). a language made up of elements of two or more other languages. A lingua franca is used as a common language by people who speak different languages and would not otherwise understand each other, especially in conducting business.

lin·gual (ling′gwəl) *adj.* **1.** of or relating to the tongue. **2.** (of speech sounds) formed chiefly with the tongue, as the letter *t.* **3.** of language or languages.

lin·gui·ne (ling gwē′nē) *also,* **lin·gui·ni.** *n.* pasta shaped into long, thin, flat noodles. [From the Italian word *linguine* meaning "little tongues," from the word *lingua* "tongue," from the Latin word *lingua* "tongue."]

lin·guist (ling′gwist) *n.* **1.** an expert in linguistics. **2.** a person who can speak or is skilled in several languages.

lin·guis·tic (ling gwis′tik) *adj.* of or relating to language or linguistics. —**lin·guis′ti·cal·ly,** *adv.*

lin·guis·tics (ling gwis′tiks) *n.* **1.** the scientific study of language. **2.** the study of the development and structure of a particular language. ▲ used with a singular verb.

Language Note

The science of **linguistics** has developed fairly recently. People have thought about language since ancient times; Hebrew, Greek, and Hindu scholars all studied language more than 2,000 years ago. But it was not until the nineteenth century that *linguists* began to examine language scientifically, by carefully and systematically studying the characteristics of many different languages. These linguists concentrated on comparing languages to determine their similarities. They learned that an ancient language no longer in existence, called Indo-European, was the basis for almost all the languages spoken in Europe, such as Greek, Spanish, Russian, and English, as well as a number of Asian languages.

In the twentieth century, linguists set out to study languages that were currently being spoken throughout the world, rather than examining past languages or those spoken only in Europe. They concentrated especially on the languages of the American Indians. From their research, they learned that many characteristics of European languages that had been assumed to be true of all language were not found in some non-European tongues. For example, one American Indian language has present, past, and future tenses for nouns, just as English does for verbs. That is, it has three different words for our word *house:* one for a house that now exists, a second for a house that once was built, and a third for one that will be built. On the other hand, another American Indian language with a different structure has no nouns at all.

The most important thing that linguists learned from these studies was that languages cannot be accurately described with such terms as "primitive" and "advanced." Each language fulfills the needs of the people who speak it. The Eskimo language may have no word for "laser" or "microscope" because these things are not important in Eskimo culture. But Eskimo has several words for "snow" because snow is such an important part of the life of the Eskimos that they need various words to describe different kinds of snow.

The conclusion that linguists have drawn from their findings is that all languages are equal. French and German are not "better" than native African languages because they have a different vocabulary with more scientific and literary terms. All languages exist in order to enable the members of a group of people to communicate thoughts, feelings, and information to one another. The things expressed and the ways in which a particular language expresses them differ according to each group's way of life. The differences between languages are only reflections of the different ways in which various groups of people live.

lin·i·ment (lin′ə mənt) *n.* a liquid rubbed on the skin to relieve pain or stiffness, as from a bruise, sore muscle, or sprain.

lin·ing (lī′ning) *n.* **1.** the surface, layer, or coating cov-

---

at; āpe; fär; câre; end; mē; it; īce; pîerce; hot; ōld; sông, fôrk; oil; out; up; ūse; rüle; pull; tûrn; chin; sing; shop; thin; this; hw in white; zh in treasure. The symbol ə stands for the unstressed vowel sound heard in about, taken, pencil, lemon, and circus.

L

ering the inside of something: *the stomach lining, the silk lining of a jacket.* **2.** a material used for this purpose.

link (lingk) *n.* **1.** one of the rings or loops of a chain. **2.** something like a link in a chain: *links of sausage.* **3.** anything that joins or connects: *a link with the past.* —*v.t.* to join by a link or links; unite; connect: *Everyone linked arms and formed a circle.* —*v.i.* to be joined by or as if by a link or links.

link·age (ling′kij) *n.* **1.** the act of linking or the state of being linked. **2.** a system or series of links.

linking verb, a verb that connects a subject with a predicate adjective or noun without expressing action. In the sentence *Your eyes are lovely,* the word *are* is a linking verb. *Appear, be,* and *seem* can function as linking verbs. Also, **copula, copulative verb.**

links (lingks) *pl. n.* another word for **golf course.**

lin·net (lin′it) *n.* a small finch of Europe and Asia having a reddish crown and breast.

li·no·le·um (li nō′lē əm) *n.* a floor covering made by putting a mixture of linseed oil, finely ground cork or wood, resins, and pigments on a backing of burlap or canvas. [Formed from the Latin words *linum* meaning "flax" and *oleum* meaning "oil."]

Li·no·type (lī′nə tīp′) *n. Trademark.* in printing, a machine for setting type, operated by a keyboard, that sets and casts a line of type in one piece of metal.

lin·seed (lin′sēd′) *n.* the seed of flax, the source of linseed oil.

linseed oil, a yellow or brown oil obtained from the seed of certain flax plants, used in making paints, varnish, printing ink, patent leather, and linoleum.

lin·sey–wool·sey (lin′zē wŭl′zē) *n., pl.* **lin·sey-wool-seys.** a strong, coarse, loosely woven fabric of wool and linen or cotton.

lint (lint) *n.* **1.** tiny bits of thread or fluff: *Lint shows readily on a dark fabric.* **2.** a soft, downy or fleecy material obtained by scraping linen fibers, formerly used as a dressing for wounds.

lin·tel (lin′təl) *n.* a horizontal part or piece set above an opening, as of a door or window, to support the structure above it.

li·on (lī′ən) *n.* **1.** a large animal of the cat family, native to Africa and southern Asia, having a tawny coat of short, coarse hair and a tufted tail. The male has a shaggy mane around the neck, head, and shoulders. **2.** a person of great strength or courage. **3.** a famous person; celebrity.

Lion
Lioness

lion and **lioness**

li·on·ess (lī′ə-nis) *n., pl.* **li·on·ess·es.** an adult female lion.

li·on·heart·ed (lī′ən här′tid) *adj.* brave; courageous.

li·on·ize (lī′ə nīz′) *v.t.,* **li·on·ized, li·on·iz·ing.** to treat as very important.

lion's share, the largest or best portion: *to receive the lion's share of an inheritance.*

lip (lip) *n.* **1.** either of the two fleshy folds forming the opening of the mouth. **2.** the edge or rim of an opening or cavity: *the lip of a crater, the lip of a pitcher.* **3.** *Botany.* the protruding part in certain plants where the calyx or corolla is divided into unequal parts, as in a snapdragon or orchid. **4.** *Slang.* disrespectful or impudent talk. —**lip′like′,** *adj.*

·to keep a stiff upper lip. to face misfortune with courage.

li·pase (lī′pās, lip′ās) *n.* an enzyme that aids in the breaking down of fats into glycerin and fatty acids.

lip·id (lip′id) *n.* any of a group of organic compounds that includes fats, oils, and other substances that are greasy to the touch and insoluble in water. Lipids, proteins, and carbohydrates are the main structural parts of most living cells. [From the Greek word *lipos* meaning "fat."]

lip–read (lip′rēd′) *v.i.,* **lip-read** (lip′red′), **lip-read·ing.** to engage in lipreading. —**lip′-read′er,** *n.*

lip·read·ing (lip′rē′ding) *n.* the act or skill of understanding what someone is saying by watching the movements of the lips, used especially by people who are deaf.

lip·stick (lip′stik′) *n.* a stick of waxlike cosmetic used to color the lips, usually in a small case.

lip-sync (lip′singk′) *also,* **lip-synch.** *v.t., v.i.,* **lip-synced, lip-sync·ing.** to move one's lips silently in synchronization with the words of a recorded song to give the impression of producing the singing oneself.

liq·ue·fac·tion (lik′wə fak′shən) *n.* the act or process of liquefying or the state of being liquefied.

liq·ue·fy (lik′wə fī′) *v.t., v.i.,* **liq·ue·fied, liq·ue·fy·ing.** to change into a liquid. —**liq′ue·fi′er,** *n.*

li·queur (li kûr′) *n.* a strong, sweet-flavored alcoholic beverage. Also, **cordial.**

liq·uid (lik′wid) *n.* a form of matter that is not solid or gaseous, characterized by the ability of its atoms or molecules to move about freely within a given area, but without the tendency to separate from one another. A liquid can take on the shape of its container, but will not necessarily fill it. —*adj.* **1.** in the form of, or having the properties of, a liquid; capable of flowing or being poured: *The medicine comes in liquid form.* **2.** clear or transparent; shining: *liquid eyes.* **3.** gracefully flowing and smooth: *the liquid motion of the ballerina's arms.* **4.** consisting of, or easily changed into, cash: *Bonds are among their liquid assets.*

liquid air, a bluish, transparent or milky liquid formed when air is put under great pressure and then cooled, used as a refrigerant.

liq·ui·date (lik′wi dāt′) *v.t.,* **liq·ui·dat·ed, liq·ui·dat·ing.** **1.** to pay off or settle (a debt). **2.** to settle the accounts of (a business). **3.** to do away with; get rid of. **4.** to murder: *The gangster was liquidated by a rival.* —**liq′ui·da′tion,** *n.*

li·quid·i·ty (li kwid′i tē) *n.* the state or quality of being liquid.

liquid measure, a unit or system of units for measuring the volume of liquids.

liquid oxygen, an extremely cold liquid obtained by putting oxygen under very great pressure and then cooling it, used as fuel in rocket engines.

liq·uor (lik′ər) *n.* **1.** an alcoholic drink that is produced by distillation, as whiskey, rather than by fermentation, as beer. **2.** any liquid, especially a liquid in which food has been cooked.

li·ra (lîr′ə) *n., pl.* **li·re** (lîr′ā). the monetary unit of Italy.

lisle (līl) *n.* **1.** a fine, strong thread, usually made of cotton fibers that have been tightly twisted and given a smooth finish, used chiefly for socks, underwear, and gloves. **2.** a knit fabric made of this thread. —*adj.* made of lisle: *lisle socks.*

lisp (lisp) *n.* a speech defect in which the sounds of *s* and *z* are mispronounced, usually in such a way that they sound like the *th* in *think* and *them,* respectively. —*v.i., v.t.* to speak with a lisp.

lis·some (lis′əm) *also,* **lis·som.** *adj.* bending or moving easily; limber; supple.

list¹ (list) *n.* a series of names, numbers, words, or other items, set down in a certain order or grouping; catalog; roll: *Make a list of the groceries we need.* —*v.t.* **1.** to make a list of: *to list items alphabetically.* **2.** to enter or include in a list: *to list a name in the telephone directory.* [From the French word *liste* with the same meaning, of Germanic origin.]

list² (list) *n.* a tilt or leaning to one side. —*v.i.* to tilt to one side: *The ship listed sharply because its cargo was loaded on one side.* [Of uncertain origin.]

list³ (list) *Archaic.* *v.i.* to listen. —*v.t.* to listen to; hear. [From the Old English word *hlystan* meaning "to listen, hear."]

lis·ten (lis'ən) *v.i.* **1.** to give attention for the purpose of hearing; try to hear: *We listened for the sound of the bell.* **2.** to pay attention: *The child refused to listen to instructions.* —**lis'ten·er,** *n.*

·**to listen in.** to listen to someone else's conversation; eavesdrop: *It is very impolite to listen in when others are talking on the telephone.*

list·ing (lis'ting) *n.* **1.** the act of making or entering in a list. **2.** an entry in a list: *a new listing in the telephone directory.* **3.** a list.

list·less (list'lis) *adj.* feeling or showing little interest in anything; lacking energy and a desire to do anything: *to feel dull and listless.* —**list'less·ly,** *adv.* —**list'less·ness,** *n.*

list price, the price of an item, as published in a catalog or price list, often reduced by discounts.

lists (lists) *pl. n.* **1.** the field or area in which knights fought tournaments. **2.** any area or place of combat, dispute, or competition.

lit (lit) a past tense and past participle of **light¹** and **light³**.

lit. **1.** liter. **2.** literary; literature.

lit·a·ny (lit'ə nē) *n.,* *pl.* **lit·a·nies.** **1.** a form of prayer consisting of a series of requests spoken by the minister to which the choir or the congregation make fixed responses. **2.** any long or repetitious series: *a litany of woes.*

li·tchi (lē'chē) *also,* **li·chee.** *n.,* *pl.* **li·tchis.** **1.** a small, round fruit of a tree that is widely grown in China, having a brittle, red outer shell and juicy white flesh that can be eaten. *Also,* **litchi nut.** **2.** the tree bearing this fruit.

li·ter (lē'tər) *also, British,* **li·tre.** *n.* a unit of capacity in the metric system, equal to one cubic decimeter, 1.05668 U.S. liquid quarts, or about 0.9080 U.S. dry quarts.

lit·er·a·cy (lit'ər ə sē) *n.* **1.** the ability to read and write. **2.** an understanding of a particular subject or field of knowledge: *computer literacy.*

lit·er·al (lit'ər əl) *adj.* **1.** following the exact words of the original; word for word: *The student prepared a literal translation of the Spanish poem.* **2.** based on, following, or giving the exact meaning. The literal meaning of the idiom "to pull one's leg" is to tug on somebody's leg. **3.** tending to take what is said in an exact manner; using little imagination: *a literal mind.* **4.** according to the facts; not exaggerated: *a literal description.* —**lit'er·al·ness,** *n.*

lit·er·al·ly (lit'ər ə lē) *adv.* **1.** in a literal manner: *to translate a story literally.* **2.** actually; really: *The city was literally destroyed by the earthquake.*

lit·er·ar·y (lit'ə rer'ē) *adj.* **1.** of or relating to literature: *literary history, a literary style.* **2.** knowing much about or occupied with literature: *a literary family.*

lit·er·ate (lit'ər it) *adj.* **1.** able to read and write. **2.** knowing much about literature and culture; well-read: *The professor was highly literate.* **3.** having an understanding of a particular subject or field of knowledge. —*n.* **1.** a person who can read and write. **2.** a person who is well-educated.

lit·er·a·ture (lit'ər ə chər, lit'ər ə chùr') *n.* **1.** works of art composed of written words; writings considered to have artistic value. **2.** all the writings dealing with a particular subject: *medical literature.* **3.** the activity or profession of writing: *to pursue a career in literature.* **4.** printed matter of any kind: *some literature on a new car.*

lithe (līth) *adj.* easily bent; flexible; pliant. —**lithe'ly,** *adv.* —**lithe'ness,** *n.*

lith·i·um (lith'ē əm) *n.* a soft, silvery metallic element, the lightest metal. It is used in purifying metals. Symbol: **Li** [Formed from the Greek word *lithos* meaning "stone." The element was discovered in rock minerals.]

lith·o·graph (lith'ə graf') *n.* a print made by lithography. —*v.t.* to produce or copy by lithography. —**lith·o·graph'ic,** *adj.*

li·thog·ra·phy (li thog'rə fē) *n.* the art or process of printing from a smooth stone or other flat surface on which a design has been drawn with a special grease crayon. Water and then ink are applied to the surface, and prints are made as the ink sticks to the crayon image but not to the moist areas. —**li·thog'ra·pher,** *n.*

lith·o·sphere (lith'ə sfîr') *n.* the crust of the earth.

Lith·u·a·ni·an (lith'ü ā'nē ən) *n.* **1.** a person who was born in or is a citizen of Lithuania. **2.** the language of Lithuania. —*adj.* of or relating to Lithuania, its people, or their language or culture.

lit·i·gant (lit'i gənt) *n.* a person carrying on a lawsuit.

lit·i·gate (lit'i gāt') *v.t.,* **lit·i·gat·ed, lit·i·gat·ing.** to make the subject of a lawsuit: *The tenants litigated their complaints against the landlord.* —*v.i.* to carry on a lawsuit. —**lit'i·ga'tor,** *n.*

lit·i·ga·tion (lit'i gā'shən) *n.* **1.** the act or process of carrying on a lawsuit. **2.** a lawsuit.

lit·mus (lit'məs) *n.* a dye obtained from any of various lichens, that turns blue in alkaline solutions and red in acid solutions.

litmus paper, a paper stained with litmus, used to determine whether something is acid or alkaline.

li·tre (lē'tər) *British.* another spelling of **liter.**

lit·ter (lit'ər) *n.* **1.** bits or scraps of paper or other rubbish scattered about carelessly; mess: *Broken bottles and other litter filled the empty lot.* **2.** young animals born at one time: *a litter of kittens.* **3.** loose straw, hay, or similar material used as bedding for animals. **4.** any absorbent, granular material used to soak up urine and moisture from feces, usually placed in a box or pan to be used by household pets, especially cats, for defecation and urination: *cat litter.*

litter *(def. 5)*

5. a vehicle made up of a couch usually enclosed by curtains and carried by people on their shoulders or by animals: *Four attendants carried the ruler's litter in the procession.* **6.** a stretcher for carrying a sick or injured person. —*v.t.* **1.** to make disordered or untidy by scattering bits of rubbish about carelessly: *to litter a street with trash.* **2.** to give birth to

---

at; āpe; fär; câre; end; mē; it; īce; pîerce; hot; ōld; sông, fôrk; oil; out; up; ūse; rüle; pùll; tûrn; chin; sing; shop; thin; this; hw in white; zh in treasure. The symbol ə stands for the unstressed vowel sound heard in about, taken, pencil, lemon, and circus.

(young). **3.** to provide (animals) with litter for bedding. —*v.i.* **1.** to scatter bits of rubbish about carelessly: *Don't litter; it's against the law.* **2.** to give birth to young.

lit·ter·bug (lit′ər bug′) *n.* *Informal.* a person who litters public places.

lit·tle (lit′əl) *adj.,* **less** or **less·er** or **lit·tler,** **least** or **lit·tlest.** **1.** small in size: *A pebble is a little stone.* **2.** short in time or distance; brief: *a little while, a little walk.* **3.** small in amount or degree; not much: *Add a little water to the mixture.* **4.** small in importance or interest; trivial: *a little problem.* **5.** small in nature, mind, or spirit; mean; narrow: *a nasty, little mind.* —*adv.,* **less, least.** to a small extent; not much; slightly: *That poet is little known outside this country.* —*n.* **1.** a small amount: *I ate only a little.* **2.** a short time or distance: *Step back a little.* —**lit′tle·ness,** *n.*
 ·**little by little.** by slow degrees; gradually.
 ·**to make little of.** to treat as unimportant.
 ·**to think little of.** to have a low opinion of; consider to be unimportant or worthless.

Little Bear, another term for **Ursa Minor.**

Little Dipper, a group of stars in the constellation Ursa Minor, forming the outline of a dipper.

little finger, the finger farthest from the thumb.

Little League, a baseball league for children under thirteen years of age.

Little Leaguer, a child who participates in Little League baseball.

little slam *Bridge.* the winning of twelve tricks in a round of play.

li·tur·gi·cal (li tûr′ji kəl) *adj.* **1.** of or relating to liturgies. **2.** used in a liturgy. Also, **li·tur·gic** (li tûr′jik). —**li·tur′gi·cal·ly,** *adv.*

lit·ur·gy (lit′ər jē) *n., pl.* **lit·ur·gies.** in various churches, the set form of public worship.

liv·a·ble (liv′ə bəl) *also,* **live·a·ble.** *adj.* **1.** fit to live in; habitable: *The old house was not livable.* **2.** worth living; endurable: *to feel that life would not be livable as a slave.*

live¹ (liv) *v.,* **lived, liv·ing.** —*v.i.* **1.** to be alive; have life: *to have lived before the turn of the century.* **2.** to continue to exist; remain alive: *The large turtle lived for one hundred years.* **3.** to support oneself: *That family lives on a small income.* **4.** to feed; subsist: *Some birds live on bugs and worms.* **5.** to make one's home; dwell: *We live on the east side of town.* **6.** to pass or spend one's life: *to live happily.* **7.** to get the fullest enjoyment from life: *They really began to live when they moved to the country.* —*v.t.* **1.** to pass or spend (one's life): *to live a life of luxury.* **2.** to practice or express in one's life: *to live a lie.* [From the Old English words *libban* and *lifian,* both meaning "to live, be alive."]
 ·**to live down.** to live in such a way that (a past mistake, such as a crime) is forgotten or forgiven.
 ·**to live up to.** to abide by or fulfill: *to live up to one's end of the bargain.*
 ·**to live with.** to bear with; endure: *to live with one's mistakes.*

live² (līv) *adj.* **1.** having life; living: *The hunter brought back a live elephant.* **2.** filled with life; energetic; lively: *a live personality.* **3.** of present interest or importance; current: *a live topic.* **4.** burning: *a live coal.* **5.** containing an explosive charge: *live ammunition.* **6.** carrying electrical current. **7.** seen or presented while actually happening, as on the stage or on radio or television: *a live performance, a live broadcast.* [Short for *alive.*]

live·a·ble (līv′ə bəl) another spelling of **livable.**

live·li·hood (līv′lē hŏŏd′) *n.* the means of staying alive or supporting life: *Their livelihood is fishing.* *They earn a livelihood by farming.*

live·long (liv′lông′) *adj.* whole; entire: *to work the livelong day.*

live·ly (līv′lē) *adj.,* **live·li·er, live·li·est.** **1.** full of life, energy, or movement; vigorous; active: *a lively walk.* **2.** gay; cheerful: *a lively tune.* **3.** stimulating; exciting: *a lively debate.* **4.** inventive or creative: *a lively imagination.* **5.** striking; vivid: *lively colors.* **6.** springing back quickly: *a lively tennis ball.* —*adv.* in a lively manner; energetically; vigorously: *to step lively.* —**live′li·ness,** *n.*

liv·en (lī′vən) *v.t.* to make more cheerful, active, or exciting: *Their arrival livened the party.* —*v.i.* (usually with *up*) to become more cheerful; brighten: *to liven up after taking a shower.*

live oak (līv) an evergreen oak tree native to the southeastern United States.

liv·er¹ (liv′ər) *n.* **1.** a large, reddish brown glandular organ that produces bile, stores carbohydrates, filters poisons from the blood, and performs various other body functions. **2.** the liver of certain animals, used as food. [From the Old English word *lifer* meaning this organ.]

liv·er² (liv′ər) *n.* a person who lives in a certain manner: *an easy liver.* [*Live¹* + *-er¹.*]

liv·er·ied (liv′ə rēd) *adj.* dressed in livery: *liveried servants.*

liv·er·leaf (liv′ər lēf′) *n.* hepatica.

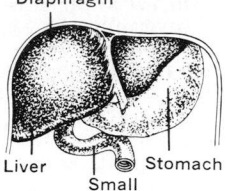
liver¹ *(def. 1)*

liv·er·wort (liv′ər wûrt′) *n.* any of various plants similar to mosses but mostly lacking stems and leaves. They are found throughout the world, growing mostly in damp, shady areas.

liv·er·wurst (liv′ər wûrst′) *n.* a sausage made mostly of liver, especially pork liver.

liv·er·y (liv′ə rē) *n., pl.* **liv·er·ies.** **1.** a uniform provided for servants: *a bellhop in livery.* **2.** any distinctive dress or uniform worn by members of a group or profession. **3.** the stabling and feeding of horses for pay. **4.** see **livery stable.**

livery stable, a stable where horses are cared for and let for hire, with or without vehicles.

lives (līvz) the plural of **life.**

live·stock (līv′stok′) *n.* domestic animals, such as cattle, horses, sheep, or pigs.

live wire (līv) **1.** a wire carrying an electrical current. **2.** *Informal.* an energetic, alert person.

liv·id (liv′id) *adj.* **1.** having a pale, usually bluish color: *a face livid with rage.* **2.** furious; enraged. **3.** having a grayish blue color from a bruise. —**liv′id·ly,** *adv.* —**liv′id·ness,** *n.*

liv·ing (liv′ing) *adj.* **1.** having life; being alive: *a living creature.* **2.** of or relating to life, or suitable for life: *Living conditions are very difficult in Antarctica.* **3.** still active or in use: *a living language.* **4.** still existing: *The elephant is the largest living land animal.* **5.** sufficient for living: *a living wage.* **6.** true to life; lifelike: *The portrait was the living image of the mayor.* —*n.* **1.** the fact or state of being alive. **2.** livelihood: *to earn one's living as a carpenter.* **3.** a manner of life: *plain living, modest living.*

living room, a room in a home for general family use or for entertaining guests.

living will, a document in which a person states whether he or she wishes to be kept alive by extraordinary medical treatment in the case of incurable illness, permanent brain damage or unconsciousness, or the like. Some states recognize living wills as legal documents.

liz·ard (liz′ərd) *n.* any of a group of scaly animals usually having a long, narrow body, four legs, and a tapering tail. Lizards are reptiles and are found in tropical and temperate regions. The chameleon and horned toad are lizards.

llamas

lla·ma (lä′mə) *n.* a cud-chewing animal of South America that is related to the camel, having a thick, woolly coat and used as a pack animal.

lla·no (lä′nō) *n., pl.* **lla·nos.** a level grassland or plain, found especially in South America.

lo (lō) *interj.* look; see: *Lo and behold!*

load (lōd) *n.* **1.** something that is carried by a vehicle, as a truck, or by a person or animal: *Each wagon is carrying a load of dirt.* **2.** the amount or quantity that can be carried: *to order a load of bricks.* **3.** something that burdens, wearies, or oppresses: *a load of guilt.* **4.** the amount of work a person or machine is expected to do: *The secretary's typing load was twenty letters a day.* **5.** the weight or pressure supported by a structure or part. **6.** a charge or amount of gunpowder or ammunition for a firearm. **7.** external resistance overcome by an engine or other power source. **8. loads,** *Informal.* a great quantity or number: *My cousin has loads of friends.* —*v.t.* **1.** to put a load on or in: *to load a shelf with books.* **2.** to place (something) on or in something for carrying: *to load cattle in a boxcar.* **3.** to weigh down; oppress: *Our teacher loaded us with homework.* **4.** to supply abundantly: *Relatives loaded the graduate with gifts.* **5.** to slant so as to prejudice the response or outcome: *to load a question.* **6.** to place something needed to begin operation into (an apparatus): *to load a camera.* **7.** to place (something) into an apparatus: *to load film into a camera, to load a computer program.* **8.** to place a charge in (a firearm). —*v.i.* **1.** to put on or receive a load. **2.** to place a charge in a firearm. —**load′er.** *n.*

load·ed (lō′did) *adj.* **1.** carrying a load: *The loaded cart was hard to move.* **2.** slanted so as to prejudice the response or outcome: *a loaded question.* **3.** *Slang.* drunk. **4.** *Slang.* very wealthy.

load·star (lōd′stär′) another spelling of **lodestar.**

load·stone (lōd′stōn′) another spelling of **lodestone.**

loaf¹ (lōf) *n., pl.* **loaves. 1.** bread molded and baked as one mass. **2.** any molded mass of food: *a meat loaf.* [From the Old English word *hlāf* meaning "bread" or "food."]

loaf² (lōf) *v.i.* to spend time doing little or nothing; idle: *My lazy cousin loafs all day.* —*v.t.* to spend (time) doing nothing. [From *loafer.*]

loaf·er (lō′fər) *n.* **1.** a person who loafs; lazy person. **2.** a shoe for informal wear, resembling a moccasin but having a sole and heel. Trademark: **Loafer.** [Perhaps a shortened form of the earlier word *landloper* meaning "vagabond."]

loam (lōm) *n.* soil that is a mixture of clay, sand, and silt, often containing decaying leaves and plants. —**loam′y,** *adj.*

loan (lōn) *n.* **1.** the act of lending. **2.** something lent, especially a sum of money lent at interest. —*v.t.* to lend: *The bank loaned them the money for a new car.*

loan shark *Informal.* a person who lends money at a very high, sometimes illegal, rate of interest.

loath (lōth, lōth) *also,* **loth.** *adj.* reluctant; unwilling: *I'm loath to go to the dentist for a checkup.*

loathe (lōth) *v.t.,* **loathed, loath·ing.** to feel disgust or strong dislike for; abhor; detest: *to loathe city life.*

loath·ing (lō′thing) *n.* disgust or strong dislike: *to have a loathing for horror movies.* —**loath′ing·ly,** *adv.*

loath·some (lōth′səm) *adj.* extremely disgusting or hateful. —**loath′some·ly,** *adv.* —**loath′some·ness,** *n.*

loaves (lōvz) the plural of **loaf¹.**

lob (lob) *v.t.,* **lobbed, lob·bing.** to hit or throw (a ball) in a high, slow arc. —*n.* a ball hit in such a manner.

lob·by (lob′ē) *n., pl.* **lob·bies. 1.** an entrance hall or large public room, as in an apartment house, hotel, or theater. **2.** a person or group that tries to influence legislators to vote in a certain way. —*v.,* **lob·bied, lob·by·ing.** —*v.i.* to try to influence legislators in their voting to favor some special group or interest. —*v.t.* **1.** to promote the passage of (a law) by lobbying. **2.** to try to influence (an official or group of officials) to do something.

lob·by·ist (lob′ē ist) *n.* a person who tries to influence legislators to favor a special group or interest.

lobe (lōb) *n.* a rounded projecting part of something: *a lobe of a leaf, the lobe of the ear.*

lobed (lōbd) *adj.* having a lobe or lobes: *a lobed leaf.*

lo·bel·ia (lō bēl′yə) *n.* any of a large group of plants found in many parts of the world, having blue, red, white, violet, or yellow flowers.

lob·lol·ly pine (lob′lol′ē) **1.** a pine tree of the southern United States, having a coarse bark. **2.** the wood of this tree.

lob·ster (lob′stər) *n.* **1.** a saltwater animal having five pairs of legs, including one pair with large pincer claws. Its body is enclosed in a hard, mottled, dark green shell that turns red when boiled. Lobsters are crustaceans. **2.** the flesh of a lobster, used as food.

lobster pot, a slatted wooden trap used to catch lobsters.

lo·cal (lō′kəl) *adj.* **1.** of or relating to a particular place: *a local newspaper, local politics.* **2.** limited or restricted; narrow: *The writer's fame is local rather than national.* **3.** stopping at all stations: *a local train.* **4.** relating to or affecting only a particular part or organ of the body: *a local inflammation, a local anesthetic.* —*n.* **1.** a train, bus, or other means of public transportation that stops at all the stations along its route. **2.** a branch or chapter of an organization, especially a labor union. **3.** someone who lives in an area: *The locals have been nervous about changes in the town.* —**lo′cal·ly,** *adv.*

lo·cale (lō kal′) *n.* a particular place, especially with reference to events or circumstances connected with it; setting: *The play's locale is London during World War II.*

lobster *(def. 1)*

L

at; āpe; fär; câre; end; mē; it; īce; pîerce; hot; ōld; sông, fôrk; oil; out; up; ūse; rüle; pull; tûrn; chin; sing; shop; thin; <u>th</u>is; hw in white; zh in treasure. The symbol ə stands for the unstressed vowel sound heard in about, taken, pencil, lemon, and circus.

lo·cal·ism (lō′kə liz′əm) *n.* a word, expression, or custom peculiar to a particular place.

lo·cal·i·ty (lō kal′i tē) *n., pl.* **lo·cal·i·ties.** a place, region, or district and its surroundings.

lo·cal·ize (lō′kə līz′) *v.t.,* **lo·cal·ized, lo·cal·iz·ing.** to keep within or restrict to a particular place: *The infection was localized in the finger.* —**lo′cal·i·za′tion,** *n.*

lo·cate (lō′kāt) *v.,* **lo·cat·ed, lo·cat·ing.** —*v.t.* **1.** to discover the exact place of: *The police were able to locate the lost child.* **2.** to show the position of: *to locate a country on a map.* **3.** to establish in a particular place; settle: *The company located its branch store in the suburbs.* —*v.i.* to establish oneself in a particular place.

lo·ca·tion (lō kā′shən) *n.* **1.** the act of locating or the state of being located. **2.** an exact position; place: *The police discovered the location of the thief's hideout.* **3.** the place where something, as a store, factory, or home, is or might be established; site: *That busy corner is a perfect location for a drugstore.* **4.** a place away from a motion-picture studio, used in filming.

loch (lok) *n. Scottish.* **1.** a lake. **2.** a narrow arm of the sea, especially one that is partly landlocked.

lo·ci (lō′sī) the plural of **locus.**

lock[1] (lok) *n.* **1.** a mechanical device used to fasten something, as a door, usually consisting of a bolt that is opened by a key having a special shape. **2.** an enclosure in a canal or other waterway, with gates at each end, in which the water level can be changed to raise or lower ships. **3.** the mechanism in a gun that explodes the charge. **4.** any of several holds in wrestling. —*v.t.* **1.** to fasten with a lock or locks: *Don't forget to lock the door.* **2.** to enclose or confine securely: *The guards locked the prisoners in the jail.* **3.** to join or link together firmly: *to lock arms.* —*v.i.* **1.** to become fastened with a lock or locks: *This door locks automatically when it is closed.* **2.** to become joined or linked together firmly: *The bumpers of the two cars locked.* [From the Old English word *loc* meaning "a bolt, bar, lock[1]."]

lock[2] (lok) *n.* **1.** a tuft or strand of hair. **2. locks.** the hair of the head. **3.** a tuft of wool, cotton, or flax. [From the Old English word *locc* meaning "hair" or "a lock of hair."]

lock·er (lok′ər) *n.* **1.** a compartment, as a metal chest or cabinet, that can be locked. **2.** a refrigerated compartment used to store frozen foods.

locker room, a room with lockers, as in a gymnasium or clubhouse, used for changing clothes and for storing clothes and equipment.

lock·et (lok′it) *n.* a small ornamental case with a hinged cover, for holding a picture, a lock of hair, or other keepsake. It is usually worn on a chain.

lock·jaw (lok′jô′) *n.* another word for **tetanus.**

lock·out (lok′out′) *n.* the closing of a plant or a business by an employer in order to force employees to accept the employer's terms.

lock·smith (lok′smith′) *n.* a person who makes, installs, or repairs locks.

lo·co·mo·tion (lō′kə mō′shən) *n.* the act or power of moving from place to place.

lo·co·mo·tive (lō′kə mō′tiv) *n.* an engine that moves on its own power, used to haul railroad cars. —*adj.* of, relating to, or capable of locomotion.

lo·co·weed (lō′kō wēd′) *n.* a plant of the western United States, containing a poison that is harmful to cattle, sheep, and horses.

lo·cus (lō′kəs) *n., pl.* **lo·ci.** **1.** a place; locality. **2.** *Mathematics.* any set of points that satisfies one or more specified conditions. The locus of all the points in a plane that are equidistant from a given point is a circle.

lo·cust (lō′kəst) *n.* **1.** any of several grasshoppers having short feelers. Locusts travel in huge swarms, destroying the crops in their path. **2.** any of certain cicadas. **3.** any

of a group of North American shrubs and trees having clusters of white to pink or purple flowers.

lo·cu·tion (lō kū′shən) *n.* **1.** a particular form of expression; phrase. **2.** a style or manner of speech.

lode (lōd) *n.* a deposit or vein containing valuable minerals: *a silver lode.*

lode·star (lōd′stär′) *also,* **load·star.** *n.* a star that serves as a guide to navigators, especially the star Polaris.

lode·stone (lōd′stōn′) *also,* **load·stone.** *n.* a piece of magnetite that has the properties of a magnet. Lodestones were used as compasses in ancient times.

lodge (loj) *n.* **1.** a small house, cabin, or hut, especially one used as a place to stay temporarily during a vacation: *a hunting lodge, a ski lodge.* **2.** a hotel, motel, or inn. **3.** a branch of an organization, as a fraternity or secret society. **4.** a meeting place for such a branch. **5.** the hut or dwelling of certain North American Indians. **6.** the den of certain wild animals, especially beavers. —*v.,* **lodged, lodg·ing.** —*v.t.* **1.** to provide with a place to stay temporarily, as for the night: *The town lodged the victims of the flood in the school gym.* **2.** to rent a room or rooms to: *Our neighbors lodge students in their homes.* **3.** to bring formally to an authority: *to lodge a complaint with the police.* **4.** to put or settle in a particular place or position; fix; embed: *The force of the shot lodged the arrow in a tree.* —*v.i.* **1.** to have a place to stay temporarily: *to lodge with friends for the night.* **2.** to occupy a rented room or rooms. **3.** to be fixed, caught, or embedded: *A pebble lodged in my shoe.*

lodge·ment (loj′mənt) another spelling of **lodgment.**

lodg·er (loj′ər) *n.* a person who rents a room or rooms, as in a private home.

lodg·ing (loj′ing) *n.* **1.** a place to stay temporarily: *The couple sought lodging for the night.* **2. lodgings.** a rented room or rooms, as in a private home.

lodg·ment (loj′mənt) *also,* **lodge·ment.** *n.* **1.** the act of lodging or the state of being lodged. **2.** something that is lodged.

loess (les, lō′əs) *n.* a yellowish brown, very finely grained deposit of silt, commonly found in river valleys.

loft (lôft) *n.* **1.** the upper story of a building, as a warehouse, often used as a storeroom or workroom. **2.** a room or space directly beneath a roof; attic. **3.** a gallery in a hall or church: *a choir loft.* **4.** see **hayloft.** **5. a.** a large room or space, usually in a former commercial building, suitable for conversion into an apartment or artist's studio. **b.** a space so converted. —*v.t.* to hit or send (an object) so that it rises in an arc: *The golfer lofted the ball high into the air.*

loft·y (lôf′tē) *adj.,* **loft·i·er, loft·i·est.** **1.** extending high in the air; towering: *lofty mountaintops.* **2.** exalted or noble in dignity, rank, character, or quality; elevated: *lofty ideals.* **3.** too proud; haughty: *a lofty manner.* —**loft′i·ly,** *adv.* —**loft′i·ness,** *n.*

log[1] (lôg, log) *n.* **1.** a piece of wood cut from a trunk or limb of a tree, stripped of branches and ready to be sawed. **2.** the record of the voyage of a ship or the flight of an aircraft. **3.** any record of progress, performance, or events: *the log of a scientific expedition.* **4.** the book in which such records are kept. Also, **logbook. 5.** a device for measuring the speed of a ship. —*v.,* **logged, log·ging.** —*v.t.* **1.** to cut down trees on (an area of land). **2.** to cut (trees) into logs. **3.** to record in a log. **4.** to cover (a certain distance), as in a ship or aircraft: *to log 150 miles in three days.* —*v.i.* to cut down trees, cut them into logs, and transport the logs to a sawmill. —*adj.* made of logs: *a log cabin.*

 •**to log off.** to break off contact with a computer program or system, as by entering a command.

 •**to log on.** to gain access to a computer program or system, as by entering a command.

log[2] (lôg, log) *n.* see **logarithm.**

lo·gan·ber·ry (lō′gən ber′ē) *n., pl.* **lo·gan·ber·ries.**

1. the tart, reddish purple fruit of a shrub grown in the United States. **2.** the thorny shrub bearing this fruit. [From the American jurist James H. *Logan* (1841–1928), who first grew this shrub.]

log·a·rithm (lô′gə rith′əm, log′ə rith′əm) *n.* the power to which a fixed number or base must be raised in order to produce a given number. The logarithm of 9 to the base 3 is 2. Also, **log.**

log·a·rith·mic (lô′gə rith′mik, log′ə rith′mik) *adj.* of or relating to a logarithm or logarithms: *logarithmic tables.*

log·book (lôg′bùk′, log′bùk′) *n.* see **log**¹ (*def. 3*).

loge (lōzh) *n.* **1.** a seating area in a theater, made up of the first few rows of the lowest balcony. **2.** a box in a theater.

log·ger (lô′gər, log′ər) *n.* **1.** a person who logs; lumberjack. **2.** a machine for handling logs.

log·ger·head (lô′gər hed′, log′ər hed′) *n.* **1.** a saltwater turtle having a large head, whose flesh and eggs are valued as food. It may weigh as much as 850 pounds (385 kilograms). **2.** a stupid person; blockhead.

   ·at loggerheads. taking part in a dispute; quarreling.

log·gia (loj′ə) *n.* an open gallery whose roof is supported by an arcade or colonnade.

log·ging (lô′ging, log′ing) *n.* the work or business of cutting down trees, cutting them into logs, and transporting the logs to a sawmill.

log·ic (loj′ik) *n.* **1.** the science dealing with the rules of correct reasoning and with proof by reasoning; science of correct reasoning. **2.** a system or method of reasoning: *I can't follow your logic.* **3** sound thinking; reason: *There is much logic in that argument.* [From the Old French word *logique* meaning "logic," from the Latin word *logica* "logic," going back to the Greek word *logikos* meaning "of reason," from the word *logos* "word" or "reason."]

loggia

log·i·cal (loj′i kəl) *adj.* **1.** of, relating to, or in agreement with logic: *a logical explanation.* **2.** following as a natural consequence; reasonably expected: *a logical result.* **3.** capable of reasoning correctly: *a logical mind.* —**log′·i·cal·ly,** *adv.*

lo·gi·cian (lō jish′ən) *n.* a person, especially a philosopher, who is skilled in logic.

lo·gis·tic (lō jis′tik) *adj.* of or relating to logistics. Also, **lo·gis′ti·cal.** —**lo·gis′ti·cal·ly,** *adv.*

lo·gis·tics (lō jis′tiks) *n.* the branch of military science dealing with the movement, supply, and maintenance of equipment and troops. ▲ used with a singular verb.

log·jam (lôg′jam′, log′jam′) *n.* **1.** a mass of logs floating in a river which have become jammed together so that they cannot move. **2.** something that blocks or obstructs: *There was a logjam of telephone orders soon after the store announced its big sale.*

lo·go (lō′gō) *n., pl.* **lo·gos.** a distinctive name, symbol, or trademark used by a company to identify its products or services. [Short for *logotype* with the same meaning, formed from the Greek word *logos* meaning "word."]

LOGO (lō′gō) *n.* a simple programming language that is especially suited to teaching children how to use computers.

log·roll·ing (lôg′rō′ling, log′rō′ling) *n.* **1.** a sport in which two persons stand on a floating log, each trying to get the other off balance and into the water by spinning the log with the feet. **2.** political bargaining among legislators, whereby political aid is given in return for a similar favor.

lo·gy (lō′gē) *adj.,* **lo·gi·er, lo·gi·est.** acting or moving slowly; heavy; sluggish.

–logy *combining form* the study or science of: *biology, theology.*

loin (loin) *n.* **1.** *usually,* **loins.** in humans and four-legged animals, the part of the body on each side of the backbone, between the hipbone and the lower ribs. **2.** a cut of meat from this part.

loin·cloth (loin′klôth′) *n.* a piece of cloth worn around the hips and over the groin and loins.

loi·ter (loi′tər) *v.i.* **1.** to linger idly or aimlessly about a place: *to loiter on a street corner.* **2.** to move slowly or with frequent pauses: *I always loiter on my way to the dentist.* —*v.t.* to waste (time); dawdle. —**loi′ter·er,** *n.*

loll (lol) *v.i.* **1.** to recline or lean in a careless, lazy, or relaxed manner: *The children lolled on the lawn.* **2.** to hang down loosely; droop: *The tired dog's tongue lolled out.* —*v.t.* to allow to hang down; let droop.

lol·li·pop (lol′ē pop′) *also,* **lol·ly·pop.** *n.* a piece of candy, especially hard sugar candy, on the end of a stick.

Lon·don·er (lun′də nər) *n.* a person who was born or is living in London.

lone (lōn) *adj.* **1.** without companions; alone; solitary: *a lone traveler.* **2.** standing apart from others; isolated: *a lone tree.* **3.** only; sole: *the lone survivor of a wreck.*

lone·ly (lōn′lē) *adj.,* **lone·li·er, lone·li·est.** **1.** solitary; lone: *a lonely hill.* **2.** unhappy from a lack of friendship or companionship; lonesome: *The coming of the dark always made him feel lonely* (Ernest Hemingway). **3.** causing such unhappiness: *a lonely room, a lonely evening.* **4.** not often visited by people; isolated; deserted: *Her car broke down on a lonely stretch of highway.* —**lone′li·ness,** *n.*

lon·er (lō′nər) *n.* a person who prefers to do something alone or to be alone rather than with other people.

lone·some (lōn′səm) *adj.* **1.** feeling unhappy because of a lack of friendship or companionship. **2.** causing such unhappiness: *a lonesome journey.* **3.** not often visited by people; deserted: *a lonesome road.*

lone wolf *Informal.* a person who mixes little with others, preferring to live and work alone or independently.

long¹ (lông) *adj.,* **long·er, long·est.** **1.** having great extent in space or time from end to end; not short: *a long highway, a long wait.* **2.** having a specified length: *The road is only two blocks long. The program was an hour long.* **3.** containing many items or entries: *a long grocery list.* **4.** (of vowels) pronounced over a relatively greater duration of time. The *e* in *be* is long. —*adv.* **1.** for a great extent of space or time: *The visitors did not stay long.* **2.** throughout the length of: *The phone rang all day long.* **3.** far from the time indicated: *long after, long ago.* —*n.* a long time: *They should be back before long.* [From the Old English word *lang* meaning "long¹."]

long² (lông) *v.i.* to have a strong or restless desire; yearn: *to long to see someone.* [From the Old English word *langian* meaning "to long for, desire."]

long., longitude.

long·boat (lông′bōt′) *n.* the largest boat carried by a sailing ship.

long·bow (lông′bō′) *n.* a large bow drawn by hand, used during the Middle Ages as a military weapon.

---

at; āpe; fär; câre; end; mē; it; īce; pîerce; hot; ōld; sông, fôrk; oil; out; up; ūse; rüle; pùll; tûrn; chin; sing; shop; thin; this; hw in white; zh in treasure. The symbol ə stands for the unstressed vowel sound heard in about, taken, pencil, lemon, and circus.

long–dis·tance (lông'dis'təns) *adj.* **1.** covering or capable of covering a long distance: *a long-distance runner.* **2.** connecting distant locations: *a long-distance telephone call.* —*adv.* by long-distance telephone: *to call long-distance.*

long distance, an operator or exchange that handles long-distance telephone calls.

lon·gev·i·ty (lon jev'i tē, lôn jev'i tē) *n.* long life.

long·hand (lông'hand') *n.* ordinary writing by hand in which the words are written out in full. —*adj.* **1.** using longhand: *The students learned longhand writing in the first grade.* **2.** written in longhand.

long·horn (lông'hôrn') *n.* one of a breed of cattle having very long horns, formerly widely raised in the southwestern United States.

long house, among the Iroquois and certain other American Indian tribes, a long, covered framework used as a dwelling in which many families lived together.

long·ing (lông'ing) *n.* a strong or restless desire; yearning: *to have a longing to travel.* —*adj.* feeling or expressing such a desire: *The hungry children cast longing glances at the sandwiches.* —**long'ing·ly,** *adv.*

lon·gi·tude (lon'ji tüd', lon'ji tūd') *n.* distance on the earth's surface, measured in degrees east and west of the prime meridian, and shown on maps and globes by lines from the North Pole to the South Pole.

lon·gi·tu·di·nal (lon'ji tü'də nəl, lon'ji tū'də nəl) *adj.* **1.** of or relating to longitude. **2.** running lengthwise: *The diagram showed a longitudinal cross section of the boat.* —**lon'·gi·tu'di·nal·ly,** *adv.*

North Pole
180°   0°
South Pole
← west
lines of **longitude**

long jump 1. a field event in which the contestant jumps for distance from a running start or from a standing position. **2.** such a jump. Also, **broad jump.**

long-lived (lông'līvd', lông'livd') *adj.* living or lasting a long time: *a long-lived friendship.*

long-play·ing (lông'plā'ing) *adj.* of or relating to a phonograph record played at 33⅓ revolutions per minute.

long-range (lông'rānj') *adj.* **1.** for or involving the future: *long-range plans.* **2.** capable of firing or traveling over long distances: *long-range guns, a long-range missile.*

long·shore·man (lông'shôr'mən) *n., pl.* **long·shore·men** (lông'shôr'mən). a person whose work is loading or unloading ships.

long shot 1. an entry in a contest or race considered to have little chance of winning. **2.** a venture promising great rewards but having little chance of success.

long·stand·ing (lông'stan'ding) *adj.* lasting a long time: *a longstanding friendship.*

long-suf·fer·ing (lông'suf'ər ing) *adj.* bearing wrongs, trouble, or pain patiently for a long time.

long-term (lông'tûrm') *adj.* **1.** planned for or involving a long period of time: *a long-term project, long-term plans.* **2.** requiring payment after a long period of time: *a long-term loan.*

long ton, see **ton** (*def. 2*).

long-wind·ed (lông'win'did) *adj.* **1.** speaking or writing at great length: *a long-winded speaker.* **2.** long and wordy in a very boring way: *a long-winded speech.* —**long'-wind'ed·ly,** *adv.* —**long'-wind'ed·ness,** *n.*

look (lŭk) *v.i.* **1.** to make use of the power of sight; use one's eyes; see: *Look carefully before you cross the street.* **2.** to direct one's eyes: *Everyone looked toward the door when it blew open.* **3.** to make a search or examination: *We'll help you look for your wallet.* **4.** to give the impression of being; seem: *You look tired.* **5.** to turn one's attention or regard; take notice: *We look at this situation in a different light now.* **6.** to face in a certain direction or have a certain view: *The windows look to the north.* —*v.t.* **1.** to have an appearance appropriate to; appear to be: *to look one's age.* **2.** to direct one's eyes upon or toward: *to look someone straight in the face.* —*n.* **1.** the act or instance of looking; glance: *Take a look at that new car.* **2.** an air or appearance: *to have a cheerful look.* **3. looks.** outward appearance: *good looks.* —**look'er,** *n.*

·**to look after.** to take care of: *We looked after our neighbors' dog while they were away.*

·**to look back on.** to recall or think about (something that happened in the past).

·**to look down on.** to have contempt for; scorn.

·**to look forward to.** to wait for or anticipate happily or eagerly.

·**to look into.** to examine; investigate.

·**to look on. a.** to be a spectator; watch: *A large crowd looked on as the firefighters battled the blaze.* **b.** to regard; consider: *I look on them as my best friends.*

·**to look out.** to take care; watch out.

·**to look out for. a.** to protect: *to look out for one's own interests.* **b.** to watch out for or be wary of: *Look out for icy patches on the road.*

·**to look over.** to examine, especially hastily.

·**to look to. a.** to attend to; take care of. **b.** to depend upon; rely on.

·**to look up. a.** to locate: *to look up a date in the encyclopedia.* **b.** to pay a visit to: *Look us up when you are in town.* **c.** *Informal.* to get better; improve: *Business is looking up.*

·**to look up to.** to respect or admire greatly.

look–a·like (lŭk'ə līk') *also,* **look·a·like.** *n.* a person or thing that closely resembles another in appearance: *My cousin and I are look-alikes.*

looking glass, another term for **mirror.**

look·out (lŭk'out') *n.* **1.** an alert or careful watch, as for someone who may come or something that may happen: *Be on the lookout for that letter.* **2.** a place, often a high place, where a watch is kept. **3.** a person or group that keeps watch: *The lookout warned the robbers that the police were coming.* **4.** *Informal.* a matter of interest or concern: *How you solve the problem is your own lookout.*

loom¹

loom¹ (lüm) *n.* a machine for weaving thread into cloth. [From the Middle English word *lome* meaning both "tool, implement" and "a weaver's loom," from the Old English word *lōma* "tool, implement."]

loom² (lüm) *v.i.* **1.** to appear indistinctly as a large, threatening shape: *An iceberg loomed in the distance through the fog.* **2.** to appear to the mind as large or ominous: *The final examinations loomed ahead.* [Of uncertain origin.]

loon¹ (lün) *n.* any of several web-footed diving birds having a slender pointed bill, small pointed wings, and short legs. Loons are noted for their laughing call. [Of Scandinavian origin.]

loon¹

loon² (lün) *n.* a crazy or foolish person. [From the Middle English word *louen* meaning "a rascal," perhaps originally from Low German or Dutch.]

loon·y (lü′nē) *Informal. adj.*, **loon·i·er, loon·i·est.** insane; crazy; foolish. —*n., pl.* **loon·ies.** a crazy or foolish person.

loop (lüp) *n.* **1.** a portion of a string, wire, or other similar material that is doubled over itself, forming a circular shape with an opening between the parts. **2.** anything resembling this: *the loops of the letter "g."* **3.** a round or bent piece of material, such as metal or cord, serving as a hook or ornament: *a belt loop.* **4.** a maneuver in which an aircraft makes a complete circle in a vertical plane. **5.** a closed electrical circuit. **6.** the repetition of a sequence of instructions in a computer program one or more times. —*v.t.* **1.** to form into a loop or loops: *to loop a rope.* **2.** to fasten with a loop or loops. **3.** to encircle with a loop: *Loop your finger with a string.* **4.** to fly (an aircraft) in a loop or loops. —*v.i.* **1.** to form a loop or loops. **2.** to move or fly in a loop or loops.

loop·hole (lüp′hōl′) *n.* **1.** a small opening in a wall, especially of a fort, to look or shoot through. **2.** a means of escape, especially a way of getting around a law or contract because of something that is unclear or left out.

loose (lüs) *adj.*, **loos·er, loos·est. 1.** not firmly attached, fastened, or fixed: *There were several loose pages in the book.* **2.** not confined; free: *The dog was loose in the fields.* **3.** not fitting tightly or snugly: *loose clothing.* **4.** not taut; slack: *loose reins.* **5.** not tied or joined together: *loose keys.* **6.** not contained in something, as a package: *loose apples.* **7.** not compact: *loose gravel, cloth with a loose texture.* **8.** not careful, accurate, or precise: *loose reasoning, a loose translation.* **9.** lacking in moral restraint: *loose behavior, a loose person.* —*adv.* in a loose manner: *to let something hang loose.* —*v.t.*, **loosed, loos·ing. 1.** to set free: *to loose a bird from a cage.* **2.** to untie; unfasten: *to loose a knot.* **3.** to make less tight; loosen. **4.** to shoot or let fly: *to loose a dart.* —**loose′ly,** *adv.* —**loose′ness,** *n.*
·**to break loose.** to run away or get away: *The prisoner broke loose from the guard.*
·**to let loose** or **to set loose** or **to turn loose.** to set free; release.

loose–joint·ed (lüs′join′tid) *adj.* **1.** having joints that are loosely formed. **2.** capable of relaxed or limber movement: *a loose-jointed dancer.*

loose–leaf (lüs′lēf′) *adj.* **1.** holding or made to hold pages with holes for easy insertion and removal: *a loose-leaf notebook.* **2.** of or designed for use with a loose-leaf notebook, binder, or the like: *loose-leaf paper.*

loos·en (lü′sən) *v.t.* **1.** to make loose or looser: *to loosen a necktie.* **2.** to set free or release: *Don't loosen the dog from the rope.* **3.** to make less severe or strict: *to loosen discipline.* —*v.i.* to become loose or looser. —**loos′en·er,** *n.*

loot (lüt) *n.* **1.** things taken by thieves in a robbery. **2.** things taken by force from an enemy during a war; booty; plunder. **3.** *Slang.* money. —*v.t.* to rob or plunder: *The soldiers looted the town. The burglars looted the store.* —*v.i.* to take booty; plunder. —**loot′er,** *n.*

lop¹ (lop) *v.t.*, **lopped, lop·ping. 1.** to cut off or remove as unnecessary: *to lop the dead branches from a tree.* **2.** to cut off parts from: *to lop trees.* [From the Middle English word *loppe* meaning "trimmed branches" or "lopped-off twigs."]

lop² (lop) *v.i.*, **lopped, lop·ping.** to hang loosely; droop. —*adj.* hanging loosely; drooping: *lop ears.* [Of uncertain origin.]

lope (lōp) *v.*, **loped, lop·ing.** —*v.i.* to run with a long, easy, often bounding stride: *The dog loped through the park.* —*v.t.* to cause to run with such a stride: *to lope a horse.* —*n.* a long, easy, often bounding stride.

lop–eared (lop′ird′) *adj.* having ears that hang down loosely: *a lop-eared hound.*

lop·sid·ed (lop′sī′did) *adj.* larger or heavier on one side than on the other; leaning or slanting to one side. —**lop′sid′ed·ly,** *adv.* —**lop′sid′ed·ness,** *n.*

lo·qua·cious (lō kwā′shəs) *adj.* tending to talk too much; talkative. —**lo·qua′cious·ly,** *adv.* —**lo·qua′cious·ness,** *n.*

lo·quac·i·ty (lō kwas′i tē) *n.* the tendency to talk too much.

lo·quat (lō′kwot, lō′kwat) *n.* **1.** a yellow or orange fruit that resembles a plum and has a slightly acid taste. Loquats are used especially in preserves. **2.** the small evergreen tree that bears this fruit.

lo·ran (lôr′an) *n.* a navigational system in which the geographical position of a ship or aircraft can be determined by using signals transmitted by three fixed radio stations. [Short for *lo*(ng-)*ra*(nge) *n*(avigation).]

lord (lôrd) *n.* **1.** a person who has power or authority over others, such as a feudal ruler. **2.** *British.* a titled nobleman or peer belonging to the House of Lords. **3. Lord.** *British.* **a.** a title or form of address for any of various noblemen or peers. The *Earl of Arran* would be referred to as *Lord Arran.* **b.** the title or form of address for certain high officials or members of the clergy: *the Lord Mayor of London.* **4. Lords.** see **House of Lords. 5. the Lord. a.** God. **b.** Jesus. [From the Old English word *hlāford* meaning "lord."]
·**to lord it over.** to behave in a haughty or domineering manner toward.

lord·ly (lôrd′lē) *adj.*, **lord·li·er, lord·li·est. 1.** of, relating to, or suited for a lord: *a lordly estate.* **2.** haughty or domineering: *a lordly manner.* —**lord′li·ness,** *n.*

lord·ship (lôrd′ship′) *n.* **1. Lordship.** *British.* the title or form of address used in speaking or referring to a lord, usually preceded by *His* or *Your.* **2.** the rank, power, or authority of a lord.

Lord's Prayer, in the Bible, a prayer given by Jesus to the Apostles, which begins with the words "Our Father." Also, **paternoster.**

Lord's Supper 1. another term for **Last Supper. 2.** another term for **Holy Communion.**

lore (lôr) *n.* **1.** the body of traditional or popular facts or beliefs on a particular subject: *nature lore.* **2.** learning; knowledge.

lor·gnette (lôrn yet′) *n.* a pair of eyeglasses or opera glasses held by a short, usually decorated handle.

lorn (lôrn) *adj.* *Archaic.* abandoned; lonely.

L

at; āpe; fär; câre; end; mē; it; īce; pîerce; hot; ōld; sông, fôrk; oil; out; up; ūse; rüle; pull; tûrn; chin; sing; shop; thin; this; hw in white; zh in treasure. The symbol ə stands for the unstressed vowel sound heard in about, taken, pencil, lemon, and circus.

lor·ry (lôr′ē, lor′ē) *n., pl.* **lor·ries. 1.** a long, flat wagon without sides, drawn by a horse. **2.** *British.* a truck.
lose (lüz) *v.,* **lost, los·ing.** —*v.t.* **1.** to have no longer because of some act or accident: *The family lost everything they owned in the fire.* **2.** to put in a place afterward forgotten; misplace: *to lose one's keys.* **3.** to fail to win: *Our team lost the game.* **4.** to fail to keep, preserve, or maintain: *to lose one's temper.* **5.** to let pass without using; fail to take advantage of: *to lose one's chance.* **6.** to fail to keep up with, especially in order to understand or see: *I lost the sense of what was said.* **7.** to wander or stray from: *The hikers lost their way in the darkness.* **8.** to let (oneself) be absorbed: *to lose oneself in a book.* **9.** to cause the loss of: *The team's many mistakes lost the game.* —*v.i.* **1.** to suffer loss: *to lose heavily on the stock market.* **2.** to be defeated: *I often lose when I play chess.*
·**to lose out.** to fail to get or achieve something.
·**to lose out on.** to fail to win, get, or take advantage of: *to lose out on an opportunity.*
los·er (lü′zər) *n.* **1.** a person or thing that loses in a game or contest: *I may not always win, but at least I try to be a cheerful loser.* **2.** *Informal.* a person or thing that loses or fails; failure; flop: *With such poor acting, that new movie is bound to be a loser.*
los·ing (lü′zing) *adj.* **1.** certain to result in a loss: *a losing battle.* **2.** failing to win; defeated: *the losing team.* —*pl. n.* **losings.** an amount lost, especially money lost in gambling.
loss (lôs) *n., pl.* **loss·es. 1.** the act or instance of losing or the state of being lost: *the loss of a race, a loss of memory.* **2.** a person, thing, or amount that is lost: *a financial loss.* **3.** the damage or disadvantage that results from losing something: *The closing of the factory was a great loss to the town.* **4. losses.** soldiers wounded, killed, or captured in action: *to sustain heavy losses during a fierce battle.*
·**at a loss. a.** puzzled; confused; perplexed: *Their rudeness left me completely at a loss.* **b.** unable: *We were at a loss to explain the disappearance of the money.*
lost (lôst) *v.* the past tense and past participle of **lose.** —*adj.* **1.** unable to be found; misplaced or missing: *a lost dog.* **2.** no longer possessed or used: *a lost fortune.* **3.** not won; defeated: *a lost game.* **4.** certain to result in a loss: *lost cause.* **5.** not used to good purpose; wasted: *a lost opportunity.* **6.** having gone astray: *We were lost in the woods.* **7.** destroyed; ruined: *a lost reputation.* **8.** absorbed; preoccupied: *to be lost in thought.* **9.** confused; bewildered: *The faces of the survivors of the crash had lost expressions.*
lot (lot) *n.* **1.** one of a set of objects, as bits of paper, wood, or straw, used to decide something by chance: *to draw lots to decide who would have the first turn.* **2.** the casting or drawing of such objects as a means of deciding something: *They chose the captain of the team by lot.* **3.** a decision or choice made in this way. **4.** something that one gets in this way; portion or share. **5.** a portion or plot of land: *The children played baseball on an empty lot.* **6.** a motion picture studio and its property. **7.** fortune or fate in life: *The lot of the poor is a hard one.* **8.** a number of persons or things considered as a unit or group: *a lazy lot of workers.* **9.** also, **lots.** *Informal.* a great number or amount: *a lot of cars, lots of gravy.* —*adv.* also, **lots.** a great deal; much: *a lot taller, a lot stronger.*
loth (lōth, lōth) another spelling of **loath.**
lo·tion (lō′shən) *n.* a liquid preparation used on the skin to heal, soothe, soften, or cleanse.
lot·ter·y (lot′ə rē) *n., pl.* **lot·ter·ies.** a way of raising money in which chances or numbered tickets are sold. Winning tickets are then drawn by lot and prizes are awarded to the winners.

lo·tus (lō′təs) *n., pl.* **lo·tus·es. 1.** the large flower of a plant related to the water lily. **2.** the plant bearing this flower, having leaves that float on the surface of water. **3.** a shrubby plant related to the pea, having red, white, or pink flowers. **4.** *Greek Legend.* a fruit supposed to cause a dreamy, contented forgetfulness in those who ate it.

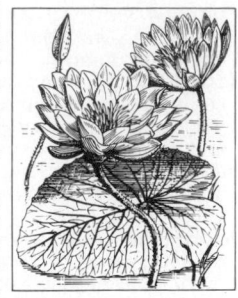
lotus (defs. 1 and 2)

loud (loud) *adj.* **1.** having a strong and powerful sound: *a loud cry, a loud noise.* **2.** producing such sound: *loud cymbals.* **3.** vehement or insistent: *loud demands.* **4.** tastelessly bright; flashy: *a loud red tie.* **5.** tending to be offensive in appearance or manner: *a loud, vulgar person.* —*adv.* in a loud manner. —**loud′ly,** *adv.* —**loud′ness,** *n.*
loud·mouth (loud′mouth′) *n., pl.* **loud·mouths** (loud′mouth̲z′, loud′mouths′). a person who annoys other people by talking too loudly or too much.
loud·speak·er (loud′spē′kər) *n.* a device that transforms an electrical signal into sound and amplifies the sound to the desired volume.
Lou·i·si·an·a Purchase (lü ē′zē an′ə) the territory purchased by the United States from France in 1803, extending from the Mississippi River to the Rocky Mountains and from Canada to the Gulf of Mexico.
lounge (lounj) *v.,* **lounged, loung·ing.** —*v.i.* **1.** to lean, sit, or lie lazily; loll: *to lounge on a sofa.* **2.** to move lazily, listlessly, or unhurriedly: *The bored children lounged about the yard.* —*v.t.* to pass (time) by lounging. —*n.* **1.** a public room where one may lounge, smoke, relax, or wait, as in a hotel, restaurant, or club. **2.** a sofa; couch.
lour (lour) another word for **lower².**
louse (lous) *n., pl.* *(def. 1)* **lice** or *(def. 2)* **lous·es. 1.** any of a large number of tiny wingless insects that live as parasites on humans and animals. **2.** *Slang.* a low, contemptible person.
lous·y (lou′zē) *adj.,* **lous·i·er, lous·i·est. 1.** infested with lice. **2.** *Informal.* disgusting; contemptible: *a lousy trick.* **3.** *Informal.* of wretched quality; terrible: *That was such a lousy movie that I'm mystified why it's so popular.* —**lous′i·ly,** *adv.* —**lous′i·ness,** *n.*
lout (lout) *n.* an awkward, stupid person; oaf.
lout·ish (lou′tish) *adj.* like a lout; awkward; clumsy. —**lout′ish·ly,** *adv.* —**lout′ish·ness,** *n.*
lou·ver (lü′vər) *also,* **lou·vre.** *n.* one of a series of horizontal, overlapping slats fitted in a window or other opening, slanted to keep out rain while letting in light and air.
Lou·vre (lü′vrə) *n.* an art museum in Paris.
lov·a·ble (luv′ə bəl) *also,* **love·a·ble.** *adj.* having qualities that tend to make one loved; worthy of being loved: *a lovable puppy.* —**lov′a·bly,** *adv.*
love (luv) *n.* **1.** a strong feeling of affection, devotion, and concern for another: *love for one's children.* **2.** a strong liking for something: *a love of music.* **3.** a beloved person; sweetheart. **4.** a thing that is loved or greatly liked: *Skiing is my great love.* **5.** in tennis, a score of zero. —*v.,* **loved, lov·ing.** —*v.t.* **1.** to have a deep affection for: *to love one's family.* **2.** to have a strong liking for: *to love good books.* —*v.i.* to be in love.

louver

·**in love.** feeling love.
·**to fall in love.** to begin to love.
love·a·ble (luv′ə bəl) another spelling of **lovable.**
love·bird (luv′bûrd′) *n.* a small parrot, often kept in a

cage as a pet. It is noted for showing great affection toward its mate.

love·less (luv′lis) *adj.* without love: *a loveless marriage.*

love·lorn (luv′lôrn′) *adj.* abandoned by one's lover; miserable because of love.

love·ly (luv′lē) *adj.,* **love·li·er, love·li·est. 1.** having beautiful qualities, as of appearance or personality. **2.** very delightful; enjoyable; pleasing: *We had a lovely time!* —**love′li·ness,** *n.*

lov·er (luv′ər) *n.* **1.** a person who loves another. **2.** a person who has a strong liking for something: *a lover of art.*

love seat, a small sofa seating two persons.

love·sick (luv′sik′) *adj.* pining or languishing because of love.

lov·ing (luv′ing) *adj.* feeling or showing love; affectionate; fond. —**lov′ing·ly,** *adv.*

loving cup, a large cup, usually with handles, presented as a prize or trophy and often bearing an inscription.

lov·ing-kind·ness (luv′ing kīnd′nis) *n.* affectionate tenderness and thoughtfulness coming from love.

low¹ (lō) *adj.* **1.** rising only slightly above the surface; not high or tall: *A low hedge surrounds the yard.* **2.** close to the ground: *a low leap, the low branches of a tree.* **3.** below the average or natural level of the ground: *a low valley.* **4.** below the usual or desired level: *The river was low after the drought.* **5.** below what is usual or desired, as in amount, force, or degree: *Food prices were low last summer.* **6.** below or inferior to others, as in rank or position: *a low grade of oil, low intelligence.* **7.** mean; vulgar; corrupt: *a low person, low language.* **8.** disapproving; critical; unfavorable: *to have a low opinion of something.* **9.** not having an adequate supply: *The store is low on canned goods.* **10.** not loud; soft: *a low whisper.* **11.** deep in pitch: *a low note.* **12.** depressed; gloomy: *Failing the test made them feel low.* **13.** feeble; weak; poor: *The patient's condition is very low.* —*adv.* **1.** near the ground or floor: *The plane flew very low.* **2.** to, in, or at a low point, degree, or level: *Prices sank low.* —*n.* **1.** a low level, place, or position: *The temperature reached a new low for this time of year.* **2.** the arrangement of gears, as in a car, that produces the lowest speed and the greatest power. **3.** an area of low barometric pressure. [From the Old Norse word *lāgr* meaning ''low.''] —**low′ness,** *n.*

·**to lie low.** to stay in hiding: *The thieves decided to lie low to avoid capture.*

low² (lō) *v.t., v.i.* to make the bellowing sound characteristic of cattle; moo. —*n.* such a sound. [From the Old English word *hlowan* meaning ''to bellow.'']

low beam, a beam of a motor vehicle headlight aimed close to the ground to illuminate nearby objects.

low·boy (lō′boi′) *n.* a low chest of drawers on short legs.

low·brow (lō′brou′) *Informal. n.* a person who lacks culture or intellectual interests. —*adj. Informal.* of, relating to, or suitable for a lowbrow.

low·down (lō′doun′) *n. Slang.* the bare facts; actual truth: *The reporter tried to get the lowdown on the mayor's past.*

low-down (lō′doun′) *adj. Informal.* mean; disgusting; contemptible: *a low-down trick.*

low·er¹ (lō′ər) *adj.* the comparative of **low¹.** —*v.t.* **1.** to take or bring down; let down: *to lower the flag, to lower a bucket into a well.* **2.** to reduce, as in height, amount, value, or degree: *to lower prices, to lower the water level in a pool.* **3.** to lessen the intensity or volume of: *Lower your voice.* **4.** to bring down in value or estimation: *Don't lower yourself by cheating.* **5.** to lessen the force or effectiveness of; weaken: *Not eating properly will lower your resistance to illness.* —*v.i.* to become lower. [*Low¹* + *-er¹.*]

low·er² (lou′ər) *v.i.* **1.** to frown; scowl. **2.** to appear dark, gloomy, or threatening. —*n.* **1.** a frown; scowl. **2.** a dark, gloomy, or threatening appearance, as of the sky. Also, **lour.** [From the Middle English word *louren* meaning ''to frown, scowl.'']

low·er-case (lō′ər kās′) *adj.* of, relating to, or printed in small letters. —*v.t.,* **low·er-cased, low·er-casing.** to set in or print with small letters.

lower case, another term for **small letters.**

low·er-class (lō′ər klas′) *adj.* of or relating to the lower class.

lower class, the portion of society, including the working class and the very poor, occupying a social and economic position below that of the middle class.

lower house *also,* **Lower House.** in a legislature having two branches, the larger and more representative branch, such as the House of Representatives in the U.S. Congress.

low·er·most (lō′ər mōst′) *adj.* lowest.

lower world, the abode of the dead; Hades.

lowest common denominator, another term for **least common denominator.**

lowest common multiple, another term for **least common multiple.**

low frequency, a radio frequency between 30 kilohertz and 300 kilohertz.

Low German 1. a form of the German language spoken predominantly in the lowlands of northern Germany. **2.** a group of Germanic languages, including Dutch and Flemish, spoken predominantly in the Low Countries.

low-key (lō′kē′) *adj.* characterized by restraint or subtlety; quiet. Also, **low-keyed** (lō′kēd′).

low·land (lō′lənd) *n.* land that is on a lower level than the surrounding land. —*adj.* of, relating to, or characteristic of such land.

low·land·er (lō′lən dər) *n.* **1.** a person who was born or is living in a lowland. **2. Lowlander.** a person who was born or is living in the Lowlands of Scotland.

low·ly (lō′lē) *adj.,* **low·li·er, low·li·est. 1.** humble in condition or quality; low in rank or importance: *a lowly cottage.* **2.** humble in manner or spirit; meek. —*adv.* in a humble manner; humbly; meekly. —**low′li·ness,** *n.*

low-pitched (lō′picht′) *adj.* **1.** having a low tone. **2.** (of a roof) having little slope.

low-pres·sure (lō′presh′ər) *adj.* **1.** having, using, or indicating a low degree of pressure: *low-pressure tires.* **2.** having low atmospheric pressure: *a low-pressure center.* **3.** calm and unhurried; relaxed: *a low-pressure sales technique.*

low profile, a manner, attitude, or way of behaving that is deliberately restrained so as not to attract attention.

low relief, another term for **bas-relief.**

low-spir·it·ed (lō′spir′i tid) *adj.* sad; depressed.

low tide 1. the tide at its lowest level. **2.** the time when this level is reached.

lox (loks) *n.* a kind of smoked salmon.

loy·al (loi′əl) *adj.* **1.** faithful in one's friendship, devotion, or regard: *a loyal friend.* **2.** faithful in one's allegiance to one's monarch, government, or country. **3.** characterized by or showing loyalty: *a loyal declaration.* —**loy′al·ly,** *adv.*

loy·al·ist (loi′ə list) *n.* **1.** a person who supports the existing monarch, leader, or government, especially during times of war or revolution. **2.** *also,* **Loyalist.** a colonist

L

who remained loyal to the British government during the American Revolution.

loy·al·ty (loi'əl tē) *n., pl.* **loy·al·ties.** **1.** the state of remaining loyal; faithfulness: *loyalty to one's country.* **2.** an instance of being loyal: *to have loyalties to two schools.*

loz·enge (loz'inj) *n.* **1.** a small tablet of sugar and other flavoring, often containing medicine. **2.** a figure shaped like a diamond.

LP *n., pl.* **LPs** or **LP's.** *Trademark.* a long-playing record.

LPN, licensed practical nurse.

Lr, the symbol for lawrencium.

LSD, a psychedelic drug that produces hallucinations and temporary changes in personality. [Short for *l*(y)*s*(ergic acid) *d*(iethylamide).]

Lt., Lieutenant.

Ltd., ltd. limited.

Lu, the symbol for lutetium.

lu·au (lü'ou') *n.* in Hawaii, a feast, often with entertainment.

lub·ber (lub'ər) *n.* **1.** a heavy, clumsy, stupid person. **2.** an awkward or inexperienced sailor; landlubber.

lu·bri·cant (lü'bri kənt) *n.* any substance, as oil or grease, used to reduce friction, as between the moving parts of a machine.

lu·bri·cate (lü'bri kāt') *v.,* **lu·bri·cat·ed, lu·bri·cat·ing.** —*v.t.* **1.** to apply oil, grease, or other lubricant to (the moving parts of a machine) in order to reduce friction: *to lubricate a door hinge.* **2.** to make slippery or smooth: *to lubricate the skin with lotion.* —*v.i.* to act as a lubricant. [From the Latin word *lubricatus,* past participle of *lubricare* meaning "to make slippery," from the word *lubricus* "slippery."] —**lu'bri·ca'tion,** *n.* —**lu'bri·ca'tor,** *n.*

lu·cent (lü'sənt) *adj.* **1.** shining; bright; luminous. **2.** clear; translucent.

lu·cid (lü'sid) *adj.* **1.** easily understood; clear: *a lucid explanation.* **2.** showing clear thinking or mental soundness; rational; sane: *a lucid person, lucid reasoning.* **3.** clear; transparent: *the pure and lucid mountain air.* **4.** shining; bright; luminous. —**lu'cid·ly,** *adv.* —**lu'cid·ness,** *n.*

lu·cid·i·ty (lü sid'i tē) *n.* the state or quality of being lucid.

Lu·ci·fer (lü'sə fər) *n.* in Christian tradition, the rebellious archangel who was cast out of heaven with his followers; Satan.

Lu·cite (lü'sīt) *n.* *Trademark.* a transparent acrylic resin available in solid or liquid form and having many uses, as in light fixtures.

luck (luk) *n.* **1.** the force or factor that seems to influence events or circumstances of a person's life for good or ill: *Luck alone won't get you a job—you'll have to look harder.* **2.** the events or circumstances so influenced: *a life filled with bad luck.* **3.** good fortune; success: *Did you have any luck in finding the glasses you had lost?*

·**to be down on one's luck.** to have bad luck.

·**to be in luck.** to have good luck.

·**to be out of luck.** to have bad luck.

luck·i·ly (luk'ə lē) *adv.* with or by a stroke of good luck; fortunately.

luck·less (luk'lis) *adj.* not having good luck; unlucky. —**luck'less·ly,** *adv.* —**luck'less·ness,** *n.*

luck·y (luk'ē) *adj.,* **luck·i·er, luck·i·est.** **1.** having good luck; fortunate. **2.** happening happily or fortunately: *a lucky meeting.* **3.** thought to bring good luck: *a lucky rabbit's foot.* —**luck'i·ness,** *n.*

lu·cra·tive (lü'krə tiv) *adj.* bringing money or profit; profitable: *a lucrative business.* —**lu'cra·tive·ly,** *adv.*

lu·cre (lü'kər) *n.* money or riches, especially when thought of as evil: *filthy lucre.*

lu·di·crous (lü'di krəs) *adj.* laughably absurd; ridiculous: *to look ludicrous in a wig.* —**lu'di·crous·ly,** *adv.*

Word Family

A variety of English words are derived from the Latin word **ludus,** meaning "a game" or "something played." A magician can create an **illusion.** A situation in a play or opera that **deludes** one of the characters may be amusing or even **ludicrous,** especially when there is **collusion** among the other characters to keep the ignorant one guessing. A musical **prelude** may be played before the performance begins, and between acts there may be an **interlude** based on one of the musical themes of the music. You may make an **allusion** to a play you've seen or read, but if your friends don't know the play, they may find your ideas **elusive.**

luff (luf) *n.* **1.** the act of sailing a ship toward the wind. **2.** the forward edge of a fore-and-aft sail. —*v.i.* to turn the bow of a ship toward the wind.

lug¹ (lug) *v.t.,* **lugged, lug·ging.** to pull or carry with effort: *We lugged the heavy trunk down the stairs.* [Of Scandinavian origin.]

lug² (lug) *n.* **1.** the projecting part by which something is gripped or held. **2.** *Slang.* a clumsy or stupid person. [Perhaps from *lug¹.*]

lug³ (lug) *n.* see **lugsail.**

lug·gage (lug'ij) *n.* the bags, boxes, trunks, or suitcases used by a traveler for carrying belongings; baggage.

lug·ger (lug'ər) *n.* a small boat having two or three masts and rigged with lugsails.

lug·sail (lug'sāl', lug'səl) *n.* a four-sided sail without a boom, held by a yard that hangs slantwise across the mast. Also, **lug.**

lu·gu·bri·ous (lü gü'brē əs, lü gū'brē əs) *adj.* very mournful or sorrowful: *The disappointed child had a lugubrious look.* —**lu·gu'bri·ous·ly,** *adv.* —**lu·gu'bri·ous·ness,** *n.*

lug·worm (lug'wûrm') *n.* a worm that burrows in the sand

lugger

along the seashore. It is often used as bait for fishing.

Luke (lük) *n.* the third Gospel of the New Testament, thought to have been written by the Evangelist Luke.

luke·warm (lük'wôrm') *adj.* **1.** slightly warm; tepid: *lukewarm bath water.* **2.** having or showing little warmth or enthusiasm; indifferent: *a lukewarm welcome.* —**luke'warm'ly,** *adv.* —**luke'warm'ness,** *n.*

lull (lul) *v.t.* to calm with soothing sounds or caresses. —*v.i.* to become calm: *The storm lulled.* —*n.* a brief period of calm, quiet, or lessening activity.

lul·la·by (lul'ə bī') *n., pl.* **lul·la·bies.** a soothing song sung to lull a child to sleep.

lum·ba·go (lum bā'gō) *n.* a pain in the lower back between the chest and the pelvis.

lum·bar (lum'bər) *adj.* of, relating to, or near the lower back or loins.

lum·ber¹ (lum'bər) *n.* timber cut as planks and boards. —*v.i.* to cut timber into lumber and get it ready for use. [Of uncertain origin.]

lum·ber² (lum'bər) *v.i.* to move in a clumsy or noisy manner: *The old wagon lumbered down the dirt road.* [From the Middle English word *lomeren* meaning "to stumble, move slowly."]

lumbering

lum·ber·ing (lum′bər ing) *n.* the business or work of cutting and preparing timber.

lum·ber·jack (lum′bər jak′) *n.* a person who cuts down trees and gets logs ready for transportation to the sawmill.

lum·ber·man (lum′bər mən) *n., pl.* **lum·ber·men** (lum′bər mən). **1.** another word for **lumberjack**. **2.** a person who works in or manages a lumberyard.

lum·ber·yard (lum′bər yärd′) *n.* a place where lumber is stored and sold.

lu·men (lü′mən) *n.* a unit of luminous flux equal to the amount of light falling on one square unit of surface area, of which each point is at a distance of one unit from a light source with an intensity of one candle.

lu·mi·nar·y (lü′mə ner′ē) *n., pl.* **lu·mi·nar·ies**. **1.** a person who is recognized or noted for high achievement: *A group of luminaries discussed the future of space science.* **2.** a light-giving body, especially the sun or the moon.

lu·mi·nes·cence (lü′mə nes′əns) *n.* the sending out of visible light without heat. Phosphorescence and fluorescence are two forms of luminescence. —**lu′mi·nes′cent,** *adj.*

lu·mi·nos·i·ty (lü′mə nos′i tē) *n., pl.* **lu·mi·nos·i·ties**. **1.** the quality or condition of being luminous. **2.** something luminous.

lu·mi·nous (lü′mə nəs) *adj.* **1.** sending out light of its own; shining: *luminous flames.* **2.** full of light; bright. **3.** clear to the mind; easily understood. —**lu′mi·nous·ly,** *adv.* —**lu′mi·nous·ness,** *n.*

lump (lump) *n.* **1.** a solid, usually irregularly shaped piece or mass: *a lump of iron ore, a lump of clay.* **2.** a small cube: *a lump of sugar.* **3.** a swelling: *to have a lump on the head.* —*adj.* **1.** formed in a lump or lumps: *lump sugar.* **2.** not divided into parts; whole or total: *We paid for the used car with a lump sum.* —*v.t.* to put, bring, or deal with together: *The campers lumped their expenses.* —*v.i.* to form into a lump or lumps; become lumpy: *The oatmeal lumped when it cooled.*

lump·ish (lum′pish) *adj.* **1.** like a lump. **2.** heavy and awkward. **3.** stupid; dull.

lump·y (lum′pē) *adj.,* **lump·i·er, lump·i·est**. **1.** covered or filled with lumps: *lumpy oatmeal.* **2.** heavy and awkward; lumpish. —**lump′i·ness,** *n.*

Lu·na (lü′nə) *n. Roman Mythology.* the goddess of the moon. In Greek mythology she was called Selene.

lu·na·cy (lü′nə sē) *n., pl.* **lu·na·cies**. **1.** madness; insanity. **2.** senseless or reckless conduct.

lu·na moth (lü′nə) a large green moth having wings with transparent spots.

lu·nar (lü′nər) *adj.* of or relating to the moon: *the lunar orbit.*

lunar eclipse, a partial or total darkening of the moon when the earth moves between the moon and the sun.

lunar module, a self-contained section of a spacecraft, designed to separate from the spacecraft as it orbits the moon and carry astronauts to and from the moon's surface.

lunar month, see **month** *(def. 4).*

lunar year, see **year** *(def. 4).*

lu·na·tic (lü′nə tik) *n.* **1.** an insane person. **2.** a senseless or reckless person. —*adj.* **1.** insane; crazy. **2.** of or for insane people: *a lunatic asylum.* **3.** extremely senseless or reckless. [From the Latin word *lunaticus* meaning "crazy, lunatic," from the word *luna* "moon." It was formerly believed that one form of insanity was related to or caused by the phases of the moon.]

lunch (lunch) *n., pl.* **lunch·es**. **1.** a light meal between breakfast and dinner, usually eaten around noon. **2.** the food prepared for such a meal. —*v.i.* to eat lunch.

lunch counter, an area where light meals are served, consisting of a counter and a row of stools.

lunch·eon (lun′chən) *n.* a lunch, especially a formal one.

lunch·eon·ette (lun′chə net′) *n.* a small restaurant or lunch counter where light meals, especially breakfast and lunch, are served.

lunch·room (lunch′rüm′, lunch′rům′) *n.* a place where light meals are served, especially a cafeteria in a school.

lung (lung) *n.* **1.** in human beings and many other animals with backbones, one of a pair of spongy organs for breathing that supply the blood with oxygen and rid the blood of carbon dioxide. **2.** a similar organ found in certain animals without backbones.

lunge (lunj) *n.* **1.** any sudden forward movement: *The catcher made a lunge for the ball.* **2.** a sudden forward thrust, as with a sword. —*v.i.,* **lunged, lung·ing**. to make a sudden forward movement: *We lunged for the falling platter.* —**lung′er,** *n.*

lung·fish (lung′fish′) *n., pl.* **lung·fish** or **lung·fish·es**. any of several fish that have a lunglike air bladder as well as gills, enabling them to breathe in or out of water. Lungfish live in freshwater swamps and marshes in Africa, South America, and Australia.

lu·pine (lü′pin) *n.* a plant related to the pea, bearing spikes of white, yellow, blue, or purple flowers.

lurch¹ (lûrch) *n., pl.* **lurch·es**. a sudden rolling or swaying to one side or from side to side: *The ship gave a lurch in the choppy water.* —*v.i.* **1.** to move jerkily and unsteadily; stagger: *to lurch to one's feet after suddenly awakening.* **2.** to roll or sway suddenly to one side or from side to side. [Of uncertain origin.]

lurch² (lûrch) *n.* **to leave in the lurch.** to leave (someone) in a difficult or embarrassing situation. [From the French word *lourch,* the name of a board game.]

lure (lůr) *n.* **1.** a powerful attraction: *the lure of a swim on a hot day.* **2.** a bait, as an artificial fly used in fishing.

Trachea

Right lung — Cross section of left lung

Bronchial tubes

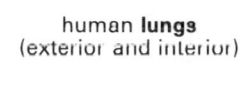

human **lungs**
(exterior and interior)

L

at; āpe; fär; câre; end; mē; it; īce; pierce; hot; ōld; sông, fôrk; oil; out; up; ūse; rüle; půll; tûrn; chin; sing; shop; thin; **th**is; hw in white; zh in treasure. The symbol ə stands for the unstressed vowel sound heard in about, taken, pencil, lemon, and circus.

—*v.t.*, **lured, lur·ing.** to attract powerfully; tempt: *The hungry child was lured to the kitchen by the smell of dinner cooking.*

lu·rid (lŭr′id) *adj.* **1.** terrible; sensational; shocking: *a lurid crime.* **2.** shining with a reddish glow or fiery glare: *a lurid fire.* —**lu′rid·ness,** *n.*

lurk (lûrk) *v.i.* **1.** to lie hidden: *A lion lurked in the underbrush, waiting for prey.* **2.** to move about in a stealthy manner.

lus·cious (lush′əs) *adj.* **1.** sweet and pleasing to the taste or smell; delicious: *ripe, luscious pears.* **2.** pleasing to the mind or to the senses: *luscious music.* —**lus′cious·ly,** *adv.* —**lus′cious·ness,** *n.*

lush (lush) *adj.* **1.** rich and abundant; luxuriant: *a lush growth of ferns.* **2.** characterized by or covered with luxuriant growth: *lush forests.* **3.** juicy and tender: *lush oranges.* **4.** luxurious; rich: *The room had a thick, lush rug.* —**lush′ly,** *adv.* —**lush′ness,** *n.*

lust (lust) *n.* **1.** strong sexual desire. **2.** any strong desire: *The miser had a lust for money.* —*v.i.* to have a strong desire: *The would-be dictator lusted after power.*

lus·ter (lus′tər) *also, British,* **lus·tre.** *n.* **1.** the quality of shining by reflected light; luminous glow; sheen: *The wax gave the kitchen floor a bright luster.* **2.** radiance; brightness: *tired eyes that had lost their luster.* **3.** splendor; glory; renown: *Brave deeds add much luster to one's reputation.* **4.** a shiny, often iridescent, glazed surface on pottery.

lus·ter·ware (lus′tər wâr′) *n.* pottery having a shiny, often iridescent, glazed surface.

lust·ful (lust′fəl) *adj.* full of or characterized by lust. —**lust′ful·ly,** *adv.* —**lust′ful·ness,** *n.*

lus·tre (lus′tər) *British.* another spelling of **luster.**

lus·trous (lus′trəs) *adj.* having a shining surface: *lustrous hair.* —**lus′trous·ly,** *adv.*

lust·y (lus′tē) *adj.,* **lust·i·er, lust·i·est.** full of strength and vigor; healthy. —**lust′i·ly,** *adv.*

lute (lūt) *n.* a stringed musical instrument having a pear-shaped body, played by plucking with the fingers or a plectrum.

lu·te·ti·um (lü tē′shē əm) *n.* a heavy, silver-white metallic element and the heaviest element of the rare-earth group. Symbol: **Lu** [From *Lutetia,* the Roman name for Paris, the hometown of its discoverer.]

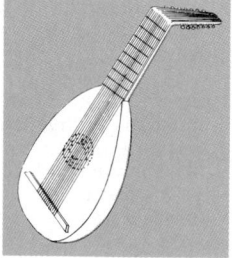

lute

Lu·ther·an (lü′thər ən) *adj.* of or relating to Martin Luther, his doctrines, or one of the Protestant churches named after him. —*n.* a member of a Lutheran Church.

lux·u·ri·ant (lug zhŭr′ē ənt, luk shŭr′ē ənt) *adj.* **1.** thick or abundant: *a luxuriant growth of rosebushes.* **2.** rich in detail or ornament: *a luxuriant imagination, luxuriant decoration.* **3.** producing in great abundance: *luxuriant soil.* —**lux·u′ri·ance,** *n.* —**lux·u′ri·ant·ly,** *adv.*

lux·u·ri·ate (lug zhŭr′ē āt′, luk shŭr′ē āt′) *v.i.,* **lux·u·ri·at·ed, lux·u·ri·at·ing.** **1.** to indulge oneself in pleasure or luxury; live luxuriously. **2.** to take great delight: *The dictator luxuriated in power.* **3.** to grow in great abundance: *The plants luxuriated in the warm, moist climate.*

lux·u·ri·ous (lug zhŭr′ē əs, luk shŭr′ē əs) *adj.* **1.** given to or liking pleasure or luxury: *to have luxurious tastes.* **2.** characterized by luxury: *a luxurious mansion.* —**lux·u′ri·ous·ly,** *adv.* —**lux·u′ri·ous·ness,** *n.*

lux·u·ry (luk′shə rē, lug′zhə rē) *n., pl.* **lux·u·ries.** **1.** something that adds to a person's comfort or pleasure in life but is not really necessary: *A mink coat is a luxury.* **2.** a way of life that gives great comfort or pleasure: *to live in luxury.* —*adj.* providing luxury: *a luxury hotel.*

-ly[1] *suffix* (used to form adverbs) **1.** in a particular manner or to a particular extent: *gladly, greatly.* **2.** in a particular position or at a particular time: *secondly, hourly, annually.* [From the Old English suffix *-lice* with the same meanings.]

-ly[2] *suffix* (used to form adjectives) **1.** like, of the nature of, or suited to: *brotherly, sisterly.* **2.** happening at specified periods of time: *weekly.* [From the Old English suffix *-lic* with the same meanings.]

ly·ce·um (lī sē′əm, lī′sē əm) *n.* **1.** a public hall in which educational programs, as concerts or lectures, are presented. **2.** an organization devoted to such educational programs. [From the Latin *Lyceum,* name of the school near Athens where Aristotle taught, from the Greek *Lykeion* with the same meaning.]

lye (lī) *n.* **1.** sodium hydroxide, used to make soap and detergents. **2.** a strong solution obtained from wood ashes, used in making soap.

ly·ing[1] (lī′ing) *v.* the present participle of **lie**[1]. —*n.* the act of telling lies. —*adj.* untruthful or deceitful.

ly·ing[2] (lī′ing) the present participle of **lie**[2].

Lyme disease (līm) a disease characterized by tiredness, chills, fever, headache, and a stiff neck, sometimes followed weeks or months later by heart and nerve abnormalities and arthritis. It is caused by a bacterium that is transmitted by the bite of a tick. [From *Lyme,* the town in Connecticut where it was first described.]

lymph (limf) *n.* a clear, colorless fluid, similar to blood in composition, that brings nourishment and oxygen to the cells and carries away waste products.

lym·phat·ic (lim fat′ik) *adj.* **1.** of, relating to, or carrying lymph: *lymphatic vessels.* **2.** dull; sluggish.

lymphatic system, the system in the body that forms white blood cells and carries lymph from the tissues to the bloodstream. The lymphatic system includes the lymphatic vessels and the lymph glands.

lymph node, any of the small nodes or bodies in the lymphatic vessels that filter out harmful substances and produce lymphocytes. Also, **lymph gland.**

lym·pho·cyte (lim′fə sīt′) *n.* one of the white blood cells formed in the lymph nodes.

lym·phoid (lim′foid) *adj.* of, relating to, or resembling lymph or the tissue of the lymph nodes.

lynch (linch) *v.t.* to seize by mob action and put to death, usually by hanging, without due process of law: *The enraged crowd lynched the suspected murderer.*

lynx (lingks) *n., pl.* **lynx** or **lynx·es.** a wildcat having long legs, a short tail, and tufted ears.

ly·on·naise (lī′ə nāz′) *adj.* cooked with finely chopped onions: *lyonnaise potatoes.*

Ly·ra (lī′rə) *n.* a constellation in the northern sky, thought to resemble a lyre in shape. It contains the bright star Vega.

lyre (līr) *n.* a stringed musical instrument, used by the ancient Greeks to accompany singing and recitation.

lyre·bird (līr′bûrd′) *n.* an Australian bird, having brown feathers. The male has a long tail that is lyre-shaped when spread.

lyr·ic (lir′ik) *adj.* **1.** of or relating to poetry that expresses strong personal emotion. **2.** writing poetry that expresses strong personal emotion: *a lyric poet.* Also, **lyr·ic·al** (lir′i kəl). —*n.* **1.** a lyric poem or lyric poetry. **2. lyrics.** the words written for a song: *That popular song has very clever lyrics.* —**lyr′i·cal·ly,** *adv.*

lyr·i·cist (lir′ə sist) *n.* a person who writes lyrics, especially one who writes the words for popular songs.

ly·sin (lī′sin) *n.* any antibody that is capable of bringing about the destruction of tissues, bacteria, or cells, especially red blood cells.

lyrebird

Mm

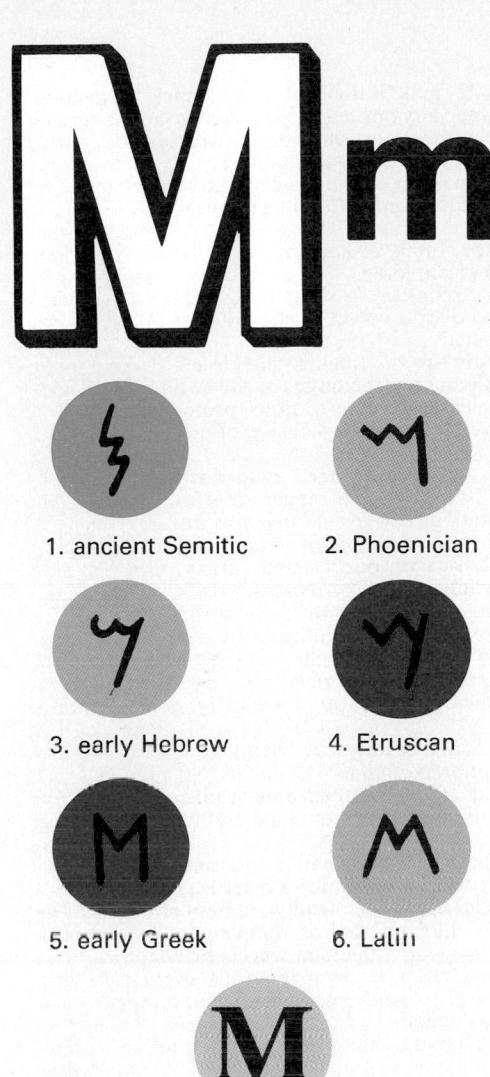

1. ancient Semitic
2. Phoenician
3. early Hebrew
4. Etruscan
5. early Greek
6. Latin
7. English

M is the thirteenth letter of the English alphabet. The way we write the capital letter **M** today is very much like the way it was written in the time of the earliest alphabets. The earliest form of this letter is the ancient Semitic letter *mem* (1), meaning "water." The shape of *mem* was altered in the early Phoenician (2) and early Hebrew (3) alphabets by being turned and making the last stroke longer. This was the form of **M** that the Etruscans borrowed around 2,800 years ago (4). The early Greeks (5) also borrowed this form of *mem* and called it *mu*. But in writing *mu*, the Greeks made the first and last strokes of the letter nearly vertical. This form was only slightly altered in the following centuries when the Romans borrowed *mu*. The form of **M** in the Latin alphabet (6) looks almost like our modern capital letter **M** (7).

m, M (em) *n., pl.* **m's, M's. 1.** the thirteenth letter of the English alphabet. **2.** the Roman numeral for 1,000.

m. 1. meridian. **2.** meter; meters. **3.** mile; miles. **4.** minute; minutes. **5.** month.

M. 1. Master. **2.** Monday. **3.** Monsieur.

ma (mä) *n. Informal.* mother.

MA, postal abbreviation for Massachusetts.

M.A., Master of Arts.

ma'am (mam) *n. Informal.* madam.

ma·ca·bre (mə kä'brə, mə kä'bər) *adj.* suggesting or dealing with death in a frightening way; gruesome; ghastly: *a macabre tale of a haunted cemetery.*

mac·ad·am (mə kad'əm) *n.* **1.** a pavement or road made largely or entirely of layers of crushed stone. **2.** the crushed stone used in such pavements or roads. [From the Scottish engineer John L. *McAdam* (1756–1836), who developed this product.]

mac·ad·am·ize (mə kad'ə mīz') *v.t.,* **mac·ad·am·ized, mac·ad·am·iz·ing.** to construct or pave (a road) with macadam. —**mac·ad·am·i·za'tion,** *n.*

ma·caque (mə kak', mə käk') *n.* any of various short-tailed monkeys of Asia and northern Africa having cheek pouches.

mac·a·ro·ni (mak'ə rō'nē) *n., pl.* **mac·a·ro·nis** or **mac·a·ro·nies.** a food made from flour paste or dough, usually in the shape of short, hollow tubes. Macaroni is prepared for eating by boiling.

mac·a·roon (mak'ə rün') *n.* a cookie made of ground almonds or coconut, egg whites, and sugar.

ma·caw (mə kô') *n.* any of several long-tailed, brilliantly colored parrots of Central and South America. The macaw has a large, strong beak with which it cracks nuts. It is the largest parrot.

Mac·beth (məkbeth') *n.* the main character in William Shakespeare's play *Macbeth.*

mace[1] (mās) *n.* **1.** a heavy club, usually having a spiked metal head, used as a weapon in the Middle Ages. **2.** an ornamental staff shaped like such a club, used as a ceremonial symbol of office or authority. [From the Old French word *mace* with the same meaning.]

mace[2] (mās) *n.* a spice made by grinding the dried outer covering of

macaw

the seed of the nutmeg. [From the Old French word *macis* meaning this spice, from the Latin word *macir* "a kind of spice from India," from the Greek word *makir* with the same meaning.]

Mace (mās) *n. Trademark.* a chemical mixture containing tear gas.

mac·er·ate (mas'ə rāt') *v.,* **mac·er·at·ed, mac·er·at·ing.** —*v.t.* **1.** to soften or separate into parts by soaking in liquid. **2.** to cause (the body) to waste away or grow thin. —*v.i.* to become macerated. **mac·er·a'tion,** *n.*

ma·chet·e (mə shet'ē, mə chet'ē) *n.* a broad, heavy knife used as a tool and weapon.

M

Mach·i·a·vel·li·an (mak′ē ə vel′ē ən) *adj.* **1.** acting according to the political theories of Niccolò Machiavelli, who wrote that a ruler could use even evil means to keep power and achieve goals. **2.** of or relating to Machiavelli or his political theories. —*n.* a follower of the political theories of Machiavelli.

mach·i·nate (mak′ə nāt′) *v.i.*, **mach·i·nat·ed, mach·i·nat·ing.** to scheme or plot slyly or secretly: *The rebels machinated to overthrow the dictator.*

mach·i·na·tion (mak′ə nā′shən) *n.* a sly, secret, or elaborate plot or scheme.

ma·chine (mə shēn′) *n.* **1.** an apparatus consisting of a number of fixed or moving parts, used to do work: *a machine for drying clothes.* **2.** a device that is used to transmit, redirect, or concentrate an applied physical force. The lever, pulley, screw, and inclined plane are among the simple machines. **3.** a group that controls a political party in a city, county, state, or other area: *the Democratic machine.* **4.** a person who acts in a mechanical way without thought, emotion, or will. —*v.t.*, **ma·chined, ma·chin·ing.** to make, shape, or finish with a machine.

ma·chine–gun (mə shēn′gun′) *v.t.*, **ma·chine-gunned, ma·chine-gun·ning.** to fire at or shoot with a machine gun.

machine gun, an automatic weapon that keeps firing as long as the trigger is pressed.

ma·chine–read·a·ble (mə shēn′rē′də bəl) *adj.* in a form that can be processed directly by a computer.

ma·chin·er·y (mə shē′nə rē) *n., pl.* **ma·chin·er·ies.** **1.** machines or machine parts: *The factory is equipped with the latest machinery.* **2.** the working parts of a particular machine: *The mechanics repaired the machinery of the elevator.* **3.** the means or working parts by which something is kept going or a desired result is obtained: *the machinery of government, the machinery of the courts.*

machine shop, a workshop where metal or other material is cut, shaped, and finished with machine tools.

machine tool, a power-driven tool used to cut or shape metal or other material.

ma·chin·ist (mə shē′nist) *n.* **1.** a person who is skilled in using machine tools. **2.** a person who designs, assembles, installs, or repairs machinery.

ma·chis·mo (mä chēz′mō) *n.* a strong or exaggerated concept of masculinity, characterized by aggressiveness and a sense of male superiority. Also, **macho.**

Mach·me·ter (mäk′mē′tər) *n.* a device that measures and shows the speed of an aircraft in relation to the speed of sound.

Mach number (mäk) *also,* **mach number.** a number expressing the ratio of the speed of a moving body in a given atmosphere to the speed of sound in the same atmosphere. If the speed of sound in a given atmosphere is 700 miles per hour (1,130 kilometers per hour), an airplane traveling at the same speed is said to be traveling at Mach 1. If the airplane is flying at twice the speed of sound in a given atmosphere, its Mach number is 2. [From the Austrian physicist Ernst *Mach* (1838–1916).]

ma·cho (mä′chō) *n., pl.* **ma·chos.** **1.** another word for **machismo.** **2.** in Spanish cultures, a strong, brave, and virile man. —*adj.* having or showing machismo; strongly masculine. [From the Spanish word *macho* meaning "male," going back to the Latin word *masculus* "male."]

mack·er·el (mak′ər əl) *n., pl.* **mack·er·el** or **mack·er·els.** a food and game fish related to the tuna, having a silvery body that is marked in metallic blue on its upper surface.

mackerel sky, a sky covered with rows of small, white, fleecy clouds resembling the patterns on the back of a mackerel.

mack·i·naw (mak′ə nô′) *n.* **1.** a short coat made of a heavy woolen fabric that is usually woven in a plaid. **2.** a thick blanket made of a heavy woolen fabric, often woven in wide bands of different colors.

mack·in·tosh (mak′in tosh′) *n., pl.* **mack·in·tosh·es.** a raincoat, especially one made of a waterproof, rubberized cloth. [From the Scottish chemist Charles *Macintosh* (1766–1843), who invented this cloth.]

mac·ra·mé (mak′rə mā′) *n.* a decorative work made by knotting thread or cord, often in geometric patterns.

mac·ro·cosm (mak′rə koz′əm) *n.* the whole world or universe.

ma·cron (mā′kron) *n.* a short horizontal line (¯) placed over a vowel to show that it has a long sound.

mac·ro·nu·cle·us (mak′rō nü′klē əs, mak′rō nü′klē əs) *n.* the larger of the two types of nuclei present in various protozoans, believed to control processes of metabolism.

mad (mad) *adj.*, **mad·der, mad·dest.** **1.** feeling or showing great anger, resentment, or irritation: *I was mad because my parents made me stay home from the party to study.* **2.** out of one's mind; crazy; insane. **3.** wildly foolish or reckless; rash: *The two teenagers had a mad plan to run away from home.* **4.** very enthusiastic: *to be mad about football.* **5.** wildly or frantically confused: *to be mad with jealousy, a mad rush for tickets to the World Series.* **6.** having rabies: *a mad dog.* —**mad′ly,** *adv.* —**mad′ness,** *n.*

·**like mad.** *Slang.* with great energy or speed: *The audience cheered like mad.*

macramé

mad·am (mad′əm) *n., pl.* **mad·ams** or **mes·dames.** lady; mistress. ▲ used as a form of respectful or polite address to a woman.

mad·ame (ma dam′, mad′əm) *n., pl.* **mes·dames.** Mrs. ▲ a French form of address for a married woman.

mad·cap (mad′kap′) *adj.* wildly reckless or foolish: *The group had the madcap idea of climbing the mountain in the snowstorm.* —*n.* a person who is madcap.

mad·den (mad′ən) *v.t.* to make very angry: *The lazy student's refusal to study maddened the teacher.* —*v.i.* to become maddened.

mad·den·ing (mad′ə ning) *adj.* causing anger, resentment, or irritation: *a maddening delay, a maddening traffic jam.* —**mad′den·ing·ly,** *adv.*

mad·der[1] (mad′ər) *n.* **1.** a climbing plant of Asia and southern Europe, having long, fleshy, red roots. **2.** a red dye made from the roots of this plant. **3.** a brilliant red color. [From the Old English word *mædere* meaning this plant.]

mad·der[2] (mad′ər) the comparative of **mad.**

mad·dest (mad′ist) the superlative of **mad.**

mad·ding (mad′ing) *adj.* Archaic. acting as if mad: *Far from the madding crowd's ignoble strife* (Thomas Gray).

made (mād) *v.* the past tense and past participle of **make.** —*adj.* produced, built, or shaped. ▲ often used in combination: *a well-made chair, a handmade sweater.*

Ma·dei·ra (mə dîr′ə) *n.* a sweet, amber-colored wine originally made on the island of Madeira.

mad·e·moi·selle (mad′ə mə zel′, mad′mwə zel′) *n., pl.* **mes·de·moi·selles** or **mad·e·moi·selles.** miss. ▲ a French form of address for an unmarried girl or woman.

made–to–or·der (mād′tü ôr′dər) *adj.* **1.** made to suit a buyer's special instructions or requirements; custom-made: *made-to-order shoes.* **2.** perfectly suited to one's tastes, abilities, needs, or wishes: *a made-to-order vacation, with lots of sun, sea, and sand.*

made–up (mād′up′) *adj.* **1.** not real or true; fictitious: *a made-up name.* **2.** having cosmetics or makeup on.

mad·house (mad′hous′) *n., pl.* **mad·hous·es** (mad′hou′ziz). **1.** formerly, a hospital or asylum for the mentally ill. **2.** a place or scene of wild uproar or confusion: *After our team won, the locker room was a madhouse.*

Mad·i·son Avenue (mad′ə sən) the U.S. advertising industry. [From *Madison Avenue* in New York City, where the offices of many advertising firms are located.]

mad·man (mad′man′, mad′mən) *n.*, *pl.* **mad·men** (mad′men′, mad′mən). a person who is, acts, or seems to be insane.

Ma·don·na (mə don′ə) *n.* **1.** Mary, the mother of Jesus. **2.** a picture or statue of the mother of Jesus.

mad·ras (mad′rəs, mə dras′) *n.* a cotton fabric usually having a plaid, checked, or striped pattern. [From *Madras,* the city in southeastern India where this fabric was first made.]

mad·ri·gal (mad′ri gəl) *n.* **1.** a short, lyric medieval poem that can be set to music. **2.** a song with parts for several voices, sung without accompaniment.

mad·wom·an (mad′wŭm′ən) *n.*, *pl.* **mad·wom·en** (mad′wim′ən). a woman who is, acts, or seems to be insane.

mael·strom (māl′strəm) *n.* **1.** a large, violent or turbulent whirlpool. **2.** something like such a whirlpool in intensity, violence, or destructive force: *the maelstrom of war.* [From the obsolete Dutch word *maelstrom* meaning "violent whirlpool," from the words *malen* "to grind" + *strom* "stream."]

maes·tro (mīs′trō) *n.*, *pl.* **maes·tros.** **1.** any noted conductor, composer, or teacher of music. **2.** a master in any art.

Ma·fi·a (mä′fē ə) *n.* **1.** a secret criminal society in Sicily. **2.** a secret criminal organization said to be related to this society and active in the United States and other countries.

mag·a·zine (mag′ə zēn′, mag′ə zēn′) *n.* **1.** a publication, usually issued weekly or monthly, containing articles, stories, pictures, or other features. **2.** a building or room for storing ammunition and explosives, as in a ship or fort. **3.** a metal container for holding bullets or cartridges so that they can be fed into the chamber of a gun for firing.

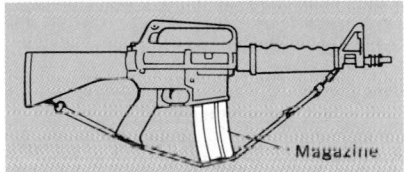

magazine *(def. 3)*

ma·gen·ta (mə jen′tə) *n.* a purplish red color. —*adj.* having the color magenta.

mag·got (mag′ət) *n.* the wormlike larva of a fly, having a thick body and no legs.

Ma·gi (mā′jī, maj′ī) *pl. n.* in the New Testament, the three wise men from the East who brought gifts to the infant Jesus.

mag·ic (maj′ik) *n.* **1.** the art or practice that has been claimed to be capable of summoning and using supernatural forces with spells, charms, rituals, and the like. **2.** the art or skill of doing tricks or producing baffling effects or illusions, especially for entertainment: *The children loved to see magic performed at parties.* **3.** an enchanting influence; mysterious charm: *the magic of the first snowfall of winter.* —*adj.* relating to, done by, or used in magic: *a magic act, a magic trick, a magic wand.*

mag·i·cal (maj′i kəl) *adj.* of, relating to, or done by or as if by magic. —**mag′i·cal·ly,** *adv.*

ma·gi·cian (mə jish′ən) *n.* **1.** an entertainer who does tricks or sleight of hand: *The audience applauded when the magician suddenly pulled two rabbits from a hat.* **2.** a person who is skilled in the use of magic; sorcerer; wizard.

magic lantern, an early kind of projector for showing slides on a screen or wall.

mag·is·te·ri·al (maj′ə stir′ē əl) *adj.* **1.** of, relating to, or suiting a person in a position of authority; commanding: *a magisterial manner.* **2.** domineering; dictatorial. **3.** of or relating to a magistrate or the office or duties of a magistrate. —**mag′is·te′ri·al·ly,** *adv.*

mag·is·tra·cy (maj′ə strə sē) *n.*, *pl.* **mag·is·tra·cies.** **1.** the office, duties, or term of a magistrate. **2.** magistrates as a group. **3.** the district of a magistrate.

mag·is·trate (maj′ə strāt′, maj′ə strit) *n.* **1.** a government officer who has the power to apply and enforce the law. **2.** a judge having limited power, such as a justice of the peace.

mag·ma (mag′mə) *n.* molten rock beneath the surface of the earth, from which lava and igneous rocks are formed.

Mag·na Car·ta (mag′nə kär′tə) *also,* **Mag·na Char·ta.** the charter that King John of England was forced to grant to his barons at Runnymede on June 15, 1215. The Magna Carta guaranteed certain civil rights and liberties to the barons, merchants, and clergy of England by limiting the power of the king.

mag·na cum lau·de (mag′nə kŭm lou′də, mag′nə-kŭm lô′dē) with high honors or praise. ▲ used to show graduation with high honors from a college or university.

mag·na·nim·i·ty (mag′nə nim′i tē) *n.*, *pl.* **mag·na·nim·i·ties.** **1.** the quality of being magnanimous. **2.** a magnanimous act.

mag·nan·i·mous (mag nan′ə məs) *adj.* generous and noble of mind and heart, especially in overlooking insults or grievances; free from pettiness: *The winning candidate was magnanimous toward the loser.* —**mag·nan′i·mous·ly,** *adv.* —**mag·nan′i·mous·ness,** *n.*

mag·nate (mag′nāt, mag′nit) *n.* a person of great power, wealth, or importance in a field of activity: *a railroad magnate, a shipping magnate.*

mag·ne·sia (mag nē′shə, mag nē′zhə) *n.* a white powder compound used especially in laxatives and as an antacid. [From the Medieval Latin word *magnesia,* from the Greek word *magnēsia,* applied to various metallic ores, from *Magnēsia,* an area of eastern Greece where this mineral was found.]

mag·ne·si·um (mag nē′zē əm, mag nē′zhəm) *n.* a very light, strong, silver-white metallic element used to make lightweight alloys. It is an essential part of chlorophyll. Symbol: **Mg** [From *magnesia.*]

mag·net (mag′nit) *n.* **1.** a piece of stone, metal, or ore that has the property of attracting iron, steel, and certain other materials. **2.** a person or thing that attracts: *That monument is a magnet for tourists.*

mag·net·ic (mag net′ik) *adj.* **1.** having the properties of a magnet; able to exert magnetism. **2.** of, relating to, producing, or caused by magnetism. **3.** of or relating to the magnetism of the earth. **4.** having the power to attract attention, followers, or the like: *The senator was a magnetic speaker.* —**mag·net′i·cal·ly,** *adv.*

magnetic field, the region around a magnet or an electric current, in which a magnetic force can be detected.

magnetic flux, the total number of lines of force in a magnetic field. Also, **flux.**

magnetic needle, a slender bar of magnetized steel, as in a compass, that points approximately toward the earth's north and south magnetic poles.

magnetic north, the direction toward which the end of a compass needle points, usually differing from true north.

magnetic pole **1.** either of the two points of a magnet where its magnetic force seems to be greatest. **2.** either of two points on the earth's surface that are the poles of the earth's magnetic field, and toward which a compass

M

at; āpe; fär; câre; end; mē; it; īce; pîerce; hot; ōld; sông, fôrk; oil; out; up; ūse; rüle; pùll; tûrn; chin; sing; shop; thin; **th**is; hw in white; zh in treasure. The symbol ə stands for the unstressed vowel sound heard in about, taken, pencil, lemon, and circus.

needle points. The north magnetic pole is at approximately 75 degrees north latitude and 101 degrees west longitude. The south magnetic pole is at approximately 69 degrees south latitude and 14 degrees east longitude.

magnetic tape, a thin tape coated with magnetically sensitive material, used to record sound, images, and data. Also, **tape.**

mag·net·ism (mag'ni tiz'əm) n. **1.** the quality of certain materials and of all electric currents that makes it possible for them to produce a magnetic field outside themselves, and to attract or repel iron, steel, and certain other materials. **2.** the branch of physics dealing with magnets, their fields of force, and their magnetic qualities. **3.** a strong power to attract, influence, or charm.

mag·net·ite (mag'ni tīt') n. a black magnetic iron ore often found in igneous and metamorphic rocks.

mag·net·ize (mag'ni tīz') v.t., **mag·net·ized, mag·net·iz·ing. 1.** to give magnetic qualities to; make into a magnet. **2.** to attract as if by a magnet; fascinate; charm. —**mag'net·i·za'tion,** n. —**mag'net·iz'er,** n.

mag·ne·to (mag nē'tō) n., pl. **mag·ne·tos.** a small generator of alternating current, using permanent magnets rather than electromagnets.

magnet school, a public school with particularly good, often specialized programs and instruction designed to attract students from all groups within a district.

magni- combining form great; large: magnify.

mag·ni·fi·ca·tion (mag'nə fi kā'shən) n. **1.** the act, process, or degree of magnifying. **2.** the state of being magnified. **3.** something that has been magnified.

mag·nif·i·cence (mag nif'ə səns) n. the state or quality of being magnificent.

mag·nif·i·cent (mag nif'ə sənt) adj. **1.** very beautiful or splendid: The house on the top of the hill has a magnificent view of the valley. **2.** very good; exceptional; outstanding. —**mag·nif'i·cent·ly,** adv.

mag·ni·fy (mag'nə fī') v., **mag·ni·fied, mag·ni·fy·ing.** —v.t. **1.** to cause to look larger than the real size: This microscope magnifies objects 1,000 times. **2.** to cause to seem greater or more important; exaggerate: Some people magnify the dangers involved in traveling by airplane. **3.** to increase the size or extent of; add to: the brisk wind magnified the cold as the storm approached. —v.i. to increase or have the power to increase the apparent size of an object. —**mag'ni·fi·er,** n.

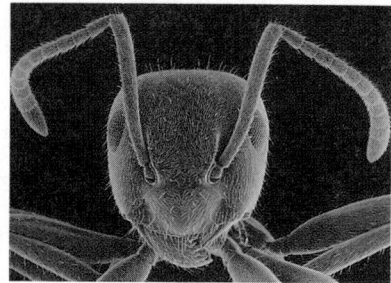

magnified view of the head of a black garden ant

magnifying glass, a lens or combination of lenses that causes something to look larger than it really is.

mag·ni·tude (mag'ni tüd', mag'ni tūd') n. **1.** size or extent, especially greatness of size or extent: the magnitude of a problem, the magnitude of an angle. **2.** importance; significance: The splitting of the atom was an achievement of great magnitude. **3.** the relative brightness of a star or other heavenly body as measured on a numerical scale.

mag·no·lia (mag nōl'yə) n. **1.** any of a group of trees and tall shrubs having large, fragrant flowers. **2.** the flower itself, growing in white, rose, purple, or yellow. [From the French botanist Pierre Magnol (1638–1715).]

mag·pie (mag'pī') n. **1.** a noisy, long-tailed bird having black-and-white markings. **2.** a person who chatters or talks constantly.

mag·uey (mag'wā) n. **1.** a Mexican plant that yields long, tough fibers used for making cord and rope and sap used in medicines and in making alcoholic beverages. **2.** the fiber obtained from such a plant.

Mag·yar (mag'yär, mäg'yär) n. **1.** a member of a people who settled in Hungary in the ninth century. **2.** the language of the Magyars; Hungarian. —adj. of or relating to the Magyars or their language; Hungarian.

ma·ha·ra·jah (mä'hə rä'jə) also, **ma·ha·ra·ja.** n. formerly, a ruling prince of an Indian state. [From the Sanskrit word mahārāja meaning "great king," from the words mahā "great, mighty" + rājā "king."]

ma·ha·ra·ni (mä'hə rä'nē) also, **ma·ha·ra·nee.** n. **1.** the wife of a maharajah. **2.** formerly, a ruling princess of an Indian state.

ma·hat·ma (mə hät'mə) n. **1.** a wise and holy person. **2.** a Hindu title of respect for a spiritual leader: Mahatma Gandhi.

Ma·hi·can (mə hē'kən) n., pl. **Ma·hi·can** or **Ma·hi·cans.** a member of a tribe of North American Indians, formerly living in the area of the upper Hudson River. Also, **Mohican.**

mah jongg (mä' jong') also, **mah-jongg, mah-jong.** a game of Chinese origin for two to four players, played with 152 decorated tiles. The object of the game is to obtain any of various winning combinations of tiles.

ma·hog·a·ny (mə hog'ə nē) n., pl. **ma·hog·a·nies. 1.** a strong, hard, reddish brown or yellowish wood of a tropical evergreen tree, widely used for making furniture and musical instruments. **2.** the tree yielding this wood. **3.** a rich reddish brown color. —adj. having the color mahogany; reddish brown.

Ma·hom·et·an (mə hom'i tən) adj., n. another word for **Muslim.**

ma·hout (mə hout') n. in India and the East Indies, an elephant driver or trainer.

maid (mād) n. **1.** a female servant. **2.** a girl or young unmarried woman.

maid·en (mā'dən) n. a girl or young unmarried woman. —adj. **1.** of, relating to, or like a maiden. **2.** unmarried: a maiden aunt. **3.** first or earliest: a ship's maiden voyage.

maid·en·hair (mā'dən hâr') n. any of a large group of delicate ferns, having slender stems and feathery fronds.

maid·en·ly (mā'dən lē) adj. characteristic of or suited to a maiden: maidenly modesty. —**mai'den·li·ness,** n.

maiden name, a woman's last name before she is married.

maid–in–wait·ing (mād'in wā'ting) n., pl. **maids-in-wait·ing.** an unmarried woman, especially a noblewoman, who attends a queen or princess.

maid of honor pl. **maids of honor. 1.** the chief unmarried female attendant of the bride at a wedding. **2.** a maid-in-waiting.

maid·ser·vant (mād'sûr'vənt) n. a female servant.

mail¹ (māl) n. **1.** letters and packages sent or received by post. **2.** a collection of such material sent or delivered at a specific time: The check should arrive in today's mail. **3.** also, **mails.** the system by which mail is collected, transported, and delivered, usually operated by the national government; postal system. —v.t. to send by mail: to mail a package. [From the Middle English word male meaning "a bag, pouch," from the Old French word male with the same meaning, referring to the pouch in which letters were carried.]

mail² (māl) n. flexible armor for protecting the body, made of interlinked rings of metal. —v.t. to cover or protect with mail. [From the Old French word maille meaning this armor, from the Latin word macula meaning "a spot" or "mesh."]

mail·box (māl'boks') n., pl. **mail·box·es. 1.** a box into which mail is deposited for collection by the post office. **2.** a box into which mail is delivered.

mail carrier, a person who carries and delivers mail.

Mail·gram (māl′gram′) *n.* *Trademark.* a letter sent by telegraph to a local post office from which it is delivered together with regular mail.

mail·man (māl′man′) *n., pl.* **mail·men** (māl′men′). a person who carries and delivers mail. Also, **postman.**

mail order, an order for merchandise that is received and filled by mail. —**mail′-or′der,** *adj.*

maim (mām) *v.t.* to injure or disfigure seriously and horribly, especially to deprive of a limb; cripple; mutilate.

main (mān) *adj.* greatest or foremost in size, extent, or importance; principal: *the main branch of a library.* —*n.* **1.** a principal pipe, duct, conduit, or cable for the passage of water, gas, sewage, or electricity. **2.** the open sea. ·**in the main.** in general; mainly: *We enjoyed the show in the main.*

main clause, another term for **independent clause.**

main·frame (mān′frām′) *n.* a large, powerful computer that can quickly perform numerous complicated calculations as well as support more than one user.

main·land (mān′land′, mān′lənd) *n.* the body of land forming the principal or largest land mass of a region, country, or continent, as distinguished from an island or peninsula: *the mainland of Greece.*

main·line (mān′līn′) *v.t., v.i.,* **main·lined, main·lin·ing.** *Slang.* to inject (a narcotic or other illegal drug) directly into a vein. —**main′lin′er,** *n.*

main·ly (mān′lē) *adv.* for the most part; chiefly: *The coin collector was interested mainly in old dimes.*

main·mast (mān′mast′, mān′məst) *n.* the principal mast of a ship.

main·sail (mān′sāl′, mān′səl) *n.* the principal sail of a ship, set on the mainmast.

main·sheet (mān′shēt′) *n.* a rope used to set the mainsail at the proper angle to the wind.

main·spring (mān′spring′) *n.* **1.** the principal spring in a mechanism, especially in a watch or clock. **2.** the main purpose, motive, or cause. *The mainspring of their lives was a desire for wealth and comfort.*

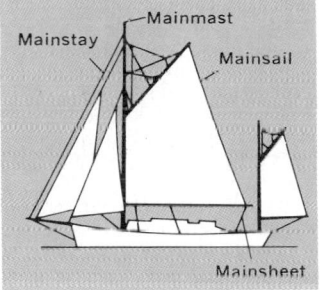

mainmast

main·stay (mān′stā′) *n.* **1.** a rope that supports or steadies the mast of a sailing ship. **2.** a person or thing that is the main support of something: *The quarterback is the mainstay of our football team.*

main·stream (mān′strēm′) *n.* the main direction or trend of development: *That senator's political beliefs are in the mainstream of American politics.*

main·tain (mān tān′) *v.t.* **1.** to go on with; continue: *to maintain a high speed on a highway.* **2.** to keep in force, operation, or proper condition: *The city maintains the streets.* **3.** to keep or hold on to: *It was hard for me to maintain my balance on the icy path. The senators maintained their position on a tax increase.* **4.** to state positively or firmly: *No matter what others may think, I still maintain that my cousin is innocent.* **5.** to provide for the support or upkeep of: *to maintain a large family on a small income.* [From the Old French word *maintenir* meaning "to preserve, maintain," going back to the Latin words *manus* "hand" and *tenēre* "to hold."]

main·te·nance (mān′tə nəns) *n.* **1.** the act of maintaining or the state of being maintained. **2.** means of support or upkeep.

main·top (mān′top′) *n.* a platform at the head of the lower section of a mainmast.

main yard, the lower yard on the mainmast of a sailing ship.

maî·tre d' (mā′tər dē′, mā′trə dē′) *n., pl.* **maî·tre d's** (mā′tər dēz′, mā′trə dēz′). **1.** a headwaiter. **2.** the manager of a hotel. **3.** a butler or steward. Also, **maî·tre d'hô·tel** (mā′tər dō tel′, mā′trə dō tel′) *n., pl.* **maî·tres d'hô·tel** (mā′tərz dō tel′, mā′trəz dō tel′). [From the French phrase *maître d'hôtel* meaning "master of the house" or "headwaiter," going back to the Latin words *magister* "master" + *de* "from" + the Medieval Latin word *hospitale* "place to receive guests."]

maize (māz) *n.* **1.** see **corn¹** (*defs. 1, 2*). **2.** the color of ripe corn; deep yellow. —*adj.* having the color maize; deep yellow.

maj., major.

ma·jes·tic (mə jes′tik) *adj.* having or showing majesty: *a majestic mountain.* Also, **ma·jes·ti·cal** (mə jes′ti kəl). —**ma·jes′ti·cal·ly,** *adv.*

maj·es·ty (maj′ə stē) *n., pl.* **maj·es·ties.** **1.** very great dignity, splendor, or grandeur: *The king and queen were seated on their thrones in all their majesty.* **2.** supreme authority or power: *the majesty of the law.* **3. Majesty.** the form of address used when speaking about or to a sovereign, preceded by *His, Her,* or *Your.*

ma·jor (mā′jər) *adj.* **1.** greater in size, amount, value, importance, or rank: *The Rockies are a major mountain system in America. My partner takes the major credit for the success of the business.* **2.** *Music.* **a.** of or relating to an interval that is a half tone greater than a minor interval: *C to D is a major second, and C to D flat is a minor second.* **b.** of, relating to, or based on a major scale: *a major chord, a major key.* —*n.* **1.** in the U.S. Army, Air Force, and Marine Corps, an officer ranking below a lieutenant colonel and above a captain. **2.** the main subject studied at a college or university: *My major is physics.* **3. majors.** *Sports.* the major leagues. —*v.i.* to study or specialize in an academic major: *to major in English.*

ma·jor-do·mo (mā′jər dō′mō) *n., pl.* **ma·jor-do·mos.** **1.** the chief steward in a royal, noble, or great household. **2.** a butler; steward.

ma·jor·ette (mā′jə ret′) *n.* another word for **drum majorette.**

major general, in the U.S. Army, Air Force, and Marine Corps, an officer ranking below a lieutenant general and above a brigadier general.

ma·jor·i·ty (mə jôr′i tē, mə jor′i tē) *n., pl.* **ma·jor·i·ties.** **1.** the larger number or part of a whole; more than half: *The majority of the students voted to have a dance.* **2.** the amount by which a larger number exceeds a smaller number; margin. **3.** a group or political party having more than half of the votes or members, as in a legislature. **4.** the age at which a person is said to have full legal rights and responsibilities, usually twenty-one.

▲ **Majority** and **plurality** both refer to a winning number of votes. A **majority** is more than half the total number of votes cast. A **plurality** is the number of votes that the winning candidate receives over the highest total of another candidate. If, in a school election in which 100 votes were cast, one student got 46 votes, a second student 29 votes, and a third 25 votes, the first student would lack a majority, but would have a plurality of 17 votes over the second.

at; āpe; fär; câre; end; mē; it; īce; pîerce; hot; ōld; sông, fôrk; oil; out; up; ūse; rūle; pu̇ll; tûrn; chin; sing; shop; thin; this; hw in white; zh in treasure. The symbol ə stands for the unstressed vowel sound heard in about, taken, pencil, lemon, and circus.

major league **1.** either of the two main groups of professional baseball teams in the United States. **2.** any league of principal importance in certain other professional sports, such as ice hockey. —**ma′jor-league′**, *adj.*

major scale, a musical scale consisting of eight tones, having half steps instead of whole steps after the third and seventh notes.

make (māk) *v.*, **made, mak·ing.** —*v.t.* **1.** to form or bring into being; construct: *The birds made a nest in the tree.* **2.** to cause to be or occur; bring about: *The slamming door made a loud noise. They made a change in their plans. The two countries made peace.* **3.** to put in a certain condition; cause to become: *The smell of food made us hungry.* **4.** to cause to act or behave in a particular manner: *Peeling the onions made my eyes water.* **5.** to cause to seem or appear: *Those jeans make you look thin.* **6.** to force or compel (a person) to do something: *The police could not make the prisoner confess.* **7.** to fashion or reach in one's mind: *to make plans, to make a decision.* **8.** to perform (an action); do: *to make a phone call, to make a speech.* **9.** to earn or gain: *to make $10.00 an hour. I made many friends this year.* **10.** to prepare or arrange for use: *to make breakfast, to make a bed.* **11.** to draw up; establish: *to make rules.* **12.** to regard as the meaning: *What do you make of this letter?* **13.** to provide: *to make room for someone.* **14.** to develop into; become: *You'll make a good doctor.* **15.** to add up or amount to; equal: *Five and five make ten. Twelve inches make one foot.* **16.** to bring about or make certain the success of: *Your singing made the show.* **17.** *Informal.* to succeed in winning a place or position on: *We made the basketball team.* **18.** to arrive at; reach: *They barely made the train.* —*v.i.* **1.** to move or set out; head: *The ship made for the nearest harbor.* **2.** to put oneself in a certain condition: *The team made ready for the game.* —*n.* **1.** a particular style or type of manufactured article; brand. **2.** the way in which a thing is made.

·**to make after.** to chase; pursue.

·**to make away with.** **a.** to steal. **b.** to kill. **c.** to get rid of or consume.

·**to make for.** **a.** to be favorable to; help: *The sunny weather made for a pleasant weekend at the beach.* **b.** to provide: *This book makes for enjoyable reading.*

·**to make it.** *Informal.* to succeed.

·**to make off with.** to carry off; steal.

·**to make out.** **a.** to write out or fill out: *to make out a shopping list, to make out a check.* **b.** to manage to see or read clearly: *I can't make out your handwriting.* **c.** to get along; succeed: *How did you make out at the job interview?* **d.** to try to prove or show: *The newspaper story made me out to be a hero.*

·**to make over.** **a.** to change or redo: *The tailor made over the jacket because it was too large.* **b.** to transfer ownership of.

·**to make up.** **a.** to be the parts of; constitute: *Nine players make up a baseball team.* **b.** to become friendly or loving again: *The two friends quarreled, but now they have made up.* **c.** to invent or create in the mind: *I made up an excuse for being late.* **d.** to put cosmetics on (the face). **e.** to take or repeat (an examination that one has missed or failed). **f.** to compensate: *I hope this gift will make up for my selfish behavior.*

make–be·lieve (māk′bi lēv′) *n.* an imagining or acting out in play; fantasy: *The story about ghosts in the house is only make-believe.* —*adj.* imaginary: *The cardboard box became a make-believe rocket ship.*

mak·er (mā′kər) *n.* **1.** a person or thing that makes something. ▲ often used in combination: *noisemaker, shoemaker, troublemaker.* **2. Maker.** God.

make·shift (māk′shift′) *n.* something used temporarily in place of the proper or usual thing: *We used a carton*

as a makeshift for a table. —*adj.* of, like, or used as a makeshift: *The sofa was a makeshift bed.*

make·up (māk′up′) *n.* **1.** cosmetics put on the face. Rouge, lipstick, eye shadow, and mascara are kinds of makeup. **2.** the cosmetics, wigs, or other articles used by a performer for his or her role. **3.** the way in which something is put together. **4.** physical, mental, or moral nature: *It isn't in my makeup to be rude to people.* **5.** an examination taken by a student for an earlier examination that he or she has missed or failed. **6.** the arrangement of type and illustrations on a page.

mal- *prefix* bad or badly; wrong or wrongly: *malpractice, malnutrition.*

Mal·a·chi (mal′ə kī′) *n.* a book of the Old Testament believed to have been written by the Hebrew prophet Malachi.

mal·a·chite (mal′ə kīt′) *n.* a bright green copper ore used for making ornaments and jewelry.

mal·ad·just·ed (mal′ə jus′tid) *adj.* poorly adjusted, especially to one's surroundings or circumstances.

mal·ad·just·ment (mal′ə just′mənt) *n.* poor adjustment, especially to one's surroundings or circumstances.

mal·a·droit (mal′ə droit′) *adj.* lacking in skill; awkward; clumsy: *a maladroit dancer.* —**mal′a·droit′ly,** *adv.* —**mal′a·droit′ness,** *n.*

mal·a·dy (mal′ə dē) *n., pl.* **mal·a·dies.** **1.** a sickness or disease. **2.** any disturbed or unwholesome condition.

mal·a·mute (mal′ə mūt′) *n.* see **Alaskan malamute.**

mal·a·prop·ism (mal′ə prop iz′əm) *n.* a funny or silly misuse of words, especially the use of one word for another having a similar sound but a different meaning. For example: *What are you incinerating* (insinuating) *by that last remark?* or *The police learned of the crime by means of a unanimous* (anonymous) *telephone call.*

ma·lar·i·a (mə lâr′ē ə) *n.* a disease characterized by chills, high fever, and sweating. Malaria is caused by microscopic parasites introduced into the bloodstream by the bite of certain mosquitoes. [From the Italian word *mal′aria* meaning this disease, from the phrase *mala aria* meaning "bad air." It was believed that *malaria* was spread by foul air coming from swamps.]

ma·lar·i·al (mə lâr′ē əl) *adj.* **1.** relating to or caused by malaria. **2.** having malaria.

Ma·lay (mā′lā) *n.* **1.** a member of a people of southeastern Asia living in the Malay Peninsula, eastern Sumatra, parts of Borneo, Singapore, and some nearby islands. · **2.** the language of the Malays. —*adj.* of or relating to the Malays, their language, or culture. Also, **Malayan.**

Words From Other Languages

For centuries the Malays have been travelers, traders, and sailors living near people who spoke other languages. The Malay language has contributed to English many words for goods first made or grown in the Pacific area.

amok	wild and out of control
bamboo	a woody plant of the grass family
compound	an enclosed area for living or work
gingham	a checked or striped cotton fabric
gong	a musical instrument with a metal disk that is struck
ketchup	a thick sauce of tomatoes and seasonings
orangutan	a reddish brown, tree-dwelling ape
paddy	a field for growing rice
sarong	a piece of cloth wrapped as a skirt

Ma·lay·an (mə lā′ən) *adj., n.* another word for **Malay.**

mal·con·tent (mal′kən tent′) *adj.* unhappy or dissatisfied, especially with a government or existing conditions. —*n.* a person who is malcontent.

male (māl) *adj.* **1.** of or relating to the sex that can fertilize female eggs and thus father young. **2.** of or characteristic of the male sex; masculine. **3.** made up of men or boys: *a male club.* **4.** of or relating to a plant that bears stamens. **5.** (of an object or device) having a part designed to be inserted into a corresponding hollow part: *a male electric plug.* —*n.* a male person, animal, or plant. —**male′ness,** *n.*

mal·e·dic·tion (mal′ə dik′shən) *n.* **1.** a curse. **2.** malicious talk; slander.

mal·e·fac·tor (mal′ə fak′tər) *n.* **1.** a person who commits a crime; criminal. **2.** an evildoer.

ma·lev·o·lence (mə lev′ə ləns) *n.* the wish for evil or harm to happen to others.

ma·lev·o·lent (mə lev′ə lənt) *adj.* doing or desiring to do evil or harm to others. —**ma·lev′o·lent·ly,** *adv.*

mal·fea·sance (mal fē′zəns) *n. Law.* wrongdoing, especially by a public official: *Police officers are guilty of malfeasance if they accept bribes.*

mal·for·ma·tion (mal′fôr mā′shən) *n.* an abnormal or faulty formation or structure, especially in a part of the body.

mal·formed (mal fôrmd′) *adj.* having an abnormal or faulty structure or formation; misshapen.

mal·func·tion (mal fungk′shən) *n.* the failure to function or work properly: *A malfunction in the carburetor caused the car to stall.* —*v.i.* to fail to function or work properly.

mal·ice (mal′is) *n.* the wish to cause harm, injury, or pain to another; spite: *With malice toward none; with charity for all* (Abraham Lincoln).

ma·li·cious (mə lish′əs) *adj.* characterized by, showing, or resulting from malice: *a malicious person, malicious gossip.* —**ma·li′cious·ly,** *adv.* —**ma·li′cious·ness,** *n.*

ma·lign (mə līn′) *v.t.* to tell damaging lies about; speak ill of; slander: *to malign someone's character.* —*adj.* harmful or evil; injurious.

ma·lig·nan·cy (mə lig′nən sē) *n., pl.* **ma·lig·nan·cies. 1.** the state or quality of being malignant. Also, **ma·lig·nance** (mə lig′nəns). **2.** any malignant disease or condition, especially a cancerous tumor.

ma·lig·nant (mə lig′nənt) *adj.* **1.** tending to spread through the body and eventually cause death: *a malignant tumor.* **2.** evil or harmful: *a malignant influence, malignant lies.* —**ma·lig′nant·ly,** *adv.*

ma·lig·ni·ty (mə lig′ni tē) *n., pl.* **ma·lig·ni·ties. 1.** the state or quality of being malign. **2.** something evil or harmful.

ma·lin·ger (mə ling′gər) *v.i.* to try to avoid work or duty, especially by pretending to be sick or injured. —**ma·lin′ger·er,** *n.*

mall (môl) *n.* **1.** a public walk or promenade that is often lined with trees. **2.** a shopping area closed off to vehicles. Also (def. 2.), **shopping mall.**

mal·lard (mal′ərd) *n., pl.* **mal·lards** or **mal·lard.** a common wild duck, the male of which has a green head, a white band around the neck, and a reddish brown breast.

mal·le·a·ble (mal′ē ə bəl) *adj.* **1.** able to be hammered, pressed, or beaten into various shapes without breaking: *a malleable metal.* **2.** easy to change or influence: *That young child has a malleable personality.* —**mal·le·a·bil·i·ty** (mal′ē ə bil′i tē), *n.*

mallard

mal·let (mal′it) *n.* **1.** a short-handled hammer with a heavy, usually wooden, head. **2.** a long-handled wooden hammer used to strike the ball in certain games, such as croquet or polo.

mal·le·us (mal′ē əs) *n., pl.* **mal·le·i** (mal′ē ī′). the largest and outermost of the three small bones in the middle ear, shaped like a hammer; hammer. See **stapes** for illustration.

mal·low (mal′ō) *n.* any of various plants having pink or white flowers.

malm·sey (mäm′zē) *n.* a sweet white wine.

mal·nour·ished (mal nûr′isht, mal nur′isht) *adj.* suffering from malnutrition; poorly fed; undernourished.

mal·nu·tri·tion (mal′nü trish′ən, mal′nū trish′ən) *n.* a condition caused by a lack of enough food or of the right kinds of food.

mal·oc·clu·sion (mal′ə klü′zhən) *n.* a condition in which the teeth of the upper and lower jaws do not meet properly.

mal·o·dor·ous (mal ō′dər əs) *adj.* having an unpleasant odor. —**mal·o′dor·ous·ly,** *adv.* —**mal·o′dor·ous·ness,** *n.*

mal·prac·tice (mal prak′tis) *n.* **1.** the improper or harmful treatment of a patient by a doctor. **2.** improper or wrong conduct in any professional or official position.

malt (môlt) *n.* **1.** a cereal grain, especially barley, steeped in warm water until it has sprouted, and then dried. Malt is used chiefly in brewing and distilling. **2.** an alcoholic beverage or liquor brewed from malt, such as beer or ale. —*v.t.* **1.** to cause (grain) to become malt. **2.** to treat or mix with malt.

malted milk 1. a powdered preparation consisting chiefly of dried milk and malted cereals. **2.** *also,* **malted.** a drink made by mixing this preparation with milk and sometimes ice cream.

Mal·tese (môl tēz′, môl tēs′) *n., pl.* **Mal·tese. 1.** a person who was born in or is a citizen of Malta. **2.** the language of Malta. —*adj.* of or relating to Malta, its people, or their language.

Maltese cat, a short-haired, bluish gray domestic cat.

Maltese cross, a cross with four arms that resemble arrowheads.

malt·ose (môl′tōs) *n.* a colorless compound formed by the action of an enzyme on starch. It is used as a foodstuff and as a sweetener.

mal·treat (mal trēt′) *v.t.* to treat badly or cruelly; abuse: *to maltreat an animal.* —**mal·treat′ment,** *n.*

ma·ma (mä′mə) *also,* **mam·ma.** *n. Informal.* mother.

mam·bo (mäm′bō) *n., pl.* **mam·bos. 1.** a Latin American dance. **2.** the music for this dance. —*v.i.* to dance the mambo.

mam·mal (mam′əl) *n.* any of a class of warm-blooded animals with backbones, the females of which have mammary glands. Almost all mammals give birth to live offspring rather than lay eggs. Human beings, dogs, elephants, porcupines, bats, cows, and whales are all mammals. —**mam·ma·li·an** (mə mā′lē ən), *adj.*

mam·ma·ry gland (mam′ə rē) a gland that produces milk, with which female mammals nourish their young.

mam·mo·gram (mam′ə gram′) *n.* an X ray of the breast to detect cancer or other abnormal conditions.

Mam·mon (mam′ən) *n.* **1.** the personification of riches and worldly gain. **2.** *usually,* **mammon.** riches regarded as an evil influence or as an object of greed.

at; āpe; fär; câre; end; mē; it; īce; pîerce; hot; ōld; sông, fôrk; oil; out; up; ūse; rüle; pull; tûrn; chin; sing; shop; thin; this; hw in white; zh in treasure. The symbol ə stands for the unstressed vowel sound heard in about, taken, pencil, lemon, and circus.

M

mam·moth (mam′əth) *n.* a large extinct prehistoric elephant that had long, upward-curving tusks and shaggy black hair. —*adj.* of immense size; huge; gigantic.

mam·my (mam′ē) *n., pl.* **mam·mies.** **1.** *Informal.* mother. **2.** formerly, a black woman who took care of white children in the southern United States.

mammoth *(n.)*

man (man) *n., pl.* **men.** **1.** an adult male human being. **2.** a member of the human race; human being; person: *All men are created equal.* **3.** human beings; the human race: *the study of man through the ages.* **4.** a male human being thought to have strength, courage, and the like. **5.** a male worker or servant. **6.** a husband: *to become man and wife.* **7.** one of the pieces used to play certain games, such as chess and checkers. —*v.t.*, **manned, man·ning. 1.** to supply with people, as for work or defense: *Soldiers manned the fort.* **2.** to take one's place or station at: *Man the torpedoes.*
·**to a man.** without exception; all: *We agree with you to a man.*

Man., Manitoba.

man·a·cle (man′ə kəl) *n.* **1.** *usually,* **manacles.** handcuffs. **2.** anything that restrains or binds. —*v.t.*, **man·a·cled, man·a·cling. 1.** to put manacles on: *Guards manacled the prisoners.* **2.** to restrain or bind; hamper.

man·age (man′ij) *v.*, **man·aged, man·ag·ing.** —*v.t.* **1.** to control or guide the affairs or operation of: *to manage a department store, to manage a political campaign.* **2.** to succeed in doing: *I'll manage to visit you before I leave.* **3.** to control or handle: *Can you manage that heavy package?* —*v.i.* to be able to succeed or get along: *I don't know how the team will manage without you.*

man·age·a·ble (man′i jə bəl) *adj.* capable of being managed: *a manageable horse.* —**man′age·a·bil′i·ty,** *n.* —**man′age·a·bly,** *adv.*

man·age·ment (man′ij mənt) *n.* **1.** the act, art, or practice of managing: *The company was bankrupted through bad management.* **2.** the person or persons who manage a business, institution, or the like: *the management of a hotel.*

man·ag·er (man′i jər) *n.* **1.** a person who manages something, especially a business: *the manager of a store, the manager of a baseball team.* **2.** a person who is skilled in managing. **3.** a person who manages the business affairs of an actor, singer, or the like. —**man′ag·er·ship′,** *n.*

man·a·ge·ri·al (man′ə jîr′ē əl) *adj.* of or relating to a manager or management: *managerial duties.*

ma·ña·na (mä nyä′nä) *Spanish. adv.* **1.** tomorrow. **2.** at some future time. —*n.* some future time.

man–at–arms (man′ət ärmz′) *n., pl.* **men–at–arms** (men′ət ärmz′). a heavily armed soldier in the Middle Ages.

man·a·tee (man′ə tē′) *n.* a sea mammal having two broad front flippers and a tail shaped like a paddle. The manatee is found in the warm coastal waters of the Atlantic Ocean.

manatee

Man·chu (man chü′) *n., pl.* **Man·chu** or **Man·chus. 1.** a member of a Mongolian people living in Manchuria, who conquered China in 1644 and established a dynasty that ruled until 1912. **2.** the language of the Manchus. —*adj.* of or relating to the Manchus or to their dynasty, language, or culture.

Man·dan (man′dan) *n., pl.* **Man·dan** or **Man·dans.** a member of a North American Indian tribe formerly living in the northern Great Plains and speaking a Siouan language.

man·da·rin (man′dər in) *n.* **1.** a member of any of the nine ranks of high public officials of imperial China. **2. Mandarin.** the principal dialect of the Chinese language. It is the official language of the People's Republic of China. **3.** see **mandarin orange.** —*adj.* of, relating to, or characteristic of a mandarin.

mandarin orange, a small, sweet orange having a thin rind that is easy to peel.

man·date (man′dāt) *n.* **1.** instruction or support given by voters to their representatives in government, expressed by the results of an election or vote. **2.** an official command, order, or charge. **3.** a commission given by the League of Nations to a member nation for the administration of a former German colony or other conquered territory. **4.** a territory so administered. —*v.t.*, **man·dat·ed, man·dat·ing. 1.** to place (a territory) under a mandate. **2.** to make mandatory; order or require: *The law mandates that toys be safe.*

man·da·to·ry (man′də tôr′ē) *adj.* **1.** required by a law, rule, order, or the like; officially commanded: *Fastening your seat belt when the plane takes off is mandatory.* **2.** of or relating to a mandate.

man·di·ble (man′də bəl) *n.* **1.** the bone of the lower jaw. **2.** the upper or lower part of a bird's beak. **3.** one of a pair of jawlike parts used for seizing and biting, on either side of the mouth opening in insects.

man·do·lin (man′də lin) *n.* a musical instrument having a pear-shaped body that is flat on one side and metal strings, usually played by plucking with a plectrum.

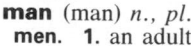

mandible *(def. 3)*

man·drake (man′drāk′) *n.* **1.** a low-growing plant having thick, fleshy roots, oval leaves, and cup-shaped flowers. **2.** the root of this plant, sometimes resembling a human body in form, formerly believed to have magical powers.

man·drel (man′drəl) *n.* **1.** a shaft, spindle, or similar piece for holding material to be shaped or worked, as on a lathe. **2.** a metal rod or core around which material may be shaped, cast, or bent.

man·drill (man′dril) *n.* a large ground-dwelling baboon of tropical western Africa. The male has brilliantly colored markings on the face and rump.

mane (mān) *n.* the long, heavy hair along the back and around the neck of certain animals, such as the horse and lion.

ma·neu·ver (mə nü′vər) *also, British,* **ma·noeu·vre.** *n.* **1.** a planned and strategic movement of troops or ships. **2.** *usually,* **maneuvers.** the training of large numbers of the armed forces under conditions that resemble combat. **3.** any skillful or clever move or plan: *political maneuvers.* —*v.t.* **1.** to cause (troops or ships) to perform a maneuver or maneuvers. **2.** to move or manage skillfully or cleverly: *I maneuvered my way through the crowd.* —*v.i.* **1.** to perform a maneuver or maneuvers. **2.** to use skillful or clever moves or plans. [From the French word *manoeuvre* meaning "action, handling" and "tactical action, maneuver," going back to the Latin words *manus* "hand, by hand" and *opere* meaning "to work."] —**ma·neu'·ver·er,** *n.*

ma·neu·ver·a·ble (mə nü'vər ə bəl) *adj.* capable of being maneuvered, especially easily: *That small airplane is more maneuverable than a big airliner.* —**ma·neu'·ver·a·bil'i·ty,** *n.*

man Friday 1. a dependable, faithful servant, aide, or follower. 2. a male employee, especially in an office, with many kinds of duties. [From *Friday,* the faithful servant and companion in Daniel Defoe's novel *Robinson Crusoe* (1719).]

man·ful (man'fəl) *adj.* having or showing a manly spirit; brave; resolute. —**man'ful·ly,** *adv.* —**man'ful·ness,** *n.*

man·ga·nese (mang'gə nēz', mang'gə nēs') *n.* a brittle, grayish white metallic element, used in the production of steel. Symbol: **Mn** [From the French word *manganèse,* from the Italian word *manganese* with the same meaning, going back to the Greek word *magnēsia,* applied to a variety of ores, from *Magnēsia,* an area of eastern Greece where manganese was found.]

mange (mānj) *n.* a contagious skin disease of cattle, horses, dogs, and other domestic animals. Mange is caused by certain mites, and is characterized by scaly pimples and often by a loss of hair.

man·ger (mān'jər) *n.* a box or trough used to hold feed for horses or cattle.

man·gle¹ (mang'gəl) *v.t.,* **man·gled, man·gling.** 1. to spoil or destroy, as by tearing or crushing; mutilate; disfigure: *The dog mangled the rubber toy by chewing on it.* 2. to make imperfect or mar; ruin; botch: *The inexperienced translator mangled the author's novel.* [From the Old French word *mangler* meaning "to mutilate, maim."]

man·gle² (mang'gəl) *n.* a machine for pressing and smoothing cloth by passing it between rollers. *v.t.,* **man·gled, man·gling.** to press or smooth with a mangle: *to mangle sheets.* [From the Dutch word *mangel* meaning this machine, going back to the Late Latin word *manganum,* a kind of catapult, from the Greek word *manganon* "a war machine."]

man·go (mang'gō) *n., pl.* **man·goes** or **man·gos.** 1. the yellowish red, oval, edible fruit of a tree of the cashew family. The mango has a sweet, spicy taste. 2. the tropical evergreen tree bearing this fruit.

mangroves

man·grove (man'grōv') *n.* any of several tropical trees found in marshy and coastal regions. Some mangroves have branches that send down roots resembling tree trunks.

man·gy (mān'jē) *adj.,* **man·gi·er, man·gi·est.** 1. having, resembling, or caused by mange: *a mangy cat.* 2. worn, dirty, and shabby; seedy: *a mangy old coat.* —**man'gi·ly,** *adv.* —**man'gi·ness,** *n.*

man·han·dle (man'han'dəl) *v.t.,* **man·han·dled, man·han·dling.** to handle or treat roughly: *The prisoners charged that the guards had manhandled them.*

man·hole (man'hōl') *n.* an opening, usually with a removable cover, through which a sewer, steam boiler, or other structure may be entered for inspection or repair.

man·hood (man'hud') *n.* 1. the state of being an adult male human being: *to reach manhood.* 2. character or qualities, such as strength and courage, considered to be manly. 3. men as a group.

man–hour (man'our') *n.* the amount of work that can be done by one person in one hour, used as a unit or standard of measurement in industry.

man·hunt (man'hunt') *n.* an intensive search for someone: *a manhunt for an escaped prisoner.*

ma·ni·a (mā'nē ə) *n.* 1. a great enthusiasm or desire: *The miser had a mania for gold coins.* 2. a form of mental illness characterized by great excitability, elation, and agitation.

ma·ni·ac (mā'nē ak') *n.* a person who is or seems wildly or violently insane; lunatic. —*adj.* another word for **maniacal.**

ma·ni·a·cal (mə nī'ə kəl) *adj.* 1. of, relating to, or characteristic of mania or a maniac: *maniacal laughter.* 2. wildly or violently insane: *a maniacal dictator.* Also, **maniac.** —**ma·ni'a·cal·ly,** *adv.*

man·ic (man'ik) *adj.* relating to, resembling, or affected by mania: *a manic personality, a manic mood, manic behavior.*

man·i·cure (man'i kyůr') *n.* the cleaning, shaping, and polishing of the fingernails. —*v.t.,* **man·i·cured, man·i·cur·ing.** 1. to give a manicure to. 2. to trim evenly, closely, or elaborately: *The gardener manicured the lawns of the park*

man·i·cur·ist (man'i kyůr'ist) *n.* a person who gives manicures.

man·i·fest (man'ə fest') *v.t.* 1. to make obvious or clear; show plainly: *I manifested my approval of the plan by nodding.* 2. to be evidence of; prove: *The firefighter's daring rescue of the child manifested great courage.* —*adj.* plainly apparent; evident; obvious. —*n.* a list of cargo or passengers for a ship or plane.

man·i·fes·ta·tion (man'ə fes tā'shən) *n.* 1. the act of manifesting or the state of being manifested. 2. something that manifests; indication; sign.

man·i·fes·to (man'ə fes'tō) *n., pl.* **man·i·fes·tos** or **man·i·fes·toes.** a public declaration of principles or goals, especially by a political group.

man·i·fold (man'ə fōld') *adj.* 1. of many kinds or varieties; multiple; diverse: *This job has manifold duties.* 2. having many parts or features: *The novel is a manifold portrait of society.* —*n.* a pipe fitting having several openings for connecting one pipe with others. The exhaust manifold of a car conducts exhaust (waste) gases from each cylinder of the engine to a single exhaust pipe.

man·i·kin (man'i kin) also, **man·ni·kin.** *n.* 1. a little man; dwarf. 2. an anatomical model of the human body, such as one used for teaching anatomy. 3. another spelling of **mannequin.**

M

at; āpe; fär; câre; end; mē; it; īce; pîerce; hot; ōld; sông, fôrk; oil; out; up; ūse; rüle; půll; tûrn; chin; sing; shop; thin; <u>th</u>is; hw in white; zh in treasure. The symbol ə stands for the unstressed vowel sound heard in about, taken, pencil, lemon, and circus.

ma·nil·a (mə nil′ə) *n.* **1.** see **Manila hemp. 2.** see **Manila paper.** —*adj.* made of Manila paper: *a manila envelope.*

Ma·nil·a hemp (mə nil′ə), a fiber obtained from the leaves of the abaca, widely used in the manufacture of rope, cord, and paper.

Manila paper, a strong, brown or yellow paper originally made from Manila hemp, used especially for bags, envelopes, and file folders.

man·i·oc (man′ē ok′) *n.* another word for **cassava** (*def. 1*).

ma·nip·u·late (mə nip′yə lāt′) *v.t.,* **ma·nip·u·lat·ed, ma·nip·u·lat·ing. 1.** to try to influence, adapt, or manage to one's own advantage: *They manipulated other people to do what they wanted.* **2.** to manage or work with the hands, especially in a skillful manner: *By manipulating a few wires, I repaired the telephone.* **3.** to change, falsify, or tamper with for one's own purpose or profit: *The cashier manipulated bank funds so that the theft would not be discovered.* —**ma·nip′u·la′tive,** *adj.* —**ma·nip′u·la′tor,** *n.*

ma·nip·u·la·tion (mə nip′yə lā′shən) *n.* the act of manipulating or the state of being manipulated.

man·i·tou (man′i tü′) *also,* **man·i·to, man·i·tu.** *n.* among the Algonquian Indians, a spirit or god that controls nature.

man·kind (*def. 1* man′kīnd′, *def. 2* man′kīnd′) *n.* **1.** human beings as a group; the human race. **2.** men as a group.

man·like (man′līk′) *adj.* **1.** suitable for a man; manly: *manlike bravery.* **2.** like a human being: *manlike apes.*

man·ly (man′lē) *adj.,* **man·li·er, man·li·est. 1.** having the qualities thought of as characteristic of a man. **2.** relating to or suitable for a man: *Football is a manly sport.* —**man′li·ness,** *n.*

man-made (man′mād′) *adj.* made by human beings, rather than formed by nature; synthetic; artificial: *There was man-made snow on the ski slope.*

man·na (man′ə) *n.* **1.** in the Old Testament, the food miraculously supplied to the Israelites during their flight from Egypt. **2.** anything that is badly needed and is unexpected: *The praise from classmates was manna to the shy student.*

manned (mand) *adj.* carrying or controlled by human beings: *a manned spacecraft.*

man·ne·quin (man′i kin) *also,* **man·i·kin.** *n.* **1.** a full-sized, usually jointed model of a human figure, used especially for displaying clothes. **2.** a woman who models clothes.

man·ner (man′ər) *n.* **1.** the way in which something happens or is done: *Please put a heading on your paper in the usual manner.* **2.** a way of acting or behaving: *The stranger's gruff manner frightened the children.* **3. manners.** ways of behaving or acting in social situations, especially polite ways of acting: *poor table manners.* **4.** kind or sort: *What manner of dog is that?* —**man′ner·less,** *adj.*

man·nered (man′ərd) *adj.* **1.** having (a specified kind of) manner or manners. ▲ used in combination: *well-mannered.* **2.** having mannerisms; stilted: *The actor gave a mannered performance.*

man·ner·ism (man′ə riz′əm) *n.* **1.** a peculiar trait or way of acting that has become habitual: *You have an annoying mannerism of rubbing your nose when you are talking.* **2.** an affected or exaggerated use of a particular manner or style: *The author's novel was full of mannerisms.*

man·ner·ly (man′ər lē) *adj.* having or showing good manners; polite. —*adv.* with good manners; politely. —**man′ner·li·ness,** *n.*

man·ni·kin (man′i kin) another spelling of **manikin** (*defs. 1 and 2*).

man·nish (man′ish) *adj.* **1.** thought to be suited to a man or men: *mannish furniture.* **2.** in a manner thought to be like that of a man or men: *She dresses in a mannish way.* —**man′nish·ly,** *adv.* —**man′nish·ness,** *n.*

ma·noeu·vre (mə nü′vər) *British. n., v.t., v.i.,* **ma·noeu·vred, ma·noeu·vring.** another spelling of **maneuver.**

man-of-war (man′əv wôr′) *n., pl.* **men-of-war.** an armed naval ship, usually rigged with sails.

man·or (man′ər) *n.* **1.** under the feudal system, an estate granted to a lord, in which part of the land was divided among serfs who paid rent to the lord in labor and goods. **2.** land largely farmed by tenants who pay rent to the owner. **3.** a mansion, especially the main house on an estate or manor.

ma·no·ri·al (mə nôr′ē əl) *adj.* of or like a manor.

man·pow·er (man′pou′ər) *n.* **1.** the total number of persons available for work, as in industry or the armed forces: *the manpower of the automobile industry.* **2.** power or force supplied by the physical work of human beings.

man·sard (man′särd) *n.* **1.** a roof having two slopes on all sides, with the lower slope almost vertical and the upper slope almost horizontal. **2.** the room or story under such a roof.

manse (mans) *n.* the home of a minister, especially of a Presbyterian minister; parsonage.

man·serv·ant (man′sûr′vənt) *n., pl.* **men·serv·ants.** a male servant.

man·sion (man′shən) *n.* a very large, stately, or imposing house.

man·slaugh·ter (man′slô′tər) *n.* **1.** the unlawful killing of a human being by another, without cold-blooded intent. **2.** the slaying of a human being by another.

man·ta (man′tə) *n.* a huge fish related to the shark, having a flat body, fins resembling wings, and a pair of fleshy horns on its head. The manta may weigh more than 3,000 pounds (1,360 kilograms). Also, **manta ray, devilfish.**

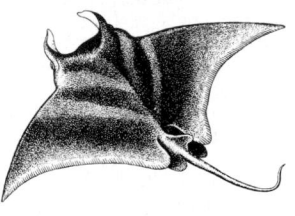

manta

man·tel (man′təl) *n.* **1.** a structure made of stone, brick, or other material that surrounds the opening of a fireplace. **2.** a shelf that is positioned above a fireplace. Also (*def. 2*), **man·tel·piece** (man′təl pēs′).

man·til·la (man til′ə, man tē′ə) *n.* a covering for the head worn by women, especially in Spain and Latin America. It is usually made of black or white lace.

man·tis (man′tis) *n., pl.* **man·tis·es** or **man·tes** (man′tēz). see **praying mantis.** [From the Greek word *mantis* meaning "prophet, seer." The way this insect holds its forelegs reminded people of a holy person praying.]

man·tle (man′təl) *n.* **1.** a loose cloak, usually without sleeves. **2.** something that covers, conceals, or envelops: *the mantle of night.* **3.** the layer of the earth's interior between the crust and the core. **4.** in mollusks, a fleshy fold of tissue that encloses the internal organs and secretes the shell. **5.** the feathers on the back and wings of a bird. —*v.t.,* **man·tled, man·tling.** to cover with or as if with a mantle; conceal; envelop: *The snow mantled the whole countryside in white.*

man·tra (man′trə) *n.* in Hinduism and Buddhism, a prayer or incantation, often thought to possess magical power.

man·u·al (man′ū əl) *adj.* **1.** relating to, done by, or involving the use of the hands: *manual crafts, manual labor.* **2.** operated by hand: *a manual control.* —*n.* a book of basic instructions or other information on a particular subject; handbook. [From the Old French word *manuel* meaning "by hand," from the Latin word *manualis*

580

"by or with the hands," from the word *manus* "hand."]
—**man'u·al·ly,** *adv.*

manual alphabet, an alphabet used to communicate with the deaf, consisting of a series of signs made with the fingers, each sign representing a letter of the written alphabet.

manual training, practical training in work involving the use of the hands, such as woodworking.

man·u·fac·ture (man'yə fak'chər) *v.t.,* **man·u·fac·tured, man·u·fac·tur·ing. 1.** to make or produce (a product), especially on a large scale by means of machinery. **2.** to make or process (a raw material) into a form or product suitable for use: *to manufacture wool into cloth.* **3.** to make up; invent: *to manufacture an excuse.* —*n.* **1.** the act or process of manufacturing. **2.** something manufactured; product. [From the French word *manufacture* meaning "a making, workmanship," going back to the Latin phrase *manu factura* "a making by hand," from the words *manus* "hand" and *facere* "to do, make."]

man·u·fac·tur·er (man'yə fak'chər ər) *n.* a person or company whose business is manufacturing.

ma·nure (mə nur', mə nyūr') *n.* a natural substance, especially the waste matter of domestic animals, used as fertilizer. —*v.t.,* **ma·nured, ma·nur·ing.** to put manure in or on. [From the Middle English word *mainouren* meaning "to till²," from the Anglo-Norman word *meinoverer* "to manage," going back to the Latin words *manus* "hand" and *operare* "to labor, work."]

man·u·script (man'yə skript') *n.* **1.** the typewritten or handwritten version of a book, article, or other work, prepared for a publisher or printer. **2.** a book or document written or copied by hand, especially one from before the invention of printing.

Manx (mangks) *n.* **1. the Manx.** the people of the Isle of Man. **2.** the language originally spoken by the Manx, now nearly extinct. —*adj.* of or relating to the Isle of Man, its people, or their language.

Manx cat, a short-haired domestic cat having long hind legs, a high, rounded rump, and, usually, no tail.

man·y (men'ē) *adj.,* **more, most.** consisting of or amounting to a large number; numerous: *The library has many books on history.* —*n.* **1.** a large number: *Many of my friends were at the picnic.* **2. the many.** the majority of people. —*pron.* a large number of persons or things: *Many were late for the party because of the storm.*

Mao·ism (mou'iz əm) *n.* the political theories, principles, and practices of Mao Zedong.

Mao·ist (mou'ist) *n.* a person who believes in or supports Maoism. —*adj.* of or relating to Mao Zedong or Maoism.

Ma·o·ri (mä ôr'ē, mou'rē) *n., pl.* **Ma·o·ri** or **Ma·o·ris. 1.** a member of a Polynesian people living in New Zealand.

2. the language of these people. —*adj.* of or relating to the Maoris, their language, or their culture.

map (map) *n.* **1.** a drawing or other representation of all or part of the earth's surface, usually showing cities, rivers, oceans, mountains, and other features. **2.** a drawing or representation of all or part of the sky, usually showing the position of the stars and planets. —*v.t.,* **mapped, map·ping.** to make a map of; represent on a map. [From the Medieval Latin phrase *mappa (mundi)* meaning "map (of the world)," from the Latin word *mappa* "napkin" or "painted cloth."]
·**off the map.** out of existence: *The enemy threatened to wipe the town off the map.*
·**to map out.** to plan in detail: *to map out a political campaign.*
·**to put on the map.** *Informal.* to make well-known: *The discovery of oil in the area put the town on the map.*

ma·ple (mā'pəl) *n.* **1.** any of a large group of trees and some shrubs growing throughout the Northern Hemisphere, usually having lobed leaves and paired winged fruits. **2.** the wood of these trees, used in the manufacture of furniture. **3.** the flavor of maple syrup or of maple sugar.

maple sugar, a sugar made by boiling down maple syrup.

maple syrup, a syrup made by boiling and concentrating the sap of the sugar maple or of any other maple tree.

mar (mär) *v.t.,* **marred, mar·ring. 1.** to spoil the appearance of; damage: *Water stains marred the table top.* **2.** to damage the quality or character of; impair: *Their rude behavior marred an otherwise enjoyable evening.*

Mar., March.

mar·a·bou (mar'ə bü') *n.* **1.** any of several storks of Africa, India, and southeastern Asia, having white, black, and gray feathers. **2.** the soft, downy feathers of this bird, often used in trimming hats. **3.** the trimming or material made from such feathers.

ma·ra·ca (mə rä'kə) *n.* a musical instrument made of a dried gourd or gourd-shaped rattle that contains seeds or pebbles, often played in pairs.

mar·a·schi·no cherry (mar'ə skē'nō, mar'ə shē'nō) a cherry preserved in a sweet syrup, often used in making drinks.

mar·a·thon (mar'ə thon') *n.* **1.** a foot race of 26 miles and 385 yards (approximately 42 kilo-

aerial view of runners in a **marathon**

meters), run over an open course. **2.** any long race or other competition testing the endurance of the participants; endurance contest: *a dance marathon.* [From the legend that a Greek messenger ran 26 miles from the battlefield at *Marathon* to Athens to announce the Athenian victory over the Persians in 490 B.C.]

ma·raud (mə rôd′) *v.i.* to roam or wander in search of plunder; make raids for booty. —*v.t.* to plunder; raid.

ma·raud·er (mə rô′dər) *n.* a person who roams in search of booty or plunder.

mar·ble (mär′bəl) *n.* **1.** a hard stone formed of crystallized limestone, usually mottled or streaked with swirls of different colors, widely used in architecture and sculpture. **2.** a piece, block, or slab of marble. **3.** something made of or resembling marble. **4.** a small, hard ball of glass or other material used in children's games. **5. marbles.** any of various games played with a number of these balls. ▲ used with a singular verb. —*adj.* made of or resembling marble. —*v.t.,* **mar·bled, mar·bling.** to color or streak in imitation of marble. [From the Old French word *marbre* meaning this stone, from the Latin word *marmor* "marble stone," from the Greek word *marmaros* "marble stone."]

march[1] (märch) *v.i.* **1.** to walk with regular, measured steps, especially in an orderly group or formation: *The soldiers marched down the avenue.* **2.** to move in a steady, deliberate, or solemn manner: *The children marched off to bed soon after supper.* **3.** to go or move forward steadily: *Time marches on.* —*v.t.* to cause (someone) to march: *The sergeant marched the troops up and down the field.* —*n., pl.* **march·es. 1.** the act of marching. **2.** the distance covered by a march: *a twenty-mile march.* **3.** a steady forward movement: *the march of time.* **4.** a regular measured step. **5.** a musical composition having a strong, steady beat and suitable for marching. [From the Old French word *marchier* meaning "to trample," of Germanic origin.] —**march′er,** *n.*

march[2] (märch) *n., pl.* **march·es.** *usually,* **marches.** a region along the border of a country; frontier. [From the Old French word *marche* meaning "boundary" or "border district," of Germanic origin.]

March (märch) *n., pl.* **March·es.** the third month of the year, having thirty-one days. [From the Anglo-Norman word *Marche* meaning this month, from the Latin phrase *Martius (mensis)* "(month) of Mars," from *Mars,* the Roman god of war.]

mar·chion·ess (mär′shə nis) *n., pl.* **mar·chion·ess·es.** *British.* another word for **marquise.**

Mar·di Gras (mär′dē grä′) **1.** the last day before Lent. Also, **Shrove Tuesday. 2.** the celebration held on or ending on this day, marked by parades and festivities.

mare[1] (mâr) *n.* the full-grown female of certain animals, such as the horse, donkey, or zebra. [From the Old English word *mere* meaning "female horse."]

ma·re[2] (mär′ā) *n., pl.* **ma·ri·a.** any of various dark, smooth lowlands on the surface of the moon or Mars. [From the Latin word *mare* meaning "sea."] These lunar features were named by the Italian astronomer Galileo (1564–1642), who thought they were seas.]

mar·ga·rine (mär′jər in, mär′jə rēn′) *n.* a food product usually made from vegetable oil with milk or water and salt, used as a substitute for butter. Also, **oleomargarine.**

mar·gin (mär′jin) *n.* **1.** the blank space around the written or printed matter on a page. **2.** the amount allowed or available in addition to what is necessary or needed: *In this rainy weather, allow a margin of fifteen minutes for driving home.* **3.** the amount or degree of difference: *We won the game by a narrow margin.* **4.** an edge or border: *the margin of a river.* **5.** the difference between the cost and selling price of merchandise. **6.** the percentage of the total purchase price of stocks and bonds

that the purchaser has to pay in cash. —*v.t.* to provide with a margin; border.

mar·gin·al (mär′jə nəl) *adj.* **1.** written or printed in the margin of a page: *marginal notes.* **2.** relating to, forming, or located near an edge or border: *the marginal territories of an empire.* **3.** barely enough: *marginal ability.* **4.** making very little profit. —**mar′gin·al·ly,** *adv.*

mar·gue·rite (mär′gə rēt′) *n.* **1.** a daisy having a yellow center surrounded by white or yellow petal-like florets. **2.** any of several other plants that resemble daisies.

ma·ri·a (mär′ē ə) the plural of **mare**[2].

mar·i·gold (mar′i gōld′) *n.* **1.** a fragrant yellow, orange, or red flower of any of a group of plants. **2.** the plant bearing this flower. **3.** any of various other plants, such as the pot marigold and the marsh marigold. [From the Middle English word *marigolde* meaning "Mary's gold," used as the name of this flower, from the words *Marie* meaning "Mary, the mother of Jesus" + *gold* meaning "gold."]

mar·i·jua·na (mar′ə wä′nə) *also,* **mar·i·hua·na.** *n.* **1.** a drug obtained from the dried flowering tops and leaves of the hemp plant. **2.** the hemp plant.

ma·rim·ba (mə rim′bə) *n.* a musical instrument resembling a large xylophone. The marimba is made up of a series of tuned wooden bars and is played by striking the bars with hand-held hammers. [Of Bantu origin.]

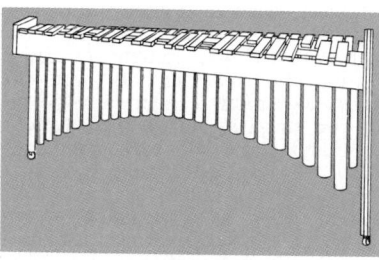

marimba

ma·ri·na (mə-rē′nə) *n.* a dock or basin with various facilities for mooring and, often, supplying and repairing small boats.

mar·i·nade (mar′ə nād′, mar′ə näd′) *n.* a mixture, usually containing vinegar or wine, oil, and various spices, in which food is soaked before cooking. —*v.t.,* **mar·i·nad·ed, mar·i·nad·ing.** to marinate.

mar·i·nate (mar′ə nāt′) *v.t.,* **mar·i·nat·ed, mar·i·nat·ing.** to soak (food) in a marinade.

ma·rine (mə rēn′) *adj.* **1.** of or relating to the sea: *marine ecology.* **2.** living in the sea: *marine animals.* **3.** of, relating to, or used in sea navigation; nautical: *a marine barometer.* **4.** of or relating to commerce or shipping on the sea; maritime. **5.** of or relating to the navy or naval affairs. —*n.* **1. Marine.** a member of the U.S. Marine Corps. **2.** a soldier serving on a ship. [From the Old French word *marine,* from the Latin word *marinus* "of the sea," from the word *mare* "sea."]

marine biologist, a student of or an expert in marine biology.

marine biology, the study of plants and animals living in the sea.

Marine Corps, a branch of the armed forces of the United States, under the Department of the Navy, that specially trains troops for overseas landing operations. Also, **Marines.**

mar·i·ner (mar′ə nər) *n.* a person who navigates or assists in navigating a ship; sailor.

mar·i·o·nette (mar′ē ə net′) *n.* a small jointed figure, often of wood, moved by strings, wires, or rods held from above.

mar·i·tal (mar′i təl) *adj.* of or relating to marriage: *marital vows, marital problems.* —**mar′i·tal·ly,** *adv.*

mar·i·time (mar′i tīm′) *adj.* **1.** bordering on, close to, or living near the sea: *a maritime town, a maritime people.* **2.** of or relating to the sea or to navigation, commerce, or shipping on the sea: *maritime law.*

mar·jo·ram (mär′jər əm) *n.* **1.** an herb related to mint. **2.** the dried leaves of this herb, used as a spice.

mark¹ (märk) *n.* **1.** any visible trace, such as a line, spot, scratch, or stain, left by an object or substance when it comes into contact with the surface of another object or substance. **2.** a sign or symbol used in writing or printing: *a mark of punctuation.* **3.** a label, seal, inscription, or stamp placed on an object to identify or distinguish it. **4.** a number or letter used to show the level or quality of a person's work: *to get high marks in school.* **5.** an indication of some quality, feature, or characteristic: *The delicate carving on the bench is a mark of good craftsmanship.* **6.** something, as a line or object, used as a guide, indicator, or point of reference: *The racers have reached the halfway mark.* **7.** something aimed at; target or goal: *The archer missed the mark.* **8.** a permanent impression or influence: *a writer who left a mark on literature.* **9.** an accepted standard: *Your work is below the mark.* **10.** the starting line of a race: *On your mark, get set, go!* —*v.t.* **1.** to make or put a mark or marks on: *The children marked the sidewalk with chalk.* **2.** to trace, form, or show the limits or boundaries of: *to mark a route on a map.* **3.** to write down, show, or represent by marks: *I marked my initials on the package.* **4.** to be a feature or characteristic of: *Formality marked the occasion.* **5.** to give or assign a mark to; grade: *The teacher marked the tests.* **6.** to pay attention to; heed: *Mark my words or you will be sorry.* [From the Old English word *mearc* meaning "a limit, boundary" and "a sign, mark¹."]
·**beside the mark** or **wide of the mark. a.** missing what is aimed at. **b.** not to the point; not relevant.
·**to hit the mark. a.** to be accurate; be right. **b.** to attain one's goal; be successful.
·**to make one's mark.** to become famous or successful.
·**to mark down. a.** to write down. **b.** to reduce the price of.
·**to mark time. a.** to move the feet as in marching, but without going forward. **b.** to perform the actions of something without really accomplishing anything.
·**to mark up.** to increase the price of.
·**to miss the mark. a.** to be inaccurate; be wrong. **b.** to fail to attain one's goal; be unsuccessful.

mark² (märk) *n.* **1.** see **deutsche mark. 2.** see **ostmark.** [From the German word *Mark* meaning this unit of money.]

Mark (märk) *n.* the second book of the New Testament, believed to have been written by the Evangelist Mark.

mark·down (märk′doun′) *n.* a reduction in the selling price of an item.

marked (märkt) *adj.* **1.** very noticeable; obvious: *There is a marked similarity between the two sisters.* **2.** singled out, as for vengeance, punishment, or death: *a marked man.* **3.** having a mark or marks.

mark·ed·ly (mär′kid lē) *adv.* in a marked manner; clearly; obviously.

mark·er (mär′kər) *n.* **1.** a person who marks. **2.** something that marks a place, as a bookmark or gravestone.

mar·ket (mär′kit) *n.* **1.** an open space or building where food products or goods are bought and sold; marketplace: *The farmer took vegetables to the market every week.* **2.** a shop or store where food products are sold: *a fish market.* **3.** a region or country where goods can be bought and sold: *The company manufactures leather goods for many foreign markets.* **4.** trade and commerce in a particular service or commodity: *the grain market.* **5.** demand for something: *There is very little market for buggy whips today.* **6.** the available supply of a particular service or commodity: *New York has a large labor market.* **7.** see **stock market.** —*v.i.* to buy food products and other household items in a market: *We go marketing every Thursday.* —*v.t.* to sell or offer for sale: *The farmer markets vegetables in town.*
·**on the market.** available for purchase: *That company*

is famous for making the best television sets on the market.
·**to be in the market for.** to be interested in buying.

mar·ket·a·ble (mär′ki tə bəl) *adj.* fit for sale; salable. —**mar′ket·a·bil′i·ty,** *n.*

mar·ket·place (mär′kit plās′) *n.* **1.** a place where food products or goods are bought and sold. **2.** business and business activities in general.

mark·ing (mär′king) *n.* **1.** a mark or marks. **2.** *also,* **markings.** the arrangement of marks and colors on a plant or animal: *a bird with red markings.* **3.** the act of making a mark or marks on something.

marks·man (märks′mən) *n., pl.* **marks·men** (märks′-mən). a person who is skilled in shooting a gun or other weapon.

marks·man·ship (märks′mən ship′) *n.* skill in shooting a gun or other weapon.

mark·up (märk′up′) *n.* an increase in the selling price of an item.

marl (märl) *n.* a clay containing calcium carbonate and, often, fragments of shells, used in making portland cement and as a fertilizer.

mar·lin (mär′lin) *n., pl.* **mar·lin** or **mar·lins.** a saltwater game fish related to the sailfish and having a long, spear-shaped bill.

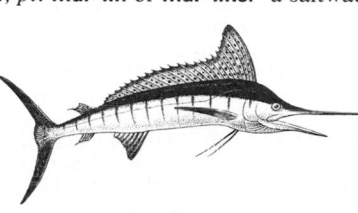

marlin

mar·line (mär′-lin) *n.* a small cord consisting of two strands loosely twisted together, used, as on ships, for winding around the ends of ropes or cables to prevent fraying.

mar·line·spike (mär′lin spīk′) *also,* **mar·lin·spike.** *n.* a pointed iron pin used to separate strands of rope, as in splicing.

mar·ma·lade (mär′mə lād′) *n.* a jam made by boiling the peel and flesh of fruit, usually citrus fruit, with sugar.

mar·mo·set (mär′mə zet′, mär′mə set′) *n.* a small monkey of Central and South America, having shaggy or soft and fine fur, long curved claws except on the big toe, and a long tail.

mar·mot (mär′mət) *n.* any of several large rodents having a coarse gray or brown coat and a bushy tail, such as the woodchuck.

ma·roon¹ (mə rün′) *n.* a dark brownish red color. —*adj.* having the color maroon. [From the French word *marron* meaning "a kind of chestnut."]

ma·roon² (mə rün′) *v.t.* **1.** to put ashore and leave on a desolate island or coast. **2.** to leave helpless and alone.

marmoset

[From the Spanish word *cimarrón* meaning "wild." The word *cimarrón* later meant "runaway slave," especially one who escaped to an island or some other remote place.]

mar·quee (mär kē′) *n.* a canopy placed over the entrance to a theater, hotel, or other building.

mar·quess (mär′kwis) *n., pl.* **mar·quess·es.** *British.* another spelling of **marquis.**

M

mar·quis (mär′kwis, mär kē′) *also, British,* **mar·quess.** *n., pl.* **mar·quis·es** or **mar·quis** (mär kēz′). a nobleman ranking next below a duke and above an earl or count.

mar·quise (mär kēz′) *n.* **1.** the wife or widow of a marquis. **2.** a woman holding in her own right the rank equal to that of a marquis.

mar·riage (mar′ij) *n.* **1.** the state of being married; wedlock: *a happy marriage.* **2.** the act of marrying. **3.** the ceremony accompanying this. **4.** a close union: *the marriage of comedy and drama in a play.*

mar·riage·a·ble (mar′i jə bəl) *adj.* suitable for marriage.

mar·ried (mar′ēd) *adj.* **1.** joined in marriage: *a married couple.* **2.** having a husband or wife. **3.** of or relating to marriage or married persons: *married life.*

mar·row (mar′ō) *n.* **1.** a soft tissue that fills the cavities and spongy parts of bones and that produces blood cells. **2.** the innermost, best, or most important part.

mar·row·bone (mar′ō bōn′) *n.* a bone containing marrow that can be eaten, used for making soups and stews.

mar·ry[1] (mar′ē) *v.,* **mar·ried, mar·ry·ing.** —*v.t.* **1.** to take as a husband or wife; wed. **2.** to join as husband and wife; unite in wedlock: *A judge will marry the couple.* **3.** to give in marriage. **4.** to join closely; unite: *The dish marries beef and peppers.* —*v.i.* **1.** to take a husband or wife; enter into marriage: *They married at a young age.* **2.** to become joined closely. [From the Old French word *marier* "to give in marriage, wed," from the Latin word *maritare* "to wed."]

mar·ry[2] (mar′ē) *interj. Archaic.* an exclamation of anger, surprise, or indignation. [From the Middle English exclamation *marie!* with the same meaning, from *Marie,* Mary, the mother of Jesus.]

Mars (märz) *n.* **1.** *Roman Mythology.* the god of war. In Greek mythology he was called Ares. **2.** the seventh largest planet of the solar system and fourth in order of distance from the sun, having two moons.

marsh (märsh) *n., pl.* **marsh·es.** an area of low, wet land covered with grasses or similar plants, such as reeds.

mar·shal (mär′shəl) *n.* **1.** an officer of a federal court who is appointed to a judicial district to perform duties similar to those of a sheriff. **2.** in some states, a law officer of a city or borough having powers similar to those of a sheriff. **3.** the head of a city police or fire department. **4.** see **field marshal. 5.** a person in charge of arranging ceremonies and processions, such as parades. —*v.t.,* **mar·shaled, mar·shal·ing;** *also, British,* **mar·shalled, mar·shal·ling. 1.** to arrange in proper or logical order: *I marshaled my arguments for the debate.* **2.** to organize or place (soldiers) in proper order: *The general marshaled the troops for battle.* [From the Old French word *mareschal* meaning "high official," going back to the Old High German word *marahscalc* "high official," earlier meaning "a groom," from the words *marah* "horse" + *scalc* "servant."]

Mar·shall Plan (mär′shəl), a U.S. plan for economic aid to western Europe after World War II. [From U.S. Secretary of State George C. *Marshall* (1880–1959), who introduced it.]

marsh gas, another term for **methane.**

marsh·land (märsh′land′) *n.* an area that has marshes or swamps.

marsh·mal·low (märsh′mel′ō, märsh′mal′ō) *n.* a soft, usually white, spongy candy made from starch, sugar, gelatin, and corn syrup and covered with powdered sugar. [From *marsh mallow.* This candy was originally made from the root of the marsh mallow.]

marsh mallow, a tall, leafy plant growing wild in eastern Europe and the eastern United States, bearing downy, oval or heart-shaped leaves and bluish to pink flowers. [From the Old English word *merscmealwe* meaning this

plant, from the words *mersc* "a marsh" + *mealwe* "the mallow plant."]

marsh marigold, any of several plants that grow in damp areas, bearing large heart- or kidney-shaped leaves and flowers often resembling buttercups. Also, **cowslip.**

marsh·y (mär′shē) *adj.,* **marsh·i·er, marsh·i·est.** relating to, containing, or like a marsh or marshes: *marshy land.* —**marsh′i·ness,** *n.*

mar·su·pi·al (mär sü′pē əl) *n.* any of various animals, such as kangaroos, wombats, and opossums, the female of which has a pouch in which the young continue to develop after birth. —*adj.* of or relating to a marsupial.

mart (märt) *n.* a trading center; market: *a new food mart.*

mar·ten (mär′tən) *n., pl.* **mar·tens** or **mar·ten. 1.** an animal resembling the weasel, having thick, soft, golden or dark brown fur. **2.** the fur of this animal, made into coats, stoles, and trimmings; sable.

marten *(def. 1)*

mar·tial (mär′shəl) *adj.* **1.** of, relating to, or suitable for war or military life: *martial music.* **2.** of or characteristic of a warrior; warlike: *a martial spirit.* [From the Latin word *Martialis* meaning "relating to Mars," from *Mars,* the Roman god of warfare.]

martial art, any of the Oriental methods of unarmed combat or self-defense, as karate or jujitsu.

martial law, military rule or authority imposed on a civilian population during a time of war or other emergency.

Mar·tian (mär′shən) *adj.* of or relating to the planet Mars. —*n.* a supposed inhabitant of the planet Mars.

mar·tin (mär′tən) *n.* any of various dark-colored swallows found throughout the world.

mar·ti·net (mär′tə net′) *n.* a person who maintains strict discipline: *The drill sergeant was a martinet.*

mar·tin·gale (mär′tən gāl′) *n.* a strap of a horse's harness attached under the belly and secured to the head. It prevents the horse from rearing or throwing back its head.

mar·ti·ni (mär tē′nē) *n.* a cocktail made with gin or vodka and dry vermouth.

Martin Luther King Day, the third Monday in January or January 15, observed as a legal holiday in some states of the United States in honor of Martin Luther King, Jr.

mar·tyr (mär′tər) *n.* **1.** a person who suffers death rather than give up his or her religious faith. **2.** a person who dies, suffers greatly, or sacrifices all for a belief, principle, or cause. **3.** a person who willingly suffers greatly or sacrifices much. —*v.t.* **1.** to make a martyr of. **2.** to cause to suffer greatly; torture or persecute.

mar·tyr·dom (mär′tər dəm) *n.* **1.** the state or condition of being a martyr. **2.** the death or suffering of a martyr. **3.** extreme pain or suffering; torture; torment.

mar·vel (mär′vəl) *n.* a wonderful or astonishing thing: *Penicillin is one of the marvels of modern medicine.* —*v.i.,* **mar·veled, mar·vel·ing;** *also, British,* **mar·velled, mar·vel·ling.** to be or become filled with wonder or astonishment: *We marveled at the acrobat's skill.*

mar·vel·ous (mär′və ləs) *also, British,* **mar·vel·lous.** *adj.* **1.** causing or exciting wonder or astonishment: *a marvelous invention.* **2.** very good: *We had a marvelous vacation.*

Marx·ism (märk′siz əm) *n.* the theories of Karl Marx.

Marx·ist (märk′sist) *n.* a person who believes in or supports Marxism. —*adj.* of or relating to Karl Marx or Marxism. Also, **Marx·i·an** (märk′sē ən).

masc., masculine.

mas·car·a (mas kar'ə) *n.* a cosmetic preparation used to color the eyelashes.

mas·cot (mas'kot) *n.* an animal, person, or thing kept to bring good luck, especially a pet animal kept by an athletic team: *The school mascot was an especially large bulldog.*

mas·cu·line (mas'kyə lin) *adj.* **1.** of, relating to, or thought to be characteristic of a man: *masculine interests.* **2.** having qualities or characteristics regarded as manly. **3.** (of a woman) mannish. **4.** *Grammar.* of or designating one of the genders or classes of words. In English, words of masculine gender apply to persons or things assumed to be male.

mas·cu·lin·i·ty (mas'kyə lin'i tē) *n.* the state or quality of being masculine.

ma·ser (mā'zər) *n.* an electronic device that produces or amplifies electromagnetic waves. [Short for *m*(icrowave) *a*(mplification by) *s*(timulated) *e*(mission of) *r*(adiation).]

mash (mash) *n., pl.* **mash·es. 1.** a feed that consists of a mixture of ground grains, fed either wet or dry to livestock or poultry. **2.** ground or crushed malt or meal combined with water, used to make beer or whiskey. **3.** any soft, pulpy mass or mixture. —*v.t.* **1.** to make into a soft, pulpy mass or mixture: *to mash potatoes.* **2.** to mix (ground malt) with hot water in making beer or whiskey. **3.** to cause to be crushed or squeezed. —**mash·er,** *n.*

American Indian
mask

African
mask

mask (mask) *n.* **1.** a covering worn over all or part of the face, used to hide or disguise one's identity: *Everyone at the costume party wore a mask.* **2.** a covering of metal, plastic, wire, or other material, worn on the face for protection, as in certain sports or occupations: *Baseball catchers wear masks.* **3.** a molded or sculptured likeness of a face, often made of plaster or clay. **4.** anything that hides, disguises, or conceals. **5.** see **gas mask.** —*v.t.* **1.** to cover with a mask: *We masked our faces for the Halloween party.* **2.** to hide, disguise, or conceal: *A high wall masked the house from the road. A smile masked my disappointment.*

masking tape, an adhesive tape that can be removed easily, used especially to cover and protect surfaces, as during painting.

mas·o·chism (mas'ə kiz'əm) *n.* an abnormal tendency to derive pleasure from being hurt, punished, or embarrassed. [From the German novelist Leopold von Sacher-*Masoch* (1836–1895), who described this behavior.]

ma·son (mā'sən) *n.* **1.** a person whose occupation is building with stone, brick, or concrete. **2. Mason.** see **Freemason.**

Ma·son–Dix·on line (mā'sən dik'sən) the boundary line between Maryland and Pennsylvania, regarded as the boundary between the free and the slave states before the Civil War. It is now a symbolic boundary between the North and South.

Ma·son·ic (mə son'ik) *adj.* of, relating to, or characteristic of Freemasons or Freemasonry.

Ma·son jar (mā'sən) a glass jar that is used for home canning. It has a wide mouth and a metal top consisting of a lid with a rubber rim that makes an airtight seal when a separate fastener is screwed on.

ma·son·ry (mā'sən rē) *n., pl.* **ma·son·ries. 1.** something built by a mason, especially in stone. **2.** the art, skill, or occupation of a mason. **3. Masonry.** see **Freemasonry.**

masque (mask) *n.* **1.** an elaborate form of dramatic entertainment popular in the sixteenth and seventeenth centuries, in which the performers often wore masks. **2.** see **masquerade** (*def. 1*).

mas·quer·ade (mas'kə rād') *n.* **1.** a social gathering at which masks and costumes are worn. **2.** a false outward show; pretense. —*v.i.* **mas·quer·ad·ed, mas·quer·ad·ing. 1.** to take part in a masquerade. **2.** to assume a false appearance or identity; disguise oneself; pose: *The car thief masqueraded as a mechanic.* —**mas'quer·ad'er,** *n.*

mass (mas) *n., pl.* **mass·es. 1.** a body of matter holding or sticking together without a particular shape: *a mass of snow.* **2.** a large quantity, amount, or number: *a mass of people.* **3.** size or bulk: *The hippopotamus has great mass.* **4.** the main or greater part; majority: *The mass of parents attended the meeting of the school board.* **5.** *Physics.* a property of matter, used as a measure of the quantity of matter a body contains. **6. the masses.** the common people. —*v.t., v.i.* to gather or form into a mass; assemble: *The police massed the crowd behind the barricades. The people massed together in front of the theater.*

Mass (mas) *also,* **mass.** *n., pl.* **Mass·es. 1.** the main ceremony of worship in the Roman Catholic and certain Anglican churches. **2.** music written for certain parts of this service.

Mass., Massachusetts.

Mas·sa·chu·set (mas'ə chü'sit) *also,* **Mas·sa·chu·sett.** *n., pl.* **Mas·sa·chu·set** or **Mas·sa·chu·sets.** a member of a North American Indian tribe formerly living in present-day Massachusetts and speaking an Algonquian language.

mas·sa·cre (mas'ə kər) *n.* a brutal, wholesale slaughter of people or animals. —*v.t.,* **mas·sa·cred, mas·sa·cring.** to kill brutally and in large numbers.

mas·sage (mə säzh', mə säj') *n.* the rubbing or kneading of parts of the body to increase circulation or relax muscles. —*v.t.,* **mas·saged, mas·sag·ing.** to give a massage to.

mass–en·er·gy equation (mas'en'ər jē) an equation, $E = mc^2$, expressing the relation of mass and energy. In the equation, E = energy, m = mass, c = the velocity of light.

mas·seur (mə sûr') *n.* a man whose occupation is giving massages.

mas·seuse (mə süs', mə süz') *n.* a woman whose occupation is giving massages.

mas·sive (mas'iv) *adj.* **1.** consisting of or forming a large mass; having great size and weight: *The vault had massive*

---

at; āpe; fär; câre; end; mē; it; īce; pîerce; hot; ōld; sông, fôrk; oil; out; up; ūse; rūle; pull; tûrn; chin; sing; shop; thin; **th**is; hw in white; zh in treasure. The symbol ə stands for the unstressed vowel sound heard in about, taken, pencil, lemon, and circus.

M

steel doors. **2.** imposing or exceedingly large, as in scope, size, degree, or intensity: *a massive bombing raid.* —**mas'sive·ly,** *adv.* —**mas'sive·ness,** *n.*

mass media *pl., sing.* **mass medium.** the various forms of public communication, such as television, newspapers, and radio, that reach large audiences.

mass meeting, a large public gathering of people to discuss, listen to discussion of, or act on some matter of common interest.

mass noun, a noun that names a general thing or idea that cannot be counted. *Mud* and *snow* are mass nouns; *hat, car,* and *dog* are not.

mass number, the total number of protons and neutrons in the nucleus of an atom.

mass–pro·duce (mas'prə düs', mas'prə düs') *v.t.,* **mass-pro·duced, mass-pro·duc·ing.** to manufacture or produce (goods) in large quantities, especially by the use of machinery and assembly lines.

mass production, the act or process of mass-producing.

mass transit, public transportation in a large city or urban area, usually consisting of some combination of buses, subways, and trains.

mast (mast) *n.* **1.** an upright pole in a sailing boat or ship to support the yards, sails, and rigging. **2.** any upright pole, as of a crane.

mas·tec·to·my (mastek'tə mē) *n., pl.* **mastec·to·mies.** surgical removal of a breast, sometimes accompanied by removal of muscles and other tissues near the breast. [From the Greek word *mastos* meaning "breast" + the English suffix *-ectomy.*]

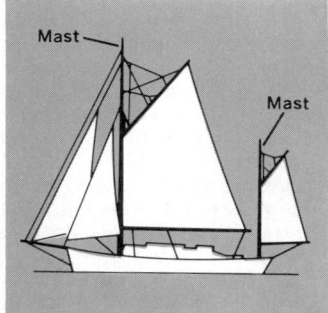

mas·ter (mas'tər) *n.*
1. a person who is in possession of or has power, control, or authority over someone or something: *The dog obeyed its master.* **2.** a person who has great skill, ability, or knowledge in something; expert: *That author is a master of the short story.* **3.** a skilled artisan or worker qualified to practice a craft or trade independently and to train apprentices. **4.** a male teacher, especially in a private school. **5.** the captain of a merchant ship. **6.** *also,* **Master.** a person who holds a master's degree. **7. Master.** a form of address used before the name of a youth or boy not considered old enough to be addressed as *Mister.* —*adj.*
1. being a master in one's craft or trade: *a master plumber.* **2.** main; principal: *a master bedroom.* **3.** of, relating to, or characteristic of a master; skilled. **4.** referring to a device or mechanism that controls, operates, or fits any of various similar devices or mechanisms: *a master switch.* —*v.t.* **1.** to gain control over; overcome; defeat: *to master one's fears.* **2.** to acquire complete knowledge or understanding of; become expert in: *to master French, to master a trade.* [From the Old English word *magister* meaning "master" and the Old French word *maistre* meaning "lord, chief, master" or "learned teacher," both from the Latin word *magister* with the same meanings.]

mas·ter·ful (mas'tər fəl) *adj.* **1.** forceful or authoritative; domineering. **2.** having or showing mastery; skillful: *The violinist gave a masterful performance.* —**mas'terful·ly,** *adv.*

master key, a key designed to open all the locks of a certain type or in a certain place, as an office building. Also, **passkey.**

mas·ter·ly (mas'tər lē) *adj.* characteristic of a master;

expert. —*adv.* in a masterly manner. —**mas'ter·liness,** *n.*

mas·ter·mind (mas'tər mīnd') *n.* a person who has or shows great intelligence, skill, and ability, especially in planning or directing a course of action. —*v.t.* to plan or direct a course of action for: *to mastermind a complicated robbery.*

Master of Arts, a master's degree given to a person who has completed an advanced course of study in the arts or social sciences.

master of ceremonies, a person who is in charge of a formal gathering or entertainment and introduces the speakers or performers.

Master of Science, a master's degree given to a person who has completed an advanced course of study in science or mathematics.

mas·ter·piece (mas'tər pēs') *n.* **1.** something, such as a work of art, done with supreme skill or craftsmanship. **2.** something thought of as a person's greatest achievement.

master's degree, a degree given to a person who has completed a course of graduate study. It ranks above a bachelor's degree and below a doctorate. Also, **master's.**

master sergeant, a noncommissioned officer of the second highest rank in the U.S. Army and Marine Corps, and of the third highest rank in the U.S. Air Force.

mas·ter·work (mas'tər wûrk') *n.* a masterpiece.

mas·ter·y (mas'tə rē) *n., pl.* **mas·ter·ies.** **1.** the state of being master; rule; control. **2.** expert skill or knowledge: *Your mastery of French will help you when you study in Paris.* **3.** the act of mastering something.

mast·head (mast'hed') *n.* **1.** the head or top of a ship's mast. **2.** a notice printed in a newspaper or magazine giving the title, publisher's name, and other information.

mas·ti·cate (mas'ti kāt') *v.t.,* **mas·ti·cat·ed, mas·ti·cat·ing.** to chew. —**mas'ti·ca'tion,** *n.*

mas·tiff (mas'tif) *n.* a large, powerful dog having a heavy head, a light brown, short-haired coat, dark ears and muzzle, and a long, tapering tail.

mas·to·don (mas'tə don') *n.* any of various extinct animals that resembled elephants with long, curving tusks. They lived all over the world and may have existed as recently as several thousand years ago in parts of North America.

mastiff

mas·toid (mas'toid) *n.* the part of the skull behind and below each ear. —*adj.* of, relating to, or near the mastoid.

mas·tur·bate (mas'tər bāt') *v.i.,* **mas·tur·bat·ed, mas·tur·bat·ing.** to stimulate the genitals, usually by hand, to produce sexual pleasure. —**mas'tur·ba'tion,** *n.*

mat¹ (mat) *n.* **1.** a small, flat piece of material, such as rubber or woven straw, used as a floor covering or placed in front of a door. **2.** a small, flat piece of material placed on a table under a vase, dish, or other object for protection or decoration. **3.** a large, thick pad or covering placed on the floor to protect wrestlers, boxers, or gymnasts. **4.** any thick, tangled mass: *a mat of hair.* —*v.,* **mat·ted, mat·ting.** —*v.t.* **1.** to cover with a mat or mats. **2.** to entangle or entwine into a thick mass. —*v.i.* to become entangled into a thick mass. [From the Old English word *matt* meaning "a mat," from the Latin word *matta* "a mat made of rushes," of Semitic origin.]

mat² (mat) *n.* a piece of cardboard or other material serving as a mount or frame for a picture, or as a border between a picture and its frame. —*v.t.,* **mat·ted, mat-**

ting. to provide (a picture) with a mat. [From the French word *mat* meaning "unpolished, dull."]

mat·a·dor (mat′ə dôr′) *n.* the person who kills the bull in a bullfight. [From the Spanish word *matador,* from the word *matar* meaning "to kill," from the Latin word *mactare* "to sacrifice" or "to slaughter."]

match¹ (mach) *n., pl.* **match·es.** **1.** a short piece of wood, cardboard, or other material coated on one end with a chemical substance that easily catches fire when rubbed or struck against something. **2.** a wick prepared to burn at an even rate, formerly used to fire guns and cannon. [From the Middle English word *mecche* meaning "candle wick," from the Old French word *meche* "wick," going back to the Greek word *myxa* "lamp wick."]

match² (mach) *n., pl.* **match·es.** **1.** a person or thing that is exactly equal to or like another; counterpart. **2.** a person or thing that can compete with or oppose another as an equal: *one's match in chess.* **3.** two persons or things that are like, or suitable for, each other: *The blue coat and the blue dress are a good match.* **4.** a game or contest between two or more persons, animals, or teams: *a wrestling match.* **5.** a marriage. **6.** a possible spouse. —*v.t.* **1.** to be like, suitable for, or equal to: *The pattern on the drapes matches that of the sofa.* **2.** to find, select, or produce a match or counterpart for: *to match socks.* **3.** to cause to be like; adapt: *Try to match your spending to your income.* **4.** to compete with or oppose as an equal; be a match for: *No one can match you in tennis.* **5.** to place in competition or opposition, as in a game or contest: *They matched the fighters according to weight.* **6.** to join in marriage. —*v.i.* to be exactly equal or alike: *These gloves do not match.* [From the Old English words *mæc* "equal" and *gemæcca* "a mate, companion, spouse."]

match·book (mach′bŭk′) *n.* a small cardboard folder containing two or more rows of safety matches and a surface for striking them.

match·box (mach′boks′) *n., pl.* **match·box·es** a small box for holding safety matches, usually with a surface for striking them.

match·less (mach′lis) *adj.* having no equal; peerless; unrivaled. —**match′less·ly,** *adv.*

match·lock (mach′lok′) *n.* formerly, a type of gun fired by igniting the powder with a slow-burning wick.

match·mak·er (mach′mā′kər) *n.* **1.** a person who arranges marriages for others. **2.** a person who arranges sports contests, such as boxing matches.

mate (māt) *n.* **1.** one of a pair: *Where is the mate to this sock?* **2.** a husband or wife. **3.** the male or female of a pair of animals that have paired or been paired for breeding. **4.** an officer on a merchant ship, ranking below the captain. **5.** an assistant to a warrant officer in the U.S. Navy. **6.** a close associate; companion. —*v.,* **mat·ed, mat·ing.** —*v.t.* **1.** to join together or match. **2.** to cause (animals) to produce offspring; pair. **3.** to join in marriage. —*v.i.* **1.** (of animals) to pair for breeding: *Birds mate in the spring.* **2.** to become joined in marriage.

ma·té (mä′tā) *n.* **1.** a greenish beverage resembling tea, made from the dried leaves and shoots of an evergreen shrub of the holly family. **2.** the leaves and shoots used to make this beverage. **3.** the shrub bearing these leaves and shoots, found in South America.

ma·ter (mā′tər) *n.* mother. [From the Latin word *mater* meaning "mother."]

ma·te·ri·al (mə tîr′ē əl) *n.* **1.** the substance of which something is or may be made or composed. **2.** something made by weaving, knitting, or otherwise arranging textile fibers; cloth; fabric. **3.** something that may be used, developed, or elaborated on, especially in making something: *material for a new novel.* **4. materials.** things needed to make or do something: *writing materials.* —*adj.* **1.** of, relating to, or consisting of matter; physical: *a material object.* **2.** of or relating to the body or physical

well-being: *material needs.* **3.** of or concerned with physical rather than spiritual things: *material success.* **4.** essential, important, or relevant: *Those facts are material to our discussion.*

ma·te·ri·al·ism (mə tîr′ē ə liz′əm) *n.* **1.** the philosophical doctrine that everything that exists is either composed of matter or depends on matter for its existence. **2.** a tendency to be overly or solely concerned with wealth, possessions, and physical comforts.

ma·te·ri·al·ist (mə tîr′ē ə list) *n.* **1.** a believer in philosophical materialism. **2.** a person who is overly or solely concerned with wealth, possessions, and physical comforts.

ma·te·ri·al·is·tic (mə tîr′ē ə lis′tik) *adj.* relating to materialism or materialists. —**ma·te′ri·al·is′ti·cal·ly,** *adv.*

ma·te·ri·al·ize (mə tîr′ē ə līz′) *v.,* **ma·te·ri·al·ized, ma·te·ri·al·iz·ing.** —*v.i.* **1.** to come into being; become actual fact; be realized: *Their dreams of success failed to materialize.* **2.** to assume or appear in bodily or visible form: *Spirits seemed to materialize before my eyes.* —*v.t.* to give material form or character to. —**ma·te′ri·al·i·za′tion,** *n.*

ma·te·ri·al·ly (mə tîr′ē ə lē) *adv.* **1.** with regard to material or physical things: *They were well-off materially.* **2.** to a great degree; considerably: *The patient's condition did not improve materially.*

ma·té·ri·el (mə tîr′ē el′) *also,* **ma·te·ri·el.** *n.* the equipment and supplies of an organized body, especially a military force.

ma·ter·nal (mə tûr′nəl) *adj.* **1.** of, relating to, or like a mother; motherly: *maternal love.* **2.** inherited or derived from one's mother. **3.** related through one's mother: *maternal grandparents.* —**ma·ter′nal·ly,** *adv.*

ma·ter·ni·ty (mə tûr′ni tē) *adj.* **1.** for pregnant women: *a maternity dress.* **2.** designed for the care of newborn babies and women during and after childbirth: *a maternity ward.* —*n.* **1.** the state of being a mother; motherhood. **2.** the qualities or characteristics of a mother; motherliness.

math (math) *n.* see **mathematics.**

math·e·mat·i·cal (math′ə mat′i kəl) *adj.* **1.** of, relating to, like, or concerned with mathematics. **2.** extremely exact; precise: *mathematical certainty.* —**math′e·mat′i·cal·ly,** *adv.*

math·e·ma·ti·cian (math′ə mə tish′ən) *n.* a student of or an expert in mathematics.

math·e·mat·ics (math′ə mat′iks) *n.* **1.** the study of numbers, quantities, shapes, sets, and operations, and of their properties and relationships. Mathematics includes arithmetic, algebra, geometry, and calculus. ▲ used with a singular verb. **2.** mathematical operations, procedures, or properties: *There is an error in your mathematics.* ▲ used with either a singular or plural verb.

mat·i·nee (mat′ə nā′) *also,* **mat·i·née.** *n.* a theatrical presentation performed in the afternoon.

ma·tins (mat′inz) *n.* **1.** the first of the seven canonical hours, or the service for it. **2.** in the Church of England, the morning prayer service. ▲ used with either a singular or plural verb.

ma·tri·arch (mā′trē ärk′) *n.* **1.** a woman who is the head of a family or tribe. **2.** a woman who dominates or has great authority in any group.

ma·tri·ar·chal (mā′trē är′kəl) *adj.* **1.** relating to, like,

at; āpe; fär; câre; end; mē; it; īce; pîerce; hot; ōld; sông, fôrk; oil; out; up; ūse; rüle; pull; tûrn; chin; sing; shop; thin; this; hw in white; zh in treasure. The symbol ə stands for the unstressed vowel sound heard in about, taken, pencil, lemon, and circus.

M

or based on a matriarchy: *a matriarchal culture.* **2.** of or relating to a matriarch.

ma·tri·ar·chy (mā′trē är′kē) *n., pl.* **ma·tri·ar·chies.** a form of society in which a woman heads a family or tribe and descent is traced through the maternal line.

ma·tri·ces (mā′trə sēz′, mat′rə sēz′) a plural of **matrix.**

mat·ri·cide (mat′rə sīd′, mā′trə sīd′) *n.* the act of killing one's mother. [From the Latin word *matricidium* with the same meaning, from the words *mater* "mother" + *-cidium* "a killing."]

ma·tric·u·late (mə trik′yə lāt′) *v.,* **ma·tric·u·lat·ed,** **ma·tric·u·lat·ing.** —*v.i.* to enroll in a college or university as a candidate for a degree: *Fifty students matriculated last fall.* —*v.t.* to admit to a college or university as a candidate for a degree. —**ma·tric′u·la′tion,** *n.*

mat·ri·mo·ni·al (mat′rə mō′nē əl) *adj.* of or relating to marriage. —**mat′ri·mo′ni·al·ly,** *adv.*

mat·ri·mo·ny (mat′rə mō′nē) *n., pl.* **mat·ri·mo·nies.** **1.** the state of being married. **2.** the rite or ceremony of marriage.

ma·trix (mā′triks, mat′riks) *n., pl.* **ma·tri·ces** or **ma·trix·es.** the place or thing in which something originates, develops, forms, or is contained. A mold for casting metal is a matrix.

ma·tron (mā′trən) *n.* **1.** a married woman, especially one who is mature in age and manner. **2.** a female attendant, supervisor, or guard, as in a jail.

ma·tron·ly (mā′trən lē) *adj.* characteristic of, suitable for, or like a matron.

matron of honor, a married woman who is the chief attendant of the bride at a wedding.

Matt., Matthew.

matte (mat) *adj.* not bright or shiny; dull: *a matte finish.* —*n.* a dull finish or surface, as on glass or paper.

mat·ted (mat′id) *adj.* **1.** entangled or entwined in a thick mass: *The dog's wet hair was matted.* **2.** covered with or made of matting.

mat·ter (mat′ər) *n.* **1.** anything that occupies space and has weight. The three common states of matter are solid, liquid, and gaseous. **2.** a particular kind or form of substance: *A plant is organic matter.* **3.** something that is the subject of discussion, concern, feeling, or action: *a legal matter, a business matter.* **4.** a difficult, unpleasant, or unsatisfactory condition or circumstance; trouble; problem: *What is the matter with my report?* **5.** importance; significance: *It's of no matter to me what you do.* **6.** written or printed material: *reading matter.* **7.** the content of something that is written or spoken: *the matter of a speech.* **8.** an amount, quantity, or extent: *It is only a matter of minutes before they arrive.* **9.** a substance given off by the body, as from a wound or abscess; pus. —*v.i.* to be of importance: *It does not matter to me what you want.*

  •**as a matter of course.** as something to be expected.
  •**as a matter of fact.** in truth; actually; truthfully: *As a matter of fact, I do know them.*
  •**no matter.** regardless of; despite: *No matter what you say, I still disagree with you.*

mat·ter–of–fact (mat′ər əv fakt′) *adj.* **1.** dealing with facts; unimaginative; practical: *a matter-of-fact description.* **2.** having or showing no emotion or feeling; disinterested: *a matter-of-fact way of speaking.* —**mat′ter-of-fact′ly,** *adv.*

Mat·thew (math′ū) *n.* the first book and Gospel of the New Testament, believed to have been written by the Apostle Matthew.

mat·ting (mat′ing) *n.* **1.** a coarse, woven fabric of grass, straw, hemp, or other fiber, used for making floor coverings and as a packing material. **2.** mats as a group.

mat·tock (mat′ək) *n.* a tool with a handle and a two-bladed head, used for loosening soil and cutting roots.

mat·tress (mat′ris) *n., pl.* **mat·tress·es.** a pad covered with strong cloth or other material, filled with hair, cotton, rubber, or other material and, often, coiled springs, and designed to fit on the frame of a bed, especially on top of a box spring.

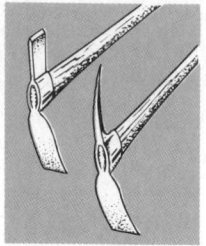

mattocks

mat·u·rate (mach′ə rāt′) *v.i.* **mat·u·rat·ed, mat·u·rat·ing.** to ripen; mature. —**mat′u·ra′tion,** *n.*

ma·ture (mə ch▹oor′, mə t▹oor′, mə tyur′) *adj.* **1.** having reached full growth or development: *mature fruit, a physically mature person.* **2.** showing the qualities or characteristics of a person who has reached full physical and mental development: *mature behavior, a mature worker.* **3.** fully developed or thought out: *a mature plan.* **4.** due for payment, as a loan or bond. —*v.,* **ma·tured, ma·tur·ing.** —*v.i.* **1.** to become fully grown or developed; reach maturity. **2.** to become due for payment: *The savings bond matures in seven years.* —*v.t.* to bring to full growth or development: *The difficult experience helped to mature the teenager.* —**ma·ture′ly,** *adv.*

ma·tu·ri·ty (mə chur′i tē, mə tur′i tē, mə tyur′i tē) *n., pl.* **ma·tu·ri·ties.** **1.** the state or quality of being mature. **2.** the time at which something, such as a loan or bond, is due for payment.

mat·zoh (mät′sə) *also,* **mat·zo.** *n.* a thin, flat piece of unleavened bread, traditionally eaten at Passover. [Hebrew *matztzāh.*]

maud·lin (môd′lin) *adj.* overly or foolishly sentimental. [From the Middle English name *Maudelaine,* Mary Magdalene. This saint was so often depicted as weeping over her sins that her name came to be used as an adjective meaning "tearful," then later "sentimental."]

maul (môl) *n.* a heavy mallet or hammer used for driving wedges, stakes, and piles. —*v.t.* **1.** to injure, as by beating, bruising, or knocking about: *The angry lion mauled the trainer.* **2.** to handle roughly or clumsily.

maun·der (môn′dər) *v.i.* **1.** to talk in a rambling, confused manner. **2.** to move or act in an aimless, dreamy, and confused manner.

mau·so·le·um (mô′sə lē′əm, mô′zə lē′əm) *n., pl.* **mau·so·le·ums** or **mau·so·le·a** (mô′sə lē′ə, mô′zə lē′ə). a stately, often large, building housing a tomb or tombs.

mauve (mōv, môv) *n.* any of various pale, purplish blue or rose colors. —*adj.* having the color mauve.

mav·er·ick (mav′ər ik) *n.* **1.** an unbranded animal, especially a calf, traditionally belonging to the first person to find and brand it. **2.** a person whose views, especially in politics, are different from those of the group to which he or she belongs. [From Samuel A. *Maverick* (1803–1870), a Texas rancher who did not brand his calves.]

ma·vis (mā′vis) *n., pl.* **ma·vis·es.** another word for **song thrush.**

maw (mô) *n.* the jaws, mouth, throat, gullet, or stomach of an animal.

mawk·ish (mô′kish) *adj.* **1.** overly sentimental. **2.** having a sickening flavor; nauseating. —**mawk′ish·ly,** *adv.* —**mawk′ish·ness,** *n.*

max., maximum.

max·i (mak′sē) *n., pl.* **max·is.** a long skirt, dress, or coat, usually one that reaches to the ankles.

max·il·la (mak sil′ə) *n., pl.* **max·il·lae** (mak sil′ē). **1.** the bone of the upper jaw. **2.** either of a pair of appendages located just behind the mandibles in insects, crabs, spiders, and other related animals.

max·il·lar·y (mak′sə ler′ē) *adj.* of, relating to, or situated near the bone of the upper jaw: *maxillary artery.* —*n., pl.* **max·il·lar·ies.** see **maxilla** (*def. 1*).

max·im (mak′sim) *n.* a short statement expressing a general truth or doctrine; precept. For example: *Haste makes waste* is a maxim.

max·i·mize (mak′sə mīz′) *v.t.,* **max·i·mized, max·i·miz·ing.** to make as great as possible; increase to the maximum.

max·i·mum (mak′sə məm) *n., pl.* **max·i·mums** or **max·i·ma** (mak′sə mə). **1.** the greatest possible amount, degree, or quantity: *It will take a maximum of three hours to drive home.* **2.** the highest point, degree, or number reached or recorded: *The temperature reached a maximum of 90° yesterday.* —*adj.* greatest possible or allowable: *The maximum permissible speed on this road is 50 miles per hour.*

may (mā) *auxiliary verb.* Present tense: *sing.* first person, **may**; second, **may** or *(archaic)* **mayst** or **mayest**; third, **may**; *pl.* **may.** Past tense: **might. 1.** used to ask for or express permission: *May I leave the table? Yes, you may.* **2.** used to express possibility or likelihood: *It may snow.* **3.** used to express desire, hope, or a wish: *May you have a happy life.* **4.** used to express opportunity or chance: *I am willing to pay all the expenses so that you may go on the trip.* ▲ See **can**[1] for usage note.

May (mā) *n.* the fifth month of the year, having thirty-one days. [From the Old French word *Mai* meaning this month, from the Latin phrase *Maius (mensis)* "(month) of May."]

Ma·ya (mä′yə) *n., pl.* **Ma·ya** or **Ma·yas. 1.** a member of a tribe of American Indians who live in southern Mexico and parts of Central America. The Maya had a well-developed civilization before they were conquered by the Spanish in the sixteenth century. **2.** the language of the Maya. —*adj.* of or relating to the Maya, their language, or their culture. Also, **Ma·yan** (mä′yən).

may·be (mā′bē) *adv.* possibly; perhaps.

May·day (mā′dā′) *n.* an international signal used by ships or aircraft as a call for help. [From the French phrase *m'aidez* meaning "Help me."]

May Day, a holiday traditionally celebrated as a spring festival. Some countries honor working people on this day with parades and other demonstrations. It falls on May 1.

may·est (mā′ist) *Archaic.* a present indicative, second person singular of **may.** ▲ used with *thou.*

Mayflower
a painting of the Mayflower

may·flow·er (mā′flou′ər) *n.* **1.** any of various plants whose flowers blossom in May, such as the trailing arbutus. **2.** **Mayflower.** the ship on which the Pilgrims came to America in 1620.

may·fly (mā′flī′) *n., pl.* **may·flies.** an insect having two pairs of finely veined wings and two or three long filaments attached to the end of the body. Adult mayflies live for a period of only a few hours to a few days.

may·hem (mā′hem, mā′əm) *n.* **1.** the crime of violently and intentionally injuring or maiming a person. **2.** a state of confusion and violent disorder.

may·n't (mā′ənt) *contr.* may not.

may·on·naise (mā′ə nāz′, mā′ə nāz′) *n.* a thick, creamy sauce or dressing made of egg yolks, oil, vinegar or lemon juice, and seasoning.

may·or (mā′ər) *n.* the official head of a city or town government. —**may′or·al,** *adj.*

may·or·al·ty (mā′ər əl tē) *n., pl.* **may·or·al·ties.** the position or term of office of a mayor.

May·pole (mā′pōl′) *also,* **may·pole.** *n.* a pole decorated with flowers and ribbons, around which people dance on May Day.

mayst (māst) *Archaic.* a present indicative, second person singular of **may.** ▲ used with *thou.*

maze (māz) *n.* **1.** a confusing network of paths or passageways, usually bordered by high walls or shrubs. **2.** a confusing network of pathways used in experiments with animals to study learning. **3.** an intricately patterned puzzle that is solved by finding a path from the starting point to the goal. **4.** a state of bewilderment, confusion, or doubt.

ma·zur·ka (mə zûr′kə, mə zùr′kə) *also,* **ma·zour·ka.** *n.* **1.** a lively Polish dance resembling the polka. **2.** the music for such a dance.

maz·y (mā′zē) *adj.* **maz·i·er, maz·i·est.** like a maze; complicated or confusing.

MB, postal abbreviation for Manitoba.

Mc, megacycle; megacycles.

M.C., Master of Ceremonies.

Md, the symbol for mendelevium.

Md., Maryland.

MD, postal abbreviation for Maryland.

M.D., Doctor of Medicine.

me (mē) *pron.* the objective case of **I.** ▲ According to the rules of traditional grammar, **I,** rather than **me,** should be used after the verb *to be.* However, **me** is often used in conversation by many good speakers and writers when they think **I** would sound too formal: *Who's there? It's only me.*

Me., Maine.

ME, postal abbreviation for Maine.

mead[1] (mēd) *n.* an alcoholic drink made from fermented honey and water and flavored with herbs. [From the Old English word *medu* meaning this drink.]

mead[2] (mēd) *n. Archaic.* a meadow. [From the Old English word *mǣd* meaning "meadow."]

mead·ow (med′ō) *n.* a piece of grassy land, often used as a pasture or for growing hay.

mead·ow·lark (med′ō lärk′) *n.* a North American songbird having a pointed, cone-shaped bill and a yellow breast with a black crescent across it.

mea·ger (mē′gər) *also,* **mea·gre.** *adj.* **1.** barely adequate in amount or quantity; scanty: *a meager meal of bread and broth.* **2.** thin; lean: *a meager figure.* —**mea′ger·ly,** *adv.* —**mea′ger·ness,** *n.*

meadowlark

meal[1] (mēl) *n.* **1.** the food served or eaten at one particular time. **2.** the time or occasion during which such food is regularly served or eaten: *Their evening meal was short.* [From the Middle

M

at; āpe; fär; câre; end; mē; it; īce; pîerce; hot; ōld; sông, fôrk; oil; out; up; ūse; rüle; pùll; tûrn; chin; sing; shop; thin; this; hw in white; zh in treasure. The symbol ə stands for the unstressed vowel sound heard in about, taken, pencil, lemon, and circus.

English word *meel* meaning "appointed time," "meal-time," and "feast, meal¹," from the Old English word *māl* "a measure," "appointed time," and "mealtime."]

meal² (mēl) *n.* **1.** a coarsely ground and unsifted grain. **2.** any similar ground substance. [From the Old English word *melu* meaning "flour, meal²."]

meal·time (mēl′tīm′) *n.* **1.** the usual time for a meal to begin: *Mealtime is 6:00.* **2.** the time during which a meal is eaten: *Don't telephone at mealtime.*

meal·y (mē′lē) *adj.,* **meal·i·er, meal·i·est. 1.** like meal; dry and grainy: *mealy potatoes.* **2.** of or containing meal. **3.** sprinkled or covered with meal. **4.** pale or sickly: *a mealy complexion.* —**meal′i·ness,** *n.*

meal·y-mouthed (mē′lē mou<u>th</u>d′, mē′lē moutht′) *adj.* unwilling to say plainly what one means; not outspoken; insincerely hesitant.

mean¹ (mēn) *v.,* **meant, mean·ing.** —*v.t.* **1.** to have in mind as a purpose or intention: *We didn't mean to hurt you.* **2.** to intend to express or indicate: *I do not know what you mean by that remark.* **3.** to have as a particular sense; be defined as: *"Do not" and "don't" mean the same thing.* **4.** to intend or design for a particular person, purpose, or use: *I meant that gift for you. That singer was meant to be a star.* **5.** to be or serve as an indication or sign of: *Smoke usually means fire.* **6.** to bring about or have as a result: *The promotion means a raise in salary.* —*v.i.* **1.** to have a specified importance or value: *Your friendship means a lot to me.* **2.** to have intentions of a particular kind; be disposed: *They mean well, despite their nosy questions.* [From the Old English word *mǣnan* meaning "to intend, have in mind."]

mean² (mēn) *adj.* **1.** lacking in kindness, compassion, or understanding: *I apologized for having been mean to them.* **2.** full of or showing spite; malicious: *a mean look.* **3.** miserly; stingy. **4.** poor in appearance; shabby. **5.** of low birth, rank, or social position. **6.** *Informal.* hard to deal with; difficult: *There is a mean curve in the road just ahead.* **7.** *Slang.* expert; excellent: *to play a mean game of golf.* [From the Old English word *mǣne* meaning "wicked, evil, mean²."] —**mean′ly,** *adv.*

  ·**no mean.** of high quality, value, or importance: *Being elected class president of the eighth grade was no mean achievement.*

mean³ (mēn) *n.* **1.** a point, state, or course of action that is halfway between two extremes. **2. means. a.** the way that something is or may be done: *to get money by dishonest means.* **b.** money, property, or other resources; wealth: *a family of means.* **3.** *Mathematics.* either the second or third term of a mathematical proportion of four terms. In *a/b = c/d, b* and *c* are the means. —*adj.* **1.** halfway between two extremes. **2.** average, as in size, quality, or degree: *The mean temperature for the month of May was 60°.* [From the Old French word *moien* meaning "middle" or "common," from the Latin word *medianus* "middle, in the middle," from the word *medius* "middle," "between."]

  ·**by all means.** without fail or hesitation.

  ·**by means of.** with the help or use of: *We crossed the river by means of the bridge.*

  ·**by no means. a.** in no way; not at all. **b.** on no account: *By no means should they be left alone.*

  ·**not by any means.** not at all.

me·an·der (mē an′dər) *v.i.* **1.** to follow a winding course: *The stream meandered through the woods.* **2.** to wander aimlessly or idly: *I meandered through the gardens.*

mean·ing (mē′ning) *n.* **1.** something that is meant as a goal or purpose: *The philosopher tried to find the meaning of life.* **2.** something that is meant to be expressed or understood, as by language; sense: *the meaning of a word.* **3.** expressiveness; suggestiveness: *a glance that is full of*

meaning. —*adj.* having meaning; expressive; significant: *a meaning smile.* —**mean′ing·ly,** *adv.*

Language Note·

Words themselves have no absolute **meaning.** Although a dog is what it is, there is no reason why it must be called dog. Indeed, Germans call the same animal *hund,* the French *chien,* and the Russians *sobaka.* The relationship between a word and the object it refers to is set by people, not by the word or by the thing. In spite of this, we can establish certain general boundaries for the meanings of words. Consider, for example, the word *beautiful* in the sentence *That's a beautiful painting.* Individual members of a language community may agree or disagree as to whether a particular painting is beautiful, but they would agree on certain features of the word *beautiful.* For instance, they would agree that *beautiful* is a term of approval rather than disapproval and that it is applied to things that produce a sense of delight. Features like these make up the generally used and understood meaning of *beautiful.*

Words have no fixed meaning. As time passes, the meaning of words can change, sometimes quite drastically. But *change* of meaning, although sometimes difficult to predict, does follow certain patterns. Four of the most common patterns of change are extension, narrowing, pejoration, and amelioration.

When the meaning of a word undergoes extension, its range is increased or broadened. The word *barn,* for example, used to mean "a storehouse for barley." Today the range of its meaning has been increased to mean "a storehouse for any kind of grain or a place for livestock." The opposite of extension is narrowing. When the meaning of a word is narrowed, its range is decreased. The word *starve* used to mean "to die"; now it means "to die of hunger." Sometimes words come to mean something worse than what they had previously meant. This is called pejoration. The word *silly* once meant "blessed" or "happy"; now it means "stupid." The opposite of pejoration is amelioration, that is, the process by which words come to mean something better than what they had previously meant. *Praise* once meant "to put a value on," which is neutral; now it means "to value highly."

When changes in meaning occur, they occur so gradually that most people do not even realize that a change has occurred. It is the job of dictionary makers to observe changes in meaning and then to record them. The dictionaries that result from this work show what words mean at a particular time.

mean·ing·ful (mē′ning fəl) *adj.* full of meaning; significant. —**mean′ing·ful·ly,** *adv.*

mean·ing·less (mē′ning lis) *adj.* without meaning; senseless: *a meaningless statement.* —**mean′ing·less·ly,** *adv.* —**mean′ing·less·ness,** *n.*

mean·ness (mēn′nis) *n.* **1.** the state or quality of being mean. **2.** a mean or spiteful act.

meant (ment) the past tense and past participle of **mean¹.**

mean·time (mēn′tīm′) *n.* the time between: *I'll be gone for an hour; in the meantime, please behave.* —*adv.* **1.** in or during the time between. **2.** at the same time.

mean·while (mēn′hwīl′, mēn′wīl′) *adv.* **1.** in or during the time between: *The train doesn't leave for an hour; meanwhile, I'm going to take a nap.* **2.** at the same time: *They went shopping; meanwhile, I cleaned the house.* —*n.* the time between.

meas., measure.

mea·sles (mē′zəlz) *n.* **1.** a highly contagious virus disease characterized by cold symptoms, fever, and a rash. 2. see **German measles**.

mea·sly (mēz′lē) *adj.*, **mea·sli·er**, **mea·sli·est**. 1. of, like, or having measles. 2. *Slang*. scanty or worthless: *They gave me a measly fifty cents for mowing the lawn.*

meas·ur·a·ble (mezh′ər ə bəl) *adj.* capable of being measured: *a measurable distance.* —**meas′ur·a·bly**, *adv.*

meas·ure (mezh′ər) *v.*, **meas·ured**, **meas·ur·ing**. —*v.t.* 1. to find the dimensions, weight, extent, quantity, or capacity of: *to measure a person's height, to measure a room.* 2. to mark off, set apart, or allot by measuring: *to measure out two cups of flour.* 3. to serve as a standard or unit of measurement for: *Degrees measure temperature.* 4. to think over carefully and choose: *to measure one's words.* —*v.i.* 1. to have a specific measurement: *The room measures 10 feet by 12 feet.* 2. to take measurements: *A carpenter must measure accurately.* —*n.* 1. the dimensions, weight, extent, quantity, or capacity of something as found by measuring. 2. a standard or unit of measurement, such as an inch, quart, or mile. 3. any standard or basis of comparison, estimation, or judgment: *Marks in school are not always a true measure of a person's intelligence.* 4. a system of measurement. 5. an instrument, container, or other device used for measuring: *a gallon measure.* 6. an amount or degree that should not be exceeded; limit: *Their generosity knows no measure.* 7. an amount, degree, or proportion: *Our success was due in large measure to your help.* 8. *also,* **measures.** a course of action or procedure used as a means to an end: *to take drastic measures.* 9. a legislative act or bill: *The measure passed both houses of Congress.* 10. *Poetry.* **a.** rhythm; meter. **b.** a metrical unit; foot. 11. *Music.* the music contained between two bar lines; bar.

·**for good measure.** as something extra.

·**to measure up.** to have the needed qualifications: *Does the applicant measure up for the job?*

·**to measure up to.** to fulfill or meet: *The movie didn't measure up to what we had expected.*

meas·ure·less (mezh′ər lis) *adj.* not capable of being measured.

meas·ure·ment (mezh′ər mənt) *n.* 1. the act or process of measuring. 2. something found or determined by measuring, such as dimensions or quantity: *The measurements of this shelf are 6 inches by 3 feet.* 3. a system of measuring.

measuring worm, another term for **inchworm**.

meat (mēt) *n.* 1. the parts of an animal used as food, especially the flesh of a cow or pig. 2. the fleshy part of anything that can be eaten: *the meat of a coconut.* 3. the main idea or most important part; substance: *the meat of a book.* 4. anything eaten for nourishment; food: *meat and drink.*

meat·y (mē′tē) *adj.*, **meat·i·er**, **meat·i·est**. 1. of, relating to, or like meat: *a meaty taste.* 2. full of meat; plump. 3. full of substance or significance: *a meaty discussion.*

Mec·ca (mek′ə) *also,* **mec·ca.** *n.* any place that is visited by many people or has a special attraction. [From *Mecca,* a city in western Saudi Arabia, the birthplace of Muhammad and a place of pilgrimage for Muslims.]

me·chan·ic (mi kan′ik) *n.* a person skilled in designing, repairing, or operating machinery: *an automobile mechanic.*

me·chan·i·cal (mi kan′i kəl) *adj.* 1. of, relating to, or involving machinery or tools: *a mechanical part, mechanical skills.* 2. produced or operated by a machine: *a mechanical toy.* 3. like or suitable for a machine; without or not requiring thought or feeling: *a mechanical task.* 4. of or relating to the science of mechanics. —**me·chan′i·cal·ly,** *adv.*

mechanical drawing 1. a drawing, usually of machinery or mechanical parts, done with the aid of rulers, scales, compasses, and similar instruments. 2. the art or process of making such a drawing.

me·chan·ics (mi kan′iks) *n.* 1. the branch of physics that deals with the conditions under which bodies and fluids move or remain at rest. 2. the body of knowledge dealing with the design, construction, operation, and care of machinery. ▲ used with a singular verb in definitions 1 and 2. 3. the mechanical or technical aspects of anything: *the mechanics of painting.* ▲ used with a plural verb in definition 3.

mech·a·nism (mek′ə niz′əm) *n.* 1. the working parts, or arrangement of parts, of a machine: *The jeweler fixed the mechanism of my watch.* 2. a system of parts resembling those of a machine: *the mechanism of the nervous system, the mechanism of government.* 3. the way, means, or process by which something is done.

mech·a·nize (mek′ə nīz′) *v.t.*, **mech·a·nized**, **mech·a·niz·ing.** 1. to equip with or convert to machinery as a means of production: *Much industry has been mechanized.* 2. to equip (a military unit or army) with tanks and other vehicles. —**mech′a·ni·za′tion,** *n.*

med. 1. medical. 2. medicine. 3. medium.

med·al (med′əl) *n.* a flat piece of metal bearing a design or inscription, often given as an award.

med·al·ist (med′ə list) *n.* 1. a person who engraves, designs, or makes medals. 2. a person who has been awarded a medal: *an Olympic gold medalist.*

me·dal·lion (mə dal′yən) *n.* 1. a large medal. 2. anything resembling this, such as a round or oval object or design.

med·dle (med′əl) *v.i.*, **med·dled**, **med·dling.** 1. to concern oneself with or interfere in the affairs of others without having been asked. 2. to handle or change something without permission; tamper: *Someone has meddled with the lock on this door.* —**med′dler,** *n.*

med·dle·some (med′əl səm) *adj.* tending to meddle. —**med′dle·some·ness,** *n.*

Mede (mēd) *n.* a person who lived in ancient Media.

Me·de·a (mi dē′ə) *n. Greek Legend.* an enchantress who helped Jason get the Golden Fleece in return for his marrying her.

me·di·a (mē′dē ə) a plural of **medium.**

me·di·ae·val (mē′dē ē′vəl, mid ē′vəl) another spelling of **medieval.**

me·di·al (mē′dē əl) *adj.* 1. of, relating to, or situated in the middle. 2. of, relating to, or being the middle number in a set or series; average.

me·di·an (mē′dē ən) *n.* 1. the middle number in a set of numbers arranged in numerical order or, where there is no middle number, the average of the two middle numbers. In the set *2, 4, 6, 8, 10,* the median is *6.* In the set *11, 25, 41, 65,* the median is *33.* 2.**a.** on a triangle, a line connecting the midpoint of any side with the intersection of the other two sides. **b.** on a trapezoid, a line connecting the midpoints of the two sides that are not parallel. —*adj.* of, relating to, or situated in the middle; medial.

me·di·ate (*v.,* mē′dē āt′; *adj.,* mē′dē it) *v.,* **me·di·at·ed**, **me·di·at·ing.** —*v.t.* 1. to bring about by coming between and working with disagreeing or opposing parties: *The lawyer mediated a settlement between the union and the owner of the factory.* 2. to settle (differences or disputes) by coming between and working with disagreeing

at; āpe; fär; câre; end; mē; it; īce; pîerce; hot; ōld; sông, fôrk; oil; out; up; ūse; rüle; pull; tûrn; chin; sing; shop; thin; this; hw in white; zh in treasure. The symbol ə stands for the unstressed vowel sound heard in about, taken, pencil, lemon, and circus.

M

or opposing parties. —*v.i.* to try to mediate an agreement or settlement between disagreeing or opposing parties. —*adj.* acting through or involving another person or thing; indirect. —**me′di·a′tion,** *n.*

me·di·a·tor (mē′dē ā′tər) *n.* a person or group that mediates.

med·ic (med′ik) *n.* *Informal.* **1.** in the armed services, an enlisted person trained to give medical assistance. **2.** a physician. **3.** a medical student or intern.

Med·i·caid (med′i kād′) *also,* **med·i·caid.** *n.* a program of the U.S. federal and individual state governments that provides health care services to people of all ages who have limited income.

med·i·cal (med′i kəl) *adj.* of or relating to doctors, medicine, or the study or practice of medicine. —**med′i·cal·ly,** *adv.*

med·dic·a·ment (mə dik′ə mənt, med′i kə mənt) *n.* a substance used to treat disease or relieve pain; medicine.

Med·i·care (med′i kâr′) *also,* **med·i·care.** *n.* a program of the U.S. federal government that provides hospital insurance to people over the age of sixty-five and certain disabled people under the age of sixty-five.

med·i·cate (med′i kāt′) *v.t.,* **med·i·cat·ed, med·i·cat·ing.** **1.** to treat with medicine. **2.** to fill with medicine; put medicine on or in: *to medicate an ointment.*

med·i·ca·tion (med′i kā′shən) *n.* **1.** a substance used to treat disease or relieve pain; medicine. **2.** the act of medicating or the state of being medicated.

me·dic·i·nal (mə dis′ə nəl) *adj.* **1.** able to heal, cure, or relieve: *a medicinal substance.* **2.** characteristic of or like medicine: *The hospital room had a medicinal smell.* —**me·dic′i·nal·ly,** *adv.*

med·i·cine (med′ə sin) *n.* **1.** a drug or other substance used to treat disease or relieve pain. **2.** the science that deals with the cause, prevention, and treatment of disease and the preservation of health. **3.** the medical profession. **4.** among North American Indians, any object or ceremony thought to have magical, healing, or curing powers.

medicine ball, a large, heavy stuffed ball thrown from one person to another for exercise.

medicine man, among North American Indians, a person believed to have magical powers; shaman.

me·di·e·val (mē′dē ē′vəl, mid ē′vəl) *also,* **me·di·ae·val.** *adj.* of, relating to, belonging to, or characteristic of the Middle Ages.

Medieval Latin, Latin, especially as a literary language, from the eighth to the fifteenth centuries A.D. Also, **Middle Latin.**

me·di·o·cre (mē′dē ō′kər) *adj.* not exceptional; ordinary; commonplace. [From the French word *médiocre,* from the Latin word *mediocris* meaning "moderate, ordinary" or "indifferent."]

me·di·oc·ri·ty (mē′dē ok′ri tē) *n., pl.* **me·di·oc·ri·ties.** **1.** the state or quality of being mediocre. **2.** mediocre ability, accomplishment, or performance. **3.** a person who has mediocre talents or ability.

med·i·tate (med′i tāt′) *v.,* **med·i·tat·ed, med·i·tat·ing.** —*v.i.* **1.** to think seriously and carefully; reflect: *to meditate on the problems of the world.* **2.** to reflect deeply on matters of spiritual importance, often as a regular religious practice. —*v.t.* to consider; plan: *The prisoners meditated their escape.*

med·i·ta·tion (med′i tā′shən) *n.* **1.** serious and careful thought. **2.** deep reflection on matters of spiritual importance, often as a regular religious practice.

med·i·ta·tive (med′i tā′tiv) *adj.* given to, showing, or characterized by meditation: *a meditative person, a meditative mood.* —**med′i·ta′tive·ly,** *adv.*

Med·i·ter·ra·ne·an (med′i tə rā′nē ən) *adj.* of, relating to, or characteristic of the Mediterranean Sea or the nearby countries and their people.

me·di·um (mē′dē əm) *n., pl.* **me·di·a** or **me·di·ums.**

1. something occupying a position between two extremes; mean: *to find a happy medium between too much work and idleness.* **2.** the substance in which something exists or functions; environment: *Most bacteria grow best in a slightly acid medium.* **3.** a means or form of communication that reaches a large audience: *Television and newspapers are media that influence our daily life.* **4.** a substance or means through, in, or by which something may act or be carried: *The atmosphere is a medium for sound waves.* **5.** *pl.* **mediums.** a person through whom the spirits of the dead supposedly communicate with the living. **6.** a material or technique used for artistic expression: *That artist's medium is watercolor.* —*adj.* intermediate, as in quantity, amount, or degree: *a dress of medium blue, a person of medium height.*

medium frequency, a radio frequency between 300 kilohertz and 3,000 kilohertz.

med·ley (med′lē) *n., pl.* **med·leys.** **1.** a confused and disordered mixture of things; jumble. **2.** a musical composition made up of various tunes or parts from other compositions.

me·dul·la (mə dul′ə) *n., pl.* **me·dul·las** or **me·dul·lae** (mə dul′ē). **1.** see **medulla oblongata.** **2.** the inner substance of an organ or part.

medulla ob·lon·ga·ta (ob′lông gä′tə) the lowest part of the brain, connected with the top of the spinal cord. It controls breathing and other involuntary functions.

Me·du·sa (mə dü′sə, mə-dü′sə) *Greek Mythology.* one of the three Gorgons, who was slain by Perseus.

meek (mēk) *adj.* **1.** patient and mild in manner or disposition; gentle. **2.** giving in or yielding easily; lacking spirit: *The clerk was too meek to insist on an overdue raise in salary.* [Of Scandinavian origin.] —**meek′ly,** *adv.* —**meek′ness,** *n.*

Medulla oblongata

meer·schaum (mîr′shəm) *n.* **1.** a soft, light, white clay mineral that is heat-resistant, used to make tobacco pipes. **2.** a tobacco pipe that has a bowl made of meerschaum. [German *Meerschaum* this mineral; literally, sea foam; because it was originally found along the seashore and was thought to be the foam of the sea hardened into stone.]

meet[1] (mēt) *v.,* **met, meet·ing.** —*v.t.* **1.** to come face to face with; come upon or across: *I met them just as I was leaving.* **2.** to make the acquaintance of; be introduced to: *Haven't I met you before?* **3.** to keep an appointment with: *I'm going to meet my friend after school.* **4.** to be present at the arrival of: *Will you be able to meet my plane next Monday?* **5.** to satisfy, fulfill, or comply with: *to meet the qualifications for a job.* **6.** to come into contact with: *The Hudson River meets the ocean at New York City.* **7.** to pay: *I couldn't meet my bills this month.* **8.** to oppose or fight with, as in battle: *The army met the enemy in the valley.* **9.** to come into the observation or notice of: *There is more work involved in this job than meets the eye.* **10.** to deal or cope with effectively; confront: *We met their criticism with indifference.* —*v.i.* **1.** to come face to face: *After avoiding each other all morning, we met in the elevator.* **2.** to be introduced; become acquainted: *That couple met at a party.* **3.** to come into contact or union; join: *Oh, East is East, and West is West, and never the twain shall meet* (Rudyard Kipling). **4.** to come together, as for business or worship: *The committee met for five hours.* **5.** to fight: *The enemies met on the battlefield.* —*n.* an assembly or gathering, as for an athletic contest: *a swimming meet.* [From the Old English word *mētan* meaning ''to come upon, find, meet¹.'']

·**to meet with. a.** to receive: *My suggestion met with approval.* **b.** to experience; undergo: *The explorers met with difficulty in the jungle.*

meet² (mēt) *adj. Archaic.* suitable; proper. [From the Old English word *gemǣte* meaning ''moderate, fit¹.'']

meet·ing (mē′ting) *n.* **1.** a gathering or assembly of people: *The head of the committee presided at the meeting.* **2.** the persons so gathered. **3.** the act of coming together: *a meeting of two minds.* **4.** the place or point where things come together; junction: *the meeting of two rivers.* **5.** a gathering or assembly of people, especially Quakers, for religious worship.

meeting house, a building used for religious worship, especially by Quakers.

mega- *combining form* **1.** large; great: *megaphone.* **2.** multiplied by a million; one million of (a specified unit): *megahertz, megacycle.*

meg·a·byte (meg′ə bīt′) *n.* 1,024 kilobytes, or 1,048,576 bytes.

meg·a·cy·cle (meg′ə sī′kəl) *n.* **1.** a unit equal to one million cycles. **2.** another word for **megahertz.**

meg·a·hertz (meg′ə hûrts′) *n., pl.* **meg·a·hertz.** a unit equal to 1 million hertz, used in measuring the frequency of electromagnetic waves. Also, **megacycle.**

meg·a·lith (meg′ə lith′) *n.* a huge stone, especially one used in prehistoric monuments.

meg·a·lo·ma·ni·a (meg′ə lō mā′nē ə) *n.* a mental disorder characterized by delusions of greatness, power, or wealth.

meg·a·lo·ma·ni·ac (meg′ə lō mā′nē ak′) *n.* a person suffering from megalomania.

meg·a·lop·o·lis (meg′ə lop′ə lis) *n., pl.* **meg·a·lop·o·lis·es.** a densely populated urban area made up of a number of adjoining cities.

meg·a·phone (meg′ə fōn′) *n.* a funnel-shaped device used to increase or direct the sound of the voice.

meg·a·ton (meg′ə tun′) *n.* a unit used to measure the explosive force of nuclear bombs, equal to the force produced by the explosion of 1 million tons (907 million kilograms) of TNT.

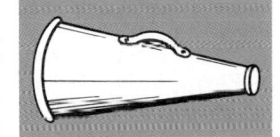

megaphone

meg·a·watt (meg′ə wot′) *n.* a unit of electrical or mechanical power equal to 1 million watts (1,341 horsepower).

mei·o·sis (mī ō′sis) *n.* in living things that reproduce sexually, the process of cell division by which the number of chromosomes in a sex cell are reduced by half.

mel·an·cho·li·a (mel′ən kō′lē ə) *n.* a mental disorder characterized by severe depression and self-criticism.

mel·an·chol·ic (mel′ən kol′ik) *adj.* **1.** melancholy; sad; depressed. **2.** of, relating to, or suffering from melancholia.

mel·an·chol·y (mel′ən kol′ē) *adj.* **1.** low in spirits; sad; depressed. **2.** suggestive of or causing sadness: *melancholy music.* —*n., pl.* **mel·an·chol·ies.** a gloomy or depressed state of mind; sadness. [From the Old French word *melancolie* meaning ''bad-humored'' or ''having a surplus of black bile,'' going back to the Greek word *melancholia* with the same meanings, from the words *melas* ''black'' + *cholē* ''bile.'' In former times, black bile was thought to be one of the four humors that made up the body and influenced a person's temperament.]

Mel·a·ne·sian (mel′ə nē′zhən) *n.* **1.** a member of a Negroid people living in Melanesia. **2.** any of the languages spoken in Melanesia. —*adj.* of or relating to Melanesia, its people, their languages, or culture.

mé·lange (mā länzh′) *n.* a mixture; medley: *a mélange of antique and modern furniture.* [From the French word *mélange,* from the Old French word *mesler* meaning ''to mix,'' going back to the Latin word *miscēre* ''to mix.'']

mel·a·nin (mel′ə nin) *n.* a dark brown pigment present in skin, hair, and other animal tissues. It helps to determine the color of the skin, hair, and eyes.

mel·a·no·ma (mel′ə nō′mə) *n.* cancer of the skin cells that produce the dark brown pigment melanin. [Formed from the Greek word *melas* meaning ''black'' + the Greek suffix *-ōma* meaning ''a tumor.'']

Mel·ba toast (mel′bə) very thin, dry slices of toast.

meld (meld) *v.t., v.i.* in card games, to place (one or more cards) on the table in a set or on another set. —*n.* **1.** the act of melding. **2.** the cards melded.

me·lee (mā′lā′, mā lā′) *also,* **mê·lée.** *n.* a confused fight involving a number of people.

mel·lif·lu·ous (me lif′lü əs) *adj.* sweetly or smoothly flowing: *a mellifluous voice.* —**mel·lif′lu·ous·ly,** *adv.*

mel·low (mel′ō) *adj.* **1.** (of fruit) soft, sweet, and juicy from ripeness. **2.** (of cheese and wine) rich, delicate, and fully aged. **3.** softened and made wise, gentle, and understanding by age and experience. **4.** full, rich, and soft: *a mellow color, a mellow tone.* —*v.t., v.i.* to make or become mellow. —**mel′low·ly,** *adv.* —**mel′low·ness,** *n.*

me·lod·ic (mə lod′ik) *adj.* **1.** relating to or containing melody. **2.** melodious; musical. —**me·lod′i·cal·ly,** *adv.*

me·lo·di·ous (mə lō′dē əs) *adj.* **1.** pleasant to hear; musical: *a melodious voice.* **2.** of, relating to, or producing melody. —**me·lo′di·ous·ly,** *adv.* —**me·lo′di·ous·ness,** *n.*

mel·o·dra·ma (mel′ə drä′mə, mel′ə dram′ə) *n.* **1.** a dramatic performance or play characterized by exaggerated emotions, sensational or overly sentimental incidents, and usually having a happy ending. **2.** such plays as a group. **3.** sensational or overly emotional writing, speech, or behavior.

mel·o·dra·mat·ic (mel′ə drə mat′ik) *adj.* **1.** of, relating to, or characteristic of melodrama: *melodramatic acting.* **2.** sensational or overly emotional: *a melodramatic plea.* —**mel′o·dra·mat′i·cal·ly,** *adv.*

mel·o·dy (mel′ə dē) *n., pl.* **mel·o·dies.** **1.** a pleasing arrangement or series of sounds. **2.** *Music.* **a.** a series of notes that makes up a complete phrase or idea; tune. **b.** the main part in a harmonized composition.

mel·on (mel′ən) *n.* a large fruit of any of several leafy vines, having a sweet, soft, juicy pulp that can be eaten. Watermelons, cantaloupes, and casabas are melons.

Mel·pom·e·ne (mel pom′ə nē) *n. Greek Mythology.* the Muse of tragedy.

melt (melt) *v.,* **melt·ed, melt·ed** or *(archaic)* **mol·ten, melt·ing.** —*v.i.* **1.** to be changed from a solid to a liquid state, especially by heating: *By the end of winter the ice on the pond had melted.* **2.** to dissolve, as in water. **3.** to disappear gradually; disperse. **4.** to pass or change by gradual degrees; blend: *The blue of the sky melted into the green landscape.* **5.** to become gentle, tender, or more understanding; soften: *My heart melted when the child began to cry.* —*v.t.* **1.** to change (something) from a solid to a liquid state, especially by heating. **2.** to dissolve (something), as in water: *to melt sugar in lemonade.* **3.** to make gentle, tender, or more understanding. —**melt′er,** *n.*

at; āpe; fär; câre; end; mē; it; īce; pîerce; hot; ōld; sông; fôrk; oil; out; up; ūse; rüle; pùll; tûrn; chin; sing; shop; thin; this; hw in white; zh in treasure. The symbol ə stands for the unstressed vowel sound heard in about, taken, pencil, lemon, and circus.

M

melt·ing point, the temperature at which a given solid changes into a liquid. The melting point of a solid is identical to its freezing point. The melting point of ice is 32 degrees Fahrenheit (0 degrees Celsius).

melt·ing pot, a country, city, or region in which people of various races and nationalities become part of an existing culture.

mem·ber (mem′bər) *n.* **1.** a person, animal, or thing belonging to a group: *The club has 200 members. The wolf is a member of the dog family.* **2.** also, **Member.** a representative of a legislative body: *a member of Congress.* **3.** *Mathematics.* **a.** either of the sides of an algebraic equation. **b.** one of the collection of objects that make up a set; element. **4.** a part of a human or animal body, especially a limb.

mem·ber·ship (mem′bər ship′) *n.* **1.** the state or condition of being a member of a group. **2.** the members of a group or organization as a whole: *The union membership voted to strike.* **3.** the number of members in a group or organization: *The club's membership increased this year.*

mem·brane (mem′brān) *n.* a thin layer of tissue that lines a cavity or passage in the body or covers a body surface.

mem·bra·nous (mem′brə nəs) *adj.* **1.** of, relating to, or resembling a membrane. **2.** forming a membrane.

me·men·to (mə men′tō) *n., pl.* **me·men·tos** or **me·men·toes.** anything serving as a reminder of someone or something; keepsake; souvenir: *The pennant is a memento of my high school days.*

mem·o (mem′ō) *n., pl.* **mem·os.** see **memorandum.**

mem·oir (mem′wär) *n.* **1.** *usually,* **memoirs. a.** a record of facts and events having to do with a particular subject or period, usually written from the writer's personal knowledge, experiences, and observations. **b.** a written account of the incidents and experiences of one's life; autobiography. **2.** an account of a person's life; biography. **3. memoirs.** a report of the proceedings of an organization or society.

mem·o·ra·bil·i·a (mem′ər ə bil′ē ə) *pl. n.* things that are worth being remembered or recorded.

mem·o·ra·ble (mem′ər ə bəl) *adj.* not to be forgotten; worthy of remembrance; notable: *a memorable event in history.* —**mem′o·ra·bly,** *adv.*

mem·o·ran·dum (mem′ə ran′dəm) *n., pl.* **mem·o·ran·dums** or **mem·o·ran·da** (mem′ə ran′də). **1.** a brief note written as a reminder. **2.** an informal letter or communication, as that sent between departments in a business office. **3.** a short document stating the terms of a legal or business agreement or transaction.

memorial
the Vietnam War Memorial in Washington, D.C.

me·mo·ri·al (mə môr′ē əl) *n.* **1.** something serving as a remembrance of some person or event, such as a monument or plaque: *The town built a memorial to honor the famous general.* **2.** a written request or statement of facts sent to a government, legislative body, or other group in authority. —*adj.* serving as a memorial; commemorative: *a memorial plaque.*

Memorial Day, a legal holiday in memory of members of the military killed in all American wars. It was originally celebrated on May 30, and is now usually celebrated on the last Monday in May. Also, **Decoration Day.**

me·mo·ri·al·ize (mə môr′ē ə līz′) *v.t.,* **me·mo·ri·al·ized, me·mo·ri·al·iz·ing. 1.** to preserve or honor the memory of. **2.** to submit a memorial to; petition.

mem·o·rize (mem′ə rīz′) *v.t.,* **mem·o·rized, mem·o·riz·ing.** to learn by heart; commit to memory. —**mem′o·ri·za′tion,** *n.* —**mem′o·riz′er,** *n.*

mem·o·ry (mem′ə rē) *n., pl.* **mem·o·ries. 1.** the mental power or ability to recall past experiences. **2.** all that one can or does recall: *I can recite the poem from memory.* **3.** someone or something remembered: *The accident is an unpleasant memory.* **4.** something that is remembered of a person or thing: *to honor the memory of those who died in war.* **5.** the period of time covered by recollection, such as that of a person or group: *an ancient time beyond the memory of the living.* **6.** remembrance; commemoration: *a prayer in memory of a parent.* **7.** the act of remembering or the state of being remembered. **8.a.** the capacity of a computer to store information that can be recalled later. **b.** the components of a computer in which this information is stored.

men (men) the plural of **man.**

men·ace (men′is) *n.* **1.** a person or thing that is a threat; danger: *The underwater reefs are a menace to ships entering the harbor.* **2.** a very annoying or troublesome person. —*v.t.,* **men·aced, men·ac·ing.** to put in danger; threaten; endanger: *The storm menaced the small ship.* —**men′ac·ing·ly,** *adv.*

me·nag·er·ie (mə naj′ə rē) *n.* **1.** a collection of wild or unusual animals kept in cages or other enclosures, usually for exhibition. **2.** the enclosure where such animals are kept.

mend (mend) *v.t.* **1.** to return to good condition or working order: *to mend a broken vase, to mend a torn curtain.* **2.** to reform, correct, or improve (something): *We were warned to mend our mischievous ways.* —*v.i.* **1.** to knit, as a broken bone; heal. **2.** to regain one's health; recover. —*n.* a mended place: *a mend in a sock's heel.*

·**on the mend.** getting better, especially in health.

men·da·cious (men dā′shəs) *adj.* **1.** given to lying; untruthful: *a mendacious person.* **2.** false; untrue: *mendacious rumors.* —**men·da′cious·ly,** *adv.*

men·dac·i·ty (men das′i tē) *n., pl.* **men·dac·i·ties. 1.** the quality of being mendacious; untruthfulness. **2.** a falsehood; lie.

men·de·le·vi·um (men′də lē′vē əm) *n.* a radioactive, metallic element produced artificially from einsteinium. Symbol: **Md** [From the Russian chemist Dmitry Ivanovich *Mendeleev* (1834–1907).]

men·di·cant (men′di kənt) *adj.* given to or characterized by begging; living on alms. —*n.* a person who lives on alms; beggar.

Men·e·la·us (men′ə lā′əs) *n. Greek Legend.* the king of Sparta whose wife, Helen, was carried off to Troy by Paris.

men·folk (men′fōk′) *also,* **men·folks.** *pl. n. Informal.* males as a group, especially all the male members of a family or other group.

men·ha·den (men hā′dən) *n., pl.* **men·ha·den.** a saltwater fish related to the herring, found in the western Atlantic. It is used as a source of animal feed, fertilizer, and oil.

me·ni·al (mē′nē əl) *adj.* **1.** degrading; lowly: *a menial* *task.* **2.** of, relating to, or suitable for a servant. —*n.* a servant who performs very lowly or humble tasks. —**me′ni·al·ly,** *adv.*

me·nin·ges (mi nin′jēz) *pl. n.,* *sing.* **me·ninx** (mē′ningks). the three membranes that enclose and protect the brain and spinal cord.

men·in·gi·tis (men′in jī′tis) *n.* a serious illness characterized by inflammation of the meninges.

me·nis·cus (mi nis′kəs) *n., pl.* **me·nis·cus·es** or **me·nis·ci** (mi nis′ī). **1.** a crescent or crescent-shaped body. **2.** the curved upper surface of a liquid in a container. The surface is concave if the liquid wets the walls of the container and convex if it does not. **3.** a lens that is convex on one side and concave on the other.

Men·non·ite (men′ə nīt′) *n.* a member of a Protestant sect founded in Holland in the sixteenth century, that rejects infant baptism, the taking of oaths, the holding of public office, and military service. [From the German word *Mennonit* meaning ''a Mennonite,'' from the Dutch religious reformer *Menno* Simons (1496–1561), who founded this sect + the German suffix *-it* ''-ite.'']

men-of-war (men′əv wôr′) the plural of **man-of-war.**

Me·nom·i·nee (mə nom′ə nē) *n., pl.* **Me·nom·i·nee** or **Me·nom·i·nees.** a member of a North American Indian tribe living in Wisconsin and speaking an Algonquian language.

men·o·pause (men′ə pôz′) *n.* the time at which menstruation permanently ceases to occur.

me·no·rah (mə nôr′ə) *n.* **1.** a candelabrum, traditionally with seven branches, used in Jewish religious services. **2.** a candelabrum with nine branches, used in the celebration of Hanukkah.

men·ser·vants (men′sûr′vənts) the plural of **manservant.**

men·ses (men′sēz) *pl. n.* another word for **menstruation.** ▲ used with either a singular or plural verb.

men·stru·al (men′strü əl) *adj.* of or relating to menstruation.

men·stru·ate (men′strü āt′) *v.i.,* **men·stru·at·ed, men·stru·at·ing.** to undergo menstruation. [From the Latin word *menstruatus,* past participle of *menstruare* meaning ''to menstruate,'' from the word *menstruus* ''monthly,'' from the word *mensis* ''month.'']

men·stru·a·tion (men′strü ā′shən) *n.* **1.** the periodic discharge of blood and bloody fluid from the uterus of a female who is not pregnant, occurring approximately every twenty-eight days in a woman between puberty and menopause. **2.** an instance of this. Also, **menses.**

men·su·ra·tion (men′shə rā′shən) *n.* **1.** the act or process of measuring. **2.** the branch of mathematics dealing with the determination of lengths, areas, and volumes.

–ment *suffix* (used to form nouns) **1.** the act or process of: *accomplishment, development.* **2.** the state or condition of being: *involvement, amazement.* **3.** the product or result of: *pavement, improvement.* **4.** the means or instrument of: *inducement.*

men·tal (men′təl) *adj.* **1.** of or relating to the mind: *mental development, mental awareness.* **2.** carried on in or performed by the mind: *mental arithmetic.* **3.** mentally ill: *a mental patient.* **4.** for the care of the mentally ill: *a mental hospital.*

mental age, the level of mental development as measured by performance on an intelligence test. A child who does as well on an intelligence test as an average ten-year-old is said to have a mental age of ten.

men·tal·i·ty (men tal′i tē) *n., pl.* **men·tal·i·ties. 1.** mental ability or power. **2.** a manner or way of thinking; outlook: *a British mentality.*

men·tal·ly (men′tə lē) *adv.* **1.** with regard to the mind: *to be mentally ill.* **2.** in or with the mind: *to add or subtract mentally.*

mental retardation, a condition in which there is a poor or incomplete development of intelligence, characterized by difficulty in learning.

men·thol (men′thôl) *n.* a white, crystalline substance obtained from peppermint oil by freezing.

men·tion (men′shən) *v.t.* to speak about or refer to briefly: *I mentioned them in my last letter.* —*n.* a brief remark or reference: *There was no mention of the robbery in today's newspaper.*

  ·not to mention. without needing to mention or consider: *That student is good-looking and smart, not to mention popular in school.*

Men·tor (men′tər) *n.* **1.** *Greek Mythology.* a loyal friend of Odysseus who was left in charge of his household and son. **2. mentor.** any wise and trusted counselor.

men·u (men′ū) *n.* **1.** a list of the food served or available in a restaurant or other eating place. **2.** the food served or available. **3.** *Computers.* a list of options, such as commands or functions, from which a user may choose while operating a computer.

me·ow (mē ou′) *also,* **mi·aow.** *n.* the cry of a cat. —*v.i.* to make such a sound.

Meph·i·stoph·e·les (mef′ə stof′ə lēz′) *n.* **1.** *German Legend.* the devil to whom Faust sold his soul. **2.** any crafty, evil person.

mer·can·tile (mûr′kən tēl′, mûr′kən tīl′) *adj.* **1.** of, relating to, or characteristic of merchants or commerce; commercial. **2.** of or relating to mercantilism.

mer·can·til·ism (mûr′kən ti liz′əm, mûr′kən tī liz′əm) *n.* an economic system developed in France and England in the sixteenth and seventeenth centuries that stressed strict government control of the national economy and believed that having more exports than imports was good because it brought in gold and silver from other countries.

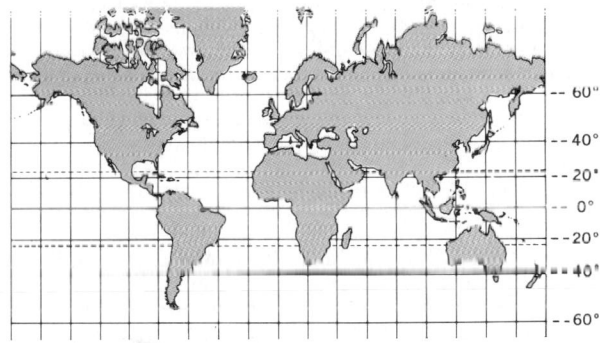

Mercator projection

Mer·ca·tor projection (mər kā′tər) a map projection developed in the sixteenth century, in which the distances between parallels of latitude gradually increase as one moves away from the equator. Though the relative sizes of areas in the higher latitudes are distorted, the Mercator projection shows compass directions as straight lines and so is ideal for navigation over small areas. [From the Flemish map maker Gerhardus *Mercator* (1512–1594), who devised this method.]

mer·ce·nar·y (mûr′sə ner′ē) *adj.* **1.** working or acting only out of a desire for money or material gain. **2.** (of a

at; āpe; fär; câre; end; mē; it; īce; pîerce; hot; ōld; sông, fôrk; oil; out; up; ūse; rüle; pùll; tûrn; chin; sing; shop; thin; **this;** hw in white; zh in treasure. The symbol ə stands for the unstressed vowel sound heard in about, taken, pencil, lemon, and circus.

M

-- 60°
-- 40°
-- 20°
-- 0°
-- 20°
-- 40°
-- 60°

soldier) serving in a foreign army for pay. —*n., pl.* **mer·ce·nar·ies.** a mercenary soldier.

mer·cer·ize (mûr′sə rīz′) *v.t.,* **mer·cer·ized, mer·cer·iz·ing.** to treat (cotton thread or fabric) with a caustic soda solution to give it more luster, strength, and absorbency and make it easier to dye. [From the English textile maker John *Mercer* (1791–1866), who invented this process.]

mer·chan·dise (*v.,* mûr′chən dīz′; *n.,* mûr′chən dīz′, mûr′chən dīs′) *n.* articles bought and sold; commodities; wares. —*v.,* **mer·chan·dised, mer·chan·dis·ing.** —*v.t.* **1.** to buy and sell; trade. **2.** to promote the sale of, as through advertising. —*v.i.* to carry on commerce; trade. —**mer′chan·dis′er,** *n.*

mer·chant (mûr′chənt) *n.* **1.** a person whose business is buying and selling merchandise for profit. **2.** a person who owns or runs a retail store; storekeeper. —*adj.* **1.** of or relating to merchants or commerce. **2.** of or relating to the merchant marine.

mer·chant·man (mûr′chənt mən) *n., pl.* **mer·chant·men** (mûr′chənt mən). a ship used in commerce.

merchant marine **1.** the commercial or trading ships of a nation as a group. **2.** the officers and crews of such ships.

mer·ci·ful (mûr′si fəl) *adj.* feeling, showing, or characterized by mercy. —**mer′ci·ful·ly,** *adv.* —**mer′ci·ful·ness,** *n.*

mer·ci·less (mûr′si lis) *adj.* without mercy; pitiless. —**mer′ci·less·ly,** *adv.* —**mer′ci·less·ness,** *n.*

mer·cu·ri·al (mər kyür′ē əl) *adj.* **1.** likely or tending to change; changeable; erratic: *a mercurial personality, mercurial moods.* **2.** of, relating to, containing, or caused by the action of mercury: *mercurial compounds, mercurial poisoning.* **3.** lively; quick. —**mer·cu′ri·al·ly,** *adv.*

Mer·cu·ro·chrome (mər kyür′ə krōm′) *n. Trademark.* a red antiseptic liquid solution that contains mercury.

Mer·cu·ry (mûr′kyə rē) *n.* **1.** *Roman Mythology.* the messenger of the gods and patron of commerce. In Greek mythology he was called Hermes. **2.** the second smallest planet of our solar system, after Pluto, and the closest planet to the sun. It is the fastest-moving planet, completing a full revolution in eighty-eight days.

mer·cu·ry (mûr′kyə rē) *n., pl.* **mer·cu·ries.** **1.** a heavy, lustrous, silvery, poisonous metallic element. It is the only metallic element that is liquid at normal room temperature. Mercury is used in electrical switches, thermometers, and barometers. Symbol: **Hg** Also, **quicksilver.** **2.** a column of mercury in a thermometer or barometer, used as an indication of temperature or atmospheric pressure: *The weather bureau reported that the mercury rose to 90° yesterday.* [From the Medieval Latin word *Mercurius* meaning this metal, the planet Mercury, and the god Mercury.]

mer·cy (mûr′sē) *n., pl.* **mer·cies.** **1.** kindness, forgiveness, or compassion toward another or others where harshness is expected or deserved; leniency: *The criminal begged the judge for mercy.* **2.** the disposition or power to be kind or forgiving: *The convicted thieves threw themselves on the mercy of the court.* **3.** something to be thankful for; blessing: *Your help was a real mercy.*

·**at the mercy of.** completely in the power of: *We were at the mercy of the enemy.*

mercy killing, another term for **euthanasia.**

mere (mîr) *adj. superlative,* **mer·est.** being nothing more or other than what is specified; only: *I was a mere child when we moved to California. I shudder at the mere sight of a spider.*

mere·ly (mîr′lē) *adv.* and nothing more; only: *Your explanations are merely poor excuses.*

mer·e·tri·cious (mer′i trish′əs) *adj.* attractive in a vulgar or deceitful way. —**mer′e·tri′cious·ly,** *adv.*

mer·gan·ser (mər gan′sər) *n.* a diving duck having a long, slender bill with saw-toothed edges and, usually, a crested head.

merge (mûrj) *v.,* **merged, merg·ing.** —*v.i.* to be united so as to become one: *The two paths merge just ahead. The two companies merged.* —*v.t.* to unite so as to become one: *The library merged the two rare book collections.*

merg·er (mûr′jər) *n.* the act of merging, especially the union of two or more corporations: *the merger of two advertising companies.*

me·rid·i·an (mə rid′ē ən) *n.* **1.** an imaginary great circle on the earth's surface passing through the North and South poles. **2.** one half of such a circle extending from pole to pole; a line or parallel of longitude. **3.** a great circle on the celestial sphere passing through the north and south celestial poles. **4.** the highest point; zenith: *the meridian of a person's career.*

me·ringue (mə rang′) *n.* **1.** a mixture of stiffly beaten egg whites and sugar, usually baked and used as a topping, as on cakes or pies. **2.** a small cake or pastry shell made of this mixture.

me·ri·no (mə rē′nō) *n., pl.* **me·ri·nos.** **1.** a sheep of a breed originally developed in Spain, having a light-colored fleece and a white face. It is raised for its wool. **2.** a fine, soft yarn or fabric made from the wool of this sheep, used for such items as suits or dresses. **3.** a knitted fabric woven from a blend of cotton and wool fibers, used for such items as hosiery and underwear.

merino *(def. 1)*

mer·it (mer′it) *n.* **1.** quality, worth, or excellence: *The author's latest book has great merit.* **2.** *also,* **merits.** something deserving praise or reward; good quality: *You may not like the plan, but it has its merits.* **3.** **merits.** the actual facts of a matter under consideration, whether good or bad: *The judge will decide the case on its merits.* —*v.t.* to be deserving of: *I feel that I merit a raise in pay.*

mer·i·to·ri·ous (mer′i tôr′ē əs) *adj.* worthy of reward or praise; having merit: *The soldier was given a medal for meritorious service.* —**mer′i·to′ri·ous·ly,** *adv.* —**mer′i·to′ri·ous·ness,** *n.*

merit system, a system in which people are hired, paid, or promoted according to their competence or performance, not strictly on the basis of seniority.

merle (mûrl) *also,* **merl.** *n.* a European blackbird.

Mer·lin (mûr′lin) *n.* in the legends of King Arthur, the wise magician who protected and counseled the young king.

mer·maid (mûr′mād′) *n.* in folklore, a sea creature having the head and body of a beautiful woman and the tail of a fish instead of legs.

mer·man (mûr′man′) *n., pl.* **mer·men** (mûr′men′). in folklore, a sea creature having the head and body of a man and the tail of a fish instead of legs.

mer·ri·ment (mer′i mənt) *n.* playfulness and gaiety; fun.

mer·ry (mer′ē) *adj.,* **mer·ri·er, mer·ri·est.** **1.** festive and cheerful; full of merriment: *a merry group of people.* **2.** characterized by festivity and rejoicing; joyous: *a merry song.* —**mer′ri·ly,** *adv.*

·**to make merry.** to be festive and jovial; celebrate.

mer·ry–an·drew (mer′ē an′drü) *n.* a clown; buffoon.

mer·ry–go–round (mer′ē gō round′) *n.* **1.** a revolving circular platform equipped with wooden animals, especially horses, and often having seats. It is ridden for amusement. Also, **carousel.** **2.** a circular platform that revolves when pushed, found in playgrounds. **3.** a rapid round; whirl: *a merry-go-round of parties during the holidays.*

mer·ry·mak·ing (mer′ē mā′king) *n.* **1.** the act of engaging in or having fun; making merry. **2.** boisterous or gay festivity: *The merrymaking after the wedding went on until late at night.* —*adj.* full of joy and fun; gay and festive. —**mer′ry·mak′er,** *n.*

me·sa (mā′sə) *n.* a flat-topped hill or mountain with steep sides descending to the plain below; high plateau. [From the Spanish word *mesa* meaning "table" and "mesa," from the Latin word *mensa* "table."]

mesa

mes·ca·line (mes′kə lēn′, mes′kə lin) *n.* a crystalline drug that produces hallucinations, derived from the dried tops of certain cactuses.

mes·dames (mā däm′) **1.** a plural of **madam**. **2.** the plural of **madame**.

mes·de·moi·selles (mād mwä zel′) a plural of **mademoiselle**.

mesh (mesh) *n., pl.* **mesh·es. 1.** one of the open spaces between the cords, threads, or wires of a net or netting. **2.** an open network consisting of interlaced cords, threads, or wires; netting. **3.** any of various fabrics consisting of an open network of interlaced threads. **4.** *also,* **meshes.** anything that entangles or traps: *They were caught in the mesh of their lies.* **5.** the interlocking or engagement of the teeth of a gear. —*v.t., v.i.* to engage or become engaged, as the teeth of a gear; interlock.
·**in mesh.** in gear; interlocked.

mes·mer·ism (mez′mə riz′əm, mes′mə riz′əm) *n.* another word for **hypnotism**. [From the Austrian physician Franz Anton *Mesmer* (1734–1815), who used hypnotism on his patients.]

mes·mer·ize (mez′mə rīz′, mes′mə rīz′) *v.t.,* **mes·mer·ized, mes·mer·iz·ing. 1.** to put in a hypnotic trance; hypnotize. **2.** to affect as deeply as by a trance: *We were mesmerized by the dazzling painting.* —**mes′mer·i·za′tion,** *n.* —**mes′mer·iz′er,** *n.*

mes·o·derm (mez′ō dûrm′, mes′ō dûrm′) *n.* the middle of the three cell layers of an embryo in an early stage of its development. The mesoderm develops into the skeletal, muscular, connective, and reproductive tissues.

mes·on (mez′on, mes′on) *n.* any of a group of subatomic particles whose mass is greater than that of an electron but less than that of a proton.

mes·o·sphere (mez′ə sfîr′, mes′ə sfîr′) *n.* the layer of the atmosphere above the stratosphere, from about 30 miles to about 50 miles (50–80 kilometers) above the earth's surface.

Mes·o·zo·ic (mez′ə zō′ik, mes′ə zō′ik) *n.* one of the major geological eras, comprising the Cretaceous, Jurassic, and Triassic periods; age of reptiles. —*adj.* of, relating to, or characteristic of this era.

mes·quite (mes kēt′) *n.* a small thorny tree or shrub that grows in desert regions from the southwestern United States to Chile, bearing small flowers, and slender seed pods containing beans used as feed for livestock.

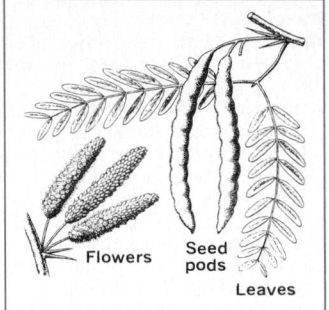

Flowers
Seed pods
Leaves

mesquite

mess (mes) *n., pl.* **mess·es. 1.** an untidy, disorderly, or dirty state or condition: *The closet is in a mess.* **2.** a person or thing that is in such a state or condition: *The room was a mess after the party.* **3.** an unpleasant, difficult, or confusing situation: *to make a mess of one's life.* **4.** an untidy or confused mass or collection; jumble: *a mess of newspapers on the floor.* **5.** an indefinite amount: *to catch a mess of fish.* **6.a.** a group of people who take meals together regularly, especially in the army or navy. **b.** the meal eaten by such a group. **c.** the place where such a meal is eaten; mess hall. —*v.i.* **1.** to interfere or tamper: *Don't mess with my typewriter.* **2.** to take one's meals in a mess hall.
·**to mess around.** to waste time or busy oneself by puttering: *We messed around in the house all day.*
·**to mess up. a.** to make dirty or untidy: *to mess up a room.* **b.** to confuse or spoil: *Your late arrival messed up our plans.*

mes·sage (mes′ij) *n.* **1.** a communication sent from one person or group to another. **2.** a formal or official communication: *the president's message to Congress.* **3.** the point of view or idea meant to be communicated: *The movie's message was that crime doesn't pay.*

mes·sen·ger (mes′ən jər) *n.* **1.** a person who picks up and delivers messages or runs errands. **2.** a person employed to deliver telegrams, letters, or parcels. **3.** a person whose work is carrying official dispatches. **4.** *Archaic.* a person or thing that tells of something to come; harbinger; forerunner.

messenger RNA, see **RNA**.

mess hall, a place where a group of people take meals together regularly, especially in the army or navy.

Mes·si·ah (mə sī′ə) *n.* **1.** in Judaism, the expected savior of the Jews promised by God. **2.** in Christianity, Jesus, regarded as the savior of the human race. **3.** *also,* **messiah.** any savior or deliverer.

Mes·si·an·ic (mes′ē an′ik) *adj.* **1.** of or relating to the Messiah. **2.** *also,* **messianic.** characteristic of a messiah.

mes·sieurs (mes′ərz) the plural of **monsieur**.

mess kit, a compact kit consisting of eating utensils and a metal container that opens to make two separate compartments for holding food, used by a soldier or camper.

mess·mate (mes′māt′) *n.* a regular companion at meals, especially in a ship's mess.

Messrs. (mes′ərz) **1.** Messieurs. **2.** the plural of **Mr.**: *Messrs. Holmes and Watson.*

mess·y (mes′ē) *adj.,* **mess·i·er, mess·i·est. 1.** being in a mess; untidy: *a messy room.* **2.** causing a mess; unpleasant or difficult: *I got the messy job of cleaning the oven.* —**mess′i·ly,** *adv.* —**mess′i·ness,** *n.*

---

at; āpe; fär; câre; end; mē; it; īce; pîerce; hot; ōld; sông; fôrk; oil; out; up; ūse; rüle; pull; tûrn; chin; sing; shop; thin; this; hw in white; zh in treasure. The symbol ə stands for the unstressed vowel sound heard in about, taken, pencil, lemon, and circus.

M

mes·ti·zo (mes tē′zō) *n., pl.* **mes·ti·zos** or **mes·ti·zoes**. a person of mixed racial ancestry, especially a person of Spanish and American Indian descent.

met (met) the past tense and past participle of **meet**[1].

met·a·bol·ic (met′ə bol′ik) *adj.* of, relating to, involving, or characterized by metabolism: *metabolic rate, metabolic changes.*

me·tab·o·lism (mə tab′ə liz′əm) *n.* the total of all the biological and chemical processes that occur in a living thing. Metabolism is the means by which food is converted into protoplasm and by which the necessary energy is provided to carry on all basic life processes, such as respiration, digestion, and cell division.

met·a·car·pal (met′ə kar′pəl) *adj.* of or relating to the metacarpus. —*n.* one of the bones of the metacarpus. See **hand** for illustration.

met·a·car·pus (met′ə kär′pəs) *n., pl.* **met·a·car·pi** (met′ə kär′pī). **1.** the part of the hand between the wrist and the fingers, having five bones. **2.** a similar part of the forelimb of an animal.

met·al (met′əl) *n.* **1.** any of a class of chemical elements, such as iron, silver, copper, or lead, that have a shiny surface, can be melted, conduct heat and electricity, and usually can be hammered into thin sheets or drawn out into wires. **2.** a mixture of such elements, as brass or bronze; alloy. **3.** a basic quality or substance; mettle.

me·tal·lic (mə tal′ik) *adj.* **1.** of or having the properties of metal. **2.** containing or yielding metal. **3.** resembling, characteristic of, or suggestive of metal: *a metallic sound.*

met·al·loid (met′ə loid′) *n.* any of a class of chemical elements that have both metallic and nonmetallic properties. —*adj.* **1.** of, relating to, or having the properties of a metalloid. **2.** resembling a metal.

met·al·lur·gist (met′ə lûr′jist) *n.* a student of or an expert in metallurgy.

met·al·lur·gy (met′ə lûr′jē) *n.* the science and technology of separating metals from ores and preparing them for use, as by refining. —**met′al·lur′gi·cal,** *adj.*

met·al·work (met′əl wûrk′) *n.* **1.** objects or structures made of metal. **2.** metalworking.

met·al·work·ing (met′əl wûr′king) *n.* the act or process of making metal objects or structures. —**met′al·work′er,** *n.*

met·a·mor·phic (met′ə-môr′fik) *adj.* **1.** of, relating to, or characterized by metamorphosis. **2.** *Geology.* of, relating to, or produced by metamorphism.

met·a·mor·phism (met′ə-môr′fiz əm) *n.* **1.** the change in the texture, structure, and mineral composition of rock caused by processes operating beneath the surface of the earth. **2.** another word for **metamorphosis.**

met·a·mor·phose (met′ə-môr′fōz) *v.,* **met·a·mor·phosed, met·a·mor·phos·ing.** —*v.t.* to cause to undergo metamorphosis or metamorphism. —*v.i.* to undergo metamorphosis or metamorphism.

met·a·mor·pho·sis (met′-ə môr′fə sis) *n., pl.* **met·a·mor·pho·ses** (met′ə môr′-fə sēz′). **1.** the process by which certain animals go

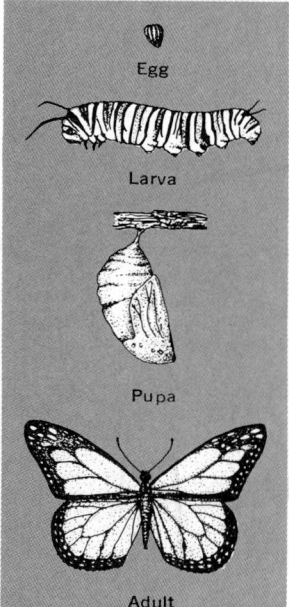

Egg

Larva

Pupa

Adult

metamorphosis of a butterfly

through changes in form, structure, or function as they develop from an immature form at birth or hatching to an adult. Caterpillars become butterflies and tadpoles become frogs through the process of metamorphosis. **2.** any complete or great change, as in form, appearance, character, or condition.

met·a·phor (met′ə fôr′) *n.* a figure of speech in which one object or idea is compared or identified with another in order to suggest a similarity between the two. For example: *The sky is a great ocean.*

Language Note

Metaphor is one of the most common figures of speech. We most often think of it as it is used in poetry and other creative writing. Poets use metaphor to give their writing a fresh, vivid quality and to surprise us by comparing one thing with another to which it is not normally related. For example, when Shakespeare wrote "All the world's a stage and all the men and women merely players," he was comparing life to a play acted in a theater and comparing people in general to actors.

We all use metaphor in our everyday speaking and writing. In fact, any new meaning of a word is a kind of metaphor. This means that from the original meaning of a word, new meanings are developed as they are used to compare different things to the original meaning. An example of this type of metaphor is our using the word *leg* to describe one of the supports of a table. If people made up a new word to describe every new thought that they had, it would be almost impossible for them to communicate with each other. Using old words to describe new ideas makes it easier for people to understand the new ideas. Because the word *memory* has been applied to the part of a computer that stores information, we can understand its function, even though a new definition of *memory* is being used. Our language has grown far more from the adoption of metaphorical meanings of existing words than it has from the creation of new words.

met·a·phor·i·cal (met′ə fôr′i kəl) *adj.* relating to or containing metaphors. —**met′a·phor′i·cal·ly,** *adv.*

met·a·phys·i·cal (met′ə fiz′i kəl) *adj.* **1.** of, relating to, or characteristic of metaphysics. **2.** hard to understand; highly abstract. —**met′a·phys′i·cal·ly,** *adv.*

met·a·phy·si·cian (met′ə fə zish′ən) *n.* a student of or an expert in metaphysics.

met·a·phys·ics (met′ə fiz′iks) *n.* the branch of philosophy that deals with the nature and meaning of reality. ▲ used with a singular verb.

me·tas·ta·sis (mə tas′tə sis) *n., pl.* **me·tas·ta·ses** (mə-tas′tə sēz′). the spread of a disease, especially a cancerous growth, from one part of the body to another.

me·tas·ta·size (mi tas′tə sīz′) *v.i.* to spread from one part of the body to another, as certain types of cancer.

met·a·tar·sal (met′ə tär′səl) *adj.* of or relating to the metatarsus. —*n.* one of the bones of the metatarsus.

met·a·tar·sus (met′ə tär′səs) *n., pl.* **met·a·tar·si** (met′-ə tär′sī). **1.** the part of the foot between the ankle and the toes, consisting of five bones. **2.** a similar part of the hind foot of a four-legged animal, or the foot of a bird.

met·a·zo·an (met′ə zō′ən) *n.* any animal whose body is composed of specialized cells grouped to form tissues and organs. All animals are metazoans except the protozoans and the sponges. —*adj.* of, relating to, or characteristic of the metazoans.

mete (mēt) *v.t.,* **met·ed, met·ing.** to distribute by or as if by measuring; allot: *to mete out punishment.*

me·te·or (mē′tē ər) *n.* matter from space that enters the earth's atmosphere, where it is heated by friction until it burns with a bright light as it travels. Also, **falling star, shooting star.**

me·te·or·ic (mē′tē ôr′ik) *adj.* **1.** of, relating to, or containing meteors. **2.** resembling a meteor; brilliant and swift: *The young senator had a meteoric rise in politics.* **3.** of, relating to, or occurring in the earth's atmosphere: *Hurricanes are meteoric phenomena.*

me·te·or·ite (mē′tē ə rīt′) *n.* a meteor that has fallen to earth.

me·te·or·oid (mē′tē ə roid′) *n.* a meteor while it is still in space, before it enters the earth's atmosphere.

me·te·or·o·log·i·cal (mē′tē ər ə loj′i kəl) *adj.* of or relating to meteorology. —**me′te·or·o·log′i·cal·ly,** *adv.*

me·te·or·ol·o·gist (mē′tē ə rol′ə jist) *n.* a student of or an expert in meteorology.

me·te·or·ol·o·gy (mē′tē ə rol′ə jē) *n.* the science dealing with the study of the atmosphere and the changes that take place within it. One important branch of meteorology is the study of weather.

me·ter¹ (mē′tər) *also, British,* **me·tre.** *n.* the fundamental unit of length in the metric system, equivalent to 3.28 feet. [From the French word *mètre* meaning this distance, from the Greek word *metron* "a measure, rule."]

me·ter² (mē′tər) *also, British,* **me·tre.** *n.* **1.** the regular arrangement of accented and unaccented or short and long syllables in a line of poetry; poetic rhythm. **2.** the regular pattern of accented notes or beats in a musical composition; musical rhythm: *Waltzes are written in triple meter.* [From the Old French word *metre* with the same meanings, from the Latin word *metrum* "poetical meter," from the Greek word *metron* "a measure, rule."]

me·ter³ (mē′tər) *n.* **1.** an instrument or device for measuring and recording the amount of gas, water, or electricity used or the rate of flow. **2.** any of various similar instruments or devices for measuring and recording time, speed, distance, or degree of intensity. —*v.t.* to measure or record by means of a meter. [From -*meter.*]

-meter *combining form* **1.** a device for measuring: *speedometer.* **2.** having a specified amount of meters: *kilometer.* **3.** having a specified number of poetic feet: *pentameter.* [From the French suffix -*mètre* with the same meanings, going back to the Greek word *metron* "a measure, rule."]

me·ter–kil·o·gram–sec·ond (mē′tər kil′ə gram′sek′-ənd) *adj.* of, relating to, or being a system of measurement in which the meter is the unit of length, the kilogram is the unit of mass, and the second is the unit of time.

meth·a·done (meth′ə dōn′) *n.* a synthetic narcotic drug used to relieve pain and as a substitute for heroin in the treatment of heroin addiction.

meth·ane (meth′ān) *n.* a colorless, odorless, highly flammable gas that is the simplest compound of carbon and hydrogen. It is the main constituent of natural gas. Also, **marsh gas.**

meth·a·nol (meth′ə nôl′) *n.* a clear, poisonous, liquid alcohol compound, used in antifreeze, shellac, and rocket fuel. Also, **methyl alcohol, wood alcohol.**

me·thinks (mi thingks′) *v.,* **me·thought.** *Archaic.* it seems to me.

meth·od (meth′əd) *n.* **1.** a way, means, or manner of doing something, especially so as to be systematic or orderly. **2.** orderliness and regularity in thought, action, or activity: *The student's preparation for the test lacked method.*

me·thod·i·cal (me thod′i kəl) *adj.* **1.** performed, arranged, or carried on in a systematic or orderly manner: *a methodical search.* **2.** characterized by systematic or orderly habits or behavior: *a very methodical housekeeper.* —**me·thod′i·cal·ly,** *adv.* —**me·thod′i·cal·ness,** *n.*

Meth·od·ism (meth′ə diz′əm) *n.* the faith, doctrines, and practices of the Methodists.

Meth·od·ist (meth′ə dist) *n.* a member of any of several branches of a Protestant denomination that had its origin in the teachings and work of John and Charles Wesley. —*adj.* of, relating to, or characteristic of Methodists or Methodism.

meth·od·ol·o·gy (meth′ə dol′ə jē) *n., pl.* **meth·od·ol·o·gies.** an orderly system of principles and methods used in a particular field.

me·thought (mi thôt′) the past tense of **methinks.**

Me·thu·se·lah (mə thü′zə lə) *n.* any very old man. [From the patriarch *Methuselah* who lived 969 years according to the Book of Genesis.]

meth·yl alcohol (meth′əl) another term for **methanol.**

me·tic·u·lous (mə tik′yə ləs) *adj.* characterized by or showing extreme or excessive concern about details. —**me·tic′u·lous·ly,** *adv.* —**me·tic′u·lous·ness,** *n.*

me·tre¹ (mē′tər) *British.* another spelling of **meter¹.**

me·tre² (mē′tər) *British.* another spelling of **meter².**

met·ric¹ (met′rik) *adj.* of, relating to, or designating the metric system: *metric measurement.* [From the French word *mètrique* with the same meaning, from the word *mètre* "meter¹."]

met·ric² (met′rik) *adj.* another word for **metrical.** [From the Latin word *metricus* meaning "metrical," from the Greek word *metrikos* "of measure," from the word *metron* "a measure, rule."]

met·ri·cal (met′ri kəl) *adj.* **1.** of, relating to, or composed in poetic meter. **2.** of, relating to, or used in measurement. —**met′ri·cal·ly,** *adv.*

met·ri·cate (met′ri kāt′) *v.t.,* **met·ri·cat·ed, met·ri·cat·ing.** to change to the metric system: *to metricate highway signs.* —**met′ri·ca′tion,** *n.*

metric system, a decimal system of measurement in which the meter is the fundamental unit of length, the kilogram is the fundamental unit of mass, and the liter is the fundamental unit of volume.

metric ton, a measure of weight equal to 1,000 kilograms or 2,204.62 pounds avoirdupois. Also, **tonne.**

met·ro (met′rō) *n., pl.* **met·ros.** a subway system in any of various cities, such as Paris and Montreal.

met·ro·nome (met′rə nōm′) *n.* a mechanical device used for indicating the exact tempo to be maintained in music. It usually has a reverse pendulum that can be adjusted to produce clicks at different tempos.

me·trop·o·lis (mə trop′ə lis) *n., pl.* **me·trop·o·lis·es.** **1.** a large city, especially one that is an important center of commerce or culture. **2.** the principal city of a particular country, state, or region. [From the Late Latin word *metropolis,* from the Greek word *mētropolis* meaning "chief city," from the words *mētēr* "mother" + *polis* "city."]

metronome

met·ro·pol·i·tan (met′rə pol′i tən) *adj.* **1.** relating to, resembling, or belonging to a metropolis: *a metropolitan police force.* **2.** consisting of or making up a metropolis and its surrounding regions: *the New York metropolitan area.* —*n.* in the Roman Catholic Church and certain Anglican and Orthodox churches, an archbishop who is head of a church province.

M

---

at; āpe; fär; câre; end; mē; it; īce; pîerce; hot; ōld; sông, fôrk; oil; out; up; ūse; rūle; pull; tûrn; chin; sing; shop; thin; <u>th</u>is; hw in white; zh in treasure. The symbol ə stands for the unstressed vowel sound heard in about, taken, pencil, lemon, and circus.

–metry *combining form* the art, science, or process of measuring: *geometry, optometry.*

met·tle (met′əl) *n.* **1.** spirit and courage. **2.** the basic quality or substance, as of a person's character.

Mev (mev) *n.* one million electron volts.

mew[1] (mū) *n.* the cry of a cat; meow. —*v.i.* to make such a sound. [Representation of the cry of a cat.]

mew[2] (mū) *n.* a gull, especially of Europe. Also, **sea mew.** [From the Old English word *mǣw* meaning this bird.]

mewl (mūl) *v.i.* to cry feebly like a baby; whimper.

mews (mūz) *pl. n.* **1.** stables built around a court or alley. **2.** a narrow street or alley, usually having houses that have been converted from stables. ▲ used with either a singular or plural verb.

Mex. 1. Mexican. **2.** Mexico.

Mex·i·can (mek′si kən) *n.* a person who was born in or is a citizen of Mexico. —*adj.* of or relating to Mexico, its people, their languages, or culture.

Mexican jumping bean, see **jumping bean.**

Mexican Spanish, the variety of the Spanish language that is used in Mexico.

Mexican War, the war fought between the United States and Mexico from 1846 to 1848.

me·zu·zah (mə zùz′ə) *also,* **me·zu·za.** *n.* in Judaism, a small container shaped like a tube, containing parchment inscribed with Biblical passages. It is usually attached to a doorpost of the home.

mez·za·nine (mez′ə nēn′) *n.* **1.** a floor or story between two main floors of a building, usually just above the ground floor. **2.** the lowest balcony in a theater or the first few rows of the balcony.

mez·zo (met′sō) *Music. adj.* half; medium; moderate. —*adv.* moderately.

mez·zo–so·pran·o (met′sō sə pran′ō) *n., pl.* **mez·zo·so·pran·os. 1.** a female voice lower than soprano and higher than alto. **2.** a singer who has such a voice. **3.** a musical part for such a voice. —*adj.* **1.** able to sing the mezzo-soprano. **2.** for the mezzo-soprano.

MF, medium frequency.

mfg., manufacturing.

Mg, the symbol for magnesium.

mg., milligram; milligrams.

Mgr. 1. Manager. **2.** Monseigneur. **3.** Monsignor.

MHG, M.H.G., Middle High German.

MHz, megahertz.

mi (mē) *n. Music.* **1.** the third note of the major scale. **2.** the note E.

mi., mile; miles.

MI, postal abbreviation for Michigan.

MIA (em′ī ā′) missing in action. —*n., pl.* **MIA's.** a member of the armed forces who cannot be found after a battle or war, either alive or dead.

mi·aow (mē ou′) another spelling of **meow.**

mi·as·ma (mī az′mə) *n., pl.* **mi·as·mas** or **mi·as·ma·ta** (mī az′mə tə). **1.** a poisonous vapor formerly believed to rise from the earth and decaying matter and pollute the air. **2.** any harmful influence, effect, or atmosphere.

mi·ca (mī′kə) *n.* any of a group of minerals that look like transparent or cloudy glass and can be separated into thin sheets, often used as insulators in electrical devices. Also, **isinglass.**

Mi·cah (mī′kə) *n.* a book of the Old Testament believed to have been written by the Hebrew prophet Micah.

mice (mīs) the plural of **mouse.**

Mich., Michigan.

Mi·chael (mī′kəl) *n.* in the Bible, an important archangel. In Christian tradition, Michael cast Satan out of heaven.

Mich·ael·mas (mik′əl məs) *n.* the Christian feast in honor of the archangel Michael. It falls on September 29.

Mic·mac (mik′mak) *n., pl.* **Mic·mac** or **Mic·macs.** a member of a North American Indian tribe formerly living in eastern Canada and speaking an Algonquian language.

mi·cra (mī′krə) a plural of **micron.**

micro– *combining form* **1.** very small; minute: *microorganism.* **2.** enlarging, magnifying, or amplifying: *microscope.* **3.** one millionth of (a specified unit): *micrometer.*

mi·crobe (mī′krōb) *n.* a microscopic living thing, especially one that causes disease.

mi·cro·bi·ol·o·gy (mī′krō bī ol′ə jē) *n.* the branch of biology that studies microorganisms. —**mi′cro·bi′o·log′i·cal,** *adj.* —**mi′cro·bi·ol′o·gist,** *n.*

mi·cro·chip (mī′krə chip′) *n.* a small chip made of semiconductor material and holding an integrated circuit. Also, **chip.**

mi·cro·coc·cus (mī′krō kok′əs) *n., pl.* **mi·cro·coc·ci** (mī′krō kok′sī). any of several varieties of bacteria that are spherical or egg-shaped.

mi·cro·com·put·er (mī′krō kəm pū′tər) *n.* a computer with less memory and capability than a minicomputer, used in homes, schools, businesses, and institutions to perform routine operations, such as word processing, work with graphics, and computerized mailings. Also, **personal computer.**

mi·cro·cop·y (mī′krə kop′ē) *n., pl.* **mi·cro·cop·ies.** a photographic copy, as of a manuscript, picture, or letter, that has been reduced in size.

mi·cro·cosm (mī′krə koz′əm) *n.* **1.** a little world; universe in miniature. **2.** anything thought of as being a miniature representation of something: *The small town was a microcosm of all of the nation.*

mi·cro·film (mī′krə film′) *n.* **1.** a photographic film, usually 35 or 16 millimeters wide, on which a newspaper or other printed matter is reproduced in miniature. **2.** a reproduction made on such film. —*v.t.* to make a microfilm of.

mi·cro·me·te·or·ite (mī′krō mē′tē ə rīt′) *n.* a tiny meteorite that, because of its size, encounters no air resistance in falling to earth.

mi·crom·e·ter[1] (mī krom′i tər) *n.* **1.** any of a group of instruments that measure very small dimensions, distances, or angles to a high degree of precision. **2.** see **micrometer caliper.** [From the French word *micromètre* meaning this instrument, from the prefix *micro-* "micro-" + *mètre* "meter[3]."]

mi·cro·me·ter[2] (mī′krō mē′tər) *n.* another word for **micron.** (*Micro-* + *meter*[1].)

micrometer caliper, a caliper having two jaws, one of which can be moved by turning a screw. It is used for making precise measurements.

mi·cron (mī′kron) *n., pl.* **mi·crons** or **mi·cra.** a unit of length equal to one millionth of a meter. Also, **micrometer.**

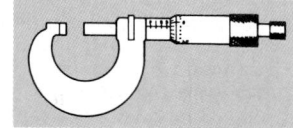

micrometer caliper

Mi·cro·ne·sian (mī′krə nē′zhən) *n.* **1.** a person who was born or is living in Micronesia. **2.** any of the languages spoken in Micronesia. —*adj.* of or relating to Micronesia, its people, their languages, or culture.

mi·cro·nu·cle·us (mī′krō nü′klē əs, mī′krō nū′klē əs) *n., pl.* **mi·cro·nu·cle·i** (mī′krō nü′klē ī′, mī′krō nū′klē-ī′) or **mi·cro·nu·cle·us·es.** the smaller of the two types of nuclei present in various protozoans, believed to control reproduction.

mi·cro·or·gan·ism (mī′krō ôr′gə niz′əm) *n.* a living thing, such as a bacterium or protozoan, that is too small to be seen with the naked eye.

mi·cro·phone (mī′krə fōn′) *n.* a device that converts sound waves to an electrical signal, used to record, transmit, or amplify sound.

microscopes

mi·cro·scope (mī'krə skōp') *n.* an instrument with a lens or combination of lenses that gives a clear magnified image of a small object viewed through it.

mi·cro·scop·ic (mī'krə skop'ik) *adj.* **1.** too small to be seen with the naked eye: *microscopic animals.* **2.** extremely small; minute. **3.** of, relating to, or done with a microscope: *a microscopic lens, a microscopic observation of cells.* **4.** as if done with a microscope; very detailed; thorough: *The jury made a microscopic examination of the evidence.* —**mi·cro·scop'i·cal·ly,** *adv.*

mi·cros·co·py (mī kros'kə pē) *n.* **1.** the process or technique of using a microscope. **2.** an investigation with a microscope.

mi·cro·sec·ond (mī'krō sek'ənd) *n.* one millionth of a second.

mi·cro·sur·ger·y (mī'krō sûr'jə rē) *n.* delicate surgery on tiny structures of the body, such as nerves and blood vessels.

mi·cro·wave (mī'krə wāv') *n.* a high-frequency electromagnetic wave having a wavelength ranging from about 1 millimeter to 30 centimeters. It is used in radar and for such purposes as long-distance transmission of television signals through the air. —*v.t.,* **mi·cro·waved, mi·cro·wav·ing.** to cook or heat in a microwave oven.

microwave oven, an oven in which food is quickly cooked with the heat produced by the action of microwaves entering the food.

mid[1] (mid) *adj.* being at or near the middle. [From the Old English word *midd* meaning "middle."]

mid[2] (mid) *also,* '**mid.** *prep. Archaic.* amid.

mid– *combining form* **1.** the middle part of: *midsummer, midweek.* **2.** being in the middle or center: *midpoint.*

mid·air (mid'âr') *n.* a point or region high in the air above the ground: *The acrobat did a spectacular flip in midair.*

Mi·das (mī'dəs) *n. Greek Legend.* a king who was given the power of turning everything he touched to gold.

mid·brain (mid'brān') *n.* the middle part of the brain.

mid·day (mid'dā') *n.* the middle of the day; noon. —*adj.* of, relating to, or occurring during the middle part of the day: *midday heat, a midday meal.*

mid·dle (mid'əl) *adj.* **1.** equally distant from the sides, ends, or outer points: *We sat in the middle row.* **2.** being or happening halfway between two things: *the middle child in a family.* **3.** average; medium: *a person of middle height.* —*n.* **1.** a point, part, or area equally distant from the sides, ends, or outer points: *the middle of the street.* **2.** a part or portion approximately halfway between the beginning and the end: *We left in the middle of the movie.* **3.** the middle part of the body; waist.

middle age, the time of life between youth and old age, often thought of as being between forty and sixty-five.

mid·dle-aged (mid'əl ājd') *adj.* **1.** in or of middle age. **2.** of or relating to persons of middle age.

Middle Ages, the period of European history between the fall of the Western Roman Empire and the beginning of the Renaissance, from about the fifth century to the middle of the fifteenth century.

middle C *Music.* **1.** the note written on the first line below the staff in the treble clef and the first line above the staff in the bass clef. **2.** the tone or key represented by this note.

mid·dle-class (mid'əl klas') *adj.* of, relating to, or characteristic of the middle class.

middle class, the part of society socially and economically above the lower class and below the upper class.

Middle Dutch, the Dutch language from the twelfth to the sixteenth centuries.

middle ear, the cavity between the eardrum and the inner ear, containing, in humans, the incus, malleus, and stapes. Also, **tympanum.**

Middle English, the English language from the twelfth through the fifteenth centuries.

Language Note

Middle English is the term language historians use to describe the English spoken from the twelfth through the fifteenth centuries. The invasion of England by French-speaking Normans in 1066 had a great effect upon the English language. *Old English,* which had been the dominant language of the country for centuries, was abandoned as the language of the rulers and the courts. For nearly two hundred years, England remained divided between a minority upper class who spoke, wrote, and ruled the country in French and a majority composed mostly of illiterate peasants who continued to speak English. For this reason, any important literature written in England during this time was written in French, the language of those who were wealthy and powerful enough to support writers.

But by the fourteenth century, even the rulers of the country had come to see themselves as English, especially since the country was then at war with France. During the fourteenth century, literature written in English began to flourish under Geoffrey Chaucer and other writers, and in the fifteenth century the Bible was first translated into English.

When English (in the form of Middle English) became reestablished, it was greatly changed from what it had been before the Norman Conquest. During the previous two hundred years, when it was primarily a spoken language, English had undergone basic changes in form and structure. Thousands of French words entered the language, particularly words used in the arts, government, law, philosophy, and military affairs. Today, about sixty percent of the words in a standard dictionary may be direct borrowings from French. Also, partly because of the French model, Middle English had far fewer inflectional endings than Old English had; for this reason, despite some archaic words and the lack of a fixed standard for spelling words, Chaucer's English seems much more familiar to us than Old English.

M

at; āpe; fär; câre; end; mē; it; īce; pîerce; hot; ōld; sông; fôrk; oil; out; up; ūse; rüle; pùll; tûrn; chin; sing; shop; thin; this; hw in white; zh in treasure. The symbol ə stands for the unstressed vowel sound heard in about, taken, pencil, lemon, and circus.

Middle French, the French language from the fourteenth to the sixteenth centuries.

Middle High German, High German from the twelfth to the mid-fourteenth centuries.

Middle Latin, another name for **Medieval Latin.**

Middle Low German, Low German from the twelfth to the sixteenth centuries.

mid·dle·man (mid′əl man′) *n., pl.* **mid·dle·men** (mid′-əl men′). **1.** a person who buys goods from the producer and sells them to the retailer or consumer. **2.** a go-between; intermediary.

mid·dle–of–the–road (mid′əl əv thə rōd′) *adj.* not taking or supporting any extreme position or side; moderate: *a middle-of-the-road politician.*

middle school, a school with classes for grades between elementary school and high school, usually from grade five or six through grade eight or nine.

mid·dle·weight (mid′əl wāt′) *n.* **1.** a boxer, wrestler, or weightlifter weighing more than a welterweight and less than a heavyweight. **2.** a person or animal of average weight.

mid·dling (mid′ling) *adj.* **1.** medium or average, as in size or amount: *a person of middling height, middling portions of food.* **2.** mediocre; second-rate: *a play with only middling performances by the actors.*

·**fair to middling.** moderately good; moderately well: *to feel fair to middling.*

mid·dy (mid′ē) *n., pl.* **mid·dies. 1.** *Informal.* a midshipman. **2.** see **middy blouse.**

middy blouse, a loosely fitting blouse designed to resemble a sailor's blouse.

midge (mij) *n.* any of various tiny flies of North America.

midg·et (mij′it) *n.* **1.** a very small but normally proportioned person. **2.** anything that is very small of its kind. —*adj.* very small.

mid·land (mid′lənd) *n.* the central or interior part of a region or country. —*adj.* of or situated in the midland: *a midland village.*

middy blouse

mid·most (mid′mōst) *adj.* being exactly in or nearest to the middle. —*adv.* in the middle or midst.

mid·night (mid′nīt) *n.* twelve o'clock at night; the middle of the night. —*adj.* **1.** of, relating to, or occurring at midnight: *a midnight train.* **2.** resembling midnight; very dark: *The dress was midnight blue.*

·**to burn the midnight oil.** to study or work late into the night.

midnight sun, the sun seen at midnight or late at night during summer in the arctic and antarctic regions.

mid·point (mid′point′) *n.* a point that is exactly in the middle of something, as a line.

mid·rib (mid′rib′) *n. Botany.* the central vein of a leaf.

mid·riff (mid′rif′) *n.* **1.** the part of the body below the breast and above the waist. **2.** the part of a woman's garment that covers this part of the body. **3.** a woman's blouse or similar garment that exposes this part of the body. **4.** see **diaphragm** (*def. 1*).

mid·ship (mid′ship′) *adj.* of, relating to, or situated in or near the middle of a ship.

mid·ship·man (mid′ship′mən) *n., pl.* **mid·ship·men** (mid′ship′mən). **1.** in the U.S. Navy, a student in training at the U.S. Naval Academy for commission as an officer. **2.** *British.* a second-year student in training on board ship for commission as an officer.

mid·ships (mid′ships′) *adv.* another word for **amidships.**

midst[1] (midst) *n.* **1.** the condition or position of being surrounded by or involved in something: *in the midst of a crowd, in the midst of trouble.* **2.** a gathering or association of people; company: *There is a traitor in our*

midst. **3.** the central or middle part. [From the Middle English word *middes* with the same meaning, from the phrase *in middes* "in the midst," from the Old English word *midde* "the middle."]

midst[2] (midst) *also,* '**midst.** *prep.* amid; amidst.

mid·stream (mid′strēm′) *n.* **1.** the middle of a stream: *to keep a boat in midstream.* **2.** the middle part of a course of action: *The debate was confusing because several of the participants changed their opinions in midstream.*

mid·sum·mer (mid′sum′ər) *n.* **1.** the middle of summer. **2.** the summer solstice, occurring about June 21. —*adj.* of, relating to, or occurring in the middle of summer.

mid·term (mid′tûrm′) *n.* **1.** the middle of a school term or semester. **2.** a test taken during the middle of a school term or semester. —*adj.* taking place during the middle of a school term or semester: *a midterm vacation.*

mid·town (mid′toun′) *n.* the central part of a city or town. —*adj.* relating to or located in midtown.

mid·way (mid′wā′) *adj.* located in the middle of the way or distance: *the midway point of a journey.* —*adv.* in or to the middle of the way or distance; halfway: *They built a bakery midway between my house and the school.* —*n.* a place where sideshows and other amusements are located, as at a carnival, circus, or fair.

mid·week (mid′wēk′) *n.* the middle of the week. —*adj.* in the middle of the week.

mid·wife (mid′wīf′) *n., pl.* **mid·wives** (mid′wīvz′). a person trained to assist women in childbirth.

mid·win·ter (mid′win′tər) *n.* **1.** the middle of winter. **2.** the winter solstice, occurring about December 22. —*adj.* of, relating to, or occurring in the middle of winter.

mid·year (mid′yîr′) *n.* the middle of the year. —*adj.* taking place during the middle of a year.

mien (mēn) *n.* a person's manner or appearance, especially as showing character or mood; bearing: *a person of gentle mien.*

miff (mif) *v.t.* to cause to be offended or annoyed: *The stranger's rudeness miffed me.*

MIG (mig) *also,* **MiG, Mig.** *n.* any of various jet fighter planes designed and built by the Soviet Union. [From *Mi*(koyan,) *G*(urevich), the last names of the Soviet aircraft engineers Artem I. Mikoyan (1905–1970) and Mikhail I. Gurevich (1892–1976).]

might[1] (mīt) *auxiliary verb* **1.** the past tense of may. **2.** used to express possibility: *What you say might be true, but I'm not sure.* **3.** used to ask permission: *Might I use your dictionary for a day or two?* **4.** used to offer a suggestion: *You might try starting over and doing it a different way.*

might[2] (mīt) *n.* **1.** great power, force, or influence: *the might of a nation.* **2.** physical power or strength: *to slam a door with all one's might.* **3.** the power or ability to do or accomplish something: *I tried with all my might not to laugh at the dumb joke.* [From the Old English word *meaht* meaning "power, might[2]."]

might·i·ly (mī′tə lē) *adv.* **1.** with great force, power, or strength. **2.** to a great degree; very much; greatly.

might·y (mī′tē) *adj.,* **might·i·er, might·i·est. 1.** having or showing great power, strength, or ability: *a mighty foe.* **2.** very great in amount, degree, intensity, or extent: *a mighty task.* —*adv. Informal.* very; greatly: *It was mighty nice of you to call me.* —**might′i·ness,** *n.*

mi·gnon·ette (min′yə net′) *n.* any of various plants that have narrow spoon-shaped leaves and tiny, often fragrant yellowish white or greenish yellow flowers in long spikes or clusters.

mi·graine (mī′grān) *n.* a severe headache, usually affecting only one side of the head and tending to recur periodically.

mi·grant (mī′grənt) *n.* **1.** a person or thing that migrates.

2. a farm laborer who moves from one region to another in search of work. Also, **migrant worker.** —*adj.* migrating; migratory.

mi·grate (mī′grāt) *v.i.*, **mi·grat·ed, mi·grat·ing. 1.** to move from one country or region to another in order to settle there. **2.** to move seasonally or periodically from one region or climate to another: *Many birds migrate south in the fall.*

mi·gra·tion (mī grā′shən) *n.* **1.** the act or instance of migrating. **2.** a group, as of people or animals, that migrate together.

migration
a flock of migrating birds

mi·gra·to·ry (mī′grə tôr′ē) *adj.* **1.** characterized by or given to migration; migrating: *migratory birds, migratory tribes.* **2.** of or relating to migration.

mi·ka·do (mi kä′dō) *also,* **Mi·ka·do.** *n., pl.* **mi·ka·dos.** the emperor of Japan.

mike (mīk) *Informal. n.* see **microphone.** *v.t.*, **miked, mik·ing.** to provide with a microphone: *The singer was not miked.*

mil (mil) *n.* a unit of length equal to one thousandth of an inch (0.254 millimeter), used in measuring the diameter of wires.

mi·la·dy (mi lā′dē) *also,* **mi·la·di.** *n., pl.* **mi·la·dies.** my lady. ▲ used in speaking or referring to an English gentlewoman or noblewoman.

milch (milch) *adj.* (of a cow) giving milk.

mild (mīld) *adj.* **1.** not extreme, harsh, or severe; moderate: *a mild winter, a mild headache.* **2.** not sharp, strong, or bitter in taste or odor: *a mild cheese.* **3.** gentle or kind in disposition, manners, or behavior. —**mild′ly,** *adv.* —**mild′ness,** *n.*

mil·dew (mil′dü′) *n.* **1.** any of various fungi that attack plants, appearing as a fine powder or fuzzy down. Mildew causes dwarfing, deformation, and loss of the affected parts of the plant. **2.** any of various fungi that appear as discolored areas on leather or other materials. —*v.t.* to cause to have mildew: *The dampness in the basement mildewed the books.* —*v.i.* to have mildew.

mile (mīl) *n.* a unit of linear measure equal to 5,280 feet, or 1,760 yards (1.6 kilometers). [From the Old English word *mīl* meaning "a mile," from the Latin phrase *milia (passuum)* "thousands of paces," from the word *mille* "thousand."]

mile·age (mī′lij) *also,* **mil·age.** *n.* **1.** the total length, extent, or distance in miles: *What's the mileage between the two towns?* **2.** the total number of miles covered or traveled in a specified period of time: *We put a lot of mileage on the car during our vacation.* **3.** the number of miles traveled by a motor vehicle on a certain amount of fuel: *Thirty miles per gallon is good mileage.* **4.** the

amount of use, service, or wear yielded by something: *The comedian got plenty of mileage from those old jokes.*

mile·post (mīl′pōst′) *n.* a post set up, as on a highway, to mark the distance in miles to a place.

mile·stone (mīl′stōn′) *n.* **1.** a stone set up, as on a highway, to mark the distance in miles to a place. **2.** an important event or development: *The invention of the telephone was a milestone in the history of communications.*

mi·lieu (mil yü′, mil ū′, mēl yü′) *n.* surroundings or environment: *That university has an intellectual milieu.*

mil·i·tant (mil′i tənt) *adj.* **1.** active or aggressive in support of a cause: *The militant protesters occupied the building.* **2.** engaged in war or fighting: *militant nations.* —*n.* a militant person. —**mil′i·tan·cy,** *n.* —**mil′i·tant·ly,** *adv.*

mil·i·ta·rism (mil′i tə riz′əm) *n.* **1.** the glorification of war, and of the military, its ideals, and its policies. **2.** a national policy of maintaining a strong military force.

mil·i·ta·rist (mil′i tər ist) *n.* a person who supports or upholds militarism. —**mil′i·ta·ris′tic,** *adj.*

mil·i·ta·rize (mil′i tə rīz′) *v.t.*, **mil·i·ta·rized, mil·i·ta·riz·ing. 1.** to train and equip for war. **2.** to fill with militarism. —**mil′i·ta·ri·za′tion,** *n.*

mil·i·tar·y (mil′i ter′ē) *adj.* **1.** of, relating to, or involving armed forces, soldiers, or war: *a military unit, military tactics, a military career.* **2.** for members of the armed forces: *a military uniform.* —*n., pl.* **mil·i·tar·ies.** the military forces of a country; armed forces. —**mil′i·tar′i·ly,** *adv.*

military academy, an educational institution equivalent to a college, in which men and women are prepared for careers as officers in the armed forces.

military police, the members of the military assigned to police duties.

military school, a school in which students follow some of the routines and disciplines typical of military life.

mil·i·tate (mil′i tāt′) *v.i.*, **mil·i·tat·ed, mil·i·tat·ing.** to act, operate, or have influence: *The wrong you have done will militate against your good reputation.*

mi·li·tia (mi lish′ə) *n.* a military force that is not professional and that may be called for service in time of emergency.

mi·li·tia·man (mi lish′ə mən) *n., pl.* **mi·li·tia·men** (mi lish′ə mən). a member of a militia.

milk (milk) *n.* **1.** a white liquid produced by female mammals in their mammary glands for the nourishment of their young. **2.** this liquid, especially as produced by cows, used as food by human beings. **3.** any liquid resembling this: *coconut milk.* —*v.t.* **1.** to draw milk from (a cow, goat, or other female mammal). **2.** to extract or take (something): *to milk information from someone.* **3.** to extract or take something from; exploit: *The blackmailer milked them of their savings.* —*v.i.* to draw milk from a cow, goat, or other female mammal.

milk·er (mil′kər) *n.* **1.** a person or machine that milks cows. **2.** a cow or other animal that gives milk.

milk·maid (milk′mād′) *n.* a woman or girl who milks cows or works in a dairy.

milk·man (milk′man′) *n., pl.* **milk·men** (milk′men′). a person who sells or delivers milk.

milk of magnesia, a milky white liquid consisting mainly of magnesia in water, used to settle the stomach or to loosen the bowels.

M

at; āpe; fär; câre; end; mē; it; īce; pîerce; hot; ōld; sông; fôrk; oil; out; up; ūse; rüle; püll; tûrn; chin; sing; shop; thin; this; hw in white; zh in treasure. The symbol ə stands for the unstressed vowel sound heard in about, taken, pencil, lemon, and circus.

milk shake, a frothy, cold drink made of milk, flavoring, and sometimes ice cream, shaken or whipped together.

milk snake, any of several king snakes of North America that are yellowish brown or pale gray with reddish blotches. Milk snakes are harmless to humans and feed chiefly on rodents and other snakes.

milk·sop (milk′sop′) *n.* an unmanly or cowardly man or boy; sissy.

milk sugar, another term for **lactose.**

milk tooth, in human beings and other mammals, one of the temporary teeth that fall out and are replaced by permanent teeth.

milk·weed (milk′wēd′) *n.* a plant containing a milky juice, and having white, red, yellow, or purple flowers and long, green pods with many seeds.

milk·white (milk′hwīt′, milk′wīt′) *adj.* having the white or bluish white color of milk.

milk·y (mil′kē) *adj.*, **milk·i·er, milk·i·est.** **1.** resembling milk, especially in color. **2.** containing or yielding milk or a substance like milk. —**milk′i·ness,** *n.*

Milky Way, a galaxy made up of more than 100 billion stars, appearing as a bright white path across the heavens. Our solar system is part of the Milky Way. Also, **Galaxy.**

milkweed

mill¹ (mil) *n.* **1.** a building or business containing machinery for grinding or crushing grain: *a flour mill, a corn mill.* **2.** a machine or device that grinds or crushes grain. **3.** any of various machines or devices for grinding or crushing something: *a pepper mill, a coffee mill.* **4.** a building or group of buildings containing machinery for manufacturing or processing materials: *a paper mill, a steel mill.* —*v.t.* **1.** to grind or crush: *to mill grain.* **2.** to stamp or cut a series of notches or ridges around the edge of (a coin or other piece of metal). —*v.i.* to move in an aimless or confused manner: *The crowd milled outside the stadium after the game ended.* [From the Old English word *mylen* meaning "a mill¹," from the Late Latin word *molina* "a mill," going back to the Latin word *mola* "a mill, millstone."]

mill² (mil) *n.* a unit of monetary value, equal to ¹/₁₀ of a cent. [Short for the Latin word *millesimus* meaning "a thousandth."]

mill·dam (mil′dam′) *n.* a dam built across a stream to raise the water level in order to supply water power for a mill.

mil·len·ni·al (mi len′ē əl) *adj.* **1.** of or relating to a thousand years. **2.** of or relating to the millennium.

mil·len·ni·um (mi len′ē əm) *n., pl.* **mil·len·ni·a** (mi len′ē ə) or **mil·len·ni·ums.** **1.** a period of a thousand years. **2.** according to the New Testament, the period of a thousand years during which Jesus will reign on earth. **3.** a period of happiness, peace, and prosperity.

mill·er (mil′ər) *n.* **1.** a person who owns or operates a mill for grinding grain. **2.** any white or grayish moth whose wings look as if they were powdered with flour.

mil·let (mil′it) *n.* **1.** a grass that is like wheat and is widely raised for its small, edible grains. **2.** the small grain of this grass.

milli– *combining form* one thousandth of (a specified unit): *milligram.*

mil·li·bar (mil′ə bär′) *n.* a unit for measuring atmospheric pressure, equal to 1,000 dynes per square centimeter.

mil·li·gram (mil′i gram′) *also, British,* **mil·li·gramme.** *n.* a metric unit of weight, equal to one thousandth of a gram.

mil·li·li·ter (mil′ə lē′tər) *also, British,* **mil·li·li·tre.** *n.*

a metric measure of capacity, equal to one thousandth of a liter, or 0.061 cubic inch.

mil·li·me·ter (mil′ə mē′tər) *also, British,* **mil·li·me·tre.** *n.* a metric measure of length, equal to one thousandth of a meter, or 0.03937 inch.

mil·li·ner (mil′ə nər) *n.* a person who designs, makes, trims, or sells women's hats.

mil·li·ner·y (mil′ə ner′ē) *n.* **1.** the articles, especially hats, sold by a milliner. **2.** the business of a milliner.

mill·ing (mil′ing) *n.* **1.** the act or process of grinding or crushing grain or some other material by a mill. **2.** the process of stamping or cutting notches or ridges around the edge of a piece of metal, such as a coin. **3.** the notches or ridges produced by this.

mil·lion (mil′yən) *n.* **1.** the cardinal number that is one thousand times one thousand. **2.** a symbol representing this number, such as 1,000,000. **3.** an indefinitely large number: *That store stocks millions of hats.* —*adj.* numbering one million: *a million dollars.*

mil·lion·aire (mil′yə nâr′) *n.* a person who has a million or more dollars, pounds, or other unit of currency.

mil·lionth (mil′yənth) *adj.* **1.** (the ordinal of million) being last in a series of one million. **2.** being one of a million equal parts. —*n.* **1.** something that is last in a series of one million. **2.** one of a million equal parts.

mil·li·pede (mil′ə pēd′) *n.* a wormlike arthropod having as many as 200 legs on a jointed body, and feeding mainly on decayed plant matter such as rotting wood. [From the Latin word *millepeda* meaning "wood louse," from the words *mille* "thousand" + *pes* "foot."]

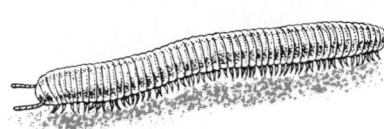

millipede

mill·pond (mil′pond′) *n.* a pond, usually formed by a dam, for supplying water power to a mill.

mill·race (mil′rās′) *n.* **1.** a current of water leading into and driving a mill wheel. **2.** the channel through which such a current runs.

mill·stone (mil′stōn′) *n.* **1.** either of a pair of circular stones between which grain or similar substances are placed for grinding. **2.** a heavy burden: *a millstone of debt.*

mill·stream (mil′strēm′) *n.* **1.** a stream whose water is used to run a mill. **2.** the water in a millrace.

mill wheel, a large wheel, usually turned by the force of falling water, that supplies mechanical power to run the machinery of a mill.

mi·lord (mi lôrd′) *n.* my lord. ▲ used in speaking or referring to an English gentleman or nobleman.

milque·toast (milk′tōst′) *n.* a weak, timid, apologetic person.

milt (milt) *n.* the sperm cells of fish, and the milky fluid containing them.

mime (mīm) *n.* **1.** a performer who portrays characters or conveys an idea or story by body movements, facial expressions, and gestures rather than by the use of speech. **2.** the art of pantomime. **3.** a drama popular among the ancient Greeks and Romans that made fun of actual persons and events. **4.** an actor in such a drama. —*v.*, **mimed, mim·ing.** —*v.t.* to act out in pantomime. —*v.i.* to act or perform as a mime. —**mim′er,** *n.*

mim·e·o·graph (mim′ē ə graf′) *n.* **1.** a machine for printing copies of material written, typed, or drawn on a stencil. **2.** a copy made by such a machine. —*v.t.* to reproduce on a mimeograph: *to mimeograph a financial report.*

mim·ic (mim′ik) *v.t.*, **mim·icked, mim·ick·ing.** **1.** to imitate the speech, manners, or gestures of, especially so as to make fun of: *You hurt my feelings by mimicking me.* **2.** to copy closely or reproduce: *That artist can mimic the* style of several famous painters. **3.** to resemble closely: *Certain insects mimic twigs.* —*n.* **1.** a person who mimics, especially a performer skilled in pantomime. **2.** something that is a copy; imitation. —*adj.* **1.** of, like, or characterized by mimicry; imitative. **2.** make-believe; pretend; mock: *a mimic battle.*

mim·ic·ry (mim′i krē) *n., pl.* **mim·ic·ries. 1.** the act, practice, or art of mimicking. **2.** the close outward resemblance of one kind of animal to another or to an object in its natural environment. Mimicry helps to protect or conceal an animal.

mi·mo·sa (mi mō′sə) *n.* a plant related to the pea, having leaves that resemble ferns and small yellow, white, pink, or purple flowers.

min. 1. minimum. **2.** minute; minutes.

minarets

min·a·ret (min′ə ret′) *n.* a tall, slender tower attached to a mosque. A crier summons worshipers to prayer from a balcony near its top.

mince (mins) *v.,* **minced, minc·ing.** —*v.t.* **1.** to cut or chop into very small, fine pieces: *The cook minced the potato.* **2.** to say or speak in a restrained or refined manner: *I don't mince words when I am annoyed.* —*v.i.* to walk in a dainty way with very short steps. —*n.* see **mincemeat.**

mince·meat (mins′mēt′) *n.* a mixture of finely chopped apples, suet, raisins, currants, sugar, spices, and some times meat, used for pies. Also, **mince.**

mince pie, a pie made with mincemeat.

minc·ing (min′sing) *adj.* dainty or refined in speech or manner. —**minc′ing·ly,** *adv.*

mind (mīnd) *n.* **1.** the part of the body where thought takes place; the center of memory, learning, and the emotions. **2.** the power or ability to know, understand, and reason: *You have a good mind and learn things quickly.* **3.** a healthy mental state; sanity: *to lose one's mind.* **4.** a way of thinking or feeling; opinion or attitude: *to have an open mind.* **5.** memory; remembrance: *The old photos brought my childhood to mind.* **6.** attention: *I can't keep my mind on what I'm doing.* **7.** desire, intention, or wish: *I have a mind to visit them next week.* **8.** a person of great intelligence: *That scientist is one of the great minds of the century.* —*v.t.* **1.** to pay attention to; be concerned or careful about: *Don't mind what I said, I was upset.* **2.** to take care of; look after; tend: *The baby-sitter will mind the children.* **3.** to obey: *Those children always mind their parents.* **4.** to object to: *I don't mind eating alone.* **5.** to look or watch out for: *Mind the broken chair.* —*v.i.* **1.** to object or care: *Do you mind if I borrow your book?* **2.** to be obedient: *The puppy must learn to mind.*

• **a piece of one's mind.** a severe scolding: *to give someone a piece of one's mind.*

• **never mind.** disregard it; it doesn't matter: *Never mind, I'll buy the tickets myself.*

• **on one's mind.** in one's thoughts.

• **to bear in mind** or **to keep in mind.** to remember.

• **to be of one mind.** to be in agreement.

• **to call to mind.** to serve as a reminder of: *That story calls to mind a funny thing that happened to us.*

• **to make up one's mind.** to come to a decision; decide: *I made up my mind to go to the party.*

mind–bog·gling (mīnd′bog′ling) *adj.* causing confusion or lack of comprehension, often because of great size, extent, or complexity: *a mind-boggling math problem.*

mind·ed (mīn′did) *adj.* **1.** favorably disposed; inclined: *Make those changes if you are so minded.* **2.** having a certain kind of mind. ▲ used in combination: *fair-minded, open-minded.*

mind·ful (mīnd′fəl) *adj.* conscious; aware: *Are you mindful of the risks involved?* —**mind′ful·ly,** *adv.* —**mind′ful·ness,** *n.*

mind·less (mīnd′lis) *adj.* **1.** lacking intelligence; stupid or foolish. **2.** without thought; heedless. —**mind′less·ly,** *adv.*

mind's eye, imagination or recollection: *In my mind's eye I saw the cabin we stayed in last summer.*

mine¹ (mīn) *pron.* the one or ones that belong or relate to me: *The brown coat is mine.* —*adj.* *Archaic.* my. ▲ used before a word beginning with a vowel or *h*, or after a noun: *mine eyes, mine heart, mother mine.* [From the Old English word *mīn* meaning "my, belonging to me."]

mine² (mīn) *n.* **1.** a large area dug into or under the ground, from which coal, mineral ores, or other materials are taken. **2.** a deposit of coal, mineral ore, or other material that may be taken from the earth. **3.** any abundant source or supply: *That book is a mine of information.* **4.** an explosive charge hidden underground or in water, used to destroy persons, equipment, or ships. —*v.,* **mined, min·ing.** —*v.t.* **1.** to take from the earth: *to mine diamonds.* **2.** to dig in (the earth) for coal, mineral ores, or other materials. **3.** to place explosive mines in or under: *The enemy mined the harbor.* —*v.i.* **1.** to dig in the earth; dig a mine: *to mine for coal.* **2.** to work in a mine. [From the Old French word *mine,* from the Medieval Latin word *mina* meaning "an underground tunnel, mine²," probably of Celtic origin.]

mine·field (mīn′fēld′) *n.* an area of land or water in which explosive mines have been laid.

min·er (mī′nər) *n.* a person who mines, especially a person whose occupation is digging in the earth for coal, mineral ores, or other materials.

min·er·al (min′ər əl) *n.* **1.** any substance in nature that has a definite chemical composition and physical form and that is not of plant or animal origin. **2.** any of various natural substances, such as water, salt, coal, petroleum, gold, and copper ore, obtained by digging in the earth. —*adj.* of, relating to, or containing a mineral or minerals: *a mineral deposit, mineral ores, mineral water.*

min·er·al·o·gist (min′ə rol′ə jist) *n.* a student of or an expert in mineralogy.

min·er·al·o·gy (min′ə rol′ə jē) *n.* the science or study of minerals. —**min·er·al·og·i·cal** (min′ər ə loj′i kəl), *adj.* —**min′er·al·og′i·cal·ly,** *adv.*

at; āpe; fär; câre; end; mē; it; īce; pîerce; hot; ōld; sông, fôrk; oil; out; up; ūse; rüle; pull; tûrn; chin; sing; shop; thin; **th**is; hw in white; zh in treasure. The symbol ə stands for the unstressed vowel sound heard in about, taken, pencil, lemon, and circus.

mineral oil, a colorless, nearly odorless, and tasteless oil obtained as a by-product of petroleum refining. Mineral oil is often used as a laxative.

Mi·ner·va (mi nûr′və) *n. Roman Mythology.* the goddess of wisdom, arts, and crafts. In Greek mythology she was called Athena.

min·e·stro·ne (min′ə strō′nē) *n.* a soup containing beans and other vegetables, pasta, and seasonings.

mine·sweep·er (mīn′swē′pər) *n.* a ship or device used to find, remove, or destroy mines.

Ming (ming) *adj.* of or relating to the Chinese dynasty that ruled from 1368 to 1644 or to the art of this period: *a Ming vase.*

min·gle (ming′gəl) *v.,* **min·gled, min·gling.** —*v.i.* **1.** to be or become mixed or joined together. **2.** to move about among others; associate freely: *We mingled with the party guests.* —*v.t.* to mix or join (something) together.

min·i (min′ē) *n., pl.* **min·is.** something that is smaller or shorter than usual, such as a minicomputer or miniskirt. —*adj.* smaller or shorter than usual: *a mini refrigerator, a mini umbrella.*

mini– *combining form* smaller or shorter than usual: *miniskirt.*

min·i·a·ture (min′ē ə chər, min′ə chər) *adj.* greatly reduced in size; very small: *a miniature rose. My neighbor builds miniature automobiles.* —*n.* **1.** a copy on a small scale: *a miniature of the Eiffel Tower.* **2.** a painting done on a very small scale and in much detail: *An artist painted a miniature of my parents.*

min·i·a·tur·ize (min′ē ə chə rīz′, min′ə chə rīz′) *v.t.,* **min·i·a·tur·ized, min·i·a·tur·iz·ing.** to make or design on a very small scale. —**min′i·a·tur·i·za′tion,** *n.*

min·i·bike (min′ē bīk′) *n.* a small, light motorcycle.

min·i·com·put·er (min′ē kəm pū′tər) *n.* a computer larger than a microcomputer but smaller than a mainframe, generally used in business, manufacturing, and scientific research.

min·i·ma (min′ə mə) a plural of **minimum.**

min·i·mal (min′ə məl) *adj.* of the smallest amount or degree; very small. —**min′i·mal·ly,** *adv.*

min·i·mize (min′ə mīz′) *v.t.,* **min·i·mized, min·i·miz·ing.** **1.** to reduce to the smallest or least possible amount or degree; make as small as possible: *The diplomats from the two countries met to minimize chances of war.* **2.** to treat as being of little importance or value: *Don't minimize your contribution to the project.* —**min′i·mi·za′tion,** *n.* —**min′i·miz′er,** *n.*

min·i·mum (min′ə məm) *n., pl.* **min·i·mums** or **min·i·ma.** **1.** the least possible or smallest amount or degree: *The mechanic will need a minimum of one week to do the job.* **2.** the lowest point, degree, or number reached or recorded: *The temperature was at its minimum for the day at six o'clock this morning.* —*adj.* least, lowest, smallest, or fewest that is possible, allowable, or reached: *Being able to type and to spell are the minimum qualifications for the secretarial job.*

minimum wage, the lowest wage that an employer may legally pay an employee.

min·ing (mī′ning) *n.* **1.** the act, process, or business of digging mines for coal, ores, gems, or other materials. **2.** the act or process of laying explosive mines.

min·ion (min′yən) *n.* a favorite, follower, or servant, especially one who acts in a slavish manner.

min·i·se·ries (min′ē sîr′ēz) *n.* a television drama broadcast in several episodes: *a six-part miniseries about the Civil War.*

min·i·skirt (min′ē skûrt′) *n.* a short skirt, usually ending several inches above the knee.

min·is·ter (min′ə stər) *n.* **1.** a person who is ordained for religious service in a church, especially a Protestant church; pastor. **2.** a person who is the head of an important governmental department: *the minister of finance.* **3.** a diplomat ranking below ambassador and acting as his or her nation's chief representative in a foreign country to which an ambassador is not sent. —*v.i.* to give aid, care, or attention: *The nurse ministered to the patient's needs.* [From the Old French word *ministre* meaning ''servant, minister,'' from the Latin word *minister* ''servant, helper, priest's assistant.'']

min·is·te·ri·al (min′ə stîr′ē əl) *adj.* **1.** of, relating to, or characteristic of religion or the ministry: *a ministerial student.* **2.** of, relating to, or characteristic of a minister of a government department. —**min′is·te′ri·al·ly,** *adv.*

min·is·trant (min′ə strənt) *adj.* serving as a minister. —*n.* a person who ministers.

min·is·tra·tion (min′ə strā′shən) *n.* **1.** the act, process, or instance of giving aid. **2.** the act of serving as a minister of religion.

min·is·try (min′ə strē) *n., pl.* **min·is·tries.** **1.** the profession or work of a minister of religion. **2.** ministers of religion as a group; the clergy. **3.** a governmental department headed by a minister. **4.** governmental ministers as a group. **5.** the act of ministering.

mink (mingk) *n., pl.* **mink** or **minks.** **1.** an animal resembling a weasel, having soft, lustrous brown fur, and living in woodlands near water. **2.** the valuable fur of this animal.

Minn., Minnesota.

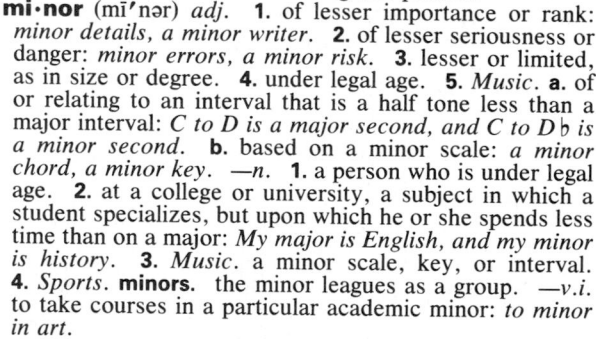

mink *(def. 1)*

min·now (min′ō) *n.* **1.** any of a group of freshwater fish widely used as bait. **2.** any very small fish.

Mi·no·an (mi nō′ən) *adj.* of or relating to the civilization of Crete from about 2500 B.C. to about 1100 B.C. —*n.* a person who lived in Crete during this period.

mi·nor (mī′nər) *adj.* **1.** of lesser importance or rank: *minor details, a minor writer.* **2.** of lesser seriousness or danger: *minor errors, a minor risk.* **3.** lesser or limited, as in size or degree. **4.** under legal age. **5.** *Music.* **a.** of or relating to an interval that is a half tone less than a major interval: *C to D is a major second, and C to D♭ is a minor second.* **b.** based on a minor scale: *a minor chord, a minor key.* —*n.* **1.** a person who is under legal age. **2.** at a college or university, a subject in which a student specializes, but upon which he or she spends less time than on a major: *My major is English, and my minor is history.* **3.** *Music.* a minor scale, key, or interval. **4.** *Sports.* **minors.** the minor leagues as a group. —*v.i.* to take courses in a particular academic minor: *to minor in art.*

mi·nor·i·ty (mə nôr′i tē, mə nor′i tē, mī nôr′i tē, mī nor′i tē) *n., pl.* **mi·nor·i·ties.** **1.** the smaller part of a group or whole: *Only a minority of the students voted.* **2.** a racial, religious, political, or other group that is different from the majority of the group of which it is a part. **3.** the state or time of being under legal age. **4.** a group or political party having fewer than half the votes or members, as in a legislature.

minor league, any league of professional sports clubs other than the major league or leagues, as in baseball or ice hockey. —**mi′nor-league′,** *adj.*

minor scale, any of three musical scales, consisting of eight tones, having half steps instead of whole steps after the second and fifth, second and seventh, or second, fifth, and seventh tones ascending the scale, and after the sixth and third or eighth, sixth, and third tones descending the scale.

Mi·nos (mī′nəs) n.   *Greek Legend.*   **1.** a king of Crete who became a judge of the dead in Hades.   **2.** the grandson of this king, and also king of Crete, who kept the Minotaur in the Labyrinth.

Min·o·taur (min′ə tôr′) n.   *Greek Legend.* a monster that was half bull and half man. It was confined by Minos in the Labyrinth until killed by Theseus.

min·ster (min′stər) n.   **1.** a church attached to a monastery.   **2.** a cathedral or other important church.

min·strel (min′strəl) n.   **1.** in the Middle Ages, a traveling musician who sang or recited poems.   **2.** a performer in a minstrel show.

minstrel show, a variety show in which white performers made up to look like blacks sing songs, dance, tell jokes, and act in humorous skits. It was popular in the United States during the nineteenth and early twentieth centuries.

min·strel·sy (min′strəl sē) n., pl. **min·strel·sies. 1.** the art of a minstrel.   **2.** a collection of songs, lyrics, and ballads, such as those sung by minstrels.

mint[1] (mint) n.   **1.** any of a group of plants, such as the peppermint or spearmint, used as a flavoring or scent.   **2.** a piece of candy flavored with mint. [From the Old English word *minte* meaning this plant, from the Latin word *menta* ''mint[1],'' from the Greek word *mintē* ''mint[1].'']   —**mint′y,** *adj.*

mint[2] (mint) n.   **1.** a place where money is coined by the government.   **2.** a very large amount of money: *They spent a mint getting the car repaired.* —*adj.* unused or seeming as if unused: *in mint condition, a mint stamp.* —*v.t.* **1.** to coin (money).   **2.** to create or invent (a phrase or word). [From the Old English word *mynet* meaning ''a coin'' or ''money,'' from the Latin word *moneta* ''mint[2]'' or ''money,'' from (Juno) *Moneta,* a title for the Roman goddess Juno, in whose temple coins were minted.]

mint·age (min′tij) n.   **1.** the act or process of coining money.   **2.** the money coined by a mint.   **3.** the cost of minting.   **4.** an impression stamped on a coin.

min·u·end (min′ū end′) n.   the number from which another is to be subtracted. In 31 − 7 = 24, the minuend is 31.

min·u·et (min′ū et′) n.   **1.** a stately, slow, and graceful dance for couples, introduced in seventeenth-century France.   **2.** music for, or in the rhythm of, this dance.

mi·nus (mī′nəs) prep. **1.** decreased by; less: *Ten minus seven is three.* **2.** without; lacking: *The dog was minus a leg because of the accident.* —*adj.* **1.** less than zero; negative.   **2.** somewhat lower than; less than: *a grade of A minus.* **3.** showing subtraction or a negative quantity: *a minus sign.* —*n., pl.* **mi·nus·es. 1.** a sign (−) showing subtraction or a negative quantity. Also, **minus sign. 2.** a negative quantity.   **3.** an unfavorable factor or quality.

min·us·cule (min′ə skūl′, mi nus′kūl) adj. very small; tiny: *a minuscule amount.*

min·ute[1] (min′it) n.   **1.** a unit of time equal to ¹⁄₆₀ of an hour; 60 seconds.   **2.** a short period of time; moment: *Can I speak to you for a minute?* **3.** a particular moment or point in time; instant: *I recognized you the minute you entered the room.* **4.** a unit of angular measurement equal to ¹⁄₆₀ of a degree.   **5. minutes.** a written record of what was said and done at a meeting or conference. [From the Old French word *minute,* from the Medieval Latin word *minuta* meaning ''minute[1]'' and ''small section,'' going back to the Latin word *minuere* ''to make smaller, lessen.'']

mi·nute[2] (mī nūt′, mī nūt′) adj.   **1.** very small; tiny: *A minute particle of dirt blew into my eye.* **2.** of small importance; trifling: *minute details.* **3.** characterized by close attention to details: *The detective made a minute examination of the room for clues.* [From the Latin word *minutus,* past participle of *minuere* meaning ''to make smaller, lessen.''] —**mi·nute′ly,** *adv.* —**mi·nute′-ness,** *n.*

min·ute·man (min′it man′) *also,* **Min·ute·man.** n., pl. **min·ute·men** (min′it men′). during the American Revolution, a volunteer soldier or armed citizen ready to fight at a minute's notice.

mi·nu·ti·ae (mi nū′shē ē′, mi nū′shē ē′) pl. n., sing. **mi·nu·ti·a** (mi nū′shē ə, mi nū′shē ə). small or unimportant details.

minx (mingks) n., pl. **minx·es.** a bold, forward girl.

Mi·o·cene (mī′ə sēn′) n.   **1.** the fourth geological epoch of the Tertiary period of the Cenozoic era. During the Miocene, early forms of horses, pigs, giraffes, elephants, and other modern animals flourished.   **2.** the strata formed in this epoch. —*adj.* of, relating to, or characteristic of this epoch.

mir·a·cle (mir′ə kəl) n.   **1.** a remarkable event thought to have been brought about by a divine or supernatural power.   **2.** an amazing or marvelous happening or thing: *the miracle of spring.*

miracle play, a religious drama popular in the Middle Ages, based on legends and stories about the saints.

mi·rac·u·lous (mi rak′yə ləs) adj. **1.** brought about by a divine or supernatural power; of the nature of a miracle.   **2.** amazing; extraordinary; incredible: *a miraculous escape.* **3.** working or having the power to work wonders: *a miraculous medicine.* —**mi·rac′u·lous·ly,** *adv.* —**mi·rac′u·lous·ness,** *n.*

mi·rage (mi räzh′) n.   an optical illusion caused by the bending of light rays by layers of air having different densities and temperatures. A common mirage is a sheet of water that is seen on a highway during a hot summer day.

Mi·ran·da warning (mə ran′də), a warning that officers of the law must give to anyone arrested or taken into custody. It must include mention of the right to remain silent, the right to consult an attorney, and the fact that anything said may be used in court against the person in custody.

mire (mīr) n.   **1.** an area of wet, soft ground; bog.   **2.** deep, soft mud; muck. —*v.,* **mired, mir·ing.** —*v.t.* **1.** to cause to sink or get stuck in mire.   **2.** to make dirty with mud or muck.   **3.** to entangle or involve: *The company's president was mired in a scandal.* —*v.i.* to sink or get stuck in mire.

mir·ror (mir′ər) n.   **1.** a smooth surface that forms images by reflecting light, especially such a surface made of glass that is coated on the back with silver or a similar material.   **2.** something that gives a true picture: *This novel by Sir Walter Scott is a mirror of life in medieval England.* —*v.t.* to reflect or picture: *The poet's moods are mirrored in his lyric verse.*

mirror image, an image or representation of something as it would appear when reflected in a mirror, with right and left sides reversed.

mirth (mûrth) n.   merriment or gaiety.

mirth·ful (mûrth′fəl) adj. full of or expressing mirth; merry. —**mirth′ful·ly,** *adv.* —**mirth′ful·ness,** *n.*

mirth·less (mûrth′lis) adj.   without mirth; joyless. —**mirth′less·ly,** *adv.* —**mirth′less·ness,** *n.*

mir·y (mīr′ē) adj., **mir·i·er, mir·i·est.** like a mire; muddy or boggy. —**mir′i·ness,** *n.*

mis– *prefix* **1.** bad or wrong: *misconduct, misconception.*   **2.** badly or wrongly: *mismanage, misquote.*   **3.** lack of: *mistrust.*

---

at; āpe; fär; câre; end; mē; it; īce; pîerce; hot; ōld; sông, fôrk; oil; out; up; ūse; rüle; pull; tûrn; chin; sing; shop; thin; this; hw in white; zh in treasure. The symbol ə stands for the unstressed vowel sound heard in about, taken, pencil, lemon, and circus.

M

mis·ad·ven·ture (mis′əd ven′chər) *n.* a mishap; misfortune.

mis·al·li·ance (mis′ə lī′əns) *n.* an association or alliance, especially a marriage, that is not proper or suitable.

mis·an·thrope (mis′ən thrōp′) *n.* a person who hates or distrusts the human race. [From the French word *misanthrope* meaning "misanthrope," from the Greek word *misanthrōpos* meaning "hating mankind," from the prefix *mis-* meaning "hating" + *anthrōpos* meaning "man, human being."] **—mis·an·throp·ic** (mis′ən throp′ ik), *adj.*

mis·an·thro·py (mis an′thrə pē) *n.* the hatred or distrust of the human race.

mis·ap·ply (mis′ə plī′) *v.t.,* **mis·ap·plied, mis·ap·ply·ing.** to apply or use badly or wrongly: *to misapply one's abilities, to misapply public funds.* **—mis·ap·pli·ca·tion** (mis′ap li kā′shən), *n.*

mis·ap·pre·hend (mis′ap ri hend′) *v.t.* to fail to understand; misunderstand.

mis·ap·pre·hen·sion (mis′ap ri hen′shən) *n.* a misunderstanding.

mis·ap·pro·pri·ate (mis′ə prō′prē āt′)*v.t.,* **mis·ap·pro·pri·at·ed, mis·ap·pro·pri·at·ing.** to take or use wrongly or dishonestly: *The politician misappropriated money from the city treasury.* **—mis′ap·pro′pri·a′tion,** *n.*

mis·be·got·ten (mis′bi got′ən) *adj.* **1.** born to a woman who is not married; illegitimate. **2.** poorly conceived, made, or done: *The misbegotten attempt to free the hostage failed.*

mis·be·have (mis′bi hāv′) *v.,* **mis·be·haved, mis·be·hav·ing.** *—v.i.* to behave badly: *The child misbehaved by writing on the wall.* *—v.t.* to conduct (oneself) badly.

mis·be·hav·ior (mis′bi hāv′yər) *also, British,* **mis·be·hav·iour.** *n.* bad or improper behavior.

mis·be·lief (mis′bi lēf′) *n.* a false or wrong belief or opinion.

misc. **1.** miscellaneous. **2.** miscellany.

mis·cal·cu·late (mis kal′kyə lāt′) *v.t., v.i.,* **mis·cal·cu·lat·ed, mis·cal·cu·lat·ing.** to figure, plan, or judge wrongly: *The general miscalculated the number of soldiers in the opposing army.* **—mis′cal·cu·la′tion,** *n.*

mis·call (mis kôl′) *v.t.* to call by a wrong name; misname.

mis·car·riage (mis kar′ij; *def. 2, also,* mis′kar′ij) *n.* **1.** a failure to achieve the intended result: *Imprisoning an innocent person is a miscarriage of justice.* **2.** the birth of an undeveloped baby that cannot live.

mis·car·ry (mis kar′ē) *v.i.,* **mis·car·ried, mis·car·ry·ing.** **1.** to fail to achieve the intended result; be unsuccessful: *The plans miscarried.* **2.** to give birth to an undeveloped baby that cannot live.

mis·cast (mis kast′) *v.t.,* **mis·cast, mis·cast·ing.** to cast in an unsuitable role: *to miscast a comedian as an evil villain.*

mis·ce·ge·na·tion (mis′ə jə nā′shən) *n.* marriage between people of different races.

mis·cel·la·ne·ous (mis′ə lā′nē əs) *adj.* **1.** of different kinds: *Miscellaneous items were scattered all over the floor.* **2.** made up of different things; varied: *I bought a miscellaneous assortment of shirts and socks.* **—mis′cel·la′ne·ous·ly,** *adv.* **—mis′cel·la′ne·ous·ness,** *n.*

mis·cel·la·ny (mis′ə lā′nē) *n., pl.* **mis·cel·la·nies.** **1.** a mixture of different things: *The child's pockets held a miscellany of string, jacks, and pennies.* **2.** a book containing different writings on various subjects.

mis·chance (mis chans′) *n.* **1.** bad luck. **2.** an unfortunate event; mishap.

mis·chief (mis′chif) *n.* **1.** an act or conduct that is often playful but causes annoyance or harm. **2.** an inclination to tease or play pranks; teasing playfulness: *Those students are full of mischief.* **3.** harm or damage. **4.** a person who causes annoyance or harm.

mis·chie·vous (mis′chə vəs) *adj.* **1.** full of mischief; playful or naughty: *a mischievous child.* **2.** showing or suggesting mischief: *a mischievous smile.* **3.** annoying, harmful, or damaging: *Mischievous rumors were spread about the new employee.* **—mis′chie·vous·ly,** *adv.* **—mis′chie·vous·ness,** *n.*

mis·ci·ble (mis′ə bəl) *adj.* capable of being mixed: *Oil and water are not miscible.* **—mis′ci·bil′i·ty,** *n.*

mis·con·ceive (mis′kən sēv′) *v.t.,* **mis·con·ceived, mis·con·ceiv·ing.** to fail to understand; have a false or mistaken idea about; misunderstand.

mis·con·cep·tion (mis′kən sep′shən) *n.* a false or mistaken idea.

mis·con·duct (*n.,* mis kon′dukt; *v.,* mis′kən dukt′) *n.* improper or wrong conduct. *—v.t.* **1.** to behave (oneself) improperly. **2.** to manage (something) badly.

mis·con·strue (mis′kən strü′) *v.t.,* **mis·con·strued, mis·con·stru·ing.** to mistake the meaning of; misinterpret: *They misconstrued my innocent remark.*

mis·count (*v.,* mis kount′; *n.,* mis′kount′) *v.t., v.i.* to count incorrectly. *—n.* an incorrect count.

mis·cre·ant (mis′krē ənt) *n.* a wicked person; villain. *—adj.* villainous.

mis·deal (*v.,* mis dēl′; *n.,* mis′dēl′) *v.t., v.i.,* **mis·dealt** (mis delt′), **mis·deal·ing.** to deal (playing cards) incorrectly. *—n.* an incorrect deal.

mis·deed (mis dēd′) *n.* a wicked act.

mis·de·mean·or (mis′di mē′nər) *also, British,* **mis·de·mean·our.** *n.* a crime less serious than a felony, usually punishable by a fine or a short term of imprisonment.

mis·di·rect (mis′di rekt′, mis′dī rekt′) *v.t.* to direct wrongly or badly. **—mis′di·rec′tion,** *n.*

mi·ser (mī′zər) *n.* a stingy person who hoards money.

mis·er·a·ble (miz′ər ə bəl) *adj.* **1.** very unhappy; wretched: *I felt so miserable I wanted to cry.* **2.** causing or marked by great discomfort or unhappiness: *miserable weather, a miserable toothache.* **3.** of little or no value; of very poor quality: *The actor gave a miserable performance.* **—mis′er·a·ble·ness,** *n.* **—mis′er·a·bly,** *adv.*

mi·ser·ly (mī′zər lē) *adj.* like or characteristic of a miser; stingy. **—mi′ser·li·ness,** *n.*

mis·er·y (miz′ə rē) *n., pl.* **mis·er·ies.** **1.** a state or condition of great unhappiness or distress: *Constant ill health can be a source of misery.* **2.** a cause or source of this: *My broken arm was a misery to me.* **3.** wretched living conditions: *The outcast lived in misery in an old shack.*

mis·fire (*v.,* mis fīr′; *n.,* mis′fīr′) *v.i.,* **mis·fired, mis·fir·ing.** **1.** to fail to fire or ignite at the proper time: *The engine misfired. The gun misfired.* **2.** to fail to have the desired effect or result: *All their plans for the trip misfired.* *—n.* the failure to fire or ignite at the proper time.

mis·fit (mis′fit′) *n.* **1.** something that does not fit properly, such as a garment of the wrong size. **2.** a person who does not fit in with other people or with his or her surroundings.

mis·for·tune (mis fôr′chən) *n.* **1.** bad luck; ill fortune: *It was my misfortune to lose my wallet.* **2.** an instance of this; unlucky accident; mishap: *The train crash was a misfortune.*

mis·giv·ing (mis giv′ing) *n.* a feeling of doubt or uneasiness: *We have misgivings about making a long trip with so little money.*

mis·gov·ern (mis guv′ərn) *v.t.* to govern or manage badly. **—mis·gov′ern·ment,** *n.*

mis·guide (mis gīd′) *v.t.,* **mis·guid·ed, mis·guid·ing.** to guide or influence wrongly; lead astray. **—mis·guid·ance** (mis gī′dəns), *n.*

mis·guid·ed (mis gī′did) *adj.* **1.** guided or influenced wrongly; misled: *The misguided expedition became lost in the jungle.* **2.** marked by mistaken ideas: *misguided advice.* **—mis·guid′ed·ly,** *adv.*

mis·han·dle (mis han'dəl) v.t., **mis·han·dled, mis·han·dling.** to handle, treat, or manage badly.

mis·hap (mis'hap) n. an unfortunate accident: *We had a mishap on the highway and lost a hubcap.*

mish·mash (mish'mash') n., pl. **mish·mash·es.** a confused mixture; jumble.

mis·in·form (mis'in fôrm') v.t. to give false information to: *The suspects misinformed the police of their whereabouts on the night of the crime.* —**mis·in·for·ma'tion,** n.

mis·in·ter·pret (mis'in tûr'prit) v.t. to interpret wrongly. —**mis·in·ter·pre·ta'tion,** n.

mis·judge (mis juj') v.t., v.i., **mis·judged, mis·judg·ing.** to judge wrongly or unfairly: *We misjudged your character.* —**mis·judg'ment;** also, **mis·judge'ment,** n.

mis·lay (mis lā') v.t., **mis·laid, mis·lay·ing.** 1. to put in a place that is later forgotten; lose: *I mislaid my keys.* 2. to lay or put down wrongly: *to mislay the carpet.*

mis·lead (mis lēd') v.t., **mis·led, mis·lead·ing.** 1. to lead or guide in the wrong direction. 2. to lead into a mistaken or wrong thought or action: *The exaggerated advertisements for the product misled us.*

mis·lead·ing (mis lē'ding) adj. causing or tending to cause a mistaken or wrong thought or action: *a misleading speech, misleading instructions.* —**mis·lead'ing·ly,** adv.

mis·man·age (mis man'ij) v.t., **mis·man·aged, mis·man·ag·ing.** to manage or handle badly: *to mismanage one's money, to mismanage a business.* —**mis·man'age·ment,** n.

mis·match (v., mis mach'; n., mis'mach') v.t. to match or join together unwisely or unsuitably: *The two boxers were mismatched. These socks are mismatched.* —n., pl. **mis·match·es.** an unwise or unsuitable match.

mis·name (mis nām') v.t., **mis·named, mis·nam·ing.** to call by a wrong name.

mis·no·mer (mis nō'mər) n. a name that is not fitting or suitable: *"Yacht" was a misnomer for the small boat.*

mis·place (mis plās') v.t., **mis·placed, mis·plac·ing.** 1. to mislay; lose: *I misplaced my notebook.* 2. to put or locate in a wrong place. 3. to place improperly or unwisely: *We misplaced our trust in them.*

mis·play (v., mis plā'; n., mis plā', mis'plā') v.t. to play badly or wrongly in a game or sport: *to misplay a hand of cards.* —n. a bad or wrong play in a game or sport.

mis·print (n., mis'print', mis print'; v., mis print') n. an error in printing. —v.t. to print incorrectly.

mis·pro·nounce (mis'prə nouns') v.t., **mis·pro·nounced, mis·pro·nounc·ing.** to pronounce (words or sounds) incorrectly or in a way that is thought of as incorrect. —**mis·pro·nun·ci·a·tion** (mis'prə nun'sē ā'shən) n.

mis·quote (mis kwōt') v.t., **mis·quot·ed, mis·quot·ing.** to quote incorrectly. —**mis·quo·ta'tion,** n.

mis·read (mis rēd') v.t., **mis·read** (mis red'), **mis·read·ing.** to read or understand incorrectly: *to misread a sign.*

mis·rep·re·sent (mis'rep ri zent') v.t. to give a false or misleading impression of; represent falsely: *The company misrepresented its product.* —**mis'rep·re·sen·ta'tion,** n.

mis·rule (mis rül') n. 1. bad, unjust, or unwise rule or government. 2. disorder; confusion. —v.t., **mis·ruled, mis·rul·ing.** to rule or govern badly, unjustly, or unwisely.

miss¹ (mis) v.t. 1. to fail to hit or reach: *The batter missed the ball.* 2. to fail to catch, meet, or get: *to miss one's bus.* 3. to fail to notice or find: *The driver missed the exit on the highway.* 4. to fail to do or accomplish: *The golfer missed a short putt.* 5. to fail to attend or be present for: *I missed an appointment with the dentist.* 6. to fail to understand: *They missed the point of the*

lecture. 7. to be sad over the absence or loss of: *The parents missed their child who was away at college.* 8. to discover the absence or loss of: *It was a long time before I missed my ring.* 9. to fail to take advantage of; let slip by: *You have missed a good opportunity.* 10. to escape: *The mountain climber just missed being struck by falling rocks.* 11. to be without; lack: *The coat is missing a button.* 12. to do or answer wrongly: *I missed two questions on the test.* —v.i. 1. to fail to hit something: *Several arrows were shot at the target, but they all missed.* 2. to be unsuccessful; fail: *Your clever plan can't miss.* 3. to misfire. —n., pl. **miss·es.** a failure to hit or reach. [From the Old English word *missan* meaning "to miss."]

miss² (mis) n., pl. **miss·es.** 1. **Miss.** a form of address used before the name of a girl or unmarried woman: *Miss Simpson.* 2. also, **Miss.** a form of address used in place of the name of a girl or unmarried woman: *May I help you, Miss?* 3. a girl or young unmarried woman. [Short for *mistress.*]

Miss., Mississippi.

mis·sal (mis'əl) n. a book containing the prayers for celebrating Mass throughout the year.

mis·shape (mis shāp') v.t., **mis·shaped, mis·shaped** or **mis·shap·en, mis·shap·ing.** to shape badly; deform.

mis·shap·en (mis shā'pən) v. a past participle of **misshape.** —adj. badly shaped; deformed.

mis·sile (mis'əl) n. 1. an object that is thrown or shot in the air, such as a stone, arrow, or bullet. 2. see **guided missile.** 3. see **ballistic missile.**

miss·ing (mis'ing) adj. 1. not to be found; lost: *The detective's job was tracing missing persons.* 2. absent or lacking: *This jigsaw puzzle has a missing piece.*

mis·sion (mish'ən) n. 1. a group of persons sent to perform a task or service: *Four rangers formed a rescue mission to reach the injured mountain climber.* 2. the task or service that a person or group of persons is sent to perform; assignment: *The spy was sent on a secret mission.* 3. the task or goal of a military force. 4. a team of diplomats assigned to a foreign country. 5. a group of missionaries sent to do religious, humanitarian, or educational work, especially in a foreign country. 6. a church or other place used by missionaries in their work. 7. **missions.** organized missionary work or activities. 8. the duty or task in life that a person feels destined to perform.

mis·sion·ar·y (mish'ə ner'ē) n., pl. **mis·sion·ar·ies.** 1. a person who is sent by a church to spread its religion among nonbelievers, especially in a foreign country: *a Protestant missionary in India.* 2. a person who goes or is sent to do humanitarian or educational work, especially in a foreign country: *That doctor served as a medical missionary in Africa.* —adj. of, relating to, or characteristic of missionaries or religious missions: *missionary zeal.*

mis·sive (mis'iv) n. a written message; letter.

mis·spell (mis spel') v.t., **mis·spelled** or **mis·spelt** (misspelt'), **mis·spell·ing.** to spell (a word) incorrectly.

mis·spend (mis spend') v.t., **mis·spent** (mis spent'), **mis·spend·ing.** to spend or use wrongly or wastefully.

mis·state (mis stāt') v.t., **mis·stat·ed, mis·stat·ing.** to state incorrectly or falsely: *to misstate one's intentions.* —**mis·state'ment,** n.

at; āpe; fär; câre; end; mē; it; īce; pierce; hot; ōld; sông, fôrk; oil; out; up; ūse; rüle; pull; tûrn; chin; sing; shop; thin; this; hw in white; zh in treasure. The symbol ə stands for the unstressed vowel sound heard in about, taken, pencil, lemon, and circus.

M

609

mis·step (mis step′) *n.* **1.** a wrong or careless step. **2.** a mistake in conduct; improper act.

miss·y (mis′ē) *n., pl.* **miss·ies.** *Informal.* see **miss².**

mist (mist) *n.* **1.** a mass or cloud of tiny droplets of water suspended in the air. **2.** something resembling mist, as a thin cloud of smoke or a fine spray from a pressurized can. **3.** a thin veil or film that blurs the vision: *a mist of tears.* **4.** something that dims or clouds: *The ancient ruler's true deeds were lost in the mist of legend.* —*v.i.* **1.** to be or become covered with or clouded by mist: *The child's eyes misted over with tears.* **2.** to rain in very fine drops; drizzle. —*v.t.* to cover or cloud with mist.

mis·take (mis tāk′) *n.* something incorrectly done, thought, or said; error: *a mistake on a test.* —*v.t.,* **mis·took, mis·tak·en, mis·tak·ing.** **1.** to identify (a person or thing) incorrectly: *They mistook me for my twin brother.* **2.** to understand incorrectly; misinterpret: *You must have mistaken my intentions.*

mis·tak·en (mis tā′kən) *v.* the past participle of **mistake.** —*adj.* based on error; wrong: *a mistaken belief.* —**mis·tak′en·ly,** *adv.*

mis·ter (mis′tər) *n.* **1. Mister.** a form of address used before the name or title of a man, usually written *Mr.*: Mr. Smith, Mr. President. **2.** *also,* **Mister.** a form of address used in place of a man's name: *Can you help me, mister?* [From a modification of the word *master* used as a title before a man's name, going back to the Latin word *magister* meaning "leader, head, teacher."]

mis·tle·toe (mis′əl tō′) *n.* **1.** a plant that lives as a parasite on the branches of various trees and has leathery, yellowish green leaves and small, round fruit. **2.** a sprig of this plant, often used as a Christmas decoration.

mis·took (mis tùk′) the past tense of **mistake.**

mis·treat (mis trēt′) *v.t.* to treat badly: *The child mistreated the kitten by pulling its tail.* —**mis·treat′ment,** *n.*

mis·tress (mis′tris) *n., pl.* **mis·tress·es.** **1.** a woman who has control of a household or estate. **2.** a female owner of an animal. **3.** *also,* **Mistress.** something that is thought of as female and has control or rule over something else: *England's navy made her mistress of the high seas.* **4.** a woman who has a romantic relationship with and is often supported by a man to whom she is not married. **5.** a female teacher, especially in England. **6. Mistress.** *Archaic.* a title of address used before the name of a woman. [From the Old French word *maistresse* meaning "lady" or "mistress of a household," feminine form of *maistre* meaning "lord, chief, master" or "learned teacher," from the Latin word *magister* with the same meanings.]

mis·tri·al (mis trī′əl) *n.* *Law.* **1.** a trial that is declared to be without legal force because of some error in the proceedings. **2.** a trial in which the jury fails to agree on a verdict.

mis·trust (mis trust′) *n.* a lack of trust or confidence. —*v.t.* to regard with suspicion or doubt. —**mis·trust′ful,** *adj.*

mist·y (mis′tē) *adj.,* **mist·i·er, mist·i·est.** **1.** of, resembling, or clouded by mist: *a misty fog.* **2.** blurred or clouded with a mist of tears; tearful: *misty eyes.* **3.** vague; indistinct: *I have a misty recollection of that day.* —**mist′i·ly,** *adv.* —**mist′i·ness,** *n.*

mis·un·der·stand (mis′un dər stand′) *v.t.,* **mis·un·der·stood** (mis′un dər stùd′), **mis·un·der·stand·ing.** to understand (someone or something) incorrectly: *I misunderstood the instructions.*

mistletoe

mis·un·der·stand·ing (mis′un dər stan′ding) *n.* **1.** the failure to understand correctly. **2.** a disagreement; quarrel: *The two friends had a slight misunderstanding.*

mis·use (*n.,* mis ūs′; *v.,* mis ūz′) *n.* a wrong or improper use: *the misuse of government funds.* —*v.t.,* **mis·used, mis·us·ing. 1.** to use wrongly; misapply. **2.** to treat badly.

mite¹ (mīt) *n.* any of a group of tiny animals related to spiders, having piercing, sucking mouth parts. Mites usually live on plants or animals and often damage stored foods. [From the Old English word *mīte* meaning "a small insect."]

mite² (mīt) *n.* **1.** a very small thing or creature. **2.** a coin of very small value. **3.** a very small amount or sum: *There was a mite of dust on the floor.* [From the Middle Dutch word *mīte* meaning "a coin with small value."]

mi·ter (mī′tər) *also,* **mi·tre.** *n.* **1.** a headdress worn by bishops and other high-ranking members of the clergy, consisting of a tall, peaked cap that can be folded flat, with two fringed strips of material hanging from the back. **2.** see **miter joint. 3.** the slanted edge on either of the pieces used to form a miter joint. —*v.t.* **1.** to join with a miter joint. **2.** to cut or shape for forming a miter joint.

miter
(n., def. 1)

miter box, a device with slotted sides used to guide a saw, as when making miter joints.

miter joint, a joint formed by cutting the ends of two pieces of wood or other material at a slant and fitting them together. Picture frames are usually made with miter joints at the corners.

mit·i·gate (mit′i gāt′) *v.t.,* **mit·i·gat·ed, mit·i·gat·ing.** to make milder or less severe or painful: *The nurse tried to mitigate the suffering of the patient.* —**mit′i·ga·ble** (mit′i gə bəl) *adj.* —**mit′i·ga′tion,** *n.* —**mit′i·ga′tor,** *n.*

mi·to·chon·dri·a (mī′tə kon′drē ə) *pl. n., sing.* **mi·to·chon·dri·on** (mī′tə kon′drē ən). very tiny structures found in the cytoplasm of nearly all cells. Mitochondria convert food molecules into energy for the cells.

mi·to·sis (mī tō′sis) *n.* a process of cell division in which the nucleus of a cell divides into two identical nuclei, and the cell itself divides equally, forming two new cells, each with the same number of chromosomes as the parent cell.

mi·tre (mī′tər) *n., v.t.,* **mi·tred, mi·tring.** another spelling of **miter.**

mitt (mit) *n.* **1.** a baseball glove, especially that worn by the catcher or the person playing first base. **2.** see **mitten** *(def. 1).* **3.** a woman's glove that does not cover the fingers.

mit·ten (mit′ən) *n.* **1.** a covering for the hand that holds the four fingers together in one part and the thumb separately in another part. **2.** see **mitt** *(def. 3).*

mix (miks) *v.,* **mixed** or **mixt, mix·ing.** —*v.t.* **1.** to put together into one mass; combine thoroughly; blend: *You mix lemon juice, sugar, and water to make lemonade.* **2.** to make or prepare by combining ingredients thoroughly: *I mixed some pancake batter.* **3.** to add as an ingredient: *to mix mushrooms into a salad.* **4.** to join or bring together: *The florist mixed red and yellow roses in a bouquet.* **5.** to produce (an audio recording) by electronically combining sounds from various sources. —*v.i.* **1.** to become mixed or be capable of being mixed: *Oil and water will not mix.* **2.** to go or belong together. **3.** to associate or get along: *The young writer wanted to mix with people from all walks of life.* —*n., pl.* **mix·es. 1.** the act, result, or product of mixing; mixture. **2.** a mixture of ingredients prepared and sold commercially: *a cake mix.*

·to mix up. a. to confuse or disorder: *I mixed up the two telephone numbers.* **b.** to involve: *We suspect that they were mixed up in the crime.*

mixed (mikst) *adj.* **1.** put together by mixing: *mixed ingredients, mixed fruits.* **2.** of or formed of different parts or qualities: *I have mixed feelings about moving to a new city.* **3.** made up of or involving persons of both sexes: *a mixed class.* **4.** made up of or involving persons of different races, religions, or national origins: *a mixed marriage.*

mixed bag *Informal.* a group of persons or things with few characteristics in common; an odd mixture or assortment: *This week has been a mixed bag, with some great days and a few not so good.*

mixed metaphor, an expression in which two or more metaphors are combined in an illogical, contradictory, or absurd way. For example: *I smell a rat, and I will nip it in the bud.*

mixed number, a number consisting of a whole number and a fraction. The number 4⅞ is a mixed number.

mixed–up (mikst′up′) *adj.* confused or disordered: *a mixed-up situation.*

mix·er (mik′sər) *n.* **1.** a person or thing that mixes, especially a machine or device for mixing. **2.** a person who gets along well with others: *Are you a good mixer at parties?* **3.** a dance, party, or other social gathering for the purpose of getting people acquainted.

mixt (mikst) a past tense and past participle of **mix.**

mix·ture (miks′chər) *n.* **1.** a product or result of mixing; combination; blend: *This batter is a mixture of milk, eggs, and flour.* **2.** the act or process of mixing: *The mixture of oil and vinegar makes a salad dressing.* **3.** *Chemistry.* two or more substances that, when put together, keep their individual properties, and are not chemically combined.

mix–up (miks′up′) *n.* a state or instance of confusion.

miz·zen (miz′ən) *also,* **miz·en.** *n.* **1.** a fore-and-aft sail set on the mizzenmast. **2.** see **mizzenmast.** —*adj.* of or relating to the mizzenmast.

miz·zen·mast (miz′ən mast′, miz′ən məst) *also,* **miz·en·mast.** *n.* **1.** the mast nearest the stern in a ship having two or three masts. **2.** the third mast from the forward end of a ship having more than three masts.

mks, MKS, m.k.s., M.K.S., meter-kilogram-second.

ml., milliliter; milliliters.

Mlle., Mademoiselle.

Mlles., Mesdemoiselles; Mademoiselles.

mm., millimeter; millimeters.

MM., Messieurs.

Mme., Madame.

Mmes. 1. Mesdames. **2.** the plural of **Mrs.**

Mn, the symbol for manganese.

MN, postal abbreviation for Minnesota.

mne·mon·ic (ni mon′ik) *adj.* **1.** helping or intended to help the memory. **2.** of or relating to memory. —*n.* something, such as a formula or phrase, that helps a person remember. —**mne·mon′i·cal·ly,** *adv.*

Mo, the symbol for molybdenum.

mo., month.

Mo., Missouri.

MO, postal abbreviation for Missouri.

M.O. 1. Medical Officer. **2.** *also,* **m.o.** money order.

mo·a (mō′ə) *n.* an extinct bird that could not fly, resembling the ostrich. It was once numerous in New Zealand.

moan (mōn) *n.* **1.** a low, mournful

moa

sound, usually expressing grief or pain. **2.** any sound resembling this: *the wind's eerie moan.* —*v.i.* **1.** to make a moan or moans. **2.** to complain: *The students moaned about having too much homework.* —*v.t.* **1.** to express or say with a moan or moans: *"I failed the test," the student moaned.* **2.** to complain about: *Don't moan your troubles to everyone you meet.*

moat (mōt) *n.* a deep, wide ditch, usually filled with water, surrounding a castle, fortress, or town as protection. —*v.t.* to surround with a moat.

mob (mob) *n.* **1.** a disorderly crowd or throng: *An angry mob gathered in front of the courthouse.* **2.** any crowd: *A mob of children came out of the school.* **3. the mob.** common people as a group; the masses. **4.** *Informal.* an organized group of gangsters. —*v.t.,* **mobbed, mobbing. 1.** to crowd around excitedly: *Fans mobbed the actors wherever they went.* **2.** to crowd to capacity: *Shoppers mobbed the store during the big sale.*

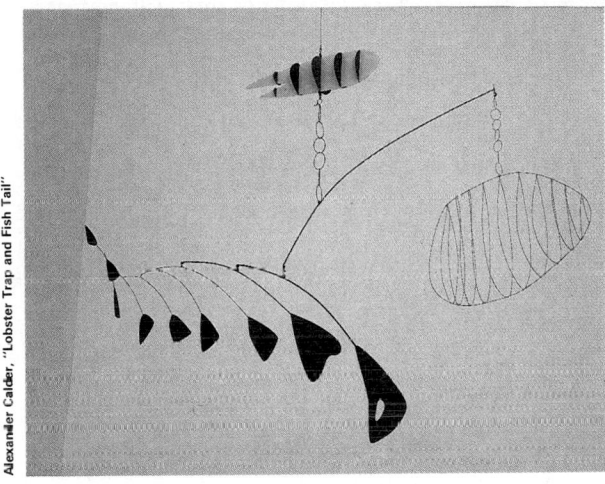

mobile *(n.)*

Alexander Calder, "Lobster Trap and Fish Tail"

mo·bile (*adj.,* mō′bəl, mō′bēl; *n.,* mō′bēl) *adj.* **1.** capable of moving or being moved: *a mobile cannon, a mobile home.* **2.** changing expression freely and quickly: *the clown's mobile features.* **3.** moving or allowing movement from one social class or group to another: *a mobile society.* —*n.* a sculpture of metal, plastic, cardboard, or other material, having parts that are hung from wires and set in motion by air currents. —**mo·bil·i·ty** (mō·bil′i tē), *n.*

–mobile *combining form* vehicle: *bookmobile.*

mobile home, a large trailer that is designed and fully equipped for use as a permanent home. Mobile homes are towed to a permanent site where they are connected to utilities.

mo·bi·lize (mō′bə līz′) *v.,* **mo·bi·lized, mo·bi·liz·ing.** —*v.t.* to organize or prepare, as for war or an emergency: *The government mobilized the army.* —*v.i.* to become organized or prepared, as for war or an emergency. —**mo′bi·li·za′tion,** *n.*

Mö·bi·us strip (mü′bē əs, mō′bē əs, mā′bē əs) *Math-*

at; āpe; fär; câre; end; mē; it; īce; pîerce; hot; ōld; sông, fôrk; oil; out; up; ūse; rüle; pull; tûrn; chin; sing; shop; thin; this; hw in white; zh in treasure. The symbol ə stands for the unstressed vowel sound heard in about, taken, pencil, lemon, and circus.

M

611

ematics. a continuous surface having only one side and one edge, formed by turning one end of a rectangular strip 180 degrees and then attaching it to the other end. [From the German mathematician August F. *Möbius* (1790–1868), who devised it.]

mob·ster (mob′stər) *n.* *Slang.* a criminal, especially one who is a member of an organized gang; gangster.

moc·ca·sin (mok′ə sin) *n.* **1.** a shoe having a soft sole and no heel, usually made from one piece of leather. Moccasins were originally worn by American Indians. **2.** any similar shoe or slipper. **3.** see **water moccasin.**

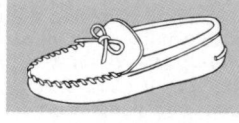

moccasin

moccasin flower, another name for **lady's-slipper.**

mo·cha (mō′kə) *n.* **1.** a choice coffee originally grown in Arabia. **2.** a flavoring made from coffee and chocolate. —*adj.* flavored with coffee or with a mixture of coffee and chocolate.

mock (mok) *v.t.* **1.** to speak to or treat with contempt; ridicule; deride: *The writer mocked the government's policies.* **2.** to imitate or mimic jokingly or rudely: *How unkind of you to mock someone's pronunciation!* **3.** to scoff at or defy: *The criminal mocked the law.* —*v.i.* to express contempt; scoff. —*adj.* not real; pretended; sham: *mock humility.* —*n.* **1.** an act of mocking or an expression of mockery. **2.** a person or thing that is mocked. —**mock′er,** *n.*

mock·er·y (mok′ə rē) *n., pl.* **mock·er·ies.** **1.** the act of mocking or a speech or action that mocks; ridicule; derision. **2.** a person or thing that is mocked. **3.** a false, offensive, or ridiculous imitation: *The trial was a mockery of justice.*

mock·ing·bird (mok′ing bûrd′) *n.* any of several North and South American birds that can imitate the calls of other birds.

mock orange, a shrub that has showy, creamy white flowers. Also, **syringa.**

mock–up (mok′up′) *also,* **mock·up.** *n.* a full-scale model of something, such as an airplane or machine, used for testing, display, or study.

mod (mod) *also,* **Mod.** *adj.* of or relating to a style that is fashionable and up-to-date, especially in an unconventional way: *mod clothing.* [Short for *modern.*]

mod·al (mō′dəl) *adj.* **1.** of or relating to a mode. **2.** in grammar, of or relating to mood.

modal auxiliary, a verb used to indicate the mood of the verb with which it is used. *May, must,* and *would* are modal auxiliaries.

mode[1] (mōd) *n.* **1.** a way or method of doing something: *Automobiles are a popular mode of transportation.* **2.** another word for **mood**[2]. [From the Latin word *modus* meaning "measure" or "manner."]

mode[2] (mōd) *n.* a current style or fashion, as of dress. [From the French word *mode* meaning "style, fashion," from the Latin word *modus* "measure" or "manner."]

mod·el (mod′əl) *n.* **1.** a copy of something, usually built on a smaller scale than the original: *I make airplane models from kits.* **2.** a figure of something to be copied in a more permanent material: *a clay model for a statue.* **3.** a person or thing that serves as an example or standard for imitation or comparison: *The U.S. Constitution was used as a model by the new nation.* **4.** a person who serves as the subject for an artist, photographer, or writer: *That senator was the model for a character in the novel.* **5.** a person who is employed to display merchandise, especially clothing. **6.** a style, design, or type: *The car was a very old model.* —*v.,* **mod·eled, mod·el·ing;** *also, British,* **mod·elled, mod·el·ling.** —*v.t.* **1.** to make or fashion after a particular pattern or model: *The sculptor modeled this statue after an ancient Greek one.* **2.** to make or form: *I modeled a unicorn in wax.*

3. to work as a model of: *to model clothes.* —*v.i.* **1.** to make a model or models: *The art students are modeling in plaster.* **2.** to work as a model: *They modeled at a fashion show.* —*adj.* **1.** designed as a copy of something: *to build a model airplane.* **2.** designed as a display of things for sale or study: *The store has a model kitchen.* **3.** worthy of serving as a model: *a model teacher.* —**mod′el·er;** *also, British,* **mod′el·ler,** *n.*

mod·el·ing (mod′ə ling) *also,* **mod·el·ling.** *n.* **1.** the act or art of making a model or models. **2.** the act or occupation of serving as a model: *a career in fashion modeling.*

mod·er·ate (*adj., n.,* mod′ər it; *v.,* mod′ə rāt′) *adj.* **1.** kept within reasonable limits; not going to extremes: *a moderate price for a coat.* **2.** of medium or average amount, degree, or quality: *moderate traffic on a highway.* **3.** not violent or intense; mild; calm: *moderate weather.* **4.** not radical or extreme: *moderate political opinions.* —*n.* a person who holds moderate views, especially in politics. —*v.,* **mod·er·at·ed, mod·er·at·ing.** —*v.t.* **1.** to keep within reasonable limits; make less extreme: *The employees moderated their demands for higher pay.* **2.** to preside over: *The professor moderated the discussion.* —*v.i.* **1.** to become less excessive, extreme, violent, or intense. **2.** to act as a moderator; preside. —**mod′er·ate·ly,** *adv.* —**mod′er·ate·ness,** *n.*

mod·er·a·tion (mod′ə rā′shən) *n.* **1.** the state or quality of being moderate. **2.** the act of moderating.

mod·e·ra·to (mod′ə rä′tō) *Music. adj.* in moderate tempo. —*adv.* at a moderate tempo. —*n., pl.* **mod·e·ra·tos.** a moderato passage or movement.

mod·er·a·tor (mod′ə rā′tər) *n.* **1.** a person or thing that moderates, especially a person who presides over a meeting or discussion. **2.** a material, such as graphite or heavy water, used to control the rate of fission in a nuclear reactor.

mod·ern (mod′ərn) *adj.* **1.** of or relating to the present or recent time: *modern art.* **2.** of or relating to the period since about 1450: *modern history.* **3.** up-to-date; not old-fashioned: *The kitchen has modern appliances.* —*n.* a person who has modern views or standards. —**mod′ern·ly,** *adv.* —**mod′ern·ness,** *n.*

modern dance, a form of dance that developed in the twentieth century, characterized by training and performance techniques that are freer and less formal than those of classical ballet.

Modern English, the English language as it has been spoken and written since about the year 1500.

Our language entered the **Modern English** period at the beginning of the sixteenth century. Several factors separate Modern English from Middle English. During the fifteenth century, the long vowels of Middle English were changed into the diphthongs we now use. If you say the name of any vowel carefully, you will hear that it really is made up of two sounds. During this period, there was also a revival of interest in classical learning. Many learned words were borrowed from Latin and Greek at this time, especially words used in the vocabularies of the arts and sciences. At the same time, the invention of the printing press helped standardize the spelling of English and make many more people able to own and read books. The spelling of English words did not become completely standardized, however, until the eighteenth century, when there was also much interest in establishing definite rules for English grammar and usage. The first dictionaries of English were compiled at this time.

From the seventeenth century on, English became a worldwide language and borrowed extensively from all of the cultures with which it came in contact. Apart from vocabulary, however, English has changed little in the past two centuries. Grammar, spelling, and sentence structure have remained basically the same as those used by the early American colonists.

mod·ern·ism (mod′ər niz′əm) *n.* something characteristic of modern times, such as a word or practice. —**mod′ern·ist,** *n.* —**mod′ern·is′tic,** *adj.*

mod·ern·ize (mod′ər nīz′) *v.,* **mod·ern·ized, mod·ern·iz·ing.** —*v.t.* to make modern; change to suit present needs: *The town modernized its hospital by installing new equipment.* —*v.i.* to become modern; adopt modern ways. —**mod′ern·i·za′tion,** *n.*

Modern Latin, the Latin language as it has been used since about the year 1500, especially in scientific writing. Also, **New Latin.**

mod·est (mod′ist) *adj.* **1.** not boastful or forward: *to be modest and not brag about one's accomplishments.* **2.** retiring; reserved: *a quiet, modest person.* **3.** having or showing a sense of what is decent or proper: *a modest swimsuit.* **4.** not grand or showy; simple: *The apartment has modest furnishings.* **5.** within reasonable limits; not extreme; moderate: *We spent only a modest sum of money on our trip.* —**mod′est·ly,** *adv.*

mod·es·ty (mod′ə stē) *n.* the state or quality of being modest.

mod·i·cum (mod′i kəm) *n.* a small or moderate amount: *They have only a modicum of talent as actors.*

mod·i·fi·ca·tion (mod′ə fi kā′shən) *n.* **1.** the act of modifying or the state of being modified. **2.** a change or alteration: *After a few slight modifications, the plan was ready to be put into effect.* **3.** the result of modifying; a modified form.

mod·i·fi·er (mod′ə fī′ər) *n.* **1.** a person or thing that modifies. **2.** *Grammar.* a word, phrase, or clause that limits the meaning of or describes another word or group of words. Adjectives and adverbs are modifiers.

mod·i·fy (mod′ə fī′) *v.t.,* **mod·i·fied, mod·i·fy·ing.** **1.** to change or alter: *The inventor modified the original design to make the machine more efficient.* **2.** *Grammar.* to limit the meaning of or describe. In the phrase *a quiet evening,* the adjective *quiet* modifies the noun *evening.* **3.** to make less severe or extreme; moderate. —**mod′i·fi′a·ble,** *adj.*

mod·ish (mō′dish) *adj.* following a current style or fashion; fashionable. —**mod′ish·ly,** *adv.* —**mod′ish·ness,** *n.*

mod·u·lar (moj′ə lər) *adj.* of, relating to, or composed of modules: *modular furniture.*

mod·u·late (moj′ə lāt′) *v.,* **mod·u·lat·ed, mod·u·lat·ing.** —*v.t.* **1.** to change or vary the tone, volume, or pitch of: *to modulate the voice.* **2.** to adjust or regulate. **3.** to vary the amplitude, frequency, or other characteristic of (a carrier wave) for the transmission of a signal. —*v.i. Music.* to pass from one key to another. —**mod′u·la′tor,** *n.* —**mod·u·la·to·ry** (moj′ə lə tôr′ē) *adj.*

mod·u·la·tion (moj′ə lā′shən) *n.* **1.** the act or process of modulating or the state of being modulated. **2.** *Music.* a passing from one key to another. **3.** the process of varying the amplitude, frequency, or other characteristic of a carrier wave for the transmission of a signal.

mod·ule (moj′ül, mod′ūl) *n.* **1.** a standard or unit of measurement. **2.** a self-contained unit or part of a spacecraft, having a specific function: *a command module.* **3.** a standardized unit that can be combined with other units, as in building a house. **4.** an instructional unit on a single topic or part of a broad topic.

Mo·gul (mō′gəl, mō′gul) *n.* **1.** any of the Mongol conquerors of India or their descendants. **2.** a Mongol or

Mongolian. **3. mogul.** a powerful or important person: *The president of that studio is a mogul of the movie industry.*

mo·hair (mō′hâr′) *n.* **1.** the long, silky hair of the Angora goat. **2.** a woven fabric made of this hair.

Mo·ham·med·an (mō ham′i dən) *adj., n.* another word for **Muslim.**

Mo·ham·med·an·ism (mō ham′i də niz′əm) *n.* see **Islam** *(def. 1).*

Mo·ha·ve (mō hä′vē) also, **Mo·ja·ve.** *n., pl.* **Mo·ha·ve** or **Mo·ha·ves.** a member of a North American Indian tribe living along the Colorado River and speaking a Siouan language.

Mo·hawk (mō′hôk) *n., pl.* **Mo·hawk** or **Mo·hawks.** a member of a tribe of Iroquois Indians formerly living along the Mohawk River.

Mo·he·gan (mō hē′gən) *n., pl.* **Mo·he·gan** or **Mo·he·gans.** a member of a North American Indian tribe formerly living in what is now southeastern Connecticut and speaking an Algonquian language. —*adj.* of or relating to the Mohegan, their language, or their culture.

Mo·hi·can (mō hē′kən) *n., pl.* **Mo·hi·can** or **Mo·hi·cans.** another spelling of **Mahican.**

Mo·ho·ro·vi·čić discontinuity (mō′hə rō′vi chich′) the boundary between the earth's two outer layers, the crust and the mantle. Its depth ranges from an average of 22 miles (35 kilometers) beneath the continents to 3–6 miles (5–10 kilometers) beneath the ocean floor. Also, **Mo·ho** (mō′hō′), *n.* [From the Croatian geologist Andrija *Mohorovičić* (1857–1936), who discovered it.]

Mohs scale (mōz) a scale for judging the hardness of minerals. The scale consists of ten standard minerals arranged in order of increasing hardness from talc, with a value of 1, to diamond, with a value of 10. The hardness of a mineral is determined by finding which mineral on the scale it can scratch, and then which mineral on the scale can scratch it. [From the German mineralogist Friedrich *Mohs* (1773–1839), who devised it.]

moi·e·ty (moi′i tē) *n., pl.* **moi·e·ties. 1.** a half. **2.** a portion; part; share.

moist (moist) *adj.* **1.** slightly wet; damp: *a moist cloth.* **2.** containing moisture; humid: *moist air.* —**moist′ly,** *adv.* —**moist′ness,** *n.*

moist·en (moi′sən) *v.t., v.i.* to make or become moist.

mois·ture (mois′chər) *n.* **1.** water or other liquid in the air or on a surface. **2.** dampness; slight wetness.

Mo·ja·ve (mō hä′vē) another spelling of **Mohave.**

mo·lar (mō′lər) *n.* in humans and most other mammals, any of the large teeth at the back of the upper and lower jaws, which have broad, irregular surfaces for grinding food. In humans there are twelve molars. [From the Latin word *molaris* meaning "a millstone" or "molar," from the word *mola* "millstone" or "mill."]

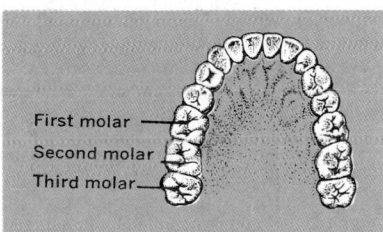

First molar

Second molar

Third molar

molars

mo·las·ses (mə las′iz) *n.* a sweet, thick, yellowish brown

M

syrup that is obtained from sugarcane as the sugar is being refined.

mold¹ (mōld) *n.* **1.** a hollow form for giving a particular shape to something in a fluid or plastic state: *The liquid plaster hardened in the mold.* **2.** something formed or made in a mold: *We served gelatin molds for dessert.* **3.** the general form; shape: *the round mold of a baby's face.* **4.** a distinctive character or type: *The pioneers were people of rugged mold.* —*v.t.* **1.** to work into a particular shape; form: *The children molded clay with their hands.* **2.** to form or make with a mold. **3.** to determine the form or nature of; influence or direct: *My parents helped to mold my personality.* [From the Old French word *molde* meaning "pattern, model," from the Latin word *modulus* "a small measure," from the word *modus* "measure" or "manner."] —**mold′er,** *n.*

mold² (mōld) *n.* **1.** any of various woolly or furry growths that form on food and on damp or decaying animal or plant matter. **2.** any of a number of fungi that cause such a growth. —*v.i.* to become covered with mold; grow moldy. [From the Middle English word *moulen* meaning "to become moldy, spoil," of Scandinavian origin.]

mold³ (mōld) *n.* a loose soil that is rich in decaying animal or plant matter. [From the Old English word *molde* meaning "dust, earth."]

mold·board (mōld′bôrd′) *n.* a curved metal plate or board in a plow that turns over the soil as it is plowed.

mold·er (mōl′dər) *v.i.* to crumble or decay; turn to dust: *The old wooden fence around the field moldered in the dense grass.* —*v.t.* to cause to crumble or decay.

mold·ing (mōl′ding) *n.* **1.** the act or process of forming or making something. **2.** something formed or made by molding; molded object. **3.** a shaped strip of wood, plaster, or other material that serves as a decorative edge, as on a wall or other surface.

mold·y (mōl′dē) *adj.,* **mold·i·er, mold·i·est.** **1.** covered with or containing fungus mold: *an old, moldy orange.* **2.** damp or stale; musty: *a moldy odor in an old house.* —**mold′i·ness,** *n.*

mole¹ (mōl) *n.* a brownish spot on the skin. [From the Old English word *māl* meaning "a spot, mark¹."]

mole² (mōl) *n.* **1.** an animal that lives in underground burrows. Moles have long claws used for digging, very small eyes, a long, pointed snout, and velvety fur. **2.** a spy who has established over time an identity as a trustworthy person and usually occupies a position vital to an enemy nation's security, as in an intelligence agency. [From the Middle English word *molle* meaning this animal, from Old English.]

moldings *(def. 3)*

mo·lec·u·lar (mə lek′yə lər) *adj.* of, relating to, or caused by molecules.

molecular weight, the sum of the atomic weights of the atoms in a molecule.

mol·e·cule (mol′ə kūl′) *n.* **1.** a particle of matter made up of two or more atoms joined by a pair of shared electrons. The molecule is the smallest unit of an element or compound that can exist without losing the chemical properties of the element or compound. **2.** any very small particle or bit: *There's not a molecule of truth in the rumor.*

mole·hill (mōl′hil′) *n.* a small mound or ridge of earth formed by a mole burrowing under the ground.

·to make a mountain out of a molehill. to give too much importance or emphasis to something that is

unimportant: *Worrying about the silly argument was making a mountain out of a molehill.*

mo·lest (mə lest′) *v.t.* **1.** to annoy or disturb; bother. **2.** to make improper sexual advances to or abuse sexually. —**mo·les·ta·tion** (mō′les tā′shən), *n.* —**mo·lest′er,** *n.*

moll (mol) *n.* *Slang.* a female companion of a gangster.

mol·lie (mol′ē) *also,* **mol·ly.** *n., pl.* **mol·lies.** any of a group of tropical fish that bear their young alive.

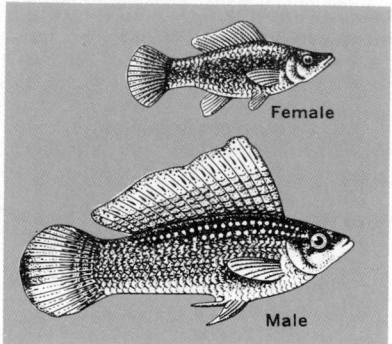

Female

Male

mollies

mol·li·fy (mol′ə fī′) *v.t.,* **mol·li·fied, mol·li·fy·ing.** to reduce the anger or strong feelings of (a person); soothe: *The clerk tried to mollify the angry customer.* —**mol′li·fi·ca′tion,** *n.*

mol·lusk (mol′əsk) *also,* **mol·lusc.** *n.* any of a large group of animals without backbones, found mainly in salt water, and including clams, oysters, and snails. Most mollusks have a soft body protected by a hard outer shell, but some mollusks, such as the squid and octopus, lack this type of shell.

mol·ly·cod·dle (mol′ē kod′əl) *n.* a weak-willed, pampered man or boy. —*v.t.,* **mol·ly·cod·dled, mol·ly·cod·dling.** to pamper; overprotect.

Mo·loch (mō′lok) *n.* in the Old Testament, a pagan god to whom parents sacrificed their children by fire.

Mo·lo·tov cocktail (mol′ə tôf′, mō′lə tof′) a makeshift bomb consisting of a breakable container filled with gasoline or other flammable liquid and a wick made of cloth or other material.

molt (mōlt) *v.i.* to shed the hair, feathers, skin, or shell and replace with a new growth. —*v.t.* to shed (an outer covering). —*n.* the act or process of molting: *The bird was in molt.*

mol·ten (mōl′tən) *v.* *Archaic.* a past participle of **melt.** —*adj.* melted or kept in a liquid state by heat: *Magma is molten rock.*

mol·to (mōl′tō) *adv.* *Music.* much; very.

mo·lyb·de·num (mə lib′də nəm) *n.* a heavy, very hard, silver-white metallic element that has a high melting point. It is used to make strong, heat-resistant alloys and missile parts. Symbol: **Mo** [Formed from the Latin word *molybdaena* meaning "galena," from the Greek word *molybdaina* "galena" or "lead²," from the word *molybdos* "lead²."]

mom (mom) *n.* *Informal.* mother.

mom–and–pop (mom′ən pop′) *adj.* being or relating to a small retail business managed by the married couple or family that owns it: *a mom-and-pop delicatessen.*

mo·ment (mō′mənt) *n.* **1.** a short period of time: *I'll be back in a moment.* **2.** a particular point in time, especially the present time: *The moment you spoke we recognized your voice.* **3.** importance; significance: *This is a question of great moment.*

mo·men·ta (mō men′tə) a plural of **momentum.**

mo·men·tar·i·ly (mō′mən ter′ə lē) *adv.* **1.** for a moment: *Our train was momentarily delayed.* **2.** at any moment; very soon: *An announcement is expected momentarily.* **3.** from moment to moment: *The swelling from the injury grew less and less momentarily.*

mo·men·tar·y (mō′mən ter′ē) *adj.* **1.** lasting only a very short time: *There was a momentary lull in the storm.*

2. occurring at every moment. **3.** occurring at any moment. —**mo′men·tar′i·ness,** *n.*

mo·men·tous (mō men′təs) *adj.* of great importance: *a momentous event.* —**mo·men′tous·ly,** *adv.* —**mo·men′tous·ness,** *n.*

mo·men·tum (mō men′təm) *n., pl.* **mo·men·ta** or **mo·men·tums.** **1.** *Physics.* the property of a moving body measured by multiplying its mass by its velocity. **2.** the force or speed resulting from motion; impetus: *The rock steadily gained momentum as it rolled down the hill.*

mom·my (mom′ē) *n., pl.* **mom·mies.** *Informal.* mother.

Mon., Monday.

mon·arch (mon′ərk) *n.* **1.** a hereditary ruler of a state or country, such as a king or queen. **2.** a large orange and black butterfly found in North America.

monarch *(def. 2)*

mo·nar·chi·cal (mə när′ki kəl) *adj.* **1.** of, relating to, or characteristic of a monarch or monarchy. **2.** ruled by or favoring a monarch or monarchy: *a monarchical society, a monarchical movement.*

mon·ar·chism (mon′ər kiz′əm) *n.* **1.** the principles of monarchy. **2.** belief in or support of monarchy as a form of government. —**mon′arch·ist,** *n.*

mon·ar·chy (mon′ər kē) *n., pl.* **mon·ar·chies.** **1.** government by a monarch: *France once had a monarchy as its form of government.* **2.** a nation or state ruled by a monarch.

mon·as·ter·y (mon′ə ster′e) *n., pl.* **mon·as·ter·ies.** **1.** a place of residence occupied by persons living together in a religious community, especially monks. **2.** the persons living in such a place. [From the Church Latin word *monasterium* meaning "monastery," from the Late Greek word *monastērion,* from the Greek word *monazein* "to live alone," from the word *monos* "alone."]

mo·nas·tic (mə nas′tik) *adj.* of, relating to, or characteristic of a monastery, monks, or their way of life: *monastic seclusion, monastic vows.* —*n.* a monk or other member of a religious order. —**mon·as·ti·cism** (mə nas′tə siz′əm), *n.*

mon·au·ral (mon ôr′əl) *adj.* of or relating to a system of sound reproduction in which the sound is heard from a single source. Also, **mono, monophonic.**

Mon·day (mun′dē, mun′dā) *n.* the second day of the week. [From the Old English word *mōnandæg* meaning "Monday," going back to the words *mōna* "moon" and *dæg* "day," a translation of the Late Latin phrase *lunae dies* "moon's day," name of the second day of the week.]

mo·ne·ran (mə nîr′ən) *n.* any of a group of one-celled organisms, such as bacteria or blue-green algae, that lack a nucleus enclosed by a membrane. Many biologists classify monerans as a kingdom alongside the plant and animal kingdoms, the fungi, and the protists. —*adj.* of or relating to a moneran or monerans.

mon·e·tar·y (mon′i ter′ē) *adj.* **1.** of or relating to the currency or coinage used by a country: *The franc is the monetary unit of France.* **2.** of or relating to money: *a monetary gift.*

mon·ey (mun′ē) *n., pl.* **mon·eys** or *(def. 5, also)* **mon·ies.** **1.** the coins and paper currency issued by a government for payment of debts and for purchase of goods and services; legal tender. **2.** anything used or serving as money. **3.** payment, gain, profit, or loss in terms of money: *The company made money on that deal.* **4.** wealth measured in terms of money: *They tried to give the impression that their family had money.* **5. moneys** or **monies.** funds collected or stored, as by a government. [From the Old French word *monoie* meaning "money," from the Latin word *moneta* "mint?" or "money," from (Juno) *Moneta,* a title for the Roman goddess Juno, in whose temple coins were minted.]

mon·ey·bag (mun′ē bag′) *n.* **1.** a bag for holding money. **2. moneybags.** *Informal.* wealthy, often miserly person.

mon·ey·chang·er (mun′ē chān′jər) *n.* a person who exchanges money, usually the money of one country for that of another.

mon·eyed (mun′ēd) *also,* **mon·ied.** *adj.* **1.** having much money; wealthy: *a moneyed family.* **2.** representing or derived from money or wealth: *moneyed influence.*

mon·ey·lend·er (mun′ē len′dər) *n.* a person who lends money and charges interest.

money order, an order for the payment of a sum of money, especially one issued by a bank or post office.

Mon·gol (mong′gəl) *n.* **1.** a member of one of the nomadic peoples now living in Mongolia. **2.** see **Mongolian.** —*adj.* see **Mongolian.**

Mon·go·li·an (mong gō′lē ən) *n.* **1.** a person who was born in or is a citizen of Mongolia. **2.** a member of the Mongoloid division of the human race. **3.** a language spoken in Mongolia and central Asia. —*adj.* **1.** of or relating to Mongolia or the Mongolian People's Republic. **2.** of or relating to the Mongols, their language, or their culture.

mon·gol·ism (mong′gə liz′əm) *n.* a word formerly used for **Down syndrome.**

Mon·gol·oid (mong′gə loid′) *adj.* **1.** of or relating to one of the major divisions of the human race, whose members have yellowish skin, brown, slanted eyes, and straight, dark hair. The Mongoloid division includes the peoples of eastern Asia and Japan, the Eskimo, and the North American Indians. **2.** of, resembling, or characteristic of Mongols or Mongolians. **3. mongoloid.** formerly, having mongolism. —*n.* **1.** a member of the Mongoloid division of the human race. **2. mongoloid.** formerly, a person having mongolism.

mon·goose (mong′güs′) *n., pl.* **mon·goos·es.** a slender, flesh-eating animal having a pointed face, a long tail, and rough, shaggy fur. The mongoose is noted for its ability to kill certain poisonous snakes, especially cobras.

mongoose

at; āpe; fär; câre; end; mē; it; īce; pîerce; hot; ōld; sông, fôrk; oil; out; up; ūse; rüle; pu̇ll; tûrn; chin; sing; shop; thin; **this**; hw in white; zh in treasure. The symbol ə stands for the unstressed vowel sound heard in about, taken, pencil, lemon, and circus.

M

mon·grel (mung′grəl, mong′grəl) *n*. **1.** an animal, especially a dog, of mixed breed. **2.** a person or thing that is a mixture of different elements. —*adj*. of mixed breed.

mon·ied (mun′ēd) another spelling of **moneyed**.

mon·ies (mun′ēz) a plural of **money**.

mon·i·tor (mon′i tər) *n*. **1.** a student in school given a special duty or responsibility, such as keeping order or taking attendance. **2.** a receiver used for checking, watching, or listening to television or radio transmissions. **3.** an instrument or device used to observe, record, or control an activity or process. **4.** a person or thing that warns, advises, or reminds. **5.** the part of a computer terminal that contains the screen on which data is displayed. —*v.t.* **1.** to check, watch, or listen to (a television or radio transmission). **2.** to watch over or supervise; oversee. **3.** to observe, record, or control by means of a monitor. —*v.i.* to serve as a monitor.

mon·i·to·ry (mon′i tôr′ē) *adj*. serving to warn: *A monitory look from the teacher made the class quiet down.*

monk (mungk) *n*. a man who has entered a religious order and is bound by religious vows.

mon·key (mung′kē) *n., pl*. **mon·keys. 1.** any of a group of animals, related to apes and humans, having long limbs and hands and feet adapted for grasping and climbing. **2.** a person who resembles a monkey in behavior or appearance, especially a mischievous or playful child. —*v.i.*, **mon·keyed, mon·key·ing.** *Informal*. to play, fool, or meddle: *Don't monkey with the machinery.*

monkey wrench, a wrench with one jaw that can be adjusted and one jaw that is fixed, used on nuts and bolts of different sizes.

monk·ish (mung′kish) *adj*. of, relating to, or like a monk or monks.

monks·hood (mungks′- hŏod′) *n*. see **aconite** *(def. 1).*

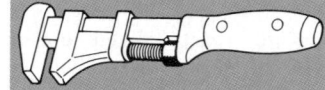

monkey wrench

mon·o[1] (mon′ō) *n*. *Informal*. see **infectious mononucleosis**.

mon·o[2] (mon′ō) *adj*. another word for **monaural**.

mono– *combining form* one; single; alone: *monoplane, monosyllabic*.

mon·o·chro·mat·ic (mon′ə krō mat′ik) *adj*. **1.** of or having only one color: *a monochromatic painting*. **2.** consisting of light of one wavelength.

mon·o·chrome (mon′ə krōm′) *n*. a painting or drawing done in a single color. —*adj*. displaying shades of a single color or gray, as a black-and-white television receiver or some computer monitors.

mon·o·cle (mon′ə kəl) *n*. an eyeglass for one eye.

mon·o·cled (mon′ə kəld) *adj*. wearing a monocle.

mon·o·cot·y·le·don (mon′ə kot′ə lē′dən) *n*. a plant that has one cotyledon, or seed leaf, in the embryo. Monocotyledons make up one of the two classes of flowering plants. Also, **mon·o·cot** (mon′ə kot′). —**mon·o·cot′y·le′don·ous,** *adj*.

mo·noc·u·lar (mə nok′yə lər) *adj*. **1.** having only one eye. **2.** using or for use by one eye: *a monocular microscope*.

mo·nog·a·mist (mə nog′ə mist) *n*. a person who practices or believes in monogamy.

mo·nog·a·mous (mə nog′ə məs) *adj*. of, relating to, or practicing monogamy.

mo·nog·a·my (mə nog′ə mē) *n*. the condition or practice of being married to only one person at a time.

mon·o·gram (mon′ə gram′) *n*. a design made by combining or interlacing two or more letters, especially the initials of one's name, used on clothing, stationery, and other items. —*v.t.*, **mon·o·gramed** or **mon·o·grammed, mon·o·gram·ing** or **mon·o·gram·ming.** to mark with a monogram.

mon·o·graph (mon′ə graf′) *n*. a scholarly book, treatise, or article written on a single subject or on a particular aspect of a subject.

mon·o·lith (mon′ə lith′) *n*. **1.** a single, usually very large block of stone, used in architecture and sculpture. **2.** a monument or other structure formed of such a block of stone.

mon·o·lith·ic (mon′ə lith′ik) *adj*. **1.** formed of, relating to, or resembling a monolith: *a monolithic pillar*. **2.** of the nature of a monolith; massive or uniform.

mo·nol·o·gist (mə nol′ə jist) *n*. a person who gives a monologue.

mon·o·logue (mon′ə lôg′, mon′ə log′) *also,* **mon·o·log.** *n*. **1.** a long speech made by one person. **2.** a dramatic or literary composition involving or performed by only one speaker. **3.** a series of jokes or humorous stories presented by a single speaker: *a comedian's monologue*.

mon·o·ma·ni·a (mon′ə mā′nē ə) *n*. **1.** a mental disorder in which a person has an obsession with one idea but otherwise appears sane. **2.** an excessive preoccupation with or enthusiasm for one idea or subject. —**mon·o·ma·ni·ac** (mon′ə mā′nē ak′), *n*. —**mon·o·ma·ni·a·cal** (mon′ə mə nī′ə kəl), *adj*.

mo·no·mi·al (mə nō′mē əl) *adj*. consisting of a single term. The expression *3x* is a monomial expression. —*n*. a monomial expression, quantity, or name.

mon·o·nu·cle·o·sis (mon′ə nü′klē ō′sis, mon′ə nū′klē- ō′sis) *n*. see **infectious mononucleosis**.

mon·o·phon·ic (mon′ə fon′ik) *adj*. **1.** *Music*. having a single melodic line with no accompaniment. **2.** another word for **monaural**.

mon·o·plane (mon′ə plān′) *n*. an airplane with only one pair of main wings.

mo·nop·o·list (mə nop′ə list) *n*. a person who has a monopoly or favors monopoly. —**mo·nop·o·lis′tic,** *adj*.

mo·nop·o·lize (mə nop′ə līz′) *v.t.*, **mo·nop·o·lized, mo·nop·o·liz·ing. 1.** to obtain or have a monopoly of or over: *That company is attempting to monopolize the textile industry.* **2.** to take exclusive control of; have all to oneself: *to monopolize a conversation, to monopolize a person's time.*

mo·nop·o·ly (mə nop′ə lē) *n., pl*. **mo·nop·o·lies. 1.** the exclusive control of something, such as manufactured goods or a service, by a person, group, or company. **2.** the right or privilege of such control granted by a government. A patent gives an inventor a monopoly over an invention for a limited number of years. **3.** something that is controlled by a monopoly. **4.** a group or company that has a monopoly. **5.** the exclusive control or possession of something: *Neither side in the controversy has a monopoly on the truth.*

mon·o·rail (mon′ə rāl′) *n*. **1.** a railway system in which the cars ride on a single rail, usually elevated above ground traffic. Cars either ride upon the rail or are suspended beneath it. **2.** the single rail for such a system.

mon·o·so·di·um glu·ta·mate (mon′ə sō′dē əm glü′- tə māt′) a white powder added to many prepared foods to improve their flavor.

mon·o·syl·lab·ic (mon′ə si lab′ik) *adj*. **1.** having only one syllable: *a monosyllabic name*. **2.** consisting of or using a word or words of one syllable: *a curt, monosyllabic reply*. —**mon′o·syl·lab′i·cal·ly,** *adv*.

mon·o·syl·la·ble (mon′ə sil′ə bəl) *n*. a word of one syllable.

mon·o·the·ism (mon′ə thē iz′əm) *n*. the doctrine or belief that there is only one God. —**mon′o·the·ist,** *n*. —**mon′o·the·is′tic,** *adj*.

mon·o·tone (mon′ə tōn′) *n*. **1.** the saying or uttering of words or sounds with no change in pitch; a single, unchanging tone in speaking: *The lecturer spoke in a dull monotone.* **2.** sameness of style, manner, or color.

mo·not·o·nous (mə not′ə nəs) *adj.* **1.** not changing, as in tone, sound, or beat: *a monotonous voice, a monotonous rhythm.* **2.** tiresome or uninteresting because of a lack of variety: *I quickly became bored with the monotonous job.* —**mo·not′o·nous·ly,** *adv.* —**mo·not′o·nous·ness,** *n.*

mo·not·o·ny (mə not′ə nē) *n.* **1.** a tiresome sameness; lack of variety: *the monotony of prison life.* **2.** a lack of change, as in tone, sound, or beat.

mon·o·treme (mon′ə trēm′) *n.* a member of a primitive order of mammals, found chiefly in Australia and New Guinea. Monotremes lay eggs like birds and reptiles but nurse their young like mammals. The platypus and the echidnas are the only monotremes.

mon·ox·ide (mon ok′sīd, mə nok′sīd) *n.* an oxide containing only one atom of oxygen in each molecule.

Mon·roe Doctrine (mən rō′) a declaration of U.S. foreign policy made by President James Monroe in 1823, opposing further European colonization or interference in the Western Hemisphere.

Mon·sei·gneur (mōn se nyûr′) *n., pl.* **Mes·sei·gneurs** (mā se nyûr′). **1.** a French title of honor given to men of high rank, such as members of the higher nobility, bishops, and cardinals. **2.** *also,* **monseigneur.** a person who bears this title.

mon·sieur (mə syûr′) *n., pl.* **mes·sieurs.** mister; sir. ▲ a French form of respectful or polite address for a man.

Mon·si·gnor (mon sēn′yər) *n., pl.* **Mon·si·gnors** or **Mon·si·gno·ri** (mon′sēn yôr′ē). **1.** a title given to certain Roman Catholic dignitaries. **2.** *also,* **monsignor.** a person who bears this title.

mon·soon (mon sün′) *n.* **1.** a seasonal wind of the Indian Ocean and southern Asia, which blows from the southwest towards the land in summer and from the northeast towards the ocean in winter. **2.** the season of the summer monsoon, characterized by heavy rains.

mon·ster (mon′stər) *n.* **1.** an imaginary creature that is large and frightening, and has an abnormal, grotesque, or horrible shape. **2.** *Biology.* an animal or plant that is abnormal in structure or appearance: *A two-headed turtle is a monster.* **3.** an imaginary creature that combines various animal and/or human features, such as a centaur or griffin. **4.** a person whose behavior is inhumanly wicked, cruel, or immoral. **5.** a person or thing that is unusually large. —*adj.* enormous; gigantic: *a monster whale.*

mon·stros·i·ty (mon stros′i tē) *n., pl.* **mon·stros·i·ties.** **1.** a monstrous person or thing. **2.** the quality or condition of being monstrous: *the monstrosity of a crime.*

mon·strous (mon′strəs) *adj.* **1.** abnormal, grotesque, or horrible in shape or character: *The dragon was a monstrous creature.* **2.** unusually large; enormous: *an error of monstrous proportions.* **3.** shocking, as in wickedness; horrible. —**mon′strous·ly,** *adv.* —**mon′strous·ness,** *n.*

Mont., Montana.

mon·tage (mon täzh′) *n.* **1.** a picture made by combining several different pictures or parts of pictures. **2.** the art or process of making such pictures. **3.** in motion pictures, a rapid sequence of changing scenes and images.

Mon·tes·so·ri method (mon′tə sôr′ē) a system of education for young children developed by Maria Montessori, emphasizing training of the child's senses through independent activity in a carefully structured classroom, so as to encourage the development of individual expression, self-discipline, and independence.

month (munth) *n.* **1.** one of the twelve parts into which the calendar year is divided. Also, **calendar month.** **2.** the time from any day of one calendar month to the corresponding day of the next month. **3.** a period of about four weeks or thirty days. **4.** the period of a complete revolution of the moon around the earth. Also (*def. 4*), **lunar month.**

month·ly (munth′lē) *adj.* **1.** done, happening, or appearing once a month: *the monthly bills, a monthly magazine.* **2.** of, relating to, or happening in a month: *monthly rainfall.* **3.** continuing or lasting a month. —*adv.* once a month; every month. —*n., pl.* **month·lies.** a magazine that is published once a month.

mon·u·ment (mon′yə mənt) *n.* **1.** a building, statue, arch, or other structure set up or constructed in memory of a person or event. **2.** a memorial stone or marker placed at a grave; tombstone. **3.** a work or achievement of lasting significance: *The discovery of penicillin was a monument in medical research.* **4.** an area or site of special importance or of great natural beauty set aside and preserved by a government.

mon·u·men·tal (mon′yə men′təl) *adj.* **1.** of lasting significance; notable: *a monumental decision of the U.S. Supreme Court.* **2.** of great size or scope; huge; colossal: *a monumental undertaking.* **3.** of, like, or serving as a monument: *A monumental work of sculpture was placed over the general's grave.* —**mon′u·men′tal·ly,** *adv.*

moo (mü) *n., pl.* **moos.** the sound made by a cow. —*v.i.,* **mooed, moo·ing.** to make such a sound; low.

mood[1] (müd) *n.* **1.** a state of mind or feeling at a particular time: *The good news put us in a happy mood.* **2.** a special quality or atmosphere, as of a place or work of art: *the restful mood of a landscape painting.* [From the Old English word *mōd* meaning "courage, heart, mind."]

mood[2] (müd) *n. Grammar.* the form of a verb that shows whether the statement refers to a fact, command, wish, or possibility. There are three moods in English: indicative, imperative, and subjunctive. Also, **mode.** [A form of *mode*[1].]

mood·y (mü′dē) *adj.,* **mood·i·er, mood·i·est. 1.** tending to have changing moods, especially gloomy or sullen moods: *a person with a moody nature.* **2.** showing or expressing a gloomy mood: *a moody answer.* —**mood′i·ly,** *adv.* —**mood′i·ness,** *n.*

| Crescent moon | Half moon | Gibbous moon | Full moon |

phases of the **moon**

moon (mün) *n.* **1.** the earth's natural satellite, visible by the sun's reflected light. The moon orbits the earth from west to east once in about 29½ days. **2.** anything resembling the moon in any of its phases, such as a crescent-shaped object or design. **3.** a satellite of any other planet: *Mars has two small moons.* **4.** a month, especially a lunar month. **5.** moonlight. —*v.i.* to move or look about dreamily or aimlessly.

moon·beam (mün′bēm′) *n.* a ray of light from the moon.

moon·light (mün′līt′) *n.* the light shining from the moon. —*adj.* **1.** lighted by the moon; moonlit. **2.** happening or done by the light of the moon: *to take a moonlight ride.* —*v.i.* to work at a second job, especially at night, in addition to one's regular job: *The police officer moon-*

at; āpe; fär; câre; end; mē; it; īce; pîerce; hot; ōld; sông, fôrk; oil; out; up; ūse; rüle; pùll; tûrn; chin; sing; shop; thin; this; hw in white; zh in treasure. The symbol ə stands for the unstressed vowel sound heard in about, taken, pencil, lemon, and circus.

M

617

lighted as a taxi driver. —**moon'light'er,** *n.* —**moon'-light'ing,** *n.*

moon·lit (mün'lit') *adj.* lighted by the moon: *a moonlit night.*

moon·scape (mün'skāp') *n.* a picture or view of the moon's surface.

moon·shine (mün'shīn') *n.* **1.** the light shining from the moon; moonlight. **2.** empty talk or ideas; nonsense. **3.** *Informal.* liquor distilled illegally.

moon·stone (mün'stōn') *n.* a pearly gemstone, a variety of feldspar.

moon·struck (mün'struk') *adj.* romantically dazed or slightly crazy because of the supposed influence of the moon.

moor¹ (mŭr) *v.t.* **1.** to secure (a ship or other craft) in place with lines or anchors, as at a dock. **2.** to fix in place; secure. —*v.i.* **1.** to secure a ship or other craft. **2.** to be secured, as by ropes and anchors: *The ship moored at the dock to unload and load cargo.* [From the late Middle English word *moren* meaning ''to moor¹.'']

moor² (mŭr) *n.* an area of open, rolling, wild land, often covered with heather and having bogs and marshes. [From the Old English word *mōr* with the same meaning.]

Moor (mŭr) *n.* a member of a people of mixed Arab and Berber descent living in northern Africa. The Moors invaded and conquered Spain in the eighth century A.D.

moor·age (mŭr'ij) *n.* **1.** a place for mooring. **2.** the act of mooring or the state of being moored. **3.** a charge for the use of moorings.

moor·ing (mŭr'ing) *n.* **1.** the act of a person or thing that moors. **2.** a device, such as a cable, rope, or anchor, by which a ship is moored. **3.** a place where a boat or a ship can be moored.

Moor·ish (mŭr'ish) *adj.* of or relating to the Moors.

moose (müs) *n., pl.* **moose.** a large, heavy mammal, the largest member of the deer family, native to the forests of northern North America, having a large head, a short neck, and a blackish brown coat with gray markings. The male has large, broad antlers.

moose

moot (müt) *adj.* open to dispute or discussion; debatable: *a moot point in an argument.*

mop (mop) *n.* **1.** a cleaning device that has a bundle of coarse yarn, cloth, sponge, or other absorbent material, fastened at the end of a long handle. **2.** any thick, tangled mass resembling this, such as a bushy head of hair. —*v.t.,* **mopped, mop·ping.** to clean with or as with a mop: *They mopped the floor before the game continued. I mopped the sweat from my forehead.*

·**to mop up. a.** *Informal.* to finish (a task). **b.** to clear out remaining enemy troops from (a captured area).

mope (mōp) *v.i.,* **moped, mop·ing.** to be gloomy and sad.

mo·ped (mō'ped) *n.* a lightweight motorbike that can be driven at low speeds or pedaled.

mop·pet (mop'it) *n.* a little child.

mo·raine (mə rān') *n.* a mass of rock deposited by a melting glacier.

mor·al (môr'əl, mor'əl) *adj.* **1.** good or virtuous in behavior or character according to a standard of right and wrong: *a moral person, a moral act.* **2.** of, relating to, or concerned with a standard of right and wrong; ethical: *a moral question.* **3.** promoting or aiding right conduct: *moral teachings.* **4.** able to judge between right and

wrong: *People are moral beings.* **5.** having an effect on or relating to the mind, thoughts, emotions, attitudes, or the like: *My friends gave me moral support while I was in the hospital.* —*n.* **1.** the lesson taught by a fable, story, or event. **2. morals.** principles or standards of right and wrong. —**mor'al·ly,** *adv.*

mo·rale (mə ral') *n.* the attitude or spirit of a person or group: *The football team's morale was low after its tenth loss.*

mor·al·ist (môr'ə list, mor'ə list) *n.* **1.** a person who teaches or writes about morals. **2.** a moralistic person.

mor·al·is·tic (môr'ə lis'tik, mor'ə lis'tik) *adj.* concerned with morals, especially tending to promote or aid right conduct: *a moralistic person, moralistic sermons.*

mo·ral·i·ty (mə ral'i tē) *n., pl.* **mo·ral·i·ties.** **1.** the moral rightness or wrongness of an act. **2.** moral conduct; virtue. **3.** a system of morals; ethics.

mor·al·ize (môr'ə līz', mor'ə līz') *v.,* **mor·al·ized, mor·al·iz·ing.** —*v.i.* to make judgments on matters of right and wrong, especially to tell people what to do in a self-righteous way. —*v.t.* **1.** to explain or interpret the lesson or moral of. **2.** to view in moral terms; regard as a question of right and wrong.

mo·rass (mə ras') *n., pl.* **mo·rass·es.** **1.** an area of low, soft, wet ground; marsh; swamp. **2.** a confusing or difficult situation.

mor·a·to·ri·um (môr'ə tôr'ē əm) *n., pl.* **mor·a·to·ri·ums** or **mor·a·to·ri·a** (môr'ə tôr'ē ə). **1.** the postponing of a legal obligation, such as the paying of a debt. **2.** the period of such a postponement. **3.** a temporary delaying or stopping of some activity: *The nations agreed to a moratorium on testing nuclear weapons.*

Mo·ra·vi·an (mô rā'vē ən) *adj.* of or relating to Moravia, its people, their language, or culture. —*n.* **1.** a person who was born in or is a citizen of Moravia. **2.** the language of Moravia, a dialect of Czech.

mo·ray (môr'ā) *n.* any of numerous saltwater eels found in warm waters and having strong jaws and sharp teeth. Also, **moray eel.**

mor·bid (môr'bid) *adj.* **1.** overly concerned with or interested in death, disease, decay, or the like: *a morbid sense of humor.* **2.** of or relating to death, disease, decay, or the like; gruesome; grisly: *a morbid graveyard scene.* **3.** relating to, caused by, or characteristic of disease: *a morbid condition of the liver.* —**mor'bid·ly,** *adv.* —**mor'bid·ness,** *n.*

mor·bid·i·ty (môr bid'i tē) *n.* **1.** the quality or state of being morbid. **2.** the rate of disease or proportion of diseased persons in a place.

mor·dant (môr'dənt) *adj.* biting or sarcastic; cutting: *a mordant wit, a mordant remark.* —*n.* **1.** any substance that serves to fix the color of a dye in cloth. **2.** an acid or other substance used in etching to eat into metal. —**mor'dan·cy,** *n.* —**mor'dant·ly,** *adv.*

more (môr) *adj.* the comparative of **much** and **many.** **1.** greater in number, quantity, intensity, or degree: *There are more students in this school now than there were last year. I need more flour for this recipe.* **2.** being an additional amount; further: *Repeat that one more time. I'll need an hour more to finish.* —*adv.* the comparative of **much.** **1.** in or to a greater extent or degree: *Be more careful. You exercise more regularly than I do.* **2.** in addition; further; again: *The kite flew up and then fell once more.* —*n.* an additional amount: *The dog wants more to eat. Say no more.*

·**more or less. a.** to an indefinite degree; somewhat: *The patient's condition has more or less improved.* **b.** just about; approximately: *We arrived more or less on time.*

mo·rel (mə rel') *n.* any of a group of fungi characterized by a cone-shaped cap with spongelike indentations.

more·o·ver (môr ō′vər) *adv.* in addition to what has been said; also: *The day was dark and cold, and moreover it was raining.*

mo·res (môr′āz) *pl. n.* the customs of a particular group or society that are considered essential to its welfare.

morgue (môrg) *n.* **1.** a place where a dead person's body is kept until it is identified, examined by autopsy, or buried. **2.** a reference library in a newspaper office in which old issues, clippings, and other sources of information are stored.

mor·i·bund (môr′ə bund′, mor′ə bund′) *adj.* in a dying state; almost lifeless.

Mor·mon (môr′mən) *n.* a member of the Church of Jesus Christ of Latter-day Saints; a follower of Mormonism. —*adj.* of or relating to Mormons or Mormonism.

Mor·mon·ism (môr′mə niz′əm) *n.* a Christian religion founded in 1830 by Joseph Smith, known officially as the Church of Jesus Christ of Latter-day Saints.

morn (môrn) *n.* see **morning**.

morn·ing (môr′ning) *n.* **1.** the first part of the day, beginning at midnight and ending at noon. **2.** dawn. —*adj.* of, relating to, or occurring in the morning: *a morning newspaper, a morning appointment.*

morning glory **1.** a trumpet-shaped flower growing mainly in blue, purple, pink, yellow, or white, and generally open only in the early morning. **2.** any of various plants bearing this flower, especially a twining vine widely grown in gardens and having oval or heart-shaped leaves.

morning star, a planet, especially Venus, visible in the eastern sky before sunrise.

mo·roc·co (mə rok′ō) *n., pl.* **mo·roc·cos.** leather that originally came from Morocco, made from goatskin and used for the bindings of fine books.

mo·ron (môr′on) *n.* **1.** a person who is mentally retarded, having a mental age of up to 12 years. ▲ now considered obsolete. **2.** a very foolish or stupid person. —**mo·ron·ic** (mə ron′ik), *adj.*

morning glory

mo·rose (mə rōs′) *adj.* bad-tempered, gloomy, or sullen. —**mo·rose·ly,** *adv.* —**mo·rose·ness,** *n.*

mor·pheme (môr′fēm) *n.* the smallest unit of language that has meaning. A morpheme may be a word, a root, or an affix.

Mor·phe·us (môr′fē əs, môr′fūs) *n. Greek Mythology.* the god of dreams.

mor·phine (môr′fēn) *n.* a powerful, habit-forming drug made from opium. Morphine is used to relieve pain. [From the French word *morphine,* from *Morpheus,* the Greek god of sleep.]

mor·pho·log·i·cal (môr′fə loj′i kəl) *adj.* of or relating to morphology. Also, **mor·pho·log·ic** (môr′fə loj′ik).

mor·phol·o·gy (môr fol′ə jē) *n., pl.* **mor·phol·o·gies.** **1.** the biological study of the structure of animals and plants. **2.** the structure of an organism. **3.** the branch of linguistics that studies how groups of sounds are joined together to make words.

mor·row (môr′ō, mor′ō) *n. Archaic.* **1.** the next day; tomorrow: *I shall say good night till it be morrow* (Shakespeare, *Romeo and Juliet*). **2.** morning.

Morse code (môrs) a code used in telegraphy in which combinations of short and long signals, or dots and dashes, are used to represent the letters of the alphabet, numerals, and punctuation marks. It was invented by Samuel F.B. Morse.

mor·sel (môr′səl) *n.* **1.** a small bite or portion of food. **2.** a small quantity or piece; fragment.

mor·tal (môr′təl) *adj.* **1.** subject to death; certain to die: *All things that live are mortal.* **2.** causing death; fatal: *a*

mortal blow, a mortal wound. **3.** fought to the death: *mortal combat.* **4.** relentless; irreconcilable: *mortal enemies.* **5.** very great or intense: *mortal fear.* **6.** of or characteristic of human beings; earthly: *a mortal weakness.* —*n.* a human being; person. —**mor′tal·ly,** *adv.*

mor·tal·i·ty (môr tal′i tē) *n.* **1.** the state or condition of being subject to death. **2.** the number of deaths in a given time in a given place; death rate: *That country has a high mortality from disease.* **3.** large-scale death or destruction, as from war or other disaster: *the horrible mortality from an earthquake.*

mortal sin, in Roman Catholic theology, a sin so serious as to separate the sinner from the favor and love of God and to result in damnation to hell unless forgiven.

mor·tar (môr′tər) *n.* **1.** a material made of a mixture of sand, water, and lime that hardens as it dries, used especially for binding bricks or stones together in a wall or other structure. **2.** a thick bowl of marble or other hard material in which substances are crushed to a powder by means of a pestle. **3.** a short cannon for firing shells at high angles. [From the Old French word *mortier* meaning both "plaster" and this bowl, from the Latin word *morarium* with both meanings.]

mortar *(def. 2)*

mor·tar·board (môr′tər bôrd′) *n.* **1.** a square, flat plate of wood or metal with a centered handle, used by masons to hold mortar. **2.** a cap attached to a square cloth-covered piece of wood or cardboard, worn at graduations and other academic exercises.

mort·gage (môr′gij) *n.* **1.** a pledge of property, given as security for the payment of a debt. **2.** a document indicating the terms of such a pledge and the manner in which the debt is to be paid. —*v.t.,* **mort·gaged, mort·gag·ing.** **1.** to pledge (property) as security for the payment of a debt: *They mortgaged their farm to the bank in return for a loan.* **2.** to give up or pledge in advance. [Old French *morgage, mortgage* literally, dead pledge; because if one did not pay off a mortgage when it was due, one lost the property (the property was "dead" to the debtor).]

mort·ga·gee (môr′gə jē′) *n.* a person to whom property is mortgaged.

mort·ga·gor (môr′gə jər) *also,* **mort·gag·er.** *n.* a person who mortgages property.

mor·tice (môr′tis) *n., v.t.,* **mor·ticed, mor·tic·ing.** another spelling of **mortise**.

mor·ti·cian (môr tish′ən) *n.* see **undertaker** *(def. 1).*

mor·ti·fi·ca·tion (môr′tə fi kā′shən) *n.* **1.** a feeling of shame, humiliation, or embarrassment. **2.** anything causing such feelings. **3.** the practice of suppressing desires and passions by strict self-discipline. **4.** the death and decay of a part of the body; gangrene.

mor·ti·fy (môr′tə fī′) *v.,* **mor·ti·fied, mor·ti·fy·ing.** —*v.t.* **1.** to cause to feel shame, humiliation, or embarrassment: *The thought of my cousin reading my diary mortifies me.* **2.** to subject to mortification. —*v.i.* to become affected with gangrene; decay. —**mor′ti·fi·er,** *n.*

mor·tise (môr′tis) *also,* **mor·tice.** *n.* a hole, as in a piece of wood, shaped to receive a tenon, or projecting part, of a second piece in order to form a strong joint.

---

at; āpe; fär; câre; end; mē; it; īce; pierce; hot; ōld; sông; fôrk; oil; out; up; ūse; rüle; pull; tûrn; chin; sing; shop; thin; **th**is; hw in white; zh in treasure. The symbol ə stands for the unstressed vowel sound heard in about, taken, pencil, lemon, and circus.

M

—*v.t.*, **mor·tised, mor·tis·ing. 1.** to join or fasten securely by means of a tenon and mortise: *to mortise two pieces of lumber.* **2.** to cut or make a mortise in.

mor·tu·ar·y (môr′chü er′ē) *n., pl.* **mor·tu·ar·ies.** a place where corpses are prepared or kept until burial or cremation. —*adj.* of or relating to death or burial.

mos., months.

mosaic *(def. 1)*

mo·sa·ic (mō zā′ik) *n.* **1.** a picture or design made by fitting together variously colored bits of stone, glass, or other hard material. **2.** the technique or process of making such designs. **3.** anything that is like a mosaic: *The novelist's life was a mosaic of interesting experiences.*

Mo·sa·ic (mō zā′ik) *adj.* of or relating to Moses or the writings or laws attributed to him.

mo·sey (mō′zē) *v.i.,* **mo·seyed, mo·sey·ing.** *Informal.* to move in a slow or leisurely way; stroll; amble: *to mosey along a street.*

Mos·lem (moz′ləm) *adj., n.* another spelling of **Muslim.**

mosque (mosk) *n.* a Muslim temple or place of worship.

mos·qui·to (mə skē′ tō) *n., pl.* **mos·qui·toes** or **mos·qui·tos.** any of a group of two-winged insects, the females of which can pierce the skin of humans and other animals and suck their blood. The bite of some mosquitoes can transmit such diseases as malaria and yellow fever.

mosquito net, a screen or covering resembling gauze, used to keep out mosquitoes and other insects, as from a tent. Also, **mosquito netting.**

moss (môs) *n., pl.* **moss·es. 1.** any of a large group of nonflowering plants growing in clusters and often forming soft, dense mats. Mosses grow mostly in damp, shady places, as on rocks, next to streams, on tree trunks, and on the ground. **2.** any of various other plants that resemble moss.

moss·y (mô′sē) *adj.,* **moss·i·er, moss·i·est. 1.** covered with moss. **2.** resembling moss.

most (mōst) *adj.* the superlative of **much** and **many. 1.** greatest in number, quantity, or degree: *Which candidate received the most votes?* **2.** the greatest part or number of; majority of: *Most young children like to play games.* —*n.* **1.** the greatest number, quantity, or degree: *That is the most I can give you.* **2.** the greatest part or number of persons: *You did more to help than most would.* —*adv.* the superlative of **much. 1.** very: *a most unusual person.* **2.** in or to the greatest extent or degree: *That is the most interesting book I have ever read.*

·**at most** or **at the most.** at the maximum: *At most, you'll get $650 for your car.*

·**for the most part.** in general; mainly.

·**to make the most of.** to use to the best advantage: *Make the most of your free time.*

–most *suffix* (used to form adjectives and adverbs in the superlative degree) most or closest to: *topmost, uppermost.*

most·ly (mōst′lē) *adv.* for the most part; mainly; chiefly: *The weather has been mostly cloudy.*

mote (mōt) *n.* a particle or speck, as of dust.

mo·tel (mō tel′) *n.* a hotel for motorists, usually located near a main road or highway. [*Mo*(tor) + (ho)*tel.*]

moth (môth) *n., pl.* **moths** (môthz, môths). **1.** any of a group of broad-winged insects resembling butterflies but different from them in flying mostly at night, in being less brightly colored, in having feathery antennae, and in having stouter bodies. **2.** see **clothes moth.**

moth·ball (môth′bôl′) *n.* a small ball of naphthalene or camphor, used to repel clothes moths from fabrics and furs.

moth–eat·en (môth′ē′tən) *adj.* **1.** eaten away or damaged by clothes moths. **2.** worn-out or old-fashioned: *a moth-eaten superstition.*

moth·er (muth′ər) *n.* **1.** a female parent. **2.** a woman who acts or is thought of as a female parent; guardian or provider. **3.** a source or origin: *The state of Virginia has been called "the Mother of Presidents."* **4.** see **mother superior. 5.** a filmy layer on the surface of fermenting vinegar, wine, or cider, formed of yeast cells and bacteria. —*adj.* **1.** being a mother: *a mother hen.* **2.** relating to or considered characteristic of a mother: *mother love.* **3.** native: *one's mother country.* **4.** bearing a relationship like that of a mother: *I work for a branch of the mother company.* —*v.t.* **1.** to give birth to; be the mother of. **2.** to treat in a motherly way, especially by being too protective. [From the Old English word *mōdor* meaning "a mother."] —**moth′er·less,** *adj.*

Mother Goose, the imaginary author of a collection of fairy tales and nursery rhymes.

moth·er·hood (muth′ər hud′) *n.* **1.** the state or role of being a mother. **2.** mothers as a group.

moth·er–in–law (muth′ər in lô′) *n., pl.* **moth·ers–in–law.** the mother of one's husband or wife.

moth·er·land (muth′ər land′) *n.* **1.** a person's native country. **2.** the country of one's ancestors.

moth·er·ly (muth′ər lē) *adj.* of, like, or considered characteristic of a mother: *motherly love.* —*adv.* in the manner of a mother. —**moth′er·li·ness,** *n.*

moth·er–of–pearl (muth′ər əv pûrl′) *n.* a hard, rainbow-colored layer lining the shells of pearl oysters and certain other mollusks. It is used for making buttons and ornaments. Also, **nacre.**

mother of vinegar, see **mother** (*n. def. 5*).

Mother's Day, a day set aside in honor of mothers, observed annually on the second Sunday of May.

mother superior, a nun who is head of a religious community of women.

mother tongue 1. a person's native language. **2.** a language from which other languages are derived: *Latin is the mother tongue of French and Spanish.*

mo·tif (mō tēf′) *n.* **1.** a recurring idea, situation, problem, or theme in a work of art, literature, or drama. **2.** a distinctive, usually repeated figure, design, or color, as in a decoration or printed pattern: *The wallpaper had a floral motif.* **3.** *Music.* a short and easily recognizable fragment of music that may be associated with a particular character or idea. Also, **motive.**

mo·tile (mō′təl) *adj. Biology.* having the power to move itself. —**mo·til·i·ty** (mō til′i tē), *n.*

mo·tion (mō′shən) *n.* **1.** the fact or process of changing position or place; movement: *the endless motion of the sea, the forward motion of a car.* **2.** the act of moving the body or one of its parts: *I signaled them with a motion of my hand.* **3.** a formal proposal or suggestion made in a court of law or other meeting or assembly: *The treasurer* *made a motion to take a vote.* —*v.i.* to make a movement of the hand or other part of the body to express one's meaning. —*v.t.* to direct with a movement or gesture: *The usher motioned me to a seat.*

mo·tion·less (mō′shən lis) *adj.* not moving or not capable of moving.

motion picture **1.** a presentation or show created by projecting a series of still photographs onto a white screen or the like at high speed, thus producing the illusion of movement or reproducing the movement originally photographed. Also, **moving picture.** **2.** a story or other subject matter photographed as a motion picture. —**mo′tion-pic′ture,** *adj.*

motion sickness, a disorder that arises when a person is subjected to a swinging or joggling motion, as in a car, ship, or aircraft. It is characterized by nausea, dizziness, and vomiting.

mo·ti·vate (mō′tə vāt′) *v.t.,* **mo·ti·vat·ed, mo·ti·vat·ing.** to provide with a motive; move to effort or action.

mo·ti·va·tion (mō′tə vā′shən) *n.* **1.** the act of motivating or the state of being motivated. **2.** something that motivates.

mo·tive (mō′tiv; *for n., def. 2* mō tēv′) *n.* **1.** a mental state, inner need, or outward goal that causes a person to act; motivation: *The police were unable to determine the motive for the crime.* **2.** another word for **motif.** —*adj.* of, relating to, or producing motion: *Wind is a motive power.*

mot·ley (mot′lē) *adj.* **1.** made up of different kinds; diverse: *a motley blend of images, a motley group of people.* **2.** of different colors: *motley autumn leaves.* —*n., pl.* **mot·leys.** a suit or costume of many different colors, especially one worn by a clown or court jester.

mo·tor (mō′tər) *n.* **1.** a machine that converts electrical energy into mechanical energy: *the motor of a fan.* **2.** any engine, especially an internal-combustion engine. **3.** *British.* an automobile. —*adj.* **1.** of, for, or relating to a motor or motor vehicle: *motor oil, a motor trip.* **2.** equipped with or driven by a motor. **3.** of or relating to that part of the nervous system that sends out impulses to control the various muscles in the body: *a motor nerve.* —*v.i.* to travel by automobile.

mo·tor·bike (mō′tər bīk′) *n.* **1.** a bicycle powered by a small motor. **2.** a light or small motorcycle.

mo·tor·boat (mō′tər bōt′) *n.* a boat powered by a motor, especially a small, open boat with an outboard motor.

mo·tor·cade (mō′tər kād′) *n.* a procession of automobiles.

mo·tor·car (mō′tər kär′) *n.* an automobile; car.

mo·tor·cy·cle (mō′tər sī′kəl) *n.* a two-wheeled vehicle that is built like a bicycle but is larger and heavier and is propelled by an internal-combustion engine. —*v.i.,* **mo·tor·cy·cled, mo·tor·cy·cling.** to ride a motorcycle; travel by motorcycle. —**mo′tor·cy′clist,** *n.*

mo·tor·ist (mō′tər ist) *n.* a person who drives a car.

mo·tor·ize (mō′tə rīz′) *v.t.,* **mo·tor·ized, mo·tor·iz·ing.** **1.** to equip or furnish with a motor: *to motorize a wheelchair.* **2.** to supply with motor-driven vehicles. —**mo′tor·i·za′tion,** *n.*

mo·tor·man (mō′tər mən) *n., pl.* **mo·tor·men** (mō′tər-mən). a person who drives or operates a subway train, streetcar, or similar vehicle.

motor scooter, a two-wheeled motorized vehicle similar in appearance to a child's scooter.

motor vehicle, any vehicle powered by a motor for use on roads and highways, such as an automobile, truck, bus, or motorcycle.

mot·tle (mot′əl) *v.t.,* **mot·tled, mot·tling.** to mark or cover with irregular spots or streaks of different colors. —*n.* a mottled coloring or pattern.

mot·to (mot′ō) *n., pl.* **mot·toes** or **mot·tos.** **1.** a brief saying that expresses a guiding idea or principle: *My motto is "Haste makes waste."* **2.** a short, appropriate statement added to something to express or symbolize its content or nature, such as a phrase inscribed on a coin, document, or monument.

mould (mōld) *British.* another spelling of **mold.**

mould·er (mōl′dər) *British.* another spelling of **molder.**

mould·ing (mōl′ding) *British.* another spelling of **molding.**

mould·y (mōl′dē) *adj.,* **mould·i·er, mould·i·est.** *British.* another spelling of **moldy.** —**mould′i·ness,** *n.*

moult (mōlt) *British.* another spelling of **molt.**

mound (mound) *n.* **1.** a bank or heap of earth or stones. **2.** any heap or pile: *a mound of garbage.* **3.** a small hill. **4.** *Baseball.* the slightly raised area in the center of the diamond from which the pitcher pitches. —*v.t.* to heap in a mound.

mount[1] (mount) *v.t.* **1.** to go up; climb: *to mount stairs.* **2.** to get up on top of: *to mount a horse.* **3.** to place on or attach to a support or stand: *to mount a camera on a tripod.* **4.** to set in place, as for display: *to mount stamps in an album.* **5.** to prepare and begin to carry out: *to mount an attack.* **6.** to provide (a theatrical presentation) with scenery, costumes, and lighting. **7.** to furnish with a horse or other animal for riding. —*v.i.* **1.** to increase or build up: *Tension mounted as the tied game neared its end.* **2.** to get up on something, as the back of a horse: *The sheriff mounted and rode off.* **3.** to rise; ascend. —*n.* **1.** a horse or other animal for riding. **2.** an album, frame, or the like, in which something is set in place, as for display. **3.** something used as a support or stand: *a mount for a microscope.* [From the Old French word *monter* meaning "to ascend," going back to the Latin word *mons* "mountain."]

mount[2] (mount) *n.* mountain. ▲ usually used before a proper name: *Mount Everest.* [From the Old English word *munt* meaning "mountain" and the Old French word *mont* "mountain," both from the Latin word *mons* "mountain."]

moun·tain (moun′tən) *n.* **1.** a mass of land rising steeply to a great height above the surrounding country. **2.** a huge heap or pile; towering mass: *a mountain of garbage.* **3.** a great quantity or amount: *a mountain of trouble.*

mountain chain, a group of mountain ranges that are roughly parallel to each other.

moun·tain·eer (moun′tə nîr′) *n.* **1.** a person who lives in a mountainous region. **2.** a person who is skilled at mountain climbing.

mountain goat, see **Rocky Mountain goat.**

mountain laurel, an evergreen shrub having glossy, oblong leaves and large clusters of flowers.

mountain lion, another term for **cougar.**

moun·tain·ous (moun′tə nəs) *adj.* **1.** having many mountains: *a mountainous island.* **2.** enormous; huge: *a mountainous pile of old newspapers.*

mountain range, a ridge or series of ridges of mountains, usually alike in origin, geological age, and form.

moun·tain·side (moun′tən sīd′) *n.* the side or slope of a mountain: *The cabin was built on the mountainside.*

Mountain Standard Time, the local time used in the west-central United States and Canada. It is 7 hours earlier than Greenwich Time.

M

at; āpe; fär; câre; end; mē; it; īce; pîerce; hot; ōld; sông, fôrk; oil; out; up; ūse; rüle; pùll; tûrn; chin; sing; shop; thin; this; hw in white; zh in treasure. The symbol ə stands for the unstressed vowel sound heard in about, taken, pencil, lemon, and circus.

moun·tain·top (mount′ən top′) *n.* the top of a mountain.

moun·te·bank (moun′tə bank′) *n.* **1.** a person who peddles quack medicines. **2.** a person who is deceitful; trickster; charlatan.

Moun·tie (moun′tē) *n. Informal.* a member of the Royal Canadian Mounted Police, the Canadian federal police force.

mount·ing (moun′ting) *n.* **1.** a support or setting: *The rifle is in its mounting on the wall.* **2.** the act of a person or thing that mounts.

mourn (môrn) *v.i.* **1.** to feel or express sorrow or grief. **2.** to lament the death of someone: *The nation mourned for the dead president.* —*v.t.* **1.** to feel or express sorrow or grief over: *The people mourned the general's death.* **2.** to complain about or lament: *The victims mourned their misfortunes.*

mourn·er (môr′nər) *n.* a person who mourns, especially a person attending a funeral.

mourn·ful (môrn′fəl) *adj.* feeling, expressing, or filled with grief or sorrow: *a mournful orphan, a mournful song.* —**mourn′ful·ly,** *adv.* —**mourn′ful·ness,** *n.*

mourn·ing (môr′ning) *n.* **1.** the act of a person who mourns. **2.** the state of feeling sorrow or grief. **3.** a display of sorrow over a person's death, especially the wearing of black. **4.** the customary clothes, draperies, and other furnishings worn or used to express such sorrow. **5.** the period during which such expression of sorrow continues.

mourning dove, a wild North American pigeon, having a mournful, cooing call.

mouse (*n.*, mous; *v.*, mouz) *n., pl.* **mice.** **1.** a small rodent usually having a pointed snout, relatively small ears, and a thin tail. **2.** a quiet or timid person. **3.** *Computers.* a hand-held device used to control the movement of the cursor on the screen. —*v.i.*, **moused, mous·ing.** to hunt for or catch mice.

mourning dove

mous·er (mou′zər) *n.* an animal, especially a cat, that catches mice.

mouse·trap (mous′trap′) *n.* a trap for catching mice.

mousse (müs) *n.* **1.** a chilled dessert consisting of whipped cream or beaten egg whites combined with a flavoring. **2.** a molded dish made with puréed fish or meat. **3.** a foamy substance used to style the hair.

mous·tache (mə stash′, mus′tash) another spelling of **mustache.**

mous·y (mou′sē) *adj.*, **mous·i·er, mous·i·est.** **1.** of, resembling, or suggesting a mouse, especially in color: *mousy brown hair.* **2.** timid and quiet as a mouse. **3.** infested with mice.

mouth (*n.*, mouth; *v.*, mouⁿth) *n., pl.* **mouths** (mouⁿthz). **1.** an opening through which an animal takes in food. In humans and most other animals with backbones it consists of a cavity containing a tongue, teeth, and gums enclosed on the outside by the lips. **2.** an opening resembling a mouth: *the mouth of a jar, the mouth of a volcano.* **3.** the part of a river where it empties into another body of water. **4.** a living thing considered as needing food: *There are five mouths to feed in our family.* —*v.t.* **1.** to pronounce or speak without believing or understanding; say or repeat automatically: *to mouth someone else's opinions.* **2.** to speak or say in a pompous, affected manner. **3.** to form by silently moving the lips: *I mouthed the words to the song.* **4.** to take, grasp, or touch with the mouth.

·**down in the mouth.** *Informal.* unhappy; sad: *You looked a little down in the mouth after losing the game.*

mouth·ful (mouth′fùl′) *n., pl.* **mouth·fuls.** **1.** an amount of food that is or can be held in the mouth at one time. **2.** a word or phrase that is difficult to pronounce: *That name is quite a mouthful.*

mouth organ, another term for **harmonica.**

mouth·piece (mouth′pēs′) *n.* **1.** a piece or part, as of a musical instrument, telephone, or cigarette, that is placed between or close to the lips. **2.** a rubber or plastic device worn by boxers, football players, and other athletes to protect the teeth. **3.** *Informal.* a person who speaks on behalf of another or others.

mouth·wash (mouth′wôsh′, mouth′wosh′) *n., pl.* **mouth·wash·es.** a liquid used to clean the mouth or to sweeten the breath.

mov·a·ble (mü′və bəl) also, **move·a·ble.** *adj.* **1.** capable of being moved. **2.** changing from one date to another in different years: *Thanksgiving is a movable holiday.* —*n.* any furnishing or piece of furniture that can be moved.

move (müv) *v.*, **moved, mov·ing.** —*v.i.* **1.** to change place, position, or direction: *to move to a different seat.* **2.** to change the location of a home or business: *to move to another city.* **3.** to go forward; advance; progress: *to move quickly through a book.* **4.** to live or circulate; be active: *The society columnist moved in a world of banquets, parties, and receptions.* **5.** to go into action: *You should move on that plan as soon as possible.* **6.** (of goods) to be sold. **7.** to leave; go: *The police officer told us to move on.* **8.** to make a formal motion, as in a court or legislative assembly: *to move for adjournment.* **9.** in games such as chess and checkers, to change the position of a playing piece. —*v.t.* **1.** to change the location, position, or direction of: *Move the chair away from the door.* **2.** to put or keep in motion: *Wind moves the windmill.* **3.** to cause or urge: *I was moved by curiosity to open the package.* **4.** to affect with emotion; stir the feelings of: *The plea for mercy moved us deeply.* —*n.* **1.** an action planned to bring about a result; piece of strategy: *Buying those stocks then was a wise move.* **2.** in games such as chess and checkers, the act of moving a playing piece, or a turn to move a piece. **3.** the act of moving; movement or motion: *I was so frightened that I couldn't make a move.*

·**on the move.** moving or traveling about: *The candidate was always on the move.*

move·a·ble (mü′və bəl) another spelling of **movable.**

move·ment (müv′mənt) *n.* **1.** the act or process of moving. **2.** a mechanism consisting of many closely associated moving parts, as in a watch. **3.** the efforts or actions of a group of people to achieve some goal: *a civil rights movement, the labor movement.* **4.** a course or tendency; trend: *a movement toward a casual, informal way of life.* **5.** *Music.* **a.** one of the main divisions or sections of a sonata, symphony, or other long musical composition. **b.** see **tempo** *(def. 1).* **c.** rhythm.

mov·er (mü′vər) *n.* **1.** a person or thing that moves. **2.** a person whose work is moving the furniture and belongings of others, especially from one house or office to another.

mov·ie (mü′vē) *n.* **1.** a motion picture. **2.** *usually,* **mov·ies.** a motion-picture theater. **3. movies.** the motion-picture industry.

mov·ing (mü′ving) *adj.* **1.** that moves: *a moving target.* **2.** that causes or produces action or motion: *You were the moving force behind the charity drive at school.* **3.** stirring or affecting the emotions; touching: *The governor made a moving plea for the hostage's life.* **4.** used or hired to move furniture and belongings: *a moving van, a moving company.* —**mov′ing·ly,** *adv.*

moving picture, another term for **motion picture.**

mow¹ (mō) *v.*, **mowed, mowed** or **mown, mow·ing.** —*v.t.* **1.** to cut (grass, grain, hay, or the like) with a scythe or machine. **2.** to cut the grass, grain, or hay from:

to mow a lawn. —*v.i.* to cut grass, grain, hay, or the like. [From the Old English word *māwan* meaning "to cut down, mow¹."]

·**to mow down.** to kill, defeat, or destroy.

mow² (mou) *n.* **1.** the part of a barn where hay and grain are stored. **2.** a pile or stack of hay or grain. [From the Old English word *mūga* with the same meaning.]

moz·za·rel·la (mot'sə rel'ə, mōt'sə rel'ə) *n.* a soft, white cheese with a slightly acid, walnut flavor.

MP **1.** Member of Parliament. **2.** Military Police.

mpg, miles per gallon.

mph, miles per hour.

Mr. (mis'tər) *pl.* **Messrs.** Mister. ▲ a form of address used before a man's name or title: *Mr. Simpson, Mr. Chairman.*

MRI, a medical technique that produces detailed pictures of organs and tissues in the body by recording the effect of a magnetic pull on hydrogen atoms found in the body's cells. It is used to study and diagnose diseases. [Short for *m*(agnetic) *r*(esonance) *i*(maging).]

Mrs. (mis'iz) *pl.* **Mmes.** ▲ a form of address used before a married woman's name: *Mrs. Simpson.*

Ms. (miz, em'es') *pl.* **Mses.** ▲ a form of address used before a married or unmarried woman's name: *Ms. Antonelli.*

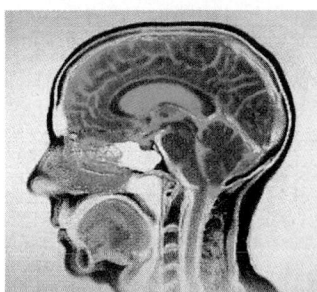

MRI image of a human head

MS **1.** *pl.* **MSS.** manuscript. **2.** multiple sclerosis.

MS, postal abbreviation for Mississippi.

M.S. *also,* **M.Sc.** Master of Science.

MSG, monosodium glutamate.

Msgr., Monsignor.

MST, Mountain Standard Time.

Mt. **1.** Mount. **2.** mountain.

MT, postal abbreviation for Montana.

mu (mu, mu) *n.* the twelfth letter of the Greek alphabet (M, μ), corresponding to the English letter M, m.

much (much) *adj.,* **more, most.** great in quantity, amount, or degree. *much money, much rain, much fun, much trouble.* —*adv.,* **more, most. 1.** to a great extent or degree: *We were much disturbed by the dog's behavior.* **2.** just about; nearly; largely· *We feel much the same as you do.* —*n.* **1.** a great amount or quantity: *Much has been written on that subject.* **2.** anything noteworthy or important: *The small house doesn't look like much, but a president was born there.*

·**to make much of.** to treat as noteworthy or important.

mu·ci·lage (mū'sə lij) *n.* **1.** a clear, brownish glue used especially on paper and cardboard. **2.** any of several gluey substances produced by certain plants.

muck (muk) *n.* **1.** any dirty, moist, sticky, or slimy substance, such as mud or manure. **2.** *Informal.* anything messy or disgusting. **3.** a black soil consisting chiefly of decayed plant matter.

muck·rake (muk'rāk') *v.i.,* **muck·raked, muck·rak·ing.** to search for and expose corruption in government or society. —**muck'rak'er,** *n.*

mu·cous (mū'kəs) *adj.* **1.** containing or secreting mucus. **2.** of or like mucus: *a mucous secretion.*

mucous membrane, a membrane that secretes mucus and that lines the mouth, throat, and other body passages and cavities open to the outside. The respiratory and digestive tracts are lined with mucous membranes.

mu·cus (mū'kəs) *n.* a slimy fluid secreted by the mucous membranes, serving to coat and protect the inner surfaces of the mouth, throat, and other body passages and cavities.

mud (mud) *n.* **1.** soft, wet, sticky earth or dirt. **2.** this earth or dirt after it has dried and hardened: *a house of mud and straw.*

mud·dle (mud'əl) *n.* a state of confusion; mess: *Don't make a muddle of your financial affairs.* —*v.,* **mud·dled, mud·dling.** —*v.t.* to bring to a state of confusion; mix up: *to muddle the issues in a debate.* —*v.i.* to think or act in a confused or bungling manner: *We muddled along, not knowing how to solve the problem.*

mud·dle–head·ed (mud'əl hed'id) *adj.* confused or bungling.

mud·dy (mud'ē) *adj.,* **mud·di·er, mud·di·est. 1.** covered or spattered with mud; full of mud: *a muddy road, a muddy raincoat.* **2.** clouded or dull with mud; not clear or pure: *a muddy pond.* **3.** vague or unclear; muddled: *a muddy style of writing.* —*v.t.,* **mud·died, mud·dy·ing. 1.** to cover or spatter with mud; get mud on: *Don't muddy your new shoes.* **2.** to make cloudy or dull: *to muddy the waters of a stream.* **3.** to make vague or unclear: *to muddy an issue.* —**mud'di·ness,** *n.*

mud puppy, a large salamander found in fresh waters of North America, having three pairs of red, external gills.

mud·sling·ing (mud'sling'ing) *n.* the practice of making malicious charges against an opponent, especially against a political rival. —**mud'sling'er,** *n.*

mu·ez·zin (mū ez'in) *n.* in Muslim communities, the public crier who calls the people to prayer.

muff (muf) *n.* **1.** a fluffy cylinder of fur or other material, designed so that one hand can be slipped in at each end for warmth. **2.** a mistake or missed opportunity. —*v.t.* to fail at or miss: *I had my chance, and I muffed it.* —*v.i.* to make a mistake or miss an opportunity.

muf·fin (muf'in) *n.* **1.** a light bread made of batter containing eggs, baked in individual portions, and often served hot. **2.** see **English muffin.**

muf·fle (muf'əl) *v.t.,* **muf·fled, muf·fling. 1.** to deaden or soften (a sound): *to muffle one's sobs behind a handkerchief.* **2.** to wrap or cover so as to deaden or soften the sound of (something): *to muffle a hammer with a towel.* **3.** to wrap up or cover for protection or warmth; bundle: *The child was all muffled up in a sweater, scarf, and heavy blanket.*

muf·fler (muf'lər) *n.* **1.** a scarf of wool or other material, worn around the neck for warmth. **2.** a device that reduces the noise from an engine exhaust, as in an automobile.

muf·ti (muf'tē) *n.* street dress or plain clothes, especially when worn by a person who usually wears a uniform.

mug (mug) *n.* **1.** a large, heavy drinking cup. **2.** the contents of a mug; as much as a mug holds: *to drink a mug of beer.* **3.** *Slang.* a person's mouth or face. —*v.,* **mugged, mug·ging.** —*v.t.* **1.** to assault (a person) with intent to rob. **2.** to photograph the face of (a suspect or criminal) for police files. —*v.i.* to make faces or exaggerated expressions; grimace. —**mug'ger,** *n.*

mug·ging (mug'ing) *n.* a crime in which someone is assaulted and robbed.

mug·gy (mug'ē) *adj.,* **mug·gi·er, mug·gi·est.** warm, humid, and stifling: *a hot, muggy day with no breeze.* —**mug'gi·ness,** *n.*

---

at; āpe; fär; câre; end; mē; it; īce; pîerce; hot; ōld; sông, fôrk; oil; out; up; ūse; rüle; pull; tûrn; chin; sing; shop; thin; this; hw in white; zh in treasure. The symbol ə stands for the unstressed vowel sound heard in about, taken, pencil, lemon, and circus.

M

mug·wump (mug′wump′) *n.* a person who is independent in politics.

Mu·ham·ma·dan·ism (mu̇ ham′ə də niz′əm) *n.* see Islam *(def. 1).*

mu·lat·to (mə lat′ō, mə lä′tō) *n., pl.* **mu·lat·toes.** **1.** a person who is of mixed white and black ancestry. **2.** a person who has one white parent and one black parent.

mul·ber·ry (mul′ber′ē, mul′bə rē) *n., pl.* **mul·ber·ries.** **1.** any of various trees bearing sweet, edible fruit similar to the blackberry. The leaves of some mulberries are fed to silkworms. **2.** the fruit of any of these trees. **3.** a dark reddish purple color. —*adj.* having the color mulberry; dark reddish purple.

mulch (mulch) *n., pl.* **mulch·es.** any of various loose, porous materials, such as straw, leaves, grass, or manure, spread around plants to protect them against loss of moisture or sharp changes in temperature, to help prevent soil erosion, or to slow the growth of weeds. —*v.t.* to cover with mulch.

mulct (mulkt) *v.t.* **1.** to punish by a fine or penalty. **2.** to swindle (someone) out of something: *Someone mulcted the old couple of their savings.* —*n.* any fine or penalty.

mule¹ (mūl) *n.* **1.** a large-eared animal produced by crossbreeding a female horse with a male donkey. Mules are frequently used as pack animals and for farm work. **2.** *Informal.* a person who is very stubborn. **3.** a machine that spins fiber into yarn and winds it on spindles. [From the Old English word *mūl* and the Old French word *mule*, both meaning this animal and both from the Latin word *mulus* "a mule¹."]

mule¹ *(def. 1)*

mule² (mūl) *n.* a slipper that leaves the back of the heel uncovered. [From the French word *mule*, from the Latin word *mulleus* meaning "a red shoe worn by magistrates."]

mule deer, a deer of western North America having a tawny gray coat and large ears.

mule skinner *Informal.* a person who drives mules.

mu·le·teer (mū′li tîr′) *n.* a person who drives mules.

mul·ish (mū′lish) *adj.* stubborn; obstinate. —**mul′ish·ly,** *adv.* —**mul′ish·ness,** *n.*

mull¹ (mul) *v.* **to mull over.** to think about at length; ponder: *The witness mulled the question over before answering.* [Probably from the Middle English word *mollen* meaning "to grind into powder," from the Old French word *moillier* "to grind," from Latin *molere* "to grind," from *mola* "millstone" or "mill¹."]

mull² (mul) *v.t.* to sweeten, heat, and add spices to (wine, cider, or another beverage). [Of uncertain origin.]

mul·lah (mul′ə, mu̇l′ə) *n.* a Muslim religious leader, especially one versed in religious law.

mul·lein (mul′ən) *also,* **mul·len.** *n.* a tall plant having coarse, woolly leaves and yellow flowers.

mul·let (mul′it) *n., pl.* **mul·lets** or **mul·let.** any of a group of saltwater and freshwater food fish having a gray, red, or striped torpedo-shaped body.

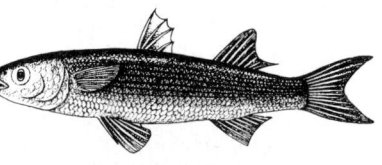

mullet

multi– *prefix* **1.** more than one or two; many: *multicolored, multitalented, multiform.* **2.** many times over: *multimillionaire.*

mul·ti·cel·lu·lar (mul′tē sel′yə lər) *adj.* composed of more than one cell; many-celled: *Human beings are multicellular organisms.*

mul·ti·col·ored (mul′ti kul′ərd) *adj.* of many or various colors: *a multicolored shirt.*

mul·ti·far·i·ous (mul′ti fâr′ē əs) *adj.* having much variety; diverse: *The students in our class have multifarious interests and hobbies.*

mul·ti·form (mul′tə fôrm′) *adj.* having many different forms or appearances.

mul·ti·lat·er·al (mul′ti lat′ər əl) *adj.* **1.** involving or participated in by three or more nations or governments: *a multilateral treaty.* **2.** having many sides; many-sided.

mul·ti·me·di·a (mul′tē mē′dē ə) *adj.* of or relating to the use of several communications media at the same time, as the use of television and newspapers for advertising or photographs and watercolors for an art collage.

mul·ti·mil·lion·aire (mul′ti mil′yə nâr′) *n.* a person who has several millions of some unit of currency, especially dollars.

mul·ti·na·tion·al (mul′tē nash′ə nəl) *adj.* **1.** of or relating to more than two nations or nationalities: *a multinational agreement, multinational society.* **2.** having business divisions and operations in more than one country: *a multinational corporation.* —*n.* a business enterprise that has divisions and operations in more than one country.

mul·ti·ple (mul′tə pəl) *adj.* made up of or involving many or more than one: *Several of the passengers in the derailed train sustained multiple fractures.* —*n.* a number that is a product of a given number and an integer. The numbers 8, 12, and 16 are multiples of 4.

mul·ti·ple–choice (mul′tə pəl chois′) *adj.* **1.** having several answers given from which the correct one is to be chosen: *a multiple-choice question.* **2.** consisting of multiple-choice questions: *a multiple-choice test.*

Language Note

Many of the words in this dictionary have **multiple meanings.** The ability of a word to convey more than one meaning is one of the basic and most important characteristics of language. It is probable that every word in our language originally had only one meaning. As civilization grew, the need to define new concepts, objects, and actions was met by borrowing words from other languages, by coining new words, or by creating new meanings for existing words. A foreign word or new word is not always immediately understood by most people. A new meaning of an existing word is clearer because the word itself is familiar and because our knowledge of the original meaning gives us a clue as to what the new meaning describes. For instance, the original meaning of the word *arm* is "the upper limb of the human body." All the other meanings of *arm* in our language developed from this meaning, such as *the arm of a monkey, the arm of a dress, the arm of a chair, an arm of the sea,* and *an arm of the government.*

Some basic words may have several hundred meanings. The word *run* is an example of a basic word whose original meaning has been extended to stand for a very large number of new meanings. If you look up the word *run* in this dictionary, you will see that we have included more than eighty meanings. There are hundreds more definitions that are rare, highly technical, or obsolete.

The process of adding new meanings to existing words has allowed the scope of our language to grow constantly while limiting the confusion that the addition of entirely new words would cause.

multiple sclerosis, a disease of the nervous system characterized by patchy destruction of the sheath that covers the nerves of the brain and spinal cord. The disease usually leads to shaking or paralysis of the muscles controlled by the affected nerves.

mul·ti·pli·cand (mul′tə pli kand′) *n.* a number or algebraic expression that is to be multiplied by another.

mul·ti·pli·ca·tion (mul′tə pli kā′shən) *n.* **1.** the process of adding a number to itself a certain number of times. **2.** the act or process of multiplying or increasing. —**mul′ti·pli·ca′tive,** *adj.*

mul·ti·plic·i·ty (mul′tə plis′i tē) *n., pl.* **mul·ti·plic·i·ties.** a great number or variety.

mul·ti·pli·er (mul′tə plī′ər) *n.* **1.** a number or algebraic expression by which another is to be multiplied. **2.** a person or thing that multiplies or causes an increase.

mul·ti·ply (mul′tə plī′) *v.,* **mul·ti·plied, mul·ti·ply·ing.** —*v.i.* **1.** to perform multiplication. **2.** to grow in number or quantity, as by reproduction: *Rabbits multiply rapidly.* —*v.t.* **1.** to perform multiplication with (numbers or algebraic expressions). **2.** to cause to increase in number or quantity.

mul·ti·ra·cial (mul′tē rā′shəl) *adj.* of, relating to, or composed of several races, peoples, or ethnic groups: *Hawaii has a multiracial society.*

mul·ti·tude (mul′ti tüd′, mul′ti tūd′) *n.* a great number of people or things: *The prophet had a multitude of followers. They have a multitude of problems.*

mul·ti·tu·di·nous (mul′ti tü′də nəs, mul′ti tū′də nəs) *adj.* of, like, or forming a multitude. —**mul′ti·tu′di·nous·ly,** *adv.*

mum[1] (mum) *adj.* silent; quiet: *Keep mum about this.* ·**mum's the word.** keep silent.

mum[2] (mum) *n.* see **chrysanthemum.** [Short for (chry·santhe)*mum.*]

mum·ble (mum′bəl) *v.,* **mum·bled, mum·bling.** —*v.t.* to speak (words) low and indistinctly with or as if with the mouth partly closed: *The shy speaker mumbled the speech.* —*v.i.* to speak low and indistinctly: *to mumble to oneself.* —*n.* a low, indistinct sound or utterance. —**mum′bler,** *n.* —**mum′bling,** *n.*

mum·ble·ty-peg (mum′bəl tē peg′) *also,* **mum·ble·dy-peg** (mum′bəl dē peg′). *n.* a game in which one or more players throw or drop a knife from various positions in such a way that it sticks in the ground. Also, **mum·bly-peg** (mum′blē peg′).

mum·bo jum·bo (mum′bo jum′bō) **1.** meaningless words or actions used in a ritual. **2.** obscure or meaningless talk that seems intended to confuse; gibberish: *I want a straight answer, not a lot of mumbo jumbo.*

mum·mer (mum′ər) *n.* **1.** a person who wears a mask or costume, as for a parade or celebration. **2.** an actor.

mum·mer·y (mum′ə rē) *n., pl.* **mum·mer·ies. 1.** an action or performance done by mummers. **2.** a ritual or ceremony that is pretentious or hypocritical.

mum·mi·fy (mum′ə fī′) *v.,* **mum·mi·fied, mum·mi·fy·ing.** —*v.t.* to make into a mummy by embalming. —*v.i.* to dry, shrivel up, or become lifeless like a mummy. —**mum′mi·fi·ca′tion,** *n.*

mum·my (mum′ē) *n., pl.* **mum·mies.** a dead body embalmed and dried for preservation, especially in the manner of the ancient Egyptians.

mumps (mumps) *n.* a contagious disease caused by a virus, characterized by painful swelling of the salivary glands at the sides of the face. ▲ used with either a singular or plural verb.

munch (munch) *v.t., v.i.* to chew or eat noisily: *to munch a carrot, to munch contentedly.*

mun·dane (mun dān′, mun′dān) *adj.* **1.** of or relating to what is practical, common, or ordinary: *the mundane problem of earning a living. They were bored by the mundane life they led.* **2.** of this world; earthly.

mung bean (mung) **1.** the edible green or yellow seed of a plant grown especially as the chief source of bean sprouts. **2.** the plant bearing this seed.

mu·nic·i·pal (mū nis′ə pəl) *adj.* of or relating to the local government or affairs of a city, town, or other community: *a municipal election.* —**mu·nic′i·pal·ly,** *adv.*

mu·nic·i·pal·i·ty (mū nis′ə pal′i tē) *n., pl.* **mu·nic·i·pal·i·ties.** a city, town, or other community having local self-government.

mu·nif·i·cent (mū nif′ə sənt) *adj.* very generous: *a munificent gift, a munificent person.* —**mu·nif′i·cence,** *n.* —**mu·nif′i·cent·ly,** *adv.*

mu·ni·tion (mū nish′ən) *n. usually,* **munitions.** military supplies, such as guns, ammunition, or bombs. —*v.t.* to provide with munitions.

a **mural** in East Los Angeles

mu·ral (myur′əl) *n.* a picture painted directly on a wall or ceiling. —*adj.* **1.** placed, fixed, or done on a wall or ceiling. **2.** of, relating to, or resembling a wall.

mur·der (mûr′dər) *n.* **1.** the unlawful and deliberate killing of a human being. **2.** *Informal.* a person or thing that is very difficult, trying, or dangerous: *It was murder to travel on the overcrowded train.* —*v.t.* **1.** to kill (a human being) unlawfully and deliberately. **2.** to abuse, mangle, or mar: *to murder the English language.* —*v.i.* to commit murder.

mur·der·er (mûr′dər ər) *n.* a person who murders or has murdered.

mur·der·ous (mûr′dər əs) *adj.* **1.** of, relating to, or characterized by murder: *a murderous attack.* **2.** capable of or threatening murder: *There was a murderous gleam in the criminal's eyes.* **3.** very difficult, trying, or dangerous: *The mountain climber undertook the murderous descent to the valley below. The teacher gave a murderous history test.* —**mur′der·ous·ly,** *adv.*

murk (mûrk) *n.* darkness or gloom.

murk·y (mûr′kē) *adj.,* **murk·i·er, murk·i·est.** dark, gloomy, or cloudy: *the murky waters of the muddy river.* —**murk′i·ness,** *n.*

mur·mur (mûr′mər) *n.* **1.** a low, continuous sound: *the murmur of the wind in the trees.* **2.** a soft, low voice or spoken sound: *a murmur of approval.* **3.** a faint sound of discontent or protest; grumble: *to accept a punishment without a murmur.* —*v.i.* **1.** to make a murmur. **2.** to

at; āpe; fär; câre; end; mē; it; īce; pîerce; hot; ōld; sông, fôrk; oil; out; up; ūse; rüle; pull; tûrn; chin; sing; shop; thin; this; hw in white; zh in treasure. The symbol ə stands for the unstressed vowel sound heard in about, taken, pencil, lemon, and circus.

M

make a faint sound of discontent or protest. —*v.t.* to say in a soft, low voice: *to murmur an apology.* —**mur′mur·er,** *n.*

mur·rain (mûr′in) *n.* any of several infectious, usually fatal diseases of cattle and other animals.

mus·cle (mus′əl) *n.* **1.** a body tissue made up of fibers that are capable of contracting to produce motion or apply force. **2.** one of the organs of the body composed of these tissues, especially one that is attached by tendons to bones and that functions to move part of the body. **3.** strength or force, especially bodily strength: *No one has the muscle to lift that heavy barrel.*

mus·cle·bound (mus′əl-bound′) *adj.* having tight or overdeveloped muscles, as from too much exercise.

Mus·co·vite (mus′kə vīt′) *n.* a person who was born or is living in Moscow or, formerly, in Russia.

mus·cu·lar (mus′kyə lər) *adj.* **1.** of, relating to, or involving muscles: *muscular coordination.* **2.** having well-developed muscles; strong: *a muscular athlete.* **3.** composed or consisting of muscle: —**mus·cu·lar·i·ty** (mus′kyə lar′i tē), *n.*

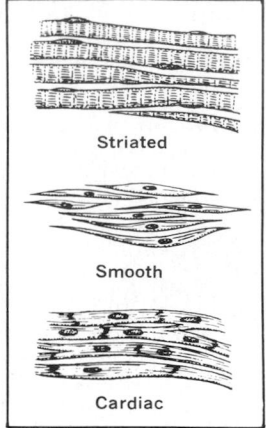

Striated

Smooth

Cardiac

types of **muscles**

muscular dys·tro·phy (dis′trə fē) a hereditary disease that is characterized by a gradual weakening and wasting away of the muscles. It commonly begins in early childhood.

muscular system, the system of muscles that move the parts of the body of an animal. Some parts of the muscular system, such as the heart, work automatically. Others, such as the skeletal muscles, are mostly under voluntary control.

mus·cu·la·ture (mus′kyə lə chər) *n.* the arrangement of the muscles in the body or in a particular part of the body.

muse (mūz) *v.i.,* **mused, mus·ing.** to think, reflect, or meditate: *to muse on the events of the day.*

Muse (mūz) *n.* **1.** *Greek Mythology.* any of the nine goddesses of the arts and sciences. **2. muse.** a spirit or other source of genius or inspiration.

mu·se·um (mū zē′əm) *n.* a building or place where objects of value or interest, as in the fields of art, science, history, or natural history, are preserved and displayed. [From the Latin word *museum* meaning "a building set apart for study," from the Greek word *mouseion* "a philosophical school and library," earlier "a shrine for the Muses," from the word *Mousa* "Muse."]

mush¹ (mush) *n., pl.* **mush·es. 1.** a thick porridge made by boiling cornmeal. **2.** any soft, thick mass. **3.** *Informal.* anything overly sentimental or romantic. [Probably a form of *mash*.]

mush² (mush) *interj.* go or go faster. ▲ said as an order to a team of dogs pulling a sled. —*v.i.* to travel by dogsled. [From the Canadian French cry *mouche!* meaning "run!"] —**mush′er,** *n.*

mush·room (mush′rüm′, mush′rùm′) *n.* any of various fungi usually shaped like an umbrella. Some mushrooms can be eaten; others are poisonous. —*v.i.* **1.** to spring up or grow suddenly and rapidly: *Buildings mushroomed all over the area.* **2.** to spread out into the shape of a mushroom: *The cloud of smoke from the explosion mushroomed in the sky.*

mush·y (mush′ē) *adj.,* **mush·i·er, mush·i·est. 1.** like mush in consistency; soft and thick. **2.** *Informal.* overly sentimental or romantic. —**mush′i·ness,** *n.*

mu·sic (mū′zik) *n.* **1.** a pleasing or harmonious combination of sounds. **2.** the art of producing and arranging pleasing and expressive combinations of sounds, usually according to principles of rhythm, melody, harmony, and the like. **3.** a musical composition: *Does the pianist know the music to that song?* **4.** the written or printed score of a musical composition: *I can read music.* **5.** any pleasant sound or series of sounds: *Your words of welcome were music to our ears.*

mu·si·cal (mū′zi kəl) *adj.* **1.** of, relating to, or producing music: *a musical instrument.* **2.** set to or accompanied by music: *a musical show.* **3.** pleasant to hear: *the musical sounds of children's laughter.* **4.** fond of or skilled in the performance of music. —*n.* a musical comedy or other musical play. —**mu′si·cal·ly,** *adv.*

musical comedy, a show or play made up of songs, dances, and spoken dialogue.

mu·si·cale (mū′zi kal′) *n.* a party or other social gathering featuring musical entertainment.

music box, a box or case containing a device that produces a tune mechanically.

music hall, an auditorium or hall for musical performances.

mu·si·cian (mū zish′ən) *n.* a person skilled in or professionally engaged in the performance or composition of music. —**mu·si′cian·ship′,** *n.*

mu·si·col·o·gy (mū′zi kol′ə jē) *n.* the study of the history, theory, and forms of music. —**mu′si·col′o·gist,** *n.*

musk (musk) *n.* **1.** an oily, strong-smelling substance obtained from a gland of the male musk deer. Musk is used in making perfumes, medicine, and soaps. **2.** any similar substance made by humans or obtained from certain other animals, such as the muskrat or civet cat. **3.** the odor of musk.

musk deer, a small hornless deer of central and eastern Asia, the male of which has a gland that secretes musk.

mus·kel·lunge (mus′kə lunj′) *n., pl.* **mus·kel·lunge.** a large, greenish brown freshwater game fish related to the pike, found especially in the Great Lakes.

mus·ket (mus′kit) *n.* a long-barreled gun fired from the shoulder, used before rifles were invented.

mus·ket·eer (mus′ki tîr′) *n.* **1.** a soldier armed with a musket. **2.** a member of the royal guard in seventeenth-century France.

mus·ket·ry (mus′ki trē) *n.* the art or skill of firing muskets or rifles.

musk·mel·on (musk′mel′ən) *n.* **1.** any of several melons that have a netted rind, sweet, juicy orange or green flesh, and small, flat seeds in the center. **2.** any trailing or climbing vine bearing such a fruit.

musk ox, an animal somewhat like a buffalo, native to northern Canada and Greenland, and having a shaggy dark brown or black coat. It gives off a musky odor during the mating season.

musk·rat (musk′rat′) *n., pl.* **musk·rat** or **musk·rats. 1.** a North American rodent that has webbed hind feet, a flat tail, a musky odor, and dark brown fur and that lives in swampy places. **2.** the fur of this animal.

musk ox

musk·y (mus′kē) *adj.,* **musk·i·er, musk·i·est.** smelling like musk: *a musky odor.* —**musk′i·ness,** *n.*

Mus·lim (muz′lim, mùz′lim, mùs′lim) *also,* **Mus·lem, Mos·lem.** *adj.* of, relating to, or characteristic of Islam or its culture. —*n.* a follower of Islam. Also, **Mohammedan, Mahometan, Mus·sul·man.** [From the Arabic word *muslim,* a participle of *aslama* meaning "he submitted himself (to God)."]

mus·lin (muz′lin) *n.* any of a large group of cotton fabrics, varying from lightweight, sheer materials used for such items as blouses to heavyweight materials used for sheets and pillowcases.

muss (mus) *Informal. v.t.* to make disordered or untidy; mess: *The sudden gust of wind mussed my hair.* —*n., pl.* **muss·es.** a disorder; mess.

mus·sel (mus′əl) *n.* **1.** a saltwater animal related to the clam, having a soft body protected by a bluish black shell of two hinged parts. **2.** a freshwater animal related to the clam, found in lakes and streams of the central United States.

Mus·sul·man (mus′əl mən) *n., pl.* **Mus·sul·mans.** *Archaic.* another word for **Muslim.**

muss·y (mus′ē) *adj.,* **muss·i·er, muss·i·est.** *Informal.* disordered or untidy; messy: *mussy hair.*

must (must) *auxiliary verb* **1.** to be obliged or bound to: *I must return the book I borrowed from the library.* **2.** to be forced or required to, as by necessity: *A person must eat to survive.* **3.** to be likely or certain to: *They must have forgotten about the meeting.* —*n.* anything necessary or essential: *Gloves are a must on such an icy day.*

mus·tache (mus′tash, mə stash′) *also,* **mous·tache.** *n.* a growth of hair on the upper lip.

mus·ta·chio (mə stash′ō) *n., pl.* **mus·ta·chios.** another word for **mustache.**

mus·tang (mus′tang) *n.* a wild horse of the American plains.

mus·tard (mus′tərd) *n.* **1.** a pungent, yellowish paste or powder made from the seeds of a plant and used as a seasoning. **2.** the plant itself, bearing yellow flowers. —*adj.* designating a family of plants growing in temperate parts of the world, including many common vegetables, such as broccoli, cabbage, and turnip.

mus·ter (mus′tər) *v.t.* **1.** to call forth from within oneself; collect or summon: *to muster up one's strength.* **2.** to gather or call together; assemble: *to muster troops.* —*n.* **1.** the act of gathering or calling troops together for military inspection or service. **2.** the list of those so gathered together.

·**to muster out.** to dismiss or discharge, especially from military service.

·**to pass muster.** to be adequate.

must·n't (mus′ənt) *contr.* must not.

mus·ty (mus′tē) *adj.,* **mus·ti·er, mus·ti·est.** **1.** having a stale or moldy odor or taste: *The damp cellar smelled musty.* **2.** out-of-date; old-fashioned: *a musty law, musty beliefs.* —**mus′ti·ness,** *n.*

mu·ta·ble (mū′tə bəl) *adj.* liable or likely to change; variable; changeable. —**mu′ta·bil′i·ty,** *n.*

mu·tant (mū′tənt) *n.* see **mutation** (*def. 2*).

mu·tate (mū′tāt) *v.i., v.t.,* **mu·tat·ed, mu·tat·ing.** to undergo or cause to undergo change, especially by mutation.

mu·ta·tion (mū tā′shən) *n.* **1.** a sudden change in a gene or a chromosome that affects the offspring and is inheritable. **2.** a new variety of animal, plant, or other organism produced by such a change. **3.** a change; variation.

mute (mūt) *adj.* **1.** unable to speak as a result of a birth defect or an injury. **2.** refusing to speak; not speaking; silent: *The defendant sat mute, never responding to the charges.* **3.** *Language.* not pronounced; silent. The *b* in *lamb* is mute. —*n.* **1.** a person who is unable to speak. **2.** a device inserted in or put on a musical instrument to muffle or soften the tone. —*v.t.,* **mut·ed, mut·ing.** to

muffle or soften the sound of: *to mute a trumpet.* —**mute′ly,** *adv.* —**mute′ness,** *n.*

mu·ti·late (mū′tə lāt′) *v.t.,* **mu·ti·lat·ed, mu·ti·lat·ing.** **1.** to deform or injure seriously, as by removing a limb; maim. **2.** to damage or disfigure; mar: *The desk was mutilated by deep scratches.* **3.** to make incomplete, imperfect, or less effective by removing an important part or parts: *The censors mutilated the film by cutting out important scenes.* —**mu′ti·la′tion,** *n.*

mu·ti·neer (mū′tə nîr′) *n.* a person who is guilty of mutiny.

mu·ti·nous (mū′tə nəs) *adj.* **1.** engaged in or planning a mutiny: *The mutinous sailors were thrown into the brig.* **2.** rebellious: *a mutinous spirit.* —**mu′ti·nous·ly,** *adv.*

mu·ti·ny (mū′tə nē) *n., pl.* **mu·ti·nies.** an open rebellion against authority, especially by sailors or soldiers against their commanding officers. —*v.i.,* **mu·ti·nied, mu·ti·ny·ing.** to engage in a mutiny; revolt against one's leaders: *Working conditions were so bad that the crew mutinied.*

mutt (mut) *n. Informal.* a dog, especially a mongrel.

mut·ter (mut′ər) *v.i.* **1.** to speak in low, unclear tones with the mouth nearly closed: *to mutter to oneself.* **2.** to complain; grumble. —*v.t.* to utter (words) in low, unclear tones. —*n.* a low, unclear sound or utterance.

mut·ton (mut′ən) *n.* the flesh from a sheep, especially one between one and two years old, used as food.

mu·tu·al (mū′chü əl) *adj.* **1.** done, felt, or expressed by each of two toward the other; reciprocal: *The two countries signed a treaty for their mutual defense. The friends showed mutual respect for each other.* **2.** of or having the same relationship toward each other: *mutual enemies.* **3.** shared; common: *They met each other through a mutual friend.* —**mu′tu·al·ly,** *adv.*

mutual fund, an investment company that sells an unlimited number of shares to the public and invests the money of its shareholders in securities.

mu·tu·al·ism (mū′chü ə liz′əm) *n.* a symbiotic relationship between two different kinds of organisms that benefits both of them. The relationship between a fungus and an alga growing together to form a lichen is an example of mutualism.

muz·zle (muz′əl) *n.* **1.** the projecting part of the head of an animal, including the nose, mouth, and jaws; snout. **2.** a device, usually made of straps or wires, put over an animal's mouth to keep it from biting or eating. **3.** the opening at the front end of a gun, out of which the bullet or other projectile leaves the weapon. —*v.t.,*

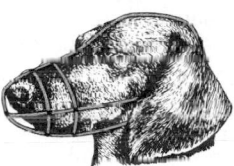

muzzle (*n. def. 2*)

muz·zled, muz·zling. **1.** to put a muzzle on. **2.** to restrain or discourage (someone) from speaking; silence.

MVP, most valuable player: *Which athlete was voted the school's MVP of the year?*

MW, megawatt.

my (mī) *adj.* of, belonging to, or done by me: *my parents, my raincoat, my work.*

my·ce·li·um (mī sē′lē əm) *n., pl.* **my·ce·li·a** (mī sē′-lē ə). the part of a mushroom or other fungus that consists of a tangled network of tiny, tubular fibers, usually lying just below the earth, wood, or other surface on which the fungus is living.

---

at; āpe; fär; câre; end; mē; it; īce; pîerce; hot; ōld; sông, fôrk; oil; out; up; ūse; rüle; pull; tûrn; chin; sing; shop; thin; **th**is; hw in white; zh in treasure. The symbol ə stands for the unstressed vowel sound heard in about, taken, pencil, lemon, and circus.

M

my·col·o·gy (mī kol′ə jē) *n.* the branch of science that studies fungi.

my·e·lin (mī′ə lin) *n.* the white, fatty substance forming a sheath around certain nerve fibers.

my·na (mī′nə) *also,* **my·nah.** *n.* any of several black or brown starlings native to Asia. Some mynas are very skillful at imitating the human voice.

my·o·pi·a (mī ō′pē ə) *n.* the inability to see things that are far away; nearsightedness. —**my·op·ic** (mī op′ik), *adj.*

myr·i·ad (mir′ē əd) *n.* a great or countless number: *Myriads of tiny creatures lived in the swampy water.* —*adj.* too numerous to count; countless.

myrrh (mûr) *n.* a fragrant, yellowish brown resin obtained from any of several tropical trees. Myrrh is used in making perfumes and products for cleaning the teeth.

myr·tle (mûr′təl) *n.* **1.** any of a group of fragrant evergreen shrubs and trees bearing shiny leaves and white or pink flowers. **2.** see **periwinkle**[1].

my·self (mī self′) *pron., pl.* **our·selves. 1.** the form of **I** or **me** used to give emphasis: *I myself mowed the whole lawn.* **2.** the form used to show that the subject **I** is the same as the direct object, indirect object, or object of a preposition: *I cut myself. I bought myself a new shirt. I'm proud of myself.* **3.** my usual, normal, or true self: *I haven't been myself since the accident.* ▲ **Myself** should not be used without **I** as the subject of a sentence, and it should not be used as an object if the subject is not **I** : *You and I* (not *myself*) *will sing. They invited you and me* (not *myself*).

mys·te·ri·ous (mi stîr′ē əs) *adj.* full of, surrounded by, or suggesting mystery; difficult or impossible to explain or understand; puzzling: *Mysterious lights had been reported at the deserted house.* —**mys·te′ri·ous·ly,** *adv.* —**mys·te′ri·ous·ness,** *n.*

mys·ter·y (mis′tə rē) *n., pl.* **mys·ter·ies. 1.** something that is not or cannot be known, explained, or understood: *The identity of the thief is still a mystery.* **2.** a thing or event that arouses curiosity or suspense because it is not fully explained or revealed: *It is a mystery to me how they can live so well on such a small income.* **3.** a book, play, motion picture, or the like involving a puzzling crime, with a plot that gradually leads to the discovery of the criminal. **4.** a puzzling or secret character or quality: *An air of mystery surrounded the auto accident.*

mystery play, a medieval religious drama based on events in the Bible, especially in the life of Jesus.

mys·tic (mis′tik) *adj.* **1.** of or relating to beliefs or practices that have hidden or secret meanings: *mystic rites.* **2.** having a hidden or secret meaning or character: *the mystic prophecies of an oracle.* **3.** of or relating to mystics or mysticism. **4.** see **mystical** (*def. 1*). —*n.* a person who believes in or practices mysticism.

mys·ti·cal (mis′ti kəl) *adj.* **1.** having a spiritual meaning that is beyond human knowledge or understanding. **2.** of or relating to mystics or mysticism. —**mys′ti·cal·ly,** *adv.*

mys·ti·cism (mis′tə siz′əm) *n.* **1.** the doctrines, beliefs, or ideas of mystics. **2.** the doctrine that knowledge of God or absolute truth may be gained through personal spiritual experience, especially by contemplation.

mys·ti·fi·ca·tion (mis′tə fi kā′shən) *n.* **1.** the act of mystifying or the state of being mystified. **2.** something that mystifies.

mys·ti·fy (mis′tə fī′) *v.t.,* **mys·ti·fied, mys·ti·fy·ing.** to bewilder or confuse; puzzle: *The criminal's escape mystified the police.*

myth (mith) *n.* **1.** a traditional story that expresses a belief of a particular people, usually involving gods and heroes. A myth may often attempt to explain a natural phenomenon, a historical event, or the origin of some custom, practice, or religious belief. **2.** such accounts or stories as a group; mythology. **3.** any imaginary or fictitious person, story, or thing: *The unicorn is a myth.* **4.** an opinion, belief, or ideal that has little or no basis in truth or fact.

myth·i·cal (mith′i kəl) *adj.* **1.** of, based on, or existing only in myths: *a mythical ruler, a mythical animal.* **2.** imaginary or fictitious: *The story gave a purely mythical account of the author's early life.* —**myth′i·cal·ly,** *adv.*

myth·o·log·i·cal (mith′ə loj′i kəl) *adj.* of, relating to, or found in mythology: *a mythological tale, a mythological creature.* —**myth′o·log′i·cal·ly,** *adv.*

my·thol·o·gy (mi thol′ə jē) *n., pl.* **my·thol·o·gies. 1.** myths and legends as a group, especially a body of myths belonging to a particular ancient religion or culture: *Greek mythology.* **2.** the study of myths.

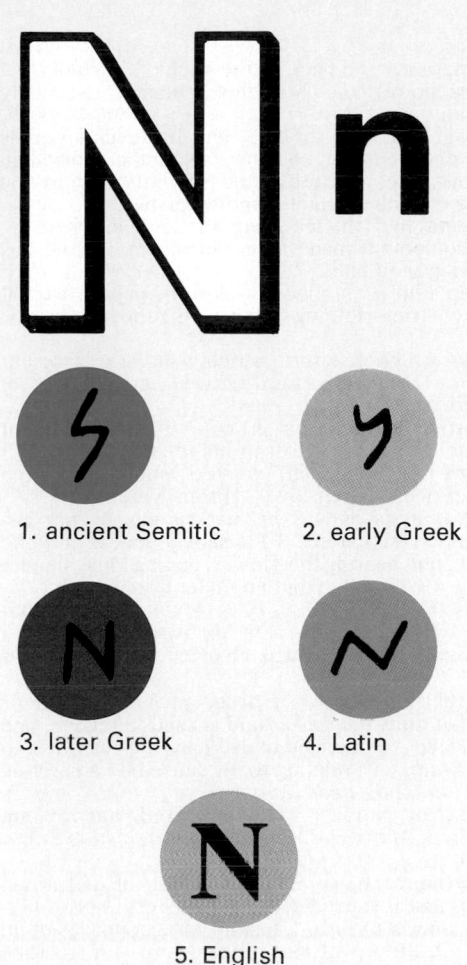

1. ancient Semitic   2. early Greek

3. later Greek   4. Latin

5. English

N is the fourteenth letter of the English alphabet. The earliest form of N was used in the ancient Semitic alphabet (1) as the letter *nun*, meaning "fish." The early Greeks borrowed *nun* and called it *nu* (2). The shape of *nu* differed from earlier forms in that the crossbar of the letter was drawn on a slant, connecting the bottom of the first vertical stroke with the top of the second. By about the fifth century B.C., the direction of the slant of the crossbar had been reversed (3). This altered form of *nu* was adopted by the Romans (4) who, by the fourth century B.C., were writing it almost exactly as we write the capital letter **N** today (5).

n, N (en) *n.*, *pl.* **n's, N's.** the fourteenth letter of the English alphabet.

n (en) *n. Mathematics.* any indefinite number.

N **1.** the symbol for nitrogen. **2.** North. **3.** Northern.

n. **1.** name. **2.** noon. **3.** north. **4.** northern. **5.** noun. **6.** number.

N. **1.** Navy. **2.** North. **3.** Northern.

Na, the symbol for sodium. [From the scientific Latin word *natrium* meaning "sodium," going back to the Arabic word *naṭrūn* "sodium carbonate," from the Greek word *nitron* "sodium carbonate," of Egyptian origin.]

N.A., North America.

nab (nab) *v.t.*, **nabbed, nab·bing.** *Informal.* **1.** to capture or arrest: *The police nabbed the thief.* **2.** to snatch or steal: *The thief nabbed my camera.*

na·bob (nā′bob) *n.* a rich and important person.

na·celle (nə sel′) *n.* an enclosed part of an aircraft that carries the engines and sometimes the crew.

na·cho (nä′chō) *n.*, *pl.* **na·chos.** a tortilla chip topped with cheese or chilies and broiled, eaten as a snack or appetizer.

na·cre (nā′kər) *n.* another word for **mother-of-pearl.** —**na·cre·ous** (nā′krē əs), *adj.*

na·dir (nā′dər) *n.* **1.** a point in the heavens directly below the place where one stands. **2.** the lowest point: *the nadir of a career.* [From the Old French word *nadir*, going back to the Arabic word *naẓīr* meaning "opposite to, against, opposite point." The nadir is opposite to the zenith.]

nag¹ (nag) *v.*, **nagged, nag·ging.** —*v.t.* **1.** to annoy with scolding or complaining: *My parents never have to nag me about my homework.* **2.** to worry or trouble: *My conscience nagged me when I cheated on the test.* —*v.i.* **1.** to annoy with ill-tempered scolding or complaining. **2.** to be a source of worry. —*n.* a person who nags. [Probably of Scandinavian origin.] —**nag′ger,** *n.*

nag² (nag) *n.* **1.** an old, broken-down horse. **2.** *Informal.* any horse. [From the Middle English word *nagge* meaning "a horse, pony."]

Na·hua·tl (nä′wä′təl) *n.* the language spoken by the Aztecs and various other Indian tribes in central Mexico and parts of Central America.

Na·hum (nā′əm, nā′həm) *n.* a book of the Old Testament containing the prophecies of Nahum.

nai·ad (nā′ad, nī′ad) *n.*, *pl.* **nai·ads** or **nai·a·des** (nā′ə-dēz′, nī′ə dēz′). *Greek and Roman Mythology.* any of the water nymphs who were believed to live in a fountain, spring, or brook.

nail (nāl) *n.* **1.** a slender piece of metal, usually pointed at one end and enlarged and flattened at the other, used to hold or fasten wood and other materials together. **2.** the thin, hard layer of dead cells that grows on the upper side of the end of a finger or toe. **3.** any similar part, such as a claw or talon. —*v.t.* **1.** to hold or fasten with a nail or nails. **2.** to hold fast or keep fixed as if with a nail: *Fear nailed us to the spot.* **3.** *Informal.* to catch or capture: *The police nailed the thief.*

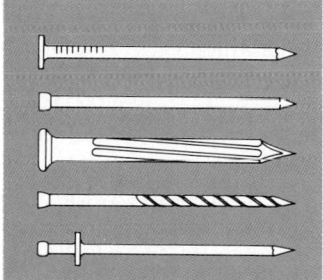

nails *(n., def. 1)*

·**to hit the nail on the head.** to say or do something exactly right.

·**to nail down.** to make certain of; secure: *to nail down a job.*

nain·sook (nān′sůk) *n.* a soft, lightweight cotton fabric.

na·ive (nä ēv′) also, **na·ïve**. adj. simple and childlike; not sophisticated; innocent: *A naive customer may sometimes be cheated.* —**na·ive′ly**; also, **na·ïve′ly**, adv. —**na·ive′ness**; also, **na·ïve′ness**, n.

na·ive·té (nä′ēv tā′, nä ē′və tā′) also, **na·ïve·té**. n. **1.** the quality or condition of being naive. **2.** a naive remark or action.

na·ked (nā′kid) adj. **1.** without clothing or covering; nude. **2.** stripped, as of vegetation, furnishings, or decoration; bare: *a naked room, a naked branch.* **3.** not covered or enclosed; exposed: *a naked light bulb, a naked wire.* **4.** without anything added; plain: *the naked truth.* —**na′ked·ly**, adv. —**na′ked·ness**, n.

naked eye, the eye unaided by a magnifying glass, telescope, or microscope: *The planet Pluto is not visible to the naked eye.*

nam·a·ble (nā′mə bəl) another spelling of **nameable.**

nam·by–pam·by (nam′bē pam′bē) adj. foolishly sentimental. —n., pl. **nam·by-pam·bies.** a namby-pamby person.

name (nām) n. **1.** a word or words by which a person, animal, place, or thing is known or referred to. **2.** a word or phrase, usually bad, used to describe a person or thing: *The bully called me names.* **3.** reputation; character: *Constant lying will give you a bad name.* **4.** outward appearance: *a democracy in name only.* —v.t., **named, nam·ing. 1.** to give a name or names to: *The young couple named their first child after a grandparent.* **2.** to mention by name; refer to by name: *The newspaper article named the people who won the awards.* **3.** to speak of; mention: *Name a few things you'd like for your birthday.* **4.** to nominate, appoint, or assign: *The President named Senator Brown to head the commission.* **5.** to determine or fix: *Name the time and I'll meet you.* —**nam′er**, n.
·in the name of. a. on behalf of. **b.** by the authority of: *The prime minister spoke officially in the name of the monarch.*
·to one's name. belonging to one: *I don't have a cent to my name.*

name·a·ble (nā′mə bəl) also, **nam·a·ble**. adj. **1.** that can be named. **2.** worthy of being mentioned; memorable.

name–drop·ping (nām′drop′ing) n. the act or practice of trying to impress other people by frequently mentioning famous or important people in a casual or familiar manner. —**name′–drop′per**, n.

name·less (nām′lis) adj. **1.** without a name: *The newborn baby was still nameless.* **2.** not known or mentioned by name; anonymous: *The article is by a nameless author.* **3.** that cannot be identified: *nameless fears.* **4.** too terrible to be mentioned: *nameless atrocities.* —**name′less·ly**, adv.

name·ly (nām′lē) adv. that is to say; specifically: *We visited two southern states, namely Florida and Georgia.*

name·sake (nām′sāk′) n. a person named after or having the same name as another.

nan·ny (nan′ē) n., pl. **nan·nies.** British. a nursemaid.

nan·ny goat (nan′ē) Informal. a female goat.

nan·o·sec·ond (nan′ə sek′ənd) n. one billionth of a second.

nap¹ (nap) n. a short sleep. —v.i., **napped, nap·ping. 1.** to sleep for a short while: *I like to nap each afternoon.* **2.** to be off guard or unprepared: *The question caught us napping.* [From the Old English word *hnappian* meaning "to slumber, sleep."]

nap² (nap) n. a soft, fuzzy finish on cloth, formed by short fibers raised on the surface. [From the Middle Dutch word *noppe* meaning "the nap of a fabric."]

na·palm (nā′päm) n. **1.** a compound used to thicken and jell gasoline. **2.** gasoline that has been thickened and jelled with this, used in incendiary bombs that break on impact and spread the flaming contents in all directions. —v.t. to attack with napalm.

nape (nāp, nap) n. the back of the neck.

na·per·y (nā′pə rē) n. household linens, especially tablecloths and napkins.

naph·tha (naf′thə, nap′thə) n. any of several liquids made from petroleum or coal tar. Naphtha is used in cleaning fluid, fuel mixtures, and solvents and in the manufacture of rubber, paints, and varnishes.

naph·tha·lene (naf′thə lēn′, nap′thə lēn′) n. a white, crystalline compound made from petroleum or coal tar, used in making mothballs.

nap·kin (nap′kin) n. a piece of cloth or paper, used at meals for protecting clothing or for wiping the lips, hands, or fingers.

na·po·le·on (nə pō′lē ən) n. a rich, usually rectangular pastry having cream or custard between crisp layers of pastry dough.

Na·po·le·on·ic (nə pō′lē on′ik) adj. of, relating to, or characteristic of Napoleon I or of his reign.

nar·cis·sism (när′sə siz′əm) n. too much admiration for or love of oneself; self-love. [From *Narcissus.*]

nar·cis·sus (när sis′əs) n., pl. **nar·cis·sus** or **nar·cis·sus·es** or **nar·cis·si** (när sis′ī) **1.** a showy yellow or white flower. **2.** a plant bearing this flower, having long, slender leaves that grow directly from an underground bulb.

Nar·cis·sus (när sis′əs) n. Greek Mythology. a handsome youth who fell in love with his own reflection in a pool. He finally died and was changed into the flower narcissus.

nar·cot·ic (när kot′ik) n. a drug, such as opium or morphine, that dulls the senses and is used to relieve pain or produce sleep. Prolonged use of narcotics can lead to addiction. —adj. of, relating to, or caused by a narcotic or narcotics: *narcotic addiction.*

nar·rate (nar′āt, na rāt′) v.t., **nar·rat·ed, nar·rat·ing.** to tell or relate: *My friend narrated an interesting story.* —**nar′ra·tor**, n.

nar·ra·tion (na rā′shən) n. **1.** the act of narrating. **2.** something that is narrated, such as a story; narrative.

nar·ra·tive (nar′ə tiv) n. **1.** a story or account, as of an experience. **2.** the act of narrating. —adj. of, relating to, or containing narration: *a narrative poem.*

nar·row (nar′ō) adj. **1.** having little width; not broad: *We jumped across the narrow stream.* **2.** limited in extent: *a narrow range of interests.* **3.** not tolerant; narrow-minded. **4.** barely successful; with little margin: *That was a narrow escape!* —v.t. to make smaller in width or extent: *The workers narrowed the sidewalk. We've narrowed the choices down to three.* —v.i. to become smaller in width or extent: *The river narrows at the bridge.* —n. also, **narrows.** a narrow part, as of a body of water, or a strait between two bodies of water: *A bridge was built across the narrows.* —**nar′row·ly**, adv. —**nar′row·ness**, n.

nar·row–gauge (nar′o gāj′) adj. **1.** (of a railroad track) having a width less than the standard width of 56½ inches (143.5 centimeters) between rails. **2.** designed for use on a narrow-gauge railroad track. Also, **nar·row·gauge.**

nar·row–mind·ed (nar′ō mīn′did) adj. having or showing a limited or prejudiced outlook; not liberal. —**nar′row-mind′ed·ly**, adv. —**nar′row-mind′ed·ness**, n.

nar·whal (när′-wəl) n. a small toothed whale native to arctic seas. The male has a long, twisted tusk.

narwhal

nar·y (nâr′ē) adj. Informal. not one: *There's nary a hope that the sunken ship will be found after the storm.*

NASA (nas′ə) National Aeronautics and Space Administration, the U.S. agency charged with developing and testing space vehicles and with conducting space exploration.

na·sal (nā′zəl) *adj.* **1.** of, from, or relating to the nose: *a nasal passage.* **2.** *Phonetics.* pronounced with the sound passing through the nose, such as the sounds *m, n,* and *ng.* —*n.* a nasal sound or letter. —**na′sal·ly,** *adv.*

na·sal·ize (nā′zə līz′) *v.t.,* **na·sal·ized, na·sal·iz·ing.** to pronounce with a nasal tone quality. —**na′sal·i·za′tion,** *n.*

nas·cent (nas′ənt, nā′sənt) *adj.* in the process of coming into being; beginning to exist or develop. —**nas′cence, nas′cen·cy,** *n.*

na·stur·tium (nə stûr′shəm) *n.* **1.** a yellow, orange, or red flower that has sharp-tasting buds and seeds sometimes used in pickling. **2.** the climbing plant bearing this flower.

nas·ty (nas′tē) *adj.,* **nas·ti·er, nas·ti·est.** **1.** resulting from hate or spite; spiteful: *a nasty rumor.* **2.** disagreeable or annoying; unpleasant: *nasty weather.* **3.** seriously harmful; severe: *a nasty fall.* **4.** morally bad; indecent: *nasty language.* —**nas′ti·ly,** *adv.* —**nas′ti·ness,** *n.*

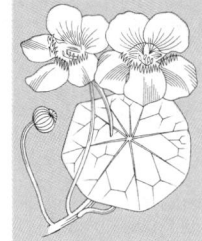

nasturtium

na·tal (nā′təl) *adj.* of, relating to, or dating from one's birth.

na·tion (nā′shən) *n.* **1.** the people living in a particular land under one government and sharing the same culture, history, and often the same language. **2.** the land where such a people live; country: *The candidate campaigned throughout the nation.* **3.** a tribe or group of tribes of North American Indians.

na·tion·al (nash′ə nəl) *adj.* of, belonging to, or characteristic of a nation as a whole: *a national election.* —*n.* a person who is a member of a nation; citizen or subject. —**na′tion·al·ly,** *adv.*

national bank **1.** in the United States, a commercial bank that is chartered by the federal government. **2.** a bank officially associated with the finances of a nation.

national debt, the total amount that is owed by a national government. The U.S. Department of the Treasury finances the national debt by selling securities backed by the credit of the government.

National Guard, a reserve military force supported by each state of the United States. It is under the control of the governor of the state but may be put under federal control by the president in time of war or national emergency.

na·tion·al·ism (nash′ə nə liz′əm) *n.* **1.** patriotic devotion to one's nation. **2.** a desire or movement for national independence.

na·tion·al·ist (nash′ə nə list) *adj.* favoring or supporting nationalism. Also, **na·tion·al·is·tic** (nash′ə nə lis′tik). —*n.* a person who favors or supports nationalism. —**na′tion·al·is′ti·cal·ly,** *adv.*

na·tion·al·i·ty (nash′ə nal′i tē) *n., pl.* **na·tion·al·i·ties.** **1.** the fact or state of belonging to a particular nation: *Their nationality is Australian.* **2.** a group of people sharing the same culture and history; nation. **3.** the condition of being a politically independent nation.

na·tion·al·ize (nash′ə nə līz′) *v.t.,* **na·tion·al·ized, na·tion·al·iz·ing.** **1.** to place under the control or ownership of a national government: *to nationalize an industry.* **2.** to extend throughout a nation; make nationwide: *to nationalize a news broadcast.* —**na′tion·al·i·za′tion,** *n.*

national monument, a natural formation, place of historic interest, or specially erected structure maintained by the U.S. government for public use.

national park

national park, an area of land, usually with great natural beauty or historical importance, maintained by the government for public use.

National Socialism, another term for **Naziism.**

na·tion·wide (nā′shən wīd′) *also,* **na·tion-wide.** *adj.* extending throughout the nation.

na·tive (nā′tiv) *n.* **1.** a person who was born in a particular place or country: *a native of France.* **2.** an original inhabitant of a region or country. **3.** an animal or plant living or growing in a particular place: *That bird is a native of South Carolina.* —*adj.* **1.** born in a particular place or country: *I am a native New Yorker.* **2.** connected with or belonging to a person by birth or birthplace: *My native language is French.* **3.** possessed from birth; natural: *native intelligence.* **4.** living or growing in a particular place: *Cactus is native to desert regions.* **5.** of, relating to, or characteristic of the original inhabitants of a region or country: *native tribal dances.* **6.** occurring or found in nature in a pure state: *Native silver is very soft.* —**na′tive·ly,** *adv.*

Native American, a member of one of the tribes of people inhabiting North and South America before Europeans arrived there; American Indian.

Language Note

Many of the words we use today came into English from languages of **Native Americans,** known as American Indian languages. When the European explorers and settlers came to America, they borrowed American Indian words because they found many new things they had not seen before, and they needed names for these things. That is how words like *tobacco, raccoon, canoe, tomato,* and *maize* entered our language. Sometimes the European settlers renamed the features of the land, but sometimes they kept the American Indian names for the rivers, lakes, and other places that they found. That is why more than half our fifty states have names that can be traced back to words used by Native Americans.

There are a great many different American Indian languages. Within the past sixty years, scholars have

N

made a careful study of these languages. From their study, they have learned many important things about how people use language. In fact, studies of languages such as those of Native Americans, which are completely unrelated to any European language, have contributed greatly to advances in the science of language.

na·tive–born (nā′tiv bôrn′) *adj.* born in the place or country indicated: *a native-born American.*

na·tiv·i·ty (nə tiv′i tē) *n., pl.* **na·tiv·i·ties.** **1. Nativity. a.** the birth of Jesus. **b.** a representation of the birth of Jesus, as in painting. **c.** Christmas. **2.** birth.

natl., national.

NATO (nā′tō) North Atlantic Treaty Organization, a military alliance of sixteen Western nations, formed in 1949.

nat·ty (nat′ē) *adj.,* **nat·ti·er, nat·ti·est.** neat, trim, and stylish: *a natty new uniform.* —**nat′ti·ly,** *adv.* —**nat′ti·ness,** *n.*

nat·u·ral (nach′ər əl) *adj.* **1.** found or produced in nature; not manufactured: *a natural metal, natural rock formations.* **2.** of or relating to nature: *A biologist is a natural scientist.* **3.** belonging to a person from birth; innate: *She has natural beauty.* **4.** having innate talents and abilities: *She is a natural athlete.* **5.** reasonable or logical; expected: *Anger was a natural reaction to the insult.* **6.** happening in the normal course of things: *to die from natural causes.* **7.** closely following nature; realistic; lifelike: *The portrait is very natural.* **8.** free from affectation; not forced or contrived: *He spoke in a natural voice. He has an open and natural manner.* **9.** *Music.* neither sharp nor flat. —*n.* **1.** *Music.* **a.** the sign (♮) used to cancel the effect of a preceding sharp or flat. **b.** a tone or note changed by this sign. **2.** *Informal.* a person who seems well-qualified because of special talents or other abilities: *That student is a natural as an athlete.* —**nat′u·ral·ness,** *n.*

natural gas, a colorless, odorless, highly flammable gas, occurring naturally in the earth. It consists mainly of methane and is used as a fuel.

natural history, the study of things in nature, such as animals, plants, and minerals.

nat·u·ral·ist (nach′ər ə list) *n.* a person who studies natural science, especially a botanist or zoologist.

nat·u·ral·is·tic (nach′ər ə lis′tik) *adj.* closely resembling nature.

nat·u·ral·ize (nach′ər ə līz′) *v.t.,* **nat·u·ral·ized, nat·u·ral·iz·ing.** **1.** to make a citizen of (a person born in a foreign country); grant citizenship to. **2.** to take in or adopt (a foreign custom or word). **3.** to adapt (an animal or plant) to another place or country. —**nat′u·ral·i·za′tion,** *n.*

nat·u·ral·ly (nach′ər ə lē) *adv.* **1.** as would be expected; of course: *Naturally I'll help you.* **2.** by nature: *to be naturally shy.* **3.** in a natural manner; without affectation: *to act naturally.*

natural number, the number 1 or any number produced by repeatedly adding 1 to it. The numbers 4, 37, and 592 are natural numbers.

natural resource, a material found in nature that is useful to humans or necessary for their survival, such as water, forests, and minerals.

natural science, any of the sciences concerned with nature, including biology, physics, chemistry, and geology.

natural selection, the process by which animals and plants having characteristics best suited to their environment tend to survive and pass those characteristics on to their offspring.

na·ture (nā′chər) *n.* **1.** the essential character and qualities of a thing: *It is the nature of fire to be hot.* **2.** *also,* **Nature.** the forces that create and control all things in the universe: *the laws of Nature.* **3.** the entire physical universe. **4.** the disposition or temperament of a person or animal: *a kindly nature.* **5.** sort; kind; variety: *I don't enjoy books of that nature.* **6.** natural plant and animal life: *We took a walk through the woods to observe nature.*

naught (nôt) *also,* **nought.** *n.* **1.** nothing: *All our plans came to naught.* **2.** zero: *Five plus naught equals five.*

naugh·ty (nô′tē) *adj.,* **naugh·ti·er, naugh·ti·est. 1.** mischievous; disobedient: *a naughty child.* **2.** in bad taste; improper: *a naughty word.* —**naugh′ti·ly,** *adv.* —**naugh′ti·ness,** *n.*

nau·sea (nô′zē ə, nô′shə) *n.* **1.** a sick feeling in the stomach; the feeling that one is going to vomit. **2.** extreme disgust; loathing. [From the Latin word *nausea* meaning "seasickness, nausea," from the Greek dialect word *nausiē* "seasickness," from the word *naus* "ship."]

nau·se·ate (nô′zē āt′, nô′shē āt′) *v.,* **nau·se·at·ed, nau·se·at·ing.** —*v.t.* to produce nausea in: *The rolling of the ship nauseated the passengers.* —*v.i.* to feel nausea. —**nau′se·at′ing·ly,** *adv.* —**nau′se·a′tion,** *n.*

nau·seous (nô′shəs, nô′zē əs) *adj.* **1.** causing nausea: *a nauseous smell.* **2.** disgusting; loathsome. **3.** sickened; nauseated: *I felt a little nauseous during the boat ride.* —**nau′seous·ly,** *adv.* —**nau′seous·ness,** *n.*

nau·ti·cal (nô′ti kəl) *adj.* of or relating to ships, sailors, or navigation. —**nau′ti·cal·ly,** *adv.*

nautical mile, a unit of distance equal to 6,076.115 feet (1,852 meters). Also, **sea mile.**

nau·ti·lus (nô′tə ləs) *n., pl.* **nau·ti·lus·es** or **nau·ti·li** (nô′tə lī′). **1.** a saltwater animal found in tropical waters, having a flattened spiral shell divided into chambers. The nautilus lives in the outermost chamber of its shell. **2.** a saltwater animal related to the octopus, the female of which has a very thin, delicate shell. Also (*def. 2*), **paper nautilus.**

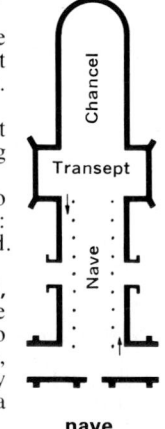

Chambers

Animal

nautilus (cutaway view)

Nav·a·ho (nav′ə hō′) *n., pl.* **Nav·a·ho** or **Nav·a·hos** or **Nav·a·hoes. 1.** a member of a tribe of North American Indians living in New Mexico, Arizona, and Utah. **2.** the language of this tribe. **3. the Navaho.** the tribe taken as a whole.

Nav·a·jo (nav′ə hō′) *n., pl.* **Nav·a·jo** or **Nav·a·jos** or **Nav·a·joes.** another spelling of **Navaho.**

na·val (nā′vəl) *adj.* **1.** of or relating to a navy: *naval supplies.* **2.** having a navy: *That country was once a great naval power.* —**na′val·ly,** *adv.*

nave (nāv) *n.* the main part of some churches, located between the side aisles.

na·vel (nā′vəl) *n.* a rounded scar in the middle of the surface of the abdomen that remains after the umbilical cord is cut. Also, **umbilicus.**

navel orange, a large, seedless, sweet orange, having a mark at one end resembling a navel.

nav·i·ga·ble (nav′i gə bəl) *adj.* **1.** able to be sailed on or through by boats or ships: *a navigable river.* **2.** capable of being steered. —**nav′i·ga·bil′i·ty,** *n.*

nav·i·gate (nav′i gāt′) *v.,* **nav·i·gat·ed, nav·i·gat·ing.** —*v.t.* **1.** to direct the course of (a boat, ship, or aircraft); pilot. **2.** to plan or direct the course of (a voyage, flight, or the like). **3.** to sail on or across (a body of water). —*v.i.* to direct the course of a boat, ship, or aircraft.

Chancel

Transept

Nave

nave

nav·i·ga·tion (nav′i gā′shən) *n.* **1.** the act or practice of navigating a boat, ship, or aircraft. **2.** the art or science of determining the position and directing the course of boats, ships, and aircraft. —**nav′i·ga′tion·al,** *adj.*

nav·i·ga·tor (nav′i gā′tər) *n.* **1.** a person who navigates. **2.** a person who has skill in or practices navigation.

na·vy (nā′vē) *n., pl.* **na·vies. 1.** all the warships of a country. **2.** *also,* **Navy. a.** the entire military sea force of a country, including ships, land bases, equipment, and personnel. **b.** the department of government in charge of this. **3.** see **navy blue.**

navy bean, a small, dried white bean.

navy blue, a very dark blue color.

navy yard, a base on land used for building or repairing naval vessels.

nay (nā) *adv.* **1.** no. **2.** not only that, but even: *They were saddened, nay, heartbroken, by the news.* —*n.* **1.** a negative vote or voter. **2.** a refusal or denial; no.

Naz·a·rene (naz′ə rēn′, naz′ə rēn′) *n.* **1.** a person who was born or is living in Nazareth. **2.** a member of a sect of early Christians. **3. the Nazarene.** Jesus.

Na·zi (nät′sē, nat′sē) *n., pl.* **Na·zis. 1.** a member or follower of the fascist political party that controlled Germany under the leadership of Adolf Hitler from 1933 to 1945. **2.** a person holding views similar to those of the Nazis.

Na·zi·ism (nät′sē iz′əm, nat′sē iz′əm) *also,* **Na·zism** (nät′siz əm, nat′siz əm). *n.* the political doctrines and practices of the Nazis, including a belief in the superiority or inferiority of various racial groups, total government control of the lives of citizens, and an aggressive foreign policy. Also, **National Socialism.**

Nb, the symbol for niobium.

NB, postal abbreviation for New Brunswick.

N.B. 1. New Brunswick. **2.** note well. [From the Latin phrase *nota bene* meaning "note well."]

NC, postal abbreviation for North Carolina.

N.C., North Carolina.

Nd, the symbol for neodymium.

ND, postal abbreviation for North Dakota.

N. Dak., North Dakota. Also, **N.D.**

Ne, the symbol for neon.

NE 1. postal abbreviation for Nebraska. **2.** northeast. **3.** northeastern.

N.E., New England.

Ne·an·der·thal (nē an′dər thôl′, nē an′dər täl′) *adj.* of, relating to, or characteristic of Neanderthal man. —*n.* see **Neanderthal man.**

Neanderthal man, any of an extinct species of prehistoric human being that lived in caves in Europe, North Africa, and parts of Asia during the early Stone Age.

Ne·a·pol·i·tan (nē′ə pol′i tən) *n.* a person who was born or is living in Naples. —*adj.* of or relating to Naples.

neap tide (nēp) the tide occurring at the first and third quarters of the moon, when there is the least difference between the levels of high and low tide.

near (nîr) *adv.* **1.** not far in time, place, or degree: *Night is drawing near.* **2.** almost; nearly: *We were near frantic with worry.* —*adj.* **1.** not distant in time, place, or degree: *Will I see you in the near future?* **2.** done or missed by only a slight margin: *We had a near escape from the fire.* **3.** closely related or associated: *They are near relatives of ours.* **4.** short and direct: *the nearest route into the city.* —*prep.* close to or by: *a house near the beach.* —*v.t.* to come or draw near to; approach: *The airplane neared the landing field.* —*v.i.* to come or draw near or nearer. —**near′ness,** *n.*

near·by (nîr′bī′) *adj.* a short distance away; close: *a nearby town.* —*adv.* not far off: *They go to school nearby.*

near·ly (nîr′lē) *adv.* **1.** almost, but not quite: *I nearly forgot your birthday. It is nearly midnight.* **2.** closely: *We are nearly related.*

near·sight·ed (nîr′sī′tid) *adj.* unable to see distant objects clearly; myopic. —**near′sight′ed·ly,** *adv.* —**near′sight′ed·ness,** *n.*

neat (nēt) *adj.* **1.** clean and orderly; tidy: *a neat room, a neat person, neat work.* **2.** attractive or pleasing in appearance: *a neat dress.* **3.** done in a clever or skillful way: *That was a neat trick.* **4.** *Informal.* wonderful; fine: *We had a neat time at the party.* —**neat′ly,** *adv.* —**neat′ness,** *n.*

neath (nēth) *also,* **′neath.** *prep. Archaic.* another word for **beneath.**

neb·bish (neb′ish) *n. Slang.* a pitiful, unfortunate, timid person. [From the Yiddish exclamation *nebach!* meaning "poor thing!" of Slavic origin.]

Nebr., Nebraska. Also, **Neb.**

neb·u·la (neb′yə lə) *n., pl.* **neb·u·lae** (neb′yə lē′) or **neb·u·las.** a bright, cloudlike mass, composed of stars or of dust and gases, visible in the night sky. —**neb′u·lar,** *adj.*

neb·u·lous (neb′yə ləs) *adj.* **1.** vague or confused; unclear: *a nebulous answer, nebulous outlines.* **2.** of or relating to a nebula or nebulae. —**neb′u·lous·ly,** *adv.* —**neb′u·lous·ness,** *n.*

nec·es·sar·i·ly (nes′ə ser′ə lē) *adv.* **1.** because of an obligation or necessity: *I don't necessarily have to leave now.* **2.** as a certain or unavoidable result: *Tall people are not necessarily good basketball players.*

nec·es·sar·y (nes′ə ser′ē) *adj.* **1.** that cannot be done without; needed; required: *Proper food and rest are necessary for good health.* **2.** that cannot be avoided; certain; inevitable: *Failure was a necessary result of their poor work.* —*n., pl.* **nec·es·sar·ies.** something that cannot be done without; necessity; essential: *the necessaries for a camping trip.*

ne·ces·si·tate (nə ses′i tāt′) *v.t.* **ne·ces·si·tat·ed, ne·ces·si·tat·ing.** to cause (something) to be needed or done; make necessary: *Their refusal to go necessitated a change of plans.* —**ne·ces′si·ta′tion,** *n.*

ne·ces·si·ty (ni ses′i tē) *n., pl.* **ne·ces·si·ties. 1.** something that cannot be done without; requirement: *The poor family could afford only the basic necessities, such as food and shelter.* **2.** the fact or condition of being necessary: *I realize the necessity of completing school.* **3.** the fact or condition of great need.

neck (nek) *n.* **1.** the part of the body of a human or animal connecting the head and the trunk. **2.** the part of a garment that fits around the neck. **3.** the narrow, upper part of a bottle, vase, or other container. **4.** a narrow strip of land, such as an isthmus or cape. **5.** the narrow part of a stringed musical instrument, such as a violin or guitar.
  ·**neck and neck.** at an equal pace; even: *The two horses were running neck and neck in the race.*
  ·**to stick one's neck out.** *Informal.* to take a chance or risk: *I stuck my neck out and criticized the student council.*

neck·er·chief (nek′ər chif) *n.* a scarf or kerchief worn around the neck.

neck·lace (nek′lis) *n.* an ornament worn around the neck, such as a string or chain of beads or gems.

at; āpe; fär; câre; end; mē; it; īce; pîerce; hot; ōld; sông; fôrk; oil; out; up; ūse; rüle; pull; tûrn; chin; sing; shop; thin; this; hw in white; zh in treasure. The symbol ə stands for the unstressed vowel sound heard in about, taken, pencil, lemon, and circus.

N

neck·line (nek'līn') *n.* the upper edge of a garment at or near the neck.

neck·tie (nek'tī') *n.* a strip of fabric worn around the neck, usually under the collar, and knotted in front. Also, **tie.**

neck·wear (nek'wâr') *n.* any of various articles of clothing that are worn around the neck, such as scarves and neckties.

nec·ro·man·cy (nek'rə man'sē) *n.* **1.** the act of predicting the future by supposedly communicating with the dead. **2.** black magic; sorcery. **—nec'ro·man'cer,** *n.*

nec·tar (nek'tər) *n.* **1.** *Greek Mythology.* the drink of the gods that made all who drank it immortal. **2.** any sweet and delicious drink. **3.** a sweet liquid formed in many flowers, used by bees in the making of honey. **—nec'tar·ous,** *adj.*

nec·tar·ine (nek'tə rēn') *n.* **1.** a variety of peach having a smooth skin. **2.** the tree that bears this fruit.

née (nā) *also,* **nee.** *adj.* *French.* born. ▲ used chiefly to show the maiden name of a married woman: *Mrs. Susan Brown, née Smith.*

need (nēd) *n.* **1.** the lack of something necessary, useful, or desired: *The team's defeat showed their need of practice.* **2.** something necessary, useful, or desired: *Food is one of our basic needs.* **3.** a necessity or obligation: *There is no need to stay any longer.* **4.** a great desire for something: *The young painter had a need for recognition.* **5.** poverty or hardship: *Their great need caused them to beg.* **6.** a time or condition of difficulty or trouble: *a friend in need.* **—v.t.** to have need of; lack; require: *to need new shoes, to need a room for the night.* **—v.i.** to be obligated; must: *You need to check your spelling more carefully.* **—auxiliary verb** used in questions and in the negative: *Need I wait for you? No, you need not wait. Nothing need be done.*

·if need be. if necessary.

need·ful (nēd'fəl) *adj.* needed; required; necessary: *needful advice.* **—need'ful·ly,** *adv.* **—need'ful·ness,** *n.*

need·i·ness (nē'dē nis) *n.* the quality or condition of being needy.

nee·dle (nē'dəl) *n.* **1.** a thin, pointed steel instrument with a hole at one end through which thread is passed, used in sewing. **2.** a pointer, as on a compass or dial. **3.** the sharp, hollow tube at the end of a hypodermic syringe. **4.** a slender rod tapered at one or both ends, used in knitting. **5.** a slender instrument of metal, usually tipped with diamond, sapphire, or other hard material, mounted in a cartridge and used to transmit sound vibrations from phonograph records; stylus. **6.** something resembling a needle in shape, such as an obelisk or pinnacle. **7.** *Botany.* the needle-shaped leaf of a fir tree, pine tree, or other coniferous tree. **—v.t., nee·dled, nee·dling.** *Informal.* to annoy, as by constant teasing. **—nee'dle·like',** *adj.*

nee·dle·point (nē'dəl point') *n.* embroidery done on canvas, usually with wool yarn.

need·less (nēd'lis) *adj.* not needed; unnecessary: *a needless expense, a needless remark.* **—need'less·ly,** *adv.* **—need'less·ness,** *n.*

nee·dle·work (nē'dəl wûrk') *n.* work done with a needle, such as embroidery.

need·n't (nē'dənt) *contr.* need not.

need·y (nē'dē) *adj.,* **need·i·er, need·i·est.** being in need or poverty: *We gave clothes, food, and toys to a needy family.*

ne'er (nâr) *adv.* *Archaic.* another word for **never.**

ne'er-do-well (nâr'dü wel') *n.* a worthless person; good-for-nothing. **—adj.** worthless; good-for-nothing.

ne·far·i·ous (ni fâr'ē əs) *adj.* wicked; evil: *nefarious deeds, a nefarious scoundrel.* **—ne·far'i·ous·ly,** *adv.* **—ne·far'i·ous·ness,** *n.*

ne·gate (ni gāt') *v.t.,* **ne·gat·ed, ne·gat·ing. 1.** to keep

from being effective; make ineffective; nullify: *That one mistake negated all their efforts.* **2.** to deny: *The new evidence uncovered is so convincing that it totally negates the prisoner's alibi.*

ne·ga·tion (ni gā'shən) *n.* **1.** the act of negating. **2.** something that negates; denial. **3.** the absence or opposite of something positive: *A lie is the negation of truth.*

neg·a·tive (neg'ə tiv) *adj.* **1.** expressing or implying denial or refusal: *Her answer was negative. He gave a negative shake of his head in reply to our question.* **2.** not helpful or constructive: *She gave only negative criticism.* **3.** not hopeful or confident: *He has a negative attitude.* **4.** less than zero: *−3 is a negative number.* **5.** *Electricity.* having more electrons than protons: *a negative charge.* **6.** *Photography.* having the areas that were light in the original subject dark, and those that were dark, light. **7.** not showing a given condition, disease, or the like: *The tests for tuberculosis were negative.* **—n. 1.** a negative image on a photographic plate or film from which prints can be made. **2.** a word or phrase that expresses denial or refusal. ''No'' and ''not'' are negatives. **3.** the side that argues against the proposition in a debate. **4.** a negative number. **—neg'a·tive·ly,** *adv.* **—neg'a·tive·ness,** *n.*

·in the negative. in a way that expresses refusal or denial: *to answer in the negative.*

neg·lect (ni glekt') *v.t.* **1.** to fail to give proper attention or care to: *She neglected her friends because she was very busy. The children neglected their pets.* **2.** to fail to do; leave undone, especially through carelessness: *I neglected my chores in the kitchen.* **—n. 1.** an act or instance of neglecting; negligence: *His neglect of the business caused its bankruptcy.* **2.** the condition of being neglected: *The old house had fallen into neglect.* **—neg·lect'er,** *n.*

neg·lect·ful (ni glekt'fəl) *adj.* characterized by or showing neglect: *I have been neglectful of my homework during the last two weeks.* **—neg·lect'ful·ly,** *adv.* **—neg·lect'ful·ness,** *n.*

neg·li·gee (neg'li zhā') *n.* a woman's loose, flowing dressing gown. [From the French word *négligé,* past participle of *négliger* meaning ''to neglect,'' from the Latin word *neglegere* ''to neglect, disregard.'' Earlier, *negligee* referred to a kind of loose robe worn by women and the informal dress a woman might wear in her house.]

neg·li·gence (neg'li jəns) *n.* **1.** the state or quality of being negligent. **2.** an act or instance of being negligent.

neg·li·gent (neg'li jənt) *adj.* **1.** habitually neglecting to do what ought to be done; neglectful: *a negligent driver.* **2.** showing carelessness or casual indifference: *a negligent reply.* **—neg'li·gent·ly,** *adv.*

neg·li·gi·ble (neg'li jə bəl) *adj.* not worth considering: *Their contribution to the project was negligible.* **—neg'li·gi·bil'i·ty,** *n.* **—neg'li·gi·bly,** *adv.*

ne·go·tia·ble (ni gō'shə bəl) *adj.* **1.** that can be sold or transferred, as a bond. **2.** open to discussion: *a negotiable demand.* **3.** that can be gone or passed over: *a negotiable hill.* **—ne·go'tia·bil'i·ty,** *n.*

ne·go·ti·ate (ni gō'shē āt') *v.,* **ne·go·ti·at·ed, ne·go·ti·at·ing. —v.t. 1.** to bring about or arrange the terms of: *The factory owners met with union leaders to negotiate a settlement of the strike.* **2.** to sell or transfer: *to negotiate securities.* **3.** to succeed in going or passing over: *The car was unable to negotiate the icy road.* **—v.i.** to have a discussion in order to bring about an agreement: *The two countries refused to negotiate.* **—ne·go'ti·a'tor,** *n.*

ne·go·ti·a·tion (ni gō'shē ā'shən) *n.* **1.** the act of negotiating. **2.** a discussion for the purpose of bringing about an agreement or sale.

Ne·gro (nē'grō) *n., pl.* **Ne·groes.** a member of the

Negroid division of the human race, including the native peoples of southern and central Africa. —*adj.* of or relating to a Negro or Negroes. [From either the Spanish or Portuguese word *negro,* going back to the Latin word *niger* meaning "black."]

Ne·groid (nē′groid) *adj.* of or relating to one of the major divisions of the human race, whose members are characterized by dark skin, tightly curled hair, and broad features. —*n.* a member of the Negroid race.

Ne·he·mi·ah (nē′ə mī′ə) *n.* the book of the Old Testament that tells the story of the Hebrew leader Nehemiah.

neigh (nā) *n.* the characteristic cry of a horse; whinny. —*v.i.* to utter a neigh; whinny.

neigh·bor (nā′bər) *also, British.* **neigh·bour.** *n.* **1.** a person who lives near another, especially a person who lives in the house next to or near one's own. **2.** a person, place, or thing located next to another: *Mexico is a neighbor of the United States.* **3.** a fellow human being; brother: *Thou shalt love thy neighbor as thyself* (Mark 12:31).

neigh·bor·hood (nā′bər hud′) *n.* **1.** a small area or district in a town or city where people live: *an Irish-American neighborhood, a tough neighborhood.* **2.** people living in the same district: *The whole neighborhood is talking about the fire.*
   ·in the neighborhood of. somewhere near; about; approximately: *Tickets to the game cost in the neighborhood of six dollars.*

neigh·bor·ing (nā′bər ing) *adj.* being next to or near; located or living nearby: *My friend comes from a neighboring town.*

neigh·bor·ly (nā′bər lē) *adj.* characteristic of a good neighbor; friendly; sociable. —**neigh′bor·li·ness,** *n.*

neigh·bour (nā′bər) *British.* another spelling of **neighbor.**

nei·ther (nē′thər, nī′thər) *conj.* **1.** not either: *When I was sick, I could neither eat nor drink.* ▲ used with **nor** before the first of two or more negative possibilities. **2.** nor: *They don't want to go; neither do I.* —*adj.* not the one nor the other; not either: *Neither team played well in the game.* —*pron.* not either one: *I tried on two hats, but neither fit me.*

nek·ton (nek′ton) *n.* the group of animals that swim freely in the ocean, including such animals as fish, octopuses, squid, and whales.

nem·a·tode (nem′ə tōd′) *adj.* of or relating to a large group of worms having a long, rounded body tapering to a point at each end; roundworm. —*n.* a nematode worm. Nematodes include many crop pests and parasites, such as the hookworm.

Nem·e·sis (nem′ə sis) *n., pl.* (defs. 2 and 3) **nem·e·ses** (nem′ə sēz′). *n.* **1.** *Greek Mythology.* the goddess of vengeance. **2. nemesis. a.** a person or thing that punishes wrongdoing. **b.** just punishment for wrongdoing. **3. nemesis.** a person or thing that causes one's defeat or failure: *Spelling has always been my nemesis.*

ne·o·dym·i·um (nē′ō dim′ē əm) *n.* a yellow metallic element of the rare-earth group, used in lasers, optical glass, and medicine. Symbol: **Nd** [Formed from the Greek word *neo* meaning "new" + the scientific Latin word *didymium,* name of a mixture of rare-earth elements containing neodymium, from the Greek word *didymos* "twin." Didymium is associated with lanthanum, another rare-earth element.]

Ne·o·lith·ic (nē′ə lith′ik) *adj.* of, relating to, or characteristic of the last period of the Stone Age, when people developed agriculture, tamed animals, and used tools and weapons made from stone.

ne·ol·o·gism (nē ol′ə jiz′əm) *n.* a new word or a new meaning of an existing word.

ne·on (nē′on) *n.* a colorless, odorless, inert nonmetallic

neon lighting

element that makes up a very small part of the air. Gaseous neon is used to fill lamps, and liquid neon is used as a cooling substance. Symbol: **Ne** [Formed from the Greek word *neos* meaning "new." It was recognized at once as a new element.]

ne·o·phyte (nē′ə fīt′) *n.* **1.** a new convert to a religion or denomination. **2.** a beginner; novice.

neph·ew (nef′ū) *n.* **1.** the son of a person's brother or sister. **2.** the son of a person's brother-in-law or sister-in-law.

ne·phri·tis (ni frī′tis) *n.* inflammation of the kidneys.

neph·ron (nef′ron) *n.* any of a large number of tiny structures in the kidney that filter water, wastes, and other substances from the blood and send them to the bladder to be excreted as urine.

nep·o·tism (nep′ə tiz′əm) *n.* the giving of special favors or jobs to relatives by a person in a high or official position. [From the French word *népotism* meaning "nepotism," from the Italian word *nepotismo,* going back to the Latin word *nepos* "grandson, descendant." *Nepotism* originally referred to the practice of certain popes who advanced their nephews to high positions.]

Nep·tune (nep′tün, nep′tūn) *n.* **1.** *Roman Mythology.* the god of the sea and brother of Jupiter. In Greek mythology he was called Poseidon. **2.** the fourth largest planet of the solar system and eighth in order of distance from the sun. It is invisible to the naked eye, but appears green when viewed through a telescope. Neptune has two known moons.

nep·tu·ni·um (nep tü′nē əm, nep tū′nē əm) *n.* a radioactive metallic element similar to uranium, produced artificially from uranium. Symbol: **Np** [From the planet *Neptune.* In the periodic table, neptunium is the next element after uranium, as the planet Neptune is the next planet beyond Uranus.]

nerd (nûrd) *n.* *Slang.* a clumsy, silly, or ineffectual person; jerk.

nerve (nûrv) *n.* **1.** a bundle of fibers carrying impulses between the brain and spinal cord and other parts of the body. **2.** courage; bravery: *It took plenty of nerve to climb that high mountain.* **3. nerves.** the nervous system

N

at; āpe; fär; câre; end; mē; it; īce; pîerce; hot; ōld; sông, fôrk; oil; out; up; ūse; rüle; pull; tûrn; chin; sing; shop; thin; this; hw in white; zh in treasure. The symbol ə stands for the unstressed vowel sound heard in about, taken, pencil, lemon, and circus.

thought of as the source of a person's state of mind: *to have unsteady nerves.* **4.** *Informal.* impudence; boldness: *You've got a lot of nerve to ask such a personal question.* **5. nerves.** emotional or physical tension; nervousness: *I always have a bad case of nerves before an exam.* —*v.t.,* **nerved, nerv·ing.** to give courage or strength to: *The athletes nerved themselves for the race.*

·**to get on one's nerves.** to make one annoyed or irritated: *Your constant bragging gets on my nerves.*

nerve cell, another term for **neuron.**

nerve fiber, any of the threadlike fibers that make up neurons.

nerve·less (nûrv′lis) *adj.* **1.** lacking strength; feeble; weak. **2.** controlled and calm; poised. **3.** *Anatomy.* having no nerves. —**nerve′less·ly,** *adv.* —**nerve′less·ness,** *n.*

nerve–rack·ing (nûrv′rak′ing) *also,* **nerve-wrack·ing.** *adj.* very irritating, upsetting, or frustrating: *a nerve-racking experience.*

nerv·ous (nûr′vəs) *adj.* **1.** having or showing restlessness, tension, or strain; jittery; jumpy: *Loud noises make me nervous.* **2.** fearful or timid: *I am very nervous about taking that exam.* **3.** of or relating to the nerves or nervous system: *a nervous disorder.* —**nerv′ous·ly,** *adv.* —**nerv′ous·ness,** *n.*

nervous breakdown, any mental or emotional disorder that leaves a person unable to lead his or her life in a normal way.

nervous system, the system that includes the brain, spinal cord, and nerves. The nervous system controls and coordinates all the activities of the body.

nerv·y (nûr′vē) *adj.,* **nerv·i·er, nerv·i·est.** *Informal.* bold and rude; sassy; impudent: *a nervy person, a nervy remark.* —**nerv′i·ness,** *n.*

–ness *suffix* **1.** the quality, state, or condition of being: *wildness, lightness.* **2.** an act or instance of being: *a kindness.*

nest (nest) *n.* **1.** a place or structure built by a bird for holding its eggs and raising its young. **2.** a place or structure used by insects, fish, turtles, or other animals for laying eggs or raising young: *a hornet's nest.* **3.** a group of birds, animals, insects, or other animals living in a nest. **4.** a cozy place or shelter. **5.** a place where something dangerous, bad, or illegal takes place: *a smuggler's nest.* **6.** a set of similar objects made so that each fits into the next largest one. —*v.i.* to build or live in a nest: *The robins nested in the oak tree beside the house.* —*v.t.* **1.** to place in a nest. **2.** to arrange (objects) in a stack with each fitting into the next largest one.

Bird's nest   Wasp's nest

nests (n., defs. 1 and 2)

nest egg **1.** a natural or artificial egg left in a nest to persuade or encourage a hen to continue laying eggs in the nest. **2.** money saved for an emergency or some future need.

nes·tle (nes′əl) *v.,* **nes·tled, nes·tling.** —*v.i.* **1.** to press or lie close; snuggle; cuddle: *The foal nestled up to its mother.* **2.** to settle oneself snugly and cozily: *We nestled by the fire.* **3.** to be located in a snug and sheltered spot: *The cabin nestled among the trees.* —*v.t.* **1.** to hold or press closely; snuggle: *I nestled the kitten in my arms.* **2.** to give protection to; shelter: *The thick forest nestled the family of deer.* —**nes′tler,** *n.*

nest·ling (nest′ling, nes′ling) *n.* a bird too young to leave the nest.

Nes·tor (nes′tər) *n.* *Greek Mythology.* the oldest and wisest of the Greek chieftains in the Trojan War.

net¹ (net) *n.* **1.** any of various fabrics made of threads, cords, or ropes that are knotted, twisted, or woven into an open, crisscross pattern. **2.** something made of such fabric, used to catch, hold, or protect: *a badminton net, a butterfly net.* **3.** a fine, openwork fabric, as that used for veils. **4.** something that captures or entangles like a net: *a net of lies.* —*v.t.,* **net·ted, net·ting.** **1.** to catch with a net: *to net a fish.* **2.** to make into net: *to net string.* **3.** to hold or protect with a net. [From the Old English word *nett* "a fishing net" or "web."] —**net′like′,** *adj.*

net¹ *(def. 2)*

net² (net) *adj.* **1.** remaining after all deductions or allowances have been made: *net income, net profit, net weight.* **2.** basic; final: *What was the net result of the meeting?* —*v.t.,* **net·ted, net·ting.** to produce or earn as a final yield or profit: *After taxes I net $15,000 per year.* —*n.* something that remains after all deductions or allowances have been made: *The business produced a yearly net of $50,000.* [From the Middle English word *net* meaning both "pure, fine" and "net²," from the Old French word *net* "pure," from the Latin word *nitidus* "bright, clear" and "neat, trim," from the word *nitēre* "to shine, be bright."]

neth·er (neth′ər) *adj.* lying below; lower: *Hell is sometimes called the nether world.*

neth·er·most (neth′ər mōst′) *adj.* lowest.

net·ting (net′ing) *n.* netted material, such as fabric or wire mesh.

net·tle (net′əl) *n.* any of a group of weedy plants whose leaves are covered with tiny hairs that sting the skin when touched. —*v.t.,* **net·tled, net·tling.** to cause annoyance to; irritate; rile: *I was nettled by their constant, noisy arguing.*

net·work (net′wûrk′) *n.* **1.** any system of lines or structures that cross: *a network of wires, a network of highways.* **2.** an interconnected system or organization: *a network of spies.* **3.** openwork material; net; netting. **4.** a group of radio or television stations connected so that they may all broadcast the same program. **5.** a system of computers linked by telephone lines.

neu·ral (nûr′əl, nyûr′əl) *adj.* of or relating to a nerve, neuron, or nervous system.

neu·ral·gia (nù ral′jə, nyù ral′jə) *n.* a sharp pain along the path of a nerve. —**neu·ral′gic,** *adj.*

neu·ri·tis (nù rī′tis, nyù rī′tis) *n.* an inflammation of a nerve or nerves.

neu·ro·log·i·cal (nûr′ə loj′i kəl, nyûr′ə loj′i kəl) *adj.* of, relating to, or affecting the nervous system.

neu·rol·o·gist (nù rol′ə jist, nyù rol′ə jist) *n.* a student of or an expert in neurology.

neu·rol·o·gy (nù rol′ə jē, nyù rol′ə jē) *n.* the branch of medicine concerned with the nervous system and its disorders.

neu·ron (nûr′on, nyûr′on) *also,* **neu·rone** (nûr′ōn, nyûr′ōn). *n.* the basic unit of the nervous system, consisting of a cell body and its fibers. The neuron receives nerve impulses and sends them to other cells. Also, **nerve cell.**

Dendrites   Axon
Nucleus
Myelin sheath
Muscle
Cell body

neuron

neu·ro·sis (nù rō′sis, nyù rō′sis) *n., pl.* **neu·ro·ses** (nù rō′sēz, nyù rō′sēz). an emotional disorder in which a person deals with the normal anxieties and concerns of life in inappropriate ways.

neu·rot·ic (nù rot′ik, nyù rot′ik) *adj.* having or characteristic of neurosis: *neurotic symptoms.* —*n.* a person who is neurotic: *The doctor treated many neurotics.* —**neu·rot′i·cal·ly**, *adv.*

neu·ro·trans·mit·ter (nùr′ō trans mit′ər, nyùr′ō transmit′ər) *n.* any of several chemical substances that transmit impulses from one nerve cell to another.

neut., neuter.

neu·ter (nü′tər, nū′tər) *adj.* **1.** *Grammar.* of or relating to the gender that is neither masculine nor feminine. **2.** having no sex organs or having undeveloped sex organs. —*n.* **1.** a neuter animal or plant. **2.** the neuter gender. **3.** a word belonging to the neuter gender.

neu·tral (nü′trəl, nū′trəl) *adj.* **1.** not taking either side in a conflict: *Switzerland was neutral during World War II.* **2.** belonging to neither side in a conflict: *a neutral zone.* **3.** having no particular shade or tint: *Gray is a neutral color.* **4.** *Chemistry.* neither acid nor base. **5.** *Electricity.* neither positive nor negative. —*n.* **1.** a person or thing that is neutral. **2.** a position of gears in which they are not interlocked and do not pass along motion from the engine to the wheels, as in an automobile. —**neu′tral·ly**, *adv.*

neu·tral·ism (nü′trə liz′əm, nū′trə liz′əm) *n.* a policy of remaining neutral, especially in foreign affairs. —**neu′tral·ist**, *adj., n.*

neu·tral·i·ty (nü tral′i tē, nū tral′i tē) *n.* the quality or state of being neutral: *The country maintained its neutrality throughout the war.*

neu·tral·ize (nü′trə līz′, nū′trə līz′) *v.t.,* **neu·tral·ized**, **neu·tral·iz·ing.** **1.** to act against the effect or force of; counteract: *to neutralize an enemy's strength, to neutralize an argument.* **2.** to keep (a country or territory) from entering into a conflict; declare neutral. **3.** *Chemistry.* to make neutral. An acid and a base neutralize each other and form a salt and water. **4.** *Electricity.* to make neutral by balancing the positive and negative charges. —**neu′tral·i·za′tion**, *n.* —**neu′tral·iz′er**, *n.*

neutral vowel, another term for **schwa.**

neu·tri·no (nü trē′nō, nū trē′nō) *n., pl.* **neu·tri·nos.** either of two stable subatomic particles having no mass or electric charge.

neu·tron (nü′tron, nū′tron) *n.* a particle that forms part of the nucleus of an atom and carries no electric charge.

Nev., Nevada.

nev·er (nev′ər) *adv.* **1.** at no time; not ever: *I have never been to Australia.* **2.** in no way or degree; not at all: *This kind of behavior will never do.*

nev·er·more (nev′ər môr′) *adv.* never again.

nev·er·the·less (nev′ər thə les′) *adv.* in spite of all; however; yet; anyway; in any case: *It looked as if it might rain; nevertheless, we went to the ball game. We had very little money in the bank, but we bought the new car nevertheless.*

new (nü, nū) *adj.* **1.** having existed only a short time; recently grown or made: *The tree has new buds. Have you heard the new school song?* **2.** seen, known, or thought of for the first time: *I found a new way to get to your house.* **3.** unfamiliar; strange: *There were many new faces in my class.* **4.** not yet accustomed or experienced: *I am still new to the job.* **5.** having recently come into a certain state, relationship, or position: *I have made many new friends.* **6.** not yet worn or used: *You need a new pair of shoes. The store sells both new and used furniture.* **7.** coming or beginning again: *a new dawn.* **8.** changed, especially for the better: *After my vacation, I felt like a new person.* **9.** further; additional: *We need a new supply of paper.* —*adv.* newly; recently; freshly. ▲ usually used in combination: *new-fallen snow, a new-found friend.* —*n.* something that is new. [From the Old English word *nīwe* meaning "new."] —**new′ness**, *n.*

Language Note

New words are constantly being added to our language. As new ideas, activities, and objects are introduced, new words or meanings that describe them must be developed. The fields of science and technology are the most common sources of new words, but slang words also make a substantial contribution to our vocabulary. Sometimes these new words fail to become a permanent part of our language. Others, however, are kept as part of our vocabulary and so are defined in dictionaries.

The increased communication produced by modern technology has helped new words come into our language at a faster rate than at any other time. Television, radio, motion pictures, and other media spread new words to a vast audience. For example, the word *AIDS* was first used in 1982, and in a very short time millions of people had added it to their vocabularies.

new·born (nü′bôrn′, nū′bôrn′) *adj.* **1.** born very recently: *A newborn baby sleeps most of the time.* **2.** born again: *newborn faith.* —*n.* a newborn baby.

new·com·er (nü′kum′ər, nū′kum′ər) *n.* a person who has recently arrived: *I'm a newcomer in town and haven't made many friends yet.*

New Deal, the domestic program of President Franklin D. Roosevelt during the 1930s that included social and economic reforms.

new·el (nü′əl, nū′əl) *n.* **1.** the post at the head or foot of a flight of stairs, supporting the handrail. Also, **newel post.** **2.** the central, upright pillar of a spiral staircase.

new·fan·gled (nü′fang′gəld, nū′fang′gəld) *adj.* recently come into fashion; modern: *a newfangled invention.*

New·found·land (nü′fənd lənd, nū′fənd lənd) *n.* a large, heavily built dog of a breed developed in Newfoundland for pulling sleds and carrying loads, having a dense, usually black coat.

Newfoundland

New Latin, another term for **Modern Latin.**

new·ly (nü′lē, nū′lē) *adv.* **1.** lately; recently: *a newly elected senator.* **2.** again; once more.

new·ly·wed (nü′lē wed′, nū′lē wed′) *n.* a person who has recently been married.

new math, a modern method of teaching mathematics that uses set theory and stresses understanding of basic mathematical concepts. Also, **new mathematics.**

new moon 1. the moon when it is not visible or when it is a thin crescent with the hollow side on the right. **2.** the period during which the new moon appears.

news (nüz, nūz) *n.* **1.** a recent event or events, especially when important or interesting: *We heard a report of the news on the radio.* **2.** a report or information of a recent

at; āpe; fär; câre; end; mē; it; īce; pîerce; hot; ōld; sông, fôrk; oil; out; up; ūse; rüle; pùll; tûrn; chin; sing; shop; thin; this; hw in white; zh in treasure. The symbol ə stands for the unstressed vowel sound heard in about, taken, pencil, lemon, and circus.

N

event or events: *There's no news from home.* ▲ used with a singular verb.

news·boy (nüz′boi′, nūz′boi′) *n.* a boy who sells or delivers newspapers.

news·cast (nüz′kast′, nūz′kast′) *n.* a radio or television program on which news is presented. —**news′·cast′er,** *n.*

news·deal·er (nüz′dē′lər, nūz′dē′lər) *n.* a person who sells newspapers and magazines.

news·girl (nüz′gûrl′, nūz′gûrl′) *n.* a girl who sells or delivers newspapers.

news·let·ter (nüz′let′ər, nūz′let′ər) *n.* a printed report of news, usually published regularly and read by a particular group of people: *a club newsletter.*

news·man (nüz′man′, nūz′man′) *n., pl.* **news·men** (nüz′men′, nūz′men′). a person who reports news, as for a newspaper or radio or television station.

news·pa·per (nüz′pā′pər, nūz′pā′pər) *n.* a publication printed on sheets of paper that are folded but not bound, containing news, editorials, feature articles, and advertising, and issued regularly, especially every day or every week.

news·pa·per·man (nüz′pā′pər man′, nūz′pā′pər man′) *n., pl.* **news·pa·per·men** (nüz′pā′pər men′, nūz′pā′pər men′). a person who works for or owns a newspaper, especially a reporter or editor.

news·pa·per·wom·an (nüz′pā′pər wùm′ən, nūz′pā′pər wùm′ən) *n., pl.* **news·pa·per·wom·en** (nüz′pā′pər wim′ən, nūz′pā′pər wim′ən). a woman who works for or owns a newspaper, especially a reporter or editor.

news·print (nüz′print′, nūz′print′) *n.* a thin paper made chiefly from wood pulp, on which newspapers are usually printed.

news·reel (nüz′rēl′, nūz′rēl′) *n.* a short motion picture dealing with recent events, usually shown in a motion picture theater.

news·stand (nüz′stand′, nūz′stand′) *n.* a stand where newspapers, magazines, and books are sold.

news·wom·an (nüz′wùm′ən, nūz′wùm′ən) *n., pl.* **news·wom·en** (nüz′wim′ən, nūz′wim′ən). a woman who reports news, as for a newspaper or radio or television station.

news·wor·thy (nüz′wûr′thē, nūz′wûr′thē) *adj.* important or interesting enough to be reported in a newscast or newspaper.

news·y (nü′zē, nū′zē) *adj.,* **news·i·er, news·i·est.** *Informal.* chatty and full of news; gossipy: *a newsy letter.*

newt (nüt, nūt) *n.* any of various small, brightly colored salamanders found living in or around water. Newts are amphibians.

New Testament, the second part of the Christian Bible, containing the life and teachings of Jesus and his disciples.

new·ton (nü′tən, nū′tən) *n.* the basic unit of force

newt

equal to the amount of force that must be applied to a mass of 1 kilogram to accelerate it 1 meter per second per second. [From the English physicist and mathematician Sir Isaac *Newton* (1642–1727).]

New·to·ni·an (nü tō′nē ən, nū tō′nē ən) *adj.* of or relating to Sir Isaac Newton or his theories or discoveries.

new wave, a style of rock music developed from and similar to punk rock but characterized by more sophisticated performance techniques and instrumentation and less violent lyrics that treat a wider range of topics.

New World, the Western Hemisphere.

New Year's Day, the first day of the year. It falls on January 1. Also, **New Year, New Year's.**

next (nekst) *adj.* following immediately in time, space,

or order: *I'll see you next week. My friend lives in the next house.* —*adv.* **1.** immediately afterward: *The children's choir will sing next.* **2.** on the first time after this one: *Visit us when you are next in town.*

·**next door.** in, at, or to a building, house, apartment, or the like that is nearest: *Who lives next door to you?*

·**next to.** **a.** almost; nearly: *Fixing the toaster was next to impossible.* **b.** beside: *I was standing next to my cousin.*

next–door (nekst′dôr′) *adj.* in or at the nearest building, house, apartment, or the like: *Our next-door neighbors share a driveway with us.*

Nez Percé (nez′ pûrs′) *n., pl.* **Nez Percé** or **Nez Percés.** a member of a North American Indian tribe formerly living in what is now the northwestern United States and southwestern Canada.

Nfld., Newfoundland.

N.G. 1. National Guard. **2.** New Guinea.

NH, postal abbreviation for New Hampshire.

N.H., New Hampshire.

Ni, the symbol for nickel.

ni·a·cin (nī′ə sin) *n.* a vitamin of the vitamin B complex, found in liver, yeast, beans, and grains, that helps to prevent and cure pellagra. Also, **nicotinic acid.**

nib (nib) *n.* **1.** the tip or point of a pen, especially a fountain pen. **2.** the projecting point of anything. **3.** a bird's bill or beak.

nib·ble (nib′əl) *v.,* **nib·bled, nib·bling.** —*v.t.* **1.** to eat by taking small, quick bites: *The mouse nibbled the cheese.* **2.** to take small, gentle bites on; bite softly: *A fish nibbled our bait.* —*v.i.* **1.** to eat with small, quick bites: *to nibble on an apple.* **2.** to take small, gentle bites: *to nibble on the end of a pencil.* —*n.* **1.** a small, quick bite, as that taken by a fish at bait. **2.** a small piece; morsel: *There's not even a nibble of the cake left.* —**nib′bler,** *n.*

nice (nīs) *adj.,* **nic·er, nic·est. 1.** agreeable or pleasant: *The weather was nice yesterday.* **2.** kind; considerate: *It was nice of you to ask us to the party.* **3.** highly satisfactory; good: *a nice piece of work.* **4.** showing or requiring accuracy, skill, or delicacy: *That artist makes nice distinctions in color.* **5.** respectable or well-bred: *a nice manner, a nice family.* [From the Old French word *nice* meaning "foolish, ignorant," from the Latin word *nescius* "ignorant," from the word *nescire* "not to know."] —**nice′ly,** *adv.* —**nice′ness,** *n.*

·**nice and.** very: *The test was nice and easy.*

ni·ce·ty (nī′si tē) *n., pl.* **ni·ce·ties. 1.** *also,* **niceties.** something that is elegant or refined: *Having a chauffeur is one of the niceties of life.* **2.** *also,* **niceties.** a small or subtle detail; fine point. **3.** the quality or state of requiring delicacy, subtlety, or accuracy.

niche (nich) *n.* **1.** a decorative, usually arch-shaped recess or hollow in a wall, often used as a setting for statues or other ornaments, such as vases or glassware. **2.** a place, position, or situation for which a person is especially suited: *I found my niche in the science department.*

nick (nik) *n.* a place on a surface or edge that has been cut or chipped: *The razor made a nick on my skin. The table top was full of nicks.* —*v.t.* to make a nick or nicks in or on.

·**in the nick of time.** at the last moment; just in time.

nick·el (nik′əl) *n.* **1.** a hard, strong, silvery metallic element that resists corrosion. It is used in alloys and electroplating. Symbol: **Ni 2.** a coin of the United States equal to five cents, or one twentieth of a dollar.

niche *(def. 1)*

[From the German word *kupfernickel* meaning "nickel ore," from the words *kupfer* "copper" + *nickel* "goblin, sprite." The color of this ore makes it look like copper.]

nickel silver, another term for **German silver.**

nick·nack (nik′nak′) another spelling of **knickknack.**

nick·name (nik′nām′) *n.* **1.** a descriptive word or phrase used in addition to or instead of a name: *Chicago's nickname is "the Windy City."* **2.** a familiar, usually shortened form of a name: *"Dan" is a nickname for Daniel.* [The Middle English phrase *a neke-name* meaning "an additional name" was formed by the mistaken division into separate words of the earlier phrase *an eke-name.* The word *eke-name* was formed from the Middle English words *eke* (from the Old English word *ēac*) meaning "also" + *name* (from the Old English word *nama*) meaning "name."] —*v.t.,* **nick·named, nick·nam·ing.** to give a nickname to.

nic·o·tine (nik′ə tēn′) *n.* a poisonous, addictive, oily substance found in the leaves, roots, and seeds of the tobacco plant.

nic·o·tin·ic acid (nik′ə tin′ik) another term for **niacin.**

niece (nēs) *n.* **1.** the daughter of one's brother or sister. **2.** the daughter of one's brother-in-law or sister-in-law.

niels·bohr·i·um (nēlz bôr′ē əm) *n.* see **hahnium.**

nif·ty (nif′tē) *adj.,* **nif·ti·er, nif·ti·est.** *Informal.* fine, dandy, or stylish: *a nifty idea, a nifty party.*

nig·gard (nig′ərd) *n.* a stingy person; miser. —*adj.* another word for **niggardly.**

nig·gard·ly (nig′ərd lē) *adj.* **1.** stingy; miserly. **2.** scanty; meager: *a niggardly amount.* —*adv.* in a niggardly manner; stingily. —**nig′gard·li·ness,** *n.*

nigh (nī) *Archaic. adv.* **1.** near; close: *The carriage drew nigh.* **2.** practically; almost: *It's nigh onto midnight.* —*adj.,* **nigh·er, nigh·est** or **next.** near; close: *The holiday season is nigh.* —*prep.* near; close to.

night (nīt) *n.* **1.** the period of darkness between the setting and the rising of the sun; time from sunset to sunrise. **2.** the beginning of night; nightfall. **3.** the darkness of night; the dark; darkness. **4.** a state or time of mental, emotional, or spiritual darkness: *In the real dark night of the soul it is always three o'clock in the morning* (F. Scott Fitzgerald).

night blindness, an inability to see normally in dim light. Night blindness is often caused by not having enough vitamin A.

night·cap (nīt′kap′) *n.* **1.** a soft, cloth cap worn in bed. **2.** *Informal.* an alcoholic drink taken before going to bed.

night·clothes (nīt′klōz′, nīt′klōthz′) *pl. n.* clothes worn in bed, such as pajamas.

night·club (nīt′klub′) *n.* a place of entertainment open until late at night, usually offering food, drink, and a show.

night crawler, another term for **earthworm.**

night·fall (nīt′fôl′) *n.* the end of the day; beginning of night: *Come home before nightfall.*

night·gown (nīt′goun′) *n.* a loose gown worn in bed by women or children.

night·hawk (nīt′hôk′) *n.* **1.** an American bird resembling the whippoorwill, having mostly gray feathers. **2.** another word for **night owl.**

night·in·gale (nī′tən gāl′, nī′ting gāl′) *n.* a small European migratory thrush having mostly reddish brown feathers and a whitish breast. Nightingales are noted for the beautiful song that the male sings.

nightingale

night–light (nīt′līt′) *n.* a small light kept burning all night, as in a bedroom, hall, or bathroom.

night·ly (nīt′lē) *adj.* done, happening, or appearing at night or every night: *to watch a nightly news broadcast.* —*adv.* at night or every night: *to call home nightly.*

night·mare (nīt′mâr′) *n.* **1.** a bad dream that causes feelings of great nervousness or fear. **2.** any experience or condition resembling a nightmare; something horrible or frightening: *Being lost in the big city was a nightmare.* —**night′mar′ish,** *adj.*

night owl *Informal.* a person who often stays up late.

night school, a school that holds classes in the evening for working adults and other people who cannot attend school during the day.

night·shade (nīt′shād′) *n.* a plant related to the tomato and the potato, having small flowers and black or red berries which may be poisonous.

night·shirt (nīt′shûrt′) *n.* a long shirt worn in bed instead of pajamas.

night·stick (nīt′stik′) *n.* a long, slender club carried by a police officer. Also, **billy, billy club.**

night·time (nīt′tīm′) *n.* the period of time between dusk and dawn.

ni·hil·ism (nī′ə liz′əm) *n.* **1.** a total rejection of all existing political and social institutions and traditional religious and moral values. **2.** any violent revolutionary movement that advocates terrorism or anarchy. —**ni′hil·ist,** *n.* —**ni′hil·is′tic,** *adj.*

Ni·ke (nī′kē) *n. Greek Mythology.* the goddess of victory, usually represented as a winged figure.

nil (nil) *n.* nothing; zero: *My knowledge of classical music is nil.*

nim·ble (nim′bəl) *adj.,* **nim·bler, nim·blest.** **1.** light and quick in movement: *a nimble dancer.* **2.** quick to understand or respond: *a nimble mind.* —**nim′ble·ness,** *n.* —**nim′bly,** *adv.*

nim·bo·stra·tus (nim′bō strā′təs, nim′bō strat′əs) *n.,* *pl.* **nim·bo·stra·tus** or **nim·bo·stra·ti** (nim′bō strā′tī, nim′bō strat′ī). a low, dark gray cloud layer, usually bringing rain or snow.

nim·bus (nim′bəs) *n.,* *pl.* **nim·bi** (nim′bī) or **nim·bus·es.** **1.** a disk or ring of light surrounding the head of a god, saint, or other holy person in a painting. **2.** a feeling of splendor or glory surrounding a person or thing. **3.** see **nimbostratus.**

nin·com·poop (nin′kəm püp′, ning′kəm püp′) *n.* *Informal.* a silly or stupid person; fool.

nine (nīn) *n.* **1.** the cardinal number that is one more than eight. **2.** a symbol representing this number, such as 9 or IX. **3.** something having this many units or things, such as a playing card or a baseball team. —*adj.* numbering one more than eight.

nine·fold (nīn′fōld′) *adj.* **1.** nine times as great or numerous. **2.** having or consisting of nine parts. —*adv.* so as to be nine times greater or more numerous.

nine·teen (nīn′tēn′) *n.* **1.** the cardinal number that is nine more than ten. **2.** a symbol representing this number, such as 19 or XIX. **3.** something having this many units or things. —*adj.* numbering nine more than ten.

nine·teenth (nīn′tēnth′) *adj.* **1.** (the ordinal of nineteen) next after the eighteenth. **2.** being one of nineteen equal parts. —*n.* **1.** something that is next after the eighteenth. **2.** one of nineteen equal parts; 1/19.

nine·ti·eth (nīn′tē ith) *adj.* **1.** (the ordinal of ninety) next after the eighty-ninth. **2.** being one of ninety equal parts. —*n.* **1.** something that is next after the eighty-ninth. **2.** one of ninety equal parts; 1/90.

N

nine·ty (nīn′tē) *n.*, *pl.* **nine·ties. 1.** the cardinal number that is nine times ten. **2.** a symbol representing this number, such as 90 or XC. —*adj.* numbering nine times ten.

nin·ny (nin′ē) *n.*, *pl.* **nin·nies.** a fool; simpleton.

ninth (nīnth) *adj.* **1.** (the ordinal of nine) next after the eighth. **2.** being one of nine equal parts. —*n.* **1.** something that is next after the eighth. **2.** one of nine equal parts; ⅑. —*adv.* in the ninth place.

ni·o·bi·um (nī ō′bē əm) *n.* a gray or silver-white metallic element that is used in alloys and superconductors. Symbol: **Nb** [From *Niobe*, the daughter of Tantalus in Greek mythology. This element is found in ores containing tantalum (named for Tantalus).]

nip¹ (nip) *v.t.*, **nipped, nip·ping. 1.** to seize, as between two surfaces, and pinch or bite: *The parrot nipped my finger.* **2.** to sever by pinching, cutting, or biting: *The gardener nipped the dead leaves off the bush.* **3.** to cause (something) to smart or sting: *The cold night air nipped their fingers.* **4.** to stop or destroy the growth of: *The late frost nipped the fruit trees.* —*n.* **1.** the act of nipping. **2.** a small portion or quantity; little bit. **3.** a sharp, biting cold; chill: *There is a nip in the air today.* **4.** a sharp or pungent flavor; tang. [From the Middle Dutch word *nipen* meaning "to bite, sever, nip off."]

·**nip and tuck.** *Informal.* so close or even as to leave the outcome in doubt: *The game was nip and tuck until the last inning.*

nip² (nip) *n.* a little drink; sip: *a nip of brandy.* [Probably from *nipperkin*, a kind of liquor bottle.]

nip·per (nip′ər) *n.* **1.** a person or thing that nips. **2. nippers.** any of various tools that grab and hold or cut, as pincers or pliers. **3.** one of the large claws of a lobster or similar animal. **4.** *Informal.* a small boy.

nip·ple (nip′əl) *n.* **1.** a small pointed or rounded projection at the center of the breast or udder that, in a female mammal, contains the opening of the milk ducts. **2.** the rubber mouthpiece of a baby's bottle. **3.** anything like a nipple in shape or use, such as a short piece of pipe threaded at each end for use as a coupling.

Nip·pon·ese (nip′ə nēz′, nip′ə nēs′) *n.*, *pl.* **Nip·pon·ese.** another name for **Japanese.** —*adj.* of or relating to Japan, its people, their language, or culture.

nip·py (nip′ē) *adj.*, **nip·pi·er, nip·pi·est. 1.** cold or chilling in a sharp, biting way: *The air is often a bit nippy in November.* **2.** tending or likely to nip.

nir·va·na (nir vä′nə) *also,* **Nir·va·na.** *n.* **1.** the highest state of bliss in Buddhism, in which all desire and suffering are extinguished, and the soul becomes a part of the supreme universal soul. **2.** any place or condition free from care or pain.

Ni·sei (nē′sā′) *n.*, *pl.* **Ni·sei.** a person who was born and educated in the United States or Canada and whose parents were immigrants from Japan.

nit (nit) *n.* the egg or young of any of various insects, such as a louse.

ni·ter (nī′tər) *also,* **ni·tre.** *n.* **1.** another word for **potassium nitrate. 2.** another word for **sodium nitrate.**

nit·pick (nit′pik′) *v.i.* to be overly concerned or critical about small details or minor faults. —**nit′pick·er,** *n.*

nit·pick·ing (nit′pik′ing) *n.*, *adj.* concerned or fussing about small faults or unimportant details: *Your constant nitpicking makes us angry.*

ni·trate (nī′trāt) *n.* **1.** a salt or ester of nitric acid. **2.** sodium nitrate or potassium nitrate used as a fertilizer. —*v.t.*, **ni·trat·ed, ni·trat·ing.** to treat or combine with nitric acid or a nitrate.

ni·tric (nī′trik) *adj.* of or containing nitrogen, especially of a higher valence.

nitric acid, a colorless, highly corrosive, liquid compound that is one of the strongest known oxidizing agents, used in the manufacturing of explosives, nitrate fertilizers, and dyes.

ni·tro·cel·lu·lose (nī′trə sel′yə lōs′) *n.* any of a number of flammable compounds made by adding a mixture of concentrated sulfuric and nitric acids to cellulose. Nitrocellulose is used in making plastics, lacquers, and explosives. Also, **cellulose nitrate.**

ni·tro·gen (nī′trə jən) *n.* a colorless, odorless, tasteless gaseous element that makes up about 78 percent of the volume of the atmosphere. Nitrogen is essential to all forms of life. It is used to produce ammonia, nitric acid, and fertilizers. Symbol: **N** [From the French word *nitrogène*, formed from the Greek prefix *nitro-* meaning "niter" + *gennan* "to produce." This element was discovered in potassium nitrate (niter).] —**ni·trog·e·nous** (nī troj′ə nəs), *adj.*

nitrogen cycle, a continuous series of chemical changes by which nitrogen circulates between air, soil, and living things. Free nitrogen in the air passes into the soil, where it is converted by bacteria into compounds that can be used by plants and animals. When the plant and animal matter decays, nitrogen is released into the air, completing the cycle.

nitrogen fixation, conversion of free nitrogen that has entered the soil into compounds that can be used by plants and animals.

ni·tro·gen–fix·ing bacteria (nī′trə jən fik′sing) bacteria that combine nitrogen in the air with other elements to produce compounds useful to plants and animals. These bacteria live in the soil or in the roots of such plants as peas and beans.

ni·tro·glyc·er·in (nī′trə glis′ər in) *also,* **ni·tro·glyc·er·ine.** *n.* a colorless, oily, liquid compound that is poisonous and very explosive. Nitroglycerin is used to treat angina.

ni·trous (nī′trəs) *adj.* **1.** of or containing nitrogen, especially of a lower valence. **2.** of or containing niter.

nitrous acid, an unstable compound of nitrogen, occurring only in solution or in the form of its salts.

nitrous oxide, a gas with a sweetish odor and taste that produces an intoxicating effect when inhaled. It is used as an anesthetic. Also, **laughing gas.**

nit·ty–grit·ty (nit′ē grit′ē) *n.* the basic part or parts; practical essentials; fundamental details: *Let's concentrate on the nitty-gritty of this plan and ignore the unimportant factors.*

nit·wit (nit′wit′) *n.* a stupid person.

nix (niks) *Slang. n.* nothing. —*adv.* no. —*interj.* watch out; stop. —*v.t.* to reject or put a stop to: *The teacher nixed their plans.*

NJ, postal abbreviation for New Jersey.

N.J., New Jersey.

NM, postal abbreviation for New Mexico.

N.M., New Mexico.

N. Mex., New Mexico.

no¹ (nō) *adv.* **1.** certainly not; not so. ▲ used to show denial, disagreement, or refusal. The word "no" sometimes makes a negative statement more emphatic: *No, I don't want to do it. No, that's not right.* **2.** not at all. ▲ used with the comparative form of an adjective: *That test was no worse than the others.* **3.** not: *whether or no.* —*interj.* used to express surprise, bewilderment, or disbelief. —*n.*, *pl.* **noes** or **nos. 1.** the saying of the word "no"; refusal; denial. **2.** a negative vote or voter. [From the Old English word *nā* with the same meanings.]

no² (nō) *adj.* **1.** not any: *There were no mistakes in your spelling test. They've had no food all day.* **2.** not a: *I am no great baseball player.* [From the Old English word *nān* or *nā* meaning "none."]

No, the symbol for nobelium.

No., no. 1. north. **2.** northern. **3.** number.

no·be·li·um (nō bē′lē əm) *n.* a radioactive metallic element produced artificially from curium. Symbol: **No** [From the Swedish chemist and industrialist Alfred B. Nobel (1833–1896).]

No·bel prize (nō bel′) any of the prizes established by Alfred Nobel to be awarded each year for accomplishments in the fields of physics, chemistry, physiology or medicine, and literature, and for the promotion of peace. A Nobel prize in economics was established later.

no·bil·i·ty (nō bil′i tē) *n., pl.* **no·bil·i·ties. 1.** a class of people in a society having high birth, rank, or title. Dukes, duchesses, earls, and countesses are among the members of the British nobility. **2.** the state or quality of being distinguished by high birth, rank, or title. **3.** the state or quality of showing greatness of character or superior merit.

no·ble (nō′bəl) *adj.*, **no·bler, no·blest. 1.** distinguished by high birth, rank, or title; aristocratic. **2.** having or showing greatness of character or superior merit; worthy: *noble sentiments, a noble cause, noble deeds.* **3.** impressive in appearance; splendid; magnificent: *a noble oak tree.* —*n.* a nobleman or noblewoman. —**no′ble·ness,** *n.* —**no′bly,** *adv.*

no·ble·man (nō′bəl mən) *n., pl.* **no·ble·men** (nō′bəl-mən). a man of noble birth, rank, or title.

no·ble·wom·an (nō′bəl wùm′ən) *n., pl.* **no·ble-wom·en** (nō′bəl wim′ən). a woman of noble birth, rank, or title.

no·bod·y (nō′bod′ē) *pron.* no person; no one: *Nobody was late.* *n., pl.* **no·bod·ies.** a person of no importance, authority, or position.

▲ In writing and formal speech, **nobody** and **no one** are used with a singular pronoun: *Nobody raised his voice. No one likes to lose his or her wallet.* In informal conversation, they are sometimes used with a plural pronoun: *Nobody called while I was out, did they?*

nock (nok) *n.* **1.** a notch at either end of a bow that holds the bowstring. **2.** a notch at the end of an arrow for receiving the bowstring. —*v.t.* **1.** to put a notch in (an arrow or bow). **2.** to fit (an arrow) to the bowstring for shooting.

noc·tur·nal (nok tûr′nəl) *adj.* **1.** of or happening at night: *nocturnal sounds, a nocturnal walk.* **2.** active at night: *The raccoon is a nocturnal animal.* **3.** (of a flower) opening at night and closing during the day. —**noc-tur′nal·ly,** *adv.*

noc·turne (nok′tûrn′) *n.* **1.** a musical composition of a dreamy, thoughtful, or romantic character that is suitable for the evening. **2.** a painting of a night scene.

nod (nod) *v.*, **nod·ded, nod·ding.** —*v.i.* **1.** to lower briefly and then raise the head, as in greeting or agreement. **2.** to let the head fall forward with a quick motion, as when sleepy: *The student sat nodding over the dull book.* **3.** to bend forward with a swaying motion: *The grasses nodded as the breeze swept over the field.* —*v.t.* **1.** to lower briefly and then raise (the head), as in greeting or agreement. **2.** to show or express by nodding: *The teacher nodded approval of my request.* —*n.* a lowering and raising of the head, as in greeting or agreement. —**nod′der,** *n.*

node (nōd) *n.* **1.** a knot, knob, or swelling. **2.** a point on a stem from which a leaf or branch grows. —**nod′al,** *adj.*

nod·ule (noj′ül) *n.* **1.** a small knot, swelling, or growth, as on a plant or animal. **2.** a small, rounded mass or lump, as of some mineral. —**nod·u·lar** (noj′ə lər), *adj.*

no·ël (nō el′) *n.* **1.** a Christmas carol. **2. Noël.** Christmas.

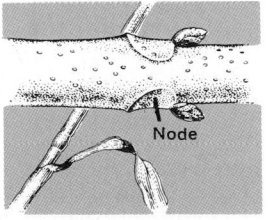

node *(def. 2)*

no–fault (nō′fôlt′) *adj.* **1.** of or relating to a form of automobile insurance under which an accident victim is compensated for damages by his or her own insurance com-

pany, without any finding of blame for the accident. **2.** of or relating to a form of divorce that requires only that the husband and wife desire to end the marriage, with no finding of blame.

no–frills (nō′frilz′) *adj.* basic and unadorned; without extras or embellishments: *a no-frills airline flight without refreshments.*

nog·gin (nog′in) *n.* **1.** a small mug or cup. **2.** a small quantity of drink, especially liquor, equal to about one fourth of a pint. **3.** *Informal.* a person's head.

noise (noiz) *n.* **1.** a sound that is loud, harsh, or unpleasant: *The noise of the traffic made it difficult to sleep.* **2.** any sound: *I heard a noise outside the window.* —*v.t.*, **noised, nois·ing.** to spread by rumor or report: *It was noised about that the coach intended to resign.* [From the Old French word *noise* meaning "uproar, noise," from the Latin word *nausea* "seasickness, nausea," from the Greek dialect word *nausiē* "seasickness," from the word *naus* meaning "ship."]

noise·less (noiz′lis) *adj.* making no noise; silent; quiet: *noiseless movements, a noiseless fan.* —**noise′less·ly,** *adv.* —**noise′less·ness,** *n.*

noise·mak·er (noiz′mā′kər) *n.* something that makes noise, especially a horn, rattle, or other device used to make noise at a celebration or party.

noi·some (noi′səm) *adj.* **1.** offensive or bad to the smell; disgusting: *a noisome odor.* **2.** harmful; injurious: *noisome fumes in the air.* —**noi′some·ly,** *adv.* —**noi′some·ness,** *n.*

nois·y (noi′zē) *adj.*, **nois·i·er, nois·i·est. 1.** making noise: *noisy children.* **2.** full of or characterized by noise: *a noisy argument.* —**nois′i·ly,** *adv.* —**nois′i·ness,** *n.*

nomads *(def. 1)*

no·mad (nō′mad) *n.* **1.** a member of a group or tribe that has no permanent home and moves from place to place in search of food or land on which to graze their animals. **2.** any person who wanders from place to place.

no·mad·ic (nō mad′ik) *adj.* of or relating to nomads; wandering: *a nomadic tribe.* —**no·mad′i·cal·ly,** *adv.*

no–man's–land (nō′manz′land′) *n.* **1.** the land between two opposing armies, not controlled by either one. **2.** an area of thought or activity that is indefinite or uncertain: *the no-man's-land between fact and fiction.*

N

at; āpe; fär; câre; end; mē; it; īce; pîerce; hot; ōld; sông, fôrk; oil; out; up; ūse; rüle; pùll; tûrn; chin; sing; shop; thin; **th**is; hw in white; zh in treasure. The symbol ə stands for the unstressed vowel sound heard in about, taken, pencil, lemon, and circus.

nom de plume (nom'də plüm') pen name. [From the French phrase *nom de plume*, from the words *nom* meaning "name" + *de* meaning "of" + *plume* meaning "pen.'"]

no·men·cla·ture (nō'mən klā'chər) *n.* a system of names or special terms, especially in an art or science: *the nomenclature of biology.* [From the Latin word *nomenclatura* meaning "calling by name," going back to the words *nomen* "name" + *calare* "to call."]

nom·i·nal (nom'ə nəl) *adj.* **1.** being so in name but not in fact; not real or actual: *The king is the nominal ruler, while the prime minister has real power.* **2.** small compared with the actual value: *a nominal cost.* **3.** *Grammar.* of, relating to, or used as a noun: *a nominal adjective.* —**nom'i·nal·ly,** *adv.*

nom·i·nate (nom'ə nāt') *v.t.,* **nom·i·nat·ed, nom·i·nat·ing. 1.** to propose as a candidate for an office or honor: *The Democrats nominated a former senator for the presidency.* **2.** to appoint to an office or duty: *The mayor nominated a new police chief.*

nom·i·na·tion (nom'ə nā'shən) *n.* the act of nominating or the state of being nominated: *Your name was placed in nomination during the meeting.*

nom·i·na·tive (nom'ə nə tiv) *Grammar. adj.* of, relating to, or designating the case of the subject of a verb, or of words agreeing with the subject. —*n.* **1.** the nominative case. **2.** a word in the nominative case. *I, they,* and *who* are nominatives.

nom·i·nee (nom'ə nē') *n.* a person who is nominated, especially as a candidate for office.

non– *prefix* opposite or lack of; not: *nonprofit, nonviolence, nonsense.*

Language Note

To understand the meaning of a word that begins with **non–** but is not defined in this dictionary, add the word "not" to the meaning of the basic word. For example, *nonliving* means "not living" and *noncommunist* means "not communist." For some nouns, it is clearer to add the phrase "the opposite of." For example, *noninvolvement* means "the opposite of involvement" and *nonbeliever* means "the opposite of (a) believer." For any important *non–* word that has a special meaning, there is an entry in this dictionary.

non·a·ge·nar·i·an (non'ə jə när'ē ən) *n.* a person who is 90 years old or between 90 and 100 years old. —*adj.* being 90 years old or between 90 and 100 years old.

non·a·gon (non'ə gon') *n.* a polygon with nine sides and nine angles.

non·al·co·hol·ic (non'al kə hô'lik) *adj.* containing no alcohol: *a nonalcoholic beverage.*

non·a·ligned (non'ə līnd') *adj.* not allied with or favoring any major power in foreign affairs; committed to neutrality as a foreign policy: *a nonaligned Third World country.* —**non'a·lign'ment,** *n.*

nonce (nons) *n.* a particular purpose or occasion. ▲ used chiefly in the phrase *for the nonce.*

nonce word, a word made up and used for a particular purpose or occasion.

non·cha·lance (non'shə läns') *n.* the state of being nonchalant.

non·cha·lant (non'shə länt') *adj.* marked by or showing a lack of interest or enthusiasm; casually indifferent. —**non'cha·lant'ly,** *adv.*

non·com (non'kom') *n. Informal.* a noncommissioned officer.

non·com·bat·ant (non'kəm bat'ənt, non kom'bə tənt) *n.* **1.** a member of the armed forces, such as a doctor or chaplain, whose normal duties do not include fighting. **2.** a civilian in wartime.

non·com·mis·sioned officer (non'kə mish'ənd) an enlisted person in the armed forces who has been promoted to a rank above other enlisted people, but who has not received a commission from the president. A sergeant and a corporal are noncommissioned officers.

non·com·mit·tal (non'kə mit'əl) *adj.* not involving or showing commitment to a particular opinion, view, or course of action: *The governor made a noncommittal statement urging further study of the problem.* —**non'com·mit'tal·ly,** *adv.*

non·com·pli·ance (non'kəm plī'əns) *n.* failure or refusal to comply.

non·con·duc·tor (non'kən duk'tər) *n.* a substance that does not easily conduct some form of energy. Most plastics are nonconductors of heat and electricity.

non·con·form·ist (non'kən fôr'mist) *n.* **1.** a person who does not hold or conform to the thoughts, actions, or beliefs held or approved by most people; unconventional person. **2.** *also,* **Nonconformist.** in English history, any Protestant who was not a member of the Church of England.

non·con·form·i·ty (non'kən fôr'mi tē) *n.* lack of conformity.

non·dair·y (non dâr'ē) *adj.* containing no milk or milk products: *a nondairy whipped topping for desserts.*

non·de·nom·i·na·tion·al (non'di nom'ə nā'shə nəl) *adj.* not restricted to a particular religious denomination: *a nondenominational service.*

non·de·script (non'di skript') *adj.* without interesting or striking characteristics or features; not distinctive.

none (nun) *pron.* **1.** no one; not one: *Several senators criticized the bill, but none voted against it.* **2.** not any: *None of the stolen money was ever recovered.* **3.** no part; nothing: *I'll have none of that foolishness!* ▲ In the past, **none** was used only or mainly with a singular verb: *None of my friends has ever been to Paris.* In current usage, **none** is also used with a plural verb: *None of the passengers were aware of the danger.* —*adv.* by no means; not at all: *Help came none too soon.*

non·en·ti·ty (non en'ti tē) *n., pl.* **non·en·ti·ties.** a person or thing of little or no importance.

non·es·sen·tial (non'i sen'shəl) *adj.* not essential; not necessary; not needed. —*n.* a person or thing that is nonessential: *When we go camping, be sure to leave all nonessentials home.*

none·the·less (nun'thə les') *adv.* nevertheless; however.

non·ex·ist·ent (non'eg zis'tənt) *adj.* not existing in reality; unreal. —**non'ex·ist'ence,** *n.*

non·fat (non'fat') *adj.* (of food) having fat or fat solids removed; containing no fats: *nonfat dry milk.*

non·fic·tion (non fik'shən) *n.* prose literature other than fiction, dealing with real situations, persons, or events. Essays and biographies are examples of nonfiction. —**non·fic'tion·al,** *adj.*

non·flam·ma·ble (non flam'ə bəl) *adj.* not likely to catch fire easily; not flammable.

non·in·ter·ven·tion (non'in tər ven'shən) *n.* a failure or refusal to intervene, especially a nation's policy or practice of not interfering in the affairs of other nations.

non·judg·men·tal (non'juj men'təl) *adj.* avoiding judgment based on one's personal principles or opinions: *a nonjudgmental decision.*

non·met·al (non met'əl) *n.* a chemical element not having the character of a metal, especially an element that tends to gain electrons and form negatively charged ions.

non·me·tal·lic (non'mi tal'ik) *adj.* **1.** not of or like metal. **2.** *Chemistry.* of or relating to a nonmetal.

no–no (nō'nō') *n., pl.* **no-nos** or **no-no's.** *Informal.* something unacceptable or improper: *Talking out loud in the library is a no-no.*

no–non·sense (nō′non′sens) *adj.* practical, serious, or businesslike: *The piano teacher asked the students to take a no-nonsense approach to practicing.*

non·pa·reil (non′pə rel′) *adj.* having no equal; matchless. —*n.* a person or thing that has no equal.

non·par·ti·san (non pär′tə zən) *also,* **non·par·ti·zan.** *adj.* not partisan, especially not supporting, belonging to, or influenced by any political party or its interests.

non·plus (non plus′) *v.t.,* **non·plused, non·plus·ing;** *also, British,* **non·plussed, non·plus·sing.** to make unable to say or do more; put at a loss; perplex; bewilder.

non·pro·duc·tive (non′prə duk′tiv) *adj.* **1.** not involved directly in the production of goods: *nonproductive sales personnel.* **2.** producing or yielding little or nothing: *nonproductive soil.* —**non′pro·duc′tive·ly,** *adv.* —**non′pro·duc′tive·ness,** *n.*

non·prof·it (non prof′it) *adj.* not operated for profit: *a nonprofit hospital.*

non·re·new·a·ble (non′ri nü′ə bəl, non′ri nū′ə bəl) *adj.* not readily replaced or capable of renewal; easily used up or exhausted: *Coal and petroleum are nonrenewable natural resources.*

non·res·i·dent (non rez′i dənt) *adj.* not living in a particular place, especially not living permanently where one works, attends school, or owns property. —*n.* a nonresident person.

non·re·stric·tive (non′ri strik′tiv) *adj. Grammar.* designating a word, clause, or phrase that describes a noun without limiting or changing the basic meaning of the sentence, and that is set off by commas. In the sentence *Officer Bridges, who is a captain in the army, was sent to Japan,* the clause *who is a captain in the army* is nonrestrictive.

non·sec·tar·i·an (non′sek târ′ē ən) *adj.* not restricted or belonging to any particular sect or religion: *a nonsectarian church service.*

non·sense (non′sens) *n.* **1.** language or behavior that is silly or makes no sense: *The little baby babbled nonsense.* **2.** language or behavior that is annoying or lacking in good sense: *I refuse to put up with any more nonsense from the children.* **3.** things of no importance or value; trifles: *Don't waste your money on that nonsense.*

non·sen·si·cal (non sen′si kəl) *adj.* making no sense; foolish; absurd: *a nonsensical statement.* **non·sen′si·cal·ly,** *adv.*

non se·qui·tur (non sek′wi tər) a statement or conclusion that does not follow logically from the statements already made or facts given. For example: *We are tired of our team losing; therefore, we will change the colors of the team's uniforms.* [From the Latin phrase *non sequitur* meaning "(it) does not follow," from the words *non* "not, no" and *sequor* "to follow."]

non·stan·dard (non stan′dərd) *adj.* **1.** of or relating to usage or language that is not considered acceptable by educated users of the language. **2.** not standard.

non·stick (non′stik′) *adj.* having a special coating to which food does not stick during cooking and that easily washes clean: *a nonstick frying pan.*

non·stop (non′stop′) *adj.* not making any intermediate stops: *a nonstop flight.* —*adv.* without stops: *We flew nonstop to Rome.*

non·un·ion (non ūn′yən) *adj.* **1.** employing people who are not union members: *a nonunion barbershop.* **2.** not belonging to a trade or labor union.

non·vi·o·lence (non vī′ə ləns) *n.* the philosophy or practice of opposing the use of all physical force or violence. —**non·vi′o·lent,** *adj.* —**non·vi′o·lent·ly,** *adv.*

non·white (non hwīt′, non wīt′) *adj.* not white; not belonging to the white race. —*n.* a person who is not white.

noo·dle¹ (nü′dəl) *n.* a narrow flat strip of dried dough made from a mixture of flour, water, and eggs. [From the German word *Nudel* meaning this food.]

noo·dle² (nü′dəl) *n.* **1.** a silly or stupid person; fool. **2.** *Slang.* the head. [Of uncertain origin.]

nook (nùk) *n.* **1.** any small recess or corner. **2.** a secluded or sheltered place: *We found a shady nook in the woods.*

noon (nün) *n.* **1.** twelve o'clock in the daytime; the middle of the day. **2.** the highest point: *In the bright wisdom of youth's breathless noon* (Percy Shelley).

noon·day (nün′dā′) *n.* see **noon** (*def. 1*). —*adj.* of or occurring at noon: *a noonday meal.*

no one, nobody. ▲ See **nobody** for usage note.

noon·time (nün′tīm′) *n.* see **noon** (*def. 1*). Also, **noontide** (nün′tīd′).

noose (nüs) *n.* **1.** a loop of rope with a slipknot that allows the loop to tighten when the end of the rope is pulled. **2.** a trap or snare. —*v.t.,* **noosed, noos·ing.** to capture with a noose; entrap.

nor (nôr) *conj.* **1.** used with *neither* or another negative word to introduce another element in a series: *Neither she nor I have seen it.* **2.** used in place of *and . . . not* to continue a negative idea: *He was not at work today, nor will he be there tomorrow.*

▲ *Or* is generally used instead of *nor* to introduce another negative idea if it is clear that the idea is negative: *The employee would not go on a vacation from work, or even take one day off.*

noose *(def. 1)*

Nor. **1.** Norman. **2.** North. **3.** Norway; Norwegian.

Nor·dic (nôr′dik) *adj.* of or relating to a people living mainly in northern Europe, especially Scandinavia, characterized by tall stature, long heads, fair skin, and blond hair. —*n.* a member of the Nordic people.

norm (nôrm) *n.* **1.** a rule, standard, or pattern, as of behavior: *the cultural norms of today's United States.* **2.** an average: *statistical norms.*

nor·mal (nôr′məl) *adj.* **1.** conforming to an accepted standard, model, or pattern; usual; standard; typical: *Heavy traffic is normal during rush hour.* **2.** having or showing average mental, physical, or emotional development, as at a particular age: *According to various tests, that child has normal intelligence.* —*n.* a usual or standard condition or level: *My temperature was two degrees above normal.*

nor·mal·cy (nôr′məl sē) *n.* another word for **normality.**

nor·mal·i·ty (nôr mal′i tē) *n.* the state or quality of being normal.

nor·mal·ize (nôr′mə līz′) *v.t.,* **nor·mal·ized, nor·mal·iz·ing.** to make normal: *The diplomats sought to normalize relations between the two hostile countries.* —**nor′mal·i·za′tion,** *n.*

nor·mal·ly (nôr′mə lē) *adv.* **1.** under normal circumstances; ordinarily; usually: *Normally the train takes twenty minutes to reach the next town.* **2.** in a normal manner: *to behave normally.*

normal school, a school that trains high school graduates to be teachers.

N

---

at; āpe; fär; câre; end; mē; it; īce; pîerce; hot; ōld; sông, fôrk; oil; out; up; ūse; rüle; pùll; tûrn; chin; sing; shop; thin; this; hw in white; zh in treasure. The symbol ə stands for the unstressed vowel sound heard in about, taken, pencil, lemon, and circus.

Nor·man (nôr′mən) *n.* **1.** a member of the Scandinavian people who invaded and conquered Normandy in the tenth century A.D. **2.** one of the descendants of these people and the French who conquered England in 1066. **3.** a native or inhabitant of Normandy. **4.** see **Norman French.** —*adj.* of or relating to Normandy or the Normans.

Norman Conquest, the conquest of England by the Normans under William the Conqueror, in 1066.

Norman French, a dialect of French spoken by the people of Normandy in the Middle Ages.

Norse (nôrs) *adj.* **1.** of or relating to ancient Scandinavia, its people, or their language or culture. **2.** another word for **Norwegian.** —*n.* **1. the Norse. a.** the ancient Scandinavians. **b.** the Norwegians. **2.** the language of Norway; Norwegian.

Norse·man (nôrs′mən) *n., pl.* **Norse·men** (nôrs′mən). a member of the people of ancient Scandinavia. Also, **North·man.**

north (nôrth) *n.* **1.** the direction to one's right as one faces the sunset. North is one of the four main points of the compass, located directly opposite south and at zero degrees. **2.** *also,* **North.** any region or place lying in this direction. **3. the North.** a region of the United States north of Maryland, the Ohio River, and Missouri, especially the Northern states that fought against the Confederacy in the Civil War. —*adj.* **1.** toward or in the north. **2.** from the north: *the north wind.* —*adv.* toward the north: *to walk north.*

north·bound (nôrth′bound′) *adj.* going north: *north-bound traffic.*

north·east (nôrth′ēst′) *n.* **1.** the direction halfway between north and east. **2.** the point of the compass indicating this direction. **3.** a region or place in this direction. **4. the Northeast.** the northeastern part of the United States, especially New England and New York. —*adj.* **1.** toward or in the northeast; northeast. **2.** from the northeast. —*adv.* toward the northeast.

north·east·er (nôrth′ēs′tər) *n.* a strong wind or storm from the northeast.

north·east·er·ly (nôrth′ēs′tər lē) *adj., adv.* **1.** toward the northeast. **2.** from the northeast: *northeasterly winds.*

north·east·ern (nôrth′ēs′tərn) *adj.* **1.** toward or in the northeast. **2.** *also,* **Northeastern.** of, relating to, or characteristic of the northeast or Northeast. **3.** coming from the northeast.

north·east·ward (nôrth′ēst′wərd) *adv.* toward the northeast. Also, **north·east·wards** (nôrth′ēst′wərdz). —*adj.* toward or in the northeast. —*n.* a northeastward direction, point, or place.

north·er·ly (nôr′thər lē) *adj., adv.* **1.** toward the north. **2.** from the north.

north·ern (nôr′thərn) *adj.* **1.** toward or in the north. **2.** *also,* **Northern.** of, relating to, or characteristic of the north or North. **3.** from the north.

north·ern·er (nôr′thər nər) *n.* **1.** a person who was born or is living in the north. **2.** *usually,* **Northerner.** a person who was born or is living in the northern part of the United States.

Northern Hemisphere, the half of the earth north of the equator.

northern lights, another term for **aurora borealis.**

north·ern·most (nôr′thərn mōst′) *adj.* farthest north.

north·land (nôrth′lənd) *n.* the land in the north, such as the northern region of a country.

North·man (nôrth′mən) *n., pl.* **North·men** (nôrth′mən). another name for **Norseman.**

north–north·east (nôrth′nôrth′ēst′) *n.* a point on the compass halfway between north and northeast. —*adj., adv.* toward the north-northeast.

north–north·west (nôrth′nôrth′west′) *n.* a point on the compass halfway between north and northwest. —*adj., adv.* toward the north-northwest.

North Pole **1.** the northernmost point on earth; the northern end of the earth's axis. **2. north pole.** the pole of a magnet that points to the north when the magnet swings freely.

North Star, another term for **Polaris.**

north·ward (nôrth′wərd) *adv.* toward the north. Also, **north·wards** (nôrth′wərdz). —*adj.* toward or in the north. —*n.* a northward direction, point, or place.

north·west (nôrth′west′) *n.* **1.** the direction halfway between north and west. **2.** the point of the compass indicating this direction. **3.** a region or place in this direction. —*adj.* **1.** toward or in the northwest; northwestern. **2.** from the northwest: *the northwest wind.* —*adv.* toward the northwest.

north·west·er (nôrth′wes′tər) *n.* a strong wind or storm from the northwest.

north·west·er·ly (nôrth′wes′tər lē) *adj., adv.* **1.** toward the northwest. **2.** from the northwest.

north·west·ern (nôrth′wes′tərn) *adj.* **1.** toward or in the northwest. **2.** *also,* **Northwestern.** of, relating to, or characteristic of the northwest or Northwest. **3.** coming from the northwest.

Northwest Passage, a supposed sea route along the north coast of North America connecting the Atlantic and Pacific oceans.

north·west·ward (nôrth′west′wərd) *adv.* toward the northwest. Also, **north·west·wards** (nôrth′west′wərdz). —*adj.* toward or in the northwest. —*n.* a northwestward direction, point, or place.

Nor·we·gian (nôr wē′jən) *n.* **1.** a person who was born in or is a citizen of Norway. **2.** the Germanic language of Norway. —*adj.* of or relating to Norway, its people, or their language or culture. Also, **Norse.**

nose (nōz) *n.* **1.** the part of the human face that contains the organ of smell and the breathing passages. **2.** the corresponding part of the head in other animals. **3.** the sense of smell: *Cats have good noses.* **4.** a prominent or projecting part of something, such as the front end of a ship or airplane. **5.** the ability to discover or learn: *That columnist has a nose for news.* —*v.,* **nosed, nos·ing.** —*v.t.* **1.** to discover or notice by smell: *The dog nosed out the rabbit.* **2.** to touch or rub with the nose; nuzzle. **3.** to push slowly or gently with or as if with the nose: *Tugboats nosed the ship into the dock.* —*v.i.* **1.** to sniff: *The puppy nosed at my arm.* **2.** to move forward, especially with caution. **3.** to pry or meddle: *to nose around for information.*

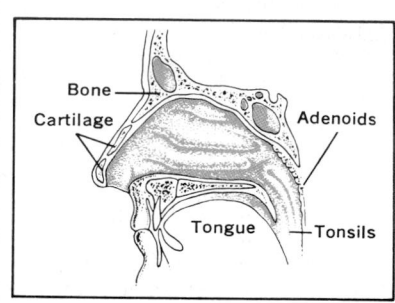

nose *(def. 1)*

(labels: Bone, Cartilage, Adenoids, Tongue, Tonsils)

　·**by a nose.** by a small margin: *I won the race by a nose.*

　·**to look down one's nose at.** to have a superior attitude toward; disdain.

　·**to nose out.** to defeat by a small margin: *to nose out another runner at the end of a race.*

　·**to turn up one's nose at.** to show scorn or contempt for.

　·**under one's nose.** plainly or clearly visible.

nose·bleed (nōz′blēd′) *n.* a bleeding from the nose.

nose cone, the cone-shaped front section of a rocket, often equipped with a heat shield.

nose·dive (nōz′dīv′) *n.* **1.** a rapid or sudden plunge downward by an aircraft, with the nose pointing toward the earth. **2.** any rapid or sudden plunge downward:

Prices on the stock market took a nosedive. —*v.i.,* **nose·dived, nose·div·ing.** to make a nosedive: *The plane flipped over and nosedived out of sight.*

nose·gay (nōz′gā′) *n.* a small bunch of flowers; bouquet.

nosh (nosh) *Slang. n., pl.* **nosh·es.** a light meal; snack: *to have a nosh with some friends.* —*v.i.* **noshed, nosh·ing.** to eat a snack.

nos·tal·gia (nos tal′jə) *n.* **1.** a sentimental longing for what is past or far away: *The faded mementos of my youth filled me with nostalgia.* **2.** a longing for one's home and family; homesickness. —**nos·tal′gic,** *adj.* —**nos·tal′gi·cal·ly,** *adv.*

nos·tril (nos′trəl) *n.* either of the two outer openings of the nose. [From the Old English word *nosthyrl* meaning "nostril," from the words *nosu* "nose" + *thyrel* "hole."]

nos·trum (nos′trəm) *n.* **1.** a patent medicine, especially one that is a quack remedy. **2.** a favorite scheme or remedy, as for curing social problems.

nos·y (nō′zē) *also,* **nos·ey.** *adj.,* **nos·i·er, nos·i·est.** *Informal.* overly curious about other people's business; prying. —**nos′i·ly,** *adv.* —**nos′i·ness,** *n.*

not (not) *adv.* at no time; in no way. ▲ used to form negative statements: *They are not home. You may not go.*

no·ta·ble (nō′tə bəl) *adj.* worthy of notice; noteworthy; remarkable: *The novelist's first book was a notable success.* —*n.* a person who is worthy of notice. —**no′ta·bly,** *adv.*

no·ta·rize (nō′tə rīz′) *v.t.,* **no·ta·rized, no·ta·riz·ing.** to witness and certify (a document) to be authentic: *The notary public notarized the will.* —**no′ta·ri·za′tion,** *n.*

no·ta·ry (nō′tə rē) *n., pl.* **no·ta·ries.** see **notary public.**

notary public, a person authorized to administer oaths and certify documents as authentic.

no·ta·tion (nō tā′shən) *n.* **1.** a system of signs or symbols used to represent values, quantities, or other facts or information: *musical notation.* **2.** the act or process of using such signs or symbols. **3.** a brief note, as in the margin of a book. **4.** the act of writing notes. —**no·ta′tion·al,** *adj.*

notch (noch) *n., pl.* **notch·es.** **1.** a wedge-shaped nick or other indentation cut into the surface or along the edge of something. **2.** a narrow pass between mountains. **3.** *Informal.* a step or degree: *Your hard work in arithmetic has made you come up several notches in my opinion.* —*v.t.* **1.** to cut a notch or notches in. **2.** to keep count of by or as if by cutting notches.

note (nōt) *n.* **1.** *usually,* **notes.** a brief record, as of a lecture, written down to help the memory: *She took notes in class. The lecturer spoke without notes.* **2.** a comment or explanation added to a text, as at the bottom of a page. **3.** a brief message or letter: *The teacher sent a note to my parents.* **4.** careful notice; regard: *His opinions are worthy of note.* **5.** distinction or importance; significance: *The judge is a person of note.* **6.** an indication or suggestion, as of an emotion: *I detect a note of bitterness in your voice.* **7.** see **promissory note. 8.** a piece of paper money or a certificate of payment issued by a government or bank. **9.** *Music.* **a.** a tone of definite pitch. **b.** a sign representing such a tone and showing its pitch and duration. **c.** the key of a piano or other similar instrument. **10.** the musical call of a bird. —*v.t.,* **not·ed, not·ing. 1.** to set down in writing; make a note of: *I noted your telephone number in my address book.* **2.** to observe carefully; regard; notice: *Please note the enclosed instructions.* **3.** to men-

Whole note	𝅝
Half note	𝅗𝅥
Quarter note	𝅘𝅥
Eighth note	𝅘𝅥𝅮
Sixteenth note	𝅘𝅥𝅯

notes *(n., def. 9b)*

tion specially; remark about: *The critic noted several of my poems.*

·**to compare notes.** to exchange points of view or ideas.

note·book (nōt′bŭk′) *n.* a book with pages for notes.

noted
the heads of four **noted** presidents sculpted into Mt. Rushmore

not·ed (nō′tid) *adj.* well-known or celebrated; famous; distinguished: *Several noted authors have written for that paper.*

note·wor·thy (nōt′wûr′thē) *adj.* worthy of notice or special attention: *a noteworthy accomplishment.* —**note′wor′thi·ly,** *adv.* —**note′wor′thi·ness,** *n.*

noth·ing (nuth′ing) *n.* **1.** no thing; not anything: *I have nothing to say about the matter. We bought nothing at the store.* **2.** no part or share: *Nothing is left of the money.* **3.** a person or thing that is of no value or importance. **4.** zero: *The final score in the game was two to nothing.* —*adv.* in no way; not at all: *You look nothing like your sister.*

·**nothing doing.** *Informal.* absolutely not.

noth·ing·ness (nuth′ing nis) *n.* **1.** the absence of matter; empty space; emptiness. **2.** the absence of existence.

no·tice (nō′tis) *v.t.,* **no·ticed, no·tic·ing.** to become aware of; pay attention to: *I noticed your car parked outside.* —*n.* **1.** the act of observing or the state of being observed: *We escaped notice by tiptoeing out of the room.* **2.** an announcement or warning: *to attack without notice.* **3.** a printed announcement: *Notices about the circus were posted all over town.* **4.** a formal announcement, as of the end of an agreement: *I gave my employer two weeks' notice before leaving for another job.* **5.** a critical review: *The play received very poor notices.*

·**to take notice of.** become aware of; pay attention to: *Take notice of the new parking regulations.*

no·tice·a·ble (nō′ti sə bəl) *adj.* easily seen or noticed: *There is a noticeable difference in the patient's appearance today.* —**no′tice·a·bly,** *adv.*

no·ti·fi·ca·tion (nō′tə fi kā′shən) *n.* **1.** the act of notifying or the state of being notified. **2.** a written or printed notice.

at; āpe; fär; câre; end; mē; it; īce; pîerce; hot; ōld; sông, fôrk; oil; out; up; ūse; rüle; pùll; tûrn; chin; sing; shop; thin; this; hw in white; zh in treasure. The symbol ə stands for the unstressed vowel sound heard in about, taken, pencil, lemon, and circus.

no·ti·fy (nō′tə fī′) v.t., **no·ti·fied, no·ti·fy·ing.** to give notice to; inform: *to notify the police of an accident, to notify customers of a sale.* —**no′ti·fi′er,** n.

no·tion (nō′shən) n. **1.** a mental image; idea: *I haven't the slightest notion of what you meant by that remark.* **2.** a theory, belief, or opinion: *a superstitious notion.* **3.** an intention or whim; desire: *I had a sudden notion to leave.* **4. notions.** small useful items, such as ribbons, pins, needles, and thread.

no·to·chord (nō′tə kôrd′) n. a stiff, supporting, rodlike structure that extends lengthwise below the spinal cord in primitive animals with backbones, and is present during the early or embryonic stage in the development of higher animals with backbones.

no·to·ri·e·ty (nō′tə rī′i tē) n. the quality or state of being notorious.

no·to·ri·ous (nō tôr′ē əs) adj. well-known for something bad; widely and unfavorably known: *a notorious criminal, a notorious liar.* —**no·to′ri·ous·ly,** adv. —**no·to′ri·ous·ness,** n.

not·with·stand·ing (not′with stan′ding, not′with stan′- ding) prep. in spite of: *The game was completed notwithstanding the bad weather.* —adv. all the same; nevertheless: *It began raining, but we continued to play notwithstanding.* —conj. in spite of the fact that; although.

nou·gat (nü′gət) n. a candy made mainly of sugar or honey and nuts.

nought (nôt) another spelling of **naught.**

noun (noun) n. a word that names or denotes something, such as a person, animal, place, thing, action, or quality, and that functions as the subject or object of a verb, or the object of a preposition. Most English nouns have a plural formed by adding -s or -es, and many have a possessive formed by adding -'s.

Language Note

We learn that a **noun** is a word that names a person, place, or thing and that an adjective is a word that modifies a noun. Nouns themselves can also be modifiers. Consider the following sentences: *I want to study to be a* computer *expert. Many of my friends are* football *fans. Is that a* library *book?* In these sentences the nouns *computer, football,* and *library* are used to modify other nouns that directly follow them. They act as modifiers in exactly the way that adjectives do. This use of a noun as a modifier is known as *attributive* use, and the nouns are said to be used *attributively.* Nouns used in this way always *precede* the noun they modify. Unlike most adjectives, nouns used attributively *cannot* follow the noun they modify. For example, with the adjective *red,* we can say *That is a red book* and *That book is red.* With the noun *library,* we can say *This book is a library book,* but we cannot say *This book is library.*

We do not often think about using nouns this way because we do it so often, and the structure of English makes such use perfectly natural.

nour·ish (nûr′ish, nur′ish) v.t. **1.** to furnish with food and other substances necessary to life and growth. **2.** to promote the development of; foster.

nour·ish·ing (nûr′ə shing, nur′ə shing) adj. promoting health and growth; providing nourishment; nutritious: *Milk, cereals, and fresh fruit and vegetables are nourishing foods.*

nour·ish·ment (nûr′ish mənt, nur′ish mənt) n. **1.** something that nourishes; sustenance: *Plants receive nourishment from nutrients in the soil.* **2.** the act of nourishing or the state of being nourished.

Nov., November.

no·va (nō′və) n., pl. **no·vas** or **no·vae** (nō′vē). a star that rapidly increases in brightness and then gradually fades to its original brightness. Novas are believed to be older stars.

nov·el¹ (nov′əl) n. a fictional story written in prose, usually fairly long and having a detailed plot. [From the Italian word *novella* meaning "new," going back to the Latin word *novus* "new."]

nov·el² (nov′əl) adj. new and unusual: *a novel idea, a novel technique.* [From the Old French word *novel,* from the Latin word *novellus* meaning "young, new," from the word *novus* "new."]

nov·el·ette (nov′ə let′) n. a short novel.

nov·el·ist (nov′ə list) n. a person who writes novels.

nov·el·ist·ic (nov′ə lis′tik) adj. of, characteristic of, or relating to novels. —**nov′el·is′ti·cal·ly,** adv.

no·vel·la (nō vel′ə) n. a short novel; novelette.

nov·el·ty (nov′əl tē) n., pl. **nov·el·ties. 1.** the quality of being new; newness. **2.** something that is new or unusual, such as a thing or event. **3. novelties.** small, inexpensive, manufactured articles, such as ornaments or toys.

No·vem·ber (nō vem′bər) n. the eleventh month of the year, having thirty days. [From the Old French word *Novembre* meaning this month, from the Latin word *November,* the ninth month of the Roman calendar, from the word *novem* "nine."]

no·ve·na (nō vē′nə) n., pl. **no·ve·nas** or **no·ve·nae** (nō vē′nē). a Roman Catholic observance consisting of prayers said for a period of nine days.

nov·ice (nov′is) n. **1.** a person who is new to an occupation, activity, or the like; beginner. **2.** a person who is admitted into a religious order for a specified period before taking vows.

no·vi·ti·ate (nō vish′ē it) also, **no·vi·ci·ate.** n. **1.** the state or period of being a novice. **2.** a novice; beginner. **3.** the quarters housing novices in a religious order.

No·vo·cain (nō′və kān′) n. *Trademark.* a drug used as a local anesthetic, especially by dentists; procaine.

now (nou) adv. **1.** at the present time: *They are now living in London. I am busy now.* **2.** without delay; at once; immediately: *You must leave now.* **3.** a very short while ago: *They arrived just now, while you were out.* **4.** under the present conditions or circumstances: *Since you missed your train, you must now wait for the next one.* **5.** at the point of time referred to; then: *The war was now over, and the soldiers could return to their families.* —conj. since: *Now that we are alone, we can speak freely.* —n. the present time; present: *The time to act is now.* —interj. used to express warning, sympathy, or reproach: *Now, watch it! Now, now, don't worry about a thing.*

·**now and again** or **now and then.** from time to time; occasionally.

now·a·days (nou′ə dāz′) adv. at the present time; these days.

no·way (nō′wā′) also, **no·ways** (nō′wāz′) adv. in no way; not at all.

no·where (nō′hwâr′, nō′wâr′) adv. to, in, or at no place; not anywhere. —n. **1.** no place. **2.** a place or state of obscurity: *The loyal employee rose from nowhere to become president of the company.*

·**nowhere near.** *Informal.* not nearly: *I'm nowhere near finished.*

no·wise (nō′wīz′) adv. in no way; noway.

nox·ious (nok′shəs) adj. **1.** very harmful to the health: *noxious gases.* **2.** morally harmful. —**nox′ious·ly,** adv. —**nox′ious·ness,** n.

noz·zle (noz′əl) *n.* a spout at the end of a hose, pipe, or the like that serves as an outlet for a liquid or gas.

Np, the symbol for neptunium.

NS, postal abbreviation for Nova Scotia.

N.S., Nova Scotia.

NT, postal abbreviation for the Northwest Territories.

N.T., New Testament.

nth (enth) *adj.* relating to or denoting an indefinitely large or small number or value: *a number raised to the nth power.*

· **to the nth degree.** to the greatest extreme; to the utmost.

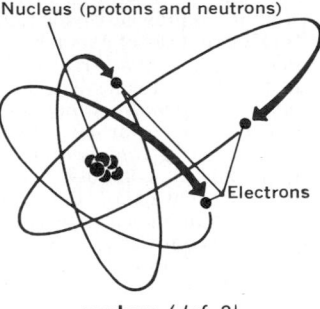

nozzle

nt. wt., net weight.

nu (nū, nü) *n.* the thirteenth letter of the Greek alphabet (N, *v*), corresponding to the English letter N, n.

nu·ance (nü′äns, nū′äns, nü äns′, nū äns′) *n.* a slight or delicate shade, as of tone, expression, or meaning.

nub (nub) *n.* **1.** a knob or bump. **2.** a small piece or lump: *a nub of a pencil, a nub of coal.* **3.** *Informal.* the main part or point, as of a story.

nub·bin (nub′in) *n.* **1.** a small or imperfect ear of corn. **2.** any small or imperfect fruit. **3.** something small that usually projects.

nub·by (nub′ē) *adj.,* **nub·bi·er, nub·bi·est.** having a rough, lumpy texture: *a nubby fabric, a nubby sweater.*

nu·bile (nü′bil, nū′bil) *adj.* of an age suitable for marriage; marriageable. —**nu·bil′i·ty,** *n.*

nu·cle·ar (nü′klē ər, nū′klē ər) *adj.* **1.** of, relating to, or forming a nucleus. **2.** of, relating to, or involving atomic nuclei or energy derived from atomic nuclei: *a nuclear chain reaction, a nuclear weapon.* **3.** of, relating to, or having atomic weapons: *The United States is a nuclear power.*

nuclear energy, energy obtained from controlled nuclear fission or fusion. Also, **atomic energy.**

nuclear family, a social unit made up of a mother and father and their child or children, as opposed to an extended family.

nuclear fission, see **fission** *(def. 2).*

nuclear fusion, see **fusion** *(def. 5).*

nuclear physics, a branch of physics that deals with the structure and properties of atomic nuclei. ▲ used with a singular verb.

nuclear power, power produced by a nuclear reactor; heat, electricity, or other forms of power obtained from nuclear energy. Also, **atomic power.**

nuclear reactor, a device in which a nuclear chain reaction can be begun, continued, and controlled. It is used for generating heat or producing useful radiation. Also, **atomic reactor.**

nuclear winter, a period of extreme cold, darkness, and destruction of life that some scientists believe would result from widespread explosions of nuclear weapons in a war and the formation of vast clouds of dust and smoke that would block heat from the sun.

nu·cle·i (nü′klē ī′, nū′klē ī′) a plural of **nucleus.**

nu·cle·ic acid (nü klē′ik, nū klē′ik) a group of complex organic compounds found in all living cells, that determine and transmit the inherited traits of all living things. The two main types are DNA and RNA.

nu·cle·o·lus (nü klē′ə ləs, nū klē′ə ləs) *n., pl.* **nu·cle·o·li** (nü klē′ə lī′, nū klē′ə lī). a small rounded body in the nucleus of a cell that contains genetic material and is involved in reproduction.

nu·cle·on (nü′klē on′, nū′klē on′) *n.* a proton or neutron, especially one that is a part of the atomic nucleus.

nu·cle·o·tide (nü′klē ə tīd′, nū′klē ə tīd′) *n.* any of various organic compounds that are the fundamental building blocks of the nucleic acids that make up DNA and RNA. Nucleotides are composed of a sugar, phosphate, and one of five different nitrogen bases.

nu·cle·us (nü′klē əs, nū′klē əs) *n., pl.* **nu·cle·i** or **nu·cle·us·es.** **1.** a central or necessary part around which other parts are grouped or collected; core: *The nucleus of the building is a large open court. These valuable books form the nucleus of a fine library.* **2.** a small, dense, usually round or oval body located near the center of a plant or animal cell, surrounded by a delicate membrane and containing most of the cell's hereditary material. The

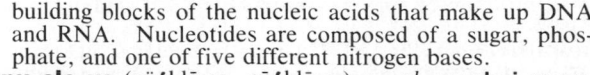

Nucleus (protons and neutrons)

Electrons

nucleus *(def. 3)*

nucleus is necessary for growth, reproduction, metabolism, and other vital activities. **3.** the positively charged central portion of an atom, containing most of the atom's mass and consisting of protons and neutrons, except in that of hydrogen, which consists of only one proton. [From the Latin word *nucleus* meaning "kernel, little nut," from the word *nux* "nut."]

nude (nüd, nūd) *adj.* without clothing or other covering; unclothed; bare. —*n.* **1.** an unclothed human figure, especially one represented in a painting or other work of art. **2.** the state of being unclothed: *in the nude.* —**nude′ly,** *adv.* —**nude′ness,** *n.*

nudge (nuj) *v.t.,* **nudged, nudg·ing.** to push gently or touch, especially in order to attract attention: *My friend nudged me with an elbow when I fell asleep in class.* —*n.* a gentle push or touch.

nu·di·ty (nü′di tē, nū′di tē) *n.* the state of being nude; nakedness.

nug·get (nug′it) *n.* **1.** a lump, especially a lump of gold as it is found in nature. **2.** something small but useful or valuable: *nuggets of information.*

nui·sance (nü′səns, nū′səns) *n.* a person, thing, or action that annoys or offends: *The child next door is a nuisance with that radio.*

null (nul) *adj.* **1.** without force or authority; invalid; ineffective: *That theory was proved to be null.* **2.** amounting to nothing; nonexistent; nil. **3.** *Mathematics.* of or relating to a set that contains no elements or members.

· **null and void.** without legal force; invalid: *After one year, this contract will be null and void.*

nul·li·fi·ca·tion (nul′ə fi kā′shən) *n.* **1.** the act of nullifying or the state of being nullified. **2.** the refusal of a state to recognize or enforce a federal law within its borders.

nul·li·fy (nul′ə fī′) *v.t.,* **nul·li·fied, nul·li·fy·ing.** **1.** to make void; declare invalid; annul: *to nullify a law.* **2.** to cause to amount to nothing; make ineffective: *Their mistake was so serious that it nullified all the good work they had done.* —**nul′li·fi′er,** *n.*

numb (num) *adj.* lacking or having lost feeling or movement: *to be numb with cold, to be numb with fear.*

---

at; āpe; fär; câre; end; mē; it; īce; pîerce; hot; ōld; sông, fôrk; oil; out; up; ūse; rüle; pull; tûrn; chin; sing; shop; thin; <u>th</u>is; hw in white; zh in treasure. The symbol ə stands for the unstressed vowel sound heard in about, taken, pencil, lemon, and circus.

N

647

—*v.t.* to make numb. —**numb'ly,** *adv.* —**numb'ness,** *n.*

num·ber (num′bər) *n.* **1.** a mathematical idea that shows how many units or objects are contained in a certain group; something that tells how many members there are in a set. **2.** a word or symbol, or group of words or symbols, representing such an idea; numeral. **3.** a specified amount, as of persons or things; total; sum: *The host increased the number of invited guests to thirty.* **4.** an unspecified amount, as of persons or things; quantity: *A number of people gathered in front of the store.* **5.** a numeral given to or identifying a person or thing: *What is the number of your hotel room?* **6.** one of the songs or other musical compositions on a program. **7.** a single issue of a magazine. **8.** *Grammar.* a form or property of a word that indicates whether the word is singular or plural. **9. numbers.** strength based on size or amount: *The army overpowered the invaders by force of numbers.* **10. numbers.** arithmetic. —*v.t.* **1.** to find out the number of; count. **2.** to give a number or numbers to. **3.** to amount to or include: *The freshman class numbers a thousand students.* **4.** to limit the number of: *The days are numbered before summer vacation ends.* —*v.i.* **1.** to amount to a group or total: *The contest winners numbered in the hundreds.* **2.** to list or recite numbers. —**num'ber·er,** *n.* ▲ See **amount** for usage note.

·**beyond number** or **without number.** too many to be counted.

num·ber·less (num′bər lis) *adj.* **1.** too many to be counted; innumerable: *The sky was filled with numberless stars.* **2.** without a number.

number line, a line on which points are identified with real numbers.

Num·bers (num′bərz) *n.* the fourth book of the Old Testament.

-4 -3 -2 -1 0 1 2 3 4

number line

numb·skull (num′-skul′) see **numskull.**

nu·mer·a·ble (nü′mər ə bəl, nū′mər ə bəl) *adj.* capable of being counted.

nu·mer·al (nü′mər əl, nū′mər əl) *n.* **1.** a symbol or a group of symbols representing a number, such as 7 or VII. **2.** a word standing for such a symbol, such as *seven.* —*adj.* of, relating to, or representing a number or numbers.

nu·mer·ate (nü′mə rāt′, nū′mə rāt′) *v.i.,* **nu·mer·at·ed, nu·mer·at·ing.** to number; count. —**nu′mer·a′tion,** *n.*

nu·mer·a·tor (nü′mə rā′tər, nū′mə rā′tər) *n.* the number above or to the left of the line in a fraction, indicating the number of equal parts being considered; dividend. In the fraction ½, 1 is the numerator.

nu·mer·i·cal (nü mer′i kəl, nū mer′i kəl) *adj.* of, relating to, or represented by a number or numbers. —**nu·mer′i·cal·ly,** *adv.*

nu·mer·ous (nü′mər əs, nū′mər əs) *adj.* **1.** forming a large number; many: *We visited them on numerous occasions.* **2.** containing a large number; large: *We have a numerous collection of antiques.* —**nu′mer·ous·ly,** *adv.* —**nu′mer·ous·ness,** *n.*

nu·mis·mat·ics (nü′miz mat′iks, nū′miz mat′iks) *n.* the collecting or study of coins, paper money, or medals. ▲ used with a singular verb. —**nu′mis·mat′ic,** *adj.* —**nu·mis·ma·tist** (nü miz′mə tist, nū miz′mə tist), *n.*

num·skull (num′skul′) also, **numb·skull.** *n.* a stupid person; blockhead.

nun (nun) *n.* a member of a religious order for women, usually living under vows in a convent and leading a life of prayer and good works.

nun·ci·o (nun′shē ō′) *n., pl.* **nun·ci·os.** a permanent ambassador representing the pope in a foreign country.

nun·ner·y (nun′ə rē) *n., pl.* **nun·ner·ies.** the residence of a group of nuns; convent.

nup·tial (nup′shəl) *adj.* of or relating to marriage or the marriage ceremony: *nuptial bliss, the nuptial feast.* —*n. usually,* **nuptials.** the marriage ceremony; wedding.

nurse (nûrs) *n.* **1.** a person who is trained to attend the sick or injured, usually under the direction of a doctor. **2.** a woman hired to take care of children; nursemaid. —*v.,* **nursed, nurs·ing.** —*v.t.* **1.** to take care of (the sick or injured); act as a nurse for. **2.** to feed (a baby) from the breast; suckle. **3.** to try to cure or heal (an illness or injury): *to nurse a sore throat with aspirin and plenty of rest.* **4.** to handle or use with care: *to nurse a weak knee by limping slightly.* **5.** to aid in the growth or development of; foster: *to nurse a small tree, to nurse a talent.* —*v.i.* **1.** to work as a nurse. **2.** to suckle a baby. **3.** to be fed from the breast.

nurse·maid (nûrs′mād′) *n.* a woman hired to take care of children.

nurs·er·y (nûr′sə rē) *n., pl.* **nurs·er·ies. 1.** a room set apart for small children, especially a baby's bedroom. **2.** a place where plants, especially trees and shrubs, are raised for sale.

nurs·er·y·man (nûr′sə rē mən) *n., pl.* **nurs·er·y·men** (nûr′sə rē mən). a person who owns or works in a nursery that raises and sells plants.

nursery rhyme, a short, rhymed poem or jingle for young children.

nursery school, another word for **preschool.**

nursing home, an institution for the long-term housing and care of people who cannot care for themselves, such as those who are chronically ill.

nurs·ling (nûrs′ling) *n.* **1.** a baby who is being nursed. **2.** a person or thing that receives careful and loving attention.

nur·ture (nûr′chər) *v.t.,* **nur·tured, nur·tur·ing. 1.** to take care of; nourish; feed. **2.** to educate, develop, or foster: *to nurture a talent.* —*n.* **1.** something that nourishes; food. **2.** an act or instance of educating, developing, or fostering. —**nur′tur·er,** *n.*

nut (nut) *n.* **1.** the dry, one-seeded fruit of a plant, having a hard, woody shell. **2.** the kernel of such a fruit. **3.** a block of metal or wood with a screw thread around an opening in the center, into which the threaded end of a bolt fits. **4.** *Slang.* a strange or crazy person. **5.** *Slang.* an enthusiast; devotee; buff: *a jazz nut.* —*v.i.,* **nut·ted, nut·ting.** to hunt for or gather nuts. —**nut′like′,** *adj.*

nut·crack·er (nut′krak′ər) *n.* **1.** a device for cracking nuts. **2.** a bird related to the crow, having a long, pointed bill. Nutcrackers feed on pine seeds and nuts.

nut·hatch (nut′hach′) *n., pl.* **nut·hatch·es.** any of various small, lively birds that can climb up and down tree trunks and walk upside down on branches. They feed on insects.

nut·meat (nut′mēt′) *n.* the edible part of a nut.

nutcracker *(def. 2)*

nut·meg (nut′meg′) *n.* **1.** a hard, aromatic seed of an evergreen tree, dried and ground or grated and used as a spice. **2.** the tree bearing this seed, having light green or yellowish green leaves and yellow flowers.

nu·tri·a (nü′trē ə, nū′trē ə) *n.* a large South American rodent that lives near water and closely resembles the beaver. It is valued for its thick, brown to black fur. Also, **coypu.**

nu·tri·ent (nü′trē ənt, nū′trē ənt) *adj.* giving nourishment; nutritious. —*n.* a nutritious substance that is needed by the body. Proteins, fats, carbohydrates, minerals, and vitamins are all nutrients.

nu·tri·ment (nü′trə mənt, nū′trə mənt) *n.* anything that nourishes; food.

nu·tri·tion (nü trish′ən, nū trish′ən) *n.* **1.** the process by which nutrients are taken and absorbed into body tissues. **2.** nourishment. **3.** the science or study of food and its effect on the body.

nu·tri·tious (nü trish′əs, nū trish′əs) *adj.* containing or giving nourishment; nourishing: *nutritious food.* —**nu·tri′tious·ly,** *adv.* —**nu·tri′tious·ness,** *n.*

nu·tri·tive (nü′tri tiv, nū′tri tiv) *adj.* **1.** giving nourishment; nutritious: *a nutritive diet.* **2.** of or relating to nutrition. —**nu′tri·tive·ly,** *adv.*

nuts (nuts) *adj. Slang.* **1.** eccentric or crazy. **2.** in love with or very enthusiastic: *I'm nuts about baseball.*

nuts and bolts, the basic facts and details; practicalities: *to learn the nuts and bolts of a business.* —**nuts-and-bolts,** *adj.*

nut·shell (nut′shel′) *n..* the hard shell of a nut.
  ·**in a nutshell.** in a few words: *The book review gave the author's ideas in a nutshell.*

nut·ty (nut′ē) *adj.,* **nut·ti·er, nut·ti·est. 1.** filled with or producing nuts. **2.** having the flavor of nuts. **3.** *Slang.* strange or crazy; nuts: —**nut′ti·ly,** *adv.* —**nut′ti·ness,** *n.*

nuz·zle (nuz′əl) *v.,* **nuz·zled, nuz·zling.** —*v.t.* to touch or rub with the nose: *The dog nuzzled its owner.* —*v.i.* to press or lie close; nestle; cuddle: *The child nuzzled against my shoulder.*

NV, postal abbreviation for Nevada.

NW, northwest; northwestern.

N.W.T., Northwest Territories.

NY, postal abbreviation for New York.

N.Y., New York.

N.Y.C., New York City.

ny·lon (nī′lon) *n.* **1.** any of a group of strong, synthetic substances that are used to make thread for fabric, bristles for brushes, handles for tools, and other products. **2.** a fabric woven with threads made from this substance. **3. nylons.** stockings that are made of nylon.

nymph (nimf) *n.* **1.** *Greek and Roman Mythology.* any of various goddesses that were believed to live in forests, hills, or rivers, and usually represented as beautiful maidens. **2.** a beautiful young woman. **3.** the larva of any of various insects, such as the dragonfly and cicada, that resembles the adult and goes through gradual changes to reach the adult stage. —**nymph′like′,** *adj.*

N.Z., New Zealand.

---

at; āpe; fär; câre; end; mē; it; īce; pîerce; hot; ōld; sông, fôrk; oil; out; up; ūse; rüle; pùll; tûrn; chin; sing; shop; thin; <u>th</u>is; hw in white; zh in treasure. The symbol ə stands for the unstressed vowel sound heard in about, taken, pencil, lemon, and circus.

N

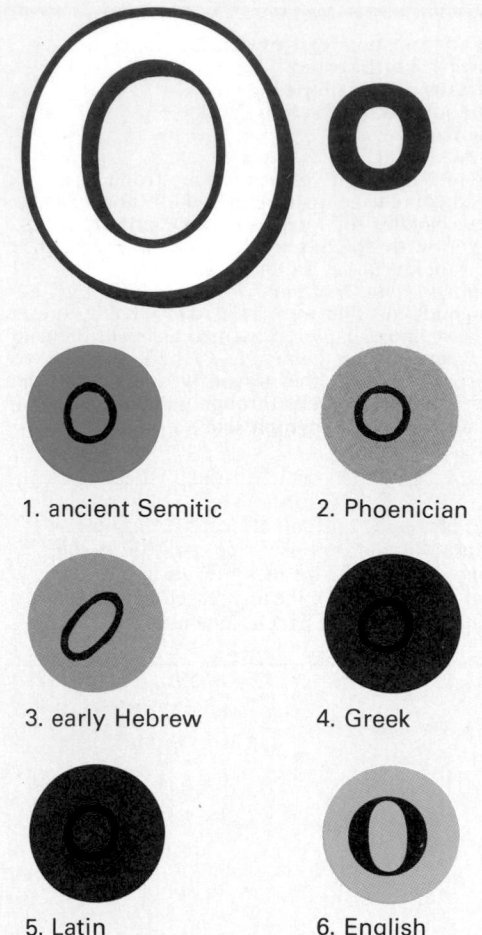

1. ancient Semitic
2. Phoenician
3. early Hebrew
4. Greek
5. Latin
6. English

O is the fifteenth letter of the English alphabet. It is one of the very few letters whose written form has remained almost unchanged throughout the history of the alphabet. The earliest form of the letter **O** was the ancient Semitic (1) letter *ayin*, meaning "eye," which stood for a breathing sound. A similar letter appeared in the Phoenician (2) and early Hebrew (3) alphabets. When the Greeks adopted *ayin* for their own alphabet, they used it to represent the short *o* sound and called it *omicron* (4). In Greek, *omicron* literally meant "small *o*" to distinguish it from the Greek letter for the long *o* sound called *omega*, meaning "great *o*." The Romans (5) borrowed *omicron* from the Greeks and by the fourth century B.C. were writing it almost exactly the way we write the capital letter **O** today (6).

o, O (ō) *n., pl.* **o's, O's.** **1.** the fifteenth letter of the English alphabet. **2.** something having the shape of this letter. **3.** zero.

O (ō) *interj.* **1.** used in formal address: *O heart, how fares it with thee now?* (Alfred, Lord Tennyson). **2.** another spelling of **oh.**

o' (ə, ō) *prep.* of: *will-o'-the-wisp.*

O, the symbol for oxygen.

oaf (ōf) *n.* a stupid, clumsy person. —**oaf'ish,** *adj.*

oak (ōk) *n.* **1.** any of a large group of trees or shrubs bearing acorns and found especially in northern temperate regions. **2.** the hard, strong wood of this tree, used for making furniture, flooring, and boats. —*adj.* made of oak: *an oak table.*

oak·en (ō'kən) *adj.* made of oak: *an oaken chair.*

oa·kum (ō'kəm) *n.* a loose fiber obtained by untwisting and picking apart old ropes. It is often used for filling up seams and cracks in a wooden boat or ship.

oar (ôr) *n.* **1.** a long, usually wooden pole with a flat or curved blade at one end, used to row or steer a boat. **2.** a person who rows a boat; rower. —*v.t.* to propel with oars; row. —*v.i.* to move by rowing.

oar·lock (ôr'lok') *n.* a device, usually Y-shaped, for holding an oar in place while rowing. Also, **rowlock.**

oars·man (ôrz'mən) *n., pl.* **oars·men** (ôrz'mən). a person who rows a boat.

OAS, Organization of American States.

o·a·sis (ō ā'sis) *n., pl.* **o·a·ses** (ō ā'sēz). **1.** a place in a desert that is fertile because it has a supply of water. **2.** any place or condition that provides refreshment or relief: *The library was an oasis of quiet in the noisy city.*

oat (ōt) *n.* **1.** *also,* **oats.** the cereal grain of a plant of the grass family. It is used as food and as fodder for horses. **2.** *also,* **oats.** the plant bearing this grain, having slender, flat, bluish green leaves.

oat·en (ō'tən) *adj.* relating to, containing, or made of oats, oatmeal, or oat straw.

oath (ōth) *n., pl.* **oaths** (ōthz, ōths). **1.** a formal declaration that is made with an appeal to God or to an honored or sacred person or thing to witness the fact that one will tell the truth or keep a promise. **2.** the use of the name of God or an honored or sacred person or thing to add emphasis or express anger. **3.** a word used in swearing; curse.

·**under oath.** bound by an oath to tell the truth.

oat·meal (ōt'mēl') *n.* **1.** a meal made by grinding or rolling oats. **2.** a cooked cereal prepared from this.

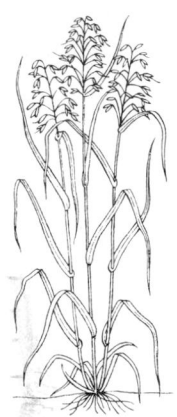

oat *(def. 2)*

O·ba·di·ah (ō'bə dī'ə) *n.* a book of the Old Testament containing prophecies attributed to the prophet Obadiah.

ob·bli·ga·to (ob'li gä'tō) *Music. adj.* (of an accompaniment or part) necessary for the performance of a composition. —*n., pl.* **ob·bli·ga·tos.** an obbligato accompaniment or part.

ob·du·ra·cy (ob'dər ə sē, ob'dyər ə sē) *n.* the state or quality of being obdurate.

ob·du·rate (ob'dər it, ob'dyər it) *adj.* **1.** not yielding; stubborn; obstinate: *an obdurate denial of the truth, an obdurate opponent.* **2.** unmoved by feelings of pity or regret; hardhearted: *an obdurate attitude.* —**ob'du·rate·ly,** *adv.* —**ob'du·rate·ness,** *n.*

o·be·di·ence (ō bē'dē əns) *n.* the act of obeying or the state of being obedient.

o·be·di·ent (ō bē'dē ənt) *adj.* tending or willing to obey or submit to something, such as a rule, order, or law: *We trained our dog to be obedient. Everyone admires an obedient child.* —**o·be'di·ent·ly,** *adv.*

o·bei·sance (ō bā′səns, o bē′səns) *n.* **1.** a movement or gesture of the body showing obedience or respect, such as a bow or curtsy. **2.** deference, respect, or regard given or shown; homage: *to pay obeisance to an important person.*

ob·e·lisk (ob′ə lisk′) *n.* a four-sided stone pillar that narrows as it rises and is shaped like a pyramid at the top. It was often used as a monument in ancient Egypt.

O·ber·on (ō′bə ron′) *n. Medieval Legend.* the king of the fairies.

o·bese (ō bēs′) *adj.* extremely fat or fleshy. —**o·bese′-ness,** *n.*

o·bes·i·ty (ō bē′si tē) *n.* the condition of being obese.

o·bey (ō bā′) *v.t.* **1.** to carry out the orders, requests, or instructions of: *to obey one's parents.* **2.** to carry out or comply with: *to obey the law, to obey orders.* **3.** to be guided or controlled by: *to obey one's conscience.* —*v.i.* to be obedient.

obis

o·bi (ō′bē) *n.* a broad sash worn with a Japanese kimono.

o·bit·u·ar·y (ō bich′ü er′ē) *n., pl.* **o·bit·u·ar·ies.** a notice of a person's death, especially in a newspaper, often including a short biography. —*adj.* relating to or recording a death.

obj. **1.** object. **2.** objection. **3.** objective.

ob·ject (*n.,* ob′jikt; *v.,* əb jekt′) *n.* **1.** anything that can be seen or touched and that can be differentiated from other things around it; material thing: *I have a large, round object in my hand. What is that object in the water?* **2.** a person or thing toward which feeling, thought, or action is directed: *The scientist's theory was the object of much criticism.* **3.** a thing desired or aimed at; purpose; goal: *The object of my telephone call was to invite you to the party.* **4.** *Grammar.* **a.** a word or group of words that receive or are affected by the action of the verb. **b.** a word or group of words that follow and are affected by a preposition. —*v.i.* **1.** to have or raise an objection: *The colonists objected to the tax on tea.* **2.** to express or feel disapproval: *We objected to their rudeness.* —**ob·jec′tor,** *n.*

ob·jec·tion (əb jek′shən) *n.* **1.** a cause or reason for opposing, disliking, or disapproving of something: *Their objection to the parade was its cost.* **2.** a feeling of opposition, dislike, or disapproval: *We left the party to show our objection to their drinking beer and behaving foolishly.*

ob·jec·tion·a·ble (əb jek′shə nə bəl) *adj.* deserving of or causing dislike or disapproval; offensive: *objectionable behavior.* —**ob·jec′tion·a·bly,** *adv.*

ob·jec·tive (əb jek′tiv) *adj.* **1.** not affected or influenced by personal feelings or opinions; without bias; detached: *The reporter tried to be as objective as possible.* **2.** having actual existence independent of the mind; real: *The child's fear of the dark isn't based on objective fact.* **3.** *Grammar.* designating the case of the object of a verb or preposition. —*n.* **1.** something toward which effort is directed. **2.** *Grammar.* **a.** the objective case. **b.** a word in this case; object. **3.** a lens or lenses nearest to the object being observed through an optical instrument, such as a telescope, microscope, or camera. —**ob·jec′tive·ly,** *adv.* —**ob·jec′tive·ness,** *n.*

ob·jec·tiv·i·ty (ob′jek tiv′i tē) *n.* the state or quality of being objective.

object lesson, a practical illustration of some principle or truth.

ob·jet d'art (ob zhä där′) *n., pl.* **ob·jets d'art** (ob zhä-där′). *French.* an object, such as a vase, that has artistic value.

ob·li·gate (ob′li gāt′) *v.t.,* **ob·li·gat·ed, ob·li·gat·ing.** to bind morally or legally, as by a contract, promise, or sense of duty: *A driver is obligated to obey the traffic laws.*

ob·li·ga·tion (ob′li gā′shən) *n.* **1.** a binding power, as of a law, promise, or sense of duty: *We are under an obligation to them for lending us the money.* **2.** something that one is morally or legally bound to do: *It is the obligation of doctors to help the sick.* **3.** the fact or condition of being grateful or indebted to another for something received: *I feel a deep sense of obligation toward my parents.* **4.** something by which one is bound, such as a promise or sense of duty or responsibility: *to feel an obligation to repay a friend's loan.*

ob·lig·a·to·ry (ə blig′ə tôr′ē) *adj.* of the nature of or being an obligation; compulsory.

o·blige (ə blīj′) *v.t.,* **o·bliged, o·blig·ing.** **1.** to bind or compel, as by moral or legal force: *I was obliged to pay for the window I broke.* **2.** to place under an obligation, as for a favor or service; make indebted or grateful: *I am obliged to you for all your help.* **3.** to do a favor or service for: *Please oblige me by returning this book to the library.*

o·blig·ing (ə blī′jing) *adj.* willing to do favors or to be of service; helpful. —**o·blig′ing·ly,** *adv.*

ob·lique (ə blēk′) *adj.* **1.** having a slanting or sloping direction, position, or course; inclined: *an oblique line.* **2.** not straightforward or direct: *an oblique answer to a question.* —*n.* something that is oblique, as a line. —**ob·lique′ly,** *adv.*

oblique angle, any angle that is not a right angle; acute angle or obtuse angle.

ob·lit·er·ate (ə blit′ə rāt′) *v.t.,* **ob·lit·er·at·ed, ob·lit·er·at·ing.** **1.** to destroy completely; remove all traces of: *The heavy rains obliterated the footprints on the path.* **2.** to blot or rub out, as writing; erase. —**ob·lit·er·a′tion,** *n.*

ob·liv·i·on (ə bliv′ē ən) *n.* **1.** the state or condition of being entirely forgotten: *That author's works have passed into oblivion.* **2.** the state or condition of forgetting completely; forgetfulness.

ob·liv·i·ous (ə bliv′ē əs) *adj.* not aware or conscious; unmindful: *to be oblivious to a noise.* —**ob·liv′i·ous·ly,** *adv.* —**ob·liv′i·ous·ness,** *n.*

ob·long (ob′lông′) *adj.* having greater length than width,

0

at; āpe; fär; câre; end; mē; it; īce; pîerce; hot; ōld; sông, fôrk; oil; out; up; ūse; rüle; pull; tûrn; chin; sing; shop; thin; **th**is; hw in white; zh in treasure. The symbol ə stands for the unstressed vowel sound heard in about, taken, pencil, lemon, and circus.

as an ellipse and certain rectangles. —*n.* an oblong figure.

ob·lo·quy (ob′lə kwē) *n., pl.* **ob·lo·quies. 1.** abusive, slanderous language addressed to or aimed at another, especially by a large number of people. **2.** the disgrace or shame resulting from such abuse.

ob·nox·ious (ob nok′shəs) *adj.* extremely annoying, disagreeable, or offensive: *That bully is an obnoxious person.* —**ob·nox′ious·ly,** *adv.* —**ob·nox′ious·ness,** *n.*

o·boe (ō′bō) *n.* a woodwind instrument having a double reed, high pitch, and a penetrating tone.

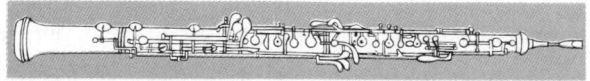

oboe

ob·scene (əb sēn′) *adj.* offensive to modesty or decency; indecent. —**ob·scene′ly,** *adv.*

ob·scen·i·ty (əb sen′i tē) *n., pl.* **ob·scen·i·ties. 1.** the state or quality of being obscene; indecency. **2.** something that is obscene, as an act, expression, or word.

ob·scure (əb skyůr′) *adj.,* **ob·scur·er, ob·scur·est. 1.** not clearly expressed; difficult to understand: *an obscure explanation.* **2.** barely perceived by the senses; not clear or distinct: *an obscure figure in a photograph.* **3.** not well-known; undistinguished: *an obscure writer.* **4.** not easily noticed or discovered; remote; hidden: *an obscure mountain village.* **5.** having little or no light; dark; dim: *an obscure corner of a cellar.* —*v.t.,* **ob·scured, ob·scur·ing. 1.** to hide from view; darken or conceal: *Fog obscured the sun.* **2.** to make difficult to understand: *The speaker's frequent use of unfamiliar words obscured the meaning.* —**ob·scure′ly,** *adv.* —**ob·scure′ness,** *n.*

ob·scu·ri·ty (əb skyůr′i tē) *n., pl.* **ob·scu·ri·ties. 1.** the state or quality of being obscure. **2.** a person or thing that is obscure.

ob·se·quies (ob′si kwēz) *pl. n.* funeral rites or services.

ob·se·qui·ous (əb sē′kwē əs) *adj.* too willing or eager to serve, please, or obey; fawning. —**ob·se′qui·ous·ly,** *adv.* —**ob·se′qui·ous·ness,** *n.*

ob·serv·a·ble (əb zûr′və bəl) *adj.* **1.** that can be observed; noticeable: *There was an observable change in temperature.* **2.** that may, should, or must be observed, celebrated, followed, or kept: *Certain formalities are observable in a court of law.* —**ob·serv′a·bly,** *adv.*

ob·serv·ance (əb zûr′vəns) *n.* **1.** the act or practice of following, keeping to, or complying with a rule or law: *The police enforce the observance of the speed limit.* **2.** the act or practice of keeping or celebrating a customary rite, ceremony, or holiday: *the observance of religious feasts.* **3.** a customary rite, ceremony, or celebration: *Birthdays are annual observances.* **4.** the act of noticing or perceiving; observation.

ob·serv·ant (əb zûr′vənt) *adj.* **1.** quick to notice or perceive; alert: *An observant reader found a misspelling in the book.* **2.** careful in observing anything required, as a rule, law, or custom: *A good citizen must be observant of the laws.* —**ob·serv′ant·ly,** *adv.*

ob·ser·va·tion (ob′zər vā′shən) *n.* **1.** the act, practice, or power of seeing and noticing: *The detective's careful observation helped to solve the crime.* **2.** the fact or condition of being observed; notice: *The thief escaped observation.* **3.** the act of examining, noting, and recording facts or occurrences, especially for scientific study: *The scientist went to the laboratory for hourly observations of the experiment.* **4.** something recorded as a result of observing: *a neatly written observation.* **5.** a remark or comment: *observations about a baseball game.* —**ob′-ser·va′tion·al,** *adj.*

ob·serv·a·to·ry (əb zûr′və tôr′ē) *n., pl.* **ob·serv·a·to·ries. 1.** a place or building furnished with telescopes and other equipment for observing, studying, and collecting information on the moon, planets, or stars. **2.** a building or place equipped for observing the weather. **3.** any place or building providing a wide view.

ob·serve (əb zûrv′) *v.t.,* **ob·served, ob·serv·ing. 1.** to see or notice: *to observe someone entering a house.* **2.** to watch carefully; regard with attention: *Observe how much parsley I add to the sauce.* **3.** to make a careful observation of, especially for a scientific purpose: *The scientist observed the behavior of the mice after they were given the drug.* **4.** to follow or comply with, as a rule or law: *to observe the speed limit.* **5.** to keep or celebrate: *to observe Thanksgiving.* **6.** to comment; remark: *"It might rain tonight,"* I observed. —**ob·serv′er,** *n.*

ob·sess (əb ses′) *v.t.* to occupy or trouble the mind of: *A fear of failure obsessed the student.*

ob·ses·sion (əb sesh′ən) *n.* **1.** the act of obsessing or the state of being obsessed. **2.** something that obsesses, as a fixed idea or desire: *Making a great deal of money is an obsession of that business executive.*

ob·ses·sive (əb ses′iv) *adj.* of, relating to, or caused by an obsession: *an obsessive interest in clothes.*

ob·sid·i·an (ob sid′ē ən) *n.* a hard, glassy rock, usually black, formed when molten lava cools.

ob·so·les·cent (ob′sə les′ənt) *adj.* going out of use; becoming out of date or obsolete: *an obsolescent word.* —**ob′so·les′cence,** *n.*

ob·so·lete (ob′sə lēt′, ob′sə lēt′) *adj.* **1.** no longer in use or practice: *Stagecoaches are obsolete.* **2.** out-of-date; old-fashioned; outmoded: *obsolete customs, obsolete slang.*

Language Note

Obsolete words are words that at one time were part of the standard English vocabulary but that are no longer used. There are various reasons why words become obsolete. Over a period of time, a concept or idea itself can become obsolete. When this happens, the words that describe such a concept or idea will most likely become obsolete, too. For example, many words that referred to knighthood are no longer used today. Rare words often become obsolete, sometimes quite soon after they are introduced into a language. Duplication of words also can cause one or the other to become obsolete. For example, Old English had a word *ei* meaning "egg." When we borrowed the Norse word *egg,* it competed with the earlier word *ei* for some time, but eventually we kept *egg* and *ei* became obsolete.

Slang words become obsolete more quickly than any other type of word. Unlike most words that are part of standard English, slang words lack a secure position in the language, and slang that is fashionable for a time may quickly fall into disuse. Very few slang words ever become a permanent part of our language.

ob·sta·cle (ob′stə kəl) *n.* a person or thing that opposes, stands in the way, or blocks progress: *The heavy snow was an obstacle to traffic.*

ob·stet·ric (ob stet′rik) *adj.* of or relating to obstetrics and childbirth. Also, **ob·stet·ri·cal** (ob stet′ri kəl).

ob·ste·tri·cian (ob′sti trish′ən) *n.* a physician specializing in obstetrics.

ob·stet·rics (ob stet′riks) *n.* the branch of medicine that deals with the care of women from the first sign of pregnancy until a few weeks after the baby is born. ▲ used with a singular verb.

ob·sti·na·cy (ob'stə nə sē) *n.*, *pl.* **ob·sti·na·cies.**
1. the state or quality of being obstinate; stubbornness.
2. an act or instance of this.

ob·sti·nate (ob'stə nit) *adj.* **1.** not yielding to argument, persuasion, or reason; stubborn; inflexible: *an obstinate person.* **2.** difficult to overcome, control, or cure: *an obstinate cough.* —**ob'sti·nate·ly,** *adv.*

ob·strep·er·ous (əb strep'ər əs) *adj.* noisy, boisterous, or unruly: *The speaker could not quiet the obstreperous heckler.* —**ob·strep'er·ous·ly,** *adv.* —**ob·strep'er·ous·ness,** *n.*

ob·struct (əb strukt') *v.t.* **1.** to block or fill with obstacles that prevent passage: *Large boulders obstructed the entrance to the cave.* **2.** to be or come in the way of: *The hat obstructed my view of the stage.* **3.** to interrupt, interfere with, or delay the progress of: *to obstruct justice.* —**ob·struc'tive,** *adj.*

ob·struc·tion (əb struk'shən) *n.* **1.** something that obstructs: *The soldiers set up blockades and other obstructions on the road to the city.* **2.** the act of obstructing or the state of being obstructed.

ob·struc·tion·ism (əb struk'shə niz'əm) *n.* the act or practice of obstructing work or progress, especially in a meeting or legislature. —**ob·struc'tion·ist,** *n.*

ob·tain (əb tān') *v.t.* to get as one's own, especially as a result of effort; gain possession of; acquire: *to obtain permission to do something.* —*v.i.* to be widespread, established, or customary: *That custom still obtains in many small towns.* —**ob·tain'a·ble,** *adj.*

ob·trude (əb trüd') *v.,* **ob·trud·ed, ob·trud·ing.** —*v.t.* **1.** to force or thrust upon another or others in a rude or bold manner: *to obtrude one's opinions on others.* **2.** to push out; thrust forward. —*v.i.* to force oneself upon another or others.

ob·tru·sion (əb trü'zhən) *n.* **1.** the act of obtruding. **2.** something obtruded.

ob·tru·sive (əb trü'siv) *adj.* tending to obtrude; forward. —**ob·tru'sive·ly,** *adv.* —**ob·tru'sive·ness,** *n.*

ob·tuse (əb tüs', əb tūs') *adj.* **1.** slow in understanding or sensing; dull or stupid. **2.** not sharp or pointed; blunt. **3.** (of a triangle) having an obtuse angle. —**ob·tuse'ly,** *adv.* —**ob·tuse'ness,** *n.*

obtuse angle, an angle that is greater than 90 degrees but less than 180 degrees.

ob·verse (*n.,* ob'vûrs; *adj.,* ob vûrs') *n.* **1.** the side of a coin or medal that bears the main design. **2.** the front or main side of anything. —*adj.* turned toward or facing the observer. —**ob·verse'ly,** *adv.*

ob·vi·ate (ob'vē āt') *v.t.,* **ob·vi·at·ed, ob·vi·at·ing.** to anticipate and prevent or remove; take care of beforehand: *to obviate a risk, to obviate a need.*

ob·vi·ous (ob'vē əs) *adj.* **1.** easily seen or understood; clearly evident: *to make one's feelings obvious.* **2.** not trying to hide one's feelings; without pretense: *to be obvious about one's anger.* —**ob'vi·ous·ly,** *adv.* —**ob'vi·ous·ness,** *n.*

oc·a·ri·na (ok'ə rē'nə) *n.* a musical wind instrument that has finger holes and produces a soft tone like that of a whistle when air is blown through the mouthpiece. Also, **sweet potato.**

oc·ca·sion (ə kā'zhən) *n.* **1.** the particular time at which something occurs: *I cannot remember the occasion when I met you.* **2.** an

Right angle   Obtuse angle

obtuse angle

ocarina

event or occurrence: *I congratulated the students on the occasion of their graduation.* **3.** an event or function thought of as being special or important: *The baby's first birthday was quite an occasion.* **4.** a favorable or suitable time; opportunity: *I don't have many occasions to be alone.* **5.** an immediate cause or reason: *The soldier's death was the occasion of much sadness.* —*v.t.* to be the cause of; bring about: *Their rudeness occasioned the quarrel.*

·**on occasion.** once in a while; at times; occasionally: *We see them on occasion.*

oc·ca·sion·al (ə kā'zhə nəl) *adj.* **1.** happening or appearing now and then; not frequent: *There will be occasional showers today.* **2.** produced or used for some special occasion or event: *The composer wrote an occasional song for the coronation.* **3.** (of furniture) not part of a set: *an occasional chair.*

oc·ca·sion·al·ly (ə kā'zhə nə lē) *adv.* once in a while; at times.

Oc·ci·dent (ok'si dənt) *n.* the countries of Europe and the Western Hemisphere.

Oc·ci·den·tal (ok'si den'təl) *also,* **oc·ci·den·tal.** *adj.* of, relating to, or characteristic of the Occident. —*n.* a member of a people native to the Occident.

oc·cip·i·tal (ok sip'i təl) *adj.* of or relating to the back part of the head or skull. —*n.* see **occipital bone.**

occipital bone, the bone located at the back of the skull.

oc·clude (ə klüd') *v.,* **oc·clud·ed, oc·clud·ing.** —*v.t.* **1.** to stop up, close, or block, as a passage or pore. **2.** to shut in, out, or off. **3.** of a chemical compound, to absorb and retain (another compound). **4.** of a mass of cold air, to force (warm air) upward from the surface of the earth. —*v.i.* of the teeth in the upper and lower jaws, to meet closely.

occluded front, a mass of air formed when a cold front collides with a warm front and pushes the warm air mass above the cold air.

oc·clu·sion (ə klü'zhən) *n.* the act of occluding or the state of being occluded.

oc·cult (ə kult', ok'ult) *adj.* **1.** of, relating to, or concerned with certain mystical arts or practices, as astrology or alchemy. **2.** beyond the range of human understanding; mysterious.

oc·cult·ism (ə kul'tiz əm, ok'əl tiz'əm) *n.* **1.** a belief in the existence of mysterious or hidden spiritual powers. **2.** the study or practice of occult arts.

oc·cu·pan·cy (ok'yə pən sē) *n.,* *pl.* **oc·cu·pan·cies.** **1.** the act of occupying or the state of being occupied. **2.** a period of time during which something is occupied: *The cabin was rented for a one-year occupancy.*

oc·cu·pant (ok'yə pənt) *n.* **1.** a person who occupies a place or position. **2.** a person having legal control or possession of a property, such as a house, office building, or apartment.

oc·cu·pa·tion (ok'yə pā'shən) *n.* **1.** the work that a person does to earn a living; profession; trade. **2.** the act of occupying or the state of being occupied. **3.** the act or process of seizing and maintaining control of enemy territory by a military force.

oc·cu·pa·tion·al (ok'yə pā'shə nəl) *adj.* of or resulting from one's occupation: *an occupational disease.*

0

at; āpe; fär; câre; end; mē; it; īce; pîerce; hot; ōld; sông, fôrk; oil; out; up; ūse; rüle; pull; tûrn; chin; sing; shop; thin; **th**is; hw in white; zh in treasure. The symbol ə stands for the unstressed vowel sound heard in about, taken, pencil, lemon, and circus.

653

oc·cu·py (ok′yə pī′) *v.t.*, **oc·cu·pied**, **oc·cu·py·ing**.
1. to take up (time or space): *Running errands occupied most of the morning.* **2.** to seize and maintain control of by military force: *Enemy troops occupied the town.* **3.** to live in; inhabit: *The family occupied a house.* **4.** to keep busy or engage: *to occupy oneself with a hobby.* **5.** to have and keep possession of: *to occupy a high government position.* —**oc′cu·pi′er**, *n.*

oc·cur (ə kûr′) *v.i.*, **oc·curred**, **oc·cur·ring**. **1.** to happen; take place; come to pass: *The explosion occurred at noon.* **2.** to appear or be found: *The same theme occurs in many novels.* **3.** to come to mind; suggest itself: *It did not occur to me to take my umbrella.*

oc·cur·rence (ə kûr′əns) *n.* **1.** the act or fact of occurring. **2.** something that occurs; incident: *There were stories of strange occurrences in the haunted house.*

o·cean (ō′shən) *n.* **1.** the whole body of salt water that covers nearly three fourths of the earth's surface. **2.** any one of the major subdivisions of this body of water, such as the Atlantic, Pacific, Indian, or Arctic Ocean.

o·ce·an·ic (ō′shē an′ik) *adj.* **1.** of, relating to, or living in the ocean: *oceanic fish.* **2.** like the ocean; vast.

o·cean·og·ra·phy (ō′shə nog′rə fē) *n.* the science of the oceans, dealing with the structure of the ocean basins, composition and movement of the waters, and oceanic life. —**o′cean·og′ra·pher**, *n.* —**o·cean·o·graph·ic** (ō′shə nə graf′ik), *adj.*

o·cel·lus (ō sel′əs) *n., pl.* **o·cel·li** (ō sel′ī). a simple kind of eye in insects and certain other animals without backbones, used to distinguish between light and dark.

o·ce·lot (os′ə lot′, ō′sə lot′) *n.* a wildcat native to Central and South America, having a yellowish coat marked with black spots, rings, and stripes.

o·cher (ō′kər) *also*, **o·chre**. *n.* **1.** a mixture of clay and iron oxides ranging in color from yellow to red, used as a pigment. **2.** a reddish yellow or brownish yellow color. —*adj.* having the color ocher.

ocelot

o′clock (ə klok′) *adv.*
1. of or according to the clock: *They will meet us at two o'clock.* **2.** a word used to indicate direction within a system in which orientation is based on the position of numbers on a clock face, with the number twelve pointed vertically or ahead: *an airplane approaching at two o'clock.* [Short for the phrase *of the clock.*]

Oct., October.

octa– *combining form* eight: *octagon.*

oc·ta·gon (ok′tə gon′) *n.* a polygon having eight sides and eight angles.

oc·tag·o·nal (ok tag′ə nəl) *adj.* having the shape of an octagon. —**oc·tag′o·nal·ly**, *adv.*

oc·tal (ok′təl) *adj.* **1.** relating to or based on the number 8. **2.** of or relating to a system of computation having the number 8 as its base.

oc·tane (ok′tān) *n.* a colorless, liquid hydrocarbon found in petroleum.

octane number, a number indicating the extent to which a motor fuel resists engine knocking. Fuel with a high octane number produces less knocking.

oc·tave (ok′tiv, ok′tāv) *n.* **1.** *Music.* **a.** the interval between the first and eighth tones or notes of the major scale. **b.** a tone or note having twice or half as many vibrations per second as the one below or above it at this interval. **c.** a combination of two tones or notes at this interval sounded together. **d.** a series of tones or notes or of keys of an instrument contained within this interval: *The singer's range is two octaves.* **2.** any group of eight.

oc·ta·vo (ok tā′vō, ok tä′vō) *n., pl.* **oc·ta·vos.** **1.** a paper or paper size, as of a book, usually measuring from 5 by 8 inches (12.7 by 20.3 centimeters) to 6 by 9½ inches (15.2 by 24.1 centimeters), formerly ⅛ of a whole printer's sheet. **2.** a book having pages this size.

oc·tet (ok tet′) *n.* **1.** *Music.* **a.** a composition for eight voices or instruments. **b.** a group of eight performers. **2.** any group of eight.

Oc·to·ber (ok tō′bər) *n.* the tenth month of the year, having thirty-one days. [From the Old French word *October,* from the Latin word *October,* the eighth month of the Roman calendar, from the word *octo* meaning "eight."]

oo·to·go·nar·i·an (ok′tə jə nâr′ē ən) *n.* a person who is eighty years old or between eighty and ninety years old. —*adj.* being eighty or between eighty and ninety years old.

oc·to·pus (ok′tə pəs) *n., pl.* **oc·to·pus·es** or **oc·to·pi** (ok′tə pī′). a saltwater animal having a soft, rounded body and eight arms, or tentacles, on which there are suckers that help it to move along the ocean bottom and to capture prey.

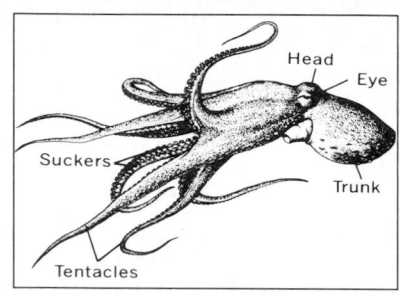

octopus

oc·u·lar (ok′yə lər) *adj.* **1.** of, relating to, or similar to the eye or eyesight. **2.** seen by the eye; visual: *ocular data.*

oc·u·list (ok′yə list) *n.* **1.** another word for **ophthalmologist.** **2.** another word for **optometrist.**

OD (ō′dē′) *n., pl.* **OD's.** *Slang.* an overdose of a drug, especially a narcotic. —*v.i.*, **OD'ed**, **OD'ing.** to take or receive an overdose of a drug.

odd (od) *adj.* **1.** differing from the usual or ordinary; strange; peculiar: *an odd remark, an odd way of dressing.* **2.** being what remains of a pair or set: *an odd shoe, an odd dish.* **3.** irregular; occasional: *I do odd jobs.* **4.** leaving a remainder of one when divided by two: *5, 7, and 187 are odd numbers.* **5.** with an indefinite amount in addition to a certain round number. ▲ often connected to a numeral by a hyphen: *I have forty-odd dollars in the bank.* **6.** left over; extra: *The odd guest at the dinner party made thirteen at the table.* —**odd′ly**, *adv.* —**odd′ness**, *n.*

odd·i·ty (od′i tē) *n., pl.* **odd·i·ties.** **1.** a person or thing that is odd or peculiar: *The collection of green flowers was an oddity.* **2.** the state or quality of being odd; strangeness.

odds (odz) *pl. n.* **1.** the difference in favor of or against something being true or happening, often stated in the form of a ratio: *The odds are ten to one against that horse winning the race.* **2.** an allowance or advantage given to the weaker opponent in a contest. **3.** a difference that favors one side over another; advantage: *The odds are against the weaker team.*

·**at odds.** in disagreement; quarreling.

odds and ends, miscellaneous or leftover items: *I bought a few odds and ends at the hardware store.*

ode (ōd) *n.* a dignified and lofty lyric poem, usually rhymed and often addressed to a person or thing.

O·din (ō′din) *n.* *Norse Mythology.* the king of the gods and god of wisdom and war. In Teutonic mythology he was called Woden.

o·di·ous (ō′dē əs) *adj.* causing hate, disgust, or repugnance; detestable: *an odious crime.* —**o′di·ous·ly**, *adv.* —**o′di·ous·ness**, *n.*

o·di·um (ō′dē əm) *n.* **1.** extreme hatred, disgust, or repugnance; detestation: *We view cruelty to animals with odium.* **2.** shame or disgrace: *the odium of being disloyal.*

o·dom·e·ter (ō dom′i tər) *n.* a device for measuring the distance traveled by a vehicle.

o·dor (ō′dər) *n.* **1.** the quality of a thing or substance that affects the sense of smell; scent. **2.** reputation or estimation. —**o′dor·less,** *adj.*

o·dor·if·er·ous (ō′də rif′ər əs) *adj.* having or giving off an odor, especially a pleasant one. —**o′dor·if′er·ous·ly,** *adv.* —**o′dor·if′er·ous·ness,** *n.*

o·dor·ous (ō′dər əs) *adj.* another word for **odoriferous.** —**o′dor·ous·ly,** *adv.* —**o′dor·ous·ness,** *n.*

O·dys·se·us (ō dis′ē əs) *n.* another name for **Ulysses.**

Od·ys·sey (od′ə sē) *n., pl.* **Od·ys·seys. 1.** an ancient Greek epic poem describing the adventures of Odysseus after the Trojan War. It is thought to have been written by Homer. **2. odyssey.** any long, adventurous journey.

Oed·i·pus (ed′ə pəs, ē′də pəs) *n. Greek Legend.* a king who fulfilled a prophecy by unknowingly killing his father and marrying his mother.

o′er (ôr) *prep., adv.* over. ▲ used in literature.

of (ov, uv; *unstressed* əv) *prep.* **1.** belonging to: *the cover of a book, the leg of a chair.* **2.** descended or coming from: *a citizen of France.* **3.** away or at a distance from: *within a yard of the finish line, five minutes of twelve.* **4.** that is or is called; named: *the city of New York.* **5.** having as a quality; characterized by: *a man of honor.* **6.** in or with regard to; concerning: *to be innocent of a crime.* **7.** as a result of; caused by: *to die of suffocation.* **8.** having; possessing: *a family of wealth.* **9.** filled with or containing: *a glass of water, a book of poetry.* **10.** from the whole number, amount, or group making up: *three members of the class.* **11.** made, created, or produced by: *the novels of Dickens, the sweet fragrance of flowers.* **12.** made from or with: *a house of stone.*

off (ôf) *prep.* **1.** so as to be no longer on or connected with; away from: *to take a book off a shelf, to jump off a horse.* **2.** not engaged in or occupied with; free from: *to be off duty.* **3.** differing from or less than the usual or normal: *That's four dollars off the marked price.* **4.** *Informal.* no longer using or eating: *a campaign to get addicts off drugs.* **5.** seaward of: *The boat is a mile off the coast.* —*adv.* **1.** so as to be no longer connected, attached, or on: *to break off a piece of bread, to take off one's coat.* **2.** so as to be no longer working, continuing, or taking place: *to call off a party, to turn a motor off.* **3.** at or to a distance: *The dog scared off the stranger.* **4.** so as to be away from work or duty: *to take the day off.* **5.** so as to divide, set apart, or form: *to mark off an area on a map.* **6.** on the way: *to start off on a trip.* —*adj.* **1.** no longer working, continuing, or taking place: *The electricity is off.* **2.** not engaged in or occupied with work or duty: *We're off for the holidays.* **3.** in a specified state or condition: *to be well off financially.* **4.** not accurate or correct: *The addition on the bill was off by three cents.* **5.** on the way; going: *The children are off to bed.* **6.** not up to the usual or normal level or standard; below average: *an off year.*
　·**off and on.** now and then; at times.
　·**off with.** take off; remove: *Off with their heads!*

of·fal (ô′fəl) *n.* **1.** the waste parts of a butchered animal. **2.** garbage; refuse.

off·beat (*n.,* ôf′bēt′; *adj.,* ôf′bēt′) *n. Music.* any weak or unaccented beat in a measure. —*adj. Informal.* differing from the usual or ordinary; strange; unconventional: *an offbeat movie.*

off-cen·ter (ôf′sen′tər) *adj.* **1.** not in the center or centered. **2.** not conventional; eccentric: *an off-center sense of humor.*

off-col·or (ôf′kul′ər) *adj.* **1.** slightly improper; not decent: *an off-color joke.* **2.** without the usual color.

of·fence (ə fens′) *British.* another spelling of **offense.**

of·fend (ə fend′) *v.t.* **1.** to cause or arouse resentment, anger, or displeasure; insult: *Your remarks offended me.* **2.** to be displeasing or disagreeable to. —*v.i.* to commit an offense; do wrong. —**of·fend′er,** *n.*

of·fense (*defs. 1–5* ə fens′; *def. 6* ô′fens) *also, British,* **of·fence.** *n.* **1.** the act of breaking or violating the law or a rule. **2.** the act of causing or arousing resentment, anger, or displeasure: *to mean no offense by a remark.* **3.** the condition of being offended; anger; displeasure: *to feel offense at cruel words.* **4.** something that offends: *Their rudeness was an offense to me.* **5.** the act of attacking or assaulting: *A knife may be used for offense.* **6.** *Sports.* the side, team, or players having possession of the ball or puck and trying to score, as in football, basketball, or hockey.
　·**to give offense.** to offend.
　·**to take offense.** to be offended.

of·fen·sive (ə fen′siv) *adj.* **1.** causing resentment, anger, or displeasure; giving offense: *offensive behavior.* **2.** unpleasant to the senses; disagreeable: *an offensive smell.* **3.** relating to or used for attack: *an offensive weapon, offensive tactics.* **4.** *Sports.* of or relating to the offense. —*n.* a position, attitude, or course of attack: *The enemy took the offensive and attacked the fort.* —**of·fen′sive·ly,** *adv.* —**of·fen′sive·ness,** *n.*

of·fer (ô′fər) *v.t.* **1.** to present for acceptance or refusal: *to offer an apology.* **2.** to express one's willingness or readiness (to do or give something); volunteer: *We offered to help.* **3.** to put forth or propose for consideration: *to offer an opinion.* **4.** to attempt or make a show of: *The enemy offered little resistance.* **5.** to suggest or propose as a price: *We offered ten dollars for the book.* **6.** to present as an act of religious worship or devotion: *to offer prayers in thanksgiving.* —*v.i.* **1.** to present itself; occur: *They'll visit if an opportunity offers.* **2.** to make an offering in religious worship or devotion. —*n.* **1.** the act of offering. **2.** something that is offered.

of·fer·ing (ô′fər ing) *n.* **1.** something that is offered, such as a contribution at a religious service. **2.** the act of making an offer.

of·fer·to·ry (ô′fər tôr′ē) *n., pl.* **of·fer·to·ries. 1.** the part of the Mass or Communion service at which the unconsecrated bread and wine are offered to God. **2.** the collection of the congregation's offerings at a religious service. **3.** the verses said or the music sung by the choir during the offerings at Mass or other religious services.

off·hand (ôf′hand′) *adv.* without previous thought or preparation: *I can't say offhand when I might arrive.* —*adj.* **1.** done, made, or said offhand: *offhand comments.* **2.** casual; informal: *an offhand manner.*

off·hand·ed (ôf′han′did) *adj.* done, made, or said offhand. —**off′hand′ed·ly,** *adv.* —**off′hand′ed·ness,** *n.*

of·fice (ô′fis) *n.* **1.** a place in which business, professional services, or clerical duties are carried on. **2.** all the people who work in such a place: *The office is having a Christmas party.* **3.** a position or post of authority, trust, or responsibility, especially in a government or corporation: *the office of vice president.* **4.** a duty, service, or responsibility of one's position or post: *to exercise the*

O

at; āpe; fär; câre; end; mē; it; īce; pîerce; hot; ōld; sông, fôrk; oil; out; up; ūse; rüle; pùll; tûrn; chin; sing; shop; thin; <u>th</u>is; hw in white; zh in treasure. The symbol ə stands for the unstressed vowel sound heard in about, taken, pencil, lemon, and circus.

offices of teacher and counselor. **5.** *also,* **Office.** an administrative unit or branch of a government. **6.** *also,* **offices.** something done for another; kindness, service, or favor: *We got the information we needed through the good offices of a friend.* **7.** *also,* **Office.** a religious ceremony for a particular occasion or purpose. [From the Old French word *office* with the same meanings, from the Latin word *officium* "a service, duty" or "function," from the words *opus* "work" and *facere* "to do."]

of·fice·hold·er (ô′fis hōl′dər) *n.* a person who holds a public office.

of·fice hours **1.** hours during which an office is normally open for business. **2.** the number of hours spent at work in an office.

of·fi·cer (ô′fə sər) *n.* **1.** a person appointed to a particular rank and position of authority in a military service, especially one holding a commission, as a general or captain. **2.** a person who holds an office or position of responsibility, as in a club or business. **3.** the captain or any of the captain's chief assistants on a boat or ship. **4.** a member of the police.

of·fi·cial (ə fish′əl) *n.* **1.** a person who holds an office or position. **2.** a person who referees or umpires a sport or game. —*adj.* **1.** of or relating to an office or position of authority: *official duties.* **2.** coming from or authorized by a proper authority: *The president made an official statement to the press.* **3.** authorized to carry out some specific function: *an official scorekeeper.* **4.** characteristic of or suitable for a person of authority; formal: *an official reception for a governor.* —**of·fi′cial·ly,** *adv.*

of·fi·ci·ate (ə fish′ē āt′) *v.i.,* **of·fi·ci·at·ed, of·fi·ci·at·ing.** **1.** to perform the duties and functions of an office or position: *The governor officiated at the opening of the new school.* **2.** to perform the duties of a member of the clergy: *to officiate at a wedding.* **3.** to act as an umpire or referee: *to officiate at a football game.*

of·fi·cious (ə fish′əs) *adj.* too forward in offering services or advice to others; meddlesome: *We have an officious neighbor who constantly interferes in everyone's business.* —**of·fi′cious·ly,** *adv.* —**of·fi′cious·ness,** *n.*

off·ing (ô′fing) *n.* that part of the sea that can be seen lying between the shore and the horizon.
·**in the offing.** in the near future: *Their wedding is in the offing.*

off–key (ôf′kē′) *adj.* **1.** higher or lower in pitch than the correct tone; out of tune: *Several people in the chorus were off-key.* **2.** not conforming to what is expected, usual, or customary; somewhat unusual: *an off-key remark.*

off–lim·its (ôf′lim′its) *adj.* prohibited as a place to be entered or patronized, especially by a particular group; out of bounds: *The school's boiler room is off-limits to all students.*

off of, off.

off–sea·son (ôf′sē′zən) *n.* a time of the year that is not a busy season for a particular activity: *Winter is the off-season for travel abroad. Summer is the off-season for the fur business.*

off·set (*v.,* ôf′set′; *n.,* ôf′set′) *v.t.,* **off·set, off·set·ting.** **1.** to balance or make up for: *The product's virtues offset its faults.* **2.** to reproduce (something) by offset printing. —*n.* **1.** something that balances or makes up for something else; compensation. **2.** a shoot or branch that grows from a root or main stem near the ground and can take root as a new plant. **3.** see **offset printing.**

offset printing, a printing process in which an inked impression is transferred from a coated zinc or aluminum plate to a cylinder covered with rubber, which then transfers it onto paper.

off·shoot (ôf′shüt′) *n.* **1.** a shoot or branch that grows from the main stem of a plant. **2.** anything that develops, grows, or branches off from something else.

off·shore (ôf′shôr′) *adj.* **1.** moving or directed away from the shore: *an offshore storm.* **2.** at a distance from the shore: *offshore fishing.* —*adv.* **1.** in a direction away from the shore. **2.** at a distance from the shore: *to anchor a ship offshore.*

off·side (ôf′sīd′) *also,* **offside.** *adj.* **1.** in football, illegally across the line of scrimmage before a play begins. **2.** in certain games, especially hockey and soccer, illegally ahead of the puck or ball in an attacking zone or area. —*adv.* in or to an offside position.

offshore oil rig

off·spring (ôf′spring′) *n., pl.* **off·spring.** the young of a person, animal, or plant.

off·stage (ôf′stāj′) *adj.* in or from that part of the stage that cannot be seen by the audience. —*adv.* away from that part of the stage that can be seen by the audience.

oft (ôft) *adv. Archaic.* often.

of·ten (ô′fən) *adv.* many times; repeatedly; frequently.

of·ten·times (ô′fən tīmz′) *adv.* frequently; often. Also, **oft·times** (ôft′tīmz′).

o·gle (ō′gəl) *v.t.,* **o·gled, o·gling.** to look or stare at in a leering or amorous way. —*n.* a leering or amorous look. —**o′gler,** *n.*

o·gre (ō′gər) *n.* **1.** in fairy tales and legends, a fearsome giant or monster that eats people. **2.** any person or thing that is cruel, brutal, or dreaded.

oh (ō) *also,* **O.** *interj.* **1.** used to express an emotion or feeling, as surprise, joy, grief, or pain. **2.** used to address a person directly: *Oh, waiter! Would you bring us the check?*

OH, postal abbreviation for Ohio.

ohm (ōm) *n.* a unit of electrical resistance equal to the resistance of a conductor in which a potential difference of one volt produces a current of one ampere. [From the German physicist Georg S. *Ohm* (1787–1854).]

ohm·me·ter (ōm′mē′tər) *n.* a device for measuring electrical resistance in a circuit.

Ohm's law (ōmz) the law stating that in electric circuits the current is directly proportional to the voltage and inversely proportional to the resistance. [From the German physicist Georg S. *Ohm* (1787–1854), who formulated this law.]

–oid *suffix* **1.** (used to form adjectives from nouns) having the form, nature, or appearance of: *spheroid.* **2.** (used to form nouns) something that resembles a certain object or has a certain quality: *planetoid.*

oil (oil) *n.* **1.** any of a large group of greasy substances that will dissolve in alcohol but not in water. Oils are liquid at normal temperatures or liquefy readily when warmed. Oil is obtained from animals, as whale oil, from vegetables, as linseed oil, and from minerals, as kerosene. **2.** another word for **petroleum. 3.** see **oil paint. 4.** see **oil painting.** —*v.t.* to cover, smear, grease, supply, or polish with oil. —**oil′er,** *n.*

oil burner, a furnace or heating unit that burns fuel oil.

oil·cloth (oil′klôth′) *n.* a waterproof fabric made by

coating cloth with oil or a similar substance. It is used for tablecloths, shelf lining, cushion covers, and the like.

oil color, another term for **oil paint.**

oil of vitriol, another term for **sulfuric acid.**

oil paint, paint that is made of pigment ground in linseed oil or another oil.

oil painting **1.** a painting done in oil paints. **2.** the art of painting in oil paints.

oil·skin (oil′skin′) *n.* **1.** a fabric that has been treated with oil or a similar substance to make it waterproof. It is used especially for garments intended to protect the wearer from rain. **2.** a garment made of this fabric.

oil slick, a film of oil floating on the surface of water.

oil well, a well that is dug or drilled in the earth to obtain petroleum.

oil·y (oi′lē) *adj.,* **oil·i·er, oil·i·est.** **1.** of, containing, or like oil: *an oily taste.* **2.** covered, smeared, or soaked with oil; greasy: *an oily rag.* **3.** too smooth or polished in speech or manner. —**oil′i·ness,** *n.*

oint·ment (oint′mənt) *n.* a soft, usually greasy substance, often medicated, applied to the skin to soothe, protect, or heal it; salve.

O·jib·wa (ō jib′wä) *n., pl.* **O·jib·wa** or **O·jib·was.** **1.** a member of a large tribe of North American Indians formerly living in the Great Lakes region, now living mainly in Minnesota, Wisconsin, and North Dakota. **2.** the language of this tribe. Also, **Chippewa.**

OK[1] (ō′kā′) *also,* **o·kay.** *Informal. adj., adv., interj.* all right: *Your idea's OK. I'm doing OK now. OK, let's go.* —*n., pl.* **OK's.** agreement or approval: *Get the treasurer's OK before spending any money.* —*v.t.,* **OK'd, OK'ing.** to approve or agree to: *to OK a plan.* [Probably made popular as a slogan of the *O. K. Club* of the Democratic Party in 1840. The club name was an abbreviation of *Old Kinderhook,* the nickname of the Democratic candidate, Martin Van Buren, who was born in Kinderhook, New York. *OK* was in use before 1840, but its origin is not known.]

OK[2], postal abbreviation for Oklahoma.

o·ka·pi (ō kä′pē) *n., pl.* **o·ka·pis** or **o·ka·pi.** an African animal related to the giraffe, having a dark purplish brown coat and black and white stripes resembling those of a zebra on the upper legs and hindquarters.

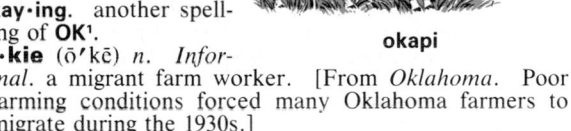

okapi

o·kay (ō′kā′) *Informal. adj., adv., interj., n., pl.* **o·kays,** *v.t.,* **o·kayed, o·kay·ing.** another spelling of **OK**[1].

O·kie (ō′kē) *n. Informal.* a migrant farm worker. [From *Oklahoma.* Poor farming conditions forced many Oklahoma farmers to migrate during the 1930s.]

Okla., Oklahoma.

o·kra (ō′krə) *n.* **1.** the soft, sticky pods of a plant, used in soups and eaten as a vegetable. **2.** the plant bearing these pods. Also, **gumbo.**

old (ōld) *adj.,* **old·er** or **eld·er, old·est** or **eld·est.** **1.** having lived or existed for a long period of time: *an old couple.* **2.** of a certain age: *Our car is three years old.* **3.** not new, recent, or current: *an old song, an old joke.* **4.** known or used in the past or for a long time; familiar: *We are old friends.* **5.** of or belonging to the ancient or remote past. **6.** former: *an old classmate.* **7.** worn with age or use; worn-out: *We gave all our old clothes to charity.* **8.** having the characteristics of an old or mature person: *old beyond one's years.* **9.** experienced, skilled, or practiced: *an old hand at sailing.* —*n.* former times: *tales of old.*

old country, a country from which a person has emigrated.

old·en (ōl′dən) *adj.* old; ancient: *stories of olden days.*

Old Church Sla·von·ic (slə von′ik) a Slavic language used in translations of the Bible as early as the ninth century A.D. It is still used in some Orthodox liturgies.

Old English **1.** the English language as it was spoken until about the year 1100. Also, **Anglo-Saxon.** **2.** a style of printing characterized by elaborate, angular letters, used especially in printing formal documents or invitations. It is the style that was used by the first printers of books.

$$\mathfrak{ABCDEFGH}$$
$$\mathfrak{nopqrstuvwxyz}$$

Old English letters

Language Note

Old English is the earliest recorded form of the English language. It was brought to Britain by Germanic tribes from northwestern Europe who invaded in the fifth century A.D. These invading tribes—the Angles, Saxons, and Jutes—conquered Britain, and their language, which is also called Anglo-Saxon, soon became the common language of what became known as England.

If you were to hear or read Old English today, it would seem like a completely foreign language. It used a complicated system of word forms, called inflections, to show how a word was used in a sentence. In contrast, Modern English has lost most of its inflections. The few inflections that we still retain include the plural of most nouns (with suffixes *-s* and *-es*), the possessive of nouns (with suffix *-'s*), and the past tense and past participles of verbs (with suffix *-ed*). Consider the Modern English sentences *The stone is heavy, He threw a stone,* and *She broke the window with a stone.* The word *stone* has the same form in all three sentences, although its position shows us when it is used as the subject, the direct object, or the object of a preposition. In Old English, each of these usages would have required a different form of the noun *stone.* All nouns had a particular gender: masculine, feminine, or neuter. The word *wheat* was considered masculine and referred to as ''he,'' the word *heart* was feminine, and the word *wife* was neuter. There were also many more verbs that changed their root vowel to indicate tense. One of the few verbs to keep this pattern is *sing, sang, sung,* which comes from Old English.

Old English was written in a form of the Latin alphabet, as is Modern English. It contains some of the earliest poetry of any Germanic language. From the time of King Alfred the Great in the ninth century, Old English was widely used among writers of history, philosophy, and religious works. When the Normans successfully invaded England in 1066, however, the country came to be ruled by kings and nobles who spoke French, and Old English ceased to be written at all.

Old English sheepdog, a dog having a long, shaggy, gray or bluish gray coat with white markings.

at; āpe; fär; câre; end; mē; it; īce; pîerce; hot; ōld; sông; fôrk; oil; out; up; ūse; rüle; pull; tûrn; chin; sing; shop; thin; **th**is; hw in white; zh in treasure. The symbol ə stands for the unstressed vowel sound heard in about, taken, pencil, lemon, and circus.

O

old–fash·ioned (ōld'fash'ənd) *adj.* **1.** keeping to or favoring old ways, ideas, or customs: *My grandparents are old-fashioned about many things.* **2.** of, relating to, or characteristic of former times; out-of-date: *an old-fashioned hat, an old-fashioned idea.*

Old French, the French language from the ninth to the thirteenth centuries A.D.

Old Glory, the flag of the United States.

old hand, a person with a great deal of experience or skill in something: *The mayor is an old hand at campaigning.*

Old High German, the form of the German language spoken in southern Germany from the eighth century to the end of the eleventh century A.D. Modern German is descended from Old High German.

Old Icelandic, the Icelandic language from the mid-twelfth century through the fourteenth century A.D.

old·ish (ōl'dish) *adj.* somewhat old.

Old Latin, the Latin language before the second century B.C.

old maid **1.** an older woman who has never been married. ▲ now usually considered offensive. **2.** *Informal.* a person who is prim, fussy, and prudish. **3.** a simple card game in which the player holding the odd queen at the end is the loser.

Old Norse, the language of Scandinavia from the eighth to the fourteenth centuries A.D., especially in its Norwegian and Icelandic forms.

Old Testament, the collection of writings that makes up the Jewish Bible and the first part of the Christian Bible. It contains an account of the Creation and early human history, the sacred agreements between God and the Hebrews, and the laws, prophecies, and religious literature of the Hebrew nation up to the second century B.C.

old–time (ōld'tīm') *adj.* of, belonging to, or characteristic of former times: *old-time movies.*

old–tim·er (ōld'tī'mər) *n.* *Informal.* **1.** a person who has been a member of a group or organization for a long time. **2.** a person who is old or elderly.

old wives' tale, a belief not based on any fact, especially a superstition.

Old–World (ōld'wûrld') *also,* **Old World.** *adj.* **1.** of, relating to, or belonging to the Old World: *Old-World customs, Old-World monkeys.* **2.** **old-world.** belonging to or characteristic of former times: *genteel, old-world manners.*

Old World, the Eastern Hemisphere, including Europe, Asia, and Africa.

o·le·an·der (ō'lē an'dər) *n.* a very poisonous evergreen shrub, having narrow, lance-shaped leaves and clusters of fragrant, funnel-shaped flowers that are red, purple, or white.

o·le·o·mar·ga·rine (ō'lē ō mär'jər in) *also,* **o·le·o·mar·ga·rin.** *n.* see **margarine.** Also, **o·le·o** (ō'lē ō').

ol·fac·to·ry (ol fak'tə rē, ōl fak'tə rē) *adj.* of or relating to the sense of smell: *an olfactory nerve.* —*n., pl.* **ol·fac·to·ries.** an olfactory organ.

ol·i·garch (ol'i gärk') *n.* any of the rulers in an oligarchy.

ol·i·gar·chic (ol'i gär'kik) *adj.* of, relating to, or ruled by an oligarchy: *an oligarchic state.* Also, **ol·i·gar·chi·cal** (ol'i gär'ki kəl).

ol·i·gar·chy (ol'i gär'kē) *n., pl.* **ol·i·gar·chies.** **1.** a form of government in which power is held by only a few people. **2.** a state having such a government. **3.** the body of persons making up such a government.

Ol·i·go·cene (ol'i gō sēn') *n.* the third geological epoch of the Tertiary period, when the first monkeys and apes appeared. —*adj.* of, relating to, or characteristic of this epoch.

ol·ive (ol'iv) *n.* **1.** a small, oily fruit of any of a group of evergreen shrubs and trees, having a single hard seed and firm flesh. It is often eaten pickled and is widely used as a source of olive oil. **2.** a shrub or tree bearing this fruit. **3.** a dull yellowish green color. Also, **olive green.** —*adj.* having the color olive.

olive branch **1.** a branch of the olive tree thought of as a symbol of peace. **2.** anything offered as a sign or token of peace or goodwill.

olive drab **1.** a dull greenish brown color. **2.** a fabric of this color. **3.** *also,* **olive drabs.** a military uniform made of this fabric.

olive oil, a clear yellow or greenish yellow oil obtained by pressing olives, used as a salad and cooking oil.

Ol·mec (ol'mek, ōl'mek) *n., pl.* **Ol·mec** or **Ol·mecs.** a member of a North American Indian tribe formerly living in what is now southern Mexico.

O·lym·pi·ad (ō lim'pē ad') *n.* **1.** a period of four years from one celebration of the Olympic games to another, by which the ancient Greeks reckoned time. **2.** a celebration of the modern Olympic games.

O·lym·pi·an (ō lim'pē ən) *adj.* **1.** of or relating to Mount Olympus or the gods who, in Greek mythology, lived there. **2.** of or relating to the plain of Olympia. **3.** like a god; majestic; exalted: *Olympian beauty.* —*n.* **1.** one of the twelve major Greek gods who lived on Mount Olympus. **2.** a person who competes in the Olympic games.

O·lym·pic (ō lim'pik) *adj.* **1.** of or relating to Mount Olympus or to the plain of Olympia. **2.** of or relating to the Olympic games. —*n.* **Olympics.** see **Olympic games.**

Olympic games **1.** in ancient Greece, a festival consisting of a series of competitions in athletics, poetry, music, and oratory. It was held every four years at Olympia in honor of Zeus. **2.** modern international athletic contests modeled on the ancient athletic games, held winter and summer every four years.

om·buds·man (om'bədz mən, om bŭdz'mən) *n., pl.* **om·buds·men** (om'bədz mən, om bŭdz'mən). a person who is employed by a government or organization to investigate and resolve complaints.

o·meg·a (ō meg'ə, ō mē'gə, ō mā'gə) *n.* **1.** the twenty-fourth and last letter of the Greek alphabet (Ω, ω), corresponding to the English long *o*. **2.** the last in a group or series; end.

om·e·let (om'lit, om'ə lit) *also,* **om·e·lette.** *n.* a dish made of beaten eggs that have been cooked in a pan and then folded over. It often has a filling of cheese or meat.

o·men (ō'mən) *n.* a sign or event that is supposed to foretell good or bad luck.

om·i·cron (om'i kron', ō'mi kron') *n.* the fifteenth letter of the Greek alphabet (O, o).

om·i·nous (om'ə nəs) *adj.* foretelling trouble or misfortune; threatening: *ominous black clouds coming in from the sea.* —**om'i·nous·ly,** *adv.* —**om'i·nous·ness,** *n.*

o·mis·sion (ō mish'ən) *n.* **1.** the act of omitting or the state of being omitted. **2.** something that is omitted.

o·mit (ō mit') *v.t.,* **o·mit·ted,** **o·mit·ting.** **1.** to leave out; fail to include: *to omit an item on a shopping list.* **2.** to fail to do or perform; neglect: *to omit mailing a letter.*

omni– *combining form* all; everywhere; universally: *omnipresent.*

om·ni·bus (om'nə bus') *n., pl.* **om·ni·bus·es.** **1.** see **bus.** **2.** a collection of works written by the same author or of writings relating to the same subject: *an omnibus of ghost stories.* —*adj.* including or covering a number of different items, cases, or instances: *The legislature passed an omnibus bill.*

om·nip·o·tence (om nip'ə təns) *n.* unlimited power or authority: *the omnipotence of a dictator.*

om·nip·o·tent (om nip'ə tənt) *adj.* having unlimited power or authority; all-powerful. —*n.* **the Omnipotent.** God. —**om·nip'o·tent·ly,** *adv.*

om·ni·pres·ent (om'nə prez'ənt) *adj.* present in all

places at the same time: *an omnipresent fear.* —**om′ni-pres′ence**, *n.*

om·nis·cient (om nish′ənt) *adj.* having unlimited knowledge; knowing everything. —*n.* **the Omniscient.** God. —**om·nis′cience**, *n.* —**om·nis′cient·ly**, *adv.*

om·ni·vore (om′nə vôr′) *n.* an organism that eats both animal and vegetable food. [From the Latin word *omnivorus* meaning "omnivorous," from the words *omnis* "all" and *vorare* "to devour."]

om·niv·o·rous (om niv′ər əs) *adj.* **1.** eating both animal and vegetable food: *Bears are omnivorous.* **2.** eating all kinds of food. **3.** taking in everything: *an omnivorous reader.* —**om·niv′o·rous·ly**, *adv.* —**om·niv′o·rous·ness**, *n.*

on (ôn, on) *prep.* **1.** in a position above and supported by; above and in contact with: *The coats are on the bed.* **2.** so as to be in contact with a surface: *Please put butter on the bread.* **3.** fastened to or suspended from: *a watch on a chain.* **4.** so as to be supported or borne by: *Stand on your toes.* **5.** in a position at, near, or next to: *Their cabin is on the lake.* **6.** in the direction of; toward; to: *Our house is on the left.* **7.** directed toward, especially in the way of attack; against: *to make war on one's enemies.* **8.** in the state, condition, or process of: *The guard was on duty.* **9.** in regard to; about; concerning: *The lecture was on monkeys.* **10.** during the time, course, or occasion of: *We left on Thursday.* **11.** connected or associated with as a member: *They are on the football team.* **12.** by means or use of: *We went for a ride on our bicycles.* —*adv.* **1.** in or into a position in contact with, supported by, or covering something: *to put one's shoes on.* **2.** forward in time or space; onward: *Please move on. Time marches on.* **3.** in or into action, operation, or movement: *to turn the water on.* **4.** in or at the present place or position: *If you don't hang on, you'll fall.* —*adj.* **1.** taking place or planned; happening or going to happen: *The game is still on.* **2.** in operation or movement: *The radio is on.*

·**and so on.** and more of the same; and so forth.
·**on and off.** from time to time; occasionally.
·**on and on.** without stopping; continuously.

ON, postal abbreviation for Ontario.

once (wuns) *adv.* **1.** one time: *once a week.* **2.** in time past; previously: *That house was once very grand.* **3.** at any time; ever: *If they once learn something, they never forget.* —*n.* one single time. *Once should be enough.* —*conj.* as soon as; when; whenever: *That game is easy, once you learn the basic rules.*

·**all at once.** all at the same time: *to do everything all at once.*
·**at once. a.** without delay; immediately: *Come here at once.* **b.** at the same time.
·**once and for all.** finally or for the last time.
·**once in a while.** from time to time; occasionally.
·**once upon a time.** at some time in the past; long ago.

on·com·ing (ôn′kum′ing, on′kum′ing) *adj.* approaching: *an oncoming train.* —*n.* approach: *the oncoming of summer.*

one (wun) *n.* **1.** the first and lowest cardinal number. **2.** a symbol representing this number, such as 1 or I. **3.** a single person or thing: *There is only one left in the box.* —*adj.* **1.** being a single person or thing: *one student, one pencil.* **2.** being a specific person, thing, or group: *The child ran from one side of the yard to the other.* **3.** some: *You'll meet the right person one day.* **4.** a certain: *The winning dog was one Fido.* **5.** the same: *They are all members of one family.* **6.** characterized by harmony, unity, or agreement: *The country spoke with one voice.* —*pron.* **1.** a specific person or thing: *One of the children was left behind.* **2.** any person or thing: *One could see that we had lost.* **3.** the same person or thing: *Frozen water and ice are one.*

·**at one.** in harmony, unity, or agreement.
·**one and all.** everyone.
·**one another.** each other: *They loved one another.*
·**one by one.** one at a time in succession.

one–horse (wun′hôrs′) *adj.* **1.** using one horse; requiring only one horse to operate: *a one-horse carriage, a one-horse farm.* **2.** *Informal.* small and unimportant: *a one-horse town.*

O·nei·da (ō nī′də) *n., pl.* **O·nei·da** or **O·nei·das. 1.** a member of a tribe of Iroquois Indians of central New York State. **2.** the language of this tribe.

one–lin·er (wun′lī′nər) *n.* a very brief joke or witty remark.

one·ness (wun′nis) *n.* the state or quality of being one; singleness or sameness.

one–on–one (wun′ôn wun′, wun′on wun′) *adj., adv.* **1.** in sports, competing as an individual against a single opposing player. **2.** involving direct communication between one person and another: *The president and the senator had a one-on-one discussion about taxes.*

on·er·ous (on′ər əs, ō′nər əs) *adj.* difficult to bear; burdensome; oppressive: *I was given the onerous task of washing all the windows in the house.*

one·self (wun′self′) *also,* **one's self.** *pron.* **1.** one's own self: *Seeing oneself on television is exciting.* **2.** one's usual or normal self: *not feeling like oneself.*

one–sid·ed (wun′sī′did) *adj.* **1.** favoring or presenting only one side; biased; partial: *a one-sided account of a trial.* **2.** unequal or uneven: *a one-sided game.* **3.** having or on one side only.

one–time (wun′tīm′) *adj.* former: *a one-time actor.*

one–to–one (wun′tə wun′) *adj.* **1.** equal on both sides: *a one-to-one exchange of letters.* **2.** *Mathematics.* relating to a rule of correspondence that pairs each element of one set with one and only one element from another set.

one–track (wun′trak′) *adj.* limited to only one idea or purpose at a time; narrow: *a one-track mind.*

one–way (wun′wā′) *adj.* **1.** moving or allowing movement in one direction only: *one-way traffic, a one-way street.* **2.** allowing travel in one direction only: *a one-way ticket.* **3.** one-sided: *a one-way conversation.*

on·go·ing (ôn′gō′ing, on′gō′ing) *adj.* continuing: *Building new housing is an ongoing program of the city.*

on·ion (un′yən) *n.* **1.** a plant bulb having a strong taste and smell, eaten as a vegetable either raw or cooked. **2.** the plant that grows from this bulb. —**on′ion·like′**, *adj.*

on·ion·skin (un′yən skin′) *n.* a thin, strong, translucent paper.

on·look·er (ôn′lŭk′er, on′lŭk′ər) *n.* a person who looks on without taking part; spectator.

on·ly (ōn′lē) *adj.* **1.** alone of its kind or class; without others; solitary: *an only child.*

onions *(def. 1)*

2. most suitable or excellent of all; best: *the only person for the job.* —*adv.* **1.** no more than; nothing but: *I have only two dollars.* **2.** no one or nothing other than: *Only you remembered that it was my birthday.* **3.** exclusively; solely: *This bus runs only on weekends.* **4.** as recently in

O

at; āpe; fär; câre; end; mē; it; īce; pierce; hot; ōld; sông, fôrk; oil; out; up; ūse; rūle; pull; tûrn; chin; sing; shop; thin; **th**is; hw in white; zh in treasure. The symbol ə stands for the unstressed vowel sound heard in about, taken, pencil, lemon, and circus.

the past as: *I saw them only last week.* —*conj.* except that; but: *I would have gone, only it was raining.*

•**only too.** very: *I am only too glad to help.*

on·o·mat·o·poe·ia (on′ə mat′ə pē′ə, on′ə mä′tə pē′ə) *n.* **1.** the forming of a name or word by imitating the natural sound associated with the thing indicated. **2.** a word formed in this way. **3.** the use of such words, as in poetry.

Language Note

Onomatopoeia is one of the ways in which new words are created. Throughout the history of language, onomatopoeia has been used to coin words needed to describe natural sounds or the sounds made by objects or actions. Many of these sounds, such as *buzz, hiss, clang, and meow,* have become a part of the standard English vocabulary. Other onomatopoetic words are made up for a special purpose or occasion and never become a permanent part of our language. A person reading or hearing such a word, however, will easily understand its meaning because the word clearly imitates a sound. For example, in the sentence *The stone fell ka-plank into the lake,* you can imagine what the word *ka-plank* means even though it is not an established English word that you might find in a dictionary.

In Greek, the word *onomatopoeia* means literally "to make names." Some scholars believe that "making names" by coining onomatopoetic words is the way language first developed. Early language may have been an attempt by people to imitate the natural sounds that they heard around them.

One of the most interesting features of such word formation is the comparison of onomatopoetic words among various languages. Because we hear the same sounds, the words are very often similar. For instance, in English we use the word *cock-a-doodle-doo* to describe the sound a rooster makes. In French the equivalent word is *cocorico,* in Spanish it is *quiquiriquí,* in German it is *kikeriki,* and in Japanese it is *kokke-kokko.*

on·o·mat·o·po·et·ic (on′ə mat′ə pō et′ik, on′ə mä′tə-pō et′ik) *adj.* relating to or of the nature of onomatopoeia.

On·on·da·ga (on′ən dô′gə, on′ən dä′gə) *n., pl.* **On·on·da·ga** or **On·on·da·gas. 1.** a member of a tribe of Iroquois Indians formerly living in central New York State, now living mainly in Canada. **2.** the language of this tribe.

on·rush (ôn′rush′, on′rush′) *n., pl.* **on·rush·es.** a rapid or violent forward flow or rush: *The house was swept from its foundations by the onrush of floodwaters.*

on·set (ôn′set′, on′set′) *n.* **1.** the beginning; start: *the onset of summer.* **2.** an attack; assault.

on·shore (ôn′shôr′, on′shôr′) *adv., adj.* on or toward the shore.

on·side (ôn′sīd′, on′sīd′) *adj., adv.* in various sports, not offside.

on·site (ôn′sīt′, on′sīt′) *adj.* carried out or located at the site where a particular activity or event takes place: *on-site training of hospital workers.*

on·slaught (ôn′slôt′, on′slôt′) *n.* a vigorous or destructive attack or assault: *The onslaught of the storm took the campers by surprise.*

Ont., Ontario.

on–the–job (ôn′thə job′, on′thə job′) *adj.* done or received while working at a job: *on-the-job-training.*

on·to (ôn′tü, on′tü) *prep.* **1.** to a position on: *The door opens onto the street. The actress walked onto the stage.* **2.** *Informal.* aware of: *I'm onto your tricks.*

o·nus (ō′nəs) *n., pl.* **o·nus·es.** a burden; responsibility.

on·ward (ôn′wərd, on′wərd) *adv.* toward a position that is ahead or in front: *They climbed onward toward the top of the mountain.* Also, **on·wards** (ôn′wərdz, on′wərdz). —*adj.* moving or directed toward a point in front; forward: *the onward rush of flood waters.*

on·yx (on′iks) *n., pl.* **on·yx·es.** a variety of quartz consisting of different-colored layers that are usually white, yellow, black, or red.

oo·dles (ü′dəlz) *pl. n. Informal.* a large amount; a lot.

ooze¹ (üz) *v.,* **oozed, ooz·ing.** —*v.i.* **1.** to leak out slowly through small openings; seep: *Blood oozed from the scrape on my knee.* **2.** to disappear gradually as if by slowly leaking out: *The team's enthusiasm oozed away after they failed to win.* —*v.t.* to give off slowly or gradually. [From the Middle English word *wosen* meaning "to exude moisture," from the Old English word *wōs* "moisture, juice."]

ooze² (üz) *n.* soft, wet mud or slime, especially at the bottom of a body of water, such as a pond. [From the Old English word *wāse* meaning "mud, slime."]

oo·zy¹ (ü′zē) *adj.,* **oo·zi·er, oo·zi·est.** slowly leaking; dripping. [*Ooze¹* + *-y.¹*]

oo·zy² (ü′zē) *adj.,* **oo·zi·er, oo·zi·est.** of or like ooze; slimy: *There was oozy mud at the bottom of the lake.* [*Ooze²* + *-y¹.*] —**oo′zi·ness,** *n.*

op., opus.

o·pac·i·ty (ō pas′i tē) *n.* the state or quality of being opaque.

o·pal (ō′pəl) *n.* any of various forms of silica that are used as gems. Opals show delicate changes of iridescent colors when they are moved in the light.

o·pal·es·cence (ō′pə les′əns) *n.* iridescent changes of colors like that of the opal.

o·pal·es·cent (ō′pə les′ənt) *adj.* showing delicate changes of iridescent colors like an opal.

o·paque (ō pāk′) *adj.* **1.** not letting light through; not transparent or translucent: *The opaque shades kept the sunlight out of the room.* **2.** not shining or lustrous; dull: *The table had an opaque finish.* **3.** hard to understand; obscure. —**o·paque′ly,** *adv.* —**o·paque′ness,** *n.*

op art (op) *also,* **Op Art.** a style of art characterized by geometric designs that play tricks on the eye.

ope (ōp) *v.t., v.i.,* **oped, op·ing.** *Archaic.* to open.

op–ed (op′ed′) *also,* **Op-ed.** *n.* a newspaper page, usually appearing opposite the editorial page, that carries articles by columnists and other writers. Also, **op-ed page.**

o·pen (ō′pən) *adj.* **1.** allowing free passage through; not shut or blocked: *an open door, an open lane on a highway.* **2.** not having its lid, door, or other cover or seal closed: *an open box, an open closet, an open envelope.* **3.** not closed in; having no surrounding barriers: *open country.* **4.** having spaces, holes, or gaps: *cloth with an open weave, an open formation of troops.* **5.** not protected; exposed: *open to attack, an open fire on a beach.* **6.** that can be used; not taken or reserved; available: *The job is still open.* **7.** able or ready to receive new ideas, facts, or views without prejudice: *to be open to suggestions.* **8.** outspoken; frank; candid: *to be open with someone.* **9.** free or accessible to the general public: *an open meeting of the city council.* **10.** not settled or determined: *Where we'll go on our vacation is an open question.* **11.** ready to do business: *That store is not open on Mondays.* —*v.t.* **1.** to cause to be open: *to open a drawer, to open a letter, to open one's mouth.* **2.** to take off a lid or other covering from: *to open a jar.* **3.** to spread out; unfold: *The captain opened the map.* **4.** to make available or accessible: *The school board opened the meeting to the whole town.* **5.** to prepare for or set into operation: *to open a bank account, to open a new movie theater.* **6.** to begin; start: *to open the meeting with a short talk.* —*v.i.* **1.** to become open: *The old door creaked as it* opened. **2.** to have an opening: *The room opened onto a terrace.* **3.** to become ready to do business: *The new store opens next week.* **4.** to begin: *The exhibition opens tomorrow.* **5.** to spread out; unfold: *The buds on the bush opened in the spring.* —*n.* **1.** an athletic contest, such as a golf tournament, in which both amateurs and professionals may take part. **2.** **the open. a.** any clear or unenclosed space or area. **b.** public or general knowledge: *Their secret is now in the open.* —**o'pen·ly,** *adv.* —**o'pen·ness,** *n.*

o·pen–air (ō'pən âr') *adj.* outdoor: *The play was performed in an open-air theater.*

open air, outdoors.

o·pen–and–shut (ō'pən ən shut') *adj.* easily settled or decided: *The lawsuit was an open-and-shut case.*

open door 1. free admission or easy access: *vocational training that provides an open door to employment.* **2.** a policy of admission to a country of all people on equal terms, as for immigration. **3.** a policy whereby a country allows equal opportunity for trade to all other countries. Also, **open-door policy** (ō'pən dôr').

o·pen·er (ō'pə nər) *n.* **1.** an instrument or device for opening closed or sealed containers, such as cans and bottles. **2.** the first item or part in any series: *Their baseball team won the opener.* **3.** a person or thing that opens.

o·pen–eyed (ō'pən īd') *adj.* **1.** having the eyes wide open, as in amazement or surprise. **2.** very watchful; alert.

o·pen–faced (ō'pən fāst') *adj.* **1.** having a face or expression thought to be frank and honest. **2.** without an upper slice of bread: *an open-faced sandwich.*

o·pen·hand·ed (ō'pən han'did) *adj.* generous in giving. —**o'pen·hand'ed·ly,** *adv.* —**o'pen·hand'ed·ness,** *n.*

o·pen·heart·ed (ō'pən här'tid) *adj.* **1.** frank; candid. **2.** generous. —**o'pen·heart'ed·ly,** *adv.* —**o'pen·heart'ed·ness,** *n.*

o·pen–hearth (ō'pən härth') *adj.* relating to or used in a process for making steel, in which a furnace reflects heat from a low roof onto the raw material, and brickwork on either side of the furnace keeps in the heat so that it can be reused.

o·pen–heart surgery (ō'pən härt') surgery performed on the heart during which the heart is opened and the blood is circulated through the body by a machine.

open house 1. a party that is open to all who wish to come. **2.** an occasion when an institution, school, or the like is open to visitors.

o·pen·ing (ō'pə ning) *n.* **1.** a vacant or empty space: *an opening in a forest, an opening in a fence.* **2.** the first steps or stage; beginning: *the opening of a book.* **3.** an unfilled job; vacancy: *an opening at the grocery store.* **4.** the first performance or occasion: *the opening of a play.* **5.** the act of becoming open. **6.** a favorable opportunity or chance.

open letter, a statement of protest, appeal, or belief written in the form of a personal letter but meant for the public. An open letter is often published in a newspaper or magazine.

o·pen–mind·ed (ō'pən mīn'did) *adj.* ready to consider new facts, ideas, views, or beliefs; unprejudiced. —**o'pen-mind'ed·ly,** *adv.* —**o'pen-mind'ed·ness,** *n.*

o·pen–mouthed (ō'pən mouthd', ō'pən moutht') *adj.* having the mouth open, as in wonder or surprise; gaping: *The tourists stared open-mouthed at the geyser.*

open primary, a direct primary election in which members of any political party are permitted to vote.

open sesame, any miraculous, swift, or unfailing means of reaching a desired result or goal: *Some people think that money is the open sesame to happiness.* [From the magic words used to open the door of the robbers' cave in the story *Ali Baba and the Forty Thieves.*]

open shop, a factory or business in which belonging to or becoming a member of a union is not a requirement for employment.

o·pen·work (ō'pən wûrk') *n.* any ornamental material containing numerous small openings.

op·e·ra[1] (op'ər ə) *n.* a play having all or most of its words sung, usually performed by solo voices, chorus, and orchestra. It is presented with costumes, scenery, acting, and, sometimes, dancing. [From the Italian word *opera* with the same meaning, from the Latin word *opera,* plural of *opus* "work, labor."]

Word Family

More than one English word is derived from the Latin word *opus,* meaning "a work," and its plural, *opera.* We use **opus** itself to refer to a work of art or scholarship, and an **opera** is a work that combines several art forms. The less serious form of opera, the **operetta,** also belongs in this family. Some projects in an **office** require the **cooperation** of many people, but one person can often handle a simple **operation** alone. Some work titles also show traces of this Latin root, such as telephone **operator** and elevator **operator.**

op·e·ra[2] (ō'pər ə, op'ər ə) a plural of **opus.**

op·er·a·ble (op'ər ə bəl) *adj.* **1.** that can be done, carried out, or used: *an old but still operable automobile.* **2.** that can be treated by surgery: *an operable condition, an operable tumor.*

opera glasses, small, low-power binoculars for use at operas, plays, or concerts.

opera house, a theater especially designed for the performance of operas.

op·er·ate (op'ə rāt') *v.,* **op·er·at·ed, op·er·at·ing.** —*v.i.* **1.** to perform or function; work: *The car's motor operates well.* **2.** to produce the intended or proper effect: *The plan operated successfully.* **3.** to perform a surgical operation: *The surgeon operated to remove an appendix.* **4.** to carry on military activities: *The guerrillas operated behind enemy lines.* —*v.t.* **1.** to cause to work: *to operate an elevator.* **2.** to manage or direct the affairs of: *to operate a business.*

opera glasses

op·er·at·ic (op'ə rat'ik) *adj.* of, relating to, or like the opera: *a trained operatic voice, operatic music.* —**op·er·at'i·cal·ly,** *adv.*

operating system, a group of programs that control the basic functioning of a computer, including the operation of other programs.

op·er·a·tion (op'ə rā'shən) *n.* **1.** the act, process, or way of performing, directing, or working: *The operation of a large business is a full-time job.* **2.** the state of being at work: *The machine is in operation.* **3.** surgical treatment performed on the body to cure a physical ailment or repair an injured part: *an operation on a broken leg.* **4.** a military movement, attack, or campaign: *an operation against the enemy.* **5.** *Mathematics.* something done to one or more

at; āpe; fär; câre; end; mē; it; īce; pîerce; hot; ōld; sông, fôrk; oil; out; up; ūse; rüle; pūll; tûrn; chin; sing; shop; thin; **th**is; hw in white; zh in treasure. The symbol ə stands for the unstressed vowel sound heard in about, taken, pencil, lemon, and circus.

0

numbers or algebraic expressions to produce a single number or algebraic expression. Addition, subtraction, multiplication, and division are the four most common operations.

op·er·a·tion·al (op′ə rā′shə nəl) *adj.* **1.** of or relating to working, performing, or directing: *a company's operational headquarters, a machine's operational efficiency.* **2.** capable of operating or being used; ready to perform some intended function: *Our new computer has been installed and is now operational.*

op·er·a·tive (op′ər ə tiv, op′rə tiv) *adj.* **1.** in operation; in force; functioning: *That law is no longer operative in this state.* **2.** relating to physical or mechanical work: *the operative part of an automobile factory.* **3.** resulting from or relating to a surgical operation: *operative techniques.* —*n.* **1.** a skilled worker. **2.** a private or secret agent or investigator.

op·er·a·tor (op′ə rā′tər) *n.* **1.** a person who operates a machine or other mechanical device: *an elevator operator, a telephone operator.* **2.** a person who owns or runs a business or factory. **3.** *Informal.* a person who is shrewd, crafty, and often dishonest in getting what he or she wants.

o·per·cu·lum (ō pûr′kyə ləm) *n., pl.* **o·per·cu·la** (ō pûr′kyə lə) or **o·per·cu·lums.** any flaplike part that covers an opening in an animal or plant, especially the protective covering over the gills of a bony fish.

op·er·et·ta (op′ə ret′ə) *n., pl.* **op·er·et·tas.** a light and amusing, often short opera in which music and song are combined with spoken dialogue and dancing.

oph·thal·mol·o·gist (of′thal mol′ə jist, op′thal mol′ə jist) *n.* a doctor who specializes in ophthalmology.

oph·thal·mol·o·gy (of′thal mol′ə jē, op′thal mol′ə jē) *n.* the branch of medicine that deals with the treatment of diseases and disorders of the eye and includes eye surgery.

o·pi·ate (ō′pē it, ō′pē āt′) *n.* **1.** a drug that contains opium, used to lessen pain and bring sleep. **2.** anything that soothes or quiets. —*adj.* **1.** made with or containing opium. **2.** bringing sleep or relaxation.

o·pine (ō pīn′) *v.t., v.i.,* **o·pined, o·pin·ing.** to hold or express as an opinion; think.

o·pin·ion (ə pin′yən) *n.* **1.** a belief or conclusion based on a person's judgment rather than on what is proven or known to be true: *It is my opinion that the mayor will be reelected.* **2.** an impression or estimation of the worth, excellence, or quality of a person or thing: *What is your opinion of that book?* **3.** a formal estimation or judgment given by an expert: *The judge wrote an opinion on the case.*

o·pin·ion·at·ed (ə pin′yə nā′tid) *adj.* stubbornly holding to one's opinions; dogmatic: *to be too opinionated to listen to someone else's point of view.*

o·pi·um (ō′pē əm) *n.* a powerful, habit-forming drug made from a white fluid contained in the unripe seed capsules of a poppy, used for relieving pain and causing sleep. Opium is the source of morphine and codeine.

o·pos·sum (ə pos′əm) *n.* a small, furry mammal that lives in trees. An opossum is a marsupial and carries its young in a pouch. When frightened, the opossum may lie still as if it were dead to discourage predators.

opossum

op·po·nent (ə pō′nənt) *n.* a person or thing that opposes, fights, or competes with another, as in a game, struggle, or discussion: *an opponent at tennis, an opponent of injustice.* —*adj.* acting or behaving in opposition; opposing: *The colors of the opponent team were blue and red.*

op·por·tune (op′ər tün′, op′ər tūn′) *adj.* **1.** suitable or appropriate for a particular purpose: *an opportune time to discuss a problem.* **2.** well-timed; timely: *an opportune offer of help.* —**op′por·tune′ly,** *adv.* —**op′por·tune′ness,** *n.*

op·por·tun·ist (op′ər tü′nist, op′ər tū′nist) *n.* a person who takes advantage of every opportunity to get what he or she wants, regardless of right or wrong. —**op′por·tun′ism,** *n.* —**op′por·tun·is′tic,** *adj.*

op·por·tu·ni·ty (op′ər tü′ni tē, op′ər tū′ni tē) *n., pl.* **op·por·tu·ni·ties.** **1.** a time or circumstance that is favorable or suitable for a particular purpose: *When the pond froze, we had a good opportunity to go ice skating.* **2.** a good chance, as to advance oneself.

op·pose (ə pōz′) *v.t.,* **op·posed, op·pos·ing.** **1.** to be against; struggle against; offer resistance to: *The older members were opposed to changing the club's rules.* **2.** to put in opposition; contrast: *Good is opposed to evil.* —**op·pos′er,** *n.*

op·po·site (op′ə zit) *adj.* **1.** placed face to face with; on the other side of or across from another person or thing; facing: *The two friends live on opposite sides of the street.* **2.** turned or moving the other way: *The two cars were traveling in opposite directions.* **3.** completely and entirely different: *Hot is opposite to cold.* —*n.* **1.** a person or thing that is opposite or contrary to another: *Summer and winter are opposites.* **2.** a word that has the opposite meaning of another word; antonym. —*prep.* across from: *Meet me opposite the drugstore.* —**op′po·site·ly,** *adv.* —**op′po·site·ness,** *n.*

op·po·si·tion (op′ə zish′ən) *n.* **1.** the act of opposing or the state of being opposed: *Your opposition to the plan surprised us. The manager was in opposition to a raise for the workers.* **2.** contrary or opposing action or feeling: *The plan for higher taxes met with opposition.* **3.** a position that is opposite to another. **4.** *also,* **Opposition.** a political party opposed to the party in power. **5.** a group of people, such as a team, that opposes someone or something: *The basketball team beat the opposition.*

op·press (ə pres′) *v.t.* **1.** to control or govern by cruel and unjust use of force or authority; tyrannize: *The army oppressed the people.* **2.** to weigh heavily on so as to depress or trouble: *Our failure oppressed us.* —**op·pres′sor,** *n.*

op·pres·sion (ə presh′ən) *n.* **1.** the act of oppressing or the state of being oppressed. **2.** something that causes difficulty, pain, or suffering; hardship; burden: *the oppression of having many debts.* **3.** the feeling of being mentally or physically weighed down.

op·pres·sive (ə pres′iv) *adj.* **1.** cruel and unjust; tyrannical: *an oppressive law.* **2.** causing a state or feeling of oppression: *The hot, muggy day was oppressive.* —**op·pres′sive·ly,** *adv.* —**op·pres′sive·ness,** *n.*

op·pro·bri·ous (ə prō′brē əs) *adj.* **1.** expressing reproach, disapproval, or disgrace; abusive: *Calling a person a coward is an opprobrious remark.* **2.** deserving reproach or disapproval; disgraceful: *opprobrious conduct.* —**op·pro′bri·ous·ly,** *adv.* —**op·pro′bri·ous·ness,** *n.*

op·pro·bri·um (ə prō′brē əm) *n.* **1.** a disgrace or reproach caused by shameful conduct. **2.** a cause of disgrace or reproach.

opt (opt) *v.i.* to make a choice; choose: *I opt to have the picnic at the seashore instead of at the lake.*

op·tic (op′tik) *adj.* of or relating to the eye or to the sense of sight. [From the Old French word *optique* with the same meaning, going back to the Greek word *optikos* meaning "relating to vision."]

op·ti·cal (op′ti kəl) *adj.* **1.** of or relating to the sense of sight: *A mirage is an optical illusion.* **2.** designed to aid sight: *A microscope is an optical instrument.* **3.** of or relating to the science of optics. —**op′ti·cal·ly,** *adv.*

optical disc, *also,* **optical disk.** a disk on which sounds, images, or computer data are stored in microscopic pits. The information can be read by a laser beam and played back through a speaker, television receiver, or computer. Also, **laser disc, laser disk.**

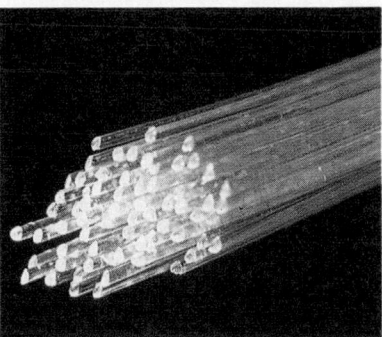

optical fibers

optical fiber, a very thin, transparent fiber of glass or plastic, used in the technology of fiber optics. Optical fibers can transmit optical images and are used in modern communications to send telephone and computer messages over long distances.

optical illusion **1.** a false impression of the appearance of something, caused by a misinterpretation of what is seen. **2.** a design, pattern, or the like that gives such a false impression.

op·ti·cian (op tish′ən) *n.* a person who makes or sells eyeglasses, contact lenses, and optical instruments.

optic nerve, the nerve that carries impulses from the eye to the brain.

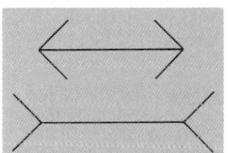

optical illusion in which two horizontal lines are equal in length although they appear unequal

op·tics (op′tiks) *n.* the branch of physics dealing with the nature and behavior of light. ▲ used with a singular verb.

op·ti·mal (op′tə məl) *adj.* best or most favorable: *The rocket was launched only when the weather was optimal.*

op·ti·mism (op′tə miz′əm) *n.* **1.** a belief that things will turn out for the best: *There was great optimism that the economy would improve.* **2.** a tendency to hope for or expect the best, or to look on the bright side of things: *cheerful and full of optimism.*

op·ti·mist (op′tə mist) *n.* a person who expects the best or looks on the bright side of things.

op·ti·mis·tic (op′tə mis′tik) *adj.* **1.** inclined to look on the bright side of things and to believe that everything will turn out for the best. **2.** hopeful (about something): *I'm optimistic about my chances of getting a job.* **3.** of or relating to optimism. —**op′ti·mis′ti·cal·ly,** *adv.*

op·ti·mum (op′tə məm) *n., pl.* **op·ti·ma** (op′tə mə) or **optimums.** the best, highest possible, or most favorable point or level: *Business profits are at an optimum.* —*adj.* best, highest possible, or most favorable.

op·tion (op′shən) *n.* **1.** the right or opportunity to choose. **2.** the act of choosing or the course of action chosen: *My option is to stay home and read.* **3.** something chosen or available for choosing. **4.** the right to buy, sell, rent, or use something for a specified price within a stated period of time.

op·tion·al (op′shə nəl) *adj.* left to one's choice; not required or automatic: *Attendance at the meeting is optional.* —**op′tion·al·ly,** *adv.*

op·tom·e·trist (op tom′i trist′) *n.* a person licensed to practice optometry.

op·tom·e·try (op tom′i trē) *n.* the practice or profession of testing the eyes for defects of vision and prescribing corrective lenses.

op·u·lent (op′yə lənt) *adj.* **1.** having much wealth; affluent: *an opulent business executive.* **2.** showing wealth or affluence: *an opulent gift, an opulent apartment.* **3.** plentiful; abundant; luxuriant: *the opulent vegetation of the jungle.* —**op′u·lence,** *n.*

o·pus (ō′pəs) *n., pl.* **op·er·a** or **o·pus·es.** a musical or literary work or composition. ▲ often abbreviated **op.** and followed by a number to identify a composer's works by the order in which they were composed or published: *Beethoven's Symphony No. 9 op. 125.* [From the Latin word *opus* meaning "work."]

or (ôr) *conj.* **1.** used to show a choice of two or more: *Is the water warm or cold? You may use red, blue, or green ink.* **2.** used to introduce the second of two choices when the first is introduced by *either* or *whether: Either write or phone me. We didn't know whether to stay or leave.* **3.** used to introduce a word or phrase meaning the same thing: *aeronautics, or the science of flight.* **4.** otherwise: *You should eat lunch, or you will be hungry.* ▲ See **nor** for usage note.

-or *suffix* **1.** (used to form nouns from verbs) a person or thing that performs the action of: *inventor, governor, elevator.*

OR, postal abbreviation for Oregon.

or·a·cle (ôr′ə kəl, or′ə kəl) *n.* **1.** a priest or priestess through whom certain ancient gods, such as Apollo, were believed to answer the questions of their worshipers. **2.** a shrine or temple of a god, such as that at Delphi, where answers were given. **3.** an answer given by a priest or priestess at such a shrine, often having a vague or hidden meaning. **4.** a person or thing that is believed to have great wisdom or authority.

o·rac·u·lar (ô rak′yə lər) *adj.* **1.** of, relating to, or like an oracle. **2.** with vague or hidden meaning: *oracular writings about the future.* —**o·rac′u·lar·ly,** *adv.*

o·ral (ôr′əl) *adj.* **1.** not written; using speech; spoken: *I gave an oral report to the class.* **2.** of or relating to the mouth: *oral hygiene.* **3.** taken into the body through the mouth: *an oral vaccine.* —**o′ral·ly,** *adv.*

oral history **1.** a historical account obtained by recording interviews with people who can give firsthand descriptions of past events: *an oral history of the civil rights movement.* **2.** the study or collection of oral histories.

or·ange (ôr′inj, or′inj) *n.* **1.** a round citrus fruit having a thick reddish yellow or yellow rind and a juicy, sweetish or acid pulp. **2.** a tropical evergreen tree bearing this fruit, having waxy white flowers. **3.** a reddish yellow color. —*adj.* **1.** having the color orange. **2.** made from or flavored with oranges: *orange juice.*

or·ange·ade (ôr′in jād′, or′in jād′) *n.* a drink made of orange juice and water and sweetened with sugar.

o·rang·u·tan (ô rang′ù tan′) *also,* **o·rang·u·tang,** **o·rang·ou·tang** (ô rang′ù tang′). *n.* a large tree-dwelling ape of the forests of Borneo and Sumatra, having very long, powerful arms, short legs, and a shaggy coat of reddish brown hair. [From the Malay phrase *ōrang ūtan* meaning "wild man," from the words *ōrang* "man" + *ūtan* "forest."]

orangutan

at; āpe; fär; câre; end; mē; it; īce; pîerce; hot; ōld; sông, fôrk; oil; out; up; ūse; rüle; pùll; tûrn; chin; sing; shop; thin; <u>th</u>is; hw in white; zh in treasure. The symbol ə stands for the unstressed vowel sound heard in about, taken, pencil, lemon, and circus.

O

o·rate (ô rāt′) *v.i.,* **o·rat·ed, o·rat·ing.** to speak in a grand, pompous, or formal manner.

o·ra·tion (ô rā′shən) *n.* a long, elaborate, formal speech, especially one given on a special occasion before a large audience.

or·a·tor (ôr′ə tər, or′ə tər) *n.* **1.** a person who delivers orations or an oration. **2.** any skilled public speaker.

or·a·tor·i·cal (ôr′ə tôr′i kəl, or′ə tôr′i kəl) *adj.* of, relating to, or characteristic of orators or oratory. —**or′a·tor′i·cal·ly,** *adv.*

or·a·to·ri·o (ôr′ə tôr′ē ō′, or′ə tôr′ē ō′) *n., pl.* **or·a·to·ri·os.** a dramatic musical composition, usually set to a religious text and performed by solo voices, chorus, and orchestra, without action, costumes, or scenery.

or·a·to·ry[1] (ôr′ə tôr′ē, or′ə tôr′ē) *n.* **1.** eloquence or skill in public speaking: *The candidate was a master of campaign oratory.* **2.** the art of public speaking. [From the Latin word *oratoria* meaning "oratorical art," from the word *orator* "a speaker, orator," from the word *orare* "to plead, argue" or "to pray."]

or·a·to·ry[2] (ôr′ə tôr′ē, or′ə tôr′ē) *n., pl.* **or·a·to·ries.** a place set aside for prayer, as a room in a convent. [From the Old French word *oratoire* meaning "a chapel for prayer," from the Late Latin word *oratorium* "place for prayer," from the Latin word *orator* "a speaker, orator," from the word *orare* "to plead, argue" or "to pray."]

orb (ôrb) *n.* **1.** something round, such as a sphere or globe. **2.** the sun, moon, or any other heavenly body. **3.** the eye or eyeball. ▲ used in literature. **4.** a small globe having a cross on the top, used as a symbol of royal power.

or·bit (ôr′bit) *n.* **1.** the path of a heavenly body as it revolves in a closed curve about another body: *the orbit of the earth around the sun.* **2.** one complete trip of a spacecraft or artificial satellite along such a path. **3.** a range of activity, influence, or knowledge. **4.** either of the bony hollows or cavities in the skull in which the eyeballs are located; eye socket. —*v.t.* **1.** to move in an orbit around: *The planet Mercury orbits the sun.* **2.** to put (a spacecraft or satellite) into an orbit. —*v.i.* to move in an orbit.

or·bit·al (ôr′bi təl) *adj.* of or relating to an orbit: *the orbital path of a spacecraft.*

or·chard (ôr′chərd) *n.* **1.** an area where fruit or nut trees are grown. **2.** a group of such trees.

or·ches·tra (ôr′kə strə) *n.* **1.** a group of musicians playing together on various instruments, usually including strings, woodwinds, brasses, and percussion instruments. **2.** the instruments played by such a group. **3.** the main floor of a theater. **4.** a usually lowered or sunken area just in front of a stage, in which the orchestra plays at the performance of an opera, ballet, or other musical show. [From the Latin word *orchestra* meaning "place in the theater where the Senate sat," from the Greek word *orchēstra* "dancing area," the place in the Greek theater where the chorus danced, from the word *orcheisthai* meaning "to dance."]

or·ches·tral (ôr kes′trəl) *adj.* of, relating to, composed for, or performed by an orchestra: *orchestral music.* —**or′ches′tral·ly,** *adv.*

or·ches·trate (ôr′kə strāt′) *v.t.,* **or·ches·trat·ed, or·ches·trat·ing.** to compose or arrange (music) for an orchestra. —**or′ches·tra′tion,** *n.* —**or′ches·tra′tor,** *n.*

or·chid (ôr′kid) *n.* **1.** any of various irregularly shaped flowers, often pale purple or white. **2.** a plant bearing this flower. **3.** a bluish purple color. —*adj.* having the color orchid; bluish purple.

or·dain (ôr dān′) *v.t.* **1.** to fix, decide, or command by decree or authority: *The law ordains the punishment of a convicted criminal.* **2.** to appoint formally to the ministry or another religious office.

or·deal (ôr dēl′, ôr′dēl) *n.* **1.** a very difficult test or painful experience: *The first day in a new school can be an ordeal.* **2.** in former times, a way of deciding whether someone was guilty or innocent of a crime by making the person undergo a dangerous or painful test. If the person was unharmed, it was believed to be proof of his or her innocence.

or·der (ôr′dər) *n.* **1.** a direction or command to do something: *a court order to release a prisoner. A soldier must obey orders.* **2.** an arrangement of things; position in a series: *Arrange the names in alphabetical order.* **3.** any fixed system or condition: *the order of the universe.* **4.** a condition in which laws and rules are obeyed: *Police restored order after the riot.* **5.** clean, neat, or proper condition: *to keep one's room in order.* **6.** a request for goods: *a grocery order.* **7.** the goods requested or supplied: *The company shipped the order by express.* **8.** a single portion of food: *an order of pie.* **9.** kind; sort: *intelligence of a high order.* **10.** a category in the classification of plants and animals that ranks higher than a family but lower than a class. **11.** a grade or rank of the clergy: *the order of deacons.* **12.** a group of persons living under the same rules, especially a religious group: *an order of monks.* **13.** a society into which a person is admitted as an honor. **14.** a fraternal organization: *a Masonic order.* **15.** any one of the three major styles of classical Greek architecture: Doric, Ionic, or Corinthian. —*v.t.* **1.** to command or direct; give an order to. **2.** to place an order for; request: *to order books by mail.* **3.** to put into proper order; give order to: *to order one's business affairs before going on vacation.* —*v.i.* to place or give an order or orders.

·**by order** or **by order of.** according to an order (given by a person with the proper authority): *by order of the president.*

·**in order. a.** in the right or proper position or condition: *The books were in order on the shelf.* **b.** in working condition. **c.** according to the rules: *Nominations for class president are now in order.*

·**in order that.** for the purpose that; so that.

·**in order to.** so as to: *to stand on a chair in order to see.*

·**in short order.** without delay; quickly.

·**on order.** having been ordered but not yet delivered: *We have a new car on order.*

·**on the order of.** similar to; like.

·**out of order. a.** not in the right or proper position or condition: *These books are out of order.* **b.** not working properly: *The telephone is out of order.* **c.** against the rules: *The chairperson ruled that the motion was out of order.* **d.** not proper or suitable for the occasion: *Their sad faces seemed out of order at the party.*

·**to call to order.** to ask to be quiet and pay attention: *The mayor called the meeting to order.*

·**to order.** according to the wishes of the buyer: *to have a suit made to order.*

·**to take orders. a.** to do what is ordered; obey. **b.** to become ordained as a member of the clergy.

ordered pair *Mathematics.* a pair of numbers or elements in which one of the pair is considered the first and the other the second.

or·der·ly (ôr′dər lē) *adj.* **1.** in a certain order or having order: *to march in an orderly line, an orderly room.* **2.** free from disturbances, trouble, or violence: *an orderly crowd.* —*n., pl.* **or·der·lies. 1.** a soldier assigned to an officer or officers for the purpose of carrying messages and doing various other tasks. **2.** a hospital worker who assists doctors and nurses. **3.** a male hospital attendant. —**or′der·li·ness,** *n.*

Order of the Garter, the oldest and most important order of knighthood in England, founded about 1350.

or·di·nal (ôr′də nəl) *adj.* of, relating to, or indicating order or position in a series. —*n.* see **ordinal number**.

ordinal number, a number that shows sequence or position in a set or collection, as first, second, third, and so forth. ▲ See **cardinal number** for usage note.

or·di·nance (ôr′də nəns) *n.* a regulation or law, especially one made by the government of a city or town: *Our city has an ordinance that prohibits littering.*

or·di·nar·i·ly (ôr′də när′ə lē, ôr′də ner′ə lē) *adv.* **1.** in most cases; usually; commonly: *Ordinarily, the museum is open on Sundays.* **2.** in a usual or normal way.

or·di·nar·y (ôr′də ner′ē) *adj.* **1.** commonly used; habitual or regular; usual: *one's ordinary tone of voice.* **2.** not distinguished in any way from others; average; everyday: *This author's book is a very ordinary novel.* —**or′di·nar′i·ness,** *n.*

 ·**out of the ordinary.** unusual; exceptional: *Such hot weather is out of the ordinary this time of year.*

or·di·nate (ôr′də nit, ôr′də nāt′) *n.* **1.** on a graph, the distance of a point from the horizontal axis measured parallel to the vertical axis. It is used to define the point in a Cartesian coordinate system. The ordinate is frequently called the *y* coordinate. See **abscissa** for illustration. **2.** a line, number, or algebraic expression representing this distance.

or·di·na·tion (ôr′də nā′shən) *n.* **1.** the ceremony of ordaining. **2.** the condition of being ordained.

ord·nance (ôrd′nəns) *n.* **1.** military weapons and equipment. **2.** the branch of a military service that obtains, stores, and issues ordnance.

Or·do·vi·cian (ôr′də vish′ən) *n.* the second geological period of the Paleozoic era, when fish, the first animals with backbones, appeared. —*adj.* of, relating to, or characteristic of this period.

ore (ôr) *n.* a rock or other mineral substance in the earth containing enough of a metal or of a useful mineral to make mining it profitable.

Ore., Oregon.

Oreg., Oregon.

o·reg·a·no (ə reg′ə nō′) *n.* any of various plants related to the mint, having fragrant leaves that are used for seasoning.

O·res·tes (ô res′tēz) *n.* *Greek Mythology.* the son of Agamemnon and Clytemnestra, who killed his mother and her lover because they had murdered his father.

or·gan (ôr′gən) *n.* **1.** a musical instrument consisting of pipes of different lengths that are sounded by air blown from a bellows. It is played by means of one or more keyboards. Also, **pipe organ.** **2.** a similar instrument whose tones are produced and amplified electrically. **3.** any of various other musical instruments, such as the reed organ. **4.** a part of an animal or plant that is composed of several kinds of tissues and that performs a specific function or functions. The heart, liver, and eyes are organs of the body. **5.** a newspaper, newsletter, or magazine published by a political party, business, or some other group or organization. **6.** a means of getting something done: *The city council is an organ of local government.*

or·gan·dy (ôr′gən dē) *also,* **or·gan·die.** *n., pl.* **or·gan·dies.** a sheer, lightweight fabric, usually made of cotton and given a crisp finish. It is used especially for dresses and curtains.

or·gan·elle (ôr′gə nəl′) *n.* a structure inside a cell that has a specialized function. Mitochondria, vacuoles, and ribosomes are typical organelles.

organ grinder, a street musician who plays a hand organ.

or·gan·ic (ôr gan′ik) *adj.* **1.** relating to, deriving from, or including living things: *Decayed leaves and grass are used as organic fertilizers.* **2.** of or relating to a body

organ: *an organic disease.* **3.** of, using, raised, or grown by methods in which chemical fertilizers, insecticides, or other artificial substances are not used: *organic farming, organic foods.* **4.** made up of related parts: *an organic whole.* **5.** of, relating to, or belonging to a class of chemical compounds including most of the compounds of carbon. Starches and proteins are organic compounds. —**or·gan′i·cal·ly,** *adv.*

organic chemistry, the branch of chemistry that deals with organic compounds.

or·gan·ism (ôr′gə niz′əm) *n.* **1.** any living thing. Animals, plants, mushrooms, protozoans, and bacteria are all organisms. **2.** something having parts that work together to form a whole: *the economic organism.*

or·gan·ist (ôr′gə nist) *n.* a person who plays the organ.

or·gan·i·za·tion (ôr′gə nə zā′shən) *n.* **1.** the act or process of organizing: *The class president was in charge of organization of the school dance.* **2.** the state or manner of being organized: *In our library the organization of books is by author.* **3.** a group of persons united or organized for a particular purpose: *a labor organization.*

Organization of American States, an organization of thirty-two Latin American and Caribbean countries and the United States, formed in 1948 to provide collective security, economic cooperation, and peaceful settlement of disputes.

or·gan·ize (ôr′gə nīz′) *v.,* **or·gan·ized, or·gan·iz·ing.** —*v.t.* **1.** to arrange in an orderly, systematic way: *to organize books on a shelf.* **2.** to put or bring together; bring into being: *to organize an amateur theater group.* **3.** to cause (employees) to form or join a labor union: *to organize steelworkers.* **4.** to cause employees of (a business or an industry) to form or join a labor union. —*v.i.* to form or join a labor union or other organization. —**or′gan·iz′a·ble,** *adj.* —**or′gan·iz′er,** *n.*

organized labor, all the members of labor unions as a group.

or·gan·za (ôr gan′zə) *n.* a transparent, lightweight fabric that looks like organdy.

or·gasm (ôr′gaz əm) *n.* the sensations felt at the height of sexual excitement.

or·gy (ôr′jē) *n., pl.* **or·gies. 1.** a wild, drunken, unrestrained revelry or party. **2. orgies.** in ancient Greece and Rome, secret rites or ceremonies that were dedicated to certain gods, such as Bacchus, and were accompanied by drunkenness and wild dancing and singing.

o·ri·el (ôr′ē əl) *n.* a bay window built out from a wall.

o·ri·ent (*n.,* ôr′ē ənt; *v.,* ôr′ē ent′) *n.* **Orient.** the countries of Asia, especially the Far East. —*v.t.* **1.** to make familiar with new surroundings or circumstances or a situation: *It took a while for the new students to orient themselves.* **2.** to get or fix the location or bearings of: *to orient oneself by the North Star.* **3.** to fix so as to be pointed or directed: *to orient a tennis court north and south, to orient fashions toward youthful buyers.*

O·ri·en·tal (ôr′ē en′təl) *also,* **o·ri·en-**

oriel

---

at; āpe; fär; câre; end; mē; it; īce; pîerce; hot; ōld; sông, fôrk; oil; out; up; ūse; rüle; pùll; tûrn; chin; sing; shop; thin; this; hw in white; zh in treasure. The symbol ə stands for the unstressed vowel sound heard in about, taken, pencil, lemon, and circus.

O

tal. *adj.* of, relating to, or characteristic of the Orient. —*n.* **1.** a person who was born or is living in the Orient. **2.** a person who is descended from one of the native peoples of the Orient. ▲ now often considered offensive for definition 2.

o·ri·en·tate (ôr′ē ən tāt′) *v.t.*, *v.i.*, **o·ri·en·tat·ed**, **o·ri·en·tat·ing.** to orient or become oriented.

o·ri·en·ta·tion (ôr′ē ən tā′shən) *n.* **1.** the act or process of orienting or the state of being oriented. **2.** an introduction to familiarize people with new surroundings or circumstances: *The college sponsored a weekend orientation for the new students.* **3.** one's awareness of one's surroundings and environment, and of other people in relation to oneself.

or·i·fice (ôr′ə fis, or′ə fis) *n.* a passage or opening, especially in the body, such as the ears, nose, and mouth.

o·ri·ga·mi (ôr′i gä′mē) *n.* the Japanese art of folding paper into the form of an animal, flower, or other object.

origami
practicing the art of origami

or·i·gin (ôr′i jin, or′i jin) *n.* **1.** the source from which something begins or comes; root or cause: *the origin of a rumor. The fire's origin was in the basement.* **2.** parentage; ancestry: *a person of Irish origin.* **3.** *Mathematics.* the point of intersection of the horizontal and vertical axes of a Cartesian coordinate system, where both coordinates equal zero.

o·rig·i·nal (ə rij′ə nəl) *adj.* **1.** not made, done, thought of, or used before; new or unusual: *an original suggestion, original research.* **2.** able to produce, do, or think of something new or unusual; inventive; creative: *an original thinker.* **3.** of, relating to, or belonging to the origin or beginning of something; first; starting: *the original owner of a house.* **4.** that is not a copy, imitation, or translation: *an original painting.* —*n.* something that is not a print, copy, imitation, or translation; something original.

o·rig·i·nal·i·ty (ə rij′ə nal′i tē) *n.* **1.** the quality of being original. **2.** the ability to be inventive or creative: *a writer of great originality.*

o·rig·i·nal·ly (ə rij′ə nə lē) *adv.* **1.** at or from the start; at first; initially: *Basketball was originally played in the United States.* **2.** in a new, fresh, or unusual manner.

original sin **1.** in Christian theology, the tendency to do evil that humans are born with and that is inherited from Adam, the first human. **2.** Adam's disobedience to God that is the cause of this tendency.

o·rig·i·nate (ə rij′ə nāt′) *v.*, **o·rig·i·nat·ed**, **o·rig·i·nat·ing.** —*v.t.* to start or bring into existence: *to originate a new card game.* —*v.i.* to come into existence; begin: *an airplane flight that originates in Boston.* —**o·rig′i·na′tion**, *n.* —**o·rig′i·na′tor**, *n.*

o·ri·ole (ôr′ē ōl′) *n.* **1.** any of various songbirds related to the crow, found from Europe to Australia. The male is usually bright orange or yellow and has black markings on the head, wings, and tail, while the female is dull greenish yellow. **2.** any of various American songbirds of similar appearance. American orioles are related to blackbirds, meadowlarks, tanagers, and grackles.

oriole

O·ri·on (ō rī′ən) *n.* a constellation on the celestial equator, thought to resemble a hunter wearing a belt with a sword attached at the side.

or·i·son (ôr′ə zən, or′ə zən) *n.* *Archaic.* a prayer.

Or·lon (ôr′lon) *n.* *Trademark.* a synthetic fiber that is widely used in making clothing, bedding, and other textile products.

or·na·ment (*n.*, ôr′nə mənt; *v.*, ôr′nə ment′) *n.* **1.** a small, often brightly colored or shiny decorative object: *a row of ornaments on the mantel.* **2.** anything used to decorate or beautify. —*v.t.* to add an ornament or ornaments to: *to ornament a dress with silver buttons.* —**or′na·men·ta′tion**, *n.*

or·na·men·tal (ôr′nə men′təl) *adj.* relating to or being an ornament: *an ornamental design on a blouse.* —*n.* a plant grown to decorate or beautify. —**or′na·men′tal·ly**, *adv.*

or·nate (ôr nāt′) *adj.* having much ornamentation: *The palace was furnished with ornate furniture.* —**or·nate′ly**, *adv.* —**or·nate′ness**, *n.*

or·ner·y (ôr′nə rē) *adj.*, **or·ner·i·er**, **or·ner·i·est.** **1.** stubborn and difficult to manage; unruly: *an ornery mule.* **2.** mean or ugly: *an ornery mood.* —**or′ner·i·ness**, *n.*

or·ni·thol·o·gist (ôr′nə thol′ə jist) *n.* a student of or an expert in ornithology.

or·ni·thol·o·gy (ôr′nə thol′ə jē) *n.* the branch of zoology that deals with the study of birds. —**or·ni·tho·log′i·cal** (ôr′nə thə loj′i kəl), *adj.*

o·ro·tund (ôr′ə tund′) *adj.* **1.** (of the voice) strong, resonant, and mellow: *The great actor spoke in orotund tones.* **2.** pompous; bombastic: *an orotund speech.*

or·phan (ôr′fən) *n.* a child whose natural parents are absent or dead and who must be brought up in an orphanage or by foster parents. —*v.t.* to make an orphan of: *The war orphaned thousands of children.*

or·phan·age (ôr′fə nij) *n.* an institution that takes in and cares for orphans.

Or·phe·us (ôr′fē əs) *n.* *Greek Mythology.* a musician renowned for the beautiful way in which he played the lyre. His playing enchanted trees and stones and tamed wild beasts.

or·ris (ôr′is, or′is) *n.*, *pl.* **or·ris·es.** any of several varieties of iris having a fragrant root.

or·ris·root (ôr′is rüt′, ôr′is rŭt′, or′is rüt′, or′is rŭt′) *n.* the violet-scented root of the orris. It is dried and powdered for use in perfume, sachets, and tooth powder.

or·tho·clase (ôr′thə klās′, ôr′thə klāz′) *n.* a hard mineral that is a type of feldspar and is found mainly in igneous rock.

or·tho·don·tics (ôr′thə don′tiks) *n.* the branch of dentistry that deals with the straightening of the teeth, often by means of braces. ▲ used with a singular verb. Also, **or·tho·don·tia** (ôr′thə don′shə).

or·tho·don·tist (ôr′thə don′tist) *n.* a dentist who specializes in orthodontics.

or·tho·dox (ôr′thə doks′) *adj.* **1.** established or accepted: *orthodox political views.* **2.** following widely used or proven methods: *an orthodox approach to education.* **3. Orthodox. a.** of, relating to, or characteristic of the Orthodox Church. **b.** of, relating to, or practicing Orthodox Judaism. [From the Late Latin word *orthodoxus* meaning "having the right faith," from the Greek word *orthodox* "having the right opinion," from the words *orthos* "straight, right" + *doxa* "opinion."]

Orthodox Church, a group of Christian churches that developed from the church of the Byzantine Empire. The Orthodox Church does not recognize the supremacy of the pope. Also, **Eastern Church, Eastern Orthodox Church.**

Orthodox Judaism, the branch of Judaism that adheres to a strict interpretation of the Torah.

or·tho·dox·y (ôr′thə dok′sē) *n., pl.* **or·tho·dox·ies. 1.** the quality or character of being orthodox. **2.** an orthodox belief or opinion.

or·tho·graph·ic (ôr′thə graf′ik) *adj.* **1.** of or relating to orthography. **2.** correct in spelling. Also, **or·tho·graph·i·cal** (ôr′thə graf′i kəl). —**or′tho·graph′i·cal·ly,** *adv.*

or·thog·ra·phy (ôr thog′rə fē) *n., pl.* **or·thog·ra·phies. 1.** the way of representing the sounds of a language by written or printed symbols. **2.** the correct spelling of words. **3.** the study of letters and spelling.

or·tho·pe·dic (ôr′thə pē′dik) *adj.* of, relating to, or used in orthopedics.

or·tho·pe·dics (ôr′thə pē′diks) *n.* the branch of medicine that deals with injuries, deformities, and diseases of the bones, tendons, ligaments, muscles, and joints. ▲ used with a singular verb.

or·tho·pe·dist (ôr′thə pē′dist) *n.* a physician who specializes in orthopedics.

Or·well·i·an (ôr wel′ē ən) *adj.* of, relating to, or characteristic of George Orwell or his writings.

–ory *suffix* **1.** (used to form adjectives from verbs or from nouns) **a.** of, relating to, or doing: *contradictory.* **b.** serving to or characterized by: *compulsory, contributory.* **2.** (used to form nouns from verbs or from other nouns) a place or instrument for: *observatory.*

o·ryx (ôr′iks) *n., pl.* **o·ryx·es** or **o·ryx.** an antelope found in desert regions of Africa and Arabia, having a gray or brown coat with black or brown markings and long, nearly straight horns.

Os, the symbol for osmium.

O·sage (ō′sāj, ō sāj′) *n.* **1.** a member of a tribe of North American Indians, originally living in parts of Kansas, Missouri, and Illinois, now living in Oklahoma. **2.** the language of this tribe. —*adj.* of or relating to these people or their language.

Os·car (os′kər) *n.* **1.** any of a group of awards given each year in the United States by the Academy of Motion Picture Arts and Sciences for achievement in acting, direction, writing, and other areas of motion-picture production. **2.** the statuette that represents such an award. Also, **Academy Award.**

os·cil·late (os′ə lāt′) *v.i.,* **os·cil·lat·ed, os·cil·lat·ing. 1.** to vibrate or swing back and forth between two points: *to oscillate like a pendulum.* **2.** *Physics.* to produce oscillation. **3.** to waver in making a choice: *The senator oscillated between voting against the bill and for it.*

os·cil·la·tion (os′ə lā′shən) *n.* **1.** the act or process of oscillating. **2.** a single movement from one point, limit, or extreme to another: *an oscillation of a pendulum.* **3.** *Physics.* the periodic fluctuation between two extremes of a quantity, such as voltage, or two extreme positions, as in a vibrating tuning fork.

os·cil·la·tor (os′ə lā′tər) *n.* **1.** a person or thing that oscillates. **2.** a device that produces electrical oscillations, or alternating current, used in radio and television transmitters and receivers. —**os·cil·la·to·ry** (os′ə lə tôr′ē), *adj.*

os·cil·lo·scope (ə sil′ə skōp′) *n.* an electronic instrument that produces a visible wave pattern on the fluorescent screen of a cathode-ray tube corresponding to the electric signals fed into it.

os·cu·late (os′kyə lāt′) *v.i., v.t.,* **os·cu·lat·ed, os·cu·lat·ing.** to kiss. —**os′cu·la′tion,** *n.*

–ose¹ *suffix* (used to form adjectives) full of, given to, or like: *grandiose, verbose.* [From the Latin suffix *-osus* meaning "full of."]

–ose² *suffix* used in chemistry to indicate a carbohydrate: *dextrose.* [From the French suffix *-ose,* from the word *glucose* "glucose."]

o·sier (ō′zhər) *n.* **1.** any of various species of willow, having flexible twigs and branches that are used in making baskets and wicker furniture. **2.** a twig of such a willow.

O·si·ris (ō sī′ris) *n. Egyptian Mythology.* the god of the lower world and judge of the dead.

os·mi·um (oz′mē əm) *n.* a very hard, heavy, bluish gray metallic element. Its alloys are used in pen points, electrical contacts, lighting filaments, and phonograph needles. Symbol: **Os** [From the Greek word *osmē* meaning "odor." Some osmium compounds have an unpleasant smell.]

os·mo·sis (oz mō′sis, os mō′sis) *n.* **1.** the movement through a membrane, such as a plant or animal cell membrane, of a more concentrated solution toward a less concentrated one. This equalizes the pressure on both sides of the membrane. **2.** any gradual process of absorbing that seems to happen without conscious effort: *to learn something by osmosis.* —**os·mot·ic** (oz mot′ik, os mot′ik), *adj.*

os·prey (os′prē, os′prā) *n., pl.* **os·preys** or **osprey.** a fish-eating hawk having brownish black feathers and a white head and undersides. Also, **fish hawk.**

os·si·fi·ca·tion (os′ə fi kā′shən) *n.* **1.** the process of changing into bone. **2.** a part that has become changed into bone.

osprey

os·si·fy (os′ə fī′) *v.,* **os·si·fied, os·si·fy·ing.** —*v.t.* **1.** to cause to change into bone. **2.** to cause to become very rigid, conservative, or conventional: *An old quarrel had ossified the cousins' dislike for each other.* —*v.i.* **1.** to change into bone. **2.** to become very rigid, conservative, or conventional: *Their opinions slowly ossified*

os·ten·si·ble (os ten′sə bəl) *adj.* put forth as actual; apparent: *an ostensible reason for doing something, but not the real reason.* —**os·ten′si·bly,** *adv.*

os·ten·ta·tion (os′tən tā′shən) *n.* a showy display meant to impress others or attract attention: *a rich family that lives without ostentation.*

os·ten·ta·tious (os′tən tā′shəs) *adj.* **1.** done to impress others or attract attention; showy: *an ostentatious tour in a new sports car.* **2.** characterized by or showing ostentation. —**os′ten·ta′tious·ly,** *adv.* —**os′ten·ta′tious·ness,** *n.*

os·te·o·path (os′tē ə path′) *n.* a person who is trained to practice osteopathy.

os·te·o·pa·thy (os′tē op′ə thē) *n.* a method of treating diseases by manipulating the bones and muscles. Osteo-

O

at; āpe; fär; câre; end; mē; it; īce; pîerce; hot; ōld; sông, fôrk; oil; out; up; ūse; rüle; pùll; tûrn; chin; sing; shop; thin; this; hw in white; zh in treasure. The symbol ə stands for the unstressed vowel sound heard in about, taken, pencil, lemon, and circus.

pathy also includes other methods of medical treatment, such as the use of drugs and surgery. —**os′te·o·path′ic,** *adj.*

os·te·o·po·ro·sis (os′tē ō pə rō′sis) *n.* a disorder in which the bones become porous and brittle because of a loss of calcium and other minerals. Osteoporosis develops gradually and is most common in older women. [Formed from the Greek words *osteon* meaning "bone" and *poros* "pore" and the suffix *-ōsis* meaning "a process or condition."]

os·tler (os′lər) another spelling of **hostler.**

ost·mark (ôst′märk′) *n.* the monetary unit of East Germany, equal to 100 pfennigs. Also, **mark.**

os·tra·cism (os′trə siz′əm) *n.* **1.** the act of ostracizing or the condition of being ostracized. **2.** in ancient Greece, temporary banishment by vote of the people.

os·tra·cize (os′trə sīz′) *v.t.,* **os·tra·cized, os·tra·ciz·ing. 1.** to cut off or exclude from a group or from society: *to ostracize a classmate for cheating.* **2.** in ancient Greece, to banish temporarily by vote of the people. [From the Greek word *ostrakizein* meaning "to banish," from the word *ostrakon* "potsherd." In ancient Athens, people voted to banish criminals by writing their names on potsherds.]

os·trich (ôs′trich, os′trich) *n., pl.* **os·trich·es.** a two-toed bird of central Africa, the largest of all living birds. It has a long neck, long, powerful legs, a small, flat head, and, in the male, large white plumes on the wings and tail that are valued as ornaments. The ostrich cannot fly, but it can run very swiftly.

Os·tro·goth (os′trə goth′) *n.* a member of the eastern branch of the Goths, who controlled Italy from A.D. 493 to 554. —**Os′tro·goth′ic,** *adj.*

O.T., Old Testament.

ostrich

O·thel·lo (ō thel′ō) *n.* the main character of Shakespeare's tragedy *Othello,* who, driven to suspicion and jealousy, murders his faithful wife.

oth·er (uth′ər) *adj.* **1.** different from the one or ones already mentioned; not the same: *If you don't accept the job, some other person will.* **2.** remaining: *The other guests have not arrived yet.* **3.** additional; further: *The thief had no other choice but to surrender.* **4.** recently past: *the other morning, the other night.* **5.** different in kind or quality: *No other color is suitable.* —*pron.* **1.** a different or additional person or thing. **2.** the remaining one or ones: *The others will join us later.* —*adv.* otherwise: *I could not feel other than surprised.*

  •**every other.** every second or alternate: *The team has practice every other day.*

oth·er·wise (uth′ər wīz′) *adv.* **1.** apart from that; in other respects: *The food ran out early, but otherwise the party was a success.* **2.** under any different circumstances; if not for that: *Fortunately the shipwrecked sailors had a life raft; they would have otherwise drowned.* **3.** in a different way or in any other way: *I cannot believe otherwise but that we shall succeed.* —*adj.* different; other: *The facts are otherwise.* —*conj.* because if not; or else: *The shingles must be fixed; otherwise, the roof will leak.*

other world, a world or existence beyond death or beyond earthly reality.

Ot·ta·wa (ot′ə wə) *n.* a member of a tribe of Algonquian-speaking Indians who lived near the Great Lakes in what is now Michigan.

ot·ter (ot′ər) *n., pl.* **ot·ters** or **ot·ter. 1.** a web-footed water animal related to and resembling the weasel and mink. It has a long, slightly flattened tail. **2.** the valuable glossy brown fur of this animal.

otter *(def. 1)*

Ot·to·man (ot′ə mən) *n., pl.* **Ot·to·mans. 1.** another name for **Turk. 2. ottoman.** a low, box-like, upholstered seat or footstool. —*adj.* another word for **Turkish.**

Ottoman Empire, a Turkish empire that lasted from 1289 to 1922 and included part of eastern Europe, the Near East, Asia Minor, northern Africa, and the eastern Mediterranean.

ouch (ouch) *interj.* used to express sudden pain.

ought[1] (ôt) *auxiliary verb* **1.** to be bound by a promise or duty: *You ought to obey the law.* **2.** to be expected or likely: *I put in new batteries, so the radio ought to work.* **3.** to be bound by what is sensible or wise: *You ought to take care of your cold.* [From the Middle English word *ought,* past participle of *owen* meaning "to own, possess," "to owe," or "to be obliged," from the Old English word *āgan* "to own, possess."]

ought[2] (ôt) another spelling of **aught**[1] and **aught**[2].

ounce[1] (ouns) *n.* **1.** a unit of weight equal to ¹⁄₁₆ pound avoirdupois (28.35 grams). **2.** a unit of weight equal to ¹⁄₁₂ pound troy (31.1 grams). **3.** see **fluid ounce. 4.** a small quantity: *The hikers didn't have an ounce of energy left by nightfall.* [From the Old French word *unce* meaning this unit of weight, from the Latin word *uncia* "a twelfth" or "twelfth part of a pound," from the word *unus* "one" or "a unit."]

ounce[2] (ouns) *n.* another word for **snow leopard.** [From the Old French word *once* meaning this animal, a form of *lonce* "snow leopard," from the Latin word *lynx* "a lynx," from the Greek word *lynx* "a lynx."]

our (our) *adj.* of or belonging to us: *They need our help.*

ours (ourz) *pron.* the one or ones belonging to us: *Their dog is larger than ours.*

our·selves (our′selvz′) *pl. pron.* **1.** the form of **we** or **us** used to give emphasis to the word it goes with: *We ourselves made the decision.* **2.** the form of **we** or **us** used to show that the subject of a verb is the same as the direct object, indirect object, or object of a preposition: *We covered ourselves with a quilt. We told ourselves it was all for the best. We took it upon ourselves to tell you.* **3.** our usual or normal selves: *After feeling very hungry all morning, we were ourselves again after having eaten.*

–ous *suffix* (used to form adjectives from nouns) of, full of, characterized by, or like: *religious, dangerous, famous, clamorous.*

oust (oust) *v.t.* to force or drive out; compel to leave; expel: *The player was ousted from the game for fighting.*

oust·er (ou′stər) *n.* the act or an instance of ousting: *The citizens demanded the ouster of the dictator.*

out (out) *adv.* **1.** from within or the inside; away from the center: *The water rushed out.* **2.** away from one's home or business: *The doctor went out on a call.* **3.** into the open air; outdoors: *The children went out to play.* **4.** from a source or container: *to pour out wine.* **5.** so as to project or extend: *The rocks jutted out into the sea.* **6.** to an end or conclusion: *to fight it out, to hear someone out.* **7.** into a condition of inactivity or extinction: *to put out the flames.* **8.** so as to be exhausted or consumed: *The supplies gave out.* **9.** into or within view, public notice, or circulation: *The sun came out. The book came out last week.* **10.** from among others: *to pick out a new coat.* **11.** *Baseball.* so as to be unsuccessful in reaching a base. —*adj.* **1.** not in control or power: *the out political party.* **2.** not in working order or condition: *That road is out because of the flood. The fire is out.* **3.** directed outward: *an out train.* **4.** outlying: *out islands.* **5.** *Informal.* no longer fashionable or popular: *That style is out this year.* **6.** *Baseball.* (of a batter or base runner) unsuccessful in reaching a base. —*prep.* **1.** from within; out from: *to look out a window.* **2.** outward on; out along: *Drive out the dirt road until you come to the highway.* —*n.* **1.** *usually,* **outs.** the people not in office or in power. **2.** a way or means of escaping or avoiding: *to look for an out.* **3.** *Baseball.* the act of putting out a batter or base runner. —*v.i.* to be revealed; come out: *The truth will out.* —*interj.* away; begone.

· **on the outs** or **at outs.** in disagreement; not friendly: *They have been on the outs since their fight.*

· **out for.** trying hard to get or do: *to be out for a raise in salary.*

· **out of.** **a.** from within: *to look out of the window.* **b.** beyond the limits, reach, or range of: *The airplane flew out of sight.* **c.** without: *The swimmer was out of breath.* **d.** so as to deprive or be deprived of: *to be swindled out of $500.* **e.** from, as material: *That house is built out of brick.* **f.** from among: *to choose one out of three.* **g.** because of; as a result of: *out of kindness.*

· **out to.** trying hard to: *to be out to earn a lot of money.*

out– *prefix* **1.** outside or outward: *outline, outcry.* **2.** more than or better than: *outgrow, outshine, outshoot.*

out·age (ou′tij) *n.* an interruption in some service or operation, as of electric power.

out–and–out (out′ən out′) *adj.* thorough; complete: *an out-and-out liar.*

out·back (out′bak′) *n.* the wild, undeveloped part of Australia.

out·bid (out′bid′) *v.t.,* **out·bid, out·bid** or **out·bid·den, out·bid·ding.** to offer a higher price than (someone else).

out·board (out′bôrd′) *adv., adj.* outside the hull of a boat or ship or farther away from the center of a boat, ship, or aircraft.

outboard motor
a boat with an outboard motor

outboard motor, an engine with a shaft that has a propeller at the end and that is attached to the outside of the stern of a small boat.

out·bound (out′bound′) *adj.* outward bound: *an outbound flight.*

out·break (out′brāk′) *n.* a sudden occurrence or outburst: *an outbreak of flu, the outbreak of World War II.*

out·build·ing (out′bil′ding) *n.* a building, such as a woodshed, barn, or garage, that is separate from a main building.

out·burst (out′bûrst′) *n.* an outpouring or explosion: *a sudden outburst of anger, an outburst of flames.*

out·cast (out′kast′) *n.* a person who is rejected or forced out of a group: *The traitor was an outcast.* —*adj.* forced out or rejected: *an outcast criminal.*

out·class (out′klas′) *v.t.* to be better or higher than in rank or quality; surpass: *to outclass other students in arithmetic.*

out·come (out′kum′) *n.* a result or consequence: *We are waiting to hear the outcome of the election.*

out·crop (*n.,* out′krop′; *v.,* out′krop′) *n.* the part of a rock layer that comes out to the surface of the ground so as to be seen or easily mined: *an outcrop of ore.* —*v.i.,* **out·cropped, out·crop·ping.** to come to the surface of the ground.

out·cry (out′krī) *n., pl.* **out·cries. 1.** a strong objection or protest: *The proposed tax caused an outcry.* **2.** a cry; shout.

out·dat·ed (out′dā′tid) *adj.* out-of-date; old-fashioned.

out·dis·tance (out′dis′təns) *v.t.,* **out·dis·tanced, out·dis·tanc·ing.** to leave behind, as in a race: *That horse easily outdistanced the other horses.*

out·do (out′dü′) *v.t.,* **out·did** (out′did′), **out·done** (out′dun′), **out·do·ing.** to do better than; exceed: *to outdo the rest of the class in geography.*

out·door (out′dôr′) *adj.* done, being, or used out in the open rather than inside a house or other building: *outdoor furniture, an outdoor game.*

out·doors (out′dôrz′) *adv.* not in a house or other building; out under the sky: *to take a walk outdoors, to eat outdoors.* —*n.* the world that is outside houses or other buildings; the open air. ▲ used with a singular verb.

out·er (ou′tər) *adj.* **1.** on the outside: *I wear warm outer clothes in winter.* **2.** far away from the center: *the outer reaches of the universe.*

outer ear, another term for **external ear.**

out·er·most (ou′tər mōst′) *adj.* most distant or farthest out.

outer space 1. the space beyond the earth's atmosphere: *Mars is in outer space.* **2.** the space between the planets or between the stars.

out·field (out′fēld′) *n.* **1.** the part of a baseball field beyond the infield and between the foul lines. **2.** the players who play in this area.

out·field·er (out′fēl′dər) *n.* a baseball player who plays a position in the outfield.

out·fit (out′fit′) *n.* **1.** a set of different articles or equipment for doing something: *a camping outfit.* **2.** a set of clothes; ensemble: *a red outfit.* **3.** *Informal.* any group or team that works together, such as a military unit. —*v.t.,* **out·fit·ted, out·fit·ting.** to provide with articles or equipment: *to outfit an expedition of explorers.* —**out′fit′ter,** *n.*

out·flank (out′flangk′) *v.t.* **1.** to outmaneuver (an opposing army or other force) by getting around its side. **2.** to get the better of (an opponent), especially by avoiding a direct assault.

out·flow (out′flō′) *n.* **1.** the act or process of flowing out. **2.** something that flows out: *an outflow of lava from a volcano.*

out·fox (out′foks′, out′foks′) *v.t.* to outwit; outsmart: *We outfoxed the other team by trying two new plays we had practiced.*

at; āpe; fär; câre; end; mē; it; īce; pîerce; hot; ōld; sông, fôrk; oil; out; up; ūse; rüle; pu̇ll; tûrn; chin; sing; shop; thin; <u>th</u>is; hw in white; zh in treasure. The symbol ə stands for the unstressed vowel sound heard in about, taken, pencil, lemon, and circus.

out·go (out'gō') *n., pl.* **out·goes.** something that goes out, especially money spent.

out·go·ing (out'gō'ing) *adj.* **1.** sociable, open, and talkative; not withdrawn or private: *An outgoing person makes friends quickly.* **2.** going out or departing: *an outgoing president.*

out·grow (out'grō') *v.t.,* **out·grew** (out'grü'), **out·grown,** **out·grow·ing.** **1.** to grow too large for: *to outgrow one's clothing.* **2.** to leave behind or lose as one grows older: *to outgrow a fear of the dark.* **3.** to grow taller or faster than.

out·growth (out'grōth') *n.* **1.** something that develops or results from something else: *Our new interest in conservation is an outgrowth of our hike last summer.* **2.** something that grows out; growth.

out·guess (out'ges') *v.t.* to guess correctly the plans of; be smarter or more clever than; outwit.

out·house (out'hous') *n., pl.* **out·hous·es** (out'hou'ziz). **1.** a small shed or stall outdoors that is used as a toilet. **2.** another word for **outbuilding.**

out·ing (ou'ting) *n.* a short pleasure trip; excursion: *The students all enjoyed the school outing.*

out·land·ish (out'lan'dish) *adj.* strange, unfamiliar, or odd: *outlandish clothes.*

out·last (out'last') *v.t.* to last longer than.

out·law (out'lô') *n.* **1.** a person who habitually breaks or defies the law; criminal. **2.** formerly, a person who was excluded from the benefits and protection of the law; fugitive or exile. —*v.t.* **1.** to make illegal; prohibit: *to outlaw the sale of certain drugs.* **2.** to declare (someone) an outlaw.

out·lay (out'lā') *n.* an investment or expenditure of money.

out·let (out'let) *n.* **1.** a place at which something escapes or comes out: *Leaves clogged the outlets of the swimming pool.* **2.** a means of expression or release: *Sports are a good outlet for one's energy.* **3.** a place in an electrical wiring system where appliances can be plugged in. **4.** a place where products are sold, especially a store that sells the goods of a single manufacturer.

out·line (out'līn') *n.* **1.** the shape or contour of an object formed by following or tracing along its outer edges: *Through the fog they saw the outline of a passing ship.* **2.** a summary or general description, especially one that organizes the contents of a story, composition, or speech. **3.** a style of drawing in which an object or scene is represented merely by its outer lines with no shading. —*v.t.,* **out·lined, out·lin·ing.** **1.** to set off or make visible: *Skyscrapers were outlined against the sky.* **2.** to summarize or give a general description of: *to outline a plan of action.* **3.** to draw the outline of.

out·live (out'liv') *v.t.,* **out·lived, out·liv·ing.** to live or last longer than.

out·look (out'lúk') *n.* **1.** a view into the future; expectation: *The weather outlook for tomorrow is not good.* **2.** a point of view or set of opinions: *an optimistic outlook on life.* **3.** a place from which a view is obtained; lookout. **4.** the view from such a place.

out·ly·ing (out'lī'ing) *adj.* located far from the center of something: *The zoo is located in an outlying district of the city.*

out·ma·neu·ver (out'mə nü'vər) *v.t.* to maneuver better than or defeat by maneuvering.

out·mod·ed (out'mō'did) *adj.* no longer in style, suitable, or useful: *an outmoded machine.*

out·most (out'mōst') *adj.* farthest out; outermost.

out·num·ber (out'num'bər) *v.t.* to exceed in number; be greater in number than: *The soldiers were greatly outnumbered by the enemy.*

out–of–bounds (out'əv boundz') *adv.* in sports, outside the legal area of play: *The ball was thrown out-of-bounds.* —*adj.* being outside the legal area of play.

out–of–date (out'əv dāt') *adj.* no longer in style or use; outmoded: *an out-of-date manner of dress.*

out–of–doors (out'əv dôrz') *adj.* another term for **outdoor.** Also, **out-of-door.** —*n., adv.* another term for **outdoors.**

out–of–the–way (out'əv thə wā') *adj.* remote; secluded: *an out-of-the-way spot.*

out·pa·tient (out'pā'shənt) *n.* a patient who receives care or treatment from a hospital, clinic, or similar institution without staying there overnight.

out·play (out'plā') *v.t.* to play better than.

out·post (out'pōst') *n.* **1.** a small military station, usually at some distance from the main force, established to keep control over an area and to guard against attack. **2.** the soldiers assigned to such a station. **3.** a remote settlement, as on a frontier.

out·pour·ing (out'pôr'ing) *n.* something that pours out or is poured out; outflow: *There were great outpourings of help for the victims of the earthquake.*

out·put (out'pút') *n.* **1.** the amount of something produced: *electrical output, work output.* **2.** the information made available by a computer.

out·rage (out'rāj') *n.* **1.** an act of extreme violence, viciousness, or cruelty: *The murder of the hostages was an outrage against humanity.* **2.** great anger or rage: *The peasants felt outrage at the attacks on their villages.* **3.** a great insult or offense: *Such behavior in public is an outrage.* —*v.t.,* **out·raged, out·rag·ing.** **1.** to cause great anger in: *The newspaper's editorial outraged the senator.* **2.** to subject to an outrage; abuse or injure greatly.

out·ra·geous (out rā'jəs) *adj.* **1.** going beyond proper limits: *an outrageous price, an outrageous demand.* **2.** shameful; offensive; shocking: *outrageous behavior.* —**out·ra·geous·ly,** *adv.*

out·rank (out'rangk') *v.t.* to be of a higher rank than: *A major outranks a captain.*

out·reach (*v.,* out'rēch'; *n., adj.* out'rēch') *v.t.* to reach or extend beyond; exceed; surpass: *During the flood, the demands for medicine and food outreached the supplies.* —*adj.* of or relating to the extending of services or benefits beyond usual limits: *an outreach program for students who don't speak English.*

out·rig·ger (out'rig'ər) *n.* **1.** an extra float and its supporting frame that can be attached to the side of a canoe to extend out into the water and prevent the boat from capsizing. **2.** a canoe equipped with an outrigger.

out·right (out'rīt') *adj.* complete; total; thorough: *an outright lie.* —*adv.* **1.** in a direct or straightforward way; openly: *Please say outright what you mean.* **2.** completely and all at once: *to pay for a house outright.* **3.** at once; immediately.

outrigger

out·run (out'run') *v.t.,* **out·ran** (out'ran'), **out·run, out·run·ning.** **1.** to run farther or faster than: *Our horse outran all the others in the race.* **2.** to go beyond; exceed: *The demand for the new book outran the store's supply.*

out·sell (out'sel') *v.t.,* **out·sold** (out'sōld'), **out·sel·ling.** **1.** to sell more merchandise than: *to outsell other salesclerks.* **2.** to be sold in greater quantities than.

out·set (out'set') *n.* the beginning; start: *the outset of a journey.*

out·shine (out'shīn') *v.t.,* **out·shone, out·shin·ing.** **1.** to shine more brightly than. **2.** to be better than; excel.

out·side (out'sīd', out'sīd', out'sīd') *n.* **1.** the outer side, surface, or part; exterior: *The outside of the house was painted white.* **2.** an area or world beyond an enclosure or boundary: *The prisoner got a letter from the*

outside. —*adj.* **1.** situated on the outside; outer: *The outside layer of paint was peeling.* **2.** coming from or acting from without: *outside influences.* **3.** extremely slight; remote: *an outside chance.* **4.** reaching the utmost limit possible: *an outside estimate of expenses.* —*adv.* on, to, or toward the outside; outdoors: *Do you want to go outside for a while?* —*prep.* **1.** beyond the walls, surfaces, or boundaries of: *They live just outside Philadelphia.* **2.** beyond the range or limits of: *The matter falls outside the jurisdiction of this court.*

‑**at the outside.** at most: *The job may take two hours at the outside.*

‑**outside of. a.** outside. **b.** with the exception of.

out·sid·er (out′sī′dər) *n.* a person who is not a member of a certain group, society, or organization.

out·skirts (out′skûrts′) *pl. n.* the regions or sections surrounding or at the edge of a specified area, as a city.

out·smart (out′smärt′) *v.t.* to outwit.

out·spo·ken (out′spō′kən, out′spō′kən) *adj.* **1.** open or frank in speech: *The senator was very outspoken on the issues.* **2.** expressed frankly or boldly: *outspoken disapproval.* —**out′spo′ken·ly,** *adv.* —**out′spo′ken·ness,** *n.*

out·spread (*adj.,* out′spred′; *v.,* out′spred′) *adj.* spread out; extended. —*v.t., v.i.* **out·spread, out·spread·ing.** to spread out; extend.

out·stand·ing (out′stan′ding) *adj.* **1.** so excellent as to stand out from others of its kind: *an outstanding athlete.* **2.** remaining to be done, settled, or paid: *an outstanding debt.* —**out′stand′ing·ly,** *adv.*

out·stay (out′stā′) *v.t.* to remain longer than or beyond the time of: *to outstay one's welcome.*

out·stretched (out′strecht′) *adj.* stretched out; extended: *to welcome a guest with outstretched arms.*

out·strip (out′strip′) *v.t.,* **out·stripped, out·strip·ping. 1.** to surpass; excel: *That state outstrips others in coal production.* **2.** to exceed: *Demand for the car outstripped its production.* **3.** to run farther or faster than, as in a race.

out·ward (out′wərd) *adv.* to or toward the outside; away; out: *The door opens outward.* —*adj.* **1.** toward the outside. **2.** relating to the outside, the visible, or the external: *There were outward changes, but the city remained essentially the same.* Also (*adv.*), **out·wards** (out′wərdz). —**out′ward·ness,** *n.*

out·ward·ly (out′wərd lē) *adv.* **1.** on or toward the outside. **2.** in appearance; seemingly: *outwardly happy.*

out·wear (out′wâr′) *v.t.,* **out·wore** (out′wôr′), **out·worn** (out′wôrn′), **out·wear·ing. 1.** to last longer or wear better than: *This fabric outwears most other materials.* **2.** to wear out or exhaust.

out·weigh (out′wā′) *v.t.* **1.** to be greater in weight than: *You outweigh me by ten pounds.* **2.** to be more important than: *The advantages outweigh the disadvantages.*

out·wit (out′wit′) *v.t.,* **out·wit·ted, out·wit·ting.** to get the better of (someone) by cunning or cleverness.

out·work (out′wûrk′) *v.t.* to work better or faster than; outdo in working.

out·worn (*v.,* out′wôrn′; *adj.,* out′wôrn′) *v.* past participle of **outwear.** —*adj.* **1.** worn out: *an outworn coat.* **2.** no longer in use; out-of-date.

o·va (ō′və) the plural of **ovum.**

o·val (ō′vəl) *adj.* **1.** shaped like an egg. **2.** shaped like an ellipse. —*n.* something having an oval shape.

Oval Office, the office of the president of the United States, located in the White House.

o·var·i·an (ō vâr′ē ən) *adj.* of, relating to, or affecting an ovary.

o·va·ry (ō′və rē) *n., pl.* **o·va·ries. 1.** the female reproductive organ that produces eggs. **2.** *Botany.* the part of a plant in which the seeds are formed.

o·vate (ō′vāt) *adj.* having an oval shape: *an ovate leaf.*

o·va·tion (ō vā′shən) *n.* an enthusiastic burst of applause or other demonstration of public approval: *The pianist received a standing ovation.*

ov·en (uv′ən) *n.* an enclosed chamber, as in a stove, that is used to heat, bake, roast, or dry objects that are placed inside.

ov·en·bird (uv′ən bûrd′) *n.* a North American warbler with brownish feathers. It builds a dome-shaped nest on the ground.

o·ver (ō′vər) *prep.* **1.** in a place or position higher than; above: *Clouds hung over the lake.* **2.** upon so as to cover or close: *Put a blanket over the sleeping child.* **3.** on the surface of: *to spread butter over bread.* **4.** to the other side of; across: *The horse jumped over the fence.* **5.** forward and down from: *to fall over a cliff.* **6.** from one end of to the other; along: *to drive over a new road.* **7.** on the other side of; beyond: *The town is over the next hill.* **8.** during; throughout: *School is closed over the holidays.* **9.** above in authority, power, or rank: *Those soldiers need a strong leader over them.* **10.** more than: *The price is over $700.* **11.** in preference to: *to be chosen over ten other candidates.* **12.** with reference to; concerning; about: *Don't get so upset over minor details.* **13.** by means of: *The news came over the radio.* —*adv.* **1.** above: *We could hear a plane flying over.* **2.** down or forward and down: *The ball rolled to the edge of the cliff and fell over.* **3.** above and beyond the top, brim, or edge: *The water boiled over.* **4.** from an erect or upright position: *The cat knocked the vase over.* **5.** so as to bring what is underneath to the top; upside down: *Turn the page over.* **6.** so as to cover or be covered: *The lake froze over.* **7.** from one side or place to the other: *Come over for dinner tonight.* **8.** on or at the other side of some intervening space: *a pal over in the next county.* **9.** once more; again: *If you don't do the job right, you'll have to do it over.* **10.** in repetition or succession: *three times over.* **11.** from beginning to end; through: *Read this contract over.* **12.** in excess; in addition; remaining: *Four goes into ten twice with two left over.* —*adj.* **1.** ended; finished: *The war was soon over.* **2.** higher or upper; in excess: *Our estimate was two dollars over.*

‑**over again.** once more: *Tell that story over again.*

‑**over and above.** in addition; besides.

‑**over and over.** again and again; repeatedly.

over- *prefix* **1.** too much, too highly, or too: *overload, overrate, overanxious.* **2.** above; higher: *overhead.* **3.** around, covering, or on top: *overgrowth, overcoat, overshot.* **4.** from above to below; down: *overthrow, overturn.*

Language Note

To understand the meaning of a word that begins with **over-** but is not defined in this dictionary, add the words "too much" or "too" to the meaning of the basic word. For example, *overcooked* means "cooked too much" and *overambitious* means "too ambitious." For any important *over-* word that has a special meaning, there is an entry in the dictionary.

at; āpe; fär; câre; end; mē; it; īce; pîerce; hot; ōld; sông; fôrk; oil; out; up; ūse; rüle; pull; tûrn; chin; sing; shop; thin; this; hw in white; zh in treasure. The symbol ə stands for the unstressed vowel sound heard in about, taken, pencil, lemon, and circus.

O

o·ver·a·bun·dance (ō′vər ə bun′dəns) n. too great an amount; excess: *An overabundance of rain this spring caused the river to flood.*

o·ver·act (ō′vər akt′) v.i., v.t. to act (a role or part) in an exaggerated or unrealistic way; overdo in acting.

o·ver·ac·tive (ō′vər ak′tiv) adj. too active: *an overactive child.* —**o′ver·ac′tive·ly,** adv.

o·ver·all (ō′vər ôl′) adj. 1. general or total: *My overall impression of them was favorable.* 2. from one end to the other: *The overall length of the car is 12 feet.*

o·ver·alls (ō′vər ôlz′) pl. n. loose-fitting trousers usually having a piece that covers the chest, with suspenders attached.

o·ver·anx·ious (ō′vər angk′shəs) adj. too anxious.

o·ver·arm (ō′vər ärm′) adj. performed with the arm raised above the shoulder; overhand: *an overarm throw.*

o·ver·ate (ō′vər āt′) the past tense of **overeat.**

o·ver·awe (ō′vər ô′) v.t., **o·ver·awed, o·ver·aw·ing.** to overcome or restrain by inspiring awe.

o·ver·bal·ance (ō′vər bal′əns) v.t., **o·ver·bal·anced, o·ver·bal·anc·ing.** 1. to cause to lose balance. 2. to be greater than in weight or importance.

o·ver·bear (ō′vər bâr′) v.t., **o·ver·bore** (ō′vər bôr′), **o·ver·borne** (ō′vər bôrn′), **o·ver·bear·ing.** to overcome or drive down, as by weight or power.

overalls

o·ver·bear·ing (ō′vər bâr′ing) adj. arrogantly superior in manner; domineering. —**o′ver·bear′ing·ly,** adv.

o·ver·bite (ō′vər bīt′) n. a condition in which the upper front teeth project out over the lower front teeth when the jaws are closed.

o·ver·board (ō′vər bôrd′) adv. over the side of a ship into the water: *The sailor slipped and fell overboard.*
 ·**to go overboard.** to go to extremes, especially because of enthusiasm or affection.

o·ver·book (o′vər bŏk′) v.t, v.i., **o·ver·booked, o·ver·book·ing.** to make reservations (for more than can be accommodated by the space available): *The airline overbooked our flight. Ten passengers were overbooked.*

o·ver·bur·den (ō′vər bûr′dən) v.t. to put too great a weight or burden on; overload.

o·ver·came (ō′vər kām′) the past tense of **overcome.**

o·ver·cast (ō′vər kast′) adj. clouded over; cloudy; dark; gloomy: *an overcast sky.* —v.t., **o·ver·cast, o·ver·cast·ing.** 1. to cover with clouds or darkness. 2. to sew (the edge of fabric) over and over with long stitches to prevent raveling. —n. 1. a covering of clouds. 2. a stitch sewn by overcasting.

o·ver·cau·tious (ō′vər kô′shəs) adj. too cautious.

o·ver·charge (v., ō′vər chärj′; n., ō′vər chärj′) v.t., **o·ver·charged, o·ver·charg·ing.** 1. to charge (someone) too high a price: *The salesclerk overcharged me on that purchase.* 2. to load or supply with too great a charge: *to overcharge an electric battery.* —n. a charge that is too great.

o·ver·cloud (ō′vər kloud′) v.t. to cover with clouds.

o·ver·coat (ō′vər kōt′) n. a heavy outer coat worn over other clothing for added warmth.

o·ver·come (ō′vər kum′) v., **o·ver·came, o·ver·come, o·ver·com·ing.** —v.t. 1. to get the better of, as in a contest or conflict; conquer: *The army overcame all opposition.* 2. to rise above or get over: *to overcome one's fear of heights.* 3. to exhaust, overwhelm, or make helpless: *I was overcome by the heat.* —v.i. to be victorious; conquer.

o·ver·con·fi·dent (ō′vər kon′fi dənt) adj. too confident. —**o′ver·con′fi·dence,** n.

o·ver·crowd (ō′vər kroud′) v.t. to put too many people

or things into: *The small apartment was overcrowded with furniture.*

o·ver·de·vel·op (ō′vər di vel′əp) v.t. 1. to develop too much. 2. to submerge (a photographic film or plate) in developing solution too long, so that it becomes too dark.

o·ver·do (ō′vər dü′) v., **o·ver·did** (ō′vər did′), **o·ver·done** (ō′vər dun′), **o·ver·do·ing.** —v.t. 1. to do or use too much; carry too far. 2. to cook (food) too much. —v.i. to do too much or go too far.

o·ver·dose (n., ō′vər dōs′; v., ō′vər dōs′, ō′vər dōs′) n. too large a dose, as of a drug. —v.i. **o·ver·dosed, o·ver·dos·ing.** —v.i. to take too large a dose, as of a drug.

o·ver·draft (ō′vər draft′) n. 1. an overdrawing of a bank account. 2. the amount overdrawn: *an overdraft of fifty dollars.*

o·ver·draw (ō′vər drô′) v.t., **o·ver·drew** (ō′vər drü′), **o·ver·drawn, o·ver·draw·ing.** 1. to write a check against (a bank account) that is larger than the account's balance or credit. 2. to exaggerate: *characters overdrawn for dramatic effect.*

o·ver·dress (ō′vər dres′) v.i., v.t. to dress in clothes that are too formal, fancy, or warm for the occasion.

o·ver·due (ō′vər dü′, ō′vər dū′) adj. 1. remaining unpaid past the assigned date of payment: *The rent is overdue.* 2. not happening or arriving, though the expected or scheduled time is past: *The birth of the young couple's baby is overdue.* 3. that should have happened sooner: *An apology is long overdue.*

o·ver·eat (ō′vər ēt′) v.i., **o·ver·ate, o·ver·eat·en, o·ver·eat·ing.** to eat too much.

o·ver·em·pha·size (ō′vər em′fə sīz′) v.t., **o·ver·em·pha·sized, o·ver·em·pha·siz·ing.** to place too much emphasis on; stress too much. —**o′ver·em′pha·sis,** n.

o·ver·es·ti·mate (v., ō′vər es′tə māt′; n., ō′vər es′tə·mit) v.t., **o·ver·es·ti·mat·ed, o·ver·es·ti·mat·ing.** to make too high an estimate of: *to overestimate the cost.* —n. an estimate that is too high. —**o′ver·es′ti·ma′tion,** n.

o·ver·ex·pose (ō′vər ek spōz′) v.t., **o·ver·ex·posed, o·ver·ex·pos·ing.** 1. to display or expose (someone or something) too much. 2. to expose (a photographic film or plate) for too long a time. —**o′ver·ex·po′sure,** n.

o·ver·feed (ō′vər fēd′) v.t., **o·ver·fed** (ō′vər fed′), **o·ver·feed·ing.** to feed too much.

o·ver·flow (v., ō′vər flō′; n., ō′vər flō′) v., **o·ver·flowed, o·ver·flowed** or **o·ver·flown, o·ver·flow·ing.** —v.i. 1. to flow beyond the usual limits: *Water from the kitchen sink overflowed onto the floor.* 2. to be so full that the contents flow over: *The bathtub overflowed.* 3. to be very full: *The parents' hearts overflowed with love for the child.* —v.t. 1. to flow over the top edge or rim of: *The river overflowed its banks.* 2. to flow or spread over; flood: *When the dam burst, water overflowed the town.* 3. to be larger than (something) can hold: *The crowd overflowed the small auditorium.* —n. 1. the act of overflowing. 2. something that overflows. 3. an outlet for excess liquid.

o·ver·grow (ō′vər grō′) v., **o·ver·grew** (ō′vər grü′), **o·ver·grown, o·ver·grow·ing.** —v.t. 1. to cover with growth; grow over: *Weeds overgrew the yard.* 2. to grow too large for; outgrow. —v.i. to grow too much or too fast.

o·ver·grown (v., ō′vər grōn′; adj., ō′vər grōn′, ō′vər·grōn′) v. past participle of **overgrow.** —adj. 1. grown too large or beyond normal size. 2. covered with weeds, vines, or other growth.

o·ver·growth (ō′vər grōth′) n. 1. excessive growth. 2. growth spreading over or covering something: *The ruins are covered by an overgrowth of vines.*

o·ver·hand (ō′vər hand′) adj. performed with the hand raised above the elbow or the arm raised above the shoulder: *an overhand pitch.* —adv., also, **o′ver·hand′ed.**

in an overhand style or manner: *to throw a baseball overhand.*

o·ver·hang (*v.*, ō′vər hang′; *n.*, ō′vər hang′) *v.*, **o·ver·hung** (ō′vər hung′), **o·ver·hang·ing.** —*v.t.* to hang out over (something): *a smooth broad highway overhung by the dark cloud of a mountain ridge* (John Updike). —*v.i.* to hang or project over something. —*n.* a part or section that overhangs; projection.

o·ver·haul (*v.*, ō′vər hôl′, ō′vər hôl′; *n.*, ō′vər hôl′) *v.t.* **1.** to examine thoroughly and make needed repairs or adjustments: *to overhaul an automobile engine.* **2.** to make far-reaching changes in: *The governor introduced legislation designed to overhaul the prison system.* **3.** to catch up with; overtake: *The coast guard cutter quickly overhauled the fishing boat.* —*n.* the act of overhauling: *The engine needs a complete overhaul.*

o·ver·head (*adv.*, ō′vər hed′; *adj.*, *n.*, ō′vər hed′) *adv.* above the level of the head: *a light burning overhead, birds flying overhead.* —*adj.* situated, operating, or moving overhead: *overhead lights.* —*n.* the general operating expenses of a business, such as rent, taxes, heating, lighting, and repairs, as opposed to costs of materials, supplies, and labor.

o·ver·hear (ō′vər hîr′) *v.t.*, **o·ver·heard** (ō′vər hûrd′), **o·ver·hear·ing.** to hear without the speaker's intention or knowledge: *to overhear a private conversation.*

o·ver·heat (ō′vər hēt′) *v.i.*, *v.t.* to become or cause to become too hot: *The car's engine overheated.*

o·ver·in·dulge (ō′vər in dulj′) *v.t.*, *v.i.*, **o·ver·in·dulged, o·ver·in·dulg·ing.** to indulge too much. —**o′ver·in·dul′gence,** *n.*

o·ver·joyed (ō′vər joid′) *adj.* very happy or joyful; filled with joy: *We were overjoyed with our success.*

o·ver·kill (ō′vər kil′) *n.* **1.** the capacity to destroy more of an enemy or opponents or inflict greater damage than is necessary for victory. **2.** something that exceeds what is suitable or required: *It was overkill when the radio station played the song twice every hour.*

o·ver·land (ō′vər land′) *adv.* by, on, or across land: *to travel overland.* —*adj.* over or across land: *an overland mail route.*

o·ver·lap (*v.*, ō′vər lap′; *n.*, ō′vər lap′) *v.*, **o·ver·lapped, o·ver·lap·ping.** —*v.t.* **1.** to rest on top of (something) and partially cover it up: *One feather overlaps another on a bird's wing.* **2.** to coincide partly with or have something in common: *Our study of English literature overlaps our study of English history.* —*v.i.* **1.** to rest on top of something, partially covering it. **2.** to coincide in part. —*n.* **1.** an instance of overlapping. **2.** a part that overlaps. **3.** the extent or amount of overlapping.

o·ver·lay (*v.*, ō′vər lā′; *n.*, ō′vər lā′) *v.t.*, **o·ver·laid, o·ver·lay·ing.** **1.** to place over or on each other: *to overlay shingles on a roof.* **2.** to cover or spread with something, such as a layer of protective or decorative material: *to overlay painted wood with shellac.* —*n.* **1.** a decorative or protective layer: *There was an overlay of gold on the rim of the mirror.* **2.** any added surface, front, or veneer: *An overlay of friendliness covered their anger.*

o·ver·load (*v.*, ō′vər lōd′; *n.*, ō′vər lōd′) *v.t.* to put too great a load or burden in or upon: *to overload a car, to overload an electrical system.* —*n.* a load or burden that is too great.

o·ver·look (*v.*, ō′vər lùk′; *n.*, ō′vər lùk′) *v.t.* **1.** to fail to see, notice, or think of: *The visitors overlooked the possibility that the family might be away.* **2.** to disregard; ignore: *to overlook an insult.* **3.** to look over or down upon from a higher place or position: *From the tower we overlooked the whole valley.* **4.** to provide a view of: *The house on the hill overlooks a river.* —*n.* a high place that provides a view of things below.

o·ver·lord (ō′vər lôrd′) *n.* a person who is the lord of other lords or rulers.

o·ver·ly (ō′vər lē) *adv.* excessively; too: *overly generous, overly careful.*

o·ver·much (ō′vər much′) *adj.*, *adv.*, *n.* too much.

o·ver·night (*adv.*, ō′vər nīt′, ō′vər nīt′; *adj.*, ō′vər nīt′) *adv.* **1.** during or through the night: *to keep watch overnight.* **2.** very quickly; suddenly: *A person's character does not change overnight.* —*adj.* **1.** for one night: *an overnight guest.* **2.** of, lasting through, or occurring during the night: *an overnight airplane ride, an overnight storm.* **3.** suitable, used, or made for short trips: *an overnight bag.* **4.** sudden; very quick: *an overnight success.*

o·ver·pass (ō′vər pas′) *n.*, *pl.* **o·ver·pass·es.** a bridge, road, or other passage that crosses above another roadway, a railroad, or some other passage.

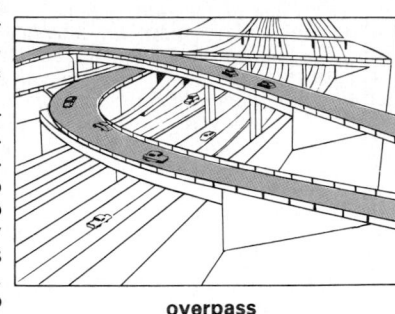

overpass

o·ver·pay (ō′vər pā′) *v.*, **o·ver·paid, o·ver·pay·ing.** —*v.t.* **1.** to pay (someone) too much. **2.** to pay more than what is required or due. —*v.i.* to pay too much: *If you overpay, ask for a refund.* —**o′ver·pay′ment,** *n.*

o·ver·play (ō′vər plā′) *v.t.* to play (a part or role) in an exaggerated manner; overact.

o·ver·pop·u·late (ō′vər pop′yə lāt′) *v.t.*, **o·ver·pop·u·lat·ed, o·ver·pop·u·lat·ing.** to fill with too many people. —**o′ver·pop′u·la′tion,** *n.*

o·ver·pow·er (ō′vər pou′ər) *v.t.* **1.** to overcome by greater strength or power: *My friend overpowered me at wrestling.* **2.** to make helpless or ineffective; overcome: *to be overpowered by feelings of sadness.*

o·ver·price (ō′vər prīs′) *v.t.*, **o·ver·priced, o·ver·pric·ing.** to set too high a price on.

o·ver·pro·duce (ō′vər prə düs′, ō′vər prə dūs′) *v.t.*, **o·ver·pro·duced, o·ver·pro·duc·ing.** to produce more (foodstuffs or other goods) than is necessary. —**o′ver·pro·duc′tion,** *n.*

o·ver·pro·tect (ō′vər prə tekt′) *v.t.* to protect or shelter too much or to a great degree. —**o′ver·pro·tec′tive,** *adj.*

o·ver·ran (ō′vər ran′) the past tense of **overrun.**

o·ver·rate (ō′vər rāt′) *v.t.*, **o·ver·rat·ed, o·ver·rat·ing.** to rate, value, or estimate too highly.

o·ver·reach (ō′vər rēch′) *v.t.* **1.** to reach or extend over or beyond. **2.** to reach past and miss. —*v.i.* to reach too far. —**o′ver·reach′er,** *n.*

·to overreach oneself. to fail by trying to do too much.

o·ver·re·act (ō′vər rē akt′) *v.i.*, **o·ver·re·act·ed, o·ver·re·act·ing.** to react to something too strongly or emotionally: *It would be overreacting to give up baseball just because you weren't chosen for the school team.* —**o′ver·re·ac′tion,** *n.*

o·ver·ride (ō′vər rīd′) *v.t.*, **o·ver·rode** (ō′vər rōd′), **o·ver·rid·den** (ō′vər rid′ən), **o·ver·rid·ing.** **1.** to set aside (an action or decision) by superior authority; cancel: *The legislature overrode the governor's veto.* **2.** to prevail

O

over; supersede: *This problem overrides all other matters.*
3. to ride over; trample.

o·ver·ripe (ō′vər rīp′) *adj.* past the point of ripeness; too ripe.

o·ver·rule (ō′vər rül′) *v.t.,* **o·ver·ruled, o·ver·rul·ing.**
1. to set aside or rule against by higher authority: *The Supreme Court overruled the decision of the lower court.*
2. to decide against or prevail over: *to overrule someone by a nearly unanimous vote.*

o·ver·run (*v.,* ō′vər run′; *n.,* ō′vər run′) *v.t.,* **o·ver·ran, o·ver·run, o·ver·run·ning.** **1.** to swarm or spread over or throughout: *The invading army overran the countryside.* **2.** to flow over: *The river overran its banks.*
3. to run or go beyond: *to overrun second base, to overrun the time allotted for one's speech.* —*n.* **1.** an act or instance of overrunning: *an overrun in the cost of a project.* **2.** an amount that is an overrun.

o·ver·seas (ō′vər sēz′) *also,* **o·ver·sea.** *adv.* over, across, or beyond the sea; abroad: *to travel overseas.*
—*adj.* **1.** employed, situated, or serving overseas: *a company's overseas representative.* **2.** of or relating to countries across the sea; foreign: *overseas trade.*

o·ver·see (ō′vər sē′) *v.t.,* **o·ver·saw** (ō′vər sô′), **o·ver·seen, o·ver·see·ing.** to watch over and manage; have charge of; direct: *to oversee the building of a canal.*

o·ver·se·er (ō′vər sē′ər) *n.* a person who oversees, especially a person who directs the work of laborers.

o·ver·shad·ow (ō′vər shad′ō) *v.t.* **1.** to be more important or significant than: *War overshadowed all the country's other problems.* **2.** to cast a shadow over; obscure; darken.

o·ver·shoe (ō′vər shü′) *n.* a shoe or boot, usually made of rubber, worn over an ordinary shoe to protect against cold, snow, water, or mud.

o·ver·shoot (ō′vər shüt′) *v.,* **o·ver·shot, o·ver·shoot·ing.** —*v.t.* **1.** to go or pass over, above, or beyond (a target, mark, or goal): *The aircraft overshot the landing field.* **2.** to shoot or project (something) over or beyond a target or goal. —*v.i.* to shoot or go too far beyond.

o·ver·shot (*v.,* ō′vər shot′; *adj.,* ō′vər shot′) *v.* past tense and past participle of **overshoot**: —*adj.* **1.** having the upper jaw projecting beyond the lower jaw. **2.** (of a water wheel) driven by water falling down from above, rather than by water flowing past.

o·ver·sight (ō′vər sīt′) *n.* **1.** a careless, unintentional mistake: *The omission of their names from the guest list was an oversight.* **2.** watchful care or direction; supervision: *We worked under the manager's oversight.*

o·ver·sim·pli·fy (ō′vər sim′- plə fī′) *v.t.,* **o·ver·sim·pli·fied, o·ver·sim·pli·fy·ing.** to make (something) appear to be much simpler than it really is:

overshot *(def. 2)*

Many economic problems are complex and must not be oversimplified. —**o′ver·sim′pli·fi·ca′tion,** *n.*

o·ver·size (ō′vər sīz′) *also,* **o·ver·sized.** *adj.* larger than the normal or usual size.

o·ver·sleep (ō′vər slēp′) *v.i.,* **o·ver·slept** (ō′vər slept′), **o·ver·sleep·ing.** to sleep beyond one's intended or usual time for waking up.

o·ver·state (ō′vər stāt′) *v.t.,* **o·ver·stat·ed, o·ver·stat·ing.** to state too strongly; exaggerate. —**o′ver·state′·ment,** *n.*

o·ver·stay (ō′vər stā′) *v.t.* to stay beyond the time or limit of: *to overstay one's welcome.*

o·ver·step (ō′vər step′) *v.t.,* **o·ver·stepped, o·ver·step·ping.** to go over or beyond (a limit); exceed: *to overstep one's authority.*

o·ver·stock (*v.,* ō′vər stok′; *n.,* ō′vər stok′) *v.t.* to supply with more than is needed. —*n.* a stock or supply that is too large.

o·ver·stuffed (ō′vər stuft′) *adj.* **1.** stuffed to excess. **2.** (of furniture) having the frame covered over with a thick padding or large amount of stuffing.

o·ver·sup·ply (*v.,* ō′vər sə plī′; *n.,* ō′vər sə plī′) *v.t.,* **o·ver·sup·plied, o·ver·sup·ply·ing.** to supply with more than is needed; overstock: *We were oversupplied with food for the camping trip.* —*n., pl.* **o·ver·sup·plies.** a supply that is too large: *an oversupply of wheat from a huge harvest.*

o·vert (ō vûrt′, ō′vûrt) *adj.* not hidden, concealed, or secret; easily observed: *The invasion of the neutral country was an overt act of aggression.* —**o·vert′ly,** *adv.*

o·ver·take (ō′vər tāk′) *v.t.,* **o·ver·took** (ō′vər tůk′), **o·ver·tak·en, o·ver·tak·ing.** **1.** to catch up with: *The police car overtook the speeding driver.* **2.** to catch up with and then pass: *Los Angeles has overtaken Chicago in population.* **3.** to come upon unexpectedly or suddenly.

o·ver·tax (ō′vər taks′) *v.t.* **1.** to place too heavy a burden on or draw too much from: *Years of war had overtaxed the country's resources.* **2.** to charge too great a tax on.

o·ver–the–coun·ter (ō′vər thə koun′tər) *adj.* (of a drug) able to be sold legally without a doctor's prescription: *Aspirin is an over-the-counter drug.*

o·ver·throw (*v.,* ō′vər thrō′; *n.,* ō′vər thrō′) *v.t.,* **o·ver·threw** (ō′vər thrü′), **o·ver·thrown, o·ver·throw·ing.** **1.** to remove from a position of power or dominance, especially by force or struggle: *The rebels overthrew the government.* **2.** to throw or knock down; overturn; upset: *to overthrow a table in rage.* **3.** to throw something, as a baseball, beyond (the intended place). —*n.* **1.** the act of overthrowing or the state of being overthrown. **2.** a throw that goes beyond the intended place.

o·ver·time (ō′vər tīm′) *n.* **1.** time worked beyond regular working hours. **2.** the pay for such extra time worked. **3.** *Sports.* an extra period of play to decide the winner of a contest that ended in a tie. —*adv.* beyond regular hours: *to work overtime.* —*adj.* of, for, or in overtime.

o·ver·tone (ō′vər tōn′) *n.* **1.** a fainter and higher tone that occurs with the fundamental tone produced by a musical instrument. Also, **harmonic. 2.** a secondary or implied meaning or quality; suggestion; hint: *an overtone of jealousy in a seemingly friendly remark.*

o·ver·ture (ō′vər chər) *n.* **1.** an orchestral musical composition that introduces a larger musical work, such as an opera. **2.** a suggestion or proposal meant to lead to some new action; offer to begin something: *a friendly overture to a new neighbor.*

o·ver·turn (ō′vər tûrn′) *v.t.* **1.** to turn or throw over; upset: *Heavy winds overturned the sailboat.* **2.** to overthrow, defeat, or destroy. —*v.i.* to be or become turned over: *The speeding car overturned on the sharp curve.*

o·ver·use (*v.,* ō′vər ūz′; *n.,* ō′vər ūs′) *v.t.,* **o·ver·used, o·ver·us·ing.** to use too much. —*n.* too much or too frequent use.

o·ver·view (ō′vər vū′) *n.* a broad, general view or survey.

o·ver·ween·ing (ō′vər wē′ning) *adj.* having or showing great arrogance, conceit, or self-importance.

o·ver·weight (ō′vər wāt′) *adj.* above the normal, desirable, or allowed weight. —*n.* more weight than is normal, desirable, or allowed.

o·ver·whelm (ō′vər hwelm′, ō′vər welm′) *v.t.* **1.** to overcome completely; overpower or crush: *Enemy forces* *overwhelmed the outpost.* **2.** to cover or bury completely. —**o′ver·whelm′ing·ly,** *adv.*

o·ver·whelm·ing (ō′vər hwel′ming, ō′vər wel′ming) *adj.* that overwhelms by great power or intensity; irresistible; overpowering: *The force of the tornado was overwhelming. The candidate was elected by an overwhelming majority.*

o·ver·work (*v.,* ō′vər wûrk′; *n.,* ō′vər wûrk′) *v.t.* to cause to work too hard; tire or exhaust with work: *to overwork a mule.* —*n.* more work than one should do or can be expected to do.

o·ver·wrought (ō′vər rôt′) *adj.* **1.** worked up to a state of excessive excitement or nervousness. **2.** too elaborate or fancy; overdone.

o·vi·duct (ō′vi dukt′) *n.* in female humans and certain other female mammals, the tube through which the egg cell passes from the ovary.

o·vip·a·rous (ō vip′ər əs) *adj.* producing eggs that hatch after they have left the body of the female. All birds and most fish and reptiles are oviparous.

o·vi·pos·i·tor (ō′və poz′i tər) *n.* an organ at the end of the abdomen of the female of certain insects and fish, by which eggs are deposited.

o·void (ō′void) *adj.* having the shape of an egg; egg-shaped. —*n.* something shaped like an egg.

o·vo·vi·vip·a·rous (ō′vō vī vip′ər əs) *adj.* producing eggs that develop inside the body of the female and hatch either inside the mother or soon after they are laid. Certain reptiles and fish and many insects are ovoviviparous.

Ovipositor

ov·u·late (ov′yə lāt′, ō′vyə lāt′) *v.i.,* **ov·u·lat·ed, ov·u·lat·ing.** to produce egg cells or discharge them from the ovary. —**ov′u·la′tion,** *n.*

ov·ule (ov′ūl, ō′vūl) *n.* **1.** a small egg, especially one in an early stage of growth. **2.** a part of a plant that develops into a seed after fertilization.

o·vum (ō′vəm) *n., pl.* **o·va.** see **egg**[1] *(def. 4).*

owe (ō) *v.,* **owed, ow·ing.** —*v.t.* **1.** to be under obligation to pay or repay (money): *to owe ten dollars to a friend, to owe the landlord two months' rent.* **2.** to be under obligation to offer or give: *I owe you an apology.* **3.** to be obliged or indebted for: *Modern physics owes a great deal to Einstein.* —*v.i.* to be in debt.

ow·ing (ō′ing) *adj.* due to be paid; unpaid; owed.
   •**owing to.** because of: *Owing to bad weather, I didn't go.*

owl (oul) *n.* any of various birds of prey having a rounded head with large, staring eyes and a hooked bill, a short, square tail, rounded wings, and soft, downy feathers. Owls usually hunt at night and feed chiefly on rodents and other small mammals.

owl·et (ou′lit) *n.* a young or small owl.

owl·ish (ou′lish) *adj.* like or resembling an owl.

own (ōn) *adj.* of, relating to, or belonging to oneself or itself: *The accident was your own fault. Their own child testified against them.* —*n.* something that belongs to oneself or itself: *That idea is better than my own.* —*v.t.* **1.** to have as one's property; have ownership of: *They own all the land between here and the river.* **2.** to acknowledge or admit: *I own that the mistake was mine.*

owl

•**of one's own.** belonging exclusively to oneself: *a pet of one's own.*

•**on one's own. a.** relying only on oneself for support or success: *Since his parents died, he has been on his own.* **b.** through one's personal efforts: *I got the job on my own.*

•**to come into one's own.** to receive the success or recognition one deserves: *She had been an artist for many years before she finally came into her own.*

•**to hold one's own.** to maintain one's position or standing, as against opposition or competition.

•**to own up.** to confess frankly and fully: *Whoever spilled soup on the new rug should own up.*

own·er (ō′nər) *n.* a person who owns something.

own·er·ship (ō′nər ship′) *n.* the state of being an owner; right of possession.

ox (oks) *n., pl.* **ox·en. 1.** the adult castrated male of domestic cattle, used as a work animal or for beef. **2.** any member of a family of large mammals that have hollow horns and chew their cuds, including cattle, buffaloes, and kudus.

ox·blood (oks′blud′) *n.* a deep red color. —*adj.* having the color oxblood; deep red.

ox·bow (oks′bō′) *n.* **1.** the wooden, U-shaped part of a yoke, placed as a collar under and around the neck of an ox. **2.** a U-shaped bend in a river.

ox·cart (oks′kärt′) *n.* a cart pulled by an ox or oxen.

ox·en (ok′sən) the plural of **ox.**

ox·ford (oks′fərd) *n.* **1.** a shoe that comes up to just below the ankle and laces over the instep. **2.** a soft, medium-weight cotton or synthetic fabric, used chiefly for shirts and blouses. Also *(def. 2),* **oxford cloth.** [From *Oxford,* England.]

Oxford gray, a very dark gray color.

ox·i·da·tion (ok′si dā′shən) *n.* the act of oxidizing or the state of being oxidized.

ox·ide (ok′sīd) *n.* a compound of oxygen and one other element.

ox·i·dize (ok′si dīz′) *v.,* **ox·i·dized, ox·i·diz·ing.** —*v.t.* to combine (a chemical substance) with oxygen; make into an oxide. —*v.i.* to become oxidized.

ox·i·diz·er (ok′si dī′zər) *n.* **1.** a substance that yields oxygen for the burning of rocket fuel or a propellant. **2.** any substance that causes oxidation.

ox·tail (oks′tāl′) *n.* the skinned tail of an ox or steer, used in cooking.

ox·y·a·cet·y·lene (ok′sē ə set′ə lēn′) *n.* a mixture of oxygen and acetylene.

oxyacetylene torch, a metal torch used for cutting and welding. It burns a mixture of oxygen and acetylene.

ox·y·gen (ok′sə jən) *n.* a colorless, odorless, tasteless gaseous element that makes up about one fifth of the air and is the most abundant element in the earth's crust. It combines with all other elements except the inert gases. Oxygen is essential to life. Symbol: **O** [From the French word *oxygène* meaning this gas, formed from the Greek words *oxys* meaning "sharp, acid" + *gennan* meaning "to produce." The French chemist Antoine Lavoisier (1743–1794) coined the word *oxygène* because he believed that oxygen was the element that formed acids.]

ox·y·gen·ate (ok′sə jə nāt′) *v.t.,* **ox·y·gen·at·ed, ox·y·gen·at·ing.** to treat, supply with, or mix with oxygen. —**ox′y·gen·a′tion,** *n.*

O

at; āpe; fär; câre; end; mē; it; īce; pîerce; hot; ōld; sông, fôrk; oil; out; up; ūse; rüle; pull; tûrn; chin; sing; shop; thin; **this**; hw in white; zh in treasure. The symbol ə stands for the unstressed vowel sound heard in about, taken, pencil, lemon, and circus.

oxygen mask
firefighters wearing oxygen masks

oxygen mask, a device worn over the nose and mouth, through which oxygen is supplied, often from a storage container.

oxygen tent, a structure resembling a small tent, usually made of a clear plastic material. It is placed over a patient's head and supplied with a flow of oxygen to aid breathing.

ox·y·he·mo·glo·bin (ok′sē hē′mə glō′bin) *n.* a bright red substance in red blood cells consisting of hemoglobin combined with oxygen. It is carried to the tissues by the arteries.

o·yez (ō′yes, ō′yez) *interj.* hear ye! ▲ used to announce that a court of law is in session and to ask for silence.

oys·ter (oi′stər) *n.* any of a group of shellfish found in shallow coastal waters, having a soft body enclosed in two irregular ear-shaped shells hinged at the narrow end. Some oysters are highly valued as food, while others are raised for the fine pearls they produce.

oyster bed, an area on the bottom of shallow coastal waters where oysters breed or are cultivated.

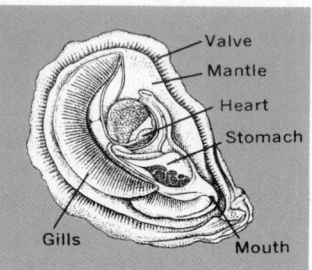

oyster

oz. *pl.* **oz.** or **ozs.** ounce.

o·zone (ō′zōn) *n.* a form of oxygen that is a pale blue gas with a distinctive odor, formed when an electric discharge passes through the air. It is used as a bleach, disinfectant, and deodorant.

ozone layer, a layer of ozone concentrated in the upper atmosphere approximately 10 miles to 30 miles (16–48 kilometers) above the earth. The ozone layer absorbs harmful ultraviolet rays, preventing them from reaching the earth's surface.

P p

1. ancient Semitic   2. Phoenician

3. early Hebrew   4. Greek

5. early Latin   6. later Latin

7. English

P is the sixteenth letter of the English alphabet. The earliest ancestor of our modern letter **P** was an ancient Semitic (1) letter that looked like a hook. This hook-shaped letter, which was called *pe*, meaning "mouth," was used, with only slight changes, in the Phoenician (2) and early Hebrew (3) alphabets. The ancient Greeks borrowed *pe* and called it *pi* (4), writing it very much as it had been written in the preceding alphabets. The Romans (5) originally adopted the Greek form of *pi* and later changed its shape by adding a closed loop at the top of the letter (6). By about 2,400 years ago, the Romans were writing this form of *pi* exactly as we write the capital letter **P** today (7).

p, P (pē) *n.*, *pl.* **p's, P's.** the sixteenth letter of the English alphabet.

p **1.** *Music*. piano. **2.** *Baseball*. pitcher.

P, the symbol for phosphorus.

p. **1.** page. **2.** part. **3.** participle. **4.** pint.

pa (pä) *n. Informal.* father; papa.

Pa, the symbol for protactinium.

Pa., Pennsylvania.

PA **1.** postal abbreviation for Pennsylvania. **2.** public-address system.

pace (pās) *n.* **1.** a single step. **2.** the distance covered in a step, often used as a measure of length averaging from 2½ to 3½ feet (75–100 centimeters). **3.** the rate of speed in walking, running, or other activity: *He quickened his pace as he neared home. She worked at a hectic pace to finish her report.* **4.** a gait of a horse in which both feet on the same side are lifted and put down together. —*v.*, **paced, pac·ing.** —*v.t.*, **1.** to walk back and forth across: *She paced the room while she waited.* **2.** to measure by paces: *He paced off 20 feet from wall to wall.* **3.** to set the rate of speed for: *The coach paced the runner.* —*v.i.* **1.** to walk with slow, steady steps. **2.** (of a horse) to move at a pace.
  ·to keep pace with. a. to keep the same speed of movement as. **b.** to maintain the same rate of progress or development as.
  ·to set the pace. a. to set the speed for others to keep up with or go beyond. **b.** to be an example for others to follow.

pace·mak·er (pās'mā'kər) *n.* **1.** a person who sets the pace in a race. **2.** a person who leads a trend or sets an example for others. **3.** an electronic device implanted in the body to control the rhythm of the heart, used in the treatment of heart disorders.

pac·er (pā'sər) *n.* **1.** a person who paces. **2.** a horse that paces.

pach·y·derm (pak'ə dûrm') *n.* any of several large, thick-skinned, hoofed animals, such as the elephant, hippopotamus, or rhinoceros.

pa·cif·ic (pə sif'ik) *adj.* **1.** making or tending to make peace: *pacific efforts.* **2.** of a peaceful nature; calm; tranquil: *pacific waters.* —**pa·cif'i·cal·ly,** *adv.*

pac·i·fi·ca·tion (pas'ə fi kā'shən) *n.* the act of pacifying or the state of being pacified.

Pa·cif·ic Standard Time (pə sif'ik) the standard time used in much of the western United States and Canada. It is 8 hours earlier than Greenwich Time.

pac·i·fi·er (pas'ə fī'ər) *n.* **1.** a person or thing that pacifies. **2.** a rubber nipple or similar object for babies to suck on.

pac·i·fism (pas'ə fiz'əm) *n.* the principle of opposition to war or other violence, and the belief that peaceful means should be used to settle differences between countries.

pac·i·fist (pas'ə fist) *n.* a person who opposes war or other violence. —**pac'i·fis'tic,** *adj.*

pac·i·fy (pas'ə fī') *v.t.*, **pac·i·fied, pac·i·fy·ing.** **1.** to make calm or quiet: *The mayor tried to pacify the angry crowd.* **2.** to make peaceful; bring peace to.

pack¹ (pak) *n.* **1.** a collection of things wrapped or tied together, especially for carrying on the back: *The camper's pack was heavy.* **2.** a package containing a certain number of similar things: *a pack of matches, a pack of gum.* **3.** a set or group of similar things: *a pack of cards.* **4.** a group of animals living or hunting together: *a pack of wolves.* **5.** a large quantity or amount: *a pack of lies.* **6.** something soaked in water or medicine and applied to a part of the body as a treatment. —*v.t.* **1.** to place in something for storing or carrying: *We packed the books in boxes.* **2.** to fill (something) with objects: *She packed her suitcase for the trip.* **3.** to crowd closely together: *The child packed the sand down with his shovel.* **4.** to fill by crowding or pressing together: *A large crowd packed the ball park.* **5.** to fill or surround tightly in order to seal or protect: *to pack a pipe joint with lead.* **6.** *Informal.* to carry or wear on one's person regularly: *The detective packs a gun.* —*v.i.* **1.** to place articles in something, such as a box or suitcase, for carrying or storing: *Have you packed for the trip yet?* **2.** to become packed or compressed: *This suit packs easily.* **3.** to press together tightly; crowd together: *People packed into the subway car.* [From the Middle Dutch word *pac* meaning "a bundle, package."]

pack² (pak) *v.t.* to select, arrange, or manipulate dishonestly or to one's own advantage: *to pack a jury.* [From the obsolete word *pack* meaning "a secret arrangement."]

pack·age (pak'ij) *n.* **1.** a thing or group of things packed, wrapped up, or bound together; parcel. **2.** a box, case, or the like in which things may be packed. **3.** a group of items considered as a unit: *The travel package includes several tours.* —*v.t.,* **pack·aged, pack·ag·ing.** to make or put into a package.

package deal **1.** an arrangement under which a group of items or services is offered or sold only as a unit: *a package deal for a trip to Canada, with transportation and meals included.* **2.** the items or services offered or sold in this way.

package store, a store that sells alcoholic beverages that can be consumed only off the premises; liquor store.

pack animal, an animal used for carrying loads, such as a horse or mule.

pack·er (pak'ər) *n.* a person or thing that packs, especially a person who owns or is employed in a business where items are packaged for sale: *a meat packer.*

pack·et (pak'it) *n.* **1.** a small package or parcel: *a packet of letters.* **2.** see **packet boat.**

packet boat, a boat that carries mail, passengers, and freight at scheduled times over a regular route, especially along a coast or river.

pack ice, a large layer of floating ice formed by pieces of ice that are pressed together and frozen into a single mass. Also, **ice pack.**

pack·ing (pak'ing) *n.* **1.** the action of a person or a thing that packs: *With careful packing, we were able to fit the clothes in the suitcase without wrinkling them.* **2.** the processing and packaging of meat or other foods for market. **3.** material placed around something else as a cushion or barrier: *We carefully removed the packing from the box of glassware.*

packing house, a place where items to be sold are packaged for sale. Also, **packing plant.**

pack rat **1.** a North American rat noted for its habit of collecting small shiny objects and leaving other objects, such as nuts or pine cones, in their place. **2.** *Informal.* a person who saves miscellaneous, often unneeded items.

pack·sad·dle (pak'sad·əl) *n.* a saddle for carrying the load on a pack animal.

pact (pakt) *n.* an agreement between persons or countries, such as a treaty: *The two warring nations signed a peace pact.*

pad¹ (pad) *n.* **1.** a cushion or soft piece of thick material, used as a stuffing or for protection or comfort. **2.** a number of sheets of paper fastened together along one edge; tablet: *a note pad, an artist's sketch pad.* **3.** one of the cushionlike parts on the underside of the toes of dogs, foxes, and certain other animals. **4.** the foot of a dog, fox, and certain other animals. **5.** a small ink-soaked block of cloth or other material, used to ink a rubber stamp. **6.** a large floating leaf of a water lily or other water plant. **7.** see **launching pad.** **8.** *Slang.* the place where a person lives, such as a room or apartment. —*v.t.,* **pad·ded, pad·ding.** **1.** to cover, stuff, or line with a pad or padding. **2.** to lengthen by adding unnecessary

material: *to pad an essay with quotations.* **3.** to add to dishonestly: *to pad an expense account with false expenditures.* [Possibly of Low German origin.]

pad² (pad) *v.i.,* **pad·ded, pad·ding.** **1.** to travel on foot. **2.** to move with soft or almost silent steps: *We took our shoes off and padded across the room.* —*n.* a soft sound, as of a footstep. [Of uncertain origin.]

pad·ding (pad'ing) *n.* **1.** any soft material, such as cotton or foam, used to make a pad. **2.** unnecessary written material added merely to lengthen.

pad·dle¹ (pad'əl) *n.* **1.** a short oar with a blade at one or both ends, used to propel a canoe or other small boat. **2.** a round or rectangular board with a short handle, used to strike the ball in table tennis and similar games. **3.** any of various flat wooden tools used for beating, stirring, or mixing. **4.** one of the broad boards set in a paddle wheel or waterwheel. —*v.,* **pad·dled, pad·dling.** —*v.t.* **1.** to propel (a canoe or other small boat) by means of a paddle or paddles. **2.** to punish by striking with a paddle; spank. —*v.i.* to propel a canoe or other small boat by means of a paddle. [From the Middle English word *padel* meaning "a long-handled spade," from the Medieval Latin word *padela* with the same meaning.] —**pad'dle·like',** *adj.* —**pad'dler,** *n.*

pad·dle² (pad'əl) *v.i.,* **pad·dled, pad·dling.** to move about or splash in shallow water. [Of uncertain origin.]

pad·dle·fish (pad'əl fish') *n., pl.* **pad·dle·fish** or **pad·dle·fish·es.** any of several species of large fish, having a long, paddle-like snout, found in the Mississippi River.

paddlefish

paddle wheel, a wheel having projecting paddles set at right angles to its circumference, used to propel a water vehicle, as a steamboat.

pad·dock (pad'ək) *n.* **1.** a small field or enclosure in which an animal can graze and exercise. **2.** an area at a racetrack where the horses are saddled and mounted.

paddy *(def. 1)*

pad·dy (pad'ē) *n., pl.* **pad·dies.** **1.** a field where rice is grown. **2.** rice in the husk.

pad·lock (pad'lok') *n.* a detachable lock with a curved bar made to be passed through an opening. —*v.t.* to fasten with a padlock.

pa·dre (pä'drā) *n.* father. ▲ used in addressing or referring to a priest in Italy, Spain, Portugal, and Latin America.

pa·el·la (pä yel′ə, pä āl′yə) *n.* a dish consisting of rice with chicken, seafood, meat, and vegetables flavored with saffron. [From the Spanish word *paella,* from the Catalan word *paella* meaning "frying pan," used as the name of this food, going back to the Latin word *patella* "a small pan or dish."]

pae·an (pē′ən) *also,* **pe·an.** *n.* a song of praise or thanksgiving.

pa·gan (pā′gən) *n.* **1.** a person who is not a Christian, Jew, or Muslim, especially a person who worships many gods. The ancient Greeks and Romans were pagans. **2.** a person who has no religion. —*adj.* of or relating to pagans or paganism. [From the Late Latin word *paganus* meaning "heathen, unbeliever," from the Latin word *paganus* "peasant, person from the country," from the word *pagus* "countryside." Christianity was adopted first in the cities of the Roman Empire, while the rural areas long held to their earlier religions.]

pa·gan·ism (pā′gə niz′əm) *n.* **1.** the beliefs, practices, and customs of pagans. **2.** the state of being a pagan.

page[1] (pāj) *n.* **1. a.** one side of a leaf of a book or letter. **b.** an entire leaf of a book or letter. **2.** the print, writing, or type used on one side of a leaf. **3.** an event or events worthy of recording: *The Civil War was perhaps the most tragic page in American history.* —*v.t.,* **paged, pag·ing.** to number the pages of. —*v.i.* to turn the pages steadily: *to page through a catalog to find an item.* [From the French word *page,* from the Latin word *pagina* "leaf of a book."]

page[2] (pāj) *n.* **1.** a male servant or attendant, especially a boy who attends a person of rank. **2.** a young person employed to serve as an attendant to members of Congress or other legislative bodies. **3.** a person employed to run errands or carry messages, as in a hotel. **4.** formerly, a boy in training for knighthood. —*v.t.,* **paged, pag·ing.** to summon or try to find (someone) by calling out a person's name or sending signals to a beeper. [From the Old French word *page* meaning "male servant."]

pag·eant (paj′ənt) *n.* **1.** a theatrical presentation that is based on or dramatizes events in history or legend. **2.** an elaborate spectacle, procession, or parade.

pag·eant·ry (paj′ən trē) *n., pl.* **pag·eant·ries. 1.** pageants as a group. **2.** an elaborate or spectacular display: *We enjoyed the pageantry of the parade.*

pag·er (pā′jər) *n.* another word for **beeper.**

pa·go·da (pə gō′də) *n.* in eastern Asia, a temple or memorial tower of several stories, often with a series of projecting roofs that curve upward from each story. [From the Portuguese word *pagode* meaning "Oriental temple," probably going back to the Persian word *buktkada* "temple of idols."]

paid (pād) *v.* the past tense and past participle of **pay**[1]. —*adj.* **1.** receiving pay: *a paid adviser.* **2.** having been paid for: *a paid political advertisement.*

pail (pāl) *n.* **1.** a round, open container, usually with a handle, used for carrying water, sand, or other materials. **2.** the amount that a pail holds; pailful.

pail·ful (pāl′fŭl′) *n., pl.* **pail·fuls.** the amount that a pail holds.

pain (pān) *n.* **1.** a feeling of strong discomfort, usually in a particular part of the body; physical distress or suffering: *I have a pain in my knee.* **2.** emotional or mental distress or suffering; anxiety; grief: *the pain of loneliness.* **3. pains.** care or

pagoda

effort: *Take great pains to assemble the model airplane neatly.* —*v.t.* to cause pain to; make suffer: *My knee pains me on damp days. The child's death pained the family.* [From the Old French word *peine* meaning "pain, suffering," from the Latin word *poena* "a penalty" or "pain," from the Greek word *poinē* "penalty."]

·on pain of or **under pain of.** at the risk of (punishment or death).

pained (pānd) *adj.* **1.** suffering from pain; hurt or distressed. **2.** showing pain: *a pained expression on one's face.*

pain·ful (pān′fəl) *adj.* **1.** causing physical or mental pain; distressing: *a painful wound, a painful subject.* **2.** requiring effort or care: *a painful decision.* —**pain′ful·ly,** *adv.* —**pain′ful·ness,** *n.*

pain·kill·er (pān′kil′ər) *n.* something that dulls or relieves pain, such as a medicine.

pain·less (pān′lis) *adj.* free from pain; causing no pain. —**pain′less·ly,** *adv.* —**pain′less·ness,** *n.*

pains·tak·ing (pānz′tā′king) *adj.* needing or showing close, careful work or attention: *a painstaking job, a painstaking worker.* —**pains′tak′ing·ly,** *adv.*

paint (pānt) *n.* **1.** a coloring material made of a pigment mixed with a liquid, such as oil or water. Paint is applied to surfaces as a protective or decorative coating. **2.** a layer or coating of such a material. **3.** a cosmetic, such as rouge, used to add color. —*v.t.* **1.** to represent on a surface with paints: *The artist painted a landscape on the canvas.* **2.** to coat or cover the surface of with paint: *The workers painted the house.* **3.** to describe vividly in words. **4.** to put on or apply with a brush or swab: *to paint a wound with antiseptic.* **5.** to color with cosmetics; apply cosmetics to: *to paint one's face with rouge.* —*v.i.* **1.** to practice the art of painting; make pictures: *I learned how to paint in art class.* **2.** to use paint.

paint·brush (pānt′brush′) *n., pl.* **paint·brush·es.** a brush for applying paint.

paint·er[1] (pān′tər) *n.* **1.** an artist who paints pictures. **2.** a person whose work is painting walls or other surfaces. [From the Old French word *peintour* meaning "one who paints," from the Latin word *pictor* "one who paints pictures," going back to the word *pingere* "to paint, color" or "to depict."]

paint·er[2] (pān′tər) *n.* a rope attached to the bow of a boat for tying it up to something. [From the Old French word *penteur* meaning "a rope on which things are hung."]

paint·er[3] (pān′tər) *n.* another word for **cougar.** [A form of *panther.*]

paint·ing (pān′ting) *n.* **1.** the act or art of applying paints to a surface: *to study painting.* **2.** a picture produced in this way.

pair (pâr) *n., pl.* **pairs** or **pair. 1.** a set of two things meant to be used together: *a pair of slippers, a pair of oars.* **2.** a single thing made up of two parts: *a pair of pliers, a pair of pants.* **3.** two persons or animals associated or working together: *a pair of police officers, a pair of horses.* **4.** a married or engaged couple. **5.** two animals mated together. **6.** in card games, two cards of the same value: *a pair of tens.* —*v.t.* to join or match (two persons or things) in a pair: *They paired the two tallest trumpeters to lead the band.* —*v.i.* to form a pair or pairs.

·to pair off. to join in a pair; form a pair.

---

at; āpe; fär; câre; end; mē; it; īce; pîerce; hot; ōld; sông, fôrk; oil; out; up; ūse; rüle; pull; tûrn; chin; sing; shop; thin; this; hw in white; zh in treasure. The symbol ə stands for the unstressed vowel sound heard in about, taken, pencil, lemon, and circus.

pais·ley (pāz′lē) *n., pl.* **pais·leys. 1.** a colorful design with curved forms on a patterned background. **2.** a fabric having such a design. —*adj.* having such a design: *a paisley shirt.* [From *Paisley,* the city in Scotland where wool shawls having this design were first made.]

Pai·ute (pī üt′, pī′üt) *n., pl.* **Pai·ute** or **Pai·utes. 1.** a member of either of two North American Indian tribes living mainly in California and Nevada. **2.** the language spoken by these tribes.

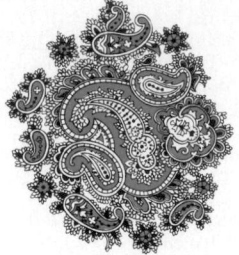

paisley design

pa·ja·mas (pə jä′məz, pə jam′əz) *also, British,* **py·ja·mas.** *pl. n.* a garment for sleeping or informal wear, consisting of a top and trousers.

Pak·i·stan·i (pak′ə stan′ē) *n., pl.* **Pak·i·stan·is** or **Pak·i·stan·i.** a person who was born in or is a citizen of Pakistan. —*adj.* of or relating to Pakistan or its people.

pal (pal) *Informal. n.* a close friend. —*v.i.,* **palled, pal·ling.** to associate as close friends.

pal·ace (pal′is) *n.* **1.** the official residence of a ruler or other high-ranking person. **2.** any large, grand residence or building.

pal·an·quin (pal′ən kēn′) *also,* **pal·an·keen.** *n.* a covered vehicle for one person, carried on the shoulders of two or more people by means of poles.

pal·at·a·ble (pal′ə tə bəl) *adj.* **1.** pleasant to the taste; pleasing in flavor. **2.** agreeable to the mind or feelings; acceptable: *a palatable solution to a problem.* —**pal′at·a·bil′i·ty,** *n.* —**pal′at·a·bly,** *adv.*

pal·ate (pal′it) *n.* **1.** the roof of the mouth. The bony part in the front is the hard palate, and the fleshy part in the back is the soft palate. **2.** the sense of taste: *food that is pleasing to the palate.*

pa·la·tial (pə lā′shəl) *adj.* of, like, or fit for a palace: *a palatial home.* —**pa·la′tial·ly,** *adv.*

pal·a·tine (pal′ə tīn′) *adj.* formerly, having royal privileges and rights in one's own territory: *a count palatine.*

pa·lav·er (pə lav′ər) *n.* **1.** idle talk; chatter. **2.** a parley or conference, especially between explorers or traders and native inhabitants. —*v.i.* to talk idly.

pale¹ (pāl) *adj.,* **pal·er, pal·est. 1.** whitish or lacking intense color; ashen; pallid: *a pale complexion.* **2.** without brightness or richness of color: *pale green.* **3.** having little light; not bright; dim: *pale moonlight.* **4.** feeble; weak: *a pale imitation.* —*v.,* **paled, pal·ing.** —*v.i.* to turn pale: *We paled when we heard the scream.* —*v.t.* to make pale. [From the Old French word *pale,* from the Latin word *pallidus* meaning "pallid, lacking in color," from the word *pallēre* "to grow pale."]

pale² (pāl) *n.* **1.** a narrow, pointed piece of wood, used for fences; stake; picket. **2.** any boundary, barrier, or limit: *behavior beyond the pale of what is right or proper.* —*v.t.,* **paled, pal·ing.** to enclose with pales; fence in. [From the Old French word *pal* meaning "a stake," from the Latin word *palus* "a stake, prop."]

pale·face (pāl′fās′) *n.* a white person. ▲ supposedly first used by North American Indians.

Pa·le·o·cene (pā′lē ə sēn′) *n.* the earliest geological epoch of the Tertiary period of the Cenozoic era, characterized by the development of many primitive mammals. —*adj.* of or relating to this epoch.

Pa·le·o·lith·ic (pā′lē ə lith′ik) *adj.* of or relating to the earliest part of the Stone Age.

pa·le·on·tol·o·gy (pā′lē ən tol′ə jē) *n.* the branch of science that studies fossils and extinct forms of life. —**pa′le·on·tol′o·gist,** *n.*

Pa·le·o·zo·ic (pā′lē ə zō′ik) *n.* a geological era that began about 600 million years ago and ended about 220

million years ago, characterized by the appearance of land plants, sea animals without backbones, fish, amphibians, and reptiles. —*adj.* of or relating to this era.

Pal·es·tine Liberation Organization (pal′ə stīn′) a coalition of Arab political and military groups formed with the purpose of establishing a Palestinian state.

Pal·es·tin·i·an (pal′ə stin′ē ən) *adj.* of or relating to Palestine. —*n.* a person who was born in Palestine or considers Palestine as his or her homeland.

pal·ette (pal′it) *n.* **1.** a thin board or tablet, usually having a hole for the thumb, on which artists place and mix their paints. **2.** the colors used by an artist or in a painting.

pal·in·drome (pal′in drōm′) *n.* a word, phrase, sentence, number, or the like that reads the same forward and backward. The word *Madam,* the sentence *Was it a cat I saw?,* and *2992* are palindromes.

pal·ing (pā′ling) *n.* **1.** a fence made of pales. **2.** pales as a group. **3.** one of the pales forming a fence.

pal·i·sade (pal′ə sād′) *n.* **1.** a fence of strong, pointed stakes placed closely together and set firmly in the ground, used for defense or protection. **2.** one of the stakes used in such a fence. **3. palisades.** a line of steep cliffs, usually rising along a river. —*v.t.,* **pal·i·sad·ed, pal·i·sad·ing.** to enclose or fortify with a palisade.

pall¹ (pôl) *n.* **1.** a heavy covering of black or purple cloth laid over a coffin, hearse, or tomb. **2.** any covering of darkness and gloom: *a thick pall of black smoke.* —*v.t.* to cover with a pall. [From the Old English word *pæll* meaning "a robe, garment" or "covering," from the Latin word *pallium* with the same meanings.]

pall² (pôl) *v.i.* to become dull or boring: *After ten minutes the television show began to pall.* [From the Middle English word *palen* meaning "to become pale," from the Old French word *paleir* "to grow pale," going back to the Latin word *pallēre* "to be pale."]

pal·la·di·um (pə lā′dē əm) *n.* a soft, silver-white metallic element, used in alloys and as a catalyst. Symbol: **Pd** [From *Pallas,* name of one of the largest asteroids. This element was isolated shortly after the asteroid was discovered.]

Pal·las (pal′əs) *n. Greek Mythology.* another name for **Athena.** Also, **Pallas Athena.**

pall·bear·er (pôl′bâr′ər) *n.* one of the persons who carry the coffin at a funeral.

pal·let (pal′it) *n.* **1.** a straw bed or mattress. **2.** any small, hard, or temporary bed, often on the floor.

pal·li·ate (pal′ē āt′) *v.t.,* **pal·li·at·ed, pal·li·at·ing. 1.** to make (an offense or fault) appear less serious. **2.** to lessen the pain or effects of (a disease or illness) without curing it. —**pal′li·a′tion,** *n.*

pal·li·a·tive (pal′ē ā′tiv, pal′ē ə tiv) *adj.* serving to palliate: *palliative drugs.* —*n.* something that palliates.

pal·lid (pal′id) *adj.* lacking color; pale.

pal·lor (pal′ər) *n.* lack of color; paleness: *The child's pallor was due to lack of sleep.*

palm¹ (päm) *n.* **1.** the inner surface of the hand from the wrist to the base of the fingers. **2.** a measure of length equal to the width of a hand, or about 3 to 4 inches (7–10 centimeters). **3.** the part of a glove or mitten covering the palm. —*v.t.* to hold or hide in the palm or hand: *to palm cards.* [From the Old French word *palme* meaning "palm of the hand," from the Latin word *palma* "palm tree" or "palm of the hand."]

·to palm off. to pass off by deceit or fraud.

palm² (päm) *n.* **1.** any of a group of tropical and subtropical trees or shrubs usually having large, featherlike or fan-

palm² *(def. 1)*

shaped leaves growing in a cluster at the top of a tall trunk. **2.** a leaf of such a tree, used as a symbol of victory or success. [From the Old English word *palm* meaning this tree, from the Latin word *palma* "palm tree" or "palm of the hand."]

pal·mate (pal′māt) *adj.* resembling a hand with the fingers spread out: *a palmate leaf.*

pal·met·to (pal met′ō) *n., pl.* **pal·met·tos** or **pal·met·toes.** a palm tree grown in the southern United States and other warm areas.

palm·ist (pä′mist) *n.* a person who practices palmistry.

palm·is·try (pä′mə strē) *n.* the practice of telling a person's fortune by studying the pattern of the lines in the palm of the hand.

Palm Sunday, the Sunday before Easter Sunday, commemorating Jesus' entry into Jerusalem, when people spread palm branches before him.

palm·y (pä′mē) *adj.,* **palm·i·er, palm·i·est. 1.** full of palm trees. **2.** flourishing; prosperous: *the palmy days of one's life.*

pal·o·mi·no (pal′ə mē′nō) *n., pl.* **pal·o·mi·nos.** a light tan horse having a cream-colored or white mane and tail.

palp (palp) *n.* in insects and some other arthropods, a jointed organ of touch or taste that is attached to the mouth.

pal·pa·ble (pal′pə bəl) *adj.* **1.** capable of being touched or felt; tangible. **2.** easily perceived by the senses or mind; obvious; noticeable: *a palpable lie, a palpable error.* —**pal′pa·bil′i·ty,** *n.* —**pal′pa·bly,** *adv.*

pal·pate (pal′pāt) *v.t.,* **pal·pat·ed, pal·pat·ing.** to examine by touch: *The doctor palpated the patient's abdomen to find the pain.* —**pal·pa′tion,** *n.*

pal·pi·tate (pal′pi tāt′) *v.i.,* **pal·pi·tat·ed, pal·pi·tat·ing. 1.** to beat at a rapid rate: *My heart palpitated from excitement.* **2.** to quiver or tremble.

pal·pi·ta·tion (pal′pi tā′shən) *n.* **1.** an abnormally rapid and often irregular beating of the heart. **2.** a quivering or trembling motion.

pal·pus (pal′pəs) *n., pl.* **pal·pi** (pal′pī). another word for **palp.**

pal·sied (pôl′zēd) *adj.* affected with palsy; trembling; shaking.

pal·sy (pôl′zē) *n., pl.* **pal·sies.** weakness or paralysis of a muscle, usually characterized by trembling. —*v.t.,* **pal·sied, pal·sy·ing.** to affect with palsy; cause to tremble.

pal·try (pôl′trē) *adj.,* **pal·tri·er, pal·tri·est.** having little or no value: *Don't leave the waiter a paltry amount of money as a tip.* —**pal′tri·ness,** *n.*

pam·pas (pam′pəz) *also,* **pam·pa.** *pl. n.* vast, treeless plains extending from the Atlantic Ocean to the Andes Mountains in Argentina and in some other areas of South America.

pam·per (pam′pər) *v.t.* to treat too well; indulge or cater to; coddle: *to pamper a child.* —**pam′per·er,** *n.*

pam·phlet (pam′flit) *n.* a short book, usually having a paper cover: *a political pamphlet.*

pam·phlet·eer (pam′fli tîr′) *n.* a person who writes or publishes pamphlets. —*v.i.* to write or publish pamphlets.

pan[1] (pan) *n.* **1.** a dish or container of metal, usually broad, shallow, and without a cover, used especially for cooking or baking. **2.** something like this, such as the container used to separate precious minerals from gravel by washing with water. **3.** a layer of hard earth underneath soft soil; hardpan. —*v.,* **panned, pan·ning.** —*v.t.* **1.** to cook in a pan. **2.** *Informal.* to criticize harshly: *The critics panned the movie.* **3.** to separate (gold or other precious minerals) from gravel by washing in a pan. —*v.i.* to wash earth or gravel in a pan in search of gold or other precious minerals: *The prospector panned for*

gold. [From the Old English word *panne* meaning "a pan[1]."]

·**to pan out.** *Informal.* to turn out well; succeed.

pan[2] (pan) *v.,* **panned, pan·ning.** —*v.t.* to move (a movie or television camera) in order to take in a wide area or follow a moving object. —*v.i.* to move a movie or television camera in this way. —*n.* the act of panning. [From *panorama.*]

Pan (pan) *n.* *Greek Mythology.* the god of forests, fields, flocks, and shepherds, represented as a man with the horns, ears, legs, and tail of a goat.

pan– *combining form* **1.** all; every: *pantheism.* **2.** *usually,* **Pan-.** of or relating to all members of a specified group or area: *Pan-American.*

pan·a·ce·a (pan′ə sē′ə) *n.* something that will cure all diseases or evils; cure-all.

pan·a·ma (pan′ə mä′) *also,* **Pan·a·ma.** *n.* a hat made from the young leaves of a tropical American plant.

Pan·a·ma·ni·an (pan′ə mā′nē ən) *n.* a person who was born in or is a citizen of Panama. —*adj.* of or relating to Panama or its people.

Pan–A·mer·i·can (pan′ə mer′i kən) *adj.* relating to the countries or people of North, Central, and South America: *Pan-American politics.*

pan·cake (pan′kāk′) *n.* a flat cake made from batter and cooked in a pan or on a griddle; griddlecake; flapjack.

pan·chro·mat·ic (pan′krō mat′ik) *adj.* sensitive to light of all colors, as a photographic film.

pan·cre·as (pan′krē əs) *n., pl.* **pan·cre·as·es.** a long, narrow gland below the stomach that sends digestive juices into the small intestine and the hormone insulin into the bloodstream. —**pan·cre·at·ic** (pan′krē at′ik), *adj.*

pan·da (pan′də) *n.* **1.** a bearlike mammal native to the bamboo forests of southwestern China, having a shaggy white coat with black markings. Also, **giant panda. 2.** a reddish brown raccoonlike mammal native to the Himalayas, having short legs, a long, bushy, ringed tail, and a white face. Also, **lesser panda, red panda.**

panda *(def. 1)*

pan·dem·ic (pan dem′ik) *n.* a widespread epidemic that afflicts most of the population in the affected area. —*adj.* (of a disease) epidemic over a large area and afflicting most of the population.

pan·de·mo·ni·um (pan′də mō′nē əm) *n.* **1.** wild disorder or uproar: *There was pandemonium in the arena when our team won.* **2.** a place of wild disorder or uproar.

pan·der (pan′dər) *n.* a person who takes advantage of or makes money from the weaknesses or vices of others. —*v.i.* to act as a pander: *The writer panders to the public taste for violence in this novel.*

Pan·do·ra (pan dôr′ə) *n.* *Greek Mythology.* the first mortal woman, whose curiosity led her to open a box into which Zeus had put all human evils and miseries, thus allowing them to escape into the world.

pane (pān) *n.* a sheet of glass or similar material placed in a window or door.

pan·e·gyr·ic (pan′ə jir′ik) *n.* **1.** a formal speech or writing praising a person or thing. **2.** lofty praise.

---

at; āpe; fär; câre; end; mē; it; īce; pîerce; hot; ōld; sông, fôrk; oil; out; up; ūse; rüle; pùll; tûrn; chin; sing; shop; thin; **this;** hw in white; zh in treasure. The symbol ə stands for the unstressed vowel sound heard in about, taken, pencil, lemon, and circus.

P

pan·el (pan′əl) *n.* **1.** a section of a door, cabinet, or other surface, set off from the surrounding surface by being raised, recessed, or bordered. **2.** a flat piece of material, as of wood or plastic, made to be joined with others. **3.** a section of fabric in a garment, as a skirt. **4.** a thin wooden board used as the surface for an oil painting. **5.** a board on which dials or other controls are mounted, as in an automobile or airplane. **6.** a group of persons whose purpose is to discuss or judge something: *a panel of experts.* **7.** a list of persons called for jury duty. —*v.t.* to furnish or decorate with panels: *The walls of the living room were paneled in walnut.*

pan·el·ing (pan′ə ling) *n.* **1.** wood or other material used to make panels. **2.** a set or series of panels.

pan·el·ist (pan′ə list) *n.* a person who serves on a panel.

panel truck, a small truck, pickup, or van with an enclosed cargo section, used especially to make deliveries and to carry small loads.

pang (pang) *n.* **1.** a sudden, sharp feeling of discomfort or pain: *pangs of hunger.* **2.** a sharp feeling of mental distress: *I felt pangs of guilt after lying to my friend.*

pan·go·lin (pan gō′lin) *n.* a scale-covered mammal, native to Africa and Asia, having sharp claws, a long tongue, and usually a long tail. Also, **scaly anteater.**

pan·han·dle (pan′han′dəl) *n.* **1.** the handle of a pan. **2.** *also,* **Panhandle.** a narrow strip of land attached to a larger area of land and resembling the handle of a pan: *the Oklahoma Panhandle.* —*v.i., v.t.* **pan·han·dled, pan·han·dling.** to beg, especially in the streets: *to panhandle for money for a meal.* —**pan′han′dler,** *n.*

pan·ic (pan′ik) *n.* **1.** a terrible, often uncontrollable fear that can spread suddenly through a group: *When the school caught fire there was a panic.* **2.** a widespread financial crisis caused by a loss of public confidence in stocks or other investments. —*v.,* **pan·icked, pan·ick·ing.** —*v.i.* to become affected with panic: *The children panicked when they realized they were lost.* —*v.t.* to affect with panic: *We were afraid that the storm would panic the horses.* [Originally from the Greek word *panikos* meaning "of the god Pan." In Greek mythology, Pan inspired fear in mortals venturing alone in the forest.] —**pan′ick·y,** *adj.*

pan·ic–strick·en (pan′ik strik′ən) *adj.* overcome by panic.

pan·ni·er (pan′ē ər) *n.* a basket for carrying goods, especially one of two baskets slung across the back of a pack animal or hung over the wheel of a bicycle.

pan·o·ply (pan′ə plē) *n., pl.* **pan·o·plies. 1.** any magnificent covering or display: *a panoply of jewels.* **2.** a complete suit of armor.

pan·o·ram·a (pan′ə ram′ə, pan′ə rä′mə) *n.* **1.** a wide or complete view of an area: *From the mountaintop we could see the vast panorama of the valley below us.* **2.** a complete survey or presentation of a subject. **3.** a picture or series of pictures unrolled and passed before the viewers, showing a continuous scene. [Formed from the prefix *pan-* + the Greek word *horama* meaning "sight," from the word *horan* "to see."]

pan·o·ram·ic (pan′ə ram′ik, pan′ə rä′mik) *adj.* of or like a panorama. —**pan′o·ram′i·cal·ly,** *adv.*

pan·pipe (pan′pīp′) *also,* **Pan·pipe.** *n.* a primitive musical instrument made of a series of reeds or tubes bound together.

pan·sy (pan′zē) *n., pl.* **pan·sies. 1.** a flower having five flat, overlapping petals and growing in a variety of colors. **2.** the plant bearing this flower.

pant (pant) *v.i.* **1.** to breathe quickly or heavily; gasp for breath: *I panted after running up the stairs.* **2.** to long eagerly; yearn: *to pant for success.* —*v.t.* to say breathlessly: *The drowning*

panpipe

swimmer panted, "Help me!" —*n.* a short, labored breath; gasp.

pan·ta·lets (pan′tə lets′) *also,* **pan·ta·lettes.** *pl. n.* long ruffled drawers formerly worn by women and girls.

pan·ta·loon (pan′tə lün′) *n.* **1.** pantaloons. tight-fitting trousers formerly worn by men. **2. Pantaloon.** a comic character in pantomime, usually a foolish old man wearing pantaloons and slippers.

pan·the·ism (pan′thē iz′əm) *n.* the religious belief that everything in nature is part of God and that God is in everything.

pan·the·ist (pan′thē ist) *n.* a person who adheres to pantheism. —**pan′the·is′tic,** *adj.* —**pan′the·is′ti·cal·ly,** *adv.*

pan·the·on (pan′thē on′) *n.* **1. Pantheon.** a round, domed temple built at Rome for all the gods, later used as a Christian church. **2.** all the gods worshiped by a people. **3.** a public building serving as a memorial or mausoleum for the famous people of a country.

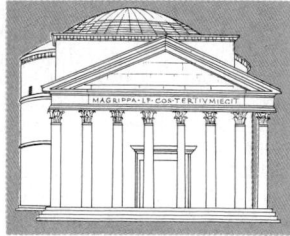

pan·ther (pan′thər) *n., pl.* **pan·thers** or **pan·ther. 1.** a large leopard having a black coat. **2.** another word for **cougar. 3.** another word for **jaguar.**

pantheon *(def. 1)*

pant·ies (pan′tēz) *pl. n.* short underpants worn by girls and women.

pan·to·mime (pan′tə mīm′) *n.* **1.** the telling of a story without speech, through the use of gestures, body movements, and facial expressions. **2.** a dramatic performance acted in this way. —*v.,* **pan·to·mimed, pan·to·mim·ing.** —*v.t.* to express in pantomime. —*v.i.* to act in pantomime. —**pan′to·mim′ist,** *n.*

pan·try (pan′trē) *n., pl.* **pan·tries.** a room or closet for storing food, utensils, china, and the like.

pants (pants) *pl. n.* **1.** another word for **trousers. 2.** another word for **underpants.**

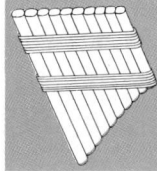

a **pantomime** performer

pant·suit (pant′süt′) *also,* **pants suit.** *n.* a woman's outfit consisting of matching jacket and slacks.

pan·ty·hose (pan′tē hōz′) *n.* a one-piece undergarment for women, combining panties and stockings.

pap (pap) *n.* a soft food prepared especially for babies or sick people.

pa·pa (pä′pə) *n.* father; daddy.

pa·pa·cy (pā′pə sē) *n., pl.* **pa·pa·cies. 1.** the office or authority of the pope. **2.** the period of a pope's reign. **3.** popes as a group. **4.** the government of the Roman Catholic Church by the pope as the supreme ruler.

pa·pal (pā′pəl) *adj.* **1.** of or relating to the pope or the papacy: *papal influence, papal reforms.* **2.** of or relating to the Roman Catholic Church.

pa·paw (pô′pô) *n.* another spelling of **pawpaw.**

pa·pa·ya (pə pä′yə) *n.* **1.** a yellowish orange fruit having a thick rind, many small green to black seeds, and a fleshy pulp with a sweet flavor. **2.** the tropical American tree bearing this fruit.

pa·per (pā′pər) *n.* **1.** a material made from wood pulp, rags, or certain grasses, usually formed in thin sheets. Paper is used for writing, printing, wrapping, and many other purposes. **2.** a piece or sheet of this material: *I wrote my name at the top of the paper.* **3.** a written report or essay: *Her history paper is due tomorrow. The scientist presented a paper on space travel.* **4.** a newspaper: *Has the paper been delivered yet?* **5. papers.** a collection of letters, journals, or other writings, especially by one person: *the Churchill papers.* **6. papers.** a collection of documents that identify a person. **7.** see **wallpaper.** —*v.t.* to cover or decorate with paper, especially wallpaper: *to paper a room.* —*adj.* **1.** made of paper: *paper flowers.* **2.** like paper: *pecans with paper shells.* **3.** existing on paper but not yet realized; theoretical: *paper profits, paper promises.* **4.** used to make paper: *paper pulp.* —**pa′per·er,** *n.* —**pa′per·y,** *adj.*
·**on paper. a.** in written or printed form. **b.** in theory: *The idea looked good on paper, but it never worked out.*

papaya *(def. 2)*

pa·per·back (pā′pər bak′) *n.* a book bound in a paper cover. —*adj.* bound in a paper cover.

pa·per·boy (pā′pər boi′) a person who sells or delivers newspapers.

paper clip, a device made of bent wire or molded plastic that holds sheets of paper together.

pa·per·girl (pā′pər gûrl′) *n.* a girl who sells or delivers newspapers.

pa·per·hang·er (pā′pər hang′ər) *n.* a person whose work is hanging wallpaper.

paper money, currency printed on paper

paper nautilus, see **nautilus** *(def. 2).*

pa·per·weight (pā′pər wāt′) *n.* a small, heavy object placed on top of loose sheets of paper to hold them down.

pa·per·work (pā′pər wûrk′) *n.* **1.** routine clerical work, especially the keeping of administrative records: *The office staff worked overtime to catch up on all the paperwork.* **2.** work done on paper, especially written forms and records: *The company has a warehouse full of old office paperwork.*

pa·pier-mâ·ché (pā′pər mə shā′) *n.* a substance made of shreds of paper mixed with glue and other materials. It can be molded when wet and hardens when dry. —*adj.* made of papier-mâché.

pa·pil·la (pə pil′ə) *n., pl.* **pa·pil·lae** (pə pil′ē) **1.** a small knoblike projection of skin containing tiny blood vessels that nourish the root of a hair. **2.** any of certain other small projections, as on the surface of the tongue.

pa·poose (pa püs′) *also,* **pap·poose.** *n.* a North American Indian baby or small child.

pap·ri·ka (pa prē′kə, pap′ri kə) *n.* a reddish orange spice made from the powdered pods of a red pepper.

Pap smear (pap) a medical test in which a small sample of cells is wiped from the cervix or vagina and studied under a microscope for abnormalities. [From the Greek-American physician George Nicolas *Papanicolaou* (1883–1962), who developed the test.]

pa·py·rus (pə pī′rəs) *n., pl.* **pa·py·ri** (pə pī′rī) **1.** a plant found growing in swamps and along rivers in northern Africa and southern Europe, having dark green, hollow stalks. **2.** a writing material made from the stems of this plant by the ancient Egyptians and other peoples. **3.** an ancient manuscript or document written on this material.

par (pär) *n.* **1.** an average or normal amount, condition, degree, or quality: *Your work is above par.* **2.** an equal level: *Her work is on a par with his.* **3.** the value of a stock printed on the stock certificate. **4.** *Golf.* the number of strokes set as a standard for playing a hole or course. —*adj.* **1.** average or normal. **2.** of or at par: *the par value of a bond.*

par. **1.** paragraph. **2.** parallel.

para–¹ *prefix* **1.** beside; near: *parallel, paraphrase.* **2.** beyond: *paradox.* **3.** disordered; abnormal: *paranoia.* **4.** subsidiary: *paramedic.* [Originally from the Greek prefix *para-,* from the word *para* with the same meanings.]

para–² *combining form* using a parachute: *paratroops.* [From *parachute.*]

par·a·ble (par′ə bəl) *n.* a short story that teaches some truth or moral lesson.

pa·rab·o·la (pə rab′ə lə) *n.* an open curve consisting of a set of points in a plane that lie at equal distances from a fixed point and a fixed line. A parabola is formed by the intersection of a cone and a plane parallel to a side of the cone.

par·a·chute (par′ə shüt′) *n.* a device resembling an umbrella, used for slowing the speed of a body falling through the air. Parachutes are employed mainly to drop a person or object safely to the ground from an aircraft. —*v.,* **par·a·chut·ed, par·a·chut·ing.** —*v.i.* to descend by parachute: *The pilot parachuted from the burning plane.* —*v.t.* to drop (something, such as troops or supplies) by parachute: *They parachuted medical supplies to the stranded troops.*

parabola

par·a·chut·ist (par′ə shü′tist) *n.* a person who uses a parachute or is skilled in parachuting.

pa·rade (pə rād′) *n.* **1.** a march or procession in honor of a person or event: *We went to the parade held for the astronauts.* **2.** a showy display, exhibition: *to make a parade of one's wealth.* **3.** a public place where people stroll. **4.** a procession of troops for display or review. —*v.,* **pa·rad·ed, pa·rad·ing.** —*v.i.* **1.** to march publicly in a procession: *The soldiers paraded through town.* **2.** to walk about to show oneself off. —*v.t.* **1.** to display in a showy manner; make a show of: *to parade one's knowledge before everyone.* **2.** to cause (troops) to march in review: *The company commander paraded the troops before the visiting dignitaries.* —**pa·rad′er,** *n.*

par·a·digm (par′ə dīm′, par′ə dim) *n.* **1.** a pattern or example. **2.** *Grammar.* a list of all the forms or inflections of a word, used as a pattern for other words of the same class.

P

par·a·dise (par'ə dīs') *n.* **1.** the dwelling place of God, the angels, and those who are saved; heaven. **2.** any place of great beauty or delight: *The tropical island seemed a paradise to the tourists.* **3.** a state of supreme happiness or bliss. **4. Paradise.** the garden of Eden.

par·a·dox (par'ə doks') *n., pl.* **par·a·dox·es.** **1.** a statement that seems to be contradictory, but in fact may be true. The statement "Liberty is the only thing you cannot have unless you are willing to give it to others" is a paradox. **2.** a statement that contradicts itself and is therefore unclear, meaningless, or untrue: *I puzzled my friends with this paradox: "All that I say is false, including this statement."* **3.** any person or thing that seems to be contradictory. —**par'a·dox'i·cal,** *adj.* —**par'a·dox'i·cal·ly,** *adv.*

par·af·fin (par'ə fin) *n.* a waxy, white substance obtained from petroleum and used for making candles and waxed paper and for sealing jars of preserves.

par·a·gon (par'ə gon') *n.* an excellent or perfect model or pattern: *You are a paragon of virtue.*

par·a·graph (par'ə graf') *n.* **1.** a distinct part of something written, consisting of one or more sentences on one particular subject or idea, and beginning on a new, usually indented line. **2.** a brief article or item, as in a newspaper. **3.** a mark (¶) used in printing and writing to indicate the beginning of a new paragraph. —*v.t.* to arrange in or divide into paragraphs: *The editor paragraphed the news story.* —**par'a·graph'er,** *n.*

par·a·keet (par'ə kēt') *also,* **par·ra·keet.** *n.* any of a group of small parrots, usually having brightly colored feathers, and often kept as pets. Parakeets are noted for their ability to imitate speech.

par·a·le·gal (par'ə lē'gəl) *n.* a person who is trained to assist lawyers and to perform certain legal tasks but who does not have a license to practice law. —*adj.* of or relating to a paralegal or paralegals.

par·al·lax (par'ə laks') *n.* the apparent change in the position of an object that occurs when the observer changes position. In astronomy parallax is used to find the distance of a star from the observer.

parakeet

par·al·lel (par'ə lel') *adj.* **1.** going in the same direction and always being the same distance apart at every point, so as never to meet: *The rails of a railroad track are parallel.* **2.** closely similar or corresponding: *parallel opinions, parallel wording.* **3.** of or relating to an electric circuit connected in parallel. —*n.* **1.** a parallel line, plane, or surface. **2.** a close similarity or correspondence: *The explorer found many parallels in the customs of the two tribes.* **3.** a comparison that shows a similarity: *The teacher drew a parallel between the two wars.* **4.** any of the imaginary lines that circle the earth parallel to the equator and show degrees of latitude. —*v.t.,* **par·al·leled, par·al·lel·ing;** *also, British,* **par·al·lelled, par·al·lel·ling.** **b.** to be or lie in a direction parallel to: *The railroad tracks paralleled the highway.* **2.** to be similar or correspond to: *The growth of the town paralleled that of the country.* —*adj.* in a parallel manner or direction: *The highway runs parallel with the river.*

·in parallel. (of an electric circuit) connected so as to form separate paths between the positive and negative terminals of the current source of each object, as each light, in the circuit.

parallel bars, two poles set parallel to each other and raised above the floor, used in gymnastics.

par·al·lel·e·pi·ped (par'ə lel'ə pī'ped) *n.* a solid form with six faces that are all parallelograms.

par·al·lel·ism (par'ə le liz'əm) *n.* **1.** the state or con-

dition of being parallel. **2.** a close similarity or correspondence.

par·al·lel·o·gram (par'ə lel'ə gram') *n.* a plane figure with four sides whose opposite sides are parallel and equal in length.

pa·ral·y·sis (pə ral'ə sis) *n., pl.* **pa·ral·y·ses** (pə ral'ə sēz'). **1.** the loss of power of movement or sensation in a part of the body. **2.** a state of inactivity or inability to act: *The war caused a paralysis of normal trade.*

par·a·lyt·ic (par'ə lit'ik) *adj.* **1.** of, relating to, or characteristic of paralysis. **2.** having paralysis. —*n.* a person who has paralysis.

par·a·lyze (par'ə līz') *v.t.,* **par·a·lyzed, par·a·lyz·ing.** **1.** to affect with paralysis; make paralytic. **2.** to make helpless, powerless, or inactive: *The bus strike paralyzed the city.*

par·a·me·ci·um (par'ə mē'shē əm, par'ə mē'sē əm) *n., pl.* **par·a·me·ci·a** (par'ə mē'shē ə, par'ə mē'sē ə). a freshwater protozoan consisting of a single cell. It is so small that it can be seen only through a microscope. The paramecium has very small hairlike structures, called cilia, that enable it to swim about and help it to sweep food into its mouth.

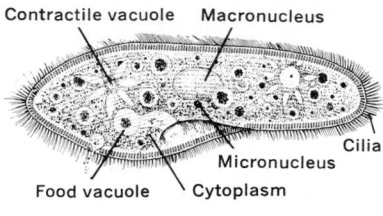

Contractile vacuole   Macronucleus
Cilia
Micronucleus
Food vacuole   Cytoplasm

paramecium

par·a·med·ic (par'ə med'ik) *n.* a person who is specially trained to assist a doctor or give first aid at the scene of an emergency.

par·a·mount (par'ə mount') *adj.* above all others, as in influence or importance; supreme.

par·a·mour (par'ə mùr') *n.* a lover, especially of a person who is married to someone else.

par·a·noi·a (par'ə noi'ə) *n.* **1.** a mental illness marked by feelings of grandeur or persecution. **2.** a tendency to distrust others and to look on everyone as an enemy.

par·a·noid (par'ə noid') *adj.* relating to, characteristic of, or affected with paranoia. —*n.* a person who is affected with paranoia. Also, **par·a·noi·ac** (par'ə noi'ak).

par·a·pet (par'ə pet') *n.* **1.** a low wall of earth or stone to protect troops from being fired upon. **2.** a low wall or railing around the edge of a balcony, roof, or other structure. —**par'a·pet'ed,** *adj.*

par·a·pher·nal·ia (par'ə fərnāl'yə) *n.* **1.** personal belongings. **2.** any equipment used for a particular purpose or activity; gear: *fishing paraphernalia.* ▲ used with a singular or plural verb.

par·a·phrase (par'ə frāz') *n.* the use of different words to express the same meaning; restatement of the meaning of a phrase or passage. —*v.t.,* **par·a·phrased, par·a·phras·ing.** to express in a par-

parapet *(def. 1)*

aphrase: *The speaker paraphrased the author's words.*

par·a·ple·gic (par'ə plē'jik) *adj.* paralyzed in both legs and all or part of the trunk of the body. —*n.* a person who is paraplegic.

par·a·pro·fes·sion·al (par'ə prə fesh'ə nəl) *n.* a person trained to assist a lawyer, teacher, nurse, or other professional, but not licensed to practice alone.

par·a·site (par'ə sīt') *n.* **1.** an animal or plant that lives on or in another animal or plant of a different species, from which it gets all or part of its food. Fleas, tapeworms, and mistletoe are parasites. **2.** a person who lives off another or who associates with another for his or her own gain while giving nothing in return.

par·a·sit·ic (par′ə sit′ik) *adj.* **1.** of or like a parasite. **2.** caused by a parasite: *Trichinosis is a parasitic disease.* Also, **par·a·sit·i·cal** (par′ə sit′i kəl).

par·a·sol (par′ə sôl′) *n.* a small, light umbrella, used for protection from the sun.

par·a·thy·roid glands (par′ə thī′roid) the small endocrine glands next to the thyroid glands, secreting a hormone that regulates the amounts of calcium and phosphorus in the blood.

par·a·troop·er (par′ə trü′pər) *n.* a member of the paratroops.

par·a·troops (par′ə trüps′) *pl. n.* a group of soldiers who are trained to parachute from airplanes into an area of battle.

par·boil (pär′boil′) *v.t.* to cook partially by boiling, usually for a short time.

par·cel (pär′səl) *n.* **1.** a thing or group of things packed together; package; bundle: *A parcel of books arrived in the mail.* **2.** a section or part, as of land. **3.** a group of similar persons or things; pack; bunch. —*v.t.* to divide into sections or parts: *to parcel land, to parcel out supplies.*

parcel post **1.** a class of mail made up primarily of packages weighing 16 ounces (0.45 kilogram) or more. **2.** the branch of the postal service handling such mail.

parch (pärch) *v.t.* **1.** to make very dry or shriveled, as by exposure to heat: *The summer sun parched the lawn.* **2.** to make very thirsty. **3.** to dry by roasting slightly: *to parch nuts.* —*v.i.* to become very dry or hot, as by exposure to heat.

parch·ment (pärch′mənt) *n.* **1.** the skin of sheep, goats, or other animals, prepared as a thin sheet and used as a writing material. **2.** a manuscript or document written on this material. **3.** any of several types of paper made to resemble this material.

par·don (pär′dən) *v.t.* **1.** to free (a person) from punishment for an offense: *The governor pardoned the condemned prisoner.* **2.** to pass over (an offense) without placing blame or requiring punishment; forgive. **3.** to excuse or overlook: *Please pardon my questions.* —*n.* **1.** a freeing from punishment for an offense, or a document granting this. **2.** a passing over an offense without placing blame or requiring punishment; forgiveness. **3.** polite excuse or toleration; *I beg your pardon if I bumped you.* —**par′don·a·ble,** *adj.* —**par′don·a·bly,** *adv.* —**par′-don·er,** *n.*

pare (pâr) *v.t.,* **pared, par·ing. 1.** to cut or peel off the outer layer or skin of: *to pare an apple with a knife.* **2.** to cut or peel off (an outer layer or part): *to pare the bark from a twig.* **3.** to reduce or make less, as if by cutting: *He pared down his essay. She tried to pare expenses.*

par·e·gor·ic (par′ə gôr′ik) *n.* a medicine containing opium and camphor, used to relieve pain and coughing and to treat diarrhea.

pa·ren·chy·ma (pə reng′kə mə) *n.* **1.** the tissue in plants made up of thin-walled cells that serve for storage, as in leaves and fruit. **2.** the essential or functional tissue of an animal organ, as distinguished from the connective tissue that supports the organ.

par·ent (pâr′ənt) *n.* **1.** a person who is a father or mother. **2.** a person who serves as a father or mother. **3.** any organism that produces offspring. **4.** a cause, origin, or source. —*adj.* of, relating to, or like a parent or parents: *a parent organization.* —*v.i., v.t.* to raise (a child or children).

par·ent·age (pâr′ən tij) *n.* descent from parents.

pa·ren·tal (pə ren′təl) *adj.* of, relating to, or characteristic of a parent: *parental duties.* —**pa·ren′tal·ly,** *adv.*

pa·ren·the·sis (pə ren′thə sis) *n., pl.* **pa·ren·the·ses** (pə ren′thə sēz′). **1.** an additional word or phrase placed in a sentence to explain or modify what is said, usually set off by curved marks. **2.** either of the curved marks ( ) used to set off such a word or phrase or to enclose symbols or numbers.

par·en·thet·i·cal (par′ən thet′i kəl) *adj.* **1.** placed within parentheses: *Each foreign word was followed by a parenthetical translation.* **2.** briefly explaining or modifying what is said. Also, **par·en·thet·ic** (par′ən thet′ik). —**par′en·thet′i·cal·ly,** *adv.*

par·ent·hood (pâr′ənt hůd′) *n.* the state of being a parent.

par·ent·ing (pâr′ən ting) *n.* **1.** the raising of a child or children. **2.** the methods used in raising children: *a course in parenting.*

par·fait (pär fā′) *n.* **1.** a dessert made of layers of ice cream, syrup, and sometimes fruit. It is usually served in a tall, slender glass. **2.** a dessert made of custard or whipped cream and syrup frozen together.

pa·ri·ah (pə rī′ə) *n.* a person who is rejected or avoided by others; outcast.

par·ing (pâr′ing) *n.* something pared off: *fingernail parings.*

Par·is (par′is) *n. Greek Legend.* the son of Priam, king of Troy. He carried off Helen, queen of Sparta, and by this act brought on the Trojan War.

par·ish (par′ish) *n., pl.* **par·ish·es. 1.** a church district with its own church and one or more assigned clergy. **2.** in Louisiana, a district corresponding to a county in other states. **3.** the people of a parish.

pa·rish·ion·er (pə rish′ə nər) *n.* a member of a parish.

Pa·ri·sian (pə rē′zhən, pə rizh′ən) *n.* a person who was born or is living in Paris, France. *adj.* of or relating to Paris or its people.

par·i·ty (par′i tē) *n.* the state or quality of being equal: *The two countries reached parity in military strength.*

park (pärk) *n.* **1.** an area of land set apart for the pleasure and use of the public, such as an open area in a city with paths, benches, and playgrounds. **2.** a large area of scenic land kept in its natural state. **3.** the grounds of a country estate, often having woods, lakes, and fields. —*v.t.* **1.** to leave (a vehicle) in a certain place where it may remain for a time: *Park the car near the house.* **2.** *Informal.* to place or leave: *Park your coat in the closet.* —*v.i.* to leave an automobile or other vehicle for a time: *You parked too close to the fire hydrant.*

par·ka (pär′kə) *n.* **1.** a hooded fur outer garment worn by Eskimos. **2.** any hooded jacket for outdoor wear.

parking lot, an area set aside for the parking of cars.

parking meter, a coin-operated timer installed near a parking space, used to regulate the length of time a vehicle may occupy the space.

Par·kin·son's disease (pär′kin sənz) a progressive disease of the central nervous system, characterized by shaking, rigidity, slowness of all voluntary movement, and weakness. [From the English physician James *Parkinson* (1755–1824), who first described it.]

park·way (pärk′wā′) *n.* a highway or wide thoroughfare

at; āpe; fär; câre; end; mē; it; īce; pîerce; hot; ōld; sông; fôrk; oil; out; up; ūse; rüle; půll; tûrn; chin; sing; shop; thin; this; hw in white; zh in treasure. The symbol ə stands for the unstressed vowel sound heard in about, taken, pencil, lemon, and circus.

P

divided by or bordered with landscaped trees, bushes, or grass.

par·lance (pär′ləns) *n.* a manner of speech; type of language: *medical parlance.*

par·lay (pär′lā, pär′lē) *v.t.* **1.** to bet (the money from a first bet plus the winnings) on one or more succeeding races or contests. **2.** to increase (money or talent) successfully: *to parlay a small inheritance into a fortune.* —*n.* a bet made by parlaying.

par·ley (pär′lē) *n., pl.* **par·leys.** a conference, especially one between enemies to decide the terms of a truce or agreement. —*v.i.* to hold a parley.

par·lia·ment (pär′lə mənt) *n.* **1.** an assembly that makes the laws of a country. **2. Parliament. a.** the legislature of Great Britain, made up of the House of Commons and the House of Lords. **b.** the legislature of Canada, made up of the House of Commons and the Senate. [From the Old French word *parlement* meaning ''a speaking, conference, council,'' from the word *parler* ''to speak,'' going back to the Late Latin word *parabola* ''speech, parable,'' from the Greek word *parabolē* ''parable, comparison,'' from the word *paraballein* meaning ''to compare.'']

par·lia·men·tar·i·an (pär′lə men târ′ē ən) *n.* a person who is expert in parliamentary procedure or debate.

par·lia·men·ta·ry (pär′lə men′tə rē) *adj.* **1.** of, relating to, or having a parliament: *a parliamentary government.* **2.** according to the rules of a parliament or other lawmaking assembly: *parliamentary procedure.* **3.** enacted by a parliament: *a parliamentary act.*

par·lor (pär′lər) *also, British,* **par·lour.** *n.* **1.** a room in a home in which visitors are received and entertained. **2.** a room or group of rooms equipped for a special purpose or business: *an ice-cream parlor.*

parlor car, a railroad passenger car with individual chairs.

Par·me·san (pär′mə zän′) *n.* a hard, dry, sharp Italian-style cheese, usually grated.

par·mi·gia·na (pär′mi zhä′nə, pär′mi jä′nə) *adj.* made or covered with Parmesan cheese: *veal parmigiana, eggplant parmigiana.* [From the Italian word *Parmigiana* meaning ''of Parma,'' used as the name of Parmesan cheese, from *Parma,* a city in northern Italy.]

pa·ro·chi·al (pə rō′kē əl) *adj.* **1.** of, relating to, or supported by a parish or church: *a parochial school.* **2.** limited in point of view; narrow: *parochial ideas.* —**pa·ro′chi·al·ly,** *adv.*

pa·ro·chi·al·ism (pə rō′kē ə liz′əm) *n.* the quality of being parochial in thinking.

parochial school, a school supported and run by a church or other religious organization.

par·o·dy (par′ə dē) *n., pl.* **par·o·dies.** a humorous imitation of something serious, such as a literary or artistic work. —*v.t.,* **par·o·died, par·o·dy·ing.** to make a parody of: *The film parodied old silent movies.*

pa·role (pə rōl′) *n.* the conditional release of a prisoner before the full sentence is served. —*v.t.,* **pa·roled, pa·rol·ing.** to release (a prisoner) from prison before the full sentence is served: *The prisoner was paroled for good behavior.*

par·ox·ysm (par′ək siz′əm) *n.* **1.** a sudden outburst or fit: *a paroxysm of laughter.* **2.** a sudden attack of a disease, usually of a recurring nature: *to suffer paroxysms of malaria every few years.*

par·quet (pär kā′, pär ket′) *n.* **1.** flooring made of pieces of wood fitted together in a geometric pattern. **2.** the main floor of a theater; orchestra. —*adj.* made of parquet: *parquet floors.*

par·quet·ry (pär′ki trē) *n., pl.* **par·quet·ries.** a geometric pattern formed by pieces of wood fitted together, used for floors.

par·ra·keet (par′ə kēt′) another spelling of **parakeet.**

par·ri·cide (par′ə sīd′) *n.* **1.** the murder of a parent or

other close relative. **2.** a person who commits such a murder. [From the Latin word *parricidium* meaning such a murder.] —**par′ri·cid′al,** *adj.*

par·rot (par′ət) *n.* **1.** any of a number of tropical birds having a hooked bill, large head, and glossy, usually brightly colored feathers. Some parrots can imitate speech and other sounds and are popular as pets. **2.** a person who repeats or imitates the words or actions of others without thinking or understanding. —*v.t.* to repeat or imitate without thinking or understanding: *Your friend parroted everything you said about the plan.* —**par′rot·like′,** *adj.*

par·ry (par′ē) *v.t.,* **par·ried, par·ry·ing. 1.** to ward off; deflect: *The fencer parried the opponent's sword.* **2.** to turn aside; evade: *The speaker parried the questions from the audience with clever replies.* —*n., pl.* **par·ries.** the act of parrying.

parrot *(def. 1)*

parse (pärs) *v.t.,* **parsed, pars·ing. 1.** to analyze (a sentence) grammatically, naming the parts of speech and their uses in the sentence. **2.** to analyze (a word in a sentence) by naming its part of speech and its use in the sentence.

Par·see (pär′sē) *also,* **Par·si.** *n.* a member of a Zoroastrian sect in India, descended from Persians who fled from Muslim persecution in the eighth century A.D.

par·si·mo·ni·ous (pär′sə mō′nē əs) *adj.* overly careful in spending money; stingy. —**par′si·mo′ni·ous·ly,** *adv.* —**par′si·mo′ni·ous·ness,** *n.*

par·si·mo·ny (pär′sə mō′nē) *n.* a tendency to be overly careful in spending money; stinginess.

pars·ley (pär′slē) *n., pl.* **pars·leys.** a plant related to the carrot, having finely divided, fragrant leaves used to flavor or garnish food. —*adj.* designating a family of plants grown throughout most parts of the world, including such vegetables as celery, carrots, and parsnips, and many herbs.

pars·nip (pär′snip) *n.* **1.** the thick, white root of a plant of the parsley family, cooked and eaten as a vegetable. **2.** the plant bearing this root, having clusters of greenish yellow flowers.

par·son (pär′sən) *n.* **1.** a member of the clergy in charge of a parish; pastor. **2.** any member of the clergy, especially a Protestant minister.

par·son·age (pär′sə nij) *n.* the house of a parson, usually provided by the church.

part (pärt) *n.* **1.** something less than the whole: *The cat finished only part of the milk. The last part of the movie is very exciting.* **2.** one of several equal portions or quantities into which a whole may be divided: *An inch is a twelfth part of a foot.* **3.** a separate piece that together with other pieces makes up a whole, as in a machine: *to assemble the parts of a bicycle.* **4.** a share, as of responsibility, work, or concern: *They all did their part to make the picnic a success.* **5.** one of the sides in a contest, dispute, or question. **6.** a dividing line made when combing one's hair: *She always wears a center part.* **7.** *usually,* **parts.** a region, place, or district: *He is going to travel in foreign parts this summer.* **8. parts.** ability; talent: *a person of many parts.* **9.** a character or role in a motion picture, play, or other performance: *I played the part of a ghost in that scene.* **10.** the words and actions of a character in a performance. **11.** one of the voices or instruments in a piece of music: *the soprano part, the piano part.* **12.** the music for one of the voices or instruments in a piece of music. —*v.t.* **1.** to separate by coming between; force, draw, or hold apart: *The referee parted the boxers.* **2.** to comb (the hair) so as to make a

part. 3. to divide into two or more portions or sections: *to part a pie with a knife.* —*v.i.* **1.** to become separated or divided into two or more pieces: *The shirt parted at the seams.* **2.** to go in different directions; go apart from one another: *They parted at the corner.* —*adv.* in part; partly. —*adj.* not full or complete; partial: *part owner of the store.*
· **for one's part.** as far as one is concerned.
· **for the most part.** mostly; generally.
· **in part.** partly.
· **part and parcel.** a necessary part or element.
· **to part from.** to go away from; leave.
· **to part with.** to give up: *to part with one's money.*
· **to take part.** to take or have a share: *They take part in school sports.*
part. 1. participle. **2.** particular.
par·take (pär tāk′) *v.i.*, **par·took, par·tak·en, par·tak·ing.** to take part; participate: *She partook in the festivities.* —**par·tak′er,** *n.*
· **to partake of. a.** to take or have a portion of: *to partake of dinner.* **b.** to have the character or quality of; resemble: *His wild acts partake of madness.*
par·the·no·gen·e·sis (pär′thə nō jen′ə sis) *n.* reproduction in which a new organism develops from an egg cell without fertilization.

Parthenon

Par·the·non (pär′thə non′) *n.* the temple of Athena on the Acropolis in Athens, Greece, built in the fifth century B.C. It is considered the finest existing example of Greek Doric architecture.
par·tial (pär′shəl) *adj.* **1.** not complete or total: *partial payment.* **2.** favoring one side, person, or group more than another; prejudiced; biased: *The umpire was partial to one of the teams.* **3.** having a strong liking for someone or something: *Our whole family is partial to traveling.* —**par′tial·ly,** *adv.*
par·ti·al·i·ty (pär′shē al′i tē) *n., pl.* **par·ti·al·i·ties. 1.** the state or quality of favoring one side, person, or group more than another; bias; prejudice: *The jury considered the case without partiality.* **2.** a strong liking or fondness: *a partiality for water sports.*
par·tic·i·pant (pär tis′ə pənt) *n.* a person who participates. —*adj.* taking part; participating.
par·tic·i·pate (pär tis′ə pāt′) *v.i.*, **par·tic·i·pat·ed, par·tic·i·pat·ing.** to take or have a part or share with others, as in an activity or quality. —**par·tic′i·pa′tion,** *n.*
par·ti·cip·i·al (pär′tə sip′ē əl) *adj.* of, based on, or used as a participle: *a participial phrase.*
par·ti·ci·ple (pär′tə sip′əl) *n.* a verb form that is used with auxiliary verbs to form certain tenses and that sometimes can function as an adjective or noun.

par·ti·cle (pär′ti kəl) *n.* **1.** a very small bit or minute amount; trace; speck: *a particle of soot, a particle of truth.* **2.** see **subatomic particle. 3.** a part of speech that expresses a relationship or function, as a preposition, conjunction, or article. **4.** a prefix or suffix.
particle accelerator, see **accelerator** (*def. 2*).
particle board, a board made from small bits of wood bonded together with glue or resin, used for wall panels, partitions, furniture, and other items usually constructed from wood.
par·ti–col·ored (pär′ti kul′ərd) *adj.* having different colors in different parts: *a parti-colored flower.*
par·tic·u·lar (pər tik′yə lər) *adj.* **1.** apart or distinct from others: *This particular suitcase is too small for such a long trip.* **2.** belonging to or characteristic of a single person or thing: *My particular hobby is collecting stamps.* **3.** unusual in some way; special; noteworthy: *That book is of particular interest to sports fans.* **4.** very careful about details; demanding; fussy: *I am very particular about how I dress.* —*n.* a single and distinct fact or part; item: *The article included the particulars of the scandal.*
· **in particular.** especially: *I like all kinds of fruit, but I like peaches in particular.*
par·tic·u·lar·i·ty (pər tik′yə lar′i tē) *n., pl.* **par·tic·u·lar·i·ties. 1.** the quality of being distinct from others. **2.** carefulness about details. **3.** a distinctive characteristic or trait. **4.** a particular item or detail.
par·tic·u·lar·ize (pər tik′yə lə rīz′) *v.*, **par·tic·u·lar·ized, par·tic·u·lar·iz·ing.** —*v.t.*, to mention in detail; treat individually; specify. —*v.i.* to give particulars; go into detail. —**par·tic′u·lar·i·za′tion,** *n.*
par·tic·u·lar·ly (pər tik′yə lər lē) *adv.* **1.** to an unusual degree; especially: *a particularly clever design.* **2.** in a detailed manner; item by item: *to discuss a problem particularly.*
part·ing (pär′ting) *n.* **1.** the act of taking leave; departure: *The children cried at their parents' parting.* **2.** a separation or division: *a parting of one's hair.* —*adj.* **1.** given, spoken, or done at parting: *a parting warning, a parting request.* **2.** leaving; departing.
par·ti·san (pär′tə zən) *also,* **par·ti·zan.** *n.* **1.** a person who strongly supports a person, idea, cause, or side: *The senator is a partisan of tax reform.* **2.** a member of a group of resistance fighters; guerrilla. —*adj.* of, relating to, or characteristic of a partisan or partisans: *partisan politics, an attack of partisan troops.*
par·ti·tion (pär tish′ən) *n.* **1.** a division into shares or distinct parts: *the partition of territory between rival states.* **2.** something that divides, especially a movable structure that separates parts of a room. —*v.t.* **1.** to divide into shares or distinct parts: *to partition land for sale.* **2.** to separate by a partition: *to partition off a place to sleep.*
par·ti·zan (pär′tə zən) another spelling of **partisan.**
part·ly (pärt′lē) *adv.* in part; in some degree; not wholly or completely: *I am only partly responsible for the damage.*
part·ner (pärt′nər) *n.* **1.** a person who shares or joins with another: *partners in crime.* **2.** a person associated with another or others in a business: *a partner in a law firm.* **3.** a person with whom one plays a game, usually on the same side: *a tennis partner.* **4.** either of two persons dancing together. **5.** a wife or husband.

at; āpe; fär; câre; end; mē; it; īce; pîerce; hot; ōld; sông, fôrk; oil; out; up; ūse; rüle; pûll; tûrn; chin; sing; shop; thin; this; hw in white; zh in treasure. The symbol ə stands for the unstressed vowel sound heard in about, taken, pencil, lemon, and circus.

P

part·ner·ship (pärt′nər ship′) *n.* **1.** the state of being a partner; association: *I started a paper route in partnership with a friend.* **2.** a business organization in which two or more persons are associated, usually sharing the profits and losses.

part of speech, any of the major grammatical classes into which the words of a language can be divided. The traditional parts of speech for English are noun, pronoun, adjective, verb, adverb, preposition, conjunction, and interjection.

Language Note

In recent years, many language scholars have been critical of the traditional method used in classifying English words according to **parts of speech**. They have pointed out that the eight traditional parts of speech are based on Greek and Latin grammar, rather than on natural English grammar. In former times, it was believed that all languages should be modeled on Latin and Greek. However, scholars now know that there are many languages in the world, including English, that cannot be classified according to the grammatical structures of Greek and Latin.

Modern scholars have done a great deal of research in an attempt to develop a system of parts of speech that truly reflects the nature of English. Although all grammarians now agree that the traditional parts of speech are not entirely adequate, there is at present no agreement as to what new system is suitable to replace the traditional one. Several different possibilities have been advanced, but none has yet been generally accepted as completely satisfactory.

For this reason, this dictionary uses the traditional parts of speech in classifying words. This is the only method that is familiar to all students, and it does not require learning any new rules or terms. A dictionary should reflect the language as it is being used, but until any new system of parts of speech becomes universally accepted, dictionaries will continue to use the traditional classes.

par·took (pär tůk′) the past tense of **partake**.
par·tridge (pär′trij) *n., pl.* **par·tridge** or **par·tridges**.
1. any of several plump game birds of Europe, Asia, and Africa, having gray, brown, and white feathers. **2.** any of various similar or related birds of the United States, such as the ruffed grouse and the bob-white.

partridge

part–time (pärt′tīm′) *adj.* for or during only part of the normal, usual, or regular working time: *a part-time job.* —*adv.* on a part-time basis: *I work part-time as a clerk in a supermarket and part-time as a waiter in a restaurant.*
par·tu·ri·tion (pär′tə rish′ən, pär′chə rish′ən) *n.* the act of giving birth; childbirth.
part·way (pärt′wā′) *adv.* part of the way; to some extent; partly: *The sun is partway out. Rewind the tape partway.*
par·ty (pär′tē) *n., pl.* **par·ties**. **1.** a gathering of people for pleasure or entertainment: *Everyone had a good time at the birthday party.* **2.** a group of people gathered together for some common purpose: *A search party was organized to find the lost child.* **3.** a group of people organized to gain political influence or control: *Each political party selected its candidate for the office of president.* **4.** a person who takes part in an action or plan: *I refuse to be a party to dishonesty.* **5.** a person or organization involved in a lawsuit or other legal matter. **6.** a person: *A certain party telephoned you twice this evening.*

party line **1.** a single telephone circuit with two or more subscribers on it. **2.** the official views and policies of a political party, especially the Communist Party.
par·ve·nu (pär′və nü′, pär′və nü′) *n.* a person who has recently or suddenly risen to a position of wealth or importance for which he or she is not fit; upstart. [French *parvenu*, the past participle of *parvenir* "to arrive at, succeed."]
Pas·cal (pas kal′) also, **PASCAL.** *n.* a computer language used for programming. [Probably from the French philosopher and mathematician Blaise *Pascal* (1623–1662).]
pas·chal (pas′kəl) *adj.* **1.** of or relating to Passover. **2.** of or relating to Easter.
pas de deux (pä′də dü′, pä′də dü′) *pl.* **pas de deux.** in ballet, a dance for two performers.
pa·sha (pə shä′) *n.* the title formerly placed after the name of a high-ranking civil or military official in the Ottoman Empire.
pass (pas) *v.i.* **1.** to go or move; proceed: *The hosts passed from table to table. Several thoughts passed through my mind.* **2.** to go or move by: *A flock of birds passed overhead. The hours passed slowly.* **3.** to extend; run: *The new subway passes under the park.* **4.** to get away or get by without notice or action: *You let a good opportunity pass.* **5.** to come to an end; cease: *As time went on, his sorrow passed.* **6.** to complete an examination, trial, or course of study successfully or satisfactorily: *The student passed after taking the test over again.* **7.** to be approved or ratified: *The bill passed easily in the Senate.* **8.** to take place; happen; occur: *We had no idea of what had passed at the meeting.* **9.** to be transferred: *The couple's property passed to their children.* **10.** to be changed: *The ice passed into water and steam.* **11.** *Sports.* to transfer the ball or puck to a teammate. **12.** to decline to bid, play, or bet in a card game. —*v.t.* **1.** to go or move by (something): *I pass the park on my way to school.* **2.** to complete (an examination, trial, or course of study) successfully or satisfactorily. **3.** to hand about or over, or spread from one person or place to another: *Please pass the salt. Did you pass the word?* **4.** to cause or allow (something) to move or go in a particular way: *to pass thread through the eye of a needle.* **5.** to go beyond; exceed; surpass: *This year's attendance may pass that of last year.* **6.** to go through, across, or over. **7.** to cause or allow to elapse; spend: *She passed the summer traveling.* **8.** to approve or ratify: *Congress passed the resolution.* **9.** to be approved or ratified by: *The bill passed the Senate.* **10.** to pronounce or express: *The judge passed sentence.* **11.** *Sports.* to transfer (the ball or puck) to a teammate.—*n., pl.* **pass·es**. **1.** a permit or written authorization to come, go, or move about freely: *No one was allowed to enter the building without showing a pass.* **2.** a ticket, usually free, entitling the holder to admission or transportation: *My friend gave me two passes to the baseball game.* **3.** a way or opening through which one can go or move, especially a narrow gap in or passage through a mountain range or ridge. **4.** a condition or situation; state of affairs: *Events had come to a critical pass.* **5.** a movement or motion of the hand or hands: *The magician made a pass over the hat and then pulled out a rabbit.* **6.** *Sports.* a transfer of the ball or puck to a teammate. —**pas′ser,** *n.*
•**to bring to pass.** to cause to happen.
•**to come to pass.** to happen.
•**to pass away. a.** to die. **b.** to spend (time) in a leisurely manner: *to pass away the hours sitting in the sun.*

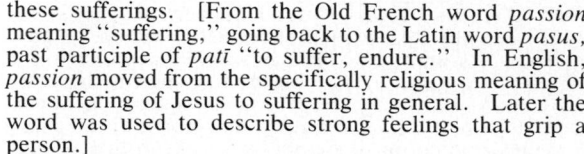

·to pass off. to cause to be accepted as genuine: *The crook tried to pass the rabbit fur off as mink.*
·to pass out. a. to give out: *to pass out pamphlets.*
b. to lose consciousness; faint.
·to pass over. to overlook or ignore.
·to pass up. to fail to take advantage of; refuse: *I passed up an offer of a summer job.*

pass·a·ble (pas′ə bəl) *adj.* **1.** fairly good; adequate; acceptable: *My knowledge of French is rusty but passable.* **2.** capable of being traveled through or across: *The dense jungle was barely passable.*

pass·a·bly (pas′ə blē) *adv.* fairly well; adequately: *to play the piano passably.*

pas·sage (pas′ij) *n.* **1.** a portion, usually short, of a written work or speech: *The author read a passage from a new story to the class.* **2.** a short section of a musical composition. **3.** a route, path, or other way by which a person or thing can pass: *air passages in a mine, a mountain passage.* **4.** a hall or passageway in a building; corridor. **5.** the right, permission, or freedom to pass, go, or travel: *The government granted them passage through the country.* **6.** a journey or voyage, especially by sea or air: *Her passage across the Pacific was rough.* **7.** passenger accommodations: *He wrote months in advance to book passage on an ocean liner.* **8.** course, progress, or advance: *the passage of time.* **9.** approval or enactment by a legislative body: *Congressional passage of such a resolution seemed unlikely.*

pas·sage·way (pas′ij wā′) *n.* a way by which a person or thing can pass, as a corridor or alley.

pass·book (pas′bŭk′) *n.* another word for **bankbook.**

pas·sé (pa sā′) *adj.* no longer in style; out-of-date.

passed ball *Baseball.* a pitch that the catcher fails to catch or control, allowing one or more base runners to advance.

pas·sen·ger (pas′ən jər) *n.* a person who travels in or on an automobile, train, airplane, ship, or other conveyance.

passenger pigeon, an extinct wild pigeon of North America.

pass·er·by (pas′ər bī′) *n., pl.* **pass·ers·by.** a person who passes or goes by: *A passerby saw the accident and described it to the police.*

pas·ser·ine (pas′ər in, pas′ə rīn′) *adj.* of or belonging to a group of perching birds, including all songbirds. More than half of all living birds belong to this group. *—n.* a passerine bird.

passenger pigeon

pass·ing (pas′ing) *adj.* **1.** going or moving by: *The crowd watched the passing circus parade. The child grew taller with the passing years.* **2.** not lasting; brief; *I had a passing fancy for collecting miniature cars.* **3.** given or done casually: *passing remarks.* **4.** allowing one to pass an examination, trial, or course of study; satisfactory: *a passing grade. —n.* **1.** the act of a person or thing that passes: *the passing of the days.* **2.** death: *the passing of the old general.* **3.** a means or place of passing or crossing, as a ford.
·in passing. incidentally: *The speaker remarked in passing that our town had many lovely parks.*

pas·sion (pash′ən) *n.* **1.** a strong or intense feeling, such as love, hate, or anger. **2.** a strong liking, desire, or enthusiasm: *a passion for baseball.* **3.** the object of strong feeling, liking, desire, or enthusiasm: *Painting was the artist's only passion.* **4.** strong love between two people. **5.** an outburst or fit of rage. **6. Passion. a.** the sufferings of Jesus following the Last Supper and ending with the Crucifixion. **b.** the chapters in the Gospels that tell of

these sufferings. [From the Old French word *passion* meaning "suffering," going back to the Latin word *pasus,* past participle of *patī* "to suffer, endure." In English, *passion* moved from the specifically religious meaning of the suffering of Jesus to suffering in general. Later the word was used to describe strong feelings that grip a person.]

pas·sion·ate (pash′ə nit) *adj.* **1.** characterized by or showing strong or intense feeling; ardent: *The senator has long been a passionate defender of freedom of speech.* **2.** showing or coming from strong or intense feeling: *The lawyer made a passionate plea for the defendant's life.* **3.** easily angered; hot-tempered. *—***pas′sion·ate·ly,** *adv.*

pas·sion·flow·er (pash′ən flou′ər) *n.* **1.** any of a group of plants that have climbing vines and large, showy flowers. **2.** the flower itself.

pas·sion·less (pash′ən lis) *adj.* without strong feeling.

Passion play also, **passion play.** a play representing the passion, death, and resurrection of Jesus.

pas·sive (pas′iv) *adj.* **1.** acted upon without responding or acting back: *They played a passive role in the student protest.* **2.** giving in without opposition or resistance; submissive: *The prisoner was passive as the judge pronounced the sentence.* **3.** *Grammar.* relating to or designating the voice of a verb whose subject receives the action expressed by the verb. In the sentence *The child was struck by an automobile, was struck* is in the passive voice. *—n.* **1.** the passive voice. **2.** a verb form in this voice. *—***pas′sive·ly,** *adv.* *—***pas′sive·ness,** *n.*

passionflower

passive resistance, a method of resisting authority or protesting against some law or act by nonviolent means, as by refusing to obey.

passive smoking, the unwanted, unavoidable inhaling of smoke in the air from someone's cigarette, cigar, or pipe.

pas·siv·i·ty (pa siv′i tē) *n.* the state or condition of being passive.

pass·key (pas′kē′) *n., pl.* **pass·keys. 1.** another word for **master key. 2.** any of various other keys, as a skeleton key or latchkey.

Pass·o·ver (pas′ō′vər) *n.* the annual Jewish feast commemorating the Exodus of the Jews from Egypt. Also, **Pesach.** [From the phrase *to pass over,* a translation of the Hebrew word *Pesah* meaning "a passing over" or "sparing," from the Biblical story in which the Egyptians were persuaded to free the captive Israelites after God had killed the first-born sons of the Egyptians but *passed over* and spared those of the Israelites.]

pass·port (pas′pôrt′) *n.* **1.** a document issued by the government of a citizen's own country giving the citizen official identification for use in travel abroad. **2.** anything that gives a person acceptance or admission: *Wealth can be a passport to society.*

pass·word (pas′wûrd′) *n.* **1.** a secret word or phrase that identifies the speaker as someone to be allowed to pass. **2.** a secret code used to gain access to a computer system, program, or file.

P

at; āpe; fär; câre; end; mē; it; īce; pîerce; hot; ōld; sông, fôrk; oil; out; up; ūse; rüle; pull; tûrn; chin; sing; shop; thin; this; hw in white; zh in treasure. The symbol ə stands for the unstressed vowel sound heard in about, taken, pencil, lemon, and circus.

past (past) *adj.* **1.** gone by; ended; over: *The days of our youth are past.* **2.** having happened or existed in time gone by: *to study the past events in the history of a country.* **3.** gone by just before the present time: *We have been on the telephone for the past hour.* **4.** having served formerly: *a past mayor.* **5.** *Grammar.* indicating a state or action in time gone by. —*n.* **1.** a time that has gone by: *Dinosaurs lived in the distant past.* **2.** something that was done or has happened in the past. **3.** *Grammar.* the past tense or a verb in the past tense. —*prep.* **1.** beyond in place; farther than: *The pitcher threw the ball past the catcher.* **2.** beyond in time; after: *It is past my bedtime.* **3.** beyond the power, scope, or limits of: *This poetry is past understanding.* **4.** beyond in amount, number, or degree: *My grandmother is past ninety.* —*adv.* so as to pass or go by: *We watched the train rumble past.*

pas·ta (pä′stə) *n.* **1.** a paste or dough made with flour, used to make macaroni, ravioli, and similar food. **2.** a dish of cooked pasta.

paste (pāst) *n.* **1.** a mixture, as of flour and water, used to stick things together. **2.** any soft, smooth, often moist mixture: *tomato paste.* **3.** a dough used for pastry. **4.** a hard, glasslike material used to make artificial or imitation gems. —*v.t.,* **past·ed, past·ing.** **1.** to stick with paste: *She pasted the photographs in her album.* **2.** to cover with something that is pasted on: *He pasted the walls of his room with posters.* **3.** *Slang.* to strike with a hard blow; punch. [From the Old French word *paste* "paste, dough," going back to the Greek word *pastē* "porridge made from barley."]

paste·board (pāst′bôrd′) *n.* a stiff material made of sheets of heavy paper pasted together or of paper pulp pressed together. —*adj.* made of pasteboard: *a pasteboard box.*

pas·tel (pa stel′) *n.* **1.** a chalklike crayon used in drawing. **2.** a picture drawn with such crayons. **3.** a pale, soft shade of a color. —*adj.* **1.** of, relating to, or drawn with pastels. **2.** having a pale, soft shade: *a dress in pastel blue.*

pas·tern (pas′tərn) *n.* the part of a horse's foot between the fetlock and the hoof.

pas·teur·ize (pas′chə rīz′) *v.t.,* **pas·teur·ized, pas·teur·iz·ing.** to heat (milk or other food) to a temperature high enough to destroy disease-producing bacteria and organisms that cause food spoilage. [From the French chemist and bacteriologist Louis *Pasteur* (1822–1895), who developed this process.]

{ Pastern

pas·time (pas′tīm′) *n.* something that makes time pass pleasantly and happily: *Playing softball is a favorite summer pastime for many Americans.*

pas·tor (pas′tər) *n.* a member of the clergy in charge of a parish or congregation. [From the Old French word *pastor,* from the Latin word *pastor* meaning "shepherd," from the traditional image of the clergy as shepherds of their "flock," or congregation.]

pas·tor·al (pas′tər əl) *adj.* **1.** of, relating to, or describing shepherds or country life: *pastoral poetry.* **2.** having the simplicity, peacefulness, charm, and other qualities usually associated with country life: *pastoral scenery.* **3.** of or relating to a pastor or his or her duties. —*n.* a poem, play, or picture that deals with shepherds or country life. —**pas′tor·al·ly,** *adv.*

pas·tor·ate (pas′tər it) *n.* **1.** the office, position, or jurisdiction of a pastor. **2.** the term or length of service of a pastor with one parish or congregation. **3.** pastors as a group.

past participle, a participle expressing a past action or state, used with auxiliary verbs to form perfect tenses of the active voice and all tenses of the passive voice. In the sentence *I have studied all day,* the word *studied* is a past participle.

past perfect 1. a verb tense expressing past action completed before another past action or before a specified past time. In the sentence *We had returned by the time our guests began to arrive,* the phrase *had returned* is in the past perfect. **2.** a verb in this tense. Also, **pluperfect.**

pas·tra·mi (pə strä′mē) *n.* a variety of highly seasoned smoked beef, usually from a shoulder cut.

pas·try (pās′trē) *n., pl.* **pas·tries.** **1.** any of several flour doughs used in making pie crusts, tarts, and other baked goods. **2.** baked foods made with such a dough. **3.** any sweet, baked food.

past tense 1. a verb tense expressing an action or state that happened or existed in the past. In the sentence *The bird flew away,* the word *flew* is in the past tense. **2.** a verb in this tense.

pas·tur·age (pas′chər ij) *n.* **1.** grass and other growing plants that livestock feed on. **2.** land used or suitable for grazing livestock.

pas·ture (pas′chər) *n.* **1.** a field or other tract of land used for the grazing of cattle, sheep, or other animals. **2.** grass and other growing plants that livestock feed on. —*v.,* **pas·tured, pas·tur·ing.** —*v.t.* to put (animals) in a pasture to graze. —*v.i.* to graze: *The farmer's children led the sheep out to pasture.*

past·y[1] (pās′tē) *adj.,* **past·i·er, past·i·est.** **1.** like paste: *a pasty mixture.* **2.** pale and sickly: *a pasty complexion.* [*Paste* + *-y*[1].]

pas·ty[2] (pas′tē) *n., pl.* **pas·ties.** a small pie with a filling, usually of meat. [From the Old French word *pasté* meaning "a meat pie," from the word *paste* "paste, dough," going back to the Greek word *pastē* "porridge made from barley."]

pat[1] (pat) *v.t.,* **pat·ted, pat·ting.** **1.** to stroke or tap gently, usually with the hand, especially in affection or approval: *I patted the dog.* **2.** to shape or smooth by striking gently with something flat. —*n.* **1.** a gentle tap or stroke. **2.** the sound made by such a tap or stroke. **3.** a small slice or molded mass: *a pat of butter.* [From the Middle English word *pat* meaning "a blow, stroke."]
•**pat on the back.** *Informal.* praise or approval.

pat[2] (pat) *adj.* **1.** exactly suitable for the purpose or occasion; fitting. **2.** Insincere; glib: *You had a pat answer to every question.* —*adv.* aptly; suitably. [From *pat*[1].]
•**to have down pat** or **to know pat.** to know perfectly or thoroughly: *I have all the answers down pat.*
•**to stand pat.** to stay firm without changing.

pat., patent; patented.

patch (pach) *n., pl.* **patch·es.** **1.** a piece of material used to mend or cover a hole, strengthen a worn spot, or decorate a garment. **2.** a pad, piece of cloth, or other covering worn or put over a wound or injured part for protection: *an eye patch.* **3.** any of the pieces of material used in making patchwork. **4.** a small area, as of a surface, that differs or stands out from the rest: *Nothing showed on the surface of the water but some patches of yellow weed* (Ernest Hemingway). **5.** a small piece of ground on which a particular plant grows: *a lettuce patch.* —*v.t.* **1.** to mend, cover, strengthen, or decorate with a patch or patches: *to patch up a torn pair of dungarees.* **2.** to fix, repair, or put together, especially in a hasty or makeshift way: *The worker patched up the roof before the rain could leak in.* **3.** to make by joining pieces together: *to patch a quilt.*
•**to patch up.** to smooth over; settle: *to patch up a quarrel.*

patchwork quilt

patch·work (pach′wûrk′) *n.* **1.** needlework consisting of pieces of material, usually of various colors or shapes, that are sewed together. **2.** something put together out of irregular or varied parts: *The report was a patchwork of many unrelated facts.* —*adj.* made of or covered with patchwork: *a patchwork quilt.*

patch·y (pach′ē) *adj.,* **patch·i·er, patch·i·est.** made up of, like, or occurring in patches. —**patch′i·ly,** *adv.* —**patch′i·ness,** *n.*

patd., patented.

pate (pāt) *n.* the head, especially the crown of the head.

pâ·té (pä tā′) *n. French.* a meat paste.

pa·tel·la (pə tel′ə) *n., pl.* **pa·tel·lae** (pə tel′ē) or **pa·tel·las.** another word for **kneecap.**

pat·ent (pat′ənt; *for adj., def. 2, also* pā′tənt) *n.* **1.** a government grant that gives a person or company an exclusive right, especially to make, use, or sell a new invention for a certain period of time. **2.** an invention that is protected by such a grant. **3.** an official document granting a right or privilege: *a patent of nobility.* —*adj.* **1.** protected by a patent. **2.** obvious; evident; clear: *a patent lie.* —*v.t.* to get a patent for; protect with a patent. **pat′ent·a·ble,** *adj.* —**pat′ent·ly,** *adv.*

pat·ent·ee (pat′ən tē′) *n.* a person to whom a patent is granted.

patent leather, a smooth, soft leather that is finished to a very high gloss.

patent medicine, any medicine that is patented and can be purchased without a prescription.

pa·ter (pā′tər) *n.* father. [From the Latin word *pater* meaning "father."]

pa·ter·nal (pə tûr′nəl) *adj.* **1.** of, relating to, or like a father; fatherly: *paternal affection.* **2.** related through one's father: *a paternal grandparent.* **3.** inherited or derived from one's father: *a paternal fortune.* —**pa·ter′nal·ly,** *adv.*

pa·ter·nal·ism (pə tûr′nə liz′əm) *n.* the principle or practice of regulating the life and supplying the needs of a group of people in a way suggestive of a father dealing with his children. —**pa·ter′nal·is′tic,** *adj.*

pa·ter·ni·ty (pə tûr′ni tē) *n.* **1.** the state of being a father; fatherhood. **2.** the identity of one's father: *The paternity of the orphan was unknown.*

pat·er·nos·ter (pā′tər nos′tər, pat′ər nos′tər) *n.* the Lord's Prayer. [From the Latin phrase *pater noster* meaning "Our Father," from the opening words of the Latin version of this prayer.]

path (path) *n., pl.* **paths** (pathz, paths). **1.** a trail or way that has been made or worn by footsteps, as through a forest. **2.** a way or road made for a specific purpose: *to shovel a path through the snow.* **3.** a course or route

taken by a person or thing: *the path of a rocket.* *A black cat crossed my path.* **4.** a way or line of action or behavior: *The writer seemed to be on the path to success.*

path., pathological; pathology.

pa·thet·ic (pə thet′ik) *adj.* **1.** arousing pity, sadness, or sympathy: *An abandoned child is a pathetic sight.* **2.** pitifully unsuccessful or inadequate: *a pathetic attempt.* —**pa·thet′i·cal·ly,** *adv.*

path·find·er (path′fīn′dər) *n.* a person who discovers or leads the way: *a pathfinder in space science.*

path·o·gen (path′ə jən) *n.* any agent, such as a virus or bacterium, that causes disease.

path·o·gen·ic (path′ə jen′ik) *adj.* causing disease: *a pathogenic organism.*

pathol., pathological; pathology.

path·o·log·i·cal (path′ə loj′i kəl) *adj.* **1.** of, relating to, or concerned with pathology: *a pathological study of blood cells.* **2.** characteristic of, caused by, or accompanying disease: *a pathological condition of the heart.* Also, **path·o·log·ic** (path′ə loj′ik). —**path′o·log′i·cal·ly,** *adv.*

pa·thol·o·gist (pə thol′ə jist) *n.* a doctor who specializes in pathology.

pa·thol·o·gy (pə thol′ə jē) *n., pl.* **pa·thol·o·gies.** **1.** the science that deals with the nature, cause, and development of disease. **2.** the abnormal condition and bodily changes resulting from a disease.

pa·thos (pā′thos) *n.* a quality in an event or work of art or literature that arouses a feeling of pity, sadness, or sympathy.

path·way (path′wā′) *n.* a path or course.

pa·tience (pā′shəns) *n.* **1.** the quality or fact of being patient, or the ability to be patient: *The crowd showed great patience as they waited in line for tickets to the game.* **2.** see **solitaire** *(def. 1).*

pa·tient (pā′shənt) *adj.* **1.** able to put up with hardship, pain, trouble, or delay calmly and without complaint or anger: *The boy was very patient when they put the cast on his broken leg.* **2.** showing or characterized by the ability to wait or put up with calmly and without anger: *She quieted the restless children with a patient smile.* **3.** quietly careful and diligent: *a patient worker.* —*n.* a person who is under the care or treatment of a doctor. —**pa′tient·ly,** *adv.*

pat·i·o (pat′ē ō′) *n., pl.* **pat·i·os.** **1.** a paved, outdoor area next to a house, used for cooking, eating, and lounging. **2.** an inner court open to the sky, as in a Spanish or Spanish-American house.

pat·ois (pat′wä) *n., pl.* **pat·ois** (pat′wäz). a regional dialect of a language.

pa·tri·arch (pā′trē ärk′) *n.* **1.** the father and head of a family or tribe. Abraham, Isaac, and Jacob were biblical patriarchs. **2.** an old man who is respected and honored.

patio *(def. 2)*

P

3. in the Roman Catholic, Orthodox, and various other Christian churches, a high-ranking bishop.

pa·tri·ar·chal (pā'trē är'kəl) *adj.* **1.** of, relating to, or characteristic of a patriarch: *patriarchal authority, a patriarchal form of government.* **2.** ruled by a patriarch: *a patriarchal tribe.*

pa·tri·ar·chy (pā'trē är'kē) *n., pl.* **pa·tri·ar·chies.** a society in which the father is the head of the family or tribe and descent is traced through the paternal line.

pa·tri·cian (pə trish'ən) *n.* **1.** a person of high social status; aristocrat. **2.** a member of one of the aristocratic families in ancient Rome. —*adj.* **1.** aristocratic; noble. **2.** of or relating to the aristocracy, especially of ancient Rome.

pat·ri·cide (pat'rə sīd') *n.* **1.** the act of killing one's father. **2.** a person who kills his or her father. [From the Late Latin word *patricidium* meaning such a murder, from the word *pater* "father" + the suffix *-cidium* "a killing."]

pat·ri·mo·ny (pat'rə mō'nē) *n., pl.* **pat·ri·mo·nies.** **1.** property inherited or handed down from one's father or ancestors. **2.** anything inherited; heritage: *Americans enjoy a patrimony of freedom of speech.* **3.** the property or endowment of a church or other religious institution.

pa·tri·ot (pā'trē ət) *n.* a person who loves and enthusiastically and loyally supports his or her country.

pa·tri·ot·ic (pā'trē ot'ik) *adj.* characterized by or showing patriotism: *a patriotic holiday.* —**pa'tri·ot'i·cal·ly,** *adv.*

pa·tri·ot·ism (pā'trē ə tiz'əm) *n.* a love for and enthusiastic and loyal support of one's country.

pa·trol (pə trōl') *v.,* **pa·trolled, pa·trol·ling.** —*v.t.* to go through or around (an area or place) for the purpose of guarding or inspecting: *The commissioner ordered additional police cars to patrol the neighborhood.* —*v.i.* to go through or around an area or place for the purpose of guarding or inspecting. —*n.* **1.** one or more persons who patrol or are assigned to patrol. **2.** a group of soldiers, ships, or airplanes sent out for combat or to find out about the enemy's position. **3.** the act of patrolling. **4.** a unit of a Boy or Girl Scout troop, usually consisting of eight scouts. [From the French word *patrouiller* meaning "to patrol," from the Middle French word *patrouillier* "to tramp about in the mud," from the Old French word *patoueil* "mire," from soldiers' slang used to describe the duties of a sentry.]

patrol car, a police car assigned to patrol a particular area. Also, **squad car.**

pa·trol·man (pə trōl'mən) *n., pl.* **pa·trol·men** (pə-trōl'mən). a police officer assigned to patrol a particular area.

patrol wagon, a specially equipped truck used by the police for carrying prisoners.

pa·tron (pā'trən) *n.* **1.** a person who supports, assists, or protects a person, cause, organization, or undertaking by the use of his or her money or influence: *a patron of the arts.* **2.** a regular customer: *a patron of a restaurant.*

pa·tron·age (pā'trə nij, pat'rə nij) *n.* **1.** the support or assistance given by a patron. **2.** the support given to a store, restaurant, or other business establishment by customers. **3.** good will or favorable treatment given with a tone of superiority. **4.** the power or system of giving out jobs, government contracts, or other political favors: *the patronage of a senator.* **5.** the political jobs or favors given out.

pa·tron·ize (pā'trə nīz', pat'rə nīz') *v.t.,* **pa·tron·ized, pa·tron·iz·ing.** **1.** to be a customer of (a store, restaurant, or other business establishment), especially on a regular basis. **2.** to treat as inferior or in a condescending manner: *Don't patronize the younger children.* **3.** to give support or assistance to; act as a patron toward.

patron saint, a saint looked on as the special guardian or protector of a person, place, or group.

pa·troon (pə trün') *n.* under Dutch colonial rule in New York and New Jersey, a person who owned a large amount of land and was given certain rights and privileges.

pat·sy (pat'sē) *n., pl.* **pat·sies.** *Slang.* a person who is easily fooled, made the object of ridicule or jokes, or taken advantage of; dupe.

pat·ter[1] (pat'ər) *v.i.* **1.** to make soft, rapid taps: *The raindrops pattered on the roof.* **2.** to move with soft, rapid steps: *We heard the children as they pattered down the stairs.* —*n.* a series of soft, rapid taps. [From *pat*[1].]

pat·ter[2] (pat'ər) *n.* rapid speech, especially the fast, glib talk of a salesperson or the like. [From the Middle English word *pateren* meaning "to rush through the paternoster," from the word *pater,* short for *paternoster.*]

pat·tern (pat'ərn) *n.* **1.** an arrangement or design of colors, shapes, or lines: *The wallpaper was printed with a pretty flower pattern.* **2.** a guide or model used in making something: *I cut the cloth according to a pattern.* **3.** an example or model worthy of being followed or copied: *You were the pattern of politeness.* **4.** a set of actions or characteristics that does not change: *The scientist studied the pattern of the monkey's behavior.* —*v.t.* to make according to a pattern or example: *The author patterned the novel after a famous legend.*

pat·ty (pat'ē) *n., pl.* **pat·ties.** a piece of food in a small, round, flat shape: *a hamburger patty.*

pau·ci·ty (pô'si tē) *n.* **1.** a small number: *There was a paucity of people in the stadium.* **2.** a scarcity; insufficiency: *That country has a paucity of land fit for farming.*

Paul Bun·yan, (pôl'bun'yən) in American folklore, a giant lumberjack known for his superhuman strength and courage.

paunch (pônch) *n., pl.* **paunch·es.** the belly or stomach, especially when protruding; potbelly.

paunch·y (pôn'chē) *adj.,* **paunch·i·er, paunch·i·est.** having a large belly. —**paunch'i·ness,** *n.*

pau·per (pô'pər) *n.* a very poor person, especially one supported by charity.

pau·per·ism (pô'pə riz'əm) *n.* the state of being very poor; poverty.

pause (pôz) *v.i.* to stop for a short time: *The rider paused to let the horse rest.* —*n.* **1.** a short stop: *After a pause because of rain, the game continued.* **2.** a short stop or break in speaking, reading, or writing: *The speaker continued the speech, after a pause for applause.* **3.** *Music.* a sign (⌢ or ⌣) placed above or below a note or rest to show that it is to be held longer.

pa·vane (pə vän', pə van') *n.* **1.** a slow, stately dance of the sixteenth century. **2.** the music for this dance.

pave (pāv) *v.t.,* **paved, pav·ing.** to cover (a road or other surface) with pavement: *The town paved the road with asphalt.*
·**to pave the way.** to prepare or lead the way; make progress easier: *This research paved the way for the discoveries of later scientists.*

pave·ment (pāv'mənt) *n.* **1.** a covering or surface of concrete, asphalt, brick, or similar material, as for a street, road, or sidewalk. **2.** the material used to make such a covering or surface. **3.** a sidewalk.

pa·vil·ion (pə vil'yən) *n.* **1.** an open, often ornamental building used for exhibition, entertainment, recreation, or shelter, as in a park or at a fair: *They went to a concert in the pavilion.* **2.** a large tent, often with a pointed top. **3.** one of a group of related buildings, as of a hospital. **4.** a projecting part of a building, often elaborately decorated.

pav·ing (pā'ving) *n.* **1.** a paved surface; pavement. **2.** the material used for pavement.

paw (pô) *n.* the foot of a four-footed animal having nails or claws. —*v.t.* **1.** to strike or scrape (something) with the paws or hooves: *The angry bull pawed the ground.* **2.** to touch or handle roughly, clumsily, or in too familiar a manner.

pawl (pôl) *n.* a catch or bar on a pivot that engages the teeth of a ratchet wheel, allowing the wheel to revolve in only one direction. See **ratchet** for illustration.

pawn¹ (pôn) *v.t.* to leave (something valuable) with a lender, especially a pawnbroker, as a pledge to repay a loan. —*n.* something left as a pledge to repay a loan. [From the Old French word *pan* meaning "something given as a pledge."]

pawn² (pôn) *n.* **1.** *Chess.* any of the pieces of lowest value, eight to each player. A pawn is able to move only one square forward at a time (or two squares on its first move) and captures by moving one square diagonally. **2.** a person or thing used by someone for personal gain or advantage: *Their friends were only pawns of their ambition to become rich.* [From the Old French word *peon* meaning this chess piece, from the Medieval Latin word *pedo* "foot soldier," going back to the Latin word *pes* "foot."]

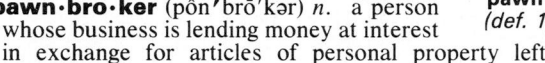

pawn²
(def. 1)

pawn·bro·ker (pôn′brō′kər) *n.* a person whose business is lending money at interest in exchange for articles of personal property left as security.

Paw·nee (pô nē′) *n., pl.* **Paw·nee** or **Paw·nees. 1.** a member of any of a group of North American Indian tribes formerly living in Nebraska, now living in Oklahoma. **2.** the language of the Pawnees.

pawn·shop (pôn′shop′) *n.* a pawnbroker's shop.

paw·paw (pô′pô) *also,* **pa·paw.** *n.* **1.** a fruit having yellow flesh and a taste like that of a banana. **2.** the tree bearing this fruit, grown mainly in the central United States.

pay (pā) *v.,* **paid, pay·ing.** —*v.t.* **1.** to give (money) in return for services or goods: *We paid fifteen dollars to have the radio fixed.* **2.** to give money to in return for services or goods: *I paid the salesclerk for the coat.* **3.** to give money in order to settle: *to pay a bill, to pay a fine.* **4.** to give in return: *This job pays two hundred dollars a week.* **5.** to be profitable to or worthwhile for: *It will pay you to plan now for the future.* **6.** to give or make: *to pay a compliment, to pay a visit to a friend.* —*v.i.* **1.** to give something in making a purchase or settling a debt; make payment. **2.** to be profitable or worthwhile. *It pays to eat a balanced diet.* —*n.* something given in return for services or goods: *The workers were on strike for higher pay.* —*adj.* operated by or made available for use by the deposit of a coin or coins: *a pay telephone.*
　•**to pay back. 1.** to repay: *Please pay back the money I lent you.* **2.** to return: *to pay back a favor.*
　•**to pay off. a.** to pay all that is owed; pay in full: *to pay off a debt.* **b.** to get even with.
　•**to pay out (payed, paying).** to slacken or let out (a rope or line).
　•**to pay up.** to pay all that is owed.

pay·a·ble (pā′ə bəl) *adj.* **1.** to be paid; due: *The bill is payable within ninety days.* **2.** made ready to be paid (to): *Make the check payable to the owner of the store.*

pay·check (pā′chek′) *n.* a check given to an employee for work done.

pay·day (pā′dā′) *n.* the day on which wages are paid: *Payday in that company is every other Friday.*

pay dirt 1. earth, ore, or similar material containing enough of a valuable substance to make mining profitable: *After years of digging for gold, the prospector finally struck pay dirt.* **2.** *Informal.* any source of profit or

success: *The toy company really hit pay dirt with its new talking dolls.*

pay·ee (pā ē′) *n.* a person to whom money has been or is to be paid.

pay·er (pā′ər) *n.* a person who pays or is responsible for paying something, as a bill.

pay·load (pā′lōd′) *n.* **1.** a cargo or part of a cargo that produces profit. **2.** in a rocket, aircraft, or spacecraft, anything carried in addition to what is essential to the operation of the craft: *The rocket carried a payload of scientific instruments for collecting data.* **3.** the warhead of a guided or ballistic missile.

pay·mas·ter (pā′mas′tər) *n.* a person in charge of paying wages or salaries.

pay·ment (pā′mənt) *n.* **1.** the act of paying: *The company required that payment be made on time.* **2.** something that is paid: *to receive weekly payment for one's work.* **3.** a reward or punishment: *The long jail sentence was just payment for that crime.*

pay·off (pā′ôf′) *n.* **1.** a payment, as of wages. **2.** a reward or punishment. **3.** *Informal.* a climax or outcome, as of a story or series of events. **4.** *Informal.* a bribe.

pay·roll (pā′rōl) *also,* **pay roll.** *n.* **1.** a list of employees to be paid, with the amount that each is to receive. **2.** the total amount of money to be paid to employees.

pay TV, a service that provides subscribers with certain television programs for a monthly payment. Cable TV is a form of pay TV. Also, **pay television.**

Pb, the symbol for lead. [Short for the Latin word *plumbum* meaning "lead²."]

p.c. 1. percent. **2.** petty cash. **3.** postcard.

PC, personal computer.

PCP, a drug used illegally as a hallucinogen, formerly used as an animal tranquilizer.

pct., percent.

pd., paid.

Pd, the symbol for palladium.

P.D., Police Department.

PE, postal abbreviation for Prince Edward Island.

pea (pē) *n.* **1.** the round, usually green seed of a pod-bearing plant, eaten as a vegetable. **2.** the plant bearing this seed.

peace (pēs) *n.* **1.** freedom from war: *years of peace between the world wars.* **2.** an agreement, treaty, or settlement to end a war or hostilities. **3.** freedom from lawlessness or other strife; public order: *Law officers were assigned to keep the peace.* **4.** calmness; tranquility: *the peace and quiet of the country.* **5.** freedom from fear or worry: *peace of mind.*
　•**at peace.** free from war or other strife.
　•**to hold one's peace** or **to keep one's peace.** to be or keep silent.

peace·a·ble (pē′sə bəl) *adj.* **1.** liking peace; avoiding strife and disturbance. **2.** characterized by peace; peaceful: *The ruler had a long and peaceable reign.* **peace′a·ble·ness,** *n.* —**peace′a·bly,** *adv.*

Peace Corps, a U.S. government agency that trains and sends volunteer workers to aid developing countries.

peace·ful (pēs′fəl) *adj.* **1.** free from war, strife, or other disturbance. **2.** not warlike or quarrelsome: *to decide a dispute by peaceful means.* **3.** calm; tranquil; serene: *a peaceful atmosphere.* —**peace′ful·ly,** *adv.* —**peace′ful·ness,** *n.*

P

at; āpe; fär; câre; end; mē; it; īce; pîerce; hot; ōld; sông, fôrk; oil; out; up; ūse; rüle; pull; tûrn; chin; sing; shop; thin; <u>th</u>is; hw in white; zh in treasure. The symbol ə stands for the unstressed vowel sound heard in about, taken, pencil, lemon, and circus.

peace·keep·ing (pēs′kē′ping) *n.* the maintenance of peace and order between hostile countries or groups within a country by an outside military force: *to use UN troops for peacekeeping.* —*adj.* relating to or charged with peacekeeping: *a peacekeeping force.*

peace·mak·er (pēs′mā′kər) *n.* a person who brings about or tries to bring about peace between others.

peace pipe, a tobacco pipe with a long decorated stem, used by North American Indians on ceremonial occasions as a symbol of peace. Also, **calumet.**

peace·time (pēs′tīm′) *n.* a period when a nation is not at war. —*adj.* of, for, or characteristic of such a period: *a peacetime army.*

peach (pēch) *n., pl.* **peach·es.** **1.** a sweet, juicy fruit having a large rough stone, or pit, and a velvety yellow or yellow-red skin. **2.** the tree bearing this fruit, having pink flowers. **3.** a yellowish pink color. —*adj.* having the color peach. —**peach′like′,** *adj.*

peach·y (pē′chē) *adj.,* **peach·i·er, peach·i·est. 1.** resembling a peach, as in color or texture. **2.** *Slang.* fine; wonderful: *a peachy idea.*

peacock *(def. 1)*

pea·cock (pē′kok′) *n., pl.* **pea·cocks** or **pea·cock. 1.** the male of the peafowl, having a fan-shaped crest, shiny blue feathers on the head, neck, and body, and a train of bright green feathers covered with large eyelike spots. When the train is raised and spread, it is fanshaped. **2.** any peafowl. **3.** a vain and showy person.

peacock blue, a bright greenish blue color.

pea·fowl (pē′foul′) *n., pl.* **pea·fowl** or **pea·fowls.** a pheasant of Asia and Africa, noted for the brilliant ornamental feathers of the male.

pea·hen (pē′hen′) *n.* a female peafowl.

pea jacket, a short, double-breasted coat of thick woolen cloth, worn especially by sailors.

peak (pēk) *n.* **1.** the pointed top of a mountain or hill. **2.** a mountain having a pointed top, usually standing alone. **3.** a sharp, tapering, or projecting point or end. **4.** the highest point or greatest level: *at the peak of one's career. Traffic reaches its peak during rush hour.* **5.** the projecting brim of a cap. —*v.* to reach a high point: *The cafeteria's business peaks at lunchtime.*

peaked¹ (pēkt) *adj.* having or ending in a peak; pointed: *a peaked roof.* [*Peak* + -*ed².*]

peak·ed² (pē′kid) *adj.* pale or sickly in appearance: *You looked rather peaked after your illness.* [Perhaps from the Middle English word *peken* meaning "to slink, move dejectedly," of uncertain origin.]

peal (pēl) *n.* **1.** a loud, long sound or series of sounds: *a peal of thunder, a peal of laughter.* **2.** a set of bells tuned to one another. —*v.i., v.t.* to sound or ring in a peal or peals: *The church bells pealed on Sunday morning.*

pe·an (pē′ən) another spelling for **paean.**

pea·nut (pē′nut′) *n.* **1.** the nutlike seed of a plant related to the pea that develops in an underground pod and has a thin brownish skin. **2.** such a pod, usually containing two of these seeds. **3.** the plant bearing this pod.

peanut butter, a spread made from ground, roasted peanuts.

peanut oil, an oil pressed from peanuts, used in cooking and in the manufacture of margarine.

pear (pâr) *n.* **1.** a usually bell-shaped fruit having a firm, sweet, juicy flesh and a smooth yellow, brown, or reddish skin. **2.** the tree bearing this fruit.

pearl (pûrl) *n.* **1.** a rounded, lustrous gem, usually white or cream-colored. Pearls are formed inside the shells of certain kinds of oysters or other similar shellfish. **2.** something that looks like a pearl. **3.** a person or thing like a pearl in beauty or value: *pearls of wisdom.* **4.** see **mother-of-pearl. 5.** see **pearl gray.** —*adj.* **1.** of, relating to, or like a pearl or pearls. **2.** having the color pearl gray.

pearl gray, a clear, pale, bluish gray color.

pearl·y (pûr′lē) *adj.,* **pearl·i·er, pearl·i·est. 1.** resembling a pearl or pearls: *pearly teeth.* **2.** adorned with pearls or mother-of-pearl. —**pearl′i·ness,** *n.*

peas·ant (pez′ənt) *n.* a member of a class of small farmers or farm laborers.

peas·ant·ry (pez′ən trē) *n.* peasants as a group.

pease (pēz) *Archaic.* pea.

peat (pēt) *n.* rotted plant matter found in bogs and swamps. Peat is used as a fertilizer and is burned as fuel.

peat moss 1. a pale green moss that grows in swamps and bogs and is the major source of peat. **2.** the residue of such mosses and other plants, used as a mulch.

peb·ble (peb′əl) *n.* a small, usually round stone that is worn smooth by water or sand. —*v.t.,* **peb·bled, peb·bling. 1.** to cover with pebbles: *to pebble a walk.* **2.** to give a rough, uneven surface to (leather or paper). —**peb′bly,** *adj.*

pe·can (pi kän′, pi kan′) *n.* **1.** an edible nut having a thin, oval shell. **2.** the large tree bearing this nut.

pec·ca·dil·lo (pek′ə dil′ō) *n., pl.* **pec·ca·dil·loes** or **pec·ca·dil·los.** a slight fault or sin.

pec·ca·ry (pek′ə rē) *n., pl.* **pec·ca·ries.** a wild, piglike mammal found from the southern United States to Argentina, having coarse, bristly hair and straight tusks that point downward.

peccary

peck¹ (pek) *n.* **1.** a unit of dry measure for fruit, vegetables, and grain, equal to 8 quarts, or ¼ bushel (8.8 liters). **2.** a container holding or measuring a peck. **3.** *Informal.* a great amount: *I got into a peck of trouble when I broke the window.* [From the Medieval Latin word *pica* meaning this unit of dry measure.]

peck² (pek) *v.t.* **1.** to strike (something) with the beak in a short, rapid movement: *The parakeet pecked the bars of its cage.* **2.** to make by striking with the beak or a pointed tool: *The chick pecked a hole through the box.* **3.** to strike at and pick up with the beak: *The hen pecked the grains of corn.* —*v.i.* to strike or try to strike with the beak in a short, rapid movement: *The parrot pecked at my finger.* —*n.* **1.** a short, rapid stroke made with the beak or a pointed tool. **2.** a hole or mark made by such a stroke. **3.** *Informal.* a quick, light kiss: *She greeted him with a peck on the cheek.* [Perhaps from a form of *pick¹.*]

pecking order 1. a pattern of social organization in a group of birds, especially poultry, in which each bird has a definite rank determined by aggressiveness. Each bird pecks at those birds that are weaker than it is, and is pecked at by those birds that are stronger. **2.** any human social organization having definite levels of rank, especially one in which rank is determined by aggressive behavior.

pec·tin (pek′tin) *n.* any of several substances that cause jams and jellies to thicken or gel, found especially in certain ripe fruits.

pec·to·ral (pek′tər əl) *adj.* of, in, or on the chest. —*n.* a pectoral organ, such as a muscle.

pe·cul·iar (pi kūl′yər) *adj.* **1.** strange or unusual; odd: *They have many peculiar habits.* **2.** belonging to a certain person, group, place, or thing: *The koala bear is peculiar to Australia.* —**pe·cul′iar·ly,** *adv.*

pe·cu·li·ar·i·ty (pi kū′lē ar′i tē) *n., pl.* **pe·cu·li·ar·i·ties. 1.** a strange or unusual feature or characteristic. **2.** a special or particular characteristic: *A long tail is a peculiarity of that breed of dog.* **3.** the state or quality of being peculiar: *The peculiarity of your answer puzzled them.*

pe·cu·ni·ar·y (pi kū′nē er′ē) *adj.* of, relating to, or consisting of money: *a pecuniary reward.*

ped·a·gog·ic (ped′ə goj′ik) *adj.* of, relating to, or characteristic of a pedagogue or pedagogy. Also, **ped·a·gog·i·cal** (ped′ə goj′i kəl). —**ped′a·gog′i·cal·ly,** *adv.*

ped·a·gogue (ped′ə gog′, ped′ə gôg′) *also,* **ped·a·gog.** *n.* **1.** any teacher. **2.** a teacher who is pedantic and narrow-minded. [From the Latin word *paedagogus* meaning "a slave who led a boy to school, a governor," from the Greek word *paidogōgos,* going back to the words *pais* "boy, child" and *agein* "to lead."]

ped·a·go·gy (ped′ə goj′ē, ped′ə gō′jē) *n.* the art, science, or profession of teaching.

ped·al (ped′əl) *n.* **1.** a foot-operated part or lever that operates, moves, or controls a machine or part of a machine, as on a bicycle or automobile. **2.** a similar part or lever worked by the foot, used to modify the sound of a musical instrument, as a piano. —*v.,* **ped·aled, ped·al·ing;** *also, British,* **ped·alled, ped·al·ling.** —*v.t.,* to work the pedals of, operate by working pedals: *to pedal a bicycle, to pedal the treadle of an old-fashioned sewing machine.* —*v.i.* to work or use a pedal or pedals: *to pedal slowly.* —*adj.* **1.** of or relating to a foot or the feet. **2.** of, relating to, or operated by a pedal or pedals.

ped·ant (ped′ənt) *n.* a person who presents his or her knowledge in a showy or dull manner, often placing too much emphasis on unimportant details and formal rules.

pe·dan·tic (pi dan′tik) *adj.* of, like, or characteristic of a pedant or pedantry: *a pedantic lecturer* —**pe·dan′ti·cal·ly,** *adv.*

ped·ant·ry (ped′ən trē) *n., pl.* **ped·ant·ries. 1.** a showy display of knowledge characteristic of a pedant. **2.** an instance of being pedantic.

ped·dle (ped′əl) *v.,* **ped·dled, ped·dling.** —*v.t.,* **1.** to sell (goods), usually in small quantities, by traveling from place to place: *to peddle vegetables from door to door.* **2.** to deal out or distribute: *to peddle rumors.* —*v.i.* to travel from place to place offering goods for sale.

ped·dler (ped′lər) *also,* **ped·lar.** *n.* a person who peddles goods.

–pede *combining form* foot; feet: *centipede.*

ped·es·tal (ped′ə stəl) *n.* **1.** a support at the base of a column, statue, or similar upright structure. **2.** any base or supporting structure, as for a tall lamp or vase.
  ·on a pedestal. in a position or condition of high, often exaggerated regard or admiration: *The children put the movie star on a pedestal.*

ped·es·tri·an (pə des′trē ən) *n.* a person who travels on foot; walker. —*adj.* **1.** of or for people traveling on foot: *a pedestrian path.* **2.** lacking originality, imagination, or excitement; commonplace or dull: *a pedestrian style of writing.* [From the Latin word

pedestal

pedester meaning "going on foot," from the word *pes* meaning "foot."]

Word Family

Many English words come from the Latin word for "foot," *pes,* and its root form *ped-.* We classify animals by their number of feet, whether **biped** or **quadruped,** and we name two of them **centipede** and **millipede** (an exaggeration). Even things with no feet at all may be named with words in this family, such as the **pedals** of a bicycle. Where there are feet, there is movement, whether it is the slow movement of a **pedestrian** or the more **expeditious** movement of a jogger. Some people mount **expeditions** into uncharted areas, while others chart their **pedigree** on a family tree. Shackles on the feet **impede** movement, and the threat of **impeachment** is an **impediment** to political wrongdoing.

pe·di·at·ric (pē′dē at′rik) *adj.* of or relating to pediatrics.

pe·di·a·tri·cian (pē′dē ə trish′ən) *n.* a doctor who specializes in pediatrics.

pe·di·at·rics (pē′dē at′riks) *n.* the branch of medicine that deals with the care of babies and children and the treatment *and prevention* of their diseases. ▲ used with a singular verb.

ped·i·cel (ped′i səl) *also,* **ped·i·cle** (ped′i kəl). *n.* the stalk of a flower, especially one supporting a single flower in a flower cluster.

ped·i·cure (ped′i kyūr′) *n.* a beauty treatment for the feet, especially a trimming and polishing of the toenails.

ped·i·gree (ped′i grē′) *n.* **1.** a line of ancestors; descent; lineage. **2.** a detailed record or list of ancestry or descent, especially of an animal; *the pedigree of a champion dog.*

ped·i·greed (ped′i grēd′) *adj.* having a recorded or known pedigree: *a pedigreed cat.*

ped·i·ment (ped′ə mənt) *n.* **1.** a triangular portion on the front of a building in the Greek architectural style. **2.** a similar ornamental part, as over a door, mantel, or window.

ped·lar (ped′lər) another spelling of **peddler**

pe·dom·e·ter (pi dom′i tər) *n.* an instrument that measures the distance covered on foot by counting the number of steps taken and multiplying by the length of a single step.

pe·dun·cle (pi dung′kəl) *n.* a stem or stalk, especially one supporting a flower cluster or bearing an individual flower.

pediment *(def. 1)*

peek (pēk) *v.i.* to look quickly, secretly, or cautiously: *I peeked into the box.* —*n.* a quick, secret, or cautious look.

peek·a·boo (pēk′ə bü′) *n.* a game played with a young child in which a person hides his or her face, then suddenly uncovers it and says "peekaboo."

peel (pēl) *n.* the skin or outer covering that has been or can be removed from certain fruits and vegetables: *a*

at; āpe; fär; câre; end; mē; it; īce; pîerce; hot; ōld; sông; fôrk; oil; out; up; ūse; rüle; pùll; tûrn; chin; sing; shop; thin; this; hw in white; zh in treasure. The symbol ə stands for the unstressed vowel sound heard in about, taken, pencil, lemon, and circus.

P

695

banana peel. —*v.t.* **1.** to remove the skin or outer covering from: *to peel a potato.* **2.** to remove or strip: *to peel a stamp off an envelope, to peel paint from a wall.* —*v.i.* **1.** to come off, as in pieces or strips: *The paint is peeling from the walls.* **2.** to lose or shed an outer covering or layer, as of skin: *Your sunburned back is peeling.* —**peel′er**, *n.*

·**to keep one's eyes peeled.** *Informal.* to be watchful; keep alert.

peep¹ (pēp) *v.i.* **1.** to look secretly, cautiously, or quickly, as through a narrow opening or from a hiding place; peek: *to peep through a crack in a wall.* **2.** to come slowly or partly into view: *The moon peeped through the clouds.* —*n.* **1.** a secret, cautious, or quick look. **2.** the first appearance: *the peep of dawn.* [From the Middle English word *peepen* meaning "to peek."]

peep² (pēp) *n.* **1.** a short, sharp sound, such as that made by a young bird; cheep. **2.** a slight sound; utterance: *Not another peep out of you!* —*v.i.* to utter a peep. [Representation of the sound of a bird.]

peep·er¹ (pē′pər) *n.* **1.** a person who peeps or spies. **2.** *Informal.* an eye. [*Peep¹* + *-er¹.*]

peep·er² (pē′pər) *n.* any of several tree frogs that make a shrill, peeping noise. [*Peep²* + *-er¹.*]

peep·hole (pēp′hōl′) *n.* a small hole or opening, especially in a door, through which one may look.

peer¹ (pîr) *n.* a person who is equal to another, as in status, social class, age, or ability; equal: *to be tried by a jury of one's peers. As a painter, she has few peers.* **2.** in Great Britain, a member of one of the five degrees of nobility; duke, marquis, earl, viscount, or baron. **3.** any titled member of the nobility. [From the Old French word *per* meaning "someone who is an equal, a match²," going back to the Latin word *par* "equal."]

peer² (pîr) *v.i.* **1.** to look closely or searchingly, as in an effort to see clearly: *We tried to peer through the darkness.* **2.** to come into view; be partly visible: *The sun peered over the mountain.* [Perhaps from the Middle English word *peeren* meaning "to be visible, be present," short for *appeeren* "to appear."]

peer·age (pîr′ij) *n.* **1.** the rank or dignity of a peer (*defs. 2 and 3*). **2.** the peers of a country thought of as a group. **3.** a book listing the peers of a country and their genealogies.

peer·ess (pîr′is) *n., pl.* **peer·ess·es. 1.** the wife or widow of a peer. **2.** a woman who holds the rank of a peer in her own right.

peer·less (pîr′lis) *adj.* without equal; matchless: *a peerless performance.* —**peer′less·ly,** *adv.* —**peer′less·ness,** *n.*

peeve (pēv) *v.t.,* **peeved, peev·ing.** to annoy; irritate; vex. —*n.* a cause of annoyance; grievance: *Rude people are one of my biggest peeves.*

pee·vish (pē′vish) *adj.* **1.** irritable and ill-tempered; cranky: *The baby sometimes gets very peevish and won't stop crying.* **2.** showing or marked by annoyance or irritation: *a peevish look.* —**pee′vish·ly,** *adv.* —**pee′·vish·ness,** *n.*

pee·wee (pē′wē′) *n.* **1.** *Informal.* an unusually small person, animal, or thing. **2.** another spelling of **pewee.**

peg (peg) *n.* **1.** a piece of wood, metal, or another hard substance that can be fitted or driven into a surface, as to fasten parts together, hang something on, or serve as a marker. **2.** a wooden, plastic, or metal pin in a stringed musical instrument that fastens and controls the tension of a string. **3.** a step or degree: *Ever since he lied to me he has come down a peg in my estimation.* **4.** *Informal.* throw, as in baseball. —*v.t.,* **pegged, peg·ging. 1.** to fasten or mark with a peg or pegs. **2.** *Informal.* to throw. **3.** *Informal.* to recognize or classify; identify: *I pegged her as a cheat from the very beginning.*

Peg·a·sus (peg′ə səs) *n. Greek Mythology.* a winged horse that carried the hero Bellerophon. It is associated with the Muses, and especially with poetry.

P.E.I., Prince Edward Island.

pe·jo·ra·tive (pi jôr′ə tiv, pi jor′ə tiv, pej′ə rā′tiv) *adj.* having an unfavorable meaning or effect; disparaging: *to use a word in a pejorative sense.* —**pe·jo′ra·tive·ly,** *adv.*

Pe·kin·ese (pē′kə nēz′, pē′kə nēs′) *n., pl.* **Pe·kin·ese.** another spelling of **Pekingese.**

Pe·king·ese (pē′kə nēz′, pē′king ēz′, pē′kə nēs′, pē′king ēs′) *also,* **Pe·kin·ese.** *n., pl.* **Pe·king·ese.** a small dog having a wrinkled, flat face, bulging eyes, and a long, silky coat.

Pe·king man (pē′king′) an extinct primitive human being whose fossil remains were found near Peking (Beijing), China.

pe·koe (pē′kō) *n.* a superior grade of black tea from India, Sri Lanka, and Java, made from the smallest tea leaves.

pelf (pelf) *n.* money or wealth.

pel·i·can (pel′i kən) *n.* any of various web-footed water birds having a long pouch beneath its bill that is used for storing fish. Most pelicans have chiefly white feathers.

pel·lag·ra (pə lag′rə) *n.* a disease caused by a lack of niacin in the diet, characterized by diarrhea, skin eruptions, and nervous disorders.

pel·let (pel′it) *n.* **1.** a small ball, as of food, medicine, or paper. **2.** a bullet or piece of shot. **3.** a ball, usually of stone, formerly used as a missile.

pelican

pell–mell (pel′mel′) *also,* **pell·mell.** *adv.* **1.** in great, disorderly haste; headlong: *The people ran pell-mell from the burning building.* **2.** in a jumbled or confused manner; without order: *Papers were scattered pell-mell about the room.* —*adj.* disorderly or hasty; headlong.

pel·lu·cid (pə lü′sid) *adj.* **1.** clear, as glass; transparent: *a pellucid stream.* **2.** easy to understand; lucid: *a pellucid writing style.*

Pel·o·pon·ne·sian War (pel′ə pə nē′zhən) the war between Athens and Sparta from 431 to 404 B.C., ending in victory for Sparta.

pelt¹ (pelt) *v.t.* **1.** to attack or strike repeatedly with or as if with missiles: *The children pelted each other with snowballs.* **2.** to beat against continuously or repeatedly: *Hail pelted the roof.* **3.** to throw or hurl repeatedly: *We pelted stones against the wall.*—*v.i.* to beat or strike heavily or continuously: *The rain pelted against the windows.* —*n.* a hard blow, as from something thrown. [From the Middle English word *pilten* meaning "to thrust, strike, beat," from Old English.]

pelt² (pelt) *n.* the hide or skin of an animal with its fur or hair, especially when removed to be used for making garments or other items. [From the Middle English word *pelt.*]

pel·vic (pel′vik) *adj.* of or relating to the pelvis.

pel·vis (pel′vis) *n., pl.* **pel·vis·es** or **pel·ves** (pel′vēz). **1.** the large, basin-shaped ring of bone that protects and supports the organs in the lower trunk of the human body, consisting of the sacrum, coccyx, ilium, ischeum, and pubis. **2.** a similar structure in other animals. [From the scientific Latin word *pelvis* meaning this structure, from the Latin word *pelvis* "a basin," from its shape.]

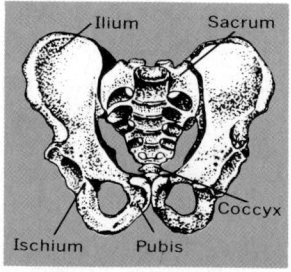

pelvis *(front view)*

pem·mi·can (pem′i kən)

also, **pem·i·can**. *n.* lean meat that is dried, pounded, mixed with melted fat to form a paste, and pressed into cakes.

pen¹ (pen) *n.* **1.** any of various instruments for writing or drawing with ink, such as a fountain pen or a ball-point pen. **2.** writing style or ability: *That author has a satiric pen.* —*v.t.*, **penned, pen·ning**. to write: *to pen a letter.* [From the Old French word *pen* meaning "feather" and "quill pen," from the Latin word *penna* "feather."]

pen² (pen) *n.* **1.** a small enclosed area used to confine animals. **2.** the animals confined to such an area. **3.** any of various small enclosed areas, as a playpen. —*v.t.*, **penned** or **pent, pen·ning**. to confine in a pen or other small area. [From the Old English word *penn* meaning "fold², enclosure."]

pen³ (pen) *n. Slang.* see **penitentiary**.

pe·nal (pē′nəl) *adj.* **1.** of or relating to punishment, especially legal punishment: *penal laws.* **2.** being or serving as punishment: *penal labor.* **3.** punishable: *a penal offense.*

pe·nal·ize (pē′nə līz, pen′ə līz′) *v.t.*, **pe·nal·ized, pe·nal·iz·ing**. to subject to a penalty or punishment. —**pe′nal·i·za′tion**, *n.*

pen·al·ty (pen′əl tē) *n., pl.* **pen·al·ties**. **1.** a punishment established or imposed for violating a law or regulation. **2.** an unpleasant or painful result of an action or condition. **3.** *Sports.* a disadvantage or punishment imposed on a player or team for breaking the rules.

penalty box, an area alongside a hockey rink where a player must sit for a certain amount of time as a penalty for breaking a rule.

pen·ance (pen′əns) *n.* **1.** a punishment, usually self-imposed, undergone to show or express sorrow and obtain forgiveness for a sin or offense. **2.** in some Christian churches, a sacrament that includes sorrow for and confession of sin, acceptance of punishment, and absolution.

pence (pens) *British.* the plural of **penny** *(def. 2).*

pen·chant (pen′chənt) *n.* a strong liking or inclination: *a penchant for gardening.*

pen·cil (pen′səl) *n.* **1.** a marking, drawing, or writing implement, usually consisting of a stick of graphite, chalk, or similar substance enclosed in a tube of wood, metal, or plastic. **2.** something like a pencil in shape or use, especially an implement having a cosmetic or medicinal use. —*v.t.*, **pen·ciled, pen·cil·ing**; *also, British,* **pen·cilled, pen·cil·ling**. to write, draw, mark, or color with a pencil.

pend·ant (pen′dənt) *n.* an ornamental object, such as a jewel, that hangs from something else. —*adj.* see **pendent**.

pend·ent (pen′dənt) *also,* **pend·ant**. *adj.* **1.** suspended; hanging: *pendent glass beads.* **2.** jutting out; overhanging. **3.** undecided or unsettled; pending. —*n.* see **pendant**.

pend·ing (pen′ding) *adj.* **1.** not yet decided or settled; unresolved: *The decision on that question is still pending.* **2.** about to happen; impending; imminent: *a pending disaster.* —*prep.* while awaiting; until: *We postponed our picnic pending a change in the weather.*

pen·du·lous (pen′jə ləs) *adj.* **1.** hanging, especially in a loose or drooping manner: *a pendulous branch of a tree.* **2.** swinging: *a pendulous motion.*

pen·du·lum (pen′jə ləm) *n.* an object hung from a fixed point and set in motion to swing back and forth, often used to regulate the movement of a clock.

Pe·nel·o·pe (pə nel′ə pē) *n. Greek and Roman Legend.* the wife of Ulysses, noted for her faithfulness during her husband's long absence.

pe·nes (pē′nēz) a plural of **penis**.

pen·e·tra·ble (pen′i trə bəl) *adj.* capable of being penetrated. —**pen′e·tra·bil′i·ty**, *n.*

pen·e·trate (pen′i trāt′) *v.*, **pen·e·trat·ed, pen·e·trat-**

ing. —*v.t.* **1.** to pass into or through, especially by force or with difficulty: *The bullet penetrated the steel plate.* **2.** to seep or spread through: *The rain penetrated my sleeping bag.* **3.** to discover the meaning of; understand: *Science has attempted to penetrate the mysteries of the universe.* —*v.i.* to pass or force a way into or through something: *The walls are so thick that almost no sound can penetrate.*

pen·e·tra·tion (pen′i trā′shən) *n.* **1.** the act or power of penetrating. **2.** the degree or extent to which something penetrates. **3.** keenness of mind; insight; discernment.

pen·guin (pen′gwin, peng′gwin) *n.* a flightless bird native to Antarctica and to the coastlines of southern continents. Penguins have webbed feet, dense feathers that are usually black or gray on the back and white on the chest, stomach, and legs, and wings that resemble flippers and are used for swimming.

pen·i·cil·lin (pen′ə sil′in) *n.* an antibiotic made from certain penicillium molds, used in the treatment of a wide variety of bacterial infections. [From the name of the mold *Penicillium,* from the Latin word *penicillus* meaning "painter's brush" and "little tail." The penicillium mold got its name because its spores looked like a brush under the microscope.]

pen·i·cil·li·um (pen′ə sil′ē əm) *n., pl.* **pen·i·cil·li·a** (pen′ə sil′ē ə) or **pen·i·cil·li·ums**. any of a group of fungi commonly found as a blue-green mold on bread, cheese, and other foods.

penguin

pen·in·su·la (pə nin′sə lə, pə nin′syə lə) *n.* a body of land almost entirely surrounded by water, projecting out from a large land mass. Most of Italy is a peninsula.

pen·in·su·lar (pə nin′sə lər, pə nin′syə lər) *adj.* of, relating to, or like a peninsula.

pe·nis (pē′nis) *n., pl.* **pe·nis·es** or **pe·nes** (pē′nēz). the male sex organ. In mammals, it is also used for urination.

pen·i·tence (pen′i təns) *n.* the state of being penitent; repentance.

pen·i·tent (pen′i tənt) *adj.* feeling or showing sorrow or regret for sin or wrongdoing; repentant: *I wrote a penitent letter apologizing for my rudeness.* —*n.* a person who is penitent, especially one who confesses a sin and receives the sacrament of penance. —**pen′i·tent·ly**, *adv.*

pen·i·ten·tial (pen′i ten′shəl) *adj.* **1.** relating to or showing penitence or repentance. **2.** relating to penance.

pen·i·ten·tia·ry (pen′i ten′shə rē) *n., pl.* **pen·i·ten·tia·ries**. a prison, especially a state or federal prison, for persons convicted of major crimes. —*adj.* **1.** punishable by imprisonment in a penitentiary: *a penitentiary offense.* **2.** of or relating to penance.

pen·knife (pen′nīf′) *n., pl.* **pen·knives** (pen′nīvz′). a small pocketknife, originally used for making or sharpening quill pens.

pen·man (pen′mən) *n., pl.* **pen·men** (pen′mən). **1.** a writer; author. **2.** a person skilled in penmanship.

P

pen·man·ship (pen′mən ship′) *n.* **1.** the style or quality of handwriting. **2.** the art or skill of handwriting.

Penn., Pennsylvania. Also, **Pa.**

pen name, a fictitious name under which an author writes; pseudonym.

pen·nant (pen′ənt) *n.* **1.** a long, usually triangular flag, used especially as a school or team emblem or, on a ship, for signaling or identification. **2.** such a flag symbolizing a victory or championship, especially in professional baseball.

pen·ni·less (pen′ē lis) *adj.* having no money; very poor. —**pen′ni·less·ness,** *n.*

pen·non (pen′ən) *n.* **1.** a distinctive banner or streamer carried at the tip of a knight's lance in the Middle Ages. **2.** any flag or banner.

Penn·syl·va·nia Dutch (pen′səl vān′yə) **1.** the descendants of German immigrants who settled in Pennsylvania in the seventeenth and eighteenth centuries. **2.** a German dialect heavily mixed with English, spoken by these people.

pen·ny (pen′ē) *n., pl.* **pen·nies** or (*def. 2*) **pence. 1.** a coin of the United States and Canada, equal to one cent or 1/100 of a dollar. **2.** a coin of the United Kingdom, equal to 1/100 of a pound, formerly equal to 1/12 of a shilling. **3.** a sum of money.

pen·ny·weight (pen′ē wāt′) *n.* a measure of weight equal to 24 grains, or 1/20 ounce troy (1.555 grams).

pen·ny–wise (pen′ē wīz′) *adj.* cautious or thrifty in small matters.

·to be penny-wise and pound-foolish. to be cautious or thrifty in small matters but wasteful in large ones.

pen·ny·worth (pen′ē wûrth′) *n.* **1.** as much as can be bought for a penny. **2.** a small amount of anything.

Pe·nob·scot (pə nob′skot) *n., pl.* **Pe·nob·scot** or **Pe·nob·scots.** a member of a North American Indian tribe living in southern Maine and speaking an Algonquian language.

pe·nol·o·gy (pē nol′ə jē) *n.* the study of the punishment and rehabilitation of criminals and the management of prisons.

pen pal, a person with whom one exchanges letters regularly, especially without having ever met: *Some of my friends have pen pals in foreign countries.*

pen·sion (pen′shən) *n.* a sum of money, other than wages, paid regularly by a former employer to a retired or disabled person who has fulfilled certain requirements or conditions. —*v.t.* to give a pension to.

·to pension off. to retire or dismiss with a pension: *The company pensioned off its veteran employees.*

pen·sion·er (pen′shə nər) *n.* a person who receives a pension.

pen·sive (pen′siv) *adj.* **1.** in deep and serious thought, often about matters of a sad nature: *The pensive judge sat silently on the bench.* **2.** characterized by or showing deep, often sad thoughtfulness: *a pensive look, a pensive mood.* —**pen′sive·ly,** *adv.* —**pen′sive·ness,** *n.*

pent (pent) *v.* a past tense and past participle of **pen².** —*adj.* closely confined; shut up.

penta– *combining form* five: *pentagon.*

pen·ta·gon (pen′tə gon′) *n.* **1.** a polygon with five sides and five angles. **2. the Pentagon.** the U.S. Department of Defense [from the *Pentagon,* its five-sided main building, in Arlington, Va.].

pen·tag·o·nal (pen tag′ə nəl) *adj.* having five sides and five angles; like a pentagon.

pen·tam·e·ter (pen tam′i tər) *n.* **1.** a line of verse consisting of five metrical feet. **2.** a verse composed of such lines. —*adj.* containing five metrical feet.

pentagons *(def. 1)*

Pen·ta·teuch (pen′tə tük′, pen′tə tūk′) *n.* the first five books of the Old Testament; Torah.

pen·tath·lon (pen tath′lən, pen tath′lon) *n.* an athletic contest in which each contestant participates in each of five different events.

Pen·te·cost (pen′ti kôst′) *n.* **1.** a Christian feast observed on the seventh Sunday after Easter, commemorating the possession of the Apostles by the Holy Ghost, considered by many the beginning of the Christian religion. Also, **Whitsunday. 2.** another word for **Shavuoth.**

pent·house (pent′hous′) *n., pl.* **pent·hous·es** (pent′hou′ziz). an apartment or other dwelling built on the roof of a building.

pent–up (pent′up′) *adj.* not expressed or released; held in; restrained: *pent-up feelings, pent-up anger.*

pe·nult (pē′nult, pi nult′) *n.* the next to last syllable in a word.

pe·nul·ti·mate (pi nul′tə mit) *adj.* **1.** next to the last. **2.** of, relating to, or occurring on the penult of a word: *a penultimate stress.* —*n.* the next to last.

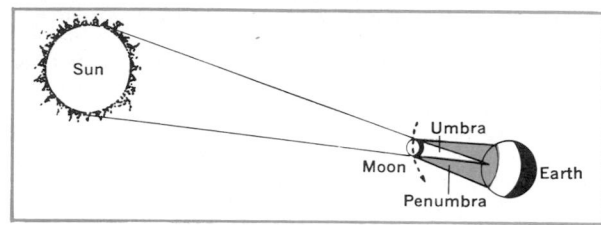

penumbra *(def. 1)*

pe·num·bra (pi num′brə) *n., pl.* **pe·num·bras** or **pe·num·brae** (pi num′brē). **1.** in an eclipse, the partial shadow between the area of total eclipse and the area of complete illumination. **2.** the grayish fringe around the dark central portion of a sunspot. **3.** the partially darkened area surrounding the completely dark central region of a shadow.

pe·nu·ri·ous (pi nùr′ē əs, pi nyùr′ē əs) *adj.* **1.** reluctant to spend or part with money; stingy; miserly. **2.** very poor; poverty-stricken: *a penurious existence.* —**pe·nu′ri·ous·ly,** *adv.* —**pe·nu′ri·ous·ness,** *n.*

pen·u·ry (pen′yə rē) *n.* extreme poverty.

pe·on (pē′on) *n.* **1.** in Spanish America, an unskilled worker or farm laborer. **2.** formerly, a person forced to work to pay off a debt. **3.** an unskilled worker of low status. [From the Spanish word *péon,* from the Medieval Latin word *pedo* "foot soldier," going back to the Latin word *pes* "foot."]

pe·on·age (pē′ə nij) *n.* **1.** the condition of being a peon. **2.** the system or practice of forcing people to work in exchange for payment of debts.

pe·o·ny (pē′ə nē) *n., pl.* **pe·o·nies. 1.** a large, showy pink, red, or white flower of any of a group of hardy plants. **2.** the plant bearing this flower, widely grown in gardens.

peo·ple (pē′pəl) *n., pl.* **peo·ple** or (*def. 2*) **peo·ples. 1.** men, women, and children; persons: *This theater can seat 500 people.* **2.** the body of persons making up a nation, race, tribe, or group: *the Israeli people, primitive peoples, the peoples of Europe.* **3.** the body of citizens of a state or other political unit: *Members of Congress are elected by the people.* **4.** the body or mass of common persons. **5.** persons in relation to a superior, such as the subjects of a ruler: *The king and queen loved their people.* **6.** human beings as distinguished from animals: *Distemper is not a disease that affects people.* **7.** *Informal.* one's family; relatives. —*v.t.,* **peo·pled, peo·pling.** to fill with people; inhabit; populate: *A great number of human beings people the earth.*

pep (pep) *n.* liveliness and high spirits; energy: *She is always full of pep in the morning.* —*v.t.,* **pepped, pep-**

ping. to make lively or cheerful; fill with energy (used with *up*): *The good news pepped him up.* [Short for *pepper.*]

pep·per (pep′ər) *n.* **1.** a hot, pungent spice of a tropical American plant. Black pepper is made from whole dried berries that are ground. White pepper is made from the dried, ground seeds of the berries with the outer coat and pulp removed. **2.** the plant that bears these berries. **3.** the red, green, or yellow sweet or hot fruit of any of a group of plants. Peppers may be eaten either raw or cooked or may be ground into spices. **4.** the plant bearing this fruit. **5.** a hot spice made from hot red peppers; cayenne. —*v.t.* **1.** to sprinkle or season with pepper. **2.** to cover or sprinkle: *The tweed fabric was peppered with flecks of red and blue.* **3.** to shower or pelt with bullets or other small objects.

peppers (*n., def. 3*)

pep·per·corn (pep′er kôrn′) *n.* the dried fruit of the black pepper, used as a spice, either whole or ground.

pepper mill, a utensil used to grind peppercorns.

pep·per·mint (pep′ər mint′) *n.* **1.** a fragrant plant related to the mint, having small purple or white flowers and toothed leaves. **2.** the oil obtained from this plant, having a minty aroma and taste and used in medicine and as a flavoring, especially in candy, chewing gum, and toothpaste. **3.** a candy or lozenge flavored with peppermint oil.

pep·per·y (pep′ə rē) *adj.* **1.** of, like, or relating to pepper; pungent: *a peppery taste.* **2.** sharp or fiery; stinging: *a peppery speech, peppery writing.* **3.** hot-tempered; testy. —**pep′per·i·ness,** *n.*

pep·py (pep′ē) *adj.,* **pep·pi·er, pep·pi·est.** *Informal.* full of pep or energy; lively. —**pep′pi·ness,** *n.*

pep·sin (pep′sin) *n.* **1.** an enzyme that is produced in the stomach and aids in the digestion of eggs, fish, meat, and other proteins. **2.** a medicine used to relieve indigestion, containing pepsin taken from the stomach of certain animals.

pep talk, a speech given for the purpose of increasing enthusiasm or confidence or boosting morale: *The coach gave the team a pep talk before the big game.*

pep·tic (pep′tik) *adj.* **1.** of, relating to, or aiding digestion. **2.** of or relating to pepsin or other digestive secretions, or resulting from their action: *a peptic ulcer.*

per (pûr; *unstressed* pər) *prep.* **1.** for each: *I earn $200 per week.* **2.** by means of; through. **3.** according to: *per instructions.*

per·ad·ven·ture (pûr′əd ven′chər) *adv.* *Archaic.* perhaps; maybe.

per·am·bu·late (pər am′byə lāt′) *v.,* **per·am·bu·lat·ed, per·am·bu·lat·ing.** —*v.t.* to walk through, around, or about (a place), especially so as to survey, inspect, or examine: *The tourists perambulated the estate.* —*v.i.* to walk about; stroll. —**per·am′bu·la′tion,** *n.*

per·am·bu·la·tor (pər am′byə lā′tər) *n.* a baby carriage.

per an·num (pər an′əm) for each year; per year; annually: *an income of $20,000 per annum.* [From the Latin phrase *per annum* meaning "for (a) year," from the words *per* "by, for, through" and *annus* "year."]

per·cale (pər kāl′) *n.* a closely woven, lightweight cotton fabric with a smooth finish, used especially for sheets.

per cap·i·ta (pər kap′i tə) for, from, or by each person: *per capita income.* [From the Latin phrase *per capita* meaning "for person," from the words *per* "by, for, through" and *caput* "head" or "person."]

per·ceive (pər sēv′) *v.t.,* **per·ceived, per·ceiv·ing.** **1.** to be or become aware of through the senses; see, hear, taste, smell, or feel: *to perceive a change in the temperature.* **2.** to take in or grasp mentally; comprehend: *I perceived that you were angry with us.*

per·cent (pər sent′) *also,* **per cent.** *n.* the number of parts in or to every hundred. Two percent of 50 is ²/₁₀₀ × 50, or 1. ▲ the symbol for percent (%) is often used with figures, as in *6% interest.*

per·cent·age (pər sen′tij) *n.* **1.** the rate or proportion of something to every hundred: *What percentage of registered voters actually voted?* **2.** a part of a whole; portion: *A large percentage of the students ride the bus to school.*

per·cen·tile (pər sen′tīl) *n.* any value in a series of values on a scale found by dividing a group into a hundred equal parts. A person with a percentile of eighty on a test has done as well as or better than eighty percent of the people taking the test.

per·cep·ti·ble (pər sep′tə bəl) *adj.* able to be perceived; noticeable: *There has been a perceptible change in the cat's behavior lately.* —**per·cep′ti·bil′i·ty,** *n.* —**per·cep′ti·bly,** *adv.*

per·cep·tion (pər sep′shən) *n.* **1.** the act or process of perceiving. **2.** the power or faculty of perceiving: *Since I am color-blind, my perception of red and green is poor.* **3.** the result of perceiving; an observation. **4.** depth of understanding; insight; perceptiveness: *a person of great perception.*

per·cep·tive (pər sep′tiv) *adj.* capable of or characterized by keen perception: *a perceptive judge of human nature.* —**per·cep′tive·ly,** *adv.* —**per·cep′tive·ness,** *n.*

perch¹ (pûrch) *n., pl.* **perch·es.** **1.** anything on which a bird can come to rest, such as a horizontal bar or branch. **2.** any raised place for sitting or standing: *The lifeguard watched the swimmers from a perch above the pool.* —*v.i.* to rest or sit on a perch; settle: *The blue jay perched on the lowest branch of the tree.* —*v.t.* to set or place on a perch: *The cat perched itself on the bookcase.* [From the Old French word *perche* "bough where birds sit" or "pole, bar," from the Latin word *pertica* "a pole, staff."]

perch² (pûrch) *n., pl.* **perch** or **perch·es.** any of a large group of freshwater food and game fish found throughout North America and in most of Europe. [From the Old French word *perche,* from the Latin word *perca,* from the Greek word *perkē,* all meaning this fish.]

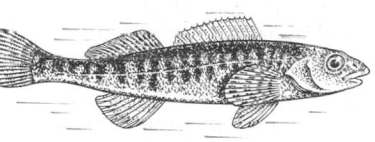

perch²

at; āpe; fär; câre; end; mē; it; īce; pîerce; hot; ōld; sông, fôrk; oil; out; up; ūse; rüle; pùll; tûrn; chin; sing; shop; thin; this; hw in white; zh in treasure. The symbol ə stands for the unstressed vowel sound heard in about, taken, pencil, lemon, and circus.

P

per·chance (pər chans′) *adv.* by chance; possibly; perhaps.

per·co·late (pûr′kə lāt′) *v.*, **per·co·lat·ed, per·co·lat·ing.** —*v.t.* **1.** to prepare in a percolator: *to percolate coffee.* **2.** to cause (a liquid) to pass through tiny spaces or holes. —*v.i.* to pass through tiny spaces or holes: *The water from the spring is pure because it has percolated through the tiny pebbles of the stream bed. The coffee is percolating.* —**per′co·la′tion,** *n.*

per·co·la·tor (pûr′kə lā′tər) *n.* a kind of coffee pot in which boiling water rises through a tube to a perforated basket containing ground coffee, and then drips back down to the bottom.

per·cus·sion (pər kush′ən) *n.* **1.** the striking of one body against another with great force; collision. **2.** the sound or vibration resulting from such a collision. **3.** the striking of sound waves upon the ear. **4.** *Medicine.* the tapping of a part of the body in order to find out about its condition from the sounds produced. **5.** musical percussion instruments as a group.

percussion cap, a device that contains a small amount of explosive powder, designed to set off a larger charge when it is struck, as by the hammer of a gun.

percussion instrument, any of various musical instruments in which tones are produced by striking one thing against another. The drum, cymbal, xylophone, and piano are percussion instruments.

per di·em (pər dē′əm) for each day; per day; daily. [From the Latin phrase *per diem* meaning ''for (a) day,'' from the words *per* ''by, for, through'' and *dies* ''day.'']

per·di·tion (pər dish′ən) *n.* **1.** the loss of one's soul; loss of heavenly salvation; eternal damnation. **2.** another word for **hell. 3.** complete loss or destruction.

per·e·grine (per′ə grin) *n.* a falcon having predominantly bluish gray feathers, formerly much used in falconry. Also, **peregrine falcon.**

per·emp·to·ry (pə remp′tə rē) *adj.* **1.** absolutely settled or determined; unconditional; final: *a peremptory court decision.* **2.** not to be disobeyed, refused, or questioned; imperative: *the dictator's peremptory orders.* **3.** imperious; dictatorial; dogmatic: *a peremptory manner.* —**per·emp′to·ri·ly,** *adv.* —**per·emp′to·ri·ness,** *n.*

per·en·ni·al (pə ren′ē əl) *adj.* **1.** lasting or existing through the year or many years: *a perennial stream that doesn't dry up during the summer.* **2.** lasting for a long time; enduring: *the perennial optimism of youth.* **3.** *Botany.* living more than two years: *perennial plants.* —*n.* a perennial plant. —**per·en′ni·al·ly,** *adv.*

per·fect (*adj., n.,* pûr′fikt; *v.,* pər fekt′) *adj.* **1.** free from any defect or imperfection; faultless: *The examination paper was perfect, without even one spelling mistake.* **2.** fully developed, formed, or done; complete: *She drew a perfect circle.* **3.** corresponding exactly to the original; accurate; correct: *That painted portrait is a perfect likeness of you.* **4.** very great; absolute; utter: *He made a perfect fool of himself!* **5.** *Grammar.* of, relating to, or designating the tenses of a verb that express action completed in the past. There are three perfect tenses in English: the present perfect, the past perfect (or pluperfect), and the future perfect. —*n. Grammar.* **1.** a perfect tense. **2.** a verb form in such a tense. —*v.t.* **1.** to make perfect or flawless. **2.** to bring to completion; complete: *The scientists finally perfected a system for space travel.*

per·fect·i·ble (pər fek′tə bəl) *adj.* capable of being made perfect. —**per·fect′i·bil′i·ty,** *n.*

per·fec·tion (pər fek′shən) *n.* **1.** the state or quality of being perfect or faultless; excellence; flawlessness: *I*

peregrine

always strive for perfection in my work. **2.** a person or thing that is regarded as being perfect or excellent: *The performance of the symphony orchestra was perfection.* **3.** the act or process of perfecting: *the perfection of a style.*

per·fec·tion·ist (pər fek′shə nist) *n.* a person who sets extremely high standards and goals for himself or herself and others; person who demands perfection.

per·fect·ly (pûr′fikt lē) *adv.* **1.** in a perfect manner; faultlessly: *This dress fits perfectly.* **2.** completely; entirely: *Today was a perfectly awful day.*

perfect number, a number that is equal to the sum of its divisors, not including the number itself. The number 28, which can be divided by 1, 2, 4, 7, and 14, is a perfect number.

perfect pitch, another term for **absolute pitch.**

per·fid·i·ous (pər fid′ē əs) *adj.* given to or characterized by perfidy; not faithful; treacherous: *a perfidious companion.* —**per·fid′i·ous·ly,** *adv.* —**per·fid′i·ous·ness,** *n.*

per·fi·dy (pûr′fi dē) *n., pl.* **per·fi·dies.** a deliberate breaking of faith; faithlessness; disloyalty.

per·fo·rate (pûr′fə rāt′) *v.t.,* **per·fo·rat·ed, per·fo·rat·ing. 1.** to make a hole or holes through; pierce: *Please perforate the carton with a knife so that the kittens can breathe.* **2.** to make a row of small holes through: *The edge of the order blank in the catalog was perforated so that it could be torn out easily.*

per·fo·ra·tion (pûr′fə rā′shən) *n.* **1.** the act of perforating or the state of being perforated. **2.** a hole made by boring or piercing through something: *perforations in a sheet of postage stamps.*

per·force (pər fôrs′) *adv. Archaic.* of or by necessity; necessarily.

per·form (pər fôrm′) *v.t.* **1.** to begin and carry out to completion; execute; do: *to perform a job, to perform an operation.* **2.** to meet or satisfy; fulfill; discharge: *to perform one's duty.* **3.** to give a performance of: *to perform a play by Shakespeare.* —*v.i.* **1.** to carry out a job, duty, task, or the like; function: *to perform well under pressure.* **2.** to give a performance: *The singer performed in New York.*

per·for·mance (pər fôr′məns) *n.* **1.** a public presentation, as of a play, musical program, or other entertainment: *The show closed after ten performances.* **2.** the act of performing or the state of being performed: *the performance of an operation.* **3.** the way in which someone or something performs; manner of performing: *The driver wanted to test the car's performance on rough roads.* **4.** something performed; accomplishment; deed: *Climbing the cliff was a daring performance.*

per·form·er (pər fôr′mər) *n.* a person who performs, especially a person who gives or takes part in public entertainment.

per·fume (*n.,* pûr′fūm, pər fūm′; *v.,* pər fūm′) *n.* **1.** a liquid with a pleasant odor, as worn by people or added as a scent to various products. **2.** a sweet or pleasant odor; fragrance: *the perfume of a flower garden.* —*v.t.,* **per·fumed, per·fum·ing.** to fill or scent with a sweet or pleasant odor: *Gardenias perfumed the air.*

per·fum·er·y (pər fū′mə rē) *n., pl.* **per·fum·er·ies. 1.** the art of making perfumes or the business of selling them. **2.** a place where perfumes are made or sold. **3.** perfume or perfumes.

per·func·to·ry (pər fungk′tə rē) *adj.* **1.** done hurriedly and as a matter of routine; mechanical; superficial: *a perfunctory greeting that lacked real warmth.* **2.** acting in such a manner; halfhearted; indifferent: *a perfunctory salesclerk.* —**per·func′to·ri·ly,** *adv.*

per·haps (pər haps′) *adv.* possibly but not certainly; maybe: *Perhaps your friend would like to join us.*

per·i·car·di·um (per′i kär′dē əm) *n., pl.* **per·i·car·di·a** (per′i kär′dē ə). the thin membranous sack that surrounds and protects the heart.

per·i·gee (per′i jē′) *n.* the point in the orbit of the moon or an artificial satellite at which it is closest to the earth.

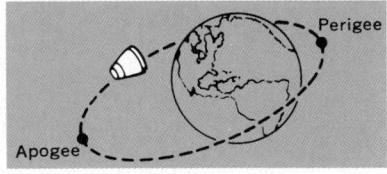

perigee

per·i·he·li·on (per′ə hē′lē ən) *n., pl.* **per·i·he·li·a** (per′ə hē′lē ə). the point in the orbit of a planet or other heavenly body at which it is closest to the sun.

per·il (per′əl) *n.* **1.** a chance or risk of injury, loss, or destruction; danger: *The general led the army bravely during a time of great peril.* **2.** something that may cause injury or damage: *Icy roads are a peril to motorists.* —*v.t.,* **per·iled, per·il·ing;** also, British, **per·illed, per·il·ling.** to expose to danger; imperil.

per·il·ous (per′ə ləs) *adj.* full of or involving peril; hazardous; dangerous: *a perilous journey.* —**per′il·ous·ly,** *adv.* —**per′il·ous·ness,** *n.*

pe·rim·e·ter (pə rim′i tər) *n.* **1.** the boundary of an area or a closed plane figure: *the perimeter of a yard, the perimeter of a square.* **2.** the length of such a boundary.

pe·ri·od (pîr′ē əd) *n.* **1.** a portion of time of a given length or marked by certain conditions or events: *They went to Europe for a period of three months. During November we had a period of relatively mild weather.* **2.** a span of historical time; era: *the colonial period in America.* **3.** a portion of time specified by the repeated occurrence of some action or event; cycle: *The changing of the guard was at regular two-hour periods.* **4.** the time that it takes a planet or satellite to make one complete revolution. **5.** a timed portion of certain games and sports: *The goal was scored in the second period of the hockey game.* **6.** one of the divisions of time in a school day: *My English class meets during the first period in the morning.* **7.** one of the divisions of geological time, a major subdivision of an era. It is characterized by certain kinds of rock formations and usually named for the place where such formations were discovered or are particularly prominent. **8.** a mark of punctuation (.) indicating the end of a sentence or an abbreviation. **9.** the time of the month when a woman is menstruating. —*adj.* of or relating to a certain past era or time: *The actors in the Shakespearean play were all dressed in elaborate period costumes.*

pe·ri·od·ic (pîr′ē od′ik) *adj.* **1.** recurring at intervals: *The team has lost most of its games, but has had periodic wins. We make periodic trips to the museum.* **2.** appearing or occurring at regular intervals: *the periodic rise and fall of the tide. The state law requires the periodic inspection of cars.* —**pe′ri·od′i·cal·ly,** *adv.*

pe·ri·od·i·cal (pîr′ē od′i kəl) *n.* a publication issued at regular intervals, usually every two weeks or every month. —*adj.* **1.** of or relating to periodicals. **2.** published at regular intervals, usually every two weeks or every month. **3.** another word for **periodic.**

periodic law, the scientific principle that the properties of the chemical elements vary at regular intervals with their atomic numbers.

periodic table, a table in which the chemical elements are arranged in order of increasing atomic numbers, with elements having similar properties arranged in vertical columns.

per·i·pa·tet·ic (per′ə pə tet′ik) *adj.* walking or traveling from place to place: *a peripatetic peddler.*

pe·riph·er·al (pə rif′ər əl) *adj.* relating to, located at, or forming the outermost part or edge: *Peripheral vision enables a person to see things at the side. We strolled along the peripheral areas of the park.* —*n. Computers.* a device, such as a printer or disk drive, that is linked to and controlled by a computer. —**pe·riph′er·al·ly,** *adv.*

peripheral nervous system, the part of the nervous system that connects the central nervous system (the brain and spinal cord) to the rest of the body. The nerves that connect the brain with organs such as the eyes and ears are part of the peripheral nervous system.

pe·riph·er·y (pə rif′ə rē) *n., pl.* **pe·riph·er·ies. 1.** the outermost part of an area; edge or border: *the periphery of an empire, the periphery of one's field of vision.* **2.** the limit or boundary of an area or surface: *the periphery of a circle.* **3.** the area just beyond a boundary; environs.

per·i·scope (per′ə skōp′) *n.* an instrument, as in a submarine or tank, for seeing objects above or obscured from the observer's line of sight. It is made up of a tube with an arrangement of prisms or mirrors that reflect the image through the tube to the eye of the observer.

per·ish (per′ish) *v.i.* **1.** to die, especially in a tragic or violent way: *Many people perished when the ship sank.* **2.** to pass from existence; disappear; vanish: *Government of the people, by the people, and for the people, shall not perish from the earth* (Abraham Lincoln).

per·ish·a·ble (per′i shə bəl) *adj.* likely to spoil or decay quickly: *Perishable foods, such as milk or butter, should be refrigerated.* —*n.* a food that is likely to spoil or decay. —**per′ish·a·bil′i·ty, per′ish·a·ble·ness,** *n.*

per·i·stal·sis (per′ə stōl′sis, per′ə stal′sis) *n., pl.* **per·i·stal·ses** (per′ə stōl′sēz, per′ə stal′sēz). the successive waves of contractions in the walls of the intestine or another tubular organ, which force the contents of the organ to move through it.

per·i·to·ne·um (per′i tə nē′əm) *also,* **per·i·to·nae·um.** *n., pl.* **per·i·to·ne·ums** or **per·i·to·ne·a** (per′i tə nē′ə) the transparent membrane that lines the walls of the abdomen and covers the organs in it.

per·i·to·ni·tis (per′i tə nī′tis) *n.* inflammation of the peritoneum.

per·i·wig (per′i wig′) *n.* a large wig, either powdered or in natural color, especially of the type worn by men in the late seventeenth and eighteenth centuries.

per·i·win·kle¹ (per′i wing′kəl) *n.* a trailing plant having shiny leaves and small trumpet-shaped flowers. [From the Old English word *pervince* meaning this plant, from the Latin word *pervinca,* this plant.]

per·i·win·kle² (per′i wing′kəl) *n.* a sea snail having a cone-shaped spiral shell. [Perhaps from the Old English word *pinewincle* meaning this animal.]

per·jure (pûr′jər) *v.t.,* **per·jured, per·jur·ing.** to make (oneself) guilty of perjury: *The district attorney proved that the witnesses had perjured themselves.* —**per′jur·er,** *n.*

per·ju·ry (pûr′jə rē) *n., pl.* **per·ju·ries.** the act of telling a lie while under oath to tell the truth.

periwinkle²

perk (pûrk) **to perk up a.** to recover one's liveliness and vigor: *We perked up when the rain*

P

at; āpe; fär; câre; end; mē; it; īce; pîerce; hot; ōld; sông, fôrk; oil; out; up; ūse; rüle; pùll; tûrn; chin; sing; shop; thin; this; hw in white; zh in treasure. The symbol ə stands for the unstressed vowel sound heard in about, taken, pencil, lemon, and circus.

stopped before our picnic. **b.** to raise smartly or briskly: *The fox perked up its ears.*

perk·y (pûr′kē) *adj.,* **perk·i·er, perk·i·est.** full of liveliness and vigor; brisk and lively: *a perky puppy.* —**perk′i·ly,** *adv.* —**perk′i·ness,** *n.*

perm (pûrm) *n. Informal.* see **permanent wave.**

per·ma·frost (pûr′mə frôst′) *n.* a layer of earth that is permanently frozen.

per·ma·nence (pûr′mə nəns) *n.* the state or quality of being permanent; durability; endurance.

per·ma·nen·cy (pûr′mə nən sē) *n., pl.* **per·ma·nen·cies. 1.** another word for **permanence. 2.** something permanent.

per·ma·nent (pûr′mə nənt) *adj.* lasting or intended to last indefinitely without change; enduring. —*n.* see **permanent wave.** —**per′ma·nent·ly,** *adv.*

permanent press, (of a fabric or garment) made in such a way that little or no ironing is required after washing.

permanent wave, a curly hairdo that lasts several months, set in the hair with a chemical solution or with heat.

per·me·a·bil·i·ty (pûr′mē ə bil′i tē) *n.* the state or quality of being permeable: *I held the cloth under a faucet to test its permeability.*

per·me·a·ble (pûr′mē ə bəl) *adj.* capable of being passed through or permeated: *This material is permeable by water. The enemy's defenses were permeable at several points.*

per·me·ate (pûr′mē āt′) *v.,* **per·me·at·ed, per·me·at·ing.** —*v.t.* **1.** to pass through the holes, pores, or openings of: *Water will not permeate this fabric.* **2.** to spread throughout; pervade: *The smells from the refinery permeated the town.* —*v.i.* to spread itself: *Fear permeated through the entire community.* —**per′me·a′tion,** *n.*

Per·mi·an (pûr′mē ən) *n.* the seventh and last geological period of the Paleozoic era, when the reptile ancestors of mammals and the ancestors of coniferous trees appeared. —*adj.* of, relating to, or characteristic of this period.

per·mis·si·ble (pər mis′ə bəl) *adj.* able to be permitted; allowable. —**per·mis′si·bly,** *adv.*

per·mis·sion (pər mish′ən) *n.* **1.** the act of permitting. **2.** a formal consent or authorization; leave: *Do I have your permission to go?*

per·mis·sive (pər mis′iv) *adj.* **1.** allowing much freedom; not strict; lenient: *a permissive parent.* **2.** granting permission; permitting; allowing: *a permissive proclamation.* —**per·mis′sive·ly,** *adv.* —**per·mis′sive·ness,** *n.*

per·mit (*v.,* pər mit′; *n.,* pûr′mit, pər mit′) *v.,* **per·mit·ted, per·mit·ting.** —*v.t.* **1.** to allow (a person) to do something; give leave to: *Permit me to be of assistance to you.* **2.** to allow (something) to be done; give consent to: *The county permits the sale of alcoholic beverages.* **3.** to give an opportunity for; admit of: *The large window permitted a good view of the mountain.* —*v.i.* to give an opportunity; allow: *I'll call you today if time permits.* —*n.* a written order or license granting permission to perform some action: *The game warden asked to see their fishing permits.*

per·mu·ta·tion (pûr′myü tā′shən) *n.* **1.** the act of rearranging; alteration. **2.** *Mathematics.* **a.** a change in the sequence of the elements of a set. **b.** any ordered arrangement of the elements of a set of objects. The sequences *abc, acb, bac,* and *cab* are permutations of the set containing *a, b,* and *c.*

per·ni·cious (pər nish′əs) *adj.* **1.** causing great harm or destruction; malicious: *Pernicious gossip ruined my reputation.* **2.** causing serious injury or death; severe or fatal: *a pernicious disease.* —**per·ni′cious·ly,** *adv.* —**per·ni′cious·ness,** *n.*

per·nick·e·ty (pər nik′i tē) another word for **persnickety.**

per·o·ra·tion (per′ə rā′shən) *n.* the final part of a speech or oration, summing up what has been said.

per·ox·ide (pə rok′sīd) *n.* **1.** a compound of a metal and oxygen, in which the oxygen atoms form a weak bond with each other. **2.** an oxide containing the highest possible proportion of oxygen. **3.** see **hydrogen peroxide.** —*v.t.,* **per·ox·id·ed, per·ox·id·ing.** to bleach (hair) by using hydrogen peroxide.

per·pen·dic·u·lar (pûr′pən dik′yə lər) *adj.* **1.** straight up and down; upright; vertical: *a perpendicular dive.* **2.** *Mathematics.* at right angles to a given line, plane, or surface. The sides of a square are perpendicular to the base. —*n.* **1.** a perpendicular line or plane. **2.** a perpendicular position. [Originally from the Latin word *perpendicularis* meaning ''vertical,'' from the word *perpendiculum* ''plumb line,'' from the words *per* ''through'' and *pendēre* ''to hang.'']

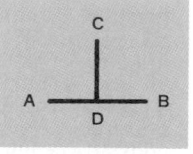

perpendicular lines

per·pe·trate (pûr′pi trāt′) *v.t.,* **per·pe·trat·ed, per·pe·trat·ing.** to commit or perform (a crime, trick, or the like): *The students perpetrated a hoax that fooled everyone.* —**per′pe·tra′tion,** *n.* —**per′pe·tra′tor,** *n.*

per·pet·u·al (pər pech′ü əl) *adj.* **1.** lasting or enduring for a very long time or forever: *a mountaintop covered by perpetual snow.* **2.** continuing throughout one's lifetime; permanent: *perpetual ownership.* **3.** continuing without interruption; unceasing: *the perpetual ebb and flow of the tide.* —**per·pet′u·al·ly,** *adv.*

per·pet·u·ate (pər pech′ü āt′) *v.t.,* **per·pet·u·at·ed, per·pet·u·at·ing.** to preserve in fact or existence; keep alive, active, or current: *The monument perpetuates the memory of those who fought in the war.* —**per·pet′u·a′tion,** *n.*

per·pe·tu·i·ty (pûr′pi tü′i tē, pûr′pi tū′i tē) *n., pl.* **per·pe·tu·i·ties. 1.** the state or quality of being perpetual; endless existence or duration. **2.** something perpetual. **·in perpetuity.** forever.

per·plex (pər pleks′) *v.t.* to fill with uncertainty; confuse; bewilder: *The cat's strange behavior perplexed us.*

per·plex·i·ty (pər plek′si tē) *n., pl.* **per·plex·i·ties. 1.** the state or condition of being perplexed; bewilderment; confusion. **2.** something that perplexes; puzzling situation or circumstances.

per·qui·site (pûr′kwə zit) *n.* an additional profit or benefit received for work besides a salary: *Free health insurance was one of the perquisites of the job.*

per se (pər sā′) *Latin.* by or in itself; intrinsically.

per·se·cute (pûr′si kūt′) *v.t.,* **per·se·cut·ed, per·se·cut·ing. 1.** to subject continually to cruel, harmful, or unjust treatment: *Many minority groups have been persecuted over the years. The heretics were persecuted for their beliefs.* **2.** to harass, vex, or annoy constantly: *The salesperson persecuted us with telephone calls.* —**per′se·cu′tor,** *n.*

▲ **Persecute** and **prosecute** should not be confused, even though they look somewhat alike. **Persecute** generally means to treat a person or group cruelly or unjustly: *Some early Christians were persecuted for their beliefs.* **Prosecute** usually refers to bringing a case before a court of law for trial: *The district attorney is prosecuting the case against the defendant.*

per·se·cu·tion (pûr′si kū′shən) *n.* the act of persecuting or the state of being persecuted.

Per·seph·o·ne (pər sef′ə nē) *n. Greek Mythology.* the goddess of vegetation and of death. She was the daughter of Zeus and Demeter and the wife of Hades, god of the underworld. In Roman mythology she was called Proserpina.

Per·se·us (pûr′sē əs) *n.* **1.** *Greek Mythology.* the hero who killed Medusa and rescued Andromeda from a sea monster. **2.** a constellation in the northern sky, between Taurus and Cassiopeia.

per·se·ver·ance (pûr′sə vîr′əns) *n.* the act or quality of persevering; persistence.

per·se·vere (pûr′sə vîr′) *v.i.*, **per·se·vered, per·se·ver·ing.** to continue steadily in a course of action or purpose in spite of difficulties or obstacles; persist: *Despite several failures, the scientist persevered with the experiment.*

Per·sian (pûr′zhən) *adj.* of or relating to Persia, its people, their language, or culture. —*n.* **1.** a person who was born in or is a citizen of Iran. **2.** a person who lived in ancient Persia. **3.** the language of ancient Persia. **4.** the language of modern Iran.

Words From Other Languages

Persian was the language of the ancient Persian Empire and is now the language of Iran.

arsenic	a metallic element used in poisons
bazaar	a marketplace
caravan	a group traveling together for safety
chess	a board game in which both players have sixteen pieces
dervish	a Muslim holy man who whirls and howls when worshiping
divan	a low couch
paradise	a heavenly place or a state of delight
peach	a fuzzy-skinned fruit with one seed
scimitar	a curved, single-edged sword
shah	a ruler of Iran or Persia
tulip	a bell-shaped flower grown from a bulb
turban	a head covering formed by wrapping a cloth around one's head or cap

Persian cat, a cat of a breed having a round head and long, silky fur, originally raised in Persia.

Persian lamb, the tightly curled fur from newborn karakul lambs.

per·si·flage (pûr′sə fläzh′) *n.* light, playful speech or writing; banter.

per·sim·mon (pər sim′ən) *n.* **1.** the fleshy fruit of any of a group of trees and shrubs, having thin orange or yellow skin and containing from one to ten flat seeds. Persimmons are sweet when they are fully ripe and may be eaten either fresh or dried. **2.** the tree or shrub bearing this fruit.

Fruit and leaves

Halved fruit

persimmon *(def. 1)*

per·sist (pər sist′) *v.i.* **1.** to continue firmly and steadily in spite of opposition or difficulty; persevere: *If you persist in misbehaving, you will be punished.* **2.** to continue to exist; endure: *The bad weather persisted all week. My cold and cough persisted throughout most of the winter.*

per·sist·ence (pər sis′təns) *n.* **1.** the act of persisting: *The salesclerk's persistence made the customer angry.* **2.** the state or quality of being persistent: *Both boxers are known for their persistence.* **3.** the power or condition of lasting; continued existence: *I worried about the persistence of my backache.* Also, **per·sist·en·cy** (pər sis′tən sē).

per·sist·ent (pər sis′tənt) *adj.* **1.** continuing firmly and steadily in spite of opposition or difficulty; persevering: *a persistent salesclerk.* **2.** lasting; continuing: *a persistent cough, persistent interruptions.* —**per·sist′ent·ly,** *adv.*

per·snick·e·ty (pər snik′i tē) *adj. Informal.* very fussy about trivial matters or details. Also, **pernickety.**

per·son (pûr′sən) *n.* **1.** a man, woman, or child; human being; individual. **2.** the living body of a human being. **3.** bodily appearance: *I try to be very neat about my person.* **4.** *Grammar.* any of three classes of personal pronoun and verb forms indicating the person speaking (the first person), the person spoken to (the second person), or the person or thing spoken of (the third person). ·**in person.** in the flesh; physically present: *The movie stars looked old when I saw them in person.*

per·son·a·ble (pûr′sə nə bəl) *adj.* having a pleasing or attractive appearance and manner: *With your personable ways you should find friends easily.* —**per′son·a·ble·ness,** *n.* —**per′son·a·bly,** *adv.*

per·son·age (pûr′sə nij) *n.* **1.** a person of distinction or importance. **2.** any person; individual. **3.** a character in a play, novel, or the like.

per·son·al (pûr′sə nəl) *adj.* **1.** of or relating to a particular person; private: *a personal matter that shouldn't be discussed in public.* **2.** done, made, or performed in person: *The mayor made a personal appearance on a television program.* **3.** of or relating to a person's body or physical appearance: *personal hygiene, personal adornments.* **4.** asking or making remarks about private matters: *The reporters became very personal in their questions.* **5.** directed to a particular person or persons, especially in a rude or offensive way: *a personal insult, a personal attack.* **6.** having the characteristics of a person, considered as a rational being, as opposed to a thing or abstraction: *a personal god.* —*n.* a short paragraph or item in a newspaper relating to a particular person or persons or to a private matter.

personal computer, another term for **microcomputer.**

personal foul, any of various violations of the rules in certain team sports, such as basketball, usually involving body contact.

per·son·al·i·ty (pûr′sə nal′i tē) *n., pl.* **per·son·al·i·ties.** **1.** the sum of the traits, habits, attitudes, and behavior of a person that makes him or her different from all others. **2.** attractive personal qualities: *She was popular at school because of her personality.* **3.** a person, especially one who is well-known or distinguished: *He is a famous television personality.*

per·son·al·ize (pûr′sə nə līz′) *v.t.*, **per·son·al·ized, per·son·al·iz·ing.** **1.** to be an example or type of; personify. **2.** to mark (property or possessions) with the name or initials of a person: *This stationery can be personalized with your initials.* **3.** to make personal: *I personalized each invitation by adding a short note.*

per·son·al·ly (pûr′sə nə lē) *adv.* **1.** not by the aid of or through others; by oneself; in person: *The senator answered my letter personally.* **2.** as far as oneself is concerned; for oneself: *Personally, I am in favor of going on a camping trip.* **3.** as an individual: *He is a friend of the family, but I don't like him personally.* **4.** as though directed toward or meant for one as a person: *I took her remarks personally and felt insulted.*

at; āpe; fär; câre; end; mē; it; īce; pîerce; hot; ōld; sông, fôrk; oil; out; up; ūse; rüle; pull; tûrn; chin; sing; shop; thin; **th**is; hw in white; zh in treasure. The symbol ə stands for the unstressed vowel sound heard in about, taken, pencil, lemon, and circus.

P

personal name, a name given to a person or by which a person is known.

Language Note

Most of the **personal names** that English-speaking people use today can be traced back to five languages or language groups: Hebrew, Teutonic, Celtic, Latin, and Greek. Formerly, people had only one name, the equivalent of our "given," or "first," name, which they were given at birth or shortly afterward. All early names had a meaning, and much importance was attached to naming because people believed that a name would affect a person's character and success in life.

At first, any word or group of words could be used as a name. Then the early Christian church declared that Christians could use only the names of saints and martyrs. Given at baptism, these names were known as *christened* names, from which our term *Christian name* comes. As Christianity spread throughout Europe and the British Isles, many of the early "pagan" names were discarded, which greatly limited the choice of names. Soon there were so many people with the same name, often several in one family, that some additional way was needed to distinguish them from one another. The use of second names, or *surnames,* then became common. These added names had been developed in families where father and son, or grandfather and grandson, had the same name. The common practice was to give an additional name after a person was older, and the name usually described some particular characteristic of the person or some circumstance of the person's life. Especially common were names describing a person's complexion or hair color, such as "the Red." In many places it was customary to derive the surname from the father's name. For example, the Scottish word *Mac* meant "son of" or sometimes "grandson or descendant of" and was added to the father's or ancestor's name to produce names such as *MacDonald.* Scandinavians often added -*son* at the end of the father's name to produce names such as *Peterson.*

The other two most common sources for surnames were a person's profession, such as *Miller* or *Smith,* and the locality in which a person lived. Names derived from a locality are the most numerous, and it was common practice to take a name from one's state, town, or county or from some natural feature near one's home.

An interesting development in modern times has been the derivation of common vocabulary words from personal names. *Silhouette, boycott, pasteurize, maverick,* and *chauvinist* are all words that were developed from people's surnames.

personal pronoun, one of a group of pronouns indicating the speaker, the person or persons addressed, or any other persons, places, or things spoken about. *I, you, he, she, it,* and *they* are personal pronouns.

per·so·na non gra·ta (pər sō′nə non grä′tə, pər sō′nə non grat′ə) a person who is not acceptable or welcome, as in a foreign country. [From the Latin phrase *persona non grata* meaning "unwelcome person," from the words *persona* "person" or "mask" + *non* "not" + *gratus* "beloved, acceptable."]

per·son·i·fi·ca·tion (pər son′ə fi kā′shən) *n.* **1.** a figure of speech in which human characteristics are given to an animal, thing, idea, or quality. For example: *A pity beyond all telling is hid in the heart of love* (William Butler Yeats). *The sun smiled down on the green meadows.* **2.** a person or thing that typifies a quality; embodiment: *That firefighter is the personification of bravery.* **3.** an imaginary or ideal person thought of as representing a thing or idea: *In Greek mythology, Poseidon was the personification of the sea.*

per·son·i·fy (pər son′ə fī′) *v.t.,* **per·son·i·fied, per·son·i·fy·ing. 1.** to regard or represent as having human characteristics: *to personify purity as an innocent child.* **2.** to typify in one's own person; be the embodiment of: *That dictator personifies evil.*

per·son·nel (pûr′sə nel′) *n.* the persons working in a business or other place of employment: *The hospital personnel includes doctors and nurses.* ▲ used with a singular or plural verb.

perspective in which parallel lines appear to meet

per·spec·tive (pər spek′tiv) *n.* **1.** the technique of representing objects on a flat surface in such a way as to give the appearance of three dimensions, depth, and distance. **2.** a picture that represents objects in this way. **3.** a scene or view from a distance; vista: *You can get an interesting perspective of the town from the church tower.* **4.** the effect of distance on the way something looks. **5.** a point of view: *Let's try to think about the problem from a different perspective.* **6.** the relation of events, ideas, facts, or the like, to one another: *If you keep things in their proper perspective, you won't worry about what is unimportant.* —*adj.* of, relating to, or represented in perspective: *a perspective drawing.*

per·spi·ca·cious (pûr′spi kā′shəs) *adj.* having keen powers of observation and judgment; discerning. —**per′spi·ca′cious·ly,** *adv.*

per·spi·cac·i·ty (pûr′spi kas′i tē) *n.* keenness of observation and judgment; discernment.

per·spi·ra·tion (pûr′spə rā′shən) *n.* **1.** moisture given off through the pores of the skin by the sweat glands; sweat: *There were beads of perspiration on the runner's brow.* **2.** the act or process of perspiring.

per·spire (pər spīr′) *v.i.,* **per·spired, per·spir·ing.** to give off perspiration; sweat.

per·suade (pər swād′) *v.t.,* **per·suad·ed, per·suad·ing.** to cause (someone) to do or believe something, as by argument: *The salesperson persuaded us to buy the car.* —**per·suad′er,** *n.*

per·sua·sion (pər swā′zhən) *n.* **1.** the act of persuading. **2.** the power or ability to persuade; persuasiveness. **3.** a firm belief; conviction: *The two friends are of different political persuasions.* **4.** a religious belief, sect, or denomination: *a minister of the Methodist persuasion.*

per·sua·sive (pər swā′siv) *adj.* able or tending to persuade: *The lawyer presented a persuasive argument in defense of the accused.* —**per·sua′sive·ly,** *adv.* —**per·sua′sive·ness,** *n.*

pert (pûrt) *adj.* **1.** showing disrespect in speech or behavior; saucy; impudent: *a pert reply.* **2.** spirited; lively.

3. trim and smart-looking: *a pert hat.* —**pert'ly,** *adv.*
—**pert'ness,** *n.*

per·tain (pər tān') *v.i.* **1.** to have reference (to); refer; relate: *The president and the cabinet discussed matters that pertained to the economy.* **2.** to belong or be connected: *The queen's son inherits the throne and all that pertains to it.*

per·ti·na·cious (pûr'tə nā'shəs) *adj.* holding firmly to a purpose, action, or opinion; stubbornly persistent. —**per'ti·na'cious·ly,** *adv.*

per·ti·nac·i·ty (pûr'tə nas'i tē) *n.* the quality of being pertinacious; stubborn persistence.

per·ti·nence (pûr'tə nəns) *n.* the quality of being pertinent; relevance.

per·ti·nent (pûr'tə nənt) *adj.* relating to the matter at hand; relevant: *You made a number of pertinent remarks on the subject we were discussing.* —**per'ti·nent·ly,** *adv.*

per·turb (pər tûrb') *v.t.* to disturb greatly; make uneasy or anxious; trouble: *I was perturbed by my friend's foolish behavior.* —**per'tur·ba'tion,** *n.*

pe·ruke (pə rük') *n.* a wig, especially of the type worn by men in the seventeenth and eighteenth centuries.

pe·rus·al (pə rü'zəl) *n.* the act of reading through or examining, especially with great care: *A careful perusal of the documents revealed several errors.*

pe·ruse (pə rüz') *v.t.,* **pe·rused, pe·rus·ing.** to read through or examine, especially with great care: *to peruse a letter.*

Pe·ru·vi·an (pə rü'vē ən) *n.* a person who was born in or is a citizen of Peru. —*adj.* of or relating to Peru, its people, their language, or culture.

Peruvian bark, see **cinchona** *(def 2).*

per·vade (pər vād') *v.t.,* **per·vad·ed, per·vad·ing.** to spread through or be present in every part of: *The scent of the perfume pervaded the room. A strong sense of humor pervades the author's writings.* —**per·va·sion** (pər vā'zhən), *n.*

per·va·sive (pər vā'siv) *adj.* tending to pervade; spreading through or permeating: *a pervasive odor.*

per·verse (pər vûrs') *adj.* **1.** willfully going against what is right, reasonable, or required; wrong: *a perverse opinion, perverse behavior.* **2.** determined to do as one pleases; stubborn; obstinate: *a perverse child who refuses to obey anyone.* **3.** morally wrong or corrupt; wicked: *O faithless and perverse generation* (Matthew 17:17). —**per·verse'ly,** *adv.* —**per·verse'ness,** *n.*

per·ver·sion (pər vûr'zhən) *n.* **1.** the act of perverting or the state of being perverted: *a perversion of facts.* **2.** any abnormal sexual act or practice.

per·ver·si·ty (pər vûr'si tē) *n., pl.* **per·ver·si·ties.** **1.** the state or quality of being perverse. **2.** an instance of this; a wrong or wicked act, habit, or thing.

per·vert (*v.,* pər vûrt'; *n.,* pûr'vûrt) *v.t.* **1.** to lead or turn from what is considered right or moral; lead astray; corrupt: *Bribery had perverted the judge's decision.* **2.** to distort the meaning of: *to pervert the truth.* **3.** to use wrongly; misuse: *to pervert one's skills.* —*n.* a person who is perverted or given to perversion, especially sexual perversion.

Pe·sach (pä'säk) *n.* see **Passover.**

pe·se·ta (pə sā'tə) *n.* the monetary unit of Spain.

pes·ky (pes'kē) *adj.,* **pes·ki·er, pes·ki·est.** *Informal.* troublesome; annoying. —**pes'ki·ly,** *adv.* —**pes'ki·ness,** *n.*

pe·so (pā'sō) *n., pl.* **pe·sos.** the monetary unit of Mexico, several South and Central American countries, Cuba, the Dominican Republic, and the Philippines.

pes·si·mism (pes'ə miz'əm) *n.* **1.** the tendency to take a gloomy view of life or to see only the bad side of things. **2.** the belief that everything naturally tends to evil.

pes·si·mist (pes'ə mist) *n.* a person who expects the worst or takes a gloomy view of life. —**pes'si·mis'tic,** *adj.* —**pes'si·mis'ti·cal·ly,** *adv.*

pest (pest) *n.* a person or thing that is troublesome, annoying, or destructive; nuisance: *Locusts, gnats, and mosquitoes are insect pests.*

pes·ter (pes'tər) *v.t.* to trouble or bother; annoy: *Ants and flies pestered the picnickers.*

pes·ti·cide (pes'tə sīd') *n.* a chemical or other substance used to destroy harmful plants or animals.

pes·tif·er·ous (pes tif'ər əs) *adj.* producing or carrying disease: *a pestiferous swamp.*

pes·ti·lence (pes'tə ləns) *n.* any highly infectious, epidemic disease, as bubonic plague.

pes·ti·lent (pes'tə lənt) *adj.* **1.** causing or tending to cause disease or death. **2.** harmful or destructive to peace, morals, or society.

pes·ti·len·tial (pes'tə len'shəl) *adj.* **1.** of, relating to, or causing a pestilence. **2.** harmful; destructive.

pes·tle (pes'əl, pes'təl) *n.* a blunt tool for pounding, grinding, or mixing substances in a mortar. See **mortar²** for illustration.

pes·to (pes'tō) *n.* a sauce usually made with basil, garlic, pine nuts, grated cheese, and olive oil, often served with pasta.

pet¹ (pet) *n.* **1.** a tame animal, such as a cat or dog, that is kept chiefly for amusement and companionship. **2.** any person who is treated with special favor or kindness; favorite: *That student is the teacher's pet.* —*adj.* **1.** kept or treated as a pet: *a pet frog.* **2.** expressing fondness or familiarity; affectionate: *a pet name.* **3.** favorite; cherished: *Getting that old car to run is their pet project.* —*v.t.,* **pet·ted, pet·ting.** to stroke, pat, or caress: *The cat purred when it was petted.* [Perhaps from *petty.*]

pet² (pet) *n.* a fit of peevishness or ill humor; discontent. [Of uncertain origin.]

pet·al (pet'əl) *n.* one of the divisions or parts, usually colored, of a flower. —**pet'aled;** *also,* **pet'alled,** *adj.* —**pet'al·like',** *adj.*

Petal

pet·cock (pet'kok') *n.* a small valve or faucet.

pe·ter (pē'tər) *v.* **to peter out.** *Informal.* to diminish gradually and disappear: *The tennis player's strength petered out toward the end of the game.*

Pe·ter (pē'tər) *n.* either of two Epistles of the New Testament thought to have been written by the Apostle Peter.

pet·i·ole (pet'ē ōl') *n.* the slender stalk by which a leaf is attached to a stem. Also, **leafstalk.**

pe·tite (pə tēt') *adj.* (usually of a woman or girl) of small size; little; tiny.

pe·ti·tion (pə tish'ən) *n.* **1.** a formal request made to a person in a position of authority: *The students signed a petition asking the principal to open the school library on weekends.* **2.** a prayer or entreaty. —*v.t.* to make a petition to: *to petition the government.* —*v.i.* to make a petition. —**pe·ti'tion·er,** *n.*

pet·it four (pet'ē fôr') *n., pl.* **pet·its fours** (pet'ē fôrz'). a very small cake covered with decorative icing.

pet·it jury (pet'ē) a jury, usually of twelve persons, selected to hear a civil or criminal case in a court of law.

---

at; āpe; fär; câre; end; mē; it; īce; pîerce; hot; ōld; sông, fôrk; oil; out; up; ūse; rüle; pull; tûrn; chin; sing; shop; thin; <u>th</u>is; hw in white; zh in treasure. The symbol ə stands for the unstressed vowel sound heard in about, taken, pencil, lemon, and circus.

pet·it larceny, another spelling of **petty larceny.**

pet·rel (pet′rəl) *n.* a hook-billed seabird usually having blackish or brownish feathers with white markings.

pe·tri dish (pē′trē) *n.* a round, shallow dish of plastic or glass with a slightly larger cover, used in the laboratory for growing bacteria and other microorganisms. [From the German bacteriologist Julius *Petri* (1852–1921), who suggested using this type of dish.]

pet·ri·fac·tion (pet′rə fak′shən) *n.* **1.** the process of petrifying or the state of being petrified. **2.** something that is petrified. Also, **pet·ri·fi·ca·tion** (pet′rə fi kā′shən).

petrified wood, a hard, stony material formed when silica replaces organic materials in wood.

pet·ri·fy (pet′rə fī′) *v.,* **pet·ri·fied, pet·ri·fy·ing.** —*v.t.* **1.** to convert (organic material) into stone or a stony substance. **2.** to paralyze with fear, astonishment, or horror. —*v.i.* to become stone or like stone.

pet·ro·chem·i·cal (pet′rō kem′i kəl) *n.* a chemical substance obtained from petroleum or natural gas, such as gasoline or kerosene. —*adj.* of or relating to such substances or the industry producing them.

pet·rol (pet′rəl) *n. British.* another word for **gasoline.**

pe·tro·le·um (pə trō′lē əm) *n.* an oily, flammable liquid made up of a mixture of hydrocarbons, usually found beneath the earth's surface. Petroleum yields such products as gasoline, diesel fuel, and lubricants. [From the Medieval Latin word *petroleum* meaning "rock oil, petroleum," going back to the Greek words *petra* "rock" and *elaion* "oil."]

petroleum jelly, a greasy whitish or yellowish substance obtained from petroleum and used as a lubricant, a rust preventive, and a base for making cosmetics and medical ointments.

PET scan (pet) an X ray that pinpoints areas of unusual metabolic activity in the brain or other parts of the body. A PET scan records bursts of energy given off by the body as it absorbs a radioactive substance that has been injected. [Short for *p(ositron) e(mission) t(omography)*.]

pet·ti·coat (pet′ē kōt′) *n.* a skirt or slip worn as an undergarment.

pet·tish (pet′ish) *adj.* ill-tempered; cross; peevish. —**pet′tish·ly,** *adv.*

pet·ty (pet′ē) *adj.,* **pet·ti·er, pet·ti·est. 1.** of little value or importance; insignificant: *a petty complaint.* **2.** mean, spiteful, or narrow-minded: *a petty person who doesn't respect the feelings of others.* **3.** minor; inferior; subordinate: *a petty government official.* [From the Middle English word *peti* meaning "small, little," from the Old French word *petit* "small."] —**pet′ti·ly,** *adv.* —**pet′ti·ness,** *n.*

petty cash, a small amount of cash kept on hand to pay minor incidental expenses, as in a business office.

petty larceny *also,* **petit larceny.** larceny in which the value of the property taken is less than an amount fixed by law.

petty officer, a noncommissioned officer in the U.S. Navy or Coast Guard.

pet·u·lant (pech′ə lənt) *adj.* ill-humored; peevish. —**pet′u·lance,** *n.* —**pet′u·lant·ly,** *adv.*

pe·tu·nia (pə tün′yə, pə tün′yə) *n.* **1.** a funnel-shaped flower sometimes having fringed or ruffled petals. **2.** the plant bearing this flower.

pew (pū) *n.* a long bench for seating worshipers in a church.

pe·wee (pē′wē′) *also,* **pee·wee.** *n.* a small American bird having dull brown or gray feathers.

pew·ter (pū′tər) *n.* **1.** an alloy, formerly made of tin, lead, and copper, now made of tin, copper, and antimony. It is used to make tableware, utensils, and ornamental objects. **2.** articles made of this alloy. —*adj.* made of pewter: *a pewter mug.*

pey·o·te (pā ō′tē) *n.* **1.** a small cactus found in dry regions from Texas to Central America. Also, **mescal. 2.** a drug that produces hallucinations, derived from this cactus; mescaline.

Pfc., private first class.

pg., page.

pH, the chemical symbol for the unit that measures the acidity or alkalinity of a substance. On a scale of 0 to 14, a pH of 7 is neutral, a pH of less than 7 is acid, and a pH of more than 7 is alkaline.

pha·e·ton (fā′ə tən) *n.* **1.** a light, low, open, four-wheeled carriage. **2.** an open automobile whose body resembles that of such a carriage.

phag·o·cyte (fag′ə sīt′) *n.* any cell, especially a white blood cell, that can ingest and destroy bacteria and other harmful material in the body.

pha·lanx (fā′langks) *n., pl.* **pha·lanx·es** or **pha·lan·ges** (fə lan′jēz). **1.** in ancient Greek and Macedonian armies, a battle formation of infantry standing in close ranks with their shields and long spears overlapping each other.

phaeton *(def. 1)*

2. a compact body of persons, animals, or things massed together, as for attack or for defense: *A phalanx of police held back the crowd.* **3.** a number of persons united for a common purpose. **4.** any of the bones in the fingers or toes. See **hand** for illustration.

phan·tasm (fan′taz əm) *n.* **1.** something seen in the imagination; unreal or fantastic idea or fancy: *the bizarre phantasms of a nightmare.* **2.** a ghost; phantom. —**phan·tas′mal,** *adj.*

phan·ta·sy (fan′tə sē) *n., pl.* **phan·ta·sies.** another spelling of **fantasy.**

phan·tom (fan′təm) *n.* **1.** something that appears to be real but is not; ghost; apparition. **2.** something existing only as an image in the mind; illusion. **3.** an appearance without force or substance: *The ruler had only the phantom of authority.* —*adj.* of the nature of a phantom; ghostly or not genuine: *a tale of a phantom ship, a phantom army.*

Phar·aoh (fâr′ō) *n.* the title of the kings of ancient Egypt.

Phar·i·see (far′ə sē′) *n.* **1.** a member of an ancient Jewish sect that was very strict in observing both the written law and the oral tradition of Judaism. **2. pharisee.** a self-righteous or hypocritical person.

phar·ma·ceu·ti·cal (fär′mə sü′ti kəl) *adj.* of or relating to a pharmacy or drugs. Also, **phar·ma·ceu·tic** (fär′mə sü′tik). —*n.* a medicinal product; drug.

phar·ma·cist (fär′mə sist) *n.* a person who is licensed to prepare drugs and fill prescriptions.

phar·ma·col·o·gy (fär′mə kol′ə jē) *n.* the branch of science that deals with the preparation, uses, and effects of drugs.

phar·ma·cy (fär′mə sē) *n., pl.* **phar·ma·cies. 1.** another word for **drugstore. 2.** the science, practice, or profession of preparing and giving out or selling drugs.

Pha·ros (fâr′os) *n.* a huge lighthouse constructed on an island in the harbor of Alexandria, Egypt, in the third century B.C.

pha·ryn·ge·al (fə rin′jē əl, far′in jē′əl) *adj.* of, relating to, or affecting the pharynx.

phar·ynx (far′ingks) *n., pl.* **pha·ryn·ges** (fə rin′jēz) or **phar·ynx·es.** the upper part of the digestive tract, made up of a short, muscular tube that connects the mouth and nasal cavity with the esophagus and windpipe.

phase (fāz) *n.* **1.** a stage of development of a person or thing: *an early phase of a disease. The child went through*

a phase during which he was ill-tempered and stubborn. **2.** a side, view, or aspect: *I am interested in all phases of stamp collecting.* **3.** *Astronomy.* the appearance of the moon or a planet at a particular time, depending on how much of its lighted side can be seen from the earth.
   ·to phase out. to eliminate in stages: *The army plans to phase out the old equipment as more modern equipment becomes available.*

Ph.D., Doctor of Philosophy.

pheas·ant (fez′ənt) *n., pl.* **pheas·ants** or **pheas·ant.** any of various long-tailed birds originally native to Asia and now found in most parts of the world, the male of which often has brilliantly colored feathers.

phe·nol (fē′nŏl) *n.* a poisonous crystalline compound used in plastics, explosives, weed killers, and drugs. It was formerly used as an antiseptic and disinfectant. Also, **carbolic acid.**

phe·nom·e·nal (fə nom′ə nəl) *adj.* **1.** of or relating to a phenomenon or phenomena. **2.** extraordinary or remarkable: *That athlete has phenomenal strength.* —**phe·nom′e·nal·ly,** *adv.*

phe·nom·e·non (fə nom′ə non′) *n., pl.* **phe·nom·e·na** (fə nom′ə nə) or **phe·nom·e·nons.** **1.** a fact, event, or condition that can be observed or perceived: *Rain and snow are phenomena of the weather.* **2.** a person or thing that is extraordinary or remarkable: *The new company's rapid success made it a phenomenon in the business world.*

phe·no·type (fē′nə tīp′) *n.* the physical appearance of an organism. The phenotype is determined by the combination of the organism's genetic makeup, or genotype, and its environment. [Formed from the Greek words *phainein* meaning "to show" + *typos* "type."]

phi (fī) *n.* the twenty-first letter of the Greek alphabet (Φ, φ).

phi·al (fī′əl) another spelling of **vial.**

phil·an·throp·ic (fil′ən throp′ik) *n.* relating to, characterized by, or engaged in philanthropy; charitable. Also, **philanthropical.** —**phil′an·throp′i·cal·ly,** *adv.*

phil·an·thro·pist (fə lan′thrə pist) *n.* a person who gives his or her money or time to good causes.

phi·lan·thro·py (fə lan′thrə pē) *n., pl.* **phi·lan·thro·pies.** **1.** a love of humanity expressed by the giving of money or time to good causes. **2.** a charitable action, service, or institution.

phi·lat·e·list (fə lat′ə list) *n.* a person who collects and studies postage stamps and related items.

phi·lat·e·ly (fə lat′ə lē) *n.* the collecting and study of postage stamps and related items. —**phil·a·tel·ic** (fil′ə tel′ik), *adj.*

Phi·le·mon (fə lē′mən) *n.* a New Testament Epistle written by Paul.

phil·har·mon·ic (fil′här mon′ik) *adj.* **1.** fond of or devoted to music. **2.** of, relating to, or presented by a musical society or an orchestra, especially a symphony orchestra: *a philharmonic concert.* —*n.* a symphony orchestra, concert, or society.

Phil·ip·pine (fil′ə pēn′) *adj.* of or relating to the Philippines or their inhabitants. Also, **Filipino.**

Phil·is·tine (fil′ə stēn′, fil′ə stīn′, fə lis′tin) *n.* **1.** in the Bible, a member of an ancient people of southwestern Palestine often mentioned in the Old Testament as enemies of the Israelites. **2.** *also,* **philistine.** a person who is uncultured or has narrow-minded ideas and tastes. —*adj.* **1.** of or relating to the Philistines. **2.** *also,* **philistine.** uncultured or narrow-minded in ideas and tastes.

phil·o·den·dron (fil′ə den′drən) *n.* a tropical American plant often having heart-shaped, glossy leaves, commonly grown as a house plant.

phi·lol·o·gist (fə lol′ə jist) *n.* a student of or an expert in philology.

phi·lol·o·gy (fə lol′ə jē) *n.* **1.** the study, criticism, and interpretation of literature and other written records. **2.** the study of languages, especially of their history and development; linguistics. —**phil·o·log·i·cal** (fil′ə loj′i-kəl), *adj.*

phi·los·o·pher (fə los′ə fər) *n.* **1.** a student of or an expert in philosophy. **2.** a person who develops or lives by a system of philosophy. **3.** a person who accepts life and its problems with calmness and understanding.

phil·o·soph·i·cal (fil′ə sof′i kəl) *adj.* **1.** of or relating to philosophy: *a philosophical essay.* **2.** of or relating to a philosopher: *philosophical thought.* **3.** accepting life and its problems with calmness and understanding. Also, **phil·o·soph·ic** (fil′ə sof′ik). —**phil′o·soph′i·cal·ly,** *adv.*

phil·os·o·phize (fə los′ə fīz′) *v.i.,* **phil·os·o·phized, phil·os·o·phiz·ing.** to think or express ideas as a philosopher does: *to philosophize about the meaning of life.* —**phi·los′o·phiz′er,** *n.*

phi·los·o·phy (fə los′ə fē) *n., pl.* **phil·os·o·phies.** **1.** the study of the basic nature and purpose of humanity, the universe, and life itself. **2.** the system of thought of a particular school or philosopher: *the philosophy of Plato.* **3.** the study of the basic principles of a branch of knowledge or of an activity: *the philosophy of history.* **4.** a person's principles and beliefs.

phil·ter (fil′tər) *n.* a magic drug or potion, especially one that is supposed to make a person fall in love.

phlegm (flem) *n.* mucus, especially in the nose or throat.

phleg·mat·ic (fleg mat′ik) *adj.* sluggish in disposition; indifferent. [From the Old French word *flaumatique* meaning "sluggish" or "full of phlegm," going back to the Greek word *phlegmatikos* "full of phlegm." In former times, *phlegm* was thought to be one of the four humors that made up the body and whose mixture determined a person's health and temperament.] —**phleg·mat′i·cal·ly,** *adv.*

phlo·em (flō′em) *n.* a layer of plant tissue that conducts food made in the leaves down to the other parts of the plant. In woody plants, it lies just under the hard outer bark. Also, **bast.**

phlox

phlox (floks) *n., pl.* **phlox·es.** an erect or trailing plant bearing showy clusters of small flowers that are white, red, pink, violet, or blue.

at; āpe; fär; câre; end; mē; it; īce; pîerce; hot; ōld; sông, fôrk; oil; out; up; ūse; rüle; pull; tûrn; chin; sing; shop; thin; this; hw in white; zh in treasure. The symbol ə stands for the unstressed vowel sound heard in about, taken, pencil, lemon, and circus.

P

pho·bi·a (fō′bē ə) *n.* a strong, irrational dread or fear of something: *a phobia about the dark.* [Formed from the Greek word *phobos* meaning "panic, flight."] —**pho′bic,** *adj.*

phoe·be (fē′bē) *n.* a small bird having gray-brown feathers with white underparts, named for the sound of its two-noted song.

Phoe·be (fē′bē) *n. Greek Mythology.* another name for Artemis as goddess of the moon.

Phoe·bus (fē′bəs) *n. Greek Mythology.* another name for Apollo as god of the sun. Also, **Phoebus Apollo.**

Phoe·ni·cian (fə nē′shən, fə nish′ən) *adj.* of or relating to Phoenicia, its people, their language, or culture. —*n.* **1.** a person who was born or lived in Phoenicia. **2.** the ancient language of Phoenicia.

phoe·nix (fē′niks) *n., pl.* **phoe·nix·es.** *Egyptian and Greek Mythology.* a legendary bird thought to live for 500 or 600 years, to die in the flames of a funeral pyre, and then to rise again from its own ashes.

phone (fōn) *Informal.* *n., v.,* **phoned, phon·ing.** see **telephone.**

pho·neme (fō′nēm) *n.* the smallest unit of speech sound that can distinguish one word from another. The words *hat* and *rat* are distinguished by the different phonemes *h* and *r.*

pho·nem·ic (fə nēm′ik) *adj.* of or relating to a phoneme or phonemes.

pho·net·ic (fə net′ik) *adj.* **1.** of or relating to speech sounds or phonetics. **2.** representing speech sounds with a set of symbols, each of which stands for a single speech sound: *a phonetic alphabet, the phonetic spelling of a word.* —**pho·net′i·cal·ly,** *adv.*

pho·ne·ti·cian (fō′ni tish′ən) *n.* a student of or an expert in phonetics.

pho·net·ics (fə net′iks) *n.* the science or study of speech sounds and their representation by symbols. ▲ used with a singular verb.

phon·ic (fon′ik) *adj.* of, relating to, or of the nature of sound, especially speech sound.

phon·ics (fon′iks) *n.* any of various methods of teaching reading by explaining how letters and groups of letters are pronounced. ▲ used with a singular verb.

phono– *also,* **phon-.** *combining form* sound; voice; speech: *phonograph.*

pho·no·graph (fō′nə graf′) *n.* a device that reproduces sounds recorded on a disk of plastic or other material.

pho·no·graph·ic (fō′nə graf′ik) *adj.* of, relating to, or produced by a phonograph.

pho·ny (fō′nē) *Informal. adj.,* **pho·ni·er, pho·ni·est.** not genuine; counterfeit; fake: *a phony diamond.* —*n., pl.* **pho·nies. 1.** something that is not genuine; fake: *The painting was a phony.* **2.** a person who is deceptive or insincere. —**pho′ni·ness,** *n.*

phos·phate (fos′fāt) *n.* **1.** a salt of phosphoric acid. **2.** a fertilizer having a high phosphorus content. **3.** a beverage made with carbonated water and flavored syrup.

phos·phor (fos′fər) *n.* a substance that gives off light when affected by a form of radiant energy, such as ultraviolet light.

phos·pho·res·cence (fos′fə res′əns) *n.* **1.** the giving off of light from a substance that has absorbed radiant energy, continuing after the source of energy is removed. **2.** a light so produced. —**phos′pho·res′cent,** *adj.*

phos·phor·ic (fos fôr′ik) *adj.* of, relating to, or containing phosphorus.

phosphoric acid, any of three acids containing phosphorus.

phos·pho·rous (fos′fər əs) *adj.* of, relating to, or containing phosphorus.

phos·pho·rus (fos′fər əs) *n.* a nonmetallic element that occurs in three forms. Yellow or white phosphorus is a poisonous, waxy solid that glows in the dark and ignites in air at normal temperatures. Red phosphorus is a less reactive, reddish brown, crystalline powder. Black phosphorus is prepared by heating yellow phosphorus under very high pressure. Phosphorus is essential to plant and animal cells. Symbol: **P** [Formed from the Greek word *phôsphoros* meaning "light-bearing," from the words *phôs* "light" and *pherein* "to bring, carry, bear." Phosphorus got its name because it glows in the dark.]

Word Family

English contains a number of words that come from the Greek word *pherein,* meaning "to bear" or "to carry." Both **phosphorus** and **phosphor** are so named because they "bear," or give off, light. The feeling of **euphoria** is one of well-being. A **semaphore** is used to carry messages to a train running at the **periphery** of an area. Liquids can be carried in an **amphora.**

pho·to (fō′tō) *n., pl.* **pho·tos.** *Informal.* see **photograph.**

photo– *combining form* **1.** of, relating to, or produced by light: *photosynthesis.* **2.** of, relating to, or produced by photography; photographic: *photocopy.*

pho·to·cop·y (fō′tə kop′ē) *v.t.,* **pho·to·cop·ied, pho·to·cop·y·ing.** to make a copy or copies of (printed matter or the like) by a photographic process. —*n., pl.* **pho·to·cop·ies.** a copy produced by such a process.

pho·to·e·lec·tric cell (fō′tō i lek′trik) an electrical device that is sensitive to light or other electromagnetic radiation, used especially in sensing devices and light meters. Also, **pho·to·cell** (fō′tō sel′).

photo finish, the finish of a race that is so close that a photograph is used to decide the winner.

pho·to·gen·ic (fō′tə jen′ik) *adj.* that is a good subject for a photograph; that photographs well: *You have a very photogenic face.*

pho·to·graph (fō′tə graf′) *n.* a picture or reproduction made by photography. —*v.t.* to take a photograph of. —*v.i.* to appear or look in a photograph: *That model always photographs well.*

pho·tog·ra·pher (fə tog′rə fər) *n.* a person who takes photographs, especially as a profession.

pho·to·graph·ic (fō′tə graf′ik) *adj.* **1.** relating to, used in, or produced by photography: *photographic equipment.* **2.** resembling a photograph, as in accuracy: *a photographic memory, a photographic style of painting.* —**pho′to·graph′i·cal·ly,** *adv.*

pho·tog·ra·phy (fə tog′rə fē) *n.* **1.** the technique of recording the image of a given area or object by the action of light on a light-sensitive surface. **2.** the art or practice of taking photographs.

pho·ton (fō′ton) *n.* the basic unit of light or other form of radiant energy, considered as a particle.

pho·to·sphere (fō′tə sfīr′) *n.* **1.** the visible surface of the sun, made up of a layer of hot gases about 250 miles (400 kilometers) thick. **2.** a similar surface on any star.

Pho·to·stat (fō′tə stat′) *n.* **1.** *Trademark.* a device for making photographic copies directly on specially prepared paper. **2.** *also,* **photostat.** a copy made by Photostat. —*v.t.* **photostat.** to make a photostat of.

pho·to·syn·the·sis (fō′tə sin′thə sis) *n.* the process by which green plants make food. In photosynthesis, carbohydrates are manufactured from carbon dioxide and water, using the energy produced when light is absorbed by chlorophyll.

pho·tot·ro·pism (fō tot′rə piz′əm, fō′tō trō′piz əm) *n.* the response of a plant or other organism to light. Plant leaves turning toward the sunlight and plant roots growing away from the sunlight are examples of phototropism.

phrase (frāz) *n.* **1.** a group of words taken as a grammatical unit or expressing a single thought, but not containing a subject and predicate. In the sentence *To achieve success is his goal, To achieve success* is a phrase. **2.** a brief, often striking expression: *"No more war"* was the *phrase the protesters chanted as they marched.* **3.** *Music.* a group of musical notes that forms a unit of melody. —*v.t.,* **phrased, phras·ing. 1.** to express in a particular way: *The defense attorney phrased the questions very carefully.* **2.** to divide or mark off (a melody, musical composition, or the like) into phrases. —**phras′al,** *adj.*

phra·se·ol·o·gy (frā′zē ol′ə jē) *n., pl.* **phra·se·ol·o·gies.** a particular style or manner of expression; choice and arrangement of words: *legal phraseology.*

phre·nol·o·gy (fri nol′ə jē) *n.* the supposed technique of judging a person's character and intelligence by studying the shape of the skull.

phy·lum (fī′ləm) *n., pl.* **phy·la** (fī′lə). one of the major subdivisions into which living things are divided. A phylum ranks below a kingdom and above a class.

phys·ic (fiz′ik) *n.* any medicine, especially a laxative.

phys·i·cal (fiz′i kəl) *adj.* **1.** of or relating to the body: *physical strength, physical fitness.* **2.** of, relating to, or containing matter: *physical things.* **3.** of or relating to matter and energy, or to the laws governing them. **4.** of or relating to nature or to natural objects: *a map of the physical features of a country.* **5.** characterized by particularly rough action: *a physical football game.* —*n.* see **physical examination.** —**phys′i·cal·ly,** *adv.*

physical education, instruction in physical activities and the care of the body.

physical examination, a medical examination to find out a person's general state of health or physical fitness for a certain activity.

physical geography, the study of the physical features of the earth, such as land formation, climate, and vegetation.

physical science, any science concerned with matter and energy and with the laws governing them, such as physics, chemistry, or astronomy.

physical therapy, the treatment of disease or injury by physical methods, such as heat, massage, or exercise. Also, **physiotherapy.**

phy·si·cian (fə zish′ən) *n.* a person who is licensed to practice medicine; medical doctor.

phys·i·cist (fiz′ə sist) *n.* a student of or specialist in physics.

phys·ics (fiz′iks) *n.* the science that deals with matter and energy, and with the laws governing them. ▲ used with a singular verb.

phys·i·og·no·my (fiz′ē og′nə mē) *n., pl.* **phys·i·og·no·mies. 1.** the features or appearance of the face: *The sailor had a rugged physiognomy.* **2.** the art of judging character from the features or appearance of the face. **3.** the general appearance of something: *the physiognomy of a mountain.*

phys·i·o·log·i·cal (fiz′ē ə loj′i kəl) *adj.* of or relating to physiology. —**phys′i·o·log′i·cal·ly,** *adv.*

phys·i·ol·o·gy (fiz′ē ol′ə jē) *n.* **1.** the science that deals with the functions of living things or of any of their parts. **2.** the functions of a living thing or of any of its parts: *the physiology of the frog.* —**phys′i·ol′o·gist,** *n.*

phys·i·o·ther·a·py (fiz′ē ō ther′ə pē) *n.* another word for **physical therapy.**

phy·sique (fi zēk′) *n.* the structure, development, or appearance of the body: *a muscular physique.*

pi (pī) *n., pl.* **pis. 1.** the sixteenth letter of the Greek alphabet (Π, π). **2.** the ratio of the circumference of a circle to its diameter, represented by the Greek letter π. Pi is approximately 3.1416.

P.I., Philippine Islands.

pi·a·nis·si·mo (pē′ə nis′ə mō′, pya nis′ə mō′) *Music. adj.* very soft: *My favorite part of the sonata is the pianissimo passage.* —*adv.* very softly.

pi·an·ist (pē an′ist, pyan′ist, pē′ə nist) *n.* a person who plays the piano, especially a skilled performer.

pi·an·o¹ (pē an′ō, pyan′ō) *n., pl.* **pi·an·os.** a musical instrument played from a keyboard. Individual keys can each produce a distinct tone when played through an array of hammers that strike tuned metal strings. Also, **pianoforte.** [Short for *pianoforte.*]

pi·a·no² (pē ä′nō, pyä′nō) *Music. adj.* soft. —*adv.* softly. [From the Italian word *piano* meaning "softly, quietly," going back to the Latin word *planus* "level, even¹, flat¹."]

pi·an·o·for·te (pē an′ə fôr′tē, pē an′ə fôr′tā, pē an′ə fôrt′) *n.* another word for **piano¹.** [From the Italian word *pianoforte,* from the earlier phrase *piano e forte* meaning "softly and loudly," from the range of loudness of this instrument.]

Grand piano

Upright piano

piano¹

pi·az·za (pē az′ə, pē ät′sə) *n.* **1.** a public square in a town, especially in Italy. **2.** a veranda; porch.

pl·ca (pī′kə) *n.* **1.** a unit of measure used in printing, equal to about ⅙ inch (4.2 millimeters). **2.** a size of type for typewriters, providing ten characters to the inch.

pic·a·dor (pik′ə dôr′) *n.* a mounted participant in a bullfight who pricks the neck of the bull with a lance in order to weaken the bull's neck muscles, so that the bull will keep its head lower during the rest of the fight.

pic·a·resque (pik′ə resk′) *adj.* of or relating to usually low-born, roguish adventurers, especially as described in fiction.

pic·a·yune (pik′ə ūn′) *adj.* **1.** of little value or importance; paltry: *a picayune sum of money.* **2.** narrow-minded; mean; petty.

pic·ca·lil·li (pik′ə lil′ē) *n.* a relish made of chopped vegetables, sugar, hot spices, and vinegar.

pic·co·lo (pik′ə lō′) *n., pl.* **pic·co·los.** a small flute having a pitch one octave higher than the ordinary flute.

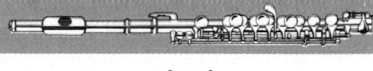

pick¹ (pik) *v.t.* **1.** to select from a number; choose:

piccolo

The city picked a site for the new museum. Have you picked out the book you want to buy? **2.** to gather with the fingers; pluck: *to pick flowers, to pick berries.* **3.** to

at; āpe; fär; câre; end; mē; it; īce; pîerce; hot; ōld; sông, fôrk; oil; out; up; ūse; rüle; pùll; tûrn; chin; sing; shop; thin; <u>th</u>is; hw in white; zh in treasure. The symbol ə stands for the unstressed vowel sound heard in about, taken, pencil, lemon, and circus.

use the fingers or a pointed instrument, such as a toothpick, in order to remove matter from: *to pick one's teeth.* **4.** to remove bit by bit with the fingers or an instrument, such as a fork: *to pick the meat from a bone.* **5.** to make or form (a hole) with a pointed instrument or tool. **6.** to pluck with the fingers or a plectrum: *to pick the strings of a guitar.* **7.** to play (a stringed instrument) by plucking the strings with the fingers or a plectrum. **8.** to cause deliberately; provoke: *to pick a fight with someone.* **9.** to steal the contents of: *A thief picked my pocket.* **10.** to open (a lock) with a pointed instrument or wire instead of a key. —*v.i.* **1.** to select, especially in a careful manner. **2.** to eat in small amounts or without appetite: *to pick at one's food.* —*n.* **1.** a choice; selection: *Take your pick of the books on the table.* **2.** the best or the choicest part or example: *That big puppy in the corner is the pick of the litter.* **3.** another word for **plectrum.** [From the Middle English word *pikken* meaning "to work with a pick²" or "to strike, hit," from Old English.] —**pick′er,** *n.*

•**to pick on.** *Informal.* to criticize or annoy; harass: *The older students picked on the new student.*

•**to pick out. a.** to see (something) as different from its surroundings or from a group; distinguish: *to pick out a friend's face in a crowd.* **b.** to play (a piece of music) by ear: *to pick out a tune on the piano.*

•**to pick up. a.** to take or lift up: *to pick up pebbles from the ground.* **b.** to make (something) neat: *Pick up your room.* **c.** to take (someone or something) into a vehicle or ship: *to pick up a hitchhiker.* **d.** to get or acquire casually or by chance: *to pick up a few dollars by doing odd jobs.* **e.** to learn: *to pick up foreign languages easily.* **f.** to go faster; accelerate: *The car's speed picked up as it went down the hill.* **g.** *Informal.* to improve; recover: *Business is picking up now that summer is over.* **h.** *Informal.* to take into custody: *Police kept a close watch on the criminals and picked them up as they were boarding a train.*

pick² (pik) *n.* **1.** a chipping or breaking tool that has a metal head, usually with one or two tips sharpened to a point, attached to a wooden handle; pickax. **2.** any of various pointed instruments or tools without a head, such as an ice pick. [From the Middle English word *pik* meaning "a spike, stake" or "pickax," from the Old English word *pīc* meaning "a pointed instrument" or "a pike²."]

pick·a·back (pik′ə bak′) *adv., adj.* another word for **piggyback.**

pick·ax (pik′aks′) *also,* **pick·axe.** *n., pl.* **pick·ax·es.** see **pick²** *(def. 1).*

picked (pikt) *adj.* **1.** specially selected: *a group of picked employees for a special project.* **2.** cleaned or cleared, as of dirt or unwanted matter.

pick·er·el (pik′ər əl) *n., pl.* **pick·er·el** or **pick·er·els.** any of several kinds of small pike with slender bodies and long snouts. It is a freshwater game and food fish of North America.

pick·et (pik′it) *n.* **1.** a pointed stake or slat usually driven into the ground to hold something in place or to build something, such as a fence. **2.** a person who stands or walks outside a place of business, government office, or other establishment to protest against something, as in a labor dispute or political demonstration. **3.** *Military.* a guard or body of troops stationed ahead of an army or outside a camp to watch for and give warning of the enemy's approach. —*v.t.* **1.** to act as or station a picket or pickets outside: *to picket an embassy.* **2.** to guard with a picket or pickets. **3.** to post as a picket. **4.** to fasten to a picket, as a horse. —*v.i.* to stand or walk about as a picket.

picket fence, a fence made of a row of pickets.

picket line

picket line, a group of people walking in a line outside a place of business, government office, or other establishment in protest against that establishment or one of its policies.

pick·ing (pik′ing) *n.* **1.** the act of a person who picks. **2. pickings. a.** that which is left over; scraps: *Only slim pickings remained on the table.* **b.** the amount or quality that can be picked: *The pickings were good at the sale.*

pick·le (pik′əl) *n.* **1.** any food, especially a cucumber, that has been preserved in a solution of salt water or vinegar. **2.** a solution of salt water or vinegar used to preserve or flavor food. **3.** *Informal.* a difficult or disagreeable situation. —*v.t.,* **pick·led, pick·ling.** to preserve or flavor in a solution of salt water or vinegar.

pick·pock·et (pik′pok′it) *n.* a thief who steals from the pockets or purses of others.

pick·up (pik′up′) *n.* **1.** the act of picking up: *a pickup of mail.* **2.** the capacity for quick acceleration: *The old car doesn't have much pickup.* **3.** a device that holds a phonograph needle and converts its vibrations into a weak electric current; cartridge. **4.** in radio and television, the reception of sound or light waves by the transmitter for conversion into electric waves. **5.** a small truck with an open, low-sided bed. Also, **pickup truck. 6.** *Informal.* an increase or improvement, as in activity or business. —*adj. Informal.* organized using whoever or whatever is at hand: *a pickup basketball game.*

pick·y (pik′ē) *adj.,* **pick·i·er, pick·i·est.** hard to please; fussy: *a picky eater.*

pic·nic (pik′nik) *n.* an outing that includes a meal eaten out-of-doors. —*v.i.,* **pic·nicked, pic·nick·ing.** to go on or have a picnic: *We picnicked in the park.* —**pic′nick·er,** *n.*

pi·cot (pē′kō) *n.* one of a series of small loops forming an ornamental edging on a piece of material, as on ribbon or lace. —*v.t.* to finish or ornament with such loops.

Pict (pikt) *n.* a member of an ancient people formerly living in northern and central Scotland.

pic·to·graph (pik′tə graf′) *n.* **1.** a picture that stands for a word or idea in a system of picture writing. **2.** a diagram, graph, or chart using pictures to represent data.

pic·to·ri·al (pik tôr′ē əl) *adj.* **1.** of, relating to, or of the nature of pictures: *pictorial art, pictorial writing.* **2.** illustrated by or containing pictures: *The school library subscribes to several pictorial publications.* **3.** very descriptive; graphic. —**pic·to′ri·al·ly,** *adv.*

pictograph
meaning
"No Bicycles"

pic·ture (pik′chər) *n.* **1.** a visual representation of something on a flat surface; drawing, painting, photograph, or the like. **2.** something presented to the eye, as an image on a motion-picture or television screen. **3.** a description in words: *The lecturer gave an excellent picture of living conditions in China.* **4.** an impression or idea: *a mental picture of life in ancient Greece.* **5.** a typical example; embodiment: *You look the picture of health.* **6.** see **motion picture. 7.** a situation: *the political picture.* —*v.t.,* **pic·tured, pic·tur·ing. 1.** to represent something visually, as in a drawing or painting; depict: *The artist pictured a child sitting in a chair.* **2.** to give a description of; describe: *The writer pictured the horror and destruction of war.* **3.** to form an impression or idea of; imagine: *Can you picture them playing football?*

Word Family

Several English words have come from the Latin word *pingere* (and its participle *pictus*), meaning "to paint." There are many ways to create a **picture** besides **painting** it. If you were a **painter**, you might decide to do a **picturesque** landscape, perhaps with a **pinto** running in the wind. **Depicting** such a scene requires the right colors, and choosing the right **pigments** shows **pictorial** skill. If you were more practical, you might do a sign instead, such as the **pictograph** for a railroad crossing.

pic·tur·esque (pik′chə resk′) *adj.* **1.** having pleasing qualities suitable for a picture: *A cottage by the sea is a picturesque setting.* **2.** striking or expressive: *picturesque speech.* —**pic′tur·esque′ly,** *adv.* —**pic′tur·esque′ness,** *n.*

picture tube, a cathode-ray tube that displays the picture on a television set. Also, **kinescope.**

picture window, a large window with a single pane of glass, usually allowing a wide view of the outdoors.

pid·dling (pid′ling) *adj.* unimportant or trivial; petty.

pid·gin (pij′ən) *n.* a mixture of two or more languages having a simplified grammar and vocabulary, used for communication between peoples who speak different languages.

pidgin English also, **Pidgin English.** any of several pidgins based on English and used especially in trade in areas of Africa, Asia, and the Pacific.

pie[1] (pī) *n.* a baked dish made of pastry with a filling of meat, fish, fruit, or other food. [From the Medieval Latin word *pica* meaning this pastry.]

pie[2] (pī) *n.* see **magpie.** [From the Old French word *pie* meaning this bird, from the Latin word *pica* "magpie."]

pie·bald (pī′bôld′) *adj.* having spots or patches, especially of black and white. —*n.* a piebald animal, especially a horse.

piece (pēs) *n.* **1.** a separated part; fragment: *a piece of broken glass.* **2.** a part of something forming a single unit or whole: *a piece of land, a piece of cake.* **3.** a single object belonging to a set or group: *a piece of luggage, a piece of china.* **4.** an artistic composition or production: *a piece of music, a literary piece.* **5.** a particular quantity or amount, as of fabric sold or work done. **6.** an instance; example: *That car is a piece of junk.* **7.** a coin: *a ten-cent piece.* **8.** any of the small objects, such as disks or figures, used in playing checkers, chess, or other board games. **9.** a gun or cannon. —*v.t.,* **pieced, piec·ing. 1.** to join the pieces of in order to construct: *to piece a story together from scattered information.* **2.** to mend by bringing together or adding a piece or pieces; patch: *to piece a ripped dress.*

·**to go to pieces. 1.** to break or fall into pieces. **2.** *Informal.* to break down emotionally.

piece·meal (pēs′mēl′) *adv.* **1.** piece by piece; a little at a time: *The book was written piecemeal over a long period of time.* **2.** into pieces or fragments: *to be torn piecemeal.* —*adj.* made or done piece by piece: *a piecemeal effort.*

piece of cake *Informal.* something very easy; a cinch: *The test was a piece of cake for those who had studied for it.*

piece of eight, an obsolete Spanish silver coin.

piece·work (pēs′wûrk′) *n.* work done and paid for by pieces completed rather than by the hour or the day. —**piece′work′er,** *n.*

pied (pīd) *adj.* having large spots of different colors.

pier (pîr) *n.* **1.** a structure built out over the water, used especially as a landing place for boats or ships. **2.** a solid support on which an arch rests, as in a bridge. **3.** the solid part of a wall between openings, as windows.

pierce (pîrs) *v.,* **pierced, pierc·ing.** —*v.t.* **1.** to penetrate or pass into or through, as with a sharp-pointed instrument: *The splinter pierced my skin.* **2.** to make a hole or opening in or through; perforate: *The pick pierced the layer of ice.* **3.** to force or break a way into or through: *The enemy's attack pierced our line of defense.* **4.** to perceive with the mind or senses; see into or through; discern: *to pierce a mystery.* **5.** to affect (the emotions) keenly; touch or move deeply: *The sad tale pierced our hearts.* **6.** to penetrate with a sharp sound: *A shout pierced the stillness of the night.* —*v.i.* to pass into or through; penetrate: *The knife did not pierce very deeply.*

pier *(def. 1)*

pierc·ing (pîr′sing) *adj.* penetrating; sharp: *a piercing scream, a piercing look.* —**pierc′ing·ly,** *adv.*

Pie·tà (pē′ä tä′) *also,* **pie·tà.** *n.* an artistic rendering of Mary holding the dead body of Jesus.

pi·e·ty (pī′i tē) *n., pl.* **pi·e·ties. 1.** reverence for God; religious devoutness; godliness. **2.** loyalty and obedience, as to one's parents. **3.** a pious act or belief.

pi·e·zo·e·lec·tric·i·ty (pī e′zō i lek tris′i tē) *n.* electricity that is produced when certain nonmetallic minerals, such as quartz or tourmaline, are stretched or compressed. [From the Greek word *piezein* meaning "to squeeze, press" + the word *electric.*] —**pi·e′zo·e·lec′tric,** *adj.*

pig (pig) *n.* **1.** a hoofed mammal, especially one of various breeds widely raised for food, having a stout, roundish body, short legs, and a blunt snout. **2.** a young swine. **3.** the flesh of a pig used as food; pork. **4.** *Informal.* a person who is dirty, greedy, or very fat. **5.** an oblong mass of metal, especially iron, cast from a smelting furnace.

pi·geon (pij′ən) *n.* **1.** any of numerous wild or domesticated birds with a stout body, small head, and thick, soft feathers. **2.** a blue and gray bird of this group, commonly found in cities and sometimes raised for food. **3.** *Slang.* a person who is easily cheated or fooled; dupe.

at; āpe; fär; câre; end; mē; it; īce; pîerce; hot; ōld; sông, fôrk; oil; out; up; ūse; rüle; pull; tûrn; chin; sing; shop; thin; <u>th</u>is; hw in white; zh in treasure. The symbol ə stands for the unstressed vowel sound heard in about, taken, pencil, lemon, and circus.

pi·geon·hole (pij′ən hōl′) *n.* **1.** a small compartment, as in a cabinet or desk, for holding papers or other articles. **2.** a small hole or place for pigeons to nest in. —*v.t.*, **pi·geon·holed, pi·geon·hol·ing. 1.** to put in a small compartment; file. **2.** to lay aside or put away and forget: *The committee pigeonholed the proposal.* **3.** to put in a category; classify: *I pigeonholed them as troublemakers.*

pi·geon–toed (pij′ən tōd′) *adj.* having the toes or feet turned inward.

pig·gish (pig′ish) *adj.* like a pig in habits or manners, especially in being greedy or dirty. —**pig′gish·ly,** *adv.* —**pig′gish·ness,** *n.*

pig·gy·back (pig′ē bak′) *adv., adj.* **1.** on the back or shoulders. **2.** of, by, or in truck trailers that are carried on railroad flatcars: *to transport goods piggyback.* Also, **pickaback.**

piggy bank, a small bank, often in the shape of a pig, used especially by children for saving coins.

pig·head·ed (pig′hed′id) *adj.* unreasonably stubborn; obstinate. —**pig′head′ed·ly,** *adv.* —**pig′head′ed·ness,** *n.*

pig iron, crude iron as it comes from the blast furnace.

pig·let (pig′lit) *n.* a little pig, especially a baby pig.

pig·ment (pig′mənt) *n.* **1.** a substance used for coloring, especially a powdered substance that is mixed with a liquid to produce a paint or dye. **2.** a substance, such as chlorophyll, that gives color to plant or animal tissues.

pig·men·ta·tion (pig′mən tā′shən) *n.* the coloration in plant or animal tissues caused by pigment.

Pig·my (pig′mē) *n., pl.* **Pig·mies.** another spelling of **Pygmy.**

pig·pen (pig′pen′) *n.* **1.** a pen for pigs. **2.** a dirty place.

pig·skin (pig′skin′) *n.* **1.** the skin of a pig. **2.** leather made of this. **3.** *Informal.* a football.

pig·sty (pig′stī′) *n., pl.* **pig·sties.** another word for **pig-pen.**

pig·tail (pig′tāl′) *n.* a braid of hair hanging down from the back or the side of the head.

pike¹ (pīk) *n.* a weapon consisting of a long wooden shaft with a pointed tip of iron or steel, formerly used by foot soldiers. [From the Old French word *pique* meaning this weapon, from the word *piquer* "to pierce, prick."]

pike² (pīk) *n.* a sharp point, such as the tip of a spear. [From the Middle English word *pike* meaning "a spike, stake" or "pickax," from the Old English word *pīc* meaning "a pointed instrument" or "a pike²."]

pike³ (pīk) *n.* a large freshwater fish of Europe, Asia, and northern North America, having a slim, tapering, olive-green body and a duck-billed snout with many sharp teeth. [From the Middle English word *pike* meaning this fish, probably from the word *pike* "pike¹."]

pike⁴ (pīk) *n.* see **turnpike.**

pik·er (pī′kər) *n. Slang.* a person who is stingy, overly cautious, or petty.

pike·staff (pīk′staf′) *n., pl.* **pike·staves** (pīk′stāvz′). **1.** the shaft of a pike. **2.** a walking stick with a metal tip at the lower end.

pi·laf (pē′läf) *also,* **pi·laff.** *n.* a dish consisting mainly of rice boiled with meat or fish and seasoned with spices. [From the Persian word *pilāw* meaning this food.]

pi·las·ter (pi las′tər) *n.* a rectangular flat column projecting slightly from a wall.

pile¹ (pīl) *n.* **1.** a number of things laid or lying one upon another; heap: *a pile of newspapers, a pile of dirt.* **2.** *Informal.* a large amount or quantity: *a pile of money, a pile of troubles.* —*v.,* **piled, pil·ing.** —*v.t.* **1.** to form into a heap or mass: *The gardener piled the dead leaves in a corner of the yard.* **2.** to accumulate: *to pile up debts.* **3.** to cover or load with a pile: *The writer piled the desk with books.* —*v.i.* **1.** to form or rise in a heap or mass: *The snow piled in drifts.* **2.** *Informal.* to move in a

confused or disorderly mass; crowd: *The whole family piled into the car.* [From the Middle English word *pile* meaning "a pillar" or "heap, pile¹," from the Old French word *pile* with the same meanings, from the Latin word *pila* "a pillar."]

pile² (pīl) *n.* a strong, slender beam of wood, steel, or concrete, driven vertically into the ground to support a structure, such as a bridge or wharf. [From the Middle English word *pile* meaning "an arrow, dart, or other sharp-pointed missile" or "a pile²," from the Old English word *pīl* "something pointed" or "pointed missile," from the Latin word *pilum* "a heavy Roman spear."]

pile³ (pīl) *n.* **1.** the raised cut or uncut loops of yarn that form the surface of a fabric, such as velvet, or of a carpet. **2.** fine, soft hair or fiber. [From the Latin word *pilus* "hair."]

pile driver, a machine for driving piles into the ground, usually consisting of a frame in which a heavy weight is suspended and then dropped on the pile.

piles (pīlz) *pl. n.* hemorrhoids. [From the Latin word *pila* meaning "ball," from the shape of hemorrhoids.]

pil·fer (pil′fər) *v.t., v.i.* to steal in small quantities. —**pil′fer·age,** *n.*

pil·grim (pil′grəm) *n.* **1.** a person who journeys to a sacred place for a religious purpose, as for penance or devotion. **2.** any traveler. **3. Pilgrim.** one of the group of English Puritans who founded Plymouth Colony in 1620. [From the Old French word *peligrin* meaning "one traveling to a sacred place for religious devotion," going back to the Latin word *peregrinus* "foreigner, foreign."]

pil·grim·age (pil′grə mij) *n.* **1.** a journey to a sacred or revered place. **2.** any long journey.

pil·ing (pī′ling) *n.* a number of piles, or a structure made up of a number of piles.

pill (pil) *n.* **1.** a pellet of medicine that is swallowed whole or chewed; tablet. **2.** something that is disagreeable but must be endured: *The loss of the election was a bitter pill for them to swallow.* **3.** *Slang.* a disagreeable or boring person.

pil·lage (pil′ij) *v.,* **pil·laged, pil·lag·ing.** —*v.t.* to rob by force, as during a war; plunder: *The soldiers pillaged the town.* —*v.i.* to take booty: *The invading army pillaged throughout the countryside.* —*n.* **1.** the act of plundering. **2.** something carried off as booty; plunder: *The pillage from the cargo ship made the pirates rich.* —**pil′lag·er,** *n.*

pil·lar (pil′ər) *n.* **1.** an upright structure that serves as a support for a building or stands alone as a monument. **2.** something resembling a pillar in shape or function. **3.** a person who is a chief supporter or important member of something: *a pillar of society.*

·from pillar to post. from one place, person, or situation to another without purpose or aim.

pill·box (pil′boks′) *n., pl.* **pill·box·es. 1.** a small box for pills. **2.** a small, low, concrete fortification defending a coast, border, or the like. **3.** a woman's small round hat.

pil·lion (pil′yən) *n.* a pad or cushion behind the saddle of a horse or the seat of a motorcycle, for another rider.

pil·lo·ry (pil′ə rē) *n., pl.* **pil·lo·ries.** a wooden frame fitted with openings to hold the head and hands, formerly used to expose a person to public ridicule as punishment for an offense. —*v.t.,* **pil·lo·ried, pil·lo·ry·ing. 1.** to put in a pillory. **2.** to expose to public ridicule or abuse: *The crooked politician was pilloried by the newspapers.*

pil·low (pil′ō) *n.* a bag or casing filled with soft material, such as feathers, down, or foam rubber, used as a support, as for the head during sleep. —*v.t.* **1.** to rest (something) on or as if on a pillow: *to pillow one's head on one's hand.* **2.** to serve as a pillow for: *Some straw pillowed the baby's head.*

pil·low·case (pil′ō kās′) *n.* a removable cloth cover for a pillow. Also, **pil·low·slip** (pil′ō slip′).

pi·lot (pī′lət) *n.* **1.** a person who operates the controls of an aircraft or spacecraft. **2.** a person who steers a ship, especially into or out of a harbor. **3.** any person who guides or leads. **4.** see **pilot light. 5.** a television program made as a test for a proposed series of shows. —*v.t.* **1.** to act as the pilot of; steer. **2.** to guide. —*adj.* trial or sample: *a pilot study.*

PILOT (pī′lət) *n.* a computer language designed for beginners, especially for children and students in the classroom.

pilot fish *also,* **pi·lot·fish** (pī′lət fish′). a small fish that usually swims along with sharks or other large fish.

pi·lot·house (pī′lət hous′) *n., pl.* **pi·lot·hous·es** (pī′lət-hou′ziz). a structure on the deck of a ship that shelters the steering equipment and the pilot.

pilot light, a small flame kept burning in order to light a gas burner when it is turned on.

pi·men·to (pi men′tō) *n., pl.* **pi·men·tos. 1.** an evergreen tree, related to the myrtle, from which allspice is obtained. **2.** another spelling of **pimiento.**

pi·mien·to (pi myen′tō, pi men′tō) *also,* **pi·men·to.** *n., pl.* **pi·mien·tos.** a mild, sweet red pepper used to stuff olives or to garnish food.

pim·per·nel (pim′pər nel′, pim′pər nəl) *n.* **1.** a small, scarlet, purple, or white flower of a plant related to the primrose. **2.** the plant bearing this flower.

pim·ple (pim′pəl) *n.* a small raised blemish on the skin, often red and sore, that contains pus. —**pim′pled, pim′ply,** *adj.*

pin (pin) *n.* **1.** a short, straight, stiff piece of wire with a point at one end and a head at the other, used to fasten or attach things. **2.** an ornament or emblem that has a pin or clasp for attaching it to clothing: *a fraternity pin.* **3.** anything like a pin in form or use, such as a safety pin, a clothespin, a hairpin, or a bobby pin. **4.** a peg of wood, plastic, or metal, used for various purposes, as for fastening things together or hanging something on. **5.** *Bowling.* a bottle-shaped piece of wood set up as a target to be knocked down by the ball. **6.** *Golf.* the staff of the flag that marks the hole on a green. **7. pins.** *Informal.* legs. —*v.t.,* **pinned, pin·ning. 1.** to fasten or attach with a pin or pins. **2.** to seize and hold fast in one spot or position: *One boxer had pinned the other against the ropes.*
　·**to be on pins and needles.** to be nervous or anxious.
　·**to pin (something) on (someone):** *Slang.* to place the blame for (something) on (someone).

pin·a·fore (pin′ə fôr′) *n.* a garment resembling an apron, covering most of a dress, worn especially by young girls.

pi·ña·ta (pēn yä′tə) *also,* **pinata.** *n.* a colorfully decorated container originally used in Latin American Christmas and birthday celebrations. It is filled with fruit, candy, and gifts, and hung from the ceiling to be broken with a stick by a child who is blindfolded.

pince–nez (pans′nā′, pins′nā′) *n., pl.* **pince-nez.** eyeglasses held on the nose by a spring. [From the French word *pince-nez,* from the words *pincer* meaning "to pinch" + *nez* "the nose," from the Latin word *nasus* "nose."]

pin·cers (pin′sərz) *also,* **pinch·ers.** *pl. n.* **1.** a gripping instrument having a pair of jaws and handles that are fastened on a pivot. **2.** a grasping claw resembling this, such as that of a crab or lobster.

pinch (pinch) *v.t.* **1.** to squeeze between two surfaces or edges, as between the forefinger and thumb: *The child pinched my arm.* **2.** to press or squeeze (something) painfully: *Don't those narrow shoes pinch your toes?* **3.** to make haggard or wrinkled: *Hunger had pinched the beggar's face.* **4.** *Slang.* to steal. **5.** *Slang.* to arrest. —*v.i.* **1.** to press or squeeze painfully; hurt. **2.** to be frugal: *The young couple pinched and saved in order to*

buy a house. —*n., pl.* **pinch·es. 1.** the act of pinching; sharp squeeze. **2.** the quantity that can be taken up between the forefinger and thumb; very small amount: *Add a pinch of sugar to the mixture.* **3.** a physical or other hardship: *Everyone felt the pinch of the new taxes.* **4.** a time of need; emergency: *I can loan you money in a pinch.* **5.** *Slang.* an arrest. [From the Old French word *pincier* meaning "to pinch."]

pinch·er (pin′chər) *n.* **1.** a person or thing that pinches. **2. pinchers.** another spelling of **pincers.**

pinch–hit (pinch′hit′) *v.i.,* **pinch-hit, pinch-hit·ting. 1.** *Baseball.* to bat in place of another player. **2.** to take someone's place; be a substitute.

pinch hitter, a person who pinch-hits.

pin·cush·ion (pin′kush′ən) *n.* a small cushion into which sewing needles and pins are stuck when not in use.

pine¹ (pīn) *n.* **1.** any of a large group of evergreen trees bearing cones and needlelike leaves. **2.** the wood of any of these trees, widely used in building and as a source of turpentine. [From the Old English word root *pīn-*, meaning "pine tree," from the Latin word *pinus* "a pine, pine tree."]

pine² (pīn) *v.i.,* **pined, pin·ing. 1.** to become weak or unhealthy, as from grief or longing: *After its owner's death, the old dog pined away.* **2.** to long intensely; yearn: *The exiles pined for their homes.* [From the Middle English word *pinen* meaning "to torment" and "to languish, pine²," from the Old English word *pīnian* "to torment," going back to the Latin word *poena* "a penalty" or "pain," from the Greek word *poinē* "penalty."]

pin·e·al body (pin′ē əl) a small organ whose function is not fully known, found in the brain of human beings and other animals with backbones. Also, **pineal gland.**

pineapple plants

pine·ap·ple (pīn′ap′əl) *n.* **1.** a large, oval fruit having

P

firm, juicy, yellow flesh that can be eaten and a hard, scaly outer covering. **2.** the plant bearing this fruit, having jagged-edged leaves and clusters of reddish or violet flowers.

pine cone, the fruit of the pine tree, covered with hard, overlapping scales. Cones from other evergreen trees are sometimes also called pine cones.

pine needle, a slender needlelike leaf of a pine tree.

pine nut, the edible seed found in the cone of any of several pine trees.

pin·y (pī′nē) *adj.,* **pin·i·er, pin·i·est.** another spelling of **piny.**

pin·feath·er (pin′feth′ər) *n.* an undeveloped feather that is just beginning to break through the skin of a young bird.

Ping–Pong (ping′pong′) *n. Trademark.* another word for **table tennis.**

pin·hole (pin′hōl′) *n.* a tiny hole made by or as if by a pin.

pin·ion¹ (pin′yən) *n.* a bird's wing, especially the last segment. —*v.t.* **1.** to prevent (a bird) from flying by clipping or binding the pinions. **2.** to clip or bind (the pinions). **3.** to bind or hold firmly: *The police officers pinioned the suspects' arms behind them with handcuffs.* [From the Old French word *pignon* meaning "a bird's wing," going back to the Latin word *penna* "feather."]

pin·ion² (pin′yən) *n.* a small wheel with cogs that lock into the cogs of a larger wheel or rack. [From the French word *pignon* with the same meaning, from the Old French word *peigne* "a comb," from the Latin word *pecten* "a comb, rake¹."]

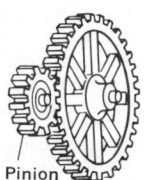

Pinion

pinion²

pink¹ (pingk) *n.* **1.** a light red color. **2.** the highest degree: *in the pink of health.* **3.** any of a group of often fragrant flowers having five or more petals, such as the carnation. **4.** a plant bearing this flower, having grayish green leaves. —*adj.* having the color pink. [Of uncertain origin.] —**pink′ish,** *adj.*

pink² (pingk) *v.t.* **1.** to pierce slightly with a sharp, pointed weapon, such as a sword. **2.** to decorate (cloth, paper, or the like) by punching tiny holes in a pattern. **3.** to cut and finish the edge of (fabric) with a series of small notches, especially with pinking shears. [From the Middle English word *pinken* meaning "to push" or "to pierce, stab," from the Old English word *pyngan* "to prick," from the Latin word *pungere* "to prick, pierce."]

pink·eye (pingk′ī′) *n.* a contagious reddening of the tissue that covers the eyeball and lines the lower and upper eyelids; conjunctivitis.

pink·ie (ping′kē) *also,* **pink·y.** *n., pl.* **pink·ies.** *Informal.* the smallest finger.

pinking shears, scissors having notched blades, used to pink fabric.

pin money, a small sum of money for minor expenses or purchases, originally an allowance given by a husband to his wife for her personal expenses.

pin·na·cle (pin′ə kəl) *n.* **1.** a high, pointed formation, such as a mountain peak. **2.** the highest point; acme: *That scientist achieved the pinnacle of success in chemistry.* **3.** *Architecture.* a small tower set above a larger structure.

pin·nate (pin′āt) *adj.* resembling a feather in shape or structure: *pinnate leaves.* —**pin′-nate·ly,** *adv.*

pi·noch·le (pē′nuk′əl, pē′nok′əl) *also,* **pi·noc·le.** *n.* a game played with a special deck of forty-eight cards having two of the ace, king, queen, jack, ten, and nine in each suit.

pinnacle
(def. 3)

pi·ñon (pin′yən, pēn yōn′) *n.* **1.** a small pine tree found in the southwestern United States. **2.** the edible nut of this tree.

pin·point (pin′point′) *v.t.* to locate, fix, or identify precisely: *The soldiers pinpointed the camp of the enemy.* —*adj.* strict; exact: *The gunners were able to fire with pinpoint accuracy.* —*n.* **1.** the point of a pin. **2.** something very small or unimportant: *In the distance we saw a pinpoint of light.*

pin·stripe (pin′strīp′) *n.* a very narrow stripe woven in a fabric: *a dark blue suit with white pinstripes.*

pint (pīnt) *n.* **1.** a unit of liquid measure equal to half a quart, or ⅛ gallon (473 milliliters). **2.** a unit of dry measure equal to half a quart, or ¹⁄₁₆ peck (550.6 milliliters).

pin·tail (pin′tāl′) *n., pl.* **pin·tail** or **pin·tails.** **1.** a long-necked duck, having long, pointed central tail feathers. **2.** a grouse of North America, having a long, pointed tail.

pin·to (pin′tō) *adj.* having spots or patches of two or more colors; mottled. —*n., pl.* **pin·tos.** a pinto horse or pony.

pin·wheel (pin′hwēl′, pin′wēl′) *n.* a toy made of colored paper or plastic in the shape of a wheel and pinned to a stick so as to revolve when spun by hand or blown upon.

pin·worm (pin′wûrm′) *n.* a small parasitic roundworm that can infest the lower intestinal tract of humans.

pin·y (pī′nē) *also,* **pine·y.** *adj.,* **pin·i·er, pin·i·est.** **1.** of, relating to, or like pine trees: *a piny fragrance.* **2.** covered with or having many pine trees: *a piny forest.*

Pin·yin (pin′yin′) *n.* a modern system of transliteration used to write Chinese words in the Latin alphabet. Pinyin replaced previous systems, including that known as Wade-Giles. The name of the former leader of the People's Republic of China is written *Mao Zedong* in Pinyin and as *Mao Tse-tung* in the Wade-Giles system. [From the Mandarin Chinese phrase *p'in yin* meaning "to spell phonetically," from the words *p'in* "to arrange" + *yin* "pronunciation" or "sound."]

pi·o·neer (pī′ə nîr′) *n.* **1.** a person who is the first or among the first to explore or settle a region. **2.** a person who is the first or among the first to open up or develop an area of thought, research, or activity: *That scientist was a pioneer in psychology.* —*v.t.* **1.** to explore or settle: *Courageous settlers pioneered the Northwest Territory.* **2.** to open up or develop. —*v.i.* to be a pioneer: *American industry pioneered in the development of mass production.* [From the French word *pionnier* meaning "a pioneer," from the Old French word *peonier* "a foot soldier, scout¹," from the word *peon* "foot soldier," or "pawn²," from the Medieval Latin word *pedo* "foot soldier," going back to the Latin word *pes* "foot."]

pi·ous (pī′əs) *adj.* **1.** deeply religious: *a pious family.* **2.** of or relating to religious devotion: *pious writings.* —**pi′ous·ly,** *adv.* —**pi′ous·ness,** *n.*

pip¹ (pip) *n.* **1.** the seed of a fruit, such as an apple or orange. **2.** *Slang.* a person or thing that is remarkable or excellent: *You sure are a pip!* [Short for *pippin.*]

pip² (pip) *n.* a contagious disease of chickens and other birds, characterized by the secretion of thick mucus in the mouth and throat. [From the Middle Dutch word *pippe* meaning "phlegm, mucus."]

pip³ (pip) *n.* any of the spots or marks on dominoes, dice, or playing cards. [Of uncertain origin.]

pipe (pīp) *n.* **1.** a tube of metal, plastic, or similar material for carrying a gas or liquid. **2.** a tube with a bowl of briar, clay, or other material at one end, used for smoking. **3.** a musical instrument in the form of a tube that is blown into at one end. **4.** one of the tubes in an organ in which tones are produced. **5.** pipes. **a.** a musical instrument made up of a series of tubes of different lengths bound together; panpipe. **b.** see **bagpipe.** —*v.,* **piped, pip·ing.** —*v.t.* **1.** to convey by means of a pipe or pipes: *The* *farmer piped water to the fields.* **2.** to supply with pipes: *The builders piped the new house for gas.* **3.** to play (music) on a pipe. **4.** to say or sing in a loud, shrill voice. —*v.i.* **1.** to make a loud, shrill sound. **2.** to play on a pipe. —**pipe′like′**, *adj.*

·**to pipe down.** *Slang.* to be quiet.

pipe dream, a vain or fanciful notion or wish: *The child's pipe dream was to be a movie star.*

pipe·line (pīp′līn′) *n.* **1.** a line of pipes for carrying gas or liquid. **2.** a route by which information or supplies are carried: *Party leaders have a direct pipeline to the governor's office.*

pipe organ, another term for **organ** *(def. 1).*

pip·er (pī′pər) *n.* a person who plays on a pipe, especially on the bagpipes.

·**to pay the piper.** to bear the responsibility for one's actions.

pi·pette (pī pet′) *n.* a slender glass tube for measuring or for transferring small amounts of liquids.

pip·ing (pī′ping) *n.* **1.** a system of pipes. **2.** the music of a pipe or pipes: *the piping of a flute.* **3.** a loud, shrill sound: *the piping of a bird.* **4.** a tubular strip of material used for trimming seams or edges of fabric. —*adj.* shrill: *a piping voice.*

·**piping hot.** very hot.

pip·it (pip′it) *n.* any of various small birds resembling a sparrow, having a thin bill and brown feathers.

pip·pin (pip′in) *n.* any of various kinds of apples. [From the Old French word *pepin* meaning "seed of certain fruits."]

pip·squeak (pip′skwēk′) *n. Informal.* a small or unimportant person or thing: *Compared to that tugboat, our little rowboat is just a pipsqueak.*

pi·quant (pē′kənt, pē′känt) *adj.* **1.** pleasantly sharp to the taste; pungent; tart: *The cook poured a piquant sauce over the meat.* **2.** interesting or stimulating: *The critic made piquant comments about the author's newest book.* —**pi′quan·cy**, *n.* —**pi′quant·ly**, *adv.*

pique (pēk) *n.* resentment caused by having one's feelings hurt or one's pride wounded: *After that insult, I returned the gift in a fit of pique.* —*v.t.*, **piqued, pi·quing. 1.** to cause a feeling of anger or resentment in; offend: *Your thoughtless remark has piqued your friend.* **2.** to arouse; excite: *The locked closet piqued my curiosity.*

pi·qué (pi kā′, pē kā′) *n.* a fabric usually made of cotton, woven with narrow, lengthwise ribs.

pi·ra·cy (pī′rə sē) *n., pl.* **pi·ra·cies. 1.** robbery of ships at sea. **2.** the use of another's work, invention, or ideas without permission or in violation of a copyright.

pi·ra·nha (pi ran′yə, pi rä′nə) *n.* a freshwater fish of tropical South America that travels in schools and feeds on other fish. Piranhas will also attack large animals, including humans.

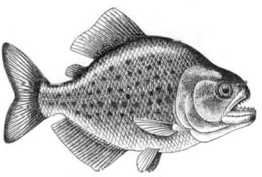
piranha

pi·rate (pī′rit) *n.* **1.** a person who robs ships at sea. **2.** a person who uses the work, invention, or ideas of another without permission or in violation of a copyright. —*v.,* **pi·rat·ed, pi·rat·ing.** —*v.t.* **1.** to rob (ships) at sea. **2.** to use (another's work, invention, or ideas) without permission or in violation of a copyright. —*v.i.* to practice piracy.

pir·ou·ette (pîr′ü et′) *n.* a rapid turning about on the toes, especially in dancing. —*v.i.,* **pir·ou·et·ted, pir·ou·et·ting.** to perform a pirouette.

Pis·ces (pī′sēz, pis′ēz) *n.* **1.** a constellation in the northern sky, thought to resemble two fish in shape. **2.** the twelfth sign of the zodiac.

pis·ta·chi·o (pi stash′ē ō′) *n., pl.* **pis·ta·chi·os. 1.** a

small, edible, greenish nut having a thin purple skin and covered by a hard gray shell. **2.** the small tree bearing this nut. **3.** the flavor of the nut. **4.** a light yellowish green color. —*adj.* having the color or flavor of pistachio.

pis·til (pis′təl) *n.* the part of a flower where seeds are produced. It is made up of the ovary, style, and stigma.

pis·til·late (pis′tə lāt′) *adj.* (of a flower) having a pistil or pistils, especially, having pistils but no stamens.

pis·tol (pis′təl) *n.* a small firearm that is held and fired with one hand.

pis·ton (pis′tən) *n.* **1.** a disk or solid cylinder that fits closely inside a sleeve or hollow cylinder, where it slides back and forth. **2.** in a brass musical instrument, a sliding valve used to change the pitch of tones.

piston ring, an expandable metal ring that fits into a groove near the top end of a piston, sealing the gap between the piston and the surrounding cylinder.

piston rod, a rod connected to a piston that transfers the motion of the piston to a shaft or other part.

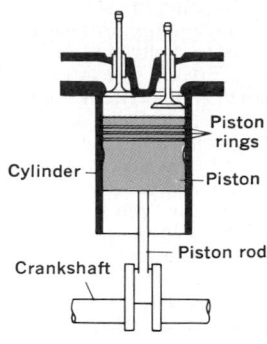
piston in a gasoline engine

(labels: Piston rings, Cylinder, Piston, Piston rod, Crankshaft)

pit¹ (pit) *n.* **1.** a hole in the ground, either natural or dug. **2.** a small hollow or scar on a surface, as a pockmark on the skin. **3.** a natural hollow in the body: *the pit under the arm.* **4.** a sunken or enclosed area for staging fights between animals. **5.** a sunken area in front of the stage of a theater for the orchestra. **6.** hell. **7.** an area beside a racetrack for servicing cars in a race. **8. the pits.** *Slang.* an unpleasant situation, place, or thing: *Cold, rainy weather is the pits.* —*v.t.,* **pit·ted, pit·ting. 1.** to make small holes in; mark with pits: *Pebbles thrown against the walls pitted the plaster.* **2.** to place in opposition; match: *They pitted the challenger against the seasoned champion.* [From the Old English word *pytt* meaning "a hole in the ground," going back to the Latin word *puteus* "a well, pit¹."]

pit² (pit) *n.* the hard stone of a fruit, such as a peach or cherry. —*v.t.,* **pit·ted, pit·ting.** to remove stones from (fruit). [From the Dutch word *pit* with the same meaning.]

pi·ta (pē′tə) *n.* a round, flat bread that can be sliced across to form a pocket and stuffed with meat, vegetables, and other fillings. [From the Modern Greek word *pita* meaning this bread.]

pit·a·pat (pit′ə pat′) *also,* **pit-a-pat.** *adv.* with quick beats or taps: *My heart went pitapat.* —*v.i.,* **pit·a·pat·ted, pit·a·pat·ting.** to go pitapat. —*n.* quick beating, or the sound made by it.

pitch¹ (pich) *v.t.* **1.** to throw, hurl, or toss: *to pitch horseshoes, to pitch pennies.* **2.** *Baseball.* to throw (the ball) to the batter. **3.** to set up; erect: *to pitch a camp, to pitch a tent.* **4.** to set on a slope; incline: *to pitch a roof.* **5.** *Music.* to set the key of: *to pitch a guitar, to pitch a tune.* —*v.i.* **1.** to fall or plunge forward: *The painter slipped and pitched off the ladder.* **2.** to slope downward. **3.** *Baseball.* **a.** to throw the ball to the

at; āpe; fär; câre; end; mē; it; īce; pîerce; hot; ōld; sông, fôrk; oil; out; up; ūse; rüle; pull; tûrn; chin; sing; shop; thin; this; hw in white; zh in treasure. The symbol ə stands for the unstressed vowel sound heard in about, taken, pencil, lemon, and circus.

P

batter. **b.** to play the position of pitcher. **4.** to plunge so that the bow and stern rise and fall: *The ship pitched in the rough sea.* —*n., pl.* **pitch·es. 1.** a throw, hurl, or toss. **2.** a point, degree, or level: *a high pitch of enthusiasm.* **3.** a downward slope: *the pitch of a roof.* **4.** *Baseball.* **a.** the act or manner of pitching the ball to the batter. **b.** the ball that is pitched. **5.** the highness or lowness of a sound or musical tone. **6.** *Slang.* a talk intended to persuade, usually using high-pressure tactics: *a sales pitch.* [From the Middle English word *picchen* meaning "to thrust; pierce," "to erect," or "to throw," from Old English.]

·**to pitch in.** *Informal.* **a.** to begin a task with promptness and energy: *Pitch in and get the housework done quickly.* **b.** to contribute money toward a common purpose: *We all pitched in to rent a boat for the holiday weekend.*

pitch² (pich) *n.* **1.** a dark, thick, sticky substance obtained from petroleum, coal tar, or wood tar, used for water-proofing and paving. **2.** a resin obtained from pine trees. —*v.t.* to cover or smear with pitch. [From the Old English word *pic* with the same meaning, from the Latin word *pix* "pitch²."] —**pitch'y,** *adv.*

pitch–black (pich'blak') *adj.* extremely black.

pitch·blende (pich'blend') *n.* a black, lumpy variety of uranium ore.

pitch–dark (pich'därk') *adj.* extremely dark.

pitched battle, a fierce, closely fought battle.

pitch·er¹ (pich'ər) *n.* **1.** a vessel with a handle and a lip or spout, used chiefly for holding and pouring liquids. **2.** the amount contained by a pitcher. [From the Old French word *pichier* meaning this container, from the Medieval Latin word *bicarius* "a goblet," from the Greek word *bikos* "a drinking bowl."]

pitch·er² (pich'ər) *n.* a person who pitches, especially the player on a baseball team who throws the ball to the batter. [*Pitch¹* + *-er¹.*]

pitcher plant, a plant having pitcher-shaped leaves that trap insects.

pitch·fork (pich'fôrk') *n.* a long-handled tool with fork-like prongs, used especially to lift and pitch hay.

pitch·out (pich'out') *n.* **1.** *Baseball.* a pitch thrown high and away from the batter to give the catcher a clear throw at a base runner attempting to steal. **2.** *Football.* a lateral pass behind the line of scrimmage, usually from the quarterback to another back.

pitch pipe, a small pipe that has a fixed note, used to give the pitch to a person who sings or plays an instrument.

pit·e·ous (pit'ē əs) *adj.* deserving or arousing pity; pitiable; pathetic. —**pit'e·ous·ly,** *adv.* —**pit'e·ous·ness,** *n.*

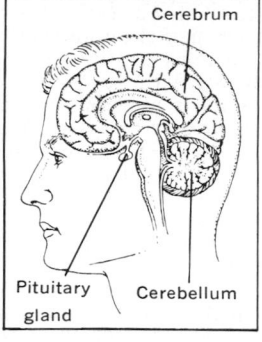
pitchfork

pit·fall (pit'fôl') *n.* **1.** a pit dug into the ground and covered over, used to catch animals. **2.** any hidden danger or difficulty.

pith (pith) *n.* **1.** soft, spongy tissue in the center of the stems of certain plants. **2.** soft tissue resembling this: *the pith of a grapefruit.* **3.** the important or essential part: *the pith of an essay.*

Pith·e·can·thro·pus (pith'i kan'thrə pəs) *n., pl.* **Pith·e·can·thro·pi** (pith'i kan'thrə pī'). another word for **Java man.**

pith·y (pith'ē) *adj.,* **pith·i·er, pith·i·est. 1.** of, like, or full of pith. **2.** short and full of meaning: *a pithy statement.* —**pith'i·ly,** *adv.* —**pith'i·ness,** *n.*

pit·i·a·ble (pit'ē ə bəl) *adj.* deserving or arousing pity: *a pitiable old beggar.* —**pit'i·a·ble·ness,** *n.* —**pit'i·a·bly,** *adv.*

pit·i·ful (pit'i fəl) *adj.* **1.** arousing pity: *a pitiful look.* **2.** arousing contempt; paltry: *a pitiful excuse.* —**pit'i·ful·ly,** *adv.* —**pit'i·ful·ness,** *n.*

pit·i·less (pit'i lis) *adj.* without pity; showing no mercy: *a pitiless attack.* —**pit'i·less·ly,** *adv.* —**pit'i·less·ness,** *n.*

pit·tance (pit'əns) *n.* a small or meager amount or allowance, as of money: *I was paid only a pittance for mowing the lawn.*

pit·ter–pat·ter (pit'ər pat'ər) *n.* the sound of quick taps or beats: *the pitter-patter of footsteps.* —*adv.* with quick taps or beats.

pi·tu·i·tar·y (pi tü'i ter'ē, pi tū'i ter'ē) *n., pl.* **pi·tu·i·tar·ies.** see **pituitary gland.** —*adj.* of or relating to the pituitary gland.

pituitary gland, a small, oval endocrine gland located beneath the brain. The pituitary gland secretes hormones that regulate body growth and the functions of many parts of the body.

pit viper, any of several poisonous snakes including the rattlesnake, copperhead, and water moccasin, having a deep pit on each side of the head for sensing heat.

pit·y (pit'ē) *n., pl.* **pit·ies. 1.** a feeling of sorrow and sympathy aroused by the unhappiness or suffering of another or others. **2.** a cause for regret: *What a pity you can't go.* —*v.t.,* **pit·ied, pit·y·ing.** to feel pity for: *We pitied the people who lost their homes in the flood.* —**pit'y·ing·ly,** *adv.*

piv·ot (piv'ət) *n.* **1.** a point, shaft, or pin that something turns on. **2.** a person or thing of importance that something depends on. **3.** the act of turning on a pivot or as if on a pivot. —*v.t.* to place on or furnish with a pivot. —*v.i.* to turn on a pivot or as if on a pivot: *I pivoted around to face the person who called my name.*

piv·ot·al (piv'ə təl) *adj.* **1.** of, relating to, or serving as a pivot. **2.** of much importance; crucial: *a pivotal matter.* —**piv'ot·al·ly,** *adv.*

pix·el (pik'səl) *n.* a small, luminous dot on a television or computer screen. Pixels are arranged in groups to form pictures, characters, and symbols. [From *pix* (short for *picture*) + *el*(ement).]

pix·ie (pik'sē) *also,* **pix·y.** *n., pl.* **pix·ies. 1.** an imaginary small or mischievous being; fairy; elf. **2.** a mischievous child.

piz·za (pēt'sə) *n.* a baked Italian dish made with a flat layer of dough topped with tomatoes, cheese, and sometimes other ingredients, such as sausages or mushrooms.

piz·ze·ri·a (pēt'sə rē'ə) *n.* a place where pizzas are prepared and sold.

piz·zi·ca·to (pit'si kä'tō) *Music. adj.* played by plucking the strings of an instrument with the finger. —*n., pl.* **piz·zi·ca·ti** (pit'si kä'tē). a note or passage of music played in this way.

pk. *pl.* **pks. 1.** pack. **2.** peak. **3.** peck.

pkg. *pl.* **pkgs.** package.

pl. 1. place. **2.** plate. **3.** plural.

plac·ard (plak'ärd) *n.* a large sign or notice made of paper or cardboard for displaying in a public place. —*v.t.* to display placards on or in: *to placard the wall of the building.*

pla·cate (plā'kāt, plak'āt) *v.t.,* **pla·cat·ed, pla·cat·ing.** to calm the hostility or anger of; pacify: *The salesclerk tried to placate the unhappy customer.* —**pla'cat·er,** *n.* —**pla·ca'tion,** *n.*

place (plās) *n.* **1.** a portion of space; location: *The vase has a place on the shelf. Here is a place to hang your coat.* **2.** an area or locality, such as a town or city: *We visited several interesting places on our trip.* **3.** a building

Cerebrum

Pituitary gland

Cerebellum

pituitary gland

or part of a building with a particular use: *The town has ten places of worship.* **4.** a house or other residence: *They have a place in the mountains.* **5.** a particular part or spot: *There is a sore place on my arm.* **6.** a particular passage in a book or other writing: *I lost my place when I dropped my book.* **7.** a space or seat for a person: *Save a place for me on the bus.* **8.** a position or standing: *That painter has an important place in the history of art.* **9.** a job: *She found a place as a sales manager.* **10.** duty or business: *It is not your place to criticize.* **11.** a position in a line, list, or the like. **12.** the position of the horse that finishes second in a race. **13.** a short street or public square. **14.** *Mathematics.* the position of a figure in a series relative to the positions of other figures. In the number *.347*, 4 is in the second decimal place. —*v.*, **placed, plac·ing.** —*v.t.* **1.** to put or set in a particular place: *Place the napkin beside the plate.* **2.** to identify by connecting with the correct location or time: *He finally placed the dentist as a childhood friend.* —*v.i.* **1.** to be in a particular position, as in a contest or race: *That poodle placed third in the dog show.* **2.** to finish first, second, or third in a contest. **3.** *Horse Racing.* to finish second in a race.
  ·**in place.** in the original, proper, or natural place.
  ·**in place of.** instead of: *Use cream in place of milk in the recipe.*
  ·**out of place. a.** not in the original, proper, or natural place. **b.** not proper; unsuitable: *Shouting is out of place in a museum.*
  ·**to take place.** to happen; occur.
pla·ce·bo (plə sē′bō) *n.*, *pl.* **pla·ce·bos** or **pla·ce·boes.** a preparation having no medical effect, used to soothe a patient, or to make comparisons when testing an active medicine. [From the Latin word *placebo* meaning "I shall please," from the word *placēre* "to please."]
place–kick (plās′kik′) *v.t.* to give a place kick to (a football). —*v.i.* to give a place kick.
place kick, a kick in which a football is placed or held nearly upright on the ground, as in attempting a field goal or an extra point.
place mat, a mat laid on a table at each place setting for protection or decoration.
place·ment (plās′mənt) *n.* **1.** the act or instance of putting or setting in a particular place. **2.** the act or function of finding suitable jobs, schools, or living quarters for people. **3.** the placing of the ball in football for a place kick.
pla·cen·ta (plə sen′tə) *n.*, *pl.* **pla·cen·tas** or **pla·cen·tae** (plə sen′tē) in many female mammals bearing young, the organ through which the unborn young, or fetus, receives food and oxygen and gives off waste. —**pla·cen′tal**, *adj.*
plac·er (plas′ər) *n.* a deposit, as of gravel or sand, that contains particles of gold or other valuable minerals.
placer mining, mining in which gravel or sand is washed to sort out gold or other valuable minerals.
place setting, the dishes, silverware, and other items needed to set a place for one person at a table.
plac·id (plas′id) *adj.* not easily excited or disturbed; calm or peaceful: *a placid disposition.* —**pla·cid′i·ty, plac′id·ness**, *n.* —**plac′id·ly**, *adv.*
plack·et (plak′it) *n.* an opening or slit at the top of a garment, as at the neckline or wrists, that makes it easy to put the garment on or take it off.
pla·gia·rism (plā′jə riz′əm) *n.* **1.** the act of copying someone else's work and passing it off as one's own. **2.** the work or ideas of another taken and passed off as one's own. —**pla′gia·rist**, *n.* —**pla′gia·ris′tic**, *adj.*
pla·gia·rize (plā′jə rīz′) *v.*, **pla·gia·rized, pla·gia·riz·ing.** —*v.t.* to take and pass off as one's own (someone else's work or ideas): *The writer plagiarized this passage from the encyclopedia.* —*v.i.* to commit plagiarism. —**pla′gia·riz′er**, *n.*

plague (plāg) *n.* **1.** any serious, often fatal disease that affects a large part of the population of an area. **2.** see **bubonic plague. 3.** a great misfortune or evil: *The land was ravaged by a plague of locusts.* **4.** a source of trouble or annoyance: *That bully is the plague of the schoolyard.* —*v.t.*, **plagued, plagu·ing. 1.** to afflict with a serious disease, misfortune, or evil: *After the storm, flooding and traffic breakdowns plagued the countryside.* **2.** to trouble or annoy: *Injuries plagued the team.*
plaice (plās) *n.*, *pl.* **plaice** or **plaic·es. 1.** a European flatfish found in the North Atlantic Ocean. **2.** any of various American flatfish.
plaid (plad) *n.* **1.** a pattern that has narrow and wide stripes of different colors crossing one another at right angles. **2.** a shawl having such a pattern. It is part of the traditional Scottish Highland dress. **3.** a fabric made with such a pattern. —*adj.* having such a pattern.
plain (plān) *adj.* **1.** clearly seen or heard; distinct: *She was in plain sight.* **2.** clearly understood; evident; obvious: *He made it plain that he did not agree.* **3.** downright; sheer: *That's just plain nonsense!* **4.** straightforward or direct; outspoken; frank: *I will be plain with you and tell you the truth.* **5.** without ornament; unadorned: *a plain black coat.* **6.** not rich or highly seasoned: *plain food.* **7.** unsophisticated or ordinary: *plain people.* **8.** not beautiful; homely: *a plain face.* —*n.* also, **plains.** an area of level or nearly level land. —**plain′ly**, *adv.* —**plain′ness**, *n.*
plain·clothes·man (plān′klōz′mən, plān′klōthz′mən) *n.*, *pl.* **plain·clothes·men** (plān′klōz′mən, plān′klōthz′mən). a police officer who wears civilian clothes while on duty.
Plains Indian, a member of any of various American Indian tribes who formerly lived on the Great Plains.
plains·man (plānz′mən) *n.*, *pl.* **plains·men** (plānz′mən). a person who lives on the plains.
plain·song (plān′sông′) *n.* medieval church music having a simple melody and sung in unison without accompaniment; Gregorian chant.
plain–spo·ken (plān′spō′kən) *adj.* open in speech; outspoken; frank.
plains·wom·an (plānz′wùm′ən) *n.*, *pl.* **plains·wom·en** (plānz′wim′ən). a woman who lives on the plains.
plaint (plānt) *n.* **1.** a complaint; grievance. **2.** *Archaic.* a lament.
plain·tiff (plān′tif) *n.* the person who brings a suit in a court of law; complainant.
plain·tive (plān′tiv) *adj.* expressing sorrow; mournful; sad: *The mourners had plaintive expressions.* —**plain′-tive·ly**, *adj.* —**plain′tive·ness**, *n.*
plait (plāte, plat) *n.* **1.** a braid, as of hair. **2.** another word for **pleat.** —*v.t.* **1.** to braid. **2.** to make by braiding: *The two friends plaited a rug.* Also, **plat. 3.** another word for **pleat.**
plan (plan) *n.* **1.** a method or way of doing something that has been thought out beforehand: *The general had a plan of attack.* **2.** something that a person intends to do: *I have no plans for this weekend.* **3.** a drawing or diagram that shows how the parts of something are to be arranged: *The architect drew up the plans for the house.* —*v.*, **planned, plan·ning.** —*v.t.* **1.** to prepare beforehand: *The general planned the defense of the city.* **2.** to have in mind; intend: *We plan to go shopping tomorrow.* **3.** to

at; āpe; fär; câre; end; mē; it; īce; pîerce; hot; ōld; sông, fôrk; oil; out; up; ūse; rüle; pùll; tûrn; chin; sing; shop; thin; this; hw in white; zh in treasure. The symbol ə stands for the unstressed vowel sound heard in about, taken, pencil, lemon, and circus.

P

make a drawing or diagram of; design: *The engineer planned a new bridge.* —*v.i.* to make a plan or plans: *to plan for a celebration.* —**plan′ner,** *n.*

pla·nar·i·an (plə när′ē ən) *n.* any of a group of flatworms living in freshwater lakes, streams, or ponds.

plane[1] (plān) *n.* **1.** a flat or level surface. **2.** a level or degree: *The student reached a high plane of achievement at school.* **3.** see **airplane.** **4.** *Geometry.* a flat surface that wholly contains every line connecting any two points on it. —*adj.* **1.** level; flat. **2.** of or relating to a plane or planes, or a figure contained in a plane: *a plane curve.* [From the Latin word *planus* meaning "level, flat[1], even[1]."]

plane[2] (plān) *n.* a hand tool with a blade that projects from the bottom, used for smoothing wood. —*v.,* **planed, plan·ing.** —*v.t.* to smooth with a plane. —*v.i.* to work with a plane. [From the Old French word *plane,* from the Late Latin word *plana* meaning this tool, going back to the Latin word *planus* "flat[1]."]

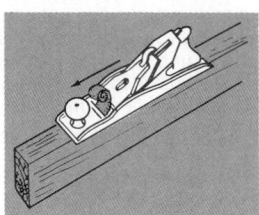

plane[2] *(n.)*

plane[3] (plān) *n.* see **plane tree.**

plane geometry, the branch of geometry that deals with plane figures.

plan·er (plā′nər) *n.* a person or thing that planes.

plan·et (plan′it) *n.* **1.** any one of the nine large bodies that revolve around the sun and shine by reflecting its light. The planets in order of their distance from the sun are Mercury, Venus, Earth, Mars, Jupiter, Saturn, Uranus, Neptune, and Pluto. **2.** any similar large celestial body. [From the Old French word *planete* meaning "a wandering star," from the Late Latin word *planeta,* from the Greek word *planētēs* meaning "wandering star, wanderer." The planets were so named because their paths seemed to wander in the sky among the stars.]

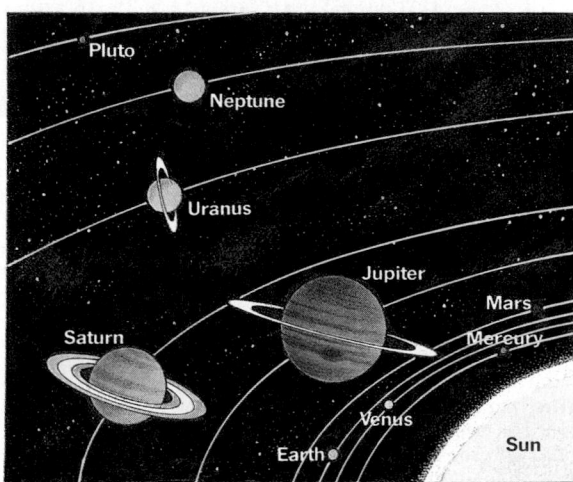

planets in the solar system

plan·e·tar·i·um (plan′i tär′ē əm) *n., pl.* **plan·e·tar·i·ums** or **plan·e·tar·i·a** (plan′i tär′ē ə). **1.** an apparatus that shows the positions and motions of stars, planets, and other heavenly bodies by projecting their images on the inside of a dome. **2.** a room or building housing such an apparatus.

plan·e·tar·y (plan′i ter′ē) *adj.* of, relating to, or resembling a planet.

plan·et·oid (plan′i toid′) *n.* another word for **asteroid.**

plane tree, any of a group of trees having smooth, brown bark that flakes off in thin layers, and bearing clusters of tiny flowers at the ends of the branches. The plane tree

of North America is also called the sycamore. [From the Old French word *plane,* from the Latin word *platanus,* from the Greek *platanos,* all meaning this tree.]

plank (plangk) *n.* **1.** a long, flat piece of sawed wood. **2.** a statement of a goal or principle forming part of the platform of a political party. —*v.t.* **1.** to cover or lay with planks. **2.** to cook and serve (steak or fish) on a board. **3.** *Informal.* to put down quickly or forcefully: *I planked down the money to pay my share of the bill.*

·**to walk the plank.** to walk blindfolded off a plank that sticks out over the water from a ship.

plank·ing (plang′king) *n.* **1.** planks as a group: *the planking on a floor.* **2.** the act of covering or laying with planks.

plank·ton (plangk′tən) *n.* very small plants and animals that drift or float in the sea or another body of water. Plankton is made up of mostly microscopic algae and protozoans. It is the basic source of food for many animals that live in the sea.

plant (plant) *n.* **1.** any of a large kingdom of living things that are not able to move about, have cell walls of cellulose, and respond slowly to stimuli. Plants have chlorophyll and are able to produce their own food by photosynthesis. Trees, flowers, mosses, liverworts, and most algae are plants. **2.** a small plant having a soft stem, as distinguished from a tree or shrub. **3.** a young tree, vine, shrub, or other plant recently planted or ready for planting. **4.** the buildings, machinery, tools, and the like used in manufacturing; factory: *an automobile plant.* **5.** equipment for a particular purpose: *a heating plant for an office building.* **6.** the buildings and equipment of a facility, as a school or hospital. **7.** *Slang.* a person or thing placed in a location in order to deceive or trick. —*v.t.* **1.** to set or place in the ground so that it will take root and grow: *to plant seeds, to plant a small tree.* **2.** to furnish (land) with growing plants. **3.** to fix or introduce in the mind; instill. **4.** to place or set firmly in position: *to plant one's feet on the ground.* **5.** *Slang.* to place (someone or something) in order to deceive or trick: *to plant fake evidence.*

plan·tain[1] (plan′tən) *n.* **1.** a large greenish yellow fruit resembling a banana. **2.** the plant bearing this fruit. [From the Spanish word *plántan* meaning "plane tree," from the Latin word *platanus,* from the Greek *platanos,* all meaning this tree.]

plan·tain[2] (plan′tən) *n.* a plant found as a common weed, bearing clusters of tiny flowers and large leaves. [From the Old French word *plantain,* from the Latin word *plantago* meaning this plant.]

plan·ta·tion (plan tā′shən) *n.* **1.** a large estate or farm where one crop is grown: *a sugar plantation.* **2.** a group of plants, such as rubber trees, grown as a crop.

plant·er (plan′tər) *n.* **1.** a person or machine that plants. **2.** a person who owns or manages a plantation. **3.** a container for growing plants.

plant louse, aphid.

plaque (plak) *n.* **1.** a flat plate or slab of hard material, such as porcelain, wood, or metal, that is ornamented or engraved for mounting on a wall. **2.** a thick, white film that forms on the surface of the teeth as a result of the growth of bacteria.

plash (plash) *v; n., pl.* **plash·es.** another word for **splash.**

plas·ma (plaz′mə) *n.* **1.** a clear yellow liquid that forms the fluid portion of blood, and in which the blood cells are suspended. **2.** *Physics.* a highly ionized gas, as found in the sun or in lightning bolts. Plasma can also be created by passing an electrical current through a gas.

plas·mo·di·um (plaz mō′dē əm) *n., pl.* **plas·mo·di·a** (plaz mō′dē ə). any of several parasitic protozoans, especially one that causes malaria in humans.

plas·ter (plas′tər) *n.* **1.** a mixture of lime, sand, and water that becomes a hard, smooth material when dry, used for coating walls and ceilings. **2.** see **plaster of Paris.**

3. a medical preparation that is spread on cloth and then applied to the body for healing purposes. —*v.t.* **1.** to cover or coat with plaster. **2.** to cover thoroughly, as if with plaster: *The workers plastered the fence with posters.* **3.** to spread thickly or abundantly: *to plaster mustard on a sandwich.* **4.** to cause to lie flat: *The rain has plastered your hair against your head.* —**plas′ter·er,** *n.*

plas·ter·board (plas′tər bôrd′) *n.* a thin, firm board composed of layers of paper and plaster, used for walls or partitions.

plaster of Par·is (par′is) powdered gypsum that is mixed with water to form a paste that dries rapidly into a hard, solid mass. It is used for making molds, casts, or copies of works of art. [From *Paris,* France, where this form of plaster was first used.]

plas·tic (plas′tik) *n.* a synthetic material that can be molded or shaped when soft. Cellophane and vinyl are plastics. —*adj.* **1.** capable of being molded or shaped: *Wax is a plastic material.* **2.** of or relating to molding or shaping: *Ceramics is a plastic art.* **3.** made of plastic: *The radio has a plastic cabinet.* —**plas′ti·cal·ly,** *adv.* —**plas·tic·i·ty** (plas tis′i tē), *n.*

plastic surgery, surgery for repairing or replacing injured or badly formed parts of the body.

plat[1] (plat) *n.* **1.** a small piece of ground; plot. **2.** a map, chart, or plan. [A form of *plot.*]

plat[2] (plat) *n., v.t.,* **plat·ted, plat·ting.** another word for **plait.**

plate (plāt) *n.* **1.** a flat or shallow dish for holding food to be served or eaten: *Set the plates on the table.* **2.** the food held by such a dish: *a plate of spaghetti.* **3.** food for one person at a meal. **4.** a dish passed to take collections, as in a church. **5.** dishes or table utensils made of or coated with a layer of silver or gold. **6.** a flat thin sheet of metal of even thickness and surface: *a plate of steel.* **7.** armor made of such pieces of metal. **8.** a piece of metal on which something is or can be engraved, such as a license plate or a plate used for printing. **9.** a print made from an engraved piece of metal, as an illustration in a book: *The art book has many color plates.* **10.** *Printing.* a cast of a page of type to be printed, such as an electrotype or a stereotype. **11.** *Photography.* a thin sheet of glass, metal, or other material coated with a substance sensitive to light, used to take photographs. **12.** *Baseball.* see **home plate. 13.** a piece of metal, plastic, or similar material with a set of artificial teeth, fitted to the gums to replace missing teeth. **14.** *Geology.* one of the large sections that form the earth's crust. **15.** a thin cut of beef from the lower end of the breast or brisket. —*v.t.,* **plat·ed, plat·ing. 1.** to coat with a layer of metal: *Plating steel with tin prevents rust from forming.* **2.** to cover with metal plates for protection. **3.** *Printing.* to make an electrotype or stereotype from (a page of type). —**plate′like′,** *adj.*

pla·teau (pla tō′) *n., pl.* **pla·teaus** or **pla·teaux** (pla-tōz′). **1.** an area of flat land raised above the surrounding land. **2.** a stage, as in development: *The economy reached a new plateau.* [From the French word *plateau* meaning "tableland," from the Old French word *plat* "flat."]

plate·ful (plāt′fül′) *n., pl.* **plate·fuls.** as much as a plate will hold, especially a large amount of food.

plate glass, a strong glass made in clear, flat sheets, used for windowpanes or mirrors.

plate·let (plāt′lit) *n.* any of the round, oval, or rod-shaped microscopic structures in the blood that aid in blood clotting.

plat·en (plat′ən) *n.* **1.** the flat plate on a printing press that presses paper against inked metal type. **2.** a cylindrical device in a typewriter or computer printer around which paper is fed. The platen holds the paper in place during typing or printing.

plate tectonics (tek ton′iks). **1.** the theory that the earth's crust consists of individual rigid plates that slowly move in various directions. Earthquakes, volcanic activity, and the formation of mountains often can be linked to forces generated at the adjacent edges of two plates moving in different directions. **2.** the branch of geology that studies this theory.

plat·form (plat′fôrm′) *n.* **1.** a raised, flat structure or flooring: *The speaker stood on a platform. We waited on the platform for the train.* **2.** a statement of principles, especially a public statement of the principles and policies of a political party.

platform tennis, a form of tennis that is played with wooden paddles and a rubber ball on a wooden platform surrounded by a high wire fence.

plat·ing (plā′ting) *n.* a thin coating or layer of metal.

plat·i·num (plat′ə nəm) *n.* a heavy, soft, silvery metallic element that is ductile, malleable, and resistant to corrosion. It is used in alloys, jewelry, and catalytic converters. Symbol: **Pt** [Formed from the Spanish word *platina* meaning "platinum," from the word *plata* "silver," referring to its color.]

plat·i·tude (plat′i tüd, plat′i tūd′) *n.* a dull, trite, or commonplace remark, especially one meant to sound original or important.

plat·i·tu·di·nous (plat′i tü′də nəs, plat′i tū′də nəs) *adj.* **1.** of, relating to, or having the nature of a platitude; trite: *a platitudinous statement.* **2.** given to or full of platitudes. —**plat′i·tu′di·nous·ly,** *adv.*

Pla·ton·ic (plə ton′ik) *adj.* **1.** of or relating to Plato or his philosophy. **2.** *also,* **platonic.** of or relating to a relationship between a man and woman that is spiritual or intellectual rather than sexual. —**Pla·ton′i·cal·ly,** *adv.*

Pla·to·nism (plā′tə niz′əm) *n.* the philosophy of Plato or his followers.

pla·toon (plə tün′) *n.* **1.** a military unit forming part of a company, usually commanded by a lieutenant. **2.** a group of football players who specialize in either offensive or defensive play and enter or leave the game as a unit. —*v.i., v.t. Sports.* to play alternately with another teammate at one position: *The manager platooned two players in the infield.*

plat·ter (plat′ər) *n.* a large, oval, flat dish for serving food, especially fish or meat: *a platter of roast beef.*

plat·y·pus (plat′ə pəs) *n., pl.* **plat·y·pus·es.** an egg laying mammal that lives along streams in Australia and Tasmania. It has a flat, wide bill that is very sensitive to touch, webbed feet, and a plump body covered with soft brown fur. Also, **duckbill, duck-billed platypus.**

platypus

plau·dit (plô′dit) *n. usually,* **plau·dits.** an expression of praise or approval: *The speaker sought the plaudits of the crowd.*

plau·si·ble (plô′zə bəl) *adj.* seeming to be true, honest, or worthy of trust: *What he says is plausible. Her excuse was plausible, but I still had doubts.* —**plau′si·bil′i·ty, plau′si·ble·ness,** *n.* —**plau′si·bly,** *adv.*

P

---

at; āpe; fär; câre; end; mē; it; īce; pîerce; hot; ōld; sông, fôrk; oil; out; up; ūse; rüle; pùll; tûrn; chin; sing; shop; thin; this; hw in white; zh in treasure. The symbol ə stands for the unstressed vowel sound heard in about, taken, pencil, lemon, and circus.

play (plā) *n.* **1.** something done for pleasure or amusement; recreation: *The children spent several hours at play.* **2.** the act or manner of carrying on a game: *The play began when the coach blew the whistle.* **3.** a move or turn to move in a game. **4.** a work of literature written to be performed on a stage; drama. **5.** a way of acting or behaving: *He is admired for his sense of fair play.* **6.** action or operation: *The engine was in full play.* **7.** a quick flickering movement: *a play of light across a surface.* **8.** freedom of movement: *The play of the wheel was hindered by the tight bolt.* —*v.i.* **1.** to do something for pleasure or amusement; have fun: *The children played in the backyard.* **2.** to act carelessly with something; toy: *Don't play with matches.* **3.** to perform in a play, movie, or television program. **4.** to be performed or presented: *What is playing on television tonight?* **5.** to act or behave in a particular way: *That politician plays rough.* **6.** to perform music or perform on a musical instrument: *The band is playing.* **7.** to give out sound or music: *The phonograph stopped playing.* **8.** to have a quick, flickering movement: *A smile played on her lips.* **9.** to be in a game: *I played for three innings.* —*v.t.* **1.** to act the part of or behave like: *He played an old sailor in the movie.* **2.** to make believe or pretend to be for pleasure or amusement: *The children played cowboys and Indians.* **3.** to do, especially in fun: *to play a trick on someone.* **4.** to cause to act or operate: *The firefighter played the hose on the burning building.* **5.** to perform on (a musical instrument): *She plays the clarinet.* **6.** to perform: *The orchestra played two symphonies.* **7.** to cause to give out sound or music: *to play one's radio.* **8.** to be in (a game or other activity): *The two friends played tennis.* **9.** to be in a game against; contend against: *Our team plays their high school in basketball.* **10.** to be in (a particular position) in a game: *Who will play first base?* **11.** to bet on: *to play the horses.* —**play'a·ble,** *adj.*
 •**in play.** *Sports.* being in use or motion: *The ball is in play.*
 •**out of play.** *Sports.* no longer in use or on the field.
 •**to play down.** to treat as of little or no importance; understate the importance of.
 •**to play into the hands of.** to act so that another gets an advantage.
 •**to play off.** to play one or more games in order to settle a tie.
 •**to play on. a.** to take advantage of: *to play on a person's sympathies.* **b.** to continue to play: *to play on despite an injury.*
 •**to play up.** to treat as of much importance; stress the importance of.
 •**to play up to.** *Informal.* to try to gain the favor of.

play·back (plā'bak') *n.* the act or process of playing a recording again, especially a sound or video tape that has just been made.

play·bill (plā'bil') *n.* a program or announcement of a play.

play·boy (plā'boi') *n.* a man who spends much of his time seeking pleasure, especially a wealthy man.

play·er (plā'ər) *n.* **1.** a person who plays in a sport or game: *a baseball player, a chess player.* **2.** a person who performs on the stage; actor. **3.** a person who performs on a musical instrument; musician: *a piano player.* **4.** a mechanical device or machine for giving out sound or music: *a record player.*

player piano, a piano played by a mechanical device.

play·fel·low (plā'fel'ō) *n.* another word for **playmate.**

play·ful (plā'fəl) *adj.* **1.** full of spirit and play; frolicsome; lively: *a playful puppy.* **2.** humorous; joking: *a playful remark.* —**play'ful·ly,** *adv.* —**play'ful·ness,** *n.*

play·go·er (plā'gō'ər) *n.* a person who goes to the theater regularly or often.

play·ground (plā'ground') *n.* an area used for outdoor recreation, especially by children.

play·house (plā'hous') *n., pl.* **play·hous·es** (plā'hou'ziz). **1.** a place where plays and the like are given; theater. **2.** a small house for children to play in.

playing card, a card used in playing games, especially one of a deck of fifty-two cards divided into four suits (clubs, diamonds, hearts, and spades) and thirteen ranks (jacks, queens, kings, aces, and the numbers from two to ten).

play·mate (plā'māt') *n.* a companion in games and other amusements.

play·off (plā'ôf') *n.* **1.** a game played to break a tie. **2.** one or more games played to decide a championship or who will play for a championship.

play·pen (plā'pen') *n.* a small, usually portable enclosure, used for a baby or small child to play in.

play·room (plā'rüm', plā'rùm') *n.* a room, usually in a home, for a child or children to play in.

play·thing (plā'thing') *n.* a thing to play with; toy: *The children's playthings were put neatly away.*

play·wright (plā'rīt') *n.* a person who writes plays.

plaza *(def. 1)*

pla·za (plä'zə, plaz'ə) *n.* **1.** a public square or open space in a city or town. **2.** a shopping area or shopping center. **3.** a service area along a superhighway.

plea (plē) *n.* **1.** an earnest request or appeal: *a plea for help.* **2.** a reason given as an explanation; excuse. **3.** *Law.* the answer given by the accused to a formal charge: *to enter a plea of not guilty.*

plea bargaining, in law, the practice of allowing the defendant in a criminal case to plead guilty to a less serious charge in order to avoid a long, costly, or difficult trial over the original charge or to obtain the defendant's testimony in prosecuting persons accused of other crimes.

plead (plēd) *v.,* **plead·ed** or **pled, plead·ing.** —*v.i.* **1.** to make an earnest request or appeal; beg: *to plead for mercy.* **2.** to argue a case in a court of law: *to plead before a jury.* —*v.t.* **1.** to give as an excuse: *to plead illness.* **2.** to argue (a case or cause) in a court of law. **3.** to give as an answer to a charge in a court of law: *to plead not guilty.*

pleas·ant (plez'ənt) *adj.* **1.** giving pleasure; pleasing; agreeable: *pleasant surroundings.* **2.** having or showing pleasing manners or behavior: *a pleasant personality.* —**pleas'ant·ly,** *adv.* —**pleas'ant·ness,** *n.*

pleas·ant·ry (plez'ən trē) *n., pl.* **pleas·ant·ries. 1.** a pleasant, courteous remark. **2.** a humorous or playful remark or action.

please (plēz) *v.,* **pleased, pleas·ing.** —*v.t.* **1.** to give pleasure to; be agreeable to: *Winning the prize really pleased her. It pleases me to see you so happy.* **2.** to be so kind as to. ▲ used to express a request or command politely: *Please close the door.* **3.** to be the will of: *May it please Your Honor to hear this testimony.* —*v.i.* **1.** to give pleasure; be agreeable: *He is trying very hard to please.* **2.** to have the will or desire; choose: *You may come back to visit whenever you please.* [From the Old French word *plaisir* meaning "to please," from the Latin word *placēre* "to please."]

pleas·ing (plē′zing) *adj.* giving pleasure; agreeable. —**pleas′ing·ly**, *adv.* —**pleas′ing·ness**, *n.*

pleas·ur·a·ble (plezh′ər e bəl) *adj.* giving pleasure: *a pleasurable experience.* —**pleas′ur·a·ble·ness**, *n.* —**pleas′ur·a·bly**, *adv.*

pleas·ure (plezh′ər) *n.* **1.** an enjoyable or delightful feeling or emotion: *He takes great pleasure in helping other people. The children's pleasure showed in their faces.* **2.** something that gives such a feeling or emotion: *It is a pleasure to be here again.* **3.** amusement that satisfies the senses or appetites. **4.** desire; will: *It is Her Majesty's pleasure that you join her.*

pleat (plēt) *n.* a lengthwise, flat fold in cloth or other material, made by doubling the material upon itself and then fastening or pressing it into place. —*v.t.* to make a pleat or pleats in; arrange in pleats. Also, **plait.**

plebe (plēb) *n.* a member of the first-year class at the U.S. Military Academy or Naval Academy.

ple·be·ian (pli bē′ən) *n.* **1.** a member of the common people in ancient Rome. **2.** a person who is ordinary, common, or vulgar. —*adj.* **1.** of or relating to the common people of ancient Rome. **2.** ordinary, common, or vulgar: *plebeian tastes in art.*

pleb·i·scite (pleb′ə sīt′) *n.* a direct vote by the people of a country or state on a single question or issue.

plec·trum (plek′trəm) *also,* **plec·tron** (plek′trən). *n., pl.* **plec·trums** or **plec·tra** (plek′trə). a small, thin piece of horn, plastic, or other material, used for plucking the strings of a guitar or similar instrument. Also, **pick.**

pled (pled) a past tense and past participle of **plead.**

pledge (plej) *n.* **1.** a solemn or formal promise: *a pledge of secrecy.* **2.** something given or held as security: *He left his watch as a pledge that he would pay the debt.* **3.** the state of being held as security: *She left her money in pledge.* **4.** something given as a token: *The rings they exchanged were pledges of their love.* **5.** an expression of good will made by drinking to a person's health; toast. —*v.t.,* **pledged, pledg·ing. 1.** to guarantee with a pledge; promise solemnly or formally: *We pledged our help. They pledged allegiance to the flag.* **2.** to bind or commit to or as by a pledge: *The traitors pledged themselves to secrecy.* **3.** to give (something) as security. **4.** to drink a toast to.

Plei·o·cene (plī′ə sēn′) another spelling of **Pliocene.**

Pleis·to·cene (plīs′tə sēn′) *n.* the first geological epoch of the Quaternary period of the Cenozoic era. During the Pleistocene, glaciers advanced, and then receded, over large areas of North and South America, Europe, and Asia, and human beings appeared. Also, **Ice Age.** —*adj.* of, relating to, or belonging to this epoch.

ple·na·ry (plē′nə rē, plen′ə rē) *adj.* **1.** attended by everyone who is a member: *The members of Congress attended a plenary session.* **2.** full; complete: *The diplomat was given plenary powers.*

plen·i·po·ten·ti·ar·y (plen′i pə ten′chē er′ē) *n., pl.* **plen·i·po·ten·ti·ar·ies.** an ambassador or other diplomat having full power to represent a government. —*adj.* having full power.

plen·i·tude (plen′i tüd′, plen′i tūd′) *n.* the quality or state of being abundant; abundance.

plen·te·ous (plen′tē əs) *adj.* in great quantity; plentiful. —**plen′te·ous·ly**, *adv.* —**plen′te·ous·ness**, *n.*

plen·ti·ful (plen′ti fəl) *adj.* **1.** in great quantity; abundant; ample: *Food was plentiful on the prosperous farm.*

2. providing or yielding an abundance: *a plentiful harvest.* —**plen′ti·ful·ly**, *adv.* —**plen′ti·ful·ness**, *n.*

plen·ty (plen′tē) *n., pl.* **plen·ties. 1.** a full supply or amount: *There's plenty of milk in the refrigerator.* **2.** more than enough food and material goods; general prosperity: *a time of plenty.* —*adj.* ample; plentiful: *One helping of meat is plenty for me.*

ple·si·o·saur (plē′sē ə sôr′) *n.* an extinct water-dwelling reptile that had a small head, a long neck, and four paddlelike limbs.

ple·si·o·saur·us (plē′sē ə sôr′əs) *n. pl.,* **ple·si·o·sau·ri** (plē′sē ə sôr′ī) or **ple·si·o·sau·rus·es.** another word for **plesiosaur.**

pleth·o·ra (pleth′ər ə) *n.* more than is needed; too much; excess.

pleu·ra (plur′ə) *n., pl.* **pleu·rae** (plur′ē). a thin membrane enclosing the lungs and lining the inner walls of the chest cavity. —**pleu′ral**, *adj.*

pleu·ri·sy (plur′ə sē) *n.* an inflammation of the pleura, often accompanied by fever, difficulty in breathing, and a painful cough. Also, **pleu·ri·tis** (plù rī′tis).

Plex·i·glas (plek′si glas′) *n. Trademark.* a strong, transparent plastic.

plex·us (plek′səs) *n., pl.* **plex·us·es** or **plex·us.** a network of fibers, as of nerves or blood vessels.

pli·a·ble (plī′ə bəl) *adj.* **1.** easily molded or bent; flexible: *Clay and wax are pliable.* **2.** easily influenced or persuaded: *a pliable personality.* —**pli′a·bil′i·ty, pli′a·ble·ness**, *n.* —**pli′a·bly**, *adv.*

pli·an·cy (plī′ən sē) *n.* the state or quality of being pliant.

pli·ant (plī′ənt) *adj.* **1.** easily bent; pliable; supple: *pliant material.* **2.** easily influenced or controlled: *a pliant person.* —**pli′ant·ly**, *adv.*

pli·ers (plī′ərz) *pl. n.* small pincers used chiefly for gripping and bending things.

plight¹ (plīt) *n.* a situation or condition, especially one that is bad: *the terrible plight of flood victims.* [From the Middle English word *plight* meaning "danger" or "condition," from both the Old English word *pliht* "danger" and the Old French word *ploit* "condition."]

plight² (plīt) *v.t.* to bind by a pledge; promise. [From the Middle English word *plighten* meaning "to pledge, promise," from the Old English word *plihtan* "to put into danger." The word referred to the penalties that would follow if a person broke a promise.]

plink (plingk) *n.* a light, sharp, high sound, such as one made on a piano. —*v.i.* to make such a sound. —*v.t.* to cause to make such a sound: *to plink a banjo.*

plinth (plinth) *n.* a slab, block, stone, or base on which a column, pedestal, or the like rests.

Pli·o·cene (plī′ə sēn′) *also,* **Plei·o·cene.** *n.* the fifth and last geological epoch of the Tertiary period of the Cenozoic era. During the Pliocene, most of the major mountain ranges were formed. —*adj.* of or relating to this epoch.

PLO, Palestine Liberation Organization.

plod (plod) *v.i.,* **plod·ded, plod·ding. 1.** to walk or move slowly and heavily; trudge: *The tired child silently plodded through the snow.* **2.** to work slowly but steadily: *The student plodded through*

plinth

at; āpe; fär; câre; end; mē; it; īce; pîerce; hot; ōld; sông, fôrk; oil; out; up; ūse; rüle; pùll; tûrn; chin; sing; shop; thin; this; hw in white; zh in treasure. The symbol ə stands for the unstressed vowel sound heard in about, taken, pencil, lemon, and circus.

the geography textbook. —*n.* the act of plodding. —**plod′der,** *n.*

plop (plop) *v.,* **plopped, plop·ping.** —*v.i.* to drop or fall heavily with a sound like that of an object dropping into water. —*v.t.* to drop or let fall so as to make such a sound. —*n.* the act or sound of plopping: *The wet clay fell on the floor with a plop.*

plot (plot) *n.* **1.** a secret plan, especially to bring about an evil or illegal purpose: *The criminals formed a plot to kidnap the banker.* **2.** the main story in a play, novel, or other literary work. **3.** a small piece of ground: *a cemetery plot.* **4.** a chart, diagram, or map. —*v.,* **plot·ted, plot·ting.** —*v.t.* **1.** to make a secret plan for: *The thieves plotted an attack on the safe.* **2.** to make a diagram or map of; chart: *The navigator plotted the ship's course.* —*v.i.* to form a plot; scheme. [From the Old English word *plot* meaning "a plot of ground."] —**plot′ter,** *n.*

plo·ver (pluv′ər, plō′vər) *n.* any of various birds that have a straight bill and a short tail and live along the shore.

plow (plou) *also,* **plough.** *n.* **1.** a farm tool for turning over or breaking up the soil for sowing or planting. A plow is usually drawn by animals or by a tractor. **2.** any of various devices resembling a plow in shape or use, such as a snowplow. —*v.t.* **1.** to break and turn up the surface of (soil) with a plow: *The farmer plowed the field.* **2.** to form or make with or as if with a plow: *We plowed our way through the crowd in front of the theater.* —*v.i.* **1.** to break and turn up soil with a plow. **2.** to move forward steadily, forcefully, or with difficulty.

plover

plow·man (plou′mən) *also,* **plough·man.** *n., pl.* **plow·men** (plou′mən). **1.** a person who guides or operates a plow. **2.** a farmer or farm worker.

plow·share (plou′shâr′) *also,* **plough·share.** *n.* the front edge or blade of a plow, which cuts the soil.

ploy (ploi) *n.* a tricky move or piece of strategy: *We thought your crying was a ploy to gain our sympathy.*

pluck (pluk) *v.t.* **1.** to pull out or off; pick: *to pluck the feathers from a chicken.* **2.** to pull out the hair or feathers from: *to pluck one's eyebrows.* **3.** to pull with sudden force or with a jerk; snatch: *He plucked the letter from her hands.* **4.** to pull on and quickly let go of (the strings of a musical instrument), causing them to sound. —*v.i.* to give a pull; grasp; tug: *The little child plucked at the drooping tablecloth.* —*n.* **1.** spirit and courage, especially in the face of danger or difficulty. **2.** the act of pulling; tug; jerk.

pluck·y (pluk′ē) *adj.,* **pluck·i·er, pluck·i·est.** having or showing spirit and courage, especially in the face of danger or difficulty. —**pluck′i·ly,** *adv.* —**pluck′i·ness,** *n.*

plug (plug) *n.* **1.** a piece of wood, rubber, or other material used to close up a hole or fill a gap. **2.** a fitting with one or more prongs, attached to the end of a wire or cable and inserted into an outlet to make an electrical connection. **3.** a cake of pressed or twisted tobacco, or a piece of it cut off for chewing. **4.** see **spark plug** (*def. 1*). **5.** *Informal.* a favorable mention of or piece of publicity about someone or something: *The product received a free plug on the television show.* **6.** *Slang.* an old or worn-out horse. —*v.,* **plugged, plug·ging.** —*v.t.* **1.** to stop or fill with or as if with a plug: *The coffee grounds plugged the kitchen drain.* **2.** *Informal.* to make favorable public mention of; publicize or advertise: *The disc jockey plugged the singer's new record.* —*v.i. Informal.* to work hard or persistently: *I kept plugging until I solved the math problem.* —**plug′ger,** *n.*

·to plug in. to insert the plug of (an electrical device) into an outlet to make a connection: *to plug in a toaster.*

plum (plum) *n.* **1.** the round or oval fruit of a tree of the rose family, having a flattened pit, soft, juicy flesh that can be eaten, and smooth reddish purple or bluish red skin. **2.** the tree bearing this fruit, having oval leaves and small white or pink flowers. **3.** something very good or desirable, such as a fine job or position. **4.** a reddish purple or bluish red color. **5.** a raisin, when added to a pudding or other dish. —*adj.* having the color plum.

plum·age (plü′mij) *n.* the feathers of a bird.

plumb (plum) *v.t.* **1.** to test or adjust by a plumb line. **2.** to measure the depth of (a body of water) with a plumb line. **3.** to discover or examine closely the dimensions, nature, or contents of: *to plumb a mystery.* **4.** to make vertical; straighten. —*adj.* **1.** vertical; straight. **2.** *Informal.* complete; total: *That's plumb nonsense.* —*adv.* **1.** in a vertical direction or line; vertically: *The wall must run plumb.* **2.** *Informal.* completely; totally: *plumb crazy.* —*n.* see **plumb bob.**

plumb bob, a weight at the end of a plumb line. Also, **plumb, plummet.**

plumb·er (plum′ər) *n.* a person who installs and repairs plumbing.

plumb·ing (plum′ing) *n.* **1.** the pipes and fixtures for bringing water into or taking water and wastes out of a building or other structure. **2.** the work that is done by a plumber.

plumb line, a line from which a weight hangs, used to measure depths, as of bodies of water, or to test whether something is vertical. Also, **plummet.**

plume (plüm) *n.* **1.** a large, fluffy, showy feather. **2.** an ornament made up of a plume or cluster of plumes, or of a feathery tuft of fluffy material. **3.** something resembling a plume: *A plume of smoke rose from the fire.* —*v.t.,* **plumed, plum·ing.** **1.** to adorn with a plume or plumes. **2.** (of a bird) to smooth (itself) with the beak; preen.

plum·met (plum′it) *v.i.* to fall or drop straight downward; plunge. —*n.* **1.** another word for **plumb bob.** **2.** another word for **plumb line.**

plump¹ (plump) *adj.* having a full or rounded form; somewhat fat or well filled out: *a plump child, a plump cushion.* —*v.t.* to make plump: *I plumped the pillows on the couch.* —*v.i.* to become plump. [Probably from the Middle Dutch word *plomp* meaning "blunt."] —**plump′ness,** *n.*

plump² (plump) *v.i.* to fall or drop heavily or suddenly: *They plumped down onto the sofa.* —*v.t.* to throw, put, or let fall heavily or suddenly. —*n.* a sudden or heavy fall or the sound of such a fall: *to hit the floor with a plump.* —*adv.* heavily or suddenly: *The book fell plump on the floor.* [Probably from the Middle English word *plumpen* meaning "to plunge into water."]

plum pudding, a boiled or steamed pudding made of flour, suet, eggs, raisins, currants, and spices.

plum·y (plü′mē) *adj.,* **plum·i·er, plum·i·est.** **1.** covered or adorned with feathers or plumes: *a plumy hat.* **2.** like a plume; feathery.

plun·der (plun′dər) *v.t.* **1.** to loot or rob, as during a war: *The Mongols plundered northern China in the thirteenth century.* **2.** to take illegally or by force; steal: *to plunder goods.* —*v.i.* to take goods or valuables by force. —*n.* **1.** something that is taken by plundering; booty; loot: *The thieves divided the plunder among themselves.* **2.** the act of plundering. —**plun′der·er,** *n.*

plunge (plunj) *v.,* **plunged, plung·ing.** —*v.t.* **1.** to put forcefully or suddenly; thrust: *to plunge one's hand into water.* **2.** to force or place suddenly into some condition or course of action: *A power failure plunged the room into darkness.* —*v.i.* **1.** to dive, fall, or move suddenly or sharply in a downward direction: *The elevator plunged three stories when the cable snapped.* **2.** to move quickly, suddenly, or with a headlong lunge. **3.** to enter or fall suddenly into some condition or course of action: *The nations plunged into war.* **4.** to go downward suddenly: *The road plunges toward the beach.* —*n.* **1.** the act or motion of plunging. **2.** *Informal.* a swim: *to go for a plunge in the pool.*

plung·er (plun′jər) *n.* **1.** a device made of a rubber suction cup attached to the end of a long handle, used to clear toilets and drains that are stopped up. **2.** any device or machine that works with a plunging or thrusting motion, especially a piston when it is part of a pump. **3.** a person or thing that plunges.

plunk (plungk) *Informal. v.t.* **1.** to pluck or strum the strings of (a musical instrument): *to plunk a banjo.* **2.** to throw or put heavily or suddenly: *I plunked down all my change.* —*v.i.* **1.** to drop or fall heavily or suddenly: *The stone plunked into the pond.* **2.** to make a twanging sound, as a banjo. —*n.* **1.** the act or sound of plunking. **2.** a heavy, direct blow.

plu·per·fect (plü pûr′fikt) *Grammar. n.* the past perfect tense. —*adj.* of, relating to, or designating the past perfect tense.

plur., plural.

plunger
(def. 1)

plu·ral (plür′əl) *adj.* **1.** of, relating to, or containing more than one. **2.** of or relating to a grammatical form showing more than one: *a plural noun, a plural verb.* —*n.* the form of a word showing more than one. *Doors* is the plural of *door,* and *women* is the plural of *woman.* —**plu′ral·ly,** *adv.*

plu·ral·i·ty (plü ral′i tē) *n., pl.* **plu·ral·i·ties.** **1.** the number of votes that a winning candidate receives over and above the number cast for the nearest opponent. **2.** the number of votes cast for any one candidate in a contest of more than two candidates, if it is greater than the number received by any other candidate, but not greater than one half of the total votes cast. **3.** the state or fact of being plural. ▲ See **majority** for usage note.

plus (plus) *prep.* **1.** increased by; added to: *Two plus two is four.* **2.** with the addition of; together with: *The set consists of a table plus chairs.* *adj.* **1.** somewhat higher than: *a grade of C plus.* **2.** favorable: *a plus factor.* **3.** more than zero; positive: *plus four.* **4.** showing addition or a positive quantity: *a plus sign.* —*n., pl.* **plus·es.** **1.** a sign (+) showing addition or a positive quantity. Also, **plus sign. 2.** a favorable factor or quality: *Your good record is a plus in your favor.* **3.** a positive quantity.

plush (plush) *adj.* showing or characterized by richness or luxury; luxurious: *Although it strained our budget, we stayed at a plush hotel.* —*n., pl.* **plush·es.** a fabric similar to but having a deeper pile than velvet, used especially for upholstery. —**plush′y,** *adj.*

Plu·to (plü′tō) *n.* **1.** *Greek Mythology.* the god of the dead and ruler of the underworld. Also, **Hades. 2.** the smallest planet in our solar system and the ninth planet in order of distance from the sun.

plu·toc·ra·cy (plü tok′rə sē) *n., pl.* **plu·toc·ra·cies. 1.** government by the wealthy. **2.** a powerful or influential class of wealthy persons.

plu·to·crat (plü′tə krat′) *n.* **1.** a person who has power or influence because of wealth. **2.** a wealthy person.

plu·to·crat·ic (plü′tə krat′ik) *adj.* relating to plutocrats or plutocracy. —**plu′to·crat′i·cal·ly,** *adv.*

plu·to·ni·um (plü tō′nē əm) *n.* a silvery, poisonous, radioactive metallic element produced artificially from uranium. It is used as a fuel in nuclear reactors and as the fission material in atomic bombs. Symbol: **Pu** [From

the planet *Pluto.* On the periodic table, this is the next element after neptunium, as Pluto is the next planet beyond Neptune.]

plu·vi·al (plü′vē əl) *adj.* of or relating to rain.

ply[1] (plī) *v.,* **plied, ply·ing.** —*v.t.* **1.** to use or apply; work with: *The carpenter plied his saw and chisel.* **2.** to work at or pursue busily or steadily; practice: *She plied her trade as a carpenter.* **3.** to provide often: *The teacher plied us with good books.* **4.** to address urgently or repeatedly: *The lawyer plied the witness with questions.* **5.** to travel regularly: *The boat plies the route from the island to the mainland.* —*v.i.* to travel the same course regularly. [Short for *apply.*]

ply[2] (plī) *n., pl.* **plies. 1.** a fold or layer, as of cloth or wood. **2.** one of the strands twisted together to make yarn, rope, or similar material. ▲ used in combination to show a certain number of layers or strands: *two-ply tissues, three-ply yarn.* [From the Old French word *pli* meaning "a fold, pleat," going back to the Latin word *plicare* "to fold up."]

Plym·outh Colony (plim′əth) the first English settlement in New England, founded by the Pilgrims at Plymouth, Massachusetts, in 1620.

Plymouth Rock 1. a rock at Plymouth, Massachusetts, on which the Pilgrims, according to tradition, disembarked in 1620. **2.** one of an American breed of domestic chickens that are raised for their meat and eggs.

ply·wood (plī′wŭd′) *n.* a construction material made of a number of thin layers of wood glued together, with the grain of one layer at right angles to the grain of the next.

Pm, the symbol for promethium.

p.m. 1. post meridiem. **2.** postmortem.

P.M. 1. Postmaster. **2.** post meridiem. **3.** Prime Minister.

PMS, premenstrual syndrome.

pneu·mat·ic (nü mat′ik, nū mat′ik) *adj.* **1.** operated by or using the force of compressed air: *a pneumatic drill.* **2.** containing or filled with air, especially compressed air: *a pneumatic tire.* **3.** of or relating to air or other gases or to pneumatics. [From the Latin word *pneumaticus* meaning "relating to wind or air," going back to the Greek word *pneuma* "wind, breath, spirit."]

pneumatic caisson, a large boxlike or cylindrical structure for laying underwater foundations, having an airtight work chamber at the bottom. Compressed air is pumped into this chamber to force out the water. Workers enter the chamber through an air lock.

pneu·mat·ics (nü mat′iks, nū-mat′iks) *n.* the branch of physics that deals with the physical properties of air and other

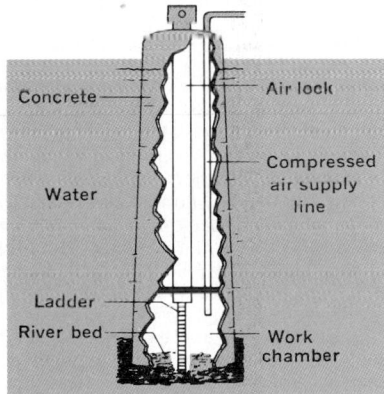

pneumatic caisson

gases and with their effect on objects. ▲ used with a singular verb.

pneu·mo·nia (nü mōn′yə, nü mōn′yə) *n.* any of several diseases involving an inflammation of the lungs, usually caused by a bacterial or viral infection.

Po, the symbol for polonium.

P.O., post office.

poach[1] (pōch) *v.t.* **1.** to cook (an egg) in simmering water or in a container placed above simmering water. **2.** to cook in simmering liquid: *to poach fish.* [From the Old French word *pochier* meaning "to put into a bag," from the word *poche* "bag," of Germanic origin.]

poach[2] (pōch) *v.i.* **1.** to hunt or fish illegally, as on someone else's property. **2.** to trespass for the purpose of hunting or fishing. —*v.t.* **1.** to take (game or fish) illegally. **2.** to trespass on (property) for the purpose of hunting or fishing. [From the Middle French word *pocher* meaning "to trespass," of Germanic origin.] —**poach′er,** *n.*

pock (pok) *n.* **1.** a swelling on the skin that is filled with pus, caused by such diseases as smallpox and acne. **2.** a scar or pit left by such a swelling. —*v.t.* to mark with pocks. Also (*n., def. 2; v.*), **pockmark.**

pock·et (pok′it) *n.* **1.** a pouch sewn into or on a garment, used especially to hold small articles. **2.** something resembling a pocket in shape or function: *There are pockets inside the suitcase for stockings and shoes.* **3.** an isolated, usually small area or group that is different in some way from a surrounding area or group: *A pocket of poverty existed in the middle of the wealthy community.* **4.** any of the pouches at the corners and sides of a pool or billiard table, into which the balls are driven. **5.** see **air pocket. 6.** a hole in the earth containing ore. **7.** *Football.* an area protected by blockers from which the quarterback makes a pass. —*adj.* made small enough or intended to be carried in a pocket: *a pocket radio.* —*v.t.* **1.** to put in a pocket: *I pocketed my change and left.* **2.** to take for one's own, especially dishonestly: *The salesclerk pocketed the day's receipts.* **3.** to hide or suppress, as an emotion: *They pocketed their pride and begged for help.*

pock·et·book (pok′it bùk′) *n.* **1.** a bag or case, often made of leather, used for carrying small articles. **2.** financial means or interests; money: *Rising food prices are a drain on everyone's pocketbook.* **3.** *also,* **pocket book.** a book, usually bound in paper, small enough to be carried in a pocket.

pock·et·ful (pok′it fùl′) *n., pl.* **pock·et·fuls.** the amount that a pocket holds.

pock·et·knife (pok′it nīf′) *n., pl.* **pock·et·knives** (pok′it nīvz′). a small knife with one or more blades that fold into the handle.

pocket money, money that is carried for small personal expenses: *We paid for our lunches with pocket money.*

pocket veto 1. the power of the president of the United States to veto a bill passed by Congress during the last ten days of a session by simply not signing the bill before Congress adjourns. **2.** a similar power exercised by a chief executive, such as a state governor.

pock·mark (pok′märk′) *n., v.t.* another word for **pock.**

pod (pod) *n.* **1.** the part of certain plants, such as a pea or bean, that carries the seeds and usually splits along two seams when it is ripe. **2.** a separate enclosed section on an aircraft, usually located beneath a wing, for storing fuel, cargo, weapons, an engine, or the like: *The airliner had four jet engine pods.* —*v.i.,* **pod·ded, pod·ding. 1.** to produce pods. **2.** to swell out into a pod.

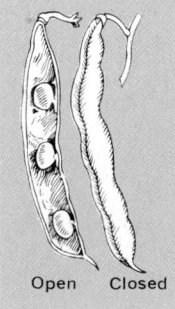

Open   Closed

pods *(def. 1)*

po·di·a·trist (pə dī′ə trist) *n.* a person who is trained in and licensed to practice podiatry. Also, **chiropodist.**

po·di·a·try (pə dī′ə trē) *n.* the branch of medicine dealing with the diagnosis, prevention, and treatment of diseases and injuries of the foot. Also, **chiropody.**

po·di·um (pō′dē əm) *n., pl.* **po·di·ums** or **po·di·a** (pō′dē ə). **1.** a raised platform from which a conductor leads an orchestra. **2.** a place or structure from which to speak to a group; lectern; rostrum.

po·em (pō′əm) *n.* **1.** a composition expressing emotion or imaginative thought, usually written in some rhythmic pattern, using language that is more condensed and vivid than that used in prose writing. Poems often use such devices as rhyme, meter, and metaphor. **2.** anything having the quality or effect of a poem: *The eagle's flight was a poem of graceful motion.*

po·e·sy (pō′ə sē) *n. Archaic.* **1.** poems as a group; poetry. **2.** the art of writing poetry.

po·et (pō′it) *n.* a person who writes poetry.

po·et·ess (pō′i tis) *n.* a woman who writes poetry. ▲ **Poet,** rather than **poetess,** is now generally used for a woman who writes poetry.

po·et·ic (pō et′ik) *adj.* **1.** of or relating to poetry: *poetic genius, poetic works.* **2.** having the quality or effect of poetry: *a poetic description.* **3.** characteristic of or like a poet. Also, **po·et·i·cal** (pō et′i kəl). —**po·et′i·cal·ly,** *adv.*

poetic justice, a suitable reward for goodness or punishment for evil: *It was poetic justice that they lost the game after trying to cheat.*

poetic license, the freedom to ignore a conventional rule, fact, or the like in order to achieve a desired artistic effect.

po·et·ics (pō et′iks) *n.* the branch of literary criticism that deals with the theory, nature, and forms of poetry. ▲ used with a singular verb.

poet laureate *pl.* **poets laureate** or **poet laureates. 1.** in Great Britain, a poet appointed for life by the king or queen to be the official poet of the royal household. The poet laureate's duties formerly included writing poems to commemorate state occasions. **2.** an official or the most highly regarded poet of a nation, state, region, or other place. The poet laureate of the United States is appointed by the head of the Library of Congress and serves for a term of one year, which may be renewed.

po·et·ry (pō′i trē) *n.* **1.** poems as a group: *The teacher read from a book of poetry.* **2.** the writing or language typical of poems. **3.** the art of writing poems. **4.** a quality or effect that is like that of poetry: *the poetry of a dancer's movements.* **5.** something that has such a quality or effect.

po·go stick (pō′gō) a toy that is like a stilt, made of a pole with footrests and a spring at its base, on which a person may move in a series of hops.

po·grom (pō grom′, pō′grəm) *n.* the organized persecution or massacre of a minority group, especially of Jews. [From the Yiddish word *pogrom,* from the Russian word *pogrom* meaning "devastation."]

poi (poi) *n.* a Hawaiian food made from a root of the taro plant that has been cooked, pounded into a paste, and fermented.

poign·ant (poin′yənt) *adj.* **1.** bringing out deep emotions, especially sadness; touching: *The magazine printed a poignant story of a soldier leaving for the war.* **2.** sharply felt; acute: *The family felt a poignant sense of loss when the pet dog died.* **3.** sharp; penetrating. —**poign′an·cy,** *n.* —**poign′ant·ly,** *adv.*

poin·set·ti·a (poin set′ē ə) *n.* a tropical American plant bearing oval leaves and small flowers surrounded by showy red, pink, or white leaves that resemble flower petals.

poinsettias

point (point) *n.* **1.** a sharp or tapering end: *the point of a pencil, the point of a knife.* **2.** a tapering piece of land that projects into the water: *A lighthouse was built on the point.* **3.** a dot or other small mark used in writing or printing, such as a decimal point or period. **4.** *Mathematics.* something having position, but no length, width, or height: *to draw a line between two points.* **5.** a particular location; place; spot: *The tourists visited all the points of interest in the city.* **6.** a position on a scale: *The boiling point of water is 100 degrees centigrade.* **7.** a stage in a process: *We worked to the point of exhaustion.* **8.** a particular moment or time: *At that point, I got up and left the room.* **9.** the main or most important part or idea: *What is the point of the story?* **10.** an object; purpose: *I don't see any point in going if the party is almost over.* **11.** an item; detail: *The general explained the plan point by point.* **12.** a special or personal quality; characteristic; trait: *Loyalty to his friends is one of his good points.* **13.** a unit of scoring in a game: *A touchdown in football counts as six points.* **14.** *Printing.* a unit for measuring type, approximately ¹/₇₂ inch (0.35 millimeter). **15.** one of the thirty-two marks showing direction on a compass. —*v.t.* **1.** to direct or aim: *The soldier pointed the gun at the target.* **2.** to direct attention to: *The sign pointed the way to the town.* **3.** to give force to; emphasize (followed by *up*): *The speaker pointed up the need for more funding.* —*v.i.* **1.** to direct attention with or as if with the finger: *The child pointed at the clown with red hair.* **2.** to direct the mind or thought in a certain direction: *All the evidence points toward their guilt.* **3.** (of a hunting dog) to show where a bird or animal is by standing still with the nose and the body facing it.

•**beside the point.** not related to the subject; irrelevant: *What you say is probably true, but it is entirely beside the point.*

•**in point.** related to the subject; relevant; pertinent: *a case in point.*

•**to make a point of.** to be determined to; insist upon: *I make a point of always being on time.*

•**to the point.** related to the subject; relevant: *The mayor's speech was brief and to the point.*

point–blank (point′blangk′) *adv.* **1.** from a very close range: *She fired the gun point-blank at the target.* **2.** plainly and bluntly; flatly: *They asked him point-blank if he had stolen the money.* —*adj.* **1.** pointed or aimed straight at the target, especially from close range: *to be exposed to point-blank fire.* **2.** very close to the target: *point-blank range.* **3.** plain and blunt: *a point-blank refusal.*

point·ed (poin′tid) *adj.* **1.** having or coming to a point or points: *a clown's pointed cap, a pointed stick.* **2.** related to the subject; to the point: *a pointed question.*

3. clearly aimed at or referring to a person, group, or thing: *a pointed comment.* **4.** emphatic; conspicuous: *a pointed display of anger.* —**point′ed·ly,** *adv.* —**point′ed·ness,** *n.*

point·er (poin′tər) *n.* **1.** a long stick used to point out things, as on a blackboard, chart, or map. **2.** any of a breed of short-haired dogs having long ears and a long, tapering tail. Pointers hunt game birds by scent and point to their location. **3.** a needle or similar device, as on a scale or meter, showing a measurement. **4.** *Informal.* a piece of information or advice; hint; suggestion: *The teacher gave me some good pointers on how to write the composition.* **5.** a person or thing that points.

point·less (point′lis) *adj.* **1.** without force, purpose, or result; useless: *a pointless attempt.* **2.** without meaning; senseless: *a pointless remark, a pointless joke.* **3.** without a sharp or tapering end. —**point′less·ly,** *adv.* —**point′less·ness,** *n.*

point of order, a question raised as to whether correct parliamentary procedure is being followed.

point of view **1.** a manner of thinking or feeling about something; attitude. **2.** the position from which something is considered or looked at.

poise (poiz) *n.* **1.** a calm, confident manner; self-assurance and composure. **2.** a state of balance; stability. —*v.,* **poised, pois·ing.** —*v.t.* to place, carry, or hold in balance: *The juggler poised the plate on the point of the stick.* —*v.i.* to be held in balance.

poi·son (poi′zən) *n.* **1.** a substance that causes serious injury, illness, or death by its chemical action on a living thing. **2.** anything that harms, corrupts, or destroys. —*v.t.* **1.** to give poison to; injure or kill with poison. **2.** to put poison in; cause to become harmful or deadly: *Dangerous bacteria poisoned the canned soup.* **3.** to have a harmful, corrupting, or destructive effect on: *to poison someone's mind with ideas of revenge.* —*adj.* able to poison; poisonous. [From the Old French word *poison* meaning "beverage" or "poison," from the Latin word *potio* "a drink," from the word *potare* "to drink."] —**poi′son·er,** *n.*

poison ivy **1.** a woody vine of North America, having shiny leaves made up of three jagged oval leaflets. It contains an oil that causes a rash when it comes in contact with the skin. **2.** the rash caused by contact with this plant.

poison oak **1.** a slender woody plant related to poison ivy and causing a similar rash. It has leaves made up of three usually oval leaflets. **2.** the rash caused by contact with this plant.

poi·son·ous (poi′zə nəs) *adj.* **1.** causing or capable of causing serious injury, illness, or death by poison: *a poisonous snake, a poisonous liquid.* **2.** having a harmful, corrupting, or destructive effect. **3.** full of anger, spite, or ill will: *a poisonous glance.* —**poi′son·ous·ly,** *adv.* —**poi′son·ous·ness,** *n.*

poison sumac **1.** a shrub or small tree related to poison ivy and causing a similar rash. It has leaves made up of from seven to thirteen oblong or oval leaflets. **2.** the rash caused by contact with this plant.

poke¹ (pōk) *v.,* **poked, pok·ing.** —*v.t.* **1.** to push into or against, as with something pointed; prod: *Please stop poking me with your finger.* **2.** to push or thrust: *I poked*

at; āpe; fär; câre; end; mē; it; īce; pîerce; hot; ōld; sông, fôrk; oil; out; up; ūse; rüle; pull; tûrn; chin; sing; shop; thin; this; hw in white; zh in treasure. The symbol ə stands for the unstressed vowel sound heard in about, taken, pencil, lemon, and circus.

my head out of the window. **3.** to make by pushing or thrusting: *The stick poked a hole in the drum.* —*v.i.* **1.** to make a pushing, thrusting, or prodding motion. **2.** to thrust forward or stick out; protrude: *A large rock poked up out of the water.* **3.** to look, search, or investigate. **4.** to intrude or meddle; pry: *to poke into someone else's business.* **5.** to move or go slowly or lazily; dawdle: *We'll be late if you don't stop poking along.* —*n.* a pushing, thrusting, or prodding motion. [From the Middle English word *poken* meaning "to nudge, push," probably from the Middle Dutch word *poken* with the same meaning.]

·**to poke fun at.** to make fun of; mock.

poke² (pōk) *n.* a bag; sack. [From the Old English word *pocca* meaning "a bag, pouch."]

poke bonnet, a bonnet having a large, deep brim that sticks out in front.

pok·er¹ (pō′kər) *n.* **1.** a metal rod for stirring a fire. **2.** a person or thing that pokes. [*Poke¹* + *-er¹*.]

pok·er² (pō′kər) *n.* any of various card games in which the players bet on the value of their hands. [Of uncertain origin.]

pok·y (pō′kē) *also,* **pok·ey.** *adj.,* **pok·i·er, pok·i·est.** extremely slow; dawdling.

poke bonnet

po·lar (pō′lər) *adj.* **1.** of or relating to a pole or poles, as of a magnet, battery, or sphere. **2.** relating to, near, or coming from the North or South Pole: *a polar expedition.* **3.** directly opposite, as in character or tendency.

polar bear, a large white bear, native to arctic regions.

Po·lar·is (pō lar′is) *n.* a star located in the northern sky. It is the outermost star in the handle of the Little Dipper. Also, **North Star, polestar.**

po·lar·i·ty (pō lar′i tē) *n., pl.* **po·lar·i·ties.** **1.** the possession of two poles at opposite ends with opposite properties, as in a magnet. **2.** the condition of being directly opposite, as in character or tendency: *political polarity.* **3.** the condition of having an electrical charge, either positive or negative.

polar bear

po·lar·ize (pō′lə rīz′) *v.t.,* **po·lar·ized, po·lar·iz·ing. 1.** to give polarity to. **2.** to cause to separate into opposing groups: *Disagreement over the government's policies threatened to polarize the country.* **3.** to act upon (light or other electromagnetic radiation) so that the vibrations of the waves are confined to a single plane or direction. —*v.i.* to become polarized. —**po·lar·i·za′tion,** *n.*

Po·lar·oid (pō′lə roid′) *n. Trademark.* **1.** a transparent plastic material capable of polarizing light, used especially in lamps and eyeglasses to reduce glare. **2.** a camera that produces a finished photograph. **3.** a photograph produced by such a camera.

pole¹ (pōl) *n.* a long, slender piece of wood, metal, or other material: *a fishing pole.* —*v.t.,* **poled, pol·ing.** to move, push, or strike with a pole: *to pole a boat down a river.* [From the Old English word *pāl* meaning "a stake, pole¹," from the Latin word *palus* meaning "stake."]

pole² (pōl) *n.* **1.** either end of the earth's axis; North Pole or South Pole. **2.** see **celestial pole.** **3.** either of two regions or parts having forces opposite to one another, as the ends of a magnet or the terminals of an electric battery.

4. *Biology.* either end of a nucleus, cell, or ovum, at or near which certain parts are symmetrically arranged. **5.** either of two principles, ideas, or the like that are directly opposite, as in character or tendency: *Their political beliefs are at opposite poles.* [From the Latin word *polus* meaning "the end of an axis, pole².]

Pole (pōl) *n.* a person who was born in or is a citizen of Poland.

pole·cat (pōl′kat′) *n.* **1.** a small, meat-eating European animal closely related to the weasel and ferret, and having long, soft gray fur. Polecats spray a foul-smelling liquid when attacked or frightened. **2.** a skunk.

po·lem·ic (pə lem′ik) *n.* **1.** an argument or discussion, especially an attack on a particular opinion, doctrine, or theory. **2. polemics.** the art or practice of argument. ▲ used with a singular verb. —*adj. also,* **po·lem·i·cal** (pə lem′i kəl). of or relating to controversy or dispute. —**po·lem′i·cal·ly,** *adv.*

pole·star (pōl′stär′) *n.* another word for **Polaris.**

pole–vault (pōl′vôlt′) *v.i.* to make a pole vault. —**pole′-vault′er,** *n.*

pole vault, an athletic field event in which the contestant vaults over a horizontal bar with the aid of a long pole.

po·lice (pə lēs′) *n.* **1.** an official force established and given power by a government to prevent and detect crime, enforce the law, and keep public order. **2.** the members of such a force as a group. ▲ used with a plural verb. **3.** any group officially given power to enforce regulations or keep order: *campus police.* —*v.t.,* **po·liced, po·lic·ing. 1.** to patrol or keep order in (an area), usually by means of police. **2.** to make (an area, as in a military camp) clean and tidy.

police dog 1. another term for **German shepherd. 2.** any dog used to aid police in their work.

po·lice·man (pə lēs′mən) *n., pl.* **po·lice·men** (pə-lēs′mən). a member of the police.

police officer, a member of a police force.

police state, a country or state in which the government seeks to control the lives of its citizens, especially by means of a secret police force.

po·lice·wom·an (pə lēs′wùm′ən) *n., pl.* **po·lice·wom·en.** (pə lēs′wim′ən). a female member of the police.

pol·i·cy¹ (pol′ə sē) *n., pl.* **pol·i·cies. 1.** a guiding principle that helps determine what decision to make: *The policy of the store was not to make refunds.* **2.** wisdom or shrewdness in the management of affairs; prudence. [From the Old French word *policie* meaning "government" or "course of action," from the Late Latin word *politia* "government," from the Greek word *politeia* "government," from the word *polis* "the Greek city-state."]

pol·i·cy² (pol′ə sē) *n., pl.* **pol·i·cies.** a written contract of insurance between an insurance company and the person or persons insured. [From the Old French word *police* meaning this contract, from the early Italian word *polizza* "written agreement," going back to the Greek word *apodeixis* "proof."]

po·li·o (pō′lē ō′) *n.* see **poliomyelitis.**

po·li·o·my·e·li·tis (pō′lē ō mī′ə lī′tis) *n.* a highly contagious disease caused by a virus. In its mild forms, it causes headache, sore throat, and fever. In its severe forms, it attacks the central nervous system and causes muscular weakness and paralysis. Also, **infantile paralysis.**

pol·ish (pol′ish) *n., pl.* **pol·ish·es. 1.** the smoothness or shininess of a surface or finish, such as that produced by rubbing or by applying a special substance; luster: *I buffed the floor to a high polish.* **2.** a preparation or substance used to shine, clean, or smooth a surface: *shoe polish.* **3.** smooth elegance of manner or style; refinement: *a sophisticated diplomat with polish and poise.* —*v.t.* **1.** to shine, clean, or smooth, as by rubbing or applying a special substance: *to polish silverware.* **2.** to make more finished or complete; improve or refine: *Polish up that speech a bit.* —*v.i.* to become smooth or glossy. —**pol′ish·er,** *n.*

·**to polish off.** *Informal.* to finish completely and quickly: *to polish off a meal, to polish off an assignment.*

Pol·ish (pō′lish) *adj.* of or relating to Poland, its people, their language, or culture. —*n.* the language of Poland.

Po·lit·bu·ro (pə lit′byŭr′ō) *n.* the highest policy-making and executive committee of the Communist Party of the Soviet Union.

po·lite (pə līt′) *adj.* **1.** having or showing good manners, consideration for others, and a regard for correct social behavior; courteous. **2.** marked by correct social behavior; refined: *polite society.* ▲ see **civil** for usage note. —**po·lite′ly,** *adv.* —**po·lite′ness,** *n.*

pol·i·tic (pol′i tik) *adj.* characterized by or showing good judgment, tact, or shrewdness: *politic advice.*

po·lit·i·cal (pə lit′i kəl) *adj.* **1.** of, relating to, or concerned with the organization or activities of government. **2.** of, relating to, or involved in politics: *a political party.* **3.** of, relating to, or characteristic of politicians. —**po·lit′i·cal·ly,** *adv.*

political science, the study of the origin, organization, principles, and operation of government. —**political scientist.**

pol·i·ti·cian (pol′i tish′ən) *n.* **1.** a person who is active in politics, especially a person who holds or seeks public office. **2.** a person who is skilled in shrewd dealings with others.

pol·i·tics (pol′i tiks) *pl. n.* **1.** the affairs or activities of a government: *state politics.* **2.** the science or art of government. **3.** general political opinions or convictions: *Those senators are liberal in their politics.* **4.** competition for positions of power within a group: *office politics.* ▲ used with a singular or plural verb.

pol·i·ty (pol′i tē) *n., pl.* **pol·i·ties.** **1.** a form, system, or method of government. **2.** any community living under some form or system of government.

pol·ka (pōl′kə, pō′kə) *n.* **1.** a lively dance that originated in Central Europe. It is danced in couples, and its basic movement consists of three steps and a hop. **2.** the music for this dance. —*v.i.,* **pol·kaed, pol·ka·ing.** to dance the polka.

pol·ka dot (pō′kə) **1.** one of a series of round dots spaced to form a pattern on fabric or other materials. **2.** a pattern or material with such dots.

poll (pol) *n.* **1.** a survey of public opinion on a given subject, usually based on questioning a sample group of people. **2.** the casting and recording of votes in an election. **3.** the total number of votes cast or recorded. **4. polls.** a place where votes are cast and recorded. **5.** a list of persons, especially those who can vote. **6.** the head, especially that part of it on which the hair grows. —*v.t.* **1.** to receive (a given number of votes) in an election: *The winner polled twice as many votes as the losing candidate.* **2.** to question (a sample group of people) to get a survey of public opinion. **3.** to record or register the votes of: *to poll a district.* **4.** to cut off, trim, or crop: *The farmer held the cow while the cowhand polled the horns of the animal. The sheepherder polled the woolen coat of the sheep.*

pol·len (pol′ən) *n.* a fine powdery material produced in the anthers of flowering plants. Grains of pollen are the male reproductive cells, and they fertilize the female reproductive cells, or ovules, to form seeds.

pol·li·nate (pol′ə nāt′) *v.t.,* **pol·li·nat·ed, pol·li·nat·ing.** to carry pollen from an anther to a stigma of (a plant).

pol·li·na·tion (pol′ə nā′shən) *n.* the transfer of pollen from the anther of a flower to the stigma of the same or another flower. Pollen grains fertilize the female reproductive cells, or ovules, in the ovary of the flower in order to form seeds.

pol·li·wog (pol′ē wog′) *also,* **pol·ly·wog.** *n.* another word for **tadpole.**

poll·ster (pōl′stər) *n.* a person who questions people to get a survey of public opinion; person who conducts public opinion polls.

poll tax, a tax on persons who are qualified to vote, which in some states formerly had to be paid before voting.

pol·lut·ant (pə lü′tənt) *n.* something that pollutes, especially industrial waste or other material that pollutes air, water, or soil.

pol·lute (pə lüt′) *v.t.,* **pol·lut·ed, pol·lut·ing. 1.** to make impure or dirty, as with harmful chemicals, gases, or other wastes: *Oil from the damaged ship polluted the river. Exhaust from automobile engines pollutes the air.* **2.** to destroy the purity of; corrupt.

pol·lu·tion (pə lü′shən) *n.* **1.** the act of polluting or the state of being polluted. **2.** something that pollutes.

Pol·lux (pol′əks) *n.* see **Castor and Pollux.**

pol·ly·wog (pol′ē wog′) *also,* **polliwog.** *n.* another word for **tadpole.**

po·lo (pō′lō) *n.* **1.** a game played on horseback by two teams of four players, using long-handled mallets with which they attempt to hit a wooden ball through the opponent's goalposts. **2.** see **water polo.**

pol·o·naise (pol′ə nāz′, pō′lə nāz′) *n.* **1.** a stately dance of Polish origin, in three-quarter time, marked by slow, gliding steps. **2.** the music for this dance. **3.** a woman's dress popular in the eighteenth century, having a fitted bodice and a full skirt, over which a separate skirt, open at the front, was worn.

po·lo·ni·um (pə lō′nē əm) *n.* a heavy, poisonous, radioactive metallic element that occurs naturally when pitchblende decays. It also can be artificially produced. Polonium was the first radioactive element to be discovered and is now used in nuclear physics research. Symbol: **Po** [From *Polonia,* Latin name for Poland, the homeland of Marie Curie, who discovered it.]

polo shirt, a sport shirt made of knitted cotton, usually close-fitting and having short sleeves.

pol·ter·geist (pōl′tər gīst′) *n.* a spirit or ghost that is said to make mysterious noises and move inanimate objects. [From the German word *Poltergeist,* from the words *poltern* meaning "to bump, knock" + *Geist* "spirit."]

pol·troon (pol trün′) *n.* a complete coward.

poly- *combining form* more than one; many; much: *polygamy, polygon.*

pol·y·es·ter (pol′ē es′tər) *n.* any of several synthetic resins, used especially in making textile fibers.

pol·y·eth·y·lene (pol′ē eth′ə lēn′) *n.* a strong, light plastic used in manufacturing bags, containers, and insulation.

po·lyg·a·mist (pə lig′ə mist) *n.* a person who practices polygamy.

po·lyg·a·mous (pə lig′ə məs) *adj.* of, relating to, or practicing polygamy. —**po·lyg′a·mous·ly,** *adv.*

po·lyg·a·my (pə lig′ə mē) *n.* the practice, custom, or condition of having more than one spouse at a time.

pol·y·glot (pol′ē glot) *n.* **1.** a person who speaks, understands, or writes several languages. **2.** a mixture or confusion of several languages. —*adj.* **1.** speaking, un-

at; āpe; fär; câre; end; mē; it; īce; pîerce; hot; ōld; sông, fôrk; oil; out; up; ūse; rüle; pùll; tûrn; chin; sing; shop; thin; <u>th</u>is; hw in white; zh in treasure. The symbol ə stands for the unstressed vowel sound heard in about, taken, pencil, lemon, and circus.

P

727

derstanding, or writing several languages. **2.** made up of or expressed in several languages.

pol·y·gon (pol′ē gon′) *n.* a closed plane figure having at least three straight sides. A square is a polygon. [From the Late Latin word *polygonum* meaning "polygon," from the Greek word *polygōnon,* from the words *poly* meaning "many, much" + *gōnia* meaning "angle."] —**po·lyg·o·nal** (pə lig′ə nəl), *adj.*

pol·y·graph (pol′ē graf′) *n.* another word for **lie detector.**

pol·y·he·dron (pol′ē hē′drən) *n., pl.* **pol·y·he·drons** or **pol·y·he·dra** (pol′ē hē′drə). a closed solid figure that is the union of plane polygons, each two adjoining polygons having a common edge. —**pol′y·he′dral,** *adj.*

pol·y·mer (pol′ə mər) *n.* **1.** any large molecule formed of smaller simple molecules

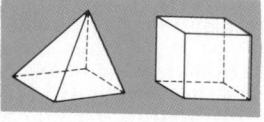

polyhedrons

linked together in long chains of repeating units. The number of molecules that unite to form a polymer may vary from a few to thousands. **2.** a substance made of polymers.

Pol·y·ne·sian (pol′ə nē′zhən) *n.* **1.** a person who was born or is living in Polynesia. **2.** the subfamily of languages spoken mainly in Polynesia and including Hawaiian, Maori, and Tahitian. —*adj.* of or relating to Polynesia, its people, their languages, or culture.

pol·y·no·mi·al (pol′ē nō′mē əl) *n. Mathematics.* an expression made up of two or more terms. —*adj.* made up of or characterized by two or more terms.

pol·yp (pol′ip) *n.* **1.** a small marine animal with a cup-shaped or sac-shaped body, having a mouth opening at one end of the body surrounded by many tentacles. **2.** a projecting growth on the surface of mucous membrane.

pol·y·phon·ic (pol′ē fon′ik) *adj. Music.* of, relating to, or composed of two or more separate melodic voices or parts.

pol·y·ploi·dy (pol′ē ploi′dē) *n.* a condition in which an organism has one or more extra sets of chromosomes. Polyploidy is often purposely bred into plants to make them larger or hardier.

pol·y·sty·rene (pol′ē stī′rēn) *n.* a clear plastic often used in packaging and insulation, as in refrigerators.

pol·y·syl·lab·ic (pol′ē si lab′ik) *adj.* **1.** made up of three or more syllables. **2.** marked by words of three or more syllables: *polysyllabic writing.* —**pol′y·syl·lab′i·cal·ly,** *adv.*

pol·y·syl·la·ble (pol′ē sil′ə bəl) *n.* a word of three or more syllables.

pol·y·tech·nic (pol′ē tek′nik) *adj.* of, relating to, or giving instruction in many crafts and applied sciences: *a polytechnic institute.*

pol·y·the·ism (pol′ē thē iz′əm) *n.* the belief in or worship of more than one god. —**pol′y·the′ist,** *n.* —**pol′y·the·is′tic,** *adj.*

pol·y·un·sat·u·rat·ed (pol′ē un sach′ə rā′tid) *adj.* (of a fat) containing more than two double bonds in its carbon chain. Polyunsaturated fats tend to be liquid in form, as certain vegetable oils, and may be associated with lower blood cholesterol levels.

pol·y·u·re·thane (pol′ē yùr′ə thān′) *n.* any of several synthetic polymers, especially a foam variety used as an insulating material and an elastic variety used in textiles that stretch.

po·made (po mād′, po mäd′) *n.* a perfumed ointment, especially one for dressing the hair. —*v.t.,* **po·mad·ed, po·mad·ing.** to dress (one's hair) with pomade.

pome (pōm) *n.* a fleshy, firm fruit that can be eaten, having several seeds. The apple and pear are pomes.

pome·gran·ate (pom′gran′it, pom′ə gran′it) *n.* **1.** the round fruit of a shrub or small tree, having a tough red rind and containing many seeds, each of which is enclosed by a juicy reddish pulp that can be eaten. **2.** the shrub or tree bearing this fruit, having red or orange trumpet-shaped flowers.

Pom·er·a·ni·an (pom′ə rā′nē ən) *n.* any of a breed of small, long-haired dogs having a head like a fox and a bushy tail that lies over the back.

pom·mel (pum′əl, pom′əl) *n.* **1.** the raised front part of a saddle, usually with a knob used as a grip. **2.** the rounded knob on the hilt of a sword, dagger, or similar weapon. —*v.t.* another spelling of **pummel.**

pomp (pomp) *n.* a stately and splendid ceremony or display; splendor; pageantry: *The newspaper described the pomp and ritual of the royal wedding.*

pom·pa·dour (pom′pə dôr′, pom′pə dùr′) *n.* **1.** a man's hair style in which the hair is combed up high and back from the forehead. **2.** a woman's hair style in which the hair is combed back from the forehead and puffed high in front, often over a pad. [From the Marquise de *Pompadour* (1721–1764), mistress of Louis XV of France, who wore her hair in this style.]

pom·pa·no (pom′pə nō′) *n., pl.* **pom·pa·nos.** a food fish found in temperate and tropical waters of North and South America. It has a flattened roundish or oval body that is usually silver in color.

pom·pom (pom′pom′) *n.* an ornamental ball or tuft of material, used especially as a decoration on clothing. Also, **pompon.**

pom·pon (pom′pon′) *n.* **1.** a small, round flower, such as a chrysanthemum. **2.** another spelling of **pompom.**

pom·pos·i·ty (pom pos′i tē) *n., pl.* **pom·pos·i·ties. 1.** the state or quality of being pompous. **2.** a pompous action, remark, or display.

pom·pous (pom′pəs) *adj.* **1.** marked by or showing too much dignity or self-importance. **2.** pretentious. —**pom′pous·ly,** *adv.* —**pom′pous·ness,** *n.*

pon·cho (pon′chō) *n., pl.* **pon·chos. 1.** a garment that is like a cloak, made of a piece of cloth with a slit or hole in the middle so that it can be slipped over the head. **2.** a waterproof garment resembling this, worn chiefly as a raincoat.

pond (pond) *n.* a body of still water, usually smaller than a lake.

pon·der (pon′dər) *v.t.* to consider or think over carefully: *They pondered what they should do next.* —*v.i.* to think carefully; muse; reflect: *to ponder over a problem.*

ponchos *(def. 1)*

pon·der·ous (pon′dər əs) *adj.* **1.** having great weight or bulk; heavy; unwieldy: *The ponderous old cart lumbered down the road.* **2.** clumsy and slow: *the ponderous movements of an elephant.* **3.** dull and labored: *The law journal was full of ponderous articles.* —**pon′der·ous·ly,** *adv.* —**pon′der·ous·ness,** *n.*

pone (pōn) *n.* see **corn pone.**

pon·gee (pon jē′) *n.* a brownish yellow, thin fabric having an uneven surface, originally hand-woven in China from silk.

pon·iard (pon′yərd) *n.* another word for **dagger.**

pons (ponz) *n.*, *pl.* **pon·tes** (pon'tēz). a band of nerve fibers in the brain connecting the cerebellum, cerebrum, and medulla oblongata.

pon·tiff (pon'tif) *n.* **1.** another word for **pope**. **2.** any high priest. **3.** any bishop.

pon·tif·i·cal (pon tif'i kəl) *adj.* of or relating to a pope, high priest, or bishop. —**pon·tif'i·cal·ly,** *adv.*

pon·tif·i·cate (*v.*, pon tif'i kāt'; *n.*, pon tif'i kit, pon tif'i kāt'). *v.i.*, **pon·tif·i·cat·ed, pon·tif·i·cat·ing.** **1.** to perform the duties of or act as a pope or bishop. **2.** to speak or act in a pompous manner. —*n.* the office or term of office of a pope or bishop.

pon·toon (pon tün') *n.* **1.** a flat-bottomed boat or similar floating structure used as a support, as in the building of floating bridges over water or in the raising of submerged vessels. **2.** the float of a seaplane.

pontoon bridge, a bridge that is supported in the water by pontoons.

po·ny (pō'nē) *n.*, *pl.* **po·nies.** **1.** a horse of any of various small breeds. **2.** any horse, especially a small one. **3.** a small liquor glass. **4.** *Informal.* a text, especially a literal translation of a foreign work, used by students, usually dishonestly, in doing schoolwork or in preparing for an exam.

pony express, a postal service in which mail was carried in relays by riders on horseback. The pony express ran between Missouri and California from 1860 to 1861.

pontoon bridge

po·ny·tail (pō'nē tāl') *also,* **pony tail.** *n.* a hair style in which the hair is drawn back and fastened behind at the back of the head, so as to hang down like a pony's tail.

pooch (püch) *n.*, *pl.* **pooch·es.** *Slang.* a dog.

poo·dle (pü'dəl) *n.* any of a breed of dogs having a thick, curly, usually solid-colored coat that is often clipped in elaborate styles.

pooh (pü) *interj.* an expression of mild dislike, displeasure, or scorn: *The tourist said "pooh!" after sniffing the strange food.*

pooh-pooh (pü'pü') *v.t.* *Informal.* to express mild dislike, displeasure, or scorn: *A small-minded person often pooh-poohs unusual ideas.*

pool¹ (pül) *n.* **1.** a small body of still, usually fresh water. **2.** an indoor or outdoor tank designed for swimming. Also, **swimming pool. 3.** a small, shallow amount of liquid on a surface: *a pool of gravy, a pool of oil.* **4.** a still, deep place in a stream or river. [From the Old English word *pōl* meaning "a pool of water."]

pool² (pül) *n.* **1.** a game played on a pool table, with the object being to drive balls into pockets by striking them with another ball. **2.** a common fund or supply, as of money or skilled people: *Many secretaries in this company work in a typing pool.* **3.** an arrangement in which a number of people share the use of something: *Many of our neighbors belong to a car pool.* **4.** the persons employed or participating in a pool. **5.** the amount that the winner gets in certain gambling games. —*v.t.* to put into a common fund or joint effort: *The members of the football team pooled their money to buy some new equipment.* [From the French word *poule* meaning "a stake in a game."]

pool·room (pül'rüm', pül'rùm') *n.* a room or place of business where pool or billiards may be played. Also, **pool hall.**

pool table, a rectangular table used in playing pool, having a smooth, level, cloth-covered surface with six pockets,

one in each of the four corners and one in the center of each long side.

poop (püp) *n.* the short deck above the main deck at the stern of a boat or ship, often forming the roof of a cabin. Also, **poop deck.**

poor (pùr) *adj.* **1.** having little or no money; needy. **2.** marked by or showing such need: *a poor neighborhood.* **3.** below a standard; inferior; bad: *poor health, poor quality.* **4.** being less than is wanted, needed, or expected; insufficient: *a poor wheat crop.* **5.** lacking skill or ability; not capable or talented: *a poor writer, a poor student.* **6.** deserving pity or compassion; unfortunate: *The poor dog had been beaten by its owner.* —*n.* **the poor.** poor or needy persons as a group. —**poor'ness,** *n.*

poor·house (pùr'hous') *n.*, *pl.* **poor·hous·es** (pùr'hou'ziz). a place kept at public expense to shelter and aid or employ poor people.

poor·ly (pùr'lē) *adv.* in a poor manner; badly: *He has performed rather poorly in school this term.* —*adj.* *Informal.* somewhat ill: *She's been feeling poorly lately.*

pop¹ (pop) *v.*, **popped, pop·ping.** —*v.i.* **1.** to make a short, sharp, explosive sound: *The champagne bottle popped when the cork was pulled.* **2.** to burst open or explode with such a sound: *The corn popped quickly.* **3.** *Informal.* to move, go, appear, or come quickly or suddenly: *She popped in to see us yesterday.* **4.** *Informal.* (of the eyes) to open wide suddenly. **5.** *Baseball.* to hit a pop fly. —*v.t.* **1.** to cause to burst with a short, sharp, explosive sound: *The pin popped the balloon.* **2.** to put or thrust quickly or suddenly: *The boy popped his head out the window.* —*n.* **1.** a short, sharp, explosive sound. **2.** a flavored, nonalcoholic beverage; soft drink. [Representation of this sound.]

pop² (pop) *adj.* *Informal.* of, relating to, or designating something popular: *pop music, a pop novel.* [Short for *popular.*]

pop³ (pop) *n.* *Informal.* another word for **father.** [A form of *papa.*]

pop⁴ (pop) *n.* *Informal.* another term for **soda** (*def. 3*). [From *pop¹.*]

pop. **1.** popular; popularly. **2.** population.

pop art, art that takes its subjects, themes, and techniques from advertising, comic strips, motion pictures, and other forms of popular culture.

pop·corn (pop'kôrn') *n.* **1.** a variety of corn having small, hard kernels that burst open when heated and puff out to form white, fluffy masses. **2.** the burst kernels of this corn, eaten as a snack.

pope (pōp) *also,* **Pope.** *n.* the bishop of Rome and supreme head of the Roman Catholic Church.

pop fly *Baseball.* a fly ball hit into or near the infield.

pop·gun (pop'gun') *n.* a toy gun that makes a loud pop when fired, especially one that fires pellets or corks by means of air compressed in the barrel.

pop·in·jay (pop'in jā') *n.* a vain, silly person who talks too much.

pop·lar (pop'lər) *n.* **1.** any of a type of fast-growing trees of the willow family, found throughout the Northern Hemisphere, having pale, ridged bark and broad leaves. **2.** the soft white wood of such a tree, often used to make shipping boxes and pulp.

pop·lin (pop'lin) *n.* a durable fabric woven with a cross-

at; āpe; fär; câre; end; mē; it; īce; pîerce; hot; ōld; sông, fôrk; oil; out; up; ūse; rüle; pùll; tûrn; chin; sing; shop; thin; ***this;*** hw in white; zh in treasure. The symbol ə stands for the unstressed vowel sound heard in about, taken, pencil, lemon, and circus.

P

729

wise rib. It is often made of cotton, and used for shirts, dresses, curtains, and pajamas.

pop·o·ver (pop′ō′vər) *n.* a very light muffin, made of flour, eggs, milk, and shortening, that puffs up and becomes hollow when baked.

pop·py (pop′ē) *n., pl.* **pop·pies. 1.** a round, showy flower often grown as a garden flower. **2.** the plant bearing this flower, containing a milky juice. One species of poppy is the source of the drug opium. **3.** a bright orange-red color. —*adj.* having the color poppy.

pop·py·cock (pop′ē kok′) *n.* completely foolish or empty talk; nonsense.

pop·u·lace (pop′yə lis) *n.* **1.** all the inhabitants of a place; population. **2.** the common people; the masses.

pop·u·lar (pop′yə lər) *adj.* **1.** pleasing to or favored by very many or most people: *a popular actor, a popular restaurant.* **2.** having many friends and acquaintances; well-liked: *Who was voted the most popular student in your class?* **3.** of, relating to, or representing the general public: *a popular election, popular government.* **4.** accepted or widespread among the general public; common: *The belief that pencils contain lead is a popular notion.* **5.** suited to the taste and intelligence of the average person or the general public: *popular music, popular literature.* **6.** suited to or within the means of ordinary people; moderate: *This model is now available at popular prices.* [From the Latin word *popularis* meaning "of the people," from the word *populus* "people."] —**pop′u·lar·ly,** *adv.*

pop·u·lar·i·ty (pop′yə lar′i tē) *n.* the quality or state of being widely liked, admired, or favored.

pop·u·lar·ize (pop′yə lə rīz′) *v.t.,* **pop·u·lar·ized, pop·u·lar·iz·ing.** to make (something) popular or understandable to the general public. —**pop′u·lar·i·za′tion,** *n.* —**pop′u·lar·iz′er,** *n.*

pop·u·late (pop′yə lāt′) *v.t.,* **pop·u·lat·ed, pop·u·lat·ing. 1.** to live in; inhabit: *The forest is populated by wildlife.* **2.** to furnish with inhabitants, as by colonization.

pop·u·la·tion (pop′yə lā′shən) *n.* **1.** the total number of people living in an area or place: *The population of that town doubled in the past decade.* **2.** the people themselves: *The entire population of the town came to watch the parade.* **3.** a distinct group of such people: *the French-speaking population of Canada.* **4.** the act or process of populating; furnishing with inhabitants.

Pop·u·list (pop′yə list) *adj.* of, relating to, or characteristic of the Populist Party. —*n.* a member or supporter of the Populist Party.

Populist Party, a political party active in the United States in the 1890s that favored the interests of farmers and workers.

pop·u·lous (pop′yə ləs) *adj.* having many inhabitants; heavily populated.

por·ce·lain (pôr′sə lin) *n.* **1.** a type of ceramic material that is hard and white. **2.** objects made of this.

porch (pôrch) *n., pl.* **porch·es. 1.** a roofed, sometimes enclosed area attached to the outside of a house. **2.** a structure forming an entrance to a building.

por·cu·pine (pôr′kyə pīn′) *n.* any of several types of rodent whose body and tail are covered with sharp spines or quills that serve as protection.

pore[1] (pôr) *n.* a very small opening, as in the skin of an animal or in the surface of a leaf, through which water, air, or the like may pass. [From the Old French word *pore,* from the Latin word *porus* meaning "a passage," from the Greek word *poros* "passage, pore."]

porcupine

pore[2] (pôr) *v.i.,* **pored, por·ing.** to read or study with great attention or care: *I pored over*

my notes while waiting for my turn to speak at the club meeting. [From the Middle English word *pouren* with the same meanings, from Old English.]

por·gy (pôr′gē) *n., pl.* **por·gies** or **por·gy.** a food and game fish found chiefly in coastal waters of the Atlantic Ocean.

pork (pôrk) *n.* the meat of a pig or hog used as food.

pork barrel *Informal.* a government project or the assigning of public funds for projects that may not be needed but that will please local voters. —**pork-bar·rel** (pôrk′-bar′əl), *adj.*

pork·er (pôr′kər) *n.* a pig or hog, especially one fattened for slaughter.

por·nog·ra·phy (pôr nog′rə fē) *n.* writing or pictures meant to arouse sexual desires. —**por·no·graph·ic** (pôr′nə graf′ik), *adj.*

po·ros·i·ty (pô ros′i tē) *n., pl.* **po·ros·i·ties.** the quality or condition of being porous.

po·rous (pôr′əs) *adj.* having or full of pores: *a porous material.* —**po′rous·ness,** *n.*

por·phy·ry (pôr′fə rē) *n., pl.* **por·phy·ries.** volcanic rock composed of two or more minerals, usually including a feldspar mineral.

por·poise (pôr′pəs) *n., pl.* **por·pois·es** or **por·poise.** a warm-blooded animal that is closely related to the dolphin and is found in all oceans except those in polar regions. The porpoise has a torpedo-shaped body that is usually black with white undersides.

porpoise

por·ridge (pôr′ij, por′ij) *n.* a soft food made by boiling oatmeal or other meal in water or milk until thickened, usually served as a breakfast dish.

por·rin·ger (pôr′in jər, por′in jər) *n.* a small, shallow bowl, usually with a short handle, for holding porridge or other food.

port[1] (pôrt) *n.* **1.** a place along a coast or waterway where boats and ships can anchor and be protected from storms; harbor. **2.** a city or town with a harbor. [From the Old English word *port* and the Old French word *port,* both with the same meaning and both from the Latin word *portus* "harbor, haven."]

port[2] (pôrt) *n.* the left side of a boat or ship as one faces forward. —*adj.* of, relating to, or located on the left side of a boat or ship. Also, **larboard.** —*v.t.* to turn or shift to the port side. [Of uncertain origin.]

port[3] (pôrt) *n.* a strong, sweet wine, usually dark red in color. [From *Oporto,* a city in Portugal that shipped this wine.]

port[4] (pôrt) *n.* **1.** see **porthole. 2.** the covering for a porthole. **3.** a point on a computer for plugging in cables that connect to peripheral devices. [From the Middle English word *porte* meaning "entrance," from the Old French word *porte* "entrance," from the Latin word *porta* "gate" or "entrance."]

port·a·ble (pôr′tə bəl) *adj.* able to be moved or carried easily, especially by hand: *a portable radio, portable furniture* —*n.* something that is portable, such as a lightweight typewriter.

por·tage (pôr′tij) *n.* **1.** the act of transporting boats or goods overland from one river or other body of water to another. **2.** the route or place over which this is done. **3.** the cost or charge for this. —*v.t., v.i.,* **por·taged, por·tag·ing.** to carry (boats or goods) over a portage.

por·tal (pôr′təl) *n.* a door, gate, or entrance, especially a large and imposing one: *the portal of a medieval cathedral.*

por·cul·lis (pôrt kul′is) *n., pl.* **port·cul·lis·es.** a heavy grating built so as to slide up and down in grooves cut in the sides of the gateway of a castle or fortress. It may be lowered quickly as a defense against assault.

por·tend (pôr tend′) *v.t.* to be a warning, sign, or indication of: *A black sky portended the coming storm.*

por·tent (pôr′tent) *n.* a warning, sign, or indication of what is to come, especially of something important or disastrous; omen.

portcullis

por·ten·tous (pôr ten′təs) *adj.* **1.** threatening; ominous. **2.** very remarkable or important: *a portentous era.* —**por·ten′tous·ly,** *adv.* —**por·ten′tous·ness,** *n.*

por·ter¹ (pôr′tər) *n.* **1.** a person who is employed to carry baggage, as at a railroad station or in a hotel. **2.** an attendant who helps passengers in a railroad car. [From the Anglo-Norman word *portour* meaning ''one who carries goods,'' going back to the Latin word *portare* ''to carry, bear¹.'']

por·ter² (pôr′tər) *n.* a person employed to do cleaning and repair work in a building, as in an apartment house; janitor. [From the Old French word *portier* meaning ''a gatekeeper,'' from the Late Latin word *portarius* with the same meaning, from the Latin word *porta* ''gate'' or ''entrance.'']

por·ter³ (pôr′tər) *n.* a dark brown, heavy, bitter beer brewed from partly charred malt. [From *porter¹*.]

por·ter·house (pôr′tər hous′) *n., pl.* **por·ter·hous·es** (pôr′tər hou′ziz). a cut of beef taken from the loin, including a portion of tenderloin. Also, **porterhouse steak.**

port·fo·li·o (pôrt fō′lē ō′) *n., pl.* **port·fo·li·os.** **1.** a portable case for holding or carrying loose papers, drawings, documents, and similar materials. **2.** the office, position, and duties of a cabinet member or a minister of state in charge of a department. **3.** a list or group of stocks, bonds, and the like, belonging to a bank, investment company, or private investor. **4.** a representative collection of an artist's or writer's works.

port·hole (pôrt′hōl′) *n.* **1.** a small, usually circular opening in the side of a boat or ship for letting in air and light. **2.** an opening in a wall, as of a fort, through which a gun can be fired. Also, **port.**

por·ti·co (pôr′ti kō′) *n., pl.* **por·ti·coes** or **por·ti·cos.** a roofed structure supported by columns or piers and open on at least one side, forming a covered walk and usually attached to a building.

por·tion (pôr′shən) *n.* **1.** a limited amount or part of something: *He spent a portion of the day running errands. I saw only a portion of the movie before I fell asleep.* **2.** a part of a whole that is given to or belongs to one person or group; share: *What is she going to do with her portion of the inheritance?* **3.** a quantity of food served to one person: *a portion of mashed potatoes.* —*v.t.* to divide (something) into portions or shares; distribute.

portico

port·land cement (pôrt′lənd) *also,* **Portland cement.** a type of cement used to make concrete that will harden underwater.

port·ly (pôrt′lē) *adj.,* **port·li·er, port·li·est.** large and heavy; corpulent. —**port′li·ness,** *n.*

port·man·teau (pôrt man′tō) *n., pl.* **port·man·teaus** or **port·man·teaux** (pôrt man′tōz). a suitcase or traveling bag, especially one made of leather and hinged at the back so as to open like a book into two sections or compartments.

por·trait (pôr′trit, pôr′trāt) *n.* **1.** a painting, photograph, or other representation of a person, usually showing only the face and upper part of the body. **2.** a picture or description in words, especially of a person.

por·trait·ist (pôr′tri tist, pôr′trā tist) *n.* a person who makes portraits; portrait painter or photographer.

por·trai·ture (pôr′tri chər) *n.* **1.** the art or practice of making portraits. **2.** a portrait.

por·tray (pôr trā′) *v.t.* **1.** to give a picture of in words; tell or write about; describe: *The writer portrayed the teacher as a kind and understanding person in this novel.* **2.** to make a picture or other likeness of: *The artist portrayed the family in a painting.* **3.** to play the part of: *I portrayed a doctor in the school play.* —**por·tray′er,** *n.*

por·tray·al (pôr trā′əl) *n.* **1.** the act or process of portraying. **2.** something that portrays.

Por·tu·guese (pôr′chə gēz′, pôr′chə gēs′) *n., pl.* **Por·tu·guese.** **1.** a person who was born in or is a citizen of Portugal. **2.** the language of Portugal, also spoken in Brazil. —*adj.* of or relating to Portugal, its people, their language, or culture.

Portuguese man-of-war, a floating colony of sea animals found in warm waters of the Atlantic Ocean. In each colony there is one animal that forms a gas-filled, floating sac, and other animals that form long tentacles with stinging cells for stunning and capturing prey.

pose (pōz) *n.* **1.** a position of the body, as for a portrait by an artist or photographer. **2.** an attitude or way of behaving assumed for effect; pretense: *His bravery is just a pose.* —*v.,* **posed, pos·ing.** —*v.i.* **1.** to hold a position, as for a portrait. **2.** to assume a false appearance or identity: *The swindler posed as a member of the nobility.* —*v.t.* **1.** to place in a particular position. **2.** to put forward; present: *The reporter posed an interesting question. Her refusal to cooperate with us poses a severe problem.* —**pos′er,** *n.*

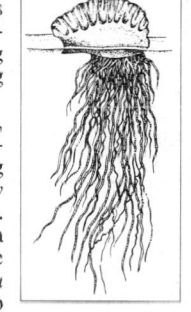

Portuguese man-of-war

Po·sei·don (pə sī′dən) *n. Greek Mythology.* the god of the sea and brother of Zeus and Hades. In Roman mythology he was called Neptune.

posh (posh) *adj. Informal.* fashionable, luxurious, or elegant: *a posh hotel.*

po·si·tion (pə zish′ən) *n.* **1.** the place where a person or thing is: *From our position at the window we could see the entire parade.* **2.** an arrangement of the body or of its parts: *an uncomfortable position.* **3.** the way in which something is placed or arranged: *the position of the chairs around the table.* **4.** one's situation or condition: *Bankruptcy left them in a difficult position.* **5.** the proper or appropriate place: *The members of the team were in position.* **6.** the way in which one looks upon or views a

---

at; āpe; fär; câre; end; mē; it; īce; pîerce; hot; ōld; sông, fôrk; oil; out; up; ūse; rüle; pùll; tûrn; chin; sing; shop; thin; this; hw in white; zh in treasure. The symbol ə stands for the unstressed vowel sound heard in about, taken, pencil, lemon, and circus.

particular issue or subject; point of view: *What is the senator's position on the treaty?* **7.** social standing or rank: *a person of high position.* **8.** a place or post of employment; job: *a position in the company's shipping department.* —*v.t.* to put in a particular place or arrangement: *We positioned the chairs in a circle.* [From the Middle French word *position,* from the Latin word *positio* meaning "a placing, situation," from the word *positus,* past participle of *ponere* meaning "to put, place, lay down."]

pos·i·tive (poz′i tiv) *adj.* **1.** admitting of no question or doubt; undeniable: *positive proof.* **2.** clearly expressed; definite; emphatic: *He answered my question with a positive "no."* **3.** confident or fully assured; certain; convinced: *Are you positive that you saw them?* **4.** showing, containing, or suggesting approval or acceptance: *a positive reply.* **5.** helpful or practical: *She made a positive contribution to the discussion.* **6.** tending or moving toward an improved condition: *There was a positive change in the student's behavior.* **7.** *Mathematics.* greater than zero: *a positive number.* **8.** *Medicine.* (of a test) indicating the presence of a particular disease, germ, or other condition. **9.** *Electricity.* having more protons than electrons: *That surface has a positive charge.* **10.** *Photography.* showing light and shade as they appear in the original subject: *a positive image.* **11.** *Grammar.* designating the form or degree of an adjective or adverb used when no comparison is made. *Fast is the positive form of the adjective fast, faster is the comparative form, and fastest is the superlative form.* —*n.* **1.** a positive photographic print, image, or picture. **2.** the positive form or degree of an adjective or adverb. **3.** something that is positive. —**pos′i·tive·ly,** *adv.* —**pos′i·tive·ness,** *n.*

poss. **1.** possession. **2.** possessive.

pos·se (pos′ē) *n.* a group of people summoned by a sheriff for help, as in capturing a criminal.

pos·sess (pə zes′) *v.t.* **1.** to hold as property; own: *He possesses great wealth.* **2.** to have as a quality, characteristic, or attribute: *She possesses much talent.* **3.** to have an overwhelming power or influence over: *What possessed you to buy that coat? A need for revenge possessed the criminal.* —**pos·ses′sor,** *n.*

pos·sessed (pə zest′) *adj.* **1.** in possession of; having: *a speaker possessed of a quick wit.* **2.** controlled by or as if by a strong emotion or evil spirit: *There was a rumor that the house was haunted and its owner possessed by a demon.* **3.** self-possession.

pos·ses·sion (pə zesh′ən) *n.* **1.** the act or fact of holding or owning; ownership: *He has possession of the property. A large amount of money comes into her possession at the age of twenty-one.* **2.** something that is held or owned: *That poor family has few possessions.* **3.** a territory that is under the rule of a foreign country. **4.** domination by or as if by an evil spirit or demon.

pos·ses·sive (pə zes′iv) *adj.* **1.** characterized by or showing a strong desire to own, keep, or dominate: *I'm very possessive about my books.* **2.** *Grammar.* relating to or designating a case of nouns and pronouns that show possession. —*n.* *Grammar.* the possessive case or a word in the possessive case. In the sentence *This is the baby's bottle, baby's* is a possessive. —**pos·ses′sive·ly,** *adv.* —**pos·ses′sive·ness,** *n.*

possessive adjective, an adjective that shows possession, formed from a personal pronoun. In the sentence *This is your book, your* is a possessive adjective.

possessive pronoun, a pronoun that shows possession, formed from a personal pronoun. In the sentence *This book is mine, mine* is a possessive pronoun.

pos·si·bil·i·ty (pos′ə bil′i tē) *n., pl.* **pos·si·bil·i·ties.** **1.** the state or fact of being possible; likelihood: *There is a possibility that we will meet them tonight.* **2.** something

possible: *Winning the championship is a possibility for our team.*

pos·si·ble (pos′ə bəl) *adj.* **1.** capable of existing, happening, being done, or being proven true: *It is possible that they are lying. It is not possible to be in two places at the same time.* **2.** capable of being used, chosen, or considered; potential: *a possible candidate for the presidency.*

pos·si·bly (pos′ə blē) *adv.* **1.** by any possibility: *Our plan can't possibly succeed.* **2.** by some possibility; perhaps: *I'll see you today, or possibly tomorrow.*

pos·sum (pos′əm) *n.* see **opossum.**

post¹ (pōst) *n.* an upright piece of wood, stone, or other solid material, usually used as a support or marker. —*v.t.* **1.** to put up (an announcement or notice) in a public place. **2.** to announce by or as if by putting up a notice: *The teacher posted the grades on the door. The authorities posted a reward.* **3.** to put up signs or notices warning against trespassing on (property): *The new owner closed the gate and posted the lot.* [From the Old English word *post,* from the Latin word *postis* meaning "the post beside a doorway."]

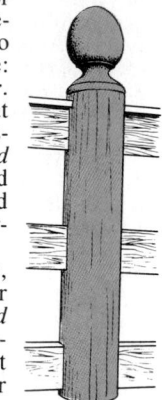

post¹ *(n.)*

post² (pōst) *n.* **1.** a place where a soldier, police officer, or the like is stationed or assigned for duty: *The guards were ordered not to leave their posts except in an emergency.* **2.** a military area with permanent buildings where soldiers are assigned for work and training; military base. **3.** a position of employment, especially a public office to which one is appointed: *The ambassador has just been assigned a new post.* **4.** see **trading post.** —*v.t.* **1.** to station at or assign to a post: *The police posted guards at all exits of the building.* **2.** to provide or put up (bail). [From the French word *poste* with the same meaning, from the early Italian word *posto* "sentry's post," going back to the Latin word *ponere* "to put, place."]

post³ (pōst) *n.* **1.** a system by which mail is collected, carried, and delivered: *to send a letter by post.* **2.** a single delivery of mail: *I received a letter in today's post.* **3.** formerly, one of a series of stations providing relays of people and horses for the carrying and delivery of mail. —*v.t.* **1.** to deposit in a mailbox or at a post office: *to post a letter.* **2.** *Informal.* to supply with information or the latest news; inform: *Keep me posted on what happens while I am away.* [From the Middle French word *poste* meaning "a relay station" or "speedy messenger," from the early Italian word *posta* "relay station."]

post– *prefix* coming afterward in time or order: *postwar.*

post·age (pōs′tij) *n.* the amount charged to send something by mail.

postage stamp, an official stamp issued and sold by a government, to be placed on mail to show payment of postage.

post·al (pōs′təl) *adj.* of, relating to, or concerning mail or its collection and delivery.

post·card (pōst′kärd′) a card, often with a picture on one side, that can be sent through the mail without an envelope. Also, **postal card.**

post chaise, a four-wheeled, horse-drawn carriage, used to carry mail and passengers from station to station.

post·date (pōst dāt′) *v.t.,* **post·dat·ed, post·dat·ing.** **1.** to date (a check, letter, or the like) with a date that is later than the actual one. **2.** to occur later than; follow in time.

post·er (pōs′tər) *n.* a large printed sign that carries a public notice or advertisement, often with a colorful illustration.

pos·te·ri·or (pos tîr′ē ər, pōs tîr′ē ər) *adj.* **1.** situated at or toward the back; rear. **2.** later in time; subsequent. —*n.* the rear; buttocks.

pos·ter·i·ty (pos ter′i tē) *n.* **1.** all generations of the future: *Posterity will judge the worth of our achievements.* **2.** all of one's descendants.

pos·tern (pōs′tərn, pos′tərn) *n.* the back door or gate, as of a castle or fortification.

post exchange, a government store at a military post that sells tax-free goods to soldiers and their families and to civilian employees.

post·grad·u·ate (pōst graj′ü it) *adj.* of, relating to, or taking a course of study after graduation from a college or school, especially after receiving a bachelor's degree. —*n.* a postgraduate student.

post·haste (pōst′hāst′) *adv.* as quickly as possible; with the utmost haste.

post·hu·mous (pos′chə məs) *adj.* **1.** published after the death of the author: *a posthumous book.* **2.** coming or happening after one's death: *a posthumous award, posthumous fame.* **3.** (of a child) born after the death of the father. —**post′hu·mous·ly,** *adv.*

pos·til·ion (pōs til′yən, pos til′yən) *also,* **pos·til·lion.** *n.* a person who guides the team of a horse-drawn carriage by riding the left lead horse.

post·im·pres·sion·ism (pōst′im presh′ə niz′əm) *n.* a style in French painting, beginning in the late nineteenth century and lasting until the early twentieth century, characterized by the work of such painters as Georges Seurat, Vincent Van Gogh, and Paul Cézanne. —**post′·im·pres′sion·ist,** *n., adj.* —**post′im·pres′sion·is′tic,** *adj.*

post·man (pōst′mən) *n., pl.* **post·men** (pōst′mən). another word for **mailman** or **mail carrier.**

post·mark (pōst′märk′) *n.* an official mark stamped on mail to cancel the postage stamp and to show the place and date of mailing. —*v.t.* to stamp with a postmark.

post·mas·ter (pōst′mas′tər) *n.* the official in charge of a post office.

postmaster general *pl.* **postmasters general.** **1.** the head of the postal service of a country. **2. Postmaster General.** the head of the postal service of the United States, appointed by the president with the approval of the Senate.

post me·ri·di·em (pōst′mə rid′ē əm) between noon and midnight. *Abbreviation,* **P.M.** [From the Latin phrase *post meridiem* meaning "after midday."]

post·mis·tress (pōst′mis′tris) *n., pl.* **post·mis·tress·es.** a woman in charge of a post office.

post·mor·tem (pōst′môr′təm) *adj.* taking place or done after a person's death: *a postmortem examination.* —*n.* a medical examination of a dead body; autopsy.

post·na·tal (pōst nā′təl) *adj.* taking place after birth: *postnatal care.*

post office **1.** the department or agency of a national government in charge of handling mail. **2.** the local branch of such a department, responsible for the collection, sorting, and distribution of mail.

post·op·er·a·tive (pōst op′ər ə tiv, pōst op′rə tiv) *adj.* done or happening after a surgical operation: *postoperative care.*

post·paid (pōst′pād′) *adj.* having the postage paid by the sender.

post·pone (pōst pōn′) *v.t.,* **post·poned, post·pon·ing.** to put off to a later time. —**post·pone′ment,** *n.*

post road, a road over which mail was carried by riders, with stations along the way that provided fresh horses.

post·script (pōst′skript) *n.* **1.** a message or note added to a letter after the writer's signature. **2.** any material added to or supplementing a composition or literary work.

pos·tu·late (*n.,* pos′chə lit; *v.,* pos′chə lāt′) *n.* a statement or principle accepted as true without proof; self-evident or universally accepted truth. —*v.t.,* **pos·tu-**

lat·ed, pos·tu·lat·ing. **1.** to accept (something) as true without proof; take for granted. **2.** to require, demand, or claim.

pos·ture (pos′chər) *n.* **1.** the way of carrying or holding the head and body; carriage: *That athlete has good posture.* **2.** a position of the body or of parts of the body: *a crouching posture.* **3.** an attitude or position: *The army assumed a defensive posture.* —*v.,* **pos·tured, pos·tur·ing.** —*v.i.* to take or assume a certain posture, especially for effect. —*v.t.* to put in a certain position; pose. —**pos′tur·al,** *adj.*

post·war (pōst′wôr′) *adj.* after a war.

po·sy (pō′zē) *n., pl.* **po·sies.** **1.** a single flower. **2.** a bouquet of flowers; nosegay.

pot (pot) *n.* **1.** a container of metal, earthenware, or other material, usually round and sometimes having one or two handles, used in cooking, for holding growing plants, and for many other purposes. **2.** the contents of or the amount contained in a pot: *I made a pot of coffee.* **3.** the amount of money bet on a single hand in a card game, especially poker. **4.** a trap, as for crabs or lobsters. **5.** *Informal.* a large sum of money. **6.** *Slang.* marijuana. —*v.t.,* **pot·ted, pot·ting.** **1.** to put into a flowerpot: *to pot a plant.* **2.** to cook or preserve (food) in a pot or jar: *to pot beef.* **3.** to shoot (game) for food rather than for sport. **·to go to pot.** to become ruined or run-down: *The estate went to pot after the owners died.*

po·ta·ble (pō′tə bəl) *adj.* fit or suitable for drinking. —*n.* something drinkable; drink.

pot·ash (pot′ash′) *n.* any of various compounds that contain potassium, used especially in fertilizers, in soaps, and in making glass. [From the earlier phrase *pot ashes.* Potash was obtained from wood *ashes* in an iron *pot.*]

po·tas·si·um (pə tas′ē əm) *n.* a very soft, light, silver-white metallic element. Its compounds are used in fertilizers, soaps, and explosives. Symbol: **K** [The English chemist Sir Humphrey Davy (1778–1829) coined the word *potassium* from the word *potass* meaning "potash," because potassium can be found in potash.]

potassium hydroxide, a caustic, white compound, used especially in making soap.

potassium nitrate, a colorless crystalline compound, used especially in gunpowder and explosives, fertilizers, and medicine. Also, **niter, saltpeter.**

po·ta·to (pə tā′tō) *n., pl.* **po·ta·toes.** **1.** the underground tuber of a leafy, low-growing plant, cultivated as a vegetable. The potato was originally grown in South America. It is a basic food in Europe, America, and other parts of the world, and is used to make a wide variety of products, such as starch, flour, and vodka. **2.** the plant bearing this tuber. **3.** see **sweet potato.**

potato chip, a very thin slice of potato, fried crisp and usually salted.

pot·bel·lied (pot′bel′ēd) *adj.* **1.** having a potbelly. **2.** having the shape of a potbelly: *a potbellied stove.*

pot·bel·ly (pot′bel′ē) *n., pl.* **pot·bel·lies.** **1.** a large, bulging belly. **2.** a person who has such a belly.

pot·boil·er (pot′boi′lər) *n. Informal.* an inferior piece of writing or art produced solely to earn money.

potbellied stove

P

po·ten·cy (pō'tən sē) *n.* the state or quality of being potent.

po·tent (pō'tənt) *adj.* having force, effectiveness, strength, or power: *a potent medicine, a potent argument.* —**po'tent·ly,** *adv.*

po·ten·tate (pō'tən tāt') *n.* a person who has great power or authority, such as a monarch or ruler.

po·ten·tial (pə ten'shəl) *adj.* capable of being or becoming; possible but not actual: *a potential leader, a potential criminal, a potential source of trouble.* —*n.* **1.** a quality or ability capable of being developed or advanced: *a novelist with great potential.* **2.** the amount of electrification of a point in an electric circuit or field in relation to some standard reference point in the same circuit or field. —**po·ten'tial·ly,** *adv.*

potential energy, the energy stored by a body due to its position or structure. A coiled spring has potential energy.

po·ten·ti·al·i·ty (pə ten'shē al'i tē) *n., pl.* **po·ten·ti·al·i·ties. 1.** a potential quality or ability. **2.** something potential; possibility.

pot·ful (pot'fùl') *n., pl.* **pot·fuls.** the amount that a pot can hold: *a potful of tea.*

pot·herb (pot'ûrb', pot'hûrb') *n.* any plant whose leaves, stems, or flowers are cooked and eaten as a vegetable, such as spinach, or are used as a seasoning, such as sage or thyme.

pot·hold·er (pot'hōl'dər) *n.* a thick cloth pad used to handle hot cooking utensils safely.

pot·hole (pot'hōl') *n.* **1.** a deep hole worn in the rock bed of a river or stream by stones and gravel whirled around by the force of the current. **2.** any deep hole, especially in the surface of a street or road.

pot·hook (pot'hùk') *n.* **1.** a hook used to hang a pot over an open fire. **2.** an iron rod with a hook at the end, used to lift hot pots, irons, or stove lids.

po·tion (pō'shən) *n.* a drink, especially one believed to have magical powers. [From the Old French word *poition* meaning "a mixture of liquids," from the Latin word *potio* "a drink," from the word *potare* "to drink."]

pot·latch (pot'lach') *n.* a feast held by certain American Indian tribes of the Pacific Northwest at which the host gives away and sometimes destroys valuable objects as a show of wealth.

pot·luck (pot'luk') *n.* whatever food may be available for a meal for which no special preparation was made: *If you stay for dinner, you'll have to take pot luck.*

pot·pie (pot'pī') *n.* **1.** a pie filled with meat or poultry and usually vegetables. **2.** a meat stew with dumplings.

pot·pour·ri (pō'pù rē') *n.* **1.** a medley, mixture, or collection: *The program consisted of a potpourri of folk songs.* **2.** a mixture of dried flower petals and spices, kept in a jar and used for fragrance, as for a room, closet, or chest of drawers.

pot roast, meat, usually beef, browned in a pot, covered, and cooked slowly in a little water, often with vegetables.

pot·sherd (pot'shûrd') *n.* a fragment of pottery, especially one found at an archaeological site.

pot·shot (pot'shot') **1.** a shot fired at random or without careful aim from close range. **2.** a shot fired to kill game for food, with little or no regard to the rules of sport. **3.** a seemingly careless criticism: *The reviewer of the new movie took several potshots at the star.*

pot·tage (pot'ij) *n.* a thick soup or broth.

pot·ter¹ (pot'ər) *n.* a person who makes pottery: *The potter makes beautiful vases.*

pot·ter² (pot'ər) another word for **putter¹.**

potter's field, a piece of ground used as a burial place for the poor and the unknown.

potter's wheel, a rotating level disk that is turned by a motor or by pumping with the foot, used by a potter to shape objects from soft clay.

potter's wheel

pot·ter·y (pot'ə-rē) *n., pl.* **pot·ter·ies. 1.** pots, vases, and other objects made from soft clay and hardened by heat. **2.** the art or technique of making pottery. **3.** a place where pottery is made.

pouch (pouch) *n., pl.* **pouch·es. 1.** a bag or sack made of a flexible material, such as leather or canvas: *The mail carrier's pouch was full of letters.* **2.** a bag-like part on the belly of the female of marsupials, such as kangaroos and opossums, in which the young are carried after birth. **3.** any baglike part, as under the bill of a pelican.

poul·tice (pōl'tis) *n.* a soft, moist mass of a substance, such as a mustard compound, heated and applied to a part of the body as a treatment for soreness or inflammation. —*v.t.,* **poul·ticed, poul·tic·ing.** to apply a poultice to.

poul·try (pōl'trē) *n.* any domestic fowl, such as chickens, turkeys, geese, or ducks, raised for their meat or eggs.

pounce (pouns) *v.i.,* **pounced, pounc·ing.** to swoop down, spring, or leap suddenly in or as if in attack: *The tiger pounced on its prey.* —*n.* the act of pouncing.

pound¹ (pound) *n., pl.* **pounds** or **pound. 1.** a unit of weight equal to 16 ounces avoirdupois (0.4536 kilogram). **2.** a unit of weight equal to 12 ounces troy, or 5,670 grains apothecaries' (0.3732 kilogram). **3.** the monetary unit of the United Kingdom, equal to 100 pence, formerly equal to twenty shillings. Also, **pound sterling. 4.** a monetary unit of various other countries, such as Ireland, Egypt, Ghana, and Israel. [From the Old English word *pund,* a measure of weight, from the Latin word *pondo* meaning "by weight," from *pondus* "a weight."]

pound² (pound) *v.t.* **1.** to hit with heavy, repeated blows: *The carpenter pounded the nail into the wall.* **2.** to make into a powder or pulp by pounding; pulverize: *Ancient peoples used stones to pound grain into meal.* —*v.i.* **1.** to strike heavy, repeated blows: *The waves pounded against the rocks.* **2.** to beat heavily: *The runner's heart was pounding.* **3.** to move heavily: *The horses pounded along the road.* —*n.* **1.** a heavy blow. **2.** the sound of this; thump; thud. [From the Old English word *pūnian* meaning "to beat, pound²."]

pound³ (pound) *n.* an enclosed place for confining animals, especially stray dogs. [From the Middle English word *pounde* with the same meaning, from the Old English word *pyndan* "to enclose, shut in."]

pound cake, a rich cake made with eggs, butter, sugar, and flour. [From the original recipe, which specified 1 pound of each ingredient.]

pound–fool·ish (pound′fü′lish) *adj.* unwise or careless about spending large sums of money.
pound sterling, see **pound**[1] (*def. 3*).
pour (pôr) *v.t.* **1.** to cause to flow in a steady stream: *to pour water from a bucket.* **2.** to speak of or reveal freely or openly: *to pour out one's anger.* —*v.i.* **1.** to flow in a steady stream: *The stream poured into the river.* **2.** to rain hard. **3.** to move or come forth in great numbers; swarm: *The people poured out of the stadium.* **4.** to act as a host by pouring beverages for guests. —*n.* a heavy rainfall; downpour. —**pour′er,** *n.*
pout (pout) *v.i.* **1.** to thrust out the lips, as in displeasure or sullenness. **2.** to be sullen; sulk. —*n.* **1.** a thrusting out of the lips, as when displeased. **2.** a fit of sullenness: *The little child was in a pout all day.*
pout·er (pou′tər) *n.* any of a breed of domestic pigeons having an enlarged crop that can be inflated with air and puffed out.
pov·er·ty (pov′ər tē) *n.* **1.** the state of being poor: *to live in poverty.* **2.** the lack of what is needed or desired: *the poverty of the soil in a desert area.* **3.** smallness of amount; scarcity: *This poem shows a poverty of imagination.*
pov·er·ty–strick·en (pov′ər tē strik′ən) *adj.* very poor; destitute.
POW (pē′ō dub′əl ū′) *n., pl.* **POW's.** a prisoner of war.
pow·der (pou′dər) *n.* **1.** fine, minute particles produced by grinding, crushing, pounding, or crumbling a dry substance. **2.** any of various preparations or substances in such a form: *soap powder.* **3.** see **gunpowder.** —*v.t.* **1.** to make into powder; pulverize. **2.** to sprinkle or cover with powder or something like powder: *to powder a rolling pin with flour.* **3.** to use powder as a cosmetic on (the face or body). —*v.i.* to become or be made into powder.
powder horn, a horn of a cow or other animal, used for carrying gunpowder.
powder puff, a soft pad for applying powder to the skin.
powder room 1. a lavatory for women in a public building. **2.** a lavatory for guests, located in the main part of a house.
pow·der·y (pou′də rē) *adj.* **1.** of or like powder: *powdery snow.* **2.** sprinkled or covered with powder. **3.** easily made into powder.
pow·er (pou′ər) *n.* **1.** the ability to do, act, or bring about a particular result or effect: *It is not in my power to help you. The president has the power to veto bills.* **2.** the ability or right to command, control, or make decisions; authority: *They have no power over you.* **3.** *also,* **powers.** a particular ability or faculty: *the power of speech.* **4.** a person or thing that has or exercises influence, control, or authority over others: *The United States is a major world power.* **5.** the political or military strength of a nation, government, or similar organization. **6.** strength; force: *There was no power behind the punch.* **7.** *Mathematics.* **a.** the number of times, indicated by an exponent, that a given number or algebraic expression is multiplied by itself. The power of 4^3 is 3; the power of y^4 is 4. **b.** the product found by multiplying a number or algebraic expression by itself a given number of times as indicated by an exponent. The second power of 5 is 25 since $5^2 = 5 \times 5 = 25$. **8.** energy or force that can do work, such as electricity. **9.** the rate at which work is done or energy is used. **10.** the capacity of a lens or combination of lenses to magnify the apparent size of an object. —*adj.* operated or driven by a motor: *power tools.* —*v.t.* to provide with power, especially mechanical power.
pow·er·boat (pou′ər bōt′) *n.* another word for **motorboat.**
pow·er·ful (pou′ər fəl) *adj.* having great strength, in-fluence, or authority: *a powerful machine, a powerful athlete, a powerful nation.* —**pow′er·ful·ly,** *adv.*
pow·er·house (pou′ər hous′) *n., pl.* **pow·er·hous·es** (pou′ər hou′ziz). **1.** another word for **power plant.** **2.** *Informal.* a person or thing having a great deal of strength or energy.
pow·er·less (pou′ər lis) *adj.* **1.** lacking the ability or authority to do or act. **2.** lacking power or strength; weak. —**pow′er·less·ly,** *adv.*
power of attorney 1. a written document giving one person the authority to act as the attorney or legal representative for another. **2.** the legal authority granted by such a document.
power plant, a building where electrical power is generated.
power saw, a saw with a cutting blade driven by a motor. Circular saws and band saws are common kinds of power saw.
pow·wow (pou′wou′) *n.* **1.** a conference of or with North American Indians. **2.** a North American Indian ceremony characterized by feasting, dancing, and rites performed for the cure of disease or success in war or hunting. **3.** *Informal.* any conference or meeting. —*v.i.* to hold a powwow.
pox (poks) *n.* any of several diseases characterized by skin eruptions, such as chicken pox or smallpox.
pp, pianissimo.
pp. **1.** pages. **2.** past participle.
p.p. **1.** parcel post. Also, **P.P. 2.** past participle. **3.** post-paid.
ppd. **1.** postpaid. **2.** prepaid.
ppr., present participle. Also, **p.pr.**
PQ, postal abbreviation for the Province of Quebec.
P.Q., Province of Quebec.
Pr, the symbol for praseodymium.
pr. **1.** pair; pairs. **2.** price.
PR **1.** postal abbreviation for Puerto Rico. **2.** Public Relations.
P.R., Puerto Rico.
prac·ti·ca·ble (prak′ti kə bəl) *adj.* **1.** capable of being put into practice; feasible: *a practicable plan.* **2.** capable of being used: *a practicable bridge.* —**prac′ti·ca·bil′-i·ty,** *n.* —**prac′ti·ca·bly,** *adv.*
prac·ti·cal (prak′ti kəl) *adj.* **1.** of, relating to, or coming from experience, action, or use rather than from thought or theory: *practical knowledge.* **2.** capable of being done, used, or carried out: *a practical method of solving a problem.* **3.** having or showing good judgment or good sense; sensible. **4.** tending or preferring to do things rather than to think or theorize about them: *a practical person.* **5.** to all intents and purposes; virtual: *Your behavior toward them was a practical insult.*
prac·ti·cal·i·ty (prak′ti kal′i tē) *n., pl.* **prac·ti·cal·i·ties.** **1.** the state or quality of being practical. **2.** something practical.
practical joke, a prank, trick, or other joke played on someone, especially in order to cause embarrassment.
prac·ti·cal·ly (prak′ti kə lē, prak′ti klē) *adv.* **1.** to all intents and purposes; virtually: *They are practically engaged.* **2.** nearly; almost: *The work is practically finished.* **3.** in a practical manner.
practical nurse, a person who has training and experi-

P

---

at; āpe; fär; câre; end; mē; it; īce; pîerce; hot; ōld; sông; fôrk; oil; out; up; ūse; rüle; pull; tûrn; chin; sing; shop; thin; this; hw in white; zh in treasure. The symbol ə stands for the unstressed vowel sound heard in about, taken, pencil, lemon, and circus.

ence in performing certain nursing duties, but lacks the training and education of a registered nurse.

prac·tice (prak′tis) *also* (v.), *British*, **prac·tise**. *n.* **1.** the repeated or continuous performance of an action in order to gain knowledge or skill: *Practice makes perfect.* **2.** a period or session during which such an action is performed: *He has football practice every afternoon.* **3.** the condition of being skilled through repeated or continuous performance of an action: *to be out of practice.* **4.** the act or process of doing, using, or carrying out something; execution: *The idea seemed good, but it did not work in practice.* **5.** the usual way of doing something; custom; habit: *She makes a practice of calling whenever she is going to be late.* **6.** the active following of or working at a profession or occupation: *the practice of medicine.* **7.** the business of a doctor or lawyer: *The new doctor has a small practice.* —*v.*, **prac·ticed**, **prac·tic·ing.** —*v.t.* **1.** to do (something) repeatedly or continuously in order to gain knowledge or skill: *I practice the piano every day.* **2.** to carry out in action; put into practice: *Practice what you preach.* **3.** to make a habit or custom of: *to practice caution.* **4.** to work at or follow as a profession or occupation: *to practice law.* —*v.i.* **1.** to perform something repeatedly or continuously in order to gain knowledge or skill. **2.** to work at or follow a profession or occupation.

prac·ticed (prak′tist) *also, British,* **prac·tised.** *adj.* skilled or expert through practice; experienced.

prac·tise (prak′tis) *British. v.*, **prac·tised, prac·tis·ing.** another spelling of **practice.**

prac·ti·tion·er (prak tish′ə nər) *n.* a person who practices a profession.

prae·tor (prē′tər) *n.* in ancient Rome, an elected magistrate or judge ranking next below a consul.

prae·to·ri·an (prē tôr′ē ən) *adj.* **1.** of or relating to a praetor. **2. Praetorian.** of or relating to the bodyguard of a Roman emperor or commander. —*n.* **1.** another word for **praetor. 2. Praetorian.** a bodyguard of a Roman emperor or commander.

prag·mat·ic (prag mat′ik) *adj.* **1.** concerned with practical results or values rather than thought or theory. **2.** of or relating to pragmatism. Also, **prag·mat·i·cal** (prag mat′i kəl). —**prag·mat′i·cal·ly,** *adv.*

prag·ma·tism (prag′mə tiz′əm) *n.* **1.** a philosophy set forth in the late nineteenth century, holding that the truth of an idea should be evaluated in terms of its practical consequences. **2.** a practical character or quality.

prag·ma·tist (prag′mə tist) *n.* a person who believes in pragmatism.

prai·rie (prâr′ē) *n.* a large, level or gently rolling grassland without trees.

prairie chicken, a grouse of the prairies of North America.

prairie dog, either of two species of burrowing rodents that live in large colonies in the plains of central North America and have a call like a dog's bark.

prairie schooner, a covered wagon used by pioneers in crossing the prairies westward.

prairie wolf, another term for **coyote.**

praise (prāz) *n.* **1.** the expression of admiration or approval. **2.** the worship or glorification of a god, ruler, or hero, especially worship of God when expressed in words or song. —*v.t.*, **praised**, **prais·ing.** **1.** to express admiration or approval of; commend: *The critics praised the author's latest novel.* **2.** to worship or glorify in words or song: *to praise God.* [From the Old French word *preisier* meaning "to price, value," going back to the Latin word *pretium* "price."] —**prais′er,** *n.*

prairie dog

praise·wor·thy (prāz′wûr′thē) *adj.* worthy of praise; commendable. —**praise′wor′thi·ly,** *adv.* —**praise′wor′thi·ness,** *n.*

pram (pram) *n. Informal.* a baby carriage; perambulator.

prance (prans) *v.i.*, **pranced, pranc·ing.** **1.** to move in a proud, lively way; strut; swagger: *The band pranced across the football field.* **2.** (of a horse) to spring forward from the hind legs. **3.** to ride on a horse that is prancing. **4.** to run, leap, or skip about in play: *The children pranced about in the yard.* —*n.* **1.** the act of prancing. **2.** a prancing movement.

prank (prangk) *n.* a mischievous or playful act. —**prank′ish,** *adj.*

prank·ster (prangk′stər) *n.* a person who plays tricks or practical jokes; mischievous person.

pra·se·o·dym·i·um (prā′sē ō dim′ē əm) *n.* a soft, slightly yellow metallic element of the rare-earth group, used to color glass, enamel, and artificial emeralds. Symbol: **Pr** [Formed from the Greek word *prasios* meaning "green" + the scientific Latin word *didymium*, name of a mixture of rare-earth elements. Praseodymium was found in the green salts of didymium.]

prate (prāt) *v.*, **prat·ed, prat·ing.** —*v.i.* to talk at length in an idle or foolish manner; chatter; babble. —*v.t.* to say in an idle or foolish manner. —*n.* idle or foolish talk; prattle. —**prat′er,** *n.*

prat·tle (prat′əl) *v.*, **prat·tled, prat·tling.** —*v.i.* to talk childishly or foolishly; babble. —*v.t.* to say or tell in a childish or foolish manner. —*n.* **1.** childish or foolish talk. **2.** a sound that is similar to baby talk. —**prat′tler,** *n.*

prawn (prôn) *n.* any of various shellfish resembling shrimp but larger, found in salt and fresh waters.

pray (prā) *v.i.* **1.** to speak to God or a god with adoration, appeal, or thanksgiving. **2.** to ask or request from God or a god: *to pray for divine guidance.* —*v.t.* **1.** to ask of or for earnestly; beg; entreat: *I pray you to stay.* **2.** to get or bring about by praying. **3.** to be so kind or obliging as to; please. ▲ used to express a request or command politely: *Pray be quiet.*

prayer (prâr) *n.* **1.** the act of praying to God or a god. **2.** something prayed for: *Their prayers were granted.* **3.** a set form of words used in praying: *a book of prayers.* **4.** *also,* **prayers.** a form of worship consisting mainly of prayers: *morning prayers.* **5.** an earnest request; entreaty.

prayer book, a book containing prayers and often other forms of religious worship.

prayer·ful (prâr′fəl) *adj.* characterized by, given to, or used in prayer; devout: *a prayerful attitude.* —**prayer′ful·ly,** *adv.* —**prayer′ful·ness,** *n.*

praying mantis, any of a group of brown or green insects related to the grasshopper, found especially in the tropics, having stout, spiny forelegs for grasping their prey. Also, **mantis.** [So named because it often holds its forelegs as though it were *praying.*]

pre– *prefix* **1.** before in place, time, or rank: *prewar, prehistoric.* **2.** in preparation for: *preschool.* [From the Old French prefix *pre-*, going back to the Latin word *prae* meaning "before, in front of."]

preach (prēch) *v.i.* **1.** to speak publicly on a religious subject;

praying mantis

deliver a sermon. **2.** to give advice, especially in a boring way: *They are always preaching to me about saving my allowance.* —*v.t.* **1.** to set forth by preaching: *The missionaries preached the glory of God.* **2.** to recommend strongly: *to preach understanding.* **3.** to deliver (a sermon).

preach·er (prē'chər) *n.* a person who preaches, especially a member of the Protestant clergy.

preach·y (prē'chē) *adj.,* **preach·i·er, preach·i·est.** *Informal.* tending to preach or suggestive of preaching; dogmatic: *a preachy editorial, a preachy writer.*

pre·am·ble (prē'am'bəl) *n.* a preliminary statement or introduction, especially one stating or explaining reasons or purposes: *the preamble of a law.*

pre·ar·range (prē'ə rānj') *v.t.,* **pre·ar·ranged, pre·ar·rang·ing.** to arrange beforehand. —**pre'ar·range'ment,** *n.*

Pre·cam·bri·an (prē kam'brē ən) *n.* the earliest geological era, comprising four fifths of the history of the earth. During the Precambrian, bacteria, algae, and other simple organisms appeared and the earth's atmosphere developed through the process of photosynthesis. By the end of the Precambrian the first animals appeared. —*adj.* of, relating to, or characteristic of this era.

pre·car·i·ous (pri kâr'ē əs) *adj.* **1.** dependent on chance or circumstance; uncertain; insecure: *a precarious investment.* **2.** dangerous; perilous: *The climber was in a precarious position on a cliff.* [From the Latin word *precarius* meaning "obtained by prayer or begging," from the word *precor* "to ask, beg, pray for."] —**pre·car'i·ous·ly,** *adv.*

pre·cau·tion (pri kô'shən) *n.* **1.** a measure taken beforehand to avoid danger, failure, loss, or harm: *We took precautions against burglary by installing a complex system of electronic alarms.* **2.** caution or care taken beforehand; foresight.

pre·cau·tion·ar·y (pri kô'shə ner'ē) *adj.* relating to, advising, or using precaution: *precautionary advice.*

pre·cede (pri sēd') *v.,* **pre·ced·ed, pre·ced·ing.** —*v.t.* to go or come before or ahead of, as in time, order, rank, or importance: *My parents preceded me through the door.* —*v.i.* to be, go, or come before.

prec·e·dence (pres'i dəns, pri sē'dəns) *n.* **1.** the act or fact of preceding, as in time, rank, or order: *Deciding on a new class treasurer will take precedence over collecting the dues.* **2.** the right to precede others because of superiority of rank or position, especially at ceremonial or formal occasions: *the precedence of a senator over a representative at a state banquet.*

prec·e·dent (*n.,* pres'i dənt; *adj.,* pri sē'dənt, pres'i-dənt) *n.* an action that may serve as an example for similar future actions: *The judge's ruling established a precedent for similar cases.* —*adj.* going or coming before; preceding.

pre·ced·ing (pri sē'ding) *adj.* going or coming before; previous: *That information is on the preceding page.*

pre·cept (prē'sept) *n.* **1.** a rule or principle intended as a guide for behavior or action. **2.** a short statement expressing a general truth or doctrine. For example: *A stitch in time saves nine.*

pre·cep·tor (pri sep'tər) *n.* a teacher; instructor.

pre·ces·sion (prē sesh'ən) *n.* the act or fact of preceding.

pre·cinct (prē'singkt') *n.* **1.** a subdivision or district of a city or town: *a police precinct, an election precinct.* **2.** a police station in such a district. **3.** *also,* **precincts.** a space or area within fixed limits: *the precincts of a university campus.*

pre·cious (presh'əs) *adj.* **1.** having great cost or value; costly: *Silver is a precious metal. Diamonds are precious stones.* **2.** beloved; dear: *a precious child.* **3.** overly elegant or refined: *precious manners.* **4.** *Informal.* very great. —*adv. Informal.* extremely; very: *The campers had precious little food remaining.* —*n.* loved one; dear; darling. —**pre'cious·ly,** *adv.* —**pre'cious·ness,** *n.*

precious stone, a rare, valuable gem, as a diamond or emerald.

prec·i·pice (pres'ə pis) *n.* a high, steep, often vertical face of rock.

pre·cip·i·tate (*v.,* pri sip'i tāt'; *n., adj.,* pri sip'i tit, pri sip'i tāt'), *v.,* **pre·cip·i·tat·ed, pre·cip·i·tat·ing.** —*v.t.* **1.** to cause to happen before expected, needed, or desired: *My hasty criticism precipitated the argument.* **2.** to throw down violently; hurl downward. **3.** *Chemistry.* to cause (a substance in a solution) to combine to form a solid substance. **4.** to cause (a vapor) to condense and fall as rain, snow, or dew. —*v.i.* **1.** (of vapor) to be condensed and fall in the form of rain, snow, or dew. **2.** *Chemistry.* to be precipitated. **3.** to fall headlong. —*n.* a solid chemical compound formed in a solution by the reaction of ions of a dissolved compound or element with ions of a compound or element added to the solution. —*adj.* **1.** falling or rushing rapidly or headlong. **2.** acting or done in a hasty or rash manner. **3.** coming suddenly or unexpectedly; abrupt: *a precipitate change in the weather.* —**pre·cip'i·tate·ly,** *adv.*

pre·cip·i·ta·tion (pri sip'i tā'shən) *n.* **1.** any form of water that falls to earth, such as rain, hail, or snow. **2.** the depositing of such moisture on the earth. **3.** the amount, as of rain or snow, deposited. **4.** the chemical process of forming solid substances in a solution. **5.** the act of precipitating or the state of being precipitated. **6.** rash or sudden haste.

pre·cip·i·tous (pri sip'i təs) *adj.* **1.** like or having a precipice or precipices; very steep: *precipitous cliffs.* **2.** hasty; rash: *a precipitous decision.* —**pre·cip'i·tous·ly,** *adv.* —**pre·cip'i·tous·ness,** *n.*

pre·cise (pri sīs') *adj.* **1.** very accurate or definite; exact: *The instructions were not very precise.* **2.** being exactly what is called for or needed; neither more nor less: *Measure out the precise amount of flour for the cake.* **3.** distinguished from others; particular; exact: *At that precise moment they entered the room.* **4.** very strict or careful, as in following rules or standards: *a rigid, precise person.* —**pre·cise'ly,** *adv.* —**pre·cise'ness,** *n.*

pre·ci·sion (pri sizh'ən) *n.* the state or quality of being precise; accuracy; exactness. —*adj.* marked by or designed for a high degree of fineness or accuracy: *a precision tool.*

pre·clude (pri klud') *v.t.,* **pre·clud·ed, pre·clud·ing.** to make impossible; prevent: *A lack of money precluded our going to the circus.*

pre·co·cious (pri kō'shəs) *adj.* developed or matured earlier than usual: *a precocious child.* [Originally from the Latin word *praecox* meaning "ripe before its time."] —**pre·co'cious·ly,** *adv.* —**pre·co'cious·ness,** *n.*

pre·coc·i·ty (pri kos'i tē) *n.* the state or quality of being precocious; early development or maturity.

pre–Co·lum·bi·an (prē'kə lum'bē ən) *adj.* of, relating to, or belonging to the time before Columbus arrived in America: *The museum has a collection of pre-Columbian art from Central America.*

pre·con·ceive (prē'kən sēv') *v.t.,* **pre·con·ceived, pre·con·ceiv·ing.** to form an idea or opinion of beforehand: *preconceived notions.*

pre·con·cep·tion (prē'kən sep'shən) *n.* an idea or opinion formed beforehand.

pre·cook (prē kůk') *v.t.* **1.** to cook beforehand for later reheating. **2.** to cook partially before the final cooking.

pre·cur·sor (pri kûr'sər) *n.* a person or thing that pre-

P

at; āpe; fär; câre; end; mē; it; īce; pîerce; hot; ōld; sông, fôrk; oil; out; up; ūse; rüle; půll; tûrn; chin; sing; shop; thin; **th**is; hw in white; zh in treasure. The symbol ə stands for the unstressed vowel sound heard in about, taken, pencil, lemon, and circus.

cedes and announces or indicates the approach of another; forerunner.

pred., predicate.

pre·date (prē dāt') *v.t.,* **pre·dat·ed, pre·dat·ing. 1.** to be or happen earlier than; precede in time. **2.** to give a date earlier than the correct one: *to predate a check.*

pred·a·tor (pred'ə tər) *n.* **1.** an animal, such as a wolf, lion, or hawk, that lives by preying on other animals. **2.** a predatory person.

pred·a·to·ry (pred'ə tôr'ē) *adj.* **1.** living by preying on other animals: *Wolves are predatory animals.* **2.** given to plundering, robbing, or exploiting others: *a predatory pirate and crew.*

pred·e·ces·sor (pred'ə ses'ər) *n.* a person who comes before another in time, especially in an office or position.

pre·des·ti·na·tion (prē des'tə nā'shən) *n.* **1.** the act of predestining or the state of being predestined. **2.** the doctrine that God has preordained the salvation or damnation of each soul.

pre·des·tine (prē des'tin) *v.t.,* **pre·des·tined, pre·des·tin·ing.** to determine, decree, or decide beforehand; foreordain.

pre·de·ter·mine (prē'di tûr'min) *v.t.,* **pre·de·ter·mined, pre·de·ter·min·ing.** to determine, decree, or decide beforehand. —**pre·de·ter'mi·na'tion,** *n.*

pre·dic·a·ment (pri dik'ə mənt) *n.* an unpleasant, trying, or difficult situation.

pred·i·cate (*n.,* pred'i kit; *v.,* pred'i kāt') *n.* the part of a sentence or clause that expresses what is said about the subject, consisting of the verb with its objects and modifiers. In the sentence *The dog ran home quickly, ran home quickly* is the predicate. —*v.t.,* **pred·i·cat·ed, pred·i·cat·ing. 1.** to found or base (an action, statement, or the like): *to predicate a belief on one's experiences.* **2.** to declare or affirm to be an attribute, quality, or property of something: *to predicate coldness of ice.* **3.** to declare or affirm. —**pred'i·ca'tive·ly,** *adv.*

predicate adjective, an adjective that follows a linking verb and refers to the subject of the verb. In the sentence *The woods are lovely, lovely* is a predicate adjective.

predicate nominative, a noun or pronoun that follows a linking verb and refers to the subject of the verb. In the sentence *You are a student, student* is a predicate nominative.

predicate noun, a noun that is a predicate nominative.

pre·dict (pri dikt') *v.t.* to announce or declare beforehand; prophesy: *to predict tomorrow's weather.* —*v.i.* to make a prediction. —**pre·dict'a·ble,** *adj.* —**pre·dict'a·bly,** *adv.*

pre·dic·tion (pri dik'shən) *n.* **1.** the act of predicting. **2.** something predicted; prophecy: *Your predictions about the election came true.*

pre·di·lec·tion (pred'ə lek'shən, prē'də lek'shən) *n.* a preference or particular liking: *a predilection for peanuts.*

pre·dis·pose (prē'dis pōz') *v.t.,* **pre·dis·posed, pre·dis·pos·ing. 1.** to make susceptible or subject to: *His poor health predisposes him to colds.* **2.** to give an inclination to; influence: *Her honesty predisposed me to like her.*

pre·dis·po·si·tion (prē'dis pə zish'ən) *n.* the state of being predisposed; inclination: *I have a predisposition to rise early in the morning.*

pre·dom·i·nance (pri dom'ə nəns) *n.* the state or quality of being predominant: *There was a predominance of nurses at the hospital meeting.*

pre·dom·i·nant (pri dom'ə nənt) *adj.* **1.** having or exerting superior power, authority, or influence over others: *Who is the predominant member of your group?* **2.** more frequent, common, or noticeable: *Red is the predominant color in that painting.* —**pre·dom'i·nant·ly,** *adv.*

pre·dom·i·nate (pri dom'ə nāt') *v.i.,* **pre·dom·i·nat·ed,**

pre·dom·i·nat·ing. 1. to have or exert superior power, authority, or influence; have control: *That child predominates over the younger ones.* **2.** to be greater than others, as in power or influence; prevail: *Bright colors predominate in this printed fabric.* —**pre·dom'i·na'tion,** *n.*

pre·em·i·nent (prē em'ə nənt) *also,* **pre·em·i·nent.** *adj.* superior to or surpassing others; outstanding: *a preeminent surgeon.* —**pre·em'i·nence;** *also,* **pre·em'i·nence,** *n.* —**pre·em'i·nent·ly;** *also,* **pre·em'i·nent·ly,** *adv.*

pre·empt (prē empt') *also,* **pre·empt.** *v.t.* **1.** to get or take possession of before others: *My parents always preempt the morning paper.* **2.** to settle on (public land) with the right to purchase it before or in preference to others. **3.** (of a radio or television program) to be presented in the place of (another): *The football game preempted the regularly scheduled program.* **4.** to take priority over: *The celebration preempted all other activities.* —**pre·emp'tion;** *also,* **pre·emp'tion,** *n.*

preen (prēn) *v.t.* **1.** (of birds) to clean and smooth (feathers) with the beak. **2.** to dress or adorn (oneself) carefully; primp. **3.** to take or show pride or satisfaction in: *They preened themselves on having made the honor roll.* —*v.i.* to primp.

pre·ex·ist (prē'eg zist') *also,* **pre·ex·ist.** *v.i.* to exist beforehand.

pre·ex·ist·ent (prē eg zis'tənt) *also,* **pre·ex·ist·ent.** *adj.* existing beforehand. —**pre'ex·ist'ence;** *also,* **pre'·ex·ist'ence,** *n.*

pre·fab (prē fab') *n.* a prefabricated house or other building.

prefabricate
constructing a prefabricated house

pre·fab·ri·cate (prē fab'ri kāt') *v.t.,* **pre·fab·ri·cat·ed, pre·fab·ri·cat·ing. 1.** to construct or manufacture in standardized parts for easy and rapid assembly: *to prefabricate houses.* **2.** to make up beforehand: *to prefabricate an excuse for being late for school.* —**pre'fab·ri·ca'tion,** *n.*

pref·ace (pref'is) *n.* an introduction to a speech, book, or similar work, often written by the author. —*v.t.,* **pre·faced, pre·fac·ing. 1.** to introduce or furnish with a preface. **2.** to serve as a preface to: *A short documentary prefaced the featured movie.*

pref·a·to·ry (pref'ə tôr'ē) *adj.* relating to, like, or serving as a preface; introductory: *prefatory remarks.*

pre·fect (prē'fekt) *n.* **1.** in ancient Rome, any of various high-ranking military or civil officials. **2.** the head administrative official of one of the departments of France. **3.** the police chief of Paris.

pre·fec·ture (prē'fek chər) *n.* the office, district, or residence of a prefect.

pre·fer (pri fûr′) v.t., **pre·ferred, pre·fer·ring.** **1.** to like better; choose above others: *I prefer tea to coffee.* **2.** to put forward or offer for consideration or decision before a court of law or other legal authority: *We didn't prefer charges, since the stolen articles were returned.*

pref·er·a·ble (pref′ər ə bəl) adj. worthy of being chosen over another or others; more desirable. —**pref′er·a·bly,** adv.

pref·er·ence (pref′ər əns) n. **1.** the act of choosing one over others. **2.** the right or opportunity of so choosing: *You may have your preference of dessert for your birthday.* **3.** a person or thing that is preferred; first choice. **4.** the favoring of one person, group, or thing over others.

pref·er·en·tial (pref′ə ren′shəl) adj. showing or giving preference: *preferential treatment.* —**pref′er·en′tial·ly,** adv.

pre·fer·ment (pri fûr′mənt) n. **1.** an advancement, as to higher rank; promotion. **2.** a position or office to which one is advanced.

preferred stock, the stock of a corporation on which dividends must be paid before they can be paid on common stock.

pre·fig·ure (prē fig′yər) v.t., **pre·fig·ured, pre·fig·ur·ing.** **1.** to show, indicate, or suggest beforehand; foreshadow: *The dark clouds prefigured a storm.* **2.** to picture or imagine to oneself beforehand. —**pre′fig·ur·a′tion,** n.

pre·fix (n., prē′fiks′; v., prē fiks′) n., pl. **pre·fix·es.** a syllable or group of syllables added to the beginning of a word, root, or stem so as to change its meaning or to form a new word. In the word *postwar, post-* is a prefix. —v.t. to put before or at the beginning: *to prefix the title "Doctor" to one's name.*

preg·nan·cy (preg′nən sē) n., pl. **preg·nan·cies.** the quality, period, or condition of being pregnant.

preg·nant (preg′nənt) adj. **1.** (of a female animal) having one or more unborn offspring in the uterus; being with child or young. **2.** full of meaning or importance: *a pregnant statement.* **3.** filled; abounding: *That remark was pregnant with meaning.*

pre·heat (prē hēt′) v.t. to heat before using: *The recipe said to preheat the oven to 350 degrees.*

pre·hen·sile (prē hen′sil) adj. adapted for grasping or holding, especially by wrapping around: *Some monkeys have prehensile tails.*

pre·his·tor·ic (prē′his tôr′ik, prē′his tor′ik) adj. of, relating to, or belonging to the period before recorded history: *prehistoric peoples, prehistoric reptiles.* Also, **pre·his·tor·i·cal** (prē′his tôr′i kəl, prē′his tor′i kəl). —**pre′his·tor′i·cal·ly,** adv.

pre·his·to·ry (prē his′tə rē) n. the events or conditions on earth before recorded history; prehistoric matters or times.

pre·judge (prē juj′) v.t., **pre·judged, pre·judg·ing.** to judge beforehand or without knowing all the facts. —**pre·judg′ment;** also, **pre·judge′ment,** n.

prej·u·dice (prej′ə dis) n. **1.** an opinion or judgment, especially an unfavorable one, formed beforehand or without knowing all the facts. **2.** hatred or intolerance of a particular group, such as members of a race or religion. —v.t., **prej·u·diced, prej·u·dic·ing.** **1.** to cause to have a prejudice: *A movie's publicity often prejudices the public and affects attendance.* **2.** to damage or injure, as by an unfair action.

prej·u·di·cial (prej′ə dish′əl) adj. causing prejudice or injury: *Your behavior was prejudicial to others.* —**prej′u·di′cial·ly,** adv.

prel·ate (prel′it) n. a high-ranking member of the clergy, as a bishop, archbishop, or cardinal.

pre·lim·i·nar·y (pri lim′ə ner′ē) adj. coming before and leading up to the main event, subject, or action: *preliminary arrangements for a party.* —n., pl. **pre·lim·i·nar·ies.** **1.** a preliminary step or action. **2.** a contest or match coming before the main one. —**pre·lim′i·nar′i·ly,** adv.

prel·ude (prel′ūd, prā′lūd) n. **1.** a preliminary or introductory event, action, or performance: *This first tragedy was a mere prelude to a life of sorrow.* **2.** Music. **a.** a composition or movement introducing another, such as that played before a religious service. **b.** a short, independent composition, often written for a keyboard instrument or an orchestra. —v.t., **prel·ud·ed, prel·ud·ing.** **1.** to serve as a prelude to. **2.** to introduce with a prelude. —v.i. to serve as a prelude.

pre·ma·ture (prē′mə chùr′, prē′mə tyùr′, prē′mə tùr′) adj. arriving, happening, or existing before the usual or proper time: *a premature baby, a premature decision.* —**pre′ma·ture′ly,** adv. —**pre′ma·ture′ness,** n.

pre·med (prē′med′) Informal. adj. see **premedical.** —n. a premedical student.

pre·med·i·cal (prē med′i kəl) adj. of, relating to, or preparing for the study of medicine.

pre·med·i·tate (prē med′i tāt′) v.t., **pre·med·i·tat·ed, pre·med·i·tat·ing.** to consider, think out, or plan beforehand: *They tried to prove that the murderer had premeditated the crime.* —**pre′med·i·ta′tion,** n.

pre·men·stru·al syndrome (prē men′strü əl) various symptoms, such as bloating, irritability, and depression, that occur in some women before the menstrual period. Also, **PMS.**

pre·mier (pri mîr′) n. a prime minister, as in certain European countries such as France and Italy. —adj. **1.** first in position, rank, or authority; chief: *the premier reason.* **2.** first in order of time; earliest.

pre·miere (pri mîr′, prim yâr′) also, **pre·mière.** n. the first formal public performance or presentation, as of a play or motion picture. —v.i., **pre·miered, pre·mier·ing.** to appear or be presented for the first time: *The movie premiered in August.* [From the Old French word *premier* meaning "first," from the Latin word *primarius* "leading, foremost," from the word *primus* "first, foremost."]

prem·ise (prem′is) n. **1.** a statement or principle that is accepted as true and from which a conclusion is drawn. **2. premises. a.** land and the buildings on it. **b.** a building or part of a building. —v.t., **prem·ised, prem·is·ing.** **1.** to mention beforehand as an introduction or explanation. **2.** to state or assume as a premise in an argument.

pre·mi·um (prē′mē əm) n. **1.** something offered free or at a lower price as an inducement to buy something else. **2.** an amount paid for insurance. **3.** a high or unusual value: *to put a premium on honesty.* **4.** an amount paid in addition to the regular or usual price, wage, or other fixed amount. —adj. of a higher grade or better quality: *premium gasoline.*

·**at a premium. a.** in great demand; valuable. **b.** at more than the normal or usual price or value: *Did you buy that new gold watch at a premium?*

pre·mo·lar (prē mō′lər) n. any of eight perma-

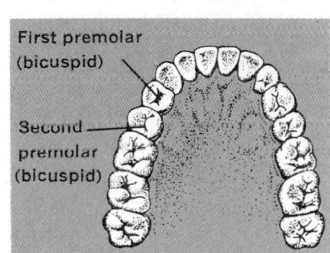

First premolar (bicuspid)

Second premolar (bicuspid)

premolars

P

nent human teeth, having double-pointed crowns and situated between the molars and the cuspids; bicuspid. —*adj.* of or relating to the premolars.

pre·mo·ni·tion (prē'mə nish'ən, prem'ə nish'ən) *n.*
1. a feeling that something is about to happen, especially something bad or harmful. **2.** a warning or sign of something to come; forewarning: *a premonition of danger.*

pre·na·tal (prē nā'təl) *adj.* of or relating to the period before birth or before giving birth.

pre·oc·cu·pa·tion (prē ok'yə pā'shən) *n.* **1.** the state of being preoccupied. **2.** anything that occupies the mind or attention: *Reading is my main preoccupation.* **3.** the act of occupying beforehand or before others.

pre·oc·cu·pied (prē ok'yə pīd') *adj.* **1.** absorbed in thought; engrossed. **2.** occupied beforehand or before others.

pre·oc·cu·py (prē ok'yə pī') *v.t.*, **pre·oc·cu·pied, pre·oc·cu·py·ing.** **1.** to take up all the attention of; engross: *Plans for the wedding preoccupied them.* **2.** to occupy or take possession of beforehand or before others.

pre·or·dain (prē'ôr dān') *v.t.* to decide or determine beforehand; predestine.

prep (prep) *n.* preparation, as for an activity, contest, or the like. —*adj.* preparatory: *prep sessions before a history test.* —*v.*, **prepped, prep·ping.** —*v.i.* to prepare for something: *We prepped for the test by studying our class notes.* —*v.t.* to get ready; prepare: *The nurse prepped the patient for surgery.*

prep. **1.** preparatory. **2.** preposition.

pre·paid (prē pād') *v.* the past tense and past participle of **prepay.** —*adj.* paid for beforehand.

prep·a·ra·tion (prep'ə rā'shən) *n.* **1.** the act or process of preparing. **2.** the state of being prepared or in readiness. **3.** an action or measure needed or taken to prepare for something: *preparations for a party.* **4.** something prepared for a specific purpose, as a medicine or food.

pre·par·a·to·ry (pri par'ə tôr'ē, prep'ər ə tôr'ē) *adj.* **1.** serving to prepare; preliminary: *a preparatory course.* **2.** undergoing preparation, as for college: *a preparatory student.*

preparatory school, a school, especially one that is private, that prepares students for college.

pre·pare (pri pâr') *v.*, **pre·pared, pre·par·ing.** —*v.t.* **1.** to make ready or fit, as for a particular purpose, event, or undertaking: *They prepared themselves for the race by practicing every day.* **2.** to put together by combining various ingredients or parts, or according to a plan: *to prepare a meal, to prepare a medicine, to prepare a speech.* —*v.i.* to get ready: *to prepare for college, to prepare for a party.* —**pre·par'er,** *n.*

pre·par·ed·ness (pri pâr'id nis) *n.* the state of being prepared.

pre·pay (prē pā') *v.t.*, **pre·paid, pre·pay·ing.** to pay or pay for in advance. —**pre·pay'ment,** *n.*

pre·pon·der·ance (pri pon'dər əns) *n.* superiority, as in quantity, weight, power, influence, or importance: *The preponderance of the data supports our theory.* Also, **pre·pon·der·an·cy** (pri pon'dər ən sē).

pre·pon·der·ant (pri pon'dər ənt) *adj.* superior or greater, as in quantity, weight, power, influence, or importance; predominant. —**pre·pon'der·ant·ly,** *adv.*

pre·pon·der·ate (pri pon'də rāt') *v.i.*, **pre·pon·der·at·ed, pre·pon·der·at·ing.** to be superior or greater, as in quantity, weight, power, influence, or importance; predominate.

prep·o·si·tion (prep'ə zish'ən) *n.* a word that shows the relationship between a noun or pronoun and another word, such as a verb or another noun. *By, into,* and *on* are prepositions in English.

prep·o·si·tion·al (prep'ə zish'ə nəl) *adj.* relating to, serving as, or having a preposition: *a prepositional phrase.*

pre·pos·sess·ing (prē'pə zes'ing) *adj.* making a

favorable impression; pleasing: *a prepossessing manner.*

pre·pos·ter·ous (pri pos'tər əs) *adj.* contrary to reason or common sense; absurd; ridiculous: *Driving a car in this storm is preposterous.* —**pre·pos'ter·ous·ly,** *adv.* —**pre·pos'ter·ous·ness,** *n.*

prep·py (prep'ē) *also,* **prep·pie.** *n., pl.* **prep·pies.** *Informal.* **1.** a student or graduate of a preparatory school. **2.** a person who dresses or behaves in a manner thought to be typical at preparatory schools. —*adj.* relating to or characteristic of preppies: *preppy clothes.*

prep school, see **preparatory school.**

pre·puce (prē'pūs) *n.* the fold of skin that covers the end of the penis before circumcision, or of the clitoris; foreskin.

pre·re·cord (prē'ri kôrd') *v.t.* to record beforehand for a later broadcast: *to prerecord a television show.*

pre·req·ui·site (prē rek'wə zit) *n.* something required or necessary before something else can follow. —*adj.* required or necessary beforehand: *a prerequisite course.*

pre·rog·a·tive (pri rog'ə tiv) *n.* a right or privilege belonging to a particular person, class, or group of persons: *Senators have the prerogative of mailing letters without paying postage.*

pres., present.

Pres., President.

pres·age (*n.,* pres'ij; *v.,* pres'ij, pri sāj') *n.* **1.** a sign or warning of a future event; omen; portent. **2.** a feeling that something is about to happen; premonition. —*v.*, **pres·aged, pres·ag·ing.** —*v.t.* **1.** to give or be a sign or warning of; portend: *The violent argument presaged a fight between the two drinkers.* **2.** to have a feeling about beforehand. **3.** to give a prophecy of; predict; foretell: *to presage the future.* —*v.i.* to make a prediction.

pres·by·ter (prez'bə tər) *n.* **1.** in the early Christian church, an elder who belonged to a council that governed a congregation. **2.** a minister or elder in a Presbyterian church or in certain other churches.

Pres·by·te·ri·an (prez'bə tîr'ē ən) *n.* a person who believes in Presbyterianism, especially a member of a Presbyterian church. —*adj.* of, relating to, or belonging to any of various Protestant denominations, especially those of English or Scottish origin, in which church government is by ministers or elders of equal rank.

Pres·by·te·ri·an·ism (prez'bə tîr'ē ə niz'əm) *n.* **1.** a system of church government by ministers or elders of equal rank. **2.** the doctrines, beliefs, and practices of the Presbyterian churches.

pres·by·ter·y (prez'bə ter'ē) *n., pl.* **pres·by·ter·ies.** **1.** in Presbyterianism, a church court having jurisdiction over the congregations in a certain area, made up of all the ministers and certain of the elders of the congregations. **2.** all the congregations under the jurisdiction of such a court. **3.** the part of a church reserved for the clergy.

pre·school (prē'skül') *adj.* of, relating to, or for a child younger than school age, usually between the ages of two and five. —*n.* a school for children too young to attend kindergarten. Also, **nursery school.** —**pre'school'er,** *n.*

pre·sci·ence (prē'shē əns) *n.* knowledge of something before it exists or happens; foreknowledge.

pre·sci·ent (prē'shē ənt) *adj.* having knowledge of something before it exists or happens.

pre·scribe (pri skrīb') *v.*, **pre·scribed, pre·scrib·ing.** —*v.t.* **1.** to set down or give as a rule or direction to be followed: *The law prescribes a speed limit of forty miles per hour on this road.* **2.** to order or recommend for use as a remedy or treatment: *The doctor prescribed an ointment for the patient's skin rash.* —*v.i.* **1.** to set down or give rules or directions; dictate. **2.** to give medical advice or a prescription.

pre·scrip·tion (pri skrip'shən) *n.* **1.** an order written by a doctor for the preparation and use of a medicine or other remedy. **2.** the medicine or remedy ordered. **3.** the act of prescribing. **4.** something that is prescribed; rule or direction.

pre·scrip·tive (pri skrip′tiv) *adj.* **1.** giving or setting down strict rules, laws, or directions. **2.** according to established use or custom. ▲See note at **descriptive** for further information.

pres·ence (prez′əns) *n.* **1.** the state or fact of being in a specific place at a given time: *The big dog's presence in the room made me uneasy.* **2.** the area immediately surrounding a person or thing: *to sign a contract in the presence of witnesses.* **3.** the appearance or bearing of a person, especially when dignified or impressive: *The royal couple have a stately presence.* **4.** something, such as a spirit, ghost, or invisible influence, felt to be present.

presence of mind, the ability to think and act calmly and intelligently in an emergency or other difficult situation: *The child who saw the robbery showed presence of mind by calling the police.*

pres·ent¹ (prez′ənt) *adj.* **1.** in a specific place at a given time: *We were not present when they arrived.* **2.** existing or going on at this time: *the present generation.* **3.** found; existing: *Oxygen is present in the air.* **4.** *Grammar.* indicating an action now taking place or a state of being now existing. —*n.* **1.** the present time; time now passing: *Are you busy at present?* **2.** *Grammar.* the present tense or a verb in the present tense. [From the Old French word *present,* from the Latin word *praesens* meaning "that which is present, what is before you," from the word *praeesse* "to be before (something)" or "to preside," from the suffix *prae-* "before, in front of" + *esse* "to be."]

pre·sent² (*v.,* pri zent′; *n.,* prez′ənt) *v.t.* **1.** to introduce to another or others; make acquainted: *May I present you to my parents?* **2.** to bring into the presence of another or others or into a particular place: *He presented his plan to the city council.* **3.** to make a gift, award, offer, or donation of; bestow: *The principal will present the diplomas.* **4.** to give to as a gift: *The author presented me with a copy of her latest book.* **5.** to suggest or bring up for consideration: *My lack of money presents a problem.* **6.** to put before the public; display; show: *The museum will present the works of a new artist.* **7.** to hand or send in; submit: *The carpenter presented a bill for the work.* —*n.* something given, as a gift or donation. [From the Old French word *presenter* meaning "to present²" or "to offer," from the Latin word *praesentare* with the same meanings, from the word *praesens,* present participle of *praeesse* "to be before (something)" or "to preside," from the prefix *prae-* "before, in front of" + *esse* "to be."]

pre·sent·a·ble (pri zen′tə bəl) *adj.* **1.** suitable or good enough to be present in company: *I cleaned and pressed my clothes to make myself presentable for the party.* **2.** fit to be seen: *to make a room presentable.* **3.** suitable to be offered or given: *to put a report in presentable form.* —**pre·sent′a·bil′i·ty,** *n.* —**pre·sent′a·bly,** *adv.*

pres·en·ta·tion (prez′en tā′shən, prē′zen tā′shən) *n.* **1.** the act of presenting or the state of being presented. **2.** an exhibition or showing, as of a play. **3.** something presented, as a gift or donation.

pres·ent-day (prez′ənt dā′) *adj.* of, belonging to, or happening at the present time; current: *present-day events.*

pre·sen·ti·ment (pri zen′tə mənt) *n.* a feeling that something is about to happen, especially something bad; premonition.

pres·ent·ly (prez′ənt lē) *adv.* **1.** in a little while; shortly: *They will arrive presently.* **2.** at the present time; currently: *Our class is presently studying Mexican history.*

pre·sent·ment (pri zent′mənt) *n.* **1.** the act of presenting. **2.** something presented; exhibition; showing.

present participle, a participle expressing a present action or state, formed with the suffix -*ing* and used especially to form the progressive tenses and as an adjective or noun. In the sentence *I am awaiting your reply,* the word *awaiting* is a present participle.

present perfect **1.** a verb tense expressing action completed at the time of speaking. In the sentence *We have seen that science fiction movie three times,* the phrase *have seen* is in the present perfect. **2.** a verb in this tense.

present tense **1.** a verb tense expressing an action or state that is happening or exists at the present time. In the sentence *You look well today,* the word *look* is in the present tense. **2.** a verb in this tense.

pre·serv·a·tive (pri zûr′və tiv) *n.* anything that preserves, especially a chemical substance added to foods to keep them from spoiling. —*adj.* tending or serving to preserve.

pre·serve (pri zûrv′) *v.t.,* **pre·served, pre·serv·ing.** **1.** to maintain or keep; make lasting: *to preserve an old house.* **2.** to prepare (food) for storage and future use, as by canning, smoking, or pickling. **3.** to protect from harm or danger; keep in safety; save: *to preserve freedom of speech.* **4.** to keep from spoiling or decaying, as with ice or chemical substances. —*n.* **1.** usually, **preserves.** fruit that has been boiled with sugar and stored in airtight containers to keep it from spoiling or fermenting. **2.** an area set aside for the protection of plant and animal life or other natural resources. —**pre·serv′a·ble,** *adj.* —**pres·er·va·tion** (prez′ər vā′shən), *n.* —**pre·serv′er,** *n.*

pre·set (prē set′) *v.t.,* **pre·set, pre·set·ting.** to adjust or set (a device or mechanism) before operation: *to preset the controls on a microwave oven.* —*adj.* set or able to be set in advance: *The radio has preset buttons for tuning in stations quickly.*

pre·side (pri zīd′) *v.i.,* **pre·sid·ed, pre·sid·ing.** **1.** to act as chairperson, as at a meeting. **2.** to have authority or control: *to preside over a business.* [From the French word *presider* meaning "to preside," from the Latin word *praesidēre* "to govern, preside, stand watch over," from the prefix *prae-* "before, in front of" + *sedēre* "to sit."] —**pre·sid′er,** *n.*

pres·i·den·cy (prez′i dən sē) *n., pl.* **pres·i·den·cies.** **1.** the office or function of president. **2.** the time during which a president holds office. **3.** *also,* **Presidency.** the office of the President of the United States.

pres·i·dent (prez′i dənt) *n.* **1.** *also,* **President.** the chief executive of a republic, as the United States. **2.** a chief officer, as of a company, college, or organization. —**pres·i·den·tial** (prez′ə den′shəl), *adj.*

pres·i·dent-e·lect (prez′i dənt i lekt′) *n.* a person who has been elected president but has not yet been inaugurated.

President's Day, the third Monday in February, observed as a legal holiday in most states of the United States in commemoration of the birthdays of George Washington and Abraham Lincoln.

pre·sid·i·o (pri sid′ē ō) *n., pl.* **pre·sid·i·os.** a fortified military post, especially one in the western or southwestern United States. [From the Spanish word *presidio* meaning "fortified military post," from the Latin word *praesidium* meaning "garrison."]

Pre·sid·i·um (pri sid′ē əm) *n.* a permanent committee of the Soviet government that acts when the Supreme Soviet is not in session.

---

at; āpe; fär; câre; end; mē; it; īce; pîerce; hot; ōld; sông, fôrk; oil; out; up; ūse; rüle; pŭll; tûrn; chin; sing; shop; thin; **th**is; hw in white; zh in treasure. The symbol ə stands for the unstressed vowel sound heard in about, taken, pencil, lemon, and circus.

P

press¹ (pres) *v.t.* **1.** to use steady force or weight on or against; push against: *to press the button of an elevator, to press one's nose against a window.* **2.** to remove (juice or other contents) by squeezing: *to press juice from lemons.* **3.** to squeeze in order to remove juice or other contents from (something): *The workers pressed the grapes to make wine.* **4.** to give a particular shape or consistency to by means of pressure: *The artist pressed the clay into a ball.* **5.** to iron: *The cleaner can also press your clothes.* **6.** to hold close; embrace; hug: *I pressed my old friend to me.* **7.** to urge strongly: *The bank pressed them to pay back the loan.* **8.** to cause difficulties for; harass: *Enemy soldiers pressed our troops from all sides.* —*v.i.* **1.** to use steady force or weight: *You have to press down on the lever to make the machine work.* **2.** to push or strain forward: *The police pressed through the crowd.* **3.** to crowd; throng: *The fans pressed about the singer.* **4.** to demand or seek urgently: *The senator pressed for passage of the civil rights bill.* —*n., pl.* **press·es. 1.** the act of pressing: *A press of the button started the washing machine.* **2.** any of various tools or machines that exert pressure, as to stamp or compress materials or to get juice from fruits or vegetables. **3.** hurry; pressure: *the press of duties.* **4.** see **printing press. 5.** a business establishment for printing or publishing. **6.** published news, as in newspapers or on radio or television: *The President's speech was described the next day in the press.* **7.** people who gather, write, distribute, or broadcast news, as reporters and journalists: *The press came to the opening of the new play.* [From the Old French word *presser* with the same meaning, going back to the Latin word *pressus,* past participle of *premere* meaning "to press¹."] —**press'er,** *n.*

press² (pres) *v.t.* to force into military service; impress. [From the obsolete word *prest* meaning "wages paid in advance," from the Old French word *prest* "a forced loan to the king."]

press agent, a person who manages publicity or public relations for a person or organization, such as for an actor or motion picture studio.

press conference, an interview given to a gathering of reporters, as by a public official or celebrity.

press·ing (pres'ing) *adj.* demanding or calling for immediate action or attention: *pressing business, a pressing problem.* —**press'ing·ly,** *adv.*

press secretary, a person who is in charge of the press conferences and public relations of a public figure.

pres·sure (presh'ər) *n.* **1.** the force exerted by one thing upon another with which it is in contact: *The pressure of the water broke the dam.* **2.** a compelling force or influence: *My parents put pressure on me to study harder.* **3.** urgent demands on one's time or energy: *You work well under pressure.* **4.** a burden or strain, as of something difficult to bear: *the pressure of grief.* **5.** *Physics.* the amount of force exerted on a unit of area. —*v.t.,* **pres·sured, pres·sur·ing.** to compel by force or influence: *The salesclerk pressured me into buying the more expensive coat.*

pressure cooker, an airtight metal pot that uses steam pressure to cook foods quickly.

pressure group, a group of people who share a common interest and try, as by lobbying, to persuade lawmakers or government officials to promote that interest.

pressure suit, an airtight suit worn at high altitudes or in space to maintain normal atmospheric pressure.

pres·sur·ize (presh'ə rīz') *v.t.,* **pres·sur·ized, pres·sur·iz·ing. 1.** to keep normal atmospheric pressure in the interior of (something, such as an airplane, spacecraft, or diving apparatus). **2.** to keep under high pressure, as the contents of an aerosol can. —**pres'sur·i·za'tion,** *n.*

pres·ti·dig·i·ta·tion (pres'ti dij'i tā'shən) *n.* sleight of hand; magic tricks. —**pres'ti·dig'i·ta'tor,** *n.*

pres·tige (pre stēzh', pre stēj') *n.* power, influence, or respect that is based on success, reputation, or achievements: *The research team's discoveries brought them prestige.*

pres·ti·gious (pre stij'əs, pre stē'jəs) *adj.* having or giving prestige; highly honored or respected: *a prestigious award given to top scientists.*

pres·to (pres'tō) *adv.* **1.** at once; immediately. **2.** *Music.* very quickly. —*adj. Music.* rapid; quick. —*n. Music.* a presto passage, movement, or piece.

pre·sum·a·ble (pri zü'mə bəl) *adj.* capable of being presumed or taken for granted; likely; probable. —**pre·sum'a·bly,** *adv.*

pre·sume (pri züm') *v.,* **pre·sumed, pre·sum·ing.** —*v.t.* **1.** to accept as true until proven to be untrue; take for granted; suppose: *I presume that you know what you are talking about.* **2.** to do or take upon oneself without permission or authority; dare: *Do you presume to tell me how to choose my friends?* —*v.i.* **1.** to be presumptuous; take liberties. **2.** to take unfair advantage: *We will leave after dinner rather than presume on your hospitality.* —**pre·sum·ed·ly** (pri zü'mid lē), *adv.* —**pre·sum'er,** *n.*

pre·sump·tion (pri zump'shən) *n.* **1.** the act of presuming. **2.** something taken for granted; assumption: *I went to the party on the presumption that you would be there.* **3.** reason or cause for presuming something. **4.** thought or behavior that is too bold or arrogant.

pre·sump·tive (pri zump'tiv) *adj.* **1.** giving a good reason for accepting or believing: *presumptive evidence.* **2.** based on presumption or likelihood; presumed. —**pre·sump'tive·ly,** *adv.*

pre·sump·tu·ous (pri zump'chü əs) *adj.* too bold or arrogant; forward; impertinent. —**pre·sump'tu·ous·ly,** *adv.* —**pre·sump'tu·ous·ness,** *n.*

pre·sup·pose (prē'sə pōz') *v.t.,* **pre·sup·posed, pre·sup·pos·ing. 1.** to take for granted; assume beforehand. **2.** to require as a necessary condition; imply: *A good musical performance presupposes much training and practice.*

pre·sup·po·si·tion (prē'sup ə zish'ən) *n.* **1.** the act of presupposing. **2.** something that is presupposed.

pre·teen (prē tēn') *also,* **pre-teen.** *n.* a child who is not yet thirteen years old, especially one nearing that age: *The town council sponsored a summer picnic for preteens.* —*adj.* of or relating to preteens: *preteen styles of clothing.*

pre·tence (prē'tens, pri tens') another spelling of **pretense.**

pre·tend (pri tend') *v.t.* **1.** to claim, especially falsely or insincerely: *I do not pretend to be an expert chess player.* **2.** to give a false appearance of; feign: *to pretend sleep.* **3.** to act out in play; make believe: *The children pretended they were sailors.* —*v.i.* **1.** to act out roles or events in play: *Children love to pretend.* **2.** to give a false appearance in order to deceive: *I am not sure if they are sick or only pretending.* **3.** to lay claim: *to pretend to a throne.* —*adj. Informal.* imaginary; not real or genuine: *a pretend playmate, a stack of pretend money.*

pre·tend·ed (pri ten'did) *adj.* claimed falsely or insincerely; not genuine; false: *a pretended friend.* —**pre·tend'ed·ly,** *adv.*

pre·tend·er (pri ten'dər) *n.* **1.** a person who makes false or insincere claims or presents a false appearance. **2.** a person who lays claim to something, especially a throne.

pre·tense (prē'tens, pri tens') *also,* **pre·tence.** *n.* **1.** a false show or appearance, especially for the purpose of deceiving: *The child used any pretense to avoid going to the dentist.* **2.** a claim, especially one that is false or insincere. **3.** false show or display; affectation: *That is without pretense.* **4.** acting out in play; fantasy.

pre·ten·sion (pri ten'shən) *n.* **1.** a claim: *pretensions to a throne.* **2.** the act of laying claim to something. **3.** a false show or display; affectation.

pre·ten·tious (pri ten'shəs) *adj.* **1.** making claims to, or presenting a false display of, some distinction or quality: *a talented but pretentious writer.* **2.** intended to show off or attract attention. —**pre·ten'tious·ly,** *adv.* —**pre·ten'tious·ness,** *n.*

pret·er·it (pret'ər it) *also,* **pret·er·ite.** *Grammar. n.* **1.** the past tense. **2.** a verb in the past tense. —*adj.* expressing past time or action: *the preterit tense.*

pre·ter·nat·u·ral (prē'tər nach'ər əl) *adj.* **1.** going beyond or differing from the natural or ordinary; extraordinary or abnormal. **2.** supernatural. —**pre'ter·nat'u·ral·ly,** *adv.*

pre·text (prē'tekst') *n.* a false reason or excuse given to hide a true reason or motive: *One guest left the boring party on the pretext of being sick.*

pret·ty (prit'ē) *adj.,* **pret·ti·er, pret·ti·est. 1.** pleasing or attractive, especially in a graceful or dainty way: *a pretty baby, a pretty flower, a pretty poem.* **2.** fine; nice. ▲ usually used ironically: *You certainly got us into a pretty mess this time.* —*adv.* fairly; rather; quite: *It was raining pretty hard when we left.* —**pret'ti·ly,** *adv.* —**pret'ti·ness,** *n.*

pret·zel (pret'zəl) *n.* a thin roll of dough that is usually baked in the form of a loose knot or a short stick and salted on the outside.

pre·vail (pri vāl') *v.i.* **1.** to be greater in power or influence; be victorious; triumph or succeed: *to prevail over the enemy in the battle.* **2.** to be widespread; persist: *Crime still prevails in our cities.*
·**to prevail on** or **to prevail upon.** to use persuasion successfully: *They prevailed on me to stay.*

pre·vail·ing (pri vā'ling) *adj.* **1.** most common or frequent: *prevailing winds.* **2.** having greater power or influence. —**pre·vail'ing·ly,** *adv.*

prev·a·lent (prev'ə lənt) *adj.* commonly or generally happening, used, or accepted; widespread: *a prevalent belief.* —**prev'a·lence,** *n.* —**prev'a·lent·ly,** *adv.*

pre·var·i·cate (pri var'i kāt') *v.i.,* **pre·var·i·cat·ed, pre·var·i·cat·ing.** to speak falsely; evade the truth; lie. —**pre·var'i·ca'tion,** *n.* —**pre·var'i·ca'tor,** *n.*

pre·vent (pri vent') *v.t.* **1.** to keep from happening or developing: *to prevent forest fires.* **2.** to keep from doing something: *The traffic noises prevented me from sleeping.* —**pre·vent'a·ble,** *also,* **pre·vent'i·ble,** *adj.*

pre·ven·tion (pri ven'shən) *n.* **1.** the act of preventing. **2.** something that prevents.

pre·ven·tive (pri ven'tiv) *adj.* serving or intended to prevent something; concerned with prevention: *to take preventive measures against disease.* —*n.* **1.** something that prevents; means of preventing. **2.** a drug or other agent used to prevent disease. Also, **pre·vent·a·tive** (pri ven'tə tiv). —**pre·ven'tive·ly,** *adv.* —**pre·ven'tive·ness,** *n.*

pre·view (prē'vū) *also,* **pre·vue.** *n.* **1.** an advance showing of a motion picture, play, or exhibition before its public opening. **2.** an advance showing of scenes from a motion picture or television program in order to advertise it. —*v.t.* to present or view in advance.

pre·vi·ous (prē'vē əs) *adj.* coming or made before; earlier: *the previous day, a previous appointment.* —**pre'vi·ous·ly,** *adv.*
·**previous to.** before: *He left previous to her arrival.*

pre·war (prē'wôr') *adj.* happening or existing before a war.

prey (prā) *n.* **1.** any animal hunted or killed by another animal for food. **2.** a person or thing that is a victim: *The couple were the prey of a mugger.* **3.** the habit or manner of hunting or killing for food: *A tiger is a beast of prey.* —*v.i.* **to prey on** or **upon. 1.** to hunt or kill for food: *Owls prey on mice.* **2.** to take advantage of; victimize: *They were preyed upon by a used car dealer.* **3.** to have a harmful or wearing effect: *to prey on the mind.*

Pri·am (prī'əm) *n. Greek Legend.* the King of Troy during the Trojan War, and the father of Hector, Paris, and Cassandra.

price (prīs) *n.* **1.** the amount of money or its equivalent for which something is bought or sold: *The price of milk may go up next year.* **2.** the cost at which something is obtained: *The war was won at the price of many lives.* **3.** a reward offered for the capture or killing of a person: *There was a price on the murderer's head.* **4.** value; worth: *jewels of great price.* —*v.t.,* **priced, pric·ing. 1.** to set a price on; fix the price of: *This meat is priced much too high.* **2.** *Informal.* to find out the price of: *to price a car.* [From the Middle English word *pris* meaning "value, price" or "reward," from the Old French word *pris* with the same meanings, from the Latin word *pretium* "money," "worth," or "reward."]

price·less (prīs'lis) *adj.* **1.** too valuable to be priced; invaluable: *a priceless painting.* **2.** *Informal.* very amusing: *That remark was priceless.*

prick (prik) *v.t.* **1.** to pierce slightly with a sharp point: *I pricked the pie's crust with a fork.* **2.** to cause a sharp physical or mental pain to; sting: *His conscience pricked him for having told a lie.* —*n.* **1.** the act of pricking. **2.** a physical or mental pain produced by or as if by pricking: *to feel the prick of a pin.* **3.** a mark or opening made by a sharp point; puncture. **4.** a pointed object or instrument, such as a thorn. —**prick'er,** *n.*
·**to prick up one's ears. a.** to raise the ears to an erect position: *The dog pricked up its ears at the sound.* **b.** to listen closely or with sudden interest.

prick·le (prik'əl) *n.* **1.** a small, sharp point, such as a thorn. **2.** a stinging or tingling sensation, as of being pricked. —*v.,* **prick·led, prick·ling.** —*v.t.* to cause a stinging or tingling sensation in. —*v.i.* to sting or tingle.

prick·ly (prik'lē) *adj.,* **prick·li·er, prick·li·est. 1.** having prickles. **2.** stinging; tingling. **3.** difficult; troublesome: *a prickly situation.* —**prick'li·ness,** *n.*

prickly heat, a skin rash characterized by redness and itching, caused by inflammation of the sweat glands.

prickly pear 1. the red or purple pear-shaped fruit of any

prickly pear

of a large group of cacti found in North and South America. **2.** the plant that bears this fruit.

at; āpe; fär; câre; end; mē; it; īce; pîerce; hot; ōld; sông, fôrk; oil; out; up; ūse; rüle; pull; tûrn; chin; sing; shop; thin; this; hw in white; zh in treasure. The symbol ə stands for the unstressed vowel sound heard in about, taken, pencil, lemon, and circus.

pride (prīd) *n.* **1.** a sense of one's personal worth or dignity; self-respect: *Despite years of poverty, the couple had kept their pride.* **2.** an exaggerated or unreasonable sense of one's worth or importance: *I knew I was wrong, but my foolish pride kept me from apologizing.* **3.** pleasure or satisfaction resulting as from an achievement or possession: *The woodcarver took pride in his work.* **4.** a person or thing that causes such pleasure or satisfaction: *The dog was its owner's pride and joy.* **5.** a family or group of lions. —*v.t.,* **prid·ed, prid·ing.** to take pride, pleasure, or satisfaction in (oneself) for: *The woman prided herself on her financial success in business.*

pried (prīd) the past tense and past participle of **pry.**

priest (prēst) *n.* **1.** in certain Christian churches, a member of the clergy or minister. **2.** a person who performs the rites of a deity: *a priest of Apollo.* [From the Old English word *prēost* meaning "priest," going back to the Church Latin word *presbyter* "priest, elder who officiates in church," from the Greek word *presbyteros* "elder," from the word *presbys* "old" or "old man."]

priest·ess (prē′stis) *n.* a woman who performs the sacred rites of a religion.

priest·hood (prēst′hŭd′) *n.* **1.** the office or duties of a priest. **2.** priests as a group.

priest·ly (prēst′lē) *adj.,* **priest·li·er, priest·li·est.** of, like, or suitable for a priest.

prig (prig) *n.* a smug, self-righteous person. —**prig′-gish,** *adj.* —**prig′gish·ness,** *n.*

prim (prim) *adj.,* **prim·mer, prim·mest.** very formal, neat, or precise; proper. —**prim′ly,** *adv.* —**prim′ness,** *n.*

pri·ma·cy (prī′mə sē) *n., pl.* **pri·ma·cies. 1.** the state of being first, as in rank or importance. **2.** the rank or dignity of a primate of a church. **3.** in the Roman Catholic Church, the supreme authority of the pope.

pri·ma don·na (prē′mə don′ə) *pl.* **pri·ma don·nas. 1.** the leading female singer in an opera company. **2.** a temperamental or vain person. [From the Italian phrase *prima donna* meaning "first lady," going back to the Latin words *primus* "first, foremost" and *domina* "lady."]

pri·mal (prī′məl) *adj.* **1.** of or relating to early times; original; primitive. **2.** of first importance; fundamental.

pri·ma·ri·ly (prī mer′ə lē) *adv.* **1.** chiefly; principally. **2.** in the first place; originally.

pri·ma·ry (prī′mer ē) *adj.* **1.** first or greatest in importance or degree; principal: *Your safety is my primary concern.* **2.** first in order, as in a series: *primary school.* **3.** first or earliest in time; primitive; elementary: *the primary phase of development.* **4.** basic; fundamental; elemental. **5.** not derived from something else; original; direct: *We consulted only primary sources in our research.* **6.** relating to the induction circuit, coil, or current in an electrically powered machine. —*n., pl.* **pri·ma·ries. 1.** an election in which contenders from the same party oppose each other for the party's nomination or for the right to run for office with the party's support. Also, **primary election. 2.** one of the primary colors. **3.** something that is first in order, importance, or degree.

primary accent 1. the main stress in the pronunciation of a word. **2.** the mark (′) used to indicate this stress.

primary color 1. any of three colors, either yellow, magenta (purplish red), or cyan (greenish blue), that can be combined in various proportions in pigments and dyes to produce all other colors. **2.** any of three colors, either orange-red, green, or blue, from which light of all other colors can be produced.

primary election, see **primary** (*n.,* def. 1).

primary school, a school providing instruction for very young pupils, usually comprising the first three or four grades of elementary school.

pri·mate (prī′māt, prī′mit) *n.* **1.** any member of the order of mammals that includes human beings, apes, monkeys, tarsiers, and lemurs. **2.** an archbishop of the highest rank in a country or in a church province.

prime (prīm) *adj.* **1.** first in importance or value; main; chief: *Your happiness is our prime concern.* **2.** first in rank, dignity, influence, or authority: *The Supreme Court is the prime legal authority.* **3.** of the best quality; excellent: *a prime cut of beef.* **4.** *Mathematics.* **a.** relating to or designating a prime number. **b.** having no common divisor except 1. —*n.* **1.** the best or most flourishing stage or condition: *the prime of a person's life. The trees were cut down before they had reached their prime.* **2.** see **prime number.** —*v.t.,* **primed, prim·ing. 1.** to make ready or prepare for use by filling or charging with something: *to prime the engine with gasoline.* **2.** to pour water into (a pump) so as to make it ready for operation. **3.** to prepare for painting, as by applying a base coat. **4.** to instruct or prepare (a person) beforehand in what he or she is to say or do: *The lawyer primed the witness.* **5.** to prepare (a gun or mine) for firing by supplying a charge of gunpowder or a primer. [From the Old French word *prime,* from the Latin word *primus* meaning "first, foremost."] —**prime′ness,** *n.*

prime meridian, the meridian that passes through Greenwich, England, designated as zero degrees longitude, and from which longitude east and west is measured.

prime minister, the highest-ranking member of a body of administrators or of a council of ministers, especially in a parliamentary government, as that of Great Britain.

prime number, a number that can be divided without a remainder only by itself and by 1, as 2, 3, 7, 13, or 29.

prim·er[1] (prim′ər) *n.* **1.** an elementary book for teaching children to read. **2.** an elementary or introductory book on any subject. [From the Middle English word *primere* meaning "a layperson's prayer book," from the Medieval Latin word *primarium* with the same meaning, going back to the Latin word *primarius* "primary, principal," from the Latin word *primus* meaning "first, foremost." Such prayer books were used to teach children to read.]

prim·er[2] (prī′mər) *n.* **1.** a flat disk or other device that is filled with a small quantity of explosive and used to set off the main charge, as in a cartridge or shell. **2.** a substance put on a surface to prepare it for painting, especially a first coat of paint applied as a base. **3.** a person or thing that primes. [*Prime* + *-er*[1].]

prime rate, the lowest rate of interest on loans offered by a bank at a particular time to its preferred customers.

prime time, the period of television broadcasting that attracts the largest number of viewers, in the United States usually considered as from 7 P.M. to 11 P.M.

pri·me·val (prī mē′vəl) *adj.* of, relating to, or belonging to the first or earliest age or ages, especially of the world; primitive. [From the Latin word *primaevus* meaning "young, youthful," from the words *primus* "first" + *aevum* "age."] —**pri·me′val·ly,** *adv.*

prim·ing (prī′ming) *n.* **1.** powder or other material used to ignite a charge. **2.** a substance put on a surface to prepare it for painting; primer.

prim·i·tive (prim′i tiv) *adj.* **1.** of, relating to, or characteristic of an early original stage, especially in the development of something: *a fossil of a primitive animal.* **2.** of, relating to, or characteristic of the earlier stages in the development of human civilization or culture: *an exhibit of primitive art.* **3.** crude or simple; unsophisticated: *primitive adobe huts.* —*n.* **1.** a member of a primitive people. **2.** an artist, often self-taught, whose work has a naive or simple quality: *That painter of rural scenes is famous as an American primitive.* —**prim′i·tive·ly,** *adv.* —**prim′i·tive·ness,** *n.*

pri·mo·gen·i·ture (prī′mə jen′i chər, prī′mə jen′i chûr′) *n.* **1.** the state or fact of being the first-born child. **2.** a system of inheritance in which the eldest son inherits his father's entire estate.

pri·mor·di·al (prī môr′dē əl) *adj.* **1.** of, relating to, or existing at or from the very beginning. **2.** fundamental; basic. —**pri·mor′di·al·ly,** *adv.*

primp (primp) *v.t., v.i.* to dress, groom, or adorn, especially with vanity.

prim·rose (prim′rōz′) *n.* **1.** a trumpet-shaped flower of any of a large group of plants, grown as a garden flower. **2.** a plant bearing this flower. **3.** a pale greenish yellow color. —*adj.* having the color primrose.

primrose

prince (prins) *n.* **1.** any male member of a royal family other than the king. **2.** a male sovereign; monarch. **3.** the ruler of a small state or territory. **4.** a high-ranking nobleman in certain countries. **5.** a person or thing that is outstanding in a group, class, or profession: *He is a prince of artists.*

prince consort, the husband of a female sovereign.

prince·dom (prins′dəm) *n.* **1.** the state or territory ruled by a prince; principality. **2.** the rank or dignity of a prince.

prince·ly (prins′lē) *adj.,* **prince·li·er, prince·li·est. 1.** of, relating to, resembling, or suitable for a prince. **2.** lavish; magnificent; sumptuous: *The house cost a princely sum.* —**prince′li·ness,** *n.*

Prince of Wales, the male heir apparent to the British throne, a title usually given to the oldest son of the sovereign.

prin·cess (prin′sis, prin′ses) *n., pl.* **prin·cess·es. 1.** any female member of a royal family other than the queen. **2.** the wife of a prince. **3.** a female sovereign.

prin·ci·pal (prin′sə pəl) *adj.* greatest or first, as in importance, rank, or value; chief: *The principal demand of the striking workers was higher pay.* —*n.* **1.** the head of an elementary or secondary school. **2.** a person who takes a leading part or plays the main role in some activity: *Who is the principal in the new play?* **3.** an original sum of money borrowed or invested, not including interest charged or income earned.

prin·ci·pal·i·ty (prin′sə pal′i tē) *n., pl.* **prin·ci·pal·i·ties. 1.** a state or territory ruled by a prince or from which a prince takes his title. **2.** the position or authority of a prince.

principal parts, the forms of a verb from which all other inflected forms can be derived. In English the principal parts are the present infinitive, the past tense, and the past participle, such as *jump, jumped, jumped* or *throw, threw, thrown.*

prin·ci·ple (prin′sə pəl) *n.* **1.** a basic truth, law, belief, or doctrine: *This government is said to be based on the principle that all people are created equal.* **2.** a rule of personal conduct: *It is my principle to answer letters promptly.* **3.** a sense of right or honorable action; integrity: *to follow the rules as a matter of principle.* **4.** a scientific rule or law concerned with or explaining how something acts or operates: *the principle of gravity.*

prin·ci·pled (prin′sə pəld) *adj.* having, characterized by, or based on ethical or moral principles.

print (print) *v.t.* **1.** to produce (a text, picture, or design) on a surface, such as paper, by applying inked type, plates, or blocks. **2.** to produce a text, picture, or design on (a surface) by applying inked type, plates, or blocks. **3.** to cause to be printed; publish: *The newspaper printed the story of the candidate's political career.* **4.** to write using letters like those made by type: *Please print your name on the application.* **5.** to produce (a photograph) by passing light through a negative onto a sensitized surface. —*v.i.* **1.** to be capable of taking an impression from type, as in a printing press. **2.** to write using letters like those made by type. **3.** to produce something by the process of printing. —*n.* **1.** printed lettering: *The book was written in large print.* **2.** a mark or indentation made by pressing or stamping: *There were prints where we had walked in the snow.* **3.** something that has been marked or formed by pressing or stamping. **4.** a picture or design printed from a block or plate. **5.** a photograph made from a negative. **6.** fabric with a design printed on it by means of dyes on engraved rollers, woodblocks, or screens. **7.** something made of such fabric. —**print′a·ble,** *adj.*
·**in print. a.** in a printed form. **b.** still being printed and available for purchase from the publisher.
·**out of print.** no longer being printed by the publisher.

printed circuit, an electrical circuit consisting of a pattern of conducting material deposited on a flat plate or base of insulating material, widely used in electronic equipment.

print·er (prin′tər) *n.* **1.** a person or thing that prints, especially a person or company whose business is printing. **2.** *Computers.* a device that produces output data in printed form.

printer's devil, see **devil** (*def. 6*).

print·ing (prin′ting) *n.* **1.** the process, business, or art of producing printed matter, especially by means of a printing press. **2.** something that is printed; printed matter. **3.** all the copies of a book or other matter printed at one time: *The first printing of the book was 20,000 copies.* **4.** writing that resembles that made by type.

printing press, a machine for producing copies by transferring ink from a metal plate, roller, or similar device to paper or other material. Also, **press.**

print·out (print′out′) also, **print-out.** *n.* the printed output of a computer.

pri·or[1] (prī′ər) *adj.* earlier or before in time, order, or importance: *He isn't coming to the party because he has a prior engagement.* [From the Latin word *prior* meaning "former, previous" or "superior."]
·**prior to.** before: *Prior to moving here, she lived in the Midwest.*

pri·or[2] (prī′ər) *n.* a monk who ranks next below an abbot in a monastery or who is the superior of a priory. [From the Old English word *prior* and the Old French word *prior,* both with the same meaning and both from the Medieval Latin word *prior* meaning this person, going back to the Latin word *prior* "former" or "superior."]

pri·or·ess (prī′ər is) *n., pl.* **pri·or·ess·es.** a nun who ranks next below an abbess in an abbey or who is the superior of a priory.

pri·or·i·ty (prī ôr′i tē, prī or′i tē) *n., pl.* **pri·or·i·ties. 1.** the condition of coming before another or others, as in order or importance. **2.** the right to have superior or special treatment: *Emergency vehicles have priority on the road.* **3.** a matter deserving or receiving special emphasis or attention: *Buying a new car was the couple's first priority.*

at; āpe; fär; câre; end; mē; it; īce; pîerce; hot; ōld; sông, fôrk; oil; out; up; ūse; rüle; pùll; tûrn; chin; sing; shop; thin; this; hw in white; zh in treasure. The symbol ə stands for the unstressed vowel sound heard in about, taken, pencil, lemon, and circus.

P

priority mail, a class of mail for packages of more than 12 ounces, handled as first-class mail in the United States.

pri·o·ry (prī′ə rē) *n., pl.* **pri·o·ries.** a religious community of monks or nuns ranking next below an abbey, governed by a prior or prioress.

prism (priz′əm) *n.* **1.** a solid having two congruent and parallel faces, and whose other faces are parallelograms. **2.** a transparent solid having this shape, used for refracting or dispersing light or for breaking it up into its component colors.

pris·mat·ic (priz mat′ik) *adj.* **1.** of, relating to, produced by, or like a prism. **2.** of varied colors.

prism *(def. 1)*

prismatic colors, the seven colors, red, orange, yellow, green, blue, indigo, and violet, that are produced when white light is passed through a prism or water droplets.

pris·on (priz′ən) *n.* **1.** a building or institution in which persons convicted or accused of crimes are confined. **2.** any place of confinement.

pris·on·er (priz′ə nər) *n.* **1.** a person confined in a prison. **2.** a person who is arrested or taken into custody. **3.** a person or thing that is restrained, deprived of freedom, or held in captivity. **4.** see **prisoner of war.**

prisoner of war, a person captured or held by the enemy in war.

pris·sy (pris′ē) *adj.,* **pris·si·er, pris·si·est.** very prim, fussy, or prudish.

pris·tine (pris′tēn) *adj.* **1.** of or relating to the earliest time, period, or condition; original; primitive: *The young couple restored the old house to its pristine state.* **2.** not corrupt; pure; unspoiled: *the pristine beauty of freshly fallen snow.*

prith·ee (prith′ē) *interj. Archaic.* I pray thee; please.

pri·va·cy (prī′və sē) *n., pl.* **pri·va·cies.** **1.** the state of being private, secluded, or isolated: *The writer needed privacy to finish the novel.* **2.** the right to be free from interference with one's private affairs: *Opening someone else's mail is an invasion of privacy.*

pri·vate (prī′vit) *adj.* **1.** belonging or restricted to a particular person or persons: *a private driveway, private property.* **2.** personal; individual: *I tell my private thoughts to no one.* **3.** not intended for general or public knowledge; confidential: *a private conversation.* **4.** not holding public office or having an official position: *The former senator retired to life as a private citizen.* **5.** secluded; isolated: *We had our picnic in a private spot.* —*n.* in the U.S. Army and Marine Corps, a soldier of the lowest rank. —**pri′vate·ly,** *adv.* —**pri′vate·ness,** *n.*

·**in private.** confidentially or secretly; privately: *The two friends spoke in private about their secret plan.*

private detective, a detective who is employed by a private person or group rather than by a police force or government agency. Also, **private investigator.**

private enterprise, another term for **free enterprise.**

pri·va·teer (prī′və tîr′) *n.* **1.** a privately owned armed ship commissioned by a government to attack enemy ships, especially merchant ships. **2.** the commander or a member of the crew of such a ship. —*v.i.* to sail on or as a privateer.

private eye *Informal.* a private detective.

private first class 1. in the U.S. Army, a soldier ranking below a corporal and above a private. **2.** in the U.S. Marine Corps, a soldier ranking below a lance corporal and above a private.

private investigator, another term for **private detective.**

private school, a school that is supported and managed by a private group rather than by the government.

pri·va·tion (prī vā′shən) *n.* **1.** the lack of the comforts or necessities of life or the condition resulting from such a lack. **2.** the act of depriving or the state of being deprived.

priv·et (priv′it) *n.* any of a group of evergreen shrubs or small trees widely used for hedges, usually having white flowers and black berries.

priv·i·lege (priv′ə lij) *n.* a special right, advantage, or benefit granted to or held by a certain person, group, or class: *The older teenagers were given the privilege of staying out late.* —*v.t.,* **priv·i·leged, priv·i·leg·ing.** to grant a privilege to.

priv·i·leged (priv′ə lijd) *adj.* **1.** having or enjoying a privilege or privileges: *a privileged group.* **2.** confidential; private; restricted: *privileged information.*

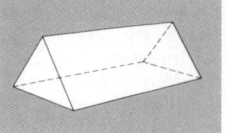

privet

priv·i·ly (priv′ə lē) *adv.* privately; secretly.

priv·y (priv′ē) *adj.* having knowledge of something secret or private: *Only three people were privy to the plot.* —*n., pl.* **priv·ies.** see **outhouse** *(def. 1).*

Privy Council, an honorary body of advisers appointed by the British sovereign.

prix fixe (prē′fiks′) *n., pl.* **prix fixes** (prē′fiks′). **1.** a complete meal served at a fixed price. **2.** the price charged for such a meal. [From the French phrase *prix fixe* meaning "fixed price," going back to the Latin words *pretium* "price, value" and *fixus,* past participle of *figere* "to fasten."]

prize¹ (prīz) *n.* **1.** something that is offered or won as a reward, especially for winning in a competition or in a game of chance. **2.** anything worth winning; something valuable. —*adj.* **1.** having won or likely to win a prize: *a prize painting.* **2.** offered or given as a prize. **3.** worthy of a prize; outstanding. [From the Middle English word *pris* meaning "value, price" or "reward," from the Old French word *pris* with the same meanings, from the Latin word *pretium* "money," "worth," or "reward."]

prize² (prīz) *n.* something seized or captured, especially an enemy ship captured at sea during wartime. [From the Old French word *prise* meaning "booty, something taken," from the word *prendre* "to take," from the Latin word *praehendere* "to seize."]

prize³ (prīz) *v.t.,* **prized, priz·ing. 1.** to value or esteem highly: *to prize a friend's advice.* **2.** to estimate the value of; appraise: *to prize one's honor above one's life.* [From the Old French word *prisier* meaning "to value, appraise," going back to the Latin word *pretium* "money," "worth," or "reward."]

prize⁴ (prīz) *v.t.,* **prized, priz·ing.** to raise or force with a lever; pry. —*n.* an instrument used for prying; lever. [From the earlier word *prize* meaning "a lever, crowbar," perhaps from *prize².*]

prize·fight (prīz′fīt′) *n.* a match between professional boxers. —**prize′fight′er,** *n.*

prize·win·ner (prīz′win′ər) *n.* a person or thing that has been awarded a prize in a competition: *An apple pie was the prizewinner at the state fair last year.*

pro¹ (prō) *adv.* in favor of; for. —*n., pl.* **pros.** a reason, argument, or person in favor of something: *The senator listed all the pros and cons of the new plan for tax reform.* [From the Latin word *pro* meaning "for, in favor."]

pro² (prō) *adj.; n., pl.* **pros.** *Informal.* professional.

pro–¹ *prefix* **1.** in favor of; supporting; in behalf of: *pro-British.* **2.** forward; forth; out: *proclaim.* **3.** in place of; acting as: *pronoun.* [Originally from the Latin prefix *pro-,* from the word *pro* meaning "for, before."]

pro–² *prefix* before in time or place: *prognosis*. [Originally from the Greek prefix *pro-*, from the word *pro* meaning "prior, before" or "forward."]

prob·a·bil·i·ty (prob′ə bil′i tē) *n.*, *pl.* **prob·a·bil·i·ties.** **1.** the state or quality of being probable; likelihood: *Bad weather increases the probability of highway accidents.* **2.** something probable or likely: *It is only a probability that they will come.* **3.** *Mathematics.* the ratio of the number of chances favoring the occurrence of a particular event to the total number of possible occurrences.
·**in all probability.** most probably; very likely.

prob·a·ble (prob′ə bəl) *adj.* **1.** likely to occur but not certain; reasonable to expect: *The experts agreed on the probable outcome of the boxing match.* **2.** likely to be true; plausible: *That's the probable answer, but it can't be proved.*

prob·a·bly (prob′ə blē) *adv.* in all likelihood; most likely.

pro·bate (prō′bāt) *n.* the act or process of legally proving a will. —*adj.* of or relating to the legal proving of a will: *a probate court.* —*v.t.,* **pro·bat·ed, pro·bat·ing.** to establish the authenticity or validity of (a will).

pro·ba·tion (prō bā′shən) *n.* **1.** a testing or trial of the ability, qualifications, or suitability of a person, as a new employee, usually for a specified period of time. **2.** *Law.* **a.** the action or practice of allowing a person convicted of an offense to remain free under close supervision, rather than be put in prison. **b.** the period of being on probation or the status of a person on probation.

pro·ba·tion·er (prō bā′shə nər) *n.* a person who is on probation.

probation officer, an officer appointed to supervise someone who is on probation.

probe (prōb) *n.* **1.** a thorough investigation or examination: *The newspaper article led to a probe into prison conditions.* **2.** a slender surgical tool for exploring a body cavity, wound, or similar opening. **3.** a device, mechanism, or object used for investigation or exploration, as a space probe. —*v.,* **probed, prob·ing.** —*v.t.* **1.** to investigate, examine, or explore thoroughly: *The police probed all the details of the crime.* **2.** to examine or explore with a probe. —*v.i.* to conduct a thorough investigation or examination: *Scientists probed into the nature of the substance.*

pro·bi·ty (prō′bi tē, prob′i tē) *n.* moral strength; integrity.

prob·lem (prob′ləm) *n.* **1.** a question, situation, or condition that is difficult, confusing, or not resolved: *Air pollution is a major problem facing our cities.* **2.** a person who is troublesome or causes difficulty: *The oldest child at camp was a problem for the counselor.* **3.** a question proposed for thinking, discussing, or solving: *an arithmetic problem.* —*adj.* being a problem; difficult to handle: *a problem child.*

prob·lem·at·ic (prob′lə mat′ik) *adj.* being, presenting, or involving a problem; uncertain. Also, **prob·lem·at·i·cal** (prob′lə mat′i kəl). —**prob′lem·at′i·cal·ly,** *adv.*

pro·bos·cis (prō bos′is, prō bos′kis) *n.*, *pl.* **pro·bos·cis·es** or **pro·bos·ci·des** (prō bos′i dēz′). **1.** a long, flexible snout, as the trunk of an elephant. **2.** the long, tubular mouth parts of certain insects, as mosquitoes and butterflies, adapted for piercing and sucking.

pro·caine (prō′kān) *n.* a synthetic drug widely used as a local anesthetic in dentistry and medicine.

pro·ce·dure (prə sē′jər) *n.* **1.** a particular course of action, especially one that follows a definite series of steps: *What is the proper procedure for leaving the building in case of fire?* **2.** the customary or established way of conducting legal, parliamentary, or similar business: *rules of parliamentary procedure.* **3.** a manner of proceeding or acting. —**pro·ce′du·ral,** *adj.*

pro·ceed (prə sēd′) *v.i.* **1.** to continue, especially after a stop or interruption: *The speaker waited for the applause to stop and then proceeded.* **2.** to begin or undertake some action or process: *The mechanic jacked up the car and then proceeded to change the tire.* **3.** to move on or forward: *The parade proceeded through town.* **4.** to be carried on or put into action: *The experiment is proceeding as planned.*

pro·ceed·ing (prə sē′ding) *n.* **1.** an action or course of action; procedure. **2. proceedings. a.** a series of actions or events; happenings. **b.** a record of business transacted at a meeting of a society or similar organization. **c.** *Law.* legal action.

pro·ceeds (prō′sēdz) *pl. n.* the money or profit derived from a commercial undertaking, especially money raised for a particular cause.

proc·ess (pros′es, prō′ses) *n.*, *pl.* **proc·ess·es.** **1.** the series of acts or operations performed in making or doing something: *the process of making a dress.* **2.** a series of continuous changes or actions leading to an end: *the process of growth.* **3.** a course or lapse: *In the process of time the job will be done.* **4.** the course of being done or going on: *The novelist is in the process of writing another book.* **5.** *Law.* **a.** a writ or summons by which a person is ordered to appear in court in a legal action. **b.** all of the proceedings in a legal action. **6.** *Biology.* an outgrowth or protruding part: *The animal had a bony process on top of its head.* —*v.t.* **1.** to handle by routine procedures: *The college staff processes new students at the beginning of each year.* **2.** to treat, make, or prepare, as by a special method: *to process cheese.* —*adj.* made or prepared by some special method: *process cheese.*

pro·ces·sion (prə sesh′ən) *n.* **1.** a continuous or steady forward movement or progression, especially in a formal, orderly, or ceremonious manner. **2.** a group of persons or things moving along in this way, often in a long line: *The wedding procession moved slowly down the aisle.* **3.** a continuous course or succession.

procession *(def. 2)*

pro·ces·sion·al (prə sesh′ə nəl) *adj.* of, relating to, or moving in a procession. —*n.* **1.** the music accompanying a procession. **2.** a book containing the hymns, prayers, and ritual used in religious processions.

process server, a person who is authorized to deliver legal documents, such as writs, summonses, and subpoenas.

at; āpe; fär; câre; end; mē; it; īce; pîerce; hot; ōld; sông; fôrk; oil; out; up; ūse; rüle; pùll; tûrn; chin; sing; shop; thin; this; hw in white; zh in treasure. The symbol ə stands for the unstressed vowel sound heard in about, taken, pencil, lemon, and circus.

P

pro·claim (prə klām′) *v.t.* **1.** to announce officially; declare publicly: *The enemy nations proclaimed a truce.* **2.** to make clear; reveal: *The child's tears proclaimed great sorrow.*

proc·la·ma·tion (prok′lə mā′shən) *n.* **1.** something that is proclaimed, especially an official public announcement. **2.** the act of proclaiming.

pro·cliv·i·ty (prō kliv′i tē) *n., pl.* **pro·cliv·i·ties.** a tendency or inclination; propensity: *The sickly child showed a proclivity to complain.*

pro·con·sul (prō kon′səl) *n.* the governor or military commander of an ancient Roman province.

pro·cras·ti·nate (prō kras′tə nāt) *v.i.,* **pro·cras·ti·nat·ed, pro·cras·ti·nat·ing.** to put off doing something until a future time, especially when this is done as a habit. —**pro·cras′ti·na′tion,** *n.* —**pro·cras′ti·na′tor,** *n.*

pro·cre·ate (prō′krē āt′) *v.t., v.i.,* **pro·cre·at·ed, pro·cre·at·ing.** to produce offspring. —**pro′cre·a′tion,** *n.*

proc·tor (prok′tər) *n.* a person appointed to keep order and supervise students during an examination at a college or university. —*v.t.* to act as proctor for (an examination).

pro·cure (prə kyūr′) *v.t.,* **pro·cured, pro·cur·ing.** **1.** to acquire or get, especially with effort: *The children procured the money to buy the present by mowing lawns.* **2.** to bring about; effect; cause. —**pro·cure′ment,** *n.*

prod (prod) *v.t.,* **prod·ded, prod·ding.** **1.** to push or jab, as with a pointed instrument. **2.** to stir to action; rouse. —*n.* **1.** a push or jab. **2.** a pointed instrument used for prodding, as a goad. **3.** something that stirs to action. —**prod′der,** *n.*

prod·i·gal (prod′i gəl) *adj.* **1.** foolishly extravagant; wasteful: *Your prodigal spending habits have put you into debt.* **2.** lavish, generous, or profuse; abundant: *prodigal talents.* —*n.* a person who is recklessly extravagant. —**prod·i·gal·i·ty** (prod′i gal′i tē), *n.* —**prod′i·gal·ly,** *adv.*

pro·di·gious (prə dij′əs) *adj.* **1.** huge or extraordinary in size, number, or degree; enormous: *The mountains rose to a prodigious height.* **2.** causing amazement; marvelous: *a prodigious feat of strength.* —**pro·di′gious·ly,** *adv.* —**pro·di′gious·ness,** *n.*

prod·i·gy (prod′i jē) *n., pl.* **prod·i·gies.** **1.** an extremely gifted or talented person, especially a child. **2.** something that causes wonder or amazement; marvel.

pro·duce (*v.,* prə düs′, prə dūs′; *n.,* prod′üs, prod′ūs, prō′düs, prō′dūs) *v.,* **pro·duced, pro·duc·ing.** —*v.t.* **1.** to make or bring into being; manufacture: *That company produces steel.* **2.** to bring forth; yield; bear: *A cow produces milk.* **3.** to bring into existence by mental or artistic effort; create: *This artist has produced many fine paintings.* **4.** to give rise to; cause: *The song produced a strong reaction from the audience.* **5.** to bring forward or present; show; furnish: *The lawyer could not produce any evidence.* **6.** to prepare (a play, motion picture, or other entertainment) for public showing, as by securing financial backing and hiring performers. —*v.i.* to bring forth or make something: *These workers produce at a very fast rate.* —*n.* **1.** something that is produced. **2.** farm products, especially fresh fruit and vegetables.

pro·duc·er (prə dü′sər, prə dū′sər) *n.* **1.** a person or thing that produces. **2.** a person in charge of producing a play, motion picture, or other entertainment. **3.** an organism, such as a plant, that uses inorganic substances to make its own food.

prod·uct (prod′əkt) *n.* **1.** anything that is produced: *dairy products.* **2.** result; consequence: *My good grades were the product of studying.* **3.** a number or algebraic expression obtained by multiplication: *12 is the product of 4 and 3.*

pro·duc·tion (prə duk′shən) *n.* **1.** the act of producing or state of being produced: *a new motion picture that is still in production.* **2.** the amount produced: *Wheat production has increased this year.* **3.** something that is produced, especially a play, motion picture, or other form of entertainment.

production line, an assembly line.

pro·duc·tive (prə duk′tiv) *adj.* **1.** producing abundantly; fertile or prolific: *productive land, a productive author.* **2.** having favorable, useful, or positive results; fruitful; effective: *Talks to end the strike had not been very productive.* **3.** yielding some product at a profit: *a productive business.* **4.** producing, tending to produce, or capable of producing: *Our club meeting was productive of good ideas for the picnic.* —**pro·duc′tive·ly,** *adv.* —**pro·duc′tive·ness,** *n.*

pro·duc·tiv·i·ty (prō′duk tiv′i tē) *n.* the state or quality of being productive.

Prof., Professor (used as a title).

prof·a·na·tion (prof′ə nā′shən) *n.* the act of profaning.

pro·fane (prō fān′, prə fān′) *adj.* **1.** showing or marked by irreverence, disrespect, or contempt for God or sacred things; blasphemous. **2.** not concerned with or relating to religion or religious matters; secular. **3.** vulgar; coarse; obscene: *profane language.* —*v.t.,* **pro·faned, pro·fan·ing.** **1.** to treat (something sacred) with disrespect or contempt; desecrate: *You have been guilty of profaning the Lord's day* (Daniel Defoe). **2.** to put to wrong, degrading, or unworthy use; abuse: *to profane one's precious time.* —**pro·fane′ly,** *adv.* —**pro·fane′ness,** *n.*

pro·fan·i·ty (prō fan′i tē, prə fan′i tē) *n., pl.* **pro·fan·i·ties.** **1.** a profane act or remark. **2.** the use of profane or vulgar language. **3.** the state or quality of being profane.

pro·fess (prə fes′) *v.t.* **1.** to claim, especially falsely or insincerely: *That student professes to know everything about sculpture.* **2.** to declare openly; affirm: *We profess ourselves to be loyal citizens.* **3.** to affirm one's faith in: *to profess Judaism.* —*v.i.* to make a declaration or affirmation.

pro·fessed (prə fest′) *adj.* **1.** alleged; pretended: *professed generosity.* **2.** openly declared: *a professed enemy.*

pro·fes·sion (prə fesh′ən) *n.* **1.** an occupation that requires special education and training, such as law or medicine. **2.** a group of persons following such an occupation: *the medical profession.* **3.** any activity considered as a profession: *the acting profession.* **4.** the act or an instance of professing; declaration: *a profession of loyalty.* **5.** the affirming of faith in a religion.

pro·fes·sion·al (prə fesh′ə nəl) *adj.* **1.** of or relating to a profession or a person in a profession: *The doctor charged a fee for professional services.* **2.** engaged in a profession: *The school's professional staff includes a nurse.* **3.** working for money in an activity not generally done as an occupation, especially a sport: *a professional golfer.* **4.** engaged in by professionals as opposed to amateurs: *professional basketball.* —*n.* **1.** a person engaged in a profession. **2.** a person working for money in an activity not generally done as an occupation, especially an athlete. **3.** a person who is skilled or expert in a particular activity or occupation. —**pro·fes′sion·al·ly,** *adv.*

pro·fes·sion·al·ism (prə fesh′ə nə liz′əm) *n.* professional methods, quality, or status.

pro·fes·sor (prə fes′ər) *n.* **1.** a teacher of the highest rank in a college, university, or other institution of higher education. **2.** *Informal.* any teacher.

pro·fes·so·ri·al (prō′fə sôr′ē əl, prof′ə sôr′ē əl) *adj.* of, relating to, or characteristic of a professor. —**pro′fes·so′ri·al·ly,** *adv.*

pro·fes·sor·ship (prə fes′ər ship′) *n.* the position or duties of a professor.

prof·fer (prof′ər) *v.t.* to present for acceptance; offer: *We proffered an apology for our lateness.* —*n.* something presented for acceptance; offer.

pro·fi·cien·cy (prə fish′ən sē) *n., pl.* **pro·fi·cien·cies.** the state or quality of being proficient; skill.

pro·fi·cient (prə fish′ənt) *adj.* highly skilled; expert; adept: *Years of practice had made the musician proficient in playing the flute.* —**pro·fi′cient·ly,** *adv.*

pro·file (prō′fīl) *n.* **1.** a side view, especially of a human face or head. **2.** an outline, drawing, or other representation of this. **3.** any outline or representation of an outline: *The mountain's jagged profile stood out against the sky.* **4.** a brief biographical sketch: *The newspaper printed a profile of the new mayor.* **5.** an analysis, usually shown by means of a graph or diagram, of some person, process, or thing: *a profile of the voters in a district.* —*v.t.,* **pro·filed, pro·fil·ing.** to make, sketch, or write a profile of.

profile *(def. 2)*

prof·it (prof′it) *n.* **1.** *also,* **profits.** the amount remaining after all the costs of a business or business transaction have been paid. **2.** *also,* **profits.** financial gain, especially return or income received from investment or property. **3.** a benefit or advantage; gain. —*v.i.* **1.** to get benefit or profit; gain: *to profit from an experience.* **2.** to be of advantage, use, or benefit. —*v.t.* to be of advantage, use, or benefit to.

prof·it·a·ble (prof′i tə bəl) *adj.* **1.** yielding a financial profit: *a profitable business.* **2.** beneficial; rewarding; useful: *a profitable experience.* —**prof′it·a·ble·ness,** *n.* —**prof′it·a·bly,** *adv.*

prof·it·eer (prof′i tîr′) *n.* a person who makes or seeks to make excessive profits, especially by selling goods at very high prices during a time of shortage. —*v.i.* to act as a profiteer.

prof·li·gate (prof′li git) *adj.* **1.** totally corrupt with regard to morals; thoroughly immoral; dissolute. **2.** recklessly extravagant or wasteful. —*n.* a profligate person. —**prof′li·ga·cy,** *n.* —**prof′li·gate·ly,** *adv.*

pro·found (prə found′) *adj.* **1.** showing or characterized by great understanding, knowledge, or insight: *a profound idea, a profound book.* **2.** coming from the depth of one's being; intensely felt: *We felt profound sorrow upon hearing of our neighbor's death.* **3.** significant; important; extensive: *The doctor's discovery will have a profound influence on mankind.* **4.** absolute; complete; thorough: *There was a profound silence when the President began to speak.* —**pro·found′ly,** *adv.* —**pro·found′ness,** *n.*

pro·fun·di·ty (prə fun′di tē) *n., pl.* **pro·fun·di·ties.** **1.** the state or quality of being profound; depth. **2.** a profound or complicated statement, idea, or matter.

pro·fuse (prə fūs′) *adj.* **1.** great or abundant in amount; plentiful: *profuse foliage, profuse bleeding.* **2.** given or giving freely, often to too great a degree; lavish: *profuse compliments.* —**pro·fuse′ly,** *adv.* —**pro·fuse′ness,** *n.*

pro·fu·sion (prə fū′zhən) *n.* **1.** a plentiful amount; abundance. **2.** extravagance; lavishness.

pro·gen·i·tor (prō jen′i tər) *n.* **1.** an ancestor from whom descent is traced; forefather. **2.** originator: *a progenitor of modern science.*

prog·e·ny (proj′ə nē) *n., pl.* **prog·e·nies.** offspring, descendants, or children as a group.

pro·ges·ter·one (prō jes′tə rōn′) *n.* a female sex hormone that in combination with estrogen prepares the uterus to receive a fertilized egg and helps to maintain pregnancy by keeping the uterus in the proper condition for the embryo. [From the prefix *pro-*[1] + the word *ge*(station) + the combining form *ster*(ol) (derived from such words as *cholesterol*) + the scientific suffix *-one* meaning a particular kind of compound.]

prog·no·sis (prog nō′sis) *n., pl.* **prog·no·ses** (prog-nō′sēz). **1.** a prediction of the probable course and outcome of a disease. **2.** any prediction or forecast.

prog·nos·tic (prog nos′tik) *adj.* **1.** of, relating to, or serving as a basis for a prognosis. **2.** foretelling; predictive. —*n.* **1.** a sign or indication of some future occurrence. **2.** a prediction or forecast.

prog·nos·ti·cate (prog nos′ti kāt′) *v.t.,* **prog·nos·ti·cat·ed, prog·nos·ti·cat·ing.** **1.** to predict on the basis of present indications; forecast; prophesy. **2.** to foreshadow. —**prog·nos′ti·ca′tion,** *n.* —**prog·nos′ti·ca′tor,** *n.*

pro·gram (prō′gram, prō′grəm) *also, British,* **pro·gramme.** *n.* **1.** a list or printed announcement, especially for some public presentation, as a play or concert, usually showing what is to be presented and who will participate. **2.** a presentation or performance, especially a television or radio show. **3.** a schedule or procedure: *The representative proposed a new program for fighting crime.* **4.** a set of organized activities or other offerings planned by or available at a particular place or institution: *That university has an excellent English program.* **5.** a series of steps specified for the solution of a particular problem, to be coded for use in a computer. **6.** a series of coded instructions used to direct a computer in the solution of a problem. —*v.t.,* **pro·grammed** or **pro·gramed, pro·gram·ming** or **pro·gram·ing.** **1.** to arrange or include in a program or schedule. **2.** to make up or work out a program for. **3.** to write a program for (a computer).

pro·gram·mer (prō′gram ər) *also,* **pro·gram·er.** *n.* a person who programs, especially a person who programs computers.

prog·ress (*n.,* prog′res; *v.,* prə gres′) *n.* **1.** forward movement: *Heavy rains slowed the explorer's progress through the jungle.* **2.** movement toward a goal or toward completion: *Are you making any progress with your book report?* **3.** development to a better or higher state; improvement: *The patient is making progress toward recovery.* —*v.i.* **1.** to move forward or onward; proceed: *The debater's argument progressed logically from one step to the next.* **2.** to move toward a goal or toward completion: *Construction of the new hospital is progressing according to schedule.* **3.** to advance to a higher or better state; improve: *to progress in one's schoolwork.*

pro·gres·sion (prə gresh′ən) *n.* **1.** the act of progressing; advance. **2.** *Mathematics.* a sequence of numbers or algebraic expressions in which there is the same relation between each quantity and the one succeeding it. **3.** a sequence or succession, as of events. **4.** *Music.* **a.** the movement from one tone or chord to another. **b.** a succession of tones or chords.

pro·gres·sive (prə gres′iv) *adj.* **1.** moving forward; advancing. **2.** proceeding steadily or step by step. **3.** favoring, supporting, or characterized by progress, reform, or improvement, especially in political or social matters: *The candidate promised progressive leadership if elected.* **4.** *Grammar.* denoting action in progress. —*n.* a person who favors or advocates progress or reform, as in political, social, or educational matters. —**pro·gres′sive·ly,** *adv.* —**pro·gres′sive·ness,** *n.*

pro·hib·it (prō hib′it) *v.t.* **1.** to forbid by authority:

at; āpe; fär; câre; end; mē; it; īce; pîerce; hot; ōld; sông, fôrk; oil; out; up; ūse; rüle; pull; tûrn; chin; sing; shop; thin; <u>th</u>is; hw in white; zh in treasure. The symbol ə stands for the unstressed vowel sound heard in about, taken, pencil, lemon, and circus.

Smoking is prohibited in this building. **2.** to prevent; hinder: *Poor health prohibits them from traveling.*

pro·hi·bi·tion (prō′ə bish′ən) *n.* **1.** the act of prohibiting. **2.** a law, order, or rule that forbids something. **3.** the forbidding by law of the manufacture, transportation, and sale of alcoholic beverages. **4. Prohibition.** the period from 1920 to 1933 during which alcoholic beverages were prohibited by federal law in the United States.

pro·hi·bi·tion·ist (prō′ə bish′ə nist) *n.* a person who favors the prohibition of alcoholic beverages.

pro·hib·i·tive (prō hib′i tiv) *adj.* **1.** so high or expensive as to make buying, paying, or using difficult or impossible: *The house was being sold at an almost prohibitive price.* **2.** prohibiting or tending to prohibit: *a prohibitive law.* Also, **pro·hib·i·to·ry** (prō hib′i tôr′ē).

proj·ect (*n.*, proj′ekt; *v.*, prə jekt′) *n.* **1.** a plan; scheme; proposal. **2.** a task or activity that is to be done; undertaking: *Our town has begun a project to improve the roads.* **3.** a housing installation, usually made up of apartment buildings, especially such housing supported by the government to provide for families with lower incomes. —*v.t.* **1.** to throw, shoot, or hurl forward. **2.** to cause (a shadow, light, or image) to fall on a surface. **3.** to cause (one's voice) to be heard clearly at a distance. **4.** to visualize or think of by using one's imagination: *to project oneself into the future.* **5.** to predict on the basis of certain given or known information: *to project the winner of an election by using a computer.* —*v.i.* **1.** to stick out; protrude: *A narrow piece of land projected into the sea.* **2.** to cause one's voice to be heard clearly at a distance.

pro·jec·tile (prə jek′təl, prə jek′tīl) *n.* an object that is designed to be shot or in some other way projected through space, as a bullet. —*adj.* **1.** capable of being thrown, shot, or hurled forward. **2.** impelling or driving forward: *the projectile force of a weapon.*

pro·jec·tion (prə jek′shən) *n.* **1.** the act of projecting. **2.** something that sticks out or projects; protruding part. **3.** the process of projecting images, as from film or a transparent slide, onto a screen or other surface. **4.** an image that is so projected. **5.** a prediction based on certain given or known information: *a computer projection of an election's outcome.*

pro·jec·tor (prə jek′tər) *n.* **1.** a device that projects images, as from film or a transparent slide, onto a screen or other surface. **2.** a person who devises projects or plans.

pro·le·tar·i·an (prō′li târ′ē ən) *adj.* of, relating to, or characteristic of the proletariat. —*n.* a member of the proletariat. [From the Latin word *proletarius* meaning ''a Roman citizen of low class,'' from the word *proles* ''offspring.'' These citizens were supposed to serve Rome by producing children.]

pro·le·tar·i·at (prō′li târ′ē ət) *n.* **1.** the working class, especially the industrial working class. **2.** in ancient Rome, the lowest class of citizens.

pro·lif·er·ate (prə lif′ə rāt′) *v.*, **pro·lif·er·at·ed, pro·lif·er·at·ing.** —*v.i.* to increase, reproduce, or grow rapidly: *The bacteria proliferated in the laboratory.* —*v.t.* to cause to increase, reproduce, or grow rapidly. —**pro·lif′er·a′tion,** *n.*

pro·lif·ic (prə lif′ik) *adj.* **1.** producing abundantly through creative or artistic effort; highly productive: *The prolific novelist had written more than thirty books.* **2.** producing offspring or fruit in abundance; fertile: *a prolific apple tree.* —**pro·lif′i·cal·ly,** *adv.*

pro·lix (prō liks′, prō′liks′) *adj.* **1.** so long and wordy as to be boring: *a prolix sermon.* **2.** inclined to speak or write in a boringly long and wordy manner. —**pro·lix′i·ty,** *n.*

pro·logue (prō′lôg′, prō′log′) *also,* **pro·log.** *n.* **1.** an introduction to a play, poem, or other literary work. **2.** any introductory or preliminary act or event.

pro·long (prə lông′) *v.t.* to make longer, especially in time; extend: *Don't prolong the suspense by not telling us what happened until tomorrow.*

pro·lon·ga·tion (prō′lông gā′shən) *n.* **1.** the act of prolonging or the state of being prolonged. **2.** something that prolongs or is prolonged.

prom (prom) *n. Informal.* a formal school or college dance.

prom·e·nade (prom′ə nād′, prom′ə näd′) *n.* **1.** a leisurely walk, especially one taken in a public place for pleasure or display. **2.** a place or area for such walking. **3.** a formal dance; ball. **4.** a march of the guests at the opening of a formal dance. **5.** a march of dancers in a square dance. —*v.i.*, **prom·e·nad·ed, prom·e·nad·ing.** **1.** to go on a promenade or leisurely walk. **2.** to perform a promenade in a square dance.

Pro·me·the·us (prə mē′thē əs) *n. Greek Mythology.* a Titan who stole fire from the gods and brought it to humankind. Zeus punished him by chaining him to a rock where an eagle ate away at his liver every day.

pro·me·thi·um (prə mē′thē əm) *n.* a radioactive, metallic element of the rare-earth group. It is produced artificially from uranium, thorium, and plutonium. Symbol: **Pm** [From *Prometheus,* the Titan of Greek mythology who brought fire to the human race. This element was discovered through the constructive use of nuclear energy.]

prom·i·nence (prom′ə nəns) *n.* **1.** the state or quality of being prominent: *the prominence of a public figure.* **2.** something prominent; projection. **3.** a cloud of glowing gas that erupts from the surface of the sun.

prom·i·nent (prom′ə nənt) *adj.* **1.** well-known or important; notable: *a prominent member of the community.* **2.** very noticeable; conspicuous: *One large oak tree was the landscape's only prominent feature.* **3.** sticking out from a surface; projecting: *The cliff had a prominent overhang.* —**prom′i·nent·ly,** *adv.*

prom·is·cu·i·ty (prom′ə skū′i tē) *n.* **1.** promiscuous or loose sexual relations or behavior. **2.** the state or quality of being promiscuous.

pro·mis·cu·ous (prə mis′kū əs) *adj.* **1.** indiscriminate, especially having sexual relations indiscriminately or with many persons. **2.** made up of varied and unrelated things, parts, or individuals. —**pro·mis′cu·ous·ly,** *adv.* —**pro·mis′cu·ous·ness,** *n.*

prom·ise (prom′is) *n.* **1.** an assurance or pledge given that one will or will not do something, or that something will or will not occur: *I made a promise that I would keep my room neat.* **2.** an indication of or reason for expecting future excellence, success, or progress: *The new drug shows promise in treating the disease. That young musician shows promise.* **3.** an indication of something that may occur or develop: *There was a promise of spring in the air.* —*v.*, **prom·ised, prom·is·ing.** —*v.t.* **1.** to declare or guarantee with a promise: *Everyone promised to keep the surprise party a secret.* **2.** to make a promise of (something): *The new owner of the apartment house promised improvements that never took place.* **3.** to give reason to expect or anticipate (something): *The clear skies promised a nice day.* —*v.i.* to make or give a promise.

Promised Land 1. in the Bible, the land of Canaan, promised by God to Abraham and his descendants. **2. promised land.** any place where final happiness is hoped or expected to be found.

prom·is·ing (prom′ə sing) *adj.* showing promise for the future: *The most promising new playwright has a very sharp wit.* —**prom′is·ing·ly,** *adv.*

prom·is·so·ry (prom′ə sôr′ē) *adj.* containing or conveying a promise: *a promissory pact.*

promissory note, a written promise to pay a particular

sum of money to a certain party at a specified future time or on demand.

prom·on·to·ry (prom'ən tôr'ē) *n., pl.* **prom·on·to·ries.** a raised portion of land extending out into a body of water.

pro·mote (prə mōt') *v.t.,* **pro·mot·ed, pro·mot·ing.** **1.** to raise in rank, position, or honor: *The private was promoted to the rank of corporal.* **2.** to aid in or contribute to the growth, development, or progress of: *Certain foods promote tooth decay.* **3.** to work for; advocate: *The young senator promoted the passage of the bill.* **4.** to advance (a student) to the next higher grade. **5.** to try to sell, make more popular, or get the necessary money for (a product, business undertaking, or the like), as by advertising.

pro·mot·er (prə mō'tər) *n.* **1.** a person or thing that promotes, advances, or furthers something. **2.** a person who organizes or promotes a business undertaking or commercial enterprise, especially a sports event.

pro·mo·tion (prə mō'shən) *n.* **1.** an advancement in rank, position, honor, or grade. **2.** the furthering of a business undertaking or commercial enterprise. **3.** the act of promoting. —**pro·mo'tion·al,** *adj.*

prompt (prompt) *adj.* **1.** acting or occurring at the proper time; on time; punctual: *They are usually prompt in arriving.* **2.** done or given without delay: *This repair shop is known for its prompt service.* **3.** quick to act; ready: *Don't be so prompt to criticize.* —*v.t.* **1.** to move to action; incite: *An odd feeling that something was wrong prompted me to return home.* **2.** to give rise to; inspire: *The scandal prompted a Senate investigation.* **3.** to supply (a performer or speaker) with words that have been forgotten or a cue that has been missed. —*n. Computers.* a message or mark displayed on a computer screen that tells the operator how to proceed. —**prompt'ly,** *adv.* —**prompt'ness,** *n.*

prompt·er (promp'tər) *n.* a person whose task is to prompt the actors in a theatrical production.

promp·ti·tude (promp'ti tüd', promp'ti tūd') *n.* the quality of being prompt; promptness.

prom·ul·gate (prom'əl gāt', prō mul'gāt) *v.t.,* **prom·ul·gat·ed, prom·ul·gat·ing.** **1.** to make known or put into effect formally and officially, especially by public declaration; proclaim: *to promulgate a new law.* **2.** to make widespread; spread. **prom'ul·ga'tion,** *n.* —**prom'ul·ga'tor,** *n.*

pron. **1.** pronoun. **2.** pronunciation.

prone (prōn) *adj.* **1.** lying with the face or front downward; prostrate. **2.** naturally inclined, disposed. *I am prone to distrust strangers.* —**prone'ly,** *adv.* —**prone'ness,** *n.*

prong (prông, prong) *n.* **1.** a sharply pointed end of a tool or implement, as of a fork. **2.** any sharply pointed projection, as of an antler.

pronged (prôngd, prongd) *adj.* having prongs.

prong·horn (prông'hôrn', prong'hôrn') *n., pl.* **prong·horn** or **prong·horns.** a cud-chewing animal resembling an antelope, found chiefly on the Rocky Mountain plains, and having slender, pronged horns. Also, **antelope, pronghorn antelope.**

pro·noun (prō'noun') *n.* a word used as a substitute for a noun or noun phrase, signifying a person, place, or thing without naming it. *I, you, he, she, who, what,* and *this* are pronouns.

pro·nounce (prə nouns')
v., **pro·nounced, pro-**

pronghorn

nounc·ing. —*v.t.* **1.** to utter (a word or sound). **2.** to utter (a word or sound) in a particular way, especially with a certain accent or according to an accepted standard. **3.** to indicate the correct manner of uttering (a word) with phonetic symbols. **4.** to declare or state, especially officially, formally, or solemnly: *The jury pronounced the defendant not guilty.* —*v.i.* **1.** to state an opinion, judgment, or decision; make a pronouncement. **2.** to utter or pronounce words. —**pro·nounce'a·ble,** *adj.*

pro·nounced (prə nounst') *adj.* clearly recognizable; strongly defined; decided.

pro·nounce·ment (prə nouns'mənt) *n.* **1.** a formal or official declaration or statement. **2.** an opinion, judgment, or decision.

pron·to (pron'tō) *adv. Informal.* quickly; promptly.

pro·nun·ci·a·tion (prə nun'sē ā'shən) *n.* **1.** the act or manner of pronouncing words. **2.** an accepted or standard way of pronouncing a word: *There are many words that have more than one pronunciation.* **3.** the phonetic representation of a word, indicating the way it is pronounced.

Language Note

There have been considerable changes in the **pronunciation** of the English language from its early forms until the present day. The pronunciation of Old English was very different from that of Modern English. Middle English pronunciation, however, was more like our own, differing mainly in the pronunciation of vowels and in the sounding of final vowels and some consonants that in Modern English are silent. Because there are obviously no living speakers of these early forms of our language, language scholars must draw their conclusions about early pronunciation by studying Middle English spelling and rhymes, statements made by writers of the period, and old books about foreign languages in which foreign sounds are given English equivalents.

By using this evidence, scholars have found that fundamental changes in English pronunciation occurred in the fifteenth and sixteenth centuries. The changes that took place during these years, which mark the difference in pronunciation between the Middle English of Geoffrey Chaucer and the Elizabethan English of William Shakespeare, are often called the *Great Vowel Shift*. The most important aspect of this shift was that all long vowels changed their pronunciation. Thus, although many Elizabethan vowel sounds are not the same as modern vowel sounds, they are still much closer to them than they are to Middle English vowels.

The pronunciation of English has been changed by distance as well as time. American English, which has its roots in the English spoken by seventeenth-century settlers, is pronounced in a different way from British English. The pronunciation of American English also varies from one part of our country to another. These differences, although noticeable, are small enough so that it is rarely difficult for a person from one part of the United States to communicate with a person from another part.

The many regional pronunciations of American English are all correct and acceptable. In this dictionary you will

at; āpe; fär; câre; end; mē; it; īce; pîerce; hot; ōld; sông, fôrk; oil; out; up; ūse; rüle; pull; tûrn; chin; sing; shop; thin; this; hw in white; zh in treasure. The symbol ə stands for the unstressed vowel sound heard in about, taken, pencil, lemon, and circus.

P

find more than one pronunciation listed for many words, such as *apricot* and *tomato*. Each of these pronunciations is equally correct. The pronunciation key, which is at the bottom of each right-hand page, will show you how a sound is pronounced in a common word that you know. These common words are pronounced differently in different parts of our country, so using this key will enable you to pronounce any word in this book according to your own accent.

Although there is no such thing as a theoretically "correct" way of saying a word, the speakers of a particular language all pronounce its words in a basically similar way. The reason for this is that people use language to communicate, and, if there were too much variation in the way different people pronounced the same word, they would have great difficulty in understanding one another.

proof (prüf) *n.* **1.** evidence that establishes a fact or shows something to be true: *The prosecutor had proof of the defendant's guilt.* **2.** a test or trial, as of the truth, quality, or strength of something. **3.** establishment of the truth or validity of something; conclusive demonstration: *The philosopher used simple logic in the proof of the statement.* **4.** the standard alcoholic content and strength of a liquor. **5.** strength with reference to this standard. **6.** *Printing.* a trial impression taken from type, blocks, or plates for the purpose of checking and making corrections or changes before printing. **7.** *Etching and Engraving.* a trial impression taken from an engraved stone, plate, or block for the purpose of examination. **8.** *Photography.* a trial print from a photographic negative.
–proof *combining form* **1.** impervious or resistant to: *waterproof, fireproof, lightproof.* **2.** safe from; protected against: *foolproof.*
proof·read (prüf′rēd′) *v.t.,* **proof·read** (prüf′red′), **proof·read·ing.** to read (written or printed material) for the purpose of finding and correcting errors. —**proof′-read′er,** *n.*
prop¹ (prop) *v.t.,* **propped, prop·ping. 1.a.** to support, hold up, or hold in position by placing something under or against: *We propped up the sagging roof with some pieces of lumber.* **b.** to support, hold up, or hold in position by placing against something: *Prop the bicycle against the wall.* **2.** to sustain; support; bolster: *The coach propped up the team's spirit after they lost the game.* —*n.* **1.** something that serves to prop up an object or hold something in place; support. **2.** a person or thing that props or sustains. [Perhaps from the Middle Dutch word *proppe* meaning "a stopper for a bottle."]
prop² (prop) *n.* see **property** (*def. 5*).
prop³ (prop) *n. Informal.* propeller.
prop·a·gan·da (prop′ə gan′də) *n.* **1.** a body of doctrines, ideas, or attitudes of a particular group promoted or spread, often in a distorted or biased form, in order to influence the point of view of others, gain supporters, or damage an opposing group. **2.** the systematic promotion or spreading of such doctrines, ideas, or attitudes.
prop·a·gan·dist (prop′ə gan′dist) *n.* a person who spreads propaganda. —*adj.* of, like, or relating to propaganda.
prop·a·gan·dize (prop′ə gan′dīz) *v.,* **prop·a·gan·dized, prop·a·gan·diz·ing.** —*v.t.* **1.** to spread by means of propaganda. **2.** to subject to propaganda. —*v.i.* to spread or carry on propaganda.
prop·a·gate (prop′ə gāt′) *v.,* **prop·a·gat·ed, prop·a·gat·ing.** —*v.i.* to multiply by reproduction; breed. —*v.t.* **1.** to cause organisms to reproduce; breed or raise. **2.** to spread or transmit from person to person, as information; disseminate: *to propagate false rumors.* —**prop′a·ga′tion,** *n.*

pro·pane (prō′pān) *n.* a colorless gas found in petroleum and natural gas, widely used as a heating fuel.
pro·pel (prə pel′) *v.t.,* **pro·pelled, pro·pel·ling. 1.** to cause to move forward or onward; put or keep in motion: *to propel an aircraft by jet engines.* **2.** to urge onward: *The explorer was propelled by a desire for fame.*
pro·pel·lant (prə pel′ənt) *also,* **pro·pel·lent.** *n.* a propelling agent or substance, especially a fuel for propelling a rocket.
pro·pel·lent (prə pel′ənt) *adj.* propelling or capable of propelling. —*n.* another spelling of **propellant.**
pro·pel·ler (prə pel′ər) *n.* a device consisting of a hub with blades mounted at an angle. When the hub revolves, the action of the blades creates a driving force that can be used to propel a boat or aircraft.
pro·pen·si·ty (prə pen′si tē) *n., pl.* **pro·pen·si·ties.** a natural tendency; inclination: *to have a propensity for overeating.*
prop·er (prop′ər) *adj.* **1.** suitable, appropriate, or correct for a given purpose: *To do good work, a carpenter must have the proper tools.* **2.** conforming to a particular or the accepted standard: *The visiting dignitary was given a proper reception.* **3.** strictly formal, neat, or respectable; prim. **4.** understood or considered in a precise or strict sense: *That area is not really part of the city proper.* **5.** *Grammar.* referring to or derived from a particular person, place, or thing.
proper adjective, an adjective that is formed from a proper noun. For example, *Australian* is a proper adjective formed from *Australia.*
proper fraction, a fraction in which the numerator is less than the denominator, such as ⅝ or ⅔.
prop·er·ly (prop′ər lē) *adv.* **1.** in a suitable, appropriate, or correct manner: *properly equipped for a fishing trip.* **2.** in accordance with a particular or accepted standard: *to be properly married.* **3.** with precision or accuracy; strictly: *Properly speaking, that book is not a novel.*
proper noun, a noun that names a particular person, place, or thing and, in English, is always capitalized when written. For example, *Elizabeth, David, Geneva,* and *Saturday* are proper nouns. Also, **proper name.**
proper subset, a set that contains fewer members than the set of which it is a subset. The proper subsets of the set [a,b] are [a], [b], and [0].
prop·er·ty (prop′ər tē) *n., pl.* **prop·er·ties. 1.** something that is owned by someone; possession: *The statue was considered town property.* **2.** a piece of real estate: *My cousins purchased some property in Florida.* **3.** the right to the possession, use, or disposal of a thing or things; ownership. **4.** a special attribute or quality of a person or thing: *A resistance to heat is one of the properties of this metal.* **5.** any movable article, except scenery and costumes, used on the set of a theatrical production; prop: *Students brought in a table, chairs, and other property needed for the school play.*
proph·e·cy (prof′ə sē) *n., pl.* **proph·e·cies. 1.** the act of telling beforehand what is to come; foretelling of the future. **2.** something that is foretold; prediction. **3.** a divinely inspired utterance or revelation. **4.** the power or ability to foretell the future.
proph·e·sy (prof′ə sī′) *v.,* **proph·e·sied, proph·e·sy·ing.** —*v.t.* to tell beforehand (what is to come); foretell; predict: *The seer prophesied that the ruler would have a long and prosperous reign.* —*v.i.* **1.** to foretell the future; make predictions. **2.** to speak as a prophet.
proph·et (prof′it) *n.* **1.** a person who speaks or claims to speak by divine inspiration or as the interpreter of divine will, especially a religious leader professing or considered to be divinely inspired. **2.** a person who foretells the future. **3.** a spokesperson, as for a cause or movement. **4. the Prophet.** another name for **Muhammad. 5. the Prophets.** those books of the Old Testament

either written by prophets or composed mainly of prophecies.

proph·et·ess (prof′i tis) *n.*, *pl.* **proph·et·ess·es.** a woman who is a prophet.

pro·phet·ic (prə fet′ik) *adj.* **1.** containing or of the nature of prophecy: *prophetic words, a prophetic warning.* **2.** of, relating to, or belonging to a prophet: *prophetic powers.* —**pro·phet′i·cal·ly,** *adv.*

pro·phy·lac·tic (prō fə lak′tik) *adj.* serving to protect against or prevent something, such as disease. —*n.* a prophylactic device, medicine, or treatment. [From the Greek word *prophylaktikos* meaning "prophylactic," from the word *prophylassein* "to be on guard against, keep watch," from the prefix *pro-* "before, in front of" + *phylassein* "to keep watch, guard."]

pro·pin·qui·ty (prō ping′kwi tē) *n.* **1.** nearness in time or place; proximity. **2.** nearness of relation; kinship.

pro·pi·ti·ate (prə pish′ē āt′) *v.t.*, **pro·pi·ti·at·ed, pro·pi·ti·at·ing.** to win over (someone, especially someone who has been offended); appease; conciliate. —**pro·pi′ti·a′tion,** *n.*

pro·pi·tious (prə pish′əs) *adj.* favorable or suitable; opportune: *It appeared to be a propitious time for our voyage.* —**pro·pi′tious·ly,** *adv.* —**pro·pi′tious·ness,** *n.*

pro·po·nent (prə pō′nənt) *n.* **1.** a person who favors or supports something; advocate: *The senator is a leading proponent of the new tax-reform program.* **2.** a person who proposes or propounds something.

pro·por·tion (prə pôr′shən) *n.* **1.** the relation of one thing to another with respect to size, number, amount, or degree; ratio: *the proportion of men to women in a profession.* **2.** a proper or balanced relation, as between parts; harmony; symmetry: *The length and height of the room were in proportion.* **3.** a part or share: *A proportion of the profits was given to each partner in the company.* **4. proportions.** dimensions or size: *the proportions of a room, a disaster of immense proportions.* **5.** the relation between two ratios in which the first of four quantities divided by the second is equal to the third divided by the fourth. For example: 8 is to 4 as 6 is to 3. —*v.t.* **1.** to cause to be in a proper or balanced relation: *The architect proportioned the width of the building to its height.* **2.** to form the parts of (a whole) so as to be in a proper or balanced relation: *to proportion a sculpture.*

pro·por·tion·al (prə pôr′shə nəl) *adj.* **1.** in or having proportion. **2.** of, relating to, or based on proportion; relative: *a proportional scale of measurements.* **3.** *Mathematics.* having the same or a constant ratio. —**pro·por′tion·al·ly,** *adv.*

pro·por·tion·ate (prə pôr′shə nit) *adj.* in proper proportion; proportional. —**pro·por′tion·ate·ly,** *adv.*

pro·pos·al (prə pō′zəl) *n.* **1.** something put forward for consideration, discussion, or acceptance, as a plan or a course of action: *The committee voted in favor of the senator's proposal.* **2.** an offer of marriage. **3.** the act of proposing.

pro·pose (prə pōz′) *v.*, **pro·posed, pro·pos·ing.** —*v.t.* **1.** to put forward for consideration, discussion, or acceptance: *The mayor proposed a new plan for settling the strike.* **2.** to suggest or present (someone), as for a position or office. **3.** to intend; plan: *The general proposes to attack the city at dawn.* **4.** to suggest (a toast). —*v.i.* to make an offer of marriage.

prop·o·si·tion (prop′ə zish′ən) *n.* **1.** something that is proposed for consideration, discussion, or acceptance; proposal, offer, or suggestion: *The company rejected the inventor's business proposition.* **2.** *Informal.* matter, undertaking, or situation: *Finding a buyer for this old car is not an easy proposition.* **3.** a statement or subject to be discussed: *The two teams prepared to debate the given proposition.* **4.** *Mathematics.* a statement of a theorem to be demonstrated or a problem to be solved. **5.** *Informal.*

a thought, idea, or possibility: *The proposition of studying all night made me quite unhappy.* —*v.t.* to make a proposal or offer to.

pro·pound (prə pound′) *v.t.* to put forward for consideration; set forth; propose: *The scientist propounded a new theory.* —**pro·pound′er,** *n.*

pro·pri·e·tar·y (prə prī′i ter′ē) *adj.* **1.** of, relating to, or characteristic of a proprietor or proprietors. **2.** made and sold by exclusive legal right, as a medicine. **3.** privately owned and operated: *a proprietary hospital.* **4.** governed by a person or persons who have been granted complete authority by a monarch or central government: *a proprietary colony.* —*n.*, *pl.* **pro·pri·e·tar·ies.** **1.** another word for **proprietor.** **2.** a group of proprietors. **3.** a proprietary medicine.

pro·pri·e·tor (prə prī′i tər) *n.* **1.** a person who has legal title or right to something, especially property; owner. **2.** an owner or operator of a small business establishment: *the proprietor of a candy store.*

pro·pri·e·ty (prə prī′i tē) *n.*, *pl.* **pro·pri·e·ties.** **1.** the quality of being proper or suitable; suitability. **2.** conformity with what is proper, especially with socially approved standards of manners and conduct. **3. the proprieties.** standards of polite behavior approved by society.

pro·pul·sion (prə pul′shən) *n.* **1.** the act or process of driving forward or propelling. **2.** something that propels.

pro·rate (prō rāt′, prō′rāt′) *v.t.*, **pro·rat·ed, pro·rat·ing.** to divide proportionately: *The three friends prorated the expenses for their party.*

pro·sa·ic (prō zā′ik) *adj.* **1.** lacking in uniqueness, freshness, or imagination; unimaginative; commonplace; ordinary: *a prosaic subject, a prosaic person.* **2.** of or like prose: *a prosaic verse style.* —**pro·sa′i·cal·ly,** *adv.* —**pro·sa′ic·ness,** *n.*

pro·sce·ni·um (prō sē′nē əm) *n.*, *pl.* **pro·sce·ni·a** (prō sē′nē ə). **1.** the part of the stage in front of the curtain. **2.** the structure, usually arched, that frames the stage opening. Also, **proscenium arch. 3.** the entire stage in an ancient theater.

proscenium *(defs. 1 and 2)*

pro·scribe (prō skrīb′) *v.t.*, **pro·scribed, pro·scrib·ing. 1.** to prohibit or condemn (something); forbid. **2.** to outlaw (someone); banish. —**pro·scrib′er,** *n.*

prose (prōz) *n.* everyday written or spoken language that is not like poetry. —*adj.* of, relating to, or written in prose: *a prose narrative.*

pros·e·cute (pros′i kūt′) *v.*, **pros·e·cut·ed, pros·e·cut·ing.** —*v.t.* **1.** to begin and carry on a criminal action against (a person, corporation, or institution) in a court of law: *to prosecute someone for theft.* **2.** to seek to obtain or enforce by legal means: *to prosecute a claim for damages.* **3.** to carry out (something), especially to completion: *to prosecute an investigation.* —*v.i.* **1.** to begin and carry on a criminal action in a court of law: *The district attorney will prosecute in the next case.* **2.** to act as prosecutor. ▲ See **persecute** for usage note.

at; āpe; fär; câre; end; mē; it; īce; pîerce; hot; ōld; sông, fôrk; oil; out; up; ūse; rüle; pùll; tûrn; chin; sing; shop; thin; this; hw in white; zh in treasure. The symbol ə stands for the unstressed vowel sound heard in about, taken, pencil, lemon, and circus.

prosecuting attorney, a public official, such as a district attorney, who institutes and conducts criminal prosecutions on behalf of a government; prosecutor.

pros·e·cu·tion (pros'i kū'shən) *n.* **1.** the act or process of beginning and carrying on a criminal action in a court of law. **2.** the person or group conducting this. **3.** the act of prosecuting.

pros·e·cu·tor (pros'i kū'tər) *n.* **1.** an attorney who represents the state or the people in criminal prosecutions. **2.** a person who begins and carries on a legal action against another.

pros·e·lyte (pros'ə līt') *n.* a person who has recently been persuaded to accept a faith or doctrine, especially a new convert to a religion. —*v.t., v.i.,* **pros·e·lyt·ed, pros·e·lyt·ing.** to proselytize.

pros·e·lyt·ize (pros'ə lə tīz') *v.t., v.i.,* **pros·e·lyt·ized, pros·e·lyt·iz·ing.** to convert or attempt to convert from one faith or doctrine to another.

Pro·ser·pi·na (prō sûr'pə nə) *also,* **Pro·ser·pi·ne** (prō-sûr'pə nē). *n. Roman Mythology.* the daughter of Jupiter and Ceres, who was carried off by Pluto, who made her queen of the underworld. She was allowed to revisit the earth for part of each year, and her return was accompanied by the coming of spring. In Greek mythology she was called Persephone.

pros·o·dy (pros'ə dē) *n., pl.* **pros·o·dies. 1.** the study or science of poetic form. **2.** a particular system of poetic form.

pros·pect (pros'pekt) *n.* **1.** the thought of something looked forward to or expected: *The child was excited by the prospect of being given a bicycle.* **2.** *usually,* **prospects.** a chance for future success. **3.** a person who shows promise of some kind, such as a possible customer or a strong contestant. **4.** a scene presented to the eye; view. —*v.i.* to search or explore: *to prospect for gold.* —*v.t.* to explore (a region): *to prospect an area for minerals.*

pro·spec·tive (prə spek'tiv) *adj.* **1.** possible or expected; future: *a prospective buyer.* **2.** of, relating to, or in the future. —**pro·spec'tive·ly,** *adv.*

pros·pec·tor (pros'pek tər, prə spek'tər) *n.* a person who explores an area for minerals, such as gold.

pros·pec·tus (prə spek'təs) *n., pl.* **pro·spec·tus·es.** a printed statement describing something, such as a proposed undertaking or work.

pros·per (pros'pər) *v.i.* to be prosperous; flourish.

pros·per·i·ty (pros per'i tē) *n.* the state of being prosperous.

pros·per·ous (pros'pər əs) *adj.* having success, wealth, or good fortune; flourishing: *a prosperous town, a prosperous family.* —**pros'per·ous·ly,** *adv.* —**pros'per·ous·ness,** *n.*

pros·ta·glan·din (pros'tə glan'din) *n.* any of a group of chemical substances formed in animal tissue and involved in various functions, such as regulating blood pressure and body temperature and stimulating contraction of the smooth muscles.

pros·tate (pros'tāt) *n.* a small organ that surrounds the urethra in male animals. It consists of glandular tissue that secretes part of the fluid that makes up semen and muscle tissue that controls the flow of urine. Also, **prostate gland.** —*adj.* of, relating to, or affecting this organ.

pros·the·sis (pros thē'sis) *n., pl.* **pros·the·ses** (prosthē'sēz). an artificial replacement for a part of the body, such as a leg, arm, or eye.

pros·ti·tute (pros'ti tūt', pros'ti tūt') *n.* **1.** a person who engages in sexual acts for money. **2.** a person who puts his or her abilities to an unworthy use, especially for money. —*v.t.,* **pros·ti·tut·ed, pros·ti·tut·ing. 1.** to sell (oneself or another) for sexual purposes. **2.** to put (oneself or one's abilities) to an unworthy use, especially for

money: *Those writers prostituted their talents by writing for second-rate television programs.*

pros·ti·tu·tion (pros'ti tū'shən, pros'ti tū'shən) *n.* **1.** the act or practice of engaging in sexual acts for money. **2.** the act of putting oneself or one's abilities to an unworthy use, especially for money.

pros·trate (pros'trāt) *v.t.,* **pros·trat·ed, pros·trat·ing. 1.** to lay or throw (oneself) face downward on the ground, as in humility or submission. **2.** to lay or throw down on the ground; flatten. **3.** to weaken or make helpless: *The disease had prostrated the patient.* —*adj.* **1.** lying face downward on the ground. **2.** lying or thrown down. **3.** completely exhausted, helpless, or overcome: *The country was left prostrate by war.*

pros·tra·tion (pros trā'shən) *n.* **1.** the act of prostrating or the state of being prostrated. **2.** extreme exhaustion.

Prot., Protestant.

prot·ac·tin·i·um (prō'tak tin'ē əm) *n.* a rare radioactive metallic element found in pitchblende. It also is produced artificially. Symbol: **Pa** [Formed from the Greek word *prōtos* meaning "first, primary" + the English word *actinium.* This element decays to form an isotope of actinium.]

pro·tag·o·nist (prō tag'ə nist) *n.* the leading character in a novel, play, or other work of literature.

pro·te·an (prō'tē ən) *adj.* taking different shapes or forms readily; variable. [From the Greek god *Proteus.*]

pro·tect (prə tekt') *v.t.* to defend or keep from harm: *Soldiers wear helmets to protect their heads.* —**pro·tect'ing·ly,** *adv.*

pro·tec·tion (prə tek'shən) *n.* **1.** the act of protecting or the state of being protected. **2.** a person or thing that protects.

pro·tec·tion·ism (prə tek'shə niz'əm) *n.* the policy of protecting and promoting a nation's domestic industries by restricting or taxing imported goods. —**pro·tec'tion·ist,** *adj., n.*

pro·tec·tive (prə tek'tiv) *adj.* protecting or intended to protect: *A turtle has a protective shell. A protective tariff is a tax on imports in order to help local industries compete.* —**pro·tec'tive·ly,** *adv.* —**pro·tec'tive·ness,** *n.*

protective coloration helps this insect avoid detection by making it resemble a leaf

protective coloration, the natural coloring of certain animals that allows them to match their natural surroundings and thus escape the notice of their enemies.

pro·tec·tor (prə tek'tər) *n.* a person or thing that protects; guardian; defender: *In Greek mythology, a fierce dragon was the protector of the Golden Fleece.*

pro·tec·tor·ate (prə tek'tər it) *n.* **1.** a weak country that is protected and controlled by a strong country. **2.** the relationship between two such countries.

pro·té·gé (prō′tə zhā′) *n.* a person who is under the care, guidance, or patronage of an influential or prominent person.

pro·tein (prō′tēn) *n.* any of a large group of organic compounds that contain nitrogen, carbon, hydrogen, and oxygen, and are present in all living cells. Proteins are the materials of cell growth and repair. [From the French word *protéine,* formed from the Greek word *prōteios* meaning "primary, prime," from the word *prōtos* "first." Scientists considered protein to be the primary, or most essential, building block of life.]

pro tem·po·re (prō tem′pə rē) *Latin.* for the time being; temporarily. Also, **pro tem** (prō′tem′).

Prot·er·o·zo·ic (prō′tər ə zō′ik) *n.* a geological division of the Precambrian era, during which the earliest animals appeared, and algae and bacteria were already present. —*adj.* of, relating to, or characteristic of the Proterozoic.

pro·test (*n.,* prō′test; *v.,* prə test′) *n.* **1.** an expression of disapproval or objection: *The demonstration was a protest against the proposed new highway.* **2.** a formal objection, especially one made in writing. —*v.i.* to express disapproval or objection: *The students protested against the closing of the library on weekends.* —*v.t.* **1.** to express disapproval of; object to: *He protested the cut in his allowance.* **2.** to declare earnestly; assert: *The accused woman protested that she knew nothing about the missing jewels.* [From the Old French word *protester* meaning "to protest," from the Latin word *protestari* "to declare publicly, testify," from the prefix *pro-* "pro-¹" + *testari* "to witness to, testify."] —**pro′test·er,** *n.*

Prot·es·tant (prot′ə stənt) *n.* a Christian who belongs to one of the non-Orthodox churches that split from the Roman Catholic Church during the Reformation, or that developed later. —*adj.* of or relating to Protestants or Protestantism. [From the French word *Protestants,* referring to a group *protesting* the Roman Catholic Church's condemnation of the Reformation, going back to the Latin word *protestari* "to protest."]

Prot·es·tant·ism (prot′ə stən tiz′əm) *n.* **1.** the doctrines, beliefs, and practices of Protestants. **2.** Protestants or the Protestant churches as a group.

prot·es·ta·tion (prot′ə sta′shən, prō′te stā′shən) *n.* **1.** the act of protesting. **2.** an earnest declaration: *protestations of loyalty.* **3.** an expression of disapproval or objection; protest: *A group of senators filibustered as a protestation against the bill.*

Pro·te·us (prō′tē əs) *n. Greek Mythology.* a sea god who could assume many different shapes.

pro·tist (prō′tist) *n.* a one-celled organism that has a nucleus surrounded by a membrane. Some protists contain chlorophyll and produce their own food; others capture food as animals do. Protists make up their own kingdom, alongside the plant and animal kingdoms, the fungi, and the monerans.

proto– *prefix* first in time; earliest; original: *protozoan, prototype.*

pro·to·a·vis (prō′tō ā′vis) *n.* an extinct, birdlike animal that had a tail and hind legs like those of a dinosaur and bones and other features similar to those of birds. It flourished in the Triassic period, before archaeopteryx.

pro·to·col (prō′tə kôl′) *n.* **1.** the customs and rules of polite behavior and order of rank observed by diplomats; diplomatic etiquette. **2.** the original copy of a treaty or other document.

pro·ton (prō′ton) *n.* a particle found in the nucleus of all atoms, having a positive electric charge equal to the negative charge of an electron. The atomic number of an atom is equal to the number of protons in its nucleus.

pro·to·plasm (prō′tə plaz′əm) *n.* a substance somewhat like jelly that is the living matter in the cells of all organisms. It consists of the cell's nucleus and cytoplasm.

pro·to·type (prō′tə tīp′) *n.* **1.** the original or model from which something is derived or on which something is based: *the prototype of a new automobile engine.* **2.** the first, early, or typical example: *The Gordian knot is a prototype of a difficult problem.*

pro·to·zo·an (prō′tə zō′ən) *n., pl.* **pro·to·zo·ans** or **pro·to·zo·a** (prō′tə zō′ə). any of a large group of single-celled microscopic protists, such as the ameba. —*adj.* of or relating to protozoans. [Formed from the Greek words *prōtos* meaning "first" and *zōion* meaning "animal."]

pro·tract (prō trakt′) *v.t.* to lengthen in time; prolong: *to protract a speech.* —**pro·trac′tion,** *n.*

pro·trac·tor (prō trak′tər) *n.* an instrument in the form of a semicircle marked off in degrees, used for measuring or drawing angles.

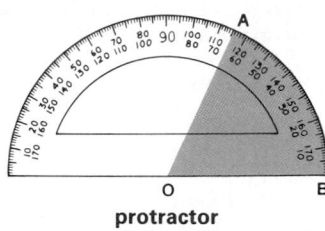

protractor
AOB = 65°

pro·trude (prō trüd′) *v.,* **pro·trud·ed, pro·trud·ing.** —*v.i.* to stick out; project: *Rocks protruded from the snow.* —*v.t.* to cause to stick out: *The snail protruded its horns.*

pro·tru·sion (prō trü′zhən) *n.* **1.** the act of protruding or the state of being protruded. **2.** something that protrudes.

pro·tu·ber·ance (prō tü′bər əns, prō tū′bər əns) *n.* **1.** something that sticks out, as a swelling or bulge. **2.** the state or condition of being protuberant.

pro·tu·ber·ant (prō tü′bər ənt, prō tū′bər ənt) *adj.* sticking out; bulging. —**pro·tu′ber·ant·ly,** *adv.*

proud (proud) *adj.* **1.** taking great personal satisfaction in something or someone (used with *of*): *The parents were proud of the baby's learning to walk.* **2.** having a sense of one's personal worth or dignity: *She was too proud to ask her friends for money.* **3.** having too high an opinion of oneself; conceited; haughty: *He was too proud to admit his mistake.* **4.** causing or feeling pleasure or satisfaction: *Winning the award was a proud moment for me.* **5.** arising from or caused by pride: *The matador had a proud look.* —**proud′ly,** *adv.*

prov., province; provincial.

prove (prüv) *v.,* **proved, proved** or **prov·en** (prü′vən), **prov·ing.** —*v.t.* **1.** to show the truth or genuineness of: *The district attorney proved the guilt of the defendant.* **2.** to show the merits or worth of: *to prove oneself as an athlete.* **3.** to test the qualities of: *to prove a new rifle.* —*v.i.* to turn out: *The play proved enjoyable.* —**prov′a·ble,** *adj.*

Pro·ven·çal (prō′vən säl′) *n.* **1.** a person who was born or is living in Provence. **2.** the language of Provence. —*adj.* of or relating to Provence, its people, their language, or culture.

prov·en·der (prov′ən dər) *n.* **1.** dry food for livestock. **2.** *Informal.* food; provisions.

prov·erb (prov′ərb) *n.* a short, popular saying that

---

at; āpe; fär; câre; end; mē; it; īce; pîerce; hot; ōld;
sông; fôrk; oil; out; up; ūse; rüle; pùll; tûrn; chin;
sing; shop; thin; this; hw in white; zh in treasure.
The symbol ə stands for the unstressed vowel sound
heard in about, taken, pencil, lemon, and circus.

expresses a truth. For example: *A stitch in time saves nine.*

pro·ver·bi·al (prə vûr′bē əl) *adj.* **1.** of, relating to, expressed in, or characteristic of a proverb: *proverbial wisdom.* **2.** commonly spoken of; well-known: *the proverbial courage of American pioneers.* —**pro·ver′bi·al·ly,** *adv.*

Prov·erbs (prov′ərbz) *n.* a book of the Old Testament containing practical advice and moral instruction.

pro·vide (prə vīd′) *v.,* **pro·vid·ed, pro·vid·ing.** —*v.t.* **1.** to give what is needed or desired; supply; furnish: *The school provided the students with books.* **2.** to give or produce: *Trees provide shelter from the sun.* **3.** to set as a condition; stipulate: *The law provides that witnesses shall be sworn before testifying.* —*v.i.* **1.** to make preparation for a future need: *to provide for one's old age.* **2.** to take care of present needs: *Wolves provide for their young cubs.* —**pro·vid′er,** *n.*

pro·vid·ed (prə vī′did) *conj.* on the condition that; if: *I'll lend you the book, provided you return it next week.*

prov·i·dence (prov′i dəns) *n.* **1.** God's care or guidance. **2.** wise management, as of resources; prudence. **3. Providence.** God.

prov·i·dent (prov′i dənt) *adj.* **1.** having a concern for the future; showing foresight. **2.** economical; thrifty. —**prov′i·dent·ly,** *adv.*

prov·i·den·tial (prov′i den′shəl) *adj.* **1.** of, relating to, or proceeding from divine providence. **2.** coming about as if through divine intervention; fortunate: *A providential rain put out the forest fire.* —**prov′i·den′tial·ly,** *adv.*

pro·vid·ing (prə vī′ding) *conj.* provided; if.

prov·ince (prov′ins) *n.* **1.** a political division of a country. Canada is made up of ten provinces and two territories. **2.** a range or sphere of activity or authority: *Judging the constitutionality of a law is within the province of the Supreme Court.* **3.** in ancient times, a territory outside Italy ruled by Rome. **4. the provinces.** regions of a country outside the capital or cultural center.

pro·vin·cial (prə vin′shəl) *adj.* **1.** of or relating to a province: *a provincial government.* **2.** characteristic of the inhabitants of a rural province; unsophisticated or unfashionable: *provincial manners.* **3.** having or showing a limited point of view; narrow-minded: *provincial attitudes.* —*n.* **1.** a person who was born or is living in a province. **2.** a narrow-minded person. —**pro·vin′cial·ly,** *adv.*

pro·vin·cial·ism (prə vin′shə liz′əm) *n.* **1.** the state or quality of being provincial, especially in manner, speech, or point of view. **2.** something that is provincial, such as a particular word, expression, or pronunciation.

prov·ing ground (prü′ving) a place for testing new devices or theories, especially a tract of land for testing military weapons and equipment.

pro·vi·sion (prə vizh′ən) *n.* **1.** the act of giving or supplying: *The coach supervised the provision of equipment to the players.* **2.** preparation for a future or possible need: *They had made little provision for their retirement.* **3.** something that is specified as a condition; stipulation: *A provision in the labor agreement called for a pay increase.* **4. provisions.** a supply of food: *The ship had provisions for three weeks.* —*v.t.* to supply with provisions.

pro·vi·sion·al (prə vizh′ə nəl) *adj.* for the time being; not permanent; temporary: *A provisional government ruled the country until elections could be held.* —**pro·vi′sion·al·ly,** *adv.*

pro·vi·so (prə vī′zō) *n., pl.* **pro·vi·sos** or **pro·vi·soes.** a statement that makes a condition; stipulation: *a proviso in a contract.*

prov·o·ca·tion (prov′ə kā′shən) *n.* **1.** the act of pro-

voking. **2.** something that angers or incites: *The attack came without provocation.*

pro·voc·a·tive (prə vok′ə tiv) *adj.* tending to provoke, especially by arousing anger, interest, or desire: *a provocative newspaper editorial.* —**pro·voc′a·tive·ly,** *adv.* —**pro·voc′a·tive·ness,** *n.*

pro·voke (prə vōk′) *v.t.,* **pro·voked, pro·vok·ing. 1.** to make angry; irritate greatly: *The insulting remark provoked her.* **2.** to stir up (a person); excite: *His rudeness provoked me to anger.* **3.** to cause by inciting; bring about deliberately: *to provoke a fight, to provoke an argument.* **4.** to call forth or bring out; arouse: *to provoke interest, to provoke thought.* —**pro·vok′ing·ly,** *adv.*

pro·vost (prō′vōst, prov′əst) *n.* **1.** a high administrative official in certain colleges or universities. **2.** the chief magistrate of a Scottish town or city. **3.** the head of a cathedral.

prow (prou) *n.* **1.** the forward part of a boat or ship; bow. **2.** something like the prow of a ship, such as the front end of an airplane.

prow·ess (prou′is) *n.* **1.** great bravery or daring, especially in battle. **2.** great ability or skill: *athletic prowess.*

prowl (proul) *v.i.* to move about quietly and secretly, as in search of prey: *The tiger prowled through the jungle.* —*v.t.* to move or roam over or through: *The gang prowled the streets at night.* —*n.* the act of prowling. —**prowl′er,** *n.*

prow *(def. 1)*

prowl car, another term for **squad car.**

prox·im·i·ty (prok sim′i tē) *n.* nearness; closeness: *I like the house where I live now because of its proximity to my job.*

prox·y (prok′sē) *n., pl.* **prox·ies. 1.** a person authorized to act for another; substitute. **2.** the act or instance of authorizing such a person: *to vote by proxy.* **3.** a document authorizing a person to act for another.

prude (prüd) *n.* a person who is overly modest or proper in behavior, dress, and speech.

pru·dence (prü′dəns) *n.* **1.** the quality of being prudent; good judgment. **2.** careful management; economy.

pru·dent (prü′dənt) *adj.* **1.** having or showing good judgment or caution; wise; sensible: *a prudent person, a prudent act.* **2.** showing careful management; economical; frugal: *a prudent use of one's money.* —**pru′dent·ly,** *adv.*

pru·den·tial (prü den′shəl) *adj.* characterized by or using good judgment or caution. —**pru·den′tial·ly,** *adv.*

prud·er·y (prü′də rē) *n., pl.* **prud·er·ies. 1.** extreme modesty. **2.** a prudish act or behavior.

prud·ish (prü′dish) *adj.* extremely modest or proper. —**prud′ish·ly,** *adv.* —**prud′ish·ness,** *n.*

prune[1] (prün) *n.* a dried plum. [From the Old French word *prune* meaning "a plum" or "a prune[1]," from the Latin word *prunum* "a plum," from the Greek word *prounē* "a plum tree."]

prune[2] (prün) *v.t.,* **pruned, prun·ing. 1.** to cut off (branches, twigs, or roots). **2.** to cut off unwanted branches, twigs, or roots from (a plant), usually to improve growth or appearance. **3.** to remove unnecessary or unwanted parts from: *The writer pruned two chapters from the story.* [From the Old French word *provigner* meaning "to prune a vine."] —**prun′er,** *n.*

pru·ri·ent (prür′ē ənt) *adj.* characterized by or having indecent thoughts. —**pru′ri·ent·ly,** *adv.*

prus·sic acid (prus′ik) another term for **hydrocyanic acid.**

pry[1] (prī) *v.i.,* **pried, pry·ing.** to look closely or curiously: *to pry into another person's affairs.* [From the Middle English word *prien* meaning "to look inquisitively, gaze upon," from Old English.]

pry[2] (prī) *v.t.,* **pried, pry·ing. 1.** to move, raise, or pull by force, as with a lever: *to pry the top off a box.* **2.** to get with much effort: *to pry information from someone.* —*n., pl.* **pries.** anything used as a lever for prying, such as a crowbar. [From the earlier word *prize* (misunderstood as a plural) meaning "a lever, crowbar," perhaps from *prize*[2].]

pry·ing (prī′ing) *adj.* overly curious: *a prying question about private matters.* —**pry′ing·ly,** *adv.*

Ps., Psalm; Psalms.

P.S. 1. postscript. **2.** public school.

psalm (säm) *n.* **1.** a sacred poem, song, or hymn. **2. Psalm.** any one of the sacred lyric poems that form the book of Psalms in the Old Testament.

psalm·ist (sä′mist) *n.* **1.** a writer or composer of psalms. **2. the Psalmist.** King David, the traditional composer of many of the Psalms.

Psalms (sämz) *n.* a book of sacred, lyric poetry in the Old Testament. ▲ used with a singular verb.

Psal·ter (sôl′tər) *n.* **1.** the Book of Psalms. **2.** a version of all or part of the Psalms arranged for liturgical or devotional use.

psal·ter·y (sôl′tə rē) *n., pl.* **psal·ter·ies.** an ancient musical instrument played by plucking its strings.

pseu·do (sü′dō) *adj.* false; pretended: *a pseudo gesture of friendship.*

pseudo– *combining form* false; pretended: *pseudonym.*

pseu·do·nym (sü′də nim) *n.* a fictitious name, especially one used by an author as a pen name: *That well-known author also writes under several pseudonyms.* [Originally from the Greek word *pseudōnymos* meaning "under a false name," from the words *pseudos* "falsehood" and *onoma* "name."]

pseu·do·pod (sü′də pod′) *n.* a temporary projection sent out from a protozoan as a means of moving about and taking in food.

pshaw (shô) *interj.* used to express scorn, impatience, or disapproval.

psi (sī, psī) *n.* the twenty-third letter of the Greek alphabet (Ψ, ψ).

psit·ta·co·sis (sit′ə kō′sis) *n.* an infectious disease of certain birds, especially parrots, that can be transmitted to people, in whom it produces a form of pneumonia.

pso·ri·a·sis (sə rī′ə sis) *n.* a chronic skin disease characterized by scaly, reddish patches on the skin.

PST, Pacific Standard Time.

Psy·che (sī′kē) *n. Greek and Roman Mythology.* a beautiful princess who fell in love with Eros. She was considered the personification of the human soul.

psy·che (sī′kē) *n.* the human soul or mind. [Originally from the Greek word *psychē* meaning "breath, soul, life."]

psy·che·del·ic (sī′ki del′ik) *adj.* of, characterized by, or causing hallucinations or a state like a trance: *a psychedelic drug.*

psy·chi·at·ric (sī′kē at′rik) *adj.* of or relating to psychiatry. Also, **psy·chi·at·ri·cal** (sī′kē at′ri kəl). —**psy′chi·at′ri·cal·ly,** *adv.*

psy·chi·a·trist (si kī′ə trist, sī kī′ə trist) *n.* a physician who specializes in the diagnosis and treatment of emotional and mental disorders.

psy·chi·a·try (si kī′ə trē, sī kī′ə trē) *n.* the branch of medicine that deals with the diagnosis and treatment of emotional and mental disorders.

psy·chic (sī′kik) *adj.* **1.** of or relating to the human soul or mind; spiritual or mental. **2.** of, relating to, or caused by supernatural influences or forces, such as telepathy: *to claim to have psychic powers.* **3.** sensitive to such influences or forces. Also, **psy·chi·cal** (sī′ki kəl). —*n.* a person who is sensitive to supernatural influences or forces. —**psy′chi·cal·ly,** *adv.*

psycho– *combining form* the mind or mental processes: *psychology.*

psy·cho·a·nal·y·sis (sī′kō ə nal′ə sis) *n.* **1.** a theory of psychology, developed by Sigmund Freud and others, that tries to explore mental processes. **2.** the methods used to explore the mind and treat emotional and mental disorders.

psy·cho·an·a·lyst (sī′kō an′ə list) *n.* a person who practices psychoanalysis. Also, **analyst.**

psy·cho·an·a·lyt·ic (sī′kō an′ə lit′ik) *adj.* of or relating to psychoanalysis. Also, **psy·cho·an′a·lyt′i·cal.** —**psy′cho·an′a·lyt′i·cal·ly,** *adv.*

psy·cho·an·a·lyze (sī′kō an′ə līz′) *v.t.,* **psy·cho·an·a·lyzed, psy·cho·an·a·lyz·ing.** to treat (someone) by psychoanalysis.

psy·cho·log·i·cal (sī′kə loj′i kəl) *adj.* **1.** of or relating to psychology. **2.** of or relating to the mind or mental processes. Also, **psy·cho·log·ic** (sī′kə loj′ik). —**psy′cho·log′i·cal·ly,** *adv.*

psy·chol·o·gist (sī kol′ə jist) *n.* a person who is trained or who specializes in psychology.

psy·chol·o·gy (sī kol′ə jē) *n., pl.* **psy·chol·o·gies. 1.** the study of the mind, the emotions, and behavior. **2.** the mental, emotional, or behavioral processes characteristic of a person or group, or relating to an experience: *the psychology of the criminal, the psychology of defeat.*

psy·cho·neu·ro·sis (sī′kō nù rō′sis, sī′kō nyü rō′sis) *n., pl.* **psy·cho·neu·ro·ses** (sī′kō nù rō′sēz, sī′kō nyü·rō′sēz). see **neurosis.**

psy·cho·path (sī′kə path′) *n.* a person afflicted with a serious mental disorder. —**psy′cho·path′ic,** *adj.*

psy·cho·sis (sī kō′sis) *n., pl.* **psy·cho·ses** (sī kō′sēz). a severe mental disorder involving loss of contact with reality.

psy·cho·so·mat·ic (sī′kō sə mat′ik) *adj.* **1.** of or relating to the relation between the mind and body. **2.** of or relating to physical symptoms and changes in the body that are the result of emotional or mental conditions: *a psychosomatic illness, the study of psychosomatic medicine.*

psy·cho·ther·a·py (sī′kō ther′ə pē) *n.* the treatment of emotional or mental disorders by psychological means, as by psychoanalysis and group therapy.

psy·chot·ic (sī kot′ik) *n.* a person afflicted with a psychosis. —*adj.* of, relating to, suffering from, or caused by a psychosis. —**psy′chot′i·cal·ly,** *adv.*

Pt, the symbol for platinum.

pt. 1. part. **2.** payment. **3.** pint. **4.** point.

ptar·mi·gan (tär′mi gən) *n., pl.* **ptar·mi·gan** or **ptar·mi·gans.** any of various grouse of northern regions, having brownish feathers and feathered legs and feet.

PT boat, a small, fast, and highly maneuverable boat armed with torpedoes. [Short for *p*(atrol) *t*(orpedo) *boat.*]

pte·rid·o·phyte (tə rid′ə fīt′) *n.* any of a group of seedless, flowerless plants, such as club mosses or ferns, that reproduce by means of spores.

P

at; āpe; fär; câre; end; mē; it; īce; pîerce; hot; ōld; sông, fôrk; oil; out; up; ūse; rüle; pùll; tûrn; chin; sing; shop; thin; this; hw in white; zh in treasure. The symbol ə stands for the unstressed vowel sound heard in about, taken, pencil, lemon, and circus.

pter·o·dac·tyl (ter′ə dak′təl) *n.* any of a group of extinct flying reptiles, having greatly enlarged fourth fingers supporting featherless, leathery wing membranes. [Formed from the Greek words *pteron* meaning "wing" + *daktylos* meaning "finger."]

pter·o·saur (ter′ə sôr′) *n.* any of a group of extinct flying reptiles, varying greatly in size and in the length of the tail. The pterodactyl was the largest pterosaur.

pterodactyl

Ptol·e·ma·ic (tol′ə mā′ik) *adj.* **1.** of or relating to the astronomer Ptolemy. **2.** of or relating to the Ptolemies who ruled Egypt.

Ptolemaic System, a theory named for the astronomer Ptolemy. It maintained that the earth is the center of the universe and that the sun, moon, and all the planets move around it.

pto·maine (tō′mān) *n.* **1.** any of various foul-smelling substances formed by the decay of food, formerly thought to be poisonous. **2.** food poisoning believed to be caused by ptomaine. Also *(def. 2),* **ptomaine poisoning.**

pty·a·lin (tī′ə lin) *n.* an enzyme in saliva that converts starch into sugar.

Pu, the symbol for plutonium.

pub (pub) *n. Informal.* a tavern or inn. [Short for *public house.*]

pu·ber·ty (pū′bər tē) *n.* the age at which a person becomes physically capable of reproducing offspring, occurring at about fourteen for boys and twelve for girls.

pu·bic (pū′bik) *adj.* of, relating to, or near the pubis.

pu·bis (pū′bis) *n., pl.* **pu·bes** (pū′bēz). the part of the hipbone that forms the front of the pelvis.

pub·lic (pub′lik) *adj.* **1.** of, relating to, or affecting the people as a whole: *public welfare.* **2.** for the use of all the people; open to all: *a public park, a public lecture.* **3.** of, relating to, or engaged in the affairs or service of a community or country: *a public official.* **4.** generally known: *The charges against the mayor have long been public.* —*n.* **1.** the people as a whole; all the people of a community, state, or country. **2.** a group of people having similar interests or tastes: *the reading public, a movie star's public.*

·**in public.** not in private; openly: *That singer has appeared in public many times.*

pub·lic–ad·dress system (pub′lik ə dres′) an electrical apparatus with microphones, amplifiers, and loudspeakers, used to amplify sound.

pub·li·can (pub′li kən) *n.* **1.** *British.* the keeper of a public house. **2.** in ancient Rome, a collector of taxes, tolls, and other public monies.

pub·li·ca·tion (pub′li kā′shən) *n.* **1.** the act of publishing: *The novel is ready for publication.* **2.** something that has been published, such as a book or magazine. **3.** public announcement: *These comments are not for publication.*

public defender, an attorney employed as a public official to defend someone who is accused of a crime but who cannot afford to hire his or her own attorney.

public house *British.* a tavern; saloon.

pub·li·cist (pub′lə sist) *n.* **1.** a person who is skilled in or who writes on law or public affairs. **2.** a person who manages publicity or public relations for an individual or organization; press agent.

pub·lic·i·ty (pu blis′i tē) *n.* **1.** information about a person or thing brought to notice or public attention: *There*

was a great deal of publicity about the space flight. **2.** public notice or attention: *The shy novelist didn't like publicity.* **3.** the means used to bring a person or thing to public notice or attention: *Who is in charge of the publicity for the school play?*

pub·li·cize (pub′lə sīz′) *v.t.,* **pub·li·cized, pub·li·ciz·ing.** to give publicity to; bring to public attention: *to publicize a new motion picture.*

pub·lic·ly (pub′li klē) *adv.* **1.** in a public manner: *Two senators publicly announced their candidacies for President.* **2.** by or in the name of the public: *That beach is publicly owned.*

public opinion, the general opinion of the people in a country, community, city, or the like.

public relations 1. the act or method of promoting goodwill for an individual or organization: *That company has poor public relations.* **2.** the business of doing such work: *to work in public relations.*

public school 1. a free elementary or secondary school supported by taxes. **2.** in Great Britain, a private boarding school.

public servant, a person who serves the public by holding a government office.

public service 1. service to the community or public by a public servant. **2.** the service provided by a public utility. **3.** something done to benefit the public: *The documentary was broadcast as a public service, with no commercials.*

pub·lic–spir·it·ed (pub′lik spir′i tid) *adj.* working for or showing a concern for the welfare of the community: *a public-spirited citizen.*

public television, broadcasting of cultural and educational television programs for the public. It is supported by donated and public funds rather than by revenues from commercial advertising.

public utility, see **utility** *(def. 2).*

public works, projects built and financed by the government for public use, such as roads, dams, or sewers.

pub·lish (pub′lish) *v.t.* **1.** to produce and issue (printed material, such as a book) for sale or distribution to the public. **2.** to print and sell the works of (a writer): *That company publishes Walt Whitman and Emily Dickinson.* **3.** to make known publicly: *Don't publish all your troubles.*

pub·lish·er (pub′li shər) *n.* a person or company whose business is the publishing of books, magazines, newspapers, and the like.

puce (pūs) *n.* a purplish brown or reddish brown color. —*adj.* having the color puce.

puck[1] (puk) *n.* a black disk of rubber or other hard material, used in playing ice hockey. [From the English dialect word *puck* meaning "to poke, hit," a form of *poke*[1].]

puck[2] (puk) *n.* **1.** a mischievous sprite; elf. **2. Puck.** a mischievous fairy or sprite in English folklore. [From the Old English word *pūca* meaning "a goblin, mischievous spirit."]

puck·er (puk′ər) *v.t.* to gather into irregular folds or wrinkles: *to pucker the sleeves of a dress in sewing, to pucker the lips.* —*v.i.* to become gathered into wrinkles: *My lips puckered from the sour lemon.* —*n.* an irregular fold or wrinkle.

puck·ish (puk′ish) *adj.* mischievous; impish.

pud·ding (pŏŏd′ing) *n.* **1.** a sweet, soft dessert that is cooked by being boiled, baked, or steamed. **2.** a similar dish that is unsweetened, served as a part of a main course: *corn pudding.*

pud·dle (pŏŏd′əl) *n.* **1.** a small, shallow pool of water, especially of muddy water: *The child liked to splash in the puddles after a rainstorm.* **2.** a small, shallow pool of any liquid: *a puddle of spilled milk.* **3.** a mixture of clay, sand, and water, used to make something watertight.

—*v.t.*, **pud·dled, pud·dling. 1.** to make muddy. **2.** to make (clay, sand, and water) into a watertight mixture. **3.** to convert (pig iron) into wrought iron. —**pud′dly,** *adj.*

pud·dling (pud′ling) *n.* the process of converting pig iron into wrought iron by removing the impurities and excess carbon in a furnace.

pudg·y (puj′ē) *adj.*, **pudg·i·er, pudg·i·est.** short and fat. —**pudg′i·ness,** *n.*

pueblo *(def. 1)*

pueb·lo (pweb′lō) *n.*, *pl.* **pueb·los. 1.** an Indian village consisting of adobe and stone houses joined in groups, found especially in the southwestern United States. **2. Pueblo.** a member of any of several Indian tribes that live in such villages, as the Hopi. [From the Spanish word *pueblo* meaning "village" or "people," from the Latin word *populus* "people."]

puer·ile (pyür′əl) *adj.* **1.** childish; silly: *puerile pranks.* **2.** of or relating to boyhood or childhood.

puff (puf) *n.* **1.** a short, sudden blast, as of air, breath, or smoke: *A puff of wind rippled the pond.* **2.** a drawing in or blowing out of smoke, as from a cigarette or pipe. **3.** something that looks soft and fluffy: *Puffs of clouds filled the sky.* **4.** a small pad for putting powder on the face or body; powder puff. **5.** a light pastry shell having a filling, such as whipped cream. **6.** a slight swelling: *The patient had puffs under the eyes from lack of sleep.* **7.** a quilted covering for a bed. —*v.i.* **1.** to blow with a puff or puffs. *Smoke puffed out of the chimney.* **2.** to breathe hard: *The climbers puffed as they reached the top of the steep hill.* **3.** to give out puffs, as of steam or smoke: *The locomotive puffed.* **4.** to take puffs: *to puff on a cigarette.* **5.** to swell with air or a liquid: *Your bruised eyebrow has puffed up.* —*v.t.* **1.** to blow or send out in a puff or puffs: *The engine puffed smoke.* **2.** to smoke (a cigar, cigarette, or pipe). **3.** to swell or make fluffy: *The wind puffed the ship's sails.*

puff adder, a very poisonous snake of Africa that puffs up its body and hisses when disturbed. It has a brown or gray body with crescent-shaped yellow markings.

puff·ball (puf′bôl′) *n.* a round fungus, similar to a mushroom, that sends out a cloud of spores when ripe.

puff·er (puf′ər) *n.* **1.** a person or thing that puffs. **2.** any of various fish that can expand their bodies with air or water until they become globelike in appearance.

puf·fin (puf′in) *n.* a sea bird of northern regions, having a large, brightly striped, triangular bill.

puff·y (puf′ē) *adj.*, **puff·i·er, puff·i·est. 1.** puffed out or up; swollen: *a puffy face.* **2.** blowing in puffs: *a puffy wind.* —**puff′i·ness,** *n.*

pug¹ (pug) *n.* **1.** a small, short-haired dog having a curled tail and wrinkled face. **2.** see **pug nose.** [Of uncertain origin.]

pug² (pug) *n. Slang.* see **pugilist.**

pu·gi·lism (pū′jə liz′əm) *n.* the art or practice of fighting with the fists; boxing.

pu·gi·list (pū′jə list) *n.* a person who fights with the fists, especially a professional boxer. —**pu′gi·lis′tic,** *adj.*

pug·na·cious (pug nā′shəs) *adj.* ready and eager to fight; quarrelsome. —**pug·na′cious·ly,** *adv.* —**pug·na′cious·ness, pug·nac·i·ty** (pug nas′ə tē), *n.*

pug nose, a short, broad, turned-up nose. Also, **pug.** —**pug′-nosed′,** *adj.*

puis·sance (pwis′əns, pū′i səns) *n.* power; strength.

puis·sant (pwis′ənt, pū′i sənt) *adj.* powerful; strong.

puke (pūk) *Slang. v.t., v.i.*, **puked, puk·ing.** to vomit. —*n.* vomit.

pul·chri·tude (pul′kri tüd′, pul′kri tüd′) *n.* physical beauty: *The model had great pulchritude.*

pule (pūl) *v.i.*, **puled, pul·ing.** to cry in a weak voice; whimper; whine. —**pul′er,** *n.*

pull (pül) *v.t.* **1.** to use force on (something) so as to cause it to move toward the force: *Two horses pulled the wagon. She pulled the closet door open.* **2.** to tug at; yank: *She pulled his sleeve to get his attention.* **3.** to tear away or remove: *to pull a tooth, to pull a branch from a tree.* **4.** to rip or tear: *The puppy pulled the blanket to pieces.* **5.** to injure or weaken by too much stretching; strain: *The baseball player pulled a shoulder muscle.* **6.** *Informal.* to carry out; bring about; do: *He was suspected of pulling the robbery.* **7.** *Informal.* to draw or attract: *That new motion picture is pulling crowds.* **8.** *Informal.* to draw out so as to use: *The bandit pulled a gun.* —*v.i.* **1.** to draw or tug: *The jockey pulled on the reins to slow up the horse.* **2.** to go, move, or proceed: *The car pulled into the driveway.* **3.** to move when pulled: *Your sled pulls easily.* **4.** to row: *They pulled toward the bank of the river.* —*n.* **1.** the act or an instance of pulling. **2.** the effort used in pulling: *It was a long, hard pull for them to reach the top of the hill.* **3.** anything used for pulling, such as a handle, knob, or rope. **4.** a drawing or attracting force: *the pull of a magnet.* **5.** *Informal.* influence or advantage: *I got my job through pull, because I knew the boss.* **6.** *Informal.* the ability to attract or appeal: *That star has great pull at the box office.* —**pull′er,** *n.*

·**to pull for.** *Informal.* to hope for the success of: *We are all pulling for the local baseball team.*

·**to pull off.** *Informal.* to accomplish in spite of difficulties.

·**to pull oneself together.** to regain one's self-control: *I know you've been through a bad experience, but you must pull yourself together.*

·**to pull through.** to get through a serious or difficult situation successfully.

·**to pull up.** to halt; stop: *The car pulled up at the curb.*

pul·let (pül′it) *n.* a young hen less than a year old.

pul·ley (pül′ē) *n.*, *pl.* **pul·leys. 1.** a grooved wheel on which a rope or chain is pulled, used to lift heavy loads or change the direction of an applied force. **2.** a simple machine consisting of such a wheel or set of such wheels mounted in a casing.

Pull·man (pül′mən) *n.* a railroad car with sleeping accommodations. [From the American industrialist George M. *Pullman* (1831–1897), who designed it.]

pull·o·ver (pül′ō′vər) *n.* a garment, such as a shirt or sweater, that is put on by being pulled over the head.

---

at; āpe; fär; câre; end; mē; it; īce; pîerce; hot; ōld; sông, fôrk; oil; out; up; ūse; rüle; pül; tûrn; chin; sing; shop; thin; <u>th</u>is; hw in white; zh in treasure. The symbol ə stands for the unstressed vowel sound heard in about, taken, pencil, lemon, and circus.

P

pul·mo·nar·y (pŭl'mə ner'ē, pŭl'mə ner'ē) *adj.* of, relating to, or affecting the lungs: *a pulmonary disease.*

pulp (pulp) *n.* **1.** the soft, juicy part of certain fruits and vegetables. **2.** the inner part of a tooth containing soft tissue, blood vessels, and nerves. **3.** any soft, moist, formless mass, such as the mixture of matted fibers of wood used in making paper. **4.** a magazine printed on a cheap grade of paper made from wood pulp, usually containing sensational stories or articles. —*v.t.* to make into pulp.

pul·pit (pŭl'pit, pŭl'pit) *n.* **1.** a raised structure from which a minister delivers a sermon. **2.** ministers as a group; the clergy.

pulp·wood (pulp'wŭd') *n.* wood used to make paper, especially pine, fir, or spruce.

pulp·y (pul'pē) *adj.,* **pulp·i·er, pulp·i·est.** of or like pulp; soft or fleshy. —**pulp'i·ly,** *adv.* —**pulp'i·ness,** *n.*

pul·sar (pul'sär) *n.* any of a number of astronomical objects that send out intense pulses of electromagnetic energy at regular intervals.

pul·sate (pul'sāt) *v.i.,* **pul·sat·ed, pul·sat·ing. 1.** to expand and contract rhythmically: *The heart pulsates.* **2.** to vibrate; quiver.

pul·sa·tion (pul sā'shən) *n.* **1.** the act of pulsating. **2.** a single beat or vibration.

pulse¹ (puls) *n.* **1.** the rhythmic expansion and contraction of the arteries caused by the pulsation of the heart as it pumps blood. **2.** any regular, rhythmical beating or vibrating: *the steady pulse of an automobile engine.* **3.** the feeling or opinion of a group: *the political pulse of the country during the last decade.* —*v.i.,* **pulsed, puls·ing.** to beat or vibrate; pulsate. [From the Old French word *pulse* with the same meaning, from the Latin word *pulsus* "a beating, striking" and "the pulse¹," from the word *pulsare* "to push, strike, beat."]

pulse² (puls) *n.* **1.** the seeds of such plants as peas, beans, or lentils, used as food. **2.** any plant yielding such seeds. [From the Old French word *pouls* meaning "edible seeds" or "porridge," from the Latin word *puls* "porridge."]

pul·ver·ize (pul'və rīz') *v.,* **pul·ver·ized, pul·ver·iz·ing.** —*v.t.* **1.** to grind or pound into powder or dust. **2.** to smash or destroy completely: *The earthquake almost pulverized the town.* —*v.i.* to become powder or dust: *The block of plaster was easy to pulverize.* —**pul'ver·i·za'tion,** *n.* —**pul'ver·iz'er,** *n.*

pu·ma (pū'mə, pü'mə) *n., pl.* **pu·mas** or **pu·ma.** another word for **cougar.**

pum·ice (pum'is) *n.* a light, porous volcanic rock used for cleaning, smoothing, or polishing. —*v.t.,* **pum·iced, pum·ic·ing.** to clean, smooth, or polish with pumice.

pum·mel (pum'əl) *also,* **pom·mel.** *v.t.,* **pum·meled, pum·mel·ing;** *also, British,* **pum·melled, pum·mel·ling.** to strike again and again with the fists: *The two boxers pummeled one another.*

pump¹ (pump) *n.* a machine for moving liquids or gases from one place to another. —*v.t.* **1.** to make (a fluid) move from one place to another by means of a pump: *to pump water into a swimming pool.* **2.** to remove fluid from: *to pump a flooded basement.* **3.** to fill with a gas, especially with air, by means of a pump: *to pump up a flat tire.* **4.** to move by forcing up and down or back and forth repeatedly: *I pumped the gas pedal, but the car would not start.* **5.** to get or try to get information from by close questioning: *The police pumped the suspects to find out where they had been on the day of the crime.* —*v.i.* to make a fluid move from place to place by means

of a pump: *A child's heart pumps faster than an adult's.* [From the Middle English word *pumpe* meaning this device, possibly from Middle Dutch.]

pump² (pump) *n.* a low-cut shoe without laces or other fasteners. [Of uncertain origin.]

pum·per·nick·el (pum'pər nik'əl) *n.* a coarse dark bread made of unsifted rye flour.

pump·kin (pump'kin, pum'kin, pung'kin) *n.* **1.** a large orange or yellow-orange fruit, having a firm outer rind and a soft pulp containing many seeds. **2.** the trailing vine bearing this fruit.

pun (pun) *n.* a humorous use of words in which a double meaning is applied to one word or to two words having the same sound. —*v.i.,* **punned, pun·ning.** to make a pun or puns.

punch¹ (punch) *v.t.* **1.** to hit (someone or something) with the fist. **2.** to operate by pressing: *to punch an elevator button.* **3.** *Informal.* to herd or drive (cattle). —*v.i.* to hit, especially with the fist. —*n., pl.* **punch·es. 1.** a blow made with the fist. **2.** *Informal.* force; vitality: *The politician's angry speech had a lot of punch.* [From the Middle English word *pouncen* meaning "to stamp metal" or "to stab, push, prod," from the Old French word *ponchonner* "to stamp" or "to thrust," going back to the Latin word *punctus* "a point," from the word *pungere* "to prick."] —**punch'er,** *n.*

·**to pull one's punches.** *Informal.* to hold oneself back from speaking or acting openly, straightforwardly, or too forcefully.

punch² (punch) *n., pl.* **punch·es.** a tool for making holes in or stamping or pressing a design on a surface. —*v.t.* to make holes in or stamp or press a design on with a punch: *to punch paper for a notebook.* [From the Middle English word *pounce* meaning "stamp, punch²," from the Old French word *ponchonner* "to stamp" or "to thrust," going back to the Latin word *punctus* "a point," from the word *pungere* "to prick."]

punch³ (punch) *n., pl.* **punch·es.** a drink made from various ingredients, usually fruit juices and an alcoholic or carbonated beverage. [From the Hindi word *pānch* meaning "five." This beverage was originally made with five ingredients.]

punch card, a card with holes punched in specific positions to provide instructions or information for a data-processing machine.

pun·cheon¹ (pun'chən) *n.* **1.** a large cask of varying capacity, holding from 70 to 120 gallons (265–454 liters). **2.** the amount contained in a puncheon. [From the Old French word *ponchon* meaning "a large cask."]

pun·cheon² (pun'chən) *n.* **1.** a broad, heavy piece of timber roughly finished on one side. **2.** see **punch².** [From the Old French word *ponchonner* "to stamp" or "to thrust," going back to the Latin word *punctus* "a point," from the word *pungere* "to prick."]

punching bag, an inflated or stuffed leather or canvas bag, usually suspended, punched for exercise or training in boxing.

punch line, the last sentence or phrase of a joke or story, which carries the humor or meaning.

punch·y (pun'chē) *adj.,* **punch·i·er, punch·i·est.** *Informal.* dizzy or groggy.

punc·til·i·o (pungk til'ē ō') *n., pl.* **punc·til·i·os. 1.** a fine point of proper or polite behavior. **2.** strict or careful attention to such fine points.

punc·til·i·ous (pungk til'ē əs) *adj.* **1.** strictly or carefully attentive to the fine points of proper or polite behavior: *He had punctilious table manners.* **2.** very careful and exact: *She was punctilious in doing her homework.* —**punc·til'i·ous·ly,** *adv.* —**punc·til'i·ous·ness,** *n.*

punc·tu·al (pungk'chü əl) *adj.* arriving at the correct time; on time; prompt: *The train was punctual.* —**punc·tu·al·i·ty** (pungk'chü al'i tē), *n.* —**punc'tu·al·ly,** *adv.*

pulpit *(def. 1)*

punc·tu·ate (pungk′chü āt′) v., **punc·tu·at·ed, punc-tu·at·ing.** —v.i. **1.** to mark (written material) with periods, commas, and other marks to make the meaning clear: *The editor punctuated the paragraph carefully.* **2.** to interrupt from time to time: *The candidate's speech was punctuated by cheers from the enthusiastic crowd.* **3.** to give emphasis to: *The politician punctuated the demand by banging on the table.* —v.i. to use punctuation marks.

punc·tu·a·tion (pungk′chü ā′shən) n. **1.** the use of periods, commas, and other marks to make the meaning of written material clear and understandable. **2.** a punctuation mark or marks.

Language Note

Punctuation is used to show the division of written language into sentences and sentence parts and to show the relationship between sentence parts. Punctuation makes the meaning of written language clear in much the same way that pauses, and the rising and falling of the voice, clarify the meaning of spoken language. When punctuation marks are not used, the meaning of what is written can be unclear.

The ancient Greeks and Romans used very little punctuation in their writing, and they had no standard or systematic rules of punctuation. The punctuation in Old English and Middle English manuscripts was also scanty and irregular. The invention of movable type around 1450 caused a vast increase in the amount of written material available to readers. As printed books became more common, people began to see the need for standardized punctuation. Printers, rather than writers, were responsible for the modern comma and other developments in punctuation that occurred at this time. The new system of punctuation proved successful, and when the First Folio of Shakespeare's plays was printed in 1632, it used the period, comma, colon, semicolon, exclamation point, question mark, and parentheses much as we use them today.

In the seventeenth and eighteenth centuries, writers began to use punctuation marks almost to excess, particularly the comma and the semicolon. This resulted in a highly complicated style of writing. This heavy use of punctuation continued up until the early nineteenth century. But about 150 years ago, certain American writers chose to write in a clearer and simpler style that used punctuation only when necessary. This trend toward simplification has continued until the present. Modern English punctuation is designed to make our written language flow like natural speech.

punctuation mark, any of various marks used to make the meaning of written material clear. Periods, commas, semicolons, colons, and question marks are punctuation marks.

punc·ture (pungk′chər) v., **punc·tured, punc·tur·ing.** —v.t. **1.** to make a hole in (something) with a sharp or pointed object; pierce: *to puncture a balloon with a pin.* **2.** to make (a hole) by piercing. **3.** to lessen in importance, spoil, or ruin as if by puncturing: *The bad news punctured our happiness.* —v.i. to become punctured. —n. **1.** a hole made by a sharp or pointed object. **2.** the act or process of puncturing.

pun·dit (pun′dit) n. **1.** a learned Brahman, especially one who is an expert in the laws, language, or religion of India. **2.** a very learned person, especially one who is an expert in a particular field.

pun·gent (pun′jənt) adj. **1.** sharp and stinging to the

taste or smell: *pungent spices, the pungent scent of ammonia.* **2.** piercing or severe: *The new book received pungent criticism from the reviewers.* —**pun′gen·cy,** n. —**pun′gent·ly,** adv.

Pu·nic (pū′nik) adj. of or relating to Carthage, its people, or their language. —n. the Semitic language of ancient Carthage.

pun·ish (pun′ish) v.t. **1.** to cause (someone) to suffer for a crime, offense, or fault: *The parents punished the naughty child.* **2.** to inflict a penalty for (an offense, crime, or fault): *The law punishes robbery.* *The school punishes cheating on a test.* **3.** to treat or handle roughly or severely: *The losing boxer was severely punished in the championship fight.* —**pun′ish·a·ble,** adj. —**pun′ish·er,** n.

pun·ish·ment (pun′ish mənt) n. **1.** the act of punishing or the state of being punished. **2.** a penalty inflicted for a crime, offense, or fault. **3.** severe treatment; rough handling: *The car took a lot of punishment on the bumpy road.*

pu·ni·tive (pū′ni tiv) adj. of, relating to, or inflicting punishment; punishing: *a punitive law.* —**pu′ni·tive·ly,** adv. —**pu′ni·tive·ness,** n.

punk¹ (pungk) n. **1.** a dry substance that burns slowly without a flame, used especially to light fireworks. **2.** dry, decayed wood, used especially as tinder. [Possibly from the Algonquian word *punk* meaning "live ashes."]

punk² (pungk) *Slang.* n. a young, contemptible, or inexperienced person. —adj. of poor quality; worthless. [Of uncertain origin.]

punk rock, a style of rock music characterized by loud, highly energetic music with fast tempos, crude instrumental techniques, and violent, often anti-establishment lyrics.

pun·ster (pun′stər) n. a person who frequently makes puns.

punt¹ (punt) n. a flat-bottomed boat with square ends, usually moved by a long pole. —v.t. **1.** to move (a boat) with a long pole. **2.** to carry in a punt. —v.i. to go or travel in a punt. [From the Old English word *punt*, from the Latin word *ponto* meaning this boat.] —**punt′er,** n.

punt² (punt) n. a kick in which a football is dropped from the hands and kicked before it reaches the ground. —v.t., v.i. to kick (a football) in this manner. [Of uncertain origin.] —**punt′er,** n.

pu·ny (pū′nē) adj., **pu·ni·er, pu·ni·est.** inferior in size, strength, or importance: *a puny calf, a puny effort.* —**pu′ni·ness,** n.

pup (pup) n. **1.** a young dog; puppy. **2.** the young of various other animals, such as the fox, wolf, or seal.

pu·pa (pū′pə) n., pl. **pu·pae** (pū′pē) or **pu·pas.** an insect in the intermediate stage of development, coming after the larva and before the adult. A caterpillar in its cocoon is a pupa. —**pu′pal,** adj.

pu·pate (pū′pāt) v.i., **pu·pat·ed, pu·pat·ing.** to change into a pupa. —**pu·pa′tion,** n.

pu·pil¹ (pū′pəl) n. a person who studies under the direction of an instructor; student. [From the Latin word *pupillus* meaning "an orphan, a ward," from the word *pupulus* "little boy" or "puppet."]

pu·pil² (pū′pəl) n. the opening in the center of the iris, through which light enters the eye. [From the Latin word *pupilla* meaning this part of the eye.]

P

at; āpe; fär; câre; end; mē; it; īce; pîerce; hot; ōld; sông, fôrk; oil; out; up; ūse; rüle; pùll; tûrn; chin; sing; shop; thin; <u>th</u>is; hw in white; zh in treasure. The symbol ə stands for the unstressed vowel sound heard in about, taken, pencil, lemon, and circus.

puppets *(def. 1)*

pup·pet (pup'it) *n.* **1.** a small, usually jointed, figure made to look like a person or animal and manipulated by the hand or by strings, wires, or rods. **2.** a person or thing that is under the complete control of another: *The legislature was only a puppet of the dictator.*

pup·pet·eer (pup'ə tîr') *n.* a person who operates puppets to entertain.

pup·pet·ry (pup'i trē) *n.* the art of making puppets or producing puppet shows.

pup·py (pup'ē) *n., pl.* **pup·pies.** a young dog.

pup tent, a small, portable tent for use by two people.

pur·blind (pûr'blīnd') *adj.* **1.** nearly blind. **2.** slow to understand. —**pur'blind'ly,** *adv.* —**pur'blind'ness,** *n.*

pur·chase (pûr'chəs) *v.t.,* **pur·chased, pur·chas·ing.** **1.** to get by paying money; buy: *My parents are going to purchase a new car.* **2.** to get by hardship, sacrifice, or suffering: *The military victory was purchased at great cost of life.* —*n.* **1.** the act of purchasing. **2.** something purchased. **3.** a firm hold or grasp to help in moving something or to keep from slipping. —**pur'chas·er,** *n.*

pur·dah (pûr'də) *n.* among some Muslims and Hindus, the practice of keeping women hidden, as by having them wear a veil.

pure (pyùr) *adj.,* **pur·er, pur·est. 1.** not mixed with anything else; unadulterated: *a scarf of pure silk.* **2.** not stained, spotted, or contaminated; clean: *pure water.* **3.** free from evil or guilt: *a pure heart.* **4.** of unmixed descent: *That cat is pure Siamese.* **5.** nothing but; sheer; utter: *That explanation of what happened is pure nonsense.* **6.** concerned with theory rather than with practical application; abstract: *Mathematics is a pure science.* —**pure'ness,** *n.*

pure·bred (pyùr'bred') *adj.* coming from ancestors of unmixed breed: *That dog is a purebred cocker spaniel.*

pu·rée (pyù rā') *n., pl.* **pu·rées. 1.** food that is put through a sieve or blender and made into a thick, moist mass. **2.** a smooth, thick soup. —*v.t.,* **pu·réed, pu·rée·ing.** to make (food) into a purée.

pure·ly (pyùr'lē) *adv.* **1.** entirely; simply: *Breaking the dish was purely accidental.* **2.** in a pure manner.

pur·ga·tive (pûr'gə tiv) *n.* a medicine that causes the bowels to empty. —*adj.* purging; cleansing.

pur·ga·to·ri·al (pûr'gə tôr'ē əl) *adj.* of or relating to purgatory.

pur·ga·to·ry (pûr'gə tôr'ē) *n., pl.* **pur·ga·to·ries. 1.** in Roman Catholic belief, a temporary place of purification, where the souls of those who have died are purged of unrepented minor sins or of major sins that have been forgiven but not wholly punished. **2.** any place or condition of temporary punishment or suffering.

purge (pûrj) *v.,* **purged, purg·ing.** —*v.t.* **1.** to cleanse or rid of whatever is unclean or undesirable. **2.** to remove undesired or disloyal persons from (a political party, government, or other organization): *The dictator purged the army of all officers thought to be planning a revolt.* **3.** to remove (undesired or disloyal persons) from a political party, government, or other organization. **4.** to free of sin or guilt. **5.** to cause (the bowels) to empty. —*v.i.* to forcibly expel urine, feces, or stomach contents, as by vomiting or taking medicines. —*n.* **1.** the act or process of purging. **2.** the elimination of undesired or disloyal persons from a political party, government, or other organization. **3.** a medicine that causes the bowels to empty; cathartic.

pu·ri·fi·ca·tion (pyúr'ə fi kā'shən) *n.* the act of purifying or the state of being purified.

pu·ri·fy (pyúr'ə fī') *v.,* **pu·ri·fied, pu·ri·fy·ing.** —*v.t.* to make pure or clean: *to purify air through filters.* —*v.i.* to become pure. —**pu'ri·fi'er,** *n.*

Pu·rim (pùr'im) *n.* an annual Jewish holiday observed in February or March, commemorating the rescue of the Persian Jews by Esther from a plot to massacre them.

pu·rine (pyúr'ēn) *n.* a chemical compound that is the fundamental base of many substances.

pur·ist (pyúr'ist) *n.* a person who is very strict about purity or correctness, especially in language: *The teacher was a purist and did not like the pupils to use slang.*

Pu·ri·tan (pyúr'i tən) *n.* **1.** a member of a sect of English Protestants in the sixteenth and seventeenth centuries who wanted simpler religious ceremonies and high standards of morality. **2. puritan.** a person who is very strict in matters of morality or religion. —*adj.* **1.** of, relating to, or characteristic of the Puritans or Puritanism. **2. puritan.** of, relating to, or characteristic of a puritan.

pu·ri·tan·i·cal (pyúr'i tan'i kəl) *adj.* **1.** very strict in matters of morality or religion: *a puritanical attitude.* **2. Puritanical.** of, relating to, or characteristic of Puritans or Puritanism. Also, **pu·ri·tan·ic** (pyúr'i tan'ik). —**pu'·ri·tan'i·cal·ly,** *adv.* —**pu'ri·tan'i·cal·ness,** *n.*

Pu·ri·tan·ism (pyúr'i tə niz'əm) *n.* **1.** the beliefs and practices of the Puritans. **2. puritanism.** great strictness in matters of morality or religion.

pu·ri·ty (pyúr'i tē) *n.* **1.** the state or quality of being pure. **2.** freedom from evil or guilt. **3.** great strictness about correctness of language.

purl¹ (pûrl) *v.i.* to flow, ripple, or swirl, especially with a murmuring sound. —*n.* a murmuring sound made by a shallow stream or brook. [Perhaps of Scandinavian origin.]

purl² (pûrl) *v.t., v.i.* to knit with reverse stitches. [Of uncertain origin.]

pur·loin (pûr loin') *v.t., v.i.* to steal. —**pur·loin'er,** *n.*

pur·ple (pûr'pəl) *n.* **1.** the color made by mixing red and blue. **2.** a cloth or robe of this color, especially one worn to show royalty or high rank. —*adj.* **1.** having the color purple. **2.** ornate in writing style: *a purple passage.*

Purple Heart, a U.S. military award given to a member of the armed forces who is wounded while in action against the enemy.

pur·port (*v.,* pər pôrt'; *n.,* pûr'pôrt) *v.t.* **1.** to claim or profess, often falsely: *He purports to be an expert on automobiles.* **2.** to intend; mean. —*n.* meaning or substance: *Her letter gives the purport of our telephone conversation.*

pur·pose (pûr'pəs) *n.* **1.** the result or goal that one wants; intention; aim: *My purpose is to go to college.* **2.** the object or reason for which something is made or done; function or use: *What is the purpose of that hook on the kitchen wall?* —*v.t.,* **pur·posed, pur·pos·ing.** to intend, resolve, or aim.

·on purpose. not by accident; intentionally.

pur·pose·ful (pûr′pəs fəl) *adj.* **1.** having a purpose or meaning; done on purpose; intentional: *a purposeful insult.* **2.** having or showing determination: *a purposeful attitude toward work.* —**pur′pose·ful·ly,** *adv.* —**pur′pose·ful·ness,** *n.*

pur·pose·less (pûr′pəs lis) *adj.* without purpose or meaning. —**pur′pose·less·ly,** *adv.* —**pur′pose·less·ness,** *n.*

pur·pose·ly (pûr′pəs lē) *adv.* on purpose; intentionally.

purr (pûr) *n.* **1.** a soft, murmuring sound made by a cat when pleased or contented. **2.** any similar sound: *the purr of an engine.* —*v.i.* to make a soft, murmuring sound. —*v.t.* to express by making a soft, murmuring sound: *to purr one's thanks.*

purse (pûrs) *n.* **1.** a woman's handbag. **2.** a small bag, pouch, or case for carrying money. **3.** money; funds. **4.** a sum of money offered as a prize or given as a gift. —*v.t.,* **pursed, purs·ing.** to draw together into wrinkles or folds; pucker: *to purse one's lips in anger.*

purs·er (pûr′sər) *n.* the officer who has charge of financial matters on board a ship.

purs·lane (pûrs′lin, pûrs′lān) *n.* a trailing plant having bright yellow flowers and fleshy stems and leaves, sometimes used as a salad green.

pur·su·ance (pər sü′əns) *n.* a carrying out: *In pursuance of our plan, we spent the summer camping.*

pur·su·ant (pər sü′ənt) *adj.* going in pursuit; pursuing. ·**pursuant to.** in accordance with: *I loaned them the money, pursuant to our agreement.*

pur·sue (pər sü′) *v.,* **pur·sued, pur·su·ing.** —*v.t.* **1.** to follow in order to overtake, capture, or kill: *The hounds pursued the fox.* **2.** to go along or hold to the course of; follow: *The class pursued their plans for the picnic.* **3.** to strive for; seek: *to pursue a goal with effort.* **4.** to continue or follow through: *to pursue the study of Spanish.* **5.** to continue to trouble, disturb, or distress: *Questions about their bravery pursued the defeated soldiers.* —*v.i.* to go in pursuit; follow. —**pur·su′er,** *n.*

pur·suit (pər süt′) *n.* **1.** the act of following in order to overtake: *The police were in pursuit of a robber.* **2.** the act of seeking: *the pursuit of wealth.* **3.** any occupation, pastime, or interest: *Collecting stamps is my favorite pursuit.*

pur·vey (pər vā′) *v.t.* to supply (food or provisions): *to purvey groceries and meats.* —**pur·vey′ance,** *n.*

pur·vey·or (pər vā′ər) *n.* a person who supplies food or provisions: *a purveyor of fruits.*

pus (pus) *n.* a thick, yellowish fluid that collects in abscesses and other infections in the body, containing bacteria and dead white blood cells.

push (push) *v.t.* **1.** to press forcefully on or against so as to move: *Push the door with your shoulder. I am pushing the baby carriage up the hill.* **2.** to urge vigorously: *That journalist always pushes reform of the city government.* **3.** to put strain or pressure on: *We were pushed for time.* **4.** to make with effort or force: *The campers pushed their way through the bushes.* **5.** to advance or expand by effort: *The settlers pushed the frontier farther west.* **6.** to make an effort to sell: *That grocery store is pushing canned goods this week.* —*v.i.* **1.** to press forcefully on or against something so as to move it: *If you push against the fence it will give way.* **2.** to move forward with effort: *to push through a crowd.* **3.** to put forth a strong or steady effort: *to push for higher wages.* —*n., pl.* **push·es. 1.** the act of pushing: *The bully gave me a push that knocked me down.* **2.** a forceful effort, attempt, or drive: *The troops made one last push to take the town.* ·**to push around.** *Informal.* to treat roughly. ·**to push off.** *Informal.* to leave; depart.

push button, a button or knob pushed to operate some device, especially by closing or opening an electric circuit.

push–but·ton (push′but′ən) *adj.* operated by a push button: *a car with push-button windows.*

push·cart (push′kärt′) *n.* a small cart pushed by hand, used especially by a peddler.

push·er (push′ər) *n.* **1.** a person or thing that pushes. **2.** *Slang.* a person who sells drugs illegally.

push·o·ver (push′ō′vər) *n. Slang.* **1.** a person who is easily defeated, fooled, or taken advantage of. **2.** anything easily done.

push–up (push′up′) *n.* an exercise in which a person lies face down and raises and lowers the body by straightening and bending the arms.

push·y (push′ē) *adj.,* **push·i·er, push·i·est.** *Informal.* forward or aggressive in an offensive manner. —**push′i·ly,** *adv.* —**push′i·ness,** *n.*

pu·sil·lan·i·mous (pū′sə lan′ə məs) *adj.* lacking courage; fainthearted; cowardly. —**pu·sil·lan′i·mous·ly,** *adv.*

puss[1] (pus) *n., pl.* **puss·es.** a cat. [Of uncertain origin.]

puss[2] (pus) *n., pl.* **puss·es.** *Slang.* the face or mouth. [From the Irish word *pus* meaning "lip" or "mouth."]

puss·y (pus′ē) *n., pl.* **puss·ies. 1.** a cat. **2.** a catkin.

puss·y·foot (pus′ē füt′) *v.i. Informal.* **1.** to move quietly, cautiously, or secretly. **2.** to act in a cautious or timid manner; be unwilling to commit oneself.

pussy willow, an American shrub or small tree bearing furry, silvery gray catkins.

pus·tule (pus′chül) *n.* **1.** a small, inflamed swelling of the skin containing pus. **2.** any similar swelling.

put (put) *v.,* **put, put·ting.** —*v.t.* **1.** to cause to be in a certain place or position; place; set; lay: *Put the package on the table. I put another log on the fire.* **2.** to cause to be in a certain condition: *The teacher's warm smile put the frightened child at ease.* **3.** to cause to undergo; subject: *to put a person to a great deal of trouble.* **4.** to set at a certain point or amount; estimate: *I put the value of the car at five hundred dollars.* **5.** to attribute; ascribe; assign: *The report put the blame on the mayor.* **6.** to express; state: *Put your question clearly.* **7.** to bring to bear; apply: *to put one's knowledge to use.* **8.** to impose: *to put a tax on imports.* **9.** to suggest for consideration or judgment: *to put a question to an audience.* **10.** to throw (the shot) with an overhand, pushing motion. —*v.i.* to go; proceed: *The ship put out to sea.* —*n.* an overhand, pushing throw. [From the Middle English word *putten* meaning "to push, strike, drive," from Old English.]

·**to put aside.** to save for later use.

·**to put away. a.** to save for later use. **b.** *Informal.* to eat or drink. **c.** to give up; abandon: *to put away childish habits.* **d.** *Informal.* to kill.

·**to put by.** to save for later use.

·**to put down. a.** to put an end to: *to put down the rebellion.* **b.** to write down: *to put down thoughts on paper.* **c.** to belittle or snub (someone).

·**to put forth. a.** to send out; sprout; grow: *The tree put forth leaves.* **b.** to exert: *to put forth great effort.*

—Catkin

pussy willow

at; āpe; fär; câre; end; mē; it; īce; pîerce; hot; ōld; sông; fôrk; oil; out; up; ūse; rüle; pùll; tûrn; chin; sing; shop; thin; this; hw in white; zh in treasure. The symbol ə stands for the unstressed vowel sound heard in about, taken, pencil, lemon, and circus.

P

·**to put forward.** to propose; present.

·**to put in. a.** *Informal.* to spend (time) in a certain way: *to put in a long day at the office.* **b.** (of a ship) to enter (a port). **c.** to make or present a request, offer, claim, or the like: *to put in for a car loan.*

·**to put off. a.** to postpone or delay: *to put off a trip.* **b.** to get rid of by delay or evasion: *to put off creditors with false promises to pay.*

·**to put on. a.** to assume or pretend: *to put on a brave front.* **b.** to present or perform: *to put on a play.* **c.** to apply: *The driver put on the brakes.*

·**to put out. a.** to extinguish: *to put out a fire, to put out the lights.* **b.** to annoy or inconvenience. **c.** to publish: *to put out a new book.* **d.** *Baseball.* to cause (a batter or base runner) to be out.

·**to put over.** *Informal.* to carry out with success: *to put over a deal.*

·**to put through. a.** to carry out with success. **b.** to cause to undergo or do: *to put someone through a lot of trouble.*

·**to put up. a.** to build: *to put up a new office building.* **b.** to preserve (food). **c.** to get food and lodging: *They put up at a motel.* **d.** to give food and lodging to: *We put up a friend for the night.* **e.** to propose or nominate: *to put up a candidate for office.* **f.** to offer: *to put up a house for sale.* **g.** to provide: *to put up the money for a project.* **h.** to show: *The lost child put up a brave front.*

·**to put upon.** to take advantage of; treat unfairly.

·**to put up to.** *Informal.* to encourage (a person) to do: *Who put those students up to that prank?*

·**to put up with.** to bear patiently; endure.

put·down (pŭt′doun′) *n.* *Slang.* a remark or action meant to belittle or snub someone.

put·on (pŭt′ôn′, pŭt′on′) *adj.* pretended; assumed: *a put-on display of grief.* —*n.* *Slang.* something meant to deceive: *Their bravery was a put-on.*

put·out (pŭt′out′) *n.* *Baseball.* the act or instance of putting out a batter or base runner.

pu·tre·fac·tion (pū′trə fak′shən) *n.* the act or process of putrefying or the state of being putrefied.

pu·tre·fy (pū′trə fī′) *v.*, **pu·tre·fied, pu·tre·fy·ing.** —*v.t.* to cause to decay or rot; make putrid. —*v.i.* to rot.

pu·trid (pū′trid) *adj.* **1.** decayed and foul-smelling; rotten: *putrid fish.* **2.** characteristic of or produced by putrefying: *a putrid smell.* —**pu′trid·ly,** *adv.* —**pu′trid·ness,** *n.*

putt (put) *n.* *Golf.* a short, rolling shot made on a putting green in an attempt to send the ball into the cup. —*v.t.* to hit (a ball) with such a stroke. —*v.i.* to hit a ball with such a stroke. [A form of *put.*]

put·tee (pŭt′ē, pu tē′) *n.* a long, narrow strip of cloth wound round the leg from ankle to knee, worn as a protection and support for the leg.

put·ter[1] (pŭt′ər) *also,* **pot·ter.** *v.i.* to work or act in an aimless or useless way: *You've puttered around all day.* —*v.t.* to waste (time) in puttering. [From the English dialect word *potter* with the same meaning, going back to the Old English word *potian* "to push, thrust, poke," of Celtic origin.] —**put′ter·er,** *n.*

putt·er[2] (pŭt′ər) *n.* **1.** a golf club with a short shaft and an upright head, used in putting. **2.** a person who putts. [*Putt* + *-er*[1].]

putting green, see green *(def. 3).*

put·ty (pŭt′ē) *n., pl.* **put·ties.** a soft, doughlike mixture of powdered chalk and linseed oil, used especially for filling cracks or attaching panes of glass. —*v.t.,* **put·tied, put·ty·ing.** to fill, fasten, or cover with putty.

put·up·on (pŭt′ə pôn′, pŭt′ə pon′) *adj.* taken advantage of; imposed upon: *The hosts felt put-upon when their guests brought several uninvited friends to dinner.*

puz·zle (puz′əl) *n.* **1.** a person or thing that confuses or bewilders: *Algebra is a real puzzle to me.* **2.** a toy or game that presents a problem to solve or a task to be done for fun: *They tried to fit together the pieces of the puzzle.* —*v.,* **puz·zled, puz·zling.** —*v.t.* to confuse or bewilder: *Your strange attitude puzzles me.* —*v.i.* to be confused or bewildered: *We puzzled over the arithmetic problem.* —**puz′zler,** *n.*

puz·zle·ment (puz′əl mənt) *n.* **1.** the state of being puzzled. **2.** something that confuses or bewilders.

Pvt., Private.

Pyg·ma·lion (pig māl′yən) *n.* *Greek Legend.* a sculptor and king of Cyprus who fell in love with the statue of a maiden he had carved.

Pyg·my (pig′mē) *also,* **Pig·my.** *n., pl.* **Pyg·mies. 1.** a member of a dark-skinned people of Africa who are usually less than five feet tall. **2.** pygmy. a very small person or thing. —*adj.* **1.** of or relating to the Pygmies. **2.** pygmy. very small. [From the Latin name *Pygmaei* meaning "the Pygmies," from the Greek name *Pygmaioi.* The Greeks took this name from the word *pygmē* meaning "the distance from the elbow to the knuckles," which was supposedly the height of a Pygmy.]

py·ja·mas (pə jä′məz, pə jam′əz) *British.* another spelling of **pajamas.**

py·lon (pī′lon) *n.* **1.** a tall steel tower that supports high-tension wires. **2.** a tower for guiding aviators, especially in a race. **3.** a monumental gateway, especially to an ancient Egyptian temple.

py·lo·rus (pī lôr′əs) *n., pl.* **py·lo·ri** (pī lôr′ī). the opening between the stomach and the duodenum. —**py·lor′ic,** *adj.*

py·or·rhe·a (pī′ə rē′ə) *also,* **py·or·rhoe·a.** *n.* an inflammation of the gums and other soft tissues that surround the teeth, resulting in the loosening of the teeth.

pyr·a·mid (pir′ə mid′) *n.* **1.** Pyramids. the massive stone structures, usually having a square base and four triangular sides that slope upward to an apex, built as tombs by the ancient Egyptians. **2.** a solid figure having a polygon for a base and triangular sides intersecting at a point. **3.** anything resembling a pyramid in form or structure: *The acrobats formed a human pyramid.* —*v.t.* to arrange or raise in the shape of a pyramid. —*v.i.* **1.** to have the shape of a pyramid. **2.** to rise or increase: *The cost of food has pyramided in recent years.*

pyramid *(n., def. 1)*

py·ram·i·dal (pi ram′i dəl) *adj.* of, relating to, or like a pyramid. —**py·ram′i·dal·ly,** *adv.*

pyre (pīr) *n.* a pile of wood or other combustible material for burning a dead body.

Py·rex (pī′reks) *n.* *Trademark.* a kind of glass that is resistant to heat, used to make cooking utensils and laboratory glassware.

pyr·i·dox·ine (pir′i dok′sēn) *n.* another word for **vitamin B₆.**

py·rite (pī′rīt) *n.* a hard, shiny, yellow compound of iron and sulfur, often mistaken for gold, used in the manufacture of sulfuric acid; fool's gold.

py·ri·tes (pī rī′tēz, pī′rīts) *pl. n.* any of various compounds of sulfur and a metal.

py·ro·ma·ni·a (pī′rə mā′nē ə) *n.* an uncontrollable desire to set fire to things.

py·ro·ma·ni·ac (pī′rə mā′nē ak′) *n.* a person who has an uncontrollable desire to set fire to things.

py·ro·tech·nic (pī′rə tek′nik) *adj.* **1.** of or relating to fireworks. **2.** brilliant and exciting like fireworks: *to play the violin with a pyrotechnic display of skill.* Also, **py·ro·tech·ni·cal** (pī′rə tek′ni kəl). —**py′ro·tech′ni·cal·ly,** *adv.*

py·ro·tech·nics (pī′rə tek′niks) *n.* **1.** the manufacture or use of fireworks. ▲ used with a singular verb. **2.** a display of fireworks. **3.** any brilliant, dazzling, or sensational display. ▲ used with a plural verb in definitions 2 and 3.

Pyr·rhic victory (pir′ik) a victory won at a huge or ruinous cost. [From the Greek king *Pyrrhus* (319–272 B.C.), who suffered heavy losses in defeating the Romans in 279 B.C.]

Py·thag·o·re·an (pi thag′ə rē′ən) *adj.* or or relating to Pythagoras, his doctrines, or his followers. —*n.* a follower of Pythagoras.

Pythagorean theorem, the theorem that in a right triangle, the square of the length of the hypotenuse is equal to the sum of the squares of the lengths of the other two sides.

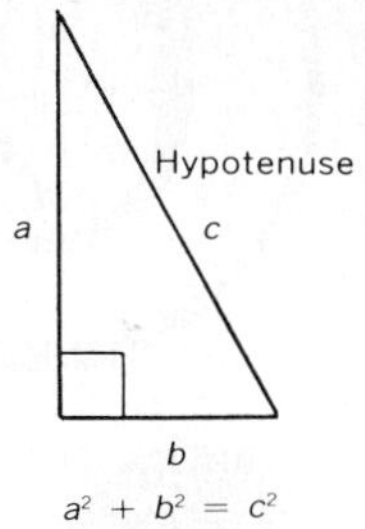

Pyth·i·as (pith′ē əs) *n.* see **Damon.**

py·thon (pī′thon) *n.* any of a group of large, nonpoisonous snakes related to the boas, that are found in Asia, Africa, the East Indies, and Australia. Pythons coil around and squeeze and suffocate their prey.

$$a^2 + b^2 = c^2$$

Pythagorean theorem

at; āpe; fär; câre; end; mē; it; īce; pîerce; hot; ōld; sông, fôrk; oil; out; up; ūse; rüle; pùll; tûrn; chin; sing; shop; thin; <u>th</u>is; hw in white; zh in treasure. The symbol ə stands for the unstressed vowel sound heard in about, taken, pencil, lemon, and circus.

P

765

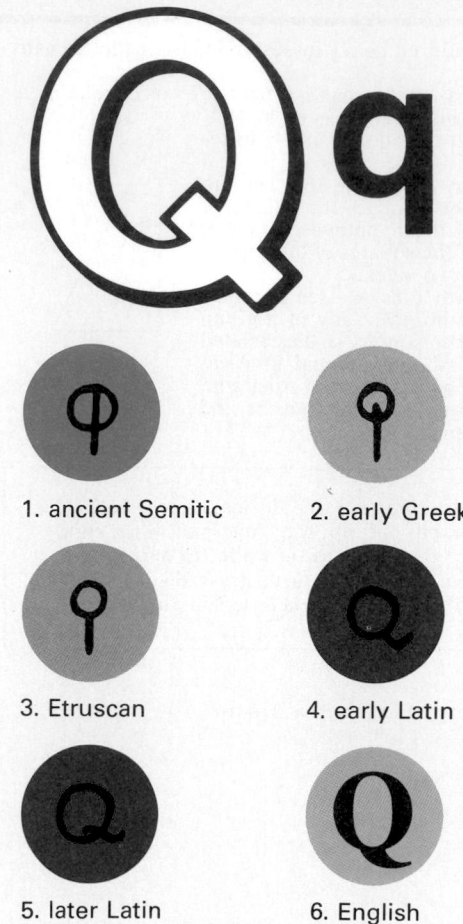

1. ancient Semitic

2. early Greek

3. Etruscan

4. early Latin

5. later Latin

6. English

Q is the seventeenth letter of the English alphabet. The oldest form of the letter **Q** was the ancient Semitic letter *koph* (1), which meant "monkey." This letter, which was pronounced like a *k* sound made at the back of the throat, was adopted by the early Greeks, who called it *koppa* (2). Because the Greeks eventually used the letter *kappa* to represent both the hard *k* sound and the Semitic *k* sound, *koppa* was dropped from later Greek alphabets. When the early Greek alphabet was borrowed by the Etruscans (3), they inherited three letters for the same hard *k* sound. Koppa, which became our letter **Q**, was used before **U**. In early Latin (4), the letter **O**, which the Etruscans did not use, sometimes followed the Latin **Q**. In classical Latin (5), **Q** was used only in combination with the letter **U**, in order to produce a *kw* sound. Our spelling rule that **Q** is followed by **U** comes from this spelling rule in Latin. By about 2,000 years ago, the Romans were writing and pronouncing the letter **Q** almost exactly as we do today (6).

q, Q (kū) *n.*, *pl.* **q's, Q's.** the seventeenth letter of the English alphabet.

q. **1.** quart. **2.** quarter; quarterly.

Q., Queen.

Q.E.D., which was to be proved or demonstrated. [Short for the Latin phrase *quod erat demonstrandum* meaning "which was to be demonstrated."]

qt. 1. quantity. **2.** quart; quarts.

quack¹ (kwak) *n.* the harsh, flat sound made by a duck. —*v.i.* to make such a sound. [Representation of the sound of a duck.]

quack² (kwak) *n.* **1.** a dishonest person who pretends to have skill as a doctor. **2.** a person with little knowledge or skill who poses as an expert; charlatan. —*adj.* relating to or characteristic of a quack or quackery; fake: *a quack doctor.* [Short for the earlier *quacksalver* meaning "a dishonest peddler of salves and ointments," from the obsolete Dutch word *quacksalver*.]

quack·er·y (kwak′ə rē) *n.*, *pl.* **quack·er·ies.** the practices or methods of a quack; fakery.

quad (kwod) *n.* **1.** see **quadrangle** *(defs. 2 and 3).* **2.** see **quadraphonic.**

quad·ran·gle (kwod′rang′gəl) *n.* **1.** a plane geometric figure having four angles and four sides; quadrilateral. **2.** a square space, especially a courtyard, partly or entirely surrounded by a building or buildings: *The classrooms are in the buildings around the quadrangle.* **3.** the building or buildings surrounding such a space.

quad·rant (kwod′rənt) *n.* **1.** a quarter of a circle, or an arc of 90 degrees. **2.** an instrument consisting of an arc with markings to show 90 degrees, used in navigation and astronomy for measuring the altitude or angular distance of an object above the horizon. **3.** any of the four parts into which a plane is divided by perpendicular coordinate axes.

quad·ra·phon·ic (kwod′rə fon′ik) *adj.* of or relating to the recording, reproduction, or transmission of sound by the use of four different channels.

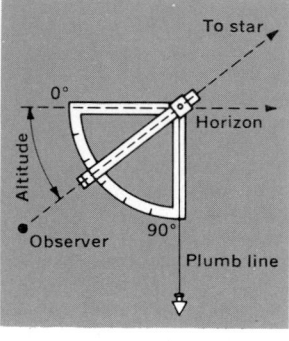

quadrant *(def. 2)*

quad·rat·ic (kwo drat′ik) *adj.* *Algebra.* of, relating to, or involving a quantity or quantities that are squared, with none that are raised to a higher power: $x^2 + 4x + 3 = 15$ is a quadratic equation. —*n.* a quadratic equation or expression.

quad·ren·ni·al (kwo dren′ē əl) *adj.* **1.** occurring every four years: *a quadrennial election.* **2.** lasting four years: *a quadrennial term of office.*

quadri– or **quadr-** or **quadru-** *combining form* four; having four: *quadrilateral, quadraphonic, quadruplet.*

quad·ri·ceps (kwod′rə seps′) *n.*, *pl.* **quad·ri·ceps** or **quad·ri·cep·ses.** the large muscle in the front of the thigh that extends the leg.

quad·ri·lat·er·al (kwod′rə lat′ər əl) *adj.* having four sides. —*n.* a polygon with four sides and four angles.

qua·drille (kwo dril′) *n.* **1.** a square dance for four couples that usually has five parts. **2.** the music for such a dance.

quad·ril·lion (kwo dril′yən) *n.* **1.** in the United States, the cardinal number that is represented by one followed by fifteen zeros. **2.** in Great Britain, the cardinal number that is represented by one followed by twenty-four zeros. —*adj.* numbering one quadrillion. —**quad·ril′lionth,** *adj., n.*

quad·ri·no·mi·al (kwod′rə nō′mē əl) *n.* in algebra, an expression with four terms.

quad·ri·ple·gic (kwod′rə plē′jik) *adj.* paralyzed in both arms and both legs. —*n.* a person who is quadriplegic.

quad·ru·ped (kwod′rə ped′) *n.* any animal having four feet. Dogs and alligators are quadrupeds. —*adj.* having four feet.

quad·ru·ple (kwo drü′pəl) *adj.* **1.** consisting of four parts or members: *a quadruple alliance.* **2.** four times as great or as many: *The value of this land is quadruple what it was twenty years ago.* —*v.,* **quad·ru·pled, quad-ru·pling.** —*v.i.* to become four times as great or as many: *The value of their farm quadrupled when the new road was built.* —*v.t.* to make four times as great or as many. —*n.* a number or amount four times as great as another.

quad·rup·let (kwo drü′plit) *n.* **1.** one of four offspring born at the same birth. **2.** any set or group of four.

quaff (kwof, kwaf) *v.t., v.i.* to drink heartily and with large swallows: *to quaff water.* —*n.* a hearty drink.

quag·mire (kwag′mīr′, kwog′mīr′) *n.* **1.** soft, muddy ground. **2.** a difficult position or situation: *to be caught in a quagmire of debts.*

qua·hog (kwô′hôg′, kwô′hog′, kō′hôg′, kō′hog′) *n.* a roundish, hard-shelled clam, found in shallow waters along the Atlantic coast of North America.

quail[1] (kwāl) *n., pl.* **quail** or **quails.** any of various game birds, having gray or brown feathers that are often speckled with white. [From the Old French word *quaile* meaning this bird.]

quail[2] (kwāl) *v.i.* to shrink back in fear: *The small child quailed when the dog growled.* [Probably from the Middle Dutch word *quelen* meaning "to grow feeble, weaken."]

European **quail**

quaint (kwānt) *adj.* **1.** charming or attractive in an old-fashioned way: *We walked along the quaint, narrow streets of the old town.* **2.** pleasingly unusual or odd: *The audience found the singer's French accent quaint.* —**quaint′ly,** *adv.* —**quaint′ness,** *n.*

quake (kwāk) *v.i.,* **quaked, quak·ing.** to shake; tremble: *to quake with terror. The clap of thunder made the house quake.* —*n.* **1.** a trembling or shaking. **2.** see **earthquake.**

Quak·er (kwā′kər) *n.* a member of the Society of Friends, a Christian sect founded in the seventeenth century. Also, **Friend.**

Quak·er·ism (kwā′kə riz′əm) *n.* the doctrines and practices of the Quakers.

qual·i·fi·ca·tion (kwol′ə fi kā′shən) *n.* **1.** the act of qualifying or the state of being qualified. **2.** any ability, accomplishment, knowledge, or condition that makes a person fit for a certain job, task, or office: *His past teaching experience was a qualification for his position as principal of the school.* **3.** something that limits or restricts: *She is, without qualification, the most intelligent person I've ever known.*

qual·i·fied (kwol′ə fīd′) *adj.* **1.** having the necessary abilities, accomplishments, or requirements: *a qualified voter, a person who is qualified for a job.* **2.** limited; restricted: *The play was at best a qualified success, receiving critical praise but drawing only small crowds.*

qual·i·fi·er (kwol′ə fī′ər) *n.* **1.** a person or thing that qualifies. **2.** a word, such as an adjective or adverb, that limits or modifies the meaning of another word.

qual·i·fy (kwol′ə fī′) *v.,* **qual·i·fied, qual·i·fy·ing.** —*v.t.* **1.** to make fit, as for a certain job, task, or office: *Your previous experience qualifies you for the job.* **2.** to limit or restrict: *I should have qualified my statement with the word "usually."* **3.** to limit or modify the meaning of

(a word or phrase): *Adjectives qualify nouns.* —*v.i.* to be or become fit.

qual·i·ta·tive (kwol′i tā′tiv) *adj.* of or relating to quality: *There was a qualitative change in the output of the team.* —**qual′i·ta′tive·ly,** *adv.*

qualitative analysis, a method of testing to determine the constituents of a chemical substance.

qual·i·ty (kwol′i tē) *n., pl.* **qual·i·ties. 1.** something that makes a person or thing what it is: *the qualities of a successful business executive. Lemons have a sour quality.* **2.** basic character; nature: *The sound of the waves had a soothing quality.* **3.** degree of excellence; grade: *Our butcher sells meat that is of a very high quality.* **4.** excellence; fineness; superiority: *That restaurant prides itself on the quality of its food.* **5.** high rank or social position.

qualm (kwäm) *n.* **1.** a twinge of conscience: *to have qualms about cheating.* **2.** a sudden feeling of uneasiness or doubt; misgiving: *I had some qualms about my first airplane flight.*

quan·da·ry (kwon′də rē) *n., pl.* **quan·da·ries.** a state of hesitation or uncertainty; dilemma; predicament.

quan·ta (kwon′tə) the plural of **quantum.**

quan·ti·ta·tive (kwon′ti tā′tiv) *adj.* **1.** of or relating to quantity. **2.** capable of being measured: *a quantitative increase.* —**quan′ti·ta′tive·ly,** *adv.*

quantitative analysis, a method of testing to determine the amounts of each constituent in a chemical substance.

quan·ti·ty (kwon′ti tē) *n., pl.* **quan·ti·ties. 1.** a number or amount: *The recipe calls for a small quantity of milk.* **2.** a large number or amount: *It is often less expensive to buy goods in quantity.* **3.** a property of a thing that can be determined by measurement, as of volume, length, or weight. **4.** an amount, number, or algebraic expression representing a mathematical value. **5.** the length of a vowel sound or syllable in pronunciation. **6.** *Music.* the length of a note or tone.

quan·tum (kwon′təm) *n., pl.* **quan·ta** (kwon′tə). *Physics.* a separate and indivisible basic unit of energy. [From the Latin word *quantum,* neuter form of *quantus* meaning "how much? how great?"]

quantum theory, the theory that energy is emitted and absorbed in quanta, rather than in a continuous manner.

quar·an·tine (kwôr′ən tēn′, kwor′ən tēn′) *n.* **1.** the isolation of persons, animals, ships, or goods infected by or exposed to an infectious disease, to prevent the spread of the disease. **2.** the place or length of time of such isolation. **3.** any enforced isolation. —*v.t.,* **quar·an·tined, quar·an·tin·ing.** to keep away from others in order to prevent the spreading of a disease.

quark (kwôrk) one of the hypothetical particles that are thought to be the basic constituents of all known atomic particles. [Coined by the American physicist Murray Gell-Mann (b. 1929) from a word in the novel *Finnegans Wake* (1939) by James Joyce.]

quar·rel (kwôr′əl, kwor′əl) *n.* **1.** an angry dispute or disagreement: *They had a quarrel about whose turn it was to wash the dishes.* **2.** a cause for such a dispute or disagreement: *I have no quarrel with your plan.* —*v.i.,* **quar·reled, quar·rel·ing;** also, *British,* **quar·relled, quar-rel·ling. 1.** to have an angry dispute or disagreement: *The children quarreled about who would ride the bicycle first.*

at; āpe; fär; câre; end; mē; it; īce; pîerce; hot; ōld; sông, fôrk; oil; out; up; ūse; rüle; pull; tûrn; chin; sing; shop; thin; this; hw in white; zh in treasure. The symbol ə stands for the unstressed vowel sound heard in about, taken, pencil, lemon, and circus.

Q

2. to find fault: *We quarreled with your methods, not your goals.* —**quar′rel·er,** *n.*

quar·rel·some (kwôr′əl səm, kwor′əl səm) *adj.* prone to quarreling; likely to dispute: *No one likes our quarrelsome neighbor.* —**quar′rel·some·ly,** *adv.* —**quar′rel·some·ness,** *n.*

quar·ri·er (kwôr′ē ər, kwor′ē ər) *n.* a person who works in a quarry.

quar·ry¹ (kwôr′ē, kwor′ē) *n., pl.* **quar·ries.** a place where stone is cut or blasted out for use in building, road construction, or the like. —*v.t.,* **quar·ried, quar·ry·ing. 1.** to cut or blast from a quarry: *to quarry marble.* **2.** to make a quarry in: *to quarry a hillside.* [From the Medieval Latin word *quareia* meaning "a stone quarry."]

quar·ry² (kwôr′ē, kwor′ē) *n., pl.* **quar·ries.** an animal that is hunted or chased; prey. [From the Old French word *cuiriee* meaning "the parts of a deer that are given to the hounds as their reward."]

quart (kwôrt) *n.* **1.** a unit of liquid measure equal to one fourth of a gallon, or two pints (0.946 liter). **2.** a unit of dry measure equal to one eighth of a peck, or two pints (1.101 liters). **3.** a container for holding or measuring a quart.

quar·ter (kwôr′tər) *n.* **1.** one of four equal or corresponding parts; one fourth: *I divided the apple into quarters.* **2.** a coin of the United States and Canada equal to twenty-five cents, or one quarter of a dollar. **3.** one fourth of an hour; fifteen minutes. **4.** one fourth of a year; three months. **5.** a part of a school or college year, usually lasting three months. **6.** a fourth part of the period of the moon's revolution around the earth, lasting about seven days: *The moon is in its first quarter.* **7.** one of the four equal time periods into which certain games, such as football or basketball, are divided. **8.** one of the four principal divisions of the compass. **9.** a section or district, as of a city or town: *Sightseers were delighted with the quaint French quarter of the city.* **10.** a person, place, or group: *The ruling came from the highest quarters.* **11. quarters. a.** a place to live; living accommodations: *the winter quarters of a circus.* **b.** an assigned position or station, as on a warship. **12.** one of the legs of a four-footed animal, with the adjoining parts: *a quarter of lamb.* **13.** mercy, especially when granted to a defeated enemy: *The judges gave no quarter to the traitor.* —*v.t.* **1.** to divide into four equal parts: *to quarter an apple.* **2.** to provide with living accommodations; lodge: *to quarter troops in tents for the night.* —*adj.* **1.** being one of four equal parts: *The four partners each received a quarter part of the profits from the business.* **2.** being equal to one fourth of a standard unit of measure: *a quarter pound of butter.*

·**at close quarters.** at close range; very close together.

quar·ter·back (kwôr′tər bak′) *n.* *Football.* a player whose position is directly behind the center, and who directs the team and calls signals for the offense.

quar·ter·deck (kwôr′tər dek′) *n.* the part of the upper deck of a ship between the stern and mainmast, used especially by officers.

quar·ter·ly (kwôr′tər lē) *adj.* done, occurring, or paid once every three months: *to figure the quarterly interest on a savings account.* —*n., pl.* **quar·ter·lies.** a magazine published four times a year, or once every three months. —*adv.* once every three months: *The payments were made quarterly.*

quar·ter·mas·ter (kwôr′tər mas′tər) *n.* **1.** in the U.S. Army, an officer responsible for providing quarters, clothing, food, equipment, and the like for troops. **2.** in the U.S. Navy, a petty officer on a ship who is in charge of navigation and certain equipment, such as compasses and signals.

quarter note *Music.* a note having one fourth the duration of a whole note.

quar·ter·staff (kwôr′tər staf′) *n., pl.* **quar·ter·staves** (kwôr′tər stāvz′). a stout pole 6 to 8 feet (1.8–2.4 meters) long, having an iron tip. It was formerly used in England as a weapon.

quar·tet (kwôr tet′) *also,* **quar·tette.** *n.* **1.** a musical composition for four voices or instruments. **2.** a musical group of four performers. **3.** any group or set of four.

quar·to (kwôr′tō) *n., pl.* **quar·tos. 1.** the page size of a book made up of sheets of paper folded twice to make four leaves, each usually about 9 by 12 inches (22.9 by 30.5 centimeters). **2.** a book composed of pages of this size.

quartz (kwôrts) *n., pl.* **quartz·es.** a very hard form of silica that occurs in crystals or in a single mass, and is colorless and transparent in its pure state. Certain impure colored varieties, as amethyst, are used as semiprecious stones. Quartz is the most common of all minerals and is the main constituent of sand.

quartz·ite (kwôrt′sīt) *n.* a granular metamorphic rock consisting chiefly of quartz.

qua·sar (kwā′zär, kwā′sär) *n.* any of various starlike celestial objects that emit extremely powerful radio waves, light, and other electromagnetic radiation. [Short for *quas*(i stell)*ar* (radio source).]

quash¹ (kwosh) *v.t.* to put down forcibly and quickly: *The army quickly quashed the insurrection.* [From the Old French word *quasser* meaning "to smash, crush, overcome entirely," from the Latin word *quassare* "to shake" or "to shatter, break to pieces."]

quash² (kwosh) *v.t.* to make void or set aside, as a law, election, or indictment: *The judge quashed the lower court's decision.* [From the Medieval Latin word *quassare* with the same meaning, from the Late Latin word *cassare* "to make void, nullify," from the Latin word *cassus* "void."]

qua·si– *combining form* resembling or similar to, but not the same as; seemingly, but not really; almost or somewhat: *quasi-successful.*

Qua·ter·na·ry (kwä′tər ner′ē) *n.* the second geological period of the Cenozoic era, including the Pleistocene and Recent epochs. —*adj.* of, relating to, or characteristic of this period.

quat·rain (kwot′rān) *n.* a stanza or poem of four lines, often with alternately rhyming lines.

qua·ver (kwā′vər) *v.i.* **1.** to tremble or shake: *The little child's voice quavered with fright.* **2.** to speak or sing with a trembling voice. —*n.* **1.** a shaking or trembling, especially of the voice. **2.** a trill produced or performed in singing or in playing a musical instrument. —**qua′ver·y,** *adj.*

quay (kē) *n.* a landing place for boats and ships, usually made of stone: *The ferry arrived at the quay at noon.*

Que., Quebec.

quea·sy (kwē′zē) *adj.,* **quea·si·er, quea·si·est. 1.** sick to one's stomach; nauseated: *The rough boat trip made us queasy.* **2.** causing or tending to cause nausea. **3.** uneasy; uncomfortable: *I had a queasy feeling that I had failed the test.* **4.** easily troubled, especially as a result of a guilty conscience. —**quea′si·ly,** *adv.* —**quea′si·ness,** *n.*

quay

que·bra·cho (kā brä′chō) *n., pl.* **que·bra·chos.** any of several tropical American trees whose bark and hard wood are used in tanning and dyeing.

Quech·ua (kech′wä) *n.* **1.** a South American Indian language, formerly spoken by the Incas, now spoken mainly in Peru, Ecuador, and parts of Bolivia and Argentina. **2.** any of the Incas that spoke this language.

queen (kwēn) *n.* **1.** the wife or widow of a king. **2.** a female sovereign of a kingdom who rules in her own right. **3.** a woman, or a place or thing, thought of as outstanding or preeminent: *That new ocean liner is the queen of the seas.* **4.** a fully developed female in a colony of bees, ants, or termites who can lay eggs. **5.** a playing card bearing a picture of a queen. **6.** *Chess.* the most powerful piece. It can move any number of spaces in any straight or diagonal line. —*v.i.* to reign as or act like a queen. —**queen'like'**, *adj.*

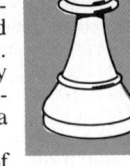

queen
(def. 6)

Queen Anne's lace, a wild species of carrot, having flat, lacy clusters of tiny white flowers.

queen consort, the wife of a reigning king.

queen·ly (kwēn'lē) *adj.*, **queen·li·er, queen·li·est.** characteristic of, like, or suitable for a queen. —*adv.* in a queenly manner. —**queen'li·ness,** *n.*

queen mother, the widow of a king who is also the mother of the reigning sovereign.

queen regent, a queen ruling in place of a king who is absent or who is unable or too young to reign.

Queen's English, see **King's English.**

queen-size (kwēn'sīz') *adj.* of or relating to a bed 60 inches wide by 80 inches long (152 centimeters by 203 centimeters), a size larger than a standard double bed but smaller than a king-size bed: *queen-size sheets.* Also, **queen-sized** (kwēn'sīzd').

queer (kwîr) *adj.* **1.** different from what is normal or expected; strange; peculiar; unusual: *That was a queer way for the dog to behave.* **2.** ill or faint: *to feel queer.* —**queer'ly,** *adv.* —**queer'ness,** *n.*

quell (kwel) *v.t.* **1.** to put down; crush; suppress: *The captain quelled the mutiny.* **2.** to put an end to; ease: *Medicine quelled the pain.*

quench (kwench) *v.t.* **1.** to satisfy; slake: *I quenched my thirst with a glass of milk.* **2.** to put out or extinguish: *The firefighters quenched the fire.* —**quench'·a·ble,** *adj.*

quer·u·lous (kwer'ə ləs) *adj.* **1.** finding fault; complaining: *The sick child was querulous about everything.* **2.** characterized as complaining: *a querulous voice.* —**quer'u·lous·ly,** *adv.* —**quer'u·lous·ness,** *n.*

que·ry (kwîr'ē) *n., pl.* **que·ries.** a question; inquiry. —*v.t.,* **que·ried, que·ry·ing. 1.** to ask about; inquire into: *My friend queried my reasons for quitting my job.* **2.** to ask a question or questions of: *The editor queried the author.* **3.** to feel doubt about the correctness or truth of: *to query a statement in an article.*

quest (kwest) *n.* **1.** a search or pursuit: *The explorer's quest for gold was in vain.* **2.** in the Middle Ages, an expedition or journey made by a knight or knights, especially one made in order to find or achieve something. **3.** a knight or knights on such an expedition or journey. —*v.i.* to go on a quest.

ques·tion (kwes'chən) *n.* **1.** something asked in order to receive a reply or find out something: *I could not answer the teacher's question.* **2.** a matter to be discussed or considered: *The meeting dealt with the question of civil rights.* **3.** a matter of dispute or doubt; controversy: *A question arose as to who owned the land.* **4.** uncertainty; doubt: *That student is, without question, the smartest one in the class.* **5.** a proposal to be voted on: *After much debate, the members of the legislature were ready for the question.* —*v.t.* **1.** to ask a question or questions of: *The police questioned the suspect.* **2.** to ask questions about; doubt; challenge: *The lawyer questioned the truth of the witness's account of the accident.* —**ques'tion·er,** *n.*

·**beside the question.** off the subject: *Your comment is beside the question.*

·**beyond question.** without doubt: *You are, beyond question, the best softball player on the team.*

·**in question.** under discussion or consideration: *The matter in question was the building of the new gymnasium.*

·**out of the question.** not to be considered or thought of.

·**to call in question.** to raise doubts about; challenge: *Don't call my honesty in question by hinting that I am lying.*

ques·tion·a·ble (kwes'chə nə bəl) *adj.* **1.** of doubtful character, honesty, respectability, or the like: *questionable behavior.* **2.** open to doubt or dispute; uncertain: *That theory is questionable.* —**ques'tion·a·bly,** *adv.*

ques·tion·ing·ly (kwes'chə ning lē) *adv.* in the manner of one who questions: *He looked at her questioningly.*

question mark, a punctuation mark (?) put at the end of a question. Also, **interrogation point.**

ques·tion·naire (kwes'chə nâr') *n.* a written or printed form consisting of a list of questions, used to get information or a sample of public opinion.

quet·zal (ket säl') *n.* a Central American bird having shiny green and bright red feathers. The male has a tail of long feathers.

Quet·zal·co·a·tl (ket säl'kō ä'təl) *n.* a god of the Aztecs and Toltecs, depicted as a serpent with feathers.

queue (kū) *n.* **1.** a braid of hair made at the back of the head. **2.** *also,* **cue.** a line of people, automobiles, or the like. —*v.i.,* **queued, queu·ing.** to form, stand, or wait in a line: *People queued up to buy tickets for the movie.*

quib·ble (kwib'əl) *v.i.,* **quib·bled, quib·bling.** to make petty or minor objections or criticisms, as to avoid the truth or main point: *The two lawyers quibbled about the terms of the contract.* —*n.* a petty objection or criticism. —**quib'bler,** *n.*

quiche (kēsh) *n.* a rich pie baked with a mixture of cheese, eggs, cream, and other ingredients: *a spinach quiche, a salmon quiche.* [From the French word *quiche,* from the German dialect word *Küche* meaning "little cake," from the German word *Küchen* "cake."]

quick (kwik) *adj.* **1.** done or happening within a very short time; rapid: *a quick glance.* **2.** moving with speed:

quetzal

at; āpe; fär; câre; end; mē; it; īce; pîerce; hot; ōld; sông, fôrk; oil; out; up; ūse; rüle; pùll; tûrn; chin; sing; shop; thin; **this**; hw in white; zh in treasure. The symbol ə stands for the unstressed vowel sound heard in about, taken, pencil, lemon, and circus.

Q

769

That secretary is a quick typist. **3.** understanding, thinking, learning, or responding easily or rapidly: *I don't have as quick a mind as you do.* **4.** easily aroused or stirred: *a quick temper.* —*n.* **1.** tender, sensitive flesh, especially that beneath a fingernail or toenail. **2.** living persons. ▲ used chiefly in the phrase *the quick and the dead.* —*adv.* quickly. [From the Old English word *cwicu* meaning "living, alive."] —**quick′ness,** *n.*

· **to cut to the quick.** to cause emotional pain or distress; hurt deeply.

quick·en (kwik′ən) *v.t.* **1.** to cause to go or move more rapidly; hasten: *He quickened his steps.* **2.** to give new life to; revive: *The camper quickened the fire by adding more wood.* **3.** to excite; stimulate: *The book quickened her interest in history.* —*v.i.* **1.** to go or move more rapidly. **2.** to return to life; revive. **3.** to show signs of life: *The earth quickened when spring arrived.*

quick–freeze (kwik′frēz′) *v.t.,* **quick-froze** (kwik′-frōz′), **quick-fro·zen** (kwik′frō′zən), **quick-freez·ing.** to freeze food so rapidly that it retains its flavor and is able to undergo long storage at low temperatures.

quick·lime (kwik′līm′) *n.* see **lime**[1].

quick·ly (kwik′lē) *adv.* with speed or haste; rapidly.

quick·sand (kwik′sand′) *n.* very deep, loose, wet sand that can engulf any heavy object that rests or moves upon it.

quick·sil·ver (kwik′sil′vər) *n.* see **mercury** (*def. 1*).

quick·step (kwik′step′) *n.* **1.** a rapid marching step. **2.** march music with a rapid tempo. **3.** a fast dance step.

quick–tem·pered (kwik′tem′pərd) *adj.* easily angered or irritated.

quick time, the normal military marching rate, consisting of 120 steps per minute.

quick–wit·ted (kwik′wit′id) *adj.* having or showing a lively or ready mind; mentally alert or keen: *a quick-witted pupil.* —**quick′-wit′ted·ly,** *adv.*

quid[1] (kwid) *n.* a piece of something to be chewed, especially tobacco. [From the Old English word *cwidu* meaning "cud."]

quid[2] (kwid) *n., pl.* **quid.** *British. Slang.* one pound sterling. [Of uncertain origin.]

qui·es·cent (kwī es′ənt) *adj.* in a state of inactivity or rest: *a quiescent frame of mind.* —**qui·es′cence,** *n.* —**qui·es′cent·ly,** *adv.*

qui·et (kwī′it) *adj.* **1.** making little or no noise: *The children were quiet while the teacher talked.* **2.** with or characterized by little or no noise: *a quiet library.* **3.** having little or no motion; still: *a quiet pond.* **4.** free from disturbance; peaceful: *a quiet evening, a quiet life.* **5.** restful or soothing, as to the eye: *The room was decorated in beige and other quiet colors.* —*n.* the quality or state of being quiet: *We enjoyed the peace and quiet of the little country town.* —*v.t.* to make quiet: *The nurse quieted the crying child.* —*v.i.* to become quiet: *The waves quieted down after the storm passed.* —**qui′et·er,** *n.* —**qui′et·ly,** *adv.* —**qui′et·ness,** *n.*

qui·e·tude (kwī′i tüd′, kwī′i tūd′) *n.* calmness or tranquility: *the quietude of the countryside.*

qui·e·tus (kwī ē′təs) *n., pl.* **qui·e·tus·es.** the final ending or settling of something: *the quietus of death.*

quill (kwil) *n.* **1.** a large, stiff feather. **2.** the hard, hollow stem of a feather. **3.** a pen made from the hollow stem of a feather. **4.** one of the sharp spines of a porcupine or hedgehog.

quilt (kwilt) *n.* a bed covering consisting of two pieces of cloth filled with soft stuffing material, such as feathers or cotton batting, and held together by lines of stitching, usually in a pattern, across the entire surface. —*v.i.* to make a quilt or quilts. —*v.t.* to stitch

quill *(def. 1)*

together with a soft lining: *to quilt a jacket for skiing.*

quilt·ing (kwil′ting) *n.* **1.** the act of making quilts or quilted work. **2.** the material used in making quilts.

quince (kwins) *n.* **1.** a pear-shaped yellow fruit of a small Asian tree, used in preserves. **2.** the tree bearing this fruit, related to the rose and having round white or pale pink flowers.

qui·nine (kwī′nīn) *n.* a bitter, colorless, crystalline drug made from the bark of the cinchona tree. It is used to treat malaria and other illnesses.

quin·sy (kwin′zē) *n.* severe inflammation of the tonsils and throat, often accompanied by the formation of an abscess.

quince branch

quint (kwint) *n. Informal.* see **quintuplet.**

quin·tes·sence (kwin tes′əns) *n.* **1.** the purest part or form of something; pure essence: *This chapter contains the quintessence of the author's thought.* **2.** the most perfect example of something: *Your behavior was the quintessence of generosity.*

quin·tet (kwin tet′) *also,* **quin·tette.** *n.* **1.** a musical composition for five voices or instruments. **2.** a musical group of five performers. **3.** any group or set of five.

quin·tu·ple (kwin tü′pəl, kwin′tə pəl) *adj.* **1.** consisting of five parts or members. **2.** five times as great or as many. —*v.,* **quin·tu·pled, quin·tu·pling.** —*v.i.* to become five times as great or as many. —*v.t.* to make five times as great or as many. —*n.* a number or amount five times as great as another.

quin·tu·plet (kwin tup′lit, kwin′tə plit) *n.* **1.** one of five offspring born at the same birth. **2.** any set or group of five. Also, *Informal.* **quint.**

quip (kwip) *n.* **1.** a clever or witty remark or saying, usually made on the spur of the moment. **2.** a sharp or sarcastic remark; taunt; gibe. —*v.i.,* **quipped, quip·ping.** to make a quip or quips.

quire (kwīr) *n.* twenty-four or twenty-five sheets of paper of the same size and quality.

quirk (kwûrk) *n.* **1.** a strange mannerism or way of acting. **2.** a sudden or unexpected twist or turn: *a quirk of fate.*

quirt (kwûrt) *n.* a flexible riding whip made of knotted rawhide thongs and having a short handle.

quis·ling (kwiz′-ling) *n.* a person who betrays his or her own country by aiding an in-

quirt

vading enemy. [From the Norwegian politician Vidkun *Quisling* (1887–1945), who betrayed his country by collaborating with the invading Germans during World War II.]

quit (kwit) *v.,* **quit** or **quit·ted, quit·ting.** —*v.t.* **1.** to stop, cease, or discontinue: *He quit studying to take a walk. It was hard to quit smoking.* **2.** to give up or abandon: *to quit a job.* **3.** to go away from; leave: *The guard did not quit the post all night long.* —*v.i.* **1.** to stop, cease, or discontinue doing something. **2.** to resign from a position: *She quit because her salary was too low.* **3.** to give up or stop trying, as in defeat or discouragement: *I quit when I realized I could not win the race.* —*adj.* free, clear, or rid of: *They are quit of all debts.*

quit·claim (kwit′klām′) *Law. n.* **1.** the giving up of one's claim, title, or right of action. **2.** a legal document in which one gives up a claim, title, or right of action. —*v.t.* to give up one's claim or title to or right of action on.

quite (kwīt) *adv.* **1.** completely; entirely; wholly: *We were not quite finished with dinner. I believe quite the opposite.* **2.** actually; really: *Climbing that mountain was*

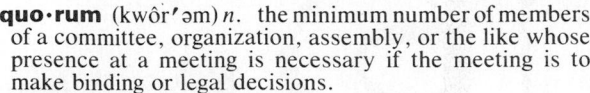

quite an accomplishment. **3.** to a considerable extent or degree; rather: *The weather is quite warm for November.*

quits (kwits) *adj.* on even terms by means of repayment or revenge: *After they made the last payment on the television set, they were quits with the store.*

·**to call it quits.** to discontinue or stop something: *After we studied all morning, we decided to call it quits.*

quit·ter (kwit′ər) *n.* a person who gives up easily.

quiv·er[1] (kwiv′ər) *v.i.* to shake slightly; shiver; tremble: *The child quivered with excitement at seeing the new bicycle.* —*n.* the act or motion of quivering: *the quiver of leaves in a breeze.* [Probably from the Middle English word *quiver* meaning ''active, quick, lively,'' from Old English.]

quiv·er[2] (kwiv′ər) *n.* a case for holding arrows. [From the Old French word *quivre* with the same meaning, of Germanic origin.]

Qui·xo·te, Don (ki hō′tē, kwik′sət) see **Don Quixote.**

quix·ot·ic (kwik sot′ik) *adj.* ridiculously chivalrous or romantic; too idealistic: *a quixotic young reformer.* [From *Don Quixote.*] —**quix·ot′i·cal·ly,** *adv.*

quiz (kwiz) *n., pl.* **quiz·zes.** a short, informal examination: *a history quiz.* —*v.t.,* **quizzed, quiz·zing.** to question; examine: *The police quizzed the suspect. The students were quizzed on last week's work.* —**quiz′zer,** *n.*

quiz show, a radio or television show in which contestants try to answer questions, usually for prizes.

quiz·zi·cal (kwiz′i kəl) *adj.* **1.** questioning; uncertain; puzzled: *The children looked quizzical because they didn't understand the question.* **2.** teasing; mocking: *a quizzical remark.* —**quiz′zi·cal·ly,** *adv.*

quoin (koin, kwoin) *n.* **1.** an outside angle of a wall or building. **2.** one of the stones forming such an angle. **3.** a wedge or wedge-shaped piece of material used in printing to lock type in a galley.

quoit (kwoit) *n.* **1. quoits.** a game played by throwing a flattened ring made of metal, rope, or another material, in an attempt to encircle or come as close as possible to a peg stuck in the ground. ▲ used with a singular verb. **2.** the flattened ring used in this game.

quon·dam (kwon′dəm) *adj.* that once was; former: *a quondam friend.*

Quon·set hut (kwon′sit) *Trademark.* a prefabricated building made of corrugated metal and supported by steel trusses, having a semicircular roof whose sides curve down to form the walls. [From *Quonset* Point, Rhode Island, where this hut was first built.]

quiver²

quo·rum (kwôr′əm) *n.* the minimum number of members of a committee, organization, assembly, or the like whose presence at a meeting is necessary if the meeting is to make binding or legal decisions.

quot., quotation.

quo·ta (kwō′tə) *n.* **1.** a fixed amount, or a share of a total, due to or required of a person, group, state, or the like: *Each soldier received a daily quota of rations. The salesclerks failed to sell their quota of shoes.* **2.** a fixed or maximum number or proportion of a certain group or category of people that are to be admitted, as to a country. [From the Medieval Latin phrase *quota (pars)* meaning ''how great (a part),'' from the Latin word *quotus* meaning ''how many?'']

quot·a·ble (kwō′tə bəl) *adj.* suitable for or worth quoting.

quo·ta·tion (kwō tā′shən) *n.* **1.** the act of quoting. **2.** a person's words quoted or repeated exactly by another person: *The book contained quotations from many authors.* **3.** a statement of the current price offered or bid for a stock, bond, or commodity. **4.** the price so stated.

quotation mark, one of a pair of punctuation marks ('' '') used chiefly to indicate the beginning and end of a quotation. Single quotation marks (' ') are usually used to indicate a quotation within another quotation.

quote (kwōt) *v.,* **quot·ed, quot·ing.** —*v.t.* **1.** to repeat or reproduce the exact words of: *The newspapers quoted the president's speech. The author frequently quoted the Constitution.* **2.** to bring forward as an example or evidence: *The driving instructor quoted the statistics on automobile accidents to the class.* **3.** to state (a price) for a stock, bond, or commodity. **4.** to enclose in quotation marks. —*v.i.* to repeat or reproduce the exact words of another: *If you're going to quote, give credit to the author.* —*n. Informal.* **1.** see **quotation. 2.** see **quotation mark.** —**quot′er,** *n.*

quoth (kwōth) *v.i. Archaic.* said or spoke.

quo·tient (kwo′shənt) *n.* a number or algebraic expression obtained by dividing one number or algebraic expression by another. In 12 ÷ 4 − 3, 3 is the quotient.

q.v., which see; look in the place just mentioned. [Short for the Latin phrase *quod vide* meaning ''which see.'']

---

at; āpe; fär; câre; end; mē; it; īce; pîerce; hot; ōld; sông, fôrk; oil; out; up; ūse; rüle; pull; tûrn; chin; sing; shop; thin; this; hw in white; zh in treasure. The symbol ə stands for the unstressed vowel sound heard in about, taken, pencil, lemon, and circus.

Q

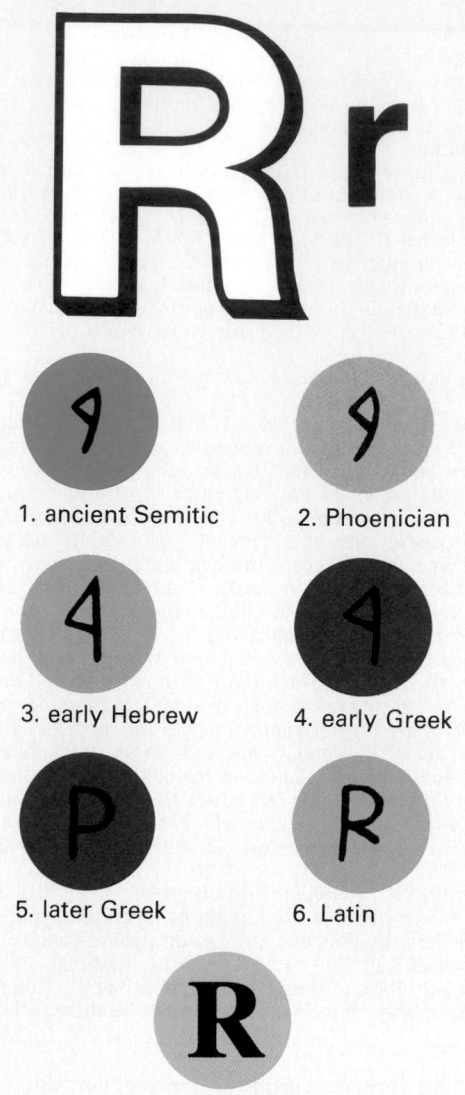

1. ancient Semitic
2. Phoenician
3. early Hebrew
4. early Greek
5. later Greek
6. Latin
7. English

R is the eighteenth letter of the English alphabet. The earliest ancestor of **R** was the letter *resh* (1), meaning "head" in the ancient Semitic alphabets. *Resh* continued to be written this way in the early Phoenician (2) and early Hebrew (3) alphabets. The ancient Greeks borrowed *resh* and called it *rho* (4). In ancient times, the Greeks wrote either from right to left or in alternating rows of right to left and left to right. Later, when they began to write from left to right, the shape of certain letters, including *rho*, was reversed (5). This new form of *rho*, which looked like our modern capital letter P, was adopted by the Romans (6). About 2,400 years ago, a stroke was added to the Latin form of *rho*, making it look very much like our modern capital letter **R** (7).

r, R (är) *n.*, *pl.* **r's, R's.** the eighteenth letter of the English alphabet.
  •**the three R's.** reading, writing, and arithmetic (humorously spelled *reading, 'riting, and 'rithmetic*).
r, roentgen.
R. 1. rabbi. **2.** Republican. **3.** river. **4.** road.
Ra (rä) *n.* a hawk-headed sun god of ancient Egypt.
Ra, the symbol for radium.
R.A., rear admiral.
rab·bi (rab'ī) *n.*, *pl.* **rab·bis** or **rab·bies.** a teacher of the Jewish religion who is usually the leader of a Jewish congregation. [From the Hebrew word *rabbī* meaning "my master," from the word *rabh* "great one, master" + the pronoun ending *-ī* "my."]
rab·bin·ate (rab'ə nit, rab'ə nāt') *n.* **1.** the office or term of office held by a rabbi. **2.** rabbis as a group.
rab·bin·i·cal (rə bin'i kəl) *adj.* of or relating to rabbis or their views, teachings, or writings.
rab·bit (rab'it) *n.* **1.** any of a group of mammals that have long ears, soft fur, and a short tail and move about by hopping. **2.** the fur of this animal.
rabbit ears *Informal.* an indoor television antenna consisting of two movable, and usually extendible, rods attached to a common base in the shape of a V.
rab·ble (rab'əl) *n.* **1.** a disorderly crowd; mob. **2. the rabble.** the common people. ▲ used to show contempt: *The Duke and Duchess refused to associate with the rabble.*
rab·ble-rous·er (rab'əl rou'zər) *n.* a person who tries to stir up people by exciting their fears, prejudices, or passions.
rab·id (rab'id) *adj.* **1.** showing too much zeal or enthusiasm in one's beliefs or actions; fanatical: *a rabid patriot. They are rabid football fans.* **2.** violent; raging; furious: *rabid with anger.* **3.** affected with rabies; mad: *a rabid fox.* —**rab'id·ly,** *adv.* —**rab'id·ness,** *n.*
ra·bies (rā'bēz) *n.* a viral disease of mammals, such as dogs and bats, that attacks the central nervous system and can be transmitted to humans by the bite of a rabid animal. Also, **hydrophobia.**
rac·coon (ra kün') *also,* **ra·coon.** *n.* **1.** a small tree-dwelling mammal of North and Central America, having brownish gray fur, black masklike facial markings, and a ringed tail. **2.** the fur of this animal.

race¹ *(def. 1)*

race¹ (rās) *n.* **1.** a contest to determine which contestant is fastest: *a running race, an automobile race.* **2.** any contest or competition: *a race for a political office.* —*v.,* **raced, rac·ing.** —*v.i.* **1.** to take part in a contest of speed: *We raced on our bicycles.* **2.** to run, move, or go rapidly: *They raced down five flights of stairs.* **3.** (of machinery) to run at high speed. —*v.t.* **1.** to try to go faster than; be in a contest of speed against: *I'll race you* to the front door. **2.** to cause to race: *We'll be racing sailboats tomorrow. The driver raced the engine of the car.* [From the Old Norse word *rās* meaning "running, race¹."]

race² (rās) *n.* **1.** a group of human beings having particular physical characteristics that are passed on from generation to generation. **2.** a group of persons sharing a common ancestry, history, nationality, or area of origin. **3.** a group of people sharing similar interests or habits. **4.** a group of animals or plants having particular characteristics that are passed on from one generation to another. [From the French word *race,* from the Italian word *razza* "a tribe, clan, race²."]

race·course (rās'kôrs') *n.* another word for **racetrack.**

race·horse (rās'hôrs') *n.* a horse that is bred and trained for racing.

ra·ceme (rā sēm', rə sēm') *n.* a simple arrangement of flowers on a stem, in which each flower grows on its own short stalk.

rac·er (rā'sər) *n.* **1.** a person or thing that races or takes part in a race, or is able to go very fast. **2.** any of several long, slender American snakes that are among the swiftest of snakes.

race·track (rās'trak') *n.* an area of ground for racing, usually oval in shape. Also, **racecourse.**

ra·cial (rā'shəl) *adj.* **1.** of, relating to, or characteristic of a race: *racial origins, racial traits.* **2.** of, relating to, or arising from relations between races: *racial prejudice, racial harmony.* —**ra'cial·ly,** *adv.*

rac·ism (rā'siz əm) *n.* **1.** a doctrine or belief that one race, especially one's own, is superior to another. **2.** a political policy or social system based on this. Also, **ra·cial·ism** (rā'shə liz'əm).

rac·ist (rā'sist) *n.* a person who believes in or supports racism. —*adj.* of or relating to racism.

rack¹ (rak) *n.* **1.** a framework or stand for hanging, showing, or storing things: *a coat rack, a display rack.* **2.** see **hayrack** *(def. 2).* **3.** an instrument of torture used to stretch a victim's body. **4.** a mechanical part with teeth on one surface that mesh with a toothed gear or wheel. —*v.t.* **1.** to cause to suffer mentally or physically; torment: *to be racked with pain.* **2.** to place in or on a rack. [From the Middle English word *rak* with the same meaning, perhaps from Old English.]

rack² (rak) *n.* **to go to rack and ruin.** to deteriorate; fall apart. [A form of *wrack.*]

rack·et¹ (rak'it) *n.* **1.** a loud or confusing noise; clamor. **2.** *Informal.* a dishonest scheme or activity for getting money by the use of bribery, extortion, fraud, or threats of violence. [Of uncertain origin.]

rack·et² (rak'it) *also,* **rac·quet.** *n.* **1.** a round or oval frame strung with a network of gut, nylon, or other material, and having a handle, used to strike a ball, as in tennis or squash. **2.** see **paddle¹** *(def. 2).* [From the Middle French word *raquette* with the same meaning, going back to the Arabic word *rāḥet* "the palm of the hand."]

rack·et·eer (rak'ə tîr') *n.* a person who organizes or takes part in a dishonest scheme or activity for getting money. —*v.i.* to organize or take part in a racket.

rac·on·teur (rak'ən tûr') *n.* a person who is skilled in telling stories. [From the French word *raconteur,* from the word *raconter* meaning "to tell," from the Old French prefix *re-* "again" + *aconter* "to tell, account."]

ra·coon (ra kün') another spelling of **raccoon.**

rac·quet (rak'it) another spelling of **racket².**

rac·quet·ball (rak'it bôl') *n.* a game similar to squash,

racket²
(def. 1)

played in a walled court with a strung racket that is shorter than a tennis racket.

rac·quets (rak'its) *n.* a game like squash, played in a court enclosed by four walls. ▲ used with a singular verb.

rac·y (rā'sē) *adj.,* **rac·i·er, rac·i·est. 1.** somewhat indecent or improper. **2.** full of spirit; spirited; lively: *a racy style of writing.* —**rac'i·ly,** *adv.* —**rac'i·ness,** *n.*

ra·dar (rā'där) *n.* a device used to locate and track distant objects by the reflection of radio waves. [Short for *ra*(dio) *d*(etecting) *a*(nd) *r*(anging).]

ra·di·al (rā'dē əl) *adj.* **1.** of, relating to, or arranged like rays or radii. **2.** having parts branching outward from a common center. —**ra'di·al·ly,** *adv.*

radial symmetry, the arrangement of similar body parts around a central point or axis, as in the starfish and sea anemone.

radial tire, a tire constructed from layers of material arranged at right angles to the direction in which the tire rolls, forming sides that flex more easily than those of a conventional tire.

ra·di·ance (rā'dē əns) *n.* the quality or state of being radiant. Also, **ra·di·an·cy** (rā'dē ən sē).

ra·di·ant (rā'dē ənt) *adj.* **1.** giving off rays of light or heat; shining brightly: *a radiant lamp.* **2.** beaming with joy, contentment, love, or the like: *a radiant smile, a radiant face.* **3.** made up of, having, or transmitted by radiation: *radiant heat.* —**ra'di·ant·ly,** *adv.*

radiant energy, energy transmitted in the form of waves, especially electromagnetic waves. X rays, visible light, heat, and radio waves are forms of radiant energy.

ra·di·ate (*v.,* rā'dē āt'; *adj.,* rā'di ət, rā'dē āt') *v.,* **ra·di·at·ed, ra·di·at·ing.** —*v.i.* **1.** to give off rays of light or heat. **2.** to issue in rays: *Heat radiates from the sun.* **3.** to move or branch outward from a center: *Streets radiated from the main square.* —*v.t.* **1.** to give off in rays: *The sun radiates light and heat.* **2.** to show (joy, contentment, love, or the like): *a face that radiates happiness.* —*adj.* **1.** having rays spreading out from a center: *a radiate flower.* **2.** radiating from a center.

ra·di·a·tion (rā'dē ā'shən) *n.* **1.** the process of giving off radiant energy in waves or particles. **2.** radiant energy given off in the form of waves or particles. **3.** the act or process of radiating.

ra·di·a·tor (rā'dē ā'tər) *n.* **1.** a heating device made up of a series of pipes or coils through which steam or hot water is made to circulate. **2.** a cooling device, as in an automobile engine. Water passes through it, losing heat quickly, and then circulates back into the engine.

rad·i·cal (rad'i kəl) *adj.* **1.** going to the root or origin; fundamental; basic: *to make a radical change in one's study habits.* **2.** favoring or supporting fundamental change, especially in political, social, and economic institutions. **3.** of or forming the root of a number or quantity. —*n.* **1.** a person who favors or supports fundamental change, as in political, social, and economic institutions. **2.** a group of atoms remaining connected and acting as a unit, often in the form of an ion, in chemical reactions. **3.** *Mathematics.* **a.** a root of a number or quantity. **b.** a radical sign. [From the Late Latin word *radicalis* meaning "having roots," from the Latin word *radix* "root, origin."] —**rad'i·cal·ly,** *adv.* —**rad'i·cal·ness,** *n.*

at; āpe; fär; câre; end; mē; it; īce; pîerce; hot; ōld; sông, fôrk; oil; out; up; ūse; rüle; pùll; tûrn; chin; sing; shop; thin; **th**is; hw in white; zh in treasure. The symbol ə stands for the unstressed vowel sound heard in about, taken, pencil, lemon, and circus.

R

rad·i·cal·ism (rad′i kə liz′əm) *n.* the support of fundamental change, as in political institutions.

radical sign *Mathematics.* the sign ($\sqrt{}$) placed above a number or an algebraic expression to show that the root of it is to be found. For example: $\sqrt[3]{8}$ = *the cube root of 8 = 2.*

rad·i·cand (rad′i kand′) *n.* the quantity under a radical sign: *9 is the radicand of $\sqrt{9}$.*

ra·di·i (rā′dē ī′) a plural of **radius.**

ra·di·o (rā′dē ō′) *n., pl.* **ra·di·os.** **1.** a means of communication involving the transmission of sound signals in the form of electromagnetic waves. **2.** an apparatus for receiving broadcasts or for sending and receiving messages by radio. **3.** radio broadcasting as a business or form of entertainment: *a career as an announcer in radio.* —*adj.* of or relating to a radio. —*v.,* **ra·di·oed, ra·di·o·ing.** —*v.t.* **1.** to send (a message) by radio. **2.** to send a radio message to. —*v.i.* to send a message by radio: *The pilot radioed for landing instructions.*

ra·di·o·ac·tive (rā′dē ō ak′tiv) *adj.* of, relating to, caused by, or showing radioactivity.

ra·di·o·ac·tiv·i·ty (rā′dē ō ak tiv′i tē) *n.* the giving off of energy in the form of alpha and beta particles and gamma rays from the nuclei of atoms during a process of disintegration, in which atoms of one element are changed into atoms of another element.

radio astronomy, the branch of astronomy that studies heavenly objects by means of the radio waves that they give off.

ra·di·o·car·bon (rā′dē ō kär′bən) *n.* See **carbon 14.**

radiocarbon dating, a technique for determining the age of organic materials, such as bones or fossils, by measuring the radioactivity of their carbon content.

radio frequency, electromagnetic frequency from about 10 kilohertz to several thousand megahertz, used especially in sending radio and television signals. —**ra′di·o·fre′quen·cy,** *adj.*

ra·di·o·gram (rā′dē ō gram′) *n.* a message sent by radio.

ra·di·o·graph (rā′dē ō graf′) *n.* a picture made on a sensitive surface by radiation other than visible light, especially by X rays. —*v.t.* to make a radiograph of.

ra·di·o·i·so·tope (rā′dē ō ī′sə tōp′) *n.* an isotope that produces radiation in the form of particles or gamma rays; a radioactive isotope. Radioisotopes are usually artificially produced and are used in biological and medical research and in some medical treatments.

ra·di·ol·o·gist (rā′dē ol′ə jist) *n.* a doctor who specializes in radiology.

ra·di·ol·o·gy (rā′dē ol′ə jē) *n.* the science that deals with the use of X rays and other forms of radiant energy in the diagnosis and treatment of diseases.

ra·di·om·e·ter (rā′dē om′i tər) *n.* **1.** a device for measuring light or other radiant energy, consisting of a glass tube containing four metal vanes blackened on one side and silvered on the other. Light or other radiant energy is absorbed by the blackened side and reflected by the other, causing the vanes to rotate. **2.** a device for measuring microwave radiation from the earth or heavenly bodies.

ra·di·o·sonde (rā′dē ō sond′) *n.* an instrument that is carried into the sky by a balloon to radio back information about meteorological conditions at high altitudes.

ra·di·o·tel·e·phone (rā′dē ō tel′ə fōn′) *n.* a telephone that uses radio waves to send sound.

ra·di·o·tel·e·scope (rā′dē ō tel′ə skōp′) *n.* a telescope that detects radio waves coming from sources in space.

radio wave, an electromagnetic wave within radio frequency.

rad·ish (rad′ish) *n., pl.* **rad·ish·es.** **1.** a fleshy red or white root that has a strong, biting taste and is usually eaten raw. **2.** the plant bearing this root.

ra·di·um (rā′dē əm) *n.* a white, highly radioactive metallic element found in pitchblende and other uranium ores. Symbol: **Ra** [Formed from the Latin word *radius* meaning "ray."]

ra·di·us (rā′dē əs) *n., pl.* **ra·di·i** or **ra·di·us·es.** **1.** a line going from the center to the outside of a circle or sphere. **2.** a circular area measured by the length of such a line: *There is no other house within a radius of three miles of here.* **3.** the shorter and thicker of the two bones of the lower arm, extending from the humerus to the wrist on the thumb side of the arm.

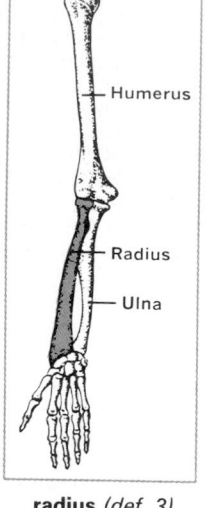

ra·don (rā′don) *n.* a colorless, radioactive gaseous element formed by the decay of radium. It is used in the treatment of cancer and is the heaviest known gas. Symbol: **Rn** [From *radium.*]

raf·fi·a (raf′ē ə) *n.* **1.** a strong fiber obtained from the leaves of a palm tree, used to make matting and baskets. **2.** the tree itself, found in Madagascar.

raf·fle (raf′əl) *n.* a lottery in which chances to win a prize are sold. —*v.t.,* **raf·fled, raf·fling.** to sell by a raffle: *The club raffled off a turkey.*

raft (raft) *n.* **1.** a flat platform that is made of logs, planks, or other similar

radius *(def. 3)*

materials which are fastened together, used for transportation on water. **2.** see **life raft.**

raft·er (raf′tər) *n.* one of the sloping beams that support a roof.

rag[1] (rag) *n.* **1.** a small piece of cloth, especially one that is torn or worn out. **2. rags.** old, worn, tattered clothing. [From the Middle English word *ragge* meaning "scrap of cloth," from Old Norse.]

rag[2] (rag) *v.t.,* **ragged, ragging.** *Slang.* **1.** to tease. **2.** to speak sharply to; scold. [Of uncertain origin.]

rafters

rag·a·muf·fin (rag′ə muf′in) *n.* a ragged, untidy person, especially a child.

rage (rāj) *n.* **1.** violent or uncontrolled anger; fury: *eyes flashing with rage.* **2.** a fit of violent anger: *to be in a rage.* **3.** great force or violence. **4.** a fad; fashion; craze. —*v.i.,* **raged, rag·ing.** **1.** to feel or show violent anger; be in a rage. **2.** to act or move with great force or violence: *The hurricane raged along the coast.*

rag·ged (rag′id) *adj.* **1.** worn into rags; tattered: *a ragged dress.* **2.** wearing tattered clothing: *a ragged beggar.* **3.** shaggy; unkempt: *ragged hair.* **4.** rough or uneven; jagged: *ragged cliffs.* —**rag′ged·ly,** *adv.* —**rag′ged·ness,** *n.*

rag·lan (rag′lən) *adj.* **1.** (of a sleeve) extending over the shoulder to the collar. **2.** having such sleeves: *a raglan coat.* [From the British general F. J. H. Somerset, Lord Raglan (1788–1855).]

ra·gout (ra gü′) *n.* a highly seasoned meat and vegetable stew.

rag·time (rag′tīm′) *n.* **1.** an American music related to early jazz, characterized by a steady, marching rhythm in the lower notes and syncopation in the upper notes or melody. **2.** the syncopated rhythm of such music.

rag·weed (rag′wēd′) *n.* any of several coarse weeds whose pollen is one of the major causes of hay fever.

rah (rä) *interj., n.* see **hurrah.**

raid (rād) *n.* **1.** a sudden, surprise entering of a place, as by the police, for the purpose of seizing illegal equipment or stolen goods and making arrests. **2.** a sudden attack by a small force of soldiers. —*v.t.* to make a raid on: *The police raided the building to seize gambling equipment.* —*v.i.* to take part in or lead a raid. —**raid′er,** *n.*

rail[1] (rāl) *n.* **1.** a long, narrow bar of wood, metal, or other material, resting horizontally on posts and used as a guard or support. **2.** a fence or railing. **3.** one of a pair of metal bars that make up a railroad track. **4.** a railroad as a means of transportation: *The company sent its products by rail.* —*v.t.* to provide or enclose with a rail or rails. [From the Old French word *reille* meaning "horizontal bar" or "ruler," from the Latin word *regula* "rule, ruler."]

rail[2] (rāl) *v.i.* to use scolding, bitter words; complain angrily or bitterly: *to rail against higher taxes.* [From the Old French word *raillier* "to mock."]

rail[3] (rāl) *n.* a small bird that has short wings, long toes, and a harsh cry, found in marshy areas. [From the Old French word *raale* meaning this bird.]

rail·ing (rā′ling) *n.* **1.** a fence or barrier made of a rail or rails. **2.** rails or the material for making rails.

rail·ler·y (rā′lə rē) *n., pl.* **rail·ler·ies.** good-natured teasing; banter.

rail·road (rāl′rōd′) *n., also,* **rail·way.** **1.** a permanent road laid with parallel metal rails fixed by ties and providing a track for trains.

rail[3]

2. an entire transportation system of such roads, including stations, trains, and property. **3.** the company that owns or manages such a system. —*v.t.* **1.** to transport by railroad. **2.** *Informal.* to rush or push through with great haste and without proper consideration: *The senators tried to railroad the bill through Congress.* **3.** *Slang.* to cause to be imprisoned on false charges or without a fair trial.

rail·way (rāl′wā′) *n.* **1.** another word for **railroad.** **2.** any set of rails for wheels.

rai·ment (rā′mənt) *n. Literary.* clothing; attire.

rain (rān) *n.* **1.** water condensed from vapor in the atmosphere, falling in drops from the sky to the earth: *Rain came through the open window.* **2.** a fall of rain; rainstorm or shower: *We were caught in the rain.* **3.** a heavy or rapid fall of anything: *a rain of missiles.* **4.** **the rains,** the rainy season, as in tropical climates. —*v.i.* **1.** (of rain) to fall: *It is raining hard.* **2.** to fall like rain: *Acorns rained down on us from the oak tree.* —*v.t.* to pour or send down like rain: *People rained confetti from windows onto the parade.*

·**to rain out,** to cause (an outdoor event) to be canceled or postponed because of rain.

rain·bow (rān′bō′) *n.* an arc of colored light showing all the colors of the spectrum in separate bands, seen in the sky opposite the sun, caused by the reflection and refraction of the sun's rays by water droplets in the air.

rain·coat (rān′kōt′) *n.* a water-repellent or waterproof coat for use when it rains.

rain date, an alternate date set for an outdoor event in case the event must be postponed because of rain.

rain·drop (rān′drop′) *n.* a drop of rain.

rain·fall (rān′fôl′) *n.* **1.** a fall or shower of rain. **2.** the amount of water falling in the form of rain, snow, sleet, or hail in a given area within a given time; precipitation.

rain forest, a dense, usually tropical forest in a region having a high annual rainfall.

rain·proof (rān′prüf′) *adj.* not letting rain in; shedding rain.

rain·storm (rān′stôrm′) *n.* a storm with rain.

rain·y (rā′nē) *adj.,* **rain·i·er, rain·i·est.** **1.** characterized by or full of rain: *a rainy night, rainy weather.* **2.** wet with rain: *rainy streets.* —**rain′i·ness,** *n.*

rainy day, a time of need: *to save money for a rainy day.*

raise (rāz) *v.t.,* **raised, rais·ing.** **1.** to move or cause to move to a higher position: *to raise your arms above your head.* **2.** to cause to rise or appear: *The bee sting raised a bump on my leg.* **3.** to move to a higher rank, position, or dignity: *The young officer was raised to the rank of major.* **4.** to increase, as in amount or volume: *to raise taxes, to raise one's voice in anger.* **5.** to gather together; collect: *The club needs to raise money.* **6.** to breed or grow: *The farmer raises wheat.* **7.** to bring up; rear: *The young couple wants to raise a family.* **8.** to bring up for consideration or discussion: *The speaker raised an important question.* **9.** to stir up; arouse: *to raise a commotion.* **10.** to cause to rise with yeast: *to raise dough.* **11.** to build; construct: *to raise a barn.* —*n.* **1.** the act of raising. **2.** an increase in amount: *a raise in salary.* —**rais′er,** *n.*

rai·sin (rā′zin) *n.* a dried sweet grape.

ra·jah (rä′jə) *also,* **ra·ja.** *n.* a ruler or prince in India or the East Indies.

rake[1] (rāk) *n.* a tool having a long handle with teeth or prongs attached at one end, used for gathering together such things as leaves or hay, or for smoothing surfaces, as clumps of soil. —*v.,* **raked, rak·ing.** —*v.t.* **1.** to gather or smooth with a rake. **2.** to collect in a large amount; amass: *to rake in money, to rake leaves.* **3.** to search carefully and thoroughly: *I raked the bureau drawers for the lost key.* **4.** to bring to attention: *The reporter raked up an old scandal.* **5.** to direct gunfire along the length of. —*v.i.* to use a rake: *I've been raking in the yard all morning.* [From the Old English word *raca* meaning this tool.]

rake[2] (rāk) *n.* an immoral man who seeks only pleasure. [Short for the obsolete *rakehell* with the same meaning, perhaps from the Middle English word *rakel* meaning "unruly, disobedient, rash[1]."]

rake[3] (rāk) *n.* a slope from the vertical, as of the mast of a ship. [Of uncertain origin.]

rak·ish[1] (rā′kish) *adj.* **1.** dashing or stylish; jaunty: *a hat worn at a rakish angle.* **2.** suggesting speed; streamlined, as a boat. [*Rake[3]* + *-ish.*]

rak·ish[2] (rā′kish) *adj.* like a rake; immoral and pleasure-loving. [*Rake[2]* + *-ish.*]

ral·ly[1] (ral′ē) *v.,* **ral·lied, ral·ly·ing.** —*v.t.* **1.** to bring together into order again; gather again: *The general rallied the scattered troops.* **2.** to bring together for a common purpose; assemble: *The club president rallied the members for the meeting.* —*v.i.* **1.** to come together into order again: *The team quickly rallied.* **2.** to unite or come together for a common purpose. **3.** to come to the aid or support of a cause or person: *The public rallied behind the president.* **4.** to recover strength or energy: *The patient rallied overnight.* **5.** in tennis and similar games, to exchange a series of strokes before a point is made. —*n., pl.* **ral·lies.** **1.** the act of rallying. **2.** a meeting for a common purpose: *a political rally.* **3.** in tennis and similar games, a series of strokes exchanged before a point

at; āpe; fär; câre; end; mē; it; īce; pierce; hot; ōld; sông, fôrk; oil; out; up; ūse; rüle; pùll; tûrn; chin; sing; shop; thin; **th**is; hw in white; zh in treasure. The symbol ə stands for the unstressed vowel sound heard in about, taken, pencil, lemon, and circus.

is made. [From the French word *rallier* meaning "to muster, assemble."]

ral·ly² (ral′ē) *v.t., v.i.,* **ral·lied, ral·ly·ing.** to tease good-naturedly; banter. [From the French word *railler* meaning "to mock," from the Old French word *raillier* "to mock."]

ram (ram) *n.* **1.** a male sheep. **2.** a device used to batter, crush, or force something, such as a battering ram. —*v.,* **rammed, ram·ming.** —*v.t.* **1.** to batter or strike against with great force; butt against: *The two ships tried to ram each other.* **2.** to force or drive down or into place: *to ram a tent stake into the ground.* **3.** to stuff or cram: *We rammed all the junk into a closet.* —*v.i.* to strike against something with great force; collide: *The last car rammed into the car ahead.* —**ram′mer,** *n.*

RAM (ram) *n.* a type of computer memory that stores data temporarily. The time required to store or retrieve data in RAM does not depend on the position of the data in the memory. [Short for *r*(andom)-*a*(ccess) *m*(emory).]

Ram·a·dan (ram′ə dän′) *n.* **1.** the ninth month of the Muslim year, a period observed by fasting each day from sunrise to sunset. **2.** the fasting observed during this period.

ram·ble (ram′bəl) *v.i.,* **ram·bled, ram·bling. 1.** to go about or move about aimlessly; roam. **2.** to talk or write in a confused and disordered way: *The speaker rambled on and never came to the point.* —*n.* a pleasant stroll or walk.

ram·bler (ram′blər) *n.* **1.** a person or thing that rambles. **2.** any of certain climbing roses with long, flexible stems.

ram·bunc·tious (ram bungk′shəs) *adj.* wild and boisterous: *a rambunctious child.* —**ram·bunc′tious·ly,** *adv.*

ram·i·fi·ca·tion (ram′ə fi kā′shən) *n.* **1.** the act or process of dividing or spreading into branches. **2.** something, such as an effect or consequence, that results from a situation or statement: *What are the ramifications of this plan?*

ram·i·fy (ram′ə fī′) *v.i.,* **ram·i·fied, ram·i·fy·ing.** to divide or spread into branches or as if into branches.

ramp (ramp) *n.* **1.** a sloping passageway or roadway connecting different levels. **2.** a movable staircase for entering or leaving an airplane.

ram·page (*n.,* ram′pāj; *v.,* ram′pāj, ram pāj′) *n.* a fit of violent or reckless behavior or action: *The bear went on a rampage and knocked over tents at the campsite.* —*v.i.,* **ram·page, ram·pag·ing.** to behave in a violent or reckless way; rage.

ramp *(def. 2)*

ramp·ant (ram′pənt) *adj.* **1.** thick or abundant; luxuriant: *a rampant growth of wild flowers.* **2.** acting or spreading without control; unchecked; unrestrained: *Flu was rampant in the town.* **3.** (of an animal on a coat of arms) rearing up on the hind legs and with the head and body in profile: *a lion rampant.* —**ramp′ant·ly,** *adv.*

ram·part (ram′pärt) *n.* **1.** a bank of earth built up around a fort or castle and sometimes supporting a wall, used for defense. **2.** anything that serves as a defense or protection.

ram·rod (ram′rod′) *n.* **1.** a rod used to ram the charge down the barrel of a gun that is loaded through the muzzle. **2.** a rod used to clean the barrel of a gun.

ram·shack·le (ram′shak′əl) *adj.* likely or seemingly ready to collapse; dilapidated; rickety: *a ramshackle old house.*

ran (ran) the past tense of **run.**

ranch (ranch) *n., pl.* **ranch·es. 1.** a large farm, especially in the western United States, used to raise large herds of cattle, sheep, or horses. **2.** any farm devoted to raising a particular crop or animal: *a goat ranch.* —*v.i.* to manage or work on a ranch. [From the American Spanish word *rancho* meaning "ranch," from the Spanish word *rancho* "hut, camp" or "small farm."]

ranch·er (ran′chər) *n.* a person who owns or works on a ranch. [From the Spanish word *ranchero,* from the word *rancho* meaning "ranch" + the suffix *-ero* "one who does," from the Latin suffix *-arius* "-ary."]

ran·cid (ran′sid) *adj.* having the unpleasant odor or taste of spoiled oil or fat: *rancid butter.* —**ran′cid·ly,** *adv.* —**ran′cid·ness,** *n.*

ran·cor (rang′kər) *n.* deep or bitter resentment; hatred; spite.

ran·cor·ous (rang′kər əs) *adj.* deeply or bitterly resentful; spiteful. —**ran′cor·ous·ly,** *adv.* —**ran′cor·ous·ness,** *n.*

ran·dom (ran′dəm) *adj.* lacking a definite plan, purpose, or pattern; happening by chance; unplanned; haphazard: *The storm left a random assortment of trees knocked down. The children's drawings seemed to be random blotches until I looked closer.* —**ran′dom·ly,** *adv.* —**ran′dom·ness,** *n.*

·**at random.** with no definite plan or purpose: *While waiting for the dentist, I picked a magazine at random from the pile.*

ran·dom–ac·cess memory (ran′dəm ak′ses) see **RAM.**

rang (rang) the past tense of **ring².**

range (rānj) *n.* **1.** the limits between which something varies: *There is a wide range in prices for television sets.* **2.** the area in which something can act or be effective: *The airplane flew beyond our range of vision. The child's range of knowledge is still limited.* **3.** the greatest distance that a gun, cannon, or other similar weapon can fire a projectile. **4.** the greatest distance that a plane, ship, or other vehicle can travel without refueling. **5.** a place set aside for shooting practice or for testing rockets and missiles. **6.** a large area of open land over which livestock roam and graze. **7.** a row or series, especially of mountains. **8.** a large kitchen appliance having burners and an oven: *a cooking range.* **9.** a region in which a particular plant or animal normally lives. —*v.,* **ranged, rang·ing.** —*v.t.* **1.** to place in a particular order; arrange: *The librarian ranged the books on the shelf.* **2.** to place in a particular position or group. **3.** to move or wander over (an area): *Cattle ranged the prairie.* —*v.i.* **1.** to vary between certain limits: *The price for that bicycle ranges between $75 and $125.* **2.** to wander or roam: *The cattle ranged over thousands of acres belonging to the huge ranch.* **3.** to stretch out in a line; extend: *Trees ranged along the road.* **4.** (of plants and animals) to live or grow in a region.

rang·er (rān′jər) *n.* **1.** see **forest ranger.** **2.** an officer assigned to patrol a region to maintain law and order. **3.** a person or thing that ranges.

rang·y (rān′jē) *adj.,* **rang·i·er, rang·i·est.** having long legs and a slender body: *a rangy youth.*

rank¹ (rangk) *n.* **1.** relative position or standing: *to have a high rank in one's class at school.* **2.** position or grade: *the rank of captain.* **3.** high position, standing, or class: *The cabinet members are officials of rank.* **4.** a line or row of soldiers standing side by side in close order. **5. ranks. a.** the common soldiers or general body of a group, as distinct from the officers. **b.** an army. **6.** *Chess.* any row of squares running across the board. —*v.t.* **1.** to arrange in a row or rows: *to rank soldiers.* **2.** to assign a position to; classify: *to rank students according to their grades.* **3.** to take precedence over;

outrank: *Lieutenants rank sergeants.* —*v.i.* to have a certain rank or position: *Shakespeare ranks high among writers.* [From the Old French word *ranc* meaning "a row¹, series," of Germanic origin.]

rank² (rangk) *adj.* **1.** growing thickly and unchecked: *a rank growth of grass.* **2.** having a strong, bad smell or taste: *rank pork, rank cigars.* **3.** utter or complete: *a rank liar.* [From the Middle English word *rank* meaning "fierce, proud," from the Old English word *ranc* "proud, showy."] —**rank′ly,** *adv.* —**rank′ness,** *n.*

rank and file 1. the common soldiers or enlisted people of an army, as distinguished from the officers. **2.** the people who make up a group, as distinguished from the leaders: *the rank and file of organized labor.*

rank·ing (rang′king) *adj.* **1.** of a high rank, as in seniority: *After a long and distinguished career in Congress, the senator had become a ranking member of the committee.* **2.** outstanding; prominent; foremost: *That playwright is one of the ranking figures in literature.*

ran·kle (rang′kəl) *v.,* **ran·kled, ran·kling.** —*v.t.* to irritate, hurt, or anger (someone) continuously. —*v.i.* to irritate, hurt, or anger: *The unkind remark rankled in my mind.*

ran·sack (ran′sak′) *v.t.* **1.** to search thoroughly: *to ransack your pockets looking for change.* **2.** to search through for valuables: *Thieves ransacked the house.*

ran·som (ran′səm) *n.* **1.** the release of a person or property for a price: *to hold someone for ransom.* **2.** the price paid or demanded. —*v.t.* **1.** to obtain the release of by paying a certain price. **2.** to release upon receiving payment of ransom.

rant (rant) *v.i.* to speak in a wild, excited, and loud way; rave. —*n.* wild, excited, and loud speech or way of speaking.

rap¹ (rap) *n.* **1.** a quick, sharp, or light knock or tap. **2.** *Slang.* punishment or blame, especially a prison sentence: *to take the rap for something you didn't do.* —*v.,* **rapped, rap·ping.** —*v.i.* to knock or tap sharply: *to rap at a door.* —*v.t.* **1.** to knock or tap sharply: *to rap a table with a pencil.* **2.** to say sharply: *to rap out a reply.* [From the Middle English word *rappe* meaning "a blow, knock," perhaps of Scandinavian origin.]

rap² (rap) *n. Informal.* the least bit: *I don't care a rap about sports.* [Of uncertain origin.]

rap³ (rap) *v.i.,* **rapped, rap·ping.** *Slang.* to discuss openly and informally: *We rapped for a few hours about sports and music.* —*adj. Slang.* involving open, informal discussion: *The students had a rap session in the dormitory, discussing politics.* —*n.* **1.** *Slang.* open and informal conversation or discussion. **2.** a style of popular music in which rhyming lyrics are spoken in a rapid, rhythmical way, set to a simple, repetitive beat. Also (def. 2), **rap music.** [Perhaps short for *repartee.*]

ra·pa·cious (rə pā′shəs) *adj.* **1.** wanting more than one's share; grasping; greedy: *a rapacious embezzler.* **2.** (of animals) living on live prey; predatory. **3.** given to taking by force; plundering: *rapacious pirates.* —**ra·pa′cious·ly,** *adv.* —**ra·pa′cious·ness,** *n.*

ra·pac·i·ty (rə pas′i tē) *n.* the quality of being rapacious.

rape¹ (rāp) *n.* **1.** the crime of forcing a person to do a sexual act against his or her will. **2.** a seizing and carrying off by force. —*v.t.,* **raped, rap·ing.** to force to do a sexual act. [From the Anglo-Norman word *raper* meaning "to abduct or rape," from the Latin word *rapere* "to seize, ravish, plunder."]

rape² (rāp) *n.* a plant whose leaves are used as fodder and whose seeds yield an oil that is used as a lubricant. [From the Latin word *rapum* meaning this plant.]

rap·id (rap′id) *adj.* moving or acting with great speed;

kayaking down **rapids**

swift: *a rapid pace, rapid development, a rapid worker.* —*n. usually,* **rapids.** a part of a river where the current is swift, caused by a steep descent of the riverbed. —**rap′id·ly,** *adv.* —**rap′id·ness,** *n.*

rapid eye movement, see REM.

rap·id–fire (rap′id fīr′) *adj.* **1.** (of guns) firing shots in rapid succession. **2.** happening quickly, one after another: *rapid-fire questions.*

ra·pid·i·ty (rə pid′i tē) *n.* the state or quality of being rapid; quickness.

rapid transit, a system of fast-moving public transportation in an urban area, such as a subway or train system.

ra·pi·er (rā′pē ər) *n.* a long, light sword having a sharp point, used for thrusting.

rap·ine (rap′in) *n.* the act of seizing and carrying off property belonging to another; plunder; pillage.

rap·port (ra pôr′) *n.* a relationship characterized by harmony or close agreement: *The teacher had good rapport with all the students.*

rap·proche·ment (ra prōsh män′) *n.* the establishing or renewing of friendly relations, as between nations.

rap·scal·lon (rap skal′yən) *n.* a rascal; rogue; scamp.

rapt (rapt) *adj.* **1.** carried away with joy or delight; enraptured. **2.** deeply absorbed: *I was so rapt in my book that I didn't hear your question.*

rap·ture (rap′chər) *n.* a feeling of great happiness, delight, or joy.

rap·tur·ous (rap′chər əs) *adj.* showing or feeling rapture. —**rap′tur·ous·ly,** *adv.*

rare¹ (râr) *adj.,* **rar·er, rar·est. 1.** seldom happening, seen, or found: *the rare experience of seeing an eclipse, a rare white peacock.* **2.** unusually fine or valuable: *a rare taste in art.* **3.** having little density; thin: *The air is rare at high altitudes.* [From the Latin word *rarus* meaning "thin, scattered" or "scarce."]

rare² (râr) *adj.,* **rar·er, rar·est.** (of meat) cooked for a short period of time. [From the Old English word *hrēr* with the same meaning.]

rare·bit (râr′bit) *n.* see **Welsh rabbit.**

rare–earth element (râr′ûrth′) any of the metallic elements with atomic numbers from 57 through 71. Also, **rare-earth metal.**

---

at; āpe; fär; câre; end; mē; it; īce; pîerce; hot; ōld; sông, fôrk; oil; out; up; ūse; rüle; pull; tûrn; chin; sing; shop; thin; this; hw in white; zh in treasure. The symbol ə stands for the unstressed vowel sound heard in about, taken, pencil, lemon, and circus.

R

rar·e·fy (râr′ə fī′) v., **rar·e·fied, rar·e·fy·ing.** —v.t. **1.** to make thinner or less dense: *to rarefy air.* **2.** to refine or purify: *to rarefy one's wit.* —v.i. to become thinner or less dense.

rare·ly (râr′lē) adv. not often; seldom: *We rarely go to the movies.*

rar·i·ty (râr′i tē) n., pl. **rar·i·ties. 1.** a person or thing that is rare: *Rain is a rarity in the desert.* **2.** the state or fact of being rare: *the rarity of trees in the city, the rarity of the air in the mountains.*

ras·cal (ras′kəl) n. **1.** a mischievous, playful person. **2.** a low, mean, dishonest person; scoundrel.

ras·cal·i·ty (ras kal′i tē) n., pl. **ras·cal·i·ties. 1.** the character or behavior of a rascal. **2.** a dishonest act.

ras·cal·ly (ras′kə lē) adj. of or characteristic of a rascal. —adv. in a rascally manner.

rash[1] (rash) adj. acting with or characterized by too much haste; reckless: *a rash youngster, a rash decision.* [From the Middle English word *rashe* meaning "unrestrained, rash[1]," probably from Old English.] —**rash′ly,** adv. —**rash′ness,** n.

rash[2] (rash) n., pl. **rash·es. 1.** a breaking out of spots on the skin. **2.** a number of related incidents occurring in a brief span: *a rash of burglaries in the neighborhood.* [From the obsolete French *rache* meaning "scurf," probably going back to the Latin word *rasus,* past participle of *radere* "to scratch."]

rash·er (rash′ər) n. a slice of bacon for frying or broiling.

rasp (rasp) v.t. **1.** to scrape or grate with a rough tool, such as a file. **2.** to grate upon; irritate: *The loud noise rasped my nerves.* **3.** to say in a rough, grating voice: *The officer rasped a command to the recruits.* —v.i. to make a rough, grating sound. —n. **1.** a rough, grating sound. **2.** a coarse file with raised, pointed projections, used on wood.

rasp·ber·ry (raz′ber′ē, raz′bə rē) n., pl. **rasp·ber·ries. 1.** the sweet red fruit of any of several plants of the rose family. **2.** the prickly plant that bears this fruit. **3.** *Slang.* a sound of disapproval or contempt made by vibrating the tongue between the lips.

raspberries

rasp·y (ras′pē) adj., **rasp·i·er, rasp·i·est.** rough; grating: *The sore throat left me with a raspy voice.*

rat (rat) n. **1.** a rodent similar to a mouse but larger, having a long snout, rounded ears, and a long, slender tail. Rats are found throughout most of the world. **2.** *Slang.* a sneaky, low person who cannot be trusted. —v.i., **rat·ted, rat·ting. 1.** to hunt for rats. **2.** *Slang.* to tell on; betray.

ra·tan (ra tan′) another spelling of **rattan.**

ratch·et (rach′it) n. **1.** a mechanism consisting of a wheel whose slanted teeth are caught by a pawl, allowing the wheel to revolve in one direction only. **2.** the pawl or the wheel of such a mechanism.

rate (rāt) n. **1.** an amount or number in relation to units of measure or a standard: *a rate of sixty miles per hour.* **2.** price or charge per unit, as of a service: *telephone rates.* **3.** a certain rank or class: *Your work is of the first rate.* —v., **rat·ed, rat·ing.** —v.t. **1.** to

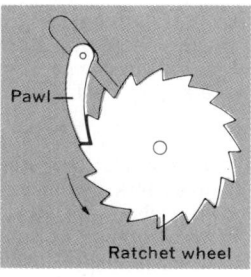
Pawl

Ratchet wheel

ratchet

estimate or set the value of: *to rate a movie as poor.* **2.** to place in a certain class or rank: *to be rated first among college football teams.* **3.** to consider; regard: *I rate this a very successful day.* **4.** *Informal.* to deserve; merit: *The manager thinks that you rate a raise.* —v.i. to have a certain rank or class.

·at any rate. in any case; at least.

rath·er (rath′ər) adv. **1.** more readily or willingly: *I would rather stay home than go out tonight.* **2.** more properly; instead: *They, rather than we, deserved to win.* **3.** more correctly: *The airplane is arriving at noon or, rather, at 12:15 p.m.* **4.** somewhat: *It is rather cold out.* **5.** on the contrary: *It is not raining; rather, the sun has come out.* —interj. *British.* certainly.

rat·i·fi·ca·tion (rat′ə fi kā′shən) n. the act of ratifying or the state of being ratified.

rat·i·fy (rat′ə fī′) v.t., **rat·i·fied, rat·i·fy·ing.** to consent to officially; approve: *Congress ratified the trade agreement.* —**rat′i·fi′er,** n.

rat·ing (rā′ting) n. **1.** a certain rank or grade: *That television show has a high rating.* **2.** an estimate of the financial position of a person or business: *a good credit rating.*

ra·ti·o (rā′shē ō′) n., pl. **ra·ti·os. 1.** a comparison between two things; proportion: *The ratio of girls to boys in the class is four to three.* **2.** *Mathematics.* the proportional relationship between two numbers or algebraic expressions expressed as a quotient. The ratio of 3 to 7 is written 3:7 or ³⁄₇.

ra·tion (rash′ən, rā′shən) n. **1.** a fixed portion or share. **2.** the daily amount of food allowed, as for a soldier. **3. rations.** food. —v.t. **1.** to give out in portions: *After the flood, food and clothes were rationed to the victims.* **2.** to supply with rations: *to ration an army.* **3.** to limit to fixed portions: *The government rationed meat during the war.*

ra·tion·al (rash′ə nəl) adj. **1.** based on or conforming to reason; sensible: *Use rational arguments to support your opinions.* **2.** able to think clearly; sane. **3.** having the ability to reason: *Humans are rational beings.* **4.** *Mathematics.* of or relating to a rational number. —**ra′tion·al·ly,** adv.

ra·tion·ale (rash′ə nal′) n. a reasonable or logical basis.

ra·tion·al·ism (rash′ə nə liz′əm) n. the practice or doctrine of depending on reason alone as the authority or guide for one's opinion, belief, or conduct.

ra·tion·al·i·ty (rash′ə nal′i tē) n. the quality or state of being rational.

ra·tion·al·ize (rash′ə nə līz′) v.t., **ra·tion·al·ized, ra·tion·al·iz·ing. 1.** to explain (one's behavior) in a way that seems reasonable but is probably untrue: *to rationalize cheating by saying that everyone else cheats.* **2.** to explain in a rational way. —**ra′tion·al·i·za′tion,** n. —**ra′tion·al·iz′er,** n.

rational number, a real number that can be expressed as a quotient of two integers or as an integer. ¾ and 5 are rational numbers.

rat·line (rat′lin) *also,* **rat·lin.** n. one of the small ropes stretching horizontally across the shrouds of a ship, used as a ladder.

rat race *Slang.* any activity, especially a competitive pattern of work, that is frantic or seemingly endless or that causes much stress: *Twelve hours of work a day can turn a good job into a rat race.*

rat·tan (ra tan′) *also,* **ra·tan.** n. **1.** the long, thin stems of a tropical palm tree, used for mats, baskets, wicker chairs, and other products. **2.** the tree having these stems. **3.** a cane or switch made from these stems.

rat·ter (rat′ər) n. an animal, such as a dog or cat, that catches rats.

rat·tle (rat'əl) v., **rat·tled, rat·tling.** —v.i. **1.** to make a quick series of short, sharp sounds: *The doors and windows rattled when the wind blew against the house.* **2.** to move with such sounds; clatter: *The old car rattled over the cobblestones.* **3.** to talk quickly and aimlessly; chatter: *The child rattled on.* —v.t. **1.** to cause to rattle. **2.** to say quickly: *to rattle off answers.* **3.** to confuse; embarrass: *to be rattled by one's own mistake.* —n. **1.** a quick series of short, sharp sounds. **2.** an object, especially a baby's toy, that makes a rattling noise when shaken. **3.** a series of rings of horny tissue at the end of a rattlesnake's tail.

rat·tler (rat'lər) n. **1.** a person or thing that rattles. **2.** a rattlesnake.

rat·tle·snake (rat'əl snāk') n. any of a group of poisonous American snakes having a series of rings of horny tissue at the end of the tail that rattle when shaken.

rat·tle·trap (rat'əl trap') n. anything old and rattling, such as an old car.

rau·cous (rô'kəs) adj. **1.** harsh; grating: *a raucous voice.* **2.** disorderly; rowdy: *The raucous party kept the neighborhood awake.* —**rau'cous·ly,** adv. —**rau'cous·ness,** n.

rattlesnake

rav·age (rav'ij) v., **rav·aged, rav·ag·ing.** —v.t. to lay waste; destroy: *The fire ravaged the town.* —v.i. to lay waste; be destructive. —n. a destructive action or its result: *The ravages of hunger could be seen in the faces of the poor.* —**rav'ag·er,** n.

rave (rāv) v.i., **raved, rav·ing.** **1.** to talk in a wild or crazy way. **2.** to talk with much or too much enthusiasm: *to rave about a new car.* —n. **1.** the act of raving. **2.** very enthusiastic approval or recommendation. —adj. very enthusiastic or approving: *The new television show received rave reviews.*

rav·el (rav'əl) v., **rav·eled, rav·el·ing;** also, British, **rav·elled, rav·el·ling.** —v.t. to cause (cloth or rope) to separate into loose threads; fray. —v.i. to become raveled; fray. —n. a loose thread or raveled part.

rav·en (rā'vən) n. a bird similar to a crow but larger, having glossy black feathers and a harsh cry. —adj. having a glossy black color.

rav·en·ing (rav'ə ning) adj. greedy; rapacious.

rav·en·ous (rav'ə nəs) adj. **1.** extremely hungry; famished. **2.** greedy; rapacious: *The ravenous mob pillaged the town.* —**rav'en·ous·ly,** adv.

raven

ra·vine (rə vēn') n. a deep, narrow valley, especially one worn by running water.

rav·ing (rā'ving) adj. **1.** wild; frenzied: *a raving lunatic.* **2.** Informal. outstanding; extraordinary: *a raving beauty.* —n. wild talk: *the raving of a delirious patient.*

rav·i·o·li (rav'ē ō'lē) n. a food made of casings of pasta filled with chopped meat, cheese, or other filling, boiled and served with a tomato sauce. ▲ used with a singular or plural verb.

rav·ish (rav'ish) v.t. **1.** to seize and carry off by force. **2.** to rape. **3.** to carry away with joy; enrapture. —**rav'ish·er,** n. —**rav'ish·ment,** n.

rav·ish·ing (rav'i shing) adj. delightful; enchanting. —**rav'ish·ing·ly,** adv.

raw (rô) adj. **1.** uncooked: *raw meat.* **2.** not refined or processed; in a natural state: *raw cotton, raw milk.* **3.** having the skin rubbed or worn off: *a raw wound.* **4.** having no experience or training: *a raw recruit.*

5. damp and cold: *raw weather.* **6.** very unfair or harsh: *a raw deal.* —**raw'ly,** adv. —**raw'ness,** n.

raw·boned (rô'bōnd') adj. having little flesh; gaunt.

raw·hide (rô'hīd') n. **1.** the untanned hide of cattle or other animals. **2.** a rope or whip made of such hide.

raw material, material not yet refined, manufactured, or processed: *Wood is the raw material of paper.*

ray[1] (rā) n. **1.** a narrow beam of light or other radiant energy: *the rays of the sun.* **2.** one of a group of lines coming from a common center. **3.** something projecting from a common center, such as an arm of a starfish. **4.** a very small amount; trace: *a ray of hope.* [From the Old French word *rai* meaning "a beam of light," from the Latin word *radius* "a shaft, beam of light."]

ray[2] (rā) n. any of a number of flat fish, related to sharks, that have a skeleton of cartilage rather than of bone. [From the Old French word *rai* meaning this fish, from the Latin word *raia* meaning this fish.]

ray·on (rā'on) n. **1.** a synthetic fiber made from cellulose. **2.** cloth or thread made of rayon.

raze (rāz) v.t., **razed, raz·ing.** to tear down; demolish: *The city razed the old buildings to make room for a park.*

ra·zor (rā'zər) n. an instrument or device used for shaving off or cutting hair.

razz (raz) v.t. Slang. to make fun of; ridicule.

Rb, the symbol for rubidium.

rbi, r.b.i. run batted in; runs batted in.

R.C. 1. Red Cross. **2.** Roman Catholic.

Rd., rd., road.

R.D., rural delivery.

RDA, the amount of a vitamin, mineral, or other nutrient that must be consumed daily to meet the nutritional needs of an average person. [Abbreviation of *r*(ecommended) *d*(aily) *a*(llowance) or *r*(ecommended) *d*(ietary) *a*(llowance).]

re[1] (rā) n. Music. **1.** the second note of the major scale. **2.** the note D. [From the Italian word *re* as the name of this note.]

re[2] (rē) prep. about; concerning. [From the Latin phrase *in re* meaning "about (this) thing," from the word *res* "thing."]

Re, the symbol for rhenium.

re- prefix **1.** again: *re-count.* **2.** back: *repel.* [From the Old French prefix *re-*, from the Latin prefix *re-* with the same meanings.]

Language Note

To understand the meaning of a word that begins with **re-** but is not defined in this dictionary, add the word "again" to the meaning of the basic word. For example, *reheat* means "heat again" and *rediscover* means "discover again."

reach (rēch) v.t. **1.** to arrive at; get as far as; come to: *We reached the house after driving for several hours.* **2.** to touch or grasp: *The small child was not able to reach the dish on the shelf.* **3.** to extend to: *Television reaches almost all American homes.* **4.** to affect: *The last act of the play really reached the audience.* **5.** to take hold of and pass: *Reach me that screwdriver.* **6.** to get in touch

at; āpe; fär; câre; end; mē; it; īce; pîerce; hot; ōld; sông, fôrk; oil; out; up; ūse; rüle; pull; tûrn; chin; sing; shop; thin; this; hw in white; zh in treasure. The symbol ə stands for the unstressed vowel sound heard in about, taken, pencil, lemon, and circus.

with; contact: *I tried to reach you by telephone.* —*v.i.*
1. to stretch the arm or hand out, as to touch or grasp: *I reached toward the ceiling.* **2.** to stretch or extend: *The drapes reached from ceiling to floor.* —*n., pl.* **reach·es.**
1. the act of reaching or stretching out. **2.** the extent or distance covered in reaching: *A person would have to have a long reach to touch that branch.* **3.** the extent or amount that a person is able to understand or do; range: *Choose a goal within your reach.*

re·act (rē akt′) *v.i.* **1.** to act in response to something; respond: *The kitten reacts to kindness by purring.* **2.** to act in opposition: *to react against a parent's strictness.* **3.** to act in return: *You and your friends are constantly reacting to each other.* **4.** to undergo a chemical reaction.

re·ac·tant (rē ak′tənt) *n.* a substance that changes chemically during a reaction.

re·ac·tion (rē ak′shən) *n.* **1.** an action in response to something: *What was your friends' reaction when they saw your new coat?* **2.** a political or social tendency to return to a former condition or state of affairs: *During the period of political reaction, the monarchy returned to power.* **3.** *Chemistry.* a process in which substances are changed chemically into new substances. **4.** *Physics.* a force equal to but opposing the force that produces it.

re·ac·tion·ar·y (rē ak′shə ner′ē) *adj.* of, relating to, or favoring a return to a former political or social condition or state of affairs. —*n., pl.* **re·ac·tion·ar·ies.** a person who favors political and social reaction.

re·ac·ti·vate (rē ak′tə vāt′) *v.t.,* **re·ac·ti·vat·ed, re·ac·ti·vat·ing.** to make active again. —**re·ac·ti·va′tion,** *n.*

re·ac·tive (rē ak′tiv) *adj.* **1.** tending to react. **2.** relating to or characterized by reaction.

re·ac·tor (rē ak′tər) *n.* see **nuclear reactor.**

read (rēd) *v.,* **read** (red), **read·ing.** —*v.t.* **1.** to look at and understand the meaning of (something written or printed): *to read a magazine.* **2.** to say aloud (something written or printed): *to read bedtime stories to children.* **3.** to understand letters or symbols in (a foreign language): *I learned to read French.* **4.** to get the meaning of; understand: *to read someone's thoughts.* **5.** to give or register (information): *The speedometer read sixty miles per hour.* **6.** *British.* to study: *to read law.* —*v.i.* **1.** to understand something written or printed: *The children haven't learned to read yet.* **2.** to say aloud something written or printed. **3.** to learn by reading: *I read about the incident in the newspaper.* **4.** to be worded in a particular way: *The two editions of the book read differently.*

  ·**to read between the lines.** to find another meaning besides the one expressed in the written or spoken words.

  ·**to read up on.** to study.

read·a·ble (rē′də bəl) *adj.* **1.** easy or interesting to read. **2.** able to be read; legible: *poor handwriting that is barely readable.* —**read′a·bil′i·ty, read′a·ble·ness,** *n.*

read·er (rē′dər) *n.* **1.** a person who reads. **2.** a schoolbook with exercises for learning and practicing reading.

read·i·ly (red′ə lē) *adv.* **1.** in a willing manner; without opposition; willingly: *The boy readily followed his friend's advice.* **2.** without difficulty; easily: *Her remark was readily understood by everyone.*

read·i·ness (red′ē nis) *n.* **1.** the quality or state of being ready. **2.** willingness. **3.** ease: *Its readiness of operation makes the machine useful.*

read·ing (rē′ding) *n.* **1.** the act or practice of a person who reads. **2.** the act or instance of saying aloud something written or printed: *The author gave a public reading of the book.* **3.** something read or to be read: *That book is interesting reading.* **4.** a personal interpretation: *The actor gave a fine reading of the role.* **5.** the information given

or amount indicated by a meter, dial, or other instrument. —*adj.* **1.** that reads: *the reading public.* **2.** made or used for reading: *reading glasses.*

re·ad·just (rē′ə just′) *v.t.* to adjust again. —*v.i.* to become adapted to again: *The former soldier tried to readjust to civilian life.* —**re′ad·just′ment,** *n.*

read–on·ly memory (rēd′ōn′lē) see **ROM.**

read·y (red′ē) *adj.,* **read·i·er, read·i·est.** **1.** prepared or fit for use or action: *The car is ready for the trip. We are ready to start the game.* **2.** mentally prepared; willing: *to be ready to work hard.* **3.** immediately liable or likely: *The dynamite is ready to explode.* **4.** quick or prompt: *a ready answer.* **5.** immediately available: *ready cash for emergencies.* —*v.t.,* **read·ied, read·y·ing.** to make ready; prepare: *The plane was readied for takeoff.*

read·y–made (red′ē mād′) *adj.* made in quantity and not to order: *ready-made dresses.*

re·a·gent (rē ā′jənt) *n.* a substance used in a chemical reaction in order to find, analyze, or produce other substances.

re·al¹ (rē′əl, rēl) *adj.* **1.** actual or true; not imagined: *The children's adventures were real; they did not make them up.* **2.** not artificial; genuine; authentic: *The flowers are real, not plastic.* **3.** *Law.* relating to or consisting of permanent or immovable things, such as lands or buildings: *real property.* —*adv. Informal.* very; extremely: *I'm real hungry.* [From the Old French word *real,* from the Medieval Latin *realis* "concerning things (in law)," from the Latin word *res* "a thing, circumstance, fact, legal situation."]

re·al² (rā äl′) *n., pl.* **re·als** or **re·a·les** (rā ä′lās). a former coin and monetary unit of Spain and various Latin American countries. [From the Spanish word *real* meaning this coin.]

real estate, land together with the buildings, trees, water, or other things that are on it and are not easily movable.

re·al·ism (rē′ə liz′əm) *n.* **1.** concern with what is actual or practical, instead of with what does not or cannot exist. **2.** in art and literature, the showing of people, things, and events as they actually appear, often in everyday life. **3.** a theory in philosophy that the real world exists with or without our awareness of it and that our senses give real knowledge of it.

re·al·ist (rē′ə list) *n.* **1.** a person who is concerned with what is actual or practical, instead of with what does not or cannot exist. **2.** an artist or writer whose work is characterized by realism. **3.** a person who believes in or follows realism in philosophy.

re·al·is·tic (rē′ə lis′tik) *adj.* **1.** showing people, things, or events as they actually appear in everyday life: *a realistic painting.* **2.** concerned with what is actual or practical: *a realistic person, a realistic attitude.* **3.** of, relating to, or characterized by realism in philosophy. —**re′al·is′ti·cal·ly,** *adv.*

re·al·i·ty (rē al′i tē) *n., pl.* **re·al·i·ties.** **1.** the state or quality of being real. **2.** a real thing, fact, or event: *The reality is that we are out of gas.*

re·al·i·za·tion (rē′ə lə zā′shən) *n.* **1.** the act of realizing or the state of being realized. **2.** something realized.

re·al·ize (rē′ə līz′) *v.t.,* **re·al·ized, re·al·iz·ing.** **1.** to understand completely: *Do you realize what you have done?* **2.** to make real, as an idea or emotion: *Their hopes were never realized.* **3.** to gain (a sum of money): *We realized $300 from the sale of the furniture.*

re·al·ly (rē′ə lē, rē′lē) *adv.* **1.** in reality or fact; actually: *Tell us what really happened.* **2.** indeed: *Really, you can't be serious!* **3.** truly; genuinely: *We spent a really pleasant day in the park.*

realm (relm) *n.* **1.** a kingdom. **2.** a field, area, or sphere, as of knowledge, activity, influence, or interest: *the realm of science, the realm of fantasy.*

real number *Mathematics.* any rational or irrational number.

re·al·tor (rē′əl tər) *n.* a real estate agent or broker. Trademark: **Realtor.**

re·al·ty (rē′əl tē) *n., pl.* **re·al·ties.** another word for **real estate.**

ream¹ (rēm) *n.* **1.** a quantity of paper of the same size and quality, varying from 480 to 516 sheets. **2. reams.** a large amount; great quantity: *The clerk had reams of office forms to check over.* [From the Old French word *reyme* meaning "a quantity of paper," from the Arabic word *rizmah* "a bundle."]

ream² (rēm) *v.t.* **1.** to create or enlarge (a hole). **2.** to remove with a reamer. [From the Middle English word *reemen* meaning "to stretch, distend," probably from Old English.]

ream·er (rē′mər) *n.* **1.** a steel tool with cutting edges, used to enlarge or shape a drilled hole. **2.** a utensil used for removing the juice from oranges, lemons, and other fruit.

reap (rēp) *v.t.* **1.** to cut down (grain). **2.** to gather (a crop) by reaping. **3.** to cut down or harvest the crop from: *to reap fields.* **4.** to receive as a reward: *The child's good behavior reaped praise.*

reap·er (rē′pər) *n.* **1.** a person who reaps. **2.** a machine used to cut and gather grain.

reaper *(def. 2)*

re·ap·pear (rē′ə pîr′) *v.i.* to appear again. —**re′ap·pear′ance,** *n.*

rear¹ (rîr) *n.* **1.** the part that is behind or in the back; back: *the rear of a room, the rear of a bus.* **2.** the part of a military force farthest from the fighting area. —*adj.* relating to or located behind or in the back: *a rear seat.* [From the Old French word *rere* meaning "behind," going back to the Latin word *retro* "backward, behind" or "formerly."]

rear² (rîr) *v.t.* **1.** to help bring to maturity; raise: *to rear children, to rear cattle.* **2.** to construct; build. **3.** to bring to an upright position; lift up. —*v.i.* (of an animal) to rise on the hind legs. [From the Old English word *rǣran* meaning "to raise, cause to rise."]

rear admiral, an officer in the U.S. Navy ranking below a vice admiral and above a captain.

re·arm (rē ärm′) *v.t., v.i.* to arm again, especially with new or better weapons. —**re·ar·ma·ment** (rē är′mə·mənt),** *n.*

re·ar·range (rē′ə rānj′) *v.t.,* **re·ar·ranged, re·ar·rang·ing.** to arrange again, especially in a different way. —**re′ar·range′ment,** *n.*

rear·view mirror (rîr′vū′) a mirror mounted ahead of the driver of an automobile, motorcycle, or other vehicle to provide the driver with a view of the road behind.

rear·ward (rîr′wərd) *adj.* located in or moving toward the rear. —*adv.* in, at, or toward the rear. Also *(adv.),* **rear·wards** (rîr′wərdz).

rea·son (rē′zən) *n.* **1.** a cause or motive: *There is no reason to be alarmed.* **2.** a statement used to justify, prove, or explain: *They could give no reason for their behavior.* **3.** the ability to think logically and clearly: *The shock caused the victim to lose all reason.* —*v.i.* **1.** to think logically and clearly: *The professor's aim was to teach students to reason.* **2.** to try to persuade or influence someone: *It was useless to reason with the mob.* —*v.t.* **1.** to think about logically and clearly: *to reason a problem out.* **2.** come to an opinion about; conclude: *We reasoned that the train would be faster than driving.* —**rea′son·er,** *n.*

·**by reason of.** due to the fact that; because of.

·**in reason** or **within reason.** fair; reasonable.

·**to stand to reason.** to be logical or reasonable: *It stands to reason that the air is cleaner in the country than in the city.*

rea·son·a·ble (rē′zə nə bəl, rēz′nə bəl) *adj.* **1.** showing or using good sense or judgment; not foolish; sensible: *a reasonable person, a reasonable conclusion.* **2.** moderate; fair: *a reasonable request.* **3.** not too expensive: *The sale price is very reasonable.* —**rea′son·a·ble·ness,** *n.* —**rea′son·a·bly,** *adv.*

rea·son·ing (rē′zə ning, rēz′ning) *n.* **1.** the process of drawing conclusions from facts. **2.** arguments or evidence; reasons.

re·as·sem·ble (rē′ə sem′bəl) *v.,* **re·as·sem·bled, re·as·sem·bling.** —*v.t.* to bring or fit together again: *to reassemble a broken toy, to reassemble a group of people.* —*v.i.* to meet or come together again.

re·as·sure (rē′ə shùr′) *v.t.,* **re·as·sured, re·as·sur·ing.** **1.** to restore confidence or courage to: *The parents reassured the frightened child.* **2.** to assure again. —**re′as·sur′ance,** *n.* **re·as·sur′ing·ly,** *adv.*

re·bate (*n.,* rē′bāt; *v.,* rē′bāt, ri bāt′) *n.* a sum of money returned from an amount that has been paid. —*v.t.,* **re·bat·ed, re·bat·ing.** to make a rebate of.

reb·el (*n., adj.,* reb′əl; *v.,* ri bel′) *n.* **1.** a person who resists or refuses to obey authority. **2. Rebel.** a person who fought on the side of the Confederacy in the Civil War. —*adj.* of a rebel or rebels: *rebel forces, a rebel victory.* —*v.i.,* **re·belled, re·bel·ling. 1.** to resist or disobey authority. **2.** to feel or show intense dislike: *My stomach rebelled against the medicine.*

re·bel·lion (ri bel′yən) *n.* **1.** an armed uprising against a legal government. **2.** resistance or defiance against any control or authority.

re·bel·lious (ri bel′yəs) *adj.* **1.** resisting or refusing to obey authority: *rebellious soldiers.* **2.** characteristic of or marked by rebellion: *a rebellious period in the history of a country.* **3.** hard to manage: *a rebellious child.* —**re·bel′lious·ly,** *adv.* —**re·bel′lious·ness,** *n.*

re·birth (rē bûrth′, rē′bûrth′) *n.* **1.** a second or subsequent birth; return to life. **2.** revival; renaissance.

re·born (rē bôrn′) *adj.* born again.

re·bound (*v.,* ri bound′; *n.,* rē′bound′, ri bound′) *v.i.* to bound back; spring back. —*n.* an act or instance of springing back: *to try to catch a ball on the rebound.*

re·buff (ri buf′) *n.* **1.** a blunt or rude rejection, as of a person's offer to help, or a request for something. **2.** a sudden, unexpected check, as to a person's plans; repulse.

at; āpe; fär; câre; end; mē; it; īce; pîerce; hot; ōld; sông, fôrk; oil; out; up; ūse; rüle; pùll; tûrn; chin; sing; shop; thin; this; hw in white; zh in treasure. The symbol ə stands for the unstressed vowel sound heard in about, taken, pencil, lemon, and circus.

R

—*v.t.* **1.** to reject bluntly or rudely. **2.** to check suddenly; repulse.

re·build (rē bild′) *v.*, **re·built** (rē bilt′), **re·build·ing.** —*v.t.* **1.** to build (something) again. **2.** to make changes in; repair or remodel. —*v.i.* to build again: *After the hurricane, the town had to rebuild.*

re·buke (ri būk′) *v.t.*, **re·buked, re·buk·ing.** to scold sharply; reprimand. —*n.* a sharp scolding; reprimand; reproof. —**re·buk′er,** *n.*

To 🔑 + **P** yourself in top SH + 🐵 ,

take a bath or shower every morning or 🛡️ .

rebus

re·bus (rē′bəs) *n.*, *pl.* **re·bus·es.** a representation of a syllable, word, or phrase using pictures or symbols whose names sound like the intended syllable or words. A picture of an eye followed by the numeral 1 is a rebus for "I won."

re·but (ri but′) *v.t.*, **re·but·ted, re·but·ting.** to disprove; refute: *to rebut an argument.* —**re·but′ter,** *n.*

re·but·tal (ri but′əl) *n.* **1.** the act of rebutting. **2.** an argument or statement that rebuts: *to deliver a rebuttal.*

re·cal·ci·trant (ri kal′si trənt) *adj.* stubborn and hard to manage; obstinate and disobedient: *The recalcitrant horse would not go into the stall.* —*n.* a person who is stubborn and hard to manage. —**re·cal′ci·trance, re·cal′ci·tran·cy,** *n.*

re·call (*v.*, ri kôl′; *n.*, ri kôl′, rē′kôl′) *v.t.* **1.** to call or bring back to mind; remember: *I don't recall your name.* **2.** to call back; summon back: *The auto manufacturer recalled the cars because of defects.* **3.** to take back; revoke: *Permission to make the trip was recalled.* —*n.* **1.** a remembering of someone or something; remembrance: *to have total recall of a conversation.* **2.** a calling back; summoning back: *the recall of an ambassador.* **3.** the taking back of something granted earlier. **4.** a special election to vote on the removal of an unwanted public official from office before his or her term is over.

re·cant (ri kant′) *v.t.* to take back formally or publicly; renounce; retract: *to recant an official statement.* —*v.i.* to take back or deny an opinion or belief: *The witness recanted under cross-examination.* —**re·can·ta·tion** (rē′kan tā′shən), *n.*

re·ca·pit·u·late (rē′kə pich′ə lāt′) *v.t.*, **re·ca·pit·u·lat·ed, re·ca·pit·u·lat·ing.** to restate or go over again briefly; summarize. —**re′ca·pit′u·la′tion,** *n.*

re·cap·ture (rē kap′chər) *v.t.*, **re·cap·tured, re·cap·tur·ing. 1.** to retake possession of; capture again. **2.** to bring back to mind: *to recapture one's youth.*

re·cast (rē kast′) *v.t.*, **re·cast, re·cast·ing. 1.** to cast again or anew. **2.** to change the form of; remodel; reconstruct: *to recast a statement.*

recd., received. Also, **rec′d.**

re·cede (ri sēd′) *v.i.*, **re·ced·ed, re·ced·ing. 1.** to move back or away: *The waves receded.* **2.** to slope or appear to slope backward: *a receding hairline.*

re·ceipt (ri sēt′) *n.* **1.** a written statement acknowledging that something, such as money, goods, or mail, has been received. **2. receipts.** the amount or quantity, especially of money, that has been received: *The store's receipts for the week were over $5,000.* **3.** the act of receiving or the state of being received. —*v.t.* **1.** to write a receipt for (money, goods, or mail). **2.** to mark (a bill or account) as paid.

re·ceiv·a·ble (ri sē′və bəl) *adj.* **1.** that can be received; acceptable. **2.** awaiting payment; due. Accounts receivable are unpaid accounts held by a creditor, rather than a debtor. —*n.* **receivables.** accounts or bills that are awaiting payment.

re·ceive (ri sēv′) *v.*, **re·ceived, re·ceiv·ing.** —*v.t.* **1.** to take (something) into one's hands or possession; get: *to receive a watch for your birthday, to receive a letter from a friend.* **2.** to take in mentally; learn; comprehend: *to be willing to receive new ideas.* **3.** to meet with; experience: *We received a shock when we heard the news.* **4.** to be subjected to; suffer: *I received a heavy blow from the collision.* **5.** to greet or welcome: *They received us at the door.* —*v.i.* **1.** to take, acquire, or get something. **2.** to greet and entertain visitors.

re·ceiv·er (ri sē′vər) *n.* **1.** a person or thing that receives. **2.** a person appointed by a court of law to take charge of and administer the property or business of others until a legal decision has been made, as when a company becomes bankrupt. **3.** a device that receives electrical impulses or radio waves and converts them into pictures or sound, as the part of a telephone held to the ear.

re·ceiv·er·ship (ri sē′vər ship′) *n.* **1.** the condition of being in the hands of a receiver. **2.** the position and functions of a receiver appointed by a court.

re·cent (rē′sənt) *adj.* **1.** done, happening, or made just before the present: *What is the most recent news?* **2.** of or belonging to a period of time not long ago; modern: *a recent period in history.* **3. Recent.** of, relating to, or characteristic of the present geological epoch, the second of the Quaternary period, during which the climate has become warmer, glaciers have melted, and modern man has flourished. Also (*def. 3*), **Holocene.** —*n.* **Recent.** the present geological epoch. Also, **Holocene.** —**re′cent·ly,** *adv.* —**re′cent·ness,** *n.*

re·cep·ta·cle (ri sep′tə kəl) *n.* a container or place used to hold something: *We use a large metal can as a receptacle for garbage.*

re·cep·tion (ri sep′shən) *n.* **1.** the act of receiving or the state of being received. **2.** the way in which a person or thing is accepted or received: *We got a very rude reception from our new neighbors.* **3.** a social gathering, especially one at which guests are formally received: *There will be a reception immediately after the wedding.* **4.** the conversion of radio or television signals into sound or pictures, especially with reference to quality: *We have been getting poor reception from our new television set.*

re·cep·tion·ist (ri sep′shə nist) *n.* a person who is employed in an office to receive calls and visitors, make appointments, and give information.

re·cep·tive (ri sep′tiv) *adj.* able or willing to receive suggestions, new ideas, or impressions: *The committee was receptive to the plan. A receptive mind grasps new concepts easily.* —**re·cep′tive·ly,** *adv.* —**re·cep′tive·ness,** *n.*

re·cep·tor (ri sep′tər) *n.* **1.** a cell or group of cells in the nervous system that receives information from other cells or from the senses. **2.** an area on the surface of a cell that is capable of combining chemically with a specific substance.

re·cess (rē′ses, ri ses′) *n.*, *pl.* **re·cess·es. 1.** a period of time during which work or other activity is temporarily stopped. **2.** a part of a wall that is set back or indented from the rest; niche. **3.** an inner or secret spot or part; hidden place: *the recesses of one's heart.* —*v.t.* **1.** to place in a recess; set back or away. **2.** to make a recess in. —*v.i.* to take a recess: *The court recessed for the afternoon.*

re·ces·sion (ri sesh′ən) *n.* **1.** the act of receding or moving back or away; withdrawal. **2.** a period of decline in business activity, shorter and less severe than a depression.

re·ces·sion·al (ri sesh′ə nəl) *adj.* of, relating to, or happening at the end of a church service: *a recessional hymn.* —*n.* **1.** a recessional hymn or music. **2.** a procession at the end of a ceremony, as of the clergy leaving the church.

re·ces·sive (ri ses′iv) *adj.* **1.** tending to go back; receding. **2.** relating to or indicating one of a pair of inherited, genetic characteristics that is dominated by the other when both are present. —*n.* a recessive hereditary characteristic.

re·charge (rē chärj′) *v.t.*, **re·charged, re·charg·ing.** to charge with electricity or electrical energy again: *to recharge a battery.*

rec·i·pe (res′ə pē′) *n.* **1.** a list of ingredients and directions for preparing food or drink. **2.** a method or formula for doing, achieving, or preparing anything: *a recipe for happiness.*

re·cip·i·ent (ri sip′ē ənt) *n.* a person or thing that receives: *the recipient of a gift.* —*adj.* receiving or able to receive; receptive.

re·cip·ro·cal (ri sip′rə kəl) *adj.* **1.** given, felt, or shown by both sides; mutual: *reciprocal respect, reciprocal hostility.* **2.** given, felt, or shown in return: *a reciprocal vow.* **3.** indicating a pronoun that expresses mutual action or relation. *One another* is a reciprocal pronoun. —*n.* *Mathematics.* a number or algebraic expression by which a given number or an algebraic expression is multiplied to produce a value of one. The reciprocal of $\frac{3}{5}$ is $\frac{5}{3}$, since $\frac{3}{5} \times \frac{5}{3} = 1$. —**re·cip′ro·cal·ly,** *adv.*

re·cip·ro·cate (ri sip′rə kāt′) *v.*, **re·cip·ro·cat·ed, re·cip·ro·cat·ing.** —*v.t.* **1.** to give, feel, or show in return: *to reciprocate love.* **2.** to give and return in exchange; interchange: *to reciprocate favors.* —*v.i.* to give, feel, or show something in return: *We showed them hospitality, but they did not reciprocate.* —**re·cip′ro·ca′tion,** *n.*

rec·i·proc·i·ty (res′ə pros′i tē) *n., pl.* **rec·i·proc·i·ties.** **1.** the quality or state of being reciprocal. **2.** a mutual interchange between countries, states, or organizations, such as the exchange of trading privileges.

re·cit·al (ri sīt′əl) *n.* **1.** a performance or concert of music or dance, often given by a single performer or devoted to the works of a single composer: *a piano recital.* **2.** the act of repeating or reading something aloud in public: *a poetry recital.* **3.** a detailed account: *a recital of the arguments for the plan.*

rec·i·ta·tion (res′i tā′shən) *n.* **1.** the act of repeating or reading something aloud in public; recital. **2.** the act of reciting a lesson. **3.** a piece to be recited.

rec·i·ta·tive (res′i tə tēv′) *n.* **1.** a style of music in which words are sung in a manner similar to speaking, found especially in operas. **2.** a passage, part, or composition in this style.

re·cite (ri sīt′) *v.*, **re·cit·ed, re·cit·ing.** —*v.t.* **1.** to repeat from memory: *to recite a poem.* **2.** to give an account of; narrate: *to recite one's life story.* —*v.i.* **1.** to repeat something memorized, especially before an audience. **2.** to repeat a lesson or answer questions in class. —**re·cit′er,** *n.*

reck·less (rek′lis) *adj.* **1.** not careful; heedless: *Reckless of the danger, they skated on the thin ice.* **2.** characterized or distinguished by such heedlessness; irresponsible: *reckless driving.* —**reck′less·ly,** *adv.* —**reck′less·ness,** *n.*

reck·on (rek′ən) *v.t.* **1.** to count or figure; calculate: *Interest on my savings account is reckoned quarterly.* **2.** to suppose to be; consider; regard: *They reckoned that experience is the best teacher.* **3.** *Informal.* to think; suppose: *I reckon that they'll come.* —*v.i.* **1.** to count, depend, or rely: *You can reckon on our support.* **2.** to make a calculation; count or figure. **3.** *Informal.* to suppose; guess. —**reck′on·er,** *n.*
·to reckon with. to take into consideration.

reck·on·ing (rek′ə ning) *n.* **1.** the act of calculating; calculation. **2.** the settlement of accounts. **3.** a bill, as at an inn or hotel. **4.** see **dead reckoning.**

re·claim (ri klām′) *v.t.* **1.** to bring back to a useful state or condition: *to reclaim land.* **2.** to get or recover from old or waste products: *to reclaim metal from a junkyard.* —**re·claim′a·ble,** *adj.*

rec·la·ma·tion (rek′lə mā′shən) *n.* the act of reclaiming or the state of being reclaimed; restoration.

re·cline (ri klīn′) *v.*, **re·clined, re·clin·ing.** —*v.i.* to lie back or down: *to recline on a couch.* —*v.t.* to cause to lie back or down.

rec·luse (rek′lüs, ri klüs′) *n.* a person who lives alone, away from other people.

rec·og·ni·tion (rek′əg nish′ən) *n.* **1.** the act of recognizing or the state of being recognized. **2.** an acknowledgment of something, especially as being true or valid. **3.** favorable attention or notice; acceptance: *to gain recognition for work with the poor.*

re·cog·ni·zance (ri kog′nə zəns) *n.* *Law.* **1.** a bond or obligation by which a person promises to perform a particular act, such as appearing for a hearing or trial. **2.** the amount of money to be forfeited if the act is not performed.

rec·og·nize (rek′əg nīz′) *v.t.*, **rec·og·nized, rec·og·niz·ing.** **1.** to know as someone or something previously seen or known; know again: *I recognized your face at once.* **2.** to identify, as from a description or a distinctive feature: *to recognize a bird by its coloring.* **3.** to be aware of or understand clearly; realize: *to recognize a fact.* **4.** to take notice of as having the right to speak, as at a formal meeting: *The chair recognized the club's treasurer.* **5.** to show or express appreciation of: *The company recognized the employee's long service with the gift of a watch.* **6.** to acknowledge the existence of (another nation), usually by establishing diplomatic relations. [Going back to the Old French word *reconoistre* meaning "to recognize," from the Latin word *recognoscere* "to examine, recognize, acknowledge," from the prefix *re-* "again" + *cognoscere* "to find out, experience, recognize."] —**rec′og·niz′a·ble,** *adj.* —**rec′og·niz′a·bly,** *adv.*

re·coil (*v.*, ri koil′; *n.*, ri koil′, rē′koil′) *v.i.* **1.** to draw or shrink back, as in fear, horror, or surprise: *to recoil at the sight of a rat.* **2.** to fly back, as from force of impact or discharge; spring back: *The gun recoiled when it was fired.* —*n.* **1.** the act of recoiling. **2.** the backward movement of a firearm when discharged.

rec·ol·lect (rek′ə lekt′) *v.t.* to call back to mind; remember: *I cannot recollect the address at the moment.* —*v.i.* to have a recollection; remember.

rec·ol·lec·tion (rek′ə lek′shən) *n.* **1.** the act or power of calling back to mind: *The victory still lives in our recollection.* **2.** a thing remembered.

re·com·bi·nant DNA (rē kom′bə nənt) DNA that re-

at; āpe; fär; câre; end; mē; it; īce; pîerce; hot; ōld; sông, fôrk; oil; out; up; ūse; rüle; pu̇ll; tûrn; chin; sing; shop; thin; th̲is; hw in white; zh in treasure. The symbol ə stands for the unstressed vowel sound heard in about, taken, pencil, lemon, and circus.

R

sults from gene-splicing, in which genetic material from one organism is inserted into the DNA of another organism.

rec·om·mend (rek′ə mend′) *v.t.* **1.** to speak of or present favorably: *Can you recommend a good restaurant?* **2.** to advise; suggest: *I recommend that you go to the doctor.* **3.** to make acceptable, pleasing, or attractive: *Your ability recommends you for the job.*

rec·om·men·da·tion (rek′ə men dā′shən) *n.* **1.** the act of recommending. **2.** anything that recommends, such as a letter. **3.** something recommended; advice: *I followed your recommendation.*

rec·om·pense (rek′əm pens′) *v.t.*, **rec·om·pensed, rec·om·pens·ing.** **1.** to pay or repay (someone), as for something done or given: *We recompensed them for their services.* **2.** to make up for; give compensation for: *The insurance company will recompense you for the damage caused by the fire.* —*n.* **1.** payment, as for something done or given; reward. **2.** compensation, as for loss or injury.

rec·on·cile (rek′ən sīl′) *v.t.*, **rec·on·ciled, rec·on·cil·ing.** **1.** to make friendly again, as after an argument or fight: *The quarreling friends are now reconciled.* **2.** to make (someone) willing to accept or become resigned to: *to reconcile oneself to failure.* **3.** to bring to an end; settle: *The referee tried to reconcile the disagreement between the two teams.* **4.** to bring into harmony; make agree: *The police officer tried to reconcile the different accounts of the accident.* —**rec′on·cil′a·ble,** *adj.* —**rec′on·cile′ment,** *n.*

rec·on·cil·i·a·tion (rek′ən sil′ē ā′shən) *n.* the act of reconciling or the state of being reconciled.

rec·on·dite (rek′ən dīt′, ri kon′dīt) *adj.* **1.** hard to understand; profound: *a recondite mathematical theory.* **2.** dealing with difficult or little-known matters: *recondite research.*

re·con·di·tion (rē′kən dish′ən) *v.t.* to restore to good condition, as by repairing or cleaning: *to recondition a car.*

re·con·nais·sance (ri kon′ə səns) *n.* an examination or survey made in order to obtain information, especially military information about an enemy.

re·con·noi·ter (rē′kə noi′tər, rek′ə noi′tər) *also, British,* **re·con·noi·tre.** *v.t.* to inspect, examine, or survey (an area or position) in order to obtain information, as for military purposes. —*v.i.* to make a reconnaissance.

re·con·noi·tre (rē′kə noi′tər, rek′ə noi′tər) *v.*, **re·con·noi·tred, re·con·noi·tring.** *British.* another spelling of **reconnoiter.**

re·con·sid·er (rē′kən sid′ər) *v.t.* to consider again, especially with the possibility of changing one's mind. —**re′con·sid′er·a′tion,** *n.*

re·con·sti·tute (rē kon′sti tüt′, rē kon′sti tūt′) *v.t.*, **re·con·sti·tut·ed, re·con·sti·tut·ing.** to constitute again, especially to restore to the original state by adding water: *to reconstitute frozen fruit juice.*

re·con·struct (rē′kən strukt′) *v.t.* **1.** to construct again; rebuild. **2.** to re-create (something that happened or existed) in the mind from available evidence or information: *The detective tried to reconstruct the crime.*

re·con·struc·tion (rē′kən struk′shən) *n.* **1.** the act of reconstructing or the state of being reconstructed. **2.** something reconstructed. **3. Reconstruction. a.** the process of reestablishing the former Confederate states in the Union after the Civil War. **b.** the period during which this process took place, from 1867 to 1877.

Re·con·struc·tion·ism (rē′kən struk′shə niz′əm) *n.* a twentieth-century movement in American Judaism that views Judaism as a religious civilization and preserves the traditional customs and observances but adapts them to modern-day living.

rec·ord (*n., adj.,* rek′ərd; *v.,* ri kôrd′) *n.* **1.** an account in writing or in another permanent form: *The school keeps*

records for each student. **2.** an official written account: *a record of a town meeting.* **3.** the facts about the activities or achievements of a person or group of people: *an outstanding academic record.* **4.** a performance, achievement, or event surpassing all others of its kind, as in sports: *a record in the 100-yard dash.* **5.** a disk on which sounds are recorded to be played back on a phonograph. —*adj.* surpassing all others of its kind: *record attendance at a ball game.* —*v.t.* **1.** to set down in permanent form, as in writing, for future use: *to record history.* **2.** to indicate; show; register: *The dial on the left records speed.* **3.** to put on magnetic tape or the like for later playback, as on a tape recorder or phonograph. **4.** to make a recording of: *to record a song.*

·**off the record.** not for publication or quotation: *The candidate's remarks at the banquet were off the record.*

·**on record.** known publicly or officially.

·**to break a record.** to surpass a previous record: *The low temperature this morning broke the record for the date.*

rec·ord–break·ing (rek′ərd brā′king) *adj.* surpassing a record established previously: *to finish a race in record-breaking time.*

re·cord·er (ri kôr′dər) *n.* **1.** a person who is employed to take notes and keep records. **2.** a machine that records sounds, as on magnetic tape. **3.** a musical wind instrument having eight finger holes to regulate pitch, and producing a tone somewhat like a flute's.

re·cord·ing (ri kôr′ding) *n.* **1.** a phonograph record, magnetic tape, or other medium that records. **2.** a sound registered on a phonograph record, magnetic tape, or other medium. **3.** the process of putting sound or visual material onto tape or the like.

record player, an instrument that reproduces sound from a phonograph record; phonograph.

re·count (ri kount′) *v.t.* to tell in detail; narrate: *to recount the experiences of youth.*

re–count (*v.,* rē′kount′; *n.,* rē′kount′) *v.t.* to count again. —*n.* a second count, especially of votes in an election.

re·coup (ri küp′) *v.t.* **1.** to make up for or get back: *to recoup one's losses.* **2.** to pay back: *The insurance company recouped the owners for their losses in the fire.*

re·course (rē′kôrs′, ri kôrs′) *n.* **1.** a turning or appealing to a person or thing for help or protection: *Our recourse when a fire breaks out is to call the fire department.* **2.** a person or thing that is turned or appealed to; resort: *My friends were my recourse when I felt lonely.*

re·cov·er (ri kuv′ər) *v.t.* **1.** to get back (something lost or stolen); regain: *The police recovered the stolen jewelry.* **2.** to make up for: *We took a shortcut to recover the time spent getting gas.* **3.** to get (oneself) back to a normal position or condition: *to slip but recover before falling.* —*v.i.* to get back to a normal position or condition: *to recover from the flu.*

re–cov·er (rē′kuv′ər) *v.t.* to cover again.

re·cov·er·y (ri kuv′ə rē) *n., pl.* **re·cov·er·ies. 1.** the act of recovering or the state of being recovered. **2.** a return to a normal or healthy condition: *a speedy recovery from the flu.*

recovery room, a hospital room where patients are taken after an operation for special care and observation.

rec·re·ant (rek′rē ənt) *adj.* **1.** not faithful; disloyal. **2.** not brave; cowardly. —*n.* an unfaithful or cowardly person.

re–cre·ate (rē′krē āt′) *v.t.*, **re–cre·at·ed, re–cre·at·ing.** to create anew.

rec·re·a·tion (rek′rē ā′shən) *n.* **1.** refreshment by means of some form of amusement or relaxation. **2.** any particular form of amusement or relaxation: *Fishing is my favorite recreation.*

rec·re·a·tion·al (rek′rē ā′shə nəl) *adj.* of or relating to recreation: *recreational activities.*

recreational vehicle, a motor vehicle designed for recreational and vacation use, usually equipped with living and sleeping facilities.

re·crim·i·nate (ri krim′ə nāt′) *v.i.*, **re·crim·i·nat·ed, re·crim·i·nat·ing.** to answer an accusation by making one in return. —**re·crim′i·na′tion,** *n.*

re·cru·des·cence (rē′krü des′əns) *n.* a new outbreak, as of a disease. —**re′cru·des′cent,** *adj.*

re·cruit (ri krüt′) *n.* **1.** a newly enlisted member of the armed forces. **2.** a new member of any group or organization. —*v.t.* **1.** to get (someone) to join the armed forces; enlist (someone) for military service. **2.** to raise or make up by enlisting: *to recruit a new army.* **3.** to hire or get the services of. —**re·cruit′er,** *n.* —**re·cruit′ment,** *n.*

rec·tal (rek′təl) *adj.* relating to, affecting, or near the rectum.

rec·tan·gle (rek′tang′gəl) *n.* a parallelogram having four right angles. [From the Medieval Latin *rectangulus* meaning ''having a right angle,'' from the Latin words *rectus* ''right'' + *angulus* ''angle.'']

rec·tan·gu·lar (rek tang′gyə lər) *adj.* shaped like a rectangle: *a rectangular piece of wood.*

rec·ti·fi·er (rek′tə fī′ər) *n.* **1.** a person or thing that rectifies. **2.** *Electronics.* a device for changing alternating current into direct current.

rec·ti·fy (rek′tə fī′) *v.t.*, **rec·ti·fied, rec·ti·fy·ing. 1.** to set or make right; amend; correct: *to rectify a mistake.* **2.** *Electronics.* to change (an alternating current) into a direct current. **3.** *Chemistry.* to refine or purify (liquids) by repeated distillation. —**rec′ti·fi·ca′tion,** *n.*

rec·ti·lin·e·ar (rek′tə lin′ē ər) *adj.* **1.** moving in or forming a straight line. **2.** made up of or bounded by straight lines.

rec·ti·tude (rek′ti tüd′, rek′ti tūd′) *n.* uprightness of moral character or conduct; righteousness.

rec·tor (rek′tər) *n.* **1.** a member of the Anglican or Episcopalian clergy who has charge of a parish. **2.** a priest in the Roman Catholic Church in charge of a seminary, college, or religious house. **3.** the chief administrator in certain schools, colleges, or universities.

rec·to·ry (rek′tə rē) *n., pl.* **rec·to·ries.** a rector's house.

rec·tum (rek′təm) *n., pl.* **rec·tums** or **rec·ta** (rek′tə). the lowest part of the large intestine, connecting the colon to the anus, where feces are stored until they are discharged from the body.

re·cum·bent (ri kum′bənt) *adj.* lying down; reclining: *The artist completed a painting of a recumbent lion.* —**re·cum′bent·ly,** *adv.*

re·cu·per·ate (ri kü′pə rāt′, ri kū′pə rāt′) *v.i.*, **re·cu·per·at·ed, re·cu·per·at·ing.** to gain back health or strength; recover: *I recuperated at home after my illness.* —**re·cu′per·a′tion,** *n.*

re·cur (ri kûr′) *v.i.*, **re·curred, re·cur·ring. 1.** to happen or appear again: *The fever recurred after two days.* **2.** to come back or return to the mind or memory: *Thoughts of home and family recurred to the lonely traveler.* **3.** to go back or return in thought or speech: *At the meeting we recurred to the subject we had discussed the week before.* —**re·cur′rence,** *n.*

re·cur·rent (ri kûr′ənt) *adj.* happening or appearing again, especially repeatedly or at intervals: *a recurrent nightmare.* —**re·cur′rent·ly,** *adv.*

re·cy·cle (rē sī′kəl) *v.t.*, **re·cy·cled, re·cy·cling.** to make (waste material) available or suitable for reuse: *to recycle old newspapers.*

red (red) *n.* **1.** the color of fresh blood. **2.** something having this color, such as a dye or paint. **3.** *also,* **Red.** *Informal.* **a.** a communist. **b.** any radical or revolutionary. —*adj.*, **red·der, red·dest. 1.** having the color red.

2. blushing; flushed: *to be red with embarrassment.* **3.** *also,* **Red.** *Informal.* **a.** communist. **b.** radical or revolutionary. —**red′ness,** *n.*

·**in the red.** losing or owing money.

red·bird (red′bûrd′) *n.* any of several birds having mainly red feathers, such as the cardinal or scarlet tanager.

red blood cell, one of the cells found in the blood of humans and other animals with backbones, containing hemoglobin, and functioning chiefly to carry oxygen to the cells and tissues and carbon dioxide back to the respiratory organs.

red–blood·ed (red′blud′id) *adj.* full of vitality; vigorous.

red·breast (red′brest′) *n.* any of various birds having a red breast, especially a robin.

red·cap (red′kap′) *n.* a porter who handles baggage, especially at a railroad station. [From the *red cap* usually worn by these porters.]

red·coat (red′kōt′) *n.* a British soldier, as during the American Revolution and the War of 1812, when the British uniform included a red coat.

Red Cross 1. an international organization founded in 1864, having as its main purpose the care and relief of the wounded and other victims of war and natural disasters, such as floods, fires, or earthquakes. **2.** any branch of this organization.

red deer 1. a reddish brown deer found in Europe and Asia. **2.** the American white-tailed deer in the summer, when its coat is reddish.

red·den (red′ən) *v.t.*, *v.i.* to make or become red.

red·dish (red′ish) *adj.* somewhat red.

re·deem (ri dēm′) *v.t.* **1.** to get or win back; regain; recover: *to redeem a pawned watch.* **2.** to exchange for money or merchandise: *to redeem trading stamps.* **3.** to make up for; compensate for: *Apologies cannot redeem such poor manners.* **4.** to set free from or deliver from a sinful state. —**re·deem′a·ble,** *adj.*

red deer

re·deem·er (ri dē′mər) *n.* **1.** a person who redeems or rescues. **2. The Redeemer.** Jesus.

re·demp·tion (ri demp′shən) *n.* **1.** the act of redeeming or the state of being redeemed. **2.** deliverance from sin.

red–faced (red′fāst′) *adj.* having a red face, especially as a result of anger or embarrassment; flushed or blushing.

red–hand·ed (red′han′did) *adj.* in the act of doing something wrong: *The detective caught the pickpocket red-handed.*

red·head (red′hed′) *n.* a person having red hair.

red–head·ed (red′hed′id) *adj.* having red hair.

red herring 1. a herring dried and smoked to a reddish color. **2.** something intended to draw attention away from the problem at hand.

red–hot (red′hot′) *adj.* **1.** red or glowing with heat; very

at; āpe; fär; câre; end; mē; it; īce; pîerce; hot; old; sông, fôrk; oil; out; up; ūse; rüle; pu̇ll; tûrn; chin; sing; shop; thin; this; hw in white; zh in treasure. The symbol ə stands for the unstressed vowel sound heard in about, taken, pencil, lemon, and circus.

R

hot. **2.** marked by or showing great intensity, as of enthusiasm or anger: *a red-hot discussion.* **3.** fresh from a source; new: *red-hot news.*

re·did (rē did′) the past tense of **redo.**

red–let·ter (red′let′ər) *adj.* especially important or happy; memorable: *a red-letter day.* [From the practice of marking religious holidays in *red letters* on church calendars.]

re·do (rē dü′) *v.t.,* **re·did, re·done, re·do·ing. 1.** to do over or again. **2.** to remodel; renovate.

red·o·lent (red′ə lənt) *adj.* **1.** having or giving off a pleasant odor; fragrant. **2.** suggestive; reminiscent: *a design redolent of the architecture of the U.S. Capitol.* —**red′o·lence,** *n.* —**red′o·lent·ly,** *adv.*

re·done (rē dun′) the past participle of **redo.**

re·dou·ble (rē dub′əl) *v.t., v.i.,* **re·dou·bled, re·dou·bling. 1.** to increase greatly. **2.** to double again.

re·doubt (ri dout′) *n.* a small enclosed fortification.

re·doubt·a·ble (ri dou′tə bəl) *adj.* inspiring fear or awe; formidable; awesome: *a redoubtable army.*

re·dound (ri dound′) *v.i.* to have an effect; contribute: *Your concern for others redounds to your credit.*

red panda, see **panda** *(def. 2).*

red pepper 1. the ripe fruit of any of a group of pepper plants, such as the sweet pepper. **2.** another term for **cayenne.**

re·dress (*v.,* ri dres′; *n.,* rē′dres′, ri dres′) *v.t.* to correct and make up for; set right; remedy: *to redress a wrong.* —*n.* **1.** something given or done to make up for an injury or wrong. **2.** the act of redressing.

red snapper, a food and game fish that is bright red in color, found in the Caribbean Sea and the Gulf of Mexico.

red·start (red′stärt′) *n.* **1.** a small European bird having a reddish tail. **2.** a fly-catching warbler of eastern North America, the male of which is black with orange or red patches.

red tape, official rules and procedures in a business or government office, usually causing inaction or delay. [From the *red tape* formerly used to tie official documents of the British government.]

red tide, a rapid increase in the number of certain one-celled organisms in a sea or lake. The great number of these organisms colors the water reddish or brownish, and the organisms produce a poison that kills fish and other aquatic animals.

re·duce (ri düs′, ri dūs′) *v.,* **re·duced, re·duc·ing.** —*v.t.* **1.** to make less or smaller, as in size, number, or degree; decrease; diminish: *to reduce the speed of an automobile, to reduce prices for a sale.* **2.** to lower in rank, position, or condition; degrade: *The sergeant was reduced to private for disobeying orders.* **3.** to bring to a particular state, form, or condition: *The fire reduced the forest to ashes.* **4.** to break down or bring to a simpler form or character: *to reduce an argument to its basic points.* **5.** *Mathematics.* to change (an expression) to a simpler form: *to reduce ⅘ to ½.* **6.** *Chemistry.* **a.** to add electrons to (the atom of an element) so that its oxidation number is decreased. **b.** to remove oxygen from (a compound). —*v.i.* **1.** to lose weight, as by dieting. **2.** to become reduced. —**re·duc′er,** *n.* —**re·duc′i·ble,** *adj.*

re·duc·tion (ri duk′shən) *n.* **1.** the act of reducing or the state of being reduced. **2.** the amount by which something is reduced: *The store is offering a 10 percent reduction on summer clothes.*

re·dun·dan·cy (ri dun′dən sē) *n., pl.* **re·dun·dan·cies. 1.** the use of more words than necessary to express an idea; wordiness. **2.** an amount that is more than enough. **3.** the quality or condition of being redundant.

re·dun·dant (ri dun′dənt) *adj.* **1.** using more words than necessary; characterized by wordiness. **2.** more than

enough; unnecessary; superfluous. —**re·dun′dant·ly,** *adv.*

red–winged blackbird (red′wingd′) a North American blackbird, the male of which has a scarlet patch at the shoulder of each wing. Also, **red·wing** (red′wing′).

red·wood (red′wu̇d′) *n.* **1.** a tall evergreen tree having a thick reddish brown bark, found only along the western coast of North America. Redwoods may grow to a height of 300 to 340 feet (90–100 meters), and some are probably more than 2,000 years old. **2.** the soft, light, reddish wood obtained from this tree. Redwood is strong and highly resistant to decay.

reed (rēd) *n.* **1.** a tall grass having long, narrow leaves and slender, jointed stems. Reeds grow chiefly around marshes and other wet areas. **2.** the stem of this grass. **3.** a musical pipe made from a reed or from some other hollow stalk or stem. **4.** *Music.* **a.** a thin piece of wood, reed, metal, or plastic, used in the mouthpiece of certain wind instruments and in the pipes of certain organs. A reed produces a musical sound when a current of air passes over it and causes it to vibrate. **b.** *also,* **reed instrument.** a musical wind instrument, such as the clarinet or oboe, whose tone is produced by the vibration of a single or double reed.

reed·bird (rēd′bûrd′) *n.* another word for **bobolink.**

reed organ, another term for **harmonium.**

reed·y (rē′dē) *adj.,* **reed·i·er, reed·i·est. 1.** having a sound like a reed instrument: *thin, reedy voices.* **2.** resembling a reed or reeds: *reedy legs.* **3.** full of reeds: *reedy marshes.* —**reed′i·ness,** *n.*

reef¹ (rēf) *n.* a ridge of sand, rock, or coral that lies at or near the surface of a sea or other body of water. [From the Dutch word *rif* with the same meaning, probably of Scandinavian origin.]

reef² (rēf) *n.* a portion of a sail that can be rolled up or let out in order to reduce the area of the sail exposed to the wind. —*v.t.* to reduce the area of (a sail) by rolling or folding up a portion and fastening it. [From the Old Norse word *rif* with the same meaning.]

reek (rēk) *v.i.* to give off or be filled with a strong, bad odor; smell strongly and unpleasantly: *The empty lot reeks from the garbage dumped there. The room reeks of stale cigar smoke.* —*n.* a strong, bad odor.

reel¹ (rēl) *n.* **1.** a spool or similar device on which lengths of rope, fishing line, motion picture film, tape, or the like can be wound: *a reel of wire.* **2.** the amount of material wound on a reel: *two reels of film.* —*v.t.* **1.** to draw or pull by winding a line on a reel: *to reel a fish in.* **2.** to wind on a reel: *to reel a rope.* [From the Old English word *hrēol* meaning "a spindle or reel¹ used to wind yarn."]

·**to reel off.** to say or write quickly and easily: *to reel off the answers.*

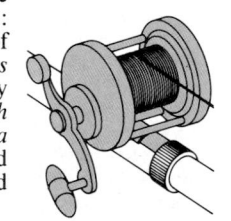

fishing **reel**

reel² (rēl) *v.i.* **1.** to be thrown off balance, as from a blow; stagger: *I reeled when the bike ran into me.* **2.** to walk or move unsteadily; totter. **3.** to turn or seem to turn round and round; whirl: *The bright lights made my head reel.* —*v.t.* to cause to reel. —*n.* a reeling movement. [From the Middle English word *relen* meaning "to whirl about" or "to stagger."]

reel³ (rēl) *n.* **1.** a lively folk dance, performed by two or more couples, in which the dancers form two lines facing each other. **2.** the music for such a dance. [Probably from *reel².*]

re·e·lect (rē′i lekt′) *also,* **re-e·lect.** *v.t.* to elect again: *The voters reelected the governor to another term in office.* —**re′e·lec′tion,** *n.*

re·en·force (rē′en fôrs′) *also,* **re-en·force.** *v.t.,* **re·en-**

forced, re·en·for·cing. another spelling of **reinforce**.

re·en·force·ment (rē'en fôrs'mənt) *also*, **re-en-force-ment**. *n.* another spelling of **reinforcement**.

re·en·list (rē'en list') *also*, **re-en-list**. *v.t., v.i.* to enlist again: *The private reenlisted for two more years of duty.* —**re'en·list'ment**; *also*, **re'-en-list'ment**, *n.*

re·en·ter (rē en'tər) *also*, **re-en-ter**. *v.t.* to enter or go into again.

re·en·try (rē en'trē) *also*, **re-en-try**. *n., pl.* **re·en·tries**. **1.** the act or instance of entering again. **2.** the return of a missile or spacecraft to the earth's atmosphere.

re·es·tab·lish (rē'e stab'lish) *also*, **re-es-tab-lish**. *v.t.* to establish again; restore. —**re'es·tab'lish·ment**; *also*, **re'-es-tab'lish·ment**, *n.*

re·ex·am·ine (rē'eg zam'in) *also*, **re-ex-am-ine**. *v.t.*, **re·ex·am·ined, re·ex·am·in·ing**. **1.** to examine again. **2.** *Law.* to question (a witness) again after cross-examination. —**re'ex·am·i'na'tion**; *also*, **re'-ex-am'i·na'tion**, *n.*

re·fec·to·ry (ri fek'tə rē) *n., pl.* **re·fec·to·ries**. a dining hall, as in a school, monastery, or other institution.

re·fer (ri fûr') *v.*, **re·ferred, re·fer·ring**. —*v.t.* **1.** to send or direct (someone), as for information or aid: *The doctor referred the patient to a surgeon.* **2.** to turn over or submit for consideration or for a recommendation or decision: *The clerk referred the problem to the owner of the store.* —*v.i.* **1.** to call or direct attention; make reference: *I was referring to the party last Friday.* **2.** to use as a source, as of information: *to refer to notes while speaking.*

ref·er·ee (ref'ə rē') *n.* **1.** an official in certain sports and games, often the chief official, who interprets and enforces the rules. **2.** a person who settles a matter or question in dispute. —*v.*, **ref·er·eed, ref·er·ee·ing**. —*v.t.* to act as a referee in: *to referee a boxing match.* —*v.i.* to act as a referee.

ref·er·ence (ref'ər əns) *n.* **1.** the act of referring. **2.** a statement that calls or directs attention; mention: *The candidate made a reference to the incumbent's record.* **3.** relation; respect; regard: *I am writing in reference to your letter of November 5.* **4.** a person or thing that is referred to; a source, as of information or aid: *The encyclopedia was my reference for the report.* **5.** a statement about a person's character or ability: *Your references indicate that you are highly qualified for the job.* **6.** a person from whom such a statement may be obtained: *to give a former teacher as a reference.* **7.** a note referring a reader to a source or sources, as of information: *The author has included a table of references at the end of the book.* —*adj.* used for information: *a reference source.*

reference book, a book, such as a dictionary, encyclopedia, atlas, or almanac, that contains information arranged in a systematic, convenient way for easy access.

ref·er·en·dum (ref'ə ren'dəm) *n., pl.* **ref·er·en·dums** or **ref·er·en·da** (ref'ə ren'də). **1.** a method of submitting public measures already enacted to the vote of the people for approval or rejection. **2.** a direct vote by the people on a public measure.

re·fer·ral (ri fûr'əl) *n.* **1.** the act of referring or an instance of referring: *a doctor's referral of a patient to a specialist, referral of a problem to someone in charge.* **2.** someone who has been referred: *The job applicant was a referral from an employment agency.*

re·fill (*v.*, rē fil'; *n.*, rē'fil') *v.t.* to fill again. —*n.* a supply of a product replacing material that filled the original container and has been used up.

re·fine (ri fīn') *v.t.*, **re·fined, re·fin·ing**. **1.** to make fine or pure; free from impure or unwanted matter: *to refine crude oil.* **2.** to make more elegant, cultured, or polished. —**re·fin'er**, *n.*

re·fined (ri fīnd') *adj.* **1.** free from coarseness and vulgarity; elegant, cultured, or polished: *refined taste in music.* **2.** free from impure or unwanted matter.

re·fine·ment (ri fīn'mənt) *n.* **1.** freedom from coarseness and vulgarity; polish. **2.** the act or process of refining. **3.** a change or addition that is meant to improve; improvement.

re·fin·er·y (ri fī'nə rē) *n., pl.* **re·fin·er·ies**. a place where some raw substance, such as crude petroleum or sugar, is refined.

re·fit (rē fit') *v.t., v.i.*, **re·fit·ted, re·fit·ting**. to make or be made fit for use again: *to refit an old ship.*

re·flect (ri flekt') *v.t.* **1.** to turn or throw back: *Because light-colored fabric reflects heat, it is often used for summer clothes.* **2.** to give back an image of; mirror: *The still water in the lake reflected our faces.* **3.** to express or represent: *a home that reflects the owner's warmth.* **4.** to bring or give back as a result; cast: *Their deeds reflected honor upon them.* —*v.i.* **1.** to think seriously or carefully; ponder: *to reflect on a question.* **2.** to bring blame or discredit: *Cowardice reflects on one's character.*

reflecting telescope, a telescope with a concave mirror that gathers light and reflects it to form an image of the object being viewed.

re·flec·tion (ri flek'shən) *n.* **1.** an image given back by a reflecting surface: *a reflection in the mirror.* **2.** something reflected or produced by reflection: *The reflection of the sun on the windshield temporarily blinded the driver.* **3.** serious or careful thinking; consideration: *Upon further reflection, I decided not to accept the job.* **4.** an observation or statement that results from such thinking. **5.** the turning back of light, heat, or sound waves. **6.** something that expresses or represents something else: *A smile is a reflection of happiness.* **7.** something that causes or brings blame or discredit. **8.** the act of reflecting or the state of being reflected.

re·flec·tive (ri flek'tiv) *adj.* **1.** given to or showing serious or careful thinking; thoughtful. **2.** that throws back light, heat, or sound waves; reflecting: *Polished silver has a reflective surface.* —**re·flec'tive·ly**, *adv.*

re·flec·tor (ri flek'tər) *n.* **1.** something that reflects. **2.** a surface or device designed to reflect light, heat, or sound waves. **3.** see **reflecting telescope**.

re·flex (rē'fleks') *n., pl.* **re·flex·es**. the response to a stimulus that happens without a person's control or effort. Blinking the eyes at a fast-approaching object is a reflex. —*adj.* relating to, produced by, or indicating a response to a stimulus that happens without a person's control or effort: *The immediate withdrawal of one's hand from a hot surface is a reflex action.*

re·flex·ive (ri flek'siv) *adj.* *Grammar.* relating to or expressing an action directed back on the subject. In the sentence *I washed myself, myself* is a reflexive pronoun and *washed* is a reflexive verb. —*n.* a reflexive verb or pronoun. —**re·flex'ive·ly**, *adv.*

re·for·est (rē fôr'ist, rē for'ist) *v.t.* to replant (an area) with trees; cover again with forest.

re·for·est·a·tion (rē'fôr ə stā'shən, rē'for ə stā'shən) *n.* the replanting of an area with trees, especially an area that has been stripped of trees by fire or timbering.

re·form (ri fôrm') *v.t.* **1.** to make a change for the better

---

at; āpe; fär; câre; end; mē; it; īce; pierce; hot; ōld; sông, fôrk; oil; out; up; ūse; rüle; pùll; tûrn; chin; sing; shop; thin; this; hw in white; zh in treasure. The symbol ə stands for the unstressed vowel sound heard in about, taken, pencil, lemon, and circus.

R

in; correct what is wrong with: *The government tried to reform the tax laws.* **2.** to cause (someone) to change for the better; rehabilitate: *to reform a criminal.* —*v.i.* to become changed for the better. —*n.* a change for the better: *a reform of the prison system.* —*adj.* **1.** of or relating to reform or correction. **2. Reform.** of, relating to, or practicing Reform Judaism. —**re·form′er,** *n.*

ref·or·ma·tion (ref′ər mā′shən) *n.* **1.** the act of reforming or the state of being reformed. **2. Reformation.** a religious movement in sixteenth-century Europe, led by Martin Luther, that began as an attempt to reform the Catholic Church and resulted in the establishment of Protestant churches.

re·form·a·to·ry (ri fôr′mə tôr′ē) *n., pl.* **re·form·a·to·ries.** an institution to which young offenders are sent, and which stresses rehabilitation rather than punishment. —*adj.* serving or intended to reform.

Reform Judaism, the branch of Judaism that rejects the strict traditional observance of religious rituals and that changes and accepts many variations in religious practice.

reform school, see **reformatory.**

re·fract (ri frakt′) *v.t.* to cause to undergo refraction. —**re·frac′tive,** *adj.*

refracting telescope, a telescope that uses a convex lens as an objective to focus light and form an image.

re·frac·tion (ri frak′shən) *n.* the bending of waves, especially light waves, as they pass from one substance to another substance having a different density, or as they pass through a substance whose density is not uniform.

re·frac·tor (ri frak′tər) *n.* **1.** something that refracts. **2.** see **refracting telescope.**

re·frac·to·ry (ri frak′tə rē) *adj.* **1.** difficult to control or manage; rebellious; obstinate: *a refractory student.* **2.** resisting treatment, as a disease. **3.** resisting heat or fusion, as certain ores or metals.

re·frain¹ (ri frān′) *v.i.* to hold oneself back; restrain oneself: *We could scarcely refrain from laughing.* [From the Old French word *refrener* meaning "to restrain."]

re·frain² (ri frān′) *n.* **1.** a phrase or verse in a song, poem, or the like, that is repeated regularly, especially at the end of each stanza; chorus. **2.** a musical setting for this. [From the Old French word *refrain,* from the word *refraindre* meaning "to resound," going back to the Latin word *refringere* "to break off," from the prefix *re-* "again" + *frangere* "to break."]

re·fresh (ri fresh′) *v.t.* **1.** to restore strength or vitality to; make fresh again; revive: *The weary children refreshed themselves with cold lemonade.* **2.** to cause to remember; prompt (the memory). —**re·fresh′er,** *n.*

re·fresh·ing (ri fresh′ing) *adj.* **1.** that refreshes: *A cold shower on a warm day is refreshing.* **2.** pleasingly different or unusual: *someone with a refreshing point of view.* —**re·fresh′ing·ly,** *adv.*

re·fresh·ment (ri fresh′mənt) *n.* **1. refreshments.** food and drink taken as a snack or light meal. **2.** something that refreshes. **3.** the act of refreshing.

re·fried beans (rē′frīd′) boiled and fried beans that are mashed, then seasoned and fried again in fat.

re·frig·er·ant (ri frij′ər ənt) *n.* any substance used in cooling or refrigeration.

re·frig·er·ate (ri frij′ə rāt′) *v.t.,* **re·frig·er·at·ed, re·frig·er·at·ing.** to make or keep cool or cold, especially to chill or freeze (food) in order to preserve it. —**re·frig′er·a′tion,** *n.*

re·frig·er·a·tor (ri frij′ə rā′tər) *n.* **1.** a closed, usually box-shaped appliance with a cooling system, used to preserve food and other perishables. **2.** any closed area, such as a room or railroad car, that is kept cool by refrigeration.

re·fu·el (rē fū′əl) *v.,* **re·fu·eled, re·fu·el·ing;** *also, Brit-*

refuel
helicopter refueling in midair

ish, **re·fu·elled, re·fu·el·ling.** —*v.t.* to supply again with fuel: *to refuel an airplane.* —*v.i.* to take on a fresh supply of fuel.

ref·uge (ref′ūj) *n.* **1.** shelter or protection, as from danger, trouble, or hardship: *The frightened puppy took refuge under the bed.* **2.** a place providing shelter, protection, or safety; haven: *The abandoned shack was our refuge during the storm.* **3.** a source of aid or relief.

ref·u·gee (ref′yù jē′, ref′yù jē′) *n.* a person who flees to safety or refuge, especially one who leaves home or homeland because of persecution, war, or danger and seeks safety in another place.

re·ful·gent (ri ful′jənt) *adj.* shining brightly; radiant. —**re·ful′gence,** *n.* —**re·ful′gent·ly,** *adv.*

re·fund (*v.,* ri fund′; *n.,* rē′fund′) *v.t.* to give or pay back: *The salesperson promised to refund the deposit if we should decide not to buy the sofa.* —*n.* **1.** the amount refunded: *a refund of five dollars.* **2.** the act or an instance of refunding.

re·fur·bish (rē fûr′bish) *v.t.* to brighten or freshen up: *to refurbish an old brass lamp.*

re·fus·al (ri fū′zəl) *n.* **1.** the act of refusing. **2.** the right or option to accept or reject something ahead of others: *to have first refusal on a sale.*

re·fuse¹ (ri fūz′) *v.,* **re·fused, re·fus·ing.** —*v.t.* **1.** to withhold acceptance of; turn down; reject: *to refuse a gift, to refuse an offer.* **2.** to withhold the giving or granting of; deny: *Every country refused asylum to the hijackers.* **3.** to be determined not to do (something); be unwilling: *You always refuse to see my point of view.* —*v.i.* to be unwilling to do something: *They can't refuse if you ask politely.* [From the Old French word *refuser* with the same meaning, from the Latin word *refusus,* past participle of *refundere* "to pour or fling back," from the prefix *re-* "back, again" + *fundere* "to pour out."]

ref·use² (ref′ūs) *n.* anything thrown away as useless or worthless; waste; rubbish. [From the Old French word *refus* meaning "waste, refuse²," from the word *refuser* "to refuse¹."]

re·fuse·nik (ri fūz′nik) *n.* a citizen of the Soviet Union who has requested to emigrate but has been denied permission by the Soviet government. [A translation of the Russian word *otkaznik* with the same meaning, from the word *otkaz* "refusal" + the suffix *-nik* "person."]

ref·u·ta·tion (ref′yù tā′shən) *n.* **1.** the act of refuting. **2.** something that refutes or disproves, as evidence or an argument.

re·fute (ri fūt′) *v.t.,* **re·fut·ed, re·fut·ing. 1.** to prove (a statement or argument) to be false or incorrect. **2.** to prove (someone) to be wrong: *The lawyer refuted the witness.* —**re·fut′a·ble,** *adj.* —**re·fut′er,** *n.*

re·gain (rē gān′) *v.t.* **1.** to get possession of again; get back; recover: *to regain one's health.* **2.** to reach again; get back to: *We regained the main highway from the side road.*

re·gal (rē′gəl) *adj.* **1.** suitable for or characteristic of a king or other ruler; stately; splendid; dignified: *a regal manner.* **2.** of or belonging to a king or other ruler; royal. —**re′gal·ly,** *adv.*

re·gale (ri gāl′) *v.,* **re·galed, re·gal·ing.** —*v.t.* **1.** to give great pleasure to; delight or entertain: *Our grandparents regaled us with stories of their childhood.* **2.** to provide a feast for. —*v.i.* to feast.

re·ga·li·a (ri gā′lē ə, ri gāl′yə) *pl. n.* **1.** the symbols or emblems of royalty, such as crowns and scepters. **2.** the symbols, emblems, or decorations of any rank, office, society, or order. **3.** splendid or fancy clothes; finery. ▲ used with a singular or plural verb.

re·gard (ri gärd′) *v.t.* **1.** to look upon or think of; consider: *to regard someone as your best friend.* **2.** to look at closely: *The guard regarded us with suspicion.* **3.** to show respect or consideration for: *to regard the rights of others.* **4.** to have relation to; have to do with; concern: *My question regards your future plans.* **5.** to pay attention to; heed: *I did not regard their warnings.* —*n.* **1.** careful thought, notice, or attention; consideration; heed: *to give no regard to the wishes of one's friends.* **2.** respect or affection. **3. regards.** best wishes: *Give my regards to your family.* **4.** a particular point; matter: *I agree with you in that regard.* **5.** a close or steady look: *I tried my first serve under my tennis teacher's careful regard.*

·**in regard to** or **with regard to.** regarding; in reference to.

re·gard·ful (ri gärd′fəl) *adj.* **1.** heedful; observant; mindful: *to be regardful of the rights of others.* **2.** respectful.

re·gard·ing (ri gär′ding) *prep.* in reference to; concerning.

re·gard·less (ri gärd′lis) *adj.* having or showing no regard or consideration; heedless; unmindful: *The acrobat was regardless of the risks involved in the difficult stunt.* —*adv.* in spite of everything; anyway: *I know you object, but I am buying the skis, regardless.* —**re·gard′less·ly,** *adv.*

re·gat·ta (ri gat′ə) *n.* a boat race or a series of boat races.

re·gen·cy (rē′jən sē) *n., pl.* **re·gen·cies.** **1.** the office, government, or power of a regent or body of regents, **2.** the period during which a regent or body of regents governs. **3. Regency.** in English history, the period from 1811 to 1820.

re·gen·er·ate (*v.,* ri jen′ə rāt′; *adj.,* ri jen′ər it) *v.,* **re·gen·er·at·ed, re·gen·er·at·ing.** —*v.t.* **1.** to cause to be morally or spiritually renewed. **2.** to give new strength, energy, or life to: *The team's victory regenerated their hopes of winning the pennant.* **3.** to reproduce or grow anew in order to replace something lost or damaged: *A lobster can regenerate a claw that has been broken off.* —*v.i.* **1.** to become formed anew; be reproduced. **2.** to be morally or spiritually renewed. —*adj.* **1.** morally or spiritually renewed. **2.** restored to a better state; renewed. —**re·gen′er·a′tion,** *n.*

re·gen·er·a·tive (ri jen′ə rā′tiv, ri jen′ər ə tiv) *adj.* **1.** of or relating to regeneration: *regenerative power.* **2.** tending to regenerate: *a regenerative species.*

re·gent (rē′jənt) *n.* **1.** a person who governs in place of a monarch who is absent, disabled, or too young. **2.** a member of a governing board, as of a state college or university or of a state educational system. —*adj.* acting as a regent: *a prince regent.*

reg·gae (reg′ā) *n.* a style of popular music of Jamaican origin that combines elements of rock 'n' roll, blues, and calypso. Reggae is characterized by the use of synco-

pation and lilting rhythms, often with lyrics of social protest. [Of uncertain origin.]

reg·i·cide (rej′ə sīd′) *n.* the act of killing a king. [From the Latin word *rex* meaning "king" + the English suffix *-cide*[1].]

re·gime (rə zhēm′, rā zhēm′) *also,* **ré·gime.** *n.* **1.** a system of government: *a dictatorial regime.* **2.** the time during which a government rules. **3.** another word for **regimen.**

reg·i·men (rej′ə mən, rej′ə men′) *n.* a regular schedule, as for diet, exercise, sleep, or study.

reg·i·ment (*n.,* rej′ə mənt; *v.,* rej′ə ment′) *n.* a military unit, usually commanded by a colonel, made up of three battalions and a headquarters, and forming part of a division. —*v.t.* to force to behave in a strict, uniform way; enforce uniformity on: *The military school regiments its students. The company regiments its workers.* —**reg′i·men·ta′tion,** *n.*

Word Family

The Latin word *regere,* meaning "to guide, direct," is the source of many English words. The officer **directing** a **regiment** usually subjects the troops to a strict **regimen.** They must always be ready to defend any **region** of the **realm.** If a **regime** that rules a nation becomes corrupt and lacks **rectitude,** the monarch might be removed and replaced by a **regent,** who would be expected to **rectify,** or **correct,** the situation. Once the nation received sound **direction** again, the popularity of the government would **surge.** There would be no worry then that **insurgents** would lead the people in a general **insurrection.**

reg·i·men·tal (rej′ə men′təl) *adj.* of or relating to a regiment. —*pl. n.* **regimentals.** **1.** the uniform of a regiment. **2.** any military uniform.

re·gion (rē′jən) *n.* **1.** a geographic area having one or more characteristics that set it apart from other areas: *a mining region, desert regions.* **2.** a large portion of a territory, space, or area: *the upper regions of the atmosphere.* **3.** a division or part of the body: *the abdominal region.* **4.** a sphere of interest or activity; a field; realm: *the region of philosophy.*

re·gion·al (rē′jə nəl) *adj.* of or relating to a particular region. —**re′gion·al·ly,** *adv.*

reg·is·ter (rej′ə stər) *n.* **1.** a formal or official record or list, as of names, facts, or events: *a register of marriages.* **2.** a book for such records: *a hotel register.* **3.** a machine that automatically records or counts, such as a cash register. **4.** in a heating or ventilating system, a grille or other device over an opening in a wall or floor, that can be opened or closed to regulate the passage of air into a room. **5.** *Music.* **a.** the range of a voice or instrument, or a particular portion of the range. **b.** a set of organ pipes controlled by one stop. —*v.t.* **1.** to enter in a register; record: *to register the names of students, to register a complaint.* **2.** to enroll formally or officially: *The volunteers registered the new voters.* **3.** to show or record, as on a scale: *The thermometer registered fifty degrees.* **4.** to show or express: *Their faces registered disappoint-*

at; āpe; fär; câre; end; mē; it; īce; pîerce; hot; ōld; sông, fôrk; oil; out; up; ūse; rüle; pull; tûrn; chin; sing; shop; thin; this; hw in white; zh in treasure. The symbol ə stands for the unstressed vowel sound heard in about, taken, pencil, lemon, and circus.

R

789

ment. **5.** to have (mail) officially recorded by paying a fee, so as to insure against loss, theft, or damage. —*v.i.* **1.** to enter one's name in a register: *to register at a hotel.* **2.** to enroll formally or officially: *The students register in September for the fall term.*

registered nurse, a nurse licensed by the state after completing certain training and education requirements.

reg·is·trar (rej′ə strär′) *n.* an official, especially at a college or university, in charge of keeping records.

reg·is·tra·tion (rej′ə strā′shən) *n.* **1.** the act of registering or the state of being registered. **2.** a document showing that something has been registered: *an automobile registration.* **3.** an entry in a register. **4.** the number of people registered, especially at a college or university; total enrollment.

reg·is·try (rej′ə strē) *n., pl.* **reg·is·tries.** **1.** a place where a register is kept; office of registration. **2.** see **register** *(def. 1).* **3.** the act of registering.

re·gress (ri gres′) *v.i.* to go back or return to an earlier or less advanced form or state; revert. —**re·gres′sion,** *n.*

re·gret (ri gret′) *v.t.,* **re·gret·ted, re·gret·ting. 1.** to feel sorry or distressed about: *to regret the loss of someone's friendship.* **2.** to remember with a feeling of loss or sadness: *to regret a lost opportunity.* —*n.* **1.** sorrow or distress: *I feel no regret for my decision.* **2.** a sense of loss or sadness. **3. regrets.** a polite apology, especially for refusing an invitation: *to send one's regrets.* —**re·gret′ta·ble,** *adj.* —**re·gret′ta·bly,** *adv.*

re·gret·ful (ri gret′fəl) *adj.* feeling or showing regret; filled with regret. —**re·gret′ful·ly,** *adv.* —**re·gret′ful·ness,** *n.*

reg·u·lar (reg′yə lər) *adj.* **1.** customary or expected; normal; usual: *The chair was moved from its regular place.* **2.** happening at fixed periods of time or according to a set schedule; unvarying; steady: *a regular summer vacation, regular train departures.* **3.** evenly shaped, spaced, or arranged: *regular teeth.* **4.** according to habit or a usual way of doing something: *a regular customer.* **5.** following a discipline; orderly: *to lead a regular life.* **6.** belonging to or making up a permanent or standing armed service: *Many early Americans were against establishing a regular army.* **7.** *Grammar.* using the most common inflectional endings, such as *-s* for nouns, *-ed* and *-ing* for verbs, and *-er* and *-est* for adjectives. *Lift* and *cook* are regular verbs. **8.** *Informal.* nice; decent; pleasant: *a regular guy.* —*n.* a soldier belonging to a permanent or standing armed service. [From the Old French word *reguler* meaning "belonging to a religious order," from the Late Latin word *regularis* "according to a (monastic) rule," from the Latin word *regula* "a rule, pattern, model," from the word *regere* "to rule, order."] —**reg′u·lar·ly,** *adv.*

reg·u·lar·i·ty (reg′yə lar′i tē) *n.* the quality or condition of being regular.

reg·u·late (reg′yə lāt′) *v.t.,* **reg·u·lat·ed, reg·u·lat·ing. 1.** to manage or control according to a set rule, principle, or system: *to regulate the economy.* **2.** to maintain at a certain level or standard; keep in adjustment: *a valve that regulates the intake of fuel in an engine.* **3.** to put or keep in good or proper working order: *to regulate a complex mechanism.* [From the Late Latin word *regulatus,* past participle of *regulare* meaning "to regulate," from the Latin word *regula* "rule, standard," from the word *regere* "to guide, determine, rule."] —**reg′u·la′tor,** *n.*

reg·u·la·tion (reg′yə lā′shən) *n.* **1.** a law, rule, or order intended to control behavior or procedure; governing rule or law: *school regulations.* **2.** the act of regulating or the state of being regulated. —*adj.* required by or in accordance with regulation: *a regulation uniform.*

reg·u·la·to·ry (reg′yə lə tôr′ē) *adj.* **1.** tending to regulate or control: *Sweating is a regulatory mechanism that*

lowers body temperature. **2.** providing or issuing regulations: *The practices of airlines are under the supervision of a government regulatory agency.*

re·gur·gi·tate (rē gûr′ji tāt′) *v.,* **re·gur·gi·tat·ed, re·gur·gi·tat·ing.** —*v.t.* to vomit. —*v.i.* to rush, pour, or flow back, as liquids, gases, or undigested food. —**re·gur′gi·ta′tion,** *n.*

re·ha·bil·i·tate (rē′hə bil′i tāt′) *v.t.,* **re·ha·bil·i·tat·ed, re·ha·bil·i·tat·ing. 1.** to restore or bring to a healthy or useful state: *to rehabilitate an injured leg.* **2.** to restore to a good condition; renovate: *to rehabilitate an abandoned cabin.* **3.** to restore the former rank, privileges, or good name of; reinstate. —**re′ha·bil′i·ta′tion,** *n.*

re·hash (*v.,* rē hash′; *n.,* rē′hash′) *v.t.* to go over or deal with again without making changes or improvements: *The lecturer simply rehashed ideas used by another lecturer yesterday.* —*n., pl.* **re·hash·es.** work or thought that is not original or creative; something rehashed: *The magazine article is a rehash of other writings on the subject.*

re·hears·al (ri hûr′səl) *n.* **1.** a period of practice in preparation for a public or official performance: *a dance rehearsal.* **2.** the act of rehearsing.

re·hearse (ri hûrs′) *v.,* **re·hearsed, re·hears·ing.** —*v.t.* **1.** to practice in preparation for a public or official performance: *to rehearse a play.* **2.** to train or improve by practice: *The director rehearsed the actors until they all knew their parts.* —*v.i.* to take part in a rehearsal.

reign (rān) *n.* **1.** the period of rule of a monarch or other ruler: *the reign of Queen Victoria.* **2.** supreme power or rule, as of a monarch; sovereignty. —*v.i.* **1.** to hold or use the power of a monarch or other ruler: *Louis XIV reigned for seventy-two years.* **2.** to have a widespread influence; prevail: *A severe famine reigned throughout the country.*

Reign of Terror, a period of the French Revolution, from about May 1793 to July 1794, during which thousands of persons were imprisoned or guillotined.

re·im·burse (rē′im bûrs′) *v.t.,* **re·im·bursed, re·im·burs·ing.** to pay back for what has been spent, used, or lost; recompense: *The company reimburses sales personnel for their traveling expenses.* —**re′im·burse′ment,** *n.*

rein (rān) *n.* **1.** either of two or more long, narrow straps attached to a bit at either side of a horse's mouth and used to control the movement of the horse. **2.** any means of guidance or control; check: *The dictator seized the reins of power.* —*v.t.* to guide, control, or check with or as if with reins: *to rein a horse, to rein one's anger.* —*v.i.* to slow down or stop a horse or other animal by means of reins: *to rein in a horse.*

·to give rein to or **to give free rein to.** to give complete freedom to: *to give rein to one's imagination.*

re·in·car·nate (rē′in kär′nāt) *v.t.,* **re·in·car·nat·ed, re·in·car·nat·ing.** to cause to undergo reincarnation.

re·in·car·na·tion (rē′in kär nā′shən) *n.* **1.** the rebirth of the soul in a new body. **2.** any similar rebirth or reappearance: *the reincarnation of a phoenix, the reincarnation of a folk tune as a hymn.*

rein·deer (rān′dîr′) *n., pl.* **rein·deer.** a large deer found in Lapland, Greenland, and other northern regions, having a white, gray, or brown coat and branched antlers.

re·in·force (rē′in fôrs′) also, **re·en·force, re-en-force.** *v.t.,* **re·in·forced, re·in·forc·ing. 1.** to strengthen by repairing or by adding new or extra parts

reindeer

or materials: *to reinforce a dam with sandbags.* **2.** to strengthen a military or naval force with additional personnel, supplies, or equipment: *to reinforce a fort.*

re·in·force·ment (rē′in fôrs′mənt) *also,* **re·en·force·ment, re-en·force·ment.** *n.* **1.** the act of reinforcing or the state of being reinforced. **2.** something that reinforces. **3. reinforcements.** additional troops, ships, or supplies to be used in a military action.

re·in·state (rē′in stāt′) *v.t.,* **re·in·stat·ed, re·in·stat·ing.** to restore to a former position or condition: *The suspended officers were reinstated after the charges against them were proved untrue.* —**re′in·state′ment,** *n.*

re·it·er·ate (rē it′ə rāt′) *v.t.,* **re·it·er·at·ed, re·it·er·at·ing.** to say or do again or repeatedly; repeat: *to reiterate an argument.* —**re·it′er·a′tion,** *n.*

re·ject (*v.,* ri jekt′; *n.,* rē′jekt′) *v.t.* **1.** to refuse to accept, believe, grant, or approve: *to reject an offer.* **2.** to throw away, set aside, or discard as marred or worthless: *The inspector rejected the chipped glasses.* **3.** to be unable to accept; expel: *The patient's body rejected the transplant.* —*n.* a person or thing that is rejected. —**re·jec′tion,** *n.*

re·joice (ri jois′) *v.,* **re·joiced, re·joic·ing.** —*v.i.* to express great joy or be filled with joy: *to rejoice at a soldier's safe return.* —*v.t.* to fill with joy; gladden: *to rejoice the spirit.*

re·join[1] (rē join′) *v.t.* **1.** to join the company of again: *to rejoin one's friends after vacation.* **2.** to join together again: *to rejoin the parts of a broken vase with glue.* [Re- + join.]

re·join[2] (ri join′) *v.i.* to answer; reply: *to rejoin sharply to criticism.* [From the Middle English word *rejoinen* meaning "to answer a legal charge," from the Old French word *rejoinder* "an answer, rejoinder."]

re·join·der (ri join′dər) *n.* an answer or reply, especially to a previous response: *My reply was met by a quick rejoinder.*

re·ju·ve·nate (ri jü′və nāt′) *v.t.,* **re·ju·ve·nat·ed, re·ju·ve·nat·ing.** to make young or vigorous again: *The vacation rejuvenated us.* —**re·ju′ve·na′tion,** *n.*

re·lapse (*n.,* rē′laps′; *v.,* rē laps′) *n.* the act of falling or slipping back into a former condition, especially the return of an illness after partial recovery. —*v.i.,* **re·lapsed, re·laps·ing.** to have a relapse.

re·late (ri lāt′) *v.,* **re·lat·ed, re·lat·ing.** —*v.t.* **1.** to report the events or details of; narrate; tell: *to relate what one has seen.* **2.** to show as having to do with; bring into relation; link: *Our teacher related our improved grades to better study habits.* —*v.i.* **1.** to be connected; apply; pertain: *How does that comment relate to what we are discussing?* **2.** to establish a close or friendly relationship with: *to relate well to children.*

re·lat·ed (ri lā′tid) *adj.* **1.** having relation; connected: *related problems.* **2.** connected by blood or marriage. —**re·lat′ed·ness,** *n.*

re·la·tion (ri lā′shən) *n.* **1.** the fact or condition of having to do with another or other things; connection between two or more things: *the relation between a good diet and a healthy body.* **2.** the position of one person or thing with respect to another: *the relation of parent to child.* **3. relations.** matters or conditions that bring one person or thing in contact with another; affairs; dealings: *business relations.* **4.** a connection formed by blood or marriage. **5.** a relative: *We have relations in Virginia.* **6.** the act or instance of narrating or telling.

re·la·tion·ship (ri lā′shən ship′) *n.* **1.** the state or condition of being related; connection; link. **2.** the condition of being connected by blood or marriage; kinship. **3.** an instance of being related or connected.

rel·a·tive (rel′ə tiv) *adj.* **1.** resulting from or judged by comparison; comparative: *to walk with relative ease after an operation.* **2.** existing or having meaning only in relation to something else, as the terms *right* and *left, big*

and *little* do. **3.** having to do with; connected with: *information relative to the case.* **4.** *Grammar.* modifying or referring to a person or thing previously mentioned. In the sentence *The person who called was my friend,* the word *who* is a relative pronoun referring to *friend.* —*n.* **1.** a person connected with another by blood or marriage: *Most of my relatives live in California.* **2.** *Grammar.* a relative word or term. —**rel′a·tive·ly,** *adv.*

·**relative to.** concerning; in regard to.

relative humidity, see **humidity** (*def. 2*).

rel·a·tiv·i·ty (rel′ə tiv′i tē) *n.* **1.** the quality, state, or fact of being relative. **2.** a theory, developed by Albert Einstein, that deals with the way in which measurements of physical quantities, such as space, time, and energy, differ when made by observers who are in motion relative to one another. It is based on the principle that all motion is relative and on the fact that the speed of light is the same with respect to all observers. The **special theory of relativity** treats the case in which the relative motion of the observers is along a straight line at a constant speed. Among its conclusions are that nothing can move faster than the speed of light and that mass and energy are equivalent. The **general theory of relativity** extends this theory to include all kinds of motion and provides an explanation for the force of gravity.

re·lax (ri laks′) *v.t.* **1.** to make less rigid or tense; loosen: *The hot bath helped to relax my muscles.* **2.** to make less strict, severe, or harsh: *The club relaxed its rules on accepting new members.* **3.** to provide release from tension or strain: *We needed a vacation to relax us.* —*v.i.* **1.** to become less rigid or tight. **2.** to become less tense, nervous, or anxious: *to relax by watching television.*

re·lax·ant (ri lak′sənt) *n.* a drug or procedure that relaxes, especially one that relaxes muscles: *Massage can be an effective relaxant.*

re·lax·a·tion (rē′lak sa′shən) *n.* **1.** the act of relaxing or the state of being relaxed. **2.** something that relaxes.

re·lay (*n.,* rē′lā; *v.,* rē′lā, ri lā′) *n.* **1.** a fresh set or team, as of workers or animals, prepared to replace or relieve another. **2.** see **relay race. 3.** an electrical switch that opens or closes in response to mechanical forces or to changes in the condition of an electric current. —*v.t.* to carry forward or pass along by or as if by relays: *to relay a message to someone.*

relay race, a race between two or more teams in which each team member in turn covers a certain distance and is then relieved by a teammate.

re·lease (ri lēs′) *v.t.,* **re·leased, re·leas·ing. 1.** to set free or loose: *to release a hostage.* **2.** to let go or cause to be free from something that holds or fastens: *to release a brake.* **3.** to relieve from duty, responsibility, or obligation: *to release someone from a promise.* **4.** to authorize or permit the publication, circulation, sale, or use of: *to release a motion picture for distribution.* **5.** to give up (a right, privilege, or claim). —*n.* **1.** the act of releasing or the state of being released. **2.** something that offers freedom or relief, as from work or tension: *to play golf as a release.* **3.** a written discharge or authorization: *The warden signed the prisoner's release.* **4.** something that is formally issued to the public: *a news release.* **5.** a device, such as a catch or button, that starts or holds a mechanism.

at; āpe; fär; câre; end; mē; it; īce; pîerce; hot; ōld; sông, fôrk; oil; out; up; ūse; rüle; pull; tûrn; chin; sing; shop; thin; *this;* hw in white; zh in treasure. The symbol ə stands for the unstressed vowel sound heard in about, taken, pencil, lemon, and circus.

791

rel·e·gate (rel′i gāt′) *v.t.*, **rel·e·gat·ed, rel·e·gat·ing.**
1. to send away or remove, especially to a lower or less important place or position: *We relegated the old toys to the attic.* **2.** to turn over (a matter or task) to another. —**rel′e·ga′tion,** *n.*

re·lent (ri lent′) *v.i.* to become less harsh or severe; soften; yield: *We begged them to change their decision, and they finally relented.*

re·lent·less (ri lent′lis) *adj.* **1.** harsh or severe; pitiless; unyielding. **2.** steady and persistent; ceaseless: *The story told of a scientist's relentless search for a vaccine.* —**re·lent′less·ly,** *adv.* —**re·lent′less·ness,** *n.*

rel·e·vant (rel′ə vənt) *adj.* connected or having to do with the matter at hand; appropriate; pertinent: *The lawyer's question about the defendant's car was relevant to the accident case.* —**rel′e·vance, rel′e·van·cy,** *n.*

re·li·a·ble (ri lī′ə bəl) *adj.* that can be depended on with confidence; trustworthy: *a reliable friend, a reliable business firm.* —**re·li′a·bil′i·ty,** *n.* —**re·li′a·bly,** *adv.*

re·li·ance (ri lī′əns) *n.* **1.** the act of relying. **2.** confidence, trust, or dependence. **3.** a person or thing that is relied on.

re·li·ant (ri lī′ənt) *adj.* having or showing reliance.

rel·ic (rel′ik) *n.* **1.** something from the past, such as an object or custom, that has survived the passage of time; remnant: *a relic of Roman civilization.* **2.** the body or part of the body of a saint, martyr, or other holy person, or some object associated with him or her, often enshrined as a memorial. **3.** something that is kept and cherished for its age or sentimental associations; memento; keepsake: *to keep a uniform as a relic of army days.*

re·lief¹ (ri lēf′) *n.* **1.** the freeing from or lessening of pain, anxiety, discomfort, or the like: *We sought relief from the heat in the air-conditioned room.* **2.** something that stops or lessens discomfort: *The cool air was a relief.* **3.** financial aid, as from government funds, to those in need: *to receive family relief, relief for flood victims.* **4.** release from a post or duty, as by a person or persons substituting for another. **5.** a person or persons who substitute for another or others: *The nurse's relief gets here at seven o'clock.* [From the Middle English word *relefe* meaning "help, assistance," and earlier "a payment made to a lord by a vassal who has gained new rank," from the word *relever* "to raise up, elevate (in rank)," going back to the Latin prefix *re-* "back, again" + *levare* "to raise." This payment was used to support various institutions and to help those in need.]

relief² *(defs. 3 and 4)*

re·lief² (ri lēf′) *n.* **1.** distinctness or prominence resulting from contrast: *The tree stood in bold relief against the sky.* **2.** a representation of the variation in height of a surface, especially as shown on a relief map. **3.** a projection of a figure or design from a flat background or other

surface, as in sculpture: *The marble block contained figures carved in relief.* **4.** a work of sculpture or design made with such a projection. **5.** the illusion of depth created in a painting or drawing by the use of line, shading, or color. [From the French word *relief* meaning "a raised figure or design on a flat surface," from the Old French word *relever* "to raise up."]

relief map, a map that shows variations in the height of a surface by means of contour lines, shading, color, or molding.

re·lieve (ri lēv′) *v.t.*, **re·lieved, re·liev·ing.** **1.** to free from or lessen (pain, anxiety, discomfort, or the like): *Gargling may relieve a sore throat.* **2.** to free from pain, anxiety, discomfort, or the like: *The good news relieved them.* **3.** to free from a post or duty by providing or serving as a substitute: *The night nurse will relieve the day nurse in an hour.* **4.** to furnish aid to: *to relieve the poor and needy.* **5.** to give variety to: *a gray day relieved by sunshine.*

re·li·gion (ri lij′ən) *n.* **1.** belief in, reverence for, or worship of God or a god or gods, who are usually thought of as having created or as ruling the universe. **2.** a particular system of such belief and worship: *the Christian religion.* **3.** something believed in or followed with great devotion or seriousness: *Success was the entrepreneur's religion.*

re·li·gious (ri lij′əs) *adj.* **1.** showing devotion to a religion; devout: *a religious person.* **2.** of or relating to religion: *religious beliefs.* **3.** very careful and exact; conscientious; strict: *a religious attention to details in one's work.* **4.** of, relating to, or belonging to an order or community bound by monastic vows. —*n., pl.* **re·li·gious.** a person bound by monastic vows, as a monk or nun. —**re·li′gious·ly,** *adv.* —**re·li′gious·ness,** *n.*

re·lin·quish (ri ling′kwish) *v.t.* **1.** to give over possession or control of; surrender; yield: *The defeated nation relinquished territory to the conquerors.* **2.** to put aside or give up; abandon: *to relinquish all claim to a sum of money.* **3.** to let go; release: *The dog would not relinquish its hold on the stick.* —**re·lin′quish·ment,** *n.*

rel·ish (rel′ish) *n., pl.* **rel·ish·es.** **1.** a mixture of spices, pickles, olives, chopped vegetables, or the like, used chiefly to flavor other food or as a side dish. **2.** interest or pleasure; enjoyment: *to open a present with relish.* **3.** anything that lends interest or pleasure to something else. —*v.t.* to take pleasure in; savor; enjoy: *to relish a meal.*

re·live (rē liv′) *v.t.*, **re·lived, re·liv·ing.** to live over again, especially in the mind: *to relive an adventure, to relive a happy time.*

re·lo·cate (rē lō′kāt, rē′lō kāt′) *v.t., v.i.*, **re·lo·cat·ed, re·lo·cat·ing.** to move to another place: *to relocate a business, to relocate in the next town.*

re·luc·tance (ri luk′təns) *n.* the state of being reluctant; lack of eagerness; hesitation or unwillingness.

re·luc·tant (ri luk′tənt) *adj.* **1.** feeling hesitation or unwillingness; unwilling; averse: *I was reluctant to leave the party.* **2.** marked by hesitation or unwillingness: *a reluctant apology.* —**re·luc′tant·ly,** *adv.*

re·ly (ri lī′) *v.i.*, **re·lied, re·ly·ing.** **1.** to have confidence; trust: *You can rely on them to be prompt.* **2.** to depend; be dependent on: *We rely on the sun for heat.*

REM (rem) *n.* the rapid shifting of the eyes under closed eyelids during the phase of sleep in which dreams occur. [Abbreviation of *r*(apid) *e*(ye) *m*(ovement).]

re·main (ri mān′) *v.i.* **1.** to continue in the same place; stay behind; abide: *You should have remained at home.* **2.** to continue unchanged; go on being: *We remained as friends for years.* **3.** to be left: *All that remains of the ancient city is ruins. If you take three apples from five apples, two remain.*

re·main·der (ri mān′dər) *n.* **1.** something that remains or is left; remaining part: *We played ball for the remainder of the day.* **2.** *Mathematics.* **a.** the number found when one number is subtracted from another. Ten subtracted from 12 leaves a remainder of 2. **b.** the number remaining when one number is divided by another. If you divide 7 by 3 you get 2 and a remainder of 1.

re·mains (ri mānz′) *pl. n.* **1.** something that is left: *the remains of an ancient city, the remains of dinner.* **2.** a dead body; corpse.

re·make (*n.*, rē′māk′; *v.*, rē māk′) *n.* something made again or anew: *a remake of an old motion picture.* —*v.t.*, **re·made** (rē mād′), **re·mak·ing.** to make again or anew.

re·mand (ri mand′) *v.t.* **1.** to send, call, or order back: *to remand troops to their base.* **2.** *Law.* **a.** to return (a prisoner or an accused person) to custody. **b.** to send (a case) back to a lower court for further proceedings. —*n.* the act of remanding or the state of being remanded.

re·mark (ri märk′) *n.* **1.** a spoken or written statement or observation, especially a brief or casual comment. **2.** the act of taking notice or observing; notice. —*v.t.* **1.** to express as an opinion or observation. **2.** to take notice of; observe; perceive. —*v.i.* to make remarks.

re·mark·a·ble (ri mär′kə bəl) *adj.* **1.** having unusual qualities; extraordinary; uncommon: *Your keen wit is remarkable.* **2.** worthy of notice or likely to be noticed: *The change in temperature was remarkable.* —**re·mark′a·ble·ness,** *n.* —**re·mark′a·bly,** *adv.*

re·mar·ry (rē mar′ē) *v.*, **re·mar·ried, re·mar·ry·ing.** —*v.i.* to marry again after being widowed or divorced. —*v.t.* to marry (a former spouse) again. —**re·mar·riage** (rē mar′ij), *n.*

re·match (rē′mach′) *n.* a second contest between two competitors; return match.

re·me·di·a·ble (ri mē′dē ə bəl) *adj.* able to be remedied. —**re·me·di·a·bly,** *adv.*

re·me·di·al (ri mē′dē əl) *adj.* providing or intending to provide a remedy or improvement: *a remedial reading program.* —**re·me′di·al·ly,** *adv.*

rem·e·dy (rem′i dē) *n., pl.* **rem·e·dies.** **1.** something that relieves, heals, or improves a disease, disorder, or the like: *a headache remedy.* **2.** something that corrects or gets rid of something bad or harmful: *Some scientists and engineers are seeking a remedy for air pollution.* —*v.t.*, **rem·o·died, rem·e·dy·ing.** **1.** to relieve, heal, or improve (a disease, disorder, or the like), as by treatment with medicine. **2.** to set or make right; correct: *to remedy conditions after a disaster.*

re·mem·ber (ri mem′bər) *v.t.* **1.** to bring back or recall to the mind or memory; recollect: *Do you remember where you put the keys?* **2.** to keep in mind or memory: *to remember a phone number.* **3.** to think of or keep in mind as worthy of affection, regard, or recognition: *I'll always remember you for your kindness.* **4.** to reward or present with a gift: *We remember our mail carrier with a gift at the holidays.* **5.** to send greetings from: *Remember me to your parents.* —*v.i.* to use the memory.

re·mem·brance (ri mem′brəns) *n.* **1.** something that is remembered; recollection: *a remembrance from childhood.* **2.** the act or power of remembering. **3.** the state of being remembered. **4.** an object, such as a gift, serving to bring someone or something to mind; memento; keepsake: *to give a bracelet as a remembrance.*

re·mind (ri mīnd′) *v.t.* to make (someone) think of something or someone; bring back to mind; cause to remember: *I reminded her to return the library book. He reminds me of an old friend.* —**re·mind′er,** *n.*

rem·i·nisce (rem′ə nis′) *v.i.*, **rem·i·nisced, rem·i·nisc·ing.** to think or tell of past experiences or events: *The two friends reminisced about their school days.*

rem·i·nis·cence (rem′ə nis′əns) *n.* **1.** a thinking of past experiences or events. **2.** *also,* **reminiscences.** a story or account of past experiences or events. **3.** something remembered; memory.

rem·i·nis·cent (rem′ə nis′ənt) *adj.* **1.** reminding or suggestive: *This landscape is reminiscent of home.* **2.** marked by or given to reminiscence: *to become reminiscent about old times.*

re·miss (ri mis′) *adj.* **1.** careless or negligent, as in one's duty; lax: *I was very remiss and failed to get my work in on time.* **2.** showing carelessness or negligence: *a remiss way of doing something.* —**re·miss′ly,** *adv.* —**re·miss′ness,** *n.*

re·mis·sion (ri mish′ən) *n.* **1.** the act of remitting or the state of being remitted. **2.** a freeing from penalty or guilt; forgiveness; pardon: *to obtain remission of one's sins.* **3.** a temporary lessening of pain or the symptoms of a disease, or the like: *The heat continued without remission. The disease is in remission.* **4.** a cancellation, as of a debt.

re·mit (ri mit′) *v.*, **re·mit·ted, re·mit·ting.** —*v.t.* **1.** to send (money) in payment. **2.** to free from the penalty or guilt of; forgive; pardon: *to remit a sin.* **3.** to do away with; cancel: *to remit punishment.* **4.** to make less; lessen; reduce. **5.** to submit or refer for consideration, decision, or action, especially to someone in authority. **6.** *Law.* to send (a case) back to a lower court for further proceedings. —*v.i.* **1.** to send money in payment. **2.** to become less; abate; diminish: *The fever remitted.* —**re·mit′ter,** *n.*

re·mit·tance (ri mit′əns) *n.* **1.** the sending of money. **2.** money sent, as a payment: *We have received your remittance of fourteen dollars.*

rem·nant (rem′nənt) *n.* **1.** a remaining piece or part; remainder: *The remnants of the meal were still on the table. The archaeologist uncovered the remnants of an ancient civilization.* **2.** a piece of cloth or carpet left over from the cutting of a larger piece, often sold at a reduced price.

re·mod·el (rē mod′əl) *v.t.*, **re·mod·eled, re·mod·cl·ing;** *also, British,* **re·mod·elled, re·mod·cl·ling.** to make over or anew; reconstruct; renovate: *The builder remodeled the store for the new owner.*

re·mon·strance (ri mon′strəns) *n.* the act or an instance of remonstrating; protest.

re·mon·strate (ri mon′strāt) *v.i.*, **re·mon·strat·ed, re·mon·strat·ing.** to present reasons against something; plead or argue in opposition: *The district attorney remonstrated with the judge against the motion to dismiss the case.*

rem·o·ra (rem′ər ə) *n.* any of a group of fish, found mainly in tropical seas, that attach themselves to sharks and other larger fish by means of a suction disk on the top of their heads. Remoras feed on parasitic crustaceans attached to their hosts or on food left over by their hosts.

re·morse (ri môrs′) *n.* a deep, painful feeling of guilt, sorrow, or distress for wrongdoing: *The teenager showed remorse for having stolen the watch.* [From the Old French phrase *remors (de conscience)* meaning "remorse (of conscience)," going back to the Latin word *remorsus,* past participle of *remordēre* meaning "to bite again, gnaw at," from the prefix *re-* "again" + *mordēre* "to bite."] —**re·morse′ful,** *adj.* —**re·morse′ful·ly,** *adv.* —**re·morse′ful·ness,** *n.*

re·morse·less (ri môrs′lis) *adj.* having no pity or re-

---

at; āpe; fär; câre; end; mē; it; īce; pîerce; hot; ōld; sông, fôrk; oil; out; up; ūse; rüle; pull; tûrn; chin; sing; shop; thin; <u>th</u>is; hw in white; zh in treasure. The symbol ə stands for the unstressed vowel sound heard in about, taken, pencil, lemon, and circus.

R

morse; merciless; cruel: *a display of remorseless cruelty.*
—**re·morse′less·ly,** *adv.* —**re·morse′less·ness,** *n.*

re·mote (ri mōt′) *adj.,* **re·mot·er, re·mot·est. 1.** located
at a distance; not near: *remote regions.* **2.** located out of
the way; secluded: *a remote house.* **3.** far removed from
the present; distant in time: *the remote past.* **4.** small in
degree; slight; faint: *There was only a remote possibility
that our team would win.* **5.** having no close connection
or bearing: *The question was remote from the subject of
the talk.* —*n.* another term for **remote control.** —**re·
mote′ly,** *adv.* —**re·mote′ness,** *n.*

remote control 1. control of a machine or apparatus,
such as a guided missile or a television set, from a distance,
especially by means of transmitted signals. **2.** a device
used for remote control. Also, **remote.**

re·mount (*v.,* rē mount′; *n.,* rē′mount′) *v.t.* to mount
(something) again: *The riders remounted their horses.
The insect collector remounted several specimens.*
—*v.i.* to mount again. —*n.* a fresh horse that takes the
place of another.

re·mov·al (ri mü′vəl) *n.* **1.** the act of removing or the
state of being removed: *The removal of the books from
the shelf took only a few minutes.* **2.** a changing of a
location, as of a business. **3.** dismissal from an office or
position: *the removal of a dishonest mayor.*

re·move (ri müv′) *v.,* **re·moved, re·mov·ing.** —*v.t.*
1. to take or move away, as from one place or position to
another: *to remove dishes from a table.* **2.** to take off or
shed: *Remove your hat when you go inside.* **3.** to do
away with; eliminate: *to remove all cause for alarm.*
4. to dismiss from an office or position. —*v.i.* to change
one's place of residence or business; move. —*n.* a
distance or space separating one person or thing from
another: *The two oases are at some remove from each
other.* —**re·mov′a·ble,** *adj.* —**re·mov′er,** *n.*

re·moved (ri müvd′) *adj.* **1.** separated by a degree in
relationship: *My first cousin's child is my first cousin once
removed.* **2.** distant; remote.

re·mu·ner·ate (ri mū′nə rāt′) *v.t.,* **re·mu·ner·at·ed,
re·mu·ner·at·ing.** to pay (someone) for any service,
loss, or expense; reward; repay: *They remunerated me
for mowing the lawn.* —**re·mu′ner·a′tion,** *n.*

re·mu·ner·a·tive (ri mū′nə rā′tiv, ri mū′nər ə tiv) *adj.*
that remunerates; profitable: *a remunerative investment.*

Re·mus (rē′məs) *n.* see **Romulus.**

ren·ais·sance (ren′ə säns′, ren′ə säns′) *n.* **1.** a renewal
of activity, interest, or enthusiasm about something; rebirth; revival: *There was a renaissance of the arts in our
town.* **2. Renaissance. a.** a revival of European art and
learning that began in Italy during the fourteenth century,
marked by a growth of interest in ancient Greek and Latin
literature and art, concern with individualism, and intellectual and scientific activity. **b.** the period of European
history during which this occurred, extending from the
fourteenth through the sixteenth centuries. **c.** a style of
art and architecture developed during this period. —*adj.*
Renaissance. of, characteristic of, or in the style of the
Renaissance. Also, **renascence.**

re·nal (rē′nəl) *adj.* of, relating to, or near the kidneys.

re·nas·cence (ri nas′əns, ri nā′səns) *n., adj.* another
word for **renaissance.**

re·nas·cent (ri nas′ənt, ri nā′sənt) *adj.* showing renewed growth or vigor; being born again.

rend (rend) *v.t.,* **rent** or **rend·ed, rend·ing. 1.** to split or
tear apart or into pieces forcibly or violently: *The wind
rent the sails of the yacht.* **2.** to divide or split as if by
tearing: *Political disagreements rent the community.*
3. to remove forcibly; wrest: *to rend a weapon from
someone's hands.* **4.** to trouble greatly: *We were rent
with anxiety.*

ren·der (ren′dər) *v.t.* **1.** to cause to be or become; make:
to render someone helpless. **2.** to give or pay as something

owed or due: *to render an apology, to render homage.*
3. to give or make available; provide: *to render aid to the
needy.* **4.** to represent or show, as in a painting. **5.** to
present and interpret in performance: *The pianist rendered
the composition in a lively manner.* **6.** to deliver
or state formally: *The jury rendered a verdict of not guilty.*
7. to reproduce or express in another language; translate:
to render an English poem into Russian. **8.** to give up;
surrender; yield: *to render one's life for a cause.* **9.** to
separate, purify, or extract by melting: *to render fat.*

ren·dez·vous (rän′də vü′) *n., pl.* **ren·dez·vous** (rän′-
də vüz′). **1.** an appointment to meet at a fixed place or
time. **2.** the place chosen for such a meeting. **3.** any
meeting or gathering place. —*v.,* **ren·dez·voused**
(rän′də vüd′), **ren·dez·vous·ing** (rän′də vü′ing). —*v.i.*
to meet by arrangement. —*v.t.* to cause to meet by
arrangement. [From the French word *rendezvous,* from
the phrase *rendez-vous* meaning "present yourself (at a
meeting)."]

ren·di·tion (ren dish′ən) *n.* **1.** an interpretation given
by a performer to a dramatic, literary, or musical composition. **2.** an interpretation or version of a text; translation: *an English rendition of Homer's Iliad.* **3.** the
act of rendering.

ren·e·gade (ren′i gād′) *n.* a person who abandons, rejects, or turns against his or her group in favor of another;
traitor. —*adj.* of, being, or like a renegade: *a renegade
soldier.*

re·nege (ri nig′, ri neg′) *v.i.,* **re·neged, re·neg·ing.
1.** to fail to fulfill a promise or commitment: *to renege on
a business deal.* **2.** in a card game, to fail to play a card
of the suit required by the rules.

re·new (ri nü′, ri nū′) *v.t.* **1.** to make new or as if new
again; restore to a previous or good condition: *to renew
the finish on a table, to renew one's spirits.* **2.** to begin
again or start over; take up again; resume: *to renew a
friendship, to renew a discussion.* **3.** to cause to continue
for another period of time: *to renew the loan of a library
book, to renew a subscription.* **4.** to replace with something new of the same sort; fill again; replenish: *The ship
renewed its provisions.*

re·new·a·ble (ri nü′ə bəl, ri nū′ə bəl) *adj.* **1.** able to
be renewed or repeated: *This prescription is renewable
three times.* **2.** able to be replaced or restored: *Lumber
is a renewable natural resource.*

re·new·al (ri nü′əl, ri nū′əl) *n.* **1.** the act of renewing
or the state of being renewed. **2.** something renewed.

ren·net (ren′it) *n.* a substance containing rennin, obtained from the stomachs of young calves and added to
milk in the making of cheese.

ren·nin (ren′in) *n.* an enzyme present in the gastric juice
of certain animals, especially young calves, that causes
milk to curdle.

re·nounce (ri nouns′) *v.t.,* **re·nounced, re·nounc·ing.
1.** to give up or abandon, especially by formal declaration:
to renounce a claim. **2.** to refuse to recognize or accept
as one's own; disown: *The angry rebels renounced their
loyalty to the government.* —**re nounce′ment,** *n.*

ren·o·vate (ren′ə vāt′) *v.t.,* **ren·o·vat·ed, ren·o·vat·ing.**
to make like new; renew: *to renovate a building.* —*v.i.*
to make changes or improvements; redecorate: *We spent
a week at home renovating.* —**ren′o·va′tion,** *n.* —**ren′-
o·va′tor,** *n.*

re·nown (ri noun′) *n.* widespread reputation; fame.

re·nowned (ri nound′) *adj.* having renown; famous.

rent¹ (rent) *n.* a payment for the use of property, especially such payment made regularly by a tenant to a
landlord or owner. —*v.t.* **1.** to get the right to use
(property) in return for the paying of rent: *to rent a car,
to rent a house.* **2.** to grant the use of (property) in return
for the paying of rent: *The store rents bicycles.* —*v.i.* to

be for rent: *The apartment rents for $500 a month.* [From the Old French word *rent* meaning "revenue from property," going back to the Latin word *renditus*, past participle of *rendere* "to yield."]

·**for rent.** available for use in return for the paying of rent.

rent² (rent) *v.* a past tense and past participle of **rend.** —*n.* **1.** an opening or hole made by rending or tearing; gap or slit: *a rent in a dress, a rent in a curtain.* **2.** a sharp division or split, as in a group or organization. [From the Middle English word *rent*, past participle of *renden* meaning "to tear¹, rip apart," from the Old English word *rendan* "to tear¹."]

rent·al (ren′təl) *n.* **1.** an amount charged, paid, or collected as rent. **2.** the act of renting. **3.** property rented or available for renting. —*adj.* of or relating to rent or renting: *a car rental agency.*

rent strike, a refusal by tenants to pay rent, usually in protest against increases in rent or against poor service.

re·nun·ci·a·tion (ri nun′sē ā′shən) *n.* the act of renouncing.

re·o·pen (rē ō′pən) *v.t., v.i.* **1.** to open again: *to reopen a bottle of soda. School reopens in September.* **2.** to begin again; resume: *We reopened the discussion.*

re·or·gan·i·za·tion (rē′ôr gə nə zā′shən) *n.* the act of reorganizing or the state of being reorganized.

re·or·gan·ize (rē ôr′gə nīz′) *v.t., v.i.,* **re·or·gan·ized, re·or·gan·iz·ing.** to organize again or anew, as in a different way: *The new management reorganized the company.*

Rep. **1.** Representative. **2.** Republic. **3.** Republican.

re·paid (ri pād′) the past tense and past participle of **repay.**

re·pair¹ (ri pâr′) *v.t.* **1.** to restore to a good condition or working order, as by replacing parts or putting together what has broken; fix; mend: *to repair a toaster. The road crew repaired the highway.* **2.** to correct or eliminate by repairing: *The plumber repairs leaks.* **3.** to bring back to a sound or healthy state; renew: *to repair damaged body tissues.* **4.** to make good; set right; remedy: *to repair a wrong.* —*n.* **1.** the act or process of repairing: *The roof is beyond repair.* **2.** the result of repairing. **3.** condition in terms of soundness or need of repairing: *to be in good repair.* [From the Old French word *reparer* meaning "to mend, fix," from the Latin word *reparare* "to recover, restore," from the prefix *re-* "back, again" + *parare* "to get ready, prepare."] —**re·pair′er,** *n.*

re·pair² (ri pâr′) *v.i.* to go: *They repair to their favorite campsite every vacation.* [From the Old French word *repairier* meaning "to return," from the Late Latin word *repatriare* "to return to one's own country," from the Latin prefix *re-* "back, again" + *patria* "native land."]

re·pair·man (ri pâr′man′) *n., pl.* **re·pair·men** (ri pâr′men′). a person whose occupation is making repairs.

rep·a·ra·ble (rep′ər ə bəl) *also,* **re·pair·a·ble** (ri pâr′ə bəl). *adj.* able to be repaired.

rep·a·ra·tion (rep′ə rā′shən) *n.* **1.** the act of giving satisfaction or making amends, as for a wrong or injury. **2.** something done or given as satisfaction or to make amends. **3. reparations.** money or material given in compensation for damage or loss in war, especially that given by a defeated nation to a victorious one.

rep·ar·tee (rep′ər tē′, re′pär tā′) *n.* **1.** an exchange of quick, witty replies. **2.** skill or quickness in making such replies. **3.** a quick, witty reply.

re·past (ri past′) *n.* a meal, or the food and drink eaten or provided at a meal.

re·pa·tri·ate (*v.,* rē pā′trē at′; *n.,* rē pā′trē it) *v.t.,* **re·pa·tri·at·ed, re·pa·tri·at·ing.** to return (someone) to the country in which he or she was born or is a citizen.

—*n.* a person who has been repatriated. —**re·pa′tri·a′tion,** *n.*

re·pay (ri pā′) *v.t.,* **re·paid, re·pay·ing.** **1.** to pay or give back: *to repay a loan.* **2.** to pay or give something back to (someone): *I'll never be able to repay you for your help.* **3.** to give, make, or do in return: *to repay a compliment.* —**re·pay′a·ble,** *adj.* —**re·pay′ment,** *n.*

re·peal (ri pēl′) *v.t.* to withdraw or cancel formally or officially; revoke: *to repeal a law.* —*n.* the act of repealing: *the repeal of a constitutional amendment.*

re·peat (ri pēt′) *v.t.* **1.** to say or utter (something already said) again: *to repeat a question.* **2.** to tell to another or others: *Don't repeat a word of what I told you.* **3.** to say again or recite from memory. **4.** to do, make, or perform again: *The tennis player repeated the serve.* —*v.i.* to say or do something again. —*n.* **1.** the act of repeating. **2.** something repeated; repetition. **3.** *Music.* **a.** a passage, section, or movement that is to be repeated. **b.** any of several signs indicating this, especially double bar lines with two dots placed at the end (:‖), and usually also at the beginning (‖:) of such a passage. —**re·peat′er,** *n.*

re·peat·ed (ri pē′tid) *adj.* said, done, or happening again and again. —**re·peat′ed·ly,** *adv.*

repeating decimal, a decimal in which a particular digit or series of digits is repeated indefinitely. 0.666 . . . and 0.1232323 . . . are repeating decimals.

re·pel (ri pel′) *v.t.,* **re·pelled, re·pel·ling.** **1.** to drive back or away: *to repel an attack.* **2.** to cause to feel dislike or disgust: *Violence repels me.* **3.** to withstand the action or effect of; resist: *This material will repel heat and moisture.* **4.** to refuse to accept or consider; reject: *to repel an offer.* **5.** to push away or force apart: *The negative poles of two magnets will repel each other.*

re·pel·lent (ri pel′ənt) *adj.* **1.** causing dislike or disgust; repugnant. **2.** resistant to something. ▲ usually used in combination: *a water repellent coat.* **3.** serving or tending to drive away. —*n.* something that repels: *a mosquito repellent.*

re·pent (ri pent′) *v.i.* to feel sorrow or deep regret for something one has done or failed to do: *The sinner repented.* —*v.t.* **1.** to feel sorrow or deep regret for: *to repent one's mistakes and resolve to be a better person.* **2.** to change one's mind about or regret: *I repented my decision to sell the house.*

re·pent·ance (ri pen′təns) *n.* **1.** sorrow or deep regret, as for sin or wrongdoing. **2.** the act or process of repenting.

re·pent·ant (ri pen′tənt) *adj.* feeling, showing, or marked by repentance; penitent. —**re·pent′ant·ly,** *adv.*

re·per·cus·sion (rē′pər kush′ən) *n.* **1.** a result or effect of an action or event; consequence: *The firing of the coach caused repercussions throughout the school.* **2.** an echo: *the repercussions of a loud noise.* **3.** a recoil or springing back: *the repercussion of a hammer after hitting an anvil.*

rep·er·toire (rep′ər twär′) *n.* **1.** the artistic works, such as plays, operas, or songs, that a performer or group of performers is ready to perform. **2.** a list of such works.

rep·er·to·ry (rep′ər tôr′ē) *n., pl.* **rep·er·to·ries.** **1.** another word for **repertoire.** **2.** a store or collection. **3.** see **repertory theater.**

repertory theater, a theatrical organization in which a

---

at; āpe; fär; câre; end; mē; it; īce; pîerce; hot; ōld; sông; fôrk; oil; out; up; ūse; rūle; pull; tûrn; chin; sing; shop; thin; this; hw in white; zh in treasure. The symbol ə stands for the unstressed vowel sound heard in about, taken, pencil, lemon, and circus.

R

permanent acting company performs different plays during a season.

rep·e·ti·tion (rep′i tish′ən) *n.* **1.** the act of repeating. **2.** something that is repeated.

rep·e·ti·tious (rep′i tish′əs) *adj.* full of, marked by, or containing repetition: *a repetitious speaker, a repetitious article.* —**rep′e·ti′tious·ly,** *adv.* —**rep′e·ti′tious·ness,** *n.*

re·pet·i·tive (ri pet′i tiv) *adj.* another word for **repetitious.**

re·place (ri plās′) *v.t.,* **re·placed, re·plac·ing. 1.** to take or fill the place of: *She will replace him as club president.* **2.** to provide or get a substitute for: *The car battery is defective and should be replaced.* **3.** to restore or return to the original or proper place; put back: *Please replace the magazine in the rack.*

re·place·ment (ri plās′mənt) *n.* **1.** a person or thing that replaces. **2.** the act of replacing or the state of being replaced.

re·play (*v.,* rē plā′; *n.,* rē′plā′) *v.t.* to play again, as a game or phonograph record. —*n.* **1.** the act of replaying something: *No one could tell if the serve was good, so the tennis umpire ordered a replay of the point.* **2.** something replayed, especially a recorded portion of a game: *In the replay you could see that the quarterback dropped the ball.*

re·plen·ish (ri plen′ish) *v.t.* **1.** to bring back to a state of fullness or completeness, as by replacing what is lacking or has been used: *to replenish one's food supplies.* **2.** to provide a new supply for: *to replenish the storage closet.* —**re·plen′ish·ment,** *n.*

re·plete (ri plēt′) *adj.* **1.** supplied in abundance; abounding: *a garden replete with brightly colored flowers.* **2.** filled with food or drink; sated.

re·ple·tion (ri plē′shən) *n.* the state or condition of being replete.

replica of a dinosaur skeleton

rep·li·ca (rep′li kə) *n.* a close or exact copy, especially one done on a smaller scale than the original: *The architects constructed a replica of the house.*

rep·li·cate (rep′li kāt′) *v.,* **rep·li·cat·ed, rep·li·cat·ing.** —*v.t.* **1.** to duplicate or repeat exactly: *to replicate a scientific experiment.* **2.** to make a model or replica of: *The museum is replicating an ancient Indian village.* —*v.i.* to duplicate or reproduce exactly by genetic processes: *DNA divides and replicates in cell division.*

rep·li·ca·tion (rep′li kā′shən) *n.* **1.** the act or process of replicating. **2.** the process, occurring during cell division, in which the DNA in the cell duplicates itself, thus ensuring that all new cells are exactly like the original.

re·ply (ri plī′) *v.,* **re·plied, re·ply·ing.** —*v.i.* **1.** to respond in speech or writing; answer: *I did not reply when questioned.* **2.** to respond by some action; react. —*v.t.* to say in response; give as a response: *They replied that they could not come to dinner.* —*n., pl.* **re·plies.** something said, written, or done in response.

re·port (ri pôrt′) *n.* **1.** an account, statement, or announcement: *a news and weather report.* **2.** an explosive sound or noise, especially that made by a rifle or pistol when fired. **3.** reputation; repute: *a teacher of good report.* **4.** rumor; common talk: *Report has it that it will snow tonight.* —*v.t.* **1.** to make or give an account, statement, or announcement of: *to report the news.* **2.** to bring charges of wrongdoing against; complain about: *to report a drunk driver to the police.* —*v.i.* **1.** to make a report: *The newspaper reported on the election.* **2.** to present oneself: *I reported for work at noon.*

report card, a written report of a pupil's grades and conduct.

re·port·ed·ly (ri pôr′tid lē) *adv.* according to report: *The senator is reportedly going to visit Russia.*

re·port·er (ri pôr′tər) *n.* **1.** a person employed to gather and report news for a newspaper or magazine, or for television or radio. **2.** a person who makes an official record of what is said in a courtroom during a trial. **3.** any person who reports.

re·pose[1] (ri pōz′) *n.* **1.** relaxation, as after activity; rest; sleep. **2.** peace and quiet; tranquillity: *the beauty and repose of the forest.* **3.** calmness or ease, as of manner; composure. —*v.i.,* **re·posed, re·pos·ing. 1.** to lie or be at rest; sleep: *to repose on the sofa.* **2.** to be supported; rest; lie: *The book reposes on the table.* **3.** to lie buried or interred. [From the Old French word *reposer* meaning "to rest," from the Late Latin word *repausare* "to rest," from the Latin prefix *re-* "back, again" + *pausa* "a pause."]

re·pose[2] (ri pōz′) *v.t.,* **re·posed, re·pos·ing.** to place, as confidence or hope in someone or something. [*Re-* + *pose.*]

re·pos·i·to·ry (ri poz′i tôr′ē) *n., pl.* **re·pos·i·to·ries.** a place or receptacle in which something is or may be stored or deposited.

re·pos·sess (rē′pə zes′) *v.t.* **1.** to possess again; regain possession of. **2.** to resume possession of (something bought on installments or credit) because the buyer has failed to make due payment: *The bank repossessed the car.* —**re·pos·ses·sion** (rē′pə zesh′ən), *n.*

rep·re·hend (rep′ri hend′) *v.t.* to criticize sharply; reprove; censure.

rep·re·hen·si·ble (rep′ri hen′sə bəl) *adj.* deserving sharp criticism or reproof. —**rep′re·hen′si·bly,** *adv.*

rep·re·hen·sion (rep′ri hen′shən) *n.* the act of reprehending; criticism; reproof.

rep·re·sent (rep′ri zent′) *v.t.* **1.** to serve as a symbol, sign, or expression of; stand for; symbolize: *In this story the witch represents evil.* **2.** to express by some symbol, character, sign, or the like: *to represent speech sounds by letters.* **3.** to speak or act for; serve as the delegate or agent of: *Two senators represent each state in Congress.* **4.** to present an image or likeness of, as in painting or sculpture. **5.** to serve as an example or instance of; typify: *The works of Dickens represent the Victorian novel.* **6.** to describe; claim to be: *They represented their restaurant as the best in the city.*

rep·re·sen·ta·tion (rep′ri zen tā′shən, rep′ri zən tā′shən) *n.* **1.** the act of representing or the state of being represented. **2.** an account, statement, or description: *The salesperson gave a favorable representation of the product.* **3.** something that represents, such as a picture or other likeness. **4.** the state, fact, or right of being represented in a legislative or deliberative assembly. **5.** a body or number of representatives.

rep·re·sen·ta·tion·al (rep′ri zen tā′shə nəl, rep′ri zən-tā'shə nəl) *adj.* of or relating to a style of art that shows objects as they appear to the eye rather than as totally abstract forms.

rep·re·sent·a·tive (rep'ri zen'tə tiv) *n.* **1.** a person who is chosen or authorized to represent another or others; delegate; agent: *The company had a representative in Rome.* **2.** a person or thing serving to typify a group, kind, or class. **3.** an elected member of a legislative assembly, especially a member of the lower house of Congress or of a state legislature. —*adj.* **1.** typifying a group, kind, or class; typical; characteristic: *The museum has a representative collection of modern art.* **2.** acting for or authorized to act for another or others. **3.** composed of representatives or based on political representation: *a representative government.* **4.** serving to represent, portray, or symbolize: *This monument is representative of the community's sentiments.*

re·press (ri pres') *v.t.* **1.** to hold back or keep under control; restrain: *to repress a smile.* **2.** to put down or put a stop to, especially by force: *to repress a revolution.* **3.** to prevent the natural development or expression of: *This child's creative talents have been repressed for too long.* **4.** to keep (painful memories or disturbing desires) in the unconscious mind. —**re·press'er,** *n.*

re·pres·sion (ri presh'ən) *n.* **1.** the act of repressing or the state of being repressed. **2.** an instance of this. **3.** a psychological process by which painful memories or disturbing desires are kept in the unconscious mind.

re·pres·sive (ri pres'iv) *adj.* tending or serving to repress. —**re·pres'sive·ly,** *adv.*

re·prieve (ri prēv') *n.* **1.** an official postponement of the carrying out of a sentence, especially a delay in the execution of a condemned person. **2.** a temporary relief or escape, as from something unpleasant or difficult. —*v.t.,* **re·prieved, re·priev·ing. 1.** to grant a reprieve to (someone), especially to delay the execution of (a condemned person). **2.** to free temporarily, as from something unpleasant or difficult.

rep·ri·mand (*n.,* rep'rə mand'; *v.,* rep'rə mand', rep'rə-mand') *v.t.* to reprove, especially formally. —*n.* a reproof, especially one formally or officially given.

re·print (*n.,* rē'print'; *v.,* rē print') *n.* a new edition of a work that has already been published. —*v.t.* to print a new edition or copy of; print again.

re·pris·al (ri prī'zəl) *n.* **1.** harm or injury done to an enemy in return for injuries or losses suffered. **2.** the act or an instance of retaliating.

re·prise (ri prīz', ri prēz') *n. Music.* the repetition of a song that has been sung previously, or of an earlier section of a composition.

re·proach (ri prōch') *v.t.* to charge with or blame for a fault or wrongdoing; reprove: *The coach reproached the team members for their poor play.* —*n., pl.* **re·proach·es. 1.** the act of reproaching; blame; reproof. **2.** an expression of this. **3.** a cause, object, or occasion of blame or disgrace: *Litter in the streets is a reproach to our city.*

re·proach·ful (ri prōch'fəl) *adj.* full of or expressing reproach: *a reproachful look.* —**re·proach'ful·ly,** *adv.*

rep·ro·bate (rep'rə bāt') *n.* a wicked or immoral person. —*adj.* given to wickedness or immorality; sinful.

rep·ro·ba·tion (rep'rə bā'shən) *n.* condemnation; censure.

re·pro·duce (rē'prə düs', rē'prə dūs') *v.,* **re·pro·duced, re·pro·duc·ing.** —*v.t.* **1.** to produce, form, or bring about again or anew: *The movie attempted to reproduce the era of the Civil War.* **2.** to make a duplicate or representation of: *to reproduce a picture.* **3.** to give rise to or produce (offspring or others of the same kind). —*v.i.* **1.** to give rise to or produce offspring or others of the same kind. **2.** to undergo reproduction: *The photograph reproduced clearly.*

re·pro·duc·tion (rē'prə duk'shən) *n.* **1.** the process by which living things give rise to or produce offspring or others of their kind. **2.** the act of reproducing or the state of being reproduced. **3.** something made by reproducing: *a reproduction of an original sculpture.*

re·pro·duc·tive (rē'prə duk'tiv) *adj.* **1.** of, used in, or relating to reproduction. **2.** reproducing; capable of reproducing. —**re'pro·duc'tive·ly,** *adv.* —**re'pro·duc'tive·ness,** *n.*

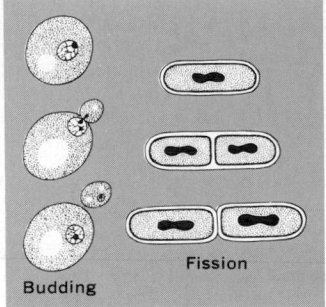

asexual **reproduction**

reproductive system, the system of organs by which living things reproduce their own kind. In mammals, the reproductive system includes the penis and the testes in males and the uterus, the vagina, and the ovaries in females.

re·proof (ri prüf') *n.* **1.** the act of reproving. **2.** an expression of criticism; scolding or reprimand.

re·prove (ri prüv') *v.t.,* **re·proved, re·prov·ing.** to blame or find fault with; scold; rebuke.

rep·tile (rep'təl, rep'tīl) *n.* any of a class of cold-blooded animals with backbones, including lizards, snakes, crocodiles, and turtles. Reptiles have dry, usually scaly skin and usually reproduce by laying eggs. —*adj.* another word for **reptilian.** [Going back to the Late Latin word *reptilis* meaning "creeping," from the Latin word *reptus,* past participle of *repere* "to creep."]

rep·til·i·an (rep til'ē ən) *adj.* **1.** of, relating to, or characteristic of a reptile or reptiles. **2.** like a reptile in appearance or behavior. —*n.* another word for **reptile.**

Repub. **1.** Republic. **2.** Republican.

re·pub·lic (ri pub'lik) *n.* **1.** a form of government in which the final authority of the state rests with voting citizens and is exercised by elected representatives of the people. **2.** a nation or state that has such a form of government. ▲ See **democracy** for usage note. [From the French word *république* meaning "republic," going back to the Latin phrase *res publica* "the state, a republic," from the words *res* "thing, property, wealth" + *publica* "public, of the people."]

re·pub·li·can (ri pub'li kən) *adj.* **1.** of, characteristic of, or like a republic. **2. Republican.** of, relating to, or characteristic of the Republican Party. **3.** supporting or advocating a republic as a form of government. —*n.* **1. Republican.** a member of the Republican Party. **2.** a person who believes in or advocates a republic as a form of government.

Republican Party, one of the two major political parties in the United States.

re·pu·di·ate (ri pū'dē āt') *v.t.,* **re·pu·di·at·ed, re·pu·di·at·ing. 1.** to reject as unjust or untrue: *to repudiate an accusation.* **2.** to refuse to have anything to do with; cast off; disown. **3.** to refuse to acknowledge or pay: *to repudiate a debt.* —**re·pu'di·a'tion,** *n.*

re·pug·nance (ri pug'nəns) *n.* extreme dislike or aversion; disgust.

---

at; āpe; fär; câre; end; mē; it; īce; pîerce; hot; ōld; sông, fôrk; oil; out; up; ūse; rüle; pùll; tûrn; chin; sing; shop; thin; this; hw in white; zh in treasure. The symbol ə stands for the unstressed vowel sound heard in about, taken, pencil, lemon, and circus.

R

re·pug·nant (ri pug′nənt) *adj.* causing extreme dislike or aversion; highly distasteful; repulsive.

re·pulse (ri puls′) *v.t.*, **re·pulsed, re·puls·ing. 1.** to beat or drive back: *Our army repulsed the enemy.* **2.** to refuse to accept; reject; rebuff: *to repulse an offer of assistance.* —*n.* **1.** the act of repulsing or the state of being repulsed. **2.** a rejection; rebuff.

re·pul·sion (ri pul′shən) *n.* **1.** extreme dislike or aversion; disgust. **2.** the act of repelling or the state of being repelled.

re·pul·sive (ri pul′siv) *adj.* **1.** causing extreme dislike or aversion; highly distasteful or offensive. **2.** tending to repel: *the repulsive force of a strong headwind.* —**re·pul′sive·ly,** *adv.* —**re·pul′sive·ness,** *n.*

rep·u·ta·ble (rep′yə tə bəl) *adj.* having a good reputation; trustworthy; respectable: *a reputable company.* —**rep′u·ta·bly,** *adv.*

rep·u·ta·tion (rep′yə tā′shən) *n.* **1.** a general or public estimation of something or someone: *That judge has a reputation for honesty.* **2.** the state of being highly regarded or esteemed: *Scandal can ruin one's reputation.*

re·pute (ri pūt′) *n.* **1.** a general or public estimation of something or someone. **2.** the state of being highly regarded or esteemed: *a store of repute.* —*v.t.*, **re·put·ed, re·put·ing.** to consider to be; suppose.

re·put·ed (ri pū′tid) *adj.* generally considered or supposed: *the reputed author of this poem.* —**re·put′ed·ly,** *adv.*

re·quest (ri kwest′) *v.t.* **1.** to express a wish or desire for; ask for: *He requested permission to leave.* **2.** to express a wish or desire to; ask: *She requested us to be on time.* —*n.* **1.** the act or an instance of requesting. **2.** something that is requested: *to grant a request.* **3.** the state of being sought after or in demand.

Req·ui·em (rek′wē əm) *n.* **1.** a Roman Catholic Mass offered for the eternal rest of the soul of one or more deceased persons, especially as part of a funeral. **2.** *also,* **requiem.** a musical setting for this. **3. requiem.** any musical composition, hymn, or service in honor of the dead.

re·quire (ri kwīr′) *v.t.*, **re·quired, re·quir·ing. 1.** to be in need of: *That cut will require medical attention.* **2.** to have as an obligation or condition: *Knitting requires much patience.* **3.** to order or compel (someone) to do something: *The customs officer required us to open our luggage.*

re·quire·ment (ri kwīr′mənt) *n.* **1.** something that is imposed as an obligation or condition: *Good grades are a requirement for getting into this college.* **2.** something that is needed: *A proper diet is one requirement for good health.*

req·ui·site (rek′wə zit) *adj.* required; necessary. —*n.* something that cannot be done without; an essential.

req·ui·si·tion (rek′wə zish′ən) *n.* **1.** an official written request or application, as for new equipment. **2.** the act of taking, as through authority: *The army's requisition of food brought hardship to the people.* —*v.t.* **1.** to put through a requisition for: *The secretary requisitioned new supplies.* **2.** to take, as through authority.

re·quit·al (ri kwī′təl) *n.* **1.** the act of requiting. **2.** something that is given or done in return: *Your sarcastic answer was a proper requital for that insult.*

re·quite (ri kwīt′) *v.t.*, **re·quit·ed, re·quit·ing. 1.** to give or pay back in kind; return: *We will requite your hospitality when you visit us.* **2.** to repay or reward.

re·run (*n.*, rē′run′; *v.*, rē run′) *n.* **1.** the showing of a filmed or taped performance, as a motion picture, after its original showing. **2.** the filmed or taped performance itself. **3.** the act of running again. —*v.t.*, **re·ran** (rē-ran′), **re·run·ning. 1.** to show as a rerun. **2.** to run again: *to rerun a race.*

re·sale (rē′sāl′) *n.* the act of selling what one has bought.

re·scind (ri sind′) *v.t.* to make void; annul; cancel: *to rescind a contract, to rescind a law.*

res·cue (res′kū) *v.t.*, **res·cued, res·cu·ing.** to save or free, as from danger: *The lifeguard rescued the drowning swimmer.* —*n.* the act of rescuing or the fact of being rescued. —**res′cu·er,** *n.*

re·search (ri sûrch′, rē′sûrch′) *n., pl.* **re·search·es.** study or investigation in a particular field, usually for the purpose of learning new facts and making new interpretations. —*v.t.* to do research on or for: *The student researched a paper for the history class.* —**re·search′er,** *n.*

re·sem·blance (ri zem′bləns) *n.* a similarity, as of physical appearance; likeness: *There is a close resemblance between the brother and sister.*

re·sem·ble (ri zem′bəl) *v.t.*, **re·sem·bled, re·sem·bling.** to be similar to, as in appearance or nature.

re·sent (ri zent′) *v.t.* to feel resentment at or toward: *to resent the high-handedness of government officials.*

re·sent·ful (ri zent′fəl) *adj.* characterized by or tending to feel resentment: *a resentful remark, a resentful loser.* —**re·sent′ful·ly,** *adv.* —**re·sent′ful·ness,** *n.*

re·sent·ment (ri zent′mənt) *n.* indignation, anger, or bitterness caused by a real or imagined offense or injury.

res·er·va·tion (rez′ər vā′shən) *n.* **1.** an arrangement by which something, such as a theater seat or hotel room, is reserved. **2.** something that is reserved: *Our reservation for dinner is at 8:00.* **3.** land set aside, as by a government, for a special purpose, as for an Indian tribe to live on or for a wildlife preserve. **4.** doubt; misgiving: *Do you have reservations about traveling alone?* **5.** something that limits; restriction: *They approved the plan without a single reservation.*

re·serve (ri zûrv′) *v.t.*, **re·served, re·serv·ing. 1.** to set aside or have set aside for a particular person or purpose or for future use: *We reserved a table for two.* **2.** to save until a later time: *Reserve your strength for another try.* **3.** to keep for oneself: *I reserve the right to make my own decisions.* —*n.* **1.** something that is set aside, as for a special purpose or future use; store; supply. **2.** the state or condition of being set aside or saved: *There was food in reserve for emergencies.* **3.** land set aside for a special purpose; a preserve. **4.** the habit of keeping one's feelings or thoughts to oneself; restraint: *You showed reserve by not losing your temper.* **5.** *Finance.* the amount of money or assets held back, as from investment, to meet emergencies or special demands. **6.** *also,* **reserves.** the part of the armed forces not on active duty but available for service in an emergency. —*adj.* kept in reserve.

re·served (ri zûrvd′) *adj.* **1.** set aside for a particular person or purpose or for future use: *These parking places are reserved for the staff.* **2.** characterized by reserve in speech and behavior. —**re·serv·ed·ly** (ri zûr′vid lē), *adv.*

re·serv·ist (ri zûr′vist) *n.* a member of a military reserve.

res·er·voir (rez′ər vwär′) *n.* **1.** a natural or artificially constructed place used for the storage of water. **2.** a receptacle or part used for the storage of a liquid or gas. **3.** a store; supply: *This book contains a reservoir of facts.*

re·side (ri zīd′) *v.i.*, **re·sid·ed, re·sid·ing. 1.** to make one's home permanently or for a time: *She resides with her brother.* **2.** to be present: *Much benefit resides in regular exercise.* —**re·sid′er,** *n.*

res·i·dence (rez′i dəns) *n.* **1.** a place where a person resides. **2.** the act or state of residing, especially in order to satisfy legal requirements: *Residence in the town enabled me to vote there.* **3.** a period of time spent residing in a place: *ten years' residence in the country.*

res·i·den·cy (rez′i dən sē) *n., pl.* **res·i·den·cies.** the period of time during which a physician receives advanced, specialized training, as at a hospital.

res·i·dent (rez′i dənt) *n.* **1.** a person who resides in a particular place. **2.** a physician serving a residency. —*adj.* **1.** residing in a particular place. **2.** residing in a place in connection with work or duty: *a resident surgeon.*

res·i·den·tial (rez′i den′shəl) *adj.* **1.** of or relating to residence: *a residential requirement for voting.* **2.** characterized by, restricted to, or suitable for residences: *a residential neighborhood.*

re·sid·u·al (ri zij′ü əl) *adj.* of, relating to, or being a residue; remaining. —*n.* *also,* **residuals.** payments made to a performer for the repeated use of a recorded appearance, as in a television show.

res·i·due (rez′i dü′, rez′i dū′) *n.* **1.** a substance remaining at the end of a separating process, such as evaporation, combustion, or filtration. **2.** anything that remains, as after a main part is taken away.

re·sign (ri zīn′) *v.i.* to give up voluntarily, as a job, position, or office: *The president had to resign because of poor health.* —*v.t.* **1.** to give up (a position or responsibility) voluntarily: *to resign a job with regret.* **2.** to make (oneself) accept without protest or complaint: *to resign oneself to an unpleasant situation.*

res·ig·na·tion (rez′ig nā′shən) *n.* **1.** the act of resigning. **2.** a formal, usually written notice that a person is resigning. **3.** the acceptance of something without protest or complaint; submission: *to suffer a loss with resignation.*

re·signed (ri zīnd′) *adj.* characterized by or showing resignation; submissive: *a resigned attitude of acceptance.* —**re·sign·ed·ly** (ri zī′nid lē), *adv.*

re·sil·ience (ri zil′yəns, ri zil′ē əns) *n.* the power or quality of being resilient. Also, **re·sil·ien·cy** (ri zil′yən sē, ri zil′ē ən sē).

re·sil·ient (ri zil′yənt, ri zil′ē ənt) *adj.* **1.** capable of springing back to the original size, shape, or position after being bent, compressed, or stretched. **2.** capable of recovering quickly or easily, as from depression or difficulty.

res·in (rez′in) *n.* **1.** any of various translucent yellow or brown sticky substances that come from certain trees, such as pine and balsam, and are used especially to improve paints and plastics and to make linoleum, glue, and rubber. **2.** any of various similar synthetic materials that are the basic ingredient of plastics. **3.** see **rosin** (*def. 1*).

res·in·ous (rez′ə nəs) *adj.* **1.** of, relating to, or resembling resin. **2.** obtained from or containing resin.

re·sist (ri zist′) *v.t.* **1.** to keep from yielding to; abstain from: *It was difficult to resist telling the secret.* **2.** to repel or oppose: *The nation was unable to resist the invasion.* **3.** to withstand the action or effect of: *This metal resists rusting.* —*v.i.* to act in opposition. —**re·sist′er,** *n.*

re·sist·ance (ri zis′təns) *n.* **1.** the act of resisting. **2.** the ability to resist something, especially disease: *You probably caught a cold because your resistance was low.* **3.** a group that works against or opposes an occupying or oppressive army or government, especially by guerrilla tactics. **4.** a force that opposes or hinders the motion of another: *Cars are streamlined to overcome the resistance of the air.* **5.** the characteristic of a substance by which it opposes the flow of electrical current, producing heat. A good conductor, such as silver, has low resistance.

re·sist·ant (ri zis′tənt) *adj.* offering resistance; resisting.

re·sist·less (ri zist′lis) *adj.* **1.** that cannot be resisted; irresistible. **2.** that does not or cannot resist.

re·sis·tor (ri zis′tər) *n.* an electronic component that adds resistance to a circuit to limit the flow of current or to produce heat, as in a toaster.

res·o·lute (rez′ə lüt) *adj.* having or showing strong determination. —**res′o·lute′ly,** *adv.* —**res′o·lute′ness,** *n.*

res·o·lu·tion (rez′ə lü′shən) *n.* **1.** the act or process of resolving or determining. **2.** something that is resolved upon; vow: *a New Year's resolution to go on a diet.* **3.** a formal statement of a decision, opinion, or course of action, presented to or adopted by an assembly. **4.** the state or quality of being resolute. **5.** the act or result of settling, explaining, or solving: *the resolution of a problem.* **6.** the act or process of breaking or changing into separate or simpler parts.

re·solve (ri zolv′) *v.,* **re·solved, re·solv·ing.** —*v.t.* **1.** to decide (to do something); determine: *I resolved not to go to the party.* **2.** to settle, explain, or solve: *to resolve a dispute.* **3.** to give a decision or opinion formally by vote, as in a legislative assembly. **4.** to break or change into simpler or separate parts: *The prism resolved the light into the colors of the spectrum.* —*v.i.* **1.** to come to a decision; decide: *The board resolved on a budget for the project.* **2.** to be broken or changed into simpler or separate parts. —*n.* **1.** strong determination or firmness of purpose. **2.** something resolved upon; resolution.

re·solved (ri zolvd′) *adj.* resolute; determined. —**re·solv·ed·ly** (ri zol′vid lē), *adv.*

res·o·nance (rez′ə nəns) *n.* **1.** the state or quality of being resonant; fullness and richness of sound: *the resonance of a grand piano.* **2.** *Physics.* **a.** the state of a mechanical or electrical system characterized by a vibration of large amplitude, occurring when an outside force is applied at a frequency equal or nearly equal to one of the natural frequencies of the system. Because of resonance, a swing will rise to a great height if it is given a regular series of pushes at the same frequency at which it swings. **b.** the vibration produced in such a state. **3.** the increasing and prolonging of sound by the similar vibration of another object, as when the tone produced by the strings of a violin is enhanced by vibrations of the instrument's wooden body.

res·o·nant (rez′ə nənt) *adj.* **1.** continuing to sound; echoing. **2.** capable of increasing or prolonging sounds: *the resonant cavity of a guitar.* **3.** having a full, rich sound: *a resonant voice.* —**res′o·nant·ly,** *adv.*

re·sort (ri zôrt′) *v.i.* **1.** to make use of or appeal to for aid, relief, protection, or support: *to resort to lying when in trouble.* **2.** to go often or by habit, as for recreation. —*n.* **1.** a place where people go, especially for recreation or relaxation: *a ski resort.* **2.** a person or thing that one makes use of or appeals to, as for protection or support: *Emergency shelters were the only resort for the flood victims.* **3.** the use of or appeal to a person or thing, as for protection or support: *to have resort to friends in an emergency.*

re·sound (ri zound′) *v.i.* **1.** to be filled with sound: *The church resounded with music.* **2.** to produce a loud, echoing, or prolonged sound: *The brass band resounded as it marched down the street.* **3.** (of sounds) to be echoed; ring: *The shouts resounded in our ears.*

re·source (rē′sôrs′, ri sôrs′, rē′zôrs′, ri zôrs′) *n.* **1.** someone or something that is made use of or called upon, as for aid or support. **2.** *usually,* **resources.** actual wealth or the means of producing wealth: *Oil is one of that country's largest natural resources.* **3.** personal ability to accomplish something: *The prisoner showed great resource in escaping.* **4.** the action or means used in an emergency or a difficult situation: *In the desert our only resource was to dig for water.*

---

at; āpe; fär; câre; end; mē; it; īce; pîerce; hot; ōld; sông, fôrk; oil; out; up; ūse; rüle; pull; tûrn; chin; sing; shop; thin; **th**is; hw in white; zh in treasure. The symbol ə stands for the unstressed vowel sound heard in about, taken, pencil, lemon, and circus.

R

re·source·ful (ri sôrs′fəl, ri zôrs′fəl) *adj.* capable of or skilled in dealing with new or difficult situations. —**re·source′ful·ly,** *adv.* —**re·source′ful·ness,** *n.*

re·spect (ri spekt′) *n.* **1.** a regard for or appreciation of the basic worth or value of someone or something: *a respect for life, a respect for the rights of other people.* **2.** recognition for superiority, as in strength or wisdom: *The chief had the respect of everyone in the village.* **3.** high or courteous regard or consideration: *to show respect for one's elders.* **4.** a specific aspect or manner; particular detail: *In some respects, I like winter more than summer.* **5.** relation; reference: *an improvement with respect to grades.* **6. respects.** courteous expressions of regard and greeting: *Please send my respects to your family.* —*v.t.* **1.** to have or feel respect for: *We respect honesty.* **2.** to show consideration for; act so as not to interfere with: *to respect someone's privacy.* **3.** to relate or refer to; concern: *The report is correct as it respects time and place.*

re·spect·a·bil·i·ty (ri spek′tə bil′i tē) *n.* the state, quality, or condition of being respectable.

re·spect·a·ble (ri spek′tə bəl) *adj.* **1.** having or showing proper or approved standards of conduct; worthy of respect: *a respectable leader.* **2.** fit to be seen or used; presentable: *a respectable suit of clothes.* **3.** better than average; reasonably good: *The amateur group put on a respectable performance.* —**re·spect′a·bly,** *adv.*

re·spect·ful (ri spekt′fəl) *adj.* full of, marked by, or showing respect, especially courteousness. —**re·spect′ful·ly,** *adv.* —**re·spect′ful·ness,** *n.*

re·spect·ing (ri spek′ting) *prep.* with respect to; concerning: *What are your views respecting politics?*

re·spec·tive (ri spek′tiv) *adj.* relating or belonging to each of two or more persons or things under consideration; particular: *The committee studied the respective advantages of each plan.*

re·spec·tive·ly (ri spek′tiv lē) *adv.* with respect to each of two or more in the order considered: *Mr. Jones and Ms. Lane are, respectively, producer and director of the film.*

re·spell (rē spel′) *v.t.* **1.** to spell again. **2.** to spell out according to a system of letters or symbols different from ordinary writing, especially a phonetic alphabet.

res·pi·ra·tion (res′pə rā′shən) *n.* **1.** the act of breathing in and out. **2.** the process by which oxygen reacts with food to release the energy living cells need to function.

res·pi·ra·tor (res′pə rā′tər) *n.* **1.** a device that supplies breathable air, used in giving artificial respiration. **2.** a device worn over the mouth, or over the nose and mouth, to prevent the breathing in of fumes, dust, or the like.

res·pi·ra·to·ry (res′pər ə tôr′ē) *adj.* of or relating to respiration or to organs used in respiration: *a respiratory disease.*

respiratory system, the system of organs and passages by which living things take in and use oxygen. In mammals, the respiratory system includes the nasal passages, the mouth, the pharynx, the larynx, the trachea, and the lungs.

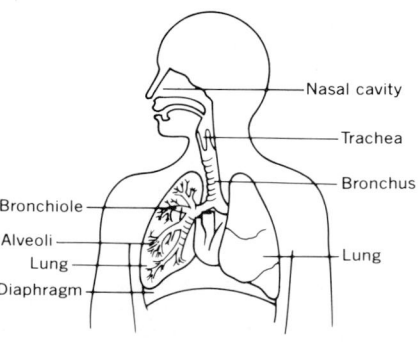

respiratory system

re·spire (ri spīr′) *v.i.,* **re·spired, re·spir·ing.** to inhale and exhale; breathe: *The patient respired irregularly.*

res·pite (res′pit) *n.* **1.** a brief or temporary period of rest or relief, as from work or unpleasantness: *Having a glass of lemonade was a pleasant respite from mowing the lawn.* **2.** a delay or postponement, as in carrying out a sentence of death.

re·splend·ence (ri splen′dəns) *n.* the state or quality of being full of splendor.

re·splend·ent (ri splen′dənt) *adj.* full of splendor; gleaming; brilliant. —**re·splend′ent·ly,** *adv.*

re·spond (ri spond′) *v.i.* **1.** to give an answer: *Please respond to my question.* **2.** to act in return; react: *The dog responded to the sudden light by blinking its eyes.* **3.** to be improved or positively affected by: *The patient responded to treatment.*

re·sponse (ri spons′) *n.* **1.** the act of responding. **2.** something said in answer: *What is your response to the question?* **3.** behavior caused by an outside influence or stimulus. **4.** words said or sung by a congregation or choir in answer to something said or sung by its leader.

re·spon·si·bil·i·ty (ri spon′sə bil′i tē) *n., pl.* **re·spon·si·bil·i·ties. 1.** the state, quality, or condition of being responsible. **2.** a job, duty, or area of concern: *Setting the table is your responsibility.*

re·spon·si·ble (ri spon′sə bəl) *adj.* **1.** accountable to someone for the performance of duty or of a certain job or task: *Congress is responsible to the electorate for making laws.* **2.** faithful to duties; trustworthy; reliable: *We need a responsible baby-sitter.* **3.** being the cause or main cause: *Careless driving is responsible for many accidents.* **4.** involving important duties: *a responsible job.* —**re·spon′si·ble·ness,** *n.* —**re·spon′si·bly,** *adv.*

re·spon·sive (ri spon′siv) *adj.* **1.** readily reacting with sympathy, warmth, or understanding: *They were responsive to their friends' misery.* **2.** of, relating to, or indicating a response: *A nod of the head is a responsive gesture.* **3.** marked by or made up of responses: *a responsive chant.* —**re·spon′sive·ly,** *adv.* —**re·spon′sive·ness,** *n.*

rest¹ (rest) *n.* **1.** a period of inactivity, relaxation, or refreshment, especially after work or physical activity: *The carpenter took a rest before finishing the job.* **2.** freedom from work, distress, or disturbance; quiet; ease: *The evening is our time of rest.* **3.** sleep: *Do you get enough rest at night?* **4.** the state of being motionless: *The plane came to rest in the field.* **5.** something that serves as a stand or support: *a book rest.* **6.** death: *to go to one's rest.* **7.** *Music.* **a.** an interval of silence between tones, lasting for the same amount of time as a note of the same name: *half rest, whole rest.* **b.** any of the various symbols indicating such a pause. —*v.i.* **1.** to relax or refresh oneself: *The children rested on the porch after the ball game.* **2.** to be quiet or at ease: *They wouldn't rest until they knew their child was safe.* **3.** to be supported, as by leaning or lying: *My hands were resting in my lap.* **4.** to be fixed or directed: *The crowd's attention rested on the strangers.* **5.** to remain without change or further action; stand: *We decided to let the matter rest.* **6.** to lie in death: *May they rest in peace.* **7.** *Law.* to stop presenting evidence in a case voluntarily: *The defense rests.* —*v.t.* **1.** to give rest to: *Rest your horse after the race.* **2.** to put, lay, or lean (something), as for support: *I rested my arm on the table.* **3.** *Law.* to stop presenting evidence in (a case) voluntarily: *Your Honor, I rest my case.* [From the Old English word *rest.*]

rest² (rest) *n.* **1.** something that remains; remainder. **2.** those remaining; others: *The rest will meet us at the theater.* ▲ used with a plural verb in definition 2. —*v.i.* to continue to be; remain: *You may rest assured that I'll be there.* [From the Middle French word *reste* meaning ''residue, remainder,'' from the Old French word *rester* ''to remain, stay,'' from the Latin word *restare* ''to stand still, remain behind,'' from the Latin prefix *re-* ''back, again'' + *stare* ''to stand.'']

re·state (rē stāt′) *v.t.*, **re·stat·ed, re·stat·ing.** to say again or in a new or different way: *During a debate, the presidential candidates restated their ideas on fighting pollution.*

res·tau·rant (res′tər ənt, res′tə ränt′) *n.* a place where food is prepared and served to customers, often at tables by a waiter or waitress.

res·tau·ra·teur (res′tər ə tûr′) *n.* a person who owns or manages a restaurant.

rest·ful (rest′fəl) *adj.* **1.** full of or giving rest: *a restful vacation.* **2.** at rest; quiet; tranquil: *a restful landscape.* —**rest′ful·ly,** *adv.* —**rest′ful·ness,** *n.*

res·ti·tu·tion (res′ti tü′shən, res′ti tū′shən) *n.* **1.** the act of restoring something that has been lost or taken away. **2.** compensation for loss or damage; reparation.

res·tive (res′tiv) *adj.* **1.** unable to rest; restless; fretful. **2.** stubborn and difficult to manage; unruly: *a restive horse.* —**res′tive·ly,** *adv.* —**res′tive·ness,** *n.*

rest·less (rest′lis) *adj.* **1.** nervous or agitated in mind or body; unable to rest: *The restless patient paced back and forth.* **2.** characterized by lack of rest; not restful: *to spend a restless night.* **3.** constantly in motion; never still: *the restless wind, the restless sea.* **4.** constantly shifting or changing from one thing to another: *a restless mind.* —**rest′less·ly,** *adv.* —**rest′less·ness,** *n.*

restoration of a Colonial village

res·to·ra·tion (res′tə rā′shən) *n.* **1.** the act of restoring or the state of being restored. **2.** something that is or has been restored. **3. Restoration. a.** the return of the English monarchy in 1660 under King Charles II. **b.** the period following this, including the reign of Charles II, from 1660 to 1685, and sometimes also the reign of James II, from 1685 to 1688.

re·stor·a·tive (ri stôr′ə tiv) *adj.* **1.** capable of restoring. **2.** relating to restoration. —*n.* something that restores.

re·store (ri stôr′) *v.t.*, **re·stored, re·stor·ing 1.** to bring back; reestablish: *The monarchy was restored ten years after the revolution.* **2.** to bring back to a former or original state or condition: *The cathedral was restored during the last century.* **3.** to return (something lost, taken, or stolen): *The police restored the jewels to their owner.* —**re·stor′er,** *n.*

re·strain (ri strān′) *v.t.* **1.** to hold in; keep in check: *Try to restrain your laughter.* **2.** to prevent from acting; hold back: *to restrain a dog from jumping on someone.* **3.** to take away the liberty of, as by confinement in prison. —**re·strain′a·ble,** *adj.*

re·straint (ri strānt′) *n.* **1.** the act of restraining or the state of being restrained. **2.** something that restrains. **3.** a holding back; reserve.

restraint of trade, interference with the free movement of goods or services or with free competition.

re·strict (ri strikt′) *v.t.* to keep within specified limits; confine: *Use of the pool is restricted to club members.*

re·strict·ed (ri strik′tid) *adj.* **1.** confined or limited: *a restricted diet.* **2.** available only to certain persons or groups; excluding certain persons or groups: *The pool is restricted to people who can swim.* **3.** intended for use only by authorized persons: *a restricted government document.*

re·stric·tion (ri strik′shən) *n.* **1.** something that restricts. **2.** the act of restricting or the state of being restricted.

re·stric·tive (ri strik′tiv) *adj.* **1.** serving or tending to restrict: *The students felt that the school's rules were too restrictive.* **2.** *Grammar.* designating a word, clause, or phrase that limits the meaning of the word it modifies and is usually not set off by commas. In the sentence *Anyone who stands up to that bully will be a neighborhood hero,* the clause *who stands up to that bully* is restrictive. —**re·stric′tive·ly,** *adv.* —**re·stric′tive·ness,** *n.*

rest room, a public bathroom in a building.

re·sult (ri zult′) *n.* **1.** something that occurs or is brought about because of an earlier action, process, or condition; effect: *The accident was the result of careless driving.* **2.** the outcome of a mathematical operation: *If you divide 4 by 2, the result is 2.* —*v.i.* **1.** to be a result: *Low grades may result from poor study habits.* **2.** to have as a result: *The trial resulted with the defendant found not guilty.*

re·sult·ant (ri zul′tənt) *adj.* occurring or brought about as a result. —*n.* **1.** a result. **2.** *Physics.* a force that is the equivalent and result of, and has the same effect as, two or more forces acting together.

re·sume (ri züm′) *v.t.*, **re·sumed, re·sum·ing. 1.** to go on after interruption: *The violinist resumed playing after the intermission.* **2.** to take or occupy again: *to resume one's former position with a company.*

ré·su·mé (rez′ù mā′, rez′ù mā′) *n.* **1.** a statement of one's qualifications and work record, used in applying for work. **2.** a summary: *The professor gave a résumé of the main points of the lecture.*

re·sump·tion (ri zump′shən) *n.* the act or instance of resuming.

re·sur·gence (ri sûr′jəns) *n.* a rising again; revival.

re·sur·gent (ri sûr′jənt) *adj.* rising or tending to rise again.

res·ur·rect (rez′ə rekt′) *v.t.* **1.** to raise (a person) from the dead; restore to life. **2.** to bring back into use or notice; restore after disuse or neglect: *to resurrect the writings of a forgotten author.*

res·ur·rec·tion (rez′ə rek′shən) *n.* **1.** the act of rising from the dead. **2.** the state of having risen from the dead. **3.** the bringing back of something after disuse or neglect; revival. **4. Resurrection.** in Christian belief, the rising again of Jesus after his death and burial.

re·sus·ci·tate (ri sus′i tāt′) *v.t.*, **re·sus·ci·tat·ed, re·sus·ci·tat·ing.** to bring back to life or consciousness. —**re·sus·ci·ta′tion,** *n.*

re·sus·ci·ta·tor (ri sus′i tā′tər) *n.* **1.** a person or thing that resuscitates. **2.** a machine or other device that resuscitates by forcing oxygen into the lungs.

re·tail (rē′tāl; *esp. for v.t., def. 2,* ri tāl′) *n.* the sale of goods or articles individually or in small quantities, directly to the consumer. —*adj.* of, relating to, or engaged in the selling of goods in this manner: *a retail store.* —*adv.* in a retail quantity or at a retail price: *to buy a*

at; āpe; fär; câre; end; mē; it; īce; pîerce; hot; ōld; sông, fôrk; oil; out; up; ūse; rüle; pull; tûrn; chin; sing; shop; thin; <u>th</u>is; hw in white; zh in treasure. The symbol ə stands for the unstressed vowel sound heard in about, taken, pencil, lemon, and circus.

R

dress retail. —*v.t.* **1.** to sell (goods or articles) individually or in small quantities, directly to the consumer: *to retail clothing.* **2.** to repeat or retell: *to retail gossip.* —*v.i.* to be sold at retail: *This shirt retails for eight dollars.* [From the Old French word *retail,* from the prefix *re-* meaning "re-" + *taillier* meaning "to cut," referring to the practice of selling goods in small, or "cut off," quantities.]

re·tail·er (rē′tā lər) *n.* a merchant or dealer who sells retail.

re·tain (ri tān′) *v.t.* **1.** to continue to have or hold; maintain or preserve: *to retain ownership of a house after a parent's death.* **2.** to hold back or contain: *The cracked jar would not retain water.* **3.** to keep in mind; remember: *to retain facts.* **4.** to employ by the payment of a fee: *to retain a lawyer.* [From the Old French word *retenir* meaning "to hold, retain," from the Latin word *retinēre* "to hold back, keep, restrain," from the Latin prefix *re-* "back, again" + *tenēre* "to hold."]

re·tal·i·ate (ri tal′ē āt′) *v.i.,* **re·tal·i·at·ed, re·tal·i·at·ing.** to return or repay in kind, especially to return a wrong or injurious act with a similar one: *When one child took all the milk, the other retaliated by taking all the cereal.* —**re·tal′i·a′tion,** *n.*

re·tal·i·a·to·ry (ri tal′ē ə tôr′ē) *adj.* of, relating to, or serving as retaliation: *a retaliatory action.*

re·tard (ri tärd′) *v.t.* to delay the progress of (an action or process); slow; hinder: *A long and serious illness can retard growth.* —*v.i.* to be slowed or delayed. —**re·tard′er,** *n.*

re·tar·da·tion (rē′tär dā′shən) *n.* **1.** the act of retarding or the state of being retarded. **2.** something that retards; impediment; hindrance. **3.** see **mental retardation.**

re·tard·ed (ri tär′did) *adj.* suffering from or marked by mental retardation.

retch (rech) *v.i.* to strain as if to vomit.

re·ten·tion (ri ten′shən) *n.* **1.** the act of retaining or the state of being retained. **2.** the ability or power to retain. **3.** the ability to remember.

re·ten·tive (ri ten′tiv) *adj.* having the ability or capacity to retain: *a retentive mind.* —**re·ten′tive·ness,** *n.*

ret·i·cence (ret′ə səns) *n.* restraint or reserve, especially in speech: *The child's reticence in class is due to shyness.*

ret·i·cent (ret′ə sənt) *adj.* restrained or reserved, especially in speech. —**ret′i·cent·ly,** *adv.*

re·tic·u·late (*v.,* ri tik′yə lāt′; *adj.,* ri tik′yə lit, ri·tik′yə lāt′) *v.,* **re·tic·u·lat·ed, re·tic·u·lat·ing.** —*v.t.* to form into, cover, or mark with a network. —*v.i.* to form a network. —*adj.* covered with or resembling a network.

ret·i·na (ret′ə nə) *n., pl.* **ret·i·nas** or **ret·i·nae** (ret′ə nē′). the inner membrane at the back of the eyeball, made up of several layers of cells that are sensitive to light and transmit the images entering the eye to the optic nerve.

reticulate leaf

ret·i·nal (ret′ə nəl) *adj.* of or relating to the retina.

ret·i·nol (ret′ə nôl′) *n.* another word for **vitamin A.**

ret·i·nue (ret′ə nü′, ret′ə nū′) *n.* a group of people, such as servants or assistants, who accompany a person of rank or authority.

re·tire (ri tīr′) *v.,* **re·tired, re·tir·ing.** —*v.i.* **1.** to withdraw oneself from business, public life, or active service: *My grandparents both retired when they were 65.* **2.** to go to bed: *We retired early last night.* **3.** to go away, as for seclusion or rest: *to retire to the country.* —*v.t.* **1.** to remove from an office, position, or active service.

2. *Baseball.* to put out (a batter or side). **3.** to pay off and cancel a bond or other debt. —**re·tire′ment,** *n.*

re·tir·ing (ri tīr′ing) *adj.* tending to avoid people or publicity; reserved; shy.

re·tort¹ (ri tôrt′) *v.i.* to make a reply, especially in a quick, witty, or sharp manner. —*n.* a quick, witty, or sharp reply. [From the Latin word *retortus,* past participle of *retorquēre* meaning "to twist back, return," from the Latin prefix *re-* "back, again" + *torquēre* "to twist."]

re·tort² (ri tôrt′) *n.* a container, usually consisting of a glass globe with a long tube extending downward, in which to distill or decompose substances by heat. [From the Old French word *retorte* meaning this container, going back to the Latin word *retortus* "bent backward," from the shape of its neck.]

re·touch (rē tuch′) *v.t.* **1.** to improve, as a painting, by additional touches or slight changes. **2.** to change (a photographic negative or print) by removing or adding details.

re·trace (rē trās′) *v.t.,* **re·traced, re·trac·ing. 1.** to go back over: *to retrace one's steps.* **2.** to trace back: *to retrace one's ancestors.*

retort²

re·tract (ri trakt′) *v.t.* **1.** to withdraw or recant (something); take back: *to retract a statement.* **2.** to draw (something) back or in: *The cat retracted its claws.* —**re·tract′a·ble,** *adj.* —**re·trac′tor,** *n.*

re·trac·tile (ri trak′təl) *adj.* capable of being drawn back or in, as the head of a turtle.

re·trac·tion (ri trak′shən) *n.* **1.** the act of retracting or the state of being retracted. **2.** a statement that retracts: *The newspaper printed a retraction of a previous article.*

re·tread (*v.,* rē tred′; *n.,* rē′tred′) *v.t.,* **re·tread·ed, re·tread·ing.** to put a new tread on (a tire). —*n.* a retreaded tire.

re·treat (ri trēt′) *v.i.* to withdraw, as from battle; draw back: *The defeated army retreated.* —*n.* **1.** the act of retreating. **2.** a place of rest or relaxation: *a summer retreat.* **3.** a signal for a military retreat. **4.** *Military.* **a.** a flag-lowering ceremony at sunset. **b.** a signal, as on a bugle, played at this ceremony.

re·trench (ri trench′) *v.t.* **1.** to cut back on: *to retrench expenses.* **2.** to put an end to or remove: *The dictator gradually retrenched the people's freedoms.* —*v.i.* to cut down expenses; economize. —**re·trench′ment,** *n.*

re·tri·al (rē trī′əl) *n.* a second trial, as of a case in a court.

ret·ri·bu·tion (ret′rə bū′shən) *n.* **1.** punishment in return for evil done. **2.** something done or given as punishment for wrongdoing.

re·trib·u·tive (ri trib′yə tiv) *adj.* serving as or characterized by retribution.

re·triev·al (ri trē′vəl) *n.* the act or process of retrieving, or the state of being retrieved.

re·trieve (ri trēv′) *v.t.,* **re·trieved, re·triev·ing. 1.** to get back; recover; regain: *The golfer retrieved the golf ball from the lake.* **2.** to bring back to a former condition; restore. **3.** to make amends for; make good: *to retrieve a mistake.* **4.** (of dogs) to locate and fetch (wounded or dead game). **5.** to get from storage, as in a computer: *We retrieved information we needed for the study.* —**re·triev′a·ble,** *adj.*

re·triev·er (ri trē′vər) *n.* any of various hardy, medium-sized dogs with thick, coarse coats. Retrievers were originally bred to retrieve game for hunters.

retro– *prefix* backward, back, or behind: *retrograde.*

ret·ro·ac·tive (ret′rō ak′tiv) *adj.* relating or applying to something that has taken place in the past: *My raise in pay is retroactive to July 1.*

ret·ro·grade (ret′rə grād′) *adj.* **1.** moving backward; reversed: *Numbers in a countdown are given in retrograde order.* **2.** becoming worse; deteriorating: *There are retrograde conditions in the poorer sections of the city.* —*v.i.,* **ret·ro·grad·ed, ret·ro·grad·ing. 1.** to move backward; reverse. **2.** to become worse; deteriorate.

ret·ro·gress (ret′rə gres′, ret′rə gres′) *v.i.* **1.** to move or go backward. **2.** to go to a worse or a less advanced condition. —**ret′ro·gres′sion,** *n.*

ret·ro·gres·sive (ret′rə gres′iv) *adj.* of or characterized by retrogression. —**ret′ro·gres′sive·ly,** *adv.*

ret·ro·rock·et (ret′rō rok′it) *n.* a rocket engine that produces thrust opposite to the motion of a spacecraft in flight in order to reduce speed, to change course, or to separate a section of the spacecraft.

ret·ro·spect (ret′rə spekt′) *n.* a thoughtful review or survey of past events: *In retrospect, we were wrong.*

ret·ro·spec·tion (ret′rə spek′shən) *n.* the act of looking back on or thinking about past events.

ret·ro·spec·tive (ret′rə spek′tiv) *adj.* **1.** looking back on or thinking about past events. **2.** applying to the past; retroactive. —*n.* an exhibit of works produced over a period of time by an artist or artists. —**ret′ro·spec′tive·ly,** *adv.*

ret·ro·vi·rus (ret′rə vī′rəs) *n., pl.* **ret·ro·vi·rus·es.** any of a group of viruses that includes the AIDS virus and certain cancer-causing viruses.

re·turn (ri tûrn′) *v.i.* **1.** to come or go back, as to a former place or condition: *to return to consciousness, to return home.* **2.** to come or go back in thought or speech: *The speaker finally returned to the subject.* **3.** to happen or appear again: *Winter returns every year.* —*v.t.* **1.** to take, bring, send, give, or put back: *to return a book to the library.* **2.** to give or pay back in the same way: *to return a visit.* **3.** to report officially: *The jury returned a verdict.* **4.** to yield: *The new tax returned only part of the money needed to build the new school.* **5.** to say in response: *Questioned closely, the witness returned, "I don't remember."* —*n.* **1.** a coming or going back: *to make a return to one's home town.* **2.** the act of happening or appearing again: *The return of winter brought hardship to the settlers.* **3.** the act of taking, sending, or putting back: *the return of a book to the library.* **4.** the act of giving or paying back in the same way: *Your prompt return of my phone call pleased me.* **5.** an official or formal report: *a tax return, election returns.* **6.** also, **returns.** yield or profit: *The returns from the cake sale were more than fifty dollars.* —*adj.* **1.** of or relating to a return: *a return ticket, a return route.* **2.** given or done in return: *a return visit.* —**re·turn′a·ble,** *adj.*

re·un·ion (rē un′yən) *n.* **1.** the act of reuniting or the state of being reunited. **2.** a social gathering of friends, classmates, or relatives after separation or absence: *My high school class is holding its tenth reunion.*

re·u·nite (rē′u nīt′) *v.,* **re·u·nit·ed, re·u·nit·ing.** —*v.t.* to bring together again: *The occasion reunited several old friends.* —*v.i.* to come together again.

re·use (*v.,* rē ūz′; *n.,* rē ūs′) *v.t.,* **re·used, re·us·ing.** to use again. —*n.* the act of using again. —**re·us′a·ble,** *adj.*

rev (rev) *n.* the revolution of an engine or motor. —*v.t.,* **revved, rev·ving.** to increase the speed of (a motor): *to rev the engine while standing still.*

rev. 1. revenue. **2.** reverse. **3.** revolution.

Rev. 1. Revelation. **2.** Reverend.

re·val·u·ate (rē val′ū āt′) *v.t.,* **re·val·u·at·ed, re·val·u·at·ing.** to set a new value for: *to revaluate currency.* —**re·val′u·a′tion,** *n.*

re·vamp (rē vamp′) *v.t.* **1.** to repair or replace the vamp of (a shoe). **2.** to patch up, renovate, or revise: *The author revamped the novel in two weeks.*

re·veal (ri vēl′) *v.t.* **1.** to make known; divulge: *to reveal a secret.* **2.** to expose to view; display; show: *The open door revealed a large living room.*

rev·eil·le (rev′ə lē) *n.* a signal on a bugle or drums to awaken troops.

rev·el (rev′əl) *v.i.,* **rev·eled, rev·el·ing;** also, British, **rev·elled, rev·el·ling. 1.** to take great pleasure: *The lottery winners reveled in their new wealth.* **2.** to make merry: *The party guests reveled all night long.* —*n.* loud merrymaking. —**rev′el·er;** also, British, **rev′el·ler,** *n.*

rev·e·la·tion (rev′ə lā′shən) *n.* **1.** the act of revealing. **2.** something revealed. **3.** a disclosure or communication of divine truth by supernatural means. **4. Revelation.** also, **Revelations.** the last book of the New Testament, believed to have been written by John. Also, **Apocalypse.**

re·venge (ri venj′) *n.* **1.** injury, harm, or punishment in return for a wrong or offense: *The victim's friends swore to get revenge on the attackers.* **2.** a desire for vengeance. —*v.t.,* **re·venged, re·veng·ing. 1.** to inflict injury, harm, or punishment in return for: *to revenge an insult.* **2.** to inflict injury, harm, or punishment on behalf of: *They vowed to revenge their parents.*

re·venge·ful (ri venj′fəl) *adj.* full of or showing revenge. —**re·venge′ful·ly,** *adv.* —**re·venge′ful·ness,** *n.*

rev·e·nue (rev′ə nū′, rev′ə nū′) *n.* **1.** the income from property or other investments or activities. **2.** the annual or current income of a government from taxation and other sources.

revenue sharing, the distribution of part of the money that a government receives from taxes to more local governments to help them pay their expenses.

re·ver·ber·ate (ri vûr′bə rāt′) *v.i.,* **re·ver·ber·at·ed, re·ver·ber·at·ing.** to be echoed; resound: *The sound of footsteps reverberated through the empty house.* —**re·ver′ber·a′tion,** *n.*

re·vere (ri vir′) *v.t.,* **re·vered, re·ver·ing.** to feel deep respect and affection for: *The children revered their grandparents.*

rev·er·ence (rev′ər əns, rev′rəns) *n.* **1.** a feeling of deepest respect and affection; veneration. **2.** an act or expression of respect, as a bow or curtsy. **3.** the state of being revered. **4. Reverence.** a title used in addressing or referring to some members of the clergy, usually preceded by *Your* or *His.* —*v.t.,* **rev·er·enced, rev·er·enc·ing.** to feel reverence for: *to reverence one's parents.*

rev·er·end (rev′ər ənd, rev′rənd) *adj.* **1.** worthy of reverence. **2. Reverend.** a form of address used in referring to a member of the clergy, usually preceded by *the.*

rev·er·ent (rev′ər ənt) *adj.* feeling or showing reverence: *to be reverent in church.* —**rev′er·ent·ly,** *adv.*

rev·er·en·tial (rev′ə ren′shəl) *adj.* feeling or showing reverence; reverent. —**rev′er·en′tial·ly,** *adv.*

rev·er·ie (rev′ə rē) also, **rev·er·y.** *n.* **1.** dreamy thinking or daydreaming of happy, pleasant things. **2.** an instance of this; daydream.

re·ver·sal (ri vûr′səl) *n.* the act of reversing or the state of being reversed: *Only a reversal of much of human behavior could bring about world peace.*

re·verse (ri vûrs′) *n.* **1.** something that is the direct opposite of something else; contrary: *Writing from right to left is the reverse of our usual practice.* **2.** a mechanism

---

at; āpe; fär; câre; end; mē; it; īce; pîerce; hot; ōld; sông, fôrk; oil; out; up; ūse; rüle; pull; tûrn; chin; sing; shop; thin; this; hw in white; zh in treasure. The symbol ə stands for the unstressed vowel sound heard in about, taken, pencil, lemon, and circus.

803

in a machine that makes it transmit force or cause movement in a direction opposite to that which is usual. **3.** the back side of something: *the reverse of a phonograph record.* **4.** the side of a coin or medal that does not bear the principal design. **5.** a change of fortune from good to bad; setback: *to suffer business reverses.* —*adj.* **1.** opposite, as in position, direction, or order. **2.** moving or causing movement in a direction opposite to that which is usual: *to put a car in reverse gear.* —*v.,* **re·versed, re·vers·ing.** —*v.t.* **1.** to turn (something) around, upside down, or inside out: *to reverse a sock.* **2.** to change to the opposite: *to reverse an opinion.* **3.** to turn or cause to turn or move in a direction opposite to that which is usual. **4.** to revoke or set aside, as a judgment; annul; revoke: *The judge reversed the original decision.* —*v.i.* to move or turn in the opposite direction. —**re·verse′ly,** *adv.* —**re·vers′er,** *n.*

re·vers·i·ble (ri vûr′sə bəl) *adj.* **1.** able to be reversed. **2.** made so as to be worn or used on either side: *a reversible jacket, a reversible fabric.* —*n.* a garment that can be worn with either side out. —**re·vers′i·bil′i·ty, re·vers′i·ble·ness,** *n.* —**re·vers′i·bly,** *adv.*

re·ver·sion (ri vûr′zhən) *n.* **1.** a return, as to a former condition, practice, or belief. **2.** the act of reversing or the state of being reversed.

re·vert (ri vûrt′) *v.i.* to return, as to a former condition, practice, or belief: *Their thoughts reverted to the days of their youth.*

rev·er·y (rev′ə rē) *n., pl.* **rev·er·ies.** another spelling of **reverie.**

re·view (ri vū′) *v.t.* **1.** to study, go over, or examine again: *to review notes in preparing for an exam.* **2.** to go over in one's mind; look back on: *He reviewed the day's events with a smile.* **3.** to write or give a critical summary or discussion of: *She was asked to review the play for the newspaper.* **4.** to consider or examine (a court action) again. **5.** to make a formal or official inspection of: *The general reviewed the troops.* —*n.* **1.** a studying, going over, or examining again: *a review of each topic in detail.* **2.** a looking back: *a review of the main events of one's childhood.* **3.** a summary or survey: *The speaker gave a review of recent political developments.* **4.** a critical summary or discussion: *The reviews of the new motion picture are not very good.* **5.** a formal or official inspection: *a review by the judges of each float in the parade.* **6.** Another spelling of **revue.**

re·view·er (ri vū′ər) *n.* **1.** a person whose business is writing articles criticizing books, plays, and the like. **2.** any person who reviews.

re·vile (ri vīl′) *v.,* **re·viled, re·vil·ing.** —*v.t.* to attack with insulting language; call names: *The defendant angrily reviled the accusers.* —*v.i.* to use insulting language. —**re·vile′ment,** *n.* —**re·vil′er,** *n.*

re·vise (ri vīz′) *v.t.,* **re·vised, re·vis·ing.** **1.** to change in order to correct or improve: *to revise a manuscript.* **2.** to make different; alter: *to revise one's opinion.* —**re·vis′er,** *n.*

re·vi·sion (ri vizh′ən) *n.* **1.** the act or process of revising. **2.** something revised: *a revision of the previous edition.*

re·viv·al (ri vī′vəl) *n.* **1.** the act of reviving or the state of being revived. **2.** an awakening or return, as of a custom, style, or the like: *the revival of manners.* **3.** an awakening or increase of interest in religion in a church, community, or denomination. **4.** a special service held to increase interest in religion.

re·viv·al·ist (ri vī′və list) *n.* a person who holds or promotes religious revivals. —**re·viv′al·ism,** *n.*

re·vive (ri vīv′) *v.,* **re·vived, re·viv·ing.** —*v.t.* **1.** to bring back to consciousness: *The firefighters revived the unconscious child.* **2.** to bring back into existence, use, currency, or awareness: *The old motion picture was revived with great success.* **3.** to give new strength, vitality, or freshness to: *A good meal revived the weary*

hikers. —*v.i.* **1.** to come back to consciousness. **2.** to show new strength, vitality, or freshness. —**re·viv′er,** *n.*

rev·o·ca·ble (rev′ə kə bəl) *adj.* able to be revoked.

rev·o·ca·tion (rev′ə kā′shən) *n.* **1.** the act or fact of revoking: *the revocation of a driver's license.* **2.** the state of being revoked.

re·voke (ri vōk′) *v.t.,* **re·voked, re·vok·ing.** to cancel or make no longer valid: *The city revoked the restaurant's license.*

re·volt (ri vōlt′) *n.* an uprising or rebellion against authority: *The farmers took part in the revolt against the government.* —*v.i.* **1.** to rebel against authority. **2.** to be disgusted or repelled. —*v.t.* to disgust or repel: *The mere thought of giving up revolts me.*

re·volt·ing (ri vōl′ting) *adj.* disgusting or repulsive; repellent: *a revolting smell.* —**re·volt′ing·ly,** *adv.*

rev·o·lu·tion (rev′ə lü′shən) *n.* **1.** the overthrow of an existing political system or form of government by those governed, usually by force, and the establishment of a new or different system of government. **2.** any sudden, far-reaching, or very great change: *Modern machines brought about a revolution in industry.* **3.** movement in a circular course around a central point or object. **4.** a spinning or turning around an axis; rotation. **5.** one complete turn of a rotating body: *The crankshaft of this engine makes up to 5,000 revolutions per minute.* **6.** the movement of one celestial body in an orbit around another, as the movement of the planets about the sun. **7.** one complete course of such a body. **8.** a cycle or series: *the revolution of the seasons.*

rev·o·lu·tion·ar·y (rev′ə lü′shə ner′ē) *adj.* **1.** relating to, of the nature of, or tending to bring a revolution. **2. Revolutionary.** of or relating to the American Revolution. —*n., pl.* **rev·o·lu·tion·ar·ies.** a person who takes part in or supports a revolution.

Revolutionary War, another term for **American Revolution.**

rev·o·lu·tion·ist (rev′ə lü′shə nist) *n.* a person who takes part in or supports a revolution; revolutionary.

rev·o·lu·tion·ize (rev′ə lü′shə nīz′) *v.t.,* **rev·o·lu·tion·ized, rev·o·lu·tion·iz·ing.** to produce a far-reaching or very great change in: *The development of the airplane revolutionized transportation.*

re·volve (ri volv′) *v.,* **re·volved, re·volv·ing.** —*v.i.* **1.** to move in a circle or orbit around a central point or object: *The planets revolve around the sun.* **2.** to spin or turn around on an axis; rotate: *Wheels revolve when in motion.* **3.** to move or happen in a cycle: *The seasons revolve.* —*v.t.* **1.** to cause to move in a circle or orbit. **2.** to cause to rotate. [From the Latin word *revolvere* meaning "to roll back, reverse" and "to revolve," from the prefix *re-* "again, back" + *volvere* "to roll."]

·**revolve around.** to have as a focus or central point; concern primarily: *The doctor's whole life revolves around the hospital.*

re·volv·er (ri vol′vər) *n.* a pistol fitted with a cylinder that holds the cartridges and revolves after each shot, thus allowing the weapon to be fired several times without reloading.

re·vue (ri vū′) *also,* **re·view.** *n.* a theatrical presentation usually consisting of songs, dances, and skits that make fun of people and recent events.

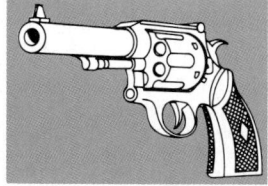

revolver

re·vul·sion (ri vul′shən) *n.* **1.** strong disgust; repugnance: *The conditions in the slums filled us with revulsion.* **2.** the act of drawing back or away; withdrawal.

re·ward (ri wôrd′) *n.* **1.** something given or received in return, as for service or merit: *The student received a medal as a reward for high marks.* **2.** money offered or given for the recovery of lost property, the capture of criminals, or the like: *We offered a reward for the return of our lost dog.* —*v.t.* **1.** to give a reward to: *The judges rewarded each winner with a medal.* **2.** to give a reward for: *Our country rewards bravery.* **3.** to be a reward for: *Success rewarded their efforts.* —**re·ward′er,** *n.*

re·word (rē wûrd′) *v.t.* to write or say again in another way; put into other words: *to reword a statement or question so that it will be better understood.*

re·work (rē wûrk′) *v.t.* to work or do over again: *to rework a mine, to rework parts of a composition.*

re·write (*v.*, rē rīt′; *n.*, rē′rīt′) *v.t.*, **re·wrote** (rē rōt′), **re·writ·ten** (rē rit′ən), **re·writ·ing.** **1.** to write again, especially in a different or improved form: *to rewrite an unsatisfactory book report.* **2.** to write a news story based on a reporter's notes or description. —*n.* **1.** a revision of something that has been written: *to do a rewrite of a term paper.* **2.** a news story written from a reporter's notes or description.

Reye's syndrome (rīz, rāz) a rare, serious disease of the brain, occurring in children, usually following a viral disease such as influenza. [From the Australian pediatrician Ralph D. K. *Reye* (1912–1978), who first described it.]

Reyn·ard (ren′ərd, rā′närd) *n.* the clever fox who outwits the other animals in certain medieval fables.

RFD, R.F.D., rural free delivery.

Rh, the symbol for rhodium.

rhap·sod·ic (rap sod′ik) *adj.* of, relating to, or characteristic of rhapsody; overly emotional or enthusiastic. Also, **rhap·sod·i·cal** (rap sod′i kəl). —**rhap·sod′i·cal·ly,** *adv.*

rhap·so·dy (rap′sə dē) *n., pl.* **rhap·so·dies.** **1.** speech or writing characterized by or expressing too much emotion or enthusiasm: *to go into rhapsodies in describing a sunset.* **2.** *Music.* an instrumental composition that is irregular in form and full of emotion.

rhe·a (rē′ə) *n.* a type of South American bird that cannot fly, resembling the ostrich and having brownish feathers.

Rhen·ish (ren′ish) *adj.* of or relating to the Rhine River or the regions bordering it.

rhe·ni·um (rē′nē əm) *n.* a soft, heavy, silver-white metallic element, with a very high melting point. Alloys containing rhenium are used in electrical contacts. Symbol: **Re** [Formed from *Rhenus*, the Latin name for the river Rhine in Germany. The name was chosen by two German scientists who discovered the element.]

rhe·o·stat (rē′ə stat′) *n.* an electrical device for varying the resistance of a circuit, used especially in switches that dim lights.

rhe·sus monkey (rē′səs) a yellowish brown monkey native to northern India, used widely in biological experiments.

rhet·o·ric (ret′ər ik) *n.* **1.** the art or skill of speaking or writing well, and the study of this art. **2.** showy, exaggerated, or insincere language in speech or writing: *The politician's speech was mere rhetoric.*

rhe·tor·i·cal (ri tôr′i kəl, ri tor′i kəl) *adj.* **1.** of, like, or relating to rhetoric. **2.** using rhetoric. —**rhe·tor′i·cal·ly,** *adv.* —**rhe·tor′i·cal·ness,** *n.*

rhetorical question, a question asked only for effect, with no answer expected: *The speaker asked the rhetorical question, "Don't we all want happiness?"*

rhet·o·ri·cian (ret′ə rish′ən) *n.* **1.** a person who is skilled in or teaches rhetoric. **2.** a person who writes or speaks in a rhetorical manner.

rheum (rüm) *n.* a watery discharge from mucous membranes, such as those in the nose.

rheu·mat·ic (rü mat′ik) *adj.* of, relating to, having, or caused by rheumatism. —*n.* a person who has rheumatism. —**rheu·mat′i·cal·ly,** *adv.*

rheumatic fever, an inflammatory disease that sometimes follows a streptococcal infection, most frequently occurring in childhood, characterized by inflammation in the joints and often serious damage to the heart.

rheu·ma·tism (rü′mə tiz′əm) *n.* any of several diseases characterized by inflammation, swelling, and stiffness of the muscles and joints.

Rh factor, a substance often present in the blood of humans and certain other mammals. Blood containing this substance, **Rh positive,** often causes severe reactions when combined with blood lacking it, **Rh negative,** as in transfusions. [From the *rh*(esus monkey). The factor was first discovered in the blood of this monkey.]

rhine·stone (rīn′stōn′) *n.* a colorless cut gem made of quartz or glass paste, used to imitate diamonds.

rhi·no (rī′nō) *n., pl.* **rhi·nos.** see **rhinoceros.**

rhi·noc·er·os (rī nos′ər əs) *n., pl.* **rhi·noc·er·os·es** or **rhi·noc·er·os.** a large, thick-skinned, plant-eating mammal of Africa and Asia, having one or two horns rising from the snout.

rhi·zome (rī′zōm) *n.* a fleshy underground stem, usually growing parallel to the surface of the ground, bearing

rhinoceros

nodes that can give rise to new plants. Also, **rootstock.**

rho (rō) *n., pl.* **rhos.** the seventeenth letter of the Greek alphabet (P, ρ), corresponding to the English letter R, r.

rho·di·um (rō′dē əm) *n.* a heavy, silver-white metallic element that resists corrosion. It is often used in alloys with platinum. Symbol: **Rh** [Formed from the Greek word *rhodon* meaning "rose¹." Many of the salts containing rhodium are red.]

rhododendron

rho·do·den·dron (rō′də den′drən) *n.* any of a large group of shrubs and trees that bear clusters of bell-shaped flowers.

rhom·bus (rom′bəs) *n., pl.* **rhom·bus·es** or **rhom·bi** (rom′bī). a parallelogram with equal sides, having two obtuse angles and two acute angles.

rhu·barb (rü′bärb) *n.* **1.** a plant having reddish leafstalks that have a slightly sour taste. **2.** the leafstalks of this

at; āpe; fär; câre; end; mē; it; īce; pîerce; hot; ōld; sông, fôrk; oil; out; up; ūse; rüle; pull; tûrn; chin; sing; shop; thin; *th*is; hw in white; zh in treasure. The symbol ə stands for the unstressed vowel sound heard in about, taken, pencil, lemon, and circus.

R

plant, cooked in pies, sauces, and other dishes. **3.** *Slang.* a heated dispute or squabble.

rhum·ba (rum′bə) *n.* another spelling of **rumba**.

rhyme (rīm) *also*, **rime**. *n.* **1.** the correspondence or repetition of similar or the same sounds, usually at the ends of lines of verse. For example: I must go down to the seas again, to the lonely sea and the *sky/* And all I ask is a tall ship and a star to steer her *by* (John Masefield). **2.** a word having a sound that is similar to or the same as another: *"Stale" is a rhyme for "pail."* **3.** verse or poetry whose lines have similar or the same sounds at the end. —*v.*, **rhymed, rhym·ing.** —*v.i.* **1.** to form or make a rhyme: *"Wide" rhymes with "side."* **2.** to compose rhyme or verse. —*v.t.* **1.** to put into rhyme: *to rhyme a fable.* **2.** to use as a rhyme: *to rhyme "hippopotamus" with "have you thought of us."* —**rhym′er,** *n.*

rhythm (ri͟th′əm) *n.* **1.** a pattern, usually regular or orderly, of sounds or movements: *the rhythm of drumbeats, the rhythm of a poem.* **2.** movement marked by such a pattern. **3.** see **meter**². **4.** *Music.* **a.** a repeated pattern of beats, formed by the different lengths of tones and by the way in which the tones are accented. **b.** a particular or characteristic form of this: *That song is written in waltz rhythm.*

rhythm and blues, a style of American popular music based on the blues and characterized by a strong rhythm and a steady beat.

rhyth·mi·cal (ri͟th′mi kəl) *adj.* of, relating to, or characterized by rhythm. Also, **rhyth·mic** (ri͟th′mik).

RI, postal abbreviation for Rhode Island.

R.I., Rhode Island.

rib (rib) *n.* **1.** one of the series of curved bones attached in pairs to the backbone and enclosing the chest cavity. **2.** a cut of meat including one or more ribs. **3.** anything resembling a rib: *the ribs of an umbrella.* **4.** a raised ridge, as in a knitted sweater or sock. **5.** the main vein of a leaf. —*v.t.*, **ribbed, rib·bing. 1.** *Informal.* to poke fun at; tease. **2.** to strengthen or support with ribs. **3.** to make raised ridges in.

rib·ald (rib′əld) *adj.* vulgar; coarse: *ribald humor.*

rib·ald·ry (rib′əl drē) *n.* ribald behavior or language.

rib·bon (rib′ən) *n.* **1.** a band of fabric, paper, or other material

ribs

used for decoration. **2.** any similar band of a flexible material: *a typewriter ribbon.* **3.** a strip: *The road was a ribbon of concrete across the desert.* **4.** a small strip of cloth used as a military decoration. —**rib′bon·like′,** *adj.*

rib cage, the protective bony framework of the chest, made up of the ribs, the sternum, and the upper part of the backbone.

ri·bo·fla·vin (rī′bə flā′vin) *n.* see **vitamin B₂**.

ri·bo·nu·cle·ic acid (rī′bō nü klē′ik, rī′bō nū klē′ik). see **RNA**.

ri·bose (rī′bōs) *n.* a simple sugar that is a component of ribonucleic acid.

ri·bo·some (rī′bə sōm′) *n.* a tiny structure in the cytoplasm of cells where protein is manufactured for cell growth and other activities.

rice (rīs) *n.* **1.** the starchy grains of a cereal grass that is an important food in many parts of the world, such as India and China. **2.** the plant bearing these grains. —*v.t.*, **riced, ric·ing.** to reduce to grains resembling rice.

rice·bird (rīs′bûrd′) *n.* another word for **bobolink**.

rice paper, a thin paper usually made from the pith of a small Asian tree.

rich (rich) *adj.* **1.** having great wealth: *a rich banker, a rich country.* **2.** well-supplied with something: *The old house was rich in memories.* **3.** productive; fertile: *rich soil, a rich imagination.* **4.** deep and full: *a rich baritone voice, a rich brown color.* **5.** (of foods) having a heavy, strong flavor or containing large amounts of nutritious, sugary, or fatty ingredients: *a rich sauce.* **6.** not thin or diluted: *a rich mixture of fuel.* —*n.* **the rich.** wealthy people, taken as a group. —**rich′ly,** *adv.* —**rich′ness,** *n.*

rich·es (rich′iz) *pl. n.* an abundance of money, land, or other valuable possessions; wealth.

Rich·ter scale (rik′tər) a scale for measuring the magnitude of earthquakes, having graded steps from 1 upward. Each successive number stands for an increase of 10 in the strength of the tremors and an increase of 30 in the amount of energy the earthquake releases. 1.5 stands for a very slight earthquake, 4.5 stands for an earthquake causing slight damage, and 8.5 stands for a very destructive earthquake. [From the American scientist Charles F. *Richter* (1900–1985), who devised this scale.]

rick (rik) *n.* a stack of hay, straw, or grain, especially one that has been covered so that rain will run off it. —*v.t.* to form into a rick or ricks.

rick·ets (rik′its) *n.* a disease of infants and children, usually caused by a lack of vitamin D, which results in faulty calcium metabolism. It is characterized by softening, and sometimes bending, of the bones and enlargement of the liver and spleen.

rick·et·y (rik′i tē) *adj.* **1.** liable to fall; shaky: *a rickety old fence.* **2.** having rickets. **3.** feeble in the joints; infirm.

rick·sha (rik′shô′) *also*, **rick·shaw.** *n.* a two-wheeled carriage with a hood, drawn by one or two persons, originally used in the Orient. Also, **jinricksha.**

ric·o·chet (rik′ə shā′, rik′ə shā′) *n.* **1.** the skipping or glancing of an object off a surface that it strikes at an angle. **2.** an object skipping or glancing in this way, as a bullet: *A bystander was hit by a ricochet during the gun battle.* —*v.i.*, **ric·o·cheted** (rik′ə shād′, rik′ə shād′), **ric·o·chet·ing** (rik′ə shā′ing, rik′ə shā′ing). to skip or glance off a surface in this manner: *The ball ricocheted off the step.*

ri·cot·ta (ri kot′ə) *n.* a soft, moist cheese resembling cottage cheese, made from milk or whey. [From the Italian word *ricotta,* going back to the Latin word *recocta,* past participle of *recoquere* meaning "to cook again," from the prefix *re-* "again" + *coquere* "to cook."]

rid (rid) *v.t.*, **rid** or **rid·ded, rid·ding.** to clear or free, as from something unpleasant or undesirable.

· **to be rid of.** to be freed from: *to be rid of debts.*

· **to get rid of. a.** to get free from: *to get rid of a cold.* **b.** to kill or drive away: *Insect spray got rid of the ants in the house.*

rid·dance (rid′əns) *n.* the act of ridding or the state of being rid.

· **good riddance.** a welcome relief from someone or something undesirable or unpleasant.

rid·den (rid′ən) the past participle of **ride**.

rid·dle¹ (rid′əl) *n.* **1.** a puzzling problem or question. **2.** a person or thing that is hard to understand. —*v.*, **rid·dled, rid·dling.** —*v.i.* to speak in riddles. —*v.t.* to solve or explain (a riddle). [From the Old English word *rædels* meaning "obscure saying" or "counsel, opinion."]

rid·dle² (rid′əl) *v.t.*, **rid·dled, rid·dling. 1.** to pierce in many places: *to riddle a target with arrows.* **2.** to sift through a coarse sieve. —*n.* a coarse sieve. [From the Old English word *hriddel* meaning "a coarse sieve."]

ride (rīd) *v.*, **rode, rid·den, rid·ing.** —*v.i.* **1.** to sit on and be carried by something in motion, such as a horse or vehicle, while controlling its movement: *I ride to school every day on my bicycle.* **2.** to travel or be carried on or in a vehicle or other conveyance: *We rode through the* countryside on the train. **3.** to proceed or be carried along, as if riding: *The ship rode over the waves.* **4.** to be carried or supported while moving: *The racing car rode on two wheels as it rounded the turn.* **5.** to carry or support a rider in a certain manner: *The car rides smoothly.* **6. ride up.** to move or work upward out of place: *This sweater rides up at the waist.* **7.** to be moored: *The ship rode at anchor in the harbor.* **8.** *Informal.* to continue unchanged or without interruption: *Let the matter ride until tomorrow.* —*v.t.* **1.** to sit on and be carried by (something) in motion, while controlling its movements: *Can you ride a horse?* **2.** to travel or be carried on or in (something): *to ride a train to Chicago.* **3.** to ride over or along: *The cowboy rode the range.* **4.** *Informal.* to harass or tease: *My friends rode me about my haircut.* —*n.* **1.** a short trip on an animal or in a vehicle: *We took a ride in the country.* **2.** any of various vehicles or devices, such as a merry-go-round or Ferris wheel, that people can ride on or in for amusement: *rides at an amusement park.* **3.** the manner in which a vehicle moves: *a smooth ride.*

rid·er (rī′dər) *n.* **1.** a person or thing that rides. **2.** an amendment or addition, as to a contract or legislative bill.

ridge (rij) *n.* **1.** the long and narrow raised part of something: *the ridge of a horse's back, the ridge of a hill.* **2.** any raised narrow strip, as on fabric: *Corduroy has ridges.* **3.** a long and narrow chain of hills or mountains. **4.** a line formed at the meeting of two sloping sides: *the ridge of a roof.* —*v.t.*, *v.i.*, **ridged, ridg·ing.** **1.** to form or make into ridges. **2.** to mark or cover with ridges.

ridge·pole (rij′pōl′) *n.* a horizontal timber or pole along the top of a roof or tent to which sloping beams or fabric are fastened.

rid·i·cule (rid′i kūl′) *v.t.*, **rid·i·culed, rid·i·cul·ing.** to point out (someone or something) as foolish or insignificant; laugh at or expose to laughter. —*n.* words or actions intended to ridicule someone or something: *Their strange behavior exposed them to ridicule.* [From the French word *ridicule*, from the Latin word *ridiculus* meaning "funny, comic," from the word *ridēre* "to laugh."]

ri·dic·u·lous (ri dik′yə ləs) *adj.* deserving or arousing ridicule; laughable; silly. —**ri·dic′u·lous·ly,** *adv.* —**ri·dic′u·lous·ness,** *n.*

rife (rīf) *adj.* **1.** happening commonly and often; widespread: *Poverty is rife in that area.* **2.** filled; abounding: *a sloppy paper rife with errors.*

riff·raff (rif′raf′) *n.* **1.** low or worthless persons. **2.** trash; rubbish.

ri·fle¹ (rī′fəl) *n.* a firearm designed to be fired from the shoulder, having spiral grooves cut into its bore to cause the bullet to spin as it is fired, increasing its accuracy. —*v.t.*, **ri·fled, ri·fling.** to cut spiral grooves in (the bore of a firearm). [From the French word *rifler* meaning "to file², scrape," referring to the grooves in the bore of a rifle.]

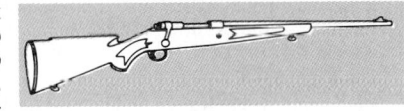

rifle¹

ri·fle² (rī′fəl) *v.t.*, **ri·fled, ri·fling.** to search through and rob; ransack: *The thief rifled the safe.* [From the Old French word *rifler* meaning "to rob, plunder," of Germanic origin.] —**ri′fler,** *n.*

ri·fle·man (rī′fəl mən) *n.*, *pl.* **ri·fle·men** (rī′fəl mən). **1.** a soldier armed with a rifle. **2.** a person skilled in the use of a rifle.

ri·fling (rī′fling) *n.* **1.** the act or process of cutting spiral grooves in the bore of a firearm. **2.** the spiral grooves of a firearm.

rift (rift) *n.* **1.** an opening made by splitting; break; fissure: *a rift in a rock.* **2.** a breach in a relationship; quarrel: *a rift between friends.* —*v.t.*, *v.i.* to split; cleave.

rig (rig) *v.t.*, **rigged, rig·ging.** **1.** to fit (a boat or ship) with masts, sails, spars, lines, and the like. **2.** to fit out; equip: *We rigged the car to carry skis.* **3.** to make or build hurriedly or as a makeshift: *to rig up a radio from spare parts.* **4.** to arrange in a dishonest way: *to rig an election.* —*n.* **1.** the arrangement of masts, sails, spars, lines, and the like on a boat or ship. **2.** apparatus or equipment used for drilling an oil well. **3.** any apparatus or equipment used for a particular purpose: *a fishing rig.* **4.** *Informal.* dress; clothing; costume. **5.** a truck or carriage that transports freight: *an 18-wheel rig carrying frozen fruit.* [Probably of Scandinavian origin.]

rig·ger (rig′ər) *n.* **1.** a person who rigs. **2.** a person who installs and repairs the rigging and hoisting gear of sailboats or ships.

rig·ging (rig′ing) *n.* **1.** all the lines of a boat or ship, as the ropes, chains, and wires, used for supporting the masts or working the sails. **2.** apparatus or equipment used for a special purpose. [From the Middle English word *rigginge* meaning "the outfitting or preparation of a ship," probably from the Middle Dutch word *rigen* with the same meaning.]

right (rīt) *adj.* **1.** free from error; correct or true; accurate: *the right answer to the arithmetic problem.* **2.** just, moral, or good: *Telling the truth was the right thing to do.* **3.** of, on, or toward the side of the body that is to the east when one is facing north: *the right hand, a right turn on a highway.* **4.** suitable; proper: *the right person for the job.* **5.** healthy; sound: *not in one's right mind.* **6.** with or having the side or surface meant to be seen: *the right side of a piece of cloth.* **7.** *also,* **Right.** relating to or having conservative or reactionary political views. —*n.* **1.** something that is just, moral, good, or true: *the triumph of right over wrong.* **2.** *also,* **rights.** a just, legal, or moral claim: *the right to free speech.* **3.** the right side or direction: *to drive on the right.* **4.** *also,* **Right.** a party or group having conservative or reactionary political views. Also, **right wing.** **5.** a blow delivered with the right hand, as in boxing. —*adv.* **1.** according to truth, fact, or reason; correctly: *You didn't spell my name right.* **2.** according to that which is just, moral, or good; so right. **3.** in a proper or suitable way: *This telephone doesn't work right.* **4.** exactly; precisely: *Put the book right here on the table.* **5.** without delay; immediately: *Let's leave right after lunch.* **6.** to or toward the right: *Turn right at the foot of the hill.* **7.** very. ▲ used as part of certain formal titles: *the right honorable senator.* **8.** in a straight line; directly: *Go right through the town.* **9.** completely: *The rain washed the dust right off the plants.* —*v.t.* **1.** to make good, just, or correct: *to right a wrong.* **2.** to put into a proper or normal position: *The crew righted the capsized boat.* —*v.i.* to get into a proper or normal position: *The boat righted slowly as the wind died down.*

•**by right** or **by rights.** properly; if justice prevails; rightly.

•**in the right.** not wrong, mistaken, or at fault.

•**right away** or **right off.** immediately: *I'll be there right away.*

at; āpe; fär; câre; end; mē; it; īce; pîerce; hot; ōld; sông, fôrk; oil; out; up; ūse; rüle; pull; tûrn; chin; sing; shop; thin; this; hw in white; zh in treasure. The symbol ə stands for the unstressed vowel sound heard in about, taken, pencil, lemon, and circus.

R

right angle, an angle of 90 degrees, formed by two lines that are perpendicular to each other.

right–an·gled (rīt′ang′gəld) *adj.* containing one or more right angles.

right·eous (rī′chəs) *adj.* **1.** doing what is right; virtuous. **2.** coming from a sense of what is right; justifiable: *to show righteous indignation at an insult.* —**right′eous·ly,** *adv.* —**right′eous·ness,** *n.*

right field *Baseball.* **1.** the right section of the outfield when viewed from home plate. **2.** the position of the player stationed in this area. —**right field·er,** *n.*

right·ful (rīt′fəl) *adj.* **1.** having a just, legal, or moral claim: *the rightful heir to a throne.* **2.** owned or held by such claim: *rightful property.* —**right′ful·ly,** *adv.* —**right′ful·ness,** *n.*

right–hand (rīt′hand′) *adj.* **1.** on or toward the right: *She drove on the right-hand side of the street.* **2.** of, for, relating to, or with the right hand. **3.** most trusted and useful: *the boss's right-hand man.*

right–hand·ed (rīt′han′did) *adj.* **1.** using the right hand more often and more easily than the left. **2.** done with the right hand: *a right-handed catch.* **3.** made to be held in or used by the right hand. **4.** turning or moving from left to right, or clockwise: *a right-handed spiral.* —*adv. also,* **right–handedly.** with the right hand: *to pitch right-handed.* —**right′hand′ed·ness,** *n.*

right·ist (rī′tist) *n.* a person who has conservative or reactionary political views. —*adj.* of, relating to, or characterized by conservative or reactionary political views.

right·ly (rīt′lē) *adv.* **1.** in a correct way; accurately: *to answer a question rightly.* **2.** properly; suitably. **3.** justly or honestly.

right of way **1.** the right of a person or thing to go first or cross in front of another or others: *A pedestrian in a crosswalk has the right of way.* **2.** a legal right to go across property belonging to another. **3.** a strip of land set aside for a specific purpose, as for railroad tracks, public roads, or power lines.

right–on (rīt′ôn′, rīt′on′) *adj. Slang.* exactly correct; perfectly right: *That weather forecast was right-on.*

right triangle, a triangle with a right angle.

right–wing (rīt′wing′) *adj.* of, relating to, or belonging to the right wing.

right wing **1.** see **right** (*n., def. 4*). **2.** a portion of a political party or other group having a more conservative or reactionary outlook than the rest.

rig·id (rij′id) *adj.* **1.** not yielding or bending; stiff: *Rigid steel girders made up the frame of the building.* **2.** strict; rigorous: *rigid discipline.* **3.** not changing; inflexible; fixed: *The requirements for membership are rigid.* —**rig′id·ly,** *adv.* —**rig′id·ness,** *n.*

ri·gid·i·ty (ri jid′i tē) *n.* the state of being rigid.

rig·ma·role (rig′mə rōl′) *n.* **1.** complicated and often foolish or unnecessary action: *to go through a lot of rigmarole to get a check cashed.* **2.** foolish or senseless talk; nonsense.

rig·or (rig′ər) *also, British,* **rig·our.** *n.* **1.** the state or quality of being strict; strictness: *the rigor of the law.* **2.** severity; harshness: *the rigor of winter, the rigors of tyranny.* **3.** exactness; precision: *the rigor of mathematics.*

rig·or mor·tis (rig′ər môr′tis) the stiffening of the muscles that begins shortly after death.

rig·or·ous (rig′ər əs) *adj.* **1.** very strict; inflexible: *rigorous rules.* **2.** severe; harsh: *the rigorous climate of the North Pole.* **3.** very exact; precise. —**rig′or·ous·ly,** *adv.* —**rig′or·ous·ness,** *n.*

rile (rīl) *v.t.,* **riled, ril·ing.** *Informal.* **1.** to irritate or annoy; provoke: *Your rudeness really riles me.* **2.** to roil (liquid).

rill (ril) *n.* a tiny stream or brook.

rim (rim) *n.* **1.** the outer edge or border of something: *a glass filled to the rim.* **2.** a strip of metal on an automobile

wheel on which the tire is fastened. —*v.t.,* **rimmed, rim·ming. 1.** to form a rim around: *The mountains rimmed the valley.* **2.** to roll around the rim of (something) without going in: *The basketball rimmed the basket and rolled out.*

rime[1] (rīm) *n., v.,* **rimed, rim·ing.** another spelling of **rhyme.**

rime[2] (rīm) *n.* frost, especially when it forms a white coating on a surface; hoarfrost. —*v.t.,* **rimed, rim·ing.** to cover with rime. [From the Old English word *hrīm* meaning ''hoarfrost.'']

rim·y (rī′mē) *adj.,* **rim·i·er, rim·i·est.** covered with rime; frosty.

rind (rīnd) *n.* a firm outer covering or skin, as of fruit or cheese.

ring[1] (ring) *n.* **1.** a continuous, closed curved line; circle. **2.** a circular band, often of precious metal, worn on a finger. **3.** any circular band, as of metal, wood, or plastic, used especially for holding or carrying something: *a napkin ring, curtain rings.* **4.** a circular course: *The children danced in a ring around the campfire.* **5.** a group of persons or things forming a circle: *The president was surrounded by a ring of bodyguards.* **6.** a circular, usually enclosed, area used especially for circus performances. **7.a.** an area used for boxing or wrestling matches. **b.** the sport of boxing: *a career in the ring.* **8.** a group of persons working together, especially for a criminal purpose: *a ring of car thieves.* **9.** any of a series of concentric layers of wood produced yearly in the trunk of a tree. **10.** *Chemistry.* a closed chain of atoms. —*v.t.* **1.** to put a ring around; enclose with a ring; encircle. **2.** to form into a ring or rings. **3.** in certain games, to throw a horseshoe, ring, or other object over: *to ring a stake.* **4.** to put a ring in the nose of: *to ring a bull.* —*v.i.* to move in a ring or spiral. [From the Old English word *hring* meaning ''circle, ring[1].''] —**ring′like′,** *adj.*

ring[2] (ring) *v.,* **rang, rung, ring·ing.** —*v.i.* **1.** to make a clear, resonant sound, as that made by a bell when struck. **2.** to cause a bell or bells to sound, especially as a signal or summons: *We rang for assistance.* **3.** to resound loudly and clearly; reverberate; echo: *The room rang with laughter.* **4.** to have a sensation, as of an echoing sound or buzzing: *My ears rang from the shrill noise.* —*v.t.* **1.** to cause (something) to ring: *The visitor rang the doorbell.* **2.** to announce or proclaim by the ringing of bells: *The chimes rang the hour.* **3.** to call on the telephone: *Ring me up when you get home.* —*n.* **1.** the act of ringing something, especially a bell. **2.** a clear, resonant sound, as that made by a bell when struck. **3.** a sound expressing a certain quality; tone: *a voice with a ring of sincerity.* **4.** *Informal.* a telephone call: *I'll give you a ring when I get home.* [From the Old English word *hringan* meaning ''to make the sound of a bell.'']

ring·bolt (ring′bōlt′) *n.* a bolt with a ring fitted into an eye in its head.

ring·er[1] (ring′ər) *n.* **1.** a person or thing that rings or encircles. **2.** a horseshoe or quoit thrown so as to encircle a stake or pin. [*Ring[1] + -er[1].*]

ring·er[2] (ring′ər) *n.* **1.** a person or thing that rings a bell, chime, or the like. **2.** *Slang.* a horse or athlete illegally entered in a contest, as by the falsification of name or age. **3.** *Slang.* a person or thing that closely resembles another: *You're a ringer for that new movie star.* [*Ring[2] + -er[1].*]

ring·lead·er (ring′lē′dər) *n.* a person who leads others, especially in wrong or unlawful acts.

ring·let (ring′lit) *n.* **1.** a coiled or curved lock of hair. **2.** *Archaic.* a small ring.

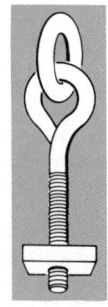

ringbolt

ring·mas·ter (ring′mas′tər) *n.* a person who introduces the acts in a circus.

ring·side (ring′sīd′) *n.* **1.** an area just outside a ring, especially the area containing the first row of seats at a boxing match. **2.** any area where a person can have a close view.

ring·worm (ring′wûrm′) *n.* any of several contagious fungous infections of the skin characterized by ring-shaped patches.

rink (ringk) *n.* **1.** a building, part of a building, or an area having a smooth, open surface, as of ice for skating. **2.** the surface itself.

rinse (rins) *v.t.,* **rinsed, rins·ing. 1.** to remove (soap or impurities) by washing with clear water: *to rinse soap off one's hands.* **2.** to remove soap or impurities from (something) by washing with clear water: *to rinse clothes.* **3.** to cleanse or wash lightly: *to rinse a blouse and hang it to dry.* —*n.* **1.** the act of rinsing. **2.** water or other liquid used for rinsing. **3.** a liquid preparation that is applied to the hair to tint or condition it.

ri·ot (rī′ət) *n.* **1.** a disorderly, often violent, disturbance or outbreak by a large crowd. **2.** *Law.* a disturbance of the peace by three or more persons acting together. **3.** a bright, lavish display: *The autumn leaves were a riot of color.* **4.** *Slang.* a person or thing that is extremely amusing. —*v.i.* to take part in a disorderly, often violent, disturbance: *The prisoners rioted.* —**ri′ot·er,** *n.*

·**to read the riot act to.** to scold harshly and warn against continuing offensive behavior or actions.

·**to run riot. a.** to behave or move wildly and without restraint. **b.** to grow in great amounts or without control: *Weeds ran riot in the garden.*

ri·ot·ous (rī′ə təs) *adj.* **1.** of, relating to, or taking part in a disorderly, often violent, disturbance. **2.** noisy or rowdy; boisterous: *riotous laughter.* —**ri′ot·ous·ly,** *adv.* —**ri′ot·ous·ness,** *n.*

rip¹ (rip) *v.,* **ripped, rip·ping.** —*v.t.* **1.** to tear (something); rend: *I ripped my trousers on the fence.* **2.** to make by ripping: *The nail ripped a hole in the tarpaulin.* **3.** to tear or cut into pieces: *to rip up a piece of paper.* **4.** to remove (something) by tearing or pulling: *to rip out a seam.* **5.** to saw or split (wood) along the grain. —*v.i.* to become torn apart. —*n.* a torn place; tear. [Probably from the Middle Dutch word *rippen* meaning "to tear¹, rip¹."]

·**to rip off.** *Slang.* **1.** to rob or steal. **2.** to cheat or swindle (someone).

rip² (rip) *n.* **1.** a stretch of rough water formed by the meeting of opposing currents. **2.** see **riptide.** [Perhaps from *rip¹.*]

rip cord, a cord with a handle that releases a parachute when pulled.

ripe (rīp) *adj.,* **rip·er, rip·est. 1.** fully grown and ready to be gathered and used as food: *The tomatoes were not yet ripe.* **2.** fully developed; mature: *ripe cheese.* **3.** advanced in years: *a ripe old age.* **4.** fully prepared and ready: *The country was ripe for revolution.* **5.** favorable or suitable: *The time is ripe.* —**ripe′ly,** *adv.* —**ripe′ness,** *n.*

rip·en (rī′pən) *v.t., v.i.* to make or become ripe: *to ripen cheese. The tomatoes ripened on the vine.*

rip–off (rip′ôf′) *n. Slang.* a theft, swindle, or example of cheating someone: *The offer for a twenty-dollar gold watch was a rip-off, because I sent my money but never received the watch.*

ri·poste (ri pōst′) *n.* **1.** *Fencing.* a quick thrust made after successfully parrying an opponent's lunge. **2.** a quick, witty, or sharp reply; retort.

rip·ple (rip′əl) *n.* **1.** a very small wave on the surface of a liquid, such as water: *The breeze made ripples on the surface of the pond.* **2.** anything resembling this: *ripples in a fabric.* **3.** a sound resembling the lapping of very small waves: *a ripple of applause.* —*v.,* **rip·pled, rip·pling.** —*v.i.* **1.** to form or have ripples: *The grass rippled gently in the wind* (Ernest Hemingway). **2.** to make a rippling sound. —*v.t.* to cause ripples on.

rip–roar·ing (rip′rôr′ing) *adj. Informal.* noisy and lively: *The children had a rip-roaring good time at the amusement park.*

rip·saw (rip′sô′) *n.* a handsaw with squared cutting edges on its teeth, used to cut wood along the grain. See **crosscut saw** for illustration.

rip·tide (rip′tīd′) *n.* a strong current of water flowing rapidly away from a shore and against another current.

Rip Van Win·kle (rip′ van wing′kəl) the hero of a story by Washington Irving. He slept for twenty years and awakened to find his village and country changed completely.

rise (rīz) *v.i.,* **rose, ris·en, ris·ing. 1.** to get up from a sitting, kneeling, or lying position; stand up: *Everyone rose when the judge entered the courtroom.* **2.** to get out of bed: *That farmer always rises early.* **3.** to move from a lower to a higher place; go upward: *Smoke rose from the chimney.* **4.** (of the sun and other heavenly bodies) to appear above the horizon. **5.** to slope upward: *The hills rise beyond the fields.* **6.** to extend upward: *That tall building rises above all the others.* **7.** to increase, as in amount, value, degree, or force: *The cost of living rose last year.* **8.** to advance, as in rank, position, or influence: *to rise to the presidency.* **9.** to reach a higher level; increase in height: *The river rose two feet.* **10.** to swell up: *The cake will rise.* **11.** to become louder or higher in pitch: *My voice rose with anger.* **12.** to have an origin; start; begin: *That river rises in the mountains.* **13.** to revolt; rebel: *The people rose against the tyrant.* **14.** to come back from death; return to life. —*n.* **1.** an upward movement; ascent: *the rise of water in a river.* **2.** an increase, as in amount, value, degree, or force: *a rise in temperature, a rise in prices.* **3.** an upward slope or direction: *the rise of a hill.* **4.** a piece of rising ground; hill: *The house was built on a rise above the river.* **5.** an advance in rank, status, or influence: *the rise of a politician.*

·**to give rise to.** to cause; begin; start: *The depression gave rise to widespread unemployment.*

·**to rise to.** to be equal to the demands of: *to rise to the occasion and score the winning goal.*

ris·en (riz′ən) the past participle of **rise.**

ris·er (rī′zər) *n.* **1.** a person or thing that rises: *Early risers are up before dawn.* **2.** the vertical part of a step.

risk (risk) *n.* a chance of loss or harm; danger: *There is great risk involved in that plan.* —*v.t.* **1.** to expose to loss or harm: *to risk one's life to save a drowning child.* **2.** to take the risk of: *to risk losing money on an investment.*

risk·y (ris′kē) *adj.,* **risk·i·er, risk·i·est.** full of risk; dangerous: *Climbing that mountain was risky. Being a race car driver is a risky profession.* —**risk′i·ness,** *n.*

risers

ris·qué (ris kā′) *adj.* slightly improper; suggestive: *a risqué story.*

ri·tar·dan·do (rē′tär dän′dō) *Music. adj.* becoming gradually slower. *n., pl.* **ri·tar·dan·dos.** a gradual slowing of tempo.

rite (rīt) *n.* **1.** a formal act or series of acts set by ritual

---

at; āpe; fär; câre; end; mē; it; īce; pîerce; hot; ōld; sông, fôrk; oil; out; up; ūse; rüle; pùll; tûrn; chin; sing; shop; thin; this; hw in white; zh in treasure. The symbol ə stands for the unstressed vowel sound heard in about, taken, pencil, lemon, and circus.

R

or tradition: *marriage rites*. **2.** a particular formal ceremony: *the rite of baptism.*

rit·u·al (rich'ü əl) *n.* **1.** a set form or procedure for the performance of a religious or solemn rite. **2.** a system or body of rites. **3.** a routine faithfully followed: *to make a ritual of exercising every morning.* —*adj.* of, relating to, or performed as a ritual. —**rit'u·al·ly,** *adv.*

rit·u·al·ism (rich'ü ə liz'əm) *n.* **1.** a strict observance of or adherence to ritual. **2.** a study of religious ritual.

ritz·y (rit'sē) *adj.*, **ritz·i·er, ritz·i·est.** *Slang.* very elegant and fashionable; posh: *a ritzy restaurant, to live in a ritzy neighborhood.* [From the *Ritz* hotels, known for their luxurious décor.]

ri·val (rī'vəl) *n.* **1.** a person who competes with another to achieve the same thing or tries to equal or do better than another; competitor: *The two friends were rivals for the prize.* **2.** a person or thing that compares favorably with or equals another: *New York has no rival for size among American cities.* —*v.t.,* **ri·valed, ri·val·ing;** also, British, **ri·valled, ri·val·ling. 1.** to try to equal or do better than; compete with. **2.** to compare favorably with or be the equal of: *London rivals New York in population.* —*adj.* being a rival; competing: *rival football teams.*

ri·val·ry (rī'vəl rē) *n.*, *pl.* **ri·val·ries. 1.** the act of rivaling; competition. **2.** the state of being rivals: *There was great rivalry between the two schools in basketball.*

rive (rīv) *v.t.,* **rived, rived** or **riv·en** (riv'ən), **riv·ing.** to split; cleave: *to rive a log with an ax.*

riv·er (riv'ər) *n.* **1.** a large stream of water that flows in a natural channel and empties into a lake, ocean, or another river. **2.** anything resembling a river, as in quantity or flow: *a river of oil.*

river basin, the land area drained by a river and its tributaries.

riv·er·bed (riv'ər bed') *n.* the bottom of the channel through which a river flows or formerly flowed.

riv·er·head (riv'ər hed') *n.* the source of a river.

riv·er·side (riv'ər sīd') *n.* the bank of a river, or the area near it.

riv·et (riv'it) *n.* a metal bolt used to make permanent fastenings, especially in metalwork and fabrics. The shaft of the rivet is put through aligned holes in materials to be joined, and the headless end is flattened to make a tight connection. —*v.t.* **1.** to fasten with a rivet or rivets. **2.** to fasten or hold firmly: *The entire audience's attention was riveted on the tightrope walker.* —**riv'et·er,** *n.*

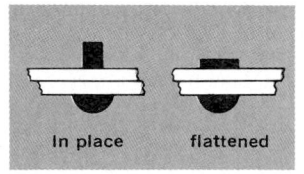

In place   flattened

rivets

riv·u·let (riv'yə lət) *n.* a tiny stream or brook.

rm. 1. ream. **2.** room.

Rn, the symbol for radon.

RN 1. registered nurse. **2.** Royal Navy.

RNA, any of various nucleic acids found in the cytoplasm and nucleus of all living cells, consisting of a long strand made up of alternating units of sugar and phosphate connected by a nitrogen base. One form of this acid, **messenger RNA,** carries the genetic information contained in DNA from the cell nucleus to the cytoplasm. Another form, **transfer RNA,** arranges amino acids so that protein is produced in the manner directed by DNA. [Short for *r*(ibo)*n*(ucleic) *a*(cid).]

roach¹ (rōch) *n.*, *pl.* **roach·es.** see **cockroach.** [Short for *cockroach.*]

roach² (rōch) *n.*, *pl.* **roach·es** or **roach. 1.** a freshwater fish related to the carp and found in lakes and rivers in northern Europe. **2.** any of several similar fish found in North America. [From the Old French word *roche* meaning this fish.]

road (rōd) *n.* **1.** a strip of pavement or cleared ground used for traveling between places; open way for the passage of vehicles, persons, or animals. **2.** any means of going or moving toward a specific goal: *the road to power.* **3.** *often,* **roads.** see **roadstead. 4.** a railroad.
  ·on the road. traveling, as for business.

road agent, formerly, a highwayman who robbed stagecoaches in the western United States.

road·bed (rōd'bed') *n.* **1.** a foundation or bed for the ties and rails of a railroad. **2.** the foundation or surface of a road.

road·block (rōd'blok') *n.* **1.** a blockade to stop traffic on a road, as that used by police to stop criminals. **2.** anything that hinders progress.

road hog *Informal.* a driver who obstructs traffic by driving in more than one lane of the road.

road map, a map that shows the streets and highways of an area: *Whenever we drive in a new city, we use a road map.*

road·run·ner (rōd'run'ər) *n.* a desert bird, related to the cuckoo, native to southwestern North America. The roadrunner has brownish black streaked feathers, a long, white-tipped tail, and a shaggy crest. It usually runs very swiftly instead of flying.

roadrunner

road·side (rōd'sīd') *n.* an area along the side of a road: *Let's pull up on the roadside and rest.* —*adj.* along the side of a road: *We stopped at a roadside vegetable stand.*

road·stead (rōd'sted') *n.* a protected area near the shore where ships may anchor. It is less sheltered than a harbor.

road·ster (rōd'stər) *n.* an open automobile with a single seat for two or more people, often with a rumble seat or luggage compartment in the rear.

road test 1. a test of a vehicle's performance under actual driving conditions. **2.** a test of the driving skill of an applicant for a driver's license.

road·way (rōd'wā') *n.* a road, especially that part over which vehicles travel.

road·work (rōd'wûrk') *n.* physical exercise or training consisting of long runs over a road or path.

roam (rōm) *v.i.* to go about without any purpose or destination, especially over a large area; wander: *to roam through the woods.* —*v.t.* to wander over or through (a place): *The wolves roamed the forest in search of food.* —**roam'er,** *n.*

roan (rōn) *adj.* reddish brown with flecks of gray or white. —*n.* **1.** a roan color. **2.** a horse of this color.

roar (rôr) *v.i.* **1.** to make a loud, deep sound or cry: *The lion roared.* **2.** to resound loudly and deeply: *The motor roared.* **3.** to move with a loud, deep noise: *The plane roared up the runway.* **4.** to laugh loudly: *The audience roared at the comedian's jokes.* —*v.t.* to shout or express in a roar: *The crowd roared its approval of the speech.* —*n.* **1.** a loud, deep sound or cry. **2.** a loud, resounding noise: *the roar of ocean waves.* —**roar'er,** *n.*

roast (rōst) *v.t.* **1.** to cook without liquid in an oven or over an open fire or hot coals: *to roast a chicken, to roast chestnuts.* **2.** to dry and brown by heat: *to roast coffee beans.* **3.** *Informal.* to criticize or ridicule severely: *The critics roasted the new play.* **4.** to make very hot. **5.** to heat (ore) with air in a furnace so as to purify, dehydrate, or oxidize. —*v.i.* **1.** to be cooked without liquid in an oven or over an open fire or hot coals. **2.** to be uncomfortably hot: *I'm roasting in this heavy coat.* —*n.* **1.** a cut of meat that has been roasted or is prepared to be roasted. **2.** an outdoor gathering at which food is cooked over an open fire or hot coals. **3.** an entertainment at which a series of speakers playfully mock a guest of honor, usually a celebrity.

roast·er (rōs′tər) *n.* **1.** a pan or appliance used for roasting. **2.** an animal suitable for roasting, especially a chicken or a young pig.

rob (rob) *v.*, **robbed, rob·bing.** —*v.t.* **1.** to take property from unlawfully by threats or by the use of violence: *They robbed the jewelry store in broad daylight.* **2.** *Informal.* to take away (property) by illegal means; steal: *Someone robbed the pencils from my desk.* **3.** to deprive (someone) of something: *The hailstorm robbed us of our crops.* —*v.i.* to commit robbery: *The gang robbed until they were caught.*

rob·ber (rob′ər) *n.* a person who robs.

rob·ber·y (rob′ə rē) *n., pl.* **rob·ber·ies.** the act of unlawfully taking another's property; theft.

robe (rōb) *n.* **1.** a long, loose outer garment, especially one worn at home or on informal occasions: *a beach robe.* **2.** *often,* **robes.** such a garment worn to show office, profession, or rank: *a judge's robes, a cleric's robe.* **3.** a blanket or other covering, as for use by spectators at outdoor sporting events. —*v.*, **robed, rob·ing.** —*v.t.* to put a robe on. —*v.i.* to put on a robe. [From the Old French word *robe* meaning this garment and "booty," of Germanic origin.]

rob·in (rob′in) *n.* **1.** a North American thrush having a reddish orange breast and a black head and tail. **2.** a smaller thrush of Europe and parts of Asia and Africa, having a brown back, a white underside, and a reddish brown breast.

Robin Hood *English Legend.* an outlaw who, with his band of men, robbed the rich in order to give help to the poor.

Rob·in·son Cru·soe (rob′in sən krü′sō) the castaway hero of Daniel Defoe's novel of the same name, published in 1719.

ro·bot (rō′bət, rō′bot) *n.* **1.** a machine designed to perform certain human tasks. **2.** a person who works or acts in a mechanical way. [From the Czech word *robot*, coined by the Czech playwright Karel Čapek (1890–1938) in his 1921 play *R. U. R. (Rossum's Universal Robots),* from the word *robota* meaning "forced labor."]

using a **robot** to handle explosives

ro·bot·ics (rō bot′iks) *n.* the science or technology of using automated or computer-controlled robots to perform routine tasks, as in a factory.

ro·bust (rō bust′, rō′bust) *adj.* **1.** having or showing strength and vigor; in good health; hardy: *a robust young athlete, a robust appetite.* **2.** requiring strength and vigor: *the robust life of a lumberjack.* **3.** rich and full-bodied: *a robust flavor.*

roc (rok) *n. Arabian Legend.* an enormous and fearsome bird of prey.

rock¹ (rok) *n.* **1.** a fragment or piece of stone: *to throw rocks into a pond.* **2.** a large mass of stone forming a cliff, peak, or reef: *The ship was dashed violently against the rocks.* **3.** *Geology.* **a.** an extensive, naturally formed mass of mineral matter that forms part of the crust of the earth. **b.** a particular kind of such matter. Granite, limestone, and slate are rocks. **4.** something resembling a rock in firmness or as a source of strength or support. [From the Old French word *roche* meaning "a large stone" or "rocky area."] —**rock′like′,** *adj.*

•**on the rocks.** *Informal.* **a.** in a state of destruction or ruin. **b.** (of a drink) served over ice.

rock² (rok) *v.t.* **1.** to move back and forth or from side to side gently: *to rock a baby in your arms.* **2.** to move or shake violently: *The earth tremor rocked the house.* **3.** to upset or unnerve: *The news of the mayor's death rocked the city.* —*v.i.* **1.** to be moved back and forth or from side to side gently: *The porch chair rocked in the breeze.* **2.** to be shaken violently: *The ship rocked in the squall.* —*n.* **1.** a rocking motion. **2. a.** see **rock 'n' roll.** **b.** a form of popular music that developed from rock 'n' roll, influenced by folk and country and western music. It is characterized especially by generally more complex lyrics and arrangements than rock 'n' roll. Also *(def. 2b),* **rock music.** [From the Middle English word *rokken* meaning "to rock a cradle" or "to move back and forth," from Old English.]

rock–and–roll (rok′ən rōl′) another spelling of **rock 'n' roll.**

rock bottom, the lowest level; very bottom: *The price of oil hit rock bottom.* —**rock′-bot′tom,** *adj.*

rock candy, clear, hard crystals of pure sugar.

rock crystal, a clear, colorless variety of quartz, used to make optical devices, jewelry, vases, and ornaments.

rock·er (rok′ər) *n.* **1.** a rocking chair. **2.** one of the two curved pieces on which a cradle, rocking chair, or other object rocks.

rock·et (rok′it) *n.* **1.** a device that is propelled by a jet of hot gases ejected in a direction opposite to the direction of motion, and that does not require air from the outside for its operation. **2.** a vehicle, missile, or projectile propelled by such a device. —*v.i.* to move or rise swiftly: *The price of food is rocketing upward.*

rock·et·ry (rok′i trē) *n.* the science of rocket design, construction, and flight.

rock garden, a garden arranged with flowers and plants on rocky ground or among rocks.

rocking chair, a chair mounted on rockers or springs, so that it can rock back and forth.

rocking horse, a toy horse mounted on rockers, large enough for a child to ride. Also, **hobbyhorse.**

rock lobster, see **spiny lobster.**

rock music, see **rock²** *(n., def. 2b).*

rock 'n' roll (rok′ ən rōl′) *also,* **rock-and-roll, rock.** **1.** a form of popular music derived from blues, country music, and jazz, characterized especially by a strong, persistent beat, electronically amplified instruments, and relatively simple lyrics and arrangements. —*adj.* of or relating to this music: *rock 'n' roll bands.* —*v.* to perform this music.

rock salt, common salt occurring in solid form, especially in large crystals; halite.

---

at; āpe; fär; câre; end; mē; it; īce; pîerce; hot; ōld; sông, fôrk; oil; out; up; ūse; rüle; pùll; tûrn; chin; sing; shop; thin; **th**is; hw in white; zh in treasure. The symbol ə stands for the unstressed vowel sound heard in about, taken, pencil, lemon, and circus.

R

rock wool, fibrous, fireproof insulating material made by blowing steam or hot air through a molten mass of rock, such as limestone.

rock·y¹ (rok′ē) *adj.,* **rock·i·er, rock·i·est. 1.** full of rocks: *a rocky hill.* **2.** like rock; hard; unyielding. [*Rock*¹ + -*y*¹.] **—rock′i·ness,** *n.*

rock·y² (rok′ē) *adj.,* **rock·i·er, rock·i·est. 1.** likely to sway or totter; shaky. **2.** doubtful; uncertain: *a rocky future.* **3.** *Informal.* physically weak or unsteady: *The fever made me feel rocky.* [*Rock*² + -*y*¹.] **—rock′i·ness,** *n.*

Rocky Mountain goat, a cud-chewing animal of the mountain ranges of western North America, having short, black horns and a thick coat of long, white hair. Also, **mountain goat.**

Rocky Mountain sheep, another term for **bighorn.**

Rocky Mountain spotted fever, an infectious disease caused by a microorganism and transmitted by the bite of a tick, characterized by high fever, headache, muscular pain, and a red or purple rash.

Rocky Mountain goat

ro·co·co (rə kō′kō) *n.* a style of interior decoration, architecture, and painting that originated in France and northern Italy and was much used during the eighteenth century, characterized especially by the use of curved forms based on objects from nature, such as shells, flowers, and leaves. —*adj.* of, relating to, or in this style.

rod (rod) *n.* **1.** a thin, straight, usually cylindrical piece of metal, wood, or other material. **2.** a slender straight stick cut from or growing on a tree or bush. **3.** see **fishing rod. 4.** a stick or bundle of sticks used to beat or punish. **5. the rod.** punishment; discipline: *Spare the rod and spoil the child* (Samuel Butler). **6.** a unit of measurement equal to 5½ yards, or 16½ feet (5.03 meters). **7.** *Slang.* a pistol or revolver. **8.** one of the rod-shaped cells on the retina of the eye that are sensitive to dim light. **9.** a staff as a symbol of authority or power. **—rod′like′,** *adj.*

rode (rōd) the past tense of **ride.**

ro·dent (rō′dənt) *n.* any of various mammals having a pair of large front teeth used for gnawing. Rats, mice, squirrels, guinea pigs, porcupines, and beavers are rodents. —*adj.* **1.** gnawing: *the rodent teeth of a beaver.* **2.** of, relating to, or characteristic of a rodent.

ro·de·o (rō′dē ō′, rō dā′ō) *n., pl.* **ro·de·os. 1.** a show in which contestants display their skills in various events, such as horseback riding, calf roping, and steer wrestling, often for cash prizes. **2.** a roundup of cattle. [From the Spanish word *rodeo* meaning "roundup," from the word *rodear* "to go around," going back to the Latin word *rota* "wheel."]

roe¹ (rō) *n.* the eggs of fish. [Perhaps from the Middle Dutch word *roch* meaning "fish eggs."]

roe² (rō) *n., pl.* **roes** or **roe.** a small deer native to the forests of Europe and northern Asia, having a coarse, reddish brown coat with a white patch over the rump. Also, **roe deer.** [From the Old English word *rā* meaning this deer.]

roe·buck (rō′buk′) *n., pl.* **roe·bucks** or **roe·buck.** a male roe deer.

roent·gen (rent′gən) *n.* the international unit for measuring the intensity of X rays or gamma rays. [From the Ger-

roe²

man physicist Wilhelm K. *Röntgen* (1845–1923), who discovered X rays.]

rog·er (roj′ər) *interj.* **1.** in radio communications, message received and understood. **2.** *Informal.* all right or OK.

rogue (rōg) *n.* **1.** a person who is dishonest and deceitful; scoundrel. **2.** a person who is mischievous and playful. **3.** a wild animal, especially an elephant, of a dangerous or savage nature, living apart from the herd.

ro·guer·y (rō′gə rē) *n., pl.* **ro·guer·ies. 1.** dishonest and deceitful actions or behavior. **2.** playfully mischievous actions or behavior.

rogues' gallery, a collection of photographs of known criminals and suspects kept by police to aid in making identifications.

ro·guish (rō′gish) *adj.* **1.** dishonest and deceitful. **2.** playfully mischievous: *a roguish wink.* **—ro′guish·ly,** *adv.* **—ro′guish·ness,** *n.*

roil (roil) *v.t.* **1.** to make (liquid) muddy or unsettled by stirring up sediment. **2.** to disturb or make angry; vex.

rois·ter (roi′stər) *v.i.* **1.** to behave or frolic in a loud or boisterous manner. **2.** to swagger. **—rois′ter·er,** *n.*

Ro·land (rō′lənd) *n.* in French and Italian literature, a hero who fought under Charlemagne and, according to legend, was killed by the Saracens in A.D. 778.

role (rōl) *also,* **rôle.** *n.* **1.** a character or part played by an actor. **2.** a part played by anyone or anything; position or function: *the role of interpreter for a group.* [From the French word *rôle* with the same meaning, from the Old French word *rolle* "a roll of paper (on which an actor's part was written)," from the Medieval Latin word *rotulus* "roll of parchment," going back to the Latin word *rota* "wheel."]

role model, a person whose behavior sets an example, especially for those who are young or impressionable: *Teachers and parents are important role models.*

roll (rōl) *v.i.* **1.** to move by turning over and over: *The ball rolled off the table.* **2.** to move or be moved on rollers or wheels: *The wagon rolled down the street.* **3.** to turn over many times: *The dog rolled in the mud.* **4.** to move or extend in a smooth, rising and falling manner: *The road rolled before us over gentle hills.* **5.** to pass or go: *The years roll on.* **6.** to turn around wholly or partially: *eyes rolling in amazement.* **7.** to rock or move from side to side; sway: *The ship rolled violently in the storm.* **8.** to make a deep, continuous sound; rumble: *The thunder rolled.* **9.** *Informal.* to make progress or start: *Let's get this project rolling.* —*v.t.* **1.** to cause to move by turning over and over: *to roll a hoop.* **2.** to move (something) by means of rollers or wheels: *to roll a bed against the wall.* **3.** to wrap (something) around on itself or on something else; shape into a ball or cylinder: *to roll up a blanket.* **4.** to enclose or wrap in a covering: *to roll a wet swimsuit in a towel.* **5.** to spread out, flatten, or make smooth with a roller: *to roll metal into sheets, to roll dough.* **6.** to cause to rock from side to side: *The strong winds rolled the boat.* **7.** to pronounce (a speech sound, especially the sound of *r*) with a trill. **8.** to turn (the eyes) around, wholly or partly. **9.** to cast (dice). —*n.* **1.** a ball or cylinder formed by winding something round and round; something rolled up: *a roll of stamps, a roll of wallpaper.* **2.** a list of names of people belonging to a group: *a class roll.* **3.** a mass of something that is rounded or cylindrical. **4.** a small cake of baked dough. **5.** any food, such as meat or cake, that is rolled up. **6.** a rolling or swaying motion: *The roll of the boat was making us dizzy.* **7.** a rapid, continuous series of short sounds, as those made by beating on a drum. **8.** a deep, continuous sound: *the roll of the surf.* **9.** see **roller. 10.** the act of rolling.

roll call, the act of calling a list of names, such as those registered in a class, to find out who is present.

roll·er (rō′lər) *n.* **1.** a cylinder on which something is rolled or wound up: *the roller of a window shade.* **2.** a cylinder that smooths, spreads out, flattens, or crushes: *a paint roller.* **3.** a small wheel on which something is rolled: *We had to put the piano on rollers to move it.* **4.** a hollow cylinder of wire mesh or plastic on which hair is rolled up. **5.** a long, swelling wave breaking on a shoreline. **6.** a person or thing that rolls.

roller coaster, an amusement ride consisting of a series of open, attached cars that move at high speeds over a track having sharp turns and steep declines.

roll·er–skate (rō′lər skāt′) *v.i.,* **roll·er-skat·ed, roll·er-skat·ing.** to skate on roller skates.

roller skate, a skate having small wheels on the bottom, used for skating on a flat surface, such as a sidewalk.

rol·lick (rol′ik) *v.i.* to behave in a carefree, joyous manner; frolic.

rol·lick·ing (rol′i king) *adj.* carefree and joyous; merry; frolicking.

rolling mill 1. a factory where metal is made into sheets, bars, or plates by being passed between heavy rollers. **2.** a machine with rollers for making metal into sheets, bars, or plates.

roller skates

rolling pin, a smooth, usually wooden cylinder, often with a handle at each end, used to roll out dough.

rolling stock, locomotives, cars, and other wheeled vehicles of a railroad.

ro·ly–po·ly (rō′lē pō′lē) *adj.* short and plump; pudgy: *a roly-poly child.* —*n., pl.* **ro·ly-po·lies.** a short, plump person or thing.

Rom. 1. Roman. **2.** Romans. **3.** Romance (languages).

ROM (rom) *n.* a type of computer memory that holds permanent data that can usually be read at high speed but to which no new data can be added.

ro·maine (rō mān′) *n.* **1.** the narrow crisp leaves of a kind of lettuce plant, forming a long loose head. **2.** the plant bearing these leaves.

Ro·man (rō′mən) *adj.* **1.** of or relating to ancient or modern Rome, its people, or their culture. **2.** of or relating to the Roman Catholic Church or its members. **3.** *usually,* **roman.** of or designating the most widely used style of type or lettering, characterized by upright letters. This sentence is in roman type. —*n.* **1.** a person who was born or is living in Rome. **2.** a person who lived in ancient Rome. **3.** *usually,* **roman.** roman type or lettering.

Roman Catholic 1. of, relating to, or characteristic of the Roman Catholic Church. **2.** a member of the Roman Catholic Church.

Roman Catholic Church, the Christian church that recognizes the pope as its supreme head.

Roman Catholicism, the beliefs, practices, and system of government of the Roman Catholic Church.

ro·mance (rō mans′, rō′mans) *n.* **1.** a love affair. **2.** a quality of love, excitement, mystery, or adventure: *The dim lights gave a sense of romance to the room.* **3.** a story or poem dealing with heroes and their deeds, especially one about knights and chivalry: *the romances of King Arthur and his knights of the Round Table.* **4.** a story about love or adventure in mysterious or faraway places; fanciful or exaggerated story. —*v.,* **ro·manced, ro·manc·ing.** —*v.i.* **1.** to behave or speak in a romantic way. **2.** to make up or tell fanciful stories. —*v.t. Informal.* to make love to; court; woo. [From the Old French word *romans* meaning both "French" and something written in French, going back to the Latin word *Romanicus* "of the Roman type," from the name *Romanus* "Roman." In Middle English, the word *romance* was used to identify a type of popular French literature. Later

it came to be used for imaginative literature, which often contained a love story.] —**ro·manc′er,** *n.*

Romance language, a language that developed directly from Latin, such as French, Italian, Spanish, Portuguese, Romanian, Catalan, and Provençal.

Roman Empire, the empire of ancient Rome, extending from Britain to North Africa to the Persian Gulf. It was begun under the Emperor Augustus in 27 B.C. and lasted until A.D. 395, when it was divided into the Eastern Roman Empire and the Western Roman Empire.

Ro·man·esque (rō′mə nesk′) *adj.* of, relating to, or in the style of architecture that was widely used in western Europe during the eleventh and twelfth centuries, characterized by massive stone construction, rounded arches and vaults, and elaborate ornamentation. —*n.* the Romanesque style of architecture.

Ro·ma·ni·an (rō mā′nē ən) *also,* **Rou·ma·ni·an, Ru·ma·ni·an.** *n.* **1.** a person who was born in or is a citizen of Romania. **2.** the language of Romania. —*adj.* of or relating to Romania, its people, their language, or culture.

Roman nose, a nose with a jutting or prominent bridge.

Roman numeral, any of the numerals I, V, X, L, C, D, M, or any combination of these, as used in the ancient Roman numbering system. I = 1, V = 5, X = 10, L = 50, C = 100, D = 500, and M = 1,000. The value of any combination of numerals is their sum, except when a smaller numeral is placed in front of a larger numeral. In such a case, the smaller is subtracted from the larger. Thus VI = 6, but IV = 4.

Ro·ma·no (rō mä′nō) *n.* a hard, dry, sharp cheese made from sheep's, cow's, or goat's milk, often grated and served over pasta and other food.

Ro·mans (rō′mənz) *n.* a book of the New Testament, an epistle from Paul to the Christians of Rome.

Ro·mansh (rō mansh′, rō mänsh′) *also,* **Ro·mansch** *n.* a small group of Romance dialects spoken in eastern Switzerland.

ro·man·tic (rō man′tik) *adj.* **1.** of, relating to, or characterized by romance: *a romantic story.* **2.** having thoughts and feelings of love and adventure: *a romantic person.* **3.** having a quality of adventure, excitement, or mystery: *the romantic life of a spy.* **4.** suitable for love or romance: *The candlelit room created a romantic atmosphere.* **5.** not practical or real; idealized: *to have romantic notions about living abroad.* **6.** *also,* **Romantic.** of or relating to romanticism in art, literature, or music. —*n.* **1.** a romantic person. **2.** a romanticist. —**ro·man′ti·cal·ly,** *adv.*

ro·man·ti·cism (rō man′tə siz′əm) *n.* a style of literature, music, and art during the last part of the eighteenth century and the first half of the nineteenth century. It is characterized by strong feeling, love of nature, and freedom of form.

ro·man·ti·cist (rō man′tə sist) *n.* a person who follows the principles of romanticism in literature, music, or art.

ro·man·ti·cize (rō man′tə sīz′) *v.,* **ro·man·ti·cized, ro·man·ti·ciz·ing.** —*v.t.* to give a romantic spirit or character to; make romantic: *to romanticize one's life.* —*v.i.* to act, talk, or think romantically.

Rom·a·ny (rom′ə nē, rō′mə nē) *n., pl.* **Rom·a·nies. 1.** a Gypsy. **2.** the language of the Gypsies. —*adj.* of or relating to the Gypsies, their language, or culture.

Ro·me·o (rō′mē ō′) *n.* the love-stricken hero of William Shakespeare's play *Romeo and Juliet.*

romp (romp) *v.i.* to play or frolic in a lively or noisy

at; āpe; fär; câre; end; mē; it; īce; pîerce; hot; ōld; sông, fôrk; oil; out; up; ūse; rüle; púll; tûrn; chin; sing; shop; thin; this; hw in white; zh in treasure. The symbol ə stands for the unstressed vowel sound heard in about, taken, pencil, lemon, and circus.

R

813

way. —*n.* lively or noisy play; frolic: *The children went for a romp in the woods.* —**romp′er,** *n.*

romp·ers (rom′pərz) *pl. n.* a loose one-piece garment worn by young children.

Rom·u·lus (rom′yə ləs) *n.* *Roman Mythology.* the founder and first king of the city of Rome. He and his twin brother, Remus, were abandoned as infants and raised by a wolf.

rood (rüd) *n.* **1.** a unit of land measure equal to 40 square rods, or ¼ acre (0.1 hectare). **2.** a cross or crucifix, especially a large crucifix over an altar.

roof (rüf, rŭf) *n.* **1.** the outer covering at the top of a building. **2.** something like a roof in position or use: *the roof of the mouth, the roof of a car.* —*v.t.* to provide or cover with a roof: *to roof a house.* —**roof′like′,** *adj.*

roof·er (rü′fər, rŭf′ər) *n.* a person who builds or repairs roofs.

roof·ing (rü′fing, rŭf′ing) *n.* the material used to build roofs.

roof·top (rüf′top′, rŭf′top′) *n.* the roof of a building: *to watch fireworks from a rooftop.*

roof·tree (rüf′trē′, rŭf′trē′) *n.* the ridgepole of a roof.

rook¹ (rŭk) *n.* a European bird that nests in colonies, closely related to and resembling the crow. —*v.t.* *Informal.* to cheat; swindle. [From the Old English word *hrōc* meaning this bird.]

rook² (rŭk) *n.* *Chess.* any of the four pieces, two to each player, that may move any number of empty spaces parallel to the sides of the board. Also, **castle.** [From the Old French word *roc* meaning this piece, going back to the Persian word *rukh* meaning this piece.]

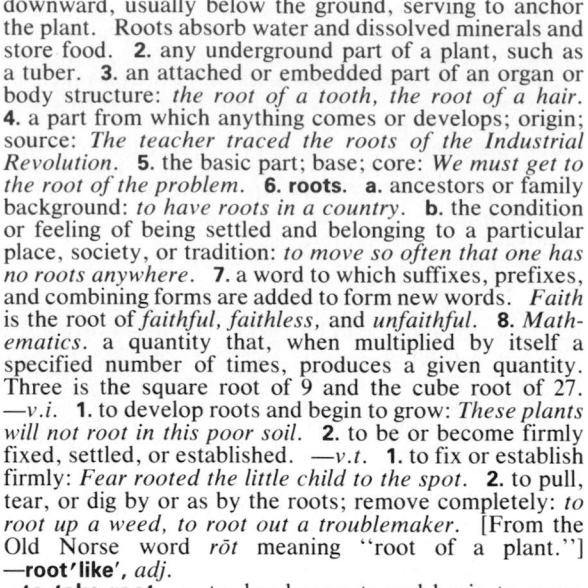

rook²

rook·er·y (rŭk′ə rē) *n., pl.* **rook·er·ies.** **1.** a breeding place or colony of rooks. **2.** a breeding place or colony of other birds or animals, such as penguins and seals.

rook·ie (rŭk′ē) *n.* *Informal.* **1.** an inexperienced recruit, as on a police force. **2.** an inexperienced athlete, especially a player in his or her first season with a professional sports team: *The rookie was chosen as the team's most valuable player.* **3.** any beginner; novice.

room (rüm, rŭm) *n.* **1.** an area that is or may be occupied by something; space: *There was no room to park the car.* **2.** an area within a house or other building that is separated or set off by walls or partitions: *a house with seven rooms.* **3.** the people in such an area: *The whole room stood up and applauded the singer.* **4.** a suitable chance or opportunity; possibility: *room for improvement.* **5.** **rooms.** living quarters; lodgings: *The student rented rooms near the campus.* —*v.i.* to live in a room or rooms; lodge: *We roomed together at college.*

room and board, lodging and meals.

room·er (rü′mər, rŭm′ər) *n.* a person who occupies a rented room or rooms in another's house; lodger.

room·ful (rüm′fŭl′, rŭm′fŭl′) *n., pl.* **room·fuls.** **1.** as much or as many as a room will hold: *a roomful of furniture.* **2.** the people or objects in a room.

rooming house, a house with furnished rooms for rent.

room·mate (rüm′māt′, rŭm′māt′) *n.* a person or persons with whom one shares a room or rooms.

room·y (rü′mē, rŭm′ē) *adj.,* **room·i·er, room·i·est.** having plenty of room; large; spacious. —**room′i·ness,** *n.*

roost (rüst) *n.* **1.** a perch on which birds rest or sleep. **2.** a building or other place for birds to rest or sleep. **3.** a place in which people rest, stay, or gather. —*v.i.* **1.** to rest or sleep on a roost as a bird does. **2.** to rest or stay for the night.

roost·er (rüs′tər) *n.* a male domestic fowl. Also, **cock.**

root¹ (rüt, rŭt) *n.* **1.** the lower part of a plant that grows downward, usually below the ground, serving to anchor the plant. Roots absorb water and dissolved minerals and store food. **2.** any underground part of a plant, such as a tuber. **3.** an attached or embedded part of an organ or body structure: *the root of a tooth, the root of a hair.* **4.** a part from which anything comes or develops; origin; source: *The teacher traced the roots of the Industrial Revolution.* **5.** the basic part; base; core: *We must get to the root of the problem.* **6. roots. a.** ancestors or family background: *to have roots in a country.* **b.** the condition or feeling of being settled and belonging to a particular place, society, or tradition: *to move so often that one has no roots anywhere.* **7.** a word to which suffixes, prefixes, and combining forms are added to form new words. *Faith* is the root of *faithful, faithless,* and *unfaithful.* **8.** *Mathematics.* a quantity that, when multiplied by itself a specified number of times, produces a given quantity. Three is the square root of 9 and the cube root of 27. —*v.i.* **1.** to develop roots and begin to grow: *These plants will not root in this poor soil.* **2.** to be or become firmly fixed, settled, or established. —*v.t.* **1.** to fix or establish firmly: *Fear rooted the little child to the spot.* **2.** to pull, tear, or dig by or as by the roots; remove completely: *to root up a weed, to root out a troublemaker.* [From the Old Norse word *rōt* meaning "root of a plant."] —**root′like′,** *adj.*

·**to take root. a.** to develop roots and begin to grow. **b.** to become firmly fixed, settled, or established.

root² (rüt, rŭt) *v.i.* **1.** to turn up or dig in the earth with the snout or nose: *The pig rooted for food.* **2.** to search for something; rummage: *We rooted through the closet for the missing shoe.* [From the Old English word *wrōtan* meaning "to dig up with the snout."]

root³ (rüt, rŭt) *v.i.* **1.** to give encouragement to a contestant or team, as by applauding or shouting: *Everyone was rooting for our team to win.* **2.** to wish success to someone or something: *We are all rooting for you to win the scholarship.* [Possibly from *root².*] —**root′er,** *n.*

root beer, a soft drink made from the juice of the roots of various plants, such as sarsaparilla or sassafras.

root canal 1. a chamber in the pulp of the root of a tooth, containing blood vessels and nerves. **2.** a procedure for treating disease in the pulp of a tooth, especially by removing the pulp and replacing it with filling.

root hair, a thin, hairlike growth on a plant root that absorbs water and dissolved minerals.

root·less (rüt′lis, rŭt′lis) *adj.* **1.** without ties to a particular place, society, or tradition. **2.** having no roots.

root·let (rüt′lit, rŭt′lit) *n.* a small root.

root·stock (rüt′stok′, rŭt′stok′) *n.* **1.** another word for **rhizome. 2.** the root onto which part of another plant is grafted.

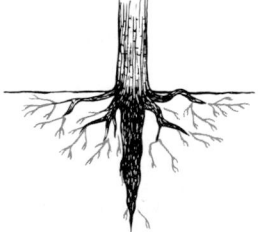

root hairs

rope (rōp) *n.* **1.** a strong cord made of twisted or intertwined strands of fiber, wire, or similar material. **2.** a number of things joined together by twisting, twining, or threading: *a rope of pearls.* **3.** a hangman's noose. **4.** a lasso. **5.** a sticky, stringy mass or thread. —*v.,* **roped, rop·ing.** —*v.t.* **1.** to tie, bind, or fasten with a rope. **2.** to separate or enclose with a rope or ropes: *to rope off a street for a parade.* **3.** to catch with a lasso. —*v.i.* to form sticky, stringy threads. —**rop′er,** *n.*

·**at the end of one's rope. 1.** at the end of one's patience. **2.** having run out of resources.

·**to learn** or **know the ropes.** *Informal.* to learn or be familiar with all the details of an operation or activity.

rop·y (rō′pē) *adj.,* **rop·i·er, rop·i·est. 1.** forming or having sticky, stringy threads: *a ropy syrup.* **2.** like a rope or cord. —**rop′i·ness,** *n.*

Roque·fort (rōk′fərt) *Trademark.* a strong, cream-colored cheese having a blue mold running through it. [From *Roquefort,* the village in southern France where it was first made.]

ro·sa·ry (rō′zə rē) *n., pl.* **ro·sa·ries. 1.** in the Roman Catholic Church, a string of beads used for counting in the saying of prayers. **2.** a series of prayers said with these beads.

rose¹ (rōz) *n.* **1.** the often fragrant flower of any of a large group of plants. Roses are usually red, pink, yellow, or white. **2.** the woody plant bearing this flower, having thorny stems. **3.** a pinkish red color. **4.** something resembling a rose in shape or form, as a rosette. —*adj.* **1.** having the color rose. **2.** designating a large family of flowering plants that grow in temperate parts of the world, many of which are cultivated for their fruit or flowers. [From the Old English word *rōse,* from the Latin word *rosa* meaning this plant.]

rose² (rōz) the past tense of **rise.**

ro·se·ate (rō′zē it, rō′zē āt′) *adj.* **1.** resembling a rose in color; rosy. **2.** full of hope or optimism; cheerful.

rose·bud (rōz′bud′) *n.* the bud of a rose.

rose·bush (rōz′bush′) *n., pl.* **rose·bush·es.** a bush or vine bearing roses.

rose–col·ored (rōz′kul′ərd) *adj.* **1.** tinted pinkish red, as eyeglasses. **2.** cheerful; optimistic; rosy: *to have a rose-colored outlook.*

rose·mar·y (rōz′mâr′ē) *n., pl.* **rose·mar·ies. 1.** the fragrant leaves of an evergreen shrub, used as a seasoning. **2.** the shrub bearing these leaves, having usually pale blue flowers.

Ro·set·ta stone (rō zet′ə) *n.* a basalt slab found in 1799 inscribed with an ancient decree written in hieroglyphics, in Greek letters, and in other characters. Comparison of the writings provided the key to deciphering Egyptian hieroglyphics. [From *Rozetta,* the town in Egypt where it was found.]

ro·sette (rō zet′) *n.* **1.** an ornament, usually made of gathered ribbon in the shape of a rose, used as a decoration or a badge of honor or office. **2.** something shaped like a rose, as a circular carved ornament used in architecture.

rose water, a preparation usually made by mixing oil of roses with water, used in cosmetics and in cooking.

rose window, a circular window, usually made up of stained glass sections that radiate from a center.

rose·wood (rōz′wüd′) *n.* **1.** a hard, strongly grained, dark red wood of any of several tropical evergreen trees, widely used to make fine furniture. **2.** the tree yielding this wood.

Rosh Ha·sha·nah (rōsh′ hə·shä′nə) the Jewish New Year, occurring in September or early October. [From the Modern Hebrew phrase *rōsh hashānāh* meaning "beginning of the year."]

ros·in (roz′in) *n.* **1.** a hard, brittle substance obtained by

Tea rose   Shrub rose

Hybrid perpetual rose

roses

rose window

heating crude turpentine and removing the surface oil. It is used in the manufacture of paints and other products, and is rubbed on the surface of certain items, such as violin bows and dancers' shoes, to make them less slippery. **2.** see **resin** (*def. 1*). —*v.t.* to rub or cover with rosin.

ros·ter (ros′tər) *n.* **1.** a list of military officers and soldiers enrolled for duty. **2.** any list of names.

ros·trum (ros′trəm) *n., pl.* **ros·trums** or **ros·tra** (ros′trə). a raised area, such as a platform or pulpit, used for public speaking.

ros·y (rō′zē) *adj.,* **ros·i·er, ros·i·est. 1.** having the color rose; pinkish red: *The baby's cheeks were rosy.* **2.** full of hope or optimism; bright: *a rosy outlook on life.* —**ros′i·ly,** *adv.* —**ros′i·ness,** *n.*

rot (rot) *v.,* **rot·ted, rot·ting.** —*v.i.* **1.** to become rotten; decay: *The apples rotted on the tree.* **2.** to become useless or worthless. —*v.t.* to cause to become rotten; decay: *The damp air in the basement rotted the food stored there.* —*n.* **1.** the process of rotting. **2.** something that is rotting or rotted. **3.** a disease of plants caused by any of various fungi or bacteria. **4.** *Informal.* nonsense; rubbish; trash.

ro·ta·ry (rō′tə rē) *adj.* **1.** turning or designed to turn around an axis; rotating. **2.** having a part or parts that rotate: *a rotary plow.* —*n., pl.* **ro·ta·ries.** another word for **traffic circle.**

rotary engine 1. an internal-combustion engine in which cylinders are arranged radially around a fixed crankshaft. **2.** any engine that produces rotation or torque directly, as a steam turbine.

ro·tate (rō′tāt) *v.,* **ro·tat·ed, ro·tat·ing.** —*v.i.* **1.** to turn around on an axis: *The earth rotates from west to east.* **2.** to change in a fixed order; alternate regularly: *The nurses rotated every eight hours.* —*v.t.* **1.** to cause to turn on an axis. **2.** to cause to change in a fixed order; alternate (something) regularly: *to rotate crops.*

ro·ta·tion (rō tā′shən) *n.* **1.** the act or process of turning on an axis. **2.** one complete turn of such a movement: *One rotation of the earth takes 24 hours.* **3.** change in a fixed order; variation according to a plan: *the rotation of crops.*

ro·ta·tor (rō′tā tər) *n.* a person or thing that rotates.

ro·ta·to·ry (rō′tə tôr′ē) *adj.* **1.** of, relating to, or characterized by rotation. **2.** causing rotation: *a rotatory muscle.*

ROTC. Reserve Officers' Training Corps, a U.S. military corps in which college and high school students are trained to become officers in the armed services.

rote (rōt) *n.* a mechanical way of doing something.
· **by rote,** in a mechanical way, without attention to meaning: *to recite a lesson by rote.*

ro·ti·fer (rō′tə fər) *n.* any of a large group of many-celled microscopic animals found in ponds and puddles, having a ring of cilia at one end that is used for locomotion and feeding. When the cilia are in motion, the ring resembles a wheel.

ro·tis·se·rie (rō tis′ə rē) *n.* a cooking device or appliance having a rotating spit on which food is roasted.

ro·to·gra·vure (rō′tə grə vyür′) *n.* **1.** a printing process in which the image to be printed is reproduced on a copper surface in a pattern of depressions. These depressions are then filled with ink and the pattern is transferred under pressure to the surface to be printed. **2.** a picture or a section of a newspaper printed by this process.

at; āpe; fär; câre; end; mē; it; īce; pîerce; hot; ōld; sông; fôrk; oil; out; up; ūse; rüle; pull; tûrn; chin; sing; shop; thin; **th**is; hw in white; zh in treasure. The symbol ə stands for the unstressed vowel sound heard in about, taken, pencil, lemon, and circus.

R

ro·tor (rō′tər) *n.* **1.** the rotating part of a motor or other machine. **2.** a set of large, revolving blades that lifts and moves a helicopter.

rot·ten (rot′ən) *adj.* **1.** having undergone decomposition or decay from the action of bacteria; decayed: *The food became rotten in storage.* **2.** likely to break, crack, or give way; weak: *rotten timbers.* **3.** very bad; disagreeable; contemptible: *a rotten movie, rotten weather.* **4.** corrupt, dishonest, or depraved: *Something is rotten in the state of Denmark* (Shakespeare, *Hamlet*). —**rot′ten·ly,** *adv.* —**rot′ten·ness,** *n.*

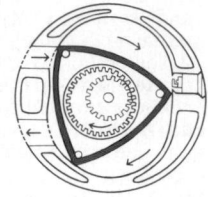

rotor *(def. 1)*

ro·tund (rō tund′) *adj.* **1.** rounded; plump: *a rotund opera star.* **2.** full-toned; deep: *a rotund voice.* —**ro·tund′ly,** *adv.* —**ro·tund′ness,** *n.*

ro·tun·da (rō tun′də) *n.* a circular building or room, especially one having a dome.

ro·tun·di·ty (rō tun′di tē) *n., pl.* **ro·tun·di·ties. 1.** the state or condition of being rotund. **2.** something round.

rou·ble (rü′bəl) another spelling of **ruble.**

rou·é (rü ā′) *n.* an immoral man; rake.

rouge (rüzh) *n.* **1.** any of various red or pink cosmetics used to color the cheeks. **2.** a red, powdery pigment, used to polish metal, gems, and glass. —*v.t.,* **rouged, roug·ing.** to color with rouge.

rough (ruf) *adj.* **1.** having an uneven surface; not smooth or level: *the rough bark of a tree, a rough country road.* **2.** characterized by or showing force, violence, or ruggedness: *Ice hockey is a rough game. The little boat battled against the rough seas.* **3.** having or showing a lack of gentleness, refinement, or politeness; harsh; rude: *rough manners, rough language.* **4.** partly, imperfectly, or hastily made or done: *a rough estimate, a rough sketch.* **5.** in a natural or crude state: *rough, unpolished gems.* **6.** difficult or unpleasant; hard: *a rough day at school.* **7.** without luxury, ease, or the usual comforts: *The pioneers in the West led a rough life.* **8.** having a shaggy or uneven texture; coarse: *The dog had a rough coat.* —*v.t.* **1.** to treat violently: *The gang roughed up several passersby.* **2.** to plan, shape, or sketch in an incomplete form: *to rough in the details of a drawing, to rough out the plan of a house.* **3.** to make rough; roughen. —*adv.* in a rough manner; roughly. —*n.* **1.** the unmowed part of a golf course surrounding the fairways and greens. **2.** a crude, coarse person; ruffian; rowdy. —**rough′ly,** *adv.* —**rough′ness,** *n.*

   ·**in the rough.** in a crude or unfinished condition: *The floor plans for our new house are still in the rough.*

   ·**to rough it.** to live without the usual comforts or conveniences: *We plan to rough it on our canoe trip.*

rough·age (ruf′ij) *n.* **1.** coarse food, such as bran or lettuce, that serves to aid the movement of food through the intestines. **2.** any rough or coarse material.

rough·en (ruf′ən) *v.t., v.i.* to make or become rough.

rough·hew (ruf′hū′) *v.t.,* **rough·hewed, rough·hewed** or **rough·hewn, rough·hew·ing.** to hew (something, as timber or stone) without smoothing or finishing. Also, **rough–hew.**

rough·house (*n.,* ruf′hous′; *v.,* ruf′hous′, ruf′houz′) *n.* rough, boisterous play. —*v.i.,* **rough·housed, rough·hous·ing.** to behave or play in a rough, boisterous way.

rough·neck (ruf′nek′) *n. Informal.* a rough, crude person; rowdy.

rough·rid·er (ruf′rī′dər) *n.* a person who breaks in or rides wild horses.

rough·shod (ruf′shod′) *adj.* having horseshoes with calks or other projections to prevent slipping.

   ·**to ride roughshod over.** to be cruel or inconsiderate to.

rou·lette (rü let′) *n.* **1.** a gambling game in which the players bet on which space of a wheel a ball will come to rest in after the wheel has been spun. **2.** a small, toothed wheel, used to make rows of marks, dots, or holes when rolled over a surface.

Rou·ma·ni·an (rü mā′nē ən) another spelling of **Romanian.**

round (round) *adj.* **1.** shaped like a globe or ball: *a round mass of clay, a round grapefruit.* **2.** shaped like a circle; circular, as a tire or hoop: *a round table.* **3.** having a curved surface or outline: *round shoulders.* **4.** not missing any parts; full; complete: *a round dozen.* **5.** full and mellow: *The piano had a rich, round tone.* **6.** pronounced with the lips formed in a nearly oval shape. The *o* in *lone* is a round vowel. **7.** see **round number. 8.** see **round trip.** —*n.* **1.** something round in shape. **2.** movement in a circle or about an axis; revolution: *the sun's round.* **3.** Also, **rounds.** a fixed or regular course or route: *an intern's rounds, the first round in the morning.* **4.** a series of actions or events: *a round of parties.* **5.** a single, sustained outburst, as from a crowd: *a round of applause.* **6.** any of various periods into which certain sports and games are divided: *a boxing match of ten rounds.* **7.** a complete game or division of a game: *a round of golf.* **8.** a short song that is sung by three or more voices, each voice beginning the song in turn at a different time. **9.** a single discharge of a gun or other firearm, or a number of guns fired simultaneously: *to fire a round in the air.* **10.** a charge of ammunition for a single shot. **11.** a cut of beef just above the hind leg between the leg and the rump. **12.** see **round dance.** —*v.t.* **1.** to make round: *to round the corners of a picture frame.* **2.** to pass or travel to the other side of; go around: *The car rounded the corner. The ship rounded the peninsula.* **3.** to express as a round number: *to round 49.8 to 50.* **4.** to make complete; finish or perfect: *We are such stuff as dreams are made on; and our little life is rounded with a sleep* (Shakespeare, *The Tempest*). *That coin rounds out my collection.* **5.** to pronounce with the lips formed in a nearly oval shape. —*v.i.* to become round. —*adv.* around: *The top spun round and round.* —*prep.* around: *The crowd gathered round the speaker.* —**round′ness,** *n.*

   ·**in the round. a.** having seats surrounding a central stage: *a theater in the round.* **b.** fully carved or sculptured on all sides, standing free from any background: *a statue in the round.*

   ·**to round up.** to drive or gather together: *to round up stray cattle, to round up all one's friends for a party.*

   ▲ In the United States, **around** is much more common than **round** as an adverb or a preposition: *They hunted around until they found the still* (William Faulkner). In British use, **round** is generally preferred: *He gripped my wrist and twisted it round* (George Orwell). The two words, however, may be used interchangeably.

round·a·bout (round′ə bout′, round′ə bout′) *adj.* not straight or direct: *a roundabout route, a roundabout way of saying something.* —*n. British.* a traffic circle.

round dance 1. a ballroom dance characterized by circular or revolving movements, as the waltz or the polka. **2.** a folk dance in which the dancers move in a circle.

roun·de·lay (roun′də lā′) *n.* **1.** a song in which a section, phrase, or line, especially the first verse, is continually repeated. **2.** a dance performed in a circle.

Round·head (round′hed′) *n.* a member of the Puritan or Parliamentary party during the English civil war from 1642 to 1652. [From the short-cropped hair of the members of this party.]

round·house (round′hous′) *n., pl.* **round·hous·es** (round′hou′ziz). **1.** a circular building with a large turntable in the center, used for housing, repairing, and turning around locomotives. **2.** a cabin on the rear part of the quarterdeck of a ship.   **3.** a blow delivered with a wide swing of the arm.

round·ish (roun′dish) *adj.*   somewhat round.

round·ly (round′lē) *adv.*   **1.** in a frank, straightforward manner; bluntly: *They refused the offer roundly.*   **2.** in a complete manner; fully; thoroughly: *to be beaten roundly.*   **3.** in a round form.

round number, a number expressed to the nearest whole number or to a multiple of five or ten.   500 is the round number for 498, and 6 is the round number for 5⅞.

round robin, a tournament, as in tennis, in which each player or team plays every other player or team.

round–shoul·dered (round′shōl′dərd) *adj.*   having the shoulders bent forward so that they appear rounded.

Round Table   **1.** a table around which King Arthur and his knights sat.   It was round to prevent quarrels about the order of seating.   **2.** King Arthur and his knights.   **3. round table.   a.** a group of persons gathered for an informal conference or discussion.   **b.** such a conference or discussion.

round–the–clock (round′thə klok′) *adj.*   another word for **around-the-clock.**

round trip, a trip to a place and back to the starting point.   —**round′-trip′,** *adj.*

round·up (round′up′) *n.*   **1.** the act of driving scattered cattle together, as for counting, branding, or selling.   **2.** the people and horses that do this.   **3.** any gathering together, as of people, objects, or facts: *a news roundup, a roundup of criminal suspects.*

round·worm (round′wûrm′) *n.*   any of a large group of worms having thin, round bodies; nematode.   Roundworms live in water and soil or as parasites in the intestines of humans and other animals.

rouse (rouz) *v.,* **roused, rous·ing.**   —*v.t.*   **1.** to awaken from sleep, unconsciousness, rest, or the like: *Sounds of thunder roused us.*   **2.** to stir up; excite: *The speaker roused the crowd to a frenzy.*   —*v.i.*   **1.** to awaken from sleep, unconsciousness, or the like.   **2.** to become active or excited.   —**rous′er,** *n.*

roust·a·bout (roust′tə bout′) *n.*   an unskilled laborer, as on a ranch or dock, or in an oil field or circus.

rout¹ (rout) *n.*   **1.** an overwhelming or complete defeat.   **2.** a disorderly flight or retreat after a defeat.   —*v.t.*   **1.** to defeat overwhelmingly: *to rout a team by ten goals.*   **2.** to put to disorderly flight or retreat: *to rout enemy troops.*   [From the Middle English word *route* meaning "a company or band of people," "a disorderly mob," or "a riot," from the Old French word *route* "a troop, company," going back to the Latin word *ruptus,* past participle of *rumpere* "to break to pieces, destroy."]

rout² (rout) *v.t.*   **1.** to uncover or find by searching; bring to view; discover: *to rout out an old coat from the closet.*   **2.** to drive or force out; make leave: *The hurricane routed us from our homes.*   **3.** to dig up with the snout.   —*v.i.*   **1.** to dig with the snout: *The pig routed about in the ground.*   **2.** to search; rummage.   [A form of *root².*]

route (rüt, rout) *n.*   **1.** a course, road, or way for travel: *a trade route.*   **2.** a regular course or territory covered by a salesman or deliveryman: *a milk route, a newspaper route.*   —*v.t.,* **rout·ed, rout·ing.**   **1.** to arrange the route for: *Our travel agent routed our cross-country trip.*   **2.** to send by a certain route; dispatch: *The company routes its goods through New York.*

rou·tine (rü tēn′) *n.*   **1.** a fixed way or method of doing something; regular procedure: *Walking the dog is part of my daily routine.*   **2.** sameness of actions or procedures: *The children were soon bored with the routine of camp life.*   **3.** a theatrical act or part of an act, such as a funny story or a dance number.   —*adj.*   **1.** according to or using routine; regular; habitual: *routine chores.*   **2.** not creative or original; commonplace; dull: *The actor gave a routine performance.*   —**rou·tine′ly,** *adv.*

rove (rōv) *v.,* **roved, rov·ing.**   —*v.i.*   to wander aimlessly from place to place; roam about: *We roved around all afternoon.*   —*v.t.*   to wander over or through: *They roved the museum looking at the paintings.*   [From the Middle English word *rowen* meaning "to shoot (arrows) randomly."]

rov·er¹ (rō′vər) *n.*   a person who roves; wanderer.   [*Rove* + *-er¹.*]

rov·er² (rō′vər) *n.*   **1.** a pirate.   **2.** a pirate ship.   [From the Middle Dutch word *rovere* meaning "a pirate."]

row¹ (rō) *n.*   **1.** a series of people or things arranged in a line; line: *a row of trees.*   **2.** a line of seats, as in a theater or classroom: *We were seated in the last row.*   **3.** a line of houses on a street.   **4.** a street lined with buildings on both sides.   [From the Old English word *ræw* meaning "a line, row¹."]

row² (rō) *v.i.*   to use oars to propel a boat.   —*v.t.*   **1.** to propel (a boat) by the use of oars.   **2.** to carry in a rowboat: *to row a person to shore.*   —*n.*   a trip in a rowboat: *It is a long row across the lake.*   [From the Old English word *rōwan* meaning "to go by water, row², sail."]

row³ (rou) *n.*   a noisy quarrel, fight, or disturbance; clamor.   [Of uncertain origin.]

row·boat (rō′bōt′) *n.*   a boat propelled by oars.

row·dy (rou′dē) *n., pl.* **row·dies.**   a rude, boisterous, disorderly person.   —*adj.,* **row·di·er, row·di·est.**   rude; boisterous; disorderly: *a rowdy crowd.*   —**row′di·ness,** *n.*

row·el (rou′əl) *n.*   a small wheel with sharp points, as on the end of a rider's spur.

row house, a house attached to other similar houses in a row.

row·lock (rō′lok′) *n.*   another word for **oarlock.**

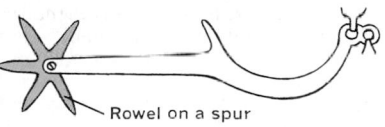

Rowel on a spur

rowel

roy·al (roi′əl) *adj.*   **1.** of or relating to a king or queen: *royal blood, a royal family.*   **2.** belonging to or serving a king or queen: *a royal palace, a royal navy.*   **3.** coming from or by a king or queen: *a royal command.*   **4.** suitable for or characteristic of a king or queen; magnificent; majestic: *a royal banquet, a royal welcome.*   —**roy′al·ly,** *adv.*

roy·al·ist (roi′ə list) *n.*   **1.** a person who supports a king or queen or a royal government.   **2. Royalist.** a supporter of King Charles I in his struggle with Parliament from 1641 to 1649; Cavalier.   **3. Royalist.** an American colonist who supported the British in the American Revolution; Tory.   —*adj.*   of or relating to a royalist.

roy·al·ty (roi′əl tē) *n., pl.* **roy·al·ties.**   **1.** a royal person, such as a king, queen, prince, or princess.   **2.** royal persons as a group.   **3.** the position or power of a king or queen: *A crown is a symbol of royalty.*   **4.** a share of the profits from the sale or performance of a work, such as a play or musical composition, paid to the author or composer.   **5.** a payment to the owner of a patent for the right to use it.

rpm, revolutions per minute.

R.R., railroad.

R.S.F.S.R., Russian Soviet Federated Socialist Republic.

RSVP, please reply.   Also, **r.s.v.p.**   [Short for the French phrase *r*(épondez) *s*('il) *v*(ous) *p*(laît) meaning "reply, if you please."]

---

at; āpe; fär; câre; end; mē; it; īce; pîerce; hot; ōld; sông, fôrk; oil; out; up; ūse; rüle; pùll; tûrn; chin; sing; shop; thin; this; hw in white; zh in treasure. The symbol ə stands for the unstressed vowel sound heard in about, taken, pencil, lemon, and circus.

rt., right.

rte., route.

Ru, the symbol for ruthenium.

rub (rub) *v.*, **rubbed, rub·bing.** —*v.t.* **1.** to apply friction or pressure over the surface of: *to rub a sore spot.* **2.** to apply or spread (something) with friction or pressure: *to rub lotion on a sunburn.* **3.** to move (an object or objects) against another or each other: *to rub two sticks together.* **4.** to subject (something) to pressure and friction in order to clean, polish, or make smooth: *to rub the silverware until it gleams.* **5.** to irritate or wear down by friction: *The elastic on my cuff is rubbing my wrist.* **6.** to remove or erase by friction or pressure: *to rub off tarnish, to rub out ink stains.* —*v.i.* **1.** to move with friction or pressure; press: *The cat rubbed gently against my leg.* **2.** to be able to be removed or erased by friction: *This ink rubs out easily.* —*n.* **1.** the act of rubbing. **2.** something that hurts or annoys, as a rude remark. **3.** difficulty or hindrance: *Aye, there's the rub* (Shakespeare, *Hamlet*). [From the Middle English word *rubben* meaning "to rub."]

　·**to rub down.** to massage: *to rub down an athlete after a game.*

　·**to rub it in.** *Slang.* to keep mentioning something that annoys or embarrasses a person.

　·**to rub the wrong way.** *Slang.* to irritate or annoy.

rub·ber¹ (rub′ər) *n.* **1.** a tough, elastic, waterproof substance produced from the milky sap of any of several tropical trees or made synthetically. **2.** an overshoe made of this substance. **3.** any of various other articles made of this substance, such as a pencil eraser. **4.** a person or thing that rubs. —*adj.* made of rubber: *a rubber ball.* [*Rub* + -*er¹*, originally referring to a pencil eraser.] —**rub′ber·like′,** *adj.*

rub·ber² (rub′ər) *n.* **1.** in bridge and other games, a series of an odd number of games, usually three, in which the final winner is the side that wins the most games. **2.** any game that breaks a tie and determines the outcome of a series of games. [Of uncertain origin.]

rubber band, an elastic loop of rubber, used to hold things together.

rub·ber·ize (rub′ə rīz′) *v.t.*, **rub·ber·ized, rub·ber·iz·ing.** to coat or treat with rubber.

rubber plant **1.** a tropical evergreen plant, widely raised as a houseplant, having a single woody stem, and thick leathery leaves. **2.** any of various plants yielding rubber.

rub·ber–stamp (rub′ər stamp′) *v.t.* **1.** to print or mark with a rubber stamp. **2.** *Informal.* to approve or endorse as a matter of routine: *The legislature rubber-stamped the resolution proposed by the governor.*

rubber stamp, a hand stamp with a raised message or design made of rubber that can be inked and used to imprint dates, names, and the like.

rub·ber·y (rub′ə rē) *adj.* like rubber; elastic.

rub·bish (rub′ish) *n.* **1.** useless waste material; refuse; trash. **2.** worthless talk or thoughts; nonsense.

rub·ble (rub′əl) *n.* **1.** rough broken pieces of solid material, as stone or rock: *The rescuers searched through the rubble of the collapsed building for survivors.* **2.** masonry made of rough, irregular stones.

rub·down (rub′doun′) *n.* a rubbing of the body; massage.

ru·bel·la (rü bel′ə) *n.* a contagious disease usually producing a pink, blotchy rash; German measles.

ru·bi·cund (rü′bi kənd) *adj.* reddish; ruddy.

ru·bid·i·um (rü bid′ē əm) *n.* a soft, light, silver-white metallic element used as a catalyst and in photoelectric cells and electron tubes. Symbol: **Rb** [Formed from the Latin word *rubidus* meaning "deep red," from the prominent red lines in its spectrum.]

ru·ble (rü′bəl) *also,* **rou·ble.** *n.* the monetary unit of the Soviet Union.

ru·bric (rü′brik) *n.* **1.** a title, chapter heading, or other division in a book or manuscript, printed in red or in a special color or design to set it off from the rest of the text. **2.** a direction or rule for the conducting of a religious ceremony, inserted in a prayer book, missal, or similar book. **3.** any established rule or guide.

ru·by (rü′bē) *n.*, *pl.* **ru·bies.** **1.** a transparent red variety of corundum, valued as a precious stone. **2.** a deep red color. —*adj.* having the color ruby.

ruck·sack (ruk′sak′, rŭk′sak′) *n.* a kind of knapsack.

ruck·us (ruk′əs) *n.* *Slang.* a loud commotion; uproar.

rud·der (rud′ər) *n.* **1.** a broad, flat, movable piece of wood, metal, or similar material, attached vertically at the rear of a boat or ship and used in steering. **2.** a similar piece at the tail of an aircraft.

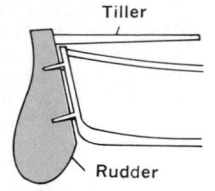

rudder *(def. 1)*

rud·dy (rud′ē) *adj.*, **rud·di·er, rud·di·est.** **1.** of or having a healthy redness: *a ruddy complexion.* **2.** tinged with red; reddish. —**rud′di·ness,** *n.*

rude (rüd) *adj.*, **rud·er, rud·est.** **1.** not polite or courteous; ill-mannered; uncivil: *a rude reply, a rude child.* **2.** roughly made or formed; showing a lack of skill or polish; crude: *People of the Stone Age used rude tools.* **3.** rough or violent; forceful: *a rude shove.* **4.** not developed or advanced; primitive: *a rude culture.* —**rude′ly,** *adv.* —**rude′ness,** *n.*

ru·di·ment (rü′də mənt) *n.* **1.** usually, **rudiments.** the first or basic principle of something: *to learn the rudiments of woodworking.* **2.** usually, **rudiments.** the beginning or early stage of something: *the rudiments of civilization.* **3.** *Biology.* an organ or part that is not completely developed, especially one that has no function in the adult individual, as the appendix.

ru·di·men·ta·ry (rü′də men′tə rē) *adj.* **1.** of or having the nature of a first principle; elementary: *rudimentary knowledge.* **2.** in a beginning or early stage of development. **3.** *Biology.* incompletely or imperfectly developed: *A penguin has rudimentary wings.*

rue¹ (rü) *v.t.*, **rued, ru·ing.** to feel sorrow or remorse for; regret: *He rued the day he left home.* —*n.* sorrow; regret. [From the Old English word *hrēowan* meaning "to make sorry."]

rue² (rü) *n.* any of a large family of strong-smelling plants, having yellow flowers. [From the Old French word *rue,* from the Latin word *ruta* meaning this herb, from the Greek word *rhytē* "a bitter herb, rue²."]

rue·ful (rü′fəl) *adj.* **1.** showing sorrow or regret: *a rueful cry.* **2.** causing sorrow or grief; pitiable: *a rueful sight.* —**rue′ful·ly,** *adv.* —**rue′ful·ness,** *n.*

ruff (ruf) *n.* **1.** a growth of distinctively marked feathers or hairs around the neck of a bird or animal. **2.** a stiff, circular cloth frill, worn as a collar by men and women in the sixteenth and seventeenth centuries.

ruffed (ruft) *adj.* having a ruff.

ruffed grouse, a North American game bird having brownish feathers and a fan-shaped tail. The male has a ruff of black feathers on each side of the neck.

ruf·fi·an (ruf′ē ən) *n.* a rough, brutal, or violent person. —*adj.* rough, brutal, and violent: *ruffian behavior.*

ruf·fle (ruf′əl) *v.*, **ruf·fled, ruf·fling.** —*v.t.* **1.** to disturb the smoothness or

ruff *(def. 2)*

order of: *The wind ruffled the water. The bird ruffled its feathers.* **2.** to disturb or upset: *Nothing could ruffle the patient teacher.* **3.** to gather (ribbon, lace, or other material) together along one edge. —*v.i.* **1.** to become disordered or uneven. **2.** to become upset. **3.** to rise or become stiff, as in anger or fright: *The bird's feathers ruffled at the sight of the fox.* —*n.* **1.** a strip of ribbon, lace, or other material gathered along one edge, used for trimming or as a border, as on garments or such items as curtains or bedspreads. **2.** a disturbance of a smooth surface.

rug (rug) *n.* **1.** a piece of heavy fabric, used to cover part of a floor. **2.** an animal hide used as a covering: *a bearskin rug.* **3.** another word for **lap robe.**

Rug·by (rug′bē) *also,* **rug·by.** *n.* a form of football played with an oval ball by two fifteen-man teams. The American form of football developed from this game. [From *Rugby,* the school in England where this game was first played.]

rug·ged (rug′id) *adj.* **1.** having a sharp, jagged outline or surface; rough and uneven: *rugged mountain peaks, a rugged coastline.* **2.** able to endure physical hardship; sturdy; robust: *a rugged mountain climber.* **3.** (of the face or its features) strong, lined, or uneven. **4.** difficult to do or endure; harsh; hard: *a rugged life, a rugged test.* —**rug′ged·ly,** *adv.* —**rug′ged·ness,** *n.*

ru·in (rü′in) *n.* **1.** destruction, decay, or collapse: *the ruin of an empire, financial ruin.* **2. ruins.** the remains of something destroyed or decayed: *the ruins of a bombed city.* **3.** something that causes destruction, decay, or collapse. —*v.t.* **1.** to bring to ruin: *The drought ruined the crops.* **2.** to spoil or harm greatly: *A sprained ankle ruined my chances of winning the race.*

ru·in·a·tion (rü′i nā′shən) *n.* **1.** the act of ruining or the state of being ruined. **2.** something that causes ruin.

ru·in·ous (rü′i nəs) *adj.* **1.** bringing or tending to bring to ruin; disastrous; destructive: *a ruinous war.* **2.** fallen to ruin; decayed; destroyed: *The garden is in a ruinous condition.* —**ru′in·ous·ly,** *adv.* —**ru′in·ous·ness,** *n.*

rule (rül) *n.* **1.** fixed principle or direction regulating behavior, procedure, or action: *the rules of baseball, the rules of etiquette, the rules of logic.* **2.** controlling power or authority; government: *the rule of a monarch.* **3.** a straight-edged instrument used for drawing straight lines or measuring; ruler. **4.** something that usually or normally occurs or is done: *A rest at midday is the rule in tropical climates.* —*v.,* **ruled, rul·ing.** —*v.t.* **1.** to have power or authority over; govern; control: *to rule a country.* **2.** to have great influence over; guide: *Fear ruled their actions.* **3.** to declare with authority: *The higher court ruled the law unconstitutional.* **4.** to mark with lines, especially by using a ruler: *to rule a piece of paper carefully.* —*v.i.* **1.** to have power or authority; govern: *to rule with justice and mercy.* **2.** to make a decision with authority: *The club ruled against accepting new members.* **3.** to be the rule: *Silence ruled in the library.* [From Old French word *reule* meaning "an order, rule of life," from the Latin word *regula* "a rule, pattern, model," from the word *regere* "to rule, order."]

•**as a rule,** usually; generally.

•**to rule out,** to decide to ignore or omit; eliminate as a choice or possibility.

rule of thumb, a general principle, guide, or estimate that is based on experience or practical knowledge instead of on scientific knowledge.

rul·er (rü′lər) *n.* **1.** a person who rules. **2.** a straight-edged strip of wood, plastic, metal, or other material marked off into measuring units, used for drawing straight lines or measuring.

rul·ing (rü′ling) *n.* a decision made with authority, as by a judge or court of law. —*adj.* **1.** having authority; governing: *the ruling class.* **2.** most commonly accepted; widespread; prevalent: *the ruling opinion in the community.* **3.** most important; dominant: *a ruling passion.*

rum (rum) *n.* **1.** an alcoholic liquor made from fermented juice, syrup, or molasses obtained from sugarcane. **2.** alcoholic drink in general.

Ru·ma·ni·an (rü mā′nē ən) another spelling of **Romanian.**

rum·ba (rum′bə) *also,* **rhum·ba.** *n.* **1.** a Cuban dance of African origin. **2.** a modern ballroom dance resembling this. **3.** the music for this dance. —*v.i.* to dance the rumba.

rum·ble (rum′bəl) *v.i.,* **rum·bled, rum·bling. 1.** to make a heavy, deep, rolling sound. **2.** to move or advance with such a sound: *The tank rumbled along the road.* —*n.* **1.** a heavy, deep, rolling sound: *the rumble of thunder.* **2.** an area in the back of a carriage used for seating or as a luggage compartment.

rumble seat, an open, folding seat in the back of certain early automobiles.

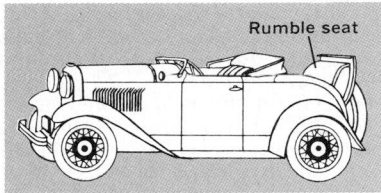

Rumble seat

ru·men (rü′min) *n., pl.* **ru·mi·na** (rü′mə nə). the first stomach of a ruminant, in which swallowed food is stored until it is chewed again as a cud.

ru·mi·nant (rü′mə nənt) *n.* any of various four-footed, hoofed animals that have a stomach consisting of four chambers and that chew the cud. Cows, sheep, deer, antelope, giraffes, and camels are ruminants. —*adj.* of or relating to a ruminant.

ru·mi·nate (rü′mə nāt′) *v.i.,* **ru·mi·nat·ed, ru·mi·nat·ing. 1.** to think deeply; meditate: *to ruminate on one's fortunes.* **2.** to chew the cud, as a cow does. —**ru′mi·na′tion,** *n.*

rum·mage (rum′ij) *v.,* **rum·maged, rum·mag·ing.** —*v.t.* **1.** to search through (something) thoroughly by moving about its contents: *I rummaged the entire attic for my scrapbook.* **2.** to find or bring forth by searching: *The children rummaged some old suits out of the trunk.* —*v.i.* to search thoroughly by moving about the contents of something: *to rummage in a toy box.* —*n.* **1.** a thorough search made by moving things about. **2.** items on sale at a rummage sale.

rummage sale, a sale of miscellaneous items, such as furniture or old clothing, usually held to raise money for some charity.

rum·my (rum′ē) *n.* any of various card games in which the players try to match their cards in sets.

ru·mor (rü′mər) *n.* **1.** a report or statement passed from person to person as truth without any evidence to support it; unverified story: *Someone started a rumor that the game had been canceled.* **2.** general talk; hearsay: *Rumor has it that the ship will leave next week.* —*v.t.* to spread or tell by rumor.

rump (rump) *n.* **1.** the back part of an animal's body where the trunk and legs are joined. **2.** a cut of beef from this part. **3.** the buttocks.

rum·ple (rum′pəl) *v.,* **rum·pled, rum·pling.** —*v.t.* to mess by wrinkling or creasing: *to rumple a jacket by sitting on it.* —*v.i.* to become messed by wrinkling or creasing: *This material rumples easily.* —*n.* an uneven crease; wrinkle.

---

at; āpe; fär; câre; end; mē; it; īce; pîerce; hot; ōld; sông, fôrk; oil; out; up; ūse; rüle; pùll; tûrn; chin; sing; shop; thin; this; hw in white; zh in treasure. The symbol ə stands for the unstressed vowel sound heard in about, taken, pencil, lemon, and circus.

R

rum·pus (rum′pəs) *n.* *Informal.* a noisy disturbance; uproar.

rumpus room, a room for play and informal parties.

run (run) *v.,* **ran, run, run·ning.** —*v.i.* **1.** to move quickly with both legs in the air for an instant during each step; proceed at a pace faster than walking: *We had to run to catch the bus.* **2.** to go or move quickly; rush; hasten: *to run for help in an emergency.* **3.** to leave rapidly; flee; escape: *The dog broke loose and ran.* **4.** to make a short or quick trip: *to run to the store for a loaf of bread.* **5.** to go or travel regularly: *The express runs hourly between Boston and New York.* **6.** to move about or pass freely or easily; go without restraint: *We always let our cats run in the house.* **7.** to take part in a race or other contest: *Seven horses ran in the derby.* *Do you plan to run for office?* **8.** to extend in a certain direction: *The road runs north for ten miles.* **9.** (of plants) to grow in a certain direction or area; creep; climb: *The ivy runs up the wall.* **10.** to be in operation; work; function: *The radio runs on batteries.* *The factory runs day and night.* **11.** to be in effect; last: *The sale will run for one week.* **12.** to pass into a particular state or condition: *If you run into trouble on your trip, call me.* **13.** to have a particular size, quality, value, or price: *Meat prices are running high.* **14.** to occur in the mind over and over: *The melody ran through my head.* **15.** to be present or common: *Dark hair runs in their family.* **16.** to flow in a stream: *The water stopped running through the pipes.* **17.** to spread or mingle when exposed to water: *The colors in the shirt ran after the first washing.* **18.** to discharge serum, mucus, or pus: *My nose ran from a cold.* **19.** to have knitted fabric break and unravel in a narrow band: *The cheaper stockings ran easily.* **20.** (of fish) to migrate upstream or from the sea for spawning, especially in a school: *The salmon are running.* —*v.t.* **1.** to move along by running: *to run the length of the field.* **2.** to perform by or as if by running: *to run a race, to run an errand.* **3.** to cause to run: *The trainer ran the horse for an hour.* **4.** to bring to a particular place, state, or condition: *to run a car off the road.* **5.** to enter in a race or other contest: *We want to run the best candidate we can find.* **6.** to cause to keep working; operate: *to run a machine.* **7.** to expose oneself to: *You ran the risk of catching a cold by going out in the rain.* **8.** to cause to move, pass, or slide easily: *to run a flag up a pole.* **9.** to be in charge or control of; manage: *to run a meeting, to run a grocery store.* **10.** to cause to flow in a stream: *to run water in a bathtub.* **11.** to cause to extend in a certain direction: *to run a pipe underneath a road.* **12.** to publish, as in a newspaper or magazine: *The company ran an advertisement in today's paper.* **13.** to cause to be presented or shown: *The theater ran the movie for one week.* **14.** to drive, force, or thrust: *to run one's hand through a window accidentally.* **15.** to suffer from; have: *to run a fever.* **16.** to flow with: *The streets ran with water after the heavy rain.* **17.** to get past or through: *The ship tried to run the blockade in the fog.* **18.** to execute or operate a computer program. —*n.* **1.** the act of running: *to take a run around the block.* **2.** a pace that is faster than a walk: *The children broke into a run when they neared the park.* **3.** a distance covered or time taken by moving at such a pace: *a one-mile run.* **4.** a short or quick trip or visit: *We took a run into town this afternoon.* **5.** a distance traveled regularly between two places, as by a train: *The conductor worked on the run between Baltimore and Washington.* **6.** a journey or trip over this distance: *The train makes four runs daily.* **7.** the freedom to move about or use: *We were given the run of the house.* **8.** a continuous series of a particular kind or class: *We had a run of rainy days during July.* **9.** a period of continuing performance or exhibition: *The play had a six-month run.* **10.** a general

direction or tendency; trend: *We were not surprised at the run of events after the scandal became known.* **11.a.** a period of operation, as of a factory or machine. **b.** an amount produced: *a run of 10,000 copies of the book.* **12.** a period of sudden demand by customers: *There was a run on the banks.* **13.** a place where stitches have broken and unraveled: *a run in a stocking.* **14.a.** a flowing movement, as of a liquid: *a run of sap.* **b.** a flow of water; stream: *There is a pretty run behind the house to fish in.* **15.** an enclosed area where animals can exercise: *The kennel had a large run for the dogs.* **16.** *Baseball.* **a.** a score made by touching home plate after touching the three bases. **b.** a point scored in this way.

·**a run for one's money. a.** strong competition. **b.** return or satisfaction for money or effort spent.

·**in the long run.** in the end; ultimately.

·**on the run. a.** constantly active or in motion. **b.** in rapid retreat or flight.

·**to run across.** to meet or come upon by chance: *I ran across an old friend on the way home.*

·**to run away with.** to win or outshine by excelling all others: *to run away with first prize.*

·**to run down. a.** to make or become weak, as in strength or health. **b.** to chase until caught or killed: *to run down a criminal, to run down an animal.* **c.** to stop operating: *The clock ran down.* **d.** to knock down by colliding with: *Did anyone see the car that ran the pedestrian down?* **e.** to say mean or bad things about: *The candidate ran down the rival party.* **f.** to find or trace by searching: *The plumber ran down the source of the trouble.*

·**to run for it.** to run in order to escape.

·**to run in. a.** to include. **b.** *Slang.* to arrest.

·**to run into. a.** to meet or come upon by chance. **b.** to collide with: *The car ran into a telephone pole.*

·**to run off. a.** to print or make copies of: *We ran off 200 copies of the newsletter.* **b.** to determine a winner (between or among contestants) by a runoff.

·**to run out.** to come to an end; be used up; expire: *The time ran out.* *My strength ran out.*

·**to run out of.** to use up the supply of: *to run out of sugar.*

·**to run out on.** to desert; forsake.

·**to run over. a.** to ride or drive over: *The car ran over the bicycle in the driveway.* **b.** to go or examine quickly: *to run over notes before giving a speech.*

·**to run through. a.** to use up quickly or in a foolish manner: *to run through a fortune in three years.* **b.** to drive into; pierce. **c.** to go over or examine quickly.

·**to run up.** to allow to accumulate: *We ran up a bill at the grocery last month.*

run·a·bout (run′ə bout′) *n.* **1.** a small motorboat. **2.** a light, open carriage or wagon.

run·a·round (run′ə round′) *n.* *Informal.* evasive or deceptive answers or action, especially in response to a question or request: *The ambassador gave the reporter the runaround when asked about violations of the treaty.*

run·a·way (run′ə wā′) *n.* **1.** a person or thing that runs away, such as a fugitive or a horse that has broken out of the driver's control. **2.** the act of running away. —*adj.* **1.** escaping from control; running away; fleeing: *a runaway horse.* **2.** brought about by running away. **3.** rising or expanding rapidly: *runaway prices, runaway inflation.*

run·back (run′bak′) *n.* a football play in which a player catches a punt or kickoff, or intercepts a pass, and carries it back toward the opposing team's goal.

run·down (run′doun′) *n.* a summary; résumé: *a run-down of current events.*

run–down (run′doun′) *adj.* **1.** in poor health; tired out; exhausted. **2.** in need of repair; dilapidated: *a run-down old mansion.* **3.** not working for lack of power, as a clock or batteries.

rune¹ (rün) *n.* **1.** a letter or character used in an ancient Germanic system of writing, found mainly in Scandinavia and England. **2.** a similar letter or character

rune¹ *(def. 1)*

that is supposed to have mysterious or magical power or meaning. [From the Danish word *rune,* from the Old Norse word *rūn* meaning both "secret, mystery" and "runic letter."] Runes were used in charms and other secret writing.]

rune² (rün) *n.* an ancient Scandinavian poem or song. [From the Finnish word *runo* meaning this sort of literature, probably from the Old Norse word *rūn* "secret, mystery" and "runic letter."]

rung¹ (rung) a past tense and past participle of **ring².**

rung² (rung) *n.* **1.** a crosspiece forming a step of a ladder. **2.** a supporting crosspiece placed between the legs or within the framework of the back of a chair. [Old English *hrung* "a pole, staff."]

ru·nic (rü′nik′) *adj.* of, relating to, or consisting of runes.

run-in (run′in′) *n.* *Informal.* a disagreement; quarrel.

run·let (run′lit) *n.* a small stream or brook; runnel.

run·nel (run′əl) *n.* a small stream or brook.

run·ner (run′ər) *n.* **1.** a person or animal that runs, such as a contestant in a race. **2.** one of the long, narrow parts on which a sled or an ice skate glides. **3.** a person who runs errands or delivers messages. **4.** a long, narrow rug or carpet, used for hallways and staircases. **5.** a narrow strip of cloth used to cover table tops, dressers, and other furniture. **6.** *Botany.* the

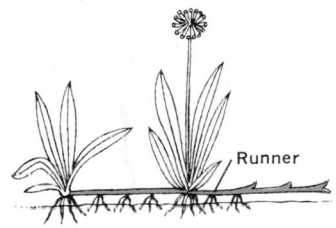

runner *(def. 6)*

slender trailing stem of certain plants that gives rise to roots that produce new plants.

run·ner-up (run′ər up′) *n., pl.* **run·ners-up.** a contestant or team that finishes in second place.

run·ning (run′ing) *n.* the act of a person or thing that runs. —*adj.* **1.** moving rapidly, proceeding at a run. **2.** flowing: *running water.* **3.** going on continuously: *a running battle.* **4.** done with or during a run: *The outfielder made a running catch.* **5.** in operation, as a machine; working: *the sound of a running motor.* **6.** discharging matter: *a running sore.* **7.** having to do with or for a run or runs: *running shoes.* —*adv.* in succession; consecutively: *I had the same dream for six nights running.*
  ·**in the running.** having a good chance to win or succeed.
  ·**out of the running.** not likely to win or succeed.

running board, a footboard, mounted below the door, along the side of some trucks and automobiles.

running knot, a knot made so as to form a noose that tightens as the line is pulled.

running mate, a person who campaigns for office on the same ticket with another, for the lesser of the two offices: *After being nominated for the presidency, the candidate chose a running mate.*

run·ny (run′ē) *adj.* **run·ni·er, run·ni·est.** **1.** tending to flow or drip; soft, melting, or watery: *runny paste, runny cheese.* **2.** discharging mucus: *a runny nose.*

run·off (run′ôf′) *n.* **1.** rain or snow not absorbed by the soil, which forms surface streams. **2.** a contest or election held in order to determine a final winner.

run-of-the-mill (run′əv thə mil′) *adj.* not special or outstanding in any way; ordinary; average.

run-on (run′ôn′, run′on′) *adj.* added to the end of printed material; not set off, as by a paragraph: *a run-on entry in a dictionary.* —*n.* something that has been added in this way.

run-on entry, an undefined word in a dictionary added at the end of an entry for a defined word. It is formed by the addition of a suffix to the defined word, and its meaning can be derived from the meaning of the defined word and the meaning of the suffix. **Ruggedness** is a run-on entry under the word **rugged.**

run-on sentence, a sentence containing two or more independent clauses that are not separated by a period, a semicolon, or conjunction. For example, *We missed the bus, we were late for school.*

runt (runt) *n.* **1.** a stunted or undersized animal or person. **2.** the smallest or weakest of a litter of puppies or other animals.

run-through (run′thrü′) *n.* a quick rehearsal, review, or examination.

runway *(def. 1)*

run·way (run′wā′) *n.* **1.** a long, narrow strip of ground, usually paved, where airplanes can take off and land. **2.** a ramp extending from a stage in a theater. **3.** a track, channel, or the like through or along which something runs.

ru·pee (rü pē′) *n.* a monetary unit and coin of India and other neighboring countries.

rup·ture (rup′chər) *n.* **1.** the act of breaking open or bursting: *the rupture of a blood vessel.* **2.** a hernia, especially one in or near the groin. **3.** a break in friendly or diplomatic relations between people or countries. —*v.*, **rup·tured, rup·tur·ing.** —*v.t.* **1.** to break open or apart; burst: *to rupture a thin membrane.* **2.** to end or break off (friendly or diplomatic relations). **3.** to affect with a hernia, especially one in or near the groin. —*v.i.* to suffer a break; burst: *A swollen appendix may rupture.* [Originally from the Latin word *ruptura* meaning "a break, fracture," from the word *ruptus,* past participle of *rumpere* meaning "to break."]

ru·ral (rûr′əl) *adj.* **1.** of, relating to, or characteristic of the country: *rural areas, rural population.* **2.** of or relating to agriculture: *a rural economy.* —**ru′ral·ly,** *adv.*

---

at; āpe; fär; câre; end; mē; it; īce; pîerce; hot; ōld;
sông, fôrk; oil; out; up; ūse; rüle; pull; tûrn; chin;
sing; shop; thin; this; hw in white; zh in treasure.
The symbol ə stands for the unstressed vowel sound
heard in about, taken, pencil, lemon, and circus.

R

rural delivery, the delivery of mail in rural or farm areas. Formerly, **rural free delivery.**

ruse (rüz, rüs) *n.* an action or plan intended to deceive; trick: *The dinner invitation was a ruse to keep the surprise party secret.*

rush¹ (rush) *v.i.* **1.** to move, go, or come with speed or haste: *He had to rush to catch the bus. Blood rushed to her head.* **2.** to act quickly and rashly: *to rush into a decision without knowing all the facts.* —*v.t.* **1.** to take, send, or cause to move with speed or haste: *The police rushed the injured child to the hospital.* **2.** to do or complete hastily: *I can't rush my work without making errors.* **3.** to attack or overcome swiftly and forcefully: *The troops planned to rush the fortress in the morning.* —*n., pl.* **rush·es.** **1.** the act of rushing; sudden swift movement: *a rush of water.* **2.** a sudden and hasty movement of many people to get to a place: *We left home at ten o'clock to avoid the morning rush.* **3.** bustling activity; being busy; haste: *the rush of a crowded department store during the Christmas season.* **4.** a sudden demand: *a rush for tickets to the championship game.* **5.** a hurried state: *to be in a rush to leave the house in the morning.* —*adj.* requiring haste; urgent: *a rush job.* [From the Anglo-Norman word *russher* meaning ''to hurry about, move quickly,'' from the Old French word *ruser* ''to put to flight,'' going back to the Latin word *recusare* ''to refuse, object.'']

rush² (rush) *n., pl.* **rush·es.** **1.** any of several plants resembling reeds or grass, found in marshy areas, having slender, often hollow stems and clusters of small green or brown flowers. **2.** the stem of any of these plants, often woven into mats, baskets, chair seats, and other products. [From the Old English word *rysc* meaning this plant.]

rush hour, one of the periods during a day when traffic is heaviest, as when many people are going to or coming from work.

rusk (rusk) *n.* **1.** a sweet or plain bread or cake baked in the oven, sliced, and then baked again to make it brown, dry, and crisp. **2.** a light, soft, sweetened biscuit.

Russ. **1.** Russia. **2.** Russian.

rus·set (rus'it) *n.* **1.** a yellowish brown or reddish brown color. **2.** any of various kinds of apples having this color. **3.** a coarse, homespun woolen fabric having this color. —*adj.* having the color russet.

Rus·sian (rush'ən) *n.* **1.** a person who was born in, or is a citizen of, Russia. **2.** the language of Russia. —*adj.* of or relating to Russia, its people, their language, or culture.

Words From Other Languages

Many Russian words used in English describe items that are part of the Russian or Soviet cultures.

balalaika	a musical instrument like a guitar, with a triangular body
borscht	a hot or cold beet soup
borzoi	a kind of long-haired hunting dog
cosmonaut	a Soviet astronaut
Cossack	a member of a southeastern Russian people known for horsemanship
glasnost	a policy of openness about Soviet social problems
mammoth	a prehistoric elephant
sable	a small mammal with fine, dark fur
samovar	a metal urn for boiling tea water
sputnik	a Soviet artificial earth satellite
steppe	a vast, grassy plain
vodka	a liquor made from potatoes or grain

Russian Church, the largest branch of the Orthodox Church, governed by a patriarch and a number of other prelates. It was the official church of imperial Russia. Also, **Russian Orthodox Church.**

Russian dressing, a dressing made of mayonnaise mixed with chili sauce or ketchup and other ingredients, such as chopped pickles or olives.

Russian Revolution, a revolution in Russia, in 1917, that ended the czarist form of government and later established the Soviet government under the leadership of the Bolsheviks headed by Lenin.

Russian wolfhound, another term for **borzoi.**

rust (rust) *n.* **1.** a reddish brown or orange coating that forms on the surface of iron or steel that has been exposed to moisture and oxygen. **2.** any of various plant diseases caused by parasitic fungi, characterized by the appearance of reddish brown or orange spots and streaks on the plants. **3.** any of the parasitic fungi causing such a disease. **4.** a reddish brown or orange color. —*v.i.* **1.** to corrode by becoming covered with rust. **2.** to become weakened or ruined through lack of use. **3.** (of a plant) to become infected with a rust. —*v.t.* to cause to become covered with rust. —*adj.* having the color rust.

rus·tic (rus'tik) *adj.* **1.** of, relating to, or characteristic of the country: *a rustic scene.* **2.** characteristic of country people or country life; simple; plain: *rustic manners.* **3.** made of rough, untrimmed trees or branches: *rustic furniture.* —*n.* a person who lives in the country: *a simple rustic.* —**rus'ti·cal·ly,** *adv.*

rus·tle (rus'əl) *v.,* **rus·tled, rus·tling.** —*v.i.* **1.** to make a series of soft, fluttering sounds, as that of papers or leaves being rubbed together or stirred about: *The leaves rustled in the wind.* **2.** *Informal.* to steal cattle. —*v.t.* **1.** to cause to make a series of soft, fluttering sounds: *The wind rustled the papers on the desk.* **2.** *Informal.* to steal (cattle). —*n.* a series of soft, fluttering sounds.

rus·tler (rus'lər) *n.* a cattle thief.

rust·y (rus'tē) *adj.,* **rust·i·er, rust·i·est.** **1.** covered or affected with rust: *a rusty nail.* **2.** consisting of or made by rust: *rusty spots on a metal chair.* **3.** having the color rust. **4.** weakened or ruined through lack of use: *My French is a bit rusty.* **5.** less skilled through lack of use: *to get rusty in math.* —**rust'i·ly,** *adv.* —**rust'i·ness,** *n.*

rut (rut) *n.* **1.** a groove or track made in the ground by a wheel or by continuous wear. **2.** a fixed way of living, thinking, or acting; boring routine. —*v.t.,* **rut·ted, rut·ting.** to make a rut in: *The heavy tractors rutted the road.*

ru·ta·ba·ga (rü'tə bā'gə, rü'tə bā'gə) *n.* a turnip having a thick yellow or white root that is used as food.

Ruth (rüth) *n.* the book of the Old Testament relating the story of Ruth, daughter-in-law of Naomi.

ru·the·ni·um (rü thē'nē əm) *n.* a hard, silvery metallic element used in electrical contacts. Symbol: **Ru** [Formed from *Ruthenia,* the Medieval Latin name for Russia, the homeland of its discoverers.]

ruth·er·for·di·um (ruth'ər fôr'dē əm) *n.* a proposed name for the artificially produced radioactive element with atomic number 104. Also, **element 104, kurchatovium, unnilquadium.** [From the English physicist Ernest *Rutherford* (1871–1937).]

ruth·less (rüth'lis) *adj.* without pity, mercy, or compassion: *a ruthless criminal.* —**ruth'less·ly,** *adv.* —**ruth'less·ness,** *n.*

RV, recreational vehicle.

–ry, a form of the suffix **-ery,** as in *revelry, jewelry.*

Ry., railway.

rye (rī) *n.* **1.** the grain of a hardy slender-stemmed plant of the grass family, used chiefly as feed for animals, and in the manufacture of flour and alcohol. **2.** the plant bearing this grain, widely cultivated and often used as a winter cover crop to prevent soil erosion.

1. ancient Semitic
2. Phoenician
3. early Hebrew
4. early Greek
5. Etruscan
6. Latin
7. English

S is the nineteenth letter of the English alphabet. The earliest form of **S** was the letter *shin*, meaning "tooth," in the ancient Semitic alphabets (1). The early Phoenician (2) and early Hebrew (3) versions of *shin* were written very much as we write the letter **W**. Between about 2,800 and 2,500 years ago, a new form of *shin* appeared in the earliest Greek alphabets. This letter (4), called *sigma*, was later adopted by the Etruscans (5). By about 2,200 years ago, the Romans (6), who borrowed the Etruscan form of *sigma*, were writing the letter **S** very much as we write it today (7).

s, S (es) *n., pl.* **s's, S's. 1.** the nineteenth letter of the English alphabet. **2.** something having the shape of this letter.

-s¹, the ending used to form the plural of most nouns: *horses.*

-s², the ending used to form the third person singular of the present indicative of most verbs: *talks, runs, eats.*

-'s¹, the ending used to form the possessive case of singular nouns, of plural nouns not ending in *s*, and of some pronouns: *a girl's dress, children's toys, anyone's hat.*

-'s² 1. a contraction of **is:** *She's three years old. He's away for the day.* **2.** a contraction of **has:** *He's already been there.* **3.** a contraction of **us:** *Let's go before it begins to rain.*

s. 1. second. **2.** shilling. **3.** singular.

S 1. South. **2.** Southern. **3.** the symbol for sulfur.

S.A. 1. Salvation Army. **2.** South Africa. **3.** South America.

Sab·bath (sab'əth) *n.* the day of the week for rest and religious worship. Sunday is the Sabbath for most Christians; Saturday is the Sabbath for Jews and certain Christian denominations.

sab·bat·i·cal (sə bat'i kəl) *n.* a period of leave from one's regular work, especially such a leave granted to a professor or teacher for travel or study. —*adj. also,* **Sabbatical.** of, relating to, or proper for the Sabbath.

sa·ber (sā'bər) *also, British,* **sa·bre.** *n.* **1.** a heavy sword with one cutting edge and a long, usually curved blade. **2.** a light fencing sword that has two cutting edges.

sa·ber–toothed tiger (sā'bər tütht') any of various large extinct animals related to the cat, that had long, curved teeth in the upper jaw. Saber-toothed tigers lived from 40 million to 12,000 years ago.

saber-toothed tiger

sa·ble (sā'bəl) *n.* **1.** any of several animals related to the weasel, especially such an animal that lives in the northern pine forests of Siberia and Europe and has a bushy tail, round ears, and soft, brown fur. **2.** the valuable fur of this animal, used for making coats. **3.** the color black. **4. sables.** black mourning clothes. —*adj.* having the color sable; black.

sab·ot (sab'ō, sa bō') *n.* **1.** a shoe carved from a single piece of wood, traditionally worn in the Netherlands, Belgium, and France. **2.** a heavy leather sandal or shoe having a thick wooden sole.

sab·o·tage (sab'ə täzh') *n.* **1.** the deliberate damage or destruction of buildings or other property, or interference with work or other activity, as at a factory, by enemy agents in order to hinder a nation's war or defense efforts. **2.** any deliberate damage or destruction that is done to hinder some activity or effort: *sabotage of machinery by dissatisfied workers.* —*v.t.,* **sab·o·taged, sab·o·tag·ing.** to damage or destroy deliberately. [From the French word *sabotage,* from *sabot* "wooden shoe" or "railroad tie." The word refers to the destruction of a railroad bed by French laborers during a strike in 1910.]

sab·o·teur (sab'ə tùr') *n.* a person who commits sabotage.

sa·bra (sä'brə) *n.* a person who was born in Israel. [From the modern Hebrew word *ṣābhār* meaning "prickly pear," a cactus common in Israel.]

sa·bre (sā'bər) *British.* another spelling of **saber.**

sac (sak) *n.* a part in a plant or animal that is shaped like a pouch or bag, and that often contains a liquid.

sac·cha·rin (sak′ər in) *n.* a white powdery chemical used as a substitute for sugar. It is very sweet but has no calories.

sac·cha·rine (sak′ər in) *adj.* **1.** overly sweet: *a saccharine smile.* **2.** of or like sugar; very sweet. —*n.* another spelling of **saccharin.**

sac·er·do·tal (sas′ər dō′təl) *adj.* of or relating to a priest or the priesthood; priestly.

sa·chem (sā′chəm) *n.* a chief of certain North American Indian tribes. A sachem inherited the position rather than being chosen for it.

sa·chet (sa shā′) *n.* a small bag or pad containing a perfumed powder or other substance, usually put in a drawer to make clothes, towels, or sheets smell sweet.

sack¹ (sak) *n.* **1.** a large bag made of coarse, strong material: *The clerks sorted the mail and put it into sacks.* **2.** any bag. **3.** a sack and what it holds: *We bought a sack of potatoes at the market.* **4.** a short, loose-fitting jacket for women and children. —*v.t.* **1.** to put into a sack or sacks. **2.** *Slang.* to fire from a job. [From the Old English word *sacc* meaning "a bag," from the Latin word *saccus* "bag," from the Greek word *sakkos* "bag," of Semitic origin.]
· **the sack.** *Slang.* **a.** dismissal from one's job: *to get the sack.* **b.** bed: *to stay in the sack all morning.*
· **to hit the sack.** *Slang.* to go to bed.

sack² (sak) *v.t.* to steal everything of value or use in a town or city that has been captured in a war; plunder. —*n.* the act of plundering a captured town or city. [From the Middle French phrase *mettre à sac* meaning "to sack², plunder," going back to the Latin word *saccus* "a bag, sack¹."]

sack³ (sak) *n.* **1.** a light-colored sherry. **2.** any of various strong, dry white wines. [From the French phrase (*vin*) *sec* meaning "dry wine," going back to the Latin word *siccus* "dry."]

sack·cloth (sak′klôth′) *n., pl.* **sack·cloths** (sak′klôths′, sak′klôthz′). **1.** a coarse cloth for making sacks; sacking. **2.** a garment made of such cloth, worn to show mourning, humility, or penitence.

sack·ful (sak′fŭl′) *n., pl.* **sack·fuls.** the amount that a sack holds.

sack·ing (sak′ing) *n.* any coarsely woven cloth, such as burlap, used for making sacks.

sa·cra (sā′krə, sak′rə) a plural of **sacrum.**

sac·ra·ment (sak′rə mənt) *n.* **1.** any of several sacred Christian rites, such as baptism and confirmation. **2.** *also,* **the Sacrament. a.** another term for **Holy Communion. b.** the consecrated bread and wine used in Holy Communion, or the bread alone. —**sac·ra·men·tal** (sak′rə men′təl), *adj.*

sa·cred (sā′krid) *adj.* **1.** associated with, set apart for, or belonging to God or a god: *sacred relics, sacred ground, a sacred name.* **2.** of or relating to religion; having a religious use or purpose: *sacred music.* **3.** regarded with the same respect or reverence as holy or religious things: *the sacred memory of our ancestors.* —**sa′cred·ly,** *adv.* —**sa′cred·ness,** *n.*

sacred cow, a person or thing not to be criticized. [From the Hindu belief that the cow is a sacred animal.]

sac·ri·fice (sak′rə fīs′) *n.* **1.** the act of offering something, such as an animal or a human life, to a god as an act of worship. **2.** an animal, person, or thing so offered: *The usual sacrifice of the ancient Greeks was an animal, such as a sheep.* **3.** the giving up of something that is valued or wanted, usually for the sake of something else: *The parents made many sacrifices in order to save money for their children's college education.* **4.** something given up. **5.** a loss of profit when something is sold for less than it is worth. **6.** see **sacrifice hit.** —*v.,* **sac·ri·ficed, sac·ri·ficing.** —*v.t.* **1.** to offer as a sacrifice to a god.

2. to give up or destroy for the sake of something else. **3.** to sell at a loss. **4.** *Baseball.* to advance (a runner or runners) by making a sacrifice hit. —*v.i.* **1.** to offer or make a sacrifice. **2.** *Baseball.* to make a sacrifice hit. [From the Old French word *sacrifice,* from the Latin word *sacrificium* meaning "offering to a god, sacrifice," from the words *sacer* "consecrated, holy" and *facere* "to do, make."]

sacrifice fly *Baseball.* a fly ball that enables a base runner to score after the ball has been caught by an opposing player.

sacrifice hit *Baseball.* a bunt that enables a base runner or runners to advance, but results in the batter being put out.

sac·ri·fi·cial (sak′rə fish′əl) *adj.* relating to, used in, or like a sacrifice. —**sac′ri·fi′cial·ly,** *adv.*

sac·ri·lege (sak′rə lij) *n.* an act that shows disrespect for or harms something sacred.

sac·ri·le·gious (sak′rə lij′əs) *adj.* of, relating to, or being a sacrilege. —**sac′ri·le′gious·ly,** *adv.* —**sac′ri·le′gious·ness,** *n.*

sac·ris·tan (sak′rə stən) *n.* a person who is in charge of a sacristy.

sac·ris·ty (sak′rə stē) *n., pl.* **sac·ris·ties.** the room or rooms in a church where the sacred vessels, robes, and other objects used in ceremonies are kept.

sac·ro·sanct (sak′rō sangkt′) *adj.* very sacred.

sa·crum (sā′krəm, sak′rəm) *n., pl.* **sa·cra** or **sa·crums.** a triangular bone located near the base of the spine. It is made up of five fused vertebrae and forms the back of the pelvis.

sad (sad) *adj.,* **sad·der, sad·dest. 1.** feeling or showing unhappiness, sorrow, or gloom: *to be sad when one's friend moves away.* **2.** causing or marked by unhappiness, sorrow, or gloom: *a sad memory, a sad day.* **3.** so bad as to arouse pity; pitiful: *The wet dog was a sad sight.* —**sad′ly,** *adv.* —**sad′ness,** *n.*

sad·den (sad′ən) *v.t., v.i.* to make or become sad.

sad·dle (sad′əl) *n.* **1.** a seat or pad for a rider, used on the back of a horse or other animal that has to carry a load. **2.** a similar padded seat, as on a motorcycle. **3.** something that looks like a saddle, such as a ridge of land between two mountain peaks. **4.** a cut of meat that comes from the back of an animal: *The cook prepared a saddle of lamb.* —*v.t.,* **sad·dled, sad·dling. 1.** to put a saddle on: *to saddle a horse.* **2.** to load or burden: *to be saddled with a responsibility.*

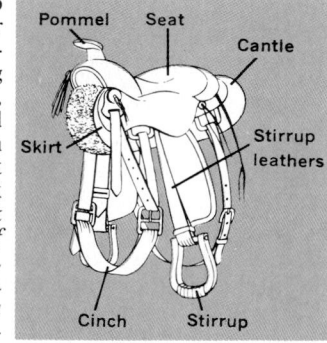

saddle (n., def. 1)

sad·dle·bag (sad′əl bag′) *n.* a bag of leather or other material, usually one of a pair of such bags that is hung from a saddle.

saddle horse, a horse trained or suitable for riding.

sad·dler (sad′lər) *n.* a person who makes, repairs, or sells saddles and harnesses.

saddle shoe, a shoe that is usually white with a band of a contrasting color over the middle portion.

saddle soap, a mild soap used to clean, soften, and preserve leather and leather articles.

sa·dism (sā′diz əm, sad′iz əm) *n.* the deriving of pleasure from causing physical or mental pain to others. [From the French word *sadisme* with the same meaning, from the Marquis de *Sade* (1740–1814), who wrote of this behavior.]

sa·dist (sā′dist, sad′ist) *n.* a person who gets pleasure from causing physical or mental pain to others.

sa·dis·tic (sə dis′tik) *adj.* relating to or showing sadism. —**sa·dis′ti·cal·ly,** *adv.*

sa·fa·ri (sə fär′ē) *n., pl.* **sa·fa·ris.** a hunting or investigative expedition, especially in Africa. [From an Arabic word meaning "trip" or "journey."]

safe (sāf) *adj.,* **saf·er, saf·est.** 1. free from harm or danger: *It's not safe to skate on that thin ice.* 2. having escaped injury; unharmed: *The soldier arrived safe at headquarters after crossing enemy lines.* 3. giving protection from harm or danger: *a safe harbor from the storm.* 4. without risk of failure or error: *a safe bet.* 5. not able to do harm or injury: *The lion is safe in its cage.* 6. not taking dangerous chances; careful: *a safe driver.* 7. *Baseball.* having reached a base without being put out. —*n.* a strong metal box or other container that can be locked, used for the safekeeping of valuables, such as jewelry and money. —**safe′ly,** *adv.* —**safe′ness,** *n.*

safe–con·duct (sāf′kon′dukt) *n.* 1. the privilege of being protected in passing through a dangerous region, such as enemy territory. 2. a paper or escort assuring this privilege.

safe–de·pos·it box (sāf′di poz′it) a box for storing valuables, especially one kept in a bank vault.

safe·guard (sāf′gärd′) *n.* something that protects: *The parents put a gate across the stairway as a safeguard for the baby. Getting enough sleep is a safeguard against sickness.* —*v.t.* to guard; protect; defend.

safe·keep·ing (sāf′kē′ping) *n.* care or protection; custody: *to leave something valuable in the safekeeping of a friend.*

safe·ty (sāf′tē) *n., pl.* **safe·ties.** 1. freedom from danger, injury, or risk; being safe. 2. a device to prevent accident or injury, such as the catch on a gun that prevents it from firing. 3. *Football.* **a.** a score of two points for the defensive team, occurring when the offensive team downs the ball behind its own goal line. **b.** a defensive player who takes the position nearest to his team's goal line. —*adj.* giving safety.

safety belt 1. a belt or harness used to fasten a person who works at great heights to a fixed object in order to prevent falling or injury. 2. another term for **seat belt.**

safety glass, a glass made by putting a layer of plastic material between two sheets of glass to prevent shattering.

safety match, a match that will light only when struck against a special surface.

safety pin, a pin bent so as to form a spring, having a guard at one end to cover and hold the point.

safety razor, a razor with a guard or guards around the blade to prevent cuts in the skin.

safety belt *(def. 1)*

safety valve 1. a device on a container, such as a steam boiler, that opens automatically to let some steam out when the pressure in the container nears a dangerous point. 2. something that helps a person get rid of too much energy or emotion: *Hitting the punching bag was a good safety valve.*

saf·flow·er (saf′lou′ər) *n.* a tall plant that looks like a thistle and has yellowish orange flowers. The seeds yield an oil used in cooking.

saf·fron (saf′rən) *n.* 1. an orange-yellow substance that is used as a dye and for flavoring food. It is made from the dried stigmas of the flowers of a type of crocus. 2. the plant bearing this substance, having fragrant purple or white flowers. 3. an orange-yellow color. —*adj.* having the color saffron; orange-yellow.

S. Afr., South Africa; South African.

sag (sag) *v.i.,* **sagged, sag·ging.** 1. to sink or hang down, especially in the middle, as from weight; droop: *The old mattress sags.* 2. to bend or hang unevenly or loosely: *The rusty gate sagged on its hinges.* 3. to lose firmness or strength; weaken: *Their courage sagged when they realized help wasn't on the way.* 4. to slow up or move down; decline: *Production sagged at the factory during the hot weather.* —*n.* 1. the act, state, or amount of sagging. 2. a place where something sags.

sa·ga (sä′gə) *n.* 1. an adventure story that originated in Iceland during the Middle Ages, usually dealing with heroes and kings of Scandinavia and their deeds. 2. any long story about adventurous or heroic deeds.

sa·ga·cious (sə gā′shəs) *adj.* very wise: *The judge's sagacious ruling satisfied both parties.* —**sa·ga′cious·ly,** *adv.* —**sa·ga′cious·ness,** *n.*

sa·gac·i·ty (sə gas′i tē) *n.* the quality of being sagacious.

sag·a·more (sag′ə môr′) *n.* among certain North American Indian tribes, an elected ruler or chief, especially one who had less power than a sachem.

sage¹ (sāj) *n.* a person who is very wise. —*adj.,* **sag·er, sag·est.** having or showing great wisdom and sound judgment: *to give sage advice.* [From the Old French word *sage* meaning "wise," going back to the Latin word *sapere* "to be wise" or "to taste, savor."] —**sage′ly,** *adv.* —**sage′ness,** *n.*

sage² (sāj) *n.* 1. a small plant related to the mint, having fragrant leaves that are used to flavor food. 2. see **sagebrush.** [From the Old French word *sauge* meaning this plant, from the Latin word *salvia* "sage²."]

sage·brush (sāj′brush′) *n.* a shrub that grows mostly on the dry plains of western North America. It has silvery white leaves and small yellow, brown, or white flowers.

Sag·it·tar·i·us (saj′i târ′ē əs) *n.* 1. a constellation in the southern sky, thought to look like an archer with a bow. 2. the ninth sign of the zodiac.

sa·go (sā′gō) *n., pl.* **sa·gos.** 1. a grainy or powdered starch obtained from the trunk and stems of various palm trees, used to thicken soups, sauces, and other foods. 2. see **sago palm.**

sage leaves

sago palm, a palm tree found in marshy areas of the East Indies. It is the major source of sago.

at; āpe; fär; câre; end; mē; it; īce; pîerce; hot; ōld; sông, fôrk; oil; out; up; ūse; rüle; púll; tûrn; chin; sing; shop; thin; this; hw in white; zh in treasure. The symbol ə stands for the unstressed vowel sound heard in about, taken, pencil, lemon, and circus.

S

sa·gua·ro (sə gwär′ō, sə wär′ō) *n., pl.* **sa·gua·ros.** *also,* **sa·hua·ro** (sə wär′ō). a very large cactus found in southern Arizona and neighboring regions, having white flowers, branches covered with heavy spines, and fruit that can be eaten.

sa·hib (sä′ib, sä′hib) *n.* sir; master. ▲ formerly used as a title of respect for Europeans in colonial India.

said (sed) the past tense and past participle of **say.**

sail (sāl) *n.* **1.** a piece of canvas or other material used on a boat or ship to catch the wind and cause the vessel to move through the water. **2.** something resembling a sail in shape, position, or use, such as an arm of a windmill. **3.** a trip or ride in a boat or other vessel: *It was a beautiful day for a sail.* —*v.i.* **1.** (of a boat or ship) to move through the water by means of a sail or sails, or by means of an engine. **2.** to travel over water in a boat or ship. **3.** to begin a voyage by water: *The ship will sail for Hawaii in two weeks.* **4.** to steer and operate a boat, especially a sailboat. **5.** to move smoothly and without difficulty: *The ballet dancer sailed through the air.* —*v.t.* **1.** to move or travel over or across (a body of water): *This ship sailed the Mediterranean last year.* **2.** to steer, manage, or navigate (a boat or ship).

sail·board (sāl′bôrd′) *n.* a very light sailboat with one mast and sail attached to a flat hull.

sail·boat (sāl′bōt′) *n.* a boat that has a sail or sails, by means of which it is moved through the water.

sail·cloth (sāl′klôth′) *n., pl.* **sail·cloths** (sāl′klôths′, sāl′klôthz′). canvas or other strong material that is used for making sails, tents, or the like.

sail·fish (sāl′fish′) *n., pl.* **sail·fish** or **sail·fish·es.** a large, tropical, saltwater fish, related to the swordfish, having a large fin resembling a sail on its back.

sail·ing (sā′ling) *n.* **1.** the art or sport of operating a boat or ship, especially a sailboat. **2.** the act of a person or thing that sails.

sail·or (sā′lər) *n.* **1.** a person whose trade or occupation is sailing or navigating boats and ships; mariner. **2.** a member of a country's navy.

saint (sānt) *n.* **1.** a very holy person, especially one honored after death as being worthy of special reverence, as in the Roman Catholic Church. **2.** a person who is very kind, patient, or unselfish. —*v.t.* to declare (someone) to be a saint; canonize.

Saint Ber·nard (bər närd′) a very large, reddish brown and white dog having a large head, a long bushy tail, and a very thick coat. The Saint Bernard is famous for rescuing people lost in the snow in the Swiss Alps. [From the hospice in the Swiss Alps founded by *Saint Bernard* of Menthon (d. 1081?), where this dog was first bred.]

Saint Bernard

saint·ed (sān′tid) *adj.* **1.** declared to be a saint; canonized. **2.** of or like a saint; pious; saintly. **3.** thought to be among the saints in heaven; deceased.

saint·hood (sānt′hůd′) *n.* **1.** the character or condition of being a saint. **2.** saints as a group.

saint·ly (sānt′lē) *adj.,* **saint·li·er, saint·li·est.** of, relating to, or proper for a saint: *saintly behavior.* —**saint′li·ness,** *n.*

Saint Pat·rick's Day (pat′riks) the day on which Saint Patrick is honored. It falls on March 17.

Saint Valentine's Day, see **Valentine's Day.**

Saint Vi·tus' dance (vī′təs siz) a disease that affects the nerves, causing the muscles in the face, arms, and legs to twitch. [From the Italian martyr *Saint Vitus* (d. 303?). It was a tradition to pray to Saint Vitus for a cure of this disease.]

saith (seth, sā′ith) *Archaic.* the third person singular present indicative of **say.**

sake[1] (sāk) *n.* **1.** good or advantage; benefit: *to move to a dry climate for the sake of one's health.* **2.** purpose; reason: *to take a new job for the sake of making more money.* [From the Middle English word *sake* meaning "dispute, lawsuit, guilt," from the Old English word *sacu* "strife, dispute."]

sa·ke[2] (sä′kē) *also,* **sa·ki.** *n.* a Japanese alcoholic beverage that is made from rice. [From the Japanese word *sake* meaning this beverage.]

sa·laam (sə läm′) *n.* **1.** in certain Asian and African countries, a greeting or gesture of respect performed by bowing low and touching the right hand to the forehead. **2.** a greeting meaning "peace," used by Muslims. —*v.i.* to make a salaam. —*v.t.* to greet with a salaam. [From the Arabic word *salām* meaning "peace."]

sal·a·ble (sā′lə bəl) *also,* **sale·a·ble.** *adj.* that can be sold. —**sal′a·bil′i·ty, sal′a·ble·ness,** *n.*

sa·la·cious (sə lā′shəs) *adj.* not decent; obscene. —**sa·la′cious·ly,** *adv.* —**sa·la′cious·ness,** *n.*

sal·ad (sal′əd) *n.* a dish, usually served cold, often made with raw vegetables, such as lettuce and tomato, and served with a dressing. When a salad makes up a whole meal, it often includes meat or fish.

salad bar, a self-service counter in a restaurant at which a variety of salads and dressings can be obtained.

sal·a·man·der (sal′ə man′dər) *n.* any of a group of animals that look like small lizards. Salamanders are amphibians with tails. They live in and near fresh water, and have smooth, moist skin.

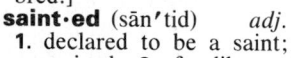

salamander

sa·la·mi (sə lä′mē) *n.* a sausage made of pork or beef and spices.

sal·a·ried (sal′ə rēd) *adj.* getting or offering a salary: *a salaried worker, a salaried position.*

sal·a·ry (sal′ə rē) *n., pl.* **sal·a·ries.** a fixed sum of money paid to someone at regular intervals for work that is done. [From the Anglo-Norman word *salarie* meaning "compensation, payment," from the Latin word *salarium* "an allowance, pension," from the earlier meaning "money given to soldiers to buy salt," from the word *sal* "salt."]

sale (sāl) *n.* **1.** a change of ownership of something from one person or group to another in exchange for money: *the sale of a house.* **2.** the offering or selling of something for less than it usually costs: *The store is having a sale on ski equipment.* **3. sales. a.** an amount sold: *Sales are up at the store.* **b.** the work or department that has to do with selling: *a job in sales.*
•**for sale.** available for purchase.
•**on sale. a.** available for purchase. **b.** available at a reduced price.

sale·a·ble (sā′lə bəl) another spelling of **salable.**

sales·clerk (sālz′klûrk′) *n.* a person who sells merchandise in a store.

sales·man (sālz′mən) *n., pl.* **sales·men** (sālz′mən). a man who sells merchandise or services.

sales·man·ship (sālz′mən ship′) *n.* skill in selling.

sales·peo·ple (salz′pē′pəl) *pl. n.* salespersons.

sales·per·son (sālz′pûr′sən) *n.* a person who sells merchandise or services.

sales tax, a tax on goods that are sold. It is usually a percentage of the selling price.

sales·wom·an (sālz′wům′ən) *n., pl.* **sales·wom·en** (sālz′wim′ən). a woman who sells merchandise or services.

sal·i·cyl·ic acid (sal′ə sil′ik) a white, crystalline organic compound used in the making of aspirin.

sa·li·ent (sā′lē ənt) *adj.* standing out from the rest; most noticeable or important: *a salient feature of the landscape, the salient points in a speech.* —*n.* the part of a fortification or line of defense that is closest to the enemy.

sa·line (sā′lēn) *adj.* **1.** of, relating to, or like salt; salty. **2.** containing salt. —*n.* a solution that has a large amount of salt. Such solutions are used in medicine, surgery, and biological experiments.

sa·lin·i·ty (sə lin′i tē) *n.* **1.** the quality or condition of being saline. **2.** the amount of salt in something: *The salinity of the bay is very high.*

Salis·bur·y steak (sôlz′ber′ē, sôlz′bə rē, salz′ber′ē, salz′bə rē) ground beef, often mixed with eggs or bread crumbs, that is formed into patties and cooked.

sa·li·va (sə lī′və) *n.* a colorless liquid that is secreted by the glands of the mouth. Saliva keeps the mouth moist, moistens food during chewing, and starts the digestion of starches.

sal·i·var·y (sal′ə ver′ē) *adj.* of, relating to, or secreting saliva: *a salivary gland.*

sal·i·vate (sal′ə vāt′) *v.i.,* **sal·i·vat·ed, sal·i·vat·ing.** to secrete saliva. —**sal′i·va′tion,** *n.*

sal·low (sal′ō) *adj.* of a sickly, yellowish color or complexion: *sallow skin.*

sal·ly (sal′ē) *v.i.,* **sal·lied, sal·ly·ing.** **1.** to start or go out briskly: *The children sallied forth into the cold night to sing carols.* **2.** to rush suddenly, as into battle: *The soldiers bravely sallied across the field.* —*n., pl.* **sal·lies.** **1.** a sudden rushing forth, especially a charge by soldiers at the enemy. **2.** a quick, witty remark. **3.** a short trip.

salm·on (sam′ən) *n., pl.* **salm·on** or **salm·ons.** **1.** a popular food fish that usually has a large, silver body with a dark back and yellowish pink flesh. Some salmon live and spawn in fresh water, but most live in salt water

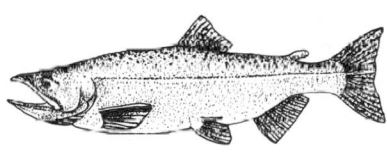

salmon *(def. 1)*

and migrate to fresh water to spawn. **2.** a yellowish pink color. —*adj.* having the color salmon; yellowish pink.

sal·mo·nel·la (sal′mə nel′ə) *n.* a common type of food poisoning that is caused by bacteria of the genus *Salmonella.*

sa·lon (sə lon′) *n., pl.* **sa·lons.** **1.** an elegant and usually large hall or room for receiving or entertaining guests. **2.** a gathering of guests in such a room. A salon is usually held so that famous people, such as artists or writers, can meet one another. **3.** a stylish shop or store, especially one that provides a special service or product: *a beauty salon.* **4.** a place to show works of art.

sa·loon (sə lün′) *n.* **1.** a place where alcoholic drinks are served; bar; tavern. **2.** a large room for public use, especially the main lounge on a passenger ship.

sal·sa (säl′sə) *n.* a Latin American dance music similar to the mambo but with elements of jazz and rock music.

sal soda, another term for **sodium carbonate** *(def. 2).*

salt (sôlt) *n.* **1.** a white substance made up of sodium and chlorine and found in seawater and in mineral deposits in the earth. It is used to season and preserve food. Formula: $NaCl$ **2.** in chemistry, any compound formed, along with water, by the reaction of an acid with a base. The salt is made up of the positive ion of the base and the negative ion of the acid. **3. salts. a.** any of various salts used as a laxative, such as Epsom salts. **b.** see **smelling salts. 4.** something that adds flavor or liveliness; zest. **5.** *Informal.* a sailor, especially an old and experienced one. —*adj.* **1.** tasting of or containing salt.

2. preserved with salt: *salt pork.* **3.** flooded with or growing in or near salt water: *a salt meadow, a salt plant.* —*v.t.* **1.** to sprinkle or season with salt. **2.** to preserve with salt or a salt solution. **3.** to add flavor or zest to; make lively: *to salt one's conversation with witty stories.*
·**to salt away.** *Informal.* to store away; save: *to salt away a fortune.*
·**with a grain of salt.** with some doubt; not too seriously: *to accept an excuse with a grain of salt.*

salt·cel·lar (sôlt′sel′ər) *n.* a shaker or dish that holds salt and is used at the table.

salt flat, an expanse of ground with deposits of salt on the surface, as the bed of a former salt lake.

salt·ine (sôl tēn′) *n.* a thin, crisp cracker sprinkled with salt.

salt lick, a natural salt deposit, or a block of salt put out in a field, that animals can lick to get the salt they need.

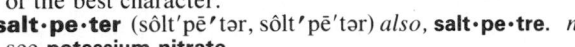

saltcellar

salt of the earth, a person or persons of the best character.

salt·pe·ter (sôlt′pē′tər, sôlt pē′tər) *also,* **salt·pe·tre.** *n.* see **potassium nitrate.**

salt·shak·er (sôlt′shā′kər) *n.* a container having a top with a hole or holes in it, used for sprinkling salt on food.

salt·wa·ter (sôlt′wô′tər) *adj.* of, relating to, or living in salt water or the sea: *saltwater fish.*

salt·y (sôl′tē) *adj.,* **salt·i·er, salt·i·est. 1.** relating to, containing, or tasting of salt. **2.** of or suggesting the sea or life at sea. **3.** witty or lively, especially in a coarse or earthy way. —**salt′i·ness,** *n.*

sa·lu·bri·ous (sə lü′brē əs) *adj.* good for a person's health; healthful: *Fresh sea air is thought to be salubrious.* —**sa·lu′bri·ous·ly,** *adv.* —**sa·lu′bri·ous·ness,** *n.*

sal·u·tar·y (sal′yə ter′ē) *adj.* **1.** good for a person's health: *Hiking is a salutary exercise.* **2.** having a good effect; beneficial: *salutary advice.*

sal·u·ta·tion (sal′yə tā′shən) *n.* **1.** the act of greeting, welcoming, or saluting by gestures or words. **2.** gestures or words used in greeting, welcoming, or saluting. **3.** a word or phrase, such as "Dear Sir," that is used to begin a letter.

sa·lu·ta·to·ri·an (sə lü′tə tôr′ē ən) *n.* the student, often the second highest in class rank, who gives the opening speech at graduation.

sa·lu·ta·to·ry (sə lü′tə tôr′ē) *adj.* of, relating to, or expressing a greeting or salutation: *a salutatory gesture.* —*n., pl.* **sa·lu·ta·to·ries.** an opening speech, especially one given at a graduation.

sa·lute (sə lüt′) *v.,* **sa·lut·ed, sa·lut·ing.** —*v.t.* **1.** to show respect for in a particular way, as by raising the right hand to the forehead: *The private saluted the commanding officer.* **2.** to greet with words or gestures of welcome or respect: *The president saluted the cheering crowd.* —*v.i.* to make a gesture of respect, especially by raising the right hand to the forehead: *The students saluted when the flag was raised.* —*n.* **1.** the act, gesture, or ceremony of saluting: *to give a salute.* **2.** the position or attitude taken when one salutes: *to stand at salute.*

Sal·va·do·ran (sal′və dôr′ən) *n.* a person who was born in or is a citizen of El Salvador. —*adj.* of or relating to

at; āpe; fär; câre; end; mē; it; īce; pîerce; hot; ōld; sông; fôrk; oil; out; up; ūse; rüle; pùll; tûrn; chin; sing; shop; thin; <u>th</u>is; hw in white; zh in treasure. The symbol ə stands for the unstressed vowel sound heard in about, taken, pencil, lemon, and circus.

S

El Salvador, its people, or their culture. Also, **Sal·va·do·ri·an** (sal′və dôr′ē ən).

sal·vage (sal′vij) *v.t.*, **sal·vaged, sal·vag·ing.** to save or rescue from being lost or destroyed: *The owner salvaged only a few pieces of furniture from the burning store.* —*n.* **1.** the act of saving a ship, its crew, or its cargo from being lost or destroyed. **2.** the ship, crew, cargo, or property that is saved. **3.** payment given to those who help save a ship, its crew, or its cargo from being lost or destroyed. **4.** the act of saving any property from being lost or destroyed. —**sal′vage·a·ble,** *adj.* —**sal′vag·er,** *n.*

sal·va·tion (sal vā′shən) *n.* **1.** a saving or freeing from difficulty, danger, destruction, or evil. **2.** a person or thing that saves or frees. **3.** the freeing of the soul from sin and from punishment for sin; redemption.

Salvation Army, an international Protestant organization engaged in preaching Christianity and helping the poor. It was founded by William Booth in 1865.

salve (sav) *n.* **1.** a soothing, often medicated substance that is put on the skin to help heal an injury and to stop pain; ointment. **2.** anything that soothes: *the salve of kindness.* —*v.t.*, **salved, sal·ving. 1.** to soothe or calm; comfort: *Words of praise can salve hurt feelings.* **2.** to put salve on: *to salve a burn.*

sal·ver (sal′vər) *n.* a tray, especially one made of metal and used for serving food or drink.

sal·vo (sal′vō) *n., pl.* **sal·vos** or **sal·voes. 1.** a firing of several guns at the same time, often as a salute. **2.** the dropping at the same time of all the bombs or missiles carried by an airplane. **3.** a sudden outburst, as of cheers.

S. Am., South America; South American.

SAM (sam) *n.* a surface-to-air missile.

Sa·mar·i·tan (sə mar′i tən) *n.* **1.** a person who lived in Samaria. **2.** see **Good Samaritan.** —*adj.* of or relating to Samaria, its people, or their culture.

sa·mar·i·um (sə mâr′ē əm) *n.* a silvery metallic element of the rare-earth group, used in the production of lasers and in nuclear reactors. Symbol: **Sm** [Formed from *samarskite,* a mineral composed of samarium and other elements, from the nineteenth-century Russian mine official Colonel von *Samarski.*]

sam·ba (sam′bə, säm′bə) *n.* **1.** a Brazilian dance of African origin. **2.** the music for this dance. —*v.i.* to dance the samba.

same (sām) *adj.* **1.** resembling another in every way; exactly alike: *The two neighbors drive the same kind of car.* **2.** being the very one; not another; identical: *That is the same person I saw yesterday.* **3.** not changed, as in character: *You are the same friendly person you've always been.* —*n.* a person or thing that is alike or identical: *My friend ordered pie, and I asked for the same.*

   ·**all the same** or **just the same.** nevertheless.
   ·**the same.** in the same manner: *They feel the same as you do about it.*

same·ness (sām′nis) *n.* **1.** the state or quality of being alike or identical. **2.** lack of variety; monotony.

S. Amer., South America; South American.

sam·i·sen (sam′ə sən) *n.* a traditional musical instrument of Japan, resembling a banjo but having three strings.

Sa·mo·an (sə mō′ən) *adj.* of or relating to Samoa, its people, or their culture. —*n.* a person who was born in or is a citizen of Samoa.

Sa·mo·a Standard Time (sə mō′ə) the local time used in American Samoa and the Midway Islands. It is 11 hours earlier than Greenwich Time.

sam·o·var (sam′ə vär′) *n.* a metal urn that has a spigot. It is used especially in Russia for boiling water for tea.

Sam·o·yed (sam′ə yed′) *n.* a dog having a thick, white coat that forms a ruff around the shoulders. It was first bred in Siberia for pulling sleds and herding reindeer.

sampan

sam·pan (sam′pan′) *n.* a small boat with a flat bottom, a large oar at the stern, and often one sail, used in China and Japan.

sam·ple (sam′pəl) *n.* a small part or piece of anything, or one item of a group, that shows the quality, nature, or characteristics of the whole: *The decorator brought a sample of the wallpaper.* —*v.t.*, **sam·pled, sam·pling.** to test, examine, or judge by taking a sample. [From the Old French word *essemple* meaning "sample, example," from the Latin word *exemplum* "a model, example."]

sam·pler[1] (sam′plər) *n.* a decorative piece of cloth embroidered with designs or letters. [From the Old French word *essemplaire* meaning "pattern, sample," from the Latin word *exemplar* "a pattern, model, example," from the word *exemplum* "a model, example."]

sam·pler[2] (sam′plər) *n.* a person who samples. [*Sample* + *-er*[1].]

sam·pling (sam′pling) *n.* the act, process, or result of testing or examination by taking a sample: *We distributed questionnaires to all the students to get a sampling of opinion about the new sports program.*

Sam·son (sam′sən) *n.* any man of great strength.

Sam·u·el (sam′ū əl) *n.* either of two books of the Old Testament, containing Hebrew history from the birth of Samuel to the death of David.

sam·u·rai (sam′ù rī′) *n., pl.* **sam·u·rai. 1.** in feudal Japan, a member of the warrior class, noted for carrying a special long sword. **2.** this warrior class.

san·a·to·ri·um (san′ə tôr′ē əm) *n., pl.* **san·a·to·ri·ums** or **san·a·to·ri·a** (san′ə tôr′ē ə). **1.** an institution for the care of patients who have tuberculosis or other diseases that require treatment over a long period of time. **2.** a health resort.

San·cho Pan·za (sän′chō pän′zə) the peasant squire of Don Quixote.

sanc·ti·fy (sangk′tə fī′) *v.t.*, **sanc·ti·fied, sanc·ti·fy·ing.**

1. to set apart as sacred or holy; reserve for religious use; consecrate: *The priest sanctified the new chapel.* **2.** to make free from sin; purify. **3.** to give religious approval to: *to sanctify marriage.* **4.** to make acceptable or give approval to. —**sanc·ti·fi·ca′tion,** *n.*

sanc·ti·mo·ni·ous (sangk′tə mō′nē əs) *adj.* pretending to be very pious or religious. —**sanc′ti·mo′ni·ous·ly,** *adv.* —**sanc′ti·mo′ni·ous·ness,** *n.*

sanc·tion (sangk′shən) *v.t.* **1.** to give approval, support, or encouragement to: *The owners did not sanction hunting on their property.* **2.** to permit, accept, or approve officially: *The court sanctioned the new law.* —*n.* **1.** official permission, acceptance, or approval. **2.** approval or encouragement that serves to make something acceptable or permissible. **3.** *usually,* **sanctions.** in international law, action by one or more countries against another country to force it to obey the law.

sanc·ti·ty (sangk′ti tē) *n., pl.* **sanc·ti·ties. 1.** piety, as of life or character; saintliness. **2.** the state or quality of being holy; sacredness: *the sanctity of a place of worship.* **3.** the state or quality of being regarded with great respect.

sanc·tu·ar·y (sangk′chü er′ē) *n., pl.* **sanc·tu·ar·ies. 1.** any place of refuge or protection. **2.** refuge or protection so provided. **3.** a holy or sacred place, such as a church or temple. **4.** the most holy part of a church or temple. **5.** a natural area where birds and animals are protected from hunters.

sanc·tum (sangk′təm) *n., pl.* **sanc·tums** or **sanc·ta** (sangk′tə). **1.** a holy or sacred place. **2.** a private room or other place where a person can be undisturbed.

sand (sand) *n.* **1.** tiny, loose grains of crushed or worn-down rocks. Sand is formed by the process of erosion. **2.** *usually,* **sands.** a region covered with this material, such as a desert or beach. —*v.t.* **1.** to scrape, smooth, or polish with sand or sandpaper: *to sand a floor.* **2.** to sprinkle or cover with sand: *to sand icy roads.*

san·dal (san′dəl) *n.* a type of light, open shoe consisting of a sole held to the foot by one or more straps or thongs.

san·dal·wood (san′dəl wúd′) *n.* **1.** the hard, yellowish, fine-grained wood of a type of evergreen tree, used for making carved boxes and fans. It also yields a fragrant oil used in perfumes and soaps. **2.** the tree from which this wood comes.

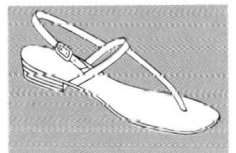

sandal

sand·bag (sand′bag′) *n.* **1.** a bag filled with sand, used as ballast in balloons and to build dams or walls for protection when there is danger of a flood or attack. **2.** a small, narrow bag filled with sand and used as a weapon. —*v.t.,* **sand·bagged, sand·bag·ging. 1.** to place sandbags in or around: *to sandbag the banks of a river.* **2.** to hit with a sandbag.

sand·bank (sand′bangk′) *n.* a ridge or mass of sand, as on a hillside or beneath shallow water.

sand·bar (sand′bär′) *also,* **sand bar.** *n.* a ridge of sand in a river or bay or along the shore, built up by the action of waves and currents.

sand·blast (sand′blast′) *v.t.* to clean, grind, or decorate a hard surface, such as glass, metal, or brick, with a high-speed stream of sand. —*n.* a high-speed stream of sand.

sand·box (sand′boks′) *n., pl.* **sand·box·es.** a large, low box filled with sand for children to play in.

sand dollar, a round, flat, spiny animal, related to sea urchins and starfish, that lives in the sandy bottom of shallow ocean waters throughout the world.

sand·er (san′dər) *n.* **1.** a machine that has a disk or belt of sandpaper, used to sand floors or woodwork. **2.** a person who sands.

sand·glass (sand′glas′) *n., pl.* **sand·glass·es.** another word for **hourglass.**

sand·lot (sand′lot′) *also,* **sand·lot.** *adj.* of or relating to games played by amateurs, as in a grassless lot: *sandlot baseball.*

sand·man (sand′man′) *n., pl.* **sand·men** (sand′men′). in folklore, a man who is said to make children sleepy by sprinkling sand on their eyes at bedtime.

sand·pa·per (sand′pā′pər) *n.* a strong, heavy paper with a coating of sand or other material, used for smoothing, polishing, or cleaning surfaces. —*v.t.* to smooth, polish, or clean by rubbing with sandpaper.

sand·pip·er (sand′pī′pər) *n.* any of various birds that live along the seashore, having a long, slender bill, long legs, and a shrill call.

sand·stone (sand′stōn′) *n.* a sedimentary rock made up mainly of grains of sand, widely used as a building material.

sandpiper

sand·storm (sand′stôrm′) *n.* a storm of high winds that carry sand through the air, commonly occurring in desert areas where loose sand is abundant.

sand·wich (sand′wich, san′-wich) *n., pl.* **sand·wich·es. 1.** two or more slices of bread with a filling of meat, cheese, or other food. **2.** something like a sandwich: *an ice-cream sandwich.* —*v.t.* to fit, place, or squeeze in tightly: *The book was sandwiched between two others.* [From the English diplomat John Montagu, fourth Earl of *Sandwich* (1718–1792), who reportedly developed the sandwich so he would not have to leave the gambling table to eat.]

sand·y (san′dē) *adj.,* **sand·i·er, sand·i·est. 1.** of, covered with, or like sand: *sandy soil, a sandy road.* **2.** yellowish red in color: *sandy hair.* —**sand′i·ness,** *n.*

sane (sān) *adj.,* **san·er, san·est. 1.** having a sound and healthy mind; not mentally ill. **2.** having or showing reason or good judgment; sensible; rational: *sane advice.* —**sane′ly,** *adv.* —**sane′ness,** *n.*

San·for·ized (san′fə rīzd′) *adj. Trademark.* (of fabric) preshrunk by a special process before being made into clothing.

sang (sang) the past tense of **sing.**

san·gui·nar·y (sang′gwə ner′ē) *adj.* **1.** involving much bloodshed; bloody: *a sanguinary battle.* **2.** eager to shed blood; bloodthirsty.

san·guine (sang′gwin) *adj.* **1.** cheerful and optimistic: *a sanguine personality, a sanguine outlook.* **2.** having a red color; ruddy: *a glowing, sanguine complexion.* —**san′guine·ly,** *adv.*

san·i·tar·i·um (san′i târ′ē əm) *n., pl.* **san·i·tar·i·ums** or **san·i·tar·i·a** (san′i târ′ē ə). **1.** a health resort. **2.** an institution for the care of patients with long-term diseases; sanatorium.

san·i·tar·y (san′i ter′ē) *adj.* **1.** of or relating to health: *Hospitals must maintain strict sanitary rules.* **2.** free from dirt or germs: *a sanitary swimming pool.* —**san·i·tar·i·ly** (san′i ter′ə lē), *adv.*

sanitary napkin, a disposable pad of absorbent material worn to absorb menstrual flow.

at; āpe; fär; câre; end; me; it; īce; pîerce; hot; ōld; sông, fôrk; oil; out; up; ūse; rüle; pùll; tûrn; chin; sing; shop; thin; this; hw in white; zh in treasure. The symbol ə stands for the unstressed vowel sound heard in about, taken, pencil, lemon, and circus.

S

san·i·ta·tion (san'i tā'shən) *n.* the protection of public health by keeping a clean and healthy environment, as by removing and disposing of sewage and garbage, controlling the population of insects and rodents, and keeping the water supply clean.

san·i·tize (san'i tīz') *v.t.,* **san·i·tized, san·i·tiz·ing.** to make (something) clean and free of dirt or germs, as by sterilizing.

san·i·ty (san'i tē) *n.* **1.** a sound and healthy state of mind. **2.** soundness of judgment; reasonableness; sensibleness.

San Jo·se scale (san'hō zā'), a tiny insect found throughout North America that is destructive to fruit trees and shrubs.

sank (sangk) a past tense of **sink.**

sans (sanz) *prep.* without.

San·skrit (san'skrit) *also,* **San·scrit.** *n.* a language of ancient India, used in literature and religion.

Words From Other Languages

Although Sanskrit is no longer a spoken language, it is the language of many ancient Indian religious books. Many of the Sanskrit words in English have to do with religion.

guru	a Hindu holy man and spiritual teacher
nirvana	in Buddhism, the highest state of bliss
pundit	a learned Brahman or an expert
sugar	a sweet food substance
swami	a Hindu mystic or religious teacher
swastika	a symbol in the shape of a cross with arms bent at right angles
yoga	a system of mental and physical discipline

San·ta Claus (san'tə klôz') in American folklore, a jolly old man with a white beard who brings presents to children at Christmas. He wears a red suit and drives a sleigh with eight reindeer. Also, **Santa.**

sap[1] (sap) *n.* **1.** a liquid that circulates through a plant and carries water, dissolved minerals, and food from one part of the plant to another. **2.** *Slang.* a person who is foolish or silly. [From the Old English word *sæp* meaning this fluid.]

sap[2] (sap) *v.t.,* **sapped, sap·ping. 1.** to weaken or destroy slowly: *The long illness sapped his strength.* **2.** to weaken by removing the underlying support of (a structure), as by digging under or wearing away the foundation. [From the Middle French word *sapper* meaning "to undermine (a fortress), dig into," from the word *sappe* "a hoe, tool for digging."]

sa·pi·ence (sā'pē əns) *n.* wisdom.

sa·pi·ent (sā'pē ənt) *adj.* wise; sage. —**sa'pi·ent·ly,** *adv.*

sap·ling (sap'ling) *n.* a young tree.

sap·o·dil·la (sap'ə dil'ə) *n.* **1.** a tall evergreen tree found in tropical America, having a heavy, fine-grained wood, and yielding chicle. **2.** the sweet fruit of this tree, having brownish yellow flesh and rough, brown skin. It is shaped like an apple and can be eaten.

sa·pon·i·fi·ca·tion (sə pon'ə fi kā'shən) *n.* a changing or being changed into soap.

sa·pon·i·fy (sə pon'ə fī') *v.,* **sa·pon·i·fied, sa·pon·i·fy·ing.** —*v.t.* to make (a fat) react with an alkali to form soap. —*v.i.* to become changed into soap by this method.

sap·per (sap'ər) *n.* a soldier who lays mines and detects and disarms enemy mines. Sappers also build fortifications and trenches.

sap·phire (saf'īr) *n.* **1.** a precious stone that is transparent and deep blue in color. **2.** a deep blue color. —*adj.* having the color sapphire; deep blue. [From the Old French word *safre,* from the Latin word *sapphirus,* from the Greek word *sappheiros,* from the Hebrew word *sappīr,* all meaning "sapphire." Hebrew may have borrowed this word from the Sanskrit word *śanipriya* meaning "(stone) dear to the planet Saturn."]

sap·py (sap'ē) *adj.,* **sap·pi·er, sap·pi·est. 1.** full of sap; juicy. **2.** *Slang.* silly; foolish: *a sappy person, a sappy story.* —**sap'pi·ness,** *n.*

sap·ro·phyte (sap'rə fīt') *n.* a plant that is not green and gets its food from dead or decaying plant or animal matter.

sap·suck·er (sap'suk'ər) *n.* any of several North American woodpeckers that feed on insects and tree sap by drilling holes in trees with their strong, pointed bills.

sap·wood (sap'wùd') *n.* the young, soft wood of a tree or other woody plant found just beneath the bark. It is made up of living cells, through which sap moves upward in the plant.

Sar·a·cen (sar'ə sən) *n.* **1.** a Muslim, especially at the time of the Crusades or during the Middle Ages. **2.** formerly, any Arab.

sa·ran (sə ran') *n.* a plastic material used especially to make strong, transparent wrappings.

sa·ra·pe (sə rä'pē) another spelling of **serape.**

sapsucker

sar·casm (sär'kaz əm) *n.* **1.** the use of sharp, bitter, taunting, or scornful remarks or language intended to hurt or make fun of someone or something: *"Right on time," said the teacher with sarcasm as the student came in late.* **2.** such a remark or language.

sar·cas·tic (sär kas'tik) *adj.* **1.** characterized by sarcasm; mocking: *sarcastic comments.* **2.** given to the use of sarcasm: *a very sarcastic person.* —**sar·cas'ti·cal·ly,** *adv.*

sar·co·dine (sär'kə dīn', sär'kə dēn') *n.* any of a group of protozoans that grasp food and move about with the aid of pseudopods. Also, **sar·co·din·i·an** (sär'kə din'ē ən), *n.*

sar·co·ma (sär kō'mə) *n., pl.* **sar·co·mas** or **sar·co·ma·ta** (sär kō'mə tə). any of various highly malignant cancers of connective tissues.

sar·coph·a·gus (sär kof'ə gəs) *n., pl.* **sar·coph·a·gi** (sär kof'ə jī') or **sar·coph·a·gus·es.** a stone coffin placed above ground. It is often ornamented with sculpture or painting.

sard (särd) *n.* reddish brown chalcedony quartz, used especially in jewelry.

sar·dine (sär dēn') *n.* a food fish that is related to the herring. Sardines are caught while young and small, and are usually packed tightly in flat cans.

sar·don·ic (sär don'ik) *adj.* mocking or sneering, often in a sarcastic way: *a harsh, sardonic laugh.* —**sar·don'i·cal·ly,** *adv.*

sardine

sar·don·yx (sär don'iks) *n.* a variety of chalcedony quartz having layers of white or black alternating with red or reddish brown, used especially in the making of cameos.

sar·gas·so (sär gas'ō) *n., pl.* **sar·gas·sos.** a seaweed that floats in large masses in the Gulf Stream and the Sargasso Sea.

sa·ri (sär′ē) *n.* an outer garment worn by women in India and Pakistan. It is made by wrapping a long piece of silk or cotton cloth around the body to form a long skirt, and by bringing one end up in front and over the shoulder to form the top.

sa·rong (sə rông′, sə rong′) *n.* an outer garment that is worn as a skirt by men and women who live on islands in the Pacific Ocean. It is made by draping a long, rectangular piece of material around the body at the waist.

sar·sa·pa·ril·la (sas′pə ril′ə, sär′sə pə-ril′ə) *n.* **1.** a climbing or trailing vine found in Mexico, Central America, and South America, having prickly stems and large heart-shaped leaves with toothed edges. **2.** the root of this vine, dried and used as a medicine, and as a flavoring for syrups and soft drinks. **3.** a soft drink flavored with this root.

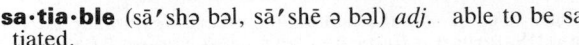

sari

sar·to·ri·al (sär tôr′ē əl) *adj.* **1.** of or relating to tailors or their work. **2.** of or relating to clothing or dress: *to appear in sartorial splendor.* —**sar·to′ri·al·ly**, *adv.*

sash[1] (sash) *n., pl.* **sash·es.** a broad band of cloth or ribbon, often worn over one shoulder or around the waist as part of a uniform. [From the Arabic word *shāsh* meaning "muslin cloth."]

sash[2] (sash) *n., pl.* **sash·es.** the frame that holds the panes of glass in a window or door. [From the French word *châssis* meaning "chassis, frame," going back to the Latin word *capsa* "box[1]."]

sa·shay (sa shā′) *v.i. Informal.* to walk or move in a noticeably nonchalant or swaggering manner.

sa·shi·mi (sä shē′mē) *n.* a Japanese dish consisting of very thin slices of raw fish, usually served with shredded horseradish and soy sauce. [From the Japanese word *sashimi* meaning this food.]

Sask., Saskatchewan.

sass (sas) *Informal. n.* back talk; impudence. —*v.t.* to talk impudently or disrespectfully to; talk back to.

sas·sa·fras (sas′ə fras′) *n., pl.* **sas·sa·fras·es.** a tree found in North America, whose roots have a bark that is used to make tea and to flavor such things as root beer and tobacco.

sas·sy (sas′ē) *adj.*, **sas·si·er, sas·si·est.** *Informal.* impudent, saucy. *The sassy child talked back to the teacher.*

sat (sat) a past tense and past participle of **sit.**

Sat., Saturday.

Sa·tan (sā′tən) *n.* the Devil. [From the Late Latin word *Satan*, from the Greek word *Satan*, from the Hebrew word *śatān*, "adversary."]

sa·tan·ic (sā tan′ik) *adj.* **1.** of or relating to Satan. **2.** very evil or cruel.

satch·el (sach′əl) *n.* a bag or small suitcase for carrying clothing, instruments, books, or other articles. It sometimes has a shoulder strap.

sate (sāt) *v.t.*, **sat·ed, sat·ing. 1.** to fill or satisfy completely: *to sate one's hunger.* **2.** to provide with more than enough; glut.

sa·teen (sa tēn′) *n.* a strong cotton fabric woven with a smooth, glossy finish so as to look like satin.

sat·el·lite (sat′ə līt′) *n.* **1.** a heavenly body that revolves in an orbit around another body larger than itself; moon. **2.** an artificial object placed in orbit around another body in space, such as the earth or the moon. **3.** a country dominated or controlled by another more powerful country. **4.** a follower or attendant of an important person. [From the French word *satellite* meaning "attendant," going back to the Latin word *satelles* "bodyguard, attendant."]

sa·tia·ble (sā′shə bəl, sā′shē ə bəl) *adj.* able to be satiated.

sa·ti·ate (sā′shē āt′) *v.t.*, **sa·ti·at·ed, sa·ti·at·ing. 1.** to provide with more than enough; cloy. **2.** to satisfy completely: *A large dinner can satiate one's hunger.* —**sa′ti·a′tion,** *n.*

sat·in (sat′in) *n.* a fabric having a smooth, glossy surface, made of silk or various synthetic fibers. —*adj.* resembling satin; smooth; glossy: *satin skin.*

sat·in·wood (sat′in wùd′) *n.* **1.** any of various kinds of wood having a satiny appearance, used for veneers. **2.** any of the trees yielding such wood.

sat·in·y (sat′ə nē) *adj.* resembling satin in softness, smoothness, or glossiness.

sat·ire (sat′īr) *n.* **1.** the use of humor, irony, or ridicule to attack or make fun of human faults or follies. **2.** a work of literature that attacks or makes fun of human faults or follies by this means.

sa·tir·i·cal (sə tir′i kəl) *adj.* **1.** of, resembling, or characterized by satire. **2.** using satire: *a satirical author.* Also, **sa·tir·ic** (sə tir′ik). —**sa·tir′i·cal·ly,** *adv.*

sat·i·rist (sat′ər ist) *n.* a person who uses satire, especially a writer of satires.

sat·i·rize (sat′ə rīz′) *v.t.*, **sat·i·rized, sat·i·riz·ing.** to attack or make fun of by means of satire.

sat·is·fac·tion (sat′is fak′shən) *n.* **1.** the act of satisfying or the state of being satisfied. **2.** the cause or means of being satisfied. **3.** something that makes up for a wrong, injury, or obligation.

sat·is·fac·to·ry (sat′is fak′tə rē) *adj.* good enough to meet a need or desire; giving satisfaction. —**sat′is·fac′to·ri·ly,** *adv.* —**sat′is·fac′to·ri·ness,** *n.*

sat·is·fy (sat′is fī′) *v.*, **sat·is·fied, sat·is·fy·ing.** —*v.t.* **1.** to meet the needs or desires of; make contented: *The team's performance in the game didn't satisfy the coach.* **2.** to supply fully with what is needed or desired: *A cold drink satisfied my thirst.* **3.** to fulfill or answer the conditions of: *to satisfy the requirements of a course.* **4.** to pay off: *to satisfy a debt.* **5.** to make up for; redress: *to satisfy a wrong.* **6.** to answer convincingly: *A prompt and precise reply satisfied the teacher.* *v.i.* to give satisfaction. —**sat′is·fi′er,** *n.*

sa·trap (sā′trap) *n.* **1.** a governor of a province in the ancient Persian empire. **2.** any official or ruler of lesser rank or position.

sat·u·rate (sach′ə rāt′) *v.t.*, **sat·u·rat·ed, sat·u·rat·ing. 1.** to fill with something to the point where no more can be absorbed, especially to soak thoroughly: *Water saturated the cloth.* **2.** to fill full or to excess: *The smell of perfume saturated the room.* **3.** *Chemistry.* to supply (a solvent or solution) with as much of a particular substance as can be dissolved in it.

sat·u·rat·ed (sach′ə rā′tid) *adj.* **1.** filled completely or soaked thoroughly. **2.** (of a solution) containing the largest amount of a substance capable of being dissolved at a given temperature and pressure. **3.** belonging to a particular class of fats that tend to be solid in form, such as lard or butter, and that most often come from animal sources. **4.** (of a color) of the highest intensity of hue; not diluted with white.

sat·u·ra·tion (sach′ə rā′shən) *n.* the act of saturating or the state of being saturated.

Sat·ur·day (sat′ər dē, sat′ər dā′) *n.* the seventh day of

at; āpe; fär; câre; end; mē; it; īce; pîerce; hot; ōld; sông, fôrk; oil; out; up; ūse; rüle; pùll; tûrn; chin; sing; shop; thin; this; hw in white; zh in treasure. The symbol ə stands for the unstressed vowel sound heard in about, taken, pencil, lemon, and circus.

S

831

the week. [From the Old English word *Sæterndæg* meaning "Saturday," from the Latin word *Saturnus* "Saturn" + the Old English word *dæg* "day."]

Sat·urn (sat′ərn) *n.* **1.** *Roman Mythology.* the god of agriculture. In Greek mythology he was called Cronus. **2.** the second largest planet of the solar system and sixth in order of distance from the sun, believed to have at least twenty-two moons. Saturn is surrounded by rings that are made up of millions of tiny ice particles.

Saturn *(def. 2)*

Sat·ur·na·li·a (sat′ər nā′lē ə) *n., pl.* **Sat·ur·na·li·a** or **Sat·ur·na·li·as.** **1.** an ancient Roman celebration in honor of Saturn that began on December 17 and continued for seven days. **2. saturnalia.** any period or occasion of merrymaking and festivity.

sat·ur·nine (sat′ər nīn′) *adj.* having or showing a gloomy or moody nature. [Originally from the Latin word *Saturnus* meaning "Saturn," from the former belief that people born under the sign of this planet had a gloomy disposition.] **—sat′ur·nine′ly,** *adv.*

sat·yr (sat′ər, sā′tər) *n. Greek Mythology.* a minor god of the countryside, represented as a man having the horns, tail, and legs of a goat. In Roman mythology it was called a faun.

sauce (sôs) *n.* **1.** a liquid or creamy blend of several ingredients served with food to add to or improve its flavor. **2.** a fruit that has been stewed into a pulp and sweetened: *cranberry sauce.* **3.** *Informal.* impudence. **—*v.t.*, sauced, sauc·ing.** to prepare or flavor with sauce.

sauce·pan (sôs′pan′) *n.* a small pot with a handle, used for cooking food.

sau·cer (sô′sər) *n.* a small shallow dish, especially one for holding a cup.

sau·cy (sô′sē) *adj.*, **sau·ci·er, sau·ci·est.** bold or rude; impudent. **—sau′ci·ly,** *adv.* **—sau′ci·ness,** *n.*

Sa·u·di (sä ü′dē, sou′dē, sô′dē) *n.* a person who was born in or is a citizen of Saudi Arabia. **—*adj.*** of or relating to Saudi Arabia, its people, or their culture. Also, **Saudi Arabian.**

sauer·kraut (sour′krout′) *n.* finely shredded cabbage that has been salted and fermented in its own juice.

Sauk (sôk) *n., pl.* **Sauk** or **Sauks.** a member of a tribe of North American Indians who formerly lived in what is now Michigan and Wisconsin.

sau·na (sô′nə, sou′nə) *n.* **1.** a bath, similar to a steambath, in which the bather is surrounded by hot, dry air. **2.** a room in which to take such a bath.

saun·ter (sôn′tər) *v.i.* to walk in a slow, relaxed way; stroll. **—*n.*** a slow, relaxed walk; stroll.

sau·ri·an (sôr′ē ən) *n.* a lizard or lizardlike reptile such as a crocodile or dinosaur. **—*adj.*** of or relating to lizards or lizardlike reptiles.

sau·sage (sô′sij) *n.* finely chopped, seasoned meat, such as pork, beef, or veal, made into patties or stuffed in a casing.

sau·té (sô tā′) *v.t.*, **sau·téed, sau·té·ing.** to cook or brown quickly in an open pan using a small amount of very hot fat. **—*n.*** food cooked in this manner. **—*adj.*** cooked or browned quickly in a small amount of very hot fat.

sau·terne (sô tûrn′) *also,* **Sau·ternes** (sô tûrn′). **—*n.*** a variety of sweet white wine.

sav·age (sav′ij) *adj.* **1.** brutal, cruel, or vicious: *savage fighting.* **2.** not civilized: *a savage custom.* **3.** not tamed; wild: *savage beasts.* **—*n.*** **1.** a person who is not civilized, especially a person belonging to a primitive people or society. **2.** a brutal, cruel, or vicious person. **sav′age·ly,** *adv.* **—sav′age·ness,** *n.*

sav·age·ry (sav′ij rē) *n., pl.* **sav·age·ries.** **1.** the state or quality of being savage. **2.** savage behavior.

sa·van·na (sə van′ə) *also,* **sa·van·nah.** *n.* a broad, grassy plain with few trees.

sa·vant (sa vänt′, sav′ənt) *n.* a person of great learning; scholar.

save¹ (sāv) *v.*, **saved, sav·ing. —*v.t.*** **1.** to free from harm; make safe: *The firefighter saved the children from the burning house.* **2.** to set aside for future use: *to save part of one's allowance each week.* **3.** to keep from being lost, spent, or wasted: *to save time.* **4.** to keep from wear or damage; safeguard; preserve: *to save a good coat for special occasions.* **5.** to deliver from sin and its consequences. **—*v.i.*** **1.** to set aside money, as for future use: *to save for a new bicycle.* **2.** to avoid expense or waste; economize: *It's difficult to save on groceries.* [From the Old French word *salver* with the same meaning, going back to the Latin word *salvus* "safe."] **—sav′er,** *n.*

save² (sāv) *prep.* except; but: *No one save the immediate family was invited to the wedding.* [From the Middle English preposition *sauf* with the same meaning, from the adjective *sauf* "safe," from the Old French word *sauf* "safe," going back to the Latin word *salvus* "safe."]

sav·ing (sā′ving) *adj.* **1.** that makes up for everything else; redeeming: *The old car's saving feature was its reliability.* **2.** thrifty; economical; frugal. **—*n.*** **1.** the act of a person or thing that saves something: *the saving of time.* **2.** something saved. **3. savings.** money saved, especially in a bank account.

savings account, a bank account for the purpose of saving money, on which interest is paid.

savings bank, a bank whose main purpose is to accept money for lending or investing, and to pay interest on it.

savings bond, a bond issued by the United States government, which a buyer may cash in for its value plus interest after a certain length of time.

sav·ior (sāv′yər) *also, British,* **sav·iour.** *n.* **1.** a person who saves from harm, danger, or destruction; person who brings salvation. **2. the Savior.** Jesus.

sa·vor (sā′vər) *also, British,* **sa·vour.** *n.* **1.** a particular taste or smell. **2.** the power to arouse interest or excitement. **—*v.t.*** **1.** to taste or smell with pleasure: *to savor a meal.* **2.** to take great delight in: *I savored the news that our team had won the championship.* **3.** to give flavor to; season. [From the Old French word *savor* meaning "taste, smell," from the Latin word *sapor* "taste, relish, flavor."] **—sa′vor·er,** *n.*

sa·vor·y¹ (sā′və rē) *also, British,* **sa·vour·y.** *adj.* **1.** agreeable to the taste or smell: *Savory odors came from the kitchen.* **2.** morally acceptable or respectable: *a savory reputation.* **3.** sharp to the taste; pungent. [From the Old French word *savoré* with the same meaning, from the word *savorer* "to taste, savor," going back to the Latin word *sapor* "taste, relish, flavor."] **—sa′vor·i·ness,** *n.*

sa·vor·y² (sā′və rē) *n., pl.* **sa·vor·ies.** a plant of the mint family used to flavor food. [From the Old English word *sætherige* and the Old French word *sarree*, both meaning this plant and both from the Latin word *satureia* "savory²." The spelling has been influenced by *savory¹*.]

sav·vy (sav′ē) *Slang. v.i.*, **sav·vied, sav·vy·ing.** to know; understand. **—*n.*** good sense, judgment, or understanding. [From the Spanish phrase *sabe (Usted)?* meaning "do (you) know?" going back to the Latin word *sapere* "to be wise" or "to taste, savor."]

saw¹ (sô) *n.* **1.** a hand or power tool having a metal blade whose edge is notched with pointed teeth, used for cutting wood, metal, or other hard materials. **2.** a machine having such a tool or tools. —*v.*, **sawed, sawed** or **sawn, saw-ing.** —*v.t.* **1.** to cut with a saw: *to saw a log in half.* **2.** to shape or form by cutting with a saw: *to saw a hole in the ice.* —*v.i.* **1.** to use a saw: *to saw along the grain of the wood.* **2.** to be cut with a saw: *This wood saws easily.* [From the Old English word *saga* meaning this tool.] —**saw'er,** *n.*

saw² (sô) the past tense of **see¹.**

saw³ (sô) *n.* a traditional and familiar saying, such as *Too many cooks spoil the broth.* [From the Old English word *sagu* meaning "a saying, story."]

saw·buck (sô'buk') *n.* **1.** a kind of sawhorse made up of two X-shaped frames. It is used to hold logs while they are being sawed. **2.** *Slang.* a ten-dollar bill.

saw·dust (sô'dust') *n.* the fine particles that fall from wood or other material as it is being sawed.

sawed–off (sôd'ôf') *adj.* **1.** having one end sawed off: *a sawed-off shotgun.* **2.** *Slang.* of less than average height; short.

saw·fish (sô'fish') *n.*, *pl.* **saw·fish** or **saw·fish·es.** a large fish of the ray family, having a long snout with sharp teeth along both edges.

saw·horse (sô'hôrs') *n.* a frame made up of a plank with two legs at each end. It is used to support boards while they are being sawed.

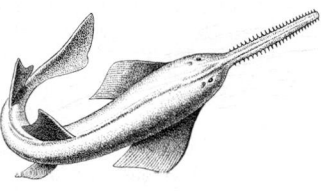

sawfish

saw·mill (sô'mil') *n.* a place where logs are sawed into lumber by machinery.

sawn (sôn) a past participle of **saw¹.**

saw·yer (sô'yər) *n.* a person whose work is sawing wood.

sax (saks) *n.*, *pl.* **sax·es.** *Informal.* saxophone.

sax·i·frage (sak'sə frij) *n.* any of a large group of plants bearing clusters of white, pink, purple, or yellow flowers.

Sax·on (sak'sən) *n.* **1.** a member or descendant of a Germanic tribe that, along with the Angles and Jutes, conquered parts of Britain in the fifth and sixth centuries A.D. **2.** a person who was born in or is a citizen of Saxony. —*adj.* **1.** of or relating to the early Saxons or Anglo-Saxons. **2.** of or relating to Saxony.

sax·o·phone (sak'sə fōn') *n.* a wind instrument having a single-reed mouthpiece, a usually curving body made of metal, and a series of keys for changing the pitch of the tones. [From the Belgian instrument maker Antoine Joseph *Sax* (1814–1894), who invented it.] —**sax'o·phon'ist,** *n.*

say (sā) *v.t.*, **said, say·ing. 1.** to speak or pronounce; utter: *I can't understand what you are saying.* **2.** to make known or express in words; state: *I didn't get a chance to say "thank you."* **3.** to state as an opinion; declare: *The worker couldn't say how much longer the job would take.* **4.** to estimate; suppose; assume: *I would say that the house is 100 years old.* **5.** to recite; repeat: *to say a prayer before lunch.* —*n.* the right or chance to speak: *Give them their say.* —*interj.* used to attract attention, express surprise, or the like: *Say! What was that noise outside?* —**say'er,** *n.*

say·ing (sā'ing) *n.* **1.** a traditional and familiar statement believed to contain truth, wisdom, or common sense. For example: *A stitch in time saves nine.* **2.** something said; statement.

saxophone

says (sez) the third person singular, present indicative of **say.**

say–so (sā'sō') *n.*, *pl.* **say-sos.** *Informal.* **1.** the authority to decide something: *We went ahead with the project on the teacher's say-so.* **2.** a person's statement or assertion: *No one's going to believe such a strange story just on your say-so.*

Sb, the symbol for antimony. [From the Latin word *stibium* meaning "antimony."]

S.B., Bachelor of Science.

Sc, the symbol for scandium.

sc. 1. scale. **2.** scene.

SC, postal abbreviation for South Carolina.

S.C., South Carolina.

scab (skab) *n.* **1.** a crust of dried blood and lymph fluid that forms a protective cover over a sore or wound during healing. **2.** *Informal.* a worker who refuses to join a labor union, especially one who works when the union workers are on strike.

scab·bard (skab'ərd) *n.* a case or sheath for the blade of a sword, bayonet, or other similar weapon.

sca·bies (skā'bēz) *n.* a contagious skin disease producing intense itching. It is caused by mites that burrow under the skin and lay eggs.

scads (skadz) *pl. n. Informal.* large quantities or numbers: *There are scads of fish in that lake.*

scaf·fold (skaf'əld) *n.* **1.** a temporary wooden or metal platform, often suspended from a roof, used to support workers and materials. **2.** a raised platform on which criminals are executed. **3.** any raised framework, stage, or stand.

scaf·fold·ing (skaf'əl ding) *n.* **1.** a scaffold or a connected series of scaffolds. **2.** the materials used to build a scaffold.

scal·a·wag (skal'ə wag') *n.* **1.** any white Southerner who helped carry out Reconstruction following the Civil War. **2.** a worthless person; rascal.

scald (skôld) *v.t.* **1.** to burn with hot liquid or steam: *The spilled coffee scalded my hand.* **2.** to clean or treat with steam or boiling liquid: *The nurse scalded the medical instruments.* **3.** to heat to a temperature just below the boiling point: *to scald milk.* —*n.* a burn caused by hot liquid or by steam.

scale¹ (skāl) *n.* **1.** a device for weighing an object by balancing it against another weight or against the force of a spring. **2. scales.** see **balance** (*def.* 4). **3.** a dish, pan, or platform of a balance. —*v.*, **scaled, scal·ing.** —*v.i.* to amount to in weight; weigh. —*v.t.* to weigh (something) in a scale or scales. [From the Old Norse word *skál* meaning "a bowl" or "one pan of a balance."]

·**to tip the scales. a.** to weigh: *The boxer tipped the scales at 200 pounds.* **b.** to have a decisive effect: *The lawyer's brilliant closing statement tipped the scales in the defendant's favor.*

scale² (skāl) *n.* **1.** one of the horny, flattened, platelike structures forming all or part of the outer covering of certain animals, such as snakes, lizards, and fish. **2.** any structure resembling this, as on the wings of some insects or on the legs of birds. **3.** a thin, flat piece or plate, as of armor. —*v.*, **scaled, scal·ing.** —*v.t.* **1.** to remove the scales from: *to scale a fish.* **2.** to remove in thin layers or scales: *to scale the bark off a branch.* —*v.i.* to peel or come off in scales; flake. [From the Medieval Latin

at; āpe; fär; câre; end; mē; it; īce; pîerce; hot; ōld; sông, fôrk; oil; out; up; ūse; rüle; pull; tûrn; chin; sing; shop; thin; this; hw in white; zh in treasure. The symbol ə stands for the unstressed vowel sound heard in about, taken, pencil, lemon, and circus.

S

word *scala* meaning "shell, scale²," of Germanic origin.] —**scale'less**, *adj.* —**scale'like'**, *adj.*

scale³ (skāl) *n.* **1.** a series of steps or degrees: *The student thought the grading scale was fair. The president's family ranks high on the social scale.* **2.** the proportion that a plan, map, or model has to what it represents: *The scale of the map is 1 inch to 200 miles.* **3.** a series of marks made along

scale³ (n., def. 6)

a line at regularly spaced intervals, used in measuring or calculating: *the scale on a ruler.* **4.** any instrument marked with such a series of marks. **5.** relative size or extent: *The painter worked on a large scale.* **6.** *Music.* a series of tones that go up or down in pitch according to fixed intervals, especially such a series within an octave: *the scale of C major.* **7.** *Mathematics.* a particular system of numbering: *the decimal scale.* —*v.t.*, **scaled, scal·ing. 1.** to climb up: *to scale a mountain.* **2.** to change or adjust by a fixed proportion or scale: *The two sides scaled down the level of fighting during the peace talks.* **3.** to make according to a scale: *to scale a drawing.* [From the Late Latin word *scala* meaning "ladder."]

scale insect, any of a group of tiny insects that live on plants. The females secrete a waxy covering resembling scales.

sca·lene (skā lēn') *adj.* (of a triangle) having three unequal sides.

scal·lion (skal'yən) *n.* a young onion whose bulb is just beginning to form. Also, **green onion.**

scal·lop (skol'əp, skal'əp) *also,* **scol·lop, es·cal·lop.** *n.* **1.** any of a group of shellfish having soft bodies enclosed by two circular hinged shells that are ridged and have wavy edges. **2.** a muscle of certain species of this animal, used as food. **3.** one of a series of curves resembling the edge of a scallop shell, forming an ornamental border, as on clothing. —*v.t.* **1.** to shape or ornament with scallops, especially by cutting: *The edges of the tablecloth were scalloped.* **2.** to bake in a casserole with a sauce, often with a topping of bread crumbs: *to scallop potatoes.*

sca·lop·pi·ne (skä'lə pē'nē, skal'ə pē'nē) *also,* **scal·lo·pi·ni.** *n.* a dish consisting of thin pieces of meat, especially veal, sauteed or fried. [From the Italian word *scaloppina* meaning "thin, boneless slices of meat," going back to the Old French word *escalope* "shell" and "thin slice of meat."]

scalp (skalp) *n.* **1.** the skin that covers the human skull, usually covered with hair. **2.** part of this skin and the attached hair, formerly cut or torn from the head of an enemy by certain North American Indians as a trophy or symbol of victory. —*v.t.* **1.** to cut or tear the scalp from. **2.** *Informal.* to buy and resell (tickets) at a very high profit: *to scalp tickets to a championship game.* —**scalp'er,** *n.*

scal·pel (skal'pəl) *n.* a small, pointed knife with a straight handle and curved cutting edge, used in surgery.

scal·y (skā'lē) *adj.,* **scal·i·er, scal·i·est. 1.** covered with or made up of scales. **2.** resembling scales. **3.** peeling or coming off in scales or flakes; flaking. —**scal'i·ness,** *n.*

scaly anteater, another term for **pangolin.**

scam (skam) *n.* *Slang.* a scheme to trick or cheat someone; a swindle.

scamp (skamp) *n.* **1.** a worthless, dishonest person; rogue. **2.** a mischievous or playful person, especially a youngster.

scam·per (skam'pər) *v.i.* **1.** to run or flee quickly: *The rabbit scampered off into the woods.* **2.** to move about playfully: *The children scampered about the yard.* —*n.* the act of scampering.

scan (skan) *v.,* **scanned, scan·ning.** —*v.t.* **1.** to look at

closely and carefully: *to scan a photograph for details.* **2.** to search or look over (a wide area) thoroughly, especially by a slow, sweeping movement: *The sailors scanned the horizon for a ship.* **3.** to glance over or go through quickly; skim: *to scan a magazine article.* **4.** to mark off or analyze (verse) according to a metrical pattern. **5.** to trace out closely spaced parallel lines on (a cathode-ray tube or other surface). —*v.i.* **1.** to scan verse. **2.** (of verse) to conform to a metrical pattern. **3.** (of a beam from an electron gun) to trace out closely spaced parallel lines that cover a surface, such as the screen of a television receiver or some other cathode-ray tube. **4.** to cover systematically with a beam, such as a laser or radar beam, to record information or create an image. —*n.* **1.** the act of scanning. **2.** the result or product of scanning.

scan·dal (skan'dəl) *n.* **1.** something that shocks people or offends their sense of right and wrong, and disgraces those associated or connected with it: *There was a scandal when it was revealed that the mayor had stolen city funds.* **2.** anger or outrage caused by this: *News of the mayor's dishonesty gave rise to a public scandal.* **3.** harmful gossip: *to spread scandal through the neighborhood.*

scan·dal·ize (skan'də līz') *v.t.,* **scan·dal·ized, scan·dal·iz·ing.** to shock or offend by doing or saying something considered immoral or improper; outrage.

scan·dal·mon·ger (skan'dəl mung'gər, skan'dəl mong'gər) *n.* a person who spreads harmful gossip.

scan·dal·ous (skan'də ləs) *adj.* **1.** causing a scandal; shocking: *scandalous behavior.* **2.** spreading gossip that harms someone's reputation: *scandalous news.* —**scan'dal·ous·ly,** *adv.* —**scan'dal·ous·ness,** *n.*

Scan·di·na·vi·an (skan'də nā'vē ən) *n.* **1.** a person who was born in or is a citizen of a Scandinavian country. **2.** the languages of Scandinavia, including Danish, Norwegian, Icelandic, and Swedish. —*adj.* of or relating to Scandinavia, its people, their language, or culture.

Words From Other Languages

Scandinavian peoples and their language began invading England in 793. Scandinavians ruled northern England for a while, and many Scandinavian words became part of the basic language of modern English. Other Scandinavian words became part of the English language much later.

bark	the outer covering of a tree
call	to say in a loud voice
die	to stop living
gale	a very strong wind
get	to obtain possession of
geyser	a natural hot spring bursting with steam and hot water
husband	the man of a married couple
kid	a young goat
law	a rule governing a people or country
leg	a limb supporting a person or animal
mink	a small mammal with soft brown fur
ransack	to search thoroughly
ski	one of a pair of snow runners
slalom	a downhill ski racing course
steak	a slice of meat to broil or fry
walrus	a large arctic mammal with tusks
window	an opening for letting in light
wrong	not true or correct

scan·di·um (skan′dē əm) *n.* a rare, very light, silver-white metallic element that is abundant in stars. Symbol: **Sc** [Formed from *Scandia,* the Latin name for Scandinavia. This element was found in rare-earth ores from Scandinavia.]

scan·ner (skan′ər) *n.* **1.** a person or thing that scans. **2.** a device that examines or records by scanning.

scan·sion (skan′shən) *n.* the analyzing or marking off of lines of verse according to a metrical pattern; scanning. In English poetry, scansion is by accented and unaccented syllables.

scant (skant) *adj.* **1.** not enough or scarcely enough; meager: *Our scant food supplies barely lasted through our camping trip.* **2.** not quite amounting to a specified measure: *a scant six miles.* —*v.t.* to furnish a scant amount of; skimp on. —**scant′ly**, *adv.* —**scant′ness**, *n.*

scant·y (skan′tē) *adj.,* **scant·i·er**, **scant·i·est**. **1.** not enough or scarcely enough; meager. **2.** small, as in size; skimpy: *a scanty bathing suit.* —**scant′i·ly**, *adv.* —**scant′i·ness**, *n.*

-scape *combining form* view; scene: *seascape, moonscape.* [From *landscape.*]

scape·goat (skāp′gōt′) *n.* a person or thing made to suffer for or bear the blame for the mistakes or wrongdoing of others.

scap·u·la (skap′yə lə) *n., pl.* **scap·u·lae** (skap′yə lē′) or **scap·u·las**. either of two flat, rectangular bones in the upper part of the back; shoulder blade.

scar (skär) *n.* **1.** any mark or discolored area left on the skin where tissue that has been damaged or destroyed by injury or disease has healed. **2.** any mark or blemish resembling this. **3.** a lasting effect on the mind produced by a distressing or tragic experience. **4.** *Botany.* a mark showing where something was attached, as where a leaf was attached to a stem. —*v.t.,* **scarred, scar·ring.** to mark with a scar or scars; leave a scar or scars upon.

scar·ab (skar′əb) *n.* **1.** any of a large group of beetles having stocky, oval bodies, especially one of a species of beetles thought of as sacred by the ancient Egyptians. **2.** a gem cut in the shape of this beetle, or a piece of jewelry bearing its image.

scarce (skârs) *adj.,* **scarc·er**, **scarc·est.** difficult to get or find: *Water is scarce in the desert.* —*adv.* scarcely. —**scarce′ness**, *n.*
·**to make (oneself) scarce.** *Informal.* to go or stay away.

scarce·ly (skârs′lē) *adv.* **1.** by a small margin; barely: *I had scarcely come in when the phone rang.* **2.** almost not; hardly: *There was scarcely a person on the street.* **3.** certainly or most probably not: *I could scarcely afford a new car on my small income.*

scar·ci·ty (skâr′si tē) *n., pl.* **scar·ci·ties**. **1.** an insufficient amount or supply. **2.** the state or quality of being scarce.

scare (skâr) *v.,* **scared, scar·ing.** —*v.t.* **1.** to cause to be afraid or alarmed; frighten: *The thunder scared the children.* **2.** to drive or force by frightening: *The dog scared the thief away.* —*v.i.* to become scared: *They don't scare easily.* —*n.* **1.** sudden fear or alarm; fright: *The sound of the explosion gave me quite a scare.* **2.** a state of widespread fear or alarm; panic: *There was a bomb scare at the store.*

scare·crow (skâr′krō′) *n.* **1.** a crude figure of a person dressed in old clothes, set in a field to frighten crows and other birds away from crops. **2.** a person resembling a scarecrow, especially a very thin or ragged person.

scarf (skärf) *n., pl.* **scarves** or **scarfs.** **1.** a square, oblong, or triangular piece of cloth worn about the neck or head for warmth, protection, or adornment. **2.** a strip of cloth used to cover the top of a piece of furniture, such as a dresser or table.

scar·let (skär′lit) *n.* a bright red or orange-red color. —*adj.* having the color scarlet.

scarlet fever, a highly contagious disease occurring most often in children, marked by a scarlet rash, high fever, and a sore throat and caused by streptococci.

scarlet tanager, a North American songbird. The male in breeding plumage is bright red with black wings and tail.

scarp (skärp) *n.* **1.** a cliff or steep slope. **2.** a wall or steep slope at the outer part of a fortification. —*v.t.* to cut or make into a steep slope; form into a scarp.

scarves (skärvz) a plural of **scarf.**

scar·y (skâr′ē) *adj.,* **scar·i·er**, **scar·i·est**. *Informal.* **1.** causing alarm, fear, or uneasiness; frightening: *a scary movie.* **2.** marked by fear: *a scary feeling.* **3.** easily scared; timid.

scat (skat) *v.i.,* **scat·ted, scat·ting.** *Informal.* to go away quickly. ▲ usually used as a command.

scath·ing (skā′thing) *adj.* very severe or harsh: *scathing sarcasm, a scathing rebuke.* —**scath′ing·ly**, *adv.*

scat·ter (skat′ər) *v.t.* **1.** to spread or throw about here and there; strew: *A gust of wind scattered the leaves all over the yard.* **2.** to cause to separate and go off in different directions; disperse: *The gunshot scattered the flock of birds.* —*v.i.* to separate and go off in different directions: *The crowd scattered when the rain began.* —**scat′ter·er**, *n.*

scat·ter·brain (skat′ər brān′) *n.* a person who does not think clearly or seriously; silly, flighty, or forgetful person.

scat·ter·brained (skat′ər brānd′) *adj.* silly, flighty, or forgetful.

scat·ter·ing (skat′ər ing) *n.* a small, scattered number or amount.

scatter rug, a small rug used to cover part of a floor. Also, **throw rug.**

scav·enge (skav′ənj) *v.,* **scav·enged, scav·eng·ing.** —*v.i.* to search, as for food or something useful: *The raccoon scavenged for a meal among the garbage cans.* —*v.t.* **1.** to find or collect by searching: *The explorers scavenged any food they could to keep alive.* **2.** to search (something) for material that can be used: *to scavenge a ship's wreckage.*

scav·en·ger (skav′ən jər) *n.* **1.** an animal, such as a vulture or hyena, that feeds on decaying plant or animal matter. **2.** a person who searches through trash or discarded material for things that can be sold or used.

sce·nar·i·o (si nâr′ē ō′) *n., pl.* **sce·nar·i·os.** **1.** a script of a motion picture, especially a preliminary script giving an outline of the plot. **2.** a plot outline of any dramatic work. **3.** an outline for an action or series of events.

sce·nar·ist (si nâr′ist) *n.* a person who writes scenarios, especially for motion pictures.

scene (sēn) *n.* **1.** the place where an action or event occurs or has occurred: *the scene of an accident.* **2.** the place and time in which the action of a story, play, or motion picture occurs; setting: *The scene of this novel is Italy during the Renaissance.* **3.** a division of an act of a play, motion picture, or the like: *We left after the first scene of the second act.* **4.** an episode in a story, play, or motion picture. **5.** something presented to the eye; view: *The scene from the window was quite beautiful.* **6.** a display of strong feeling or unpleasant behavior, especially in public: *The angry child made a scene in the*

---

at; āpe; fär; câre; end; mē; it; īce; pîerce; hot; ōld; sông, fôrk; oil; out; up; ūse; rüle; pull; tûrn; chin; sing; shop; thin; <u>th</u>is; hw in white; zh in treasure. The symbol ə stands for the unstressed vowel sound heard in about, taken, pencil, lemon, and circus.

S

835

restaurant. **7.** a field of activity or interest: *the political scene.*
·**behind the scenes.** in private; secretly.

scen·er·y (sē′nə rē) *n., pl.* **scen·er·ies. 1.** the general appearance or visible features of a place, especially when striking or pleasing: *They drove to the mountains to look at the scenery.* **2.** backdrops or other structures used to create the setting of a play, motion picture, or the like.

sce·nic (sē′nik; *occasionally,* sen′ik) *adj.* **1.** of, relating to, or full of natural scenery; picturesque: *a scenic route through the mountains.* **2.** of or relating to stage scenery or effects.

scent (sent) *n.* **1.** a smell, especially an agreeable or delicate one: *the scent of lilacs.* **2.** a characteristic smell left behind by an animal or human, used in tracking. **3.** the trail or track by which someone or something can be traced or detected: *Some misleading clues threw the police off the scent of the gang.* **4.** the sense of smell. **5.** see **perfume** *(def. 1).* —*v.t.* **1.** to sense or know by smell: *The dogs scented the rabbit.* **2.** to get a hint or vague idea of: *to scent trouble.* **3.** to make fragrant: *The perfumed soap scented the drawer.*

scep·ter (sep′tər) *also, British,* **scep·tre.** *n.* **1.** a rod or staff carried by a king or queen and serving as a symbol of royal office or power. **2.** royal office or power.

scep·tic (skep′tik) *n.* another spelling of **skeptic.** —**scep′ti·cal,** *adj.* —**scep′ti·cal·ly,** *adv.*

scep·ti·cism (skep′tə siz′əm) another spelling of **skep·ticism.**

sched·ule (skej′ül) *n.* **1.** a list of the times when certain events are to take place: *a program schedule, a schedule of train departures.* **2.** a plan or group of things to do, or of events to occur at or during a particular time: *a busy social schedule.* **3.** the time planned upon or shown, as in a schedule: *The train was running behind schedule because of an accident.* **4.** a written or printed table or list, as of rates or prices: *a schedule of postal rates.* —*v.t.,* **sched·uled, sched·ul·ing. 1.** to place in or on a schedule: *The airline scheduled additional flights for the holidays.* **2.** to plan or arrange for a specified time: *I scheduled an appointment with my dentist for Friday.*

sche·mat·ic (skē mat′ik) *adj.* of, relating to, or in the form of a diagram or scheme; diagrammatic: *a schematic drawing.* —**sche·mat′i·cal·ly,** *adv.*

sche·ma·tize (skē′mə tīz′) *v.t.,* **sche·ma·tized, sche·ma·tiz·ing.** to form or arrange according to a scheme.

scheme (skēm) *n.* **1.** a program or course of action for doing something; plan: *a scheme for remodeling the house.* **2.** an underhanded or secret plan; plot: *The thieves have a scheme for robbing the bank.* **3.** an orderly arrangement of related parts or things; system; design: *to choose a color scheme for decorating a room.* —*v.,* **schemed, schem·ing.** —*v.t.* to plan (something), especially in an underhanded or secret way; plot. —*v.i.* to make a plan; plot. —**schem′er,** *n.*

scher·zo (sker′tsō) *n., pl.* **scher·zos** or **scher·zi** (sker′tsē). a playful, lively, or humorous movement or passage in a work of music, such as a symphony.

schism (siz′əm, skiz′əm) *n.* **1.** a division into opposing groups, especially a division within a church or other religious body. **2.** a sect or group that is formed by such a division.

schis·mat·ic (siz mat′ik, skiz mat′ik) *adj.* relating to or causing a schism. —*n.* a person who causes or takes part in a schism.

schist (shist) *n.* a rock that is easily split because of its layered structure. It has a high mica content.

schiz·o·phre·ni·a (skit′sə frē′nē ə) *n.* any of a group of mental disorders characterized by a severe withdrawal from reality, illogical thought processes, hallucinations, and delusions.

schiz·o·phren·ic (skit′sə fren′ik) *n.* a person who is suffering from schizophrenia. —*adj.* of, relating to, or characteristic of schizophrenia.

schmaltz (shmälts, shmôlts) *n. Informal.* extreme sentimentality, as in music or literature. [From the Yiddish word *shmalts* meaning "melted fat," from the German word *Schmalz* with the same meaning.]

schnau·zer (shnou′zər) *n.* a sturdy, short-haired dog having small, pointed ears and beardlike whiskers.

schol·ar (skol′ər) *n.* **1.** a person having much knowledge of, or considered to be an authority in, a particular field: *a noted Shakespearean scholar.* **2.** a person having much knowledge and an interest in learning and study. **3.** a person holding a scholarship. **4.** a person who attends school; student.

schnauzer

schol·ar·ly (skol′ər lē) *adj.* **1.** of, characteristic of, or suited to a scholar: *a scholarly life.* **2.** of, relating to, or based on much knowledge and learning: *a scholarly book.* **3.** having the qualities of a scholar; learned: *a scholarly person.* —**schol′ar·li·ness,** *n.*

schol·ar·ship (skol′ər ship′) *n.* **1.** a grant of financial aid given to a student to help defray the cost of studies: *The winner of the essay contest received a college scholarship.* **2.** knowledge acquired by study; learning: *The book shows the considerable scholarship of its author.*

scho·las·tic (skə las′tik) *adj.* of or relating to schools, scholars, or education: *scholastic standing, a scholastic award.* —**scho·las′ti·cal·ly,** *adv.*

school¹ (skül) *n.* **1.** a place for teaching and learning. **2.** a department or division of a college or university for instruction in a specialized field: *the school of medicine.* **3.** an institution for instruction in a particular field or skill: *an art school, a dancing school.* **4.** the building or group of buildings of a school. **5.** a period or time of instruction at a school: *There is no school today because of the holiday.* **6.** the process of being educated at school. **7.** the students, faculty, and other staff members of a school: *The entire school was gathered in the auditorium.* **8.** a group of people following the same methods, styles, or beliefs: *Claude Monet belongs to the impressionist school of painting.* —*v.t.* **1.** to train or teach, as in a school; educate. **2.** to bring under control; discipline: *Doctors must school themselves to be calm during emergencies.* [From the Old English word *scolu* meaning "a place for teaching and learning," from the Latin word *schola* "leisure given to learning," "a group of students," or "place for learning," from the Greek word *scholē* "leisure time," or "a gathering for learning."]

school² (skül) *n.* a large group of fish or water animals of the same kind swimming together: *a school of tuna, a school of porpoises.* [From the Middle Dutch word *schole* meaning "a group, troop."]

school board, a group of persons elected or appointed by the citizens of a community to oversee the public schools of the area.

school·book (skül′bùk′) *n.* a book used for study in schools; textbook.

school·boy (skül′boi′) *n.* a boy attending school.

school·child (skül′chīld′) *n., pl.* **school·chil·dren** (skül′chil′drən). a child attending school.

school day **1.** a day when school is in session: *Election day is not a school day in most states.* **2.** the part of a day in which school is in session: *The school day ends at 3 P.M.*

school·girl (skül′gûrl′) *n.* a girl attending school.

school·house (skül′hous′) *n., pl.* **school·hous·es** (skül′hou′ziz). a building used as a school.

school·ing (skü′ling) *n.* training at school; education: *to have little schooling.*

school·mas·ter (skül′mas′tər) *n.* a man who teaches in or heads a school.

school·mate (skül′māt′) *n.* a companion at school.

school·mis·tress (skül′mis′tris) *n., pl.* **school·mis·tress·es.** a woman who teaches in or heads a school.

school·room (skül′rüm′, skül′rüm′) *n.* a room in a school in which classes are held.

school·teach·er (skül′tē′chər) *n.* a person who teaches in a school, especially below the college level.

school·work (skül′wûrk′) *n.* lessons or assignments given to a student at school.

school·yard (skül′yärd′) *n.* a yard or playground of a school.

school year, that part of the year during which school is in session, usually from September to June.

schooner *(def. 1)*

schoon·er (skü′nər) *n.* **1.** a ship that has two or more masts and fore-and-aft sails. **2.** a large beer glass.

schot·tische (shot′ish) *n.* **1.** a dance resembling the polka. **2.** the music for this dance.

schuss (shùs, shüs) *v.i.* to ski down a straight, steep course without decreasing speed.

schwa (shwä) *n.* **1.** a vowel sound occurring in many syllables in English that are pronounced without any stress, such as the *a* in *ago* or the *o* in *lemon.* **2.** the symbol (ə) representing this sound. Also, **neutral vowel.**

sci. **1.** science. **2.** scientific.

sci·at·ic (sī at′ık) *adj.* **1.** of, relating to, or affecting the ischium, or lowest portion of the hipbone. **2.** affecting the hip or the sciatic nerve.

sci·at·i·ca (sī at′i kə) *n.* pain in the area of the sciatic nerve and its branches, usually caused by injury or infection.

sciatic nerve, the largest nerve of the body, extending along the back part of the thigh and lower leg.

sci·ence (sī′əns) *n.* **1.** the body of knowledge and theory dealing with things in nature and the universe, and with the forces that create, shape, and form them. Science is based on facts that are obtained from experiments and careful study. **2.** any particular branch of this body of knowledge, such as physics, chemistry, or biology. **3.** any activity or skill that may be studied like a science: *Some say that chess is a science, not just a game.*

science fiction, a story or stories based on actual or imaginary happenings or discoveries in science, usually dealing with such subjects as travel in space and life in the future.

sci·en·tif·ic (sī′ən tif′ik) *adj.* **1.** of, relating to, derived from, or used in science: *a scientific theory.* **2.** based on or using the principles and methods of science; systematic; exact: *to take a scientific approach to a problem.*

sci·en·tif·i·cal·ly (sī′ən tif′i kə lē, sī′ən tif′i klē) *adv.* in a scientific manner.

scientific method, the method of research used by scientists, in which a problem is stated, a hypothesis is formed, data are collected through observation or experimentation, and the hypothesis is proved or disproved by analysis of the data.

sci·en·tist (sī′ən tist) *n.* a student of or an expert in science, especially a person who engages in some branch of science as a profession: *a laboratory scientist, a teaching scientist.*

sci-fi (sī′fī′) *Informal. n.* science fiction. —*adj.* of or relating to science fiction.

scim·i·tar (sim′i tər) *also,* **scim·i·ter.** *n.* a curved, single-edged sword of Asian origin.

scin·til·la (sin til′ə) *n.* a very small amount; trace: *There was not a scintilla of truth in that story.*

scin·til·late (sin′tə lāt′) *v.,* **scin·til·lat·ed, scin·til·lat·ing.** —*v.i.* **1.** to be brilliant: *That author's stories scintillate with wit.* **2.** to give off sparks or flashes of light; sparkle: *The rushing stream scintillated in the morning sun.* —*v.t.* to give off as a flash or flashes. —**scin′til·la′tion,** *n.*

scin·til·la·ting (sin′tə lā′ting) *adj.* brilliant; animated: *a scintillating conversation.*

sci·on (sī′ən) *n.* **1.** *also,* **cion.** a bud, or a branch having one or more buds, cut from a plant and used for grafting onto the stock of another plant. **2.** a descendant; heir: *the wealthy scion of a noble family.*

scis·sor (siz′ər) *v.t.* to cut with scissors. —*n.* see **scissors.**

scis·sors (siz′ərz) *pl. n.* a cutting instrument having two blades with looped handles that are fastened together by a bolt and form a cutting edge when they are closed over each other.

scle·ra (sklîr′ə) *n., pl.* **scle·ras.** a tough, white membrane covering all of the surface of the eyeball, except for the cornea.

scle·ro·sis (skli rō′sis) *n., pl.* **scle·ro·ses** (skli rō′sēz). the abnormal hardening of a tissue or part of the body, such as the wall of an artery.

scoff (skof, skôf) *v.i.* to express ridicule or contempt; mock; jeer: *to scoff at a foolish suggestion.* —*n.* a mocking expression. —**scoff′er,** *n.*

scoff·law (skof′lô′, skôf′lô′) *n.* a person who disregards the law, as by not paying fines or taxes.

scold (skōld) *v.t.* to find fault with; speak sharply to; reprimand: *The teacher scolded the class for talking in the library.* —*n.* a person who scolds.

sco·li·o·sis (skō′lē ō′sis) *n.* an abnormal sideways curving of the spine.

scol·lop (skol′əp) another spelling of **scallop.**

at; āpe; fär; câre; end; mē; it; īce; pîerce; hot; ōld; sông, fôrk; oil; out; up; ūse; rüle; pùll; tûrn; chin; sing; shop; thin; this; hw in white; zh in treasure. The symbol ə stands for the unstressed vowel sound heard in about, taken, pencil, lemon, and circus.

S

sconce (skons) *n.* a wall bracket or fixture used for holding a candle or other light.

scone (skōn) *n.* a small, often round biscuit.

scoop (skūp) *n.* **1.** a utensil shaped like a small shovel, used chiefly for taking up loose material or powdery substances, such as flour or sugar. **2.** a utensil shaped like a deep, rounded cup attached to a handle, used for taking up portions of food, such as ice cream. **3.** a large bucket of a dredge or steam shovel, used for taking up and depositing a load, as of dirt. **4.** the amount taken up in a scoop: *to ask for a scoop of ice cream.* **5.** a dipping or sweeping movement: *to pick up the pebbles with a scoop of the hand.* **6.** *Informal.* a news story reported first or exclusively, as by a newspaper, magazine, television network, or television network. —*v.t.* **1.** to take up or out with a scoop. **2.** to gather with a sweeping motion: *I scooped up my books and left the house.* **3.** *Informal.* to get the better of (another newspaper, magazine, television network, or reporter) by reporting a news story first or exclusively.

sconce

scoop·ful (skūp′fůl′) *n., pl.* **scoop·fuls.** the amount that a scoop holds: *three scoopfuls of ice cream.*

scoot (skūt) *v.i.* *Informal.* to go hurriedly; dart: *The rabbit scooted off into the woods.*

scoot·er (skū′tər) *n.* **1.** a vehicle having a narrow footboard mounted on two wheels and a handle for steering. It is made to move by pushing one foot against the ground while resting the other foot on the board. **2.** see **motor scooter.**

scope (skōp) *n.* **1.** the range within which something applies or extends; area covered: *That topic is not within the scope of today's discussion.* **2.** the range of a person's ability to understand or act; grasp: *The article on nuclear physics was beyond my scope.* **3.** opportunity or room for expression, development, or action.

-scope *combining form* an instrument for viewing or examining: *microscope.*

scorch (skôrch) *v.t.* **1.** to burn slightly so as to change the appearance or taste of: *The hot iron scorched the tablecloth. The cook scorched the pudding.* **2.** to dry up or wither with heat; parch: *The hot summer sun scorched the grass.* —*n., pl.* **scorch·es.** a slight burn.

scorch·er (skôr′chər) *n.* **1.** *Informal.* a very hot day. **2.** a person or thing that scorches.

score (skôr) *n.* **1.** a record of points made in a game or contest: *The score after six innings was 5 to 4.* **2.** the number of points made by one side or person in such a game or contest. **3.** a grade or rating on a test or examination: *What was your score on the spelling test?* **4.** a set or group of twenty: *a score of years.* **5.** **scores.** a large number; very many: *Scores of people flock to the beach every summer.* **6.** a debt, grievance, or wrong to be settled or revenged. **7.** account; ground; basis: *You have nothing to fear on that score.* **8.** a notch, line, or other mark. **9.** written or printed music. **10.** the music for a motion picture, stage production, or the like. —*v.,* **scored, scor·ing.** —*v.t.* **1.** to make or gain (points) in a game or contest. **2.** to keep a record of points made in (a game or contest). **3.** to check and give a grade to: *The teacher scored the examination.* **4.** to make a particular grade: *Several students scored 100 percent on the spelling test.* **5.** to make notches, lines, or other marks on. **6.** to criticize severely: *The newspapers scored the mayor for the town's financial problems.* **7.** to arrange (music), as for a particular voice or instrument: *The composer scored the sonata for piano and guitar.* —*v.i.* **1.** to make or

gain a point or points in a game or contest. **2.** to achieve an advantage or success. —**scor′er,** *n.*

score·board (skôr′bôrd′) *n.* a large board on which the score of a game or contest, and often other important information, is shown.

score·card (skôr′kärd′) *n.* a card on which the scores of players in a game or contest are recorded.

score·keep·er (skôr′kē′pər) *n.* a person who keeps the score during a game or contest.

scorn (skôrn) *n.* a feeling of hatred or contempt for someone or something considered low, bad, or vile: *to feel scorn for a dishonest politician.* —*v.t.* **1.** to treat or consider as low, bad, or vile; despise: *to scorn a coward.* **2.** to refuse or reject with contempt: *to scorn an offer.*

scorn·ful (skôrn′fəl) *adj.* showing or feeling scorn; contemptuous. —**scorn′ful·ly,** *adv.* —**scorn′ful·ness,** *n.*

Scor·pi·o (skôr′pē ō′) *n.* **1.** a constellation in the southern sky, thought to resemble a scorpion in shape. **2.** the eighth sign of the zodiac.

scor·pi·on (skôr′pē ən) *n.* any of a group of animals related to the spider, having a long, segmented tail that ends in a poisonous stinger. Scorpions are found in temperate and tropical regions.

Scot (skot) *n.* a person who was born in or is a citizen of Scotland. ▲ **Scot, Scotsman,** and **Scotswoman** are preferred as nouns referring to the people of Scotland, who object to the nouns *Scotchman* and *Scotchwoman.*

scotch (skoch) *v.t.* **1.** to put an end to; crush: *The army was sent to scotch the rebellion.* **2.** to injure so as to make harmless.

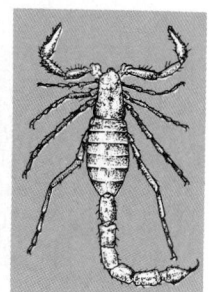
scorpion

Scotch (skoch) *n.* **1.** see **Scottish** (*def.* 1). **2.** *also,* **scotch.** a whiskey distilled in Scotland. —*adj.* another term for **Scottish.** ▲ See **Scottish** for usage note.

Scotch·man (skoch′mən) *n., pl.* **Scotch·men** (skoch′-mən). another word for **Scotsman.** ▲ See **Scot** for usage note.

Scotch tape, a cellulose tape, usually transparent and with adhesive on only one side, used for fastening and sealing. Trademark: **Scotch.**

Scotch terrier, another term for **Scottish terrier.**

Scotch·wom·an (skoch′wům′ən) *n., pl.* **Scotch·wom·en** (skoch′wim′ən). another word for **Scotswoman.** ▲ see **Scot** for usage note.

scot-free (skot′frē′) *adj.* free from injury, loss, punishment, or other penalty: *The bank robber got away scot-free.*

Scot·land Yard (skot′lənd) **1.** the police department of London, especially the branch that investigates crime. **2.** its headquarters.

Scots (skots) *adj.* another term for **Scottish.** —*n.* see **Scottish** (*def.* 2).

Scots·man (skots′mən) *n., pl.* **Scots·men** (skots′mən). see **Scot.** Also, **Scotchman.**

Scots·wom·an (skots′wům′ən) *n., pl.* **Scots·wom·en** (skots′wim′ən). a woman who was born in or is a citizen of Scotland.

Scot·tie (skot′ē) another term for **Scottish terrier.**

Scot·tish (skot′ish) *n.* **1. the Scottish.** the people of Scotland. **2.** the dialect of English spoken in Scotland. Also (*def.* 2), **Scots, Scottish English.** —*adj.* of, relating to, or characteristic of Scotland, its people, their language, or culture. ▲ **Scottish, Scots,** and **Scotch** are the adjectives that refer to Scotland. **Scottish** and **Scots** are preferred when referring to the people of Scotland, who object to the adjective *Scotch.* **Scotch** is acceptable when referring to things from Scotland, as in such combinations as *Scotch plaid* and *Scotch whisky.*

Scottish Gaelic, the form of Gaelic spoken in Scotland.

Scottish terrier, a small, short-legged dog having a large head, pointed ears, and a rough coat of black, gray, or light tan hair. It is believed to be the oldest breed of dog native to Britain. Also, **Scotch terrier, Scottie.**

Scottish terrier

scoun·drel (skoun′drəl) *n.* a wicked, base, or dishonest person; villain; rogue. —**scoun′drel·ly,** *adj.*

scour¹ (skour) *v.t.* **1.** to rub (something) vigorously in order to clean, wash, or brighten it: *to scour a pot with a pad of steel wool.* **2.** to remove by rubbing in this manner: *to scour the tarnish off an old silver cup.* **3.** to clean, clear, or wear away, as with flowing water: *The water from melting snow scoured a channel down the mountainside.* —*v.i.* to rub vigorously in order to clean, wash, or brighten. —*n.* the act of scouring. [From the Middle Dutch word *scūren* meaning "to clean."]

scour² (skour) *v.t.* to go or move over or through, especially in making a thorough search: *Police scoured the countryside for the missing child.* [From the Middle English word *scuren* meaning "to rush about searching," from the word *scour* "an attack," of Scandinavian origin.]

scourge (skûrj) *n.* **1.** a whip; lash. **2.** a cause of much suffering or destruction: *War has been a scourge of humanity for centuries.* —*v.t.,* **scourged, scourg·ing. 1.** to whip; lash. **2.** to punish or criticize severely. **3.** to cause suffering or destruction to; afflict; ravage.

scout¹ (skout) *n.* **1.** a person or thing sent out to gather and bring back information, such as a soldier, ship, or aircraft sent out during wartime to gather information about the enemy. **2.** a person sent out to find new talent, especially in sports or entertainment. **3.** *also,* **Scout,** a member of the Boy Scouts or Girl Scouts. —*v.i.* to make a search; hunt: *We scouted around to see what we could find to eat.* —*v.t.* to look at or explore in order to obtain information: *The two soldiers went ahead to scout the enemy camp.* [From the Old French word *escouter* meaning "to hear, listen to," going back to the Latin word *auscultare* "to listen attentively."]

scout² (skout) *v.t.* to reject with scorn: *to scout someone's idea as ridiculous.* [Of Scandinavian origin.]

scout·ing (skou′ting) *also,* **Scout·ing.** *n.* the activities of the Boy Scouts or Girl Scouts.

scout·mas·ter (skout′mas′tər) *n.* the adult leader of a troop of scouts, especially of Boy Scouts.

scow (skou) *n.* a large, flat-bottomed boat with square ends. It is usually pushed or towed and is used chiefly for carrying freight.

Scow

scowl (skoul) *n.* an expression of anger or disapproval; a sullen or angry frown. —*v.i.* to have a look of anger or disapproval; frown angrily: *to scowl at a rude person.* —*v.t.* to express with a scowl: *to scowl an objection to something.*

scrab·ble (skrab′əl) *v.i.,* **scrab·bled, scrab·bling. 1.** to scratch or scrape about with hands, feet, or paws: *The dog scrabbled in the dirt for the bone.* **2.** to struggle; strive.

scrag (skrag) *n.* **1.** a thin, scrawny person or animal.

2. a lean, bony piece of meat, especially of mutton or veal.

scrag·gly (skrag′lē) *adj.,* **scrag·gli·er, scrag·gli·est.** having a ragged, sparse, or rough appearance: *a scraggly beard, a scraggly lawn.*

scrag·gy (skrag′ē) *adj.,* **scrag·gi·er, scrag·gi·est. 1.** thin and bony; scrawny. **2.** rough or jagged in appearance; scraggly. —**scrag′gi·ness,** *n.*

scram (skram) *v.i.,* **scrammed, scram·ming.** *Slang.* to leave quickly or immediately. ▲ usually used as a command.

scram·ble (skram′bəl) *v.,* **scram·bled, scram·bling.** —*v.t.* **1.** to mix together in a confused way; mix up: *to scramble the pieces of a jigsaw puzzle.* **2.** to fry (eggs) with the whites and yolks mixed together. **3.** to alter (a message-carrying wave) so that only a special receiver can reproduce the message. —*v.i.* **1.** to make one's way quickly or frantically: *The hikers scrambled down the rocks along the stream.* **2.** to struggle or compete with others: *Many countries were scrambling to increase exports.* **3.** to get airplanes into the air on short notice to intercept enemy aircraft. —*n.* **1.** the act of moving or climbing quickly or frantically. **2.** a struggle or competition: *There was a scramble for the best seats in the theater.* —**scram′bler,** *n.*

scrap¹ (skrap) *n.* **1.** a small piece or fragment; bit: *The wastebasket was full of scraps of paper.* **2. scraps.** leftover or discarded bits of food. **3.** used or discarded metal that may be used again by melting and refining: *to sell an old car for scrap.* **4.** any material that is left over or discarded as trash, or that can be reprocessed for reuse. —*v.t.,* **scrapped, scrap·ping. 1.** to discard or abandon as useless, worthless, or ineffective: *to scrap an idea.* **2.** to make scrap of: *to scrap an old battleship.* [From the Old Norse word *skrap* meaning "leftovers from a meal" or "a tidbit."]

scrap² (skrap) *Informal. n.* a noisy quarrel or disagreement. —*v.i.,* **scrapped, scrap·ping.** to take part in a scrap; fight: *The dog and the cat scrapped.* [Perhaps a form of *scrape.*] —**scrap′per,** *n.*

scrap·book (skrap′buk′) *n.* a book with blank pages on which pictures, newspaper clippings, or other items may be pasted.

scrape (skrāp) *v.,* **scraped, scrap·ing.** —*v.t.* **1.** to injure or damage the surface of by rubbing against something sharp or rough: *to fall and scrape one's knee, to scrape a fender against a tree.* **2.** to draw, move, or rub (something) roughly or forcefully or with a harsh, grating sound: *to scrape a chair on the floor.* **3.** to move or rub roughly or with a harsh, grating sound on or across (something): *The spoon scraped the bottom of the pot.* **4.** to rub (a surface), as with something sharp or abrasive, in order to remove an outer layer or make smooth or clean: *to scrape dinner plates.* **5.** to remove by rubbing in this manner: *to scrape old paint off a wall.* **6.** to collect, gather, or produce with difficulty or serious effort: *to scrape up some money for a trip.* —*v.i.* **1.** to move or rub roughly or with a harsh, grating sound: *The car's broken exhaust pipe scraped along the ground.* **2.** to manage or make one's way barely or with difficulty: *The couple scraped by on their small income.* —*n.* **1.** a mark made on a surface by scraping. **2.** a harsh, grating sound made by scraping. **3.** the act of moving or rubbing roughly or with a harsh, grating sound. **4.** a difficult,

at; āpe; fär; câre; end; mē; it; īce; pîerce; hot; ōld; sông, fôrk; oil; out; up; ūse; rüle; pull; tûrn; chin; sing; shop; thin; **this**; hw in white; zh in treasure. The symbol **ə** stands for the unstressed vowel sound heard in about, taken, pencil, lemon, and circus.

S

troublesome, or unpleasant situation: *to be in a scrape and need help.* [From the Old Norse word *skrapa* with the same meaning.]

scrap·er (skrā′pər) *n.* **1.** any of various tools or devices for cleaning or smoothing a surface, or for removing paint or other matter. **2.** a person or thing that scrapes.

scrap·ple (skrap′əl) *n.* a boiled mixture of ground pork, cornmeal or flour, and seasonings, which is chilled until firm and then sliced and fried.

scrap·py[1] (skrap′ē) *adj.*, **scrap·pi·er, scrap·pi·est.** made up of scraps or fragments; fragmentary. [*Scrap*[1] + *-y*[1].] —**scrap′pi·ness,** *n.*

scrap·py[2] (skrap′ē) *adj.*, **scrap·pi·er, scrap·pi·est.** *Informal.* **1.** full of fighting spirit; aggressive: *a scrappy puppy.* **2.** inclined to scrap or quarrel; quarrelsome. [*Scrap*[2] + *-y*[1].] —**scrap′pi·ly,** *adv.* —**scrap′pi·ness,** *n.*

scratch (skrach) *v.t.* **1.** to cut, mark, or mar with something rough, sharp, or pointed: *The broken glass scratched the table top.* **2.** to scrape, tear, or wound with the nails or claws: *The cat scratched the dog's nose.* **3.** to rub or scrape in order to relieve itching: *to scratch someone's back.* **4.** to cause to feel itchy or irritated: *This wool scarf scratches my neck.* **5.** to strike out or cancel: *Scratch that name off the list.* **6.** to write or draw by scraping or cutting into a surface: *to scratch someone's initials on a tree.* **7.** to write hurriedly or carelessly: *to scratch a note.* **8.** to withdraw (an entry) from a race or other competition: *to scratch a horse.* —*v.i.* **1.** to dig, scrape, or wound, as with the nails or claws: *The chickens scratched in the dirt for corn.* **2.** to rub or scrape a part of the body to relieve itching. **3.** to rub with a harsh, grating sound: *We could hear the puppy scratching at the door.* **4.** to become cut, marked, or scraped: *a plastic that scratches easily.* —*n., pl.* **scratch·es. 1.** a mark made by scratching: *a scratch on a table, a scratch on one's leg.* **2.** a harsh, grating sound: *The scratch of the branch against the windowpane startled us.* —*adj.* used for quick, rough, or informal writing or sketching: *scratch paper.*

·**from scratch.** from the beginning; from nothing: *They started a successful business from scratch.*

scratch test, any of various tests to show if a person is allergic to something, made by rubbing a particular substance into small scratches made in the skin.

scratch·y (skrach′ē) *adj.*, **scratch·i·er, scratch·i·est. 1.** causing itching: *a scratchy wool sweater.* **2.** making a harsh, grating sound: *a scratchy phonograph record.* **3.** not regular or even: *scratchy handwriting.* —**scratch′i·ly,** *adv.* —**scratch′i·ness,** *n.*

scrawl (skrôl) *v.t.* to write or draw (something) hastily or carelessly in a sprawling, irregular way: *to scrawl a note.* —*n.* irregular, sprawling, almost unreadable handwriting. —**scrawl′er,** *n.*

scraw·ny (skrô′nē) *adj.*, **scraw·ni·er, scraw·ni·est.** thin, bony, or undersized; skinny: *a scrawny old mule.* —**scraw′ni·ness,** *n.*

scream (skrēm) *v.i.* **1.** to make a loud, shrill, piercing cry, especially from fright or pain. **2.** to shout or speak loudly or shrilly. —*v.t.* to utter with a loud, shrill, piercing sound: *to scream a plea for help.* —*n.* **1.** a loud, shrill, piercing cry or sound: *a scream of terror, the scream of a train whistle.* **2.** *Informal.* a very funny person or thing. —**scream′er,** *n.*

scream·ing (skrē′ming) *adj.* **1.** boldly striking; startling: *a screaming headline, a screaming red color.* **2.** uttering screams. **3.** *Informal.* very funny: *a screaming comedy.* —**scream′ing·ly,** *adv.*

screech (skrēch) *v.i.* to make a shrill, high-pitched sound. —*v.t.* to make or express with a shrill, high-pitched sound: *to screech a warning.* —*n., pl.* **screech·es.** a shrill, high-pitched sound: *the screech of brakes.*

screech owl

screech owl, a small brown or gray North American owl having tufts of feathers on its forehead and a wavering, whistling call.

screech·y (skrē′chē) *adj.*, **screech·i·er, screech·i·est.** like a screech; shrill: *a screechy voice.*

screen (skrēn) *n.* **1.** mesh or netting, usually of wire and enclosed in a frame: *a window screen, a screen in front of a fireplace.* **2.** a frame or a series of frames hinged together, often used as a room divider or as an ornament. **3.** anything that serves to separate, conceal, or protect. **4.** a surface that reflects light, on which motion pictures or slides may be projected. **5.** a surface on which the image is displayed in a cathode-ray tube, such as that of a television, computer monitor, or radar set. **6.** the motion-picture industry; motion pictures: *The play was adapted for the screen.* **7.** a sieve used for sifting or grading gravel, sand, and the like. —*v.t.* **1.** to provide with a screen: *They screened the porch to keep out insects.* **2.** to hide or protect with or as if with a screen: *We screened our eyes from the sun with our hands.* **3.** to sift or grade by passing through a screen: *to screen gravel.* **4.** to block, remove, or filter as if by a screen: *The earth's atmosphere screens out much of the sun's radiation.* **5.** to examine carefully or systematically, especially so as to make a selection: *The personnel manager screened applicants for the job.* **6.** to show (a motion picture) on a screen. —**screen′er,** *n.* —**screen′like′,** *adj.*

screen·play (skrēn′plā′) *n.* a script written for television or motion pictures.

screen test, a short scene filmed to test a person's ability as a television or motion-picture actor.

screen·writ·er (skrēn′rī′tər) *n.* a writer of screenplays.

screw (skrü) *n.* **1.** a fastening device consisting of a rod, usually made of metal, that has a spiraling thread or groove cut into it and a head, usually slotted, at one end. It is driven into place by being twisted or turned, as with a screwdriver. **2.** a simple machine, consisting of a cylinder with a spiraling thread cut into it, to be fitted into a hole or socket cut with a matching thread. **3.** something like a screw in shape or function. **4.** a twist or turn of a screw. **5.** the propeller of a boat or ship. —*v.t.* **1.** to attach or fasten with a screw or screws: *The worker screwed a lock to the door.* **2.** to insert, attach,

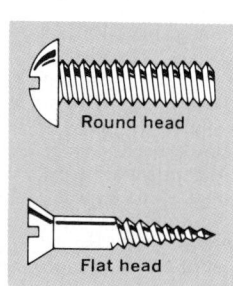

Round head

Flat head

screws *(n., def. 1)*

or fix (a screw or other threaded or grooved object) in place by a twisting or turning motion: *Screw the cap back on the tube of toothpaste.* **3.** to twist out of shape; contort: *to screw up one's mouth with displeasure.* **4.** to call forth or gather with difficulty; muster: *to screw up one's courage and ask for a raise.* —*v.i.* **1.** to become attached or fastened by means of a screw or screws: *The towel rack screws to the wall.* **2.** to become inserted, attached, or fixed in place by a twisting or turning motion: *The light bulb screws into the socket.* —**screw′like′**, *adj.*

·**to have a screw loose.** *Informal.* to be odd, eccentric, or crazy.

·**to put the screws on.** *Informal.* to exert pressure or force on.

screw·ball (skrü′bôl′) *n.* **1.** *Informal.* an odd, eccentric, or crazy person. **2.** *Baseball.* a pitch that breaks in a direction opposite to a curve ball. —*adj.* eccentric; irrational: *a screwball plan that will never succeed.*

screw·driv·er (skrü′drī′vər) *n.* a tool for turning screws.

screw propeller, a device consisting of a hub with blades mounted at an angle, used to propel certain boats and aircraft.

screw·y (skrü′ē) *adj.,* **screw·i·er, screw·i·est.** *Informal.* odd; crazy; eccentric. —**screw′i·ness,** *n.*

scrib·ble (skrib′əl) *v.,* **scrib·bled, scrib·bling.** —*v.t.* to write or draw (something) carelessly or hastily: *to scribble notes while trying to speak.* —*v.i.* to make meaningless marks: *to scribble on a pad.* —*n.* writing, drawing, or marks made by scribbling. —**scrib′bler,** *n.*

scribe (skrīb) *n.* **1.** before the invention of printing, a person whose profession was writing down or copying letters, manuscripts, contracts, or other documents **2.** a public clerk or secretary. **3.** a writer; author. **4.** a teacher who interpreted the Mosaic law among the ancient Hebrews. —*v.t.,* **scribed, scrib·ing.** to mark with a scriber or other pointed instrument.

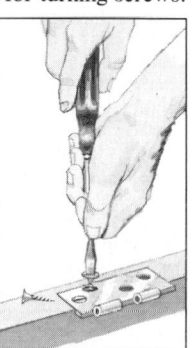

screwdriver

scrib·er (skrī′bər) *n.* a pointed steel tool for marking on material, such as wood or metal, that is to be cut.

scrim (skrim) *n.* a loosely woven cotton or linen fabric used especially for curtains and bunting.

scrim·mage (skrim′ij) *n.* **1.** *Football.* the play that occurs from the time the ball is snapped back until it is called dead. **2.** a practice session taking the form of a game, as in football and other sports. —*v.i.,* **scrim·maged, scrim·mag·ing.** to participate in a scrimmage. [This word is a variant of the word *skirmish,* from the Old French word *escaramuch* meaning "small battle, skirmish," going back to a Germanic word meaning "to defend."]

·**line of scrimmage.** in football, the imaginary line separating the two teams at the beginning of a play.

scrimp (skrimp) *v.i.* to be very sparing or economical: *to scrimp and save for a new bike.* —*v.t.* to be very sparing of or with.

scrimp·y (skrim′pē) *adj.,* **scrimp·i·er, scrimp·i·est.** skimpy; scanty; meager.

scrim·shaw (skrim′shô′) *n.* **1.** the art of carving or engraving designs, often nautical scenes or motifs, on whalebone, ivory, or shell. This work was done especially by sailors during long whaling or other voyages. **2.** articles decorated in this way. —*v.t.* to carve or engrave into scrimshaw. —*v.i.* to make scrimshaw.

scrip (skrip) *n.* **1.** a certificate, token, or the like issued in place of money, to be exchanged for goods or services. **2.** paper money issued for temporary use in times of emergency.

script (skript) *n.* **1.** writing in which the letters are joined together; cursive handwriting. **2.** any of various styles of type resembling this. **3.** a writing system or style: *Babylonian script, Gothic script.* **4.** a typed or written text of a play, motion picture, or radio or television program, that is used by the performers, director, and other members of the production staff.

Scrip·tur·al (skrip′chər əl) *also,* **scrip·tur·al.** *adj.* of, based on, or according to Scripture or any sacred writings.

Scrip·ture (skrip′chər) *n.* **1.** *also,* **the Scriptures.** the books of the Old and New Testaments; the Bible. **2.** *also,* **scripture.** a book or body of writings sacred to a religion.

scrive·ner (skriv′nər) *n. Archaic.* a clerk; scribe.

scrod (skrod) *n.* a young cod or haddock prepared for cooking.

scroll (skrōl) *n.* **1.** a roll of parchment, paper, silk, or other material, especially one with writing on it, often wound around a rod or a pair of rods so as to be conveniently used or stored. **2.** a figure or ornamental design resembling a partly unrolled scroll, such as the curved head on a violin. —*v.i. Computers.* to move characters displayed on a computer screen horizontally or vertically, as in locating specific information: *to scroll slowly through an alphabetical file.* —**scroll′-like′,** *adj.*

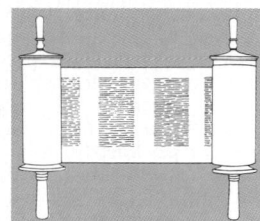

scroll (def. 1)

scroll saw, a saw having a narrow blade with fine teeth, used to cut curved or intricate patterns in thin wood.

scroll·work (skrōl′wûrk′) *n.* ornamental work consisting chiefly of scroll-like patterns, especially such work cut with a scroll saw.

Scrooge (skrüj) *also,* **scrooge.** *n.* a nasty, mean-tempered miser. [From the mean-tempered miser Ebenezer Scrooge in Charles Dickens's story *A Christmas Carol* (1843).]

scro·tum (skrō′təm) *n., pl.* **scro·ta** (skrō′tə) or **scro·tums.** the external sac of skin and muscle that contains the testicles in most male mammals.

scrounge (skrounj) *Slang. v.,* **scrounged, scroung·ing.** —*v.t.* **1.** to get, collect, or gather with effort or difficulty or by foraging: *to scrounge up money to buy a ticket.* **2.** to borrow (something) without intending to return or repay: *to scrounge a meal.* —*v.i.* to search; forage: *I scrounged around in the drawer and found my gloves.*

scrub¹ (skrub) *v.,* **scrubbed, scrub·bing.** —*v.t.* **1.** to rub vigorously in order to wash or clean: *to scrub a floor.* **2.** to remove by such rubbing: *to scrub the ink stains off a shirt.* **3.** to cleanse (a gas or vapor) of impurities. **4.** *Informal.* to postpone or cancel: *to scrub a missile launch.* —*v.i.* to wash or clean something by hard rubbing. —*n.* the act of scrubbing. [Probably of Scandinavian origin.]

scrub² (skrub) *n.* **1.** low, stunted trees or shrubs. **2.** an undersized person, animal, or thing. **3.** a player who is not a member of the first or regular team. —*adj.* **1.** undersized, stunted, or inferior: *a scrub tree, scrub cows.* **2.** relating to, made up of, or played by players not on the first or regular team. [From the Middle English word *scrub,* a form of *shrubbe* meaning "shrub."]

at; āpe; fär; câre; end; mē; it; īce; pîerce; hot; ōld; sông, fôrk; oil; out; up; ūse; rüle; pull; tûrn; chin; sing; shop; thin; this; hw in white; zh in treasure. The symbol ə stands for the unstressed vowel sound heard in about, taken, pencil, lemon, and circus.

841

scrub·ber (skrub′ər) *n.* a person or thing that scrubs, especially an apparatus for cleansing gas of impurities.

scrub·by (skrub′ē) *adj.,* **scrub·bi·er, scrub·bi·est.** **1.** undersized, stunted, or inferior: *a scrubby bush.* **2.** covered with or consisting of scrub. **3.** unfair or mean; shabby: *a scrubby trick.* —**scrub′bi·ness,** *n.*

scruff (skruf) *n.* the back of the neck or the skin covering it: *to grab someone by the scruff of the neck.*

scruff·y (skruf′ē) *adj.,* **scruff·i·er, scruff·i·est.** worn or dirty; shabby.

scrump·tious (skrump′shəs) *adj. Informal.* very pleasing or delightful, especially to the taste; delectable.

scru·ple (skrü′pəl) *n.* **1.** a feeling of doubt, hesitancy, or uneasiness of mind that arises from a person's conscience and often restrains or inhibits action: *to have no scruples about spreading rumors.* **2.** a very small amount or portion. **3.** an apothecaries' weight equal to 20 grains, or ¹⁄₂₄ of an ounce (1.295 grams). —*v.i.,* **scru·pled, scrupling.** to hesitate because of scruples; have scruples.

scru·pu·lous (skrü′pyə ləs) *adj.* **1.** having or showing a strict regard for what is right: *to be scrupulous about telling the truth.* **2.** very careful of small details; painstaking: *scrupulous neatness, a scrupulous report.* —**scru′pu·lous·ly,** *adv.* —**scru′pu·lous·ness,** *n.*

scru·ti·nize (skrü′tə nīz′) *v.t.,* **scru·ti·nized, scru·ti·niz·ing.** to look at or examine closely or critically; inspect carefully or minutely: *The immigration officer scrutinized the passport.* —**scru′ti·niz′er,** *n.*

scru·ti·ny (skrü′tə nē) *n., pl.* **scru·ti·nies.** close, critical study, examination, or inquiry; careful inspection: *The suspect's movements were under the scrutiny of the police.*

scu·ba (skü′bə) *n.* a portable underwater breathing device consisting of one or more cylinders of compressed air that are fastened on a diver's back, and a hose or hoses for transmitting the air to a mouthpiece. —*adj.* of or relating to a scuba or to scuba diving: *a scuba tank, scuba equipment.* [Short for *s*(elf) *c*(ontained) *u*(nderwater) *b*(reathing) *a*(pparatus).]

scuba diver, a person who engages in scuba diving.

scuba diving, swimming underwater for long periods of time with a scuba.

scud (skud) *v.i.,* **scud·ded, scud·ding.** **1.** to run or move swiftly: *The clouds scudded across the sky.* **2.** *Nautical.* to run before a gale with little or no sail set. —*n.* **1.** the act of scudding or moving swiftly. **2.** light clouds, spray, or rain driven swiftly before the wind. [Of Scandinavian origin.]

scuff (skuf) *v.t.* to scratch, mar, or roughen the surface of by scraping or wear: *to scuff one's shoes on the gravel.* —*v.i.* **1.** to walk by dragging the feet; shuffle: *The child scuffed along to school.* **2.** to

scuba diving

become scratched, marred, or roughened by scraping or wear: *This tile scuffs easily.* —*n.* the act of scuffing.

scuf·fle (skuf′əl) *n.* a confused, often rough struggle or fight: *Their angry shouts and pushing started a scuffle.* —*v.i.,* **scuf·fled, scuf·fling.** to struggle or fight at close quarters in a rough, confused manner.

scull (skul) *n.* **1.** an oar used to propel a boat by working it from side to side over the stern. **2.** one of a pair of light oars used together, one on each side of a boat, by a single rower. **3.** a small boat propelled by sculls, especially a light racing boat propelled by one or more rowers. —*v.t., v.i.* to propel (a boat) by a scull or sculls. —**scull′er,** *n.*

scul·ler·y (skul′ə rē) *n., pl.* **scul·ler·ies.** a place, often a small room adjoining a kitchen, where cooking utensils are cleaned and stored and other kitchen chores are done.

scul·lion (skul′yən) *n. Archaic.* **1.** a servant employed to wash cooking utensils and do other menial work in a kitchen. **2.** a low, contemptible person; wretch.

sculpt (skulpt) *v.t., v.i.* to sculpture: *to sculpt a statue.*

sculp·tor (skulp′tər) *n.* a person who produces sculpture.

sculp·tur·al (skulp′chər əl) *adj.* of, relating to, or like sculpture.

sculp·ture (skulp′chər) *n.* **1.** the act or process of making figures or designs, as by carving or chiseling stone or marble, modeling in clay or wax, or casting in bronze or a similar metal. **2.** a figure or design so made. **3.** such figures or designs as a group. —*v.,* **sculp·tured, sculptur·ing.** —*v.t.* **1.** to carve or otherwise form (a figure or design) by means of sculpture. **2.** to make a sculpture of. **3.** to ornament or cover with sculpture. —*v.i.* to produce sculpture.

scum (skum) *n.* **1.** a filmy layer that forms on or rises to the surface of a liquid or body of water: *A green scum floated in the harbor.* **2.** a low, vile, despicable person or persons. —*v.i.,* **scummed, scum·ming.** to become covered with or form scum: *The pond scummed over.*

scum·my (skum′ē) *adj.,* **scum·mi·er, scum·mi·est.** **1.** covered with, containing, or like scum. **2.** low; vile; despicable.

scup (skup) *n., pl.* **scup** or **scups.** a commercially important food fish found along the eastern coast of the United States.

scup·per (skup′ər) *n.* a hole in the side of a ship that allows water to drain off the deck. [Of uncertain origin.]

scup·per·nong (skup′ər nông′, skup′ər nong′) *n.* a pale green grape that tastes like a plum, grown in the southeastern United States.

scurf (skûrf) *n.* **1.** dead, flaky skin, especially dandruff. **2.** any scaly or flaky matter sticking to a surface.

scur·ril·i·ty (skə ril′i tē) *n., pl.* **scur·ril·i·ties.** **1.** the quality of being scurrilous. **2.** something that is scurrilous.

scur·ri·lous (skûr′ə ləs) *adj.* indecent and coarse; vulgar: *scurrilous language, a scurrilous attack on a person's character.* —**scur′ri·lous·ly,** *adv.* —**scur′ri·lous·ness,** *n.*

scur·ry (skûr′ē) *v.i.,* **scur·ried, scur·ry·ing.** to go or move hurriedly: *The deer scurried off into the woods.* —*n., pl.* **scur·ries.** the act of scurrying.

scur·vy (skûr′vē) *n.* a disease caused by a lack of vitamin C in the diet, characterized by spongy and bleeding gums, bleeding under the skin, and extreme weakness. —*adj.,* **scur·vi·er, scur·vi·est.** mean and vile; contemptible; base.

scut (skut) *n.* a short tail, as of a rabbit or deer.

scut·tle¹ (skut′əl) *v.t.,* **scut·tled, scut·tling.** **1.** to cause (a boat or ship) to sink by cutting, boring, or uncovering an opening in the bottom, deck, or sides. **2.** to abandon or destroy: *to scuttle one's plans.* —*n.* **1.** an opening, especially in the deck, side, or compartment of a ship, usually having a movable cover. **2.** a lid or cover for such an opening. [From the Middle English word *skottell* meaning "a hatch" or "opening," from the Old French word *escoutille* with the same meaning, probably of Germanic origin.]

scut·tle² (skut′əl) *n.* see **coal scuttle.** [From the Old English word *scutel* meaning "a dish, bowl," from the Latin word *scutella* "a metal food tray."]

scut·tle³ (skut′əl) *v.i.,* **scut·tled, scut·tling.** to go or move with short, rapid steps: *Crabs scuttled across the sand.* —*n.* a short, hurried run. [A form of the English dialect word *scuddle* with the same meaning, from the word *scud.*]

scut·tle·butt (skut′əl but′) *n. Informal.* rumor; gossip.

Scyl·la (sil′ə) *n. Greek Mythology.* a monster having six heads and twelve feet, that lived in a cave on the Strait of Messina, opposite the monster Charybdis. Sailors passing through the strait risked being drowned by Charybdis or snatched from their ships and devoured by Scylla.
·**between Scylla and Charybdis.** caught between two dangers, neither of which can be avoided without confronting the other.

scythe (sīth) *n.* an implement consisting of a long, curved blade attached at an angle to a long, bent handle, used for mowing, cutting, or reaping. —*v.t.,* **scythed, scyth·ing.** to mow or cut with a scythe: *to scythe grass.*

SD, postal abbreviation for South Dakota.

S. Dak., South Dakota. Also, **S.D.**

Se, the symbol for selenium.

SE, s.e., southeast; southeastern.

sea (sē) *n.* **1.** the continuous body of salt water that covers nearly three fourths of the earth's surface; the ocean. **2.** a large portion of this, partly enclosed by land, such as the Caribbean Sea or the Aegean Sea. **3.** a large inland body of salt or fresh water, such as the Sea of Galilee or the Caspian Sea. **4.** the condition of the ocean's surface, especially with regard to the motion of the waves: *a calm sea, a stormy sea.* **5.** a large, heavy swell or wave: *The ship foundered in rough seas.* **6.** an overwhelming quantity or number: *a sea of troubles.* **7.** see **mare².** —*adj.* of or relating to the sea: *a sea breeze, a sea animal.*
·**at sea. a.** out on the ocean. **b.** at a loss, in confusion.

sea anemone, any of a group of marine animals, related to jellyfish, that attach themselves to rocks, wharves, and other objects. Sea anemones have numerous, brightly colored tentacles that bear stinging cells and are used to stun prey.

sea bass (bas) any of a group of saltwater fish that have spiny fins and are important food and game fish.

sea·bed (sē′bed′) *n.* the ground at the bottom of the sea; ocean bed.

Sea·bee (sē′bē′) *n.* a member of a U.S. Navy construction battalion that is made up of skilled workers of all trades who build and maintain various installations, such as shipyards and ammunition depots. [A form of *C.B.,* the abbreviation of *C*(onstruction) *B*(attalion).]

sea·bird (sē′bûrd′) *n.* a bird whose principal habitat is the open ocean, such as an albatross or petrel.

sea biscuit, another term for **hardtack.**

sea·board (sē′bôrd′) *n.* land near or bordering on the sea; seacoast: *the Atlantic seaboard.*

sea breeze, a breeze blowing inland from the sea.

sea·coast (sē′kōst′) *n.* land near or bordering on the sea.

sea cow **1.** an extinct sea-dwelling mammal, related to the dugong and manatee, with a huge body, front flippers, and a flat, broad tail. **2.** see **dugong.** **3.** see **manatee.**

sea cucumber, a cucumber-shaped animal found in coastal waters. It has a flexible body with several tentacles around the mouth that are used to capture food.

sea dog, a sailor, especially an old or experienced one.

sea·far·er (sē′fâr′ər) *n.* a person engaged in seafaring, especially a sailor.

sea·far·ing (sē′fâr′ing) *adj.* **1.** following the sea as a business or calling: *a seafaring merchant.* **2.** of or relating to the sea or to life or work as a sailor. **3.** traveling on the sea: *a seafaring ship.* Also, **seagoing.** —*n.* **1.** the life or work of a sailor. **2.** travel by sea.

sea·food (sē′fūd′) *n.* saltwater fish or shellfish used for food.

sea·girt (sē′gûrt′) *adj.* surrounded by the sea.

sea·go·ing (sē′gō′ing) *adj.* **1.** designed, suitable, or used for sea travel. **2.** another word for **seafaring.**

sea green, a medium bluish green color.

sea gull, see **gull¹.**

sea horse **1.** any of various slender fish found in warm and temperate seas, having a head that resembles that of a horse and a tail that is used for clinging to underwater plants. **2.** another term for **walrus.** **3.** a mythical sea creature, half fish and half horse.

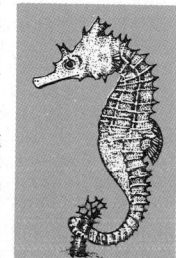

sea horse
(def. 1)

seal¹ (sēl) *n., pl.* **seals** or **seal.** **1.** any of several sea mammals having a long body, a muscular neck, and limbs that are modified to form flippers. Some seals are hunted for their valuable fur. **2.** the skin or fur of such an animal. **3.** leather made from the hide of such an animal. —*v.i.* to hunt seals, especially for their fur. [From the Old English word *seolh* meaning this animal.] —**seal′er,** *n.*

seal² (sēl) *n.* **1.** the impression of a design, figure, or word stamped on wax, paper, or other soft material to show ownership or authenticity, intended to officially represent a person, institution, or governing body. **2.** the representation of such an impression, or a disk or wafer of wax, paper, or other material bearing such an impression, put on a document to prove authenticity or to close or fasten it tightly. **3.** a stamp, die, ring, or other object engraved with a design, figure, or word, used to make such impressions. **4.** something that fastens securely, closes completely, or makes airtight or watertight: *the seal on an envelope, the seal on a jar.* **5.** a decorative gummed stamp or sticker. —*v.t.* **1.** to fasten or close securely, as to make airtight or watertight: *to seal an envelope.* **2.** to fill or obstruct; stop up: *The painter sealed the cracks in the wall.* **3.** to shut in or confine; enclose tightly: *They sealed the documents in a strongbox.* **4.** to confirm, conclude, or settle: *to seal a bargain with a handshake.* **5.** to put beyond doubt, question, or reversal; decide definitely: *The testimony of the eyewitness sealed the defendant's fate.* **6.** to place a seal on, as to prove authenticity: *The notary sealed the application, as required by law.* [From the Old French word *seel* meaning "a guarantee," from the Latin word *sigillum* "a sign, mark¹" or "seal²," from the word *signum* "a sign, mark¹" or "seal².''] —**seal′er,** *n.*

at; āpe; fär; câre; end; mē; it; īce; pîerce; hot; ōld; sông, fôrk; oil; out; up; ūse; rüle; pu̇ll; tûrn; chin; sing; shop; thin; th̲is; hw in white; zh in treasure. The symbol ə stands for the unstressed vowel sound heard in about, taken, pencil, lemon, and circus.

sea legs *Informal.* the ability to walk steadily aboard ship, especially on rough seas.

sea level, the mean level of the surface of the sea, especially halfway between mean high and low water. Land elevations and sea depths are measured as so many feet above or below sea level.

sealing wax, a mixture usually made of shellac and turpentine, that softens when heated but quickly hardens as it cools. It is used to seal letters, packages, and jars.

sea lion, any of various large seals with ears, found chiefly in the Pacific Ocean.

seal·skin (sēl'skin') *n.* the skin or fur of certain seals that are hunted for their pelts.

seam (sēm) *n.* **1.** a line formed by sewing together the edges of two or more pieces of cloth, leather, or similar material: *the seam of a dress.* **2.** a similar line, groove, or ridge formed by joining edges, as of planks or layers of bricks. **3.** any mark, line, or ridge resembling a seam. **4.** a thin layer or stratum: *a seam of coal, a seam of rock.* —*v.t.* **1.** to join together by sewing. **2.** to mark with a seam or seams; furrow: *Time had seamed the old sailor's face.* —*v.i.* to become furrowed; crack open. —**seam'less,** *adj.*

sea lion

sea·man (sē'mən) *n., pl.* **sea·men** (sē'mən). **1.** a sailor; mariner. **2.** in the U.S. Navy and Coast Guard, an enlisted person of any of the three lowest grades.

sea·man·ship (sē'mən ship') *n.* skill in and knowledge of managing or sailing a boat or ship.

sea mew, see **mew²**.

sea mile, another term for **nautical mile.**

seam·stress (sēm'stris) *n., pl.* **seam·stress·es.** a woman who is skilled at sewing, especially one whose occupation is sewing.

seam·y (sē'mē) *adj.,* **seam·i·er, seam·i·est.** **1.** dismal, squalid, or low in status; sordid: *the seamy side of life.* **2.** having or showing seams. —**seam'i·ness,** *n.*

sé·ance (sā'äns) *n.* a meeting in which a group of people try to communicate with the spirits of the dead through the help of a medium.

sea otter, a dark brown otter found along the western coast of North America and around offshore islands of the Pacific, having broad hind feet that resemble flippers. It is the largest of all otters and the only one that lives in salt water.

sea·plane (sē'plān') *n.* an airplane, especially one equipped with floats, that is designed to take off from and land on water. Also, **hy·droplane** (def. 2).

sea·port (sē'pôrt') *n.* **1.** a port or harbor for seagoing vessels. **2.** a city or town having such a port or harbor.

seaplane

sear (sîr) *v.t.* **1.** to burn the surface of; char; scorch: *to sear a steak.* **2.** to dry up or wither: *The hot sun seared the grass.* **3.** to harden or make callous: *The war seared the young soldier's feelings.* —*n.* a mark made by searing or burning. —*adj. Archaic.* dried; sere.

search (sûrch) *v.t.* **1.** to look through or explore carefully and thoroughly in order to find something: *We searched the whole gymnasium for the lost basketball.* **2.** to look into or examine carefully and closely; probe: *to search one's heart for forgiveness.* —*v.i.* to look carefully and thoroughly: *to search through one's pockets, to search for a lost cat.* —*n., pl.* **search·es.** the act of searching: *They found the missing child after a long search.* —**search'er,** *n.*

search·ing (sûr'ching) *adj.* **1.** very observant and penetrating: *a searching glance.* **2.** examining and probing carefully: *searching questions.* —**search'ing·ly,** *adv.*

search·light (sûrch'līt') *n.* **1.** a device that projects a strong beam of light. **2.** such a beam of light.

search warrant, a court order authorizing the search of a house or other building for wanted persons or stolen or unlawfully held property.

sea·scape (sē'skāp') *n.* **1.** a picture or painting showing a view of the sea. **2.** a view of the sea.

sea serpent, any of various legendary sea monsters resembling a snake.

sea·shell (sē'shel') *n.* the shell of a sea animal, such as an oyster or clam.

sea·shore (sē'shôr') *n.* land near or bordering on the sea.

sea·sick (sē'sik') *adj.* nauseated and dizzy as a result of the rolling motion of a boat or ship. —**sea'sick'ness,** *n.*

sea·side (sē'sīd') *n.* land bordering on the sea; seashore.

sea snake, any of a group of poisonous snakes found in the inshore seas of Asia, having a tail that resembles a fin.

sea·son (sē'zən) *n.* **1.** one of the divisions of the year, as determined by the position of the earth in its orbit around the sun. The four seasons, spring, summer, autumn, and winter, are characterized chiefly by differences in weather, temperature, and the number of hours of daylight. **2.** a period or time of the year with reference to the weather conditions that characterize it: *the dry season, the monsoon season.* **3.** any period or time of the year marked by a particular activity or thing: *the football season, the opera season.* **4.** a proper, suitable, or usual time. —*v.t.* **1.** to add seasoning in order to bring out, heighten, or improve flavor: *to season meat with salt and pepper.* **2.** to add zest or interest to: *The teacher seasoned the lecture with anecdotes.* **3.** to make suitable for use, as by drying or aging: *to season timber.* **4.** to condition or make fit through experience. **5.** to make accustomed: *to season troops to battle.* —*v.i.* to become more suitable for use. [From the Old French word *seson* meaning "season of the year," going back to the Latin word *satio* meaning "sowing" or "seed-time." Originally, *season* meant "the season of spring, planting time." Later this word came to mean any particular period of time or portion of the year.]

·**in season. a.** available or in the best condition for eating: *Peaches are in season.* **b.** legally permitted to be hunted or caught: *Deer are now in season.*

·**out of season.** not in season.

sea·son·a·ble (sē'zə nə bəl) *adj.* **1.** usual for or in keeping with the time of year: *Seasonable temperatures are expected through Friday.* **2.** done, happening, or coming at the right or proper time; timely. —**sea'son·a·ble·ness,** *n.* —**sea'son·a·bly,** *adv.*

sea·son·al (sē'zə nəl) *adj.* affected by, characteristic of, or happening at a certain season or seasons: *Harvesting cherries provides only seasonal employment.* —**sea'son·al·ly,** *adv.*

sea·son·ing (sē'zə ning) *n.* **1.** something used to bring out, heighten, or improve the flavor of food, as a spice, herb, or condiment. **2.** something that adds zest or interest.

season ticket, a ticket for a seat for an entire season or series of scheduled performances, as of sporting events or concerts.

seat (sēt) *n.* **1.** something to sit on, such as a chair, stool, or bench. **2.** a place to sit: *Those who arrive late will have to find seats on the floor.* **3.** that part of an object on which one sits: *the seat of a chair.* **4.** that part of the body on which one sits or the part of the clothes covering it: *the seat of a pair of trousers.* **5.** a membership or official position: *a seat in the Senate, a seat on the stock exchange.* **6.** a reserved place for sitting: *We have two seats for the afternoon performance.* **7.** a center or source: *A college is a seat of learning. The capital is the seat of government for the country.* **8.** a manner of sitting, as on horseback. —*v.t.* **1.** to place on or lead to a seat; assign a seat to: *I carefully seated the child on a stool. The ushers seated all the wedding guests.* **2.** to have seats for: *The auditorium seats 200 people.* **3.** to put a seat in or on. **4.** to fit in place firmly or properly.

seat belt, a strap or set of straps that may be buckled to hold a person in the seat of an automobile or other vehicle in case of a crash or jolt. Also, **safety belt.**

seat·ing (sē′ting) *n.* **1.** the arrangement of seats: *The new auditorium has excellent seating for 600 people.* **2.** the assignment of seating: *The host paid great attention to the seating of guests at the table.* **3.** the act of conducting to or providing with seats: *Ushers are responsible for the seating of wedding guests.*

sea urchin, any of a group of sea animals having a shell covered with hard, movable spines.

sea wall, a strong wall or embankment made to prevent waves from wearing away the shoreline or to act as a breakwater.

sea·ward (sē′wərd) *adj.* toward the sea: *a seaward course.* —*adv.* also, **sea·wards** (sē′wərdz). in the direction of the sea: *The explorers walked seaward.*

sea·wa·ter (sē′wô′tər) *n.* the salt water of a sea or ocean.

sea·way (sē′wā′) *n.* **1.** a route over the sea; shipping lane. **2.** an inland waterway deep and wide enough for large ships. **3.** the headway of a ship or boat.

sea·weed (sē′wēd′) *n.* any of various plants or algae living in the sea.

sea·wor·thy (sē′wûr′thē) *adj.* fit or safe to sail on the sea: *a seaworthy ship.* —**sea′wor′thi·ness,** *n.*

se·ba·ceous (si bā′shəs) *adj.* **1.** of or relating to oil or fat; oily; greasy. **2.** secreting oil or fat.

sebaceous gland, any of the glands of the skin that secrete an oily substance to the skin and hair.

sec, secant.

sec, 1. second. **2.** secondary. **3.** secretary. **4.** section.

se·cant (sē′kant, sē′kənt) *n.* **1.** *Trigonometry.* **a.** (of either acute angle of a right triangle) the ratio of the length of the hypotenuse to the length of the side adjacent to the angle. **b.** a straight line drawn from the center of a circle through one end point of an arc to the tangent drawn from the other end point of the same

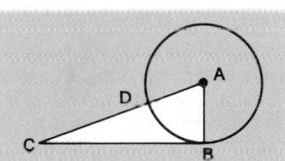

secant of angle $A = AC/AB$

arc. **2.** *Geometry.* a line intersecting a curve at two or more points. —*adj.* that intersects; intersecting.

se·cede (si sēd′) *v.i.,* **se·ced·ed, se·ced·ing.** to withdraw formally, especially as a group, from an organization, usually to form an alternative organization. [From the Latin word *secedere* meaning "to withdraw," from the prefix *se-* "apart, aside" + *cedere* "to go, depart, retire."]

se·ces·sion (si sesh′ən) *n.* **1.** an act or instance of seceding. **2.** also, **Secession.** the withdrawal of eleven Southern states from the Union in 1860 and 1861, leading to the Civil War.

se·ces·sion·ist (si sesh′ə nist) *n.* **1.** a person who favors or supports secession. **2.** a member of a group that

secedes. —*adj.* relating to, favoring, or supporting secession or the beliefs or principles of secessionists.

se·clude (si klüd′) *v.t.,* **se·clud·ed, se·clud·ing.** to keep apart or remove from the company of others; isolate: *to seclude oneself in a room to study.*

se·clud·ed (si klü′did) *adj.* **1.** shut off or screened from view: *The yard was secluded from the street by trees.* **2.** kept apart or removed from others; solitary: *to lead a secluded life.* —**se·clud′ed·ness,** *n.*

se·clu·sion (si klü′zhən) *n.* the act of secluding or the state of being secluded.

sec·ond¹ (sek′ənd) *adj.* **1.** (the ordinal of the number two) next after the first: *Our team finished in second place.* **2.** additional or other; another: *a second helping of potatoes, a second chance.* **3.** below the first or best: *the second pitcher on the baseball team.* **4.** *Music.* of, relating to, or performing a part lower in pitch than or subordinate to another: *second violin, second soprano.* **5.** of or relating to the forward gear next above first or low in a motor vehicle. —*adv.* in the group or position next after the first: *to finish second in a race.* —*n.* **1.** a person or thing that is next after the first: *I was the second to arrive at the party.* **2.** a person who aids or supports another, as in a duel or prizefight. **3.** *also,* **seconds.** goods below the first or best quality: *These towels are seconds.* **4.** the forward gear next above first or low in a motor vehicle. **5.** *Music.* **a.** a note that is one degree above a given note. D is the second of C. **b.** an interval of one degree. **c.** a combination of two notes that are separated by this interval. —*v.t.* **1.** to approve or support formally; endorse: *to second a motion to adjourn.* **2.** to give support, encouragement, or assistance to: *The city council seconded the mayor's efforts to have a new hospital built.* [From the Old French word *second,* from the Latin word *secundus* meaning "subsequent, following, second¹," from the Latin word *sequi* "to follow."] —**sec′ond·er,** *n.*

sec·ond² (sek′ənd) *n.* **1.** a unit of time equal to ¹⁄₆₀ of a minute or ¹⁄₃₆₀₀ of an hour. **2.** any very short interval of time: *It will take me only a second to put on my coat.* **3.** ¹⁄₆₀ of a minute or ¹⁄₃₆₀₀ of a degree of angular measurement. [From the Medieval Latin word *secundum* meaning this portion of a degree or of time.]

Second Advent, another term for **Second Coming.**

sec·ond·ar·y (sek′ən der′ē) *adj.* **1.** coming from or based on something that is original or primary; derived: *information from secondary sources.* **2.** coming below or after the first in order, place, importance, or time: *a secondary fact.* **3.** not main or chief; less important: *a secondary cause.* **4.** of or relating to an electrical coil in which a current is produced by induction when the current in a primary coil changes. —**sec′ond·ar′i·ly,** *adv.*

secondary accent 1. the weaker of the two stresses in any word that has two accented or stressed syllables. The third syllable of **sec′ond·ar′y** has a secondary accent. **2.** the mark (′) showing this accent.

secondary color, any color that results from the mixing of two primary colors, such as green or orange.

secondary school, a school providing instruction after elementary or grade school, made up of grades seven, eight, or nine through twelve.

secondary sex characteristic, any of the physical

at; āpe; fär; câre; end; mē; it; īce; pîerce; hot; ōld; sông; fôrk; oil; out; up; ūse; rüle; pull; tûrn; chin; sing; shop; thin; this; hw in white; zh in treasure. The symbol ə stands for the unstressed vowel sound heard in about, taken, pencil, lemon, and circus.

S

845

features not related to reproduction that are characteristic of each sex and usually appear at puberty, such as breast development or beard growth.

sec·ond-best (sek'ənd best') *adj.* next or inferior to the best.

sec·ond-class (sek'ənd klas') *adj.* **1.** less than the first or best; inferior: *a second-class baseball player*. **2.** of or relating to a class of mail consisting primarily of newspapers and magazines. **3.** of or relating to a form of travel ranking next in price or luxury below first class. —*adv.* by second-class mail or travel accommodations: *The tourist traveled second-class.*

second class 1. by means of second-class travel accommodations. **2.** by means of second-class mail.

Second Coming, the expected return of Jesus on Judgment Day to judge the living and the dead. Also, **Second Advent.**

sec·ond-de·gree burn (sek'ənd di grē'), a burn of the outer and second layers of the skin; a burn that causes blistering.

sec·ond-guess (sek'ənd ges') *v.t.* to make judgments about (some decision or the person who made it) after the results of that decision are known.

sec·ond·hand (sek'ənd hand') *adj.* **1.** owned, used, or worn by someone else: *a secondhand car*. **2.** not obtained from the original source; derivative; borrowed: *secondhand knowledge of an incident from eyewitness reports*. **3.** dealing in used goods: *a secondhand furniture store*. —*adv.* in a secondhand manner; indirectly: *We heard the facts secondhand.*

second hand, the hand or pointer of a clock or watch that shows seconds as it moves around the dial.

second lieutenant, a commissioned officer of the lowest rank in the U.S. Army, Air Force, or Marine Corps, ranking below a first lieutenant.

sec·ond·ly (sek'ənd lē) *adv.* in the second place.

second nature, a habit or quality that is so deeply fixed that it seems to be part of a person's nature.

second person, the form of a pronoun or verb that indicates the person being addressed. In the sentence *You were out when I called, you* and *were* are in the second person.

sec·ond-rate (sek'ənd rāt') *adj.* not best in some quality or degree; mediocre or inferior: *The team played second-rate defense and lost the game.*

se·cond-string (sek'ənd string') *adj.* **1.** playing for a team as an alternate or substitute: *a second-string fullback*. **2.** not preferred or best; mediocre; second-rate.

second wind, renewed energy after a brief rest: *Now that I've got my second wind, we can finish chopping the logs.*

se·cre·cy (sē'krə sē) *n.* **1.** the state of being secret or being kept secret. **2.** the ability or practice of keeping secrets.

se·cret (sē'krit) *adj.* **1.** known only to oneself or a few; kept from general knowledge: *a secret password, a secret report, a secret plan*. **2.** acting in a hidden way: *a secret agent, a secret organization*. **3.** dependable in keeping to oneself what one knows; reticent. —*n.* **1.** something known only to oneself or a few and kept from general knowledge: *to keep a secret*. **2.** a hidden reason or explanation: *the secret of success*. **3.** a cause or process not readily understood or explained; mystery: *the secrets of nature*. [From the Latin word *secretus* meaning "hidden, concealed," from the word *secernere* "to separate, dissociate" or "set apart."] —**se'cret·ly,** *adv.*
  ·**in secret.** not openly or in public; in private: *to meet in secret.*

secret agent 1. a member of a secret service. **2.** a spy.

sec·re·tar·i·al (sek'ri târ'ē əl) *adj.* of or relating to a secretary or a secretary's duties.

sec·re·tar·i·at (sek'ri târ'ē it) *n.* **1.** the administrative department of an organization: *the secretariat of the United Nations*. **2.** the officials who keep records or perform secretarial duties. **3.** the office or position of a secretary, especially the secretary of a government department.

sec·re·tar·y (sek'ri ter'ē) *n., pl.* **sec·re·tar·ies. 1.** a person employed to handle correspondence, keep records, and the like for an individual or company. **2.** an officer of an organization or company responsible for important records and correspondence. **3.** a person who heads an executive department of a government: *the Secretary of Agriculture*. **4.** a piece of furniture having a writing surface, drawers or compartments, and often bookshelves.

secretary bird, a large, long-legged African bird having a crest of feathers at the back of its head. [Named because its crest reminded people of the quill pens that secretaries of former times used to stick behind their ears.]

secretary (def. 4)

sec·re·tar·y-gen·er·al (sek'-ri ter'ē jen'ər əl) *n., pl.* **sec·re·tar·ies-gen·er·al.** the chief administrative officer of a secretariat.

se·crete[1] (si krēt') *v.t.,* **se·cret·ed, se·cret·ing.** to produce by means of secretion: *Some glands secrete hormones.* [From *secretion*.]

se·crete[2] (si krēt') *v.t.,* **se·cret·ed, se·cret·ing.** to put in a hiding place; hide away: *to secrete documents in a safe.* [A form of the obsolete verb to *secret*, from *secret*.]

se·cre·tion (si krē'shən) *n.* **1.** the process by which a cell or gland in an organism produces and releases a particular substance for use by the organism. **2.** the substance so produced. **3.** the act of secreting; hiding. [From the Latin word *secretio* meaning "a separation, dividing," from the word *secernere* "to separate, dissociate" or "set apart."]

se·cre·tive (sē'kri tiv, si krē'tiv) *adj.* **1.** of, characterized by, or indicating secrecy or concealment: *a secretive smile.* **2.** another word for **secretory.** —**se'cre·tive·ly,** *adv.* —**se'cre·tive·ness,** *n.*

se·cre·to·ry (si krē'tə rē) *adj.* relating to, producing, or causing secretion.

secret police, a police force that operates mainly in secret, often using terrorism to suppress opposition to its government's political policies.

Secret Service 1. a division of the U.S. Treasury Department that protects the president and other important people and enforces federal laws against counterfeiting U.S. currency and bonds. **2. secret service.** a government department or bureau that makes secret investigations.

secs. 1. seconds. **2.** sections.

sect (sekt) *n.* **1.** a religious body, especially a small group separated from a large, established church. **2.** any relatively small group that shares the same principles, beliefs, or opinions.

sect., section.

sec·tar·i·an (sek târ'ē ən) *adj.* **1.** of, relating to, or limited to one small and narrow group: *sectarian ideas*. **2.** of or relating to a religious sect: *a sectarian college*. —*n.* a person who belongs to a religious sect.

sec·tar·i·an·ism (sek târ′ē ə niz′əm) *n.* the practice of being sectarian.

sec·tion (sek′shən) *n.* **1.** a part of something separated or cut off from the rest; portion: *to plant vegetables in one section of a garden.* **2.** a division of something written: *the sports section of a newspaper.* **3.** a part, piece, or unit that fits together with others: *The plumber replaced a leaky section of the pipe.* **4.** a distinctive part of a nation, community, area, or group of people: *the financial section of a city, the violin section of an orchestra.* **5.** a drawing or other representation of something as it would appear if cut through to show its inner structure. **6.** the act of cutting. **7.** a measure of public land equal to one square mile, or 640 acres (259 hectares), and making up 1/36 of a township. —*v.t.* to divide, as by separating or cutting into parts: *The farmer sectioned off the pasture from the rest of the farm.*

sec·tion·al (sek′shə nəl) *adj.* **1.** of, coming from, or characteristic of different regions or areas: *sectional interests.* **2.** made up of several sections or parts fitting into one another: *a sectional cabinet.* —**sec′tion·al·ly,** *adv.*

sec·tion·al·ism (sek′shə nə liz′əm) *n.* too great a concern for the local interests of a particular region or area.

sec·tor (sek′tər) *n.* **1.** a particular division or part: *the industrial sector of a country.* **2.** *Geometry.* a plane figure bounded by two radii of a circle and the intercepted arc. **3.** a distinct military area within which a military unit operates and for which it is responsible. **4.** *Computers.* a part of one of the circular tracks on a disk where data are stored.

sec·u·lar (sek′yə lər) *adj.* **1.** of or relating to affairs considered separately from church or religion; worldly: *secular education, secular interests.* **2.** (of clergy) living in an outside community, not in a monastery or other religious community: *a secular priest.* —**sec′u·lar·ly,** *adv.*

sec·u·lar·ize (sek′yə lə rīz′) *v.t.,* **sec·u·lar·ized, sec·u·lar·iz·ing.** to make secular; separate from religion or religious institutions. —**sec′u·lar·i·za′tion,** *n.*

se·cure (si kyùr′) *adj.* **1.** not likely to be taken away; certain or guaranteed: *a secure job.* **2.** safe from danger or harm, as of loss or attack: *The cellar was a secure place to be during the hurricane.* **3.** free from worry, care, or fear: *to feel secure about one's future.* **4.** not likely to give way; stable: *The house stands on a secure foundation.* —*v.t.,* **se·cured, se·cur·ing. 1.** to get; obtain: *I secured two tickets to the football game.* **2.** to put or fasten firmly: *to secure doors and windows for the night.* **3.** to bring about; effect: *The lawyer secured the prisoner's release by putting up bail.* **4.** to make safe; guard; protect: *The gold shipments were secured against theft by armed guards.* [From the Latin word *securus* meaning "safe, secure, sure," from the words *se* "apart, without" + *cura* "care."] —**se·cure′ly,** *adv.* —**se·cure′ness,** *n.*

se·cu·ri·ty (si kyùr′i tē) *n., pl.* **se·cu·ri·ties. 1.** protection from danger, as of loss or attack: *the security of a fortress.* **2.** freedom from worry, care, or fear: *Their savings account gave the couple a feeling of security.* **3.** measures taken to guard against something, such as crime: *Security is provided by a high fence around the property.* **4.** *usually,* **securities.** a stock or bond certificate: *to sell securities through a broker.* **5.** property given as a pledge, as for repayment of a loan. **6.** a person who agrees to be financially responsible for another.

security blanket 1. a blanket or other familiar object carried around by a child to give a feeling of security. **2.** any person or thing that gives a sense of comfort or security.

secy. *also,* **sec′y.** secretary.

se·dan (si dan′) *n.* an automobile with two or four doors and a full-width seat in both the front and the back.

sedan chair, an enclosed chair suspended on poles carried by two men, as one used in the seventeenth and eighteenth centuries.

sedan chair

se·date (si dāt′) *adj.* quiet and serious; calm: *a sedate judge.* —*v.t.,* **se·dat·ed, se·dat·ing.** to calm, as with a sedative: *to sedate a patient.* —**se·date′ly,** *adv.* —**se·date′ness,** *n.*

se·da·tion (si dā′shən) *n.* **1.** the state of being sedated: *The patient is under sedation.* **2.** the act of sedating.

sed·a·tive (sed′ə tiv) *n.* a drug or medicine that lessens nervousness, excitement, or distress. —*adj.* lessening nervousness, excitement, or distress; soothing; calming.

sed·en·tar·y (sed′ən ter′ē) *adj.* **1.** not used to physical exercise, activity, or movement: *a sedentary person.* **2.** requiring little or no physical activity: *Most office jobs are sedentary.* **3.** remaining in one area; not migratory: *sedentary birds.* —**sed′en·tar′i·ness,** *n.*

Se·der (sā′dər) *n.* in Judaism, a religious service and ceremonial feast held during Passover to commemorate the Exodus from Egypt.

sedge (sej) *n.* any of a large group of grassy plants growing in marshes and other wet areas.

sed·i·ment (sed′ə mənt) *n.* **1.** matter that settles to the bottom of a liquid; dregs. **2.** *Geology.* solid matter, such as rocks or earth, deposited by water, ice, or wind.

sed·i·men·tar·y (sed′ə men′tə rē) *adj.* **1.** of or relating to sediment. **2.** formed by the deposit of sediment: *sedimentary rock.*

sed·i·men·ta·tion (sed′ə mən tā′shən) *n.* the act or process of depositing sediment.

se·di·tion (si dish′ən) *n.* a speech or action causing discontent or rebellion against the existing government.

se·di·tious (si dish′əs) *adj.* **1.** taking part in or guilty of sedition. **2.** of, relating to, or containing sedition: *a seditious document, a seditious speech.* —**se·di′tious·ly,** *adv.*

se·duce (si dūs′, si dūs′) *v.t.,* **se·duced, se·duc·ing. 1.** to tempt or persuade to do wrong: *The witness was seduced by bribes to give false evidence at the trial.* **2.** to persuade to engage in sexual intercourse. —**se·duc′er,** *n.*

se·duc·tion (si duk′shən) *n.* **1.** the act of seducing or the state of being seduced. **2.** something that seduces.

se·duc·tive (si duk′tiv) *adj.* tending to seduce; alluring; enticing. —**se·duc′tive·ly,** *adv.* —**se·duc′tive·ness,** *n.*

sed·u·lous (sej′ə ləs) *adj.* working industriously; diligent: *The sedulous employee spent many evenings and weekends in the office.* —**sed′u·lous·ly,** *adv.*

see¹ (sē) *v.,* **saw, seen, see·ing.** —*v.t.* **1.** to become aware of or notice with the eyes; look at: *I cannot see the road signs in this fog.* **2.** to be aware of with the mind; understand: *I do not see why you have to leave so*

---

at; āpe; fär; câre; end; mē; it; īce; pîerce; hot; ōld; sông, fôrk; oil; out; up; ūse; rüle; pùll; tûrn; chin; sing; shop; thin; this; hw in white; zh in treasure. The symbol ə stands for the unstressed vowel sound heard in about, taken, pencil, lemon, and circus.

S

847

soon. **3.** to attend as a spectator: *to see a movie.* **4.** to regard; judge; view: *My friend and I see things the same way.* **5.** to find out: *See who is at the door.* **6.** to make sure: *We will see that you leave on time.* **7.** to go with; accompany; escort: *to see someone to the door.* **8.** to visit or meet: *to see friends, to see a doctor.* **9.** to receive, as for a visit, interview, or examination: *The doctor does not see patients on Thursdays.* **10.** to experience or undergo: *to see service in the Army.* **11.** to be marked or characterized by: *That corner has seen many car accidents.* **12.** to predict or foresee: *I see many years of trouble ahead.* —*v.i.* **1.** to have or use the power of sight: *A blind person cannot see.* **2.** to understand; comprehend. **3.** to judge or discover: *See for yourself.* [From the Old English word *sēon* with the same meanings.]

·**to see off.** to go with (someone) to the departure point: *to see a friend off at the airport.*

·**to see out.** to continue with to the end; finish.

·**to see through. a.** to continue with to the end. **b.** to watch over in time of difficulty. **c.** to understand the true character or meaning of.

·**to see to.** to attend to; take care of.

see² (sē) *n.* the office or jurisdiction of a bishop. [From the Old French word *sé* meaning "the seat or residence of a bishop," from the Latin word *sedes* "seat."]

seed (sēd) *n., pl.* **seeds** or **seed. 1.** the part of a plant that develops from a usually fertilized ovule and contains the developing embryo of a new plant. **2.** any part of a plant from which a new plant will grow, such as a tuber, bulb, or spore. **3.** the origin or beginning from which something larger will grow or develop: *the seeds of rebellion.* **4.** *Archaic.* children, descendants, or offspring. —*v.t.* **1.** to sow (land) with seeds: *to seed a field with alfalfa.* **2.** to remove the seeds from: *to seed a watermelon.* **3.** *Sports.* to place (tournament contestants) so that stronger competitors will not meet each other in the early rounds. **4.** to spray (clouds) with dry ice or other chemical substances in order to produce rain. —*v.i.* to produce seeds. —**seed′like′,** *adj.*

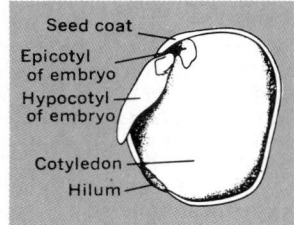

seed (n., def. 1)

Seed coat
Epicotyl of embryo
Hypocotyl of embryo
Cotyledon
Hilum

seed·case (sēd′kās′) *n.* the part of a flowering plant that contains the seeds, such as a pod or capsule.

seed coat, the protective outer covering of a seed.

seed·er (sē′dər) *n.* **1.** a person who sows or plants seeds. **2.** a device for sowing seeds. **3.** a device for removing seeds, as from fruit.

seed leaf, the leaf forming part of the embryo in a seed; cotyledon.

seed·ling (sēd′ling) *n.* **1.** any young plant grown from a seed. **2.** a young tree less than three feet high.

seed money, money designated to start a new project and to help it grow.

seed pearl, a very small pearl.

seed·y (sē′dē) *adj.,* **seed·i·er, seed·i·est. 1.** looking shabby or run-down: *a seedy restaurant, a seedy old coat.* **2.** having many seeds. —**seed′i·ly,** *adv.* —**seed′i·ness,** *n.*

see·ing (sē′ing) *conj.* in view of the fact; considering: *Seeing that it is late, we should go home.* —*n.* the ability to see; sight. —*adj.* having sight; able to see.

Seeing Eye dog, *also,* **seeing eye dog.** another term for **guide dog.** Trademark: **Seeing Eye.**

seek (sēk) *v.,* **sought, seek·ing. 1.** to go in search of; try to find; look for: *The company is seeking new employees.* **2.** to try; attempt: *Every candidate seeks to win.* **3.** to desire or try to get; ask for: *to seek aid.*

—*v.i.* to search; make inquiry: *Seek and ye shall find* (Matthew 7:7). —**seek′er,** *n.*

seem (sēm) *v.i.* **1.** to give the feeling of being; appear to be: *to seem much older than one really is.* **2.** to be true so far as one can tell: *The child seems happy in the new home. It seems to be about to rain.* **3.** to appear to oneself: *I seem to hear faint footsteps.*

seem·ing (sē′ming) *adj.* appearing to be true, as far as one can tell: *The city has made seeming improvements in garbage collection.* —**seem′ing·ly,** *adv.*

seem·ly (sēm′lē) *adj.,* **seem·li·er, seem·li·est.** suitable, as to a purpose or occasion; proper: *It is not seemly to speak loudly in a library.* —**seem′li·ness,** *n.*

seen (sēn) the past participle of **see¹.**

seep (sēp) *v.i.* to spread or flow slowly, as through openings or pores: *Water seeped steadily from the cracked pipe.*

seep·age (sē′pij) *n.* **1.** the act or process of seeping. **2.** something that seeps.

seer (sîr) *n.* a person who is believed to have the power of foreseeing future events. —**seer′ess,** *n.*

seer·suck·er (sîr′suk′ər) *n.* a lightweight fabric, usually woven with alternating plain and crinkled stripes, and used chiefly for summer clothing and children's wear.

see·saw (sē′sô′) *n.* **1.** a playground device made of a plank supported at the middle so that when a person is seated on each end, one end goes up as the other goes down. Also, **teeter-totter. 2.** any up-and-down or back-and-forth action or movement: *the seesaw of political power.* —*v.i.* **1.** to move up and down on a seesaw. **2.** to move or act up and down or back and forth.

seethe (sēth) *v.i.,* **seethed, seeth·ing. 1.** to be very disturbed or agitated: *to seethe with rage.* **2.** to rise, surge, or form bubbles, as if boiling: *The waves seethed around the rocks.*

seg·ment (*n.,* seg′mənt; *v.,* seg′ment, seg ment′) *n.* **1.** any of the parts into which a thing is or may be divided; division; section: *the segments of an orange.* **2.** *Geometry.* **a.** a part of a plane figure cut off by a line, such as the part of a circle bounded by an arc and a chord. **b.** the part of a sphere cut off by a plane or by parallel planes. —*v.t.* to divide into segments.

seg·men·tal (seg men′təl) *adj.* of, relating to, or composed of segments. —**seg·men·tal·ly,** *adv.*

seg·men·ta·tion (seg′mən tā′shən) *n.* **1.** the act or process of dividing into segments. **2.** *Biology.* the division of a cell into many cells, as in a fertilized egg; cleavage.

se·go (sē′gō) *n., pl.* **se·gos. 1.** the bell-shaped flower of a plant found in the deserts of the western United States, usually white with pink, purple, or greenish yellow markings. **2.** the plant that bears this flower.

seg·re·gate (seg′ri gāt′) *v.,* **seg·re·gat·ed, seg·re·gat·ing.** —*v.t.* **1.** to set apart from others or the rest; isolate: *to segregate a patient with a contagious disease.* **2.** to impose segregation on (a racial group or social facilities): *to segregate schools.*

sego (def. 1)

—*v.i.* **1.** to become separate or separated; go apart. **2.** to have or practice racial segregation. [From the Latin word *segregatus,* past participle of *segregare* meaning "to separate, exclude," from the prefix *se-* "apart, aside" + *grex* "flock."]

seg·re·ga·tion (seg′ri gā′shən) *n.* **1.** the practice of separating one racial group, especially blacks, from another or from the rest of society by making them use different schools and social facilities or live in certain areas. **2.** the act of segregating or the state of being segregated.

seg·re·ga·tion·ist (seg'ri gā'shə nist) *n.* a person who practices or supports racial segregation.

sei·gneur (sēn yûr', sān yûr') *n.* a feudal nobleman, especially the lord of a manor.

seine

seine (sān) *n.* a fishing net, especially a long one that hangs vertically in the water, supported by floats on its upper edge and kept taut by weights on the bottom edge. —*v.t., v.i.,* **seined, sein·ing.** to catch (fish) with a seine. —**sein'er,** *n.*

seis·mic (sīz'mik) *adj.* of, caused by, or subject to earthquakes.

seismo– *combining form* of or relating to earthquakes: *seismology.*

seis·mo·graph (sīz'mə graf') *n.* an instrument that records the location, direction, intensity, and duration of earthquakes and other earth vibrations.

seis·mol·o·gy (sīz mol'ə jē) *n.* the study of earthquakes and other earth vibrations.

seize (sēz) *v.t.,* **seized, seiz·ing.** **1.** to take hold of suddenly and forcibly; grab on to: *The dog seized the bone.* **2.** to take away or get control or possession of by force or authority: *The soldiers seized the fortress.* **3.** to capture or arrest: *The police seized the criminal.* **4.** to take advantage of: *to seize an opportunity.* **5.** to have a sudden and powerful effect on; possess: *Panic seized the crowd when the fire broke out.*

·to seize on or **to seize upon,** to take hold of suddenly: *to seize on an idea.*

sei·zure (sē'zhər) *n.* **1.** the act of seizing. **2.** a sudden attack of a disease: *a seizure of epilepsy.*

sel·dom (sel'dəm) *adv.* not often; on few occasions; rarely: *We seldom go to the movies.*

se·lect (si lekt') *v.t.* to take or pick out from among many; choose: *Select the book you want to read from the library.* —*v.i.* to make a selection; choose. —*adj.* **1.** picked or chosen because of special ability or fitness: *to coach a select group of athletes.* **2.** of high quality; choice: *select apples.* **3.** careful in selecting; discriminating.

se·lec·tion (si lek'shən) *n.* **1.** the act of selecting or the state of being selected. **2.** a person or thing that is selected. **3.** a person or thing that may be selected: *the selections on a menu.* **4.** *Biology.* see **natural selection.**

se·lec·tive (si lek'tiv) *adj.* able to select or careful in selecting. —**se·lec'tive·ly,** *adv.*

selective breeding, a process of mating the most desirable offspring of a variety of plant or breed of animal to maintain the best possible stock. Selective breeding is especially used with horses, dogs, and cattle.

selective service, compulsory military service of persons selected according to age and fitness.

se·lec·tiv·i·ty (si lek tiv'i tē) *n.* the state or quality of being selective.

se·lect·man (si lekt'mən) *n., pl.* **se·lect·men** (si-lekt'mən). a member of the board that governs a town in most New England states.

se·lec·tor (si lek'tər) *n.* **1.** a person or thing that selects. **2.** a dial, switch, or other device used to control or select different operations of a machine.

Se·le·ne (sə lē'nē) *n. Greek Mythology.* the goddess of the moon. In Roman mythology she was called Luna.

se·le·ni·um (sə lē'nē əm) *n.* a metalloid element that conducts electricity when light shines on it. It is used in photoelectric cells and xerography and as a semiconductor. Symbol: **Se** [Formed from the Greek word *selēnē* meaning "moon." Selenium was named by analogy to the related element tellurium, which was named for the earth.]

self (self) *n., pl.* **selves.** **1.** one's own person as distinguished from all others. **2.** the qualities or characteristics of a person or thing. **3.** personal interests, welfare, advantage, or the like. —*adj.* of the same material as a garment or article itself: *curtains with a self lining.*

self- *prefix* **1.** of or for oneself or itself: *self-confidence, self-conscious.* **2.** by oneself or itself: *self-educated.* **3.** to oneself: *self-addressed.*

Language Note

To understand the meaning of a word that begins with **self-** but is not defined in this dictionary, add the words "oneself" or "itself" to the meaning of the basic word. For example, *self-inflicted* means "inflicted by oneself" and *self-regulating* means "regulating itself." For any important *self-* word that has a special meaning, there is an entry in the dictionary.

self-ad·dressed (self'ə drest') *adj.* addressed to oneself: *a self-addressed envelope.*

self-ap·point·ed (self'ə poin'tid) *adj.* appointed by oneself alone, without the consent or support of others.

self-as·sur·ance (self'ə shùr'əns) *n.* firm trust in one's own ability, position, or worth.

self-as·sured (self'ə shùrd') *adj.* having firm trust in one's own ability, position, or worth.

self-cen·tered (self'sen'tərd) *adj.* preoccupied with one's own thoughts, interests, or activities to the point of selfishness. —**self'-cen'tered·ness,** *n.*

self-clean·ing (self'klē'ning) *adj.* cleaning itself by mechanical means: *a self-cleaning oven.*

self-con·fi·dent (self'kon'fi dənt) *adj.* having confidence or faith in one's own ability or worth. —**self'-con'fi·dence,** *n.* —**self'-con'fi·dent·ly,** *adv.*

self-con·scious (self'kon'shəs) *adj.* **1.** uncomfortably aware of one's own actions, words, or thoughts, especially in the presence of others; shy and embarrassed among others. **2.** showing such awareness: *a self-conscious laugh.* **3.** aware of one's own being, actions, or nature. —**self'-con'scious·ly,** *adv.* —**self'-con'scious·ness,** *n.*

self-con·tained (self'kən tānd') *adj.* **1.** reserved or restrained in behavior. **2.** having all that is necessary in oneself or itself; complete: *a self-contained machine.*

at; āpe; fär; câre; end; mē; it; īce; pîerce; hot; ōld; sông, fôrk; oil; out; up; ūse; rüle; půll; tûrn; chin; sing; shop; thin; this; hw in white; zh in treasure. The symbol ə stands for the unstressed vowel sound heard in about, taken, pencil, lemon, and circus.

S

849

self‑con‑trol (self′kən trōl′) *n.* control over one's own actions or emotions.

self‑de‑fense (self′di fens′) *n.* defense or protection of oneself, as against attacks or threats.

self‑de‑ni‑al (self′di nī′əl) *n.* the practice of sacrificing one's own desires and interests for the sake of others or for a goal or ideal.

self‑de‑struct (self′di strukt′) *v.i.* to destroy itself: *The missile was designed to self-destruct if it veered off course.*

self‑de‑ter‑mi‑na‑tion (self′di tûr′mə nā′shən) *n.* **1.** the act of making one's own decisions without outside influence. **2.** the right of a people to choose the form of government they shall have.

self‑dis‑ci‑pline (self′dis′ə plin) *n.* stern control or discipline of oneself, one's actions, or one's feelings.

self‑ed‑u‑cat‑ed (self′ej′ə kā′tid) *adj.* educated by reading books or studying on one's own, with little or no formal classroom schooling.

self‑em‑ployed (self′em ploid′) *adj.* earning income from one's own business rather than from an employer.

self‑es‑teem (self′e stēm′) *n.* proper regard for or awareness of one's own worth and abilities as a person; self‑respect.

self‑ev‑i‑dent (self′ev′i dənt) *adj.* needing no proof or explanation; evident in itself.

self‑ex‑plan‑a‑to‑ry (self′ek splan′ə tôr′ē) *adj.* needing no extra explanation or details; containing or being its own explanation: *The diagram is self-explanatory.*

self‑ex‑pres‑sion (self′ek spresh′ən) *n.* the expression of one's own thoughts, feelings, or true personality.

self‑gov‑ern‑ing (self′guv′ər ning) *adj.* ruled by its own people rather than by an outside authority; having or exercising self‑government: *The colony gained its independence and became self-governing.*

self‑gov‑ern‑ment (self′guv′ern mənt) *n.* government or rule of a group by its own members rather than by an outside authority: *Many former colonies in Africa achieved self-government in the 1960s.*

self‑help (self′help′) *n.* the practice or process of helping oneself, especially in solving personal problems without the help of professional counseling, as by reading or by meeting with other people seeking to solve the same problem. —*adj.* of, relating to, or offering self‑help: *a self-help book, a self-help group.*

self‑im‑por‑tant (self′im pôr′tənt) *adj.* having an exaggerated opinion of one's own importance. —**self′‑im‑por′tance,** *n.*

self‑im‑prove‑ment (self′im prüv′mənt) *n.* improvement of oneself through one's own efforts.

self‑in‑dul‑gent (self′in dul′jənt) *adj.* giving in to one's own weaknesses, feelings, or desires. —**self′‑in‑dul′‑gence,** *n.*

self‑in‑ter‑est (self′in′tər ist, self′in′trist) *n.* **1.** personal advantage. **2.** the practice of regarding one's own welfare more than the welfare of others.

self‑ish (sel′fish) *adj.* concerned for or serving one's own desires and interests above all others: *a selfish person, a selfish attitude.* —**self′ish‑ly,** *adv.* —**self′ish‑ness,** *n.*

self‑less (self′lis) *adj.* having little or no thought for oneself; unselfish. —**self′less‑ly,** *adv.* —**self′less‑ness,** *n.*

self‑made (self′mād′) *adj.* **1.** made by oneself or itself. **2.** rising to wealth or success through one's own efforts: *a self-made millionaire.*

self‑pit‑y (self′pit′ē) *n.* a feeling of pity for oneself.

self‑pol‑li‑na‑tion (self′pol′ə nā′shən) *n.* the transfer of pollen from the anthers to the stigmas of the same flower or of another flower on the same plant.

self‑por‑trait (self′pôr′trit) *n.* a portrait of oneself made by oneself.

self‑pos‑sessed (self′pə zest′) *adj.* in control of oneself; composed.

self‑pos‑ses‑sion (self′pə zesh′ən) *n.* control of oneself; composure.

self‑pres‑er‑va‑tion (self′prez′ər vā′shən) *n.* an instinctive desire to protect oneself from injury, death, or danger.

self‑pro‑pelled (self′prə peld′) *adj.* containing the means to propel itself, as an automobile.

self‑re‑li‑ant (self′ri lī′ənt) *adj.* relying on one's own resources or abilities. —**self′‑re‑li′ance,** *n.*

self‑re‑spect (self′ri spekt′) *n.* proper regard for or awareness of one's own worth and capabilities as a person; self‑esteem.

self‑re‑spect‑ing (self′ri spek′ting) *adj.* having self‑respect.

self‑re‑straint (self′ri strānt′) *n.* control over one's own reactions to or feelings about events; self‑control: *You showed great self-restraint by not getting angry about the damage to your car.* —**self′‑re‑strained′,** *adj.*

self‑right‑eous (self′rī′chəs) *adj.* thinking that one's own actions and beliefs are more moral or right than those of others. —**self′‑right′eous‑ly,** *adv.* —**self′right′‑eous‑ness,** *n.*

self‑sac‑ri‑fice (self′sak′rə fīs′) *n.* the giving up or ignoring of one's own interests and desires for the sake of duty or the welfare of another. —**self′‑sac′ri‑fic′ing,** *adj.*

self‑same (self′sām′) *adj.* exactly the same; identical.

self‑sat‑is‑fac‑tion (self′sat′is fak′shən) *n.* satisfaction with oneself or one's own achievements.

self‑sat‑is‑fied (self′sat′is fīd′) *adj.* feeling or showing satisfaction with oneself or one's achievements.

self‑seek‑ing (self′sē′king) *adj.* concerned mainly with furthering one's own selfish interests; selfish. —*n.* self‑ishness.

self‑serve (self′sûrv′) *adj.* intended for or allowing self‑service: *a self-serve pump at the gas station.*

self‑ser‑vice (self′sûr′vis) *n.* the act or process of serving oneself. —*adj.* having or requiring self‑service: *a self-service store, a self-service elevator.*

self‑stick (self′stik′) *adj.* having its own adhesive; able to stick to a surface without the addition of glue, paste, or moisture: *self-stick mailing labels.*

self‑styled (self′stīld′) *adj.* called or considered so by oneself alone: *a self-styled expert.*

self‑suf‑fi‑cient (self′sə fish′ənt) *adj.* capable of providing for oneself without help from others; independent. —**self′‑suf‑fi′cien‑cy,** *n.*

self‑sup‑port‑ing (self′sə pôr′ting) *adj.* supporting or providing for oneself without outside help.

self‑taught (self′tôt′) *adj.* taught by oneself without aid from others.

self‑will (self′wil′) *n.* insistence on having one's own way; stubbornness; obstinacy.

self‑willed (self′wild′) *adj.* stubborn about having one's own way; unmindful of the wishes of others.

self‑wind‑ing (self′wīn′ding) *adj.* (of a clock or watch) not needing to be wound by hand; wound automatically.

sell (sel) *v.,* **sold, sell‑ing.** —*v.t.* **1.** to give in return for money; accept money in payment for: *to sell a car.* **2.** to offer for sale; deal in: *Does this store sell shoes?* **3.** to bring about or promote the sale of: *Advertising sells new products.* **4.** to persuade (someone) to do, approve, or accept something: *Did you sell the bank on giving you a loan to buy a new car?* **5.** to convince someone to do, approve, or accept (something) by using persuasive methods. —*v.i.* **1.** to sell goods, property, or the like, especially to engage in selling things for a living. **2.** to be offered for sale or be sold: *This coat sells for $150.* **3.** to gain acceptance or approval: *That idea will never sell.*

·**to sell out. a.** to dispose of completely by selling: *The store sold out its stock of sweaters.* **b.** *Informal.* to betray: *The spy sold out to the other side by providing secret information.*

sell·er (sel′ər) *n.* **1.** a person who sells. **2.** something that is sold, especially something that is in great demand.

sell·out (sel′out′) *n.* **1.** the act of selling out. **2.** a performance or event for which all tickets have been sold.

selt·zer (selt′sər) *n.* **1.** water that has been filtered, carbonated, and bottled for sale, usually containing no flavoring. **2.** naturally effervescent spring water with a high mineral content.

sel·vage (sel′vij) *also,* **sel·vedge.** *n.* the narrow, tightly woven edge on a fabric that prevents raveling.

selves (selvz) the plural of **self.**

se·man·tic (si man′tik) *adj.* **1.** of, based on, or concerned with the meanings of words. **2.** of or having to do with semantics. —**se·man′ti·cal·ly,** *adv.*

se·man·tics (si man′tiks) *pl. n.* **1.** the branch of linguistics that deals with the meanings of words, especially with regard to their historical development and change. **2.** the meaning of words or the interpretation of their meaning: *an argument over semantics.* ▲ used with a singular verb.

sem·a·phore (sem′ə fôr′) *n.* **1.** a method of signaling that uses two flags, one held in each hand. Different positions of the arms represent the letters of the alphabet. **2.** an apparatus for signaling, such as a post with movable arms or an arrangement of lights or flags. —*v.i., v.t.,* **sem·a·phored, sem·a·phor·ing.** to signal by semaphore.

sem·blance (sem′bləns) *n.* **1.** outward appearance, often one that is false: *The witness's testimony had a semblance of truth but was actually a complete lie.* **2.** a likeness, image, or copy.

semaphore
(def. 2)

se·men (sē′mən) *n.* a fluid produced by the testes that contains the male reproductive cells.

se·mes·ter (si mes′tər) *n.* one of two terms into which a school or college year is divided.

semi- *prefix* **1.** half: *semicircle.* **2.** in part; partly; not completely: *semiofficial.* **3.** happening twice within a specified time period: *semimonthly.*

sem·i·an·nu·al (sem′ē an′ū əl) *adj.* happening twice a year, especially at six-month intervals. —**sem′i·an′nu·al·ly,** *adv.*

sem·i·ar·id (sem′ē ar′id) *adj.* of or relating to an area having little rainfall, especially one having an average annual rainfall of less than 20 inches.

sem·i·au·to·mat·ic (sem′ē ô′tə mat′ik) *adj.* **1.** partly automatic. **2.** (of firearms) firing one shot each time the trigger is pulled, without reloading or cocking.

sem·i·cir·cle (sem′ē sûr′kəl) *n.* half a circle or something arranged in or resembling half a circle. —**sem′i·cir′cu·lar,** *adj.*

semicircular canal, any of three curved tubes of membrane in the inner ear that help the body maintain balance.

sem·i·co·lon (sem′ē kō′lən) *n.* a mark of punctuation (;) that shows a grammatical separation stronger than that shown by a comma, but not as strong as that shown by a period.

sem·i·con·duc·tor (sem′ē kən duk′tər) *n.* **1.** a material, such as germanium or silicon, whose ability to conduct an electric current is greater than that of an insulator, but less than that of a conductor. Semiconductors are used in transistors. **2.** an electronic component made from such a material. —**sem′i·con·duct′ing,** *adj.*

sem·i·con·scious (sem′ē kon′shəs) *adj.* not completely conscious. —**sem′i·con′scious·ly,** *adv.* —**sem′i·con′scious·ness,** *n.*

sem·i·fi·nal (sem′ē fī′nəl) *adj.* immediately preceding the final match, as in a tournament. —*n.* a semifinal match.

sem·i·fi·nal·ist (sem′ē fī′nə list) —*n.* a person who takes part in a semifinal match.

sem·i·month·ly (sem′ē munth′lē) *adj.* appearing or happening twice a month. —*n., pl.* **sem·i·month·lies.** something that appears or takes place twice a month, such as a magazine. —*adv.* twice a month. ▲ See **bimonthly** for usage note.

sem·i·nal (sem′ə nəl) *adj.* **1.** of, relating to, or containing semen or seed. **2.** influential as a source of ideas: *a seminal theory, a seminal thinker.*

sem·i·nar (sem′ə när′) *n.* **1.** a group of advanced students, as at a university, doing independent study or research under supervision. **2.** a meeting in which such a group reports and discusses a specialized subject.

sem·i·nar·y (sem′ə ner′ē) *n., pl.* **sem·i·nar·ies. 1.** a school that trains students to be priests, ministers, or rabbis. **2.** a school or academy at or beyond the high school level, especially a boarding school for young women.

Sem·i·nole (sem′ə nōl′) *n., pl.* **Sem·i·nole** or **Sem·i·noles.** a member of a group of North American Indians, originally living in Florida and now mostly in Oklahoma.

sem·i·of·fi·cial (sem′ē ə fish′əl) *adj.* having some degree of authority; partly official.

sem·i·pre·cious (sem′ē presh′əs) *adj.* (of gems and minerals) valuable but having less value than precious stones. Garnets, amethysts, and turquoise are semiprecious stones.

sem·i·pro·fes·sion·al (sem′ē prə fesh′ə nəl) *adj.* **1.** working part-time at a job and receiving a salary or expenses: *a semiprofessional athlete.* **2.** of, relating to, or engaged in by part-time workers who receive a salary or expenses: *semiprofessional football.* —*n.* a person engaged as a semiprofessional worker.

sem·i·skilled (sem′ē skild′) *adj.* possessing or requiring limited skill or training: *semiskilled workers, semiskilled labor.*

sem·i·sol·id (sem′ē sol′id) *adj.* solid in part only; partly solid, as some gelatinlike substances. —*n.* a semisolid substance.

Sem·ite (sem′īt) *n.* a member of a group of peoples speaking related languages, living mainly in the Middle East and parts of Africa. The ancient Hebrews, Phoenicians, and Assyrians were Semites. In modern times, Jews, Arabs, Syrians, and a number of Ethiopians are called Semites.

Se·mit·ic (sə mit′ik) *adj.* of or relating to Semites. —*n.* a language group that includes Hebrew and Arabic.

sem·i·tone (sem′ē tōn′) *n. Music.* see **half step.**

sem·i·trail·er (sem′ē trā′lər) *n.* **1.** a trailer with no front wheels, designed to be attached to a tractor. **2.** a truck consisting of a tractor and a semitrailer.

sem·i·trop·i·cal (sem′ē trop′i kəl) *adj.* nearly tropical; subtropical.

---

at; āpe; fär; câre; end; mē; it; īce; pierce; hot; ōld; sông; fôrk; oil; out; up; ūse; rüle; pull; tûrn; chin; sing; shop; thin; <u>th</u>is; hw in white; zh in treasure. The symbol ə stands for the unstressed vowel sound heard in about, taken, pencil, lemon, and circus.

S

sem·i·week·ly (sem′ē wēk′lē) *adj.* appearing or happening twice a week: *a semiweekly newspaper.* —*n., pl.* **sem·i·week·lies.** a publication that is issued twice a week. —*adv.* twice a week. ▲ See **biweekly** for usage note.

sem·o·li·na (sem′ə lē′nə) *n.* the hard, coarsely ground kernels of wheat that are left after flour has been ground and sifted, used in making soup, pudding, and pasta.

Sen. 1. Senate. 2. Senator.

sen·ate (sen′it) *n.* 1. a governing or lawmaking council or assembly. 2. **Senate. a.** the upper house of the legislature of the United States or of most states of the United States. **b.** a similar house in other countries. 3. the ruling council of upper-class citizens in ancient Rome. [From the Old French word *senat* meaning "a legislative council of elders," from the Latin word *senatus* with the same meaning, from the word *senex* meaning "old" or "old man."]

sen·a·tor (sen′ə tər) *also,* **Sen·a·tor.** *n.* a member of a senate.

sen·a·to·ri·al (sen′ə tôr′ē əl) *adj.* of, relating to, or befitting a senator or a senate: *a senatorial debate.*

send (send) *v.t.,* **sent, send·ing.** 1. to cause to go to a certain place or from one place to another: *to send a letter to Boston, to send a spacecraft into orbit.* 2. to cause to go into a certain state or condition: *to send a person into a rage.* 3. to cause to come or be: *The music sent chills up and down my back.* —**send′er,** *n.*
·**to send for. a.** to ask (someone) to come; summon: *Did you send for the police?* **b.** to ask that something be brought or sent: *We sent for a free booklet.*

send–off (send′ôf′) *n. Informal.* a demonstration of goodwill in honor of the start of a journey, new career, or the like.

Sen·e·ca (sen′i kə) *n.* a member of the largest tribe of the Iroquois confederation of North American Indians, formerly living in western New York State.

sen·es·chal (sen′ə shəl) *n.* an official in medieval times who was in charge of a royal or noble household.

se·nile (sē′nīl) *adj.* 1. suffering the weakness that often occurs in old age, especially weakness of mental powers. 2. of, having to do with, or caused by old age. [From the Latin word *senilis* meaning "old, aged," from the word *senex* "old" and "old man."]

se·nil·i·ty (si nil′i tē) *n.* 1. the mental and, sometimes, physical weakness of old age. 2. the state of being old.

sen·ior (sēn′yər) *adj.* 1. the older of two. ▲ often used after the name of a father whose son has the same name: *Robert Smith, Senior.* 2. of relatively old age: *a senior member of the legal profession.* 3. of higher position or rank, especially after long service or experience: *senior officers of the army, a senior senator.* 4. of or relating to the final year of high school or college. —*n.* 1. a person who is older than another: *My cousin is my senior by three years.* 2. a student in the final year of high school or college. 3. a person of higher position or rank.

senior citizen, an elderly person, especially one who is over 65 years old or past the age of retirement.

senior high school, a school attended after junior high school, usually including grades nine or ten through twelve.

sen·ior·i·ty (sēn yôr′i tē, sēn yor′i tē) *n.* 1. the state of being more advanced than another or others in age, position, or length of service. 2. special consideration or privileges given a person in a job or office, because of age, position, or length of service.

sen·na (sen′ə) *n.* 1. the dried leaves of any of several tropical plants, used in making a laxative. 2. a plant bearing these leaves.

se·ñor (sen yôr′) *n., pl.* **se·ño·res** (sen yôr′ās). sir; mister. ▲ the Spanish form of respectful or polite address for a man.

se·ño·ra (sen yôr′ə) *n.* madam. ▲ the Spanish form of respectful or polite address for a married woman.

se·ño·ri·ta (sen′yə rē′tə) *n.* miss. ▲ the Spanish form of respectful or polite address for an unmarried girl or woman.

sen·sa·tion (sen sā′shən) *n.* 1. the process of feeling or being aware of things by means of the senses: *the sensation of sight, the sensation of touch.* 2. a feeling or impression arising from some particular condition or set of circumstances: *a sensation of fear.* 3. a state of great excitement or interest: *The political scandal caused a nationwide sensation.* 4. a person or thing that causes great excitement or interest: *The young guitarist was a singing sensation.*

sen·sa·tion·al (sen sā′shə nəl) *adj.* 1. arousing or intended to arouse great excitement or interest: *a sensational newspaper story.* 2. of or having to do with the senses. 3. *Informal.* outstanding or extraordinary; spectacular: *A sensational play had the crowd cheering.* —**sensa′tion·al·ly,** *adv.*

sen·sa·tion·al·ism (sen sā′shə nə liz′əm) *n.* sensational language or writing intended to excite or stimulate an audience or the public.

sense (sens) *n.* 1. any of the special powers by which a living being can be aware of its environment or changes in its own body. Sight, hearing, smell, taste, and touch are the five senses. 2. feeling or awareness; impression: *a sense of security.* 3. the ability to appreciate or understand: *a good sense of humor.* 4. speech, thought, or action that is reasonable or intelligent. 5. reasonableness; wisdom: *What is the sense of worrying about something that cannot be changed?* 6. judgment; intelligence: *a person of good sense.* 7. *also,* **senses.** normal, sound mental ability: *to finally come to one's senses.* 8. meaning, as of a word or statement: *There are many different senses of the word "run."* —*v.t.,* **sensed, sensing.** to be aware or conscious of; feel; understand: *We sensed the tension in the locker room before the final game.*
·**in a sense.** from one aspect; in one way.
·**to make sense.** to be reasonable or logical; have an understandable meaning: *This paragraph doesn't make sense as you have written it.*

sense·less (sens′lis) *adj.* 1. lacking wisdom, intelligence, or reason; foolish: *senseless spending of money.* 2. unconscious: *The blow knocked me senseless.* 3. meaningless: *senseless political slogans.* —**sense′-less·ly,** *adv.* —**sense′less·ness,** *n.*

sense organ, any of the organs that receive and are affected by stimuli, such as light, sound, or heat, including the eyes, ears, nose, and taste buds.

sen·si·bil·i·ty (sen′sə bil′i tē) *n., pl.* **sen·si·bil·i·ties.** 1. the power to feel or perceive. 2. *also,* **sensibilities.** refined or delicate feeling: *The vulgar novel offended their sensibilities.* 3. sensitiveness in feeling or perception.

sen·si·ble (sen′sə bəl) *adj.* 1. having, showing, or characterized by good sense or sound judgment; reasonable; wise: *a sensible individual, a sensible decision.* 2. easily perceived, noticed, or detected by the mind or senses. 3. aware or conscious: *to be sensible of another person's feelings.* —**sen′si·ble·ness,** *n.* —**sen′si·bly,** *adv.*

sen·si·tive (sen′si tiv) *adj.* 1. easily or readily affected by: *eyes that are very sensitive to sunlight.* 2. easily damaged, hurt, or irritated: *A baby's skin is very sensitive.* 3. responsive to outside stimuli: *The film is sensitive to light.* 4. quick to take offense or be hurt; touchy: *They were sensitive about their failure to make the team.* 5. keenly aware of or responsive to other people's feelings, problems, and the like. —**sen′si·tive·ly,** *adv.* —**sen′si·tive·ness,** *n.*

sensitive plant 1. a shrubby tropical American plant

whose leaflets fold up when touched. **2.** any of various other plants sensitive to touch.

sen·si·tiv·i·ty (sen'si tiv'i tē) *n.* the state, condition, or degree of being sensitive: *to show great sensitivity to the hardships of others.*

sen·si·tize (sen'si tīz') *v.t.,* **sen·si·tized, sen·si·tiz·ing.** to make sensitive.

sen·sor (sen'sər) *n.* any of various devices used to measure or detect light, radiation, heat, or other stimuli, and to transmit a resulting electrical impulse, as for operating a control.

sen·so·ry (sen'sə rē) *adj.* of, relating to, or conveying sensation: *a sensory nerve.*

sen·su·al (sen'shü əl) *adj.* **1.** enjoying and seeking the pleasures of the body or senses. **2.** physically pleasing or appealing. **3.** of or relating to stimulation of the body or senses rather than the spirit or intellect. **—sen·su·al·i·ty** (sen'shü al'i tē), *n.* **—sen'su·al·ly,** *adv.*

sen·su·ous (sen'shü əs) *adj.* **1.** of, relating to, or affecting the senses. **2.** enjoying the pleasures of the senses; sensual. **—sen'su·ous·ly,** *adv.* **—sen'su·ous·ness,** *n.*

sent (sent) the past tense and past participle of **send.**

sen·tence (sen'təns) *n.* **1.** a group of words or, sometimes, a single word that makes a statement, asks a question, or otherwise expresses a complete thought. A sentence is a separate grammatical unit, and it usually has a subject and a predicate. *The dog and cat* is not a sentence. *The dog and cat are fighting* is a sentence. **2.** *Law.* **a.** a judgment by a court or judge setting the punishment of a defendant after conviction. **b.** the punishment itself. **3.** *Mathematics.* any statement that expresses a relationship between numbers. A sentence may be true, such as $5 + 3 = 8$, false, such as $6 - 2 = 3$, or neither true nor false, such as $x + 4 > 7$. A **closed sentence** has no unknown quantities, such as $3 + 2 = 5$; an **open sentence** contains at least one variable, such as $3a + 6 = 15$. **—v.t., sen·tenced, sen·tenc·ing.** to set the punishment of: *The judge sentenced the criminal to a term of three years in prison.*

sen·ten·tious (sen ten'shəs) *adj.* **1.** short and meaningful; pithy. **2.** inclined to speak in a pompous or moralizing manner. **3.** tending to use trite phrases or proverbs. **—sen·ten'tious·ly,** *adv.* **—sen·ten'tious·ness,** *n.*

sen·tient (sen'shənt) *adj.* having the power of feeling.

sen·ti·ment (sen'tə mənt) *n.* **1.** a mental attitude or point of view; opinion: *Popular sentiment is against the new tax law.* **2.** an expression of feeling or emotion: *I appreciate the sentiment, but you didn't have to buy me a gift.* **3.** refined or tender emotion. **4.** emotion that is exaggerated, overdone, or foolish.

sen·ti·men·tal (sen'tə men'təl) *adj.* **1.** characterized by or showing emotion or feeling: *a sentimental love song.* **2.** influenced by or inclined to be moved by feeling rather than by reason: *a sentimental person.* **3.** appealing to the emotions: *The candidate made a sentimental plea for support.* **4.** relating to or based on sentiment: *to save old clothes for sentimental reasons.* **5.** characterized by exaggerated or foolish emotion. **—sen'ti·men'tal·ly,** *adv.*

sen·ti·men·tal·ism (sen'tə men'tə liz'əm) *n.* **1.** the quality or state of being sentimental. **2.** the tendency to be influenced by feeling rather than by reason.

sen·ti·men·tal·ist (sen'tə men'tə list) *n.* a person who is sentimental.

sen·ti·men·tal·i·ty (sen'tə men tal'i tē) *n., pl.* **sen·ti·men·tal·i·ties.** **1.** the quality or state of being sentimental. **2.** the tendency to be influenced by feeling rather than by reason. **3.** an expression of exaggerated or excessive emotion.

sen·ti·nel (sen'tə nəl) *n.* a person stationed to keep watch and alert others of danger; guard; sentry.

sen·try (sen'trē) *n., pl.* **sen·tries.** a person, especially a soldier, stationed to keep watch and alert others of danger; guard.

sentry box, a small building or booth for sheltering a sentry on duty.

se·pal (sē'pəl) *n.* one of the leaflike divisions of the calyx of a flower, usually green but sometimes, as in the tulip, the same color as the petals.

sep·a·ra·ble (sep'ər ə bəl) *adj.* able to be separated.

sep·a·rate (*v.,* sep'ə rāt'; *adj.,* sep'ər it, sep'rit) *v.,* **sep·a·rat·ed, sep·a·rat·ing.** **—v.t. 1.** to keep apart; be a barrier between; divide: *A fence separates the garden from the sidewalk.* **2.** to set or place apart: *to separate black socks from white socks, to separate fact from fantasy.* **3.** to divide or sort into individual parts or elements: *to separate a tangle of threads.* **—v.i. 1.** to come apart; withdraw; part: *We separated and each of us took a different path.* **2.** (of a married couple) to live apart but without a divorce. **—adj. 1.** set apart or divided from others: *two separate rooms.* **2.** different; distinct: *Those are separate problems and cannot be handled in the same way.* **3.** single; individual: *each separate item on a list.* **—sep'a·rate·ly,** *adv.*

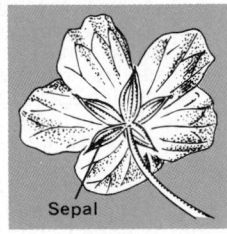

sepals of
a geranium

sep·a·ra·tion (sep'ə rā'shən) *n.* **1.** the act of separating or the state of being separated. **2.** the point at which two or more objects or parts are divided from each other; division. **3.** a condition in which a husband and wife live apart by agreement or by a court order.

sep·a·ra·tism (sep'ər ə tiz'əm, sep'rə tiz'əm) *n.* the principle of supporting or favoring separation from a political or religious body.

sep·a·ra·tist (sep'ər ə tist, sep'rə tist) *n.* a person who supports or favors separation from a political or religious body.

sep·a·ra·tor (sep'ə rā'tər) *n.* **1.** a person or thing that separates. **2.** an apparatus for separating one thing from another, as cream from milk.

se·pi·a (sē'pē ə) *n.* **1.** a dark brown pigment made from the inky fluid secreted by the cuttlefish. **2.** a dark brown color. **—adj.** having the color sepia; dark brown.

sep·pu·ku (se pü'kü) *n.* another word for **hara-kiri.**

Sept., September.

Sep·tem·ber (sep tem'bər) *n.* the ninth month of the year, having thirty days. [From the Old French word *Septembre* meaning this month, from the Latin word *September,* the seventh month of the Roman calendar, from the word *septem* "seven."]

sep·tet (sep tet') *also,* **sep·tette.** *n.* **1.** a musical composition for seven voices or seven instruments. **2.** a musical group of seven performers. **3.** any group or set of seven persons or things.

sep·tic (sep'tik) *adj.* **1.** of or causing infection. **2.** caused by infection.

sep·ti·ce·mi·a (sep'tə sē'mē ə) *n.* a disease caused by the circulation of bacteria and their toxins in the bloodstream; blood poisoning.

septic tank, an underground tank in which sewage is decomposed by the action of bacteria.

---

at; āpe; fär; câre; end; mē; it; īce; pîerce; hot; ōld; sông, fôrk; oil; out; up; ūse; rüle; pull; tûrn; chin; sing; shop; thin; <u>th</u>is; hw in white; zh in treasure. The symbol ə stands for the unstressed vowel sound heard in about, taken, pencil, lemon, and circus.

S

sep·tum (sep′təm) *n.*, *pl.* **sep·ta** (sep′tə). a dividing wall, membrane, or partition in an animal or plant structure. A septum separates the two nostrils of the nose.

sep·ul·cher (sep′əl kər) *also, British,* **sep·ul·chre.** *n.* a burial place, especially a vault or tomb.

se·pul·chral (sə pul′krəl) *adj.* **1.** of or relating to a sepulcher or tomb. **2.** of or relating to burial or the dead. **3.** deep, dark, and dismal; funereal.

se·quel (sē′kwəl) *n.* **1.** a literary work that is complete in itself but continues the story of a previous work. **2.** something that follows. **3.** something that comes as a result; consequence.

se·quence (sē′kwəns) *n.* **1.** the coming of one thing after another; succession: *A strange sequence of events led to the accident.* **2.** the order in which things occur or are arranged: *alphabetical sequence.* **3.** a group, collection, or series of connected things: *a sequence of arithmetic exercises.*

se·quent (sē′kwənt) *adj.* following in sequence.

se·ques·ter (si kwes′tər) *v.t.* **1.** to withdraw or remove from the world at large; hide away: *to sequester oneself in a mountain cabin.* **2.** *Law.* to take and hold (property) until a debt or claim is settled.

se·ques·tra·tion (sē′kwes trā′shən) *n.* **1.** the act of sequestering or the state of being sequestered. **2.** the act or process of taking property into custody until a debt or claim is settled.

se·quin (sē′kwin) *n.* a small, thin disk put on cloth or clothes as decoration.

se·quoi·a (si kwoi′ə) *n.* **1.** a giant evergreen tree of central California and Oregon that has thick, spongy, reddish brown bark and sharply pointed leaves. Sequoias are among the oldest and largest of trees. **2.** see **redwood** *(def. 1).*

se·ra (sîr′ə) a plural of **serum.**

se·ragl·io (si ral′yō) *n.*, *pl.* **se·ragl·ios.** a portion of a Muslim house that has been reserved for women; harem.

se·ra·pe (sə rä′pē) *n.* *also,* **sa·ra·pe.** an outer garment like a cloak or poncho, often brightly colored, worn chiefly by men in Mexico and in other Latin-American countries.

ser·aph (ser′əf) *n.*, *pl.* **ser·a·phs** or **ser·a·phim** (ser′ə fim′). an angel of high rank. —**se·raph·ic** (si raf′ik), *adj.*

Serb (sûrb) *n.* **1.** a person who was born in or is a citizen of Serbia. **2.** Serbo-Croatian as it is written and spoken in Serbia. —*adj.* another word for **Serbian.**

Ser·bi·an (sûr′bē ən) *adj.* of or relating to Serbia, its people, their language, or culture. —*n.* another word for **Serb.**

Ser·bo–Cro·a·tian (sûr′bō krō ā′shən) *n.* a Slavic language spoken mainly by the Serbs and Croats of Yugoslavia. —*adj.* of or relating to this language.

sere (sîr) *adj.* withered; dry.

ser·e·nade (ser′ə nād′) *n.* a song or other musical performance played and sung personally for someone as an expression of love or admiration. —*v.*, **ser·e·nad·ed,** **ser·e·nad·ing.** —*v.t.* to perform a serenade for (someone). —*v.i.* to sing or play a serenade. —**ser′e·nad′er,** *n.*

ser·en·dip·i·ty (ser′ən dip′i tē) *n.*, *pl.* **ser·en·dip·i·ties.** the act or ability of making fortunate discoveries by accident.

se·rene (sə rēn′) *adj.* **1.** peaceful; calm; tranquil: *a serene mountain village.* **2.** clear and bright: *a serene sky.* —**se·rene′ly,** *adv.*

se·ren·i·ty (sə ren′i tē) *n.* the state or quality of being serene; peacefulness.

serf (sûrf) *n.* **1.** in the Middle Ages, a peasant bound to the land or to the service of the landlord. A serf could neither leave at will nor be forced off the land, and was sold only along with the land. **2.** any slave.

serf·dom (sûrf′dəm) *n.* **1.** the state or condition of being a serf. **2.** the practice or institution of working the land with serfs.

serge (sûrj) *n.* any of a group of fabrics woven with slanting ribs, used especially for suits.

ser·geant (sär′jənt) *n.* **1.** in the U.S. Army and Marine Corps, a noncommissioned officer in one of five grades above a corporal. **2.** in the U.S. Air Force, a noncommissioned officer in one of six grades above an airman first class. **3.** a police officer ranking above an officer assigned to patrol and below a captain or lieutenant. [From the Middle English word *sergeant* meaning "servant, attendant," from the Old French word *serjant,* going back to the Latin word *servire* "to serve."]

sergeant at arms *pl.* **sergeants at arms.** an official charged with preserving order in a legislative assembly or court of law.

sergeant major *pl.* **sergeants major** or **sergeant majors.** in the U.S. Army and Marine Corps, a noncommissioned officer of the highest grade.

se·ri·al (sîr′ē əl) *n.* a long story broken up into parts that are televised, broadcast, or published one at a time. The end of each part usually leads to the next part, so that the audience or reader is interested in learning what will happen. —*adj.* **1.** of or relating to a serial: *The novel appeared in the magazine in serial form.* **2.** of, relating to, or arranged in a series. —**se′ri·al·ly,** *adv.*

se·ri·al·ize (sîr′ē ə līz′) *v.t.*, **se·ri·al·ized, se·ri·al·iz·ing.** to televise, broadcast, or publish as a serial.

serial number, a number assigned to a person or thing, as to a member of the armed forces or an automobile engine, for the purpose of identification.

se·ries (sîr′ēz) *n.*, *pl.* **se·ries. 1.** a number or group of similar or related things or events coming one after another: *a series of announcements, a series of meetings, a series of baseball games.* **2.** a set of things that go together to make a whole, often in a certain order: *a series of physical exercises.* **3.** a television program seen each day or each week.

·in series. (of electrical devices or circuits) arranged with the positive electrode of one connected to the negative electrode of the next, so that the same current flows through all devices or circuits.

se·ri·ous (sîr′ē əs) *adj.* **1.** of, characterized by, or showing deep and earnest thought; grave; solemn: *a serious person. The judge gave serious consideration to the case.* **2.** not joking; in earnest; sincere: *Were you serious when you said that?* **3.** requiring thought or consideration; weighty; important: *a serious literary work, a serious problem.* **4.** causing concern or anxiety; dangerous: *a serious illness.* —**se′ri·ous·ly,** *adv.* —**se′ri·ous·ness,** *n.*

sequoia *(def. 1)*

854

ser·mon (sûr′mən) *n.* **1.** a public talk delivered by a member of the clergy for the purpose of giving religious or moral instruction. **2.** any long, serious talk dealing with morals, correct behavior, or the like.

ser·mon·ize (sûr′mə nīz′) *v.i.*, **ser·mon·ized, ser·mon·iz·ing. 1.** to deliver a sermon. **2.** to speak at length in a dogmatic or moralizing way.

Sermon on the Mount, Jesus' sermon to his disciples, containing important principles of Christianity, including the Beatitudes.

se·rous (sîr′əs) *adj.* **1.** of, relating to, or producing serum. **2.** like serum: *a serous fluid.*

ser·pent (sûr′pənt) *n.* **1.** a snake, especially an extremely large or poisonous one. **2.** a monster or creature like a snake, such as a dragon. **3.** a sly or wicked person.

ser·pen·tine (sûr′pən tēn′, sûr′pən tīn′) *adj.* **1.** winding about like a snake's body: *a serpentine path through a garden.* **2.** of or resembling a snake or serpent. **3.** sly or wicked. —*n.* a mineral, usually green with a greasy texture, used as a source of magnesium compounds.

ser·rat·ed (ser′ā tid) *adj.* jagged or saw-toothed, as the edges of a saw or of certain leaves: *a knife with a serrated edge.* Also, **ser·rate** (ser′āt).

se·rum (sîr′əm) *n., pl.* **se·rums** or **se·ra** (sîr′ə). **1.** the clear, thin fluid that separates from the blood when a clot forms. **2.** any clear fluid in the body, such as lymph. **3.** a liquid used to prevent a disease by producing immunity to it. It is obtained from the blood of an animal that has been made immune to the disease.

serv·ant (sûr′vənt) *n.* **1.** a person who is employed in a household to perform certain duties, such as cooking or cleaning. **2.** a person who is dedicated to the service of someone or something, such as a religion, government, or cause: *a servant of the people.*

serve (sûrv) *v.,* **served, serv·ing.** —*v.t.* **1.** to set (food or drink) on a table or before a person or persons: *to serve dinner at six o'clock.* **2.** to set food or drink before (a person or persons): *The cook served us at once.* **3.** to supply regularly or continuously, as with a service or product: *The bakery serves us with fresh bread daily.* **4.** to act as a servant to; attend or wait upon; work for: *The cook served the same family for years.* **5.** to give assistance to: *The salesclerk offered to serve us.* **6.** to honor, obey, or worship: *to serve God.* **7.** to pass (a specified period of time), as in military service, public office, or imprisonment: *The senator served two terms in the state legislature.* **8.** to be of use or service to; meet the requirements of: *The house is too small to serve the needs of a large family.* **9.** in tennis, badminton, and other racket games and volleyball, to put (the ball or shuttlecock) in play. **10.** *Law.* **a.** to present (a court order or writ) to a person. **b.** to present with a court order or writ: *to serve a person with a summons.* —*v.i.* **1.** to set food or drink before a person or persons. **2.** to perform a duty or duties, as of an office: *to serve on a jury, to serve as mayor.* **3.** to be of use; suffice: *The sofa served as a bed.* **4.** to be favorable or suitable. **5.** in tennis, badminton, and other racket games and volleyball, to put the ball or shuttlecock in play. —*n.* **1.** in tennis, badminton, and other racket games and volleyball, the act, instance, or manner of serving a ball or shuttlecock. **2.** a player's turn at serving.

·**to serve one right.** to be just what one deserves.

serv·er (sûr′vər) *n.* **1.** a person who serves. **2.** something that is used in serving, as a tray.

ser·vice (sûr′vis) *n.* **1.** an act or means of serving or helping; conduct that contributes to the welfare or advantage of another person or persons: *to devote one's life to service to the community.* **2.** a system or means of providing something useful or necessary, especially for the general public: *a taxi service, the electrical service.* **3.** *usually,* **services.** useful work: *the services of a plumber.*

4. the repair, maintenance, or replacement of goods that have been sold to customers: *to take a hair dryer back to a store for service.* **5.** the manner of serving food: *The service is very good in that restaurant.* **6.** a religious ceremony or ritual: *a burial service.* **7.** one of the branches of the armed forces: *to spend four years in the service.* **8.** duty in any such branch: *to see active service in the navy.* **9.** a branch or department of public employment: *the foreign service.* **10.** the persons employed in this. **11.** a set of things required for table use, such as silver or dishes: *a service for eight.* **12.** in tennis, badminton, and other racket games and volleyball, the act, instance, or manner of putting the ball or shuttlecock in play. —*v.t.,* **ser·viced, ser·vic·ing. 1.** to make or keep fit for use: *to service an automobile.* **2.** to supply service to. —*adj.* **1.** of, relating to, or used by those in service: *a service entrance.* **2.** of or relating to the armed forces; military: *a service revolver.* **3.** of or relating to economic activity other than the production of goods: *the service industries.*
·**at one's service.** ready to serve or help one.
·**of service.** of use or assistance; useful; helpful.

ser·vice·a·ble (sûr′və sə bəl) *adj.* **1.** capable of giving useful service; helpful; beneficial. **2.** wearing well in long or hard use; durable: *a serviceable fabric.* —**ser′-vice·a·bil′i·ty,** *n.* —**ser′vice·a·bly,** *adv.*

serv·ice·man (sûr′vis man′) *n., pl.* **serv·ice·men** (sur′vis men′). **1.** a member of the armed forces. **2.** a person whose work is repairing machinery or equipment.

service station, another term for **gas station.**

serv·ice·wom·an (sûr′vis wùm′ən) *n., pl.* **serv·ice·wom·en** (sûr′vis wim′ən). a female member of the armed forces.

ser·vile (sûr′vəl, sûr′vīl) *adj.* **1.** acting like a slave; submissive. **2.** of, relating to, or appropriate for a slave or slaves: *servile work.* —**ser′vile·ly,** *adv.*

ser·vil·i·ty (sər vil′i tē) *n.* the quality or condition of being servile.

serv·ing (sûr′ving) *n.* **1.** a portion of food; helping. **2.** the act of a person or thing that serves. —*adj.* used in serving food: *a serving spoon.*

ser·vi·tude (sûr′vi tüd′, sûr′vi tūd′) *n.* **1.** the condition of being a slave; slavery; bondage. **2.** forced labor as a punishment.

ses·a·me (ses′ə mē) *n.* **1.** a small, oval seed of a tropical plant native to India, used mainly in baked goods and candies. **2.** the plant bearing this seed.

ses·sile (ses′əl) *adj.* **1.** permanently attached; not moving or swimming about: *Sea anemones are sessile organisms.* **2.** attached directly to the base rather than by a stem or stalk: *sessile leaves.*

ses·sion (sesh′ən) *n.* **1.** a meeting, as of a court, council, or legislature, to carry on business. **2.** a series of such meetings. **3.** the period or term of such a meeting or meetings. **4.** the period of time during which classes are conducted in a school or college. **5.** a meeting held for any purpose or activity: *a recording session.*
·**in session.** in the process of meeting or being conducted: *Court is now in session.*

set (set) *v.,* **set, set·ting.** —*v.t.* **1.** to place in some location or position; put: *to set a lamp on a table.* **2.** to put in the correct or desired place, position, or condition: *The doctor set the broken bone.* **3.** to arrange (the hair), as with rollers or clips, so as to take on a desired style.

at; āpe; fär; câre; end; mē; it; īce; pîerce; hot; ōld; sông, fôrk; oil; out; up; ūse; rüle; pùll; tûrn; chin; sing; shop; thin; **th**is; hw in white; zh in treasure. The symbol ə stands for the unstressed vowel sound heard in about, taken, pencil, lemon, and circus.

S

4. to prepare or arrange for use: *to set a trap, to set the table for a meal.* **5.** to arrange scenery and properties on (a stage) for a presentation. **6.** to adjust or regulate: *to set one's watch.* **7.** to cause to be in a certain condition: *to set a prisoner free, to set a log on fire.* **8.** to cause to be in a firm, settled, or fixed position or condition: *to set one's jaw, to set one's mind on doing something.* **9.** to determine or fix firmly; establish: *Have they set a date for the meeting?* **10.** to place in a certain category or rank: *Many critics set Shakespeare above all other English writers.* **11.** to establish as the highest or greatest level or achievement: *to set a record in the high jump.* **12.** to present or provide for others to follow: *to set a good example.* **13.** to cause to take a particular direction; direct: *The captain set the ship's course for Australia.* **14.** to place in a frame or mounting: *to set a diamond.* **15.** to adorn or ornament: *to set a crown with jewels.* **16.** *Printing.* **a.** to arrange (type) for printing. **b.** to put into type: *to set a manuscript.* **17.** *Music.* to write, adapt, or fit (words) to music: *to set a poem to music.* —*v.i.* **1.** to go down below the horizon: *At what time will the sun set today?* **2.** to become firm or hard: *The concrete set after a few hours.* **3.** (of a broken bone) to mend properly. **4.** to become fast or permanent, as a dye or color. **5.** to hang or fit: *That jacket sets well on you.* **6.** (of a hen) to sit on eggs. —*adj.* **1.** fixed or decided beforehand; established: *The electrician charged a set fee.* **2.** fixed in a certain position; rigid: *a set smile.* **3.** stubbornly unchanging; obstinate: *to be set in one's ways.* **4.** determined; intent: *to be set on doing something.* **5.** ready; prepared: *We are all set to leave on our trip.* —*n.* **1.** the act of setting or the state of being set. **2.** a group of persons or things associated or belonging together: *the younger set, a set of furniture, a chess set.* **3.** *Mathematics.* a collection of numbers, points, objects, or other things that are grouped together or have a certain property in common that distinguishes them from all other things not within the collection: *The number 12 is a member of the set of even numbers from 10 to 20.* **4.** a complete unit of scenery, properties, and structures used for a scene in a play, motion picture, or television program. **5.** a sending or receiving apparatus assembled as a unit for radio, television, telephone, or other means of communication. **6.** a group of six or more games making up a unit of a match in tennis. **7.** the position or form of the body or of a part of it: *I could tell you were tired by the set of your shoulders.* **8.** the way something fits or hangs, as an article of clothing: *the set of a coat.*

•**to set about.** to begin to do; start.

•**to set against. a.** to cause to be hostile or unfriendly toward. **b.** to balance or compare.

•**to set aside. a.** to place apart or to one side, as for later use; reserve; save. **b.** to discard, dismiss, or reject. **c.** to declare null and void; overrule; annul: *to set aside a verdict.*

•**to set back. a.** to hinder or check. **b.** *Informal.* to cost (a person) a certain sum of money: *Those three items set me back fifty dollars.*

•**to set down. a.** to record in writing or printing. **b.** to ascribe; attribute.

•**to set forth. a.** to make known; state; declare: *The speaker set forth some new ideas on health care.* **b.** to start out on a journey.

•**to set in.** to begin to take place: *Cold weather set in early this year.*

•**to set off. a.** to make more noticeable by contrast: *Dark hair sets off a fair complexion.* **b.** to start out or begin, as on a course or journey. **c.** to explode: *to set off fireworks.* **d.** to cause to begin: *to set off an argument.* **e.** to place apart from others.

•**to set on** or **to set upon.** to attack or urge to attack: *The bees set on the bear that broke into the hive.*

•**to set out. a.** to start out on a journey or course. **b.** to

begin to do something; undertake a task: *I set out to prove the theory.*

•**to set to. a.** to begin; start working. **b.** to start fighting: *The puppies set to over a bone.*

•**to set up. a.** to raise to a position of authority or power. **b.** to assemble, erect, or prepare for use: *to set up a tent.* **c.** to establish; found: *to set up an organization.* **d.** to claim to be: *to set oneself up as an expert in politics.*

set·back (set′bak′) *n.* a defeat or other check to progress.

set·tee (se tē′) *n.* a bench or small sofa with a high back and, usually, arms.

set·ter (set′ər) *n.* **1.** any of several long-haired hunting dogs having drooping ears and a soft, silky coat. A setter is trained to stand in a rigid position and point toward the game being hunted. **2.** a person or thing that sets.

set theory, a branch of mathematics dealing with sets, their properties, and their relationships.

setter *(def. 1)*

set·ting (set′ing) *n.* **1.** a thing in which something, such as a jewel, is set. **2.** the place and time of a dramatic or literary work: *The setting of the novel is London during World War II.* **3.** the scenery and other properties for a play. **4.** the surroundings of anything; background; environment: *a cabin in a forest setting.* **5.** music composed for a particular story, poem, or the like. **6.** the number of eggs that a hen sits on for hatching at one time. **7.** the act of a person or thing that sets. **8.** dishes, silverware, and the like used to set one place at a table. **9.** the position of or regulation specified by a control, dial, or other instrument.

set·tle¹ (set′əl) *v.,* **set·tled, set·tling.** —*v.t.* **1.** to determine or decide; come to agreement about; resolve: *to settle an argument.* **2.** to arrange in an orderly manner; put into order: *I must settle all my affairs before leaving.* **3.** to pay or satisfy: *to settle an account.* **4.** to colonize: *French colonists settled Louisiana.* **5.** to place in a proper or desired position; adjust: *to settle oneself on a couch.* **6.** to make tranquil or calm; compose: *Eating a cracker might settle your stomach.* **7.** to cause (a liquid) to become clear. **8.** to cause to sink: *The rain settled the dust.* —*v.i.* **1.** to decide, select, or agree: *We finally settled on the kind of car we want.* **2.** to establish a home or residence: *to settle in a small town.* **3.** to come to rest; alight. **4.** to sink gradually. [From the Middle English word *setlen* meaning "to seat" or "to bring to rest," from the Old English word *setlan* "to seat," from the word *setl* "a seat."]

•**to settle down. a.** to become calm or composed: *After the excitement of the fire drill, it took the class a long time to settle down.* **b.** to direct steady effort and attention: *to settle down to studying.* **c.** to be established in a more regular life, especially as a result of marriage.

set·tle² (set′əl) *n.* a long bench or seat for two or more people, with arms and a high back. [From the Old English word *setl* meaning "seat."]

set·tle·ment (set′əl mənt) *n.* **1.** the act of settling or the state of being settled. **2.** the deciding or determining of something in doubt or debate; decision or agreement: *The strike ended when the two sides reached a settlement.* **3.** a small village or group of houses. **4.** the establishment of people in

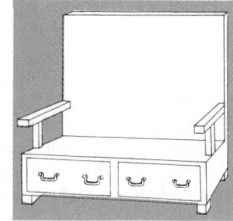
settle²

a new country or region; colonization. **5.** a colony, especially in its earlier stages. **6.** an adjustment or payment, as of claims. **7.** see **settlement house.**

settlement house, an institution that provides counseling, recreation, food, and other services to the residents of a poor neighborhood.

set·tler (set′lər) *n.* a person who is among the first to settle in a new country or region.

set·up (set′up′) *n.* the way in which a thing is arranged or organized; plan or structure of something: *the setup of a business.*

sev·en (sev′ən) *n.* **1.** the cardinal number that is one more than six. **2.** a symbol representing this number, such as 7 or VII. **3.** something having this many units or things, as a playing card. —*adj.* numbering one more than six.

sev·en·fold (sev′ən fōld′) *adj.* **1.** seven times as great or as numerous. **2.** having or consisting of seven parts. —*adv.* so as to be seven times greater or more numerous.

seven seas, all the oceans and seas of the world: *The old sailor had sailed the seven seas.*

sev·en·teen (sev′ən tēn′) *n.* **1.** the cardinal number that is seven more than ten. **2.** a symbol representing this number, such as 17 or XVII. **3.** something having this many units or things. —*adj.* numbering seven more than ten.

sev·en·teenth (sev′en tēnth′) *adj.* **1.** (the ordinal of seventeen) next after the sixteenth. **2.** being one of seventeen equal parts. —*n.* **1.** something that is next after the sixteenth. **2.** one of seventeen equal parts; 1/17.

sev·enth (sev′ənth) *adj.* **1.** (the ordinal of seven) next after the sixth. **2.** being one of seven equal parts. —*n.* **1.** something that is next after the sixth. **2.** one of seven equal parts; 1/7. **3.** *Music.* **a.** a note that is a total of five whole steps and one half step above a given note. B is the seventh of C. **b.** an interval of five whole steps and one half step. **c.** a combination of two notes that are separated by this interval. —*adv.* in the seventh place.

sev·en·ti·eth (sev′ən tē ith) *adj.* **1.** (the ordinal of seventy) next after the sixty-ninth. **2.** being one of seventy equal parts. —*n.* **1.** something that is next after the sixty-ninth. **2.** one of seventy equal parts; 1/70.

sev·en·ty (sev′ən tē) *n., pl.* **sev·en·ties. 1.** the cardinal number that is seven times ten. **2.** a symbol representing this number, such as 70 or LXX. —*adj.* numbering seven times ten.

Seven Wonders of the World, the seven most remarkable structures of ancient times, usually listed as the pyramids of Egypt, the hanging gardens of Babylon, the Colossus of Rhodes, the mausoleum at Halicarnassus, the temple of Diana (Artemis) at Ephesus, the statue of Zeus by Phidias at Olympia, and the Pharos (lighthouse) of Alexandria.

sev·er (sev′ər) *v.t.* **1.** to separate by cutting or breaking; cut apart or off: *The loggers severed the branches from the tree.* **2.** to end or break off: *to sever diplomatic relations with another country.* —*v.i.* to become separated; be divided into parts. —**sev′er·a·ble,** *adj.*

sev·er·al (sev′ər əl, sev′rəl) *adj.* **1.** more than two but not many: *to sleep for several hours.* **2.** individual; different: *After the party, the guests went their several ways.* —*n.* more than two but not many; a few: *The shepherd found several of the stray sheep.*

sev·er·al·ly (sev′ər ə lē, sev′rə lē) *adv.* separately; individually.

sev·er·ance (sev′ər əns, sev′rəns) *n.* the act of severing or the state of being severed; separation.

se·vere (sə vîr′) *adj.,* **se·ver·er, se·ver·est. 1.** very strict or stern; harsh: *severe laws.* **2.** stern or grim in manner or appearance: *a severe face.* **3.** serious; dangerous; grave: *a severe illness, a severe wound.* **4.** plain or simple; without ornament: *a severe style of dressing.*

5. causing great discomfort; sharp or violent: *severe pain, severe cold.* **6.** difficult; rigorous: *a severe test.* —**se·vere′ly,** *adv.* —**se·vere′ness,** *n.*

se·ver·i·ty (sə ver′i tē) *n., pl.* **se·ver·i·ties. 1.** strictness or sternness; harshness: *the severity of a punishment.* **2.** seriousness: *the severity of an illness.* **3.** simplicity of style or taste: *severity of dress.* **4.** sharpness or violence: *the severity of a storm.*

sew (sō) *v.,* **sewed, sewed** or **sewn, sew·ing.** —*v.i.* to work with needle and thread or with a sewing machine. —*v.t.* **1.** to fasten, join, or attach with stitches: *to sew a button on a jacket.* **2.** to make or mend by means of a needle and thread or a sewing machine: *to sew a dress.* **3.** to close with stitches: *to sew up a wound.*

sew·age (sü′ij) *n.* the waste matter carried off by sewers and drains.

sew·er[1] (sü′ər) *n.* an underground pipe or channel used for carrying off waste water and refuse. [From the Old French word *esseweur* meaning ''drainage channel,'' going back to the Latin words *ex* ''out, out of'' and *aqua* ''water.'']

sew·er[2] (sō′ər) *n.* a person or thing that sews. [*Sew* + *-er*[1].]

sew·er·age (sü′ər ij) *n.* **1.** a system of sewers, including pipes, treatment plants, and other devices. **2.** the removal of water and waste materials through a system of sewers.

sew·ing (sō′ing) *n.* **1.** work done with a needle and thread or with a sewing machine. **2.** something to be sewed. **3.** the act of a person who sews.

sewing machine, a mechanical device for sewing fabric and other materials, usually powered by a small electric motor.

sewn (sōn) a past participle of **sew.**

sex (seks) *n., pl.* **sex·es. 1.** either of the two divisions, male or female, into which human beings and most other organisms are divided according to their functions in the process of reproduction. **2.** all the characteristics that determine whether an organism is male or female. **3.** the fact or character of being male or female. **4.** the activities that are part of the process of reproduction. **5.** sexuality.

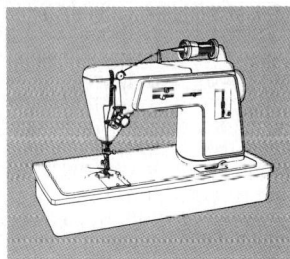

sewing machine

sex chromosome, either of the two types of chromosomes that contain the genes that determine the sex of an offspring; X chromosome or Y chromosome. A female germ cell always has an X chromosome; a male germ cell may have either an X chromosome or a Y chromosome. A combination of germ cells resulting in a fertilized cell with two X chromosomes produces a female organism; a male results from an X chromosome and Y chromosome combination.

sex gland, a gonad.

sex·ism (sek′siz əm) *n.* discrimination based on a person's sex, as in employment or politics.

sex·ist (sek′sist) *adj.* of, relating to, or exhibiting sexism: *sexist behavior.*

---

at; āpe; fär; câre; end; mē; it; īce; pîerce; hot; ōld; sông, fôrk; oil; out; up; ūse; rüle; pull; tûrn; chin; sing; shop; thin; <u>th</u>is; hw in white; zh in treasure. The symbol ə stands for the unstressed vowel sound heard in about, taken, pencil, lemon, and circus.

S

sex-linked (seks′lingkt′) *adj.* (of an inherited trait) determined by a gene carried by a sex chromosome: *Color blindness is a sex-linked trait.*

sex·tant (sek′stənt) *n.* an instrument used mainly in navigation for measuring the altitude of the sun or a star to determine the position of the observer.

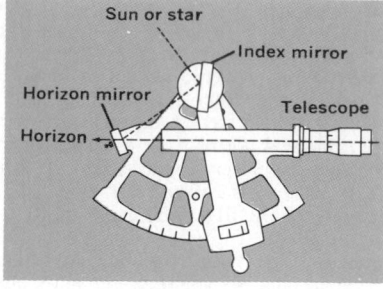

sextant

sex·tet (seks tet′) *also,* **sex·tette.** *n.* **1.** a musical composition for six voices or instruments. **2.** a musical group of six performers. **3.** any group or set of six persons or things, such as a team of ice hockey players.

sex·ton (sek′stən) *n.* a person employed by a parish to take care of church property. The duties of a sexton sometimes also include ringing the church bell and arranging burials.

sex·u·al (sek′shü əl) *adj.* **1.** of or relating to sex or the sexes: *sexual instincts, sexual behavior.* **2.** involving the union of male and female germ cells: *sexual reproduction.* —**sex′u·al·ly,** *adv.*

sexual intercourse, human sexual activity in which male and female genital organs are joined.

sex·u·al·i·ty (sek′shü al′i tē) *n.* **1.** the condition of being distinguished by sex; sexual quality. **2.** the possession and expression of sexual feelings.

sexually transmitted disease, a disease passed from one person to another by sexual activity; venereal disease.

Sgt., Sergeant.

shab·by (shab′ē) *adj.,* **shab·bi·er, shab·bi·est. 1.** faded and dingy from wear or exposure: *a shabby coat.* **2.** neglected; run-down: *a shabby house.* **3.** wearing worn and faded clothes; seedy: *a shabby person.* **4.** mean, unfair, or dishonorable: *a shabby act, shabby treatment.* —**shab′bi·ly,** *adv.* —**shab′bi·ness,** *n.*

shack (shak) *n.* a small, roughly built hut or cabin.

shack·le (shak′əl) *n.* **1.** a metal band fastened around the ankle or wrist of a prisoner, usually one of a pair connected by a chain; fetter. **2.** *usually,* **shackles.** anything that hinders or restrains freedom of action or thought: *the shackles of censorship.* **3.** any of various devices for fastening or coupling. —*v.t.,* **shack·led, shack·ling. 1.** to put a shackle or shackles on; fetter. **2.** to hinder or restrain.

shad (shad) *n., pl.* **shad** or **shads.** any of several food fish related to herring. They are found in the coastal waters of Europe and North America and swim up streams to spawn.

shade (shād) *n.* **1.** partial darkness caused by something cutting off rays of light, as from the sun: *The old elm tree cast shade on the lawn.* **2.** a place or area sheltered or cut off from light, especially from the sun: *to rest in the shade.* **3.** something that shuts out or reduces light: *Please pull down the shades in the living room. I bought a new shade for the lamp.* **4.** the degree of darkness in color: *The dress was a deep shade of green.* **5.** a dark part or surface, as in a painting. **6.** small degree or amount; trace: *a shade of doubt.* **7.** a small difference; nuance: *a shade of meaning.* **8.** a spirit; ghost. —*v.,* **shad·ed, shad·ing.** —*v.t.* **1.** to shelter, screen, or protect from glare, heat, or light: *The umbrella shaded us from the hot sun.* **2.** to mark (a drawing, painting, or the like)

with various degrees of darkness: *The painter shaded the figures in the background of the picture.* —*v.i.* to change or vary slightly or by degrees: *The colors in the painting shaded from deep green to bright yellow.*

shad·ing (shā′ding) *n.* **1.** the representing of different degrees of light and dark in a painting, drawing, or the like, to give a feeling of depth or shadow. **2.** a small degree of change or difference. **3.** a shelter from light or heat.

shad·ow (shad′ō) *n.* **1.** a relatively dark area produced when rays of light are blocked by a person or thing: *to sit in the cool shadows of a forest.* **2.** the dark image or figure cast by a person or thing blocking these light rays: *The shadow of the maple tree fell across the yard.* **3.** a darker or shaded portion of a picture. **4.** a ghost; phantom. **5.** something unreal or imaginary. **6.** a faint image or representation: *The event was a shadow of things to come.* **7.** a slight degree or suggestion; faintest trace: *There is not a shadow of a doubt about the facts.* **8.** a person who follows another closely and secretly, such as a detective. **9.** sadness; gloom; unhappiness: *Their defeat cast a shadow over the team's spirits.* **10. the shadows.** darkness. —*v.t.* **1.** to cast a shadow on or over; cover with a shadow. **2.** to follow closely and secretly: *The detective shadowed the suspect.* **3.** to make gloomy; sadden.

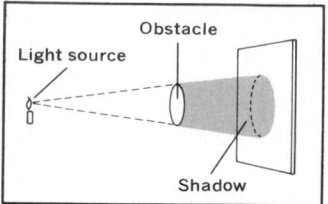

shadow *(n., def. 1)*

shad·ow·y (shad′ō ē) *adj.,* **shad·ow·i·er, shad·ow·i·est. 1.** full of shadow or shade; shady: *a shadowy corner.* **2.** like a shadow; dim; unclear: *a shadowy figure.*

shad·y (shā′dē) *adj.,* **shad·i·er, shad·i·est. 1.** sheltered from the sun; full of shade; shaded: *We picnicked in a shady spot under a tree.* **2.** giving shade: *a shady tree.* **3.** *Informal.* of doubtful honesty; disreputable: *a shady business deal.* —**shad′i·ly,** *adv.* —**shad′i·ness,** *n.*

shaft (shaft) *n.* **1.** a long, slender body connected to the head of an arrow or spear. **2.** an arrow or spear. **3.** something aimed like an arrow or spear: *shafts of criticism.* **4.** a ray or beam: *bright shafts of morning light.* **5.** either of the two wooden poles between which a horse or other draft animal is harnessed to pull a carriage or other vehicle. **6.** the long, straight handle of any of various tools or implements, such as a hammer, golf club, or hockey stick. **7.** a bar in a machine that supports rotating parts or transmits motion to other parts. **8.** a deep passage, usually vertical, from ground level to an underground excavation, as in a mine. **9.** a passage like a well, as for an elevator. **10.** the part of a column between the base and capital.

shag (shag) *n.* **1.** rough, matted hair, wool, or the like. **2.** a long, rough nap on cloth, as wool or cotton. **3.** a cloth or article, such as a rug, having such a nap: *A small shag lay next to the sofa.*

shag·bark (shag′bärk′) *n.* **1.** a hickory tree of Canada and the eastern United States, having shaggy gray bark that peels off in long strips. **2.** the wood of this tree, used as timber.

shag·gy (shag′ē) *adj.,* **shag·gi·er, shag·gi·est. 1.** covered with or having

shagbark

long, rough hair or wool: *A sheepdog is a shaggy animal.*
2. long, bushy, and rough: *shaggy eyebrows.* **3.** having a
long, rough nap: *a shaggy rug.*

shah (shä) *n.* the title of the former hereditary ruler of
Iran.

shake (shāk) *v.,* **shook, shak·en, shak·ing.** —*v.t.* **1.** to
cause to move quickly to and fro, up and down, or from
side to side: *Shake the bottle to mix its contents.* **2.** to
throw, bring, or remove with such movements: *The dog
shook the water from its back.* **3.** to cause to tremble,
vibrate, or quiver: *The passing train shook the house.*
4. to weaken or make less firm: *The district attorney could
not shake the witness's testimony.* **5.** to move or stir the
feelings of; upset; disturb: *The news of the accident shook
us all.* **6.** *Informal.* to get rid of or avoid: *to shake a bad
habit.* —*v.i.* **1.** to move quickly to and fro, up and down,
or from side to side: *The house shakes when the trains
go by.* **2.** to tremble; quiver: *The kitten was shaking with
fright when we found it.* —*n.* **1.** the act of shaking: *a
shake of the finger.* **2. the shakes.** *Informal.* a trembling
or shivering, as from fever or chills.
· **to shake down.** *Slang.* to get money from (someone)
dishonestly.
· **to shake hands.** to grasp (another's hand), as in greeting
or agreement.
· **to shake off.** to get rid of or away from.
· **to shake up. a.** to disturb mentally or physically; shock.
b. to change (something) suddenly and thoroughly.

shak·en (shā′kən) the past participle of **shake.**

shak·er (shā′kər) *n.* **1.** a container having a top with
holes, as for sprinkling salt or pepper. **2.** any of various
other devices or machines used for shaking: *a cocktail
shaker.* **3.** a person who shakes.

Shak·er (shā′kər) *n.* a member of an American religious
sect practicing communal living and celibacy. [Named
because the members of this sect used to dance with
shaking movements at their prayer meetings.]

Shake·spear·e·an (shāk spîr′ē ən) *also,* **Shake·spear-
i·an.** *adj.* of, relating to, or like Shakespeare or his
works.

shake-up (shāk′up′) *n.* a sudden, thorough change in
organization, as of a business or government: *The president's cabinet shake-up surprised everyone.*

shako
members of a marching band wearing **shakos**

shak·o (shak′ō) *n., pl.* **shak·os.** a high, stiff military hat
with a visor and, usually, a plume attached in front.

shak·y (shā′kē) *adj.,* **shak·i·er, shak·i·est. 1.** trembling;
shaking: *shaky writing.* **2.** liable to break down
or give way; unsound: *a shaky bridge.* **3.** not to be

depended on: *shaky information.* —**shak′i·ly,** *adv.*
—**shak′i·ness,** *n.*

shale (shāl) *n.* a fine-grained rock, formed from hardened
clay in very thin layers that separate easily.

shall (shal) *auxiliary verb.* Present tense: *sing.,* first
person, **shall;** second, **shall** or *(archaic)* **shalt;** third, **shall;**
pl., **shall.** Past tense: *sing.,* first person, **should;** second,
should or *(archaic)* **shouldest** or **shouldst;** third, **should;**
pl., **should. 1.** in the first person, used to express future
time: *I shall be glad to help you.* **2.** in the second and
third persons, used to express determination, obligation,
or compulsion: *They shall do as they are told.* **3.** in all
persons, used in direct questions when *shall* is expected
in the answer: *Shall we leave tomorrow? Yes, we shall.*
▲ According to the rules of traditional grammar, **shall** is
used with the first person to express the simple future
tense: *When shall we three meet again* (Shakespeare,
Macbeth), and **will** is used with the second and third
persons: *Some say the world will end in fire* (Robert
Frost).

In the same way, it has traditionally been considered
correct to use *will* with the first person, and *shall* with
the second and third persons, to show determination or
obligation: *I will not retreat a single inch and I will be
heard* (William Lloyd Garrison). *We here highly resolve
. . . that this nation . . . shall have a new birth of freedom*
(Abraham Lincoln).

However, this distinction between *shall* and *will* is
subtle and somewhat difficult to grasp, and it has never
been faithfully observed, even by the best speakers and
writers. For example: *We shall never surrender* (Winston
Churchill) shows determination, and *Show me a hero and
I will write you a tragedy* (F. Scott Fitzgerald) expresses
the simple future tense.

In current American usage, *shall* and *will* are used
interchangeably, with *will* being much more common.
Shall is common in British English, but to many American
speakers it sounds too formal or artificial.

shal·lop (shal′əp) *n.* a small open boat with sails or
oars.

shal·lot (shə lot′, shal′ət) *n.* **1.** a small bulb or clove of
a plant closely related to the onion, used to flavor foods.
2. the small plant that grows from this bulb.

shal·low (shal′ō) *adj.* **1.** of little depth; not deep: *a
shallow pond.* **2.** lacking depth of thought, reasoning,
knowledge, or feeling: *a shallow mind.* —*n. usually,*
shallows. a shallow area in a body of water. —**shal′-
low·ly,** *adv.* —**shal′low·ness,** *n.*

sha·lom (shə lōm′) *interj.* a traditional Jewish expression of greeting or farewell. [From the Hebrew word
shālōm meaning "peace."]

shalt (shalt) *Archaic.* the second person singular, present
tense of **shall.** ▲ used with *thou.*

sham (sham) *n.* **1.** something false intended to appear
genuine or true; fraud; counterfeit: *Their friendliness is
all sham.* **2.** a person who falsely takes on a certain
character for the purpose of deceiving. —*adj.* not real
or true; pretended; false: *a sham battle, sham diamonds.*
—*v.,* **shammed, sham·ming.** —*v.t.* **1.** to take on the
appearance of; feign: *to sham illness.* **2.** to make an
imitation of. —*v.i.* to pretend.

at; āpe; fär; câre; end; mē; it; īce; pîerce; hot; ōld;
sông; fôrk; oil; out; up; ūse; rüle; pull; tûrn; chin;
sing; shop; thin; this; hw in white; zh in treasure.
The symbol ə stands for the unstressed vowel sound
heard in about, taken, pencil, lemon, and circus.

S

859

sha·man (shä′mən, shā′mən) *n.* in certain tribal religions, a person who is believed to be able to influence good and evil spirits to cure illness, bring rain, and the like; medicine man.

sham·ble (sham′bəl) *v.i.*, **sham·bled, sham·bling.** to walk awkwardly or unsteadily; shuffle. —*n.* a shambling walk or gait: *The old horse moved at a shamble.*

sham·bles (sham′bəlz) *pl. n.* **1.** a place or condition of great disorder or confusion: *The unruly children left the house in a shambles.* **2.** a scene of slaughter or of great bloodshed. ▲ used with a singular verb.

shame (shām) *n.* **1.** a painful feeling of guilt or embarrassment caused by having done something wrong, indecent, or foolish: *to feel shame.* **2.** dishonor; disgrace: *to bring shame to one's entire family.* **3.** a person or thing that brings or causes disgrace: *Widespread corruption was the shame of the city government.* **4.** a thing to be sorry about: *It was a shame that we did not win the race.* —*v.t.*, **shamed, sham·ing.** **1.** to cause to feel shame; make ashamed; embarrass. **2.** to bring disgrace upon; dishonor. **3.** to force or drive by shame or fear of shame: *The more experienced soldiers shamed the new recruit into volunteering.*
·**for shame.** shame on you; how shameful.
·**to put to shame. a.** to bring disgrace upon; cause to feel ashamed. **b.** to outdo another or others.

shame·faced (shām′fāst′) *adj.* **1.** bashful; shy. **2.** showing shame; ashamed: *a shamefaced look.*

shame·ful (shām′fəl) *adj.* causing shame; disgraceful. —**shame′ful·ly,** *adv.* —**shame′ful·ness,** *n.*

shame·less (shām′lis) *adj.* **1.** having no sense of shame; immodest. **2.** without shame. —**shame′less·ly,** *adv.* —**shame′less·ness,** *n.*

sham·poo (sham pü′) *v.t.*, **sham·pooed, sham·poo·ing. 1.** to wash (the hair or scalp) with soap and water or a special preparation. **2.** to wash the hair and scalp of. **3.** to clean (upholstery or rugs) with any of various cleaning preparations. —*n.*, *pl.* **sham·poos. 1.** the act of shampooing. **2.** any special preparation for use in shampooing.

sham·rock (sham′rok′) *n.* **1.** a plant having leaves composed of three leaflets, especially the clover. **2.** such a leaf used as the national emblem of Ireland.

shang·hai (shang′hī) *v.t.*, **shang·haied, shang·hai·ing. 1.** to make (someone) unconscious by drugs, liquor, or a blow in order to force the person onto a ship to serve as a sailor. **2.** to cause to do something against one's will, especially by trickery or force. [From the earlier practice of acquiring sailors against their will for voyages to *Shanghai.*]

Wood sorrel   White clover

shamrocks

shank (shangk) *n.* **1.** a part of the leg in humans between the knee and the ankle. **2.** a similar part in certain animals and birds. **3.** the entire leg. **4.** a cut of meat from the leg of an animal. **5.** the part of an instrument or tool that connects the working part with a handle or with the part by which it is held or moved.

shan't (shant) *contr.* shall not.

shan·tey (shan′tē) *n.*, *pl.* **shan·teys.** another spelling of **chantey.**

shan·tung (shan′tung′, shan′tung′) *n.* a soft, textured fabric made of silk, rayon, or cotton. [From *Shantung,* the province in northeast China where this cloth originated.]

shan·ty¹ (shan′tē) *n.*, *pl.* **shan·ties.** a crude, flimsily built hut or cabin. [Probably from the word *chantier* meaning "lumber camp shanty¹" in the dialect of French

spoken in Canada, from the French word *chantier* "lumber yard" or "gantry."]

shan·ty² (shan′tē) *n.*, *pl.* **shan·ties.** another spelling of **chantey.**

shape (shāp) *n.* **1.** an outward form or outline; contour; figure: *All circles have the same shape. Clay can be molded into many shapes.* **2.** condition: *to be in bad shape after an accident.* **3.** good physical condition: *to keep in shape by exercising.* **4.** a definite, regular, or proper form or arrangement; order: *Let's get the room in shape before the guests arrive.* —*v.*, **shaped, shaping.** —*v.t.* **1.** to give form to; fashion; mold: *to shape dough into loaves.* **2.** to adapt in form; adjust; modify: *to shape pillows. Don't shape your ideas just to agree with ours.* **3.** to give definite direction or character to: *to shape one's life.* —*v.i.* to take on a definite form, order, or plan; develop: *Things are shaping up nicely.*
·**to take shape.** to have or take on a definite form, order, or plan: *Our plans for a vacation are beginning to take shape.*

shape·less (shāp′lis) *adj.* **1.** without definite or regular shape: *a shapeless mound of earth.* **2.** having no beauty or elegance of form; unshapely; unattractive. —**shape′less·ly,** *adv.* —**shape′less·ness,** *n.*

shape·ly (shāp′lē) *adj.*, **shape·li·er, shape·li·est.** having a beautiful or elegant shape; well-formed. —**shape′li·ness,** *n.*

shard (shärd) *n.* a fragment of some brittle material, as of glass or pottery; potsherd.

share¹ (shâr) *n.* **1.** the part that is given or belongs to one individual: *I spent my share of the money.* **2.** one of the equal parts into which the ownership of a company or corporation is divided: *to own fifty shares of stock.* —*v.*, **shared, shar·ing.** —*v.t.* **1.** to use, enjoy, or take part in together or in common: *to share an apartment, to share someone's happiness.* **2.** to divide into portions and give to others as well as to oneself: *to share one's sandwich with a friend.* —*v.i.* to have a share; take part: *We all shared in the fun at the party.* [From the Old English word *scearu* meaning "a cutting" or "share¹."]

share² (shâr) *n.* another word for **plowshare.** [From the Old English word *scear* meaning "plowshare."]

share·crop·per (shâr′krop′ər) *n.* a tenant farmer who farms land for the owner in return for a share of the crop that the land yields.

share·hold·er (shâr′hōl′dər) *n.* another word for **stockholder.**

shark¹ (shärk) *n.* any of numerous saltwater fish having skeletons of cartilage rather than bone, with usually gray rough skin, a deeply forked tail, and a large mouth on the underside of the head with several rows of sharp teeth.

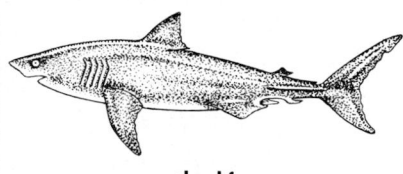

shark¹
great white **shark**

Sharks eat other fish and some species will attack humans. [From the Middle English word *shark,* of uncertain origin.]

shark² (shärk) *n.* a dishonest person who takes advantage of others; swindler. [Probably from the German word *Schurke* meaning "rogue."]

sharp (shärp) *adj.* **1.** having a fine cutting edge or point; well-suited for cutting or piercing: *a sharp blade, a sharp knife.* **2.** having a pointed end; not rounded or blunt: *The mountain has a sharp peak.* **3.** involving an abrupt or sudden change in direction: *to make a sharp turn, a sharp curve.* **4.** harsh, biting, or severe: *sharp words.*

5. keenly affecting the senses or emotions: *sharp pangs of hunger.* **6.** (of food) having a biting taste: *sharp cheese.* **7.** high-pitched; shrill: *a sharp cry of pain.* **8.** clear or distinct, as in outline or contour: *That camera takes sharp pictures.* **9.** having the ability to feel or perceive quickly: *a sharp eye for details.* **10.** shrewd or clever: *to be sharp at cards.* **11.** watchful; alert; vigilant: *Keep a sharp lookout.* **12.** rapid; brisk; energetic: *a sharp pace.* **13.** *Slang.* strikingly attractive; stylish: *You really look sharp in that new suit.* **14.** *Music.* **a.** raised a half step in pitch. **b.** above the true and proper pitch; too high. **c.** (of a key) having sharps in the signature. —*adv.* **1.** at the moment specified; promptly; exactly: *We must leave at 1:30 sharp.* **2.** in a sharp manner: *Look sharp or you will miss the turn.* **3.** above the true pitch in music: *to sing sharp.* —*n. Music.* **1.** a note or tone one half step above a given note or tone. **2.** the symbol (♯) which, when placed before a note or on a degree of the staff, shows that the pitch is to be played or sung a half step higher. —**sharp′ly,** *adv.* —**sharp′ness,** *n.*

sharp·en (shär′pən) *v.t., v.i.* to make or become sharp or sharper: *to sharpen a pencil.* —**sharp′en·er,** *n.*

sharp·shoot·er (shärp′shü′tər) *n.* a person who is skilled in shooting, especially with a rifle.

shat·ter (shat′ər) *v.t.* **1.** to break (something, especially a hard or brittle thing) into pieces, as by a sudden blow: *to shatter a glass.* **2.** to destroy completely or damage greatly: *The candidate's hopes were shattered by defeat.* —*v.i.* to break suddenly into pieces; go to pieces: *The glass shattered when it hit the floor.*

shave (shāv) *v.,* **shaved, shaved** or **shav·en, shav·ing.** —*v.t.* **1.** to remove hair from with a razor: *to shave one's face, to shave one's legs.* **2.** to cut (hair) down close to the skin with a razor: *to shave a beard off.* **3.** to cut down the surface of by removing thin shavings or parings: *The carpenter shaved the edge of the board.* **4.** to cut off in thin slices or parings: *That appliance shaves ice.* **5.** to cut very closely, as a lawn. **6.** to touch slightly or come very near touching; graze. —*v.i.* to remove hair with a razor. —*n.* the act of shaving: *a quick shave.*

shav·en (shā′vən) *v.* a past participle of **shave.** —*adj.* **1.** shaved. **2.** closely cut or trimmed, as grass.

shav·er (shā′vər) *n.* **1.** a person who shaves. **2.** any device for shaving. **3.** *Informal.* a youngster; boy.

shav·ing (shā′ving) *n.* **1.** a very thin piece or slice, especially of wood. **2.** the act or process of removing hair or trimming a surface with a razor.

Sha·vu·oth (shə vü′əs, shä vü ōt′) also, **Sha·vu·ot.** *n.* a Jewish holiday, originally a spring harvest festival, commemorating the giving of the Commandments to Moses. Also, **Feast of Weeks.**

shawl (shôl) *n.* a square or oblong piece of fabric, usually worn over the shoulders.

Shaw·nee (shô nē′) *n., pl.* **Shaw·nee** or **Shaw·nees.** **1.** a member of a tribe of Algonquian Indians, formerly living in the East, South, and Midwest, now living mainly in Oklahoma. **2.** the language of this people.

shay (shā) *n.* a light, two-wheeled carriage; chaise.

she (shē) *pron.* **1.** a female person or animal that has been mentioned or spoken about before: *My aunt said that she would be glad to join us.* **2.** something thought of as female: *She is the fastest boat we ever saw.* **3.** any woman or girl: *She who listens learns.* —*n., pl.* **shes.** a female person or animal.

sheaf (shēf) *n., pl.* **sheaves.** **1.** one of the bundles in which stalks of cereal plants, such as wheat, are bound after reaping. **2.** any bundle of things of the same kind: *a sheaf of papers.*

shear (shîr) *v.t.,* **sheared, sheared** or **shorn, shear·ing.** **1.** to clip or cut with shears, scissors, or a similar sharp instrument: *to shear the grass close to the ground.* **2.** to cut the wool or hair from: *to shear sheep.* **3.** to cut off; remove by clipping: *to shear fleece.* —**shear′er,** *n.*

shears (shîrz) *pl. n.* **1.** any of various, usually large, cutting instruments resembling scissors. **2.** large scissors.

sheath (shēth) *n., pl.* **sheaths** (shēthz). **1.** a case for the blade of a sword, knife,

shear
shearing a sheep

or the like. **2.** any similar covering, such as a membrane covering a muscle. **3.** a tight, close-fitting dress. —*v.t.* to sheathe.

sheathe (shēth) *v.t.,* **sheathed, sheath·ing.** **1.** to put into a sheath or scabbard: *to sheathe a sword.* **2.** to enclose or protect in a case or covering.

sheath·ing (shē′thing) *n.* **1.** something that covers or protects, such as the first covering of boards on a house or one of the metal plates on the bottom of a ship. **2.** the act of a person who sheathes.

sheave (shēv) *v.t.,* **sheaved, sheav·ing.** to gather and bind into a sheaf or sheaves.

sheaves (shēvz) the plural of **sheaf.**

shed[1] (shed) *n.* a small structure used for storage or shelter: *a tool shed.* [Probably from the Old English word *scead* "shade" or "protection, shelter."]

shed[2] (shed) *v.,* **shed, shed·ding.** —*v.t.* **1.** to cause to flow; let fall; let pour: *to shed tears.* **2.** to throw off or lose by natural process: *The snake shed its skin. The trees are beginning to shed their leaves.* **3.** to send out; radiate: *The lilacs shed their fragrance throughout the room. The investigation shed new light on the problem.* **4.** to get rid of: *to shed extra weight, to shed one's fears.* —*v.i.* **1.** to throw off or lose a covering, especially by natural process: *Our dog sheds a lot.* **2.** to fall off or drop: *Leaves shed in the fall.* [From the Old English word *scēadan* meaning "to divide, separate" or "scatter."]

she′d (shēd) *contr.* **1.** she had. **2.** she would.

sheen (shēn) *n.* a lustrous brightness; gloss; shininess: *the sheen of a polished marble floor.* —**sheen′y,** *adj.*

sheep (shēp) *n., pl.* **sheep.** **1.** any of various cud-chewing mammals related to the goat, many of which are widely raised for fleece, meat, milk, and skin. **2.** a person who is timid, meek, or easily led. —**sheep′like′,** *adj.*

---

at; āpe; fär; câre; end; mē; it; ice; pierce; hot; ōld; sông, fôrk; oil; out; up; ūse; rüle; pùll; tûrn; chin; sing; shop; thin; **th**is; hw in white; zh in treasure. The symbol ə stands for the unstressed vowel sound heard in about, taken, pencil, lemon, and circus.

S

sheep·cote (shēp′kōt′) *n.* a shed or similar shelter for sheep.

sheep·dog (shēp′dôg′) *n.* **1.** see **Old English sheepdog**. **2.** any dog that has been trained to guard, drive, or tend sheep, such as a collie. Also (*def. 2*), **shepherd dog**.

sheep·fold (shēp′fōld′) *n.* an enclosure for sheep, such as a pen.

sheep·herd·er (shēp′hûr′dər) *n.* a person who raises or tends a large number of sheep, especially on open land.

sheep·ish (shē′pish) *adj.* **1.** awkwardly bashful or embarrassed: *a sheepish grin.* **2.** like a sheep; timid or meek. —**sheep′ish·ly,** *adv.* —**sheep′ish·ness,** *n.*

sheep·skin (shēp′skin′) *n.* **1.** the skin of a sheep, especially one prepared with the wool on it, often used for clothing. **2.** leather or parchment made from the skin of a sheep. **3.** *Informal.* a diploma.

sheer¹ (shîr) *adj.* **1.** very thin and fine; nearly transparent: *a sheer fabric.* **2.** unmixed with anything else; complete or total: *to drop from sheer exhaustion.* **3.** utter; downright: *sheer nonsense.* **4.** straight up or straight down; steep: *From the cliff there was a sheer drop of 200 feet.* —*adv.* **1.** completely; quite; altogether. **2.** very steeply up or down. [From the Middle English word *shire* meaning "bright, fair" or "pure," from the Old English word *scīr* "clear, bright."] —**sheer′ly,** *adv.* —**sheer′ness,** *n.*

sheer² (shîr) *v.i.* to turn from a course; swerve: *The ship sheered away from the rocks.* —*v.t.* to cause to turn from a course. —*n.* a moving away of a ship or boat from its course. [Probably from the Middle English word *sheren* meaning "to cut, divide" or "to swerve," from the Old English word *sceran* "to cut, shear."]

sheet¹ (shēt) *n.* **1.** a large piece of fabric used as a bed covering. **2.** any broad, thin piece or object: *a sheet of clear plastic.* **3.** a single oblong or square piece of paper or parchment for writing or printing on. **4.** a broad, flat expanse or surface: *sheets of flame, a sheet of water.* —*v.t.* **1.** to furnish with a sheet or sheets. **2.** to cover with a sheet: *Snow sheeted the ground.* [From the Old English word *scīte* meaning "a linen cloth, sheet¹."]

sheet² (shēt) *n.* a rope or chain attached to one or both of the lower ends of a sail, used to adjust or control the sail. [From the Old English word *scēata* meaning "corner, angle" or "sheet²."]

sheet·ing (shē′ting) *n.* fabric used for bed sheets.

sheet lightning, lightning appearing as bright, broad flashes, as from within a cloud or beyond the horizon.

sheet metal, metal in thin, flat pieces.

sheet music, music printed on unbound sheets of paper.

sheik (shēk, shāk) *also,* **sheikh.** *n.* **1.** the leader of an Arab clan, tribe, or other large group. **2.** a Muslim religious leader, especially the superior of a religious community.

sheik·dom (shēk′dəm, shāk′dəm) *also,* **sheikh·dom.** *n.* a region governed by a sheik.

shek·el (shek′əl) *n.* **1.** any of various ancient units of weight, especially one used by the Babylonians, Phoenicians, Hebrews, and Assyrians, equal to about ½ ounce (about 14 grams). **2.** an ancient silver coin of the Hebrews weighing one shekel. **3.** the unit of money used by Israel.

shel·duck (shel′duk′) *n.* **1.** any of several large ducks that resemble geese, found in Europe, North Africa, and Asia. **2.** any of various similar ducks, especially the merganser. Also, **shel·drake** (shel′drāk′).

shelduck (def. 1)

shelf (shelf) *n., pl.* **shelves. 1.** a thin, flat piece of wood, metal, stone, or other material, fastened horizontally to a wall or frame to hold things, such as books or dishes. **2.** anything like a shelf, such as a sandbar, reef, or projecting ledge of rock. [From the Old English word *scilf* meaning "a ledge, shelf."]

·**on the shelf.** put away or aside as done with or not needed: *The plan to build a new gym is on the shelf for the time being.*

shelf life, the length of time that a product remains fresh or suitable for sale and use: *Milk has a short shelf life compared with dry cereal.*

shell (shel) *n.* **1.** a hard or tough outer covering of any of various animals, such as the turtle, lobster, or snail. **2.** the material of which such a covering is made. **3.** any similar covering, as of a seed, fruit, or egg. **4.** something like a shell, such as the framework of a building or a rounded piece of pastry for holding filling. **5.** shyness; reserve: *Friendliness can make people come out of their shells.* **6.** a metal projectile fired by cannon and other artillery, designed to explode at or in a target or in the air. **7.** a cartridge for a shotgun or rifle. **8.** a long, light racing boat propelled by oars. **9.** *Physics.* any of several energy levels occupied by electrons as they orbit the nucleus of an atom. —*v.t.* **1.** to remove the shell, husk, or pod of: *to shell peanuts.* **2.** to remove grains from the ear or cob of: *to shell corn.* **3.** to subject to artillery fire; bombard with shells. —**shell′like′,** *adj.*

she'll (shēl) *contr.* **1.** she shall. **2.** she will.

shel·lac (shə lak′) *n.* **1.** a liquid preparation made of lac dissolved in alcohol, used as a varnish on floors, furniture, or similar surfaces. **2.** the lac itself when not dissolved, used in making certain insulating materials. —*v.t.,* **shel·lacked, shel·lack·ing.** to coat or treat with shellac: *to shellac a floor.*

shell·fish (shel′fish′) *n., pl.* **shell·fish** or **shell·fish·es.** any animal having a shell and living in water, especially a mollusk or crustacean. Shrimps, lobsters, clams, and oysters are shellfish.

shell shock, a nervous or mental disorder resulting from combat in war.

shel·ter (shel′tər) *n.* **1.** something that covers or protects, as from weather, danger, or attack: *The school was turned into a temporary shelter for victims of the flood.* **2.** protection; refuge: *We found shelter in an abandoned house during the snowstorm.* —*v.t.* **1.** to provide cover or protection for; shield: *The canopy sheltered us from the rain.* **2.** to take under one's protection: *to shelter a homeless family.* —*v.i.* to find or take shelter.

shelve¹ (shelv) *v.t.,* **shelved, shelv·ing. 1.** to place on a shelf: *to shelve books.* **2.** to put away or aside as done with or not needed: *to shelve a plan.* **3.** to furnish with shelves: *to shelve a wall.* [From *shelf.*]

shelve² (shelv) *v.t.,* **shelved, shelv·ing.** to slope gradually. [Of uncertain origin.]

shelves (shelvz) the plural of **shelf.**

shelv·ing (shel′ving) *n.* **1.** material for shelves, such as wood or metal. **2.** shelves as a group: *The library had shelving for 10,000 books.*

she·nan·i·gan (shə nan′i gən) *usually,* **shenanigans.** *n. Informal.* nonsense or trickery.

She·ol (shē′ōl) *n.* in the Old Testament, the dwelling place of the spirits of the dead; underworld.

shep·herd (shep′ərd) *n.* **1.** a person who takes care of a flock of sheep. **2.** a spiritual leader; pastor. —*v.t.* **1.** to tend as a shepherd. **2.** to watch over or guide like a shepherd: *The teacher shepherded the children onto the bus.*

shepherd dog, another term for **sheepdog** (*def. 2*).

shep·herd·ess (shep′ər dis) *n.*, *pl.* **shep·herd·ess·es.** a woman or girl who takes care of a flock of sheep.

sher·bet (shûr′bit) *n.* a frozen dessert made of fruit juice, water, sweeteners, and small amounts of egg whites or milk. [From the Turkish word *sherbet* and the Persian word *sharbat*, both names for a cool drink made of fruit juice, going back to the Arabic word *sharbah* "a drink."]

sher·iff (sher′if) *n.* the chief law enforcement officer of a county, who is in charge of keeping the peace, serving court orders, maintaining the jails, and other administrative functions. [From the Middle English word *shirreve* meaning "the high official of a county who represented the king," from the Old English word *scīrgerefa* with the same meaning, from the words *scīr* "district" or "shire" + *gerefe* "royal official."]

Sher·lock Holmes (shûr′lok hōmz′) a fictional British detective, noted for his remarkable powers of observation, analysis, and deduction, the main character in mystery stories by Sir Arthur Conan Doyle.

Sher·pa (shûr′pə) *n.*, *pl.* **Sher·pa** or **Sher·pas.** a member of a people of Tibetan origin living in the Himalayas in Nepal, famous as guides and porters for mountain climbers.

sher·ry (sher′ē) *n.*, *pl.* **sher·ries.** a strong wine that varies in color from pale amber to dark brown, and in taste from dry to sweet.

she's (shēz) *contr.* **1.** she is. **2.** she has.

Shet·land pony (shet′lənd), a small, hardy pony of a breed that originated in the Shetland Islands. It has a rough coat and a long mane and tail.

Shetland sheepdog, a dog closely resembling the collie, but smaller.

shew (shō) *n.*, *v.*, **shewed, shewn, shewing.** *Archaic.* another spelling of **show.**

SHF, superhigh frequency.

Shetland pony

Shi·a (shē′ə) *n.* the smaller of the two principal sects of Islam. The Shia sect considers Ali, Muhammad's son-in-law, as the true successor of Muhammad.

shib·bo·leth (shib′ə lith) *n.* **1.** a catchword, slogan, or custom of a certain group, political party, or class of people, especially one frequently repeated or followed unthinkingly. **2.** any characteristic, as of speech or usage, that distinguishes a group. [From the Hebrew word *shibbōleth* meaning "flowing stream." According to the Book of Judges in the Bible, *shibboleth* was used as a password because the enemy, speaking a different dialect, could not pronounce the *sh-* sound but would mispronounce it as *s-.*]

shied (shīd) the past tense and past participle of **shy².**

shield (shēld) *n.* **1.** a piece of armor carried on the arm for defense in battle. **2.** a person or thing that defends or protects, as against danger, injury, or distress: *to use an umbrella as a shield against the rain.* **3.** something shaped like a shield, such as a police officer's badge. **4.** another word for **escutcheon.** —*v.t.* to shield, protect, or defend: *to shield one's eyes from the glare of the sun.*

shi·er (shī′ər) a comparative of **shy¹.**

shi·est (shī′ist) a superlative of **shy¹.**

shift (shift) *v.t.* **1.** to move from one person, place, or position to another: *to shift the furniture in the living room.* **2.** to switch or change: *to shift one's position on capital punishment.* **3.** to change (gears) from one arrangement to another, as in driving an automobile.

—*v.i.* **1.** to move, as from one place or position to another: *to shift uneasily in a chair.* **2.** to change gears from one arrangement to another, as in driving an automobile. —*n.* **1.** a movement from one person, place, or position to another: *a shift from one side of a boat to the other.* **2.** a switch or change, as in attitude: *a shift in policy.* **3.** a group of workers who work during a particular period of time: *The day shift at the factory is just arriving.* **4.** the working time of such a group. **5.** a gearshift, especially in an automobile. **6.** a loosely fitting dress designed to fall with straight lines from the shoulders to the hips.
·**to shift for oneself.** to get along by oneself.

shift·less (shift′lis) *adj.* lacking in ambition or energy; good-for-nothing; lazy. —**shift′less·ly,** *adv.* —**shift′less·ness,** *n.*

shift·y (shif′tē) *adj.*, **shift·i·er, shift·i·est. 1.** not to be trusted or believed; dishonest; tricky. **2.** showing trickery or dishonesty: *shifty eyes.* —**shift′i·ly,** *adv.* —**shift′i·ness,** *n.*

Shi·ite (shē′īt) *n.* a follower of the Shia sect of Islam. —*adj.* of or pertaining to the Shia sect of Islam.

shil·le·lagh (shə lā′lē, shə lā′lə) *also,* **shil·la·lah.** *n.* a short stick or cudgel, traditionally made in Ireland from the wood of a blackthorn or oak.

shil·ling (shil′ing) *n.* **1.** a former coin of the United Kingdom, equal to ¹/₂₀ of a pound. **2.** the unit of money used by Kenya, Tanzania, and Uganda.

shil·ly-shal·ly (shil′ē shal′ē) *v.i.*, **shil·ly-shal·lied, shil·ly-shal·ly·ing. 1.** to be undecided or hesitant. **2.** to waste time; dawdle.

shim·mer (shim′ər) *v.i.* to shine with a faint, wavering light; glimmer. —*n.* a faint, wavering light; glimmer; gleam. —**shim′mer·y,** *adj.*

shim·my (shim′ē) *n.*, *pl.* **shim·mies. 1.** an unusual shaking or vibration. **2.** a dance characterized by much shaking of the body, popular in the 1920s. —*v.i.*, **shim·mied, shim·my·ing. 1.** to shake; vibrate. **2.** to shake the body, as in dancing the shimmy.

shin (shin) *n.* **1.** the front part of the leg from the knee to the ankle. **2.** a similar part in certain animals and birds. —*v.i.*, **shinned, shin·ning.** to climb by using the hands or arms and the feet or legs in grasping or pulling: *to shin up a tree.* [From the Old English word *scinu* with the same meaning.]

shin·bone (shin′bōn′) *n.* the inner and thicker of the two bones of the leg, extending from the knee to the ankle; tibia.

shin·dig (shin′dig′) *n.* *Slang.* a festive or noisy social gathering, such as a dance or party.

shine (shīn) *v.*, **shone** or (*v.t.*) **shined, shin·ing.** —*v.i.* **1.** to give out or send out light or brightness: *The sun shone all day.* **2.** to be bright or gleam with reflected light; glow: *The newly waxed floor shone. The child's face was shining with excitement.* **3.** to be outstanding; excel: *to shine in math.* —*v.t.* **1.** to put a gloss or polish on: *I shined my shoes.* **2.** to cause to shine: *to shine a flashlight.* —*n.* **1.** light or brightness; radiance. **2.** luster or sheen, as of an object reflecting light. **3.** fair weather; sunshine: *Let's go on a hike, come rain or shine.* **4.** a polish given to shoes. **5.** *Informal.* a liking; fancy: *to take a shine to someone.*

at; āpe; fär; câre; end; mē; it; īce; pierce; hot; ōld; sông, fôrk; oil; out; up; ūse; rüle; pùll; tûrn; chin; sing; shop; thin; this; hw in white; zh in treasure. The symbol ə stands for the unstressed vowel sound heard in about, taken, pencil, lemon, and circus.

S

shin·er (shī'nər) *n.* **1.** a person or thing that shines. **2.** *Informal.* a black eye.

shin·gle[1] (shing'gəl) *n.* **1.** a thin piece of wood or other material, such as asphalt, applied to roofs and outside walls in overlapping rows. **2.** *Informal.* a small signboard, especially outside the office of a doctor or lawyer. **3.** a very short haircut. —*v.t.*, **shingled, shin·gling. 1.** to cover with shingles: *to shingle a roof.* **2.** to cut (the hair) very short. [From the late Old English word *scingul*, a form of *scindel* meaning "a wooden tile for roofing," from the Latin word *scindula* "a split piece of wood," "shingle[1]."]

shingles[1] *(def. 1)*

shin·gle[2] (shing'gəl) *n.* loose gravel made up of flattened pebbles and stones, such as that found on beaches. [Probably of Scandinavian origin.]

shin·gles (shing'gəlz) *n.* a virus infection characterized by painful irritation of groups of nerves and the eruption of blisters. ▲ used with a singular verb. [From the Middle English word *schingles* meaning this disease, from the Medieval Latin word *cingulus* meaning this disease, from the Latin word *cingulus* "a belt, girdle," from the word *cingere* "to gird" or "to surround."]

shin·ing (shī'ning) *adj.* **1.** sending out or reflecting light; bright. **2.** outstanding; distinguished: *a shining example of honesty.* —**shin'ing·ly,** *adv.*

shin·ny[1] (shin'ē) *v.i.,* **shin·nied, shin·ny·ing.** to climb by the use of the hands or arms and the feet or legs in pulling or grasping: *to shinny up a tree.* [From *shin*.]

shin·ny[2] (shin'ē) *n.* a game resembling hockey, played with a curved stick and a ball or block of wood. [Possibly from the cry *shin ye!* made during the game.]

shin·splints (shin'splints') *pl. n.* tiny rips in the muscles of the front of the lower leg, sometimes caused by persistent running or jumping on hard surfaces.

Shin·to (shin'tō) *n.* **1.** the native religion of Japan, marked by worship of nature, reverence of ancestors and ancient heroes, and belief in the divinity of the emperor. **2.** a person who follows or believes in this religion.

Shin·to·ism (shin'tō iz'əm) *n.* the Shinto religion.

shin·y (shī'nē) *adj.,* **shin·i·er, shin·i·est. 1.** shining; bright. **2.** worn to a glossy smoothness: *The seat of the trousers was shiny from wear.* —**shin'i·ness,** *n.*

ship (ship) *n.* **1.** any large seagoing vessel. **2.** the crew of such a vessel. **3.** an airplane, airship, or spacecraft. **4.** a sailing vessel having three or more masts. —*v.,* **shipped, ship·ping.** —*v.t.* **1** to send or transport, as by ship, rail, or truck: *The store shipped our new furniture by truck.* **2.** (of a boat or ship) to take on (water) over the side. **3.** to put (an object) in its proper place for use on a boat or ship: *to ship a mast.* —*v.i.* **1.** to go on board a ship; embark. **2.** to enlist as a member of the crew of a ship: *The young sailor shipped as a deck hand.* **3.** (of certain perishable foods) to withstand shipment: *Some fruit does not ship well.* ▲ See **boat** for usage note.

–ship *suffix* (used to form nouns) **1.** the quality, state, or condition of being: *friendship.* **2.** the office, position, or rank of: *ambassadorship.* **3.** the art or skill of being: *horsemanship.*

ship biscuit, another term for **hardtack.**

ship·board (ship'bôrd') *n.* **on shipboard.** aboard a ship: *Is everything loaded on shipboard?*

ship·build·er (ship'bil'dər) *n.* a person who builds or designs ships.

ship·build·ing (ship'bil'ding) *n.* **1.** the act of building ships. **2.** the art or business of building ships.

ship·load (ship'lōd') *n.* all that a ship can hold or carry.

ship·mas·ter (ship'mas'tər) *n.* a person in command of a ship.

ship·mate (ship'māt') *n.* a fellow sailor on a ship.

ship·ment (ship'mənt) *n.* **1.** the act of shipping goods. **2.** something shipped: *A shipment of vegetables arrived at the market.*

ship·per (ship'ər) *n.* a person or company that ships goods.

ship·ping (ship'ing) *n.* **1.** the act or business of sending or transporting goods, as by ship or railroad. **2.** ships as a group, especially those belonging to a particular port, country, or company: *Greek shipping.* **3.** the total tonnage of such ships.

ship·shape (ship'shāp') *adj.* in good or proper order; neat. —*adv.* in a shipshape manner.

ship·worm (ship'wûrm') *n.* any of a group of mollusks resembling worms, having long, slender bodies and two shells. Shipworms cause damage by burrowing into wharves or ship timbers.

ship·wreck (ship'rek') *n.* **1.** the destruction or loss of a ship. **2.** the remains of a wrecked ship; wreckage. **3.** total failure, destruction, or loss: *the shipwreck of one's dreams.* —*v.t.* **1.** to cause (a ship) to be destroyed or lost. **2.** to ruin; destroy. —*v.i.* (of a ship) to be destroyed or lost: *The tanker shipwrecked off the coast of England.*

ship·yard (ship'yärd') *n.* a place containing docks, workshops, and warehouses where ships can be built, equipped, and repaired.

shire (shīr) *n.* in Great Britain, a county.

shirk (shûrk) *v.t.* to avoid or neglect doing (something that should be done): *to shirk one's duties.* —**shirk'er,** *n.*

shirr (shûr) *v.t.* **1.** to gather (fabric) by means of a series of parallel threads. **2.** to bake (eggs) in a dish with butter.

shir·ring (shûr'ing) *n.* a shirred arrangement of fabric.

shirt (shûrt) *n.* **1.** any of various garments for the upper part of the body, usually having a collar, sleeves, and buttons down the front. **2.** an undershirt. —**shirt'like',** *adj.*

shirt·ing (shûr'ting) *n.* fabric used for making shirts or blouses.

shirt·waist (shûrt'wāst') *n.* **1.** a tailored dress having a top that resembles a shirt. **2.** a tailored blouse.

shirring

shish ke·bab (shish'kə bob') *also,* **shish ka·bob, shish ke·bob.** cubes of meat and often onions, tomatoes, or green peppers, broiled on skewers. Also, **kabob, kebab, kebob.**

Shi·va (shē'və) *n. also,* **Siva.** the Hindu god who personifies the destructive forces of the universe and, with Brahma and Vishnu, forms the Hindu trinity.

shiv·er[1] (shiv'ər) *v.i.* to shake, as with cold or fear; tremble: *They shivered in the cool night air.* —*n.* **1.** the act of shivering. **2.** a shivering sensation: *The ghost story sent shivers up my spine.* [From the Middle English word *chiveren* with the same meaning.]

shiv·er[2] (shiv'ər) *v.t.* to cause to break into fragments or splinters; shatter. —*v.i.* to break into fragments or splinters; shatter: *The glass shivered when it hit the floor.* —*n.* a small broken bit; fragment. [From the Middle English word *shiveren* meaning "to shatter, smash."]

shiv·er·y (shiv'ə rē) *adj.* **1.** shivering, as from cold or fear; trembling. **2.** causing shivers: *a shivery tale of horror.* **3.** inclined to shiver, as from cold.

shoal[1] (shōl) *n.* **1.** a sandbank or sandbar seen at low tide. **2.** any area, as in a river or the ocean, where the water is shallow. —*v.i.* to become shallow: *The lake shoals near the shore.* —*v.t.* to make shallow. —*adj.* of little depth; shallow. [Probably a form of the Middle English word *shold* meaning "a shallow place," from the Old English word *sceald* "a shallow place."]

shoal² (shōl) *n.* a school of fish. —*v.i.* (of fish) to collect in a shoal. [From the Old English word *scolu* meaning "a multitude, crowd."]

shoat (shōt) *also,* **shote.** *n.* a young pig that has been weaned.

shock¹ (shok) *n.* **1.** a sudden, violent disturbance of the mind or emotions: *The news of the accident was a shock to us.* **2.** a feeling caused by the passage of an electric current through the body. **3.** a sudden, violent shake, blow, or impact, as of an explosion or earthquake. **4.** a serious weakening of the body or mind following a severe physical or emotional injury. Shock is characterized by a weak pulse, cold skin, an ashen complexion, and a great drop in blood pressure that prevents enough blood from reaching the body's tissues. —*v.t.* **1.** to disturb the mind or emotions of: *The sudden death of the president shocked the nation.* **2.** to give an electric shock to. [From the French word *choc* with the same meaning, from the word *choquer* "to strike, knock against."] —**shock′er,** *n.*

shock² (shok) *n.* a bundle, as of wheat or corn, set upright in a field. —*v.t.* to gather into a shock or shocks. [From the Middle English word *shok* meaning "a bundle of sheaves," from Old English.]

shock³ (shok) *n.* a thick, bushy mass, as of hair. [Probably from *shock²*, because of its resemblance to a bundle of grain.]

shock ab·sorb·er (ab sôr′bər, ab zôr′bər), a device, as in automobiles, airplanes, or machines, that lessens the jarring or shaking effect of sudden impacts or bumps.

shock·ing (shok′ing) *adj.* **1.** offensive, distasteful, or revolting: *a shocking movie.* **2.** causing horror or surprise: *shocking news.* —**shock′ing·ly,** *adv.*

shock troops, troops specially chosen and trained to make sudden attacks.

shock wave, a disturbance of the atmosphere created by an aircraft, rocket, or other body traveling at supersonic speed.

shod (shod) the past tense and past participle of **shoe.**

shod·dy (shod′ē) *adj.* **shod·di·er, shod·di·est. 1.** poorly made or done; inferior: *a shoddy piece of work.* **2.** mean or nasty; *shoddy treatment.* **3.** worn-out; shabby; seedy: *The old rug looks very shoddy.* **4.** made of wool fibers reclaimed from woolen waste or other remnants. —*n.,* *pl.* **shod·dies. 1.** wool fibers reclaimed from woolen waste or other remnants. **2.** cloth made of such fibers. —**shod′di·ly,** *adv.* —**shod′di·ness,** *n.*

shoe (shü) *n.* **1.** any of various outer coverings, usually of leather, that protect and support the human foot. **2.** something resembling a shoe in shape, position, or function. **3.** see **horseshoe. 4.** a curved metal piece in a brake that presses against the wheel to slow or stop it. —*v.t.,* **shod, shoe·ing. 1.** to provide with a shoe or shoes. **2.** to provide or protect the end or edge of something with a metal covering.

·**in someone's shoes.** in another person's position or place.

shoe·horn (shü′hôrn′) *n.* a curved device inserted at the back of a shoe to help slip the heel into the shoe.

shoe·lace (shü′lās′) *n.* a cord for fastening a shoe.

shoe·mak·er (shü′mā′kər) *n.* a person who makes or repairs shoes and other footwear.

shoe·shine (shü′shīn′) *n.* the act or result of cleaning and polishing a pair of shoes.

shoe·string (shü′string′) *n.* another word for **shoelace.**

·**on a shoestring.** with very little money or resources: *The young artist was living on a shoestring.*

shoe tree, a device put in a shoe to preserve the shape of the shoe when it is not being worn.

sho·far (shō′fär, shō′fər) *n.* a ram's horn blown like a trumpet in various Jewish religious services, especially during Rosh Hashanah and Yom Kippur.

sho·gun (shō′gən) *n.* one of the military commanders who ruled Japan from 1192 to 1867.

shone (shōn) a past tense and past participle of **shine.**

shoo (shü) *interj.* a sound used to frighten or drive away a person or animal. —*v.,* **shooed, shoo·ing.** —*v.t.* to frighten or drive away by making this sound. —*v.i.* to make such a sound.

shook (shuk) the past tense of **shake.**

shoot (shüt) *v.,* **shot, shoot·ing. 1.** to wound or kill (a person or animal) with a bullet, arrow, or the like. **2.** to send forth or discharge (a missile) from a weapon, such as a gun or bow: *to shoot arrows at a target.* **3.** to cause to discharge or explode: *to shoot a gun, to shoot off fireworks.* **4.** to send forth or direct rapidly or suddenly: *The snake shot out its tongue. The child shot a nervous look at the guest.* **5.** to pass rapidly down, through, or over: *to shoot the rapids of a river.* **6.** to propel (a ball, puck, marble, or other object) toward a target or goal. **7.** to score, as points or a goal, in this way. **8.** to photograph or film, as for television or a motion picture: *They are going to shoot the final scene today.* **9.** to mark with streaks of color: *black hair shot with gray.* **10.** to slide into or out of a fastening: *to shoot the bolt of a door.* **11.** to play, as pool or craps. —*v.i.* **1.** to send forth or discharge a bullet, arrow, or other missile from a weapon. **2.** (of a weapon) to send forth a missile in a certain way: *This rifle shoots high.* **3.** to go or move suddenly or rapidly; dart: *The horse shot forward. Sparks were shooting from the fireworks.* **4.** to propel a ball, puck, marble, or other object toward a target or goal. **5.** to extend; project: *This piece of land shoots out into the bay.* —*n.* **1.** a new or young growth, as from a bud; sprout. **2.** the part of a plant that bears leaves and buds. —**shoot′er,** *n.*

shooting star, another term for **meteor.**

shop (shop) *n.* **1.** a small store where merchandise is sold retail: *a dress shop, a pet shop.* **2.** a place where a particular type of work is done: *a barber's shop.* **3.** a place where things are made or repaired: *I took the broken radio to the shop.* —*v.i.* **shopped, shop·ping.** to visit stores to look at, price, or buy merchandise: *The three friends shop together often.*

·**to talk shop.** to talk about matters that relate to one's work.

shop·keep·er (shop′kē′pər) *n.* a person who owns or manages a shop: *That shopkeeper is always on the lookout for anyone who might be a shoplifter.*

shop·lift (shop′lift′) *v.t., v.i.* to steal (merchandise) from a store while pretending to be a customer.

shop·lift·er (shop′lif′tər) *n.* a person who steals merchandise from a store while pretending to be a customer: *Shoplifters will be prosecuted.*

shop·lift·ing (shop′lif′ting) *n.* the act of stealing merchandise from a store while pretending to be a customer.

shop·per (shop′ər) *n.* a person who visits stores to look at, price, or buy merchandise; customer. *The department stores are always mobbed with Christmas shoppers on the day after Thanksgiving.*

---

at; āpe; fär; câre; end; mē; it; īce; pîerce; hot; ōld; sông, fôrk; oil; out; up; ūse; rüle; pùll; tûrn; chin; sing; shop; thin; <u>th</u>is; hw in white; zh in treasure. The symbol ə stands for the unstressed vowel sound heard in about, taken, pencil, lemon, and circus.

S

shopping bag, a bag used to carry purchases, especially a strong bag with handles.

shop·ping–bag lady (shop'ing bag') see **bag lady.**

shopping center, a place or area, especially in the suburbs, consisting of a group of stores, shops, and other facilities.

shopping mall, see **mall** (def. 2).

shop·talk (shop'tôk') *n.* conversation about matters relating to one's work, especially after working hours: *Let's not have any shoptalk at the dinner table.*

shop·worn (shop'wôrn') *adj.* **1.** soiled, frayed, or damaged from being displayed or handled in a store. **2.** worn out, as from overuse: *a shopworn phrase.*

shore¹ (shôr) *n.* **1.** the land along the edge of an ocean, lake, or large river. **2.** land: *Those sailors are now stationed on shore.* **3.** *also,* **shores.** country: *one's native shore.* [Probably from the Middle Dutch word *schore* with the same meaning.]

shore² (shôr) *v.t.,* **shored, shor·ing.** to support with a timber or beam: *to shore up an unsteady wall.* —*n.* a prop, especially a timber or beam, placed against the side of a structure as a temporary support. [From the Middle Dutch word *schoren* meaning "to support, prop up."]

shore·bird (shôr'bûrd') *n.* any of various birds that frequent shores and riverbanks, such as plovers and sandpipers.

shore·line (shôr'līn') *n.* the outline or contour of a shore.

Shore Patrol, a detail of the U.S. Navy, Coast Guard, or Marine Corps, acting as military police on shore.

shores²

shore·ward (shôr'wərd) *adv., adj.* in the direction of the shore.

shorn (shôrn) *v.* a past participle of **shear.** —*adj.* **1.** sheared: *shorn lambs.* **2.** stripped; deprived: *to be shorn of one's wealth and power.*

short (shôrt) *adj.* **1.** having little length; not long: *short hair.* **2.** having relatively little height; not tall: *a short person.* **3.** not long in time: *a short wait, a short trip.* **4.** using few words; concise; brief: *a short statement.* **5.** not having enough; lacking: *to be short of funds.* **6.** inadequate in amount: *We had a short supply of food.* **7.** rudely brief or abrupt; curt: *to be short with someone.* **8.** (of dough or pastry) rich and flaky due to the addition of shortening. **9.** (of vowels) relatively brief in duration, such as the *i* in *bit.* —*adv.* **1.** suddenly; abruptly: *to stop short.* **2.** not quite up to; on the near side of: *The player kicked the ball short of the goal line.* —*n.* **1.** something short. **2.** see **short subject. 3.** see **short circuit. 4. shorts. a.** short pants that reach to or almost to the knee. **b.** similar pants worn as an undergarment by men or boys. —*v.t.* to make a short circuit in. —*v.i.* to have a short circuit. —**short'ness,** *n.*

 ·**for short.** as a shortened or shorter form: *Leslie is called Les for short.*

 ·**in short.** in summary; briefly.

 ·**short for.** as a shortened or shorter form of: *"Cab" is short for "taxicab."*

 ·**short of.** less than: *Nothing short of winning will please that swimmer.*

short·age (shôr'tij) *n.* **1.** too small an amount or supply; lack: *a shortage of funds.* **2.** the amount by which anything is lacking: *The bank teller discovered a shortage of twenty dollars.*

short·bread (shôrt'bred') *n.* a crumbly, rich cookie made of flour, sugar, and shortening.

short·cake (shôrt'kāk') *n.* a dessert consisting of a rich biscuit or cake covered or filled with fruit, such as strawberries, and usually topped with whipped cream.

short·change (shôrt'chānj') *v.t.,* **short·changed, short·chang·ing. 1.** to give less than the proper change to: *The cashier shortchanged me by one dollar.* **2.** to swindle; cheat. —**short'chang'er,** *n.*

short–cir·cuit (shôrt'sûr'kit) *v.t.* to cause a short circuit in. —*v.i.* to have a short circuit.

short circuit, an electrical circuit, usually formed accidentally, that has abnormally low resistance, thus resulting in an excessive flow of current through it. A short circuit may blow a fuse or cause a fire. Also, **short.**

short·com·ing (shôrt'kum'ing) *n.* a fault or failure; defect: *Being constantly late is a serious shortcoming.*

short·cut (shôrt'kut') *also,* **short cut.** *n.* **1.** a way that is shorter than the ordinary way. **2.** any way or means that saves time or effort.

short·en (shôr'tən) *v.t.* **1.** to make short or shorter. **2.** to make rich or flaky by adding shortening. —*v.i.* to become short or shorter.

short·en·ing (shôr'tə ning) *n.* **1.** any of various fats, such as butter, lard, or vegetable oil, used in cooking. **2.** the act, process, or result of making or becoming short or shorter: *"Phone" is a shortening of "telephone."*

short·fall (shôrt'fôl') *n.* **1.** a failure to reach an amount that is needed or wanted; a falling short: *a shortfall in the year's grain harvest.* **2.** the amount by which something falls short; deficit; shortage: *a fifty-dollar shortfall in the club's budget.*

short·hand (shôrt'hand') *n.* a method of rapid handwriting or typing in which words are replaced by symbols, characters, or letters. —*adj.* **1.** using shorthand. **2.** written in shorthand.

shorthand for *As we have not heard from you*

short–hand·ed (shôrt'han'did) *adj.* lacking the necessary or usual number of workers, assistants, or the like: *The football team was shorthanded because of numerous injuries.*

short·horn (shôrt'hôrn') *n.* one of a breed of beef cattle with short horns, originally bred in northern England.

short·lived (shôrt'līvd', shôrt'livd') *adj.* living or lasting only a short time.

short·ly (shôrt'lē) *adv.* **1.** in a short time; presently; soon: *The doctor will see you shortly.* **2.** in a few words; briefly. **3.** in a rude or abrupt manner; curtly.

short–or·der (shôrt'ôr'dər) *adj.* relating to or specializing in food that is cooked quickly to order: *a short-order restaurant, a short-order cook.*

short–range (shôrt'rānj') *adj.* **1.** not reaching far into the future: *short-range plans.* **2.** capable of doing something, as firing or traveling, only over a short distance: *short-range guns.*

short shrift, hasty treatment showing little interest, concern, or mercy: *The shopkeeper gave short shrift to the beggar.*

 ·**to make short shrift of.** to take care of quickly.

short·sight·ed (shôrt'sī'tid) *adj.* **1.** not having or showing foresight: *a shortsighted plan.* **2.** nearsighted; myopic. —**short'sight'ed·ly,** *adv.* —**short'sight'ed·ness,** *n.*

short·stop (shôrt'stop') *n. Baseball.* **1.** the infield position between second and third base. **2.** a player playing this position.

short story, a work of fiction that has a single theme, a full plot, and a limited number of characters, and is shorter in length than a novel.

short subject, a short film, such as a documentary or cartoon. Also, **short.**

short–tem·pered (shôrt'tem'pərd) *adj.* easily or quickly angered; quick-tempered.

short–term (shôrt'tûrm') *adj.* **1.** planned for, covering,

866

or involving a short period of time: *short-term goals, a short-term forecast.* **2.** requiring payment or becoming effective after a short period of time: *a short-term loan, a short-term investment.*

short ton, see **ton** (*def. 1*).

short·wave (shôrt′wāv′) *n.* a radio wave of 60 meters or less.

short–wind·ed (shôrt′win′did) *adj.* suffering from shortness of breath: *The horse was short-winded after the race.*

Sho·sho·ne (shə shō′nē, shō shō′nē) *also*, **Sho·sho·ni.** *n., pl.* **Sho·sho·ne** or **Sho·sho·nes. 1.** a member of a tribe of North American Indians living in Idaho, Montana, Nevada, Oregon, Wyoming, and Utah. **2.** the language of this tribe.

shot¹ (shot) *n.* **1.** a discharge of a firearm or other weapon: *Did you hear a shot?* **2.** the act of shooting. **3.** a person who shoots: *The police officer is a good shot.* **4.** tiny balls of lead or steel that are contained in a cartridge and discharged by a shotgun. **5.** a single ball of lead used as ammunition for a gun or cannon. **6.** the launching of a rocket or missile toward a particular target: *a moon shot.* **7.** an injection given with a needle or syringe; hypodermic. **8.** the distance over which something, such as a missile or sound, can travel; reach; range. **9.** an aim or stroke in certain games: *I took a practice shot at the basket.* **10.** a photograph. **11.** a single piece of motion-picture film or magnetic tape recording a continuous action, taken by one camera from one angle. **12.** the heavy metal ball used in the shot put. **13.** *Informal.* a small amount of liquor, often drunk in one gulp. [From the Old English word *scot* meaning "shooting, a shot."]

shot² (shot) *v.* the past tense and past participle of **shoot.** —*adj.* **1.** streaked or woven so as to have a mixture of colors: *a scarf of red silk shot with blue.* **2.** *Informal.* completely worn out or ruined: *These old shoes are shot.*

shote (shōt) another spelling of **shoat.**

shot·gun (shot′gun′) *n.* a gun designed to fire cartridges that release a quantity of shot when discharged.

shot put, an athletic event in which a shot is thrown for distance.

should (shŭd) *auxiliary verb* a past tense of **shall. 1.** used to express an obligation or duty. *I should study harder.* **2.** used to express a condition: *If anyone should call, say that I'll be back in an hour.* **3.** used to express probability or expectation: *They should be here by five o'clock.* **4.** used to lessen the bluntness or directness of a statement: *I should not do that sort of thing if I were you.* **5.** used to express advice: *You should bandage that cut.*

shoul·der (shōl′dər) *n.* **1.** the part on either side of the body from the base of the neck to the upper arm or forelimb. **2. shoulders.** both shoulders and the part of the back connecting them. **3.** the portion of a garment covering the shoulders: *I ripped my sweater at the shoulder.* **4.** the front quarter of an animal. **5.** an edge or border on either side of a road or highway. **6.** any projecting part or slope: *the shoulder of a hill.* —*v.t.* **1.** to force by pushing with the shoulder or shoulders: *to shoulder one's way through a crowd.* **2.** to take upon oneself, as a burden; assume: *to shoulder the blame, to shoulder responsibility.* **3.** to place on and support or carry with the shoulder or shoulders: *to shoulder a trunk.* —*v.i.* to push forward or force one's way with the shoulder or shoulders.

 ·shoulder to shoulder. a. side by side and close together: *to stand shoulder to shoulder.* **b.** in cooperation: *to work shoulder to shoulder.*

 ·straight from the shoulder. honestly; frankly; candidly.

shoulder blade, either of two flat, triangular bones in the upper part of the back; scapula.

shoulder strap 1. a strap worn over the shoulder to hold up a garment or to carry a purse, bag, or the like. **2.** an ornamental cloth strip fastened on the shoulder of a uniform, usually to indicate rank.

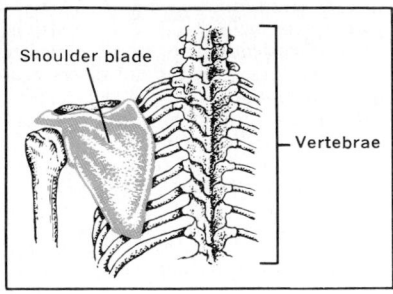
Shoulder blade
Vertebrae

should·n't (shŭd′ənt) *contr.* should not: *You shouldn't be afraid of meeting strangers.*

shouldst (shŭdst) *Archaic.* the second person singular, past tense of **shall.** ▲ used with **thou.**

shout (shout) *v.i.* to cry out loudly; yell: *to shout for help.* —*v.t.* to express by a shout: *Shout the alarm!* —*n.* a loud cry or yell. —**shout′er,** *n.*

 ·to shout down. to silence by shouting: *The crowd shouted down the speaker at the meeting.*

shove (shuv) *v.*, **shoved, shov·ing.** —*v.t.* **1.** to move along by pushing or pressing from behind; push: *Shove the chair against the table.* **2.** to push or press roughly: *People were shoving each other to get closer to the movie star.* —*v.i.* to push or press roughly. —*n.* a strong push.

 ·to shove off. a. to push a boat away from the shore. **b.** *Informal.* to leave.

shov·el (shuv′əl) *n.* **1.** a tool with a broad blade attached to a long handle, used for digging up and moving loose material, such as soil, snow, or gravel. **2.** any large power-driven machine for digging up and moving loose material, such as coal or dirt. **3.** a shovelful. —*v.*, **shov·eled, shov·el·ing;** *also, British*, **shov·elled, shov·el·ling.** —*v.t.* **1.** to dig up and move with a shovel: *to shovel dirt.* **2.** to dig or clear with a shovel: *to shovel a path in the snow.* **3.** to move or throw in large quantities as if with a shovel: *to shovel food into one's mouth.* —*v.i.* to use a shovel.

shov·el·er (shuv′ə lər) *also, British*, **shov·el·ler.** *n.* **1.** a person or thing that shovels. **2.** any of several freshwater ducks having a broad, flat bill.

shov·el·ful (shuv′əl fül′) *n., pl.* **shov·el·fuls.** the amount that a shovel can hold.

show (shō) *v.*, **showed, shown** or **showed, show·ing.** —*v.t.* **1.** to bring to sight or view; display: *Please show your tickets at the door. The theater showed the movie last week.* **2.** to make known or clear by one's behavior; reveal: *to show anger by yelling.* **3.** to point out or lead: *to show the way.* **4.** to register, as on a scale: *The thermometer shows the temperature to be quite high.* **5.** to explain to: *to show someone how to change a tire.* **6.** to demonstrate or explain: *I'll show how it can be done.* **7.** to grant or give; bestow: *to show mercy to a prisoner, to show favor to a friend.* —*v.i.* **1.** to be in sight or view; appear: *The scar on my arm doesn't show.* **2.** to be made known: *Your kindness shows in the help you gave us.* —*n.* **1.** something shown; exhibition or display: *an art*

at; āpe; fär; câre; end; mē; it; īce; pîerce; hot; ōld; sông, fôrk; oil; out; up; ūse; rüle; pull; tûrn; chin; sing; shop; thin; **this**; hw in white; zh in treasure.
The symbol ə stands for the unstressed vowel sound heard in about, taken, pencil, lemon, and circus.

S

show, a dog show. **2.** any entertainment, especially in a theater or on radio or television. **3.** a display meant to attract attention: *a show of wealth.* **4.** appearance; sign: *There was little show of recognition when we met.* **5.** a false or misleading appearance; pretense: *to put on a show of friendliness.* **6.** the act of showing: *We will vote by a show of hands.*
  •**for show.** in order to attract attention; for effect.
  •**to show off. a.** to display in a proud or showy manner: *to show off a new suit.* **b.** to behave in such a way as to call attention to oneself: *The little child is always showing off.*
  •**to show up. a.** to reveal; expose: *You showed them up for what they really are.* **b.** *Informal.* to make an appearance: *We will leave without them if they don't show up soon.*

show bill, a poster advertising a play or other entertainment.

show·boat (shō′bōt′) *n.* a river steamboat having a theater and troupe of performers on board for providing entertainment.

show business, the entertainment industry, including television, motion pictures, theater, circuses, and concerts.

show·case (shō′kās′) *n.* **1.** a glass case for displaying and protecting articles, as in a store or museum. **2.** a place or means for displaying something, especially attractively: *That television program is a showcase for new talent.*

show·down (shō′doun′) *n.* a meeting that forces a matter to a climax or conclusion.

show·er (shou′ər) *n.* **1.** a brief fall of rain. **2.** a fall of anything in large number: *a shower of tears, a shower of sparks.* **3.a.** a bath in which water is sprayed on a person from an overhead nozzle. **b.** a room or apparatus for such a bath. Also, **shower bath.** **4.** an abundant or large quantity or supply: *a shower of criticism.* **5.** a party for someone, such as a future bride or mother, to which gifts are brought. —*v.i.* **1.** to rain or fall in a shower. **2.** to bathe by taking a shower. —*v.t.* **1.** to wet with water or other liquid; sprinkle; spray. **2.** to cause to fall in a shower. **3.** to give or grant lavishly: *to shower compliments on a person.* —**show′er·y,** *adj.*

shower bath, see **shower** *(defs. 3a, 3b).*

show·ing (shō′ing) *n.* **1.** the act or instance of bringing to view; presentation. **2.** a performance, as in a contest or test: *to make a poor showing in a race.*

show·man (shō′mən) *n., pl.* **show·men** (shō′mən). **1.** a person who produces, presents, or manages a theatrical show. **2.** a person who acts or presents something in a dramatic or showy way.

show·man·ship (shō′mən ship′) *n.* the skill of a showman.

shown (shōn) a past participle of **show.**

show–off (shō′ôf′) *n.* **1.** a person who shows off; exhibitionist. **2.** the act of showing off.

show·piece (shō′pēs′) *n.* something thought of or shown as a fine example of its kind.

show·room (shō′rüm′, shō′rum′) *n.* a room used for the display of merchandise: *a furniture showroom.*

show·y (shō′ē) *adj.,* **show·i·er, show·i·est. 1.** making a striking display: *showy flowers.* **2.** bright or loud in a tasteless way; gaudy; flashy: *a showy dresser.* —**show′i·ly,** *adv.* —**show′i·ness,** *n.*

shrank (shrangk) a past tense of **shrink.**

shrap·nel (shrap′nəl) *n., pl.* **shrap·nel. 1.** a thin-walled shell filled with small lead fragments or balls that are scattered over a large area when the shell explodes. **2.** scattered fragments from an exploding shell or bomb. [From

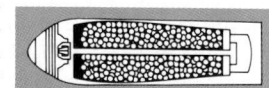
shrapnel *(def. 1)*

the English general Henry *Shrapnel* (1761–1842), who invented it.]

shred (shred) *n.* **1.** a very small piece or narrow strip torn or cut off: *Shreds of paper covered the floor.* **2.** a small amount; particle; scrap; bit: *There is not a shred of truth in that story.* —*v.t.,* **shred·ded** or **shred, shred·ding.** to tear or cut into shreds: *to shred cabbage for a salad.*

shrew (shrü) *n.* **1.** a very small mammal related to the mole, found in nearly all parts of the world. It has a long, pointed snout, short, rounded ears, and usually brownish fur. **2.** a bad-tempered, nagging woman.

shrewd (shrüd) *adj.* clever or keen, especially in practical matters; astute: *a shrewd politician, a shrewd judge of character.* —**shrewd′ly,** *adv.* —**shrewd′ness,** *n.*

shrew·ish (shrü′ish) *adj.* like a shrew; bad-tempered. —**shrew′ish·ly,** *adv.* —**shrew′ish·ness,** *n.*

shriek (shrēk) *n.* a loud, shrill cry or sound: *the shriek of a whistle, shrieks of laughter.* —*v.i.* to make a loud, shrill cry or sound. —*v.t.* to utter with a shriek.

shrift (shrift) *n.* **1.** *Archaic.* a confession made to a priest or the absolution given by a priest. **2.** see **short shrift.**

shrike

shrike (shrīk) *n.* a bird of prey having a large head, a strong, hooked beak, and a long tail.

shrill (shril) *adj.* **1.** sharp and high-pitched in sound. **2.** making such a sound: *a shrill whistle.* —*v.i.* to make a shrill sound: *The bagpipes shrilled.* —*v.t.* to utter with a shrill sound. —**shrill′ness,** *n.* —**shril′ly,** *adv.*

shrimp (shrimp) *n., pl.* **shrimp** or **shrimps. 1.** any of a number of long-tailed shellfish, usually found in salt water, and often used as food. **2.** *Slang.* a person who is very short.

shrine (shrīn) *n.* **1.** a case or other container for sacred relics; reliquary. **2.** the tomb of a saint. **3.** a holy place, or a place set aside for the worship of a god, saint, or other sacred being. **4.** a place or thing revered for its history or past association: *The battlefield at Gettysburg is a national shrine.*

shrink (shringk) *v.,* **shrank** or **shrunk, shrunk** or **shrunk·en, shrink·ing.** —*v.i.* **1.** to become smaller because of heat, cold, or moisture: *Woolen cloth shrinks in hot water.* **2.** to draw back, as in fear, horror, or disgust: *to shrink from a terrible sight.* **3.** to become less; reduce; diminish: *The population of the town has shrunk in recent years.* —*v.t.* to cause to become smaller or less: *Hot water shrank my new sweater.* —*n.* **1.** the act of shrinking. **2.** *Slang.* a psychiatrist. —**shrink′a·ble,** *adj.* —**shrink′er,** *n.*

shrink·age (shring′kij) *n.* **1.** the act of shrinking.

2. the amount of shrinking. **3.** a lessening, as in quantity or value; depreciation.

shrink–wrap (shringk′rap′) *v.t.*, **shrink-wrapped, shrink-wrap·ping.** to wrap or package (an article) in a plastic film that, when heated, shrinks to fit tightly. —*n.* the plastic film used in this process.

shrive (shrīv) *v.*, **shrove** or **shrived, shriv·en** or **shrived, shriv·ing.** *Archaic.* —*v.t.* **1.** to hear the confession of and grant absolution to. **2.** to rid (oneself) of sin by confessing and doing penance. —*v.i.* **1.** to make confession to a priest. **2.** to hear confessions.

shriv·el (shriv′əl) *v.*, **shriv·eled, shriv·el·ing;** *also, British,* **shriv·elled, shriv·el·ling.** —*v.i.* to shrink and become wrinkled or curled up: *The flowers shriveled and died because they were not watered.* —*v.t.* to cause to shrivel: *Exposure to the heat of the sun shriveled the plant.*

shriv·en (shriv′ən) a past participle of **shrive.**

shroud (shroud) *n.* **1.** a cloth or garment used to wrap a dead body for burial. **2.** something that covers or hides: *A shroud of clouds covered the mountain-top.* **3.** a rope or wire giving support to a mast on a boat or ship. —*v.t.* **1.** to clothe for burial. **2.** to cover so as to conceal; obscure; veil: *Mist shrouded the harbor. The affair was shrouded in secrecy.*

shrove (shrōv) a past tense of **shrive.**

Shrove Tuesday, the day before Ash Wednesday.

shrub (shrub) *n.* a woody plant that is smaller than a tree and has many stems that branch at or near the ground. [From the Old English word *scrybb* meaning "a shrub" or "underbrush."]

shrouds *(def. 3)*

shrub·ber·y (shrub′ə rē) *n., pl.* **shrub·ber·ies. 1.** a group of shrubs: *New shrubbery was planted in the park.* **2.** a plot of ground planted with shrubs.

shrub·by (shrub′ē) *adj.*, **shrub·bi·er, shrub·bi·est. 1.** of or resembling a shrub: *a shrubby plant.* **2.** made up of or covered with shrubs.

shrug (shrug) *v.t., v.i.*, **shrugged, shrug·ging.** to raise or draw up (the shoulders), as to show doubt or lack of interest. —*n.* the act of shrugging: *to dismiss an insult with a shrug.*

shrunk (shrungk) a past tense and past participle of **shrink.**

shrunk·en (shrung′kən) *v.* a past participle of **shrink.** —*adj.* shriveled up; made smaller.

shuck (shuk) *n.* **1.** the outer covering of corn or certain nuts. **2.** the shell of an oyster or clam. —*v.t.* **1.** to remove the shucks from. **2.** *Informal.* to take off; remove: *to shuck one's clothes.* —**shuck′er,** *n.*

shud·der (shud′ər) *v.i.* to tremble suddenly, as from horror, disgust, or cold. —*n.* the act of shuddering. —**shud′der·ing·ly,** *adv.*

shuf·fle (shuf′əl) *v.*, **shuf·fled, shuf·fling.** —*v.t.* **1.** to drag (the feet) along the ground or floor. **2.** to mix (playing cards) so as to rearrange them. **3.** to mix about or move (something) from one place to another: *to shuffle papers.* —*v.i.* **1.** to walk by dragging the feet: *to shuffle down the street.* **2.** to mix playing cards so as to rearrange them. **3.** to mix or move things about from one place to another. **4.** to move, act, or do something in a clumsy, careless, or hasty manner: *to shuffle through one's homework.* —*n.* **1.** the act of shuffling the feet. **2.** the act of shuffling playing cards. **3.** the right or turn to shuffle playing cards. —**shuf′fler,** *n.*

shuf·fle·board (shuf′əl bôrd′) *n.* **1.** a game played by pushing disks with a cue on a smooth level surface marked off in scoring areas. **2.** the marked surface on which this game is played.

shul (shŭl, shừl) *n.* a synagogue.

shun (shun) *v.t.*, **shunned, shun·ning.** to keep away from; avoid: *to shun city life for the quiet of the country.* —**shun′ner,** *n.*

shunt (shunt) *v.t.* **1.** to move or turn aside or away. **2.** to switch (a train) from one track to another. **3.** to carry or divert (part of an electric current) by means of a shunt. —*v.i.* to move or turn aside or away. —*n.* **1.** the act of shunting. **2.** a railroad switch. **3.** a conductor joining two points in an electric circuit that provides an electrical bypass for part of the current. —**shunt′er,** *n.*

shush (shush) *interj.* be quiet; hush. —*v.t.* to quiet or silence.

shut (shut) *v.*, **shut, shut·ting.** —*v.t.* **1.** to move (something) into a closed position so as to block an entrance, passageway, or opening: *to shut a window.* **2.** to bring together the parts; close; fold: *to shut an umbrella, to shut a book.* **3.** to confine or enclose: *to shut an animal in a cage.* **4.** to stop the operation of: *to shut a store, to shut a mine.* **5.** to prevent the passage or flow of: *to shut off water.* —*v.i.* to become shut.
　·to shut out. *Sports.* to prevent (the opposing team) from scoring in a contest, as in a baseball game.
　·to shut up. *Informal.* **a.** to quiet or silence (someone). **b.** to become silent.

shut·down (shut′doun′) *n.* the stopping of work, as in a factory.

shut·in (shut′in′) *adj.* confined to a house or hospital. —*n.* a person who is confined to a house or hospital, as by illness.

shut·out (shut′out′) *n. Sports.* **1.** the preventing of the opposing team from scoring. **2.** a game in which one team does not score.

shut·ter (shut′ər) *n.* **1.** a movable panel or screen for a door or window, used to shut out light or to give protection or privacy. **2.** a device that opens and closes the lens opening of a camera. **3.** a person or thing that shuts. —*v.t.* to provide or cover with shutters: *to shutter windows.*

shut·tle (shut′əl) *n.* **1.** a device on a loom that carries the yarn back and forth across or through the yarn strung on the loom. **2.** any of various devices that hold and carry thread, as in a sewing machine. **3.** a vehicle, such as a bus, subway train, or airplane, that makes frequent trips back and forth between two points. **4.** see **space shuttle. 5.** a moving or traveling back and forth between two points: *a diplomatic shuttle.* —*v.*, **shut·tled, shut·tling.** —*v.t.* to move (something) back and forth. —*v.i.* to move back and forth: *The taxi shuttled between the airport and the hotel.*

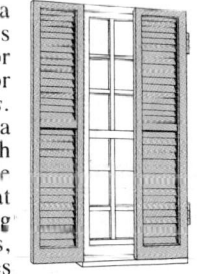

shutters
(def. 1)

shut·tle·cock (shut′əl kok′) *n.* a cone-shaped object with feathers inserted into a rounded cork or plastic base, used in the game of badminton. Also, **bird.**

shy¹ (shī) *adj.*, **shy·er** or **shi·er, shy·est** or **shi·est. 1.** uncomfortable in the presence of others; bashful; retiring: *to be shy around strangers.* **2.** showing a lack of

---

at; āpe; fär; câre; end; mē; it; īce; pîerce; hot; ōld; sông, fôrk; oil; out; up; ūse; rüle; pừll; tûrn; chin; sing; shop; thin; <u>th</u>is; hw in white; zh in treasure. The symbol ə stands for the unstressed vowel sound heard in about, taken, pencil, lemon, and circus.

S

courage; easily frightened; timid. **3.** cautious or distrustful; wary. **4.** *Informal.* lacking; short: *shy of money.* —*v.i.,* **shied, shy·ing. 1.** to move back or aside suddenly, as in fear; start: *The horse shied at the loud noise.* **2.** to draw back, as from caution, dislike, or doubt: *to shy away from something unpleasant.* [From the Old English word *scēoh* meaning "timid, fearful."] —**shy′ly,** *adv.* —**shy′ness,** *n.*

shy² (shī) *v.t.,* **shied, shy·ing.** to throw (something) with a jerk; fling; toss. —*n., pl.* **shies.** a quick, jerking throw. [Of uncertain origin.]

Shy·lock (shī′lok′) *n.* **1.** the demanding moneylender in Shakespeare's play *The Merchant of Venice.* **2.** any severe and demanding creditor.

shy·ster (shī′stər) *n.* *Slang.* a lawyer or other person who is professionally unethical or unscrupulous.

si (sē) *n.* *Music.* another word for **ti.**

Si, the symbol for silicon.

Si·a·mese (sī′ə mēz′, sī′ə mēs′) *adj.; n., pl.* **Si·a·mese.** another word for **Thai.**

Siamese cat, a breed of cat originally from Siam (now Thailand), having a slender body covered with short, tan or grayish hair that is darker on the ears, nose, tail, and limbs.

Siamese twins, identical twins who are born joined together. [From the joined *twins* Eng and Chang (1811–1874), who were born in *Siam* (now Thailand).]

Si·be·ri·an husky (sī bîr′ē ən) a sturdy breed of dog having a brushlike tail and a soft, gray, tan, white, or black coat.

sib·i·lant (sib′ə lənt) *adj.* having a hissing sound. —*n.* a consonant pronounced with a hissing sound, such as *s* or *sh.* —**sib′i·lance,** *n.*

sib·ling (sib′ling) *n.* a brother or sister.

Siamese cat

sib·yl (sib′əl) *n.* **1.** *Greek and Roman Mythology.* any of various women who could predict the future. **2.** any female prophet.

sic¹ (sik) *adv.* *Latin.* thus; so. ▲ used to show that a word or phrase in a quotation that seems to be an obvious mistake is an exact copy of the original. For example: The note read "I've taken the dog to the veteran aryan" *[sic].* [From the Latin word *sic* meaning "so, thus."]

sic² (sik) *also,* **sick.** *v.t.,* **sicked** or **sicced, sick·ing** or **sic·cing. 1.** to set upon; attack. ▲ used as a command, especially to a dog. **2.** to cause to attack: *to sic a dog on someone.* [A form of the command *seek!*]

Si·cil·ian (si sil′yən) *n.* **1.** a person who was born in or is a citizen of Sicily. **2.** the dialect of Italian spoken in Sicily. —*adj.* of or relating to Sicily, its people, their dialect, or culture.

sick¹ (sik) *adj.* **1.** suffering from some disease; having poor health; ill. **2.** suffering from nausea; nauseated. **3.** of or for sick people. **4.** showing sickness: *a sick look.* **5.** completely weary: *to be sick of one's job.* **6.** annoyed or disgusted; chagrined: *Such cruel gossip makes me sick.* **7.** gruesome or morbid in some way: *a sick joke.* [From the Old English word *sēoc* meaning "ill."]

sick² (sik) another spelling of **sic².**

sick bay, a hospital or dispensary, especially on a ship.

sick·bed (sik′bed′) *n.* a bed on which a sick person lies.

sick·en (sik′ən) *v.t., v.i.* to make or become sick.

sick·en·ing (sik′ə ning) *adj.* suffering from or causing nausea or disgust. —**sick′en·ing·ly,** *adv.*

sick·ish (sik′ish) *adj.* **1.** somewhat sick. **2.** slightly sickening. —**sick′ish·ly,** *adv.* —**sick′ish·ness,** *n.*

sick·le (sik′əl) *n.* a hand tool made up of a sharp, curved blade attached to a short handle, used for cutting grass, grain, or weeds.

sickle cell anemia, a hereditary blood disease that occurs mainly in blacks, characterized by abnormal red blood cells that tend to become sickle-shaped and useless when deprived of oxygen.

sick·ly (sik′lē) *adj.,* **sick·li·er, sick·li·est. 1.** usually or always sick; in poor health. **2.** of, characteristic of, or causing sickness: *a sickly complexion, a sickly climate.* **3.** suffering from or causing nausea; sickening: *sickly smells.* **4.** faint; feeble; weak: *a sickly smile.* —*adv.* in a sick manner. —**sick′li·ness,** *n.*

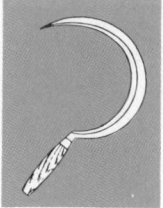

sickle

sick·ness (sik′nis) *n.* **1.** the state of being sick. **2.** a particular disease or illness. **3.** nausea.

side (sīd) *n.* **1.** one of the surfaces or lines that bound an object or figure: *A triangle has three sides.* **2.** either of the two surfaces or lines of an object or figure connecting the front and back, and the top and bottom: *the sides of a car.* **3.** either of two surfaces of a flat object, such as a piece of paper: *One side of the cloth is smoother than the other.* **4.** either of two parts of a place lying to the right or left of a central line or point: *Put the chairs on the left side of the room.* **5.** any of various parts of a region or place lying beyond a particular, usually central, line or point: *the west side of town.* **6.** either the right or left part of the body of a person or animal. **7.** the area or space next to one's person: *Come stand at my side.* **8.** a region or area separated from another by an object, space, or line: *both sides of the Atlantic.* **9.** either of two opposing groups or persons: *Their side won the game.* **10.** an aspect, attitude, or point of view: *Look at all sides of the question.* **11.** a line of descent: *She is my second cousin on my father's side.* —*adj.* **1.** at or near one side: *a side door.* **2.** coming from or directed toward one side. **3.** less important; secondary: *side issues.* —*v.t.,* **sid·ed, sid·ing.** to provide with sides or siding.

•**on the side.** in addition to one's main job or duties.

•**side by side.** next to one another.

•**to side with.** to agree with; support.

side·arm (sīd′ärm′) *adj.* thrown with the arm almost parallel with the ground: *a sidearm pitch.* —*adv.* with a sidearm motion: *to throw sidearm.*

side arm, a weapon carried on the side, such as a sword or revolver.

side·board (sīd′bôrd′) *n.* a piece of dining-room furniture used especially for storing tableware and linen.

side·burns (sīd′bûrnz′) *n., pl.* hair growing down the sides of a man's face, especially when worn as short whiskers with the rest of the beard shaved off. [A form of *burnsides* meaning these whiskers, from the U.S. Civil War general Ambrose *Burnside* (1824–1881), who wore such whiskers.]

side·car (sīd′kär′) *n.* a small one-wheeled car attached to the side of a motorcycle and used for carrying a passenger.

sid·ed (sī′did) *adj.* having a side or sides. ▲ used in combination: *one-sided.*

side effect, any effect of a drug that may occur in addition to the drug's intended effect. Some side effects are harmful and in some cases cause the use of the drug to be discontinued.

side·kick (sīd′kik′) *n.* *Slang.* a close friend, companion, or associate.

side·light (sīd′līt′) *n.* **1.** a light coming from the side. **2.** incidental or additional information or knowledge concerning some subject: *One speaker added interesting sidelights to the discussion.*

side·line (sīd′līn′) n. **1.** either of two lines that mark the side limits of the playing area in certain sports, such as football or basketball. **2. sidelines.** the area just beyond these lines. **3.** work additional to one's usual job or duties: *The young teacher's sideline is coaching basketball.* **4.** a line of goods additional to that regularly sold by a store.

side·long (sīd′lông′) adj. directed to the side: *a sidelong glance.* —adv. toward the side.

si·de·re·al (sī dîr′ē əl) adj. **1.** of or relating to the stars. **2.** determined or measured by means of the stars.

sidereal year, see **year** (def. 3).

side·sad·dle (sīd′sad′əl) n. a woman's saddle made so that the rider sits with both legs on the same side of the horse. —adv. on a sidesaddle.

side·show (sīd′shō′) n. a show connected to or part of a larger entertainment or exhibition.

side·split·ting (sīd′split′ing) adj. **1.** causing uncontrollable laughter; extremely funny; hilarious: *a sidesplitting joke.* **2.** uncontrollable; convulsive: *sidesplitting laughter.*

side·step (sīd′step′) v., **side·stepped, side·step·ping.** —v.t. to avoid by or as if by stepping aside: *to sidestep a decision.* —v.i. **1.** to step to one side. **2.** to avoid a responsibility, decision, or difficulty. —**side′step′per,** n.

side·stroke (sīd′strōk′) n. a swimming stroke performed while the swimmer lies on his or her side and extends one arm forward while pushing backward with the other.

side·swipe (sīd′swīp′) v.t., **side·swiped, side·swip·ing.** to strike with a blow along the side, as in passing: *The truck sideswiped a parked car when it skidded.* —n. a blow made on or along the side.

side·track (sīd′trak′) v.t. **1.** to turn aside from what is most important: *to be sidetracked from one's work by a long phone call.* **2.** to shift (a train) to a siding. —n. a railroad siding.

side·walk (sīd′wôk′) n. a walk along the side of a street or road for pedestrians.

side·ward (sīd′wərd) adj. moving or directed toward one side. —adv. also, **sidewards.** toward one side.

side·ways (sīd′wāz′) adv. **1.** toward or from one side. **2.** with one side forward: *to walk sideways through a narrow doorway.* —adj. moving or directed toward one side. Also (adv., adj.), **side·way** (sīd′wā′), **side·wise** (sīd′wīz′).

side·wind·er (sīd′wīn′dər) n. a rattlesnake found in the southwestern United States and Mexico that moves sideways and has hornlike knobs over each eye.

sid·ing (sī′ding) n. **1.** a short railroad track connected by a switch to a main track. **2.** wood, metal, or other material forming the outside covering of a frame building.

si·dle (sī′dəl) v.i., **si·dled, si·dling.** to move sideways, especially in a sly manner. —n. a sideways movement.

siege (sēj) n. **1.** the surrounding of a fortified enemy position for a long period of time in order to cut off supplies and force surrender. **2.** any long attempt to overcome something. **3.** a long, distressing or tiring period, as of illness: *a siege of pneumonia.*

Sieg·fried (sēg′frēd′) n. *Germanic Legend.* a hero who killed a dragon and gained a golden treasure.

si·en·na (sē en′ə) n. **1.** brown earth used as a yellowish brown pigment in its natural state **(raw sienna)** or as a reddish brown pigment after being roasted **(burnt sienna). 2.** a yellowish brown or reddish brown color. —adj. having the color sienna; yellowish brown or reddish brown.

si·er·ra (sē er′ə) n. a chain of rugged hills or mountains with sharp, jagged peaks that look like the teeth of a saw. [From the Spanish word *sierra* meaning "saw" and also "a ridge of mountains," from the Latin word *serra* "a saw."]

si·es·ta (sē es′tə) n. an afternoon nap or rest, especially one taken during the hottest part of the day in Spain and certain other Latin American countries. [From the Spanish word *siesta*, from the Latin phrase *sexta (hora)* meaning "sixth (hour of the day)." Since the Roman day began at sunrise, the sixth hour occurred approximately at midday.]

sieve (siv) n. a utensil or device having a bottom made of wire mesh or with holes punched into it, used for sifting or draining. —v.t., **sieved, siev·ing.** to pass (a substance) through a sieve; sift.

sift (sift) v.t. **1.** to separate by passing through a sieve: *to sift sand from gravel.* **2.** to remove lumps from or make lighter by passing through a sieve: *to sift flour.* **3.** to sprinkle by shaking through a sieve: *to sift flour into a batter.* **4.** to examine closely: *to sift evidence.* —v.i. **1.** to sift something. **2.** to fall loosely as if through a sieve: *Dust sifted through the cracks.* —**sift′er,** n.

sigh (sī) v.i. **1.** to make a long, deep breathing sound, as from sadness, weariness, or relief. **2.** to make a sound like that of a sigh: *The wind sighed in the rafters of the old barn.* **3.** to wish earnestly; yearn; long: *to sigh for a friend's return.* —v.t. to express with a sigh. —n. the act or sound of sighing: *a sigh of relief.* —**sigh′er,** n.

sight (sīt) n. **1.** the faculty or power of seeing; vision: *Glasses can improve your sight.* **2.** the act or instance of seeing: *Our first sight of the mountain was from miles away.* **3.** the range of one's vision: *Keep the surprise out of the children's sight.* **4.** something seen; view: *The sunset was a beautiful sight.* **5.** usually, **sights.** something striking or worth seeing: *the sights of Philadelphia.* **6.** personal judgment or opinion; regard: *In your friend's sight, you can do nothing wrong.* **7.** any of various devices used as an aid in observing or aiming, as on a surveying instrument or firearm. **8.** *Informal.* something messy or unpleasant to look at: *The room was a sight after the party.* —v.t. **1.** to perceive with the eyes; see: *The hikers sighted a clearing in the forest.* **2.** to aim by means of a sight or sights.

·at sight or **on sight.** as soon as seen; immediately: *We bought the car on sight.*

sight·ed (sī′tid) adj. having sight; able to see; not blind: *The library is designed to be used by both blind and sighted students.*

sight·less (sīt′lis) adj. unable to see; blind. —**sight′less·ness,** n.

sight·ly (sīt′lē) adj., **sight·li·er, sight·li·est. 1.** pleasing to the eye; comely. **2.** presenting a fine view. —**sight′li·ness,** n.

sight–read (sīt′rēd′) v.t., v.i., **sight-read** (sīt′red′), **sight-read·ing.** to read (a text or sheet music) without having previously seen or studied it.

sight·see (sīt′sē′) v.i., v.t., **sight·saw, sight·see·ing.** to visit or tour places of interest: *We spent the day sightseeing in the capital.*

sight·see·ing (sīt′sē′ing) n. the act or instance of visiting places of interest. —adj. used for or engaged in visiting places of interest: *a sightseeing bus, a sightseeing tour.*

sight·se·er (sīt′sē′ər) n. a person who visits places of interest; tourist.

---

at; āpe; fär; câre; end; mē; it; īce; pîerce; hot; ōld; sông, fôrk; oil; out; up; ūse; rüle; pùll; tûrn; chin; sing; shop; thin; this; hw in white; zh in treasure. The symbol ə stands for the unstressed vowel sound heard in about, taken, pencil, lemon, and circus.

S

871

sig·ma (sig′mə) *n.* the eighteenth letter of the Greek alphabet (Σ, σ, ς), corresponding to the English letter S, s.

sign (sīn) *n.* **1.** something that shows or suggests some state, quality, condition, or feeling: *There were signs of wear on the carpet.* **2.** a motion, gesture, or action that expresses an idea or gives a command or warning: *A nod is a sign of agreement.* **3.** a lettered plate, board, or the like, bearing a notice or advertisement: *The sign on the door said "Closed for the day."* **4.** something that stands for an object, relationship, idea, or the like; symbol: *The dove is a sign of peace.* **5.** a warning or indication of what is to come; portent; omen: *Dark clouds were a sign of stormy weather.* **6.** a trace: *There is no sign of them anywhere.* **7.** one of the twelve divisions of the zodiac: *My sign is Libra.* —*v.t.* **1.** to put one's signature to (something), especially to confirm or show agreement: *If the artist signed the painting, it must be genuine.* **2.** to put as a signature: *to sign one's name to a check.* **3.** to hire by means of a contract or other written agreement: *The team signed the quarterback for the year.* **4.** to communicate or express by gesture, as in sign language. —*v.i.* **1.** to write one's signature: *Sign on the bottom of the page.* **2.** to accept employment or be hired by means of a contract or other written agreement. **3.** to communicate by sign language. —**sign′er,** *n.*

·**to sign off.** to cease television or radio transmission.

·**to sign up.** to join an organization or group, such as a branch of military service.

Word Family

A number of English words have come from the Latin word *signum,* meaning "a sign" or "token." The world is full of **signs,** and they **signify** various things. The **seal** of a ruler is one particularly **significant** token of authority. Usually, it consists of a **design** that includes the **insignia** of the ruler. Pressed in wax on a document, it **signals** the approval of a law or decree, which might include the **consignment** of a person to prison or the **assignment** of an officer to a new post. Like all signs, its **significance** depends on the situation. If the ruler **designates** a successor and **resigns** from office, the seal of the former ruler becomes **insignificant.**

sig·nal (sig′nəl) *n.* **1.** something that serves to warn, direct, inform, or instruct: *The flashing light was a signal that a train was coming.* **2.** an action or happening that serves to bring about or stir up something: *The king's harsh edict was a signal for revolt.* **3.** an electric current that transmits sounds or pictures to receiving equipment. —*v.,* **sig·naled, sig·nal·ing;** *also, British,* **sig·nalled, sig·nal·ling.** —*v.t.* **1.** to make a signal or signals to: *The shipwrecked sailors signaled a passing ship for help.* **2.** to communicate or make known by a signal or signals: *The bell signaled a warning.* —*v.i.* to make a signal or signals. —*adj.* **1.** used as a signal: *a signal light.* **2.** remarkable; striking; notable: *a signal event in history.*

sig·nal·ize (sig′nə līz′) *v.t.,* **sig·nal·ized, sig·nal·iz·ing. 1.** to make notable or striking. **2.** to point out clearly.

sig·nal·ly (sig′nə lē) *adv.* in a signal manner; remarkably; notably.

sig·nal·man (sig′nəl mən, sig′nəl man′) *n., pl.* **sig·nal·men** (sig′nəl mən, sig′nəl men′). a person whose job is sending signals, as on a railroad or ship, or in the armed forces.

sig·na·ture (sig′nə chər) *n.* **1.** the name of a person, or a mark representing the person's name, written in his or her own handwriting. **2.** a melody, sound effect, or visual effect that identifies a radio or television program. **3.** *Music.* a symbol or group of symbols at the beginning of a staff to indicate pitch or meter.

sign·board (sīn′bôrd′) *n.* a board bearing a notice or advertisement.

sig·net (sig′nit) *n.* **1.** a small seal, especially one used to stamp a document. **2.** an impression made by a signet.

sig·nif·i·cance (sig nif′i kəns) *n.* **1.** special value or importance: *The 4th of July has great significance for Americans.* **2.** something that is meant; meaning: *What is the significance of that remark?*

sig·nif·i·cant (sig nif′i kənt) *adj.* **1.** having special value or importance: *a significant event in one's life.* **2.** having a meaning; signifying something. **3.** having or expressing a special or hidden meaning; suggestive: *a significant look.* —**sig·nif′i·cant·ly,** *adv.*

sig·ni·fi·ca·tion (sig′nə fi kā′shən) *n.* **1.** something that is meant; meaning: *the signification of a word.* **2.** the act of signifying; communication.

sig·ni·fy (sig′nə fī′) *v.,* **sig·ni·fied, sig·ni·fy·ing.** —*v.t.* **1.** to be a sign, symbol, or indication of; represent; mean: *A smile signifies happiness.* **2.** to show by signs, speech, or actions: *to signify disapproval by frowning.* —*v.i.* to be of importance; matter.

sign language

sign language, a system of communication in which gestures are used instead of speech. Sign language is used especially by the deaf.

si·gnor (sēn yôr′) *also,* **si·gnior.** *n., pl.* **si·gno·ri** (sēn yôr′ē) *or* **si·gnors.** mister; sir. ▲ the Italian form of respectful or polite address for a man, usually used before the name.

si·gno·ra (sēn yôr′ə) *n., pl.* **si·gno·re** (sēn yôr′ā). madam; Mrs. ▲ the Italian form of respectful or polite address for a married woman.

si·gno·re (sēn yôr′ā) *n., pl.* **si·gno·ri** (sēn yôr′ē). mister; sir. ▲ the Italian form of respectful or polite address for a man, used in direct address without the name.

si·gno·ri·na (sēn′yô rē′nə) *n., pl.* **si·gno·ri·ne** (sēn′yô rē′nā). miss. ▲ the Italian form of respectful or polite address for an unmarried girl or woman.

sign·post (sīn′pōst′) *n.* **1.** a post with a sign or signs on it to give information or directions. **2.** something that serves as a guide, indication, or clue.

Sikh (sēk) *n.* a follower of a religion developed about A.D. 1500 that combines elements of both Hinduism and Islam.

si·lage (sī′lij) *n.* green fodder that has been preserved in a silo by fermenting. Also, **ensilage.**

si·lence (sī′ləns) *n.* **1.** the absence of sound; complete quiet; stillness. **2.** the state of being or keeping silent: *to* *listen in silence.* —*v.t.,* **si·lenced, si·lenc·ing. 1.** to cause to be or keep silent; bring to silence: *to silence a noisy classroom.* **2.** to put a stop to; suppress: *The dictator tried to silence all criticism.*

si·lenc·er (sī′lən sər) *n.* **1.** a person or thing that silences. **2.** a device shaped like a tube and attached to the front of a gun barrel to deaden the sound of the gun being fired.

si·lent (sī′lənt) *adj.* **1.** marked by the absence of sound; completely quiet; still: *the silent desert.* **2.** not speaking or making a sound: *to remain silent while someone else speaks.* **3.** not given to speaking; taciturn: *a shy, silent child.* **4.** not uttered or expressed; unspoken: *There was much silent opposition to the new rules.* **5.** free from activity; inactive: *A silent volcano was located in the center of the island.* **6.** (of a motion picture) having no soundtrack. **7.** (of a letter) not pronounced in speech, as the *k* in *know* or the *e* in *give.* —**si′lent·ly,** *adv.*

sil·hou·ette (sil′ü et′) *n.* **1.** the outline of a figure or object filled in with solid color, usually black. **2.** a dark outline seen against a lighter background. —*v.t.,* **sil·hou·et·ted, sil·hou·et·ting.** to cause to appear in or as if in a silhouette: *The tree was silhouetted against the sky.* [From the French word *silhouette,* from the French Minister of Finance Étienne de *Silhouette* (1709–1767).]

sil·i·ca (sil′i kə) *n.* silicon dioxide, a hard, transparent mineral that occurs naturally as quartz. It is used to make glass and ceramics. [From the Latin word *silex* meaning "flint" or "quartz." Quartz is crystalline silica.]

sil·i·cate (sil′i kit, sil′i kāt′) *n.* any of various compounds containing silicon, oxygen, metal, and sometimes hydrogen. Glass, clay, and many rocks are made of silicates.

sil·i·con (sil′i kən, sil′i kon′) *n.* a nonmetallic element that occurs in the form of either brown powder or dark gray or black crystals. Silicon is the second most abundant element in the earth's crust. Silicon crystals are used as semiconductors in electronic devices. Symbol: **Si** [Formed from the word *silica* and the ending *-on.* Silicon is found in silica.]

sil·i·cone (sil′i kōn′) *n.* any of various compounds composed of chains of silicon and oxygen atoms to which organic radicals are attached. Because silicones are unaffected by extremes of temperature, they are used as oils, plastics, and synthetic rubbers and in various industrial processes.

sil·i·co·sis (sil′i kō′sis) *n.* a chronic disease of the lungs caused by the long-term inhalation of air containing particles of certain silicon compounds.

silk (silk) *n.* **1.** a soft, shiny fiber spun by silkworms. **2.** a strong, shiny fabric made from these fibers, used for such items as scarves, ties, and blouses. **3.** anything like silk in appearance or texture: *the silk on an ear of corn.* —*adj.* of, resembling, or relating to silk.

silk·en (sil′kən) *adj.* **1.** made of silk. **2.** like silk in appearance or texture; silky: *long, silken hair.*

silk·worm (silk′wûrm′) *n.* the caterpillar of a moth originally domesticated in China. The cocoon that it spins is the source of silk fiber.

silk·y (sil′kē) *adj.,* **silk·i·er, silk·i·est.** like silk in appearance or texture; smooth, soft, and lustrous. —**silk′i·ly,** *adv.* —**silk′i·ness,** *n.*

sill (sil) *n.* **1.** the part across the bottom of a door or window. **2.** a horizontal beam that forms the foundation of a structure.

sil·ly (sil′ē) *adj.,* **sil·li·er, sil·li·est. 1.** lacking in judgment or common sense; stupid: *a silly person.* **2.** absurd; ridiculous: *a silly notion.* **3.** *Informal.* stunned; dazed, as by a blow: *The blast knocked them silly.* —**sil′li·ness,** *n.*

si·lo (sī′lō) *n., pl.* **si·los. 1.** a tall, cylindrical tower of metal or other material for the storage and fermentation of green fodder. **2.** a deep hole in the ground for storing and launching missiles.

silt (silt) *n.* fine sand, clay, or similar matter carried by water and deposited as sediment. —*v.t.* to fill or choke (something) with silt: *Heavy rains silted the river.* —*v.i.* to become filled or choked with silt. —**silt′y,** *adj.*

Si·lu·ri·an (si lúr′ē ən) *n.* the third geological period of the Paleozoic era, during which the first land plants appeared. —*adj.* of, relating to, or characteristic of this period.

sil·van (sil′vən) another spelling of **sylvan.**

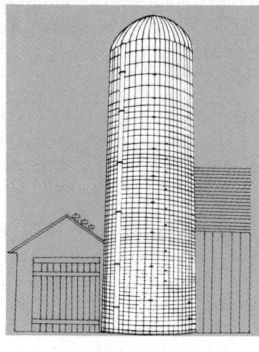

silo (def. 1)

sil·ver (sil′vər) *n.* **1.** a soft, shiny, white metallic element that is ductile, malleable, and the best conductor of heat and electricity of any metal. Its alloys are used in the manufacture of coins, jewelry, and tableware. Symbol: **Ag** **2.** this metal used as a commodity or as a standard of currency. **3.** coins, especially those made from silver; change. **4.** articles made of or coated with a thin layer of silver, such as tableware. **5.** the color of silver. —*adj.* **1.** made of or coated with a thin layer of silver: *silver spoons.* **2.** like silver, as in color or shine: *silver paint.* **3.** of or marking the twenty-fifth year or event in a series: *a silver wedding anniversary.* —*v.t.* **1.** to coat with a thin layer of silver. **2.** to give (something) the color or shine of silver: *The moonlight silvered the waters of the lake.* —*v.i.* to become silver or silvery in color. [From the Old English word *seolfor* meaning this metal.]

sil·ver·fish (sil′vər fish′) *n., pl.* **sil·ver·fish** or **sil·ver·fish·es. 1.** a small white or gray wingless insect. It is a common household pest that feeds on wallpaper, bookbindings, and other starchy materials. **2.** a white or silver goldfish. **3.** any of several silvery fishes, such as the tarpon.

sil·ver·plate (sil′vər plāt′) *v.t.,* **sil·ver·plat·ed, sil·ver·plat·ing.** to coat with a thin layer of silver.

silver plate, articles made of silver or coated with a thin layer of silver, such as tableware.

sil·ver·smith (sil′vər smith′) *n.* a person who makes or repairs articles of silver.

sil·ver·tongued (sil′vər tungd′) *adj.* smooth and effective in speech; eloquent: *a silver-tongued orator.*

sil·ver·ware (sil′vər wâr′) *n.* **1.** articles made of silver or coated with a thin layer of silver, especially tableware. **2.** table utensils made of metal other than silver.

sil·ver·y (sil′və rē) *adj.* **1.** having the shiny whiteness of silver. **2.** having a soft and clear musical sound. **3.** made of or coated with a layer of silver. —**sil′ver·i·ness,** *n.*

sim·i·an (sim′ē ən) *adj.* of, relating to, or resembling an ape or monkey. —*n.* an ape or monkey.

sim·i·lar (sim′ə lər) *adj.* **1.** having or bearing a marked resemblance; alike: *The designs of the two houses are similar.* **2.** *Geometry.* having corresponding angles that

at; āpe; fär; câre; end; mē; it; īce; pîerce; hot; ōld; sông, fôrk; oil; out; up; ūse; rüle; pull; tûrn; chin; sing; shop; thin; this; hw in white; zh in treasure. The symbol ə stands for the unstressed vowel sound heard in about, taken, pencil, lemon, and circus.

S

are equal and corresponding sides that are in proportion: *similar triangles.* —**sim′i·lar·ly,** *adv.*

sim·i·lar·i·ty (sim′ə lar′i tē) *n.,* pl. **sim·i·lar·i·ties.** **1.** the quality or state of being similar; likeness. **2.** instance or point of likeness: *There are many similarities between the twins.*

sim·i·le (sim′ə lē) *n.* a figure of speech in which one object or idea is compared with another in order to suggest that they are alike. For example: *a face that shines like the sun, hands as cold as ice.*

si·mil·i·tude (si mil′i tüd′, si mil′i tūd′) *n.* similarity; likeness.

sim·mer (sim′ər) *v.i.* **1.** (of a liquid or something in a liquid) to cook at, or just below, the boiling point. **2.** to make a murmuring sound, as a liquid does when it begins to boil. **3.** to be on the verge of breaking forth: *to simmer with anger.* —*v.t.* to cook at, or just below, the boiling point. —*n.* the state or process of simmering.

·**to simmer down. a.** to become calm: *to simmer down after an argument.* **b.** to reduce the amount of liquid by boiling slowly: *to thicken a sauce by simmering it down for half an hour.*

si·mo·ny (sī′mə nē, sim′ə nē) *n.* the act or practice of buying or selling sacred things, such as promotions or positions in the church. [From the Late Latin word *simonia* meaning this practice, from the sorcerer *Simon Magus,* who offered the Apostle Peter money in order to obtain a power given by God.]

si·moom (si müm′) *also,* **si·moon** (si mün′). *n.* a hot, dry, sandy wind of the Arabian and African deserts.

sim·per (sim′pər) *v.i.* to smile in a silly, self-conscious way. —*n.* a silly, self-conscious smile.

sim·ple (sim′pəl) *adj.,* **sim·pler, sim·plest.** **1.** easily done, used, or understood: *a simple task, a simple arithmetic problem.* **2.** consisting of only one part or one unit; unmixed: *simple facts, a simple substance.* **3.** with nothing added; mere; pure: *the simple truth.* **4.** without ornament; unadorned; plain: *a simple style of writing, a simple design.* **5.** without pride or sophistication; artless; natural: *a simple and unaffected person.* **6.** straightforward; honest; sincere: *a simple heart, a simple manner.* **7.** without rank; humble or common: *a simple laborer.* **8.** lacking in judgment or common sense; foolish. —**sim′ple·ness,** *n.*

simple fraction, another term for **common fraction.**

simple machine, one of the basic devices used as an aid in doing work. The lever, the wheel and axle, the inclined plane, the wedge, and the screw are simple machines.

sim·ple·mind·ed (sim′pəl mīn′did) *adj.* **1.** uneducated, foolish, or stupid. **2.** weak-minded. **3.** unsophisticated; artless.

simple sentence, a sentence made up of one independent clause without a dependent clause. For example: *I like to walk quickly.*

sim·ple·ton (sim′pəl tən) *n.* a silly or stupid person; fool.

sim·plic·i·ty (sim plis′i tē) *n.,* pl. **sim·plic·i·ties.** **1.** the state or quality of being simple. **2.** a lack of ornament; plainness: *Their clothes show simplicity and good taste.* **3.** straightforwardness; sincerity. **4.** a lack of common sense; foolishness or stupidity.

sim·pli·fi·ca·tion (sim′plə fi kā′shən) *n.* **1.** the act of simplifying or the state of being simplified. **2.** a result of this.

sim·pli·fy (sim′plə fī′) *v.t.,* **sim·pli·fied, sim·pli·fy·ing.** to make simple: *to simplify an arithmetic problem, to simplify a design.* —**sim′pli·fi′er,** *n.*

sim·plis·tic (sim plis′tik) *adj.* oversimplifying or tending to oversimplify a problem or issue: *Your solution is too simplistic for such a complex problem.*

sim·ply (sim′plē) *adv.* **1.** in a clear, unpretentious, or straightforward manner: *to speak simply and to the point.* **2.** without ornament; plainly: *The room was decorated simply.* **3.** merely; only: *Returning someone's call is simply a matter of politeness.* **4.** to the fullest or highest degree; absolutely: *That rose garden is simply lovely.*

sim·u·late (sim′yə lāt′) *v.t.,* **sim·u·lat·ed, sim·u·lat·ing.** **1.** to give the false appearance of; pretend: *to keep up morale by simulating hope.* **2.** to have the appearance of; imitate: *That painted panel simulates marble.* —**sim′u·la′tive,** *adj.* —**sim′u·la′tor,** *n.*

sim·u·la·tion (sim′yə lā′shən) *n.* **1.** the act or process of simulating. **2.** something that simulates; imitation.

si·mul·cast (sī′məl kast′) *v.t.,* **si·mul·cast** or **si·mul·cast·ed, si·mul·cast·ing.** to broadcast simultaneously on both television and radio, with the radio carrying only the audio portion of the program. —*n.* a program broadcast in this way.

si·mul·ta·ne·ous (sī′məl tā′nē əs) *adj.* existing, happening, or done at the same time: *simultaneous events.* —**si′mul·ta′ne·ous·ly,** *adv.*

sin (sin) *n.* **1.** the willful breaking of God's law. **2.** an instance of this. **3.** an action that is felt to be wrong: *It's a sin to waste food.* —*v.i.,* **sinned, sin·ning. 1.** to break God's law; commit sin. **2.** to commit an offense of any kind.

sin, sine.

since (sins) *adv.* **1.** from then till now: *The neighbors left last week and have been away since.* **2.** at some time between then and now: *The child was sick last month but has since recovered.* —*prep.* **1.** continuously after the time of: *They have been gone since five o'clock.* **2.** during the time following: *There have been many changes in the town since my grandparents' time.* —*conj.* **1.** during the period following the time when: *They haven't seen their teachers since they graduated.* **2.** continuously from the time when: *I have lived abroad since I was ten years old.* **3.** in view of the fact that; because: *Since the car isn't working, we'll have to take a bus.*

sin·cere (sin sîr′) *adj.,* **sin·cer·er, sin·cer·est.** without falseness; honest; true: *a sincere wish, a sincere friend.* —**sin·cere′ly,** *adv.*

sin·cer·i·ty (sin ser′i tē) *n.* the state or quality of being sincere.

sine (sīn) *n.* (of either acute angle of a right triangle) the ratio of the length of the side opposite the angle to the length of the hypotenuse.

si·ne·cure (sī′ni kyúr′, sin′i kyúr′) *n.* a position or job that demands little or no work or responsibility, especially one with a good salary.

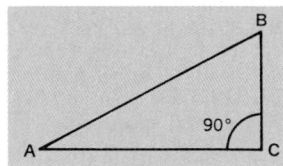

sine of angle *A* = *BC/AB*

sin·ew (sin′ū) *n.* **1.** a tendon. **2.** muscular power or strength. **3.** *also,* **sinews.** a source of power or strength.

sin·ew·y (sin′ū ē) *adj.* **1.** characteristic of or containing sinews; tough; stringy: *a sinewy cut of meat.* **2.** physically strong or powerful; muscular: *a sinewy runner.*

sin·ful (sin′fəl) *adj.* full of or marked by sin; wicked; corrupt. —**sin′ful·ly,** *adv.* —**sin′ful·ness,** *n.*

sing (sing) *v.,* **sang** or **sung, sung, sing·ing.** —*v.i.* **1.** to utter words or sounds with musical tones; perform a song: *The star of this musical sings well.* **2.** to produce musical sounds: *The birds sang in the trees.* **3.** to tell of or praise something in song or verse: *The poet sang of the army's great victory.* **4.** to make a whistling, ringing, or humming sound: *The steam sang as it escaped from the pipe.* —*v.t.* **1.** to utter or perform with musical tones: *The*

874

whole class sang the national anthem. **2.** to bring to a particular state or condition by or with singing: *to sing a child to sleep.* **3.** to recite in a singing voice; intone: *to sing a prayer during a religious service.* **4.** to proclaim enthusiastically: *to sing someone's virtues.* —*n.* a gathering of people for the purpose of singing together: *We went to the community sing.*

·**to sing out.** *Informal.* to call or cry out loudly.

sing., singular.

singe (sinj) *v.t.,* **singed, singe·ing. 1.** to burn slightly: *The hot iron singed the shirt.* **2.** to burn the ends or tips of (hair). **3.** to remove feathers or bristles from by burning: *The cook singed the turkey before roasting it.* —*n.* **1.** the act of singeing. **2.** a slight burn.

sing·er (sing'ər) *n.* **1.** a person who sings, especially a trained or professional vocalist. **2.** a bird that sings.

Sin·gha·lese (sing'gə lēz', sing'gə lēs') *n., pl.* **Sin·gha·lese.** another word for **Sinhalese.**

sin·gle (sing'gəl) *adj.* **1.** only one: *A single chair stood against the wall.* **2.** of or designed for the use of one person only: *a single room at a hotel.* **3.** not married. **4.** (of a flower) having only one row or set of petals. —*n.* **1.** a single person or thing. **2.** something that is for one person only, such as a hotel room or a ticket. **3.** *Baseball.* a hit that allows the batter to reach first base safely. **4. singles.** a match between two persons, as in tennis. —*v.,* **sin·gled, sin·gling.** —*v.t.* to select or separate from others (usually with *out*): *I singled out the black kitten as my favorite.* —*v.i. Baseball.* to hit a single. —**sin'gle·ness,** *n.*

single–breast·ed (sing'gəl bres'tid) *adj.* (of clothes, especially coats or jackets) having a row of buttons or other fastenings on one side only.

single file, a line of persons or things one behind another.

sin·gle–hand·ed (sing'gəl han'did) *adj.* **1.** without the help or support of anyone. **2.** having, using, or needing only one hand. —**sin'gle·hand'ed·ly,** *adv.*

sin·gle–mind·ed (sing'gəl mīn'did) *adj.* **1.** having only one aim or purpose. **2.** faithful; steadfast. —**sin'gle·mind'ed·ly,** *adv.* —**sin'gle·mind'ed·ness,** *n.*

sin·gle·tree (sing'gəl trē') *n.* another word for **whiffletree.**

sin·gly (sing'glē) *adv.* **1.** one at a time; individually; separately: *to consider each item singly.* **2.** without the aid of another or others; single-handedly.

sing·song (sing'sông') *n.* **1.** a monotonous rhythm or tone, as in speaking. **2.** verse, song, or speech marked by this. —*adj.* having a monotonous rhythm or tone.

sin·gu·lar (sing'gyə lər) *adj.* **1.** out of the ordinary; unusual or remarkable; extraordinary: *a singular diamond ring, a singular event.* **2.** strange or peculiar; odd: *singular behavior.* **3.** of or relating to a grammatical form showing only one person or thing: *"Am" is a singular verb.* —*n.* the form of a word showing only one person or thing.

sin·gu·lar·i·ty (sing'gyə lar'i tē) *n., pl.* **sin·gu·lar·i·ties. 1.** the state or quality of being singular. **2.** something that is singular.

Sin·ha·lese (sin'hə lēz', sin'hə lēs') *n., pl.* **Sin·ha·lese. 1.** a member of the people who make up the majority of the population of Sri Lanka. **2.** the language spoken by the Sinhalese. —*adj.* of or relating to Sri Lanka, the Sinhalese, or their language. Also, **Singhalese.**

sin·is·ter (sin'ə stər) *adj.* **1.** threatening or suggesting evil; ominous: *The dark old house looked sinister at night.* **2.** malicious or evil: *a sinister plot, a sinister laugh.* [From the Middle English word *sinistre* meaning "unlucky," from the Latin word *sinister* "left[1]," on the left side," from the ancient belief that the left side is unlucky or evil.]

sink (singk) *v.,* **sank** or **sunk, sunk** or **sunk·en, sink·ing.** —*v.i.* **1.** to go down below a surface partially or com-

pletely: *The wheels of the car sank into the mud. The ship sank after the collision.* **2.** to go down or appear to go down to a lower level, especially gradually: *The water in the pond sank three feet last summer. The sun sank behind the mountain.* **3.** to become less, as in volume, force, degree, or intensity: *The spy's voice sank to a whisper.* **4.** to become less in value; decline: *The store's reputation has sunk in our opinion.* **5.** to pass or fall gradually into a certain state or condition: *to sink into a deep sleep.* **6.** to penetrate deeply: *The stain sank into the cloth.* —*v.t.* **1.** to cause to go down below a surface: *A violent storm sank the old ship.* **2.** to cause to go down to a lower level. **3.** to make less, as in volume, force, degree, or intensity. **4.** to excavate or dig: *to sink a well.* **5.** to force, lay, or bury in the ground: *The workers sank the pipeline.* **6.** *Basketball.* to toss (the ball) into the basket. **7.** *Golf.* to putt (the ball) into the hole. —*n.* **1.** a basin of metal or porcelain, usually connected to a water supply, used for washing. **2.** a low area or hollow in a land surface where water collects. —**sink'a·ble,** *adj.*

sink·er (sing'kər) *n.* **1.** a person or thing that sinks. **2.** a weight used to sink a fishing line.

sink·hole (singk'hōl') *n.* a hole worn straight down in rock, especially limestone, by dripping water.

sin·less (sin'lis) *adj.* free from sin; without sin. —**sin'less·ly,** *adv.* —**sin'less·ness,** *n.*

sin·ner (sin'ər) *n.* a person who sins.

Sino– *combining form* Chinese: *Sino-Soviet relations.*

sin·u·os·i·ty (sin'ū os'i tē) *n., pl.* **sin·u·os·i·ties. 1.** the state or quality of being sinuous. **2.** a curve or bend.

sin·u·ous (sin'ū əs) *adj.* full of curves or bends: *a sinuous line, the sinuous course of a brook.* —**sin'u·ous·ly,** *adv.* —**sin'u·ous·ness,** *n.*

si·nus (sī'nəs) *n., pl.* **si·nus·es.** any of the hollow cavities in the front of the skull that connect with the nose. The sinuses serve to make the skull lighter and protect the brain from blows.

si·nus·i·tis (sī'nə sī'tis) *n.* the inflammation of a sinus or sinuses.

Si·on (sī'ən) another spelling of **Zion.**

Siou·an (sü'ən) *n.* a family of North American Indian languages, including Sioux, Osage, and Crow. —*adj.* of or relating to this language family.

Sioux (sü) *n., pl.* **Sioux** (sü, süz). see **Dakota.**

sip (sip) *v.t., v.i.,* **sipped, sip·ping.** to drink a very small amount of (a liquid) at a time; drink little by little: *to sip a hot drink.* —*n.* **1.** the amount of liquid sipped at one time. **2.** the act of sipping.

si·phon (sī'fən) also, **sy·phon.** *n.* **1.** a bent tube with one side longer than the other, used to transfer a liquid from one container to another one at a lower level by means of atmospheric pressure. **2.** a tubelike organ of certain animals, as the clam, used for drawing in and expelling liquids. —*v.t.* to draw off through or as through a siphon. —*v.i.* to pass through a siphon.

sir (sûr) *n.* **1.** mister. ▲ a form of respectful or polite address used in place of the name of a man: *May I help you,*

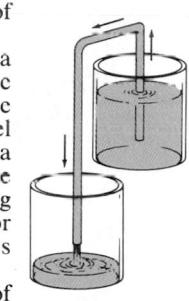

siphon
(def. 1)

---

at; āpe; fär; câre; end; mē; it; īce; pîerce; hot; ōld; sông, fôrk; oil; out; up; ūse; rüle; pull; tûrn; chin; sing; shop; thin; this; hw in white; zh in treasure. The symbol ə stands for the unstressed vowel sound heard in about, taken, pencil, lemon, and circus.

S

sir? **2. Sir.** title and form of address for a knight or baronet.

sire (sīr) *n.* **1.** the male parent of a four-legged animal, such as a horse. **2.** a father or forefather. **3. Sire.** ▲ a form of address used in speaking to a king or nobleman. —*v.t.,* **sired, sir·ing.** to be the male parent of: *Our neighbor's dog sired a litter of puppies.*

si·ren (sī′rən) *n.* **1.** a device for making a loud, shrill sound by the escape of compressed air through a rotating shutter, used as a signal or warning: *a fire siren.* **2. Siren.** *Greek Mythology.* one of several sea nymphs, part bird and part woman, whose singing lured sailors to their destruction. **3.** a charming but dangerous woman.

Sir·i·us (sir′ē əs) *n.* the brightest star in the sky. Also, **Dog Star.**

sir·loin (sûr′loin′) *n.* a cut of beef from the upper part of the loin.

si·roc·co (si rok′ō) *n., pl.* **si·roc·cos. 1.** a hot, dry wind blowing northward from North Africa across the Mediterranean Sea and into southern Europe, where it becomes warm and humid. **2.** any hot, oppressive wind.

sir·rah (sir′ə) *n. Archaic.* fellow. ▲ form of address used to show contempt for a man or boy.

sir·up (sir′əp, sûr′əp) another spelling of **syrup.**

sis (sis) *n. Informal.* sister.

sis·al (sī′səl, sis′əl) *n.* **1.** a coarse, strong fiber obtained from the leaves of any of several tropical American plants, used to make rope and bags. Also, **sisal hemp. 2.** the plant yielding this fiber.

sis·sy (sis′ē) *n., pl.* **sis·sies. 1.** a boy or man whose behavior is considered not to be manly. **2.** a coward.

sis·ter (sis′tər) *n.* **1.** a girl or woman having the same parents as another person. **2.** a fellow woman or girl. **3.** a woman who is a fellow member of a church, club, or sorority. **4.** a woman who is a member of a religious order for women; nun.

sis·ter·hood (sis′tər hŏŏd′) *n.* **1.** the state or quality of being a sister or sisters; relationship between sisters. **2.** a group of women who are united by some common aim or interest or bound by vows to a religious organization.

sis·ter–in–law (sis′tər in lô′) *n., pl.* **sis·ters–in–law. 1.** the sister of one's husband or wife. **2.** the wife of one's brother. **3.** the wife of the brother of one's husband or wife.

sis·ter·ly (sis′tər lē) *adj.* relating to, characteristic of, or befitting a sister; kind; affectionate. —**sis′ter·li·ness,** *n.*

Sis·tine Chapel (sis′tēn) a chapel in the Vatican in Rome, noted for its frescoes by Michelangelo.

Sis·y·phus (sis′ə fəs) *n. Greek Mythology.* a king noted for his craftiness, who was punished in the Underworld by having to push a huge rock to the top of a hill, from which it would roll back down, thus forcing him to begin again.

sit (sit) *v.,* **sat, sit·ting.** —*v.i.* **1.** to be in a position in which the weight of the body rests on the buttocks, while the rest of the body bends at the hips and, usually, the knees. **2.** to rest on a perch; roost: *The bird sat on a branch.* **3.** (of a chicken) to cover eggs in order to hatch them; brood. **4.** to be placed: *The hut sits in the middle of a forest.* **5.** to hold a particular pose for an artist or photographer; model: *to sit for a portrait.* **6.** to be or remain unused or inactive: *The car sat in the garage for a year.* **7.** to hold a session: *The legislature sits in the fall.* **8.** to bear down as a burden; weigh: *Old age sits lightly upon my grandparents.* **9.** to fit: *The dress sits well on your shoulders.* —*v.t.* **1.** to cause to sit; seat: *The guests sat themselves around the table.* **2.** to keep one's seat on (a horse).

·**to sit in on.** to attend or take part in: *A newspaper reporter sat in on the committee meeting.*

·**to sit on.** to be a member of (a committee, jury, legislative body, or the like).

·**to sit out.** to take no part in: *We sat out the last waltz.*

·**to sit up. a.** to delay retiring until after one's usual bedtime. **b.** to become attentive or alert: *to sit up in surprise.*

si·tar (si tär′) *n.* a stringed musical instrument of India, having a long neck and a rounded body, made from a gourd or hollowed-out wood and played by plucking the strings.

sit·com (sit′kom′) *n. Informal.* see **situation comedy.**

sit–down strike (sit′doun′) a strike in which the strikers remain at their jobs but do not work until an agreement is reached.

sitar

site (sīt) *n.* **1.** the position or location of a town, city, building, or the like: *The village occupied a mountain site.* **2.** the place where something happened: *Gettysburg, in southeastern Pennsylvania, is the site of one of the most famous battles of the American Civil War.*

sit–in (sit′in′) *n.* a protest demonstration in which persons sit in a public place and stay there until their demands are agreed to or considered. —*v.i.,* **sat-in, sit-ting-in.** to take part in a sit-in.

sit·ter (sit′ər) *n.* **1.** a person or thing that sits. **2.** see **baby-sitter.**

sit·ting (sit′ing) *n.* **1.** the act of a person or thing that sits. **2.** the period of time that a person sits for or is occupied with a particular purpose: *I read the entire book in one sitting.* —*adj.* pertaining to or used for sitting: *a sitting position.*

sitting duck *Informal.* a person or thing that is very vulnerable; easy target.

sitting room, a room used for sitting, as in a home, hotel, or club.

sit·u·ate (sich′ü āt′) *v.t.,* **sit·u·at·ed, sit·u·at·ing.** to give a position to; place: *to situate a house on top of a hill.*

sit·u·a·tion (sich′ü ā′shən) *n.* **1.** a condition or state of affairs: *The lack of sales at the store created a difficult financial situation. What is the political situation in that country?* **2.** a location; position: *The situation of the barn is to the left of the house.* **3.** the work in which one is engaged or employed. —**sit′u·a′tion·al,** *adj.*

situation comedy, a television or radio comedy series in which the same characters appear in different situations in successive episodes.

sit–up (sit′up′) *n.* an exercise in which a person lies with the back flat, bends at the waist into a sitting position, and then returns to a lying position.

Si·va (sē′və, shē′və) another spelling of **Shiva.**

six (siks) *n., pl.* **six·es. 1.** the cardinal number that is one more than five. **2.** a symbol representing this number, such as 6 or VI. **3.** something having this many units or things, such as a playing card. —*adj.* numbering one more than five.

six·fold (siks′fōld′) *adj.* **1.** six times as great or numerous. **2.** having or consisting of six parts. —*adv.* so as to be six times greater or more numerous: *The company's sales increased sixfold.*

Six Nations, see **Iroquois.**

six·pence (siks′pəns) *n.* a former coin of the United Kingdom, equal to six pennies.

six·shoot·er (siks′shü′tər) *n. Informal.* a revolver that can be fired six times without being reloaded.

six·teen (siks′tēn′) *n.* **1.** the cardinal number that is six more than ten. **2.** a symbol representing this number, such as 16 or XVI. **3.** something having this many units or things. —*adj.* numbering six more than ten.

six·teenth (siks′tēnth′) *adj.* **1.** (the ordinal of sixteen) next after the fifteenth. **2.** being one of sixteen equal parts. —*n.* **1.** something that is next after the fifteenth. **2.** one of sixteen equal parts; ¹⁄₁₆.

sixteenth note *Music.* a note having one-sixteenth the time value of a whole note.

sixth (siksth) *adj.* **1.** (the ordinal of six) next after the fifth. **2.** being one of six equal parts. —*n.* **1.** something that is next after the fifth. **2.** one of six equal parts; ¹⁄₆. **3.** *Music.* **a.** a note that is a total of four whole steps and one half step above a given note. *A* is the sixth of *C*. **b.** an interval of four whole steps and one half step. **c.** a combination of two notes that are separated by this interval. —*adv.* in the sixth place.

sixth sense, a seeming ability to know or sense things that could not be known or sensed with the five senses; intuition.

six·ti·eth (siks′tē ith) *adj.* **1.** (the ordinal of sixty) next after the fifty-ninth. **2.** being one of sixty equal parts. —*n.* **1.** something that is next after the fifty-ninth. **2.** one of sixty equal parts; ¹⁄₆₀.

six·ty (siks′tē) *n., pl.* **six·ties. 1.** the cardinal number that is six times ten. **2.** a symbol representing this number, such as 60 or LX. —*adj.* numbering six times ten.

siz·a·ble (sī′zə bəl) *also,* **size·a·ble.** *adj.* somewhat large: *a sizable two-story house, a sizable donation.*

size[1] (sīz) *n.* **1.** the amount of length, breadth, or height that something has: *the size of a room, the size of a tree.* **2.** greatness of extent; bigness: *The only building of any size in our town is the courthouse.* **3.** amount or number: *the size of an inheritance.* **4.** a measurement for classifying a manufactured article according to size: *What size shoe do you wear?* **5.** *Informal.* the true state of affairs; actual circumstances: *That's the size of it.* —*v.t.,* **sized, siz·ing. 1.** to classify according to size: *to size eggs.* **2.** to make of a certain or required size: *The jeweler sized the ring to fit my finger.* [From the Middle English word *sise* meaning "amount" or "a standard of measurement," from the Old French word *sise* with the same meanings, short for *assise* "a legislative session" or "ordinance, law."]

   to size up. to make an estimate; form an opinion of: *The mayor sized up the political situation before running for governor.*

size[2] (sīz) *n.* any of various glues or pastes used to coat or glaze the surface of a fabric or paper. Also, **siz·ing** (sī′zing). —*v.t.,* **sized, siz·ing.** to treat or coat with size. [Of uncertain origin.]

sized (sīzd) *adj.* having a stated size. ▲ used in combination: *small-sized, full-sized.*

siz·zle (siz′əl) *v.i.,* **siz·zled, siz·zling. 1.** to make a hissing sound, especially when burning or frying: *The hamburgers sizzled in the pan.* **2.** to be very hot: *It's sizzling outside.* —*n.* a hissing sound: *the sizzle of wet twigs burning.*

SK, postal abbreviation for Saskatchewan.

skald (skôld) *n.* an ancient Scandinavian poet; bard.

skate[1] (skāt) *n.* **1.** see **ice skate. 2.** see **roller skate.** —*v.i.,* **skat·ed, skat·ing.** to glide or move along on skates. [From the Dutch word *schaats* meaning "a skate[1]," of Old French origin.] —**skat′er,** *n.*

skate[2] (skāt) *n., pl.* **skates** or **skate.** a fish related to the shark and ray, found in warm and temperate seas, having two broad side fins that are shaped like wings. [From the Old Norse word *skata* meaning this fish.]

skate·board (skāt′bôrd′) *n.* a low, flat board having wheels attached to the bottom, ridden usually with the rider balancing in a standing position.

skein (skān) *n.* **1.** a continuous strand of yarn or thread

coiled in a bundle. **2.** something like this: *a skein of hair.*

skel·e·tal (skel′i təl) *adj.* of, relating to, forming, or like a skeleton.

skel·e·ton (skel′i tən) *n.* **1.** the framework of bones supporting the body of an animal with a backbone. **2.** a supporting framework or structure, as of a building or ship. **3.** an outline, as of a literary work; sketch. **4.** a very thin or gaunt person or animal.

skeleton key, a key that opens a number of different locks.

skep·tic (skep′tik) *also,* **scep·tic.** *n.* **1.** a person who doubts or questions the truth of beliefs or conclusions accepted by most people. **2.** a person who tends to be doubtful or questioning, especially about the statements of others. **3.** a person who doubts religious beliefs.

skep·ti·cal (skep′ti kəl) *also,* **scep·ti·cal.** *adj.* **1.** characterized by or showing doubt; disbelieving: *a skeptical question.* **2.** of, relating to, or characteristic of skeptics or skepticism. —**skep′ti·cal·ly,** *adv.*

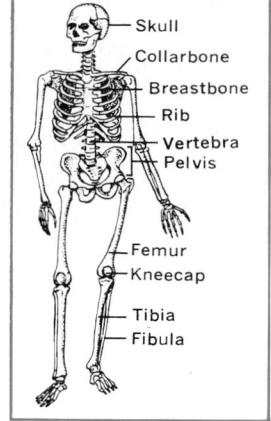

human **skeleton**

skep·ti·cism (skep′tə siz′əm) *also,* **scep·ti·cism.** *n.* **1.** a doubting or questioning attitude or state of mind. **2.** doubt about religious beliefs.

sketch (skech) *n., pl.* **sketch·es. 1.** a rough, unfinished, or quick drawing: *The artist made several sketches of the model before starting the painting.* **2.** a short description or plan giving the main features of something; outline. **3.** a brief, informal literary composition. **4.** a short scene or play, as in a revue, musical comedy, or other theatrical program. —*v.t.* to make a sketch of: *The painter sketched the old barn.* —*v.i.* to make a sketch or sketches. —**sketch′er,** *n.*

sketch·book (skech′bŭk′) *n.* a pad or book used for sketching or drawing.

sketch·y (skech′ē) *adj.,* **sketch·i·er, sketch·i·est. 1.** not detailed or finished: *I drew a sketchy outline of what I planned to paint.* **2.** incomplete or fragmentary; imperfect; slight: *The dazed driver could give only a sketchy account of the accident.* —**sketch′i·ly,** *adv.* —**sketch′i·ness,** *n.*

skew (skū) *v.i.* to veer away from a straight line; swerve; twist: *The railroad tracks skew to the left after crossing the river.* —*v.t.* **1.** to cause to turn aside from a straight line; set at an angle. **2.** to slant or twist the meaning of; distort: *The witnesses skewed their testimony to favor the defendant.* —*adj.* **1.** having a part that turns aside from a straight line. **2.** not symmetrical. —*n.* a turning from a straight line.

skew·er (skū′ər) *n.* a long pin of wood or metal used to hold meat together while cooking. —*v.t.* to fasten or pierce with or as if with a skewer.

---

at; āpe; fär; câre; end; mē; it; īce; pîerce; hot; ōld; sông, fôrk; oil; out; up; ūse; rüle; pull; tûrn; chin; sing; shop; thin; this; hw in white; zh in treasure. The symbol ə stands for the unstressed vowel sound heard in about, taken, pencil, lemon, and circus.

S

ski (skē) *n.* **1.** one of a pair of long, narrow runners, usually of wood or metal, curving upward at the front and designed to be fastened to a boot for gliding over snow. **2.** see **water ski.** —*v.,* **skied, ski·ing.** —*v.i.* to glide or travel on skis, especially as a sport. —*v.t.* to glide or travel over on skis: *to ski a steep slope.* —**ski′er,** *n.*

skid (skid) *n.* **1.** the act of sliding or slipping, usually sideways, as over an icy or wet surface. **2.** a device, such as a wedge of wood or metal, placed against the wheel of a vehicle to prevent it from moving. **3.** a plank or frame used as a track on which something heavy may be slid or pushed along. **4.** a runner that is part of the landing gear of certain aircraft. —*v.,* **skid·ded, skidding.** —*v.i.* **1.** to slide or slip, usually sideways: *The car skidded on the icy road.* **2.** (of a wheel on a moving vehicle) to slide without turning. —*v.t.* **1.** to prevent (a wheel) from moving by applying a skid. **2.** to haul, slide, move, or place on a skid or skids.

·**on the skids.** *Slang.* rapidly declining in power, value, quality, or prestige: *The actor's career was on the skids.*

skid row *Slang.* a section of a city where vagrants and derelicts live or gather, made up mostly of cheap rooming houses and bars.

skies (skīz) the plural of **sky.**

skiff (skif) *n.* a small, light boat propelled by motor, sail, or oars.

skiing

ski·ing (skē′ing) *n.* the act or sport of gliding or traveling on skis.

ski jump **1.** a steep, snow-covered ramp, track, or course ending abruptly above a long slope, designed for long-distance jumping by skiers. **2.** a jump made by a skier over such a course.

ski lift, an apparatus for carrying skiers up a slope, usually consisting of a motor-operated cable with seats attached.

skill (skil) *n.* **1.** the power or ability to do something, resulting from training, practice, knowledge, or experience; proficiency: *to show great skill in playing the violin.* **2.** a particular power or ability: *reading skills.*

skilled (skild) *adj.* **1.** having or showing skill or compe-

tence; proficient: *a skilled musician.* **2.** having or requiring special ability or training: *skilled labor.*

skil·let (skil′it) *n.* a shallow pan with a handle, used for frying; frying pan.

skill·ful (skil′fəl) *also, British,* **skil·ful.** *adj.* having, showing, or involving skill: *a skillful chess player.* —**skill′ful·ly,** *adv.* —**skill′ful·ness,** *n.*

skim (skim) *v.,* **skimmed, skim·ming.** —*v.t.* **1.** to remove floating matter from (a liquid): *The cook skimmed the soup while it simmered.* **2.** to remove (floating matter) from a liquid. **3.** to glance over or read quickly: *to skim a newspaper for a special article.* **4.** to move or glide lightly and swiftly over or across: *to skim across the ice.* **5.** to throw so as to glide or bounce lightly along a surface: *to skim a stone across a lake.* —*v.i.* **1.** to move or glide lightly and swiftly over or across a surface. **2.** to take a quick glance at something. —*adj.* that has been skimmed.

skim·mer (skim′ər) *n.* **1.** a person or thing that skims. **2.** a utensil, especially a shallow ladle having a wire mesh or a flat bowl punched with holes, used to skim liquids. **3.** any of various gull-like birds that search for food by skimming the water with their lower beak. **4.** a wide-brimmed hat, usually of straw, with a flat crown.

skimmer *(def. 3)*

skim milk *also,* **skimmed milk.** milk from which the cream has been removed.

skimp (skimp) *v.i.* to be very sparing or thrifty: *The cook skimped on the meat in the stew.* —*v.t.* **1.** to perform (a task) carelessly, hastily, or with poor material. **2.** to be very sparing or thrifty with: *Don't skimp the gravy with the mashed potatoes.*

skimp·y (skim′pē) *adj.,* **skimp·i·er, skimp·i·est.** **1.** less than what is needed; not enough; scanty: *a skimpy supper.* **2.** very sparing or thrifty: *a skimpy person.* —**skimp′i·ly,** *adv.* —**skimp′i·ness,** *n.*

skin (skin) *n.* **1.** the outer covering of an animal's body. **2.** such an outer covering removed from an animal; pelt or hide. **3.** anything resembling skin in appearance, nature, or function: *the skin of an apple.* **4.** a container made of animal skin, used for holding liquids, especially wine. —*v.t.,* **skinned, skin·ning.** **1.** to remove the skin from: *to skin a rabbit.* **2.** to injure the surface of or remove a portion of skin from, especially by scraping: *to fall and skin one's elbow.*

·**by the skin of one's teeth.** by a very small amount; barely: *I passed the test by the skin of my teeth.*

·**to get under one's skin.** *Informal.* to be or become annoying or irritating.

skin–deep (skin′dēp′) *adj.* only on the surface; superficial; shallow: *Beauty is only skin-deep.*

skin–dive (skin′dīv′) *v.i.,* **skin-dived** or **skin-dove** (skin′dōv′), **skin-dived, skin-div·ing.** to engage in skin diving.

skin diving, underwater swimming for extended periods of time, usually with a face mask and flippers, and sometimes with oxygen tanks or a snorkel so that the swimmer can remain under water longer. —**skin diver,** *n.*

skin·flint (skin′flint′) *n.* a very stingy person; miser.

skin·ner (skin′ər) *n.* **1.** a person who deals in animal skins, especially one who removes and treats animal skins and furs. **2.** a driver of mules, horses, or other animals used for hauling loads.

skin·ny (skin′ē) *adj.,* **skin·ni·er, skin·ni·est.** very thin; lean. —**skin′ni·ness,** *n.*

skin·tight (skin′tīt′) *adj.* fitting tightly: *skintight pants.*

skip (skip) *v.,* **skipped, skip·ping.** *v.i.* **1.** to spring or bound along, hopping lightly on one foot and then on the other: *The children skipped down the path.* **2.** to pass from one point to another, leaving out or paying little attention to what lies between: *to skip over a chapter in a book.* **3.** to bounce along or across a surface; skim. —*v.t.* **1.** to jump or spring lightly over: *to skip rope.* **2.** to leave out or pass over or by: *I skipped the math problems I couldn't do.* **3.** to cause to bounce along or across a surface; skim. **4.** *Informal.* to leave (a place) hurriedly or in secret: *The dishonest banker skipped town.* —*n.* **1.** a light springing, bounding, or jumping step. **2.** the act of passing over or leaving out.

skip·per¹ (skip′ər) *n.* the captain of a ship, especially of a small trading, fishing, or pleasure boat. [From the Middle Dutch word *schipper* with the same meaning, from the word *schip* "ship."]

skip·per² (skip′ər) *n.* **1.** a person or thing that skips. **2.** any of a group of butterflies that fly with quick, darting movements. [*Skip* + *-er¹*.]

skir·mish (skûr′mish) *n., pl.* **skir·mish·es. 1.** a brief fight between small groups of persons or small bodies of troops. **2.** any brief or minor conflict. —*v.i.* to take part in a skirmish. —**skir′mish·er,** *n.*

skirt (skûrt) *n.* **1.** a woman's or girl's garment that is fastened around the waist or hips and hangs down to varying lengths. **2.** that part of a dress or similar garment that hangs from the waist down. **3.** a rim, edge, or outer margin: *Deer came to the skirts of the field.* **4.** one of the flaps hanging from the side of a saddle. —*v.t.* **1.** to lie along or form the border or edge of: *Trees skirted the field.* **2.** to move or run along the border or edge of; pass around rather than go through: *The highway skirted the town.* **3.** to avoid discussing or dealing with: *The speaker skirted the controversial issue.* —*v.i.* to move along or be near the border or edge of something.

skit (skit) *n.* a short, usually humorous play.

skit·ter (skit′ər) *v.i.* to glide or skim lightly and quickly over a surface. —*v.t.* to cause to skitter.

skit·tish (skit′ish) *adj.* **1.** easily frightened or excited; jumpy: *a skittish horse.* **2.** not dependable; fickle: *a skittish young child.* —**skit′tish·ly,** *adv.* —**skit′tish·ness,** *n.*

skit·tle (skit′əl) *n.* **1. skittles.** a form of ninepins in which a wooden disk or ball is used to knock down the pins. ▲ used with a singular verb. **2.** a pin used in this game.

skoal (skōl) *interj.* to your health. ▲ used as a toast.

skul·dug·ger·y (skul′dug′ə rē) *n.* underhanded or deceitful actions; trickery.

skulk (skulk) *v.i.* **1.** to move in a sneaking or sly way. **2.** to stay out of sight, especially in order to avoid work or danger; hide oneself: *to skulk in the woods to avoid mowing the lawn.* —*n.* a person who skulks. —**skulk′er,** *n.*

skull (skul) *n.* **1.** the bony framework of the head in an animal with a backbone. It consists of the bones that enclose the brain and support the face. **2.** the human head considered as the seat of thought, intelligence, or understanding: *Can't you get it through your skull that you are wrong?*

skull and crossbones, the representation of a human skull above two crossed bones, a symbol

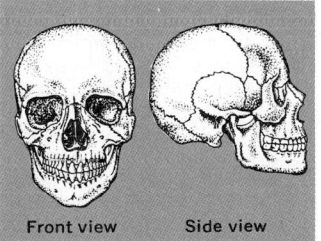

Front view   Side view

human **skull**

of death once used on the flags of pirate ships, now used chiefly as a warning sign, as on bottles of poison.

skull·cap (skul′kap′) *n.* a close-fitting cap without a brim.

skunk (skungk) *n.* **1.** a small, black animal with a bushy tail, usually having white stripes along its back. It sprays a liquid with a strong, very unpleasant smell when frightened or attacked. **2.** the fur of this animal. **3.** *Informal.* a mean, hateful person.

skunk cabbage, a weedy marsh plant found in eastern North America that gives off a foul smell when it is bruised.

sky (skī) *n., pl.* **skies. 1.** the upper atmosphere, appearing as a great arch over the earth and having a light blue color on clear days. **2.** *also,* **skies.** the condition or appearance of the sky: *sunny skies.* **3.** heaven.

·**to the skies.** to the highest point, level, or degree: *to praise someone to the skies.*

sky blue, light blue, like the color of the clear sky.

sky·dive (skī′dīv′) *v.i.,* **sky·dived** or **sky·dove, sky·dived, sky·div·ing.** to engage in skydiving. —**sky′div′er,** *n.*

sky·div·ing (skī′dī′ving) *n.* the act or sport of parachuting from an airplane and falling as far as safely possible before opening the parachute.

sky·high (skī′hī′) *adv.* **1.** to a very high point, level, or degree: *The cost of living rose sky-high.* **2.** into pieces; to bits; apart: *The explosion blew the building sky-high.* —*adj.* very high: *sky-high prices.*

sky·jack (skī′jak′) *v.t. Informal.* to hijack (an airplane), especially a commercial airliner. [*Sky* + (hi)*jack.*] —**sky′jack′er,** *n.*

Sky·lab (skī′lab′) *n.* a U.S. space station used for scientific experiments, launched into orbit around the earth in 1973. It fell from orbit in 1979.

sky·lark (skī′lärk′) *n.* a lark of Europe, Asia, and northern Africa, having dull brown feathers with black and whitish markings, noted for its melodious song while in flight. —*v.i.* to frolic about; play.

sky·light (skī′līt′) *n.* a window in a roof or ceiling for letting in daylight.

sky·line (skī′līn′) *n.* **1.** the outline of buildings, mountains, or other objects seen against the sky. **2.** the line at which the earth and sky seem to come together; horizon.

sky·rock·et (skī′rok′it) *n.* a small rocket that explodes high in the air, giving off a shower of colored sparks and lights, used chiefly in fireworks displays. —*v.i.* to rise rapidly, suddenly, or greatly: *Apartment rents in the city are skyrocketing.* —*v.t.* to cause to rise rapidly, suddenly, or greatly: *Higher food prices skyrocketed the cost of living.*

sky·scrap·er (skī′skrā′pər) *n.* a very tall building.

sky·ward (skī′wərd) *adv. also,* **sky·wards** (skī′wərdz). toward or in the direction of the sky: *The rocket flew skyward.* —*adj.* toward the sky: *a skyward glance.*

sky·writ·ing (skī′rī′ting) *n.* **1.** the act or process of forming words or symbols in the sky by releasing a trail of smoke or the like from an airplane. **2.** the words or symbols so formed. —**sky′writ′er,** *n.*

slab (slab) *n.* **1.** a broad, flat, and usually thick piece of some material: *a slab of stone.* **2.** a rough outside piece cut from a log.

slack¹ (slak) *adj.* **1.** not tight or firm; loose: *a slack rope, a slack grip.* **2.** slow in motion; unhurried; sluggish: *to walk at a slack pace.* **3.** not busy or lively: *The department store's business was slack after the big sale.* **4.** careless or lazy: *a slack worker.* —*n.* **1.** the part that is slack or

at; āpe; fär; câre; end; mē; it; īce; pierce; hot; ōld; sông; fôrk; oil; out; up; ūse; rüle; pull; tûrn; chin; sing; shop; thin; **this**; hw in white; zh in treasure. The symbol ə stands for the unstressed vowel sound heard in about, taken, pencil, lemon, and circus.

S

hangs loose: *the slack in a rope.* **2.** a period of little or no activity; lull: *a slack in business.* —*v.t.* to slacken: *The sailor slacked the rope.* —*v.i.* to be or become slack: *The wind slacked.* —*adv.* in a slack or loose manner. [From the Old English word *slæc* meaning "careless," "lax" or "sluggish."] —**slack′ly,** *adv.* —**slack′ness,** *n.*

slack² (slak) *n.* small bits of coal remaining after coal is screened or sifted. [Probably from the Middle Dutch word *slacke* with the same meaning.]

slack·en (slak′ən) *v.t.* **1.** to make slower: *to slacken one's pace.* **2.** to make loose: *to slacken wire.* **3.** to make less; lessen: *to slacken production at a factory.* —*v.i.* **1.** to become slower. **2.** to become loose. **3.** to become less, as in force or intensity: *My interest in poetry slackened after I left school.*

slack·er (slak′ər) *n.* a person who avoids or attempts to avoid work, duty, or responsibility.

slacks (slaks) *pl. n.* trousers for casual wear.

slag (slag) *n.* waste material left after metal is separated from its ore by smelting.

slain (slān) the past participle of **slay.**

slake (slāk) *v.t.*, **slaked, slak·ing. 1.** to relieve or satisfy; quench: *The cool water slaked the runner's thirst.* **2.** to cause a chemical change in (lime) by treating it with water.

slaked lime, a white compound formed by treating lime with water, used in mortar and cement.

sla·lom (slä′ləm, slal′əm) *n.* a downhill skiing race over a zigzag course that is marked by poles. [From the Norwegian word *slalåm* meaning "sloping track," from the words *sla* "sloping" + *låm* "track, path."]

slam¹ (slam) *v.*, **slammed, slam·ming.** —*v.t.* **1.** to close forcefully and with a loud noise: *to slam a car door.* **2.** to strike, throw, put, or move (something) with force and a loud noise: *The batter slammed the ball into right field.* **3.** *Informal.* to criticize harshly or severely. —*v.i.* **1.** to close with force and a loud noise: *The wind made the door slam.* **2.** to strike or move forcefully and noisily: *The shutters slammed against the side of the house.* —*n.* **1.** a forceful and noisy closing or striking. **2.** the noise made by this. [Of Scandinavian origin.]

slam² (slam) *n.* the winning of twelve or all thirteen tricks in a round of bridge; little slam or grand slam. [Of uncertain origin.]

slan·der (slan′dər) *n.* **1.** a false and malicious statement spoken about another that is damaging to his or her reputation or well-being: *The slander destroyed the senator's chance of reelection.* **2.** the uttering or spreading of such a statement. —*v.t.* to utter false and malicious statements about; injure by spreading slander against. —**slan′der·er,** *n.*

slan·der·ous (slan′dər əs) *adj.* **1.** containing slander: *slanderous statements.* **2.** uttering or spreading slander. —**slan′der·ous·ly,** *adv.*

slang (slang) *n.* **1.** a kind of language that expresses ideas in an unconventional, often striking manner. **2.** the vocabulary of a particular group, class, or profession; jargon: *military slang.*

Language Note

Slang can give freshness and variety to everyday speaking and writing. Modern English slang consists mainly of new words and new meanings of existing words. Slang words tend to remain slang for only a relatively short period of time because most slang words either quickly disappear from use or become a part of the Standard English vocabulary.

If you have ever read a novel, listened to a popular song, or seen a film that is more than twenty-five years old, you have probably noticed some words and expres-

sions that seem strange. Examples of this type of outdated slang are *the bee's knees* and *the cat's pajamas,* meaning "wonderful" or "the best," and *skiddoo,* meaning "go away." Among the words that once were slang but are now part of Standard English are *kidnap, skyscraper, jazz, blimp,* and *soap opera.* In a few cases, such as the terms *beat it,* meaning "go away," and *kooky,* meaning "zany," a slang expression has existed in our language for a long time but has remained slang.

The words that we use in slang are often a good indication of social history and general attitudes. For example, many of the former and current slang terms that describe money, such as *cabbage, dough,* and *bread,* show that in our society money appears to have the same importance for survival as food does.

Slang comes into our language in various ways. Many slang expressions have come from the jargon, or special language, of a particular profession, age group, or region. Among the most important sources of such slang has been the military, because it is composed of a large number of people from all parts of the country and all backgrounds who temporarily share a common experience. Other slang terms have come from the secret language of some part of society. While most of the language of criminals is unfamiliar to us, it has provided us with the word *grand,* meaning "a thousand dollars," among other terms. Today, much slang comes from computer jargon, including the use of the prefix *mega-* to mean "a huge amount of something" or "a very large (something)."

The communications media, particularly radio and television, have been responsible for the wide and rapid spread of slang terms. The media have also been responsible for shortening the life of slang terms, because when a slang term becomes common and overused, it loses its fresh and vivid quality and eventually ceases to be used as slang.

The American poet Carl Sandburg described slang as "language which takes off its coat, spits on its hands— and goes to work." Slang is essentially an oral, often spontaneous form of language, and as such, its fresh simplicity functions well. However, the expression of subtle or complex ideas requires the more precise language of Standard English. Slang certainly has a place in our spoken language as a colorful supplement to Standard English, but it ought not be considered a replacement for Standard English.

slang·y (slang′ē) *adj.*, **slang·i·er, slang·i·est. 1.** of the nature of, characterized by, or containing slang. **2.** given to the use of slang: *a slangy writer.* —**slang′i·ness,** *n.*

slant (slant) *v.i.* to have or take a direction that slopes away from the horizontal or vertical, or from a straight line or course: *The barn roof slants toward the ground.* —*v.t.* **1.** to cause to slant: *to slant a ladder against the wall.* **2.** to present in a way that supports a particular opinion or bias, or appeals to a particular interest: *to slant a magazine toward young people.* —*n.* **1.** a slanting direction, line, surface, or plane; inclination; angle: *The picture hung on a slant.* **2.** a point of view; attitude; opinion: *The speech offered a new slant on the problem of drug addiction.*

slant·wise (slant′wīz′) *adv.* also, **slant·ways** (slant′wāz′). in a slanting direction or position; at a slant. —*adj.* not straight up and down; slanting.

slap (slap) *n.* **1.** a sharp, quick blow, especially with the open hand or with something flat. **2.** the sound made by such a blow. —*v.t.* **1.** to strike with a sharp, quick blow, especially with the open hand or with something flat: *to slap a fly with a swatter.* **2.** to put or throw noisily, forcefully, or carelessly: *The child slapped the books down on the table.* —*v.i.* to strike or beat with a slap: *The waves slapped against the side of the boat.*

slap·dash (slap′dash′) *adj.* hasty and careless: *a slap-dash piece of work.* —*adv.* in a hasty and careless manner. —*n.* hasty and careless work or action.

slap·stick (slap′stik′) *n.* comedy characterized by loud, exaggerated, rough action. —*adj.* characterized by or relating to slapstick: *slapstick humor.*

slash (slash) *v.t.* **1.** to cut with a forceful, sweeping stroke or strokes, as with a sharp instrument: *to slash a path through a jungle.* **2.** to strike with a whip; lash. **3.** to cut slits in (a garment), as to show underlying material of a different color. **4.** to reduce sharply or drastically: *to slash production costs.* **5.** to criticize severely. —*v.i.* to make a forceful, sweeping stroke or strokes with a knife or other sharp instrument. —*n., pl.* **slash·es. 1.** a forceful, sweeping stroke: *the slash of a whip.* **2.** a cut or gash on the skin or other surface made by such a stroke. **3.** an ornamental slit in a garment. **4.** a sharp or drastic reduction: *a slash in prices.* —**slash′er,** *n.*

slat (slat) *n.* a thin, narrow, flat strip of wood, metal, or other material: *the slats of a Venetian blind.* —*v.t.,* **slat·ted, slat·ting.** to provide or make with slats.

slate (slāt) *n.* **1.** a fine-grained, bluish gray rock that splits easily into thin sheets or layers. **2.** a thin piece of this rock, used especially to make roofing tiles and blackboards. **3.** a small writing tablet, usually held in the hand. **4.** the record of a person's past actions or performance: *That candidate has a clean slate.* **5.** a list of candidates proposed for nomination or election. **6.** a dull, dark, bluish gray color. —*adj.* having the color slate; bluish gray. —*v.t.,* **slat·ed, slat·ing. 1.** to cover with slate or a substance like slate. **2.** to put on a list of candidates. **3.** to schedule or designate: *The conference was slated for June.*

slat·tern (slat′ərn) *n.* an untidy, slovenly woman or girl.

slat·tern·ly (slat′ərn lē) *adj.* relating to or characteristic of a slattern; slovenly; untidy. —*adv.* in a slovenly manner. —**slat′tern·li·ness,** *n.*

slat·y (slā′tē) *adj.,* **slat·i·er, slat·i·est. 1.** of, relating to, containing, or resembling slate. **2.** having the color of slate; bluish gray.

slaugh·ter (slô′tər) *n.* **1.** the act of killing an animal or animals for food. **2.** brutal or violent killing, especially of a large number of persons; massacre. —*v.t.* **1.** to kill (an animal or animals) for food; butcher. **2.** to kill (persons) in a brutal or violent manner; massacre. —**slaugh′ter·er,** *n.*

slaugh·ter·house (slô′tər hous′) *n., pl.* **slaugh·ter·hous·es** (slô′tər hou′ziz). a place where animals are butchered for food.

Slav (släv, slav) *n.* a member of a group of peoples speaking related languages and living mainly in eastern, southeastern, and central Europe. Poles, Czechs, Slovaks, Bulgarians, Russians, and Ukrainians are Slavs.

slave (slāv) *n.* **1.** a person who is the property of another person. **2.** a person who is under the control of some influence or person: *a slave to a habit.* **3.** a person who works, or is made to work, hard and long. —*v.i.,* **slaved, slav·ing.** to work hard and long: *The writer slaved for weeks to finish the book.* [From the Old French word *esclave* meaning "slave," from the Medieval Latin word *sclavus* "slave," from the tribal name *Sclavus* "a Slav." In the Middle Ages, many Slavs were conquered and enslaved.] —**slave′like′,** *adj.*

slave driver 1. a person who is in charge of slaves at work. **2.** any harsh or very demanding employer or taskmaster.

slave·hold·er (slāv′hōl′dər) *n.* a person who owns slaves.

slav·er¹ (slā′vər) *n.* **1.** a person who deals in slaves. **2.** a ship used to transport slaves. [*Slave* + *-er¹*.]

slav·er² (slav′ər) *v.i.* to let saliva run out from the mouth; drool; slobber. —*n.* saliva running out from the mouth.

[From the Middle English word *slaveren* meaning "to drool," of Scandinavian origin.]

slav·er·y (slā′və rē) *n.* **1.** the institution or practice of owning slaves **2.** the condition of being a slave. **3.** the condition of being under the control of some influence or person: *the slavery of drug addiction.* **4.** hard or exhausting work; drudgery.

Slav·ic (slä′vik, slav′ik) *adj.* of or relating to the Slavs, their languages, or their cultures. —*n.* the group of languages spoken by the Slavs. Also (*adj., n.*), **Slavon·ic** (slə von′ik).

slav·ish (slā′vish) *adj.* **1.** of, like, or befitting a slave or slaves: *slavish work, a slavish habit.* **2.** not original; imitative: *a slavish copy of a famous painting.* —**slav′ish·ly,** *adv.* —**slav′ish·ness,** *n.*

slaw (slô) *n.* see **coleslaw.**

slay (slā) *v.t.,* **slew, slain, slay·ing.** to kill by violent means, as in war. —**slay′er,** *n.*

slea·zy (slē′zē) *adj.,* **slea·zi·er, slea·zi·est. 1.** (of cloth) thin or flimsy. **2.** of poor quality; shoddy; cheap: *a sleazy hotel.* —**slea′zi·ness,** *n.*

sled (sled) *n.* **1.** a vehicle on runners that is used to carry people or loads over snow and ice; sledge. **2.** a small, similar vehicle having a wooden frame, used for sport in sliding down snow-covered slopes. —*v.,* **sled·ded, sled·ding.** —*v.i.* to ride or be carried on a sled. —*v.t.* to carry on a sled.

sled·ding (sled′ing) *n.* **1.** the act of riding on or using a sled. **2.** the condition of the ground for the use of sleds: *The heavy snow made for good sledding.*

·**hard sledding.** difficult conditions affecting the course or progress of any action: *It looks like hard sledding from now on.*

sledge¹ (slej) *n.* a sled or sleigh. —*v.,* **sledged, sledging.** —*v.i.* to ride or be carried on a sled or sleigh. —*v.t.* to carry on a sled or sleigh. [From the Dutch word *sleedse* meaning this vehicle.]

sledge² (slej) *n., v.t.,* **sledged, sledg·ing.** see **sledgehammer.** [From the Old English word *slecg* with the same meaning.]

sledge·ham·mer (slej′ham′ər) *n.* a heavy hammer with a long handle, usually held with both hands. —*v.t.* to strike with such a hammer. —*adj.* like a sledgehammer; powerful; smashing: *a sledgehammer punch.*

sleek (slēk) *adj.* **1.** smooth and glossy: *The cat has sleek black fur.* **2.** having a healthy, well-groomed, or well-fed ap-

a **sleek** airplane

S

pearance: *a sleek horse.* **3.** having a trim, uncluttered design. **4.** polished in manner or speech. —*v.t.* to make smooth and glossy; polish. —**sleek′ly,** *adv.* —**sleek′ness,** *n.*

sleep (slēp) *n.* **1.** a natural condition of rest occurring in humans and other animals at regular intervals, characterized by total or partial unconsciousness and a lack of voluntary movement. **2.** a period of sleep: *I had a good sleep last night.* **3.** any condition of inactivity or lessened consciousness that resembles sleep, such as death or a hypnotic trance. —*v.,* **slept, sleep·ing.** —*v.i.* **1.** to be or fall asleep: *The baby slept peacefully.* **2.** to be in a condition like sleep. —*v.t.* to provide or be able to provide with places for sleeping: *This cabin sleeps six people.*

sleep·er (slē′pər) *n.* **1.** a person or thing that sleeps: *a light sleeper.* **2.** an unknown or unimportant person or thing that unexpectedly or suddenly attains success, fame, or importance. **3.** another word for **sleeping car. 4.** a strong horizontal beam used as a support, especially a railroad tie.

sleeping bag, a long, warmly lined or padded bag, often waterproof, used for sleeping outdoors.

sleeping car, a railroad car having sleeping berths for passengers; Pullman. Also, **sleeper.**

sleeping pill, a pill or capsule containing a drug that causes sleep.

sleeping sickness, an infectious disease, often fatal, characterized by headaches, high fever, convulsions, and coma. It is most common in tropical Africa and is spread by the bite of the tsetse fly.

sleep·less (slēp′lis) *adj.* **1.** unable to sleep. **2.** without sleep: *a sleepless night.* **3.** always in motion or action. —**sleep′less·ly,** *adv.* —**sleep′less·ness,** *n.*

sleep·walk·ing (slēp′wô′king) *n.* the act or practice of walking about while asleep; somnambulism. —**sleep′-walk′er,** *n.*

sleep·y (slē′pē) *adj.,* **sleep·i·er, sleep·i·est. 1.** ready for, in need of, or inclined to sleep; drowsy. **2.** of or characterized by drowsiness: *sleepy eyes.* **3.** characterized by lack of activity; dull; quiet: *a sleepy little village.* —**sleep′i·ly,** *adv.* —**sleep′i·ness,** *n.*

sleep·y·head (slē′pē hed′) *n. Informal.* a sleepy person.

sleet (slēt) *n.* frozen or partially frozen rain. —*v.i.* to shower sleet. —**sleet′y,** *adj.*

sleeve (slēv) *n.* **1.** the part of a garment that covers all or part of the arm. **2.** a tubelike part of a machine that fits over another part. —**sleeve′less,** *adj.*
·**up one's sleeve.** secretly in reserve for use when needed: *to have a trick up one's sleeve.*

sleigh (slā) *n.* a vehicle on runners, usually drawn by a horse, used for traveling over snow or ice. —*v.i.* to ride or travel in a sleigh.

sleight (slīt) *n.* **1.** skill or dexterity in doing or making something. **2.** a clever trick or deception.

sleight of hand 1. skill and dexterity in using the hands, especially in performing tricks or feats with the hands.

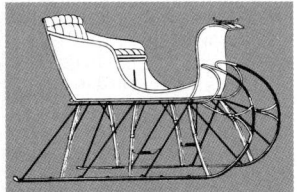

sleigh

2. tricks or feats requiring such skill, such as those performed by a magician or juggler.

slen·der (slen′dər) *adj.* **1.** thin, especially in an attractive or graceful way: *slender fingers.* **2.** having a small circumference in proportion to height or length: *a slender pole.* **3.** small in size, amount, extent, or degree: *The candidate won the election by a slender margin.* —**slen′der·ly,** *adv.* —**slen′der·ness,** *n.*

slept (slept) the past tense and past participle of **sleep.**

sleuth (slüth) *n.* a detective or investigator. —*v.i.* to act as a detective or investigator.

slew¹ (slü) the past tense of **slay.**

slew² (slü) *also,* **slue.** *v.t.* to cause to turn or twist about, especially on a pivot or fixed point: *The driver slewed the steering wheel sharply to the left.* —*v.i.* to turn or twist about; swing around. —*n.* **1.** the act of slewing. **2.** the position attained by slewing. [Of uncertain origin.]

slew³ (slü) *n.* see **slough¹** *(def. 2).*

slew⁴ (slü) *n. Informal.* a large number or group; great amount: *A whole slew of people came to the party.* [From the Irish Gaelic word *sluagh* with the same meaning.]

slice (slīs) *n.* **1.** a thin, flat piece cut from a larger object: *a slice of bread.* **2.** any of various implements having a thin, broad blade, such as a spatula. **3.** *Sports.* **a.** a stroke that causes a ball to curve off to the right if the player is right-handed, or to the left if the player is left-handed. **b.** the course followed by such a ball. —*v.,* **sliced, slic·ing.** —*v.t.* **1.** to cut into slices or pieces: *to slice a cake.* **2.** to remove in the form of a slice or slices: *to slice off a piece of cheese.* **3.** to move through or across like a knife: *The bow of the boat sliced the waves.* **4.** *Sports.* to hit (a ball) so that it makes a slice. —*v.i.* **1.** to move or cut like a knife: *The speeding boat sliced through the waves.* **2.** *Sports.* **a.** to hit a ball with a slice. **b.** (of a ball) to curve in a slice. —**slic′er,** *n.*

slick (slik) *adj.* **1.** smooth and glossy; sleek: *slick, wet hair.* **2.** smooth and slippery: *The roads were slick with ice.* **3.** cleverly or skillfully thought out, done, or said: *a slick solution to a problem.* **4.** shrewd or sly in thought, action, or speech: *a slick gambler.* **5.** having or showing skill that is only superficial or that lacks any real meaning: *a slick style of writing.* —*n.* **1.** a smooth or slippery area on a surface: *a slick of oil on water.* **2.** *Informal.* a magazine printed on glazed or coated paper. —*v.t. Informal.* **1.** to make sleek, smooth, or glossy. **2.** to make neat, trim, or tidy: *to slick up a messy room.* —**slick′ly,** *adv.* —**slick′ness,** *n.*

slick·er (slik′ər) *n.* **1.** a raincoat made of oilskin, plastic, or a similar material. **2.** *Informal.* a clever, sly person.

slide (slīd) *v.,* **slid** (slid), **sliding.** —*v.i.* **1.** to move or pass smoothly along a surface: *The wet bar of soap slid across the floor.* **2.** to shift, fall, or move suddenly from a position, as by loss of balance: *As I crossed the icy walk, my feet slid out from under me.* **3.** to pass or move smoothly, quietly, or gradually: *My friend slid into the seat next to me.* **4.** *Baseball.* to throw oneself along the ground toward a base, usually feet first, in order to avoid being tagged out by a fielder. —*v.t.* **1.** to cause to move or pass smoothly along a surface: *to slide a box along the floor.* **2.** to put or move smoothly, quietly, or gradually: *to slide a note under a door.* —*n.* **1.** the act of sliding: *to take a slide down a hill on a sled.* **2.** a smooth, usually inclined track, channel, or surface for sliding: *The children played on the slide in the playground.* **3.** a small plate of glass on which something is placed for examination under a microscope. **4.** a small, transparent photograph to be magnified and projected on a screen. **5.** the fall of a mass of rock, snow, or other matter down a slope. **6.** such a mass of matter. **7.** a part that operates by sliding, such as the U-shaped section of tubing on a trombone that is pushed in or out to change the pitch of the tones.
·**to let slide.** to let go by; neglect: *to let one's homework slide.*

slide projector, a device consisting of a light bulb and lens to project the enlarged image of a photographic slide onto a screen or wall.

slid·er (slī′dər) *n.* **1.** a person or thing that slides. **2.** *Baseball.* a fast pitch that curves sharply for a short distance.

slide rule, a device having a ruler and a central sliding piece marked with logarithmic scales, used for mathematical calculations.

sli·er (slī′ər) a comparative of **sly.**

sli·est (slī′ist) a superlative of **sly.**

slight (slīt) *adj.* **1.** small in quantity, degree, or strength: *There is only a slight possibility that we will lose the game.* **2.** of small importance: *a slight problem.* **3.** slender or thin; delicate: *a person with a slight build.* —*v.t.* **1.** to treat as unimportant or with disrespect; snub or insult: *They slighted their neighbors when they didn't invite them to the party.* **2.** to do carelessly; neglect: *to slight one's work.* —*n.* disrespectful or insulting treatment. —**slight′ly,** *adv.* —**slight′ness,** *n.*

slight·ing (slī′ting) *adj.* showing disrespect; insulting: *a slighting remark.* —**slight′ing·ly,** *adv.*

sli·ly (slī′lē) another spelling of **slyly.**

slim (slim) *adj.,* **slim·mer, slim·mest. 1.** small in thickness in proportion to height or length; slender; thin: *The fashion model had a slim build.* **2.** small in amount, degree, or extent: *a slim chance of victory.* —*v.t., v.i.,* **slimmed, slim·ming.** to make or become slim or slender: *Exercise can help slim the body.* —**slim′ly,** *adv.* —**slim′ness,** *n.*

slime (slīm) *n.* **1.** wet, soft, sticky mud. **2.** any disgusting or filthy substance. **3.** a thin, sticky substance given off by certain animals, such as snails.

slime mold, an organism that alternates between a stage during which it releases spores (as a fungus does) and a stage during which it looks like a small mass of jelly. Slime molds live on dead wood or other decaying matter and sometimes as parasites on potato, cabbage, or other plants.

slim·y (slī′mē) *adj.,* **slim·i·er, slim·i·est. 1.** covered with slime. **2.** of or like slime. **3.** disgusting or filthy; foul. —**slim′i·ly,** *adv.* —**slim′i·ness,** *n.*

sling (sling) *n.* **1.** a device for hurling stones, usually consisting of a piece of leather with a string fastened to each end. **2.** see **slingshot. 3.** a loop of cloth hanging from the neck to support an injured arm or hand. **4.** a strap for carrying a rifle or other object over the shoulder. **5.** a device, such as a chain or rope formed into a loop, used for raising, lowering, carrying, or hanging heavy objects. **6.** the act of slinging or hurling; throw. —*v.t.,* **slung, sling·ing. 1.** to hurl with or as if with a sling; throw; fling: *to sling a rock.* **2.** to hang with a sling or strap: *A guitar was slung over the singer's shoulder.* **3.** to hang or throw loosely: *to sling a hammock between two trees.* **4.** to raise, lower, carry, or hang by means of a sling. —**sling′er,** *n.*

sling·shot (sling′shot′) *n.* a Y-shaped piece of wood or metal, with an elastic band fastened to the tips of the prongs, used to shoot stones or other small objects.

slink (slingk) *v.i.,* **slunk, slink·ing.** to move in a quiet or stealthy manner: *The fox slunk closer to its prey.*

slip[1] (slip) *v.,* **slipped** or (*archaic*) **slipt, slip·ping.** —*v.i.* **1.** to lose one's balance or footing; slide suddenly or accidentally: *to slip on icy steps.* **2.** to move or slide out of place or out of control: *The bottle slipped out of my hands.* **3.** to move or go quietly or stealthily: *The tiger slipped through the jungle without a sound.* **4.** to pass unnoticed: *Another month slipped by.* **5.** to be said or made known unintentionally (usually with *out*): *Don't let the secret slip out.* **6.** to decline, fall, or become worse: *Prices on the stock market slipped sharply last year.* **7.** to put on or take off clothing, especially quickly or easily: *to slip into one's pajamas.* **8.** to make a mistake: *I slipped on the test's last question.* —*v.t.* **1.** to cause to move with a smooth, sliding motion: *to slip a ring off one's finger.* **2.** to put or give quietly or quickly: *to slip someone a note.* **3.** to fail to be remembered or noticed

by: *The name of the new student has slipped my mind.* **4.** to put on or take off (clothing), especially quickly or easily: *to slip a sweater on.* —*n.* **1.** the act of slipping. **2.** a mistake or error. **3.** a woman's undergarment, usually of a light material, such as nylon. **4.** a pillowcase. **5.** a space between wharves or piers where ships can dock. [From the Middle Low German word *slippen* meaning "to glide smoothly."]

·**to give (someone) the slip.** to escape from: *The fox gave the hounds the slip.*

·**to slip one over on.** to take advantage of; trick.

·**to slip up.** to make a mistake or error.

slip[2] (slip) *n.* **1.** a small shoot or twig cut from a plant, used for grafting or planting. **2.** a long, thin piece or strip of some material. **3.** a small printed piece of paper: *a bank deposit slip.* **4.** a slender or young person: *a mere slip of a child.* —*v.t.,* **slipped, slip·ping.** to cut a shoot or twig from (a plant) for grafting or planting. [From the Middle Dutch word *slippe* meaning "a cut or split."]

slip·cov·er (slip′kuv′ər) *n.* a removable cover, usually of cloth, for a piece of furniture, such as a sofa or chair.

slip·knot (slip′not′) *n.* **1.** a knot made so that it will slip along the rope or line around which it is tied. **2.** a knot made so that it can be easily undone by pulling on either of the free ends.

slip–on (slip′ôn′, slip′on′) *adj.* (of an article of clothing) easily put on or removed. —*n.* a slip-on article of clothing.

slipknot
(def. 1)

slip·o·ver (slip′ō′vər) *adj.* (of an article of clothing) easily put on or removed by drawing over the head: *a slipover vest, a slipover sweater.* —*n.* a slipover article of clothing.

slip·page (slip′ij) *n.* **1.** the act of slipping. **2.** the amount or extent of slipping: *The president was worried about a possible slippage in popularity.*

slip·per (slip′ər) *n.* a light, low shoe that is easily slipped on or off the foot, worn chiefly indoors.

slip·per·y (slip′ə rē) *adj.,* **slip·per·i·er, slip·per·i·est. 1.** causing or likely to cause slipping or sliding: *Freezing rain made the roads slippery.* **2.** likely to slip or slide, as from the grasp: *The wet fish was too slippery to hold.* **3.** not to be relied or depended on; tricky. **4.** able to slip away or escape easily: *a slippery thief.* —**slip′per·i·ness,** *n.*

slip·shod (slip′shod′) *adj.* **1.** carelessly made or done: *to do a slipshod job in building a chair.* **2.** untidy or slovenly in appearance.

slip·stream (slip′strēm′) *n.* a current of air driven back by the revolving propeller of an aircraft.

slipt (slipt) *Archaic.* a past tense of **slip**[1].

slip–up (slip′up′) *n. Informal.* a mistake or error.

slit (slit) *n.* a long, narrow, usually straight cut or opening: *Sunlight came through the slits in the Venetian blinds.* —*v.t.,* **slit, slit·ting.** to cut or make a slit or slits in.

slith·er (slith′ər) *v.i.* **1.** to move along with a sliding or gliding motion: *The snake slithered under a rock.* **2.** to slip or slide, as on a loose or slippery surface. —*v.t.* to cause to slither or slide.

slith·er·y (slith′ə rē) *adj.* slippery or slick.

sliv·er (sliv′ər) *n.* a slender, often pointed piece that has

at; āpe; fär; câre; end; mē; it; īce; pîerce; hot; ōld; sông, fôrk; oil; out; up; ūse; rüle; pull; tûrn; chin; sing; shop; thin; this; hw in white; zh in treasure. The symbol ə stands for the unstressed vowel sound heard in about, taken, pencil, lemon, and circus.

S

been broken, cut, or torn off; splinter: *a sliver of wood, a sliver of glass.* —*v.t., v.i.* to cut or break into slivers.

slob (slob) *n. Informal.* a sloppy, dirty, or crude person.

slob·ber (slob'ər) *v.i.* **1.** to let saliva, food, or liquid run or spill from the mouth; slaver. **2.** to speak or write in an overly sentimental way; gush. —*v.t.* to wet or smear with saliva, food, or liquid running from the mouth. —*n.* **1.** saliva, food, or liquid running from the mouth. **2.** overly sentimental speech or writing. —**slob'ber·y**, *adj.*

sloe (slō) *n.* **1.** see **blackthorn. 2.** the small, tart, blue-black fruit of the blackthorn.

slog (slog) *v.*, **slogged, slog·ging.** —*v.i.* **1.** to move with great effort; plod: *to slog through mud.* **2.** to work hard: *to slog through a long homework assignment.* —*v.t.* to make (one's way) with great effort.

slo·gan (slō'gən) *n.* **1.** a phrase, statement, or motto used by a group, such as a club or political party, or by an individual, such as a candidate for political office. **2.** a phrase used in advertising or in promoting a product, business, or service. [From the Scottish Gaelic word *sluaghghairm* meaning "battle cry," from the words *sluagh* "host, band" + *gairm* "cry."]

sloop (slüp) *n.* a fore-and-aft-rigged sailboat with a single mast, a mainsail, and a jib.

slop (slop) *n.* **1.** liquid that has been spilled or splashed. **2.** soft, watery mud or snow; slush. **3.** unappetizing or distasteful food or liquid. **4.** *also,* **slops.** waste food used to feed pigs or other animals; swill. **5.** any liquid waste. —*v.*, **slopped, slop-ping.** —*v.i.* **1.** to spill or splash: *The water in the pail slopped all over the floor.* **2.** to walk or move with splashes through mud, slush, or water. —*v.t.* **1.** to cause (a liquid) to spill or splash. **2.** to spill or splash liquid upon. **3.** to feed slop to

sloop

(animals): *The farmer's chores included slopping the pigs.*

slope (slōp) *v.*, **sloped, slop·ing.** —*v.i.* to lie or move at an angle from the horizontal or vertical; take a slanting direction: *The road slopes toward the river.* —*v.t.* to cause to slope; make with a slope: *The builders sloped the roof of the house.* —*n.* **1.** a stretch of ground that is not flat or level: *The house was built on a slope.* **2.** any slanting line, surface, position, or direction. **3.** the degree or amount of such a slant: *The roof has a steep slope.* **4.** *Mathematics.* **a.** the degree of inclination measured by the tangent of an angle formed by a line and the x-axis. **b.** (of a point on a plane curve) the slope of the line that is tangent to a curve at a point.

slop·py (slop'ē) *adj.*, **slop·pi·er, slop·pi·est. 1.** very wet, muddy, or slushy: *The roads were wet and sloppy.* **2.** spotted or splashed with liquid or slop: *a sloppy floor.* **3.** careless; slipshod: *a sloppy job.* **4.** very untidy; messy: *a sloppy room.* **5.** *Informal.* too sentimental; maudlin. —**slop'pi·ly**, *adv.* —**slop'pi·ness**, *n*

slosh (slosh) *v.i.* to move clumsily or splash about: *to slosh through mud.* —*v.t.* to stir or splash: *The child sloshed the milk around in the glass.*

slot (slot) *n.* **1.** a narrow, usually straight opening or groove: *A mailbox has a slot for letters.* **2.** *Informal.* a place or position, as in a schedule or sequence: *That television program is in the ten o'clock time slot.* —*v.t.*, **slot·ted, slot·ting.** to make or cut a slot in.

sloth (slôth, slōth) *n.* **1.** dislike of work or exertion; laziness. **2.** any of several slow-moving, tree-dwelling mammals of the tropical forests of Central and South America, having long limbs, curved claws, and coarse, shaggy hair.

sloth *(def. 2)*

sloth·ful (slôth'fəl, slōth'fəl) *adj.* characterized by sloth; lazy; idle. —**sloth'ful·ly**, *adv.* —**sloth'ful·ness**, *n.*

slot machine, a gambling or vending machine that is operated by depositing a coin through a slot.

slouch (slouch) *v.i.* **1.** to sit, stand, or walk with an awkward, drooping posture, or in an overly loose manner. **2.** to hang or bend down; droop. —*n., pl.* **slouch·es. 1.** a drooping of the head and shoulders while sitting, standing, or walking; awkward or drooping posture. **2.** *Informal.* an awkward, lazy, or untidy person: *You are no slouch at tennis.*

slouch hat, a soft, usually felt hat with a broad brim that turns down easily.

slouch·y (slou'chē) *adj.*, **slouch·i·er, slouch·i·est.** slouching: *a slouchy posture.* —**slouch'i·ly**, *adv.* —**slouch'i·ness**, *n.*

slough[1] (*defs. 1, 3*, slou; *def. 2*, slü) *n.* **1.** a place full of soft, deep mud. **2.** *also,* **slew, slue.** a swamp, marsh, or bog, especially one that is part of a backwater. **3.** a state of dejection or discouragement. [From the Old English word *slōh* meaning "a hollow filled with mire."] —**slough'y**, *adj.*

slough[2] (sluf) *n.* **1.** the outer skin shed by a snake. **2.** anything that has been shed or cast off. —*v.t.* to shed or cast: *to slough off sadness.* —*v.i.* to be shed or cast off. [From the Middle English word *slughe* with the same meaning.]

Slo·vak (slō'vak, slō'väk) *n.* **1.** a member of a Slavic people living predominantly in Slovakia and closely related to the Czechs and the Moravians. **2.** the Slavic language of these people, closely related to Czech. —*adj.* of or relating to Slovakia, its people, their language, or culture.

slov·en (sluv'ən) *n.* a person who is untidy or careless, especially in dress or appearance.

Slo·vene (slō'vēn) *n.* **1.** a member of a Slavic people living in Slovenia and closely related to the Serbs and Croats. **2.** the Slavic language of these people, closely related to Serbo-Croatian. —*adj.* of or relating to Slovenia, its people, their language, or culture.

slov·en·ly (sluv'ən lē) *adj.*, **slov·en·li·er, slov·en·li·est.** untidy or careless, especially in dress or appearance: *to look slovenly in a wrinkled and spotted suit.* —*adv.* in a slovenly manner. —**slov'en·li·ness**, *n.*

slow (slō) *adj.* **1.** acting, moving, or happening with little speed; not fast or quick: *a slow reader, slow progress.* **2.** taking a long or longer time than usual: *a slow trip, a slow game.* **3.** indicating a time behind the true time: *My watch is always slow.* **4.** not quick to learn or understand: *a slow student.* **5.** not active; sluggish: *Business is slow after a big sale.* **6.** not prompt, hasty, or easily moved: *slow to answer letters, slow to anger.* **7.** not suitable for rapid movement: *Because of all the rain the day before, the race was run on a slow track.* —*adv.* in a slow manner; slowly: *Drive slow through the town.* —*v.t., v.i.* to make or become slow or slower (often with *down* or *up*): *to slow down a car. The car slowed up.* —**slow'ly**, *adv.* —**slow'ness**, *n.*

slow·down (slō'doun') *n.* a deliberate slowing down of the rate of production by workers or management.

slow·ish (slō'ish) *adj.* somewhat slow.

slow‑mo·tion (slō′mō′shən) *adj.* **1.** of or relating to a motion-picture or videotape sequence photographed at high speed and projected or played back at normal speed so that the action appears to be slower than normal. **2.** moving, operating, or proceeding at less than normal speed: *slow-motion traffic, a slow-motion waltz.*

slow·poke (slō′pōk′) *n. Informal.* a person who moves, works, or acts at a very slow pace.

slow‑wit·ted (slō′wit′id) *adj.* slow to understand or learn.

sludge (sluj) *n.* **1.** mud or mire, especially a muddy deposit at the bottom of a body of water. **2.** any muddy or slushy mass or mixture, such as sediment from the treatment of sewage. **3.** broken or half-formed ice, as on the sea. —**sludg′y,** *adj.*

slue¹ (slü) *v.t., v.i.,* **slued, slu·ing;** *n.* another spelling of **slew².**

slue² (slü) *n.* see **slough¹** *(def. 2).*

slug¹ (slug) *n.* **1.** any of several mollusks closely resembling a snail, but either lacking a shell or having only a partly developed one. A slug moves slowly by sliding on a thin layer of slime. **2.** any slow-moving or sluggish person or thing. **3.** a small piece or lump of metal, especially a piece of lead or other metal for firing from a gun. **4.** a piece of metal shaped like, and used in place of, a coin, especially one used illegally, as in a vending machine or pay telephone. [From the Middle English word *slugge* meaning "sluggard," of Scandinavian origin.]

slug¹ *(def. 1)*

slug² (slug) *Informal. v.t.,* **slugged, slug·ging.** to strike hard, as with the fist: *The batter slugged the ball over the fence.* —*n.* a heavy blow, as with the fist. [Perhaps from *slug¹.*]

slug·gard (slug′ərd) *n.* a person who is lazy or idle. —*adj.* lazy or idle; slothful.

slug·ger (slug′ər) *n. Informal.* a person who slugs, especially a hard-hitting baseball player or a prizefighter able to throw hard punches.

slug·gish (slug′ish) *adj.* **1.** having little motion, speed, or activity: *a sluggish river.* **2.** showing a lack of vigor, energy, or alertness: *a sluggish mind.* **3.** not acting or functioning with full or usual energy or efficiency: *My car's engine is sluggish on cold mornings.* —**slug′gish·ly,** *adv.* —**slug′gish·ness,** *n.*

sluice (slüs) *n.* **1.** an artificial channel for conducting water, having a gate or valve for controlling the rate of flow. **2.** the gate or valve of such a channel. **3.** the water controlled by such a gate or valve. **4.** a long, sloping trough through which water is run, as for separating gold ore or floating logs. —*v.t.,* **sluiced, sluic·ing. 1.** to draw off by means of or through a sluice: *to sluice water.* **2.** to wash (gold) from ore, dirt, or gravel with water running through or from a sluice. **3.** to wash with a rush of water; drench. **4.** to float (logs) in a sluice.

slum (slum) *n. also,* **slums.** a crowded section of a city, characterized by poverty, run-down housing, and unclean living conditions. —*v.i.,* **slummed, slum·ming. 1.** to visit a slum, as out of curiosity. **2.** to visit a group or place considered to be of lower social status.

slum·ber (slum′bər) *v.i.* **1.** to sleep or doze: *The baby slumbered peacefully.* **2.** to be quiet, calm, or inactive: *The town slumbered under the afternoon sun.* —*v.t.* to pass or spend in sleeping: *to slumber away the day.* —*n.* **1.** a light sleep or doze. **2.** a quiet, calm, or inactive state. —**slum′ber·er,** *n.*

slum·ber·ous (slum′bər əs) *also,* **slum·brous** (slum′brəs). *adj.* **1.** sleepy or drowsy. **2.** causing sleep or drowsiness.

slum·lord (slum′lôrd′) *n.* a landlord of run-down housing, especially one who charges unfairly high rents.

slump (slump) *v.i.* **1.** to fall or sink suddenly or heavily: *The dazed boxer slumped to the floor.* **2.** to take a drooping posture; slouch: *to slump in one's seat.* **3.** to become worse or decline, as in activity, performance, or value: *The football team slumped badly after its star quarterback was injured.* —*n.* **1.** a sharp, sudden decline: *a slump in sales. The baseball player was in a batting slump.* **2.** the act of slumping.

slung (slung) the past tense and past participle of **sling.**

slunk (slungk) the past tense and past participle of **slink.**

slur (slûr) *v.t.,* **slurred, slur·ring. 1.** to pass over hurriedly or carelessly: *to slur over many facts in a hastily written report.* **2.** to speak slightingly of; insult: *to slur a person's reputation.* **3.** to pronounce indistinctly, as

slur *(n., def. 3b)*

by running sounds together: *to slur one's words.* **4.** *Music.* **a.** to play or sing (two or more tones of different pitch) in a smooth, connected manner. **b.** to mark (a note) with a slur. —*n.* **1.** a slighting or insulting remark. **2.** an indistinct pronunciation of words. **3.** *Music.* **a.** a combination of two or more slurred tones. **b.** a curved mark indicating this.

slurp (slûrp) *v.t., v.i.* to drink, sip, or eat (something) noisily.

slush (slush) *n.* **1.** partially melted snow or ice. **2.** soft mud; mire. **3.** silly, sentimental speech or writing; drivel. —**slush′i·ness,** *n.* —**slush′y,** *adj.*

slut (slut) *n.* **1.** a sexually immoral woman. **2.** a dirty, slovenly woman.

sly (slī) *adj.,* **sli·er** or **sly·er, sli·est** or **sly·est. 1.** showing or characterized by cleverness, shrewdness, or craftiness: *a sly trick.* **2.** able to deceive or trick; clever; devious: *The sly fox managed to elude the hounds.* **3.** mischievous in a playful way: *a sly glance.* —**sly′ly,** *adv.* —**sly′ness,** *n.*

•**on the sly.** in a stealthy way; secretly: *The friends met on the sly to plan the surprise party.*

Sm. the symbol for samarium.

smack¹ (smak) *v.t.* **1.** to press together and open (the lips) rapidly so as to make a sharp sound. **2.** to strike or slap sharply, as with the open hand. **3.** to kiss loudly or noisily. —*v.i.* **1.** to smack the lips. **2.** to strike something forcibly and noisily: *The car skidded and smacked into the fence.* —*n.* **1.** a sharp sound made by smacking the lips. **2.** a sharp blow or slap, as with the open hand. **3.** a loud or noisy kiss. —*adv. Informal.* **1.** in a sudden, violent manner: *to fall smack into the pool.* **2.** squarely or directly: *to run smack into the very person you were trying to avoid.* [Perhaps of Dutch or Low German origin.]

smack² (smak) *n.* **1.** a slight taste or flavor: *The pudding had a smack of cinnamon.* **2.** a suggestion or trace. —*v.i.* **1.** to have a taste or flavor: *The meat smacks of garlic.* **2.** to have a suggestion or trace: *actions that smack of dishonesty.* [From the Old English word *smæc* meaning "taste, savor."]

smack³ (smak) *n.* a small sailboat, usually fore-and-aft-

at; āpe; fär; câre; end; mē; it; īce; pîerce; hot; ōld; sông; fôrk; oil; out; up; ūse; rüle; pùll; tûrn; chin; sing; shop; thin; this; hw in white; zh in treasure. The symbol ə stands for the unstressed vowel sound heard in about, taken, pencil, lemon, and circus.

S

rigged, used chiefly for fishing. [Probably from the Dutch word *smak* meaning this vessel.]

small (smôl) *adj.* **1.** not large or great in size, amount, degree, or number, especially in comparison with others of the same kind: *a small car, a small crowd, a small town.* **2.** not important; trivial: *a small problem.* **3.** carrying on business in a limited way: *a small retailer, a small investor.* **4.** soft or weak; low: *The shy child replied in a small voice.* **5.** mean or selfish: *It was small of them not to pay their share of the cost.* —*n.* a small or narrow part: *the small of the back.* —**small′ness,** *n.*

small arms, firearms, such as pistols or rifles, that can be carried easily and held in the hand when fired.

small calorie, see **calorie** *(def. 1).*

small capital, a capital letter of slightly smaller size than the regular letter used. THIS SENTENCE IS IN SMALL CAPITALS.

small change 1. coins of small value, such as dimes or nickels. **2.** something of small value or importance.

small–claims court (smôl′klāmz′), a special court established by a state or municipality to hear and decide lawsuits involving amounts of money smaller than a specified sum. Small-claims courts use simplified procedures in order to speed their decisions.

small fry 1. a young or small child or children. **2.** people or things of little or no importance.

small game, small wild animals and birds hunted for sport.

small intestine, the part of the digestive track extending from the stomach to the large intestine, in which food broken up in the stomach is digested and absorbed. It consists of the duodenum, the jejunum, and the ileum.

small·ish (smô′lish) *adj.* somewhat small.

small letter, a letter that is not a capital letter.

small–mind·ed (smôl′mīn′did) *adj.* having or showing a narrow, selfish, or petty outlook; prejudiced. —**small′-mind′ed·ly,** *adv.* —**small′-mind′ed·ness,** *n.*

small·pox (smôl′poks′) *n.* an acute, highly contagious disease caused by a virus and characterized by fever and skin eruptions that often leave permanent pit-shaped scars. Vaccination has wiped out smallpox all over the world.

small talk, light conversation about everyday or unimportant matters.

smart (smärt) *adj.* **1.** clever or intelligent; bright: *a smart student.* **2.** neat and trim: *The children looked very smart in their school uniforms.* **3.** stylish or fashionable: *a smart outfit, a smart restaurant.* **4.** brisk or vigorous; lively: *The soldiers marched at a smart pace.* —*v.i.* **1.** to cause sharp, stinging pain: *The soap smarted in my eyes.* **2.** to feel sharp, stinging pain: *My face smarted from the icy cold wind.* **3.** to feel hurt or distress: *to smart from criticism.* —*n.* a sharp, stinging pain. —**smart′ly,** *adv.* —**smart′ness,** *n.*

smart al·eck (al′ik) *Informal.* a person who is offensively conceited and cocky. —**smart′-al′eck·y,** *adj.*

smart·en (smär′tən) *v.t., v.i.* to make or become smart or smarter.

smash (smash) *v.t.* **1.** to break (something) into pieces with noise and violence: *The ball smashed the window.* **2.** to strike with a hard blow: *The batter smashed the ball over the fence.* **3.** to destroy, crush, or defeat completely: *The attack smashed the enemy's defenses.* —*v.i.* **1.** to break into pieces: *The plate slipped from my hand and smashed on the floor.* **2.** to move with force or violence; crash: *The cart rolled down the hill and smashed into the tree.* —*n., pl.* **smash·es. 1.** the act of smashing. **2.** the sound of smashing: *the smash of glass.* **3.** a violent collision; smashup. **4.** a complete or crushing defeat or disaster: *the smash of one's hopes.* **5.** *Informal.* a complete success. —*adj. Informal.* completely successful: *The new play is a smash hit.* —**smash′er,** *n.*

smash·ing (smash′ing) *adj. Informal.* extremely good; tremendous: *Her debut as an actress was a smashing success.*

smash·up (smash′up′) *n.* **1.** a violent collision, as of automobiles; crash. **2.** a complete collapse, failure, or defeat.

smat·ter·ing (smat′ər ing) *n.* superficial or very slight knowledge: *to have only a smattering of Spanish.*

smear (smîr) *v.t.* **1.** to cover, spread, or make dirty with something wet, sticky, or greasy: *The child smeared the wall with toothpaste.* **2.** to spread or coat with (something wet, sticky, or greasy): *to slip and smear mud on one's clothes.* **3.** to cause to become blurred or indistinct, as by rubbing with the hand: *to smear a signature.* **4.** to damage or harm the reputation of: *to smear a political opponent.* —*v.i.* to be or become smeared: *The wet paint smeared when I touched it.* —*n.* **1.** a mark or stain made by smearing: *There is a smear of dirt on your cheek.* **2.** an attack on a person's reputation; slander. **3.** a small quantity of a substance, such as blood, placed on a slide for examination under a microscope.

smell (smel) *v.,* **smelled** or **smelt, smell·ing.** —*v.t.* **1.** to recognize or become aware of by means of the nose and its nerves; detect the odor of: *Do you smell something burning?* **2.** to test or sample by smelling: *to smell food to see if it is fresh.* **3.** to sense the presence of: *to smell danger.* —*v.i.* **1.** to have or give off an odor: *The kitchen smells of onions.* **2.** to have or give off an unpleasant odor: *Rotten meat smells.* **3.** to use the sense of smell. —*n.* **1.** the sense by which odors are recognized or detected. **2.** the quality of a thing or substance that makes it able to be recognized by the sense of smell; odor: *the smell of the sea.* **3.** the act of smelling. **4.** a suggestion, hint, or feeling of something: *The smell of victory increased the team's desire to win.* —**smell′er,** *n.*

smelling salts, a preparation based on ammonia, inhaled to relieve headaches or faintness.

smell·y (smel′ē) *adj.,* **smell·i·er, smell·i·est.** *Informal.* having or giving off an unpleasant or offensive smell.

smelt¹ (smelt) *v.t.* **1.** to melt (ore) to separate the metal from it. **2.** to refine (metal) in this manner. [From the Dutch or Low German word *smelten* with the same meaning.]

smelt² (smelt) *n., pl.* **smelts** or **smelt.** any of a group of slender, silvery food fish found in cold or temperate waters of the Northern Hemisphere. [From the Old English word *smelt* meaning this fish.]

smelt³ (smelt) a past tense and past participle of **smell.**

smelt·er (smel′tər) *n.* **1.** a person whose work or business is smelting ore or metal. **2.** a place where ore or metal is smelted. **3.** a furnace for smelting.

smid·gen (smij′ən) *n. Informal.* a very small amount; bit: *a smidgen of honey, a smidgen of skill.*

smi·lax (smī′laks) *n., pl.* **smi·lax·es.** a climbing African vine having stiff, shiny branches and tiny greenish white flowers that ripen into small red berries.

smile (smīl) *n.* an expression of the face formed by an upward turning of the corners of the mouth, showing various feelings, as happiness, amusement, friendliness, sympathy, or contempt. —*v.,* **smiled, smil·ing.** —*v.i.* **1.** to have, show, or give a smile: *The clown's antics made the children smile.* **2.** to show approval or favor: *Fortune smiled upon our plans.* —*v.t.* **1.** to express with a smile: *to smile one's gratitude.* **2.** to change or accomplish by smiling: *to smile away tears.* —**smil′er,** *n.* —**smil′ing·ly,** *adv.*

smilax

smirch (smûrch) *v.t.* **1.** to stain, soil, or discolor with dirt, grime, or a similar substance. **2.** to bring dishonor or disgrace upon: *to smirch a person's reputation.* —*n.*, *pl.* **smirch·es. 1.** a dirty spot or stain; smudge. **2.** a blot or stain on a person's reputation or honor.

smirk (smûrk) *v.i.* to smile in an affected, self-satisfied, or silly manner. —*n.* an affected, self-satisfied, or silly smile.

smite (smīt) *v.t.*, **smote, smit·ten** or **smit** (smit) or **smote, smit·ting. 1.** to strike hard with the hand or with a weapon. **2.** to afflict or attack suddenly and with a disastrous effect: *to be smitten by disease.* **3.** to affect suddenly or strongly with some powerful feeling, such as love, fear, or remorse. —**smit'er,** *n.*

smith (smith) *n.* **1.** a person who makes or repairs metal objects. **2.** see **blacksmith.**

smith·er·eens (smith'ə rēnz') *pl. n. Informal.* little pieces or fragments; bits: *The explosion blew the building to smithereens.*

smith·y (smith'ē, smith'ē) *n., pl.* **smith·ies. 1.** the workshop of a smith, especially a blacksmith's shop; forge. **2.** a blacksmith.

smit·ten (smit'ən) a past participle of **smite.**

smock (smok) *n.* a loose outer garment, usually resembling a long shirt, worn to protect clothing. —*v.t.* to ornament with smocking.

smock·ing (smok'ing) *n.* a decorative pattern formed by gathering fabric with rows of stitches, often with a honeycomb design.

smog (smog) *n.* a combination of smoke and fog, found especially in the air over industrial areas. [A blend of *smoke* and *fog.*] —**smog'gy,** *adj.*

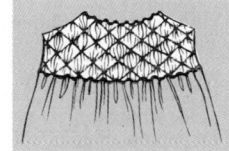

smocking

smoke (smōk) *n.* **1.** a cloud of solid matter in a gas produced by burning something, such as wood or coal. It can be seen because of the carbon particles suspended in it. **2.** anything like this, such as steam or mist. **3.** the act of smoking tobacco. **4.** a cigarette, cigar, or pipe. —*v.*, **smoked, smok·ing.** —*v.i.* **1.** to send out or produce smoke: *We could see a chimney smoking in the distance.* **2.** to draw the smoke of a cigarette, cigar, or pipe into the mouth, and often the lungs, and then breathe it out. —*v.t.* **1.** to draw in and breathe out the smoke of (a cigarette, cigar, or pipe). **2.** to cure or preserve (meat or fish) by exposure to smoke: *to smoke ham.*

·to smoke out. a. to force into the open with smoke: *to smoke out a skunk from under a house.* **b.** to drive or bring out of hiding or secrecy: *to smoke out a plot against the government.*

smoke detector, an electronic device that sounds an alarm when it detects smoke. Also, **smoke alarm.**

smoke·house (smōk'hous') *n., pl.* **smoke·hous·es** (smok'hou'ziz). a building where meat or fish is treated with smoke to preserve and flavor it.

smoke·less (smōk'lis) *adj.* having or giving off little or no smoke.

smok·er (smō'kər) *n.* **1.** a person or thing that smokes, especially a person who smokes tobacco. **2.** see **smoking car. 3.** an informal social gathering for men.

smoke screen 1. a thick cloud of smoke to conceal a military force or movement from the enemy. **2.** anything used to conceal or deceive.

smoke·stack (smōk'stak') *n.* a pipe or funnel for the escape of smoke or gases, as on a factory, ship, or locomotive.

smoking car, a railroad car or compartment where smoking is permitted. Also, **smoker.**

smok·y (smō'kē) *adj.*, **smok·i·er, smok·i·est. 1.** giving off smoke, especially too much smoke: *a smoky fire, a*

smoky chimney. **2.** filled with smoke: *a smoky room, smoky air.* **3.** like smoke, as in color or taste: *smoky sausages, a cat with smoky eyes.* —**smok'i·ly,** *adv.* —**smok'i·ness,** *n.*

smol·der (smōl'dər) *also,* **smoul·der.** *v.t.* **1.** to burn and smoke with little or no flame: *The coals of the dying fire smoldered.* **2.** to exist or continue in a hidden or pent-up state: *Resentment against the dictator smoldered among the people.* **3.** to show hidden or pent-up emotion: *Their eyes were smoldering with disappointment when I told them they were not invited to the party.* —*n.* a smoldering fire or the smoke produced by such a fire.

smooth (smūth) *adj.* **1.** having a surface that is not uneven or rough: *smooth skin, a smooth new road.* **2.** even, easy, or gentle in movement: *The pilot made a smooth landing.* **3.** free from difficulties, obstacles, or trouble: *We made smooth progress on our plans.* **4.** able, skillful, or polished: *a smooth dancer, a smooth talker.* **5.** not harsh in sound or taste: *That radio announcer has a smooth voice.* —*v.t.* **1.** to make smooth, even, or level: *to smooth dirt around plants.* **2.** to free from difficulties or obstacles; make easy: *to smooth a person's way to success in business.* **3.** to calm; soothe: *to smooth someone's temper.* —*v.i.* to become smooth. —*adv.* in a smooth manner; smoothly. —**smooth'ly,** *adv.* —**smooth'ness,** *n.*

·to smooth over. to make less unpleasant or serious: *to smooth over a quarrel. Try as you may, you cannot smooth over all of your problems.*

smooth·bore (smūth'bôr') *adj.* (of a firearm) having no spiral grooves cut into the inside of the barrel or bore; not rifled. —*n.* a firearm having an ungrooved barrel or bore.

smor·gas·bord (smôr'gəs bôrd') *also,* **smör·gås·bord.** *n.* a large assortment of food, such as appetizers, meats, fish, and cheese, usually arranged on a table so that people may serve themselves. [From the Swedish word *smörgåsbord* meaning "buffet," from the words *smörgås* "bread and butter" + *bord* "table."]

smote (smōt) the past tense and a past participle of **smite.**

smoth·er (smuth'ər) *v.t.* **1.** to prevent from breathing in air; kill by depriving of air: *The skier was almost smothered when buried by the avalanche of snow.* **2.** to cause (a fire) to go out or die down by covering it so as to cut off oxygen: *The firefighters smothered the blaze by shoveling dirt on it.* **3.** to cover thickly: *to smother a steak with onions.* **4.** to conceal or hold back: *to smother a yawn, to smother feelings of jealousy.* —*v.i.* **1.** to be prevented from breathing in air. **2.** to die from being deprived of air. —*n.* something that smothers, such as a dense cloud of smoke or dust.

smoul·der (smōl'dər) another spelling of **smolder.**

smudge (smuj) *v.*, **smudged, smudg·ing.** —*v.t.* **1.** to soil or smear; make dirty: *to smudge a white shirt with grimy hands.* **2.** to fill (a planted area) with dense smoke to drive away insects or protect against frost. —*v.i.* to be or become smudged or smeared: *A freshly painted wall smudges easily.* —*n.* **1.** a mark or stain made by smearing or smudging: *The child's dirty hand left a smudge on the wall.* **2.** a smoky fire built to drive away insects or protect against frost. **3.** the thick smoke produced by such a fire. —**smudg'y,** *adj.*

at; āpe; fär; câre; end; mē; it; īce; pîerce; hot; ōld; sông, fôrk; oil; out; up; ūse; rüle; pûll; tûrn; chin; sing; shop; thin; this; hw in white; zh in treasure. The symbol ə stands for the unstressed vowel sound heard in about, taken, pencil, lemon, and circus.

S

smudge pots

smudge pot, a pot or similar vessel for burning a fuel to produce smudge.

smug (smug) *adj.,* **smug·ger, smug·gest.** feeling or showing too much satisfaction with oneself; complacent: *a smug person, a smug attitude.* —**smug′ly,** *adv.* —**smug′ness,** *n.*

smug·gle (smug′əl) *v.t.,* **smug·gled, smug·gling. 1.** to take into or out of a country or state secretly and unlawfully, as goods on which the required duties have not been paid: *to smuggle illegal drugs.* **2.** to bring, take, or transport secretly or stealthily: *to smuggle a cat into the hospital.* —*v.i.* to take part in smuggling. —**smug′gler,** *n.*

smut (smut) *n.* **1.** a substance that darkens or soils; soot; dirt. · **2.** a spot or stain made by soot or dirt; smudge. **3.** obscene language or writing. **4.** any of several fungus diseases of plants, commonly affecting cereal grains, such as corn and wheat. It is characterized by the appearance of black, powdery masses or spores. —*v.t.,* **smut·ted, smut·ting.** to mark or stain with smut.

smut·ty (smut′ē) *adj.,* **smut·ti·er, smut·ti·est. 1.** soiled with smut; dirty. **2.** obscene: *smutty language.* **3.** (of plants) diseased with smut. —**smut′ti·ness,** *n.*

Sn, the symbol for tin. [Short for the Latin word *stannum* meaning "tin."]

snack (snak) *n.* a small quantity of food or drink, especially a light meal eaten between regular meals. —*v.i.* to eat a snack.

snack bar, an eating place where snacks are served, especially at a counter.

snaf·fle (snaf′əl) *n.* a slender, jointed horse's bit. Also, **snaf·fle·bit** (snaf′əl bit′). —*v.t.,* **snaf·fled, snaf·fling.** to provide or control with a snaffle.

snag (snag) *n.* **1.** a sharp, jagged, or rough projecting part: *A snag on the old fence tore my coat.* **2.** a branch, stump, or trunk of a tree held fast in the bottom of

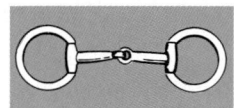

snaffle *(n.)*

a lake, river, or the like. Snags are a danger to boats. **3.** a tear or hole made by a sharp projection. **4.** an unexpected or hidden obstacle or difficulty: *Their plans for a picnic hit a snag when it began to rain.* —*v.,* **snagged, snag·ging.** —*v.t.* **1.** to catch, tear, or damage on a snag: *to snag a coat on a nail.* **2.** to hinder; block. **3.** to clear (a lake, river, or the like) of snags. **4.** *Informal.* to catch by quick action: *The outfielder leaped up and snagged the fly ball.* —*v.i.* to be or become caught on or hindered by a snag: *The fishing line snagged on an overhanging branch.* —**snag′gy,** *adj.*

snag·gle·tooth (snag′əl tüth′) *n., pl.* **snag·gle·teeth** (snag′əl tēth′). a tooth that sticks out or is broken or irregular. —**snag·gle·toothed** (snag′əl tütht′, snag′əl-tüthd′), *adj.*

snail (snāl) *n.* **1.** any of a large group of slow-moving mollusks found in water and on land. Snails have soft bodies protected by spirally coiled shells. **2.** a slow-moving or lazy person.

snake (snāk) *n.* **1.** any of a group of reptiles having long, scaly bodies without legs. Some snakes have a poisonous bite. **2.** a sly, evil, or unreliable person. **3.** a plumbing tool used to clear clogged drains, made up of a long, very flexible metal wire or rod. —*v.,* **snaked, snak·ing.** —*v.i.* to move, crawl, or curve like a snake: *The river snaked through the hills.* —*v.t.* to drag or pull (something, such as a log): *The lumberjacks snaked the newly cut logs through the forest to the river.*

snake·skin (snāk′skin′) *n.* **1.** the skin of a snake. **2.** leather made from such a skin.

snak·y (snā′kē) *adj.,* **snak·i·er, snak·i·est. 1.** of or relating to a snake or snakes. **2.** having a form or movement like that of a snake; winding; twisting: *a snaky river.* **3.** sly; evil. **4.** overrun or infested with snakes: *a snaky swamp.* —**snak′i·ly,** *adv.* —**snak′i·ness,** *n.*

snap (snap) *v.,* **snapped, snap·ping.** —*v.i.* **1.** to make a sudden, sharp sound: *The dry wood snapped and crackled as it burned.* **2.** to break suddenly, usually with a sharp sound: *The twig snapped when I stepped on it.* **3.** to close or move into place swiftly and with a sharp sound: *The lock snapped shut.* **4.** to give way suddenly under strain or tension: *The strong wind caused the string of the kite to snap.* **5.** to try to bite or seize by closing the jaws suddenly: *The fish snapped at the bait.* **6.** to seize or snatch suddenly or eagerly: *to snap at an opportunity to go to Europe.* **7.** to speak harshly, abruptly, or angrily: *I'm sorry I snapped at you.* **8.** to move or act quickly and smartly: *The soldier snapped to attention as the general approached.* —*v.t.* **1.** to break or cut suddenly with a sharp sound: *The big fish snapped the fishing line.* **2.** to speak harshly, abruptly, or angrily: *The sergeant snapped a command to the soldiers.* **3.** to cause to make a sudden, sharp sound: *to snap one's fingers.* **4.** to close, fasten, or move into place swiftly and with a sharp sound: *to snap a lock closed.* **5.** to bite suddenly (often with *up*): *The fish snapped up the bait.* **6.** to take (a photograph): *to snap pictures of one's family.* **7.** *Football.* to put (the ball) into play by sending it back from the line of scrimmage to a member of the backfield: *The center snapped the ball to the quarterback.* —*n.* **1.** a sharp sound made by breaking: *The stem of the glass broke with a snap.* **2.** the act of snapping or breaking. **3.** a fastener that works with a snapping sound: *to fasten the snaps of a sleeping bag.* **4.** a sudden snatch or bite: *The fish went after the bait with a snap.* **5.** a brief spell or period, especially of cold weather. **6.** a thin, crisp cookie, as a gingersnap. **7.** see **snapshot. 8.** *Informal.* something of little or no difficulty: *That spelling test was a snap.* —*adj.* **1.** made or done hastily or with little thought: *a snap judgment, a snap decision.* **2.** *Informal.* of little or no difficulty: *Algebra will be a snap course for you.*

·**to snap out of it.** *Informal.* to change from a state or attitude suddenly: *Don't be upset about losing the game; try to snap out of it.*

snap·dra·gon (snap′drag′ən) *n.* **1.** a usually red, purple, or white flower growing on spikes, widely grown as a garden flower. **2.** the plant bearing this flower.

snap·per (snap′ər) *n.* **1.** a person or thing that snaps. **2.** see **snapping turtle. 3.** any of a large group of brightly colored food and game fish found in warm seas, such as the red snapper.

snapping turtle, a freshwater turtle found in North and Central America, having powerful jaws.

snapping turtle

snap·pish (snap'ish) *adj.* **1.** curt, sharp, and ill-tempered in speech or manner; irritable: *a snappish reply.* **2.** inclined to snap or bite, as a dog. —**snap'pish·ly,** *adv.* —**snap'pish·ness,** *n.*

snap·py (snap'ē) *adj.*, **snap·pi·er, snap·pi·est. 1.** *Informal.* lively; brisk: *to walk at a snappy pace.* **2.** *Informal.* smart in appearance; stylish: *a snappy dresser.* **3.** snappish in speech or manner; easily annoyed. —**snap'pi·ly,** *adv.* —**snap'pi·ness,** *n.*

snap·shot (snap'shot') *n.* an informal photograph.

snare¹ (snâr) *n.* **1.** a trap for catching small animals, usually consisting of a noose that jerks tight around the animal when triggered. **2.** anything that tricks or entraps: *the snare of easy money.* —*v.t.,* **snared, snar·ing.** to catch with or as if with a snare: *The trapper snared a fox. The police snared the jewel thief only a few days after the robbery.* [From the Old English word *snearu* meaning "a noose, snare¹," probably from the Old Norse word *snara* "a halter, snare¹."]

snare² (snâr) *n.* one of the wires or strings stretched across the bottom of a snare drum. [Probably from the Dutch word *snaar* meaning "cord."]

snare drum, a small drum having wires or strings that are stretched across the lower head and produce a rattling sound when the drum is struck.

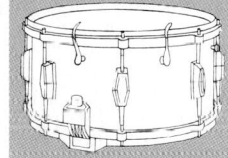

snare drum

snarl¹ (snärl) *v.i.* **1.** to growl angrily while baring the teeth: *The dog snarled at the stranger.* **2.** to speak angrily: *The grocer snarled at the clumsy clerk.* —*v.t.* to say with a snarl: *to snarl disapproval.* —*n.* an angry growl. [A form of the earlier word *snar* meaning "to growl," probably a representation of the sound of growling.] —**snarl'er,** *n.*

snarl² (snärl) *n.* **1.** a tangled or knotted mass, as of hair. **2.** a confused or disordered state or situation: *Because of the flooding, the roads were in a snarl.* —*v.t.* **1.** to make tangled or knotted: *The wind and rain had snarled my hair.* **2.** to make confused or disordered: *The fierce storm snarled traffic for hours.* —*v.i.* to become snarled: *The yarn snarled and was hard to untangle.* [From the Middle English word *snarle* with the same meaning, from the word *snare* "snare¹."]

snatch (snach) *v.t.* to seize or grasp suddenly or quickly: *The birds snatched the crumbs from the windowsill.* —*v.i.* to attempt to seize or grasp something suddenly or quickly: *The thief snatched at the purse.* —*n., pl.* **snatch·es. 1.** the act of snatching. **2.** a brief period of time: *to sleep only in snatches.* **3.** a small amount, part, or portion; bit: *We heard only snatches of their conversation.* —**snatch'er,** *n.*

sneak (snēk) *v.,* **sneaked** or **snuck, sneak·ing.** —*v.i.* **1.** to move or go in a quiet, secret, or cunning manner: *to sneak into the backstage area of a theater.* **2.** to behave in a sly or secret manner. —*v.t.* to move, take, get, or put in a sly or secret manner: *to sneak a kitten into a hospital.* —*n.* **1.** a person who sneaks, especially a sly, dishonest person. **2.** the act of sneaking. —*adj.* done, planned, or acting in a sly or secret manner: *a sneak thief.*

sneak·er (snē'kər) *n.* **1.** a shoe often made of canvas and having rubber soles, worn especially for sports. **2.** a person who sneaks; sneak.

sneak·ing (snē'king) *adj.* **1.** cunning; underhanded. **2.** not made known; secret: *a sneaking suspicion.* —**sneak'ing·ly,** *adv.*

sneak·y (snē'kē) *adj.,* **sneak·i·er, sneak·i·est. 1.** like or having the characteristics of a sneak: *to be too sneaky to be trusted.* **2.** sly, underhanded, or dishonest: *a sneaky trick.* —**sneak'i·ly,** *adv.* —**sneak'i·ness,** *n.*

sneer (snîr) *n.* **1.** a facial expression showing hatred or contempt; scornful look. **2.** a remark that shows hatred or contempt; scornful comment. —*v.i.* to have or show a sneer. —*v.t.* to say with a sneer: *to sneer a reply to an insult.* —**sneer'er,** *n.*

sneeze (snēz) *v.i.,* **sneezed, sneez·ing.** to drive or force one's breath out through the nose and mouth in a sudden, violent way. —*n.* the act of sneezing. —**sneez'er,** *n.* —**sneez'y,** *adj.*

snick·er (snik'ər) *n.* a sly laugh, usually expressing scorn or disrespect. —*v.i.* to laugh in such a manner: *to snicker loudly at an unsuccessful magic trick.* Also, **snigger.**

snide (snīd) *adj.,* **snid·er, snid·est.** unkind in a sly or sarcastic way: *a snide remark.*

sniff (snif) *v.i.* **1.** to take in air through the nose in a short breath that makes a sound, as in smelling something: *The cat sniffed at its food.* **2.** to express disdain or contempt by sniffing. —*v.t.* **1.** to take in through the nose: *to sniff the clean mountain air.* **2.** to smell by sniffing: *to sniff a flower.* —*n.* **1.** the act or sound of sniffing. **2.** something sniffed; scent; smell.

snif·fle (snif'əl) *v.i.,* **snif·fled, snif·fling.** to breathe noisily through the nose, as when crying; sniff repeatedly. —*n.* **1.** the act or sound of sniffling. **2. the sniffles.** a condition causing sniffling, such as a head cold.

snig·ger (snig'ər) *n., v.i.* another word for **snicker.**

snip (snip) *v.,* **snipped, snip·ping.** —*v.t.* **1.** to cut with scissors or shears in short, quick strokes. **2.** to remove (something) by cutting in this way: *The gardener snipped several buds from the rosebush.* —*v.i.* to cut with short, quick strokes. —*n.* **1.** the act or sound of snipping. **2.** a small cut made by snipping. **3.** a small piece that is snipped off.

snipe (snīp) *n., pl.* **snipes** or **snipe.** a long-billed bird that lives in marshes and bogs. It has a striped head and brownish feathers with black-and-white patterns. —*v.i.,* **sniped, snip·ing. 1.** to shoot at a person or persons from a hidden place. **2.** to attack with criticism, especially in a snide manner. **3.** to hunt or shoot snipe.

snipe (n.)

snip·er (snī'pər) *n.* a person who shoots at another or others from a hidden place.

snip·pet (snip'it) *n.* a small piece or part; bit; scrap.

snip·py (snip'ē) *adj.,* **snip·pi·er, snip·pi·est.** *Informal.* curt or sharp in a rude or insulting way. Also, **snip·pet·y** (snip'i tē). —**snip'pi·ness,** *n.*

snitch (snich) *Slang. v.i.* to be an informer; tattle: *to snitch on someone.* —*v.t.* to steal; swipe. —*n., pl.* **snitch·es.** a person who snitches; informer; tattletale. Also, **snitch·er** (snich'ər).

at; āpe; fär; câre; end; mē; it; īce; pîerce; hot; ōld; sông, fôrk; oil; out; up; ūse; rüle; pull; tûrn; chin; sing; shop; thin; this; hw in white; zh in treasure. The symbol ə stands for the unstressed vowel sound heard in about, taken, pencil, lemon, and circus.

S

889

sniv·el (sniv′əl) *v.i.*, **sniv·eled, sniv·el·ing;** *also, British,* **sniv·elled, sniv·el·ling. 1.** to cry with sniffling. **2.** to have a running nose. **3.** to complain in a whining manner. —*n.* the act of sniveling. —**sniv′el·er;** *also, British,* **sniv′el·ler,** *n.*

snob (snob) *n.* **1.** a person who admires or tries to imitate people with wealth or social position; one who wants to be regarded as rich or socially important. **2.** a person who has little regard or respect for people who are supposedly inferior in intelligence, achievement, or taste: *That author is an intellectual snob.*

snob·ber·y (snob′ə rē) *n., pl.* **snob·ber·ies.** snobbish character or conduct.

snob·bish (snob′ish) *adj.* of, relating to, or like a snob: *a snobbish attitude.*

snood (snüd) *n.* a small net or netlike bag, sometimes forming part of a hat, worn by women to keep their hair in place.

snoop (snüp) *Informal. v.i.* to look or go about in a sneaking, sly way; prowl or pry: *A stray dog has been snooping around the house.* —*n.* a person who snoops. —**snoop′er,** *n.*

snoot·y (snü′tē) *adj.,* **snoot·i·er, snoot·i·est.** *Informal.* stuck-up or snobbish. —**snoot′i·ly,** *adv.* —**snoot′i·ness,** *n.*

snooze (snüz) *Informal. v.i.,* **snoozed, snooz·ing.** to take a short nap; doze. —*n.* a nap; doze.

snore (snôr) *v.i.,* **snored, snor·ing.** to make harsh or noisy sounds in sleep by breathing through the open mouth or through the mouth and nose. —*n.* the act or sound of snoring. —**snor′er,** *n.*

snor·kel (snôr′kəl) *n.* **1.** a tubular device in a submarine that can be extended above the surface of the water. It is used to take in fresh air and get rid of stale air and exhaust fumes. **2.** a tube permitting a person to breathe while swimming with the face under the water. —*v.i.* to swim using a snorkel.

snort (snôrt) *v.i.* **1.** to force air violently and noisily through the nostrils. **2.** to make any similar sound. **3.** to express contempt or anger by snorting. —*v.t.* to utter or express with a snort. —*n.* the act or sound of snorting. —**snort′er,** *n.*

snout (snout) *n.* **1.** the part of an animal's head that projects forward and includes the nose, mouth, and jaws. **2.** something similar to an animal's snout in shape or use.

snow (snō) *n.* **1.** soft, white crystals or flakes of ice formed by the freezing of water vapor in the air. **2.** a fall of snow; snowstorm: *The snow ended during the night.* **3.** a layer or accumulation of snow: *The snow is deeper over here.* **4.** something that resembles snow. —*v.i.* to fall as snow. —*v.t.* **1.** to cause to fall like snow. **2.** to cover or shut in with or as if with snow: *The farm was snowed in for two days.*

 ·to snow under. to overwhelm: *The store was snowed under with requests for the new album.*

snow·ball (snō′bôl′) *n.* **1.** a mass of snow pressed into a ball. **2.** any of several shrubs having large clusters of white flowers resembling such a mass of snow. —*v.t.* to throw snowballs at. —*v.i.* to grow rapidly in size, as a rolling snowball does: *That business has snowballed into a huge industry.*

snow·bank (snō′bangk′) *n.* a large mound or drift of snow.

snow–blind (snō′blīnd′) *adj.* affected with snow blindness.

snow blindness, a temporary or partial blindness caused by the sun's glare reflected from snow.

snow·bound (snō′bound′) *adj.* shut in by a heavy fall of snow.

snow bunting, a small bird of cold northern regions, having mostly black and white plumage.

snow·cap (snō′kap′) *n.* a cap or crest of snow, as on a mountain peak. —**snow′capped′,** *adj.*

snow·drift (snō′drift′) *n.* a heap or mass of snow piled up by the wind.

snow·drop (snō′drop′) *n.* a plant native to Europe and Asia that blooms in the early spring and bears a single white and green flower.

snow·fall (snō′fôl′) *n.* **1.** a fall of snow. **2.** the amount of snow that falls during a given period or in a particular area.

snow·flake (snō′flāk′) *n.* one of the small ice crystals that fall as snow.

snow leopards

snow leopard, a large cat of the mountains of central Asia, having gray or buff fur marked with black broken rings. Also, **ounce.**

snow line, a line above which a particular area, such as a mountain slope, is always covered with snow.

snow·man (snō′man′) *n., pl.* **snow·men** (snō′men′). a figure roughly resembling that of a person, made by shaping a mass of snow.

snow·mo·bile (snō′mō bēl′) *n.* a motorized vehicle usually having runners or skis for travel on snow.

snow·plow (snō′plou′) *n.* a device or vehicle for clearing away snow, as from a road or sidewalk.

snow·shoe (snō′shü′) *n.* a light wooden frame strung with a webbing of rawhide or other material, fastened to the foot for walking over deep snow without sinking in. —*v.i.,* **snow·shoed, snow·shoe·ing.** to walk or travel by means of snowshoes. —**snow′sho′er,** *n.*

snowshoe hare, a North American hare having white fur in winter and brown fur in summer. In winter, its large hind feet, covered with fluffy hairs, enable it to travel over deep snow. Also, **snowshoe rabbit.**

snow·slide (snō′slīd′) *n.* an avalanche of snow.

snow·storm (snō′stôrm′) *n.* a heavy fall of snow with strong winds.

snow·suit (snō′süt′) *n.* a child's outer garment that has a heavy lining for cold weather.

snow–white (snō′hwīt′, snō′wīt′) *adj.* white as snow.

snow·y (snō′ē) *adj.,* **snow·i·er, snow·i·est. 1.** covered with snow: *the snowy peaks of the Alps.* **2.** bringing or including snow: *snowy weather.* **3.** resembling snow: *snowy blossoms.* —**snow′i·ness,** *n.*

snub (snub) *v.t.,* **snubbed, snub·bing. 1.** to treat with disrespect, scorn, or contempt: *to snub former friends by ignoring them.* **2.** to control or stop (an animal or thing) suddenly by winding an attached rope or line around a post: *The sailor snubbed the boat to the dock.* —*n.* disrespectful or scornful treatment. —*adj.* (of the nose) short and slightly turned up. —**snub′ber,** *n.*

snub–nosed (snub′nōzd′) *adj.* having a snub nose.

snuck (snuk) a past tense and past participle of **sneak.**

snuff¹ (snuf) *v.t.* **1.** to breathe in through the nose. **2.** to sniff at; smell. —*v.i.* to sniff. —*n.* a preparation of tobacco in powder form taken into the nose by snuffing. [From the Dutch word *snuffen* meaning "to breathe through the nose."]

·**up to snuff.** *Informal.* in good order or condition: *sloppy work that isn't up to snuff.*

snuff² (snuf) *v.t.* **1.** to cut or pinch off the burned end of (a candle wick). **2.** to put out: *to snuff a candle.* —*n.* the burned part of a candle wick. [From the Middle English word *snoffe* meaning "a burnt candle wick."]

·**to snuff out. a.** to put out: *to snuff out a candle.* **b.** to put an end to suddenly and completely: *Losing the game snuffed out the team's hopes of winning the championship.*

snuff·box (snuf'boks') *n., pl.* **snuff·box·es.** a small box for holding snuff.

snuff·ers (snuf'ərz) *pl. n.* an instrument resembling scissors, used for putting out the flame or removing the burned wick of a candle.

snuf·fle (snuf'əl) *v.*, **snuf·fled, snuf·fling.** —*v.i.* to breathe noisily because of partly stopped nasal passages. —*v.t.* to utter or say in a nasal tone. —*n.* **1.** the act or sound of snuffling. **2.** a nasal tone of voice. —**snuf'fler,** *n.*

snug (snug) *adj.*, **snug·ger, snug·gest. 1.** comfortable and warm; cozy: *a snug bed, a snug cabin.* **2.** fitting closely or tightly: *a snug sweater.* —*adv.* in a snug manner. —**snug'ly,** *adv.* —**snug'ness,** *n.*

snug·gle (snug'əl) *v.*, **snug·gled, snug·gling.** —*v.i.* to draw close, as for warmth, protection, or to show affection: *The bears snuggled against each other in the cave.* —*v.t.* to hold closely and comfortably, as for warmth or protection or to show affection; cuddle: *Everybody wanted to snuggle the cute little kitten.*

so¹ (sō) *adv.* **1.** in such a manner: *Write the words so.* **2.** to such an extent or degree: *It was so cold we stayed indoors.* **3.** very; extremely: *I am so glad.* **4.** very much: *They loved their parents so.* **5.** for this or that reason; accordingly; therefore: *We were tired and so we went home early.* **6.** too; also: *I sing and so does my cousin.* **7.** *Informal.* such being the case; as it seems: *So, you didn't like the cake I baked.* —*adj.* in accordance with fact; true: *Say it isn't so.* —*conj.* in order that: *Please turn out the light so I can sleep.* —*pron.* **1.** the same: *That is a lazy dog and will always be so.* **2.** more or less: *We will be gone for a month or so.* —*interj.* used to express surprise or displeasure: *So! We meet again.* [From the Old English word *swā* with the same meaning.]

·**so as.** in order to: *to run home so as not to be late.*

·**so that.** in order that: *We left then so that we would be home early.*

so² (sō) *n.* see **sol.**

So. 1. South. **2.** Southern.

soak (sōk) *v.t.* **1.** to make very wet; drench: *The sudden, heavy rain soaked the field.* **2.** to take in; absorb (usually with *up*): *The ground soaked up the heavy rainfall.* **3.** to cause (something) to stay in water or other liquid: *to soak a sprained ankle.* **4.** *Slang.* to charge too much; overcharge: *The mechanic soaked us for the car repair.* —*v.i.* **1.** to become thoroughly wet. **2.** to stay in a liquid: *Leave the dishes in the sink to soak.* —*n.* the act of soaking or the state of being soaked.

so-and-so (sō'ən sō') *n., pl.* **so-and-sos.** someone or something not named.

soap (sōp) *n.* **1.** a substance used for washing and cleansing, usually made by treating fats with an alkali. **2.** *Informal.* see **soap opera.** —*v.t.* to rub, cover, or treat with soap.

soap·box (sōp'boks') *n., pl.* **soap·box·es. 1.** a box or crate in which soap is packed. **2.** an empty box used as a platform for making a speech, especially on a public street.

soapbox derby, a contest for children in which they coast down a sloped track in unpowered racing cars that they have made.

soap bubble, a bubble formed from soapy water.

soap opera, a television or radio serial characterized by emotional, sentimental, and melodramatic situations, usually presented in the daytime.

soap·stone (sōp'stōn') *n.* a soft stone having a soapy feel.

soap·suds (sōp'sudz') *pl. n.* the suds from soapy water.

soap·y (sō'pē) *adj.*, **soap·i·er, soap·i·est. 1.** containing soap: *soapy water.* **2.** covered with soap: *soapy dishes.* **3.** resembling soap; smooth or slippery. —**soap'i·ly,** *adv.* —**soap'i·ness,** *n.*

soar (sôr) *v.i.* **1.** to fly upward or rise high into the air: *The bird soared overhead.* **2.** to rise to a great height, as a mountain or building. **3.** to go or move upward in position or status; rise sharply: *The price of meat soared.* **4.** to rise above the common or everyday: *The inventor's imagination soared.*

sob (sob) *v.*, **sobbed, sob·bing.** —*v.i.* to cry with short, irregular gasps. —*v.t.* **1.** to utter with a sob or sobs: *to sob out a sad story.* **2.** to put, bring, or send by sobbing: *to sob oneself to sleep.* —*n.* the act or sound of sobbing.

so·ber (sō'bər) *adj.* **1.** not drunk. **2.** grave or sedate in character or nature; serious; solemn: *to lead a sober life.* **3.** not bold or gaudy, as colors or clothes; somber: *The banker wore a sober gray suit.* —*v.t., v.i.* to make or become sober. —**so'ber·ly,** *adv.* —**so'ber·ness,** *n.*

so·bri·e·ty (sə brī'i tē) *n., pl.* **so·bri·e·ties. 1.** the state or quality of being sober. **2.** gravity; seriousness; solemnity.

so·bri·quet (sō'bri kā', sō'bri ket') *also,* **sou·bri·quet.** *n.* a nickname.

so-called (sō'kôld') *adj.* called thus, especially wrongly: *My so-called best friend would not help me.*

soc·cer (sok'ər) *n.* a game in which two teams of eleven players each attempt to move a round ball into a goal by kicking it or by striking it with any part of the body except the hands and arms. [A shortened form of *association football,* the formal British name of this game.]

so·cia·bil·i·ty (sō'shə bil'i tē) *n.* the state or quality of being sociable.

so·cia·ble (sō'shə bəl) *adj.* **1.** liking to be with others; fond of company; friendly: *a sociable person.* **2.** characterized by companionship and friendly conversation: *The club has a sociable atmosphere.* —*n.* an informal gathering; social. —**so'cia·bly,** *adv.*

so·cial (sō'shəl) *adj.* **1.** of or relating to human beings as a group: *social harmony. The family is a social unit.* **2.** of or relating to fashionable or high society: *one's social position, a social event.* **3.** of, relating to, or furthering companionship or friendly relations: *a social club, a social visit.* **4.** enjoying the company of others; friendly; sociable. **5.** (of animals) living in organized communities, as ants, bees, or baboons do. —*n.* an informal social gathering, as for the members of a church.

social climber, a person who attempts to gain social prominence, especially by associating with people of a higher social status.

social democracy, the principles and beliefs of a social democrat.

social democrat, a member of a political party that

---

at; āpe; fär; câre; end; mē; it; īce; pîerce; hot; ōld; sông; fôrk; oil; out; up; ūse; rüle; pùll; tûrn; chin; sing; shop; thin; **this;** hw in white; zh in treasure. The symbol ə stands for the unstressed vowel sound heard in about, taken, pencil, lemon, and circus.

S

favors a gradual, peaceful, and democratic change from capitalism to socialism.

so·cial·ism (sō'shə liz'əm) *n.* **1.** an economic system based on government or public ownership of the basic means of production, such as land and factories, and control of the distribution of food and goods. **2.** the policies or practices of those who favor or support such a system.

so·cial·ist (sō'shə list) *n.* **1.** a person who favors or supports socialism. **2.** *also,* **Socialist.** a member of a Socialist Party. —*adj.* see **socialistic.**

so·cial·is·tic (sō'shə lis'tik) *adj.* **1.** of, relating to, or resembling socialism. **2.** favoring or supporting socialism. —**so'cial·is'ti·cal·ly,** *adv.*

Socialist Party, a political party that favors socialism.

so·cial·ite (sō'shə līt') *n.* a member of fashionable society; socially prominent person.

so·cial·ize (sō'shə līz') *v.,* **so·cial·ized, so·cial·iz·ing.** —*v.t.* **1.** to make socialistic: *to socialize medicine, to socialize a country.* **2.** to cause to become sociable. —*v.i.* to take part in social activities; associate with others: *too busy to socialize much.* —**so'cial·i·za'tion,** *n.*

so·cial·ly (sō'shə lē) *adv.* **1.** in a social way: *Do you know them socially?* **2.** as a part of society; with regard to society: *a socially prominent family.* **3.** by or from society.

social science **1.** the study of society and the activities and relationship of people and groups within society. **2.** a particular field of study dealing with society, such as sociology, psychology, history, political science, or economics.

social security **1.** any system that provides assistance for a person or a family through government programs paid for by taxes. **2.** *also,* **Social Security.** a system of insurance maintained by the U.S. government for making payments to people who are old, retired, or handicapped.

social studies, a course of study in an elementary or secondary school that includes geography, history, and political science.

social work, any activity or service that seeks to improve the conditions in a society by helping people, such as those who are old, poor, or handicapped.

social worker, a person who does social work, especially as a profession.

so·ci·e·ty (sə sī'i tē) *n., pl.* **so·ci·e·ties.** **1.** human beings as a group; all people. **2.** a group of people forming a community and having common interests, traditions, and culture: *Colonial America was a largely agricultural society.* **3.** a group of people gathered together or associated for a common purpose or interest: *a literary society.* **4.** the wealthy or aristocratic members of a community; fashionable people as a group. **5.** companionship; company: *to enjoy a friend's society.* —*adj.* of or relating to fashionable society: *the society column of a newspaper.*

Society of Friends, a Christian religious group founded by George Fox in England about 1650, having no ritual, clergy, or formal worship service, and opposed to all forms of violence, including war. Its members are commonly called Quakers.

Society of Jesus, the religious order of the Jesuits.

so·ci·o·log·i·cal (sō'sē ə loj'i kəl) *adj.* **1.** of or relating to sociology. **2.** of or relating to society: *Hunger is a sociological problem.* —**so'ci·o·log'i·cal·ly,** *adv.*

so·ci·ol·o·gist (sō'sē ol'ə jist) *n.* an expert in sociology.

so·ci·ol·o·gy (sō'sē ol'ə jē) *n.* the science or study of human society, including its history, its different forms, and its institutions.

sock¹ (sok) *n.* a short stocking, especially one reaching

above the ankle but below the knee. [From the Old English word *socc* meaning "a kind of shoe" or "sock¹," from the Latin word *soccus* "a slipper" or "sock¹."]

sock² (sok) *Slang. v.t.* to hit or strike hard, especially with the fist. —*n.* a hard blow or punch. [Probably of Scandinavian origin.]

sock·et (sok'it) *n.* an opening or hollow part or place into which something fits: *a socket for a light bulb.*

So·crat·ic (sə krat'ik) *adj.* of or relating to Socrates, his philosophy, or his followers.

sod (sod) *n.* **1.** the surface of the ground, especially when covered with grass. **2.** a piece of this grassy surface, usually cut in a square or strip, and held together by roots. —*v.t.,* **sod·ded, sod·ding.** to cover with sod.

so·da (sō'də) *n.* **1.** any of a group of compounds that contain sodium, such as baking soda or washing soda. **2.** see **soda water.** **3.** a soft drink made with soda water and flavoring. Also, **soda pop, pop.** **4.** a beverage containing soda water, flavoring, and ice cream. [From the Medieval Latin word *soda.*]

soda fountain, a counter, as in a restaurant or store, having equipment for preparing and serving soft drinks, sodas, sundaes, ice cream, and the like.

so·dal·i·ty (sō dal'i tē) *n., pl.* **so·dal·i·ties.** a society, especially one of the Roman Catholic Church, having religious or charitable aims.

soda pop, another term for **soda** *(def. 3).*

soda water, a bubbling drink consisting of water charged under pressure with carbon dioxide gas. Also, **club soda.**

sod·den (sod'ən) *adj.* **1.** filled with water or moisture; soaked through: *The ground became sodden after the rain.* **2.** damp and heavy: *The cake is sodden because it wasn't baked enough.* —**sod'den·ly,** *adv.* —**sod'den·ness,** *n.*

so·di·um (sō'dē əm) *n.* a very light, soft, silver-white metallic element that is very reactive and may ignite in water. Its compounds are used widely in industry. Common table salt is a sodium compound. Symbol: **Na** [From *soda.*]

sodium ben·zo·ate (ben'zō āt') a white powder that is the sodium salt of benzoic acid. It is used chiefly as a food preservative.

sodium bicarbonate, a white, crystalline compound with a slightly salty taste, used especially in cooking as a leaven and in medicine as an antacid. Also, **baking soda, bicarbonate of soda.**

sodium carbonate **1.** a white, powdery compound used in making glass, soap, and paper. **2.** a crystalline form of this compound. Also *(def. 2),* **sal soda, washing soda.**

sodium chloride, see **salt** *(def. 1).*

sodium fluoride, a white, poisonous, solid compound used in the fluoridation of water, as an insecticide, and in rat poisons.

sodium hydroxide, a white, solid compound used in making rayon, soap, and detergents. Also, **caustic soda.**

sodium nitrate, a colorless, crystalline compound used in making explosives and fertilizer.

sodium thi·o·sul·fate (thī'ō sul'fāt) a colorless or white crystalline salt used in dyeing and in photography to fix negatives. Also, **hyposulfite.**

so·fa (sō'fə) *n.* a long, upholstered seat with a back and arms; couch.

soft (sôft) *adj.* **1.** easily shaped or worked; readily yielding to the touch; not hard: *soft clay, a soft bed.* **2.** not hard for its kind: *soft wood.* **3.** smooth or fine to the touch; not rough or coarse: *soft skin.* **4.** not loud or harsh; quiet: *a soft voice.* **5.** not glaring, sharp, or harsh to the sight; subdued: *soft lighting.* **6.** mild and agreeable; gentle: *a soft breeze.* **7.** having sympathy; tender; kind: *a soft heart.* **8.** lacking strength; flabby; weak: *soft muscles.*

9. (of water) free from mineral salts that interfere with the ability of soap to make suds and clean. **10.** *Phonetics.* **a.** (of *c*) pronounced with the sound of *s*, as in *city*. **b.** (of *g*) pronounced with the sound of *j*, as in *gem*. —*adv.* in a soft manner; gently. —**soft′ly**, *adv.* —**soft′ness**, *n.*

soft·ball (sôft′bôl′) *n.* **1.** a game like baseball but played on a smaller field with a larger and softer ball that is pitched underhand. **2.** the ball used in this game.

soft–boiled (sôft′boild′) *adj.* (of eggs) boiled for only a short time, so that the white and yolk are not firm.

soft coal, another term for **bituminous coal.**

soft drink, a beverage that contains no alcohol, especially a carbonated beverage.

soft·en (sô′fən) *v.t.*, *v.i.* to make or become soft or softer. —**soft′en·er**, *n.*

soft–heart·ed (sôft′här′tid) *adj.* sympathetic; tender; kind. —**soft′-heart′ed·ness**, *n.*

soft landing, a landing of a spacecraft on the moon or on another body in outer space at a slow speed to keep from damaging the vehicle or its contents.

soft palate, the soft part of the palate. The soft palate is the part of the roof of the mouth located behind the back teeth.

soft rock, rock music with a subdued beat and instrumentation and an emphasis on melody and lyrics.

soft shoulder, the soft earth along the edge of a paved road.

soft–spo·ken (sôft′spō′kən) *adj.* **1.** speaking with a soft, low voice: *a soft-spoken person.* **2.** spoken softly: *a soft-spoken criticism.*

soft spot 1. a weak, sensitive, or vulnerable part: *an economic soft spot, a soft spot in a defense system.* **2.** particular fondness; tender regard: *a soft spot for puppies.*

soft·ware (sôft′wâr′) *n.* written or printed programs, information, and the like used in a computer, as distinguished from its physical equipment.

soft·wood (sôft′wùd′) *n.* **1.** any of a large group of trees bearing cones and having needlelike leaves, such as pines, firs, and spruces. **2.** the wood of such a tree, used chiefly for building. **3.** any soft, light, easily cut wood.

soft·y (sôf′tē) *n.*, *pl.* **soft·ies.** *Informal.* a weak or overly sentimental person.

sog·gy (sog′ē) *adj.*, **sog·gi·er**, **sog·gi·est.** **1.** filled with water or moisture; soaked. *soggy ground.* **2.** damp and heavy, as poorly baked bread. —**sog′gi·ness**, *n.*

soil[1] (soil) *n.* **1.** the part of the earth's surface in which plants grow. **2.** a land, country, or region: *to land on foreign soil, a person's native soil.* [From the Anglo-Norman word *soil* meaning "land."]

soil[2] (soil) *v.t.* **1.** to make dirty: *to soil one's clothes with grease.* **2.** to bring disgrace or dishonor to; sully: *Gossip can soil a person's reputation.* —*v.i.* to become soiled or dirty: *White gloves soil easily.* —*n.* a dirty mark or place; spot; stain. [From the Old French word *soiller* meaning "to wallow in filth," from the word *soil* "pigsty."]

soi·ree (swä rā′) *also*, **soi·rée.** *n.* a party or other social gathering taking place in the evening.

so·journ (sō′jûrn, sō jûrn′) *v.i.* to live in a place for a brief time: *We sojourned in Paris during our trip to Europe.* —*n.* a brief stay. —**so′journ·er**, *n.*

sol (sōl) *n. Music.* **1.** the fifth note of the major scale. **2.** the note G. Also, **so.**

Sol (sol) *n.* **1.** *Roman Mythology.* the god of the sun. In Greek mythology he was called Helios. **2.** the sun.

sol·ace (sol′is) *n.* **1.** relief from sorrow or disappointment; comfort: *to find solace in a friend's company.* **2.** a person or thing that gives such relief: *Your sympathy was a solace during my grief.* —*v.t.*, **sol·aced**, **sol·ac·ing.** to relieve from sorrow or disappointment; comfort; console.

so·lar (sō′lər) *adj.* **1.** relating to, produced by, or coming from the sun: *solar heat.* **2.** produced from, operated by, or using solar energy: *a solar house.* [From the Latin word *solaris* meaning "of the sun," from the word *sol* "sun."]

solar battery, a device that changes the radiant energy of the sun into electricity.

solar cell, a device consisting of a thin slice of silicon or other semiconductor material that converts sunlight directly into electrical energy: *Satellites in space are powered by solar cells.*

solar collector, a device that collects heat from the rays of the sun and transmits it to a liquid, such as water or a chemical solution, that is circulated to heat a building, make hot water, or make steam to generate electricity.

solar eclipse, the partial or total blocking of the sun's light by the moon as it passes between the sun and earth.

solar flare, a sudden eruption of gas on the surface of the sun, often associated with sunspots. Radiation from solar flares can cause disturbances in the earth's magnetic field.

so·lar·i·um (sə lâr′ē əm) *n.*, *pl.* **so·lar·i·a** (sə lâr′ē ə). a glass-enclosed room, porch, or balcony where people can sit in the sun, as in a hospital.

solar panels on the roof of a house

solar panel, a group of solar cells arranged on a panel, used to convert sunlight directly into electrical energy.

solar plexus, a large network of nerves located just behind the stomach.

solar system, the sun and all the celestial bodies that revolve around it. It includes the planets and their moons or satellites, as well as asteroids, comets, and meteors.

solar wind, a stream of electrically charged particles that flows from the corona of the sun in all directions through space.

solar year, see **year** (*def. 2*).

sold (sōld) the past tense and past participle of **sell.**

sol·der (sod′ər) *n.* any metal that can be used when melted for joining metal surfaces or parts. —*v.t.* to join, fasten, or repair with solder. —*v.i.* to perform work with solder. —**sol′der·er**, *n.*

at; ape; fär; câre; end; me; it; ice; pierce; hot; old; sông, fôrk; oil; out; up; ūse; rüle; pùll; tûrn; chin; sing; shop; thin; this; hw in white; zh in treasure. The symbol ə stands for the unstressed vowel sound heard in about, taken, pencil, lemon, and circus.

S

893

sol·dier (sōl′jər) *n.* **1.** a person who serves in an army, especially one who is not an officer. **2.** a brave, skilled, or experienced warrior. —*v.i.* to be a soldier; serve in an army. [From the Old French word *soldier* meaning "warrior" or "mercenary," from the word *sould* "pay."]

sol·dier·ly (sōl′jər lē) *adj.* relating to or characteristic of a soldier.

soldier of fortune 1. a person who will serve in any army for money, adventure, or pleasure. **2.** any restless, adventurous person.

sol·dier·y (sōl′jə rē) *n.* **1.** soldiers as a group. **2.** military knowledge or training; military science.

sole[1] (sōl) *n.* **1.** the bottom surface of the foot. **2.** the part of a shoe, boot, sock, or other footwear that covers the sole. —*v.t.,* **soled, sol·ing.** to furnish with a sole: *to sole shoes.* [From the Old French word *sole* meaning "bottom of the foot," from the Latin word *solea* "a sandal."]

sole[2] (sōl) *adj.* **1.** only: *the sole survivors of a shipwreck.* **2.** being the only one; single: *the sole heir to a fortune.* **3.** limited or belonging to a single person or group; exclusive: *The film company bought sole rights to the novel.* [From the Old French word *sol* meaning "alone, solitary, singular," from the Latin word *solus* "alone, solitary."]

sole[3] (sōl) *n., pl.* **soles** or **sole. 1.** any of a group of small flatfish with small eyes and mouth found in warm and temperate seas. The European sole is an important food fish. **2.** any of various other flatfish that can be eaten, such as the flounder. [From the Old French word *sole* meaning this fish, from the Latin word *solea* meaning this fish, earlier "a sandal," from its appearance.]

sol·e·cism (sol′ə siz′əm) *n.* **1.** an error in grammar or in the choice of words. **2.** an error in social behavior. [From the Latin word *soloecismus* with the same meaning, from the Greek word *soloikismos* "solecism," from *soloikos* "of *Soloi*," a city in Asia Minor whose dialect of Greek was considered to be inferior.]

sole custody, custody of a child by only one parent after a divorce or separation.

sole·ly (sōl′lē) *adv.* **1.** without any other; by oneself or itself; alone: *The driver is solely to blame for the accident.* **2.** entirely; exclusively: *to work solely for the good of others.*

sol·emn (sol′əm) *adj.* **1.** serious and earnest; grave; sober: *a solemn judge, a solemn mood.* **2.** having much dignity or majesty: *a solemn occasion, a solemn and imposing building.* **3.** having to do with religion or religious observances; sacred. **4.** done with or accompanied by formality or ceremony: *a solemn oath.* —**sol′emn·ly,** *adv.* —**sol′emn·ness,** *n.*

so·lem·ni·ty (sə lem′ni tē) *n., pl.* **so·lem·ni·ties. 1.** the state or quality of being solemn; seriousness; gravity. **2.** *also,* **solemnities.** a solemn ceremony.

sol·em·nize (sol′əm nīz′) *v.t.,* **sol·em·nized, sol·em·niz·ing. 1.** to celebrate with a formal ceremony or by a ritual: *to solemnize a religious holiday.* **2.** to perform (a ceremony): *to solemnize a marriage.* —**sol′em·ni·za′tion,** *n.*

so·le·noid (sō′lə noid′) *n.* a coil of wire that produces a magnetic field when an electric current is passed through it. The solenoid is the basis for all electromagnets.

so·lic·it (sə lis′it) *v.t.* to seek to obtain; ask for earnestly: *The department store used an expensive advertising campaign to solicit additional business.* —**so·lic′i·ta′tion,** *n.*

so·lic·i·tor (sə lis′i tər) *n.* **1.** a person who solicits, especially a person who seeks business or trade. **2.** in

Great Britain, a lawyer who deals with clients but does not appear in court.

so·lic·it·ous (sə lis′i təs) *adj.* **1.** full of concern: *to be solicitous in asking about someone's health.* **2.** eager; desirous; anxious: *solicitous to please one's elders.* —**so·lic′it·ous·ly,** *adv.* —**so·lic′it·ous·ness,** *n.*

so·lic·i·tude (sə lis′i tüd′, sə lis′i tūd′) *n.* the state of being concerned.

sol·id (sol′id) *adj.* **1.** having shape and hardness; not liquid or gaseous: *Melted wax becomes solid when it cools.* **2.** free from empty spaces; completely filled with matter: *These metal bars are solid, not hollow.* **3.** not loose; compact; firm: *The ground is frozen solid.* **4.** of one material, color, or character; unmixed: *The ring is made of solid gold.* **5.** structurally sound or firm: *The building has a solid foundation.* **6.** of sound character; reliable: *a solid citizen.* **7.** sound; sensible: *a solid investment in government bonds, a solid argument based on fact.* **8.** united, as in opinion or support; unanimous: *The candidate received solid backing from the political party.* **9.** complete; uninterrupted: *to sleep for twelve solid hours.* **10.** *Mathematics.* having the three dimensions of length, width, and thickness: *Cubes, spheres, and pyramids are solid figures.* —*n.* **1.** a form of matter having shape and hardness. **2.** *Mathematics.* a figure having length, width, and thickness, as a cube, sphere, or pyramid. —**sol′id·ly,** *adv.* —**sol′id·ness,** *n.*

sol·i·dar·i·ty (sol′i dar′i tē) *n.* agreement among the members of a group, as in opinion, objectives, or interests.

solid geometry, a branch of geometry dealing with three-dimensional figures.

so·lid·i·fy (sə lid′ə fī′) *v.t., v.i.,* **so·lid·i·fied, so·lid·i·fy·ing. 1.** to make or become solid: *The heat of the sun solidified the mud into hard clay. The water solidified into ice.* **2.** to make or become firmly united: *The signing of the trade agreement solidified relations between the two countries.* —**so·lid′i·fi·ca′tion,** *n.*

so·lid·i·ty (sə lid′i tē) *n.* the state or quality of being solid.

sol·id–state (sol′id stāt′) *adj.* **1.** of or relating to the branch of physics that deals with the structure and properties of solids, especially crystals. **2.** of or relating to electronic devices made with transistors or other semiconductors.

so·lil·o·quize (sə lil′ə kwīz′) *v.i.,* **so·lil·o·quized, so·lil·o·quiz·ing.** to talk to oneself.

so·lil·o·quy (sə lil′ə kwē) *n., pl.* **so·lil·o·quies. 1.** the act of talking to oneself. **2.** a speech made by a character in a play to reveal the speaker's thoughts to the audience but not to the other characters in the play.

sol·i·taire (sol′i târ′) *n.* **1.** any of a number of card games for one person. Also, **patience. 2.** a single gem, especially a diamond set by itself in a ring.

sol·i·tar·y (sol′i ter′ē) *adj.* **1.** living or being alone: *a solitary traveler.* **2.** made, done, or spent alone: *a solitary life.* **3.** not often visited; secluded; lonely: *a solitary cabin.* **4.** single: *Not a solitary person came to visit.* —*n., pl.* **sol·i·tar·ies. 1.** a person who chooses to live alone, away from other people; hermit. **2.** *Informal.* see **solitary confinement.** —**sol′i·tar′i·ly,** *adv.* —**sol′i·tar′i·ness,** *n.*

solitary confinement, a punishment in which a prisoner is kept isolated from all other inmates.

sol·i·tude (sol′i tüd′, sol′i tūd′) *n.* **1.** the state of being or living alone; loneliness: *to wander in the solitude of the woods.* **2.** a lonely or unvisited place. [From the Old French word *solitude,* from the Latin word *solitudo* meaning "being alone, being desolate," from the word *solus* "alone, single."]

so·lo (sō′lō) *n., pl.* **so·los. 1.** a musical work or section of a musical work for or by a single voice or instrument, with or without accompaniment. **2.** any action done by one person alone, as an airplane flight. —*adj.* **1.** com-

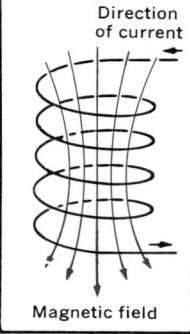

Direction of current

Magnetic field

solenoid

posed, arranged for, or performed by a single voice or instrument. **2.** made or done by one person alone: *a solo flight.* —*v.i.,* **so·loed, so·lo·ing. 1.** to make a flight alone in an airplane, especially for the first time. **2.** to perform alone.

so·lo·ist (sō′lō ist) *n.* a person who performs a solo, especially a musical solo.

Sol·o·mon (sol′ə mən) *n.* any very wise man. [From *Solomon,* the tenth-century B.C. king of Israel known for his wisdom.]

So·lon (sō′lən, sō′lon) *also,* **solon.** *n.* a wise lawmaker. [From the Athenian lawgiver *Solon* (638?–559? B.C.), known for his wisdom.]

so long *Informal.* good-bye.

sol·stice (sol′stis, sōl′stis) *n.* either of the two times during the year when the sun appears farthest from the equator. In the Northern Hemisphere, the sun appears farthest north of the equator during the summer solstice, on or about June 21, and farthest south of the equator during the winter solstice, on or about December 22.

sol·u·ble (sol′yə bəl) *adj.* **1.** able to be dissolved in another substance. **2.** able to be solved: *a soluble problem.* —**sol′u·bly,** *adv.*

sol·ute (sol′ūt) *n.* a substance that is dissolved in a solution: *In a solution of sugar and water, sugar is the solute and water is the solvent.*

so·lu·tion (sə lü′shən) *n.* **1.** the act, process, or method of solving a problem: *to use a computer in the solution of a mathematical puzzle.* **2.** an answer to a problem; explanation: *the solution to a riddle.* **3.** a mixture of two or more substances. Solutions are usually formed by solids, liquids, or gases dissolved in liquids.

solution set *Mathematics.* the set of all the values that satisfy an equation. Also, **truth set.**

solv·a·ble (sol′və bəl) *adj.* able to be solved.

solve (solv) *v.t.,* **solved, solv·ing.** to find the solution to; provide an answer for: *to solve a problem.* —**solv′er,** *n.*

sol·ven·cy (sol′vən sē) *n.* the state of being solvent.

sol·vent (sol′vənt) *adj.* **1.** able to pay all debts: *That new business is now profitable and solvent.* **2.** having the power to dissolve; causing solution. —*n.* a substance that dissolves another substance or substances to form a solution. Solvents are usually liquids.

so·mat·ic (sō mat′ik) *adj.* **1.** of or relating to the body or body tissues: *the somatic effects of a disease.* **2.** of, relating to, or affecting any of the cells in the body except the germ cells.

somatic cell, any cell of the body other than a germ cell.

som·ber (som′bər) *also,* **som·bre.** *adj.* **1.** dark and gloomy: *a cloudy, somber sky.* **2.** melancholy or depressing: *a somber mood.* —**som′ber·ly,** *adv.* —**som′ber·ness,** *n.*

som·brer·o (som brâr′ō) *n., pl.* **som·brer·os.** a hat with a broad brim, worn especially in Mexico and the southwestern United States.

some (sum) *adj.* **1.** being certain ones not named or known: *Some people don't like to travel. Some birds cannot fly.* **2.** being of a certain number or amount not given: *The accident happened some weeks ago. Please have some potatoes.* **3.** *Informal.* remarkable; striking: *That was some game yesterday!* —*pron.* **1.** certain ones not named or known: *Some of the students like to draw.* **2.** a certain number or amount: *We kept some of the apples and gave the rest away.* —*adv.* **1.** approximately; about: *The club has some forty members.* **2.** *Informal.* somewhat: *The patient's condition has improved some.*

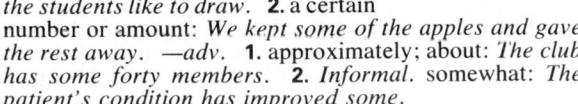

sombrero

–some[1] *suffix* (used to form adjectives) characterized by, tending to, or tending to be (what is indicated by the stem): *tiresome, bothersome.* [From the Old English suffix *-sum* with the same meaning.]

–some[2] *suffix* used to form nouns indicating a group of a specified number: *threesome, foursome.* [From the Middle English pronoun *sum* meaning "some, one," from the Old English word *sum* "some, one."]

–some[3] *combining form* body: *chromosome.* [Originally from the Greek word *sōma* meaning "body."]

some·bod·y (sum′bod′ē) *pron.* a person who is not named or known; someone: *Somebody has forgotten to close the window.* —*n., pl.* **some·bod·ies.** a person who is important or famous. ▲ **Somebody** and **someone** are both singular. In writing and in formal speech, they are used with a singular pronoun. In conversation, however, these words are often used with a plural pronoun: *Somebody left their* (rather than *his* or *her*) *pencil on my desk.*

some·day (sum′dā′) *adv.* at some future time: *We'll have lunch someday.*

some·how (sum′hou′) *adv.* in a way not known or stated: *We must get the car fixed somehow. The dog got into the garden somehow.*

some·one (sum′wun′) *pron.* a person who is not named or known; somebody: *Someone will have to mail these letters.* ▲ See **somebody** for usage note.

some·place (sum′plās′) *adv. Informal.* somewhere: *We'll have dinner someplace near the theater.*

som·er·sault (sum′ər sôlt′) *n.* a roll in which the body turns heels over head. —*v.i.* to perform a somersault.

som·er·set (sum′ər set′) *n.* a somersault. —*v.i.,* **som·er·set·ted, som·er·set·ting.** to somersault.

some·thing (sum′thing′) *pron.* a certain thing not named or known; some thing: *Something is wrong with the car.* —*n.* an important person or thing: *A new bike was really something when I was a kid.* —*adv.* to some extent; somewhat: *Your house is something like ours.*

some·time (sum′tīm′) *adv.* at a time not named or known: *I bought the book sometime last spring.* —*adj.* having been formerly; former: *a sometime movie star.*

some·times (sum′tīmz′) *adv.* now and then; at times: *Sometimes we spend the weekend in the country.*

some·way (sum′wā′) *also,* **some·ways** (sum′wāz′). *adv.* in some way; somehow. *We must be able someway to repay you for your kindness.*

some·what (sum′hwut′, sum′hwot′, sum′wut′, sum′-wot′) *adv.* to some extent; rather: *to be somewhat upset.* —*n.* some part, amount, or degree: *That movie was somewhat of a disappointment.*

some·where (sum′hwâr′, sum′wâr′) *adv.* **1.** in, at, or to some place not named or known: *They now live somewhere in California. Those gloves I lost have got to be somewhere around here.* **2.** at some time or amount: *The book costs somewhere around fifteen dollars.* —*n.* a place that is not named or known.

som·nam·bu·lism (som nam′byə liz′əm) *n.* the act or habit of walking about while asleep; sleepwalking.

som·nam·bu·list (som nam′byə list) *n.* a person who walks about while asleep. —**som·nam′bu·lis′tic,** *adj.*

som·no·lence (som′nə ləns) *n.* sleepiness; drowsiness.

som·no·lent (som′nə lənt) *adj.* **1.** sleepy; drowsy. **2.** tending to cause sleep. —**som′no·lent·ly,** *adv.*

at; āpe; fär; câre; end; mē; it; īce; pîerce; hot; ōld; sông, fôrk; oil; out; up; ūse; rüle; pull; tûrn; chin; sing; shop; thin; **th**is; hw in white; zh in treasure. The symbol ə stands for the unstressed vowel sound heard in about, taken, pencil, lemon, and circus.

S

son (sun) *n.* **1.** a male child considered in relation to one or both of his parents. **2.** a male descendant: *the sons of Adam.* **3.** a male person regarded as the product of a certain country or place: *a son of Ireland, a son of the soil.* **4.** a familiar term of address to a boy or man from an older person. **5. the Son.** Jesus.

so·nar (sō'när) *n.* an instrument used to detect underwater objects and to determine their location by means of sound waves reflected from or produced by the objects. [Short for *so*(und) *n*(avigation) *a*(nd) *r*(anging).]

so·na·ta (sə nä'tə) *n.* a musical composition for one or two instruments, often written for the piano. It usually has three or four movements.

song (sông) *n.* **1.** a musical composition for one or more voices. **2.** a poem that can be set to music. **3.** the act or art of singing. **4.** any melodious sound or series of sounds, as the call of a bird.
 ·**for a song.** at a very low price; very cheaply: *I bought this painting for a song.*

song·bird (sông'bûrd') *n.* a bird that has a musical call, such as a canary.

song·less (sông'lis) *adj.* having no song; unable to sing: *a songless bird.*

Song of Solomon, a book of the Old Testament, once thought to have been written by Solomon. Also, **Song of Songs.**

song sparrow, a common North American sparrow having brownish feathers marked with dark brown streaks. It is noted for its song.

song·ster (sông'stər) *n.* **1.** a person who sings. **2.** a writer of songs or poems. **3.** a songbird.

song·stress (sông'stris) *n., pl.* **song·stress·es.** a female singer, especially of popular songs.

song thrush, a European thrush having brown feathers and a yellow-and-white breast marked with brown spots. Also, **mavis.**

song·writ·er (sông'rī'tər) *n.* a person who writes music, words, or both for songs, especially popular songs.

son·ic (son'ik) *adj.* **1.** of, relating to, or using sound: *sonic vibrations.* **2.** of or relating to the speed at which sound travels through the air, approximately 740 miles per hour (1,190 kilometers per hour) at sea level.

sonic barrier, another term for **sound barrier.**

sonic boom, a loud, explosive noise caused by an aircraft traveling at or above the speed of sound.

son–in–law (sun'in lô') *n., pl.* **sons-in-law.** the husband of a person's daughter.

son·net (son'it) *n.* a poem that has fourteen lines and one of a number of rhyme patterns.

son·net·eer (son'i tîr') *n.* a person who writes sonnets.

son·ny (sun'ē) *n.* a young boy. ▲ often used as a familiar form of address to a young boy.

son·o·gram (son'ə gram', sō'nə gram') *n.* a record of ultrasonic waves reflected by an organ or other object inside the body. A sonogram provides an image of the shape, location, and movement of the organ or object.

so·nor·i·ty (sə nôr'i tē, sə nor'i tē) *n.* the state or quality of being sonorous.

so·no·rous (se nôr'əs) *adj.* **1.** making or able to make sound, especially a deep, full, or rich sound. **2.** (of sound) loud, deep, or resonant. **3.** having an impressive quality or style: *sonorous phrases.* —**so·no'rous·ly,** *adv.* —**so·no'rous·ness,** *n.*

soon (sün) *adv.* **1.** in the near future; before long; shortly: *Visit us again soon.* **2.** ahead of the expected time; early: *The guests arrived too soon.* **3.** without delay; promptly; quickly: *I'll come as soon as I can.* **4.** readily; willingly: *I would as soon do it now as later.*

soot (sut, süt) *n.* a black, powdery material, composed mostly of carbon. It is formed during the burning of such fuels as wood, coal, or oil. —*v.t.* to soil or cover with soot.

sooth (süth) *Archaic. n.* truth; reality. —*adj.* true; real.

soothe (süth) *v.,* **soothed, sooth·ing.** —*v.t.* **1.** to bring to a quiet or calm state; comfort: *The soft music soothed my nerves.* **2.** to ease or relieve: *The medicine soothed the pain.* —*v.i.* to have a soothing effect. —**sooth'er,** *n.*

sooth·ing (sü'thing) *adj.* tending to produce a quiet or calm state; calming; quieting: *The mother spoke soft and soothing words.* —**sooth'ing·ly,** *adv.*

sooth·say·er (süth'sā'ər) *n.* a person who claims to be able to foretell future events.

sooth·say·ing (süth'sā'ing) *n.* **1.** the act or practice of foretelling future events. **2.** an instance of this; prediction; prophecy.

soot·y (sut'ē, sü'tē) *adj.,* **soot·i·er, soot·i·est. 1.** covered or soiled with soot: *sooty buildings.* **2.** of, relating to, or making soot: *a sooty layer of dirt.* —**soot'i·ly,** *adv.* —**soot'i·ness,** *n.*

sop (sop) *n.* **1.** a piece of food, such as bread, soaked or dipped in a liquid, such as milk or gravy. **2.** anything given to pacify or quiet, or as a bribe. —*v.t.,* **sopped, sop·ping. 1.** to soak or dip in a liquid: *to sop bread in milk.* **2.** to take up (water or other liquid) by absorption (usually with *up*): *to sop up gravy with bread.* **3.** to wet thoroughly; drench.

soph., sophomore.

soph·ism (sof'iz əm) *n.* an argument that appears to be true but is actually false, especially one used to mislead.

soph·ist (sof'ist) *n.* a person who argues in a clever way so as to appear to be right, but who is actually wrong.

so·phis·ti·cate (*v.,* sə fis'ti kāt'; *n.,* sə fis'ti kit, sə-fis'ti kāt') *v.t.,* **so·phis·ti·cat·ed, so·phis·ti·cat·ing. 1.** to cause to have worldly knowledge and experience; make less natural or simple. **2.** to make complicated. —*n.* a sophisticated person.

so·phis·ti·cat·ed (sə fis'ti kā'tid) *adj.* **1.** having worldly knowledge and experience; not naive: *a sophisticated traveler.* **2.** for sophisticated people: *sophisticated entertainment.* **3.** developed to a highly complex level: *sophisticated electronic equipment.*

so·phis·ti·ca·tion (sə fis'ti kā'shən) *n.* **1.** the quality or character of being sophisticated; sophisticated ideas, tastes, or ways. **2.** the act of sophisticating.

soph·ist·ry (sof'ə strē) *n., pl.* **soph·ist·ries. 1.** a way of reasoning that is clever but unsound. **2.** a clever but false argument; sophism.

soph·o·more (sof'ə môr') *n.* a student in the second year of a four-year high school or college.

soph·o·mor·ic (sof'ə môr'ik) *adj.* **1.** of, relating to, or characteristic of a sophomore or sophomores. **2.** characteristic of, like, or being an overly self-confident, immature person: *sophomoric attitudes.*

sop·o·rif·ic (sop'ə rif'ik, sō'pə rif'ik) *adj.* **1.** causing or tending to cause sleep: *a soporific drug.* **2.** sleepy; drowsy. —*n.* something that causes sleep.

sop·ping (sop'ing) *adj.* thoroughly wet; soaked; drenched.

sop·py (sop'ē) *adj.,* **sop·pi·er, sop·pi·est.** soaked through with water or other liquid: *soppy clothes.*

so·pran·o (sə pran'ō, sə prä'nō) *n., pl.* **so·pran·os. 1.** the highest singing voice of women and boys. **2.** a singer who has such a voice. **3.** a musical instrument that has a similar range. **4.** a musical part for such a voice or instrument. —*adj.* **1.** able to sing or play soprano: *a soprano voice, a soprano saxophone.* **2.** for a soprano: *a soprano part.*

sor·bet (sôr'bit, sôr bā') *n.* a frozen dessert similar to sherbet but made without egg whites or milk. [From the French word *sorbet,* from the Italian word *sorbetto* meaning this food, from the Turkish word *sherbet* "a drink made from sweetened fruit juice," going back to the Arabic word *sharbah* "a drink."]

sor·cer·er (sôr′sər ər) *n.* a person who practices sorcery.

sor·cer·y (sôr′sə rē) *n., pl.* **sor·cer·ies.** the use of supernatural powers or magic, especially to do harm to another person; witchcraft.

sor·did (sôr′did) *adj.* **1.** dirty or filthy; foul: *sordid living conditions.* **2.** having a base or degraded character; mean; vile: *the sordid details of a crime.* —**sor′did·ly,** *adv.* —**sor′did·ness,** *n.*

sore (sôr) *adj.,* **sor·er, sor·est. 1.** painful or sensitive to the touch, as an injured or diseased part of the body: *muscles sore from exercise.* **2.** feeling physical pain, as from wounds or bruises: *The athlete was sore after the rough game.* **3.** causing sadness, grief, or misery: *The impoverished family is in sore need.* **4.** causing annoyance or anger; annoying: *The increase in taxes is a sore point with the taxpayers.* **5.** *Informal.* annoyed; angry; offended: *Are you still sore at them for not inviting you to their party?* —*n.* **1.** an area of the body where the skin is broken or bruised and painful or sensitive to the touch. **2.** any source of pain, anger, sorrow, or distress. —**sore′ly,** *adv.* —**sore′ness,** *n.*

sore·head (sôr′hed′) *n. Informal.* a person who is easily angered, annoyed, or offended.

sor·ghum (sôr′gəm) *n.* **1.** any of a group of tall tropical grasses widely grown for grain, syrup, and fodder. **2.** a syrup made from the juices of this plant.

so·ror·i·ty (sə rôr′i tē, sə ror′i tē) *n., pl.* **so·ror·i·ties.** a social organization of girls or women, especially one having chapters in various colleges.

sor·rel¹ (sôr′əl, sor′əl) *n.* any of a group of plants bearing long, branching clusters of small, greenish or reddish flowers and heart-shaped leaves. The leaves of some kinds of this plant are eaten in salads. [From the Old French word *surele* meaning this plant, from the word *sur* "sour," of Germanic origin.]

sorghum *(def. 1)*

sor·rel² (sôr′əl, sor′əl) *n.* **1.** a reddish brown color. **2.** a horse of this color. —*adj.* having the color sorrel; reddish brown. [From the Old French word *sorel* with the same meanings, from the word *sor* "chestnut brown."]

sor·row (sor′ō) *n.* **1.** sadness, grief, or distress caused by loss, injury, disappointment, or trouble: *to be filled with sorrow over a friend's death.* **2.** the cause of this: *The puppy's death was a sorrow to the family.* —*v.i.* to feel or express sorrow; be sad. —**sor′row·er,** *n.*

sor·row·ful (sor′ō fəl) *adj.* **1.** full of sorrow; sad: *a sorrowful funeral procession.* **2.** showing sorrow: *a sorrowful look.* —**sor′row·ful·ly,** *adv.* —**sor′row·ful·ness,** *n.*

sor·ry (sor′ē) *adj.,* **sor·ri·er, sor·ri·est. 1.** feeling sorrow, pity, sympathy, or regret: *I was sorry to hear of your illness.* **2.** poor in value or quality; worthless: *That was a sorry attempt at a joke.* **3.** causing pity; wretched; miserable: *The flooded town was a sorry sight.* —**sor′ri·ness,** *n.*

sort (sôrt) *n.* **1.** a group of persons or things that are alike or similar; class; kind; type: *This sort of plant usually grows in sandy soil.* **2.** character; nature: *Remarks of that sort will only make the other team angry.* **3.** a particular kind of person: *You're not a bad sort.*

—*v.t.* to place, arrange, or separate according to kind or type: *to sort mail, to sort socks by color.*
   •**of sorts.** of a poor or average kind: *a musician of sorts.*
   •**out of sorts.** feeling slightly ill or peevish.
   •**sort of.** *Informal.* somewhat: *to act sort of strange.*

sor·tie (sôr′tē) *n.* **1.** a sudden attack upon the enemy by troops that are hemmed in or surrounded. **2.** a single round trip of an aircraft on a combat mission.

so·rus (sôr′əs) *n., pl.* **so·ri** (sôr′ī). one of the dotlike clusters of spores usually located on the underside of the frond of a fern.

SOS (es′ō′es′) **1.** a radio signal of distress, used especially by ships and airplanes. **2.** any call or signal for help.

so-so (sō′sō′) *adj.* not very good or bad; mediocre: *Skiing conditions were only so-so in the spring.* —*adv.* in an indifferent or mediocre manner; passably.

sot (sot) *n.* a person who habitually drinks too much liquor.

sot·to vo·ce (sot′ō vō′chē) in a low tone of voice, so as not to be overheard. [From the Italian phrase *sotto voce* meaning "under the voice," going back to the Latin words *subtus* "below, beneath" and *vox* "voice."]

sou (sü) *n.* a former French coin of small value.

sou·bri·quet (sō′brə kā′, sō′bri ket′) another spelling of **sobriquet.**

souf·flé (sü flā′) *n.* a baked dish made light and fluffy by adding beaten egg whites before baking. —*adj.* made light and fluffy by or in cooking.

sough (sou, suf) *v.i.* to make a rushing or sighing sound: *The wind soughed through the branches overhead.* —*n.* a rushing or sighing sound.

sought (sôt) the past tense and past participle of **seek.**

soul (sōl) *n.* **1.** the nonphysical part of humans that is thought to control their thinking, feelings, and actions. Many people believe that the soul separates from the body at death and lives forever. **2.** the emotional part of humans; seat of deep feeling: *Winning the lead role filled the actor's soul with happiness.* **3.** the most important part of anything; that which gives life or spirit: *the soul of wit.* **4.** a person who leads or inspires: *The vigorous mayor was the soul of the town's revival.* **5.** a person who is thought to represent or embody a certain quality; personification: *the soul of honesty.* **6.** a person: *Not a soul was about at midnight.* **7.** a deeply felt and strongly conveyed emotion, especially of a performer or artist.

soul food, food traditionally eaten by American blacks, especially in the South, such as chitterlings, pigs' knuckles, corn bread, and turnip greens.

soul·ful (sōl′fəl) *adj.* full of or showing deep feeling: *a soulful gaze, soulful poetry.* —**soul′ful·ly,** *adv.* —**soul′ful·ness,** *n.*

soul·less (sōl′lis) *adj.* having no soul; lacking deep feelings. —**soul′less·ly,** *adv.*

sound¹ (sound) *n.* **1.** vibrations that are carried through the air, water, or another medium, and produce sensation in the ear. **2.** a sensation produced in the ear by such vibrations. **3.** something that is heard: *the sound of music.* **4.** the distance over which a sound may be heard. **5.** one of the noises made by the vocal organs that make up human speech. **6.** a mental impression left by something that is heard or read; implication: *The patient didn't like*

at; āpe; fär; câre; end; mē; it; īce; pîerce; hot; ōld; sông, fôrk; oil; out; up; ūse; rüle; pull; tûrn; chin; sing; shop; thin; **th**is; hw in white; zh in treasure. The symbol ə stands for the unstressed vowel sound heard in about, taken, pencil, lemon, and circus.

S

the sound of the doctor's report. **7.** meaningless noise. —*v.i.* **1.** to make or give forth a sound: *The bell sounded.* **2.** to give a certain impression; seem: *Your explanation sounds reasonable.* —*v.t.* **1.** to cause to make a sound: *The driver sounded the horn.* **2.** to announce by a sound: *to sound a retreat, to sound a warning.* **3.** to say so it can be heard; pronounce: *to sound a syllable.* **4.** to examine or test by causing to give forth sounds: *The doctor sounded the patient's chest for signs of pneumonia.* [From the Old French word *son* with the same meaning, from the Latin word *sonus* "a noise, sound¹."]
·**to sound off.** *Informal.* **a.** to call out one's name or serial number in a military formation. **b.** to speak in a loud, offensive, or complaining way: *to be always sounding off about something.*

sound² (sound) *adj.* **1.** free from damage, defect, or decay: *The house has a sound foundation.* **2.** free from injury or illness; healthy: *a sound mind in a sound body.* **3.** stable or safe; reliable: *Buying the house was a sound investment.* **4.** based on truth, fact, or reason; sensible: *sound reasoning.* **5.** legally valid. **6.** morally good; honest; upright: *a person of sound character.* **7.** (of sleep) deep and unbroken. —*adv.* in a sound manner; soundly: *to be sound asleep.* [From the Old English word *gesund* meaning "healthy, whole."] —**sound'ly,** *adv.* —**sound'ness,** *n.*

sound³ (sound) *v.t.* **1.** to measure the depth of (water), as by letting down a line with a weight on the end or by echoing sound off the bottom. **2.** to measure (depth) in this way. **3.** to try to learn the opinions and attitudes of (often with *out*): *Sound out the other members of the club about the proposal.* —*v.i.* **1.** to measure the depth of water. **2.** (of a whale or fish) to go deep under water; dive swiftly downward. [From the Old French word *sonder* with the same meaning, from the word *sonde* "sounding line," of Germanic origin.]

sound⁴ (sound) *n.* **1.** a long, narrow passage of water between larger bodies of water or between the mainland and an island. **2.** a long inlet or arm of the sea. [From the Old English word *sund* meaning "sea, water" and "the act of swimming."]

sound barrier, a sudden, sharp increase in resistance which the air presents to an aircraft as its speed nears the speed of sound. Also, **sonic barrier.**

sound·board (sound'bôrd') *n.* see **sounding board** (*def. 1*).

sound box also, **sound·box** (sound'boks'). the hollow chamber in some musical instruments, as violins and acoustical guitars, in which the sound resonates.

sound effects, artificially produced sounds, as of rain or hoofbeats, used to imitate the sounds required in a play, motion picture, or radio or television program.

sound·er¹ (soun'dər) *n.* a person or thing that makes a sound. [*Sound¹* + -*er¹*.]

sound·er² (soun'dər) *n.* a person or thing that measures the depth of water. [*Sound³* + -*er¹*.]

sound·ing¹ (soun'ding) *adj.* **1.** causing or making a sound. **2.** giving forth a deep, full sound; resounding. [*Sound¹* + -*ing²*.]

sound·ing² (soun'ding) *n.* **1.** the act of measuring the depth of water, as by letting down a line with a weight on the end. **2.** *also,* **soundings.** the depth of water so measured. **3. soundings.** a place where the water is shallow enough to allow a sounding line to reach bottom. **4.** an investigation of conditions in space or in the atmosphere at a given altitude, usually made with a rocket. [*Sound³* + -*ing¹*.]

sounding board 1. a thin, resonant board of wood in a musical instrument, as a piano or violin, for increasing the fullness of its tone. Also, **soundboard. 2.** a structure hung behind or over a stage to reflect sound toward the audience. **3.** any means of spreading an idea or opinion:

That newspaper column is a sounding board for the editor's opinions. **4.** a person or group on whom one tests one's opinions, ideas, or plans: *The officers of the club are the president's sounding board.*

sound·less (sound'lis) *adj.* having or making no sound; silent. —**sound'less·ly,** *adv.*

sound·proof (sound'prüf') *adj.* not letting sound pass in or out: *a soundproof room.* —*v.t.* to make soundproof: *to soundproof a building.*

sound·track (sound'trak') *also,* **sound track.** *n.* **1.** a narrow strip along one edge of a motion-picture film that carries the sound recording. **2.** a recording of the musical score of a play or motion picture.

sound wave, a series of vibrations carried through a medium, such as air or water, especially one that can be heard by the human ear.

soup (süp) *n.* a liquid food made by cooking meat, vegetables, fish, or other ingredients in water or a broth.
·**in the soup.** *Slang.* in trouble: *If you use my bicycle without permission, you will really be in the soup.*
·**to soup up.** *Slang.* to increase the power of (a motor, engine, or motor vehicle).

soup·y (sü'pē) *adj.,* **soup·i·er, soup·i·est.** thick and liquid like soup.

sour (sour, sou'ər) *adj.* **1.** having a sharp, acid taste, as lemon or lime juice. **2.** having an acid taste because of fermentation: *The milk is sour.* **3.** distasteful or disagreeable; unpleasant: *a sour odor.* **4.** having or showing an irritable or sullen nature; bad-tempered; peevish: *a sour expression.* **5.** (of soil) having too much acid. —*v.t., v.i.* to make or become sour: *The milk soured in the hot sun.* —**sour'ly,** *adv.* —**sour'ness,** *n.*

source (sôrs) *n.* **1.** a place or thing from which something comes, develops, or derives: *The dam is a source of electrical power.* **2.** a spring, lake, or other body of water that is the place where a river or stream begins. **3.** a person or thing that gives information or evidence: *What sources did you use for your report?*

sour·dough (sour'dō') *n.* **1.** a fermented dough used in making bread. **2.** a prospector or pioneer in western Canada or Alaska.

sour grapes, an attitude or remark of scorn, dislike, or criticism toward something because one cannot have it.

sou·sa·phone (sü'zə fōn') *n.* a large, circular tuba with a wide flaring bell that faces forward, used chiefly in brass bands. [From the U.S. composer and bandmaster John Philip Sousa (1854–1932.)]

souse (sous) *v.,* **soused, sous·ing.** —*v.t.* **1.** to put or plunge into water or other liquid. **2.** to make soaking wet; drench: *They were soused by the thunderstorm.* **3.** to soak in vinegar or brine; pickle. —*v.i.* to be or become plunged or soaked in water or other liquid. —*n.* **1.** a pickled food, such as the feet of a pig. **2.** the liquid used in pickling; brine.

sousaphone

898

south (south) *n.* **1.** the direction to the left as a person faces the sunset. South is one of the four main points of the compass and is located directly opposite north. **2.** *also,* **South.** any region or place lying in this direction. **3. the South.** a region of the United States south of Pennsylvania, the Ohio River, and Missouri, especially the states that fought for the Confederacy in the Civil War. —*adj.* **1.** toward or in the south: *We live on the south side of the street.* **2.** from the south: *a south wind.* —*adv.* toward the south.

South African 1. of or relating to southern Africa. **2.** of or relating to the Republic of South Africa. **3.** a person who was born in or is a citizen of the Republic of South Africa.

South African Dutch, see **Afrikaans.**

south·bound (south'bound') *adj.* going south: *a southbound train.*

south·east (south'ēst') *n.* **1.** the direction halfway between south and east. **2.** the point of the compass indicating this direction. **3.** a region or place in this direction. **4. the Southeast.** the southeastern part of the United States. —*adj.* **1.** toward or in the southeast; southeastern. **2.** from the southeast: *a southeast wind.* —*adv.* toward the southeast.

south·east·er (south'ēs'tər) *n.* a strong wind or storm from the southeast.

south·east·er·ly (south'ēs'tər lē) *adj., adv.* **1.** toward the southeast: *sailing in a southeasterly direction.* **2.** from the southeast.

south·east·ern (south'ēs'tərn) *adj.* **1.** toward or in the southeast: *a southeastern town.* **2.** of, relating to, or characteristic of the southeast or Southeast. **3.** from the southeast.

south·east·ward (south'ēst'wərd) *adv.* toward the southeast: *We are flying southeastward now.* Also, **south·east·wards** (south'ēst'wərdz). —*adj.* toward or in the southeast: *Let's hike toward the mountain southeastward of us.* —*n.* a southeastward direction, point, or place.

south·er (sou'thər) *n.* a strong wind from the south.

south·er·ly (suth'ər lē) *adj., adv.* **1.** toward the south: *a southerly direction, to travel southerly.* **2.** from the south: *a southerly breeze.*

south·ern (suth'ərn) *adj.* **1.** toward or in the south: *a room with a southern view.* **2.** *also,* **Southern.** of, relating to, or characteristic of the south or South. **3.** from the south: *a southern wind.*

Southern Cross, a southern constellation having four bright stars in the form of a cross.

south·ern·er (suth'ər nər) *n.* **1.** a person who was born or is living in the south. **2.** *usually,* **Southerner.** a person who was born or is living in the southern part of the United States.

Southern Hemisphere, the half of the earth south of the equator.

southern lights, another term for **aurora australis.**

south·ern·most (suth'ərn mōst') *adj.* farthest south.

south·land (south'lənd, south'land') *also,* **Southland.** *n.* land in the south, such as the southern region of a country.

south·paw (south'pô') *Slang. n.* a person who is left-handed, especially a left-handed baseball pitcher. —*adj.* left-handed.

South Pole 1. the southernmost point on the earth; southern end of the earth's axis. **2. south pole.** the pole of a magnet that points to the south when the magnet swings freely.

south–south·east (south'south'ēst') *n.* a point on the compass halfway between south and southeast. —*adj., adv.* toward the south-southeast.

south–south·west (south'south'west') *n.* a point on the compass halfway between south and southwest. —*adj., adv.* toward the south-southwest.

south·ward (south'wərd) *adv.* toward the south: *to travel southward.* Also, **south·wards** (south'wərdz). —*adj.* toward or in the south. —*n.* a southern direction, point, or place: *The river flows to the southward.*

south·west (south'west') *n.* **1.** the direction halfway between south and west. **2.** the point of the compass indicating this direction. **3.** a region or place in this direction. **4. the Southwest.** the southwestern part of the United States, especially Oklahoma, Texas, New Mexico, Arizona, and southern California. —*adj.* **1.** toward or in the southwest; southwestern. **2.** from the southwest: *a southwest wind.* —*adv.* toward the southwest: *to sail southwest.*

south·west·er (south'wes'tər, sou'wes'tər) *also,* **sou'·west·er.** *n.* **1.** a heavy wind or storm from the southwest. **2.** a waterproof hat with a broad brim that widens in the back to protect the neck in stormy weather, worn especially by sailors.

south·west·er·ly (south'wes'tər lē) *adj., adv.* **1.** toward the southwest. **2.** from the southwest.

south·west·ern (south'wes'tərn) *adj.* **1.** toward or in the southwest. **2.** of, relating to, or characteristic of the southwest or Southwest. **3.** from the southwest.

south·west·ward (south'west'wərd) *adj., adv.* toward or in the southwest. —*n.* a southwest direction, point, or place. Also (*adv.*), **south·west·wards** (south'west'wərdz).

sou·ve·nir (sü'və nîr', sü'və nîr') *n.* something that is kept as a reminder of a person, place, or event; keepsake; memento: *to save a ticket stub from the circus as a souvenir.* [From the French word *souvenir* meaning "a remembrance," from *souvenir* "to remember," from the Latin word *subvenire* "to assist, relieve" or "to come to mind," from the prefix *sub-* "under, after, next to" + *venire* "to come."]

sou·vla·ki (sü vlä'kē) *n.* a Greek dish consisting of lamb that has been broiled on a skewer. Also, **sou·vla·ki·a** (sü vlä'kē ə). [From the Modern Greek word *souvlákia* meaning "a little spit²," from the word *souvla* "a skewer."]

sou'west·er (sou'wes'tər) another spelling of **southwester.**

sov·er·eign (sov'rən, sov'ər ən) *n.* **1.** the supreme ruler of a monarchy, such as a king or queen. **2.** a former British gold coin worth one pound. —*adj.* **1.** having supreme power, rank, or authority: *a sovereign ruler.* **2.** not controlled by others; independent: *a sovereign state.* **3.** superior to all others; supreme: *a sovereign right.* **4.** effective or powerful, as a cure or remedy. [From the Old French word *soverain* with the same meaning, going back to the Latin word *super* "above, on top of."]

sov·er·eign·ty (sov'rən tē, sov'ər ən tē) *n., pl.* **sov·er·eign·ties.** **1.** supreme authority: *The dictator wrested sovereignty from the elected leaders.* **2.** the power of self-government; independence. **3.** a state, community, or other political unit that is politically independent. **4.** the rank, dominion, or authority of a sovereign.

so·vi·et (sō'vē et') *n.* **1.** a unit of government in the Soviet Union. Soviets are councils that pass laws and govern at local levels, as in cities and towns, and at provincial and national levels. Members of soviets are

---

at; āpe; fär; câre; end; mē; it; īce; pîerce; hot; ōld; sông, fôrk; oil; out; up; ūse; rüle; pùll; tûrn; chin; sing; shop; thin; <u>th</u>is; hw in white; zh in treasure. The symbol ə stands for the unstressed vowel sound heard in about, taken, pencil, lemon, and circus.

S

899

elected by the people. **2. the Soviets.** the government or people of the Soviet Union. *—adj.* **1.** relating to a soviet or government by soviets. **2. Soviet.** relating to the Soviet Union. [From the Russian word *sovet* meaning "council."]

sow¹ (sō) *v.*, **sowed, sown** or **sowed, sow·ing.** *—v.t.* **1.** to spread or scatter (seed) over the ground; plant. **2.** to spread or scatter seed on or upon (land). **3.** to spread; implant: *to sow suspicion.* *—v.i.* to spread or scatter seed over the ground. [From the Old English word *sāwan* with the same meanings.] **—sow'er,** *n.*

sow² (sou) *n.* an adult female pig. [From the Old English word *sugu* meaning this animal.]

sow bug (sou) see **wood louse** (*def.* 1).

sown (sōn) a past participle of **sow¹.**

sox (soks) *pl. n.* socks.

soy (soi) *n.* **1.** a salty, dark brown sauce made from fermented soybeans, used especially in Chinese and Japanese cooking. Also, **soy sauce. 2.** see **soybean.**

soy·bean (soi'bēn') *n.* **1.** the seed of a bushy Asian plant. It is rich in oil and protein and is used for fodder and soil improvement. Oil and meal from the seeds are also used in making many food and chemical products. **2.** the plant bearing this seed.

soy sauce, see **soy** (*def.* 1).

spa (spä) *n.* **1.** a mineral spring. **2.** a place where such springs exist, especially a resort. [From *Spa*, Belgium, a town famous as a resort with mineral springs.]

space (spās) *n.* **1.** an unlimited expanse that includes the entire universe. The planet earth and everything and everyone on it exists in space. **2.** the region beyond the earth's atmosphere; outer space: *to launch a rocket into space.* **3.** the distance or area between or within points or objects: *a space between buildings.* **4.** a particular area set apart or available for some purpose: *a parking space.* **5.** a period of time: *We worked for the space of an hour.* **6.** any blank or empty place, as between lines in a book. **7.** *Music.* the space between the lines of the staff. *—adj.* of, relating to, or for use in outer space, especially as a field of exploration: *space research, space food.* *—v.t.,* **spaced, spac·ing. 1.** to arrange with spaces in between; separate by spaces: *The builder spaced the houses far apart.* **2.** to divide into spaces.

space capsule, see **capsule** (*def.* 2).

space·craft (spās'kraft') *n., pl.* **space·craft.** any vehicle, with or without a pilot or crew, designed to be orbited around the earth or launched into outer space. Also, **spaceship.**

space·flight (spās'flīt') *n.* a flight into or in outer space.

space·man (spās'man') *n., pl.* **space·men** (spās'men'). an astronaut.

space medicine, the branch of medicine that deals with the mental and physical health of astronauts flying outside the earth's atmosphere and gravity.

space platform, another term for **space station.**

space·port (spās'pôrt') *n.* a place where spacecraft are tested, launched, or maintained.

space probe, an artificial satellite or other spacecraft equipped with instruments designed to collect information about outer space.

space·ship (spās'ship') *n.* another word for **spacecraft.**

space shuttle, a reusable manned space vehicle that is launched into orbit like a rocket and returns to earth to land like an airplane.

space station, an artificial satellite made to orbit the earth and support a crew, used for observation or as a launching site for further space travel. Also, **space platform.**

space·suit (spās'süt') *n.* a pressurized suit worn by astronauts to protect them from conditions in outer space, such as lack of oxygen and air pressure, radiation, and cold.

space–time (spās'tīm') *n.* space thought of as having four dimensions within which any event may be precisely located. Three of these are the ordinary space dimensions, length, breadth, and thickness, and the fourth is time.

space·walk (spās'wôk') *n.* a period of activity in which an astronaut in space is outside a spacecraft.

spacewalk

spac·ing (spā'sing) *n.* **1.** the act of a person or thing that spaces. **2.** the way spaces are arranged. **3.** a space or spaces, as between printed words.

spa·cious (spā'shəs) *adj.* **1.** having much space: *spacious rooms.* **2.** having a broad range; vast: *spacious skies.* **—spa'cious·ly,** *adv.* **—spa'cious·ness,** *n.*

spade¹ (spād) *n.* a tool used for digging. A spade has a heavy, flat, iron blade that can be pressed into the ground with the foot, and a long handle. *—v.t.,* **spad·ed, spad·ing.** to dig or cut with a spade: *to spade a garden.* [From the Old English word *spadu* meaning this tool.]

·to call a spade a spade. to call something by its right name; speak frankly and truly.

spade² (spād) *n.* **1.** a playing card marked with one or more black figures shaped like this: ♠ **2. spades.** the suit of such playing cards. [From either the Italian word *spada* or the Spanish word *espada*, both meaning "broadsword" and both from the Latin word *spatha* "a kind of broadsword" or "a spatula," from the Greek word *spathē* "a tool or weapon with a broad blade."]

spa·dix (spā'diks) *n., pl.* **spa·di·ces** (spā'də sēz') a thick or fleshy spike of tiny flowers, usually enclosed in a spathe.

spa·ghet·ti (spə get'ē) *n.* a white or yellowish starchy food consisting of a mixture of wheat flour and water shaped into long strings and cooked by boiling. It is thinner than macaroni and not hollow. [From the Italian word *spaghetti* meaning "little strings or cords," from the word *spago* "cord."]

spake (spāk) *Archaic.* a past tense of **speak.**

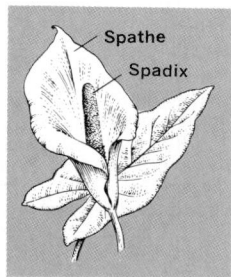

spadix

span¹ (span) *n.* **1.** the distance from the tip of the thumb to the tip of the little finger when the hand is fully spread out, considered as nine inches when used as a unit of measure. **2.** the full extent, amount, or reach of anything: *the span of a person's life.* **3.** the distance between two supports, as of an arch, beam, or bridge. **4.** a part or section between two supports. **5.** a short space of time. —*v.t.,* **spanned, span·ning. 1.** to measure by the hand with the thumb and little finger extended. **2.** to extend over or across: *That highway spans the state.* **3.** to provide with something that extends over or across: *to span a river with a bridge.* [From the Old English word *spann* meaning "breadth of the hand."]

span² (span) *n.* a pair of mules or other draft animals driven together in harness. [From the Dutch word *span.*]

span·gle (spang′gəl) *n.* **1.** a small, thin, often circular piece of glittering metal or plastic used for decoration, especially on clothing. **2.** any small, glittering object. —*v.,* **span·gled, span·gling.** —*v.t.* to decorate with or as if with spangles; cause to glitter. —*v.i.* to sparkle with or as if with spangles; glitter.

Span·iard (span′yərd) *n.* a person who was born in or is a citizen of Spain.

span·iel (span′yəl) *n.* a small or medium-sized dog of any of various breeds, usually having short legs, long, drooping ears, and a silky, wavy coat. [From the Old French word *espaignol* meaning "Spanish dog, spaniel," going back to the Latin word *Hispania* "Spain." This dog was originally bred in Spain.]

Span·ish (span′ish) *n.* **1.** the people of Spain as a group. **2.** a Romance language spoken in Spain and Spanish America. —*adj.* of or relating to Spain, its people, their language, or culture.

Words From Other Languages

Spanish words entered the English language through Spain, Mexico, and other Spanish-speaking countries of the Americas. Some words of Spanish origin, like *alligator* and *lariat,* took on English spellings and pronunciations. Others, like *fiesta* and *pueblo,* kept their Spanish spellings.

alligator	a large reptile related to the crocodile
bonanza	a rich mine of ore or source of wealth
bravado	a show of false daring or boldness
burrito	a flour tortilla wrapped around a filling and baked
canyon	a deep valley with steep sides
Chicano	an American of Mexican birth or descent
enchilada	a corn tortilla wrapped around a filling and covered with sauce
fiesta	a festival, party, or holiday
lariat	a long rope with a noose; a lasso
lasso	a long rope with a noose; a lariat
mesa	a flat-topped hill or mountain
mosquito	a small insect that bites
patio	an outdoor terrace for relaxing
pinto	a spotted horse or pony
ranch	a large farm for raising animals
sierra	a range of sharp, jagged mountains
siesta	an afternoon nap or rest
taco	a stiff, fried or baked tortilla with a filling
tortilla	a thin, unleavened pancake of cornmeal and water

Span·ish–A·mer·i·can (span′ish ə mer′i kən) *n.* **1.** a person who was born or is living in Spanish America. **2.** a person living in the United States who is of Spanish or Spanish-American descent. —*adj.* **1.** of or relating to Spain and America or to Spain and the United States. **2.** of or relating to Spanish America, its people, their language, or culture.

Spanish–American War, the war between the United States and Spain in 1898.

Spanish Armada, a fleet sent against England in 1588 by Philip II of Spain. It was defeated by the English and later mostly destroyed by storms. Also, **the Armada.**

Spanish moss, a grayish green flowering plant that grows in long, slender, hanging strands on the branches of certain trees in the southern United States and tropical America.

Spanish moss

spank (spangk) *v.t.* to strike with the open hand or a flat object, especially on the buttocks, as punishment. —*n.* a blow with the open hand or a flat object.

spank·ing¹ (spang′king) *n.* a series of slaps with the open hand or a flat object, given as punishment to a child. [*Spank* + *-ing¹.*]

spank·ing² (spang′king) *adj.* **1.** very large, great, or fine: *a spanking new bicycle.* **2.** (of a breeze) brisk and fresh. **3.** moving with a quick, vigorous pace: *a spanking trot.* [Of uncertain origin.]

spar¹ (spär) *n.* a pole that holds and stretches out a sail of a ship. A yard, a boom, and a gaff are kinds of spars. —*v.t.,* **sparred, spar·ring.** to furnish (a ship) with spars. [From the Middle English word *sparre* meaning "a pole, spar."]

spar² (spär) *v.i.,* **sparred, spar·ring. 1.** to box, especially for practice. **2.** to argue cautiously or in a restrained way, as if to test one's opponent. [From the Middle English word *sparren* meaning "to thrust or strike rapidly," probably from the Old English word *sperran* "to strike."]

spar³ (spär) *n.* any of various shiny minerals that split easily into flakes or chips. [From the Low German word *spar.*]

SPAR (spär) *also,* **Spar.** *n.* a member of the women's reserve of the U.S. Coast Guard. [Short for the Latin motto of the U.S. Coast Guard, *s*(emper) *par*(atus), meaning "always ready."]

spare (spâr) *v.t.,* **spared, spar·ing. 1.** to leave unhurt or uninjured; show mercy to: *The hunter spared the young deer.* **2.** to save or free from pain, sorrow, or trouble; show consideration for: *to spare someone's feelings.* **3.** to do without; give away or give up: *Can you spare a cup of sugar? Could you spare a few minutes to help me?* **4.** to have left over or in reserve: *We caught the train with only a minute to spare.* **5.** to be sparing of; use in small amounts: *Please give me some more meat, but spare the gravy.* —*adj.,* **spar·er, spar·est. 1.** extra or held in reserve; free: *a spare tire, a spare room, spare time.* **2.** not fat; thin; lean: *a spare figure.* **3.** scanty; meager:

at; āpe; fär; câre; end; mē; it; īce; pîerce; hot; old; sông, fôrk; oil; out; up; ūse; rüle; pull; tûrn; chin; sing; shop; thin; this; hw in white; zh in treasure. The symbol ə stands for the unstressed vowel sound heard in about, taken, pencil, lemon, and circus.

S

a spare meal, a spare diet. —n. **1.** something extra or held in reserve, as a spare tire. **2.** *Bowling.* **a.** the knocking down of all the pins in one frame with two rolls of the ball. **b.** the score so made. —**spare′ly,** *adv.* —**spare′ness,** *n.*

spare·ribs (spâr′ribz′) *pl. n.* a cut of pork consisting of the thin end of the ribs with most of the meat trimmed off.

spar·ing (spâr′ing) *adj.* careful in spending or using; frugal. —**spar′ing·ly,** *adv.*

spark (spärk) *n.* **1.** a small, hot, glowing particle, as is thrown off from a fire. **2.** a short flash of light produced by a discharge of electricity. **3.** the discharge itself, especially the discharge of a spark plug. **4.** any sparkle or flash of light. **5.** something that moves to action; motivating force: *A remark I made was the spark that touched off our argument.* **6.** a small amount; trace: *a spark of interest.* —*v.i.* to throw off or produce sparks. —*v.t.* to move into action; activate or incite: *to spark a revolt. The quarterback's enthusiasm sparked the team to victory.*

spark gap, an open space between electrodes through which a discharge of electricity may pass.

spar·kle (spär′kəl) *v.i.,* **spar·kled, spar·kling. 1.** to shine, as if giving off sparks: *The jewels sparkled. The baby's eyes sparkled with merriment.* **2.** to give off sparks. **3.** to be brilliant and lively: *Their conversation sparkled with wit.* **4.** to bubble, as champagne or soda water. —*n.* **1.** a sparkling appearance or quality: *the sparkle of clear blue ocean waters.* **2.** brilliance or liveliness. **3.** a small spark or glowing particle.

spar·kler (spär′klər) *n.* **1.** a person or thing that sparkles. **2.** a firework that burns slowly and throws off a brilliant shower of sparks.

spark plug 1. a device that is fitted into the cylinder of an internal-combustion engine and ignites the mixture of fuel and air by means of an electric spark. **2.** *Informal.* a person who inspires or leads some activity or undertaking: *The captain is the spark plug of the team.*

spar·row (spar′ō) *n.* any of numerous small, seed-eating birds having a short, thick, cone-shaped bill, a medium-length tail, mainly brown feathers, and a gray or white belly. —**spar′row·like′,** *adj.*

sparrow hawk, another term for **kestrel.**

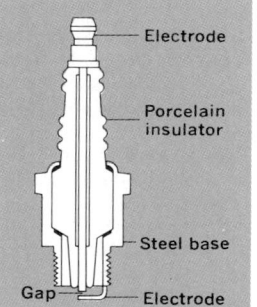

spark plug *(def. 1)*

Electrode
Porcelain insulator
Steel base
Gap
Electrode

sparse (spärs) *adj.,* **spars·er, spars·est.** thinly spread or distributed; not crowded or dense: *a sparse population, a hospital room with sparse furnishings.* —**sparse′ly,** *adv.* —**sparse′ness,** *n.*

spar·si·ty (spär′si tē) *n.* an uncrowded condition or lack: *a sparsity of people, a sparsity of grocery stores.*

Spar·tan (spär′tən) *adj.* **1.** relating to Sparta, its people, or their culture. **2.** severely simple, stern, or highly disciplined, like the people and life of Sparta: *the Spartan life of an athlete in training.* —*n.* **1.** a person who lived in Sparta. **2.** a person who has Spartan characteristics.

spasm (spaz′əm) *n.* **1.** a sudden, involuntary contraction of a muscle or group of muscles. **2.** any sudden, brief burst of energy, activity, or feeling: *a spasm of fear.*

spas·mod·ic (spaz mod′ik) *adj.* **1.** relating to or characterized by a spasm or spasms. **2.** resembling a spasm; sudden, violent, and temporary: *a spasmodic burst of energy.* **3.** happening irregularly; fitful: *spasmodic at-*

tempts to learn to play the piano. —**spas·mod′i·cal·ly,** *adv.*

spas·tic (spas′tik) *adj.* **1.** relating to, characterized by, or suffering from a spasm or spasms. **2.** suffering from spastic paralysis. —*n.* a person who is suffering from spastic paralysis. —**spas′ti·cal·ly,** *adv.*

spastic paralysis, a form of paralysis in which the affected muscles are tense and rigid and the reflexes are abnormal and exaggerated.

spat[1] (spat) *n.* **1.** a petty quarrel; slight argument. **2.** a light slap or slapping sound. —*v.i.,* **spat·ted, spat·ting. 1.** to have a petty argument; quarrel. **2.** to strike with a slapping or splashing sound. [Of uncertain origin.]

spat[2] (spat) a past tense and past participle of **spit**[1].

spat[3] (spat) *n.* a short covering of cloth or leather worn over the instep of a shoe and the ankle. [Short for *spatterdash,* a long legging formerly worn to keep trousers from being spattered with mud.]

spat[4] (spat) *n.* **1.** the spawn of an oyster or similar shellfish. **2.** a young oyster. —*v.i.,* **spat·ted, spat·ting.** (of oysters) to spawn. [Of uncertain origin.]

spate (spāt) *n.* a sudden or strong flood, as of words or emotion: *a spate of new proposals to curb drug abuse.*

spathe (spāth) *n.* a leaf or leaflike part, often large, enclosing a flower cluster or spadix.

spa·tial (spā′shəl) *adj.* **1.** relating to space. **2.** existing or happening in space. —**spa′tial·ly,** *adv.*

spat·ter (spat′ər) *v.t.* **1.** to scatter in drops or small particles: *to spatter paint on a canvas.* **2.** to splash with drops or small particles: *The mud spattered their shoes.* —*v.i.* **1.** to send out or throw off drops or small particles. **2.** to fall or strike in or as if in a shower: *Hailstones spattered on the house.* —*n.* **1.** the act of spattering. **2.** the sound made by this: *the spatter of raindrops on a roof.* **3.** a splash or spot of something spattered: *There were spatters of grease on the stove.*

spat·u·la (spach′ə lə) *n.* a small tool with a flat, flexible blade. Spatulas are used for spreading or mixing thick, soft substances, such as paint or cake batter, and for lifting food, such as an egg, from a frying pan.

spav·in (spav′in) *n.* a disease of the hock joint of horses, causing stiffness and lameness. —**spav′ined,** *adj.*

spawn (spôn) *n.* the eggs of certain animals that live in the water, such as fish or frogs. —*v.t.* **1.** to produce (eggs or offspring). **2.** to give birth to; produce. —*v.i.* to deposit eggs or sperm into the water, as fish do.

spay (spā) *v.t.* to remove the ovaries of (an animal), usually to prevent reproduction.

S.P.C.A., Society for the Prevention of Cruelty to Animals.

speak (spēk) *v.,* **spoke** or (*archaic*) **spake, spo·ken, speaking.** —*v.i.* **1.** to utter words; talk: *The baby hasn't learned to speak yet.* **2.** to make known or convey an idea, fact, or feeling: *Please speak to the teacher about your problem.* **3.** to converse. **4.** to deliver a speech: *The author spoke before a large audience.* —*v.t.* **1.** to give voice to; utter: *to speak words of sympathy.* **2.** to use or be able to use in speaking: *to speak Spanish fluently.* **3.** to make known or convey; express: *to speak the truth.*

•**so to speak.** to say in other words: *What you're saying, so to speak, is that they are wrong.*

•**to speak for. a.** to speak on behalf of; represent: *The captain spoke for the entire team at the meeting.* **b.** to ask for; choose: *The puppy had already been spoken for.*

•**to speak out** or **to speak up. a.** to speak loudly and clearly enough to be understood. **b.** to say what one really believes.

•**to speak well for.** to give a good impression of: *Your manners speak well for your parents.*

speak·eas·y (spēk′ē′zē) *n., pl.* **speak·eas·ies.** *Slang.* a place that illegally sells alcoholic drinks, as during Prohibition.

speak·er (spē′kər) *n.* **1.** a person who speaks, especially a person who makes a public speech. **2.** *usually,* **Speaker.** the presiding officer in a legislative assembly: *the Speaker of the House of Representatives.* **3.** see **loudspeaker.**

speak·er·ship (spē′kər ship′) *n.* the position of presiding officer in a legislative assembly.

speak·ing (spē′king) *adj.* **1.** using or involving speech or talking: *The senator has a speaking engagement tomorrow.* **2.** expressive, suggestive, or striking: *a speaking likeness.* —*n.* the act or utterance of a person who speaks.

spear (spîr) *n.* **1.** a weapon consisting of a sharp-pointed head attached to a long shaft, used for thrusting or throwing. **2.** a slender stalk, as of grass: *asparagus spears.* —*v.t.* to stab, penetrate, or take hold with or as if with a spear. —*v.i.* (of a plant) to send forth shoots or stems; sprout. —**spear′like′,** *adj.*

spear·head (spîr′hed′) *n.* **1.** the sharp-pointed head of a spear. **2.** a person or group that leads: *The paratroopers were the spearhead of the invasion.* —*v.t.* to lead: *to spearhead a campaign.*

spear·man (spîr′mən) *n., pl.* **spear·men** (spîr′mən). a person who is armed with a spear.

spear·mint (spîr′mint′) *n.* **1.** a fragrant plant that has leaves shaped like the head of a spear. **2.** an aromatic oil from this plant, used as a flavoring.

spe·cial (spesh′əl) *adj.* **1.** not common; unusual; exceptional: *a special talent for singing.* **2.** differing from others by some distinguishing quality or character: *They are special friends of mine.* **3.** made, arranged, or designed for a particular occasion, purpose, or person: *a special broadcast.* —*n.* **1.** something made, designed, or used for a particular occasion or purpose: *Did you see the special on hurricanes on television?* **2.** a sale at lower prices or something offered at these prices: *a special on winter coats.* —**spe′cial·ly,** *adv.*

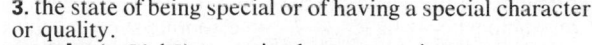

spearmint *(def. 1)*

special delivery, delivery of mail by a special messenger, in advance of the regular delivery, for an extra fee.

special education, the teaching or training of students with special learning needs, such as handicapped and gifted children.

special interest group, a group of people who promote a single cause or interest, as by seeking to enact or change laws that affect the cause or interest.

spe·cial·ist (spesh′ə list) *n.* a person who specializes in a particular branch of a profession or field of study, especially a doctor who practices a particular branch of medicine: *a specialist in heart surgery.*

spe·cial·i·za·tion (spesh′ə lə zā′shən) *n.* the act of specializing or the state of being specialized.

spe·cial·ize (spesh′ə līz′) *v.,* **spe·cial·ized, spe·cial·iz·ing.** —*v.i.* **1.** to concentrate on a particular product, activity, branch of a profession, or field of study. **2.** *Biology.* to become adapted to a special function or environment. —*v.t.* to adapt or limit to a specific purpose, use, or function.

spe·cial·ty (spesh′əl tē) *n., pl.* **spe·cial·ties.** **1.** a particular branch of a profession, trade, or field of study that a person concentrates on. **2.** a particular product or service that a store or business sells, or something that it does very well: *The restaurant's specialty is Italian food.*

3. the state of being special or of having a special character or quality.

spe·cie (spē′shē) *n.* coined money; coin.

spe·cies (spē′shēz) *n., pl.* **spe·cies.** **1.** *Biology.* **a.** a subdivision of a genus in the classification of living things. Members of a species have certain permanent characteristics in common and are able to mate with other members of the same species. **b.** an organism belonging to such a subdivision. **2.** a distinct kind or type; sort: *a strange species of humor.* **3. the species.** the human race.

spe·cif·ic (spi sif′ik) *adj.* **1.** explicitly named; definite; precise: *a specific offer, a specific amount.* **2.** belonging exclusively to; peculiar to: *the specific characteristics of a region.* **3.** of or relating to a species of plant or animal. —*n.* **1.** something that has a specific effect or result, such as a medicine used to prevent or treat a particular disease. **2.** *usually,* **specifics.** particulars; details: *Let's discuss the general situation first and then turn to the specifics.*

spe·cif·i·cal·ly (spi sif′i kə lē, spi sif′i klē) *adv.* in a specific manner; explicitly: *Your friend specifically said to look in your locker for the book.*

spec·i·fi·ca·tion (spes′ə fi kā′shən) *n.* **1.** the act of specifying. **2.** an item or article specified, as in a plan or contract. **3.** *usually,* **specifications.** a detailed list and description of the exact dimensions, materials, and methods to be used in building something.

specific gravity, the ratio of the density of a given substance to the density of another substance used as a standard. Water is used as the standard for solids and liquids, and air is used for gases.

specific heat, the amount of heat necessary to raise the temperature of one gram of a given substance by one degree centigrade.

spec·i·fy (spes′ə fī′) *v.t.,* **spec·i·fied, spec·i·fy·ing.** **1.** to mention in a precise and definite way; describe in detail: *to specify a place where a meeting will be held.* **2.** to set down as a specification: *The architect specified oak for the floors.*

spec·i·men (spes′ə mən) *n.* **1.** a single person or thing considered to be typical of its class or group; example. **2.** a sample, as of blood, taken for medical analysis.

spe·cious (spē′shəs) *adj.* seemingly true, reasonable, or attractive, but actually false: *The incorrect conclusion resulted from specious reasoning.* —**spe′cious·ly,** *adv.* —**spe′cious·ness,** *n.*

speck (spek) *n.* **1.** a very small bit; particle: *There was not a speck of dirt anywhere after we finished cleaning.* **2.** a small spot, stain, or mark: *The paint left specks on the wallpaper.* —*v.t.* to mark with specks; speckle.

speck·le (spek′əl) *n.* a small spot or mark, as on fur or skin. —*v.t.,* **speck·led, speck·ling.** to mark or cover with speckles: *Little drops of paint speckled the floor.*

specs (speks) *pl. n. Informal.* **1.** spectacles. **2.** specifications.

spec·ta·cle (spek′tə kəl) *n.* **1.** something seen, especially an impressive or unusual sight: *The sunrise over the valley was a beautiful spectacle.* **2.** a public display or performance, especially on a grand scale: *The circus parade was a delightful spectacle.* **3. spectacles.** a pair of eyeglasses.

•**to make a spectacle of oneself.** to behave badly or foolishly in public.

---

at; āpe; fär; câre; end; mē; it; īce; pîerce; hot; ōld; sông; fôrk; oil; out; up; ūse; rüle; pull; tûrn; chin; sing; shop; thin; <u>th</u>is; hw in white; zh in treasure. The symbol ə stands for the unstressed vowel sound heard in about, taken, pencil, lemon, and circus.

S

spec·tac·u·lar (spek tak′yə lər) *adj.* of, relating to, or resembling a spectacle. —*n.* an elaborate show, such as a long and lavishly made movie. —**spec·tac′u·lar·ly,** *adv.*

spec·ta·tor (spek′tā tər) *n.* a person who watches but does not take part; member of an audience; observer.

spec·ter (spek′tər) *also, British,* **spec·tre.** *n.* **1.** a visible spirit of a dead person; ghost. **2.** something that threatens or causes fear: *The treaty banished the specter of war.*

spec·tra (spek′trə) a plural of **spectrum.**

spec·tral (spek′trəl) *adj.* **1.** of or resembling a specter; ghostly: *The tree cast spectral shadows on the window.* **2.** of, relating to, or produced by a spectrum.

spec·tre (spek′tər) *British.* another spelling of **specter.**

spec·tro·scope (spek′trə skōp′) *n.* an instrument that separates white light into a spectrum by causing the light to pass through a series of lenses and a prism or through a similar device.

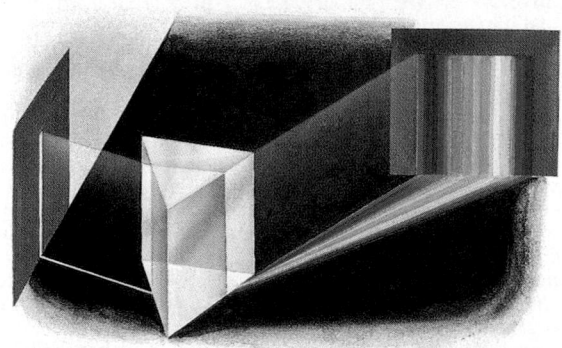

spectrum

spec·trum (spek′trəm) *n., pl.* **spec·tra** or **spec·trums.** a band of colors into which white light is separated according to wavelength by being passed through a prism or other material. The colors of the spectrum are red, orange, yellow, green, blue, indigo, and violet.

spec·u·late (spek′yə lāt′) *v.i.,* **spec·u·lat·ed, spec·u·lat·ing. 1.** to think carefully or seriously about; think of reasons or answers for; reflect; conjecture: *to speculate about the motives of others, to speculate on the outcome of an election.* **2.** to take risks or gamble on a business opportunity, as by buying or selling stock or real estate in the hope of making a large profit.

spec·u·la·tion (spek′yə lā′shən) *n.* **1.** the act of thinking carefully or seriously about something; reflection. **2.** a conclusion or opinion reached by conjecture; guess. **3.** the act or practice of speculating in stocks, land, or the like.

spec·u·la·tive (spek′yə lā′tiv, spek′yə lə tiv) *adj.* **1.** given to serious thinking; thoughtful: *the speculative mind of a brilliant scientist.* **2.** theoretical rather than practical: *ideas that are very speculative.* **3.** involving or involved in financial speculation: *speculative stocks.* —**spec′u·la′tive·ly,** *adv.* —**spec′u·la′tive·ness,** *n.*

spec·u·la·tor (spek′yə lā′tər) *n.* a person who speculates, especially in business.

sped (sped) a past tense and past participle of **speed.**

speech (spēch) *n., pl.* **speech·es. 1.** the ability to express an idea, thought, or feeling by the use of spoken words. **2.** the act of speaking: *to express one's thoughts in speech.* **3.** something spoken, especially before an audience: *a candidate's acceptance speech.* **4.** a way in which someone speaks: *Your speech is very British.* **5.** a particular idiom, dialect, or language: *Southern speech.* **6.** the study of speaking correctly, clearly, and effectively, especially in public.

speech·less (spēch′lis) *adj.* **1.** temporarily unable to speak because of emotion or shock: *We sat speechless with anger listening to the bigot's remarks.* **2.** not expressed or capable of being expressed in words: *speechless anxiety.* **3.** not having the power of speech; mute; dumb. —**speech′less·ly,** *adv.* —**speech′less·ness,** *n.*

speed (spēd) *n.* **1.** quickness of motion; swiftness: *to run with all the speed one can muster.* **2.** rate of motion; velocity: *to drive at a safe speed.* **3.** quickness or rate of action or performance: *to regulate the speed of a drill.* **4.** a gear or combination of gears, as in the transmission of an automobile. **5.** the sensitivity of a photographic film, paper, or plate to light. **6.** the amount of light that a camera lens lets through, indicated by its f number. —*v.,* **sped** or **speed·ed, speed·ing.** —*v.i.* **1.** to move or act rapidly or quickly: *to speed through one's chores.* **2.** to drive a motor vehicle faster than is safe or legally permitted. —*v.t.* to cause to move rapidly or quickly; give speed to: *We helped speed the wrapping of the presents.*

speed·boat (spēd′bōt′) *n.* a motorboat built to travel at high speeds.

speed·er (spē′dər) *n.* a person or thing that speeds, especially a person who drives a motor vehicle faster than is safe or legally permitted.

speed limit, the maximum or minimum speed that is legally permitted on a given road.

speed·om·e·ter (spē dom′i tər) *n.* a device for measuring the speed of a vehicle in miles per hour or kilometers per hour.

speed–read·ing (spēd′rē′ding) *n.* the practice of reading at a speed much faster than average and with understanding by controlling one's eye movements, skimming, concentrating on the text, and other methods.

speed·up (spēd′up′) *n.* an increase in speed, output, or work.

speed·way (spēd′wā′) *n.* **1.** a road for driving at high speeds. **2.** a track for motorcycle or automobile races.

speed·well (spēd′wel′) *n.* any of several low-growing plants having small pink, blue, or white flowers.

speed·y (spē′dē) *adj.,* **speed·i·er, speed·i·est. 1.** moving rapidly; swift: *a speedy runner.* **2.** without delay; prompt: *a speedy reply.* —**speed′i·ly,** *adv.* —**speed′i·ness,** *n.*

spe·le·ol·o·gist (spē′lē ol′ə jist) *n.* an expert in the study and exploration of caves.

spe·le·ol·o·gy (spē′lē ol′ə jē) *n.* the study and exploration of caves.

spell¹ (spel) *v.,* **spelled** or **spelt, spell·ing.** —*v.t.* **1.** to write or name the letters of (a word) in their correct order. **2.** (of letters) to form (a word): *D-o-g spells dog.* **3.** to mean; signify: *The rain spelled relief for the drought-stricken farms.* —*v.i.* to form a word or words by letters. [From the Middle English word *spellen* meaning "to read slowly, one letter at a time," from the Old French word *espeller* with the same meaning, of Germanic origin.]

 ·to spell out. to explain clearly or in detail: *to spell out exactly what is meant by a statement.*

spell² (spel) *n.* **1.** a word or phrase having magic power. **2.** a state of enchantment or fascination: *the spell of beautiful music.* [From the Old English word *spell* meaning "a story, discourse, narrative."]

spell³ (spel) *n.* **1.** a brief, indefinite period of time: *We sat outside for a spell.* **2.** a period of weather of a specified sort: *a dry spell.* **3.** an attack or bout of something, as an illness: *a dizzy spell.* —*v.t.,* **spelled, spell·ing.** to relieve by taking a turn: *The two friends spelled each other at the wheel during the long drive.* [Perhaps from the Old English word *spala* meaning "a substitute, representative." A substitute replaces a worker for "a spell."]

spell·bind (spel′bīnd′) *v.t.,* **spell·bound, spell·bind·ing.** to hold under or as if under a magic spell. —**spell′bind′er,** *n.*

spell·bound (spel′bound′) *adj.* held as if by a magic spell; entranced; rapt: *an acrobat's spellbound audience.*

spell·er (spel′ər) *n.* **1.** a person who spells words. **2.** a textbook used to teach spelling to students.

spell·ing (spel′ing) *n.* **1.** the way a word is spelled; orthography. **2.** the act of a person who spells.

Language Note

Spelling is the method we use to represent words with the letters of the alphabet. In an ideal system of spelling, each letter of the alphabet would always correspond to one and only one speech sound, and each speech sound would always be represented by one and only one letter. Such a system would be completely phonetic. Certain languages, such as Italian and German, have spelling systems that are close to being phonetic and are therefore relatively easy to learn. In other languages, including English, spelling is often not phonetic and can be quite difficult to master. The difficulties we have in spelling English are partly caused by the fact that we have a larger number of speech sounds than letters of the alphabet with which to present them. For instance, the letter *u* is used in English to represent a variety of speech sounds, as in the words *cube, rule,* u*p, busy, quite, bull, out, ought, through,* and *bury.* The reverse situation, in which a speech sound is represented by various letters and combinations of letters, is another reason that it is difficult to spell English words. The *sh* sound is represented in at least twelve different ways: s*hift, motion,* s*ure, tissue, special, machine, ocean, conscience,* sch*wa, nauseous, mansion,* and *mission.*

The irregularity of English spelling has several historical causes. Although English is a Germanic language, the alphabet that we use comes from Latin. While the alphabet was adequate for Latin, which had a smaller range of speech sounds than English, it is far from adequate for our own language. English sounds that did not have corresponding letters in the Latin alphabet were represented by combining these letters in different ways. The phonetic quality of Old English and Middle English spelling was the result of a lack of standardization; words were spelled according to the dialect and pronunciation of the writer. The invention of the printing press in the fifteenth century produced a greater degree of standardization, which, although it enabled people to read more easily, tended to fix spelling so that it could not change as pronunciation changed. Spelling remains relatively constant because it is preserved in written language in books. Spoken language, however, continually changes. The changes in pronunciation from Old English to Middle English, and then from Middle English to Modern English, were not accompanied by corresponding changes in spelling. As a result, spellings that were once phonetic now very often do not represent speech sounds. Also, the English language has borrowed a great many words from foreign languages. These words often retain their original spelling, although their pronunciation has altered. This process has given us such oddly spelled words as *beauty, gneiss,* and *psychology.*

Attempts were made to standardize English spelling in the eighteenth and nineteenth centuries, particularly by writers of dictionaries. In modern times, the greatest emphasis has been on the reforming and simplifying of spelling, rather than on standardizing. Several new alphabets have been proposed, but they have not had widespread acceptance.

One of the best-known supporters of spelling reform was the Irish writer George Bernard Shaw. To point out the irregularity of our spelling, Shaw humorously suggested that the word *fish* should be spelled *ghoti,* combining the *gh* from *cough,* the *o* from *women,* and the *ti* from *nation.* Although this spelling looks silly to us, it is not much more illogical than the spelling of many other English words. Because of this basic lack of logic and regularity in English spelling, the only way to learn to spell correctly is to learn those rules of spelling that generally hold true and to memorize the spelling of the great number of words that do not follow the rules. Using your dictionary will help you to remember these spellings and so be able to use written language correctly.

---

spelling bee, a competition that is won by the person or team spelling the most words correctly.

spelt (spelt) a past tense and past participle of **spell**[1].

spe·lunk·er (spi lung′kər) *n.* a person who explores caves. [Formed from the Greek word *spēlynx* meaning "cave" + the English suffix -*er*[1].]

spend (spend) *v.,* **spent, spend·ing.** —*v.t.* **1.** to pay out (money): *to spend ten dollars on a scarf.* **2.** to pass (time) in a specified manner or place: *to spend a week in the mountains.* **3.** to give; devote: *to spend one's energy on community activities.* **4.** to wear out: *The storm spent itself at sea.* —*v.i.* to pay out or use up money or other possessions. —**spend′er,** *n.*

spend·thrift (spend′thrift′) *n.* a person who spends money foolishly, extravagantly, or wastefully. —*adj.* lavish or wasteful; extravagant.

spent (spent) *v.* the past tense and past participle of **spend.** —*adj.* worn-out; exhausted: *a spent runner.*

sperm (spûrm) *n., pl.* **sperm** or **sperms.** **1.** a male reproductive cell; spermatozoon. Also, **sperm cell. 2.** the fluid containing the male reproductive cells; semen.

sper·ma·cet·i (spûr′mə set′ē, spûr′mə sē′tē) *n.* a white, waxy substance that comes from sperm oil, used to make cosmetics and to waterproof paper and fabrics.

sper·ma·to·phyte (spûr mat′ə fīt′) *n.* any plant that produces seeds.

sper·ma·to·zo·on (spûr′mə tə zō′ən) *n., pl.* **sper·ma·to·zo·a** (spûr′mə tə zō′ə). a male reproductive cell; male gamete; sperm.

sperm oil, a yellow oil derived from the sperm whale, used as a lubricant.

sperm whale, a large-toothed whale having a massive, barrel-shaped head. Also, **cachalot.**

spew (spū) *v.t.* to cast up, throw out, or discharge; eject; vomit: *The smokestacks of the steel plant spewed out sooty clouds of black smoke.* —*v.i.* to vomit. —*n.* something that is spewed.

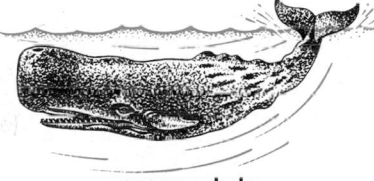

sperm whale

sp. gr., specific gravity.

---

at; āpe; fär; câre; end; mē; it; īce; pîerce; hot; ōld; sông, fôrk; oil; out; up; ūse; rūle; pull; tûrn; chin; sing; shop; thin; **th**is; hw in white; zh in treasure. The symbol ə stands for the unstressed vowel sound heard in about, taken, pencil, lemon, and circus.

sphag·num (sfag′nəm) *n.* any of a group of pale green mosses found growing in bogs and marshes.

sphere (sfîr) *n.* **1.** a round, three-dimensional figure having all the points of its surface at an equal distance from the center. **2.** a body having this shape; ball; globe. **3.** a field, extent, or range of interest, influence, knowledge, or activity: *Chemistry is outside my sphere of knowledge.* **4.** social class, rank, or position: *one's sphere in society.* **5.** any of various celestial bodies, such as stars or planets. **6.** see **celestial sphere.**

spher·i·cal (sfer′i kəl, sfîr′i kəl) *adj.* **1.** shaped like a sphere; globular: *a spherical shape.* **2.** of or relating to a sphere or spheres. —**spher′i·cal·ly,** *adv.*

sphe·roid (sfîr′oid) *n.* a three-dimensional figure that resembles a sphere in shape but is not perfectly round.

sphinc·ter (sfingk′tər) *n.* a circular band of muscle that surrounds a passage or opening in the body and contracts or expands to close or open it.

the Sphinx

sphinx (sfingks) *n., pl.* **sphinx·es** or **sphin·ges** (sfin′jēz). **1.** *Egyptian Mythology.* a creature having the head of a human and the body of a lion. **2. the Sphinx.** a large statue of this creature at Giza in Egypt. **3. Sphinx.** *Greek Mythology.* a winged monster having the head of a woman and the body of a lion, who asked a riddle and killed all those who could not guess the answer. **4.** a person who is mysterious and hard to understand.

sphyg·mo·ma·nom·e·ter (sfig′mō mə nom′i tər) *n.* an instrument for measuring blood pressure in the arteries. It is usually attached to an inflatable cuff, which is wrapped around the upper arm, inflated, and then slowly deflated while the pulse in the arm is monitored with a stethoscope.

spice (spīs) *n.* **1.** any of various substances used to season food, such as pepper and cloves. Spices come from plants. **2.** something that adds zest or interest: *Variety is the spice of life.* —*v.t.,* **spiced, spic·ing. 1.** to season with a spice or spices. **2.** to add zest or interest to: *to spice one's conversation with funny stories.*

spice·bush (spīs′bush′) *n., pl.* **spice·bush·es.** a shrub found in swamps in eastern North America, bearing clusters of small yellowish flowers.

spick–and–span (spik′ən span′) *adj.* fresh, neat, and clean: *a spick-and-span house.*

spic·ule (spik′ūl) *n.* a small needlelike structure that forms the skeleton of some sponges and other aquatic invertebrates.

spic·y (spī′sē) *adj.,* **spic·i·er, spic·i·est. 1.** seasoned with spice: *spicy food.* **2.** resembling spice; pungent or fragrant: *The soap has a spicy smell.* **3.** slightly improper; risqué: *a spicy story.* —**spic′i·ness,** *n.*

spi·der (spī′dər) *n.* any of a group of small animals without backbones, having a body divided into two parts and four pairs of legs. Spiders are able to spin silken threads for making cocoons and webs. They are classified as arachnids. —**spi′der·like′,** *adj.*

spider monkey, a monkey of tropical America, having long limbs and a long tail that can be used for gripping.

spi·der·web (spī′dər web′) *n.* a web of silken threads spun by a spider.

spi·der·y (spī′də rē) *adj.* resembling a spider or a spider's web; long and thin or delicate: *spidery handwriting, spidery legs.*

spider

spied (spīd) the past tense and past participle of **spy.**

spiel (spēl, shpēl) *n. Slang.* a speech, often long or extravagant, intended to persuade or to sell; pitch: *a sales spiel in a commercial.* [From the German word *spiel* meaning "game," from the German word *spielen* "to play."]

spiff·y (spif′ē) *adj.* **spiff·i·er, spiff·i·est.** *Slang.* smart in dress or appearance; dapper; neat: *You look very spiffy in that new suit.*

spig·ot (spig′ət) *n.* **1.** another word for **faucet. 2.** a small wooden plug or peg for stopping the opening of a barrel or cask.

spike¹ (spīk) *n.* **1.** a large, heavy nail. **2.** any sharp-pointed object or projection. **3.** one of several sharp-pointed metal projections attached to the sole and heel of a shoe to prevent slipping, worn in golf, baseball, track and field, and other sports. —*v.t.,* **spiked, spik·ing. 1.** to fasten or provide with spikes: *to spike railroad ties together.* **2.** to cut or pierce with a sharp-pointed object. **3.** to stand in the way of or put an end to; block; thwart: *to spike a rumor before it spreads.* [From the Middle English word *spyke* meaning "a large nail," probably of Scandinavian origin.]

spike² (spīk) *n.* **1.** an ear of grain. **2.** a long cluster of flowers in which the flowers grow along a single stalk. [From the Latin word *spica* meaning "a point" or "ear of grain."]

spike·let (spīk′lit) *n.* a small cluster of flowers, as on the spike of a stalk of grass.

spike·nard (spīk′nərd, spīk′närd) *n.* **1.** an East Indian plant having fragrant roots and stems. In ancient times a sweet-smelling ointment was made from this plant. **2.** a woodland herb of eastern North America, having spicy, aromatic roots and clusters of small greenish flowers.

spik·y (spī′kē) *adj.* **1.** having a spike or spikes: *a spiky fence.* **2.** resembling a spike: *spiky thorns.*

spile (spīl) *n.* **1.** a wooden plug for stopping the opening of a barrel or cask. **2.** a small spout for taking sap from a sugar maple. **3.** a strong post driven into the ground as a support; pile. —*v.t.,* **spiled, spil·ing.** to support or stop up with a spile.

spill¹ (spil) *v.,* **spilled** or **spilt, spill·ing.** —*v.t.* **1.** to cause or allow (something) to fall, flow, or run out of a container: *to spill gravy on a tablecloth, to spill cereal from a box.* **2.** to shed (blood). **3.** *Informal.* to cause to tumble or fall off something. **4.** *Informal.* to reveal; divulge: *to spill a secret.* —*v.i.* to flow or run out: *Water spilled all over the floor. The crowd spilled into the street.* —*n.* **1.** the act of spilling. **2.** the amount spilled: *The oil spill covered several miles of the bay.* **3.** *Informal.* a tumble or fall: *to take a bad spill off a bike.* [From the Middle English word *spillen* meaning "to spill a liquid," "to shed blood," or "to ruin, spoil," from the Old English word *spillan* "to destroy."]

spill² (spil) *n.* a thin strip of wood or folded piece of paper, used to light a fire. [Of uncertain origin.]

spill·way (spil′wā′) *n.* a channel that allows surplus water to run off, as from a reservoir.

spilt (spilt) a past tense and past participle of **spill¹**.

spin (spin) *v.*, **spun, spin·ning.** —*v.t.* **1.** to draw out and twist (fibers) into thread. **2.** to form or make (thread) in this way. **3.** to form (a silken thread, web, or cocoon) from a substance that is secreted from the body and hardens when exposed to air, as spiders and silkworms do. **4.** to cause to turn or revolve rapidly; twirl: *The child was spinning a top.* **5.** to extend in length or time; prolong; draw out (often with *out*): *They spun out the debate on minor points.* **6.** to tell: *to spin ghost stories.* —*v.i.* **1.** to turn or revolve rapidly; whirl: *The dancers spun to the music.* **2.** to make by spinning, as thread. **3.** to have a sensation of revolving rapidly; feel dizzy: *All that noise made my head spin.* **4.** to go or move rapidly: *The racing car spun into the lead.* —*n.* **1.** the act of spinning or the state of being spun: *the spin of a wheel.* **2.** a short ride in a motor vehicle, as for pleasure. **3.** another word for **tailspin.**

spin·ach (spin′ich) *n.* **1.** the dark green leaves of a garden plant, eaten as a vegetable, either cooked or raw. **2.** the plant itself, grown in many temperate regions.

spi·nal (spī′nəl) *adj.* of, relating to, or affecting the spinal column or the spinal cord: *a spinal injury.* —*n.* an anesthetic injected into the spinal column, which makes a person insensible to pain in part of the body while remaining conscious: *The patient was given a spinal before the surgery.*

spinal column, a series of bones joined in a column that encloses the spinal cord and forms the supporting structure of the body. Also, **spine, backbone.**

spinal cord, a thick band of nerve tissue extending down from the brain through the spinal column. The spinal cord conducts impulses to and from the brain and acts as a center for simple reflexes.

spin·dle (spin′dəl) *n.* **1.** a round, tapered stick weighted at one end and turned by hand, used to twist fibers into thread. **2.** any rod that turns or serves as an axis on which something turns, such as a shaft or axle. **3.** a spike set upright in a base for holding papers. **4.** *Biology.* a mass of fibers formed between the centrioles, along which the chromosomes move during cell division. —*v.,*

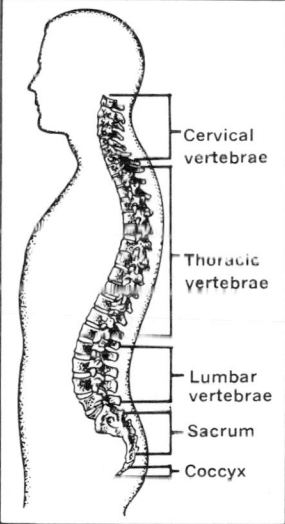

spinal column

spin·dled, spin·dling. —*v.i.* to grow into a long, slender stalk, shape, or body. —*v.t.* **1.** to form into a spindle. **2.** to make holes in (paper) with or as if with a spindle.

spin·dle–leg·ged (spin′dəl leg′id, spin′dəl legd′) *adj.* having spindlelegs. Also, **spin·dle-shanked** (spin′dəl-shangkt′).

spin·dle·legs (spin′dəl legz′) *sing. n. Informal.* a person with long, slim legs. Also, **spin·dle·shanks** (spin′dəl shangks′).

spin·dling (spind′ling) *adj.* tall and slender: *spindling pines.*

spin·dly (spind′lē) *adj.*, **spin·dli·er, spin·dli·est.** having a tall, slender shape; spindling: *a spindly basketball player.*

spin·drift (spin′drift′) *n.* the spray blown from the sea by heavy winds. Also, **spoondrift.**

spine (spīn) *n.* **1.** see **spinal column. 2.** anything resembling or functioning as a backbone, such as the back of a book. **3.** any stiff, pointed projection on a plant or animal, such as a thorn, or the quill of a porcupine.

spine·less (spīn′lis) *adj.* **1.** lacking a spinal column; invertebrate. **2.** of a plant or animal, lacking stiff, pointed projections. **3.** lacking or showing a lack of courage or willpower: *a spineless hypocrite, a spineless decision.* —**spine′less·ly,** *adv.* —**spine′less·ness,** *n.*

spin·et (spin′it) *n.* **1.** a stringed keyboard instrument resembling a small harpsichord, having one keyboard and one string for each musical tone. **2.** a small upright piano.

spin·na·ker (spin′ə kər) *n.* a large sail that billows out when filled, used on a boat when sailing before the wind.

spin·ner·et (spin′ə ret′) *n.* an organ by which various animals without backbones, such as spiders and silkworms, spin silken threads.

spinning jenny, a hand-operated spinning machine having more than one spindle so that a number of threads can be spun at once.

spinning wheel, a machine consisting of a large wheel and a spindle, used to spin fibers into thread.

spin–off (spin′ôf′) *also,* **spin·off.** *n.* **1.** a work derived from an earlier one,

spinnaker

as a television series based on a character or situation that originated in a successful earlier series. **2.** a product or enterprise derived from another field: *This new plastic used in eyeglass lenses is a spin-off of the technology developed for the aerospace industry.*

spin·ster (spin′stər) *n.* an older woman who has never been married.

spin·y (spī′nē) *adj.*, **spin·i·er, spin·i·est.** **1.** having or covered with spines. **2.** resembling a spine or thorn; sharp.

spiny anteater, another term for **echidna.**

spiny lobster, a shellfish that can be eaten, similar to the common lobster, but having sharp spines on the body and lacking large pincer claws. Also, **rock lobster.**

spi·ra·cle (spī′rə kəl, spir′ə kəl) *n.* an opening for breathing, such as one of the paired openings on the abdomen of an insect or spider or the blowhole of a whale.

spi·ral (spī′rəl) *n.* **1.** a plane curve traced by a point moving around a fixed point while continuously increasing or decreasing its distance from it. **2.** a three-dimensional curve that winds around the surface of a cylinder or cone; helix. **3.** something having the shape or form of a spiral. **4.** a slow, continuous increase or decrease: *the upward spiral of prices.* —*adj.* having the shape or form of a spiral: *a spiral staircase.* —*v.i., v.t.,* **spi·raled, spi·ral·ing;** *also, British,* **spi·ralled, spi·ral·ling.** to take or cause to take a spiral form or course: *Smoke from the campfire spiraled into the treetops.* —**spi′ral·ly,** *adv.*

at; āpe; fär; câre; end; mē; it; īce; pîerce; hot; ōld; sông, fôrk; oil; out; up; ūse; rüle; pull; tûrn; chin; sing; shop; thin; this; hw in white; zh in treasure. The symbol ə stands for the unstressed vowel sound heard in about, taken, pencil, lemon, and circus.

S

spire¹ (spīr) *n.* **1.** a tall structure that tapers to a point, built on the top of a tower. **2.** any tapering and pointed object or formation. [From the Old English word *spīr* meaning "the spiked top of a plant."]

spire² (spīr) *n.* **1.** a spiral or single twist of a spiral. **2.** the upper portion of a spiral shell. [From the Latin word *spira* meaning "a coil, something wound," from the Greek word *speira* "a coil, something wound."]

spi·ril·lum (spī ril′əm) *n., pl.* **spi·ril·la** (spī-ril′ə). any of a genus of spiral-shaped bacteria that move using flagella, some of which cause a fever and are spread by rats. See **bacteria** for illustration.

spir·it (spir′it) *n.* **1.** the part of humans that is not physical, and is thought to control their thoughts and feelings, and to live forever; soul. **2.** the moral, mental, or emotional part of human nature: *to be concerned with things of the spirit.* **3.** a supernatural being, often thought to haunt living people; specter; ghost. **4.** a person who has a certain character or temperament: *a noble spirit, a brave spirit.* **5.** a characteristic quality, mood, or tendency: *the adventurous spirit of an explorer.* **6.** the real meaning or intent: *the spirit of the law.* **7.** liveliness: *to dance with spirit.* **8.** enthusiasm, devotion, and loyalty: *school spirit.* **9. spirits.** a mental state or attitude: *The team members were in good spirits after winning the game.* **10.** *usually,* **spirits.** any distilled alcoholic beverage. —*v.t.* to remove or carry off secretly or mysteriously: *Someone spirited the dog away during the night.*

spir·it·ed (spir′i tid) *adj.* full of spirit; lively; vigorous: *a spirited horse.* —**spir′it·ed·ly,** *adv.* —**spir′it·ed·ness,** *n.*

spir·it·less (spir′it lis) *adj.* without enthusiasm or energy; lacking spirit; listless.

spir·i·tu·al (spir′i chü əl) *adj.* **1.** of or relating to the human soul. **2.** of, relating to, or concerned with things of the spirit. **3.** of, relating to, or concerned with religious matters; sacred. —*n.* a religious folk song or hymn, especially one originated by blacks in the southern United States. —**spir′i·tu·al·ly,** *adv.*

spir·i·tu·al·ism (spir′i chü ə liz′əm) *n.* the belief that the dead communicate with the living, especially through a medium.

spir·i·tu·al·ist (spir′i chü ə list) *n.* a person who believes in or supports spiritualism. —**spir′i·tu·al·is′tic,** *adj.*

spir·i·tu·al·i·ty (spir′i chü al′i tē) *n., pl.* **spir·i·tu·al·i·ties.** devotion to or concern with things of the spirit rather than with material things; state or quality of being spiritual.

spir·i·tu·ous (spir′i chü əs) *adj.* **1.** containing alcohol. **2.** produced by distillation.

spi·ro·chete (spī′rə kēt′) *n.* any of a large family of spiral-shaped bacteria that live in stagnant water and have flagella. The spirochete family includes the organism that causes syphilis.

spi·ro·gy·ra (spī′rə jī′rə) *n.* any of various freshwater green algae having spiral chloroplasts that are sometimes visible as pond scums.

spirt (spûrt) another spelling of **spurt.**

spit¹ (spit) *v.,* **spit** or **spat, spit·ting.** —*v.i.* **1.** to force out saliva from the mouth. **2.** to make a popping or hissing noise, as hot oil or grease. —*v.t.* **1.** to force out from the mouth. **2.** to force out or utter in a violent or noisy manner: *to spit insults.* —*n.* **1.** saliva. **2.** the act of spitting. [From the Old English word *spyttan* with the same meaning.] —**spit′ter,** *n.*

spire¹
(def. 1)

spit² (spit) *n.* **1.** a slender, pointed rod on which meat is roasted over a fire. **2.** a narrow point of land extending into the sea. —*v.t.,* **spit·ted, spit·ting.** to pierce or thrust through with a spit. [From the Old English word *spitu* meaning this rod.]

spit·ball (spit′bôl′) *n.* **1.** a wad of folded and chewed paper. **2.** an illegal pitch in baseball, in which the ball is moistened, as with saliva, before being thrown.

spite (spīt) *n.* a feeling of ill will or resentment toward another; malice: *to spread rumors out of spite.* —*v.t.,* **spit·ed, spit·ing.** to irritate, hurt, or humiliate: *Those two argue just to spite each other.*

·**in spite of.** regardless; despite: *We went sailing in spite of the bad weather.*

spite·ful (spīt′fəl) *adj.* filled with spite; malicious. —**spite′ful·ly,** *adv.* —**spite′ful·ness,** *n.*

spit·fire (spit′fīr′) *n.* a quick-tempered, fiery person.

spitting image, exact likeness: *a child who is the spitting image of a parent.*

spit·tle (spit′əl) *n.* saliva; spit.

spit·toon (spi tün′) *n.* a receptacle for spit; cuspidor.

spitz (spits) *n., pl.* **spitz·es.** a small, stocky dog having a pointed muzzle, small, erect ears, a fluffy tail that curls over the back, and a thick white or spotted coat.

splash (splash) *v.t.* **1.** to scatter or throw (a liquid) about: *to splash paint on the floor.* **2.** to wet, soil, or stain with a liquid or other substance by scattering or throwing: *to splash one's face with water. A passing car splashed my coat with mud.* **3.** to mark or decorate by or as if by splashing: *The wallpaper was splashed with bright colors.* —*v.i.* **1.** to cause a liquid to scatter about. **2.** to fall, strike, or move with a splash or splashes: *The diver splashed into the water.* —*n., pl.* **splash·es.** **1.** the act or sound of splashing: *The stone hit the water with a splash.* **2.** an irregular spot or patch, as of color: *The horse had a splash of white on its forehead.* **3.** a sensation or stir: *The playwright made quite a splash on Broadway.* —**splash′er,** *n.*

·**to splash down. a.** (of a spacecraft or missile) to land in a body of water. **b.** to land in a body of water in a spacecraft: *The astronauts splashed down in the Pacific.*

splash·down (splash′doun′) *n.* the landing of a spacecraft in a body of water.

splash·y (splash′ē) *adj.,* **splash·i·er, splash·i·est.** **1.** making a splash or splashes. **2.** full of irregular spots or patches; blotchy; spotty. **3.** creating a sensation or stir; showy: *a splashy display of colors.*

splat·ter (splat′ər) *v., n.* another word for **spatter.**

splay (splā) *adj.* **1.** spread or spreading out; broad. **2.** awkward or awkwardly formed; clumsy. —*n.* a sloping surface, especially in the opening of a window or door. —*v.t.* **1.** to spread out; extend. **2.** to make slanting; bevel.

spleen (splēn) *n.* **1.** a large, oval organ near the stomach that serves to produce white blood cells, break down old red blood cells, and filter blood. **2.** ill temper; malice; spite: *to be full of spleen.*

splen·did (splen′did) *adj.* **1.** having or marked by brilliance or magnificence: *a splendid display of colors, the splendid interior of a palace.* **2.** impressive; illustrious; glorious: *a splendid achievement.* **3.** very good; excellent: *Having a surprise party was a splendid idea.* [From the Latin word *splendidus* meaning "bright, shining," from the word *splendēre* "to shine, be radiant."] —**splen′did·ly,** *adv.* —**splen′did·ness,** *n.*

splay *(n.)*

splen·dor (splen'dər) n. **1.** a great display, as of riches or beautiful objects; magnificence; pomp: *the splendor of the royal palace.* **2.** great brightness; brilliance: *the splendor of the setting sun.*

sple·net·ic (spli net'ik) adj. **1.** of or relating to the spleen. **2.** ill-tempered; malicious; spiteful.

splice (splīs) v.t., **spliced, splic·ing. 1.** to unite or join by weaving together the strands of the ends of: *to splice two ropes.* **2.** to join together (film or magnetic tape) at the ends. **3.** to join together (pieces of timber) by overlapping. **4.** to join (genes or DNA segments) from different organisms to form new genetic combinations. —n. the joint or union made by splicing. —**splic'er,** n.

splint (splint) n. **1.** a device made of wood, metal, or other material, used to hold in place and protect a fractured, dislocated, or broken bone. **2.** a thin, flexible strip of wood, such as is used in weaving baskets.

splin·ter (splin'tər) n. a thin, sharp, usually small piece chipped or broken off from something hard or brittle. —v.t., v.i. to break or split into splinters. —adj. of or pertaining to people who break away from the main body because of disagreement: *a splinter group of a political party.* —**splin'ter·y,** adj.

split (split) v., **split, split·ting.** —v.t. **1.** to break apart or divide lengthwise or in layers: *to split logs.* **2.** to divide or break up into separate parts or portions: *The three partners split the profits of the business.* **3.** to burst or tear open or apart: *to bend over and split one's pants at the seams.* **4.** to divide (the stock of a company) into a larger number of shares. —v.i. **1.** to break apart lengthwise or in layers: *Slate and mica split easily.* **2.** to become divided; separate: *The search party split into two groups.* **3.** (of stock) to be or become split. —n. **1.** the act of splitting or the state of being split. **2.** a division in a group: *The controversial issue caused a split in the political party.* **3.** also, **splits.** a movement or exercise in dancing or calisthenics in which a person slides to the floor or leaps in the air with the legs spread apart. —adj. **1.** divided lengthwise or in layers. **2.** broken up; separated: *The miners worked a split shift of four hours each.* —**split'ter,** n.

split infinitive, an infinitive having a word or phrase placed between *to* and the verb. For example: *They decided to not work at all.*

split–lev·el (split'lev'əl) adj. having two or more levels separated by half flights of stairs: *a split level house.* —n. a house designed in this way.

split second, an extremely brief period of time; instant.

split ticket 1. a ballot cast for candidates of more than one political party. **2.** a slate of candidates from more than one political party.

split·ting (split'ing) adj. very severe: *a splitting headache.*

splotch (sploch) n., pl. **splotch·es.** a large, irregular spot; blot; stain. —v.t. to mark or cover with splotches. —**splotch'y,** adj.

splurge (splûrj) v.i., **splurged, splurg·ing.** to spend money with little or no attention to cost; indulge oneself in spending too much money: *to splurge on expensive clothes.* —n. the act or period of spending too much money.

splut·ter (splut'ər) v.i. **1.** to speak in a rapid, indistinct way, as when confused, angry, or excited. **2.** to make popping or hissing sounds, as food being fried; sputter. —v.t. to utter or express indistinctly: *to splutter an apology.* —n. a spluttering noise. —**splut'ter·er,** n.

spoil (spoil) v., **spoiled** or **spoilt, spoil·ing.** —v.t. **1.** to cause damage or harm to (something); injure or ruin: *The weeds spoiled the look of the lawn. A snowstorm spoiled our plans for the weekend.* **2.** to weaken or damage the character of: *to spoil a child.* —v.i. to become unfit for

use: *The meat spoiled when we left it out of the refrigerator all night.* —n. usually, **spoils. 1.** goods or property seized by force, especially in war; booty; plunder. **2.** jobs or other favors given to supporters of a victorious political party.

·to be spoiling for. to be eager or anxious for, as a fight.

spoil·age (spoi'lij) n. **1.** the act of spoiling or the state of being spoiled. **2.** something that has spoiled. **3.** the amount that has spoiled.

spoil·er (spoi'lər) n. a person or thing that causes spoilage.

spoil·sport (spoil'spôrt') n. a person whose behavior or attitude spoils the pleasure of others.

spoils system, the system or practice of distributing jobs or other favors to supporters of a victorious political party.

spoilt (spoilt) a past tense and past participle of **spoil.**

spoke[1] (spōk) a past tense of **speak.**

spoke[2] (spōk) n. **1.** one of the bars or rods that connect the rim of a wheel to its hub. **2.** a rung of a ladder. [From the Old English word *spāca* meaning this part of a wheel.]

spo·ken (spō'kən) v. the past participle of **speak.** —adj. **1.** uttered or expressed in speech; oral: *a spoken promise.* **2.** speaking in a certain way. ▲ used in combination: *a well-spoken person, a soft-spoken person.*

Language Note

Spoken language and **written language** are often quite different. In our own development as children, as well as in the historical development of language, speech comes before writing.

Besides seeming more natural, spoken language can be accompanied by gestures, facial expressions, and, most important, changes in the tone and pitch of the voice that help us to communicate our ideas clearly. The vocabulary of spoken language tends to be less formal than that of written language, often containing a great many colorful idioms and slang terms.

When spoken language acquires the kind of permanent quality that written language has, as when a person speaks into the microphone of a tape recorder, a more formal way of speaking is often adopted. Spoken language also becomes more like written language when gestures and expressions cannot be used to convey meaning, as when a person is speaking on the telephone to someone who obviously cannot see him or her.

In earlier times, written language was considered to be superior to the spoken tongue, and it was believed that the proper standard for language was the written form. More recently, people have begun to reject the formality of written language as the only standard for communication. Written language will always be more restrictive than spoken language because conventions of spelling and punctuation are necessary for the writer to be understood.

---

spoke·shave (spōk'shāv') n. a carpenter's tool having a blade between two handles, used to plane wood.

---

at; āpe; fär; câre; end; mē; it; īce; pîerce; hot; ōld; sông, fôrk; oil; out; up; ūse; rüle; pull; tûrn; chin; sing; shop; thin; this; hw in white; zh in treasure. The symbol ə stands for the unstressed vowel sound heard in about, taken, pencil, lemon, and circus.

S

909

spokes·man (spōks′mən) *n., pl.* **spokes·men** (spōks′-mən). a person who speaks on behalf of another person or a group.

spokes·per·son (spōks′pûr′sən) *n.* a person who speaks on behalf of another or others, as for a company or organization.

spokes·wom·an (spōks′wum′ən) *n., pl.* **spokes-wom·en** (spōks′wim′ən). a woman who speaks on behalf of another person or a group.

sponge (spunj) *n.* **1.** any of a large group of water animals that live in colonies attached to rocks or other solid objects and have porous bodies that absorb water easily. Sponges are of various sizes, shapes, and colors. **2.** the absorbent skeleton of certain sponges, used for washing or other purposes. **3.** an article made from any of various substances, such as rubber or plastic, resembling this skeleton in structure or use. **4.** an absorbent pad, as of gauze or prepared cotton, used in surgery. **5.** *Informal.* another word for **sponger** (*def. 1*). —*v.*, **sponged, spong·ing.** —*v.t.* **1.** to cleanse or rub with a wet sponge: *to sponge a floor.* **2.** to remove with a sponge: *to sponge crayon marks off a wall.* **3.** to absorb. **4.** *Informal.* to get without paying: *to sponge a meal from someone.* —*v.i.* **1.** to absorb liquid, as a sponge. **2.** *Informal.* to live at the expense of another or others: *to sponge off a rich relative.*

sponge bath, a bath taken by washing with a wet sponge or damp cloth without the use of a shower or bathtub.

sponge cake, a light cake made with eggs, sugar, flour, and flavoring, but without shortening.

spong·er (spun′jər) *n.* **1.** *Informal.* a person who makes a practice of living at the expense of another or others. Also, **sponge.** **2.** a person or boat that gathers sponges.

spon·gy (spun′jē) *adj.*, **spon·gi·er, spon·gi·est.** of or resembling a sponge; porous; absorbent. —**spon′gi·ness,** *n.*

spon·sor (spon′sər) *n.* **1.** a person who assumes responsibility or support for another person or thing. **2.** a person or organization that finances some event or entertainment, such as a radio or television program. **3.** a person who answers for an infant at baptism, making the required promises and professions of faith; godfather or godmother. —*v.t.* to act as sponsor for.

spon·sor·ship (spon′sər ship′) *n.* the act of sponsoring.

spon·ta·ne·i·ty (spon′tə nē′i tē, spon′tə nā′i tē) *n.* the fact, quality, or condition of being spontaneous.

spon·ta·ne·ous (spon tā′nē əs) *adj.* **1.** arising from or caused by a natural impulse or desire; not planned or forced: *spontaneous laughter.* **2.** arising or happening without an outside cause; having an internal cause or origin. —**spon·ta′ne·ous·ly,** *adv.*

spontaneous combustion, the bursting into flames of something, such as oily rags, because of the buildup of heat from slow oxidation.

spoof (spüf) *Informal. n.* **1.** a light parody; takeoff. **2.** a trick or deception; hoax. —*v.t.* **1.** to do a parody or spoof of; satirize lightly. **2.** to trick or deceive.

spook (spük) *Informal. n.* a ghost; specter. —*v.t.* to frighten; scare.

spook·y (spü′kē) *adj.*, **spook·i·er, spook·i·est.** *Informal.* causing fear or uneasiness; scary: *a spooky old ruin.*

spool (spül) *n.* **1.** a small piece of wood, plastic, or other material shaped like a cylinder, around which thread, wire, or tape may be wound. **2.** the amount of thread, wire, or tape wound on a spool. —*v.t.* to wind on a spool.

spoon (spün) *n.* **1.** a wooden, metal, or plastic utensil consisting of a handle with a small, shallow bowl at the end, used in preparing, serving, or eating food. **2.** something resembling this in shape or function. —*v.t.* to lift or transfer with a spoon: *to spoon one's soup into the mouth.*

spoon·bill (spün′bil′) *n.* any of several long-legged wading birds having a long, flat bill with a tip shaped like a spoon.

spoon·drift (spün′drift′) *n.* another word for **spindrift.**

spoon–feed (spün′fēd′) *v.t.*, **spoon-fed, spoon-feed·ing. 1.** to feed with a spoon: *to spoon-feed a baby.* **2.** to spoil by indulging too much; pamper; coddle: *to spoon-feed a misman-aged business with large government loans.* **3.** to teach or treat in a way that does not allow for independent thought and action: *to spoon-feed students.*

spoon·ful (spün′ful′) *n., pl.* **spoon·fuls.** the amount that can be held by a spoon: *three spoonfuls of baking soda.*

spoonbill

spoor (spür) *n.* a track or trail, especially of a wild animal.

spo·rad·ic (spə rad′ik) *adj.* **1.** happening from time to time; occasional: *sporadic bursts of energy.* **2.** appearing by itself in widely separate places. **3.** (of a disease) occurring in isolated cases; not epidemic. —**spo·rad′i·cal·ly,** *adv.*

spo·ran·gi·um (spə ran′jē əm) *n., pl.* **spo·ran·gi·a** (spə ran′jē ə). in certain plants, fungi, algae, and bacteria, a sac in which spores are produced; spore case.

spore (spôr) *n.* **1.** a tiny reproductive body formed by some plants and microscopic animals. **2.** a bacterial cell that has grown a tough outer wall that is highly resistant to chemicals, heat, or cold.

spore case, another term for **sporangium.**

spo·ro·phyte (spôr′ə fīt′) *n.* in the life cycle of plants, a plant or generation of plants in which asexual spores are produced.

spo·ro·zo·an (spôr′ə zō′ən) *n.* any of a group of parasitic protozoans that produce spores, such as the plasmodium that causes malaria. —*adj.* of, relating to, or designating this group.

spor·ran (spôr′ən, spor′ən) *n.* a large pouch or purse worn from the belt in front of a kilt.

sport (spôrt) *n.* **1.** any game that requires physical activity and involves some skill, such as baseball, bowling, tennis, golf, or fishing. **2.** any pastime or activity that provides pleasure or recreation; amusement; diversion: *Running for fun is a great sport.* **3.** playfulness or jest; fun: *I said that only in sport and did not mean to hurt your feelings.* **4.** *Informal.* **a.** a person with regard to his or her ability to accept teasing, criticism, or defeat: *a good sport.* **b.** a person who acts or plays fairly and accepts defeat graciously: *to be a real sport.* —*v.i.* **1.** to amuse oneself; play; frolic. **2.** to make fun; treat lightly; joke; trifle. —*v.t. Informal.* to wear, display, or show off: *to sport a*

new suit, to sport a mustache. —*adj.* also, **sports.**
1. of or relating to sports: *a sports event.* **2.** suitable for informal wear: *sport clothes.*

sport·ing (spôr′ting) *adj.* **1.** of, relating to, or suitable for sports: *a sporting event.* **2.** characteristic of a sportsman or sportswoman; fair: *That was very sporting of you.* **3.** of or relating to gambling, especially on a sports event. **4.** *Informal.* involving risk: *a sporting chance.* —**sport′ing·ly,** *adv.*

spor·tive (spôr′tiv) *adj.* frolicsome; playful; lively. —**spor′tive·ly,** *adv.* —**spor′tive·ness,** *n.*

sports car, a small, low automobile capable of high speeds, usually seating two passengers.

sports·cast (spôrts′kast′) *n.* a radio or television broadcast of a sports event. —**sports′cast·er,** *n.*

sports·man (spôrts′mən) *n., pl.* **sports·men** (spôrts′mən). **1.** a person who is interested in or engages in sports, especially outdoor sports, such as fishing, hunting, or riding. **2.** a person who plays fairly and accepts defeat graciously. —**sports′man·like′,** *adj.*

sports·man·ship (spôrts′mən ship′) *n.* **1.** conduct worthy of a sportsman or sportswoman, such as fair play or the ability to accept defeat graciously. **2.** skill in sports.

sports·wear (spôrts′wâr′) *n.* clothing designed for informal wear.

sports·wom·an (spôrts′wŭm′ən) *n., pl.* **sports·wom·en** (spôrts′wim′ən). **1.** a woman who is interested in or engages in sports, especially outdoor sports. **2.** a woman who plays fairly and accepts defeat graciously.

sports·writ·er (spôrts′rī′tər) *n.* a person who writes about sports or sports events, especially for a newspaper or magazine.

sport·y (spôr′tē) *adj.,* **sport·i·er, sport·i·est.** *Informal.* **1.** characteristic of a sportsman or sportswoman; sporting. **2.** loud or flashy, especially in dress.

spot (spot) *n.* **1.** a difference in color or texture of an area, produced by dirt or other foreign matter: *The mechanic's shirt was covered with spots of grease.* **2.** a flaw or blemish: *a spot on one's reputation.* **3.** a small mark or part differing from the surrounding area, as in color or material: *My dog is white with black spots.* **4.** place; location: *This is a pleasant spot for a picnic.* —*v.,* **spot·ted, spot·ting.** —*v.t.* **1.** to mark with a spot or spots: *The mud spotted the rug.* **2.** to locate or pick out with the eyes; recognize: *We spotted them easily in the crowd.* **3.** to blemish; disgrace: *to spot a person's reputation.* **4.** to place in a particular location. —*v.i.* to become spotted: *This fabric will spot easily.* —*adj.* paid on delivery: *spot cash.*

   ·**in a spot.** in a difficult, disagreeable, or embarrassing situation.

   ·**on the spot. a.** at the place indicated: *We were on the spot a long time before the parade began.* **b.** at once; immediately: *The seller demanded payment on the spot.* **c.** in an awkward position: *to put someone on the spot by asking a personal question.*

   ·**to hit the spot.** *Informal.* to be exactly right or exactly what is needed: *A cold drink hits the spot on a hot day.*

spot–check (spot′chek′) *v.t.* to make a quick examination of samples selected at random.

spot check, a quick check of samples selected at random.

spot·less (spot′lis) *adj.* **1.** absolutely clean; immaculate: *a spotless kitchen.* **2.** having no flaws or blemishes: *a spotless reputation.* —**spot′less·ly,** *adv.* —**spot′less·ness,** *n.*

spot·light (spot′līt′) *n.* **1.** a strong beam of light shone on a particular person, place, or object, as on a performer in a theater. **2.** a lamp projecting such a light. **3.** public attention: *The scientists were in the spotlight after their unexpected discovery.*

spot·ted (spot′id) *adj.* marked or covered with spots.

spot·ty (spot′ē) *adj.,* **spot·ti·er, spot·ti·est. 1.** marked or covered with spots; spotted. **2.** not regular or consistent: *spotty attendance.* —**spot′ti·ly,** *adv.* —**spot′ti·ness,** *n.*

spouse (spous) *n.* a married person; husband or wife.

spout (spout) *v.t.* **1.** to force out (a liquid) in a stream or spray; spurt: *The elephant spouted water from its trunk.* **2.** *Informal.* to say in a wordy, conceited manner: *They are always spouting advice to other people.* —*v.i.* **1.** to gush or pour out: *Water spouted from the fire hydrant.* **2.** to discharge a liquid continuously or in spurts. **3.** *Informal.* to speak in a wordy, conceited manner (usually with *off*): *to spout off about one's accomplishments.* —*n.* **1.** a tube or lip projecting from a vessel that channels liquid when it is poured: *the spout of a teapot.* **2.** a faucet or similar device through which liquid flows. **3.** a jet or column, as of water. —**spout′er,** *n.*

sprain (sprān) *n.* an injury caused by a violent or sudden wrenching or twisting of the ligaments around a joint: *to suffer a wrist sprain.* —*v.t.* to cause a sprain in: *to trip and sprain an ankle.*

sprang (sprang) a past tense of **spring.**

sprat (sprat) *n.* **1.** a bluish green saltwater fish found off the Atlantic coast of Europe, used for food. **2.** any of various related fish, such as a young herring.

sprawl (sprôl) *v.i.* **1.** to lie or sit with the body and limbs stretched out in an awkward or careless manner: *The tired swimmers sprawled on the sand.* **2.** to spread out in a straggling manner: *Dozens of houses sprawled across the hillside.* —*v.t.* to cause to spread out in an awkward, careless, or straggling manner. —*n.* the act or position of sprawling.

spray¹ (sprā) *n.* **1.** water or other liquid in the form of fine particles or droplets: *the spray from a waterfall.* **2.** anything resembling this, such as fine particles or small objects discharged through the air: *A spray of arrows stuck in the target.* **3.** any of various liquids forced out in a stream of fine particles by an atomizer, pressurized can, or other device: *a spray for killing ants.* **4.** the device holding such a liquid: *a deodorant spray, a paint spray.* —*v.t.* **1.** to apply spray to (a surface): *to spray a wall with paint.* **2.** to apply a spray of: *to spray perfume.* **3.** to discharge a spray in: *to spray a room with disinfectant.* —*v.i.* to scatter or force out spray. [From the Middle Dutch word *spraeyen* meaning "to sprinkle."] —**spray′er,** *n.*

spray² (sprā) *n.* **1.** a slender branch of a plant with its leaves, flowers, or fruit; sprig. **2.** an ornament, pattern, or design resembling this. [From the Middle English word *spray.*]

spray can, a can in which a gas under pressure is used to release a paint, insecticide, or other liquid in the form of a fine mist or spray.

spray gun, a device that forces out a spray of a liquid, such as paint or insecticide.

spread (spred) *v.,* **spread, spread·ing.** —*v.t.* **1.** to unfold, open up, or stretch out: *We spread the blanket out on the ground. The bird spread its wings.* **2.** to cover with a thin layer of something: *to spread a roll with jam.* **3.** to

at; āpe; fär; câre; end; mē; it; īce; pîerce; hot; ōld; sông, fôrk; oil; out; up; ūse; rüle; půll; tûrn; chin; sing; shop; thin; this; hw in white; zh in treasure. The symbol ə stands for the unstressed vowel sound heard in about, taken, pencil, lemon, and circus.

S

put as a thin covering: *to spread butter on toast.* **4.** to distribute or scatter over an area: *The farmer spread fertilizer on the ground.* **5.** to extend over a period of time: *We spread the work over three days.* **6.** to cause to become more widely known: *to spread a rumor.* **7.** to set (a table) for a meal; place food on. —*v.i.* **1.** to be placed, distributed, or scattered over an area; extend: *The rash spread along the child's arm. The fire spread through the forest.* **2.** to be put as a thin covering. **3.** to become more widely known; circulate: *Word spread quickly about the accident.* **4.** to be pushed apart. —*n.* **1.** the act of spreading. **2.** the amount or extent that something opens up or stretches: *the spread of a bird's wings.* **3.** a cloth covering, especially for a bed. **4.** printed material, such as an advertisement, that covers two facing pages or several columns in a magazine or newspaper. **5.** soft food that can be spread, such as butter or cheese. **6.** *Informal.* a lavish display of food; feast. **7.** *Informal.* a ranch or farm. —**spread'er,** *n.*

spread eagle, a representation of an eagle with its legs and wings spread out, used as an emblem of the United States.

spree (sprē) *n.* **1.** a period of excessive, unchecked participation in an activity: *a shopping spree.* **2.** lively frolic.

spri·er (sprī'ər) a comparative of **spry.**

spri·est (sprī'ist) a superlative of **spry.**

sprig (sprig) *n.* **1.** a shoot, twig, or branch of a plant with its leaves, flowers, or fruit: *a sprig of parsley.* **2.** a pattern or ornament resembling this.

spright·ly (sprīt'lē) *adj.,* **spright·li·er, spright·li·est.** lively; merry; gay: *a sprightly tune.* —**spright'li·ness,** *n.*

spring (spring) *v.,* **sprang** or **sprung, sprung, spring·ing.** —*v.i.* **1.** to move forward or jump up quickly; leap: *When the captain came in, the soldiers sprang to attention.* **2.** to appear or arise suddenly: *A breeze sprang up from the southwest.* **3.** to shift or move by or as if by elastic force: *The rubber band sprang back into shape. The door sprang shut.* **4.** to come into being or grow suddenly or rapidly: *The weeds are springing up everywhere.* **5.** to become warped, cracked, or split:

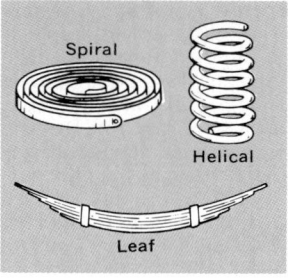

springs (n., def. 2)

The wooden door sprang from the humidity. —*v.t.* **1.** to cause to work or operate suddenly: *to spring a trap.* **2.** to present or produce suddenly or unexpectedly: *to spring a surprise.* **3.** to cause to warp, crack, or split. **4.** to develop: *The radiator has sprung a leak.* —*n.* **1.** the act of springing; leap. **2.** an elastic device, such as a spiral-shaped piece of metal, that recovers its original shape when released after being bent, compressed, or stretched. **3.** the quality of being light, bouncing, or flexible; springiness: *a spring in one's step.* **4.** a place where underground water flows out of the earth. **5.** the season of the year coming between winter and summer. In the Northern Hemisphere it extends from about March 21 to about June 21. **6.** a source or origin. —*adj.* **1.** of, relating to, or suitable for the season of spring: *spring rain, spring clothing.* **2.** having a spring or springs: *a spring mattress.*

spring·board (spring'bôrd') *n.* **1.** another word for **div·ing board. 2.** a flexible board used in tumbling. **3.** something that provides a starting or moving force: *A sharp mind can be the springboard to success.*

spring·bok (spring'bok') *n., pl.* **spring·bok** or **spring·boks.** a small antelope native to the plains of southern Africa, having horns and a tan-and-white coat. When frightened, springboks spring into the air.

spring fever, a feeling of laziness or listlessness that is commonly associated with the coming of spring.

spring·tide (spring'tīd') *n.* another word for **spring·time.**

spring tide, the tide that has the greatest rise and ebb, occurring at or soon after the new or full moon.

spring·time (spring'tīm') *n.* the season of spring.

spring·y (spring'ē) *adj.,* **spring·i·er, spring·i·est.** having a light, bouncing, or flexible quality: *a springy step, a springy mattress.* —**spring'i·ly,** *adv.* —**spring'i·ness,** *n.*

springbok

sprin·kle (spring'kəl) *v.,* **sprin·kled, sprin·kling.** —*v.t.* **1.** to scatter (a liquid or other substance) in small drops or particles: *The baker sprinkled flour over the rolls.* **2.** to scatter small drops or particles of a liquid or other substance on: *to sprinkle flowers with water.* —*v.i.* to rain lightly. —*n.* **1.** a light rain. **2.** a small quantity of something; sprinkling.

sprin·kler (spring'klər) *n.* **1.** any of various devices for sprinkling a lawn. **2.** an outlet of a sprinkler system.

sprinkler system 1. an automatic system for extinguishing fires in buildings. **2.** a system of pipes or hoses for sprinkling a lawn, garden, or other area.

sprin·kling (spring'kling) *n.* a small quantity falling or scattered over an area or a period of time: *just a sprinkling of rain, a sprinkling of humor in a speech.*

sprint (sprint) *n.* a short race at full speed. —*v.i.* to run at full speed, especially for a short distance: *The runners sprinted for the last sixty yards.* —**sprint'er,** *n.*

sprit (sprit) *n.* a small spar extending diagonally from the mast to the upper corner of a fore-and-aft sail.

sprite (sprīt) *n.* an elf, fairy, or goblin.

sprit·sail (sprit'sāl', sprit'səl) *n.* a sail spread and supported by a sprit.

sprock·et (sprok'it) *n.* **1.** any of the projections on the rim of a wheel that are arranged to engage the links of a chain. **2.** a wheel with sprockets. Also, **sprocket wheel.**

sprout (sprout) *v.i.* **1.** to put forth young growth or buds; begin to grow: *The seeds we planted have finally sprouted.* **2.** to develop, grow, or appear suddenly or rapidly: *Many stores have sprouted up near the new apartments.* —*v.t.* to cause to sprout: *The plant sprouted new leaves.* —*n.* **1.** a new or young growth on a plant. **2. sprouts. a.** young shoots of mung beans, alfalfa, or the like, eaten as a vegetable. **b.** see **Brussels sprouts.**

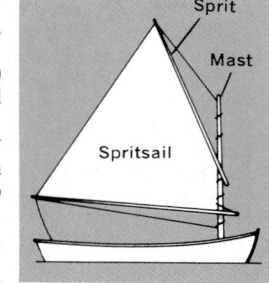

sprit

spruce[1] (sprüs) *n.* **1.** a cone-bearing evergreen tree related to the pine, having short, needle-shaped leaves and drooping cones, found in cold and temperate regions of the Northern Hemisphere. **2.** the wood of this tree, used for construction and paper pulp. [From the earlier *Spruce fir* meaning "fir tree from Prussia," from the Middle English *Sprus* or *Prus* "Prussia."]

spruce² (sprüs) *v.t., v.i.,* **spruced, spruc·ing.** to make or become neat or trim (usually with *up*): *to spruce up a room.* —*adj.,* **spruc·er, spruc·est.** having a neat or trim appearance. [Perhaps from *Spruce leather*, a fine leather from Prussia, from the Middle English *Sprus* or *Prus* meaning "Prussia."] —**spruce′ly,** *adv.* —**spruce′ness,** *n.*

sprung (sprung) a past tense and the past participle of **spring.**

spry (sprī) *adj.,* **spry·er** or **spri·er, spry·est** or **spri·est.** lively and nimble: *a spry pair of dancers.* —**spry′ly,** *adv.* —**spry′ness,** *n.*

spud (spud) *n.* **1.** a narrow, sharp tool resembling a spade, used for digging up weeds or removing bark from trees. **2.** *Informal.* a potato.

spume (spūm) *n.* foam; froth. —*v.i.,* **spumed, spum·ing.** to foam; froth.

spu·mo·ni (spù mō′nē) *also,* **spu·mo·ne.** *n.* an Italian ice cream with layers of different flavors and colors, often containing fruit or nuts. [From the Italian word *spumone* meaning this food, from the word *spuma* meaning "foam," from the Latin word *spuma* "foam."]

spun (spun) the past tense and past participle of **spin.**

spunk (spungk) *n. Informal.* courage, spirit, and determination; pluck.

spunk·y (spung′kē) *adj.,* **spunk·i·er, spunk·i·est.** *Informal.* characterized by or having courage, spirit, and determination; plucky: *a spunky little dog.* —**spunk′i·ly,** *adv.* —**spunk′i·ness,** *n.*

spur (spûr) *n.* **1.** a pointed device worn on the heel of a horse rider's boot, used to urge a horse forward. **2.** something that urges to action: *Your encouragement was a spur to my success.* **3.** something that resembles a spur, such as the sharp, hard projection on the leg of a rooster. **4.** a ridge or mountain projecting from the main mountain range. **5.** a short side track of a railroad connected with the main track. —*v.t.,* **spurred, spur·ring. 1.** to urge forward with a spur or spurs. **2.** to urge on; stimulate; incite: *The crowd's cheers spurred the team to victory.*

·**on the spur of the moment.** without preparation; on an impulse: *to change plans on the spur of the moment.*

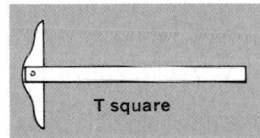
spur (n., def. 1)

spu·ri·ous (spyùr′ē əs) *adj.* not genuine or authentic; false: *a spurious passport, a spurious claim.* —**spu′ri·ous·ly,** *adv.* —**spu′ri·ous·ness,** *n.*

spurn (spûrn) *v.t.* to reject with contempt or disdain; scorn: *to spurn the offer of a bribe.*

spurred (spûrd) *adj.* fitted with or having spurs.

spurt (spûrt) *also,* **spirt.** *v.i.* **1.** to gush or pour out suddenly or forcibly in a stream; spout: *The water spurted from the broken pipe.* **2.** to make or show a sudden, brief effort: *The car spurted ahead as soon as the traffic light turned green.* —*v.t.* to force out suddenly or forcibly in a stream. —*n.* **1.** a sudden gush, especially of liquid. **2.** a sudden, brief spell, as of activity or effort: *to work in spurts.*

sput·nik (sput′nik, spùt′nik) *n.* any of several artificial earth satellites launched by the Soviet Union. The first was *Sputnik I*, launched on October 4, 1957. [From the Russian word *sputnik* meaning both "traveling companion" and "satellite."]

sput·ter (sput′ər) *v.i.* **1.** to make popping, spitting, or hissing noises: *The motor sputtered and then stopped.*

2. to utter words or sounds in a confused or hasty manner: *to sputter in anger.* **3.** to throw out or spit small bits of food or saliva, as when speaking excitedly. —*v.t.* **1.** to throw out or spit small bits of (food or saliva), as when speaking excitedly. **2.** to utter (words or sounds) in a confused or hasty manner: *to sputter nonsense.* —*n.* **1.** the act or noise of sputtering. **2.** confused or hasty speech. —**sput′ter·er,** *n.*

spu·tum (spū′təm) *n.* saliva mixed with matter coughed up from the lungs or windpipe.

spy (spī) *n., pl.* **spies. 1.** a person who is employed by a government to discover secret information about another government. **2.** a person who watches others secretly or who gathers secret information about others. —*v.,* **spied, spy·ing.** —*v.i.* **1.** to act as a spy: *to spy on the enemy.* **2.** to make a search or investigation; pry. —*v.t.* to catch sight of; observe; notice: *We spied a ship on the horizon.*

spy·glass (spī′glas′) *n., pl.* **spy·glass·es.** a small telescope.

sq., square.

squab (skwob) *n.* a young pigeon.

squab·ble (skwob′əl) *v.i.,* **squab·bled, squab·bling.** to argue noisily, especially over something of little importance: *The children squabbled over who would ride the bicycle first.* —*n.* a petty argument or dispute. —**squab′bler,** *n.*

squad (skwod) *n.* **1.** a military unit usually composed of ten soldiers and commanded by a noncommissioned officer. **2.** a small group of persons organized for a particular purpose or function: *a police squad.*

squad car, another term for **patrol car.**

squad·ron (skwod′rən) *n.* **1.** any of various military units, as of airplanes or ships. **2.** any large organized body or group.

squal·id (skwol′id) *adj.* **1.** having a gloomy, wretched, poverty-stricken appearance: *a squalid beggar, squalid slums.* **2.** morally bad; sordid: *the squalid details of a scandal.* —**squal′id·ly,** *adv.* —**squal′id·ness,** *n.*

squall¹ (skwôl) *n.* a sudden, strong gust of wind, often accompanied by rain, sleet, or snow. —*v.i.* to blow a squall; storm. [Probably of Scandinavian origin.]

squall² (skwôl) *v.i.* to cry or scream loudly and harshly: *The child fell and began to squall.* —*n.* a loud, harsh cry or scream. [Perhaps a representation of the sound of a cry.]

squall·y (skwô′lē) *adj.,* **squall·i·er, squall·i·est.** marked by squalls; stormy; gusty: *squally seas.*

squal·or (skwol′ər) *n.* the condition of being squalid; wretchedness or sordidness.

squa·mous (skwā′məs) *adj.* like or formed of scales.

squan·der (skwon′dər) *v.t.* to spend or use in a wasteful or extravagant manner: *to squander a fortune.*

square (skwâr) *n.* **1.** a plane figure having four sides of equal length and four right angles. **2.** something having this shape: *the squares of a checkerboard.* **3.** an open space in a city or town bounded by streets on all sides, often planted with grass, trees, or flowers, and used as a park. **4.** any similar open space, especially one formed by the intersection

T square

square *(n., def. 5)*

at; āpe; fär; câre; end; mē; it; īce; pierce; hot; ōld; sông, fôrk; oil; out; up; ūse; rüle; pùll; tûrn; chin; sing; shop; thin; this; hw in white; zh in treasure. The symbol ə stands for the unstressed vowel sound heard in about, taken, pencil, lemon, and circus.

S

of several streets. **5.** an L-shaped or T-shaped instrument used for drawing or measuring right angles. **6.** *Mathematics.* the product of a number multiplied by itself: *Twenty-five is the square of five.* **7.** *Slang.* a very conventional or conservative person who does not know or follow the latest trends or fashions. —*adj.,* **squar·er, squar·est. 1.** having four sides of equal length and four right angles. **2.** resembling a square in form: *a square box.* **3.** of a specified length on each of four sides of a square: *a field one hundred yards square.* **4.** forming a right angle: *a square corner.* **5.** fair or just; honest: *a square deal.* **6.** on equal terms; even: *When you pay me back we'll be square.* **7.** straightforward or direct: *a square denial.* **8.** *Slang.* too conventional or conservative. —*v.,* **squared, squar·ing.** —*v.t.* **1.** to form with four equal sides and four right angles; make or form like a square. **2.** to bring to or as if to the form of a right angle: *to square one's shoulders.* **3.** to mark out or divide into squares. **4.** to cause to agree or conform; adjust: *to square a story with the facts.* **5.** to adjust so as to leave no balance; settle: *to square an account.* **6.** *Mathematics.* to multiply (a number) by itself. —*v.i.* to agree; conform; fit: *The suspect's story doesn't square with the known facts.* —*adv.* so as to be at or form right angles. —**square′ly,** *adv.* —**square′ness,** *n.*

·**on the square. a.** at right angles. **b.** *Informal.* in a fair or just way; honestly.

·**to square off.** *Informal.* to prepare to fight.

square centimeter, a unit of area equal to the area of a rectangle measuring 1 centimeter on each side; 0.155 square inch.

square dance 1. a dance performed by groups of four or more couples who are arranged in a square at the beginning of the dance. **2.** an event or social gathering with square dances.

square foot, a unit of area equal to the area of a rectangle measuring 1 foot on each side; 0.0929 square meter.

square inch, a unit of area equal to the area of a rectangle measuring 1 inch on each side; 6.45 square centimeters.

square kilometer, a unit of area equal to the area of a rectangle measuring 1 kilometer on each side; 100 hectares, 247.1 acres, or 0.386 square mile.

square knot, a knot formed by two interlaced loops going in opposite directions.

square meal, a complete or substantial meal.

square measure, a system used to measure area in terms of a unit in the form of a square.

square meter, a unit of area equal to the area of a rectangle measuring 1 meter on each side; 10.764 square feet, or 1.196 square yards.

square mile, a unit of area equal to the area of a rectangle measuring 1 mile on each side; 640 acres, or 2.59 square kilometers.

square one *Informal.* the very beginning; the starting point: *Our plan didn't work out, so we're back to square one.*

square–rigged (skwâr′rigd′) *adj.* having square sails as the principal sails.

square–rig·ger (skwâr′rig′ər) *n.* a square-rigged ship.

square root, a number that produces a given number when multiplied by itself: *The square root of 36 is 6.*

square shooter *Informal.* one who is honest and direct in dealing with others.

square yard, a unit of area equal to the area of a rectangle measuring 1 yard on each side; 9 square feet, or 0.836 square meter.

squash¹ (skwosh) *v.t.* **1.** to beat or press into a soft or flat mass; crush: *to squash a cardboard box under one's feet.* **2.** to force or squeeze into a small area; cram; crowd: *to squash four people in the back seat of a car.*

3. to put down or suppress forcibly and completely: *to squash a revolt.* —*v.i.* to be or become crushed. —*n., pl.* **squash·es. 1.** a crushed or crowded mass. **2.** the act or sound of squashing. **3.** a game played in a walled court with rackets and a rubber ball. [From the Middle French word *esquasser* meaning "to smash, crush, overcome entirely," from the Latin word *quassare* "to shake" or "to shatter, break to pieces."]

squash² (skwosh) *n., pl.* **squash·es. 1.** the round or oblong fruit of any of a group of plants related to the gourd, cooked and eaten as a vegetable, or used as food for livestock. **2.** a plant bearing this fruit. [Short for the Algonquian word *isquoutersquash* meaning this vegetable.]

squash² *(def. 1)*

squash·y (skwosh′ē) *adj.,* **squash·i·er, squash·i·est. 1.** easily squashed: *squashy tomatoes.* **2.** soft and wet: *squashy soil.*

squat (skwot) *v.i.,* **squat·ted** or **squat, squat·ting. 1.** to crouch or sit with the knees bent and drawn close to or under the body: *to squat down to pet a cat.* **2.** to settle on land without having right or title to it. —*adj.* short and thick; low and broad.

squat·ter (skwot′ər) *n.* **1.** a person or thing that squats. **2.** a person who settles on land to which he or she has no right or title. Squatters are sometimes given title to land after having lived on it for a certain period of time.

squat·ty (skwot′ē) *adj.,* **squat·ti·er, squat·ti·est.** another word for **squat.**

squaw (skwô) *n.* a North American Indian woman or wife.

squawk (skwôk) *v.i.* **1.** to utter a shrill, harsh cry, as a gull or parrot. **2.** *Informal.* to complain or protest loudly or noisily: *The child squawked at having to take a nap.* —*n.* **1.** a shrill, harsh cry, such as that uttered by a gull or parrot. **2.** *Informal.* a loud complaint or protest. —**squawk′er,** *n.*

squeak (skwēk) *n.* a short, thin, high-pitched sound or cry. —*v.i.* **1.** to make or utter a squeak: *The rusty gate squeaked when it was opened.* **2.** to accomplish, get, or earn something by a narrow margin: *to squeak through an exam.* —**squeak′er,** *n.*

squeak·y (skwē′kē) *adj.,* **squeak·i·er, squeak·i·est.** tending to squeak; squeaking: *a squeaky door.*

squeal (skwēl) *v.i.* **1.** to make or utter a loud, shrill cry or sound: *to squeal with delight.* **2.** *Slang.* to betray a confidence; turn informer: *The crooks squealed on each other.* —*n.* a loud, shrill cry or sound. —**squeal′er,** *n.*

squeam·ish (skwē′mish) *adj.* **1.** easily sickened or nauseated: *to be squeamish about the sight of blood.* **2.** easily offended or shocked; prudish. —**squeam′ish·ly,** *adv.* —**squeam′ish·ness,** *n.*

squee·gee (skwē′jē) *n.* a T-shaped implement with a rubber or leather edge, used in wiping off or spreading liquid on flat, smooth surfaces, as in washing windows.

squeeze (skwēz) *v.,* **squeezed, squeez·ing.** —*v.t.* **1.** to apply strong pressure to (something): *to squeeze a tube of toothpaste.* **2.** to obtain (something) by or as if by applying strong pressure; extract: *to squeeze juice from an orange, to squeeze a contribution from someone.* **3.** to press or hug, as in sympathy or affection: *to squeeze someone's hand.* **4.** to force by pressure; thrust forcibly: *to squeeze a book onto a crowded shelf.* —*v.i.* **1.** to apply pressure. **2.** to be capable of being squeezed; yield to pressure. **3.** to pass or force one's way by squeezing: *to squeeze into a seat.* —*n.* **1.** the act of squeezing;

application of pressure: *to give someone's hand a squeeze.* **2.** pressure, as of a crowd of people; crush: *There is always a squeeze in the subway during rush hour.* **—squeez'a·ble,** *adj.* **—squeez'er,** *n.*

squelch (skwelch) *v.t.* **1.** to stamp out or eliminate forcibly and completely; crush; quash: *The dictatorship had squelched all opposition.* **2.** *Informal.* to silence or subdue, as with a crushing or sarcastic remark. **—***n., pl.* **squelch·es.** *Informal.* a crushing or sarcastic remark. **—squelch'er,** *n.*

squib (skwib) *n.* **1.** a short, witty written or spoken attack on someone or something; lampoon. **2.** a small firework that burns with a hissing noise and then explodes. **3.** a broken firecracker that burns but does not explode.

squid (skwid) *n., pl.* **squids** or **squid.** a sea animal having a round, tubelike body, a pair of fins, and ten arms. It is related to the cuttlefish and the octopus.

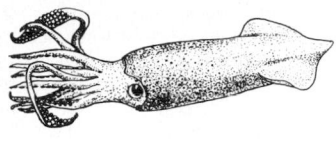

squid

squig·gle (skwig'əl) *n.* a wavy or twisting line; wriggly mark or twist: *I drew a few squiggles in my notebook as I listened to the long, boring lecture.*

squint (skwint) *v.i.* **1.** to close the eyes partially: *to squint in bright sunlight.* **2.** to look sideways. **3.** to be cross-eyed. **—***v.t.* to close (the eyes) partially: *Smoke made me squint my eyes.* **—***n.* **1.** the act or habit of squinting. **2.** the condition of being cross-eyed.

squire (skwīr) *n.* **1.** an English country gentleman or landowner. **2.** in feudal society, a young nobleman who, in preparation for his own knighthood, attended a knight. **3.** a man who escorts a woman. **—***v.t.,* **squired, squir·ing.** to escort (a woman).

squirm (skwûrm) *v.t.* **1.** to turn or twist the body: *to squirm in one's seat.* **2.** to show or feel discomfort, uneasiness, or mental distress: *The lawyer's clever questions made the witness squirm.* **—***n.* the act or motion of squirming. **—squirm'y,** *adj.*

squir·rel (skwûr'əl) *n.* **1.** any of various small rodents, usually having a slender body and a long, bushy tail. Squirrels live in trees and feed chiefly on nuts. **2.** the gray, reddish, or dark brown fur of this animal.

squirrel *(def. 1)*

squirt (skwûrt) *v.t.* **1.** to force out (liquid) though a narrow opening in a thin jet or stream: *to squirt oil on a rusty hinge.* **2.** to wet by squirting a liquid: *to squirt someone with a hose.* **—***v.i.* **1.** to come out in a thin jet or stream: *The ink squirted from the fountain pen.* **2.** to force out a thin stream of liquid. **—***n.* **1.** the act of squirting. **2.** a thin jet or stream. **3.** something used for squirting liquid, such as a syringe. **4.** *Informal.* a rude, brash young person.

Sr, the symbol for strontium.

Sr. 1. Senior. **2.** Señor. **3.** Sister.

St. 1. saint. **2.** strait. **3.** street.

stab (stab) *v.,* **stabbed, stab·bing. —***v.t.* **1.** to pierce or wound with a pointed weapon. **2.** to thrust or drive (a pointed instrument or weapon) into something: *to stab a fork into meat.* **3.** to wound the feelings of. **—***v.i.* to thrust with a pointed weapon. **—***n.* **1.** a thrust made with a pointed weapon. **2.** a wound or puncture made by stabbing. **3.** a sharp but momentary sensation or feeling; pang: *a stab of pain, a stab of regret.* **4.** *Informal.* an

attempt; effort; try: *Even though it was a difficult job, I made a stab at it.* **—stab'ber,** *n.*

sta·bil·i·ty (stə bil'i tē) *n., pl.* **sta·bil·i·ties. 1.** the state of being stable. **2.** consistency or steadiness, as of character or purpose. **3.** permanence.

sta·bi·lize (stā'bə līz') *v.t.,* **sta·bi·lized, sta·bi·liz·ing. 1.** to make stable, firm, or steady. **2.** to prevent from changing; keep steady: *The president declared that stronger measures were needed to stabilize prices.* **—sta'·bi·li·za'tion,** *n.*

sta·bi·liz·er (stā'bə lī'zər) *n.* **1.** a person or thing that stabilizes. **2.** a gyroscopic device in a ship, airplane, or the like that keeps it steady in rough water or air.

sta·ble[1] (stā'bəl) *n.* **1.** a building, especially one with stalls, where horses or cattle are kept and fed. **2.** *also,* **stables.** the race horses belonging to a particular owner or establishment. **—***v.t.,* **sta·bled, sta·bling.** to put or keep in a stable. [From the Old French word *estable* meaning this building, from the Latin word *stabulum* "humble dwelling" or "stable[1]," from *stare* "to stand."]

sta·ble[2] (stā'bəl) *adj.* **1.** not easily moved, shaken, or overthrown; firm: *a stable platform, a stable government.* **2.** reliable, constant, and sure; predictable; steady: *a stable personality.* **3.** continuing without much change; permanent; enduring: *to enjoy stable health.* **4.** (of chemical compounds) resistant to chemical change; not easily decomposed. [From the Old French word *estable* meaning "established, firm, reliable," from the Latin word *stabilis* "firm, steady, steadfast," from *stare* "to stand."] **—sta'bly,** *adv.*

stac·ca·to (stə kä'tō) *adj.* **1.** *Music.* having or produced with breaks between tones; disconnected; abrupt. **2.** composed of or characterized by abrupt and sharp emphasis, sound, or movement: *staccato gunfire.* **—***adv.* in a staccato manner.

stack (stak) *n.* **1.** a large, rectangular or cone-shaped pile of hay, straw, or grain. **2.** a pile of things arranged in an orderly way: *a stack of plates, a stack of records.* **3.** a smokestack or chimney. **4.** a rack in which books are arranged above one another on shelves. **5. stacks.** an area in a library in which most of the books are kept. **6.** a number of rifles standing muzzle upward against each other. **7.** *Informal.* a large quantity: *The applicant had a stack of recommendations.* **—***v.t.* **1.** to gather or arrange in a stack: *to stack books.* **2.** to arrange (playing cards) beforehand so that they will come up in a certain order: *to stack a deck.*

stack *(def. 6)*

sta·di·um (stā'dē əm) *n., pl.* **sta·di·ums** or **sta·di·a** (stā'dē ə). a large, usually roofless, oval or U-shaped structure surrounding an open area, used for athletic events and other purposes, such as concerts or rallies, and having rows of seats for spectators. [From the Latin word *stadium* meaning "running track," from the Greek word *stadion* "racetrack," earlier "a unit of measurement (about 600 feet)."]

at; āpe; fär; câre; end; mē; it; īce; pîerce; hot; ōld; sông, fôrk; oil; out; up; ūse; rüle; pull; tûrn; chin; sing; shop; thin; this; hw in white; zh in treasure. The symbol ə stands for the unstressed vowel sound heard in about, taken, pencil, lemon, and circus.

S

staff (staf) *n., pl.* **staffs** or *(defs. 1, 5)* **staves.** **1.** a stick, rod, or pole, often used as an aid in walking, as a weapon, or as a symbol of authority. **2.** another word for **flagpole. 3.** the entire group or a particular group of permanent employees working in an institution, business, or organization: *the staff of a hospital, the nursing staff, the president's advisory staff.* **4.** military personnel with administrative duties who usually do not take part in combat. **5.** *Music.* the five horizontal lines and four spaces on which musical notation is made. —*v.t.* to provide (an office, establishment, military unit, or the like) with officers or employees.

staff *(def. 5)*

stag (stag) *n.* **1.** a full-grown male deer. **2.** the male of various other animals. **3.** a man who goes to a social gathering unaccompanied by a woman. —*adj.* for or attended by men only: *a stag party.* —*adv.* not accompanied by a person of the opposite sex: *to go stag to a dance.*

stage (stāj) *n.* **1.** a raised platform or similar structure in a theater or hall, on which a performance takes place. **2.** the theater as a profession: *to leave the stage to act in movies.* **3.** a place where some important event takes place; scene of action: *Gettysburg was the stage of a major battle of the Civil War.* **4.** a step, period, or degree in a process, progression, or development: *Very few symptoms appeared in the early stages of the disease.* **5.** the distance traveled between two places of rest on a road or journey; part of a journey: *The first stage of our trip took us across the Atlantic Ocean.* **6.** see **stagecoach. 7.** one of the self-propelled sections of a rocket that can be separated from the rest of the vehicle. —*v.t.,* **staged, stag·ing. 1.** to put, arrange, or exhibit on or as if on a stage: *to stage a play.* **2.** to conduct, engage in, or carry on: *The protesters planned to stage a demonstration.*

stage·coach (stāj'kōch') *n., pl.* **stage·coach·es.** a horse-drawn coach that formerly traveled on a regular schedule over a fixed route, carrying passengers, mail, and baggage.

stage·hand (stāj'hand') *n.* in the theater, a person who moves scenery, sets up props, controls lighting, and performs certain other duties.

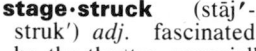

stagecoach

stage·struck (stāj'-struk') *adj.* fascinated by the theater, especially with the hope of becoming an actor or actress.

stag·ger (stag'ər) *v.i.* **1.** to move unsteadily or with a swaying motion; totter; reel: *to stagger under a heavy load.* **2.** to become confused or overwhelmed: *to stagger at a seemingly impossible task.* —*v.t.* **1.** to cause to totter or reel: *The punch staggered the fighter.* **2.** to confuse or overwhelm: *an act of bravery that staggers the imagination.* **3.** to schedule, arrange, or distribute in a continuous or overlapping order: *to stagger traffic lights, to stagger work shifts.* **4.** to arrange in a zigzag pattern or manner. —*n.* **1.** the act or motion of staggering. **2.** a staggered pattern or arrangement. **3.** **staggers.** any of several diseases of the central nervous system in cattle and other domestic animals that cause sudden falls and a staggering gait. ▲ used with a singular verb. —**stag'ger·ing·ly,** *adv.*

stag·ing (stā'jing) *n.* the direction and presentation of a theatrical production or similar entertainment.

stag·nant (stag'nənt) *adj.* **1.** still or motionless, as air or water. **2.** foul from standing still: *a pool of stagnant water.* **3.** not active, changing, or developing; inactive or dull: *Life in the small town was often stagnant.* —**stag'nant·ly,** *adv.*

stag·nate (stag'nāt) *v.i.,* **stag·nat·ed, stag·nat·ing. 1.** to be or become foul from standing still: *The water stagnated in the pond.* **2.** to stop growing, changing, or developing; be or become inactive or dull: *Don't let your mind stagnate over summer vacation.* —**stag·na'tion,** *n.*

staid (stād) *adj.* conservative or sober in character or style; sedate; serious. —**staid'ly,** *adv.* —**staid'ness,** *n.*

stain (stān) *n.* **1.** a spot or streak produced on or in something by another substance; mark or discoloration: *an ink stain, grass stains.* **2.** a liquid dye, pigment, or other colored solution used especially in coloring wood: *to apply a brown stain to a floor.* **3.** moral blemish; dishonor: *a stain on one's reputation.* —*v.t.* **1.** to spot or streak with another substance: *I stained the carpet when I spilled my drink.* **2.** to cause or be capable of causing a stain on or in: *Tomato sauce stains cotton clothing.* **3.** to color or treat with a dye, pigment, or other colored solution: *to stain a wooden bookcase.* **4.** to bring dishonor upon; taint; blemish. —*v.i.* **1.** to be or become stained: *This material stains easily.* **2.** to cause or be capable of causing a stain: *Be careful when you eat the blueberries, because they stain.* —**stain'er,** *n.*

stained glass, glass that has been colored, cut into various shapes and sizes, and assembled to form a picture or design for use especially in church windows. —**stained'-glass',** *adj.*

stained glass

stain·less (stān'lis) *adj.* having no stains; spotless.

stainless steel, an alloy of steel with large amounts of chromium and nickel. It resists rust and heat, is strong, durable, and easy to shape, and is used for tableware, cooking and serving utensils, appliances, and structural parts.

stair (stâr) *n.* **1.** *usually,* **stairs.** a series or flight of steps for passing from one level or floor to another: *We climbed the stairs to the attic.* **2.** a step or one of a series of steps.

stair·case (stâr'kās') *n.* a flight or a series of flights of stairs with its supporting framework.

stair·way (stâr'wā') *n.* another word for **staircase.**

stair·well (stâr'wel') *n.* the vertical space enclosing a staircase.

stake (stāk) *n.* **1.** a stick or post sharpened at one end for driving into the ground, used as a support, boundary mark, or post. **2.** the post to which a person was bound for execution by burning. **3.** *also,* **stakes.** something that is risked in a wager or gambling game, such as money. **4.** an emotional or financial interest: *As the star of the play, you have a great stake in its success.* —*v.t.,* **staked, stak·ing. 1.** to mark the boundaries of (land) with or as if with stakes; claim or reserve. **2.** to fasten or tie to a stake; support with a stake: *to stake tomato plants.* **3.** to gamble or risk: *to stake one's savings on a business venture.*

·at stake. in question or danger: *The firefighters acted quickly because many lives were at stake.*

·to pull up stakes. to move on or away; leave: *After years of city life, we pulled up stakes and moved to the country.*

sta·lac·tite (stə lak′tīt) *n.* a formation resembling an icicle, hanging down from the ceiling of a cave. It is usually composed of calcium carbonate deposited by water seeping through the rock above.

sta·lag·mite (stə lag′mīt) *n.* a formation resembling a cone, built up on the floor of a cave by calcium carbonate in water dripping from the ceiling.

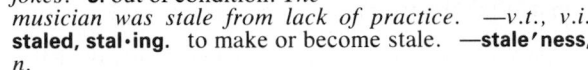

Stalactites

Stalagmites

stale (stāl) *adj.*, **stal·er, stal·est.** **1.** no longer fresh: *The old bread was so stale that we could not eat it.* **2.** having lost its novelty or interest: *stale jokes.* **3.** out of condition: *The musician was stale from lack of practice.* —*v.t., v.i.* **staled, stal·ing.** to make or become stale. —**stale′ness,** *n.*

stale·mate (stāl′māt′) *n.* **1.** a draw in chess that results when the player whose turn it is cannot make a move without putting his or her king in check. **2.** any position or situation in which no further action is possible; deadlock; standstill. —*v.t.,* **stale·mat·ed, stale·mat·ing.** to bring to a stalemate; place in a deadlock.

stalk¹ (stôk) *n.* **1.** the main stem of a plant. **2.** the stem of any plant part. **3.** a supporting part: *the stalk of a crayfish's eye.* [From the Middle English word *stalke* meaning this part of a plant.]

stalk² (stôk) *v.t.* **1.** to hunt, track, or pursue stealthily: *The tiger stalked its prey.* **2.** to move menacingly or stealthily through: *The fugitive stalked the streets.* —*v.i.* to walk in a stiff, determined manner: *to stalk out of a room.* —*n.* the act of stalking. [From the Old English suffix *-stealcian*, found in the word *bestealcian* meaning "to proceed stealthily."] —**stalk′er,** *n.*

stall (stôl) *n.* **1.** a compartment in a barn or stable for a horse, cow, or other animal. **2.** a booth or counter for setting up wares for sale. **3.** an enclosed seat in the chancel of a church, usually reserved for the clergy. **4.** *Informal.* something used to delay or prevent an action; delaying tactic. —*v.t.* **1.** to delay or prevent from acting: *The store owner stalled the robber until the police arrived.* **2.** to hinder or block the motion or progress of: *The damaged track stalled the train for an hour.* **3.** to cause (an engine, automobile, or the like) to stop running. **4.** to put or keep (an animal) in a stall. —*v.i.* **1.** to make delays; be evasive: *to stall for time.* **2.** to stop running: *The old car's engine stalls frequently on cold days.*

stal·lion (stal′yən) *n.* a male horse, especially one used for breeding.

stal·wart (stôl′wərt) *adj.* **1.** strong or brave: *a stalwart hero.* **2.** firm or unwavering, as in support of a cause; resolute. —*n.* a stalwart person. —**stal′wart·ly,** *adv.* —**stal′wart·ness,** *n.*

sta·men (stā′mən) *n.* the part of a flower that produces pollen. It consists of a slender stalk, called the filament, with an enlarged pollen-bearing tip called the anther.

stam·i·na (stam′ə nə) *n.* the moral or physical ability to withstand fatigue, disease, or hardship; endurance: *A long-distance runner must have stamina.*

stam·i·nate (stam′ə nit, stam′ə nāt′) *adj.* **1.** having a stamen or stamens. **2.** having stamens but no pistils.

stam·mer (stam′ər) *v.i.* to speak haltingly, especially by repeating a letter or sound. —*v.t.* to say or utter with a stammer: *to stammer an excuse for being late.* —*n.* an instance of stammering. —**stam′mer·er,** *n.*

stamp (stamp) *v.t.* **1.** to bring down (the foot or feet) forcefully and heavily: *The dancers stamped their feet to the music.* **2.** to strike forcefully with the sole of the foot: *to stamp the ground.* **3.** to mark (with an impression, design, or the like): *to stamp one's initials on stationery.* **4.** to mark (something) with a device that imprints or cuts a design, letters, or the like: *The salesclerk stamped the bill to show it had been paid.* **5.** to impress deeply; fix: *The canoe trip was forever stamped in our memory.* **6.** to put a postage stamp or other official mark on: *to stamp a letter.* **7.** to pound or crush, as ore. —*v.i.* **1.** to strike the foot forcefully down upon the ground: *to stamp on the floor.* **2.** to walk forcefully with heavy steps: *to stamp out of a room in anger.* —*n.* **1.** a device or tool for impressing or cutting a design, letters, or the like on paper, wax, metal, or another surface. **2.** an impression or design made with such a device. **3.** a postage stamp. **4.** any similar stamped or printed paper issued by a government and placed on something to show that a tax or other charge has been paid. **5.** an official mark or seal: *a royal stamp.* **6.** a distinguishing mark or impression: *The author's work bears the stamp of a vivid imagination.* **7.** a heavy metal block used to crush rock, ore, or the like. **8.** the act of stamping. —**stamp′er,** *n.*

·to stamp out. to put out, stop, or eliminate: *to stamp out a campfire, to stamp out crime.*

stam·pede (stam pēd′) *n.* **1.** a sudden scattering or headlong flight of frightened animals, such as a herd of cattle or horses. **2.** a sudden scattering or headlong flight of a mob or crowd: *There was a stampede toward the exit when the fire broke out in the theater.* —*v.,* **stam·ped·ed, stam·ped·ing.** —*v.i.* to be part of a stampede. —*v.t.* to cause to stampede: *The rustlers stampeded the cattle.*

stance (stans) *n.* **1.** a manner or way of standing, especially the particular position taken by an athlete while playing. **2.** an attitude; viewpoint: *a conservative political stance.*

stanch¹ (stônch, stänch) also, **staunch.** *v.t.* **1.** to stop or check the flow of (blood or other liquid). **2.** to stop or check the flow of blood or other liquid from (a wound or other opening). [From the Old French word *estanchier* "to stop a flow," going back to the Latin word *stans,* present participle of *stare* "to stand."]

stanch² (stônch, stänch) *adj.* another spelling of **staunch¹**. —**stanch′ly,** *adv.* —**stanch′ness,** *n.*

stan·chion (stan′shən) *n.* **1.** an upright pillar or bar used as a support. **2.** a device for restricting the movements of animals, such as dairy cows, usually consisting of a pair of bars loosely fitting around the neck. —*v.t.* **1.** to provide with or support by stanchions. **2.** to fasten (dairy cows) with stanchions.

stand (stand) *v.,* **stood, stand·ing.** —*v.i.* **1.** to be in an upright position on one's feet: *We had to stand because*

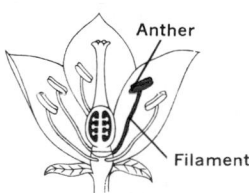

Anther

Filament

stamen

at; āpe; fär; câre; end; mē; it; īce; pîerce; hot; ōld; sông, fôrk; oil; out; up; ūse; rüle; pùll; tûrn; chin; sing; shop; thin; this; hw in white; zh in treasure. The symbol ə stands for the unstressed vowel sound heard in about, taken, pencil, lemon, and circus.

S

there were no seats. **2.** to rise to one's feet: *The congregation stood to sing the hymn.* **3.** to be or remain upright: *A ladder stood against the side of the barn.* **4.** to have location or position; be situated; lie: *The village stands at the foot of the hill.* **5.** to hold a particular place, as of degree, rank, or class: *to stand in first place among a candidate's supporters.* **6.** to be in a particular state or condition: *The window stood open.* **7.** to remain unchanged or in force; hold good: *The rule against chewing gum in the classroom still stands.* **8.** to take or have a certain position, attitude, or opinion: *to stand as an opponent of legalizing gambling.* **9.** to collect and remain: *Water stood in the gutter.* —*v.t.* **1.** to set in an upright position: *Stand the barrel on its end.* **2.** to put up with; tolerate: *I can't stand all this noise.* **3.** to undergo without damage; withstand: *Those gloves have stood the test of time and wear.* **4.** to be subjected to; undergo: *to stand trial.* —*n.* **1.** a position, attitude, or opinion: *What is the candidate's stand on taxes?* **2.** determined effort for or against something: *to take a stand against smoking.* **3.** a stop or halt, especially for battle: *The troops made a stand at the entrance to the valley.* **4.** a place where or in which someone or something stands. **5.** a rack or similar structure for placing things: *an umbrella stand.* **6.** a booth, counter, or stall for carrying on a business: *a newspaper stand.* **7.** *also,* **stands.** a raised platform or similar structure, usually having several tiers on which one can sit or stand: *We watched the baseball game from the stands.* **8.** see **witness stand. 9.** a group of trees or plants: *A stand of trees grew on the hill.*

·**to stand a chance.** to have a chance or likelihood: *Our team stands a chance of winning.*

·**to stand by. a.** to take the side of; support; defend: *My friends stood by me during the crisis.* **b.** to be or become ready, as for use or action.

·**to stand for. a.** to represent; symbolize; mean: *Uncle Sam stands for the United States.* **b.** to favor, as a position, attitude, or opinion: *That candidate stands for improving the school.* **c.** *Informal.* to permit; tolerate: *My parents won't stand for disrespect.*

·**to stand in for.** to be a substitute for.

·**to stand off.** to repel or keep at a distance: *The police formed a line and stood off the rioters.*

·**to stand out. a.** to jut out; project; protrude. **b.** to be prominent or noticeable: *to stand out in a crowd.*

·**to stand up. a.** to rise to or be on one's feet. **b.** to withstand wear, hardship, pressure, or the like; last.

·**to stand up for.** to take the side of; support; defend.

stand·ard (stan′dərd) *n.* **1.** anything accepted or used to set an example or serve as a model: *The army has strict standards of dress and conduct.* **2.** an established measure: *The meter is an international standard.* **3.** a flag, figure, or other object used as an emblem: *the standard of a regiment.* **4.** an upright support or part: *the standard of a lamp.* —*adj.* **1.** serving or fitted to serve as a standard: *a standard measure of weight.* **2.** having widely accepted excellence or authority: *a standard book on dogs.* **3.** widely used; usual: *standard practices.* **4.** conforming to the speech or writing that is generally accepted as correct or preferred: *standard spelling.*

Standard English, the English language as written and spoken by educated people and clearly understood by the majority of speakers of English. It follows generally conservative conventions of spelling, grammar, and vocabulary as used in major dictionaries and other publications.

stand·ard·ize (stan′dər dīz′) *v.t.,* **stand·ard·ized, stand·ard·iz·ing.** to make standard; regulate by a standard: *to standardize machine parts.* —**stand′ard·i·za′tion,** *n.*

standard of living, the average level of goods, services,

luxuries, and the like available to a person, group, or country.

standard time, time for any region based on its longitudinal distance from Greenwich, England. The earth is divided into twenty-four time zones. In North America and U.S. territory in the Pacific Ocean, the standard time zones are Atlantic, Eastern, Central, Mountain, Pacific, Alaska, Hawaii-Aleutian, and Samoa.

stand·by (stand′bī′) *n., pl.* **stand·bys. 1.** a person or thing that can be depended on in an emergency. **2.** a person or thing kept ready to be used as a replacement or substitute.

stand·ee (stan dē′) *n.* a person who stands because there are no vacant seats, as in a theater, train, or the like.

stand–in (stand′in′) *n.* **1.** a person who takes the place of a motion-picture or television actor or actress while lights, cameras, and other technical equipment are being set up and adjusted, or during scenes involving dangerous action. **2.** any person who substitutes for another.

stand·ing (stan′ding) *adj.* **1.** upright or on end; straight; erect: *standing corn, a standing collar.* **2.** done from or in an upright position: *a standing ovation.* **3.** continuing in existence, operation, or effect: *a standing rule, a standing committee.* —*n.* **1.** status, grade, or rank, as in a profession or society; reputation: *amateur standing, scholastic standing.* **2.** duration: *a friendship of long standing.*

stand·off·ish (stand′ôf′ish) *adj.* lacking warmth or friendliness; reserved; aloof.

stand·pipe (stand′pīp′) *n.* a large vertical pipe or tower used to store water, usually standing on high ground so as to provide pressure in a water system, such as that on the roof of an apartment house or factory.

stand·point (stand′point′) *n.* a position from which things are viewed and judged; point of view.

stand·still (stand′stil′) *n.* a halt; stop: *The strike brought work at the steel mill to a standstill.*

stank (stangk) a past tense of **stink.**

stan·nic (stan′ik) *adj.* of, relating to, or containing tin, especially in its higher oxidation state of + 4.

stan·nous (stan′əs) *adj.* of, relating to, or containing tin, especially in its lower oxidation state of + 2.

stan·za (stan′zə) *n.* in poetry, a group of lines arranged in any of various patterns according to meter, rhyme, and the like.

sta·pes (stā′pēz) *n., pl.* **sta·pes** or **sta·pe·des** (stə-pē′dēz, stā′pə dēz′). the innermost of the three small bones in the middle ear; stirrup.

staph·y·lo·coc·cus (staf′ə-lə kok′əs) *n., pl.* **staph·y·lo·coc·ci** (staf′ə lə kok′sī). any of a group of spherical bacteria that form irregular clusters. Diseases such as impetigo and pneumonia are caused by various types of staphylococci.

sta·ple¹ (stā′pəl) *n.* **1.** a small, bent piece of thin wire used for fastening together papers, fabrics, or other thin materials. **2.** a U-shaped piece of metal with pointed ends, driven into something for fastening, as to support a hook or to hold wire fencing to a post. —*v.t.,* **sta·pled, sta·pling.** to secure, fasten, or attach with a staple or staples. [From the Old English word *stapol* meaning "a post."]

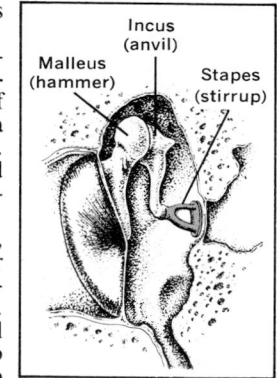

stapes and other bones of the middle ear

sta·ple² (stā′pəl) *n.* **1.** a basic product in widespread use or demand: *Flour, salt, and sugar are staples.* **2.** a major product grown or manufactured in a country or region: *Rice is a staple of southern China.* **3.** a basic or major element; substantial part. **4.** raw material. **5.** a textile fiber used in the manufacture of yarn. —*adj.* **1.** basic or major: *staple industries.* **2.** regularly produced, used, or sold in large quantities for the market: *a staple crop.* [From the Old French word *estaple* meaning "market."]

sta·pler (stā′plər) *n.* a small device for driving wire staples, especially to fasten paper and other thin materials together.

star (stär) *n.* **1.** any heavenly body that appears as a bright point of light in the night sky. **2.** *Astronomy.* a large, round heavenly body that shines by its own light, as distinguished from planets with their satellites, and from comets and meteors. **3.** a geometric figure usually having five or more points radiating from a center. **4.** an asterisk. **5.** a person who is outstanding in some field: *a baseball star.* **6.** an actor, singer, or other performer who plays the lead in a play, motion picture, television program, or the like: *the star of a show.* —*v.,* **starred, star·ring.** —*v.t.* **1.** to set or ornament with stars. **2.** to mark with an asterisk: *to star a passage in a book.* **3.** to present (a performer) in a leading role: *That movie starred my favorite actor.* —*v.i.* **1.** to perform a leading part: *to star in a play.* **2.** to perform outstandingly: *The pitcher starred in the game.* —*adj.* **1.** most prominent; leading: *a star performer, a star football player.* **2.** of or relating to a star or stars. —**star′like′,** *adj.*

star·board (stär′bərd) *n.* the right side of a boat or ship as one faces forward. —*adj.* of, relating to, or on the right side of a boat or ship.

starch (stärch) *n., pl.* **starch·es.** **1.** a white, granular carbohydrate manufactured and stored in all green plants. **2.** any food rich in starch, such as rice, corn, and wheat products. **3.** any of various substances, including natural starch, used for stiffening cloth. —*v.t.* to stiffen with starch: *to starch shirts.*

starch·y (stär′che) *adj.,* **starch·i·er, starch·i·est.** **1.** of, resembling, or containing starch: *a starchy diet.* **2.** stiffened with starch: *starchy curtains.* **3.** stiff in manner; formal: *The government reception was a starchy affair.* —**starch′i·ness,** *n.*

star·dom (stär′dəm) *n.* the state of being a star performer: *The actor achieved stardom very quickly.*

stare (stâr) *v.,* **stared, star·ing.** —*v.i.* to look intently with the eyes wide open. —*v.t.* to affect in a particular way by staring. *n.* the act of staring. —**star′er,** *n.*

•**to stare down.** to make uneasy or embarrassed by staring: *The speaker stared down the heckler.*

star·fish (stär′fish′) *n., pl.* **star·fish** or **star·fish·es.** any of a group of flattened, star-shaped sea animals, usually having five tapering arms. Starfish have no backbone and are classified as echinoderms.

star·gaze (stär′gāz′) *v.i.,* **star·gazed, star·gaz·ing.** **1.** to gaze at or study the stars. **2.** to daydream. —**star′gaz′er,** *n.*

starfish

stark (stärk) *adj.* **1.** absolute or unqualified; complete: *stark fools, stark madness.* **2.** harsh, grim, or severe: *stark weather, a stark look.* **3.** barren or desolate; bare: *a stark room, a stark landscape.* **4.** rigid; stiff. —*adv.* absolutely; completely: *stark raving mad.* —**stark′ly,** *adv.* —**stark′ness,** *n.*

star·let (stär′lit) *n.* in motion pictures, an inexperienced actress or singer who is being given training and publicity by her studio.

star·light (stär′līt′) *n.* the light from a star or stars. —*adj.* another word for **starlit.**

star·ling (stär′ling) *n.* any of various birds found in most parts of the world, usually having a stout body, pointed wings, and a short tail. The starling was brought to the United States from Europe.

star·lit (stär′lit′) *adj.* lighted by the stars. Also, **starlight.**

Star of David, a six-pointed star, a symbol of Judaism and of the nation of Israel.

star·ry (stär′ē) *adj.,* **star·ri·er, star·ri·est.** **1.** studded with or lighted by stars: *a starry night.* **2.** shining like a star or stars; bright: *crystal goblets with starry glints of light.* **3.** shaped in the form of a star.

star·ry-eyed (stär′ē īd′) *adj.* wishful or trusting: *a starry-eyed optimist.*

Stars and Stripes, the flag of the United States, consisting of alternating red and white stripes representing the thirteen original colonies and, in the upper left corner, a blue field that now contains fifty white stars, representing the fifty states.

Star of David

Star–Span·gled Banner (stär′spang′gəld) *n.* **1.** the national anthem of the United States, the words of which were written by Francis Scott Key during the War of 1812. **2.** the flag of the United States.

start (stärt) *v.i.* **1.** to make a beginning; set out: *to start on a science project.* **2.** to begin; commence: *The movie starts at ten o'clock.* **3.** to make a sudden movement, as from surprise or fear: *The baby started at the loud noise.* **4.** to spring or leap suddenly from a hiding place: *A deer started from the bushes as we walked by.* **5.** to become loose: *The planks of the boat started from the sea's pounding.* —*v.t.* **1.** to begin (something); commence: *to start a journey.* **2.** to put into action; set in motion: *to start an engine.* **3.** to set up or give rise to; establish or originate: *to start a business, to start a rumor.* **4.** to help (someone) begin something: *A good education may start you on the road to success.* **5.** to drive from a hiding place; rouse: *The hunting dog started the birds from the bush.* **6.** to cause to loosen: *The vibrations started nails from the walls.* **7.** to enter in a contest: *The owners started their horse in the race.* —*n.* **1.** the beginning, as of a course of action, movement, or journey: *to get an early start on a trip.* **2.** a sudden movement, as from surprise or fear: *I gave a start when my friend tapped me on the shoulder.* **3.** help for beginning something: *The gift of fifty dollars gave the child a start on a savings account.* **4.** the advantage gained by beginning first, as in a race.

start·er (stär′tər) *n.* **1.** a person who begins something. **2.** the beginning of a process, activity, or series. **3.** a device that starts an engine. **4.** a person whose work is seeing that public conveyances leave on schedule: *a bus starter.* **5.** a person who gives the signal for starting a race. **6.** any of the competitors starting in a race.

star·tle (stär′təl) *v.,* **star·tled, star·tling.** —*v.t.* to arouse or excite suddenly, as with surprise, fright, or astonishment: *The loud noise startled the baby.* —*v.i.* to become startled. —*n.* sudden surprise, fright, or astonishment.

star·tling (stärt′ling) *adj.* causing sudden surprise, fright, or astonishment: *startling news.* —**star′tling·ly,** *adv.*

star·va·tion (stär vā′shən) *n.* the act of starving or the state of being starved.

---

at; āpe; fär; câre; end; mē; it; īce; pîerce; hot; ōld; sông, fôrk; oil; out; up; ūse; rüle; pull; tûrn; chin; sing; shop; thin; this; hw in white; zh in treasure. The symbol ə stands for the unstressed vowel sound heard in about, taken, pencil, lemon, and circus.

S

starve (stärv) *v.*, **starved, starv·ing.** —*v.i.* **1.** to suffer from or die of hunger: *The victims of the famine were starving.* **2.** to need or desire greatly: *The orphaned child starved for affection.* **3.** *Informal.* to feel hungry: *I haven't had lunch, and I'm starving.* —*v.t.* **1.** to cause to suffer or die because of hunger. **2.** to bring to a specified condition by starving: *to starve a besieged enemy into surrendering.* [From the Old English word *steorfan* meaning "to die." *To starve* has changed its meaning over the years. In Old English, it meant "to die," no matter how, though it soon came to mean "to die from hunger" and later "to suffer from lack of food."]

starve·ling (stärv′ling) *n.* a starving person, animal, or plant. —*adj.* weak from a lack of food; starving; hungry.

stash (stash) *Informal. v.t.* to store or hide for safekeeping or future use. —*n., pl.* **stash·es.** something stored or hidden.

state (stāt) *n.* **1.** the condition of a person or thing: *The parents were in a state of anxiety about their lost child. The patient is in a good state of mind.* **2.** position, rank, or standing: *one's state in life.* **3.** *also,* **State.** a body of people living together under one government; nation; commonwealth: *The continent of Africa has many new, independent states.* **4.** *also,* **State.** one of the constituents of some nations that have federal governments: *Hawaii is a state of the United States.* **5.** the territory of a state or nation. **6.** *also,* **State.** civil government, authority, or organization: *That diplomat is involved in important affairs of state.* **7.** one of the three conditions, solid, liquid, or gas, in which matter exists. **8. the States.** the United States. —*v.t.,* **stat·ed, stat·ing. 1.** to express or explain fully in words; declare; represent: *to state an opinion, to state a problem.* **2.** to set; fix: *The bulletin stated a time for the next meeting.* —*adj.* **1.** *also,* **State.** of or relating to a state: *a state tax, a state highway.* **2.** of or relating to national or state government: *state policy, state affairs.* **3.** of, relating to, or for ceremonious or official occasions; formal: *a state reception.* **4.** designated to represent a state: *a state flower.*

state·craft (stāt′kraft′) *n.* the art of conducting state affairs; statesmanship.

state·hood (stāt′hŏŏd′) *n.* the condition of being a state, especially a state of the United States.

state·house (stāt′hous′) *also,* **State House.** *n., pl.* **state·hous·es** (stāt′hou′ziz). a building in which the legislature of a state of the United States meets.

state·less (stāt′lis) *adj.* having no citizenship or nationality: *stateless refugees.*

state·ly (stāt′lē) *adj.,* **state·li·er, state·li·est.** majestic; dignified: *a stately building, a stately monarch.* —**state′li·ness,** *n.*

state·ment (stāt′mənt) *n.* **1.** the act or manner of stating something: *accurate statement of the facts is essential.* **2.** something stated: *The suspects made false statements to the police. The president issued a statement on tax reform to the press.* **3.** a report or summary of financial matters: *a bank statement, a corporation's statement of profit and loss.*

state-of-the-art (stāt′əv thē ärt′) *adj.* using or incorporating the latest technology; being at the most advanced or up-to-date stage of development: *a state-of-the-art computer system, state-of-the-art space technology.*

state·room (stāt′rŭm′, stāt′rŏŏm′) *n.* a private room on a ship or a compartment on a railroad train.

state·side (stāt′sīd′) *also,* **State·side.** *adj.* of or in the continental United States. —*adv.* to, toward, or in the continental United States.

states·man (stāts′mən) *n., pl.* **states·men** (stāts′mən). a person who shows skill or wisdom in conducting public or national affairs. —**states′man·like′,** *adj.*

states·man·ship (stāts′mən ship′) *n.* skill in conducting public or national affairs.

states' rights 1. rights or powers not delegated to the U.S. federal government nor prohibited to the states under the Constitution. **2.** the doctrine that the powers of the federal government should impinge to a lesser degree on the powers of the various state governments.

state·wide (stāt′wīd′) *also,* **state-wide.** *adj.* happening throughout a state: *a statewide building boom, statewide elections.*

states·wom·an (stāts′wŭm′ən) *n., pl.* **states·wom·en** (stāts′wim′ən). a woman who shows skill or wisdom in conducting public or national affairs.

stat·ic (stat′ik) *adj.* **1.** showing little or no growth, change, or movement; that remains the same: *a static population.* **2.** *Mechanics.* of or relating to bodies at rest or to forces in equilibrium. **3.** *Physics.* acting by weight without producing motion: *static pressure.* **4.** of or relating to charges of electricity that have accumulated on a body and do not move about. Static electricity can be produced by combing dry hair with a dry comb. —*n.* electrical charges in the atmosphere, such as those produced by lightning, that may be picked up by a radio receiver and heard as crackling or hissing sounds. —**stat′i·cal·ly,** *adv.*

stat·ics (stat′iks) *n.* the branch of mechanics that deals with bodies at rest or in equilibrium under the action of various forces. ▲ used with a singular verb.

sta·tion (stā′shən) *n.* **1.** a building or place set up as a headquarters for a business, public service, or the like: *a first-aid station.* **2.** a regular stopping place along a route, as of a bus or train line; terminal; depot. **3.** the place in which one stands in the performance of some duty; assigned post. **4.** the social position of an individual: *The judge has a high station in life.* **5.** a place where radio or television programs are recorded and transmitted. **6.** a specific channel used for a broadcast. —*v.t.* to assign to a station; place in a post or position: *A police officer is stationed at the intersection to direct traffic.*

sta·tion·ar·y (stā′shə ner′ē) *adj.* **1.** having a fixed place or position; permanent: *The desks in the room were stationary.* **2.** not moving: *The elevator was stationary.* **3.** unchanging in character, condition, or quantity.

station break, a pause in a radio or television broadcast to identify the network or station or to make an announcement.

sta·tion·er (stā′shə nər) *n.* a person who sells stationery.

sta·tion·er·y (stā′shə ner′ē) *n.* **1.** writing paper and envelopes. **2.** materials used in writing, such as pens, pencils, or paper and office supplies.

sta·tion·mas·ter (stā′shən mas′tər) *n.* a person in charge of a railroad or bus station.

station wagon, an automobile having one or more folding or removable rear seats and a tailgate used for loading and unloading passengers or luggage.

sta·tis·tic (stə tis′tik) *n.* a numerical fact that is collected and used as information about a particular subject.

sta·tis·ti·cal (stə tis′ti kəl) *adj.* of, relating to, consisting of, or based on statistics: *a statistical problem, a statistical analysis.* —**sta·tis′ti·cal·ly,** *adv.*

stat·is·ti·cian (stat′ə stish′ən) *n.* a person who is expert in compiling and interpreting statistics.

sta·tis·tics (stə tis′tiks) *n.* **1.** the science of collecting, classifying, and interpreting numerical data as it is related to a particular subject. ▲ used with a singular verb. **2.** the numerical data itself. ▲ used with a plural verb.

sta·tor (stā′tər) *n.* a stationary part in or about which a moving part revolves, as in a motor or dynamo.

stat·u·ar·y (stach′ü er′ē) *n., pl.* **stat·u·ar·ies. 1.** statues as a group. **2.** the art of carving statues.

statue of Abraham Lincoln

stat·ue (stach′ü) *n.* a representation, often life-size or larger, of a human or animal figure that has been carved, cast, or modeled in stone, bronze, clay, or another material.

Statue of Liberty, a monumental statue situated on an island in New York Harbor that depicts liberty as a crowned woman holding a torch aloft. The Statue of Liberty was given to the United States by France.

stat·u·esque (stach′ü esk′) *adj.* resembling a statue, as in size, grace, or dignity; stately.

stat·u·ette (stach′ü et′) *n.* a small statue.

stat·ure (stach′ər) *n.* **1.** the height of a person or animal in a normal standing position: *a person of average stature.* **2.** level, as of achievement or mental growth; standing: *moral stature.*

sta·tus (stā′təs, stat′əs) *n.,* *pl.* **sta·tus·es. 1.** state; condition: *the status of the nation's economy.* **2.** relative place or rank, especially social or professional standing. **3.** the character or condition of a person or thing as determined by law: *a person's marital status.*

status quo (kwō) the existing or present state of affairs.

stat·ute (stach′üt) *n.* **1.** a law enacted by a legislative body. **2.** a written rule or law regulating an organization, such as a university or corporation.

statute mile, see mile.

stat·u·to·ry (stach′ə tôr′ē) *adj.* of, relating to, set by, or punishable under statute: *a statutory offense.*

staunch¹ (stônch) *also,* **stanch.** *adj.* **1.** loyal and dependable: *a staunch friend.* **2.** strongly built or constructed: *a staunch ship, a staunch argument.* [From the Old French word *estanche* meaning "reliable, watertight," from *estanchier* "to stop a flow," going back to the Latin word *stans,* present participle of *stare* "to stand."] —**staunch′ly,** *adv.* —**staunch′ness,** *n.*

staunch² (stônch) another spelling of **stanch¹.**

stave (stāv) *n.* **1.** any long, narrow, flexible strip of wood, such as one of those that form the sides of a barrel. **2.** a rod, pole, or staff. **3.** a rung, as of a ladder or chair. **4.** a verse or stanza, as of a poem. **5.** see **staff** (*def. 5*). —*v.,* **staved** or **stove,** **stav·ing.** —*v.t.* **1.** to smash or break a hole in (usually followed by *in*): *A rock stove in the hull of the ship.* **2.** to furnish with a stave or staves:

staves of a barrel

to stave a barrel. —*v.i.* to be smashed in or punctured.
•**to stave off.** to ward off or prevent: *to stave off a blow.*

staves (stāvz) a plural of **staff.**

stay¹ (stā) *v.,* **stayed, stay·ing.** —*v.i.* **1.** to remain or continue in a specified place or condition: *to stay home, to stay young.* **2.** to live in a place, especially for a short period of time: *They stayed at a hotel while visiting the city.* **3.** to cease movement or activity; stop. **4.** to linger; wait: *We could not stay for the last act.* **5.** *Informal.* to last or endure, as in a race or contest. —*v.t.* **1.** to remain for the duration of: *to stay the night in a motel.* **2.** to put off; defer: *The judge stayed the sentence until the following day.* **3.** to check or stop, especially temporarily: *The poor family had barely enough food to stay their hunger.* —*n.* **1.** the act of staying or remaining: *a short stay in town.* **2.** a break or delay of action; stop; halt: *The governor requested a stay on raises for all state employees in an effort to reduce the budget.* **3.** *Law.* a delay in the execution of an order of a court of law. [From the Old French word *ester* meaning "to stand, stay¹," from the Latin word *stare* "to stand."]

stay² (stā) *n.* **1.** something used to support, strengthen, or sustain; prop; brace. **2.** a piece of plastic or other stiff material, inserted in shirt collars and other garments to give shape and support. **3. stays.** a corset. —*v.t.,* **stayed, stay·ing.** to support, strengthen, or sustain. [From the Middle French word *estayer* meaning "to prop up, support."]

stay³ (stā) *n.* **1.** a strong rope, usually of wire, used to support a mast on a boat or ship. **2.** any rope or chain used for a similar purpose. —*v.t.,* **stayed, stay·ing.** to secure or steady with a stay or stays. [From the Old English word *stæg* with the same meaning.]

staying power, the ability to endure; stamina: *the staying power needed to run a marathon.*

stay·sail (stā′sāl, stā′səl) *n.* a sail, usually triangular, that is attached to a stay.

STD, sexually transmitted disease.

Ste., Sainte (in names of persons or places).

stead (sted) *n.* a place or position usually or previously occupied by another: *My friend worked in my stead.*
•**to stand in good stead.** to be of use or service to; be advantageous to.

stead·fast (sted′fast′) *adj.* **1.** not changing; unwavering; faithful: *steadfast loyalty to a cause.* **2.** direct; steady: *a steadfast gaze.* —**stead′fast′ly,** *adv.* —**stead′fast′ness,** *n.*

stead·y (sted′ē) *adj.,* **stead·i·er, stead·i·est. 1.** kept at an even rate; regular or uniform: *a steady pace.* **2.** firm or sure in movement or position; not shaking or faltering: *The artist had a steady hand.* **3.** regular or permanent: *a steady customer, a steady job.* **4.** reliable; dependable: *a steady worker.* **5.** not easily upset; calm: *steady nerves.* —*v.t.,* *v.i.,* **stead·ied, stead·y·ing.** to make or become steady. —*adv.* in a steady manner; steadily. —**stead′i·ly,** *adv.* —**stead′i·ness,** *n.*
•**to go steady.** to date someone regularly and exclusively.

steady state theory, the theory that matter in the universe is constantly being created to replace matter that is being destroyed. The universe itself keeps the same basic properties it has always had.

at; āpe; fär; câre; end; mē; it; īce; pîerce; hot; ōld; sông, fôrk; oil; out; up; ūse; rüle; pull; tûrn; chin; sing; shop; thin; **this**; hw in white; zh in treasure. The symbol ə stands for the unstressed vowel sound heard in about, taken, pencil, lemon, and circus.

S

steak (stāk) *n.* a cut of meat or fish cut for cooking by broiling or frying.

steal (stēl) *v.*, **stole, sto·len, steal·ing.** —*v.t.* **1.** to take from another secretly and without right or permission: *The paintings were stolen from the museum.* **2.** to take by surprise or in a tricky way: *to steal an hour off from work.* **3.** to move or place secretly or unobserved: *We stole the presents into the room.* **4.** *Baseball.* to gain (the next base) without the help of a hit or error. —*v.i.* **1.** to commit or practice theft. **2.** to move or pass secretly, slowly, or without being seen: *A smile stole over the child's face.* **3.** *Baseball.* to steal a base. —*n.* **1.** the act of stealing; theft. **2.** *Baseball.* the act of stealing a base. **3.** *Informal.* a bargain: *The used car was a steal at $1,000.* —**steal'er,** *n.*

stealth (stelth) *n.* secret action, procedure, or manner of behavior: *The spy obtained the information by stealth.*

stealth·y (stel'thē) *adj.*, **stealth·i·er, stealth·i·est.** moving or acting in a secret manner. —**stealth'i·ly,** *adv.* —**stealth'i·ness,** *n.*

steam (stēm) *n.* **1.** water converted into the form of a gas, especially by heat. It is used to provide heat for buildings and to power engines and other machinery. **2.** power, heat, or other energy generated by steam. **3.** a mist formed when water vapor cools: *There was steam on the window above the sink.* **4.** *Informal.* energy; initiative: *to start a project on one's own steam.* —*v.t.* to treat or expose to steam, as in cooking or cleaning: *to steam clams, to steam the wrinkles from a suit.* —*v.i.* **1.** to give off steam or vapor: *The fabric steamed from the heat of the iron.* **2.** to rise in the form of or become steam. **3.** to be covered by condensed vapor or mist: *My eyeglasses steamed up in the warm air.* **4.** to move or travel by steam: *The vessel steamed into port.* **5.** *Informal.* to be angry.

·**to let off steam** or **to blow off steam.** *Informal.* to release pent-up emotions, energy, or tensions.

steam·boat (stēm'bōt') *n.* any of various steam-driven boats, especially in lakes and rivers.

steam engine, an engine using the energy of steam to do mechanical work. The steam expands within a cylinder to drive a piston in a back-and-forth motion.

steam·er (stē'mər) *n.* **1.** a boat driven by steam; steamship. **2.** a thin-shelled clam, usually cooked by steaming. **3.** a special container in which something is steamed, especially a large pot for steaming clams.

steam fitter, a person who installs and repairs steam pipes, fittings, and other heating equipment.

steam·roll·er (stēm'rō'lər) *also,* **steam roller.** *n.* **1.** a vehicle moving on heavy rollers, used in road work, as for leveling freshly laid pavement or smoothing earth. Many were once steam-powered. **2.** any force or power that is large and powerful and can overwhelm opposition. —*v.i.* *Informal.* to move with overwhelming force or organization: *The presidential campaign steamrollered through the South.* —*v.t.* **1.** to overwhelm or suppress ruthlessly; defeat: *to steamroller all opposition.* **2.** to level or smooth with a steamroller.

steam·ship (stēm'ship') *n.* a large, ocean-going ship propelled by steam power.

steam shovel, a power-driven digging machine having a single large bucket or scoop at the end of a long beam. Many such machines were once steam-powered.

steam turbine, a turbine using steam as a source of energy.

steam·y (stē'mē) *adj.*, **steam·i·er, steam·i·est.** **1.** giving off, covered by, or filled with steam: *a steamy window.* **2.** uncomfortably

steam shovel

warm; humid: *steamy weather.* —**steam'i·ly,** *adv.* —**steam'i·ness,** *n.*

steed (stēd) *n.* *Literary.* a horse, especially a high-spirited riding horse.

steel (stēl) *n.* **1.** any alloy of iron mixed with carbon and often other elements to increase hardness and strength. **2.** something made from steel, such as a sword. **3.** a quality characteristic of steel, such as hardness or strength: *The tightrope walker had muscles of steel.* —*adj.* **1.** made of steel. **2.** of or relating to the production of steel: *a steel mill.* **3.** resembling steel: *steel nerves.* —*v.t.* **1.** to cover with steel, as by edging or plating. **2.** to cause to be strong and hard like steel: *to steel oneself for bad news.*

steel band, a musical group that uses percussion instruments made from steel oil drums. Steel bands are traditional to Trinidad and other Caribbean islands.

steel wool, fine threads of steel matted together in a pad or tuft, used for polishing or cleaning.

steel·work·er (stēl'wûr'kər) *n.* a person who works in a steel mill.

steel·works (stēl'wûrks') *n.* a plant where steel is made. ▲ used with a singular or plural verb.

steel·y (stē'lē) *adj.*, **steel·i·er, steel·i·est.** **1.** made of steel. **2.** resembling or suggesting steel: *steely eyes.* —**steel'i·ness,** *n.*

steel·yard (stēl'yärd', stil'yərd) *n.* a weighing device made up of a bar with the object to be weighed at one end and a movable weight at the other. The weight is slid along the bar until a balance is reached, and the correct weight is registered on a scale marked off on the bar.

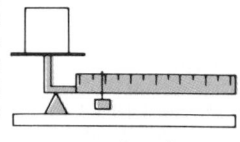

steelyard

steep¹ (stēp) *adj.* **1.** having a very sharp face or slope: *a steep stairway, to climb the steeper side of a mountain.* **2.** *Informal.* too much or too high; unreasonable: *The lawyer demanded a steep fee from the client.* [From the Old English word *stēap* meaning "lofty, high, tall."] —**steep'ly,** *adv.* —**steep'ness,** *n.*

steep² (stēp) *v.t.* **1.** to soak in liquid so as to soften, clean, or extract something, such as flavor: *to steep tea leaves.* **2.** to involve deeply or absorb; saturate: *The abandoned house was steeped in mystery.* —*v.i.* to undergo soaking in liquid. [From the Middle English word *stepen* meaning "to soak in liquid," of Scandinavian origin.]

steep·en (stē'pən) *v.t., v.i.* to make or become steeper: *The path gradually steepened as we climbed higher.*

stee·ple (stē'pəl) *n.* a high tower with a spire at the top, built on the roof of a church or other building.

stee·ple·chase (stē'pəl chās') *n.* a race on a course that has barriers, ditches, and other obstacles over which the contestants must jump.

stee·ple·jack (stē'pəl jak') *n.* a person whose work is climbing steeples, towers, and other tall structures to paint them or to make repairs.

steer¹ (stîr) *v.t.* **1.** to guide the course of (a vessel or vehicle), as with a wheel, handle, or the like. **2.** to set and follow (a course): *to steer a course for the West Indies.* **3.** to direct; guide; channel: *The police steered the candidate through the crowd.* —*v.i.* **1.** to guide a vessel or vehicle. **2.** to follow or direct one's course: *The captain is steering for the island.* **3.** to be guided, as by a wheel or a person: *The truck does not steer easily.* —*n.* *Slang.* a piece of advice;

steeple

suggestion; tip: *to be given a bum steer*. [From the Old English word *stēoran* meaning "to guide a vessel, direct."]
·**to steer clear of.** to avoid completely; shun.

steer² (stîr) *n.* a castrated bull raised for beef. [From the Old English word *stēor* meaning this animal.]

steer·age (stîr′ij) *n.* **1.** formerly, the portion of a passenger ship occupied by those passengers paying the cheapest fare. **2.** the act of steering.

steering wheel, a wheel turned by the driver to direct the course of a vehicle or vessel.

steers·man (stîrz′mən) *n., pl.* **steers·men** (stîrz′mən). a person who steers a ship; helmsman.

steg·o·sau·rus (steg′ə sôr′əs) *n., pl.* **steg·o·sau·ri** (steg′ə sôr′ī) or **steg·o·sau·rus·es.** a large dinosaur that had a spiked tail and two rows of bony plates along its back. [Formed from the Greek words *stegein* meaning "to cover, conceal" and *sauros* meaning "lizard." The name refers to the bony plates along this reptile's back.]

stegosaurus

stein (stīn) *n.* a beer mug, usually holding about a pint (about 470 milliliters).

stel·lar (stel′ər) *adj.* **1.** of, relating to, or resembling a star or stars: *stellar light.* **2.** of or relating to a star performer: *a stellar part in a play.* **3.** very important or outstanding: *a stellar achievement.*

St. El·mo's fire (el′mōz) *n.* a discharge of electricity, often during a thunderstorm, that appears as a bright glow around objects, such as the masts of a ship or the wings of an aircraft. [From *St. Elmo* (d. 303), patron saint of sailors.]

stem¹ (stem) *n.* **1.** the main supporting part of a plant, from which smaller stalks, leaves, or flowers may grow. **2.** a stalk that joins a leaf, flower, or fruit to the plant or tree it grows on. **3.** something resembling this in shape or purpose: *the stem of a wine glass, the stem of a pipe.* **4.** the part of a word to which affixes and inflectional endings are added to change the meaning of the word. *Swim* is the stem of *swimming, swims,* and *swimmer.* **5.** the bow of a boat or ship. —*v.,* **stemmed, stem·ming.** —*v.t.* to remove the stem of or from: *to stem a cluster of grapes.* —*v.i.* to begin, develop, or be descended: *Many health problems stem from poor eating habits.* [From the Old English word *stemn* meaning "a tree trunk," "stalk of a plant," or "prow."]
·**from stem to stern.** from one end to the other; thoroughly: *The house had to be cleaned from stem to stern.*

stem² (stem) *v.t.,* **stemmed, stem·ming.** **1.** to stop or restrain by or as if by damming; stanch: *to stem the flow of blood with a bandage.* **2.** to make progress or headway against. [From the Old Norse word *stemma* with the same meanings.]

stemmed (stemd) *adj.* **1.** having a stem. ▲ used chiefly in combination: *long-stemmed roses.* **2.** having the stem removed: *stemmed and pitted cherries.*

stench (stench) *n., pl.* **stench·es.** a very strong, foul odor.

sten·cil (sten′səl) *n.* **1.** a thin sheet, as of metal or paper, in which a pattern is cut. The sheet is put on top of something that is to be decorated, and only the cut-out areas allow paint or ink through to the surface. **2.** a printing or design produced by using a stencil. —*v.t.,*

sten·ciled, sten·cil·ing; *also, British,* **sten·cilled, sten·cil·ling.** to mark or paint with a stencil.

ste·nog·ra·pher (stə nog′rə fər) *n.* a person who is skilled at taking shorthand or at typing in it.

sten·o·graph·ic (sten′ə graf′ik) *adj.* of, relating to, or using stenography.

ste·nog·ra·phy (stə nog′rə fē) *n.* the act, skill, or method of taking or typing in shorthand.

sten·to·ri·an (sten tôr′ē ən) *adj.* extremely loud: *to speak in stentorian tones.* [From *Stentor,* a messenger in Greek legend who had a voice as loud as that of fifty men.]

step (step) *n.* **1.** the movement of raising the foot and putting it down in a new position, as in walking, climbing, dancing, or the like: *The dancer has a light step.* **2.** the distance covered in one such movement. **3.** any short distance: *The store is only a few steps from our house.* **4.** any place to put the foot in going up or coming down, as a stair or the rung of a ladder. **5. steps.** a flight of stairs. **6.** an action or one of a series of actions leading to a particular goal or result: *The signing of the agreement was a step toward peace.* **7.** a degree or stage in a series: *to bring a project one step nearer to completion.* **8.** the sound made by putting the foot down: *The deer heard my step and ran away.* **9.** a footprint: *The new snow covered our steps.* **10.** a rhythm or pattern of walking, dancing, marching, or the like: *to keep in step.* **11.** *Music.* an interval corresponding to one degree on the staff or in a scale. —*v.,* **stepped, step·ping.** —*v.i.* **1.** to move by taking a step or steps: *to step to the rear of a bus.* **2.** to put or press the foot: *to step on a piece of broken glass.* —*v.t.* **1.** to put or move (the foot) in taking a step. **2.** to measure by taking step: *to step off twenty paces.*
·**step by step.** little by little; gradually.
·**to step down. 1.** to resign from a position. **2.** to decrease, as in rate or speed.
·**to step on it.** to go fast; hurry up.
·**to step up.** to increase; accelerate: *The company had to step up production to fill all the orders.*
·**to watch one's step.** to act or move more carefully.

step– *combining form* related by the remarriage of a parent, rather than by blood: *stepchild.*

step·broth·er (step′bruth′ər) *n.* a son of one's stepparent by a former marriage.

step·child (step′child′) *n., pl.* **step·chil·dren** (step′chil′drən). a child of one's husband or wife by a former marriage; stepdaughter or stepson.

step·daugh·ter (step′dô′tər) *n.* a daughter of one's husband or wife by a former marriage.

step·fa·ther (step′fä′thər) *n.* the husband of one's mother after the death or divorce of one's father.

step·lad·der (step′lad′ər) *n.* a ladder that stands by itself on four legs and has flat steps instead of rungs.

step·moth·er (step′muth′ər) *n.* the wife of one's father after the death or divorce of one's mother.

step·par·ent (step′pâr′ənt) *n.* a stepfather or stepmother.

steppe (step) *n.* **1.** any of the vast, treeless plains extending from southeastern Europe into central Siberia. **2.** any vast, treeless plain. [From the Russian word *step'* with the same meaning.]

step·ping·stone (step′ing stōn′) *also,* **stepping stone.** *n.* **1.** a stone or one of a series of stones on which to

S

step, as in crossing a stream. **2.** an opportunity or means of progressing toward some goal or aim: *The Senate has often been a steppingstone to the presidency.*

step·sis·ter (step′sis′tər) *n.* a daughter of one's stepparent by a former marriage.

step·son (step′sun′) *n.* a son of one's husband or wife by a former marriage.

step–up (step′up′) *n.* an increase in intensity, amount, or activity: *a step-up in activity, a step-up in sales.*

–ster *suffix* (used to form nouns) **1.** a person who makes, uses, or is occupied with: *punster, prankster.* **2.** a person who is: *youngster.* **3.** a person who is related or belongs to: *gangster.*

ster·e·o (ster′ē ō′, stir′ē ō) *n., pl.* **ster·e·os.** **1.** a high-fidelity system designed for stereophonic sound reproduction. **2.** stereophonic sound. —*adj.* see **stereophonic.**

ster·e·o·phon·ic (ster′ē ə fon′ik, stir′ē ə fon′ik) *adj.* of or relating to a system of sound reproduction in which the sound is heard from two or more sources. In stereophonic recording, sound is picked up by two or more separate microphones and reproduced through two or more separate loud speakers, thus creating a more natural effect.

ster·e·op·ti·con (ster′ē op′ti kən, stir′ē op′ti kən) *n.* a slide projector that can project two overlapping pictures at the same time or in quick succession, so as to produce a fading of one into the other.

ster·e·o·scope (ster′ē ə skōp′, stir′ē ə skōp′) *n.* an optical instrument having two lenses through which one sees two views of a picture taken from different angles. This gives the illusion of seeing it in three dimensions.

ster·e·o·scop·ic (ster′ē ə skop′ik, stir′ē ə skop′ik) *adj.* of, for, relating to, or capable of vision or recording or reproduction of images seeming to have three dimensions.

ster·e·o·type (ster′ē ə tīp′, stir′ē ə tīp′) *n.* **1.** a metal plate used in printing that is cast from a mold of the original raised surface of type. **2.** an oversimplified or conventional image of a certain person, group, issue, or the like. A stereotype is thought to be a typical example of something. A cowboy wearing a white hat and riding a white horse is a stereotype of the hero of Western movies. —*v.t.,* **ster·e·o·typed, ster·e·o·typ·ing.** **1.** to make a stereotype of. **2.** to develop a fixed, conventional view of. —**ster′e·o·typ′er,** *n.*

ster·e·o·typed (ster′ē ə tīpt′, stir′ē ə tīpt′) *adj.* **1.** having or showing no originality or individual character; conventional. **2.** printed from stereotype plates.

ster·ile (ster′əl) *adj.* **1.** not able to reproduce; not fertile; barren. **2.** not able to produce or support plants; arid: *a dry and sterile desert region.* **3.** free from bacteria and dirt: *sterile bandages, sterile milk bottles.* **4.** lacking imagination; conventional; stale: *sterile writing.* —**ster′ile·ly,** *adv.*

ste·ril·i·ty (stə ril′i tē) *n.* the condition of being sterile.

ster·i·li·za·tion (ster′ə lə zā′shən) *n.* **1.** the act or process of sterilizing. **2.** the state of being sterilized.

ster·i·lize (ster′ə līz′) *v.t.,* **ster·i·lized, ster·i·liz·ing.** to make sterile. —**ster′i·liz′er,** *n.*

ster·ling (stûr′ling) *n.* **1.** a silver alloy containing 92.5 percent pure silver; sterling silver. **2.** something made of sterling silver. **3.** British money. —*adj.* **1.** containing 92.5 percent pure silver. **2.** made of sterling silver. **3.** made up of, relating to, or payable in British money. **4.** very worthy; excellent: *a sterling reputation.*

stern¹ (stûrn) *adj.* **1.** severe or strict. **2.** showing extreme displeasure; harsh: *to speak in a stern voice.* **3.** grim or forbidding; gloomy: *a stern look.* **4.** resolute; unwavering: *stern resolve.* [From the Old English word *stirne* meaning "hard, austere, severe."] —**stern′ly,** *adv.* —**stern′ness,** *n.*

stern² (stûrn) *n.* the rear part of a boat or ship. [Probably from the Old Norse word *stjörn* meaning "rudder, helm".]

ster·num (stûr′nəm) *n., pl.* **ster·nums** or **ster·na** (stûr′nə). the flat, narrow bone in the center of the chest to which the ribs are joined; breastbone. —**ster′nal,** *adj.*

stern·wheel·er (stûrn′hwē′lər, stûrn′wē′lər) *n.* a steamboat propelled by a single paddle wheel at the stern.

ster·oid (ster′oid, stir′oid) *n.* any of a group of organic compounds, secreted by animals and plants, that are important in regulating metabolism, in the development of sexual characteristics, and in producing certain vitamins and other useful substances. Steroids include cholesterol, digitalis, vitamin D, estrogen, and androgen. Some steroids, such as cortisone, are made synthetically and used in medicine to fight inflammation. [From *ster*(ol) + *-oid*.]

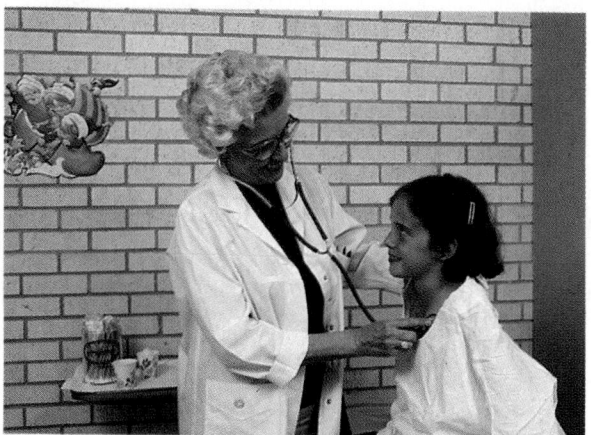

stethoscope

steth·o·scope (steth′ə skōp′) *n.* an instrument used to listen to sounds made by organs of the body, especially sounds of the lungs and heart.

ste·ve·dore (stē′və dôr′) *n.* a person whose work is loading and unloading cargo from ships.

stew (stü, stū) *v.t.* to cook (food) slowly by simmering. —*v.i.* **1.** to be cooked by slow simmering: *The cook let the meat stew for half an hour.* **2.** *Informal.* to be angry or worried; fret. —*n.* **1.** food cooked by stewing, especially a mixture of meat and vegetables cooked together. **2.** *Informal.* a state of anger or worry: *to be in a stew about a lost dog.*

stew·ard (stü′ərd, stū′ərd) *n.* **1.** a person who manages the property, finances, or affairs of another person. **2.** a person in charge of food and other services, as on a ship, airplane, or train, or for a club or hotel. **3.** a man who waits on the passengers of a ship, airplane, or train.

stew·ard·ess (stü′ər dis, stū′ər dis) *n., pl.* **stew·ard·ess·es.** a woman who waits on passengers on a ship, airplane, or train.

stew·ard·ship (stü′ərd ship′, stū′ərd ship′) *n.* **1.** the position or duties of a steward. **2.** responsibility for wise use or protection: *The speaker talked about the stewardship of our natural resources.*

stick¹ (stik) *n.* **1.** a long, thin piece of wood. **2.** anything resembling a stick, especially in shape: *a stick of dynamite.* **3.** an implement used to hit a ball or puck in any of various games: *a hockey stick.* **4.** a lever that controls the up-

and-down and side-to-side movement of an airplane. **5. the sticks.** *Informal.* any place that is far from a city or town, especially a place thought of as being very rural. [From the Old English word *sticca* meaning "a peg, stick¹."]

stick² (stik) *v.,* **stuck, stick·ing.** —*v.t.* **1.** to stab or puncture (something) with a pointed object: *The child stuck the balloon with a pin.* **2.** to push the point or end of (something) into something else: *to stick a tack in a bulletin board.* **3.** to fasten or attach with a pin or nail: *to stick a notice on a wall.* **4.** to fasten or attach by means of an adhesive, such as glue: *to stick a stamp on an envelope.* **5.** to put into a specified place or position: *to stick out one's tongue.* **6.** to keep from proceeding; detain; delay: *Our car was stuck in traffic for an hour.* **7.** *Informal.* to puzzle; confuse: *You stuck me on that question.* —*v.i.* **1.** to be or become fixed in place by having the end or point embedded in something: *The splinter stuck in my foot.* **2.** to extend; protrude: *A white handkerchief stuck out from the coat pocket.* **3.** to continue something, as a course of action: *to stick to a job until it is finished.* **4.** to remain faithful or loyal: *to stick to a bargain, to stick by one's friends.* **5.** to become or remain closely attached or associated: *If we don't stick together, we'll get lost in this crowd.* **6.** to hold fast because glued or as if glued: *The wet shirt stuck to my back. The drawer stuck when I tried to open it.* **7.** to follow closely: *We should stick to the main road since we're not sure of the way.* —*n.* a poke, thrust, or stab with or as if with a pointed object: *Someone in the crowd gave me a stick in the ribs with an elbow.* [From the Old English word *stician* meaning "to stab, pierce."]

·**to be stuck on.** *Informal.* to be in love with or very fond of.

·**to stick around.** *Informal.* to stay or wait nearby.

·**to stick out.** *Informal.* to be obvious or conspicuous.

·**to stick up.** *Informal.* to rob, especially at gunpoint.

·**to stick up for.** *Informal.* to support or defend.

stick·er (stik′ər) *n.* **1.** a label or other printed paper with glue on the back: *That sticker on the bumper is a parking permit.* **2.** a burr, thorn, or the like.

stick·le (stik′əl) *v.i.* **stick·led, stick·ling.** to argue, hesitate, or raise objections over trifles.

stick·le·back (stik′əl bak′) *n., pl.* **stick·le·backs** or **stick·le·back.** a fish that has sharp bony spines on the back and bony plates instead of scales on the sides.

stick·ler (stik′lər) *n.* a person who stubbornly insists that something be done in an exact, strict way: *to be a stickler for neatness.*

stick·pin (stik′pin′) *n.* an ornamental pin worn in a necktie or ascot.

stick·up (stik′up′) *n.* *Slang.* a robbery, as at gunpoint.

stick·y (stik′ē) *adj.,* **stick·i·er, stick·i·est. 1.** tending to stick or hold fast: *a sticky piece of gum.* **2.** coated or covered with glue or other adhesive: *a sticky poster.* **3.** hot and humid; muggy: *sticky summer weather.* **4.** difficult to deal with; touchy: *a sticky problem to solve.* —**stick′i·ly,** *adv.* —**stick′i·ness,** *n.*

sties (stīz) the plural of **sty¹** and **sty².**

stiff (stif) *adj.* **1.** not easily bent; not flexible: *The new leather belt was very stiff.* **2.** unable to move easily without pain or difficulty: *My back was stiff after sitting for so many hours.* **3.** not natural, easy, or graceful in manner or movement; formal: *a stiff bow.* **4.** harsh; severe: *The judge handed down a stiff sentence.* **5.** unusually high: *a stiff price.* **6.** requiring great effort to succeed in or overcome; difficult: *stiff competition, a stiff examination in mathematics.* **7.** not liquid or fluid; thick: *Beat the egg whites until they are stiff.* **8.** not working or moving smoothly or easily, as parts of machinery. **9.** having a strong, steady force: *a stiff breeze.*

10. strong or potent: *a stiff dose of medicine.* —*n.* *Slang.* **1.** a dead body; corpse. **2.** a very dull, staid, and unresponsive person. **3.** a person: *You're a lucky stiff.* —*adv.* **1.** so as to be rigid or unmovable: *The handle was frozen stiff.* **2.** so as to feel or seem unable to move: *to be scared stiff. I was bored stiff.* —**stiff′ly,** *adv.* —**stiff′ness,** *n.*

stiff·en (stif′ən) *v.t., v.i.* to make or become stiff or stiffer. —**stiff′en·er,** *n.*

stiff-necked (stif′nekt′) *adj.* unyielding; stubborn: *a stiff-necked refusal to agree.*

sti·fle (stī′fəl) *v.,* **sti·fled, sti·fling.** —*v.t.* **1.** to prevent or interfere with the growth or progress of: *to stifle someone's creative talent.* **2.** to hold back: *to stifle a yawn, to stifle the urge to laugh.* **3.** to kill by depriving of air. —*v.i.* **1.** to feel smothered because of a lack of air, as in a stuffy room. **2.** to die of suffocation.

stig·ma (stig′mə) *n., pl.* **stig·mas** or **stig·ma·ta** (stig-mä′tə, stig′mə tə) **1.** a mark of shame or disgrace: *to suffer the stigma of a humiliating defeat.* **2.** a spot on the skin that bleeds. **3.** the part of the pistil of a plant on which pollen grains are deposited and where they germinate. **4. stigmata.** marks or wounds that appear on the same places on a person's body as the five wounds on the crucified body of Jesus.

stig·ma·tize (stig′mə tīz′) *v.t.,* **stig·ma·tized, stig·ma·tiz·ing.** to mark as shameful or disgraceful: *to be stigmatized by an association with criminals.*

stile (stīl) *n.* **1.** a step or series of steps that enable a person to climb over a wall or fence. **2.** see **turnstile.**

sti·let·to (stə let′ō) *n., pl.* **sti·let·tos** or **sti·let·toes. 1.** a dagger with a very narrow blade. **2.** a small, pointed instrument used for making eyelets in embroidery.

still¹ (stil) *adj.* **1.** without movement; motionless: *The water was still after the storm.* **2.** without sound; silent: *Be still and listen.* —*v.t.* **1.** to make silent; quiet. **2.** to calm, as fears. —*v.i.* to become still or calm. —*n.* **1.** quiet; silence; calm: *in the still of the night.* **2.** a single photograph, especially one made from a single frame of motion-picture film. —*adv.* **1.** without movement; motionless: *Sit still.* **2.** at or up to the time indicated; as before: *We still live there.* **3.** in increasing amount or degree; beyond this: *Still greater things were expected from them.* **4.** even then; nevertheless: *Though I dieted, I still could not lose weight.* —*conj.* despite that; yet: *It's raining; still I'd like to go.* [From the Old English word *stille* meaning "not moving" or "quiet."] —**still′ness,** *n.*

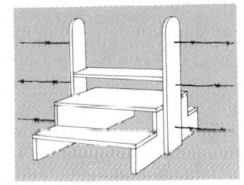

stile *(def. 1)*

still² (stil) *n.* **1.** an apparatus for distilling liquids, especially alcoholic liquors. **2.** see **distillery.** [From the Middle English word *stillen,* short for *distillen,* from the Old French word *distiller,* from the Latin word *destillare,* all meaning "to distill," from the prefix *de-* "out, out of" + *stillare* "to trickle, drip."]

still·born (stil′bôrn′) *adj.* dead at birth.

still life *pl.* **still lifes.** a painting or photograph of inanimate objects, such as bowls of fruit or flowers.

stilt (stilt) *n., pl.* **stilts** or *(def. 3)* **stilt. 1.** one of a pair of

---

at; āpe; fär; câre; end; mē; it; īce; pîerce; hot; ōld; sông; fôrk; oil; out; up; ūse; rüle; pùll; tûrn; chin; sing; shop; thin; **th**is; hw in white; zh in treasure. The symbol ə stands for the unstressed vowel sound heard in about, taken, pencil, lemon, and circus.

S

long poles, each having a footrest attached at some distance from the bottom end, allowing the wearer to walk with the feet above the ground. Stilts are worn by clowns in circuses to make them seem tall and are also used as toys by children. **2.** one of the posts used to support a building, pier, or other structure above ground or water. **3.** a water bird that has a slender bill, long, thin legs, and mainly white feathers.

stilt·ed (stil′tid) *adj.* stiffly dignified or formal: *a stilted style of writing.*

stim·u·lant (stim′yə lənt) *n.* **1.** a drug, drink, or other substance that speeds up the activity of the mind or body: *The caffeine in coffee acts as a stimulant.* **2.** anything that moves to action; stimulus: *Reading is a stimulant to the imagination.*

stim·u·late (stim′yə lāt′) *v.*, **stim·u·lat·ed, stim·u·lat·ing.** —*v.t.* **1.** to move to greater action or effort: *Warm spring days stimulated us to work in the garden.* **2.** to act as a stimulus or stimulant to (the mind or body). —*v.i.* to act as a stimulus or stimulant. —**stim′u·la′tion,** *n.*

stim·u·lus (stim′yə ləs) *n., pl.* **stim·u·li** (stim′yə lī′). **1.** something that moves or incites to action or effort. **2.** anything that produces a response in or influences the activity of the mind or body.

sting (sting) *v.*, **stung, sting·ing.** —*v.t.* **1.** to prick painfully with a sharp, usually pointed organ or object: *The bee stung me on the foot.* **2.** to cause to feel a sharp, smarting pain: *The medicine stung my cut finger.* **3.** to cause to suffer sharp mental or emotional pain: *The harsh criticism stung the young artist.* **4.** to goad or incite suddenly and sharply: *Insults stung the neighbor into making an angry reply.* —*v.i.* **1.** to have, use, or wound with a stinger, as certain insects. **2.** to cause or feel sharp physical or mental pain: *Her finger stung where she had cut it.* —*n.* **1.** the act of stinging. **2.** a wound or a smarting, burning sensation resulting from this. **3.** something that causes sharp mental or physical pain: *a sting of regret.* **4.** see **stinger** *(def. 1).* —**sting′ing·ly,** *adv.*

sting·er (sting′ər) *n.* **1.** a sharp, usually pointed organ with which an insect or animal inflicts a sting. **2.** anything that stings.

sting·ray (sting′rā′) *n.* a large fish having a flat body and a whiplike tail with two sharp, poisonous spines that can inflict a painful wound.

stin·gy (stin′jē) *adj.*, **stin·gi·er, stin·gi·est. 1.** reluctant or unwilling to give or share something, such as money; not generous. **2.** meager in amount; scanty; meager: *a stingy portion of food.* —**stin′gi·ly,** *adv.* —**stin′gi·ness,** *n.*

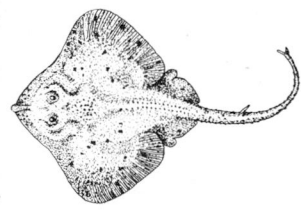
stingray

stink (stingk) *n.* **1.** a strong, foul smell; disgusting odor. **2.** *Slang.* a great fuss, disturbance, or outcry: *There was quite a stink over who was to blame for the accident.* —*v.*, **stank** or **stunk, stunk, stink·ing.** —*v.i.* **1.** to give off or have a strong, bad smell: *That dead fish stinks.* **2.** to be extremely offensive or hateful. **3.** *Slang.* to be of an extremely low quality: *That play stinks.* —*v.t.* to cause to stink.

stink·er (stingk′ər) *n.* **1.** a person or thing that stinks. **2.** *Informal.* a nasty, untrustworthy, or disagreeable person: *to be a real stinker about borrowing things.*

stint (stint) *v.t.* to limit, as in amount or degree; be stingy with: *to stint one's praise.* —*v.i.* to be stingy or sparing. —*n.* **1.** a share of work or duty to be done: *to serve a two-year stint in the army.* **2.** limitation; restriction: *to strive for perfection without stint.*

sti·pend (stī′pend) *n.* a fixed or regular pay or allowance, such as one given to a student on a scholarship or fellowship.

stip·ple (stip′əl) *v.t.*, **stip·pled, stip·pling. 1.** to paint, draw, or engrave by using dots or light, short touches instead of strokes or lines. **2.** to produce slight, gradual changes in shade or color in (something) by painting, drawing, or engraving in this way. —*n. also,* **stip·pling** (stip′ling). **1.** the art or technique of producing a painting, drawing, or engraving by using dots or light, short touches. **2.** the effect produced by this technique.

stip·u·late (stip′yə lāt′) *v.t.*, **stip·u·lat·ed, stip·u·lat·ing.** to demand or specify as a condition of agreement: *The agreement stipulated the actor's approval of the movie script.*

stip·u·la·tion (stip′yə lā′shən) *n.* **1.** the act of stipulating. **2.** a term or condition of an agreement or contract; something stipulated: *a contract complicated by many stipulations.*

stip·ule (stip′ūl) *n.* one of a pair of small leaflike structures found at the base of certain leaves.

stir (stûr) *v.*, **stirred, stir·ring.** —*v.t.* **1.** to mix (something, such as a liquid) by a continuous circular movement: *to stir paint.* **2.** to urge on or instigate; provoke: *to stir someone to action.* **3.** to excite to deep feeling or emotion; affect strongly; move: *The lawyer's plea for mercy stirred the*

Stipules

jury. **4.** to rouse or call forth: *I tried to stir you from your nap.* **5.** to cause to move, especially slightly: *The breeze stirred the fallen leaves.* —*v.i.* **1.** to make a slight movement: *The sleeping child didn't stir all night.* **2.** to move about or begin to move about; be active: *We heard someone stirring in the kitchen.* **3.** to be roused or called forth. **4.** to be capable of being stirred: *The paste hardened too much to stir.* —*n.* **1.** commotion or excitement; disturbance: *The movie star's appearance created quite a stir.* **2.** a slight or momentary movement: *A gust of wind made a stir in the curtains.* **3.** the act of stirring, as with a spoon. —**stir′rer,** *n.*

stir–fry (stûr′frī′) *v.t.*, **stir–fried, stir–fry·ing.** to fry quickly in very little oil over high heat while stirring rapidly: *to stir-fry fresh vegetables.*

stir·ring (stûr′ing) *adj.* **1.** inspiring or exciting; thrilling: *to play a stirring tune.* **2.** active; lively. —**stir′ring·ly,** *adv.*

stir·rup (stûr′əp, stir′əp) *n.* **1.** one of a pair of metal, wooden, or leather loops or rings, flattened at the bottom and suspended from a saddle, used to support a rider's foot in mounting and riding. **2.** the innermost of the three bones in the middle ear, shaped somewhat like a stirrup; stapes.

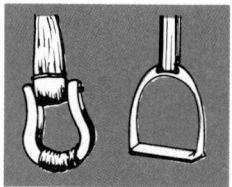
stirrups *(def. 1)*

stitch (stich) *n., pl.* **stitch·es. 1.** one complete movement of a threaded needle in and out of fabric, as in sewing, or through skin and flesh, as in surgery. **2.** a movement made to knot or loop yarn or thread on needles, as in knitting. **3.** a single loop or knot of thread or yarn made by a stitch. **4.** a particular method of arranging the thread, as in sewing or knitting. **5.** a sudden, sharp pain, especially in the side or back. **6.** *Informal.* a piece of clothing. **7.** *Informal.* slightest bit: *I didn't do a stitch of work all day.* —*v.t.* to make, fasten, join, or mend with stitches: *to stitch up a hole.* —*v.i.* to make stitches; sew.

stoat (stōt) *n.* the ermine, especially when in its brown summer coat.

stock (stok) *n.* **1.** the total amount of goods that a merchant or commercial establishment keeps on hand for sale: *This store has a large stock of fishing equipment.* **2.** a quantity of something accumulated or held in reserve; store: *The squirrel was putting away a stock of nuts for the winter.* **3.** domestic animals raised or kept on a farm or ranch, such as cattle, sheep, or pigs; livestock. **4.** ancestry or descent: *a person of Scandinavian stock.* **5.** a family or other related group of plants or animals. **6.** a liquid in which meat, poultry, or fish has been boiled, used as a base for gravies, soups, or sauces. **7.** *Finance.* **a.** ownership or partial ownership of a company or corporation as represented by shares that it is authorized to issue. **b.** such shares held by an individual or group. **c.** see **stock certificate**. **8.** the raw material from which something is made. **9. stocks.** a wooden frame with holes for confining the ankles and sometimes the wrists. It was formerly used to punish minor crimes. **10.** the wooden or metal support or handle of a tool or weapon, to which the working parts are attached. **11.** a stem of a plant onto which a graft is made. **12.** a tree, plant, or plant part that furnishes cuttings for grafting. **13.** the trunk or main stem of a tree or other plant. **14.** the crosspiece below the ring of an anchor. **15.** *Theater.* **a.** see **stock company** (*def.* 2). **b.** the repertoire of a stock company. **16.** any of a group of plants bearing stiff, showy spikes of broad, petaled flowers. —*v.t.* **1.** to supply or furnish with stock or a stock: *They stocked the cabin with enough food for the weekend.* **2.** to have or keep a supply of, especially for future use or sale: *That hardware store stocks all kinds of tools.* **3.** to supply with livestock: *to stock a farm.* **4.** to provide with wild animals, fish, or other game, especially for private or restricted hunting or fishing: *to stock a lake.* —*v.i.* to lay in a stock or supply: *to stock up for a party.* —*adj.* **1.** regularly kept in stock: *a stock size.* **2.** commonly or constantly used or brought forward; commonplace: *a stock phrase.* **3.** employed in handling or taking care of goods or merchandise: *a stock clerk.*

·**in stock.** on hand for use or sale: *The store does not have any fans in stock in winter.*

·**out of stock.** not on hand for use or sale.

·**to put stock in** or **to take stock in.** to have faith, trust, or confidence in.

·**to take stock. a.** to make an inventory of the goods one has on hand for use or sale. **b.** to make an estimate or examination: *Near the end of college, many students take stock of their plans for the future.*

stock·ade (sto kād′) *n.* **1.** a defensive barrier made of strong, usually tall, posts set upright in the ground, usually forming an enclosure. **2.** any similar barrier or enclosure. **3.** a military prison. —*v.t.,* **stock·ad·ed, stock·ad·ing.** to surround or fortify with a stockade.

stock·bro·ker (stok′brō′kər) *n.* a person who buys and sells stock or other securities for others.

stock certificate, a certificate issued by a company or corporation as evidence of a stockholder's ownership of a particular number of shares.

stock company 1. a company or corporation whose capital is divided into shares. **2.** a theatrical troupe playing regularly at a particular theater in a variety of productions.

stock exchange 1. a place where stocks and bonds are bought and sold. **2.** an association of stockholders who deal in the buying and selling of stocks and bonds.

stock·hold·er (stok′hōl′dər) *n.* a person who owns stock in a company or corporation; shareholder.

stock·ing (stok′ing) *n.* **1.** a close-fitting, knitted covering for the foot and leg, often made of sheer fabric and sold as a pair, worn especially by women. **2.** anything resembling this.

stocking cap, a knitted cap, usually having a pointed end that is worn flopped over toward the back.

stock·man (stok′mən) *n., pl.* **stockmen** (stok′mən). a person who raises livestock.

stock market 1. a place where stocks and bonds are bought and sold. **2.** the business carried on in such a place.

stock·pile (stok′pīl′) *n.* a supply of foodstuffs, raw materials, or other items accumulated and held in reserve for future use during an emergency or shortage: *a stockpile of medical supplies.* —*v.,* **stock·piled, stock·pil·ing.** —*v.t.* to accumulate a stockpile of: *to stockpile canned goods.* —*v.i.* to accumulate a stockpile.

stock·room (stok′rüm′, stok′rüm′) *n.* a room in which stocks of goods are stored.

stock–still (stok′stil′) *adj.* motionless: *to stand stock-still.*

stock·y (stok′ē) *adj.,* **stock·i·er, stock·i·est.** having a solid, sturdy, and compact build; thickset. —**stock′i·ly,** *adv.* —**stock′i·ness,** *n.*

stock·yard (stok′yärd′) *n.* an enclosure made up of pens and sheds where livestock is kept before being slaughtered or shipped to market.

stodg·y (stoj′ē) *adj.,* **stodg·i·er, stodg·i·est. 1.** extremely old-fashioned and stuffy: *someone so stodgy as to disapprove of late hours.* **2.** lacking freshness or interest; commonplace; dull: *a stodgy speech.* **3.** (of food) heavy and thick; indigestible. —**stodg′i·ly,** *adv.* —**stodg′i·ness,** *n.*

sto·gy (stō′gē) also, **sto·gie.** *n., pl.* **sto·gies.** a long, slender, inexpensive cigar.

sto·ic (stō′ik) *n.* a person who is apparently indifferent to or unaffected by pain or pleasure. —*adj.* also, **sto·i·cal** (stō′i kəl). indifferent to or unaffected by pain or pleasure. [From the Latin word *stoicus* meaning "relating to Stoic philosophy," from the Greek word *stōikos,* from *Stoa Poikile* meaning "the Painted Porch," the name of the place in ancient Athens where the philosopher Zeno (335?–263? B.C.) taught.]

stoke (stōk) *v.t.,* **stoked, stok·ing. 1.** to stir up and feed fuel to (a fire or furnace). **2.** to tend (a fire or furnace).

stoke·hold (stōk′hōld′) *n.* a room or compartment on a steamship containing the furnaces or boilers.

stoke·hole (stōk′hōl′) *n.* **1.** a hole through which fuel is fed into a furnace. **2.** another word for **stokehold.**

stok·er (stō′kər) *n.* **1.** a person who tends and supplies fuel to a furnace or boiler, as on a steamship or locomotive. **2.** a mechanical device that supplies fuel to a furnace.

STOL (stol) an airplane that needs only a short distance to take off and land. [Short for *s*(hort) *t*(ake) *o*(off and) *l*(anding).]

stole¹ (stōl) the past tense of **steal.**

stole² (stōl) *n.* **1.** a woman's long scarf, usually of fur, worn around the shoulders with the ends hanging down in front. **2.** a long narrow strip of silk or other material, worn around the neck by a member of the clergy during certain religious services. [From the Old English word *stole,* from the Latin word *stola* meaning "a long upper garment" and "ceremonial stole²," from the Greek word *stolē* "garment, robe."]

---

at; āpe; fär; câre; end; mē; it; īce; pîerce; hot; ōld; sông, fôrk; oil; out; up; ūse; rüle; pull; tûrn; chin; sing; shop; thin; this; hw in white; zh in treasure. The symbol ə stands for the unstressed vowel sound heard in about, taken, pencil, lemon, and circus.

S

sto·len (stō′lən) the past participle of **steal**.

stol·id (stol′id) *adj.* having or showing little or no emotion; not easily moved or stirred; impassive: *to maintain a stolid expression whether happy or sad.* —**stol′id·ly**, *adv.*

sto·lid·i·ty (stə lid′i tē) *n.* the state or condition of being stolid.

sto·lon (stō′lən) *n. Botany.* a stem that trails along the ground and takes root at the nodes or the tip to form a new plant; runner.

sto·ma (stō′mə) *n., pl.* **sto·ma·ta** or **sto·mas.** a small opening or pore, especially on a plant leaf, through which gases and water vapor pass in or out.

stom·ach (stum′ək) *n.* **1.** in humans and other animals with backbones, the muscular baglike organ of the alimentary canal that receives swallowed food from the esophagus, lubricates it, mixes it, and begins the digestion of proteins and fats. **2.** a similar part in certain animals without backbones, such as lobsters and insects. **3.** the part of the body containing the stomach; abdomen; belly. **4.** an inclination or liking; desire: *to have no stomach for violence.* —*v.t.* to put up with; tolerate; endure: *I can't stomach such rude behavior from them.*

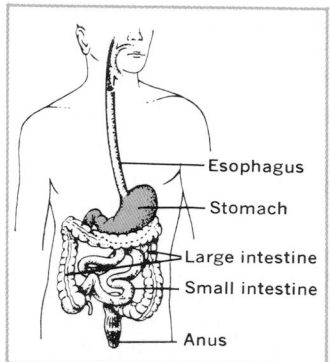

stomach *(def. 1)*

Esophagus
Stomach
Large intestine
Small intestine
Anus

stom·ach·ache (stum′ək āk′) *n.* a pain in or near the region of the stomach.

stom·ach·er (stum′ə kər) *n.* a former ornamental garment covering the stomach and chest, often extending in a V-shape to below the waistline. It was worn especially by women in the sixteenth and seventeenth centuries.

stomach pump, a suction pump with a long flexible tube, used to empty the contents of the stomach, as when a person has swallowed poison.

sto·ma·ta (stō′mə tə, stom′ə tə) a plural of **stoma**.

stomp (stomp) *v.t.* **1.** to tread heavily or violently on or upon: *to stomp the floor in anger.* **2.** to bring down (the foot or feet) forcefully and heavily; stamp: *to stomp one's feet on the floor.* —*v.i.* to tread heavily or violently: *to stomp angrily out of a room.*

stone (stōn) *n., pl.* **stones** or *(def. 7)* **stone.** **1.** a hard, naturally formed mass of mineral matter; rock. **2.** a small fragment or piece of this. **3.** a piece of stone that has been shaped or cut for a particular purpose, as for building, marking a grave, or paving a road. **4.** a precious stone; gem. **5.** a hardened mass of matter found in certain organs of the body, such as the gallbladder or kidney. **6.** the hard inner layer enclosing the seed of certain fruits, such as the cherry, peach, or avocado. **7.** a unit of weight of varying value. In Great Britain it is equal to 14 pounds avoirdupois (6.35 kilograms). —*adj.* **1.** made or built of stone: *a stone house, a stone wall.* **2.** made of stoneware. —*v.t.,* **stoned, ston·ing. 1.** to pelt or kill with stones. **2.** to furnish, fit, pave, or line with stones: *to stone a road.* **3.** to remove the stones from (fruit): *to stone peaches for canning.*

Stone Age, the earliest known stage in the development of civilization, characterized by the use of stone tools and weapons.

stone–blind (stōn′blīnd′) *adj.* completely blind.

stone·cut·ter (stōn′kut′ər) *n.* a person or thing that cuts or carves stone.

stoned (stōnd) *adj. Slang.* under the influence of alcohol or a drug; drunk or drugged.

stone–deaf (stōn′def′) *adj.* completely deaf.

Stone·henge (stōn′henj′) *n.* a structure in southern England erected by a prehistoric people, consisting mainly of a circular arrangement of giant stone blocks. It is now in ruins.

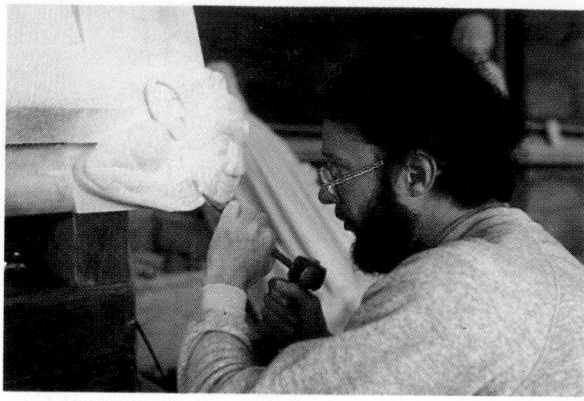

stonemason

stone·ma·son (stōn′mā′sən) *n.* a person who cuts stone or builds structures in stone.

stone's throw, a short distance: *Their house is just a stone's throw from here.*

stone·ware (stōn′wâr′) *n.* pottery made of a mixture of finely ground clay and stone and baked at a very high temperature.

stone·work (stōn′wûrk′) *n.* **1.** something made of stone. **2.** the art, process, or technique of working in stone. **3. stoneworks.** a place where stone is cut and prepared. ▲ used with a singular or plural verb. —**stone′work′er,** *n.*

ston·y (stō′nē) *adj.,* **ston·i·er, ston·i·est. 1.** showing no emotion; cold; unfeeling: *a stony stare.* **2.** having or feeling no emotion: *a stony heart.* **3.** full of or covered with stones. **4.** hard as stone. —**ston′i·ly,** *adv.* —**ston′i·ness,** *n.*

stood (stŭd) the past tense and past participle of **stand**.

stooge (stüj) *n. Informal.* **1.** an entertainer who assists a comedian, as by feeding lines, heckling from the audience, or serving as the butt of jokes. **2.** anyone who is used or taken advantage of by another; dupe.

stool (stül) *n.* **1.** an individual seat supported on legs or a pedestal, usually having no back or arms. **2.** a low backless and armless bench, used as a support for the feet or legs when sitting, or for the knees when kneeling. **3.** waste matter emitted from the bowels.

stool pigeon 1. a pigeon used as a decoy to trap other pigeons. **2.** *Slang.* any person acting as an informer or decoy, especially for the police.

stoop¹ (stüp) *v.i.* **1.** to bend the body forward and downward, often with the knees bent: *She stooped to pick up the paper she had dropped.* **2.** to stand or walk with the head and shoulders bent forward: *The old man stoops when he walks.* **3.** to lower or degrade oneself to do or use something: *Don't stoop to cheating in order to pass the test.* —*v.t.* to bend (one's head or other part of the body) forward. —*n.* **1.** a forward bending of the head and shoulders: *to walk with a stoop.* **2.** the act of bending forward and downward. [From the Old English word *stūpian* meaning "to bend, stoop¹."]

stoop² (stüp) *n.* a structure at the entrance of a building or house, made up of a number of steps leading up to a raised platform. [From the Dutch word *stoep* meaning "threshold, flight of steps."]

stop (stop) *v.*, **stopped, stop·ping.** —*v.t.* **1.** to prevent from moving, operating, acting, or progressing: *to stop a car, to stop a clock, to stop traffic.* **2.** to prevent from continuing; end: *to stop the spread of a fire, to stop the advance of floodwaters.* **3.** to keep (a person) from carrying out an action; hold back; restrain: *to stop a baby from crawling everywhere.* **4.** to obstruct or close up (a hole, passage, or cavity), as by stuffing something into it or placing something over it: *to stop a leak.* **5.** to close (a bottle or other vessel) by blocking its mouth with a plug or other stopper: *to stop up a bottle.* **6.** to keep from: *Please stop making so much noise.* **7.** *Music.* to close (a finger hole) or press down on (a string) in order to produce a desired tone. —*v.i.* **1.** to come to an end; discontinue: *The music stopped at midnight.* **2.** to come to a standstill or halt: *to stop in the middle of a speech to answer a question.* **3.** to halt during one's journey: *We will stop at this motel for the night.* —*n.* **1.** the act of stopping or the state of being stopped: *to come to a stop at the light.* **2.** a place at which a stop is made: *a bus stop.* **3.** something that stops or hinders. **4.** a punctuation mark. **5.** *Music.* **a.** a graduated set of organ pipes operated by one lever. **b.** a lever operating such a set of pipes. **c.** any mechanical part or device used to stop a string or finger hole. **6.** a device or part of a device that checks or controls movement or action in a mechanism.

stop·gap (stop′gap′) *n.* something devised or used to supply a need temporarily; temporary substitute.

stop·light (stop′līt′) *n.* **1.** another word for **traffic light. 2.** a light on the rear end of a vehicle that lights up when the brakes are applied.

stop·o·ver (stop′ō′vər) *n.* a brief visit or stay, especially overnight, at a place during the course of a journey: *We had a stopover in Paris on our trip to Italy.*

stop·page (stop′ij) *n.* **1.** the act of stopping or the state of being stopped: *Stoppage of the drain caused the sink to overflow.* **2.** something that blocks or obstructs.

stop·per (stop′ər) *n.* **1.** something, such as a cork or plug, used to close or stop up an opening in a bottle or other vessel. **2.** a person or thing that stops or arrests the movement, action, or progress of something. —*v.t.* to close with a stopper.

stop·watch (stop′woch′) *n.*, *pl.* **stop·watch·es.** a watch used to record exact intervals of time, as the duration of races, having a button that can be pressed to stop the hands or display instantly.

stor·age (stôr′ij) *n.* **1.** the act of storing goods or other items, as in a warehouse. **2.** the state of being stored. **3.** a place for storing goods or other items: *That sofa has been in storage for a year.* **4.** the charge for storing, as in a warehouse. **5.** *Computers.* **a.** the storing of data, as on a disk. **b.** the device or location where data are stored.

storage battery, a battery that produces an electric current by a chemical reaction and can be recharged by an electric current.

store (stôr) *n.* **1.** a place or establishment in which a variety of goods are kept for sale: *a grocery store, a hardware store, a clothing store.* **2.** a quantity of something put away or held in reserve for future use: *a store of medical supplies, to have a great store of energy.* **3. stores.** supplies, as of food or equipment. **4.** see **storehouse.** —*v.t.*, **stored, stor·ing. 1.** to put away or hold in reserve for future use: *The squirrel is storing nuts for the winter.* **2.** to put in a warehouse or other place for safekeeping: *to store furniture.* **3.** to provide or furnish; supply.

　·**in store.** in reserve; forthcoming: *There is a surprise in store for you when you get home.*

　·**to set store by.** to regard; value; esteem: *The doctor sets little store by home remedies.*

store·front (stôr′frunt′) *n.* **1.** the front side of a store facing a street, often having windows for the display of merchandise. **2.** a room or rooms behind a storefront; especially when used for a special purpose: *a political campaign headquarters set up in a storefront.* —*adj.* established in or operating from a storefront: *a storefront church, a storefront clinic.*

store·house (stôr′hous′) *n.*, *pl.* **store·hous·es** (stôr′hou′ziz). **1.** a place or building where things are stored. **2.** a large supply or source: *My history teacher was a storehouse of information.*

store·keep·er (stôr′kē′pər) *n.* a person who owns or runs a store.

store·room (stôr′rüm′, stôr′rům′) *n.* a room in which things are stored.

sto·rey (stôr′ē) *n.*, *pl.* **sto·reys.** another spelling of **story².**

sto·ried¹ (stôr′ēd) *adj.* celebrated or recorded in stories, history, or legend: *Daniel Boone is a storied hero.* [*Story¹* + *-ed².*]

sto·ried² (stôr′ēd) *adj.* having or divided into stories or floors. ▲ usually used in combination: *a six-storied building.* [*Story²* + *-ed².*]

stork (stôrk) *n.*, *pl.* **storks** or **stork.** any of various long-legged wading birds having a long neck, a large, strong bill, and, usually, black, white, and gray feathers.

storm (stôrm) *n.* **1.** any disturbed state of the atmosphere, usually accompanied by strong winds and some form of precipitation, such as rain or snow. **2.** a sudden or violent outburst, as of emotion or excitement: *a storm of tears.* **3.** a violent disturbance or upheaval: *The scandal over school funds caused a storm of protest in town.* **4.** a sudden, violent attack, especially on a fortified position: *The enemy took the hill by storm.* **5.** a heavy discharge or shower of objects, such as missiles: *a storm of arrows.* —*v.i.* **1.** to rain, snow, sleet, hail, or otherwise precipitate heavily: *It stormed all day Friday.* **2.** to move or rush violently or angrily: *The angry customer stormed out of the store.* —*v.t.* to make a sudden, violent attack on: *The rebels stormed the gates of the palace.*

stork

storm cellar, an underground shelter for use during cyclones, tornadoes, or the like.

storm center 1. the center of a cyclone, an area of low atmospheric pressure and relative calm. **2.** any focal point or center of trouble, commotion, or controversy.

storm door, an additional door outside an ordinary door, used for protection against storms or other severe weather.

storm petrel, a small seabird usually having black or brownish feathers with white markings. According to superstition, its presence indicates an approaching storm. Also, **stormy petrel.**

storm window, an additional window outside an ordinary window, used for protection against storms or other severe weather.

storm·y (stôr′mē) *adj.*, **storm·i·er, storm·i·est. 1.** affected by, characterized by, or subject to storms: *stormy weather, stormy seas.* **2.** characterized by violent or intense emotion or activity: *The new tax bill led to a*

---

at; āpe; fär; câre; end; mē; it; īce; pîerce; hot; ōld; sông, fôrk; oil; out; up; ūse; rüle; půll; tûrn; chin; sing; shop; thin; this; hw in white; zh in treasure. The symbol ə stands for the unstressed vowel sound heard in about, taken, pencil, lemon, and circus.

S

stormy debate in Congress. —**storm′i·ly**, *adv.*
—**storm′i·ness**, *n.*

stormy petrel, another term for **storm petrel.**

sto·ry¹ (stôr′ē) *n., pl.* **sto·ries.** **1.** a narrative or account of an event or series of events that have happened or are supposed to have happened. **2.** a narrative or account, often untrue, intended to entertain the reader or hearer. **3.** an account or statement of the facts of a matter or case: *According to their story, you started the argument.* **4.** *Informal.* a falsehood; lie. [From the Anglo-Norman word *estorie* meaning "history, tale," from the Latin word *historia* "a narrative, tale" or "history," from the Greek word *historia* "information" or "history."]

sto·ry² (stôr′ē) *also,* **sto·rey.** *n., pl.* **sto·ries.** **1.** one of the horizontal structural divisions of a building, extending from the floor to the ceiling or roof above. **2.** a set of rooms on the same floor level of a building. [From the Medieval Latin word *historia* meaning "picture" or "story²," from the Latin word *historia* "a narrative, tale" or "history"; perhaps from the practice of having scenes that told a story painted on the windows of each floor of a building.]

sto·ry·book (stôr′ē buk′) *n.* a book containing a story or stories, especially for children. —*adj.* occurring in or resembling something in a storybook; romantic: *a storybook marriage.*

sto·ry·tell·er (stôr′ē tel′ər) *n.* a person who tells or writes stories.

stoup (stüp) *n.* a basin containing holy water at or near the entrance of a church.

stout (stout) *adj.* **1.** having a thick, bulky figure; thickset; fat. **2.** having courage; brave. **3.** having strength and vigor; physically strong; robust. **4.** solid in structure, substance, or material. —*n.* a strong, very dark, heavy ale. —**stout′ly**, *adv.* —**stout′ness**, *n.*

stout–heart·ed (stout′här′tid) *adj.* valiant; brave; courageous: *stout-hearted warriors.* —**stout′-heart′ed·ly**, *adv.* —**stout′-heart′ed·ness**, *n.*

stove¹ (stōv) *n.* **1.** a kitchen appliance used for cooking that burns gas or electricity and has burners, usually an oven, and sometimes a storage compartment. **2.** any of various heating or cooking devices that use wood, coal, gas, or electricity. [From the Middle Dutch word *stove* meaning "a heated room."]

stove² (stōv) a past tense and past participle of **stave.**

stove·pipe (stōv′pīp′) *n.* **1.** a pipe, usually of sheet metal, used to carry smoke, fumes, and noxious gases from a stove. **2.** *Informal.* a tall silk hat.

stow (stō) *v.t.* **1.** to put or pack away, especially in a neat, compact manner: *The sailors stowed the cargo and supplies in the ship's hold.* **2.** to fill by packing; load: *We stowed the trunk of the car with our luggage.*

·**to stow away.** to be a stow-away.

stow·a·way (stō′ə wā′) *n.* a person who hides on a ship or airplane, especially in order to obtain free passage.

strad·dle (strad′əl) *v.,* **strad-dled, strad·dling.** —*v.t.* **1.** to sit, stand, or walk with one leg on each side of: *to straddle a fence, to straddle a horse.* **2.** to appear to favor both sides of (an issue): *to straddle the question of raising*

stovepipe *(def. 1)*

taxes. **3.** to spread (the legs) wide apart. —*v.i.* **1.** to sit, stand, or walk with the legs wide apart. **2.** to appear to favor both sides of an issue. **3.** (of the legs) to be wide apart. —*n.* the act of straddling. —**strad′dler**, *n.*

Strad·i·var·i·us (strad′ə vâr′ē əs) *n.* a violin, viola, or cello made by Stradivari.

strafe (strāf) *v.t., v.i.,* **strafed, straf·ing.** to attack (troops, ships, or other targets) with machine-gun or rocket fire from low-flying aircraft. [From the World War I German slogan *Gott strafe England!* meaning "God punish England!" from the word *strafen* "to punish."]

strag·gle (strag′əl) *v.i.,* **strag·gled, strag·gling.** **1.** to wander or move about in an irregular, rambling manner: *The exhausted hikers straggled through the woods.* **2.** to stray from or lag behind the main course or body: *The slower runners straggled behind.* **3.** to arrive or depart separately and at irregular intervals: *Late vote totals straggled in all night.* —**strag′gler**, *n.*

strag·gly (strag′lē) *adj.,* **strag·gli·er, strag·gli·est.** spread out or scattered in an irregular, rambling manner: *straggly vines.*

straight (strāt) *adj.* **1.** moving in the same direction without a curve, bend, or other irregularity: *a straight line.* **2.** not curly, wavy, or kinky: *straight hair.* **3.** not crooked or stooping; erect: *to stand with a straight back.* **4.** in proper arrangement, order, or condition: *The clerk tried to keep the counter straight. The new teacher couldn't keep the twins' names straight.* **5.** truthful; frank; candid: *a straight answer.* **6.** without interruption; unbroken; continuous: *The pianist practiced two hours straight.* **7.** strictly following or supporting the platform, policy, and candidates of a particular political party: *to vote a straight Democratic slate.* **8.** not mixed, altered, or diluted, as an alcoholic liquor. —*adv.* **1.** in a straight line, course, or manner: *Go straight down Main Street.* **2.** without delay; immediately: *I went straight home after the concert.* —**straight′ly**, *adv.* —**straight′ness**, *n.*

·**straight away** or **straight off.** without delay; immediately.

straight angle, an angle of 180 degrees.

straight·a·way (*adv.,* strāt′ə wā′; *adj., n.,* strāt′ə wā′) *adv.* at once; immediately. —*adj.* extending in a straight line or course. —*n.* a straight course or part, especially of a race-course.

straight·edge (strāt′ej′) *n.* see **ruler** *(def. 2).*

straight·en (strā′tən) *v.t.* **1.** to make straight: *Straighten your hat.* **2.** to restore to the proper order, arrangement, or condition: *I straightened up my desk.* —*v.i.* to become straight. —**straight′en·er**, *n.*

straight face, a face that shows no emotion: *The comedian told the joke with a straight face.*

straight–faced (strāt′fāst′) *adj.* showing no emotion.

straight·for·ward (strāt′fôr′wərd) *adj.* **1.** honest; frank; sincere: *a straightforward answer.* **2.** proceeding or directed straight ahead. —*adv. also,* **straightforwards.** in a straightforward manner or course. —**straight′for′ward·ly**, *adv.* —**straight′for′ward·ness**, *n.*

straight man, an entertainer who performs with a comedian, especially by giving cues and serving as the butt of jokes.

straight ticket **1.** a ballot cast for candidates of one political party. **2.** a slate of candidates from one political party.

straight·way (strāt′wā′) *adv.* at once; immediately.

strain¹ (strān) *v.t.* **1.** to draw or pull tight; stretch: *The weight of the cargo strained the ropes.* **2.** to injure or weaken by excessive stretching or overexertion: *to strain a muscle while running.* **3.** to use or push to the utmost: *We strained our voices to be heard above the noise of the engine.* **4.** to stretch beyond proper, normal, or legitimate limits. **5.** to press or pour through a strainer, sieve, or other filtering device: *to strain freshly squeezed orange juice to remove the pulp.* —*v.i.* **1.** to make violent and continuous effort to do or achieve something; exert oneself to the utmost: *to strain to reach a goal.* **2.** to pull with force: *The horse strained at the rope.* —*n.* **1.** extreme physical force or pressure: *The roof collapsed under the strain of the heavy snow.* **2.** an injury or impairment caused by excessive stretching or overexertion: *muscle strain.* **3.** extreme mental or emotional pressure or tension: *The soldier broke under the strain of combat.* **4.** the act of straining or the state of being strained. [From the Old French word *estraindre* meaning "to stretch, wring," from the Latin word *stringere* "to bind, press together."]

strain² (strān) *n.* **1.** line of descent; ancestry; stock. **2.** a group of animals or plants having distinguishing characteristics and forming a part or subdivision of a larger group: *a new strain of yellow and white roses.* **3.** an inherited or characteristic quality or tendency: *a strain of nobility.* **4.** *also,* **strains.** a musical passage; tune. [From the Old English word *strēon* meaning "lineage, generation."]

strained (strānd) *adj.* not natural; forced: *a strained smile.*

strain·er (strā′nər) *n.* **1.** any of various utensils or devices, such as a colander or sieve, into which things are poured to separate liquids from solids. **2.** a person or thing that strains.

strait (strāt) *n.* **1.** a narrow waterway or channel connecting two larger bodies of water. **2.** *also,* **straits.** a position or circumstance of difficulty, distress, or need: *to be in desperate financial straits.*

strait·en (strā′tən) *v.t.* **1.** to cause to be in need or difficulty, especially for money. **2.** to make narrow or confining.

strait·jack·et (strāt′jak′it) *also,* **strait jacket.** *n.* a canvas garment resembling a jacket, having long sleeves that wrap around the body. It is used to confine the arms of a violent patient or prisoner.

strait–laced (strāt′lāst′) *adj.* excessively strict or rigid in morals or manners; prudish.

strand¹ (strand) *v.t.* **1.** to drive or run (a boat or ship) aground. **2.** to leave in a difficult or helpless position, especially in a strange or isolated place: *The cancellation of our flight stranded us at the airport with very little money.* —*n.* land bordering a body of water; shore or beach. [From the Old English word *strand* meaning "a shore, beach."]

strand² (strand) *n.* **1.** one of the threads, wires, or fibers twisted together to form a rope, cord, or other line: *frayed strands of rope.* **2.** any single thread, hair, or similar structure: *a strand of spaghetti, strands of hair.* **3.** a string of things joined together by twisting, twining, or threading: *a strand of pearls.* [Of uncertain origin.]

strange (strānj) *adj.,* **strang·er, strang·est. 1.** differing from the usual or ordinary; remarkable or odd: *The dark, empty house gave me a strange feeling.* **2.** not known, seen, or experienced before; unfamiliar: *That part of town is strange to me.* **3.** ill at ease; uncomfortable: *I would feel strange asking them such a favor.* **4.** unaccustomed to or inexperienced in: *to be strange to a new job.* —**strange′ly,** *adv.* —**strange′ness,** *n.*

stran·ger (strān′jər) *n.* **1.** a person with whom one is not acquainted or familiar. **2.** a foreigner, outsider, or newcomer. **3.** a person who is ignorant of, unacquainted with, or unaccustomed to something specified: *The new students are strangers to the school's policies.*

stran·gle (strang′gəl) *v.,* **stran·gled, stran·gling.** *v.t.* **1.** to kill or attempt to kill by squeezing the throat to stop breathing; throttle. **2.** to suffocate or choke in any manner.

3. to hold back; stifle: *to strangle a laugh.* —*v.i.* to become strangled. —**stran′gler,** *n.*

stran·gu·la·tion (strang′gyə lā′shən) *n.* the act of strangling or the state of being strangled.

strap (strap) *n.* **1.** a long, narrow, flexible strip of leather, cloth, or other material, often having a buckle or other fastener, used for securing or holding things together or in position. **2.** a narrow metal band used to fasten or hold things together or in position. —*v.t.,* **strapped, strapping. 1.** to fasten, secure, or support with a strap: *to strap on a backpack.* **2.** to beat with a strap.

strap·ping (strap′ing) *adj. Informal.* tall and sturdy; robust: *a strapping young athlete.*

stra·ta (strā′tə, strat′ə) a plural of **stratum.**

strat·a·gem (strat′ə jəm) *n.* a scheme, trick, or maneuver designed to outwit, deceive, or surprise an enemy or obtain an advantage.

stra·te·gic (strə tē′jik) *adj.* **1.** of or relating to strategy: *a strategic decision to withdraw.* **2.** important or necessary to strategy, especially military strategy: *Having superior weapons gave the troops a strategic advantage.* —**stra·te′gi·cal·ly,** *adv.*

strat·e·gist (strat′i jist) *n.* a person who is trained or skilled in strategy, especially military strategy.

strat·e·gy (strat′i jē) *n., pl.* **strat·e·gies. 1.** the art or science of planning and directing large-scale military operations and campaigns. **2.** the skillful use of planning, as in business or politics. **3.** a plan or device designed to achieve a specific goal or advantage: *What strategy does the company intend to use to sell the new product?*

strat·i·fi·ca·tion (strat′ə fi kā′shən) *n.* **1.** the act of stratifying or the state of being stratified. **2.** a stratified structure or formation, as of rock.

strat·i·fy (strat′ə fī) *v.,* **strat·i·fied, strat·i·fy·ing.** —*v.t.* **1.** to form or arrange in layers or strata. **2.** to divide into groups or classes, as according to common social or economic characteristics. *to stratify society.* —*v.i.* to form strata.

stra·to·cu·mu·lus (strā′tō kū′myə ləs, strat′ō kū′myə ləs) *n., pl.* **stra·to·cu·mu·lus** or **stra·to·cu·mu·li** (strā′tō kū′myə lī′, strat′ō kū′myə lī′) a broad, flattened, low-level cloud that may form several layers. See **cloud** (def. 1).

strat·o·sphere (strat′ə sfir′) *n.* the layer of the atmosphere above the troposphere and below the mesosphere, extending from an average of 8 miles (13 kilometers) to about 30 miles (50 kilometers) above the earth's surface. Ozone formed in the upper part of this region protects the earth from ultraviolet radiation from the sun.

strat·o·spher·ic (strat′ə sfer′ik) *adj.* of or relating to the stratosphere.

stra·tum (strā′təm, strat′əm) *n., pl.* **stra·ta** or **stra·tums. 1.** a horizontal layer of material, such as rock or soil, especially one having several parallel layers placed or lying one on top of the other: *The diggers broke through the first stratum of rock.* **2.** a group or class having certain social or economic characteristics in common: *In former times peasants were the lowest stratum of society.*

stra·tus (strā′təs, strat′əs) *n., pl.* **stra·ti** (strā′tī, strat′ī) or **stra·tus.** a low-level, grayish, watery cloud having a foggy appearance. See **cloud** (def. 1).

---

at; āpe; fär; câre; end; mē; it; īce; pîerce; hot; ōld; sông, fôrk; oil; out; up; ūse; rüle; pull; tûrn; chin; sing; shop; thin; **this**; hw in white; zh in treasure. The symbol ə stands for the unstressed vowel sound heard in about, taken, pencil, lemon, and circus.

S

straw (strô) *n.* **1.** the dry stalks or stems of any of various grains, such as rye, oats, wheat, or barley, after they have been threshed. Straw is used especially as bedding for livestock and for making hats, baskets, and other woven products. **2.** a single one of such stalks or stems. **3.** a long, slender tube, as of paper or plastic, used for sucking up a liquid. **4.** something of little value or importance; trifle; whit: *to not care a straw about something.* —*adj.* **1.** made of straw: *a straw hat.* **2.** resembling straw, as in color.

making **straw** brooms

straw·ber·ry (strô′ber′ē, strô′bə rē) *n., pl.* **straw·ber·ries.** **1.** a sweet, juicy, usually red fruit of any of a group of plants. **2.** a low-growing plant bearing this fruit, having many slender stalks and grown in temperate regions of the world.

straw man **1.** a bundle of straw made to resemble the figure of a person. **2.** something, as an imaginary enemy or a weak argument, set up by a person deliberately so that he or she may easily defeat or refute it: *The novel contained no political argument, and the critic's review set up a straw man only to knock it down.*

straw vote, an unofficial vote taken to estimate a consensus or division of opinion on some issue. Also, **straw poll.**

stray (strā) *v.i.* **1.** to wander from a given course or group or beyond proper limits: *The puppy strayed from the yard.* **2.** to wander or move about idly or without direction; rove: *The grazing sheep strayed over the mountainside.* **3.** to turn from a course that is thought to be morally right or good; err. —*adj.* **1.** wandering, lost, or homeless: *a stray puppy.* **2.** found or occurring randomly or occasionally; scattered or isolated: *There are a few stray hairs on my coat.* **3.** off or turning from the proper or intended course: *An innocent bystander was hit by a stray bullet.* —*n.* a lost or homeless animal or person.

streak (strēk) *n.* **1.** a long, thin, irregularly shaped mark, line, or band differing in color or texture from the material or surface of which it forms a part: *to have streaks of gray in one's hair.* **2.** a slight trace or tendency: *a streak of genius, a streak of madness.* **3.** a temporary run; brief period: *a streak of bad luck.* —*v.t.* to mark with a streak or streaks; form streaks on or in: *a face streaked with dirt.* —*v.i.* **1.** to form a streak or streaks. **2.** to become streaked: *The window streaked with droplets of rain.* **3.** to move, run, or go at great speed: *The ambulance streaked down the street.*

streak·y (strē′kē) *adj.,* **streak·i·er, streak·i·est.** **1.** marked with, characterized by, or occurring in streaks. **2.** of uneven quality or character; inconsistent: *a streaky performer, a streaky run of luck.* —**streak′i·ly,** *adv.* —**streak′i·ness,** *n.*

stream (strēm) *n.* **1.** a body of running water, especially a small river. **2.** a steady flow or current of any fluid or gas: *a stream of air.* **3.** any continuous, uninterrupted movement: *a stream of people, a stream of words.* —*v.i.* **1.** to flow or issue in a stream: *Tears streamed down the child's face. Light streamed into the room when I opened the curtains.* **2.** to pour forth a stream: *The runner came off the track streaming with perspiration.* **3.** to move along steadily or smoothly; flow: *The audience streamed out of the auditorium.* **4.** to wave, float, or extend outward: *The banners of the marchers streamed in the wind.* —*v.t.* to pour out, discharge, or emit in a stream: *The deep cut streamed blood.*

stream·er (strē′mər) *n.* **1.** a long, narrow flag or banner. **2.** any long, narrow strip of material: *Paper streamers were hanging from the ceiling.*

stream·let (strēm′lit) *n.* a little stream.

stream·line (strēm′līn′) *v.t.,* **stream·lined, stream·lin·ing.** **1.** to design or build so that there is the least possible resistance to air or water: *to streamline the design of an automobile.* **2.** to make more modern or efficient: *to streamline the administration of government.* —*adj.* see **streamlined.**

stream·lined (strēm′līnd′) *adj.* **1.** designed or built so as to offer the least possible resistance to air or water. **2.** having a trim, compact design: *streamlined furniture.* **3.** efficient and smooth-running: *a streamlined procedure.*

street (strēt) *n.* **1.** a public way in a city or town, usually with sidewalks and buildings on one or both sides: *a treelined street, a street of shops.* **2.** the part of such a way for vehicles, not including the sidewalks and buildings: *Be careful crossing the street.* **3.** the people who live, work, or gather in a street: *The whole street went to the meeting of the town council.* [From the Old English word *stræt* meaning "street, paved road," from the Late Latin word *strata* meaning "paved road," from the word *stratum,* past participle of *sternere* meaning "to lay out, lay (stones) for a pavement."]

street·car (strēt′kär′) *n.* a public passenger vehicle that runs on rails in city streets. Also, **tram, trolley, trolley car.**

strength (strengkth, strength, strenth) *n.* **1.** the state or quality of being strong; power, force, or energy: *to build up one's strength by lifting weights.* **2.** the power to withstand or resist attack, force, strain, or stress without breaking or yielding: *to test the strength of a rope.* **3.** the degree of concentration, intensity, or effectiveness: *the strength of an electric current, the strength of a drug.* **4.** military power derived from numbers of soldiers, equipment, or resources: *The nation's armed forces are at full strength.* **5.** a person or thing that strengthens; source of power or force.

·on the strength of. based or depending on: *The defendant was convicted of fraud on the strength of the witnesses' testimony.*

strength·en (strengk′thən, streng′thən, stren′thən) *v.t., v.i.* to make or become strong or stronger. —**strength′en·er,** *n.*

stren·u·ous (stren′ū əs) *adj.* **1.** requiring or characterized by great effort or exertion: *a strenuous task.* **2.** very active or energetic; vigorous: *strenuous opposition.* —**stren′u·ous·ly,** *adv.* —**stren′u·ous·ness,** *n.*

strep (strep) *adj. Informal.* streptococcal: *a strep infection.*

strep throat, a serious infection of the throat caused by a streptococcus and characterized by fever and the presence of pus in the throat.

strep·to·coc·cal (strep′tə kok′əl) *adj.* of, relating to, or caused by streptococci: *a streptococcal bacterium.*

strep·to·coc·cus (strep′tə kok′əs) *n., pl.* **strep·to·coc·ci** (strep′tə kok′sī). any of a group of spherical bacteria that multiply by dividing in one direction only, thus tending to form chains. Diseases such as scarlet fever, rheumatic fever, pneumonia, and strep throat are caused by various kinds of streptococci.

stress (stres) *n., pl.* **stress·es.** **1.** mental or emotional strain or pressure: *to fall ill from the stress of worry.* **2.** a special meaning, emphasis, or importance attached to something: *to put stress on good table manners.* **3.** the relative emphasis given to a particular sound, syllable, or word in speech. In the word *employ,* the stress is on the second syllable. **4.** a force or pressure that is applied to something: *the stress of heavy traffic on a bridge.* —*v.t.* **1.** to place special meaning, emphasis, or importance on: *to stress the need for conservation of natural resources.* **2.** to pronounce (a syllable, word, or words) with a particular stress. **3.** to apply force or pressure to.

stress mark, see **accent** *(def. 2).*

stress test, a medical procedure that tests the health of the heart by monitoring its function while the patient exercises.

stretch (strech) *v.t.* **1.** to straighten or spread out to full length or width: *to stretch one's arms and legs.* **2.** to hold out; put forth: *to stretch one's arms out in greeting.* **3.** to cause to reach or extend, as from one place to another or across a given area: *to stretch a clothesline across a yard.* **4.** to strain; pull: *The runner stretched a leg muscle.* **5.** to extend beyond proper or natural limits: *to stretch the rules.* **6.** to widen, lengthen, or pull out of shape by force: *to stretch a sweater.* **7.** to cause to last; prolong: *to stretch a visit out for two weeks.* **8.** to exaggerate: *to stretch the truth.* —*v.i.* **1.** to lie down and extend the body to full length: *to stretch out on a bed.* **2.** to straighten or spread out one's body or limbs to full length: *Many people in the audience got up and stretched during the intermission.* **3.** to extend from one place to another or across space: *The road stretches for another thirty miles.* **4.** to become widened, lengthened, or pulled out of shape without tearing or breaking: *Rubber stretches.* —*n., pl.* **stretch·es.** **1.** an unbroken space or area; extent: *a quiet stretch of river.* **2.** an unbroken period of time: *a stretch of two years.* **3.** the act of stretching or the state of being stretched. **4.** the quality of being elastic; elasticity: *This rubber band has lost its stretch.* **5.** the straight part of a racecourse. —*adj.* made of material having elastic qualities: *stretch gloves, stretch stockings, stretch pants.*

stretch·er (strech'ər) *n.* **1.** a piece of canvas or similar material stretched across a frame, used for carrying a sick, injured, or dead person. **2.** any of various devices used to stretch, such as the frame on which an artist's canvas is spread. **3.** a person or thing that stretches.

strew (strü) *v.t.* **strewed, strewed** or **strewn, strew·ing.** **1.** to spread or throw about at random; scatter: *to strew hay on a barn floor.* **2.** to cover with something spread or thrown about in this way: *The street was strewn with scraps of paper and other litter.* **3.** to be scattered over: *Confetti strewed the floor.*

stri·at·ed (strī'ā tid) *adj.* marked by or having narrow grooves, bands, or streaks of distinctive color or texture, especially in a parallel arrangement: *striated rock.*

stri·a·tion (strī ā'shən) *n.* the state or condition of being striated: *the striation of the walls of the canyon.*

strick·en (strik'ən) *v.* a past participle of **strike.** —*adj.* **1.** strongly affected or overwhelmed, as by sorrow, disease, or misfortune: *stricken with grief.* **2.** struck or wounded: *a stricken animal.*

strict (strikt) *adj.* **1.** following or demanding that others follow rules or regulations in a rigid, exact manner: *a strict teacher.* **2.** closely enforced or followed: *The hospital has strict visiting hours.* **3.** exact; precise: *a strict interpretation of the rules.* **4.** complete; absolute: *plans to be*

striated column

kept in strict confidence. —**strict'ly,** *adv.* —**strict'ness,** *n.*

Word Family

An important group of English words have developed from the Latin word *stringere,* meaning "to bind, tie together." **Strict** rules can help tie the parts of a complex project together and can help promote cooperation among those working on the project. Sometimes **stringent** rules can be too **restrictive** and put a **strain** on people, but even greater **distress** results when rules are not followed. Without rules, a project may fall into dire **straits,** and its leader may be **constrained** to institute rules that establish order, encourage order, and regain prestige.

stric·ture (strik'chər) *n.* **1.** unfavorable or severe criticism; censure: *the stricture of the opposition party.* **2.** something that limits, confines, or restrains: *the narrow stricture of the rules.* **3.** an abnormal closing or narrowing of some duct or tube of the body.

stride (strīd) *v.,* **strode, strid·den** (strid'ən), **strid·ing.** —*v.i.* **1.** to walk with long, sweeping steps: *The teacher strode into the room.* **2.** to pass with a single long step: *to stride over a mud puddle.* —*v.t.* **1.** to sit or stand with one leg on each side of; straddle; bestride: *to stride a horse.* **2.** to move over, along, or through with long, sweeping steps. —*n.* **1.** a long, sweeping step: *the graceful stride of a trained runner.* **2.** the distance covered by such a step: *It is but a few strides to the lunchroom.* **3.** *usually,* **strides.** progress or improvement: *Great strides have been made in medical research.*

  ·**to take in one's stride.** to adjust to or deal with without difficulty, effort, or hesitation.

stri·dent (strī'dənt) *adj.* making or having a harsh, shrill, grating sound: *a strident mass of cars and taxis honking in the evening rush hour.* —**stri'dence, stri'den·cy,** *n.* —**stri'dent·ly,** *adv.*

strife (strīf) *n.* **1.** bitter conflict, fighting, or trouble. **2.** a contest or struggle between rivals to gain superiority.

strike (strīk) *v.,* **struck, struck** or **strick·en, strik·ing.** —*v.t.* **1.** to give a blow to; hit: *to strike someone in anger.* **2.** to deal; inflict: *to strike a blow.* **3.** to come against with force: *The car skidded and struck a tree.* **4.** to cause to come against with force; hit: *to strike one's head in a fall.* **5.** to set on fire by rubbing or hitting: *to strike a match.* **6.** to erase, cancel, or otherwise remove: *You can strike my name off the list of those coming to the party.* **7.** to make an attack on; assault: *Our troops struck the enemy camp at dawn.* **8.** to give the impression of being; appear to: *That child struck me as being very bright.* **9.** to assume: *to strike a pose for the camera.* **10.** to give or announce (time) by ringing or otherwise sounding: *The clock struck twelve.* **11.** to find suddenly or unexpectedly; discover: *to strike oil.* **12.** to cause (a feeling or emotion) to penetrate or affect deeply: *The shriek struck terror into their hearts.* **13.** to stop work at (a factory, company, or the like) until certain demands are met, such as higher pay or better working conditions. **14.** to arrive at or make: *to strike a bargain.* **15.** to come to or fall upon: *The sound of music struck our ears.*

at; āpe; fär; câre; end; mē; it; īce; pîerce; hot; ōld; sông, fôrk; oil; out; up; ūse; rüle; pull; tûrn; chin; sing; shop; thin; this; hw in white; zh in treasure. The symbol ə stands for the unstressed vowel sound heard in about, taken, pencil, lemon, and circus.

S

16. to make or form by pressing or stamping: *to strike coins.* **17.** to lower or take down, as a sail or flag: *The ship struck its sails.* —*v.i.* **1.** to come into violent contact; hit: *My head struck against the door when I slipped.* **2.** to make an attack: *The troops will strike at dawn.* **3.** to stop work until certain demands are met, such as higher pay or better working conditions: *The factory workers will strike tomorrow if a settlement is not reached tonight.* **4.** to make a sound, as by ringing: *The chimes struck at midnight.* **5.** (of fish) to seize the bait. —*n.* **1.** the act of striking; blow. **2.** a work stoppage until certain demands are met: *a nationwide strike of railroad workers.* **3.** a sudden or unexpected discovery, as of oil or ore: *a gold strike.* **4.** *Baseball.* **a.** a pitched ball that a batter swings at and misses. **b.** a pitched ball that is not swung at but is judged by the umpire to be within the strike zone. **c.** a foul ball that is not caught by a fielder, unless there are already two strikes against the batter. **5.** *Bowling.* **a.** the act of knocking down all the pins with the first ball rolled. **b.** a score made in this way. **6.** a seizing of the bait by a fish.

·**to strike out. a.** to begin, as an undertaking or journey: *We struck out for home at dawn.* **b.** *Baseball.* to put out or be put out by a strikeout.

·**to strike up.** to begin; start: *The strangers struck up a conversation.*

strike·break·er (strīk′brā′kər) *n.* a person who continues to work during a strike, takes the place of a worker on strike, or supplies workers to take the place of strikers.

strike·out (strīk′out′) *n. Baseball.* an out resulting from three strikes charged against a batter.

strik·er (strī′kər) *n.* **1.** a worker who takes part in a strike. **2.** a person or thing that strikes.

strike zone *Baseball.* an area directly over home plate and between the batter's knees and armpits, through which a pitched ball that is not swung at must pass in order to be judged a strike.

strik·ing (strī′king) *adj.* making a strong impression on the mind or senses; impressive: *There was a striking similarity between two of the paintings at the art exhibit.* —**strik′ing·ly,** *adv.*

string (string) *n.* **1.** a slender line consisting of twisted or intertwined strands of fiber, wire, or similar material. **2.** anything like this, such as a strip of cloth used for tying parts together: *the strings of an apron.* **3.** a set or number of things joined together by or arranged on a string: *a string of pearls, a string of Christmas tree lights.* **4.** a series or row of persons, things, or events: *a string of traffic signals, a string of robberies.* **5.** *usually,* **strings.** *Informal.* a limitation or condition connected with something: *There are no strings attached to my offer of a loan.* **6.** a thin strand of wire, gut, nylon, or other material used to produce tones in certain musical instruments, such as guitars or pianos. **7. strings.** musical instruments played on such strings with a bow or by plucking, as the violin, viola, and cello, especially when such instruments are considered as a group in an orchestra or ensemble. **8.** a group of players on an athletic team who are ranked together as a unit, usually according to ability: *to play on the third string of a football team.* **9.** a part of a plant resembling a string: *to pull the strings off green beans.* —*v.t.,* **strung, string·ing.** **1.** to put on a string: *to string beads.* **2.** to provide with a string or strings: *to string a guitar.* **3.** to cause to reach from one place to another or across a given area: *to string a clothesline across a yard.* **4.** to arrange in a row or series: *Workers strung lights around the construction site.* **5.** to remove fibers or strings from: *to string beans.*

·**to pull strings.** to use one's power or influence in order to get what one wants.

·**to string along.** *Informal.* **a.** to fool or deceive. **b.** to agree or cooperate.

string bean, a long, green bean, related to the kidney bean, the pod of which is eaten as a vegetable. Also, **green bean.**

stringed instrument, a musical instrument, such as a cello, violin, harp, or guitar, that has strings which produce tones when they are played with a bow or plucked.

strin·gent (strin′jənt) *adj.* **1.** rigidly maintained, enforced, or followed; rigorous: *stringent requirements, stringent procedures.* **2.** persuasive or convincing: *a stringent argument.* **3.** characterized by or resulting from scarcity or from a lack of available funds: *to adopt stringent economic restrictions.* —**strin′gen·cy,** *n.* —**strin′gent·ly,** *adv.*

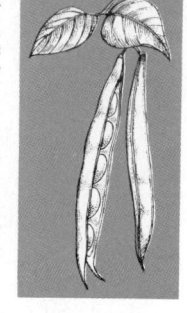

string beans

string·er (string′ər) *n.* **1.** a person or thing that strings. **2.** a long horizontal beam supporting the vertical crosspieces of a framework or structure. **3.** a part-time or local correspondent for a news publication or news service.

string·y (string′ē) *adj.,* **string·i·er, string·i·est.** **1.** having or consisting of tough fibers: *stringy celery.* **2.** like string; thin: *stringy hair.* **3.** forming strings: *stringy cheese.*

strip[1] (strip) *v.,* **stripped** or **stript, strip·ping.** —*v.t.* **1.** to remove or pull off the clothing or other covering from: *We are stripping the beds to wash the sheets.* **2.** to remove or pull off: *to strip bark from a tree, to strip off one's clothes.* **3.** to take away the rights, honors, or possessions of; divest. **4.** to rob or plunder: *The burglars stripped the house.* **5.** to damage or break the threads or teeth of (a bolt, gear, screw, or the like). —*v.i.* to undress. [From the Old English word suffix *-strȳpan,* as found in *bestrȳpan* meaning "to rob, spoil, strip[1]."]

strip[2] (strip) *n.* **1.** a long, narrow piece of something: *a strip of paper, a strip of land.* **2.** see **airstrip. 3.** see **comic strip.** [Perhaps from the Middle Low German word *strippe* meaning "a strap."]

stripe[1] (strīp) *n.* **1.** a long, narrow band that is different in color or texture from the material or surface around it: *The cloth had white stripes on a red background.* **2.** any of various strips of cloth worn on the sleeve of a uniform to indicate rank, length of service, or some other distinction: *a police sergeant with three stripes.* **3.** a particular kind of character; sort: *a person of a generous stripe.* —*v.t.,* **striped, strip·ing.** to mark with a stripe or stripes. [Probably a form of *strip*[2].]

stripes[1] on a raccoon's tail

stripe[2] (strīp) *n.* a stroke or lash, as with a rod or whip. [Of uncertain origin.]

striped (strīpt, strī′pid) *adj.* having or marked with a stripe or stripes: *a striped material.*

strip·ling (strip′ling) *n.* a youth; lad.

strip mine, a mine worked by removing surface material in successive strips to expose a mineral or ore. —**strip′-mine′,** *v.t., v.i.* —**strip mining,** *n.*

stript (stript) a past tense and past participle of **strip**[1].

strive (strīv) *v.i.,* **strove** or **strived, striv·en** (striv′ən), **striv·ing.** to make a great or strenuous effort: *to strive for perfection.*

strobe (strōb) *n.* **1.** a device that emits a very brief, intense flash of light, used as a light source in photography and as a warning signal. **2.** see **stroboscope**.

stro·bo·scope (strō′bə skōp′) *n.* an instrument that flashes a brief, intense light at regular intervals, allowing moving objects to be seen as if they were standing still. [From the Greek word *strobos* meaning "a whirling" + the English suffix *-scope*.] —**stro·bo·scop·ic** (strō′bə skop′ik), *adj.*

strode (strōd) the past tense of **stride**.

stroke¹ (strōk) *n.* **1.** the act of striking; blow: *to split wood with one stroke of the ax.* **2.** an action or event having a powerful or unexpected effect: *a stroke of misfortune.* **3.** a brilliant or inspired act, achievement, or idea: *a stroke of genius.* **4.** the sound produced by striking: *We heard the stroke of the gong.* **5.** time indicated by striking, as of a clock: *They left at the stroke of three.* **6.** a single unbroken or complete movement, as of the hand, an instrument, or something held in the hand: *the stroke of an oar.* **7.** a mark made by a pen, pencil, brush, or other implement: *The artist made the drawing with a few strokes of a pen.* **8.** a sudden weakness or paralysis, with or without loss of consciousness, caused by rupture, spasm, or blockage of blood vessels in the brain; apoplexy. **9.** a combination of repeated arm and leg movements for moving the body through water in swimming. **10.** *Sports.* **a.** the act or instance of striking the ball, as in golf or tennis. **b.** the manner in which this is done. **11.** a beat, as of the heart. **12.** a rower who sets the rhythm for a team of rowers. —*v.t.,* **stroked, strok·ing.** (of a rower) to set the rhythm for (other rowers). [From the Middle English word *stroke* meaning "a blow."]

stroke² (strōk) *v.t.,* **stroked, strok·ing.** to rub gently or caressingly with the hand, usually repeatedly and in the same direction: *to stroke a puppy's head.* —*n.* a light, caressing movement of the hand. [From the Old English word *strācian* meaning "to rub gently."]

stroll (strōl) *v.i.* to walk in a leisurely or idle manner: *We strolled through the park.* —*v.t.* to walk along or through in a leisurely or idle manner. —*n.* a leisurely walk.

stroll·er (strō′lər) *n.* **1.** a small baby carriage in which a child sits and is wheeled about. **2.** a person who strolls.

strong (strông) *adj.* **1.** having great muscular power; physically powerful: *strong arms, a strong athlete.* **2.** having good health: *The patient is not strong enough to go out yet.* **3.** having or using great influence, power, or authority: *a strong ruler, a strong government.* **4.** able to resist or withstand attack, strain, stress, or force: *a strong fort, a strong piece of furniture.* **5.** firm in mind, character, will, or purpose; morally powerful or courageous: *to be strong enough to resist temptation.* **6.** persuasive or effective; convincing: *a strong argument.* **7.** having a sharp, bitter, or offensive taste or odor: *a strong cheese, a strong tobacco.* **8.** moving with great force or speed: *strong winds, a strong undertow.* **9.** having a great degree of intensity, force, or power: *cheese with a strong smell.* **10.** containing much alcohol. **11.** having a large amount of proper or essential ingredients: *I like strong tea so I let it steep a long time when I make it.* **12.** of a specified numerical force: *an army 10,000 strong.* —*adv.* in a strong manner; vigorously; powerfully. —**strong′ly,** *adv.*

strong·box (strông′boks′) *n., pl.* **strong·box·es.** a strongly made chest or safe, used for storing money, documents, and other valuables.

strong·hold (strông′hōld′) *n.* **1.** a place fortified against attack or danger. **2.** a place where a particular idea or way of thinking is predominant or strong: *Universities are often strongholds of new thinking.*

stron·ti·um (stron′shē əm, stron′tē əm) *n.* a soft, silvery metallic element used in compounds for fireworks or flares and in television picture tubes. Symbol: **Sr** [From *Strontian*, the town in Scotland where ore containing it was first found.]

strontium 90, a radioactive isotope of strontium used in radiology and nuclear batteries. It is found in dangerous amounts in fallout from nuclear explosions.

strop (strop) *n.* a flexible strip of material, such as leather or canvas, used to sharpen razors. —*v.t.,* **stropped, strop·ping.** to sharpen on a strop.

stro·phe (strō′fē) *n.* a group of lines of poetry; stanza.

strove (strōv) a past tense of **strive**.

struck (struk) the past tense and a past participle of **strike**.

struc·tur·al (struk′chər əl) *adj.* **1.** of or relating to structure: *a structural weakness in a building.* **2.** used in or necessary to building or construction: *a structural beam.* —**struc′tur·al·ly,** *adv.*

struc·ture (struk′chər) *n.* **1.** anything that is built or constructed, such as a building or bridge: *That antenna is the tallest structure in the city.* **2.** the way in which something is built, arranged, or organized: *the structure of a society, the grammatical structure of a language.* **3.** the arrangement or interrelation of the parts or elements that make up a thing: *to study the structure of a cell.* **4.** an organized body or combination of connected and dependent parts or elements: *The brain is a complex structure.* —*v.t.,* **struc·tured, struc·tur·ing.** to build or construct: *to structure a bridge, to structure an argument.*

stru·del (strü′dəl, shtrü′dəl) *n.* a pastry made with a filling wrapped in a very thin sheet of dough and baked: *apple strudel, cheese strudel.* [From the German word *Strudel* meaning "whirlpool," used as the name of this food.]

strug·gle (strug′əl) *v.i.,* **strug·gled, strug·gling.** **1.** to make a great effort; strive: *to struggle to pass final examinations.* **2.** to make one's way with great effort: *The skiers struggled through the heavy snowdrifts.* **3.** to fight; battle: *The two dogs struggled for the bone.* —*n.* **1.** a very great or strenuous effort. *It was a struggle to understand the arithmetic problem.* **2.** a battle or fight. *Once cornered, the suspect gave up without a struggle.*

strum (strum) *v.,* **strummed, strum·ming.** —*v.t.* to play, especially in an idle, monotonous, or unskillful manner: *to strum a banjo, to strum a tune.* —*v.i.* to play a stringed musical instrument, especially in an idle, monotonous, or unskillful manner. —*n.* the act or sound of strumming. —**strum′mer,** *n.*

strum·pet (strum′pit) *n.* a prostitute.

strung (strung) the past tense and past participle of **string**.

strut¹ (strut) *v.i.,* **strut·ted, strut·ting.** to walk in a vain, pompous, or arrogant manner. —*n.* a vain, pompous, or arrogant way of walking. [From the Old English word *strūtian* meaning "to stand out stiffly, project."] —**strut′ter,** *n.*

at; āpe; fär; câre; end; mē; it; īce; pîerce; hot; ōld; sông, fôrk; oil; out; up; ūse; rüle; pull; tûrn; chin; sing; shop; thin; this; hw in white; zh in treasure. The symbol ə stands for the unstressed vowel sound heard in about, taken, pencil, lemon, and circus.

S

strut² (strut) *n.* a bar, brace, or other supporting piece in an architectural framework. —*v.t.*, **strut·ted, strut·ting.** to brace or support with a strut or struts. [Probably from *strut¹*.]

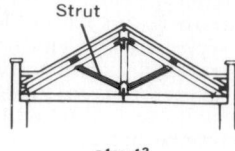

Strut

strut²

strych·nine (strik′nin, strik′nīn) *n.* a very bitter, colorless, toxic substance, formerly used in medicine to stimulate the nervous system.

stub (stub) *n.* **1.** a short piece that remains after something has been worn away, removed, cut, or broken off: *a cigar stub, the stub of a pencil.* **2.** the remaining or detachable portion, as of a check, ticket, or bill, that provides a record or receipt of payment. **3.** a short, thick, projecting piece or part. **4.** the stump of a tree trunk or plant stem. —*v.t.*, **stubbed, stub·bing.** to strike (one's toe or foot) accidentally against something: *to stub one's toe on a chair in the dark.*

stub·ble (stub′əl) *n.* **1.** short stalks of grain and certain other plants left standing in the ground after the crop has been harvested. **2.** anything resembling this, such as a short growth of beard. —**stub′bly,** *adv.*

stub·born (stub′ərn) *adj.* **1.** not giving in to argument, persuasion, or reason; obstinate: *a stubborn person.* **2.** done or carried on in an unyielding, obstinate way: *a stubborn refusal to cooperate.* **3.** hard to overcome or deal with: *a stubborn cough.* —**stub′born·ly,** *adv.* —**stub′born·ness,** *n.*

stub·by (stub′ē) *adj.*, **stub·bi·er, stub·bi·est. 1.** short and thick: *a stubby tail, stubby toes.* **2.** short, thick, and bristly: *a stubby beard.* **3.** covered with or consisting of stubs or stubble: *a stubby field.* —**stub′bi·ness,** *n.*

stuc·co (stuk′ō) *n., pl.* **stuc·coes** or **stuc·cos. 1.** plaster or cement used for covering outside walls or for ornamenting inside walls. **2.** ornamental work made of stucco. —*v.t.*, **stuc·coed, stuc·co·ing.** to cover or ornament with stucco: *to stucco a wall.*

stuck (stuk) the past tense and past participle of **stick².**

stuck–up (stuk′up′) *adj. Informal.* conceited or snobbish.

stud¹ (stud) *n.* **1.** a nail head, knob, or similar object, usually of metal, fixed to and sticking out from a surface, used especially as an ornament. **2.** an ornamental fastener resembling a button, used on the front of men's formal shirts. **3.** a vertical post, as in the framework of a wall, to which horizontal boards, plasterboard, and the like are nailed. —*v.t.*, **stud·ded, stud·ding. 1.** to set or ornament with studs: *to stud a bracelet with diamonds.* **2.** to be scattered or spread over: *Stars studded the sky.* **3.** to provide with or support by a vertical post or posts. [From the Old English word *studu* meaning "a post, pillar."]

stud² (stud) *n.* **1.** a male animal, especially a horse, kept for breeding. **2.** a group of animals, especially horses, selected and raised for breeding. [From the Old English word *stōd* "a place for breeding horses."]

stu·dent (stü′dənt, stū′dənt) *n.* **1.** a person attending a school, college, or university. **2.** a person devoted to study or investigation of a particular subject: *a student of language.*

stud·ied (stud′ēd) *adj.* carefully planned; deliberate; intentional: *We were surprised by our guest's studied rudeness.* —**stud′ied·ly,** *adv.* —**stud′ied·ness,** *n.*

stu·di·o (stü′dē ō′, stū′dē ō′) *n., pl.* **stu·di·os. 1.** a place where a sculptor, painter, musician or photographer works. **2.** a place for instruction in and practice of one of the performing arts: *a dance studio.* **3.** a place where motion pictures are filmed. **4.** a place where radio and television programs are performed or recorded. **5.** a place where music is recorded.

studio couch, an upholstered couch, usually without arms, that can be used as a bed.

stu·di·ous (stü′dē əs, stū′dē əs) *adj.* **1.** given to or fond of study and learning: *a studious researcher.* **2.** showing careful or earnest consideration or attention: *The new mayor promised to make a studious effort to find a solution to the problem.* —**stu′di·ous·ly,** *adv.* —**stu′di·ous·ness,** *n.*

stud·y (stud′ē) *v.*, **stud·ied, stud·y·ing.** —*v.t.* **1.** to apply the mind in order to gain a knowledge of; try to learn: *to study medicine, to study history.* **2.** to look at closely or critically; examine: *to study a map.* **3.** to look or inquire into; investigate: *to study ways of reducing air pollution.* **4.** to give careful thought and consideration to: *I will study the matter and give you my opinion.* **5.** to try to learn by memorizing: *The actor studied the part before the audition.* —*v.i.* **1.** to apply the mind in order to gain knowledge: *to study for the ministry.* —*n., pl.* **stud·ies. 1.** the act or process of studying: *the study of mathematics, the enjoyment of study.* **2.** a careful or critical examination or investigation: *a study of recent advances in medicine.* **3.** something that is studied or to be studied; branch of learning: *Computer science is a new field of study.* **4.** a room in a house used or set apart for study, reading, writing, or the like. **5.** a sketch, design, or plan for an artistic work, or for some detail or portion of it.

stuff (stuf) *n.* **1.** the substance or material that a thing is made of: *What kind of stuff is in this pillow?* **2.** an indefinite or vague substance or matter: *Can you get this black stuff off my shirt?* **3.** basic character or qualities: *The general was made of stern stuff and would not surrender.* **4.** worthless or useless matter or things: *That closet is full of stuff.* —*v.t.* **1.** to pack or cram full; fill: *to stuff a trunk with old clothes.* **2.** to force or thrust (something) tightly, as into a container: *to stuff papers into an envelope.* **3.** to block or stop up by thrusting something tightly in; plug: *to stuff one's ears with cotton.* **4.** to fill with too much food: *Stop stuffing yourself.* **5.** *Cooking.* to fill (poultry or other food) with stuffing. **6.** to fill the skin of (a dead animal) to restore its natural appearance. **7.** to put fraudulent votes into (a ballot box).

stuffed shirt *Informal.* a person who is extremely pompous or formal and exhibits self-importance.

stuff·ing (stuf′ing) *n.* **1.** material used for filling or packing something: *The stuffing is coming out of the pillow.* **2.** a food mixture, as of seasoned bread crumbs or rice, used to fill poultry or other food.

stuff·y (stuf′ē) *adj.*, **stuff·i·er, stuff·i·est. 1.** lacking fresh air; close: *a stuffy room.* **2.** very strait-laced; formal; pompous: *a stuffy manner.* **3.** stopped up: *a stuffy nose.* **4.** lacking freshness or interest; dull; boring: *a stuffy speech.* —**stuff′i·ly,** *adv.* —**stuff′i·ness,** *n.*

stul·ti·fy (stul′tə fī′) *v.t.*, **stul·ti·fied, stul·ti·fy·ing.** to make useless, weak, or foolish: *Boring teachers can stultify one's ambition to learn.* —**stul′ti·fi·ca′tion,** *n.*

stum·ble (stum′bəl) *v.i.*, **stum·bled, stum·bling. 1.** to lose one's balance or trip while walking or running: *I stumbled over the sleeping cat.* **2.** to move or walk unsteadily or awkwardly: *to stumble around a dark room.* **3.** to behave, act, or speak in a clumsy, awkward way: *to stumble over a difficult word, to stumble through a speech because of nervousness.* **4.** to make a mistake or blunder. **5.** to discover accidentally or unexpectedly: *The detective stumbled on an important clue.* —*n.* **1.** the act of stumbling. **2.** a mistake or blunder; slip. —**stum′bling·ly,** *adv.*

stumbling block, something that stands in the way of or prevents progress; hindrance; obstruction.

stump (stump) *n.* **1.** the lower part of a tree trunk or plant stem remaining in the ground after the main part is cut off. **2.** the part of anything that remains after the main or more important part has been removed, as the remaining part of an amputated arm or leg. **3.** a place or platform for a political speech. —*v.t.* **1.** *Informal.* to cause to be at a loss; perplex; baffle: *This problem has really stumped me.* **2.** to travel about and make political speeches in: *The candidate for senator stumped the southern part of the state.* —*v.i.* **1.** to walk stiffly, heavily, or noisily: *to stump across the floor.* **2.** to travel about making political speeches.

stump·y (stum′pē) *adj.*, **stump·i·er, stump·i·est. 1.** short and thick like a stump: *a stumpy tail.* **2.** (of land) abounding with tree stumps: *stumpy marshland.* —**stump′i·ness,** *n.*

stun (stun) *v.t.,* **stunned, stun·ning. 1.** to daze or make unconscious, as by a blow. **2.** to overwhelm, shock, or bewilder: *The unexpected news stunned me.*

stung (stung) the past tense and past participle of **sting.**

stunk (stungk) a past tense and the past participle of **stink.**

stun·ning (stun′ning) *adj.* **1.** *Informal.* extremely attractive or good-looking: *a stunning person, a stunning outfit.* **2.** that stuns, such as a blow or loud noise. —**stun′ning·ly,** *adv.*

stunt¹ (stunt) *v.t.* **1.** to stop or hinder the growth or development of: *You will stunt the tree if you don't give it enough room to grow.* **2.** to check or hinder (growth, development, or progress): *A poor diet stunted the child's growth.* [Perhaps of Scandinavian origin.]

stunt²
an aerialist performing stunts
on a tightrope

stunt² (stunt) *Informal. n.* an act that is done to attract attention, especially one requiring or showing strength, skill, or daring: *The acrobat performed dangerous stunts on the high trapeze.* —*v.i.* to perform a stunt or stunts. [Of uncertain origin.]

stu·pe·fac·tion (stü′pə fak′shən, stū′pə fak′shən) *n.* **1.** the act of stupefying or the state of being stupefied. **2.** overwhelming astonishment; amazement.

stu·pe·fy (stü′pə fī′, stū′pə fī′) *v.t.,* **stu·pe·fied, stu·pe·fy·ing. 1.** to make stupid, senseless, or inactive; dull the senses of: *The blow stupefied the boxer.* **2.** to amaze or astound; overwhelm: *The daring stunt stupefied the audience.*

stu·pen·dous (stü pen′dəs, stū pen′dəs) *adj.* causing amazement or astonishment; overwhelming: *a stupendous reversal of fortune.* —**stu·pen′dous·ly,** *adv.* —**stu·pen′dous·ness,** *n.*

stu·pid (stü′pid, stū′pid) *adj.* **1.** lacking ordinary intelligence; slow-witted; dumb. **2.** dull; uninteresting; boring: *We did nothing but sit around at that stupid party.* **3.** showing or characterized by a lack of intelligence or common sense: *a stupid answer.* —**stu′pid·ly,** *adv.* —**stu′pid·ness,** *n.*

stu·pid·i·ty (stü pid′i tē, stū pid′i tē) *n., pl.* **stu·pid·i-**

ties. **1.** lack of intelligence or common sense. **2.** a stupid statement, act, or the like.

stu·por (stü′pər, stū′pər) *n.* a partly conscious condition; lessening of the power to feel: *to be in a stupor after an operation.*

stur·dy (stûr′dē) *adj.,* **stur·di·er, stur·di·est. 1.** having strength; strong; hardy: *sturdy pioneers.* **2.** solidly built: *a sturdy log cabin.* **3.** hard to overcome; not yielding: *The enemy put up a sturdy defense.* —**stur′di·ly,** *adv.* —**stur′di·ness,** *n.*

stur·geon (stûr′jən) *n., pl.* **stur·geons** or **stur·geon.** any of a group of fish found in fresh and salt waters, having rows of bony, pointed scales, and valued as a source of caviar.

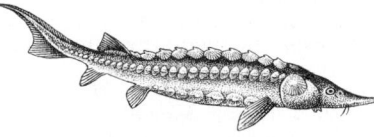
sturgeon

stut·ter (stut′ər) *v.i.* to speak haltingly with frequent, repeated sounds or syllables; stammer. —*v.t.* to utter with a series of repeated sounds or syllables: *to stutter an apology.* —*n.* **1.** an instance of stuttering. **2.** a tendency to stutter: *to speak with a stutter.* —**stut′ter·er,** —**stut′ter·ing·ly,** *adv.*

sty¹ (stī) *n., pl.* **sties. 1.** a pen or enclosure where pigs are kept; pigpen; pigsty. **2.** any filthy place; hovel: *The abandoned shack was a sty.* [From the Old English word *stig* meaning "a wooden enclosure, sty¹."]

sty² (stī) *n., pl.* **sties.** an inflamed swelling on the edge of the eyelid, resembling a small boil. [Short for *styan* with the same meaning, from the Old English word *stigend,* present participle of *stīgan* "to ascend, mount¹," because it swells from the eyelid.]

Styg·i·an (stij′ē ən) *adj.* **1.** of, relating to, or characteristic of the mythological river Styx, or the lower world in which it flows. **2.** like the river Styx; black or gloomy.

style (stīl) *n.* **1.** a particular mode or fashion, especially of dress: *a coat in the latest style.* **2.** elegance; tastefulness: *to live in style, to dance with style.* **3.** a particular way of doing or making something: *poetry in the style of Wordsworth, a building in classic Greek style.* **4.** see **stylus** *(def. 1).* **5.** *Botany.* the part of the pistil of a flower, shaped like a stalk, extending from the ovary to the stigma. **6.** special rules, as of spelling, punctuation, or capitalization, followed by a particular author, publisher, or printer. —*v.t.,* **styled, styl·ing. 1.** to design according to a mode or fashion: *to style a fall wardrobe.* **2.** to change in order to conform to an accepted or particular style of printing or writing: *to style a manuscript.*

styl·ish (stī′lish) *adj.* according to current or accepted style; fashionable: *That department store has very stylish clothes.* —**styl′ish·ly,** *adv.* —**styl′ish·ness,** *n.*

styl·ist (stī′list) *n.* **1.** a writer or speaker who is distinguished for excellence or mastery of style. **2.** a person who designs or advises on styles, as in fashion or furnishing: *a hair stylist.*

sty·lis·tic (stī lis′tik) *adj.* of or relating to style, especially artistic style. —**sty·lis′ti·cal·ly,** *adv.*

styl·ize (stī′līz) *v.t.,* **styl·ized, styl·iz·ing.** to make (something, such as a manuscript or an artistic work) follow the rules of a particular style.

---

at; āpe; fär; câre; end; mē; it; īce; pîerce; hot; ōld; sông, fôrk; oil; out; up; ūse; rüle; pull; tûrn; chin; sing; shop; thin; **this;** hw in white; zh in treasure. The symbol ə stands for the unstressed vowel sound heard in about, taken, pencil, lemon, and circus.

S

sty·lus (stī′ləs) *n.*, *pl.* **sty·li** (stī′lī) or **sty·lus·es.**
1. *also,* **style.** an instrument with a
pointed or rounded head, used to
write on soft materials, such as wax.
2. a phonograph needle that transforms vibrations from the grooves on
a record into an electric current that
is amplified and turned into sound.

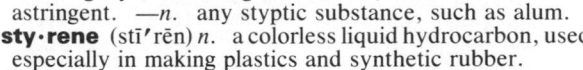

sty·mie (stī′mē) *also,* **sty·my.** *v.t.,*
sty·mied, sty·mie·ing. to bring to
or keep at a standstill; frustrate; block:
All their efforts were stymied.

stylus *(def. 1)*

styp·tic (stip′tik) *adj.* able to stop
bleeding by contracting the tissues;
astringent. —*n.* any styptic substance, such as alum.

sty·rene (stī′rēn) *n.* a colorless liquid hydrocarbon, used
especially in making plastics and synthetic rubber.

Sty·ro·foam (stī′rə fōm′) *n.* *Trademark.* a type of poly-
styrene foam containing many tiny air bubbles and used
as a lightweight insulating material.

Styx (stiks) *n.* *Greek Mythology.* the river surrounding
Hades, across which Charon ferried the souls of the dead.

sua·sion (swā′zhən) *n.* the act or an instance of convincing or urging; persuasion: *moral suasion.*

suave (swäv) *adj.* having or showing a smooth, polite
manner. —**suave′ly,** *adv.* —**suave′ness, suav′i·ty,** *n.*

sub (sub) *Informal.* *n.* **1.** see **substitute. 2.** see **submarine.** —*v.i.,* **subbed, sub·bing.** to act as a substitute.

sub– *prefix* **1.** under; below; beneath: *submarine.*
2. nearly; less than: *subtropical.* **3.** used to express a
further division or distinction: *subdivide.* **4.** partially;
slightly: *subacid.* **5.** lower in position: *subdeacon.* **6.** of
minor importance or size: *subcommittee, subhead.*

sub. **1.** subscription. **2.** substitute. **3.** suburban.

sub·al·tern (sub ôl′tərn) *n.* **1.** a person of subordinate
rank or position; aide. **2.** an officer in the British army,
ranking below a captain. —*adj.* having a subordinate
rank or position.

sub·a·tom·ic (sub′ə tom′ik) *adj.* of or relating to something smaller than an atom or something happening within
an atom.

subatomic particle, any of a number of particles smaller
than an atom that are the most basic constituents of nature
yet known. Electrons, protons, and neutrons are subatomic particles. Also, **elementary particle.**

sub·com·mit·tee (sub′kə mit′ə) *n.* a committee formed
from and acting under a main committee for some special
purpose.

sub·con·scious (sub kon′shəs) *adj.* **1.** existing in the
mind but only partially perceived by the consciousness:
a subconscious wish. **2.** not completely conscious.
—*n.* the part of the mind that retains experiences and
feelings that are difficult to bring back to awareness, often
because awareness of them would be painful or produce
anxiety. —**sub·con′scious·ly,** *adv.* —**sub·con′scious-
ness,** *n.*

sub·con·ti·nent (sub kon′tə nənt) *n.* a large land mass
that is smaller than a continent, especially a large section
of a continent regarded as a distinct geographical or
political unit: *the Indian subcontinent of Asia.*

sub·con·tract (*n.,* sub kon′trakt, sub′kon′trakt; *v.,*
sub′kən trakt′) *n.* a contract made after another contract,
carrying out all or part of the original contract: *Our builder
gave a subcontract to a plumber to install all the bathrooms
in the house.* —*v.t.* to contract to carry out (all or part
of a previous contract).

sub·cu·ta·ne·ous (sub′kū tā′nē əs) *adj.* under the surface of the skin. —**sub′cu·ta′ne·ous·ly,** *adv.*

sub·di·vide (sub′di vīd′, sub′di vīd′) *v.,* **sub·di·vid·ed,
sub·di·vid·ing.** —*v.t.* to divide or separate (a part of a

whole) after a previous division: *to subdivide a tract of
land into building lots.* —*v.i.* to be divided again after
previous divisions.

sub·di·vi·sion (sub′di vizh′ən, sub′di vizh′ən) *n.*
1. the act of subdividing or the state of being subdivided.
2. one of the parts into which a larger part has been
divided. **3.** an area of land divided into lots for building
homes.

sub·due (səb dü′, səb dū′) *v.t.,* **sub·dued, sub·du·ing.**
1. to bring under control; overcome: *The police subdued
the angry crowd.* **2.** to bring into subjection; conquer: *to
subdue an enemy.* **3.** to reduce the intensity, strength, or
force of; tone down; soften: *The new curtains subdued
the brightness of the room.* —**sub·du′er,** *n.*

sub·fam·i·ly (sub fam′ə lē, sub′fam′ə lē) *n.,* *pl.* **sub-
fam·i·lies.** a subdivision of a family: *a subfamily of
plants.*

sub·head (sub′hed′) *n.* **1.** a subordinate heading or title,
as in a book, chapter, or article. **2.** one of the subdivisions
into which a main heading or title is broken up.

sub·head·ing (sub′hed′ing) *n.* another word for **subhead.**

sub·hu·man (sub hū′mən) *adj.* belonging to or characteristic of any living thing considered to be lower than
the human species.

subj. **1.** subject. **2.** subjective. **3.** subjunctive.

sub·ject (*n., adj.,* sub′jikt; *v.,* səb jekt′) *n.* **1.** something
that is the basis of thought, discussion, or investigation;
topic: *The subject under discussion today is the causes
of the American Revolution.* **2.** a branch or field of
study: *English was my favorite subject in school.*
3. *Grammar.* a word, phrase, or clause that performs the
action of the verb or, if the verb is in the passive voice,
receives the action of the verb. In the sentences *He ran
fast* and *He was hit, He* is the subject. **4.** a person or
thing that is under the authority, control, or influence of
another: *The people were loyal subjects of the crown.*
5. a person or thing that undergoes or experiences something: *The scientist used mice as subjects in the experiments. The mayor was the subject of much criticism.*
—*adj.* **1.** under the authority, control, or influence of:
The employees are subject to the rules of the company.
2. liable; prone: *to be subject to various allergies.*
3. dependent or conditional upon: *You may go, subject to
your parents' approval.* —*v.t.* **1.** to bring under influence
or control. **2.** to cause to undergo or experience; expose:
to subject a person to ridicule.

sub·jec·tion (səb jek′shən) *n.* **1.** the act of bringing
under the control or influence of another. **2.** the condition
of being under the control or influence of another.

sub·jec·tive (səb jek′tiv) *adj.* **1.** of, existing in, or coming from the person who is thinking, based solely on the
individual's own feelings, thoughts, and experiences.
2. in literature and art, based on or expressing the feelings,
thoughts, and experiences of the artist or author.
3. *Grammar.* designating the case of the subject of a verb.
—**sub·jec′tive·ly,** *adv.*

sub·jec·tiv·i·ty (sub′jek tiv′i tē) *n.* the quality, condition, or tendency of viewing things solely in relation to
one's own feelings, thoughts, or experiences.

subject matter **1.** the main body of facts or ideas under
discussion or consideration. **2.** the body of ideas presented
in a book, speech, or the like, as distinguished from form
or style.

sub·ju·gate (sub′jə gāt′) *v.t.,* **sub·ju·gat·ed, sub·ju-
gat·ing.** to bring or have under one's control or dominance; subdue. [From the Latin word *subjugatus,* past
participle of *subjugare* meaning "to bring under the yoke,"
from the prefix *sub-* "under, from below" and *jugum* "a
yoke."] —**sub′ju·ga′tion,** *n.*

sub·junc·tive (səb jungk′tiv) *n.* **1.** the mood of a verb that indicates an act or state as possible, conditional, contrary to fact, or dependent, rather than as actual. In the sentence *If I were you, I would not go, were* is in the subjunctive. **2.** a verb form in this mood. —*adj.* of or relating to this mood.

sub·king·dom (sub king′dəm, sub′king′dəm) *n.* *Biology.* a subdivision of a kingdom.

sub·lease (*n.,* sub′lēs′; *v.,* sub lēs′) *n.* an agreement signed by a tenant transferring to another person all or part of the tenant's rights under a lease. —*v.t.* **subleased, sub·leas·ing.** to give or obtain a sublease for.

sub·let (sub let′, sub′let′) *v.t.,* **sub·let, sub·let·ting.** to give or obtain a sublease for (some property or business); sublease.

sub·li·mate (*v.,* sub′lə māt′; *n.,* sub′lə mit, sub′lə māt′) *v.t.,* **sub·li·mat·ed, sub·li·mat·ing. 1.** to act upon (something) so as to refine or purify: *Alchemists tried to sublimate base metals into gold.* **2.** to subject (thoughts or impulses) to sublimation. **3.** to sublime (a substance). —*n.* any material resulting when a substance is sublimed.

sub·li·ma·tion (sub′lə mā′shən) *n.* **1.** the act or process of sublimating or subliming. **2.** something that has been sublimated or sublimed.

sub·lime (sə blīm′) *adj.* noble or grand in manner, expression, or appearance; lofty: *sublime scenery, a sublime poem.* —*n.* something that is noble or grand in manner, expression, or appearance. —*v.,* **sub·limed, sub·lim·ing.** —*v.t.* to cause (a substance) to change directly from a solid to a gaseous state, or from a gaseous to a solid state, without passing through a liquid state; sublimate. —*v.i.* to change directly from a solid to a gaseous state, or from a gaseous to a solid state, without first becoming a liquid. Mothballs and dry ice sublime.

sub·lim·i·ty (sə blim′i tē) *n.* the state or quality of being sublime; loftiness; grandeur.

sub·ma·chine gun (sub′mə shēn′) a portable, lightweight, automatic or semiautomatic gun that is designed for shooting from the hip or shoulder.

sub·mar·ine (*n.,* sub′mə ren′; *adj.,* sub′mə rēn′) *n.* **1.** a ship that can navigate under water, used as an attack or reconnaissance vessel, or for oceanographic research. **2.** another word for **hero** (*def. 4*). —*adj.* below the surface of the sea: *submarine plants.*

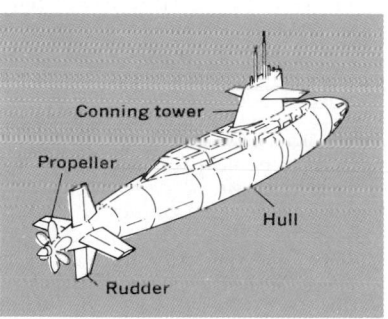

Conning tower
Propeller
Hull
Rudder

submarine *(det. 1)*

sub·merge (səb mûrj′) *v.,* **submerged, sub·merg·ing.** —*v.t.* **1.** to place under or cover with some liquid, especially water: *The flood almost submerged the town.* **2.** to overshadow; obscure: *The merit of the idea was submerged by fighting for who got the credit.* —*v.i.* to sink out of sight by going beneath the surface of a liquid: *The submarine submerged quickly.* —**sub·mer′gence,** *n.*

sub·merse (səb mûrs′) *v.t.,* **sub·mersed, sub·mers·ing.** another word for **submerge.**

sub·mers·i·ble (səb mûr′sə bəl) *adj.* that can be submerged.

sub·mer·sion (səb mur′zhən) *n.* the act of submerging or the state of being submerged.

sub·mis·sion (səb mish′ən) *n.* **1.** the act of yielding to some power or authority: *submission to the court's deci-*sion. **2.** humbleness; meekness: *to yield in submission to stronger forces.* **3.** the act of presenting something for consideration or decision: *submission of a proposal.*

sub·mis·sive (səb mis′iv) *adj.* tending to yield to power or authority; meek; humble. —**sub·mis′sive·ly,** *adv.* —**sub·mis′sive·ness,** *n.*

sub·mit (səb mit′) *v.,* **sub·mit·ted, sub·mit·ting.** —*v.i.* to yield oneself to some power or authority; give up; surrender: *to have the courage not to submit to the enemy.* —*v.t.* **1.** to present for the consideration or decision of another or others: *I submitted my term paper early.* **2.** to put forward as an opinion or proposition; propose: *I submit that the defendant is not guilty.* **3.** to yield (oneself) to some power or authority.

sub·nor·mal (sub nôr′məl) *adj.* less than usual, average, or normal, especially in intelligence. —**sub′nor·mal′i·ty,** *n.* —**sub·nor′mal·ly,** *adv.*

sub·or·bit·al (sub ôr′bi təl) *adj.* (of a missile, spacecraft, space flight, or the like) not making a complete orbit.

sub·or·der (sub′ôr′dər) *n.* a subdivision of an order.

sub·or·di·nate (*adj., n.,* sə bôr′də nit; *v.,* sə bôr′də nāt′) *adj.* **1.** lower in rank, grade, class, or the like: *a subordinate officer.* **2.** having less importance; dependent; secondary: *a subordinate position.* —*n.* a person or thing that is subordinate. —*v.t.,* **sub·or·di·nat·ed, sub·or·di·nat·ing.** to cause to be, or treat as, subordinate. —**sub·or′di·na′tion,** *n.*

subordinate clause, another term for **dependent clause.**

subordinating conjunction, a conjunction, such as *if* or *when,* that introduces a dependent clause.

sub·orn (sə bôrn′) *v.t.* **1.** to cause (a witness) to give false testimony in a court of law. **2.** to influence (a person) to commit a misdeed, especially through bribery. —**sub·or·na·tion** (sub′ôr nā′shən), *n.* —**sub·orn′er,** *n.*

sub·poe·na (sə pē′nə) *also,* **sub·pe·na.** *n.* an official document ordering a person to appear in a court of law; summons. —*v.t.,* **sub·poe·naed, sub·poe·na·ing.** to summon to a court of law by a subpoena: *to subpoena a witness.* [From the Latin phrase *sub poena* meaning "under penalty," the opening words of this legal writ.]

sub·scribe (səb skrīb′) *v.,* **sub·scribed, sub·scrib·ing.** —*v.i.* **1.** to agree to receive and pay for: *to subscribe to a magazine, to subscribe for theater tickets.* **2.** to promise to give or contribute a definite amount of money: *to subscribe to the hospital drive.* **3.** to sign one's name at the end of something to signify one's approval or agreement: *to subscribe to a petition demanding better public transportation.* **4.** to give one's assent or approval: *I heartily subscribe to your suggestion.* —*v.t.* to promise to give or pay: *Each member subscribed twenty-five dollars to the charity.* —**sub·scrib′er,** *n.*

sub·script (sub′skript′) *n.* a character, as a number, letter, or symbol, usually of relatively small size, printed or written beneath or on the lower half of a line. In the formula H_2O, 2 is a subscript. —*adj.* printed or written beneath or on the lower half of the line.

sub·scrip·tion (səb skrip′shən) *n.* **1.** the right to receive something, obtained by paying a certain sum of money. **2.** a sum of money given or contributed, as to a charity. **3.** a fund raised through the contributions of a number of persons.

---

at; āpe; fär; câre; end; mē; it; īce; pierce; hot; ōld; sông, fôrk; oil; out; up; ūse; rüle; pull; tûrn; chin; sing; shop; thin; this; hw in white; zh in treasure. The symbol ə stands for the unstressed vowel sound heard in about, taken, pencil, lemon, and circus.

S

sub·sec·tion (sub′sek′shən) *n.* a part or division of a section.

sub·se·quent (sub′si kwənt) *adj.* coming or happening after or as a result: *Subsequent events proved that they had made a good choice.* —**sub′se·quent·ly,** *adv.*

sub·serve (səb sûrv′) *v.t.,* **sub·served, sub·serv·ing.** to be important or useful in assisting (someone or something).

sub·ser·vi·ent (səb sûr′vē ənt) *adj.* **1.** slavishly submissive or obedient in behavior or attitude. **2.** important or useful in promoting an end or purpose: *Ending debate was subservient to passing the bill quickly.* —**sub·ser′vi·ence,** *n.* —**sub·ser′vi·ent·ly,** *adv.*

sub·set (sub′set′) *n. Mathematics.* a set whose members are all contained within another given set. The subsets of the set {a,b} are {a,b}, {a}, {b}, and {0}.

sub·side (səb sīd′) *v.i.,* **sub·sid·ed, sub·sid·ing. 1.** to sink to a low or lower level, especially to the normal or usual level: *The flood waters subsided.* **2.** to decrease in volume, activity, or intensity; abate: *After a short time my anger subsided.* —**sub·sid·ence** (səb sīd′əns, sub′səd əns), *n.*

sub·sid·i·ar·y (səb sid′ē er′ē) *adj.* **1.** serving to help, assist, or supplement: *a subsidiary source of income.* **2.** subordinate or secondary: *a goal subsidiary to the main objective.* **3.** relating to, consisting of, or depending on a subsidy or subsidies. —*n., pl.* **sub·sid·i·ar·ies. 1.** a company owned or controlled by another company, usually resulting from the parent company's ownership of all or a majority of the other company's stock. **2.** any subsidiary person or thing.

sub·si·dize (sub′si dīz′) *v.t.,* **sub·si·dized, sub·si·diz·ing.** to aid or support with a subsidy: *The government subsidizes farmers who agree not to produce certain crops.* —**sub′si·di·za′tion,** *n.* —**sub′si·diz′er,** *n.*

sub·si·dy (sub′si dē) *n., pl.* **sub·si·dies.** a contribution, especially of money, often given by a government as a supplement or assistance.

sub·sist (səb sist′) *v.i.* **1.** to maintain existence; support life; exist: *The lost explorers barely managed to subsist on the fruits and berries they could find.* **2.** to exist or continue to exist; remain; abide: *The custom of marriage has subsisted through the ages.*

sub·sist·ence (səb sis′təns) *n.* **1.** the state or condition of supporting life; continued existence. **2.** the means of supporting life; support; livelihood: *The farmer's subsistence depended on enough rain.*

sub·soil (sub′soil′) *n.* the layer of soil lying immediately beneath the surface soil.

sub·son·ic (sub son′ik) *adj.* of, relating to, or moving at a speed that is less than that of sound.

sub·spe·cies (sub′spē′shēz, sub spē′shēz) *n., pl.* **sub·spe·cies.** a subdivision of a species, especially a grouping of plants or animals within a species.

sub·stance (sub′stəns) *n.* **1.** that which a thing consists of; matter; material: *Diamonds and graphite are different forms of the same substance.* **2.** material or matter of a particular kind: *a radioactive substance.* **3.** the real or essential thing or part, especially of something written or spoken: *What was the substance of the speech?* **4.** solid quality; density; body: *The thick soup has substance.* **5.** the quality of being real, rather than imaginary: *There is no substance to this accusation.* **6.** material possessions; wealth; means: *a person of substance.*

sub·stand·ard (sub stan′dərd) *adj.* less than or below the usual or normal standard: *The government tried to eliminate substandard housing.*

sub·stan·tial (səb stan′shəl) *adj.* **1.** of considerable amount or importance; ample: *a substantial profit, a substantial meal.* **2.** firmly or strongly based or constructed: *a substantial house.* **3.** having wealth; wealthy:

a substantial business. **4.** having actual existence or form; not imaginary; real. —**sub·stan·ti·al·i·ty** (səbstan′-shē al′i tē), *n.*

sub·stan·tial·ly (səb stan′shə lē) *adv.* **1.** in the main; essentially: *The newspaper story was substantially accurate.* **2.** actually; really: *The plan for a new city hall was substantially realized after several years.* **3.** strongly or solidly; firmly: *The house is substantially built.*

sub·stan·ti·ate (səb stan′shē āt′) *v.t.,* **sub·stan·ti·at·ed, sub·stan·ti·at·ing.** to give factual evidence in order to prove; verify: *Can you substantiate your account of the accident?* —**sub·stan′ti·a′tion,** *n.*

sub·stan·tive (sub′stən tiv) *n. Grammar.* a noun or pronoun, or a group of words used as a noun substitute. —*adj.* **1.** *Grammar.* **a.** used as a noun or noun substitute. **b.** denoting the verb of existence, *to be.* **2.** substantial or solid; real. —**sub′stan·tive·ly,** *adv.*

sub·sta·tion (sub′stā′shən) *n.* a subsidiary station, as of a post office.

sub·sti·tute (sub′sti tüt′, sub′sti tyüt′) *n.* a person or thing that acts or is used in the place of another: *Margarine is a substitute for butter.* —*v.,* **sub·sti·tut·ed, sub·sti·tut·ing.** to put in the place of another: *The coach substituted me for the injured player.* —*v.i.* to take the place of another: *The student teacher substituted for our regular teacher.* —*adj.* taking the place of another: *a substitute teacher.*

sub·sti·tu·tion (sub′sti tü′shən, sub′sti tyü′shən) *n.* the act of substituting or the state of being substituted.

sub·stra·tum (sub strā′təm, sub strat′əm) *n., pl.* **sub·stra·ta** (sub strā′tə, sub strat′ə) or **sub·stra·tums. 1.** a substance that lies under another, especially a layer of earth beneath the surface layer. **2.** a basis or foundation: *Experiments were the substratum for the scientist's theory.*

sub·ter·fuge (sub′tər fūj′) *n.* a device or trick used to conceal one's true purpose or to escape a difficult situation: *The false alarm was a subterfuge to divert our attention.*

sub·ter·ra·ne·an (sub′tə rā′nē ən) *adj.* **1.** being, located, or happening below the surface of the earth; underground: *a subterranean tunnel, subterranean life.* **2.** existing out of sight; done secretly: *a subterranean plot.*

sub·ti·tle (sub′tī′təl) *n.* **1.** a secondary or additional title, as of a book or article. **2.** a word or words printed at the bottom of a motion picture screen, used to translate a foreign language being spoken in a film.

sub·tle (sut′əl) *adj.* **1.** having a faint, delicate quality, so as to be nearly impossible to perceive: *a subtle odor, a subtle laugh.* **2.** capable of seeing or understanding fine distinctions; perceptive: *a subtle mind.* **3.** deceitfully cunning; crafty; sly: *a subtle plan to trick someone.* **4.** difficult to solve or understand: *a subtle problem.* —**sub′tle·ness,** *n.* —**sub′tly,** *adv.*

sub·tle·ty (sut′əl tē) *n., pl.* **sub·tle·ties. 1.** the quality of being subtle. **2.** something that is subtle.

sub·tract (səb trakt′) *v.t.* to take away or deduct (a number) from another number: *If you subtract 3 from 7, you have 4.* —*v.i.* to perform the process of subtraction. —**sub·tract′er,** *n.*

sub·trac·tion (səb trak′shən) *n.* the act or process of figuring the difference between two numbers.

sub·trac·tive (səb trak′tiv) *adj.* of or relating to subtraction.

sub·tra·hend (sub′trə hend′) *n.* the number that is to be subtracted from another. In the equation $11 - 4 = 7$, 4 is the subtrahend.

sub·trop·i·cal (sub trop′i kəl) *adj.* of or relating to regions bordering on the tropics; having a nearly tropical climate.

sub·trop·ics (sub trop′iks) *n., pl.* subtropical regions.

sub·urb (sub′ûrb) *n.* **1.** a residential district close to or on the outer edge of a city. **2. the suburbs.** an area consisting of such districts. ▲ usually used with a plural verb. [From the Latin word *suburbium* meaning "country close to the city," from the prefix *sub-* "near, under" + *urbs* "city."]

sub·ur·ban (sə bûr′bən) *adj.* of, relating to, or characteristic of a suburb: *a quiet suburban street.*

sub·ur·ban·ite (sə bûr′bə nīt′) *n.* a person who lives in the suburbs.

sub·ur·bi·a (sə bûr′bē ə) *n.* **1.** the suburbs and/or the people living in them, thought of as a group. **2.** the interests, activities, or viewpoints thought to be characteristic of people living in suburbs.

sub·ver·sion (səb vûr′zhən) *n.* the act of subverting or the state of being subverted.

sub·ver·sive (səb vûr′siv) *adj.* attempting or tending to overthrow, undermine, or destroy: *a subversive speech, subversive activities.* —*n.* a person who attempts to overthrow, undermine, or destroy a belief or a government or other established institution.

sub·vert (səb vûrt′) *v.t.* **1.** to bring about the destruction of; overthrow; destroy: *to subvert a dictatorship.* **2.** to undermine the loyalty, faith, or principles of; corrupt: *The gangster tried to subvert the judge with a bribe.* —**sub·vert′er,** *n.*

sub·way (sub′wā′) *n.* **1.** a railway that runs wholly or partly underground, especially one in a large city. **2.** *British.* an underground passage.

subway
Passengers boarding a **subway** train

suc·ceed (sək sēd′) *v.i.* **1.** to have the desired result; turn out well: *Our plan succeeded.* **2.** to accomplish what is attempted or planned; do well: *to succeed in fixing a broken radio.* **3.** to come next in the place of the person or thing that came before: *After the death of the president, the vice president succeeded to the office.* —*v.t.* to take the place of; come next after: *I succeeded my best friend as treasurer of the club.*

suc·cess (sək ses′) *n., pl.* **suc·cess·es. 1.** a favorable result or ending: *The success of my science project pleased my teacher.* **2.** the gaining of wealth, position, or fame: *great success in business.* **3.** a person or thing that succeeds or is successful: *The party was a big success.*

suc·cess·ful (sək ses′fəl) *adj.* having, achieving, or resulting in success: *a successful person, a successful book.* —**suc·cess′ful·ly,** *adv.* —**suc·cess′ful·ness,** *n.*

suc·ces·sion (sək sesh′ən) *n.* **1.** a group of people or things following one after another in time or place; sequence; series: *a succession of misfortunes.* **2.** the coming of one person or thing after another. **3.** the right of being next in line for an office, rank, or the like that is held by another. **4.** the order or line of persons having such a

right: *The succession to the throne included the young prince and his three cousins.*

·in succession. one after another; in orderly sequence: *an estate that passed, in succession, from grandfather, father, to son.*

suc·ces·sive (sək ses′iv) *adj.* coming one after another in an uninterrupted order. —**suc·ces′sive·ly,** *adv.* —**suc·ces′sive·ness,** *n.*

suc·ces·sor (sək ses′ər) *n.* a person or thing that follows or takes the place of another, especially a person who succeeds or is in line to succeed another in some office, rank, or the like.

suc·cinct (sək singkt′) *adj.* expressed in few words; brief and concise; terse: *a succinct style of writing.* —**suc·cinct′ly,** *adv.* —**suc·cinct′ness,** *n.*

suc·cor (suk′ər) *also, British,* **suc·cour.** *n.* help; assistance; aid: *to give succor to the homeless.* —*v.t.* to give help, assistance, or aid to.

suc·co·tash (suk′ə tash′) *n.* corn kernels and lima beans cooked together.

Suc·coth (sŏk′əs, sü kōt′) *also,* **Suc·cot.** another spelling of **Sukkoth.**

suc·cour (suk′ər) *British.* another spelling of **succor.**

suc·cu·lent (suk′yə lənt) *adj.* **1.** full of juice; juicy: *a succulent orange.* **2.** having thick, fleshy leaves and stems that can hold large amounts of water: *Many succulent plants grow well in deserts.* —*n.* a succulent plant: *A cactus is a succulent.* —**suc′cu·lence,** *n.*

suc·cumb (sə kum′) *v.i.* **1.** to give way; yield: *to succumb to a temptation.* **2.** to die: *to succumb to pneumonia.*

such (such) *adj.* **1.** of the same kind or degree: *Have you ever heard such a story?* **2.** of that particular kind or degree: *Such an old car was next to useless.* **3.** of a similar kind or degree; like: *We bought lettuce, tomatoes, and such items for a salad.* **4.** of an extreme degree, quantity, or kind: *It was such a surprise.* —*pron.* a person or thing of the same kind or degree as that or those already mentioned: *pens, pencils, and such.*

·as such. a. as a person or thing of the kind that has already been mentioned: *A lawyer, as such, should have a good knowledge of the law.* **b.** in itself: *Success, as such, does not always bring happiness.*

·such and such. of indefinite name, location, or the like: *The accident took place on such and such a date.*

·such as. a. of the same or particular kind or degree: *A person such as that will surely succeed.* **b.** for example: *The pet store had dogs, such as dachshunds and poodles.*

suck (suk) *v.t.* **1.** to draw (something) into the mouth with the lips and tongue: *to suck milk through a straw.* **2.** to draw a liquid from (something) with the mouth: *to suck an orange.* **3.** to hold in the mouth and lick: *to suck a cough drop.* **4.** to draw in or absorb by the use of suction: *The vacuum cleaner sucked the dust out of the corners of the room.* —*v.i.* to draw milk from a breast or a bottle; suckle. —*n.* the act of sucking.

suck·er (suk′ər) *n.* **1.** a person or thing that sucks. **2.** any of a group of toothless freshwater fish having fleshy, sucking lips on the underside of the head. **3.** an organ of any of certain animals, such as octopuses, barnacles, or certain parasites, used for sucking or for attaching to

at; āpe; fär; câre; end; mē; it; īce; pîerce; hot; ōld;
sông, fôrk; oil; out; up; ūse; rüle; pull; tûrn; chin;
sing; shop; thin; **th**is; hw in white; zh in treasure.
The symbol ə stands for the unstressed vowel sound
heard in about, taken, pencil, lemon, and circus.

S

941

something by suction. **4.** a shoot growing from the underground stem or root of a plant. **5.** *Informal.* a piece of candy that is held in the mouth and licked, such as a lollipop. **6.** *Slang.* a person who can easily be cheated, fooled, or taken advantage of.

suck·le (suk′əl) *v.,* **suck·led, suck·ling.** —*v.t.* **1.** to give milk to from the breast, udder, or the like. **2.** to bring up; nurture. —*v.i.* to drink milk from the breast, udder, or the like: *A child suckled at its mother's breast.*

suck·ling (suk′ling) *n.* an infant or young animal that is not yet weaned. —*adj.* **1.** young and inexperienced. **2.** not yet weaned: *a suckling pig.*

su·crose (sü′krōs) *n.* a crystalline organic compound with a sweet taste, obtained especially from sugar beets and sugarcane and used for sweetening foods; common sugar.

suc·tion (suk′shən) *n.* **1.** a force created by a complete or partial vacuum that draws a gas or liquid into a space from which all or part of the air or liquid has been removed. **2.** the act or instance of drawing a liquid or gas into a space where a partial vacuum has been created. —*adj.* causing, relating to, using, or done by suction: *a suction pump.*

Su·da·nese (sü′də nēz′, sü′də nēs′) *n., pl.* **Su·da·nese.** a person who was born in or is a citizen of the country of Sudan, or a native of the region. —*adj.* of, relating to, or characteristic of the country or region of Sudan, its people, or their culture.

sud·den (sud′ən) *adj.* **1.** done or happening without warning; unexpected: *The sudden arrival of guests forced us to change our plans.* **2.** quick or abrupt; hasty: *to make a sudden decision. The car came to a sudden stop.* —**sud′den·ness,** *n.*

·**all of a sudden.** all at once; unexpectedly.

sud·den·ly (sud′ən lē) *adv.* without warning; unexpectedly.

suds (sudz) *pl. n.* **1.** a frothy mass of bubbles that forms on the top of water containing soap. **2.** soapy water: *Wash the sweater in warm suds.* **3.** any foam or froth.

sud·sy (sud′zē) *adj.,* **suds·i·er, suds·i·est.** full of soap-suds.

sue (sü) *v.,* **sued, su·ing.** —*v.t.* to start a suit against in a court of law: *to sue a careless driver.* —*v.i.* **1.** to take legal action: *to sue for damages.* **2.** to appeal or plead: *to sue for forgiveness.* —**su′er,** *n.*

suede (swād) *also,* **suède.** *n.* **1.** a soft leather that has a velvety nap. **2.** a fabric made with a short nap on one side to resemble this leather. Also *(def. 2),* **suede cloth.** —*adj.* also, **sueded.** of, resembling, or made of suede: *a suede jacket; a sueded finish.* [From the phrase *suede gloves,* translation of the French phrase *gants de Suède* meaning "gloves of Sweden."]

su·et (sü′it) *n.* the hard fat from around the kidneys and loins of cattle and sheep, used in cooking.

suf·fer (suf′ər) *v.i.* **1.** to have or be subject to pain, sorrow, or distress: *I'm suffering from a headache. They suffered without a complaint.* **2.** to undergo loss or damage; be hurt: *Lack of studying caused my schoolwork to suffer.* —*v.t.* **1.** to feel or be subject to; undergo: *to suffer embarrassment when speaking before strangers.* **2.** to allow or permit: *Suffer the little children to come unto me* (Mark 10:14). **3.** to bear up under; put up with; tolerate: *Our teacher will not suffer noise in the classroom.* —**suf′fer·er,** *n.*

suf·fer·ance (suf′ər əns) *n.* approval or consent given only by failure to prevent.

suf·fer·ing (suf′ər ing) *n.* **1.** the act or instance of undergoing pain, sorrow, or distress. **2.** the condition of a person who suffers.

suf·fice (sə fīs′) *v.,* **suf·ficed, suf·fic·ing.** —*v.i.* to be sufficient or enough: *One suitcase will suffice for the trip.* —*v.t.* to be enough for; satisfy: *A light lunch will suffice me.*

suf·fi·cien·cy (sə fish′ən sē) *n., pl.* **suf·fi·cien·cies.** **1.** an adequate amount or quanity: *a sufficiency of supplies.* **2.** the state or quality of being enough or sufficient; adequacy.

suf·fi·cient (sə fish′ənt) *adj.* as much as is necessary or needed; enough; adequate: *One blanket will provide sufficient warmth.* —**suf·fi′cient·ly,** *adv.*

suf·fix (suf′iks) *n., pl.* **suf·fix·es.** a syllable or syllables added at the end of a word to form another word of different meaning or function, such as *-ness* in *badness, -ly* in *quickly,* and *-er* in *painter.* —*v.t.* to add at the end, especially as a suffix.

suf·fo·cate (suf′ə kāt′) *v.,* **suf·fo·cat·ed, suf·fo·cat·ing.** —*v.t.* **1.** to kill by preventing breathing. **2.** to interrupt or hinder the breathing of: *The small, crowded room was suffocating us.* **3.** to smother; stifle; extinguish: *to suffocate a fire.* —*v.i.* **1.** to die from an interrupted or insufficient supply of air. **2.** to be or become stifled or smothered; choke. —**suf′fo·ca′tion,** *n.*

suf·fra·gan (suf′rə gən) *n.* a bishop who assists another bishop.

suf·frage (suf′rij) *n.* **1.** the right or privilege of voting; franchise: *Women in the United States won suffrage in 1920.* **2.** the act of casting a vote; voting. **3.** a vote, especially in favor of a candidate for office.

suf·fra·gette (suf′rə jet′) *n.* a woman who strongly supports suffrage for women.

suf·fra·gist (suf′rə jist) *n.* a person who favors extending the right to vote, especially to women.

suf·fuse (sə fūz′) *v.t.,* **suf·fused, suf·fus·ing.** to spread through or over, as with a light, color, or emotion: *a room suffused with sunshine, eyes suffused with tears, a face suffused with happiness.* —**suf·fu′sion,** *n.*

sug·ar (shug′ər) *n.* **1.** any of several white or brown crystalline forms of the organic compound sucrose, obtained mainly from sugarcane and sugar beets, and used for sweetening foods. **2.** any of a group of carbohydrates having a relatively simple molecular structure, including sucrose, glucose, fructose, maltose, and lactose. —*v.t.* **1.** to mix, cover, sprinkle, or sweeten with sugar: *to sugar cookies, to sugar coffee.* **2.** to disguise to make more pleasant; sugarcoat. [From the Old French word *sugar,* from the Medieval Latin word *zuccarum,* from the Arabic word *sukkar,* from the Persian word *shakar,* from the Sanskrit word *śarkarā,* all meaning "sugar."]

sugar beet, a leafy plant whose long, thick, yellow or white roots are a major source of sugar.

sug·ar·cane (shug′ər kān′) *n.* a tall grass with jointed stems containing a sweet juice that is a major source of sugar.

sug·ar·coat (shug′ər kōt′) *v.t.* **1.** to cover with sugar: *to sugarcoat a cookie.* **2.** to disguise or soften (something unpleasant) in order to make it more pleasant or acceptable: *to sugarcoat criticism with some kind words.*

sug·ar-free (shug′ər frē′) *adj.* containing no sugar: *a sugar-free soft drink.*

sug·ar·loaf (shug′ər lōf′) *n.* **1.** a cone-shaped, hard mass of refined sugar. **2.** something having the shape of a sugarloaf, such as a hill.

sugar maple, a maple tree of eastern North America whose sap is the major source of maple syrup.

sugarcane

sug·ar·plum (shug′ər plum′) *n.* a small, usually round piece of candy.

sug·ar·y (shug′ə rē) *adj.* **1.** of, consisting of, or like sugar: *a sugary sweetness.* **2.** sweetly or insincerely flattering: *to hide anger with a sugary smile.* —**sug′ar·i·ness,** *n.*

sug·gest (səg jest′, sə jest′) *v.t.* **1.** to offer or mention for consideration or action; propose: *I suggest we meet* *again tomorrow.* **2.** to bring or call to mind: *a perfume that suggests roses.* **3.** to express or show indirectly; hint: *The heavy sigh suggested disappointment.*

sug·gest·i·ble (səg jes′tə bəl, sə jes′tə bəl) *adj.* **1.** easily influenced by suggestion. **2.** able to be suggested. —**sug·ges′ti·bil′i·ty,** *n.*

sug·ges·tion (səg jes′chən, sə jes′chən) *n.* **1.** the act or instance of suggesting: *We left at their suggestion.* **2.** something that is suggested: *The suggestion of a picnic was popular with everyone.* **3.** the process by which something is brought to mind through an association or connection with something else: *The cold wind carried a suggestion of the winter to come.* **4.** a very small indication; trace; hint: *There is a suggestion of garlic in the sauce.*

sug·ges·tive (səg jes′tiv, sə jes′tiv) *adj.* **1.** giving a suggestion or hint: *The architecture of the building was suggestive of the Gothic style.* **2.** tending to bring to mind ideas or actions: *a talk suggestive of ways to raise money.* **3.** tending to suggest something improper or indecent. —**sug·ges′tive·ly,** *adv.* —**sug·ges′tive·ness,** *n.*

su·i·cid·al (sü′ə sī′dəl) *adj.* **1.** of, relating to, or causing suicide: *suicidal tendencies.* **2.** apt to cause disaster to oneself; ruinous: *a suicidal climb to the summit of a mountain.* **3.** having a definite inclination to suicide: *a suicidal individual, suicidal behavior.* —**su′i·cid′al·ly,** *adv.*

su·i·cide¹ (sü′ə sīd′) *n.* **1.** the act or instance of intentionally killing oneself. **2.** the destruction of one's own interests or aims, as in business or politics. [From the Latin word *sui* meaning "of oneself" + the suffix *-cidum* meaning "a killing."]

su·i·cide² (sü′ə sīd′) *n.* a person who has intentionally killed himself or herself. [From the Latin word *sui* meaning "of oneself" + the suffix *-cida* meaning "a killer."]

suit (süt) *n.* **1.** a set of garments designed to be worn together, especially a jacket with a matching pair of trousers or skirt. **2.** the act, process, or proceeding in a court of law for the correction of a wrong or for the enforcement of a claim. **3.** any of the four sets of playing cards in a deck: spades, hearts, diamonds, or clubs. **4.** the act or instance of wooing or appealing. **5.** a set of similar or matched things used or intended to be used together. —*v.t.* **1.** to meet the requirements of; be correct or adapted to: *The family bought a house that suited its needs.* **2.** to make right for; adapt: *The orchestra suited its music to the occasion.* **3.** to be flattering to: *That color suits you well.* **4.** to be convenient or agreeable to; please; satisfy: *This book suits my taste. I will come when it suits you.* **5.** *Archaic.* to furnish with clothes; dress. —*v.i.* to be suitable, fitting, or convenient.

·**to follow suit. a.** to play a card of the same suit as the card led. **b.** to do the same thing as another.

·**to suit oneself.** to act in the way one wishes.

suit·a·ble (sü′tə bəl) *adj.* that suits a particular purpose, object, or occasion: *suitable clothes for a party, a suitable time for a meeting.* —**suit′a·bil′i·ty, suit′a·ble·ness,** *n.* —**suit′a·bly,** *adv.*

suit·case (süt′kās′) *n.* a rigid, usually rectangular bag used for carrying clothes and other articles when traveling; valise.

suite (swēt; *def. 2, also* süt) *n.* **1.** a group of connected rooms considered as a unit, as in a hotel. **2.** a set of matching furniture: *a living room suite.* **3.** any set of similar or matched things, used or intended to be used together. **4.** *Music.* **a.** an instrumental composition made up of a series of dance tunes in the same or related keys. **b.** an instrumental composition made up of a series of short movements, often adapted from a longer work.

suit·or (sü′tər) *n.* **1.** a man who courts or woos a woman.

2. a person who institutes a lawsuit. **3.** a person who pleads or petitions.

su·ki·ya·ki (sü′kē yä′kē, skē yä′kē) *n.* a Japanese dish made of thin strips of meat and vegetables sautéed quickly, usually at the dining table. [From the Japanese word *sukiyaki* meaning "slices of beef."]

Suk·koth (sùk′əs, sü kōt′) *also,* **Suk·kot, Suc·coth, Suc·cot.** *n.* a Jewish holiday that begins five days after Yom Kippur. It commemorates the wandering of the Israelites and celebrates the harvest.

sul·fa drug (sul′fə) any of a group of synthetic drugs that stop or slow the growth of certain bacteria, used to treat infections. Also, **sulfa.**

sul·fate (sul′fāt) *also,* **sul·phate.** *n.* a salt of sulfuric acid.

sul·fide (sul′fīd) *also,* **sul·phide.** *n.* a compound obtained when sulfur is heated with another element.

sul·fur (sul′fər) *also,* **sul·phur.** *n.* a yellow nonmetallic element that occurs in both free and combined forms. Sulfur is abundant in nature and is used to make sulfuric acid, to process rubber, and to manufacture fungicides, fertilizers, and gunpowder. Symbol: S [From the Anglo-Norman word *sulfere* meaning this element, from the Latin word *sulfur* "sulfur."]

sulfur dioxide, a colorless gas with a sharp, irritating odor, used to make sulfuric acid, and serving as a bleaching agent, refrigerant, and food preservative.

sul·fu·ric (sul fyùr′ik) *also,* **sul·phu·ric.** *adj.* **1.** of or relating to sulfur. **2.** containing sulfur in its higher valence.

sulfuric acid, a colorless, oily, very reactive liquid compound containing sulfur, hydrogen, and oxygen, used in the manufacture of numerous chemical products.

sul·fur·ous (sul′fər əs, sul fyùr′əs) *also,* **sul·phur·ous.** *adj.* **1.** of or relating to sulfur. **2.** containing sulfur in its lower valence. **3.** like burning sulfur, as in odor. **4.** of or resembling the fires of hell; infernal.

sulk (sulk) *v.i.* to be silent or withdrawn as a sign of bad humor or anger. —*n.* **1.** the state of sulking: *to be in a sulk.* **2.** **the sulks.** a display or mood of sulking. ▲ usually used with a plural verb.

sulk·y (sul′kē) *adj.,* **sulk·i·er, sulk·i·est.** stubbornly silent or withdrawn as a display of bad humor or anger: *a sulky child.* —*n., pl.* **sulk·ies.** a light, two-wheeled, one-horse carriage seating one passenger, used especially for harness racing. —**sulk′i·ly,** *adv.* —**sulk′i·ness,** *n.*

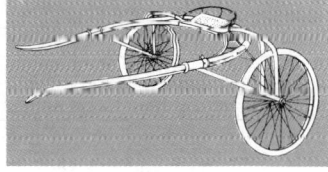

sulky (n.)

sul·len (sul′ən) *adj.* **1.** withdrawn or gloomy because of bad humor or anger; sulky; morose: *a sullen person, a sullen attitude.* **2.** dismal or gloomy: *a gray, sullen sky.* —**sul′len·ly,** *adv.* —**sul′len·ness,** *n.*

sul·ly (sul′ē) *v.t.,* **sul·lied, sul·ly·ing.** **1.** to stain the honor or purity of; defile or disgrace: *The scandal sullied the family name.* **2.** to stain; soil: *Mud sullied the hem of the coat.*

sul·phate (sul′fāt) another spelling of **sulfate.**

sul·phide (sul′fīd) another spelling of **sulfide.**

---

at; āpe; fär; câre; end; mē; it; īce; pîerce; hot; ōld; sông, fôrk; oil; out; up; ūse; rüle; pùll; tûrn; chin; sing; shop; thin; **th**is; hw in white; zh in treasure. The symbol ə stands for the unstressed vowel sound heard in about, taken, pencil, lemon, and circus.

S

sul·phur (sul′fər) another spelling of **sulfur**.

sul·phu·ric (sul fyŭr′ik) another spelling of **sulfuric**.

sul·phur·ous (sul′fər əs, sul fyŭr′əs) another spelling of **sulfurous**.

sul·tan (sul′tən) *n.* in a Muslim country, a sovereign or ruling monarch. Turkey and Morocco were formerly ruled by sultans.

sul·tan·a (sul tan′ə) *n.* **1.** the wife, mother, sister, or daughter of a sultan. **2.** a small, white, seedless grape dried to make white raisins and also used to make wine.

sul·tan·ate (sul′tə nāt′) *n.* **1.** a country or other area ruled by a sultan. **2.** the office or reign of a sultan.

sul·try (sul′trē) *adj.,* **sul·tri·er, sul·tri·est.** extremely hot and humid; sweltering: *the sultry tropics.* —**sul′tri·ness,** *n.*

sum (sum) *n.* **1.** a result obtained from addition. **2.** the whole quantity; entirety: *the sum of all our efforts.* **3.** an amount of money: *Large sums were spent on repairs.* **4.** *Informal.* an arithmetic problem, especially a list of numbers to be added. **5.** summary; gist: *That's the sum of it.* —*v.t.,* **summed, sum·ming.** to find the numerical sum of; total.

  ·**to sum up.** to tell or present briefly; summarize: *The newscaster summed up the events of the day.*

su·mac (shü′mak) *also,* **su·mach.** *n.* **1.** any of a large group of trees, shrubs, and vines having a milky juice that is sometimes poisonous. Poison sumac and poison ivy are sumacs. **2.** the dried leaves of certain of these trees or shrubs, yielding tannin, a substance used in processing leather.

Su·me·ri·an (sü mîr′ē ən, sü mer′ē ən) *adj.* of or relating to Sumer, its people, their language, or their culture. —*n.* **1.** a person who lived in Sumer. **2.** the extinct language of Sumer, preserved in inscriptions on rocks and tablets and providing the oldest known written records, dating to 4000 B.C. It is of unknown origin.

sum·ma cum lau·de (sum′ə kum lô′də, sùm′ə kùm lou′dē) with highest honors or praise. ▲ A Latin phrase used on diplomas to show graduation with highest honors from a college or university.

sum·mar·i·ly (sə mer′ə lē, sum′ər ə lē) *adv.* in a summary manner; briefly or quickly: *to be summarily dismissed from a job.*

sum·ma·rize (sum′ə rīz′) *v.t.,* **sum·ma·rized, sum·ma·riz·ing.** to make a summary of; state briefly: *to summarize the main points of a speech.*

sum·ma·ry (sum′ə rē) *n., pl.* **sum·ma·ries.** a short statement or brief account containing the main points of something: *a summary of the plot of a play.* —*adj.* **1.** containing the main points; concise; brief: *to give a summary statement of a plan.* **2.** performed rapidly without hesitation or formality: *Ignoring safety rules resulted in the employee's summary dismissal.*

sum·ma·tion (sə mā′shən) *n.* **1.** the final part of an argument, in which the facts are reviewed and a conclusion is given: *The defense will now give its summation to the jury.* **2.** the act or process of finding the total; addition. **3.** a result of addition; total.

sum·mer (sum′ər) *n.* the season of the year coming between spring and autumn. In the Northern Hemisphere it extends from about June 21 to about September 22. —*adj.* of, relating to, or suitable for summer: *a summer vacation, summer clothes.* —*v.i.* to spend the summer: *We summered at the seashore.*

sum·mer·house (sum′ər hous′) *n., pl.* **sum·mer·hous·es** (sum′ər hou′ziz). a small, roofed, usually simple building situated in a garden or park, used as a shady retreat in summer.

summer solstice, the time of year, about June 21 in the Northern Hemisphere, when the sun appears the farthest north from the equator.

sum·mer·time (sum′ər tīm′) *n.* the summer season.

sum·mer·y (sum′ə rē) *adj.* like or suitable for summer: *summery weather, a summery dress.*

sum·mit (sum′it) *n.* **1.** the highest part or point; acme: *the summit of a career.* **2.** the highest level, as of government or political authority: *to have a meeting at the summit.* —*adj.* of, for, or concerning the highest level of government or political authority, especially the heads of state: *a summit conference on nuclear disarmament.*

sum·mon (sum′ən) *v.t.* **1.** to send for or request the presence of, especially with authority: *When the burglary was discovered, we summoned the police.* **2.** to order to appear in court by means of a summons; issue a summons to: *to summon a witness to give testimony.* **3.** to call together; convene; convoke: *to summon a council.* **4.** to bring or urge to action; rouse: *to summon up one's courage.* —**sum′mon·er,** *n.*

sum·mons (sum′ənz) *n., pl.* **sum·mons·es. 1.** a notice, signal, or command to appear somewhere or to do something. **2.** *Law.* a document ordering someone to appear in court.

sump (sump) *n.* **1.** a pit or reservoir for collecting liquid, such as water, oil, or sewage. **2.** a pit or well at the bottom of a mining shaft to collect water so that it can be pumped out.

sump·tu·ous (sump′chü əs) *adj.* costly and magnificent; lavish: *a sumptuous apartment, a sumptuous dinner.* —**sump′tu·ous·ly,** *adv.* —**sump′tu·ous·ness,** *n.*

Sum·ter, Fort (sum′tər) a fort in the harbor of Charleston, South Carolina. On April 12, 1861, the Civil War began when Confederate forces attacked this fort.

sun (sun) *n.* **1.** the star that is the central body of the solar system, around which the earth and other planets revolve and from which they receive light and heat. The sun has an average distance from earth of about 93 million miles (150 million kilometers), a diameter of about 865,000 miles (1,392,000 kilometers), and a mass of about 333,000 times that of the earth. **2.** light and heat from the sun; sunshine: *Too much sun at one time can produce a painful burn.* **3.** any star that is the center of a planetary system. —*v.,* **sunned, sun·ning.** —*v.t.* **1.** to expose to the rays of the sun: *We sunned ourselves on the beach.* **2.** to warm or dry in the sun. —*v.i.* to expose oneself to the rays of the sun: *to sun on a terrace.*

Sun., Sunday.

sun·bath (sun′bath′) *n., pl.* **sun·baths** (sun′bathz′, sun′baths′). exposure of the body to the rays of the sun or a sunlamp.

sun·bathe (sun′bāth′) *v.i.,* **sun·bathed, sun·bath·ing.** to bask in the sun; take a sunbath: *to sunbathe on the beach.* —**sun′bath·er,** *n.*

sun·beam (sun′bēm′) *n.* a beam of sunlight.

sun·block (sun′blok′) *n.* a substance applied to the skin that prevents sunburn by blocking out the sun's ultraviolet rays.

sun·bon·net (sun′bon′it) *n.* a woman's bonnet having a broad brim that protects the face and a flap that protects the neck from sunlight.

sun·burn (sun′bûrn′) *n.* an inflammation of the skin caused by overexposure to sunlight or a sunlamp. —*v.,* **sun·burned** or **sun·burnt, sun·burn·ing.** —*v.t.* to overexpose to the sun or a sunlamp; affect with sunburn: *to sunburn one's back at the beach.* —*v.i.* to become affected with sunburn: *to sunburn easily.*

sun·dae (sun′dē, sun′dā) *n.* ice cream served with a topping, such as syrup, nuts, or fruit.

Sun·day (sun′dē, sun′dā) *n.* the first day of the week and the Sabbath for most Christians. [From the Old English word *Sunnandæg* meaning "Sunday," going back to the words *sunna* "sun" and *dæg* "day."]

Sunday school 1. a school usually connected with a church and held on Sunday for religious instruction. 2. the pupils and teachers of such a school.

sun·der (sun′dər) *v.t.* to cause to divide; sever: *Distance sundered their friendship for years.* —*v.i.* to become divided; separate.

sun·dew (sun′dū, sun′dü′) *n.* any of a group of plants having leaves covered with sticky, hairlike structures that trap and digest insects.

sundial

sun·di·al (sun′dī′əl) *n.* a device that shows the time of the day by the position and length of the shadow that the sun casts on a flat, usually round surface marked with numbers.

sun·down (sun′doun′) *n.* another word for **sunset**.

sun·dries (sun′drēz) *pl. n.* numerous, assorted small items: *The drugstore sold medicines, newspapers, candy, and sundries.*

sun·dry (sun′drē) *adj.* more than one; several; various: *There were sundry aspects to the problem.*

sun·fish (sun′fish′) *n.*, *pl.* **sun·fish** or **sun·fish·es**. 1. any of several small fresh-water fish found in North America. 2. a large fish found in temperate or tropical seas, having a flattened, oval body and weighing up to 2,000 pounds (about 900 kilograms).

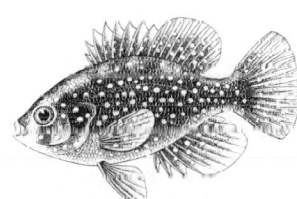

sunfish *(def. 1)*

sun·flow·er (sun′flou′ər) *n.* 1. a large flower of any of several tall plants, having rays of petals surrounding a yellow or purplish brown disk. 2. a plant bearing this flower. Sunflowers, which are found chiefly in North America, can reach a height of 12 feet (3.7 meters).

sung (sung) a past tense and the past participle of **sing**.

sun·glass·es (sun′glas′iz) *pl. n.* eyeglasses having shaded or tinted lenses to protect the eyes from the sun's glare.

sun god, any god identified with the sun.

sunk (sungk) a past tense and a past participle of **sink**.

sunk·en (sung′kən) *v.* a past participle of **sink**. —*adj.* 1. having sunk below the surface of the water or ground: *sunken treasure, sunken rock.* 2. situated below the surrounding area: *a sunken living room.* 3. abnormally hollow: *sunken cheeks.*

sun·lamp (sun′lamp′) *n.* a lamp that gives off ultraviolet radiation, used for tanning the skin.

sun·less (sun′lis) *adj.* without sunlight; dark or gloomy.

sun·light (sun′līt′) *n.* the light of the sun.

sun·lit (sun′lit′) *adj.* lighted by the sun.

Sun·ni (sun′ē) *n.* the larger of the two principal sects of Islam. It regards the traditional sayings and practices of Muhammad as part of Muslim law and considers the first four caliphs as the true successors of Muhammad.

Sun·nite (sun′īt) *n.* a follower of the Sunni sect of Islam. —*adj.* of or relating to the Sunni sect of Islam.

sun·ny (sun′ē) *adj.*, **sun·ni·er**, **sun·ni·est**. 1. full of or warmed by sunlight: *a sunny room.* 2. cheerful; happy; bright: *a sunny disposition, a sunny smile.* —**sun′ni·ly,** *adv.* —**sun′ni·ness,** *n.*

sun parlor, a room or porch with glass walls or large windows for letting in sunlight. Also, **sun porch, sun room.**

sun·rise (sun′rīz′) *n.* 1. the apparent rising of the sun above the horizon at the beginning of the day. 2. the time when the sun rises: *Farmers usually begin their chores before sunrise.* Also, **sunup.**

sun·set (sun′set′) *n.* 1. the apparent descent of the sun below the horizon at the end of the day. 2. the time when the sun sets. Also, **sundown.**

sun·shade (sun′shād′) *n.* something that is used to provide protection from the sun, such as an awning or parasol.

sun·shine (sun′shīn′) *n.* 1. the shining of the sun; direct sunlight. 2. cheerfulness; happiness; brightness: *There is much sunshine in a happy child's life.* —**sun′shin·y,** *adj.*

sun·spot (sun′spot′) *n.* one of the dark spots that occur in groups on the surface of the sun at regular intervals.

sun·stroke (sun′strōk′) *n.* an illness caused by over-exposure to the rays of the sun, causing weakness, fever, and sometimes unconsciousness.

sun·tan (sun′tan′) *n.* a brown color of the skin resulting from exposure to sunlight or a sunlamp; tan.

sun·up (sun′up′) *n.* another word for **sunrise**.

sun·ward (sun′wərd) *adj.* directed toward the sun. —*adv.* toward the sun. Also (*adv.*), **sun·wards** (sun′wərdz).

sup[1] (sup) *v.i.*, **supped, sup·ping.** to eat the evening meal. [From the Old French word *souper* with the same meaning, from the word *soup* meaning "a sop," of Germanic origin.]

sup[2] (sup) *v.t.*, **supped, sup·ping.** to take (liquid) in small quantities; sip. —*n.* a sip of a liquid. [From the Old English word *sūpan* meaning "to sip liquid."]

su·per (sü′pər) *n. Informal.* 1. a superintendent in an apartment house. 2. a performer having a very small part with no lines to say; supernumerary; extra. —*adj. Slang.* very good; excellent.

super– *prefix* 1. over; above: *superstructure, supersede.* 2. higher or greater; superior: *superhighway, superpower.* 3. to an excessive extent or degree: *supersensitive, superabundant.*

su·per·a·bun·dant (sü′pər ə bun′dənt) *adj.* more than is necessary or wanted; too abundant; excessive. —**su′per·a·bun′dance,** *n.*

su·per·an·nu·at·ed (sü′pər an′ū ā′tid) *adj.* 1. retired from service with a pension because of age or infirmity. 2. too old for use or work.

su·perb (sü pûrb′) *adj.* 1. having nobility or grandeur; magnificent; splendid: *a superb building.* 2. elegant; rich: *a superb wardrobe.* 3. of superior quality; very fine:

---

at; āpe; fär; câre; end; mē; it; īce; pîerce; hot; ōld; sông, fôrk; oil; out; up; ūse; rüle; pull; tûrn; chin; sing; shop; thin; this; hw in white; zh in treasure. The symbol ə stands for the unstressed vowel sound heard in about, taken, pencil, lemon, and circus.

S

The concert pianist gave a superb performance. —su·perb′ly, *adv.*

su·per·car·go (sü′pər kär′gō) *n., pl.* **su·per·car·goes** or **su·per·car·gos.** an officer on board a merchant ship who is in charge of the cargo and the business interests of the voyage.

su·per·charge (sü′pər chärj′) *v.t.,* **su·per·charged, su·per·charg·ing.** to increase the power of (an engine) with a supercharger.

su·per·charg·er (sü′pər chär′jər) *n.* a device for increasing the power of an internal-combustion engine by compressing air or a mixture of fuel and air and forcing it into the cylinder at a pressure greater than that of the surrounding atmosphere.

su·per·cil·i·ous (sü′pər sil′ē əs) *adj.* having or showing too much pride or scorn; haughty; arrogant. —su′per·cil′i·ous·ly, *adv.* —su′per·cil′i·ous·ness, *n.*

su·per·com·put·er (sü′pər kəm pū′tər) *n.* a type of mainframe computer capable of extremely rapid calculation for solving complex mathematical problems.

su·per·con·duc·tiv·i·ty (sü′pər kon′duk tiv′i tē) *n.* the ability of certain metals, alloys, and ceramic materials to conduct electricity at low temperatures with almost no resistance.

su·per·con·duc·tor (sü′pər kən duk′tər) *n.* a metal, alloy, or ceramic material that at very low temperatures conducts electricity with almost no resistance.

su·per·cool (sü′pər kül′) *v.t.* to cool (a liquid) below its freezing point without causing solidification.

su·per·e·rog·a·to·ry (sü′pər i rog′i tôr′ē) *adj.* **1.** going beyond what is needed or wanted. **2.** not necessary; excessive; superfluous: *supererogatory embellishments.*

su·per·fi·cial (sü′pər fish′əl) *adj.* **1.** of, relating to, or located on the surface: *a superficial wound, a superficial resemblance.* **2.** lacking depth or thoroughness; shallow: *a superficial person, superficial research.* —su′per·fi′cial·ly, *adv.*

su·per·fi·ci·al·i·ty (sü′pər fish′ē al′i tē) *n., pl.* **su·per·fi·ci·al·i·ties. 1.** the state or quality of being superficial. **2.** something superficial.

su·per·fine (sü′pər fīn′) *adj.* **1.** extremely fine in quality; of the best kind: *superfine cloth.* **2.** too refined or subtle: *superfine distinctions.* **3.** consisting of extremely fine particles or parts: *superfine sugar.*

su·per·flu·i·ty (sü′pər flü′i tē) *n., pl.* **su·per·flu·i·ties. 1.** the state of being superfluous. **2.** a greater quantity than is needed or wanted; excess. **3.** something that is superfluous: *to waste a great deal of money on expensive superfluities.*

su·per·flu·ous (sù pûr′flü əs) *adj.* **1.** more than is needed or wanted: *superfluous ornamentation, superfluous words in a letter.* **2.** needless; unnecessary: *a superfluous warning.* —su·per′flu·ous·ly, *adv.* —su·per′flu·ous·ness, *n.*

su·per·heat (sü′pər hēt′) *v.t.* **1.** to heat to an extremely high temperature; overheat. **2.** to raise the temperature of (a liquid) above its normal boiling point without causing vaporization. **3.** to raise the temperature of (vapor or steam) to increase its pressure. —*n.* **1.** the state of being superheated. **2.** the amount by which a vapor is superheated.

superhigh frequency (sü′pər hī′) a radio frequency between 3,000 and 30,000 megahertz.

su·per·high·way (sü′pər hī′wā′) *n.* a highway designed for high speeds, usually having four or more lanes with a center strip separating traffic going in opposite directions.

su·per·hu·man (sü′pər hū′mən, sü′pər ū′mən) *adj.* **1.** beyond what is human; divine: *of superhuman origin.* **2.** beyond the ordinary human ability or power: *a super-*

human effort, superhuman strength. —su′per·hu′man·ly, *adv.*

su·per·im·pose (sü′pər im pōz′) *v.t.,* **su·per·im·posed, su·per·im·pos·ing.** to place (something) over or on top of something else: *to superimpose tracing paper over a picture.*

su·per·in·tend (sü′pər in tend′) *v.t.* to direct or control the work or operation of; manage: *to superintend a building project.* —su′per·in·tend′ence, *n.*

su·per·in·tend·en·cy (sü′pər in ten′dən sē) *n., pl.* **su·per·in·tend·en·cies.** the position, duty, or authority of a superintendent.

su·per·in·tend·ent (sü′pər in ten′dənt) *n.* **1.** a person who directs the work or operation of something, such as a group of workers, an institution, or a business: *a superintendent of police, a superintendent of a school.* **2.** a person who manages and is responsible for the maintenance of an apartment building or office building.

su·pe·ri·or (sə pîr′ē ər) *adj.* **1.** higher or greater than the normal or average in degree or quality; exceptional: *superior talent, a superior piece of writing.* **2.** higher in status, rank, or office: *a superior officer.* **3.** greater in quantity: *The small army surrendered to the superior force.* **4.** haughty; disdainful: *a superior attitude.* **5.** (of an organ or part) higher in place or position; above in relation to another structure: *The lungs are superior to the intestines.* —*n.* **1.** a person who is higher than others, as in status, rank, or office: *The lieutenant was the police sergeant's superior.* **2.** the head of an abbey, monastery, or other religious community. —su·pe′ri·or·ly, *adv.*

su·pe·ri·or·i·ty (sə pîr′ē ôr′i tē, sə pîr′ē or′i tē) *n.* the state or quality of being superior: *They demonstrated superiority by winning first place.*

superl., superlative.

su·per·la·tive (sə pûr′lə tiv) *adj.* **1.** of the highest degree or quality; going beyond all others; supreme. **2.** *Grammar.* denoting the third or highest degree of quality, quantity, or relation that can be expressed by an adjective or adverb. *Fastest* is the superlative degree of the adjective *fast.* —*n.* **1.** a person or thing that goes beyond all others; highest example. **2.** *Grammar.* **a.** the superlative degree. **b.** a word or group of words that expresses this degree. *Best* is the superlative of *good.* —su·per′la·tive·ly, *adv.* —su·per′la·tive·ness, *n.*

su·per·man (sü′pər man′) *n., pl.* **su·per·men** (sü′pər-men′). a man with strength or intelligence beyond what is normal.

su·per·mar·ket (sü′pər mär′kit) *n.* a self-service store, usually large, carrying a wide selection of food and other household items.

su·per·nal (sù pûr′nəl) *adj.* **1.** relating to a higher world; heavenly. **2.** of, relating to, or existing in the sky: *a supernal phenomenon.* —su·per′nal·ly, *adv.*

su·per·nat·u·ral (sü′pər nach′ər əl) *adj.* **1.** of or relating to a realm or existence beyond or exceeding the power of the natural world: *supernatural forces.* **2.** of or relating to ghosts or spirits. —*n.* a person or thing that exists beyond the natural world. —su′per·nat′u·ral·ly, *adv.*

su·per·nat·u·ral·ism (sü′pər nach′ər ə liz′əm) *n.* **1.** the state or quality of being supernatural. **2.** a belief in supernatural forces or beings.

su·per·no·va (sü′pər nō′və) *n., pl.* **su·per·no·vas** or **su·per·no·vae** (sü′pər nō′vē). **1.** the explosion of a star in which the center of the star collapses under gravity, the outer layers are blown off at high speeds, and the brightness of the star increases greatly before fading. **2.** a star that explodes in this way.

su·per·nu·mer·ar·y (sü′pər nü′mə rer′ē, sü′pər nū′-mə rer′ē) *adj.* greater in number than is usual, expected, or needed; additional; extra. —*n., pl.* **su·per·nu·mer·ar·ies. 1.** a person or thing that is extra. **2.** a performer in a play or film who has a minor part with no lines to speak.

su·per·pose (sü′pər pōz′) *v.t.,* **su·per·posed, su·per·pos·ing.** to superimpose.

su·per·pow·er (sü′pər pou′ər) *n.* one of the powerful nations that dominate world affairs, especially through the possession of nuclear weapons.

su·per·sat·u·rate (sü′pər sach′ə rāt) *v.t.,* **su·per·sat·u·rat·ed, su·per·sat·u·rat·ing.** to add to or concentrate in (a solution) more than can normally be held at a given pressure and temperature. If a solution is supersaturated it becomes very unstable.

su·per·script (sü′pər skript) *adj.* written above. —*n.* a character or symbol written, printed, or set above and to one side of another. In *a²*, the symbol ² is a superscript.

su·per·scrip·tion (sü′pər skrip′shən) *n.* something written on the top or outside of something, especially an address on a letter or package.

su·per·sede (sü′pər sēd′) *v.t.,* **su·per·sed·ed, su·per·sed·ing. 1.** to take the place of; replace: *Diesel and electric trains have superseded steam-driven trains.* **2.** to take the job or office of; succeed: *You may eventually supersede your boss as manager of the company.* [From the Old French word *superseder* meaning "to refrain from," from the Latin word *supersedēre* "to preside over" or "to refrain from, desist," from the prefix *super-* "above" + *sedēre* "to sit."] —**su′per·sed′er,** *n.*

su·per·sen·si·tive (sü′pər sen′si tiv) *adj.* too sensitive; hypersensitive: *The child is supersensitive and cries easily.* —**su′per·sen′si·tive·ly,** *adv.* —**su′per·sen′si·tive·ness,** *n.*

su·per·son·ic (sü′pər son′ik) *adj.* of, relating to, or traveling at a speed greater than the speed of sound in air, approximately 740 miles (1,190 kilometers) per hour at sea level.

su·per·star (sü′pər stär′) *n.* a person who is thought to surpass the most outstanding people in a field or profession, such as acting, sports, or popular music; an exceptionally successful star: *a television superstar.* **2.** any exceptionally successful or outstanding person or thing: *a superstar among cars, a superstar of racehorses.*

su·per·sti·tion (sü′pər stish′ən) *n.* **1.** a belief or set of beliefs based on an unreasoning fear of the unknown. **2.** a particular practice based on such a belief or set of beliefs. *Throwing spilled salt over one's shoulder to avoid bad luck is a superstition.*

su·per·sti·tious (sü′pər stish′əs) *adj.* **1.** having superstitions: *a superstitious person.* **2.** of, relating to, or characterized by superstition: *superstitious beliefs.* —**su′per·sti′tious·ly,** *adv.* —**su′per·sti′tious·ness,** *n.*

su·per·struc·ture (sü′pər struk′chər) *n.* **1.** the part of a building above the foundation. **2.** the part of a ship, especially a warship, above the main deck.

su·per·tax (sü′pər taks′) *n., pl.* **su·per·tax·es.** another word for **surtax.**

su·per·vene (sü′pər vēn′) *v.i.* **su·per·vened, su·per·ven·ing.** to take place, especially as something additional or unexpected: *Bad health supervened and kept me from making the trip.*

su·per·vise (sü′pər vīz′) *v.t.,* **su·per·vised, su·per·vis·ing.** to watch over in order to guide, direct, or control; oversee: *to supervise workers.*

su·per·vi·sion (sü′pər vizh′ən) *n.* **1.** the act or process of supervising. **2.** care or management.

su·per·vi·sor (sü′pər vī′zər) *n.* a person who supervises.

su·per·vi·so·ry (sü′pər vī′zə rē) *adj.* of or relating to a supervisor or supervision.

su·pine (sü pīn′) *adj.* **1.** lying on the back with the face turned upward: *a supine position.* **2.** not caring; apathetic; lazy. —**su·pine′ly,** *adv.* —**su·pine′ness,** *n.*

sup·per (sup′ər) *n.* **1.** the last meal of the day, eaten in the evening. **2.** a social or community event where such a meal is served: *a church supper.*

sup·plant (sə plant′) *v.t.* to take the place of: *The automobile has supplanted the horse as a means of transportation.*

sup·ple (sup′əl) *adj.,* **sup·pler, sup·plest. 1.** easily bent or folded without breaking or cracking; flexible: *the supple twig of a tree. This shirt has a soft, supple collar.* **2.** able to yield or adapt to changes in people, ideas, or surroundings; adaptable: *a supple mind.* [From the Old French word *souple* with the same meaning, from the Latin word *supplex* "humble, submissive."] —**sup′ple·ly;** *also,* **sup′ply,** *adv.* —**sup′ple·ness,** *n.*

sup·ple·ment (*n.,* sup′lə mənt; *v.,* sup′lə ment′) *n.* something added to improve or complete something else: *We take vitamins as a dietary supplement. The school library receives an annual supplement to the encyclopedia.* —*v.t.* to add or form a supplement to.

sup·ple·men·ta·ry (sup′lə men′tə rē) *adj.* serving as a supplement. Also, **sup·ple·men·tal** (sup′lə men′təl).

supplementary angle, an angle that is added to another angle to make the sum of the two angles 180 degrees.

sup·pli·ant (sup′lē ənt) *n.* a person who supplicates. —*adj.* asking humbly and earnestly; imploring; beseeching; begging: *suppliant pleas for assistance.* —**sup′pli·ance,** *n.*

sup·pli·cant (sup′li kənt) *n.* a person who supplicates. —*adj.* asking humbly and earnestly; beseeching; begging.

Angle A 135°   Angle B 45°

supplementary angles

sup·pli·cate (sup′li kāt′) *v.,* **sup·pli·cat·ed, sup·pli·cat·ing.** —*v.t.* **1.** to make a humble and earnest request for: *to supplicate mercy from God.* **2.** to ask humbly and earnestly of; beseech: *to supplicate a judge for a pardon.* —*v.i.* to make a humble and earnest request, as by prayer. —**sup′pli·ca′tor,** *n.*

sup·pli·ca·tion (sup′li kā′shən) *n.* **1.** the act of supplicating. **2.** an earnest request or humble prayer: *to address a supplication for mercy to the governor.*

sup·pli·ca·to·ry (sup′li kə tôr′e) *adj.* making supplication.

sup·pli·er (sə plī′ər) *n.* a person or thing that supplies.

sup·ply¹ (sə plī′) *v.t.,* **sup·plied, sup·ply·ing. 1.** to make available (what is wanted or needed): *The reservoir supplies water to the community. A reference book supplies information.* **2.** to provide (someone) with what is wanted or needed: *The book supplied me with the correct answer.* —*n., pl.* **sup·plies. 1.** the amount needed or available for use; stock; store: *The store has a new supply of pencils.* **2.** *usually,* **supplies.** needed things, such as food, clothing, or equipment, that are set aside and held for use: *The army was cut off from its supplies.* **3.** the quantity of a

at; āpe; fär; câre; end; mē; it; īce; pïerce; hot; ōld; sông, fôrk; oil; out; up; ūse; rüle; pull; tûrn; chin; sing; shop; thin; this; hw in white; zh in treasure. The symbol ə stands for the unstressed vowel sound heard in about, taken, pencil, lemon, and circus.

S

commodity available for sale at a certain price at a given time. [From the Old French word *soupleier* meaning "to add to" or "to provide for," from the Latin word *supplēre* "to fill up, complete," from the prefix *sub-* "under, from below" + *plēre* "to fill."]

sup·ply² (sup′lē) *adv.* in a supple manner. [*Supple* + *-ly¹*.]

sup·port (sə pôrt′) *v.t.* **1.** to hold up; keep from falling: *Brackets support the shelves. That small chair won't support your weight.* **2.** to provide for: *to support a family. We doubt that the planet can support life.* **3.** to back; uphold: *The senator did not support either of the candidates.* **4.** to comfort or strengthen: *Religious faith often supports people in times of grief.* **5.** to show to be true; verify: *There is no evidence to support the theory of life on Mars.* —*n.* **1.** the act of supporting or the state of being supported. **2.** a person or thing that supports.

sup·port·a·ble (sə pôr′tə bəl) *adj.* able to be supported; bearable; endurable. —**sup·port′a·bly**, *adv.*

sup·port·er (sə pôr′tər) *n.* **1.** a person who supports, especially a person who aids or approves: *an ardent supporter of the president.* **2.** something that supports, such as a garter.

sup·por·tive (sə pôr′tiv) *adj.* **1.** providing support or reinforcement: *a supportive arch, supportive testimony.* **2.** providing approval, aid, or encouragement: *supportive parents, to be supportive of one's friends.*

sup·pose (sə pōz′) *v.t.*, **sup·posed, sup·pos·ing. 1.** to imagine or take to be possible for the sake of argument: *Just suppose that you were able to go with us.* **2.** to hold as an opinion; believe to be probable: *I suppose that I have enough money to make the trip.* **3.** to expect or require: *The plane is supposed to arrive at nine o'clock.*

sup·posed (sə pōzd′, sə pō′zid) *adj.* considered to be true, real, or possible, often wrongly: *The supposed explanation proved not to be true.* —**sup·pos·ed·ly** (sə pō′zid lē) *adv.*

sup·po·si·tion (sup′ə zish′ən) *n.* **1.** something supposed; assumption: *the supposition that the weather will be warm.* **2.** the act of supposing.

sup·pos·i·to·ry (sə poz′i tôr′ē) *n.*, *pl.* **sup·pos·i·to·ries.** a medical substance in solid form, usually in the shape of a cone or cylinder, made to be inserted into the rectum or vagina.

sup·press (sə pres′) *v.t.* **1.** to put an end to or to put down by force; crush: *The government suppressed the revolt.* **2.** to hold or keep in; restrain: *to suppress a laugh.* **3.** to prevent or forbid the telling or publishing of; censor: *The government suppressed the news story because it contained secret information.* —**sup·press′i·ble**, *adj.* —**sup·pres′sor;** *also,* **sup·press′er,** *n.*

sup·pres·sion (sə presh′ən) *n.* the act of suppressing or the state of being suppressed.

sup·pres·sive (sə pres′iv) *adj.* tending to suppress.

sup·pu·rate (sup′yə rāt′) *v.t.*, **sup·pu·rat·ed, sup·pu·rat·ing.** to form or give forth pus.

sup·pu·ra·tion (sup′yə rā′shən) *n.* **1.** the formation of pus. **2.** pus.

su·pra·re·nal gland (sü′prə rē′nəl) another term for **adrenal gland.**

su·prem·a·cy (sə prem′ə sē) *n.* the quality or condition of being supreme.

su·preme (sə prēm′) *adj.* **1.** greatest in rank, authority, or power: *The president is the supreme executive officer.* **2.** greatest in importance, degree, or quality; utmost: *supreme artistry, supreme wisdom, a supreme effort.* **3.** ultimate; final; last: *the supreme sacrifice.* [From the Latin word *supremus* meaning "highest, topmost," from the word *superus* "situated above," from the word *super* "above."] —**su·preme′ly**, *adv.*

Supreme Being, God.

Supreme Court 1. the highest court in the United States, with the power to hear appeals from lower courts and to declare laws unconstitutional. **2.** the highest court in some states of the United States. **3.** the highest court in some other countries, such as Denmark.

Supreme Soviet, the legislature of the Soviet Union, consisting of two houses, one of which is elected according to population and the other of which is elected by the various national groups.

Supt., superintendent.

sur– *prefix* over; above; beyond: *surcharge, surpass.*

sur·cease (sûr sēs′) *n.* *Archaic.* an end: *the surcease of pain.*

sur·charge (*n.,* sûr′chärj′; *v.,* sûr chärj′, sûr′chärj′) *n.* **1.** a charge added to the usual amount: *a tax surcharge.* **2.** an additional mark printed over a postage stamp to raise its value. —*v.t.*, **sur·charged, sur·charg·ing. 1.** to charge an extra amount. **2.** to overcharge. **3.** to print an additional mark on (postage stamps) to raise their value, instead of issuing new stamps.

sur·cin·gle (sûr′sing′gəl) *n.* a belt or band around the body of a horse or pack animal to hold down a saddle, blanket, or pack.

sur·coat (sûr′kōt′) *n.* an outer coat, especially a short garment worn over armor during the Middle Ages.

surd (sûrd) *n.* an irrational number that is a root of a positive whole number or the quotient of positive whole numbers. The numbers $\sqrt{3}$ and $\sqrt{3/5}$ are surds.

sure (shūr) *adj.,* **sur·er, sur·est. 1.** firmly believing in something; having or showing no doubt; confident: *I am sure that my answer is right.* **2.** bound to be or happen; inevitable; certain: *That horse is a sure winner. My best friend is sure to be at the party.* **3.** not liable to give way; steady; firm: *to have a sure grip on the bat.* **4.** worthy of trust; dependable: *a sure friend.* —*adv.* *Informal.* surely. —**sure′ness,** *n.*

•**for sure.** without doubt.

•**to make sure.** to be certain: *We must make sure that all our facts are correct before we release the report to the press.*

surcoat

sure·fire (shūr′fīr′) *adj.* *Informal.* not able to fail: *a surefire scheme.*

sure·foot·ed (shūr′fūt′id) *adj.* not liable to stumble or fall: *a surefooted horse.* —**sure′foot′ed·ness,** *n.*

sure·ly (shūr′lē) *adv.* **1.** without doubt; truly; positively: *They will surely be there.* **2.** firmly; steadily: *a heavy beam fitting surely in place.*

sur·e·ty (shūr′i tē) *n.,* *pl.* **sur·e·ties. 1.** security, as against loss or damage: *a deposit as a surety against damage.* **2.** a person who agrees to be responsible for the debts or actions of another. **3.** the state of being sure; assurance; certainty.

surf (sûrf) *n.* the swell of the sea or the splash of its waves breaking on the shore or upon a reef. —*v.i.* to ride on the crest of a wave, usually on a surfboard. —**surf′er,** *n.*

sur·face (sûr′fis) *n.* **1.** the upper or outer part of a thing: *the earth's surface, the surface of a lake.* **2.** outer appearance: *The problem seemed simple on the surface.* —*adj.* **1.** of, on, or relating to a surface: *a surface scratch on the table.* **2.** without much depth; superficial: *a surface explanation.* —*v.,* **sur·faced, sur·fac·ing.** —*v.i.* to come or rise to the surface: *The submarine surfaced.* —*v.t.* to cover or finish the surface of: *The workers surfaced the road with asphalt.*

surf·board (sûrf′bôrd′) *n.* a long, flat board used to ride on the crest of a wave. —*v.i.* to engage in surfing.

surf·cast·ing (sûrf′kas′ting) *n.* the sport of fishing by casting a line into the surf from the shore.

sur·feit (sûr′fit) *v.t.* to feed or supply to excess; sate; satiate: *surfeited lions lazing in the sun.* —*n.* **1.** an excessive amount or supply: *An abundant harvest yielded a surfeit of food.* **2.** the act or instance of taking an excessive amount, as of food or drink. **3.** disgust or discomfort caused by this.

surf·ing (sûr′fing) *n.* a sport in which a person rides the crest of a wave into the shore, usually on a surfboard.

surfboard

surge (sûrj) *v.i.,* **surged, surg·ing. 1.** to move with a sudden, heaving motion: *The crowd surged forward to catch a glimpse of the visiting celebrity.* **2.** to increase or rise suddenly: *The crime rate surged during the heat wave.* —*n.* **1.** a heaving motion like that of waves. **2.** a sudden increase or onset: *a surge of electric current.* **3.** a rolling swell or wave.

sur·geon (sûr′jən) *n.* a doctor of medicine who specializes in surgery.

Surgeon General *pl.* **Surgeons General. 1.** the chief medical officer of one of the armed services of the United States. **2.** the chief medical officer of the U.S. Public Health Service.

sur·ger·y (sûr′jə rē) *n., pl.* **sur·ger·ies. 1.** the branch of medicine that deals with the removal or repair of injured or diseased parts of the body. **2.** the removal or repair of injured or diseased parts of the body: *perform surgery to remove a bone chip.* **3.** a room or suite of rooms in a hospital where this is done. [From the Middle French word *cirurgie* meaning "surgery," from the Latin word *chirugia* "surgery," from the Greek word *cheirourgos* meaning "working with the hand," from the words *cheir* "hand" + *ergon* "work."]

sur·gi·cal (sûr′ji kəl) *adj.* of, relating to, or used in surgery: *surgical procedures, surgical instruments.* —**sur′gi·cal·ly,** *adv.*

sur·ly (sûr′lē) *adj.,* **sur·li·er, sur·li·est.** ill-tempered and rude; sullen and unfriendly: *a surly person, a surly demand.* —**sur′li·ness,** *n.*

sur·mise (*v.,* sər mīz′; *n.,* sər mīz′, sûr′mīz) *v.,* **surmised, sur·mis·ing.** —*v.t.* to arrive at an idea or opinion about with little or no evidence; guess: *When we didn't see your coat, we surmised that you had left.* —*v.i.* to guess. —*n.* an idea or opinion based on little or no evidence.

sur·mount (sər mount′) *v.t.* **1.** to overcome; conquer: *to surmount difficulties.* **2.** to climb up or get over: *to surmount a wall.* **3.** to stand, lie, or be above; top; crown: *A dome surmounts the building.* —**sur·mount′a·ble,** *adj.*

sur·name (sûr′nām′) *n.* **1.** a last name or family name. **2.** an added name or nickname: *Czar Ivan IV was given the surname "the Terrible."* —*v.t.,* **sur·named, sur·nam·ing.** to give a surname to; call by a surname.

sur·pass (sər pas′) *v.t.* **1.** to go beyond; be better than; excel: *That athlete surpasses the other members of the team in ability.* **2.** to be beyond the range or reach of; exceed: *success surpassing expectations.* —**sur·pass′a·ble,** *adj.* —**sur·pass′ing·ly,** *adv.*

sur·plice (sûr′plis) *n.* a white garment with wide sleeves worn by members of the clergy and choir members in certain churches.

sur·plus (sûr′plus′, sûr′pləs) *n., pl.* **sur·plus·es.** an amount or quantity above what is used or needed; excess: *a crop surplus, a surplus of dishes.* —*adj.* over and above what is used or needed: *surplus army goods.*

sur·prise (sər prīz′) *v.t.,* **sur·prised, sur·pris·ing. 1.** to cause to feel sudden wonder or astonishment: *to surprise someone with an unexpected gift.* **2.** to come upon suddenly or unexpectedly; take or catch unawares: *to surprise a thief.* **3.** to attack or capture suddenly and without warning: *They surprised the enemy with a night attack.* —*n.* **1.** the state or feeling of being surprised; sudden feeling of wonder. **2.** something that causes this feeling: *The gift was a delightful surprise.* **3.** the act of surprising.

sur·pris·ing (sər prī′zing) *adj.* causing surprise or wonder; unexpected: *The home team experienced a surprising defeat.* —**sur·pris′ing·ly,** *adv.*

sur·re·al (sə rē′əl) *adj.* **1.** having the qualities of surrealism; surrealistic: *surreal art, surreal writing.* **2.** having some of the qualities of a dream; unreal; bizarre; eerie: *surreal fantasies, a surreal world.*

sur·re·al·ism (sə rē′ə liz′əm) *n.* a movement in twentieth-century art and literature emphasizing subconscious reality and the importance of dreams and fantasy.

sur·re·al·ist (sə rē′ə list) *n.* an artist or writer whose work is characterized by surrealism.

sur·re·al·is·tic (sə rē′ə lis′tik) *adj.* of, relating to, or characteristic of surrealism. —**sur·re·al·is′ti·cal·ly,** *adv.*

sur·ren·der (sə ren′dər) *v.t.* **1.** to give over possession or control of to another or others: *The soldiers surrendered the fort to the enemy.* **2.** to yield (oneself) to an emotion, influence, or course of action: *to surrender oneself to sorrow.* —*v.i.* to give oneself up: *The outlaw surrendered to the sheriff.* —*n.* the act of surrendering.

sur·rep·ti·tious (sûr′əp tish′əs) *adj.* **1.** done by secret, sly means: *a surreptitious meeting.* **2.** acting in a secret, sly way: *a surreptitious investigator.* —**sur·rep·ti′tious·ly,** *adv.* —**sur·rep·ti′tious·ness,** *n.*

sur·rey (sûr′ē) *n., pl.* **sur·reys.** a light, four-wheeled carriage with two seats, usually covered with a top. [From *Surrey,* the county in England where it was first made.]

sur·ro·gate (sûr′ə gāt′, sûr′ə git) *n.* **1.** a person or thing that is substituted for another; substitute: *The guardian was the orphan's surrogate parent.* **2.** in some states, a judge having charge of such matters as guardianships and wills.

surrey

sur·round (sə round′) *v.t.* **1.** to be on all sides of; form a circle around: *A crowd surrounded the movie star's car.* **2.** to cause to be encircled; enclose or confine: *to surround the yard with a fence, to surround enemy troops and prevent their escape.*

sur·round·ings (sə roun′dingz) *pl. n.* the objects, influences, or conditions of a place or way of life: *Vacationers sought out the peaceful surroundings of farm villages.*

---

at; āpe; fär; câre; end; mē; it; īce; pîerce; hot; ōld; sông; fôrk; oil; out; up; ūse; rüle; pull; tûrn; chin; sing; shop; thin; this; hw in white; zh in treasure. The symbol ə stands for the unstressed vowel sound heard in about, taken, pencil, lemon, and circus.

S

sur·tax (sûr′taks′) *n., pl.* **sur·tax·es.** an additional or extra tax, especially one added to the normal income tax. Also, **supertax.**

sur·veil·lance (sər vā′ləns) *n.* **1.** a close watch kept over a person, group, or place in order to gather information: *The police have the suspect under constant surveillance.* **2.** a close watch for the purpose of supervision and control: *The new staff members worked under the manager's surveillance.*

sur·vey (*v.,* sər vā′; *n.,* sûr′vā, sər vā′) *v.t.* **1.** to view or examine as a whole: *From the tower you can survey the entire city below.* **2.** to examine or inspect in detail: *The authorities surveyed the damage after the tornado.* **3.** to find the shape, area, and boundaries of (a region or tract of land) by taking measurements. —*v.i.* to survey land. —*n., pl.* **sur·veys. 1.** a detailed study or examination: *A survey was conducted to find out how many people used the product.* **2.** a general view: *This college course is a survey of American literature.* **3.** the act or process of surveying land.

sur·vey·ing (sər vā′ing) *n.* the act, science, or occupation of making land surveys.

sur·vey·or (sər vā′ər) *n.* a person or thing that surveys, especially a person whose work is surveying land.

sur·viv·al (sər vī′vəl) *n.* **1.** the act of surviving or the state of having survived: *The accident victims owed their survival to the rescue squad.* **2.** a person or thing that survives, such as a custom or ritual from the past.

sur·vive (sər vīv′) *v.,* **sur·vived, sur·viv·ing.** —*v.t.* **1.** to live longer than; outlive: *to survive other members of one's family.* **2.** to live or be active through and after: *Two people survived the automobile accident.* —*v.i.* to continue to live or remain active; endure: *Those plants won't survive without sunlight.*

sur·vi·vor (sər vī′vər) *n.* a person or thing that survives.

sus·cep·ti·bil·i·ty (sə sep′tə bil′i tē) *n., pl.* **sus·cep·ti·bil·i·ties. 1.** the quality or condition of being susceptible. **2. susceptibilities.** strong and sensitive feelings. ▲ usually used with a plural verb.

sus·cep·ti·ble (sə sep′tə bəl) *adj.* **1.** easily affected or influenced by; sensitive: *A susceptible person is easily moved by other people's troubles. Small children are often susceptible to colds.* **2.** able to undergo or experience: *My opinion is susceptible to change.* —**sus·cep′ti·ble·ness,** *n.* —**sus·cep′ti·bly,** *adv.*

sushi

su·shi (sü′shē) *n.* a Japanese dish of cold, cooked rice topped or wrapped with garnishes, as of raw fish or seaweed.

sus·pect (*v.,* sə spekt′; *n.,* sus′pekt′; *adj.,* sus′pekt′, sə spekt′) *v.t.* **1.** to consider true, likely, or possible: *I suspect they have already left for the day.* **2.** to think (someone) guilty with little or no proof: *The police suspected the escaped convict of the crime.* **3.** to have doubts about; lack confidence in; distrust: *I suspect their sincerity.* —*v.i.* to have suspicions. —*n.* a person who is suspected, especially of having committed a crime. —*adj.* open to or viewed with distrust; suspected: *Their motives are suspect.*

sus·pend (sə spend′) *v.t.* **1.** to attach from above so as to hang down: *to suspend a swing from a tree branch.* **2.** to hold in place as if attached from above: *Bits of matter were suspended in the water.* **3.** to make no longer effective or binding, especially for a time: *to suspend someone's driver's license.* **4.** to cause to stop for a time; interrupt: *to suspend payments on a car.* **5.** to keep out or prevent from attending for a time, usually as a punishment: *The principal suspended the unruly student from school.* —*v.i.* to stop for a time.

sus·pend·ers (sə spen′dərz) *pl. n.* a pair of straps worn over the shoulders and attached to the waistband of trousers or a skirt, usually worn instead of a belt to hold up the garment.

sus·pense (sə spens′) *n.* **1.** a state of being undecided or in doubt: *We were all in suspense, wondering who had won the contest.* **2.** the worry or tension resulting from this. —**sus·pense′ful,** *adj.*

sus·pen·sion (sə spen′shən) *n.* **1.** the act of suspending or the state of being suspended. **2.** a mixture made up of small solid particles or liquid droplets in a liquid. The particles will separate out if the suspension is allowed to stand. **3.** the state or condition of the particles or droplets in such a mixture: *Dirt particles are held in suspension in muddy water.* **4.** a stopping for a time; interruption: *a suspension of telephone service after the storm.*

suspension bridge, a bridge suspended from cables or chains hung between towers.

suspension bridge

sus·pi·cion (sə spish′-ən) *n.* **1.** the act or instance of suspecting something wrong or bad with little or no proof; feeling of distrust or uncertainty: *Suspicions were aroused by the witness's hesitant answer.* **2.** a feeling or impression: *I have a suspicion that you are right.* **3.** the state or condition of being suspected: *Such an honest person is above suspicion.* **4.** a slight trace or suggestion: *The smell of smoke gave a suspicion of fire.*

sus·pi·cious (sə spish′əs) *adj.* **1.** tending to arouse suspicion; questionable: *There were a number of suspicious people near the scene of the crime.* **2.** inclined to suspect; distrustful: *to be suspicious of strangers.* **3.** expressing or indicating suspicion: *They gave the stranger a suspicious glance.* —**sus·pi′cious·ly,** *adv.* —**sus·pi′cious·ness,** *n.*

sus·tain (sə stān′) *v.t.* **1.** to keep up or in effect: *to sustain interest in an exciting story.* **2.** to keep up the spirits or courage of; keep from despair; comfort: *A positive outlook will sustain you in times of challenge.* **3.** to supply with food, clothing, or other needed things; support: *The supplies will sustain the explorers for many months.* **4.** to keep from sinking or falling; support from below: *These posts are needed to sustain the platform.* **5.** to undergo or experience, as loss or injury: *to sustain a broken arm in an accident.* **6.** to accept or uphold as true or just: *The judge sustained the defense attorney's objection.* **7.** to prove; confirm: *These new facts sustain* *our earlier opinion.* —**sus·tain′a·ble,** *adj.* —**sus·tain′er,** *n.*

sus·te·nance (sus′tə nəns) *n.* **1.** something that sustains or supports life, especially food. **2.** the act of sustaining or the state of being sustained.

su·ture (sü′chər) *n.* **1.** the act or method of joining together the edges of a cut or wound by or as if by stitching. **2.** one of the stitches or fastenings of thread, wire, or other material so used. **3.** a line or seam formed in joining two surfaces, such as that of a wound sewed together.

su·ze·rain (sü′zer in, sü′zə rān′) *n.* **1.** in feudalism, a lord to whom vassals gave their services in return for the use of a part of his land. **2.** a country that has control of another country, but allows it to have its own government.

su·ze·rain·ty (sü′zər in tē, sü′ze rān′tē) *n., pl.* **su·ze·rain·ties.** the power or position of a suzerain.

svelte (svelt) *adj.* slender and graceful; lithe: *Exercise and proper diet help maintain a svelte figure.* [From the French word *svelte*, from the Italian word *svelto*, both with the same meaning.]

SW, S.W., southwest.

swab (swob) *also,* **swob.** *n.* **1.** a small piece of cotton, sponge, or other material, usually at the tip of a small stick, used to apply medication or cosmetics and to clean certain parts of the body, as the ears. **2.** a mop used on ships to clean decks or other surfaces. —*v.t.,* **swabbed, swab·bing.** to clean, treat, or apply with a swab: *to swab a cut with ointment.*

swad·dle (swod′əl) *v.t.,* **swad·dled, swad·dling. 1.** to wrap or bind with bandages. **2.** to wrap (an infant) in swaddling clothes. —*n.* a band of cloth or bandage used for swaddling.

swaddling clothes, long, narrow bands of cloth formerly wrapped around newborn infants. Also, **swaddling bands.**

swag (swag) *n.* *Slang.* stolen goods or profits; booty.

swag·ger (swag′ər) *v.i.* **1.** to walk or behave in a bold, rude, or arrogant manner: *The winning team swaggered off the field.* **2.** to boast; brag. —*n.* a swaggering movement or manner. —**swag′ger·er,** *n.*

swagger stick, a short, light cane carried especially by army officers.

Swa·hi·li (swä hē′lē) *n.* a Bantu language containing words borrowed from Arabic. It is spoken mainly in central and eastern Africa.

swain (swān) *n.* **1.** a lover; suitor. **2.** a country youth. ▲ used especially in literature.

swal·low¹ (swol′ō) *v.t.* **1.** to cause (something, such as food) to pass from the mouth to the stomach. **2.** to take in as if by swallowing: *The darkness swallowed them. The earthquake swallowed up an entire building.* **3.** to take back; retract: *to swallow one's words.* **4.** to keep from expressing; suppress: *to swallow one's pride.* **5.** to put up with; accept without protest; tolerate: *to swallow an insult.* **6.** *Informal.* to accept without question: *They swallowed my explanation willingly.* —*v.i.* to perform the act or motion of swallowing. —*n.* **1.** the act of swallowing. **2.** the quantity swallowed at one time: *a swallow of tea.* [From the Old English word *swelgan* with the same meaning.] —**swal′low·er,** *n.*

swal·low² (swol′ō) *n.* any of a group of small migratory birds having a slender body and sometimes a deeply forked tail. [From the Old English word *swealwe* meaning this bird.]

swal·low·tail (swol′ō tāl′) *n.* **1.** a deeply forked tail, such as that of certain kites or certain butterflies, resembling the tail of a barn swallow. **2.** see **swallow-tailed coat.**

swal·low–tailed coat (swol′ō tāld′) a coat with tails, used for formal wear or as part of a costume.

swam (swam) a past tense of **swim.**

swa·mi (swä′mē) *n.* a Hindu mystic or religious teacher.

swamp (swomp) *n.* an area of low-lying, wet land that is usually covered with dense vegetation, such as grasses, trees, and shrubs. —*v.t.* **1.** to overwhelm, as with difficulties or work; burden: *to be swamped with much homework.* **2.** to drench or cover with water: *The spring floods swamped the area.* **3.** to sink or fill (a boat or ship) with water. —*v.i.* **1.** to be overwhelmed or burdened. **2.** (of a boat or ship) to become filled with water: *The rowboat swamped in the storm.*

swamp·land (swomp′land′) *n.* land covered with swamps.

swamp·y (swom′pē) *adj.,* **swamp·i·er, swamp·i·est.** of or resembling a swamp or swamps.

swan (swon) *n.* any of several large, graceful, long-necked birds having a broad, flat bill and webbed feet.

swan dive, a dive in which the arms are extended straight out to the side, with the back arched, the arms being brought together in front of the head just before entering the water.

swan

swank·y (swang′kē) *adj.,* **swank·i·er, swank·i·est.** *Slang.* having much elegance; stylish; posh: *a swanky hotel.* Also, **swank** (swangk). —**swank′i·ly,** *adv.* —**swank′i·ness,** *n.*

swans·down (swonz′doun′) *n.* **1.** the soft down of a swan. **2.** a fine, thick, soft fabric made from wool or cotton, used for such items as infants' wear.

swan song 1. the song that, according to legend, a swan sings just before it dies. **2.** a final work, as by an artist, musician, or actor at the end of a career or before death.

swap (swop) *also,* **swop.** *v.,* **swapped, swap·ping.** *Informal.* —*v.t.* to exchange (something) for something else; trade: *I wanted to swap a pair of skates for a baseball glove.* —*v.i.* to trade: *to be willing to swap.* —**swap′per,** *n.*

sward (swôrd) *n.* land covered with grass; lawn; meadow.

swarm (swôrm) *n.* **1.** a large group of insects or other small animals flying or moving about together: *a swarm of flies around the garbage.* **2.** a group of bees, led by the queen of a hive, that flies off together to start a new colony. **3.** a great number of people or animals: *Swarms of shoppers filled the stores in December.* —*v.i.* **1.** (of bees) to fly off together to start a new colony. **2.** to come together or move in a large mass or group: *The audience swarmed out of the theater.* **3.** to be filled or overrun; teem: *The river swarmed with fish.* —*v.t.* to fill with a throng or multitude; crowd.

swarth·y (swôr′t͟hē, swôr′thē) *adj.,* **swarth·i·er, swarth·i·est.** having a dark color or complexion: *swarthy skin.* Also *(archaic),* **swart** (swôrt), **swarth** (swôrth). —**swarth′i·ly,** *adv.* —**swarth′i·ness,** *n.*

swash (swosh) *v.t.* to dash (water or other liquid) about; splash. —*v.i.* to strike or wash with a splash, as waves do. —*n., pl.* **swash·es.** the swashing action or sound of water.

at; āpe; fär; câre; end; mē; it; īce; pîerce; hot; ōld; sông, fôrk; oil; out; up; ūse; rüle; pull; tûrn; chin; sing; shop; thin; t͟his; hw in white; zh in treasure. The symbol ə stands for the unstressed vowel sound heard in about, taken, pencil, lemon, and circus.

S

swash·buck·ler (swosh′buk′lər) *n.* a bragging, swaggering adventurer or soldier.

swash·buck·ling (swosh′buk′ling) *adj.* like a swashbuckler.

swas·ti·ka (swos′ti kə) *n.* **1.** a symbol or ornament having the shape of a cross with the arms bent in the center at right angles, used in both ancient and modern times. **2.** this symbol, with the arms bent clockwise, used as an emblem of the Nazi party. [From the Sanskrit word *svastika,* the name for this symbol, from the word *svasti* meaning ''well-being, fortune.'' The swastika is an ancient symbol of good fortune.]

swat (swot) *v.,* **swat·ted, swat·ting.** —*v.t.* to hit (someone or something) with a quick, sharp blow: *to swat a mosquito.* —*v.i.* to hit someone or something with a quick, sharp blow: *to swat at a fly.* —*n.* a short, sharp blow. —**swat′ter,** *n.*

swatch (swoch) *n., pl.* **swatch·es.** a small sample of a particular cloth or other material.

swath (swoth) *also,* **swathe.** *n.* **1.** the area covered by a single sweep of a scythe or other mowing tool or machine. **2.** a width or strip of grass or other grain cut in one such sweep. **3.** a long broad belt, strip, or path: *a swath of color.*

·**to cut a wide swath.** to make a big impression: *The candidate's style cut a wide swath with the audience.*

swathe (swa̱th) *v.t.,* **swathed, swath·ing.** **1.** to bind or wrap: *to swathe an arm with bandages.* **2.** to surround; enclose: *The coast was swathed in fog.* —*n.* a wrapping or binding; bandage.

sway (swā) *v.i.* **1.** to move or swing back and forth or from side to side: *The dancers swayed in time to the music. The trees swayed in the wind.* **2.** to lean or turn to one side: *The car swayed off the road after taking a sharp turn.* —*v.t.* **1.** to cause to move or swing back and forth or from side to side. **2.** to cause to waver or turn aside: *Nothing would sway me from my convictions.* **3.** to cause to be directed or controlled in a certain way; influence: *The speaker swayed the audience with a forceful speech.* —*n.* **1.** the act of swaying. **2.** influence, control, or rule: *The dictator held sway over the entire country.*

sway·back (swā′bak′) *n.* a sagging condition of the back, as of a horse, usually because of overwork.

sway·backed (swā′bakt′) *adj.* having a sagging back.

swear (swâr) *v.,* **swore, sworn, swear·ing.** —*v.i.* **1.** to make a solemn statement with an appeal to God or to some other sacred being or object: *The witnesses in the trial had to swear before they could testify.* **2.** to make a solemn promise. **3.** to use profane language. —*v.t.* **1.** to state (something) solemnly with an appeal to God or some other sacred being or object: *The witness swore the required oath.* **2.** to promise (something) in a solemn manner: *I swear that I'm telling the truth.* **3.** to cause to take an oath; bind by an oath: *to be sworn to defend the country.*

·**to swear by. a.** to name (someone or something) when taking an oath. **b.** to place great confidence in.

·**to swear in.** to bring into office by administering an oath: *The judge swore in the mayor.*

·**to swear off.** *Informal.* to promise to give up: *to swear off a bad habit.*

·**to swear out.** to get (a warrant for arrest) by making a charge under oath.

swear·word (swâr′wûrd′) *n.* a profane word used in cursing or swearing.

sweat (swet) *n.* **1.** a clear, salty fluid formed by glands beneath the skin and given off through the pores of the skin; perspiration: *The runner's shirt was soaked in sweat.* **2.** a moisture given off by something or gathered on its surface by condensation: *a cold pipe covered with sweat.*

3. the act of giving off sweat through the pores of the skin. **4.** *Informal.* an emotional state, such as worry, impatience, or anger: *You needn't get into a sweat over the problem.* —*v.,* **sweat** or **sweat·ed, sweat·ing.** —*v.i.* **1.** to give off sweat through the pores of the skin; perspire. **2.** to gather moisture from the surrounding air by condensation: *The glass of ice water sweated in the hot, humid air.* **3.** *Informal.* to work hard; drudge; toil: *to sweat over a difficult decision.* —*v.t.* **1.** to give off (moisture), as from pores. **2.** to cause to sweat. **3.** to cause to give off moisture. **4.** to get rid of by sweating: *to sweat off several pounds by working in the yard.* **5.** to cause to work hard; overwork: *The supervisor at the factory sweated the workers.*

·**to sweat out.** *Slang.* to wait anxiously or impatiently for: *to sweat out the results of a test.*

sweat·er (swet′ər) *n.* a knitted garment, often of wool, for the upper part of the body.

sweat gland, a small gland beneath the skin that gives off sweat.

sweat·pants (swet′pants′) *n.* loose-fitting pants made of an absorbent material and drawn in at the ankles and waist, used when exercising to prevent chill and induce sweating.

sweat·shirt (swet′shûrt′) *n.* a loose-fitting, absorbent shirt worn during athletic exercise.

sweat·shop (swet′shop′) *n.* a factory or workshop where workers are employed for long hours, at low wages, or under poor conditions.

sweat suit, a suit for exercising, consisting of a sweatshirt and sweatpants.

sweat·y (swet′ē) *adj.,* **sweat·i·er, sweat·i·est.** **1.** covered with, stained with, or smelling of sweat: *sweaty hands, sweaty sneakers.* **2.** causing sweat: *hard, sweaty labor.* —**sweat′i·ly,** *adv.* —**sweat′i·ness,** *n.*

Swede (swēd) *n.* a person who was born in or is a citizen of Sweden.

Swed·ish (swē′dish) *n.* **1.** the people of Sweden as a group. **2.** the language of Sweden. —*adj.* of or relating to Sweden, its people, their language, or their culture.

sweep (swēp) *v.,* **swept, sweep·ing.** —*v.t.* **1.** to clear or clean with a broom, brush, or the like: *to sweep a floor.* **2.** to remove or collect with a broom, brush, or the like: *to sweep bread crumbs up.* **3.** to pass over or through with a swift, continuous movement: *The sailor's eyes swept the horizon for a sign of land.* **4.** to move, bring, or carry with a swift movement: *The flood swept away everything in its path.* —*v.i.* **1.** to clear or clean a surface with a broom, brush, or the like. **2.** to move or pass along with a swift movement: *The wind swept through the trees.* —*n.* **1.** the act of sweeping. **2.** any swift, sweeping movement: *a sweep of the hand.* **3.** a turn, bend, or curve: *the sweep of a dome.* **4.** the reach or range of a sweeping movement: *the sweep of a telescope as it scans the sky.* **5.** a person who sweeps, especially a chimney sweep. **6.** a long oar used to steer or propel a boat or ship. **7.** a victory in every game of a series. **8. sweeps.** see **sweepstakes.**

sweep·er (swē′pər) *n.* a person or thing that sweeps floors or other surfaces.

sweep·ing (swē′ping) *adj.* **1.** moving, passing, or curving over a wide area: *a sweeping arc.* **2.** covering a wide area; extensive: *sweeping reforms.* —*n.* **1. sweepings.** things swept up; trash; rubbish. ▲ used with a plural verb. **2.** the act of a person or thing that sweeps. —**sweep′ing·ly,** *adv.*

sweep·stakes (swēp′stāks′) *n.* **1.** a lottery in which the winners are determined by the running of a horse race. **2.** a horse race run for this purpose. **3.** any lottery or contest. **4.** any of the prizes awarded in a lottery or similar contest. ▲ used with a singular or plural verb.

sweet (swēt) *adj.* **1.** having a taste like that of sugar or honey. **2.** pleasing to the senses: *The flower has a sweet fragrance.* **3.** not sour or salted: *sweet cream, sweet butter.* **4.** having or marked by pleasing, agreeable, or kindly qualities: *a sweet disposition.* —*n.* **1.** a sweet dish, especially a dessert. **2. sweets.** sweet food, such as cake or candy. ▲ used with a plural verb. **3.** a person who is dear; darling. —**sweet′ly,** *adv.* —**sweet′ness,** *n.*

sweet·bread (swēt′bred′) *n.* the pancreas or thymus gland of an animal, especially of a calf or lamb, when used as food.

sweet·bri·er (swēt′brī′ər) *also,* **sweet·bri·ar.** *n.* a rosebush bearing pink flowers and small scarlet fruit. Also, **eglantine.**

sweet corn, a variety of corn with kernels having a high sugar content, grown chiefly for human consumption.

sweet·en (swē′tən) *v.t., v.i.* to make or become sweet or sweeter.

sweet·en·er (swē′tə nər) *n.* something that sweetens, such as sugar or honey.

sweet·en·ing (swē′tə ning) *n.* **1.** something that sweetens; sweetener. **2.** the act or process of making something sweet.

sweet flag, a fragrant plant whose root yields an aromatic oil used in liqueurs and perfumes.

sweet·heart (swēt′härt′) *n.* a person who is loved by and loves another: *They've been sweethearts for years.*

sweet·ish (swē′tish) *adj.* somewhat sweet.

sweet marjoram 1. the dried leaves of a fragrant plant, used as a spice. **2.** the plant bearing these leaves, grown as a garden herb.

sweet·meat (swēt′mēt′) *n.* any sweet food, such as candy, cake, or candied or preserved fruit.

sweet pea 1. a fragrant flower growing in a variety of colors. **2.** the plant bearing this flower, having a rough, hairy stem and pairs of short, oval or oblong leaflets.

sweet pepper 1. the mild-flavored fruit of a kind of pepper plant, usually having a bell shape and eaten in its ripe (red) or unripe (green) state. **2.** the plant bearing this fruit.

sweet potato 1. a fleshy root of a long, trailing vine, having soft orange flesh, cooked and eaten as a vegetable. **2.** the vine bearing this root, widely grown in warm areas throughout the world, having violet or pink flowers.

sweet tooth, a fondness for sweets.

sweet william *also,* **sweet William.** a plant widely grown for its pink, purple, red, and white flowers with fringed petals.

swell (swel) *v.,* **swelled, swelled** or **swol·len, swell·ing.** —*v.i.* **1.** to increase in size: *The sponge swelled as it absorbed the water.* **2.** to bulge out: *The sails swelled in the breeze.* **3.** to increase in amount, degree, intensity, or force: *Attendance swelled at the evening concerts.* **4.** to rise above the ordinary level: *Heavy rains made the river swell.* **5.** *Informal.* to become filled with pride or other emotion: *The victorious general's head swelled with pride.* —*v.t.* **1.** to cause to increase in size; enlarge: *The infection swelled my hand.* **2.** to cause to bulge out: *The wind swelled the sails.* **3.** to cause to increase in amount, degree, intensity, or force: *New members swelled the rolls of the club.* —*n.* **1.** the act of swelling or the state of being swollen. **2.** a part that is swollen. **3.** a piece of land that rises gradually and evenly above the surrounding level. **4.** an unbroken wave or waves; billow; surge. **5.** *Music.* **a.** a gradual increase in volume immediately followed by a gradual decrease. **b.** the sign (<>) indicating this. **6.** *Informal.* a person of high social position, espe-

cially a person who is fashionably dressed. —*adj. Slang.* **1.** excellent; fine. **2.** elegant; stylish.

swell·ing (swel′ing) *n.* **1.** the act or process of increasing, as in size: *the swelling of a river after heavy rains.* **2.** an abnormal enlargement of some part of the body: *The mosquito bite caused a swelling on my arm.*

swel·ter (swel′tər) *v.i.* to sweat or grow tired or weak in great heat; suffer from heat. —*n.* a sweltering condition.

swel·ter·ing (swel′tər ing) *adj.* very hot: *a sweltering summer day.* —**swel′ter·ing·ly,** *adv.*

swept (swept) the past tense and past participle of **sweep.**

swept·back (swept′bak′) *adj.* (of the wings of an aircraft) extending back to form an acute angle with the main part or body of the aircraft.

swerve (swûrv) *v.,* **swerved, swerv·ing.** —*v.i.* to turn aside suddenly: *The car swerved to avoid running into the motorcycle.* —*v.t.* to turn aside: *The driver swerved the truck.* —*n.* the act of swerving.

swift (swift) *adj.* **1.** moving or able to move with great speed; fleet: *a swift runner.* **2.** happening quickly or without delay: *a swift kick.* —*adv.* fast: *to run swift and hard.* —*n.* any of a group of birds resembling swallows, having narrow wings and dark gray, brown, or bluish feathers. —**swift′ly,** *adv.* —**swift′ness,** *n.*

swig (swig) *Informal.* *n.* a large swallow or gulp. —*v.t., v.i.,* **swigged, swig·ging.** to drink in large swallows or gulps. —**swig′ger,** *n.*

swill (swil) *n.* a mixture of liquid and solid food used to feed animals, especially slop fed to swine. —*v.t.* **1.** to drink freely or to excess; guzzle. **2.** to feed (hogs or other animals) with swill.

swim (swim) *v.,* **swam** or **swum, swim·ming.** —*v.i.* **1.** to move along in the water by moving the body or parts of the body. **2.** to float on water or other liquid: *peaches swimming in cream.* **3.** to be covered or flooded with water or other liquid: *The child's eyes swam with tears.* **4.** to have a dizzy feeling; whirl: *All this noise makes my head swim.* —*v.t.* to swim across or through: *to swim a lake.* —*n.* the act, period, or distance of swimming: *a quick swim.* —**swim′mer,** *n.*

swim bladder, another term for **air bladder** (*def. 1*).

swim·mer·et (swim′ə ret′) *n.* one of the appendages on the abdomen of lobsters and many other crustaceans, used for swimming and for carrying eggs.

swim·ming (swim′ing) *n.* the act of a person or thing that swims. *adj.* **1.** of, relating to, or used for swimming or swimmers: *a swimming coach.* **2.** habitually moving in or on the water: *a swimming insect.* **3.** dizzy or lightheaded: *a swimming feeling.*

swim·ming·ly (swim′ing lē) *adv.* very well; smoothly: *The two friends get along swimmingly.*

swimming pool, see **pool**[1] (*def. 2*).

swim·suit (swim′süt′) *n.* a garment worn for swimming; bathing suit.

swin·dle (swin′dəl) *v.t.,* **swin·dled, swin·dling.** to take away money or property rightfully belonging to (someone) by fraud; defraud of money or property: *They tried to swindle people into buying worthless land.* —*n.* the act of swindling; fraud. —**swin′dler,** *n.*

swine (swīn) *n., pl.* **swine. 1.** any of a group of animals, such as the pig or boar, having a long snout, cloven hoofs,

at; āpe; fär; câre; end; mē; it; īce; pîerce; hot; ōld; sông, fôrk; oil; out; up; ūse; rüle; pùll; tûrn; chin; sing; shop; thin; <u>th</u>is; hw in white; zh in treasure. The symbol ə stands for the unstressed vowel sound heard in about, taken, pencil, lemon, and circus.

S

953

and thick, bristly skin. **2.** a stupid, crude, or beastly person.

swine·herd (swīn′hûrd′) *n.* a person who tends swine.

swing (swing) *v.*, **swung**, **swing·ing**. —*v.t.* **1.** to cause to move back and forth with a steady motion. **2.** to cause to turn on or as if on a hinge or pivot: *to swing a door shut.* **3.** to move or lift in a curved, sweeping motion: *to swing a bat at the ball.* **4.** to cause to turn: *to swing a car off the highway onto the dirt road.* **5.** to hang freely: *a lamp that swings on a hook.* **6.** *Informal.* to manage or bring about successfully: *to swing public opinion to one's side.* —*v.i.* **1.** to move back and forth with a steady motion: *The child likes to swing on the hammock.* **2.** to turn on or as if on a hinge or pivot: *The gate swung open. The car swung onto the road.* **3.** to move something in a curved, sweeping motion: *The batter swung at the ball and missed.* **4.** to walk or move freely and rhythmically: *The marching band went swinging down the avenue.* —*n.* **1.** the act of swinging: *the swing of a pendulum.* **2.** the distance covered in swinging: *The pendulum made a long swing.* **3.** a seat hung by ropes or chains in which a person may move back and forth. **4.** a free, rhythmic movement or gait: *There is a swing in the dancer's walk.* **5.** a sweeping blow or stroke: *a swing of an ax.* **6.** a form of jazz developed in the 1930s. —**swing′er,** *n.*

swin·ish (swī′nish) *adj.* like a swine; stupid, crude, or beastly. —**swin′ish·ly,** *adv.* —**swin′ish·ness,** *n.*

swipe (swīp) *n. Informal.* a sweeping stroke or glancing blow: *The cat took a swipe at the ball of yarn.* —*v.t.,* **swiped, swip·ing.** **1.** *Informal.* to hit with a sweeping stroke or glancing blow. **2.** *Slang.* to steal; snatch: *to swipe a pocketbook.*

swirl (swûrl) *v.i.* to move with a circular, twisting motion; whirl: *A gust of wind made the leaves swirl.* —*v.t.* to cause to whirl; twist. —*n.* **1.** a circular, twisting motion. **2.** something having a twisted shape; curl: *We decorated the cake with chocolate swirls.*

swish (swish) *v.i.* to move with or make a soft, muffled sound: *The silk banners swished in the breeze.* —*v.t.* to cause to swish: *The cow stood silently swishing its tail.* —*n., pl.* **swish·es.** a swishing movement or sound: *the swish of a cat's tail.*

Swiss (swis) *n., pl.* **Swiss.** a person who was born in or is a citizen of Switzerland. —*adj.* of or relating to Switzerland, its people, or their culture.

Swiss chard (shärd) a type of beet often grown for its large leaves and fleshy stalks, both of which may be cooked and eaten as a vegetable.

Swiss cheese, a firm, pale yellow cheese having many large holes.

switch (swich) *n., pl.* **switch·es.** **1.** a slender rod, twig, or stick used for whipping. **2.** a stroke or lash given with this: *a switch across the back.* **3.** the act of changing, shifting, or turning aside: *to make a switch from coffee to tea.* **4.** a device used to open or close an electric circuit: *Flick the switch to turn on the lights.* **5.** an apparatus for shifting trains from one track to another. —*v.t.* **1.** to beat, strike, or whip with a switch. **2.** to move or swing suddenly: *The cat switched its tail in anger.* **3.** to change, shift, or turn aside: *to switch channels on the television set.* **4.** to exchange: *The two friends switched coats.* **5.** to connect or disconnect by means of a switch: *to switch the lights on.* **6.** to move (a train) from one track to another; shunt. —*v.i.* to change, shift, or turn aside: *to switch to another class.* —**switch′er,** *n.*

switch·back (swich′bak′) *n.* a road, trail, or railroad track that climbs a steep course in a series of sharp turns or zigzags.

switch·blade (swich′blād′) *n.* a pocketknife with a spring-operated blade that flips out quickly when a button on the side of the handle is pressed.

switch·board (swich′bôrd′) *n.* a control panel with switches or openings for plugs, used to connect or disconnect electric circuits, as for telephone lines.

switch hitter, a baseball player who can bat both left-handed and right-handed.

switch·man (swich′mən) *n., pl.* **switch·men** (swich′-mən). a person in charge of one or more switches on a railroad.

switch·yard (swich′yärd′) *n.* a railroad yard where railroad cars are brought together to form a train, and where trains are switched from one track to another.

swiv·el (swiv′əl) *n.* **1.** a link or other fastening device that allows attached parts to turn freely. **2.** a base or support placed upon a pivot, on which something, such as a chair or stool, can be turned. —*v.,* **swiv·eled, swiv·el·ing;** *also, British,* **swiv·elled, swiv·el·ling.** —*v.i.* to turn on or as if on a swivel: *to swivel around on a piano stool.* —*v.t.* **1.** to turn (something) on or as if on a swivel: *to swivel one's chair around.* **2.** to secure with a swivel.

swivel chair, a chair whose seat revolves on a swivel.

swol·len (swō′lən) *v.* a past participle of **swell.** —*adj.* made larger by or as if by swelling: *a bruised and swollen finger.*

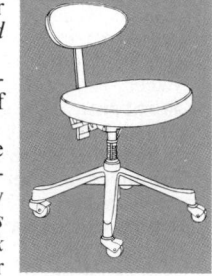

swivel chair

swoon (swün) *v.i.* to lose consciousness briefly; faint. —*n.* the act of swooning.

swoop (swüp) *v.i.* to rush or come down with a sudden, sweeping movement, as a bird diving on its prey (often followed by *down*): *Outlaws swooped down from the hills to attack the stagecoach.* —*v.t.* to seize or remove suddenly; scoop (usually followed by *up*): *The infielder swooped up the ball and threw.* —*n.* the act of swooping: *The cat pounced and caught the mouse in one swoop.*

sword (sôrd) *n.* **1.** a weapon of metal with a hilt and a straight or curved pointed blade, used for thrusting or cutting. **2.** force or the use of force, as in war: *The pen is mightier than the sword* (Edward Bulwer-Lytton). —**sword′like′,** *adj.*

sword·fish (sôrd′fish′) *n., pl.* **sword·fish** or **sword-fish·es.** a large saltwater food and game fish, having a long, flattened, swordlike snout and a streamlined body.

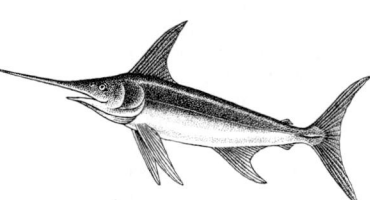

swordfish

sword·play (sôrd′plā′) *n.* the act or technique of using a sword.

swords·man (sôrdz′mən) *n., pl.* **swords·men** (sôrdz′mən). **1.** a person who is armed with a sword, such as a soldier. **2.** a person who is skilled in the use of a sword.

sworn (swôrn) the past participle of **swear.**

swum (swum) the past participle and a past tense of **swim.**

swung (swung) the past tense and past participle of **swing.**

syc·a·more (sik′ə môr′) *n.* **1.** a tree found in eastern North America, having smooth, brown bark that flakes off in thin layers, leaving irregular patches on the trunk. Also, **buttonwood. 2.** a fig tree found in Egypt and Asia Minor, bearing sweet fruit that can be eaten.

syc·o·phant (sik′ə fənt) *n.* a person who flatters powerful or important people as a means of gaining favor or influence. —**syc·o·phan·tic** (sik′ə fan′tik), *adj.*

syl·lab·ic (si lab′ik) *adj.* **1.** of, relating to, or made of a syllable or syllables. **2.** relating to a consonant that forms a separate syllable by itself without the help of a vowel, such as the *l* in *rattle.* —**syl·lab′i·cal·ly,** *adv.*

syl·lab·i·cate (si lab′i kāt′) *v.t.,* **syl·lab·i·cat·ed, syl·lab·i·cat·ing.** to divide into syllables; syllabify. —**syl·lab′i·ca′tion,** *n.*

syl·lab·i·fy (si lab′ə fī′) *v.t.,* **syl·lab·i·fied, syl·lab·i·fy·ing.** to divide into syllables. —**syl·lab′i·fi·ca′tion,** *n.*

syl·la·ble (sil′ə bəl) *n.* **1.** a word or part of a word pronounced with a single uninterrupted sounding of the voice. The words *bit* and *break* have one syllable; the word *amazement* has three. **2.** a letter or group of letters used in writing and printing to represent this, serving to show where a word may be hyphenated at the end of a line.

syl·la·bus (sil′ə bəs) *n., pl.* **syl·la·bus·es** or **syl·la·bi** (sil′ə bī′). a brief summary or outline of something, as a course of study.

syl·lo·gism (sil′ə jiz′əm) *n.* **1.** a form of reasoning having two statements or premises and a conclusion that is logically drawn from them. If the premises are accepted as true, it must follow that the conclusion is true. For example: All dogs have four legs; a collie is a dog; therefore, a collie has four legs. **2.** reasoning based on deduction; deductive reasoning.

sylph (silf) *n.* **1.** a slender, graceful girl or young woman. **2.** an imaginary being supposed to inhabit the air.

syl·van (sil′vən) *also,* **sil·van.** *adj.* **1.** of, located, or living in a wood or woods: *a sylvan deity.* **2.** formed by or filled with trees; wooded; woody: *a sylvan grove.*

sym·bi·o·sis (sim′bī ō′sis, sim′bē ō′sis) *n., pl.* **sym·bi·o·ses** (sim′bī ō′sēz, sim′bē ō′sēz). the close, and often helpful, association of two living beings that are not alike. The association between termites and the protozoans that live in their stomachs and intestines is an example of symbiosis. The protozoans break down the cellulose eaten by the termite so that it can be digested, and the termite, in turn, provides all the protozoans' nourishment. [From the German word *symbiose* from the Greek word *symbiosis* meaning "state of living together," from the word *symbioun* "to live together," from the prefix *syn-* "together" *bios* "life."]

sym·bi·ot·ic (sim′bī ot′ik, sim′bē ot′ik) *adj.* of, relating to, or characterized by symbiosis.

sym·bol (sim′bəl) *n.* **1.** something that stands for or represents something else: *The dove is the symbol of peace. A gold ring is a symbol of marriage.* **2.** a letter or other written figure used to represent something, as in chemistry or mathematics: *C is the symbol for carbon.*

sym·bol·ic (sim bol′ik) *adj.* **1.** serving as a symbol: *The owl is symbolic of wisdom and learning.* **2.** relating to, expressed by, or containing a symbol or symbols: *That poet writes symbolic poetry.* Also, **sym·bol·i·cal** (sim bol′i kəl). —**sym·bol′i·cal·ly,** *adv.*

sym·bol·ism (sim′bə liz′əm) *n.* **1.** the use of symbols, as in art or literature, to represent or express things or ideas. **2.** a system of symbols: *In the symbolism used by the early Christians, the fish represents Christ.*

sym·bol·ist (sim′bə list) *n.* a person who uses or is skilled in the use of symbolism, especially an artist or writer.

sym·bol·ize (sim′bə līz′) *v.,* **sym·bol·ized, sym·bol·iz·ing.** —*v.t.* **1.** to be or serve as a symbol of; represent: *A lily symbolizes purity.* **2.** to represent by a symbol or symbols: *Writing symbolizes the sounds that we make in speaking.* —*v.i.* to use symbols. —**sym′bol·i·za′tion,** *n.*

sym·met·ri·cal (si met′ri kəl) *adj.* having or showing symmetry. See **asymmetrical** for illustration. Also, **sym·met·ric** (si met′rik). —**sym·met′ri·cal·ly,** *adv.*

sym·me·try (sim′i trē) *n., pl.* **sym·me·tries.** **1.** an arrangement of parts that are alike on either side of a central line, as in the structure of a leaf, or around a central point, as in the structure of a starfish. **2.** beauty, proportion, and harmony of form.

sym·pa·thet·ic (sim′pə thet′ik) *adj.* **1.** feeling or expressing sympathy: *a sympathetic friend, a sympathetic statement.* **2.** in agreement with; in favor of: *to be sympathetic to someone's plans.* —**sym′pa·thet′i·cally,** *adv.*

sym·pa·thize (sim′pə thīz′) *v.i.,* **sym·pa·thized, sym·pa·thiz·ing.** **1.** to feel or express compassion: *to sympathize with another's hurt feelings.* **2.** to agree with the feelings, ideas, or aims of; be in accord: *I sympathize with the candidate's efforts for reform.* —**sym′pa·thiz′ing·ly,** *adv.*

sym·pa·thy (sim′pə thē) *n., pl.* **sym·pa·thies.** **1.** the ability to share the feelings of another or others: *The coach has sympathy for his players.* **2.** sorrow for the unhappiness or suffering of another or others: *The newspaper story aroused much sympathy for the victims of the hurricane.* **3.** the state or condition of having the same interests or tastes: *Those friends get along so well because they are in complete sympathy.* **4.** agreement; support: *I am in sympathy with the striking workers.*

sym·phon·ic (sim fon′ik) *adj.* of, relating to, or like a symphony or symphony orchestra.

sym·pho·ny (sim′fə nē) *n., pl.* **sym·pho·nies.** **1.** a composition for an orchestra, usually having three or four movements. **2.** see **symphony orchestra.** **3.** harmony, as of sounds, forms, or colors.

symphony orchestra, a large orchestra for playing symphonies and other compositions, usually having string, brass, woodwind, and percussion sections.

sym·po·si·um (sim pō′zē əm) *n., pl.* **sym·po·si·ums** or **sym·po·si·a** (sim po′ze ə). **1.** a meeting or conference for the discussion of a particular subject. **2.** a collection of opinions or comments on a particular subject, especially a published group of essays or articles.

symp·tom (simp′təm) *n.* **1.** something that indicates or accompanies a disease or other disorder. *A sore throat and runny nose are often symptoms of a cold.* **2.** anything serving as an indication of something: *The disappearance of fish in a river is usually a symptom of water pollution.*

symp·to·mat·ic (simp′tə mat′ik) *adj.* **1.** indicating or accompanying a disease or other disorder: *Repeated coughing may be symptomatic of tuberculosis.* **2.** serving as an indication of something: *A falling barometer is symptomatic of bad weather.* —**symp′to·mat′i·cal·ly,** *adv.*

syn. 1. synonym. **2.** synonymous.

syn·a·gogue (sin′ə gog′, sin′ə gôg′) *n.* **1.** a congregation of Jews assembled for religious instruction and worship. **2.** a building used for such instruction and worship. [From the Old French word *synagoge,* from the Latin Latin word *synagoga,* both meaning "synagogue," from the Greek word *synagōgē* meaning "assembly, synagogue," from the word *synagein* "to bring together,

at; āpe; fär; câre; end; mē; it; īce; pîerce; hot; ōld; sông, fôrk; oil; out; up; ūse; rüle; pu̇ll; tûrn; chin; sing; shop; thin; <u>th</u>is; hw in white; zh in treasure. The symbol ə stands for the unstressed vowel sound heard in about, taken, pencil, lemon, and circus.

S

assemble," from the prefix *syn-* "together" + *agein* "to drive, lead."]

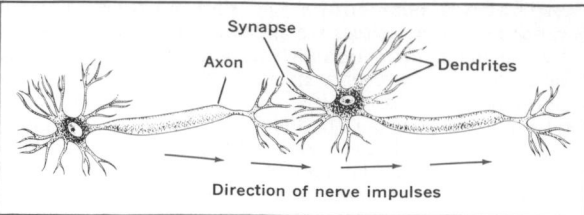

Synapse

Axon

Dendrites

Direction of nerve impulses

synapse

syn·apse (sin'aps, si naps') *n.* the point at which a nerve impulse is transmitted from one nerve cell to another.

syn·chro·nism (sing'krə niz'əm) *n.* the condition or quality of happening at the same time; coincidence.

syn·chro·nize (sing'krə nīz') *v.*, **syn·chro·nized, syn·chro·niz·ing.** —*v.i.* to happen at the same time; coincide: *The closing of the old store synchronized with the opening of the new shopping center.* —*v.t.* **1.** to cause to happen or operate at the same rate and exactly together: *to synchronize the sound and the action of a motion picture.* **2.** to make (timepieces) agree in keeping or indicating time: *The referees synchronized their watches before the game.* —**syn'chro·ni·za'tion,** *n.* —**syn'chro·niz'er,** *n.*

syn·chro·nous (sing'krə nəs) *adj.* **1.** happening at the same time: *synchronous events.* **2.** happening or operating at the same rate of speed: *synchronous gears.* —**syn'chro·nous·ly,** *adv.*

syn·chro·tron (sing'krə tron') *n.* a machine for accelerating subatomic particles, such as protons, to very high speeds by means of a magnetic field. The magnetic field is made stronger as the speed of the particles increases, so as to hold them in a stable orbit.

syn·co·pate (sing'kə pāt') *v.t.*, **syn·co·pat·ed, syn·co·pat·ing.** **1.** *Music.* to treat or modify (a tone or passage) by stressing one or more normally unaccented beats in a measure. **2.** to shorten (a word) by leaving out one or more sounds or letters, such as *sou'wester* for *southwester.*

syn·co·pa·tion (sing'kə pā'shən) *n.* *Music.* the stressing of one or more normally unaccented beats in a measure.

syn·di·cate (*n.*, sin'di kit; *v.*, sin'di kāt') *n.* **1.** a group of persons or companies brought together for a business purpose, especially one requiring a large amount of money. **2.** an organization that sells material, such as special articles and photographs, for publication in a number of newspapers or periodicals at the same time. —*v.*, **syn·di·cat·ed, syn·di·cat·ing.** —*v.t.* **1.** to bring together in order to form a syndicate. **2.** to sell (an article, column, comic strip, or the like) for publication in a number of newspapers or periodicals at the same time. —*v.i.* to form a syndicate. —**syn'di·ca'tion,** *n.*

syn·drome (sin'drōm) *n.* a group of symptoms that together are characteristic of a particular disease or disorder.

syn·fu·el (sin'fū'əl) *n.* a gaseous or liquid fuel manufactured from coal or extracted from other mineral resources.

syn·od (sin'əd) *n.* a council or assembly of church officials. —**syn'od·al,** *adj.*

syn·o·nym (sin'ə nim) *n.* a word that has the same or nearly the same meaning as another word. *Large* is a synonym of *big; leap* is a synonym of *jump.* See **antonym** for further information.

syn·on·y·mous (si non'ə məs) *adj.* being the same or very similar in meaning: *The words "bravery," "valor,"* "gallantry," and "courage" are synonymous. —**syn·on'y·mous·ly,** *adv.*

syn·op·sis (si nop'sis) *n.*, *pl.* **syn·op·ses** (si nop'sēz). a brief statement giving a review or outline of a book, speech, play, or similar work; summary: *The newspaper review of the television program included a synopsis of the story.*

syn·tac·tic (sin tak'tik) *adj.* of, relating to, or according to the rules of syntax. Also, **syn·tac·ti·cal** (sin·tak'ti kəl). —**syn·tac'ti·cal·ly,** *adv.*

syn·tax (sin'taks) *n.* the way in which words are put together to form sentences and phrases; relationship and arrangement of words in a sentence.

syn·the·sis (sin'thə sis) *n.*, *pl.* **syn·the·ses** (sin'thə-sēz'). **1.** the combining of separate parts or elements so as to form a whole. A chemical synthesis is made by combining two or more substances to form a new one. **2.** the whole that is formed in this manner: *The book is a synthesis of the professor's research in three different fields.*

syn·the·size (sin'thə sīz') *v.t.*, **syn·the·sized, syn·the·siz·ing.** **1.** to combine so as to form a whole. **2.** to produce by chemical synthesis: *to synthesize rubber.*

synthesizer *(def. 2)*

syn·the·siz·er (sin'thə sī'zər) *n.* **1.** a person or thing that synthesizes. **2.** an electronic device with a keyboard that can imitate the sounds made by many musical instruments and also produce sounds not obtainable from ordinary instruments.

syn·thet·ic (sin thet'ik) *adj.* **1.** made artificially by chemical synthesis; not occurring naturally; artificial: *Nylon is a synthetic fiber.* **2.** without genuine emotion; not real: *a synthetic smile.* **3.** of, relating to, or having the nature of a synthesis. Also, **syn·thet·i·cal** (sin·thet'i kəl). —*n.* something synthetic: *This fabric is a synthetic.* —**syn·thet'i·cal·ly,** *adv.*

synthetic fuel, see **synfuel.**

syph·i·lis (sif'ə lis) *n.* a serious infectious disease that is caused by a type of spirochete. If not treated properly and quickly, the disease progresses in severity and can damage the heart, blood vessels, spinal cord, eyes, or brain.

syph·i·lit·ic (sif'ə lit'ik) *adj.* of, relating to, or affected with syphilis. —*n.* a person who is affected with syphilis.

sy·phon (sī'fən) another spelling of **siphon.**

Syr·i·an (sîr'ē ən) *n.* a person who was born in or is a citizen of Syria. —*adj.* of or relating to Syria, its people, or their culture.

sy·rin·ga (sə ring'gə) *n.* another word for **mock orange.**

sy·ringe (sə rinj′) *n.* **1.** a device made up of a nozzle and a rubber bulb for drawing in and then forcing out a liquid in a thin stream. Syringes are used especially for injecting fluids into the body and cleansing wounds. **2.** see **hypodermic syringe.** —*v.t.,* **sy·ringed, sy·ring·ing. 1.** to inject (a liquid) with a syringe. **2.** to cleanse (a wound or part of the body) with a syringe: *The doctor syringed my ear canal.*

syringe *(def. 1)*

syr·inx (sir′ingks) *n., pl.* **sy·rin·ges** (sə rin′jēz) or **syr·inx·es. 1.** another word for **panpipe. 2.** the vocal organ of birds.

syr·up (sir′əp, sûr′əp) *also,* **sir·up.** *n.* a sweet, thick liquid, often made by boiling sugar with water or fruit juice. Some syrups contain medication, as for a cough. —**syr′up·like′,** *adj.*

syr·up·y (sir′ə pē, sûr′ə pē) *also,* **sir·up·y.** *adj.* of or like syrup.

sys·tem (sis′təm) *n.* **1.** a group of things or parts related or combined in such a way as to form a whole: *a heating system, a system of roads, a public school system.* **2.** a group of organs or parts of the body that have a similar structure and act together to perform a function: *the digestive system.* **3.** the entire body: *The patient's system was greatly weakened by the long illness.* **4.** a set of facts, rules, laws, beliefs, or principles: *a system of philosophy, a system of government.* **5.** an orderly method.

sys·tem·at·ic (sis′tə mat′ik) *adj.* **1.** of, relating to, or done by a system: *a systematic philosophy of life, a systematic study.* **2.** having an orderly method; methodical: *a systematic person.* Also, **sys·tem·at·i·cal** (sis′tə mat′i kəl). —**sys′tem·at′i·cal·ly,** *adv.*

sys·tem·a·ti·za·tion (sis′tə mə tə zā′shən) *n.* **1.** the act or process of systematizing. **2.** something systematized.

sys·tem·a·tize (sis′tə mə tīz′) *v.t.,* **sys·tem·a·tized, sys·tem·a·tiz·ing.** to form into or arrange according to a system: *to systematize office files.* —**sys′tem·a·tiz′er,** *n.*

sys·tem·ic (sis tem′ik) *adj.* **1.** of or relating to a system or systems. **2.** of, relating to, or affecting the body as a whole: *the systemic circulation of the blood, a systemic infection.*

sys·to·le (sis′tə lē) *n.* the period of contraction of the heart, during which the blood is forced out of the heart or from one chamber of the heart into another. These periods alternate rhythmically with the diastole, or period of relaxation. —**sys·tol·ic** (sis tol′ik), *adj.*

---

at; āpe; fär; câre; end; mē; it; īce; pîerce; hot; ōld; sông, fôrk; oil; out; up; ūse; rüle; pùll; tûrn; chin; sing; shop; thin; this; hw in white; zh in treasure. The symbol ə stands for the unstressed vowel sound heard in about, taken, pencil, lemon, and circus.

S

T t

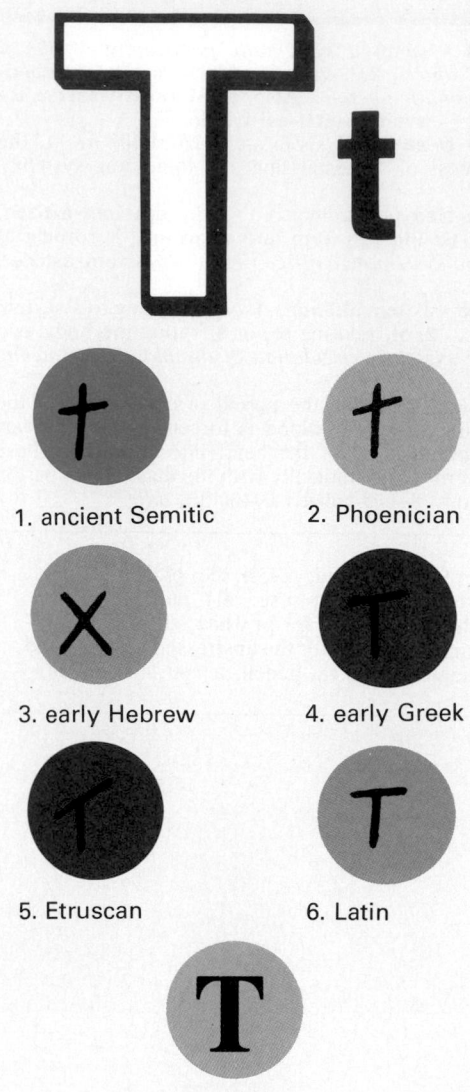

1. ancient Semitic
2. Phoenician
3. early Hebrew
4. early Greek
5. Etruscan
6. Latin
7. English

T is the twentieth letter of the English alphabet. The earliest ancestor of **T** was the letter *taw,* meaning "mark" in the ancient Semitic alphabets (1). The ancient Semitic *taw* and the Phoenician (2) and early Hebrew (3) versions of it were written as either a lower case *x* or *t* is written today. *Taw* was the last letter of these early alphabets. The early Greeks borrowed *taw* and called it *tau* (4). *Tau* was adopted, with only slight changes, in the Etruscan alphabet (5). By the fourth century B.C., the Romans (6) were writing their form of *tau* almost exactly the way we write a capital letter **T** today (7).

t, T (tē) *n., pl.* **t's, T's.** **1.** the twentieth letter of the English alphabet. **2.** something having the shape of this letter.
•**to a T.** perfectly or exactly: *That suit fits you to a T.*
t. **1.** teaspoon; teaspoons. **2.** ton; tons.
T, temperature.
T. **1.** tablespoon. **2.** Territory. **3.** Tuesday.
Ta, the symbol for tantalum.
tab (tab) *n.* **1.** a small flap, strip, or other attachment projecting from an object, used especially as an aid to opening, fastening, or handling: *Pull the tab on the soda can to open it.* **2.** a small extension on a card or the edge of a paper, for use in filing or indexing. **3.** a small ornamental flap or loop on a garment. **4.** *Informal.* a bill to be paid; check: *to pay the tab for a meal in a restaurant.* **5.** see **tabulator** (*def. 1*). —*v.i.,* **tabbed, tab·bing.** to operate a tabulator on a computer or typewriter.
•**to keep tabs on** or **to keep a tab on.** *Informal.* to watch closely; check up on: *The teacher kept tabs on the children in the playground during recess.*
tab·ard (tab'ərd) *n.* a short, loose outer garment resembling a coat, worn by knights over their armor.
Ta·bas·co (tə bas'kō) *n.* *Trademark.* a hot, pungent sauce made from a kind of red pepper.
tab·by (tab'ē) *n., pl.* **tab·bies.** **1.** a domestic cat having a brown or gray coat with dark stripes. **2.** any domestic cat, especially a female. [From the French word *tabis* meaning "striped taffeta," going back to the Arabic word *'attābī* "striped taffeta," from *Al-'Attābīya,* a section of Baghdad where such cloth was first made. Tabby cats were so named because of their stripes.]

tabby *(def. 1)*

tab·er·nac·le (tab'ər nak'əl) *n.* **1.** a place of worship, especially one for a large body of worshipers. **2. Tabernacle.** a portable tent containing the Ark of the Covenant, which was used as a place of worship by the Israelites during their wanderings from Egypt to Palestine. **3.** in the Roman Catholic and some Anglican churches, a container to hold the consecrated host.
ta·ble (tā'bəl) *n.* **1.** a piece of furniture consisting of a flat, horizontal surface supported by one or more legs. **2.** such a table upon which food is served: *The child left the table before the meal was over.* **3.** the food served at a table or any other place: *a lavish table.* **4.** the people seated at a table: *The table next to us was very noisy.* **5.** an orderly arrangement of facts or information, usually in a list: *a table of contents in a book, a table of measurements.* **6.** a tableland; plateau. **7.** a thin, flat slab, as of stone or metal, used especially for writing; tablet. —*v.t.,* **ta·bled, ta·bling.** **1.** to form into a list; tabulate: *to table population figures.* **2.** to postpone discussion or consideration of: *The committee tabled the proposal to close the library on Saturdays.* [From the Old English word *tabule* and the Old French word *table,* both meaning "table" and both from the Latin word *tabula* "board, tablet, list¹."]
•**to turn the tables.** to reverse the situation completely.
•**under the table.** secretly and illegally: *to pay money under the table in return for a politician's support.*
tab·leau (ta blō') *n., pl.* **tab·leaux** (ta blōz') or **tab·leaus.** **1.** a vivid and striking description. **2.** a silent and motionless representation of a scene, painting, or event by a person or persons posed in appropriate costume: *a tableau of the signing of the Declaration of Independence.*
ta·ble·cloth (tā'bəl klôth') *n., pl.* **ta·ble·cloths** (tā'bəl klôthz', tā'bəl klôths'). a cloth for covering a table, especially at meals.

ta·ble d'hôte (tä′bəl dōt′) *n., pl.* **ta·bles d'hôte** (tä′-bəlz dōt′). a complete meal served at a fixed price.

ta·ble·land (tā′bəl land′) *n.* an elevated, flat land area; plateau.

table salt, see salt (*def.* 1).

ta·ble·spoon (tā′bəl spün′) *n.* **1.** a spoon, larger than a teaspoon or dessert spoon, used especially for serving and measuring. **2.** the amount one tablespoon will hold. It is a standard cooking measurement equal to 3 teaspoons, or ½ fluid ounce (14.8 milliliters).

ta·ble·spoon·ful (tā′bəl spün fül′) *n., pl.* **ta·ble·spoon·fuls.** the amount a tablespoon holds; tablespoon.

tab·let (tab′lit) *n.* **1.** a number of sheets of writing paper fastened together at one edge; pad. **2.** a small, flat piece of material, such as medicine, soap, or candy. **3.** a thin, flat slab, as of wood or stone, used for writing or drawing. **4.** a slab of stone or metal bearing an inscription.

table tennis, a game similar to tennis, played on a table with a small plastic ball and wooden paddles. Also, **Ping-Pong.**

ta·ble·ware (tā′bəl wâr′) *n.* articles placed on a table for use at meals, such as dishes, glasses, and silverware.

tab·loid (tab′loid) *n.* a newspaper with pages half the size of an ordinary newspaper page, having brief news articles and many pictures, especially one having stories of a sensational nature. —*adj.* condensed or shortened.

ta·boo (tə bü′, ta bü′) *also,* **ta·bu.** *n., pl.* **ta·boos.** **1.** the system or practice of placing a sacred prohibition on certain things or acts. Among certain Polynesian peoples, it is believed that grave danger, misfortune, or death will come directly to anyone who breaks a taboo. **2.** any prohibition or restriction, especially one set by social custom or convention. —*adj.* **1.** prohibited or restricted under a taboo. **2.** prohibited or forbidden for any reason: *During Prohibition the sale of alcoholic beverages was taboo.* —*v.t.,* **ta·booed, ta·boo·ing.** to put under a taboo; ban; prohibit. [From the Polynesian word *tabu* meaning "sacred" and "set apart."]

ta·bor (tā′bər) *n.* a small drum, especially one formerly used to accompany oneself on a pipe or fife.

tab·u·lar (tab′yə lər) *adj.* **1.** having a broad, flat surface. **2.** of or arranged in lists or tables: *a tabular presentation of facts.*

tab·u·late (tab′yə lāt′) *v.t.,* **tab·u·lat·ed, tab·u·lat·ing.** to arrange in lists or columns; put into a table: *to tabulate statistics.* —**tab′u·la′tion,** *n.*

tab·u·la·tor (tab′yə lā′tər) *n.* **1.** a key on a typewriter or computer, used for arranging material in columns. **2.** a machine that tabulates.

ta·chom·e·ter (ta kom′i tər, tə kom′-i tər) *n.* a device for measuring the speed of rotation of a shaft of an engine. [Formed from the Greek word *tachos* meaning "speed" + the English suffix -*meter*.]

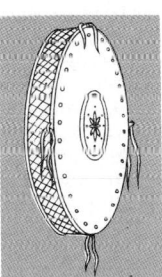

tabor

tac·it (tas′it) *adj.* **1.** not openly expressed but understood or implied: *The principal's smile was tacit approval of our suggestion.* **2.** without words; unspoken; silent: *a tacit prayer.* —**tac′it·ly,** *adv.*

tac·i·turn (tas′i tûrn′) *adj.* not inclined to speak very much; silent or reserved. —**tac′i·tur′ni·ty,** *n.* —**tac′i·turn′ly,** *adv.*

tack (tak) *n.* **1.** a small nail with a sharp point and a broad, flat head. **2.** a sewing stitch that can be easily removed, used in fastening. **3.** a course of action: *We decided to take a new tack in dealing with the problem.* **4.** *Nautical.* **a.** the direction of a ship with respect to the wind. When the wind is on a ship's starboard, or right side, the ship is on a starboard tack. **b.** the change of a ship's direction to take advantage of side winds. **c.** a zigzag course against the wind. **d.** one of a series of movements of a ship in a zigzag course against the wind. **5.** *Nautical.* **a.** a rope holding in place a corner of some sails, as the lower forward corner of a fore-and-aft sail. **b.** a corner so held in place. —*v.t.* **1.** to fasten with a tack or tacks: *The teacher tacked the poster to the wall.* **2.** to sew or fasten with stitches that can be easily removed: *to tack a bow on a dress.* **3.** to add or attach as something extra: *to tack an amendment onto a bill.* **4.** *Nautical.* **a.** to change the course (of a boat or ship) by turning its head to the wind. **b.** to navigate (a boat or ship) against the wind by a series of tacks. —*v.i.* to tack a boat or ship.

tack·le (tak′əl) *n.* **1.** the equipment or gear used for some activity, such as fishing. **2.** a system of ropes and pulleys for hoisting, lowering, or pulling heavy loads, such as those used on a ship to raise, lower, and move the sails. **3.** *Football.* **a.** either of the two players who line up between the guard and the end. **b.** the position played by either of these players. **c.** the act of stopping and bringing a ball carrier to the ground. **4.** the act of seizing, stopping, and bringing to the ground. —*v.t.,* **tack·led, tack·ling.** **1.** to deal with; work on: *How do you think we should tackle this problem?* **2.** to seize and force to the ground in order to stop: *The police officer tackled the fleeing thief.* **3.** *Football.* to bring (a ball carrier) to the ground. —**tack′ler,** *n.*

tackle (*n., def.* 1)

tack·y¹ (tak′ē) *adj.,* **tack·i·er, tack·i·est.** sticky: *tacky paint.* [*Tack* meaning "to attach" + -*y¹*.] —**tack′i·ness,** *n.*

tack·y² (tak′ē) *adj.,* **tack·i·er, tack·i·est.** *Informal.* cheap, dowdy, or shabby: *a tacky dress.* [Of uncertain origin.] —**tack′i·ness,** *n.*

ta·co (tä′kō) *n., pl.* **ta·cos.** a food of Mexican origin consisting of a fried tortilla wrapped around a filling, as of cheese, ground beef, or chicken.

tact (takt) *n.* the ability to deal with people or situations without offending anyone.

at; āpe; fär; câre; end; mē; it; īce; pîerce; hot; ōld; sông, fôrk; oil; out; up; ūse; rüle; püll; tûrn; chin; sing; shop; thin; **th**is; hw in white; zh in treasure. The symbol ə stands for the unstressed vowel sound heard in about, taken, pencil, lemon, and circus.

T

959

tact·ful (takt′fəl) *adj.* having or showing tact: *a tactful secretary, a tactful reply.* —**tact′ful·ly,** *adv.* —**tact′ful·ness,** *n.*

tac·tic (tak′tik) *n.* **1.** a plan of action or any means to achieve a goal. **2.** a method of arranging and using military forces in action. See also **tactics.**

tac·ti·cal (tak′ti kəl) *adj.* **1.** of or relating to tactics, especially military tactics. **2.** characterized by or showing clever planning and maneuvering. —**tac′ti·cal·ly,** *adv.*

tac·ti·cian (tak tish′ən) *n.* a person skilled in tactics.

tac·tics (tak′tiks) *n.* **1.** the art or science of using and maneuvering military forces and equipment in combat. ▲ used with a singular verb. **2.** such use or maneuvering of military forces. **3.** any methods or devices used to achieve a goal: *campaign tactics.* ▲ used with a plural verb in definitions 2 and 3.

tac·tile (tak′təl, tak′tīl) *adj.* **1.** of or relating to touch: *The skin receives tactile sensations.* **2.** having the sense of touch: *The whiskers of a cat are tactile organs.* **3.** capable of being felt by touch; tangible. [Originally from the Latin word *tactilis* meaning "tangible, touchable," from the word *tactus,* past participle of *tangere* "to touch."]

tact·less (takt′lis) *adj.* having or showing no tact; lacking diplomacy: *a tactless comment.* —**tact′less·ly,** *adv.* —**tact′less·ness,** *n.*

tad·pole (tad′pōl′) *n.* a frog or toad in the larval stage when it lives in the water and has gills, a slender tail, and no legs. Also, **polliwog.** [From the Middle English word *taddepol* meaning this animal, from the words *tadde* "toad" + *pol* "head."]

taf·fe·ta (taf′i tə) *n.* a shiny, somewhat stiff fabric, usually woven out of silk or rayon. [From the Old French word *taffetas* meaning "a shiny silk cloth," going back to the Persian word *tāftah* "silken or linen cloth."]

taff·rail (taf′rāl′) *n.* a rail around the stern of a ship.

taf·fy (taf′ē) *n., pl.* **taf·fies.** a chewy candy made of brown sugar or molasses mixed with butter. It is boiled down and then pulled until it holds its shape.

tag¹ (tag) *n.* **1.** a piece of paper, plastic, or other material attached to or hanging loosely from something for the purpose of identifying or labeling it: *a name tag, a price tag.* **2.** a part or piece hanging from or loosely attached to something else. **3.** a hard tip or binding on a string, as at the end of a shoelace. **4.** a saying or quotation used in speech or writing for emphasis, ornament, or effect. —*v.t.,* **tagged, tag·ging.** to attach an identifying tag to: *to tag a suitcase.* [From the Middle English word *tagge* meaning "a tatter, loose piece of cloth," probably of Scandinavian origin.]

·**to tag along.** to follow closely: *The dog tagged along after the children.*

tag² (tag) *n.* **1.** a game in which one player, usually called "it," chases the other players until he or she touches one. The player who is touched then becomes "it" and must chase the others. **2.** *Baseball.* the act of putting out a runner by touching the runner with the ball or with the hand holding the ball. —*v.t.,* **tagged, tag·ging. 1.** to touch or tap, as in the game of tag. **2.** *Baseball.* to put out (a base runner) by touching the runner with the ball or with the hand holding the ball. [Of uncertain origin.]

Ta·ga·log (tä gä′ləg) *n., pl.* **Ta·ga·log** or **Ta·ga·logs. 1.** a member of a Malay people who make up part of the native population of the Philippines. **2.** the language of these people.

Ta·hi·tian (tə hē′shən) *n.* **1.** a person who was born in or is a citizen of Tahiti. **2.** the language of Tahiti. —*adj.* of or relating to Tahiti, its people, their language, or culture.

tai·ga (tī′gə) *n.* any of the northernmost forests of cone-bearing trees in North America, Europe, and Asia.

tail (tāl) *n.* **1.** the hindmost part of an animal's body, especially a flexible part that extends beyond the main part of the body. **2.** anything resembling a tail in shape: *the tail of a comet.* **3.** the rear part of an aircraft. **4.** the rear, bottom, or last part of anything: *the tail of a bicycle.* **5. tails.** the reverse side of a coin. ▲ used with a singular verb. **6. tails.** a man's formal evening wear. ▲ usually used with a plural verb. —*v.t.* **1.** to provide with a tail. **2.** *Informal.* to follow closely and secretly: *The detective tailed the suspect.* —*adj.* at or coming from the rear: *the tail feathers of a bird.* —**tail′less,** *adj.* —**tail′like′,** *adj.*

·**to turn tail.** to run away from danger or trouble.

tail·board (tāl′bôrd′) *n.* another word for **tailgate.**

tail end 1. the rear or hindmost part: *the tail end of a truck.* **2.** the concluding part or end: *the tail end of a meeting.*

tail·gate (tāl′gāt′) *n.* a board, gate, or other closure at the rear of a truck, wagon, station wagon, or other vehicle that can be let down or removed for loading or unloading. —*v.i., v.t.,* **tail·gat·ed, tail·gat·ing.** *Informal.* to drive too closely behind another vehicle.

tail·light (tāl′līt′) *n.* a warning light, usually red, at the rear of a vehicle.

tai·lor (tā′lər) *n.* a person who makes, alters, or mends clothing, especially outer garments. —*v.t.* **1.** to make as a tailor: *to tailor a suit to fit properly.* **2.** to make, alter, or adapt to meet a special requirement or need: *The television program was tailored to the needs of young children.* —*v.i.* to work as a tailor. [From the Old French word *tailleur* meaning "tailor," from the word *taillier* "to cut," going back to the Latin word *talea* "a cutting" or "twig."]

tai·lor·ing (tā′lər ing) *n.* **1.** the workmanship or skill of a tailor. **2.** the business or occupation of a tailor.

tail·piece (tāl′pēs′) *n.* a part or piece that is the end or that is added on at the end.

tail·pipe (tāl′pīp′) *n.* a pipe for carrying and discharging the exhaust gases from an engine, as in an automobile.

tail·race (tāl′rās′) *n.* a channel that carries water away from a waterwheel.

tail·spin (tāl′spin′) *n.* **1.** the rapid, spiraling descent of an airplane, with the nose pointing downward and moving in a smaller circle than the tail. **2.** *Informal.* a sudden plunge into a state of confusion or anxiety.

tail·wind (tāl′wind′) *n.* a wind blowing in the same direction that something, such as an aircraft or ship, is moving.

taint (tānt) *v.t.* to spoil, blemish, or damage: *The lawyer's reputation was tainted by scandal.* —*v.i.* to become tainted; spoil. —*n.* a touch of decay or damage: *The meat had a taint.*

Taj Ma·hal (täzh′mə häl′) a mausoleum of white marble in Agra, India, considered to be one of the most beautiful examples of Islamic architecture.

take (tāk) *v.,* **took, tak·en, tak·ing.** —*v.t.* **1.** to get hold of, as with the hand; grasp: *to take a person's hand, to take a book from a shelf.* **2.** to get possession of: *to take control of a business.* **3.** to bring into one's possession by force; catch; capture: *The invading army took many prisoners.* **4.** to win or earn, as in a contest: *This painting took first prize.* **5.** to subscribe to: *to take a newspaper.* **6.** to choose; select: *Take a card from the deck.* **7.** to occupy: *Please take a seat near the front.* **8.** to carry with one; bring: *We took two suitcases on the trip.* **9.** to move away; remove: *Take the trash to the town dump.* **10.** to remove by death: *The harsh winter took the lives of many settlers.* **11.** to subtract; deduct: *to take 3 from 5.* **12.** to conduct; lead: *This staircase will take you to an exit.* **13.** to use as a means of transportation: *We took the train home.* **14.** to escort: *to take one's date to a* party. **15.** to make use of or find: *The fleeing deer took refuge in the forest.* **16.** to receive into the body, as by swallowing or inhaling: *to take medicine, to take a breath of fresh air.* **17.** to do, perform, or accomplish: *Let's take a walk.* **18.** to undertake or take part in: *to take a test, to take tennis lessons.* **19.** to receive; accept: *Please take my advice.* **20.** to endure; withstand: *Over the years this suitcase has taken a lot of punishment.* **21.** to undergo; suffer: *Our team really took a beating in that game.* **22.** to have a sense of; feel: *to take pride in doing a job well.* **23.** to need; require: *It takes practice to learn how to play the guitar.* **24.** to please or charm; captivate: *to take one's fancy.* **25.** to record by writing: *The secretary took notes at the meeting.* **26.** to make by photography: *to take someone's picture.* **27.** to determine by some special method: *to take attendance, to take a person's temperature.* **28.** *Grammar.* to be used with in a construction: *A transitive verb takes a direct object.* **29.** *Slang.* to swindle; cheat. —*v.i.* **1.** to be effective; work: *The vaccination did not take.* **2.** (of a seed or plant) to begin to grow. —*n.* **1.** the act of taking. **2.** something that is taken. **3.** the amount or quantity taken: *a meager take of fish.* **4.** *Informal.* profit or receipts, as from a show or sporting event. **5.** a portion of a movie, television program, or recording that is photographed or recorded without interruption. ▲ See **bring** for usage note. —**tak′er,** *n.*

•**to take after.** to resemble in appearance, character, or actions: *Do you take after your father or your mother?*
•**to take back.** to retract: *I take back what I just said.*
•**to take down.** to record in writing: *The reporter took down everything that was said.*
•**to take for.** to suppose to be, especially mistakenly.
•**to take in.** **a.** to receive; admit: *to take in boarders.* **b.** to reduce in size; make smaller: *to take in pants around the waist.* **c.** to understand: *to take in the facts.* **d.** *Informal.* to deceive; cheat: *to be taken in by a misleading advertisement.* **e.** to include: *The new county will take in parts of four other counties.* **f.** *Informal.* to go to see: *to take in a movie.*
•**to take it.** to assume; believe: *I take it you're ready to begin.*
•**to take off.** **a.** to remove: *Take off your hat.* **b.** to rise up in flight: *The airplane took off.*
•**to take on.** **a.** to hire; employ: *The farmer took on a new hand.* **b.** to deal with or handle; undertake: *to take on a new responsibility.* **c.** to adopt or acquire; answer: *to take on the likeness of a bird.*
•**to take out.** **a.** to get; obtain: *to take out a loan.* **b.** *Informal.* to escort, as on a date.
•**to take over.** to assume ownership, control, or management of: *to take over a business.*
•**to take to.** **a.** to go to, as for escape: *to take to the hills, to take to one's bed.* **b.** to form a liking for: *to take to a person.*
•**to take up.** **a.** to make shorter or smaller: *to take up a hem.* **b.** to begin learning: *to take up knitting.* **c.** to occupy or consume: *This table takes up too much space.* **d.** to undertake: *to take up a collection.*
•**to take up with.** *Informal.* to become friendly with.
tak·en (tā′kən) the past participle of **take.**
take·off (tāk′ôf′) *n.* **1.** the act of leaving the ground, especially in beginning an airplane flight. **2.** *Informal.* an imitation, usually humorous or satirical; parody.
take-out (tāk′out′) *adj.* relating to or providing food that is to be taken away from the place of sale and eaten elsewhere: *a restaurant with take-out service.* Also, **carry-out.**
take·o·ver (tāk′ō′vər) *n.* the assumption or seizure of ownership, control, responsibility, or authority: *a government takeover of the steel industry.*

tak·ing (tā′king) *adj.* attractive; captivating: *a taking smile.* —*n.* **1.** the act of a person who takes. **2.** *also,* **takings.** something that is taken, especially money or receipts.
talc (talk) *n.* a soft, smooth mineral used in making powders and as an ingredient in ceramics, electrical insulators, paints, and rubber. [From the French word *talc,* from the Arabic word *talq* with the same meaning.]
tal·cum powder (tal′kəm) a fine powder made of white talc, often medicated, used on the face and body. Also, **talcum.**
tale (tāl) *n.* **1.** a story or account of an event or series of events; narrative: *a tale of life at sea.* **2.** a story that is untrue; falsehood.
tale·bear·er (tāl′bâr′ər) *n.* a person who deliberately spreads secrets or rumors. —**tale′bear′ing,** *n.*
tal·ent (tal′ənt) *n.* **1.** a special natural ability or aptitude: *to have musical talent.* **2.** a person or persons having talent: *The director was always looking for new acting talent.* **3.** any of various ancient units of weight and money. [Originally from the Greek word *talanton,* a unit of weight or money. The sense of *talent* as "ability" comes from Jesus' parable of the talents in the gospel of Matthew.]
tal·ent·ed (tal′ən tid) *adj.* having, showing, or characterized by talent: *a talented pianist.*
tal·is·man (tal′is mən) *n., pl.* **tal·is·mans.** **1.** an engraved stone, ring, or other object believed to have magic power to keep away evil and bring good fortune. **2.** anything regarded as having magic power. [From the French word *talisman,* going back to the Greek word *telesma* meaning "consecrated object."]
talk (tôk) *v.i.* **1.** to express ideas or information by means of speech; speak; converse: *Can I talk to you about something?* **2.** to express ideas or information by some other means: *to talk in sign language.* **3.** to consult or confer: *to talk with a doctor.* **4.** to spread rumors; gossip. **5.** *Informal.* to reveal information: *The prisoner refused to talk.* —*v.t.* **1.** to make the subject of one's speech; discuss: *to talk business.* **2.** to use in speaking: *to talk Spanish.* **3.** to bring, persuade, or cause by speech: *We talked them out of leaving.* —*n.* **1.** an expression of ideas in speech; conversation: *The two friends had a long talk.* **2.** an informal speech or lecture: *The professor gave a talk about Africa.* **3.** a formal discussion; conference: *peace talks.* **4.** rumor or gossip: *That story is just idle talk.* **5.** the subject of conversation or gossip: *The new show is the talk of the town.* **6.** *Informal.* a particular way of speaking: *baby talk.*
•**to talk back.** to give a rude reply.
•**to talk down to.** to speak to in a condescending manner.
•**to talk over.** to discuss.
talk·a·tive (tô′kə tiv) *adj.* tending to talk a great deal. —**talk′a·tive·ly,** *adv.* —**talk′a·tive·ness,** *n.*
talk·er (tô′kər) *n.* **1.** a person who talks. **2.** a talkative person.
talk·ing-to (tô′king tü′) *n., pl.* **talk·ing-tos.** *Informal.* a sharp scolding: *That child needs a good talking-to.*
talk show, a television or radio program in which guests are interviewed and often engage in discussions with the host or members of the audience.
tall (tôl) *adj.* **1.** of more than average height; not short

at; āpe; fär; câre; end; mē; it; īce; pîerce; hot; ōld; sông, fôrk; oil; out; up; ūse; rüle; pull; tûrn; chin; sing; shop; thin; **this;** hw in white; zh in treasure. The symbol ə stands for the unstressed vowel sound heard in about, taken, pencil, lemon, and circus.

T

or low: *a tall youngster, a tall tree*. **2.** having a specified height: *to be five feet tall*. **3.** unusually large in amount or degree: *a tall price, a tall order*. **4.** *Informal.* exaggerated so as to be unbelievable: *a tall story*. —**tall′ness,** *n.*

tal·lith (tä′lis, tä lēt′) *n. Judaism.* a shawl worn by Jewish men during prayer services, having fringes at the four corners.

tal·low (tal′ō) *n.* the fat from cattle and sheep, used chiefly for making candles, soap, and margarine.

tal·ly (tal′ē) *n., pl.* **tal·lies. 1.** an account, reckoning, or score. **2.** formerly, a piece of wood with notches that indicated an amount, as of a debt or payment. **3.** anything on which a record or account is kept. —*v.,* **tal·lied, tal·ly·ing.** —*v.t.* to keep or make a count or record: *The grocer tallied up our bill.* —*v.i.* to correspond; agree: *The witness's story of the accident does not tally with the facts.*

tal·ly·ho (tal′ē hō′) *interj.* used by hunters to indicate the sighting of a fox.

Tal·mud (tal′məd, täl′mùd) *n.* the collection of Jewish civil and canonical law.

tal·on (tal′ən) *n.* the claw of a bird or other animal, especially of a bird of prey.

ta·lus (tā′ləs) *n., pl.* **ta·li** (tā′lī). another word for **anklebone.**

tam (tam) *n.* see **tam-o′-shanter.**

ta·ma·le (tə mä′lē) *n.* a food of Mexican origin made of cornmeal, chopped meat, and red peppers, rolled up in cornhusks and cooked. [From the Mexican Spanish word *tamal* meaning this food, from the Nahuatl word *tamalli* "tamale."]

tam·a·rack (tam′ə rak′) *n.* **1.** a North American larch tree valued for its wood. **2.** the wood of this tree, used especially for fence posts, telephone poles, and railroad ties.

tam·a·rind (tam′ə rind′) *n.* **1.** a tropical tree that bears clusters of small, yellow flowers and juicy fruit. **2.** its sharp-tasting fruit, used to make drinks and in foods.

tam·a·risk (tam′ə risk′) *n.* any of a group of shrubs and small trees of western Europe, Africa, and Asia, having tiny leaves and clusters of pink or white flowers.

tam·bou·rine (tam′bə rēn′) *n.* a shallow, one-headed drum having metal disks loosely mounted in the rim, usually played by shaking or by striking with the knuckles.

tame (tām) *adj.,* **tam·er, tam·est. 1.** taken by humans from a state of native wildness and domesticated: *a tame elephant.* **2.** not ferocious, fearful, or shy; gentle: *The deer was tame enough to let us photograph it.* **3.** not lively, forceful, or exciting; dull: *a tame football game.* —*v.,* **tamed, tam·ing.** —*v.t.* **1.** to take from a wild state and make tame: *to tame a wild stallion.* **2.** to bring under control; subdue: *to tame an unruly mob.* —*v.i.* to become tame: *The circus elephants tamed quickly.* —**tame′ly,** *adv.* —**tame′ness,** *n.* —**tam′er,** *n.*

Tam·il (tam′əl) *n., pl.* **Tam·ils** or **Tam·il. 1.** a member of a people living in southern India, Sri Lanka, and Malaysia. **2.** the language of the Tamils.

tam-o′-shan·ter (tam′ə shan′tər) *n.* a soft, woolen cap of Scottish origin, with a wide, flat, circular crown and a fitted headband, often having a pompom in the center. [From *Tam o' Shanter,* hero of the poem "Tam o' Shanter" (1791) by Robert Burns.]

tamp (tamp) *v.t.* **1.** to force or pound down by a series of light blows or taps; pack down: *to tamp dirt around a*

tambourine

new fence post. **2.** to pack (a drilled hole) with sand or dirt after an explosive charge has been placed in the hole.

tam·per (tam′pər) *v.i.* **1.** to interfere or meddle, usually with a harmful effect: *Someone has been tampering with the radio.* **2.** to try to influence or corrupt: *to tamper with a jury.* —**tam′per·er,** *n.*

tam·pon (tam′pon) *n.* a compressed plug of cotton or other absorbent material, especially one used to absorb menstrual flow.

tan (tan) *v.,* **tanned, tan·ning.** —*v.t.* **1.** to make (a hide or skin) into leather by soaking it in tannin or a similar solution. **2.** to make brown by exposure to the sun or a sunlamp: *Long hours in the sun tanned the farmer's face and arms.* **3.** *Informal.* to beat severely. —*v.i.* to become brown by exposure to the sun or a sunlamp. —*n.* **1.** a yellowish brown color. **2.** a brown color given to a person's skin by exposure to the sun or a sunlamp. **3.** tannin or a similar tanning agent. **4.** see **tanbark.** —*adj.,* **tan·ner, tan·nest.** having the color tan.

tan·a·ger (tan′ə jər) *n.* any of various small, brightly colored birds, found chiefly in Central and South America, having a cone-shaped bill.

tan·bark (tan′bärk′) *n.* any bark yielding tannin, as of the oak or hemlock tree. After the tannin has been removed, tanbark is used as a covering, as for circus rings.

tan·dem (tan′dəm) *adv.* one behind the other; in single file: *to march tandem.* —*adj.* arranged or having parts or participants arranged one behind the other: *tandem seats, a tandem bicycle.* —*n.* **1.** a bicycle having two or more seats, handlebars, and sets of pedals, one behind the other. **2.** a team of horses harnessed one behind the other. **3.** a two-wheeled carriage drawn by two or more horses so harnessed.

·in tandem. in a tandem arrangement.

tang (tang) *n.* **1.** a sharp taste, flavor, or odor: *the tang of a crisp, red apple.* **2.** a slight trace or suggestion; hint: *a tang of regret.* **3.** the projecting part of a blade, as of a chisel, file, or sword, to which the handle is fitted.

tan·ge·lo (tan′jə lō′) *n., pl.* **tan·ge·los.** a fruit produced by crossing a tangerine and a grapefruit.

tan·gent (tan′jənt) *adj.* **1.** in contact; touching. **2.** *Geometry.* touching a curve or surface at only one point but not intersecting. —*n.* **1.** *Geometry.* a tangent line, curve, or surface. **2.** *Trigonometry.* (of an acute angle of a right triangle) the ratio of the length of the side opposite the acute angle to the length of the side adjacent to the angle. **3.** an abrupt change in thought, discussion, or course of action; digression: *to go off on a tangent.* [From the Latin word *tangens,* present participle of *tangere* meaning "to touch."]

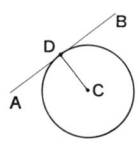

tangent
AB is
tangent
at D

tan·gen·tial (tan jen′chəl) *adj.* **1.** of or relating to a tangent. **2.** not relevant; digressive: *a tangential question.* **3.** only slightly connected. —**tan·gen′tial·ly,** *adv.*

tan·ge·rine (tan′jə rēn′) *n.* **1.** a sweet, juicy, reddish orange citrus fruit having a skin that is easily peeled. **2.** a tree bearing this fruit, widely grown in the United States. **3.** a reddish orange color. —*adj.* having the color tangerine. [Short for *tangerine orange,* the earlier name of this fruit, from the French word *Tanger* meaning "Tangier," the city in Morocco from which this fruit was first imported.]

tan·gi·ble (tan′jə bəl) *adj.* **1.** capable of being touched; perceptible to the touch; material: *A book is a tangible object.* **2.** capable of being measured or appraised for value: *A house and its land are tangible assets.* **3.** capable of being understood or grasped by the mind; definite; real: *tangible proof.* —*n., pl.* **tangibles.** property that can be

ap·praised for value; material assets. —**tan′gi·bil′i·ty,** *n.* —**tan′gi·bly,** *adv.*

tan·gle (tang′gəl) *v.,* **tan·gled, tan·gling.** —*v.t.* **1.** to twist together into a disordered mass; snarl: *The wind tangled my hair.* **2.** to catch or involve in something that hampers, obstructs, or confuses: *The fly was tangled in the spider's web. The heavy rain tangled traffic on the highway.* —*v.i.* **1.** to be or become entangled: *The branches tangled as they grew.* **2.** *Informal.* to fight, quarrel, or argue: *The children tangled over who would go first.* —*n.* **1.** a jumbled, knotted, or twisted mass: *a tangle of yarn.* **2.** a confused or jumbled condition. **3.** *Informal.* a fight or quarrel; argument: *to get into a tangle over whose turn it is.*

tan·go (tang′gō) *n., pl.* **tan·gos.** **1.** a ballroom dance of Latin American origin, characterized by long gliding steps. **2.** the music for such a dance. —*v.i.,* **tan·goed, tan·go·ing.** to dance the tango.

tang·y (tang′ē) *adj.,* **tan·gi·er, tan·gi·est.** having a tang. —**tang′i·ness,** *n.*

tank (tangk) *n.* **1.** a large container for holding a liquid or gas: *an oxygen tank, an oil tank.* **2.** the amount that a tank can hold; tankful: *a tank of gasoline.* **3.** *Military.* a fully enclosed, armored combat vehicle equipped with machine guns and cannon, and moving on continuous metal treads or tracks. —*v.t.* to place, store, or process in a tank.

tank·ard (tang′kərd) *n.* a large drinking cup having a handle and a hinged lid.

tank·er (tang′kər) *n.* a ship, truck, or airplane equipped with tanks for carrying oil or other liquid freight.

tank·ful (tangk′fül′) *n., pl.* **tankfuls.** the amount that a tank can hold.

tank top, a sleeveless upper garment with a wide opening at the neck and wide shoulder straps, similar to the top of a one piece bathing suit.

tan·ner (tan′ər) *n.* a person whose work or business is the tanning of hides.

tan·ner·y (tan′ə rē) *n., pl.* **tan·ner·ies.** a place where hides and skins are tanned and finished as leather.

tan·nic acid (tan′ik) a yellowish or brownish mixture of chemical compounds found in the bark and wood of many trees, used in tanning hides and in the preparation of ink, rubber, and medicine.

tan·nin (tan′in) *n.* **1.** another word for **tannic acid. 2.** any of various other substances used to tan hides.

tan·ning (tan′ing) *n.* the art or process of converting hide or skins into leather.

tan·sy (tan′zē) *n., pl.* **tan·sies.** a strong-smelling plant having yellow flowers and feathery leaves, formerly used in cooking and in medicines.

tan·ta·lize (tan′tə līz′) *v.t.,* **tan·ta·lized, tan·ta·liz·ing.** to tease or torment by tempting with something that is out of reach. [From *Tantalus,* in reference to his punishment.] —**tan′ta·liz′er,** *n.* —**tan′ta·liz′ing,** *adj.* —**tan′ta·liz′ing·ly,** *adv.*

tan·ta·lum (tan′tə ləm) *n.* a heavy, very hard, gray metallic element that has a very high melting point and that resists corrosion. It is used in alloys for missile and aircraft parts and surgical instruments. It is also used in electronic devices. Symbol: **Ta** [From *Tantalus,* a reference to the difficulties the discoverer of this element experienced in trying to dissolve it in acid.]

Tan·ta·lus (tan′tə ləs) *n. Greek Mythology.* a son of Zeus, who served his own son as a meal to the gods. He was punished in Hades by being immersed in water that moved away as he bent down to drink it, and by being surrounded with delicious fruit that rose up beyond his grasp as he reached up to eat it.

tan·ta·mount (tan′tə mount′) *adj.* having as much importance, value, force, or effect; equivalent: *The lack of opposition to the plan was tantamount to acceptance.*

tan·trum (tan′trəm) *n.* an outburst of bad temper or anger.

Tao·ism (tou′iz əm) *n.* one of the principal Chinese religions, characterized by an emphasis on living in harmony with nature and one's fellow human beings.

Tao·ist (tou′ist) *n.* a believer in Taoism. —*adj.* of, relating to, or characteristic of Taoism or Taoists.

tap¹ (tap) *v.,* **tapped, tap·ping.** —*v.t.* **1.** to strike (something) lightly: *to tap someone on the arm.* **2.** to strike lightly and usually repeatedly with: *The teacher tapped a pencil for attention.* **3.** to make, do, or produce by striking lightly and repeatedly: *to tap a beat with one's foot.* —*v.i.* to strike with a light blow or blows: *to tap on a desk with a ruler.* —*n.* **1.** a light or gentle blow: *I felt a tap on my shoulder.* **2.** the sound made by such a blow: *repeated taps of raindrops against a window.* **3.** a piece of metal placed on the heel or sole of a shoe or boot, as for tap-dancing. [From the Old French word *taper* meaning "to strike lightly," of Germanic origin.]

tap² *(v.t., def. 1)*

tap² (tap) *n.* **1.** a device consisting of a valve and a handle that opens or closes it, used to turn on or off a flow of liquid, as from a pipe or keg. **2.** a long peg or plug used to close a hole in a cask or other vessel containing liquid. **3.** a place for connecting electrical devices or additional wires to a flow of current. **4.** a tool screwed into an opening or hole to make internal screw threads. —*v.t.,* **tapped, tap·ping. 1.** to pierce (something) in order to draw liquid from: *to tap the trunk of a sugar maple tree for sap.* **2.** to pull out the tap from (a barrel, cask, or other container). **3.** to draw off (liquid) from a source: *to tap the vinegar in a cask.* **4.** to draw upon or make use of: *We have just begun to tap the vast resources of the oceans.* **5.** to make a connection on in order to draw from (a water, gas, or electric line). **6.** to cut into and connect with secretly, so as to obtain information; wiretap: *to tap a telephone.* [From the Old English word *tæppa* meaning "a valve, tap²."]

·on tap. a. (of a beer or liquor) in a tapped keg or cask and ready to be drawn off and served. **b.** *Informal.* ready for use; available.

---

at; āpe; fär; câre; end; mē; it; īce; pîerce; hot; ōld; sông, fôrk; oil; out; up; ūse; rüle; pùll; tûrn; chin; sing; shop; thin; **th**is; hw in white; zh in treasure. The symbol ə stands for the unstressed vowel sound heard in about, taken, pencil, lemon, and circus.

T

tap–dance (tap′dans′) *v.i.*, **tap-danced, tap-danc·ing.** to perform a tap dance. —**tap′danc′er**, *n.*

tap dance, a dance in which the steps and the rhythm are emphasized by loud taps made by the dancer's foot, toe, or heel.

tape (tāp) *n.* **1.** a long, narrow strip of woven fabric, such as that used to bind seams. **2.** a long, narrow strip of paper, plastic, or other material, coated with a sticky substance for fastening, binding, or repairing. **3.** any long, narrow strip of metal, plastic, paper, or other material. **4.** a strip of material that can be magnetized, on which sound, light, or information can be recorded. Also, **magnetic tape. 5.** a thin strip of string, cloth, or other material stretched across the finish line of a race. —*v.t.*, **taped, tap·ing. 1.** to fasten, bind, or decorate with tape: *to tape a sprained ankle.* **2.** to record on magnetic tape: *to tape an interview, to tape a television program.* **3.** to measure with a tape measure.

tape deck, a device that plays back recorded magnetic tapes and sends the recorded signal to other devices for reproduction. The signal may be reproduced on a video screen or by loudspeakers. Some tape decks can also record signals.

tape measure, a long strip of cloth, plastic, or flexible steel marked with units of length, used for measuring.

ta·per (tā′pər) *v.t.* to make gradually narrower toward one end: *The tailor tapered the trousers.* —*v.i.* **1.** to become gradually narrower toward one end: *The candle tapers to a point.* **2.** to decrease gradually; diminish: *Sales tapered off after the holidays.* —*n.* **1.** a small or slender candle. **2.** a gradual decrease of thickness or width: *the taper of a spire.*

tape–re·cord (tāp′ri kôrd′) *v.t.* to record on magnetic tape.

tape recorder, a device for recording sound on a tape coated with magnetically sensitive material. Most tape recorders are also equipped to play back the sound recorded.

tape recording 1. the act or process of recording sound on magnetic tape. **2.** a tape on which sound has been recorded.

tap·es·try (tap′ə strē) *n.*, *pl.* **tap·es·tries. 1.** a heavy woven fabric decorated with designs or pictures often showing historical or mythological events. Tapestries are used as wall hangings and to cover floors and furniture. **2.** any of various fabrics made to resemble tapestry, used for upholstery and garments.

tape·worm (tāp′wûrm′) *n.* any of a group of flatworms that, in the adult stage, are parasites in the intestines of humans and certain other animals.

tap·i·o·ca (tap′ē ō′kə) *n.* a starchy substance obtained from the root of the cassava plant, used in cooking to make pudding and to thicken sauces and soups. [From either the Portuguese or Spanish word *tapioca* meaning this food, both of which come from an American Indian language spoken along the east coast of South America.]

ta·pir (tā′pər) *n.*, *pl.* **ta·pirs** or **ta·pir.** a large, hoofed animal somewhat like a pig, found in Latin America and southeastern Asia. The tapir has a heavy, rounded body and a short, flexible snout.

tap·room (tap′rüm′, tap′rùm′) *n.* a barroom or tavern.

tapir

tap·root (tap′rüt′, tap′rüt′) *n.* the main downward-growing root of a plant from which other small, branch roots may develop.

taps (taps) *n.* a bugle call regularly played at the end of the day in military camps to indicate that all lights must be turned off, and also sounded at military funerals and memorial services. ▲ used with a singular verb.

tar¹ (tär) *n.* a thick, dark, sticky substance obtained chiefly by the distillation of coal or wood, used widely to pave roads and as a waterproofing material. —*v.t.*, **tarred, tar·ring.** to smear, coat, or cover with tar: *to tar a highway.* [From the Old English word *teoru* meaning "gum, resin, tar¹."] —**tar′like′**, *adj.*
·**to tar and feather.** to pour heated tar over (someone) and then cover with feathers as a punishment.

tar² (tär) *n. Informal.* a sailor. [Short for *tarpaulin*, an earlier term for "sailor."]

tar·an·tel·la (tar′ən tel′ə) *n.* **1.** a lively southern Italian dance, usually performed by a single couple. It was once believed to be a cure for the bite of the tarantula. **2.** the music for such a dance. [From the Italian word *tarantella* meaning "from *Taranto*, Italy," used as the name of this dance.]

ta·ran·tu·la (tə ran′chə lə) *n.*, *pl.* **ta·ran·tu·las** or **ta·ran·tu·lae** (tə ran′chə lē′). any of a group of hairy spiders found chiefly in tropical and semitropical regions. Tarantulas have a bite that is painful but usually not dangerous to humans. [From the Medieval Latin word *tarantula*, from *Taranto*, the city in Italy where these spiders were commonly found.]

tarantula

tar·dy (tär′dē) *adj.*, **tar·di·er, tar·di·est. 1.** coming or happening after the set or appropriate time; late: *The student was punished for always being tardy.* **2.** moving or happening slowly: *We were tardy in making preparations for the trip.* —**tar′di·ly**, *adv.* —**tar′di·ness**, *n.*

tare¹ (târ) *n.* **1.** a kind of vetch grown chiefly as food for livestock. **2.** the seed of this plant. **3.** in the New Testament, a weed harmful to crops. [From the Middle English word *tare.*]

tare² (târ) *n.* a deduction made from the total weight of something sold to allow for the weight of the container. [From the Old French word *tare*, going back to the Arabic word *taraha* meaning "something rejected, thrown away."]

tar·get (tär′git) *n.* **1.** an object that is aimed at in shooting practice and competitions. A padded disk marked with circles is a target used in archery. **2.** anything that is the object of a military attack: *a bombing target.* **3.** a person or thing that is the object of ridicule, criticism, or abuse: *The inexperienced candidate was an easy target for the opposition.* **4.** a person or thing that is the object of an action or effort: *to be the target of an advertising campaign, a business that is the target of a takeover.*

tar·iff (tar′if) *n.* **1.** a list or system of duties or taxes imposed by a government on imports or exports. **2.** a duty or rate of duty so imposed: *a low tariff on cameras.* **3.** any list of rates or prices, as at a hotel. [From the French word *tarif* meaning "rate" or "list of prices," going back to the Arabic word *ta′rīf* "information."]

tarn (tärn) *n.* a small mountain lake or pool.

tar·nish (tär′nish) *v.t.* **1.** to dull the luster of or discolor, as by exposure to air or dirt: *Long exposure to the air tarnished our brass doorknob.* **2.** to stain or disgrace; sully: *The scandal tarnished the family name.* —*v.i.* to become dull or discolored, as by exposure to air or dirt: *The silver will tarnish if left uncovered and exposed to the air.* —*n.* **1.** a coating or surface resulting from tarnishing. **2.** the loss of luster.

ta·ro (tär′ō, tar′ō) *n.*, *pl.* **ta·ros. 1.** a tropical plant of Hawaii and other Pacific islands having a starchy root. **2.** the root of this plant, used to make poi, or cooked and eaten like a potato.

tar pa·per *also* **tar·pa·per** (tär′pā′pər) *n.* heavy paper coated with tar, used especially as a building and waterproofing material.

tar·pau·lin (tär pô′lin, tär′pə lin) *n.* waterproofed canvas or other material, such as nylon, used as a protective covering for boats, athletic fields, or other objects exposed to the weather.

tar·pon (tär′pən) *n., pl.* **tar·pon** or **tar·pons.** a large, silvery game fish found in coastal waters of the Atlantic Ocean and sometimes in fresh water.

tar·ra·gon (tar′ə gon) *n.* **1.** a bushy European plant whose fragrant leaves are used as a seasoning. **2.** the leaves themselves.

tar·ry[1] (tar′ē) *v.i.,* **tar·ried, tar·ry·ing. 1.** to delay in doing something: *We must not tarry if we want to arrive on time.* **2.** to remain in a place; stay: *The tourists tarried a while in Rome before going on to their next stop.* [From the Middle English word *tarien* meaning "to hinder, delay."]

tar·ry[2] (tär′ē) *adj.,* **tar·ri·er, tar·ri·est.** of, like, or covered with tar: *the tarry surface of a road.* [*Tar*[1] + *-y*[1].] —**tar′ri·ness,** *n.*

tar·sal (tär′səl) *adj.* of or relating to the tarsus, or ankle.

tar·si·er (tär′sē ā′) *n.* a tree-dwelling mammal native to the East Indies, having large eyes and ears, long fingers and toes, and a long, thin tail.

tar·sus (tär′səs) *n., pl.* **tar·si** (tär′sī). the ankle, made up of seven small bones in the human being.

tart[1] (tärt) *adj.* **1.** sharp in taste; not sweet; sour: *The unripe apple has a tart flavor.* **2.** sharp in tone or meaning; biting: *a tart remark.* [From the Old English word *teart* meaning "sharp, severe, tart[1]."] —**tart′ly,** *adv.* —**tart′ness,** *n.*

tart[2] (tärt) *n.* a pastry shell containing a filling, such as custard or fruit, with or without a top crust: *We bought apricot tarts at the French bakery.* [From the Old French word *tarte* meaning this pastry.]

tar·tan (tär′tən) *n.* **1.** a plaid woolen fabric woven with one of the distinctive patterns of the Scottish Highland clans. **2.** the plaid pattern itself. **3.** any fabric with a similar design. *adj.* of, like, or made of tartan: *a tartan scarf.*

tar·tar (tär′tər) *n.* **1.** a brownish deposit on the teeth caused by a combination of food particles and various salts. **2.** a substance that collects in wine casks.

Tar·tar (tär′tər) *n.* another word for Tatar.

tartar sauce, a sauce made of mayonnaise and chopped pickles, capers, onions, olives, and the like, served especially with seafood.

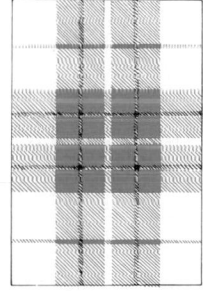

tartan (def. 2)

Tar·ta·rus (tär′tər əs) *n. Greek Mythology.* **1.** a region deep in the underworld where wicked people were punished for their crimes after death. **2.** the land of the dead; underworld.

task (task) *n.* **1.** a piece of work to be done, especially one assigned by one person to another. **2.** a tiring or burdensome job or duty: *Writing that long report was quite a task.* —*v.t.* to put a strain on; burden: *Their constant complaining tasks my patience.* [From the Norman French word *tasque* meaning "tax," "work," or "task," going back to the Medieval Latin word *taxare* "to impose a tax."]

·**to take to task.** to scold; reprimand: *The sergeant took the soldiers in the unit to task for neglecting their duties.*

task force 1. a number of military units brought together under one commander for a particular mission. **2.** any group that is formed or brought together to deal with a particular problem: *a task force on unemployment.*

task·mas·ter (task′mas′tər) *n.* a person who assigns and closely supervises the carrying out of tasks.

tas·sel (tas′əl) *n.* **1.** a hanging ornament made up of a group of threads, cords, or similar materials bound together at one end. **2.** anything resembling this in shape, such as the flower cluster of a corn plant. —*v.,* **tas·seled, tas·sel·ing;** *also, British,* **tas·selled, tas·sel·ling.** —*v.t.* to attach a tassel or tassels to. —*v.i.* (of corn) to put forth tassels.

tassels on a corn plant

taste (tāst) *n.* **1.** the sense by which the flavor of something is perceived or distinguished. **2.** a particular sensation perceived by this sense. The four basic tastes are sweet, bitter, sour, and salty. **3.** a small amount eaten or sampled: *May I have a taste of your salad?* **4.** a brief experience of anything; sample: *The preview gave a taste of what the television series would be like.* **5.** a preference; liking: *That house is not to my taste.* **6.** the ability to recognize and appreciate what is excellent, beautiful, or appropriate: *to have good taste in music.* **7.** the way in which such ability is shown: *to dress in good taste.* —*v.,* **tast·ed, tast·ing.** —*v.t.* **1.** to perceive or distinguish the flavor of (something) by means of the sense of taste: *I can taste the garlic in the sauce.* **2.** to take (something) into the mouth in order to test the flavor; sample: *Taste the soup to see if it needs more pepper.* **3.** to experience, especially briefly or for the first time: *The dictator tasted power only briefly before being overthrown.* —*v.i.* to have a particular flavor: *The sauce tastes too sweet.*

taste bud, any of a cluster of cells located chiefly in the lining of the tongue and mouth and functioning as organs of taste.

taste·ful (tāst′fəl) *adj.* having or showing a good sense of what is excellent, beautiful, or appropriate: *a tasteful outfit.* —**taste′ful·ly,** *adv.* —**taste′ful·ness,** *n.*

taste·less (tāst′lis) *adj.* **1.** without flavor; bland: *tasteless leftovers.* **2.** having or showing little or no sense of what is excellent, beautiful, or appropriate: *a tasteless remark.* —**taste′less·ly,** *adv.* —**taste′less·ness,** *n.*

tast·er (tās′tər) *n.* a person who tastes, especially one who is employed to judge the quality of tea or wine.

tast·y (tās′tē) *adj.,* **tast·i·er, tast·i·est.** pleasing to the sense of taste; flavorful; savory: *a tasty piece of homemade bread.* —**tast′i·ly,** *adv.* —**tast′i·ness,** *n.*

tat (tat) *v.,* **tat·ted, tat·ting.** —*v.t.* to make by tatting. —*v.i.* to make tatting.

Ta·tar (tä′tər) *n.* **1.** a member of the tribes of Mongols and Turks who overran parts of Asia and Europe during the Middle Ages. **2.** a member of a Turkish people descended from them, now living chiefly in parts of the Soviet Union in central and western Asia. **3.** the language of these people. —*adj.* of or relating to the Tatars, their language, or their culture. Also, **Tartar.**

at; āpe; fär; câre; end; mē; it; īce; pîerce; hot; ōld; sông; fôrk; oil; out; up; ūse; rüle; pŭll; tûrn; chin; sing; shop; thin; this; hw in white; zh in treasure. The symbol ə stands for the unstressed vowel sound heard in about, taken, pencil, lemon, and circus.

tat·ter (tat′ər) *n.* **1.** a torn, ragged piece or shred of something: *The sail was ripped to tatters by the wind.* **2. tatters.** torn or ragged clothing: *to be dressed in tatters.* —*v.t.* to tear into pieces or shreds; make ragged.

tat·tered (tat′ərd) *adj.* **1.** hanging or torn in shreds: *a tattered shirt.* **2.** dressed in torn or ragged clothes: *a tattered beggar.*

tat·ting (tat′ing) *n.* **1.** the art or process of making a delicate lace by looping and knotting cotton or linen thread with a special shuttle. **2.** the lace made in this way, used for doilies, collars, and trimmings.

tat·tle (tat′əl) *v.,* **tat·tled, tat·tling.** —*v.i.* **1.** to reveal the secrets, activities, or private affairs of another. **2.** to talk idly; chatter. —*v.t.* to tell or reveal by gossiping. —*n.* idle talk or chatter; gossip. —**tat′tler,** *n.*

tat·tle·tale (tat′əl tāl′) *n. Informal.* a person who deliberately reveals secrets; telltale.

tat·too¹ (ta tü′) *n., pl.* **tat·toos.** **1.** a military signal, as on a bugle, given at night to call soldiers or sailors to return to their quarters. **2.** military exercises given as entertainment. **3.** a rapid, continuous beating or tapping: *the tattoo of rain on a roof.* [From the Dutch word *taptoe* with the same meaning.]

tat·too² (ta tü′) *v.t.,* **tat·tooed, tat·too·ing.** **1.** to mark (the skin) permanently with colored figures or designs, usually by pricking it with a pointed instrument that has been dipped in pigment. **2.** to mark (figures or designs) on the skin in this way. —*n., pl.* **tat·toos.** a figure or design made by tattooing. [Of Polynesian origin.] —**tat·too′er,** *n.*

tau (tou, tô) *n.* the nineteenth letter of the Greek alphabet (T, τ), corresponding to the English letter T, t.

taught (tôt) the past tense and past participle of **teach.**

taunt (tônt) *v.t.* **1.** to mock or reproach with insults or scornful language: *The crowd taunted the team for its poor performance.* **2.** to get or provoke by taunting: *The children taunted the dog into a fit of barking.* —*n.* an insulting or scornful remark.

taupe (tōp) *n.* a dark gray color, tinged with brown, purple, or yellow. —*adj.* having the color taupe.

Tau·rus (tôr′əs) *n.* **1.** a constellation in the northern sky, thought to resemble a bull in shape. **2.** the second sign of the zodiac.

taut (tôt) *adj.* **1.** tightly drawn or stretched; not slack or loose: *The acrobats made sure the tightrope was taut.* **2.** showing tension or strain; tight: *My nerves are taut.* **3.** in good condition; orderly; tidy: *a taut ship.* —**taut′ly,** *adv.* —**taut′ness,** *n.*

tau·tog (tô tôg′) *n.* a fish found in Atlantic coastal waters of the United States, used as food.

tau·tol·o·gy (tô tol′ə jē) *n., pl.* **tau·tol·o·gies.** **1.** the useless repetition of an idea in different words. For example: *Those comments are irrelevant and have nothing to do with the subject.* **2.** a statement that is necessarily true because it includes all possibilities. For example: *Either it will rain tomorrow or it will not.*

tav·ern (tav′ərn) *n.* **1.** a place where alcoholic beverages are sold to be drunk on the premises; bar. **2.** a lodging place or inn.

taw (tô) *n.* **1.** a marble used by a player for shooting in a game of marbles. **2.** the line from which the players shoot in this game.

taw·dry (tô′drē) *adj.,* **taw·dri·er, taw·dri·est.** cheap and gaudy; tasteless; showy: *a tawdry display of wealth.* [From the earlier phrase *tawdry lace,* a kind of cheap necklace sold at a fair celebrating *St. Audrey* (d. A.D. 679).] —**taw′dri·ness,** *n.*

taw·ny (tô′nē) *adj.,* **taw·ni·er, taw·ni·est.** brownish yellow: *The lion has a tawny mane.* —**taw′ni·ness,** *n.*

tax (taks) *n., pl.* **tax·es.** **1.** money that must be paid by people for the support of the government. **2.** a heavy burden or demand; strain: *The long hike was a tax on my*

strength. —*v.t.* **1.** to place or impose a tax on: *The government taxes the income of its citizens.* **2.** to make a heavy demand on; strain: *to tax one's brain trying to solve a problem.* **3.** to reprove or accuse: *to tax someone for being constantly late.*

tax·a·ble (tak′sə bəl) *adj.* subject or liable to taxation: *Most purchases of food are not taxable.*

tax·a·tion (tak sā′shən) *n.* **1.** the act or system of imposing and collecting taxes. **2.** an amount of money raised by taxes.

tax–ex·empt (taks′eg zempt′) *adj.* not subject to taxes.

tax·i (tak′sē) *n., pl.* **tax·is** or **tax·ies.** see **taxicab.** —*v.i.,* **tax·ied, tax·i·ing** or **tax·y·ing.** **1.** to ride in a taxicab: *We taxied to the theater.* **2.** (of an aircraft) to move slowly along the ground or over the surface of water: *The airplane taxied out to the runway before taking off.*

tax·i·cab (tak′sē kab′) *n.* an automobile for public hire, usually having a meter that records the fare to be paid.

tax·i·der·mist (tak′si dûr′mist) *n.* a person whose work or business is taxidermy.

tax·i·der·my (tak′si dûr′mē) *n.* the art of preparing and stuffing the skins of dead animals and mounting them in lifelike positions.

tax·i·me·ter (tak′sē mē′tər) *n.* the meter in a taxicab that shows the fare due.

tax·is (tak′sis) *n., pl.* **tax·es** (tak′sēz). an involuntary movement made by an animal in response to a specific stimulus.

tax·o·nom·ic (tak′sə nom′ik) *adj.* of, relating to, or according to taxonomy.

tax·on·o·my (tak son′ə mē) *n.* **1.** the science of describing, classifying, and naming living things. **2.** the classification of living things on the basis of characteristics they have in common. Taxonomic classification fits an organism into a series of categories ranging from the general to the specific: kingdom, phylum or division, class, order, family, genus, species.

tax·pay·er (taks′pā′ər) *n.* a person who pays or is subject to a tax.

Tay–Sachs disease (tā′saks′). a genetic disease in which the body is unable to make an enzyme that is needed to break down fat. [From the English physician Warren *Tay* (1843–1927) and the American neurologist Bernard *Sachs* (1858–1944), who discovered this disease.]

Tb, the symbol for terbium.

TB, tuberculosis.

T–bill (tē′bil′) *n.* see **Treasury bill.**

T–bone steak (tē′bōn′) a loin steak containing some tenderloin and a T-shaped bone. Also, **T-bone.**

tbs., tablespoon; tablespoons. Also, **tbsp.**

Tc, the symbol for technetium.

Te, the symbol for tellurium.

tea (tē) *n.* **1.** a drink made from the dried and prepared leaves of an Asian shrub. **2.** the dried leaves used to make this drink. **3.** the shrub bearing these leaves, having fragrant, drooping, white flowers, grown mainly in China, Japan, and India. **4.** any of various similar drinks made from the leaves of certain other plants or substances: *sage tea, beef tea.* **5.** *British.* a light meal in the late afternoon, usually consisting of bread and butter, cakes, and similar food served with tea. **6.** a reception or other social gathering, usually occurring in the afternoon, at which tea and other refreshments are served.

tea bag, a small, porous bag of thin paper or cloth, containing shredded or ground tea leaves for soaking in hot water to make tea.

teach (tēch) *v.,* **taught, teach·ing.** —*v.t.* **1.** to give knowledge to, especially through lessons or formal schooling; instruct: *to teach a class of students, to teach someone to play the piano.* **2.** to give lessons or instruction in: *to teach history, to teach swimming.* **3.** to cause or help to learn: *The accident taught me to be more careful.* —*v.i.* to act or be employed as a teacher; give instruction: *My cousin teaches at an elementary school.*

teach·a·ble (tē′chə bəl) *adj.* **1.** capable of being taught: *I don't think common sense is teachable.* **2.** capable of or interested in learning: *The smart dog was very teachable.* —**teach′a·bil′i·ty,** *n.*

teach·er (tē′chər) *n.* a person who teaches, especially as an occupation.

teacher's aide, a person hired to assist the teachers of a school, especially in the classroom.

teach·ing (tē′ching) *n.* **1.** the act, work, or occupation of a teacher. **2.** *also,* **teachings.** something that is taught: *the teachings of a religion.*

tea·cup (tē′kup′) *n.* **1.** a cup in which tea is served. **2.** see **teacupful.**

tea·cup·ful (tē′kup fül′) *n., pl.* **tea·cup·fuls.** the amount that a teacup will hold, usually 4 fluid ounces (118.3 milliliters).

tea·house (tē′hous′) *n., pl.* **tea·hous·es** (tē′hou′ziz). a public place, especially in China and Japan, where tea and other light refreshments are served.

teak (tēk) *n.* **1.** a hard, yellowish brown wood used in shipbuilding and in the manufacture of furniture and flooring. Also, **teakwood.** **2.** a tree bearing this wood, found in Asia, western Africa, and tropical America. It has large, oval leaves and small, white or bluish flowers. [From the Portuguese word *teca* meaning this wood, from *tēkka,* the name for this wood in a language of southwest India.]

tea·ket·tle (tē′kct′əl) *n.* a covered kettle with a spout and handle, used to boil water.

teak·wood (tēk′wùd′) *n.* see **teak** (*def. 1*).

teal (tēl) *n., pl.* **teal** or **teals.** any of several small, short-necked ducks that live in rivers or marshes.

team (tēm) *n.* **1.** a group making up one side in an athletic contest or other competition: *a hockey team, a debating team.* **2.** any group working together in some joint action: *a comedy team, a team of engineers.* **3.** two or more horses or other animals harnessed together, as to pull a wagon or plow. —*v.t.* **1.** to bring or join together in a team: *to team horses.* **2.** to haul or transport by means of a team: *to team logs.* —*v.i.* to work together; form a team (often with *up*): *The children teamed up to collect money for charity.*

teal

team·mate (tēm′māt′) *n.* a fellow member of a team.

team·ster (tēm′stər) *n.* **1.** a person whose work or occupation is driving a truck. **2.** a person whose work or occupation is driving a team of horses or other draft animals.

team·work (tēm′wûrk′) *n.* the cooperative effort or action on the part of a number of people working together, especially to achieve a common goal: *The winners displayed great teamwork.*

tea·pot (tē′pot′) *n.* a pot with a lid, spout, and handle, used for making and serving tea.

tear[1] (târ) *v.,* **tore, torn, tear·ing.** —*v.t.* **1.** to pull apart or into pieces: *to tear a rag in half, to tear one's jacket on a nail, to tear up a sheet of paper.* **2.** to make by tearing: *I accidentally tore a hole in my coat.* **3.** to wound by tearing: *The thorn tore my skin.* **4.** to pull, pluck, or remove by force: *The storm tore many leaves and twigs off the tree.* **5.** to force as if by pulling: *We couldn't tear our eyes away from the movie.* **6.** to disrupt, divide, or split into sides: *The country was torn by civil war.* **7.** to distress greatly; torment: *My mind was torn by doubt.* —*v.i.* **1.** to become torn: *The coat tore on the picket fence.* **2.** to move with great haste or energy: *The children*

tore out of the house. —*n.* **1.** a torn part or place, such as a split or hole: *You should sew the tear in your sleeve.* **2.** the act of tearing. [From the Old English word *teran* meaning "bite, cut, tear[1]."]

·**to tear down.** to take apart; demolish.

·**to tear into.** *Informal.* to attack vigorously.

tear[2] (tîr) *n.* **1.** a drop of the clear, slightly salty fluid that flows from the eye, as in weeping. **2. tears.** the act of weeping: *to burst into tears.* —*v.i.* to shed tears: *The smoky air made my eyes tear.* [From the Old English word *tēar* with the same meaning.]

tear·drop (tîr′drop′) *n.* a single tear.

tear·ful (tîr′fəl) *adj.* **1.** full of or shedding tears; weeping: *tearful eyes.* **2.** causing tears; sad: *a tearful story.* —**tear′ful·ly,** *adv.* —**tear′ful·ness,** *n.*

tear gas (tîr) any of various gases that irritate the eyes, causing a flow of tears and temporary blindness.

tear·jerk·er (tîr′jûr′kər) *n. Slang.* something intended to arouse great sadness or sympathy, especially a very sentimental movie, play, story, or song: *That novel is a real tearjerker.*

tea·room (tē′rüm′, tē′rùm′) *n.* a small room or restaurant where beverages and light meals are served.

tease (tēz) *v.,* **teased, teas·ing.** —*v.t.* **1.** to provoke, annoy, or make fun of playfully or mischievously: *It's cruel to tease an animal.* **2.** to fluff (hair) by combing or brushing in strokes from the end of a strand toward the scalp. **3.** to raise a nap on (cloth). **4.** to separate the fibers of in preparation for spinning: *to tease wool.* —*v.i.* to engage in teasing someone. —*n.* **1.** a person who teases. **2.** the act of teasing.

teas·er (tē′zər) *n.* **1.** a person or thing that teases. **2.** *Informal.* something difficult, puzzling, or annoying: *That arithmetic problem was a real teaser.*

tea·spoon (tē′spün′) *n.* **1.** a spoon that is smaller than a tablespoon or soup spoon, used especially to stir something into a cup of tea or coffee. **2.** the amount one teaspoon will hold, a standard cooking measurement equivalent to ⅓ of a tablespoon, or 1⅓ fluid drams (4.93 milliliters).

tea·spoon·ful (tē′spün fül′) *n., pl.* **tea·spoon·fuls.** the amount that a teaspoon will hold; teaspoon.

teat (tet) *n.* a small projection on the breast or udder, through which milk is drawn; nipple.

tech. **1.** technical. **2.** technology.

tech·ne·ti·um (tek nē′shē əm) *n.* a silver-gray, radioactive metallic element produced artificially from uranium and plutonium and believed to occur naturally in the earth when molybdenum is struck by neutrinos. It was the first element to be made artificially. Symbol: Tc [Formed from the Greek word *technetos* meaning "artificial," going back to the word *technē* "art, craft." The element was created by a special "art," bombarding with atomic particles in a cyclotron.]

tech·nic (tek′nik) *n.* a method of procedure; technique.

tech·ni·cal (tek′ni kəl) *adj.* **1.** relating to, involving, or characteristic of some science, art, profession, or other field: *technical training, the technical language of engineering.* **2.** of or relating to engineering, applied science, or the mechanical or industrial arts: *a technical school.* **3.** of, relating to, or showing technique: *The musician has technical ability but little imagination.* **4.** according to a strict interpretation of rules and principles: *If you really want to be technical, the player should have been dis-*

at; āpe; fär; câre; end; mē; it; īce; pîerce; hot; ōld; sông, fôrk; oil; out; up; ūse; rüle; pùll; tûrn; chin; sing; shop; thin; **th**is; hw in white; zh in treasure. The symbol ə stands for the unstressed vowel sound heard in about, taken, pencil, lemon, and circus.

T

967

qualified altogether, not just penalized. —**tech′ni·cal·ly**, *adv.* —**tech′ni·cal·ness**, *n.*

tech·ni·cal·i·ty (tek′ni kal′i tē) *n., pl.* **tech·ni·cal·i·ties.** **1.** a point or detail, as of law: *The lawyer won the case on a legal technicality.* **2.** the state or quality of being technical.

tech·ni·cian (tek nish′ən) *n.* **1.** a person who is skilled in some science, art, or profession, especially a person trained to deal with specialized equipment or processes: *a medical technician, a lighting technician.* **2.** a person who is skilled in technique, such as a writer, artist, or musician: *That painter is a good technician but lacks originality.*

tech·ni·col·or (tek′ni kul′ər) *n.* **1. Technicolor.** *Trademark.* a process used for filming a motion picture in color by superimposing primary colors to make a final print. **2.** bright, vivid color. —*adj.* strikingly colorful; brilliant; intense.

tech·nique (tek nēk′) *n.* a method or manner of bringing about a desired result in a science, art, sport, or profession: *the techniques of painting, a new technique for recording music.* [From the French word *technique,* going back to the Greek word *technikos* meaning "technical."]

tech·no·log·i·cal (tek′nə loj′i kəl) *adj.* of, relating to, or involving technology: *Sending astronauts to the moon was a great technological achievement.* —**tech′no·log′i·cal·ly,** *adv.*

tech·nol·o·gist (tek nol′ə jist) *n.* a person who specializes in technology.

tech·nol·o·gy (tek nol′ə jē) *n., pl.* **tech·nol·o·gies.** **1.** the use of scientific knowledge for practical purposes, especially in industry: *the contribution of technology to industry.* **2.** the methods, processes, and devices obtained or resulting from such use: *modern technology.* **3.** any use of materials or objects to serve human needs: *computer technology.*

ted·dy bear (ted′ē) *also,* **Ted·dy bear.** a toy resembling a small bear, usually stuffed with soft material and covered with furlike fabric. [From *Teddy,* a nickname of President Theodore Roosevelt (1858–1919). In a political cartoon, Roosevelt was shown sparing the life of a bear cub while hunting.]

Te De·um (tā dā′əm, tē dē′əm) **1.** in the Roman Catholic and Anglican churches, a hymn of praise and thanksgiving sung at morning services or on special occasions. **2.** the music for this hymn. [From the Latin phrase *Te Deum (laudamus)* meaning "Thee, O God (we praise)," the opening words of this hymn.]

te·di·ous (tē′dē əs, tē′jəs) *adj.* causing weariness and boredom because of length, dullness, or the like; boring: *a tedious job.* —**te′di·ous·ly,** *adv.* —**te′di·ous·ness,** *n.*

te·di·um (tē′dē əm) *n.* the state of being tedious.

tee (tē) *n. Golf.* **1.** a small peg of wood, plastic, or other material, on which a golf ball is placed to be driven at the start of play for each hole. **2.** a usually raised area from which a player starts play for each hole. —*v.t.,* **teed, tee·ing.** to place (a golf ball) on a tee.
 ·**to tee off.** to drive a golf ball from a tee.

teem[1] (tēm) *v.i.* to be at the point of overflowing; be full; abound; swarm: *The creek teemed with trout. I'm teeming with ideas for the party.* [From the Middle English word *teemen* meaning "to bring forth," from the Old English word *tīman* "to bring forth offspring."]

teem[2] (tēm) *v.i.* to flow in a stream; pour: *The rain teemed down all day.* [From the Middle English word *temen* meaning "to pour," from the Old Norse word *tœma* "to empty."]

teen (tēn) *adj.* see **teenage.** —*n.* see **teenager.**

teen·age (tēn′āj′) *also,* **teen-age, teen·aged, teen-aged.** *adj.* relating to or characteristic of people in their teens.

teen·ag·er (tēn′ā′jer) *also,* **teen-ag·er.** *n.* a person who is between thirteen and twenty years of age.

teens (tēnz) *pl. n.* **1.** the years from thirteen to nineteen, as of a person's life or a century. **2.** the numbers thirteen to nineteen.

tee·ny (tē′nē) *adj.,* **tee·ni·er, tee·ni·est.** *Informal.* extremely small; tiny. Also, **teen·sy** (tēn′sē).

tee·pee (tē′pē) another spelling of **tepee.**

tee shirt, another spelling of **T-shirt.**

tee·ter (tē′tər) *v.i.* **1.** to walk or move unsteadily and uncertainly, often with a swaying motion, as if about to fall: *The acrobat teetered on the tightrope.* **2.** to move back and forth in an uncertain way; waver: *The country teetered on the brink of war.* —*n.* a teetering movement.

tee·ter–tot·ter (tē′tər tot′ər) *n.* another word for **seesaw** *(def. 1).*

teeth (tēth) the plural of **tooth.**

teethe (tēth) *v.i.,* **teethed, teeth·ing.** to grow or develop teeth; cut one's teeth.

tee·to·tal·er (tē′tō′tə lər) *n.* a person who never drinks alcoholic beverages.

Tef·lon (tef′lon) *n. Trademark.* a chemical polymer that is somewhat slippery and has a surface that does not stick to most substances. It is commonly used as a coating for cooking utensils.

teg·u·ment (teg′yə mənt) *n.* an outer covering.

tel. **1.** telegram. **2.** telegraph. **3.** telephone.

tele– *combining form* **1.** at a distance; far: *telepathy.* **2.** of or relating to television: *telecast.*

tel·e·cast (tel′i kast′) *v.t.,* **tel·e·cast** or **tel·e·cast·ed, tel·e·cast·ing.** to broadcast (a program) by television; televise. —*n.* a program broadcast by television.

tel·e·com·mu·ni·ca·tion (tel′i kə mū′ni kā′shən) *n.* **1.** the sending of messages or other information over long distances by electronic means, as by telegraph, television, or telephone. **2.** a message sent in this way. **3. telecommunications.** the science and technology of telecommunication. ▲ used with a singular verb for definition 3.

tel·e·gram (tel′i gram′) *n.* a message that is sent by telegraph.

tel·e·graph (tel′i graf′) *n.* the system, process, or equipment used for sending messages over a distance with coded electrical impulses. —*v.t.* **1.** to send (a message) by telegraph. **2.** to send a message to by telegraph.

te·leg·ra·pher (tə leg′rə fər) *n.* a person whose work is sending and receiving messages by telegraph.

tel·e·graph·ic (tel′i graf′ik) *adj.* **1.** of, relating to, or sent by telegraph. **2.** like a telegram in style; brief or concise. Also, **tel·e·graph·i·cal** (tel′i graf′i kəl). —**tel′e·graph′i·cal·ly,** *adv.*

te·leg·ra·phy (tə leg′rə fē) *n.* the operation or use of telegraphs to send messages.

tel·e·mar·ket·ing (tel′ə mär′ki ting) *n.* the selling of products or services by telephone.

te·lem·e·ter (tə lem′i tər) *n.* an electronic instrument, as on a spacecraft, for measuring temperature, radiation, or the like, and sending the information to a distant receiving station.

te·lem·e·try (tə lem′i trē) *n.* **1.** the branch of engineering dealing with the measurement of temperature, radiation, or the like, for sending to a distant receiving station. **2.** the process of making physical measurements and relaying the data obtained to a distant receiving station.

tel·e·path·ic (tel′ə path′ik) *adj.* of, relating to, or sent by telepathy. —**tel′e·path′i·cal·ly,** *adv.*

te·lep·a·thy (tə lep′ə thē) *n.* the apparent communication of one mind with another directly, without the use of speaking, writing, or gesturing.

tel·e·phone (tel′ə fōn′) *n.* **1.** an electrical system for sending sound or speech over distances. **2.** an instrument used in such a system, equipped with a transmitter, a receiver, and often a dial or buttons for directing calls. —*v.t.,* **tel·e·phoned, tel·e·phon·ing. 1.** to communicate with by telephone: *I will telephone you tomorrow.* **2.** to send by telephone: *to telephone a message.*

telephones *(n., def. 2)*

telephone book, a book containing an alphabetical list of the names of telephone subscribers, their addresses, and their telephone numbers. Also, **telephone directory.**

telephone number, an identifying number assigned to a telephone, used for making a call to that telephone.

tel·e·phon·ic (tel′ə fon′ik) *adj.* of, relating to, or sent by a telephone.

te·leph·o·ny (tə lef′ə nē) *n.* the science or method of sending messages by telephone.

tel·e·pho·to lens (tel′ə fō′tō) a camera lens that enlarges the image of a distant object.

Tel·e·prompt·er (tel′ə promp′tər) *n. Trademark.* a television set placed before a speaker or performer on which a magnified script is displayed line by line.

tel·e·scope (tel′ə skōp′) *n.* an instrument for making distant objects, such as heavenly bodies, appear nearer and larger. Optical telescopes may use lenses or mirrors in various combinations to produce a magnified image to be viewed or photographed. —*v.t.,* **tel·e·scoped, tel·e·scop·ing. 1.** to drive together or into one another like the tubes of certain telescopes: *The collision telescoped the two railroad cars.* **2.** to make shorter or smaller; condense; abridge; compress: *to telescope a three-volume book into one.*

telescope *(n.)*

tel·e·scop·ic (tel′ə skop′ik) *adj.* **1.** of, relating to, or characteristic of a telescope: *a telescopic lens.* **2.** seen or obtained by means of a telescope: *a telescopic view of a planet.* **3.** visible only through a telescope: *a telescopic galaxy.* **4.** able to see at a great distance; far-seeing. **5.** consisting of parts that can slide into one another, like the tubes of some telescopes. —**tel′e·scop′i·cal·ly,** *adv.*

tel·e·thon (tel′ə thon′) *n.* a long television program during which callers pledge money, as to a charity.

Tel·e·type (tel′i tīp′) *n. Trademark.* communications equipment by which a message typed on one teletypewriter is sent over an electrical circuit to another teletypewriter, which types out the message. —*v.t.,* **tel·e·typed, tel·e·typ·ing.** to send (a message) by teletypewriter.

tel·e·type·writ·er (tel′i tīp′rī′tər) *n.* a keyboard machine that looks like a typewriter, used for receiving and sending messages over an electrical circuit.

tel·e·vise (tel′ə vīz′) *v.t.,* **tel·e·vised, tel·e·vis·ing.** to send by television: *All the major networks televised the president's speech.*

tel·e·vi·sion (tel′ə vizh′ən) *n.* **1.** a system of sending and receiving images and sounds by changing them into signals, which are turned back into picture and sound by the receiving set. **2.** a device in which such images are received and reproduced. **3.** the industry, medium, or art of television broadcasting. —*adj.* of or relating to television.

tel·ex (tel′eks) *n.* **1.** a system for sending and receiving messages using a teletypewriter. **2.** the equipment used in such a system. **3.** a message sent or received in such a system. —*v.t.* **1.** to send (a message) by this system. **2.** to send a telex to (someone).

tell (tel) *v.,* **told, tell·ing.** —*v.t.* **1.** to give a detailed account of; narrate: *to tell a fairy tale to a child.* **2.** to put or express in written or spoken words: *to tell a lie.* **3.** to give information to; let know: *Tell us about your vacation.* **4.** to make known, especially something that is confidential; reveal; disclose: *to tell a secret.* **5.** to give an order, command, or direction to: *to tell someone to be quiet.* **6.** to distinguish; discern; determine: *The jeweler can tell a real diamond from a fake.* —*v.i.* **1.** to give an account: *The old sailors told of their many adventures.* **2.** to reveal something secret; report; inform: *If you misbehave, I'll tell.* **3.** to serve as evidence; be an indication: *Though they said nothing to each other, their eyes told of their love.* **4.** to have or produce an effect: *The strain is beginning to tell.*

·**to tell off.** *Informal.* to scold severely; reprimand.
·**to tell on.** *Informal.* to inform on.

Tell, William (tel) a legendary hero of Swiss independence who was forced to shoot an apple off his son's head with a bow and arrow.

tell·er (tel′ər) *n.* **1.** a person who relates, narrates, or informs: *a teller of tall stories.* **2.** a person who counts. **3.** a person who is employed in a bank and receives or gives out money over a counter.

tell·ing (tel′ing) *adj.* having the intended or desired effect; striking; forceful: *a telling blow, a telling style.* —**tell′ing·ly,** *adv.*

tell·tale (tel′tāl′) *n.* a person who deliberately reveals secrets; tattletale. —*adj.* revealing what is not intended to be known or seen: *A telltale fingerprint unmasked the thief.*

tel·lu·ri·um (te lur′ē əm) *n.* a lustrous, silver-white element having some metallic properties. It is a semiconductor and is used in stainless steel, lead alloys, and ceramics. Symbol: **Te** [Formed from the Latin word *tellus* meaning "the earth."]

te·mer·i·ty (tə mer′i tē) *n.* too much boldness; rashness: *That busybody had the temerity to tell me I was nosy.*

temp. 1. temperature. **2.** temporary.

tem·per (tem′pər) *n.* **1.** a tendency to become angry or

at; āpe; fär; câre; end; mē; it; īce; pîerce; hot; ōld; sông, fôrk; oil; out; up; ūse; rüle; pull; tûrn; chin; sing; shop; thin; this; hw in white; zh in treasure. The symbol ə stands for the unstressed vowel sound heard in about, taken, pencil, lemon, and circus.

T

969

irritated: *to have quite a temper and anger easily.* **2.** an angry state of mind; rage: *to be in a temper after a trying day.* **3.** a usual frame of mind; temperament: *The child has a sunny temper and is seldom cross.* **4.** control over the emotions; self-control; composure: *to lose one's temper.* **5.** the degree of hardness or strength of a substance, especially a metal, given by mixing it with another substance or by treating it in a particular way. —*v.t.* **1.** to lessen the severity or harshness of; moderate; soften: *to temper justice with mercy.* **2.** to bring (a substance) to a proper or desired degree of hardness or strength, by mixing it with another substance or by treating it in a particular way: *to temper steel with heat.*

tem·per·a·ment (tem′pər ə mənt, tem′prə mənt) *n.* the emotional makeup of a person, especially the way a person usually thinks, acts, or responds to other people or to situations: *a calm temperament.*

tem·per·a·men·tal (tem′pər ə men′təl, tem′prə men′təl) *adj.* **1.** showing moodiness, sensitivity, or irritability: *a temperamental actor.* **2.** relating to or caused by temperament: *a child's temperamental outburst.* **3.** not dependable; unpredictable: *a temperamental machine.* —**tem′per·a·men′tal·ly,** *adv.*

tem·per·ance (tem′pər əns, tem′prəns) *n.* **1.** moderation or self-restraint of any kind. **2.** the practice of drinking alcoholic beverages moderately or not at all.

tem·per·ate (tem′pər it, tem′prit) *adj.* **1.** characterized by temperance in behavior. **2.** generally free from extremes of temperature: *a temperate climate.* —**tem′per·ate·ly,** *adv.* —**tem′per·ate·ness,** *n.*

Temperate Zone, either of the two zones of the earth characterized by a temperate climate with four distinct seasons. One zone lies north of the equator between the Arctic Circle and the Tropic of Cancer, the other south of the equator between the Tropic of Capricorn and the Antarctic Circle.

tem·per·a·ture (tem′pər ə chər, tem′prə chər) *n.* **1.** the degree of heat or coldness of a body or substance as measured by a thermometer or other graduated scale. **2.** *Informal.* an abnormally high body temperature; fever: *I have a temperature, so I am staying home today.*

tem·per·a·ture–hu·mid·i·ty index (tem′pər ə chər–hū mid′i tē, tem′prə chər hū mid′i tē) a value computed from measurements of atmospheric temperature and humidity, intended to represent the degree of comfort or discomfort caused by the combination of the two.

tem·pered (tem′pərd) *adj.* **1.** having a particular disposition. ▲ used in combination: *an even-tempered person.* **2.** treated so as to have the desired degree of hardness or strength: *tempered steel.* **3.** changed or softened by the addition of some other substance or quality; lessened.

tem·pest (tem′pist) *n.* **1.** a violent windstorm, usually accompanied by rain, hail, snow, or thunder. **2.** any violent commotion or disturbance; tumult.

tem·pes·tu·ous (tem pes′chü əs) *adj.* characteristic of a tempest; turbulent; violent; stormy: *tempestuous winds, a tempestuous mob.* —**tem·pes′tu·ous·ly,** *adv.* —**tem·pes′tu·ous·ness,** *n.*

tem·plate (tem′plit) *also,* **tem·plet.** *n.* **1.** a pattern or gauge used as a guide in bringing a piece of a work to a desired shape. **2.** a short piece of stone or timber used to receive and distribute pressure, as of a beam or girder.

tem·ple[1] (tem′pəl) *n.* **1.** any building dedicated to the worship of a god or gods. **2. Temple.** any of three buildings built at different times in Jerusalem as the center of Jewish worship. **3.** see **synagogue** (def. 2). [From the Old English word *tempel* and the Old French word *temple,* both with the same meaning and both from the Latin word *templum* meaning "a sanctuary, shrine."]

tem·ple[2] (tem′pəl) *n.* the flattened part on either side of the forehead, above the cheekbone and in front of the ear. [From the Old French word *temple* with the same meaning, going back to the Latin word *tempora* "the temples of the head."]

tem·plet (tem′plit) *n.* another spelling of **template.**

tem·po (tem′pō) *n., pl.* **tem·pos** or **tem·pi** (tem′pē). **1.** *Music.* the relative speed at which a musical composition, movement, or passage is or should be played. **2.** a characteristic pace or speed: *the fast tempo of life in a modern city.*

tem·po·ral[1] (tem′pər əl) *adj.* **1.** of or relating to time. **2.** lasting for a short time; temporary: *the temporal beauty of youth.* **3.** of or relating to this life on earth; material; worldly: *temporal pleasures.* **4.** not religious; secular; civil; lay: *spiritual and temporal power.* [From the Latin word *temporalis* meaning "of time" or "temporary," from the word *tempus* "time."]

tem·po·ral[2] (tem′pər əl) *adj.* of, relating to, or near one or both temples of the head. [From the Late Latin *temporalis* with the same meaning, from the Latin word *tempora* "the temples[2]."]

tem·po·rar·y (tem′pə rer′ē) *adj.* lasting, existing, or used for a limited time only; not permanent: *a temporary shelter, a temporary job.* [From the Latin word *temporarius* meaning "lasting a brief time," from the word *tempus* "time."]

tem·po·rize (tem′pə rīz′) *v.i.,* **tem·po·rized, tem·po·riz·ing.** **1.** to delay or put off immediate action or decision, so as to avoid arguments or gain time. **2.** to change one's acts or opinions in order to fit the time or circumstances.

tempt (tempt) *v.t.* **1.** to try to persuade (someone) to do something that is sinful, illegal, or foolish. **2.** to cause (someone) to think of doing or to want to do something: *Hunger tempted the refugee to steal food.* **3.** to attract strongly; lure: *The unappetizing food didn't tempt us.* **4.** to act in a reckless or bold way toward; provoke; defy: *to tempt fate.*

temp·ta·tion (temp tā′shən) *n.* **1.** the act of tempting or the state of being tempted. **2.** something that tempts: *The rich food was a temptation for the dieter.*

tempt·er (temp′tər) *n.* a person who tempts.

tempt·ing (temp′ting) *adj.* producing temptation; attractive: *a tempting offer.* —**tempt′ing·ly,** *adv.*

tempt·ress (temp′tris) *n., pl.* **tempt·ress·es.** a woman who tempts.

tem·pu·ra (tem pŭr′ə) *n.* a Japanese dish made with shrimp, other seafood, vegetables, or combinations of these ingredients, dipped in batter and fried in deep fat.

ten (ten) *n.* **1.** the cardinal number that is one more than nine. **2.** a symbol representing this number, such as 10 or X. **3.** something having this many units or things, such as a playing card. —*adj.* numbering one more than nine.

ten·a·ble (ten′ə bəl) *adj.* capable of being held, maintained, or defended: *a tenable situation, a tenable theory.* —**ten′a·bil′i·ty,** *n.* —**ten′a·bly,** *adv.*

te·na·cious (tə nā′shəs) *adj.* **1.** holding firmly: *a tenacious grip.* **2.** tending to stick to another substance; adhesive: *Tar is tenacious.* **3.** not easily pulled or broken apart: *It was hard to plow the tenacious soil.* **4.** stubborn; obstinate: *a tenacious person.* **5.** tending to retain: *a tenacious memory.* —**te·na′cious·ly,** *adv.* —**te·na′cious·ness,** *n.*

te·nac·i·ty (tə nas′i tē) *n.* the state or quality of being tenacious.

ten·an·cy (ten′ən sē) *n., pl.* **ten·an·cies.** **1.** the occupancy of property for which rent is paid; state of being a tenant. **2.** the period of time during which a tenant occupies property. **3.** the property occupied by a tenant.

ten·ant (ten′ənt) *n.* **1.** a person who pays rent to occupy or use the property of another, such as land, a house, apartment, or office. **2.** an occupant or inhabitant of any place: *the present tenant of the White House.* —*v.t.* to hold or occupy as a tenant; inhabit.

Word Family

English contains many words that can be traced back to the Latin verb *tenere,* meaning "to hold." A person who rents an apartment is a **tenant,** "holding" a place to live or work. A teacher who **obtains** a position in a university **continues** research until receiving **tenure.** Sometimes teachers send students to **detention** after school in order to **maintain** discipline. A **lieutenant** is the officer who "holds the place" of a superior officer and acts on that officer's behalf. Television may **entertain** us for a few hours, but it does not **contain** all that is necessary to **sustain** us throughout our lives. Many people have **tenets** they believe in deeply and often hold on to them **tenaciously.** Large land masses that are "held together" are called **continents.**

tenant farmer, a farmer who works land owned by another and pays rent in cash or with a share of the crops.

ten·ant·ry (ten′ən trē) *n., pl.* **ten·ant·ries. 1.** all the tenants of an estate or other property. **2.** the state of being a tenant; tenancy.

Ten Commandments, the ten rules for living and for worshiping that God presented to Moses on Mount Sinai in the Bible.

tend[1] (tend) *v.i.* **1.** to be likely or apt: *My cat is fat because it tends to overeat. They tend to be optimistic.* **2.** to lead to some state or condition: *The difficult negotiations seem to be tending toward collapse.* **3.** to move, extend, or be directed in a particular direction: *The path tends toward the left around the tree.* [From the Middle English word *tenden* meaning "to be inclined towards," from the Old French word *tendre* "to stretch in a certain direction," from the Latin word *tendere* "to stretch, extend" or "to be inclined toward."]

tend[2] (tend) *v.t.* **1.** to take care of the needs of; care for; watch over: *to tend a sick person, to tend crops.* **2.** to be in charge of or work at; manage or operate: *to tend a machine, to tend a store.* —*v.i. Informal.* to give heed; pay attention: *tend to an important matter, tend to one's business.* [Short for *attend.*]

tend·en·cy (ten′dən sē) *n., pl.* **tend·en·cies.** a natural or usual inclination: *to have a tendency to make friends easily. My car's engine has a tendency to stall.*

ten·der[1] (ten′dər) *adj.* **1.** soft or delicate; not tough or hard: *tender beef.* **2.** not hardy, robust, or strong; fragile: *the tender petals of a flower.* **3.** having the delicacy of youth; fresh; immature: *Three is a tender age.* **4.** not rough; light; gentle: *a tender touch.* **5.** showing or characterized by warmth of feeling; kind or loving; affectionate: *tender memories.* **6.** very sensitive; easily hurt; sore: *My arm was still tender after the cut healed.* **7.** sensitive to the feelings of others; sympathetic; compassionate: *a tender heart.* **8.** requiring careful, tactful handling or treatment: *a tender subject.* [From the Old French word *tendre* with the same meaning, from the Latin word *tener* "soft, delicate, tender[1]."] —**ten′der·ly,** *adv.* —**ten′der·ness,** *n.*

ten·der[2] (ten′dər) *v.t.* **1.** to present formally; offer: *to tender one's resignation from a job.* **2.** *Law.* to offer in payment of a debt, claim, or other obligation. —*n.* **1.** a formal offer: *a tender of marriage, a tender to purchase shares of a company's stock.* **2.** something that is offered, especially money offered in payment of a debt, claim, or other obligation. [From the Old French word *tendre* meaning "to stretch in a certain direction," from the Latin

word *tendere* "to stretch, extend" or "to be inclined toward."]

ten·der[3] (ten′dər) *n.* **1.** a person who cares for, attends to, or manages someone or something. **2.** a small boat or ship that is used to serve a large vessel, as by carrying supplies or passengers between the vessel and the shore. **3.** a railroad car that is attached to the rear of a steam locomotive, used to carry fuel and water. [*Tend*[2] + *-er*[1].]

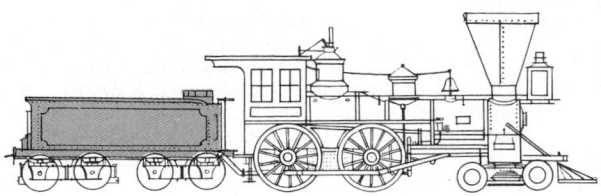

tender[3] *(def. 3)*

ten·der·foot (ten′dər fŏŏt′) *n., pl.* **ten·der·foots** or **ten·der·feet** (ten′dər fēt′). **1.** a person who is a newcomer to ranch or frontier life of the West, and is unused to the hardships or rough conditions of such life. **2.** any inexperienced person; novice. **3. Tenderfoot.** a boy who is in the lowest rank of the Boy Scouts.

ten·der-heart·ed (ten′dər här′tid) *adj.* easily moved to pity, love, or sorrow; compassionate; sympathetic. —**ten′der-heart′ed·ly,** *adv.* —**ten′der-heart′ed·ness,** *n.*

ten·der·ize (ten′də rīz′) *v.t.,* **ten·der·ized, ten·der·iz·ing.** to make (meat) tender, as by pounding, marinating, or applying a tenderizer.

ten·der·iz·er (ten′də rī′zər) *n.* any substance put on meat to make it tender.

ten·der·loin (ten′dər loin′) *n.* the tenderest part of the loin of beef, pork, or other meat.

ten·don (ten′dən) *n.* a strong cord or band of tissue that attaches a muscle to a bone or other part of the body.

ten·dril (ten′drəl) *n.* **1.** a thin, leafless, often spirally coiling part by which a climbing plant, such as the grape, twines around or clings to a tree trunk, wall, or other object for support. **2.** something resembling this: *wispy tendrils of hair.*

ten·e·ment (ten′ə mənt) *n.* **1.** an apartment building or rooming house that is poorly built or maintained and usually overcrowded, especially one that is located in a slum. **2.** any house or building to live in, especially one that is rented or intended for rent. **3.** a room or set of rooms occupied by a tenant as a separate dwelling.

ten·et (ten′it) *n.* a doctrine, principle, or belief held to be true by an individual or group.

ten·fold (ten′fōld′) *adj.* **1.** ten times as great or numerous. **2.** having or consisting of ten parts. —*adv.* so as to be ten times greater or more numerous.

ten-gal·lon hat (ten′gal′ən) a wide-brimmed felt hat with a high crown, worn especially in the southwestern United States.

Tenn., Tennessee.

Tennessee Valley Authority, see TVA.

ten·nis (ten′is) *n.* **1.** a racket game in which two or four

at; āpe; fär; câre; end; mē; it; īce; pîerce; hot; ōld; sông, fôrk; oil; out; up; ūse; rüle; pùll; tûrn; chin; sing; shop; thin; this; hw in white; zh in treasure. The symbol ə stands for the unstressed vowel sound heard in about, taken, pencil, lemon, and circus.

T

971

players hit a light, fabric-covered rubber ball back and forth over a low net stretched across the center of a level, rectangular court of grass, clay, concrete, or other material. **2.** any of several similar and related games.

ten·on (ten′ən) *n.* a projecting part on the end of a timber or other piece of wood cut so as to fit into a corresponding hole, or mortise, in another piece to form a joint. —*v.t.* **1.** to cut a tenon in (a piece of wood). **2.** to join (two pieces of wood) with a tenon and mortise joint.

ten·or (ten′ər) *n.* **1.** a general or usual tendency, course, or direction: *the quiet tenor of country life.* **2.** the general meaning or effect of something spoken or written; drift: *The sad tenor of your letter worried me.* **3.** *Music.* **a.** a male singing voice with a range that is higher than baritone and lower than countertenor. **b.** a singer who has such a voice. **c.** a musical instrument that has a similar range. **d.** a musical part for such a voice or instrument. —*adj. Music.* **1.** able to sing or play, or designed to play, the tenor: *a tenor voice, a tenor saxophone.* **2.** for the tenor.

ten·pin (ten′pin′) *n.* **1. tenpins.** the game of bowling. ▲ used with a singular verb. **2.** a pin used in this game.

tense¹ (tens) *adj.*, **tens·er, tens·est. 1.** stretched or drawn tight; strained; taut: *tense muscles.* **2.** undergoing or showing mental or emotional strain: *a tense individual, a tense look.* **3.** characterized by or causing strain or suspense: *a tense situation, a tense scene in a movie.* —*v.t., v.i.,* **tensed, tens·ing.** to make or become tense: *The cat tensed at the sudden noise.* [From the Latin word *tensus,* past participle of *tendere* "to stretch, extend" or "to be inclined toward."] —**tense′ly,** *adv.* —**tense′ness,** *n.*

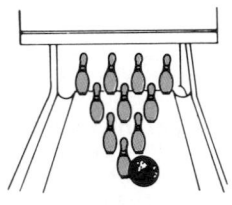
tenpins

tense² (tens) *n.* **1.** a form of a verb that shows the time of its action or state of being. *We sit* is in the present tense. *We sat* is in the past tense. *We will sit* is in the future tense. **2.** a set of such forms for a particular tense. The present tense of the verb *go* is: *I go, you go, he, she, or it goes, we go, you go, they go.* [From the Middle English word *tens* meaning "time" or "tense²," from the Old French word *tens* with the same meanings, from the Latin word *tempus* "time."]

ten·sile (ten′səl) *adj.* **1.** of or relating to tension: *the tensile strain on a rope, the tensile strength of steel.* **2.** capable of being stretched: *a tensile metal.*

ten·sion (ten′shən) *n.* **1.** the act of stretching or the state of being stretched. **2.** mental or emotional strain. **3.** any strained state or relationship: *tension between nations.*

ten·sor (ten′sər, ten′sôr) *n.* any muscle that stretches or tenses a part of the body.

tent (tent) *n.* **1.** a collapsible, portable shelter, usually of canvas, supported by one or more poles and fastened by cords attached to pegs in the ground. **2.** anything that resembles this in form or use. —*v.i.* to live or camp in a tent; encamp.

ten·ta·cle (ten′tə kəl) *n.* **1.** any of various long, slender, flexible growths on the head or about the mouth of certain animals, used for feeling, grasping, and moving. An octopus has eight tentacles. **2.** something resembling a tentacle: *a city government held in the tentacles of a corrupt mayor.* **3.** *Botany.* a sensitive, hairlike growth on the leaves of some plants.

ten·ta·tive (ten′tə tiv) *adj.* **1.** made, done, or proposed as a trial or experiment; not definite or final: *tentative plans, a tentative proposal for a class project.* **2.** showing

hesitancy or uncertainty: *a tentative smile.* —**ten′ta·tive·ly,** *adv.* —**ten′ta·tive·ness,** *n.*

tent caterpillar, any of a group of destructive caterpillars that spin large, tentlike, silken webs in the branches of trees.

ten·ter (ten′tər) *n.* a framework or machine on which cloth is stretched so as to dry evenly without shrinking. —*v.t.* to stretch (cloth) on a tenter.

ten·ter·hook (ten′tər hůk′) *n.* a sharp hooked nail used for fastening cloth on a tenter.

·**on tenterhooks.** in a state of suspense or anxiety.

tenth (tenth) *adj.* **1.** (the ordinal of ten) next after the ninth. **2.** being one of ten equal parts. —*n.* **1.** something that is next after the ninth. **2.** one of ten equal parts; 1/10. —*adv.* in the tenth place.

ten·u·ous (ten′ū əs) *adj.* **1.** thin or delicate; slender, as a thread. **2.** having little strength, substance, or importance; weak; flimsy: *a tenuous argument.* —**ten′u·ous·ly,** *adv.* —**ten′u·ous·ness,** *n.*

ten·ure (ten′yər) *n.* **1.** the act or right of holding or possessing something, such as property, a title, or office. **2.** the length of time during which something is held: *The tenure of the presidency is four years.* **3.** the terms under which something is held. **4.** the status of permanent position that is granted to an employee, such as a teacher or civil servant, after specified requirements are fulfilled.

te·pee (tē′pē′) *also,* **tee·pee.** *n.* a cone-shaped tent, usually of animal skins, used by North American Indians, especially the Plains Indians.

tep·id (tep′id) *adj.* moderately or slightly warm; lukewarm: *tepid water.* —**tep′id·ly,** *adv.* —**tep′id·ness,** *n.*

ter·bi·um (tûr′bē əm) *n.* a very soft, silver-gray, metallic element of the rare-earth group. It is used in lasers. Symbol: **Tb** [From the letters *-terb-* in the name *Ytterby,* the Swedish town where it was discovered.]

tepee

term (tûrm) *n.* **1.** a word or phrase having an exact meaning in some particular field: *legal terms, scientific terms.* **2.** any word or phrase used in an exact sense: *"Darling" is a term of affection.* **3. terms.** a particular manner of speaking or the kind of language used: *to answer the question in vague terms.* **4.** a definite or limited period of time; time during which something lasts: *the term of a lease, a term of office.* **5.** a division of a school year: *the spring term.* **6. terms.** a relationship between people: *to be on good terms with someone.* **7. terms.** the conditions according to which something is to be done: *the terms of a peace treaty.* **8.** *Mathematics.* **a.** each of the quantities that make up a fraction or ratio, or form a series or progression. **b.** each of the quantities connected by plus or minus signs in an algebraic expression. —*v.t.* to apply a particular term to; name; designate: *to term someone reliable, to term an event a disaster.*

·**to come to terms.** to reach an agreement: *The two sides came to terms and the strike was ended.*

ter·ma·gant (tûr′mə gənt) *n.* a loud, quarrelsome, scolding woman; shrew. —*adj.* quarrelsome or scolding.

ter·mi·na·ble (tûr′mə nə bəl) *adj.* capable of being ended: *a terminable contract.* —**ter′mi·na·ble·ness,** *n.*

ter·mi·nal (tûr′mə nəl) *adj.* **1.** at, forming, or coming at the end, end part, or boundary of something: *a terminal flower on a stem, the terminal payment on a loan.* **2.** ending in death: *a terminal disease.* —*n.* **1.** an end part; end. **2.** the point on an electric circuit where a connection can be made. **3.** a device for making such a connection. **4.** a station at either end of a railroad, bus, air, or other transportation line. **5.** a device or combination of devices used with a computer to enter, retrieve, or edit information, such as a keyboard and monitor. [From the Latin word *terminalis* meaning "of the end," from the word *terminus* "end" or "limit."]

ter·mi·nate (tûr′mə nāt′) *v.*, **ter·mi·nat·ed, ter·mi·nat·ing.** —*v.t.* **1.** to bring to an end; put an end to: *to terminate a marriage by divorce.* **2.** to come at the end of; form the conclusion of: *A song terminated the ceremony.* **3.** to form the boundary of; bound; limit: *The river terminates the property.* —*v.i.* to come to an end: *The show terminates at eleven o'clock.* —**ter′mi·na′tion,** *n.*

ter·mi·nol·o·gy (tûr′mə nol′ə jē) *n., pl.* **ter·mi·nol·o·gies.** the terms or system of terms used in an art, science, trade, or other specialized subject: *legal terminology, the terminology of chemistry.*

ter·mi·nus (tûr′mə nəs) *n., pl.* **ter·mi·nus·es** or **ter·mi·ni** (tûr′mə nī′). **1.** a point or place at which something comes to an end; end or goal. **2.** either end of a railroad, bus, air, or other transportation line.

ter·mite (tûr′mīt) *n.* any of a group of insects that live in colonies, having whitish bodies and dark heads. Termites feed on wood, paper, and other organic material, causing great damage to buildings, furniture, and some crops. Also, **white ant.**

tern (tûrn) *n.* a web-footed seabird closely related to the gull, but having a more slender body, narrow wings, a deeply forked tail, and, usually, white and gray feathers, with a black patch on the head.

tern

terr., territory.

ter·race (ter′is) *n.* **1.** a balcony of a house or apartment building. **2.** an open, usually paved or tiled area next to a house, used for lounging, outdoor cooking or dining, and parties. **3.** a raised, level platform of earth with a vertical or sloping front or side, especially one of a series of such levels placed one above the other. **4.** a group of houses or apartments built on a raised or sloping area of land. **5.** a street on which such a row of houses or apartments faces. **6.** the flat roof of a house, especially an Oriental or Spanish house. —*v.t.*, **ter·raced, ter·rac·ing.** to form into or provide with a terrace or terraces: *to terrace a hillside.*

ter·ra cot·ta (ter′ə kot′ə) **1.** a hard, durable, brownish orange earthenware used especially for vases, statuettes, or as a facing for buildings. **2.** something made of this substance. **3.** a brownish orange color. —*adj.* **1.** having the color terra cotta; brownish orange. **2.** made of terra cotta: *a terra cotta figurine.*

ter·ra fir·ma (ter′ə fûr′mə) solid ground; dry land.

ter·rain (tə rān′, te rān′) *n.* a region or tract of land, especially with regard to its natural features or suitability for some special purpose, such as farming: *hilly terrain, rocky terrain.*

ter·ra·pin (ter′ə pin′) *n.* any of a group of North American turtles found in fresh or partly salt water, especially the diamondback. The flesh of the terrapin is often eaten as food.

ter·rar·i·um (tə râr′ē əm) *n., pl.* **ter·rar·i·ums** or **ter·rar·i·a** (tə râr′ē ə). a small enclosure or container, often of glass, used for growing plants or raising small land animals, such as snakes, turtles, or lizards.

ter·res·tri·al (tə res′trē əl) *adj.* **1.** of, relating to, or representing the earth: *terrestrial magnetism, a terrestrial globe.* **2.** relating to or consisting of land, as distinct from water or air: *the terrestrial areas of the world.* **3.** growing in the ground or land: *a terrestrial plant.*

4. living on land, rather than in the air, water, or trees: *The deer is a terrestrial animal.* **5.** of or relating to this world; worldly; earthly. —**ter·res′tri·al·ly,** *adv.*

ter·ri·ble (ter′ə bəl) *adj.* **1.** causing terror or awe; dreadful; awful: *The volcano erupted with a terrible roar.* **2.** very violent or severe; causing great distress or pain: *a terrible automobile accident.* **3.** *Informal.* very bad or unpleasant: *terrible food.* **4.** *Informal.* very great; excessive: *a terrible bore.* [From the Middle French word *terrible* meaning "causing terror or awe," from the Latin word *terribilis* with the same meaning, from the word *terrēre* "to frighten."] —**ter′ri·ble·ness,** *n.* —**ter′ri·bly,** *adv.*

ter·ri·er (ter′ē ər) *n.* any of various lively, rugged, usually small dogs having a smooth or wiry coat, such as the fox terrier or Scottish terrier. Terriers were originally used to hunt animals that burrow in the ground, but are now kept chiefly as pets.

terrier (fox terrier)

ter·rif·ic (tə rif′ik) *adj.* **1.** *Informal.* unusually great, intense, or severe: *terrific pain, a terrific hardship.* **2.** *Informal.* extremely good; excellent; wonderful: *That's a terrific idea.* **3.** causing great fear or dread; terrifying; dreadful. —**ter·rif′i·cal·ly,** *adv.*

ter·ri·fy (ter′ə fī′) *v.t.*, **ter·ri·fied, ter·ri·fy·ing.** to fill with terror; frighten or alarm greatly. —**ter′ri·fy′ing·ly,** *adv.*

ter·ri·to·ri·al (ter′i tôr′ē əl) *adj.* **1.** of, relating to, or belonging to land or territory: *That country has made territorial claims.* **2.** relating to or restricted to a particular district or region: *a territorial government.* **3.** *also,* **Territorial.** relating to a territory of the United States. —**ter′ri·to′ri·al·ly,** *adv.*

territorial waters, coastal and inland waters under the jurisdiction of a state or nation, traditionally ocean waters within 3 miles (4.8 kilometers) of shore but now generally ocean waters within 12 miles (19.3 kilometers) or 200 miles (322 kilometers) for economic development for nations.

ter·ri·to·ry (ter′i tôr′ē) *n., pl.* **ter·ri·to·ries.** **1.** any large area of land; region: *unexplored territory, territory held by an enemy.* **2.** land and waters under the jurisdiction of a state, nation, or ruler: *The Yukon is a territory of Canada.* **3.** a district or area assigned to a salesperson or agent. **4.** a field or sphere of action, thought, or interest: *Agriculture and horticulture cover some of the same territory.* **5.** formerly, a part of the United States not having the status of a state but having its own legislature. Hawaii was a territory of the United States until 1959. **6.** *Zoology.* a particular area, such as a breeding or nesting ground, in which one or more animals live and from which they keep out intruders of the same or other species.

ter·ror (ter′ər) *n.* **1.** an overpowering or intense fear. **2.** a person or thing that causes intense fear: *The cruel dictator was a terror to the people.* **3.** *Informal.* an annoying or troublesome person or thing, especially a child.

---

at; āpe; fär; câre; end; mē; it; īce; pîerce; hot; ōld; sông, fôrk; oil; out; up; ūse; rüle; pŭll; tûrn; chin; sing; shop; thin; this; hw in white; zh in treasure. The symbol ə stands for the unstressed vowel sound heard in about, taken, pencil, lemon, and circus.

T

ter·ror·ism (ter′ə riz′əm) *n.* the use of terror, violence, or threats of violence to intimidate or frighten a people into submission.

ter·ror·ist (ter′ər ist) *n.* a person who uses or approves of terrorism. —*adj.* of, relating to, or characteristic of terrorism or terrorists: *terrorist methods.* Also, **ter·ror·is·tic** (ter′ə ris′tik).

ter·ror·ize (ter′ə rīz′) *v.t.,* **ter·ror·ized, ter·ror·iz·ing.** 1. to fill with extreme fear; overcome with terror: *The sight of the fox terrorized the chickens.* 2. to control, rule, or force through the use of terror: *to terrorize hostages into submission.* —**ter′ror·i·za′tion,** *n.*

ter·ry cloth (ter′ē) a fabric having uncut loops on both sides, especially a highly absorbent cotton cloth, used chiefly for towels and robes.

terse (tûrs) *adj.,* **ters·er, ters·est.** brief and to the point; concise: *a terse reply.* —**terse′ly,** *adv.* —**terse′ness,** *n.*

ter·tian (tûr′shən) *adj.* recurring every other day. —*n.* a tertian fever or ague.

Ter·ti·ar·y (tûr′shē er′ē) *n.* the first geological period of the Cenozoic era, during which high mountain systems, such as the Alps, Rockies, and Himalayas, were formed and modern mammals and plants appeared. —*adj.* 1. of, relating to, or characteristic of this period. 2. **tertiary.** third in rank, order, or place.

test (test) *n.* 1. a set of questions, problems, or exercises intended to determine a person's knowledge, skill, or intelligence: *a spelling test.* 2. any method or means of determining the nature, genuineness, or quality of something: *a blood test, a swimming test. Their friendship has withstood the test of time.* 3. *Chemistry.* a procedure for detecting the presence of an ingredient in a substance or determining what the substance is: *a test for carbon dioxide.* —*v.t.* 1. to subject to a test of any kind; give a test to; try: *to test a class, to test a car, to test a person's loyalty.* 2. to subject to a chemical test. —*v.i.* to take or give a test: *to test for a job, to test for acidity.* —**test′er,** *n.*

Test., Testament.

tes·ta·ment (tes′tə mənt) *n.* 1. in law, a will, especially one disposing of personal property. ▲ now used chiefly in the phrase *last will and testament.* 2. **Testament.** either of the two main divisions of the Christian Bible; Old Testament or New Testament.

tes·ta·men·ta·ry (tes′tə men′tə rē) *adj.* 1. relating to a will or the administration or settlement of a will. 2. given by or contained in a will: *The estate was disposed of according to the deceased's testamentary instructions.* 3. done in accordance with a will.

tes·tate (tes′tāt) *adj.* having made or left a legally valid will.

tes·ta·tor (tes′tā tər) *n.* a person who has died and left a legally valid will.

test ban, an agreement among nations not to test nuclear weapons, especially in the atmosphere.

tes·tes (tes′tēz) the plural of **testis.**

tes·ti·cle (tes′ti kəl) *n.* one of the pair of male reproductive glands in humans and most other animals, producing sperm and male sex hormones and enclosed in a scrotum in most mammals; testis. [From the Latin word *testiculus* meaning "a testicle," from the word *testis* "witness (of masculinity)" or "testicle."]

tes·ti·fy (tes′tə fī′) *v.,* **tes·ti·fied, tes·ti·fy·ing.** —*v.i.* 1. to give evidence under oath in a court of law: *The witness testified during the trial.* 2. to serve as evidence; be proof: *Possession of the stolen goods testified to the defendant's guilt.* 3. to bear witness: *I will testify to your honesty.* 4. to express a personal belief, especially the belief that one has been saved through the grace of God. —*v.t.* to declare under oath in a court of law: *The witness testified that the defendant owned the gun.*

tes·ti·mo·ni·al (tes′tə mō′nē əl) *n.* 1. a letter or statement affirming the superior character or quality of some-one or something; recommendation: *The satisfied customer gave a testimonial for the product.* 2. something given or done to show respect, admiration, or appreciation: *The retiring employee was given a watch as a testimonial for years of service.* —*adj.* relating to or being a testimonial: *a testimonial dinner.*

tes·ti·mo·ny (tes′tə mō′nē) *n., pl.* **tes·ti·mo·nies.** 1. a statement made under oath by a witness in a court of law, usually in answer to questioning by a lawyer. 2. proof or demonstration; evidence: *The farmer's rugged hands were testimony of years of hard work.* 3. an open declaration of one's faith.

tes·tis (tes′tis) *n., pl.* **tes·tes.** a testicle.

tes·tos·ter·one (tes tos′tə rōn′) *n.* a hormone produced by the testes that controls the development of male sexual characteristics, such as beard growth, muscle development, and deepening of the voice. [From the words *test(is)* + *ster(ol)* (as used in such words as *cholesterol*) + the scientific suffix *-one* meaning a particular kind of compound.]

test pilot, a pilot who tests new or experimental aircraft.

test tube, a thin transparent glass tube closed at one end, used in chemical and biological experiments.

test–tube baby (test′tūb′, test′tūb′) a baby conceived by the union of an ovum and sperm outside the body in a laboratory. The fertilized ovum is later placed inside the mother's uterus to develop normally.

tes·ty (tes′tē) *adj.,* **tes·ti·er, tes·ti·est.** showing or characterized by irritability; impatient or cross: *a testy patient.* —**tes′ti·ly,** *adv.* —**tes′ti·ness,** *n.*

tet·a·nus (tet′ə nəs) *n.* an acute, often fatal, disease caused by the toxin of a certain bacillus that usually enters the body through a puncture wound. Tetanus is characterized by violent spasms and stiffness of certain muscles, especially those of the neck and jaw. Also, **lockjaw.**

tete-à-tête (tāt′ə tāt′) *n.* a private or intimate conversation between two people. —*adv.* (of two people) together in private: *to dine tête-à-tête.* —*adj.* for or between two people in private; intimate: *Their dinner was a tête-à-tête affair.* [From the French phrase *tête-à-tête* meaning "head to head."]

teth·er (teth′ər) *n.* a rope or chain used to fasten a horse, donkey, or other animal so that it is confined within certain limits. —*v.t.* to fasten or confine with a tether: *to tether a horse to a tree.*

·**at the end of one's tether.** at the end or limit of one's resources, patience, or endurance.

tetra– or **tetr-** *combining form* four: *tetrameter.*

te·tram·e·ter (te tram′i tər) *n.* 1. a line of verse consisting of four metrical feet. 2. a verse composed of such lines. —*adj.* containing four metrical feet.

Teu·ton (tū′tən, tū′tən) *n.* 1. a member of an ancient tribe that lived in parts of what is now northern Germany. 2. a member of any of several groups of northern European peoples, including the Germans, Dutch, Scandinavians, and English. 3. a person who was born in Germany or who is of German descent; German.

Teu·ton·ic (tū ton′ik, tū ton′ik) *adj.* 1. of or relating to the ancient Teutons. 2. of or relating to any of the Teutons of northern Europe, their languages, or cultures. 3. of or relating to Germany or the Germans; German. 4. of or relating to the Germanic family of languages. —*n.* another word for **Germanic.**

Tex., Texas.

text (tekst) *n.* 1. the main body of matter on a written or printed page, as distinguished from headings, illustrations, notes, or appendixes. 2. the original or actual words of a writer or speaker. A text is often changed slightly when it is revised, condensed, or translated. 3. a short passage or verse from the Bible, quoted or used as the subject of a sermon. 4. any subject on which one writes or speaks; theme; topic. 5. see **textbook.**

text·book (tekst'bùk') *n.* a book used in the study of a particular subject, especially in a school: *a history textbook, an algebra textbook.*

tex·tile (teks'tīl, teks'təl) *n.* **1.** a fabric made by weaving, knitting, or otherwise arranging yarn, thread, or other fibers. **2.** any material that can be made into such a fabric, such as cotton, wool, or nylon. —*adj.* relating to textiles or their manufacture: *the textile industry.*

tex·tu·al (teks'chü əl) *adj.* relating to, based on, or contained in a text: *This history book has many textual errors.* —**tex'tu·al·ly,** *adv.*

tex·ture (teks'chər) *n.* **1.** the look or feel of a woven fabric resulting from the arrangement, quality, or size of its threads: *Silk has a smooth texture.* **2.** the characteristic arrangement of the parts of anything; composition; structure: *the rough texture of sandpaper.*

-th *suffix* used to form ordinal numbers: *seventh.*

Th, the symbol for thorium.

Thai (tī) *n.* **1.** a person who was born in or is a citizen of Thailand. **2.** the official language of Thailand. —*adj.* of or relating to Thailand, its people, their language, or culture. Also, **Siamese.**

thal·a·mus (thal'ə məs) *n., pl.* **thal·a·mi** (thal'ə mī'). a large, oblong mass in the brain, composed largely of gray matter, that relays nerve impulses from one part of the brain to another.

thal·li·um (thal'ē əm) *n.* a soft, bluish gray, poisonous metallic element. It is used in ant and rat poisons. Symbol: **Tl** [Formed from the Greek word *thallos* meaning "green twig." Thallium exhibits characteristic bright green lines in its spectrum.]

thal·lo·phyte (thal'ə fīt') *n.* any of a large group of plantlike organisms, such as algae, fungi, and bacteria, that lack roots, stems, or leaves.

thal·lus (thal'əs) *n., pl.* **thal·li** (thal'ī) or **thal·lus·es.** a plantlike organism not divided into distinct roots, stems, and leaves.

than (thăn; *unstressed* thən) *conj.* **1.** in comparison with: *You are shorter than I. I would rather listen to music than study.* **2.** except; but: *to respect no opinion other than one's own.* —*prep.* compared to: *a city than which there is none more beautiful.*

▲ In formal usage, **than** is used as a conjunction in sentences in which things are compared. The word introduced by *than* may take the form of either the nominative or objective case, depending on how it is used in the sentence: *I am taller than she (is). The story amused me more than (it amused) him.* In informal usage, *than* is sometimes used as a preposition, with the word following *than* being in the objective case: *My friend spent more money than me.*

thane (thān) *n.* **1.** in English history, a man who held lands from the king in return for military service, especially a member of a class ranking above ordinary freemen but below the nobility. **2.** in Scottish history, a lord or baron, especially the chief of a clan.

thank (thangk) *v.t.* **1.** to express gratitude or appreciation to, as for something given or done; give thanks to: *I thanked them for the gift. Thank you for your help.* **2.** to consider or hold responsible; credit or blame: *You have only yourself to thank for failing the test.*

thank·ful (thangk'fəl) *adj.* feeling or expressing thanks; grateful: *to be thankful for help with one's homework.* —**thank'ful·ly,** *adv.* —**thank'ful·ness,** *n.*

thank·less (thangk'lis) *adj.* **1.** not likely to be rewarded or appreciated: *a thankless task.* **2.** not feeling or showing gratitude; ungrateful: *a spoiled, thankless child.* —**thank'less·ly,** *adv.* —**thank'less·ness,** *n.*

thanks (thangks) *interj.* I thank you: *Thanks for the ride.* —*pl. n.* **1.** an expression of gratitude: *to give thanks.* **2.** a feeling of gratitude: *to show one's thanks.*

·**thanks to.** as a result or consequence of; because of: *Thanks to your efforts, the party was a success.*

thanks·giv·ing (thangks'giv'ing) *n.* **1.** the act of giving thanks. **2.** an expression of thanks, especially a prayer of thanks to God.

Thanksgiving **1.** a legal holiday in the United States celebrated on the fourth Thursday in November as a day of thanksgiving and feasting. It observes the memory of the harvest feast celebrated by the Pilgrims in 1621. **2.** a similar holiday celebrated in Canada on the second Monday of October. Also, **Thanksgiving Day.**

that (thăt) *adj., pl.* **those.** **1.** used to indicate a person or thing mentioned or understood: *Who wrote that book?* **2.** used to indicate something that is more distant than or contrasted with another thing: *I prefer this coat to that one. This problem is more difficult than that one.* —*pron., pl.* **those** **1.** used to indicate a person or thing already mentioned or understood: *That is the person who did it. That was the best movie I have seen this year.* **2.** used to indicate something that is more distant than or contrasted with another thing: *I prefer this dress to that.* **3.** who, whom, or which: *the family that lives next door.*

▲ **That** may be used of people, animals, or things; **which** may refer to either animals or things; **who** and **whom** refer only to people. —*conj.* **1.** used to introduce a subordinate clause: *I think that my friend will accept the job.* **2.** used to show reason or cause: *I'm sorry that you can't come to the party.* **3.** used to show result: *to eat so much that one becomes ill.* —*adv.* to such an extent or degree; so: *How could you sing that well after only one lesson?*

▲ In formal usage, a distinction is often made between **that** and **which** in relative clauses. **That** is preferred when introducing a restrictive clause: *New York is the only American city that has more than seven million people.* **Which** is preferred when introducing a nonrestrictive clause: *New York, which has more than seven million people, is our largest city.* However, many good speakers and writers do not follow this distinction and use *which* interchangeably with *that.* *Which* is used especially when *that* appears elsewhere in the sentence and its double usage might be clumsy or confusing.

thatch roof

thatch (thach) *n., pl.* **thatch·es** **1.** straw, reeds, or similar material used to cover a roof. **2.** a roof or roofing of such

T

material. **3.** anything resembling such a covering: *a thick thatch of hair.* —*v.t.* to cover with thatch.

that'll (that′əl) *contr.* **1.** that will. **2.** that shall.

that's (thats) *contr.* that is.

thaw (thô) *v.i.* **1.** to go from a frozen state to a liquid or unfrozen state; become free of frost or ice; melt: *The ice on the road thawed from the heat of the sun.* **2.** to become free of the feeling of being very cold: *The ice skaters thawed out before a large fire.* **3.** (of the weather or temperature) to become warm enough to melt ice or snow. **4.** to grow less stiff and cold in manner; become more friendly: *The new student's chilly manner thawed after we became friends.* —*v.t.* to cause to thaw: *The sun thawed the snow on the roof.* —*n.* **1.** the act or process of thawing. **2.** a period of weather warm enough to melt ice and snow: *the spring thaw.*

the[1] (*before a consonant,* thə; *before a vowel,* thē) *definite article.* **The** refers to a particular person, thing, or group. Some special uses of **the** are: **1.** to indicate a particular one or ones previously mentioned or understood: *Close the door. Give me the book.* **2.** to show that a thing is unique: *the sun, the past, the Amazon River.* **3.** to show that a thing is best known, most important, or greatest: *the place to go for a winter vacation.* **4.** to make a singular noun general: *The lion is found in Africa. You play the bugle well.* **5.** in place of a possessive pronoun: *A stone hit me on the arm.* **6.** before an adjective to make it function as a noun: *a home for the aged.* **7.** as part of a title: *the Queen of Sweden, the Duke of Edinburgh.* [From the Old English word *thē.*]

the[2] (*before a consonant,* thə; *before a vowel,* thē) *adv.* to that degree; by that much: *The sooner you finish it the better.* [From the Old English word *thȳ* meaning "by that," from the word *thæt* "that."]

the·a·ter (thē′ə tər) *also,* **the·a·tre.** *n.* **1.** a building or other place where plays or motion pictures are presented. **2.** a place resembling this, such as a room having rows of seats that is used for surgical demonstrations. **3.** the writing and performing of plays; drama: *the French theater, the modern theater.* **4.** a place where some action takes place; field of operations: *a theater of war.* [From the Latin word *theatrum* meaning "playhouse, theater," from the Greek word *theatron* "a place for viewing, playhouse."]

the·at·ri·cal (thē at′ri kəl) *adj.* **1.** relating to or characteristic of the theater or actors: *a theatrical performance.* **2.** like a performance on stage; exaggerated; not natural: *a theatrical display of grief.* —*n.* **theatricals.** theatrical performances, especially by amateurs. —**the·at′ri·cal·ly,** *adv.*

thee (thē) *sing. pron.* the objective case of **thou.**

theft (theft) *n.* the act or instance of stealing; larceny.

their (thâr) *adj.* of or belonging to them: *their house, their work, their friends.*

theirs (thârz) *pron.* the one or ones that belong or relate to them: *Our car is new; theirs is old.*

the·ism (thē′iz əm) *n.* **1.** a belief in one personal God as creator and ruler of the universe. **2.** a belief in the existence of a god or gods.

the·ist (thē′ist) *n.* a person who adheres to theism. —**the·is′tic,** *adj.*

them (them; *unstressed* thəm) *pl. pron.* the objective case of **they:** *Will you meet them at the station?*

the·mat·ic (thē mat′ik) *adj.* of or relating to a theme or themes.

theme (thēm) *n.* **1.** the main subject or idea of something: *The theme of the book was courage.* **2.** a short essay or written composition: *We were assigned five themes in our English class.* **3.** *Music.* **a.** the principal melody in a musical composition. **b.** a melody on which variations are made.

them·selves (them selvz′, thəm selvz′) *pl. pron.* **1.** the form of **they** or **them** used to give emphasis to the word it goes with: *They had to do the job themselves.* **2.** the form of **them** used to show that the subject is the same as the direct object, indirect object, or object of a preposition: *They blamed themselves for the tragedy. They had to laugh at themselves over their mistake.* **3.** their normal or average selves: *The players on the losing team were certainly not themselves today.*

then (then) *adv.* **1.** at that time: *I was much thinner then.* **2.** immediately or soon afterward; next: *The play ended and then the curtain went down.* **3.** at another time: *Sometimes the car will run smoothly; then it will stall at every corner.* **4.** in that case; if that is so; therefore: *If you don't want that book, then give it to me.* **5.** in addition; besides: *The price is right, and then I really need a new coat.* —*adj.* being or acting as such at that time; of that time: *The then ambassador to France was present at the conference.* —*n.* that time: *I hope to have it finished before then.*

 ·**now and then.** once in a while; occasionally: *Now and then we spend an evening together.*

 ·**then and there.** at that very time; immediately: *Our friends decided to stop smoking then and there.*

thence (thens) *adv.* **1.** from that place; from there: *The bank is two blocks thence.* **2.** from that time; after that: *We saw them again a few weeks thence.* **3.** for that reason; consequently; therefore: *They committed a crime, thence they must be punished.*

thence·forth (thens′fôrth′) *adv.* from that time on; after that. Also, **thence·for·ward** (thens′fôr′wərd).

the·oc·ra·cy (thē ok′rə sē) *n., pl.* **the·oc·ra·cies.** **1.** a government in which God or a god is considered the supreme ruling power. **2.** government by a priesthood or other religious authority. **3.** a country or group ruled in such a way.

the·o·crat·ic (thē′ə krat′ik) *adj.* of or relating to a theocracy.

the·od·o·lite (thē od′ə līt′) *n.* an instrument used in surveying for measuring horizontal and vertical angles.

the·o·lo·gian (thē′ə lō′jən) *n.* an expert in theology.

the·o·log·i·cal (thē′ə loj′i kəl) *adj.* of or relating to theology: *a theological seminary.* —**the·o·log′i·cal·ly,** *adv.*

the·ol·o·gy (thē ol′ə jē) *n., pl.* **the·ol·o·gies.** **1.** the study of the nature and being of God and God's relationship to humans and the universe. **2.** a particular system of religion or religious beliefs, especially of a Christian church.

the·o·rem (thē′ər əm) *n.* **1.** any statement or proposition that is not self-evident but can be proved to be true. **2.** a statement in mathematics that has been proved or can be proved.

the·o·ret·i·cal (thē′ə ret′i kəl) *adj.* **1.** of or relating to a theory: *a theoretical explanation.* **2.** not based on fact or experience; hypothetical: *My knowledge of chess is almost purely theoretical, since I have only played once.* **3.** given to theorizing; speculative: *a brilliant professor with a theoretical mind.* Also, **the·o·ret·ic** (thē′ə ret′ik). —**the′o·ret′i·cal·ly,** *adv.*

the·o·re·ti·cian (thē′ər i tish′ən) *n.* a person who theorizes, especially a person who specializes in the theory of a science or art rather than in its practical application.

the·o·rist (thē′ər ist) *n.* a person who theorizes.

the·o·rize (thē′ə rīz′) *v.i.,* **the·o·rized, the·o·riz·ing.** to form a theory or theories; speculate: *to theorize about life on other planets.*

the·o·ry (thē′ə rē) *n., pl.* **the·o·ries.** **1.** an idea or ideas that explain a group of facts or an event; assumption that has been proved to be true: *the theory of relativity.* **2.** the rules, facts, or methods of an art, science, or profession rather than the actual practice or application:

Not all politicians have a good understanding of political theory. **3.** an assumption or guess based on some evidence but not proved: *Have you any theory as to what caused the sudden rise in prices?* [From the Late Latin *theoria* meaning "an analysis of facts," from the Greek word *theōria* with the same meaning, from the word *theōrein* "to look at, inspect."]

ther·a·peu·tic (ther'ə pū'tik) *adj.* of or relating to the treatment or cure of diseases or disorders: *therapeutic medicine, the therapeutic effects of a warm, dry climate.* —**ther'a·peu'ti·cal·ly,** *adv.*

ther·a·peu·tics (ther'ə pū'tiks) *n.* a branch of medical science dealing with the treatment of disease. ▲ used with a singular verb.

ther·a·pist (ther'ə pist) *n.* a person who gives therapy, especially a doctor or other person who specializes in a particular kind of therapy.

ther·a·py (ther'ə pē) *n., pl.* **ther·a·pies.** the treatment of a disease or a physical or mental disorder by any of various methods.

there (thâr) *adv.* **1.** at or in that place: *Stay there. Put the box down there.* **2.** to, toward, or into that place: *We walked there after lunch.* **3.** at that point, as in time or action: *There the speaker paused.* **4.** about that matter or issue: *I agree with you there.* —*pron.* used as a function word: **1.** to introduce a sentence or clause in which the verb comes before the real subject: *There is no more milk.* The verb may be either singular or plural, depending on the subject: *There is someone at the door. There are thirty-one days in March.* **2.** to call attention to someone or something: *There is the noon whistle.* —*n.* that place: *Do you know the way home from there?* —*interj.* used to express various emotions, as satisfaction or sympathy: *There, there! Don't worry.*

there·a·bouts (thâr'ə bouts') *adv.* near that place, time, number, amount, or degree: *They live in Chicago or thereabouts. Each stone weighs five pounds or thereabouts.* Also, **there·a·bout** (thâr'ə bout').

there·af·ter (thâr af'tər) *adv.* from then on; after that; afterward: *The sun shone the first day of their vacation, but it rained every day thereafter.*

there·at (thâr at') *adv.* **1.** at that place or time; there. **2.** because of that.

there·by (thâr bī') *adv.* **1.** by that means: *That driver finished first in the race, thereby winning the championship.* **2.** in that connection: *The shipwrecked crew barely made it to shore, and thereby hangs a tale.*

there·for (thâr fôr') *adv.* for or in return for this, that, or it: *The bank agreed to lend me the money and issued a check therefor.*

there·fore (thâr'fôr') *adv.* for this or that reason; as a result: *The runner sprained an ankle and therefore could not race.*

there·from (thâr frum', thâr from') *adv.* from this, that, or it.

there·in (thâr in') *adv.* **1.** in or into that place, time, or thing: *The fire destroyed the warehouse and all the property therein.* **2.** in that particular point or respect; in that matter: *There are no maps of that region; therein lies the danger of the expedition.*

there·of (thâr uv', thâr ov') *adv.* **1.** of that or it: *The new law applies to the town and the residents thereof.* **2.** from that or it.

there·on (thâr ôn', thâr on') *adv.* **1.** on or upon that or it. **2.** immediately after that; thereupon.

there's (thârz) *contr.* there is.

there·to (thâr tü') *adv.* to that place or thing.

there·to·fore (thâr'tə fôr') *adv.* before or until that time; up to then.

there·un·der (thâr un'dər) *adv.* under or beneath this, that, or it.

there·un·to (thâr un'tü) *adv.* to that place or thing.

there·up·on (thâr'ə pôn', thâr'ə pon') *adv.* **1.** immediately after that; at once. **2.** as a consequence of that; therefore. **3.** with reference to that; upon that.

there·with (thâr with', thâr with') *adv.* **1.** with this, that, or it. **2.** immediately after that; thereupon.

ther·mal (thûr'məl) *adj.* of, relating to, or causing heat or warmth: *a thermal unit, thermal baths.* —*n.* a rising current of warm air: *The vulture circled in the thermal to gain altitude.* —**ther'mal·ly,** *adv.*

thermal spring, a spring with water that is hotter than the surrounding ground water.

thermo– *combining form* heat: *thermoelectricity.*

ther·mo·dy·nam·ic (thûr'mō dī nam'ik) *adj.* of or relating to thermodynamics.

ther·mo·dy·nam·ics (thûr'mō dī nam'iks) *n.* the branch of physics that deals with the relationship between heat and other forms of energy, especially mechanical energy, and the conversion of one of these forms into another. ▲ used with a singular verb.

ther·mo·e·lec·tric (thûr'mō i lek'trik) *adj.* of or relating to thermoelectricity.

ther·mo·e·lec·tric·i·ty (thûr'mō i lek tris'i tē) *n.* electricity produced by the direct action of heat.

ther·mom·e·ter (thər mom'i tər) *n.* a device for measuring temperature. The most common thermometer is a thin glass tube containing a column of mercury or colored alcohol that rises or falls as it expands or contracts from changes in temperature.

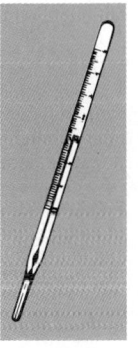

ther·mo·nu·cle·ar (thûr'mō nü'klē ər, thûr'mō nü'klē ər) *adj.* **1.** of or relating to the fusion of atomic nuclei at temperatures of millions of degrees, as in the sun or a hydrogen bomb. **2.** of or relating to thermonuclear weapons: *thermonuclear warfare.*

ther·mo·plas·tic (thûr'mə plas'tik) *adj.* becoming soft and pliable when subjected to heat, without any change in its original properties, as certain plastics or resins. —*n.* a thermoplastic substance.

ther·mos (thûr'məs) *n., pl.* **ther·mos·es.** thermometer a container in which liquids can be kept hot or cold for many hours, usually consisting of an outer container of metal enclosing one glass bottle within another, with a vacuum between the two bottles to keep the contents from losing or gaining heat. Also, **thermos bottle, vacuum bottle.**

ther·mo·stat (thûr'mə stat') *n.* an instrument that automatically regulates temperature, as in a furnace, oven, refrigerator, or room.

the·sau·rus (thə sôr'əs) *n., pl.* **the·sau·ri** (thə sôr'ī) or **the·sau·rus·es.** **1.** a book that lists words in groups of synonyms and antonyms. **2.** a book that lists words or information about one particular subject: *a thesaurus of music.* **3.** a treasury or storehouse. [From the Latin word *thesaurus* meaning "treasure" or "storehouse," from the Greek word *thēsauros* with the same meaning.]

these (thēz) the plural of **this.**

The·se·us (thē'sē əs, thē'süs) *n. Greek Legend.* a hero and, later, king of Athens, who killed the Minotaur and escaped from the Labyrinth with the help of Ariadne.

the·sis (thē'sis) *n., pl.* **the·ses** (thē'sēz). **1.** a statement

---

at; āpe; fär; câre; end; mē; it; īce; pîerce; hot; ōld; sông; fôrk; oil; out; up; ūse; rüle; púll; tûrn; chin; sing; shop; thin; this; hw in white; zh in treasure. The symbol ə stands for the unstressed vowel sound heard in about, taken, pencil, lemon, and circus.

T

or proposition that is presented and then defended, especially in a debate. **2.** an essay or dissertation on a specific topic or theme, especially one presented by a candidate for an academic degree: *a doctoral thesis.*

thes·pi·an (thes′pē ən) *also,* **Thes·pi·an.** *adj.* of or relating to drama; dramatic. —*n.* an actor. [From the sixth-century B.C. Greek poet *Thespis,* the supposed originator of ancient Greek tragedy.]

Thes·sa·lo·ni·ans (thes′ə lō′nē ənz) *n.* either of two books of the New Testament consisting of epistles written by Saint Paul. ▲ used with a singular verb.

the·ta (thā′tə, thē′tə) *n.* the eighth letter of the Greek alphabet (Θ, θ).

The·tis (thē′tis) *n. Greek Legend.* a sea nymph who was the mother of Achilles.

thews (thūz) *pl. n.* muscles; sinews.

they (thā) *pl. pron.* nominative, **they;** possessive, **their, theirs;** objective, **them. 1.** the persons or things mentioned before: *The twins were late because they missed the train.* **2.** people in general; any persons: *They say that our team will probably win today.*

they'd (thād) *contr.* **1.** they had. **2.** they would.

they'll (thāl) *contr.* **1.** they will. **2.** they shall.

they're (thâr) *contr.* they are.

they've (thāv) *contr.* they have.

THI, temperature-humidity index.

thi·a·mine (thī′ə min) *also,* **thi·a·min.** *n.* another word for **vitamin B₁.**

thick (thik) *adj.* **1.** having relatively great distance from one surface or side to the opposite one; not thin: *a thick piece of wood, a thick steak.* **2.** measured from one side or surface to the other: *That stone wall is three feet thick.* **3.** not pouring or flowing easily: *thick soup.* **4.** growing, being, or happening close together, or having its parts close together: *thick underbrush, a thick beard.* **5.** very noticeable; heavy: *to speak with a thick German accent.* **6.** *Informal.* mentally dull; stupid. —*adv.* so as to be thick; thickly: *Cut the steak thick.* —*n.* **1.** the thickest part of anything. **2.** a part or place of greatest intensity or activity: *to be in the thick of the fight.* —**thick′ly,** *adv.*

·**through thick and thin.** through good times and bad; under any circumstances.

thick·en (thik′ən) *v.t., v.i.* **1.** to make or become thick or thicker. **2.** to make or become more intense or complex, as the plot of a story. —**thick′en·er,** *n.*

thick·en·ing (thik′ə ning) *n.* **1.** something added to a liquid to thicken it. **2.** the act of making or becoming thick. **3.** a thickened place or part.

thick·et (thik′it) *n.* a dense growth, as of shrubs or bushes.

thick·head·ed (thik′hed′id) *adj.* slow to learn or understand; stupid; dull. —**thick′head′ed·ness,** *n.*

thick·ness (thik′nis) *n., pl.* **thick·ness·es. 1.** the state or quality of being thick. **2.** the dimension of a solid between its two opposite surfaces, as distinguished from its length or width. **3.** a layer or sheet, as of paper.

thick·set (thik′set′) *adj.* **1.** having a short, stocky build. **2.** planted, placed, or growing close together.

thick–skinned (thik′skind′) *adj.* **1.** having a thick skin, as certain fruit. **2.** insensitive to criticism, ridicule, or reproach.

thief (thēf) *n., pl.* **thieves.** a person who steals, especially secretly and without using force.

thieve (thēv) *v.t., v.i.* **thieved, thiev·ing.** to steal, especially secretly and without using force.

thiev·er·y (thē′və rē) *n., pl.* **thiev·er·ies.** the act, instance, or practice of stealing.

thieves (thēvz) the plural of **thief.**

thiev·ish (thē′vish) *adj.* **1.** inclined to stealing. **2.** characteristic of or like a thief; furtive; sly: *a thievish manner.*

thigh (thī) *n.* the part of the leg between the hip and the knee.

thigh·bone (thī′bōn′) *n.* the long bone of the upper leg, extending from the pelvis to the knee; femur.

thim·ble (thim′bəl) *n.* a small metal cap that is worn on the finger to protect it when pushing the needle through material in sewing.

thin (thin) *adj.,* **thin·ner, thin·nest. 1.** having relatively little distance from one surface or side to the opposite one; not thick: *a thin piece of wood, thin paper.* **2.** not plump or fat; lean: *a long, thin face.* **3.** flowing or pouring easily; watery: *a thin gravy.* **4.** easily seen through; not convincing; flimsy: *a thin excuse.* **5.** less dense than is usual or not dense: *thin*

thimble

air. **6.** having a faint, often shrill sound; weak: *a small, thin voice.* —*adv.* so as to be thin; thinly: *Slice the ham thin.* —*v.t., v.i.,* **thinned, thin·ning.** to make or become thin or thinner. —**thin′ly,** *adv.* —**thin′ness,** *n.*

thine (thīn) *Archaic. pron.* **1.** belonging to you. **2.** the one or ones belonging to you. —*adj.* thy; your. ▲ used in place of *thy* before a word beginning with a vowel or *h*: *Drink to me only with thine eyes* (Ben Jonson).

thing (thing) *n.* **1.** that which has or can be thought of as having existence; any matter, substance, object, or being: *They didn't know what the thing was. Knowledge is a thing to be cherished.* **2.** an inanimate object, as distinguished from a living being: *A stone is a thing.* **3.** a living being, especially when thought of in terms of pity, affection, or contempt: *The lost child was a sad little thing.* **4.** any act, fact, idea, or statement: *That was a terrible thing to do! Say the first thing that comes into your mind.* **5. things.** the general state of affairs: *Things have changed since you've been gone.* **6. things.** possessions; belongings: *I put all my things in a box.* **7. the thing.** the latest or proper style or fashion.

think (thingk) *v.,* **thought, think·ing.** —*v.i.* **1.** to use the mind, as in forming opinions or using judgment: *A person should think before making an important decision.* **2.** to have in the mind as an opinion, belief, or attitude: *to think of someone as clever.* **3.** to occupy one's thoughts with something or someone; reflect: *I'll have to think about it before I decide.* **4.** to have in mind the idea of doing something: *We're thinking of going to Europe this summer.* **5.** to call to mind or remember: *I could not think of the incident without smiling.* **6.** to have care or consideration: *Don't always think of yourself first.* **7.** to form an image or idea in the mind: *Who thought of the first alphabet?* —*v.t.* **1.** to form or have in the mind: *to think good thoughts.* **2.** to hold the opinion that; consider: *I think we should go home.* **3.** to arrive at a decision, conclusion, or answer regarding: *Think it through carefully before you give me your final decision.* —**think′er,** *n.*

think·a·ble (thing′kə bəl) *adj.* capable or worthy of being considered; conceivable; possible.

thin·ner (thin′ər) *n.* a liquid used to thin a substance: *Turpentine is used as a thinner for some paints.*

thin–skinned (thin′skind′) *adj.* **1.** having a thin skin: *a thin-skinned fruit.* **2.** very sensitive to criticism, ridicule, or reproach; easily hurt or offended.

third (thûrd) *adj.* **1.** (the ordinal of three) next after the second. **2.** being one of three equal parts. —*n.* **1.** something that is next after the second. **2.** one of three equal parts; ⅓. **3.** *Music.* **a.** a note that is a total of two whole steps above a given note. E is the third of C. **b.** an interval of two whole steps. **c.** a combination of two notes that are separated by this interval. **4.** the third forward gear, as of an automobile. —*adv.* in the third place.

third–class (thûrd′klas′) *adj.* **1.** next below or inferior to second-class. **2.** of or relating to a class of mail that includes all printed matter except newspapers and magazines and meets certain governmental limits, as of weight. **3.** of or relating to a class of travel accommodations on a ship or other conveyance, usually the least expensive.

third class **1.** third-class travel accommodations. **2.** third-class mail.

third degree *Informal.* harsh questioning and treatment of a prisoner to obtain information or a confession.

third–de·gree burn (thûrd′di grē′) a burn that affects all the layers of the skin and, sometimes, the tissues under the skin.

third person, the form of a pronoun or verb that indicates the person or thing spoken of. In the sentence *Whenever he sees her she is nice to him,* the words *he, sees, her, she, is,* and *him* are in the third person.

Third Reich (rīk) Germany under the rule of the Nazis, from 1933 to 1945.

Third World 1. the developing nations of the world. **2.** the nations of the world that are not aligned with the policies of either the United States or the Soviet Union.

thirst (thûrst) *n.* **1.** an uncomfortable feeling of dryness in the mouth and throat caused by a desire or need to drink fluids. **2.** the desire or need to drink: *to have an insatiable thirst.* **3.** a strong or powerful desire; craving: *a thirst for power, a thirst for learning.* —*v.i.* **1.** to want something to drink; be thirsty. **2.** to have a strong desire: *to thirst for knowledge.*

thirst·y (thûrs′tē) *adj.,* **thirst·i·er, thirst·i·est.** **1.** feeling the need to drink something. **2.** lacking water or moisture; parched; arid: *thirsty farmland.* **3.** having a strong desire: *The young scholar was thirsty for knowledge.* —**thirst′i·ly,** *adv.* —**thirst′i·ness,** *n.*

thir·teen (thûr′tēn′) *n.* **1.** the cardinal number that is three more than ten. **2.** a symbol representing this number, such as 13 or XIII. *adj.* numbering three more than ten.

thir·teenth (thûr′tēnth′) *adj.* **1.** (the ordinal of thirteen) next after the twelfth. **2.** being one of thirteen equal parts. —*n.* **1.** something that is next after the twelfth. **2.** one of thirteen equal parts; ⅟₁₃.

thir·ti·eth (thûr′tē ith) *adj.* **1.** (the ordinal of thirty) next after the twenty-ninth. **2.** being one of thirty equal parts. —*n.* **1.** something that is next after the twenty-ninth. **2.** one of thirty equal parts; ⅟₃₀.

thir·ty (thûr′tē) *n., pl.* **thir·ties.** **1.** the cardinal number that is three times ten. **2.** a symbol representing this number, such as 30 or XXX. —*adj.* numbering three times ten.

thir·ty–sec·ond note (thûr′tē sek′ənd) *Music.* a note having a time value equal to one thirty-second of a whole note.

this (this) *adj., pl.* **these.** **1.** used to indicate a person or thing that is present, nearby, understood, or mentioned: *This house is ten years old. This roast beef is delicious.* **2.** used to indicate something that is nearer than or contrasted with another thing: *This hat is cheaper than that one.* —*pron., pl.* **these.** **1.** used to indicate a person or thing that is present, nearby, understood, or just mentioned: *Is this your coat? This is a serious matter.* **2.** used to indicate something that is nearer than or contrasted with another thing: *This is mine; that is yours.* **3.** something about to be said or explained: *This is what I mean.* —*adv.* to this extent or degree; so: *Is it this hot every day?*

this·tle (this′əl) *n.* a prickly plant that has red or purple flowers. —**this′·tle·like′,** *adj.*

this·tle·down (this′əl doun′) *n.* the silky down on the flower of a thistle.

thith·er (thith′ər) *adv. Archaic.* to or toward that place; in that direction.

tho (thō) *also,* **tho′.** *conj., adv.* another spelling of **though.**

thole (thōl) *n.* a peg or pair of pegs on the upper edge of either side of a boat, used to hold an oar in rowing. Also, **thole·pin** (thōl′pin′).

thong (thông, thong) *n.* **1.** a narrow strip of leather or other material, used especially as a fastening. **2.** a sandal that is held to the foot by a thong that fits between the first two toes and is often connected to a strap that runs over the top or along the sides of the foot. **3.** the lash of a whip.

thistle

Thor (thôr) *n. Norse Mythology.* the god of thunder.

tho·rac·ic (thô ras′ik) *adj.* of, relating to, or located in or near the thorax.

tho·rax (thôr′aks) *n., pl.* **tho·rax·es** or **tho·ra·ces** (thôr′ə sēz′). **1.** in humans and certain other animals with backbones, the part of the body extending from the base of the neck to the diaphragm, containing the heart, lungs, and ribs. **2.** the section of an insect's body that contains the wings and legs, extending from the head to the abdomen. [From the Latin word *thorax* meaning "chest, thorax," from the Greek word *thōrax* with the same meaning.]

tho·ri·um (thôr′ē əm) *n.* a heavy, silver-white, radioactive metallic element used to make photoelectric cells. Symbol: Th [From the Norse god *Thor.*]

thorn (thôrn) *n.* **1.** a short, sharp-pointed growth on a branch or stem, as of a rose. **2.** any of various trees or shrubs bearing thorns. **·thorn in one's side.** a cause of annoyance or worry.

thorn·y (thôr′nē) *adj.,* **thorn·i·er, thorn·i·est.** **1.** full of thorns; spiny; prickly. **2.** difficult or irritating: *a thorny problem.*

thor·ough (thûr′o) *adj.* **1.** done or carried out completely; omitting nothing: *a thorough search, a thorough cleaning.* **2.** extremely accurate and conscientious, especially with regard to details: *Those scientists were very thorough in their research.* —**thor′ough·ly,** *adv.* —**thor′ough·ness,** *n.*

thor·ough·bred (thûr′ə bred′) *n.* **1.** an animal, such as a horse or dog, that is of pure or unmixed breed or stock.

at; āpe; fär; câre; end; mē; it; īce; pîerce; hot; ōld; sông, fôrk; oil; out; up; ūse; rüle; pull; tûrn; chin; sing; shop; thin; this; hw in white; zh in treasure. The symbol ə stands for the unstressed vowel sound heard in about, taken, pencil, lemon, and circus.

T

979

2. Thoroughbred. a horse descended from a breed first developed at the end of the eighteenth century by crossing English mares with any one of three specific Arabian stallions. Thoroughbreds are trained chiefly for horse racing. **3.** a person of good breeding and education. —*adj.* **1.** of pure or unmixed breed or stock. **2. Thoroughbred.** relating to or being a Thoroughbred.

thor·ough·fare (thûr′ə fâr′) *n.* a public road or street that is open at both ends, especially one that is a major route of travel.

thor·ough·go·ing (thûr′ə gō′ing) *adj.* thorough; complete: *a thoroughgoing liar.*

those (thōz) the plural of **that.**

thou (thou) *sing. pron. Archaic.* the one spoken to; you. ▲ used in the nominative case.

though (thō) *conj.* **1.** in spite of the fact that: *I was late for work, though I got up early.* **2.** but; yet; however: *The meal was good, though it could have been better.* —*adv.* nonetheless; however: *They won't help you; you can count on us, though.*

thought (thôt) *v.* the past tense and past participle of **think.** —*n.* **1.** the act or process of thinking: *to be lost in thought.* **2.** something that one thinks; idea: *What are your thoughts on the subject?* **3.** the way of thinking or the ideas of a particular group, time, or place: *modern thought, scientific thought.* **4.** careful notice, attention, or consideration: *Please give some thought to the problem.* **5.** something that is intended; aim: *Our only thought was to put out the fire.*

thought·ful (thôt′fəl) *adj.* **1.** expressing, showing, or having a regard for others and their feelings; considerate: *a thoughtful person, a thoughtful gift.* **2.** engaged in or full of thought; meditative: *a thoughtful look.* **3.** showing careful attention or consideration: *a thoughtful question.* —**thought′ful·ly,** *adv.* —**thought′ful·ness,** *n.*

thought·less (thôt′lis) *adj.* **1.** having or showing little or no regard for others and their feelings; inconsiderate: *The thoughtless remark hurt my feelings.* **2.** showing a lack of thought; careless: *a thoughtless error.* —**thought′less·ly,** *adv.* —**thought′less·ness,** *n.*

thou·sand (thou′zənd) *n.* **1.** the cardinal number that is ten times a hundred. **2.** a symbol representing this number, such as 1,000 or M. —*adj.* numbering ten times a hundred.

thou·sandth (thou′zəndth) *adj.* **1.** (the ordinal of thousand) next after the 999th. **2.** being one of a thousand equal parts. —*n.* **1.** something that is next after the 999th. **2.** one of a thousand equal parts; 1/1000.

Thra·cian (thrā′shən) *adj.* of or relating to ancient Thrace or its people. —*n.* a person who was born or lived in ancient Thrace.

thrall (thrôl) *n.* **1.** a person who is enslaved; slave; serf. **2.** the condition of being enslaved or like a slave: *a debtor in thrall to the bank.*

thrall·dom (thrôl′dəm) *also,* **thral·dom.** *n.* the condition of being enslaved.

thrash (thrash) *v.t.* **1.** to give a beating to. **2.** to defeat completely; overwhelm. **3.** another word for **thresh.** —*v.i.* **1.** to make wild, flailing movements; toss violently: *The children thrashed about in the pool trying to catch the ball.* **2.** another word for **thresh.**
  ·**to thrash out.** to discuss thoroughly and bring to a conclusion: *The company and the union thrashed out a new contract.*

thrash·er (thrash′ər) *n.* **1.** a person or thing that thrashes. **2.** a North American songbird, closely related to the mockingbird, having a curved bill, a long tail, short wings, and mainly brown feathers.

thrash·ing (thrash′ing) *n.* a severe beating.

thread (thred) *n.* **1.** a very fine, thin cord made of two or more fibers, as of cotton, wool, or silk, twisted together.

It is used in sewing and in weaving cloth. **2.** anything resembling thread, as in thinness or length: *A thread of paint trickled down the wall.* **3.** anything that runs through the whole of something and connects its parts: *the thread of a story.* **4.** a spiral ridge running continuously around a screw, bolt, or nut. —*v.t.* **1.** to pass a thread through: *to thread a needle.* **2.** to string together on or as if on a thread: *to thread beads.* **3.** to pass or proceed through in a winding or twisting manner: *hair threaded with a rope of pearls.* **4.** to make (one's way) in a winding or twisting manner: *to thread one's way through a crowd.* **5.** to cut a thread on, in, or around (a screw or nut). —*v.i.* **1.** to pass or proceed in a winding or twisting manner: *The stream threads among the hills.* **2.** to form a fine thread when dropped from a spoon, as boiling syrup that has reached a certain consistency. —**thread′like′,** *adj.*

thread·bare (thred′bâr′) *adj.* **1.** having the nap worn off so the threads show through; worn; shabby: *threadbare upholstery.* **2.** wearing threadbare clothes; seedy. **3.** old and worn-out; stale: *a threadbare joke.*

thread·y (thred′ē) *adj.,* **thread·i·er, thread·i·est. 1.** made of or resembling thread. **2.** weak and thin: *a thready voice.* —**thread′i·ness,** *n.*

threat (thret) *n.* **1.** an expression of the intention to inflict punishment, harm, or pain. **2.** a person or thing that is a source of misfortune, danger, or harm: *This disease is a threat to cattle.* **3.** a sign or possibility of something that might happen, such as misfortune or danger: *Farmers live under the threat of drought.*

threat·en (thret′ən) *v.t.* **1.** to make a threat against: *The terrorist threatened the hostage.* **2.** to be a threat to; endanger: *The drought threatened the farmer's crop.* **3.** to be an indication of: *The dark clouds threaten rain.* **4.** to make a threat of: *to threaten to call the police.* —*v.i.* **1.** to use or utter threats. **2.** to be or pose a threat; menace. —**threat′en·ing·ly,** *adv.*

three (thrē) *n.* **1.** the cardinal number that is one more than two. **2.** a symbol representing this number, such as 3 or III. **3.** something having this many units or things, as a playing card. —*adj.* numbering one more than two.

three–di·men·sion·al (thrē′di men′shə nəl) *adj.* **1.** of, relating to, or having three dimensions. **2.** having or giving the illusion of depth.

three·fold (thrē′fōld′) *adj.* **1.** three times as great or numerous. **2.** having or consisting of three parts. —*adv.* so as to be three times greater or more numerous.

three·score (thrē′skôr′) *adj.* three times twenty; sixty.

three·some (thrē′səm) *n.* a group of three persons.

Three Wise Men, another name for the **Magi.**

thren·o·dy (thren′ə dē) *n., pl.* **thren·o·dies.** a song or poem of lamentation, especially one written for the funeral of an important person.

thresh (thresh) *v.t.* **1.** to separate the grain from (a cereal grass) with a threshing machine or by beating with a flail. **2.** to separate (grain) from straw or chaff in this manner. **3.** to give a beating to; thrash. —*v.i.* **1.** to thresh grain. **2.** to toss violently; thrash.

thresh·er (thresh′ər) *n.* **1.** a person or thing that threshes. **2.** a machine that threshes grain. Also, **threshing machine. 3.** a large shark having a very long tail that it thrashes about in the water in order to drive together schools of the small fish that form its diet.

thresher *(def. 3)*

thresh·old (thresh′ōld) *n.* **1.** a piece of wood, stone, or metal that forms the bottom of a door frame. **2.** a point of entering or beginning: *to be on the threshold of a new* *career in business.* **3.** the point below which a stimulus cannot be felt or does not produce a reaction: *to have a high threshold for pain.*

threw (thrü) the past tense of **throw.**

thrice (thrīs) *adv.* three times.

thrift (thrift) *n.* careful management of money and other resources; frugality.

thrift·less (thrift′lis) *adj.* not thrifty; wasteful.

thrift shop, a store selling secondhand items, especially clothing, at low prices and often for a charity.

thrift·y (thrif′tē) *adj.,* **thrift·i·er, thrift·i·est.** very careful in the use and management of money and other resources; avoiding waste or extravagance; frugal. —**thrift′i·ly,** *adv.* —**thrift′i·ness,** *n.*

thrill (thril) *n.* **1.** a pleasurable or exciting feeling or sensation: *the thrill of owning a new car.* **2.** something that produces such a feeling or sensation: *My first airplane trip was a thrill for me.* —*v.t.* to fill with pleasure or excitement: *The parade thrilled the crowd.* —*v.i.* **1.** to have a sudden feeling of pleasure or excitement. **2.** to tremble; quiver. —**thrill′ing·ly,** *adv.*

thrill·er (thril′ər) *n.* **1.** a play, story, book, or the like that causes feelings of excitement or suspense. **2.** a person or thing that thrills.

thrive (thrīv) *v.i.,* **thrived** or **throve, thrived** or **thriv·en** (thriv′ən), **thriv·ing. 1.** to be successful or fortunate: *The new supermarket has thrived.* **2.** to grow very well; be very healthy: *The plant thrived in the sunlight.*

throat (thrōt) *n.* **1.** the area behind and below the mouth, containing the pharynx, the upper part of the esophagus, the larynx, and the upper part of the trachea. **2.** the front of the neck, extending from below the chin to the collarbone. **3.** any narrow opening resembling the throat: *the throat of a carburetor.*

throat·y (thrō′tē) *adj.,* **throat·i·er, throat·i·est.** produced deep in the throat; husky: *a throaty laugh.* —**throat′i·ness,** *n.*

throb (throb) *v.i.,* **throbbed, throb·bing. 1.** to beat heavily and fast, as the heart; pound. **2.** to vibrate or sound with a strong, steady rhythm: *The drums throbbed in the night.* —*n.* **1.** the act of throbbing. **2.** a beat or vibration; pulsation: *a heart throb.*

throe (thrō) *n.* **1. throes.** a condition of extreme pain, anguish, or struggle: *in the throes of death, the throes of despair.* **2.** also, **throes.** a violent spasm or pang, especially of pain: *the throes of hunger.*

throm·bo·sis (throm bō′sis) *n.,* *pl.* **throm·bo·ses** (throm bō′sēz). the formation of a clot of blood in a blood vessel or the heart that stops the flow of blood.

throm·bus (throm′bəs) *n.,* *pl.* **throm·bi** (throm′bī). a clot of blood that forms in the circulatory system, sometimes obstructing the flow of blood.

throne (thrōn) *n.* **1.** a chair on which a sovereign, pope, bishop, or other dignitary sits during state or ceremonial occasions. **2.** royal power or authority; sovereignty. [From the Latin word *thronus* meaning "elevated seat, throne," from the Greek word *thronos* with the same meaning.]

throng (thrông, throng) *n.* a large number of people or things assembled or crowded together. —*v.i.* to move or assemble in a group or large numbers; crowd: *The people thronged to the county fair.* —*v.t.* **1.** to fill (a place); crowd into: *Spectators thronged the courtroom.* **2.** to crowd around; press in on: *Fans thronged the popular singer.*

throt·tle (throt′əl) *n.* **1.** a valve that controls or regulates the supply of steam in a steam engine or turbine or the supply of fuel vapor in an internal-combustion engine. **2.** a lever or pedal that operates such a valve. —*v.t.,* **throt·tled, throt·tling. 1.** to kill by choking; strangle. **2.** to stop the flow or action of; suppress: *The army throttled the rebellion by cutting the lines of supply.*

3. to reduce or shut off the flow of (steam or fuel vapor) in an engine. **4.** to reduce the speed of (an engine) in this way.

through (thrü) *prep.* **1.** from the beginning to the end of: *to read through a book in one day.* **2.** in one side or end and out the opposite or other side or end: *to drive a nail through a board.* **3.** in or to various parts or places in: *We plan to travel through Europe this summer.* **4.** in the midst of; among: *to wander through the trees.* **5.** because of: *to lose one's job through constant tardiness.* **6.** by means of: *We got the news through our friend.* **7.** having finished or done with: *Is your cousin through college yet?* —*adv.* **1.** from one side or end to the opposite or other side or end: *The farmer opened the barnyard gate and the cattle went through.* **2.** from beginning to end: *to read a letter through.* **3.** to a conclusion or the end: *to carry a project through.* **4.** along the whole distance; all the way: *The river runs through to the mill.* **5.** throughout; completely: *to be soaked through.* —*adj.* **1.** having arrived at a point of completion; finished: *Are you through with your homework?* **2.** no longer having relations, dealings, or connections: *to be through with politics forever.* **3.** allowing free or unobstructed passage: *a through street.* **4.** going or allowing a person to go the whole distance with few or no stops and no changes: *a through train.* ·**through and through.** completely: *to be a coward through and through.*

through·out (thrü out′) *prep.* **1.** in every part of; everywhere in: *That author is famous throughout the country.* **2.** during the whole time or course of: *Close friends visited me throughout my illness.* —*adv.* **1.** in or to every place or part; everywhere: *Are your facts correct throughout?* **2.** from beginning to end.

through·way (thru′wā′) another spelling of **thruway.**

throve (thrōv) a past tense of **thrive.**

throw (thrō) *v.,* **threw, thrown, throw·ing.** —*v.t.* **1.** to send up into or through the air with the hand or hands: *to throw a ball. Please throw me a towel.* **2.** to cause to fall to the ground: *The horse threw its rider.* **3.** to put carelessly or hurriedly: *I threw a coat on and ran out the door.* **4.** to put or place in a specified position, state, or condition: *to throw a crowd into confusion.* **5.** to direct or project; cast: *to throw someone a nasty look.* **6.** to move (a lever or switch) so as to connect or disconnect parts of a mechanism. **7.** to lose or shed: *The horse threw a shoe.* **8.** *Informal.* to lose (a game, race, or other contest) on purpose. **9.** *Informal.* to give (a party, dance, or the like). —*v.i.* to send something up into or through the air with the hand or hands. —*n.* **1.** the act of throwing; toss. **2.** the distance that something is or may be thrown: *a long throw.* **3.** a scarf, shawl, or coverlet. —**throw′er,** *n.*

·**to throw away. a.** to dispose of; discard. **b.** to waste; squander: *to throw away a fortune by gambling.* **c.** to fail to take advantage of: *to throw away an opportunity.*
·**to throw in.** to add or include as a bonus.
·**to throw off. a.** to rid or free oneself of. **b.** to give off; emit.
·**to throw out. a.** to reject; discard. **b.** to offer, as a hint or suggestion. **c.** *Baseball.* to put out (a base runner) by throwing the ball to a defensive player at the base toward which the base runner is running.

at; āpe; fär; câre; end; mē; it; īce; pîerce; hot; ōld; sông, fôrk; oil; out; up; ūse; rüle; pull; tûrn; chin; sing; shop; thin; this; hw in white; zh in treasure. The symbol ə stands for the unstressed vowel sound heard in about, taken, pencil, lemon, and circus.

T

·**to throw over.** to forsake; abandon.

·**to throw up. a.** *Informal.* to vomit. **b.** to build rapidly: *to throw up a dike against a flood.* **c.** to give up; abandon: *to throw up a project for lack of funds.*

throw·a·way (thrō′ə wā′) *n.* **1.** a handbill or leaflet meant to be thrown away after reading. **2.** anything meant to be thrown away after use, such as a disposable bottle, can, or other container. —*adj.* designed or meant to be thrown away after use; disposable: *throwaway containers.*

throw·back (thrō′bak′) *n.* **1.** a reversion to an earlier or ancestral type or character. **2.** an instance of this.

thrown (thrōn) the past participle of **throw.**

throw rug, another term for **scatter rug.**

thru (thrü) another spelling of **through.**

thrum (thrum) *v.,* **thrummed, thrum·ming.** —*v.t.* to play (a stringed instrument), especially in a monotonous or unskilled manner; strum. —*v.i.* **1.** to drum or tap idly or repeatedly with the fingers. **2.** to thrum a stringed instrument. —*n.* a monotonous sound produced by thrumming.

thrush (thrush) *n., pl.* **thrush·es.** any of numerous songbirds, including the robin, bluebird, wood thrush, and nightingale.

thrust (thrust) *v.,* **thrust, thrust·ing.** —*v.t.* **1.** to push or shove suddenly or with force: *I thrust the money into my pocket.* **2.** to put forcibly into some condition, position, or situation: *to thrust oneself into an argument.* —*v.i.* **1.** to make a stab or lunge, as with a pointed instrument or weapon: *to thrust with a knife.* **2.** to make or force one's way, as through a crowd. —*n.* **1.** a sudden, forceful push or drive: *The army made a thrust into enemy territory.* **2.** a stab. **3.** the force that pushes a rocket or jet engine in a certain direction, created when hot gases rush out in the opposite direction through a nozzle. **4.** the driving force made by a propeller as it turns.

thrush (wood thrush)

thru·way (thrü′wā′) *also,* **through·way.** *n.* a wide, usually divided highway that allows rapid and direct travel between distant places.

thud (thud) *n.* **1.** a dull, heavy sound. **2.** a heavy blow producing such a sound. —*v.i.,* **thud·ded, thud·ding.** to make a thud when falling or striking against something.

thug (thug) *n.* a rough, brutal, and often violent person; ruffian. [From the Hindi word *thag* meaning "thief," originally referring to a member of a religious society in northern India that robbed and strangled people.]

thu·li·um (thü′lē əm) *n.* a soft metallic element of the rare-earth group. It is used in portable X-ray equipment. Symbol: **Tm** [From *Thylē*, the Greek name for Europe's northernmost lands. Thulium was discovered in rare-earth ores from Scandinavia.]

thumb (thum) *n.* **1.** the short, thick finger of the human hand next to the index finger. **2.** a corresponding digit in monkeys and other primates. **3.** the part of a glove or mitten that covers the thumb. —*v.t.* **1.** to turn and glance at the pages of; leaf: *to thumb a magazine.* **2.** *Informal.* to get by hitchhiking: *to thumb a ride.* —*v.i. Informal.* to hitchhike.

·**all thumbs.** clumsy, as when using the hands.

·**thumbs down.** a sign or gesture showing disapproval or rejection.

·**thumbs up.** a sign or gesture showing approval or acceptance.

·**under the thumb of.** completely under the power, control, or influence of.

thumb index, a series of labels or indentations on the outside edges of the pages of a book to mark the different sections.

thumb·nail (thum′nāl′) *n.* the nail of the thumb. —*adj.* very brief; concise: *a thumbnail report of what happened.*

thumb·screw (thum′skrü′) *n.* **1.** a screw made so that it can be turned by the thumb and a finger. **2.** formerly, an instrument of torture used to crush the thumbs.

thumb·tack (thum′tak′) *n.* a tack with a round, flat head, designed to be pressed into a wall, board, or the like by the thumb.

thump (thump) *n.* **1.** a heavy blow, as with a blunt object. **2.** the heavy, hollow sound made by such a blow. —*v.t.* to beat or hit so as to make a heavy, hollow sound: *to thump one's head against a low ceiling.* —*v.i.* **1.** to produce a thump when falling or striking against something. **2.** to beat heavily and rapidly; throb: *My heart thumped when they announced the winner.* —**thump′er,** *n.*

thumbscrew (def. 1)

thun·der (thun′dər) *n.* **1.** a rumbling or explosive sound made when a lightning discharge heats and expands the air in its path. **2.** any noise resembling thunder: *the thunder of cannons, the thunder of applause.* —*v.i.* **1.** to give forth or produce thunder. **2.** to make a noise resembling thunder: *The train thundered into the station.* **3.** to make loud or strong denunciations or threats. —*v.t.* to express loudly or strongly, especially in a threatening manner.

thun·der·bolt (thun′dər bōlt′) *n.* **1.** a flash of lightning accompanied by a clap of thunder. **2.** something that is sudden, unexpected, and terrible.

thun·der·clap (thun′dər klap′) *n.* **1.** a loud crash or burst of thunder. **2.** something that is sudden, unexpected, and violent.

thun·der·cloud (thun′dər kloud′) *n.* a dark, billowing, electrically charged cloud that produces thunder and lightning.

thun·der·head (thun′dər hed′) *n.* one of the round, swelling cloud masses that often develop into a thundercloud.

thun·der·ous (thun′dər əs) *adj.* producing a noise like thunder: *thunderous applause.* —**thun′der·ous·ly,** *adv.*

thun·der·show·er (thun′dər shou′ər) *n.* a rain shower accompanied by thunder and lightning.

thun·der·storm (thun′dər stôrm′) *n.* a storm accompanied by thunder and lightning, and usually rain.

thun·der·struck (thun′dər struk′) *adj.* stunned or shocked, as with disbelief or surprise; astonished; amazed.

Thurs., Thursday. Also, **Thur.**

Thurs·day (thûrz′dē, thûrz′dā) *n.* the fifth day of the week. [From the Old English word *Thūrsdæg* meaning "Thursday," from the Old Norse word *Thōrsdagr,* from the words *Thōr* "Thor," the Norse god of thunder + *dagr* "day."]

thus (thus) *adv.* **1.** in this, that, or the following way: *Written thus, the directions are easy to understand.* **2.** as a result; consequently; therefore: *I did not study and thus failed the test.* **3.** to this extent or degree: *We have not heard from them thus far.*

thwack (thwak) *v.t.* to hit hard with something flat; whack. —*n.* a sharp, powerful blow with something flat.

thwart (thwôrt) *v.t.* to prevent from doing or succeeding; oppose successfully: *Nothing can thwart that diver's quest for the championship.* —*n.* a crosswise seat in a boat. —*adj.* lying or extending across something; transverse. —*adv., prep. Archaic.* across; athwart.

thy (thī) *pron. Archaic.* of or belonging to you; your.

thyme (tīm) *n.* a small plant related to the mint. Its leaves are used to season food.

thy·mus (thī′məs) *n.* an endocrine gland, located at the base of the neck. Also, **thymus gland.**

thy·roid (thī′roid) *n.* **1.** see **thyroid gland. 2.** see **thyroid cartilage. 3.** a medicine obtained from the dried thyroid glands of certain animals. —*adj.* of, relating to, or characteristic of the thyroid gland or thyroid cartilage. [Originally from the Greek phrase *thyreoeidēs (chondros)* meaning ''shield-shaped (cartilage), thyroid,'' from the word *thyreoeidēs* meaning ''shield-shaped,'' from the word *thyreos* ''a shield shaped like a door,'' from the word *thyra* ''door.'']

thyroid cartilage, the largest cartilage of the larynx, which covers and protects the thyroid gland and forms the Adam's apple.

thyroid gland, an endocrine gland that secretes thyroxin, located in front of and on either side of the trachea.

thy·rox·in (thī rok′sin) *n.* a hormone obtained from the thyroid gland or made synthetically. It is important in regulating the rate at which body cells change food and oxygen into energy and heat. Also, **thy·rox·ine** (thī-rok′sēn).

thy·self (thī self′) *pron. Archaic.* yourself.

ti (tē) *n. Music.* **1.** the seventh note of the major scale. **2.** the note B.

Ti, the symbol for titanium.

ti·ar·a (tē ar′ə, tē är′ə) *n.* **1.** an ornament resembling a crown, worn on the head. Tiaras are often decorated with jewels. **2.** the triple crown worn by the pope.

Ti·bet·an (ti bet′ən) *n.* **1.** a person who was born in or is a citizen of Tibet. **2.** the language of Tibet. —*adj.* of or relating to Tibet, its people, their language, or their culture.

Tibetan Buddhism, the form of Buddhism that developed in Tibet, recognizing the spiritual and political leadership of the monk named as the Dalai Lama.

tib·i·a (tib′ē ə) *n., pl.* **tib·i·ae** (tib′ē ē′) or **tib·i·as. 1.** the inner and thicker of the two bones of the leg, extending from the knee to the ankle; shinbone. **2.** the corresponding bone in the legs of birds and certain other animals.

tic (tik) *n.* a habitual, involuntary twitching of a muscle, especially in the face.

tick¹ (tik) *n.* **1.** a light, clicking sound, such as that made by a watch or a clock. **2.** a dot, slash, or other mark, often used in checking off items in a series. —*v.i.* **1.** to make a light, clicking sound, such as that made by a clock. **2.** (of time) to pass: *The minutes ticked away as we waited.* **3.** *Informal.* to work; function; go: *What makes that person tick?* —*v.t.* to mark or indicate with a slash or other mark: *to tick names off a list.* [From the Middle English word *tek* meaning ''a light tap¹.'']

tick² (tik) *n.* **1.** any of a group of very small, wingless animals that look like and are related to spiders. Ticks attach themselves to the skin of humans and animals and suck their blood. Some ticks transmit diseases. **2.** any of various insects that are parasites of horses, sheep, cattle, and deer. [From the Middle English word *teke* meaning this animal.]

tick³ (tik) *n.* the cloth covering or case of a mattress or pillow. [Probably from the Middle Dutch word *tīke* meaning ''pillow case,'' from the Latin word *theca* ''a cover, sheath,'' from the Greek word *thēkē* ''a case.'']

tick·er (tik′ər) *n.* **1.** something that ticks. **2.** a device that prints prepared stock market reports or news on a paper tape. **3.** a similar device that displays such information electronically. **4.** *Slang.* the heart. **5.** *Slang.* a watch.

ticker tape, the paper tape or ribbon on which a ticker prints stock market reports or news.

Femur

Fibula

Tibia

Foot

tibia
(det. 1)

tick·et (tik′it) *n.* **1.** a card or piece of paper that shows that the person who holds it has the right to receive certain services or privileges: *We bought the tickets for our flight.* **2.** a card, tag, or other piece of paper attached to something to show its price, who owns it, or the like. **3.** a list or group of candidates belonging to a particular political party, to be voted on in an election. **4.** a legal summons ordering a person to pay a fine or appear in court, especially for a traffic violation: *to get a ticket for speeding.* —*v.t.* **1.** to attach a ticket to: *They ticketed our baggage at the airport. The police officer ticketed that car for illegal parking.* **2.** to serve with a legal summons: *to ticket a driver for not stopping at a red light.*

tick·ing (tik′ing) *n.* a strong, durable fabric of closely woven cotton or linen, used especially to make covers for mattresses and pillows.

tick·le (tik′əl) *v.,* **tick·led, tick·ling.** —*v.t.* **1.** to touch (a person or a part of the body) so as to produce a tingling sensation, often causing laughter. **2.** to please, amuse, or excite agreeably; delight: *The smell of food from the kitchen tickled our taste buds. The children were tickled by the clown's antics.* —*v.i.* to feel or produce a tingling sensation. —*n.* **1.** the act of tickling or the state of being tickled. **2.** a tickling sensation: *A tickle in my throat made me cough.* —**tick′ler,** *n.*

tick·lish (tik′lish) *adj.* **1.** sensitive to tickling: *a ticklish person.* **2.** requiring caution, tact, and careful handling; delicate: *a ticklish situation.* **3.** easily offended; sensitive; touchy. —**tick′lish·ness,** *n.*

tic-tac-toe (tik′tak tō′) *also,* **tick-tack-toe.** *n.* a game played with a diagram having nine squares, in which two players alternately put X's and O's in the squares. The winner is the first person to complete a row of three X's or O's.

tid·al (tī′dəl) *adj.* of, relating to, or affected by tides: *a tidal basin, tidal ebb and flow.*

tidal wave 1. a huge, powerful ocean wave caused by an underwater earthquake; tsunami. **2.** any great movement or show of strong feeling: *A tidal wave of joy swept the crowd when the firefighters rescued the child.*

tid·bit (tid′bit′) *n.* a small, choice piece, as of food or gossip.

tid·dly·winks (tid′lē winks′) *n.* a game in which the players try to shoot small colored disks into a little cup by snapping them on the edge with a larger disk. ▲ used with a singular verb.

tide (tīd) *n.* **1.** the regular rise and fall of the ocean and bodies of water connected to it, caused by the gravitational pull of the moon and the sun. High tide occurs at a given place about every twelve hours and twenty-five minutes, with low tide occurring halfway between each high tide. **2.** a general trend or tendency: *The tide of public opinion turned against the corrupt mayor.* **3.** anything that tends to rise and fall or increase and decrease: *A tide of tourists swept through the town every summer.*

·to tide over. to aid in getting along during a difficult period or until a specific time: *This money should tide you over until payday.*

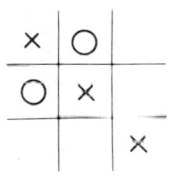

tic-tac-toe

at; āpe; fär; câre; end; mē; it; īce; pîerce; hot; old; sông, fôrk; oil; out; up; ūse; rüle; pùll; tûrn; chin; sing; shop; thin; **th**is; hw in white; zh in treasure. The symbol ə stands for the unstressed vowel sound heard in about, taken, pencil, lemon, and circus.

T

·**to turn the tide.** to reverse a condition or situation, especially to a more favorable one.

tide·land (tīd′land′) *n.* land that is covered and then uncovered by the rise and fall of the tides.

tide·wa·ter (tīd′wô′tər) *n.* **1.** a body of water affected by tides. **2.** low-lying coastal land whose waters are affected by tides. **3.** water that floods land at high tide. —*adj.* of, relating to, or situated along a tidewater: *a tidewater estate.*

ti·dings (tī′dingz) *pl. n.* news; information: *The messenger brought good tidings.*

ti·dy (tī′dē) *adj.*, **ti·di·er, ti·di·est. 1.** clean and neat; well-organized: *a tidy kitchen, a tidy person.* **2.** *Informal.* quite large; considerable: *We managed to save a tidy sum of money.* —*v.t., v.i.*, **ti·died, ti·dy·ing.** to arrange (things or oneself) in a clean and neat manner (often with *up*): *to tidy up one's room.* —*n., pl.* **ti·dies.** a small decorative covering placed over the back or arms of a chair or sofa to keep it from becoming soiled or worn. —**ti′di·ness,** *n.*

tie (tī) *v.*, **tied, ty·ing.** —*v.t.* **1.** to fasten with a rope, string, or similar material: *to tie a bundle of newspapers with a cord.* **2.** to fasten with a knot or bow: *to tie a shoe.* **3.** to make a knot or bow in: *to tie one's shoelaces.* **4.** to make (a knot or bow). **5.** to draw together or join closely: *Mutual interests tied us together.* **6.** to restrain or restrict; confine: *A long illness tied him to his bed.* **7.** to equal the score or total of (an opponent). **8.** to equal (a score or total). **9.** *Music.* to unite (notes) by a curved line written above or below two notes of the same pitch. —*v.i.* **1.** to be fastened with a rope, string, or similar material: *The baby wears a bib that ties around the neck.* **2.** to make the same score; be equal: *The two teams tied for first place.* —*n.* **1.** a cord, string, or similar material used to tie things. **2.** anything that unites or joins together: *The business partners have long been bound by ties of friendship.* **3.** see **necktie. 4.** an equal score: *The game ended in a tie.* **5.** a competition that ends with an equal score; draw: *The game was a tie.* **6.** a part of a structure, such as a beam or rod, that holds together or strengthens other parts. **7.** one of the crosspieces, usually of wood, to which railroad rails are fastened. **8.** *Music.* a curved line written above or below and connecting two notes of the same pitch, indicating that they should be played or sung as one long note.

tie *(n., def. 8)*

·**to tie down.** to restrict or confine: *The new baby tied down the parents.*

·**to tie in.** to connect, especially by being relevant or consistent: *The book I read ties in with the term paper I am writing.*

·**to tie up. a.** to fasten with a rope or the like. **b.** to prevent free action or movement: *An accident tied up traffic for an hour.* **c.** to keep in use or to keep busy and not free for anything else: *to tie up the phone for hours. The family's money was tied up in real estate.*

tie–dye (tī′dī′) *v.t.*, **tie–dyed, tie–dye·ing.** to dye (cloth) by the process of tie-dyeing.

tie–dye·ing (tī′dī′ing) *n.* a process of dyeing cloth in which parts of the cloth are folded and tied so that they will not be exposed to the dye, thereby producing a mottled appearance.

tier (tir) *n.* one of a series of layers or rows, as of seats, arranged one above another: *The bleachers are arranged in two tiers.*

tie–up (tī′up′) *n.* **1.** a stoppage or slowdown of work, action, or progress: *The accident caused a traffic tie-up at the corner.* **2.** *Informal.* a connection or association.

tiff (tif) *n.* a slight quarrel or spat.

tigers

ti·ger (tī′gər) *n.* a large, meat-eating Asian mammal of the cat family. It has a yellow coat marked with black or brown stripes. [From the Old English word *tigras* meaning "tigers," from the Latin word *tigris* "a tiger," from the Greek word *tigris* "a tiger."] —**ti′ger·like′,** *adj.*

tiger beetle, any of a group of brightly colored beetles that prey on other insects and whose larvae live in sandy soil.

tiger cat 1. any of several small, tigerlike wildcats, such as the ocelot. **2.** a domestic cat having striped markings, especially a tabby.

ti·ger·ish (tī′gər ish) *adj.* like a tiger in manner or appearance; fierce.

tiger lily, a slender plant that is grown for its showy, trumpet-shaped flowers, which are reddish orange spotted with black.

tiger moth, any of a large group of moths with striped or spotted wings.

tight (tīt) *adj.* **1.** fastened or held firmly; secure: *This window is too tight to open.* **2.** having the parts or units of which it is made close together; compact: *a fabric with a tight weave.* **3.** of such close construction or fit that a liquid or gas cannot pass through. **4.** pulled or stretched as far as possible: *Keep the clothesline tight between the poles.* **5.** fitting the body closely, especially too closely: *a tight belt.* **6.** having or allowing little time or space to spare: *a tight schedule.* **7.** difficult to deal with or manage: *to be in a tight spot.* **8.** strict; severe: *The government kept tight controls on public spending.* **9.** evenly matched; close: *a tight race.* **10.** *Informal.* not generous, especially with money; stingy. **11.** *Slang.* intoxicated; drunk. **12.** difficult to get; scarce: *Jobs are tight right now.* —*adv.* in a tight manner; firmly; securely: *to close a jar tight.* —**tight′ly,** *adv.* —**tight′ness,** *n.*

·**to sit tight.** to hold onto one's position or opinion; take no action.

tight·en (tīt′ən) *v.t., v.i.* to make or become tight or tighter.

tight–fist·ed (tīt′fis′tid) *adj.* stingy; miserly.

tight–lipped (tīt′lipt′) *adj.* **1.** having the lips closed tightly. **2.** quiet or secretive.

tight·rope (tīt′rōp′) *n.* a tightly stretched wire, cable, or rope placed high above the ground, on which acrobats perform.

tights (tīts) *pl. n.* a skintight garment, usually covering the lower part of the body.

tight·wad (tīt′wod′) *n.* *Slang.* a stingy person; miser.

ti·gress (tī′gris) *n., pl.* **ti·gress·es.** a female tiger.

tike (tīk) another spelling of **tyke.**

til·de (til′də) *n.* **1.** in Spanish, a diacritical mark (˜) used over *n* to indicate the pronunciation *ny*, as in *señor* (sen yôr′). **2.** in Portuguese, the same mark, used over the vowels *a* and *o* to indicate nasal pronunciation.

tile (tīl) *n.* **1.** a thin, often decorated slab, as of baked clay, porcelain, or linoleum, used for covering roofs, floors, or walls. **2.** tiles as a group; tiling. **3.** a piece used in playing various games, as dominoes. **4.** a short pipe, as of clay or concrete, used as a drain. —*v.t.,* **tiled, til·ing.** to cover with tiles.

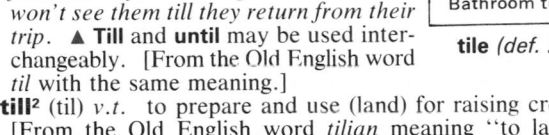

Roof tile

Bathroom tile

tile *(def. 2)*

til·ing (tī′ling) *n.* **1.** tiles as a group. **2.** the act of covering with tiles. **3.** something covered with or made of tiles.

till¹ (til) *prep.* **1.** up to the time of: *Wait till tomorrow before calling.* **2.** before (a specified time): *My grandparents won't arrive till Sunday.* —*conj.* **1.** up to the time when or that: *Wait till you hear from me before writing.* **2.** before: *We won't see them till they return from their trip.* ▲ **Till** and **until** may be used interchangeably. [From the Old English word *til* with the same meaning.]

till² (til) *v.t.* to prepare and use (land) for raising crops. [From the Old English word *tilian* meaning "to labor, strive to obtain."] —**till′a·ble,** *adj.*

till³ (til) *n.* a drawer or other container in which money is kept, as in a store. [From the Anglo-Norman word *tylle* meaning "a box for valuables."]

till·age (til′ij) *n.* **1.** the cultivation of land. **2.** land that is under cultivation. Also, **tilth.**

till·er¹ (til′ər) *n.* a bar or handle used to turn the rudder of a boat. [From the Old French word *teilier* meaning "a weaver's beam," going back to the Latin word *tela* "a weaver's beam," "the warp of a loom," or "a web."]

till·er² (til′ər) *n.* a person or thing that tills land. [*Till²* + *-er¹.*]

tilt (tilt) *v.t.* **1.** to raise one end or side of; put at an angle; tip: *Don't tilt your chair so far back or you will fall over.* **2.** to point or thrust (a lance) in a joust. **3.** to charge (an opponent) in a joust. —*v.i.* **1.** to slope or tip; incline. **2.** to take part in a joust. **3.** to charge or attack in joust. **4.** to attack in any way: *The young lawyer tilted at injustice.* —*n.* **1.** a sloping position; angle: *The tilt of the table made everything roll off.* **2.** a medieval contest between two knights on horseback who were usually armed with long lances; joust. **3.** any fight or confrontation that is like a joust between knights: *The courageous reporter engaged in journalistic tilts against dishonest city officials.* •**full tilt.** at full speed: *The car crashed full tilt against the wall.*

tilth (tilth) *n.* another word for **tillage.**

tim·ber (tim′bər) *n.* **1.** wood suitable for building, carpentry, or other forms of construction. **2.** a single piece of wood used in construction; beam: *Heavy timbers support the second floor.* **3.** one of the curved pieces leading from the keel and forming part of the framework of a ship. **4.** trees as a group. **5.** see **timberland.** —*interj.* a cry to warn others that a tree is being felled. —*v.t.* to cover, support, or supply with timber: *to timber an underground passage.*

tim·bered (tim′bərd) *adj.* **1.** covered with growing trees; wooded: *a heavily timbered region.* **2.** built or made of timber.

tim·ber·land (tim′bər land′) *n.* land covered with trees, especially trees that are to be cut for lumber.

tim·ber·line (tim′bər līn′) *n.* another word for **tree line.**

timber wolf, a gray wolf of the forest regions of Canada and the northern United States.

timber wolf

tim·bre (tim′bər, tam′bər) *n.* the special quality of sound, apart from pitch and volume, that distinguishes one voice or musical instrument from another.

tim·brel (tim′brəl) *n.* a tambourine or similar instrument.

time (tīm) *n.* **1.** an indefinite extent during which events, conditions, and actions happen, exist, or continue in succession: *The changing seasons show the passing of time.* **2.** an exact point in time, especially as shown by a clock or calendar: *What time is it?* **3.** a definite or specific point in time: *The senator has no comment at this time.* **4.** a favorable, right, usual, or appointed point in time: *It's time for lunch.* **5.** a definite or specific part or portion of time: *Summer is the warmest time of the year.* **6.** a portion of time available, necessary, or taken for some purpose: *I have no time to argue with you. The runner's time for the mile was four minutes.* **7.** a system of measuring or determining time: *sidereal time.* **8.** *also,* **times.** a portion of time in history: *the time of the Civil War, medieval times.* **9.** a period of time considered in terms of someone's personal experience: *I had a hard time finding a job.* **10.** one of a number of repeated or recurring actions or instances: *We have visited the library many times.* **11.** a period worked or to be worked by an employee. **12.** the pay received for this period. **13.** *Music.* rhythm, tempo, or meter, especially of a particular kind of musical composition: *waltz time.* —*v.t.,* **timed, tim·ing. 1.** to regulate, adjust, or arrange according to time: *The light was timed to go off at midnight.* **2.** to measure or determine the time, duration, or rate of: *to time a runner.* **3.** to choose the time or occasion for: *The mayor's announcement was timed to affect the coming election.* —*adj.* **1.** of or relating to time. **2.** regulated, adjusted, or devised to operate at a certain time: *a time lock.*
•**against time.** in an attempt to finish within or before a certain time: *The rescuers were working against time in their search for the survivors of the shipwreck.*
•**at the same time.** however; nevertheless.
•**at times.** sometimes; occasionally.
•**behind the times.** no longer in fashion; out-of-date.
•**for the time being.** for the present; for now.
•**from time to time.** now and then; occasionally.
•**in good time. a.** at the proper time; within reasonable time: *You will be told about the changes in good time.* **b.** when or sooner than expected; quickly: *We finished the work in good time and took a longer break than usual.*
•**in no time.** almost instantly; very quickly.
•**in time. a.** before it is too late: *We got to the station in time to catch the train.* **b.** in the course of time; eventually: *In time, all this will be forgotten.* **c.** in the correct rhythm or tempo: *to clap in time to music.*
•**on time. a.** at the correct or appointed time: *Did you get to school on time?* **b.** by paying in installments over a period of time: *to buy a car on time.*

at; āpe; fär; câre; end; mē; it; īce; pierce; hot; ōld; sông, fôrk; oil; out; up; ūse; rüle; pull; tûrn; chin; sing; shop; thin; **this;** hw in white; zh in treasure. The symbol ə stands for the unstressed vowel sound heard in about, taken, pencil, lemon, and circus.

T

·**time after time** or **time and again**. repeatedly.

·**to keep time**. to record time, as a clock.

·**to make time**. to move quickly, as in attempting to recover lost time.

time clock, a clock with a mechanism for recording the arrival and departure time of an employee.

time exposure 1. the exposure of a photographic film for a relatively long period of time, often for several seconds or more. **2.** a photograph made by such an exposure.

time–hon·ored (tīm'on'ərd) *adj.* revered, respected, or observed because of age or long usage: *a time-honored custom.*

time·keep·er (tīm'kē'pər) *n.* a person or thing that keeps, measures, or records time.

time·less (tīm'lis) *adj.* **1.** unaffected by the passage of time; eternal. **2.** referring to or characteristic of no particular time. —**time'less·ly,** *adv.*

time line, a representation of times or dates as points on a line, used to show the relationship of past events.

time·ly (tīm'lē) *adj.,* **time·li·er, time·li·est.** happening at a suitable or appropriate time; well-timed. —**time'li·ness,** *n.*

time-out (tīm'out') *n.* **1.** *Sports.* a short period of time during which play is stopped. **2.** any brief stopping of work or activity; break.

time·piece (tīm'pēs') *n.* any device that records, measures, or keeps time, especially a watch or clock.

tim·er (tī'mər) *n.* **1.** a person or thing that measures, records, or keeps time. **2.** a device in an internal-combustion engine that causes the spark to be produced in the cylinder at the right instant.

times (tīmz) *prep.* multiplied by: *Two times two equals four.*

time·sav·ing (tīm'sā'ving) *adj.* lessening the time needed to do something: *The microwave oven is a timesaving kitchen appliance.*

time–shar·ing (tīm'shâr'ing) *also,* **time shar·ing.** *n.* **1.** *Computers.* an arrangement by which a large computer can simultaneously serve several users at different terminals. **2.** an arrangement by which two or more people share in the ownership or rental of a house or other dwelling and occupy the dwelling at different times of the year, as for vacations.

time signature *Music.* a sign on a staff, usually expressed as a fraction, showing the meter or rhythm of the music that follows.

time·ta·ble (tīm'tā'bəl) *n.* a list of the times at which a series of events are to be done or happen, especially a schedule showing the arrival and departure times of trains, buses, boats, or airplanes.

time signature for three-quarter time

time·worn (tīm'wôrn') *adj.* **1.** showing the effects of time or long use. **2.** used too frequently; trite: *a timeworn joke.*

time zone, any of the twenty-four longitudinal regions of fifteen degrees each into which the earth is divided for measuring standard time from the prime meridian at Greenwich, England.

tim·id (tim'id) *adj.* marked by or showing a lack of courage, boldness, or self-confidence; shy: *The timid child hid whenever a visitor came to the house.* —**ti·mid'i·ty, tim'id·ness,** *n.* —**tim'id·ly,** *adv.*

tim·ing (tī'ming) *n.* the act of determining and using the right moment or speed for some action in order to produce the desired effect: *That batter has poor timing and usually strikes out.*

tim·or·ous (tim'ər əs) *adj.* marked by or showing a lack of courage, boldness, or self-confidence; timid. —**tim'or·ous·ly,** *adv.* —**tim'or·ous·ness,** *n.*

tim·o·thy (tim'ə thē) *n.* a tall, stout grass having smooth, hollow stems with clusters of tiny flowers at the tips. It is grown for hay and is sometimes used for grazing.

Tim·o·thy (tim'ə thē) *n.* either of two books of the New Testament consisting of epistles or letters written to Timothy by the Apostle Paul.

tim·pa·ni (tim'pə nē) *also,* **tym·pa·ni.** *pl. n.* kettledrums, especially those played in an orchestra. [From the Italian word *timpani* meaning "kettledrums," going back to the Latin word *tympanum* "drum" or "timbrel, tambourine," from the Greek word *tympanon* with the same meanings.] —**tim'pa·nist,** *n.*

tin (tin) *n.* **1.** a soft, silver-white metallic element that does not easily rust or corrode. It is used to coat sheet steel for cans and is alloyed with copper to make bronze. Symbol: **Sn 2.** see **tin plate. 3.** any object made of tin, such as a baking sheet. **4.** *British.* see **can²**

timothy

(def. 2). —*adj.* made of tin. —*v.t.,* **tinned, tin·ning. 1.** to cover, coat, or plate (something) with tin. **2.** *British.* to preserve or pack in tin cans; can: *to tin peaches.* [From the Old English word *tin.*]

tinc·ture (tingk'chər) *n.* **1.** a solution, usually in alcohol, containing a drug or other medicine. **2.** a small amount; trace; hint: *a tincture of sadness in one's voice.* **3.** a tinge of color; tint: *a tincture of blue in the night sky.* —*v.t.,* **tinc·tured, tinc·tur·ing. 1.** to give a tinge of a particular quality or character to. **2.** to tint; stain.

tin·der (tin'dər) *n.* any substance that burns easily, especially something used to start a fire from a spark, such as dry twigs.

tin·der·box (tin'dər boks') *n., pl.* **tin·der·box·es. 1.** a box used for holding the materials needed to start a fire, such as flint or coal. **2.** any place or situation that could become a source of strife or trouble.

tine (tīn) *n.* a sharp, projecting point or prong, as of a fork.

tin·foil (tin'foil') *n.* a very thin sheet of tin or other metal, such as aluminum, used as a wrapping.

ting (ting) *n.* a clear, high-pitched, metallic sound, such as that made by a small bell. —*v.i., v.t.* to make or cause to make a clear, high-pitched, metallic sound.

tinge (tinj) *v.t.,* **tinged, tinge·ing** or **ting·ing. 1.** to color slightly; tint; stain. **2.** to affect with a slight trace, touch, or flavor of some other quality or characteristic. —*n.* **1.** a faint trace of color. **2.** a small amount; touch; trace: *There was a tinge of autumn in the air.*

tin·gle (ting'gəl) *v.,* **tin·gled, tin·gling.** —*v.i.* **1.** to have a slight vibrating or stinging sensation, as from sudden excitement, cold, or a slap. **2.** to cause such a sensation. —*v.t.* to cause to tingle. —*n.* a tingling sensation.

tink·er (ting'kər) *n.* **1.** a craftsperson, usually one who wanders from place to place, who mends pots, pans, and other metal household utensils. **2.** a person who can do many different kinds of repair work. **3.** an unskillful or clumsy worker; bungler. —*v.i.* **1.** to busy oneself in a trifling or aimless way; putter: *to tinker with an old clock.* **2.** to work in an unskillful or clumsy manner. **3.** to work as a tinker; mend household utensils.

tin·kle (ting'kəl) *v.,* **tin·kled, tin·kling.** —*v.i.* to produce clear, light, ringing sounds. —*v.t.* to cause to tinkle. —*n.* a clear, light, ringing sound.

tin·ner (tin'ər) *n.* **1.** a person who works in a tin mine. **2.** a person who works with or buys and sells tin; tinsmith.

tin·ny (tin′ē) *adj.*, **tin·ni·er, tin·ni·est. 1.** of, relating to, or containing tin. **2.** having a metallic flavor, sound, or quality: *The canned juice had a tinny taste.* —**tin′ni·ness,** *n.*

tin plate, thin sheets of metal, especially iron or steel, coated with tin.

tin·sel (tin′səl) *n.* **1.** very thin strips of glittering metallic material, used for ornamentation, especially on Christmas trees. **2.** anything showy or attractive but having little or no real worth. **3.** a fabric woven with metallic threads, as of silver or gold. —*v.t.*, **tin·seled, tin·sel·ing;** *also,* *British,* **tin·selled, tin·sel·ling.** to trim with tinsel. —*adj.* **1.** made of, like, or decorated with tinsel. **2.** showy or attractive but having little or no real worth. [From the Middle French word *estincelle* meaning "a spark, flash," going back to the Latin word *scintilla* "a spark."]

tin·smith (tin′smith′) *n.* a person who works with or buys and sells tin or tinware.

tint (tint) *n.* **1.** a shade or variety of a color: *There are tints of red in your hair.* **2.** a delicate, pale color. —*v.t.* to add or give a slight color to: *The children tinted the Easter eggs.*

tin·type (tin′tīp′) *n.* a photograph made on an iron plate that is coated with tin and treated with a substance that is sensitive to light.

tin·ware (tin′wâr′) *n.* articles made of tin plate.

ti·ny (tī′nē) *adj.*, **ti·ni·er, ti·ni·est.** very small or slight.

–tion *suffix* (used to form nouns) **1.** the action or process of: *adoption.* **2.** the state or condition of being: *humiliation.* **3.** the result of: *contamination.*

tip¹ (tip) *n.* **1.** the extreme or outermost point or end of anything: *to scuff the tip of one's shoe.* **2.** a small piece or part attached to or forming the end of something: *the tip of a pen.* —*v.t.*, **tipped, tip·ping. 1.** to furnish with a tip. **2.** to cover, decorate, or serve as the tip of. [From the Middle English word *tip.*]

tip² (tip) *v.*, **tipped, tip·ping.** —*v.t.* **1.** to raise one end or side of. **2.** to cause to fall or tumble; overturn (often with *over*): *I accidentally tipped over the chair.* **3.** to raise or touch (one's hat) in greeting. —*v.i.* **1.** to be in or assume a sloping position or direction; tilt. **2.** to fall or topple (often with *over*). *The ashtray tipped over.* —*n.* an inclined position; tilt. [From the Middle English word *tippen* meaning "to overturn" or "to tilt."]

tip³ (tip) *n.* **1.** a gift of money given in return for some service: *to give a bellhop a tip for carrying a suitcase.* **2.** a piece of useful information given privately or secretly, especially by an expert: *a tip from a stockbroker.* **3.** any useful or helpful hint or suggestion: *The mechanic gave me some tips about the care of my car.* —*v.*, **tipped, tip·ping.** —*v.t.* to give a gift of money to for some service: *to tip a porter for carrying one's bags at the airport.* —*v.i.* to give a tip or tips. [Of uncertain origin.] —**tip′per,** *n.*

·to tip off. *Informal.* to give private or secret information to: *A friend tipped me off about a good place to buy a used car.*

tip·pet (tip′it) *n.* **1.** a covering that is like a scarf, worn about the neck and shoulders with loose ends hanging down in front. **2.** in the Anglican Church, a long black scarf worn over the robe of a member of the clergy. **3.** formerly, a long, narrow hanging part, as of a hood or sleeve.

tip·ple (tip′əl) *v.t.*, *v.i.*, **tip·pled, tip·pling.** to drink (alcoholic beverages) regularly and frequently in small amounts. —*n.* an alcoholic beverage. —**tip′pler,** *n.*

tip·ster (tip′stər) *n. Informal.* a person who gives or sells private or secret information, especially to people who bet on horse races or the like.

tip·sy (tip′sē) *adj.*, **tip·si·er, tip·si·est. 1.** slightly drunk. **2.** inclined to tip; unsteady; shaky. —**tip′si·ly,** *adv.* —**tip′si·ness,** *n.*

tip·toe (tip′tō′) *v.i.*, **tip·toed, tip·toe·ing.** to move or walk on the tips of one's toes; walk quietly or stealthily.

tip·top (tip′top′) *Informal. n.* the highest point or part. —*adj.* **1.** located at the highest point. **2.** of the highest quality; first-rate; excellent.

ti·rade (tī′rād′, tī′rād) *n.* a long, strongly expressed or very emotional speech, especially one containing abuse or criticism.

tire¹ (tīr) *v.*, **tired, tir·ing.** —*v.t.* **1.** to weaken or exhaust the strength or energy of; make weary; fatigue: *Reading in the dim light tired my eyes.* **2.** to exhaust the attention, interest, or patience of; bore: *The long speech tired the children.* —*v.i.* **1.** to become fatigued or weary: *to tire easily.* **2.** to become bored: *The children tired of the new game quickly.* [From the Old English word *tēorian* meaning "to exhaust, cease" or "to cause to fail."]

tire² (tīr) *also, British,* **tyre.** *n.* a band, usually of rubber, either solid or filled with air, around the rim of a wheel. Tires absorb shock and provide traction. [From the Middle English word *tire* meaning "equipment," "ornament," or "metal hoop around the outside of a wheel," short for *atire* "attire."]

tired (tīrd) *adj.* worn-out; weary; exhausted. —**tired′ly,** *adv.* —**tired′ness,** *n.*

tire·less (tīr′lis) *adj.* never wearying; untiring: *a tireless worker.* —**tire′less·ly,** *adv.* —**tire′less·ness,** *n.*

tire·some (tīr′səm) *adj.* tedious; boring; tiring: *tiresome details.* —**tire′some·ly,** *adv.* —**tire′some·ness,** *n.*

ti·ro (tī′rō) *n., pl.* **ti·ros.** another spelling of **tyro.**

'tis (tiz) *contr.* it is.

tis·sue (tish′ü) *n.* **1.** in animals and plants, a group of similar cells performing the same function. In the human body there are four basic types of tissues: epithelium, connective tissue, muscle, and the tissue forming the nervous system. **2.** a soft, thin, absorbent piece of paper, usually made up of two layers. It is used especially as a handkerchief. **3.** see **tissue paper. 4.** a woven fabric, usually having a light, gauzy texture. **5.** network; web: *a tissue of lies.* [From the Middle English word *tissu* meaning "a rich fabric," from the Old French word *tissu* with the same meaning, going back to the Latin word *texere* "to weave."]

tissue paper, a very thin, nearly transparent paper, used for wrapping or packing.

tit¹ (tit) *n.* **1.** see **titmouse. 2.** any of various small birds, such as the pipit. [From the Middle English word *titmose* meaning this bird, from the word *tit* "small creature" + *mose* "titmouse," from the Old English word *māse* "titmouse."]

tit² (tit) *n.* a teat. [A form of the word *teat*, both from the Old English word *tit* meaning "breast."]

Ti·tan (tī′tən) *n.* **1.** *Greek Mythology.* any of a race of giants who were the offspring or descendants of Uranus and Gaea. They ruled the world until overthrown by the Olympian gods. **2. titan.** a person who has great size, strength, or power.

Ti·ta·ni·a (ti tā′nē ə) *n. Medieval Legend.* the queen of the fairies.

---

at; āpe; fär; câre; end; mē; it; īce; pîerce; hot; ōld; sông; fôrk; oil; out; up; ūse; rūle; pûll; tûrn; chin; sing; shop; thin; this; hw in white; zh in treasure. The symbol ə stands for the unstressed vowel sound heard in about, taken, pencil, lemon, and circus.

T

ti·tan·ic (tī tan′ik) *adj.* **1.** having great size, strength, or power. **2. Titanic.** of, relating to, or like the Titans.

ti·ta·ni·um (tī tā′nē əm) *n.* a light, strong, silver-white metallic element found in the earth's crust and on the moon. It is used to make structural parts of aircraft and spacecraft. Symbol: **Ti** [From *Titan*.]

tit for tat, something equal given in return; blow for blow.

tithe (tīth) *n.* **1.** one tenth of a person's yearly income, paid in either labor or money, especially for the support of the church and the clergy. **2.** one tenth of anything. **3.** any small tax, tribute, or levy. **4.** a very small part. —*v.t.,* **tithed, tith·ing. 1.** to impose a tax of a tenth on. **2.** to give one tenth of (one's yearly income), especially for the support of the church and the clergy.

tit·il·late (tit′ə lāt′) *v.t.,* **tit·il·lat·ed, tit·il·lat·ing. 1.** to excite or stimulate agreeably: *to titillate the imagination.* **2.** to produce a tickling sensation in. —**tit′·il·la′tion,** *n.*

tit·lark (tit′lärk′) *n.* see **pipit.**

ti·tle (tī′təl) *n.* **1.** the name by which a particular thing is identified, known, or referred to, such as a book, painting, poem, song, or the like. **2.** a word or group of words attached to the name of a person or family as an expression of respect, or to show rank, occupation, status, and the like. Madam, Lord, Lady, Professor, Doctor, and Sergeant can be titles. **3.** a championship: *the heavyweight boxing title.* **4.** *Law.* **a.** a right that a person has to the ownership of property: *to have title to a house.* **b.** something that serves as evidence of such a right, as a deed. **c.** the means by which one gets such a right. **5.** an established or recognized right; just claim. —*v.t.,* **ti·tled, ti·tling.** to give a title to; call: *I titled the essay "My Country."*

ti·tled (tī′təld) *adj.* having a title: *titled nobility.*

title page, a page at the beginning of a book, usually containing the title of the book and the names of the author and publisher.

title role, a role or character in a play, motion picture, or other theatrical presentation for which the presentation is named: *the two title roles in* Romeo and Juliet.

tit·mouse (tit′mous′) *n., pl.* **tit·mice** (tit′mīs′). any of various small songbirds. Also, **tit.**

tit·ter (tit′ər) *v.i.* to laugh in a restrained or nervous way. —*n.* a restrained or nervous laugh.

tit·tle (tit′əl) *n.* **1.** a very small part or amount; tiny quantity. **2.** a small diacritical mark, as over a letter, in writing or printing. The dot over a *j* is a tittle.

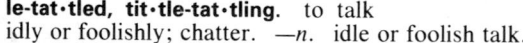
titmouse

tit·tle–tat·tle (tit′əl tat′əl) *v.i.,* **tit·tle-tat·tled, tit·tle-tat·tling.** to talk idly or foolishly; chatter. —*n.* idle or foolish talk.

tit·u·lar (tich′ə lər) *adj.* **1.** having the title or name of an office but not the powers or duties that go with it; nominal: *The former president was the titular leader of the political party.* **2.** of or relating to a title role. —**tit′u·lar·ly,** *adv.*

Ti·tus (tī′təs) *n.* a book of the New Testament consisting of an epistle written to Titus by Paul.

tiz·zy (tiz′ē) *n., pl.* **tiz·zies.** *Slang.* a state of great excitement, agitation, or confusion.

Tl, the symbol for thallium.

Tm, the symbol for thulium.

TN, postal abbreviation for Tennessee.

TNT, a yellow, crystalline compound, widely used as a high explosive.

to (tü; *unstressed* tù, tə) *prep.* **1.** in the direction of; toward: *Turn to the left.* **2.** in the direction of and reaching: *We took the train to Chicago. The tree fell to the ground.*

3. as far as: *We were caught in the rain without umbrellas and got wet to the skin.* **4.** on, upon, or against: *Tack the carpet to the floor.* **5.** toward or into a condition of: *The glass was smashed to bits.* **6.** so as to cause or result in: *To our surprise, they agreed with us.* **7.** for the purpose of; for: *The police came to our aid.* **8.** until: *The store is open from nine to six.* **9.** before: *It's five minutes to three.* **10.** as compared with: *Our team won by a score of three to one.* **11.** making up; comprising: *There are four cups to a quart.* **12.** belonging with or used with: *Where is the vest to this suit?* **13.** regarding; about; concerning: *That is all there was to it.* **14. To** is also used: **a.** for indicating the receiver of an action: *I gave the letter to the mail carrier.* **b.** for introducing the infinitive form of a verb: *I learned to swim last summer.* ▲ in this sense *to* is often used alone when the verb is understood from the rest of the statement: *You may go home when you want to.* —*adv.* **1.** forward: *The boat turned to.* **2.** into a shut or closed position: *Be sure to slam the door to.*

toad (tōd) *n.* any of various animals related to and resembling frogs, having rough, dry, bumpy skin and living most of the time on land rather than in water. Toads are tailless amphibians.

toad

toad·stool (tōd′stül′) *n.* any of various mushrooms, especially one that is thought to be poisonous or that has a bad taste.

toad·y (tō′dē) *n., pl.* **toad·ies.** a person who flatters another for personal gain; fawning person. —*v.i.,* **toad·ied, toad·y·ing.** to be or behave like a toady: *to toady to one's superiors.*

to and fro, forward and backward.

toast[1] (tōst) *n.* sliced bread browned by heat. —*v.t.* **1.** to brown by heating, as in a toaster or over a fire. **2.** to warm thoroughly, as before a fire or heater: *to toast one's feet.* —*v.i.* to become toasted: *Bread toasts much more quickly in the new toaster.* [From the Old French word *toster* meaning "to roast," going back to the Latin word *tostus,* past participle of *torrēre* "to bake, burn, parch."]

toast[2] (tōst) *n.* **1.** the act of drinking in honor of or to the health of a person or thing: *There were several toasts to the bride and groom.* **2.** the person or thing that is honored in this way: *The senator was the toast of the banquet.* —*v.t.* to drink to the honor or to the health of: *At midnight the friends toasted the New Year.* —*v.i.* to propose or drink a toast or toasts. [From the earlier use of this word to mean "a beautiful woman, belle" to whose health a toast was drunk; probably from *toast*[1].]

toast·er (tōs′tər) *n.* a device, usually electrical, for toasting bread.

toast·mas·ter (tōst′mas′tər) *n.* a person who proposes the toasts and introduces the guests and speakers at a formal dinner or other gathering.

to·bac·co (tə bak′ō) *n., pl.* **to·bac·cos. 1.** the prepared leaves of any of various plants, used for smoking and chewing and as snuff. **2.** any of these plants, having large leaves covered with hairs, and pink, white, or red flowers that are shaped like a funnel. **3.** products prepared from the leaves of these plants, such as cigars, cigarettes, or snuff.

to·bac·co·nist (tə bak′ə nist) *n.* a dealer in tobacco.

tobacco leaves

toboggan *(n.)*

to·bog·gan (tə bog′ən) *n.* a long, flat-bottomed sled without runners, having a curled-up front end. Toboggans are used for coasting on snow or for transporting goods. —*v.i.* **1.** to coast or ride on a toboggan. **2.** to decline or decrease rapidly, as in value. [Originally from the Algonquian word *tobâgun* meaning "a skin-covered sledge."]

toc·sin (tok′sin) *n.* **1.** a signal or alarm sounded on a bell. **2.** a bell or other signal that is used to sound an alarm.

to·day (tə dā′) *also,* **to-day.** *n.* the present day, time, or age. —*adv.* **1.** on or during the present day. **2.** at the present time; nowadays; currently: *Fashions today are different from what they were a hundred years ago.*

tod·dle (tod′əl) *v.i.,* **tod·dled, tod·dling.** to walk or move with short, unsteady steps, as a child who is just learning to walk. —*n.* the act of toddling.

tod·dler (tod′lər) *n.* a small child, especially one who is just learning to walk.

tod·dy (tod′ē) *n., pl.* **tod·dies. 1.** a drink made with brandy or other liquor, hot water, spices, sugar, and a slice of lemon. **2.** a drink made from the fermented sap of certain kinds of East Indian palm trees. **3.** the sap of these trees.

to do (tə dü′) *n., pl.* **to-dos.** *Informal.* bustle or fuss; commotion.

toe (tō) *n.* **1.** any of the five separate parts at the end of the foot. **2.** the part of a stocking, shoe, or other piece of footwear that covers the toes. **3.** the forward part of a foot or hoof. **4.** anything resembling a toe in shape, position, or function. —*v.,* **toed, toe·ing.** —*v.t.* **1.** to furnish with a toe or toes. **2.** to drive (a nail) at an angle. **3.** to fasten or attach by nails driven in this way. —*v.i.* to turn the toes in a specific direction.
 ·to be on one's toes. to be physically or mentally alert and ready for whatever may happen.

toed (tōd) *adj.* having toes, especially a specific number or kind of toes. ▲ usually used in combination: *a three-toed sloth, square-toed shoes.*

toe·nail (tō′nāl′) *n.* **1.** a nail that grows on a toe. **2.** a nail driven at an angle. —*v.t.* to fasten or attach with nails driven at an angle.

tof·fee (tô′fē, tof′ē) *also,* **tof·fy.** *n.* a hard, chewy candy made of butter, sugar, and often nuts.

tof·fy (tô′fē, tof′ē) *n., pl.* **tof·fies.** another spelling of **toffee.**

to·fu (tō′fü) *n.* a soft, white food made from mashed soybeans, formed into a cake, used especially in Asian and vegetarian cooking. Also, **bean curd.** [From the Japanese word *tōfu.*]

tog (tog) *Informal. n.* **togs.** clothes. —*v.t.,* **togged, tog·ging.** to dress or array.

to·ga (tō′gə) *n.* a loose outer garment draped over the entire body, covering the left arm and leaving the right arm bare, worn by male citizens of ancient Rome. The approximate social position of a man could be determined by the color and ornamentation of the toga he wore.

to·geth·er (tə geth′ər) *adv.* **1.** one with the other; with one another; in company: *The bride and groom walked down the aisle together.* **2.** in or into one gathering, company, mass, or body: *The whole school will meet together next week.* **3.** in or into contact, combination, or association with each other: *Mix the flour and water together.* **4.** in or into agreement, harmony, or cooperation: *Let's try to get together on this problem.* **5.** considered as a whole: *That elephant weighs more than all of us together.* **6.** at the same time; simultaneously: *The firecrackers all exploded together.*

tog·gle (tog′əl) *n.* **1.** a pin, bolt, or rod put through the eye of a rope or the link of a chain to prevent slipping, to tighten, or to secure an attachment. **2.** an ornamental, oblong button sewn on clothing or other items and serving as a fastening when inserted through a loop or similar opening. **3.** an electric switch that opens and closes a circuit as a lever is moved up and down. Also *(def. 3),* **toggle switch.** —*v.t.,* **tog·gled, tog·gling.** to fasten or furnish with a toggle or toggles.

toil[1] (toil) *n.* hard and exhausting work or effort. —*v.i.* **1.** to do hard and exhausting work, especially for a considerable length of time: *The workers toiled to build the railroad.* **2.** to move with difficulty, weariness, or pain. [From the Middle English word *toilen* meaning "to struggle, argue," from the Norman French word *toiler* with the same meaning.] —**toil′er,** *n.*

toil[2] (toil) *n.* something that ensnares or entangles, as a net: *The drug smugglers were caught in the toils of the law.* Also, **toils** (toilz). [From the Old French word *toile* meaning "a net," from the Latin word *tela* "a weaver's beam," "the warp of a loom," or "a web."]

toi·let (toi′lit) *n.* **1.** a fixture consisting of a water-filled basin usually having a lid, a hinged seat, and a flushing device connected to a water tank, used for the elimination and disposal of human waste. **2.** a room containing such a fixture; bathroom. **3.** the act or process of washing, dressing, and grooming oneself. **4.** a person's dress; attire. —*adj.* of, relating to, or for the toilet.

toi·let·ry (toi′li trē) *n., pl.* **toi·let·ries.** any of various articles, such as soap or cologne, used in grooming oneself.

toilet water, a scented liquid serving as a light perfume, as for use after a bath; cologne.

toil·some (toil′səm) *adj.* requiring hard work; tiresome; laborious.

toil·worn (toil′wôrn′) *adj.* exhausted or worn out by toil or hard work.

to·ken (tō′kən) *n.* **1.** something that serves to indicate or represent some fact, event, object, or feeling; sign; symbol: *This gift is a token of our appreciation.* **2.** something given as an expression of affection or as a memento. **3.** a piece of metal resembling a coin, used as a substitute for money, as in paying for transportation fares. —*adj.* having little or no value, force, or effect: *a token fee, token resistance.*
 ·by the same token. in an equivalent manner; likewise.

at; āpe; fär; câre; end; mē; it; īce; pierce; hot; ōld; sông, fôrk; oil; out; up; ūse; rüle; pull; tûrn; chin; sing; shop; thin; **this;** hw in white; zh in treasure. The symbol ə stands for the unstressed vowel sound heard in about, taken, pencil, lemon, and circus.

T

told (tōld) the past tense and past participle of **tell**.
·**all told.** counting all; in all: *They invited fifty people all told.*

tol·er·a·ble (tol′ər ə bəl) *adj.* **1.** capable of being endured; bearable: *a tolerable pain.* **2.** moderately good; passable: *a tolerable performance.* —**tol′er·a·bly.** *adv.*

tol·er·ance (tol′ər əns) *n.* **1.** the ability or willingness to accept or respect the behavior, customs, opinions, or beliefs of others. **2.** the act of tolerating. **3.** the ability to resist or endure the effects of something, such as a drug or poison, that is given in larger and larger amounts. **4.** the power or ability to endure something, such as pain. **5.** an allowable deviation from a specified standard, as in the weight of coins or in the size of a machine part.

tol·er·ant (tol′ər ənt) *adj.* **1.** inclined to accept or respect the behavior, customs, opinions, or beliefs of others. **2.** capable of resisting or enduring the effects of something, such as a drug or poison. —**tol′er·ant·ly,** *adv.*

tol·er·ate (tol′ə rāt′) *v.t.* **tol·er·at·ed, tol·er·at·ing.** **1.** to allow to exist or be done without prohibiting or interfering: *to tolerate the practice of different religions.* **2.** to suffer or endure; put up with; bear: *How can you tolerate all that noise while you work?* **3.** to develop or have tolerance for (a drug, poison, or the like). [From the Latin word *toleratus,* past participle of *tolerare* meaning "to endure, sustain."]

tol·er·a·tion (tol′ə rā′shən) *n.* **1.** the act or practice of tolerating. **2.** recognition of an individual's right to certain freedoms and privileges, especially freedom of worship.

toll¹ (tōl) *v.i.* (of a bell) to sound with slow, regular strokes; peal. —*v.t.* **1.** to cause (a bell) to sound with slow, regular strokes. **2.** to announce or summon by tolling: *The bells tolled the beginning of the church service.* —*n.* **1.** the act of tolling a bell. **2.** the sound made by a bell being tolled. [From the Middle English word *tollen* meaning "to sound a bell."]

toll² (tōl) *n.* **1.** a tax or fixed fee paid for the right or privilege to use something, such as a bridge or highway. **2.** a charge for a particular service rendered, such as the transmission of a long-distance telephone call. **3.** a number of people or things lost, destroyed, or damaged: *The hurricane took a heavy toll of lives.* [From the Old English word *toll* meaning "a tax, toll²," from the Late Latin word *telonium* "a tollbooth," from the Greek word *telōnion* "a tollbooth," going back to the word *telos* "a tax, toll²."]

toll·booth (tōl′būth′) *n., pl.* **toll·booths** (tōl′būthz′, tōl′būths′). a booth, as at a tollgate, where a toll is collected.

toll·gate (tōl′gāt′) *n.* a gate or other barrier used to block passage until a toll is paid.

Tol·tec (tōl′tek, tol′tek) *n.* a member of an Indian nation that lived in Mexico from the eleventh to the thirteenth century. —*adj.* of, like, or relating to the Toltecs or their culture.

tol·u·ene (tol′ū ēn′) *n.* a flammable, aromatic hydrocarbon compound made from petroleum, used in airplane fuel and as a solvent.

tom (tom) *n.* the male of certain animals, especially a cat or turkey.

tom·a·hawk (tom′ə hôk′) *n.* a light ax used as a weapon or tool by North American Indians. —*v.t.* to attack, strike, or kill with a tomahawk.

to·ma·to (tə mā′tō, tə mä′tō) *n., pl.* **to·ma·toes.** **1.** the juicy red, green, or yellow fruit of a plant related to the potato, having a smooth skin and eaten either raw or cooked. **2.** the plant bearing this fruit, having yellow flowers.

tomb (tüm) *n.* **1.** a vault or chamber in which a dead body is placed. **2.** any place of burial.

tom·boy (tom′boi′) *n.* a young girl who enjoys activities and interests that are usually considered to be perferred by boys.

tomb·stone (tüm′stōn′) *n.* a stone placed at the head of a grave, usually inscribed with the dead person's name and dates of birth and death.

tom·cat (tom′kat′) *n.* a male cat.

tome (tōm) *n.* **1.** a book, especially a large or scholarly one. **2.** one of a set of books containing several volumes.

tom·fool (tom′fül′) *adj.* extremely stupid or foolish. —*n.* a person who acts in a stupid or foolish manner.

tom·fool·er·y (tom′fü′lə rē) *n., pl.* **tom·fool·er·ies.** foolish or absurd behavior; nonsense.

to·mor·row (tə môr′ō, tə mor′ō) *n.* **1.** the day after today: *Tomorrow is my birthday.* **2.** some indefinite time in the future: *The world of tomorrow will be very different.* —*adv.* on the day after today: *We are going away tomorrow.*

tom·tit (tom′tit′) *n.* any of various small birds, such as the titmouse and wren.

tom-tom (tom′tom′) *n.* any of various small drums, usually beaten with the hands.

ton (tun) *n.* **1.** a unit of weight equal to 2,000 pounds avoirdupois (907.2 kilograms) in the United States and Canada. **2.** a unit of weight equal to 2,240 pounds avoirdupois (1,016 kilograms) in Great Britain. **3.** see **metric ton. 4.** *Informal.* an extremely large quantity of anything: *I have a ton of work to do.*

ton·al (tō′nəl) *adj.* of or relating to tone or tonality.

to·nal·i·ty (tō nal′i tē) *n., pl.* **to·nal·i·ties. 1.** *Music.* **a.** the melodic and harmonic relation existing between the tones of a scale or musical system. **b.** a particular scale or system of tones; key. **2.** the arrangement of tones or colors in a painting.

tone (tōn) *n.* **1.** any sound considered with reference to its pitch, quality, duration, or volume. **2.** the quality of sound: *This stereo has good tone.* **3.** *Music.* **a.** a sound having definite pitch and character. **b.** a whole step. **4.** a particular style or manner of speaking or writing: *a friendly tone of voice.* **5.** a general or prevailing character, style, or tendency, as of thought or behavior: *The tone of the meeting was serious.* **6.** a degree of tension or firmness, as of muscle. **7.** the effect of the combination of light, shade, and color in a picture: *a silvery tone.* **8.** a tint or shade of a particular color: *The painter used various tones of blue.* —*v.,* **toned, ton·ing.** —*v.t.* **1.** to give a particular tone or quality to, as in sound or color. **2.** to change or correct the color of. —*v.i.* to harmonize in color.
·**to tone down.** to soften or lessen, as in volume, intensity, or severity.
·**to tone up.** to increase or gain, as in strength, intensity, or vitality.

tone arm, the arm of a phonograph that holds the cartridge.

tone-deaf (tōn′def′) *adj.* unable to distinguish differences in musical pitch. —**tone′-deaf′ness,** *n.*

tong (tong, tông) *v.t.* to grasp, hold, or handle with tongs.

tongs (tongz, tôngz) *pl. n.* any of various devices for grasping objects, usually having two curved arms connected by a pivot.

tongue (tung) *n* **1.** a movable organ attached to the floor of the mouth, used for tasting, swallowing, and, in humans, for talking. **2.** an animal's tongue prepared and used for food. **3.** a spoken language or dialect: *My native tongue is English.* **4.** a manner of speaking, especially in re-

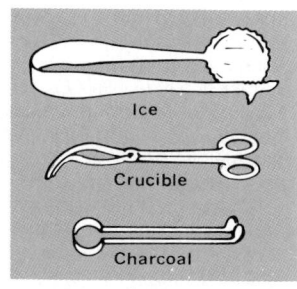

Ice

Crucible

Charcoal

tongs

gard to meaning or intent: *a sarcastic tongue.* **5.** the ability to speak; power of speech: *I was so shy I couldn't find my tongue to answer the teacher.* **6.** anything resembling the human tongue in shape, position, or function, such as a tapering jet of flame. **7.** a narrow strip of land projecting into a body of water. **8.** a strip of leather or other material lying under the laces or fastenings of a shoe or boot.

　•**on the tip of one's tongue.** about to be remembered or spoken: *The new student's name is on the tip of my tongue.*
　•**to hold one's tongue.** to keep from speaking; be silent.
　•**tongue in cheek.** with sarcasm or irony: *to speak tongue in cheek about the joys of homework.*

tongue-in-cheek (tung′in chēk′) *adj.* sarcastic or ironic: *a tongue-in-cheek remark.*

tongue-tied (tung′tīd′) *adj.* unable to speak or express oneself, as from fear, shyness, or embarrassment.

tongue twister, a word, phrase, or sentence that is difficult to pronounce distinctly and rapidly, usually because of the repetition of a sound or sounds. *Round the rugged rock the ragged rascal ran* and *Peter Piper picked a peck of pickled peppers* are tongue twisters.

ton·ic (ton′ik) *n.* **1.** anything that refreshes, invigorates, or strengthens: *The cool weather was a tonic after the hot spell.* **2.** a medicine or drug that invigorates or strengthens. **3.** *Music.* a note on which a scale or system of tones is based. **4.** a carbonated beverage containing quinine, used for mixing with liquor, such as gin or vodka. **5.** a liquid preparation for the hair or scalp. —*adj.* **1.** refreshing; bracing; invigorating. **2.** of or relating to tone or tones. **3.** *Music.* of, relating to, or based on a tonic: *a tonic chord.*

to·night (tə nīt′) *n.* **1.** the night of this day: *The morning paper says tonight will be rainy.* **2.** the present night; this night: *Tonight has been cool so far.* —*adv.* on or during the present or coming night.

ton·nage (tun′ij) *n.* **1.** the carrying capacity of a ship, expressed in tons. **2.** the total amount of shipping, as of a port or nation, in terms of carrying capacity. **3.** a duty, tax, or similar charge levied on ships at so much per ton of cargo. **4.** weight measured in tons, as of goods shipped or produced.

tonne (tun) *n.* another word for **metric ton.**

ton·sil (ton′səl) *n.* any of several masses of spongy tissue located in the mouth or throat of humans and other mammals that help protect the body against infection, especially, in humans, the pair of these spongy masses found on each side of the throat at the back of the tongue.

ton·sil·lec·to·my (ton′sə lek′tə mē) *n., pl.* **ton·sil·lec·to·mies.** the surgical removal of a tonsil or tonsils.

ton·sil·li·tis (ton′sə lī′tis) *n.* inflammation of a tonsil or tonsils.

ton·so·ri·al (ton sôr′ē əl) *adj.* of or relating to a barber or a barber's work.

ton·sure (ton′shər) *n.* **1.** a shaving of a part or all of the head of a man entering the priesthood or a monastic order. **2.** the part of the head so shaven. —*v.t.,* **ton·sured, ton·sur·ing.** to shave the head of.

too (tü) *adv.* **1.** in addition; besides; also: *Your friend is very bright and a good worker, too.* **2.** more than enough: *There were too many people in the room.* **3.** exceedingly; very: *I was not too sorry to see them go.* **4.** *Informal.* indeed. ▲ used for emphasis: *You will too do it!*

took (tuk) the past tense of **take.**

tool (tül) *n.* **1.** any of various devices held in the hand and used in doing work, such as a hammer, wrench, or saw. **2.** a power-driven instrument or machine used to cut and shape machinery parts. **3.** the cutting or shaping part of such an instrument or machine. **4.** a person who is used by another; dupe. **5.** anything used in or necessary

to the carrying out of an action, profession, or trade: *A good library is a very helpful tool in a school.* —*v.t.* **1.** to work, shape, or mark with a tool. **2.** to provide (a factory or plant) with machinery or tools for production. —*v.i.* to work with a tool or tools.

tool·box (tül′boks′) *n., pl.* **tool·box·es.** a box for storing or carrying tools.

toot (tüt) *v.t.* to cause (a horn, whistle, or the like) to sound with a short, quick blast or blasts. —*v.i.* to produce a short, quick blast or blasts. —*n.* **1.** a short, quick blast, such as that produced by a horn. **2.** the act of producing such a sound.

tooth (tüth) *n., pl.* **teeth.** **1.** in human beings and certain other animals with backbones, one of the hard structures set in the jaws and supported by the gums, used especially for biting and chewing. A human adult has thirty-two permanent teeth. **2.** a similar structure in certain animals without backbones. **3.** something resembling a tooth in shape, position, or use, such as one of the projecting pieces on a comb. —*v.t.* **1.** to furnish with teeth: *to tooth a saw.* **2.** to make jagged, as an edge. —**tooth′like′,** *adj.*

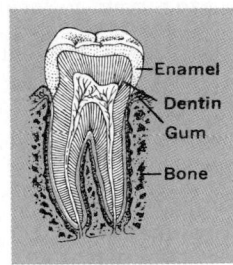

human **tooth**

　•**armed to the teeth.** completely or fully armed.
　•**in the teeth of.** in the face of; in opposition to.
　•**to fight tooth and nail.** to fight with all one's strength.
　•**to get one's teeth into** or **to sink one's teeth into.** to become completely involved in; get a firm grasp of.
　•**to put teeth into.** to give force or effect to: *to put teeth into a law.*

tooth·ache (tüth′āk′) *n.* a pain in a tooth, the teeth, or the area surrounding the teeth.

tooth·brush (tüth′brush′) *n., pl.* **tooth·brush·es.** a small, narrow brush with a long handle, used for cleaning the teeth.

toothed (tütht) *adj.* **1.** having teeth, especially of a specific kind or number. ▲ usually used in combination: *a saber-toothed tiger.* **2.** having notches; serrated; jagged: *a toothed leaf.*

tooth·less (tüth′lis) *adj.* **1.** having no teeth. **2.** without force or effect; ineffectual: *a toothless law.*

tooth·paste (tüth′pāst′) *n.* a paste for cleaning teeth.

tooth·pick (tüth′pik′) *n.* a small, narrow sliver of wood, plastic, or similar material, used to remove food or other matter from between the teeth.

tooth·some (tüth′səm) *adj.* **1.** pleasing to the taste; tasty. **2.** attractive; pleasant.

top¹ (top) *n.* **1.** the highest part of anything: *the top of a flagpole, the top of a page.* **2.** the cover or lid of something, or a part forming a cover: *a box top.* **3.** a garment for the upper half of the body, usually part of a two-piece outfit: *a pajama top.* **4.** the part of certain plants that grows above the ground. **5.** the highest or leading position or rank: *to graduate at the top of one's class.* **6.** the highest pitch or degree: *to scream at the top of one's voice.* **7.** a platform around the head of a lower mast of a ship, used as a place to stand on for

at; āpe; fär; câre; end; mē; it; īce; pîerce; hot; ōld; sông, fôrk; oil; out; up; ūse; rüle; pull; tûrn; chin; sing; shop; thin; this; hw in white; zh in treasure. The symbol ə stands for the unstressed vowel sound heard in about, taken, pencil, lemon, and circus.

T

extending the rigging of the top mast. —*adj.* **1.** of or at the top: *the top drawer, the top floor of a building.* **2.** first or highest in rank, position, or quality; foremost: *the top person in a field, the top executive in a company.* **3.** greatest or maximum in degree or amount: *to drive at top speed.* —*v.t.*, **topped, top·ping. 1.** to provide with a top or cover; put a top on: *I topped the chest with a carved lid.* **2.** to serve as, be at, or form the top of: *A cover tops the trash can.* **3.** to reach or go beyond the top of. **4.** to surpass; exceed: *a joke that topped all the others.* **5.** to cut off or remove the top of: *to top a tree before cutting it down.* **6.** to hit (a ball) above the center, as in golf or tennis. [From the Old English word *topp* meaning "the highest part, top¹."]
·**to top off.** to complete, especially by adding a finishing touch: *to top off a concert with an encore.*

top² (top) *n.* a toy usually having a rounded body that tapers to a point on which it is spun. [From the late Old English word *top* meaning this toy.]

to·paz (tō′paz) *n.* a lustrous crystalline mineral, occurring in a variety of colors and used as a gem, especially in the yellow variety.

top·coat (top′kōt′) *n.* a lightweight overcoat.

top·flight (top′flīt′) *adj.* excellent or superior; first-rate.

top²

top·gal·lant (top′gal′ənt, tə gal′ənt) *n.* the mast, sail, rigging, or the like above the topmost. —*adj.* of or relating to the topgallant.

top hat, a hat usually made of silk, having a high, cylindrical crown and a small brim, usually worn by men on formal occasions.

top·heav·y (top′hev′ē) *adj.* too heavy at the top.

top·ic (top′ik) *n.* the subject of a speech, discussion, written composition, or the like. [Originally from the Greek *Topika,* the title of a work by Aristotle, going back to the word *topos* meaning "place" or "rhetorical topic." Topics were "places" people went to for ideas.]

top hat

top·i·cal (top′i kəl) *adj.* **1.** relating to or dealing with matters of current or local interest: *a topical speech, a topical book.* **2.** of, relating to, or belonging to a specific area or place; local. **3.** *Medicine.* relating to, applied to, or affecting a particular part or organ of the body: *a topical antibiotic ointment.*

top·knot (top′not′) *n.* **1.** a knot, tuft, or crest of hair or feathers on the top of the head. **2.** a bow or other ornament worn on the top of the head.

top·mast (top′mast′) *n.* the second section of a mast above the lower mast.

top·most (top′mōst′) *adj.* at the very top; uppermost; highest.

top·notch (top′noch′) *also,* **top-notch.** *adj. Informal.* first-rate or superior.

to·pog·ra·pher (tə pog′rə fər) *n.* an expert in topography.

top·o·graph·i·cal (top′ə graf′i kəl) *adj.* of, relating to, or involving topography: *a topographical map, a topographical survey.* Also, **top·o·graph·ic** (top′ə graf′ik). —**top′o·graph′i·cal·ly,** *adv.*

to·pog·ra·phy (tə pog′rə fē) *n., pl.* **to·pog·ra·phies.** the detailed description or drawing of the natural and artificial surface features of a place or area, such as hills, valleys, lakes, roads, and bridges.

top·ping (top′ing) *n.* a sauce, frosting, or other garnish put on food: *a dessert topping.*

top·ple (top′əl) *v.,* **top·pled, top·pling.** —*v.i.* **1.** to fall forward; tumble: *The bookcase is shaky and could topple.*

2. to lean or hang over, as if about to fall. —*v.t.* to cause to fall or tumble; overturn: *to topple a lamp, to topple a government.*

tops (tops) *adj. Informal.* the very best; first-rate.

top·sail (top′sāl′, top′səl) *n.* **1.** on a square-rigged ship, the square sail next above the lowest sail on a mast. **2.** on a fore-and-aft-rigged ship, the square or triangular sail above the gaff of a lower sail.

top-se·cret (top′sē′krit) *adj.* of, relating to, or containing highly confidential information.

top·side (top′sīd′) *n.* the upper part of a ship's side, especially above the water line. —*adv. also,* **topsides.** to or on the upper portions of a ship; on deck.

top·soil (top′soil′) *n.* the top or upper part of the soil that contains most of the materials essential to plant growth, including minerals and humus.

top·sy–tur·vy (top′sē tûr′vē) *adv.* **1.** in reverse of the usual or natural order; upside down. **2.** in or into a state of utter confusion or disorder. —*adj.* **1.** turned upside down. **2.** utterly confused or disordered.

toque (tōk) *n.* **1.** a small, close-fitting woman's hat with a soft crown and either a small, rolled brim or no brim at all. **2.** a small plumed hat with a brim, worn by men and women in the sixteenth century.

To·rah (tôr′ə) *n. Judaism.* **1.** the first five books of the Old Testament; Pentateuch. **2.** the hand-written scrolls containing the Pentateuch, used in a synagogue during services. **3.** *also,* **torah.** the whole body of Jewish teaching, thought, and literature. [From the Hebrew word *tōrāh* meaning "instruction" or "law."]

torch (tôrch) *n., pl.* **torch·es.** **1.** a flaming light, usually consisting of a stick of wood, or some material soaked in a substance that will burn, wound around the end of a stick. **2.** any of various hand-held devices producing a very hot flame, used especially in welding. **3.** something considered to be a source or symbol of enlightenment, inspiration, or guidance: *the torch of liberty.* **4.** *British.* a flashlight.

torch·bear·er (tôrch′bâr′ər) *n.* **1.** a person who carries a torch. **2.** a person who is a source of enlightenment, truth, or inspiration.

torch·light (tôrch′līt′) *n.* the light given off by a torch or torches.

tore (tôr) the past tense of **tear¹.**

tor·e·a·dor (tôr′ē ə dôr′) *n.* see **matador.**

to·re·ro (tə rãr′ō) *n., pl.* **to·re·ros.** a matador, especially one who fights on foot.

tor·ment (*v.,* tôr ment′; *n.,* tôr′ment) *v.t.* **1.** to cause (someone) great mental or physical pain or suffering. **2.** to worry, annoy, or aggravate: *The dog tormented the cat.* —*n.* **1.** extreme mental or physical pain or suffering; agony. **2.** the source of such pain or suffering.

tor·men·tor (tôr men′tər) *also,* **tor·ment·er.** *n.* a person or thing that torments.

torn (tôrn) the past participle of **tear¹.**

tor·na·do (tôr nā′dō) *n., pl.* **tor·na·does** or **tor·na·dos.** a column of air darkened by dirt and shaped like a funnel, extending down from a mass of dark, black clouds and rotating at speeds of up to 500 miles per hour (800 kilometers per hour). Tornadoes travel rapidly and suck up and destroy things in their path.

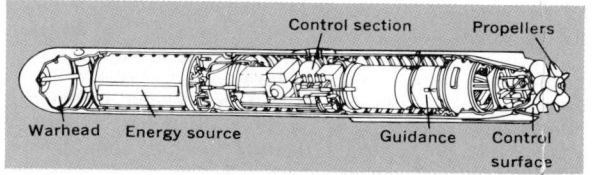

torpedo *(def. 1)*

tor·pe·do (tôr pē′dō) *n., pl.* **tor·pe·does.** **1.** a large, self-driven, underwater missile shaped like a cigar, that can be launched from ships, submarines, or airplanes. Torpedoes are often used for underwater attack against enemy ships. **2.** a type of firework that explodes when thrown against a hard surface. —*v.t.*, **tor·pe·doed, tor·pe·do·ing.** to damage or sink with or as if with a torpedo.

torpedo boat, see **PT boat.**

tor·pid (tôr′pid) *adj.* **1.** sluggish; dull. **2.** dormant, as an animal in hibernation. **3.** lacking the power of motion or feeling; numb. —**tor·pid′i·ty,** *n.* —**tor′pid·ly,** *adv.*

tor·por (tôr′pər) *n.* the state or quality of being torpid.

torque (tôrk) *n.* a force that causes or tends to cause something to turn or twist. [From the Latin word *torquēre* meaning ''to twist.'']

tor·rent (tôr′ənt) *n.* **1.** a violent, swiftly flowing stream, especially of water. **2.** a violent, overwhelming flow of anything: *a torrent of insults.*

tor·ren·tial (tô ren′chəl) *adj.* of, resembling, or caused by a torrent: *a torrential rainfall.*

tor·rid (tôr′id, tor′id) *adj.* **1.** subjected to or parched by the intense heat of the sun: *the torrid regions of the world.* **2.** intensely hot or burning; scorching: *a torrid climate.* **3.** passionate; ardent: *a torrid love story.* —**tor·rid′i·ty,** *n.*

Torrid Zone, a warm region between the Tropic of Cancer and the Tropic of Capricorn; tropics.

tor·sion (tôr′shən) *n.* **1.** the act of twisting or the state of being twisted. **2.** a strain put on an object when one end is twisted in one direction while the other end is held firm or twisted in the opposite direction.

tor·so (tôr′sō) *n., pl.* **tor·sos. 1.** the trunk of the human body. **2.** a statue of this.

tort (tôrt) *n. Law.* any wrong or injury that does not involve breach of contract and for which the wronged person or party may sue in a civil court.

tor·til·la (tôr tē′yə) *n.* a thin, round, unleavened cake made from water and cornmeal and baked on a griddle.

tor·toise (tôr′təs) *n.* a turtle that lives on land.

tor·toise·shell (tôr′təs shel′) *adj.* **1.** made of tortoise shell. **2.** having the mottled yellow and brown colors of tortoise shell.

tortoise shell 1. the hard, mottled, yellow and brown material making up the outer shell of certain turtles. It is used especially to make combs, small decorative objects, and furniture inlay. **2.** any of a group of butterflies with mottled yellow, brown, and black coloration.

tor·tu·ous (tôr′chü əs) *adj.* **1.** having many twists, turns, or bends; winding: *a tortuous road.* **2.** not direct, straightforward, or frank; devious: *a long, tortuous explanation for being late.* —**tor′tu·ous·ly,** *adv.* —**tor′tu·ous·ness,** *n.*

tor·ture (tôr′chər) *v.t.*, **tor·tured, tor·tur·ing. 1.** to subject to severe physical abuse or cruelty. **2.** to cause to suffer extreme mental or physical pain or suffering: *Nightmares of the accident tortured the survivors.* —*n.* **1.** the act of causing severe physical abuse or cruelty. **2.** a source or cause of extreme mental or physical pain or suffering. —**tor′tur·er,** *n.*

tor·tur·ous (tôr′chər əs) *adj.* relating to, characterized by, or causing torture: *a torturous punishment.*

To·ry (tôr′ē) *n., pl.* **To·ries. 1.** a member of a political party in Great Britain that favored rule by the king and the preservation of the established Anglican Church. Since 1832, it has been known as the Conservative Party. **2.** any American colonist who remained loyal to England at the time of the American Revolution. **3.** *also,* **tory.** any person or group that is conservative in politics. —*adj.* of, relating to, or like a Tory or Tories.

toss (tôs) *v.t.* **1.** to throw lightly up into or through the air, especially with the hand or hands: *Please toss me a towel.* **2.** to fling or move back and forth: *The waves*

tossed the little boat. **3.** to lift quickly or suddenly: *The horse tossed its head.* **4.** to mix (a salad) lightly, especially so as to coat with a dressing. **5.** to cause to fall to the ground: *The horse tossed its rider.* **6.** to throw (a coin) into the air so as to decide something by the side that lands upward. —*v.i.* **1.** to move about restlessly, especially in one's sleep: *to toss and turn all night.* **2.** to be flung or moved back and forth. **3.** to throw a coin into the air so as to decide something by the side that lands upward. —*n., pl.* **toss·es. 1.** the act of tossing. **2.** the distance over which something is or can be tossed.

·to toss off. a. to do quickly, casually, and easily: *to toss off a note to a friend.* **b.** to drink or eat all at once.

toss-up (tôs′up′) *also,* **toss·up.** *n.* an even chance or possibility: *It's a toss-up whether or not it will rain today.*

tos·ta·da (tō stä′də) *n.* a tortilla fried in deep fat, usually topped with a mixture of meat, beans, and raw vegetables. [From the Mexican Spanish word *tostada* meaning this food, from the word *tostado,* past participle of *tostar* ''to toast, fry,'' going back to the Latin word *tostus,* past participle of *torrēre* ''to make dry.'']

tot (tot) *n.* **1.** a small child. **2.** a small amount of something, as an alcoholic beverage.

to·tal (tō′təl) *adj.* **1.** being, relating to, or making up a whole; full; entire: *I paid the total amount of the bill.* **2.** absolute; complete; utter: *The trip was a total disaster; everything that could go wrong did go wrong. Those rude comments showed a total lack of respect.* —*n.* the whole amount; sum: *Add them all together and you get a total of 450.* —*v.*, **to·taled, to·tal·ing;** *also, British,* **to·talled, to·tal·ling.** —*v.t.* **1.** to compute or find the sum of; add up: *The waiter will total the bill.* **2.** to reach to the sum of: *The damage to the basement from the flood totaled $4,000.* **3.** *Slang.* to destroy completely; wreck: *The car was totaled in the crash.* —*v.i.* to amount; add up: *The bill totals to ten dollars.*

to·tal·i·tar·i·an (tō tal′i tär′ē ən) *adj.* of or relating to totalitarianism. —*n.* a person who favors or supports totalitarianism.

to·tal·i·tar·i·an·ism (tō tal′i tär′ē ə niz′əm) *n.* a system of government in which one political party aims at total control over the lives of the people under it, as by using a powerful secret police, restricting meetings and assemblies, and censoring or prohibiting books, newspapers, radio and television broadcasts, and other forms of communication.

to·tal·i·ty (tō tal′i tē) *n., pl.* **to·tal·i·ties. 1.** the total amount; whole; sum. **2.** the state of being whole or complete.

to·tal·ly (tō′tə lē) *adv.* completely; entirely; wholly: *We were totally unprepared for the May blizzard.*

tote (tōt) *v.t.*, **tot·ed, tot·ing.** *Informal.* to haul or carry: *to tote heavy packages home from the store.* —**tot′er,** *n.*

tote bag, a large handbag, used especially to carry small packages and other items.

to·tem (tō′təm) *n.* **1.** among North American Indians, an animal, plant, or other natural object taken as the emblem of a clan or other family group. **2.** a representation of this, especially one carved and painted on poles.

---

at; āpe; fär; câre; end; mē; it; īce; pîerce; hot; ōld; sông, fôrk; oil; out; up; ūse; rüle; pùll; tûrn; chin; sing; shop; thin; **th**is; hw in white; zh in treasure. The symbol ə stands for the unstressed vowel sound heard in about, taken, pencil, lemon, and circus.

T

totem pole, a pole consisting of carved and painted representations of totems, erected in front of a dwelling by certain American Indians of the northwestern Pacific coast.

tot·ter (tot′ər) *v.i.* **1.** to walk or move with weak or unsteady steps: *The baby tottered across the room.* **2.** to shake or sway as if about to fall or collapse; be unsteady: *The glass tottered on the edge of the table.* —*n.* the act of tottering.

tou·can (tü′kan) *n.* any of various fruit-eating tropical American birds having a heavy body, a very large beak with serrated edges, and brightly colored feathers.

totem pole

touch (tuch) *v.t.* **1.** to bring a hand, finger, or other part of the body on or against: *to touch a hot stove and burn one's hand.* **2.** to bring (something) against or into contact with something else: *to touch a match to paper.* **3.** to be against; come into contact with: *Their hands touched ours.* **4.** to affect the emotions or feelings of: *The news of their death touched us deeply.* **5.** to have an effect or bearing on; concern: *The new taxes will touch everyone.* **6.** to use or partake of: *The child did not touch any lunch.* **7.** to color slightly; tinge: *hair touched with gray.* **8.** to injure or mar slightly: *The plants were touched by the frost.* **9.** to compare with; equal: *No one can touch that student in spelling.* **10.** to arrive at or visit in passing: *I am going ashore when we touch port.* —*v.i.* **1.** to come into or be in contact: *Our hands touched.* **2.** to make a brief stop in passing: *The freighter will touch at New York.* —*n., pl.* **touch·es.** **1.** the sense by which objects are perceived through direct contact with a part of the body. **2.** the quality of an object as perceived by touching or coming into contact with it: *the soft touch of silk.* **3.** the act or instance of touching: *The balloon burst at the touch of the pin.* **4.** a slight sign or indication: *a touch of genius.* **5.** a small amount; little bit: *a touch of salt, a touch of rheumatism.* **6.** a light stroke, especially one made to change or improve something: *The artist put the final touch to the painting.* **7.** communication or contact: *Have you kept in touch with your friends during the summer?* **8.** a distinctive manner or way of doing something: *The room showed the touch of a decorator.* **9.** the manner of striking or touching the keys of a keyboard instrument or machine, as a piano or typewriter. [From the Old French word *tochier* meaning ''to touch, tap.'']

 ·**to touch down.** (of an aircraft) to land.
 ·**to touch off.** **a.** to cause to explode; ignite. **b.** to cause to happen: *A misunderstanding touched off the argument.*
 ·**to touch on.** to deal with or mention briefly or in passing: *The politician's speech touched on many issues.*
 ·**to touch up.** to improve by making slight changes: *to touch up a painting.*

touch–and–go (tuch′ən gō′) *adj.* of uncertain outcome: *The game was touch-and-go up to the last few seconds.*

touch·back (tuch′bak′) *n.* *Football.* a play in which a team gains possession of the ball from an opponent behind its own goal line, and the ball is declared dead. The team with the ball begins the next play at its twenty-yard line.

touch·down (tuch′doun′) *n.* **1.** *Football.* **a.** a scoring play worth six points, made by being in possession of the ball on or beyond the goal line that the opposing team defends. **b.** a score made in this way. **2.** the act of landing an aircraft. **3.** the moment of contact with the ground of a landing aircraft.

touched (tucht) *adj.* **1.** emotionally stirred; moved: *They were touched by the lost child's tears.* **2.** *Informal.* slightly unbalanced mentally.

touch football, a form of football in which a ball carrier is stopped by being touched with one or both hands rather than by being tackled.

touch·ing (tuch′ing) *adj.* stirring or appealing to the emotions or feelings: *a touching scene in a play.* —*prep.* with respect to; as to; concerning. —**touch′ing·ly,** *adv.*

touch·stone (tuch′stōn′) *n.* **1.** a hard, black stone, as basalt or jasper, used to test the fineness of an alloy of gold or silver, by comparing the color of the streak made on the stone by the alloy with the streak made by an alloy of known fineness. **2.** anything used to test the quality, value, or genuineness of something.

touch terminal, a computer terminal into which the user enters data by touching fingers to the screen rather than using a keyboard or mouse.

touch–tone (tuch′tōn′) *adj.* of or relating to a telephone apparatus with which calls are made by pushing buttons that electronically reproduce the tone of the number being called. —*n.* a touch-tone system or apparatus.

touch·y (tuch′ē) *adj.,* **touch·i·er, touch·i·est.** **1.** easily offended; very sensitive: *The players are touchy about their defeat.* **2.** requiring caution, tact, and careful handling: *a touchy situation.* —**touch′i·ly,** *adv.* —**touch′i·ness,** *n.*

tough (tuf) *adj.* **1.** able to withstand great pressure or strain without breaking: *Canvas is a tough fabric.* **2.** difficult to cut, tear, or chew: *a tough piece of meat.* **3.** able to endure great strain, hardship, or difficulty: *The pioneers in the West had to be tough.* **4.** harsh; stern: *The traffic laws in this town are tough.* **5.** difficult to do, deal with, or accomplish: *a tough job, a tough question.* **6.** rough; brutal; violent: *a tough neighborhood.* **7.** *Informal.* unhappy or unfortunate: *a tough life.* —*n.* a rough, brutal, and often violent person; ruffian; thug. —**tough′ly,** *adv.* —**tough′ness,** *n.*

tough·en (tuf′ən) *v.t., v.i.* to make or become tough or tougher.

tou·pee (tü pā′) *n.* a small wig worn to cover baldness.

tour (tür) *n.* **1.** a journey in which many places are visited, usually for short periods of time: *We took a tour of the Greek islands last summer.* **2.** a short journey or trip: *to make a tour of a museum.* **3.** a circuit or journey, as of a theatrical company or speaker, made to a number of places in order to give performances or lectures. **4.** a period of time in which some required task or service is fulfilled: *a tour of duty in the military service.* —*v.t.* to make a tour of or through: *They toured France on their vacation.* —*v.i.* to go on tour.

tour de force (tür′də fôrs′) *pl.* **tours de force** (tür′də fôrs′). a feat of unusual strength, skill, or ingenuity.

tour·ism (tür′iz əm) *n.* **1.** the business of providing services for tourists. **2.** traveling for pleasure.

tour·ist (tür′ist) *n.* a person who travels for pleasure. —*adj.* of or for tourists: *Our state has a tourist bureau.*

tourist class, the least expensive class of accommodation, as on an airplane.

tour·ma·line (tûr′mə lin) *n.* a glassy or lustrous mineral containing boron and aluminum, occurring in a variety of colors. Red and green tourmalines are often used as gems.

tour·na·ment (tûr′nə mənt, tûr′nə mənt) *n.* **1.** a series of contests involving two or more persons or teams: *a chess tournament, a tennis tournament.* **2.** a formal medieval combat between two mounted knights armed with lances or other weapons.

tour·ney (tûr′nē, tûr′nē) *n., pl.* **tour·neys.** another word for **tournament.**

tour·ni·quet (tûr′ni kit) *n.* a device, such as a rubber tube or a tight bandage, used to stop bleeding by pressing on a blood vessel.

tou·sle (tou′zəl) *v.t.,* **tou·sled, tou·sling.** to put into disorder; make messy; dishevel: *The wind tousled my hair.* —*n.* a disheveled mass, especially of hair.

tout (tout) *Informal. v.i.* to try to get customers, employment, or support, especially in a brash way: *The campaign manager touted for votes.* —*v.t.* **1.** to praise or publicize in an exaggerated way. **2.** to give or sell information about (a racehorse) to a better. —*n.* a person who touts. —**tout′er,** *n.*

tow¹ (tō) *v.t.* to pull, drag, or draw behind, especially with a rope, chain, or the like. —*n.* **1.** the act of towing or the state of being towed. **2.** something that is towed. **3.** see **towline.** [From the Old English word *togian* meaning "to pull, draw."]

tow² (tō) *n.* coarse, shorter fibers of flax or hemp used to make yarn and twine. [From the Old English prefix *tow-* as found in such words as *towcræft* meaning "skill in weaving or spinning."]

to·ward (tôrd, tə wôrd′) *prep.* **1.** in the direction of: *The puppy ran toward the house.* **2.** with respect to; concerning; regarding: *What are your feelings toward our plan?* **3.** near in time; shortly before: *The snow stopped toward morning.* **4.** as a help to; in order to get: *to save one's allowance toward a new bicycle.* Also, **to·wards** (tôrdz, tə wôrds′).

tow·boat (tō′bōt′) *n.* another word for **tugboat.**

tow·el (tou′əl) *n.* a piece of absorbent material, especially paper or terry cloth, used for wiping or drying. —*v.t.,* **tow·eled, tow·el·ing;** *also, British,* **tow·elled, tow·el·ling.** to wipe or dry with a towel: *to towel oneself after swimming.*

　·to throw in the towel. *Informal.* to give up; admit defeat: *to throw in the towel and go home after fishing without a bite.*

tow·er (tou′ər) *n.* a tall but fairly narrow structure, often forming a part of and rising above a church, castle, or other building. —*v.i.* to rise or extend to a great height: *The skyscraper towered above the skyline.*

tow·er·ing (tou′ər ing) *adj.* **1.** very tall; lofty: *Towering palm trees lined the beach.* **2.** very great; outstanding: *the towering genius of Beethoven.* **3.** very violent or intense: *a towering rage.*

Tower of London, a historic fortress and prison on the north bank of the Thames, in London, England.

tow·head (tō′hed′) *n.* a person having very pale blond hair. —**tow′head′ed,** *adj.*

tow·hee (tou′hē′, tō′hē′) *n.* any of several North American songbirds resembling a large sparrow.

tow·line (tō′līn′) *n.* a rope, chain, or the like used for towing.

tower

town (toun) *n.* **1.** a group of houses and public and private buildings, larger than a village but smaller than a city. **2.** any densely populated place: *Boston is a very old town.* **3.** the people of a town: *The town elected a new mayor.* **4.** the business or industrial section of a town or city: *to go into town to shop.*

town crier, formerly, a person employed to make public proclamations or announcements in the streets of a town.

town hall, a building that houses the offices of officials of a town or is used for town meetings.

town house **1.** a house in a town or city, especially one owned by a person who has a house in the country. **2.** a house attached to other similar houses in a row; row house.

town·ie (tou′nē) *also,* **town·y.** *n., pl.* **town·ies.** *Informal.* **1.** a person who lives in town; townsman. **2.** a person who lives permanently in a college town, as distinguished from a student or teacher at the college.

town meeting **1.** a meeting of the people who live in a town. **2.** in New England, a meeting of the qualified voters of a town to act upon town business.

town·ship (toun′ship′) *n.* **1.** a division of a county, having some of the powers of municipal government. **2.** in surveys of public land, an area containing thirty-six sections of 1 square mile each (2.59 square kilometers each).

towns·man (tounz′mən) *n., pl.* **towns·men** (tounz′mən). **1.** a person who lives in a town. **2.** a person who lives in one's own town.

towns·peo·ple (tounz′pē′pəl) *pl. n.* the people of a town.

tow·path (tō′path′) *n., pl.* **tow·paths** (tō′pathz′, tō′-paths′). a path along the bank of a canal or river, used in towing boats.

tow·rope (tō′rōp′) *n.* a rope used in towing, especially a hawser or cable used for towing boats.

tow truck, a truck with towing equipment for moving disabled or wrecked vehicles. Also, **wrecker.**

tox·e·mi·a (tok sē′mē ə) *also,* **tox·ae·mi·a.** *n.* blood poisoning caused by toxins.

tox·ic (tok′sik) *adj.* **1.** of, relating to, or caused by poison: *a toxic reaction.* **2.** poisonous: *a toxic drug.*

tox·ic·i·ty (tok sis′i tē) *n.* the state or quality of being toxic.

tox·i·col·o·gist (tok′si kol′ə jist) *n.* an expert in toxicology.

tox·i·col·o·gy (tok′si kol′ə jē) *n.* the science that deals with the nature, effects, and detection of poisons and the treatment of poisoning.

toxic shock syndrome, a rare bacterial disease in which the patient suffers a high fever, a sunburn-like rash, stomach upset, and a sudden drop in blood pressure.

tox·in (tok′sin) *n.* any poisonous product of animal or vegetable cells. The toxins produced by harmful bacteria cause the symptoms of many diseases.

toy (toi) *n.* **1.** an object for a child to play with. **2.** something of little or no value or importance. —*v.i.* to play or trifle: *to toy with a pencil, to toy with the idea of going on a trip.* —*adj.* **1.** of, like, or used as a toy. **2.** smaller than is usual or standard, as certain breeds of dog.

trace¹ (trās) *n.* **1.** something left behind showing that some person, place, thing, or event has existed or taken

at; āpe; fär; câre; end; mē; it; īce; pîerce; hot; ōld; sông, fôrk; oil; out; up; ūse; rüle; pull; tûrn; chin; sing; shop; thin; this; hw in white; zh in treasure. The symbol ə stands for the unstressed vowel sound heard in about, taken, pencil, lemon, and circus.

place: *The archaeologist found traces of an ancient temple.*
2. a track made by the passage of someone or something, as a footprint or tire mark. **3.** a very small amount: *I tasted a trace of mint in the drink. There was a trace of sarcasm in the speaker's tone.* **4.** a line drawn by a recording instrument, such as an electrocardiograph. —*v.*, **traced, trac·ing.** —*v.t.* **1.** to follow the track, trail, or path of; pursue: *to trace a missing person.* **2.** to follow the course, development, or history of: *to trace the origin of a word.* **3.** to mark out: *to trace a figure in the sand, to trace a route on a map.* **4.** to copy (something) by following lines as seen through a transparent sheet placed over it. —*v.i.* to have its origin; go back in time: *Their friendship traces back to childhood.* [From the Old French word *tracier* meaning "to mark"" or "to follow a path," going back to the Latin word *tractus*, past participle of *trahere* meaning "to draw, pull."] —**trace'a·ble,** *adj.*

trace² (trās) *n.* either of the two straps, ropes, or chains by which the harness of a draft animal is attached to the vehicle it pulls. [From the Old French word *trais* meaning these straps, going back to the Latin word *tractus,* past participle of *trahere* meaning "to draw, pull."]

trac·er (trā′sər) *n.* **1.** a person or thing that traces. **2.** any of various devices for making tracings of drawings. **3.** any inquiry sent from place to place to locate someone or something that is missing. **4.** an easily detected and located substance, usually a radioisotope, that is put into some system, as the human body, to study the movements and biological or chemical processes inside the system. **5.** a projectile, such as a bullet or shell, treated with a chemical compound that causes its path to be marked by a trail of fire or smoke.

trac·er·y (trā′sə rē) *n., pl.* **trac·er·ies.** ornamental work forming geometric or curved patterns, used especially in stonework or embroidery.

tracery

tra·che·a (trā′kē ə) *n., pl.* **tra·che·ae** (trā′kē ē′). the tube extending from the larynx to the bronchi; windpipe. —**tra·che·al,** *adj.*

tra·che·ot·o·my (trā′kē ot′ə mē) *n., pl.* **tra·che·ot·o·mies.** a surgical operation in which an opening is made through the neck into the trachea, usually performed when air cannot flow normally to the lungs because of an obstruction in the throat.

tra·cho·ma (trə kō′mə) *n.* a chronic, contagious bacterial disease of the eye, characterized by inflammation and granulation of the eyelids. It is common in tropical regions and can lead to blindness if not treated.

track (trak) *n.* **1.** a mark or set of marks left behind by a person, animal, or object in motion: *There were tire tracks in the snow. The deer's tracks were easy to follow.* **2.** a course along which anything moves; path; route: *the track of a storm, a track through the woods.* **3.** a course of action or way of proceeding: *Your answer is not quite correct, but you are on the right track.* **4.** a rail or set of parallel rails on which a vehicle, such as a railroad car, travels. **5.** a course laid out for racing. **6.** see **track and field. 7.** one of the continuous metal belts on which a bulldozer, tank, or similar vehicle runs; tread. **8.** a band on a magnetic tape, on which sounds, images, or data are stored. —*v.t.* **1.** to follow the tracks or scent of: *to track wild game.* **2.** to discover, pursue, or learn by following tracks: *to track down an old friend.* **3.** to observe and record the path of: *to track a hurricane, to track a space vehicle.* **4.** to make marks with (something) carried on one's feet: *to track mud on a carpet.* —**track′er,** *n.*

·**in one's tracks.** *Informal.* exactly where one is at the moment: *The explosion stopped me in my tracks.*
·**to keep track of.** to keep informed about or in contact with: *to keep track of old friends.*
·**to lose track of.** to fail to keep informed about or in contact with.

track and field, a group of competitive sports events involving running, jumping, walking, and throwing, such as the pole vault, shot put, and hurdles.

track·less (trak′lis) *adj.* **1.** without or unmarked by paths or trails: *a trackless wilderness.* **2.** not running on tracks or rails.

track meet, an athletic contest made up of track and field events.

tract¹ (trakt) *n.* **1.** a stretch or expanse of land; area; region: *a tract of woodland.* **2.** a group of parts or organs in the body that together have a particular function: *the digestive tract, the urinary tract.* [From the Latin word *tractus* meaning "a drawing out."]

tract² (trakt) *n.* a booklet or pamphlet, especially one on a religious or political subject. [Latin *tractātus* "handling, treatment."]

trac·ta·ble (trak′tə bəl) *adj.* **1.** easily controlled, managed, or influenced; docile: *a tractable horse.* **2.** easily worked or handled; malleable: *a tractable metal.* —**trac′ta·bil′i·ty,** *n.* —**trac′ta·bly,** *adv.*

trac·tion (trak′shən) *n.* **1.** the act of drawing or pulling something, such as a vehicle or load, along a road or other surface. **2.** the state of being drawn or pulled. **3.** the power used for drawing or pulling: *steam traction.* **4.** the friction that causes a body to hold firmly to a surface. A deep tread in tires provides better traction on snow-covered roads. [From the Medieval Latin word *tractio* meaning "act of drawing," from the Latin word *tractus*, past participle of *trahere* "to draw, pull."]

trac·tor (trak′tər) *n.* **1.** a motor vehicle usually having rubber tires or treads. It is used especially on farms for pulling harvesting machinery and plows and for hauling heavy loads. **2.** a truck having a powerful motor and a driver's cab, used to pull a trailer with a heavy load.

tractor *(def. 1)*

trade (trād) *n.* **1.** the business of buying and selling; exchange of goods; commerce: *foreign trade, domestic trade.* **2.** the exchange of one thing for another; swap: *to make a trade of a pair of roller skates for a baseball mitt.* **3.** something that a person does to earn a living, especially a job requiring manual or mechanical skill: *to learn the trade of an electrician.* **4.** people or firms engaged in the same business or occupation: *the building trade.* **5.** regular customers; clientele: *That clothing store caters to a fashionable trade.* **6. trades.** see **trade wind.** —*v.*, **trad·ed, trad·ing.** —*v.i.* **1.** to engage in buying and selling; be in commerce: *That store trades in electrical appliances.* **2.** to exchange one thing for another. **3.** to do business; shop: *We trade at the local grocery store.* —*v.t.* **1.** to exchange or swap: *to trade places with a friend at the theater.* **2.** to buy and sell.

·**to trade in.** to give in exchange as payment or part payment for something else.
·**to trade on.** to take advantage of: *to trade on someone's friendship.*

trade–in (trād′in′) *n.* a used car, appliance, or the like, given or received as payment or part payment for a new one.

trade·mark (trād′märk′) *n.* a mark, picture, word, phrase, or the like, used to identify and distinguish the goods or services of a manufacturer or merchant. A trademark is usually registered with the government and cannot be used by anyone else. —*v.t.* **1.** to place a trademark on. **2.** to register as a trademark.

trade name 1. a name, often registered as a trademark, used to identify and distinguish the goods or services of a manufacturer or merchant. **2.** the name by which an article, service, or the like is commonly known to the trade. **3.** the name under which a firm carries on business.

trad·er (trā′dər) *n.* **1.** a person whose business is buying and selling. **2.** a ship used in trading.

trade school, see **vocational school.**

trades·man (trādz′mən) *n., pl.* **trades·men** (trādz′mən). a person who carries on trade; shopkeeper.

trades·peo·ple (trādz′pē′pəl) *pl. n.* people who carry on a trade; shopkeepers.

trade union *also, British,* **trades union. 1.** a labor union made up of workers in a particular trade or craft. **2.** any labor union.

trade wind, either of two winds that blow steadily toward the equator. The trade wind north of the equator comes from the northeast. The trade wind south of the equator comes from the southeast.

trading post, a store or station set up by a trader or trading company in a sparsely settled or frontier region, where the local people can obtain goods, often in exchange for local products.

trading stamp, a stamp given to a customer as a bonus for buying something in a store. Trading stamps can be exchanged in various quantities for merchandise.

tra·di·tion (trə dish′ən) *n.* **1.** the handing down of knowledge, beliefs, customs, or the like from one generation to another. **2.** the knowledge, beliefs, customs, or the like handed down in this way: *Tradition says the Pilgrims landed at Plymouth Rock.* [From the Middle French word *tradition,* from the Latin word *traditio* meaning both ''a handing over'' and ''tradition,'' from *traditus,* past participle of *tradere* ''to hand over'' and ''betray.'']

tra·di·tion·al (trə dish′ə nəl) *adj.* of, coming from, or in accordance with tradition: *Thanksgiving is a traditional American holiday.* —**tra·di′tion·al·ly,** *adv.*

tra·duce (trə dūs′, trə dōōs′) *v.t.,* **tra·duced, tra·duc·ing.** to speak falsely or maliciously of; slander. —**tra·duc′er,** *n.*

traf·fic (traf′ik) *n.* **1.** automobiles, boats, people, or the like moving along or through an area or route: *There was little traffic on the highway in the early morning hours.* **2.** an exchange of goods, especially for profit; buying and selling; trade. **3.** dealing or bargaining in something illegal or improper: *The police attempted to stop drug traffic in the city.* **4.** the business done by a railroad, steamship, or other transportation line. **5.** the number of passengers or amount of freight transported by such a line. —*v.i.,* **traf·ficked, traf·fick·ing.** to carry on trade, especially illegally; deal: *to traffic in stolen goods.* —**traf′fick·er,** *n.*

traffic circle, a circular intersection for two or more roads around which traffic moves in one direction, allowing vehicles to enter or leave any of the roads without disturbing the flow of traffic. Also, **rotary.**

traffic light, a signal, usually with red and green and sometimes amber or yellow lights, that controls the flow of traffic by changing color or by blinking on and off, especially at an intersection. Also, **traffic signal, stoplight.**

tra·ge·di·an (trə jē′dē ən) *n.* an actor who specializes in playing tragic roles.

trag·e·dy (traj′i dē) *n., pl.* **trag·e·dies. 1.** a drama in which life is viewed or treated seriously, usually having a sad ending. **2.** any work of literature that is like a dramatic tragedy. **3.** a sad, dreadful, or disastrous event: *The mine explosion was a tragedy that took the lives of seven miners.* [From the Latin word *tragoedia* meaning ''a tragic drama,'' from the Greek word *tragōidia* with the same meaning, from the words *tragos* ''goat'' and *ōidē* ''song.'']

trag·ic (traj′ik) *adj.* **1.** of, relating to, or like tragedy, especially dramatic tragedy: *The play had a tragic ending.* **2.** very sad, dreadful, or disastrous: *a tragic accident, a tragic decision.* Also, **trag·i·cal** (traj′i kəl). —**trag′i·cal·ly,** *adv.*

trag·i·com·e·dy (traj′i kom′i dē) *n., pl.* **trag·i·com·e·dies.** a drama containing both tragic and comic elements, usually having a happy ending.

trail (trāl) *n.* **1.** a passage or path through a wild or uninhabited region. **2.** a mark, scent, or path made by an animal or person: *The dog lost the fox's trail at the river's edge.* **3.** something that follows along behind: *The old car gave off a trail of fumes.* —*v.t.* **1.** to follow behind, especially in a careless or lagging manner: *The onlookers trailed the parade down the street.* **2.** to drag or draw along or behind: *The children trailed their kites on the ground.* **3.** to follow the track or scent of: *The police trailed the thieves to their hideout.* **4.** to be behind or losing, as in a contest or game. —*v.i.* **1.** to hang down or be drawn behind: *The coat was too long and trailed along the floor.* **2.** to move or flow slowly; drift: *The audience trailed in after the intermission.* **3.** to grow over or along the ground or other surface: *Ivy trailed along the side of the building.* **4.** to be losing, as in a contest or game: *Our team trailed in the fifth inning but went on to win.* **5.** to lessen gradually (usually with *off* or *away*): *Conversation trailed off as the evening wore on.*

trail·blaz·er (trāl′blā′zər) *n.* **1.** a person who marks a trail for others; pathfinder. **2.** a pioneer in any field: *a trailblazer in medicine.*

trail·er (trā′lər) *n.* **1.** a person or thing that trails. **2.** a vehicle without a motor, designed to be pulled by a car, truck, or similar vehicle. It is used for transporting goods or the like. **3.** a similar vehicle equipped to be used as a home or office.

trailing arbutus, an evergreen vine that grows along the ground in shady areas and bears clusters of small, very fragrant pink or white blossoms.

train (trān) *n.* **1.** a connected line of railroad cars. **2.** a group of people, animals, or vehicles traveling together, especially in a long line or procession: *a mule train.* **3.** a connected series or succession, as of events or ideas: *to follow a train of thought.* **4.** a series of events, circumstances, or conditions coming from or following something: *The hurricane left wrecked boats and flooded homes in its train.* **5.** something that is drawn along behind, especially that part of a dress or robe that trails on the ground behind the wearer. **6.** a group of attendants; following; retinue: *The king and queen were accompanied by a train of servants.* **7.** a series of interconnected mechanical parts for transmitting motion, such as the wheels and pinions of a watch. —*v.t.* **1.** to develop or mold the character, thoughts, and behavior of; bring up; rear: *to train a child to respect the rights of others.* **2.** to make able or skilled by instruction and practice, as in a particular field or profession: *to train a new editor.* **3.** to

at; āpe; fär; câre; end; mē; it; īce; pîerce; hot; ōld; sông, fôrk; oil; out; up; ūse; rüle; pull; tûrn; chin; sing; shop; thin; this; hw in white; zh in treasure. The symbol ə stands for the unstressed vowel sound heard in about, taken, pencil, lemon, and circus.

T

prepare physically, as with a regular drill, diet, and exercise: *to train a gymnast.* **4.** to instruct (an animal) so as to make it obedient or capable of doing certain tasks or tricks. **5.** to cause to grow or lie in a desired form or direction: *to train one's hair to curl under, to train ivy to grow up a wall.* **6.** to focus or direct; aim: *to train a rifle at a target.* —*v.i.* to undergo and follow a course of instruction or discipline: *to train for a race, to train for a job.* [From the Middle French word *trainer* meaning ''to drag behind, trail.'']

train·ee (trā nē′) *n.* a person who is undergoing training, especially vocational or military training.

train·er (trā′nər) *n.* **1.** a person who trains, especially a person who is responsible for the physical training and conditioning of an athlete, race horse, or the like. **2.** a device used in training.

train·ing (trā′ning) *n.* **1.** the act, process, or method of a person who trains. **2.** the state of being trained.

train·load (trān′lōd′) *n.* the amount that a train can carry.

train·man (trān′mən) *n., pl.* **train·men** (trān′mən). a person who works for a railroad, such as a conductor.

traipse (trāps) *v.i.,* **traipsed, traips·ing.** *Informal.* to walk about idly or aimlessly.

trait (trāt) *n.* an aspect, quality, or characteristic, as of a person's character: *bravery, honesty, and other noble traits, a genetic trait.*

trai·tor (trā′tər) *n.* **1.** a person who commits treason. **2.** a person who betrays any trust.

trai·tor·ous (trā′tər əs) *adj.* **1.** of, relating to, or like a traitor. **2.** of, relating to, or like treason: *a traitorous act.* —**trai′tor·ous·ly,** *adv.*

tra·jec·to·ry (trə jek′tə rē) *n., pl.* **tra·jec·to·ries.** the curved path followed by a bullet, ballistic missile, meteor, or the like, moving through space or the atmosphere.

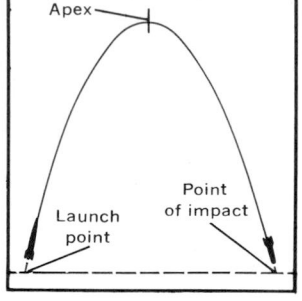

trajectory

tram (tram) *n.* *British.* **1.** another word for **streetcar.** **2.** a four-wheeled vehicle that runs on tracks, used to carry coal in a mine.

tram·mel (tram′əl) *n.* **1.** *also,* **trammels.** anything that hinders freedom, action, or progress: *At the good news, they shook off the trammels of despair.* **2.** a shackle for hobbling a horse and training it to amble. **3.** a hook in a fireplace for hanging pots over the fire. **4.** a net for catching birds or fish. —*v.t.,* **tram·meled, tram·mel·ing;** *also, British,* **tram·melled, tram·mel·ling.** **1.** to hinder the freedom, action, or progress of; impede. **2.** to entangle in a net; ensnare.

tramp (tramp) *v.i.* **1.** to walk with a firm, heavy step: *to tramp into a house in overshoes.* **2.** to travel on foot; walk: *to tramp across the countryside.* **3.** to travel or wander as a tramp or vagabond. —*v.t.* **1.** to press or compress by stepping heavily upon; trample: *to tramp the grass.* **2.** to travel over or through on foot: *The hikers tramped the forest.* —*n.* **1.** a person who wanders or travels from place to place, has no permanent home or means of support, and usually begs for food, money, or temporary work. **2.** the sound of a heavy step: *We could hear the tramp of the marching soldiers.* **3.** a long walk; hike. **4.** a cargo ship, especially a steamship, that does not trade regularly between fixed ports, but takes cargo wherever obtainable and for any port. —**tramp′er,** *n.*

tram·ple (tram′pəl) *v.,* **tram·pled, tram·pling.** —*v.t.* **1.** to tread on so heavily as to injure, crush, or destroy:

Do not trample the flowers. **2.** to treat cruelly or harshly: *When the people rebelled, the dictator trampled them.* —*v.i.* to tread heavily. —*n.* the act of trampling. —**tram′pler,** *n.*

trampoline

tram·po·line (tram′pə lēn′, tram′pə lēn′) *n.* a piece of gymnastic equipment used for acrobatic tumbling, usually consisting of canvas attached by springs to a metal frame on legs.

tram·way (tram′wā′) *n.* *British.* **1.** a streetcar track. **2.** a railway used in a coal mine for hauling loads.

trance (trans) *n.* **1.** a semiconscious state resembling sleep, as that produced by hypnotism. **2.** a dazed or stunned state; stupor. **3.** a state of deep mental absorption or concentration.

tran·quil (trang′kwəl) *adj.* free from disturbance; calm; peaceful: *a tranquil childhood. The lake was smooth and tranquil.* —**tran′quil·ly,** *adv.*

tran·quil·ize (trang′kwə līz′) *v.t.,* *v.i.,* **tran·quil·ized, tran·quil·iz·ing.** to make or become tranquil.

tran·quil·iz·er (trang′kwə lī′zər) *also,* **tran·quil·liz·er.** *n.* any of certain drugs that produce a calming effect by reducing tension, anxiety, or the like.

tran·quil·i·ty (trang kwil′i tē) *also,* **tran·quil·li·ty.** *n.* the state or quality of being tranquil.

trans– *prefix* **1.** across; through; over: *transatlantic.* **2.** so as to change completely: *transform.*

trans. **1.** transactions. **2.** transitive. **3.** transportation.

trans·act (tran sakt′, tran zakt′) *v.t.* to conduct and carry through, especially business affairs: *to transact the sale of a house.* —*v.i.* to do business. —**trans·ac′tor,** *n.*

trans·ac·tion (tran sak′shən, tran zak′shən) *n.* **1.** the act of transacting or the state of being transacted. **2.** something that is or has been transacted, especially a business deal. **3.** **transactions.** a published record of the proceedings of a society, club, or the like.

998

trans·at·lan·tic (trans'at lan'tik) *adj.* **1.** crossing or spanning the Atlantic Ocean: *a transatlantic telephone call, a transatlantic flight.* **2.** on the opposite side of the Atlantic Ocean.

tran·scend (tran send') *v.t.* **1.** to pass or go beyond the limits of; exceed: *The idea of infinity transcends human understanding.* **2.** to be greater or better than in some respect or quality; surpass: *This painting transcends the artist's earlier works.*

tran·scend·ence (tran sen'dəns) *n.* the act of transcending or the state of being transcendent.

tran·scend·ent (tran sen'dənt) *adj.* **1.** surpassing or excelling others; superior; preeminent. **2.** beyond ordinary or natural limits; transcendental. —**tran·scend'ent·ly,** *adv.*

tran·scen·den·tal (tran'sen den'təl) *adj.* **1.** superior; transcendent. **2.** beyond or contrary to human experience or to what is natural; supernatural. **3.** *Mathematics.* not capable of being a solution of a rational algebraic equation. Pi is a transcendental number. —**tran'scen·den'tal·ly,** *adv.*

tran·con·ti·nen·tal (trans'kon tə nen'təl) *adj.* **1.** crossing or spanning a continent: *a transcontinental highway.* **2.** on the opposite side of a continent.

tran·scribe (tran skrīb') *v.t.,* **tran·scribed, tran·scrib·ing.** **1.** to make a written or typewritten copy of; rewrite or type: *to transcribe the minutes of the meeting from shorthand notes.* **2.** to arrange or adapt (a musical composition) for a different voice or instrument. **3.** to make a recording of (a radio program or the like) to be broadcast later. **4.** to represent (speech sounds) by phonetic symbols. **5.** to form a strand of RNA using the genetic information in a strand of DNA as a pattern. —**tran·scrib'er,** *n.*

tran·script (tran'skript') *n.* a written or typewritten copy: *The judge reviewed the transcript of the trial.*

tran·scrip·tion (tran skrip'shən) *n.* **1.** the act of transcribing. **2.** a transcript; copy. **3.** an adaptation or arrangement of a musical composition for another voice or instrument. **4.** a recording, as on magnetic tape, of a radio program or the like to be broadcast later. **5.** a representation of speech sounds by phonetic symbols. **6.** the process of forming a strand of RNA using the genetic information in a strand of DNA as a pattern.

tran·sept (tran'sept) *n.* **1.** the part forming the arms of a cross in a church that is built in the shape of a cross. **2.** either side of this part.

trans·fer (*v.,* trans fûr', trans'fər; *n.,* trans'fər) *v.,* **trans·ferred, trans·fer·ring.** —*v.t.* **1.** to move or remove from one person, place, or the like to another: *to transfer money from one pocket to another.* **2.** to give or sell the title or possession of to another: *to transfer property from parents to children.* **3.** to convey (a drawing, design, pattern, or the like) from one surface to another. —*v.i.* **1.** to transfer oneself: *to transfer to a new school.* **2.** to be transferred: *The office will transfer to new quarters.* **3.** to switch from one bus, train, airplane, or the like, to another, usually with little or no extra charge: *to transfer at Chicago.* —*n.* **1.** the act of transferring or the state of being transferred: *the transfer of property by a will.* **2.** something that is transferred, especially a drawing, design, pattern, or the like moved from one surface to another. **3.** a ticket allowing a passenger to continue a journey on another vehicle, usually with little or no extra charge. **4.** the place or means of transferring. [From the Latin word *transferre* meaning "to transfer, transport," from the prefix *trans-* "across" + the word *ferre* "to bear, carry."] —**trans·fer'a·ble,** *adj.*

trans·fer·ence (trans fûr'əns) *n.* the act of transferring or the state of being transferred.

transfer RNA, see **RNA.**

trans·fig·u·ra·tion (trans fig'yə rā'shən) *n.* **1.** the act of transfiguring or the state of being transfigured. **2.** the **Transfiguration. a.** in the New Testament, the miraculous change in the appearance of Jesus that took place on a mountain in the presence of the Apostles Peter, James, and John. **b.** the church festival commemorating this event. It falls on August 6.

trans·fig·ure (trans fig'yər) *v.t.,* **trans·fig·ured, trans·fig·ur·ing.** **1.** to change the outward appearance of; change in form or figure: *The new paint transfigured the old cabin.* **2.** to give a glorified appearance to; glorify.

trans·fix (trans fiks') *v.t.* **1.** to make motionless, as from awe or fear: *They were transfixed by the sight of the Statue of Liberty.* **2.** to pierce through with a sharpened instrument; impale: *The collector transfixed the dead butterfly with a pin.*

trans·form (trans fôrm') *v.t.* **1.** to change in shape, form, or appearance: *A little paint will soon transform this old car.* **2.** to change the character, condition, or nature of: *The chemist transformed the solid into a liquid.* **3.** to change (one form of energy) into another, as mechanical energy into electricity, or electric energy into light or heat. **4.** to change (an electric current) to a higher or lower voltage or to direct or alternating current.

trans·for·ma·tion (trans'fər mā'shən) *n.* the act of transforming or the state of being transformed.

trans·form·er (trans fôr'mər) *n.* **1.** a person or thing that transforms. **2.** a device for transferring electric energy from one alternating current circuit to another, usually with a change in voltage and current.

trans·fuse (trans fūz') *v.t.,* **trans·fused, trans·fus·ing.** **1.** to pour (a liquid) from one container into another; transfer by pouring. **2.** to transfer (blood) from one individual to another.

trans·fu·sion (trans fū'zhən) *n.* the act of transfusing, especially the transfer of blood from one individual to another.

trans·gress (trans gres') *v.i.* to break or violate a law, commandment, or the like, sin. —*v.t.* **1.** to break or violate (a law, commandment, or the like). **2.** to go beyond (a limit or bound): *a restriction that transgresses the rights of the individual.* —**trans·gres'sor,** *n.*

trans·gres·sion (trans gresh'ən) *n.* the act or instance of transgressing, especially the breaking of a law or commandment.

tran·ship (tran ship') *v.t.,* **tran·shipped, tran·ship·ping.** another spelling of **transship.** —**tran·ship'ment,** *n.*

tran·sience (tran'shəns) *n.* the state or quality of being transient.

tran·sient (tran'shənt) *adj.* **1.** being or remaining only for a short time; not lasting or durable; transitory: *transient fame, transient beauty.* **2.** stopping only for a short time; passing through: *a transient hotel guest.* —*n.* a person or thing that is transient, especially a person who passes through a place or stays in it only for a short time: *This boarding house caters to transients.* **tran'sient·ly,** *adv.*

tran·sis·tor (tran zis'tər) *n.* **1.** a very small electronic device containing semiconductors, which is used instead of electron tubes to control and to increase the strength of electric current in television sets, computers, and other electronic equipment. **2.** see **transistor radio.**

tran·sis·tor·ize (tran zis'tə rīz') *v.t.,* **tran·sis·tor·ized, tran·sis·tor·iz·ing.** to equip with transistors.

at; āpe; fär; câre; end; mē; it; īce; pîerce; hot; ōld; sông, fôrk; oil; out; up; ūse; rüle; pùll; tûrn; chin; sing; shop; thin; this; hw in white; zh in treasure. The symbol ə stands for the unstressed vowel sound heard in about, taken, pencil, lemon, and circus.

999

transistor radio, a radio, usually portable and battery-operated, whose components include transistors instead of electron tubes.

trans·it (tran'sit, tran'zit) *n.* **1.** the act or instance of passing across or through; movement from one place or point to another: *We were delayed in transit by traffic.* **2.** the act of carrying or the state of being carried from one place or point to another: *The transit of fresh fruit to markets must be done quickly.* **3.** a transition or change. **4.** a telescope used in surveying to measure horizontal and vertical angles. **5.** *Astronomy.* **a.** the passage of a planet directly between the earth and the sun so that it can be seen as a black dot moving across the disk of the sun. **b.** the passage of a celestial body across the celestial meridian. —*v.t.* to pass across or through.

tran·si·tion (tran zish'ən) *n.* **1.** a passage from one state, position, condition, or activity to another: *the transition from childhood to adolescence.* **2.** *Music.* **a.** a change of key. **b.** a passage connecting two parts, themes, or the like. —**tran·si'tion·al,** *adj.* —**tran·si'tion·al·ly,** *adv.*

tran·si·tive (tran'si tiv, tran'zi tiv) *adj.* (of verbs) taking a direct object to complete the action of the sentence. In the sentence *I hit the ball,* hit is a transitive verb. —*n.* a verb that is transitive.

tran·si·to·ry (tran'si tôr'ē, tran'zi tôr'ē) *adj.* lasting for only a short time: *The beauty of cut flowers is transitory.*

trans·late (trans lāt') *v.,* **trans·lat·ed, trans·lat·ing.** —*v.t.* **1.** to express in or change into another language: *to translate an American play into German.* **2.** to explain by using other words, terms, or signs: *The scientist's theory can be translated into simpler terms.* **3.** to change from one place, form, or condition to another: *to translate dreams into reality.* —*v.i.* **1.** to act as translator: *The guide translated for the tourists.* **2.** to be able to be translated: *Jokes often do not translate well into another language.* [From the Latin word *translatus,* past participle of *transferre* meaning "to transfer, transport," from the prefix *trans-* "across" + the word *ferre* "to bear, carry."] —**trans·lat'a·ble,** *adj.*

trans·la·tion (trans lā'shən) *n.* **1.** the act of translating or the state of being translated. **2.** something that is produced as a result of translating, especially a literary work that has been translated from the language in which it was originally written.

trans·la·tor (trans lā'tər, trans'lā tər) *n.* a person who translates.

trans·lit·er·ate (trans lit'ə rāt') *v.t.,* **trans·lit·er·at·ed, trans·lit·er·at·ing.** to change (letters or words of one alphabet) into characters of another alphabet that have corresponding sounds. —**trans·lit·er·a'tion,** *n.*

trans·lu·cence (trans lü'səns) *n.* the state or quality of being translucent. Also, **trans·lu·cen·cy** (trans'lü'-sən sē).

trans·lu·cent (trans lü'sənt) *adj.* allowing light to pass through, but not allowing objects on the other side to be clearly seen. Frosted glass is translucent. —**trans·lu'cent·ly,** *adv.*

trans·mi·grate (trans mī'grāt) *v.i.,* **trans·mi·grat·ed, trans·mi·grat·ing.** (of a soul) to pass to another body at death. —**trans'mi·gra'tion,** *n.*

trans·mis·si·ble (trans mis'ə bəl) *adj.* capable of being transmitted.

trans·mis·sion (trans mish'ən) *n.* **1.** the act of transmitting or the state of being transmitted. Also, **transmittal. 2.** something that is transmitted, such as a television picture or a telegram. **3.** in an automobile, a series of gears and mechanical devices for transmitting power from the engine to the driving wheels. **4.** the sending out of signals, as in radio or television communication.

trans·mit (trans mit') *v.t.,* **trans·mit·ted, trans·mit·ting. 1.** to send or cause to go from one person or place to another: *to transmit a disease.* **2.** to communicate or convey: *to transmit greetings from afar.* **3.** to pass on by inheritance or heredity; hand down: *Genes are transmitted from one generation to another by chromosomes.* **4.** to cause (something, such as light, heat, or sound) to pass through a medium: *A tuning fork transmits sound waves through the air.* **5.** (of a medium) to allow (something, such as light, heat, or sound) to pass through: *Water transmits sound.* **6.** to send out (signals) on electromagnetic waves.

trans·mit·tal (trans mit'əl) *n.* the act of transmitting or the state of being transmitted.

trans·mit·ter (trans mit'ər) *n.* **1.** a person or thing that transmits. **2.** a device that produces radio or television signals for sending from an antenna. **3.** a device in a telegraph or telephone that changes the messages into electrical impulses that can be carried over wires.

trans·mu·ta·tion (trans'mū tā'shən) *n.* **1.** the act of transmuting or the state of being transmuted. **2.** *Physics.* the conversion of one element into another by a change in its nuclear structure.

trans·mute (trans mūt') *v.t.,* **trans·mut·ed, trans·mut·ing.** to change in form, nature, or quality.

trans·o·ce·an·ic (trans'ō shē an'ik) *adj.* **1.** crossing or spanning an ocean: *a transoceanic voyage.* **2.** on the opposite side of the ocean.

tran·som (tran'səm) *n.* **1.** a window above a door or other window, usually hinged to a horizontal bar. **2.** a horizontal bar that divides a window or separates a door or window from a window above.

tran·son·ic (tran son'ik) *also,* **trans·son·ic.** *adj.* of, relating to, or moving at a speed just above or just below the speed of sound.

trans·pa·cif·ic (trans'pə sif'ik) *adj.* **1.** crossing or spanning the Pacific Ocean. **2.** on the opposite side of the Pacific Ocean.

trans·par·en·cy (trans pâr'ən sē, trans par'ən sē) *n., pl.* **trans·par·en·cies. 1.** the state or quality of being transparent: *the transparency of cellophane.* Also *(def. 1),* **trans·par·ence** (trans pâr'əns, trans par'əns). **2.** something transparent, especially a photographic slide.

transom *(def. 1)*

trans·par·ent (trans pâr'ənt, trans par'ənt) *adj.* **1.** allowing light to pass through, so that objects on the other side can be clearly seen. The lenses in a pair of eyeglasses or the panes of a window are transparent. **2.** easily understood or seen through; obvious: *a transparent lie. Their insincerity is transparent.* [From the Medieval Latin word *transparens,* present participle of *transparēre* meaning "to show through," going back to the Latin prefix *trans-* "across" + the word *parēre* "to show oneself."] —**trans·par'ent·ly,** *adv.* —**trans·par'ent·ness,** *n.*

tran·spi·ra·tion (tran'spə rā'shən) *n.* the act or process of transpiring, especially the giving off of waste products in the form of vapor by a living organism.

tran·spire (tran spīr') *v.,* **tran·spired, tran·spir·ing.** —*v.i.* **1.** to happen; occur: *It was impossible to predict what would transpire by the end of the book.* **2.** to become known; come to light: *It finally transpired that the fire was set by vandals.* **3.** to give off waste products in the form of vapor, as through the pores of the skin. —*v.t.* to give off (waste products) in the form of vapor.

trans·plant (*v.,* trans plant'; *n.,* trans'plant') *v.t.* **1.** to remove (a plant) from one place and plant it again in another. **2.** to move from one place to another; transport:

The rancher transplanted the entire herd to a new pasture.
3. to transfer (skin, an organ, or the like) from one person or animal to another or from one part of the body to another. —*v.i.* to be capable of being transplanted. —*n.* **1.** something that is transplanted: *The transplant flourished in new soil. The patient received a kidney transplant.* **2.** the act or process of transplanting. —**trans·plant′a·ble,** *adj.* —**trans′plan·ta′tion** (trans′-plan tā′shən), *n.* —**trans·plant′er,** *n.*

trans·port (*v.,* trans pôrt′; *n.,* trans′pôrt) *v.t.* **1.** to bring or carry from one place or person to another: *to transport freight by ship.* **2.** to carry away by strong emotion: *The beautiful music transported us.* **3.** to punish (a criminal) by sending her or him abroad to a penal colony. —*n.* **1.** the act of transporting: *The transport of supplies was halted during the labor strike.* **2.** a ship used to carry military personnel. **3.** an airplane used to transport passengers, mail, or freight. **4.** the state or condition of being carried away by strong emotion: *a transport of delight.* —**trans·port′a·ble,** *adj.* —**trans·port′er,** *n.*

trans·por·ta·tion (trans′pər tā′shən) *n.* **1.** the act of transporting or the state of being transported. **2.** a means of transporting: *Do you need transportation to school?* **3.** the cost of transporting, especially for traveling by bus, train, or the like: *Transportation to and from work was several dollars each way.*

trans·pose (trans pōz′) *v.t.,* **trans·posed, trans·pos·ing.** **1.** to reverse the order of; interchange: *The typist accidentally transposed the initials JFK to KFJ.* **2.** to move (something) from one place or time to another: *The author transposed a medieval story to the twentieth century.* **3.** to write or perform (music) in a key other than the original or given key. **4.** to transfer (an algebraic term) from one side of an equation to the other, changing the plus or minus sign to maintain equality. —**trans·pos′er,** *n.*

trans·po·si·tion (trans′pə zish′ən) *n.* **1.** the act of transposing or the state of being transposed. **2.** something that has been transposed. Also, **trans·po·sal** (trans-pō′zəl). —**trans′po·si′tion·al,** *adj.*

trans·ship (trans ship′) *also,* **tran·ship,** *v.t.,* **trans·shipped, trans·ship·ping.** to transfer (cargo) from one ship, train, truck, or the like, to another. —**trans·ship′ment,** *n.*

trans·son·ic (trans son′ik) another spelling of **transonic.**

tran·sub·stan·ti·a·tion (tran′səb stan′shē ā′shən) *n.* **1.** the transformation of one substance into another. **2.** the doctrine that the bread and wine of the Holy Communion service become the body and blood of Jesus, although the appearance and taste are unchanged.

trans·ver·sal (trans vûr′səl) *n.* a line that intersects two or more lines.

trans·verse (trans vûrs′) *adj.* lying across or in a crosswise direction. —*n.* something that is transverse. —**trans·verse′ly,** *adv.*

trap (trap) *n.* **1.** a device used for catching game or other animals. **2.** any trick used to catch a person unawares: *The lawyer's question was a trap that made the witness sound uncertain.* **3.** a bend in a pipe, usually U-shaped or S-shaped, that fills with liquid to form a seal, as to keep air in the pipe or to prevent the return flow of a gas. **4.** a device used to hurl clay pigeons or the like into the air for target shooting. **5.** in certain games, an obstacle or hazard, especially a sand trap in a golf course. —*v.,* **trapped, trap·ping.** —*v.t.* **1.** to catch in a trap; entrap: *The hunters trapped the bear.* **2.** to furnish

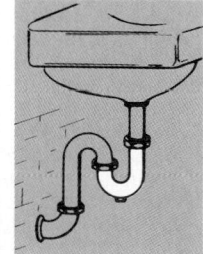

trap (n., def. 3)

or provide with a trap or traps. **3.** to stop and hold (gas, liquid, or the like) with a trap. —*v.i.* to set traps for game; be a trapper.

trap·door (trap′dôr′) *n.* a hinged or sliding door in a floor, ceiling or roof.

tra·peze (tra pēz′, trə pēz′) *n.* a short swinging horizontal bar suspended from two ropes, used in gymnastics and acrobatics.

tra·pe·zi·um (trə pē′zē əm) *n., pl.* **tra·pe·zi·ums** or **tra·pe·zi·a** (trə pē′zē ə). a figure having four sides with none of the sides parallel.

tra·pe·zi·us (trə pē′zē əs) *n., pl.* **tra·pe·zi·us·es** or **tra·pe·zi·i** (trə pē′zē ī′). a wide, flat muscle located on each side of the neck, shoulders, and back. The trapezius moves the shoulder and the head.

trap·e·zoid (trap′ə zoid′) *n.* a figure having four sides with only two sides parallel. [From the Greek word *trapezoe-idēs* meaning "shaped like a trapezium," from the word *trapeza* "table."]

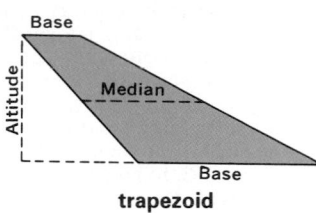

trapezoid

trap·per (trap′ər) *n.* a person who traps wild animals, especially for their fur.

trap·pings (trap′ingz) *pl. n.* **1.** an ornamented cloth or covering spread over the harness or saddle of a horse. **2.** outer or superficial adornments: *The king and queen wore purple robes and other trappings of royalty.*

trap·shoot·ing (trap′shü′ting) *n.* a sport in which shooters fire shotguns at clay pigeons hurled into the air from traps. —**trap′shoot′er,** *n.*

trash (trash) *n.* **1.** worthless or discarded objects or matter. **2.** worthless or foolish talk, writing, ideas, or the like. **3.** a low, worthless person or persons.

trash·y (trash′ē) *adj.,* **trash·i·er, trash·i·est.** of, like, or containing trash; worthless; inferior: *a trashy movie.* —**trash′i·ness,** *n.*

trau·ma (trô′mə, trou′mə) *n., pl.* **trau·mas** or **trau·ma·ta** (trô′mə tə, trou′mə tə). **1.** a severe and painful emotional shock, usually having a lasting effect on the personality. **2.** a bodily wound or injury.

trau·mat·ic (trô mat′ik, trou mat′ik) *adj.* of, relating to, like, or caused by a trauma.

trav·ail (trə vāl′, trav′āl) *n.* **1.** difficult or tiring labor. **2.** intense pain or suffering, especially when caused by great hardship: *The wartime years were a period of travail for many.* —*v.i.* to exert oneself; work hard; toil.

trav·el (trav′əl) *v.,* **trav·eled, trav·el·ing;** *also, British,* **trav·elled, trav·el·ling.** —*v.i.* **1.** to go from one place to another; make a journey: *We traveled through Ireland.* **2.** to go from place to place as a traveling salesman. **3.** to pass or be transmitted from one point to another: *Sound waves travel through water.* **4.** to associate with: *to travel with a bad crowd.* —*v.t.* to move or journey over or through; make a tour of: *The candidate traveled the country making speeches.* —*n.* **1.** the act of traveling from one place to another. **2. travels.** a long trip to many different places; journey: *We met many interesting people in our travels.*

trav·eled (trav′əld) *also, British,* **trav·elled.** *adj.*

at; āpe; fär; câre; end; mē; it; īce; pîerce; hot; ōld; sông, fôrk; oil; out; up; ūse; rüle; pull; tûrn; chin; sing; shop; thin; this; hw in white; zh in treasure. The symbol ə stands for the unstressed vowel sound heard in about, taken, pencil, lemon, and circus.

T

1. having done much traveling, especially to foreign countries. **2.** (of a road, route, or the like) used by many travelers.

trav·el·er (trav′ə lər) *also, British,* **trav·el·ler.** *n.* **1.** a person who travels. **2.** *British.* a traveling salesman.

traveler's check, a check for a fixed amount of money which is bought for use in place of cash, especially by travelers. The buyer signs the check at the time of purchase and then signs again when using it as payment or converting it to cash.

traveling salesman, a person, usually working for a firm, who travels from place to place selling or taking orders for goods.

trav·e·logue (trav′ə lôg′, trav′ə log′) *also,* **trav·e·log.** *n.* **1.** a lecture describing a trip, as to a foreign country, often illustrated with slides or films. **2.** a motion picture about a particular country or region.

trav·erse (trav′ərs, trə vûrs′) *v.,* **trav·ersed, trav·ers·ing.** —*v.t.* **1.** to pass across, over, or through: *The climbers traversed the mountain range.* **2.** to go back and forth over or along; cross and recross: *The airline traverses the country from coast to coast.* —*v.i.* **1.** to move or go along, across, or back and forth: *The skier traversed down the slope.* **2.** to go or turn from side to side; pivot. —*n.* **1.** the act of traversing or crossing. **2.** a distance traversed or crossed. **3.** something put or lying across, such as a rung of a ladder. —**trav′ers·a·ble,** *adj.* —**trav′ers·er,** *n.*

trav·es·ty (trav′ə stē) *n., pl.* **trav·es·ties. 1.** a distorted or ridiculous imitation: *The jury's unfair verdict was a travesty of justice.* **2.** in literature, a mocking treatment of a serious work or subject. —*v.t.,* **trav·es·tied, trav·es·ty·ing.** to make fun of by a travesty.

tra·vois (trə voi′, trav′oi) *n., pl.* **tra·vois.** a V-shaped sled formerly used by Indians of the Great Plains, made up of a platform or net supported by two long poles. The front ends of the poles were harnessed to a horse, dog, or other draft animal, and the rear ends of the poles were dragged along the ground.

trawl (trôl) *n.* **1.** a strong net, usually shaped like a bag, towed over the ocean bottom to catch fish. **2.** a long line usually resting near the ocean floor and supported by buoys, having short lines with baited hooks every few feet along its length. It is used to catch fish. —*v.i.* to fish with a trawl.

trawl·er (trô′lər) *n.* **1.** a fishing boat used for trawling. **2.** a person who fishes with a trawl.

tray (trā) *n.* a flat, shallow vessel with a slightly raised rim, used for carrying, storing, or displaying things.

treach·er·ous (trech′ər əs) *adj.* **1.** likely to betray a trust; traitorous; disloyal: *a pirate ship with a treacherous crew of scoundrels.* **2.** dangerous; hazardous: *Many ships have been sunk on that treacherous reef.* —**treach′er·ous·ly,** *adv.* —**treach′er·ous·ness,** *n.*

treach·er·y (trech′ə rē) *n., pl.* **treach·er·ies.** the betrayal of a trust.

trea·cle (trē′kəl) *n. British.* another word for **molasses.**

tread (tred) *v.,* **trod, trod·den** or **trod, tread·ing.** —*v.t.* **1.** to walk on, along, or over; step upon: *to tread the path home.* **2.** to press with the feet; trample: *The dog trod the flowers.* **3.** to form by walking: *The children trod a path across the lawn.* **4.** to put down or oppress; subdue; crush. —*v.i.* **1.** to move on foot; walk or step: *to tread heavily across the room.* **2.** to trample: *Don't tread on the grass.* —*n.* **1.** the act, manner, or sound of treading: *the creak of a heavy tread on the stairs.* **2.** the outer, grooved surface of an automobile tire: *Most of the tread has been worn off this old tire.* **3.** the horizontal part of a step in a staircase. **4.** the part of a wheel that touches the ground or rails. **5.** the part of the sole of a shoe that touches the ground. **6.** one of the continuous metal belts on which a tank, bulldozer, or similar vehicle runs; track.

•**to tread water** (past tense **tread·ed**). to keep the head above water while staying in an upright position, usually by moving the feet up and down in a walking motion.

trea·dle (tred′əl) *n.* a lever or pedal worked by the foot to provide motion for operating a machine, such as a sewing machine. —*v.i.,* **trea·dled, trea·dling.** to work a treadle.

tread·mill (tred′mil′) *n.* **1.** a device turned by animals or persons walking on moving steps attached to a wheel, or treading on an endless sloping belt. It is used to produce motion for doing work or as a device for exercising. **2.** any monotonous, tiresome routine or activity.

treadmill *(def. 1)*

trea·son (trē′zən) *n.* the betrayal of one's country, especially by giving aid to the enemy in wartime.

trea·son·a·ble (trē′zə nə bəl) *adj.* of, relating to, involving, or like treason. Also, **trea·son·ous** (trē′zə nəs).

treas·ure (trezh′ər) *n.* **1.** a store of valuables, such as money or jewels; accumulated riches. **2.** a person or thing that is greatly valued or considered precious: *I believe that my good health is my greatest treasure.* —*v.t.,* **treas·ured, treas·ur·ing.** to consider as being of great value; cherish: *to treasure one's parents.* [From the Old French word *tresor* meaning "treasure," from the Latin word *thesaurus* meaning "treasure" or "storehouse," from the Greek word *thēsauros* with the same meaning.]

treas·ur·er (trezh′ər ər) *n.* a person who is entrusted with the care and spending of funds, as of a business, club, or the like.

treas·ure-trove (trezh′ər trōv′) *n.* **1.** *Law.* money, jewels, or other valuables that have been found, and whose owner is not known. **2.** any valuable discovery.

treas·ur·y (trezh′ə rē) *n., pl.* **treas·ur·ies. 1.** a place where funds, especially public funds, are deposited and stored. **2.** funds, as of a corporation or government. **3. Treasury.** a governmental department that is in charge of the collection of taxes and the management of a country's finances. **4.** a place where treasure is kept. **5.** a person or thing that is thought of as a rich or ample source: *The book is a treasury of information about the Civil War.*

Treasury bill, a U.S. government bond paying no interest but sold to the public at less than its face value and usually becoming due at its face value in 91 to 182 days.

treat (trēt) *v.t.* **1.** to act or behave toward in a particular way: *to treat children with kindness. The judge treated each defendant fairly.* **2.** to deal with in a particular way: *The teacher treated the subject in great detail.* **3.** to deal with in a speech or writing; discuss: *The article treated the development of space travel.* **4.** to give medical

attention to: *The doctor treated the patient's broken leg.*
5. to subject to a process or application, as for altering or improving: *to treat cloth with a chemical to make it waterproof.* **6.** to pay for or provide the entertainment for; give food, drink, or the like to: *to treat a friend to a good meal.* —*v.i.* **1.** to deal with a subject in speech or writing: *a book that treats of ancient history.* **2.** to pay for another's food, drink, or the like. —*n.* **1.** food, drink, or the like given or paid for by another. **2.** something that gives unexpected or unusual pleasure: *Going to the circus was a treat for us.* **3.** the act of treating or entertaining. —**treat'er,** *n.*

trea·tise (trē'tis) *n.* a book or other piece of writing dealing in a formal way with some subject: *a treatise on the nature of democratic government.*

treat·ment (trēt'mənt) *n.* **1.** the act, process, or manner of treating. **2.** a course of action or means used to treat something, especially the care and medicine prescribed to treat an illness.

trea·ty (trē'tē) *n., pl.* **trea·ties.** a formal agreement, especially one between nations: *A peace treaty was signed by all the countries involved in the war.*

tre·ble (treb'əl) *adj.* **1.** three times as much or as many; triple. **2.** of, relating to, or for the highest musical instrument or voice; soprano. —*n.* a soprano voice, part, or instrument. —*v.t.,* **tre·bled, tre·bling.** to make three times as much or as many. —**tre'bly,** *adv.*

treble clef, the clef placed on the second line of the staff, showing that that line corresponds to the note G above middle C. Also, **G clef.** See **clef** for illustration.

tree (trē) *n.* **1.** a plant having a single stem or trunk made up of a solid, permanent, woody tissue, and branches and leaves at some distance above the ground. **2.** any of various bushes, shrubs, or other plants, such as the banana, that are like a tree in size or shape. **3.** any structure or device that is like a tree in shape. **4.** a diagram resembling a tree with its branches: *a family tree of one's ancestors.* —*v.t.,* **treed, tree·ing.** to chase or force into or up a tree: *The hounds treed a raccoon.* —**tree'less,** *adj.* —**tree'like',** *adj.*

•**up a tree** in an awkward, difficult, or embarrassing position or situation.

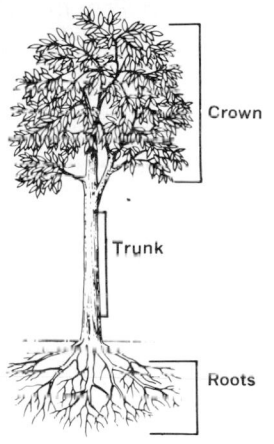

Crown

Trunk

Roots

tree *(def. 1)*

tree fern, any of various tropical, treelike ferns characterized by large fronds and, usually, thick, upright stems.

tree frog, any of a group of small frogs usually living in trees in temperate and tropical regions. Most tree frogs have sticky pads on their feet for climbing.

tree heath, a shrub or small tree found in the Mediterranean region, having fragrant, round, white flowers. Also, **briar.**

tree house, a platform or playhouse, usually for children, built in the branches of a tree.

tree line (trē'līn') *n.* an imaginary line on mountains and in polar regions above which or beyond which trees do not grow: *The change from coniferous forest to tundra is marked by the tree line.* Also, **timberline.**

tree of heaven, another term for **ailanthus.**

tre·foil (trē'foil') *n.* **1.** any of several plants related to the pea, having leaves that usually are made up of three oval leaflets. **2.** any of various clovers. **3.** an ornament, used especially in architecture, consisting of three arcs resembling the leaves of a clover.

trek (trek) *v.i.,* **trekked, trek·king.** to travel or journey, especially in a slow, difficult manner. —*n.* a journey, especially one that is slow or difficult.

trel·lis (trel'is) *n., pl.* **trel·lis·es.** a structure of crossed strips, as of wood, spaced widely apart to support growing vines. —*v.t.* to furnish or support with a trellis.

trel·lis·work (trel'is wûrk') *n.* open-work made from, consisting of, or like a trellis.

trem·a·tode (trem'ə tōd') *n.* see **fluke³** *(def. 2).*

trem·ble (trem'bəl) *v.i.,* **trem·bled, trem·bling.** **1.** to shake, as with cold, weakness, fear, or anger. **2.** to have a slight, vibrating motion, as from a jarring force: *The ground trembled as the distant volcano erupted.* **3.** to be filled with nervousness or fear: *to tremble at the thought of how dangerous the storm was.* —*n.* the act of trembling. —**trem'bling·ly,** *adv.* —**trem'bly,** *adj.*

tre·men·dous (tri men'dəs) *adj.* **1.** of very great size, amount, or intensity: *a tremendous wave, a tremendous appetite.* **2.** *Informal.* extraordinary or wonderful; astounding: *The landing of astronauts on the moon was a tremendous achievement.* **3.** terrible; dreadful: *Tremendous tragedies have occurred in times of war.*

trellis

trem·o·lo (trem'ə lō') *n., pl.* **trem·o·los.** *Music.* **1.** a trembling or vibrating effect produced by rapidly repeating a single tone or by rapidly alternating two tones. **2.** a device or stop in an organ that is used to produce such an effect.

trem·or (trem'ər) *n.* **1.** a rapid shaking or vibrating movement: *a tremor caused by an earthquake.* **2.** a shaking or trembling, especially of the body or a limb. **3.** a nervous thrill caused by emotion or excitement: *A tremor of anticipation went through the crowd as the final inning began.*

trem·u·lous (trem'yə ləs) *adj.* **1.** marked or affected by trembling; shaking: *to speak in a tremulous voice.* **2.** lacking firmness or courage; timid; wavering: *to be tremulous when quick action is needed.* —**trem'u·lous·ly,** *adv.* —**trem'u·lous·ness,** *n.*

trench (trench) *n., pl.* **trench·es.** **1.** a long, narrow ditch; deep furrow. *A trench was dug in the field to help irrigate it.* **2.** a long, narrow ditch with the earth piled up in front, used especially to protect soldiers in combat. —*v.t.* to dig a trench or trenches in.

trench·ant (tren'chənt) *adj.* **1.** sharp; cutting; biting: *trenchant wit.* **2.** forceful or effective: *a trenchant argument.* —**trench'an·cy,** *n.* —**trench'ant·ly,** *adv.*

trench coat, a loose-fitting, double-breasted raincoat having a belt around the waist and straps at the shoulders and wrists.

trench·er (tren'chər) *n.* formerly, a wooden platter or board on which food, especially meat, was carved and served.

trench·er·man (tren'chər mən) *n., pl.* **trench·er·men** (tren'chər mən). a person who eats with a hearty appetite.

trench mouth, an acute inflammation of the mouth and

T

gums, caused by certain bacteria, and marked by painful, bleeding gums.

trend (trend) *n.* a general direction, tendency, or course: *a trend in fashions toward brighter colors, a conservative trend in politics.* —*v.i.* to have or go in a general direction or course; be inclined; tend: *Prices have trended upward.*

trep·i·da·tion (trep′i dā′shən) *n.* **1.** nervous or fearful anticipation; anxiety: *to face a test with trepidation.* **2.** a vibrating motion; trembling; tremor.

tres·pass (tres′pəs, tres′pas′) *v.i.* **1.** *Law.* to unlawfully enter the property of another: *The hunter trespassed on a farm.* **2.** to encroach or intrude on a person's time, privacy, or the like. **3.** to commit a sin. —*n., pl.* **tres·pass·es.** **1.** a wrong or sin. **2.** *Law.* an illegal act, especially unlawful entry of another's property. [From the Old French word *trespasser* meaning "to cross over" or "go across," going back to the Latin prefix *trans-* "across" and the word *passus* "a step."] —**tres′pass·er,** *n.*

tress (tres) *n., pl.* **tress·es.** **1.** a curl, tuft, or strand of human hair. **2. tresses.** long hair, especially when worn loose or flowing.

tres·tle (tres′əl) *n.* **1.** a short beam or bar supported by four legs, used as support. **2.** a framework used to support a railroad bridge or other raised structure.

trey (trā) *n.* a playing card, die, or domino having three marks.

tri– *combining form* **1.** having or involving three: *triangle, tricycle.* **2.** coming or happening every three: *triweekly.*

tri·ad (trī′ad) *n.* **1.** a group of three persons or things. **2.** *Music.* a chord of three tones, especially one consisting of a given tone with the third and fifth tones above it.

trestle *(def. 2)*

tri·al (trī′əl) *n.* **1.** an examination of a case in a court of law. **2.** the state of being tried or tested: *to be given a job on trial.* **3.** a difficult test of one's strength, patience, or faith; hardship. **4.** a source or cause of pain or trouble: *That barking dog has been a constant trial to its owner.* **5.** the act of making an effort; attempt; try. —*adj.* of, for, or relating to a trial: *a trial effort, a trial lawyer.*

trial and error, the practice of trying one thing after another until a desired result is achieved: *I found the right diet for me by trial and error.*

tri·an·gle (trī′ang′gəl) *n.* **1.** a plane figure with three sides and three angles. **2.** something shaped like a triangle. **3.** a musical instrument made of a metal bar bent into the shape of a triangle, producing a high tone like a bell when struck. **4.** a group of three persons or things.

triangle *(def. 1)*

tri·an·gu·lar (trī ang′gyə lər) *adj.* **1.** of, relating to, or resembling a triangle. **2.** of, relating to, or consisting of three persons or things.

tri·an·gu·la·tion (trī ang′gyə lā′shən) *n.* a method used in surveying to determine the relative position of three points on the earth's surface. If one side and two angles of the triangle formed by the points are measured, the remaining sides and angle can be calculated.

Tri·as·sic (trī as′ik) *n.* the earliest geological period of the Mesozoic era, about 230 million years ago, during which there was much volcanic activity and dinosaurs appeared. —*adj.* of, relating to, or characteristic of this period.

tri·ath·lon (trī ath′lon) *n.* an athletic competition consisting of a long-distance race involving swimming, bicycling, and running.

trib·al (trī′bəl) *adj.* of, relating to, or characteristic of a tribe or tribes: *a tribal society, tribal customs.* —**trib′al·ly,** *adv.*

tribe (trīb) *n.* **1.** a group of people connected by common ancestry, culture, social customs, and, usually, the same political system: *The ancient Jewish nation was composed of twelve tribes.* **2.** any group of people, usually distinguished by a common characteristic, interest, or the like. **3.** a group of animals or plants.

tribes·man (trībz′mən) *n., pl.* **tribes·men** (trībz′mən). a member of a tribe.

trib·u·la·tion (trib′yə lā′shən) *n.* **1.** a condition of severe distress or misery; suffering: *The flood brought much tribulation to the town.* **2.** something that causes such distress or misery.

tri·bu·nal (trī bū′nəl, tri bū′nəl) *n.* **1.** a court of justice. **2.** any place of judgment.

trib·une¹ (trib′ūn) *n.* **1.** an official in ancient Rome appointed to protect the rights and interests of the common people. **2.** a protector or defender of the rights of the public; champion of the people. [From the Latin word *tribunus* meaning "a commander" or "tribal leader," from the word *tribus* "tribe."]

trib·une² (trib′ūn) *n.* a raised platform, stand, or seat, such as a pulpit. [From the French word *tribune,* from the Italian word *tribuna* meaning this official, from the Latin word *tribunal* "a raised judgment seat used by tribunes," from the word *tribunus* "tribune¹."]

trib·u·tar·y (trib′yə ter′ē) *n., pl.* **trib·u·tar·ies.** **1.** a river or stream that flows into a larger body of water: *The Tennessee River is a major tributary of the Ohio River.* **2.** a person or group that pays tribute. —*adj.* **1.** flowing into a larger body of water. **2.** subject to paying tribute; taxed.

trib·ute (trib′ūt) *n.* **1.** anything done, given, or observed as a sign of devotion, gratitude, or respect: *The enthusiastic applause was a tribute to the singer's performance.* **2.** money paid by one ruler or nation to another to show submission or to ensure peace or protection. **3.** any payment given under force.

trice¹ (trīs) *v.t.,* **triced, tric·ing.** to pull up and secure with a rope: *to trice a sail.* [From the Middle English word *trisen* meaning "to hoist," from the Middle Dutch word *trisen* with the same meaning.]

trice² (trīs) *n.* a very short time; instant; moment: *I'll have that fixed in a trice.* [From the Middle English word *trise* meaning "a tug, pull," from the word *trisen* "to hoist, pull."]

tri·ceps (trī′seps) *n., pl.* **tri·ceps** or **tri·ceps·es.** a muscle at the back of the upper arm that, when contracted, straightens the arm.

tri·cer·a·tops (trī ser′ə tops′) *n., pl.* **tri·cer·a·tops·es.** a plant-eating dinosaur that lived in North America and had one long horn over each eye, a shorter horn on the snout, and a bony shield projecting from the skull over the back of the neck.

triceratops

tri·chi·na (tri kī′nə) *n., pl.* **tri·chi·nae** (tri kī′nē). a parasitic roundworm that lives in humans and animals.

trich·i·no·sis (trik′ə nō′sis) *n.* a parasitic disease caused by trichinae, which enter the human body from infected pork that has not been well cooked. The adult worms lodge in the intestines, while the larvae form cysts in the muscles, resulting in nausea, diarrhea, and muscle pain.

trick (trik) *n.* **1.** something done or meant to deceive or cheat: *The misleading advertisement was a trick to draw customers.* **2.** a show of skill or cleverness, especially one meant to amuse: *to teach a dog many tricks.* **3.** the particular act or skill of doing something easily and successfully; knack: *A good speaker knows the trick of getting the listener's attention.* **4.** a mischievous act; practical joke; prank: *to play tricks on others.* **5.** a habit, trait, or practice; mannerism: *the annoying trick of not answering when called.* **6.** a group of cards made up of one card played from each player's hand. **7.** such a group of cards considered as a unit of score. —*v.t.* to deceive or cheat with a trick: *The swindler tricked them out of their savings.* —*v.i.* to practice trickery or deception. —*adj.* **1.** relating to or involving a trick or deception. **2.** inclined to give way or collapse: *The accident left the athlete with a trick knee.*
·**to do the trick.** to do what is wanted or needed: *The medicine really did the trick.*

trick·er·y (trik′ə rē) *n., pl.* **trick·er·ies.** the act or instance of deceiving or cheating; deceitful behavior.

trick·le (trik′əl) *v.,* **trick·led, trick·ling.** —*v.i.* **1.** to flow or fall drop by drop or in a thin stream: *The rain trickled down the window. Blood trickled from the cut in his arm.* **2.** to move or go in a very slow, irregular way: *The children trickled into the classroom after recess.* —*v.t.* to cause to trickle. —*n.* **1.** the act of trickling. **2.** a slow stream or movement: *Only a trickle of customers were shopping in the store.*

trick·ster (trik′stər) *n.* a person who plays tricks or practices trickery.

trick·y (trik′ē) *adj.,* **trick·i·er, trick·i·est.** **1.** given to or marked by tricks or trickery; crafty; wily: *a tricky sales pitch for a used car.* **2.** having unseen or unexpected difficulties; requiring cautious action or handling: *a tricky situation, a tricky question.* —**trick′i·ly,** *adv.* —**trick′i·ness,** *n.*

tri·col·or (trī′kul′ər) *also,* **tri·col·ored.** *adj.* having three colors. —*n.* **1.** a flag having three colors. **2.** *also,* **Tricolor.** the national flag of France, having three equal vertical bands of red, white, and blue.

tri·cot (trē′kō) *n.* **1.** a lightweight, knitted fabric made by hand or machine from wool, nylon, or rayon. **2.** a worsted fabric made of wool.

tri·cus·pid (trī kus′pid) *adj.* having three cusps or points. —*n.* any tooth that has three cusps or points.

tri·cy·cle (trī′si kəl) *n.* **1.** a three-wheeled vehicle having two wheels in the back and one in the front, driven by pedals and steered with handlebars. **2.** a motorcycle with three wheels arranged similarly.

tri·dent (trī′dənt) *n.* a spear with three prongs.

tried (trīd) *v.* the past tense and past participle of **try.** —*adj.* proved, as by experience or examination; tested: *a tried and true remedy.*

tri·en·ni·al (trī en′ē əl) *adj.* **1.** lasting or continuing for three years. **2.** done or taking place every three years. —*n.* **1.** an event that takes place every three years. **2.** a third anniversary. —**tri·en′ni·al·ly,** *adv.*

tri·er (trī′ər) *n.* a person or thing that tries.

tri·fle (trī′fəl) *n.* **1.** something of little or no value or importance; unimportant matter or thing: *There's no sense*

tricycle *(def. 1)*

arguing over trifles. **2.** a small amount; bit: *to be a trifle annoyed with a silly mistake.* **3.** a dessert made of sponge cake, having a layer of custard, fruit, or jam, and topped with whipped cream or meringue. —*v.,* **tri·fled, tri·fling.** —*v.t.* **1.** to treat something as having little value or importance; treat lightly: *to trifle with important business matters.* **2.** to handle or treat in an idle, careless manner: *to trifle with one's keys.* —*v.t.* to pass or spend (time, money, or the like) in an idle or foolish way; waste. —**tri′fler,** *n.*

tri·fling (trī′fling) *adj.* having little or no value or importance; unimportant; small: *a trifling matter.* —**tri′fling·ly,** *adv.*

trig·ger (trig′ər) *n.* **1.** a small lever on a gun or other firearm that, when pulled back or pressed with the finger, causes the firearm to discharge. **2.** any similar device, such as a lever that is pressed or pulled to start a process or mechanism. —*v.t.* to start or cause: *Jealousy triggered that angry outburst.*

tri·glyph (trī′glif′) *n.* a part of a Doric frieze, consisting of a projecting block or tablet with two vertical grooves.

trig·o·no·met·ric (trig′ə nə met′rik) *adj.* of or relating to trigonometry. —**trig′o·no·met′ri·cal·ly,** *adv.*

trig·o·nom·e·try (trig′ə nom′i trē) *n.* the branch of mathematics dealing with the relations between the sides and angles of triangles, and also with the properties of these relations.

trill (tril) *n.* **1.** a quavering, trembling, usually high-pitched sound: *the chirping trill of a bird.* **2.** *Music.* a rapid alternation of two notes either a whole step or a half step apart. —*v.t.* to sing, play, or utter (something) with a trill. —*v.i.* to sing, play, or utter a trill.

tril·lion (tril′yən) *adj.* **1.** in the United States, the cardinal number that is represented by one followed by 12 zeros. **2.** in Great Britain, the cardinal number that is represented by one followed by 18 zeros. —*adj.* numbering one trillion. —**tril′lionth,** *adj., n.*

tril·li·um (tril′ē əm) *n.* any of a group of plants related to the lily, having leaves in arrangements of three, and bearing flowers with three oval petals.

tri·lo·bate (trī lō′bāt) *adj.* having three lobes, as certain leaves.

tri·lo·bite (trī′lə bīt′) *n.* an extinct sea animal that lived hundreds of millions of years ago, having a small, segmented body divided into three lobes.

trillium

tril·o·gy (tril′ə jē) *n., pl.* **tril·o·gies.** a group of three complete plays, operas, novels, or the like that together make a related series.

trim (trim) *v.t.,* **trimmed, trim·ming. 1.** to make neat and orderly, especially by cutting parts off: *to trim one's hair, to trim a rosebush.* **2.** to remove (a part or object) in order to make neat or orderly: *to trim the thorns on a rose, to trim unnecessary items off a budget.* **3.** to add ornaments or decorations to; decorate: *to trim a cake, to trim a Christmas tree.* **4.** to balance (a boat or ship) as by arranging the cargo or ballast. **5.** to adjust (yards or sails) for sailing. —*n.* **1.** ornamentation or decoration: *The napkin had a lace trim.* **2.** the state or condition of being fit, ready, or in good order: *The swimmer was in*

at; āpe; fär; câre; end; mē; it; īce; pîerce; hot; ōld; sông; fôrk; oil; out; up; ūse; rüle; pùll; tûrn; chin; sing; shop; thin; this; hw in white; zh in treasure. The symbol ə stands for the unstressed vowel sound heard in about, taken, pencil, lemon, and circus.

T

1005

trim for the race. **3.** the condition of a ship with reference to its fitness for sailing. **4.** woodwork used as a decoration on a building, especially moldings around windows or doors. —*adj.*, **trim·mer, trim·mest.** in good order or condition: *How do you keep your clothes so neat and trim?* —**trim′ly,** *adv.* —**trim′mer,** *n.* —**trim′ness,** *n.*

tri·mes·ter (trī mes′tər) *n.* a period or term made up of three months, especially one of the three terms into which the academic year is sometimes divided.

trim·e·ter (trim′i tər) *n.* **1.** a line of verse consisting of three metrical feet. **2.** a verse composed of such lines. —*adj.* containing three metrical feet.

trim·ming (trim′ing) *n.* **1.** anything used as a decoration or ornament: *The dress had lace trimming on the sleeves.* **2. trimmings.** pieces or parts cut off in trimming something. **3. trimmings.** *Informal.* things that traditionally or usually go with or accompany something: *a parade with bands, floats, and all the trimmings.*

tri·month·ly (trī munth′lē) *adj.* done or taking place every three months.

Trin·i·ty (trin′i tē) **1.** In Christian theology, the union of the Father, the Son, and the Holy Ghost as three divine persons in the single being of God. **2. trinity.** *pl.* **trin·i·ties.** any combination or group of three persons or things.

trin·ket (tring′kit) *n.* **1.** any small ornament or fancy article, especially a piece of costume jewelry. **2.** anything of little value or importance; trifle.

tri·no·mi·al (trī nō′mē əl) *adj.* consisting of three terms: *a trinomial equation.* —*n.* a mathematical expression consisting of three terms joined by plus or minus signs. The expression $4x + 7y − 1$ is a trinomial.

tri·o (trē′ō) *n., pl.* **tri·os. 1.** a musical composition for three voices or instruments. **2.** three musicians performing such a composition. **3.** any group of three persons or things.

tri·ode (trī′ōd) *n.* an electron tube consisting of an anode and a cathode, and a grid that controls the flow of electrons between them.

tri·ox·ide (trī ok′sīd) *n.* an oxide having three atoms of oxygen in each molecule.

trip (trip) *n.* **1.** the act of traveling or going from one place to another, especially over a fairly long distance: *to take a trip to Europe, to go on a camping trip.* **2.** a fall or stumble caused by striking one's foot against an object or by losing one's footing. **3.** a light, quick step. **4.** a spring, catch, or other device that releases a part, as in setting a mechanism in operation. **5.** an error or blunder; slip. —*v.*, **tripped, trip·ping.** —*v.i.* **1.** to strike the foot against something so as to stumble or fall: *to trip over the edge of a rug.* **2.** to make an error or blunder: *to trip on a question in the test.* **3.** to move with quick, light steps; prance: *to trip merrily along a path.* —*v.t.* **1.** to cause to fall or stumble: *The rock tripped me.* **2.** to cause to make a mistake or commit a blunder: *The reporters tried to trip the mayor with their questions.* **3.** to operate (a mechanism) by releasing a spring, catch, or other device. **4.** to release (a spring, catch, or other device) in order to set a mechanism in operation.

tri·par·tite (trī pär′tīt) *adj.* **1.** divided into three parts. **2.** having three corresponding parts or copies. **3.** of, relating to, or made by three parties: *a tripartite trade agreement.*

tripe (trīp) *n.* **1.** the walls of the first and second stomachs of certain animals, especially the ox, used as food. **2.** *Informal.* anything of such poor quality as to be useless or worthless.

trip·ham·mer (trip′ham′ər) *n.* a power-driven hammer that is raised by machinery and then tripped by a device and allowed to fall.

tri·ple (trip′əl) *adj.* **1.** consisting of three parts. **2.** three times as much or as many; multiplied by three.

—*n.* **1.** a number or amount that is three times as much as another. **2.** *Baseball.* a hit that enables a batter to reach third base safely. —*v.*, **tri·pled, tri·pling.** —*v.t.* to make three times as much or as many: *The company tripled its earnings in one year.* —*v.i.* **1.** to become three times as much or as many: *The population of the town tripled in ten years.* **2.** *Baseball.* to hit a triple.

triple play *Baseball.* a play during which three outs are made.

tri·plet (trip′lit) *n.* **1.** one of three children or animals born at the same birth. **2.** any set or group of three. **3.** *Music.* a group of three notes of equal time value to be performed in the time of two. **4.** three successive lines of rhyming verse, usually of equal length.

triple time, musical time or rhythm having three beats to the measure, the accent falling on the first beat.

trip·li·cate (*adj., n.,* trip′li kit; *v.,* trip′li kāt′) *adj.* three times as much or as many; triple. —*n.* one of three identical things, especially copies of printed matter. —*v.t.*, **trip·li·cat·ed, trip·li·cat·ing.** to multiply by three; triple. —**trip′li·ca′tion,** *n.*

• **in triplicate.** in three identical copies.

tri·ply (trip′lē) *adv.* in a triple degree, amount, or manner.

tripods *(def. 1)*

tri·pod (trī′pod′) *n.* **1.** a three-legged stand for supporting a camera, surveying instrument, or the like. **2.** a pot, stool, table, or similar structure resting on three legs.

trip·ping (trip′ing) *adj.* moving quickly and lightly: *tripping footsteps.* —**trip′ping·ly,** *adv.*

trip·tych (trip′tik) *n.* **1.** a painting or carving consisting of three panels hinged together, especially one that has a religious subject and is used as an altarpiece. **2.** a set of three writing tablets tied or hinged together, used in ancient times.

tri·reme (trī′rēm) *n.* an ancient galley, especially a warship, with three tiers of oars along each side.

tri·sect (trī sekt′) *v.t.* to divide into three parts, especially into three equal parts: *to trisect an angle.* —**tri·sec′tion,** *n.*

trite (trīt) *adj.,* **trit·er, trit·est.** lacking originality or freshness because of constant repetition; hackneyed: *"Clear as crystal"* and *"in this day and age"* are trite phrases. —**trite′ly,** *adv.* —**trite′ness,** *n.*

trit·i·um (trit′ē əm, trish′ē əm) *n.* a radioactive isotope of hydrogen, containing one proton and two neutrons. The fusion of tritium with deuterium releases the explosive force of the hydrogen bomb.

Tri·ton (trī′tən) *n.* *Greek Mythology.* a sea god who was half man and half fish.

tri·umph (trī′umf) *n.* **1.** an outstanding success, achievement, or victory: *The discovery of penicillin is a medical triumph of the twentieth century.* **2.** great joy caused by victory or success: *the triumph on a winner's face.* **3.** in ancient Rome, a procession and public celebration honoring a victorious commander and army. —*v.i.* **1.** to achieve a victory; be successful; win: *to triumph over the enemy.* **2.** to rejoice or celebrate because of victory or success. [From the Latin word *triumphus* meaning "triumph" or "triumphal procession."]

tri·um·phal (trī um′fəl) *adj.* of, relating to, like, or celebrating a triumph or victory: *a triumphal procession.*

tri·um·phant (trī um′fənt) *adj.* **1.** victorious or successful: *Our team was triumphant in the match.* **2.** rejoicing because of victory or success: *The winning team gave a triumphant cheer.* —**tri·um′phant·ly,** *adv.*

tri·um·vir (trī um′vər) *n., pl.* **tri·um·virs** or **tri·um·vi·ri** (trī um′və rī′). in ancient Rome, one of the members of a triumvirate.

tri·um·vi·rate (trī um′vər it) *n.* **1.** government by three persons, especially in ancient Rome. **2.** the position or term of office of a triumvir. **3.** any group or association of three persons.

triv·et (triv′it) *n.* **1.** a three-legged stand or support used for holding pots over a fire. **2.** a metal or ceramic plate, often having three short legs, placed under hot plates or dishes on a table.

triv·i·a (triv′ē ə) *pl. n.* unimportant or insignificant facts, matters, or information; trifles. ▲ used with either a singular or plural verb.

triv·i·al (triv′ē əl) *adj.* **1.** having little or no importance or significance; trifling: *Don't worry about such a trivial problem.* **2.** commonplace; everyday. —**triv′i·al·ly,** *adv.*

triv·i·al·i·ty (triv′ē al′i tē) *n., pl.* **triv·i·al·i·ties.** **1.** the quality or state of being trivial. **2.** a thing or matter of little importance or significance; something trivial.

tri·week·ly (trī wēk′lē) *adv.* **1.** every three weeks. **2.** three times a week. —*adj.* **1.** happening or done every three weeks. **2.** happening or done three times a week. —*n., pl.* **tri·week·lies.** a newspaper, magazine, or the like issued triweekly.

tro·che (trō′kē) *n.* a lozenge containing medicine.

tro·chee (trō′kē) *n.* a metrical foot consisting of two syllables, the first accented, or long, and the second unaccented, or short. For example: *Pe′ ter Pe′ ter pump′ kin eat′ er.*

trod (trod) a past tense and a past participle of **tread.**

trod·den (trod′ən) a past participle of **tread.**

Tro·jan (trō′jən) *adj.* of or relating to Troy or its people. —*n.* **1.** a person who lived in Troy. **2.** a person who shows great courage, energy, or strength.

Trojan Horse **1.** *Greek Mythology.* in the Trojan War, a large wooden horse left behind by the Greeks when they pretended to abandon their siege of Troy. It contained hidden soldiers who, when the Trojans had brought it into the city, emerged and slaughtered the inhabitants. **2.** something or someone accepted, as into an organization, that may destroy or harm from within.

Trojan War *Greek Legend.* the war between the Greeks and the Trojans that lasted ten years and ended in the destruction of Troy.

troll¹ (trōl) *v.i.* **1.** to fish with a moving line, usually by trailing the line behind the boat. **2.** to sing in a full, rich voice. —*v.t.* **1.** (of several singers) to sing the parts of (a song) in succession, as in a round. **2.** to sing (something) in a full, rich voice. —*n.* **1.** a song whose parts are sung in succession; round. **2.** a fishing line or lure used for trolling. [From the Middle English word *trollen* meaning "to ramble, roll," from the Old French word *troller* "to run here and there."]

troll² (trōl) *n. Scandinavian Folklore.* a dwarf or a giant who lives underground or in a mountain cave. [From the Old Norse word *troll* meaning "a giant, demon."]

trol·ley (trol′ē) *n., pl.* **trol·leys.** **1.** a small grooved wheel or pulley that moves along an overhead wire to pick up electricity for an electric streetcar, train, or bus. **2.** see **trolley car.**

trolley car, an electric streetcar that gets its current from an overhead wire by means of a trolley.

trol·lop (trol′əp) *n.* a cheap, low, or vulgar woman.

trom·bone (trom bōn′, trom′bōn) *n.* a brass musical instrument that has a long, U-shaped tube with a flaring end and another tube that may be slid back and forth to change the pitch of the tones. —**trom·bon′ist,** *n.*

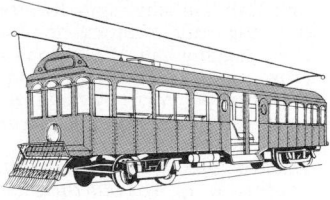

trolley car

troop (trüp) *n.* **1.** a group of persons: *A troop of students filed into the auditorium.* **2.** formerly, a cavalry unit of the U.S. Army corresponding to an infantry company. **3. troops.** members of the armed forces as a group: *The government sent troops to patrol the border.* **4.** *usually,* **troops.** a flock or swarm. **5.** a unit of Boy or Girl Scouts, usually consisting of several patrols of sixteen to thirty-two members. **6.** another spelling of **troupe.** —*v.i.* to walk or march in a group, especially in orderly fashion: *The players trooped onto the field.*

troop·er (trü′pər) *n.* **1.** a soldier in a troop of cavalry. **2.** a mounted police officer. **3.** a state police officer. **4.** another spelling of **trouper.**

troop·ship (trüp′ship′) *n.* a ship used to transport troops.

tro·phy (trō′fē) *n., pl.* **tro·phies.** **1.** a cup, bowl, statuette on a pedestal, or similar object, usually awarded for some achievement, such as winning a sports contest or other competition. **2.** something taken and kept as a reminder or proof of victory or achievement.

trop·ic (trop′ik) *n.* **the tropics.** *also,* **the Tropics.** a region of the earth lying between the Tropic of Cancer and the Tropic of Capricorn; Torrid Zone. —*adj.* of or relating to the tropics; tropical.

trop·i·cal (trop′i kəl) *adj.* of, relating to, found in, or characteristic of the tropics: *tropical plants.*

tropical fish, any of many varieties of small fish, usually brightly colored, that are native to tropical waters, breed very fast, and are often kept in home aquariums.

Tropic of Cancer **1.** an imaginary line parallel to the equator at latitude 23°27′ north, that marks the northernmost distance from the equator at which the sun appears to be overhead at noon. **2.** the circle of the celestial sphere corresponding to this, parallel to the celestial equator.

Tropic of Capricorn **1.** an imaginary line parallel to the equator at latitude 23°27′ south, that marks the southernmost distance from the equator at which the sun appears to be overhead at noon. **2.** the circle of the celestial sphere corresponding to this, parallel to the celestial equator.

tro·pism (trō′piz əm) *n.* the tendency of an animal or

---

at; āpe; fär; câre; end; mē; it; īce; pîerce; hot; ōld; sông, fôrk; oil; out; up; ūse; rüle; pull; tûrn; chin; sing; shop; thin; this; hw in white; zh in treasure. The symbol ə stands for the unstressed vowel sound heard in about, taken, pencil, lemon, and circus.

T

plant to turn or grow in response to an outside stimulus. —**tro·pis·tic** (trō pis′tik), *adj.*

trop·o·sphere (trop′ə sfîr′) *n.* the layer of the atmosphere nearest the earth's surface, extending to an average altitude of about 8 miles (13 kilometers). Most clouds form in the troposphere.

trot (trot) *n.* **1.** the gait of a horse or other four-legged animal, between a walk and a gallop, in which the left hind foot and the right forefoot are lifted together, and then the left forefoot and right hind foot are lifted. **2.** the jogging gait of a human being, between a walk and a run. —*v.*, **trot·ted, trot·ting.** —*v.i.* **1.** to ride or move at a trot: *The horse trotted around the corral.* **2.** to move quickly; hurry: *The child trotted to the grocery store.* —*v.t.* to cause to trot.
·**to trot out.** *Informal.* to bring out, as for inspection or approval: *to trot out the pictures of one's trip.*

troth (trôth, trōth) *n.* a promise of faithfulness, as in marriage or betrothal.
·**to plight one's troth.** to promise oneself in marriage.

trot·ter (trot′ər) *n.* **1.** a horse that trots, especially one bred and trained for trotting races. **2.** a foot, as of a calf, sheep, or pig, used as food.

trou·ba·dour (trü′bə dôr′) *n.* one of a group of lyric poets who flourished from the eleventh to the thirteenth centuries in southern Europe, especially in France, and who were famous for songs about love and chivalry.

trou·ble (trub′əl) *n.* **1.** difficulty, danger, or distress: *The people in the valley will be in trouble if the dam breaks.* **2.** something that causes a problem: *The trouble is that the plan will not work.* **3.** extra work or effort; pains: *The teacher went to much trouble to make the explanation clear.* **4.** a disease or illness; ailment: *kidney trouble.* **5.** a disturbance or disorder; turmoil: *There was trouble at the factory when the workers went on strike.* —*v.*, **trou·bled, trou·bling.** —*v.t.* **1.** to put into a state of distress; worry; disturb. **2.** to put (someone) to extra effort; inconvenience: *May I trouble you for a glass of water?* **3.** to cause physical pain; hurt; afflict: *to be troubled by ulcers.* —*v.i.* to take pains; bother.

trou·ble·mak·er (trub′əl mā′kər) *n.* a person or thing that is a cause of trouble.

trou·ble·shoot·er (trub′əl shü′tər) *n.* a person who specializes in locating and solving troubles, problems, and difficulties.

trou·ble·some (trub′əl səm) *adj.* causing distress, inconvenience, or annoyance: *a troublesome cough, a troublesome neighbor.*

trou·blous (trub′ləs) *adj.* **1.** full of troubles: *troublous times.* **2.** causing trouble; troublesome.

trough (trôf) *n.* **1.** a long, deep, narrow receptacle like a bin, used especially for holding water. **2.** a channel or gutter, as under or along the eaves of a roof, used for carrying water. **3.** a low point, as on a graph. **4.** a long, narrow hollow or depression, as between two mountain ridges or two ocean waves.

trounce (trouns) *v.t.*, **trounced, trounc·ing.** to beat soundly in a contest.

troupe (trüp) *also,* **troop.** *n.* a group or company, especially of touring actors, singers, or circus performers. —*v.i.*, **trouped, troup·ing.** to go on a tour with such a group.

troup·er (trü′pər) *also,* **troop·er.** *n.* **1.** a person who faces up to problems or difficulties or goes on in spite of them. **2.** an experienced actor or performer. **3.** a member of a troupe.

trou·sers (trou′zərz) *pl. n.* a garment for the lower part of the body, reaching from the waist or hips to the ankles, and divided so as to cover each leg separately.

trous·seau (trü′sō, trü sō′) *n., pl.* **trous·seaux** (trü′sōz, trü sōz′) *or* **trous·seaus.** all the items brought by a bride to her new home, such as clothing, linen, and silver.

trout (trout) *n., pl.* **trout** *or* **trouts.** any of a group of freshwater food and game fish related to the salmon, including the lake trout and brook trout.

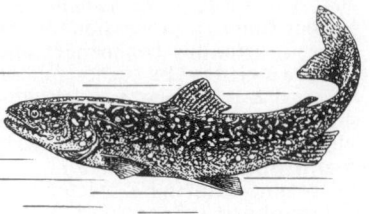

trout

trow (trō) *v.i.* *Archaic.* to be of the opinion; suppose; think.

trow·el (trou′əl) *n.* **1.** a hand tool with a flat, rectangular or triangular blade, used for spreading and smoothing plaster, mortar, or the like. **2.** a digging tool like a scoop, with a narrow, curved, pointed blade, used in gardening.

troy weight (troi) a standard system of weights used for gems and precious metals.

tru·an·cy (trü′ən sē) *n., pl.* **tru·an·cies.** the act or practice of being truant.

tru·ant (trü′ənt) *n.* **1.** a student who is absent from school without permission. **2.** a person who shirks or neglects work or duties; idle or lazy person. —*adj.* **1.** of, relating to, or characteristic of truants: *truant behavior.* **2.** being a truant: *a truant worker.*
·**to play truant. a.** to be absent from school without permission. **b.** to shirk or neglect one's work or duties.

truce (trüs) *n.* a temporary halt to fighting by mutual agreement, often in order to reach a final settlement.

truck¹ (truk) *n.* **1.** a motor vehicle designed to carry heavy loads, especially one with a cab in front for the driver, and a trailer or open area in the rear for freight. **2.** a small frame with two wheels at one end and handles at the other, used to move large, heavy boxes and other objects. **3.** a low rectangular frame on four wheels, often motorized, used for moving heavy loads; dolly. **4.** a set of two or more pairs of wheels mounted closely together in a swiveling frame, as on a railroad car or locomotive. —*v.t.* to transport on a truck or trucks: *to truck fresh vegetables to market.* —*v.i.* to drive a truck or engage in trucking. [Perhaps from the Latin word *trochus* meaning ''an iron hoop,'' from the Greek word *trochos* ''a wheel.'']

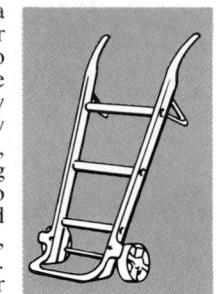

truck¹ *(def. 2)*

truck² (truk) *n.* **1.** vegetables raised for sale in a market. **2.** *Informal.* dealings: *We will have no truck with such unpleasant neighbors.* **3.** *Informal.* trash or rubbish. [From the Old French word *troquer* meaning ''to barter, exchange.'']

truck·er (truk′ər) *n.* **1.** a person or firm owning or operating a trucking business. **2.** a person whose job is driving a truck.

truck farm, a farm on which vegetables are raised for sale in a market.

truck·ing (truk′ing) *n.* the business or process of transporting goods by truck.

truck·le (truk′əl) *v.*, **truck·led, truck·ling.** —*v.i.* **1.** to be subservient or meek: *to truckle to a bully.* **2.** *Archaic.* to move on rollers or casters. —*v.t.* *Archaic.* to cause to move on rollers or casters.

truckle bed, another term for **trundle bed.**

truc·u·lence (truk′yə ləns) *n.* truculent behavior.

truc·u·lent (truk′yə lənt) *adj.* **1.** savage, fierce, or ferocious: *truculent warriors.* **2.** harsh or scathing: *a truculent speech.* **3.** hostile and belligerent. —**truc′u·lent·ly,** *adv.*

trudge (truj) *v.*, **trudged, trudg·ing.** —*v.i.* to go on foot in a steady, slow manner; plod: *to trudge up a hill.* —*v.t.* to travel over (a place or distance) in a steady, slow manner: *The hikers trudged the last mile in the rain.* —*n.* a difficult, tiring walk: *a long trudge back home.*

true (trü) *adj.*, **tru·er, tru·est.** **1.** agreeing with or correctly representing reality or fact; not false, fictitious, or wrong: *a true story.* **2.** having the proper qualities or characteristics of: *a true friend.* **3.** actually being what it seems or is claimed to be; real; genuine: *true gold.* **4.** faithful to someone or something; loyal: *to be true to one's old friends.* **5.** conforming closely to an original, standard, or type: *a true copy.* **6.** legitimate; rightful: *the true heir to an estate.* **7.** accurately fitted or placed: *a true door frame.* **8.** determined with reference to the earth's axis rather than the magnetic poles: *true north.* —*adv.* **1.** in a true manner: *to speak true.* **2.** without change from the previous generation: *to breed true.* —*v.t.*, **trued, tru·ing** or **true·ing.** to place, adjust, or fit accurately: *to true a bent bicycle wheel.* —**true′ness,** *n.*

·**to come true.** to become real or actual.

true–blue (trü′blü′) *adj.* steady in loyalty or faith; staunch: *a true-blue friend.*

truf·fle (truf′əl) *n.* **1.** any of a group of fungi shaped like a small potato and growing underground. Truffles are valued as a food. **2.** a soft chocolate candy.

tru·ism (trü′iz əm) *n.* a statement that is so obviously true that no one would argue with it. For example: *Happiness is more pleasant than sorrow.*

tru·ly (trü′lē) *adv.* **1.** in a true manner; sincerely; genuinely: *I am truly sorry that I hurt your feelings.* **2.** in fact; indeed; really: *You're truly the best friend I have.* **3.** accurately; correctly: *a model truly built from the original ship.*

trump[1] (trump) *n.* **1.** a suit of playing cards that outranks the other suits during the playing of a hand. **2.** any card of this suit. —*v.t.* to play a trump card on (another card or a trick) —*v.i.* to play a trump card. [A form of *triumph.*]

trump[2] (trump) *v.* **to trump up.** to make up in order to deceive; fabricate: *to trump up an excuse.* [Possibly from *trump*[1].]

trump·er·y (trum′pə rē) *n.*, *pl.* **trump·er·ies.** something that appears to be valuable but is really worthless.

trum·pet (trum′pit) *n.* **1.** a brass musical instrument made up of a cylindrical metal tube coiled into a long loop and flaring out at the end, the tones of which are varied by the pressure of the player's lips or by the use of three

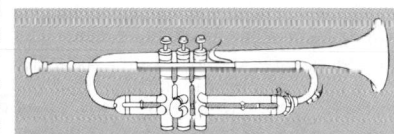

trumpet *(n., def. 1)*

valves. **2.** something resembling a trumpet in shape. **3.** a sound like that of a trumpet, such as the cry of an elephant. —*v.i.* **1.** to blow a trumpet. **2.** to make a sound like that of a trumpet. —*v.t.* **1.** to sound or produce on a trumpet. **2.** to announce or proclaim widely and loudly as if with a trumpet; herald. —**trum′pet·er,** *n.*

trumpet creeper, a woody climbing vine bearing clusters of orange and scarlet trumpet-shaped flowers. Also, **trumpet vine.**

trun·cate (trung′kāt) *v.t.*, **trun·cat·ed, trun·cat·ing.** to make smaller by removing a part of. —*adj.* having or seeming to have a part or section missing or cut off: *a truncate leaf.* —**trun·ca′tion,** *n.*

trun·cheon (trun′chən) *n.* **1.** a club, especially a long, slender, sturdy one, as used by police. **2.** a staff carried as a symbol of office or authority. —*v.t.* to beat with a truncheon; club.

trun·dle (trun′dəl) *v.*, **trun·dled trun·dling.** —*v.t.* to cause to roll along by pushing: *to trundle a bicycle rather than ride it.* —*v.i.* to move or go on rollers or wheels. —*n.* **1.** a small wheel or caster. **2.** see **trundle bed.**

trundle bed, a low, movable bed that may be pushed under another bed for storage. Also, **truckle bed.**

trunk (trungk) *n.* **1.** the main stem of a tree, as distinguished from its branches. **2.** a large, rectangular box with a hinged lid, used for transporting and storing things. **3.** the baggage compartment of an automobile. **4.** a long flexible snout, especially of an elephant. **5. trunks.** short pants, such as those worn

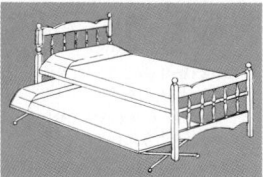

trundle bed

by swimmers, that reach from the waist to the upper thigh. **6.** the main body of a human being or animal, considered apart from the arms, legs, or neck. **7.** see **trunk line.**

trunk line **1.** the main line of a transportation system, as of a railroad. **2.** a line that connects telephone exchanges and carries many calls at once.

truss (trus) *n.*, *pl.* **truss·es.** **1.** a framework of wood or metal, usually consisting of triangular units, used to span an opening or support a heavy load, as of a bridge or roof. **2.** a device, usually consisting of a pad attached to a belt, used for support in cases of hernia. —*v.t.* **1.** to bind or tie; fasten: *to truss a turkey before cooking it.* **2.** to support or strengthen with a truss or trusses, as a roof or bridge.

trust (trust) *v.t.* **1.** to have faith or confidence in the truthfulness, honesty, ability, reliability, or justice of: *to trust one's parents, to trust a surgeon to operate.* **2.** to rely upon or believe: *They trusted the weather report when they decided to have a picnic.* **3.** to commit to someone's care; entrust: *to trust a child to a baby sitter.* **4.** to give business credit to: *The grocer trusted me for this week's food.* **5.** to feel sure of; expect with confidence: *I trust that you will get here on time.* —*v.i.* **1.** to have faith or confidence: *to trust in one's own judgment.* **2.** to feel sure: *You are being honest, I trust.* —*n.* **1.** faith or confidence in the truthfulness, honesty, ability, reliability, or justice of someone or something. **2.** keeping or custody; care: *Their dog was left in my trust for the weekend.* **3.** the fact or state of being trusted: *The president holds a position of great power and trust.* **4.** a person or thing that is believed or believed in. **5.** a usually illegal business combination or monopoly of many companies or corporations, that can control the production or distribution of a commodity or service, fix prices, and eliminate competition. **6.** property held and managed by one person or organization for the benefit of another: *to place money in a trust.*

trus·tee (trus tē′) *n.* a person or organization that manages the property or affairs of another person, company, or institution.

trus·tee·ship (trus tē′ship′) *n.* **1.** the office or duties of a trustee. **2.** the administrative authority over a trust territory given to a country by the United Nations. **3.** the territory so administered.

trust·ful (trust′fəl) *adj.* full of trust; trusting. —**trust′ful·ly,** *adv.* —**trust′ful·ness,** *n.*

---

at; āpe; fär; câre; end; mē; it; īce; pîerce; hot; ōld; sông, fôrk; oil; out; up; ūse; rüle; pùll; tûrn; chin; sing; shop; thin; this; hw in white; zh in treasure. The symbol ə stands for the unstressed vowel sound heard in about, taken, pencil, lemon, and circus.

T

trust fund, property, such as money, securities, or the like, held by a trustee, usually a bank.

trust·ing (trus′ting) *adj.* full of trust: *a trusting friend.* —**trust′ing·ly,** *adv.*

trust territory, a territory, such as a former colony, that is administered by a country under the supervision of the United Nations.

trust·wor·thy (trust′wûr′thē) *adj.* able to be trusted or worthy of trust. —**trust′wor′thi·ness,** *n.*

trust·y (trus′tē) *adj.,* **trust·i·er, trust·i·est.** able to be trusted or relied on. —*n., pl.* **trust·ies.** a convict who is given certain duties and special privileges because of good behavior.

truth (trüth) *n., pl.* **truths** (trüthz, trüths). **1.** something that is true: *to tell the truth.* **2.** the state or quality of being true, accurate, or sincere: *to doubt the truth of a statement.* **3.** an accepted or proven fact, principle, or the like: *a mathematical truth.*
·in truth. really; actually.

truth·ful (trüth′fəl) *adj.* **1.** usually or habitually telling the truth: *a truthful person.* **2.** honest: *a truthful witness.* **3.** conforming to truth, fact, or reality: *a truthful story of frontier life.* —**truth′ful·ly,** *adv.* —**truth′ful·ness,** *n.*

truth set, another term for **solution set.**

try (trī) *v.,* **tried, try·ing.** —*v.t.* **1.** to make an effort to do or accomplish; attempt; undertake: *I tried moving the heavy sofa myself.* **2.** to test the effect or operation of: *Try the brakes before you drive down the hill.* **3.** to investigate or examine in a court of law: *to try an accused person, to try a case.* **4.** to attempt to open: *The visitor tried the door, but it was locked.* **5.** to subject to trials or suffering; afflict: *The drought sorely tried the farmer.* **6.** to subject to strain; tax: *to try someone's patience.* —*v.i.* to make an effort; attempt; undertake. —*n., pl.* **tries.** an attempt; effort: *The mountain climbers made one more try to reach the top before nightfall.*
·to try on. to put on (an article of clothing) to test its fit or looks.
·to try out for. to demonstrate one's skill or ability in order to qualify as a member of: *to try out for a team.*

try·ing (trī′ing) *adj.* hard to bear or endure with patience; difficult; annoying: *a trying day, a trying person.*

try·out (trī′out′) *also,* **tryouts.** *n.* a period or session of testing during which people who are trying out for something, such as parts in a play or positions on a team, are judged for skill or ability.

try·pan·o·some (tri pan′ə sōm′) *n.* any of a group of microscopic protozoans that move by means of a flagellum and are parasites in the blood and spinal fluid of humans and other vertebrates, often causing serious diseases such as sleeping sickness. Trypanosomes are transmitted from one animal to another by insects.

tryp·sin (trip′sin) *n.* an enzyme in the pancreatic juice that digests proteins.

try square, an L-shaped instrument used in carpentry for laying out and testing right angles.

tryst (trist) *n.* **1.** a prearranged meeting, especially between lovers; rendezvous. **2.** an arrangement to meet at a specified time and place.

tsar (zär) another spelling of **czar.**

tsa·ri·na (zä rē′nə) another spelling of **czarina.**

tset·se fly (tset′sē, tsē′tsē) *also,* **tzet·ze fly.** any of a group of African flies that suck the blood of humans and animals. Certain types of tsetse flies transmit sleeping sickness to human beings and other diseases to animals. Also, **tsetse, tzetze.**

T–shirt (tē′shûrt′) *also,* **t-shirt, tee shirt.** *n.* **1.** a light, close-fitting undershirt with short sleeves. **2.** an outer shirt resembling this, worn for casual wear or for sports.

tsp., teaspoon.

T square, a T-shaped tool used by architects and engineers to draw parallel straight lines, made of a long straight piece and a short crosspiece that slides along the edge of a drawing board to serve as a guide.

tsu·na·mi (tsü nä′mē) *n.* a swift, powerful ocean wave caused by an underwater earthquake and causing great destruction to any land area it strikes; tidal wave.

Tu., Tuesday.

tub (tub) *n.* **1.** see **bathtub. 2.** a large, open container, as for washing clothes. **3.** a round container, often of wood or metal, used for holding butter, honey, fat, or other products. **4.** the amount a tub will hold. **5.** something that is like a tub, especially an old, clumsy boat or ship.

tu·ba (tü′bə, tū′bə) *n.* a very large brass musical instrument that produces a deep, mellow tone.

tuba

tub·by (tub′ē) *adj.,* **tub·bi·er, tub·bi·est.** shaped like a tub; short and broad; fat. —**tub′bi·ness,** *n.*

tube (tüb, tūb) *n.* **1.** a hollow cylinder of glass, rubber, metal or other material, as a test tube or inner tube, usually used to hold or carry liquids or gases. **2.** anything resembling a tube, as in shape or use, as the bronchial tubes. **3.** a container of soft metal, plastic, or other material, having a cap on, used for packaging toothpaste, shampoo, and other products. **4.** an underground or underwater tunnel through which a train or subway runs. **5.** see **electron tube. 6. the tube.** *Informal.* television. —**tube′like′,** *adj.*

tube foot, one of many, small tubelike structures on the underside of starfish and most other echinoderms, used for grasping and locomotion.

tuber (tü′bər, tū′bər) *n.* the thick, fleshy portion of an underground stem, such as a potato, bearing buds from which new plants grow.

tu·ber·cle (tü′bər kəl, tū′bər kəl) *n.* **1.** a small, rounded swelling, as on a bone or plant. **2.** a swelling caused by tuberculosis.

tu·ber·cu·lar (tu̇ bûr′kyə lər, tyu̇ bûr′kyə lər) *adj.* **1.** of, relating to, or having tuberculosis. **2.** of, relating to, or having tubercles.

tu·ber·cu·lin (tu̇ bûr′kyə lin, tyu̇ bûr′kyə lin) *n.* a liquid prepared from cultures of the bacteria that cause tuberculosis, used in the diagnosis and treatment of the disease.

tu·ber·cu·lo·sis (tu̇ bûr′kyə lō′sis, tyu̇ bûr′kyə lō′sis) *n.* **1.** an infectious disease caused by a bacterium that may affect any organ of the body, especially the lungs or joints. It is characterized by the formation of tubercles on the affected parts. **2.** tuberculosis of the lungs. Also (*def. 2*), **consumption.**

tu·ber·cu·lous (tu̇ bûr′kyə ləs, tyu̇ bûr′kyə ləs) *adj.* of, relating to, or having tuberculosis; tubercular.

tube·rose (tūb′rōz′, tūb′rōz′) *n.* a Mexican plant that grows from a tuber, having fragrant, waxy, white flowers.

tu·ber·ous (tū′bər əs, tū′bər əs) *adj.* **1.** of, like, or bearing a tuber or tubers: *Potatoes are tuberous plants.* **2.** covered with many rounded swellings.

tub·ing (tū′bing, tū′bing) *n.* **1.** an object or material in the form of a tube: *plastic tubing for garden hoses.* **2.** tubes as a group. **3.** a length or piece of tube: *This tubing has a hole in it.*

tu·bu·lar (tū′byə lər, tū′byə lər) *adj.* **1.** consisting of tubes: *the tubular frame of a modern chair.* **2.** of, relating to, or shaped like a tube: *the tubular body of a worm.*

tu·bule (tū′būl, tū′būl) *n.* a small tube or tubelike structure.

tuck (tuk) *v.t.* **1.** to push or fold the edge or ends of (something), so as to hold snugly in place: *to tuck a sheet under a mattress.* **2.** to put into a tight or narrow place: *The wasps' nest was tucked underneath the rafters.* **3.** to hide from view or knowledge; store away or conceal: *There were many old things tucked in the attic.* **4.** to cover snugly: *to tuck a child in bed.* **5.** to sew a tuck or tucks in (material or a garment). —*v.i.* to sew a tuck or tucks in material or a garment. —*n.* a fold sewed in a garment, as to shape or shorten.

tuck·er[1] (tuk′ər) *n.* **1.** formerly, a covering of lace, linen, or other light material worn around the neck and shoulders. **2.** a person or thing that tucks. [*Tuck* + *-er*[1].]

tuck·er[2] (tuk′ər) *v.t. Informal.* to make tired or weary: *We were all tuckered out after the long hike.* [From the obsolete word *tuck* meaning "to reproach" + the former suffix *-er* indicating repeated action.]

Tu·dor (tū′dər, tū′dər) *adj.* of or relating to a style of architecture that flourished in England during the reign of the Tudor monarchs.

Tues., Tuesday.

Tues·day (tūz′dē, tūz′dā, tūz′dē, tūz′dā) *n.* the third day of the week. [From the Old English word *Tīwesdæg* meaning "Tuesday," going back to the words *Tīw* "Tiw," the Old English god of war + *dagr* "day."]

tu·fa (tū′fə, tū′fə) *n.* any of various porous rocks formed from material deposited by water.

tuff (tuf) *n.* a rock formed from compressed volcanic ash or dust.

tuf·fet (tuf′it) *n.* a hassock or footstool.

tuft (tuft) *n.* **1.** a dense cluster of flexible fibers, such as feathers, yarn, or hair, bound together or attached at one end and loose and bushy at the other. **2.** a small group or clump, as of trees or bushes. **3.** a cluster of threads sewn through a mattress, pillow, quilt, or the like, to keep the padding in place. —*v.t.* to decorate or provide with a tuft or tufts.

tug (tug) *v.,* **tugged, tug·ging.** —*v.i.* **1.** to give a pull on something: *The child tugged at my coat to get my attention.* **2.** to strain to pull or haul: *The horse tugged harder, and finally the log began to move.* —*v.t.* **1.** to give a pull on: *to tug someone's arm.* **2.** to pull or haul with force: *to tug a heavy trunk across a room.* **3.** to tow with a tugboat. —*n.* **1.** a hard pull: *I felt a tug on my fishing line.* **2.** see **tugboat.** **3.** one of the straps of a harness.

tug·boat (tug′bōt′) *n.* a small, powerful boat used to push or tow other boats or ships. Also, **towboat.**

tugboat

tug of war **1.** a game in which two players or teams pull at opposite ends of something, such as a rope, with each trying to force the other either to let go or to be dragged out of place. **2.** any struggle or contest between opposite forces.

tu·i·tion (tū ish′ən, tū ish′ən) *n.* **1.** the amount of money paid by a student for instruction, especially at a college, university, or private school. **2.** teaching; instruction.

tu·lip (tū′lip, tū′lip) *n.* **1.** a cup-shaped flower of any of a group of plants related to the lily. **2.** a plant bearing these flowers, having thick leaves which rise directly from an underground bulb.

tulip tree, a large North American tree having yellowish green flowers that resemble tulips, and soft wood used to make furniture and other products.

tulle (tūl) *n.* a fine, stiff net fabric of silk, rayon, or nylon, used in making veils and in dressmaking.

tum·ble (tum′bəl) *v.,* **tum·bled, tum·bling.** —*v.i.* **1.** to fall, especially in an awkward, rolling manner: *The apples tumbled as the cart overturned.* **2.** to roll or toss about: *The clothes tumbled in the dryer.* **3.** to perform acrobatic feats, such as somersaults or handstands. **4.** to go or move in a hurried, disorderly manner: *The children tumbled out the door.* —*v.t.* to cause to tumble or fall. —*n.* **1.** the act of tumbling; fall. **2.** a state of disorder or confusion; tangle. **3.** a gymnastic feat, such as a somersault.

tum·ble–down (tum′bəl doun′) *adj.* in a run-down condition; falling apart: *a tumble-down old barn.*

tum·bler (tum′blər) *n.* **1.** a person who performs gymnastic feats, such as somersaults or leaps; acrobat. **2.** a drinking glass having a flat bottom and no handle. **3.** a rotating drum, especially in an automatic clothes dryer, in which objects are tumbled. **4.** a lever in a lock that must be moved to the correct height by the key in order to release the bolt.

tum·ble·weed (tum′bəl wēd′) *n.* any of several bushy plants of western North America that break off from their roots, usually in autumn, and are blown about by the wind.

tum·brel (tum′brəl) *also,* **tum·bril.** *n.* **1.** a farmer's cart with a body that can be tilted backward to empty out the load. **2.** a cart used to carry condemned prisoners to be executed, used especially during the French Revolution.

tumbleweed

tu·mes·cence (tū mes′əns, tū mes′əns) *n.* **1.** a swollen condition. **2.** a swollen part or organ.

tu·mes·cent (tū mes′ənt, tū mes′ənt) *adj.* swollen or becoming swollen.

tu·mid (tū′mid, tū′mid) *adj.* **1.** abnormally enlarged; swollen. **2.** (of language) pretentious and using big words; pompous.

tum·my (tum′ē) *n., pl.* **tum·mies.** *Informal.* stomach.

tu·mor (tū′mər, tū′mər) *also, British,* **tu·mour.** *n.* an abnormal growth formed in the body from normal tissue that grows at an abnormally fast rate. [From the Latin word *tumor* meaning "tumor" or "swelling," from the word *tumēre* "to swell."] —**tu′mor·ous;** *also, British,* **tu′mour·ous,** *adj.*

---

at; āpe; fär; câre; end; mē; it; īce; pîerce; hot; ōld; sông, fôrk; oil; out; up; ūse; rūle; pūll; tûrn; chin; sing; shop; thin; this; hw in white; zh in treasure. The symbol ə stands for the unstressed vowel sound heard in about, taken, pencil, lemon, and circus.

T

tu·mult (tü′məlt, tū′məlt) *n.* **1.** a din or commotion; uproar. **2.** a very strong disturbance, as of the mind or emotions.

tu·mul·tu·ous (tü mul′chü əs, tū mul′chü əs) *adj.* **1.** excited and noisy; disorderly: *a tumultuous meeting.* **2.** disturbed or upset: *tumultuous emotions.* **3.** stormy; turbulent: *tumultuous waves.* —**tu·mul′tu·ous·ly,** *adv.* —**tu·mul′tu·ous·ness,** *n.*

tun (tun) *n.* **1.** a large cask or barrel used for holding liquids, especially wine, ale, or beer. **2.** a liquid measure equal to 252 gallons (954 liters).

tu·na (tü′nə) *n., pl.* **tu·na** or **tu·nas.** **1.** any of several large food and game fish related to the mackerel, found in tropical and temperate seas throughout the world. Also, **tunny.** **2.** the flesh of the tuna, rich in vitamin A. It is used for food. Also, **tuna fish.**

tun·a·ble (tü′nə bəl, tū′nə bəl) *also,* **tune·a·ble.** *adj.* capable of being tuned: *a tunable musical instrument.*

tun·dra (tun′drə) *n.* a vast, treeless plain in the northernmost parts of Asia, Europe, and North America, having an arctic or subarctic climate and a layer of permanently frozen soil several inches below the surface. [From the Russian word *tundra,* from the Lapp word *tundar* meaning "tundra."]

tune (tün, tūn) *n.* **1.** a series of musical notes that make up a melody or theme: *to whistle a popular tune.* **2.** the quality or condition of being at the proper pitch or key: *The old piano is badly out of tune.* **3.** the quality or condition of agreement or accord: *Your statement was in tune with what others were saying.* —*v.,* **tuned, tun·ing.** —*v.t.* **1.** to adjust to a standard of pitch; put in tune: *to tune a piano.* **2.** to put (a vehicle or machine) into proper working order, as by lubrication or adjustment of parts: *to tune an engine.*

　·to the tune of. *Informal.* to the sum or extent of: *The repairs cost us to the tune of two hundred dollars.*

　·to tune in. to adjust a radio or television set so as to receive (a particular station, program, or signal).

　·to tune out. to adjust a radio or television set so as to get rid of (interference or the like).

　·to tune up. 1. to bring musical instruments to a standard pitch: *The orchestra tuned up before the concert.* **2.** to put (a vehicle or machine) into proper working order: *to tune up a car.*

tune·ful (tün′fəl, tūn′fəl) *adj.* full of melody; musical. —**tune′ful·ly,** *adv.* —**tune′ful·ness,** *n.*

tune·less (tün′lis, tūn′lis) *adj.* having no musical quality. —**tune′less·ly,** *adv.*

tun·er (tü′nər, tū′nər) *n.* **1.** a person or thing that tunes, especially one employed to properly tune musical instruments: *a piano tuner.* **2.** the part of a radio receiver or a separate device that selects desired radio signals and directs them to an amplifier.

tung·sten (tung′stən) *n.* a gray, very hard metallic element that has the highest melting point and boiling point of any element. It is used in making filaments for electric lamps and electron tubes. Also, **wolfram.** Symbol: **W** [From the Swedish word *tungsten,* from the words *tung* "heavy" + *sten* "stone."]

tu·nic (tü′nik, tū′nik) *n.* **1.** a garment resembling a long shirt reaching to the knee or below, worn by the ancient Greeks and Romans. **2.** a garment resembling a blouse, often belted and reaching to the hips or below. **3.** a short, close-fitting jacket, often worn as part of a military or police uniform.

tuning fork, a steel instrument with two prongs that vibrates at a constant rate when struck, producing a tone of perfect pitch. It is used in tuning certain musical instruments.

tunic
(def. 3)

tun·nel (tun′əl) *n.* a long, narrow, tubelike passageway beneath the ground or water, or under the main part of a structure: *a subway tunnel, a tunnel through the side of a mountain.* —*v.,* **tun·neled, tun·nel·ing;** *also, British,* **tun·nelled, tun·nel·ling.** —*v.i.* to make a passageway under or through something, as by digging: *to tunnel under a wall.* —*v.t.* **1.** to make by tunneling: *The prisoners tunneled an escape route.* **2.** to make a tunnel under, through, or in: *The mole tunneled the lawn.* —**tun′nel·er;** *also, British,* **tun′nel·ler,** *n.*

tun·ny (tun′ē) *n., pl.* **tun·nies** or **tun·ny.** another word for **tuna** *(def. 1).*

tu·pe·lo (tü′pə lō′, tū′pə lō′) *n., pl.* **tu·pe·los. 1.** a tree bearing tiny greenish flowers that ripen into small fruits. **2.** its wood, used to make flooring and crates.

Tu·pi–Gua·ra·ni (tü pē′gwär′ə nē′) *n.* **1.** a member of any of various South American Indian tribes living in Brazil. **2.** a family of languages spoken by South American Indians living along the Amazon River in Brazil. It is the second largest Indian language family in South America.

tur·ban (tûr′bən) *n.* **1.** a head covering worn especially by Muslims of southern Asia and by Sikhs, consisting of a long scarf that is wound around the head or around a cap. **2.** any similar headdress, such as a scarf worn wound around the head by women.

tur·bid (tûr′bid) *adj.* **1.** thick with suspended matter; not clear; muddy: *turbid floodwaters.* **2.** characterized by confusion; muddled; disordered: *turbid emotions.* —**tur·bid′i·ty, tur′bid·ness,** *n.* —**tur′bid·ly,** *adv.*

tur·bine (tûr′bin, tûr′bīn) *n.* any of various motors or

turbans
(def. 1)

engines that use the force of a steadily moving stream of gas, vapor, or liquid against slanted blades to turn a rotor. [From the French word *turbine,* from the Latin word *turbo* meaning "something that spins, whirlwind."]

tur·bo (tûr′bō) *n., pl.* **tur·bos.** see **turbocharger.**

turbo– *combining form* of, relating to, or operated by a turbine: *turbojet.*

tur·bo·charg·er (tûr′bō chär′jər) *n.* a supercharger that is driven by the pressure of an engine's exhaust gases.

tur·bo·jet (tûr′bō jet′) *n.* **1.** a jet propulsion engine in which air is taken in, compressed, mixed with fuel, and then ignited, producing hot, high-pressure gases that turn the turbine that drives the compressor. The hot exhaust provides thrust. **2.** an airplane propelled by such an engine.

tur·bo·prop (tûr′bō prop′) *n.* **1.** a turbojet engine in which the power of the exhaust gases is used to drive a propeller. **2.** an airplane propelled by a turboprop engine or engines.

tur·bot (tûr′bət) *n.*, *pl.* **tur·bot** or **tur·bots.** a large European flatfish, valued as food.

tur·bu·lence (tûr′byə ləns) *n.* the state or quality of being turbulent. Also, **tur·bu·len·cy** (tûr′byə lən sē).

tur·bu·lent (tûr′byə lənt) *adj.* of, causing, or marked by commotion, disorder, or violence; not calm or smooth; agitated: *turbulent waters, a turbulent period of history.* —**tur′bu·lent·ly,** *adv.*

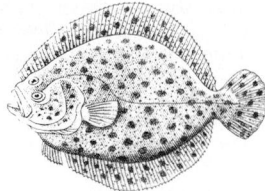

turbot

tu·reen (tə rēn′) *n.* a deep dish with a cover, used for serving food, especially soup.

turf (tûrf) *n.* **1.** the surface layer of soil, containing small plants and grasses, their matted roots, and the soil clinging to them. **2.** a separate clump or clumps of this layer, as for replanting. **3.** peat, especially a piece used for fuel. **4.** *Informal.* anything, such as a special status or position or a certain territory, that is jealously guarded and controlled by one person or group. **5. the turf.** the sport of horse racing.

tur·gid (tûr′jid) *adj.* **1.** swollen or distended. **2.** pompous; bombastic: *turgid prose.* —**tur·gid′i·ty, tur′gid·ness,** *n.*

Turk (tûrk) *n.* **1.** a person who was born in or is a citizen of Turkey. **2.** a person who speaks a Turkic language.

Turk. 1. Turkey. **2.** Turkish.

tur·key (tûr′kē) *n.*, *pl.* **tur·keys** or **tur·key. 1.** any of various long-necked birds related to the pheasant, having mainly reddish brown feathers. Most varieties have been domesticated and are raised for food. **2.** the flesh of a turkey used as food. [From *Turkey*, the country in Asia Minor, which exported a different bird that was confused with the species we now call the turkey.]

turkey vulture, a brownish black vulture native to North, Central, and South America, having a bare, reddish head. Also, **turkey buzzard.**

turkey *(def. 1)*

Tur·kic (tûr′kik) *n.* any of various languages spoken by the Turks of Turkey and various Tatar tribes.

Turk·ish (tûr′kish) *n.* the language of Turkey. —*adj.* of or relating to Turkey, its people, their language, or culture.

Turkish Empire, another name for **Ottoman Empire.**

Turkish towel also, **turkish towel.** a thick towel made of terry cloth.

tur·mer·ic (tûr′mər ik) *n.* **1.** a yellow powder with a sharp, bitter taste, obtained from the root of an Asian plant. It is used as a seasoning and as a coloring agent. **2.** the plant yielding this powder, bearing pale yellow flowers.

tur·moil (tûr′moil) *n.* a state of confused agitation or commotion; turbulence: *the turmoil of war.*

turn (tûrn) *v.i.* **1.** to move around; rotate or revolve: *The earth turns. The blades of a fan turn like a boat's propeller.* **2.** to move partly around: *The key turned in the lock.* **3.** to change direction; go in a different direction: *The truck turned onto the highway. The river turns south in the canyon.* **4.** to change or reverse to the opposite direction: *Soon our luck will turn for the better.* **5.** to curve or bend: *The corners of the clown's mouth turned up in a broad smile.* **6.** to change in nature or condition: *The leaves turned yellow. The snow turned to rain.* **7.** to become spoiled, rancid, or sour: *The milk turned*

because we left it out of the refrigerator too long. **8.** to change position in order to attack or resist: *The lion turned on its trainer.* **9.** to take on an attitude of hostility: *to turn against an old friend.* **10.** to direct one's effort or attention: *to turn to the job at hand.* **11.** to be or become dizzy or nauseated: *to have one's stomach turn at the sight of blood.* —*v.t.* **1.** to cause to revolve, as a wheel. **2.** to cause to move partly around: *to turn a doorknob.* **3.** to change the course or direction of: *The driver turned the car to the left.* **4.** to cause to curve, curl, or bend: *The tailor turned the edges of the cloth under.* **5.** to twist or wrench: *to turn one's ankle.* **6.** to reverse; invert: *to turn pancakes on a griddle.* **7.** to go or get around or beyond: *to turn a corner.* **8.** to cause to change; transform: *The hot sun turned the grass brown.* **9.** to make sick; cause nausea or disgust in: *The rich food turned my stomach.* **10.** to direct; aim: *to turn one's energies to completing a job.* **11.** (of age, time, or amount) to be or have passed beyond: *to turn fourteen.* **12.** to shape by rotating against a cutting tool, as a lathe: *to turn the legs for a table.* —*n.* **1.** the act of turning. **2.** a change in position or direction: *Make a left turn at the corner.* **3.** the place of changing direction: *a turn in the highway.* **4.** time, occasion, or opportunity that follows another or others in rotation: *It's the catcher's turn to bat.* **5.** an act or deed: *My friend did me a good turn.* **6.** a change in condition or nature: *The patient took a turn for the better.* **7.** *Informal.* a sudden shock or fright: *The blast gave me quite a turn!*

•**at every turn.** in every instance; constantly.

•**by turns.** one after another.

•**in turn.** in proper sequence or order.

•**out of turn. a.** not in proper sequence or order. **b.** *Informal.* improperly or impolitely: *Do not speak out of turn.*

•**to a turn.** perfectly: *The roast was cooked to a turn.*

•**to take turns.** to go in proper or alternating order: *The two friends took turns riding the bicycle.*

•**to turn down. a.** to reject or refuse: *to turn down an invitation.* **b.** to lessen the volume or intensity of: *Please turn down your radio.* **c.** to fold over: *to turn down the blankets on a bed.*

•**to turn in. a.** *Informal.* to go to bed. **b.** to inform on or hand over: *to turn a criminal in to the police.*

•**to turn off. a.** to cause to stop flowing, such as water, gas, or electricity. **b.** to cause to stop operating: *Turn off the radio when you leave the room.*

•**to turn on. a.** to cause to flow, such as water, gas, or electricity. **b.** to cause to operate: *to turn on a lamp.*

•**to turn out. a.** to produce: *The machine turns out fifty copies per minute.* **b.** to show up; appear: *A large crowd turned out for the football game.* **c.** to have a certain result; end: *How did the story turn out?* **d.** to put out; extinguish: *to turn out a light.*

•**to turn over. a.** (of an engine) to begin to operate. **b.** to give, transfer, or return: *to turn over a business to one's partner.* **c.** to think about; consider carefully: *to turn an idea over in one's mind.*

•**to turn to. a.** to begin to work: *The campers turned to and built a fire.* **b.** to appeal or apply to for help or support: *to turn to a friend.*

•**to turn up. a.** to appear: *The sweater I misplaced turned up at school.* **b.** to discover or search out: *The police*

at; āpe; fär; câre; end; mē; it; īce; pîerce; hot; ōld; sông, fôrk; oil; out; up; ūse; rüle; pùll; tûrn; chin; sing; shop; thin; this; hw in white; zh in treasure. The symbol ə stands for the unstressed vowel sound heard in about, taken, pencil, lemon, and circus.

T

1013

turned up new evidence in the case. **c.** to increase the volume or intensity of: *Turn up the radio if you can't hear it.*

turn·buck·le (tûrn′buk′əl) *n.* a sleeve or coupling with internal threads that holds together the threaded ends of two rods and can be turned to widen or narrow the gap between the rod ends.

turn·coat (tûrn′kōt′) *n.* a person who switches loyalty; traitor or renegade.

turn·er (tûr′nər) *n.* **1.** a person or thing that turns. **2.** a person who turns or makes things on a lathe.

turning point, the point at which a decisive or important change takes place; critical point; crisis.

tur·nip (tûr′nip) *n.* **1.** the white or yellow root of a plant of the mustard family, cooked and eaten as a vegetable. **2.** the plant bearing this root, having small, bright yellow flowers in clusters and soft, prickly leaves.

turn·key (tûrn′kē′) *n., pl.* **turn·keys.** a person who has charge of the keys of a prison or jail; jailer.

turnbuckle

turn·off (tûrn′ôf′) *n.* an exit leading off a main road to a side road.

turn·out (tûrn′out′) *n.* **1.** a gathering of people for some specific occasion: *There was a poor turnout for the football game because of the rainy weather.* **2.** the amount produced; output: *The new machine increased the factory's turnout.* **3.** the act of turning out. **4.** a section of a road that has been widened to enable vehicles to pass or park.

turn·o·ver (tûrn′ō′vər) *n.* **1.** a small pie made by folding half the crust over a filling and upon the other half. **2.** the number of workers who leave their jobs and are replaced by others during a given period. **3.** the number of times that the stock of goods of a firm is sold and replaced during a given period. **4.** the total amount of business done in a given period: *From a turnover of $15,000 for a week, the flower shop derived a profit of $3,000.*

turn·pike (tûrn′pīk′) *n.* **1.** a road, especially a large highway, that has, or used to have, a tollgate or tollbooth. **2.** any highway.

turn·stile (tûrn′stīl′) *n.* a revolving gate or movable bar at an exit or entrance, that lets people pass through one at a time.

turn·ta·ble (tûrn′tā′bəl) *n.* **1.** a revolving device used to turn things around, especially a circular railroad platform with tracks used to turn locomotives or cars around. **2.** a flat platform on a phonograph that revolves to play records rested upon it.

tur·pen·tine (tûr′pən tīn′) *n.* **1.** a thick, sticky substance secreted by certain species of pine trees. **2.** a colorless, combustible liquid obtained by distilling this substance, widely used as a thinner for paints and as a solvent for polishes.

tur·pi·tude (tûr′pi tüd′, tûr′pi tūd′) *n.* a shameful wickedness, depravity; baseness: *moral turpitude.*

tur·quoise (tûr′kwoiz, tûr′koiz) *n.* **1.** an opaque mineral, usually greenish blue, having a waxy luster and valued as a gem. **2.** a greenish blue color. —*adj.* having the color turquoise; greenish blue.

tur·ret (tûr′it) *n.* **1.** a small tower, usually forming part of a larger structure. **2.** an armored, usually revolving, structure used to house antiaircraft guns or cannons and their gunners, as on a ship or tank. **3.** a strong, transparent, often bubble-shaped structure on a military aircraft, used to protect a gunner.

tur·ret·ed (tûr′i tid) *adj.* having a turret or turrets.

tur·tle (tûr′təl) *n.* any of a group of reptiles found on land and in fresh and salt water, having a low, wide body enclosed in a hard, protective shell, and a toothless beak with sharp-edged jaws. On the average, turtles have a longer life span than any other animal with a backbone, some living to an age of 130 years.

turtle

tur·tle·dove (tûr′təl duv′) *n.* any of several small wild doves, having a long tail and a soft, cooing call.

tur·tle·neck (tûr′təl nek′) *n.* **1.** a high, often turned over, collar that fits snugly around the neck. **2.** a garment, especially a sweater, having such a collar.

Tus·can (tus′kən) *n.* **1.** a person who was born in or is a citizen of Tuscany. **2.** any of several Italian dialects spoken in Tuscany, especially that spoken in Florence. **3.** the standard literary form of the Italian language. *adj.* of or relating to Tuscany or its people.

Tus·ca·ro·ra (tus′kə rôr′ə) *n., pl.* **Tus·ca·ro·ra** or **Tus·ca·ro·ras.** a member of a tribe of Iroquois Indians formerly living in what is now North Carolina, now living in New York.

tusk (tusk) *n.* **1.** a long, pointed, projecting tooth, usually one of a pair, of certain animals, such as elephants, walruses, or wild boars. **2.** any long, pointed, projecting tooth or part that is like a tooth. —*v.t.* to dig up or gore with tusks.

tusk·er (tus′kər) *n.* an animal having well-developed tusks, especially an elephant or wild boar.

tus·sah (tus′ə) *n.* **1.** a coarse brownish or yellowish silk. **2.** an Asiatic silkworm that produces this silk.

tus·sle (tus′əl) *n.* **1.** a disorderly physical fight or struggle; scuffle. **2.** any disorderly conflict or struggle: *The election this fall will be a real tussle.* —*v.i.,* **tus·sled, tus·sling.** to engage in a disorderly physical fight or struggle: *The bear cubs tussled with each other in play.*

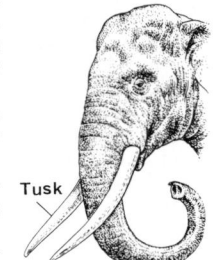

Tusk

tusks on an elephant

tus·sock (tus′ək) *n.* a clump, tuft, or matted growth, as of hair or grass.

tut (tut) *interj.* used to express impatience, contempt, annoyance, or rebuke.

tu·te·lage (tü′tə lij, tū′tə lij) *n.* **1.** the office or function of a guardian; guardianship. **2.** the act of teaching. **3.** the state of being under a tutor or guardian.

tu·te·lar·y (tü′tə ler′ē, tū′tə ler′ē) *also,* **tu·te·lar** (tü′tə lər, tū′tə lər). *adj.* **1.** having the position of a guardian; protective. **2.** of or relating to a guardian: *tutelary powers.*

tu·tor (tü′tər, tū′tər) *n.* **1.** a teacher or other person who gives private instruction to a student. **2.** *British.* a college official who supervises and advises undergraduate students. —*v.t.* to act as a tutor to, especially by giving private instruction. —*v.i.* to act or work as a private instructor.

tu·to·ri·al (tü tôr′ē əl, tū tôr′ē əl) *adj.* of, relating to, or involving a private instructor or instruction: *The school had an afternoon tutorial program.* —*n.* **1.** a class or session instructed by a tutor for one student or a small group of students. **2.** *Computers.* a program or manual that instructs a user in the proper operation of a piece of hardware or software.

tut·ti–frut·ti (tü′tē frü′tē) *adj.* containing or made with various candied fruits or fruit flavorings: *tutti-frutti punch.*

tu·tu (tü′tü) *n.* a very short, full skirt, usually consisting of many layers of sheer fabric, worn by ballerinas.

tux (tuks) *n., pl.* **tux·es.** *Informal.* see **tuxedo.**

tux·e·do (tuk sē′dō) *also,* **Tux·e·do.** *n., pl.* **tux·e·dos.** a man's formal suit, usually dark in color, having a jacket without tails and trousers with a single stripe of satin or similar material along the outer side of each leg. [From *Tuxedo* Park, New York, a wealthy and exclusive community in the nineteenth century, where this suit was popular.]

tutu

TV, television.

TVA, Tennessee Valley Authority, an independent agency of the U.S. government, established in 1933 for water control and development of resources, especially electrical power, along the Tennessee River and its major tributaries in seven southern states.

TV dinner, a prepared meal frozen in a tray, needing only to be heated before being served.

twad·dle (twod′əl) *n.* silly or idle talk; prattle. —*v.i.,* **twad·dled, twad·dling.** to talk in a childish or foolish manner. —**twad′dler,** *n.*

twain (twān) *Archaic. adj.* two. —*n.* two; pair: *Oh, East is East, and West is West, and never the twain shall meet* (Rudyard Kipling).

twang (twang) *n.* **1.** a sharp, metallic, ringing sound, such as that made by plucking a string on a guitar or other musical instrument. **2.** a sharp, nasal tone of voice. —*v.i.* to make a sharp, metallic, ringing sound: *The wire twanged when it broke.* —*v.t.* to cause to make a sharp, metallic sound.

'twas (twuz, twoz) *contr.* it was.

tweak (twēk) *v.t.* to pinch and pull sharply with a twisting motion. —*n.* a sharp, twisting pinch.

tweed (twēd) *n.* **1.** a rough fabric, usually made of wool, woven with yarns of two or more colors. **2. tweeds.** clothes made of this fabric.

twee·dle·dum and twee·dle·dee (twē′dəl dum′ ən twē′dəl dē′) two persons or things between which there is almost no difference.

tweet (twēt) *n.* a thin, chirping sound, such as that made by a small or young bird. —*v.i.* to utter a tweet or tweets.

tweet·er (twē′tər) *n.* a loudspeaker designed to reproduce high-frequency sound signals.

tweez·ers (twē′zərz) *pl. n.* small pincers for plucking out hairs or splinters or picking up tiny objects.

twelfth (twelfth) *adj.* **1.** (the ordinal of twelve) next after the eleventh. **2.** being one of twelve equal parts. —*n.* **1.** something that is next after the eleventh. **2.** one of twelve equal parts; ¹⁄₁₂.

Twelfth night, the evening of, or the night before, the twelfth night after Christmas.

twelve (twelv) *n.* **1.** the cardinal number that is two more than ten. **2.** a symbol representing this number, such as 12 or XII. **3.** something having this many units or things. **4. the Twelve.** the twelve disciples of Jesus chosen by him to preach his gospel. Also, **the Twelve Apostles.** —*adj.* numbering two more than ten.

twelve·month (twelv′munth′) *n.* a period of twelve months; year.

twen·ti·eth (twen′tē ith) *adj.* **1.** (the ordinal of twenty) next after the nineteenth. **2.** being one of twenty equal parts. —*n.* **1.** something that is next after the nineteenth. **2.** one of twenty equal parts; ¹⁄₂₀.

twen·ty (twen′tē) *n., pl.* **twen·ties.** **1.** the cardinal number that is two times ten. **2.** a symbol representing this number, such as 20 or XX. —*adj.* numbering two times ten.

twen·ty–one (twen′tē wun′) *n.* another word for **blackjack.**

twice (twīs) *adv.* **1.** on two occasions or in two instances; two times: *to do a job twice.* **2.** doubly: *twice as many.*

twice–told (twīs′tōld′) *adj.* **1.** having been told two times. **2.** having been told many times; stale; trite: *twice-told tales.*

twid·dle (twid′əl) *v.,* **twid·dled, twid·dling.** —*v.t.* to turn or twirl (something) idly: *to twiddle a locket on a chain.* —*v.i.* **1.** to play with something in an idle manner: *to twiddle with one's hair.* **2.** to be busy about trifles. —*n.* a light, twirling motion, as of the thumbs.

twig (twig) *n.* a small branch or shoot of a tree or other woody plant.

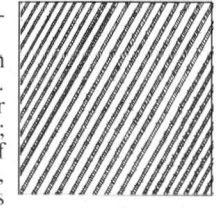

twilight
New York City during twilight

twi·light (twī′līt′) *n.* **1.** a soft, hazy light reflected from the sun just after sunset and, sometimes, just before sunrise. **2.** the period during which this light is seen: *to take a stroll during twilight.* **3.** any soft, faint light. **4.** a period or condition marked by the decline of glory, success, achievement, or the like: *the twilight of a career.* —*adj.* of, relating to, or occurring at twilight.

twill (twil) *n.* **1.** a weave characterized by parallel diagonal ridges. **2.** a strong, durable fabric having such a weave.

twilled (twild) *adj.* woven with parallel diagonal ridges on the surface.

twin (twin) *n.* **1.** one of two children or animals born at the same birth. **2.** either of two persons, animals, or things that are similar or identical; mate. —*adj.* **1.** being two or one of two born at the same birth. **2.** having, forming, or being one of two things that are similar or identical: *The castle*

twill *(def. 1)*

at; āpe; fär; câre; end; mē; it; īce; pîerce; hot; ōld; sông, fôrk; oil; out; up; ūse; rüle; pùll; tûrn; chin; sing; shop; thin; this; hw in white; zh in treasure. The symbol ə stands for the unstressed vowel sound heard in about, taken, pencil, lemon, and circus.

1015

had twin turrets. —*v.i.*, **twinned, twin·ning.** to give birth to twins.

twine (twīn) *n.* **1.** a strong string or cord made of two or more strands twisted together. **2.** something formed by twisting two or more strands, threads, or the like together. —*v.*, **twined, twin·ing.** —*v.t.* **1.** to twist together. **2.** to form by twisting together. **3.** to wind or coil (something) around something else: *The gardener twined the ivy around the trellis.* **4.** to cover or wrap in this way: *to twine a pole with ribbons.* —*v.i.* to extend, move, or grow in a winding manner or course: *Vines twined over the walls.*

twinge (twinj) *n.* **1.** a sudden, sharp pain: *a twinge of arthritis.* **2.** a sudden, sharp feeling of mental or emotional distress: *a twinge of pity, a twinge of conscience.* —*v.i.*, **twinged, twing·ing.** to feel a twinge.

twin·kle (twing′kəl) *v.i.*, **twin·kled, twin·kling.** **1.** to shine with or give flashes of light: *The stars twinkled in the sky.* **2.** (of the eyes) to be bright, as with amusement or pleasure. **3.** to move lightly and quickly. —*n.* **1.** a flicker or flash of light. **2.** brightness of the eyes, as in amusement or pleasure. **3.** a very brief period of time; twinkling: *It was done in a twinkle.*

twin·kling (twing′kling) *n.* **1.** a very brief period of time; moment; instant. **2.** a flicker or flash of light; twinkle.

twirl (twûrl) *v.t.* to cause to rotate or spin rapidly: *to twirl a baton.* —*v.i.* to rotate or spin rapidly. —*n.* **1.** the act of twirling or the state of being twirled. **2.** something having a curled or spiral shape. —**twirl′er,** *n.*

twist (twist) *v.t.* **1.** to wind (two or more strands, threads, or the like) around each other. **2.** to make or form in this way: *to twist a rope from single strands.* **3.** to rotate or turn: *to twist a lid off a jar.* **4.** to form into a spiral, as by turning the ends in opposite directions. **5.** to change the natural or usual shape or position of; contort; distort: *to twist one's face into a grimace.* **6.** to injure (a part of the body) in this way; sprain: *to fall and twist one's ankle.* **7.** to change or distort the meaning of: *to twist someone's words.* —*v.i.* **1.** to turn so as to face in a different direction. **2.** to move in or follow a winding course: *The new highway twists through the mountains.* **3.** to become wound or turned: *The thin gold wire twisted easily.* **4.** to become sprained. —*n.* **1.** a curve, bend, or turn: *There is a twist in the road ahead.* **2.** the act of twisting or the state of being twisted: *with a twist of the magician's wrist the cards disappeared.* **3.** something having a curled or spiral shape. **4.** an unexpected change in the usual or ordinary: *The movie ended with a surprising twist.* **5.** a thread, cord, or rope made of two or more strands that are twisted together.

twist·er (twis′tər) *n.* **1.** a person or thing that twists. **2.** *Informal.* a tornado.

twit (twit) *v.t.*, **twit·ted, twit·ting.** to tease or taunt, especially by reminding of past errors or embarrassments.

twitch (twich) *v.i.* to move with a sudden, unintentional jerk. —*v.t.* to pull with a sudden tug or jerk. —*n., pl.* **twitch·es.** **1.** a sudden, involuntary muscle contraction. **2.** a sudden, sharp pull or tug; jerk.

twit·ter (twit′ər) *n.* **1.** a series of short, light, chirping sounds made by a bird or birds. **2.** a state or condition of nervous agitation or excitement: *to be in a twitter before a test.* —*v.i.* to utter a series of light, chirping sounds, as a bird.

twixt (twikst) *also,* **'twixt.** *prep.* between; betwixt.

two (tü) *n., pl.* **twos.** **1.** the cardinal number that is one more than one. **2.** a symbol representing this number, such as 2 or II. **3.** something having this many units or things, such as a playing card. —*adj.* numbering one more than one.

two bits *Informal.* twenty-five cents; quarter.

two–by–four (tü′bī fôr′) *n.* **1.** a rough piece of lumber that is 2 inches thick and 4 inches wide (5.1 centimeters

by 10.2 centimeters), used especially in building. **2.** a finished piece of lumber that is 1⅝ inches thick and 3⅝ inches wide (4.1 centimeters by 9.2 centimeters), used especially in building.

two–faced (tü′fāst′) *adj.* **1.** having two faces or aspects. **2.** deceitful or hypocritical: *a two-faced liar.*

two–fist·ed (tü′fis′tid) *adj.* powerful, strong, or virile.

two–fold (tü′fōld′) *adj.* **1.** two times as great or numerous. **2.** having or consisting of two parts: *a twofold plan.* —*adv.* so as to be two times greater or more numerous.

two–ply (tü′plī′) *adj.* **1.** composed or consisting of two layers, thicknesses, or strands: *two-ply tissue.* **2.** consisting of two webs woven into each other: *a two-ply carpet.*

two·some (tü′səm) *n.* **1.** two persons together; couple. **2.** something played or done by two persons, such as a round of golf played by two people.

two–step (tü′step′) *n.* **1.** a ballroom dance consisting of sliding steps in 2/4 time. **2.** the music for such a dance.

two–time (tü′tīm′) *v.t.*, **two-timed, two-tim·ing.** *Slang.* to be unfaithful to or deceive, especially in love. —**two′-tim′er,** *n.*

two–way (tü′wā′) *adj.* **1.** moving or allowing movement in two directions: *two-way traffic, a two-way street.* **2.** allowing communication in two directions, especially by being able to transmit and receive: *a two-way radio.*

TX, postal abbreviation for Texas.

-ty¹ *suffix* multiplied by ten: *sixty, seventy.* [From the Old English suffix *-tig* with the same meaning.]

-ty² *suffix* (used to form nouns) the state, condition, or quality of being: *safety, subtlety.* [From the Old French suffix *-te* with the same meaning, from the Latin suffix *-tas.*]

ty·coon (tī kün′) *n.* a wealthy, powerful person in business, industry, or finance.

ty·ing (tī′ing) the present participle of **tie.**

tyke (tīk) *also,* **tike.** *n.* **1.** *Informal.* a small child, especially one who is mischievous. **2.** a mongrel dog; cur.

tym·pa·ni (tim′pə nē) *pl. n.* another spelling of **timpani.**

tym·pan·ic (tim pan′ik) *adj.* **1.** of or relating to the eardrum or the middle ear. **2.** relating to or resembling a drum.

tympanic membrane, a thin membrane that separates the external ear from the middle ear; eardrum.

tym·pa·nist (tim′pə nist) *n.* a member of an orchestra who plays a kettledrum and, usually, other percussion instruments.

tym·pa·num (tim′pə nəm) *n., pl.* **tym·pa·na** (tim′pə-nə) or **tym·pa·nums.** **1.** another word for **eardrum.** **2.** another word for **middle ear.**

type (tīp) *n.* **1.** a particular kind, class, or group sharing certain common traits or characteristics: *What type of car do they own?* **2.** a person or thing that shows the characteristic qualities of a kind, class, or group; typical or perfect example. **3.** *Printing.* **a.** a rectangular piece or block of metal or wood on one surface of which there is a raised letter, numeral, or other symbol that forms a printing surface. **b.** such pieces or blocks as a group. **4.** a printed or typewritten character or characters: *The book was printed in large type.* **5.** a design or other ornamental figure on either side of a coin or medal. **6.** a blood group. —*v.*, **typed, typ·ing.** —*v.t.* **1.** to write (something) with a typewriter: *to type a letter.* **2.** to identify or determine the type of (a blood sample). **3.** to place in a particular class or group: *I wrongly typed my quiet neighbor as unfriendly.* —*v.i.* to write on a typewriter.

type·script (tīp′skript′) *n.* material that has been typewritten.

type·set·ter (tīp′set′ər) *n.* **1.** a person or business that sets type or text for printing. Also, **compositor.** **2.** a machine that sets type or text for printing.

type·set·ting (tīp′set′ing) *n.* the act or process of setting type for printing. —*adj.* used or adapted for setting type: *a typesetting machine.*

type·write (tīp′rīt′) *v.,* **type·wrote** (tīp′rōt′), **type·writ·ten** (tīp′rit′ən), **type·writ·ing.** —*v.t.* to write (something) with a typewriter. —*v.i.* to use a typewriter; type.

type·writ·er (tīp′rī′tər) *n.* a machine used to produce clear writing that is like print. It is made up of a set of keys that, when struck, impress letters on paper through an inked ribbon either by electronic or mechanical means.

type·writ·ing (tīp′rī′ting) *n.* **1.** the act or process of using a typewriter. **2.** something that is done or produced on a typewriter.

ty·phoid (tī′foid) *n.* see **typhoid fever.** —*adj.* of, relating to, like, or typical of typhoid fever.

typhoid fever, an infectious, sometimes fatal, fever characterized by intestinal inflammation and rose-colored spots on the skin. It is caused by a bacillus taken into the body in food or drink.

ty·phoon (tī fün′) *n.* a tropical hurricane occurring in the western Pacific Ocean, usually during the months of July, August, September, and October.

ty·phus (tī′fəs) *n.* any of a group of infectious diseases characterized by severe headache, high fever, and a spotted rash. It is caused by germs carried by fleas or lice.

typ·i·cal (tip′i kəl) *adj.* **1.** conforming to, showing, or indicating the qualities, attributes, or nature characteristic of a particular type: *a typical student, a typical tourist.* **2.** of the nature of or constituting a type; characteristic; usual: *that joyful manner typical of young children.* —**typ′i·cal·ly,** *adv.*

typ·i·fy (tip′ə fī′) *v.t.,* **typ·i·fied, typ·i·fy·ing. 1.** to have or show the common or usual characteristics of; exemplify. **2.** to serve as a symbol of; represent; symbolize. —**typ′i·fi·ca′tion,** *n.*

typ·ist (tī′pist) *n.* a person who types, especially a person whose job is operating a typewriter.

ty·pog·ra·pher (tī pog′rə fər) *n.* see **printer** (*def. 1*).

ty·po·graph·i·cal (tī′pə graf′i kəl) *adj.* of or relating to typography: *a typographical error.* Also, **ty·po·graph·ic** (tī′pə graf′ik). —**ty′po·graph′i·cal·ly,** *adv.*

ty·pog·ra·phy (tī pog′rə fē) *n.* **1.** the act, art, or process of producing printed matter, especially by means of a printing press. **2.** the arrangement, appearance, or style of printed matter.

ty·ran·ni·cal (ti ran′i kəl) *adj.* of, relating to, or like a tyrant; cruel and unjust. Also, **ty·ran·nic** (ti ran′ik). —**ty·ran′ni·cal·ly,** *adv.*

tyr·an·nize (tir′ə nīz′) *v.,* **tyr·an·nized, tyr·an·niz·ing.** —*v.i.* **1.** to use power in a cruel and unjust way (often with *over*): *The dictator tyrannized over the people.* **2.** to rule as a tyrant. —*v.t.* to treat or govern tyrannically.

ty·ran·no·sau·rus (ti ran′ə sôr′əs) *n., pl.* **ty·ran·no·sau·rus·es.** a huge meat-eating dinosaur of North America that walked upright on its hind legs. Also, **ty·ran·no·saur** (ti ran′ə sôr′).

tyr·an·nous (tir′ə nəs) *adj.* cruel and unjust; tyrannical. —**tyr′an·nous·ly,** *adv.*

tyr·an·ny (tir′ə nē) *n., pl.* **tyr·an·nies. 1.** the cruel and unjust use of force, power, or authority. **2.** any oppressive or unjustly severe rule or government by one person.

ty·rant (tī′rənt) *n.* **1.** a person who uses power or authority in a cruel and unjust way. **2.** a person who has absolute power and rules or governs in a cruel and unjust way; absolute ruler; despot. **3.** in ancient Greece, an absolute ruler who got authority illegally.

tyre (tīr) *British.* another spelling of **tire²**.

Tyr·i·an (tir′ē ən) *adj.* of or relating to ancient Tyre or its people.

ty·ro (tī′rō) *also,* **ti·ro.** *n., pl.* **ty·ros.** a person who is just beginning to learn to do something; beginner; novice.

tzar (zär) another spelling of **czar.**

tza·ri·na (zä rē′nə) another spelling of **czarina.**

tzet·ze fly (tset′sē, tsē′tsē) another spelling of **tsetse fly.** Also, **tzetze.**

---

at; āpe; fär; câre; end; me; it; ice; pierce; hot; old; sông, fôrk, oil, out, up, ūse, rüle, pull, tûrn, chin, sing; shop; thin; this; hw in white; zh in treasure. The symbol ə stands for the unstressed vowel sound heard in about, taken, pencil, lemon, and circus.

T

U u

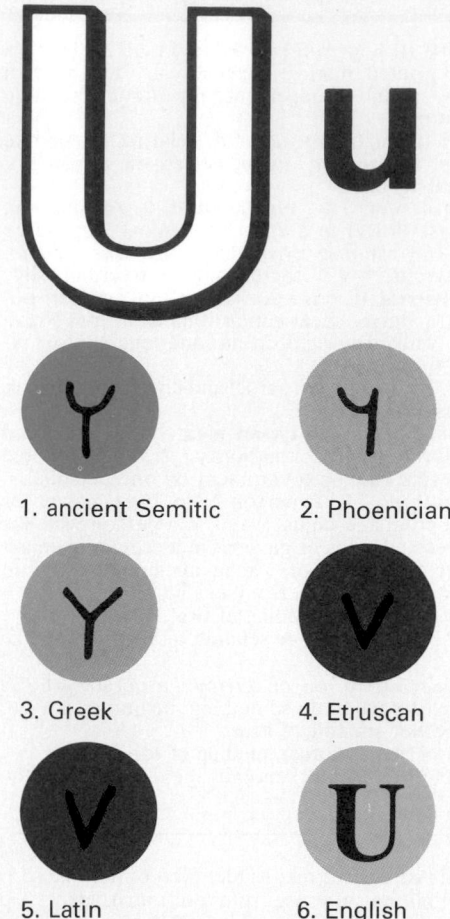

1. ancient Semitic
2. Phoenician
3. Greek
4. Etruscan
5. Latin
6. English

U is the twenty-first letter of the English alphabet. **U, W,** and **J** are the only letters that we use today that did not come from Latin or an earlier alphabet. The letter **U** developed as a variation of the letter **V.** Their earliest ancestor was the ancient Semitic letter *waw* (1), which depicted a hook and stood for the *w* sound, as the *w* in the English word *water*. When the Phoenicians (2) borrowed *waw*, they used it to represent both the consonant sound *w* and the vowel sound *ü*, as heard in the English word *rude*. The Greeks adopted *waw* and called it *upsilon* (3), writing it like our modern capital letter **y** and using it only for the *ü* sound. When this letter was borrowed by the Etruscans (4), they used it to represent both the vowel and consonant sounds, and changed its shape to look like our modern capital letter **V.** This was adopted without change in the Latin alphabet (5). About 1,000 years ago, two forms of this V-shaped letter were being used in writing: **V** at the beginning of a word and a new letter, **U,** in the middle of a word. Later, the letter **U** came to be used exclusively for a *u* sound and was written almost exactly as we write it today (6).

u, U (ū) *n., pl.* **u's, U's. 1.** the twenty-first letter of the English alphabet. **2.** something having the shape of this letter.

U, the symbol for uranium.

U., University.

UAR, United Arab Republic.

u·biq·ui·tous (ū bik′wi təs) *adj.* being everywhere at once, or seeming to be everywhere at once: *the ubiquitous picnic ant.* —**u·biq′ui·tous·ly,** *adv.* —**u·biq′ui·tous·ness,** *n.*

u·biq·ui·ty (ū bik′wi tē) *n.* the state of being ubiquitous.

U–boat (ū′bōt′) *n.* a German submarine, especially one used in World War I or II.

ud·der (ud′ər) *n.* a large sac hanging from the underside of certain female mammals, such as cows, containing the milk-producing glands and teats through which milk can be drawn by nursing or milking.

UFO, unidentified flying object.

ugh (ug, u) *interj.* a grunt or exclamation expressing disgust or horror.

ug·ly (ug′lē) *adj.,* **ug·li·er, ug·li·est. 1.** very unattractive or unpleasant to the eye: *an ugly scar, an ugly painting.* **2.** causing disgust; disagreeable; offensive: *an ugly story, ugly rumors.* **3.** likely to cause trouble or harm; ominous: *an ugly storm.* **4.** bad-tempered: *an ugly mood.* **5.** morally offensive or disgusting: *an ugly prejudice.* —**ug′li·ness,** *n.*

UHF, ultrahigh frequency.

U.K., United Kingdom.

u·kase (ū′kās′) *n.* **1.** an official proclamation or decree; edict. **2.** formerly, a decree or order having the force of law, issued by the czar or by the czarist government in Russia.

U·krain·i·an (ū krā′nē ən) *n.* **1.** a person who was born in or is a citizen of the Ukraine. **2.** a Slavic language spoken mostly in the Ukraine. It is closely related to Russian. —*adj.* of or relating to the Ukraine, its people, their language, or culture.

u·ku·le·le (ū′kə lā′lē) *n.* a small guitar having four strings, associated with Hawaiian music.

ul·cer (ul′sər) *n.* an open sore on the skin or on a membrane such as the stomach lining.

ul·cer·ate (ul′sə rāt′) *v.t., v.i.,* **ul·cer·at·ed, ul·cer·at·ing.** to make or become ulcerous.

ul·cer·a·tion (ul′sə rā′shən) *n.* **1.** the act or process of ulcerating or the state of being ulcerated. **2.** an ulcerous condition; ulcer.

ul·cer·ous (ul′sər əs) *adj.* **1.** relating to or like an ulcer or ulcers. **2.** affected with an ulcer or ulcers.

ul·na (ul′nə) *n., pl.* **ul·nae** (ul′nē) or **ul·nas. 1.** the larger of the two bones of the forearm, extending from the elbow to the wrist. **2.** a corresponding bone in the forelimb of other animals with backbones.

ul·ster (ul′stər) *n.* a very long, heavy overcoat, often with a belt and a cape. [From *Ulster,* Ireland, where it was first made.]

ul·te·ri·or (ul tîr′ē ər) *adj.* **1.** beyond what is shown or expressed; hidden: *ulterior motives.* **2.** farther off: *ulterior regions.*

ul·ti·ma (ul′tə mə) *n.* the last syllable of a word.

ul·ti·ma·ta (ul′tə mā′tə) a plural of **ultimatum.**

ul·ti·mate (ul′tə mit) *adj.* **1.** coming at the end; final: *the ultimate cost, the ultimate goal.*

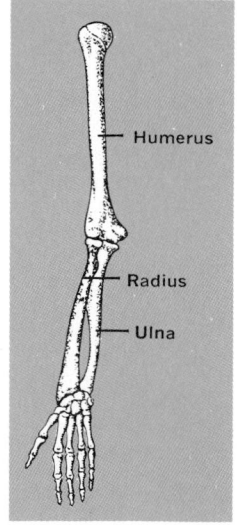

— Humerus

— Radius

— Ulna

ulna *(def. 1)*

2. greatest possible: *ultimate courage.* **3.** earliest or farthest possible: *the ultimate origin of life, the ultimate limits.* —*n.* something that is complete or final and cannot be surpassed: *the ultimate in luxury.*

ul·ti·mate·ly (ul′tə mit lē) *adv.* in the end; finally.

ul·ti·ma·tum (ul′tə mā′təm) *n., pl.* **ul·ti·ma·tums** or **ul·ti·ma·ta.** a final offer, demand, or proposal that implies the threat of punishment, a break in relations, or the use of force if it is rejected.

ul·tra (ul′trə) *adj.* going beyond what is usual or moderate; excessive; extreme. —*n.* a person who has extreme views; extremist.

ultra– *prefix* **1.** beyond what is usual or moderate; excessively; extremely: *ultraconservative.* **2.** on the other side of; beyond: *ultraviolet.* **3.** beyond the range or limits of: *ultrasonic.*

ultrahigh frequency, a radio frequency between 300 and 3,000 megahertz.

ul·tra·ma·rine (ul′trə mə rēn′) *n.* a deep blue color. **2.** a blue coloring matter, originally made from the gem lapis lazuli. —*adj.* having the color ultramarine; deep blue.

ul·tra·son·ic (ul′trə son′ik) *adj.* of, relating to, or indicating sound waves having a frequency beyond the range or limits of human hearing, usually above 20,000 hertz.

ul·tra·sound (ul′trə sound′) *n.* **1.** sound waves at ultrasonic frequencies. **2.** *Medicine.* the application of ultrasonic waves, as to provide certain types of therapy or to produce images of internal structures of the body.

ul·tra·vi·o·let (ul′trə vī′ə lit) *adj.* **1.** (of electromagnetic radiation) having wavelengths shorter than those of visible light but longer than those of X rays, ranging from 40 to 4,000 angstroms. Ultraviolet rays are present in sunlight. **2.** of, using, or producing ultraviolet radiation.

U·lys·ses (u lis′ēz) *n. Greek and Roman Legend.* a king of Ithaca and leader in the Trojan War. Ulysses was forced to wander for ten years after the fall of Troy until the gods finally permitted him to return home. He was called Odysseus by the Greeks.

um·bel (um′bəl) *n.* a flower cluster in which the flower stalks grow out of a common center at the top of the stem.

um·ber (um′bər) *n.* **1.** brown earth, used as a brown pigment. **2.** a brown color. —*adj.* having the color umber.

um·bil·i·cal cord (um bil′i kəl) a cordlike structure that connects the navel of an unborn baby to the placenta of the mother's womb.

um·bil·i·cus (um bil′i kəs, um′bə lī′kəs) *n.* another word for **navel.**

um·bra (um′brə) *n., pl.* **um·bras** or **um·brae** (um′brē). **1.** *Astronomy.* the cone-shaped shadow cast by the moon in a solar eclipse or by the earth in a lunar eclipse, in the direction away from the sun. **2.** any shaded area or shadow.

um·brage (um′brij) *n.* a feeling of resentment, especially at an imagined insult; offense: *to take umbrage at a critical remark.*

um·brel·la (um brel′ə) *n.* **1.** a device used to give protection from rain or sun, made of a circular piece of cloth or other material attached to narrow ribs radiating from a long central rod. **2.** something resembling an umbrella in shape or function, such as a group of military aircraft sent up to protect land or sea forces. [From the Italian word *ombrella* meaning "a device for protection from sun or rain," from the word *ombra* "shade," from the Latin word *umbra* "shadow, shade."]

umbrella tree, an American magnolia tree having long leaves and spreading branches that cause it to look like an open umbrella.

u·mi·ak (ū′mē ak′) *n.* a large, open Eskimo boat made of skins stretched over a wooden frame.

um·laut (ŭm′lout) *n.* a diacritical mark (¨) written over a vowel in some foreign words, indicating that the vowel is to be pronounced in a certain way.

um·pire (um′pīr) *n.* an official who rules on plays in certain sports and games, such as baseball. —*v.,* **umpired, um·pir·ing.** —*v.t.* to act as an umpire of: *to umpire a softball game.* —*v.i.* to act as an umpire. [From the phrase *an umpire,* from a mistaken division of the earlier phrase *a numpire.* The word *numpire* comes from two Old French words meaning "not" and "peer" or "partner." An *umpire* was originally a third person called in to settle a dispute or to decide a contest between two others. The umpire was not part of the argument or contest.]

un–[1] *prefix* (used to form adjectives, adverbs, and nouns) the opposite of: *uncooked, unbeliever.* [From the Old English prefix *un-* with the same meaning.]

un–[2] *prefix* **1.** (used to form verbs from verbs) **a.** to do the opposite of: *unfasten.* **b.** to make stronger the action of: *unloose.* **2.** (used to form verbs from nouns) **a.** to release, remove, or free from: *unearth.* **b.** to cause to cease to be: *unman.* [From the Old English prefix *un-,* a form of *and-* with the same meanings.]

UN, United Nations.

un·a·bashed (un′ə basht′) *adj.* not ashamed, embarrassed, or easily confused: *unabashed defiance.* —**un·a·bash·ed·ly** (un′ə bash′id lē) *adv.*

un·a·bat·ed (un′ə bā′tid) *adj.* at full strength. *unabated force.* —**un′a·bat′ed·ly,** *adv.*

un·a·ble (un ā′bəl) *adj.* lacking the required power, skills, or qualifications: *I am unable to type.*

un·a·bridged (un′ə brijd′) *adj.* not shortened; complete: *an unabridged edition of a book.*

un·ac·cent·ed (un ak′sen tid) *adj.* not accented. In the word *ago,* the *a* is unaccented.

un·ac·com·pa·nied (un′ə kum′pə nēd′) *adj.* **1.** without a companion or escort; alone: *to go unaccompanied to the theater.* **2.** *Music.* without accompaniment.

un·ac·com·plished (un′ə kom′plisht) *adj.* **1.** not skilled: *to be unaccomplished as a public speaker.* **2.** not completed.

un·ac·count·a·ble (un′ə koun′tə bəl) *adj.* **1.** that cannot be accounted for. **2.** not liable to be called to account. —**un′ac·count′a·bly,** *adv.*

un·ac·cus·tomed (un′ə kus′təmd) *adj.* **1.** not used to: *City children are unaccustomed to country life.* **2.** unfamiliar; unusual: *The last-place team played with unaccustomed skill.*

U

un·ac·quaint·ed (un'ə kwān'tid) *adj.* **1.** not known to someone or to each other. **2.** not familiar: *The new student is unacquainted with school rules.*

unadorned furniture

un·a·dorned (un'ə dornd') *adj.* not decorated; simple; plain.

un·a·dul·ter·at·ed (un'ə dul'tə rā'tid) *adj.* not diluted or mixed; pure: *unadulterated foods.*

un·ad·vis·ed·ly (un'ad vī'zid lē) *adv.* in a rash, thoughtless manner; imprudently: *an unadvisedly quick answer.*

un·af·fect·ed[1] (un'ə fek'tid) *adj.* not influenced; unmoved: *The judge was unaffected by the defendant's pleas.* [*Un-*[1] + *affected*[1].]

un·af·fect·ed[2] (un'ə fek'tid) *adj.* genuine; sincere: *an unaffected manner.* [*Un-*[1] + *affected*[2].] **—un'af·fect'ed·ly,** *adv.* **—un'af·fect'ed·ness,** *n.*

un·aid·ed (un ā'did) *adj.* without help or support.

un·al·lied (un'ə līd') *adj.* not joined by treaty, agreement, or common purpose.

un·al·ter·a·ble (un ôl'tər ə bəl) *adj.* that cannot be changed: *unalterable plans.* **—un'al'ter·a·bly,** *adv.*

un·al·tered (un ôl'tərd) *adj.* not changed.

un–A·mer·i·can (un'ə mer'i kən) *adj.* not according to the American character, traditions, or ideals.

u·na·nim·i·ty (ū'nə nim'i tē) *n.* the state of being in complete agreement.

u·nan·i·mous (ū nan'ə məs) *adj.* **1.** in complete agreement: *The club members were unanimous in their support of the project.* **2.** characterized by or showing complete agreement: *The vote was unanimous.* [From the Latin word *unanimis* meaning "of one mind, unanimous," from the words *unus* "one" + *anima* "mind."] **—u·nan'i·mous·ly,** *adv.* **—u·nan'i·mous·ness,** *n.*

un·an·swer·a·ble (un an'sər ə bəl) *adj.* **1.** that cannot be answered; having no known answer. **2.** that cannot be argued against or disproved: *an unanswerable theory.*

un·ap·proach·a·ble (un'ə prō'chə bəl) *adj.* **1.** difficult to know or deal with; unfriendly: *an unapproachable person.* **2.** that cannot be approached: *The mountain cabin is unapproachable in winter.* **—un'ap·proach'·a·ble·ness,** *n.* **—un'ap·proach'a·bly,** *adv.*

un·armed (un ärmd') *adj.* without weapons.

un·asked (un askt') *adj.* **1.** without being asked: *They came unasked to the party.* **2.** not asked for: *unasked advice.*

un·as·sail·a·ble (un'ə sā'lə bəl) *adj.* **1.** that cannot be questioned or denied: *an unassailable argument.* **2.** that cannot be successfully attacked: *an unassailable fortress.*

un·as·sum·ing (un'ə sü'ming) *adj.* modest in nature or manner; not bold or forward: *the unassuming manner of a perfect guest.* **—un'as·sum'ing·ly,** *adv.*

un·at·tached (un'ə tacht') *adj.* **1.** not fastened, joined, or connected: *The last piece of the structure was still unattached.* **2.** not engaged or married.

un·at·tend·ed (un'ə ten'did) *adj.* **1.** not accompanied or escorted; alone. **2.** not done or taken care of; neglected: *to leave the housework unattended.*

un·a·vail·ing (un'ə vā'ling) *adj.* futile; useless: *Their efforts to stop the fire were unavailing.* **—un'a·vail'·ing·ly,** *adv.*

un·a·void·a·ble (un'ə voi'də bəl) *adj.* that cannot or could not be avoided: *an unavoidable delay, an unavoidable problem.* **—un'a·void'a·bly,** *adv.*

un·a·ware (un'ə wâr') *adj.* not aware: *We were unaware of their dislike for us.*

un·a·wares (un'ə wârz') *adv.* without warning; unexpectedly; suddenly: *The storm caught us unawares.*

un·bal·anced (un bal'ənst) *adj.* **1.** not balanced: *The unbalanced load caused one side of the car to sag.* **2.** not having a sound mind; mentally ill: *an unbalanced person.* **3.** not adjusted so that the debit and credit are equal: *an unbalanced budget.*

un·bar (un bär') *v.t.,* **un·barred, un·bar·ring.** to remove the bars from; unbolt; open.

un·bear·a·ble (un bâr'ə bəl) *adj.* that cannot be endured; intolerable: *unbearable pain, unbearable suspense.* **—un·bear'a·ble·ness,** *n.* **—un·bear'a·bly,** *adv.*

un·beat·a·ble (un bē'tə bəl) *adj.* that cannot be defeated or surpassed: *an unbeatable tennis player.*

un·beat·en (un bē'tən) *adj.* **1.** never defeated or surpassed: *an unbeaten team.* **2.** not walked over: *an unbeaten path.* **3.** not shaped or mixed by beating: *unbeaten gold, an unbeaten egg.*

un·be·com·ing (un'bi kum'ing) *adj.* **1.** not flattering or attractive: *The color green is unbecoming to your complexion.* **2.** not suitable or appropriate: *to use unbecoming language.* **—un'be·com'ing·ly,** *adv.*

un·be·knownst (un'bi nōnst') *also,* **un·be·known** (un'bi nōn') *adj., adv. Informal.* not known: *Unbeknownst to us, our friends had left the city.*

un·be·lief (un'bi lēf') *n.* a lack of belief, especially in matters of religion.

un·be·liev·a·ble (un'bi lē'və bəl) *adj.* not to be believed; incredible: *an unbelievable story.* **—un'be·liev'a·bly,** *adv.*

un·be·liev·er (un'bi lē'vər) *n.* **1.** a person who does not believe in a particular religion or in any religion. **2.** a person who doubts; skeptic.

un·be·liev·ing (un'bi lē'ving) *adj.* **1.** doubting; skeptical. **2.** lacking religious belief or beliefs. **—un'be·liev'ing·ly,** *adv.*

un·bend (un bend') *v.,* **un·bent, un·bend·ing.** **—*v.t.*** **1.** to straighten (something curved or crooked). **2.** to free from effort or strain: *to unbend one's mind.* **3.** to unfasten, untie, or cast loose: *to unbend a sail.* **—*v.i.*** **1.** to become free of strain; relax: *The shy newcomer was able to unbend in the warm and friendly group.* **2.** to become straight or almost straight.

un·bend·ing (un ben'ding) *adj.* **1.** that cannot or will not relax; unyielding: *an unbending will.* **2.** not bending; stiff.

un·bent (un bent') the past tense and past participle of **unbend.**

un·bi·ased (un bī'əst) *also, British,* **un·bi·assed.** *adj.* free from bias; fair: *an unbiased judge.*

un·bid·den (un bid'ən) *adj.* **1.** not asked or invited: *Several unbidden guests showed up at the party.* **2.** not commanded or ordered.

un·bind (un bīnd') *v.t.,* **un·bound, un·bind·ing.** **1.** to release from bonds; set free. **2.** to remove or undo (something that binds); loose: *to unbind a bandage.*

un·blem·ished (un blem'isht) *adj.* free from flaw or blemish: *an unblemished complexion, an unblemished reputation.*

un·blessed (un blest′) *also,* **un·blest.** *adj.* **1.** not blessed or consecrated. **2.** cursed; evil; unholy.

un·blush·ing (un blush′ing) *adj.* **1.** without shame; shameless; brazen: *an unblushing pride in one's accomplishments.* **2.** not blushing or reddening.

un·bolt (un bōlt′) *v.t.* to open by drawing back bolts.

un·bolt·ed (un bōl′tid) *adj.* not fastened by bolts: *an unbolted door.*

un·born (un bôrn′) *adj.* not yet born: *an unborn child.*

un·bos·om (un bŏoz′əm) *v.t.* **1.** to tell (something burdensome): *to unbosom one's sorrows to an old friend.* **2.** to unburden (oneself), as of thoughts, secrets, or feelings.

un·bound (un bound′) *v.* the past tense and past participle of **unbind.** —*adj.* **1.** not tied: *an unbound package.* **2.** without a binding or cover: *an unbound book.*

un·bound·ed (un boun′did) *adj.* having no limits or bounds; boundless; measureless: *unbounded space.*

un·bowed (un boud′) *adj.* not bowed, as by defeat.

un·break·a·ble (un brā′kə bəl) *adj.* that cannot be broken: *unbreakable glass.*

un·bri·dled (un brī′dəld) *adj.* **1.** uncontrolled; ungoverned: *unbridled fury.* **2.** not wearing or fitted with a bridle: *an unbridled pony.*

un·bro·ken (un brō′kən) *adj.* **1.** not broken; whole; intact: *unbroken windows.* **2.** not interrupted; continuous: *an unbroken chain of events.* **3.** not beaten or surpassed: *an unbroken record of victories.* **4.** not used to a harness or rider; untamed: *an unbroken horse.* **5.** not weakened, subdued, or humbled: *an unbroken spirit.* **6.** not violated; kept: *an unbroken promise.* —**un·bro′ken·ly,** *adv.* —**un·bro′ken·ness,** *n.*

un·buck·le (un buk′əl) *v.t.,* **un·buck·led, un·buck·ling.** to undo or unfasten the buckle or buckles of: *to unbuckle a belt.*

un·bur·den (un bûr′dən) *v.t.* **1.** to free or relieve by telling something burdensome: *to unburden oneself to a friend.* **2.** to rid oneself of (something burdensome); reveal: *to unburden one's troubles.*

un·but·ton (un but′ən) *v.t.* to open by unfastening the button or buttons of.

un·called–for (un kôld′fôr′) *adj.* not fit, proper, or necessary; not warranted: *an uncalled-for comment, uncalled-for behavior.*

un·can·ny (un kan′ē) *adj.* **1.** strange and eerie; weird: *There were uncanny sounds in the deserted old house.* **2.** unusually good: *an uncanny knack for doing crossword puzzles.* —**un·can′ni·ly,** *adv.* —**un·can′ni·ness,** *n.*

un·cap (un kap′) *v.t.,* **un·capped, un·cap·ping.** to take off the cap of: *I uncapped a bottle of soda.*

un·ceas·ing (un sē′sing) *adv.* without end; continuous: *the unceasing flow of a river, an unceasing barrage of questions.* —**un·ceas′ing·ly,** *adv.*

un·cen·sored (un sen′sərd) *adj.* not censored: *an uncensored movie.*

un·cer·e·mo·ni·ous (un′ser ə mō′nē əs) *adj.* **1.** without courtesy; abrupt; curt: *an unceremonious departure.* **2.** characterized by a lack of ceremony; informal. —**un′cer·e·mo′ni·ous·ly,** *adv.* —**un′cer·e·mo′ni·ous·ness,** *n.*

un·cer·tain (un sûr′tən) *adj.* **1.** not known, established, or settled for sure; doubtful: *The outcome of the game is still uncertain.* **2.** that cannot be depended on; subject to change; variable: *uncertain weather.* **3.** not clearly defined; vague: *uncertain noises.* —**un·cer′tainly,** *adv.* —**un·cer′tain·ness,** *n.*

·**in no uncertain terms.** very clearly indeed; emphatically: *I gave my opinion of the performance in no uncertain terms.*

un·cer·tain·ty (un sûr′tən tē) *n., pl.* **un·cer·tain·ties.** **1.** the state or quality of being uncertain. **2.** something that is uncertain: *Tomorrow's weather is always an uncertainty.*

un·chain (un chān′) *v.t.* to release from a chain or chains; set free.

un·change·a·ble (un chān′jə bəl) *adj.* that does not change or cannot be changed: *the unchangeable dryness of the desert.* —**un·change′a·bly,** *adv.*

un·changed (un chānjd′) *adj.* not changed.

un·chang·ing (un chān′jing) *adj.* not changing.

un·charged (un chärjd′) *adj.* having no electric charge.

un·char·i·ta·ble (un char′i tə bəl) *adj.* not generous or forgiving; severe; harsh: *an uncharitable attitude.* —**un·char′i·ta·ble·ness,** *n.* —**un·char′i·ta·bly,** *adv.*

un·chart·ed (un chär′tid) *adj.* not shown on a map or chart; unexplored; unknown: *The explorers discovered several uncharted islands.*

un·chaste (un chāst′) *adj.* not pure, virtuous, or modest; not chaste.

un·checked (un chekt′) *adj.* **1.** not halted or controlled: *the unchecked advance of floodwaters, unchecked anger.* **2.** not verified or corrected: *unchecked test papers.*

un·chris·tian (un kris′chən) *adj.* **1.** not in accord with Christian teachings or ideals: *an unchristian remark.* **2.** not of the Christian religion.

un·cial (un′shəl) *adj.* of or relating to a style of writing having letters similar to, but more rounded than, modern letters. It is found in Greek and Latin manuscripts dating from about the fourth to the ninth century A.D.

ABCDEFGHJKL MNOPQRSTU

uncial letters

un·civ·il (un siv′əl) *adj.* not polite or courteous; rude: *an uncivil reply.* —**un·civ′il·ly,** *adv.*

un·civ·i·lized (un siv′ə līzd′) *adj.* not civilized; savage: *uncivilized behavior.*

un·clad (un klad′) *adj.* not clothed or dressed; nude.

un·clasp (un klasp′) *v.t.* **1.** to open or loosen the clasp of: *to unclasp a bracelet.* **2.** to release from a grasp or embrace.

un·clas·si·fied (un klas′ə fīd′) *adj.* not secret: *an unclassified report.*

un·cle (ung′kəl) *n.* **1.** the brother of a person's father or mother. **2.** the husband of a person's aunt.

un·clean (un klēn′) *adj.* **1.** not clean; dirty; foul. **2.** not morally pure: *unclean thoughts.* —**un·clean′ness,** *n.*

un·clean·ly[1] (un klēn′lē) *adj.* not cleanly; unclean. [*Un-*[1] + *cleanly*[1].]

un·clean·ly[2] (un klēn′lē) *adv.* in an unclean manner. [*Un-*[1] + *cleanly*[2].]

un·clear (un klîr′) *adj.* not clear or obvious: *Your writing is unclear.*

un·clench (un klench′) *v.t., v.i.* to open or become opened from a clenched position.

Uncle Sam (sam) **1.** the figure or personification used to symbolize the government or people of the United States. **2.** the government or people of the United States. [From a fanciful expansion of the abbreviation *U.S.* meaning "United States."]

un·cloak (un klōk′) *v.t.* **1.** to remove a cloak or cover from. **2.** to reveal; expose: *to uncloak a plot.*

un·clothed (un klōth̄d′) *adj.* not clothed; stripped; naked.

---

at; āpe; fär; câre; end; mē; it; īce; pîerce; hot; ōld; sông, fôrk; oil; out; up; ūse; rüle; pull; tûrn; chin; sing; shop; thin; <u>th</u>is; hw in white; zh in treasure. The symbol ə stands for the unstressed vowel sound heard in about, taken, pencil, lemon, and circus.

U

un·coil (un koil′) *v.t.* to unwind. —*v.i.* to become unwound.

un·com·fort·a·ble (un kumf′tə bəl, un kum′fər tə bəl) *adj.* **1.** causing discomfort: *an uncomfortable mattress.* **2.** feeling discomfort: *I was uncomfortable in those tight shoes.* —**un·com′fort·a·ble·ness,** *n.* —**un·com′fort·a·bly,** *adv.*

un·com·mon (un kom′ən) *adj.* rare; unusual: *Rain is uncommon in the desert.* —**un·com′mon·ly,** *adv.* —**un·com′mon·ness,** *n.*

un·com·mu·ni·ca·tive (un′kə mū′ni kā tiv, un′kə mū′ni kə tiv) *adj.* not telling things readily; reticent: *a shy, uncommunicative child.* —**un′com·mu′ni·ca′tive·ly,** *adv.* —**un′com·mu′ni·ca′tive·ness,** *n.*

un·com·pli·men·ta·ry (un′kom plə men′tə rē, un′kom plə men′trē) *adj.* insulting: *an uncomplimentary remark.*

un·com·pro·mis·ing (un kom′prə mī′zing) *adj.* not open to change or compromise; unyielding: *a firm and uncompromising attitude.* —**un′com′pro·mis′ing·ly,** *adv.*

un·con·cern (un′kən sûrn′) *n.* **1.** a lack of interest or concern. **2.** freedom from care or anxiety.

un·con·cerned (un′kən sûrnd′) *adj.* not interested or concerned: *to be unconcerned with someone else's problems.* —**un·con·cern·ed·ly** (un′kən sûr′nid lē), *adv.*

un·con·di·tion·al (un′kən dish′ə nəl) *adj.* not limited by a condition or conditions; absolute: *unconditional obedience, an unconditional guarantee.* —**un′con·di′tion·al·ly,** *adv.*

un·con·firmed (un′kən fûrmd′) *adj.* not firmly established or proved: *unconfirmed reports.*

un·con·nec·ted (un′kə nek′tid) *adj.* not joined or fastened together; separate: *The school consists of two unconnected buildings.* —**un′con·nec′ted·ly,** *adv.* —**un′con·nec′ted·ness,** *n.*

un·con·quer·a·ble (un kong′kər ə bəl) *adj.* that cannot be overcome: *unconquerable courage, an unconquerable army.* —**un′con′quer·a·bly,** *adv.*

un·con·scion·a·ble (un kon′shə nə bəl) *adj.* **1.** not influenced, guided, or restrained by conscience; shameful; outrageous: *an unconscionable deed, an unconscionable liar.* **2.** beyond what is reasonable or just; excessive: *an unconscionable price.* —**un′con′scion·a·bly,** *adv.*

un·con·scious (un kon′shəs) *adj.* **1.** temporarily without consciousness: *The driver was unconscious after the accident.* **2.** not knowing; unaware: *to be unconscious of one's appearance.* **3.** not done on purpose; accidental: *an unconscious error, an unconscious bad habit.* —*n.* the part of the mind that contains wishes, fears, and the like that a person is not aware of but that influence one's thoughts and behavior. —**un·con′scious·ly,** *adv.* —**un·con′scious·ness,** *n.*

un·con·sti·tu·tion·al (un′kon sti tü′shə nəl, un′kon sti tū′shə nəl) *adj.* not in keeping with the constitution of a country, state, or group, especially the Constitution of the United States. —**un′con·sti·tu′tion·al·ly,** *adv.*

un·con·sti·tu·tion·al·i·ty (un′kon sti tü′shə nal′i tē, un′kon sti tū′shə nal′i tē) *n.* the state or quality of being unconstitutional.

un·con·trol·la·ble (un′kən trō′lə bəl) *adj.* that cannot be held in check or restrained: *uncontrollable laughter.* —**un′con·trol′la·bly,** *adv.*

un·con·trolled (un′kən trōld′) *adj.* that is not held in check or restrained: *an uncontrolled temper.*

un·con·ven·tion·al (un′kən ven′shə nəl) *adj.* not following convention; out of the ordinary: *unconventional clothing.* —**un′con·ven′tion·al·ly,** *adv.*

un·con·ven·tion·al·i·ty (un′kən ven′shə nal′i tē) *n.* the state or quality of being unconventional.

un·cork (un kôrk′) *v.t.* to draw or remove the cork from.

un·count·ed (un koun′tid) *adj.* **1.** too many to count;

innumerable: *Uncounted numbers of people attended the rally.* **2.** not counted: *A few votes were still uncounted.*

un·cou·ple (un kup′əl) *v.t.,* **un·cou·pled, un·cou·pling.** to disconnect; unfasten: *to uncouple railroad cars.*

un·couth (un küth′) *adj.* **1.** lacking culture or refinement; crude: *uncouth manners.* **2.** awkward or clumsy. —**un·couth′ly,** *adv.* —**un·couth′ness,** *n.*

un·cov·er (un kuv′ər) *v.t.* **1.** to lay bare or make known; bring to light; disclose: *The detective uncovered some new clues.* **2.** to remove the cover or covering from: *The cook uncovered the dish.* **3.** to remove a hat from (one's head) as a sign of respect. —*v.i.* to remove a hat from one's head as a sign of respect.

un·cross (un krôs′) *v.t.* to change from a crossed position: *to uncross one's legs.*

un·crys·tal·lized (un kris′tə līzd′) *adj.* not crystallized.

unc·tion (ungk′shən) *n.* **1.** the act of anointing as part of a religious or other ritual. **2.** a substance used in anointing, such as oil. **3.** something that soothes or comforts. **4.** exaggerated emotion, as in language.

unc·tu·ous (ungk′chü əs) *adj.* **1.** characterized by exaggerated emotion; too suave: *an unctuous person, unctuous flattery.* **2.** like oil or ointment; slippery to the touch; greasy. —**unc′tu·ous·ly,** *adv.* —**unc′tu·ous·ness,** *n.*

un·cul·ti·vat·ed (un kul′tə vā′tid) *adj.* **1.** not prepared for growing crops: *uncultivated soil.* **2.** not cultured or refined: *an uncultivated person.*

un·cured (un kyûrd′) *adj.* **1.** not made well or healthy: *an uncured patient.* **2.** not prepared for use, as by drying: *uncured tobacco.*

un·curl (un kûrl′) *v.t.* to take the curl out of; straighten: *to uncurl one's hair.* —*v.i.* to become straightened.

un·cut (un kut′) *adj.* **1.** not cut: *uncut flowers.* **2.** not shortened or edited; unabridged: *an uncut version of a film.* **3.** not changed or shaped by cutting: *an uncut diamond.*

un·dat·ed (un dā′tid) *adj.* not marked with a date.

un·daunt·ed (un dôn′tid) *adj.* not discouraged or frightened; fearless: *Undaunted by the cold and the darkness, we continued to hike through the snow.* —**un·daunt′ed·ly,** *adv.*

un·de·cid·ed (un′di sī′did) *adj.* **1.** not having one's mind made up: *I am still undecided about what to write for my book report.* **2.** not yet settled: *The outcome of the election is still undecided.* —**un′de·cid′ed·ly,** *adv.* —**un′de·cid′ed·ness,** *n.*

un·de·clared (un′di klârd′) *adj.* not announced or proclaimed: *an undeclared war.*

un·de·feat·ed (un′di fē′tid) *adj.* not defeated: *The school basketball team was undefeated this season.*

un·de·fined (un′di fīnd′) *adj.* not defined: *an undefined word.*

un·dem·o·crat·ic (un′dem ə krat′ik) *adj.* not agreeing with or supporting the ideals or principles of democracy; not democratic.

un·de·mon·stra·tive (un′di mon′strə tiv) *adj.* not given to showing affection or feeling; reserved: *The family was undemonstrative in public but affectionate at home.* —**un′de·mon′stra·tive·ness,** *n.*

un·de·ni·a·ble (un′di nī′ə bəl) *adj.* that cannot be denied or doubted: *The police had undeniable evidence of the thief's guilt.* —**un′de·ni′a·bly,** *adv.*

un·de·pend·a·ble (un′di pen′də bəl) *adj.* that cannot be depended on; not dependable: *an old, undependable car.*

un·der (un′dər) *prep.* **1.** in a place down from or lower than; beneath: *I put the paper under a pile of books. Look under the bed for your shoe.* **2.** below the surface of: *The splinter went under the skin.* **3.** in a position so as to be covered or protected by: *to stand under an* umbrella. **4.** less than: *We drove 20 miles per hour under the speed limit.* **5.** subject to the authority of: *The veterans served under that general during the war.* **6.** subject to the force or action of: *The metal beam is under great pressure. The fire is under control.* **7.** bound by: *The witness gave testimony under oath.* **8.** in the process of: *Our new house is under construction.* **9.** according to: *Under the new rules, no one can use the tennis courts for more than one hour.* **10.** because of; considering: *We can't go under such circumstances.* **11.** during the reign, rule, or administration of: *The Peace Corps was founded under President Kennedy.* **12.** within the particular group or category of: *The article on diamonds was under "precious stones."* —*adv.* in or into a position down from or lower than something: *The raft was sucked under by the whirlpool.* —*adj.* lower in position, rank, degree, or amount: *the under surface of a leaf.*

under– *combining form* **1.** located below: *underpass.* **2.** located beneath the surface of: *underground.* **3.** less than is usual or needed: *underweight, underage.* **4.** lower or inferior, as in rank: *undergraduate.*

un·der·age (un′dər āj′) *adj.* not of the usual or legal age.

un·der·arm (un′dər ärm′) *adj.* **1.** of, relating to, or used in the armpit; under the arm: *underarm perspiration.* **2.** see **underhand** (*def. 1*). —*n.* the hollow under the arm at the shoulder; armpit. —*adv.* see **underhand** (*def. 1*).

un·der·bel·ly (un′dər bel′ē) *n.*, *pl.* **un·der·bel·lies.** **1.** the underside of something, especially the lower abdominal region of an animal. **2.** a weak or vulnerable part.

un·der·bid (un′dər bid′) *v.t.*, **un·der·bid, un·der·bid·ding.** to bid lower than (a competitor).

un·der·brush (un′dər brush′) *n.* a growth of bushes, shrubs, or similar plants beneath the large trees in a forest or woods.

un·der·charge (*v.*, un′dər chärj′; *n.*, un′dər chärj′) *v.t.*, **un·der·charged, un·der·charg·ing. 1.** to charge (someone) too small a price. **2.** to supply or load with too small a charge, as a gun. —*n.* too small a charge.

un·der·clothes (un′dər klōz′, un′dər klō*th*z′) *pl.* *n.* another word for **underwear.**

un·der·cloth·ing (un′dər klō′*th*ing) *n.* another word for **underwear.**

un·der·coat (un′dər kōt′) *n.* **1.** a layer of short hairs hidden by the fur on an animal's body. **2.** a layer of varnish, paint, or the like put on a surface before the final coat.

un·der·cov·er (un′dər kuv′ər) *adj.* working or done in secret: *an undercover agent for the government.*

un·der·cur·rent (un′dər kûr′ənt) *n.* **1.** a current, as of air or water, under another current or below a surface. **2.** an underlying feeling or emotion: *an undercurrent of fear.*

un·der·cut (*v.*, un′dər kut′, un′dər kut′; *n.*, un′dər kut′) *v.t.*, **un·der·cut, un·der·cut·ting. 1.** to sell or work for lower payment than (a competitor). **2.** to diminish one's power or authority; weaken. **3.** to cut under or away, as in carving. —*n.* the act or result of cutting under or away.

un·der·de·vel·oped (un′dər di vel′əpt) *adj.* **1.** not completely or properly developed: *underdeveloped muscles.* **2.** behind in growth or development, especially industrial or economic development: *an underdeveloped nation.*

un·der·dog (un′dər dôg′) *n.* **1.** a person who is thought most likely to lose, as in a contest or game. **2.** a victim of political or social injustice.

un·der·done (un′dər dun′) *adj.* not completely or properly cooked: *an underdone roast.*

un·der·es·ti·mate (*v.*, un′dər es′tə māt′; *n.*, un′dər es′tə mit, un′dər es′tə māt′) *v.t.*, **un·der·es·ti·mat·ed, un·der·es·ti·mat·ing. 1.** to estimate at too low an amount: *Don't underestimate the cost of such a long trip.* **2.** to place too low a value on; have too low an opinion of: *We underestimated the other team's ability.* —*n.* too low an estimate.

un·der·ex·pose (un′dər ek spōz′) *v.t.*, **un·der·ex·posed, un·der·ex·pos·ing.** to expose (a photographic film or plate) to too little light, or to light for too short a period of time, to produce a good picture.

un·der·ex·po·sure (un′dər ek spō′zhər) *n.* the act, process, or result of underexposing.

un·der·feed (un′dər fēd′) *v.t.*, **un·der·fed** (un′dər fed′), **un·der·feed·ing.** to feed too little.

un·der·foot (un′dər fůt′) *adv.* **1.** in the way: *The baby's toys are always underfoot.* **2.** beneath the foot or feet; on the ground: *It was icy underfoot.*

un·der·gar·ment (un′dər gär′mənt) *n.* an article of underwear.

un·der·go (un′dər gō′) *v.t.*, **un·der·went, un·der·gone** (un′dər gôn′, un′dər gon′), **un·der·go·ing. 1.** to pass through; experience: *The neighborhood is undergoing a change for the better.* **2.** to bear up under; endure: *to undergo a serious operation.*

un·der·grad·u·ate (un′dər graj′ü it) *n.* a college or university student who has not yet received a degree.

un·der·ground (*adj., adv.*, un′dər ground′; *n.*, un′dər·ground′) *adj.* **1.** below the surface of the earth: *an underground passage.* **2.** hidden; secret: *an underground political movement.* —*n.* **1.** a group working secretly to resist or overthrow the government in power or enemy occupation. **2.** a place or space below the surface of the earth, such as a tunnel. **3.** *British.* subway (*def. 1*). —*adv.* **1.** below the surface of the earth: *The workers dug a tunnel underground.* **2.** in or into hiding; in secret: *The rebellious troops went underground to avoid capture.*

underground railroad, before the U.S. Civil War, a system by which opponents of slavery in the United States secretly helped runaway slaves reach freedom by transporting or escorting them to Canada or the Free States.

un·der·growth (un′dər grōth′) *n.* a growth of small plants beneath the large trees of a forest; underbrush.

un·der·hand (un′dər hand′) *adv.* **1.** also, **underarm.** with the hand held below the level of the elbow or shoulder: *to toss a ball underhand.* **2.** slyly; secretly. —*adj.* **1.** done with the hand held below the level of the elbow or shoulder: *an underhand pitch.* **2.** another word for **underhanded.**

un·der·hand·ed (un′dər han′did) *adj.* done in a secret, sly manner; deceitful: *an underhanded trick.* —**un′der·hand′ed·ly,** *adv.* —**un′der·hand′ed·ness,** *n.*

un·der·lie (un′dər lī′) *v.t.*, **un·der·lay** (un′dər lā′), **un·der·lain** (un′dər lān′), **un·der·ly·ing. 1.** to be located below: *Rocky soil underlies the rich topsoil.* **2.** to be the basis or cause of: *What reasons underlay their actions?*

un·der·line (*v.*, un′dər līn′; *n.*, un′dər līn′) *v.t.*, **un·der·lined, un·der·lin·ing. 1.** to draw a line or lines under. **2.** to emphasize; stress: *to underline the need for caution.* —*n.* a line drawn under words for emphasis or to indicate italics.

un·der·ling (un′dər ling) *n.* a person who is lower in rank than another or others and must take orders.

un·der·lip (un′dər lip′) *n.* the lower lip.

at; āpe; fär; câre; end; mē; it; īce; pîerce; hot; ōld; sông, fôrk; oil; out; up; ūse; rüle; půll; tûrn; chin; sing; shop; thin; *th*is; hw in white; zh in treasure. The symbol ə stands for the unstressed vowel sound heard in about, taken, pencil, lemon, and circus.

U

un·der·ly·ing (un′dər lī′ing) *adj.* **1.** lying below: *an underlying foundation of concrete.* **2.** basic or fundamental: *underlying principles.*

un·der·mine (un′dər mīn′) *v.t.,* **un·der·mined, un·der·min·ing. 1.** to weaken or destroy slowly and secretly: *Poor eating habits can undermine one's health.* **2.** to weaken by wearing away at the foundation or base of; erode: *The river undermined the bank.* **3.** to dig a mine or passage under; dig below.

un·der·most (un′dər mōst′) *adj., adv.* lowest in place or position; bottom.

un·der·neath (un′dər nēth′) *prep.* **1.** in a lower place or position than; on the underside of: *The puppy rolled the ball underneath the chair.* **2.** under the appearance of: *Underneath their stern manner, they are really nice people.* —*adv.* lower than something; on the underside: *We packed the heavier items underneath.*

un·der·nour·ish (un′dər nûr′ish) *v.t.* to give too little food to. —**un′der·nour′ish·ment,** *n.*

un·der·pants (un′dər pants′) *pl. n.* pants or shorts worn underneath a person's outer clothes.

underpass

un·der·pass (un′dər pas′) *n., pl.* **un·der·pass·es.** a passage or road that goes underneath a bridge or the like.

un·der·pay (un′dər pā′) *v.t.,* **un·der·paid, un·der·pay·ing.** to pay too little or less than deserved.

un·der·pin·ning (un′dər pin′ing) *n.* **1.** the materials or structure used to support or strengthen a building, wall, or the like from below. **2.** anything that supports: *Education is the underpinning of a democracy.*

un·der·priv·i·leged (un′dər priv′ə lijd) *adj.* lacking advantages and/or opportunities because of poverty: *an underprivileged child.*

un·der·rate (un′dər rāt′) *v.t.,* **un·der·rat·ed, un·der·rat·ing.** to rate too low; underestimate: *That player's ability has been underrated by the press.*

un·der·score (*v.,* un′dər skôr′; *n.,* un′dər skôr′) *v.t.,* **un·der·scored, un·der·scor·ing.** to draw a line or lines under; underline. —*n.* a line drawn under a word or words for emphasis or to indicate italics; underline.

un·der·sea (un′dər sē′, un′dər sē′) *adj.* existing, done, or designed for use beneath the surface of the sea: *undersea vegetation, undersea exploration.* —*adv.* also, **under·seas.** beneath the surface of the sea: *to travel undersea in a submarine.*

un·der·sec·re·tar·y (un′dər sek′ri ter′ē) *n., pl.* **un·der·sec·re·tar·ies.** an official who ranks directly below the secretary of a government department.

un·der·sell (un′dər sel′) *v.t.,* **un·der·sold** (un′dər sōld′), **un·der·sell·ing.** to sell at a lower price than (a competitor).

un·der·shirt (un′dər shûrt′) *n.* a shirt with short sleeves or no sleeves, worn under a person's outer clothes.

un·der·shot (un′dər shot′) *adj.* **1.** (of a waterwheel) driven by water passing beneath. **2.** having the lower jaw sticking out beyond the upper jaw: *The bulldog has an undershot jaw.*

un·der·side (un′dər sīd′) *n.* the bottom side or surface.

un·der·signed (un′dər sīnd′) *adj.* **1.** having signed one's name at the end of a document. **2.** signed at the end of a document: *undersigned names.* —*n.* **the undersigned.** the person or persons who have signed a document.

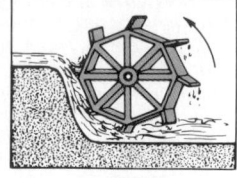

undershot
waterwheel

un·der·sized (un′dər sīzd′) *adj.* having less than the normal or usual size: *an undersized cat.*

un·der·skirt (un′dər skûrt′) *n.* a petticoat worn under a skirt.

un·der·stand (un′dər stand′) *v.,* **un·der·stood, un·der·stand·ing.** —*v.t.* **1.** to grasp the meaning of; be clear about: *I don't understand what you mean.* **2.** to be in sympathy or agreement with: *The two friends understand each other completely.* **3.** to know well; comprehend: *I don't understand Russian.* **4.** to have as an opinion; assume; conclude: *Am I to understand that you are not going to go with us?* **5.** to take as agreed or settled: *I understand that I can return the tickets before the performance and still get my money back.* —*v.i.* **1.** to grasp the meaning of something: *Even though I've explained it several times, they still don't understand.* **2.** to be told or assume: *You are going to Colorado, or so I understand.* **3.** to be sympathetic: *If you are unable to come, I will understand.*

un·der·stand·a·ble (un′dər stan′də bəl) *adj.* able to be understood: *an understandable explanation.* —**un′der·stand′a·bly,** *adv.*

un·der·stand·ing (un′dər stan′ding) *n.* **1.** the grasping of the meaning of something: *a thorough understanding of a situation.* **2.** thorough knowledge or mastery: *The class's understanding of arithmetic pleased the teacher.* **3.** opinion; conclusion: *It was my understanding that you would bring your camera.* **4.** sympathy or agreement: *They finally reached an understanding after their quarrel.* **5.** the ability to understand; intelligence: *That scientist is a person of superior understanding.* —*adj.* feeling or showing sympathy; sympathetic: *an understanding manner.* —**un′der·stand′ing·ly,** *adv.*

un·der·state (un′dər stāt′) *v.t.,* **un·der·stat·ed, un·der·stat·ing.** to tell about or state too weakly or with too little emphasis.

un·der·state·ment (un′dər stāt′mənt) *n.* a statement that tends to make something seem less important or less dramatic than it really is.

un·der·stood (un′dər stood′) *v.* the past tense and past participle of **understand.** —*adj.* **1.** agreed or settled upon: *It's understood, then, that we'll meet at four o'clock.* **2.** omitted but implied in a statement: *In the sentence "I'm willing if you are," the word "willing" is understood after "are."*

un·der·stud·y (un′dər stud′ē) *n., pl.* **un·der·stud·ies.** an actor or other performer who learns someone else's part in order to be a replacement. —*v.,* **un·der·stud·ied, un·der·stud·y·ing.** —*v.t.* **1.** to learn (a part) in order to replace the regular actor or performer. **2.** to act as an understudy to (an actor or performer). —*v.i.* to be an understudy.

un·der·take (un′dər tāk′) *v.t.,* **un·der·took, un·der·tak·en, un·der·tak·ing. 1.** to set about to do: *to undertake a journey by train.* **2.** to agree to or accept (something, as a task): *to undertake a patient's care.*

un·der·tak·er (*def. 1,* un′dər tā′kər; *def. 2,* un′dər tā′kər) *n.* **1.** a person whose job or business is arranging funerals and preparing dead people for burial. **2.** a person who undertakes something, such as a task.

un·der·tak·ing (*def. 1,* un′dər tā′king; *def. 2,* un′dər-tā′king) *n.* **1.** something undertaken, as a task: *Writing a book is a big undertaking.* **2.** the business of an undertaker.

un·der·tone (un′dər tōn′) *n.* **1.** a low tone: *The two friends spoke in an undertone during the movie.* **2.** a feeling or emotion that is partly hidden: *We sensed an undertone of anger in their words.* **3.** a soft color or a color seen through other colors: *The painting has an undertone of blue.*

un·der·took (un′dər tůk′) the past tense of **undertake.**

un·der·tow (un′dər tō′) *n.* a strong current flowing below the surface of the water, in a direction that is opposite to the direction of the surface current.

un·der·val·ue (un′dər val′ū) *v.t.,* **un·der·val·ued, un·der·val·u·ing.** to underestimate or underrate: *Don't undervalue your own ability.*

un·der·wa·ter (un′dər wô′tər) *adj.* lying, used, or performed below the surface of the water: *an underwater plant.* —*adv.* below the surface of the water: *to swim underwater.*

un·der·wear (un′dər wâr′) *n.* clothing worn under a person's outer clothes, usually next to the skin.

un·der·weight (un′dər wāt′) *adj.* weighing too little. —*n.* weight that is below what is normal or desirable.

un·der·went (un′dər went′) the past tense of **undergo.**

un·der·world (un′dər wûrld′) *n.* **1.** the part of society involved in crime, especially organized crime. **2.** also, **Underworld.** the dwelling place of the dead; Hades.

un·der·write (un′dər rīt′) *v.,* **un·der·wrote** (un′dər rōt′), **un·der·writ·ten** (un′dər rit′ən), **un·der·writ·ing.** —*v.t.* **1.** to agree to be responsible for financially; support with money: *to underwrite the production of a play.* **2.** to sign (an insurance policy), and thus take on the obligation to pay for any losses or damage. **3.** to assume financial risk under the terms of an insurance policy; insure. **4.** to agree to buy (an issue of stocks or bonds to be sold to the public) on a specified date and at a specified price. **5.** to write underneath (something). —*v.i.* to act as or carry on the business of an underwriter.

un·der·writ·er (un′dər rī′tər) *n.* **1.** *Insurance.* **a.** a person or company that underwrites insurance. **b.** an employee of an insurance company who determines risks and sets policy rates. **2.** a person or company that underwrites an issue of stocks or bonds.

un·de·served (un′di zûrvd′) *adj.* not deserved: *undeserved punishment.* —**un·de·serv·ed·ly** (un′di zûr′vid-lē), *adv.*

un·de·sir·a·ble (un′di zīr′ə bəl) *adj.* not desirable or pleasing; objectionable: *an undesirable place to live.* —*n.* a person thought to be undesirable. —**un′de·sir′a·bly,** *adv.*

un·de·terred (un′di tûrd′) *adj.* not discouraged from doing something: *undeterred by the threat of punishment.*

un·de·vel·oped (un′di vel′əpt) *adj.* **1.** not completely developed: *undeveloped muscles, undeveloped talent.* **2.** not developed or fully used: *an undeveloped area, undeveloped resources.*

un·did (un did′) the past tense of **undo.**

un·dies (un′dēz) *pl. n. Informal.* underwear, especially women's or children's underpants.

un·dis·cov·ered (un′dis kuv′ərd) *adj.* not discovered: *an undiscovered treasure, undiscovered talent.*

un·dis·guised (un′dis gīzd′) *adj.* not hidden; open; obvious: *undisguised dislike, undisguised affection.*

un·dis·mayed (un′dis mād′) *adj.* not filled with fear or discouragement; not dismayed: *The speaker was undismayed by the audience's lack of interest.*

un·dis·put·ed (un′dis pū′tid) *adj.* not questioned or opposed: *an undisputed claim to an inheritance.*

un·dis·tin·guished (un′dis ting′gwisht) *adj.* not famous or dignified; not distinguished: *an undistinguished writer.*

un·dis·turbed (un′dis tûrbd′) *adj.* not disturbed: *undisturbed peace. We slept undisturbed through the night.*

un·di·vid·ed (un′di vī′did) *adj.* not divided; whole; entire: *to give a speaker one's undivided attention.*

un·do (un dü′) *v.t.,* **un·did, un·done, un·do·ing. 1.** to loosen (a fastening); unfasten; untie: *He undid his necktie.* **2.** to open or unwrap: *She undid the package.* **3.** to do away with or reverse (what has been done): *The fire undid the work of six months. We tried to undo the harm that we had caused.* **4.** to cause the ruin or downfall of; destroy: *Their foolishness has undone them.* —**un·do′er,** *n.*

un·do·ing (un dü′ing) *n.* **1.** a doing away with or reversing of what has been done. **2.** ruin or downfall; destruction: *He brought about his own undoing.* **3.** the cause of ruin or downfall: *Her stubbornness will prove her undoing.* **4.** a loosening or opening.

un·done¹ (un dun′) *adj.* not finished; not done: *to leave a job undone.* [*Un-¹* + *done.*]

un·done² (un dun′) *v.* the past participle of **undo.** —*adj.* unfastened; untied; open.

un·doubt·ed (un dou′tid) *adj.* accepted as true; not doubted. —**un·doubt′ed·ly,** *adv.*

un·dreamed-of (un drēmd′uv′, un drēmd′ov′) *adj.* not thought possible; unimaginable: *undreamed-of riches.* Also, **un·dreamt-of** (un dremt′uv′, un dremt′ov′).

un·dress (un dres′) *v.t.* to remove the clothes or covering from: *The child undressed the doll.* —*v.i.* to remove one's clothes. —*n.* **1.** partial dress or dress not suited for public wear. **2.** casual or informal clothing.

un·due (un dü′, un dū′) *adj.* **1.** going beyond what is necessary; excessive: *to drive with undue speed, to take undue advantage of someone.* **2.** not just, right, or proper: *Eleven o'clock at night is an undue hour to pay a visit.*

un·du·lant (un′jə lənt) *adj.* moving in waves; having a wavy outline or form.

un·du·late (*v.,* un′jə lāt′; *adj.,* un′jə lit, un′jə lāt′) *v.,* **un·du·lat·ed, un·du·lat·ing.** —*v.i.* **1.** to move in waves or like a wave: *The cornstalks undulated in the wind.* **2.** to have a wavy outline, form, or appearance: *The farmer's land undulates across hills and valleys.* —*v.t.* **1.** to cause to move in waves or like a wave. **2.** to give a wavy outline, form, or appearance to. —*adj.* having a wavy outline, form, or appearance, as a leaf. Also, **un·du·lat·ed** (un′jə lā′tid).

un·du·la·tion (un′jə lā′shən) *n.* **1.** a movement in waves; wavelike motion. **2.** a wavy outline, form, or appearance.

un·du·ly (un dü′lē, un dū′lē) *adv.* unnecessarily or excessively: *unduly concerned, unduly critical.*

un·dy·ing (un dī′ing) *adj.* without end; immortal; eternal: *undying devotion.*

un·earned (un ûrnd′) *adj.* **1.** not received for work or service: *unearned income.* **2.** not deserved: *an unearned scolding.* **3.** not yet earned: *unearned interest on savings.*

un·earth (un ûrth′) *v.t.* **1.** to dig up out of the earth: *The dog unearthed its buried bone.* **2.** to bring to light by searching; discover; reveal: *The detective unearthed several new clues.*

un·earth·ly (un ûrth′lē) *adj.* **1.** strange or weird: *an*

at; āpe; fär; câre; end; mē; it; īce; pîerce; hot; ōld; sông, fôrk; oil; out; up; ūse; rüle; půll; tûrn; chin; sing; shop; thin; **th**is; hw in white; zh in treasure. The symbol ə stands for the unstressed vowel sound heard in about, taken, pencil, lemon, and circus.

U

unearthly cry. **2.** not of this world; supernatural: *an unearthly being.* —**un·earth′li·ness,** *n.*

un·eas·y (un ē′zē) *adj.,* **un·eas·i·er, un·eas·i·est. 1.** lacking ease of mind; worried; anxious: *My parents feel uneasy about my staying out so late.* **2.** restless; uncomfortable; tense: *an uneasy sleep.* **3.** embarrassed or awkward: *an uneasy laugh, an uneasy silence.* —**un·eas′i·ly,** *adv.* —**un·eas′i·ness,** *n.*

un·ed·u·cat·ed (un ej′ə kā′tid) *adj.* lacking education, especially formal education; not educated: *an uneducated person.*

un·e·mo·tion·al (un′i mō′shə nəl) *adj.* not showing emotion: *an unemotional individual, an unemotional speech.* —**un′e·mo′tion·al·ly,** *adv.*

un·em·ploy·a·ble (un′em ploi′ə bəl) *adj.* not able to be employed. —*n.* an unemployable person.

un·em·ployed (un′em ploid′) *adj.* **1.** without a job; out of work. **2.** not being put to use: *unemployed talents.* —*n.* **the unemployed.** people out of work.

un·em·ploy·ment (un′em ploi′mənt) *n.* **1.** the state of being unemployed; lack of employment. **2.** the number of people who are out of work: *The government reported a sharp decline in unemployment.*

unemployment insurance, a government program that provides regular payments for a limited period to workers who have lost their jobs.

un·end·ing (un en′ding) *adj.* having or seeming to have no end; endless: *an unending thirst for adventure.*

un·en·force·a·ble (un′en fôr′sə bəl) *adj.* not able to be enforced: *unenforceable laws.*

un·e·qual (un ē′kwəl) *adj.* **1.** not the same: *unequal portions, sleeves of unequal length, unequal opportunities.* **2.** not well or equally matched; unfair: *an unequal partnership, an unequal contest.* **3.** lacking the needed strength or ability; not fit or qualified: *to be unequal to the job.* **4.** not regular or even; uneven: *There was an unequal distribution of heat in the room.* —**un·e′qually,** *adv.*

un·e·qualed (un ē′kwəld) *also, British,* **un·e·qualled.** *adj.* not matched or surpassed; unrivaled: *an unequaled level of talent.*

un·e·quiv·o·cal (un′i kwiv′ə kəl) *adj.* having a meaning that is clear and easily understood; not equivocal: *an unequivocal denial, an unequivocal statement.* —**un′·e·quiv′o·cal·ly,** *adv.*

un·err·ing (un ûr′ing, un er′ing) *adj.* **1.** making no mistakes; faultless: *unerring judgment, unerring good taste.* **2.** not going astray or missing the mark: *the unerring flight of an arrow toward the target.* —**un·err′ing·ly,** *adv.*

un·eth·i·cal (un eth′i kəl) *adj.* not ethical: *unethical conduct. It is unethical for a doctor to refuse to treat a sick person.*

un·e·ven (un ē′vən) *adj.* **1.** not straight: *the uneven hem of a coat.* **2.** not smooth or flat; jagged: *the uneven surface of a rock.* **3.** not of the same kind or quality throughout: *uneven color.* **4.** (of a number) odd: *The numbers 1, 3, 5, and 7 are uneven.* **5.** not well-matched or balanced; unfair; one-sided: *an uneven game.* —**un·e′ven·ly,** *adv.* —**un·e′ven·ness,** *n.*

un·e·vent·ful (un′i vent′fəl) *adj.* without anything important or exciting happening; routine; ordinary: *an uneventful trip.* —**un′e·vent′ful·ly,** *adv.*

un·ex·am·pled (un′eg zam′pəld) *adj.* without like or equal; unparalleled; unique: *unexampled generosity.*

un·ex·cep·tion·a·ble (un′ek sep′shə nə bəl) *adj.* beyond criticism or reproach: *an unexceptionable candidate, unexceptionable behavior.* —**un′ex·cep′tion·a·bly,** *adv.*

un·ex·pect·ed (un′ek spek′tid) *adj.* not expected; coming or happening without warning; unforeseen: *an unexpected delay, unexpected kindness.* —**un′ex·pect′ed·ly,** *adv.* —**un′ex·pect′ed·ness,** *n.*

un·fail·ing (un fā′ling) *adj.* **1.** never weakening or changing; constant: *unfailing devotion.* **2.** always certain; trustworthy: *an unfailing cure.* **3.** never running short or stopping: *an unfailing supply of food.* —**un·fail′ing·ly,** *adv.*

un·fair (un fâr′) *adj.* **1.** not fair or just: *an unfair criticism.* **2.** not following accepted rules or standards: *unfair business practices.* —**un·fair′ly,** *adv.* —**un·fair′ness,** *n.*

un·faith·ful (un fāth′fəl) *adj.* **1.** not truly loyal or devoted; untrustworthy: *an unfaithful friend.* **2.** not true to marriage vows: *an unfaithful spouse.* **3.** not accurate or exact: *an unfaithful translation.* —**un·faith′ful·ly,** *adv.* —**un·faith′ful·ness,** *n.*

un·fa·mil·iar (un′fə mil′yər) *adj.* **1.** not well known or recognizable; strange: *This handwriting is unfamiliar to me.* **2.** not having knowledge of or experience with: *I am unfamiliar with that book.* —**un′fa·mil′iar·ly,** *adv.*

un·fa·mil·i·ar·i·ty (un′fə mil′ē ar′i tē) *n.* a lack of familiarity.

un·fash·ion·a·ble (un fash′ə nə bəl) *adj.* not in fashion; not stylish. —**un·fash′ion·a·bly,** *adv.*

un·fas·ten (un fas′ən) *v.t.* to detach or undo the fastenings of; open: *to unfasten a coat, to unfasten a suitcase.* —*v.i.* to become opened.

un·fath·om·a·ble (un fath′ə mə bəl) *adj.* **1.** that cannot be measured: *the unfathomable depths of the sea.* **2.** that cannot be fully understood: *unfathomable motives.*

un·fath·omed (un fath′əmd) *adj.* **1.** not measured: *The ship sailed over an unfathomed sea.* **2.** not fully understood: *The mystery has remained unfathomed.*

un·fa·vor·a·ble (un fā′vər ə bəl) *adj.* **1.** not in a person's favor; disadvantageous: *We formed an unfavorable impression of the neighborhood.* **2.** not approving; critical: *The play received unfavorable reviews.* **3.** denying something desired or requested; negative: *I received an unfavorable reply to my request.* —**un·fa′vor·a·ble·ness,** *n.* —**un·fa′vor·a·bly,** *adv.*

un·feel·ing (un fē′ling) *adj.* **1.** not showing sympathy or compassion; hardhearted; cruel: *an unfeeling person, unfeeling words.* **2.** not able to feel: *unfeeling trees, an unfeeling statue.* —**un·feel′ing·ly,** *adv.* —**un·feel′ing·ness,** *n.*

un·feigned (un fānd′) *adj.* not pretended; genuine; sincere: *unfeigned enthusiasm.* —**un·feign·ed·ly** (un fā′nid lē), *adv.*

un·fet·ter (un fet′ər) *v.t.* to free from bondage or restraint; liberate.

un·fin·ished (un fin′isht) *adj.* **1.** not brought to an end; not concluded or completed: *an unfinished speech, an unfinished job.* **2.** not finished, as with paint or varnish; not treated or processed; rough: *unfinished furniture, unfinished fabric.*

un·fit (un fit′) *adj.* **1.** not suited to some end or purpose: *This food is unfit to eat.* **2.** not qualified: *unfit for public office.* **3.** in poor condition; unhealthy: *to be unfit for hard work.* —*v.t.,* **un·fit·ted** or **un·fit, un·fit·ting.** to make unfit. —**un·fit′ness,** *n.*

un·flag·ging (un flag′ing) *adj.* not failing; untiring: *unflagging efforts to succeed.* —**un·flag′ging·ly,** *adv.*

un·fledged (un flejd′) *adj.* **1.** lacking knowledge or experience: *an unfledged poet.* **2.** (of a young bird) without feathers needed for flight.

un·flinch·ing (un flin′ching) *adj.* not drawing back or away from danger, pain, or other hardship: *unflinching courage.* —**un·flinch′ing·ly,** *adv.*

un·fold (un fōld′) *v.t.* **1.** to open or spread out (something folded): *to unfold clean sheets for the bed.* **2.** to make known gradually: *The general unfolded a plan of battle.* —*v.i.* **1.** to become open or spread out, as the petals of a flower. **2.** to become known gradually: *The story unfolded in an exciting manner.*

un·forced (un fôrst′) *adj.* **1.** not brought about by force;

voluntary. **2.** not done by an effort; not strained; natural: *an unforced smile.*

un·fore·seen (un'fôr sēn') *adj.* not known or guessed beforehand; unexpected: *unforeseen difficulties.*

un·for·get·ta·ble (un'fər get'ə bəl) *adj.* not to be forgotten; memorable: *an unforgettable experience.* —**un'for·get'ta·bly,** *adv.*

un·for·giv·a·ble (un'fər giv'ə bəl) *adj.* not able to be forgiven: *an unforgivable insult.*

un·formed (un fôrmd') *adj.* **1.** having no definite form; shapeless: *wet, unformed clay.* **2.** not fully developed: *an unformed argument.*

un·for·tu·nate (un fôr'chə nit) *adj.* **1.** having or causing bad luck; unlucky: *an unfortunate traveler, an unfortunate happening.* **2.** improper or unsuitable: *an unfortunate choice of words.* —*n.* a person who is unfortunate. —**un·for'tu·nate·ly,** *adv.*

un·found·ed (un foun'did) *adj.* without basis in fact or reality; groundless: *an unfounded rumor, unfounded superstitions.*

un·fre·quent·ed (un'fri kwen'tid, un frē'kwən tid) *adj.* hardly ever visited: *an unfrequented area of wilderness.*

un·friend·ly (un frend'lē) *adj.,* **un·friend·li·er, un·friend·li·est. 1.** feeling or showing dislike, coldness, or hostility; not friendly: *an unfriendly neighbor, an unfriendly manner.* **2.** not favorable or pleasant: *an unfriendly climate.* —**un·friend'li·ness,** *n.*

un·fruit·ful (un früt'fəl) *adj.* **1.** not producing desired or useful results; unsuccessful: *an unfruitful attempt.* **2.** not producing fruit or offspring; barren: *an unfruitful season, an unfruitful marriage.* —**un·fruit'ful·ness,** *n.*

un·furl (un fûrl') *v.t.* to open or spread out; unroll: *to unfurl a flag.* —*v.i.* to become spread out.

un·fur·nished (un fûr'nisht) *adj.* not furnished, as with furniture: *an unfurnished apartment.*

un·gain·ly (un gān'lē) *adj.,* **un·gain·li·er, un·gain·li·est.** not graceful; awkward; clumsy: *an ungainly puppy.* —**un·gain'li·ness,** *n.*

un·gen·er·ous (un jen'ər əs) *adj.* **1.** not generous; stingy: *an ungenerous person, an ungenerous amount.* **2.** lacking kindness or sympathy: *an ungenerous remark.* —**un·gen'er·ous·ly,** *adv.* —**un·gen'er·ous·ness,** *n.*

un·god·ly (un god'lē) *adj.,* **un·god·li·er, un·god·li·est.** not feeling or showing a reverence for God or religious laws; impious; sinful. —**un·god'll·ness,** *n.*

un·gov·ern·a·ble (un guv'ər nə bəl) *adj.* impossible to control or hold in check; not governable: *an ungovernable mob, an ungovernable temper.* —**un·gov'ern·a·bly,** *adv.*

un·grace·ful (un grās'fəl) *adj.* not graceful; awkward: *ungraceful movements.* —**un·grace'ful·ly,** *adv.* —**un·grace'ful·ness,** *n.*

un·gra·cious (un grā'shəs) *adj.* not kind or courteous; impolite; rude. —**un·gra'cious·ly,** *adv.* —**un·gra'cious·ness,** *n.*

un·gram·mat·i·cal (un'grə mat'i kəl) *adj.* not following the accepted rules or standards of grammar.

un·grate·ful (un grāt'fəl) *adj.* **1.** not thankful for kindness or favors received: *ungrateful for our efforts to help.* **2.** disagreeable; unpleasant: *Telling them that they did not make the team was an ungrateful task.* —**un·grate'ful·ly,** *adv.* —**un·grate'ful·ness,** *n.*

un·ground·ed (un groun'did) *adj.* **1.** without basis in fact or reality: *ungrounded suspicions, ungrounded hopes.* **2.** without knowledge or instruction; not educated: *to be ungrounded in mathematics.*

un·grudg·ing (un gruj'ing) *adj.* without envy or other reservation; wholehearted; unstinting: *to accept a rival's ungrudging praise.* —**un·grudg'ing·ly,** *adv.*

un·guard·ed (un gär'did) *adj.* **1.** without guard or protection: *an unguarded building.* **2.** without caution; careless: *to reveal a secret in an unguarded moment.* —**un·guard'ed·ly,** *adv.* —**un·guard'ed·ness,** *n.*

un·guent (ung'gwənt) *n.* a salve or ointment.

un·gu·late (ung'gyə lit) *adj.* having hoofs. —*n.* a hoofed animal, such as a cow, horse, or sheep.

un·hal·lowed (un hal'ōd) *adj.* **1.** not made holy: *unhallowed ground.* **2.** sinful; wicked.

un·hand (un hand') *v.t.* to release from the grasp; let go.

un·hap·py (un hap'ē) *adj.,* **un·hap·pi·er, un·hap·pi·est. 1.** without happiness or joy; sad: *an unhappy child.* **2.** not fortunate; unlucky: *an unhappy mistake.* **3.** not suitable or appropriate: *an unhappy choice of colors.* —**un·hap'pi·ly,** *adv.* —**un·hap'pi·ness,** *n.*

un·harmed (un härmd') *adj.* not harmed: *to escape from a burning building unharmed.*

un·health·ful (un helth'fəl) *adj.* not good for a person's health. —**un·health'ful·ly,** *adv.* —**un·health'ful·ness,** *n.*

un·health·y (un hel'thē) *adj.,* **un·health·i·er, un·health·i·est. 1.** not in good health, sick; sickly: *an unhealthy condition.* **2.** causing poor health: *an unhealthy climate, unhealthy eating habits.* **3.** harmful to a person's morals; unwholesome: *an unhealthy influence.* —**un·health'i·ly,** *adv.* —**un·health'i·ness,** *n.*

un·heard (un hûrd') *adj.* **1.** not heard: *The child's cries went unheard.* **2.** not given a hearing: *an unheard appeal.*

un·heard-of (un hûrd'uv', un hûrd'ov') *adj.* **1.** outrageous; ridiculous: *unheard-of prices, unheard-of behavior.* **2.** not known or happening before; unknown: *Traveling across the Atlantic Ocean in six hours was unheard-of fifty years ago.*

un·heed·ed (un hē'did) *adj.* not paid attention to; disregarded: *unheeded advice.*

un·hes·i·tat·ing (un hez'i tā'ting) *adj.* without hesitation or delay; immediate; prompt: *an unhesitating reply.* —**un·hes'i·tat'ing·ly,** *adv.*

un·hinge (un hinj') *v.t.,* **un·hinged, un·hing·ing. 1.** to remove from hinges: *The carpenter unhinged the door.* **2.** to throw into confusion or disorder; unsettle: *The shock of the accident unhinged the victim's mind.*

un·hitch (un hich') *v.t.* to set loose; unfasten: *The farmer unhitched the mule from the wagon.*

un·ho·ly (un hō'lē) *adj.,* **un·ho·li·er, un·ho·li·est. 1.** not holy; unhallowed: *unholy ground.* **2.** sinful; wicked; immoral. **3.** *Informal.* dreadful; terrible: *The children made an unholy racket building the doghouse.* —**un·ho'li·ness,** *n.*

un·hook (un hùk') *v.t.* **1.** to remove from a hook: *to unhook a fish.* **2.** to unfasten the hooks of. —*v.i.* to become unhooked.

un·hoped-for (un hōpt'fôr') *adj.* not expected or anticipated: *unhoped-for success.*

un·horse (un hôrs') *v.t.,* **un·horsed, un·hors·ing.** to throw (a rider) from a horse.

un·hur·ried (un hûr'ēd) *adj.* without haste; not hurried: *We ate an unhurried meal.* —**un·hur'ried·ly,** *adv.*

un·hurt (un hûrt') *adj.* not hurt: *to be unhurt by a fall.*

uni– *combining form* only one; single: *unicellular.*

u·ni·cam·er·al (ū'ni kam'ər əl) *adj.* having or made up of one legislative chamber or house: *The state of Nebraska has a unicameral legislature.*

---

at; āpe; fär; câre; end; mē; it; īce; pîerce; hot; ōld; sông, fôrk; oil; out; up; ūse; rüle; pùll; tûrn; chin; sing; shop; thin; **th**is; hw in white; zh in treasure. The symbol ə stands for the unstressed vowel sound heard in about, taken, pencil, lemon, and circus.

U

u·ni·cel·lu·lar (ū′nə sel′yə lər) *adj.* having or consisting of a single cell: *The ameba is a unicellular animal.*

u·ni·corn (ū′ni kôrn′) *n.* a legendary animal usually represented in art as a white horse with a long, pointed horn in the middle of its forehead.

unicycles

u·ni·cy·cle (ū′nə sī′kəl) *n.* a vehicle made up of a single wheel and operated by foot pedals, often having a seat or bar mounted on a shaft. It is used chiefly by acrobats, entertainers, and gymnasts.

un·i·den·ti·fied (un′ī den′tə fīd′) *adj.* that has not been identified; unknown: *An unidentified person was seen leaving the building.*

unidentified flying object, something seen in the sky that cannot be identified or explained. Also, **UFO.**

u·ni·fi·ca·tion (ū′nə fi kā′shən) *n.* the act of unifying or the state of being unified.

u·ni·form (ū′nə fôrm′) *adj.* **1.** without change; always the same; unvarying: *The house is heated at a uniform temperature. The walls of the room are painted a uniform color.* **2.** showing little or no difference: *All the houses in the neighborhood are uniform in design.* —*n.* the special or official clothes worn by the members of a group: *a nurse's white uniform.* —*v.t.* to provide with a uniform: *One police officer was uniformed, while the other wore civilian clothes.* —**u′ni·form′ly,** *adv.* —**u′ni·form′ness,** *n.*

u·ni·form·i·ty (ū′nə fôr′mi tē) *n., pl.* **u·ni·form·i·ties.** the state, quality, or instance of being uniform: *uniformity of appearance.*

u·ni·fy (ū′nə fī′) *v.t.,* **u·ni·fied, u·ni·fy·ing.** to combine or make into a whole; cause to be one; unite: *A common language and culture unified the people of the country.* —**u′ni·fi′er,** *n.*

u·ni·lat·er·al (ū′nə lat′ər əl) *adj.* of, affecting, or done by one person or group only: *a unilateral withdrawal of troops.* —**u′ni·lat′er·al·ly,** *adv.*

un·i·mag·i·na·ble (un′i maj′ə nə bəl) *adj.* unable to be imagined; hard to imagine: *unimaginable wealth.* —**un′i·mag′i·na·bly,** *adv.*

un·i·mag·i·na·tive (un′i maj′ə nə tiv) *adj.* not having imagination or creativity: *an unimaginative play, an unimaginative writer.* —**un′i·mag′i·na·tive·ly,** *adv.*

un·im·peach·a·ble (un′im pē′chə bəl) *adj.* not to be called into question; above reproach or blame; faultless: *an unimpeachable reputation.* —**un′im·peach′a·bly,** *adv.*

un·im·por·tant (un′im pôr′tənt) *adj.* not having any special value or meaning; not important: *an unimportant incident, an unimportant mistake.* —**un′im·port′ance,** *n.*

un·in·hab·it·ed (un′in hab′i tid) *adj.* not lived in: *The old house has been uninhabited for years.*

un·in·hib·it·ed (un′in hib′i tid) *adj.* lacking or having few inhibitions: *an uninhibited expression of joy.* —**un′in·hib′i·ted·ly,** *adv.*

un·in·spired (un′in spīrd′) *adj.* not having originality, imagination, or creativity; not inspired; dull: *an uninspired performance.*

un·in·tel·li·gi·ble (un′in tel′i jə bəl) *adj.* not capable of being made out or understood: *unintelligible handwriting.* —**un′in·tel′li·gi·bil′i·ty,** *n.* —**un′in·tel′li·gi·bly,** *adv.*

un·in·ten·tion·al (un′in ten′shə nəl) *adj.* not done on purpose. —**un′in·ten′tion·al·ly,** *adv.*

un·in·ter·est·ed (un in′tris tid, un in′tə res′tid) *adj.* not interested; unconcerned; indifferent.

▲ **Uninterested** means "not interested." **Disinterested** means "impartial," or "not taking sides in something": *to be uninterested in the hockey game* means to have no interest in the game; *to be a disinterested observer of the hockey game* means not to care which team wins.

un·in·ter·est·ing (un in′tris ting, un in′tə res′ting) *adj.* not interesting: *I found the book uninteresting.*

un·in·ter·rupt·ed (un′in tə rup′tid) *adj.* without interruption; unbroken; continuous. —**un′in·ter·rupt′ed·ly,** *adv.*

un·in·vit·ed (un′in vī′tid) *adj.* not invited: *an uninvited guest.*

un·in·vit·ing (un′in vī′ting) *adj.* not tempting or attractive: *The stale cake looked uninviting.*

un·ion (ūn′yən) *n.* **1.** the act of uniting or the state of being united: *the union of two companies through a merger.* **2.** something formed by uniting two or more things: *The Confederacy was a union of southern states.* **3.** an association of workers organized to protect and further the interests of its members; labor union. **4. the Union. a.** the United States of America. **b.** those states that remained a part of the federal government during the Civil War. **5.** the act of marrying or the state of being married; marriage. **6.** the emblem on a flag symbolizing unity, such as the three crosses on the British flag or the blue rectangle covered with stars on the U.S. flag. **7.** *Mathematics.* a set made up of all the elements of two or more sets, without repetition of any element. Union is represented by the symbol ∪. For the sets {1,2,3} and {3,4,7}, ∪ = {1,2,3,4,7}. **8.** a coupling device for connecting machinery parts, such as pipes or rods.

un·ion·ism (ūn′yə niz′əm) *n.* **1.** the support of or belief in a union or unions or membership in a union, especially a labor union. **2. Unionism.** support of the federal government during the Civil War.

un·ion·ist (ūn′yə nist) *n.* **1.** a person who belongs to a labor union or believes in unionism. **2. Unionist.** a supporter of the federal government during the Civil War.

un·ion·ize (ūn′yə nīz′) *v.t.,* **un·ion·ized, un·ion·iz·ing. 1.** to organize into a union; cause to join a union: *to unionize workers.* **2.** to put under the rules of a union: *to unionize an industry.* —**un′ion·i·za′tion,** *n.*

union jack 1. *usually,* **Union Jack.** the flag of the United Kingdom. **2.** any flag that consists of the emblem from a national flag.

union shop, a factory or business in which employees either belong to a union or are required to join a union within a certain period after they are hired.

u·nique (ū nēk′) *adj.* **1.** not having an equal; being unsurpassed: *a unique achievement.* **2.** being the only one of its kind; single; sole: *Each person is a unique individual.* **3.** *Informal.* highly unusual, rare, or noteworthy; remarkable: *a unique experience.* —**u·nique′ly,** *adv.* —**u·nique′ness,** *n.*

▲ **Unique** originally meant "one of a kind," and therefore it could not be logically qualified with words such as *more* or *most: Franklin D. Roosevelt's election to the presidency for four terms is unique.* However, because there are very few things that are only one of a kind, many people now use *unique* to mean "highly unusual" or "remarkable'' with a qualifying adverb: *This situation is very unique. That style of painting is quite unique.*

u·ni·sex (ū′nə seks′) *adj.* making no distinction as to sex; suitable for both males and females: *a unisex haircut salon, unisex clothing.*

u·ni·son (ū′nə sən, ū′nə zən) *n.* **1.** complete or perfect agreement. **2.** *Music.* sameness in pitch, as of two or more tones or voices: *The altos and tenors sang in unison.* [From the Middle French word *unison* meaning ''a note that has the same pitch as another,'' from the Medieval Latin word *unisonus* meaning ''having the same sound,'' going back to the Latin word *unus* ''one'' and *sonus* ''sound.'']

u·nit (ū′nit) *n.* **1.** a single person, thing, or group, especially one that is a basic part of a larger group: *a medical unit of an army. Each apartment building contains fifty dwelling units.* **2.** a piece of equipment having a special purpose: *a refrigeration unit.* **3.** any fixed quantity or amount that is considered as a standard of measurement: *An hour is a unit of time. A kilometer is a unit of length.* **4.** *Mathematics.* the smallest whole number; one.

U·ni·tar·i·an (ū′ni târ′ē ən) *n.* **1.** *also,* **unitarian.** a person who does not believe in the doctrine of the Trinity or the divinity of Jesus, but who believes instead that God exists as one being. **2.** a member of a denomination holding these beliefs. —*adj.* of or relating to Unitarians or Unitarianism.

U·ni·tar·i·an·ism (ū′ni târ′ē ə niz′əm) *n.* the beliefs of Unitarians.

u·ni·tar·y (ū′ni ter′ē) *adj.* **1.** of or relating to a unit or units: *unitary measure.* **2.** like a unit.

u·nite (ū nīt′) *v.,* **u·nit·ed, u·nit·ing.** —*v.t.* to bring or put together: *The two families were united by marriage.* —*v.i.* **1.** to be brought together; join together: *The countries united to form a single nation.* **2.** to join together for a common purpose: *All the towns in the county united in an effort to improve education.*

u·nit·ed (ū ni′tid) *adj.* **1.** brought or put together; joined together: *united in opposition to legislation.* **2.** of, formed by, or produced by joint action: *a united effort.* **3.** in agreement or harmony. —**u·nit′ed·ly,** *adv.* —**u·nit′ed·ness,** *n.*

United Nations, an international organization, founded in 1945, including as members most of the nations of the world. It seeks to maintain world peace, promote cooperation among nations, and encourage respect for international law. Its headquarters are located in New York City, in Manhattan.

unit price, a price, especially of a grocery item, given as the cost for some standard unit of measurement, such as per ounce or per pound. It is used for cost comparison of products sold in packages of different sizes.

unit pricing, a way of pricing foods that shows not only the total price but also a unit price.

u·ni·ty (ū′ni tē) *n., pl.* **u·ni·ties. 1.** the state or fact of being one. **2.** the state or quality of being in harmony or agreement: *a unity of purpose.* **3.** the arrangement of the parts in a work of art or literature to produce a single design or effect. **4.** *Mathematics.* the number one.

univ. 1. universal. **2.** universally. **3.** university.

u·ni·valve (ū′nə valv′) *n.* a mollusk whose shell is made up of a single part, or valve, such as the snail. —*adj.* having a single shell.

u·ni·ver·sal (ū′nə vûr′səl) *adj.* **1.** of or shared by all: *There was universal joy when the war ended.* **2.** existing everywhere or affecting everything: *It is a universal law of physics that all atoms are constantly in motion.*

U·ni·ver·sal·ist (ū′nə vûr′sə list) *n.* a person who belongs to a denomination that teaches that all human beings will be saved.

u·ni·ver·sal·i·ty (ū′nə vər sal′i tē) *n., pl.* **u·ni·ver·sal·i·ties.** the state or quality of being universal.

universal joint, a coupling that allows the parts it connects to move in any direction, especially one that transmits rotary motion from one shaft to another not in line with it.

universal joint

u·ni·ver·sal·ly (ū′nə vûr′sə lē) *adv.* in a universal manner; in every instance or place; without exception: *The new documentary film was universally praised by audiences and by the critics.*

Universal Product Code, a code consisting of a series of bars that can be read by an automatic scanning device. The bars carry such information as the name and price of the product bearing the code.

u·ni·verse (ū′nə vûrs′) *n.* **1.** all that exists, including the earth, the heavens, and all of space; entire physical world. **2.** an area or sphere of activity in its totality. **3.** *Mathematics.* a set that contains all the objects or sets under consideration at any one time. Also *(def. 3),* **universal set.**

u·ni·ver·si·ty (ū′nə vûr′si tē) *n., pl.* **u·ni·ver·si·ties.** an institution of higher education, usually including one or more colleges and graduate and professional schools.

un·just (un just′) *adj.* not fair or moral; not just: *an unjust decision.* —**un·just′ly,** *adv.* —**un·just′ness,** *n.*

un·jus·ti·fi·a·ble (un jus′tə fī′ə bəl) *adj.* that cannot be justified. —**un·jus′ti·fi′a·bly,** *adv.*

un·kempt (un kempt′) *adj.* **1.** not combed or groomed: *shaggy, unkempt hair.* **2.** not neat or clean in appearance: *an unkempt room.*

un·kind (un kīnd′) *adj.* not kind; cruel: *an unkind remark.* —**un·kind′ness,** *n.*

un·kind·ly (un kīnd′lē) *adv.* in an unkind manner: *to treat a stranger unkindly.* —*adj.* unkind; cruel.

un·know·a·ble (un nō′ə bəl) *adj.* not able to be known; not knowable.

un·known (un nōn′) *adj.* **1.** not part of a person's knowledge; unfamiliar: *That actor's name is unknown to me.* **2.** not discovered or identified: *an unknown island.* —*n.* a person or thing that is unknown.

un·lace (un lās′) *v.t.,* **un·laced, un·lac·ing.** to undo the laces of.

un·latch (un lach′) *v.t.* to unfasten or open by releasing a latch: *to unlatch a door.* —*v.i.* to become unlatched.

un·law·ful (un lô′fəl) *adj.* against the law; illegal: *an unlawful act.* —**un·law′ful·ly,** *adv.* —**un·law′ful·ness,** *n.*

un·lead·ed (un led′id) *adj.* not containing lead compounds, which can contribute to air pollution when burned: *unleaded gasoline.*

un·learn (un lûrn′) *v.t.,* **un·learned** or **un·learnt** (un·lûrnt′), **un·learn·ing.** to rid the mind of (something learned); forget.

un·learn·ed (*def. 1,* un lûr′nid; *def. 2,* un lûrnd′) *adj.* **1.** not having or showing much knowledge or education: *an unlearned child who could not read.* **2.** not gotten by learning or study: *an unlearned sense of direction.*

un·leash (un lēsh′) *v.t.* **1.** to let loose from a leash: *to unleash a dog.* **2.** to let loose: *The hurricane unleashed its fury.*

un·leav·ened (un lev′ənd) *adj.* not made with any leav-

---

at; āpe; fär; câre; end; mē; it; īce; pîerce; hot; ōld; sông, fôrk; oil; out; up; ūse; rüle; pùll; tûrn; chin; sing; shop; thin; this; hw in white; zh in treasure. The symbol ə stands for the unstressed vowel sound heard in about, taken, pencil, lemon, and circus.

U

ening agent, such as yeast: *to eat unleavened bread during Passover.*

un·less (un les′) *conj.* except on the condition that; if not: *Unless you return the books that you have, you cannot borrow any more.*

un·let·tered (un let′ərd) *adj.* **1.** not educated; ignorant: *an unlettered beginner.* **2.** not able to read or write; illiterate.

un·li·censed (un lī′sənst) *adj.* **1.** having no license: *an unlicensed driver.* **2.** done without permission; unauthorized: *unlicensed behavior.*

un·like (un līk′) *prep.* **1.** different from: *Unlike some of my friends, I enjoy dancing.* **2.** not typical of: *It is unlike you to be rude.* —*adj.* not the same or equal; different: *A deer and a mouse are unlike animals.* —**un·like′ness**, *n.*

un·like·ly (un līk′lē) *adj.*, **un·like·li·er, un·like·li·est.** **1.** not likely: *It is unlikely that it will rain today.* **2.** not likely to succeed; unpromising: *That is an unlikely scheme.* —**un·like′li·ness**, *n.*

un·lim·it·ed (un lim′i tid) *adj.* without limits or restrictions: *This pass gives you unlimited use of the pool all summer.*

un·lined (un līnd′) *adj.* without lines: *a sheet of unlined paper.*

un·list·ed (un lis′tid) *adj.* not included on a list; not listed: *an unlisted telephone number.*

un·load (un lōd′) *v.t.* **1.** to take off (a load): *The workers unloaded freight from the ship.* **2.** to remove a load from: *The driver unloaded the truck.* **3.** to remove ammunition from (a firearm): *to unload a gun.* **4.** to give expression to: *to unload one's troubles.* **5.** *Informal.* to get rid of; dispose of: *We unloaded the old furniture at an auction.* —*v.i.* to discharge a load: *The ship unloaded in Boston.*

un·lock (un lok′) *v.t.* **1.** to open or undo the lock of: *This key will unlock the door.* **2.** to open or release as if by undoing a lock: *to unlock a grip on someone's arm.* **3.** to furnish a solution to; disclose: *to unlock a mystery.* —*v.i.* to become unlocked.

un·looked–for (un lukt′fôr′) *adj.* not expected.

un·loose (un lüs′) *v.t.*, **un·loosed, un·loos·ing.** **1.** to let loose; set free; release: *to unloose a bird from its cage.* **2.** to relax; loosen: *The sailor unloosed the tight hold on the rope.*

un·loos·en (un lü′sən) *v.t.* another word for **unloose.**

un·luck·y (un luk′ē) *adj.*, **un·luck·i·er, un·luck·i·est.** **1.** not having good luck; unfortunate: *an unlucky contestant.* **2.** marked by or causing bad luck: *Last year was an unlucky season for the team. Some people believe that thirteen is an unlucky number.* —**un·luck′i·ly**, *adv.* —**un·luck′i·ness**, *n.*

un·man (un man′) *v.t.*, **un·manned, un·man·ning.** to make less strong or manly; weaken; discourage.

un·man·age·a·ble (un man′i jə bəl) *adj.* not able to be managed or controlled: *an unmanageable puppy.*

un·manned (un mand′) *adj.* without a crew: *an unmanned spacecraft.*

un·man·ner·ly (un man′ər lē) *adj.* having or showing bad manners; rude: *an unmannerly outburst of harsh language.* —*adv.* impolitely; rudely. —**un·man′ner·li·ness**, *n.*

un·mar·ried (un mar′ēd) *adv.* not married.

un·mask (un mask′) *v.t.* **1.** to remove a mask or disguise from. **2.** to reveal the true nature of; expose: *The newspaper reporter unmasked the plot.* —*v.i.* to remove one's mask or disguise.

un·mean·ing (un mē′ning) *adj.* **1.** without meaning; senseless: *unmeaning utterances.* **2.** showing no intelligence; vacant: *an unmeaning expression on one's face.*

un·meet (un mēt′) *adj.* not fit, proper, or suitable.

un·men·tion·a·ble (un men′shə nə bəl) *adj.* not fit for discussion; shameful: *an unmentionable disgrace.*

un·mer·ci·ful (un mûr′si fəl) *adj.* having or showing no mercy; merciless; cruel: *unmerciful punishment.* —**un·mer′ci·ful·ly**, *adv.* —**un·mer′ci·ful·ness**, *n.*

un·mind·ful (un mīnd′fəl) *adj.* not aware or careful; heedless; forgetful: *to be unmindful of what other people might think.* —**un·mind′ful·ly**, *adv.*

un·mis·tak·a·ble (un′mis tā′kə bəl) *adj.* that cannot be mistaken; obvious; plain: *an unmistakable note of anger in someone's voice.* —**un′mis·tak′a·bly**, *adv.*

un·mit·i·gat·ed (un mit′i gā′tid) *adj.* **1.** not lessened or softened; not made less intense: *unmitigated cold, unmitigated fear.* **2.** downright; thorough; utter: *an unmitigated liar.*

un·mor·al (un môr′əl, un mor′əl) *adj.* not having or interested in moral standards; amoral. —**un·mor′al·ly**, *adv.*

un·moved (un müvd′) *adj.* **1.** not moved. **2.** not affected or disturbed: *to be unmoved by an urgent plea.*

un·named (un nāmd′) *adj.* not named.

un·nat·u·ral (un nach′ər əl) *adj.* **1.** going against or different from the usual in nature; not natural: *The cat grew to an unnatural size.* **2.** shocking to natural feelings; monstrous; inhuman: *unnatural cruelty.* **3.** not genuine; contrived; artificial: *an unnatural smile.* —**un·nat′u·ral·ly**, *adv.* —**un·nat′u·ral·ness**, *n.*

un·nec·es·sar·y (un nes′ə ser′ē) *adj.* not needed; needless: *unnecessary trifles.* —**un·nec′es·sar′i·ly**, *adv.*

un·nerve (un nûrv′) *v.t.*, **un·nerved, un·nerv·ing.** to take away the courage or self-control of; make less calm: *The lawyer's questions unnerved the witness.*

un·nil·en·ni·um (ū′nə len′ē əm) *n.* a proposed name for the artificially produced radioactive element with atomic number 109. Proposed symbol: **Une**

un·nil·hex·i·um (ū′nəl hek′sē əm) *n.* a proposed name for the artificially produced radioactive element with atomic number 106. Also, **element 106.** Proposed symbol: **Unh** [Formed from the Latin words *unus* meaning ''one'' + *nil* meaning ''nothing, zero'' + the Greek word *hex* meaning ''six.'' The atomic number of this element is 106.]

un·nil·oc·ti·um (ū′nə lok′tē′əm) *n.* a proposed name for the artificially produced radioactive element with atomic number 108. Proposed symbol: **Uno**

un·nil·pen·ti·um (ū′nəl pen′tē əm) *n.* see **hahnium.** [Formed from the Latin words *unus* meaning ''one'' + *nil* meaning ''nothing, zero'' + the Greek word *pente* meaning ''five.'' The atomic number of this element is 105.]

un·nil·qua·di·um (ū′nəl kwod′ē əm) *n.* see **rutherfordium.** [Formed from the Latin words *unus* meaning ''one'' + *nil* meaning ''nothing, zero'' + the prefix *quadri-* meaning ''four.'' The atomic number of this element is 104.]

un·nil·sep·ti·um (ū′nəl sep′tē əm) *n.* a proposed name for the artificially produced radioactive element with atomic number 107. Also, **element 107.** Proposed symbol: **Uns**

un·num·bered (un num′bərd) *adj.* **1.** not marked with a number or numbers: *unnumbered pages.* **2.** countless: *There are unnumbered stars in the sky.*

un·ob·served (un′əb zûrvd′) *adj.* **1.** not noticed or perceived: *to slip into the house unobserved.* **2.** not complied with or obeyed: *an unobserved law.* **3.** not kept: *an unobserved holiday.*

un·ob·tru·sive (un′əb trü′siv) *adj.* that does not cause notice or disturbance; inconspicuous: *plain, unobtrusive clothing.* —**un′ob·tru′sive·ly**, *adv.* —**un′ob·tru′sive·ness**, *n.*

un·oc·cu·pied (un ok′yə pīd′) *adj.* **1.** without an occupant; vacant: *an unoccupied apartment.* **2.** not held by troops or enemy forces: *unoccupied territory.* **3.** not busy; unemployed; idle: *an unoccupied salesclerk.*

un·of·fi·cial (un′ə fish′əl) *adj.* not official: *an unofficial announcement.* —**un′of·fi′cial·ly,** *adv.*

un·o·pened (un ō′pənd) *adj.* not opened: *an unopened package.*

un·op·posed (un′ə pōzd′) *adj.* not opposed: *The district attorney was unopposed in campaigning for reelection.*

un·or·gan·ized (un ôr′gə nīzd′) *adj.* **1.** not formed into an orderly arrangement or whole; not organized: *The club is still unorganized.* **2.** not organized into a union: *The workers in that plant are unorganized.*

un·or·tho·dox (un ôr′thə doks′) *adj.* going against accepted beliefs, opinions, customs, or doctrines; not orthodox: *unorthodox teachings, unorthodox behavior.*

un·pack (un pak′) *v.t.* **1.** to empty the contents of: *to unpack a suitcase.* **2.** to remove from a container or packaging: *I unpacked the glassware from the box.* **3.** to remove a pack or burden from; unload: *to unpack a mule.* —*v.i.* to unpack something, such as luggage.

un·paid (un pād′) *adj.* **1.** not yet paid: *unpaid wages, an unpaid fine.* **2.** serving without pay; unsalaried: *an unpaid volunteer.*

un·par·al·leled (un par′ə leld′) *adj.* without equal; matchless; unsurpassed: *an unparalleled achievement.*

un·par·don·a·ble (un pär′də nə bəl) *adj.* not able to be excused or forgiven: *an unpardonable act of cruelty.*

un·pas·teur·ized (un pas′chə rīzd′) *adj.* not pasteurized: *unpasteurized milk.*

un·pa·tri·ot·ic (un pā′trē ot′ik) *adj.* not showing patriotism; not patriotic.

un·pin (un pin′) *v.t.,* **un·pinned, un·pin·ning. 1.** to remove a pin or pins from. **2.** to open, loose, or unfasten by removing a pin or pins: *to unpin a hem.*

un·pleas·ant (un plez′ənt) *adj.* not pleasing; offensive; disagreeable: *an unpleasant odor.* —**un·pleas′ant·ly,** *adv.*

un·pleas·ant·ness (un plez′ənt nis) *n.* **1.** the condition or quality of being unpleasant. **2.** something unpleasant, such as a quarrel.

un·plug (un plug′) *v.t.,* **un·plugged, un·plug·ging. 1.** to remove the plug of (an electrical appliance) from an outlet; disconnect: *to unplug a toaster.* **2.** to remove a stopper or other blockage: *to unplug a sink.*

un·pol·lut·ed (un′pə lü′tid) *adj.* not polluted, as by wastes: *The river was clear and unpolluted.*

un·pop·u·lar (un pop′yə lər) *adj.* not generally liked or accepted; not popular: *to hold unpopular opinions.* —**un·pop′u·lar·ly,** *adv.*

un·pop·u·lar·i·ty (un′pop yə lar′i tē) *n.* the state or condition of being unpopular.

un·prac·ticed (un prak′tist) *also, British,* **un·prac·tised.** *adj.* **1.** lacking experience, practice, or skill: *an unpracticed lawyer.* **2.** not put into practice: *to try an unpracticed technique.*

un·prec·e·dent·ed (un pres′i den′tid) *adj.* not known or done before; without parallel or precedent: *The first landing on the moon was an unprecedented event.*

un·pre·dict·a·ble (un′pri dik′tə bəl) *adj.* not able to be predicted: *The weather is unpredictable at this time of year.* —**un′pre·dict′a·ble·ness,** *n.* —**un′pre·dict′a·bly,** *adv.*

un·prej·u·diced (un prej′ə dist) *adj.* without prejudice; unbiased.

un·pre·med·i·tat·ed (un′prē med′i tā′tid) *adj.* not planned or thought out beforehand; not premeditated.

un·pre·pared (un′pri pârd′) *adj.* **1.** not ready; not prepared: *to be unprepared for a test.* **2.** that has not been prepared beforehand: *The mayor gave an unprepared speech.*

un·pre·pos·sess·ing (un′prē pə zes′ing) *adj.* not making a good impression: *to seem awkward and unprepossessing at first sight.*

un·pre·ten·tious (un′pri ten′shəs) *adj.* not pretentious; modest; simple: *an unpretentious compact car.* —**un′pre·ten′tious·ly,** *adv.* —**un′pre·ten′tious·ness,** *n.*

un·prin·ci·pled (un prin′sə pəld) *adj.* having or showing a lack of moral principles; unscrupulous: *The unprincipled rascal tried to cheat everyone.*

un·print·a·ble (un prin′tə bəl) *adj.* not fit for publication.

un·pro·fes·sion·al (un′prə fesh′ə nəl) *adj.* **1.** going against the standards or rules of a profession: *A scientist who claims false facts is guilty of unprofessional conduct.* **2.** not relating to, characteristic of, or connected with a profession: *an unprofessional opinion, an unprofessional performance.* —**un′pro·fes′sion·al·ly,** *adv.*

un·prof·it·a·ble (un prof′i tə bəl) *adj.* **1.** not useful or rewarding; fruitless: *an unprofitable meeting.* **2.** producing no financial profit: *The failing business is unprofitable.* —**un·prof′it·a·bly,** *adv.*

un·qual·i·fied (un kwol′ə fīd′) *adj.* **1.** not having the necessary or proper qualifications; unfit: *unqualified to vote, unqualified to practice medicine.* **2.** not limited or restricted: *The writer's first novel was an unqualified success.*

un·quench·a·ble (un kwen′chə bəl) *adj.* **1.** not able to be satisfied: *an unquenchable thirst.* **2.** not able to be put out: *an unquenchable fire.*

un·ques·tion·a·ble (un kwes′chə nə bəl) *adj.* beyond doubt or question: *The judge is a person of unquestionable fairness.* —**un·ques′tion·a·bly,** *adv.*

un·ques·tioned (un kwes′chənd) *adj.* not open to or called into question; not doubted: *unquestioned fact.*

un·qui·et (un kwī′it) *adj.* **1.** marked by or causing an uneasy feeling; anxious: *unquiet thoughts.* **2.** marked by unrest, disturbance, or disorder: *unquiet times.* —**un·qui′et·ly,** *adv.* —**un·qui′et·ness,** *n.*

un·quote (un kwōt′) *v.i.,* **un·quot·ed, un·quot·ing.** to close or end a quotation.

▲ **Unquote** is used with *quote* in speech to show when another person is being quoted. The words *quote* and *unquote* before and after a statement have the same function as quotation marks do in writing. For example: *They said, quote, "We had no knowledge of the plan," unquote, but I don't think they are telling the truth.*

un·rav·el (un rav′əl) *v.,* **un·rav·eled, un·rav·el·ing;** *also, British,* **un·rav·elled, un·rav·el·ling.** —*v.t.* **1.** to separate or untangle the threads of; to unravel a ball of yarn. **2.** to separate and make clear the parts of; solve; reveal: *We tried to unravel the plot of the story.* —*v.i.* to become unraveled.

un·read (un red′) *adj.* **1.** not yet read: *an unread manuscript.* **2.** having little or no education; ignorant: *an unread person.*

un·read·y (un red′ē) *adj.* not ready.

un·re·al (un rē′əl) *adj.* not real; imaginary; fictitious.

un·re·al·is·tic (un′rē ə lis′tik) *adj.* **1.** not according to reality: *an unrealistic painting.* **2.** not practical: *an unrealistic attitude.*

un·re·al·i·ty (un′rē al′i tē) *n., pl.* **un·re·al·i·ties. 1.** the state or quality of being unreal. **2.** an unreal thing, fact, or event; something unreal: *ghosts and other unrealities.*

un·rea·son·a·ble (un rē′zə nə bəl, un rēz′nə bəl) *adj.* **1.** not showing or using good sense or judgment; not reasonable: *It is unreasonable to insist on going first all the time.* **2.** going beyond what is moderate; excessive:

---

at; āpe; fär; câre; end; mē; it; īce; pîerce; hot; ōld; sông, fôrk; oil; out; up; ūse; rüle; pull; tûrn; chin; sing; shop; thin; this; hw in white; zh in treasure. The symbol ə stands for the unstressed vowel sound heard in about, taken, pencil, lemon, and circus.

U

1031

The prices at that restaurant are unreasonable. **—un·rea′son·a·ble·ness,** *n.* **—un·rea′son·a·bly,** *adv.*

un·rea·son·ing (un rē′zə ning, un rēz′ning) *adj.* not showing or controlled by reason: *unreasoning anger.* **—un·rea′son·ing·ly,** *adv.*

un·re·cord·ed (un′ri kôr′did) *adj.* not recorded.

un·re·fined (un′ri fīnd′) *adj.* 1. not made free of impurities: *unrefined petroleum.* 2. not cultured: *an unrefined person.*

un·re·gen·er·ate (un′ri jen′ər it) *adj.* 1. not morally or spiritually reborn: *an unregenerate sinner.* 2. resisting change; stubborn: *an unregenerate advocate of old ways of doing things.*

un·re·lent·ing (un′ri len′ting) *adv.* 1. not changing, yielding, or softening, as from pity; harsh: *to be unrelenting in one's criticism.* 2. not lessening or easing, as in intensity, effort, or speed: *That job involves unrelenting pressure.* **—un′re·lent′ing·ly,** *adv.*

un·re·li·a·ble (un′ri lī′ə bəl) *adj.* not to be trusted; untrustworthy: *If you don't finish your work, you'll be called unreliable.* **—un′re·li·a·bil′i·ty, un′re·li·a·ble·ness,** *n.* **—un′re·li·a·bly,** *adv.*

un·re·mit·ting (un′ri mit′ing) *adj.* never ceasing; constant: *unremitting effort to reach the goal.* **—un′re·mit′ting·ly,** *adv.*

un·re·quit·ed (un′ri kwī′tid) *adj.* not returned in kind: *unrequited love.*

un·re·served (un′ri zûrvd′) *adj.* 1. done or given without reservation or restriction; unqualified; full: *unreserved approval.* 2. free from reserve; candid; open: *an unreserved manner.* **—un·re·serv·ed·ly** (un′ri zûr′vid lē) *adv.*

un·rest (un rest′) *n.* restlessness; dissatisfaction; discontent: *political unrest over higher taxes.*

un·re·strained (un′ri strānd′) *adj.* not held in check or under control; not restrained: *loud, unrestrained laughter.* **—un·re·strain·ed·ly** (un′ri strā′nid lē) *adv.*

un·ripe (un rīp′) *adj.* 1. not fully ripened or developed; immature: *unripe peaches.* 2. not ready; unprepared: *The child was unripe for such weighty responsibilities.* **—un·ripe′ness,** *n.*

un·ri·valed (un rī′vəld) *also, British,* **un·ri·valled.** *adj.* having no rival or equal; matchless; supreme: *unrivaled beauty.*

un·roll (un rōl′) *v.t.* 1. to open, spread out, or expand (something rolled up): *to unroll a sleeping bag.* 2. to unfold; display; reveal: *to unroll a new plan.* **—v.i.** to become unrolled.

un·ruf·fled (un ruf′əld) *adj.* not ruffled or disturbed: *unruffled waters, an unruffled state of mind.*

un·ruled (un rüld′) *adj.* 1. not controlled or governed: *an unruled temper.* 2. not marked with lines: *unruled paper.*

un·ru·ly (un rü′lē) *adj.,* **un·ru·li·er, un·ru·li·est.** difficult to control or manage: *unruly hair, an unruly crowd.* **—un·ru′li·ness,** *n.*

un·sad·dle (un sad′əl) *v.t.,* **un·sad·dled, un·sad·dling.** 1. to remove the saddle from (a horse). 2. to cause to fall from a horse; unhorse.

un·safe (un sāf′) *adj.* not safe: *Those narrow mountain roads are unsafe.*

un·said (un sed′) *v.* the past tense and past participle of **unsay.** **—adj.** not spoken or expressed: *Some things are better left unsaid.*

un·san·i·tar·y (un san′i ter′ē) *adj.* not clean or sanitary.

un·sat·is·fac·to·ry (un′sat is fak′tə rē) *adj.* not good enough to meet a need or desire; not satisfactory: *unsatisfactory work.* **—un′sat·is·fac′to·ri·ly,** *adv.*

un·sat·is·fied (un sat′is fīd′) *adj.* not satisfied: *an unsatisfied thirst.*

un·sat·u·rat·ed (un sach′ə rā′tid) *adj.* 1. *Chemistry.* (of a solution) that can dissolve more of a substance; not saturated. 2. (of a compound) that can join with other elements without giving up original components. 3. (of a fat) containing more than one double bond in its carbon chain. Unsaturated fats tend to be liquid in form and most often come from plant sources.

un·sa·vor·y (un sā′və rē) *also, British,* **un·sa·vour·y.** *adj.* 1. unpleasant to the taste or smell: *spoiled and unsavory meat.* 2. morally bad: *an unsavory reputation.* 3. having no flavor; tasteless. **—un·sa′vor·i·ness,** *n.*

un·say (un sā′) *v.t.,* **un·said, un·say·ing.** to take back or cancel (what has been said).

un·scathed (un skāthd′) *adj.* in no way harmed or hurt; uninjured: *to walk away from an accident unscathed.*

un·sci·en·tif·ic (un′sī ən tif′ik) *adj.* not based on or using the principles and methods of science; not scientific: *Astrology is unscientific.* **—un′sci·en·tif′i·cal·ly,** *adv.*

un·scram·ble (un skram′bəl) *v.t.,* **un·scram·bled, un·scram·bling.** to make sense out of or put in order: *I tried to unscramble the mess I found in the desk drawer.*

un·screw (un skrü′) *v.t.* 1. to loosen, unfasten, or remove by turning: *to unscrew the top from a tube of toothpaste.* 2. to remove the screw or screws from. **—v.i.** to become unscrewed: *The lid of this jar unscrews easily.*

un·scru·pu·lous (un skrü′pyə ləs) *adj.* showing no regard for what is right or wrong; without scruples: *The unscrupulous merchant overcharged us.* **—un·scru′pu·lous·ly,** *adv.* **—un·scru′pu·lous·ness,** *n.*

un·seal (un sēl′) *v.t.* 1. to break or remove the seal of: *to unseal an envelope.* 2. to free from some constraining influence.

un·search·a·ble (un sûr′chə bəl) *adj.* not able to be searched or explored; mysterious. **—un·search′a·bly,** *adv.*

un·sea·son·a·ble (un sē′zə nə bəl) *adj.* 1. not characteristic of or right for the season: *Such warm weather is unseasonable for December.* 2. not done, happening, or coming at the right or proper time: *Midnight is an unseasonable hour to visit someone.* **—un·sea′son·a·ble·ness,** *n.* **—un·sea′son·a·bly,** *adv.*

un·sea·soned (un sē′zənd) *adj.* 1. not flavored with seasoning: *unseasoned food.* 2. not disciplined or experienced: *unseasoned workers.* 3. not properly aged: *unseasoned wood.*

un·seat (un sēt′) *v.t.* 1. to remove from a seat, especially to throw from a saddle: *The horse unseated its rider.* 2. to remove from an office or position: *to unseat a corrupt judge.*

un·seem·ly (un sēm′lē) *adj.,* **un·seem·li·er, un·seem·li·est.** not right or proper for the time or place: *It is unseemly to tell a joke during a funeral service.* **—adv.** in an unseemly manner. **—un·seem′li·ness,** *n.*

un·seen (un sēn′) *adj.* 1. not noticed or observed: *to come into a room unseen.* 2. not visible: *an unseen ghostly presence.*

un·self·ish (un sel′fish) *adj.* not selfish; generous: *The unselfish children shared their toys with each other.* **—un·self′ish·ly,** *adv.* **—un·self′ish·ness,** *n.*

un·set·tle (un set′əl) *v.t.,* **un·set·tled, un·set·tling.** 1. to trouble or upset; confuse; disturb: *The bad experience unsettled our confidence.* 2. to change or move; displace; disrupt.

un·set·tled (un set′əld) *adj.* 1. not peaceful, calm, or orderly; disturbed; disrupted: *Unsettled conditions followed the great flood.* 2. not determined or decided; unresolved: *an unsettled question.* 3. not paid or settled: *an unsettled debt.* 4. not occupied, inhabited, or populated: *an unsettled region of the frontier.*

un·shak·a·ble (un shā′kə bəl) *also,* **un·shake·a·ble.** *adj.* not easily weakened or shaken; firm: *an unshakable conviction.*

un·shak·en (un shā′kən) *adj.* not shaken: *unshaken faith.*

un·sheathe (un shēth′) *v.t.,* **un·sheathed, un·sheath·ing.** to draw from a sheath or scabbard; bare: *to unsheathe a sword.*

un·shod (un shod′) *adj.* without shoes: *an unshod horse.*

un·sight·ly (un sīt′lē) *adj.,* **un·sight·li·er, un·sight·li·est.** unpleasant to the sight: *Unsightly litter was strewn about the city park.* **—un·sight′li·ness,** *n.*

un·skilled (un skild′) *adj.* **1.** lacking skill, training, or experience: *an unskilled actor.* **2.** not needing skill or training: *an unskilled job.* **3.** showing a lack of skill: *an unskilled drawing.*

un·skill·ful (un skil′fəl) *also, British,* **un·skil·ful.** *adj.* not having or showing skill; not skillful; clumsy: *unskillful handling of a delicate situation.* **—un·skill′ful·ly,** *adv.* **—un·skill′ful·ness,** *n.*

un·snap (un snap′) *v.t.,* **un·snapped, un·snap·ping.** to undo the snap or snaps of; unfasten.

un·snarl (un snärl′) *v.t.* to free from a snarl or snarls: *to unsnarl hair by gentle combing.*

un·so·cia·ble (un sō′shə bəl) *adj.* not liking to be with others; not friendly: *an unsociable person.* **—un·so′cia·ble·ness,** *n.* **—un·so′cia·bly,** *adv.*

un·so·phis·ti·cat·ed (un′sə fis′ti kā′tid) *adj.* **1.** not having worldly knowledge and experience; lacking worldliness; naive: *an unsophisticated youth.* **2.** not complex; simple: *an unsophisticated mechanical device.* **—un′so·phis′ti·cat′ed·ly,** *adv.* **—un′so·phis′ti·ca′tion,** *n.*

un·sought (un sôt′) *adj.* not asked for or expected; not sought: *unsought help, an unsought prize.*

un·sound (un sound′) *adj.* **1.** not strong or solid; weak: *The foundation of the house is unsound and may crumble.* **2.** not based on truth, fact, or good judgment; not accurate or sensible: *unsound advice.* **3.** physically or mentally unhealthy; diseased: *unsound teeth.* **4.** not stable or safe; not reliable: *to make an unsound investment.* **—un·sound′ly,** *adv.* **—un·sound′ness,** *n.*

un·spar·ing (un spâr′ing) *adj.* **1.** very generous; lavish: *unsparing efforts.* **2.** unmerciful; harsh; severe: *unsparing criticism.* **—un·spar′ing·ly,** *adv.*

un·speak·a·ble (un spē′kə bəl) *adj.* **1.** not able to be described or expressed in words: *unspeakable pleasure.* **2.** extremely bad or evil: *an unspeakable act, unspeakable behavior.* **—un·speak′a·bly,** *adv.*

un·spoiled (un spoild′) *adj.* not spoiled: *The scenery along the road is unspoiled by billboards or signs.*

un·spo·ken (un spō′kən) *adj.* not described or expressed in words; not spoken: *an unspoken agreement.*

un·sports·man·like (un spôrts′mən līk′) *adj.* not having or showing such qualities or characteristics as fair play and the ability to accept defeat graciously.

un·spot·ted (un spot′id) *adj.* **1.** not marked by spots: *The glassware came out of the dishwasher unspotted.* **2.** without moral fault or defect: *an unspotted reputation.*

un·sta·ble (un stā′bəl) *adj.* **1.** not firmly fixed; easily moved; not stable: *an unstable platform, an unstable chair.* **2.** not settled or steady in character; apt to change: *an unstable government.* **3.** emotionally unsettled or troubled: *an unstable person.* **4.** *Chemistry.* readily changed into another compound, element, or isotope. **—un·sta′ble·ness,** *n.* **—un·sta′bly,** *adv.*

un·stead·y (un sted′ē) *adj.* **1.** not firm; shaky: *The ladder is unsteady.* **2.** not kept at an even rate: *Gasoline prices have been unsteady.* **3.** changeable in habits or behavior; not reliable: *a nervous and unsteady worker.* **—un·stead′i·ly,** *adv.* **—un·stead′i·ness,** *n.*

un·stop (un stop′) *v.t.,* **un·stopped, un·stop·ping.** **1.** to remove a stopper from: *to unstop a bottle of wine.* **2.** to free from something that blocks: *to unstop a drain.*

un·strap (un strap′) *v.t.,* **un·strapped, un·strap·ping.** to remove, unfasten, or loosen the strap or straps of: *to unstrap a saddle.*

un·stressed (un strest′) *adj.* not stressed in speech: *an unstressed syllable.*

un·string (un string′) *v.t.,* **un·strung, un·string·ing.** **1.** to remove or loosen the string or strings of: *to unstring a violin.* **2.** to remove from a string: *to unstring beads.* **3.** to upset emotionally; unnerve: *We were unstrung by the confusion.*

un·stud·ied (un stud′ēd) *adj.* not forced or contrived; natural: *unstudied friendliness.*

un·sub·stan·tial (un′səb stan′shəl) *adj.* **1.** not firm, strong, or solid: *unsubstantial fabric.* **2.** without material substance or form; unreal. **—un′sub·stan′tial·ly,** *adv.*

un·suc·cess·ful (un′sək ses′fəl) *adj.* not meeting with success; not successful: *an unsuccessful attempt, an unsuccessful artist.* **—un′suc·cess′ful·ly,** *adv.*

un·suit·a·ble (un sü′tə bəl) *adj.* not suitable or fit for the time or occasion: *Light clothing is unsuitable for cold weather.* **—un·suit′a·bly,** *adv.*

un·suit·ed (un sü′tid) *adj.* not suited or fit: *A weak person is unsuited for heavy physical labor.*

un·sul·lied (un sul′ēd) *adj.* not stained or soiled; not sullied: *an unsullied reputation.*

un·sung (un sung′) *adj.* **1.** not honored or celebrated: *unsung heroes.* **2.** not sung.

un·sup·port·ed (un′sə pôr′tid) *adj.* **1.** not held up: *an unsupported roof.* **2.** not provided for: *an unsupported family.* **3.** not receiving backing: *an unsupported political view.* **4.** not shown to be true; not verified: *an unsupported statement.*

un·sure (un shŭr′) *adj.* not sure: *to be unsure of one's chances.*

un·sus·pect·ed (un′sə spek′tid) *adj.* **1.** not under suspicion. **2.** not imagined or thought of: *an unsuspected talent.*

un·sus·pect·ing (un′sə spek′ting) *adj.* having no suspicion; trusting. **—un′sus·pect′ing·ly,** *adv.*

un·sym·met·ri·cal (un′si met′ri kəl) *adj.* not balanced or symmetrical; asymmetrical: *an unsymmetrical design.* **—un′sym·met′ri·cal·ly,** *adv.*

un·sym·pa·thet·ic (un′sim pə thet′ik) *adj.* not feeling or showing sympathy; not sympathetic: *to be unsympathetic to the problems of others.*

un·tan·gle (un tang′gəl) *v.t.,* **un·tan·gled, un·tan·gling.** **1.** to free from a tangle or tangles. **2.** to clear up; explain: *The police tried to untangle the mystery surrounding the kidnapping.*

un·taught (un tôt′) *adj.* **1.** not gotten by learning or teaching; natural: *an untaught art, an untaught talent.* **2.** not instructed or educated; ignorant.

un·ten·a·ble (un ten′ə bəl) *adj.* that cannot be supported or defended: *an untenable theory, an untenable position.*

un·thank·ful (un thangk′fəl) *adj.* not grateful or thankful.

un·think·a·ble (un thing′kə bəl) *adj.* not able to be thought of or considered: *It is unthinkable that all disease will be wiped out.*

un·think·ing (un thing′king) *adj.* **1.** showing or marked by carelessness or thoughtlessness: *an unthinking remark.* **2.** lacking the ability to think: *an unthinking beast.* **—un·think′ing·ly,** *adv.*

un·thought–of (un thôt′uv′, un thôt′ov′) *adj.* not thought of or imagined: *an unthought-of possibility.*

---

at; āpe; fär; câre; end; mē; it; īce; pierce; hot; ōld; sông, fôrk; oil; out; up; ūse; rüle; pull; tûrn; chin; sing; shop; thin; this; hw in white; zh in treasure. The symbol ə stands for the unstressed vowel sound heard in about, taken, pencil, lemon, and circus.

U

un·ti·dy (un tī′dē) *adj.*, **un·ti·di·er, un·ti·di·est.** not neat or orderly; messy: *an untidy desk.* —**un·ti′di·ly,** *adv.* —**un·ti′di·ness,** *n.*

un·tie (un tī′) *v.*, **un·tied, un·ty·ing.** —*v.t.* **1.** to loosen or undo (something knotted or tied): *to untie a knot.* **2.** to free: *to untie a person's hands.* —*v.i.* to become untied.

un·til (ən til′, un til′) *prep.* **1.** up to the time of: *Wait until evening before you telephone your cousin.* **2.** before: *Tickets are not available until Wednesday.* —*conj.* **1.** up to the time when: *Wait here until I get back.* **2.** before: *The store couldn't deliver the furniture until the snow melted and the roads were clear.* **3.** to the place, extent, or degree that: *Keep driving straight until you reach the intersection.* ▲ **Until** and **till** may be used interchangeably.

un·time·ly (un tīm′lē) *adj.* **1.** coming or happening before the right or usual time: *an untimely death.* **2.** coming or happening at the wrong time: *an untimely visit.* —*adv.* at a bad time or too soon. —**un·time′li·ness,** *n.*

un·tir·ing (un tīr′ing) *adj.* not tiring; persistent: *untiring patience, untiring efforts.* —**un·tir′ing·ly,** *adv.*

un·to (un′tü) *prep.* Archaic. to.

un·told (un tōld′) *adj.* **1.** too great or too many to be counted or measured: *untold suffering, untold numbers.* **2.** not told: *an untold adventure.*

un·touch·a·ble (un tuch′ə bəl) *adj.* **1.** forbidden to the touch. **2.** beyond criticism: *an untouchable masterpiece.* **3.** out of reach. **4.** disagreeable or dangerous to the touch. —*n.* also, **Untouchable.** in India, a member of the lowest caste, whose touch was formerly thought to defile members of higher castes.

un·touched (un tucht′) *adj.* **1.** not touched. **2.** not used or eaten: *The food remained untouched.* **3.** not moved: *How can anyone remain untouched by their sufferings?*

un·to·ward (un tôrd′, un′tə wôrd′) *adj.* **1.** marked by or causing trouble; unfortunate: *an untoward comment.* **2.** difficult to manage or control; unruly: *an untoward child.*

un·tried (un trīd′) *adj.* **1.** not proved or tested, as by experience or use: *an untried worker, an untried machine.* **2.** not brought before a court of law for judgment: *an untried case.*

un·trod (un trod′) *adj.* not walked on: *untrod paths.*

un·true (un trü′) *adj.* **1.** not true; incorrect; false: *an untrue remark.* **2.** not faithful or loyal: *to be untrue to one's friends.* **3.** not measured correctly; not accurate. —**un·tru′ly,** *adv.*

un·truth (un trüth′) *n.* **1.** something untrue; lie. **2.** the quality or condition of being untrue; falsity.

un·truth·ful (un trüth′fəl) *adj.* **1.** not truthful; not true: *an untruthful remark.* **2.** given to lying: *an untruthful person.* —**un·truth′ful·ly,** *adv.* —**un·truth′ful·ness,** *n.*

un·tu·tored (un tü′tərd, un tü′tərd) *adj.* not educated; untaught.

un·twine (un twīn′) *v.*, **un·twined, un·twin·ing.** —*v.t.* to undo (something twined or tangled). —*v.i.* to become untwined.

un·twist (un twist′) *v.t.* to undo (something twisted). —*v.i.* to become untwisted: *The rope untwisted by itself.*

un·used (*defs. 1 and 2,* un ūzd′; *def. 3,* un ūst′) *adj.* **1.** not in use; not put to use: *an unused shelf in a bookcase.* **2.** never having been used; new; fresh: *an unused postage stamp, an unused toothbrush.* **3.** not accustomed: *to be unused to the quiet of the country.*

un·u·su·al (un ū′zhü əl) *adj.* not usual, common, or ordinary; rare: *Seeing an eclipse is an unusual experience.* —**un·u′su·al·ly,** *adv.* —**un·u′su·al·ness,** *n.*

un·ut·ter·a·ble (un ut′ər ə bəl) *adj.* too deep or great to be put into words: *unutterable joy.*

un·var·nished (un vär′nisht) *adj.* **1.** not covered with varnish. **2.** stated without embellishment; plain; unadorned: *the unvarnished truth.*

un·veil (un vāl′) *v.t.* to remove a veil or covering from: *The sculptor unveiled a new statue.* —*v.i.* to remove a veil.

un·voiced (un voist′) *adj.* **1.** not stated: *an unvoiced objection.* **2.** (of a consonant) spoken without vibration of the vocal cords, such as the *t* sound in *toll.*

un·war·rant·ed (un wôr′ən tid, un wor′ən tid) *adj.* without basis; unjustified: *an unwarranted opinion.*

un·war·y (un wâr′ē) *adj.* not watchful or careful; careless: *The dishonest storekeeper cheated the unwary customer.* —**un·war′i·ly,** *adv.* —**un·war′i·ness,** *n.*

un·wel·come (un wel′kəm) *adj.* not received with pleasure; not welcome: *an unwelcome guest.*

un·well (un wel′) *adj.* not well; ill; sick.

un·wept (un wept′) *adj.* **1.** not mourned. **2.** (of tears) not shed.

un·whole·some (un hōl′səm) *adj.* **1.** harmful to the body; unhealthy: *an unwholesome diet.* **2.** harmful to morals: *unwholesome entertainment.* —**un·whole′some·ly,** *adv.* —**un·whole′some·ness,** *n.*

un·wield·y (un wēl′dē) *adj.* difficult to handle, manage, or use; cumbersome: *an unwieldy package.* —**un·wield′i·ness,** *n.*

un·will·ing (un wil′ing) *adj.* **1.** not wanting to do or be something; not willing; reluctant: *to be unwilling to go on a trip.* **2.** not done, said, or given readily: *unwilling testimony.* —**un·will′ing·ly,** *adv.* —**un·will′ing·ness,** *n.*

un·wind (un wīnd′) *v.*, **un·wound, un·wind·ing.** —*v.t.* **1.** to undo or reverse the winding of; unroll: *The nurse unwound the bandages.* **2.** to straighten or untangle the twisted parts of: *to unwind a tangle of string.* —*v.i.* **1.** to become unrolled or untangled. **2.** to become free from tension; relax: *to unwind by reading a good book.*

un·wise (un wīz′) *adj.* showing a lack of wisdom or good sense; not wise; foolish: *It is unwise to leave the door unlocked.* —**un·wise′ly,** *adv.*

un·wit·ting (un wit′ing) *adj.* not knowing; unaware: *an unwitting accomplice to a crime.* —**un·wit′ting·ly,** *adv.*

un·wont·ed (un wôn′tid, un wōn′tid, un wun′tid) *adj.* not customary; unusual: *The rookie played with unwonted poise.* —**un·wont′ed·ly,** *adv.*

un·world·ly (un wûrld′lē) *adj.* devoted to spiritual matters instead of to the interests or pleasures of this world. —**un·world′li·ness,** *n.*

un·wor·thy (un wûr′the) *adj.* **1.** not worthy or deserving: *I feel unworthy of such praise.* **2.** not suiting or becoming: *Such cruel remarks were unworthy of a friend.* —**un·wor′thi·ly,** *adv.* —**un·wor′thi·ness,** *n.*

un·wound (un wound′) the past tense and past participle of **unwind.**

un·wrap (un rap′) *v.*, **un·wrapped, un·wrap·ping.** —*v.t.* to remove a wrapping from; open; undo: *to unwrap a package.* —*v.i.* to become unwrapped.

un·writ·ten (un rit′ən) *adj.* **1.** not written or put in writing: *unwritten testimony.* **2.** accepted by custom; traditional: *an unwritten law.*

un·yield·ing (un yēl′ding) *adj.* not giving way; firm: *to be unyielding in one's demands.*

un·yoke (un yōk′) *v.t.*, **un·yoked, un·yok·ing.** **1.** to release from a yoke: *to unyoke an ox.* **2.** to separate; part.

up (up) *adv.* **1.** from a lower or higher place, level, or position: *to climb up to the top of the ladder, to look up to see the airplane.* **2.** in, on, or to a higher place: *Put the dishes up on the top shelf. They are spending the summer up in the mountains.* **3.** to a higher point or degree: *My weight went up during the summer. Please turn the sound up on the television.* **4.** above the surface

or horizon: *The diver came up for air. The sun came up at six o'clock.* **5.** in or to an upright position: *Sit up straight.* **6.** out of bed: *I got up at seven o'clock.* **7.** in or into a closed state: *Button up your coat. The bird was shut up in a cage.* **8.** in the lead; ahead: *That team is two games up in the pennant race.* **9.** for each side; apiece: *The score is four up.* **10.** in a northern direction; north: *From Virginia, we drove up to Pennsylvania.* —*adj.* **1.** going upward: *Take the up escalator.* **2.** at a higher point or degree: *Prices are up again this month.* **3.** risen above the horizon: *The sun is up.* **4.** awake or out of bed: *They won't be up until nine o'clock.* **5.** being presented or considered: *The house is up for sale. The mayor is up for reelection.* **6.** at an end: *Your time is up.* **7.** ahead: *Our team is two games up.* **8.** *Baseball.* at bat. **9.** *Informal.* going on: *What's up?* —*prep.* to or toward a place higher or farther along: *The spider climbed up the wall. The motorboat went up the river.* —*n.* **1.** an upward movement; ascent: *the ups and downs of a roller coaster ride.* **2.** a change for the good; time of good fortune: *the ups and downs of life.* —*v.t.,* **upped, up-ping.** to make higher or larger; increase: *The store has upped prices on many items during the past year.*
   •**up against.** facing; confronting: *The team is up against great odds.*
   •**up on.** *Informal.* well-informed about: *to be up on current events.*
   •**up to. a.** *Informal.* about to do: *What are you up to?* **b.** as far as: *What chapter is the teacher up to in the book?* **c.** capable of; equal to: *Are you up to such an important job?* **d.** dependent upon, as for a decision: *It is up to you to make the change.*

up-and-com-ing (up'ən kum'ing) *adj.* likely to succeed; promising: *an up-and-coming young actor.*

up-beat (up'bēt') *n. Music.* an unaccented beat, especially the last beat of a measure, indicated by an upward movement of the conductor's hand.

up-braid (up brād') *v.t.* to scold harshly: *The parents upbraided the children for not doing their chores.*

up-bring-ing (up'bring'ing) *n.* the care and training received during childhood and youth: *a strict upbringing.*

UPC, Universal Product Code.

up-coun-try (up'kun'trē) *also,* **up-coun-try.** *n.* the interior of a region or country. —*adj.* of or coming from the upcountry. —*adv.* toward or in the upcountry.

up-date (*v.,* up dāt', up'dāt'; *n.,* up'dāt') *v.t.,* **up-dat-ed, up-dat-ing. 1.** to make current or up-to-date: *to update a history textbook by adding new information.* **2.** to inform (someone) of current facts or recent events: *Please update me on the latest developments.* —*n.* **1.** an act of updating: *An update on the weather is broadcast every hour.* **2.** up-to-date information; an up-to-date report or version: *Give me an update on family happenings.*

up-draft (up'draft') *n.* an upward movement of air.

up-end (up end') *v.t.* to set, stand, or turn on end: *to upend an empty cup.* —*v.i.* to become upended.

up-front (up'frunt') *adj.* **1.** *Informal.* outspoken and direct: *to be up-front about a disagreement.* **2.** paid in advance: *an up-front fee for services.*

up-grade (*v.,* up grād', up'grād'; *n.,* up'grād') *v.t.,* **up-grad-ed, up-grad-ing.** to raise to a higher grade or standard: *The manufacturing firm decided to upgrade its products.* —*n.* **1.** an upward slope, as of a hill or road. **2.** an improved version or model: *an upgrade of a software program.*
   •**on the upgrade.** becoming better; improving: *My marks in history are on the upgrade.*

up-heav-al (up hē'vəl) *n.* **1.** the act of upheaving or the state of being upheaved: *the upheaval of the ground during an earthquake.* **2.** an instance of this. **3.** a violent disturbance or change: *social upheavals.*

up-heave (up hēv') *v.,* **up-heaved, up-heav-ing.** —*v.t.* to lift or throw up, as by force or pressure from beneath. —*v.i.* to be lifted, thrown, or forced up.

up-held (up held') the past tense and past participle of **uphold.**

up-hill (up'hil') *adj.* **1.** going upward on a hill; directed or sloping upward: *We took the uphill path.* **2.** presenting difficulties; hard: *Winning the championship was an uphill battle for the team.* —*adv.* up a hill; upward: *to ride a bicycle uphill.*

up-hold (up hōld') *v.t.,* **up-held, up-hold-ing. 1.** to support, approve, or agree with: *to speak out for principles that one upholds.* **2.** to keep from falling; hold up: *The posts uphold the porch roof.* —**up-hold'er,** *n.*

up-hol-ster (up hōl'stər, ə pōl'stər) *v.t.* to fit with padding, cushions, or coverings: *to upholster a sofa.*

up-hol-ster-er (up hōl'stər ər, ə pōl'stər ər) *n.* a person whose work is upholstering furniture.

up-hol-ster-y (up hōl'stə rē, ə pōl'stə rē) *n., pl.* **up-hol-ster-ies. 1.** material used in upholstering. **2.** the business or craft of upholstering.

up-keep (up'kēp') *n.* **1.** the keeping of something in good condition; maintenance: *Money is needed for the upkeep of the city parks.* **2.** the cost of such maintenance: *The upkeep on the estate is very high.*

up-land (up'lənd, up'land') *n. also,* **uplands.** land that is on a higher level than the land surrounding it. —*adj.* of, relating to, or located on such land.

up-lift (*v.,* up lift'; *n.,* up'lift') *v.t.* **1.** to raise to a higher moral or social level: *It is uplifting to help those in need.* **2.** to lift up; elevate. —*n.* **1.** the act, process, or result of lifting up. **2.** a movement to improve the moral or social level of a person, group, or community.

up-most (up'mōst') *adj.* another word for **uppermost.**

up-on (ə pôn', ə pon') *prep.* on.

up-per (up'ər) *adj.* **1.** higher: *the upper story of a house, the upper register of a voice.* **2.** (of places) on higher ground, farther north, or farther inland: *the upper towns of a state.* —*n.* the part of a shoe or boot above the sole.

up-per-case (up'ər kās') *adj.* of, relating to, or printed or written in capital letters. —*v.t.,* **up-per-cased, up-per-cas-ing.** to set in or print with capital letters.

upper case, in printing, capital letters.

up-per-class (up'ər klas') *adj.* of or relating to the upper class.

upper class, the portion of society occupying the highest social and economic position, above the middle class and lower class.

up-per-cut (up'ər kut') *n.* a blow in boxing directed upward from beneath, as to an opponent's chin. —*v.t.,* **up-per-cut, up-per-cut-ting.** to strike (an opponent) with an uppercut.

upper hand, a position of control; advantage: *Our team easily gained the upper hand in the last part of the game.*

upper house *also,* **Upper House.** in a legislature having two branches, the smaller and less representative branch, such as the Senate in the U.S. Congress.

up-per-most (up'ər mōst') *adj.* **1.** highest: *the uppermost floors of a building.* **2.** having the most importance; foremost: *to be uppermost in someone's thoughts.* Also,

---

at; āpe; fär; câre; end; mē; it; īce; pîerce; hot; ōld; sông; fôrk; oil; out; up; ūse; rüle; pùll; tûrn; chin; sing; shop; thin; this; hw in white; zh in treasure. The symbol ə stands for the unstressed vowel sound heard in about, taken, pencil, lemon, and circus.

U

upmost. —*adv.* in the highest or most important place, position, or rank.

up·pi·ty (up'i tē) *adj. Informal.* displaying an attitude of exaggerated self-importance; snobbish.

up·raise (up rāz') *v.t.,* **up·raised, up·rais·ing.** to raise or lift up.

up·right (up'rīt') *adj.* **1.** in a vertical position; straight up; erect: *an upright column.* **2.** having or showing good character and high morals: *an upright person.* —*n.* something in a vertical position, as an upright timber or beam. —*adv.* in a vertical position: *to place a chair upright.* —**up'right·ly,** *adv.* —**up'right·ness,** *n.*

upright piano, a piano having the strings arranged vertically in a rectangular case.

up·rise (up rīz') *v.i.,* **up·rose, up·ris·en** (up riz'ən), **up·ris·ing.** **1.** to arise or get up. **2.** to rise to a higher position, as from below the horizon.

up·ris·ing (up'rī'zing) *n.* a revolt against a government or other authority; rebellion.

up·roar (up'rôr') *n.* **1.** a state of noisy or confused excitement, disorder, or agitation: *The class was in an uproar.* **2.** the sound of this:

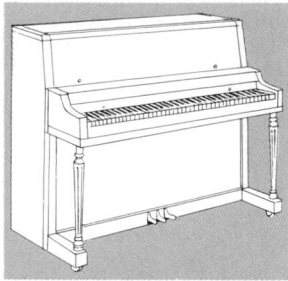

upright piano

We heard an uproar coming from around the corner.

up·roar·i·ous (up rôr'ē əs) *adj.* **1.** making, causing, or marked by an uproar: *The brave explorers were given an uproarious welcome.* **2.** loud, noisy, and unrestrained: *The room filled with uproarious laughter.* **3.** causing hearty laughter; hilarious: *an uproarious comedy.* —**up·roar'i·ous·ly,** *adv.* —**up·roar'i·ous·ness,** *n.*

up·root (up rüt', up rut') *v.t.* **1.** to tear or pull up by the roots: *The tractor uprooted the bushes.* **2.** to cause to leave familiar surroundings; displace: *The flood uprooted many families.* **3.** to remove or destroy completely; eliminate: *to uproot the source of the disease.*

an **uprooted** tree

up·rose (up rōz') the past tense of **uprise.**

up·set (*v., adj.,* up set'; *n.,* up'set') *v.t.,* **up·set, up·set·ting.** **1.** to turn, tip, or knock over; topple; capsize: *I accidentally upset the pitcher of lemonade.* **2.** to throw into confusion or disorder: *The unexpected delay upset my plans.* **3.** to make anxious or uneasy; distress: *Bad news upset the family.* **4.** to disturb physically; make sick: *Overeating at the party upset my stomach.* **5.** to defeat unexpectedly: *The novice tennis player upset the club champion.* —*adj.* **1.** turned, tipped, or knocked

over: *The upset glass of water spilled all over me.* **2.** confused or disordered: *an upset train schedule.* **3.** anxious or uneasy; distressed: *I was upset about missing the plane.* **4.** physically disturbed; made sick: *an upset stomach.* —*n.* **1.** the defeat of an opponent favored to win: *The young tennis player's victory in the final was quite an upset.* **2.** a throwing into confusion or disorder: *Delay caused an upset of our plans.* **3.** anxiety; distress. **4.** physical disturbance: *a stomach upset.* **5.** a turning, tipping, or knocking something over.

up·shot (up'shot') *n.* the final result; conclusion; outcome.

up·side down (up'sīd') **1.** in such a way that the upper side or part becomes the under or lower side or part: *You are holding the map upside down.* **2.** in or into complete disorder or confusion: *I turned my room upside down looking for the keys.*

up·si·lon (ūp'sə lon', up'sə lon') *n.* the twentieth letter of the Greek alphabet (Υ, υ).

up·stage (up'stāj') *adv.* at or toward the rear of a stage. —*adj.* of or relating to the rear of a stage. —*v.t.,* **up·staged, up·stag·ing.** **1.** to draw audience attention away from (another actor) to oneself. **2.** to draw attention to oneself at the expense of (another): *to upstage someone with a funny remark.*

up·stairs (up'stârz') *adv.* **1.** toward the top of a staircase; up the stairs: *to run upstairs.* **2.** on or to an upper floor or level: *They are watching television upstairs.* —*adj.* of, relating to, or located on an upper floor or floors: *an upstairs apartment.* —*n.* the upper floor or floors: *The upstairs of the house is not yet finished.*

up·stand·ing (up stan'ding) *adj.* honest in character and behavior; respectable; honorable: *a fine, upstanding member of the community.*

up·start (up'stärt') *n.* **1.** a person who is bold and conceited. **2.** a person of humble origins who suddenly becomes wealthy or important and, often, behaves in an arrogant way toward others; parvenu.

up·state (up'stāt') *adj.* of or relating to that part of a state lying farther inland or north of a large city: *We took a vacation in upstate New York.* —*adv.* in, to, or toward such a region: *We plan to drive upstate for the weekend.*

up·stream (up'strēm') *adv.* toward or at the source of a stream; against the current: *to fish upstream, to row a boat upstream.* —*adj.* toward or at a point upstream.

up·surge (up'sûrj') *n.* a sudden increase or rise: *There was an upsurge of interest in politics in the town around election time.* —*v.i.,* **up·surged, up·surg·ing.** to surge up; increase; rise.

up·swing (up'swing') *n.* **1.** an upward swing or movement. **2.** a marked increase or improvement, as in activity: *Business in that growing town is on the upswing.*

up·take (up'tāk') *n.* **1.** *Informal.* understanding; comprehension: *to be quick on the uptake.* **2.** a flue or shaft for drawing up air or smoke, as from a mine.

up·tight (up'tīt') *adj. Slang.* **1.** tense; uneasy; anxious: *I was uptight over the math test this afternoon.* **2.** overly strict, formal, or conventional; straitlaced: *uptight manners.*

up–to–date (up'tə dāt') *adj.* **1.** using or including the latest developments, facts, or information: *We use an up-to-date almanac.* **2.** having or showing the latest style; fashionable; modern: *up-to-date designer clothes.*

up·town (*adv., n.,* up'toun'; *adj.,* up'toun') *adv.* to, toward, or in the upper part of a town or city: *We have moved uptown.* —*adj.* of, relating to, or in the upper part of a town or city: *uptown traffic, the uptown bus.* —*n.* the upper part of a town or city.

up·turn (up'tûrn') *n.* an upward turn or trend, especially toward better conditions: *After I began studying, my grades took an upturn.*

up·ward (up'wərd) *adv.* **1.** from a lower to a higher place or position: *He looked upward.* **2.** toward a higher or greater amount, degree, or rank: *The cost of living has climbed upward.* **3.** toward or into a later time or greater age: *From childhood upward, the musician had taken piano lessons.* **4.** more; over: *Tickets go for five dollars and upward.* **5.** toward the interior, source, or origin: *The explorers followed the river upward.* —*adj.* moving from a lower to a higher place, level, or condition: *an upward trend.* —*up'ward·ly, adv.*
·**upward of** or **upwards of.** more than: *There were upwards of fifty people at the party.*

up·wards (up'wərdz) *adv.* upward.

u·ran·i·nite (yū ran'ə nīt') *n.* a rare mineral that is the main ore of uranium. A common variety is pitchblende.

u·ra·ni·um (yū rā'nē əm) *n.* a heavy, silvery, radioactive metallic element that is important as a source of nuclear energy. Symbol: **U** [From the planet *Uranus,* which had been recently discovered, going back to the Greek word *ouranos* meaning "heavenly."]

uranium 235, a uranium isotope used as fuel for the chain reaction that releases the energy in nuclear fission. It is the only naturally occurring material that undergoes nuclear fission.

uranium 238, a uranium isotope that is the most abundant naturally occurring isotope of uranium.

U·ra·nus (yūr'ə nəs, yū rā'nəs) *n.* **1.** *Greek Mythology.* the god who was the earliest ruler of the universe and was associated with the sky. He was the father of the Titans. **2.** the third largest planet of the solar system and seventh in order of distance from the sun. It has fifteen known moons and a complex of rings.

ur·ban (ûr'bən) *adj.* of, in, relating to, or characteristic of a city or city life: *urban expansion, urban problems, an urban population.*

ur·bane (ûr bān') *adj.* refined and courteous: *The senator is an urbane, cultured individual.* [From the Latin word *urbanus* meaning "of a city" or "refined, polished," from the word *urbs* "a city, town." It was believed that manners were more refined in cities than in the country.] —*ur·bane'ly, adv.* —*ur·bane'ness, n.*

ur·ban·i·ty (ûr ban'i tē) *n.* the quality of being urbane.

ur·ban·ize (ûr'bə nīz') *v.,* **ur·ban·ized, ur·ban·iz·ing.** —*v.t.* to make urban: *The builders are urbanizing the countryside around the large city.* —*v.i.* to become urban. —*ur'ban·i·za'tion, n.*

urban renewal, the planned rehabilitation and reconstruction of deteriorating urban areas, chiefly through the demolition of slums and the building of public housing. It is usually carried out under a government-subsidized program.

ur·chin (ûr'chin) *n.* **1.** a small, mischievous child. **2.** see **sea urchin.**

Ur·du (ûr'dü, ûr'dü) *n.* an Indo-European language spoken by Muslims in Pakistan and in parts of India.

–ure *suffix* (used to form nouns from verbs) **1.** the act, process, state, or result: *exposure, enclosure.* **2.** a function or a group performing a function: *legislature.*

u·re·a (yū rē'ə) *n.* a colorless substance that is found in urine and is also made synthetically. It is a product of the breakdown of protein in the body. Synthetic urea is used in fertilizers and in the manufacture of plastics and explosives.

u·re·ter (yū rē'tər) *n.* either of two tubes that carry urine from the kidneys to the bladder.

u·re·thra (yū rē'thrə) *n., pl.* **u·re·thras** or **u·re·thrae** (yū rē'thrē). the tube that carries urine from the bladder to the outside of the body.

urge (ûrj) *v.t.,* **urged, urg·ing. 1.** to try to convince or persuade; plead or reason with: *The teacher urged the class to visit the library.* **2.** to drive or force on; influence; spur: *The jockey urged the racehorse to the finish line.*

3. to speak or argue strongly for; recommend or support earnestly: *The concerned citizens urged prison reform.* —*n.* a strong impulse or desire: *a sudden urge to see a movie.*

ur·gen·cy (ûr'jən sē) *n.* the quality or condition of being urgent: *The mayor addressed the traffic problem with some urgency.*

ur·gent (ûr'jənt) *adj.* **1.** calling for immediate action or attention; compelling; pressing: *The president of the company had urgent business to attend to.* **2.** insistent or earnest, as in pleading: *The director of the hospital made an urgent appeal for funds.* —*ur'gent·ly, adv.*

u·ri·nal (yūr'ə nəl) *n.* **1.** a wall fixture used for urinating. **2.** a container for urine, as one used by a bedridden patient.

u·ri·nal·y·sis (yūr'ə nal'ə sis) *n., pl.* **u·ri·nal·y·ses** (yūr'ə nal'ə sēz'). a chemical or microscopic analysis of urine, often used to diagnose diseases of the urinary system.

u·ri·nar·y (yūr'ə ner'ē) *adj.* **1.** of or relating to urine. **2.** of, relating to, or involving the organs that produce and discharge urine.

urinary system, the system of organs that produce and excrete urine. In mammals, the urinary system is composed of the kidneys, the ureters, the bladder, and the urethra.

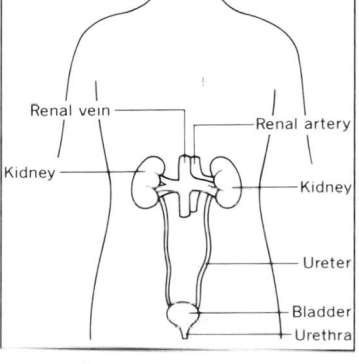

u·ri·nate (yūr'ə nāt') *v.i.,* **u·ri·nat·ed, u·ri·nat·ing.** to discharge urine. —*u'ri·na'tion, n.*

urinary system

u·rine (yūr'in) *n.* a clear, usually yellowish fluid containing waste material that is carried from the kidneys, stored in the bladder, and discharged from the body through the urethra.

urn (ûrn) *n.* **1.** a vase with a foot or pedestal, especially one used to hold the ashes of the dead. **2.** a closed vessel having a spigot, used for making, heating, or serving hot drinks: *a coffee urn.*

Ur·sa Major (ûr'sə) a constellation in the northern sky, containing the stars of the Big Dipper, thought to resemble a large bear in shape. Also, **Great Bear.**

Ursa Minor, a constellation in the northern sky, containing the bright star Polaris and the stars of the Little Dipper, thought to resemble a small bear in shape. Also, **Little Bear.**

Porcelain urn   Coffee urn

urns

us (us; *unstressed* əs) *pron.* the objective case of **we.**

at; āpe; fär; câre; end; mē; it; īce; pîerce; hot; ōld; sông, fôrk; oil; out; up; ūse; rüle; pùll; tûrn; chin; sing; shop; thin; this; hw in white; zh in treasure. The symbol ə stands for the unstressed vowel sound heard in about, taken, pencil, lemon, and circus.

U

U.S., United States.

USA, United States Army.

U.S.A., United States of America.

us·a·ble (ū′zə bəl) *also,* **use·a·ble.** *adj.* capable of being used; fit or convenient for use: *The empty can is still usable as a wastebasket.* —**us′a·bil′i·ty, us′a·ble·ness,** *n.* —**us′a·bly,** *adv.*

USAF, United States Air Force.

us·age (ū′sij, ū′zij) *n.* **1.** the act or manner of using, treating, or handling something; treatment; use: *My shoes get hard usage.* **2.** the customary or usual way in which a language is used, or in which its words and sounds are used. **3.** a customary practice: *That ceremony is a usage that has lasted in the village for centuries.*

Language Note

In language, the term **usage** means the way people use words and expressions in speaking and writing. In former times, it was believed that usage should follow the established, conservative rules of traditional grammar. Many such rules, however, do not reflect the way English is actually used, even among the most highly educated people. Often these rules have been derived from the grammatical rules of Latin, making them poorly suited to the natural structure of English. Some have been based on artificial and arbitrary judgments, rather than on a scientific examination of the English language itself.

Linguists believe strongly that statements about usage should be based on the way language is actually used, not on the way some people think it should be used. A modern approach to a description of usage might contain such information as how a word or phrase is used, by whom it is used, in what situations it is used, and how widely it is considered acceptable. A note regarding the sentence *This car won't run no more* might state that most educated speakers and writers would regard the sentence as *unacceptable* and would not use it themselves. It is important to learn what is considered *acceptable* usage so that we know what impression we convey when we speak and write the English language.

USCG, United States Coast Guard.

use (*v.,* ūz; *n.,* ūs) *v.t.,* **used, us·ing. 1.** to employ for a particular purpose or end: *May I use your scissors? I used the encyclopedia to check some facts.* **2.** to exhaust the whole or entire supply of: *We used up all the bread at breakfast.* **3.** to take often or by habit: *to use milk in the tea.* **4.** to act or behave toward; treat: *The judges used all the contestants fairly.* —*n.* **1.** the act of using: *That teacher encourages the use of the dictionary.* **2.** the state or condition of being used: *The classroom is in use until afternoon.* **3.** the quality that makes something suitable for a purpose; usefulness: *What's the use of worrying about it now?* **4.** a need or occasion for using: *Do you have any use for these empty bottles?* **5.** the purpose for which something is used; function: *This tool has many uses.* **6.** the right or privilege to use something: *I have the use of my cousin's bicycle for the weekend.* **7.** a manner or way of using: *Show me the proper use of the sewing machine.* **8.** the power or ability to use something: *I lost the use of my hand when I broke my finger.* —**us′er,** *n.*

·**to have no use for.** *Informal.* to dislike: *to have no use for lazy people.*

·**to make use of.** to use; utilize; employ: *to make good use of one's money.*

·**to put to use.** to use to advantage: *That vacant lot could be put to use as a baseball field.*

·**used to. a.** formerly did: *I used to like hiking. We used*

to vacation in the mountains. **b.** familiar with; accustomed to: *The city children are not used to country life.*

use·a·ble (ū′zə bəl) *adj.* another spelling of **usable.** —**use′a·bil′i·ty, use′a·ble·ness,** *n.* —**use′a·bly,** *adv.*

used (ūzd) *adj.* having been put to use or owned by another or others; not new: *used clothing, a used car.*

use·ful (ūs′fəl) *adj.* serving a good use or purpose; helpful: *How can I make myself useful?* —**use′ful·ly,** *adv.* —**use′ful·ness,** *n.*

use·less (ūs′lis) *adj.* **1.** serving no purpose; having no use: *The car is useless without a motor.* **2.** not bringing about any result; vain; futile: *It is useless to struggle against such odds.* —**use′less·ly,** *adv.* —**use′less·ness,** *n.*

us·er–friend·ly (ū′zər frend′lē) *adj.* easy to use, especially by someone who is inexperienced: *a user-friendly computer program.*

ush·er (ush′ər) *n.* a person who leads people to their seats, as in a church, theater, or stadium. —*v.t.* **1.** to act as an usher to; conduct; escort: *The waiter ushered the group to a table.* **2.** to mark the beginning or occurrence of: *We ushered the New Year in with a party.* —*v.i.* to act as an usher.

USMC, United States Marine Corps.

USN, United States Navy.

USRDA, see **RDA.**

USS 1. United States Ship. **2.** United States Senate.

USSR, Union of Soviet Socialist Republics.

u·su·al (ū′zhü əl) *adj.* **1.** happening often or regularly; common: *Such heat is usual for July.* **2.** according to custom or habit; customary; expected: *The dentist charged me the usual fee for cleaning my teeth.* —**u′su·al·ly,** *adv.* —**u′su·al·ness,** *n.*

·**as usual.** in the regular or customary way: *The farmer got up at five o'clock, as usual.*

u·su·rer (ū′zhər ər) *n.* a person who lends money, especially at a very high or unlawful rate of interest.

u·su·ri·ous (ū zhür′ē əs) *adj.* **1.** practicing usury: *a usurious lender.* **2.** of, relating to, or characterized by usury: *a usurious contract.* —**u·su′ri·ous·ly,** *adv.* —**u·su′ri·ous·ness,** *n.*

u·surp (ū sûrp′, ū zûrp′) *v.t.* to seize and hold without legal right or authority; take possession of by force: *The rebel army usurped control of the government.* —**u·surp′er,** *n.*

u·sur·pa·tion (ū′sər pā′shən, ū′zər pā′shən) *n.* the act of usurping.

u·su·ry (ū′zhə rē) *n., pl.* **u·su·ries. 1.** the act or practice of lending money at a very high or unlawful rate of interest. **2.** a very high or unlawful rate of interest.

UT, postal abbreviation for Utah.

Ute (ūt) *n., pl.* **Ute** or **Utes. 1.** a member of any of various tribes of Indians formerly living in what is now Utah, Colorado, and New Mexico. **2.** the language of the Utes.

u·ten·sil (ū ten′səl) *n.* an article or object that is useful or necessary in doing or making something: *cooking utensils, writing utensils.*

u·ter·ine (ū′tər in, ū′tə rīn′) *adj.* of or relating to the uterus.

u·ter·us (ū′tər əs) *n., pl.* **u·ter·i** (ū′tə rī′). a hollow muscular organ found in most female mammals that holds and nourishes the young until birth; womb.

u·til·i·tar·i·an (ū til′i tãr′ē ən) *adj.* **1.** of or relating to usefulness. **2.** made for or concerned with usefulness instead of beauty: *a stark building of purely utilitarian design.*

u·til·i·ty (ū til′i tē) *n., pl.* **u·til·i·ties. 1.** the state or quality of being useful; usefulness: *The utility of education is in the building of the mind.* **2.** a company that provides an important service to the public, as by supplying gas, electricity, or water. Also, **public utility. 3.** the service provided by such a company.

u·ti·lize (ū′tə līz′) *v.t.*, **u·ti·lized, u·ti·liz·ing.** to take full advantage of; put to good use: *The cook utilized leftover scraps of the roast to make a hash.* —**u′ti·liz′a·ble,** *adj.* —**u′til·i·za′tion,** *n.* —**u′ti·liz′er,** *n.*

ut·most (ut′mōst′) *adj.* **1.** of the greatest or highest degree or amount: *We have the utmost respect for your opinion. This work is of the utmost importance.* **2.** being or located at the farthest limit or point; most remote: *the utmost corners of the universe.* —*n.* the most or greatest possible, as in degree or amount: *The teachers did their utmost to set a good example.* Also, **uttermost.**

u·to·pi·a (ū tō′pē ə) *also,* **U·to·pi·a.** *n.* **1.** an ideal place or society in which people live together in peace and happiness. **2.** any idealistic plan having the goal of bringing peace and happiness to all people. [From the ideal society on the imaginary island of *Utopia* in Sir Thomas More's satire *Utopia* (1516). More coined the name *Utopia* from the Greek prefix *ou-* meaning "no, not" and the word *topos* meaning "a place"; hence, it means "no place."]

u·to·pi·an (ū tō′pē ən) *also,* **U·to·pi·an.** *adj.* **1.** fine in theory but not possible or practical in reality: *utopian schemes.* **2.** of or like a utopia: *a utopian community, utopian literature.* —*n.* a person who supports or works for impractical or visionary reforms.

u·to·pi·an·ism (ū tō′pē ə niz′əm) *also,* **U·to·pi·an·ism.** *n.* the beliefs or ideals of a utopian.

ut·ter¹ (ut′ər) *v.t.* to give voice to; express aloud: *to utter a sigh.* [Possibly from Middle Dutch *ūteren.*]

ut·ter² (ut′ər) *adj.* complete or perfect; total: *The room was in utter darkness. The project was an utter failure.* [Old English *ūtera, ūterra, ūttra* "outer."] —**ut′ter·ly,** *adv.*

ut·ter·ance (ut′ər əns) *n.* **1.** something uttered or expressed in words. **2.** the act of uttering; vocal expression: *to give utterance to one's joy.* **3.** the manner of speaking: *a soft utterance.*

ut·ter·most (ut′ər mōst′) *adj., n.* another word for **utmost.**

U–turn (ū′tûrn′) *n.* a change in a vehicle's direction to the opposite direction, such that the path of the vehicle is shaped like the letter U: *We made a U-turn when we realized we were going the wrong way.*

UV, ultraviolet.

u·vu·la (ū′vyə lə) *n., pl.* **u·vu·las** or **u·vu·lae** (ū′vyə- lē′). a small, cone-shaped piece of flesh that hangs from the soft palate, above and behind the tongue.

---

at; āpe; fär; câre; end; mē; it; īce; pîerce; hot; ōld; sông, fôrk; oil; out; up; ūse; rüle; půll; tûrn; chin; sing; shop; thin; **this**; hw in white; zh in treasure. The symbol ə stands for the unstressed vowel sound heard in about, taken, pencil, lemon, and circus.

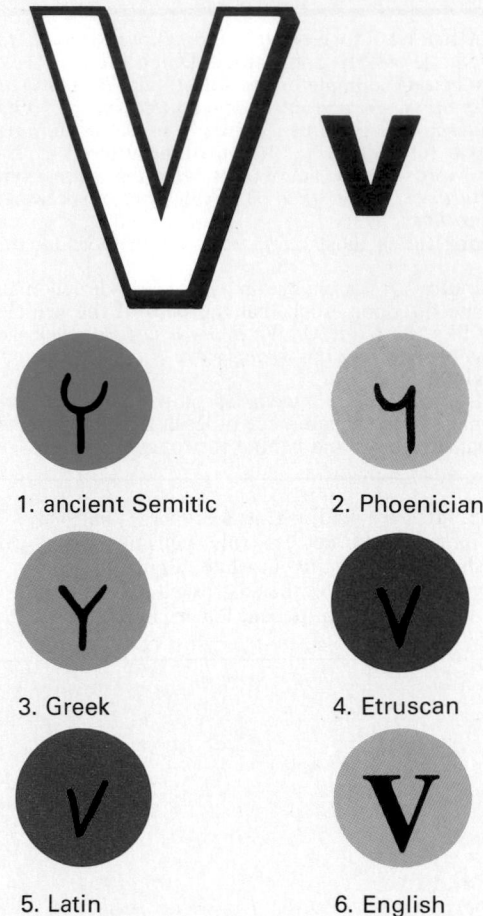

1. ancient Semitic
2. Phoenician
3. Greek
4. Etruscan
5. Latin
6. English

V is the twenty-second letter of the English alphabet. The earliest form of the letter **V** is the ancient Semitic letter *waw* (1), which depicted a hook and stood for the *w* sound, as the *w* in the English word *water*. When the Phoenicians (2) borrowed *waw*, they used it to represent both the consonant sound *w* and the vowel sound *ü*, as heard in the English word *rude*. The Greeks adopted *waw* and called it *upsilon* (3), writing it as the capital letter **Y** is written today and using it for only the *ü* sound. The Etruscans (4), changed the shape of *upsilon* and used it to represent both the vowel and consonant sounds, as did the Romans in the Latin alphabet (5). About 1,000 years ago, two forms of this V-shaped letter were being used in writing: **V** at the beginning of a word and a new letter, **U**, in the middle of a word. During the Renaissance, the letter **V** came to be used more and more for the consonant sound in the pronunciation of English, French, Italian, and other European languages. Today, we write our modern capital **V** (6) much as the Etruscans wrote it 2,800 years ago.

v, V (vē) *n., pl.* **v's, V's.** **1.** the twenty-second letter of the English alphabet. **2.** something having the shape of this letter. **3.** the Roman numeral for 5.

v. **1.** verb. **2.** verse. **3.** versus.

V **1.** the symbol for vanadium. **2.** vector. **3.** velocity. **4.** victory. **5.** volt; volts.

V. **1.** Venerable. **2.** Vicar. **3.** Viscount.

Va., Virginia.

VA, postal abbreviation for Virginia.

va·can·cy (vā′kən sē) *n., pl.* **va·can·cies.** **1.** an unoccupied or empty space, especially an apartment or room for rent: *The superintendent said that the apartment building had no vacancies.* **2.** an unfilled post, position, or office: *The bookkeeper's retirement left a vacancy in the accounting department.* **3.** the state or condition of being vacant; emptiness.

va·cant (vā′kənt) *adj.* **1.** containing no one or nothing; unoccupied or empty: *a vacant lot, a vacant seat.* **2.** not filled, as a post, position, or office. **3.** lacking or showing a lack of intelligence or awareness: *a vacant mind, a vacant stare.* **4.** free from activity; idle: *vacant hours.* —**va′cant·ly,** *adv.*

va·cate (vā′kāt) *v.,* **va·cat·ed, va·cat·ing.** —*v.t.* **1.** to cease to occupy; leave empty: *The tenant decided to vacate the apartment.* **2.** to give up (a post, position, or office). —*v.i.* to leave a place or position vacant.

va·ca·tion (vā kā′shən) *n.* a period of rest and freedom from some activity, especially a period of paid free time granted to an employee. —*v.i.* to take or spend a vacation: *Last year they vacationed in Spain.* —**va·ca′tion·er,** *n.*

vac·ci·nate (vak′sə nāt′) *v.t.,* **vac·ci·nat·ed, vac·ci·nat·ing.** to introduce a vaccine into the body in order to protect against a specific disease, such as smallpox.

vac·ci·na·tion (vak′sə nā′shən) *n.* **1.** the act or practice of vaccinating; treatment with a vaccine. **2.** a scar left by a vaccination: *to have a vaccination on one's arm.*

vac·cine (vak sēn′, vak′sēn) *n.* a substance, such as a killed or weakened bacteria or virus, that stimulates antibody production by the body and produces immunity against a particular disease. [Formed from the Latin word *vaccinus* meaning "of or from a cow," from the word *vacca* meaning "cow." The treatment was named for *(virus) vaccinus,* the scientific Latin name for cowpox.]

vac·il·late (vas′ə lāt′) *v.i.,* **vac·il·lat·ed, vac·il·lat·ing.** **1.** to move to and fro; sway unsteadily; waver. **2.** to waver in mind; be uncertain: *to vacillate between going to a meeting and staying home.* —**vac′il·la′tion,** *n.*

va·cu·i·ty (va kū′i tē) *n., pl.* **va·cu·i·ties.** **1.** the state or quality of being empty; emptiness: *the vacuity of outer space.* **2.** an empty space; vacuum; void. **3.** emptiness of mind. **4.** something that is foolish or meaningless.

vac·u·ole (vak′ū ōl′) *n.* a small cavity in a living cell, usually filled with fluid and serving to store food.

vac·u·ous (vak′ū əs) *adj.* **1.** containing nothing; empty. **2.** lacking intelligence; foolish: *a vacuous statement.* —**vac′u·ous·ly,** *adv.*

vac·u·um (vak′ū əm, vak′ūm) *n., pl.* **vac·u·ums** or *(defs. 1–3)* **vac·u·a** (vak′ū ə). **1.** a space completely empty of matter. Although a perfect vacuum is possible in theory, it has never been produced in an experiment. **2.** a space from which almost all gas, vapor, and other matter has been removed. **3.** a state of isolation from the reality, events, or influences of the outside world: *The hermit lives in a vacuum.*

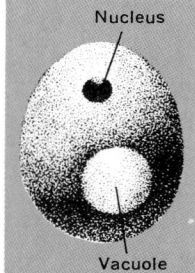

vacuole

4. see **vacuum cleaner.** —*v.t., v.i.* to clean with a vacuum cleaner.

vacuum bottle, another term for **thermos.**

vacuum cleaner, an apparatus for cleaning carpets, floors, upholstery, or the like, that operates by means of suction.

vac·u·um-packed (vak′ū əm pakt′, vak′ūm pakt′) *adj.* packed in a sealed container from which most of the air has been removed to maintain freshness.

vacuum tube, another term for **electron tube.**

vag·a·bond (vag′ə bond′) *n.* a person who wanders from place to place, having no regular home. —*adj.* of, relating to, or characteristic of a vagabond or a vagabond's way of life: *The hobo led a vagabond existence.*

va·gar·y (və gâr′ē, vā′gə rē) *n., pl.* **va·gar·ies.** an unusual or unpredictable act, idea, or happening: *the vagaries of life.* ▲ usually used in the plural.

va·gi·na (və jī′nə) *n., pl.* **va·gi·nas** or **va·gi·nae** (və-jī′nē). the canal in female mammals that leads from the uterus to the genital opening and through which the fetus passes during birth.

vag·i·nal (vaj′ə nəl, və jī′nəl) *adj.* of or relating to the vagina.

va·gran·cy (vā′grən sē) *n., pl.* **va·gran·cies.** the condition of being a vagrant: *to be arrested for vagrancy.*

va·grant (vā′grənt) *n.* a person who has no regular home or employment and wanders about from place to place; vagabond. —*adj.* **1.** of, relating to, or characteristic of a vagrant or a vagrant's way of life. **2.** wandering from place to place. —**va′grant·ly,** *adv.*

vague (vāg) *adj.,* **va·guer, va·guest. 1.** not definitely or clearly expressed: *They made a vague promise that they would visit us someday.* **2.** not clearly felt or known: *a vague idea. I had a vague feeling of uneasiness.* **3.** not having a definite form or outline; not clear or distinct: *We could see only the vague outline of the building through the fog.* —**vague′ly,** *adv.* —**vague′ness,** *n.*

vain (vān) *adj.* **1.** overly concerned with or proud of one's appearance, abilities, or accomplishments; conceited: *Don't be so vain that you won't admit you were wrong.* **2.** not successful or effective: *The mechanic made a vain effort to repair the automobile.* **3.** of no real significance or worth; empty: *One went through the vain motions, but it was mostly a waste of life* (Henry James). —**vain′ly,** *adv.*

　·**in vain. a.** without success; useless: *All attempts at rescue were in vain.* **b.** without proper respect; lightly; irreverently: *to take God's name in vain.*

vain·glo·ri·ous (vān′glôr′ē əs) *adj.* too vain, proud, or boastful: *a vainglorious statement, to be vainglorious about one's accomplishments.* —**vain′glo′ri·ous·ly,** *adv.* —**vain′glo′ri·ous·ness,** *n.*

vain·glo·ry (vān′glôr′ē, vān′glôr′ē) *n.* too much vanity, pride, or boastfulness.

val·ance (val′əns) *n.* **1.** a short drapery or piece of wood or metal hung across the top of a window, as for decoration or to hide curtain fixtures. **2.** a short drapery hanging from a shelf, table, frame of a bed, or the like, often reaching to the floor.

vale (vāl) *n.* a valley or dale.

val·e·dic·to·ri·an (val′i dik tôr′ē ən) *n.* a student, usually ranking highest in the class, who delivers the valedictory at a graduation exercise.

val·e·dic·to·ry (val′i dik′tə rē) *n., pl.* **val·e·dic·to·ries.** a farewell address, especially one delivered at a graduation exercise. —*adj.* of, relating to, or expressing a farewell.

va·lence (vā′ləns) *n.* the combining capacity of an element or radical, determined by the number of electrons that an atom will lose or gain in forming a chemical compound. The sum of the valences of the elements or radicals in the compound must equal zero. For example,

sodium has a valence of $+1$ and chlorine has a valence of -1 in sodium chloride, or common salt (NaCl).

Va·len·ci·ennes (və len′sē enz′) *n.* a fine lace, usually having a floral design. Also, **Valenciennes lace.** [From *Valenciennes,* the city in France where this lace was first made.]

val·en·tine (val′ən tīn′) *n.* **1.** a greeting card or gift sent on Valentine's Day, usually as an expression of affection for one's sweetheart. **2.** a sweetheart, especially a sweetheart chosen on Valentine's Day.

Valentine's Day, the day named in honor of Saint Valentine, traditionally observed by the sending of valentines. It falls on February 14. Also, **Saint Valentine's Day.**

va·le·ri·an (və lîr′ē ən) *n.* **1.** a drug having a strong odor, obtained from the roots of a plant, and formerly used to treat nervous conditions. **2.** the plant that produces this drug, having small white, pink, or lavender flowers.

val·et (val′it, val′ā) *n.* **1.** a man's male servant who performs various personal services for his employer, such as caring for his clothes and helping him dress. **2.** an employee, as of a hotel, who performs personal services for guests, such as getting clothes cleaned and pressed.

Val·hal·la (val hal′ə) *n. Norse Mythology.* the great hall to which heroes and warriors slain in battle were taken by the Valkyries, so that they could feast at the table of Odin.

val·iant (val′yənt) *adj.* brave; courageous: *a valiant fighter, a valiant defense of freedom.* —**val′iant·ly,** *adv.* —**val′iant·ness,** *n.*

val·id (val′id) *adj.* **1.** soundly based on facts or evidence; true: *The experiment proved that the scientist's theory was valid.* **2.** having the desired result; effective: *a valid method of treatment.* **3.** acceptable under the law; legally binding: *a valid driver's license.* —**val′id·ly,** *adv.*

val·i·date (val′i dāt′) *v.t.,* **val·i·dat·ed, val·i·dat·ing. 1.** to make or declare legally valid: *to validate election results.* **2.** to prove to be valid, true, or correct; confirm: *The clerk validated my birth certificate.*

va·lid·i·ty (və lid′i tē) *n., pl.* **va·lid·i·ties.** the quality, state, or fact of being valid: *We doubted the validity of the speaker's argument.*

va·lise (və lēs′) *n.* a small piece of luggage; suitcase.

Val·kyr·ie (val kîr′ē, val′kə rē) *n. Norse Mythology.* any of a group of beautiful warrior maidens who were the attendants of Odin, and who took heroes slain in battle to Valhalla.

val·ley (val′ē) *n., pl.* **val·leys. 1.** a region of low land between hills, mountains, or other high land, usually having a river or stream flowing through it. **2.** an area of land drained by a river system; river basin: *the Nile valley.*

val·or (val′ər) *n.* outstanding courage; great bravery: *to be decorated for valor in combat.*

val·or·ous (val′ər əs) *adj.* having or showing valor; brave; courageous. —**val′or·ous·ly,** *adv.*

val·u·a·ble (val′ū ə bəl, val′yə bəl) *adj.* **1.** having great value; worth much money: *a valuable oil painting, a valuable piece of property.* **2.** of great use, worth, or importance: *valuable advice, a valuable friend.* —*n. usually,* **valuables.** personal property that has value, such as a piece of jewelry.

---

at; āpe; fär; câre; end; mē; it; īce; pîerce; hot; ōld; sông, fôrk; oil; out; up; ūse; rüle; pùll; tûrn; chin; sing; shop; thin; <u>th</u>is; hw in white; zh in treasure. The symbol ə stands for the unstressed vowel sound heard in about, taken, pencil, lemon, and circus.

V

val·u·a·tion (val′ū ā′shən) *n.* **1.** the act or process of estimating the value or price of something: *Valuation of the property required an inspection of the buildings.* **2.** an estimated value or price.

val·ue (val′ū) *n.* **1.** relative or considered worth, usefulness, importance, or merit: *The museum purchased the antique chair for its historical value. The old schoolmates placed great value on their friendship.* **2.** monetary worth: *The value of land has gone up in recent years.* **3. values.** the principles or standards of a person or group; ideals: *Their high values kept them from doing what is wrong.* **4.** the exact meaning, as of a word: *What value does the word have in this context?* **5.** a numerical quantity: *Find the value of y if $y^2 = 25$.* **6.** *Music.* the relative length of a tone or rest as shown by a note or other symbol. For example, the value of a whole note is twice that of a half note. —*v.t.,* **val·ued, val·u·ing. 1.** to estimate the monetary value of; appraise: *The jeweler valued the necklace at one thousand dollars.* **2.** to consider as having worth, importance, or merit: *to value someone's friendship.*

val·ued (val′ūd) *adj.* considered as having worth, importance, or merit; highly regarded; esteemed: *a valued friend, a valued possession.*

val·ue·less (val′ū lis) *adj.* having no value; worthless.

valve (valv) *n.* **1.** any of various devices used to control the flow of liquids or gases by controlling a passage with a movable part. **2.** the movable part of such a device. **3.** a fold in a membrane lining a hollow organ that allows a fluid, such as blood, to flow in one direction and prevents it from flowing in the opposite direction: *a heart valve.* **4.** a device in certain brass musical instruments, such as a trumpet, for changing the pitch of the tone. **5.** one of the pair of hinged shells of an oyster, clam, or similar animal.

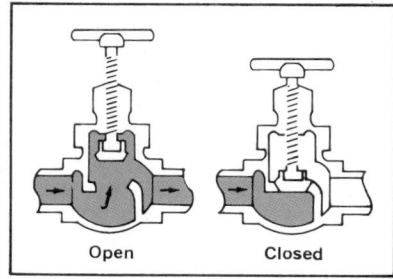

valve (defs. 1 and 2)

va·moose (va müs′) *v.i.,* **va·moosed, va·moos·ing.** *Slang.* to leave quickly; go away hastily. [From the Spanish word *Vamos!* meaning "Let us go!"]

vamp (vamp) *n.* the upper front part of a shoe or boot, covering the instep and sometimes the toes. —*v.t.* **1.** to provide with a vamp; repair with a new vamp. **2.** to patch up; repair.

vam·pire (vam′pīr) *n.* **1.** in folklore, a corpse that leaves its grave at night to suck the blood of sleeping persons. **2.** person who ruthlessly preys on or takes advantage of others. **3.** see **vampire bat.**

vampire bat 1. any of various bats of Central and South America that feed on the blood of warm-blooded animals. **2.** any of various other bats that are mistakenly believed to feed on blood.

van¹ (van) a large, covered truck or other vehicle, used for transporting furniture, goods, or animals. [Short for *caravan.*]

van² (van) *n.* see **vanguard.**

va·na·di·um (və nā′dē əm) *n.* a strong, silver-white, metallic element that resists corrosion. It is used in making steel alloys. Symbol: **V** [From *Vana-dīs,* the name given to the Norse goddess of beauty, Freya, from the Old Norse word *Vanr* meaning "one of the gods" + *dīs* meaning "sister" or "maiden." The element was so named because of the beautiful colors of its ores.]

Van Al·len radiation belt (van al′ən) a region of intense radiation encircling the earth at high altitudes, consisting of electrons and protons trapped by the earth's magnetic field. Also, **Van Allen belt.** [From the American physicist James A. *Van Allen* (b. 1914).]

van·dal (van′dəl) *n.* **1.** a person who willfully damages or destroys public or private property. **2. Vandal.** a member of a Germanic tribe that ravaged Gaul, Spain, and northern Africa in the fourth and fifth centuries A.D., and sacked Rome in A.D. 455.

van·dal·ism (van′də liz′əm) *n.* willful damage to or destruction of public or private property.

van·dal·ize (van′də līz′) *v.t.,* **van·dal·ized, van·dal·iz·ing.** to damage or destroy (property) willfully.

Van·dyke (van dīk′) *n.* a short, pointed beard. [From the Flemish painter Sir Anthony *Van Dyke* (1599–1641). Such beards often appear in his portraits.]

vane (vān) *n.* **1.** a weathervane; weathercock. **2.** a blade or flat or curved part like a blade, as of a windmill or propeller.

van·guard (van′gärd′) *n.* **1.** the part of an army that moves ahead of the main force. **2.** the leading or foremost position of a social, political, or other movement: *in the vanguard of the reform movement.*

va·nil·la (və nil′ə) *n.* **1.** a flavoring obtained from the seed pods of a climbing tropical orchid, widely used in candies, ice cream, and cookies. **2.** the seed pod from which this flavoring is obtained. Also, **vanilla bean. 3.** the orchid bearing these pods.

van·ish (van′ish) *v.i.* **1.** to pass from sight, especially suddenly or quickly; disappear: *The airplane vanished in the clouds.* **2.** to cease to exist: *All hope of winning the game vanished when our star player was injured.*

van·i·ty (van′i tē) *n., pl.* **van·i·ties. 1.** too much concern with or pride in one's appearance, abilities, deeds, or the like; conceit. **2.** the quality of being futile or useless: *to realize the vanity of attempting to gain revenge.* **3.** see **vanity case. 4.** see **dressing table.**

vanity case, a woman's small case for carrying cosmetics, toiletries, and other articles.

van·quish (vang′kwish) *v.t.* **1.** to defeat or conquer, as in battle. **2.** to overcome (a feeling): *Knowledge vanquishes fear of the unknown.* —**van′quish·er,** *n.*

van·tage (van′tij) *n.* **1.** a favorable or superior position. **2.** see **vantage point.**

vantage point, a position that allows a clear or favorable view: *We could see the whole valley from our vantage point on the mountain.*

vap·id (vap′id) *adj.* dull or lifeless; insipid; uninteresting: *a vapid conversation.* —**vap′id·ly,** *adv.*

va·por (vā′pər) *n.* **1.** visible particles of matter suspended in the air, such as mist or smoke. **2.** the gaseous state of a substance that is a liquid or a solid under normal conditions of temperature and pressure: *Vapor rose from the boiling water.*

va·por·ize (vā′pə rīz′) *v.,* **va·por·ized, va·por·iz·ing.** —*v.t.* to change (something) into vapor. —*v.i.* to change into vapor: *The magician's rabbit vaporized before our eyes.* —**va′por·i·za′tion,** *n.*

va·por·iz·er (vā′pə rī′zər) *n.* a device for changing a liquid into a vapor, especially such a device for vaporizing a liquid medicine to be inhaled.

va·por·ous (vā′pər əs) *adj.* **1.** containing or full of vapor; misty: *Vaporous breezes blew in from the ocean.* **2.** like, resembling, or characteristic of vapor: *The vaporous fabric fluttered in the wind.*

vanes of a windmill

va·que·ro (vä kâr′ō) *n., pl.* **va·que·ros.** a cowboy, especially of Mexico, South America, or the southwestern United States.

var·i·a·ble (vâr′ē ə bəl) *adj.* **1.** likely or liable to change; changeable: *variable weather.* **2.** able to be changed: *a variable-speed motor.* —*n.* **1.** something that varies or is variable. **2.** *Mathematics.* **a.** a quantity that can have any of a set of values. **b.** a symbol representing such a quantity. —**var′i·a·bil′i·ty, var′i·a·ble·ness,** *n.* —**var′i·a·bly,** *adv.*

var·i·ance (vâr′ē əns) *n.* **1.** the act or result of varying. **2.** difference; discrepancy: *a variance of a few inches.* **·at variance.** in disagreement: *That account of the accident is at variance with the facts.*

var·i·ant (vâr′ē ənt) *adj.* different or varying, as from another or others of the same kind: *The word "centre" is a variant spelling of "center."* —*n.* something that is variant, such as a different spelling or pronunciation of the same word.

var·i·a·tion (vâr′ē ā′shən) *n.* **1.** the act, fact, or process of varying: *a variation in diet.* **2.** the extent or amount to which something varies: *The scientist noted a temperature variation of thirteen degrees.* **3.** something that is based on but differs somewhat from another thing: *The new play is a variation of an earlier play by the author.* **4.** *Music.* the repetition of a theme or tune with changes or additions, as in melody, harmony, rhythm, or key, especially one of a series of such repetitions.

var·i·cel·la (var′ə sel′ə) *n.* another word for **chicken pox.**

var·i·col·ored (vâr′i kul′ərd, vâr′i kul′ərd) *adj.* having various colors; variegated.

var·i·cose (var′i kōs′) *adj.* abnormally swollen: *varicose veins.*

var·ied (vâr′ēd) *adj.* **1.** consisting of different or various kinds, items, or parts: *a varied menu.* **2.** changed; altered.

var·i·e·gat·ed (vâr′ē i gā′tid) *adj.* **1.** marked or streaked with different colors; varied in color. **2.** having or characterized by variety: *The bouquet was a variegated selection of flowers.*

va·ri·e·ty (və rī′i tē) *n., pl.* **va·ri·e·ties. 1.** the state or quality of being various or varied; change or difference; diversity. *A job that lacks variety may soon become boring.* **2.** a number or collection of different things: *to purchase a variety of items at the supermarket.* **3.** a different kind or form of something: *a new variety of synthetic fabric.* **4.** a group of related plants or animals forming a small part of a larger group, especially a subdivision of a species.

variety show, a show, as on stage or television, with songs, dances, and comedy sketches.

var·i·ous (vâr′ē əs) *adj.* **1.** different from one another; of different kinds: *People of various backgrounds applied for the job.* **2.** more than one; several; many: *We spent the night at various towns on our long trip.* —**var′i·ous·ly,** *adv.*

var·let (vär′lit) *n. Archaic.* a scoundrel; knave.

var·mint (vär′mint) *n. Informal.* a troublesome or objectionable animal or person.

var·nish (vär′nish) *n., pl.* **var·nish·es. 1.** a liquid preparation usually made up of resins dissolved in alcohol or mixed with an oil, such as linseed oil. Varnish is used to produce a hard, clear coating, as on a wood surface. **2.** the glossy coating produced by such a preparation. **3.** an outward show or appearance, especially one that is deceptive; pretense: *A varnish of smooth manners disguised the swindler's true character.* —*v.t.* **1.** to apply varnish to; cover with varnish. **2.** to cover with a deceptive appearance.

var·si·ty (vär′si tē) *n., pl.* **var·si·ties.** the main team that represents a university, college, or school in an athletic or other competition.

var·y (vâr′ē) *v.,* **var·ied, var·y·ing.** —*v.t.* **1.** to change or make different: *to vary speed according to road conditions.* **2.** to give variety to; diversify: *to vary one's diet.* —*v.i.* **1.** to be or become changed: *The temperature outside varies from day to day.* **2.** to be different; differ: *The flowers in the garden vary in color.* **3.** *Mathematics.* to be subject to change; be variable.

vas·cu·lar (vas′kyə lər) *adj.* of, composed of, or containing vessels that carry blood, sap, or other animal or plant fluid.

vas de·fe·rens (vas′def′ə renz′) *pl.* **va·sa de·fe·ren·ti·a** (vā′sə def′ə ren′shē ə). the duct that carries sperm from the testis to the urethra.

vase (vās, vāz, väz) *n.* a rounded container that is usually of greater height than width. It is used chiefly for holding flowers or for decoration.

va·sec·to·my (va sek′tə mē) *n., pl.* **va·sec·to·mies.** an operation in which the tubes through which sperm pass from the testes to the urethra are cut, used as a form of birth control in men.

Vas·e·line (vas′ə lēn′, vas′ə lēn′) *n. Trademark.* a jellylike substance made from petroleum, used as an ointment and dressing.

vas·sal (vas′əl) *n.* **1.** under feudalism, a subject of a lord. Vassals received land and protection from the lord in return for their loyal support and service, especially military service. **2.** a servant; slave. —*adj.* of, relating to, or characteristic of a vassal.

vas·sal·age (vas′ə lij) *n.* **1.** the state or condition of being a vassal. **2.** the duties or services required of a vassal. **3.** the land held by a vassal. **4.** servitude.

vast (vast) *adj.* very great, as in extent, size, or amount: *a vast expanse of land, a vast number of people.* —**vast′ly,** *adv.* —**vast′ness,** *n.*

vat (vat) *n.* a large tank or container used for holding liquids.

vats used in dyeing

Vat·i·can (vat′i kən) *n.* **1.** the official residence of the pope in Vatican City. **2.** the government or authority of the pope.

vaude·ville (vôd′vil, vô′də vil) *n.* theatrical entertainment popular in the United States in the late nineteenth and early twentieth centuries. A performance usually included a variety of short acts by singers, jugglers, comedians, and the like.

---

at; āpe; fär; câre; end; mē; it; īce; pîerce; hot; ōld; sông, fôrk; oil; out; up; ūse; rūle; pull; tûrn; chin; sing; shop; thin; this; hw in white; zh in treasure. The symbol ə stands for the unstressed vowel sound heard in about, taken, pencil, lemon, and circus.

V

vault¹ *(def. 4)*

vault¹ (vôlt) *n.* **1.** an arched structure of stone, brick, or concrete serving as a roof or ceiling. **2.** something resembling such a structure: *the vault of the sky.* **3.** an underground compartment or room used as a cellar or storeroom. **4.** a well-protected or fortified room or compartment, as in a bank, used for the safekeeping of valuables or money. **5.** a burial chamber; tomb. —*v.t.* **1.** to cover or provide with a vault. **2.** to build in the shape of a vault: *The ceiling was vaulted.* [From the Old French word *volt* meaning "a vaulted chamber."]

vault² (vôlt) *v.t.* to jump over, especially with the aid of the hands or a pole: *to vault a fence.* —*v.i.* to jump; spring: *to vault over a wall.* —*n.* the act of vaulting; jump; leap. [From the Old French word *volter* meaning "to leap, spring."] —**vault'er,** *n.*

vaunt (vônt) *v.i.* to boast; brag. —*v.t.* to boast of; brag about: *to vaunt one's athletic ability.* —*n.* a boast or brag.

VCR, a device for recording and playing back images and accompanying sounds on videocassettes. Also, **videocassette recorder, videotape recorder.** [Short for *v(ideo) c(assette) r(ecorder).*]

VD, venereal disease.

VDT, video display terminal.

veal (vēl) *n.* the flesh of a calf, used as food.

vec·tor (vek'tər) *n.* a mathematical quantity that has both magnitude and direction, such as velocity. A vector is usually represented by an arrow showing the direction of the force.

veer (vîr) *v.i.* to change in direction or course; shift; turn: *At the bottom of the hill the road veers sharply to the left.* —*v.t.* to change the direction or course of. —*n.* a change in direction or course; swerve: *A veer to the right avoided the tree.*

Ve·ga (vē'gə, vā'gə) *n.* a bright white star, the brightest star in the constellation Lyra.

veg·e·ta·ble (vej'tə bəl, vej'i tə bəl) *n.* **1.** the part of a plant used as food, eaten cooked or raw. The roots, leaves, flowers, stems, seeds, pods, and fruit of certain plants are eaten as vegetables. **2.** the plant from which such a part comes. **3.** any plant. —*adj.* **1.** of, relating to, or made from plants or parts of plants: *a roadside vegetable stand, vegetable stew.* **2.** like a plant; dull or inactive: *a vegetable existence.*

veg·e·tar·i·an (vej'i târ'ē ən) *n.* a person who eats only plants and plant products and who eats no meat, fish, or fowl, usually for health or moral reasons. —*adj.* **1.** relating to, supporting, or practicing vegetarianism. **2.** made up entirely of vegetables: *a vegetarian diet.*

veg·e·tar·i·an·ism (vej'i târ'ē ə niz'əm) *n.* the practices or principles of vegetarians.

veg·e·tate (vej'i tāt') *v.i.,* **veg·e·tat·ed, veg·e·tat·ing.** **1.** to grow or develop in the way plants do. **2.** to lead a dull or inactive life: *I spent the weekend just vegetating at home.*

veg·e·ta·tion (vej'i tā'shən) *n.* **1.** plant life: *a region of lush vegetation.* **2.** the act or process of vegetating.

veg·e·ta·tive (vej'i tā'tiv) *adj.* **1.** of or relating to plants, plant life, or plant growth: *Sunlight is necessary to the vegetative process.* **2.** growing or capable of growing as plants do. **3.** dull or inactive.

ve·he·ment (vē'ə mənt) *adj.* **1.** showing or characterized by intensity of feeling; passionate; ardent: *a vehement reply, vehement devotion.* **2.** violent; forceful: *a vehement show of force.* —**ve'he·mence,** *n.* —**ve'he·ment·ly,** *adv.*

ve·hi·cle (vē'i kəl) *n.* **1.** a device designed or used for transporting persons or goods. An automobile, sled, or carriage is a vehicle. **2.** the means by which something is expressed, communicated, or achieved: *Poetry is a vehicle of self-expression.* **3.** a liquid with which pigment is mixed to make paint.

ve·hic·u·lar (vē hik'yə lər) *adj.* **1.** of, relating to, or for vehicles: *vehicular traffic.* **2.** serving as a vehicle.

veil (vāl) *n.* **1.** a piece of lightweight fabric, as of lace, silk, or net, worn especially by women over the head and shoulders, or as a covering for the face. **2.** anything that hides or conceals: *a veil of mist, a veil of secrecy.* —*v.t.* to cover, conceal, or disguise with a veil: *to veil one's irritation with a smile.* —**veil'like',** *adj.*

vein (vān) *n.* **1.** one of the vessels that carry blood from all parts of the body to the heart. **2.** one of the bundles of vascular tissue that form the framework of a leaf. **3.** one of the branching tubular structures that serve to stiffen and strengthen the wing of an insect. **4.** a deposit of a mineral that forms in rock: *a vein of silver.* **5.** a streak or marking of a different color, as in marble

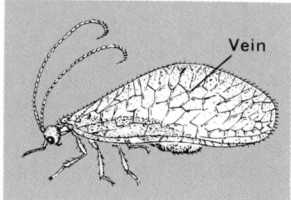

vein *(def. 3)*

or wood. **6.** a quality, mood, or attitude: *a story written in a humorous vein.* —*v.t.* to provide or mark with veins. —**vein'like',** *adj.*

Vel·cro (vel'krō) *n. Trademark.* a material consisting of one strip of nylon fabric containing many tiny nylon hooks and another strip containing matching loops; when pressed together, the two strips adhere. Velcro is widely used as a fastener on garments and luggage.

veld (velt) *also,* **veldt.** *n.* a region of open grassland in South Africa, having scattered bushes and trees.

vel·lum (vel'əm) *n.* **1.** a fine parchment prepared from calfskin, lambskin, or kidskin, used for writing or for binding fine books. **2.** a paper made to resemble such parchment.

ve·loc·i·pede (və los′ə pēd′) *n.*   **1.** an early form of bicycle or tricycle.   **2.** a child's tricycle.

ve·loc·i·ty (və los′i tē) *n., pl.* **ve·loc·i·ties.**   **1.** rapidity of motion; speed.   **2.** *Physics.* the rate of motion in a particular direction in relation to time.

ve·lour (və lŭr′) *also,* **ve·lours** (və lŭr′) *n., pl.* **ve·lours** (və lŭr′, və lŭrz′).   a soft, thick, closely woven fabric having a finish like velvet, used for clothing, draperies, upholstery, and other items.

vel·vet (vel′vit) *n.*   **1.** a fabric made of silk, rayon, nylon, or other fiber, having a smooth, thick pile.   **2.** the soft skin that covers the growing antlers of a deer.   —*adj.*   **1.** made of or covered with velvet.   **2.** like velvet in smoothness or softness.

vel·vet·een (vel′vi tēn′) *n.*   a cotton fabric made with a short, thick pile so that it resembles velvet.

vel·vet·y (vel′vi tē) *adj.*   **1.** smooth and soft like velvet: *The baby's cheeks felt velvety.*   **2.** smooth to the taste, as some liquors.

ve·na ca·va (vē′nə kā′və) *n., pl.* **ve·nae ca·vae** (vē′nē kā′vē).   either of the two large veins that return blood from the upper and lower parts of the body to the right atrium of the heart.

ve·nal (vē′nəl) *adj.*   **1.** willing to be bribed; open to bribery; corruptible: *a venal public official.*   **2.** able to be gotten or influenced by bribery: *a venal decision by a judge.*   **3.** characterized by corruption.   —**ve′nal·ly,** *adv.*

ve·nal·i·ty (vē nal′i tē) *n., pl.* **ve·nal·i·ties.**   the state or instance of being venal.

ve·na·tion (vē nā′shən, və nā′shən) *n.*   an arrangement or system of veins, as in a leaf or an insect's wing.

vend (vend) *v.t.*   to offer for sale; sell.

ven·det·ta (ven det′ə) *n.*   **1.** a feud in which the relatives of a murdered or injured person seek vengeance on the wrongdoer or members of the wrongdoer's family.   **2.** any bitter feud or dispute in which there is a desire for vengeance.

vending machine, a machine operated by inserting a coin in a slot, used for selling candy, cigarettes, or various other small items.

ven·dor (ven′dər) *also,* **vend·er.** *n.*   a person who sells or peddles; seller: *a fruit vendor, an ice-cream vendor.*

ve·neer (və nîr′) *n.*   **1.** a thin layer of fine wood or other material used in covering a surface or making plywood: *The pine table had a veneer of mahogany.*   **2.** an outward appearance, especially one that is deceptive: *They tried to hide their resentment behind a veneer of friendliness.*   —*v.t.*   **1.** to cover (a surface) with a thin layer of fine wood or other material.   **2.** to glue together (layers of wood) to make plywood.   **3.** to give an attractive outward appearance to.

ven·er·a·ble (ven′ər ə bəl) *adj.*   **1.** deserving respect or reverence, as by reason of age, character, or position: *a venerable scholar.*   **2.** worthy of respect because of age or historic or religious importance: *the venerable traditions of a university.*   —**ven′er·a·bly,** *adv.*

ven·er·ate (ven′ə rāt′) *v.t.,* **ven·er·at·ed, ven·er·at·ing.**   to regard with deep respect or reverence: *American Indian cultures venerated nature.*

ven·er·a·tion (ven′ə rā′shən) *n.*   **1.** the act of venerating or the state of being venerated.   **2.** a feeling of deep respect or reverence: *veneration for soldiers who died in war.*

ve·ne·re·al disease (və nîr′ē əl) any of several diseases, such as syphilis and gonorrhea, transmitted by sexual acts with an infected person; sexually transmitted disease.   [From the Latin word *venereus* meaning "relating to love" (from the Roman goddess of love, *Venus*) + the English suffix *-al*[1].]

Ve·ne·tian (və nē′shən) *adj.*   of or relating to Venice, its people, or their culture.   —*n.*   a person who was born in or is a citizen of Venice.

Venetian blind, a shade, especially for a window, made of a series of overlapping horizontal slats.   The slats can be opened or closed, and the shade can be raised or lowered by means of attached cords.

Venetian blind

venge·ance (ven′jəns) *n.*   the act of causing injury to another person in return for an injury or wrong; revenge: *to take vengeance for a blow struck in anger.*
   ·with a vengeance. a. with great force, intensity, or violence: *The tornado tore up houses with a vengeance.*   **b.** to an unusual extent; extremely: *During the milk shortage the price of milk rose with a vengeance.*

venge·ful (venj′fəl) *adj.*   full of or showing a desire for vengeance; seeking revenge: *a vengeful enemy.*   —**venge′ful·ly,** *adv.*   —**venge′ful·ness,** *n.*

ve·ni·al (vē′nē əl) *adj.*   that may be excused or forgiven; not very serious; pardonable: *a venial crime.*   —**ve·ni·al·i·ty** (vē′nē al′ə tē), *n.*

venial sin, in Roman Catholic theology, a sin that does not separate the sinner from the favor and love of God nor result in damnation to hell if not forgiven.

ven·i·son (ven′ə sən, ven′ə zən) *n.*   the flesh of a deer, used as food.

ven·om (ven′əm) *n.*   **1.** a poison produced by some animals, such as certain snakes or spiders, usually introduced into the body of a victim by a bite or sting.   **2.** malice; spite: *Their sarcastic comments were filled with venom.*

ven·om·ous (ven′ə məs) *adj.*   **1.** able to inflict a poisonous wound, especially by biting or stinging: *a venomous snake.*   **2.** containing or full of venom: *a venomous bite.*   **3.** malicious; spiteful: *a venomous remark.*   —**ven′om·ous·ly,** *adv.*   —**ven′om·ous·ness,** *n.*

ve·nous (vē′nəs) *adj.*   **1.** of, relating to, or characterized by veins.   **2.** of or relating to the blood returning to the heart through the veins.   Venous blood carries carbon dioxide in place of oxygen.

vent[1] (vent) *n.*   **1.** a hole or other small opening for the escape or passage of a gas, liquid, or the like.   **2.** a means of escape; outlet; expression: *to give vent to one's fury.*   —*v.t.*   **1.** to give expression to: *to vent one's criticism.*   **2.** to provide with a vent or outlet.   **3.** to allow to escape through an opening: *to vent steam by opening a valve.*   [From the Old French word *esventer* meaning "to let out air," going back to the Latin suffix *-ex* "out, out of" and *ventus* "wind."]

vent[2] (vent) *n.*   a slit in a garment, as at the back of a coat.   [From the Old French word *fente* "a slit in a garment," from the word *fendre* meaning "to split, split open," from the Latin word *findere* "to separate, divide."]

ven·ti·late (ven′tə lāt′) *v.t.,* **ven·ti·lat·ed, ven·ti·lat·ing.**   **1.** to let air into; circulate fresh air in: *to ventilate a musty room by opening the windows.*   **2.** to bring to public notice; discuss publicly: *to ventilate a political issue.*

---

at; āpe; fär; câre; end; mē; it; īce; pîerce; hot; ōld; sông, fôrk; oil; out; up; ūse; rüle; pull; tûrn; chin; sing; shop; thin; <u>th</u>is; hw in white; zh in treasure. The symbol ə stands for the unstressed vowel sound heard in about, taken, pencil, lemon, and circus.

V

ven·ti·la·tion (ven′tə lā′shən) *n.* **1.** the act of ventilating or the state of being ventilated. **2.** a system or means of letting in or circulating fresh air: *The open window provided good ventilation.*

ven·ti·la·tor (ven′tə lā′tər) *n.* an apparatus for letting in or circulating fresh air, or for getting rid of foul or stale air.

ven·tral (ven′trəl) *adj.* of or relating to the abdomen or belly; abdominal: *the ventral fins of a fish.*

ven·tri·cle (ven′tri kəl) *n.* either of the two lower chambers or cavities of the heart, which receive blood from the atria and pump it into the arteries.

ven·tril·o·quism (ven tril′ə kwiz′əm) *n.* the art or practice of speaking or producing sounds without moving the lips, so that the sound seems to be coming from some source other than the speaker.

ven·tril·o·quist (ven tril′ə kwist) *n.* a person who practices ventriloquism, especially an entertainer who appears to carry on a conversation with a dummy. [From the Late Latin word *ventrioquus* meaning "a ventriloquist," from the Latin words *venter* "belly" and *loqui* "to speak." The word reflects the illusion that the voice of a ventriloquist comes from the belly rather than from the mouth.]

ven·ture (ven′chər) *n.* an undertaking that involves some risk or danger: *It was a foolhardy business venture that was sure to fail.* —*v.,* **ven·tured, ven·tur·ing.** —*v.t.* **1.** to expose to risk or danger: *to venture all one's savings on an uncertain business scheme.* **2.** to run the risk of; brave: *to venture a storm.* **3.** to express at the risk of criticism, objection, or the like: *May I venture a word of advice?* —*v.i.* to do or undertake something despite the risk or danger involved; dare: *The children ventured out onto the ice and almost fell through.*

ven·ture·some (ven′chər səm) *adj.* **1.** willing or inclined to take risks; bold; daring: *The venturesome teenagers went into the unexplored cave.* **2.** involving risk or danger; hazardous: *a venturesome journey.*

ven·tur·ous (ven′chər əs) *adj.* **1.** looking for adventure; bold; adventurous. **2.** risky or dangerous; hazardous.

ven·ue (ven′ū) *n. Law.* **1.** the place where a crime or other happening that is the cause of legal action takes place. **2.** the county, district, or locality where a jury must be called and where a trial must be held.

Ve·nus (vē′nəs) *n.* **1.** *Roman Mythology.* the goddess of love and beauty. In Greek mythology she is called Aphrodite. **2.** the sixth largest planet of the solar system and second in order of distance from the sun.

Ve·nus's-fly·trap (vē′nə siz flī′trap′) *n.* a plant native to moist, sandy regions of North and South Carolina, having leaves with two lobes that snap shut to trap insects. Also, **Venus flytrap.**

ve·ra·cious (və rā′shəs) *adj.* **1.** truthful; honest; true: *a veracious witness.* **2.** accurate; true: *a veracious account.* —**ve·ra′cious·ly,** *adv.* —**ve·ra′cious·ness,** *n.*

ve·rac·i·ty (və ras′i tē) *n., pl.* **ve·rac·i·ties. 1.** truthfulness; honesty: *to question the veracity of a witness.* **2.** accuracy; correctness: *to double-check figures for veracity.*

ve·ran·da (və ran′də) *also,* **ve·ran·dah.** *n.* an open porch, usually roofed, extending along one or more sides of a house.

verb (vûrb) *n.* a word belonging to that part of speech that expresses action, existence, or occurrence. Verbs

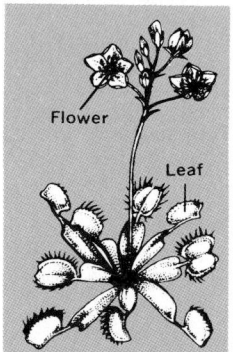

Flower

Leaf

Venus's-flytrap

usually form the main element in a predicate. *Be, fly, want,* and *spend* are verbs.

ver·bal (vûr′bəl) *adj.* **1.** of, relating to, or made up of words: *verbal communication.* **2.** expressed in speech; not written: *a verbal agreement.* **3.** word for word; literal: *a verbal translation.* **4.** *Grammar.* of, relating to, or derived from a verb: *In English "-ed" is a common verbal ending, as in "wanted" or "reached."* —*n. Grammar.* a noun or adjective that is derived from a verb. Gerunds, infinitives, and participles are verbals. —**ver′bal·ly,** *adv.*

ver·bal·ize (vûr′bə līz′) *v.,* **ver·bal·ized, ver·bal·iz·ing.** —*v.t.* to express in words: *to verbalize one's feelings.* —*v.i.* to be wordy. —**ver′bal·i·za′tion,** *n.*

ver·ba·tim (vər bā′tim) *adv.* word for word; in exactly the same words: *The newspaper printed the senator's speech verbatim.* —*adj.* word for word: *a verbatim translation.*

ver·be·na (vər bē′nə) *n.* any of a large group of trailing or loosely branching plants with clusters of small flowers.

ver·bi·age (vûr′bē ij) *n.* the use of more words than necessary; wordiness.

ver·bose (vər bōs′) *adj.* using more words than necessary; wordy: *a verbose speaker.* —**ver·bose′ly,** *adv.* —**ver·bos·i·ty** (vər bos′i tē), *n.*

ver·dant (vûr′dənt) *adj.* **1.** green with vegetation: *a verdant meadow.* **2.** green in color. —**ver′dant·ly,** *adv.*

ver·dict (vûr′dikt) *n.* **1.** the decision of a jury in a trial: *The jurors agreed on a verdict of guilty.* **2.** any decision or conclusion on some matter; judgment: *the verdict of public opinion.*

ver·di·gris (vûr′di grēs′) *n.* **1.** a poisonous mixture consisting of blue or green crystals that are formed when copper reacts with acetic acid. It is used as a paint pigment and insecticide. **2.** a greenish coating that forms on copper, brass, or bronze objects.

ver·dure (vûr′jər) *n.* **1.** the fresh, green color of growing vegetation. **2.** green vegetation.

verge¹ (vûrj) *n.* **1.** the edge or border of something. **2.** a point beyond which something happens or begins: *The frightened child was on the verge of tears.* —*v.i.,* **verged, verg·ing.** to be on the verge; border: *Your simple solution verges on genius.* [From the earlier meaning of "a rod indicating authority or office," from the Old French word *verge* "a rod, stick," from the Latin word *virga* "a rod, stick." The sense of *verge* meaning "a limit, boundary" came from phrases such as *within the verge* or *beyond the verge* meaning "within (beyond) the limit of authority."]

verge² (vûrj) *v.i.,* **verged, verg·ing.** to tend; incline; approach: *The bird's color is dark red, verging on purple.* [From the Latin word *vergere* meaning "to bend, incline."]

ver·i·fi·a·ble (ver′ə fī′ə bəl) *adj.* able to be verified.

ver·i·fi·ca·tion (ver′ə fi kā′shən) *n.* the act of verifying or the state of being verified.

ver·i·fy (ver′ə fī′) *v.t.,* **ver·i·fied, ver·i·fy·ing. 1.** to prove (something) to be true; confirm: *Several witnesses verified my account of the incident.* **2.** to check or test the accuracy or truth of: *The scientist's tests verified the results of the experiment.*

ver·i·ly (ver′ə lē) *adv. Archaic.* in truth; really.

ver·i·si·mil·i·tude (ver′ə si mil′i tüd′, ver′ə si mil′i-tūd′) *n.* the appearance of being true; closeness to truth.

ver·i·ta·ble (ver′i tə bəl) *adj.* true; actual; real: *Returning the money was veritable proof of the student's honesty.* —**ver′i·ta·bly,** *adv.*

ver·i·ty (ver′i tē) *n., pl.* **ver·i·ties. 1.** the state or quality of being true, real, or accurate. **2.** a true statement or fact; truth. **3. the verities.** things assumed to be universally true.

ver·mi·cel·li (vûr′mə sel′ē, vûr′mə chel′ē) *n.* a pasta made into long, slender threads that are thinner than spaghetti.

ver·mi·form (vûr′mə fôrm′) *adj.* shaped like a worm.
vermiform appendix, see **appendix** *(def. 1).*
ver·mil·ion (vər mil′yən) *also,* **ver·mil·lion.** *n.* **1.** a bright red color. **2.** a bright red pigment. —*adj.* having the color vermilion; bright red.
ver·min (vûr′min) *n., pl.* **ver·min.** **1.** any of various small insects or animals that are harmful, destructive, or troublesome, such as lice, fleas, or rats. **2.** a low or vile person or persons.
ver·mouth (vər müth′) *n.* a white wine flavored with herbs, used especially in making cocktails.
ver·nac·u·lar (vər nak′yə lər) *n.* **1.** the language native to the people of a certain country or locality. **2.** the common, everyday language of the people. **3.** the vocabulary used by the people of a particular profession or trade. —*adj.* **1.** (of a language or dialect) native to or used by the people of a certain country or locality. **2.** of, in, or using the everyday language of the people: *Mark Twain wrote using a vernacular style.*

Language Note

Although some form of English has been the **vernacular,** or everyday language, of England since the Anglo-Saxon invasions in the fifth and sixth centuries A.D., English was at various times considered unsuitable for use as the language of the court, the nobility, religion, and learning. Because nearly all of the learned men of ancient Britain were part of the Church, the vast majority of their writing was done in Latin, the language of the Church. The greatest contribution to the development of the vernacular as the language for English writing was made by Alfred the Great, an Anglo-Saxon king who ruled in the late ninth century. Alfred assigned various authors the task of translating major philosophical, religious, and historical works into Old English, the vernacular of that time, and he even undertook some of the work himself. Alfred also began the Anglo-Saxon Chronicle, a vernacular history of Britain from the time of Caesar to his own day. This work was continued for more than 250 years after his death. English continued to be used in the writing of sermons, moral lessons, lives of the saints, commentaries on the Bible, and various other works.

The Norman invasion in 1066 brought the French language to Britain. Norman French became the language of the court, the military, and learning (along with Latin). English survived as the spoken language of the common people. The vernacular did not return to official favor until 1362, when the formal opening of Parliament was conducted in English for the first time. In the same century, English (which we would now call Middle English) flourished in two ways. A wealth of first-rate literature appeared in English, most notably the works of the poet Chaucer. Another great step in the advancement of the vernacular came when the religious reformer John Wycliffe supervised the first translation of the Bible into English. During the late Middle Ages, vernacular literatures also arose in France, Germany, Italy, and Spain.

The revival of interest in Greek and Latin during the fifteenth and sixteenth centuries temporarily reversed the trend toward the universal acceptance of the vernacular. Scholars of that period thought that Greek and Latin were superior to English and more beautiful. English was not dominated by these other languages, however. Instead it grew by adding many new words from Latin and Greek, and the vernacular became even more widely accepted as suitable for most cultural, political, and intellectual activities.

ver·nal (vûr′nəl) *adj.* **1.** of, relating to, or happening in spring: *the vernal equinox.* **2.** like or suggesting spring; fresh or youthful: *the vernal spirit of youth.*
vernal equinox, the equinox that takes place about March 21. It marks the beginning of spring in the Northern Hemisphere.
ver·ni·er (vûr′nē ər) *n.* **1.** a short scale that slides along a longer scale and indicates subdivisions of it, used to make very fine measurements. Also, **vernier scale. 2.** a device used to make very fine adjustments in precision instruments. [From the French mathematician Pierre Vernier (1580–1637), who devised this scale.]

a **versatile** musician

ver·sa·tile (vûr′sə təl) *adj.* **1.** able to do many different things well: *a versatile athlete who can play most games with skill.* **2.** having many uses or functions: *a versatile tool.* —**ver′sa·til′i·ty,** *n.*
verse (vurs) *n.* **1.** an arrangement of words according to a particular meter or pattern, often in rhyme; poetry. **2.** a single line of poetry. **3.** a poem. **4.** a section of a poem, song, or similar composition, especially a stanza: *to sing the first verse of a hymn.* **5.** a particular type of poetic structure: *iambic verse.* **6.** one of the short divisions into which the chapters of the Bible are divided.
versed (vûrst) *adj.* learned or experienced; knowledgeable; skilled: *The English teacher is also versed in American history.*
ver·si·fi·ca·tion (vûr′sə fi kā′shən) *n.* **1.** the writing of verses. **2.** the art, practice, or theory of writing verses. **3.** a poetic form or style; metrical structure.
ver·si·fy (vûr′sə fī′) *v.,* **ver·si·fied, ver·si·fy·ing.** —*v.t.* **1.** to change from prose into verse form. **2.** to tell or describe in verse. —*v.i.* to compose verses. —**ver′si·fi′er,** *n.*
ver·sion (vûr′zhən) *n.* **1.** an account or description presented from a particular point of view: *Please tell us your version of the accident.* **2.** a translation from one language into another: *the English version of a French novel.* **3.** *also,* **Version.** a translation of the Bible or a part of the Bible: *the King James Version.* **4.** a different or changed form of something: *Congress passed a revised version of the bill.* **5.** an adaptation, as of a literary work: *the movie version of a novel.*

at; āpe; fär; câre; end; mē; it; īce; pîerce; hot; ōld; sông, fôrk; oil; out; up; ūse; rüle; pull; tûrn; chin; sing; shop; thin; this; hw in white; zh in treasure.
The symbol ə stands for the unstressed vowel sound heard in about, taken, pencil, lemon, and circus.

V

ver·sus (vûr′səs) *prep.* **1.** against: *It was the seniors versus the freshmen in the basketball game.* **2.** in contrast to; as an alternative to: *a life of hard work versus one of inactivity.*

vert., vertical.

ver·te·bra (vûr′tə brə) *n., pl.* **ver·te·brae** (vûr′tə brē′) or **ver·te·bras.** any of the small bones that make up the backbone.

ver·te·bral (vûr′tə brəl) *adj.* **1.** of, relating to, or of the nature of a vertebra or the vertebrae. **2.** composed of or having vertebrae.

ver·te·brate (vûr′tə brāt′, vûr′tə brit) *adj.* **1.** having a backbone: *vertebrate animals.* **2.** of, relating to, or characteristic of animals with backbones: *vertebrate anatomy.* —*n.* any of a large group of animals, including fish, amphibians, reptiles, birds, and mammals, having a backbone, a skeleton of bone or cartilage, and a brain enclosed in a skull.

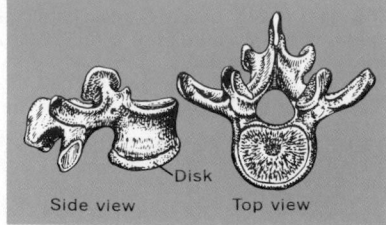

human **vertebra**

ver·tex (vûr′teks) *n., pl.* **ver·ti·ces** or **ver·tex·es.** **1.** the highest point of something; apex: *the vertex of a mountain.* **2.** *Geometry.* **a.** the point of a triangle, pyramid, or the like, opposite to the base. **b.** the point of intersection of the sides of an angle.

ver·ti·cal (vûr′ti kəl) *adj.* at a right angle to the plane of the horizon; upright; perpendicular: *a vertical climb up the face of a cliff.* —*n.* something vertical, such as a line or plane. —**ver′ti·cal·ly,** *adv.*

ver·ti·ces (vûr′tə sēz′) a plural of **vertex.**

ver·ti·go (vûr′ti gō′) *n.* a condition in which a person has a sensation of whirling about; dizziness; giddiness.

verve (vûrv) *n.* liveliness or enthusiasm; energy; spirit.

ver·y (ver′ē) *adv.* **1.** in a high degree; to a great extent; extremely: *to be very strong, to feel very sorry.* **2.** truly; absolutely; exactly: *the very best dancer.* —*adj.,* **ver·i·er, ver·i·est. 1.** identical; same: *This is the very textbook we used last term.* **2.** mere: *The very idea of getting up early made them miserable.* **3.** actual: *The thief was caught in the very act of stealing.* **4.** exact; precise: *Your gift was the very thing I needed.* **5.** absolute; complete; utter: *Our expenses have been reduced to the very minimum.* [From the Old French word *verai* meaning "true," going back to the Latin word *verus* "true."]

very high frequency, a radio frequency between 30 and 300 megahertz.

very low frequency, a radio frequency between 3 and 30 kilohertz.

ves·i·cle (ves′i kəl) *n.* any small sac, cavity, or cyst, especially one filled with fluid.

ve·sic·u·lar (və sik′yə lər) *adj.* of, relating to, or like a vesicle or vesicles.

ves·per (ves′pər) *n.* **1.** the bell that calls people to vespers. **2.** an evening prayer, hymn, or religious service. **3. Vesper.** the planet Venus when it appears as the evening star. —*adj.* **1.** of or relating to evening. **2.** of or relating to vespers: *a vesper service.*

ves·pers (ves′pərz) *also,* **Ves·pers.** *n.* **1.** the sixth of the seven canonical hours or the service for it. **2.** any religious service that is held in the late afternoon or early evening. ▲ used with a plural or singular verb.

ves·sel (ves′əl) *n.* **1.** a ship or large boat: *The ocean liner was a huge vessel.* **2.** a hollow container, as for liquids. **3.** a duct or tube that carries a body fluid, such as a vein or artery. **4.** a tubular structure in plants for conducting water.

vest (vest) *n.* a short, sleeveless garment, often buttoning in front and often worn under a jacket. —*v.t.* **1.** to clothe, as with vestments. **2.** to give authority, power, or the like to: *The club president is vested with the right to call special meetings.* **3.** to place in the control of: *All power to tax is vested in Congress.* —*v.i.* **1.** to clothe oneself, as with vestments. **2.** (of authority, power, or the like) to be or become vested.

Ves·ta (ves′tə) *n. Roman Mythology.* the goddess of the hearth and the hearth fire.

ves·tal (ves′təl) *n.* **1.** see **vestal virgin. 2.** a chaste woman; virgin. —*adj.* **1.** of or relating to the goddess Vesta. **2.** of or relating to the vestal virgins. **3.** chaste; pure.

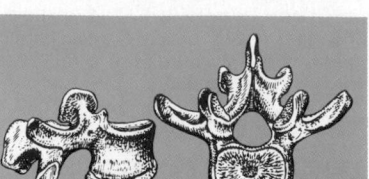

vest *(n.)*

vestal virgin, any of six virgin priestesses who watched over the sacred fire of Vesta in her temple in ancient Rome.

vest·ed (ves′tid) *adj.* **1.** *Law.* not depending on anything; fixed; settled: *a vested right.* **2.** clothed, especially in church vestments.

ves·ti·bule (ves′tə būl′) *n.* **1.** an entrance hall or passage between the outer door and the interior of a building; lobby. **2.** an enclosed space serving as a passage between one railroad passenger car and another. **3.** any small body cavity that leads to another cavity or canal, especially the cavity in the inner ear leading to the cochlea.

ves·tige (ves′tij) *n.* **1.** a trace, sign, or visible evidence of something that no longer exists: *The archaeologist discovered vestiges of an ancient temple.* **2.** *Biology.* a part or organ in a plant or animal that is not fully developed or useful, but once served a useful purpose in an earlier form of the plant or animal.

ves·tig·i·al (ves tij′ē əl) *adj.* of, relating to, or of the nature of a vestige: *a vestigial tail.*

vest·ment (vest′mənt) *n.* **1.** any of various garments worn by members of the clergy in the performance of religious services. **2.** a garment, especially an official or ceremonial robe or gown.

ves·try (ves′trē) *n., pl.* **ves·tries. 1.** a room in a church where the clergy put on their vestments and where the vestments and other articles used in religious services are kept. **2.** a room in a church or an attached building, used for Sunday school, prayer meetings, and the like. **3.** in parishes of the Anglican churches, a committee that manages the financial affairs of the parish.

ves·try·man (ves′trē mən) *n., pl.* **ves·try·men** (ves′trē mən). a member of an Anglican vestry.

ves·ture (ves′chər) *n.* **1.** clothing; garments. **2.** something that covers; covering.

vet¹ (vet) *n. Informal.* a veterinarian.

vet² (vet) *n. Informal.* a veteran.

vetch (vech) *n., pl.* **vetch·es.** any of a large group of climbing plants related to the pea, grown chiefly for food for cattle and sheep and to enrich the soil.

vet·er·an (vet′ər ən) *n.* **1.** a person who has had a great deal of experience, as in an occupation, office, or position: *The actor was a veteran of stage and screen.* **2.** a person who has served in the armed forces. —*adj.* **1.** having had a great deal of experience, as in an occupation: *a* *veteran newspaper reporter, a veteran teacher.* **2.** having had a great deal of experience in warfare or military matters: *veteran troops.*

Veterans Day, a legal holiday honoring veterans who have fought for the United States, formerly called Armistice Day. It is celebrated on November 11.

vet·er·i·nar·i·an (vet′ər ə när′ē ən) *n.* a person trained and licensed to give medical or surgical treatment to animals.

vet·er·i·nar·y (vet′ər ə ner′ē) *adj.* of or relating to the medical or surgical treatment of animals: *veterinary medicine, veterinary care.* —*n., pl.* **vet·er·i·nar·ies.** another word for **veterinarian.**

ve·to (vē′tō) *n., pl.* **ve·toes. 1.** the power of a president, governor, or other executive to reject a bill passed by a legislative body. **2.** the use of this power. **3.** any prohibition or refusal of consent by a person in authority. —*v.t.,* **ve·toed, ve·to·ing. 1.** to reject by a veto: *The president vetoed the bill passed by Congress.* **2.** to refuse to give consent to: *My parents vetoed any idea I had of buying a new bicycle.* [From the Latin word *veto* meaning ''I forbid.''] —**ve′to·er,** *n.*

vex (veks) *v.t.* **1.** to annoy or irritate, especially with petty matters: *The talkative student's constant interruptions vexed the teacher.* **2.** to trouble; torment; agitate: *sleep vexed by constant pain, land vexed with drought.*

vex·a·tion (vek sā′shən) *n.* **1.** the act of vexing or the state of being vexed; annoyance: *a look of vexation.* **2.** something that vexes: *This old car has always been a vexation to me.*

vex·a·tious (vek sā′shəs) *adj.* causing or tending to cause vexation; annoying: *a vexatious sales tax, vexatious problems.*

VHF, very high frequency.

v.i., intransitive verb.

VI, postal abbreviation for the Virgin Islands.

V.I., Virgin Islands.

vi·a (vī′ə, vē′ə) *prep.* by way of: *We drove home via the turnpike.*

vi·a·ble (vī′ə bəl) *adj.* **1.** capable of living: *a viable embryo.* **2.** capable of growing: *a viable seed.* **3.** capable of being used or done; workable; practical: *a viable plan.* —**vi′a·bil′i·ty,** *n.*

viaduct

vi·a·duct (vī′ə dukt′) *n.* a bridge that carries a road or railroad, as over a highway or valley.

vi·al (vī′əl) *also,* **phi·al.** *n.* a small glass bottle for holding a liquid, especially perfume or medicine.

vi·and (vī′ənd) *n.* **1.** an article of food. **2. viands.** choice food; delicacies: *a gift basket of tender viands.*

vi·brant (vī′brənt) *adj.* **1.** full of life, energy, and enthusiasm: *a vibrant personality.* **2.** vibrating: *a vi-*

brant string. **3.** resounding; resonant: *a vibrant sound.* —**vi′bran·cy,** *n.* —**vi′brant·ly,** *adv.*

vi·brate (vī′brāt) *v.,* **vi·brat·ed, vi·brat·ing.** —*v.i.* **1.** to move back and forth or up and down rapidly: *The strings of a guitar vibrate when plucked.* **2.** to respond or react emotionally; thrill: *The audience vibrated with excitement as the show began.* **3.** (of sounds) to echo; resound: *The explosion vibrated through the tunnel.* —*v.t.* to cause to move back and forth and up and down rapidly: *to vibrate a string.*

vi·bra·tion (vī brā′shən) *n.* **1.** the act of vibrating or the state of being vibrated: *Vibration of a string produces a sound.* **2.** *Physics.* a continuing, periodic, usually rapid motion of the particles of an elastic body or medium back and forth in alternate directions from a central point. **3.** a rapid movement back and forth or up and down; quivering; shaking: *the vibrations of the ground during a mild earthquake.*

vi·bra·to (vi brä′tō) *n., pl.* **vi·bra·tos.** *Music.* a trembling effect caused by a fast, very slight variation of the pitch of a musical tone.

vi·bra·tor (vī′brā tər) *n.* something that vibrates, especially an electrical device used in massage.

vi·bra·to·ry (vī′brə tôr′ē) *adj.* of, relating to, or producing vibration: *vibratory sensations.*

vi·bur·num (vī bûr′nəm) *n.* any of a group of shrubs or trees bearing clusters of white or pink flowers.

vic·ar (vik′ər) *n.* **1.** in the Church of England, a parish priest who receives a salary. **2.** in the Protestant Episcopal Church, a member of the clergy in charge of a chapel in a parish. **3.** any of various Roman Catholic prelates who represent the pope or a bishop. **4.** a person who acts as the representative of another.

vic·ar·age (vik′ər ij) *n.* **1.** the residence of a vicar. **2.** the rank, duties, or salary of a vicar.

vi·car·i·ous (vī kâr′ē əs) *adj.* **1.** done or endured for another: *vicarious punishment.* **2.** substituting for or representing another: *a vicarious agent.* **3.** experienced or enjoyed by an imagined sharing in the experience of another: *My friend's award gave me vicarious pleasure.* —**vi·car′i·ous·ly,** *adv.* —**vi·car′i·ous·ness,** *n.*

vice¹ (vīs) *n.* **1.** an immoral or harmful habit or practice: *Cheating and lying are vices.* **2.** immoral conduct; wickedness: *Vice is the opposite of virtue.* [From the Old French word *vice,* from the Latin word *vitium* meaning ''fault, error.'']

vice² (vīs) *British.* another spelling of **vise.**

vice– *prefix* a person who is subordinate to and acts in place of: *vice-principal.*

vice admiral, an officer in the U.S. Navy, ranking below an admiral and above a rear admiral.

vice presidency, *also,* **vice-pres·i·den·cy** (vīs′prez′i·dən sē) *n.* the office or function of vice president.

vice president, *also,* **vice-pres·i·dent** (vīs′prez′i dənt) *n.* an officer ranking second to a president and acting in the president's place when necessary. —**vice presidential** *also,* **vice′-pres′i·den′tial,** *adj.*

vice·roy (vīs′roi′) *n.* **1.** a governor of a province, kingdom, or colony, ruling as the deputy of a sovereign. **2.** an orange-and-black butterfly of North America that closely resembles, but is smaller than, the monarch butterfly.

vi·ce ver·sa (vī′sə vûr′sə) the opposite or reverse in

at; āpe; fär; câre; end; mē; it; īce; pierce; hot; old; sông, fôrk; oil; out; up; ūse; rüle; pull; tûrn; chin; sing; shop; thin; <u>th</u>is; hw in white; zh in treasure. The symbol ə stands for the unstressed vowel sound heard in about, taken, pencil, lemon, and circus.

V

order or relation; the other way around: *My friend helps me and vice versa.*

vi·chy·ssoise (vish′ē swäz′) *n.* a thick, creamy soup containing potatoes and leeks, usually served chilled.

vi·cin·i·ty (və sin′i tē) *n., pl.* **vi·cin·i·ties.** the area near or surrounding a particular place; neighborhood: *There are several parks in the vicinity of our house.*

vi·cious (vish′əs) *adj.* **1.** marked by wickedness; evil; depraved: *Kidnapping is a vicious crime.* **2.** full of malice; spiteful: *vicious lies, a vicious attack.* **3.** having an extremely bad disposition; savagely fierce: *a vicious dog.* **4.** intense; severe: *a vicious storm.* —**vi′cious·ly,** *adv.* —**vi′cious·ness,** *n.*

vicious circle, a situation in which the solving of a problem gives rise to another problem, which itself cannot be solved without bringing back the original problem.

vi·cis·si·tude (vi sis′i tüd′, vi sis′i tūd′) *n. usually,* **vicissitudes.** a change in a situation or condition: *the vicissitudes of a person's life, the vicissitudes of the weather.*

vic·tim (vik′təm) *n.* **1.** a person who is injured, killed, or ruined: *the victim of an automobile accident, a victim of lies and slander.* **2.** a person who is cheated or tricked: *the victim of a swindler.* **3.** a person or animal sacrificed to a god.

vic·tim·ize (vik′tə mīz′) *v.t.,* **vic·tim·ized, vic·tim·iz·ing. 1.** to make a victim of; inflict harm upon: *to be victimized by harsh living conditions.* **2.** to swindle; cheat: *to be victimized by an unscrupulous lawyer.* —**vic′tim·i·za′tion,** *n.*

vic·tor (vik′tər) *n.* a person who wins or conquers, as in a contest, struggle, or armed conflict.

vic·to·ri·a (vik tôr′ē ə) *n.* a low, four-wheeled carriage having a folding top, seats for two passengers, and a raised seat in front for the driver. [From Queen *Victoria* of England (1819–1901).]

victoria

Vic·to·ri·an (vik tôr′ē-ən) *adj.* **1.** of or relating to Queen Victoria of England or to the period of her reign: *Victorian literature, Victorian architecture.* **2.** of, relating to, or having characteristics associated with English people of Victorian England, such as prudishness or stuffiness. —*n.* a person who lived during the reign of Queen Victoria.

vic·to·ri·ous (vik tôr′ē əs) *adj.* **1.** having achieved a victory, as in a contest or armed conflict: *The victorious army was welcomed home.* **2.** of or relating to victory: *a victorious day for the home team.* —**vic·to′ri·ous·ly,** *adv.* —**vic·to′ri·ous·ness,** *n.*

vic·to·ry (vik′tə rē) *n., pl.* **vic·to·ries.** the defeat of an opponent or enemy, as in a contest or armed conflict: *Our basketball team won a decisive victory. The Allies achieved a great victory in World War II.*

Vic·tro·la (vik trō′lə) *n. Trademark.* a type of phonograph.

vict·ual (vit′əl) *n. usually,* **victuals.** food or provisions. —*v.t.,* **vict·ualed, vict·ual·ing.** to supply with food: *to victual a ship.*

vi·cu·ña (vī kü′nə, vī kū′nə, vī kü′nyə) *also,* **vi·cu·na.** *n., pl.* **vi·cu·ñas** or **vi·cu·ña. 1.** a small South American animal related to the llama, having a slender, graceful body and a long neck. It is highly valued for its silky wool coat. **2.** a fabric made from the wool of this animal.

vid·e·o (vid′ē ō′) *adj.* of or relating to the transmission or reception of television images. —*n.* **1.** the visual part of television. **2.** another word for **television. 3.** a program or performance, as of a popular song, recorded on video-

tape. [Formed from the Latin word *vudēre* meaning "to see" + the final *-o* of the English word *audio.*]

vid·e·o·cas·sette (vid′ē ō kə set′) *n.* a length of videotape, either blank or previously recorded, enclosed in a standard cassette for recording or playback.

videocassette recorder, another term for **VCR.**

vid·e·o·disc (vid′ē ō disk′) *also,* **vid·e·o·disk.** an optical disc that carries a recording of the sound and images of a motion picture or other program, designed for playback on special equipment and display on a television screen.

video display terminal a computer terminal consisting of a monitor and often a keyboard.

video game, any of various games in which a player or players move images on a cathode-ray tube, such as a television screen or computer monitor, by means of various devices, such as a joystick or keyboard.

vid·e·o·tape (vid′ē ō tāp′) *n.* **1.** magnetic tape used to record and play back images and accompanying sounds, as those of a television program. **2.** a length of such tape, as housed in a cassette. —*v.t.,* **vid·e·o·taped, vid·e·o·tap·ing.** to record on videotape.

videotape recorder, another term for **VCR.**

vie (vī) *v.i.,* **vied, vy·ing.** to be rivals; compete: *The tennis stars vied with each other for first place.*

Vi·en·nese (vē′ə nēz′, vē′ə nēs′) *n., pl.* **Vi·en·nese.** a person who was born in or is a citizen of Vienna. —*adj.* of, relating to, or characteristic of the city of Vienna or its people.

Vi·et·cong (vē′et kông′, vē′et kong′) *also,* **Viet Cong.** *n.* **1.** the Communist military force formed to wage guerrilla warfare in the former country of South Vietnam. **2.** a member of this group. [Short for the Vietnamese phrase *Viêt Nam cong-san* meaning "Vietnamese Communist."]

Vi·et·minh (vē′et min′) *also,* **Viet Minh.** *n.* the Communist party in Vietnam.

Vi·et·nam·ese (vē et′nə mēz′, vē et′nə mēs′) *n., pl.* **Vi·et·nam·ese. 1.** a person who was born in or is a citizen of Vietnam. **2.** the language of Vietnam. —*adj.* of or relating to Vietnam, its people, their language, or culture.

Vi·et·nam War (vē′et näm′) a civil war between rival governments in Vietnam, from 1954 to 1975. The United States participated on the side of South Vietnam, which finally lost to North Vietnam and its allies. Direct involvement by the United States lasted from the early 1960s until the U.S. withdrawal in 1975.

view (vū) *n.* **1.** the act of looking or seeing; sight: *The sailors' first view of land came after many weeks at sea.* **2.** a range of vision: *The airplane soon passed out of view.* **3.** something that is seen or can be seen: *We have a lovely view of the lake from our window.* **4.** a drawing, painting, print, or photograph: *The photographer took several views of the old lighthouse.* **5.** a particular way of thinking about something; attitude; opinion: *The two friends had different views on politics.* **6.** goal; aim: *to have a view to being a doctor.* —*v.t.* **1.** to look at or see: *Many people viewed the museum exhibit.* **2.** to think about; consider: *to view someone's behavior with concern.*

•**in view. a.** in sight: *We thought we heard footsteps, but there was no one in view.* **b.** under consideration: *Keep the future in view when you make your decision.*

•**in view of.** in consideration of; considering: *In view of the unfavorable weather, we should call off the picnic.*

•**on view.** open to the public; on exhibition: *The new automobiles are on view this week.*

•**with a view to.** with the aim or object of: *to save money with a view to buying a telescope.*

view·er (vū′ər) *n.* **1.** a person who views something, especially a person who watches television. **2.** any of several devices used to look at photographic slides or scientific specimens.

view·find·er (vū′fīn′dər) *n.* see **finder** (*def. 2*).

view·point (vū′point′) *n.* a way of thinking; point of view; mental attitude.

vig·il (vij′əl) *n.* **1.** the act or period of remaining awake to guard or observe something: *to keep vigil all night over a sick child.* **2.** a night or day spent in prayer, especially in preparation for a holy day. **3.** the day and night before a solemn feast day, as before Christmas. **4.** also, **vigils.** the prayers or religious services held on such a night or day.

vig·i·lance (vij′ə ləns) *n.* alertness; watchfulness: *Vigilance can prevent accidents.*

vig·i·lant (vij′ə lənt) *adj.* alert; watchful: *a vigilant nurse.* —**vig′i·lant·ly,** *adv.*

vig·i·lan·te (vij′ə lan′tē) *n.* **1.** a member of a group of persons who, without legal authority, take it upon themselves to punish criminals and maintain order. **2.** a person who acts alone who engages in such activities.

vi·gnette (vin yet′) *n.* **1.** a brief literary description or dramatic sketch. **2.** an ornamental design or illustration on the title page of a book or at the beginning or end of a chapter.

vig·or (vig′ər) *n.* **1.** active power or force: *The mayor campaigned with great vigor.* **2.** healthy strength: *the vim and vigor of youth.*

vig·or·ous (vig′ər əs) *adj.* full of, characterized by, or done with vigor: *vigorous exercise, a vigorous protest.* —**vig′or·ous·ly,** *adv.*

vi·king (vī′king) *also,* **Vi·king.** *n.* a member of the seafaring raiders from Scandinavia who attacked and plundered the coasts of Europe from the eighth to the eleventh centuries and who made long voyages to North America.

vile (vīl) *adj.,* **vil·er, vil·est. 1.** morally base; evil; immoral: *a criminal's vile deeds.* **2.** foul; disgusting; repulsive: *a vile odor, vile language.* **3.** degrading; mean; lowly: *the vile position of a slave.* **4.** very bad; unpleasant: *vile weather.* —**vile′ly,** *adv.* —**vile′ness,** *n.*

vil·i·fy (vil′ə fī′) *v.t.,* **vil·i·fied, vil·i·fy·ing.** to speak or write evil of; slander: *The newspaper editorial vilified the presidential candidate.* —**vil′i·fi·ca′tion,** *n.* —**vil′i·fi′er,** *n.*

vil·la (vil′ə) *n.* a large and luxurious house, especially one located in the country, on the outskirts of a city, or at the seashore.

vil·lage (vil′ij) *n.* **1.** a small community or group of houses, usually smaller than a town. **2.** the inhabitants of a village.

vil·lag·er (vil′i jər) *n.* a person who lives in a village.

vil·lain (vil′ən) *n.* **1.** a wicked, evil, or criminal person: *The villain got away with the crime.* **2.** such a person represented as a character in a novel or play: *The villain tried to discredit the hero.* **3.** another spelling of **villein.** —**vil′lain·ous,** *adj.* —**vil′lain·ous·ly,** *adv.*

vil·lain·y (vil′ə nē) *n., pl.* **vil·lain·ies. 1.** the actions or conduct of a villain; extreme wickedness; evil: *The noble knight fought all manner of villainy.* **2.** a villainous act or deed.

vil·lein (vil′ən) *also,* **vil·lain.** *n.* in feudalism, a peasant attached by rights to a plot of land but owing complete obedience to the lord. A villein was regarded as a freeman in relations with all persons other than the lord.

vil·lus (vil′əs) *n., pl.* **vil·li** (vil′ī). any of the small, hairlike projections on the surface of a mucous membrane, especially the membrane of the small intestine. The villi absorb certain nutrients.

vim (vim) *n.* energy, strength, or enthusiasm: *to be full of vim and vigor in the morning.*

vin·di·cate (vin′di kāt′) *v.t.,* **vin·di·cat·ed, vin·di·cat·ing. 1.** to clear (someone) of suspicion or charges of

wrongdoing: *The testimony of witnesses vindicated the accused.* **2.** to maintain or defend (a right or claim) against opposition. **3.** to justify: *The effectiveness of the treatment vindicated our confidence in the doctor.*

vin·di·ca·tion (vin′di kā′shən) *n.* **1.** the act of vindicating or the state of being vindicated. **2.** something that vindicates: *The success of the project was a vindication of our support.*

vin·dic·tive (vin dik′tiv) *adj.* having, showing, or coming from a desire for revenge; vengeful: *The opponents exchanged vindictive criticism.* —**vin·dic′tive·ly,** *adv.* —**vin·dic′tive·ness,** *n.*

vine (vīn) *n.* **1.** a plant with a long, usually slender stem, that grows along the ground or attaches itself to a tree, wall, or other support and grows upward. **2.** a vine on which grapes grow; grapevine.

vin·e·gar (vin′i gər) *n.* a sour liquid consisting chiefly of acetic acid, made by fermenting cider, wine, malt, or the like. It is used in flavoring or preserving food. [From the Old French word *vinaigre* meaning "vinegar," from the words *vin* "wine" + *aigre* "sour." The fermentation process that yields wine, if allowed to proceed, will sour the wine, producing vinegar.]

vin·e·gar·y (vin′i gə rē) *adj.* **1.** of or like vinegar: *a vinegary taste.* **2.** bad-tempered; sour: *a vinegary expression.*

vine·yard (vin′yərd) *n.* an area in which grapes are grown.

vin·tage (vin′tij) *n.* **1.** the wine produced from a particular crop of grapes. **2.** a year's crop of grapes. **3.** *Informal.* goods, articles, or items of some particular period or time: *a car of 1930 vintage.* —*adj.* of unusually high quality or merit; choice: *a vintage wine.*

vint·ner (vint′nər) *n.* a person who sells wines and liquors.

vi·nyl (vī′nəl) *n.* any of several flexible, shiny plastics used in floor tiles, raincoats, phonograph records, and many other products.

vi·ol (vī′əl) *n.* any of various stringed musical instruments that are similar to the violin and usually have six strings. Viols were used chiefly in the sixteenth and seventeenth centuries, and were later replaced by violins, violas, and the like.

vi·o·la (vē ō′lə) *n.* a stringed musical instrument of the violin family, slightly larger and lower in pitch than the violin.

vi·o·late (vī′ə lāt′) *v.t.,* **vi·o·lat·ed, vi·o·lat·ing. 1.** to fail to obey or keep; break: *to violate a law, to violate a peace treaty, to violate a promise.* **2.** to treat disrespectfully; desecrate; defile: *The vandals violated the church.* **3.** to break in upon; interrupt; disturb: *to violate someone's privacy.* **4.** to rape. —**vi′o·la′tor,** *n.*

vi·o·la·tion (vī′ə lā′shən) *n.* **1.** the act of violating or the state of being violated: *a violation of a peace treaty.* **2.** an instance of violating: *The driver received a summons for a traffic violation.*

vi·o·lence (vī′ə ləns) *n.* **1.** strong physical force or roughness used to injure or harm: *The mugger used violence in snatching the victim's briefcase.* **2.** a violent or destructive action: *the violence of a hurricane.* **3.** harm or injury caused by violent action or treatment: *The townspeople suffered violence in the wake of the*

---

at; āpe; fär; câre; end; mē; it; īce; pierce; hot; ōld; sông, fôrk; oil; out; up; ūse; rūle; pull; tûrn; chin; sing; shop; thin; this; hw in white; zh in treasure. The symbol ə stands for the unstressed vowel sound heard in about, taken, pencil, lemon, and circus.

V

storm. **4.** intensity of feeling or emotion: *We were shocked by the violence of the outburst.*

vi·o·lent (vī′ə lənt) *adj.* **1.** acting with, characterized by, or resulting from strong physical force or roughness: *to suffer a violent death.* **2.** caused by or showing intense feeling or emotion; passionate: *a violent temper.* **3.** characterized by great intensity or force; severe; extreme: *a violent wind.* —**vi′o·lent·ly,** *adv.*

vi·o·let (vī′ə lit) *n.* **1.** a small purple, white, or rose-colored flower of a plant found in Europe, Africa, and Asia. **2.** the plant bearing this flower. **3.** a bluish purple color. —*adj.* having the color violet.

vi·o·lin (vī′ə lin′) *n.* a musical instrument having four strings, played with a bow. It is the principal member of a family of stringed instruments that includes the viola and cello.

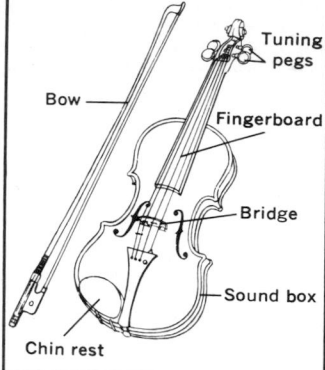

Tuning pegs
Bow
Fingerboard
Bridge
Sound box
Chin rest

violin

vi·o·lin·ist (vī′ə lin′ist) *n.* a person who plays the violin.

vi·ol·ist (vē ō′list) *n.* a person who plays the viola.

vi·o·lon·cel·list (vī′ə lən chel′ist) *n.* see **cellist.**

vi·o·lon·cel·lo (vī′ə lən chel′ō) *n., pl.* **vi·o·lon·cel·los.** see **cello.**

VIP, V.I.P. *Informal.* very important person.

vi·per (vī′pər) *n.* **1.** any of a group of poisonous snakes having a pair of sharp, hollow fangs through which venom is injected. **2.** a spiteful or treacherous person.

vi·per·ous (vī′pər əs) *adj.* **1.** of, like, or relating to a viper or vipers. **2.** spiteful or treacherous: *a viperous attack on one's character.*

vi·ra·go (vi rä′gō) *n., pl.* **vi·ra·goes** or **vi·ra·gos.** a bad-tempered, sharp-tongued woman.

vi·ral (vī′rəl) *adj.* of, relating to, or caused by a virus: *viral pneumonia.*

vi·re·o (vir′ē ō′) *n., pl.* **vir·e·os.** any of various small North American songbirds having green, yellow, brown, or gray feathers.

vir·gin (vûr′jin) *n.* **1.** a person, especially a girl or woman, who has never had sexual intercourse. **2. the Virgin.** the Virgin Mary. —*adj.* **1.** of, relating to, being, or suitable for a virgin. **2.** pure; spotless: *virgin snow.* **3.** not yet used; untouched: *a forest of virgin timber.*

vir·gin·al (vûr′jə nəl) *adj.* of, relating to, or suitable for a virgin.

Vir·gin·ia creeper (vûr jin′yə) a North American climbing vine having dull, oval, toothed leaflets and clusters of tiny green flowers. Also, **woodbine.**

Virginia reel, an American folk dance in which partners form two lines facing each other and perform a variety of steps.

vir·gin·i·ty (vər jin′i tē) *n.* the condition of being a virgin.

Vir·go (vûr′gō) *n.* **1.** a constellation in the northern sky, thought to resemble a young girl holding a spike of wheat. **2.** the sixth sign of the zodiac.

vir·ile (vir′əl) *adj.* **1.** manly; masculine: *The speaker had a deep, virile voice.* **2.** vigorous; forceful:

Virginia creeper

enthusiastic and virile support for a plan. **3.** capable of fathering children.

vi·ril·i·ty (və ril′i tē) *n.* the state or quality of being virile.

vi·rol·o·gy (vī rol′ə jē) *n.* the branch of microbiology that deals with viruses and the diseases caused by them.

vir·tu·al (vûr′chü əl) *adj.* being so in reality, though not in fact or name: *The president's assistant was the virtual head of the company.*

vir·tu·al·ly (vûr′chü ə lē) *adv.* in almost every way; practically: *Years of war had virtually destroyed the countryside.*

vir·tue (vûr′chü) *n.* **1.** moral excellence; righteousness; goodness: *Virtue is a quality of saints.* **2.** a particular type of moral excellence: *Honesty is a great virtue.* **3.** any good quality or trait of character: *You have the virtue of being a good listener.* **4.** chastity, especially of a woman. **5.** the power or strength to produce effects: *Inoculations have the virtue of preventing disease.* [From the Old French word *virtu* meaning "strength" or "moral excellence," from the Latin word *virtus* "manly strength, courage" or "excellence, virtue," from the word *vir* "man, male."]
  ·by virtue of. because of; by reason of; on the strength of: *They succeeded by virtue of practice and perseverance.*

vir·tu·os·i·ty (vûr′chü os′i tē) *n., pl.* **vir·tu·os·i·ties.** the skill, style, or art of a virtuoso.

vir·tu·o·so (vûr′chü ō′sō) *n., pl.* **vir·tu·o·sos** or **vir·tu·o·si** (vûr′chü ō′sē). **1.** a person who is exceptionally skilled in one of the fine arts, especially in music. **2.** a person who is exceptionally skilled in any activity.

vir·tu·ous (vûr′chü əs) *adj.* **1.** characterized by or showing virtue; righteous; good: *a virtuous person, virtuous deeds.* **2.** chaste; pure. —**vir′tu·ous·ly,** *adv.* —**vir′tu·ous·ness,** *n.*

vir·u·lence (vir′yə ləns) *n.* the quality or state of being virulent.

vir·u·lent (vir′yə lənt) *adj.* **1.** extremely poisonous or harmful: *a virulent infection.* **2.** extremely bitter or spiteful; full of hostility and hate: *a virulent speech.* —**vir′u·lent·ly,** *adv.*

vi·rus (vī′rəs) *n., pl.* **vi·rus·es.** any of a group of microscopic particles composed of a core of nucleic acid and an outer coat of protein. Viruses are smaller than any known bacteria and can reproduce and grow only in living cells, where they cause many diseases in humans, animals, and plants. [Formed from the Latin word *virus* meaning "venom" or "medicinal secretion."]

vi·sa (vē′zə) *n.* an official endorsement stamped on a person's passport by an official of a country, granting the holder of the passport permission to enter or leave the country.

vis·age (viz′ij) *n.* **1.** the face or facial expression of a person: *a worried visage.* **2.** the outward aspect or appearance of anything: *the sweet visage of a warm summer afternoon.*

vis·cer·a (vis′ər ə) *pl. n.* the soft organs inside the body, such as the heart, stomach, liver, intestines, and kidneys.

vis·cer·al (vis′ər əl) *adj.* **1.** of or relating to the viscera. **2.** arising from or caused by deep emotions or feelings: *a visceral reaction to danger.*

vis·cid (vis′id) *adj.* thick and gluey or sticky: *a viscid substance.*

vis·cos·i·ty (vis kos′i tē) *n., pl.* **vis·cos·i·ties.** the state or quality of being viscous: *The viscosity of oil diminishes with heat.*

vis·count (vī′kount′) *n.* in Great Britain and certain other countries, a nobleman who ranks just below an earl or count and just above a baron.

vis·count·ess (vī′koun′tis) *n., pl.* **vis·count·ess·es.**

1. the wife or widow of a viscount. **2.** a woman who holds a rank equal to that of a viscount.

vis·cous (vis′kəs) *adv.* (of a liquid) thick and gluey or sticky: *Molasses is more viscous than maple syrup.*

vise (vīs) *also, British,* **vice.** *n.* a tool with two jaws that are open and closed by turning a screw. It is used to hold an object firmly in place while it is being worked on.

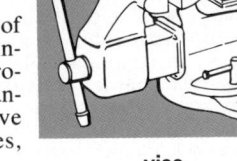

vise

Vish·nu (vish′nü) *n.* one of the three chief divinities of Hinduism, believed to be the protector and preserver of humanity. Vishnu is said to have been reincarnated many times, especially as Krishna.

vis·i·bil·i·ty (viz′ə bil′i tē) *n.*, *pl.* **vis·i·bil·i·ties. 1.** the state or quality of being visible: *The high visibility of yellow makes it a good color for school buses.* **2.** the distance that the eye can see when affected by physical conditions, such as light or weather: *Visibility is only a quarter of a mile today because of the fog.*

vis·i·ble (viz′ə bəl) *adj.* **1.** that can be seen; perceptible to the eye: *The house is visible from the road.* **2.** evident; apparent; obvious: *a long speech with no visible point to make, visible means of livelihood.* —**vis′i·bly,** *adv.*

Vis·i·goth (viz′i goth′) *n.* a member of the westernmost branch of the Goths that invaded the Roman Empire in the fourth century A.D. and settled in France and Spain.

vi·sion (vizh′ən) *n.* **1.** the act or power of seeing; sense of sight: *A person's vision usually changes with age. Glasses help my vision.* **2.** something that is or has been seen, especially someone or something of great beauty: *The garden was a vision of loveliness.* **3.** the ability to plan ahead; foresight: *a ruler of great vision.* **4.** something imagined; mental image: *The young writer had visions of success and fame.* **5.** a conception; view: *an unrealistic vision of the world.* **6.** something perceived in a dream, trance, or similar state: *The prophet had a vision of heaven.*

vi·sion·ar·y (vizh′ə ner′ē) *adj.* **1.** of, relating to, or seen in a vision: *the visionary splendors of paradise.* **2.** having visions: *a visionary saint.* **3.** having or characterized by impractical ideas or plans. *The visionary reformer advocated a society without any government or laws.* **4.** not able to be put into practice; not practicable; unrealistic: *a visionary scheme.* —*n.,* *pl.* **vi·sion·ar·ies. 1.** a person who has visions. **2.** a person whose ideas or plans are impractical.

vis·it (viz′it) *v.t.* **1.** to go to see (a person or persons) for social, business, or other reasons: *to visit a relative, to visit the dentist.* **2.** to go to (a place) for sightseeing: *The family visited Quebec last summer.* **3.** to stay with as a guest: *They visited friends for the weekend.* **4.** to go or come to see in an official or professional capacity: *The mayor will visit several of the city's hospitals tomorrow.* **5.** to come upon; afflict; assail: *A plague visited the country.* —*v.i.* **1.** to call on or stay with someone as a guest. **2.** *Informal.* to converse; chat: *to sit and visit for a few hours.* —*n.* the act or instance of visiting: *to pay a visit to a neighbor.*

vis·it·ant (viz′i tənt) *n.* a visitor, especially one thought to come from the spiritual world.

vis·it·a·tion (viz′i tā′shən) *n.* **1.** the act of visiting, especially an official visit for the purpose of inspection or examination. **2.** a punishment or reward sent by God.

visiting card, another term for **calling card.**

vis·i·tor (viz′i tər) *n.* a person who pays a visit.

vi·sor (vī′zər) *also,* **vi·zor.** *n.* **1.** the projecting brim on the front of a cap, designed to shade the eyes from the sun. **2.** in ancient armor, the movable front piece of a helmet that could be lowered to cover the upper part of the face. **3.** a projecting part attached above the windshield on the inside or outside of an automobile, truck, or other vehicle, designed to shield the eyes from glare.

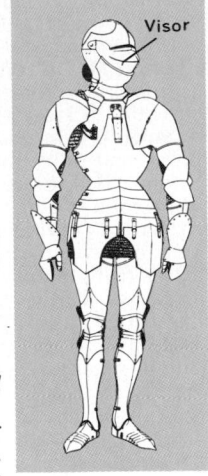

visor *(def. 2)*

vis·ta (vis′tə) *n.* **1.** a view, especially one seen through an opening or passage: *a vista of a lake.* **2.** a mental view of a series of events: *new vistas of peace and prosperity.*

vis·u·al (vizh′ü əl) *adj.* **1.** of, relating to, resulting from, or used in sight: *the visual sense, a visual nerve.* **2.** that can be seen; visible: *visual beauty.* —**vis′u·al·ly,** *adv.*

visual aid, any of various devices or materials involving the sense of sight, such as a chart, motion picture, videotape, or slide, used to aid or improve learning.

vis·u·al·ize (vizh′ü ə līz′) *v.t.,* **vist·u·al·ized, visu·al·iz·ing.** to form a mental image of: *The parents tried to visualize what their children would look like when grown.* —**vis′u·al·i·za′tion,** *n.*

vi·tal (vī′təl) *adj.* **1.** of, relating to, or characteristic of life: *vital forces, vital processes.* **2.** necessary to or supporting life: *the vital organs.* **3.** full of life and vigor; energetic: *a vital personality.* **4.** of greatest importance; essential: *The teacher's support is vital to the success of our project.* **5.** deadly; fatal: *a vital wound.* [From the Old French word *vital* meaning "having or supporting life," from the Latin word *vitalis* "of life," from the word *vita* "life."] —**vi′tal·ly,** *adv.* —**vi′tal·ness,** *n.*

vi·tal·i·ty (vī tal′i tē) *n., pl.* **vi·tal·i·ties. 1.** mental or physical vigor or energy: *a person of great vitality.* **2.** the power to live or continue living: *The great vitality of American society comes from its freedom.* **3.** the power to endure, continue, or survive: *New industry was necessary to ensure the vitality of the small country.*

vi·tal·ize (vī′tə līz′) *v.t.,* **vi·tal·ized, vi·tal·iz·ing. 1.** to put vitality or liveliness into: *to vitalize an old political issue.* **2.** to give life to. —**vi′tal·i·za′tion,** *n.*

vi·tals (vī′təlz) *pl. n.* **1.** the parts or organs of the body necessary or vital to life. **2.** the parts or features essential to the operation or existence of something.

vi·ta·min (vī′tə min) *n.* any of a group of organic compounds needed in very small amounts to maintain the health and normal functioning of the body.

vitamin A, any of several vitamins necessary for good vision at night, normal development of cells, and healthy skin. It is found in foods of animal origin, such as liver, whole milk, and eggs. A lack of vitamin A causes night blindness. Also, **retinol.**

vitamin B₁, a vitamin necessary for the normal release of energy from carbohydrates. It is found in meat, beans, peas, and nuts. A lack of vitamin B₁ causes beriberi. Also, **thiamine.**

---

at; āpe; fär; câre; end; mē; it; īce; pîerce; hot; ōld; sông, fôrk; oil; out; up; ūse; rüle; pull; tûrn; chin; sing; shop; thin; this; hw in white; zh in treasure. The symbol ə stands for the unstressed vowel sound heard in about, taken, pencil, lemon, and circus.

V

vitamin B₂, a vitamin necessary for metabolism and growth. It is found in liver, eggs, milk, and meats. Also, **riboflavin.**

vitamin B₆, a vitamin important in the utilization of protein in the body. It is found in cereal grains, yeast, and liver. Also, **pyridoxine.**

vitamin B₁₂, a complex vitamin that contains cobalt and is necessary for the formation of blood cells and for growth. It is found in high amounts in liver.

vitamin B complex, a group of vitamins found in yeast, liver, and other foods, including vitamin B₁ (thiamine), vitamin B₂ (riboflavin), vitamin B₆ (pyridoxine), vitamin B₁₂, biotin, niacin, and folic acid.

vitamin C, a vitamin compound that aids in the formation of connective tissues and prevents scurvy. It is found in citrus fruits and is made synthetically. A lack of vitamin C causes scurvy. Also, **ascorbic acid.**

vitamin D, any of several vitamins necessary for normal bone and tooth formation. It is found in fish-liver oils and is manufactured in the body by the action of sunlight on cholesterol. A lack of vitamin D causes rickets.

vitamin E, any of a group of vitamin compounds that are necessary for healthy cell membranes. It is found chiefly in green, leafy vegetables, cereals, grains, and certain vegetable oils.

vitamin G, former name of **vitamin B₂.**

vitamin H, former name of **biotin.**

vitamin K, any of several vitamins necessary for the clotting of blood. It is found chiefly in green, leafy vegetables and in tomatoes.

vi·ti·ate (vish′ē āt′) *v.t.*, **vi·ti·at·ed, vi·ti·at·ing. 1.** to impair the quality of; spoil: *The ugly, broken fence vitiated the beauty of the garden.* **2.** to make legally ineffective, such as a contract; invalidate. **—vi′ti·a′tion,** *n.*

vit·re·ous (vit′rē əs) *adj.* **1.** of, relating to, resembling, or of the nature of glass. **2.** made from glass: *vitreous china.* **3.** of or relating to the vitreous humor.

vitreous humor, the transparent, jellylike substance that fills the eyeball behind the lens.

vit·ri·fy (vit′rə fī′) *v.t., v.i.,* **vit·ri·fied, vit·ri·fy·ing.** to change into glass or a glassy substance: *The heat of the volcanic lava vitrified rocks in its wake.*

vit·ri·ol (vit′rē əl) *n.* **1.** a sulfate of copper, iron, lead, or zinc. Copper sulfate is blue; iron sulfate is green; lead sulfate and zinc sulfate are white. **2.** another word for **sulfuric acid. 3.** something that is harsh, sharp, or bitter, such as speech or writing: *The speech attacking the candidate's opponent was full of vitriol.*

vit·ri·ol·ic (vit′rē ol′ik) *adj.* **1.** of, like, or derived from vitriol. **2.** very harsh, sharp, or bitter: *vitriolic language.*

vi·tu·per·ate (vī tü′pə rāt′, vī tū′pə rāt′) *v.t.,* **vi·tu·per·at·ed, vi·tu·per·at·ing.** to speak harshly or abusively to or about; berate. **—vi·tu′per·a′tion,** *n.*

vi·tu·per·a·tive (vī tü′pə rā′tiv, vī tü′pər ə tiv, vī tū′pə rā′tiv, vī tū′pər ə tiv) *adj.* harsh or abusive: *vituperative speech.* **—vi·tu′per·a′tive·ly,** *adv.*

vi·va (vē′və) *interj. Italian, Spanish.* (long) live (a person or thing named). ▲ used as a shout of acclaim.

vi·va·cious (vi vā′shəs, vī vā′shəs) *adj.* full of life; lively or gay; animated: *a vivacious personality.* **—vi·va′cious·ly,** *adv.* **—vi·va′cious·ness,** *n.*

vi·vac·i·ty (vi vas′i tē, vī vas′i tē) *n.* liveliness or gaiety; animation: *a young crowd full of vivacity and charm.*

vive (vēv) *interj. French.* (long) live (a person or thing named). ▲ used as a shout of acclaim.

viv·id (viv′id) *adj.* **1.** (of colors) bright or intense; brilliant: *a vivid blue and yellow striped shirt.* **2.** clear and distinct; sharp: *I have a vivid recollection of the accident.* **3.** producing clear or lifelike images in the mind: *The writer gave a vivid description of the battle.* **4.** active; lively: *a vivid imagination.* **—viv′id·ly,** *adv.* **—viv′id·ness,** *n.*

viv·i·fy (viv′ə fī′) *v.t.,* **viv·i·fied, viv·i·fy·ing. 1.** to give life to; animate. **2.** to make vivid: *to vivify a room with bright colors.*

vi·vip·a·rous (vī vip′ər əs) *adj.* bringing forth living young, rather than eggs. Most mammals are viviparous.

viv·i·sect (viv′ə sekt′) *v.t.* to perform vivisection on (a living animal).

viv·i·sec·tion (viv′ə sek′shən) *n.* a surgical operation, dissection, or the like, performed on a living animal for the purpose of scientific study or experiment.

viv·i·sec·tion·ist (viv′ə sek′shə nist) *n.* a person who practices or supports vivisection.

vix·en (vik′sən) *n.* **1.** female fox. **2.** an ill-tempered or quarrelsome woman.

viz., namely. [Short for the Latin word *videlicet* meaning "evidently, clearly," from the phrase *videre licet* "it is easy to see."]

vi·zier (vi zîr′) *also,* **vi·zir.** *n.* in Muslim countries, a high official of the government, especially a minister of state.

vi·zor (vī′zər) another spelling of **visor.**

VLF, very low frequency.

vo·cab·u·lar·y (vō kab′yə ler′ē) *n., pl.* **vo·cab·u·lar·ies. 1.** all the words used or understood by a particular person or group, or used in a particular field of knowledge: *the vocabulary of science.* **2.** a list of words or of words and phrases, usually arranged in alphabetical order and defined or translated. **3.** all the words of a language. [From the Middle French word *vocabulaire* meaning "collection of words," going back to the Latin word *vocabulum* "defining word, term," from the word *vocare* "to call."]

Language Note

The **vocabulary** of English is one of the largest, if not the largest, of all languages. An unabridged English dictionary may contain as many as 600,000 entries. If the words found in scientific, technical, legal, slang, and other specialized dictionaries are added to this number, the total would probably be over 3 million words.

There are obviously more words in the English vocabulary than any one person could hope to use or learn. Some linguists estimate that the average educated adult has a vocabulary that is relatively small, perhaps between 35,000 and 70,000 words. Others believe the true figure is over 100,000. The variation in the estimates may be caused by the difference between people's working vocabulary, which is made up of the words that they would normally use, and their recognition vocabulary, which is made up of those words that they can recognize but would not normally use themselves. Whichever figure is accepted, most of what we say and write uses only a small fraction of the vocabulary available to us. The entire King James Bible, for example, has been estimated at somewhere between 16,000 and 25,000 different words.

The range of people's vocabulary depends greatly on their interests, background, profession, and education. Having a good vocabulary allows people to express themselves clearly. The only way to develop such a vocabulary is to listen and read carefully. If you come across a word that is unfamiliar to you, looking it up in your dictionary will help you to make it part of your vocabulary.

vo·cal (vō′kəl) *adj.* **1.** of, relating to, or expressed by the voice: *vocal sounds.* **2.** performed by or intended for the voice: *vocal music.* **3.** readily expressing one's views or opinions in speech: *to be vocal in one's criticism.* **—vo′cal·ly,** *adv.*

vocal cords, either of two pairs of membranes in the larynx. The passage of air from the lungs through the lower pair causes them to vibrate, thus producing the sound of the voice.

vo·cal·ic (vō kal′ik) *adj.* **1.** consisting mainly or completely of vowel sounds. **2.** of, relating to, or resembling a vowel sound.

vo·cal·ist (vō′kə list) *n.* a singer.

vo·cal·ize (vō′kə līz′) *v.,* **vo·cal·ized, vo·cal·iz·ing.** —*v.t.* to make vocal; utter or express with the voice: *to vocalize an objection.* —*v.i.* to produce sound with the voice; sing or speak. —**vo′cal·i·za′tion,** *n.*

vo·ca·tion (vō kā′shən) *n.* **1.** an occupation or profession; trade: *Teaching and medicine are vocations that require special training.* **2.** a strong desire to pursue a certain career: *a sense of vocation.* **3.** the work or career that a person feels called to do or is especially suited for.

vo·ca·tion·al (vō kā′shə nəl) *adj.* **1.** of or relating to a vocation or occupation: *vocational training.* **2.** of, relating to, or providing training or education in a skill, trade, or occupation, or guidance in choosing an occupation: *a vocational school, a vocational counselor.* —**vo·ca′tion·al·ly,** *adv.*

vo·cif·er·ous (vō sif′ər əs) *adj.* making or characterized by a loud outcry; clamorous: *a vociferous crowd, vociferous objections.* —**vo·cif′er·ous·ly,** *adv.* —**vo·cif′er·ous·ness,** *n*

vod·ka (vod′kə) *n.* a colorless alcoholic liquor, originally made in Russia, distilled from fermenting grain or potatoes.

vogue (vōg) *n.* **1.** the accepted fashion at a particular time: *Powdered wigs were in vogue during the 1700's.* **2.** popular acceptance or favor; popularity: *Those books had a great vogue several years ago.*

voice (vois) *n.* **1.** sound produced through the mouth, especially sound produced by the vocal organs of a human being, as in speaking or singing. **2.** the ability to produce such sound: *A bad cold made me lose my voice.* **3.** the quality, condition, or tone of vocal sound: *a soft voice, a high-pitched voice.* **4.** a sound resembling or suggesting vocal utterance: *the voice of the wind, the voice of thunder.* **5.** something likened to human speech: *the voice of conscience.* **6.** the right or privilege of expressing an opinion, view, or choice: *Citizens must have a voice in government.* **7.** an expressed opinion, choice, or wish: *A good public official listens to the voice of the people.* **8.** expression: *to give voice to one's feelings.* **9.** any of the vocal or instrumental parts in a musical composition. **10.** a singer: *a chorus of twenty voices.* **11.** *Grammar.* a form of a verb that shows whether its subject is active or passive. —*v.t.,* **voiced, voicing. 1.** to give utterance to; express: *to voice an opinion, to voice an objection.* **2.** *Phonetics.* to utter (a speech sound) with vibration of the vocal cords.

•**with one voice,** unanimously.

Word Family

A number of English words can be traced back to two closely related Latin words: *vox,* meaning "voice," and *vocare,* meaning "to speak." With our **voice,** we may **vocalize** using **vowel** sounds. Or we may speak out to **advocate** a particular action, **invoking** the help of our friends and perhaps **provoking** our opponents. If we have a sizable **vocabulary,** we may put it to use to **evoke** a desired response. We can **avow** what we believe or **vouch** for someone else's position, but if we choose not to commit ourselves we can **equivocate** on an issue. Our **vocation** is the work we feel called to, but some things we do as only hobbies, or **avocations.**

---

voice–ac·ti·vat·ed (vois′ak′tə vā′tid) *adj.* operated by means of the human voice: *a voice-activated door opener.*

voice box, see **larynx.**

voiced (voist) *adj.* **1.** having a voice. **2.** expressed by the voice. **3.** *Phonetics.* uttered with vibration of the vocal cords: *B is a voiced consonant.*

voice·less (vois′lis) *adj.* **1.** having no voice; mute. **2.** *Phonetics.* not voiced: *P is a voiceless consonant.* —**voice′less·ly,** *adv.*

void (void) *adj.* **1.** having no legal force; not legally valid: *The contract was declared void by the court.* **2.** not occupied by or containing matter; empty: *void space.* **3.** lacking or devoid: *a statement void of meaning.* —*n.* **1.** empty space; vacuum: *the void of outer space.* **2.** a feeling of emptiness or loss: *a void in one's life after a friend moves away.* —*v.t.* **1.** to make void or of no effect; cancel: *to void an agreement.* **2.** to empty or discharge. —**void′a·ble,** *adj.*

voile (voil) *n.* a lightweight, sheer fabric, usually made of cotton or wool, used for curtains, dresses, and other items.

vol., volume.

vol·a·tile (vol′ə təl) *adj.* **1.** tending to change readily into vapor, especially at ordinary temperatures; evaporating quickly: *Alcohol is a volatile liquid.* **2.** tending to change easily; changeable: *a volatile temperament.* **3.** easily aroused or disturbed; unstable: *an angry, volatile crowd.* —**vol′a·til′i·ty,** *n.*

vol·can·ic (vol kan′ik) *adj.* **1.** of, relating to, or characteristic of a volcano or volcanoes: *a volcanic eruption.* **2.** having or characterized by a volcano or volcanoes: *a volcanic island.* **3.** produced by or discharged from a volcano: *volcanic rock.* **4.** violent; explosive: *a volcanic outburst of anger.*

an erupting **volcano**

vol·ca·no (vol kā′nō) *n., pl.* **vol·ca·noes** or **vol·ca·nos. 1.** an opening in the surface of the earth through which molten rock, gases, and rock fragments are forced out. **2.** a cone-shaped hill or mountain around such an opening, built up by the material forced out. [From the Italian word *volcano,* from the Latin word *Volcanus* Vulcan, the Roman god of fire.]

vole (vōl) *n.* any of various gray or brown rodents closely

---

at; āpe; fär; câre; end; mē; it; īce; pîerce; hot; ōld; sông, fôrk; oil; out; up; ūse; rüle; pull; tûrn; chin; sing; shop; thin; this; hw in white; zh in treasure. The symbol ə stands for the unstressed vowel sound heard in about, taken, pencil, lemon, and circus.

V

related to the lemmings, having a plump body, small round ears, and a short tail.

vo·li·tion (və lish′ən) *n.* an act or power of willing or deciding: *The children helped with the dishes of their own volition.*

vol·ley (vol′ē) *n., pl.* **vol·leys. 1.** the discharge of a number of weapons at one time: *a volley from the artillery brigade.* **2.** the stones, arrows, bullets, or other missiles so discharged: *A volley of arrows met the advancing soldiers.* **3.** a burst or outburst of a number of things at once or in rapid succession: *The referee's decision met with a volley of protests.* **4.** *Tennis.* the return of a ball before it touches the ground. **5.** a sequence of hitting a ball back and forth over a net without interruption, as in tennis. —*v.i.,* **vol·leyed, vol·ley·ing. 1.** to be discharged in a volley. **2.** *Tennis.* to return the ball before it touches the ground. **3.** to hit the ball back and forth over the net, as in tennis.

vol·ley·ball (vol′ē bôl′) *n.* **1.** a game in which two teams placed in position on either side of a high net hit a round, inflated ball back and forth over the net with their hands, without letting it touch the ground. **2.** the ball used in this game.

volt (vōlt) *n.* a unit for measuring the force that makes electrons move in an electric current. One volt causes a current of one ampere to flow through a resistance of one ohm. [From the Italian physicist Alessandro *Volta* (1745–1827), who experimented with electricity.]

vol·tage (vōl′tij) *n.* electromotive force expressed in volts.

vol·ta·ic cell (vol tā′ik) a cell that produces electricity through the chemical action of two plates or rods of different metals in an electrolyte.

volt·me·ter (vōlt′mē′tər) *n.* an instrument for measuring the voltage between two points in an electric circuit.

vol·u·ble (vol′yə bəl) *adj.* speaking much and with a smooth, easy flow of words; fluent; talkative: *a voluble party guest.* —**vol′u·bil′i·ty,** *n.* —**vol′u·bly,** *adv.*

vol·ume (vol′ūm) *n.* **1.** a collection of written or printed pages bound together; book. **2.** one of a set or series of related books: *the fourth volume of an encyclopedia.* **3.** a number of issues of a magazine or newspaper, usually all the issues that are published in one year. **4.** the amount of space occupied in three dimensions, measured in cubic units: *the volume of liquid in a container.* **5.** an amount or quantity: *The volume of business fell off during the summer months.* **6.** the quantity or intensity of sound; loudness: *Please turn down the volume of the radio.*

vol·u·met·ric (vol′yə met′rik) *adj.* of or relating to measurement by volume.

vo·lu·mi·nous (və lü′mə nəs) *adj.* **1.** of great size or bulk; large: *the voluminous sails of a large ship.* **2.** forming or filling a large volume or many volumes: *the voluminous works of Dickens.* —**vo·lu′mi·nous·ly,** *adv.*

vol·un·tar·y (vol′ən ter′ē) *adj.* **1.** performed, done, or made of one's own free will: *a voluntary confession.* **2.** doing something of one's own free will, often without pay: *voluntary workers in a hospital.* **3.** controlled by the will: *voluntary muscles.* **4.** done on purpose; not accidental: *voluntary manslaughter.* **5.** supported by private contributions rather than by public funds: *a voluntary hospital.* —**vol·un·tar·i·ly** (vol′ən ter′ə lē), *adv.*

vol·un·teer (vol′ən tîr′) *n.* **1.** a person who offers to serve or do something willingly or by choice, often without pay: *The campaign staff consisted chiefly of volunteers. The teacher asked for volunteers to decorate the classroom.* **2.** a person who enters military service willingly or by choice, rather than as a result of being drafted. —*v.i.* to serve or offer one's services of one's own free will: *to volunteer for the army.* —*v.t.* to give or offer readily: *to volunteer an answer to the question.* —*adj.* **1.** of, relating to, or consisting of volunteers: *a volunteer*

fire department. **2.** serving as a volunteer: *a volunteer firefighter.*

vo·lup·tu·ar·y (və lup′chü er′ē) *n., pl.* **vo·lup·tu·ar·ies.** a person who indulges in sensual or luxurious pleasures.

vo·lup·tu·ous (və lup′chü əs) *adj.* **1.** having a full and shapely form: *a voluptuous beauty.* **2.** giving or characterized by sensual pleasure or luxury: *voluptuous surroundings, voluptuous habits.* —**vo·lup′tu·ous·ly,** *adv.* —**vo·lup′tu·ous·ness,** *n.*

vom·it (vom′it) *v.i.* **1.** to discharge the contents of the stomach through the mouth; throw up. **2.** to be thrown out with force: *Cinder and ash vomited out of the chimney.* —*v.t.* **1.** to discharge (the contents of the stomach) through the mouth. **2.** to throw out or discharge in large quantities or with force; spew: *The volcano vomited forth lava.* —*n.* the matter discharged in vomiting.

voo·doo (vü′dü) *n., pl.* **voo·doos. 1.** a set of mysterious religious rites characterized by a belief in sorcery and the power of charms. It originated in West Africa and is still practiced in the West Indies and elsewhere. **2.** a person who practices these rites. —*adj.* of or relating to voodoo.

voo·doo·ism (vü′dü iz′əm) *n.* the beliefs and practices of voodoo.

vo·ra·cious (və rā′shəs) *adj.* **1.** eating or craving large amounts of food; ravenous: *a voracious animal, a voracious appetite.* **2.** unable to be satisfied in some activity: *a voracious reader.* —**vo·ra′cious·ly,** *adv.* —**vo·rac′i·ty,** *n.*

vor·tex (vôr′teks) *n., pl.* **vor·tex·es** or **vor·ti·ces** (vôr′tə sēz′). a whirling mass, as of water or air, moving in a circle or spiral, that sucks nearby objects into its center; whirlpool or whirlwind.

vo·ta·ress (vō′tə ris) *n., pl.* **vo·ta·ress·es.** a female votary.

vo·ta·ry (vō′tə rē) *n., pl.* **vo·ta·ries. 1.** a person bound by a vow or vows, especially a monk, nun, or other person in religious life. **2.** a person devoted to a particular pastime, study, or activity; devotee: *a votary of tennis.*

vote (vōt) *n.* **1.** the formal expression of a wish or choice, in some matter to be decided: *to cast one's vote in the presidential election.* **2.** the means by which such a choice is expressed, such as a ballot or show of hands. **3.** a choice or decision so made: *The Senate vote was in favor of the bill.* **4.** the right or privilege of expressing such a choice; suffrage: *The nineteenth amendment to the Constitution gave women the vote.* **5.** the number of votes cast: *The vote was light in the election.* **6.** a group of votes or voters considered together: *the labor vote.* —*v.,* **vot·ed, vot·ing.** —*v.i.* to express one's opinion or choice by a vote; cast a vote: *to vote for a candidate for governor.* —*v.t.* **1.** to support or choose by a vote; cast a vote for: *to vote the Democratic or Republican ticket.* **2.** to grant or establish by a vote: *Congress voted the necessary funds for the project.* **3.** to declare: *The critics voted the show a success.* —**vot′er,** *n.*

·to vote down. to defeat by voting: *The committee voted down the proposal.*

·to vote in. to elect: *The candidate was voted in by a small margin.*

voting machine, a machine that automatically records and counts votes cast on it.

vo·tive (vō′tiv) *adj.* given, offered, or performed in fulfillment of a vow: *a votive offering.*

vouch (vouch) *v.i.* **1.** to give one's word or assurance: *I can vouch for my friend's honesty.* **2.** to serve as a guarantee: *These papers will vouch for my identity.*

vouch·er (vou′chər) *n.* **1.** a document, such as a canceled check or receipt, that serves as proof of payment. **2.** a person who vouches.

vouch·safe (vouch sāf′) *v.t.,* **vouch·safed, vouch·saf·ing.** to be kind enough to grant; deign: *to vouchsafe a prompt reply.*

vow (vou) *n.* a solemn promise or pledge: *marriage vows. The members of some religious orders take a vow of poverty.* —*v.t.* to promise or pledge solemnly: *to vow revenge, to vow loyalty.* —*v.i.* to make a vow.

vow·el (vou′əl) *n.* **1.** a voiced speech sound produced by not blocking the passage of air through the mouth, and forming a syllable or part of a syllable. **2.** a letter of the alphabet that represents such a sound, such as *a, e, i, o, u,* and sometimes *y.* —*adj.* of or relating to a vowel or vowels.

voy·age (voi′ij) *n.* **1.** a journey by water, usually one over the sea or other large body of water. **2.** any long journey: *a voyage to the moon.* —*v.i.*, **voy·aged, voy·ag·ing.** to make a voyage; go on a journey: *The group of explorers voyaged across the ocean.* —**voy′a·ger,** *n.*

V.P., vice president.

vs., versus.

v.t., transitive verb.

Vt., Vermont.

VT, postal abbreviation for Vermont.

Vul·can (vul′kən) *n. Roman Mythology.* the god of fire and of metalworking.

vul·can·ite (vul′kə nīt′) *n.* a hard, tough rubber that resembles ebony, used for such items as combs and toys.

vul·can·ize (vul′kə nīz′) *v.t.*, **vul·can·ized, vul·can·iz·ing.** to treat (rubber) with sulfur or other compounds and heat, in order to increase its strength and elasticity. [From the Roman god of fire *Vulcan.*] —**vul′can·i·za′tion,** *n.*

vul·gar (vul′gər) *adj.* **1.** showing or characterized by a lack of good breeding, refinement, or taste; coarse; crude: *a vulgar joke, a vulgar expression.* **2.** of, relating to, or characteristic of the common people: *the vulgar or vernacular tongue.* **3.** common; familiar; customary: *the vulgar dandelion.* —**vul′gar·ly,** *adv.*

vul·gar·ism (vul′gə riz′əm) *n.* a word, phrase, or expression that is used mostly by people without education, and is not considered acceptable in standard usage.

vul·gar·i·ty (vul gar′i tē) *n., pl.* **vul·gar·i·ties. 1.** the state or quality of being vulgar; lack of good breeding, refinement, or taste. **2.** something that is vulgar, such as an offensive action or expression.

vul·gar·ize (vul′gə rīz′) *v.t.*, **vul·gar·ized, vul·gar·iz·ing. 1.** to make coarse or crude: *to vulgarize language.* **2.** to express (something difficult) in a form that most people can understand; popularize: *to vulgarize recent discoveries in astronomy.*

Vulgar Latin, a vernacular form of ancient Latin, the main source of the Romance languages.

Vul·gate (vul′gāt) *n.* the Latin version of the Bible, translated in great part by St. Jerome and completed about A.D. 383. The Vulgate is the official Bible of the Roman Catholic Church and the basis of other translations.

vul·ner·a·ble (vul′nər ə bəl) *adj.* **1.** capable of being physically wounded or damaged; easily hurt: *The athlete's injured knee was a most vulnerable spot.* **2.** capable of being hurt emotionally; sensitive: *The shy youngster was very vulnerable to criticism.* **3.** open to attack; not sufficiently protected: *The open harbor was vulnerable in a storm.* —**vul′ner·a·bil′i·ty,** *n.* —**vul′ner·a·bly,** *adv.*

vul·pine (vul′pīn′) *adj.* of, relating to, or like a fox.

vul·ture (vul′chər) *n.* **1.** any of several large birds of prey having dark, dull feathers and a bald head and neck. Vultures feed chiefly on dead animals. **2.** a greedy, ruthless person: *Some so-called friends are vultures.*

vul·va (vul′və) *n., pl.* **vul·vae** (vul′vē) or **vul·vas.** the external parts of the female genital organs.

vy·ing (vī′ing) the present participle of **vie.**

vulture *(def. 1)*

at; āpe; fär; câre; end; mē; it; īce; pîerce; hot; ōld; sông, fôrk; oil; out; up; ūse; rüle; pùll; tûrn; chin; sing; shop; thin; this; hw in white; zh in treasure. The symbol ə stands for the unstressed vowel sound heard in about, taken, pencil, lemon, and circus.

V

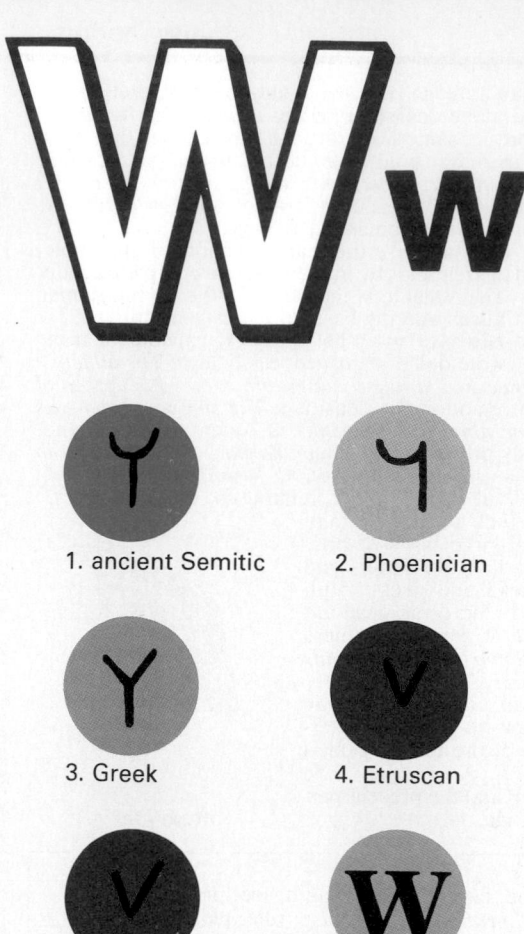

1. ancient Semitic   2. Phoenician

3. Greek   4. Etruscan

5. Latin   6. English

W is the twenty-third letter of the English alphabet. Like **U** and **J**, it did not come from Latin or from an earlier alphabet. **W** developed as a variation of the letter **V**, whose earliest ancestor was the ancient Semitic letter *waw* (1). The Phoenicians (2) borrowed *waw*, and later the Greeks adopted this letter and called it *upsilon* (3), writing it as the capital letter **Y** is written today. *Upsilon* was borrowed by the Etruscans (4), who wrote it as we write our modern capital letter **V**. This letter was adopted without change in the Latin alphabet (5). About 1,000 years ago, two forms of this V-shaped letter were being used in writing: **V** at the beginning of a word and a new letter, **U**, in the middle of a word. Later, when **V** began to be used to stand for only the consonant sound *v*, there was no longer a letter in the alphabet that represented the *w* sound. By writing two **V**'s or two **U**'s, Norman scribes soon combined these pairs of letters into a new letter that they called "double U." This new letter was written almost exactly the way we write the capital letter **W** today (6).

w, W (dub′əl ū′) *n., pl.* **w's, W's.** **1.** the twenty-third letter of the English alphabet. **2.** something having the shape of this letter.

w. **1.** week. **2.** weight. **3.** width.

W **1.** watt; watts. **2.** the symbol for tungsten. [From the German word *Wolfram* meaning "tungsten."] **3.** West. **4.** Western.

W. **1.** Wales. **2.** Wednesday. **3.** Welsh.

WA, postal abbreviation for the state of Washington.

wab·ble (wob′əl) *n.; v.t., v.i.,* **wab·bled, wab·bling.** another spelling of **wobble.**

wack·y (wak′ē) *also,* **whack·y.** *adj.,* **wack·i·er, wack·i·est.** *Slang.* strange or crazy, especially in a silly way.

wad (wod) *n.* **1.** a small, tightly packed mass or lump of soft material: *a wad of cotton, a wad of chewing gum, a wad of paper.* **2.** *Informal.* a tight roll of paper money, especially a large amount of money. **3.** a round plug used to hold the powder in place in a gun or cannon. —*v.t.,* **wad·ded, wad·ding.** **1.** to roll, press, or pack into a wad: *to wad paper and throw it in the wastebasket.* **2.** to stuff, pad, or pack with wadding.

wad·ding (wod′ing) *n.* a soft material used for stuffing, padding, or packing.

wad·dle (wod′əl) *v.i.,* **wad·dled, wad·dling.** to walk or move with short steps, swaying the body from side to side: *The duck waddled across the yard.* —*n.* a swaying or rocking walk. —**wad′dler,** *n.*

wade (wād) *v.,* **wad·ed, wad·ing.** —*v.i.* **1.** to walk in or through water, mud, or the like: *We waded across the creek.* **2.** to move or make one's way slowly and with difficulty: *The secretary had to wade through a pile of papers to find the missing letter.* —*v.t.* to walk through or cross by wading: *to wade a brook.* —*n.* the act of wading.

·**to wade in** or **to wade into.** *Informal.* to attack, approach, or begin with energy and enthusiasm.

Wade–Giles (wād′jīlz′) *n.* see **Pinyin.**

wad·er (wā′dər) *n.* **1.** a person who wades. **2.** any of various long-legged birds that wade about in shallow water searching for food, such as the crane, heron, or stork. **3. waders.** high, waterproof boots, or a pair of pants having such boots attached, worn especially when fishing in shallow water.

wa·di (wä′dē) *n.* **1.** a ravine in the deserts of Africa or Asia, through which a stream flows after a rainfall. **2.** a stream flowing through such a ravine.

wa·fer (wā′fər) *n.* **1.** a thin, crisp cookie or cracker, often sweetened and flavored. **2.** a thin disk of unleavened bread used in Holy Communion in the Roman Catholic and other churches. **3.** any thin disk, as of chocolate. **4.** a small, thin disk of paper or dried paste used for sealing letters, fastening documents, or the like.

waf·fle (wof′əl) *n.* a crisp batter cake having a surface patterned with square-shaped indentations, cooked in a waffle iron.

waffle iron, a cooking utensil consisting of two hinged metal plates with square-shaped projections, used to make waffles.

waft (waft, wäft) *v.i.* to float or be carried through the air or over water: *The smell of freshly brewed coffee wafted through the open door.* —*v.t.* to carry lightly and gently through the air or over water: *The evening breeze wafted the scent of land out to the ship.* —*n.* **1.** a light breeze; current of air. **2.** something, such as an odor, carried through the air: *I detected a waft of fresh-cut grass in the air.*

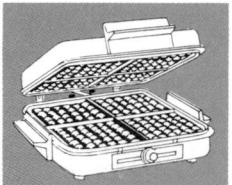

waffle iron

wag[1] (wag) *v.,* **wagged, wag·ging.** —*v.t.* to cause to move rapidly and repeatedly up and down or from side to side: *The friendly dog wagged its tail at the visitors.* —*v.i.* **1.** to move rapidly and repeatedly up and down or from side to side.   **2.** to move constantly in lively talk: *The news of their engagement made tongues wag at the office.* —*n.* the act of wagging; wagging motion. [From the Middle English word *waggen* with the same meaning.]

wag² (wag) *n.* a person who jokes and jests. [Of uncertain origin.]

wage (wāj) *n.* **1.** *often,* **wages.** payment for work done or services given: *Government workers receive their wages every two weeks.* **2. wages.** something given in return. ▲ used with a singular or plural verb: *For the wages of sin is death* (Romans 6:23). —*v.t.,* **waged, wag·ing.** to carry on or engage in: *to wage a war against crime.*

wage earner, a person who works for wages.

wa·ger (wā′jər) *n.* **1.** an agreement or promise to give or pay something to another person if that person is right about something and you are wrong; bet. **2.** something pledged or bet. —*v.t.* to pledge or risk in a wager; bet. —*v.i.* to make a wager; bet. —**wa′ger·er,** *n.*

wag·ger·y (wag′ə rē) *n., pl.* **wag·ger·ies. 1.** mischievous merrymaking. **2.** a jest or joke.

wag·gish (wag′ish) *adj.* **1.** fond of playing jokes. **2.** of, relating to, or characteristic of a wag or waggery: *a waggish sense of humor.* —**wag′gish·ly,** *adv.* —**wag′gish·ness,** *n.*

wag·gle (wag′əl) *v.t., v.i.,* **wag·gled, wag·gling.** to move or cause to move rapidly and repeatedly up and down or from side to side; wag. —*n.* the act of waggling; waggling motion.

wag·on (wag′ən) *n.* **1.** any of various four-wheeled vehicles, usually drawn by a horse or horses, used especially for carrying heavy loads. **2.** a child's low, rectangular, four-wheeled vehicle. **3.** a light truck or van that is used for carrying small loads: *a delivery wagon, a repair wagon.* **4.** see **station wagon. 5.** see **patrol wagon.**

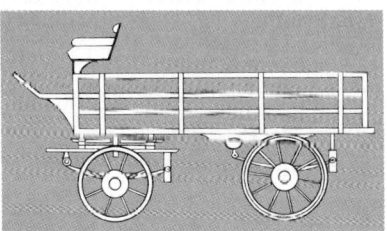
wagon (def. 1)

·**on the wagon.** *Informal.* no longer drinking alcoholic beverages.

wag·on·er (wag′ə nər) *n.* a person who drives a wagon.

wag·on·load (wag′ən lōd′) *n.* the amount that a wagon carries.

wagon train, a line or group of covered wagons traveling together.

waif (wāf) *n.* **1.** a person having no home, family, or friends, especially a lost child. **2.** anything that is without a home, such as a stray animal.

wail (wāl) *v.i.* **1.** to make a long, mournful cry, especially as an expression of grief or pain: *The baby wailed all afternoon.* **2.** to make a sound resembling this: *A siren was wailing in the street.* —*v.t.* to grieve over; bewail. —*n.* **1.** a long, mournful cry: *the wail of a lost child.* **2.** any sound resembling this. —**wail′er,** *n.*

wain (wān) *n. Archaic.* a wagon.

wain·scot (wān′skət, wān′skōt) *n.* a wood lining for inside walls, especially a paneled lining on the lower part of a wall. —*v.t.,* **wain·scot·ed, wain·scot·ing;** *also, British,* **wain·scot·ted, wain·scot·ting.** to line with a wainscot.

wain·scot·ing (wān′skō′ting) *n.* **1.** another word for **wainscot. 2.** the material used for a wainscot.

waist (wāst) *n.* **1.** the part of the human body between the ribs and the hips. **2.** a garment or part of a garment that covers this part of the body. **3.** the middle, narrow part of anything, such as the middle part of a violin or bell. **4.** the slender middle part of the body of an insect, such as a wasp or ant.

waist·band (wāst′band′) *n.* a band of material that encircles the waist, especially one that is attached to the top of a skirt or trousers.

waist·coat (wes′kət, wāst′kōt′) *n. British.* another word for **vest.**

waist·line (wāst′līn′) *n.* **1.** an imaginary line encircling the narrowest part of the waist: *a waistline of 30 inches.* **2.** the part of a garment that encircles this part of the body or falls just above or below it.

wait (wāt) *v.i.* **1.** to remain in a place so as to be ready for something or because something is expected: *Wait until you hear from me before leaving. I had to wait a long time for the bus this morning.* **2.** to look forward to something: *to wait for the day of one's graduation.* **3.** to be delayed: *Dinner will have to wait until the meat is done.* **4.** to perform the work of a waiter, waitress, or the like. —*v.t.* **1.** to remain in a place so as to be ready for (something): *to wait one's turn patiently.* **2.** *Informal.* to put off; delay: *We cannot wait dinner after 8:00.* —*n.* **1.** the act of waiting. **2.** a period of waiting: *There will be a two-hour wait before the next plane.*

·**to lie in wait.** to remain in hiding in order to attack.

·**to wait on** or **to wait upon. a.** to serve or help: *There were no clerks to wait on us at the store.* **b.** to visit formally: *A group of foreign ministers waited on the president.*

wait·er (wā′tər) *n.* a person whose job is serving food and drink, as in a restaurant.

wait·ing (wā′ting) *n.* the act of a person who waits: *Waiting is always tiresome.*

·**in waiting.** in attendance on a king, queen, or other member of a royal family.

waiting list, a list of the names of people who are waiting for something: *There is a long waiting list for apartments in the new building.*

waiting room, a room or area provided for the use of people who are waiting, as at an airport or doctor's office.

wait·ress (wā′tris) *n., pl.* **wait·ress·es.** a woman whose job is serving food and drink, as in a restaurant.

waive (wāv) *v.t.,* **waived, waiv·ing. 1.** to give up voluntarily: *to waive a right, to waive a privilege.* **2.** to put aside for the present; defer: *to waive a question.*

waiv·er (wā′vər) *n.* **1.** the voluntary giving up of something, as a legal right. **2.** a document that states this.

wake¹ (wāk) *v.,* **waked** or **woke, waked** or **wo·ken, wak·ing.** —*v.i.* **1.** to stop sleeping: *We woke at the sound of the alarm clock.* **2.** to become aware, active, or aroused: *The townspeople eventually woke to their responsibilities.* —*v.t.* **1.** to rouse from sleep: *Be quiet or you'll wake the baby.* **2.** to make active or aroused; stir up: *The news report waked the people to the danger.* —*n.* a watch or vigil over the body of a dead person before burial. [From the Old English words *wacan* meaning "to awaken" and *wacian* meaning "to watch, remain awake."]

wake² (wāk) *n.* **1.** the track left by a boat, ship, or other object moving through water: *The wake of the speedboat rocked the canoe.* **2.** a track or path left by anything that has passed: *the wake of a storm.* [Of Scandinavian origin.]

at; āpe; fär; câre; end; mē; it; īce; pîerce; hot; ōld; sông, fôrk; oil; out; up; ūse; rüle; pùll; tûrn; chin; sing; shop; thin; this; hw in white; zh in treasure. The symbol ə stands for the unstressed vowel sound heard in about, taken, pencil, lemon, and circus.

W

·in the wake of. a. following close behind: *Many traders came in the wake of the gold rush.* **b.** as a result or consequence of: *Much suffering followed in the wake of the war.*

wake·ful (wāk'fəl) *adj.* **1.** unable to sleep: *The hurricane blowing outside kept me wakeful.* **2.** without sleep: *The sick child spent a wakeful night.* **3.** watchful; vigilant: *a wakeful sentry.* —**wake'ful·ness,** *n.*

wak·en (wā'kən) *v.t.* **1.** to stop from sleeping; wake. **2.** to make active or aroused; stir up: *The book wakened new interest in conservation.* —*v.i.* to stop sleeping: *We wakened when the alarm sounded.*

wale (wāl) *n.* **1.** one of a series of ridges or ribs on the surface of certain fabrics, such as corduroy. **2.** one of several thick planks fastened horizontally to the sides of a boat or ship. **3.** a raised mark on the skin, such as one made by the lash of a whip; welt. —*v.t.,* **waled, wal·ing.** to raise a wale or wales on, as by whipping.

walk (wôk) *v.i.* **1.** to move by placing one foot on the ground before lifting the other: *You walk too fast.* **2.** to move on foot for exercise or for pleasure: *We walk after dinner almost every night.* **3.** to move in a way that resembles walking: *The toy duck walked across the floor.* **4.** to behave or live in a particular manner: *to walk in peace.* **5.** *Baseball.* (of a batter) to go to first base as a result of having been pitched four balls. —*v.t.* **1.** to move through, over, or across on foot: *I walked the streets in search of a restaurant.* **2.** to go with on foot: *I'll walk you to the door.* **3.** to make or help to walk: *to walk a dog, to walk a horse.* **4.** *Baseball.* (of a pitcher) to allow (a batter) to advance to first base by pitching four balls. —*n.* **1.** the act or an instance of walking, especially for exercise or for pleasure: *Let's take a walk.* **2.** the distance to be walked, often measured in the time required: *The beach is only a ten-minute walk from here.* **3.** a manner of walking: *a fast, bouncy walk.* **4.** a place set apart for walking: *The walk was covered with snow.* **5.** a particular social position or profession: *People from all walks of life live in this neighborhood.* **6.** *Baseball.* the act or fact of allowing a batter to advance to first base by pitching four balls.

·to walk off with. a. to win, as a prize. **b.** to steal: *to walk off with someone else's bike.*

·to walk out. to go on strike.

·to walk out on. *Informal.* to abandon; desert.

walk·er (wô'kər) *n.* **1.** a person or thing that walks. **2.** something used to help a person walk, especially an enclosed metal framework.

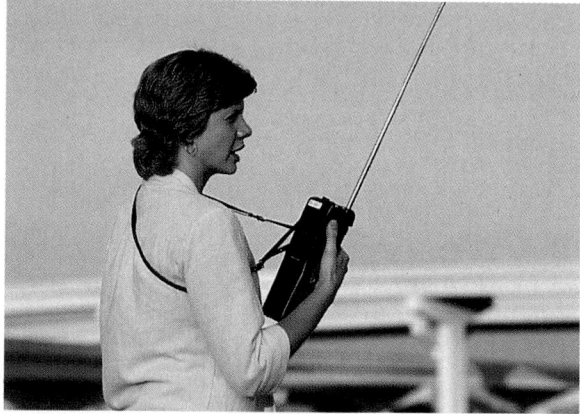

walkie-talkie

walk·ie–talk·ie (wô'kē tô'kē) *n., pl.* **walk·ie–talk·ies.** a small, portable, two-way radio.

walking stick 1. a stick or cane carried in the hand as an aid in walking or hiking. **2.** any of a group of brown or green insects that have long legs and a slender body that resembles a stick or twig.

Walk·man (wôk'mən, wôk'man') *n. Trademark.* a portable, battery-operated cassette player and/or radio with headphones.

walk–on (wôk'ôn', wôk'on') *n.* a very small part in a play, movie, or show.

walk·out (wôk'out') *n.* **1.** a strike in which workers leave their place of work. **2.** the act of walking out of a meeting or the like, especially as an expression of protest.

walk·o·ver (wôk'ō'vər) *n. Informal.* an easy victory.

walk–up (wôk'up') *n.* **1.** an apartment or office above the first floor in a building having no elevator. **2.** an apartment house or building having no elevator.

walk·way (wôk'wā') *n.* a place or passage set apart for walking.

wall (wôl) *n.* **1.** an upright structure of stone, plaster, wood, brick, or similar material, that forms the side of a building or room, or that divides or protects an area. **2.** the side or inner surface of something, such as a part of the body; lining: *the wall of the stomach.* **3.** something that resembles or acts as a wall: *a wall of fire, a wall of hatred.* —*v.t.* to form the side of, divide, protect, or block with a wall or walls: *to wall in a courtyard, to wall off a bedroom in an attic, to wall up an old entrance.*

wal·la·by (wol'ə bē) *n., pl.* **wal·la·bies** or **wal·la·by.** any of various small and medium-sized kangaroos that live in Australia and New Zealand.

wall·board (wôl'bôrd') *n.* a building material made of wood pulp or a similar substance pressed into large sheets, used instead of wood or plaster to cover walls or ceilings.

walled (wôld) *adj.* having or surrounded by walls: *a medieval walled city.*

wal·let (wol'it, wô'lit) *n.* a flat folding case, usually of leather, used for holding money, cards, photographs, and the like.

wall·eye (wôl'ī') *n.* **1.** an eye that turns outward away from the nose. **2.** an eye whose cornea is opaque or whose iris has little or no color. **3.** a large staring eye, as that of certain fish. **4.** a freshwater fish found in lakes and streams of eastern North America. Walleyes have large, staring eyes, and are caught for food and sport. Also (def. 4), **walleyed pike.**

wall·eyed (wôl'īd') *adj.* having walleyes.

walleyed pike, see **walleye** (def. 4).

wall·flow·er (wôl'flou'ər) *n.* **1.** *Informal.* a person who does not take part in a dance or party, usually because of shyness or unpopularity. **2.** a plant that bears dense clusters of fragrant yellow or orange flowers.

Wal·loon (wo lün') *n.* **1.** a member of a people living mainly in central and southern Belgium. **2.** the language of this people, a dialect of French.

wal·lop (wol'əp) *Informal. v.t.* **1.** to give a beating to; thrash. **2.** to hit hard; smack; sock: *The batter walloped the ball over the fence.* **3.** to overcome, as in a contest; defeat easily. —*n.* **1.** a forceful blow. **2.** the power to deliver such a blow.

wal·low (wol'ō) *v.i.* **1.** to toss or roll about in something: *Pigs wallow in mud. The children wallowed in the pile of leaves.* **2.** to take great pleasure; revel: *to wallow in self-pity.* **3.** to have a great amount of something: *to be wallowing in money.* —*n.* **1.** the act of wallowing. **2.** a place where an animal, such as a pig, goes to wallow.

wall·pa·per (wôl'pā'pər) *n.* decorative paper used to cover inside walls. —*v.t.* to put wallpaper on the walls of: *to wallpaper the kitchen.*

Wall Street, the banks and financiers who control or influence the economy of the United States. [From *Wall*

Street in New York City, where the New York Stock Exchange and other financial institutions are located.]

wall–to–wall (wôl'tə wôl') *adj.* **1.** covering the entire surface of a floor: *wall-to-wall carpeting.* **2.** completely occupying an area, space, or time period: *The movie was two hours of wall-to-wall excitement.*

wal·nut (wôl'nut') *n.* **1.** a sweet, oily, edible nut enclosed in a hard shell that is divided into halves. **2.** the tree that produces this nut. **3.** the wood of a walnut tree. [From the Old English word *wealhhnutu* meaning "walnut, foreign nut," from the words *wealh* "a foreigner" + *hnutu* "nut." *Wealh* is the name the Anglo-Saxons gave to the Celts. Today this word survives in the Modern English word *Welsh*.]

wal·rus (wôl'rəs, wol'rəs) *n., pl.* **wal·rus·es** or **walrus.** a large mammal that lives in water in Arctic regions. The walrus resembles but is larger than a seal, and has a thick neck, a pair of long ivory tusks, and a tough hide. Also, **sea horse.**

walrus

waltz (wôlts) *n., pl.* **waltzes. 1.** a dance in triple time having an accent on the first beat, performed by couples who whirl and glide across the dance floor. **2.** the music for this dance. —*v.i.* **1.** to dance a waltz. **2.** to move in a lively and confident manner, as if dancing: *to waltz out of a room.* —*v.t.* to lead in a waltz: *I waltzed my partner about the dance floor.* —**waltz'er,** *n.*

wam·pum (wom'pəm, wôm'pəm) *n.* **1.** small, polished beads made from shells and strung together or woven into belts, collars, or necklaces. It was used by certain tribes of North American Indians as money. **2.** *Slang.* money. [Short for the Algonquian word *wampompeag* meaning "white strings (of money.)"]

wan (won) *adj.,* **wan·ner, wan·nest. 1.** not having a natural or healthy color; pale: *a wan complexion.* **2.** showing illness or weariness; weak: *a wan smile.* —**wan'ly,** *adv.* —**wan'ness,** *n.*

wand (wond) *n.* **1.** a slender rod, especially a rod used by a magician. **2.** a short staff used as a symbol of office or authority.

wan·der (won'dər) *v.i.* **1.** to go or move about aimlessly; roam: *We wandered all over the countryside.* **2.** to go at a slow, relaxed pace; stroll: *Toward evening the cattle wandered homeward.* **3.** to lose one's way or go astray: *The small child wandered off in the store.* **4.** to become easily distracted from the matter at hand: *The speaker wandered off the subject.* **5.** to follow a winding course; meander: *The river wandered through the hills.* —*v.t.* to go or move about aimlessly: *The homeless youth wandered the streets.* —**wan'der·er,** *n.*

wan·der·lust (won'dər lust') *n.* a strong urge to travel, especially in a slow, relaxed manner with no fixed destination.

wane (wān) *v.i.,* **waned, wan·ing. 1.** to become less or smaller, as in size, brightness, or strength: *The moon waned. My enthusiasm for sports has waned.* **2.** to become less, as in power, importance, or influence: *The institution of monarchy has waned in our times.* **3.** to draw to a close: *The day waned.* —*n.* **1.** the act of waning; becoming smaller or less. **2.** a period of waning.

wan·gle (wang'gəl) *v.,* **wan·gled, wan·gling.** *Informal.* —*v.t.* to bring about or get through cleverness, trickery, or deceit: *With flattering words I wangled an invitation to the party.* —*v.i.* to use cleverness, trickery, or deceit, especially to get something for oneself.

Wan·kel engine (wang'kəl) a type of internal-combustion rotary engine that has a triangular rotor inside an elongated combustion chamber. [From the German engineer Felix *Wankel* (b. 1902), who designed it.]

want (wont, wônt) *v.t.* **1.** to have a desire or wish for: *She wants a better job. He wants to travel.* **2.** to have too little of or be without; lack: *a student who wants confidence.* **3.** to need; require: *The stew wants seasoning.* **4.** to look for in order to capture: *The robber was wanted by the police.* —*v.i.* to be needy or poor. —*n.* **1.** a lack or need: *a want of money.* **2.** the condition of being without the necessities of life: *a family in want.* **3.** something that is needed or desired: *to have many wants.*

want ad, another term for **classified ad.**

want·ing (won'ting, wôn'ting) *adj.* **1.** missing; lacking: *What is wanting in this room is more furniture.* **2.** not having something necessary; deficient: *to be wanting in experience.* —*prep.* **1.** not having; without: *a pot wanting a handle.* **2.** minus; less: *a month wanting two days.*

wan·ton (won'tən) *adj.* **1.** showing or resulting from a complete lack of feeling for others; marked by extreme thoughtlessness or ill will: *wanton cruelty, a wanton attack.* **2.** having loose morals; immoral. **3.** not controlled; unruly: *a wanton growth of weeds.* —*n.* a person who behaves in an immoral way. —**wan'ton·ly,** *adv.* —**wan'ton·ness,** *n.*

wap·i·ti (wop'i tē) *n., pl.* **wap·i·ti** or **wap·i·tis.** an elk of North America.

war (wôr) *n.* **1.** an armed conflict between countries or different groups within a country. **2.** any active opposition or struggle; fight: *a war against disease.* **3.** the profession or science of armed conflict: *The general is well-schooled in war.* —*v.i.,* **warred, war·ring.** to engage in war; fight. —*adj.* of, relating to, or used in war: *a war dance, war rations.*

War Between the States, another name for the **Civil War.**

war·ble (wôr'bəl) *v.,* **war·bled, war·bling.** —*v.i.* **1.** to sing with quavers or trills, as a bird. **2.** to make a melodic, warbling sound: *The shallow stream warbled as it flowed over the pebbles.* —*v.t.* to sing with quavers or trills: *to warble a tune.* —*n.* a trilling, quavering sound, such as the song of a bird.

war·bler (wôr'blər) *n.* **1.** any of various small songbirds found in North and South America, often having brightly colored feathers. **2.** a person who warbles.

war bonnet, a ceremonial headdress worn by certain North American Indians, especially the Plains Indians. It is usually made of eagle feathers, and each feather represents an act of bravery or other honor earned by the wearer.

warbler *(def. 1)*

war crime, any violation of the international laws and customs governing warfare, such as ill-treatment of prisoners or civilians, or unnecessary plunder or destruction of property.

ward (wôrd) *n.* **1.** a room or division of a hospital containing a number of patients: *a children's ward.* **2.** a division of a jail or prison. **3.** a person who is under the care or control of a court or guardian, such as an orphan.

---

at; āpe; fär; câre; end; mē; it; īce; pîerce; hot; ōld; sông, fôrk; oil; out; up; ūse; rüle; pull; tûrn; chin; sing; shop; thin; **th**is; hw in white; zh in treasure. The symbol ə stands for the unstressed vowel sound heard in about, taken, pencil, lemon, and circus.

W

1061

4. an administrative division of a town or city. —*v.t.* **to ward off.** to turn back or repel: *to ward off an attack.*

-ward *suffix* in the direction of: *downward, southward.*

ward·en (wôr′dən) *n.* **1.** a person whose job it is to care for or guard someone or something, especially a person in charge of a prison. **2.** an official who enforces certain laws, as in a game preserve.

ward·er (wôr′dər) *n.* a person who guards a door, gate, or tower.

ward·robe (wôrd′rōb′) *n.* **1.** a collection of clothing, such as all the clothes belonging to one person. **2.** a piece of furniture or closet for keeping clothes.

-wards a form of the *suffix* -ward.

ware (wâr) *n.* **1. wares.** articles for sale: *The shopkeepers displayed their wares.* **2.** a specific kind of manufactured article. ▲ used mainly in combination: *glassware, tableware.* **3.** pots and other objects made of fired clay; pottery: *ceramic ware.*

ware·house (wâr′hous′) *n., pl.* **ware·hous·es** (wâr′hou′ziz). a building where merchandise is stored.

war·fare (wôr′fâr′) *n.* the act of fighting a war; armed conflict.

war·head (wôr′hed′) *n.* the part in the front of a missile or torpedo that contains the explosive charge.

war–horse (wôr′hôrs′) *n.* **1.** a horse trained for use in battle; charger. **2.** *Informal.* a person who is very experienced, as from having been in many battles or struggles.

war·i·ly (wâr′ə lē) *adv.* in a cautious manner, cautiously: *The bear approached the trap warily.*

war·i·ness (wâr′ē nis) *n.* the state or quality of being cautious.

war·like (wôr′līk′) *adj.* **1.** fond of war; quick to go to war: *a warlike nation.* **2.** threatening war; hostile: *a warlike atmosphere.* **3.** of, relating to, or characteristic of war: *warlike exploits.*

war·lock (wôr′lok′) *n.* a male witch; sorcerer; wizard.

war·lord (wôr′lôrd′) *n.* a strong military leader who controls a territory.

warm (wôrm) *adj.* **1.** having a moderate degree of heat; somewhat hot; not cold: *a warm bath, a warm room.* **2.** having a feeling of heat: *to be warm from a fever.* **3.** giving off or holding in heat: *the warm sun, warm clothing.* **4.** full of enthusiasm, kindness, or affection: *warm thanks, a warm person.* **5.** excited or heated; lively: *a warm debate.* **6.** newly made; fresh: *The fox's trail was still warm.* **7.** (of colors) suggesting heat or warmth, as red and yellow. —*v.t.* **1.** to make warm or comfortably heated: *They warmed themselves by the fire.* **2.** to inspire with affectionate, kindly feelings: *The sight of home warmed their hearts.* —*v.i.* **1.** to become warm. **2.** to become affectionate or kindly toward someone or something: *The children warmed to their new neighbors after the first few weeks.* —**warm′ly,** *adv.* —**warm′ness,** *n.*

  ·**to warm up. a.** to make warm, as by heating: *to warm up rolls for dinner.* **b.** to get ready by practicing or exercising: *The runner warmed up before the race.* **c.** to make or become more friendly or enthusiastic: *The timid kitten finally warmed up to me.* **d.** to run (an engine or machine) until it reaches the right condition or temperature for operating.

warm–blood·ed (wôrm′blud′id) *adj.* having blood that stays at almost the same temperature, even though the temperature of the air or other surroundings changes. Birds and mammals are warm-blooded.

warm front, the forward edge of a mass of warm air that is pushing back a mass of cold air.

warm–heart·ed (wôrm′här′tid) *adj.* having or showing sympathy, kindness, or affection: *a warm-hearted person.* —**warm′-heart′ed·ly,** *adv.* —**warm′-heart′ed·ness,** *n.*

warming pan, a large, covered, long-handled pan that holds hot coals, formerly used to warm beds.

war·mon·ger (wôr′mung′gər, wôr′mong′gər) *n.* a person who favors or tries to bring about war.

warmth (wôrmth) *n.* **1.** the state or quality of being warm: *the warmth of the sun, the warmth of a woolen blanket.* **2.** enthusiasm or excitement; zeal: *The clowns were encouraged by the warmth of the crowd's applause.* **3.** kindness or affection; friendliness: *the warmth of a person's smile.*

warm–up (wôrm′up′) *n.* **1.** the act of practicing or exercising to get ready for some event: *We watched the warm-up of the pitchers before the baseball game.* **2.** the act of running an engine or machine until it reaches the right temperature or condition for operating.

warn (wôrn) *v.t.* **1.** to put on guard by giving notice beforehand, as of approaching danger; caution: *A radio bulletin warned the townspeople of the approaching hurricane.* **2.** to give advice to; counsel: *The doctor warned the patient to avoid salty food.* **3.** to give notice to; make aware of; signal: *The blinking red light warned drivers to stop.* **4.** to notify to keep at a distance: *The notice warned people away from the condemned building.* —*v.i.* to give a warning: *The lighthouse warned of danger ahead.*

warn·ing (wôr′ning) *n.* **1.** notice or advice given beforehand, as of approaching danger: *The darkened sky gave warning of the approaching tornado.* **2.** something that serves to warn: *The sign was a warning to trespassers.* —*adj.* serving to warn: *a warning signal.* —**warn′ing·ly,** *adv.*

War of 1812, the war between the United States and Great Britain lasting from 1812 to 1815.

War of Independence, another name for the **American Revolution.**

warp (wôrp) *v.t.* **1.** to bend, curve, or twist out of shape: *The dampness of the room had warped the guitar.* **2.** to turn from what is correct or right; twist: *Prejudice can warp a person's judgment.* **3.** to move (a ship) by pulling on a line or cable that is fastened to something, such as a dock or anchor. —*v.i.* to be or become bent, curved, or twisted. —*n.* **1.** a bend, curve, or twist, especially in a piece of wood: *The warp in the boards made them unsuitable for building.* **2.** threads running lengthwise in a woven fabric. **3.** a line or cable used in moving a ship.

war·path (wôr′path′) *n., pl.* **war·paths** (wôr′pathz′, wôr′paths′). the route taken by a group of North American Indians engaged in war.

  ·**on the warpath. a.** taking part in or getting ready for war. **b.** ready for a fight; angry.

war·plane (wôr′plān′) *n.* an airplane designed and built for use in war.

war·rant (wôr′ənt, wor′ənt) *n.* **1.** something that gives a good reason or justification for some action or conclusion: *There is no warrant for such a rude remark.* **2.** a document that authorizes something, such as an arrest or the payment of money. —*v.t.* **1.** to approve officially; authorize; sanction: *The law warrants the arrest of dangerous criminals.* **2.** to give a good reason for: *These few facts do not warrant your conclusion.* **3.** to guarantee: *The car dealer warranted the new car for one year.* **4.** to state positively: *I warrant they are the ones who did it.*

warrant officer, an officer of the armed forces who receives a certificate of appointment rather than a commission, and who ranks between a commissioned officer and an enlisted person.

war·ran·ty (wôr′ən tē, wor′ən tē) *n., pl.* **war·ran·ties.** **1.** a written statement or assurance given by a seller to a buyer that the seller's product is as described or that it will be repaired or replaced if proven defective within a

1062

certain period of time; guarantee. **2.** an authorization or justification; warrant.

war·ren (wôr′ən, wor′ən) *n.* **1.** a place where rabbits or other small animals live and breed. **2.** a very crowded place where many people live.

war·ri·or (wôr′ē ər, wor′ē ər) *n.* a person who fights or who is experienced in fighting battles.

war·ship (wôr′ship′) *n.* a ship designed and built for use in war.

wart (wôrt) *n.* **1.** a small, hard lump that grows on the skin, caused by a virus. **2.** a similar growth on a plant. —**wart′like′,** *adj.*

wart·hog (wôrt′hôg′, wôrt′hog′) *n.* an African wild hog having wartlike growths on the sides of its head, two pairs of curved tusks, and a dark coat with bristles and long, coarse hairs.

warthog

war·time (wôr′tīm′) *n.* a period of war.

wart·y (wôr′tē) *adj.,* **wart·i·er, wart·i·est. 1.** having or covered with warts. **2.** of or resembling warts.

war·y (wâr′ē) *adj.,* **war·i·er, war·i·est. 1.** always on the alert; watchful: *a wary watchdog.* **2.** characterized by caution; guarded: *a wary reply, a wary expression.* —**war′i·ly,** *adv.*

was (wuz, woz; *unstressed* wəz) the first and third person singular, past tense of **be.**

wash (wôsh, wosh) *v.t.* **1.** to make (something) free of dirt, germs, or the like, usually by using soap and water on it: *to wash one's face, to wash dishes.* **2.** to remove by using water or soap and water: *I washed a gravy stain out of the tablecloth.* **3.** to wear away or destroy by the action of water: *Rain gradually washed away the hillside.* **4.** to sweep or carry away by the action of water: *The sailor was washed overboard.* **5.** to make wet or moist: *The waves washed the deck with salt water.* **6.** to cover with a thin coat, as of ink or paint. —*v.i.* **1.** to clean oneself: *to wash before each meal.* **2.** to clean clothes, usually with soap and water. **3.** to undergo washing without damage: *This new fabric washes well.* **4.** to flow or beat with a splashing sound: *We could hear the waves washing on the rocks.* —*n., pl.* **wash·es. 1.** the act of washing or the state of being washed. **2.** the quantity of articles, such as clothes, washed at one time: *I hung the wash on the line this morning.* **3.** a flow or rush of water, or the sound made by this. **4.** a liquid used for a particular purpose: *a wash for an infected eye.* **5.** a disturbance in the water or air caused by a moving ship or airplane. **6.** a thin coat, as of ink or paint.

· **to wash down. a.** to clean from top to bottom: *to wash down walls.* **b.** to drink something with (food or medicine) in order to make swallowing easier: *to wash a pill down with orange juice.*

· **to wash one's hands of.** to refuse to have any more to do with.

· **to wash out. a.** to clean the inside of, as with soap and water: *to wash out the bathtub.* **b.** to destroy or carry away by the action of moving water: *The flood washed out the bridge.* **c.** to be removed by using water or soap and water: *The food stains washed out quickly.* **d.** to fail or cause to fail completely: *The collapse of the stock market washed out the stockbroker's business.*

· **to wash up. a.** to wash one's face and hands, as before dinner. **b.** to clean dishes and cooking utensils after a meal. **c.** to ruin or be ruined: *After a steady decline in sales, the company was all washed up and went bankrupt.*

Wash., Washington.

wash·a·ble (wô′shə bəl, wosh′ə bəl) *adj.* that can be washed without damage: *a washable sweater.*

wash–and–wear (wôsh′ən wâr′, wosh′ən wâr′) *adj.* (of a fabric or garment) that requires little or no ironing after washing.

wash·ba·sin (wôsh′bā′sin, wosh′bā′sin) *n.* another word for **washbowl.**

wash·board (wôsh′bôrd′, wosh′bôrd′) *n.* a board with a ridged surface on which clothes are rubbed during washing.

wash·bowl (wôsh′bōl′, wosh′bōl′) *n.* a bowl, basin, or sink used to hold water for washing or shaving. Also, **washbasin, washstand.**

wash·cloth (wôsh′klôth′, wosh′klôth′) *n.* a small cloth used for washing one's body or face. Also, **washrag.**

washed–out (wôsht′out′, wosht′out′) *adj.* **1.** that has faded, as from age or washing: *a dull, washed-out plaid shirt.* **2.** *Informal.* without strength or energy; exhausted: *We felt washed-out after a day walking in the sun.*

washed–up (wôsht′up′, wosht′up′) *adj. Informal.* all through, especially due to failure; finished.

wash·er (wô′shər, wosh′ər) *n.* **1.** a person or thing that washes. **2.** any of various appliances for washing, such as a washing machine. **3.** a flat ring of metal, rubber, or other material, used under a nut or around a bolt or the like to prevent friction or leakage or to give a tighter fit: *You need a new washer to keep that tap from leaking.*

wash·er·wom·an (wô′shər wùm′ən, wosh′ər wùm′ən) *n., pl.* **wash·er·wom·en** (wô′shər wim′ən, wosh′ər wim′ən). a woman who is employed to wash clothes; laundress. Also, **washwoman.**

wash·ing (wô′shing, wosh′ing) *n.* **1.** the act of cleaning with water: *Washing and ironing are done once a week.* **2.** the number of articles, such as clothes, washed at one time.

washing machine, an appliance for washing clothes, linen, and the like.

washing soda, see **sodium carbonate** (*def.* 2).

Wash·ing·ton's Birthday (wô′shing tənz, wosh′ing tənz) the anniversary of the birthday of George Washington, observed as a legal holiday on February 22 or on the third Monday in February in some states of the United States.

wash·out (wôsh′out′, wosh′out′) *n.* **1.** the carrying away of something, such as part of a road, by the action of water. **2.** the channel or hole resulting from this. **3.** *Informal.* a failure.

wash·rag (wôsh′rag′, wosh′rag′) *n.* another word for **washcloth.**

wash·room (wôsh′rüm′, wôsh′rüm′, wosh′rüm′, wosh′rùm′) *n.* a building or room having a toilet and washing facilities; lavatory.

wash·stand (wôsh′stand′, wosh′stand′) *n.* **1.** a piece of furniture, such as a table, for holding a basin and pitcher used for washing. **2.** another word for **washbowl.**

wash·tub (wôsh′tub′, wosh′tub′) *n.* a large tub used for soaking or washing clothes or household linen.

wash·wom·an (wôsh′wùm′ən, wosh′wùm′ən) *n., pl.* **wash·wom·en** (wôsh′wim′ən, wosh′wim′ən). another word for **washerwoman.**

was·n't (wuz′ənt, woz′ənt) *contr.* was not.

at; āpe; fär; câre; end; mē; it; īce; pîerce; hot; ōld; sông, fôrk; oil; out; up; ūse; rüle; pùll; tûrn; chin; sing; shop; thin; **th**is; hw in white; zh in treasure. The symbol ə stands for the unstressed vowel sound heard in about, taken, pencil, lemon, and circus.

W

wasp (wosp) *n.* any of numerous winged insects that have slender bodies and narrow waists. The female can give a painful sting. Most wasps live and work alone, although a few species, like the hornets and yellow jackets, are social insects and live in colonies.

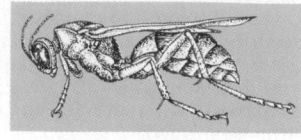

wasp

WASP (wosp) *n.* an American who is a Protestant white of English or northern European descent, regarded as a typical member of the most privileged class in the United States. ▲ sometimes used to show dislike. [Short for *W*(hite) *A*(nglo-)*S*(axon) *P*(rotestant).]

wasp·ish (wos′pish) *adj.* **1.** of, resembling, or like a wasp. **2.** quick to become angry; bad-tempered. —**wasp′ish·ly,** *adv.* —**wasp′ish·ness,** *n.*

was·sail (wos′əl) *n.* **1.** an expression used when making a toast, especially to someone's health. **2.** an alcoholic drink usually made of ale or wine with sugar, spices, or roasted apples added. **3.** a festive party where drinks are served and toasts are made. —*v.i.* **1.** to take part in or drink a wassail. **2.** to go from house to house at Christmas singing carols. —*v.t.* to drink to the health of; toast. [The Middle English word *wassail* came from the words of a toast *wæs hail!* meaning ''Be healthy!'' This toast was borrowed from the Old Norse phrase *ves heill* ''Be healthy!''] —**was′sail·er,** *n.*

wast (wost) *Archaic.* the second person singular, past tense of **be.**

wast·age (wās′tij) *n.* **1.** loss by use, wear, decay, or the like: *great wastage of natural resources.* **2.** something lost in this way.

waste (wāst) *v.,* **wast·ed, wast·ing.** —*v.t.* **1.** to use or spend in a careless or useless way: *to waste time.* **2.** to use up, wear away, or exhaust: *The long illness had wasted the elderly patient's strength.* **3.** to destroy; ruin: *The advancing army wasted everything in its path.* —*v.i.* to lose energy, strength, health, or the like: *The homeless kitten wasted away from lack of food and care.* —*n.* **1.** the act of wasting or the state of being wasted: *The trip was a waste of time.* **2.** a wild or desolate place where there are few or no living things. **3.** a slow process of wearing away. **4.** worthless material; refuse: *kitchen waste.* **5.** undigested material eliminated from the body. —*adj.* **1.** left over, rejected, or thrown away as worthless: *a pile of waste material.* **2.** of, relating to, or for waste: *a waste receptacle.* **3.** having few or no living things; desolate.
  ·**to go to waste.** to fail to be used properly or at all: *Our careful planning for the boat trip went to waste when it rained.*
  ·**to lay waste.** to destroy; devastate.

waste·bas·ket (wāst′bas′kit) *n.* a basket or other container used for useless scraps of paper or other trash.

waste·ful (wāst′fəl) *adj.* using or spending in a careless or useless way. —**waste′ful·ly,** *adv.* —**waste′ful·ness,** *n.*

waste·land (wāst′land′) *n.* a barren piece of land or area where there are few or no living things, such as a desert or polar region.

waste·pa·per (wāst′pā′pər) *n.* paper that is no longer useful and has been or is to be thrown away.

wast·er (wās′tər) *n.* a person or thing that wastes, spends, or uses up things in a careless or useless way.

wast·ing (wās′ting) *adj.* that slowly weakens or destroys: *a wasting illness, a wasting drought.*

was·trel (wās′trəl) *n.* **1.** a wasteful person; spendthrift. **2.** an idle, worthless person; good-for-nothing.

watch (woch) *v.t.* **1.** to look at (someone or something) with attention: *The children watched television all afternoon.* **2.** to keep guard over: *The soldier watched the enemy captives.* **3.** to take care of; tend: *The shepherds watched their flocks.* —*v.i.* **1.** to look with attention; observe closely: *Watch carefully while I show you how to hold the golf club.* **2.** to be on the alert; wait expectantly: *I watched for the right moment to make my request.* **3.** to remain awake at night, especially at the bedside of a person who is sick. **4.** to do duty as a guard; keep guard. —*n., pl.* **watch·es.** **1.** a small device for telling time, usually worn on the wrist. **2.** the act of watching; close observation. **3.** one or more persons whose work it is to protect or guard someone or something: *The night watch patrolled the factory.* **4.** the period of time during which a guard is on duty: *The sailor volunteered for the ten-to-midnight watch.* **5.** the act of remaining awake, especially to take care of someone or something; vigil: *to maintain a watch at a sick child's bedside.* —**watch′er,** *n.*
  ·**to watch out.** to be on the alert; be careful.

watch·band (woch′band′) *n.* a band or strap of leather, metal, or the like, used to fasten a watch to the wrist.

watch·dog (woch′dôg′) *n.* **1.** a dog kept to guard a house, property, or the like, and to give warning of the approach of intruders. **2.** any person or thing that serves as a protector or guardian for another or others: *The government agency was a watchdog for consumers against dishonest business practices.*

watch·ful (woch′fəl) *adj.* on the alert; vigilant; wary: *a watchful sentry.* —**watch′ful·ly,** *adv.* —**watch′ful·ness,** *n.*

watch·mak·er (woch′mā′kər) *n.* a person who makes, cleans, and repairs watches. —**watch′mak′ing** *n.*

watch·man (woch′mən) *n., pl.* **watch·men** (woch′mən). a person whose work it is to guard a building, property, or the like when the owner or tenant is away, especially during the night.

watch·tow·er (woch′tou′ər) *n.* a tower or tall building from which a guard or sentinel keeps watch.

watch·word (woch′wûrd′) *n.* **1.** a secret word or phrase that identifies the speaker or allows him or her to pass a guard; password. **2.** a slogan or motto of some group.

wa·ter (wô′tər) *n.* **1.** a liquid compound of hydrogen and oxygen that has no color, odor, or taste in its pure state. It is found on the earth in the form of oceans, lakes, and rivers, and it also occurs in a frozen state as ice and a gaseous state as steam and vapor. Water has a freezing point of 0 degrees Celsius (32 degrees Fahrenheit) and a boiling point of 100 degrees Celsius (212 degrees Fahrenheit). Formula: H_2O **2.** *also,* **waters.** any body of water, such as a sea, lake, or river: *We swam in the warm Florida waters.* **3.** any liquid given forth by the body, such as tears, saliva, or urine. **4.** any liquid preparation that contains or resembles water: *toilet water, ammonia water.* **5.** a wavy, lustrous sheen on fabric or metal. —*v.t.* **1.** to put water into or upon: *to water the plants every day. The valley is watered by the melting snow from the mountains.* **2.** to give water to: *Farmers water their cattle every day.* **3.** to dilute or weaken with water (often with *down*): *to water down an alcoholic drink.* **4.** to make a wavy, lustrous sheen on (fabric or metal): *to water silk.* —*v.i.* **1.** to get or take in water: *The ship put into port to water. The cattle watered at the river.* **2.** to give forth water from the body, as in the form of tears or saliva: *The smoke made their eyes water. My mouth watered at the thought of dinner.*
  ·**in hot water.** in trouble.
  ·**to hold water.** to be logical, sound, or true: *The lawyer's argument didn't hold water.*
  ·**to throw cold water on.** to discourage or forbid: *to throw cold water on a scheme.*

water bird, any bird that lives on or near the water.

wa·ter·borne (wô′tər bôrn′) *adj.* **1.** carried on or by water; floating: *waterborne flowers drifting in the lake.* **2.** carried by ship or by boat.

wa·ter·buck (wô′tər buk′) *n.* any of several antelopes that live near rivers or marshes in southeastern Africa. A waterbuck has a coat of long, coarse hair that may range from yellowish brown to nearly black.

water buffalo, a black Asian buffalo having long horns that curve backward. The water buffalo is raised for its milk and is used as a beast of burden.

water bug 1. any of various bugs that live on or under the surface of ponds and streams. **2.** the common cockroach, often found in or near sinks and other damp places.

water chestnut 1. the fruit, tuber, or corm of a plant that lives in water. The water chestnut has a nutlike taste and is widely used in Oriental cooking. **2.** the plant bearing this fruit.

water closet, see **toilet** (*defs. 1, 2*).

wa·ter·col·or (wô′tər kul′ər) *n.* **1.** a paint made by mixing pigment with water. **2.** the art or technique of painting with watercolors. **3.** a picture or design made with watercolors. —*adj.* of, relating to, or made with watercolors.

water cooler, a device for cooling and dispensing drinking water, often operated by electricity.

wa·ter·course (wô′tər kôrs′) *n.* **1.** any stream of flowing water, such as a river or brook. **2.** an artificial or natural channel of water, such as a canal or riverbed.

wa·ter·craft (wô′tər kraft′) *n.* **1.** skill in sailing boats or in performing water sports. **2.** a boat or ship. **3.** boats or ships as a group.

wa·ter·cress (wô′tər kres′) *n., pl.* **wa·ter·cress·es.** a plant that grows in water and has sharp-tasting leaves that are used in salads or as a garnish.

waterfall

wa·ter·fall (wô′tər fôl′) *n.* a flow of water falling from a high place.

wa·ter·fowl (wô′tər foul′) *n., pl.* **wa·ter·fowl** or **wa·ter·fowls.** a water bird, especially a swimming bird, such as a duck or goose, that is hunted as game.

wa·ter·front (wô′tər frunt′) *n.* **1.** the part of a city or town that is located beside the harbor of a river or ocean, especially where there are docks and shipping facilities. **2.** land or real estate next to a lake, river, or the like.

water gap, a gorge or valley in a mountain ridge through which a stream flows.

water hole, a hole or hollow place in the ground in which water collects, such as a pond or pool.

watering can, a container used for sprinkling water on plants.

watering place 1. a place where water may be obtained, as for drinking or for watering cattle. **2.** a resort with mineral springs.

water lily, any of a large group of plants that grow in freshwater ponds and lakes. The leaves and flowers of water lilies float on or stand above the surface of the water.

water lily

water line 1. a line where the surface of the water touches the hull of a boat or ship. **2.** one of several stripes painted around a ship's hull to show how far it sinks when it is loaded or unloaded.

wa·ter·logged (wô′tər lôgd′, wô′tər logd′) *adj.* **1.** so full of water that it becomes heavy and unmanageable: *a waterlogged ship.* **2.** thoroughly saturated with water: *a waterlogged mine, waterlogged earth.*

Wa·ter·loo (wô′tər lü′) *n.* any crushing or final defeat: *to meet one's Waterloo.* [From the battle of *Waterloo,* Belgium, where Napoleon I was finally defeated on June 18, 1815.]

water main, a large main pipe or pipeline used for supplying water to a particular area.

wa·ter·man (wô′tər mən) *n., pl.* **wa·ter·men** (wô′tər-mən). a man who works on or with boats.

wa·ter·mark (wô′tər märk′) *n.* **1.** a line or mark that shows how high the water of a river, lake, or ocean tide has risen. **2.** a distinctive mark or design that is impressed on certain kinds of paper, such as stationery, and is visible when the paper is held up to a light. —*v.t.* to impress (paper) with a watermark.

wa·ter·mel·on (wô′tər mel′ən) *n.* **1.** a large, juicy melon having a thick green rind and watery pulp that is pink, red, yellow, or white. **2.** the vine bearing this melon.

water mill, a mill or machine whose source of power is moving water.

water moccasin, a poisonous snake that lives in swamps and other wet regions of the southeastern United States. It has an olive or black body marked with faint crossbars. When alarmed it lifts its head and shows the inside of its white mouth. Also, **cottonmouth.**

water of crystallization, water combined in crystals with another compound. When heated, the water evaporates, causing the crystals to crumble into a powdery substance.

water polo, a water sport played with a large ball by two teams of seven swimmers each. The object is to throw or push the ball into the opponent's goal.

water power, power generated by the force of moving water.

wa·ter·proof (wô′tər prüf′) *adj.* that will not let water pass through, especially after having been treated or coated with a substance that prevents water from entering. —*n. British.* a raincoat. —*v.t.* to make waterproof: *to waterproof a garment.*

---

at; āpe; fär; câre; end; mē; it; īce; pîerce; hot; ōld; sông, fôrk; oil; out; up; ūse; rüle; pull; tûrn; chin; sing; shop; thin; this; hw in white; zh in treasure. The symbol ə stands for the unstressed vowel sound heard in about, taken, pencil, lemon, and circus.

W

water rat **1.** any of various rodents that live on the banks of streams or lakes. **2.** another term for **muskrat.**

wa·ter–re·pel·lent (wô′tər ri pel′ənt) *adj.* having a surface or finish that repels water but is not completely waterproof.

wa·ter·shed (wô′tər shed′) *n.* **1.** a ridge or other high land area separating two different river basins. **2.** the total land area from which water drains into a stream, river, or lake.

wa·ter·ski (wô′tər skē′) *v.i.,* **wa·ter·skied, wa·ter·ski·ing.** to glide over the surface of water on water skis while being pulled by a towline attached to a boat. —**wa′ter·ski′er,** *n.* —**wa′ter·ski′ing,** *n.*

water ski, one of a pair of wooden skis wider and shorter than snow skis, used in water-skiing.

water snake, any of various nonpoisonous snakes living in fresh water.

wa·ter·spout (wô′tər spout′) *n.* **1.** a pipe or nozzle that carries away unneeded water, especially one that runs from the roof down the side of a building to carry off rainwater. **2.** the end of a pipe from which water pours when the pipe is opened. **3.** a tornado occurring over a body of water, appearing as a long, dark funnel extending from the clouds down toward the surface of the water.

water table, the upper surface of a zone in the ground that is completely saturated with water.

wa·ter·tight (wô′tər tīt′) *adj.* **1.** so closely constructed or fitted as to prevent water from passing in or out. **2.** so planned or worded as to be free from error and clearly understood: *a watertight argument.*

water tower **1.** a very large tower used to store a water supply. **2.** a fire-fighting apparatus for throwing water on the upper stories of tall buildings.

water vapor, water in its gaseous state, but below the boiling point, especially as found in the atmosphere. Fog is a form of water vapor.

wa·ter·way (wô′tər wā′) *n.* **1.** a water route for the passage of ships. **2.** a channel for the passage of water.

wa·ter·wheel (wô′tər hwēl′, wô′tər wēl′) *n.* a wheel turned by the weight or pressure of water falling on it or flowing under it, used to provide power.

water wings, a waterproof device filled with air, worn under the arms to keep the body floating while learning to swim.

wa·ter·works (wô′tər wûrks′) *pl. n.* **1.** the entire system for the distribution of water to a city or town, including reservoirs, buildings, machinery, and pipes. **2.** a building in such a

waterwheel

system in which the machinery for pumping and filtering water is located. ▲ used with a singular or plural verb.

wa·ter·y (wô′tə rē) *adj.* **1.** of, relating to, or consisting of water: *the watery depths of the ocean.* **2.** full of or saturated with water: *The heavy rain made the ground very watery.* **3.** containing too much water: *a watery gravy.* **4.** pale, as if diluted by water; weak: *watery colors.*

watt (wot) *n.* a unit of electrical or mechanical power in the metric system. It is equal to a rate of 1 joule of work per second (0.0013 horsepower). [From the Scottish engineer and inventor James *Watt* (1736–1819).]

watt·age (wot′ij) *n.* **1.** electrical power expressed in watts. **2.** the number of watts of electrical power needed to run an appliance.

watt–hour (wot′our′) *n.* a unit of electrical energy, equal to the work done by 1 watt acting for 1 hour, or 3,600 joules.

wat·tle (wot′əl) *n.* **1.** a framework or structure made of poles, branches, twigs, or the like woven together, used especially in building walls, fences, or roofs. **2.** the material used to make such a framework or structure. **3.** the fleshy, often brightly colored fold of skin hanging down from the neck or throat of certain fowl, such as turkeys, and other animals. —*v.t.,* **wat·tled, wat·tling.** **1.** to build (something) by weaving together twigs, branches, or the like: *to wattle a roof for a grass hut.* **2.** to form into a network or bind together by weaving or interlacing: *to wattle branches to form a roof.* —**wat′tled,** *adj.*

wave (wāv) *v.,* **waved, wav·ing.** —*v.i.* **1.** to sway freely back and forth or up and down; move with a rippling or swaying motion, as stalks of wheat in the wind. **2.** to fall or lie in curves or rows that curve first one way then the other: *hair that waves beautifully when brushed.* **3.** to gesture by moving the hand or arm up and down, as in a greeting, farewell, or signal. —*v.t.* **1.** to cause to move back and forth or up and down: *The people along the road waved their flags as the parade passed by.* **2.** to express or signal by waving something, especially the hand: *to wave good-bye.* **3.** to give a curving form, appearance, or pattern to: *to wave hair by setting it in curlers.* —*n.* **1.** a curving or rippling movement or swell on the surface of a body of liquid, especially the sea. **2.** anything resembling this in movement or shape: *There were waves in the wallpaper where the glue didn't stick properly.* **3.** the act of waving, especially with the hand or something held in the hand: *a wave of a magician's wand.* **4.** a sudden rush or increase of anything: *Last week we had a terrible heat wave.* **5.** a curve or series of curves, as in the hair. **6.** *Physics.* a vibration or disturbance that travels through a solid, liquid, or gas, such as a sound wave. —**wave′like′,** *adj.*

wave·length (wāv′lengkth′, wāv′length′, wāv′lenth′) *n.* *Physics.* the distance between any two like points of a wave. For example, the distance between the two highest points of a wave is one wavelength.

wave·let (wāv′lit) *n.* a small wave; ripple.

wa·ver (wā′vər) *v.i.* **1.** to move unsteadily up and down or from side to side; sway; totter: *The ladder wavered and toppled over.* **2.** to flicker; quiver: *Light from the candle wavered in the breeze.* **3.** to hesitate or show doubt; be uncertain: *to waver between two choices.* **4.** to become unsteady; falter: *Their resolve to see the project completed never wavered.* —*n.* the act of wavering. —**wa′ver·ing·ly,** *adv.*

wav·y (wā′vē) *adj.,* **wav·i·er, wav·i·est.** curving in movement or shape; full of waves: *wavy hair.* —**wav′i·ness,** *n.*

wax¹ (waks) *n., pl.* **wax·es.** **1.** any of various fatty substances that come from plants or animals, such as beeswax or the wax that forms inside the ear. **2.** any of various natural mineral substances resembling this, such as paraffin. **3.** any of various substances that contain a wax, used to polish furniture, cars, and the like. —*v.t.* to cover, treat, or polish with wax: *to wax floors.* —*adj.* made of or resembling wax. [From the Old English word *weax* meaning "beeswax."] —**wax′like′,** *adj.*

wax² (waks) *v.i.* **1.** to increase gradually, as in size, brightness, or strength: *The moon waxes and wanes.* **2.** to grow or become: *to wax eloquent about the beauty of the countryside.* [From the Old English word *weaxan* meaning "to grow, increase."]

wax bean, a yellow string bean with a waxy appearance.

waxed paper, another term for **wax paper.**

wax·en (wak′sən) *adj.* **1.** made of, covered, or treated with wax: *a deep waxen shine on a table.* **2.** resembling wax; pale: *a waxen complexion.*

wax myrtle, any of various tall shrubs or trees having fragrant leaves, and small grayish berries coated with a white wax that is used in making candles and soap.

wax paper, a paper that is coated with paraffin so that it keeps out moisture, used as a protective wrapping. Also, **waxed paper.**

wax·wing (waks′wing′) *n.* a small songbird that has a crest on its head, a short, thick bill, and a red, waxy material on some of its feathers.

wax·work (waks′wûrk′) *n.* **1.** something made of wax, especially an ornament or a human figure. **2. waxworks.** a place for showing wax figures of famous persons. ▲ used with a singular or plural verb.

wax·y (wak′sē) *adj.,* **wax·i·er, wax·i·est. 1.** resembling wax, as in texture or appearance: *The plastic flowers looked waxy.* **2.** made of, covered, or treated with wax. —**wax′i·ness,** *n.*

waxwing

way (wā) *n.* **1.** a course of action or method to be followed in order to do or attain something: *a way to solve a problem, a good way to make friends.* **2.** a road, path, or the like, leading from one place to another: *The fallen branch blocked the way. That road is the quickest way to town.* **3.** a direction, as of motion: *The hurricane is heading this way.* **4.** a movement or passage along a particular route or in a particular direction: *Can you find your way back to school?* **5.** distance: *They walked a long way before finding the house.* **6.** also, **ways.** a usual style of behaving or speaking: *Our neighbor has strange ways.* **7.** a typical or characteristic style of doing something: *a special way of smiling.* **8.** something that a person desires to have or do; wish: *You can't always have your way.* **9.** a particular detail or feature; respect: *In many ways, the plan is a good one.* **10.** space enough to pass: *Make way so that the truck can get by us.* **11.** the course of action that one follows in life. **12.** *Informal.* a condition or state: *to be in a bad way financially.* **13.** *Informal.* a neighborhood, region, or area: *Few people visit out our way.* —*adv.* **1.** at a distance; far: *clouds floating way up in the sky.* **2.** to a great degree or point: *The water came way up the beach.*

·**by the way.** incidentally: *By the way, we're leaving at four o'clock.*

·**by way of. a.** by a route that includes; via: *We're going to Florida by way of Tennessee.* **b.** as a means or method of: *to send a note by way of an apology.*

·**in the way.** in a position that blocks or slows progress: *Please don't stand in the way.*

·**out of the way. a.** so as not to block or hinder: *Move your bicycle out of the way of the garage door.* **b.** in a place that is far away or hard to reach: *Their summer house is out of the way.* **c.** not proper; wrong: *to say nothing out of the way.*

·**to give way. a.** to back down; yield: *to give way in an argument.* **b.** to break down or collapse: *The bridge gave way under the heavy load.*

·**to go out of the way** or **to go out of one's way.** to do something that is not easy or convenient: *to go out of one's way to help a friend.*

·**under way.** in progress or motion: *The plane got under way after an hour's delay. The plans for the party are well under way.*

way·far·er (wā′fâr′ər) *n.* a traveler, especially a person who travels on foot.

way·far·ing (wā′fâr′ing) *adj.* traveling, especially on foot.

way·lay (wā′lā′, wā′lā′) *v.t.,* **way·laid, way·lay·ing. 1.** to lie in wait for in order to seize or attack: *The gang of thieves waylaid the traveler by the bridge.* **2.** to wait for and stop (a person): *The police chief was waylaid by reporters asking about the crime.* —**way′lay′er,** *n.*

-ways *suffix* used to form adverbs that show direction, position, or manner: *sideways.*

way·side (wā′sīd′) *n.* the land bordering a road or path: *Wildflowers grew by the wayside.* —*adj.* of, relating to, or located beside a road or path: *a wayside inn.*

·**to go by the wayside.** to be postponed or put aside.

way station, a small station between main stations, as on a railroad.

way·ward (wā′wərd) *adj.* **1.** refusing to do what is right; wrongheaded and disobedient: *a wayward child.* **2.** following no fixed rule or pattern; irregular. —**way′ward·ly,** *adv.* —**way′ward·ness,** *n.*

we (wē) *pl. pron.* nominative, **we;** possessive, **our, ours;** objective, **us. 1.** the persons who are speaking or writing: *We won the game. We are glad to meet you.* **2.** a single person who is speaking or writing officially, such as an author, judge, or king or queen.

weak (wēk) *adj.* **1.** liable to fall, fail, or collapse under strain: *The legs of the chair are weak. The weak bridge swayed under the weight of the trucks.* **2.** not having vigor or strength, as from age, illness, or fatigue: *The invalid is too weak to sit up.* **3.** not having the usual or required ability, power, or authority: *a weak leader. Their team was weaker than ours.* **4.** not supported by truth, facts, or reason; not sound or convincing: *The lawyer gave a weak defense of the criminal.* **5.** lacking willpower or strength of character: *a weak person who wouldn't stand up for what is right.* **6.** lacking intensity or power; faint: *The light was too weak to read by.* **7.** lacking the full amount or strength; diluted: *weak tea.* **8.** lacking in knowledge: *I am weak in science.* **9.** *Phonetics.* (of a syllable) having no stress or only light stress. **10.** *Grammar.* (of a verb) forming the past tense and past participle by the addition of a consonant or consonants to the stem, as in *bake, baked, baked,* not by the change of a vowel.

weak·en (wē′kən) *v.t., v.i.* to make or become weak or weaker: *I weakened the tea by adding water. The runner weakened near the finish line.*

weak·fish (wēk′fish′) *n., pl.* **weak·fish** or **weak·fish·es.** a saltwater fish found in the coastal waters of eastern North America, used for food.

weak·ling (wēk′ling) *n.* a person who is physically, mentally, or morally weak. —*adj.* weak; feeble.

weak·ly (wēk′lē) *adv.* in a weak manner. —*adj.,* **weak·li·er, weak·li·est.** not healthy or strong; weak; feeble.

weak-mind·ed (wēk′mīn′did) *adj.* **1.** lacking mental strength or firmness of will: *a weak-minded administrator.* **2.** feeble-minded.

weak·ness (wēk′nis) *n., pl.* **weak·ness·es. 1.** the state or quality of being weak. **2.** an example of this; weak

at; āpe; fär; câre; end; mē; it; īce; pîerce; hot; ōld; sông, fôrk; oil; out; up; ūse; rūle; pull; tûrn; chin; sing; shop; thin; this; hw in white; zh in treasure. The symbol ə stands for the unstressed vowel sound heard in about, taken, pencil, lemon, and circus.

W

point. **3.** a special liking; fondness: *I have a weakness for ice cream.* **4.** something for which one has a special liking: *Buying records is my weakness.*

weal¹ (wēl) *n.* well-being, happiness, or prosperity: *a law passed for the public weal.* [From the Middle English word *wele,* from Old English *wela* with the same meaning.]

weal² (wēl) *n.* a ridge or bump on the skin, as that made by a whip or stick; welt. [A form of *wale.*]

wealth (welth) *n.* **1.** a great quantity of money or valuable possessions; riches. **2.** a great quantity of anything: *The new mayor has a wealth of ideas for improving our city.*

wealth·y (wel′thē) *adj.,* **wealth·i·er, wealth·i·est.** having wealth.

wean (wēn) *v.t.* **1.** to make (a child or young animal) used to food other than the mother's milk: *We weaned our puppies when they were six weeks old.* **2.** to cause (a person) to give up gradually a habit, practice, or interest: *to be weaned from biting one's nails.*

weap·on (wep′ən) *n.* **1.** anything used in a fight to attack or defend, such as a gun or knife: *Many animals use their teeth and claws as weapons.* **2.** any means used to gain success in a contest or struggle: *The defense lawyer used every legal weapon available to win the case.*

wear (wâr) *v.,* **wore, worn, wear·ing.** —*v.t.* **1.** to carry or have on the body: *to wear clothes, to wear a bracelet.* **2.** to have or show; display: *to wear one's hair long, to wear a frown.* **3.** to damage or use up, as by scraping or rubbing: *to wear a carpet.* **4.** to cause or make, as by scraping or rubbing: *I wore a hole in my sock.* **5.** to bring to a certain condition: *to wear a suit to rags.* —*v.i.* **1.** to last or hold out: *The fabric did not wear well.* **2.** to become damaged through use or age: *These shoes have started to wear.* **3.** to come to a certain condition: *My patience is wearing thin.* **4.** to pass or advance, especially slowly: *The day wore on.* —*n.* **1.** the act of wearing or the state of being worn: *This suit has had five years of hard wear.* **2.** an article or articles of clothing: *This store sells only children's wear.* **3.** damage caused by use or age: *This rug shows signs of wear.* **4.** lasting quality; durability: *There are several years of wear left in this coat.* —**wear′a·ble,** *adj.* —**wear′er,** *n.*

·**to wear down. a.** to overcome gradually by continuous effort: *to wear down someone's resistance.* **b.** to damage or make less, as in size, by wear: *Heavy driving wore down the tread of the tires.*

·**to wear off.** to become less gradually: *The effects of the aspirin wore off after several hours.*

·**to wear out. a.** to use until no longer fit or able to be used: *to wear out a battery.* **b.** to tire or exhaust: *The three-hour hike wore us out.*

wear and tear, damage undergone through use or passage of time.

wear·ing (wâr′ing) *adj.* **1.** of, relating to, or made for wear: *Coats and suits are wearing apparel.* **2.** exhausting; tiring: *a wearing experience.*

wea·ri·some (wîr′ē səm) *adj.* causing weariness; tiresome; tedious: *The movie was long and wearisome.* —**wea′ri·some·ly,** *adv.*

wea·ry (wîr′ē) *adj.,* **wea·ri·er, wea·ri·est.** **1.** extremely tired, as from hard labor; fatigued: *We were weary after a long day's hike.* **2.** causing or characterized by fatigue; tedious; tiring: *a weary journey.* **3.** having one's interest or patience exhausted: *to grow weary listening to the same complaints.* —*v.,* **wea·ried, wea·ry·ing.** —*v.t.* to exhaust the strength of; make weary; fatigue: *The trip wearied us.* —*v.i.* to become weary: *The child wearied quickly.* —**wea′ri·ly,** *adv.* —**wea′ri·ness,** *n.*

wea·sel (wē′zəl) *n., pl.* **wea·sels** or **wea·sel.** **1.** any of various small meat-eating mammals, having a slender body, short legs, a long neck, and a soft, thick, brownish coat. **2.** a sneaky person.

weasel *(def. 1)*

weath·er (weth′ər) *n.* **1.** the condition of the atmosphere at a given time and place: *The weather has been very cold this winter. Tomorrow's weather will be warm and clear.* **2.** unpleasant or stormy conditions: *We put up more boards on the cabin to keep out the weather.* —*v.t.* **1.** to expose to the weather, especially in order to dry, bleach, or condition: *to weather lumber.* **2.** to bear up against or overcome; come safely through: *to weather a storm, to weather a crisis.* **3.** to pass or sail to the windward of. —*v.i.* to become changed through exposure to the weather: *The house shingles weathered to a soft gray.* —*adj.* windward.

·**under the weather.** *Informal.* not well; ailing.

weath·er–beat·en (weth′ər bē′tən) *adj.* **1.** worn or badly damaged by exposure to the weather: *a weather-beaten old barn.* **2.** seasoned or hardened by exposure to the weather: *The old sailor had a weather-beaten face.*

weath·er·cock (weth′ər kok′) *n.* a weather vane having the shape of a rooster.

weath·er·glass (weth′ər glas′) *n., pl.* **weath·er·glass·es.** any of various instruments, such as a barometer, that show the state of the weather.

weath·er·ing (weth′ər ing) *n.* the action of the weather upon something exposed to it.

weath·er·man (weth′ər man′) *n., pl.* **weath·er·men** (weth′ər men′). a person who studies and forecasts the weather.

weath·er·proof (weth′ər prüf′) *adj.* capable of resisting the harmful forces of the weather: *weatherproof paint.* —*v.t.* to make weatherproof.

weather station, a station where observations of the weather are made and recorded every day.

weath·er–strip (weth′ər strip′) *v.t.,* **weath·er–stripped, weath·er–strip·ping.** to fit or secure with weather stripping.

weather stripping 1. a narrow strip of metal, felt, or other material put around the openings of a door or window to keep out the wind and cold. Also, **weather strip.** **2.** such strips as a group.

weather vane, a device that is moved by the wind and shows the direction in which the wind is blowing.

weave (wēv) *v.,* **wove** or *(def. 6)* **weaved, wo·ven, wove** or *(def. 6)* **weaved, weav·ing.** —*v.t.* **1.** to lace together: *to weave yarn into cloth.* **2.** to form or make by lacing together threads, yarn, or strips of straw or other material: *to weave a basket, to weave cloth.* **3.** to spin (a web or cocoon). **4.** to unite into a connected whole: *The author wove several different themes into the essay.* **5.** to make by putting together different things or parts: *to weave stories from one's experiences.* **6.** to move or make by turning and twisting: *to weave one's way through a crowd.* —*v.i.* to form or make something by weaving. —*n.* a particular method or pattern of weaving: *an open weave.*

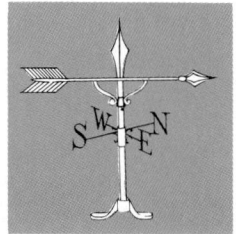
weather vane

weav·er (wē′vər) *n.* a person who weaves or whose work is weaving.

weav·er·bird (wē′vər bûrd′) *n.* any of a large number of songbirds that often weave nests of grasses and straw.

web (web) *n.* **1.** something woven, especially a whole piece of cloth in the process of being woven or just removed from a loom. **2.** a network of fine threads spun by a spider; cobweb. **3.** any complex structure or network: *a web of streets, a web of lies.* **4.** skin or membrane, especially between the toes of a swimming bird. —**web′like′**, *adj.*

web *(def. 2)*

webbed (webd) *adj.* having or joined by a web or webbing: *Geese have webbed feet.*

web·bing (web′ing) *n.* **1.** a strong, narrow band of woven fabric, made of cotton, hemp, or other fibers, used for seat belts, harness straps, and other items. **2.** anything forming a web or webs.

web–foot·ed (web′fŭt′id) *adj.* having the toes joined by a web: *Ducks are web-footed animals.*

wed (wed) *v.*, **wed·ded, wed·ded** or **wed, wed·ding.** —*v.t.* **1.** to take as one's husband or wife; marry. **2.** to join as husband and wife; unite in wedlock. **3.** to join closely; unite: *a performance that weds acting and singing.* —*v.i.* to take a husband or wife; marry.

we'd (wed) *contr.* **1.** we had. **2.** we would. **3.** we should.

Wed., Wednesday.

wed·ded (wed′id) *adj.* **1.** in a married state: *a happily wedded couple.* **2.** having to do with marriage: *to live in wedded bliss.* **3.** closely joined: *two groups wedded by a common interest.* **4.** deeply involved; devoted: *employees wedded to their work.*

wed·ding (wed′ing) *n.* **1.** a marriage ceremony. **2.** the anniversary of a marriage: *A silver wedding is a celebration of twenty-five years of marriage.*

wedge (wej) *n.* **1.** a solid, triangular or tapered piece of wood or metal that can be used to separate, split, or lift objects: *I used an iron wedge to split logs into firewood.* **2.** something resembling this in shape: *a wedge of cheese.* **3.** anything that divides in some way: *The struggle over the inheritance drove a wedge between members of the family.* —*v.*, **wedged, wedg·ing.** —*v.t.* **1.** to separate or split by driving a wedge into: *The worker wedged the floor boards apart.* **2.** to fasten or fix in place with a wedge or wedges: *to wedge the door open with a piece of wood.* **3.** to drive, push, or crowd: *to wedge a book into place on the shelf.* —*v.i.* to force one's way: *to wedge into a seat on the train.*

Wedg·wood (wej′wŭd′) *n. Trademark.* earthenware pottery usually characterized by a blue or green tinted background and white, raised ornament. [From the English potter Josiah *Wedgwood* (1730–1795), famous for such earthenware.]

wed·lock (wed′lok′) *n.* the state of being married; matrimony.

Wednes·day (wenz′dē, wenz′dā) *n.* the fourth day of the week. [From the Old English word *Wōdnesdæg* meaning "Wednesday," going back to the words *Wōden,* king of the gods in Germanic mythology, and *dæg* "day."]

wee (wē) *adj.*, **we·er, we·est. 1.** very small; little: *a wee baby in a cradle.* **2.** early: *in the wee hours of the morning.*

weed¹ (wēd) *n.* a plant that is either useless or harmful and grows where it is not wanted. —*v.t.* to remove weeds from: *to weed a lawn.* —*v.i.* to remove weeds. [From the Old English word *wēod* meaning this sort of plant.]

  ·to weed out. to remove (something that is useless or harmful): *to weed out old clothes from a closet.*

weed² (wēd) *n.* **1. weeds.** the clothes worn by someone in mourning, especially a widow. **2.** a token of mourning, such as a black band worn on the arm. [From the Old English word *wæd* meaning "a garment."]

weed·er (wē′dər) *n.* **1.** a person who weeds. **2.** a tool or device for removing weeds.

weed·y (wē′dē) *adj.*, **weed·i·er, weed·i·est. 1.** full of weeds. **2.** of, relating to, or resembling a weed or weeds.

week (wēk) *n.* **1.** a period of seven days, usually considered to begin with Sunday. **2.** the hours or days in a seven-day period usually spent at work or school: *My parents both work a 40-hour week. I don't have much time to do errands during the week.*

week·day (wēk′dā′) *n.* any day of the week except Saturday and Sunday.

week·end (wēk′end′) *n.* the period extending from Friday night or Saturday morning until Sunday night or Monday morning. —*adj.* of, relating to, or happening during a weekend: *a weekend golf game.* —*v.i.* to spend a weekend: *to weekend in the country.*

week·ly (wēk′lē) *adj.* **1.** of, for, or relating to a week or weekdays: *a weekly supply of groceries.* **2.** done, happening, or issued once a week: *The children made their weekly telephone call to their grandmother.* —*n., pl.* **week·lies.** a newspaper, magazine, or the like issued once a week. —*adv.* once each week; every week: *to shop weekly.*

weep (wēp) *v.*, **wept, weep·ing.** —*v.i.* **1.** to show grief, joy, or other strong emotion by shedding tears: *to weep for joy. The sad news made us weep.* **2.** to feel sorrow or grief; mourn: *to weep over a loss.* **3.** to drip or leak; ooze: *The faucet in the bathroom sink weeps constantly.* —*v.t.* **1.** to shed or let flow in drops: *to weep salty tears.* **2.** to bring to a particular condition by weeping: *to weep oneself to sleep.* **3.** to weep or mourn for. —**weep′er**, *n.*

weeping willow, a wide-spreading tree having pale green leaves and greenish branches that droop almost to the ground.

wee·vil (wē′vəl) *n.* any of a group of destructive beetles that have a long, downward-curving snout. Weevils feed on many crops, such as cotton and grain.

weft (weft) *n.* the crosswise threads in weaving; woof.

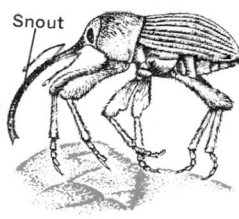

Snout

weevil

at; āpe; fär; câre; end; mē; it; īce; pîerce; hot; ōld; sông; fôrk; oil; out; up; ūse; rüle; pùll; tûrn; chin; sing; shop; thin; this; hw in white; zh in treasure. The symbol ə stands for the unstressed vowel sound heard in about, taken, pencil, lemon, and circus.

W

weigh (wā) *v.t.* **1.** to measure the weight of, as on a scale or balance: *The grocer weighed the tomatoes. The doctor weighed the baby.* **2.** to measure out (an amount of something) according to weight (often with *out*): *The shopkeeper weighed out a pound of cherries.* **3.** to think about or examine thoughtfully and carefully: *to weigh the advantages and disadvantages of a plan, to weigh one's words before speaking.* —*v.i.* **1.** to have, amount to, or be equal to a specified weight: *The car weighs 3,744 pounds.* **2.** to be important; matter: *The student's grades weighed heavily with the scholarship committee.* **3.** to be oppressive or burdensome: *A feeling of guilt weighed heavily on the sinner's conscience.* —**weigh′er,** *n.*
  ·**to weigh anchor.** to raise an anchor from the bottom and start to sail.
  ·**to weigh down.** to lie heavily on; oppress or burden: *The heavy snowfall weighed down the branches of the trees.*
  ·**to weigh in.** to be weighed, as before a boxing match or other contest: *The champion weighed in at 200 pounds.*
weight (wāt) *n.* **1.** the amount of heaviness of something: *My weight is exactly 100 pounds.* **2.** the quality of any mass or body that results from the pull of gravity upon it: *The weight of helium is less than the weight of air, causing a helium-filled balloon to rise.* **3.** a system of units for expressing weight: *troy weight.* **4.** any unit of weight, such as a ton. **5.** a piece of metal or similar material having a particular weight, used as a standard in weighing. **6.** any heavy thing: *I need a weight to keep papers from blowing off the desk.* **7.** a burden or load; pressure: *the weight of financial problems.* **8.** strong influence; importance: *an opinion that carries weight with one's friends.* —*v.t.* **1.** to add weight to; load with additional weight: *We weighted the cartons with rocks.* **2.** to burden heavily, as with a weight; oppress: *to be weighted down with troubles.*
  ·**to throw one's weight around.** to use one's power or authority, especially in an unfair way.
weight·less (wāt′lis) *adj.* **1.** having little or no weight: *weightless feathers.* **2.** (of a body) having no apparent weight due to the absence of the pull of gravity, as in outer space. —**weight′less·ness,** *n.*
weight·lift·ing (wāt′lif′ting) *n.* the exercise or sport of lifting heavy weights, usually barbells. —**weight′lift′er,** *n.*
weight·y (wā′tē) *adj.,* **weight·i·er, weight·i·est. 1.** of great weight; heavy: *a weighty object.* **2.** hard to bear; burdensome: *a weighty responsibility.* **3.** very serious; important: *a weighty decision, a weighty matter.* —**weight′i·ness,** *n.*
weir (wîr) *n.* **1.** a dam built in a river to raise the level of the water. **2.** a fence of stakes put in a stream or channel to catch fish.
weird (wîrd) *adj.* **1.** different from the usual or expected; strange; bizarre; odd: *weird behavior, a weird person.* **2.** suggesting or having to do with the supernatural; difficult to explain or understand; mysterious: *Weird sounds were heard coming from the deserted house.* [From the Middle English word *wyrde* meaning "having the power to control fate," going back to the Old English word *wyrd* "fate, fortune."] —**weird′ly,** *adv.* —**weird′ness,** *n.*
Weird Sisters, another name for the **Fates.**
welch (welch, welsh) another spelling of **welsh.**
wel·come (wel′kəm) *v.t.,* **wel·comed, wel·com·ing. 1.** to greet (someone) with pleasure and hospitality: *We welcomed them into our club.* **2.** to receive or accept graciously or with pleasure: *to welcome the news of a cousin's engagement to be married.* —*n.* a glad and friendly greeting; kind or hospitable reception. —*adj.* **1.** received kindly and with pleasure: *a welcome visitor.* **2.** giving pleasure or satisfaction: *a welcome compliment.*

3. free to use, have, or enjoy: *You are welcome to the telephone.* **4.** under no obligation. ▲ used chiefly in the phrase *you're welcome,* as a response to being thanked for something.
  ·**to wear out one's welcome.** to stay too long or visit too often.
weld (weld) *v.t.* **1.** to join (a substance, such as metal or plastic) to another by heating and softening it until it can be hammered and pressed or fused. **2.** to join closely together; unite: *The friends were welded together by their interest in sports.* —*v.i.* to be capable of being welded. —*n.* **1.** the point at which two things are joined by welding. **2.** the act or process of welding or the state of being welded. —**weld′er,** *n.*
wel·fare (wel′fâr′) *n.* **1.** the condition of being or doing well, as in health or finances: *The visitor asked about the welfare of my parents and grandparents.* **2.** financial aid or other assistance given to people in need; relief. It is usually distributed by one or more departments of the government.
welfare state, a state, nation, or government that ensures the well-being of its people by providing such benefits as health and unemployment insurance, guaranteed minimum wages, and subsidized housing.
welfare work, work done by the government, private agencies, and individuals to provide money, food, and services to people in need.
welfare worker, a person who does welfare work, especially as a profession.
wel·kin (wel′kin) *n. Archaic.* the sky; heavens.
well[1] (wel) *adv.,* **bet·ter, best. 1.** in a good or satisfactory way: *Do you sing well? I did not sleep well last night.* **2.** in a thorough or complete way: *Be sure to mix the ingredients well.* **3.** to a considerable extent or degree: *That animal weighs well over 200 pounds. Our dog ran well ahead of us on the way to town.* **4.** in a close or personal way: *Do you know them well?* **5.** under the circumstances; reasonably: *I can't very well accept your offer.* **6.** clearly; easily; perfectly: *I remember our trip well.* —*adj.* **1.** in good health: *Come back safe and well.* **2.** fortunate; good: *It is well that you called before we went out.* —*interj.* used to express surprise, doubt, or resignation, or to introduce another thought: *Well! How nice to see you. Well, I think it's time to leave.* [From the Old English word *wel* with the same meaning.]
  ·**as well. a.** in addition; also: *My cousin plays the flute, and the guitar and drums as well.* **b.** with the same outcome or effect; equally: *You might as well travel with us as go alone.*
  ·**as well as. a.** in addition to; besides: *We toured France as well as England.* **b.** to the same extent or degree as: *You can dance as well as the rest of us.*
well[2] (wel) *n.* **1.** a hole or pit made in the ground to obtain water or oil. **2.** a natural spring or fountain. **3.** something resembling a well in shape or function: *There was a well for ink in the old desk. An encyclopedia is a well of information.* **4.** an enclosed space in a building, often going through several floors, such as a shaft for stairs or for an elevator. —*v.i.* to spring; rise; fill: *Tears welled up in the baby's eyes.* [From an Old English word *will* meaning "a spring, well[2]."]
we'll (wēl) *contr.* we shall; we will.
well–ad·vised (wel′ad vīzd′) *adj.* acting with or showing good judgment: *You would be well-advised to leave before the snowstorm begins.*
well–ap·point·ed (wel′ə poin′tid) *adj.* properly or excellently furnished or equipped: *The school principal has a well-appointed office.*
well·a·way (wel′ə wā′) *interj. Archaic.* alas.
well–bal·anced (wel′bal′ənst) *adj.* **1.** nicely or evenly balanced; properly adjusted or regulated: *a well-balanced diet.* **2.** sensible or sane: *a well-balanced personality.*

well–be·haved (wel′bi hāvd′) *adj.* characterized by good conduct or manners: *a well-behaved youngster.*

well–be·ing (wel′bē′ing) *n.* health, happiness, and prosperity; welfare.

well·born (wel′bôrn′) *adj.* born of an aristocratic family.

well–bred (wel′bred′) *adj.* **1.** having or showing good manners or training; polite; tasteful: *a well-bred child, thoughtful of others.* **2.** (of an animal) coming from good stock or pedigree.

well–de·fined (wel′di fīnd′) *adj.* clear and precise, as in marking or outline: *a model with well-defined features.*

well–de·vel·oped (wel′di vel′əpt) *adj.* **1.** thought out or done in a thorough or very good way: *a well-developed plan.* **2.** having or showing good physical form: *The weightlifter had well-developed arms.*

well–done (wel′dun′) *adj.* **1.** performed well; skillfully done. **2.** (of food) thoroughly cooked.

well–fa·vored (wel′fā′vərd) *adj.* good-looking; handsome.

well–fed (wel′fed′) *adj.* properly or fully nourished.

well–fixed (wel′fikst′) *adj. Informal.* not lacking in money; financially secure.

well–found·ed (wel′foun′did) *adj.* based on solid evidence, good judgment, or sound reasoning: *a well-founded argument.*

well–groomed (wel′grümd′) *adj.* carefully and attractively dressed and groomed; neat.

well–ground·ed (wel′groun′did) *adj.* **1.** thoroughly familiar with the fundamental principles of a subject: *well-grounded in mathematics.* **2.** based on sound evidence or reasoning; well-founded.

well–heeled (wel′hēld′) *adj. Informal.* having a lot of money; rich.

well–in·formed (wel′in fôrmd′) *adj.* **1.** having much knowledge and information on a wide variety of subjects: *Democracy is based on a well-informed citizenry.* **2.** having correct or much information on a particular subject: *The doctor is well-informed about heart trouble.*

well–known (wel′nōn′) *adj.* **1.** famous; renowned: *a well-known scientist.* **2.** generally, widely, or fully known: *well-known facts.*

well–made (wel′mād′) *adj.* that has been made or developed in a careful, skillful, or strong way: *a well-made chair, a well-made movie.*

well–man·nered (wel′man′ərd) *adj.* having or showing good manners; polite.

well–mean·ing (wel′mē′ning) *adj.* **1.** intending to be helpful or good: *a well-meaning neighbor.* **2.** coming or resulting from good intentions: *a well-meaning remark.*

well–nigh (wel′nī′) *adv.* very nearly; almost.

well–off (wel′ôf′) *adj.* **1.** fairly wealthy; financially secure: *Their parents are well-off.* **2.** in a position where things are good or going well: *I knew I was well-off, so I decided not to change my job.*

well–read (wel′red′) *adj.* knowledgeable through having read many books.

well–round·ed (wel′roun′did) *adj.* **1.** having knowledge or interest in a wide variety of fields or subjects: *a well-rounded student.* **2.** made up of a wide variety of fields or subjects: *a well-rounded education.*

well–spo·ken (wel′spō′kən) *adj.* **1.** having educated and refined speech. **2.** said or delivered with style and polish: *a well-spoken rebuttal.*

well·spring (wel′spring′) *n.* **1.** a natural spring; fountainhead. **2.** the source of something, especially an unending source: *The professor seemed to be a wellspring of knowledge.*

well–thought–of (wel′thôt′uv′, wel′thôt′ov′) *adj.* having a good reputation; respected: *a well-thought-of member of the community.*

well–timed (wel′tīmd′) *adj.* happening or done at the correct or suitable time: *a well-timed entrance.*

well–to–do (wel′tə dü′) *adj.* having more than enough money; prosperous.

well–wish·er (wel′wish′ər) *n.* a person who wishes good fortune, success, or health, as to another person, a cause, or the like.

well–worn (wel′wôrn′) *adj.* **1.** showing evidence of much use or wear: *a well-worn jacket.* **2.** used too much; trite: *a well-worn phrase.*

welsh (welsh, welch) *also,* **welch.** *v.i. Informal.* **1.** to fail to pay what is owed, especially after losing a bet: *to welsh on a bet.* **2.** to fail to fulfill a promise or commitment: *to welsh on an agreement.* —**welsh′er,** *n.*

Welsh (welsh, welch) *adj.* of or relating to Wales, its people, their language, or culture. —*n.* **1.** the Celtic language of the Welsh people. **2.** the people of Wales.

Welsh cor·gi (kôr′gē) a short-legged dog having a fox-like face and a coat of stiff hair.

Welsh·man (welsh′mən, welch′mən) *n., pl.* **Welsh·men** (welsh′mən, welch′mən). a person who was born in or is a citizen of Wales.

Welsh rabbit, melted cheese mixed with beer, ale, or milk, seasoned, and served warm over toast or crackers. Also, **Welsh rarebit.**

welt (welt) *n.* **1.** a strip of material, especially a cord, sewn on an edge or in a seam of a garment or item, such as upholstery, usually for strengthening or decorating. **2.** a strip of leather or other material between the upper part and the sole of a shoe. **3.** a ridge or bump on the skin, such as one made by a stick or whip. —*v.t.* **1.** to put a welt on or in. **2.** *Informal.* to beat so as to raise welts on the skin.

wel·ter (wel′tər) *v.i.* **1.** to roll or toss about; wallow: *The pigs weltered in the mud. The boat was weltering on the stormy sea.* **2.** to be soaked or drenched in some liquid: *The hikers weltered in the rain.* —*n.* **1.** a rolling and tossing motion: *The welter of the waves kept us awake.* **2.** confusion; turmoil: *a welter of crowds at a fair, a welter of errors and inconsistencies.*

wel·ter·weight (wel′tər wāt′) *n.* a boxer or wrestler who weighs less than a middleweight and more than a lightweight.

wen (wen) *n.* a benign tumor or cyst on the skin, especially on the scalp.

wench (wench) *n., pl.* **wench·es. 1.** a girl or young woman. **2.** a female servant. **3.** an immoral woman.

wend (wend) *v.t.,* **wend·ed, wend·ing.** to make (one's way); go on (one's way); *to wend one's way through a crowded street.*

went (went) the past tense of **go.**

wept (wept) the past tense and past participle of **weep.**

were (wûr) **1.** the plural past tense and the second person singular, past tense of **be. 2.** the subjunctive of **be:** *If I were you, I wouldn't do that.*

we're (wir) *contr.* we are.

weren't (wûrnt, wûr′ənt) *contr.* were not.

were·wolf (wir′wulf′, wâr′wulf′) *also,* **wer·wolf.** *n., pl.* **were·wolves** (wir′wulvz′, wâr′wulvz′). in European folklore, a human being who sometimes turns into a wolf. [From the Old English word *werwulf* meaning "wolfman," from the words *wer* "man" + *wulf* "wolf."]

wert (wûrt) *v.i. Archaic.* were.

Wes·ley·an (wes′lē ən) *n.* a member or disciple of the

---

at; āpe; fär; câre; end; mē; it; īce; pîerce; hot; ōld; sông; fôrk; oil; out; up; ūse; rüle; pull; tûrn; chin; sing; shop; thin; this; hw in white; zh in treasure. The symbol ə stands for the unstressed vowel sound heard in about, taken, pencil, lemon, and circus.

W

church founded by John Wesley; Methodist. —*adj.* of or relating to John Wesley or to Methodists or Methodism.

west (west) *n.* **1.** the direction a person faces when watching the sun set. West is one of the four main points of the compass, located directly opposite east. **2.** *also,* **West.** any region or place lying in this direction. **3.** **the West. a.** a region of the United States west of the Mississippi River. **b.** the countries of Europe and the Americas as distinguished from those of Asia. **c.** the United States, Western Europe, and other non-Communist countries bound together by military and economic alliances. —*adj.* **1.** toward or in the west. **2.** from the west: *a west wind.* —*adv.* toward the west.

west·bound (west′bound′) *adj.* going west: *a west-bound train.*

west·er·ly (wes′tər lē) *adj., adv.* **1.** toward the west: *The plane took off in a westerly direction.* **2.** from the west: *a westerly wind. The storm came westerly.*

west·ern (wes′tərn) *adj.* **1.** toward or in the west. **2.** *also,* **Western.** of, relating to, or characteristic of the west or the West. **3.** from the west. —*n.* a novel, short story, motion picture, or the like dealing with frontier life in the western United States, especially with the life of cattle ranchers and the early settlers.

Western Church 1. the part of the Roman Catholic Church that recognizes the supremacy of the pope. **2.** the Roman Catholic, Anglican, and Protestant churches of western Europe and the Americas as a group.

west·ern·er (wes′tər nər) *n.* **1.** a person who was born or is living in the west. **2.** *usually,* **Westerner.** a person who was born or is living in the western part of the United States.

Western Hemisphere, the half of the earth that includes North and South America.

west·ern·ize (wes′tər nīz′) *v.t.,* **west·ern·ized, west·ern·iz·ing.** to cause to adopt certain customs, methods, or characteristics of Europe and the Americas: *Many peoples and countries of Asia were westernized in the twentieth century.* —**west′ern·i·za′tion,** *n.*

west·ern·most (wes′tərn mōst) *adj.* farthest west.

Western Roman Empire, see **Roman Empire.**

West Indian 1. of or relating to the West Indies. **2.** a person who was born in the West Indies or is a citizen of one of the countries or territories of the West Indies.

West·min·ster Abbey (west′min′stər) a Gothic church in London, England. It is the traditional site of coronations and contains the tombs of many English monarchs, political leaders, writers, and national heroes.

west·ward (west′wərd) *adv.* toward the west: *We will be driving westward for several hours.* Also, **west·wards** (west′wərdz). —*adj.* toward or in the west. —*n.* a westward direction, point, or place.

wet (wet) *adj.,* **wet·ter, wet·test. 1.** covered, soaked, or moist with water or other liquid: *a wet bathing suit, eyes wet with tears.* **2.** not yet dry: *A footprint was made in the wet cement.* **3.** marked by rainfall; rainy: *Spring is sometimes a wet season.* **4.** *Informal.* permitting or in favor of the manufacture and sale of alcoholic beverages: *a wet county.* —*v.,* **wet** or **wet·ted, wet·ting.** —*v.t.* to make wet: *Wet the ground before planting.* —*v.i.* to become wet or moist. —*n.* **1.** water or other moisture; wetness. **2.** rainy weather; rain. —**wet′ly,** *adv.* —**wet′ness,** *n.*

wet blanket *Informal.* a person or thing that has a depressing effect, as by discouraging others from having fun.

wet cell, in electricity, a cell having a liquid electrolyte.

weth·er (we<u>th</u>′ər) *n.* a castrated male sheep.

wet·land (wet′land′) *n.* an area of swamp, marsh, or other wet surface.

wet suit, a close-fitting, one-piece garment worn for warmth while swimming, skin-diving, or surfing.

we've (wēv) *contr.* we have.

whack (hwak, wack) *n.* **1.** a sharp, resounding blow. **2.** the sound made by such a blow. **3.** *Informal.* a chance or try at something: *I'll take a whack at fixing the toaster.* —*v.t., v.i.* to hit or slap with a sharp, resounding blow. ·**out of whack.** *Informal.* not working properly; broken: *The television set is out of whack.*

whack·y (hwak′ē, wak′ē) *adj.,* **whack·i·er, whack·i·est.** another spelling of wacky.

whale¹ (hwāl, wāl) *n., pl.* **whales** or **whale. 1.** any of various large mammals that live in all oceans and certain fresh waters. A whale has a fishlike body, horizontal tail fins, and flippers. Some whales are hunted for their oil, flesh, and bone. **2.** *Informal.* something very large or impressive: *There was a whale of a crowd at the game.* —*v.i.,* **whaled, whal·ing.** to hunt whales. [From the Old English word *hwæl* meaning this animal.]

whale² (hwāl, wāl) *v.t.,* **whaled, whal·ing.** *Informal.* to beat; thrash. [Of uncertain origin.]

whale·boat (hwāl′bōt′, wāl′bōt′) *n.* a long, narrow rowboat, pointed at both ends, formerly used in whaling.

whale·bone (hwāl′bōn′, wāl′bōn′) *n.* **1.** an elastic, horny material similar to fingernails, forming thin plates that grow in place of teeth on certain whales. Also, **ba·leen′. 2.** a thin strip of this material, formerly used for stiffening corsets or other items.

whal·er (hwā′lər, wā′lər) *n.* **1.** a person whose work is whaling. **2.** a ship or boat used in whaling.

whal·ing (hwā′ling, wā′ling) *n.* the act, business, or work of hunting whales.

wharf

wharf (hwôrf, wôrf) *n., pl.* **wharves** or **wharfs.** a structure built along a shore to be used as a landing place for boats and ships; dock.

wharf·age (hwôr′fij, wôr′fij) *n.* **1.** a space at a wharf or the use of a wharf or wharves, as for mooring a ship, loading or unloading cargo, or storing goods. **2.** the charge for using a wharf or wharves. **3.** wharves as a group.

wharves (hwôrvz, wôrvz) a plural of **wharf.**

what (hwut, hwot, wut, wot; *unstressed* hwət, wət) *pron.* **1.** which specific thing or things, action or actions, or the like: *What do you want to do? What is the date of the game?* **2.** that which: *They knew what I was thinking.* **3.** anything that; whatever: *Choose what you want for dinner.* **4.** how much: *What do you think we should charge for our work?* —*adj.* **1.** which one or ones: *What books are missing from the shelf?* **2.** whatever: *Take what food you will need for the picnic.* **3.** how surprising, great,

absurd, or the like: *What trouble I had parking the car!*
—*adv.* **1.** in what respect; how much: *What does it matter?*
2. which reason; why: *What did you do that for?* —*interj.*
an exclamation used to show surprise, disbelief, anger, or
the like.

  •**and what not.** and all kinds of other things; and so
  forth.

  •**what if.** what would happen if; suppose that.

  •**what's what.** *Informal.* the real state of affairs.

  •**what with.** taking into consideration; because of: *What
  with the ice and snow, they decided not to drive home.*

what·ev·er (hwət ev′ər, wət ev′ər) *pron.* **1.** anything
that: *Order whatever you want to eat.* **2.** no matter what:
Whatever you say, they still won't do it. **3.** *Informal.*
what: *Whatever is that noise?* —*adj.* **1.** any that: *Take
whatever books you want to read.* **2.** of any type, sort,
or character; at all: *No person whatever could be that
cruel.*

what·not (hwut′not′, hwot′not′, wut′not′, wot′not′) *n.*
a set of open shelves, as for holding ornaments or books.

what's (hwuts, hwots, wuts, wots) *contr.* **1.** what is.
2. what has.

what·so·ev·er (hwut′sō ev′ər, hwot′sō ev′ər, wut′sō-
ev′ər, wot′sō ev′ər) *pron., adj.* whatever.

wheal (hwēl, wēl) *n.* a ridge or swelling on the skin, as
from an insect bite or hives.

wheat (hwēt, wēt) *n.* **1.** a cereal grass having a thin,
hollow, jointed stem and long,
narrow, grasslike leaves. It is
a major food source for humans
and animals. **2.** the tiny grain
of this plant, used to make flour
and other foods.

wheat·en (hwē′tən, wē′tən)
adj. made of wheat.

wheat germ, the embryo of
the wheat kernel separated
from flour in milling. It is
rich in vitamins and is used as
a cereal and to enrich other
foods.

whee·dle (hwē′dəl, wē′dəl)
v.t., **whee·dled, whee·dling.**
1. to persuade or try to persuade, as with flattery or the
like: *to wheedle a friend into
doing a favor.* **2.** to get by
wheedling: *to wheedle money
out of someone.* —**whee′dler,** *n.* —**whee′dling·ly,** *adv.*

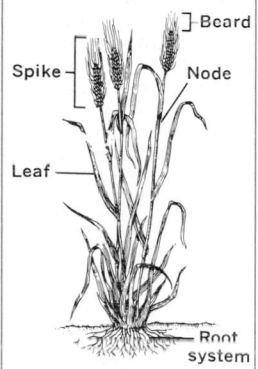

wheat plant

wheel (hwēl, wēl) *n.* **1.** a circular frame having a hub
connected to the rim by spokes. A wheel can turn on a
central axis, and is used on vehicles and certain machines.
2. any of a number of mechanical devices that use a wheel
or wheellike part, such as a potter's wheel or spinning
wheel. **3.** *usually,* **wheels.** the guiding, controlling, or
moving forces: *the wheels of business.* **4. wheels.** *Slang.*
an automobile. —*v.i.* **1.** to turn on an axis; pivot: *The
basketball player wheeled around quickly to make a shot.*
2. to move with a circular motion: *Seagulls wheeled
overhead.* **3.** to roll or move along on wheels: *to wheel
down the highway.* —*v.t.* **1.** to move or carry on wheels:
*to wheel a shopping cart around a supermarket, to wheel
a load of cement.* **2.** to cause to turn on an axis. **3.** to
provide with wheels.

  •**at the wheel. a.** doing the steering or driving. **b.** in
  control.

wheel·bar·row (hwēl′bar′ō, wēl′bar′ō) *n.* a boxlike
vehicle with one or two wheels at the front end and two
handles at the back, used to move small loads, as of sand,
dirt, or bricks.

wheel·base (hwēl′bās′, wēl′bās′) *n.* the distance measured in inches between the center of the front wheel and

the center of the rear wheel on the same side of an
automobile or similar vehicle.

wheel·chair (hwēl′chār′, wēl′chār′) *n.* a chair mounted
on wheels, used to help sick or
physically handicapped people
move about without using their
legs.

wheel·er-deal·er (hwē′lər dē′-
lər, wē′lər dē′lər) *n.* *Slang.* a
person who is shrewd and aggressive in scheming, bargaining, and
making deals, especially in business or politics.

wheel·house (hwēl′hous′, wēl′-
hous′) *n., pl.* **wheel·hous·es**
(hwēl′hou′ziz, wēl′hou′ziz). an
enclosed structure on the bridge
or deck of a ship that shelters
the steering wheel and the pilot; pilothouse.

wheelchair

wheel·wright (hwēl′rīt′, wēl′rīt′) *n.* a person who makes
or repairs wheels, or wheeled vehicles such as carriages
and wagons.

wheeze (hwēz, wēz) *v.i.,* **wheezed, wheez·ing.** **1.** to
breathe or utter a hoarse, whistling sound: *I wheeze badly
when I have a cold.* **2.** to make a similar whistling sound:
The old bus wheezed when it climbed the hill.
—*n.* the act of wheezing.

wheez·y (hwē′zē, wē′zē) *adj.,* **wheez·i·er, wheez·i·-
est.** having or making a wheezing sound: *a wheezy cough.*
—**wheez′i·ly,** *adv.* —**wheez′i·ness,** *n.*

whelk (hwelk, welk) *n.* any of various large snails that
live in salt water and have spiral shells.

whelm (hwelm, welm) *v.t.* **1.** to cover with water. **2.** to
overwhelm.

whelp (hwelp, welp) *n.* **1.** the young of certain animals,
such as dogs, bears, or lions. **2.** an impudent child or
youth. —*v.i.* to give birth to whelps.

when (hwen, wen) *adv.* at what or which time: *When
did you arrive?* —*conj.* **1.** at the time that: *Come when
I call you.* **2.** at any time that: *When I am embarrassed
my face gets red.* **3.** at what or which time; and then:
The children played until noon, when they had lunch.
4. although: *You wore only a sweater when you should
have worn a heavy coat.* **5.** considering that: *How can I
go when I haven't been invited?* —*pron.* what time;
which time: *Since when have you known about that?*
—*n.* the time or occasion: *the where and when of an
accident.*

whence (hwens, wens) *adv.* from what place or source;
from where. —*conj.* from what place, source, or cause:
*They set out last week for the coast, whence news of their
safe arrival reached us.*

whence·so·ev·er (hwens′sō ev′ər, wens′sō ev′ər) *adv.,
conj.* *Archaic.* from whatever place, source, or cause.

when·e'er (hwen âr′, wen âr′) *adv., conj.* *Archaic.*
whenever.

when·ev·er (hwen ev′ər, wen ev′ər) *adv., conj.* at
whatever time: *You may come whenever you like.*

when·so·ev·er (hwen′sō ev′ər, wen′sō ev′ər) *adv., conj.*
whenever.

where (hwâr, wâr) *adv.* **1.** in or at what place: *Where
did you put the camera?* **2.** to what place: *Where did
they go?* **3.** from what place or source: *Where did you*

---

at; āpe; fär; câre; end; mē; it; īce; pîerce; hot; ōld;
sông, fôrk; oil; out; up; ūse; rüle; pull; tûrn; chin;
sing; shop; thin; this; hw in white; zh in treasure.
The symbol ə stands for the unstressed vowel sound
heard in about, taken, pencil, lemon, and circus.

W

get that book? **4.** in or at which: *This is the restaurant where we will eat.* **5.** in what way or respect; how: *Where can we be of the most help?* —*conj.* **1.** in the place in which; at the place at which: *The car is where you parked it.* **2.** in or at which place: *Let's go inside where we can sit down.* **3.** in the case, condition, circumstances, or respect in which: *They are very protective where their friends are concerned.* —*n.* the place; scene; locality: *I don't know the when or where of the accident.*

where·a·bouts (hwâr′ə bouts′, wâr′ə bouts′) *adv.* near or in what location: *Whereabouts did you last see them?* —*n.* the location of a person or place: *The police established the whereabouts of the suspect.* ▲ used with a singular or plural verb.

where·as (hwâr az′, wâr az′) *conj.* **1.** considering that; since: *The document began "Whereas the committee has resolved . . ."* **2.** while on the contrary: *My friend likes yellow whereas I prefer green.*

where·at (hwâr at′, wâr at′) *Archaic. adv.* at what. —*conj.* whereupon.

where·by (hwâr bī′, wâr bī′) *conj.* by which or by means of which: *The mile and the kilometer are the basic units whereby we measure long distances.*

where·fore (hwâr′fôr′, wâr′fôr′) *adv.* for what reason; why. —*conj.* for which reason; therefore. —*n.* the reason: *the whys and wherefores of a decision.*

where·from (hwâr from′, hwâr frum′, wâr from′, wâr-frum′) *adv., conj. Archaic.* from which; whence.

where·in (hwâr in′, wâr in′) *conj.* in which. —*adv.* in what regard; how: *Wherein did we fail?*

where·of (hwâr uv′, hwâr ov′, wâr uv′, wâr ov′) *adv., conj.* of what, which, or whom: *Do you know whereof you speak when you say that they are responsible?*

where·on (hwâr ôn′, hwâr on′, wâr ôn′, wâr on′) *adv. Archaic.* on what. —*conj.* on which: *the rock whereon I sit.*

where·so·ev·er (hwâr′sō ev′ər, wâr′sō ev′ər) *adv., conj. Archaic.* wherever.

where·to (hwâr tü′, wâr tü′) *Archaic. conj.* to which or whom. —*adv.* for what purpose.

where·up·on (hwâr′ə pon′, hwâr′ə pon′, wâr′ə pon′, wâr′ə pon′) *conj.* at which time; after which: *They waited for me to finish speaking, whereupon they left.* —*adv. Archaic.* upon what or which.

wher·ev·er (hwâr ev′ər, wâr ev′ər) *adv.* where: *Wherever did you buy that suit?* —*conj.* in, at, or to whatever place: *I'll go wherever you go.*

where·with (hwâr with′, hwâr with′, wâr with′, wâr-with′) *adv., conj. Archaic.* with what or which.

where·with·al (hwâr′with ôl′, wâr′with ôl′) *n.* necessary means or resources, especially money.

wher·ry (hwer′ē, wer′ē) *n., pl.* **wher·ries. 1.** a light rowboat used to transport passengers and goods on rivers. **2.** a light rowboat for one person, used for racing.

whet (hwet, wet) *v.t.,* **whet·ted, whet·ting. 1.** to sharpen by grinding, scraping, or rubbing: *The barber whetted the razor on a leather strop.* **2.** to make keen; stimulate: *The article whetted my interest in the subject.* —*n.* the act of whetting.

wheth·er (hweth′ər, weth′ər) *conj.* **1.** used to introduce the first of two choices or alternatives: *You must decide whether to take the train or to go by plane.* **2.** if it be the case that: *Write to us whether you will come to visit next month.* **3.** either: *Whether from bravery or stubbornness, they did not give in.*

whet·stone (hwet′stōn′, wet′stōn′) *n.* a stone for sharpening knives or tools.

whew (hwū) *interj.* an exclamation used to express relief, surprise, dismay, or the like.

whey (hwā, wā) *n.* the watery part of milk that separates from the curd when milk coagulates, as during the process of making cheese.

which (hwich, wich) *pron.* **1.** what one or ones: *Which of the books did you like best?* **2.** any one or ones that; whichever: *Choose which you prefer.* **3.** used in a clause referring to a thing or things mentioned before: *This jacket, which I bought three years ago, still looks new.* **4.** used in place of *that* in a clause providing information that defines or restricts a thing or things mentioned before: *The team which finishes first will receive the trophy.* ▲ See **that** for usage note. **5.** used after a preposition in defining or restricting a thing or things mentioned before: *The house in which we live is across the street.* **6.** a thing, circumstance, or event that: *You are late, which reminds me that you were late yesterday too.* —*adj.* **1.** what one or ones: *Which house is yours?* **2.** being the thing or things previously mentioned: *We spent four years in France, during which time we learned to speak French.* ▲ See **that** for usage note.

which·ev·er (hwich ev′ər, wich ev′ər) *pron., adj.* **1.** any one that: *Buy whichever you like best. You can have whichever picture you want.* **2.** no matter which: *Whichever road you follow, you will arrive home.*

which·so·ev·er (hwich′sō ev′ər, wich′sō ev′ər) *pron., adj.* whichever.

whiff (hwif, wif) *n.* **1.** a sudden, light puff, breath, or gust, as of air: *A whiff of smoke rose from the small campfire.* **2.** a slight smell or odor: *a whiff of perfume.* —*v.t.* **1.** to move with a puff or gust. **2.** to breathe; sniff. —*v.i.* to blow or be carried in a puff or gust.

whif·fle·tree (hwif′əl trē′, wif′əl trē′) *n.* the crossbar to which the traces of a harness are fastened, as in a horse-drawn carriage or plow. Also, **singletree, whippletree.**

Whig (hwig, wig) *n.* **1.** a member of a former British political party in the eighteenth and early nineteenth centuries, that favored reform and opposed the Tory party. Since 1832, it has been known as the Liberal Party. **2.** an American colonist who supported the Revolution against England. **3.** a member of a U.S. political party formed about 1834 in opposition to the Democratic Party. It split in 1852 over the issue of slavery and was later succeeded by the Republican Party.

while (hwīl, wīl) *n.* **1.** a period of time, usually a short period of time: *We stopped walking and rested for a while.* **2. the while.** during the time: *I read all the while I waited.* —*conj.* **1.** during or in the time that: *Did anyone call while I was away?* **2.** at the same time that; although: *While they are my neighbors, I don't know them well.* —*v.t.,* **whiled, whil·ing.** to pass or spend (time or a period of time) in a leisurely, pleasant manner (often with *away*): *It is nice to while away a warm summer afternoon at the beach.*

   ·worth one's while. worth one's time and effort; rewarding: *Painting the house myself is not worth my while.*

whi·lom (hwī′ləm, wī′ləm) *Archaic. adj.* former. —*adv.* formerly.

whilst (hwīlst, wīlst) *conj.* while.

whim (hwim, wim) *n.* a sudden or unexpected notion or fanciful idea: *I had a whim to go for a walk in the rain.*

whim·per (hwim′pər, wim′pər) *v.i.* to cry with weak, broken sounds: *The hungry puppy whimpered.* —*v.t.* to utter with a weak, broken crying sound: *to whimper an apology.* —*n.* a whimpering cry or sound. —**whim′·per·er,** *n.* —**whim′per·ing·ly,** *adv.*

whim·sey (hwim′zē, wim′zē) *n., pl.* **whim·seys.** another spelling of **whimsy.**

whim·si·cal (hwim′zi kəl, wim′zi kəl) *adj.* **1.** full of or characterized by odd or fanciful notions: *a whimsical story about a cat that could fly.* **2.** fanciful or odd. —**whim′si·cal·ly,** *adv.*

whim·si·cal·i·ty (hwim′zi kal′i tē, wim′zi kal′i tē) *n.,* *pl.* **whim·si·cal·i·ties. 1.** the quality or state of being whimsical. **2.** a whimsical idea, notion, or action.

whim·sy (hwim′zē, wim′zē) *also,* **whim·sey.** *n., pl.* **whim·sies. 1.** an odd or fanciful notion. **2.** odd, curious, or fanciful humor, as in literature: *a story full of whimsy.*

whine (hwīn, wīn) *v.,* **whined, whin·ing.** —*v.i.* **1.** to make a muted, plaintive cry or sound, as from pain, discomfort, or fear: *The puppies whined because they were hungry.* **2.** to complain in an annoying or childish way. —*v.t.* to say with a low, plaintive cry or sound: *The tired child whined a complaint.* —*n.* the act or sound of whining. —**whin′er,** *n.* —**whin′ing·ly,** *adv.*

whin·ny (hwin′ē, win′ē) *v.,* **whin·nied, whin·ny·ing.** —*v.i.* to neigh, especially in a low, gentle manner: *The colt whinnied for its mother.* —*v.t.* to express with such a sound. —*n., pl.* **whin·nies.** the act or sound of whinnying.

whip (hwip, wip) *v.,* **whipped** or **whipt, whip·ping.** —*v.t.* **1.** to strike with a lash, rod, strap, or the like: *Animals and slaves used to be cruelly whipped by their masters.* **2.** to drive, urge, or force with or as if with lashes or blows: *The coach only had a week to whip the volleyball team into shape.* **3.** to strike like a whip or lash: *The wind whipped our faces.* **4.** to beat (a substance, such as cream or eggs) to a froth or foam. **5.** to move, take, throw, or the like suddenly and rapidly: *to whip a gun out of a holster.* **6.** *Informal.* to defeat, as in a contest or fight: *Our team whipped the champions of the league.* —*v.i.* **1.** to go, come, move, or turn suddenly and rapidly: *The ambulance whipped around the corner at high speed.* **2.** to move with a flapping or thrashing motion: *The flag whipped in the wind.* —*n.* **1.** a flexible rod or thong attached to a handle, used especially for driving animals or inflicting punishment. **2.** a whipping or lashing blow, stroke, or motion. **3.** a member of a legislative assembly chosen by his or her party to assist the party leader and to direct the party's tactics and maintain discipline. **4.** a dessert or other dish made with whipped ingredients, especially cream or eggs. —**whip′like′,** *adj.* —**whip′per,** *n.*

·to whip up. a. to arouse or excite: *The speaker's words whipped up the angry mob.* **b.** to make or prepare quickly: *to whip up a snack from leftovers.*

whip·cord (hwip′kôrd′, wip′kôrd′) *n.* **1.** a strong, twisted cord, used for the lashes of whips. **2.** a tough fabric woven with diagonal ribs.

whip hand 1. the hand in which the whip is held in driving. **2.** a position of control or advantage.

whip·lash (hwip′lash′, wip′lash′) *n., pl.* **whip·lash·es. 1.** the lash of a whip. **2.** an injury to the neck resulting from a sudden backward or forward movement of the head. Whiplash often results when a person is riding in an automobile that strikes something or is struck.

whip·per·snap·per (hwip′ər snap′ər, wip′ər snap′ər) *n.* an impudent person, especially a young person.

whip·pet (hwip′it, wip′it) *n.* a slender dog that looks somewhat like a small greyhound, having a short, smooth coat. The whippet is often used for racing.

whip·ple·tree (hwip′əl trē′, wip′əl trē′) *n.* another word for **whiffletree.**

whip·poor·will (hwip′ər wil′, wip′ər wil′) *n.* a plump North American bird having mottled brown, tan, and black feathers. It is active at night and has a call that sounds like its name.

whipt (hwipt, wipt) a past tense and past participle of **whip.**

whippet

whir (hwûr, wûr) *also,* **whirr.** *v.i., v.t.,* **whirred, whir·ring.** to move or operate with a whizzing or buzzing sound. —*n.* a whizzing or buzzing sound: *the whir of an electric motor.*

whirl (hwûrl, wûrl) *v.i.* **1.** to revolve or turn rapidly: *The blades of the fan whirled around and around.* **2.** to turn around or aside suddenly or quickly: *I whirled about when I heard the noise.* **3.** to move or go swiftly: *The explosion sent fragments of rock whirling through the air.* **4.** to have a feeling of spinning; feel dizzy or confused: *The dazzling lights made my head whirl.* —*v.t.* **1.** to cause to revolve or turn rapidly; spin: *The bully grasped me by the shoulder and whirled me around.* **2.** to move, carry, or drive swiftly, especially in a circular course: *The breeze whirled the leaves around as they fell.* —*n.* **1.** the act of whirling or spinning; whirling movement or motion. **2.** a confused or dizzy condition: *My mind was in a whirl.* **3.** a rapid round of activities or events: *a whirl of parties.* **4.** *Informal.* a try: *I didn't know how to ice-skate, but I wanted to give it a whirl anyway.* —**whirl′er,** *n.*

whirl·i·gig (hwûr′li gig′, wûr′li gig′) *n.* **1.** a toy that whirls or spins about, such as a pinwheel. **2.** see **merry-go-round** (defs. 1, 2). **3.** something that moves or seems to move in a whirling motion.

whirl·pool (hwûrl′pül′, wûrl′pül′) *n.* a current of water having a swift or violent circular motion, usually occurring in rapidly moving bodies of water; eddy.

whirl·wind (hwûrl′wind′, wûrl′wind′) *n.* **1.** a rapidly or violently rotating column of air. **2.** anything resembling a whirlwind, as in swiftness of motion: *With a whirlwind of engagements, the circus toured the country each summer.* —*adj.* very swift; hasty: *a whirlwind tour of the city.*

whirr (hwûr, wûr) another spelling of **whir.**

whish (hwish, wish) *n., pl.* **whish·es.** a soft, rushing sound; swish. —*v.i.* to move with such a sound.

whisk (hwisk, wisk) *v.t.* **1.** to sweep or brush with swift, light strokes: *I whisked the crumbs off the table.* **2.** to move or cause to move swiftly or abruptly: *A taxicab whisked us to the airport.* **3.** to whip or beat, as eggs. —*v.i.* to move swiftly or lightly: *to whisk out the door.* —*n.* **1.** a quick, light sweeping motion or movement: *With a whisk of the hand the judge dismissed the lawyer's request.* **2.** see **whisk broom. 3.** a wire kitchen utensil used especially for whipping cream or eggs.

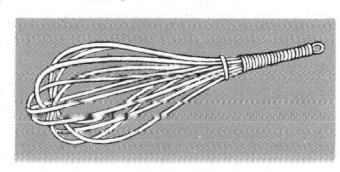

whisk
(n., def 3)

whisk broom, a small, short-handled broom used especially for brushing clothes.

whisk·er (hwis′kər, wis′kər) *n.* **1.** **whiskers.** the hair growing on a man's face; beard or a part of the beard. **2.** a single hair of a beard. **3.** one of the long, stiff hairs growing near the mouth of certain animals, such as dogs, cats, and rats. **4.** *Informal.* a very small margin: *The runner won the race by a whisker.* —**whisk′ered,** *adj.*

whis·key (hwis′kē, wis′kē) *n., pl.* **whis·keys. 1.** a strong alcoholic liquor distilled from fermenting grain, such as rye, corn, barley, or wheat. **2.** a drink of such liquor.

at; āpe; fär; câre; end; mē; it; īce; pîerce; hot; ōld; sông, fôrk; oil; out; up; ūse; rüle; pull; tûrn; chin; sing; shop; thin; this; hw in white; zh in treasure. The symbol ə stands for the unstressed vowel sound heard in about, taken, pencil, lemon, and circus.

W

[Short for earlier *usquebaugh* meaning this liquor, from Gaelic *uisgebeatha* literally, water of life.]

whis·ky (hwis′kē, wis′kē) *n., pl.* **whis·kies.** another spelling of **whiskey.**

whis·per (hwis′pər, wis′pər) *v.i.* **1.** to speak very softly or cautiously, as when telling secrets: *The people around us whispered so that we couldn't hear what they were saying.* **2.** to make a soft, rustling sound, as leaves blown by a breeze. —*v.t.* to say very softly or cautiously: *to whisper a secret.* —*n.* **1.** a very soft spoken sound: *to talk in whispers. You shouldn't speak in the library above a whisper.* **2.** something whispered, such as a rumor or secret. **3.** a soft, rustling sound. **4.** a small amount; hint: *There is a whisper of garlic in this sauce.* —**whis′per·er,** *n.*

whist (hwist, wist) *n.* a card game for four players divided into teams of two, played with a full deck of fifty-two cards. It was the forerunner of bridge.

whis·tle (hwis′əl, wis′əl) *v.,* **whis·tled, whis·tling.** —*v.i.* **1.** to make a clear, shrill sound by forcing breath through partly closed lips or through the teeth. **2.** to produce or send out a sound like this: *The kettle whistled when the water boiled.* **3.** to move with a shrill sound: *A bullet whistled past the soldier's head. The wind whistled through the trees.* —*v.t.* **1.** to produce by whistling: *to whistle a melody.* **2.** to call, signal, or direct by whistling: *The police officer whistled traffic to a halt.* —*n.* **1.** a device designed or used to produce a whistling sound: *a football referee's whistle, a factory whistle.* **2.** a whistling sound. —**whist′ler,** *n.*

whit (hwit, wit) *n.* a tiny amount; bit: *I don't feel a whit tired. The news did not surprise us one whit.*

white (hwīt, wīt) *adj.,* **whit·er, whit·est. 1.** having the lightest of all colors; having the color of fresh snow; opposite of black: *a white shirt.* **2.** light in color: *the white meat of a turkey.* **3.** pale; ashen; pallid: *a face white with fear.* **4.** silvery or pale gray: *white hair.* **5.** of, relating to, or belonging to a light-skinned people; Caucasian. **6.** not harmful: *white magic.* **7.** snowy: *a white Christmas.* **8.** not written or printed upon; blank. **9.** pure; innocent. —*n.* **1.** the lightest of all colors, reflecting all the visible rays of the spectrum; the opposite of black. White is the color of fresh snow. **2.** a white paint, dye, or the like. **3.** something that is white or light-colored, such as the albumen of an egg or the white part of an eyeball. **4.** a member of a light-skinned people; Caucasian. **5.** *also,* **whites.** white clothing or a white uniform. —*v.t.,* **whit·ed, whit·ing.** *Archaic.* to whiten. —**white′ness,** *n.*

white ant, another term for **termite.**

white blood cell, a colorless cell found in the blood, that protects the body by destroying microorganisms and foreign substances. Also, **leukocyte, white corpuscle.**

white·cap (hwīt′cap′, wīt′kap′) *n.* a wave with a crest of white foam.

white–col·lar (hwīt′kol′ər, wīt′kol′ər) *adj.* of or relating to workers employed in professional, clerical, or other fields that usually do not involve manual labor. [From the traditional white shirts worn by many of these workers.]

white corpuscle, another term for **white blood cell.**

white dwarf, a star that has collapsed to about the size of the earth and has exhausted nearly all of its thermonuclear energy.

white elephant, something that is expensive or burdensome to keep and, although often rare or unique, is of little value or use to the owner: *Their large old house was a white elephant.*

white feather, a sign or symbol of cowardice. [From the superstition that a white feather in the tail of a gamecock is a sign of a poor fighter.]

white·fish (hwīt′fish′, wīt′fish′) *n., pl.* **white·fish** or **white·fish·es.** any of several silvery white fish related to the salmon, found in freshwater lakes and streams in northern Europe, Asia, and North America, and used for food.

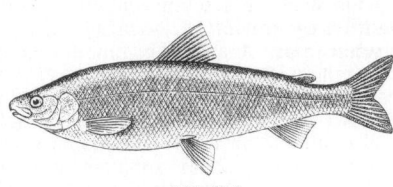

whitefish

white flag, a white flag, banner, or piece of cloth, used to indicate surrender or truce.

white gold, an alloy of gold and, usually, nickel, used for jewelry. It looks like platinum.

White·hall (hwīt′hôl′, wīt′hôl′) *n.* the British government. [From *Whitehall* Street in London, where many offices of the British government are located.]

white heat 1. an extreme degree of heat at which a substance, such as a metal, glows white. **2.** a condition of extreme emotion, excitement, or activity: *the white heat of anger.*

white–hot (hwīt′hot′, wīt′hot′) *adj.* **1.** glowing white with heat. **2.** extremely angry or excited.

White House 1. the official residence of the president of the United States, in Washington, D.C. **2.** the executive branch of the U.S. government.

white lie, a lie that is told to be polite or kind, or to conceal a minor mistake or misdeed.

white matter, the part of the brain and spinal cord consisting chiefly of nerve fibers covered with myelin and having a white appearance.

whit·en (hwī′tən, wī′tən) *v.t., v.i.* to make or become white or whiter: *Bleach whitens clothing. The streets whitened with snow.*

white oak 1. any of various oak trees, especially a large oak of eastern North America noted for its strong, heavy wood. **2.** the wood of any of these trees.

white paper, an official government report on a particular subject.

white pepper, a hot, pungent spice that is made from the dried, ground seeds of the berries of the pepper plant.

white pine 1. a tall pine tree of eastern North America, having bluish green needles and slender cones. **2.** the soft wood of this tree.

White Russian, another term for **Byelorussian.**

white–tailed deer (hwīt′tāld′, wīt′tāld′) a North American deer with a tawny coat and a bushy tail that is white on the underside.

white tie 1. a white bow tie, worn with men's formal evening wear. **2.** men's formal evening wear.

white·wall (hwīt′wôl′, wīt′wôl′) *n.* an automobile tire with a white band on its outer side.

white·wash (hwīt′wôsh′, hwīt′wosh′, wīt′wôsh′, wīt′wosh′) *n., pl.* **white·wash·es. 1.** a white paintlike substance made of a mixture of slaked lime, water, and white chalk. It is used to whiten walls, wood fences, and other surfaces. **2.** the act of covering up something, such as a mistake or wrongdoing: *The mayor's whitewash of the scandal angered the citizens.* **3.** *Sports.* a defeat in which the loser fails to score any points. —*v.t.* **1.** to coat or cover with whitewash. **2.** to cover up or gloss over (something, as a mistake or wrongdoing). **3.** *Sports.* to defeat (an opponent) without allowing the loser to score any points.

white·wa·ter (hwīt′wô′tər, wīt′wô′tər) *adj.* relating to or performed on white water: *whitewater canoeing, the whitewater section of a river.*

white water, churning, frothy, turbulent water, as in the rapids of a river.

whith·er (hwi<u>th</u>′ər, wi<u>th</u>′ər) *adv., conj. Archaic.* to what place; where.

whit·ing[1] (hwī′ting, wī′ting) *n., pl.* **whit·ing** or **whit·ings.** a silvery fish found in Atlantic coastal waters and used for food. [From the Middle Dutch word *witinc* meaning this fish, from the word *wit* "white."]

whit·ing[2] (hwī′ting, wī′ting) *n.* white chalk, powdered and washed, used especially as a pigment. [*White* + *-ing*[1].]

whit·ish (hwī′tish, wī′tish) *adj.* somewhat white: *a whitish bird.*

Whit·sun·day (hwit′sun′dē, hwit′sun′dā, wit′sun′dē, wit′sun′dā) *n.* the seventh Sunday after Easter; Pentecost.

Whit·sun·tide (hwit′sən tīd′, wit′sən tīd′) *n.* the week beginning with Whitsunday, especially the first three days of this week.

whit·tle (hwit′əl, wit′əl) *v.,* **whit·tled, whit·tling.** —*v.t.* **1.** to cut shavings or small bits or pieces from with a knife: *to whittle wood.* **2.** to make or shape (something) in this way: *to whittle a bird from a piece of soap.* **3.** to reduce or diminish gradually: *to whittle down one's expenses.* —*v.i.* to whittle wood or the like. —**whit′tler,** *n.*

whiz (hwiz, wiz) also, **whizz.** *v.,* **whizzed, whiz·zing.** —*v.i.* **1.** to make a hissing, humming, or buzzing sound, especially while moving swiftly through the air: *The plane whizzed over the rooftops. The automobile whizzed past us.* **2.** to move or go through or by very quickly: *I whizzed through my homework.* —*v.t.* to cause to move with a buzzing sound: *The child whizzed the toy truck across the floor.* —*n., pl.* **whiz·zes.** **1.** a whizzing sound or movement. **2.** *Slang.* a person having great skill or ability in some particular field or activity: *My best friend is a whiz at crossword puzzles.*

whittling

who (hü) *pron.* possessive, **whose;** objective, **whom.** **1.** what or which person or persons: *Who gave you that book?* **2.** that. ▲ used to introduce a relative clause when the preceding noun is a person or persons: *The author who wrote this play has an excellent sense of humor.* **3.** the person or persons that; whoever: *Who steals my purse steals trash* (Shakespeare, *Othello*).

▲ In formal speech and writing, **who** is used in the nominative case and **whom** in the objective case: *To whom am I speaking? Whom do you suspect of the crime?* However, in speech and informal writing, **who** is often used instead of **whom:** *Who did you call on the phone? Do you know who the committee named as its secretary?* See **that** for an additional usage note.

whoa (hwō, wō) *interj.* stop. ▲ used chiefly as a command to a horse.

who'd (hüd) *contr.* **1.** who would. **2.** who had.

who·dun·it (hü dun′it) *n. Informal.* a mystery story, especially one that centers on the gradual discovery of the criminal's identity.

who·ev·er (hü ev′ər) *pron.* **1.** any person who; whatever person: *Whoever wants to come to the party is welcome.* **2.** no matter who: *Whoever the artist is, I like the painting.* **3.** what person; who: *Whoever told you such a ridiculous story?*

whole (hōl) *adj.* **1.** made up of the entire amount, quantity, number, or extent: *Did you read the whole book? I have been away the whole week.* **2.** having all its parts; complete; entire: *A whole deck consists of fifty-two cards.* **3.** not divided into parts or pieces; in one unit: *The whale swallowed the small fish whole.* **4.** not damaged, injured, or broken; intact; sound: *The doll was still whole after it fell down the stairs.* **5.** *Mathematics.* not fractional; integral. —*n.* **1.** all the parts or elements that together make up a thing; entire amount, quantity, number, or extent: *I spent the whole of my allowance on a record album.* **2.** a combination of parts or elements forming a complete entity or system. —**whole′ness,** *n.*

·on the whole. all things considered; in general.

whole–grain (hōl′grān′) *adj.* being, having, or related to flour or other grain products that include the entire ground kernel of the grain with the outer husk or bran: *whole-grain bread.*

whole·heart·ed (hōl′här′tid) *adj.* complete, sincere, or enthusiastic: *I will give you my wholehearted support.* —**whole′heart′ed·ly,** *adv.* —**whole′heart′ed·ness,** *n.*

whole note, a musical note having a time value equal to four quarter notes or two half notes.

whole number, a number that tells how many complete things there are. *1, 2, 3,* and *0* are examples of whole numbers; ¾ and other fractions are not whole numbers.

whole·sale (hōl′sāl′) *n.* the selling of goods in large quantities, usually to retailers for resale. —*adj.* **1.** of, relating to, or engaged in the selling of goods in large quantities, usually to retailers for resale: *It is usually cheaper to buy at wholesale prices.* **2.** widespread and complete: *the wholesale slaughter of war.* —*adv.* in a wholesale quantity or at a wholesale price. —*v.,* **whole·saled, whole·sal·ing.** —*v.t.* to sell (goods) wholesale. —*v.i.* to be sold wholesale.

whole·sal·er (hōl′sā′lər) *n.* a merchant or dealer in wholesale goods.

whole·some (hōl′səm) *adj.* **1.** good for the health; healthful: *wholesome food.* **2.** of value to the mind or character; worthwhile: *wholesome entertainment.* **3.** showing good health: *a wholesome youngster.* —**whole′some·ness,** *n.*

whole step *Music.* an interval consisting of two adjacent half steps. Also, **whole tone.**

whole–wheat (hōl′hwēt′, hōl′wēt′) *adj.* **1.** made of the entire wheat kernel: *whole-wheat flour.* **2.** made with whole-wheat flour: *whole-wheat bread.*

who'll (hül) *contr.* **1.** who will. **2.** who shall.

whol·ly (hō′lē, hōl′lē) *adv.* entirely; completely. *The company was wholly owned by one family.*

whom (hüm) *pron.* the objective case of **who.** ▲ See **who** for usage note.

whom·ev·er (hüm ev′ər) *pron.* the objective case of **whoever.**

whom·so·ev·er (hüm′sō ev′ər) *pron.* the objective case of **whosoever.**

---

at; āpe; fär; câre; end; mē; it; īce; pîerce; hot; ōld; sông, fôrk; oil; out; up; ūse; rüle; pull; tûrn; chin; sing; shop; thin; this; hw in white; zh in treasure. The symbol ə stands for the unstressed vowel sound heard in about, taken, pencil, lemon, and circus.

W

whoop (hüp, hwüp, wüp; *esp. for n., def. 3,* hüp, húp) *n.*
1. a loud cry or shout, as of joy or enthusiasm.
2. the cry of an owl or certain other birds; hoot. **3.** a
loud, gasping sound that follows a fit of coughing in the
disease whooping cough. —*v.i.* to utter a whoop or
whoops: *to whoop for joy.* —*v.t.* **1.** to utter or express
with a whoop or whoops: *to whoop one's joy.* **2.** to urge
on, drive, or call with whoops or shouts.
·**to whoop it up.** *Slang.* to celebrate noisily; have fun.
whoop·ing cough (hü'ping, húp'ing) a highly contagious, infectious disease, caused by a bacterium and
characterized by fits of coughing that end with a loud,
gasping sound, or whoop. Whooping cough usually occurs
in infants and young children.
whoop·ing crane (hü'ping, hwü'ping, wü'ping) a nearly
extinct crane having a white body, black-tipped wings, a
red face, and a loud whooping call. It is the tallest of all
North American birds.
whop·per (hwop'ər, wop'ər) *n. Informal.* **1.** something
very large: *That fish you caught is a whopper!* **2.** a big
or elaborate lie.
whore (hôr) *n.* another word for **prostitute.**
whorl (hwûrl, hwôrl, wûrl, wôrl) *n.* **1.** *Botany.* a circular
arrangement of parts, such as leaves, around the same
point on a stem. **2.** *Zoology.* one of
the turns of a spiral shell. **3.** any of
the circular ridges of a fingerprint.
4. anything resembling a coil or spiral
in form or appearance.
who's (hüz) **1.** who is. **2.** who has.
whose (hüz) *pron.* the possessive
case of **who** and **which.**
who·so (hü'sō) *pron.* whoever.
who·so·ev·er (hü'sō ev'ər) *pron.*
whoever.

whorl *(def. 3)*

why (hwī, wī) *adv.* **1.** for what cause,
reason, or purpose: *Why are you laughing?* **2.** for which:
The reason why the friends broke up is not known.
—*conj.* **1.** the cause, reason, or purpose for which: *Do
you know why the visitors left early?* **2.** because of which;
for which: *I see no reason why you shouldn't go.* —*n.,
pl.* **whys.** a cause, reason, or purpose. —*interj.* used
to express surprise, hesitation, or other feeling: *Why, look
who's here!*
WI, postal abbreviation for Wisconsin.
W.I. 1. West Indies. **2.** West Indian.
wick (wik) *n.* a cord or thin bundle of fibers, as in an oil
lamp or candle, that draws up the fuel to be burned.
wick·ed (wik'id) *adj.* **1.** morally bad; evil. **2.** mischievous; sly: *to be a wicked tease.* **3.** causing or likely
to cause harm, trouble, or discomfort: *to have a wicked
cold.* —**wick'ed·ly,** *adv.* —**wick'ed·ness,** *n.*
wick·er (wik'ər) *n.* **1.** slender, flexible twigs woven
together, used in making baskets, furniture, and the like.
2. see **wickerwork.** —*adj.* made of or covered with
wicker: *a wicker basket.*
wick·er·work (wik'ər wûrk') *n.* something made of
wicker.
wick·et (wik'it) *n.* **1.** a small door
or gate, especially one that is part
of or near a larger one. **2.** a small
window or opening. **3.** in cricket,
either of the two sets of three
stakes that form the targets for the
bowler. **4.** in croquet, any of the
arches through which the ball must
be hit, usually made of wire.
wick·i·up (wik'ē up') *n.* a loosely
built hut often made of a circular
frame of poles that is covered with
brush. It has been used by certain
North American Indian tribes.

wickerwork

wide (wīd) *adj.,* **wid·er, wid·est. 1.** extending over or
made up of a very large area: *a wide lawn.* **2.** having a
greater extent from side to side than is usual: *This coat
has wide lapels.* **3.** having a specified extent from side
to side: *This room is twelve feet wide.* **4.** great in amount,
range, or extent: *This store carries a wide assortment of
products.* **5.** fully opened or extended: *eyes wide with
excitement.* **6.** far or away from a specified point or
object: *The arrow fell wide of the mark.* —*adv.* **1.** over
a large area; extensively: *to travel far and wide.* **2.** to a
large or the full extent: *to open a window wide.* **3.** far or
away from something aimed at: *The hockey player shot
the puck wide and missed the goal.* —**wide'ly,** *adv.*
—**wide'ness,** *n.*
wide–a·wake (wīd'ə wāk') *adj.* **1.** fully awake. **2.** paying attention to what is happening; alert: *wide-awake to
the dangers nearby.*
wide–eyed (wīd'īd') *adj.* with the eyes wide open, as
in wonder, disbelief, or surprise.
wid·en (wī'dən) *v.t., v.i.* to make or become wide or
wider: *to widen a road. The children's eyes widened in
surprise.*
wide·spread (wīd'spred') *adj.* **1.** occurring, distributed, or prevalent over a wide area or among many
people: *a widespread epidemic, a widespread rumor.*
2. widely extended: *widespread arms.*
widg·eon (wij'ən) another spelling of **wigeon.**
wid·ow (wid'ō) *n.* a woman whose husband is dead,
especially one who has not married again. —*v.t.* to
cause to become a widow.
wid·ow·er (wid'ō ər) *n.* a man whose wife is dead,
especially one who has not married again.
wid·ow·hood (wid'ō húd') *n.* the state or period of
being a widow.
widow's peak, a V-shaped point in a hairline, formed by
hair growing down in the middle of the forehead. [Perhaps
from its resemblance to the projecting front of the type of
bonnet formerly worn by widows.]
width (width, with) *n.* **1.** the measurement of something
from side to side; size in terms of wideness; breadth.
2. a piece of something, especially of cloth, having a
certain width: *We need two widths of curtain material to
cover the window.*
width·wise (width'wīz', with'wīz') *adv.* in the direction of the width; from side to side.
wield (wēld) *v.t.* **1.** to handle or use, as a weapon or
tool: *The logger had good experience wielding an axe.*
2. to exercise, as influence or power: *The judge wielded
authority fairly.* —**wield'er,** *n.*
wie·ner (wē'nər) *n.* another word for **frankfurter.** Also,
wie·ner·wurst (wē'nər wûrst'). [Short for the German
word *Wienerwurst* meaning this food, from the words
Wiener meaning "of Vienna" (from *Wien,* the German
name for the city of Vienna) + *wurst* "sausage."]
wife (wīf) *n., pl.* **wives.** a married woman. —**wife'ly,**
adj.
wig (wig) *n.* a covering for the head made of hair or of
a synthetic material resembling hair.
wig·eon (wij'ən) *also,* **widg·eon.** *n., pl.* **wi·geons** or
wi·geon. any of several freshwater ducks, having mainly
brown or gray feathers.
wig·gle (wig'əl) *v.,* **wig·gled, wig·gling.** —*v.i.* to move
with short, quick, jerky movements, as from side to side:
The tadpole wiggles as it swims. —*v.t.* to cause to
wiggle: *to wiggle one's toes.* —*n.* the act of wiggling; a
wiggling movement. —**wig'gly,** *adj.*
wig·gler (wig'lər) *n.* **1.** a person or thing that wiggles.
2. a mosquito larva; wriggler.
wight (wīt) *n. Archaic.* a human being; person.
wig·wag (wig'wag') *v.t., v.i.,* **wig·wagged, wig·wag-**

ging. 1. to move (something) back and forth. **2.** to send (a message) by waving flags, lights, or the like according to a code. —*n.* **1.** the act or practice of sending messages by waving flags, lights, or the like according to a code. **2.** a message so sent. —**wig'wag'ger,** *n.*

wig·wam (wig'wom, wig'wôm) *n.* a hut used by certain North American Indians, usually made with
an arched framework of
poles covered with bark
or leaves.

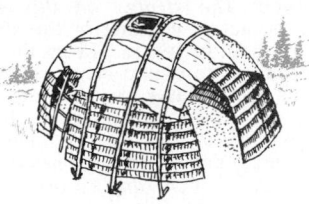

wigwam

wild (wīld) *adj.* **1.** not
brought under the con-
trol of human beings; in
a state of nature: *There
are still wild horses in
that valley.* **2.** growing
without human assist-
ance: *wild plants.* **3.** not inhabited or cultivated: *the wild prairie.* **4.** uncivilized; savage: *wild tribes.* **5.** unre-
strained or disorderly; uncontrolled: *the wild flight of a frightened animal.* **6.** not disciplined; unruly: *a wild party.* **7.** not neat or orderly in appearance; disheveled: *wild hair.* **8.** characterized by violent or intense activity; turbulent: *the wild sea.* **9.** reckless, crazy, or fantastic: *a wild idea.* **10.** wide of the mark: *a wild shot, a wild throw.* **11.** *Informal.* extremely enthusiastic or excited: *The audience was wild about the new singer.* **12.** (of a card) having any value the player chooses. —*n.* also, **wilds.** an uninhabited or uncultivated place. —*adv.* in a wild manner. —**wild'ly,** *adv.* —**wild'ness,** *n.*

·**to run wild.** to be free from any form of control or restraint.

wild boar, a wild hog native to Europe, Asia, and North America, having a coarse, gray-brown coat and a pair of short tusks.

wild·cat (wīld'kat') *n.* **1.** any of various small, wild members of the cat family, including the bobcat and lynx. **2.** an ill-tempered or spiteful person. **3.** an oil well drilled to find out whether there is oil at a given spot. —*adj.* **1.** unsound or reckless: *a wildcat bank, a wildcat scheme.* **2.** unauthorized or illegal: *The union leaders denounced the wildcat strike.* —**wild'cat'ter,** *n.*

wil·de·beest (wil'də bēst') *n.,* *pl.* **wil·de·beests** or **wil·de·beest.** another word for **gnu.**

wil·der·ness (wil'dər nis) *n.,* *pl.* **wil·der·ness·es. 1.** a wild or desolate place where no people live. **2.** a confused or bewildering collection or group of things: *a wilderness of tall buildings.*

wild·fire (wīld'fīr') *n.* a fire that spreads quickly and is not easily put out.

·**like wildfire.** very quickly and widely: *The rumor spread like wildfire through the town.*

wild·flow·er (wild'flou'ər) also, **wild flower.** *n.* **1.** any flower of a plant that grows wild, as in a field or woods. **2.** a plant bearing such a flower.

wild·fowl (wild'foul') *n.,* *pl.* **wild·fowl** or **wild·fowls.** a game bird, especially a wild duck or goose.

wild–goose chase (wīld'güs') a foolish or hopeless pursuit or endeavor.

wild·life (wīld'līf') *n.* living things, especially wild animals that live naturally in an area.

wild pitch *Baseball.* a pitch that is thrown beyond the catcher's reach and allows a base runner to advance.

wild rice, a tall aquatic grass that grows in North America and bears edible grains.

Wild West, the western frontier region of the United States, noted for its rough and lawless conditions during the nineteenth century.

wild·wood (wīld'wúd') *n.* a forest that has not been cut or cultivated and is in its natural state.

wile (wīl) *n.* a trick or stratagem meant to deceive or lure: *The spy used all kinds of wiles to obtain secret information.* —*v.t.,* **wiled, wil·ing.** to tempt; lure.

wil·i·ness (wī'lē nis) *n.* the state or quality of being wily.

will¹ (wil) Present tense: *sing.,* first person, **will;** second, **will** or *(archaic)* **wilt;** third, **will;** *pl.,* **will.** Past tense: *sing.,* first person, **would;** second, **would** or *(archaic)* **wouldst;** third, **would;** *pl.,* **would.** *auxiliary verb* **1.** to be about to; going to: *I will see you later.* **2.** to be willing to: *I will do the job if you promise to help.* **3.** to be obliged or bound to; must: *They will do as they are told.* **4.** to be able to; can: *This chair will not support your weight.* **5.** to be accustomed to; do habitually: *A cat will clean itself by licking its fur.* —*v.i.* to wish; desire: *Help me move this chair, if you will.* ▲ See **shall** for usage note. [From the Old English word *willan* with the same meanings.]

will² (wil) *n.* **1.** the power or capacity of free, conscious choice: *a decision made of one's own will, a person of high spirit and strong will.* **2.** the ability to determine or control one's actions: *I don't have the will to stop biting my nails.* **3.** a fixed resolution; purpose: *a patient's will to live.* **4.** a preferred course of action; wish: *What is your will in the matter?* **5.** *Law.* a document giving the final settlement of a person's property after he or she dies. —*v.t.* **1.** to decide on, choose, or bring about by using one's will: *You can succeed if you will it.* **2.** to influence (someone) to do something by using one's will. **3.** to give away (property) by a will: *to will one's estate to relatives.* —*v.i.* to use one's will. [From the Old English word *willa* meaning "purpose, determination, will²."]

·**at will.** when or as one wishes.

will·ful (wil'fəl) also, **wil·ful.** *adj.* **1.** determined to do as one pleases; obstinate; stubborn: *a willful youngster.* **2.** deliberate; intentional: *a willful waste.* —**will'ful·ly,** *adv.* —**will'ful·ness,** *n.*

will·ing (wil'ing) *adj.* **1.** favorably disposed; ready: *will-
ing to work.* **2.** characterized by cheerful readiness: *a willing helper.* **3.** cheerfully given, accepted, or accomplished: *willing service.* —**will'ing·ly,** *adv.* —**will'ing-
ness,** *n.*

will–o'–the–wisp (wil'ə thə wisp') *n.* **1.** a faint light seen at night hovering over marshes. **2.** something deceptive or illusive, such as a hope or goal.

wil·low (wil'o) *n.* any of a group of trees and shrubs, such as the weeping willow or pussy willow, usually having slender leaves and branches, and tiny flowers growing on furry spikes called catkins.

wil·low·y (wil'ō ē) *adj.* **1.** graceful and slender: *a tall willowy fashion model.* **2.** abounding with willows.

will·pow·er (wil'pou'ər) *n.* the ability to control one's actions; resoluteness of will: *It takes willpower to follow a strict diet.*

wil·ly–nil·ly (wil'ē nil'ē) *adv.* whether one is willing or not; willingly or unwillingly: *You must do it, willy-nilly.* —*adj.* indecisive; vacillating: *a willy-nilly person.*

wilt¹ (wilt) *v.i.* **1.** to fade or droop; become limp; wither: *The flowers wilted quickly once they were cut.* **2.** to lose energy, strength, or courage: *to wilt after a long walk in the summer heat.* —*v.t.* to cause to wilt: *The hot, dry weather wilted the flowers.* [A form of dialectal *welk* "to wither."]

at; āpe; fär; câre; end; mē; it; īce; pîerce; hot; ōld;
sông; fôrk; oil; out; up; ūse; rüle; púll; tûrn; chin;
sing; shop; thin; **th**is; hw in white; zh in treasure.
The symbol ə stands for the unstressed vowel sound
heard in about, taken, pencil, lemon, and circus.

W

wilt² (wilt) *Archaic.* the second person singular, present indicative of **will¹.** ▲ used with *thou.*

wil·y (wī′lē) *adj.,* **wil·i·er, wil·i·est.** full of wiles; cunning; crafty: *a wily swindler.*

wimp (wimp) *n.* *Slang.* a person who is timid, weak, spineless, or ineffectual.

wim·ple (wim′pəl) *n.* a cloth covering for the head and neck, formerly worn by women out-of-doors, still worn by some nuns.

wimp·y (wim′pē) *adj.* **wimp·i·er, wimp·i·est.** *Slang.* characteristic of a wimp; timid; ineffectual. —**wimp′i·ly,** *adv.*

win (win) *v.,* **won, win·ning.** —*v.i.* **1.** to be victorious over others: *A skilled player often wins at cards.* **2.** to finish first in a race: *The horse won by a head.* **3.** to succeed in some effort or endeavor: *We won in our campaign to have the rule changed.* —*v.t.* **1.** to be victorious in: *to win a battle, to win a court case.* **2.** to receive in or as if in a contest: *to win a vacation for two, to win a prize for the best essay.* **3.** to get by effort or merit: *to win respect, to win favor with a teacher.* **4.** to get the good will, favor, or support of; persuade (often with *over*): *The missionary won many converts. The lawyer won over the jury with a moving defense.* **5.** to persuade (someone) to marry or return one's love. **6.** to attain or reach, especially after long effort: *The disabled boat won the shore.* —*n.* *Informal.* a victory: *The pitcher had a record of ten wins and no losses.*

wince (wins) *v.i.,* **winced, winc·ing.** to draw back or away slightly, as from something painful, dangerous, or unpleasant; flinch: *Many students in the class winced at the very mention of final exams.* —*n.* the act of wincing.

winch (winch) *n., pl.* **winch·es. 1.** a machine for hoisting or pulling, consisting of a drum around which cord or chain is wound. **2.** a crank, handle, or lever by which a revolving machine is turned.

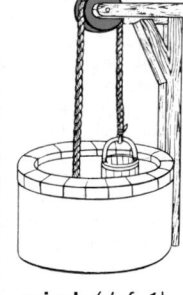

winch *(def. 1)*

wind¹ (wind) *n.* **1.** air in motion over the surface of the earth; natural movement or current of air. **2.** a strong or destructive natural movement of air; gale. **3.** air set in motion artificially, as by a fan or other moving object. **4.** moving air carrying an odor, especially of a person or animal being hunted; scent: *The dogs followed the wind of the fox.* **5.** any compelling force or influence: *the winds of social change.* **6.** the ability to breathe; breath: *The blow knocked the wind out of me.* **7.** empty, meaningless talk; chatter. **8. winds. a.** wind instruments. **b.** the players of these instruments, making up a section of an orchestra. —*v.t.,* **wind·ed, wind·ing. 1.** to cause to be out of breath, as from physical effort: *Climbing the long flight of stairs winded us.* **2.** to find or detect by scent: *The dogs winded the fox.* **3.** to allow to rest in order to recover breath: *The coach driver winded the horses after the long ride uphill.* [From the Old English word *wind.*]
 ·**in the wind.** happening or going to happen: *an uprising was in the wind.*
 ·**to get wind of.** to learn or hear information or hints about: *If the teacher gets wind of the party, the surprise will be ruined.*

wind² (wīnd) *v.,* **wound** or *(archaic)* **wind·ed, wind·ing.** —*v.t.* **1.** to wrap (something) around on itself or on something else: *to wind yarn into a ball. I wound the scarf around my neck.* **2.** to cover or entwine, as by wrapping or coiling: *to wind one's hair with ribbons.* **3.** to cause to move or proceed first in one direction and then another: *The driver wound the ambulance through the city traffic.* **4.** to make (one's way) by moving first in one direction and then another. **5.** to adjust or put (a

mechanism, such as a clock) into action by turning or coiling some part of it. —*v.i.* **1.** to move in one direction and then another; go in a crooked or bending course: *The new highway winds around the mountain.* **2.** to twine, turn, or coil around or about something: *The roses wound around the trellis.* **3.** to be capable of being turned or coiled: *The strings on this guitar wind easily.* —*n.* **1.** the act of winding or the state of being wound. **2.** a turn, coil, or twist. [From the Old English word *windan* meaning "to twist, weave, wind²."]
 ·**to wind down. a.** to come gradually to an end: *The party was winding down.* **b.** to bring gradually to an end: *I will try to wind down my work schedule.* **c.** to relax; unwind: *Jogging around the park helps them wind down after the day's work.*
 ·**to wind up. a.** to bring to an end; finish: *Let's wind up the work today.* **b.** to come to an end: *The meeting wound up at six o'clock.* **c.** to bring to a state of readiness or excitement; arouse: *The kids are all wound up about going to the baseball game.* **d.** (of a baseball pitcher) to make movements with the body or parts of the body in preparation for pitching the ball.

wind·bag (wind′bag′) *n.* *Informal.* a person who talks much but says little of importance or interest.

wind·break (wind′brāk′) *n.* a structure, such as a fence or growth of trees or shrubs, that serves as a protection from the wind.

wind·break·er (wind′brā′kər) *n.* a short jacket made of any of various tightly woven fabrics that resist the passage of air. Trademark: Windbreaker.

wind·burn (wind′bûrn′) *n.* an irritation of the skin caused by exposure to the wind. —**wind′burned′,** *adj.*

wind–chill factor (wind′chil′) a measure of the combined effect on the body of low temperature and wind speed: *The temperature is 0° with a wind-chill factor of −20°.*

wind·fall (wind′fôl′) *n.* **1.** an unexpected advantage, opportunity, or gain, especially a financial gain. **2.** a fruit that falls from the tree before it is harvested, especially one that is blown down by the wind.

wind·flow·er (wind′flou′ər) *n.* see **anemone** *(def. 1).*

wind·ing (wīn′ding) *n.* **1.** the act of a person or thing that winds. **2.** the state of being wound. **3.** a bend, turn, or curve or a series of these. **4.** something that winds or coils, such as a wire. —*adj.* **1.** full of bends or turns, as a road or stream; rambling: *a winding mountain highway.* **2.** curving about a central core; spiraling: *a winding staircase.*

wind instrument (wind) a musical instrument sounded by air being blown into it, such as the flute, clarinet, trumpet, or tuba.

wind·jam·mer (wind′jam′ər) *n.* **1.** a merchant sailing ship. **2.** a member of its crew.

wind·lass (wind′ləs) *n., pl.* **wind·lass·es.** a kind of winch that is turned by a hand crank, used chiefly to lift anchors and buckets in wells.

wind·mill (wind′mil′) *n.* a machine that converts wind power to mechanical power, consisting of a number of vanes or slats radiating from a central axis that is rotated by the wind as it strikes the vanes. Windmills are now used chiefly to pump water.

windmill

win·dow (win′dō) *n.* **1.** an opening in the wall or roof of a building or vehicle for admitting light or air, usually fitted with a movable sash and one or more panes of glass. **2.** the framework that holds the panes of glass in a window; sash: *I can't get this window open.* **3.** a windowpane: *We broke the window playing ball.* **4.** anything like a window in shape or use, such as a transparent patch on an envelope through which the address on an enclosure is read.

window box, a long, narrow box on or near a window sill or ledge, used for growing flowering plants.

window dressing 1. the act or art of decorating store windows with attractive merchandise displays. **2.** the displays themselves or the merchandise used to create such displays. **3.** anything that is made to seem or is used to make something else seem more attractive, profitable, or acceptable than it really is.

win·dow·pane (win′dō′pān′) *n.* a single pane of glass in a window.

win·dow–shop (win′dō shop′) *v.i.,* **win·dow–shopped, win·dow–shop·ping.** to look at merchandise in store windows or displays without actually buying anything. —**win′dow-shop′per,** *n.*

window sill, the horizontal part across the bottom of a window.

wind·pipe (wind′pīp′) *n.* a tube that extends from the larynx to the bronchi and carries air to and from the lungs; trachea.

wind·row (wind′rō′) *n.* a long row of hay, straw, or grain raked together to dry before being collected.

wind·shield (wind′shēld′) *n.* a transparent screen, usually of glass, attached in front of the occupants of an automobile, motorcycle, or other vehicle to protect against wind.

wind·sock (wind′sok′) *also,* **wind sock.** *n.* a long, cone-shaped sack hung on a pole or mast, that shows the direction of the wind blowing through it. Also, **wind sleeve.**

Wind·sor Castle (win′zər) the chief residence of English monarchs since the Norman Conquest, in Windsor, England.

wind·storm (wind′stôrm′) *n.* a storm with high winds but little or no rain or other precipitation.

wind tunnel (wind) a chamber in which air is forced over a scale model of an aircraft or some other object, producing the same effect that would occur if the object itself were moving through the air.

wind–up (wīnd′up′) *n.* **1.** the act of winding up; conclusion, finish: *the wind-up of a political campaign.* **2.** the movements made by a baseball pitcher before pitching.

wind·ward (wind′wərd) *adj.* located on or moving toward the side from which the wind is blowing. —*n.* the side or direction from which the wind is blowing: *to sail to windward.* —*adv.* into the wind.

wind·y (win′dē) *adj.,* **wind·i·er, wind·i·est. 1.** characterized by or having much wind: *a windy night.* **2.** exposed to or swept by the wind: *a windy beach.* **3.** wordy, boastful, or boring in content or manner: *a windy speech, a windy lecturer.* —**wind′i·ly,** *adv.* —**wind′i·ness,** *n.*

wine (wīn) *n.* **1.** the fermented juice of grapes, used as an alcoholic beverage. **2.** the fermented juice of other fruits or plants: *blackberry wine.* **3.** a dark purplish red color, similar to the color of certain wines. —*v.,* **wined, win·ing.** —*v.t.* to furnish with wine. —*v.i.* to drink wine. —*adj.* having the color wine; dark purplish red.

wine cellar 1. a place for the storing and aging of wine. **2.** a stock, store, or selection of wine: *The restaurant had an extensive wine cellar to choose from.*

wine press 1. a machine for pressing the juice from grapes. **2.** a vat in which juice is pressed from grapes.

Wine·sap (wīn′sap′) *n.* a bright red apple with white flesh.

wing (wing) *n.* **1.** a structure that enables a bird, insect,

bat, or other flying animal to fly, corresponding to the forelimb in other animals. **2.** the corresponding structure in animals that cannot fly, such as the ostrich or penguin. **3.** anything like a wing in shape or use. **4.** one of the main lifting and supporting surfaces of an airplane. **5.** a structure attached to the side of a house or other building, or considered as a separate section: *to add a new wing to a school, the children's wing of a hospital.* **6.** the part on either side of a stage that is not seen by the audience: *The actors waited in the wings.* **7.** *Sports.* **a.** either of two positions on either side of the center in ice hockey and certain other goal games. **b.** a player who plays such a position. **8.** a division or faction of an organization representing a particular point of view: *the radical wing of a political party.* **9.** a tactical unit of the U.S. Air Force, together with its supporting units. **10. wings.** an insignia awarded to certain personnel of military aircraft, such as pilots or bombardiers, when they have completed their training. —*v.t.* **1.** to do or accomplish by flight: *The bird winged its way back to the nest.* **2.** to cause to fly as if on wings; give speed to. **3.** to furnish with wings; equip for flight. **4.** to wound, as a bird, in the wing. **5.** to wound slightly: *A branch broke off and winged the farmer in the arm.* —*v.i.* to fly; soar: *The plane winged through the sky.* —**wing′like′,** *adj.*

· **on the wing.** in flight; flying: *geese on the wing.*

· **to take wing.** to fly away.

· **under one's wing.** under one's protection or care.

wing case, one of a pair of hardened forewings that form a protective covering over the hind wings of certain insects, such as the beetle. Also, **wing cover.**

winged (wingd, wing′id) *adj.* **1.** having wings or a winglike part or parts: *a winged bat.* **2.** moving or passing as if on wings: *winged hours.*

wing·less (wing′lis) *adj.* having no wings or only incompletely developed wings.

wingspan

wing·span (wing′span′) *n.* the distance between the fully extended tips of the wings of a bird, insect, or airplane.

wing·spread (wing′spred′) *n.* another word for **wingspan.**

W

wink (wingk) *v.i.* **1.** to close and open the eyelid of one eye quickly, especially as a sign or signal. **2.** to close and open the eyelids of both eyes quickly; blink. **3.** to shine with flashes of light; twinkle: *The lights of the ship winked in the distance.* —*v.t.* **1.** to close and open (an eye or the eyes) quickly. **2.** to signal or express by winking: *to wink one's approval.* —*n.* **1.** the act of winking. **2.** the time required to wink; very short time; instant: *I didn't get a wink of sleep last night.* **3.** a sign or signal conveyed by winking. **4.** a gleam or twinkle.

win·ner (win′ər) *n.* a person or thing that wins: *Who was the winner of the contest?*

win·ning (win′ing) *adj.* **1.** that wins or results in victory or success: *the winning number in a lottery, to score the winning goal in a game.* **2.** charming, pleasing, or attractive: *a winning smile.* —*n.* **1.** the act of a person who wins; victory. **2. winnings.** something that is won, especially money. —**win′ning·ly**, *adv.*

win·now (win′ō) *v.t.* **1.** to expose (grain) to wind or a current of air to blow away the chaff. **2.** to blow away (chaff) in this way. **3.** to separate or remove; sort out: *The lawyer tried to winnow the essential facts from the great mass of evidence.* —*v.i.* to separate grain from chaff.

win·some (win′səm) *adj.* attractive or pleasing; charming: *a winsome smile.* —**win′some·ly**, *adv.* —**win′some·ness**, *n.*

win·ter (win′tər) *n.* the season of the year coming between fall and spring. In the Northern Hemisphere it extends from about December 22 to about March 21. —*adj.* of, relating to, or suitable for winter: *winter sports, winter clothes, a winter vacation.* —*v.i.* to spend or pass the winter: *to winter in Florida.*

win·ter·green (win′tər grēn′) *n.* **1.** a small evergreen plant of North America, having bright red berries and aromatic leaves. **2.** the oil of this plant, used in medicine or for flavoring. **3.** the flavor of this oil or something having this flavor.

win·ter·ize (win′tə rīz′) *v.t.*, **win·ter·ized**, **win·ter·iz·ing.** to prepare or make fit for winter weather: *to winterize an automobile.*

winter solstice, the time of year, about December 22 in the Northern Hemisphere, when the sun appears the farthest south from the equator.

win·ter·time (win′tər tīm′) *n.* the winter season.

win·try (win′trē) *adj.*, **win·tri·er**, **win·tri·est. 1.** of, like, or characteristic of winter: *wintry weather.* **2.** lacking warmth, cheer, or friendliness: *a wintry welcome.* —**win′tri·ness**, *n.*

wipe (wīp) *v.t.*, **wiped**, **wip·ing. 1.** to rub, usually with something soft, as a towel or mop, in order to clean or dry: *You wash the dishes, and I will wipe them.* **2.** to remove by or as if by rubbing: *to wipe up spilled milk. Wipe that grin off your face!* **3.** to rub, move, or apply on or over a surface: *Please wipe your shoes on the mat before going in the house.* —*n.* an act or instance of wiping.

·**to wipe out. a.** to kill or destroy completely: *The epidemic wiped out a large part of the population.* **b.** to ruin financially: *The failure of the local bank wiped out many businesses in town.*

wip·er (wī′pər) *n.* a person or thing that wipes, especially a device designed or used for wiping: *a windshield wiper.*

wire (wīr) *n.* **1.** metal drawn into a thin strand, thread, or rod. **2.** a length of such metal, used chiefly as a conductor of electricity. It is usually made of copper and surrounded by an insulating covering. **3.** a unit consisting of several strands of wire wound together; cable. **4.** a telegraph: *to communicate by wire.* **5.** a telegram: *Send us a wire as soon as you get there.* —*adj.* made of or

like wire: *a wire brush.* —*v.*, **wired**, **wir·ing.** —*v.t.* **1.** to furnish or provide with a network or system of wires: *to wire a house.* **2.** to fasten with a wire or wires: *to wire parts together.* **3.** to send by telegraph: *to wire a message.* **4.** to send a telegram to. —*v.i.* to telegraph: *We'd better wire ahead for reservations.*

wire·haired (wīr′hârd′) *adj.* having coarse, stiff, or wiry hair: *a wirehaired dog.*

wire·less (wīr′lis) *adj.* **1.** having no wire or wires. **2.** *British.* of or relating to a radio. —*n., pl.* **wire·less·es. 1.** a wireless telegraph or telephone system. **2.** *British.* a radio.

wire service, a news-gathering agency that supplies news, photographs, and the like to newspapers, magazines, and radio and television stations.

wire·tap (wīr′tap′) *v.*, **wire·tapped**, **wire·tap·ping.** —*v.i.* to tap a telephone or telegraph wire to obtain information or evidence. —*v.t.* to tap (a telephone or telegraph wire). —*n.* **1.** an act or instance of wiretapping. **2.** a device used in wiretapping.

wire·worm (wīr′wûrm′) *n.* the slender, smooth-skinned larva of certain beetles, which destroys the roots and seeds of such crops as cotton, peas, and corn.

wir·ing (wīr′ing) *n.* a network or system of wires, especially for carrying electric current.

wir·y (wīr′ē) *adj.*, **wir·i·er**, **wir·i·est. 1.** made or consisting of wire. **2.** like wire; stiff: *wiry hair.* **3.** (of persons or animals) lean and strong: *The young athlete is very wiry.* —**wir′i·ness**, *n.*

Wis., Wisconsin.

wis·dom (wiz′dəm) *n.* **1.** the ability to know or judge what is right, good, and true: *a judge of great wisdom.* **2.** common sense or sound judgment: *Wisdom dictates care in the use of natural resources.* **3.** knowledge; learning: *all the wisdom of the ages.* [From the Old English word *wīsdōm*, from the word *wīs* "wise, intelligent" + the suffix *-dōm* "-dom."]

wisdom tooth, the last molar tooth on either side of the upper and lower jaws in humans, usually appearing between the ages of seventeen and twenty-five.

wise¹ (wīz) *adj.*, **wis·er**, **wis·est. 1.** having the ability to know or judge what is right, good, and true: *The teacher was a wise judge of character.* **2.** having or showing common sense or sound judgment; sensible: *That was not a very wise decision.* **3.** having knowledge or information; informed. **4.** *Slang.* rude and bold; impudent; fresh. [From the Old English word *wīs* with the same meanings.] —**wise′ly**, *adv.*

wise² (wīz) *n.* a way; manner. ▲ used chiefly in the phrases *in no wise, in this wise, in any wise.* [From the Old English word *wīse.*]

–wise *suffix* (used to form adverbs from nouns or adjectives) in a (specified) manner, direction, or position: *likewise, clockwise.*

wise·a·cre (wīz′ā′kər) *n.* a person who puts on false airs of knowledge or wisdom.

wise·crack (wīz′krak′) *n.* a short, insulting or sarcastic remark. —*v.i.* to make a wisecrack or wisecracks. —**wise′crack′er**, *n.*

wise guy *Slang.* a conceited and cocky person, especially one who makes flippant or annoying remarks; wiseacre; know-it-all; smart aleck.

wish (wish) *n., pl.* **wish·es. 1.** a longing or strong need or desire for something: *a child's wish to be loved, a student's wish to learn.* **2.** an expression of such a need or desire: *The members of the graduating class received everyone's good wishes for their future success.* **3.** something that is wished for: *to get one's wish.* —*v.t.* **1.** to have a wish or longing for; desire: *I wish I could play the piano. Don't you wish to travel?* **2.** to desire (a person or thing) to be in a particular state or condition: *I wish winter were over.* **3.** to express or have a wish or desire for: *We wish you the best of luck.* **4.** to bid, as a greeting: *to wish someone good morning.* **5.** to impose; force: *I would not wish that task on anyone.* —*v.i.* **1.** to have or feel a wish: *to wish for happiness.* **2.** to make a wish: *to wish upon a star.* —**wish′er,** *n.*

wish·bone (wish′bōn′) *n.* a forked bone in front of the breastbone of most birds. [From the custom in which two people make wishes and then together break this bone in two, the wish supposedly being granted to the one holding the longer piece.]

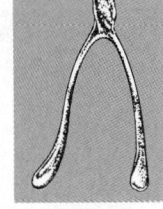

wishbone

wish·ful (wish′fəl) *adj.* having, showing, or based on a wish: *a wishful look, wishful thinking.* —**wish′ful·ly,** *adv.* —**wish′ful·ness,** *n.*

wish·y-wash·y (wish′ē wô′shē, wish′-ē wosh′ē) *adj. Informal.* **1.** lacking in strength of character or firmness of will: *a wishy-washy person who cannot make decisions.* **2.** thin or watery.

wisp (wisp) *n.* **1.** a small bunch, as of hair. **2.** a small or slight bit, piece, or the like: *a wisp of smoke.* **3.** a person or thing that is small, frail, or delicate: *a wisp of a child.* —**wisp′y,** *adj.*

wist (wist) *Archaic.* the past tense and past participle of **wit²**.

wis·te·ri·a (wi stîr′ē ə) *also,* **wis·tar·i·a** (wi stär′ē ə). *n.* a woody vine found in Asia and the United States, bearing long, drooping clusters of white, blue, pink, or purple flowers.

wist·ful (wist′fəl) *adj.* sadly longing; yearning: *The music put us in a wistful mood.* —**wist′ful·ly,** *adv.* —**wist′ful·ness,** *n.*

wit¹ (wit) *n.* **1.** the ability to make clever, amusing, or striking comments about persons, things, or situations: *The comedian's wit made us laugh at the world's troubles.* **2.** a person having such ability. **3.** *usually,* **wits. a.** the ability to think and reason; good sense: *to live by one's wits.* **b.** sanity; ability to think clearly: *to be scared out of one's wits.* [From the Old English word *wit* meaning "understanding, intelligence, mind."]

•**at one's wits' end.** at a loss as to what to do.

•**to have one's wits about one** or **to keep one's wits about one.** to be or stay calm or alert, as in an emergency: *Try to keep your wits about you if trouble arises.*

wit² (wit) *v.t., v.i.,* **wist, wit·ting.** *Archaic.* to be or become aware; know; learn. [From the Old English word *witan* meaning "to know, have knowledge" or "to be wise¹."]

•**to wit.** that is to say; namely.

witch (wich) *n., pl.* **witch·es. 1.** person, especially a woman, who practices magic, usually black magic, or is believed to have a pact with the devil; sorceress. **2.** an ugly, ill-natured old woman; hag.

witch·craft (wich′kraft′) *n.* the practices or power of a witch; sorcery.

witch doctor, in certain primitive societies or religions, a person believed to have magical powers; shaman.

witch·er·y (wich′ə rē) *n., pl.* **witch·er·ies. 1.** witchcraft; sorcery. **2.** the power to charm; fascination.

witch hazel 1. any of a small group of trees and shrubs found in North America, China, and Japan, having a scaly bark and bearing small clusters of usually yellow flowers in the fall or early spring. **2.** a lotion made from the leaves and bark of a species of witch hazel.

witch hunt *Informal.* an investigation of persons supposedly undertaken to uncover subversion or disloyalty, but actually done to weaken political opposition.

witch·ing (wich′ing) *adj.* **1.** of, relating to, or suitable

for witchcraft: *Midnight is the witching hour.* **2.** bewitching; enchanting.

with (with, with) *prep.* **1.** in the company of: *We went with our friends.* **2.** next to; alongside of: *I sat with my family.* **3.** into: *We mixed chocolate syrup with the milk.* **4.** having as a possession or characteristic: *to travel with an umbrella, a dog with a limp.* **5.** by means of; using: *to fish with a pole, to eat with a fork.* **6.** in a manner characterized by: *to dance with grace.* **7.** in addition to: *We had milk with our dinner.* **8.** in the service, employment, or association of: *to be with a large law firm.* **9.** in regard or relation to: *They are pleased with the results of the election.* **10.** in the charge or keeping of: *to leave valuables with a hotel manager.* **11.** in the opinion of: *It is fine with me if you want to go.* **12.** on account of; because of: *to tremble with fear.* **13.** from: *to part with old magazines.* **14.** in opposition to; against: *to quarrel with someone over money.* **15.** in spite of; notwithstanding: *With all the advertising, the product still wouldn't sell.* **16.** in proportion to: *My anger grew with each insult.* **17.** in support of; on the side of: *Are you with us or against us?*

with– *prefix* **1.** in opposition; against: *withstand.* **2.** back; away: *withdraw, withhold.*

with·al (with ôl′, with ôl′) *adv.* in addition; besides; also: *The letter was interesting, and instructive withal.*

with·draw (with drô′, with drô′) *v.,* **with·drew** (with-drü′, with drü′), **with·drawn, with·draw·ing.** —*v.t.* **1.** to draw back or away: *to withdraw troops from a border.* **2.** to take away; remove: *to withdraw a product from the market, to withdraw money from the bank.* **3.** to take back; retract: *to withdraw an offer of help.* —*v.i.* **1.** to move or go back or away; retire; retreat: *After dinner, the guests withdrew to the living room.* **2.** to remove oneself: *to withdraw from an election, to withdraw from school.*

with·draw·al (with drô′əl, with drô′əl) *n.* **1.** the act of withdrawing or the state of being withdrawn. **2.a.** the process of stopping the use of an addictive drug. **b.** the process by which a person becomes physically and psychologically adjusted to deprivation of such a drug.

with·drawn (with drôn′, with drôn′) *v.* the past participle of **withdraw.** —*adj.* very shy or reserved: *a withdrawn child.*

withe (with, with, wīth) *n.* a tough, flexible twig, usually of willow, used for binding or tying.

with·er (with′ər) *v.i.* to dry up or shrivel, as from heat or loss of moisture: *The flowers withered soon after they were cut.* —*v.t.* **1.** to cause to dry up or shrivel: *The intense summer heat withered the crops.* **2.** to cause to feel ashamed or embarrassed, as by harsh words or a scornful glance: *to wither someone with an angry look.*

with·ers (with′ərz) *pl. n.* the highest part of the back of a horse or similar animal, between the shoulder blades.

with·hold (with hōld′, with hōld′) *v.t.,* **with·held** (with-held′, with held′), **with·hold·ing. 1.** to refuse to give, grant, or allow: *to withhold judgment, to withhold payment on a check.* **2.** to hold back or check; restrain: *to withhold one's anger.*

withholding tax, the part of an employee's wages or salary taken out by the employer for income tax.

with·in (with in′, with in′) *prep.* **1.** in or into the inner or interior part or parts of; in the space bounded or

W

enclosed by: *The children played within the fence of the playground.* **2.** inside the limits of, as in time, space, amount, or degree: *to return within an hour.* **3.** in the scope, range, or influence of: *That was the worst storm within memory. That's not within the judge's jurisdiction.* —*adv.* **1.** in or into the inner or interior part or parts; inside. **2.** indoors. —*n.* the inner part or place.

with·out (wi<u>th</u> out′, with out′) *prep.* **1.** not having; lacking: *to go without sleep, to be without money.* **2.** so as to neglect or avoid: *to leave without saying good-bye.* **3.** unaccompanied by: *to travel without luggage.* **4.** at, on, or to the outer or exterior part or parts of; outside of; beyond. —*adv.* **1.** with something absent or lacking: *to go without.* **2.** on the outer or exterior part or parts; outside. **3.** outdoors. —*n.* the outer part or place.

with·stand (with stand′, wi<u>th</u> stand′) *v.t.*, **with·stood** (with stŭd′, wi<u>th</u> stŭd′), **with·stand·ing.** to hold out against or oppose successfully: *The house withstood the storm. I could not withstand the temptation to take a second helping.*

wit·less (wit′lis) *adj.* lacking intelligence or sense; foolish. —**wit′less·ly,** *adv.* —**wit′less·ness,** *n.*

wit·ness (wit′nis) *n., pl.* **wit·ness·es. 1.** a person who has personally seen or heard something and can therefore give a firsthand account of it. **2.** a person who testifies to some fact, occurrence, or the like in a court of law under oath. **3.** a person who is present at a transaction, such as the signing of a contract or will, or at a ceremony, such as a wedding, and can give evidence as to its authenticity. **4.** evidence; testimony. —*v.t.* **1.** to be present to see or hear; observe personally: *to witness an argument.* **2.** to be the time or scene of: *This century has witnessed outstanding scientific achievements.* **3.** to sign (a document) as a witness. **4.** to serve or give as evidence or proof of: *The neatness of the house witnessed the care and work that had been done.*

·**to bear witness.** to give or serve as evidence or testimony.

wit·ted (wit′id) *adj.* having wit or mental capacity (of a certain kind). ▲used in combination: *slow-witted, quick-witted, sharp-witted.*

wit·ti·cism (wit′ə siz′əm) *n.* a witty saying or remark.

wit·ty (wit′ē) *adj.*, **wit·ti·er, wit·ti·est.** having or characterized by wit; cleverly amusing: *a witty writer, a witty reply.* —**wit′ti·ly,** *adv.* —**wit′ti·ness,** *n.*

wives (wīvz) the plural of **wife.**

wiz·ard (wiz′ərd) *n.* **1.** a person, especially a man, who practices magic to control or influence events, people, or phenomena; magician; sorcerer. **2.** an extraordinarily clever or skillful person: *a financial wizard.* [From the Middle English word *wysard* meaning "sage, wise man," from the Old English word *wīs* "wise[1], intelligent."]

wiz·ard·ry (wiz′ərd rē) *n.* **1.** the art or methods of a wizard; magic; sorcery. **2.** great skill or cleverness.

wiz·ened (wiz′ənd) *adj.* dried out; shriveled; withered: *a wizened complexion.*

wk. *pl.* **wks. 1.** week. **2.** work.

wob·ble (wob′əl) *also,* **wab·ble.** *v.i.,* **wob·bled, wob·bling. 1.** to move or sway unsteadily from side to side: *This old chair wobbles. The tire wobbled after the blowout.* **2.** to shake or quiver; tremble: *The singer's voice wobbled on the old phonograph record.* **3.** to be unable to choose between different opinions, feelings, or courses of action; waver. —*n.* an unsteady, swaying movement: *the wobble of a top as it falls.*

wob·bly (wob′lē) *also,* **wab·bly.** *adj.* tending to wobble; unsteady; shaky: *This table has wobbly legs.*

Wo·den (wō′dən) *n. Teutonic Mythology.* the king of the gods. In Norse mythology he was called Odin.

woe (wō) *n.* **1.** great sadness or suffering; sorrow; grief:

a tale of woe. **2.** great trouble or misfortune; disaster: *economic woes.* —*interj.* alas.

woe·be·gone (wō′bi gôn′, wō′bi gon′) *also,* **wo·be·gone.** *adj.* showing great sorrow or grief; mournful: *a woebegone expression.*

woe·ful (wō′fəl) *adj.* **1.** characterized by, expressing, or full of woe; sorrowful; sad: *a woeful look.* **2.** pitiful; deplorable: *woeful inadequacies, woeful poverty.* —**woe′ful·ly,** *adv.* —**woe′ful·ness,** *n.*

wok

wok (wok) *n.* a bowl-shaped metal pan used especially in Chinese cooking to fry and steam food. [From the Cantonese word *wôk* meaning this kind of pan.]

woke (wōk) a past tense of **wake**[1].

wo·ken (wō′kən) a past participle of **wake**[1].

wold (wōld) *n.* a high, open tract of rolling land.

wolf (wùlf) *n., pl.* **wolves. 1.** any of various wild animals related to the dog, found chiefly in the cold regions of the Northern Hemisphere, having a pointed muzzle, a bushy tail, and usually gray fur. **2.** the fur of such an animal. **3.** a person who is cruel, greedy, or destructive. —*v.t.* to eat quickly and ravenously: *The hungry child wolfed down the food.* —**wolf′like′,** *adj.*

·**to cry wolf.** to raise a false alarm.

·**to keep the wolf from the door.** to ward off hunger or want.

wolf (def. 1)

wolf·hound (wùlf′hound′) *n.* any of various large dogs originally bred for hunting wolves, such as the Irish wolfhound or the borzoi.

wolf·ish (wùl′fish) *adj.* characteristic of or like a wolf; greedy or cruel: *a wolfish appetite.* —**wolf′ish·ly,** *adv.* —**wolf′ish·ness,** *n.*

wolf·ram (wùl′frəm) *n.* another word for **tungsten.**

wolfs·bane (wùlfs′bān′) *n.* another word for **aconite.**

wol·ver·ine (wùl′və rēn′) *also,* **wol·ver·ene.** *n.* a meat-eating mammal related to the weasel, native to northern regions, having dark brown fur with pale bands.

wolves (wùlvz) the plural of **wolf.**

wom·an (wùm′ən) *n., pl.* **wom·en. 1.** an adult female human being. **2.** adult female human beings as a group; the female part of the human race. —*adj.* **1.** having to do with a woman or women.

wolverine

2. female: *a woman lawyer.* [From the Old English word *wifman* meaning "woman," from the words *wīf* "adult woman" + *man* "human being." In Old English, the word *wīf* meant "any adult human female" whether or not she was married.]

wom·an·hood (wum′ən hud′) *n.* **1.** the state of being an adult female human being: *She has not yet reached womanhood.* **2.** the characteristics or qualities thought to be womanly. **3.** women as a group: *Womanhood fought for the right to vote.*

wom·an·ish (wum′ə nish) *adj.* **1.** of, for, or characteristic of a woman. **2.** like a woman; effeminate. —**wom′an·ish·ness,** *n.*

wom·an·kind (wum′ən kīnd′) *n.* women as a group.

wom·an·like (wum′ən līk′) *adj.* having the qualities of or suitable for a woman; womanly.

wom·an·ly (wum′ən lē) *adj.* **1.** having the qualities thought of as characteristic of women. **2.** relating to or suitable for a woman: *a womanly style of dress.* —**wom′an·li·ness,** *n.*

womb (wūm) *n.* **1.** a hollow muscular organ found in most female mammals, which holds and nourishes the young until birth; uterus. **2.** any protective, nurturing place or surroundings.

wom·bat (wom′bat) *n.* a burrowing mammal of Australia that is active at night and has a stocky body and a coarse coat of black or yellowish brown hair. The female wombat has a pouch for carrying her young after birth.

wom·en (wim′ən) the plural of **woman.**

wom·en·folk (wim′ən fōk′) *also,* **wom·en·folks.** *pl. n.* women as a group, especially all the female members of a family or other group.

women's rights *also,* **woman's rights.** the rights of women to opportunities and privileges equal with those of men.

won (wun) a past tense and the past participle of **win.**

won·der (wun′dər) *n.* **1.** something that causes astonishment, curiosity, or admiration: *The Egyptian pyramids are wonders of the ancient world. It's a wonder you can hear anything in all this noise.* **2.** a feeling, attitude, or state caused by this: *We watched with wonder as the comet streaked across the sky.* —*v.i.* **1.** to want to know or learn; be curious or doubtful: *I wondered about the unsolved mystery.* **2.** to feel or express admiration and astonishment: *We all wondered at the runner's strength and endurance.* —*v.t.* to want to know or learn about; be curious or doubtful about: *I wonder what we're having for dinner.* —**won′der·ing·ly,** *adv.*

won·der·ful (wun′dər fəl) *adj.* **1.** causing wonder; astonishing: *a wonderful sight, a wonderful invention.* **2.** very good; excellent: *We spent a wonderful day in the country last Sunday.* —**won′der·ful·ly,** *adv.* —**won′der·ful·ness,** *n.*

won·der·land (wun′dər land′) *n.* **1.** a wonderful place, region, or scene: *a winter wonderland.* **2.** a wonderful imaginary realm or fantasy world.

won·der·ment (wun′dər mənt) *n.* **1.** the state or emotion of wonder: *The group of tourists stood in wonderment amidst the ancient ruins.* **2.** something that causes wonder.

won·drous (wun′drəs) *adj.* wonderful: *a wondrous accomplishment.* —*adv.* Archaic. extraordinarily; wonderfully. —**won′drous·ly,** *adv.* —**won′drous·ness,** *n.*

wont (wônt, wōnt, wunt) *adj.* accustomed; used: *We are wont to stay at home on Sundays.* —*n.* a usual practice; habit: *It is their wont to rise very early each morning.*

won't (wōnt) *contr.* will not.

wonted (wôn′tid, wōn′tid, wun′tid) *adj.* accustomed; customary: *to sit at one's wonted place.*

won·ton (won′ton) *also,* **won ton.** *n.* in Chinese cook-ing, a dumpling filled with chopped meat, fish, or vegetables, eaten with soup or fried in deep fat. [From the Cantonese word *wan t'an* meaning this kind of dumpling.]

woo (wū′) *v.t.* **1.** to seek the love or affection of, especially with the intent to marry; court. **2.** to try to win over: *The company wooed new employees with promises of high salaries.* **3.** to try to obtain or gain; seek: *The governor wooed public support for the new housing plan.* —*v.i.* to seek the love or affection of a person, especially with the intent to marry.

wood (wud) *n.* **1.** the hard material that makes up the greater part of the stems and branches of trees and shrubs, located beneath the bark: *Much of the wood in that old tree had rotted.* **2.** this material, sometimes with the bark still on, cut or prepared for use, as for building, fuel, or paper manufacture; timber; lumber: *These stairs are made of wood.* **3.** *often,* **woods.** a dense growth of trees; forest; grove. **4.** something made of wood, such as a woodwind instrument. **5.** a golf club with a wooden head. —*adj.* **1.** made or consisting of wood; wooden: *a wood bucket.* **2.** made or suitable for using, holding, storing, or cutting wood: *a wood saw.* **3.** living or growing in woods.

·**out of the woods.** *Informal.* finally clear or free from danger, hazard, or other difficulty.

wood alcohol, another term for **methanol.**

wood·bine (wud′bīn′) *n.* **1.** any of various climbing shrubs or vines, especially the European honeysuckle, bearing flowers that are red or purple on the outside. **2.** another name for **Virginia creeper.**

wood·carv·er (wud′kär′vər) *n.* a person who carves objects out of wood.

wood·carv·ing (wud′kär′ving) *n.* **1.** the art or technique of carving wood. **2.** an object carved of wood.

wood·chuck (wud′chuk′) *n.* a short-legged North American burrowing rodent having a stocky body and coarse brown or gray fur. Also, **groundhog.** [From the Cree Indian word *wuchak* meaning "marten, weasel." The formation of *woodchuck* was also influenced by the resemblance of the sound of the first part of the word *wuchak* to the word *wood.*]

woodchuck

wood·cock (wud′kok′) *n., pl.* **wood·cocks** or **wood·cock.** any of several game birds that are native to forests of North America, Europe, and Asia, having a plump body, a long, slender bill, and buff, brown, and black feathers.

wood·craft (wud′kraft′) *n.* **1.** skill and knowledge in things relating to the woods and survival in the woods, such as hunting or camping. **2.** the art, process, or skill of working with wood.

wood·cut (wud′kut′) *n.* **1.** a block of wood engraved so that all the wood is cut away except the design to be printed. **2.** a print or impression that is made from such a block.

wood·cut·ter (wud′kut′ər) *n.* a person whose work is cutting trees or chopping wood.

---

at; āpe; fär; câre; end; mē; it; īce; pîerce; hot; ōld; sông, fôrk; oil; out; up; ūse; rüle; pull; tûrn; chin; sing; shop; thin; **th**is; hw in white; zh in treasure. The symbol ə stands for the unstressed vowel sound heard in about, taken, pencil, lemon, and circus.

W

wood·ed (wŭd′ĭd) *adj.* having trees or woods: *We had a picnic in a wooded area at the edge of town.*

wood·en (wŭd′ən) *adj.* **1.** made or consisting of wood: *a wooden ladder.* **2.** stiff; clumsy; awkward: *to walk with a wooden gait.* **3.** without warmth or life; lifeless; dull: *a wooden expression.* —**wood′en·ly,** *adv.* —**wood′en·ness,** *n.*

wood·land (*n.,* wŭd′lănd′, wŭd′lənd; *adj.,* wŭd′lənd) *n.* land covered with woods or trees. —*adj.* of, relating to, or living in the woods.

wood louse **1.** any of several small crustaceans that have flat, oval bodies with seven pairs of legs, and live in dark, damp places, feeding on decaying wood, leaves, and other matter. Also, **sow bug. 2.** any of various small insects living in dark places, as in the woodwork of houses.

wood·man (wŭd′mən) *n., pl.* **wood·men** (wŭd′mən). another spelling of **woodsman.**

wood nymph *Greek Mythology.* a nymph living in or guarding woods and trees.

wood·peck·er (wŭd′pek′ər) *n.* any of various strong-billed birds that live in forests throughout the world, having stiff, pointed tail feathers and curved nails for clinging to trees. The woodpecker feeds chiefly on insects in trees, which it obtains by drilling holes in bark and wood with its bill.

woodpecker

wood·pile (wŭd′pīl′) *n.* a pile of wood, especially of wood cut and stacked for use as fuel.

wood pulp, wood reduced to pulp by chemical or mechanical means, used especially for making paper.

wood·shed (wŭd′shĕd′) *n.* a shed for storing wood, especially firewood.

woods·man (wŭdz′mən) *also,* **woodman.** *n., pl.* **woods·men** (wŭdz′mən). **1.** a person, such as a hunter or trapper, who lives or works in the woods and who is skilled in woodcraft. **2.** a woodcutter; lumberjack.

woods·y (wŭd′zē) *adj.,* **woods·i·er, woods·i·est.** of, relating to, suitable for, or like the woods: *a woodsy fragrance.*

wood tar, a tar obtained from wood by distillation, used in pitch, medicines, and preservatives.

wood thrush, a large thrush found throughout the eastern United States, having brown and white feathers and a rust-colored head, and known for its flutelike song.

wood·wind (wŭd′wĭnd′) *n.* **1.** any of various musical instruments, including the flute, oboe, clarinet, and saxophone, consisting of a tube through which a column of air passes, and having holes in the tube that are opened and closed to vary the pitch of the tones produced. **2. woodwinds.** the section of an orchestra consisting of these instruments. —*adj.* of, for, or made up of these instruments: *the woodwind section of an orchestra.*

wood·work (wŭd′wûrk′) *n.* objects or parts made of wood, especially the wooden parts on the inside of a house, such as moldings, doors, and window frames.

wood·work·ing (wŭd′wûr′kĭng) *n.* the art, process, or occupation of making or shaping things of wood.

wood·y (wŭd′ē) *adj.,* **wood·i·er, wood·i·est. 1.** consisting of or containing wood. **2.** covered with or full of trees: *a woody island.* **3.** characteristic of or like wood: *a plastic with a woody texture.* —**wood′i·ness,** *n.*

woof[1] (wŭf, wo͞of) *n.* **1.** the threads that run from side to side in a woven fabric, crossing the lengthwise threads of the warp. **2.** texture, as of a fabric. [From the Old English word *ōwef* meaning "the woof."]

woof[2] (wŭf) *n.* a deep bark or barklike sound. —*v.i.* to make such a sound. [Representation of this sound.]

woof·er (wŭf′ər) *n.* a loudspeaker designed to reproduce low-frequency sound signals.

wool (wŭl) *n.* **1.** the soft, dense, usually curly hair of sheep and certain other animals, such as the Angora goat, alpaca, or llama, used to make yarn and fabric. **2.** a strong yarn or fabric made from this hair. **3.** any substance resembling the fleece of sheep in texture, such as short, curly human hair or the furry covering on certain plants. —*adj.* of, relating to, or made of wool: *a wool coat.*

·to pull the wool over (someone's) eyes. to trick or deceive (someone).

wool·en (wŭl′ən) *also,* **wool·len.** *adj.* **1.** made of wool: *a woolen blanket.* **2.** of or relating to wool. —*n. usually,* **woolens.** a cloth or garment made of wool.

wool·gath·er·ing (wŭl′gath′ər ĭng) *n.* useless or idle thinking, especially daydreaming. —*adj.* given to daydreaming; absent-minded.

wool·len (wŭl′ən) another spelling of **woolen.**

wool·ly (wŭl′ē) *also,* **wool·y.** *adj.,* **wool·li·er, wool·li·est. 1.** consisting of or like wool: *a woolly fabric.* **2.** covered with wool or something with a similar texture: *a woolly stuffed animal.* **3.** not clear or well-defined; confused; fuzzy: *woolly thinking.* —*n., pl.* **wool·lies.** *usually,* **wool·lies.** a garment made of wool, especially a knitted undergarment. —**wool′li·ness,** *n.*

wool·y (wŭl′ē) *adj.,* **wool·i·er, wool·i·est,** *n., pl.* **wool·ies.** another spelling of **woolly.** —**wool′i·ness,** *n.*

wooz·y (wo͞o′zē, wŭz′ē) *adj.,* **wooz·i·er, wooz·i·est.** *Informal.* dizzy or dazed. —**wooz′i·ly,** *adv.* —**wooz′i·ness,** *n.*

word (wûrd) *n.* **1.** a sound or combination of sounds having meaning and forming a unit of language: *I didn't hear your words.* **2.** a written or printed character or set of characters representing such a unit: *the words on a page.* **3.** a short conversation or discussion: *I'd like a word with you before you leave.* **4.** a brief remark or statement: *a word of advice.* **5.** assurance; promise: *I give you my word that I will be there.* **6.** information or news; message: *Have you received any word from them?* **7.** a signal or password: *Just give the word and we'll begin.* **8.** a command; order: *The ship captain's word had to be obeyed.* **9. words.** an angry discussion; argument. **10. the Word.** the Bible; Scripture. —*v.t.* to express in words: *to word one's reply carefully.*

·by word of mouth. by means of spoken language; orally: *to pass on a message by word of mouth.*

·in a word. in short; briefly.

·in so many words. precisely and plainly.

·to eat one's words. to have to take back something that one has said.

·to take the words out of one's mouth. to say exactly what one was going to say.

·word for word. in exactly the same words.

word·book (wûrd′bŭk′) *n.* a book containing a list of words, with definitions or explanations, such as a dictionary.

word·ing (wûr′dĭng) *n.* the style or manner of expressing something in words: *The wording of that sentence is confusing.*

word·less (wûrd′lĭs) *adj.* **1.** not using words; silent: *a wordless greeting.* **2.** that cannot be expressed in words: *wordless sorrow.* —**word′less·ly,** *adv.* —**word′less·ness,** *n.*

word of honor, a promise given as a pledge of one's honor.

word processing, the creation, storing, and processing of texts by a computer and suitable program.

word·y (wûr′dē) *adj.,* **word·i·er, word·i·est.** using or containing too many words: *a wordy author, a wordy essay.* —**word′i·ly,** *adv.* —**word′i·ness,** *n.*

wore (wôr) the past tense of **wear.**

work (wûrk) *n.* **1.** physical or mental effort directed toward accomplishing or achieving a definite end or purpose; labor: *to put a lot of work into a project.* **2.** what a person does to earn a living; occupation; profession: *the work of an accountant, the work of newspaper reporters.* **3.** an opportunity for earning a living; employment: *to be looking for work.* **4.** something to be done; undertaking; project: *Each person was assigned work for the week.* **5.** something that is being accomplished or produced, especially as part of one's occupation: *Teachers often take their work home with them.* **6.** something accomplished or produced; finished product: *a work of art, works of literature, works of music.* **7.** the way in which something is accomplished or produced; workmanship: *The vase shows careful work.* **8.** a place of employment: *You can call me at work.* **9.** *usually,* **works.** things done; feats; deeds: *to be known for one's good works.* **10. works. a.** a place for industrial labor, such as a factory, plant, or mill. ▲ usually used with a singular verb. **b.** the moving parts of a machine or other device, such as a watch. **c.** engineering structures, such as dams, docks, or bridges. **11.** *Physics.* the expenditure of energy in moving mass a given distance, measured by the product of the magnitude of the force and the distance the mass is moved in the direction of the force. —*adj.* of, for, or relating to work: *a work stoppage, work clothes.* —*v.,* **worked** or **wrought, work·ing.** —*v.i.* **1.** to put forth mental or physical effort in order to accomplish a definite end or purpose; labor: *to work hard for a living.* **2.** to be employed in some business, occupation, or profession: *to work in a hospital as a nurse.* **3.** to perform a function properly; operate: *This typewriter works well.* **4.** to move gradually so as to arrive at a specified state: *The ropes worked loose.* —*v.t.* **1.** to cause to perform a function or work: *to work a machine.* **2.** to carry on one's trade, business, or operation in: *The bus driver worked the north side of town.* **3.** to cause to produce or be productive: *The old farmer still works the land.* **4.** to do or accomplish; bring about; cause: *This medicine almost works miracles.* **5.** to shape, handle, or process for a particular purpose: *to work copper, to work dough.* **6.** to get or achieve by effort: *We worked our way upstream.* **7.** to solve: *to work a math problem.* **8.** to act upon the emotions of; excite; rouse: *The speaker worked the crowd into a rage.*
  •**out of work.** without a job; unemployed.
  •**to make short work of.** to do or accomplish quickly.
  •**to work in.** to put in or insert: *Can you work in this sentence at the bottom of the page?*
  •**to work off.** to get rid of by effort; discharge: *to work off an obligation.*
  •**to work on** or **to work upon.** to try to have an influence on; try to persuade.
  •**to work out. a.** to develop or improve: *Work out your ideas before you begin to write.* **b.** to solve: *to work out a problem.* **c.** to come to an end; result: *How did your meeting work out?* **d.** to do exercises or practice: *to work out every day to stay fit.*
  •**to work up. a.** to develop or plan: *to work up an idea.* **b.** to stir up; excite; rouse: *to relax after being worked up from too much excitement.*

work·a·ble (wûr'kə bəl) *adj.* **1.** able to be carried out or accomplished: *a workable plan.* **2.** able to be worked: *workable clay.*

work·a·day (wûr'kə dā') *adj.* **1.** commonplace; ordinary: *the workaday world.* **2.** of, relating to, or suitable for workdays: *one's workaday clothes.*

work·bench (wûrk'bench') *n., pl.* **work·bench·es.** a table used for working, as by a carpenter or mechanic.

work·book (wûrk'bʊk') *n.* **1.** a book or manual prepared for use by students, containing problems, questions, or exercises based on a particular textbook or relating to a particular course of study. **2.** a book containing a record of work planned or completed.

work·day (wûrk'dā') *n.* **1.** a day on which work is ordinarily done, as distinguished from Sunday or a holiday. **2.** that part of a day in which work is done: *The workday ends at five o'clock.*

work·er (wûr'kər) *n.* **1.** a person who works: *a fast worker, fellow workers on a project.* **2.** a person who earns a living by working, especially in manual or industrial work: *a farm worker, a factory worker.* **3.** one of the females in a colony of insects, such as bees, ants, or termites, that cannot reproduce, but perform various services for the colony.

workers' compensation, insurance payments provided by law for wage earners who are injured at work. Also, **workmen's compensation.**

work·horse (wûrk'hôrs') *n.* **1.** a horse used for heavy labor, as distinguished from a horse for racing or riding. **2.** a person who works very hard and tirelessly, especially on very difficult tasks.

work·house (wûrk'hous') *n., pl.* **work·hous·es** (wûrk'hou'ziz). **1.** a house of correction for petty offenders, who are made to work in gangs repairing roads or railways. **2.** formerly, in Great Britain, an institution for sheltering and giving work to poor people.

work·ing (wûr'king) *adj.* **1.** that works: *a working telephone.* **2.** engaged in work, especially for a living: *working people.* **3.** that is enough for use: *to have a working knowledge of Russian.* **4.** of, relating to, occupied by, or used for working: *working conditions, working hours.* —*n.* **1.** the manner in which something works; method of operation: *I do not understand the working of this machine.* **2.** *usually,* **workings.** the part of a mine where excavation is being done.

working class, the class of people who do industrial or manual labor and are dependent upon wages for their livelihood.

work·ing·man (wûr'king man') *n., pl.* **work·ing·men** (wûr'king men'). a man who works, especially one who works for a living with his hands or with machines.

working papers, official documents authorizing the employment of aliens or minors.

work·load (wûrk'lōd') *also,* **work load.** *n.* the amount of work assigned to a worker, department, or machine over a specified period of time.

work·man (wûrk'mən) *n., pl.* **work·men** (wûrk'mən). a worker, especially a craftsman or laborer.

work·man·like (wûrk'mən līk') *adj.* characteristic of or suitable for a good worker; well-executed; skillful: *a workmanlike job.*

work·man·ship (wûrk'mən ship') *n.* **1.** the art or skill of a workman. **2.** the manner in which work is done: *The workmanship of this table is very fine.* **3.** the product of skilled work: *That vase is a fine piece of workmanship.*

work·men's compensation (wûrk'mənz) another term for **workers' compensation.**

work·out (wûrk'out') *n.* **1.** a period of practice, exercise, or other physical activity: *an athlete's daily workout.* **2.** a trial or test to determine suitability, fitness, or the like: *to give a new bicycle a workout.*

---

at; āpe; fär; câre; end; mē; it; īce; pîerce; hot; ōld; sông, fôrk; oil; out; up; ūse; rüle; pʊll; tûrn; chin; sing; shop; thin; <u>th</u>is; hw in white; zh in treasure. The symbol ə stands for the unstressed vowel sound heard in about, taken, pencil, lemon, and circus.

W

work·room (wûrk′rüm′, wûrk′rùm′) *n.* a room in which work is done.

workroom

work·shop (wûrk′shop′) *n.* **1.** a shop or building in which work, especially manual or mechanical work, is done: *a cabinetmaker's workshop.* **2.** a discussion group devoted to a particular subject or field of study: *a workshop in child care, a workshop for poets.*

work·ta·ble (wûrk′tā′bəl) *n.* a table used for working, as by a tailor or carpenter.

world (wûrld) *n.* **1.** the earth: *to take a voyage around the world.* **2.** *also,* **World.** a particular part of the earth: *the Western World.* **3.** all that exists; the whole of creation; the universe. **4.** all the human inhabitants of the earth as a group; humanity: *The world would be at risk in a nuclear war.* **5.** all the inhabitants of a community, state, or country; the public in general: *Now the whole world knows the secret.* **6.** a particular civilization or period of human history: *the world of the Greeks, the Elizabethan world.* **7.** any sphere or area of human concern, pursuit, or activity: *the world of art, the world of fashion.* **8.** a particular group of people sharing certain interests or activities: *the business world.* **9.** matters, concerns, interests, or pleasures of this life and the people devoted to or associated with them: *to live apart from the world.* **10.** a division of living things: *the plant world.* **11.** any planet or other heavenly body. **12.** any place or condition of existence: *the world of today, the world to come.* **13.** *Informal.* a large number or quantity; a great deal: *The vacation did us a world of good.*

world·ly (wûrld′lē) *adj.,* **world·li·er, world·li·est. 1.** devoted to the matters, concerns, interests, or pleasures of this world: *worldly desires.* **2.** of or relating to this world; earthly; secular: *worldly pursuit of riches.* **3.** worldly-wise; sophisticated: *a worldly traveler.* —**world′li·ness,** *n.*

world·ly-wise (wûrld′lē wīz′) *adj.* wise in the ways or affairs of this world.

world power, a country that has considerable influence in or effect upon world affairs.

World Series *also,* **world series. 1.** a series of baseball games played every year between the winning teams in the two major professional leagues after the regular season has ended. It determines the championship of U.S. professional baseball. **2.** any similar series of events that determines a champion.

world war, a war involving the major powers of the world and extending over a large area.

World War I, a war fought chiefly in Europe, from 1914 to 1918, between England, France, Russia, the United States, and their allies on one side and Germany, Austria-Hungary, and their allies on the other.

World War II, a war fought chiefly in Europe, Asia, and Africa, and in the Atlantic and Pacific Oceans, from 1939 to 1945, between England, France, the Soviet Union, the United States, China, and their allies on one side and Germany, Italy, Japan, and their allies on the other.

world-wea·ry (wûrld′wîr′ē) *adj.* tired of the world or of living.

world·wide (wûrld′wīd′) *adj.* extending over all the world: *That pianist has achieved worldwide fame.*

worm (wûrm) *n.* **1.** any of various long, slender, legless animals without backbones. True worms include the flatworms, roundworms, and annelids. **2.** anything like a worm, as in appearance or movement: *the worm of a screw thread.* **3.** a person who is an object of scorn, disgust, or pity; weak, miserable, or pathetic person. **4. worms.** any of several diseases caused by parasitic worms in the body, especially in the intestines. —*v.i.* to move as a worm does; wriggle: *to worm through a narrow window.* —*v.t.* **1.** to move or bring about by moving as a worm: *The child wormed a path through the grass.* **2.** to bring about by stealth or guile: *to worm one's way into someone's favor.* **3.** to get or achieve by stealth or guile: *to worm a secret out of someone.* **4.** to free from worms: *to worm a puppy.* —**worm′like′,** *adj.*

worm-eat·en (wûrm′ē′tən) *adj.* **1.** gnawed or bored by worms; wormy: *worm-eaten vegetables.* **2.** old, worn-out, or out-of-date: *worm-eaten ideas.*

worm gear, a gear that is turned by a revolving shaft with a single spiral thread.

worm·hole (wûrm′hōl′) *n.* a hole made by a burrowing worm, as in wood or fruit.

worm·wood (wûrm′wùd′) *n.* **1.** any of several aromatic plants having small flowers and deeply indented leaves, especially one that yields an oil used in making absinthe and certain medicines. **2.** something that is bitter or unpleasant: *the wormwood of defeat.*

worm·y (wûr′mē) *adj.,* **worm·i·er, worm·i·est. 1.** containing or full of worms: *a wormy tomato.* **2.** like a worm. —**worm′i·ness,** *n.*

worn (wôrn) *v.* the past participle of **wear.** —*adj.* **1.** damaged by use or wear; threadbare: *pants worn at the knees.* **2.** showing the effects of illness, fatigue, or anxiety; exhausted: *a worn, weary expression.*

worn-out (wôrn′out′) *adj.* **1.** unfit for use because of long or harmful use or wear: *worn-out shoes.* **2.** thoroughly exhausted or fatigued: *worn-out from travel.*

wor·ri·some (wûr′ē səm) *adj.* **1.** causing worry or anxiety: *a worrisome experience.* **2.** given to worry: *a worrisome person.*

wor·ry (wûr′ē) *v.,* **wor·ried, wor·ry·ing.** —*v.i.* **1.** to feel anxious or troubled about something: *My parents worry if I am not home by dark.* **2.** to pull or tear at something, as with the teeth: *The puppy worried at the blanket.* —*v.t.* **1.** to cause to feel anxious or troubled; make uneasy: *Your constant coughing worries me.* **2.** to bother; pester; annoy: *Stop worrying me with annoying questions.* **3.** to bite at, shake, or tear with the teeth: *The dog worried the bone.* —*n., pl.* **wor·ries. 1.** the act of worrying or the state of being worried; mental uneasiness or distress. **2.** a cause of mental uneasiness or distress; source of anxiety: *Young children don't have many worries.* [From the Middle English word *worien* meaning "to seize by the throat, strangle," from the Old English word *wyrgan* "to strangle."]

wor·ry·wart (wûr′ē wôrt′) *n. Informal.* a person who tends to worry excessively and unnecessarily.

worse (wûrs) *adj.* the comparative of **bad** and **ill. 1.** of more inferior quality, condition, ability, or value: *The soup at the diner was bad, but the stew was worse.* **2.** more unfavorable, distressing, or unpleasant: *The weather today is even worse than it was yesterday.* **3.** more harmful, damaging, or severe: *The flooding is worse than*

I have ever seen it. **4.** in poorer health; less well: *The patient is worse since yesterday.* —*adv.* in a worse way or manner: *I am feeling worse now than before.* —*n.* something that is worse.

wors·en (wûr′sən) *v.t., v.i.* to make or become worse.

wor·ship (wûr′ship) *n.* **1.** respect, honor, or reverence given to God or a god, or to someone or something considered sacred: *the worship of Jesus.* **2.** the expression of such respect, honor, or reverence, especially religious services consisting of prayers and other acts in honor of God: *The singing of hymns is a traditional mode of worship.* **3.** a great or intense devotion or regard; adoration: *the worship of wealth and power.* **4. Worship.** *British.* a title of honor or respect used in speaking or referring to magistrates and certain other dignitaries. ▲ usually preceded by *Your.* —*v.,* **wor·shiped** or **wor·shipped, wor·ship·ing** or **wor·ship·ping.** —*v.t.* **1.** to pay respect, honor, or reverence to: *to worship God.* **2.** to have a great or intense devotion to or regard for; adore: *a singer worshiped by loyal fans.* —*v.i.* to take part in worship, especially to attend or take part in a religious service. —**wor′ship·er;** *also,* **wor′ship·per,** *n.*

wor·ship·ful (wûr′ship fəl) *adj.* **1.** showing or feeling reverence, respect, or adoration; worshiping. **2. Worshipful.** *British.* deserving of honor or respect; honorable. ▲ used as a title in speaking or referring to persons of rank.

worst (wûrst) *adj.* the superlative of **bad** and **ill.** **1.** most inferior in quality, condition, ability, or value: *That is the worst book I have ever read.* **2.** most unfavorable, distressing, or unpleasant: *This is the worst news I've heard all day.* **3.** most harmful, damaging, or severe: *That was the worst storm I had ever seen.* —*adv.* in the worst way or manner. —*n.* something that is worst. —*v.t.* to get the better of; defeat: *We worsted the opposing basketball team by ten points.*

·**if worst comes to worst.** if the worst possible thing happens.

·**in the worst way.** *Informal.* very much: *I want to go to the party in the worst way.*

wor·sted (wus′tid, wûr′stid) *n.* **1.** a smooth yarn made from long wool fibers that are combed parallel and twisted tightly, used in making such fabrics as gabardine. **2.** a tightly woven wool fabric made from such yarn and having a smooth, hard surface. —*adj.* consisting of or made from worsted: *a worsted coat.*

worth (wûrth) *prep.* **1.** deserving of, meriting. *That classic novel is worth reading more than once.* **2.** having the same value as: *an old coin worth thirty dollars.* **3.** having property or wealth amounting to: *a person worth a million dollars.* —*n.* **1.** the quality that makes a person or thing useful, desirable, or important; merit or excellence: *a novel of little worth.* **2.** the value of something in money: *The painting's worth was estimated at several million dollars.* **3.** the amount of something that can be had for a specific sum: *fifty cents' worth of apples.* **4.** wealth; riches.

worth·less (wûrth′lis) *adj.* not having worth or value: *worthless advice, a worthless scoundrel.* —**worth′less·ly,** *adv.* —**worth′less·ness,** *n.*

worth·while (wûrth′hwīl′, wûrth′wīl′) *adj.* having sufficient value or importance to be worth the time, effort, or money spent: *Building a new library was a worthwhile expense for the community.*

wor·thy (wûr′thē) *adj.,* **wor·thi·er, wor·thi·est.** **1.** having worth or value: *to contribute to a worthy charity.* **2.** having sufficient worth or value; deserving: *a leader worthy of our support.* —*n., pl.* **wor·thies.** a person of importance, merit, or distinction: *Washington and Lincoln are worthies of American history.* —**wor′thi·ly,** *adv.* —**wor′thi·ness,** *n.*

would (wud) *auxiliary verb.* a past tense of **will**[1]. **1.** used to express a condition: *If you would help, we would finish much sooner.* **2.** used to express future time: *We wondered if you would be on time.* **3.** used to express strong preference or willingness: *I would rather go hungry than beg.* **4.** used to express a choice: *I would never have taken the apartment if it weren't for the low rent.* **5.** used to express intention or determination: *They promised that they would return before long.* **6.** used to express longing or desire: *Would that I were with them now!* **7.** used to express probability or possibility: *Being late would make me uncomfortable.* **8.** used to express a request: *Would you be kind enough to open the door for me?* **9.** used to express customary or habitual action: *During the summer we would sit on the beach for hours.*

would–be (wud′bē′) *adj.* **1.** desiring or claiming to be: *a would-be artist.* **2.** intended to be: *The would-be short story turned into a novel.*

would·n't (wud′ənt) *contr.* would not.

wouldst (wudst) *Archaic.* the second person singular, past tense of **will**[1]. ▲ used with *thou.*

wound[1] (wünd) *n.* **1.** an injury to any part of the body, especially one in which the skin is torn, cut, or pierced. **2.** an injury to the feelings, pride, or the like. —*v.t.* **1.** to injure by tearing, cutting, or piercing the skin: *The falling rock wounded the hiker severely.* **2.** to hurt or injure: *to wound someone's pride deeply.* [From the Old English word *wund* with the same meaning.]

wound[2] (wound) a past tense and past participle of **wind**[2].

wove (wōv) a past tense and past participle of **weave.**

wo·ven (wō′vən) a past participle of **weave.**

wow (wou) *interj.* used to express surprise, wonder, pleasure, or similar feeling.

wpm, words per minute.

wrack (rak) *n.* **1.** destruction. ▲ used chiefly in the phrase *wrack and ruin.* **2.** seaweed or other sea plants cast ashore.

wraith (rāth) *n.* **1.** the ghost of a person, which, when seen while the person is living, is thought to indicate that he or she will soon die. **2.** a ghost; specter.

wran·gle (rang′gəl) *v.i.* **wran·gled, wran·gling.** to argue or dispute, especially in a noisy or angry manner: *The children wrangled about who would go first.* **2.** in the western United States, to herd, round up, or tend (horses or other livestock). —*n.* a noisy or angry argument; dispute: *caught up in a wrangle over who should pay.*

wran·gler (rang′glər) *n.* **1.** a person who wrangles. **2.** in the western United States, a person who herds or tends horses or other livestock; cowboy.

wrap (rap) *v.t.,* **wrapped** or **wrapt, wrap·ping. 1.** to fold or place (a covering) around someone or something, as for protection: *to wrap a blanket around a sleeping child.* **2.** to cover in this way: *to wrap a baby in a blanket.* **3.** to cover, especially with paper, and make secure: *to wrap a package, to wrap a present.* **4.** to cover or surround so as to obscure or conceal: *The skyscraper was wrapped in fog.* **5.** to take up completely; engross: *to be wrapped in thought.* **6.** to clasp or fold: *to wrap one's arms around a loved one.* **7.** *Informal.* to bring to an end; conclude: *The detective wrapped up the case in two days. I guess that wraps up the work for today.* —*n.* an outer covering or garment, as a shawl.

at; āpe; fär; câre; end; mē; it; īce; pîerce; hot; ōld; sông, fôrk; oil; out; up; ūse; rüle; pull; tûrn; chin; sing; shop; thin; this; hw in white; zh in treasure. The symbol ə stands for the unstressed vowel sound heard in about, taken, pencil, lemon, and circus.

W

•**under wraps.** in concealment or secrecy: *The plan was kept under wraps.*

•**wrapped up in.** absorbed or involved in: *to be wrapped up in one's work.*

wrap·per (rap′ər) *n.* **1.** paper or other material in which something is wrapped or enclosed: *a gum wrapper.* **2.** a person or thing that wraps packages, parcels, or the like. **3.** a long, loose dressing gown, robe, or similar garment.

wrap·ping (rap′ing) *n.* *usually,* **wrappings.** paper or other material designed or used for wrapping packages or other objects.

wrapt (rapt) a past tense and past participle of **wrap.**

wrap-up (rap′up′) *n. Informal.* a brief summarizing report, as of news.

wrath (rath) *n.* extreme or violent anger; rage: *to provoke someone's wrath.*

wrath·ful (rath′fəl) *adj.* full of, resulting from, or showing wrath: *Wrathful citizens demanded an end to rising taxes.* —**wrath′ful·ly,** *adv.* —**wrath′ful·ness,** *n.*

wreak (rēk) *v.t.* **1.** to inflict or exact: *to wreak havoc, to wreak vengeance.* **2.** to give free expression to; vent: *The mob wreaked its anger on the innocent bystander.*

wreath (rēth) *n., pl.* **wreaths** (rēthz, rēths). **1.** a ring of flowers or leaves woven or twined together, worn on the head as a mark of honor or victory, placed on a grave as a memorial, or used as a decoration. **2.** any spiral or curving shape or form resembling this: *Wreaths of smoke rose from the chimney.*

wreathe (rēth) *v.t.,* **wreathed, wreath·ing. 1.** to form or shape into a wreath. **2.** to decorate, encircle, or crown with a wreath or wreaths: *The children wreathed the front door at Christmas.* **3.** to envelop; cover: *a face wreathed in smiles.*

wreck (rek) *v.t.* **1.** to cause the physical destruction or ruin of: *to wreck a car in an accident.* **2.** to destroy, ruin, or put an end to: *The sudden rain wrecked our plans for the picnic.* **3.** to tear down or dismantle, as an old building. —*n.* **1.** the act of wrecking or the state of being wrecked; destruction. **2.** the remains of anything, especially a ship, automobile, or airplane, that has been destroyed, damaged, or disabled: *The wreck was towed to the junkyard.* **3.** a person in poor physical or mental condition: *a nervous wreck.* **4.** something in poor or broken-down condition, or in a state of disorder: *The town was a wreck from the tornado.*

wreck·age (rek′ij) *n.* **1.** the remains of anything that has been wrecked; debris: *After the flooding subsided the streets were filled with wreckage.* **2.** the act of wrecking or the state of being wrecked.

wreck·er (rek′ər) *n.* **1.** a person or thing that wrecks. **2.** a person whose work is tearing down or demolishing buildings. **3.** another word for **tow truck. 4.** a person, boat, or ship employed to recover wrecked or disabled ships or their cargoes.

wren (ren) *n.* any of various songbirds having a slender bill, short, rounded wings, a short tail, and brownish feathers that are usually marked with brown, black, or white.

wrench (rench) *n., pl.* **wrench·es. 1.** a sharp or violent twist, turn, or pull: *With a sudden wrench the dog broke the leash.* **2.** an injury or strain, as of the back, caused by a sudden or violent twisting, turning, or jerking motion; sprain. **3.** a sharp, usually sudden, mental or emotional distress or pain: *Moving away from old friends was a real wrench to the family.* **4.** any of various tools having fixed or movable jaws, used especially for gripping and turning a nut, bolt, or pipe. —*v.t.* **1.** to twist, turn, or pull with a sudden sharp or violent motion: *I wrenched the nail out of the wall.* **2.** to injure or strain by twisting or turning suddenly or violently: *to wrench one's back in a fall.*

wrest (rest) *v.t.* **1.** to pull, twist, or take away by force or violence: *to wrest a bone from a dog.* **2.** to seize by force or violence: *The rebels tried to wrest power from the dictator.* **3.** to obtain or extract by great effort: *The farmers wrested a bare existence from the barren land.* **4.** to twist; distort; pervert: *to wrest a candidate's words from their intended meaning.*

wres·tle (res′əl) *v.,* **wres·tled, wres·tling.** —*v.i.* **1.** to take part in the sport or activity of wrestling; grapple: *Two children were wrestling on the ground.* **2.** to struggle or contend, especially in order to gain mastery: *to wrestle with a problem, to wrestle with one's conscience.* —*v.t.* **1.** to take part in wrestling with: *to wrestle a bear.* **2.** to move or force by wrestling: *to wrestle an opponent to the ground.* —*n.* **1.** the act or action of wrestling. **2.** a struggle. —**wres′tler,** *n.*

wres·tling (res′ling) *n.* a sport or activity in which two opponents struggle hand to hand, especially in an attempt to throw or force the other to the ground.

wretch (rech) *n., pl.* **wretch·es. 1.** an unfortunate or unhappy person. **2.** an evil or contemptible person.

wretch·ed (rech′id) *adj.* **1.** very unhappy; deeply distressed: *to feel wretched after failing a test.* **2.** characterized by or causing great unhappiness or discomfort: *to lead a wretched existence, the wretched living conditions in the slums.* **3.** evil or contemptible; despicable: *a wretched tyrant.* **4.** poor or inferior in ability, quality, or the like: *a wretched tennis player.* —**wretch′ed·ly,** *adv.* —**wretch′ed·ness,** *n.*

wri·er (rī′ər) the comparative of **wry.**

wri·est (rī′ist) the superlative of **wry.**

wrig·gle (rig′əl) *v.,* **wrig·gled, wrig·gling.** —*v.i.* **1.** to twist or turn from side to side with short, quick movements; squirm: *The bored children were wriggling in their seats.* **2.** to move or proceed with a wriggling motion: *The caterpillar wriggled up the side of the tree.* **3.** to make one's way by tricky or shifty means: *to wriggle out of trouble.* —*v.t.* **1.** to cause to wriggle. **2.** to bring, get, or make by wriggling: *The explorers wriggled their way into the cave.* —*n.* a wriggling movement or action: *to crawl with a wriggle.* —**wrig′gly,** *adj.*

wrig·gler (rig′lər) *n.* **1.** a person or thing that wriggles. **2.** the larva of a mosquito; wiggler.

wright (rīt) *n.* a person who makes, constructs, or creates something. ▲ used chiefly in combination: *wheelwright, playwright.*

wring (ring) *v.t.,* **wrung, wring·ing. 1.** to squeeze or twist so as to force out liquid: *to wring wet clothes.* **2.** to force out (liquid) in this way: *to wring water from a wet bathing suit.* **3.** to get by forceful or constant effort: *to wring the truth out of someone.* **4.** to clasp and press or twist (the hands) together. **5.** to twist or squeeze forcefully or violently: *to wring the neck of a chicken.* **6.** to cause to feel great sadness or pity; torment: *Their misery wrung our hearts.* —*n.* the act of wringing; twist or squeeze.

wring·er (ring′ər) *n.* a person or thing that wrings, especially a device or machine for squeezing water out of wet clothes.

wrin·kle (ring′kəl) *n.* **1.** a small fold, ridge, or crease in a normally smooth surface: *to iron out the wrinkles in a shirt.* **2.** a small furrow, crease, or line in the skin, as is caused by aging. —*v.,* **wrin·kled, wrin·kling.** —*v.t.* to form or make a wrinkle or wrinkles in: *to wrinkle one's brow.* —*v.i.* to become wrinkled: *This fabric won't wrinkle.*

wrist (rist) *n.* **1.** the joint that connects the hand and arm, or the area surrounding this joint. **2.** the eight small bones that make up this joint; carpus.

wrist·band (rist′band′) *n.* a band, as of a sleeve, that goes around the wrist.

wrist·watch (rist′woch′) *n., pl.* **wrist·watch·es.** a watch worn on a band or strap around the wrist.

writ[1] (rit) *n.* **1.** a legal document ordering the person or persons named in it to do or to not do something. **2.** something written; writing. [From the Old English word *writ* meaning "something written" or "Scripture."]

writ[2] (rit) *Archaic.* a past tense and past participle of **write**.

write (rīt) *v.,* **wrote** or (*archaic*) **writ, writ·ten** or (*archaic*) **writ, writ·ing.** —*v.t.* **1.** to mark or form (letters, words, symbols, or the like) on a surface, as with a pen or pencil. **2.** to form the letters, words, or symbols of: *to write one's name, to write a formula.* **3.** to express, describe, or communicate in or by writing: *to write one's thoughts in a diary.* **4.** to be the author or composer of: *to write short stories.* **5.** to send a letter to: *Please write us when you get home.* **6.** to fill in with the required written information: *to write a check.* **7.** to draw up in legal form: *to write a will.* **8.** to show or indicate plainly: *to have love written all over one's face.* **9.** *Computers.* to store data on a medium, as a disk. —*v.i.* **1.** to form letters, words, or symbols on paper or another surface. **2.** to be an author or writer. **3.** to compose or send a letter: *I'll write as soon as I can.* **4.** to produce writing of a certain quality: *to write clearly.*

·**to write down.** to put into writing.

·**to write in.** to vote for (a person not listed on a ballot) by inserting a person's name.

·**to write off. a.** to cancel or remove from an account: *to write off a debt.* **b.** to regard or acknowledge as a loss or failure: *to write off a project.*

·**to write out. a.** to put into writing: *to write out one's thoughts.* **b.** to write in full: *to write out a speech from one's notes.*

·**to write up.** to describe or set down in writing, especially in a detailed account: *The reporter wrote up the interview and submitted it to the editor.*

write–in (rīt′in′) *n.* a vote cast for a person not listed on a ballot by inserting the person's name. —*adj.* of or relating to such a vote or votes: *a write-in campaign.*

writ·er (rī′tər) *n.* **1.** a person who writes: *the writer of a letter.* **2.** a person whose occupation or profession is writing: *a short-story writer.*

write–up (rīt′up′) *n.* a written account or description.

writhe (rīth) *v.i.,* **writhed, writh·ing. 1.** to move the body with a twisting or turning motion, as in great pain: *The injured hockey player writhed in pain.* **2.** to suffer great mental or emotional distress or discomfort: *to writhe in anguish over a lost dog.*

writ·ing (rī′ting) *n.* **1.** the act of a person who writes. **2.** handwriting; penmanship: *Your writing is always neat and legible.* **3.** a written form: *I'd like this agreement put in writing.* **4.** something written: *There was writing all over the wall.* **5.** a novel, play, or other literary work: *to read the writings of Mark Twain.* **6.** the occupation or profession of a writer or author. **7.** the style, form, or art of literary composition.

Language Note

Writing is one of humanity's greatest inventions because it enables us to record language in a permanent form and to store vast amounts of information. Writing has existed for only a small part of total human history, and yet almost all human technological, intellectual, and cultural achievements have come about after the invention of writing. Only by means of written language can we pass on the full measure of our knowledge to later generations.

The first form of writing was *pictographs,* which are pictures that are drawn to represent something. If you wanted to represent the sun in pictographs, you would draw a *picture* of the sun rather than write the letters *s-u-n*. The system of pictographs is limited to representing things that can be drawn. In order to express ideas and feelings, another system, called *ideographs,* was developed. Ideographs are also pictures, but they convey more than just the appearance of an object. In a system of ideographs, a picture of the sun could mean "warmth," "light," "day," or any of the other things that we associate with the sun. Chinese writing is the only modern system that is still based on such symbols.

An important advance in writing came when the connection between the thing or object and the word that names it was broken. Language is really a set of symbols. A dog is a dog, whether it is called *canis* in Latin, *perro* in Spanish, *hund* in German, *sobaka* in Russian, or *dog* in English. What was needed in writing is the means to represent the *word* that names something, be it a dog or anything else, rather than to symbolize the thing itself. The first system to do this was *logographs,* or *logograms,* which are symbols that not only show the appearance of an object, but also represent the *sound* of the word used for it. The next step is to have the written symbols represent not whole words, but only sounds. In this way the symbols themselves can be combined to form any word. When the symbols represent the sounds of a syllable, the system is known as a *syllabary.* When the symbols represent individual speech sounds, the system is known as an *alphabet.* An ideal alphabet would have only one sound represented by each symbol.

English uses a modified form of the Latin alphabet, containing 26 letters. Even though there are more sounds in English than there are letters to represent them, our alphabet makes it possible to write any conceivable word in our language.

writ·ten (rit′ən) a past participle of **write**.

wrong (rông) *adj.* **1.** not correct or accurate; untrue: *a wrong answer.* **2.** not just, moral, or good: *It would be wrong to betray a friend's trust.* **3.** not appropriate, suitable, or proper: *Now is the wrong time to ask for a favor.* **4.** not in proper or normal working order; out of order: *There is something wrong with my watch.* **5.** not meant, wanted, or necessary: *a wrong turn on the road.* **6.** of or relating to the side or surface not meant to be seen: *the wrong side of a fabric.* —*n.* something that is wrong, such as an unjust, immoral, or harmful action: *The sinners repented the wrongs they had committed.* —*adv.* in a wrong way or manner: *to guess wrong, to pronounce a word wrong.* —*v.t.* to treat in an unjust, wrong, or harmful manner; do wrong to: *to wrong a friend.* [From the Old English word *wrang* meaning "something wrong" or "unjust action," from the Old Norse word *rungr* "awry, crooked, unjust."] —**wrong′ly,** *adv.* —**wrong′ness,** *n.*

·**in the wrong.** wrong, mistaken, or at fault: *You were in the wrong in that argument.*

·**to go wrong. a.** to turn out badly or take place incorrectly: *Something went wrong with the experiment.* **b.** to begin to do evil or immoral things. **c.** to make a mistake; err.

at; āpe; fär; câre; end; mē; it; īce; pîerce; hot; ōld; sông, fôrk; oil; out; up; ūse; rüle; pull; tûrn; chin; sing; shop; thin; this; hw in white; zh in treasure. The symbol ə stands for the unstressed vowel sound heard in about, taken, pencil, lemon, and circus.

W

1091

wrong·do·er (rông′dü′ər) *n.* a person who does something wrong.

wrong·do·ing (rông′dü′ing) *n.* the act of doing something wrong.

wrong·ful (rông′fəl) *adj.* **1.** wrong, unjust, or injurious. **2.** unlawful; illegal: *a wrongful act of vandalism.* —**wrong′ful·ly,** *adv.* —**wrong′ful·ness,** *n.*

wrong·head·ed (rông′hed′id) *adj.* stubbornly or unreasonably keeping wrong opinions, judgments, or ideas. —**wrong′head′ed·ly,** *adv.*

wrote (rōt) a past tense of **write.**

wroth (rôth) *adj.* angry; wrathful.

wrought (rôt) *v.* a past tense and past participle of **work.** *adj.* **1.** made or formed: *a skillfully wrought desk.* **2.** (of metals) shaped by hammering.

·wrought up. agitated; excited: *to get wrought up over a delay.*

wrought iron, an extremely pure form of iron that is tough, easily worked and welded, and relatively resistant to corrosion.

wrung (rung) the past tense and past participle of **wring.**

wry (rī) *adj.,* **wri·er, wri·est. 1.** made by twisting or distorting the features: *a wry smile.* **2.** funny in an ironic, bitter, or perverse way: *a wry sense of humor.* —**wry′ly,** *adv.* —**wry′ness,** *n.*

wt., weight.

wurst (wûrst) *n.* a sausage.

WV, postal abbreviation for West Virginia.

W. Va., West Virginia.

WY, postal abbreviation for Wyoming.

Wyo., Wyoming.

1. early Greek **2. later Greek**

3. Etruscan **4. Latin**

5. English

X is the twenty-fourth letter of the English alphabet. The earliest form of **X** was probably an ancient Greek letter (1) that was written like a plus sign or like a modern X, usually called a "cross sign." The Greeks gave it two different pronunciations: a *ks* sound in the Western Greek alphabet and a *kh* sound in the Eastern Greek alphabet. This letter was adopted, with only slight changes, in the classical Greek (2) and Etruscan (3) alphabets. The Romans (4), who adapted their alphabet from the Western Greek and Etruscan alphabets, gave their "cross sign" letter a *ks* pronunciation. By the fourth century B.C., the letter **X** of the Latin alphabet was written almost exactly as we write it today (5).

x, X (eks) *n.*, *pl.* **x's, X's. 1.** the twenty-fourth letter of the English alphabet. **2.** something having the shape of this letter. **3.** the Roman numeral for ten. **4.** an unknown person or thing. **5.** *Mathematics.* **a.** a mark used to indicate multiplication: *4 × 10 = 40.* **b.** an unknown quantity or variable: *3x = 6.* **6.** a mark used in place of a signature by a person who cannot write. **7.** a mark used to indicate a particular point or place on a map or diagram.

Xan·thip·pe (zan tip′ē) *n.* any scolding, nagging woman; shrew. [From *Xanthippe* (469?–399? B.C.), famous for nagging her husband, Socrates.]

x–ax·is (eks′ak′sis) *n.*, *pl.* **x–ax·es** (eks′ak′sēz). the horizontal axis on a graph, along which the abscissa is measured.

X chromosome, one of a pair of chromosomes that determine sex in nearly all animals and most higher plants. A fertilized egg cell with two X chromosomes produces a female organism. A fertilized egg cell with an X chromosome and a Y chromosome produces a male organism.

Xe, the symbol for xenon.

xe·bec (zē′bek) *n.* a small, three-masted ship, formerly used in the Mediterranean Sea by pirates.

xe·non (zē′non) *n.* a rare, inert gaseous element that is approximately five times heavier than air. It is used in lasers and vacuum tubes and as a light source in certain types of motion-picture projection lamps. Symbol: **Xe** [Formed from the Greek word *xenos* meaning "strange," because xenon is a rare gas.]

xen·o·pho·bi·a (zen′ə fō′bē ə) *n.* a fear of strangers or of anything strange or foreign.

xe·rog·ra·phy (zi rog′rə fē) *n.* a process for making photographic copies of texts or pictures, in which a positive image of the material to be copied is projected onto an electrically charged surface. A black plastic powder adheres to areas of the surface to form a permanent image.

Xe·rox (zir′oks) *n.*, *pl.* **Xe·rox·es.** *Trademark.* **1.** a photocopier that uses the process of xerography. **2. xerox.** a photocopy made by the process of xerography. —*v.t.* to make a photocopy of by means of xerography.

Xho·sa (kō′sə) *n.*, *pl.* **Xho·sa** or **Xho·sas. 1.** a member of a Bantu people living mainly in southern South Africa. **2.** the language of the Xhosa, closely related to Zulu. Also, **Xosa.**

xi (zī, sī) *n.* the fourteenth letter of the Greek alphabet (Ξ, ξ).

X·mas (kris′məs, eks′məs) *n.*, *pl.* **X·mas·es.** see **Christmas.**

Xo·sa (kō′sə) *n.*, *pl.* **Xo·sa** or **Xo·sas.** another spelling of **Xhosa.**

X–ray (eks′rā′) *v.t.* to examine, photograph, or treat with X rays: *to X-ray a broken bone.* —*adj.* relating to or performed by means of X rays: *X-ray treatment, X-ray inspection of metals.*

X ray 1. an invisible, high-frequency, shortwave, electromagnetic radiation that can pass through substances that visible light cannot penetrate. It is used in medical diagnosis of internal disorders, such as broken bones, and in treating certain diseases, such as cancer. **2.** a photograph made by X rays.

xy·lem (zī′ləm, zī′lem) *n.* the woody tissue of plants that serves to carry water and dissolved nutrients from the roots to other parts of the plant and also helps to support the plant.

xy·lo·phone (zī′lə fōn′) *n.* a musical instrument consisting of a stand on which a row or rows of wooden bars of graduated length are mounted. It is usually sounded by striking the bars with small wooden mallets.

X

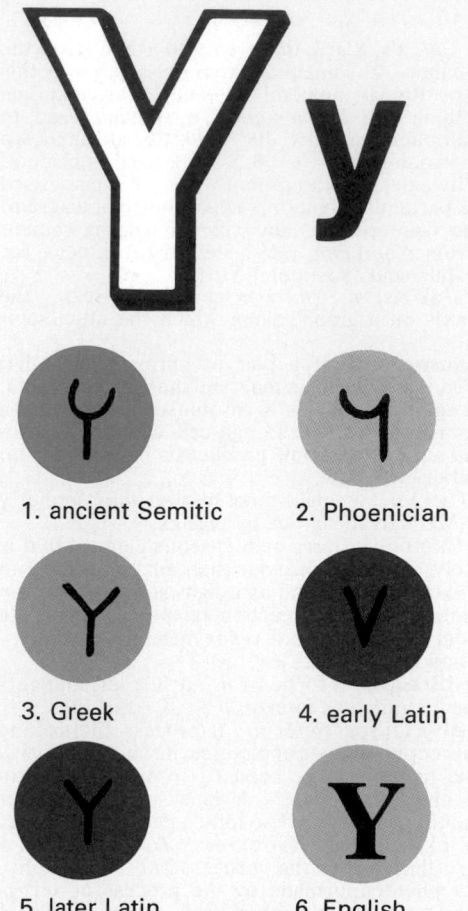

Y y

1. ancient Semitic
2. Phoenician
3. Greek
4. early Latin
5. later Latin
6. English

Y is the twenty-fifth letter of the English alphabet. The letter **Y** has the same early history as the letter **V**, coming from the ancient Semitic letter *waw* (1), which depicted a hook. This letter was borrowed first by the Phoenicians (2), and then by the ancient Greeks (3), who called it *upsilon* and wrote it very much like a modern capital **Y**. In the Latin alphabet, *upsilon* was adopted twice. It was first borrowed to form the Latin letter **V** (4) that became the source of our modern letters **U, V,** and **W**. About 2,000 years ago, *upsilon* was again adopted into the Latin alphabet (5) in order to represent this letter in words that had been borrowed from the Greek language. This later form of *upsilon*, written like the capital letter **Y**, gave us the modern letter **Y** (6).

Unlike the other letters of the English alphabet, **Y** commonly functions as both a vowel, as in *funny* and *cry*, and a consonant, as in *yesterday* and *young*. The letter **Y** was first used as a consonant to replace an obsolete Old English letter. Because of this, most of the words we use that begin with **Y** have come from Old English or Middle English.

y, Y (wī) *n., pl.* **y's, Y's. 1.** the twenty-fifth letter of the English alphabet. **2.** something having the shape of this letter. **3.** *Mathematics.* an unknown quantity or variable: $4y = 20$.

Y, the symbol for yttrium.

y-, 1. yard. **2.** year.

-y¹ *suffix* (used to form adjectives) **1.** characterized by: *rainy, funny.* **2.** containing; full of: *juicy, sooty.* **3.** inclined to: *itchy, thirsty.* **4.** somewhat like: *sugary, powdery, chilly.* **5.** resembling; like: *flowery, icy.* [From the Old English suffix *-ig* with the same meaning.]

-y² *suffix* (used to form nouns) **1.** little: *puppy, kitty.* **2.** dear: *aunty, daddy.* [From the Middle English suffix *-ie* with the same meanings.]

-y³ *suffix* (used to form nouns) state or quality: *jealousy, honesty.* [From the Middle English suffix *-ie*, from the Old French suffix *-ie*, from the Latin suffix *-ia*, from the Greek suffix *-ia*, all with the same meaning.]

yacht (yot) *n.* any of various small ships used especially for pleasure trips or racing. —*v.i.* to cruise or race in a yacht. [From the obsolete Dutch word *jaght*, short for *jaghtschip* meaning "a ship for chasing," from the words *jagen* "to chase" + *schip* "ship."]

Yah·weh (yä′wə) *n.* a name for God used in the Old Testament, based on a transliteration of the Hebrew letters symbolizing God's name.

yak¹ (yak) *n.* a long-haired ox of Tibet and central Asia, having a large hump at the shoulder and curved horns, used as a beast of burden. [From the Tibetan word *gyag* meaning this animal.]

yak¹

yak² (yak) *v.i.,* **yakked, yak·king.** *Slang.* to talk too much or idly; chatter. [Representation of the sound of talking.]

yam (yam) *n.* **1.** the root of a trailing tropical vine, used as food. **2.** the vine that bears this root, having large leaves and spikes of small, greenish flowers. **3.** a large, reddish sweet potato.

yank (yangk) *Informal. v.t.* to give a sharp, sudden pull to; jerk; tug: *I yanked the stuck door open.* —*v.i.* to pull sharply and suddenly: *The child kept yanking at the doll's hair.* —*n.* a sharp, sudden pull.

Yank (yangk) *n. Informal.* Yankee.

Yan·kee (yang′kē) *n.* **1.** a person who was born or is living in New England. **2.** a person who was born or is living in any of the Northern states. **3.** a person who fought on the side of the Union in the Civil War. **4.** any person who was born or is living in the United States. —*adj.* of or relating to Yankees.

Yankee Doo·dle (dü′dəl) a song made popular by American soldiers during the Revolutionary War.

yap (yap) *n.* **1.** a brief, sharp, or shrill bark; yelp: *the constant yap of a puppy.* **2.** *Slang.* noisy talk. —*v.i.,* **yapped, yap·ping. 1.** to bark sharply or shrilly; yelp. **2.** *Slang.* to talk noisily.

yard¹ (yärd) *n.* **1.** an area of ground next to or surrounding a house or other building. **2.** an enclosed area of ground used for a special purpose, as for keeping livestock or for carrying on some work or business. **3.** an area next to a railroad station, used for storing, switching, or servicing trains. [From the Old English word *geard* meaning "enclosure" or "garden, yard¹."]

yard² (yärd) *n.* **1.** a measure of length equal to 36 inches, or 3 feet (0.9144 meter). **2.** a long rod tapering toward the ends, fastened across a mast to support a sail. [From the Old English word *gyrd* meaning "a twig, staff, rod."]

yard·age (yär′dij) *n.* the amount or length of something measured in yards: *Our football team gained more yardage than theirs did.*

yard·arm (yärd′ärm′) *n.* either end of a yard supporting a square sail.

yard goods, fabric that is sold by the yard.

yard·mas·ter (yärd′mas′tər) *n.* a person who is in charge of a railroad yard.

yard sale, another term for **garage sale.**

yard·stick (yärd′stik′) *n.* **1.** a flat strip of wood, plastic, or metal one yard long, used in measuring. **2.** any standard used in making a judgment, evaluation, or comparison: *a yardstick for judging quality.*

yar·mul·ke (yär′məl kə, yä′məl kə) *n.* a skullcap worn by Jewish men and boys, especially during religious services.

yarn (yärn) *n.* **1.** thread spun from natural or synthetic fibers, such as cotton, wool, silk, or nylon, used in weaving or knitting. **2.** *Informal.* a long, exaggerated, or made-up story: *The old sailor told many yarns about life at sea.* —*v.i. Informal.* to tell a yarn or yarns.

yar·row (yar′ō) *n.* any of a large group of plants having finely divided leaves and clusters of small yellow, white, or pink flowers.

yaw (yô) *v.i.* **1.** (of a ship) to turn temporarily and unintentionally from a straight course. **2.** (of an aircraft, spacecraft, or projectile) to turn to the right or left on its vertical axis. —*n.* the act of turning from a straight course.

yawl (yôl) *n.* **1.** a sailboat or small yacht with a large mainmast forward and a smaller mast astern. **2.** a ship's small boat, usually rowed by a crew of four or six.

yawn (yôn) *v.i.* **1.** to open the mouth wide with a deep breath because of drowsiness, boredom, or weariness. **2.** to be or draw wide open: *The steep canyon yawned before us.* —*v.t.* to say or express with a yawn: *to yawn an answer.* —*n.* the act of yawning: *The tired student stifled a yawn.*

yaws (yôz) *n.* a contagious disease occurring chiefly in children, characterized by growths and sores on the skin. Yaws is a tropical disease that is caused by a bacterium. ▲ used with a singular verb.

y-ax·is (wī′ak′sis) *n., pl.* **y-ax·es** (wī′ak′sēz). the vertical axis on a graph, along which the ordinate is measured.

Yb, the symbol for ytterbium.

Y chromosome, one of a pair of chromosomes that determine sex in nearly all animals and most higher plants. A fertilized egg cell with a Y chromosome produces a male organism.

y·clept (ē klept′) also, **y·cleped.** *adj. Archaic.* called; named.

yd., yard; yards.

ye[1] (yē) *pron. Archaic.* the ones spoken to. [From the Old English word *gē* meaning "you" (plural).]

ye[2] (thē, yē) *Archaic.* the[1]. [From the use of the letter *y* as a substitute for an obsolete letter representing *th* in Old and Middle English.]

yea (yā) *adv.* **1.** yes: *All those in favor of the motion say "yea."* ▲ used in agreeing to or affirming something, especially in voting orally. **2.** *Archaic.* indeed; truly. ▲ used to introduce a sentence or statement. —*n.* an affirmative vote or voter.

year (yîr) *n.* **1.** a period of time consisting of 365 or 366 days, reckoned from January 1 to December 31, and divided into twelve months of fifty-two weeks. Also, **calendar year. 2.** the interval of time between one vernal equinox and the next, equal to 365 days, 5 hours, 48 minutes, and 46 seconds. Also, **solar year. 3.** the interval of time required for the earth to complete one revolution around the sun, measured against the relatively fixed background of the stars, equal to 365 days, 6 hours, 9 minutes, and 9.54 seconds. Also, **sidereal year. 4.** a period of twelve lunar months or 354 days. Also, **lunar year. 5.** any period of twelve months: *We met exactly a year ago on May 1st.* **6.** a part of a year devoted to a particular activity: *the school year.* **7.** the period of time in which any planet completes one revolution around the sun. **8. years. a.** age, especially old age: *to get on in years.* **b.** time, especially a long time: *We've been going there for years.*

·**year after year.** every year.

·**year by year.** with each succeeding year.

·**year in, year out.** every year; continuously.

year·book (yîr′bük′) *n.* **1.** a book published every year, usually containing information about or a summary of the events of the previous year. **2.** a book issued by a graduating class of a high school or college, usually containing photographs of the class and information about its activities and achievements.

year·ling (yîr′ling) *n.* an animal that is one year old or in its second year. —*adj.* one year old: *a yearling calf.*

year·long (yîr′lông′) *adj.* lasting for a year.

year·ly (yîr′lē) *adj.* **1.** happening or returning once a year: *to take a yearly vacation.* **2.** performed during a year; lasting a year. **3.** measured by the year: *a yearly salary.* —*adv.* once a year; annually: *I see my doctor yearly.*

yearn (yûrn) *v.i.* **1.** to feel a strong and deep desire: *to yearn for the carefree days of youth.* **2.** to feel deep pity; be moved with compassion: *It made my heart yearn to think of the lost kitten.*

yearn·ing (yûr′ning) *n.* an earnest or deep desire. —**yearn′ing·ly,** *adv.*

year–round (yîr′round′) *adj., adv.* throughout the year: *a year-round vacation spot, to live somewhere year-round.*

yeast (yēst) *n.* **1.** a substance consisting of very tiny cells of various fungi that cause fermentation in mixtures containing sugar. Yeast is used in raising bread, making beer and wine, and other processes. **2.** a single plant or cell forming this substance. **3.** see **yeast cake. 4.** foam; froth; spume.

yeast cake 1. yeast compressed with flour or meal into a small cake, used especially in baking and brewing. **2.** a cake or similar baked food leavened with yeast.

yell (yel) *v.i.* to cry out loudly, as in pain or anger: *to yell for help, to yell from fright.* —*v.t.* to say with a yell: *to yell an answer across the room.* —*n.* **1.** a strong, loud cry, as of pain or anger; scream. **2.** a rhythmic chant or cheer shouted by a group, as at a school or college sports event.

yel·low (yel′ō) *n.* **1.** the color of egg yolks, butter, or ripe lemons. **2.** a paint or dye having this color. **3.** the yolk of an egg. —*adj.* **1.** having the color yellow. **2.** having a yellowish complexion. **3.** *Informal.* not brave; cowardly. —*v.i.* to become yellow: *The newspapers have yellowed with age.* —*v.t.* to make yellow. —**yel′low·ness,** *n.*

yel·low·bird (yel′ō bûrd′) *n.* any of various birds with yellow feathers, such as the American goldfinch and the yellow warbler.

yellow fever, a contagious, often fatal disease of tropical regions, caused by a virus transmitted by the bite of a mosquito and characterized by high fever, vomiting, jaundice, and hemorrhaging. Also, **yellow jack.**

yel·low·ham·mer (yel′ō ham′ər) *n.* **1.** a finch of Europe and Asia, having black, brown, and yellow feathers and a short, cone-shaped bill. **2.** a flicker of North

at; āpe; fär; câre; end; mē; it; īce; pîerce; hot; ōld; sông, fôrk; oil; out; up; ūse; rüle; pùll; tûrn; chin; sing; shop; thin; this; hw in white; zh in treasure. The symbol ə stands for the unstressed vowel sound heard in about, taken, pencil, lemon, and circus.

Y

America, having brown feathers with yellow markings on the wings and tail.

yel·low·ish (yel′ō ish) *adj.* somewhat yellow.

yellow jack 1. another term for **yellow fever. 2.** a yellow flag used as a sign of quarantine, as on a ship.

yellow jacket, any of several wasps that have yellow markings.

yellow pages *also,* **Yellow Pages.** a telephone directory printed on yellow paper that lists businesses and services under general categories.

yellow warbler, a small American warbler. The male has yellow feathers with brown streaks.

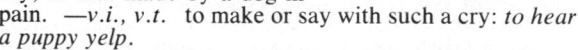
yellow jacket

yelp (yelp) *n.* a short, shrill cry, as that made by a dog in pain. —*v.i., v.t.* to make or say with such a cry: *to hear a puppy yelp.*

yen¹ (yen) *n., pl.* **yen.** a monetary unit of Japan. [From the Japanese word *yen.*]

yen² (yen) *Informal. n.* a sharp desire or longing; craving: *a yen to travel.* —*v.i.,* **yenned, yen·ning.** to yearn or long for. [Chinese *yan* "opium, a craving for opium."]

yeo·man (yō′mən) *n., pl.* **yeo·men** (yō′mən). **1.** a naval petty officer who performs clerical or administrative duties. **2.** in England, a person who owns and farms a small amount of land.

yeo·man·ry (yō′mən rē) *n.* yeomen as a group.

yes (yes) *adv.* **1.** as you say or ask; it is so. ▲ used to show acceptance, agreement, consent, or affirmation: *Yes, you are right. Yes, you may borrow my book.* **2.** in addition to that; moreover. ▲ used to emphasize a preceding statement by repeating or adding to it: *You are a good baseball player, yes, the best on the school team.* —*n., pl.* **yes·es. 1.** a saying of the word "yes"; positive reply. **2.** an affirmative vote or voter.

ye·shi·va (yə shē′və) *n., pl.* **ye·shi·vas** or **ye·shi·voth** (yə shē′vōt). **1.** an Orthodox Jewish parochial school. **2.** an Orthodox Jewish institution of higher learning.

yes man *Informal.* a person who always agrees with his or her superior.

yes·ter·day (yes′tər dē, yes′tər dā′) *n.* **1.** the day before today: *Yesterday was a beautiful day.* **2.** the recent past: *the automobiles of yesterday.* —*adv.* **1.** on the day before today: *Was it yesterday we saw you at the fair?* **2.** recently: *It seems that they were babies only yesterday.*

yes·ter·year (yes′tər yîr′) *n.* **1.** the year before this year; last year. **2.** the past.

yet (yet) *adv.* **1.** at the present time; now: *not yet old enough to vote.* **2.** up to the present time; thus far: *You have never yet been late for a meeting.* **3.** continuously up to this or that time: *The farmer rose early and is working yet.* **4.** at some future time; eventually: *The mystery will be solved yet.* **5.** after all the time that has or had gone by: *Aren't you finished eating yet?* **6.** in the time remaining: *There is yet a chance that we will win.* **7.** in addition: *There are three days yet to go until my vacation.* **8.** even; still: *It will be colder yet before spring comes.* **9.** nevertheless; however: *The judge was stern, yet completely fair.* —*conj.* nevertheless; however: *The road map seemed clear enough, yet we soon got lost.*

·**as yet.** up to now: *I have not as yet received the package you sent me.*

yet·i (yet′ē) *n.* another word for the **abominable snowman.**

yew (ū) *n.* **1.** any of a small group of evergreen trees and shrubs of Europe and Asia, having scaly reddish brown bark and flattened, needle-shaped leaves. **2.** the wood of this tree, used especially in making archery bows.

Yid·dish (yid′ish) *n.* a Germanic language spoken predominantly by Jews in Europe, Israel, and North and South America. Yiddish, which is written in the Hebrew alphabet, is derived from a dialect of German that was spoken in the Middle Ages, with the addition of many words from Hebrew, and from various Slavic and Romance languages. —*adj.* of or relating to this language.

yield (yēld) *v.t.* **1.** to give forth; produce: *This rich land will yield a large crop. That mine yields silver.* **2.** to give in return, as for an investment: *My bank account yields interest each year.* **3.** to give up (something); surrender: *The defeated troops yielded the town to the enemy.* **4.** to give or grant: *The driver of the car yielded the right of way to the pedestrians.* —*v.i.* **1.** to give up; surrender; submit: *Our troops refused to yield to the enemy forces.* **2.** to give in; consent: *We yielded to their argument.* **3.** to give way, as to force or pressure: *The lock was old and yielded when we pushed the door.* **4.** to give place, as through inferiority: *to yield to no one in patriotism.* —*n.* **1.** an amount yielded; product: *The yield of wheat was large this year.* **2.** a return, as from an investment.

yield·ing (yēl′ding) *adj.* tending to yield; submissive; obedient: *The child has a yielding nature.*

yip (yip) *n.* a yelp, especially of a dog. —*v.i.,* **yipped, yip·ping.** to give a short, sharp cry; yelp.

yo·del (yō′dəl) *v.i.* to sing with frequent alternating changes between the natural voice and a falsetto voice. —*v.t.* to sing (something) with frequent alternating changes between the natural voice and a falsetto voice. —*n.* the act or sound of yodeling. —**yo′del·er,** *n.*

yo·ga (yō′gə) *also,* **Yo·ga.** *n.* a system of mental and physical discipline practiced by Hindus in order to become free of the senses and the external world and reach ultimate reality. It is also practiced by non-Hindus to improve mental and physical health and concentration.

yo·ghurt (yō′gərt) another spelling of **yogurt.**

yo·gi (yō′gē) *n.* a person who practices or is a follower of yoga.

yo·gurt (yō′gərt) *also,* **yo·ghurt.** *n.* a semisolid food made from milk to which bacterial culture has been added, and often flavored or sweetened.

yoke (yōk) *n., pl.* (*defs. 1, 3–6*) **yokes** or (*def. 2*) **yoke. 1.** a wooden frame consisting of a long, curved bar fitted with two hoops by which two work animals are joined together. **2.** a pair of animals, especially oxen, joined together by a yoke. **3.** any of various similar devices, such as a frame carried on the shoulders and designed to carry a pail or other burden at either end. **4.** a force or influence that oppresses or enslaves; burden: *people under the yoke of tyranny.* **5.** something that joins or unites; bond; tie: *the yoke of friendship.* **6.** the top section of a garment, usually consisting of a flat, smooth-fitting piece of fabric, as around the neck and shoulders of a blouse. —*v.t.,* **yoked, yok·ing. 1.** to put a yoke on. **2.** to harness or attach (a work animal) to a yoke: *to yoke oxen for plowing.* **3.** to join or unite with a yoke. **4.** to join closely: *to be yoked in marriage.*

yoke·fel·low (yōk′fel′ō) *n.* a mate or partner.

yo·kel (yō′kəl) *n.* a country fellow. ▲ usually used to show contempt.

yolk (yōk) *n.* **1.** the yellow substance of an egg, as distinguished from the albumen, or white part. **2.** the greasy material in unprocessed sheep's wool.

Yom Kip·pur (yom kip′ər, yōm′kē pùr′) in Judaism, a day of fasting and atonement for sins, observed on the tenth day of the first month of the Jewish calendar. Also, **Day of Atonement.**

yon (yon) *adj., adv. Archaic.* yonder.

yond (yond) *adj., adv. Archaic.* yonder.

yon·der (yon′dər) *adv.* in that place; over there. —*adj.* being at a distance, but within sight: *The cattle are in yonder field.*

yore (yôr) *adv.* **of yore.** long ago; in the past: *in days of yore.*

York·ist (yôr′kist) *adj.* of or relating to the English house of York. —*n.* a member or supporter of the house of York.

York·shire pudding (yôrk′shər) a batter often baked with roasting meat to catch the drippings, frequently served with roast beef.

Yorkshire terrier, a small dog having a coat of long, straight, silky hair that is dark steel-blue and tan.

you (ū; *unstressed* yə) *pron.* **1.** the person or persons spoken or written to: *Do you want to go? I'll meet you at six o'clock.* **2.** a person; one; anyone: *You have to be careful when handling dynamite.* ▲ In formal speaking or writing, *one* is preferred to *you* as an indefinite pronoun: *One can never be sure what the future will bring.*

you–all (yū ôl′, yôl) *pron. Informal.* you. ▲ used chiefly in the southern United States in referring to two or more persons.

you'd (ūd) *contr.* **1.** you had. **2.** you would.

you'll (ūl; *unstressed* yül) *contr.* **1.** you will. **2.** you shall.

young (yung) *adj.,* **young·er** (yung′gər), **young·est** (yung′gist). **1.** having lived or existed for a short time; in the early part of life or growth; not old: *A colt is a young horse.* **2.** having or showing the characteristics or look of a young person; fresh; vigorous: *a young body, to act young for one's age.* **3.** of, relating to, or belonging to the early part of life: *to remember fondly one's young years.* **4.** recently begun, formed, or made; in an early stage of progress or development: *a young nation.* **5.** not as old as another with the same name: *I have decided to follow in the footsteps of other family members by becoming a doctor.* **6.** having little experience, skill, or practice: *The new lawyer is too young to become a partner of the firm.* —*n.* **1.** young people as a group: *That kind of music is popular with the young.* **2.** young offspring, especially of animals: *Monkeys take special care of their young.* —**young′ness,** *n.*

•**with young.** pregnant.

young·ish (yung′ish) *adj.* somewhat young.

young·ling (yung′ling) *n.* a young person, animal, or plant.

young·ster (yung′stər) *n.* a young person; child or youth.

your (yur, yôr; *unstressed* yər) *adj.* of, belonging, or relating to you: *your sister, your house, your idea.* ▲ **Your** is used in some formal titles: *Your Majesty, Your Excellency, Your Honor.* It is also used informally to refer to people in general: *your typical teacher. Your greatest problem in this city is air pollution.*

you're (yur, yôr; *unstressed* yər) *contr.* you are.

yours (yürz, yôrz) *pron.* **1.** belonging or relating to you: *This book is yours.* ▲ often used with *of: I am a great admirer of yours.* **2.** the thing or things belonging or relating to you: *My final grade was good, but yours was even better.*

your·self (yür self′, yôr self′, yər self′) *pron., pl.* **your·selves** (yür selvz′, yôr selvz′, yər selvz′). **1.** the form of **you** used to give emphasis: *You yourself know that I deserve the credit.* **2.** the form of **you** used to show that the subject is the same as the direct object, indirect object, or object of a preposition: *Don't burn yourself. Tell yourself everything will turn out well. Can you do this by yourself?* **3.** your usual or normal self: *You have not been yourself these past few weeks.*

youth (ūth) *n., pl.* **youths** (ūths, ū*th*z). **1.** the condition or quality of being young: *Exercise is a good way to keep one's youth.* **2.** the time of life between childhood and adulthood. **3.** an early period in the development or existence of anything: *George Washington was president during the youth of the nation.* **4.** young people as a

group: *Our hope lies in youth.* ▲ used with a plural verb. **5.** a young person, especially a young man.

youth·ful (ūth′fəl) *adj.* **1.** still young in years; having youth: *a youthful person.* **2.** characteristic of youth: *youthful energy.* **3.** belonging to or suitable for young people: *a youthful outfit.* —**youth′ful·ly,** *adv.* —**youth′ful·ness,** *n.*

you've (ūv; *unstressed* yüv) *contr.* you have.

yowl (youl) *n.* a long, mournful cry, such as that of a dog; howl; wail. —*v.i.* to make such a cry.

yo-yo (yō′yō) *n., pl.* **yo-yos.** a toy consisting of two disks connected at their center by a pin around which a string is wound. The yo-yo is lowered and raised by unwinding and rewinding it on the string.

yr. **1.** year; years. **2.** your.

yrs. **1.** years. **2.** yours.

YT, postal abbreviation for the Yukon Territory.

Y.T., Yukon Territory.

yt·ter·bi·um (i tûr′bē əm) *n.* a soft, silvery metallic element of the rare-earth group. It is used in alloys and lasers. Symbol: **Yb** [From the letters *ytterb-* in the name *Ytterby,* the Swedish town where this element was discovered.]

yt·tri·um (it′rē əm) *n.* a dark gray metallic element used in color television tubes. Symbol: **Y** [From the letters *yttr-* in the name *Ytterby,* the Swedish town where this element was discovered.]

yu·an (ū än′) *n., pl.* **yu·an.** the monetary unit of China.

yuc·ca (yuk′ə) *n.* any of a group of plants of the warmer regions of North America, having a woody stem and spearlike leaves and bearing clusters of white or violet, bell-shaped, drooping flowers.

yucca

Yu·go·slav (ū′gō släv′) *also,* **Ju·go·slav.** *n.* a person who was born in or is a citizen of Yugoslavia. —*adj.* of or relating to Yugoslavia or its people.

Yule (ūl) *n.* **1.** another word for **Christmas. 2.** the season of Christmas; Christmastide.

yule log, a large log burned at Christmas.

Yule·tide (ūl′tīd′) *n.* the season of Christmas; Christmastide.

yup·pie (yup′ē) *also,* **yup·py.** *n.* a member of the group of young, college-educated people holding well-paid jobs, often in the professions, commonly believed to be ambitious and to have expensive, stylish tastes. [Short for *y*(oung) *u*(rban) *p*(rofessional).]

at; āpe; fär; câre; end; mē; it; īce; pîerce; hot; ōld; sông, fôrk; oil; out; up; ūse; rüle; pull; tûrn; chin; sing; shop; thin; *th*is; hw in white; zh in treasure. The symbol ə stands for the unstressed vowel sound heard in about, taken, pencil, lemon, and circus.

Y

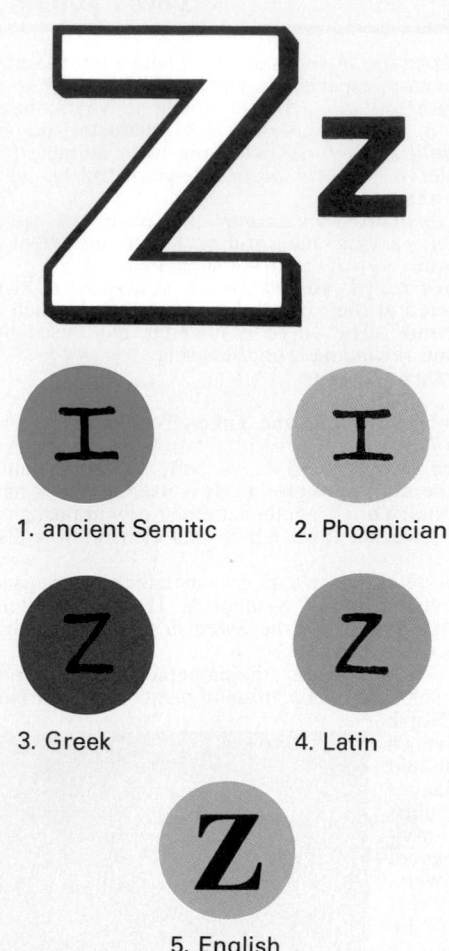

1. ancient Semitic   2. Phoenician

3. Greek   4. Latin

5. English

Z is the twenty-sixth and last letter of the English alphabet. The earliest form of the letter **Z** was the letter *zayin*, probably meaning "weapon" or "balance" in the ancient Semitic (1) and Phoenician (2) alphabets. When the Greeks adopted *zayin*, they altered its shape and called it *zeta* (3). *Zed*, which is what **Z** is called in many English-speaking countries, comes from the name of this Greek letter. The Romans (4) borrowed *zeta* to represent this letter as it appeared in Greek words which they borrowed. The Romans made only the slightest changes in its shape, writing it very much as we write the capital letter **Z** today (5).

z, Z (zē) *n., pl.* **z's, Z's. 1.** the twenty-sixth and last letter of the English alphabet. **2.** something having the shape of this letter.

z., Z., zone.

za·ny (zā′nē) *adj.,* **za·ni·er, za·ni·est.** funny in an odd or ridiculous way. —*n., pl.* **za·nies. 1.** a fool; simpleton. **2.** a clown; buffoon.

zeal (zēl) *n.* an intense desire or devotion; earnest enthusiasm: *to do a job with zeal, to have the zeal of a reformer.*

zeal·ot (zel′ət) *n.* a person who shows too much zeal.

zeal·ous (zel′əs) *adj.* filled with or characterized by zeal: *a zealous worker, a zealous patriot.* —**zeal′ous·ly,** *adv.* —**zeal′ous·ness,** *n.*

zebras

ze·bra (zē′brə) *n., pl.* **ze·bras** or **ze·bra.** any of several wild animals of eastern and southern Africa, related to the horse, having a light-colored coat with black stripes, a short, stiff mane, and a long tail ending in a tuft of hair.

ze·bu (zē′bū) *n.* a domesticated animal of Asia and Africa, related to the ox, having a large hump over the shoulders.

Zech·a·ri·ah (zek′ə rī′ə) *n.* a book of the Old Testament believed to have been written by the Hebrew prophet Zechariah.

zed (zed) *n. British.* the letter z.

Zen (zen) *n.* **1.** a Buddhist sect that differs from other Buddhist sects by stressing enlightenment through intuition and contemplation rather than through the scriptures. **2.** the beliefs of this sect.

ze·nith (zē′nith) *n.* **1.** the point in the heavens directly above the place where a person stands. **2.** the highest or greatest point: *This performance was the zenith of the musician's career.*

Zeph·a·ni·ah (zef′ə nī′ə) *n.* a book of the Old Testament believed to have been written by the Hebrew prophet Zephaniah.

zeph·yr (zef′ər) *n.* **1.** the west wind. **2.** any soft, gentle wind. **3.** any of various lightweight, soft yarns or fabrics.

zep·pe·lin (zep′ə lin) *also,* **Zep·pe·lin.** *n.* a large dirigible having a rigid, cigar-shaped body. [From the German army officer Count Ferdinand von *Zeppelin* (1838–1917), who invented this craft.]

ze·ro (zîr′ō) *n., pl.* **ze·ros** or **ze·roes. 1.** the number that leaves any number unchanged when it is added to it; number of members in the empty set. **2.** the symbol representing this number; 0. **3.** a point on a scale, such as a thermometer, from which something is measured: *The Celsius temperature scale places the freezing point at zero.* **4.** a temperature corresponding to zero on the scale of a thermometer: *It's ten degrees below zero outside and beginning to snow.* **5.** the total absence of quantity; nothing: *The business lost no money, but its profit was* *zero.* **6.** the lowest point: *The politician's popularity dropped to zero after the scandal.* —*adj.* **1.** of, relating to, being, or at zero: *Zero temperature, zero degrees.* **2.** none at all: *Zero effort gives zero results.* —*v.t.,* **ze·roed, ze·ro·ing.** to adjust (an instrument) to a zero point. [From the Italian word *zero,* going back to the Arabic word *ṣifr* meaning "zero in arithmetic, empty."] **·to zero in on. a.** to bring a gun or the like into a desired position for aiming and concentrating fire at (something): *The bomber zeroed in on the target.* **b.** to direct attention toward: *to zero in on a problem.*

zero gravity, the condition of a body not subject to any gravitational attraction; weightlessness.

zero hour 1. a set or appointed time, as for the beginning of a military operation. **2.** a time set for the beginning of any important action; critical turning point.

zero population growth, a condition in which the size of a population remains constant because the birth rate is equal to the death rate.

zest (zest) *n.* **1.** keen enjoyment or excitement; relish: *a zest for life.* **2.** a pleasant or exciting quality, flavor, or the like: *This spice will add zest to the stew.* [From the French word *zeste* meaning "an orange peel or a lemon peel," originally referring to a piece of orange or lemon peel used as a flavoring.]

zest·ful (zest'fəl) *adj.* characterized by zest: *a zestful outlook on life.* —**zest'ful·ly,** *adv.* —**zest'ful·ness,** *n.*

ze·ta (zā'tə, zē'tə) *n.* the sixth letter of the Greek alphabet (Z, ζ).

Zeus (züs) *n. Greek Mythology.* the supreme god, ruler of the heavens and the earth, whose chief weapon was the thunderbolt. In Roman mythology he was called Jupiter.

zig·gu·rat (zig'ù rat') *n.* a temple of the type built by ancient Assyrians and Babylonians, consisting of a tower in the form of a stepped pyramid with multiple stories. [From the Assyrian word *zigguratu* meaning "height" or "pinnacle."]

zig·zag (zig'zag') *adj.* having or moving with a series of short, sharp turns or angles in alternating directions: *the zigzag pattern of the saw's teeth.* —*adv.* in a zigzag manner. —*n.* **1.** a zigzag line, course, or pattern. **2.** one of the short runs or angles of a zigzag pattern. —*v.i.,* **zig·zagged, zig·zag·ging.** to form or move in a zigzag: *The road zigzagged through the mountains.*

zil·lion (zil'yən) *n. Informal.* a very large, indefinite number: *I have a zillion things to do before the party.*

zinc (zingk) *n.* a blue-white metallic element, used in alloys and dry-cell batteries and in galvanizing iron. Symbol: **Zn** [From the German word *Zink* meaning this metal.]

zinc oxide, a white, powdery compound, used especially in paints and cosmetics and as an antiseptic.

zing (zing) *n.* **1.** a high-pitched humming or buzzing sound. **2.** *Informal.* vitality; zest; vigor. —*v.i.* to make a high-pitched humming or buzzing sound, especially in moving rapidly: *An arrow zinged through the air.*

zin·ni·a (zin'ē ə) *n.* **1.** the showy flower of any of a small group of plants, growing in all colors except blue and green. **2.** a plant bearing this flower, widely cultivated as a garden plant. [From the German botanist Johann Gottfried *Zinn* (1727–1759).]

Zi·on (zī'ən) also, **Si·on.** *n.* **1.** a hill in Jerusalem on which the royal palace of David and the Temple were built. **2.** the Jewish people or nation; Israel. **3.** the kingdom of heaven. **4.** any place or institution believed to be under God's special protection, especially the Christian church.

Zi·on·ism (zī'ə niz'əm) *n.* a movement to establish a national homeland for Jews in Palestine, resulting in the creation of the state of Israel in 1948 and continuing after that time to support the emigration of Jews and their settlement in Israel.

Zi·on·ist (zī'ə nist) *n.* a person who supports Zionism. —*adj.* of or relating to Zionism or Zionists.

zip (zip) *n.* **1.** a sudden, sharp, hissing sound, as of a flying bullet. **2.** *Informal.* energy; vitality; vim. **3.** *Informal.* see **zip code.** —*v.i.,* **zipped, zip·ping. 1.** to make or move with a sudden, sharp, hissing sound. **2.** *Informal.* to move or act with energy or speed: *to zip around a corner.* —*v.t.* to fasten or close with a zipper.

zip code also, **ZIP Code, Zip Code.** a number having five or nine digits, written directly after the address on a letter, package, or other piece of mail, quickly identifying the U.S. postal delivery area to which it is to be sent. [Short for *Z*(one) *I*(mprovement) *P*(rogram).]

zip·lock bag (zip'lok') a plastic bag that can be sealed by means of interlocking strips along the open edges, used typically for storing food.

zip–out (zip'out') *adj.* able to be removed by means of a zipper: *a coat with a zip-out lining.*

zip·per (zip'ər) *n.* a fastening consisting of two rows of interlocking teeth that may be joined or separated by a sliding device, used especially on clothing, boots, and luggage.

zip·py (zip'ē) *adj.,* **zip·pi·er, zip·pi·est.** *Informal.* full of energy; lively: *a zippy little tune.*

zir·con (zûr'kon) *n.* a crystalline mineral used in nuclear reactors and as a semiprecious gem. [From the German word *zircon,* from the French word *jargon* meaning this mineral, going back to the Persian word *zargūn* "golden." Some zircon formations are yellowish.]

zir·co·ni·um (zər kō'nē əm) *n.* a gray, scaly or powdery metallic element used in explosives and nuclear reactors and in the bonding of metals to ceramics. Symbol: **Zr** [From *zircon.* Zircon contains this element.]

zith·er (zith'ər, zith'ər) *n.* a musical instrument consisting of a shallow, wooden sound box over which are stretched thirty to forty-five strings, sounded by plucking the strings with a plectrum and the fingers.

zi·ti (zē'tē) *n.* pasta in the form of short, hollow tubes, similar to but larger than macaroni. [From the Italian word *ziti* meaning "boys," used as the name of this pasta.]

Zn, the symbol for zinc.

zo·di·ac (zō'dē ak') *n.* **1.** an imaginary belt in the heavens extending approximately eight degrees on each side of the path that the sun appears to follow and including the paths of the moon and all the planets except Pluto. The zodiac is divided into twelve parts, called signs, with each part named after a constellation. **2.** a figure or diagram representing the zodiac and its signs and symbols, used in astrology. [From the Old French word *zodiaque* meaning "imaginary belt in the heavens containing twelve constellations," from the Latin word *zodiacus* "zodiac," from the Greek phrase *zōidakos (kyklos)* meaning "(circle) of animal figures," from the word *zōion* "animal, figure, living being," from the word *zōē* "life." The zodiac was so named because

zither

at; āpe; fär; câre; end; mē; it; īce; pîerce; hot; ōld; sông, fôrk; oil; out; up; ūse; rüle; pùll; tûrn; chin; sing; shop; thin; this; hw in white; zh in treasure. The symbol ə stands for the unstressed vowel sound heard in about, taken, pencil, lemon, and circus.

Z

1099

the ancient Greeks imagined that they saw animals and other figures in its constellations.]

zo·di·a·cal (zō dī′ə kəl) *adj.* of, relating to, or in the zodiac: *a zodiacal sign.*

zom·bie (zom′bē) *n., pl.* **zom·bies. 1.** in voodoo belief, a dead person who has been brought back to life and is completely subject to the will of a sorcerer. **2.** *Slang.* a person who behaves in a sluggish or mechanical manner.

zon·al (zō′nəl) *adj.* of, relating to, or marked by a zone or zones.

zone (zōn) *n.* **1.** any of the five regions of the earth's surface divided according to the climate found there, comprising two Frigid Zones, two Temperate Zones, and the Torrid Zone. **2.** any region, area, or section that is distinguished from surrounding or adjoining areas by some quality, condition, or use: *a flood zone.* **3.** a section of a city regulated by certain restrictions, especially regarding building: *There were no factories in the residential zone.* **4.** in the U.S. postal system, one of a set of circular areas going outward from a mailing point, by which parcel post charges are determined. **5.** a U.S. postal delivery service area identified by a Zip Code, usually having a central post office. —*v.t.,* **zoned, zon·ing.** to divide into zones: *to zone a city into business and residential areas.*

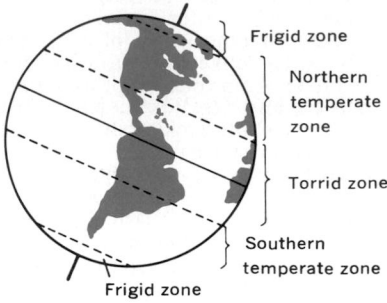

Frigid zone
Northern temperate zone
Torrid zone
Southern temperate zone
Frigid zone

zones *(def. 1)*

zon·ing (zō′ning) *n.* a system of districting in cities that regulates the construction and use of buildings in certain areas.

zoo (zü) *n., pl.* **zoos.** a park, garden, or similar place where animals are kept for exhibition.

zo·o·log·i·cal (zō′ə loj′i kəl) *adj.* **1.** of or relating to zoology. **2.** of or relating to animals: *a zoological study of the Arctic.* —**zo′o·log′i·cal·ly,** *adv.*

zoological garden, see **zoo.**

zo·ol·o·gist (zō ol′ə jist) *n.* an expert in zoology.

zo·ol·o·gy (zō ol′ə jē) *n.* **1.** the science that deals with the origin, development, structure, functioning, and classification of all forms of animal life. **2.** the animal life found in a particular region: *the zoology of the desert.*

zoom (züm) *v.i.* **1.** to move or climb suddenly and swiftly, as in an airplane. **2.** to make or move with a loud, low-pitched humming sound: *The train zoomed by us.* —*v.t.* to cause (an airplane) to zoom. —*n.* the act or sound of zooming.

zoom lens, a single lens, as on a television, motion-picture, or still camera, whose focal length can be varied, allowing distant shots or close-ups.

Zo·ro·as·tri·an (zôr′ō as′trē ən) *adj.* of or relating to Zoroaster or the religion he founded. —*n.* a person who believes in or practices Zoroastrianism.

Zo·ro·as·tri·an·ism (zôr′ō as′trē ə niz′əm) *n.* the religious system founded by Zoroaster, which stresses an ethical way of life and the final triumph of good over evil.

zounds (zoundz) *interj. Archaic.* an oath used to express surprise or anger.

Zr, the symbol for zirconium.

zuc·chi·ni (zü kē′nē) *n., pl.* **zuc·chi·ni** or **zuc·chi·nis.** a green summer squash shaped like a cucumber, eaten as a vegetable.

Zu·lu (zü′lü) *n., pl.* **Zu·lu** or **Zu·lus. 1.** a member of a group of Bantu people in southeastern Africa. **2.** the language of this people. —*adj.* of or relating to the Zulu, their language, or their culture.

Zu·ñi (zü′nē, zün′yē) *n., pl.* **Zu·ñi** or **Zu·ñis. 1.** a member of a tribe of North American Indians now living in western New Mexico who dwell in pueblos. **2.** the language of this tribe.

zwie·back (swī′bäk′, zwī′bäk′) *n.* a kind of bread that is often sweetened and flavored, as with cinnamon, baked, and then sliced and toasted until it is crisp and dry.

zy·gote (zī′gōt) *n.* an egg cell that has been fertilized by sperm, before the start of the development of the embryo.

Biographical Names

This section lists the names of people and dynasties that are important in history, contemporary life, or the biblical tradition. The main biographical entry gives the most widely used form and spelling of a person's name. People with the same family name are listed within a single entry. Names or parts of names that are not usually used appear in parentheses. Names such as nicknames, pseudonyms, and titles are shown in italics within the main entry. Variant spellings of names are shown in boldface in the main entry and are also listed separately as cross-references to the main entry.

In a main entry, the name of the person is followed by the pronunciation of the person's family name, the birth and death dates, the nationality, and a brief description. Dates in parentheses are the years during which a person reigned or held office.

Aa·ron (âr′ən) in the Old Testament, elder brother of Moses and the first high priest of the Hebrews.

A·bel (ā′bəl) in the Old Testament, second son of Adam and Eve, killed by his older brother Cain.

A·bra·ham (ā′brə ham′, ā′brə həm) patriarch and progenitor of the Hebrews.

Ab·sa·lom (ab′sə ləm) in the Old Testament, the favorite son of David who rebelled against his father.

A·dam (ad′əm) in the Old Testament, the first man and the husband of Eve.

Ad·ams (ad′əmz) **1. John.** 1735–1826, second president of the United States (1797–1801). **2. John Quincy.** 1767–1848, sixth president of the United States (1825–1829); son of John Adams. **3. Samuel.** 1722–1803, patriot during the American Revolution.

A·de·nau·er, Konrad (ad′ə nou′er) 1876–1967, West German chancellor (1949–1963).

Aes·chy·lus (es′kə ləs) 525–456 B.C., Greek dramatist.

Ae·sop (ē′səp, ē′sop) 620?–560 B.C., Greek writer of fables.

Ag·as·siz, Louis (ag′ə sē) 1807–1873, U.S. zoologist and geologist, born in Switzerland.

A·hab (ā′hab) d. 853? B.C., king of Israel (874?–853? B.C.).

Ai·ley, Alvin (ā′lē) 1931– , U.S. choreographer.

Akh·e·na·ton (ä′kə nä′tən) see **Ikhnaton.**

A·ki·hi·to (ä′kē hē′tō) 1933– , emperor of Japan (1989–).

Al·bert, Prince (al′bərt) 1819–1861, consort of Queen Victoria of Great Britain.

Al·cott, Louisa May (ôl′kət, ôl′kot) 1832–1888, U.S. author.

Al·den, John (ôl′dən) 1599?–1687, Puritan settler in Plymouth Colony.

Al·drin, Edwin Eugene, Jr. (ôl′drin) 1930– , U.S. astronaut.

Al·ex·an·der III (al′ig zan′dər) 1845–1894, czar of Russia (1881–1894).

Al·ex·an·der VI (al′ig zan′dər) 1431–1503, pope (1492–1503).

Al·ex·an·der Nev·sky (al′ig zan′dər nev′skē, nef′skē) 1220–1263, Russian hero.

Al·ex·an·der the Great (al′ig zan′dər) 356–323 B.C., king of Macedonia (336–323 B.C.), general of Greece, and conqueror of Persia.

Al·len, Ethan (al′ən) 1738–1789, colonial soldier during the American Revolution.

Al·len·de Gos·sens, Salvador (ä yen′dā gō′sens) 1908–1973, president of Chile (1970–1973).

A·men·ho·tep IV (ä′mən hō′tep) see **Ikhnaton.**

A·mos (ā′məs) eighth century B.C., Hebrew prophet.

A·mund·sen, Roald (ä′mən sən) 1872–1928, Norwegian explorer.

An·der·sen, Hans Christian (an′dər sən) 1805–1875, Danish author of fairy tales.

An·der·son (an′dər sən) **1. Marian.** 1902– , U.S. contralto. **2. Sherwood.** 1876–1941, U.S. writer.

An·drew (an′drü) in the New Testament, one of the twelve Apostles of Jesus, and brother of Peter.

An·dro·pov, Yuri Vladimirovich (an drō′pəf) 1914–1984, Soviet politician, president of U.S.S.R. (1982–1984), and first secretary of Communist Party (1982–1984).

An·gel·i·co, Fra (an jel′i kō′) 1387–1455, Italian painter and Dominican monk; born *Guido di Pietro.*

An·ge·vin (an′jə vin) see **Plantagenet.**

Anne (an) 1665–1714, queen of Great Britain (1702–1714).

An·tho·ny, Susan B. (an′thə nē) 1820–1906, U.S. social reformer and leader of the movement for women's suffrage.

An·to·ny, Marc or **Mark** (an′tə nē) see **Marc Antony.**

Ap·ple·seed, Johnny (ap′əl sēd′) 1774?–1845, U.S. frontiersman noted for sowing apple seeds; born *John Chapman.*

A·qui·nas, Saint Thomas (ə kwī′nəs) 1225?–1274, Italian philosopher and theologian.

A·qui·no, Corazon Cojuangco (ä kē′nō) 1933– , president of the Republic of the Philippines (1986–).

Ar·a·fat, Yasir (ar′ə fat′) 1929– , Palestinian leader.

Arc, Jeanne d' (ärk) see **Joan of Arc.**

Ar·chi·me·des (är′kə mē′dēz) 287?–212 B.C., Greek mathematician, physicist, and inventor.

Ar·is·tot·le (ar′ə stot′əl) 384–322 B.C., Greek philosopher.

Ark·wright, Sir Richard (ärk′rīt′) 1732–1792, English inventor and industrialist.

Arm·strong (ärm′strông′) **1. Louis.** 1900–1971, U.S. jazz musician; nicknamed *Satchmo.* **2. Neil Alden.** 1930– , U.S. astronaut, the first person to set foot on the moon.

Ar·nold (är′nəld) **1. Benedict.** 1741–1801, colonial general in the American Revolution who turned traitor. **2. Matthew.** 1822–1888, English poet and essayist.

Ash·er (ash′ər) **1.** in the Old Testament, a son of Jacob. **2.** one of the twelve tribes of Israel descended from him.

A·so·ka or **A·sho·ka** (ə sō′kə; ə shō′kə) d. 233? B.C., emperor of India (268?–233? B.C.).

---

at; āpe; fär; câre; end; mē; it; īce; pîerce; hot; ōld; sông, fôrk; oil; out; up; ūse; rüle; pull; tûrn; chin; sing; shop; thin; **th**is; hw in white; zh in treasure. The symbol ə stands for the unstressed vowel sound heard in about, taken, pencil, lemon, and circus.

A·ta·huall·pa or **A·ta·hual·pa** (ä'tə wäl'pə) king of the Incas (1502?–1533).

At·ti·la (at'ə lə, ə til'ə) A.D. 406?–453, king of the Huns.

Au·du·bon, John James (ô'də bon') 1785–1851, American ornithologist and artist.

Au·gus·tine, Saint (ô'gə stēn', ô gus'tin) A.D. 354–430, bishop of Hippo (A.D. 396–430) and a Father of the Church.

Au·gus·tus (ô gus'təs) 63 B.C.–A.D. 14, first emperor of Rome (27 B.C.–A.D. 14); full name *Gaius Julius Caesar Octavianus*. Also, **Octavian**.

Au·re·li·us (ô rē'lē əs, ô rēl'yəs) see **Marcus Aurelius Antoninus**.

Aus·ten, Jane (ôs'tən) 1775–1817, English novelist.

Bach, Johann Sebastian (bäk) 1685–1750, German composer and organist.

Ba·con, Francis (bā'kən) 1561–1626, English essayist, statesman, and philosopher.

Bal·an·chine, George (bal'ən chēn', bal'ən chēn') 1904–1983, Russian-American choreographer.

Bal·bo·a, Vasco Núñez de (bal bō'ə) 1475?–1517, Spanish explorer.

Bald·win, James (Arthur) (bôld'win) 1924–1987, U.S. writer.

Bal·four, Arthur James (bal'fûr) 1848–1930, British prime minister (1902–1905).

Ban·ne·ker, Benjamin (ban'i kər) 1731–1806, U.S. scientist, writer, and a surveyor of Washington, D.C.

Ba·rab·bas (bə rab'əs) in the New Testament, the condemned thief who was released by Pontius Pilot to satisfy the demand of the crowd that he and not Jesus should be spared from crucifixion.

Bar·num, P(hineas) T(aylor) (bär'nəm) 1810–1891, U.S. showman.

Bar·thol·di, Frédéric Auguste (bär thol'dē) 1834–1904, French sculptor.

Bar·thol·o·mew (bär thol'ə mū') in the New Testament, one of the twelve Apostles of Jesus.

Bar·ton, Clara (bär'tən) 1821–1912, U.S. humanitarian, founder of the American Red Cross.

Ba·sie, Count (bā'sē) 1904–1984, U.S. jazz pianist and conductor; real name *William Basie*.

Bau·de·laire, Charles (bō'də lâr') 1821–1867, French poet and critic.

Bea·cons·field, earl of (bē'kənz fēld') see **Disraeli, Benjamin**.

Beau·re·gard, Pierre Gustave Toutant (bō'ri gärd') 1818–1893, Confederate general in the U.S. Civil War.

Beau·voir, Simone de (bō vwär') 1908–1986, French author.

Beck·ett, Samuel (bek'it) 1906– , Irish author.

Bee·cher, Henry Ward (bē'chər) 1813–1887, U.S. clergyman, lecturer, and author.

Bee·tho·ven, Ludwig van (bā'tō vən) 1770–1827, German composer.

Be·gin, Menachem (bā'gin) 1913– , Israeli prime minister (1977–1983).

Bell, Alexander Graham (bel) 1847–1922, U.S. inventor of the telephone, born in Scotland.

Be·nét, Stephen Vincent (bə nā') 1898–1943, U.S. author.

Ben–Gu·ri·on, David (ben gùr'ē ən) 1886–1973, Israeli prime minister (1949–1953; 1955–1963); born *David Grün*.

Ben·ja·min (ben'jə min) **1.** in the Old Testament, the youngest son of Jacob and Rachel. **2.** one of the twelve tribes of Israel descended from him.

Benz, Karl (benz) 1844–1929, German engineer.

Bern·stein, Leonard (bûrn'stīn') 1918– , U.S. conductor and composer.

Bes·se·mer, Sir Henry (bes'ə mər) 1813–1898, English inventor and industrialist.

Bhut·to, Benazir (bü'tō) 1953– , prime minister of Pakistan (1988–).

Bish·op, Elizabeth (bish'əp) 1911–1979, U.S. poet.

Bis·marck, Otto von (biz'märk') 1815–1898, German statesman.

Blake, William (blāk) 1757–1827, English poet, artist, and philosopher.

Bo·as, Franz (bō'az) 1858–1942, U.S. anthropologist.

Boc·cac·ci·o, Giovanni (bō kä'chē ō') 1313–1375, Italian writer and humanist.

Bohr, Niels (bôr) 1885–1962, Danish physicist.

Bol·eyn, Anne (bùl'in, bù lin') 1507?–1536, queen of England; second wife of Henry VIII; mother of Elizabeth I.

Bo·lí·var, Simón (bol'ə vər, bō lē'vär) 1783–1830, Venezuelan statesman, soldier, and revolutionary leader.

Bo·na·parte (bō'nə pärt') Corsican family including the brothers **1.** Jérôme. 1784–1860, king of Westphalia (1807–1813). **2.** Joseph. 1768–1844, king of Naples (1806–1808), king of Spain (1808–1813). **3.** Louis. 1778–1846, king of Holland (1806–1810); father of Napoleon III. **4.** Lucien. 1775–1840, politician. **5.** Napoleon. see **Napoleon I**.

Boole, George (bül) 1815–1864, English mathematician.

Boone, Daniel (bün) 1734–1820, American frontiersman.

Booth (büth) **1.** Edwin Thomas. 1833–1893, U.S. actor and theatrical producer. **2.** John Wilkes. 1838–1865, U.S. actor and assassin of Abraham Lincoln. **3.** William. 1829–1912, English evangelist, founder of the Salvation Army.

Bor·ges, Jorge Luis (bôr'hes) 1899–1986, Argentinian writer.

Bosch, Hieronymus (bosh) 1450?–1516, Flemish painter.

Bos·well, James (boz'wel') 1740–1795, Scottish author and lawyer; biographer of Samuel Johnson.

Bo·tha, P(ieter) W(illem) (bō'tə) 1916– , South African prime minister (1978–).

Bou·lan·ger, Nadia (bü'län jä', bü'län zhä') 1887–1979, French conductor, musician, and teacher.

Bourke–White, Margaret (bûrk'hwīt', bûrk'wīt') 1904–1971, U.S. photojournalist.

Boyle, Robert (boil) 1627–1691, British physicist and chemist.

Brad·dock, Edward (brad'ək) 1695–1755, British general in the French and Indian War.

Brad·ford, William (brad'fərd) 1590?–1657, Pilgrim leader and a governor of Plymouth Colony.

Brad·street, Anne Dudley (brad'strēt') 1612?–1672, American poet.

Brahe, Tycho (brä, brä'hē) 1546–1601, Danish astronomer.

Brahms, Johannes (brämz) 1833–1897, German composer.

Braille, Louis (brāl) 1809–1852, French teacher, inventor of braille.

Bran·deis, Louis Dembitz (bran'dīs) 1856–1941, U.S. lawyer; associate justice of the U.S. Supreme Court.

Brant, Joseph (brant) 1742–1807, Mohawk chief. Also, **Thayendanegea**.

Braque, Georges (bräk) 1882–1963, French painter.

Breck·in·ridge, John Cabell (brek'ən rij') 1821–1875, U.S. politician, Confederate officer in the U.S. Civil War.

Brezh·nev, Leonid Ilyich (brezh'nef) 1906–1982, Soviet politician, general secretary of the Communist Party (1964–1982), president of the U.S.S.R. (1979–1982).

Broglie, Louis Victor de (broi) 1892–1987, French physicist.

Bron·të (bron'tē, bron'tā) English family of novelists including the sisters **1.** Anne. 1820–1849. **2.** Charlotte. 1816–1855. **3.** Emily. 1818–1848.

Brown, John (broun) 1800–1859, U.S. abolitionist.

Brue·ghel, Pieter (broi'gəl, brü'gəl) 1525?–1569, Flemish painter.

Bru·tus, Marcus Junius (brü'təs) 85?–42 B.C., Roman scholar, soldier, politician, and assassin of Julius Caesar.

Bry·an, William Jennings (brī'ən) 1860–1925, U.S. politician.

Bry·ant, William Cullen (brī′ənt) 1794–1878, U.S. poet and editor.

Bu·chan·an, James (bū kan′ən) 1791–1868, fifteenth president of the United States (1857–1861).

Bud·dha (bud′ə, bü′də) 563?–483 B.C. founder of Buddhism. Also, **Siddhartha, Gautama** or **Gautama Buddha**, and **Gotama** or **Gotama Buddha**.

Buffalo Bill, see Cody, William Frederick.

Bunche, Ralph Johnson (bunch) 1904–1971, U.S. statesman, educator, and United Nations official.

Bun·yan, John (bun′yən) 1628–1686, English author and preacher.

Bur·bank, Luther (bûr′bangk′) 1849–1926, U.S. nurseryman and plant breeder.

Bur·ger, Earl Warren (bûr′gər) 1907– , U.S. Supreme Court chief justice (1969–1986).

Bur·goyne, John (bər goin′) 1722–1792, British general in the American Revolution.

Burns, Robert (bûrnz) 1759–1796, Scottish poet.

Burr, Aaron (bûr) 1756–1836, U.S. politician and lawyer.

Bush, George (Herbert Walker) (bush) 1924– , forty-first president of the United States (1989–).

Byrd, Richard Evelyn (bûrd) 1888–1957, U.S. explorer, pioneer aviator, and author.

By·ron, Lord (bī′rən) 1788–1824, English poet.

Cab·ot (kab′ət) **1. John.** 1450?–1498, English explorer. **2. Sebastian.** 1476?–1557, English explorer; son of John Cabot.

Ca·bri·ni, Saint Frances Xavier (kə brē′nē) 1850–1917, U.S. nun, first American citizen to be canonized.

Cae·sar, Gaius Julius (sē′zər) 100?–44 B.C., Roman statesman and general.

Cai·a·phas (kā′ə fəs, kī′ə fəs) in the New Testament, the Jewish high priest who presided at the council that condemned Jesus.

Cain (kān) in the Old Testament, the oldest son of Adam and Eve and murderer of his brother Abel.

Cal·der, Alexander (kôl′dər) 1898–1976, U.S. sculptor.

Cal·houn, John Caldwell (kal hün′) 1782–1850, U.S. political leader.

Cal·vin, John (kal′vin) 1509–1564, French theologian.

Ca·mus, Albert (ka mü′) 1913–1960, French philosopher, author, and critic.

Ca·pet, Hugh (kā′pit, kap′it) A.D. 938?–996, king of France (A.D. 987–996); founder of the Capetian dynasty.

Ca·pe·tian (kə pē′shən) dynasty that ruled France (A.D. 987–1328).

Ca·ra·vag·gio, Michelangelo Merisi da or **Amerigi da** (kar′ə vä′jō) 1573–1610, Italian painter.

Car·lyle, Thomas (kär līl′) 1795–1881, Scottish essayist, historian, and social philosopher.

Car·ne·gie, Andrew (kär′ni gē) 1835–1919, U.S. steel manufacturer and philanthropist.

Car·o·lin·gi·an (kar′ə lin′jē ən) Frankish dynasty that ruled in France (A.D. 751–987), Germany (A.D. 751–911), and Italy (A.D. 751–887).

Car·roll, Lewis (kar′əl) 1832–1898, English author and mathematician; pen name of *Charles L. Dodgson.*

Car·son (kär′sən) **1. Kit.** 1809–1868, U.S. frontiersman and scout; nickname of *Christopher Carson.* **2. Rachel.** 1907–1964, U.S. marine biologist and writer.

Car·ter, Jimmy (kär′tər) 1924– , thirty-ninth president of the United States (1977–1981); full name *James Earl Carter.*

Car·tier (kär′tyā, kär′tē ā′) **1. Jacques.** 1491–1557, French navigator. **2. Sir George Étienne.** 1814–1873, Canadian statesman.

Cart·wright, Edmund (kärt′rīt′) 1743–1823, English clergyman and inventor.

Ca·ru·so, Enrico (kə rü′sō) 1873–1921, Italian tenor.

Car·ver (kär′vər) **1. George Washington.** 1864–1943, U.S. botanist and educator. **2. John.** 1576–1621, first governor of Plymouth Colony (1620–1621).

Cas·satt, Mary (kə sat′) 1845–1926, U.S. painter.

Cas·tro, Fidel (kas′trō) 1926– , Cuban revolutionary leader, premier of Cuba (1959–).

Ca·ther, Willa Sibert (kath′ər) 1873–1947, U.S. novelist.

Cath·er·ine I (kath′ər in, kath′rin) 1684?–1727, empress of Russia (1725–1727); wife of Peter I.

Cath·er·ine II (kath′ər in, kath′rin) see **Catherine the Great.**

Cath·er·ine de′ Med·i·ci (kath′ər in də med′i chē′, kath′rin) 1519?–1589, Italian-born queen of France (1547–1559).

Cath·er·ine the Great (kath′ər in, kath′rin) 1729–1796, empress of Russia (1762–1796). Also, **Catherine II.**

Cav·en·dish, Henry (kav′ən dish′) 1731–1810, English physicist and chemist.

Cax·ton, William (kak′stən) 1422?–1491, English printer.

Cel·li·ni, Benvenuto (chə lē′nē) 1500–1571, Florentine sculptor, goldsmith, and author.

Cer·van·tes, Miguel de (sər van′tēz) 1547–1616, Spanish author.

Cé·zanne, Paul (sā zan′) 1839–1906, French painter.

Cham·ber·lain, (Arthur) Neville (chām′bər lən) 1869–1940, British prime minister (1937–1940).

Cham·plain, Samuel de (sham plān′) 1567–1635, French explorer.

Chap·lin, Charles Spenser (chap′lin) 1899–1977, British film actor and director; known as *Charlie Chaplin.*

Char·le·magne (shär′lə mān′) A.D. 742?–814, king of the Franks (A.D. 768–814); as Charles I, emperor of the Holy Roman Empire (A.D. 800–814). Also, **Charles the Great.**

Charles, Prince (chärlz) 1948– , prince of Wales; son of Elizabeth II.

Charles I (chärlz) 1600–1649, king of England, Scotland, and Ireland (1625–1649).

Charles II (chärlz) 1630–1685, king of England, Scotland, and Ireland (1660–1685).

Charles V (chärlz) 1500–1558, emperor of the Holy Roman Empire (1519–1558); as Charles I, king of Spain (1516–1556).

Charles Mar·tel (chärlz′ mär tel′) A.D. 688?–741, ruler of the Franks (A.D. 720–741); grandfather of Charlemagne.

Charles the Great (chärlz) see **Charlemagne.**

Chau·cer, Geoffrey (chô′sər) 1340?–1400, English poet.

Che·khov, Anton (chek′ôf) 1860–1904, Russian author.

Che·ops (kē′ops) see Khufu.

Cher·nen·ko, Konstantin Ustinovich (chər nyeng′kō) 1911–1985, Soviet leader, general secretary of the Communist Party (1984–1985).

Chiang Kai-shek (chang′ kī shek′) 1887–1975, Chinese general and political leader, president of the Republic of China (Taiwan) (1950–1975).

Ch′in (chin) see Qin.

Ch′ing (ching) see Qing.

Cho·pin, Frédéric François (shō′pan) 1810–1849, Polish pianist and composer.

Chou (jō) see Zhou.

Chou En-lai (jō′en lī′) 1898–1976, Chinese Communist political leader. Also, **Zhou Enlai.**

Chur·chill (chûr′chil) **1. John.** 1650–1722, English general and duke of Marlborough. **2. Sir Winston Leonard Spencer.** 1874–1965, English statesman and writer, prime minister of England (1940–1945; 1951–1955).

---

at; āpe; fär; câre; end; mē; it; īce; pîerce; hot; ōld; sông, fôrk; oil; out; up; ūse; rüle; pùll; tûrn; chin; sing; shop; thin; this; hw in white; zh in treasure. The symbol ə stands for the unstressed vowel sound heard in about, taken, pencil, lemon, and circus.

Cic·e·ro, Marcus Tullius (sis'ə rō') 106–43 B.C., Roman orator, writer, and statesman.

Cid, El (sid) A.D. 1040?–1099, Spanish soldier and national hero; born *Rodrigo Díaz de Bivar.*

Clark (klärk) **1. George Rogers.** 1752–1818, U.S. general and frontiersman. **2. Joe.** 1939– , Canadian prime minister (1979–1980); full name *Charles Joseph Clark.* **3. William.** 1770–1838, U.S. soldier and explorer with Meriwether Lewis; brother of George Rogers Clark.

Clay, Henry (klā) 1777–1852, U.S. statesman.

Clem·ens, Samuel Langhorne (klem'ənz) see **Twain, Mark.**

Cle·o·pa·tra (klē'ə pa'trə) 69–30 B.C., queen of Egypt (51–49 B.C. ; 48–30 B.C.).

Cleve·land, (Stephen) Grover (klēv'lənd) 1837–1908, twenty-second and twenty-fourth president of the United States (1885–1889; 1893–1897).

Clin·ton, De Witt (klin'tən) 1769–1828, U.S. statesman.

Co·chise (kō chēs') 1815?–1874, Apache chief.

Co·dy, William Frederick (kō'dē) 1816–1917, U.S. scout and showman; known as *Buffalo Bill.*

Co·han, George M(ichael) (kō'han) 1878–1942, U.S. actor, dramatist, and producer.

Co·lum·bus, Christopher (kə lum'bəs) 1451?–1506, Italian explorer.

Con·fu·cius (kən fū'shəs) 551?–479? B.C., Chinese philosopher, founder of Confucianism.

Con·stan·tine the Great (kon'stən tēn') A.D. 274?–337, Roman emperor (A.D. 324–337).

Cook, James (kŭk) 1728–1779, English navigator.

Coo·lidge, Calvin (kü'lij) 1872–1933, thirtieth president of the United States (1923–1929).

Coo·per, James Fenimore (kü'pər) 1789–1851, U.S. novelist and social critic.

Co·per·ni·cus, Nicolaus (kə pûr'ni kəs) 1473–1543, Polish astronomer.

Cop·land, Aaron (kōp'lənd) 1900– , U.S. composer.

Cop·ley, John Singleton (kop'lē) 1738–1815, American painter.

Corn·wal·lis, Charles (kôrn wäl'is) 1738–1805, British general in the American Revolution.

Co·ro·na·do, Francisco Vásquez de (kôr'ə nä'dō) 1500?–1544, Spanish explorer.

Cor·tés, Hernán (kôr tez') 1485–1547, Spanish conqueror of Mexico. Also, **Hernando Cortéz.**

Crane, Stephen (krān) 1871–1900, U.S. author.

Crazy Horse 1849?–1877, Sioux chief.

Crick, Francis Harry Compton (krik) 1916– , British biophysicist.

Crock·ett, David (krok'it) 1786–1836, U.S. frontiersman; known as *Davy Crockett.*

Crom·well, Oliver (krom'wel') 1599–1658, English statesman and soldier.

Cu·rie (kyù rē') **1. Marie Sklodowska.** 1867–1934, Polish-French chemist and physicist. **2. Pierre.** 1859–1906, French physicist and chemist; husband of Marie Curie.

Cus·ter, George Armstrong (kus'tər) 1839–1876, U.S. Army officer.

Cy·rus the Great (sī'rəs) d. 529 B.C., king of Persia (558?–529 B.C.), founder of the Persian empire.

da Ga·ma, Vasco (də gam'ə) 1469?–1524, Portuguese navigator.

Da·guerre, Louis–Jacques–Mandé (də gâr') 1789–1851, French set painter who invented the daguerreotype.

Dan (dan) **1.** in the Old Testament, a son of Jacob. **2.** one of the twelve tribes of Israel descended from him.

Dan·iel (dan'yəl) sixth century B.C., Hebrew prophet.

Dan·te (dän'tā) 1265–1321, Italian poet. Also, **Dante Alighieri.**

Dare, Virginia (dâr) b. 1587, first child born of English parents in North America.

Da·ri·us I (də rī'əs) 549?–485? B.C., king of Persia (521–485? B.C.). Also, **Darius the Great.**

Dar·row, Clarence S(eward) (dar'ō) 1857–1938, U.S. lawyer.

Dar·win, Charles (där'win) 1809–1882, English naturalist.

Da·vid (dā'vid) 1040?–970? B.C., king of Israel (1010?–970? B.C.); father of Solomon.

da Vin·ci, Leonardo (də vin'chē) see **Leonardo da Vinci.**

Da·vis, Jefferson (dā'vis) 1808–1889, U.S. political leader, president of the Confederate States of America (1861–1865).

De·bus·sy, Claude (deb'yù sē', də bū'sē) 1862–1918, French composer.

De·gas, Edgar (dā gä') 1834–1917, French painter.

de Gaulle, Charles (di gôl') 1890–1970, French general and political leader, president (1959–1969).

De·la·croix, (Ferdinand Victor) Eugène (del'ə krwä') 1798–1863, French painter.

De la Ma·drid Hur·ta·do, Miguel (də lä mə drid' hər-tä'dō) 1934– , president of Mexico (1982–1988).

De Mille (də mil') **1. Agnes George.** 1908– , U.S. choreographer, dancer, and writer. **2. Cecil B(lount).** 1881–1959, U.S. motion-picture director and producer.

Deng Xiao·ping (dung'shou'ping') 1904– , Chinese communist leader (1977–). Also, **Teng Hsiao-ping.**

Des·cartes, René (dā kärt') 1596–1650, French philosopher and mathematician.

De So·to, Hernando (də sō'tō) 1500?–1542, Spanish explorer. Also, **Hernán** or **Fernando De Soto.**

De Va·le·ra, Eamon (dev'ə lâr'ə) 1882–1975, Irish political leader, born in the United States.

de Ve·ga, Lope (də vā'gə) see **Lope de Vega.**

Di·as, Bartolomeu (dē'äsh) 1450?–1500, Portuguese navigator. Also, **Bartholomew Diaz.**

Dí·az, Porfirio (dē'äs, dē'äz) 1830–1915, president of Mexico (1877–1880; 1884–1911).

Dick·ens, Charles (dik'ənz) 1812–1870, English novelist.

Dick·in·son, Emily (dik'ən sən) 1830–1886, U.S. poet.

Die·fen·ba·ker, John George (dē'fən bā'kər) 1895–1979, Canadian prime minister (1957–1963).

Dis·rae·li, Benjamin, earl of Beaconsfield (diz rā'lē) 1804–1881, English statesman.

Dodg·son, Charles L. (doj'sən) see **Carroll, Lewis.**

Dom·i·nic, Saint (dom'ə nik) 1170–1221, Spanish priest and founder of the Dominicans.

Donne, John (dun) 1573?–1631, English poet.

Dos·to·ev·sky, Fyodor Mikhailovich (dos'tə yef'skē) 1821–1881, Russian novelist and short-story writer.

Doug·las, Stephen A. (dug'ləs) 1813–1861, U.S. statesman.

Doug·lass, Frederick (dug'ləs) 1817–1895, U.S. abolitionist and editor.

Doyle, Sir Arthur Conan (doil) 1859–1930, British writer.

Drake, Sir Francis (drāk) 1540?–1596, English admiral and explorer.

Drei·ser, Theodore (drī'sər, drī'zər) 1871–1945, U.S. novelist.

Dry·den, John (drī'dən) 1631–1700, English author.

Du Bois, W(illiam) E(dward) B(urghardt) (dü bois') 1868–1963, U.S. educator and civil rights leader.

Du·champ, Marcel (dü shämp', dü shämp') 1887–1968, French artist.

Du Pont, Eleuthère Irénée (dü pont', dū pont', dü'pont', dū'pont') 1771–1834, U.S. industrialist, born in France.

Dü·rer, Albrecht (dùr'ər) 1471–1528, German artist.

Ea·kins, Thomas (ā'kənz) 1844–1916, U.S. artist.

East·man, George (ēst'mən) 1854–1932, U.S. industrialist and inventor who developed photographic processes.

Ed·ward VII (ed'wərd) 1841–1910, king of England (1901–1910); son of Queen Victoria.

Ed·ward VIII (ed'wərd) 1894–1972, king of England (1936) who abdicated and received the title of Duke of Windsor.

Ein·stein, Albert (īn'stīn) 1879–1955, German-American physicist.

Ei·sen·how·er, Dwight David (ī'zən hou'ər) 1890–1969, U.S. general, thirty-fourth president of the United States (1953–1961).

Ei·sen·stein, Sergei Mikhailovich (ī'zən stīn') 1898–1948, Russian film director.

El Gre·co (el grek'ō) 1541?–1614, Spanish painter, born in Crete as *Domenikos Theotokopoulos*.

E·li·jah (i lī'jə) ninth century B.C., Hebrew prophet.

El·i·ot (el'ē ət) **1. George**. 1819–1880, English novelist; born *Mary Ann Evans*. **2. T(homas) S(tearns)**. 1888–1965, English poet, essayist, and critic.

E·lish·a (i lish'ə) ninth century B.C., Hebrew prophet.

E·liz·a·beth I (i liz'ə bəth) 1533–1603, queen of England (1558–1603); daughter of Henry VIII and Anne Boleyn.

E·liz·a·beth II (i liz'ə bəth) 1926– , queen of Great Britain and Northern Ireland (1952–); daughter of George VI.

El·ling·ton, Duke (el'ing tən) 1899–1974, U.S. composer, conductor, and pianist; full name *Edward Kennedy Ellington*.

Em·er·son, Ralph Waldo (em'ər sən) 1803–1882, U.S. essayist, poet, and philosopher.

Eng·els, Friedrich (eng'gəlz) 1820–1895, German socialist writer.

E·phra·im (ē'frē əm, ē'frəm) **1.** in the Old Testament, the younger son of Joseph. **2.** one of the twelve tribes of Israel descended from him.

E·ras·mus, Desiderius (i raz'məs) 1466?–1536, Dutch author and humanist.

Er·ic·son or **Er·ic·sson, Leif** (er'ik sən) fl. A.D. 1000, Norse explorer; son of Eric the Red.

Er·ic the Red (er'ik) b. A.D. 950?, Norse explorer.

E·sau (ē'sô) in the Old Testament, son of Isaac and Rebecca, younger twin brother of Jacob.

Es·ther (es'tər) in the Old Testament, a Jewish woman chosen to be queen by the king of Persia.

Eu·clid (ū'klid) 323?–285 B.C., Greek mathematician.

Eve (ēv) in the Bible, the first woman and the wife of Adam.

E·ze·ki·el (i zē'kē əl) sixth century B.C., Hebrew prophet.

Ez·ra (ez'rə) fifth century B.C., Hebrew scribe and prophet.

Faulk·ner, William (fôk'nər) 1897–1962, U.S. author.

Fer·di·nand V (fûr'də nand') 1452–1516, king of Castile (1476–1504); as Ferdinand II, king of Aragon (1479–1516); as Ferdinand III, king of Naples (1504–1516); husband of Isabella I.

Fer·mi, Enrico (fâr'mē) 1901–1954, Italian-American physicist.

Fill·more, Millard (fil'môr') 1800–1874, thirteenth president of the United States (1850–1853).

Fitz·ger·ald, F(rancis) Scott (Key) (fits jer'əld) 1896–1940, U.S. novelist and short-story writer.

Flem·ing, Sir Alexander (flem'ing) 1881–1955, Scottish bacteriologist.

Ford (fôrd) **1. Gerald R(udolph)**. 1913– , thirty-eighth president of the United States (1974–1977). **2. Henry**. 1863–1947, U.S. automobile manufacturer.

Fos·ter, Stephen Collins (fôs'tər) 1826–1864, U.S. composer of popular songs.

Fran·cis Fer·di·nand (fran'sis fûr'də nand') 1863–1914, archduke of Austria.

Fran·cis of As·si·si, Saint (fran'sis; ə sē'zē) 1181?–1226, Italian friar, founder of the Franciscan order.

Fran·co, Francisco (fräng'kō) 1892–1975, Spanish general, dictator of Spain (1939–1975).

Frank, Anne (frangk) 1929–1945, German-Dutch victim of the Nazis, known for her diary.

Frank·lin (frang'klin) **1. Benjamin**. 1706–1790, American scientist, author, statesman, and inventor. **2. Rosalind Elsie**. 1920–1958, English chemist and molecular biologist.

Fred·er·ick I (fred'ər ik, fred'rik) **1.** 1123?–1190, emperor of the Holy Roman Empire (1155–1190), German king (1152–1190). Also, **Frederick Barbarossa**. **2.** 1657–1713, king of Prussia (1701–1713).

Fred·er·ick II (fred'ər ik, fred'rik) **1.** 1194–1250, emperor of the Holy Roman Empire (1220–1250), king of Sicily (1197–1250), German king (1212–1220), king of Jerusalem (1229–1250). **2.** see **Frederick the Great**.

Fred·er·ick Bar·ba·ros·sa (fred'ər ik bär'bə ros'ə, fred'rik) see **Frederick I**, *def. 1*.

Fred·er·ick the Great (fred'ər ik, fred'rik) 1712–1786, king of Prussia (1740–1786). Also, **Frederick II**.

Fré·mont, John Charles (frē'mont) 1813–1890, U.S. explorer, soldier, and politician.

Freud, Sigmund (froid) 1856–1939, Austrian physician and neurologist, founder of psychoanalysis.

Frost, Robert (frôst) 1874–1963, U.S. poet.

Ful·ton, Robert (fül'tən) 1765–1815, U.S. inventor.

Gad (gad) **1.** in the Old Testament, a son of Jacob. **2.** one of the twelve tribes of Israel descended from him.

Ga·ga·rin, Yuri (gə gär'in) 1934–1968, Soviet cosmonaut; first person to travel in outer space.

Gage, Thomas (gāj) 1721–1787, British general in the American Revolution.

Ga·len, Claudius (gā'lən) A.D. 130–200?, Greek physician and physiologist.

Gal·i·le·o (gal'ə lā'ō) 1564–1642, Italian astronomer, physicist, and mathematician; full name *Galileo Galilei*.

Gan·dhi (gän'dē) **1. Indira**. 1917–1984, Indian prime minister (1966–1977; 1980–1984). **2. Mohandas Karamchand**. 1869–1948, Indian political, social, and religious leader; called *Mahatma Gandhi*. **3. Rajiv**. 1944– , Indian prime minister (1984–).

Gar·cí·a Lor·ca, Federico (gär sē'ə lôr'kə) 1899–1936, Spanish poet and dramatist.

Gar·cí·a Már·quez, Gabriel (gär sē'ə mär'kes) 1928– , Colombian writer.

Gar·field, James Abram (gär'fēld') 1831–1881, twentieth president of the United States (1881).

Gar·i·bal·di, Giuseppe (gar'ə bôl'dē) 1807–1892, Italian patriot and general.

Gar·rick, David (gar'ik) 1717–1779, English actor, theater manager, and playwright.

Gar·ri·son, William Lloyd (gar'ə sən) 1805–1879, U.S. editor and abolitionist.

Gar·vey, Marcus Moziah, Jr. (gär'vō) 1887–1940, Jamaican black nationalist leader.

Gates, Horatio (gāts) 1728–1806, American general in the American Revolution.

Gau·ta·ma (gô'tə mə, gou'tə mə) see **Buddha**.

Gen·ghis Khan (jeng'gis kän') 1162–1227, Mongol conqueror of central Asia. Also, **Jenghis** or **Jenghiz Khan**.

George (jôrj) **1. David Lloyd**. see **Lloyd George, David**. **2. Saint**. d. A.D. 303, Christian martyr.

George I (jôrj) 1660–1727, king of England (1714–1727).

George III (jôrj) 1738–1820, king of England (1760–1820).

George V (jôrj) 1865–1936, king of England (1910–1936); son of Edward VII.

George VI (jôrj) 1895–1952, king of Great Britain and Northern Ireland (1936–1952); son of George V.

Ge·ron·i·mo (jə ron'ə mō') 1829?–1909, Apache chief.

at; āpe; fär; câre; end; mē; it; īce; pîerce; hot; ōld; sông, fôrk; oil; out; up; ūse; rüle; pull; tûrn; chin; sing; shop; thin; this; hw in white; zh in treasure. The symbol ə stands for the unstressed vowel sound heard in about, taken, pencil, lemon, and circus.

Gersh·win, George (gûrsh'win) 1898–1937, U.S. composer.

Get·ty, J(ean) Paul (get'ē) 1892–1976, U.S. business executive.

Gil·bert, Sir William S(chwenck) (gil'bərt) 1836–1911, English librettist who collaborated with the composer Sir Arthur Sullivan.

Giot·to (jot'ō) 1266?–1337, Italian painter.

Gis·card d'Es·taing, Valéry (zhēs kär' des tang') 1926– , French president (1974–1981).

Glad·stone, William Ewart (glad'stōn') 1809–1898, British statesman, prime minister (1868–1874; 1880–1885; 1886; 1892–1894).

Glenn, John Herschel, Jr. (glen) 1921– , U.S. astronaut and politician; first American to orbit the earth.

Goe·thals, George Washington (gō'thəlz) 1858–1928, U.S. army engineer.

Goe·the, Johann Wolfgang von (gûr'tə) 1749–1832, German poet, playwright, novelist, and scientist.

Gogh, Vincent van (gō) see **van Gogh, Vincent**.

Gold·smith, Oliver (gōld'smith') 1730–1774, English poet, novelist, and playwright.

Go·li·ath (gə lī'əth) in the Old Testament, the Philistine giant whom David killed.

Gom·pers, Samuel (gom'pərz) 1850–1924, U.S. labor leader.

Good·year, Charles (gùd'yîr') 1800–1860, U.S. inventor and discoverer of the process of vulcanizing rubber.

Gor·ba·chev, Mikhail Sergeevich (gôr'bə chəf) 1931– , Soviet general secretary of the Communist Party (1985–).

Go·ta·ma (gô'tə mə) see **Buddha**.

Go·ya y Lu·ci·en·tes, Francisco José (goi'yə ē lü'sē·en'tās) 1746–1828, Spanish painter and etcher.

Gra·ham, Martha (grā'əm) 1894– , U.S. choreographer and dancer.

Grant, Ulysses S(impson) (grant) 1822–1885, U.S. general, eighteenth president of the United States (1869–1877).

Gree·ley, Horace (grē'lē) 1811–1872, U.S. journalist, author, and politician.

Greene, Nathanael (grēn) 1742–1786, American general in the American Revolution.

Greg·o·ry I, Saint (greg'ə rē) A.D. 540?–604, pope (A.D. 590–604). Also, **Gregory the Great**.

Grieg, Edvard (grēg) 1843–1907, Norwegian composer.

Grif·fith, D(avid) W(ark) (grif'ith) 1875–1948, U.S. motion-picture director and producer.

Grimm (grim) two German brothers who collaborated as philologists and folklorists. **1. Jakob.** 1785–1863. **2. Wilhelm.** 1786–1859.

Gro·my·ko, Andrei Andreievich (grə mē'kō) 1909– , Soviet diplomat and statesman.

Gu·ten·berg, Johann (gü'tən bûrg') 1400?–1468, German printer.

Habs·burg (haps'bûrg') see **Hapsburg**.

Hai·le Se·las·sie (hī'lē sə las'ē) 1892–1975, emperor of Ethiopia (1930–1936; 1941–1974).

Hale, Nathan (hāl) 1755–1776, American patriot.

Hal·ley, Edmund (hal'ē) 1863–1914, English astronomer.

Ham·il·ton, Alexander (ham'əl tən) 1757–1804, American statesman.

Ham·mar·skjöld, Dag (ham'ər shùld') 1905–1961, Swedish statesman, secretary-general of the United Nations (1953–1961).

Ham·mu·ra·bi (hä'mù rä'bē) eighteenth century B.C., Babylonian king.

Han (hän) dynasty that ruled China (206 B.C.–A.D. 220).

Han·cock, John (han'kok) 1737–1793, American statesman, first signer of the Declaration of Independence.

Han·del, George Frederick (han'dəl) 1685–1759, British composer, born in Germany.

Han·dy, W(illiam) C(hristopher) (han'dē) 1873–1958, U.S. musician, composer, and compiler of blues music.

Han·ni·bal (han'ə bəl) 247?–183? B.C., Carthaginian general.

Han·o·ver (han'ō vər) royal family that ruled Great Britain (1714–1901).

Haps·burg or **Habs·burg** (haps'bûrg') family that ruled Austria (1282–1918), the Holy Roman Empire (1438–1806), Spain (1516–1700), and Hungary (1526–1918).

Har·ding, Warren Gamaliel (här'ding) 1865–1923, twenty-ninth president of the United States (1921–1923).

Har·dy, Thomas (här'dē) 1840–1928, English author.

Har·ri·son (har'ə sən) **1. Benjamin.** 1833–1901, twenty-third president of the United States (1889–1893). **2. William Henry.** 1773–1841, ninth president of the United States (1841); grandfather of Benjamin Harrison.

Har·vey, William (här'vē) 1578–1657, English physiologist.

Haw·king, Stephen W(illiam) (hô'king) 1942– , British physicist.

Haw·thorne, Nathaniel (hô'thôrn') 1804–1864, U.S. novelist and short-story writer.

Hay·dn, Franz Joseph (hī'dən) 1732–1809, Austrian composer.

Hayes, Rutherford B(irchard) (hāz) 1822–1893, nineteenth president of the United States (1877–1881).

Hearst, William Randolph (hûrst) 1863–1951, U.S. editor and newspaper publisher.

He·gel, Georg Wilhelm Friedrich (hā'gəl) 1770–1831, German philosopher.

Hen·ry (hen'rē) **1. Joseph.** 1797–1878, U.S. physicist. **2. O.** see **O. Henry**. **3. Patrick.** 1736–1799, American statesman, orator, and patriot.

Hen·ry II (hen'rē) **1.** 1133–1189, king of England (1154–1189). **2.** 1519–1559, king of France (1547–1559).

Hen·ry IV (hen'rē) **1.** 1367–1413, king of England (1399–1413). **2.** 1553–1610, king of France (1589–1610); as Henry III, king of Navarre (1572–1610).

Hen·ry V (hen'rē) 1387–1422, king of England (1413–1422).

Hen·ry VII (hen'rē) 1457–1509, king of England (1485–1509).

Hen·ry VIII (hen'rē) 1491–1547, king of England (1509–1547), founder of the Church of England.

Hen·ry of Na·varre (hen'rē; nə vär') see **Henry IV, def. 2.**

Hen·ry the Navigator (hen'rē) 1394–1460, Portuguese prince.

Her·od (her'əd) dynasty that ruled Palestine (37? B.C.–A.D. 100?).

Her·od An·ti·pas (her'əd an'tə pas') 20 B.C.?–A.D. 39, ruler of Judea (4 B.C.–A.D. 39); son of Herod the Great.

He·rod·o·tus (hi rod'ə təs) 484–425 B.C., Greek historian.

Her·od the Great (her'əd) 73–4 B.C., king of Palestine (37–4 B.C.).

Her·schel (hûr'shəl) British family of astronomers including **1. Caroline Lucretia.** 1750–1848, sister of Sir William Herschel. **2. Sir John Frederick William.** 1792–1871, son of Sir William Herschel. **3. Sir William.** 1738–1822.

Hi·a·wa·tha (hī'ə wä'thə) sixteenth century, chieftain, probably Mohawk, credited with founding the Iroquois confederation.

Hick·ok, Wild Bill (hik'ok) 1837–1876, U.S. frontier marshal; born *James Butler Hickok*.

Hip·poc·ra·tes (hi pok'rə tēz') 460?–370? B.C., Greek physician.

Hi·ro·hi·to (hîr'ō hē'tō) 1901–1989, emperor of Japan (1926–1989).

Hitch·cock, Sir Alfred Joseph (hich'kok) 1899–1980, British film director.

Hit·ler, Adolf (hit'lər) 1889–1945, chancellor of Germany (1933–1945), born in Austria.

Hobbes, Thomas (hobz) 1588–1679, English philosopher.

Ho Chi Minh (hō′chē′min′) 1890?–1969, president of North Vietnam (1954–1969).

Ho·hen·stau·fen (hō′ən shtou′fən) German royal family that ruled the Holy Roman Empire (1138–1208; 1212–1254).

Ho·hen·zol·lern (hō′ən zol′ərn) German royal family prominent from the eleventh century to 1918 that ruled Brandenburg (1415–1918), Prussia (1525–1918), and Germany (1871–1918).

Hol·bein (hōl′bīn) **1. Hans (the Elder).** 1460?–1524, German painter. **2. Hans (the Younger).** 1497–1543, German painter and engraver; son of Hans Holbein the Elder.

Holmes (hōmz) **1. Oliver Wendell.** 1809–1894, U.S. author and physician. **2. Oliver Wendell, Jr.** 1841–1935, associate justice of the Supreme Court (1902–1932); son of Oliver Wendell Holmes.

Ho·mer (hō′mər) eighth century? B.C., Greek poet, reputed author of the *Iliad* and *Odyssey*.

Ho·mer, Winslow (hō′mər) 1836–1910, U.S. painter.

Hook·er, Thomas (hŭk′ər) 1586–1647, English Puritan clergyman and one of the founders of Connecticut.

Hoo·ver, Herbert Clark (hü′vər) 1874–1964, thirty-first president of the United States (1929–1933).

Hor·ace (hôr′is) 65–8 B.C., Roman poet and satirist.

Ho·se·a (hō zē′ə) eighth century B.C., Hebrew prophet.

Hous·ton, Samuel (hūs′tən) 1793–1863, U.S. frontiersman and statesman, president of the Republic of Texas (1836–1838; 1841–1844).

Howe, Elias (hou) 1819–1867, U.S. inventor of the sewing machine.

Hud·son (hud′sən) **1. Henry.** d. 1611, English navigator and explorer of North America. **2. W(illiam) H(enry).** 1841–1922, English naturalist and writer.

Hughes (hūz) **1. Charles Evans.** 1862–1948, U.S. Supreme Court chief justice (1930–1941). **2. Langston.** 1902–1967, U.S. poet. **3. Ted.** 1930– , British poet.

Hu·go, Victor (hū′gō) 1802–1885, French author.

Hume, David (hūm) 1711–1776, Scottish philosopher and historian.

Hus·sein I (hü sān′) 1935– , king of Jordan (1953–).

Hutch·in·son, Anne (huch′ən sən) 1591–1643, American religious leader.

Hux·ley (huks′lē) English family including **1. Aldous.** 1894–1963, author. **2. Thomas Henry.** 1825–1895, biologist; grandfather of Aldous Huxley.

Ib·sen, Henrik Johan (ĭb′sən) 1828–1906, Norwegian dramatist.

Ig·na·tius of Loy·o·la, Saint (ig nā′shəs; loi ō′lə) see **Loyola, Saint Ignatius of.**

Ikh·na·ton (ik nä′tən) d. 1354? B.C., king of Egypt (1379–1362 B.C.). Also, **Akhenaton** and **Amenhotep IV.**

In·no·cent III (in′ə sənt) 1161?–1216, pope (1198–1216).

Ir·ving, Washington (ûr′ving) 1783–1859, U.S. author.

I·saac (ī′zək) in the Old Testament, the son of Abraham and Sarah, and the father of Jacob and Esau.

Is·a·bel·la I (iz′ə bel′ə) 1451–1504, Spanish queen of Castile; wife of Ferdinand V.

I·sai·ah (ī zā′ə) eighth century B.C., Hebrew prophet.

Is·car·i·ot, Judas (is kar′ē ət) see **Judas,** *def. 1.*

Is·ra·el (iz′rē əl, iz′rā əl) in the Old Testament, the name given to Jacob after he wrestled with the angel.

Is·sa·char (is′ə kär′) **1.** in the Old Testament, a son of Jacob and Leah. **2.** one of the twelve tribes of Israel descended from him.

I·van III (ī′vən) 1440–1505, ruler of Russia (1462–1505). Also, **Ivan the Great.**

I·van IV (ī′vən) 1530–1584, czar of Russia (1533–1584). Also, **Ivan the Terrible.**

Ives, Charles Edward (īvz) 1874–1954, U.S. composer.

Jack·son (jak′sən) **1. Andrew.** 1767–1845, seventh president of the United States (1829–1837). **2. Thomas.** 1824–1863, Confederate general in the U.S. Civil War; known as *Stonewall Jackson.*

Ja·cob (jā′kəb) in the Old Testament, the son of Isaac and Rebecca, twin brother of Esau, and husband of Leah and Rachel; ancestor of the twelve tribes of Israel.

James (jāmz) **1.** d. A.D. 43?, one of the twelve Apostles of Jesus, son of Zebedee, brother of John; called *James the Greater.* **2.** in the New Testament, a person identified as the brother of Jesus, probably the author of the Epistle of James; called *James the Less.*

James (jāmz) **1. Henry.** 1843–1916, U.S. author and critic. **2. William.** 1842–1910, U.S. psychologist and philosopher; brother of Henry James.

James I (jāmz) 1566–1625, king of England (1603–1625); as James VI, king of Scotland (1567–1625).

James II (jāmz) 1633–1701, king of England, Scotland, and Ireland (1685–1688).

Jay, John (jā) 1745–1829, U.S. statesman and first chief justice of the U.S. Supreme Court (1789–1795).

Jeanne d'Arc (zhän därk′) see **Joan of Arc.**

Jef·fer·son, Thomas (jef′ər sən) 1743–1826, third president of the United States (1801–1809).

Jen·ghis or **Jen·ghiz Khan** (jeng′gis; jeng′giz) see **Genghis Khan.**

Jen·ner, Edward (jen′ər) 1749–1833 English physician.

Jer·e·mi·ah (jer′ə mī′ə) 628?–586 B.C., Hebrew prophet.

Je·rome, Saint (jə rōm′) A.D. 342?–420, monk, Father of the Church, and author of the Vulgate.

Je·sus (jē′zəs) 4? B.C.–A.D. 29?, considered by Christians to be the Messiah and the Son of God. Also, **Jesus Christ.**

Joan of Arc (jōn) 1412–1431, French national heroine. Also, **Jeanne d'Arc.**

Job (jōb) in the Old Testament, a man who patiently accepted the trials with which God tested his faith.

John (jon) **1.** one of the Apostles of Jesus, brother of James the Greater, and reputed author of the Gospel of John, three Epistles, and the book of Revelation. **2.** see **John the Baptist. 3.** 1167?–1216, king of England (1199–1216) who signed the Magna Carta (1215).

John XXIII (jon) 1881–1963, pope (1958–1963).

John Paul I (jon′ pôl′) 1912–1978, pope (1978).

John Paul II (jon′ pôl′) 1920– , pope (1978–).

John·son (jon′sən) **1. Andrew.** 1808–1875, seventh president of the United States (1865–1869). **2. Lyndon Baines.** 1908–1973, thirty-sixth president of the United States (1963–1969). **3. Samuel.** 1709–1784, English writer, critic, and lexicographer.

John the Baptist (jon) d. A.D. 29?, in the New Testament, Jewish teacher, the forerunner and baptizer of Jesus, beheaded by Herod Antipas.

Jol·li·et or **Jo·li·et, Louis** (jō′lē et′, zhōl yā′) 1645–1700, French-Canadian explorer.

Jo·nah (jō′nə) in the Old Testament, a Hebrew prophet who was swallowed by a large fish and three days later cast up on land unharmed.

Jones (jōnz) **1. Inigo.** 1573–1652, English architect. **2. John Paul.** 1747–1792, American naval hero in the American Revolution; see *John Paul.*

Jon·son, Ben (jon′sən) 1573?–1637, English author.

Jo·seph (jō′zəf, jō′səf) **1.** in the Old Testament, older son of Jacob and Rachel. **2.** in the New Testament, husband of Mary, the mother of Jesus.

Jo·seph, Chief (jō′zəf, jō′səf) 1840?–1904, Nez Percé chief.

---

at; āpe; fär; câre; end; mē; it; īce; pîerce; hot; ōld; sông, fôrk; oil; out; up; ūse; rüle; pull; tûrn; chin; sing; shop; thin; <u>th</u>is; hw in white; zh in treasure. The symbol ə stands for the unstressed vowel sound heard in about, taken, pencil, lemon, and circus.

Josh·u·a (josh′ü ə) in the Old Testament, the successor of Moses who led the Israelites into Canaan.

Joyce, James (jois) 1882–1941, Irish author.

Juan Car·los I (hwän kär′lōs) 1938– , king of Spain (1975–).

Juá·rez, Benito Pablo (wär′ez) 1806–1872, Mexican statesman, president of Mexico (1858–1865; 1867–1872).

Ju·dah (jü′də) **1.** in the Old Testament, son of Jacob and Leah. **2.** one of the twelve tribes of Israel descended from him.

Ju·das (jü′dəs) **1.** in the New Testament, the Apostle who betrayed Jesus for thirty pieces of silver. Also, **Judas Iscariot. 2.** in the New Testament, one of the twelve Apostles of Jesus; brother of the Apostle James.

Jude (jüd) the reputed author of the book of Jude in the New Testament; sometimes identified with Judas, the brother of the Apostle James.

Jul·ius Cae·sar (jül′yəs sē′zər) see **Caesar, Gaius Julius.**

Jung, Carl Gustav (yùng) 1875–1961, Swiss psychiatrist.

Jus·tin·i·an I (jus tin′ē ən) A.D. 483–565, emperor of the Byzantine Empire (A.D. 527–565).

Ka·me·ha·me·ha I (kə mā′ə mā′ə) 1753?–1819, king of the Hawaiian Islands (1810–1819).

Kant, Immanuel (kant, känt) 1724–1804, German philosopher.

Keats, John (kēts) 1795–1821, English poet.

Kel·ler, Helen Adams (kel′ər) 1880–1968, U.S. writer and lecturer who was deaf and blind from infancy.

Kel·vin, Lord (kel′vin) 1824–1907, British physicist; born *William Thomson.*

Ken·ne·dy, John Fitzgerald (ken′i dē) 1917–1963, thirty-fifth president of the United States (1961–1963).

Ken·yat·ta, Jomo (ken yä′tə) 1893?–1978, president of Kenya (1964–1978).

Kep·ler, Johannes (kep′lər) 1571–1630, German astronomer.

Key, Francis Scott (kē) 1779–1843, lawyer and author of *The Star-Spangled Banner,* the U.S. national anthem.

Keynes, John Maynard (kēnz) 1883–1946, English economist.

Kho·mei·ni, Ruhollah (kō mā′nē, hō mā′nē) 1902– , ruler of the Islamic Republic of Iran (1979–).

Khrush·chev, Nikita (krüsh′chef) 1894–1971, premier of the Soviet Union (1958–1964).

Khu·fu (kü′fü) king of Egypt (2650?–2630? B.C.). Also, **Cheops.**

King (king) **1. Martin Luther, Jr.** 1929–1968, U.S. clergyman and civil rights leader. **2. William Lyon Mackenzie.** 1874–1950, Canadian prime minister (1921–1925; 1926–1930; 1935–1948).

Kip·ling, Rudyard (kip′ling) 1865–1936, English author.

Knox, John (noks) 1505?–1572, Scottish religious reformer, founder of Presbyterianism.

Koch, Robert (kōk) 1843–1910, German bacteriologist.

Kohl, Helmut (kōl) 1930– , chancellor of West Germany (1982–).

Ku·blai Khan (kü′blī kän′) 1215?–1294, Mongol emperor of China (1260–1294); grandson of Genghis Khan.

La·fa·yette, marquis de (laf′ē et′, laf′ ā et′) 1757–1834, French statesman and general in the American Revolution.

La Fon·taine, Jean de (lä fon ten′) 1621–1695, French poet and writer of fables.

Lamb, Charles (lamb) 1775–1834, English essayist.

Lan·cas·ter (lang′kə stər) royal family that ruled England (1399–1461).

Lao–tsu (lou′dzu′) b. 600? B.C., Chinese philosopher, reputed founder of Taoism. Also, **Lao-tze** and **Lao-tse.**

La Salle, René Cavelier, sieur de (lə sal′) 1643–1687, French explorer.

La·voi·sier, Antoine Laurent (lə vwä zyā′) 1743–1794, French chemist and physician.

Laz·a·rus (laz′ər əs) in the New Testament, a man who Jesus brought back to life.

Le·ah (lē′ə, lā′ə) in the Old Testament, Jacob's first wife.

Lea·key (lē′kē) family of anthropologists and paleontologists including **1. Louis Seymour Bazett.** 1903–1972, British. **2. Mary (Douglas).** 1913– , British; wife of Louis Leakey. **3. Richard.** 1944– , Kenyan; son of Mary and Louis Leakey.

Lee, Robert E(dward) (lē) 1807–1870, Confederate general in the U.S. Civil War.

Leeu·wen·hoek, Anton van (lā′vən hùk′) 1632–1732, Dutch naturalist.

Len·in, Vladimir Ilyich (len′in) 1870–1924, Russian revolutionary leader, founder of the Soviet Union; born *Vladimir Ilych Ulyanov;* also called *Nikolai Lenin.*

Le·o X (lē′ō) 1475–1521, pope (1513–1521).

Le·o·nar·do da Vin·ci (lē′ə när′dō də vin′chē) 1452–1519, Italian artist and scientist.

Le·vi (lē′vī) **1.** in the Old Testament, son of Jacob and Leah. **2.** one of the twelve tribes of Israel descended from him.

Lew·is (lü′is) **1. John L(lewellyn).** 1880–1969, U.S. labor leader. **2. Meriwether.** 1774–1809, U.S. explorer with William Clark. **3. Sinclair.** 1885–1951, U.S. novelist.

Li·li·u·o·ka·la·ni (lē lē′ü ō kä lä′nē) 1838–1917, last queen of the Hawaiian Islands (1891–1893).

Lin·coln, Abraham (ling′kən) 1809–1865, sixteenth president of the United States (1861–1865).

Lind·bergh, Charles A(ugustus) (lind′bûrg′) 1902–1974, U.S. aviator.

Lin·nae·us, Carolus (lə nē′əs) 1707–1778, Swedish naturalist and botanist.

Li Po (lē′bō′) A.D. 701–762, Chinese poet. Also, **Li Tai Po** and **Li T'ai Po.**

Lis·ter, Joseph (lis′tər) 1827–1912, English surgeon.

Liszt, Franz (list) 1811–1886, Hungarian composer and pianist.

Li Tai Po or **Li T'ai Po** (lē′ tī′ bō′) see **Li Po.**

Liv·ing·stone, David (liv′ing stən) 1813–1873, Scottish missionary and explorer in Africa.

Lloyd George, David (loid′ jôrj′) 1863–1945, British statesman.

Locke, John (lok) 1632–1704, English philosopher.

Lon·don, Jack (lun′dən) 1876–1916, U.S. author.

Long·fel·low, Henry Wadsworth (long′fel′ō) 1807–1882, U.S. poet.

Lo·pe de Ve·ga (lō′pā də vā′gə) 1562–1635, Spanish dramatist and poet; born *Lope Félix de Vega Carpio.*

Lot (lot) in the Old Testament, a nephew of Abraham whose wife looked back at the destruction of Sodom and was changed into a pillar of salt.

Lou·is XIV (lü′ē) 1638–1715, king of France (1643–1715); called *the Sun King.*

Lou·is XV (lü′ē) 1710–1774, king of France (1715–1774).

Lou·is XVI (lü′ē) 1754–1793, king of France (1774–1792).

Lou·is XVIII (lü′ē) 1755–1824, king of France (1814–1824); successor of **Napoleon I.**

Low·ell, James Russell (lō′əl) 1819–1891, U.S. poet, essayist, and critic.

Loy·o·la, Saint Ignatius of (loi ō′lə) 1491?–1556, Spanish ecclesiastic, founder of the Jesuits.

Luke (lük) in the New Testament, a physician and a companion of Paul; one of the Evangelists, the reputed author of Acts.

Lu·ther, Martin (lü′thər) 1483–1546, German theologian and a leader of the Protestant Reformation.

Ly·sen·ko, Trofim Denisovich (li seng′kō) 1898–1976, Soviet scientist.

Mac·Ar·thur, Douglas (mə kär′thər) 1880–1964, U.S. general.

Mac·ca·bees (mak′ə bēz′) family of Jewish patriots that ruled Judea in the second and first centuries B.C.

Mac·ca·be·us or **Mac·ca·bae·us, Judas** (mak′ə be′əs) d. 160? B.C., Jewish patriot and military leader.

Mac·don·ald, Sir John Alexander (mək don′əld) 1815–1891, first prime minister of the Dominion of Canada (1867–1873; 1878–1891).

Mac·Don·ald, Ramsay (mək don′əld) 1866–1937, British prime minister (1924; 1929–1931; 1931–1935).

Ma·chi·a·vel·li, Niccolò (mak′ē ə vel′ē) 1469–1527, Florentine author and statesman.

Mac·ken·zie (mə ken′zē) **1. Sir Alexander.** 1764?–1820, Scottish fur trader and explorer in Canada. **2. Alexander.** 1822–1892, Canadian statesman, prime minister (1873–1878). **3. William Lyon.** 1795–1861, Canadian journalist and insurgent leader.

Mac·Leish, Archibald (mə klēsh′) 1892–1982, U.S. poet, dramatist, and critic.

Mad·i·son, James (mad′ə sən) 1751–1836, fourth president of the United States (1809–1817).

Mag·da·len or **Mag·da·lene** (mag′də lən; mag′də lēn′) see **Mary Magdalene.**

Ma·gel·lan, Ferdinand (mə jel′ən) 1480?–1521, Portuguese explorer and navigator.

Ma·hom·et (mə hom′it) see **Muhammad.**

Mal·a·chi (mal′ə kī′) fifth century B.C., Hebrew prophet.

Mal·colm X (mal′kəm eks′) 1925–1965, U.S. civil rights leader; born *Malcolm Little.*

Mam·e·luke (mam′ə lük′) military class that ruled Egypt (1250?–1517) and remained powerful until 1811.

Ma·nas·seh (mə nas′ə) **1.** in the Old Testament, the elder son of Joseph. **2.** one of the twelve tribes of Israel descended from him.

Man·chu (man chü′) see **Qing.**

Man·co Ca·pac (mäng′kō kä päk′) 1500?–1544, last emperor of the Inca (1534–1544).

Man·de·la, Nelson Rolihlala (man del′ə) 1918– , South African political leader.

Mann (*def. 1*, man; *def. 2*, män, man) **1. Horace.** 1796–1859, U.S. educator. **2. Thomas.** 1875–1955, German author.

Mao Ze·dong (mou′ dze dùng′) 1893–1976, Chinese political leader, founder of the People's Republic of China. Also, **Mao Tse-tung.**

Marc or **Mark An·to·ny** (märk′ an′tə ne) 83?–30 B.C., Roman general and political leader, friend of Caesar.

Mar·co·ni, Guglielmo (mär kō′nē) 1874–1937, Italian electrical engineer.

Mar·co Po·lo (mär′kō pō′lō) 1254–1324, Italian traveler.

Mar·cos, Ferdinand Edralin (mär′kōs) 1917– , president of the Republic of the Philippines (1965–1986).

Mar·cus Au·re·li·us An·to·ni·nus (mär′kəs ô rē′lē-əs an′tə nī′nəs) A.D. 121–180, Roman emperor (A.D. 161–180) and philosopher.

Mark (märk) in the New Testament, a disciple of Peter and Paul; one of the Evangelists.

Mark An·to·ny (märk′an′tə nē) see **Marc Antony.**

Mar·lowe, Christopher (mär′lō) 1564–1593, English dramatist and poet.

Mar·quette, Jacques (mär ket′) 1637–1675, French missionary, priest, and explorer.

Mar·shall (mär′shəl) **1. George Catlett.** 1880–1959, U.S. general, statesman, and secretary of state (1947–1949). **2. John.** 1755–1835, U.S. Supreme Court chief justice (1801–1835). **3. Thurgood.** 1908– , U.S. Supreme Court associate justice (1967–).

Mar·tí, José (mär tē′) 1853–1893, Cuban poet and patriot.

Mar·y (mâr′ē) in the New Testament, the mother of Jesus.

Mar·y, Queen of Scots (mâr′ē) 1542–1587, queen of Scotland (1542–1567). Also, **Mary Stuart.**

Mar·y I (mâr′ē) 1516–1558, queen of England (1553–1558); wife of Philip II of Spain; known as *Bloody Mary.* Also, **Mary Tudor.**

Mar·y Mag·da·lene or **Mag·da·len** (mâr′ē mag′də-lēn′; mag′də lən) in the New Testament, a woman from whom Jesus cast out seven devils; often identified with the repentant sinner who anointed the feet of Jesus.

Mas·sa·soit (mas′ə soit′) 1580?–1661, American Indian chief, friend of Roger Williams.

Math·er, Cotton (math′ər) 1663–1728, American Puritan clergyman and writer.

Ma·tisse, Henri (ma tēs′) 1869–1954, French painter.

Mat·thew (math′ū) in the New Testament, one of the twelve Apostles of Jesus; one of the Evangelists.

Max·i·mil·ian (mak′sə mil′yən) 1832–1867, archduke of Austria; emperor of Mexico (1864–1867).

Mc·Clel·lan, George B. (mə klel′ən) 1826–1885, Union general in the U.S. Civil War.

Mc·Cor·mick, Cyrus Hall (mə kôr′mək) 1809–1884, U.S. inventor of the reaping machine.

Mc·Kin·ley, William (mə kin′lē) 1843–1901, twenty-fifth president of the United States (1897–1901).

Mead, Margaret (mēd) 1901–1978, U.S. anthropologist.

Med·i·ci (med′i chē′) powerful family of Florence including **1. Catherine de′.** see **Catherine de′ Medici.** **2. Cosimo de′.** 1389–1464, ruler of Florence and patron of the arts. **3. Lorenzo de′.** 1449–1492, ruler of Florence and patron of the arts; called *the Magnificent.*

Mei·ji (mā′jē′) see **Mutsuhito.**

Me·ir, Golda (me ir′) 1898–1978, Israeli leader, prime minister (1969–1974); born in Russia as *Golda Mabovitch.*

Meit·ner, Lise (mīt′nər) 1878–1968, German physicist.

Mel·ville, Herman (mel′vil) 1819–1891, U.S. writer.

Menck·en, H(enry) L(ouis) (meng′kən) 1880–1956, U.S. writer and editor.

Men·del, Gregor (men′dəl) 1822–1884, Austrian monk and botanist.

Mer·ca·tor, Gerhardus (mər kā′tər) 1512–1594, Flemish geographer, cartographer, and mathematician.

Mer·o·vin·gi·an (mer′ə vin′je ən) Frankish dynasty that ruled in Gaul and Germany (A.D. 500?–751?).

Me·thu·se·lah (mə thü′zə lə) in the Old Testament, a man who lived 969 years.

Mi·cah (mī′kə) eighth century B.C., Hebrew prophet.

Mi·chel·an·ge·lo (mī′kəl an′jə lō′) 1475–1564, Italian sculptor, painter, architect, and poet; full name *Michelangelo Buonarroti.*

Mies van der Ro·he, Ludwig (mēs′ van dər rō′ə) 1886–1969, German-American architect.

Mill, John Stuart (mil) 1806–1873, English philosopher and economist.

Mil·lay, Edna St. Vincent (mi lā′) 1892–1950, U.S. poet.

Mil·ton, John (mil′tən) 1608–1674, English poet.

Ming (ming) dynasty that ruled China (1368–1644).

Min·u·it, Peter (min′ū it) 1580–1638, Dutch administrator of New Netherland who bought Manhattan from the Indians.

Mitch·ell, Maria (mich′əl) 1818–1889, U.S. astronomer.

Mit·ter·rand, François (mē′tə rand′) 1916– , French president (1981–).

Mo·ham·med (mō ham′id, mō hä′mid) see **Muhammad.**

Mo·lière (mōl yâr′) 1622–1673, French dramatist and comic actor; born *Jean-Baptiste Poquelin.*

Mo·net, Claude (mō nā′) 1840–1926, French painter.

Mon·roe, James (man rō′) 1758–1831, fifth president of the United States (1817–1825).

---

at; āpe; fär; câre; end; mē; it; īce; pîerce; hot; ōld; sông, fôrk; oil; out; up; ūse; rüle; pull; tûrn; chin; sing; shop; thin; **th**is; hw in white; zh in treasure. The symbol ə stands for the unstressed vowel sound heard in about, taken, pencil, lemon, and circus.

1109

Mon·tes·so·ri, Maria (mon'tə sôr'ē) 1870–1952, Italian physician and educator.

Mon·te·zu·ma II (mon'tə zü'mə) 1480?–1520, ruler of the Aztecs (1502?–1520).

Mont·gol·fi·er (mont gol'fē ər) two French brothers who invented the first practical balloon. **1. Jacques Étienne.** 1745–1799. **2. Joseph Michel.** 1740–1810.

More, Sir Thomas (môr) 1478–1535, English statesman, writer, and martyr.

Mor·gan (môr'gən) **1. Sir Henry.** 1635?–1688, English privateer. **2. J(ohn) P(ierpont).** 1837–1913, U.S. financier.

Morse, Samuel F(inley) B(reese) (môrs) 1791–1872, U.S. inventor and artist.

Mo·ses (mō'ziz) in the Old Testament, prophet and lawgiver of the Israelites who led them from Egypt to Canaan.

Mo·ses, Grandma (mō'ziz) 1860–1961, U.S. painter; real name *Anna Mary Robertson Moses.*

Mott, Lucretia (mot) 1793–1880, U.S. feminist, abolitionist, and social reformer.

Mo·zart, Wolfgang Amadeus (mō'tsärt) 1756–1791, Austrian composer.

Mu·bar·ak, Muhammad Hosni (mü bär'ək) 1929– , president of Egypt (1981–).

Mu·ham·mad (mù ham'əd) A.D. 570?–632, Arab religious teacher and political and military leader; founder of Islam. Also, **Mohammed** and **Mahomet.**

Mul·ro·ney, Brian (mul rō'nē) 1939– , Canadian prime minister (1984–).

Mu·ra·sa·ki Shi·ki·bu (mùr'ə sä'kē shē'kē bü') A.D. 978?–1031?, Japanese writer.

Mus·so·li·ni, Benito (mü'sə lē'nē) 1883–1945, Italian Fascist dictator (1922–1943).

Mu·tsu·hi·to (mü'tsù hē'tō) 1852–1912, emperor of Japan (1867–1912). Also, **Meiji.**

Naph·ta·li (naf'tə lī') **1.** in the Old Testament, a son of Jacob. **2.** one of the twelve tribes of Israel descended from him.

Na·po·le·on I (nə pō'lē ən) 1769–1821, emperor of France (1804–1915); full name *Napoleon Bonaparte.*

Na·po·le·on III (nə pō'lē ən) 1808–1873, emperor of France (1852–1870); born *Charles Louis Napoleon Bonaparte;* nephew of Napoleon I.

Na·po·le·on Bo·na·parte (nə pō'lē ən bō'nə pärt') see **Napoleon I.**

Neb·u·chad·nez·zar II (neb'ə kəd nez'ər) d. 562 B.C., king of Babylon (605–562 B.C.).

Nef·er·ti·ti (nef'ər tē'tē) 1372?–1350 B.C., queen of Egypt; wife of Ikhnaton.

Ne·he·mi·ah (nē'hə mī'ə, nē'ə mī'ə) Hebrew leader who rebuilt the walls of Jerusalem, governor of Judea (445?–432? B.C.).

Neh·ru, Jawaharlal (nā'rü) 1889–1964, Indian statesman, prime minister (1947–1964); father of Indira Gandhi.

Ne·ro (nîr'ō) A.D. 37–68, Roman emperor (A.D. 54–68).

New·man, John Henry (nü'mən, nū'mən) 1801–1890, English theologian, philosopher, and cardinal.

New·ton, Sir Isaac (nü'tən, nū'tən) 1642–1727, English mathematician and physicist.

Nich·o·las, Saint (nik'ə ləs) fourth century A.D., bishop in Asia Minor, patron saint of children, often identified with Santa Claus.

Nich·o·las II (nik'ə ləs) 1868–1918, czar of Russia (1894–1917).

Nietz·sche, Friedrich Wilhelm (nē'chə) 1844–1900, German philosopher.

Night·in·gale, Florence (nī'tən gāl') 1820–1910, English nurse, regarded as the founder of modern nursing.

Ni·jin·sky, Vaslav (ni zhin'skē) 1890–1950, Russian ballet dancer.

Nix·on, Richard Milhous (nik'sən) 1913– , thirty-seventh president of the United States (1969–1974).

No·ah (nō'ə) in the Old Testament, patriarch chosen by God to build an ark in which he, his family, and a pair of every kind of living creature would survive the flood.

No·bel, Alfred Bernhard (nō bel') 1833–1896, Swedish chemist and industrialist who established the Nobel prizes.

Nye·re·re, Julius Kambarage (ni rär'ē) 1921– , president of Tanzania (1964–).

O·ba·di·ah (ō'bə dī'ə) sixth century B.C., Hebrew prophet.

O'Ca·sey, Sean (ō kā'sē) 1880–1964, Irish dramatist.

O'Con·nor, Sandra Day (ō kon'ər) 1930– , U.S. Supreme Court associate justice (1981–).

Oc·ta·vi·an (ok tā'vē ən) see **Augustus.**

O·gle·thorpe, James Edward (ō'gəl thôrp') 1696–1785, English general who founded Georgia.

O. Hen·ry (ō hen'rē) 1862–1910, U.S. short-story writer; pen name of *William Sidney Porter.*

O'Keeffe, Georgia (ō kēf') 1887–1986, U.S. painter.

O·liv·i·er, Laurence (ō liv'ē ā') 1907– , English actor, director, and producer.

O·mar Khay·yam (ō'mär kī yäm') d. 1123?, Persian poet, astronomer, and mathematician.

O'Neill, Eugene (Gladstone) (ō nēl') 1888–1953, U.S. dramatist.

Op·pen·hei·mer, J. Robert (op'ən hī'mər) 1904–1967, U.S. physicist.

Or·te·ga Sa·a·ve·dra, Daniel (ôr tā'gə sä'ä vä'drə) 1945– , Nicaraguan president (1985–).

Or·well, George (ôr'wel') 1903–1950, English novelist and essayist, born in India; pen name of *Eric Blair.*

Ot·to I (ot'ō) A.D. 912–973, king of the Germans (A.D. 936–973), first emperor of the Holy Roman Empire (A.D. 962–973). Also, **Otto the Great.**

Ov·id (ov'id) 43 B.C.–A.D. 17?, Roman poet.

Ow·ens, Jesse (ō'ənz) 1913–1980, U.S. athlete; nickname of *James Cleveland Owens.*

Pad·er·ew·ski, Ignace Jan (pad'ə ref'skē) 1860–1941, Polish pianist, composer, and statesman.

Pag·a·ni·ni, Niccolò (pag'ə nē'nē) 1782–1840, Italian violinist and composer.

Paige, Satchel (pāj) 1906–1982, U.S. baseball player; nickname of *Leroy Robert Paige.*

Paine, Thomas (pān) 1737–1809, American patriot, writer, and political theorist.

Pa·le·stri·na, Giovanni Pierluigi da (pal'ə strē'nə) 1526?–1594, Italian composer.

Pan·cho Vil·la (pän'chō vē'ə) see **Villa, Francisco.**

Par·nell, Charles Stewart (pär nel') 1846–1891, Irish political leader.

Pas·teur, Louis (pas tûr') 1822–1895, French chemist and bacteriologist.

Pat·rick, Saint (pat'rik) A.D. 389?–461?, Christian missionary, patron saint of Ireland.

Paul (pôl) d. A.D. 68?, Christian missionary and theologian.

Paul VI (pôl) 1897–1978, pope (1963–1978).

Pau·ling, Linus Carl (pô'ling) 1901– , U.S. chemist.

Pav·lov, Ivan Petrovich (pav'lov) 1849–1936, Russian physiologist.

Pav·lo·va, Anna Pavlovna (pav'lə və, pav lō'və) 1882–1931, Russian ballerina.

Penn, William (pen) 1644–1718, English Quaker, founder of Pennsylvania.

Pé·rez de Cué·llar, Javier (per'ez də kwā'yär) 1920– , Peruvian diplomat, secretary-general of the United Nations (1982–).

Per·i·cles (per'i klēz') 495?–429 B.C., Athenian statesman, orator, and general.

Pe·rón, Juan Domingo (pə rōn') 1895–1974, Argentine army officer and politician, president of Argentina (1946–1955; 1973–1974).

Per·ry (per'ē) **1. Oliver Hazard.** 1785–1819, U.S. naval commander. **2. Matthew Calbraith.** 1794–1858, U.S. naval officer; brother of Oliver Hazard Perry.

Per·shing, John Joseph (pûr'shing) 1860–1948, U.S. general.

Pe·ter (pē′tər) d. A.D. 67?, one of the twelve Apostles of Jesus; brother of Andrew. Also, **Simon Peter.**

Pe·ter I (pē′tər) 1672–1725, czar of Russia (1682–1725). Also, **Peter the Great.**

Pe·trarch (pē′trärk) 1304–1374, Italian poet and scholar.

Phid·i·as (fid′ē əs) 490?–432? B.C., Greek sculptor.

Phil·ip (fil′ip) in the New Testament, one of the twelve Apostles of Jesus.

Phil·ip II (fil′ip) **1.** 382–336 B.C., king of Macedonia (359–336 B.C.); father of Alexander the Great. **2.** 1165–1223, king of France (1180–1223). Also, **Philip Augustus. 3.** 1527–1598, king of Spain (1556–1598).

Phil·ip IV (fil′ip) 1268–1314, French king (1285–1314); called *the Fair.*

Phil·ip Au·gus·tus (fil′ip ô gus′təs) see **Philip II.**

Phil·lips, Wendell (fil′ips) 1811–1884, U.S. social reformer.

Pi·cas·so, Pablo (pi kä′sō) 1881–1973, Spanish artist.

Pierce, Franklin (pîrs) 1804–1869, fourteenth president of the United States (1853–1857).

Pi·late, Pontius (pī′lət) Roman governor of Judea (A.D. 26–36).

Pitt (pit) **1. William.** 1708–1778, English statesman; 1st earl of Chatham; called *the Elder Pitt.* **2. William.** 1759–1806, English statesman and prime minister (1783–1801; 1804–1806); called *the Younger Pitt;* son of the Elder Pitt.

Pi·us IX (pī′əs) 1792–1878, pope (1846–1878).

Pi·us XI (pī′əs) 1857–1939, pope (1922–1939).

Pi·us XII (pī′əs) 1876–1958, pope (1939–1958).

Pi·zar·ro, Francisco (pi zär′ō) 1471?–1541, Spanish conqueror of Peru.

Plan·tag·e·net (plan taj′ə nit) family that ruled England (1154–1399). Also, **Angevin.**

Pla·to (plā′tō) 428?–347? B.C., Greek philosopher.

Plu·tarch (plü′tärk) A.D. 46?–120?, Greek biographer.

Po·ca·hon·tas (pō′kə hon′təs) 1595?–1617, American Indian princess, reputed to have saved the life of Captain John Smith; daughter of Powhatan.

Poe, Edgar Allan (pō) 1809–1849, U.S. author and critic.

Polk, James Knox (pōk) 1795–1849, eleventh president of the United States (1845–1849).

Po·lo, Marco (pō′lō) see **Marco Polo.**

Pom·pi·dou, Georges Jean Raymond (pom′pi dü′) 1911–1974, French politician, premier (1962–1968), and president (1969–1974).

Ponce de Le·ón, Juan (pons′ də lā ōn′, pons′də lē′ən) 1460?–1521, Spanish explorer.

Pon·ti·ac (pon′tē ak′) 1720?–1769, Ottawa chief.

Pope, Alexander (pōp) 1688–1744, English poet and satirist.

Por·ter, William Sidney (pôr′tər) see **O. Henry.**

Pound, Ezra (pound) 1885–1972, U.S. poet, critic, and translator.

Pow·ha·tan (pou′ə tan′, pou hat′ən) 1550?–1618, American Indian chief; father of Pocahontas.

Priest·ley, Joseph (prēst′lē) 1733–1804, English chemist and theologian.

Pro·kof·iev, Sergei Sergeyevich (prə kof′yəf) 1891–1953, Russian composer.

Ptol·e·my (tol′ə mē) Greek dynasty that ruled Egypt (323–30 B.C.).

Ptol·e·my, Claudius (tol′ə mē) second century A.D., Greek astronomer, geographer, and mathematician.

Puc·ci·ni, Giacomo (pü chē′nē) 1858–1924, Italian composer of operas.

Pu·las·ki, Casimir (pə las′kē) 1748–1779, Polish nobleman who aided the colonists in the American Revolution.

Pu·lit·zer, Joseph (pul′i tsər) 1847–1911, U.S. journalist and newspaper publisher.

Py·thag·o·ras (pi thag′ər əs) 580?–500? B.C., Greek mathematician and philosopher.

Qad·da·fi, Muammar al– (kə dä′fē) 1942– , Libyan politician leader (1969–).

Qin (chin) dynasty that ruled China (221–206 B.C.). Also, **Ch'in.**

Qing (ching) Mongol dynasty that ruled China (1644–1912). Also, **Ch'ing** and **Manchu.**

Ra·chel (rā′chəl) in the Old Testament, the second wife of Jacob and the mother of Joseph and Benjamin.

Rach·ma·ni·noff, Sergei Vasilyevich (räk mä′nə-nôf′) 1873–1943, Russian composer and pianist.

Ra·leigh, Sir Walter (rô′lē, rä′lē) 1552?–1618, English courtier, colonizer, statesman, and author.

Ra·ma·nu·jan, Srinivasa (rä mä′nù jən) 1889–1920, Indian mathematician.

Ram·e·ses or **Ram·ses** (ram′ə sēz′; ram′sēz) any of eleven kings reigning in Egypt (1320?–1090? B.C.), especially **Rameses II** (reigned 1304–1237 B.C.).

Ram·say, William (ram′zē) 1852–1916, English chemist.

Ran·dolph (ran′dolf) **1.** A(sa) **Philip.** 1889–1979, U.S. labor leader. **2. Edmund.** 1753–1813, U.S. statesman.

Ra·pha·el (rä′fī el′, raf′ē əl, rä′fē əl) 1483–1520, Italian painter.

Rea·gan, Ronald Wilson (rā′gən) 1911– , fortieth president of the United States (1981–1989).

Re·bec·ca (ri bek′ə) in the Old Testament, the wife of Isaac and the mother of Esau and Jacob.

Reed, Walter (rēd) 1851–1902, U.S. army surgeon and microbiologist.

Rehn·quist, William Hubbs (ren′kwist) 1924– , U.S. Supreme Court chief justice (1986–).

Rem·brandt (rem′brant) 1606–1669, Dutch painter and etcher; full name *Rembrandt Harmenszoon van Rijn.*

Re·noir, Pierre Auguste (ren wär′) 1841–1919, French painter.

Reu·ben (rü′bən) **1.** in the Old Testament, the oldest son of Jacob and Leah. **2.** one of the twelve tribes of Israel descended from him.

Re·vere, Paul (rə vîr′) 1735–1818, American patriot and craftsman.

Reyn·olds, Sir Joshua (ren′əldz) 1723–1792, English painter.

Rich·ard I (rich′ərd) 1157–1199 king of England (1189–1199); known as *Richard the Lion-Hearted* and *Richard Coeur de Lion.*

Rich·ard II (rich′ərd) 1367–1400, king of England (1377–1399).

Rich·ard III (rich′ərd) 1452–1485, king of England (1483–1485).

Ri·che·lieu, Cardinal (rish′ə lü′, rish′ə lū′) 1585–1642, French statesman; full name *Armand Jean du Plessis de Richelieu.*

Ri·ve·ra, Diego (ri vâr′ə) 1886–1957, Mexican artist.

Robe·son, Paul (rōb′sən) 1898–1976, U.S. singer and actor.

Rob·in·son, Jackie (rob′in sən) 1919–1972, U.S. baseball player; full name *Jack Roosevelt Robinson.*

Ro·cham·beau, comte de (rō′sham bō′) 1725–1807, French marshal, commander of the French forces during the American Revolution.

Rock·e·fel·ler (rok′ə fel′ər) U.S. family including **1. John D.** 1839–1937, industrialist and philanthropist. **2. Nelson A.** 1908–1979, political leader; grandson of John D. Rockefeller.

Ro·din, Auguste (rō dan′) 1840–1917, French sculptor.

Roeb·ling, John Augustus (rō′bling) 1806–1869, U.S. engineer.

---

at; āpe; fär; câre; end; mē; it; īce; pîerce; hot; ōld; sông, fôrk; oil; out; up; ūse; rüle; pùll; tûrn; chin; sing; shop; thin; <u>th</u>is; hw in white; zh in treasure. The symbol ə stands for the unstressed vowel sound heard in about, taken, pencil, lemon, and circus.

Roent·gen or **Rönt·gen, Wilhelm Konrad** (rent'gən) 1845–1923, German physicist.

Ro·ma·nov (rō'mə nôf') dynasty that ruled Russia (1613–1917).

Ro·ma·nov, Mikhail (rō'mə nôf') 1596–1645, czar of Russia (1613–1645), founder of the Romanov dynasty.

Roose·velt (rōz'velt) U.S. family including **1. (Anna) Eleanor.** 1884–1962, humanitarian, writer, and diplomat; wife of Franklin D. Roosevelt. **2. Franklin Delano.** 1882–1945, thirty-second president of the United States (1933–1945). **3. Theodore.** 1858–1919, twenty-sixth president of the United States (1901–1909).

Ross, Betsy (rôs) 1752–1836, American woman reputed to have made the first American flag; born *Elizabeth Griscom.*

Rous·seau (rü sō') **1. Henri.** 1844–1910, French painter. **2. Jean Jacques.** 1712–1778, French philosopher and writer, born in Switzerland.

Ru·bin·stein, Artur or **Arthur** (rü'bin stīn') 1886–1982, U.S. pianist, born in Poland.

Rus·sell, Bertrand (rus'əl) 1872–1970, English philosopher and mathematician.

Ruth, Babe (rüth) 1895–1948, U.S. baseball player; nickname of *George Herman Ruth.*

Ruth·er·ford, Lord Ernest (ru_th_'ər fərd) 1871–1937, English physicist.

Sa·bin, Albert Bruce (sā'bin) 1906– , U.S. physician and microbiologist, born in Poland.

Sac·a·ja·we·a or **Sac·a·ga·we·a** (sak'ə jə wē'ə; sak'ə gə wē'ə) 1788?–1812? (or 1784?), Shoshone guide and interpreter for Meriwether Lewis and William Clark.

Sa·dat, Anwar al– (sə dät', sə dat') 1918–1981, Egyptian president (1970–1981).

Sa·kha·rov, Andrei Dmitriyovich (sä'kə rôf') 1921– , Soviet physicist and human rights advocate.

Sa·li·nas de Gor·ta·ri, Carlos (sə lē'nəs dä gôr tär'ē) 1948– , president of Mexico (1988–).

Salk, Jonas Edward (sôk, sôlk) 1914–, U.S. physician and microbiologist.

Sam·son (sam'sən) in the Old Testament, judge of Israel who was renowned for his strength.

Sam·u·el (sam'ū əl) in the Old Testament, judge and prophet of Israel.

Sand·burg, Carl (sand'bûrg') 1878–1967, U.S. poet and biographer.

San·ta An·na, Antonio López de (san'tə an'ə) 1795–1876, Mexican general.

Sap·pho (saf'ō) 620?–565 B.C., Greek poet.

Sar·ah (sâr'ə) in the Old Testament, the wife of Abraham and mother of Isaac.

Sar·gent, John Singer (sär'jənt) 1856–1925, U.S. painter.

Sar·tre, Jean Paul (sär'trə, särt) 1905–1980, French philosopher.

Saul (sôl) **1.** in the Old Testament, the first king of Israel. **2.** in the New Testament, the name of the Apostle Paul before his conversion to Christianity. Also, **Saul of Tarsus** (tär'səs).

Schil·ler, Johann Christoph Friedrich von (shil'ər) 1759–1805, German dramatist, poet, and historian.

Schlie·mann, Heinrich (shlē'män') 1822–1890, German archaeologist.

Scho·pen·hau·er, Arthur (shō'pən hou'ər) 1788–1860, German philosopher.

Schu·bert, Franz (Peter) (shü'bərt) 1797–1828, Austrian composer.

Schweit·zer, Albert (shwīt'sər) 1875–1965, Alsatian doctor, philosopher, Protestant missionary in Africa.

Scip·i·o Af·ri·ca·nus (sip'ē ō af'ri kan'əs) **1. the Elder.** 234?–183 B.C., Roman general. **2. the Younger.** 185?–129 B.C., Roman statesman and general; son of Scipio Africanus the Elder.

Scott (skot) **1. Dred.** 1795?–1858, black American slave whose suit for freedom led to a Supreme Court decision in 1857 that extended slavery to all U.S. territories. **2. Sir Walter.** 1771–1832, Scottish author.

Sel·juk (sel'jük) a Turkish family that established several dynasties in western Asia during the eleventh and twelfth centuries. The Seljuks were Muslims and fought the Crusaders.

Se·quoy·ah or **Se·quoi·a** (si kwoi'ə) 1766?–1843, Cherokee scholar and silversmith who invented the Cherokee writing system; known as *George Gist* and *George Guess.*

Ser·ra, Junípero (ser'ə) 1713–1784, Spanish Franciscan missionary in California and Mexico.

Se·ton, Saint Elizabeth Ann Bayley (sē'tən) 1774–1821, U.S. Roman Catholic nun.

Seu·rat, Georges (sü rä') 1859–1891, French painter.

Sew·ard, William Henry (sü'ərd) 1801–1872, U.S. statesman.

Sfor·za (sfôr'tsä) powerful family that ruled Milan (1450–1500; 1521–1535).

Shake·speare, William (shāk'spîr) 1564–1616, English poet and dramatist.

Shaw, George Bernard (shô) 1856–1950, Irish playwright, critic, and social theorist.

She·ba, Queen of (shē'bə) in the Old Testament, a beautiful and wealthy queen who visited Solomon.

Shel·ley (shel'ē) **1. Mary Wollstonecraft.** 1797–1851, English novelist; wife of Percy Bysshe Shelley. **2. Percy Bysshe.** 1792–1822, English poet.

Shep·ard, Alan Bartlett, Jr. (shep'ərd) 1923– , U.S. astronaut, first American to travel in outer space.

Sher·i·dan (sher'i dən) **1. Philip Henry.** 1831–1888, Union general in the U.S. Civil War. **2. Richard Brinsley.** 1751–1816, British dramatist and statesman.

Sher·man, William Tecumseh (shûr'mən) 1820–1891, Union general in the U.S. Civil War.

Shos·ta·ko·vich, Dmitri (shos'tə kō'vich) 1906–1975, Soviet composer.

Sid·dhart·ha (si där'tə) see **Buddha.**

Si·kor·sky, Igor Ivanovich (si kôr'skē) 1889–1972, Russian-American engineer.

Sim·e·on (sim'ē ən) **1.** in the Old Testament, a son of Jacob and Leah. **2.** one of the twelve tribes of Israel descended from him.

Si·mon (sī'mən) **1.** in the New Testament, the original name of the Apostle Peter. **2.** in the New Testament, one of the twelve Apostles of Jesus; called *the Canaanite.*

Si·mon Pe·ter (sī'mən pē'tər) see **Peter.**

Sitting Bull, 1834?–1890, Sioux chief.

Smith (smith) **1. Captain John.** 1580?–1631, English adventurer, explorer, and writer. **2. Joseph.** 1805–1844, U.S. religious leader, founder of the Mormon Church.

Soc·ra·tes (sok'rə tēz') 469–399 B.C., Greek philosopher.

Sol·o·mon (sol'ə mən) tenth century B.C., king of Israel (973?–933? B.C.); son of David.

Sol·zhe·nit·syn, Aleksandr Isayevich (sōl'zhə-nēt'sin) 1918– , Soviet writer.

Song (sûng) dynasty that ruled China (A.D. 960–1260). Also, **Sung.**

Soph·o·cles (sof'ə klēz') 496?–406? B.C., Greek dramatist.

Sou·sa, John Philip (sü'zə) 1854–1932, U.S. composer.

Spen·ser, Edmund (spen'sər) 1552–1599, English poet.

Spin·o·za, Baruch or **Benedict** (spi nō'zə) 1632–1677, Dutch philosopher.

Squan·to (skwon'tō) 1585?–1622, Patuxet who befriended the Pilgrims of Plymouth Colony. Also, **Tsquantum** and **Tisquantum.**

Sta·lin, Joseph Vissarionovich (stä'lin) 1879–1953, Soviet politician, secretary-general of the Communist Party (1924–1953), premier of U.S.S.R. (1941–1953).

Stan·dish, Myles or **Miles** (stan'dish) 1584?–1656, Pilgrim leader and American colonist.

Stan·i·slav·sky, Konstantin (stan′ə släv′skē) 1863–1938, Russian stage director and actor; stage name of *Konstantin Sergeyevich Alexeyev.*

Stan·ley, Sir Henry Morton (stan′lē) 1841–1904, British journalist and explorer.

Steele, Sir Richard (stēl) 1672–1729, English essayist.

Stein, Gertrude (stīn) 1874–1946, U.S. writer.

Stein·beck, John (stīn′bek′) 1902–1968, U.S. novelist.

Steu·ben, Baron Frederick William von (stü′bən, stü′bən) 1730–1794, Prussian general who aided the colonists in the American Revolution.

Ste·ven·son (stē′vən sən) **1. Adlai E(wing).** 1900–1965, U.S. politician. **2. Robert Louis.** 1850–1894, Scottish novelist and poet.

Stone, Lucy (stōn) 1818–1893, U.S. leader in the women's rights movement.

Stowe, Harriet Beecher (stō) 1811–1896, U.S. author.

Stra·di·va·ri, Antonio (strad′ə vâr′ē) 1644?–1737, Italian violin maker.

Strauss (strous) **1. Johann.** 1804–1849, Austrian composer. **2. Johann.** 1825–1899, Austrian composer; son of Johann Strauss. **3. Richard.** 1864–1949, German composer.

Stra·vin·sky, Igor (strə vin′skē) 1882–1971, Russian composer.

Stu·art (stü′ərt, stū′ərt) royal family that ruled Scotland (1371–1714) and England (1603–1714).

Stu·art (stü′ərt, stū′ərt) **1. Gilbert.** 1755–1828, American painter. **2. James Ewell Brown.** 1833–1864, Confederate general in the U.S. Civil War; known as *Jeb Stuart.* **3. Mary.** see **Mary, Queen of Scots.**

Stuy·ve·sant, Peter (stī′və sənt) 1592–1672, Dutch colonial administrator in America.

Su·har·to (sü här′tō) 1921– , president of Indonesia (1967–).

Sul·li·van (sul′ə vən) **1. Sir Arthur.** 1842–1900, English composer who collaborated with the librettist Sir William S. Gilbert. **2. John L(awrence).** 1858–1918, U.S. boxer. **3. Louis Henry.** 1856–1924, U.S. architect.

Sung (sùng) see **Song.**

Sun Yat-Sen (sùn′ yät′sen′) 1866–1925, Chinese revolutionary leader and statesman.

Swift, Jonathan (swift) 1667–1745, English author and satirist.

Szi·lard, Leo (sil′ärd) 1898–1964, U.S. nuclear physicist.

Tac·i·tus (tas′i təs) A.D. 55?–117, Roman historian.

Taft, William Howard (taft) 1857–1930, twenty-seventh president of the United States (1909–1913), chief justice of the U.S. Supreme Court (1921–1930).

Tam·er·lane or **Tam·bur·laine** (tam′ər lān′; tam′bər lān′) 1336?–1405, Mongol conqueror of central Asia and eastern Europe.

Tang or **T'ang** (täng) dynasty that ruled China (A.D. 618–906).

Tay·lor, Zachary (tā′lər) 1784–1850, U.S. general, twelfth president of the United States (1849–1850).

Tchai·kov·sky, Peter Ilyich (chī kof′skē) 1840–1893, Russian composer.

Te·cum·seh (tə kum′sə) 1768?–1813, Shawnee chief.

Teng Hsiao-ping (dung′shou′ping′) see **Deng Xiaoping.**

Ten·ny·son, Alfred, Lord (ten′ə sən) 1809–1892, English poet.

Thack·er·ay, William Makepeace (thak′ə rē) 1811–1863, English novelist.

Thant, U (thant, thänt) 1909–1975, Burmese diplomat, secretary-general of the United Nations (1961–1971).

Thatch·er, Margaret Hilda (thach′ər) 1925– , British political leader, prime minister (1979–).

Thay·en·da·ne·ge·a (thä′ən dan′ə gē′ə) see **Brant, Joseph.**

Thes·pis (thes′pis) sixth century B.C., Greek dramatist.

Thom·as (tom′əs) in the New Testament, one of the twelve Apostles of Jesus.

Thom·as, Dylan (tom′əs) 1914–1953, Welsh poet.

Thomp·son, Sir John Sparrow David (tomp′sən) 1844–1894, Canadian prime minister (1892–1894).

Tho·reau, Henry David (thə rō′) 1817–1862, U.S. writer, philosopher, and naturalist.

Thu·cyd·i·des (thü sid′i dēz′) 460?–400? B.C., Greek historian.

Tim·o·thy (tim′ə thē) in the New Testament, a disciple of Paul.

Tin·dal or **Tin·dale, William** (tin′dəl) see **Tyndale, William.**

Ti·squan·tum (ti skwon′təm) see **Squanto.**

Ti·tian (tish′ən) 1477?–1576, Venetian painter.

Tocque·ville, Alexis de (tōk′vil′) 1805–1859, French political theorist.

Tol·stoy, count Leo Nikolayevich (tōl′stoi) 1828–1910, Russian novelist and philosopher.

Tos·ca·ni·ni, Arturo (tos′kə nē′nē) 1867–1957, Italian conductor.

Tou·louse–Lau·trec, Henri de (tü lüz′ lō trek′) 1864–1901, French painter and illustrator.

Tous·saint L'Ou·ver·ture, Pierre Dominique (tüsant′ lü′vər tür′) 1743?–1803, Haitian revolutionary leader. Also, **François Dominique Toussaint L'Ouverture.**

Toyn·bee, Arnold Joseph (toin′bē) 1899–1975, English historian.

Trot·sky, Leon (trot′skē) 1879–1940, Russian revolutionary leader; born *Lev Davidovich Bronstein.*

Tru·deau, Pierre Elliott (trü dō′) 1919– , prime minister of Canada (1968–1979; 1980–1984).

Tru·man, Harry S (trü′mən) 1884–1972, thirty-third president of the United States (1945–1953).

Truth, Sojourner (trüth) 1797?–1883, U.S. abolitionist; real name *Isabella Van Wagener.*

Tsquan·tum (skwon′təm) see **Squanto.**

Tub·man, Harriet (tub′mən) 1820?–1913, U.S. abolitionist and conductor on the Underground Railroad.

Tu·dor (tü′dər, tü′dər) royal family that ruled England (1485–1603).

Tur·ge·nev, Ivan Sergeevich (tùr gā′nyəf) 1818–1883, Russian author.

Tur·ner (tûr′nər) **1. John Napier.** 1929– , Canadian prime minister (1984). **2. Nat.** 1800–1831, U.S. slave and revolutionary.

Tut·ankh·a·men (tü′täng kä′mən) king of Egypt (1361?–1352 B.C.).

Tu·tu, Desmond Mpilo (tü′tü) 1931– , South African prelate and civil rights leader.

Twain, Mark (twān) 1835–1910, U.S. author and humorist; pen name of *Samuel Langhorne Clemens.*

Ty·ler, John (tī′lər) 1790–1862, tenth president of the United States (1841–1845).

Tyn·dale, William (tin′dəl) 1492?–1536, English religious reformer and translator of the Bible. Also, **Tindal** and **Tindale.**

Ur·ban II (ûr′bən) A.D. 1042–1099, pope (1088–1099).

U Thant (ü thant′, ü thänt′) see **Thant, U.**

Val·en·tine, Saint (val′ən tīn′) d. A.D. 270?, Christian martyr.

Va·lé·ry, Paul (val′ə rē′) 1871–1945, French poet.

Val·ois (val wä′) dynasty that ruled France (1328–1589).

at; āpe; fär; câre; end; mē; it; īce; pîerce; hot; ōld; sông, fôrk; oil; out; up; ūse; rüle; pùll; tûrn; chin; sing; shop; thin; this; hw in white; zh in treasure. The symbol ə stands for the unstressed vowel sound heard in about, taken, pencil, lemon, and circus.

Van Bu·ren, Martin (van byür′ən) 1782–1862, eighth president of the United States (1837–1841).

Van Dyck or **Van·dyke, Sir Anthony** (van dīk′) 1599–1641, Flemish painter.

van Gogh, Vincent (van gō′) 1853–1890, Dutch painter.

Ve·ga, Lope de (vā′gə) see **Lope de Vega.**

Ve·láz·quez or **Ve·lás·quez, Diego Rodríguez de Silva y** (ve läs′kez) 1599–1660, Spanish painter.

Ver·di, Giuseppe (vâr′dē) 1813–1901, Italian composer of operas.

Ver·gil (vûr′jəl) 70–19 B.C., Roman poet. Also, **Virgil.**

Ver·meer, Jan (vər mîr′) 1632–1675, Dutch painter; full name *Jan van der Meer van Delft.*

Ves·puc·ci, Amerigo (ves pü′chē) 1454–1512, Italian explorer, for whom America was named.

Vic·to·ri·a (vik tôr′ē ə) 1819–1901, queen of Great Britain and Ireland (1837–1901), empress of India (1876–1901).

Vil·la, Francisco (vē′ə) 1877–1923, Mexican revolutionary; also known as *Pancho Villa;* real name *Doroteo Arango.*

Vin·ci, Leonardo da (vin′chē) see **Leonardo da Vinci.**

Vir·gil (vûr′jəl) see **Vergil.**

Vol·ta, Alessandro (vōl′tə) 1745–1827, Italian physicist.

Vol·taire (vōl târ′) 1694–1778, French philosopher, historian, and author; pen name of *François Marie Arouet.*

Wag·ner, Richard (väg′nər) 1813–1883, German composer.

Wald·heim, Kurt (wôld′hīm′, väld′hīm) 1918– , Austrian diplomat, secretary-general of the United Nations (1972–1982), president of Austria (1986–).

War·ren (wôr′ən, wor′ən) **1. Earl.** 1891–1974, U.S. Supreme Court chief justice (1953–1969). **2. Robert Penn.** 1905– , U.S. writer.

Wash·ing·ton (wô′shing tən, wosh′ing tən) **1. Booker T.** 1856–1915, U.S. educator. **2. George.** 1732–1799, American general in the American Revolution, first president of the United States (1789–1797). **3. Martha.** 1731–1802, American, wife of George Washington.

Watt, James (wot) 1736–1819, Scottish inventor.

Web·ster (web′stər) **1. Daniel.** 1782–1852, U.S. statesman. **2. Noah.** 1758–1843, American lexicographer, author, and editor.

Wel·ling·ton, duke of (wel′ing tən) 1769–1852, British soldier and statesman; born *Arthur Wellesley.*

Wells, H(erbert) G(eorge) (welz) 1866–1946, English novelist and social philosopher.

Wel·ty, Eudora (wel′tē) 1909– , U.S. writer.

Wes·ley (wes′lē, wez′lē) **1. Charles.** 1707–1788, English religious reformer, co-founder of Methodism with John Wesley. **2. John.** 1703–1791, English religious leader, co-founder of Methodism with his brother Charles Wesley.

West·ing·house, George (wes′ting hous′) 1846–1914, U.S. inventor.

Wheat·ley, Phillis (hwēt′lē, wēt′lē) 1753?–1784, American poet.

Whis·tler, James Abbott McNeill (hwis′lər, wis′lər) 1834–1903, U.S. painter and etcher.

Whit·man, Walt (hwit′mən, wit′mən) 1819–1892, U.S. poet.

Whit·ney, Eli (hwit′nē, wit′nē) 1765–1825, U.S. inventor.

Whit·ti·er, John Greenleaf (hwit′ē ər, wit′ē ər) 1807–1892, U.S. poet and abolitionist.

Wick·liffe or **Wic·lif, John** (wik′lif) see **Wycliffe, John.**

Wilde, Oscar (wīld) 1854–1900, Irish author.

Wil·der, Thornton Niven (wīl′dər) 1897–1975, U.S. playwright and novelist.

Wil·kins, Roy (wil′kənz) 1901–1981, U.S. civil rights leader.

Wil·liam I (wil′yəm) 1027?–1087, king of England (1066–1087); known as *William the Conqueror.*

Wil·liams (wil′yəmz) **1. Roger.** 1603–1684, founder of Rhode Island. **2. Tennessee.** 1914–1983, U.S. dramatist; pen name of *Thomas Lanier Williams.* **3. William Carlos.** 1883–1963, U.S. poet and physician.

Wil·son (wil′sən) **1. Edmund.** 1895–1972, U.S. social and literary critic. **2. Harold.** 1916– , British political leader, prime minister (1964–1970; 1974–1976). **3. Woodrow.** 1856–1924, twenty-eighth president of the United States (1913–1921).

Wind·sor (win′zər) **1.** name of the British royal family, adopted in 1917. **2. duke of.** see **Edward VIII.**

Win·throp (win′thrəp) family of colonial leaders in America, including **1. John.** 1588–1649, first governor of the Massachusetts Bay Colony. **2. John.** 1606–1676, governor of Connecticut (1657; 1659–1676); son of John Winthrop.

Witt·gen·stein, Ludwig Josef Johan (vit′gən shtīn′) 1889–1951, Austrian philosopher.

Wolfe (wúlf) **1. James.** 1727–1759, English military commander. **2. Thomas.** 1900–1938, U.S. novelist.

Words·worth, William (wûrds′wûrth′) 1770–1850, English poet.

Wright (rīt) **1. Frank Lloyd.** 1869–1959, U.S. architect. **2. Orville,** 1871–1948, and **Wilbur,** 1867–1912, U.S. inventors and pioneers in aviation; brothers. **3. Richard.** 1908–1960, U.S. writer.

Wyc·liffe, John (wik′lif) 1320–1384, English religious reformer. Also, **Wickliffe** and **Wiclif.**

Xa·vi·er, Saint Francis (zā′vē ər, ig zā′vē ər) 1506–1552, Spanish Jesuit missionary.

Xen·o·phon (zen′ə fən) 430?–355 B.C., Greek historian.

Xer·xes (zûrk′sēz) 519?–465 B.C., king of Persia (485?–465 B.C.).

Yeats, William Butler (yāts) 1865–1939, Irish poet and dramatist.

York (yôrk) **1.** family that ruled England (1461–1485), a branch of the royal house of Plantagenet. **2. duke of.** 1341–1402, son of Edward III; born *Edmund Langley.*

Young, Brigham (yung) 1801–1877, U.S. Mormon leader.

Yuan or **Yüan** (ū än′) Mongol dynasty that ruled China (1260–1368).

Zach·a·ri·ah (zak′ə rī′ə) in the New Testament, the father of John the Baptist.

Za·pa·ta, Emiliano (sä pä′tə) 1879?–1919, Mexican revolutionary.

Zeb·e·dee (zeb′ə dē′) in the New Testament, the father of the Apostles James and John.

Zeb·u·lun (zeb′yə lən) **1.** in the Old Testament, a son of Jacob and Leah. **2.** one of the twelve tribes of Israel descended from him.

Zech·a·ri·ah (zek′ə rī′ə) seventh century B.C., Hebrew prophet.

Zeng·er, John Peter (zeng′ər) 1697–1746, American printer, editor, and publisher.

Ze·no (zē′nō) 336?–262 B.C., Greek philosopher.

Zeph·a·ni·ah (zef′ə nī′ə) seventh century B.C., Hebrew prophet.

Zep·pe·lin, Count Ferdinand von (zep′ə lin) 1838–1917, German soldier and designer of airships.

Zhao Zi·yang (jou′ zù yäng′) 1919– , general secretary of the Chinese Communist Party (1987–).

Zhou (jō) dynasty that ruled China (1027–256 B.C.). Also, **Chou.**

Zhou En·lai (jō′ en lī′) see **Chou En-lai.**

Zo·la, Émile (zō′lə) 1840–1902, French novelist and critic.

Zo·ro·as·ter (zôr′ō as′tər) 628?–551 B.C., Persian religious teacher, founder of Zoroastrianism.

Zwing·li, Huldreich (zwing′lē) 1484–1531, Swiss religious reformer.

Geographical Names

This section lists the names of countries, states, cities, regions, continents, oceans, mountains, rivers, and other geographical features, as well as places of historical importance. The main geographical entry contains pronunciation, descriptive information, and population figures. When area, height, and length are given in an entry, metric equivalents are included. Capitals are listed for each country. Postal and traditional abbreviations, as well as capitals, are listed for U.S. states. Former names and less frequently used official names are listed as cross-references to the main entry. Adjectives and nouns formed from geographical names are included at the end of the entry. For example, **Kentuckian** can be found under the entry **Kentucky**.

Entries are listed alphabetically under the geographical name and not under a descriptive term, such as *Lake, Mount,* or *Cape,* which is part of the place name. For example, Mount Everest is listed as **Everest, Mount,** and Lake Superior as **Superior, Lake**.

Aa·chen (ä′kən) a city in West Germany, west of the Rhine, once the capital of Charlemagne's empire. Pop., 239,200. Also, **Aix-la-Chapelle**.

Aar·hus (ôr′hüs) a port city of Denmark. Pop., 245,900.

A·ba·dan (ä′bä dän′) a port city in southwestern Iran. Pop., 296,081.

Ab·er·deen (ab′ər dēn′) a city on the east coast of Scotland. Pop., 215,200.

Ab·i·djan (ab′i jän′) a port city and the former capital of the Ivory Coast, in the southeastern part of the country. Pop., 1,500,000.

Ab·i·lene (ab′ə lēn′) a city in west-central Texas. Pop., 112,000.

A·bu Dha·bi (ä′bü dä′bē, ä′bü thä′bē) **1.** the largest and most populous sheikdom in the United Arab Emirates. Area, 26,000 sq. mi. (67,340 sq. km.). Pop., 670,125. **2.** the capital of the United Arab Emirates and of the sheikdom of Abu Dhabi. Pop., 242,975.

A·bu·ja (ə bü′jə) the planned new capital of Nigeria, in the central part of the country. Pop., 15,000.

Ab·ys·sin·i·a (ab′ə sin′ē ə) see **Ethiopia**. —**Ab·ys·sin·i·an**, *adj., n.*

A·ca·di·a (ə kā′dē ə) a former French colony in eastern Canada, consisting of the present-day Maritime Provinces. —**A·ca·di·an**, *adj., n.*

A·ca·pul·co (ak′ə pül′kō, ä′kə pül′kō) a resort city on the southwestern coast of Mexico. Pop., 301,902.

Ac·cad (ak′ad, ä′käd) see **Akkad**.

Ac·cra (ə krä′, ak′rə) *also,* **Ak·kra.** the capital and largest city of Ghana, on the southern coast of the country. Pop., 633,880.

A·con·ca·gua (ak′ən kä′gwə) a mountain in western Argentina, in the Andes, the highest in South America and the Western Hemisphere. Height, 22,831 ft. (6,959 m.).

A·da·na (ä′də nə) a city in southern Turkey. Pop., 777,554.

Ad·dis Ab·a·ba (ad′is ab′ə bə) the capital and largest city of Ethiopia, in the central part of the country. Pop., 1,412,577.

Ad·e·laide (ad′ə lād′) a city in southern Australia, the capital of the state of South Australia. Pop., 882,520.

A·den (ad′ən, ä′dən) **1.** the capital of Southern Yemen, a port city on the Gulf of Aden. Pop., 176,100. **2. Gulf of.** a western inlet of the Arabian Sea, between southern Arabia and eastern Africa.

A·dri·at·ic (ā′drē at′ik) a sea between Italy and Yugoslavia, an arm of the Mediterranean. Also, **Adriatic Sea**.

Ae·ge·an (i jē′ən) a sea between Greece and Turkey, an arm of the Mediterranean. Also, **Aegean Sea**.

Aet·na, Mount (et′nə) see **Etna, Mount**.

Af·ghan·i·stan (af gan′ə stan′) a landlocked country in south-central Asia. Capital, Kabul. Area, 251,826 sq. mi. (652,229 sq. km.). Pop., 20,000,000.

Af·ri·ca (af′ri kə) a continent south of Europe, between the Atlantic and Indian oceans. Area, 11,704,000 sq. mi. (30,313,360 sq. km.). Pop., 626,000,000.

A·ga·na (ä gä′nyə) the capital of Guam. Pop., 896.

Ag·in·court (aj′in kôrt′) a village in northern France, the site of an English victory over the French in 1415.

A·gra (ä′grə) a city in north-central India, the site of the Taj Mahal. Pop., 694,191.

Ah·med·a·bad (ä′mə də bäd′) *also,* **Ah·mad·a·bad.** a city in west-central India. Pop., 2,059,725.

Ah·waz (ä wäz′) a city in southwestern Iran. Pop., 471,000. Also, **Ah·vaz** (ä väz′).

Aix-la-Cha·pelle (āks′la sha pel′) see **Aachen**.

Ak·kad (ak′ad, ä′käd) *also,* **Ac·cad. 1.** an ancient region in the northern part of Mesopotamia. **2.** an ancient city in central Mesopotamia, on the Euphrates River.

Ak·kra (ə krä′, ak′rə) see **Accra**.

Ak·ron (ak′rən) a city in northeastern Ohio. Pop., 222,000.

Al·a·bam·a (al′ə bam′ə) a state in the southeastern United States, at the southern end of the Appalachian Mountains and on the Gulf of Mexico. Capital, Montgomery. Area, 51,705 sq. mi. (133,916 sq. km.). Pop., 4,052,000. Abbreviation, **Ala.**; postal abbreviation, **AL** —**Al′a·bam′an, Al′a·bam′i·an**, *adj., n.* ▲ *Alabama* comes from *Alibamu,* the name of a tribe of the Creek Indians. This name was later used for the river near the tribal village and for the territory in which the river was located, which became the state.

A·las·ka (ə las′kə) the largest state of the United States, on the extreme northwestern peninsula of North America. Capital, Juneau. Area, 591,004 sq. mi. (1,530,700 sq. km.). Pop., 534,000. Abbreviation, **Alas.**; postal abbreviation,

---

at; āpe; fär; câre; end; mē; it; īce; pîerce; hot; ōld; sông, fôrk; oil; out; up; ūse; rüle; pull; tûrn; chin; sing; shop; thin; this; hw in white; zh in treasure. The symbol ə stands for the unstressed vowel sound heard in about, taken, pencil, lemon, and circus.

AK —**A·las′kan,** *adj., n.* ▲ The area now known as Alaska used to be called "Russian America" before the United States purchased the territory in 1867. Its name was then changed to *Alaska,* a word meaning "mainland" in the language of the inhabitants of the Aleutian Islands. This name was used to distinguish the Alaskan peninsula from the inhabitants' island homes.

Al·ba·ni·a (al bā′nē ə) a country in southeastern Europe, on the Balkan Peninsula. Capital, Tiranë. Area, 11,100 sq. mi. (28,749 sq. km.). Pop., 3,320,000.

Al·ba·ny (ôl′bə nē) the capital of New York, in the eastern part of the state. Pop., 101,727.

Al·ber·ta (al bûr′tə) a province of Canada, in the western part of the country. Capital, Edmonton. Area, 225,285 sq. mi. (583,488 sq. km.). Pop., 2,375,278.

Al·bu·quer·que (al′bə kûr′kē) the largest city in New Mexico, in the north-central part of the state. Pop., 367,000.

Al·ca·traz (al′kə traz′) an island in San Francisco Bay, the site of a former U.S. penitentiary of the same name.

A·lep·po (ə lep′ō) a city in northwestern Syria. Pop., 985,413.

A·leu·tian Islands (ə lü′shən) a chain of U.S. islands in the northern Pacific, extending southwest from Alaska. Land area, 6,391 sq. mi. (16,553 sq. km.). Also, **A·leu·tians** (ə lü′shənz).

Al·ex·an·dri·a (al′ig zan′drē ə) 1. a port city in Egypt, on the Mediterranean in the northeastern part of the country. It was founded by Alexander the Great in 332 B.C. Pop., 2,821,000. 2. a city in northern Virginia, a residential suburb of Washington, D.C. Pop., 108,000.

Al·ge·ri·a (al jîr′ē ə) a country in northern Africa, on the Mediterranean. Capital, Algiers. Area, 919,595 sq. mi. (2,381,751 sq. km.). Pop., 24,700,000. —**Al·ge′ri·an,** *adj., n.*

Al·giers (al jîrz′) the capital of Algeria, a port on the Mediterranean. Pop., 1,721,607. Also, **El Djazair, El Djezair.**

Al·le·ghe·ny (al′i gā′nē) a river in western Pennsylvania and southwestern New York, joining the Monongahela at Pittsburgh to form the Ohio. Length, 325 mi. (523 km.).

Al·len·town (al′ən toun′) a city in southeastern Pennsylvania. Pop., 104,000.

Al·ma-A·ta (äl′mə ə tä′) a city in the south-central Soviet Union. Pop., 1,088,000.

Al Maw·sil (äl mō sēl′) see **Mosul.**

Alps (alps) a mountain system in south-central Europe, extending in an arc from the Mediterranean coast near the French-Italian border to the Balkan Peninsula.

Al·sace–Lor·raine (al′sās lô rān′) a region in eastern France, on the German and Swiss borders, the subject of territorial dispute between France and Germany during the nineteenth and twentieth centuries.

Al·tai Mountains (al′tī) a mountain system in central Asia, in the southern Soviet Union, northwestern China, and northwestern Mongolia.

Am·a·ril·lo (am′ə ril′ō) a city in northwestern Texas. Pop., 166,000.

Am·a·zon (am′ə zon′) the longest river in South America and, by volume, the largest in the world, flowing from the Andes across Brazil into the Atlantic. Length, 4,000 mi. (6,436 km.).

A·mer·i·ca (ə mer′i kə) 1. the United States. 2. North America or South America. 3. North, Central, and South America considered as a whole. Also, **the Americas** *(def. 3).* —**A·mer′i·can,** *adj., n.* ▲ *America* derives from the Latin form of the name of the Italian navigator *Amerigo* Vespucci (1454–1512). A mapmaker gave Vespucci credit for discovering the New World and put this name on an early map.

American Samoa, an island group in Samoa, administered by the United States. Capital, Pago Pago. Land area, 76 sq. mi. (197 sq. km.). Pop., 38,000.

Am·man (ä män′) the capital of Jordan, in the northwestern part of the country. Pop., 777,500.

Am·ster·dam (am′stər dam′) the capital and largest city of the Netherlands, in the west-central part of the country. Pop., 679,140.

A·mu Dar·ya (ä′mü där′yə) a river in central Asia, principally in the Soviet Union, flowing into the Aral Sea. Length, 1,578 mi. (2,539 km.).

A·mur (ä mŏŏr′) a river in northeastern Asia, forming part of the boundary between the Soviet Union and China. Length, 2,761 mi. (4,442 km.).

An·a·heim (an′ə hīm′) a city in southwestern California. Pop., 241,000.

An·a·to·li·a (an′ə tō′lē ə) see **Asia Minor.** —**An′a·to′li·an,** *adj., n.*

An·chor·age (ang′kər ij) a port city in southern Alaska, the largest city in the state. Pop., 235,000.

An·da·lu·sia (an′də lü′zhə) a historic region of southern Spain, now divided into eight provinces. —**An′da·lu′sian,** *adj., n.*

An·des (an′dēz) the longest mountain system in the world, extending along the west coast of South America.

An·dor·ra (an dôr′ə) 1. a small country in southwestern Europe, between France and Spain. Area, 175 sq. mi. (453 sq. km.). Pop., 41,000. 2. the capital of this country. Pop., 16,200.

Angel Falls, the world's highest waterfall, in southeastern Venezuela. Height, 3,212 ft. (979 m.).

Angel Island, the largest island in San Francisco Bay, an entry point for Asian immigrants to the United States from 1910 to 1940.

An·go·la (ang gō′lə) a country on the west coast of southern Africa. Capital, Luanda. Area, 481,350 sq. mi. (1,246,697 sq. km.). Pop., 9,730,000.

An·guil·la (ang gwil′ə) a British island in the West Indies, one of the Leeward Islands. Area, 35 sq. mi. (91 sq. km.). Pop., 7,000.

An·jou (an′jü) a region and former province in western France, in the Loire valley.

An·ka·ra (ang′kər ə) the capital of Turkey, in the west-central part of the country. Pop., 2,235,035.

An·na·ba (ä′nə bä′) a port city in northeastern Algeria, on the Mediterranean. Pop., 313,174.

An·nap·o·lis (ə nap′ə lis) the capital of Maryland, in the central part of the state. It is the site of the United States Naval Academy. Pop., 31,740.

Ann Arbor, a city in southeastern Michigan. Pop., 108,000.

An·shan (än′shän′) a city in northeastern China. Pop., 1,280,000.

An·ta·nan·a·ri·vo (än′tə nä′nə rē′vō) the capital of Madagascar, in the central part of the country. Pop., 700,000. Formerly, **Tananarive.**

Ant·arc·ti·ca (ant ärk′ti kə, ant är′ti kə) an ice-covered continent surrounding the South Pole and lying mainly within the Antarctic Circle. Area, approx. 5,400,000 sq. mi. (13,986,000 sq. km.). Also, **the Ant·arc·tic** (ant ärk′tik, ant är′tik).

Antarctic Ocean, a body of water surrounding Antarctica, consisting of the southernmost parts of the Atlantic, Pacific, and Indian oceans.

An·tie·tam (an tē′təm) a creek in northwestern Maryland, the site of one of the bloodiest battles of the Civil War, in 1862.

An·ti·gua and Bar·bu·da (an tē′gə, an tē′gwə; bär-bü′də) an island nation in the Leeward Islands of the West Indies, including the islands of Antigua and Barbuda. Capital, St. John's. Land area, 171 sq. mi. (443 sq. km.). Pop., 84,000.

An·til·les (an til′ēz) the islands of the West Indies excluding the Bahamas, divided into the Greater Antilles and the Lesser Antilles.

Ant·werp (ant′wûrp) a port city in northern Belgium. Pop., 490,524.

A·pi·a (ä pē′ə) the capital of Western Samoa. Pop., 33,170.

Ap·pa·la·chi·an Mountains (ap′ə lā′chē ən, ap′ə lach′ē ən) the principal mountain system in eastern North America, extending from southeastern Canada to north-central Alabama. Also, **Ap·pa·la·chi·ans** (ap′ə lā′chē ənz, ap′ə lach′ē ənz).

Ap·po·mat·tox (ap′ə mat′əks) a town in central Virginia where the Confederate general Robert E. Lee formally surrendered to the Union general U. S. Grant on April 9, 1865, ending the Civil War.

A·qa·ba, Gulf of (ä′kə bə) a gulf at the northeastern end of the Red Sea, between the Sinai Peninsula and Saudi Arabia.

Aq·ui·taine (ak′wi tān′) a historic region in southwestern France.

A·ra·bi·a (ə rā′bē ə) a large peninsula in southwestern Asia. Area, approx. 1,000,000 sq. mi. (2,590,000 sq. km.). Also, **Arabian Peninsula.**

A·ra·bi·an Sea (ə rā′bē ən) the northwestern part of the Indian Ocean, between India and Arabia.

Ar·a·gon (ar′ə gon′) a historic region and former kingdom in northeastern Spain.

Ar·al Sea (ar′əl) an inland saltwater lake in the southwestern Soviet Union.

Ar·a·rat (ar′ə rat′) a mountain in eastern Turkey, traditionally identified as the landing place of Noah's Ark. Height, 16,806 ft. (5,122 m.). Also, **Mount Ararat.**

Ar·ca·di·a (är kā′dē ə) a mountainous region of ancient Greece, traditionally noted for the idyllic existence of its inhabitants.

Arc·tic, the (ärk′tik, är′tik) an ice-covered region surrounding the North Pole.

Arctic Ocean, an ocean north of the Arctic Circle and surrounding the North Pole. Also, **Arctic Sea.**

Ar·gen·ti·na (är′jən te′nə) a country in southern South America. Capital, Buenos Aires. Area, 1,073,400 sq. mi. (2,780,106 sq. km.). Pop., 32,400,000.

Ar·gos (är′gəs) an ancient city in south-central Greece.

Ar·i·zo·na (ar′ə zō′nə) a state in the southwestern United States, bordering on Mexico. Capital, Phoenix. Area, 160,113 sq. mi. (414,693 sq. km.). Pop., 3,319,000. Abbreviation, **Ariz.**; postal abbreviation, **AZ** —**Ar′i·zo′nan,** *adj., n.* ▲ *Arizona* comes from an Indian phrase meaning "little spring" or "place of the small spring" and originally referred to a very small area now south of the Mexican border. With the discovery of silver, this area became famous, and its name was applied to the surrounding region as well. The name *Arizona* was later used for the territory where this region was located, which eventually became a state.

Ar·kan·sas (*def. 1,* är′kən sô′; *def. 2,* är′kən sô′, är kan′zəs) **1.** a state in the south-central United States. Capital, Little Rock. Area, 53,187 sq. mi. (137,754 sq. km.). Pop., 2,372,000. Abbreviation, **Ark.**; postal abbreviation, **AR 2.** a river flowing from west-central Colorado into the Mississippi. Length, 1,459 mi. (2,348 km.). —**Ar·kan·san** (är kan′zən) *adj., n.* ▲ *Arkansas* comes from an Indian name for a tribe that lived near the Arkansas River. French explorers later used the word as the name of the river itself, and still later it was used as the name of the state.

Ar·ling·ton (är′ling tən) **1.** a county in northern Virginia, a residential suburb of Washington, D.C. It is the site of Arlington National Cemetery, one of the largest U.S. national cemeteries. Pop., 160,113. **2.** a city in northeastern Texas. Pop., 250,000.

Ar·me·ni·a (är mē′nē ə) **1.** a republic in the southwestern Soviet Union, bordering on Turkey and Iran. Official name: **Armenian Soviet Socialist Republic.** Area, 11,500 sq. mi. (29,785 sq. km.). Pop., 3,369,000. **2.** an ancient country in northeastern Asia Minor, now a region consisting of Soviet Armenia and parts of eastern Turkey and northwestern Iran.

A·ru·ba (ə rü′bə) an island in the Leeward Islands, a dependency of the Netherlands. Capital, Oranjestad. Area, 74 sq. mi. (192 sq. km.). Pop., 69,000.

As·cen·sion (ə sen′shən) a British island in the southern Atlantic, west of Africa. Area, 34 sq. mi. (88 sq. km.). Pop., 1,007.

A·sia (ā′zhə) the largest continent, bounded on the west by the Ural Mountains, the Caucasus, and the Black, Mediterranean, and Red seas, on the south by the Indian Ocean, and on the east by the Pacific. Area, 17,120,000 sq. mi. (44,340,800 sq. km.). Pop., 3,090,000,000.

Asia Minor, a peninsula in western Asia, bounded by the Black and Mediterranean seas. It includes most of the Asian part of Turkey. Area, 287,000 sq. mi. (743,330 sq. km.). Also, **Anatolia.**

As·ma·ra (az mär′ə) a city in northern Ethiopia. Pop., 275,385.

As·syr·i·a (ə sir′ē ə) an ancient empire in southwestern Asia, extending at its height into Egypt.

As·tu·ri·as (ə stur′ē əs) a region and former kingdom in northwestern Spain. Area, 4,207 sq. mi. (10,896 sq. km.).

A·sun·ción (ä′sün syōn′) the capital and largest city of Paraguay, an inland port in the southwestern part of the country. Pop., 455,517.

Ath·a·bas·ca (ath′ə bas′kə) *also,* **Ath·a·bas·ka. 1.** a river in Alberta, Canada, flowing north into Lake Athabasca. Length, 765 mi. (1,231 km.). **2. Lake.** a lake in Canada, on the northern Alberta-Saskatchewan border.

Ath·ens (ath′ənz) the capital of Greece, in the eastern part of the country. It was once the most important and powerful of the ancient Greek city-states. Pop., 885,737.

At·lan·ta (at lan′tə) the capital and largest city of Georgia, in the northwest-central part of the state. Pop., 422,000.

At·lan·tic (at lan′tik) an ocean separating Europe and Africa from North and South America. Also, **Atlantic Ocean.** —**At·lan′tic,** *adj.*

At Ta·if (ät′ tä ēf′) a city in western Saudi Arabia. Pop., 300,000. Also, **Taif.**

Auck·land (ôk′lənd) a port city on North Island, in northern New Zealand. Pop., 143,600.

Augs·burg (ôgz′bûrg′) a city in southern West Germany. Pop., 245,300.

Au·gus·ta (ô gus′tə) the capital of Maine, in the southern part of the state. Pop., 21,819.

Au·ro·ra (ô rôr′ə) a city in north-central Colorado, a residential suburb of Denver. Pop., 218,000.

Ausch·witz (oush′vits) the German name for **Oswlecim,** a city in southern Poland. It was the site of the largest Nazi concentration camp during World War II. Pop., 42,700.

Aus·tin (ôs′tin) the capital of Texas, in the south-central part of the state. Pop., 467,000.

Aus·tral·a·sia (ôs′trəl ā′zhə) an extensive area in the southwestern Pacific including Australia, Tasmania, New Zealand, New Guinea, and certain smaller islands in the immediate vicinity. —**Aus′tral·a′sian,** *adj., n.*

Aus·tra·lia (ôs trāl′yə) **1.** a continent southeast of Asia, between the Indian and Pacific oceans. It is the smallest of the continents. Area, 2,941,526 sq. mi. (7,618,552 sq. km.). Pop., 16,500,000. **2.** a country including this continent and the island of Tasmania. Capital, Canberra. Area, 2,967,909 sq. mi. (7,686,884 sq. km.). Pop., 16,937,300.

at; āpe; fär; câre; end; mē; it; īce; pîerce; hot; ōld; sông, fôrk; oil; out; up; ūse; rüle; pull; tûrn; chin; sing; shop; thin; this; hw in white; zh in treasure. The symbol ə stands for the unstressed vowel sound heard in about, taken, pencil, lemon, and circus.

Australian Capital Territory, a federal territory in the southeastern part of Australia. It includes Canberra, the capital of the country. Area, 939 sq. mi. (2,432 sq. km.). Pop., 244,500.

Aus·tri·a (ôs′trē ə) a landlocked country in central Europe, mainly in the Alps. Prior to World War I, it was the center of Austro-Hungary. Capital, Vienna. Area, 32,377 sq. mi. (83,856 sq. km.). Pop., 7,510,000. —**Aus′tri·an,** *adj., n.*

Aus·tro–Hun·ga·ry (ôs′trō hung′gə rē) a former dual monarchy in central Europe, including what are now Austria, Hungary, and parts of Czechoslovakia, Poland, Romania, Italy, and Yugoslavia. It was broken up at the end of World War I. Also, **Aus·tri·a-Hun·ga·ry** (ôs′trē ə-hung′gə rē), **Aus′tro-Hun·ga·ri·an Empire.** —**Aus′tro-Hun·ga′ri·an,** *adj., n.*

A·vi·gnon (a vēn yōn′) a historic city in southeastern France. It was the papal seat from 1309 to 1377. Pop., 89,132.

A·zer·bai·jan (ä′zər bī jän′) *also,* **A·zer·bai·dzhan.** **1.** a republic of the Soviet Union, south of the Caucasus on the west coast of the Caspian Sea and bordering Iran. Official name: **Azerbaijan Soviet Socialist Republic.** Area, 33,436 sq. mi. (86,599 sq. km.). Pop., 6,718,000. **2.** the part of Iran bordering this republic.

A·zores (ə zôrz′, ā′zôrz) an island group in the northern Atlantic, west of and belonging to Portugal. Land area, 894 sq. mi. (2,315 sq. km.). Pop., 252,200.

A·zov, Sea of (az′ôf) a northern arm of the Black Sea, in the western Soviet Union.

Az Zar·qa (äz zär′kə) a city in northern Jordan. Pop., 265,700. Also, **Zarka, Zarqa.**

Bab·y·lon (bab′ə lon′) an ancient city of Mesopotamia, on the Euphrates, the capital of Babylonia and later of the Chaldean empire. Babylon was noted for its wealth, magnificence, and wickedness.

Bab·y·lo·ni·a (bab′ə lō′nē ə) an ancient empire in lower Mesopotamia that flourished from about 1900 B.C. until 538 B.C., when it was conquered by the Persians.

Baf·fin Bay (baf′in) an inlet of the northern Atlantic, west of Greenland and east of Baffin Island.

Baffin Island, a large Canadian island west of Greenland, at the mouth of Hudson Bay. Area, approx. 200,000. sq. mi. (518,000 sq. km.).

Bagh·dad (bag′dad) *also,* **Bag·dad.** the capital of Iraq, in the east-central part of the country, on the Tigris River. Pop., 2,200,000.

Ba·ha·mas (bə hä′məz) an island country in the West Indies, located off the southeastern coast of Florida. Capital, Nassau. Land area, 5,380 sq. mi. (13,934 sq. km.). Pop., 230,000. Also, **Bahama Islands.** —**Ba·ha·mi·an** (bə hä′mē ən, bə hä′mē ən) *adj., n.*

Bah·rain (bä rān′) *also,* **Bah·rein.** an Arab emirate consisting of more than 30 islands in the Persian Gulf, west of Qatar. Capital, Manama. Land area, 240 sq. mi. (622 sq. km.). Pop., 503,000.

Bai·kal, Lake (bī käl′) *also,* **Lake Bay·kal.** a lake in the southeast-central Soviet Union. It is the deepest freshwater lake in the world.

Bai·ri·ki (bī rē′kē) the capital of Kiribati, an island in the Tarawa atoll. Pop., 1,956.

Ba·ja California (bä′hə) a long, narrow peninsula in northwestern Mexico, separating the Gulf of California from the Pacific. Area, 55,634 sq. mi. (144,092 sq. km.). Also, **Lower California.**

Bak·ers·field (bā′kərz fēld′) a city in southern California. Pop., 150,000.

Bakh·ta·ran (bäk′tə rän′) a city in western Iran. Pop., 532,000. Formerly, **Kermanshah.**

Ba·ku (bä kü′) a port city in the southwestern Soviet Union, on the west coast of the Caspian Sea. Pop., 1,722,000.

Ba·kwan·ga (bə kwäng′gə) see **Mbuji-Mayi.**

Bal·e·ar·ic Islands (bal′ē ar′ik) a Spanish island group in the western Mediterranean. Land area, 1,936 sq. mi. (5,014 sq. km.). Pop., 6,572.

Ba·li (bä′lē) an island in Indonesia, east of Java. Area, 2,147 sq. mi. (5,561 sq. km.).

Bal·kan Peninsula (bôl′kən) a peninsula in southern Europe, bordered by the Black and Aegean seas on the east and the Adriatic on the west.

Balkan States, the countries on the Balkan Peninsula: Yugoslavia, Romania, Bulgaria, Albania, and Greece. Also, **the Balkans.**

Bal·tic Sea (bôl′tik) an inland sea in northern Europe, bordered by East Germany and Poland on the south, Denmark and Sweden on the west, and Finland and the Soviet Union on the east. Also, **the Baltic.** —**Bal′tic,** *adj.*

Baltic States, Estonia, Latvia, and Lithuania. —**Bal′tic,** *adj.*

Bal·ti·more (bôl′tə môr′) the largest city in Maryland, a port on the Chesapeake Bay. Pop., 753,000.

Ba·ma·ko (bä′mə kō′) the capital of Mali, in the southwestern part of the country. Pop., 502,000.

Ban·dar Se·ri Be·ga·wan (bun′dər ser′ē bə gä′wən) the capital of Brunei, on the northeastern coast of the country. Pop., 17,400.

Ban·dung (bän′düng) a city in Indonesia, in western Java. Pop., 1,462,637.

Ban·ga·lore (bang′gə lôr′) a city in southern India. Pop., 2,476,355.

Bang·kok (bang′kok) the capital and largest city of Thailand, in the south-central part of the country. Pop., 5,153,902. Also, **Krung Thep.**

Ban·gla·desh (bang′glə desh′) *also,* **Ban·gla Desh.** a country located at the north end of the Bay of Bengal and largely surrounded by India. It was formerly the province of **East Pakistan.** Capital, Dhaka. Area, 55,598 sq. mi. (143,999 sq. km.). Pop., 112,000,000.

Ban·gui (bäng′gē) the capital of the Central African Republic, in the southwestern part of the country. Pop., 350,000.

Ban·jul (bän′jùl) the capital of Gambia, in the western part of the country. Pop., 44,536.

Banks·town (bangks′toun′) a city in southeastern Australia, in New South Wales. Pop., 152,636.

Ban·nock·burn (ban′ək bûrn′) a village in central Scotland, near which Scottish troops under Robert the Bruce defeated the English on June 24, 1314, thereby ending English control of Scotland until modern times.

Bar·ba·dos (bär bā′dōs) an island nation in the Lesser Antilles, the easternmost island of the West Indies. Capital, Bridgetown. Area, 166 sq. mi. (430 sq. km.). Pop., 259,000.

Bar·ba·ry Coast (bär′bə rē) the Mediterranean coast of the Barbary States.

Barbary States, Morocco, Algeria, Tunisia, and the region of Tripoli when under Turkish control, used as a refuge by pirates from the sixteenth to the early nineteenth century.

Bar·bu·da (bär bü′də) see **Antigua and Barbuda.**

Bar·ce·lo·na (bär′sə lō′nə) a port city in northeastern Spain. Pop., 1,754,900.

Bar·ents Sea (bar′ənts) the part of the Arctic Ocean north of Norway and the Soviet Union.

Ba·ri (bär′ē) a city in southeastern Italy, a port on the Adriatic. Pop., 365,630.

Bar·qui·si·me·to (bär′kə sə mā′tō) a city in northwestern Venezuela. Pop., 504,000.

Bar·ran·quil·la (bär′ən kē′yə) the chief seaport of Colombia, on the Caribbean, in the northern part of the country. Pop., 891,545.

Bar·row, Point (bar′ō) a small Alaskan peninsula, the northernmost point of the United States.

Ba·sel (bä′zəl) a city in northwestern Switzerland, on the Rhine. Pop., 174,606. Also, **Basle** (bäl).

Bas·ra (bus′rə) a port city in southeastern Iraq. Pop., 616,700.

Basse·terre (bäs târ′) the capital and largest city of St. Kitts-Nevis. Pop., 15,000.

Ba·taan (bə tan′) a peninsula in the Philippines, west of Manila, where U.S. troops surrendered to the Japanese in 1942.

Bat·on Rouge (bat′ən rüzh′) the capital of Louisiana, in the south-central part of the state. Pop., 241,000.

Ba·var·i·a (bə vâr′ē ə) the largest state of West Germany, in the southeastern part of the country. At various times in history it was a duchy, a kingdom, and a republic. Area, 27,240 sq. mi. (70,552 sq. km.). Pop., 10,993,400.

Ba·ya·món (bī′ə mōn′) a city in northeastern Puerto Rico. Pop., 185,087.

Bay·kal, Lake (bī käl′) see **Baikal, Lake.**

Beau·fort Sea (bō′fərt) an arm of the Arctic Ocean, bordering northern Alaska and northwestern Canada.

Beau·mont (bō′mont) a port city in southeastern Texas. Pop., 120,000.

Bei·jing (bā′jing′) the capital of the People's Republic of China, in the northeastern part of the country. Also called **Peking,** it was formerly known as **Peiping** (1928–1949). Pop., 5,860,000.

Bei·ra (bā′rə) the chief port of Mozambique, in the southeastern part of the country, on an arm of the Indian Ocean. Pop., 230,744.

Bei·rut (bā rüt′) the capital and largest city of Lebanon, in the west-central part of the country, on the Mediterranean. Pop., 509,000.

Be·lau (bə lou′) see **Palau.**

Be·lém (bə lem′) a port city in northeastern Brazil. Pop., 1,120,777.

Bel·fast (bel′fast) the capital and largest city of Northern Ireland, on the eastern coast of the country. Pop., 301,600.

Bel·gium (bel′jəm) a country in northwestern Europe, on the North Sea. Capital, Brussels. Area, 11,783 sq. mi. (30,518 sq. km.). Pop., 9,940,000.

Bel·grade (bel′grād) the capital and largest city of Yugoslavia, an inland port in the eastern part of the country. Pop., 1,470,073.

Be·lize (be lēz′) a country on the northeastern coast of Central America, on the Caribbean, formerly **British Honduras.** Capital, Belmopan. Area, 8,866 sq. mi. (22,963 sq. km.). Pop., 178,000.

Belize City, the largest city in Belize, located in the northern part of the country. Pop., 47,000.

Bel·mo·pan (bel′mō pän′) the capital of Belize, in the north-central part of the country. Pop., 4,500.

Be·lo Ho·ri·zon·te (bel′ō hôr′ə zon′te) a city in southeastern Brazil. Pop., 2,122,073.

Be·na·res (bə när′is) see **Varanasi.**

Ben·gal (ben′gôl, beng′gəl) **1.** a former province and historic region of northeastern British India, now divided between India and Bangladesh. **2. Bay of.** the northeastern part of the Indian Ocean, between Burma and the peninsula of India.

Ben·gha·zi (ben gä′zē) also, **Ben·ga·si.** a port city in the northeastern part of Libya. Pop., 367,600.

Be·nin (be nēn′) a country in western Africa, on the Gulf of Guinea. Capital, Porto-Novo. Area, 44,484 sq. mi. (115,214 sq. km.). Pop., 4,590,000. Formerly, **Dahomey.**

Ber·gen (bûr′gən) a port city in southwestern Norway. Pop., 207,912.

Ber·ing Sea (bîr′ing, ber′ing) the northernmost arm of the Pacific, between Siberia and Alaska.

Bering Strait, a strait between Siberia and Alaska, connecting the Bering Sea with the Arctic Ocean.

Berke·ley (bûr′klē) a city in western California. Pop., 104,000.

Ber·lin (bər lin′) the former capital of Germany, now in East Germany and divided into **West Berlin** and **East Berlin.**

Ber·mu·da (bər mū′də) a British island group in the northern Atlantic, about 600 miles east of North Carolina. Land area, 21 sq. mi. (54 sq. km.). Pop., 57,000. Also, **Ber·mu·das** (bər mū′dəz).

Bern (bûrn, bern) also, **Berne.** the capital of Switzerland, in the west-central part of the country. Pop., 138,574.

Beth·le·hem (beth′lə hem) a town in the West Bank, near Jerusalem. It was the birthplace of Jesus. Pop., 25,000.

Bho·pal (bō päl′) a city in central India, the site of one of the worst industrial accidents in history. Pop., 671,018.

Bhu·tan (bü tän′) a country of south-central Asia, in the Himalayas, bounded by China and India. Capital, Thimbu. Area, 17,954 sq. mi. (46,501 sq. km.). Pop., 1,540,000.

Bie·le·feld (bē′lə felt′) a city in central West Germany. Pop., 300,800.

Big Island, see **Hawaii** (*def.* 2).

Bi·ki·ni (bi kē′nē) an atoll in the Marshall Islands, the former site of U.S. nuclear weapons tests.

Bil·ba·o (bil bä′ō) a port city in northern Spain, near the Bay of Biscay. Pop., 433,030.

Bil·lings (bil′ingz) a city in south-central Montana, on the Yellowstone River. Pop., 66,842.

Bi·lox·i (bə luk′sē, bə lok′sē) a city in southeastern Mississippi. Pop., 49,311.

Bir·ming·ham (*def.* 1, bûr′ming ham′; *def.* 2, bûr′ming-əm) **1.** the largest city of Alabama, in the north-central part of the state. Pop., 278,000. **2.** a city in west-central England. Pop., 1,007,500.

Bis·cay, Bay of (bis′kā) a broad inlet of the northern Atlantic, between western France and northern Spain.

Bis·marck (biz′märk) the capital of North Dakota, in the south-central part of the state. Pop., 44,585.

Bismarck Archipelago, a large island group in the western Pacific, just east of New Guinea, a part of Papua New Guinea. Land area, approx. 19,000 sq. mi. (49,000 sq. km.).

Bis·sau (bi sou′) the capital of Guinea-Bissau. Pop., 109,486.

Black Forest, a mountainous forested region in southwestern West Germany.

Black Sea, an inland sea between Europe and Asia, bordered by the Soviet Union, Turkey, Bulgaria, and Romania.

Black·town (blak′toun′) a city in southeastern Australia, in New South Wales. Pop., 181,139.

Blan·tyre (blan′tīr) a city in southern Malawi. Pop., 229,000.

Block Island, an island at the eastern end of Long Island Sound, part of Rhode Island. Area, approx. 11 sq. mi. (28 sq. km.).

Bloem·fon·tein (blüm′fən tān′) the judicial capital of the Republic of South Africa, in the central part of the country. Pop., 104,381.

Blue Nile, a river in eastern Africa, flowing through northwestern Ethiopia and eastern Sudan, a tributary of the Nile. Length, 850 mi. (1,368 km.).

Blue Ridge Mountains, an eastern range of the Appalachian Mountains, extending from northeastern West Virginia to northern Georgia. Also, **Blue Ridge.**

Bo·bo Diou·las·so (bō′bō dü las′ō) a city in western Burkina Faso. Pop., 231,162.

Bo·chum (bō′kəm) a city in western West Germany, in the Ruhr valley. Pop., 382,041.

---

at; āpe; fär; câre; end; mē; it; īce; pîerce; hot; ōld; sông, fôrk; oil; out; up; ūse; rüle; pull; tûrn; chin; sing; shop; thin; <u>th</u>is; hw in white; zh in treasure. The symbol ə stands for the unstressed vowel sound heard in about, taken, pencil, lemon, and circus.

Bo·go·tá (bō'gə tä') the capital and largest city of Colombia, in the west-central part of the country. Pop., 3,967,988.

Bo·he·mi·a (bō hē'mē ə) a historic region and former kingdom, in western Czechoslovakia. Area, approx. 20,000 sq. mi. (51,800 sq. km.).

Boi·se (boi'zē, boi'sē) the capital of Idaho, in the southwestern part of the state. Pop., 108,000.

Bo·liv·i·a (bə liv'ē ə) a landlocked country in west-central South America. Capitals, La Paz and Sucre. Area, 424,165 sq. mi. (1,098,587 sq. km.). Pop., 7,110,000.

Bo·lo·gna (bə lōn'yə) a city in northern Italy. Pop., 437,203.

Bol·ton (bōl'tən) a city in northwestern England. Pop., 261,200.

Bom·bay (bom bā') the largest city and chief port of India, on the western coast of the country. Pop., 8,243,405.

Bonn (bon) the capital of West Germany, in the western part of the country. Pop., 292,600.

Bor·deaux (bôr dō') a port city in southwestern France. Pop., 208,159.

Bor·ne·o (bôr'nē ō') a large island in the Malay Archipelago, divided into Sarawak and Sabah (which are part of Malaysia), Kalimantan (which is part of Indonesia), and Brunei. Area, 290,000 sq. mi. (751,100 sq. km.).

Bos·ni·a and Her·ze·go·vi·na (boz'nē ə; hûrt'sə gə vē'nə) a republic of Yugoslavia, in the west-central part of the country. Area, approx. 19,740 sq. mi. (51,130 sq. km.). Pop., 4,124,008. Also, **Bosnia-Herzegovina.**

Bos·po·rus (bos'pər əs) a strait connecting the Black Sea and the Sea of Marmara, separating European and Asian Turkey.

Bos·ton (bôs'tən) the capital of Massachusetts, in the eastern part of the state. Pop., 562,994.

Both·ni·a, Gulf of (both'nē ə) the northern arm of the Baltic Sea, between Sweden and Finland.

Bot·swa·na (bot swä'nə) a country in central southern Africa. Capital, Gaborone. Area, 224,700 sq. mi. (581,973 sq. km.). Pop., 1,280,000.

Boua·ké (bwä kā') a city of the Ivory Coast, in the central part of the country. Pop., 275,000.

Brad·ford (brad'fərd) a city in north-central England. Pop., 463,500.

Brah·ma·pu·tra (brä'mə pü'trə) a large river in southern Asia, flowing from southwestern Tibet to the Bay of Bengal. Length, 1,770 mi. (2,848 km.).

Bramp·ton (bramp'tən) a city in southern Ontario, Canada. Pop., 188,498.

Bra·si·lia (brə zēl'yə) the capital of Brazil, in the east-central part of the country. Pop., 1,576,657.

Bra·sov (brä shôv') a city in central Romania. Pop., 351,493.

Bra·ti·sla·va (brä'tə slä'və) a city in southern Czechoslovakia, on the Danube. Pop., 409,100.

Bra·zil (brə zil') the largest country in South America, on the Atlantic in the northeastern part of the continent. Capital, Brasilia. Area, 3,286,488 sq. mi. (8,512,004 sq. km.). Pop., 147,000,000.

Braz·za·ville (braz'ə vil') the capital of the Republic of the Congo, in the southeastern part of the country. Pop., 595,102.

Breed's Hill (brēdz) see **Bunker Hill.**

Brem·en (brem'ən) a port city in northern West Germany. Pop., 528,900.

Bre·scia (bresh'ə) a city in north-central Italy. Pop., 200,790.

Bres·lau (brez'lou) see **Wroclaw.**

Bridge·port (brij'pôrt') a city in southwestern Connecticut. Pop., 142,000.

Bridge·town (brij'toun') the capital and largest city of Barbados. Pop., 7,600.

Bris·bane (briz'bān, briz'bən) a port city in eastern Australia, the capital of Queensland. Pop., 942,836.

Bris·tol (bris'təl) a port city in southwestern England. Pop., 393,800.

Brit·ain (brit'ən) see **Great Britain.**

British Columbia, the westernmost province of Canada, on the Pacific. Capital, Victoria. Area, 366,255 sq. mi. (948,600 sq. km.). Pop., 2,889,207.

British Honduras, see **Belize.**

British Isles, an island group off the western coast of continental Europe, including Great Britain, Ireland, and many smaller islands.

British West Indies, formerly, British island possessions in the West Indies, including the Bahamas, Windward Islands, Leeward Islands, and British Virgin Islands.

Brit·ta·ny (brit'ə nē) a historic region in northwestern France, between the English Channel and the Bay of Biscay.

Br·no (bûr'nō) a city in central Czechoslovakia. Pop., 383,443. Also, *German,* **Brünn.**

Brom·berg (brom'bûrg) see **Bydgoszcz.**

Bronx, The (brongks) a borough of New York City. Area, 43 sq. mi. (111 sq. km.).

Brook·lyn (bruk'lin) a borough of New York City. Area, 79 sq. mi. (205 sq. km.).

Browns·ville (brounz'vil) a city in southernmost Texas. Pop., 102,000.

Bru·nei (brü nī') a small country on the northern coast of Borneo. Capital, Bandar Seri Begawan. Area, 2,226 sq. mi. (5,765 sq. km.). Pop., 269,000.

Brünn (brün) see **Brno.**

Bruns·wick (brunz'wik) a city in northeastern West Germany. Pop., 250,700.

Bru·sa (brü'sə) see **Bursa.**

Brus·sels (brus'əlz) the capital of Belgium, in the central part of the country. Pop., 137,738.

Bu·ca·ra·man·ga (bü'kər ə mäng'gə) a city in northern Colombia. Pop., 342,169.

Bu·cha·rest (bü'kə rest') the capital and largest city of Romania, in the southern part of the country. Pop., 1,989,823.

Bu·chen·wald (bü'kən wôld', bü'kən väld') a village in East Germany, the site of a Nazi concentration camp during World War II.

Bu·da·pest (bü'də pest') the capital and largest city of Hungary, in the north-central part of the country. Pop., 2,075,990.

Bue·nos Ai·res (bwā'nəs ī'rəs, bwā'nəs âr'ēz) the capital and largest city of Argentina, on the eastern coast of the country. Pop., 2,922,829.

Buf·fa·lo (buf'ə lō') a port city in western New York, on Lake Erie. Pop., 325,000.

Bu·jum·bu·ra (bü'jəm bùr'ə) the capital and chief port of Burundi, on Lake Tanganyika in the western part of the country. Pop., 229,980.

Bu·la·wa·yo (bùl'ə wä'ō) a city in southwestern Zimbabwe. Pop., 413,814.

Bul·gar·i·a (bul gâr'ē ə, bùl gâr'ē ə) a country in southeastern Europe, in the east-central part of the Balkan Peninsula. Capital, Sofia. Area, 42,823 sq. mi. (110,912 sq. km.). Pop., 9,210,000.

Bull Run, a stream near Manassas in northeastern Virginia, site of two Civil War battles, in 1861 and 1862, in which the Union forces were defeated.

Bunker Hill, a hill in eastern Massachusetts, near Boston. The Battle of Bunker Hill, in 1775, was the first major battle of the American Revolution, but it was actually fought on nearby Breed's Hill.

Bur·gun·dy (bûr'gən dē) a historic region in east-central France, at various times an independent kingdom, a duchy, and a province of France.

Bur·ki·na Fa·so (bər kē'nə fä'sō) a country in western Africa, north of Ghana. Capital, Ouagadougou. Area, 105,869 sq. mi. (274,201 sq. km.). Pop., 7,710,000. Formerly, **Upper Volta.**

Bur·ling·ton (bûr′ling tən) **1.** the largest city in Vermont, in the northwestern part of the state. Pop., 37,712. **2.** a city in Ontario, Canada, in the southeastern part of the province. Pop., 116,675.

Bur·ma (bûr′mə) a country in southeastern Asia. Capital, Rangoon. Area, 261,228 sq. mi. (676,581 sq. km.). Pop., 40,000,000.

Bur·na·by (bûr′nə bē) a city in southwestern British Columbia. Pop., 145,161.

Bur·sa (bûr′sə) a city in northwestern Turkey, a former capital of the Ottoman Empire. Pop., 612,510. Also, **Brusa.**

Bu·run·di (bə run′dē) a landlocked country in east-central Africa. Capital, Bujumbura. Area, 10,745 sq. mi. (27,830 sq. km.). Pop., 5,290,000.

Byd·goszcz (bid′gôsh) a city in northwest-central Poland. Pop., 366,400. Also, *German,* **Bromberg.**

Bye·lo·rus·sia (byel′ō rush′ə) a republic of the Soviet Union, in the westernmost part of the country, bordering Poland. Official name: **Byelorussian Soviet Socialist Republic.** Area, 80,155 sq. mi. (207,601 sq. km.). Pop., 10,002,000. Also, **White Russia.** —**Bye′lo·rus′sian,** *adj., n.*

By·zan·ti·um (bi zan′tē əm) an ancient Greek city that became the capital of the Roman Empire and was renamed Constantinople.

Ca·bin·da (kə bin′də) a territory of Angola in western equatorial Africa, on the Atlantic, separated from the main portion of the country by Zaire. Area, 2,807 sq. mi. (7,270 sq. km.). Pop., 81,265.

Cá·diz (kə diz′, kä′diz) a city in southwestern Spain. Pop., 156,328.

Ca·glia·ri (käl′yə rē) the largest city of the Italian island of Sardinia. Pop., 223,487.

Cai·ro (kī′rō) the capital of Egypt, in the northeastern part of the country. It is the largest city in Africa. Pop., 6,205,000.

Cal·ais (kal′ā, ka lā′) a seaport on the northern coast of France, the continental European city closest to England. Pop., 78,820.

Cal·cut·ta (kal kut′ə) a port city in northeastern India, the former capital of British India. Pop., 3,305,006.

Cal·ga·ry (kal′gə rē) a city in southwestern Canada, in the province of Alberta. Pop., 636,104.

Ca·li (kä′lē) a city in western Colombia. Pop., 1,347,810.

Cal·i·for·nia (kal′ə fôr′nyə) **1.** the most populous state of the United States, on the Pacific coast. Capital, Sacramento. Area, 158,706 sq. mi. (411,049 sq. km.). Pop., 26,981,000. Abbreviation, **Calif.**; postal abbreviation, **CA 2. Gulf of.** a long inlet of the Pacific, just south of California, separating Baja California from the Mexican mainland. —**Cal′i·for′nian,** *adj., n.* ▲ *California* was originally the name of an imaginary island described as rich in gold and jewels in a Spanish romance written about 1500. When the Spanish explorers landed on the southern tip of the Baja California peninsula, they believed it was an island and named it after the island in the story. When other Spanish explorers traveled northward, they extended the name to include the northern territory, calling the northern part Alta, or Upper, California and the peninsula Baja, or Lower, California. When the northern territory became part of the United States, it was known simply as *California,* and it kept that name when it was admitted as a state.

Ca·llao (kə you′) a city on the west coast of central Peru, the major seaport of the country. Pop., 264,133.

Ca·lo·o·can (kal′ə ō′kän) a city in the Philippines, in the north-central part of the country. Pop., 467,816.

Cal·va·ry (kal′və rē) a hill near ancient Jerusalem where Jesus was crucified. Also, **Golgotha.**

Ca·ma·güey (kam′ə gwā′) a city in east-central Cuba. Pop., 245,235.

Cam·bo·di·a (kam bō′dē ə) a country in southeastern Asia. It is officially known as **Kampuchea.** Capital, Phnom

Penh. Area, 69,898 sq. mi. (181,036 sq. km.). Pop., 8,060,000.

Cam·bridge (kām′brij) **1.** a city in eastern Massachusetts. Pop., 95,322. **2.** a city in eastern England. Pop., 100,200.

Cam·den (kam′dən) a city in southwestern New Jersey, on the Delaware River. Pop., 84,910.

Cam·er·oon (kam′ə rün′) a country in west-central Africa, consisting of most of the territory of the former Cameroons. Capital, Yaoundé. Area, 183,569 sq. mi. (475,444 sq. km.). Pop., 11,000,000.

Cam·er·oons (kam′ə rünz′) two former United Nations trust territories, one under French administration, now Cameroon; and the other under British administration, now divided between Cameroon and Nigeria.

Cam·pi·nas (kam pē′nəs) a city in southeastern Brazil. Pop., 845,047.

Ca·naan (kā′nən) a region in Palestine, between the Jordan River and the Mediterranean.

Can·a·da (kan′ə də) a country in northern North America, bordering the United States. Capital, Ottawa. Area, 3,849,670 sq. mi. (9,970,645 sq. km.). Pop., 26,200,000. —**Ca·na·di·an** (kə nā′dē ən) *adj., n.*

Canal Zone, a strip of territory across the Isthmus of Panama, extending approximately five miles on each side of the Panama Canal. It was administered by the United States from 1903 to 1979, when nearly all of it was returned to Panamanian control. Area, approx. 553 sq. mi. (1,432 sq. km.). Also, **Panama Canal Zone.**

Canary Islands, a Spanish island group in the northern Atlantic, off the northwestern coast of Africa. Land area, 2,807 sq. mi. (7,270 sq. km.). Pop., 1,426,422. Also, **Canaries.**

Ca·nav·er·al, Cape (kə nav′ər əl) the site of the main U.S. launching and testing center for missiles and spacecraft, located on the Atlantic coast of Florida.

Can·ber·ra (kan ber′ə) the capital of Australia, in the southeastern part of the nation. Pop., 219,331.

Can·ter·bur·y (kan′tər ber′ē, kan′tər bə rē) a city in southeastern England. The site of a famous cathedral, it is the seat of the spiritual leader of the Church of England. Pop., 36,000.

Can·ton (*def. 1,* kan′ton; *def. 2,* kan′tən) **1.** see **Guangzhou. 2.** a city in northeastern Ohio. Pop., 93,077.

Cape Town (kāp′ toun′) *also,* **Cape·town.** the legislative capital of the Republic of South Africa, a port city on the southwestern coast of the country. Pop., 776,617.

Cape Verde (vûrd) **1.** see **Verde, Cape. 2.** an island country in the northern Atlantic, west of Cape Verde. Capital, Praia. Land area, 1,557 sq. mi. (4,033 sq. km.). Pop., 358,000. Formerly, **Cape Verde Islands.**

Ca·rac·as (kə rä′kəs) the capital and largest city of Venezuela, in the northern part of the country. Pop., 3,041,000.

Car·diff (kär′dif) the capital and chief city of Wales. Pop., 278,900.

Car·ib·be·an (kar′ə bē′ən, kə rib′ē ən) **1.** a sea bounded on the north and east by the West Indies, on the west by Central America, and on the south by South America. Also, **Caribbean Sea. 2. the Caribbean.** the region consisting of this sea and those lands in and around it. —**Car′ib·be′an,** *adj.*

Carls·bad Caverns (kärlz′bad) the largest known net-

---

at; āpe; fär; câre; end; mē; it; īce; pîerce; hot; ōld; sông, fôrk; oil; out; up; ūse; rüle; pùll; tûrn; chin; sing; shop; thin; this; hw in white; zh in treasure. The symbol ə stands for the unstressed vowel sound heard in about, taken, pencil, lemon, and circus.

1121

work of underground caverns in the world, located in southeastern New Mexico.

Carls·ruh·e (kärlz′ə) see **Karlsruhe.**

Car·o·li·na (*defs. 1, 2,* kar′ə lī′nə; *def. 3,* kär′ə lē′nə) **1.** a former British colony on the southern Atlantic coast of North America, divided into North Carolina and South Carolina in 1729. **2. the Carolinas.** North Carolina and South Carolina. **3.** a city in northeastern Puerto Rico. Pop., 147,835.

Car·o·line Islands (kar′ə līn′) an archipelago of more than 500 islands in the western Pacific north of New Guinea, administered by the United States and including Palau and the Federated States of Micronesia. Land area, approx. 525 sq. mi. (1,360 sq. km.).

Car·son City (kär′sən) the capital of Nevada, in the western part of the state. Pop., 32,022.

Car·ta·ge·na (kär′tə jē′nə) a port city in northwestern Colombia. Pop., 531,426.

Car·thage (kär′thij) an ancient city and state in northern Africa, on the site of modern Tunisia. It was founded by the Phoenicians, destroyed by the Romans in 146 B.C., and rebuilt by the Romans in 44 B.C.

Cas·a·blan·ca (kas′ə blang′kə) the largest city and chief port of Morocco, in the northwestern part of the country. Pop., 2,139,204.

Cascade Range, a mountain range in the western United States, extending from northern California through Oregon and into Washington.

Cash·mere (kash′mîr, kazh′mîr) see **Kashmir.**

Cas·per (kas′pər) a city in central Wyoming. Pop., 51,016.

Cas·pi·an Sea (kas′pē ən) an inland sea in the southern Soviet Union, bordering northern Iran. It is the largest inland body of water in the world.

Cas·tile (kas tēl′) a region and former kingdom in north-central and central Spain.

Cas·tries (kas′trēz) the capital and largest city of St. Lucia. Pop., 50,798.

Cat·a·li·na (kat′ə lē′nə) see **Santa Catalina.** Also, **Catalina Island.**

Cat·a·lo·ni·a (kat′ə lō′nē ə) a historic region and former principality in the northeastern corner of Spain.

Ca·ta·nia (kə tän′yə) a port city on the eastern coast of the Italian island of Sicily. Pop., 376,312.

Ca·thay (ka thā′) *Archaic.* China.

Cau·ca·sus (kô′kə səs) a mountain range in the southern Soviet Union between the Black and Caspian seas, traditionally regarded as part of the boundary between Europe and Asia.

Cawn·pore (kôn′pôr) see **Kanpur.**

Cay·enne (kī en′, kā en′) the capital and largest city of French Guiana, a port on the northern coast of the department. Pop., 38,135.

Cay·man Islands (kā′mən) three British islands in the Greater Antilles, northwest of Jamaica. Land area, 100 sq. mi. (259 sq. km.). Pop., 22,000.

Ce·bu (sā bü′) a port city in the south-central Philippines. Pop., 490,281.

Cedar Rapids, a city in eastern Iowa. Pop., 108,000.

Cel·e·bes (sel′ə bēz′) see **Sulawesi.**

Central African Republic, a landlocked country in central Africa. Capital, Bangui. Area, 240,535 sq. mi. (622,986 sq. km.). Pop., 2,840,000.

Central America, a region between the Pacific and the Caribbean, occupying the long isthmus of North America that links that continent with South America. It includes Guatemala, Belize, El Salvador, Honduras, Nicaragua, Costa Rica, and Panama. Area, 205,087 sq. mi. (531,175 sq. km.). —**Central American.**

Central Valley, a valley in central California, including the San Joaquin and Sacramento river valleys. Length, 450 mi. (724 km.).

Ceu·ta (sā ü′tə) a port city on the Mediterranean, a Spanish enclave in northern Morocco. Pop., 68,822.

Cey·lon (si lon′, sā lon′) see **Sri Lanka.** —**Cey·lo·nese** (sē′lə nēz′, sē′lə nēs′) *adj., n.*

Chad (chad) **1.** a country in north-central Africa. Capital, Ndjamena. Area, 495,800 sq. mi. (1,284,122 sq. km.). Pop., 5,530,000. **2. Lake.** a large lake in north-central Africa, at the southern edge of the Sahara.

Chal·de·a (kal dē′ə) *also,* **Chal·dae·a.** an ancient region in southernmost Babylonia, on the Tigris and Euphrates rivers, in what is now southern Iraq.

Cham·pagne (sham pān′) a region in northeastern France, formerly a province.

Cham·plain, Lake (sham plān′) a lake on the border between New York and Vermont, extending into southwestern Quebec.

Chang (chäng) see **Yangtze.** Also, **Chang Jiang** (chäng′ jyäng′).

Chang·chun (chäng′chûn′) a city in northeastern China. Pop., 1,480,000.

Channel Islands, a British island group off the coast of France in the English Channel, including Jersey and Guernsey. Land area, 75 sq. mi. (194 sq. km.). Pop., 138,100.

Cha·pul·te·pec (chə pul′tə pek′) a rocky hill in Mexico City, Mexico, captured by U.S. forces in 1847 in the last major battle of the Mexican War.

Char·le·roi (shär′lə roi′) a city in southern Belgium. Pop., 210,324.

Charles·ton (chärlz′tən) **1.** the capital of West Virginia, in the western part of the state. Pop., 63,968. **2.** a port city in southeastern South Carolina. Pop., 69,510.

Char·lotte (shär′lət) the largest city of North Carolina, in the southern part of the state. Pop., 352,000.

Charlotte A·ma·lie (ə mäl′yə) the capital and largest city of the Virgin Islands of the United States, on the island of St. Thomas. Pop., 11,842.

Char·lotte·town (shär′lət toun′) the capital and largest city of Prince Edward Island, Canada, a port on the southern coast of the province. Pop., 15,766.

Châ·teau–Thier·ry (sha tō tē rē′) a town in northern France where American and French troops halted the German advance on Paris in 1918 during World War I. Pop., 14,557.

Chat·ta·noo·ga (chat′ə nü′gə) a city in southern Tennessee, on the Tennessee River. Pop., 162,000.

Cheek·to·wa·ga (chēk′tə wä′gə) a city in western New York. Pop., 100,400.

Chem·nitz (kem′nits) see **Karl-Marx-Stadt.**

Cheng·chow (jung′jō′) see **Zhengzhou.**

Cheng·du (chung′dü′) *also,* **Cheng·tu.** a city in south-central China. Pop., 1,590,000.

Che·sa·peake (ches′ə pēk′) a city in southeastern Virginia. Pop., 134,000.

Chesapeake Bay, an arm of the Atlantic, on the eastern coast of the United States, in Virginia and Maryland.

Chey·enne (shī en′, shī an′) the capital and largest city of Wyoming, in the southeastern part of the state. Pop., 47,283.

Chi·ca·go (shi kä′gō) the largest city of Illinois, a port in the northeastern part of the state, located on Lake Michigan. Pop., 3,010,000.

Chi·chén It·zá (chē′chən ēt′sə) an ancient Mayan city in southeastern Mexico, on the Yucatán peninsula.

Chick·a·mau·ga (chik′ə mô′gə) a creek flowing from northwestern Georgia into the Tennessee River, the site of a Confederate victory in 1863 during the Civil War.

Chi·cla·yo (chi klī′ō) a city in northwestern Peru, near the Pacific coast. Pop., 213,095.

Chi·hua·hua (chi wä′wə) a city in northern Mexico. Pop., 385,603.

Chil·e (chil′ē) a country on the southwestern coast of South America. Capital, Santiago. Area, 292,135 sq. mi. (756,630 sq. km.). Pop., 12,800,000. —**Chil′e·an,** *adj., n.*

Chim·bo·te (chim bō'tē) a city in northwestern Peru, near the Pacific coast. Pop., 223,341.

Chi·na (chī'nə) **1. People's Republic of.** a country in eastern Asia. It is the most populous country in the world. Capital, Beijing. Area, 3,691,500 sq. mi. (9,560,985 sq. km.). Pop., 1,110,000,000. Also, **Communist China, Mainland China, Red China. 2. Republic of.** see **Taiwan.**

Chi·nan (jē'nän') see **Jinan.**

Chit·ta·gong (chit'ə gong') a port in southeastern Bangladesh, near the Bay of Bengal. Pop., 980,000.

Chong·jin (chung'jin') a seaport in western North Korea. Pop., 300,000.

Chong·qing (chung'ching') a port city in west-central China, on the Yangtze River. Pop., 2,080,000. Also, **Chungking.**

Christ·church (krīst'chûrch') a city in New Zealand, on the eastern coast of South Island. Pop., 161,700.

Christmas Island, an island south of Java in the Indian Ocean, administered by Australia. Area, approx. 52 sq. mi. (135 sq. km.). Pop., 3,000.

Chuk·chi Sea (chŭk'chē) the part of the Arctic Ocean north of the Bering Strait, between Asia and North America.

Chu·la Vis·ta (chü'lə vis'tə) a city in the southwestern corner of California, near San Diego. Pop., 119,000.

Chung·king (chŭng'king') see **Chongqing.**

Chur·chill (chûr'chil) a river in central Canada that flows east through Saskatchewan and Manitoba into the Hudson Bay. Length, 1,000 mi. (1,609 km.).

Cin·cin·nat·i (sin'sə nat'ē) a port city in southwestern Ohio, on the Ohio River. Pop., 370,000.

Ciu·dad Juá·rez (sē'ü däd' wär'ez) a city in northern Mexico, on the Rio Grande opposite El Paso, Texas. Pop., 544,496. Also, **Juárez.**

Cleve·land (klēv'lənd) a city in Ohio, a port in the northeastern part of the state, on Lake Erie. Pop., 536,000.

Cnos·sus (nos'əs, kə nos'əs) see **Knossos.**

Co·cha·bam·ba (kō'chə büm'bə) a city in west-central Bolivia. Pop., 317,251.

Cod, Cape (kod) a long, hook-shaped peninsula in eastern Massachusetts, famous as a summer vacation spot.

Co·logne (kə lōn') a city in the western part of West Germany, near Bonn. Pop., 919,300.

Co·lom·bi·a (kə lum'bē ə) a country in northwestern South America, on the Pacific and the Caribbean. Capital, Bogotá. Area, 440,831 sq. mi. (1,141,752 sq. km.). Pop., 31,200,000. **—Co·lom'bi·an,** adj., n.

Co·lom·bo (kə lum'bō) the capital and chief port of Sri Lanka, on the west coast of the island. Pop., 623,000.

Col·o·rad·o (kol'ə rad'ō, kol'ə rä'dō) **1.** a state in the western United States. Capital, Denver. Area, 104,091 sq. mi. (269,596 sq. km.). Pop., 3,267,000. Abbreviation, **Colo.;** postal abbreviation, **CO 2.** a river flowing from northern Colorado into the Gulf of California. Length, 1,450 mi. (2,333 km.). **—Col'o·rad'an,** adj., n. ▲ *Colorado* comes from a Spanish word meaning ''reddish colored,'' used originally as the name of a river in New Mexico and Arizona that has a reddish appearance and flows into the Colorado River. Later the name was applied to the Colorado River itself. The territory that later became the state was named after the Colorado River.

Colorado Springs, a city in central Colorado, the site of the United States Air Force Academy. Pop., 273,000.

Co·lum·bi·a (kə lum'bē ə) **1.** a river that flows into the Pacific, forming most of the border between Washington and Oregon. Length, 1,214 mi. (1,953 km.). **2.** the capital of South Carolina, in the central part of the state. Pop., 100,385. **3.** the United States.

Co·lum·bus (kə lum'bəs) **1.** the capital of Ohio, in the central part of the state. Pop., 566,000. **2.** a city in western Georgia. Pop., 180,000.

Communist China, see **China** (def. 1).

Com·o·ros (kom'ə rōz') an island country off the southeastern coast of Africa. Capital, Moroni. Land area, 838 sq. mi. (2,170 sq. km.). Pop., 502,000.

Con·a·kry (kon'ə krē) the capital and chief port of Guinea, in the western part of the country. Pop., 600,000.

Con·cord (defs. 1, 3, kong'kərd, def. 2, kon'kôrd, kong'kərd) **1.** a town in eastern Massachusetts, site of one of the first battles of the American Revolution, on April 19, 1775. Pop., 6,400. **2.** the capital of New Hampshire, in the southern part of the state. Pop., 30,400. **3.** a city in western California, northeast of Oakland. Pop., 106,000.

Confederate States of America, a political union formed by the eleven Southern states that seceded from the United States in 1860 and 1861. They were Alabama, Arkansas, Florida, Georgia, Louisiana, Mississippi, North Carolina, South Carolina, Tennessee, Texas, and Virginia. Also, **the Confederacy.**

Con·go (kong'gō) **1.** a long river in central Africa, flowing from southeastern Zaire into the Atlantic. Length, 2,900 mi. (4,666 km.). Also, **Zaire. 2. Republic of the.** a country in west-central Africa, west of the country of Zaire. Capital, Brazzaville. Area, 132,000 sq. mi. (341,880 sq. km.). Pop., 1,940,000. **3. Democratic Republic of the.** see **Zaire** (def. 1).

Con·nect·i·cut (kə net'i kət) **1.** a state in the northeastern United States, the southernmost of the New England states. Capital, Hartford. Area, 5,018 sq. mi. (12,997 sq. km.). Pop., 3,189,000. Abbreviations, **Conn., Ct.;** postal abbreviation, **CT 2.** the longest river in New England, flowing from northern New Hampshire into Long Island Sound. Length, 407 mi. (655 km.). ▲ *Connecticut* comes from an Algonquian word meaning ''beside the long tidal river,'' indicating the area near the mouth of the Connecticut River. Settlers used the name for the entire river and later for nearby settlements and the colony that contained them, which eventually became the state.

Con·stan·tine (kon'stən tēn') a city in northeastern Algeria. Pop., 448,578. Also, **Qacentina.**

Con·stan·ti·no·ple (kon'stan tə nō'pəl) the capital of the Byzantine and Ottoman empires, now the city of **Istanbul.**

Continental Divide, an elevation of land in North America formed by the various peaks of the Rocky Mountains, separating rivers flowing eastward from those flowing westward. Also, **Great Divide.**

Cook Islands, a group of islands east of Australia in the western part of the southern Pacific, a possession of New Zealand. Land area, approx. 90 sq. mi. (235 sq. km.). Pop., 20,000.

Co·pen·ha·gen (kō'pən hā'gən) the capital of Denmark. It is the largest city in Denmark and a major northern European port. Pop., 478,615.

Coral Sea, a southwestern arm of the Pacific, off the coast of northeastern Australia. It was the site of an American victory over the Japanese in 1942, during World War II.

Cor·di·ller·as (kôr dil'ər əz, kôr'də lyâr'əs) **1.** a mountain system extending from Alaska to Cape Horn, including the Rocky Mountains in North America and the Andes in South America. **2.** that part of this system located in South America; the Andes. **3.** that part of this system located in North America.

---

at; āpe; fär; câre; end; mē; it; īce; pîerce; hot; ōld; sông; fôrk; oil; out; up; ūse; rüle; pull; tûrn; chin; sing; shop; thin; this; hw in white; zh in treasure. The symbol ə stands for the unstressed vowel sound heard in about, taken, pencil, lemon, and circus.

Cór·do·ba (kôr′də bə) **1.** a city in southwestern Spain. Pop., 225,562. **2.** a city in north-central Argentina. Pop., 993,055. Also, **Cor·do·va** (kôr′də və).

Cor·inth (kôr′inth) a port city in southern Greece. It was a major commercial and artistic center in ancient times. Pop., 22,658.

Cor·pus Chris·ti (kôr′pəs kris′tē) a port city in southern Texas. Pop., 264,000.

Cor·reg·i·dor (kə reg′i dôr′) a fortified island in the Philippines, site of a surrender by U.S. forces to the Japanese in 1942, during World War II.

Cor·si·ca (kôr′si kə) a French island in the Mediterranean, southeast of France. Area, approx. 3,352 sq. mi. (8,682 sq. km.). Pop., 234,640. —**Cor′si·can**, *adj., n.*

Cos·ta Ri·ca (kos′tə rē′kə) a country in Central America, between Nicaragua and Panama. Capital, San José. Area, 19,730 sq. mi. (51,101 sq. km.). Pop., 2,870,000. —**Cos′ta Ri′can.**

Côte d'I·voire (kōt dē vwär′) see **Ivory Coast.**

Co·to·nou (kō′tə nü′) a port city in southern Benin. Pop., 215,000.

Co·to·pax·i (kō′tə pak′sē) a volcano in the Andes, in north-central Ecuador. It is one of the highest active volcanos in the world. Height, 19,347 ft. (5,897 m.).

Cov·en·try (kuv′ən trē) a city in south-central England. During the English civil war, Royalists were sent there to be imprisoned. Pop., 312,200.

Crac·ow (krak′ou) see **Kraków.**

Crater Lake, a lake in the crater of a prehistoric volcano, in southwestern Oregon. It is the deepest lake in the United States.

Crete (krēt) a Greek island in the eastern Mediterranean, southeast of mainland Greece. Area, 3,235 sq. mi. (8,379 sq. km.). Pop., 501,082.

Cri·me·a (krī mē′ə) a peninsula in the southwestern Soviet Union, on the northern coast of the Black Sea. Area, 10,000 sq. mi. (25,900 sq. km.).

Cro·a·tia (krō ā′shə) a historic region that is now a republic of Yugoslavia, in the northwestern part of the country. Area, approx. 21,830 sq. mi. (56,540 sq. km.). Pop., 4,601,469.

Cu·ba (kū′bə) an island country in the Caribbean, the largest and westernmost island of the West Indies. Capital, Havana. Area, 42,804 sq. mi. (110,862 sq. km.). Pop., 10,400,000. —**Cu′ban**, *adj., n.*

Cú·cu·ta (kü′kü tä′) a city in northern Colombia. Pop., 443,093.

Cu·lia·cán (kü lyä kän′) a city in northwestern Mexico. Pop., 304,826.

Cu·ra·çao (kyúr′ə sō′) the principal island of the Netherlands Antilles group, off the coast of Venezuela. Area, 171 sq. mi. (443 sq. km.). Pop., 165,000.

Cu·ri·ti·ba (kùr′i tē′bə) a city in southern Brazil. Pop., 1,285,027.

Cus·co (küs′kō) see **Cuzco.**

Cush (kùsh, kush) *also,* **Kush.** in the Bible, a land inhabited by the descendants of Ham. It is usually identified with present-day Ethiopia.

Cuz·co (küs′kō) *also,* **Cus·co.** a city in southern Peru, in the Andes. It was the capital of the Incan empire. Pop., 89,563.

Cy·prus (sī′prəs) an island country south of Turkey in the eastern Mediterranean, divided since 1974 into separate Greek and Turkish zones. Capital, Nicosia. Area, 3,572 sq. mi. (9,251 sq. km.). Pop., 697,000.

Czech·o·slo·va·ki·a (chek′ə slə vä′kē ə) a landlocked country in central Europe. Capital, Prague. Area, 49,381 sq. mi. (127,897 sq. km.). Pop., 15,800,000.

Dac·ca (dak′ə) see **Dhaka.**

Dach·au (dä′kou) a city in southern West Germany, near Munich, the site of a Nazi concentration camp.

Da·ho·mey (də hō′mē) see **Benin.** —**Da·ho′man**, *adj., n.*

Dai·ren (dī′ren′) see **Dalian** *(def. 2).*

Da·kar (dä kär′) the capital and largest city of Senegal. Pop., 1,341,000.

Da·ko·ta (də kō′tə) **1.** a former territory of the United States, consisting of what is now North Dakota and South Dakota. **2. the Dakotas.** North Dakota and South Dakota.

Da·lian (dä′lyän′) **1.** a municipality in northeastern China, formed by the merger of the cities of Dalian and Lushun. Pop., 1,630,000. Formerly, **Luda. 2.** a port city in northeastern China, now part of the municipality of Dalian. It was called Dairen during the Japanese occupation. Pop., 1,380,000.

Dal·las (dal′əs) a city in northeastern Texas. Pop., 1,004,000.

Dal·ma·tia (dal mā′shə) a region in western Yugoslavia, on the coast of the Adriatic Sea.

Da·mas·cus (də mas′kəs) the capital and largest city of Syria, one of the oldest continuously inhabited cities in the world. Pop., 1,259,000.

Da Nang (də nang′) *also,* **Da·nang.** a port city in central Vietnam, on the South China Sea. Pop., 318,655.

Dan·ube (dan′ūb) the second longest river in Europe, flowing eastward from the southern part of West Germany to the Black Sea. Length, 1,776 mi. (2,858 km.). —**Dan·u′bi·an**, *adj.*

Dan·zig (dan′sig) see **Gdansk.**

Dar·da·nelles (där′də nelz′) a narrow strait between European and Asian Turkey, connecting the Aegean Sea with the Sea of Marmara. In ancient times it was known as the Hellespont.

Dar es Sa·laam (där′ es sə läm′) a capital and the largest city of Tanzania, in the eastern part of the country. Pop., 757,346.

Dar·ling (där′ling) the longest river in Australia, flowing southwest through western New South Wales to the Murray River. Length, 1,702 mi. (2,739 km.).

Dar·win (där′win) a seaport in northern Australia, the capital of Northern Territory. Pop., 56,482.

Da·vao (dä vou′) a port city in the southeastern Philippines. Pop., 610,375.

Dav·en·port (dav′ən pôrt′) a city in eastern Iowa. Pop., 103,264.

Day·ton (dā′tən) a city in southwestern Ohio. Pop., 179,000.

Dead Sea, a salt lake between Israel and the West Bank on the west and Jordan on the east.

Death Valley, a deep desert basin in southeastern California. It is the hottest and driest place in the United States and contains the lowest point in the Western Hemisphere.

Deb·re·cen (deb′rə tsən) a city in eastern Hungary. Pop., 211,823.

Del·a·ware (del′ə wâr′) **1.** a state in the eastern United States. Capital, Dover. Area, 2,045 sq. mi. (5,297 sq. km.). Pop., 633,000. Abbreviation, **Del.;** postal abbreviation, **DE 2.** a river in the eastern United States, flowing from southeastern New York State between Pennsylvania and New Jersey into the Delaware Bay. Length, 280 mi. (451 km.). —**Del′a·war′e·an**, *n.* ▲ An English captain named the Delaware Bay after Thomas West, Lord *De la Warr* (1577–1618), the first governor of the colony of Virginia. Later English settlers transferred the name to the three lower counties of Pennsylvania, which became the state of Delaware.

Delaware Bay, an inlet of the Atlantic between Delaware and New Jersey.

Del·hi (del′ē) a city in northern India, near New Delhi. Pop., 4,884,234.

Del·phi (del′fī) an ancient city in central Greece, the site of the Delphic oracle.

Den·mark (den′märk) a country in northern Europe, between the North and Baltic seas. Capital, Copenhagen. Area, 16,633 sq. mi. (43,079 sq. km.). Pop., 5,120,000.

Den·ver (den'vər) the capital and largest city of Colorado, in the north-central part of the state. Pop., 505,000.

Der·by (dûr'bē; *British,* där'bē) a city in central England. Pop., 215,200.

Der·ry (der'ē) see **Londonderry.**

Des Moines (də moin') the capital and largest city of Iowa, in the south-central part of the state. Pop., 192,000.

De·troit (di troit') the largest city in Michigan, in the southeastern part of the state. Pop., 1,086,000.

Devil's Island, an island off the coast of French Guiana, formerly a French penal colony.

Dha·ka (dak'ə) *also,* **Dacca.** the capital and largest city of Bangladesh, in the central part of the country. Pop., 2,365,695.

Di·e·go Gar·ci·a (dē ä'gō gär sē'ə) a British island in the Indian Ocean.

District of Columbia, a federal district in the eastern United States between Maryland and Virginia, consisting of the city of Washington, the capital of the United States. It is conventionally known as Washington, D.C. Area, 69 sq. mi. (179 sq. km.). Pop., 626,000. Abbreviation, **D.C.;** postal abbreviation, **DC**

Dja·kar·ta (jə kär'tə) see **Jakarta.**

Dji·bou·ti (ji bü'tē) **1.** a country in east Africa, on the Gulf of Aden. Capital, Djibouti. Area, 8,960 sq. mi. (23,206 sq. km.). Pop., 414,000. **2.** the capital of Djibouti. Pop., 200,000.

Dne·pro·pe·trovsk (nep'rō pi trôfsk') a city in the southwestern Soviet Union, in the Ukraine. Pop., 1,166,000.

Dnie·per (nē'pər) a river flowing through the European part of the Soviet Union into the Black Sea. Length, 1,368 mi. (2,201 km.).

Dnies·ter (nēs'tər) a river flowing through the European part of the Soviet Union into the Black Sea. Length, 840 mi. (1,352 km.).

Do·do·ma (dō'də mə) a capital of Tanzania, in the central part of the country. Pop., 24,500.

Do·ha (dō'hä) the capital of Qatar. Pop., 180,000.

Dom·i·ni·ca (dom'ə nē'kə, də min'i kə) a country in the eastern West Indies, one of the Windward Islands. Capital, Roseau. Area, 290 sq. mi. (751 sq. km.). Pop., 80,000.

Do·min·i·can Republic (də min'i kən) a country in the central West Indies, occupying the eastern part of the island of Hispaniola. Capital, Santo Domingo. Area, 18,704 sq. mi. (48,443 sq. km.). Pop., 6,820,000.

Don (don) a river flowing through the western Soviet Union to the Sea of Azov. Length, 1,224 mi. (1,969 km.).

Do·netsk (də netsk') a city in the Soviet Union, in the eastern Ukraine. Pop., 1,081,000.

Dort·mund (dôrt'mənd) a city in northwestern West Germany. Pop., 575,200.

Dou·a·la (dü ä'lə) *also,* **Duala.** a port city in southwestern Cameroon, the largest city in the country. Pop., 841,000.

Do·ver (dō'vər) **1.** the capital of Delaware, in the central part of the state. Pop., 23,507. **2.** a port town in southeastern England, noted for its white cliffs. Pop., 33,700. **3. Strait of.** a strait separating southeastern England from northern France and connecting the English Channel with the North Sea.

Dres·den (drez'dən) a city in southern East Germany. Pop., 519,769.

Du·a·la (dü ä'lə) see **Douala.**

Du·bai (dü bī') **1.** one of the sheikdoms of the United Arab Emirates, on the Persian Gulf. Capital, Dubai. Area, 1,500 sq. mi. (3,885 sq. km.). Pop., 419,104. **2.** the capital of Dubai. Pop., 265,702.

Dub·lin (dub'lin) the capital and largest city of Ireland, in the eastern part of the country. Pop., 915,115.

Dud·ley (dud'lē) a borough in west-central England. Pop., 300,800.

Duis·burg (düs'bûrg) a city in northwestern West Germany. Pop., 520,200.

Dun·kirk (dun'kûrk) *also,* **Dun·kerque.** a seaport in northern France, scene of the evacuation of Allied troops in 1940. Pop., 73,120.

Du·que de Ca·xi·as (dü'kə də kä shē'əs) a city in southeastern Brazil. Pop., 666,128.

Dur·ban (dûr'bən) a port city in the eastern part of the Republic of South Africa. Pop., 634,301.

Dur·ham (dûr'əm) a city in north-central North Carolina. Pop., 114,000.

Düs·sel·dorf (dü'səl dôrf') a city in northwestern West Germany. Pop., 563,000.

East Berlin, the capital of East Germany, located in the east-central part of the country. Pop., 1,215,586.

East China Sea, an arm of the Pacific between eastern China and the Ryukyu Islands.

Easter Island, a Chilean island in the southeastern Pacific, noted for its enormous stone statues.

East Germany, a country in north-central Europe. Official name: **German Democratic Republic.** Capital, East Berlin. Area, 41,828 sq. mi. (108,335 sq. km.). Pop., 16,900,000.

East Indies **1.** the Netherlands East Indies, sometimes including India and peninsular Southeast Asia. **2.** see **Malay Archipelago.** Also, **East India.**

East Los Angeles, a city in southern California. Pop., 110,017.

East Pakistan, see **Bangladesh.**

East York (yôrk) a borough of metropolitan Toronto, Canada. Pop., 101,085.

Ec·ua·dor (ek'wə dôr') a country on the northwestern coast of South America. Capital, Quito. Area, 109,484 sq. mi. (283,564 sq. km.). Pop., 10,500,000. **—Ec'ua·do'-ri·an,** *adj., n.*

Ed·in·burgh (ed'ən bûr'ō) the capital of Scotland, in the east-central part of the country. Pop., 439,700.

Ed·mon·ton (ed'mən tən) the capital and largest city of Alberta, Canada, in the south-central part of the province. Pop., 573,982.

E·gypt (ē'jipt) a country in northeastern Africa. Ancient Egypt was the center of one of the world's earliest and greatest civilizations. Capital, Cairo. Area, 386,662 sq. mi. (1,001,455 sq. km.). Pop., 51,400,000.

El Aa·iún (el' ä ün') the capital of Western Sahara, in the northwestern part of the territory. Pop., 20,000.

El·ba (el'bə) an Italian island located between Italy and Corsica, the site of Napoleon Bonaparte's exile in 1814 and 1815. Area, 85 sq. mi. (220 sq. km.). Pop., 28,600.

El·be (el'bə) a river flowing from Czechoslovakia through East and West Germany into the North Sea. Length, 720 mi. (1,158 km.).

El·brus, Mount (el'brüs) the highest peak of Europe, in the Caucasus Mountains in the southwestern Soviet Union. Height, 18,510 ft. (5,642 m.).

El Dje·za·ir (el' jə zä ir') *also,* **El Dja·za·ir.** see **Algiers.**

E·liz·a·beth (i liz'ə bəth) a city in northeastern New Jersey. Pop., 107,000.

Elles·mere Island (elz'mîr) a large Canadian island in the Arctic Ocean, northwest of Greenland. It is the northernmost island of Canada. Area, 82,119 sq. mi. (212,688 sq. km.).

El·lis Island (el'is) a small island in upper New York Bay, the chief U.S. immigrant reception center from 1892 to 1943.

El Pas·o (el pas'ō) a city in westernmost Texas, on the Rio Grande. Pop., 492,000.

---

at; āpe; fär; câre; end; mē; it; īce; pîerce; hot; ōld; sông, fôrk; oil; out; up; ūse; rüle; pùll; tûrn; chin; sing; shop; thin; <u>th</u>is; hw in white; zh in treasure. The symbol ə stands for the unstressed vowel sound heard in about, taken, pencil, lemon, and circus.

El Sal·va·dor (el sal′və dôr′) a country in western Central America. Capital, San Salvador. Area, 8,248 sq. mi. (21,362 sq. km.). Pop., 6,090,000. Also, **Salvador.**

Eng·land (ing′glənd) the largest political division of the United Kingdom, in the southern part of the island of Great Britain. Capital, London. Area, 50,363 sq. mi. (130,440 sq. km.). Pop., 47,254,500.

English Channel, a narrow body of water between England and France, connecting the North Sea with the Atlantic Ocean.

Equatorial Guinea, a country in west-central Africa, on the Gulf of Guinea. Capital, Malabo. Area, 10,831 sq. mi. (28,052 sq. km.). Pop., 430,000.

Er·furt (âr′fərt) a city in southwestern East Germany. Pop., 216,046.

E·rie (ir′ē) **1. Lake.** the southernmost of the Great Lakes, on the U.S.-Canadian border. **2.** a city in northwestern Pennsylvania, on Lake Erie. Pop., 115,000.

Erie Canal, a waterway across New York State, connecting the Hudson River with Lake Erie. The canal is now part of the New York State Barge Canal.

Es·fa·han (es′fə hän′) a city in west-central Iran, the capital of Persia during the seventeenth and eighteenth centuries. Pop., 927,000. Also, **Isfahan.**

Es·sen (es′ən) a city in northwestern West Germany. Pop., 662,000.

Es·to·ni·a (es tō′nē ə) a republic of the Soviet Union, in the northwestern part of the country, on the Baltic Sea. Official name: **Estonian Soviet Socialist Republic.** Area, 17,400 sq. mi. (45,066 sq. km.). Pop., 1,541,000.

E·thi·o·pi·a (ē′thē ō′pē ə) a country in eastern Africa. Capital, Addis Ababa. Area, 483,000 sq. mi. (1,250,970 sq. km.). Pop., 48,700,000. Formerly, **Abyssinia.** —**E′thi·o′pi·an,** *adj., n.*

Et·na, Mount (et′nə) *also,* **Mount Aet·na.** a high, active volcano in the northeastern part of the Italian island of Sicily. Height, 10,902 ft. (3,323 m.).

E·to·bi·coke (i tō′bi kōk′) a city in southern Ontario, Canada. Pop., 302,973.

Eu·gene (ū jēn′) a city in western Oregon. Pop., 105,000.

Eu·phra·tes (ū frā′tēz) a river in southwestern Asia, flowing from east-central Turkey through Syria and Iraq into the Persian Gulf. It joins the Tigris River in southeastern Iraq. Length, 1,510 mi. (2,430 km.).

Eur·ope (yùr′əp) a continent between Asia and the Atlantic. Area, 4,063,000 sq. mi. (10,523,170 sq. km.). Pop., 706,000,000.

Ev·ans·ville (ev′ənz vil′) a city in southwestern Indiana. Pop., 129,000.

Ev·er·est, Mount (ev′ər əst) the highest mountain in the world, located in the Himalayas on the border between Nepal and Tibet. Height, 29,028 ft. (8,848 m.).

E·ver·glades (ev′ər glādz′) an extensive region of marshlands and swamps in southern Florida.

Eyre, Lake (âr) a saltwater lake in the state of South Australia, the largest lake in Australia.

Faer·oe Islands (fâr′ō) a group of Danish islands in the northern Atlantic, between the Shetland Islands and Iceland. Land area, 540 sq. mi. (1,400 sq. km.). Pop., 42,000.

Fai·sa·la·bad (fī sä′lə bäd′) a city in northeastern Pakistan. Pop., 1,104,209. Formerly, **Lyallpur.**

Falk·land Islands (fôk′lənd) an island group in the southern Atlantic, east of the southern tip of Argentina. A British dependency, they are also claimed by Argentina. Land area, approx. 4,700 sq. mi. (12,200 sq. km.). Pop., 2,000. Also, **Malvinas.**

Fall Line, the boundary east of the Appalachian Mountains between the Atlantic coastal plain and the Piedmont region.

Far East, the countries of eastern Asia, including Japan, China, and North and South Korea.

Far·go (fär′gō) the largest city in North Dakota, in the eastern part of the state. Pop., 61,383.

Federated States of Micronesia, a group of Pacific islands in the Caroline Islands, administered by the United States as a part of the Trust Territory of the Pacific Islands. Capital, Kolonia. Land area, 271 sq. mi. (702 sq. km.). Pop., 95,000.

Fertile Crescent, a crescent-shaped region of fertile land extending from the eastern coast of the Mediterranean to the northern coast of the Persian Gulf. It was the site of several early civilizations.

Fez (fez) *also,* **Fes.** a city in north-central Morocco. Pop., 448,823.

Fi·ji (fē′jē) a country consisting of some 800 islands north of New Zealand, in the southwestern Pacific. Capital, Suva. Land area, 7,078 sq. mi. (18,332 sq. km.). Pop., 738,000. Also, **Fiji Islands.**

Fin·land (fin′lənd) **1.** a nation in northeastern Europe, on the Baltic Sea. Capital, Helsinki. Area, 130,119 sq. mi. (337,008 sq. km.). Pop., 4,893,748. **2. Gulf of.** an arm of the Baltic Sea between Finland and Estonia.

Flan·ders (flan′dərz) a historic region of northwestern Europe, in western Belgium, northern France, and the southwestern Netherlands.

Flint, a city in southeastern Michigan. Pop., 146,000.

Flor·ence (flôr′əns, flor′əns) a city in central Italy. It was one of the world's greatest centers of Renaissance art. Pop., 430,738.

Flor·i·da (flôr′i də, flor′i də) a state mostly on the southeastern peninsula of the United States. Capital, Tallahassee . Area, 58,664 sq. mi. (151,940 sq. km.). Pop., 11,675,000. Abbreviation, **Fla.**; postal abbreviation, **FL** —**Flor′i·dan, Flo·rid·i·an** (flə rid′ē ən) *adj., n.* ▲ *Florida* is a Spanish word meaning "flowery." The name was given to this region by the Spanish explorer Ponce de León, who landed there during *Pasqua florida,* the Spanish festival of flowers, which takes place at Easter.

Florida Keys, a chain of small islands off the southern coast of Florida.

For·mo·sa (fôr mō′sə) another name for the island of **Taiwan.**

For·ta·le·za (fôr′tə lā′zə) a city on the northeastern coast of Brazil. Pop., 1,588,709.

Fort Knox (noks) a military reservation in northern Kentucky, the site of the U.S. gold bullion depository.

Fort–La·my (fôr lä mē′) see **Ndjamena.**

Fort Lau·der·dale (lô′dər dāl′) a city in southeastern Florida. Pop., 149,000.

Fort Wayne (wān) a city in northeastern Indiana. Pop., 173,000.

Fort Worth, a city in northeastern Texas. Pop., 430,000.

France (frans) a country in western Europe. Capital, Paris. Area, 211,208 sq. mi. (547,029 sq. km.). Pop., 55,300,000.

Frank·fort (frangk′fərt) the capital of Kentucky, in the north-central part of the state. Pop., 25,973.

Frank·furt (frangk′fərt) a city in central West Germany. Pop., 598,000. Also, **Frank·furt am Main** (frängk′fùrt äm mīn′).

Fred·er·icks·burg (fred′ər iks bûrg′) a city in northeastern Virginia, the site of a Confederate victory in the Civil War, in 1862. Pop., 15,322.

Fred·er·ic·ton (fred′ər ik tən) the capital of New Brunswick, Canada, in the southern part of the province. Pop., 44,352.

Free·town (frē′toun′) the capital of Sierra Leone, a port city on the Atlantic. Pop., 469,776.

Fre·mont (frē′mont) a city in western California, near San Francisco. Pop., 154,000.

French Guiana, a French overseas department on the northeastern coast of South America. Capital, Cayenne. Area, 34,750 sq. mi. (90,003 sq. km.). Pop., 90,000.

French Indochina, a former French dependency in Southeast Asia, consisting of what are now the countries of Vietnam, Laos, and Cambodia.

French Polynesia, a French possession in the southeastern Pacific, consisting of several island groups, including Tahiti and the other Society Islands. Land area, approx. 1,544 sq. mi. (4,000 sq. km.). Pop., 178,000.

Fres·no (frez′nō) a city in central California. Pop., 285,000.

Fu·ku·o·ka (fū′kü ō′kə) a city in Japan, on the northern part of the island of Kyushu. Pop., 1,088,588.

Ful·ler·ton (fŭl′ər tən) a city in southern California. Pop., 109,000.

Fu·na·fu·ti (fū′nə fü′tē) the capital of the country of Tuvalu, in the central Pacific. Pop., 2,810.

Fun·dy, Bay of (fun′dē) an inlet of the Atlantic in southeastern Canada, noted for its very high tides.

Fu·shun (fū′shùn′) a city in northeastern China. Pop., 1,240,000.

Ga·bon (ga bōn′) a country on the west coast of central Africa. Capital, Libreville. Area, 103,347 sq. mi. (267,669 sq. km.). Pop., 1,250,000. —**Gab·o·nese** (gab′ə nēz′, gab′ə-nēs′) *adj., n.*

Ga·bo·ro·ne (gä′bə rō′nē, gä′bə rōn′) the capital of Botswana, in the southeastern part of the country. Pop., 72,200.

Ga·lá·pa·gos Islands (gə lä′pə gōs′) island group in the eastern Pacific, west of and belonging to Ecuador. Land area, 3,029 sq. mi. (7,845 sq. km.). Pop., 8,370.

Gal·i·lee (gal′ə lē′) **1.** a small region in northernmost Palestine. **2. Sea of.** a small, freshwater lake between northeastern Israel and the Golan Heights. Also (*def. 2*), **Lake Tiberias, Lake Kinneret.**

Gal·lip·o·li (gə lip′ə lē) a peninsula in northwestern Turkey, forming the northern shore of the Dardanelles.

Gam·bi·a (gam′bē ə) a country on the western coast of Africa, largely surrounded by Senegal. Capital, Banjul. Area, 4,361 sq. mi. (11,295 sq. km.). Pop., 700,000.

Gan·ges (gan′jēz) a river in northern India and Bangladesh, flowing from the Himalayas to the Bay of Bengal. It is considered sacred by the Hindus. Length, 1,560 mi. (2,510 km.).

Garden Grove, a city in southern California. Pop., 135,000.

Gar·land (gär′lənd) a city in northeastern Texas. Pop., 177,000.

Gar·y (gâr′ē, gar′ē) a city in northwestern Indiana. Pop., 137,000.

Gas·co·ny (gas′kə nē) a historic region and former province of France, in the southwestern part of the country.

Gates·head (gāts′hed′) a city in northeastern England. Pop., 212,200.

Gaul (gôl) an ancient region in western Europe, consisting of what is now France, Belgium, northern Italy, and parts of West Germany, Switzerland, and the Netherlands.

Ga·za (gä′zə) a historic city in the Gaza Strip. It was once a major Philistine city.

Gaza Strip, a territory between Egypt and Israel on the southeastern coast of the Mediterranean, formerly part of the British mandate of Palestine. It was under Egyptian control from 1949 to 1967, when it was occupied by Israel. Area, 146 sq. mi. (378 sq. km.). Pop., 535,000.

Gdansk (gə dänsk′) a port city in northern Poland, formerly the free city of Danzig. Pop., 468,600.

Gee·long (ji lông′) a seaport in southeastern Australia, in the state of Victoria. Pop., 125,279.

Gel·sen·kir·chen (gel′zən kir′kən) a city in western West Germany, in the Ruhr region. Pop., 286,500.

Ge·ne·va (jə nē′və) **1.** a city in southwestern Switzerland. Pop., 159,895. **2. Lake.** a narrow, crescent-shaped lake between southwestern Switzerland and eastern France.

Gen·o·a (jen′ō ə) a port city in northwestern Italy. Pop., 735,600.

Gent (gent) see **Ghent.**

George·town (jôrj′toun′) the capital and largest city of Guyana, a port on the northern coast of the country. Pop., 78,500.

Geor·gia (jôr′jə) **1.** a state in the southeastern United States. Capital, Atlanta. Area, 58,910 sq. mi. (152,577 sq. km.). Pop., 6,104,000. Abbreviation, **Ga.;** postal abbreviation, **GA 2.** a republic of the Soviet Union, in the southwestern part of the country, bordering Turkey and the Black Sea, formerly an independent country. Official name: **Georgian Soviet Socialist Republic.** Area, 26,900 sq. mi. (69,671 sq. km.). Pop., 5,239,000. —**Geor′gian,** *adj., n.* ▲ Georgia was named after King George II (1683–1760) of England, who authorized a group of trustees to start a colony in what is now the southern part of the U.S. state.

German Democratic Republic, see **East Germany.**

Ger·ma·ny (jûr′mə nē) a former country in north-central Europe, divided since 1949 into **West Germany** and **East Germany.**

Geth·sem·a·ne (geth sem′ə nē′) in the New Testament, a garden on the Mount of Olives, east of Jerusalem, the scene of Jesus' agony and arrest.

Get·tys·burg (get′iz bûrg′) a town in southern Pennsylvania, the site of a decisive Union victory in 1863 during the Civil War. Pop., 7,194.

Gha·na (gä′nə) a country in western Africa, on the Gulf of Guinea. Capital, Accra. Area, 92,098 sq. mi. (238,534 sq. km.). Pop., 15,500,000.

Ghent (gent) *also,* **Gent.** a port city in northwestern Belgium. Pop., 236,540.

Gi·bral·tar (ji brôl′tər) **1.** a British crown colony and seaport near the southern tip of Spain, the site of a naval base. Area, approx. 2 sq. mi. (5 sq. km.). Pop., 32,000. **2. Rock of.** a great rock formation in this colony, known to ancient geographers as one of the Pillars of Hercules. **3. Strait of.** a body of water connecting the Mediterranean with the Atlantic, separating the northern tip of Morocco from the southern tip of Spain.

Gi·za (gē′zə) *also,* **Gi·zeh.** a city in northern Egypt, on the Nile near Cairo. It is the site of the Sphinx and the Pyramids. Pop., 1,608,400.

Glas·gow (glas′gō, glaz′gō) the largest city and chief port of Scotland, in the southern part of the country. Pop., 733,800.

Glen·dale (glen′dāl′) **1.** a city in southwestern California. Pop., 154,000. **2.** a city in central Arizona. Pop., 126,000.

Go·bi (gō′bē) a large desert in southeastern Mongolia and northern China. Area, approx. 500,000 sq. mi. (1,295,000 sq. km.).

Godt·håb (got′hob′) see **Nuuk.**

God·win Aus·ten, Mount (god′win ôs′tən) the second highest mountain in the world, located on the China-India border in the Karakoram Range of northern Kashmir. Height, 28,250 ft. (8,611 m.). Also, **K2.**

Goi·â·ni·a (goi ä′nē ə) a city in central Brazil. Pop., 928,046.

Go·lan Heights (gō′län) a hilly region of southwestern Syria, occupied by Israel after the 1967 Arab-Israeli War and annexed by Israel in 1981. Area, 454 sq. mi. (1,176 sq. km.).

Gold Coast, a city in southern Queensland, Australia, on the Pacific. Pop., 135,437.

Gol·go·tha (gol′gə thə) see **Calvary.**

Go·mor·rah (gə môr′ə) see **Sodom.**

Gond·wa·na·land (gond wä′nə land′) a vast prehistoric southern continent that included what is now Antarctica, Australia, Africa, India, and South America; it is thought

---

at; āpe; fär; câre; end; mē; it; īce; pîerce; hot; ōld; sông, fôrk; oil; out; up; ūse; rüle; pùll; tûrn; chin; sing; shop; thin; this; hw in white; zh in treasure. The symbol ə stands for the unstressed vowel sound heard in about, taken, pencil, lemon, and circus.

to have split up into the present continents in the Mesozoic era. Also, **Gond·wa·na** (gond wä′nə).

Good Hope, Cape of, a cape at the southernmost tip of Africa, on the Atlantic.

Gor·ki (gôr′kē) *also,* **Gor·ky.** a city in the European Soviet Union, on the Volga River. Pop., 1,405,000.

Gö·te·borg (yü′tə bôr′yə) a port city in southwestern Sweden. Pop., 425,495.

Gra·na·da (grə nä′də) a historic city in southern Spain, formerly the capital of a Moorish kingdom. It is the site of the Alhambra palace. Pop., 262,182.

Gran Cha·co (grän chä′kō) a vast, lowland region in south-central South America. Area, approx. 250,000 sq. mi. (647,500 sq. km.).

Grand Bank, a shoal off the eastern coast of Newfoundland, in the northern Atlantic. It is a major fishing area. Also, **Grand Banks.**

Grand Canyon, a large canyon in northwestern Arizona on the upper course of the Colorado River, regarded as one of the most spectacular natural wonders of the world.

Grand Rapids, a city in western Michigan. Pop., 187,000.

Graz (gräts) a city in southern Austria. Pop., 243,166.

Great Barrier Reef, the largest barrier reef in the world, along the northeastern coast of Australia.

Great Basin, a vast region in the western United States, consisting mostly of arid or semiarid land, characterized by numerous small basins separated by short mountain ranges. It lies between the Sierra Nevada and the Rocky Mountains and includes most of Nevada. Area, approx. 200,000 sq. mi. (518,000 sq. km.).

Great Bear Lake, a lake in the western part of the Northwest Territories, Canada.

Great Britain 1. see **United Kingdom.** 2. an island off the western coast of Europe that includes England, Scotland, and Wales, the largest of the British Isles. Area, 94,216 sq. mi. (244,019 sq. km.). Also, **Britain.**

Great Divide, see **Continental Divide.**

Greater Antilles, an island group of the West Indies, including Cuba, Jamaica, Hispaniola, and Puerto Rico.

Greater London, see **London** (*def. 1*).

Great Lakes, a group of five large, freshwater lakes along the border between the United States and Canada, including Lakes Superior, Michigan, Huron, Erie, and Ontario.

Great Plains, a vast plateau region in western North America, extending from Alberta, Canada, to Texas and consisting mostly of flat or rolling, generally treeless plains.

Great Salt Lake, a lake in northwestern Utah, the largest salt lake in North America.

Great Slave Lake, a lake in the southwestern part of the Northwest Territories, Canada.

Great Smoky Mountains, a mountain range in the southeastern United States, between Tennessee and North Carolina, part of the Appalachian Mountains. Also, **Great Smokies, Smoky Mountains.**

Greece (grēs) a country at the southern end of the Balkan Peninsula. Ancient Greece was a great intellectual and artistic center and a major influence on Western culture. Capital, Athens. Area, 50,944 sq. mi. (131,945 sq. km.). Pop., 10,072,000.

Green·land (grēn′lənd) a Danish island northeast of the mainland of North America, lying mostly within the Arctic Circle. It is the largest island in the world. Capital, Nuuk. Area, 840,000 sq. mi. (2,175,600 sq. km.). Pop., 55,000.

Greens·bor·o (grēnz′bûr′ō) a city in north-central North Carolina. Pop., 177,000.

Green·wich (gren′ich) a borough of Greater London, England, the former site of an astronomical observatory. The prime meridian passes through Greenwich. Pop., 211,800.

Greenwich Village, a section of lower Manhattan, New York City, noted as an artists′ and writers′ quarter.

Gre·na·da (gri nä′də) an island country in the West Indies, one of the Windward Islands. Capital, St. George′s. Area, 133 sq. mi. (344 sq. km.). Pop., 119,000.

Gren·a·dines (gren′ə dēnz′) an island group in the Windward Islands of the West Indies, divided politically between Grenada and St. Vincent and the Grenadines.

Gua·da·la·ja·ra (gwä′də lə här′ə) a city in southwestern Mexico. Pop., 1,626,152.

Gua·dal·ca·nal (gwä′dəl kə nal′) a mountainous island in the southwestern Pacific, one of the Solomon Islands. It was the scene of prolonged and bitter fighting between American and Japanese forces in World War II. Area, 2,500 sq. mi. (6,475 sq. km.).

Gua·de·loupe (gwä′də lüp′) a French department in the West Indies, consisting of two islands in the Leeward Islands. Land area, 687 sq. mi. (1,779 sq. km.). Pop., 338,000.

Guam (gwäm) an island in the western Pacific, east of the Philippines. It is administered by the United States. Capital, Agana. Area, 209 sq. mi. (541 sq. km.). Pop., 121,000.

Guang·zhou (gwäng′jō′) a seaport in southeastern China. Pop., 2,570,000. Also, **Canton.**

Guan·tá·na·mo Bay (gwän tä′nə mō′) an inlet of the Caribbean in southeastern Cuba, the site of a U.S. naval base.

Gua·rul·hos (gwä rül′yüs) a city in southeastern Brazil. Pop., 717,723.

Gua·te·ma·la (gwä′tə mä′lə) 1. the northernmost country of Central America. Capital, Guatemala City. Area, 42,042 sq. mi. (108,889 sq. km.). Pop., 8,940,000. 2. see **Guatemala City.** —**Gua·te·ma′lan,** *adj., n.*

Guatemala City, the capital and largest city of Guatemala, in the southern part of the country. Pop., 754,243.

Guay·a·quil (gwä′yə kēl′) the largest city and chief port of Ecuador, in the western part of the country. Pop., 1,509,108.

Guern·sey (gûrn′zē) a British island in the English Channel, off the coast of France, one of the Channel Islands. Area, approx. 25 sq. mi. (65 sq. km.).

Gui·a·na (gē an′ə, gī an′ə) a region in northeastern South America on the Atlantic, including Guyana, French Guiana, Suriname, and parts of Venezuela and Brazil.

Guin·ea (gin′ē) 1. a country on the Atlantic in western Africa. Capital, Conakry. Area, 94,926 sq. mi. (245,858 sq. km.). Pop., 6,710,000. 2. **Gulf of.** a large, open arm of the Atlantic along the west-central coast of Africa.

Guin·ea–Bis·sau (gin′ē bē sou′) a country on the Atlantic in western Africa. Capital, Bissau. Area, 13,948 sq. mi. (36,125 sq. km.). Pop., 966,000.

Guj·ran·wa·la (güj′rən wä′lə) a city in northeastern Pakistan. Pop., 600,993.

Gulf States 1. the five Southern states bordering the Gulf of Mexico: Florida, Alabama, Mississippi, Louisiana, and Texas. 2. those countries in or bordering on the Persian Gulf: Iran, Iraq, Kuwait, Saudi Arabia, Bahrain, Qatar, the United Arab Emirates, and Oman.

Gulf Stream, a warm ocean current flowing northeast across the northern Atlantic, from the Gulf of Mexico along the eastern coast of North America to the northern coast of Europe.

Guy·an·a (gī an′ə) a country on the northeastern coast of South America. Capital, Georgetown. Area, 83,000 sq. mi. (214,970 sq. km.). Pop., 1,020,000.

Hague, The (hāg) a city in the western Netherlands, the seat of the national government. Pop., 443,961.

Hai·dar·a·bad (hī′dər ə bad′) see **Hyderabad.**

Hai·fa (hī′fə) a port city in northwestern Israel, on the Mediterranean Sea. Pop., 224,700.

Hai·nan (hī′nän′) a Chinese island in the South China Sea. Area, 13,200 sq. mi. (34,188 sq. km.).

Hai·phong (hī′fong′) a seaport in northeastern Vietnam, near the Gulf of Tonkin. Pop., 330,755.

Hai·ti (hā'tē) a country in the Caribbean, on the western part of the island of Hispaniola. Capital, Port-au-Prince. Area, 10,714 sq. mi. (27,749 sq. km.). Pop., 5,620,000.

Hal·i·car·nas·sus (hal'i kär nas'əs) an ancient city in southwestern Asia Minor, the site of the famous mausoleum that was one of the Seven Wonders of the World.

Ha·li·fax (hal'ə faks') a port city in southeastern Canada, the capital of Nova Scotia. Pop., 113,577.

Hal·le (hä'lə) a city in west-central East Germany. Pop., 235,169.

Ham·burg (ham'bûrg') a port city in northern West Germany, on the Elbe River. Pop., 1,585,900.

Ham·il·ton (ham'əl tən) **1.** a port city in southeastern Ontario, Canada, at the western end of Lake Ontario. Pop., 306,728. **2.** the capital and chief city of Bermuda. Pop., 1,676.

Hamp·ton (hamp'tən) a city in southeastern Virginia. Pop., 126,000.

Hampton Roads, a channel of the Chesapeake Bay in southeastern Virginia, the site of the battle in 1862 between the Union ironclad *Monitor* and the Confederate ironclad *Virginia* (the renamed *Merrimac*).

Hang·zhou (häng'jō') a port city in eastern China. Pop., 1,250,000. Also, **Hang·chow** (hang'chou').

Han·kou (hang'kou') a former city in east-central China, now part of Wuhan.

Ha·noi (ha noi') the capital of Vietnam, a port in the northeastern part of the country. Pop., 819,913.

Han·o·ver (han'ō vər) *also,* **Han·no·ver. 1.** a historic region and former province of Prussia, in the northern part of present-day West Germany. **2.** a city in northern West Germany. Pop., 510,800.

Han·yang (hän'yäng') a former city in east-central China, now part of Wuhan.

Ha·ra·re (hə rär'ā) the capital and largest city of Zimbabwe, in the northeastern part of the country. Pop., 656,011. Formerly, **Salisbury.**

Har·bin (här'bin') a city in northeastern China. Pop., 2,630,000.

Har·lem (här'ləm) a district of New York City, in Manhattan, including one of the largest black communities in the United States.

Har·pers Ferry (här'pərz) a town in northeastern West Virginia, the site of John Brown's raid on a government arsenal in 1859.

Har·ris·burg (har'is bûrg') the capital of Pennsylvania, in the southeastern part of the state. Pop., 53,264.

Hart·ford (härt'fərd) the capital of Connecticut, in the central part of the state. Pop., 138,000.

Has·tings (hās'tingz) a city in southeastern England, on the English Channel, the site of William the Conqueror's decisive victory over the Saxons in 1066.

Hat·ter·as, Cape (hat'ər əs) a cape on an island off the eastern coast of North Carolina.

Ha·van·a (hə van'ə) the capital and chief port of Cuba, on the northwestern coast of the island. Pop., 1,972,363. Also, **La Habana.**

Ha·vre (hä'vər, hä'vrə) see **Le Havre.**

Ha·wai·i (hə wī'ē) **1.** a state of the United States, made up of the Hawaiian Islands. It is the only island state and the only state not on the North American continent. Capital, Honolulu. Land area, 6,425 sq. mi. (16,641 sq. km.). Pop., 1,062,000. Postal abbreviation, **HI 2.** the largest of the Hawaiian Islands. Area, 4,021 sq. mi. (10,414 sq. km.). Also *(def. 2)*, **Big Island. —Ha·wai'ian,** *adj., n.* ▲ *Hawaii* was originally the name of the largest island in the state. The name comes from the Polynesians' traditional name for the mythical homeland of their ancestors.

Ha·wai·ian Islands (hə wī'ən) an island chain in the north-central Pacific. Formerly, **Sandwich Islands.**

Hay·ward (hā'wərd) a city in western California. Pop., 102,000.

Heb·ri·des (heb'ri dēz') a Scottish island group off the northwestern coast of Scotland. Land area, 2,812 sq. mi. (7,283 sq. km.).

Hel·e·na (hel'ə nə) the capital of Montana, in the west-central part of the state. Pop., 23,938.

Hel·les·pont (hel'əs pont') see **Dardanelles.**

Hel·sin·ki (hel'sing kē) the capital and largest city of Finland, on the southern coast of the country. Pop., 484,263.

Her·cu·la·ne·um (hûr'kyə lā'nē əm) a partially excavated ancient city in southwestern Italy, near Naples, buried when Mount Vesuvius erupted in A.D. 79.

Hesse (hes) a historic German region, now a state of West Germany, in the central part of the country.

Hi·a·le·ah (hī'ə lē'ə) a city in southeastern Florida. Pop., 162,000.

High·lands (hī'ləndz) a rugged, mountainous region of northern and central Scotland.

Him·a·la·yas (him'ə lā'əz) the highest mountain system in the world, extending across central Asia from the northeastern border of Afghanistan through northern India and southern Tibet to the northwestern border of Burma. Also, **Him·a·la·ya Mountains** (him'ə lā'ə). **—Him'a·la'yan,** *adj.*

Hin·du Kush (hin'dü kŭsh') a mountain system of central Asia, largely in northeastern Afghanistan.

Hir·o·shi·ma (hîr'ə shē'mə, hi rō'shə mə) a port city in southwestern Japan, on the island of Honshu. On August 6, 1945, the first atomic bomb used in World War II was dropped on this city. Pop., 899,399.

His·pa·nio·la (his'pən yō'lə) an island in the Caribbean, divided into the Dominican Republic and Haiti. Area, approx. 30,000 sq. mi. (77,700 sq. km.).

Ho·bart (hō'bärt) the capital of the Australian island state of Tasmania. Pop., 128,603.

Ho Chi Minh City (hō'chē'min') the largest city in Vietnam, a seaport in the southern part of the country. Pop., 2,441,185. Formerly, **Saigon.**

Hok·kai·do (ho kī'dō) the northernmost and second largest island of Japan. Area, 30,144 sq. mi. (78,073 sq. km.).

Hol·land (hol'ənd) **1.** a historic region in northwestern Europe, now part of the Netherlands. **2.** see **Netherlands, the.**

Hol·ly·wood (hol'ē wŭd') **1.** a section of Los Angeles, noted as the traditional home of the U.S. motion-picture and television industries **2.** a city in southeastern Florida, on the Atlantic near Miami. Pop., 121,000.

Holy Land, see **Palestine** *(def. 1)*

Homs (hômz, hôms) a city in western Syria. Pop., 346,871.

Hon·du·ras (hon dúr'əs, hon dyúr'əs) a country in northern Central America, with coastlines on the Caribbean and the Pacific. Capital, Tegucigalpa. Area, 43,277 sq. mi. (112,087 sq. km.). Pop., 4,950,000. **—Hon·du'ran,** *adj., n.*

Hong Kong (hong'kong') a British crown colony off the southeastern coast of China. It will return to Chinese control after 1997. Area, 412 sq. mi. (1,067 sq. km.). Pop., 5,940,000.

Ho·ni·a·ra (hō'nē är'ə) the capital of the Solomon Islands, on the northern part of the island of Guadalcanal. Pop., 30,499.

Ho·no·lu·lu (hon'ə lü'lü) the capital and largest city of Hawaii, on the southern coast of Oahu. Pop., 372,000.

at; āpe; fär; câre; end; mē; it; īce; pîerce; hot; ōld; sông, fôrk; oil; out; up; ūse; rüle; pùll; tûrn; chin; sing; shop; thin; this; hw in white; zh in treasure. The symbol ə stands for the unstressed vowel sound heard in about, taken, pencil, lemon, and circus.

1129

Hon·shu (hon′shü) the largest island of Japan. Area, 88,936 sq. mi. (230,344 sq. km.).

Horn, Cape, a cape on an island of Tierra del Fuego, forming the southernmost tip of South America.

Hous·ton (hūs′tən) a city in southeastern Texas. Pop., 1,729,000.

How·rah (hou′rə) a city in northeastern India. Pop., 744,429.

Huang He (hwäng′hŭ′) a large river in China, flowing from Tibet to the Yellow Sea. Length, 3,395 mi. (5,463 km.). Also, **Hwang Ho, Yellow River.**

Hud·son (hud′sən) a river in eastern New York, flowing southward into New York Bay. Length, 306 mi. (492 km.).

Hudson Bay, a large inland sea in northeastern Canada.

Hue (hwā) *also,* **Hué.** a seaport in central Vietnam. Pop., 168,865.

Hull (hul) a port city in northeastern England. Pop., 258,000. Also, **Kingston-upon-Hull.**

Hun·ga·ry (hung′gə rē) a landlocked country in east-central Europe. Capital, Budapest. Area, 35,920 sq. mi. (93,033 sq. km.). Pop., 10,700,000.

Hunt·ing·ton (hun′ting tən) a port city in western West Virginia, on the Ohio River. Pop., 63,684.

Huntington Beach, a city in southern California, on the Pacific. Pop., 184,000.

Hunts·ville (hunts′vil′) a city in northern Alabama. Pop., 163,000.

Hu·ron, Lake (hyùr′ən, hyùr′on) the second largest of the Great Lakes, on the U.S.-Canadian border.

Hwang Ho (hwäng′hō′) see **Huang He.**

Hy·der·a·bad (hī′dər ə bad′) *also,* **Hai·dar·a·bad.** **1.** a city in south-central India. Pop., 2,187,262. **2.** a city in southeastern Pakistan. Pop., 702,539.

Iasi (yäsh, yä′shē) a city in northeastern Romania. Pop., 313,060.

I·ba·dan (ē bä′dän) a large city in southwestern Nigeria. Pop., 1,009,400.

I·ba·gué (ē′bä gā′) a city in central Colombia. Pop., 265,598.

I·be·ri·a (ī bîr′ē ə) a large peninsula in southwestern Europe, between the Atlantic and the Mediterranean, occupied by Spain and Portugal. Also, **I·be·ri·an Peninsula** (ī bîr′ē ən).

Ice·land (īs′lənd) an island country in the northern Atlantic, between Greenland and Norway. Capital, Reykjavik. Area, 39,800 sq. mi. (103,082 sq. km.). Pop., 252,000. —**Ice·land·er** (īs′lan′dər) *n.*

I·da·ho (ī′də hō′) a state in the western United States. Capital, Boise. Area, 83,564 sq. mi. (216,431 sq. km.). Pop., 1,002,000. Abbreviation, **Ida.;** postal abbreviation, **ID** —**I′da·ho′an,** *adj., n.* ▲ *Idaho* probably comes from an Apache name for the Comanche Indians. The name was first used in what is now Colorado, but the United States Senate officially designated another territory in the West as *Idaho,* a name that was kept when the territory became a state.

Il·i·um (il′ē əm) the Latin name for **Troy.**

Il·li·nois (il′ə noi′, il′ə noiz′) a state in the north-central United States. Capital, Springfield. Area, 56,345 sq. mi. (145,934 sq. km.). Pop., 11,552,000. Abbreviation, **Ill.;** postal abbreviation, **IL** —**Il′li·nois′an,** *adj., n.* ▲ *Illinois* is the French form of an Algonquian word meaning "men," used as the name of an American Indian tribe that lived in what is now the state.

In·chon (in′chon′) a port city in northwestern South Korea, on the Yellow Sea. Pop., 1,084,700.

Independence, a city in western Missouri. Pop., 113,000.

In·di·a (in′dē ə) **1.** a country in southern Asia. Capital, New Delhi. Area, 1,269,345 sq. mi. (3,287,604 sq. km.). Pop., 813,000,000. **2.** a large peninsular region of southern Asia, bounded by the Arabian Sea, Indian Ocean, and Bay of Bengal, and including India, Pakistan, and Bangladesh.

In·di·an·a (in′dē an′ə) a state in the north-central United States. Capital, Indianapolis. Area, 36,185 sq. mi. (93,719 sq. km.). Pop., 5,504,000. Abbreviation, **Ind.;** postal abbreviation, **IN** —**In·di·an·i·an** (in′dē an′ē ən) *adj., n.* ▲ *Indiana* comes from a Modern Latin word meaning "Indian." The name was first used by a group of land developers who called themselves the Indiana Company. The name was later used for a territory that included a large section of the Northwest Territory because there were many Indians living in the region. Part of this territory later became the state of Indiana.

In·di·an·ap·o·lis (in′dē ə nap′ə lis) the capital and largest city of Indiana, in the central part of the state. Pop., 720,000.

Indian Ocean, an ocean south of Asia, between Africa and Australia.

In·do·chi·na (in′dō chī′nə) **1.** a peninsula in southeastern Asia between the Bay of Bengal and the South China Sea, consisting of the Malay Peninsula and the nations of Vietnam, Burma, Laos, Cambodia, and Thailand. **2.** see **French Indochina.** —**In·do·chi·nese** (in′dō chī nēz′, in′dō chī nēs′) *adj., n.*

In·do·ne·sia (in′də nē′zhə) a country in southeastern Asia, composed of islands in the Malay Archipelago, including Java, Sumatra, and part of Borneo, and the western part of the island of New Guinea. Capital, Jakarta. Area, 741,034 sq. mi. (1,919,278 sq. km.). Pop., 179,000,000.

In·dore (in dôr′) a city in central India. Pop., 829,327.

In·dus (in′dəs) a river flowing from Tibet through Kashmir and Pakistan into the Arabian Sea. Length, 1,800 mi. (2,896 km.).

In·gle·wood (ing′gəl wùd′) a city in southwestern California. Pop., 103,000.

Inner Mongolia, an autonomous region of China, in the northern part of the country. Area, 456,638 sq. mi. (1,182,692 sq. km.). Pop., 20,070,000.

I·o·ni·a (ī ō′nē ə) an ancient region on the western coast of Asia Minor, colonized by the ancient Greeks.

I·o·ni·an Sea (ī ō′nē ən) the part of the Mediterranean between Greece and Albania on the east and southern Italy and Sicily on the west.

I·o·wa (ī′ə wə) a state in the north-central United States. Capital, Des Moines. Area, 56,275 sq. mi. (145,752 sq. km.). Pop., 2,851,000. Abbreviation, **Ia.;** postal abbreviation, **IA** —**I′o·wan,** *adj., n.* ▲ *Iowa* comes from *Ouaouia,* the shortened French version of a Dakota Indian name for another tribe that lived in what is now Iowa. Pioneers used *Iowa* as the name of a river in the region where the tribe lived. Later the name was used for the territory where the river and region were located, part of which eventually became the state.

I·poh (ē′pō) a city in western Malaysia. Pop., 300,300.

I·ran (i ran′) a country in southwestern Asia. Capital, Tehran. Area, 636,300 sq. mi. (1,648,017 sq. km.). Pop., 49,900,000. Formerly, **Persia.**

I·raq (i rak′) a country in southwestern Asia. Capital, Baghdad. Area, 169,235 sq. mi. (438,319 sq. km.). Pop., 18,200,000. —**I·ra·qi** (i rak′ē) *adj., n.*

Ire·land (īr′lənd) **1.** one of the British Isles, divided politically into the Republic of Ireland and Northern Ireland. Area, 32,596 sq. mi. (84,424 sq. km.). **2. Republic of.** a country in northwestern Europe, occupying most of the island of Ireland. Capital, Dublin. Area, 27,136 sq. mi. (70,282 sq. km.). Pop., 3,800,000.

I·ri·an Ja·ya (îr′ē ən jä′yə) a province of Indonesia, consisting of western New Guinea and its offshore islands. Area, 162,885 sq. mi. (421,872 sq. km.). Pop., 1,268,600.

I·rish Sea, (ī′rish) an arm of the Atlantic between Ireland and England.

Ir·tysh (îr tish′) a river of central Asia, flowing northwest and north from the Altai Mountains in China to the Ob River in Siberia. Length, 2,747 mi. (4,420 km.).

Ir·ving (ûr′ving) a city in northeastern Texas. Pop., 129,000.

Is·fa·han (is'fə hän') see **Esfahan**.

Is·lam·a·bad (is lä'mə bäd') the capital of Pakistan, in the northern part of the country. Pop., 204,364.

Is·ra·el (iz'rā əl, iz'rē əl) a country in southwestern Asia at the eastern end of the Mediterranean. Capital, Jerusalem. Area, 7,990 sq. mi. (20,694 sq. km.). Pop., 4,550,000.

Is·tan·bul (is'tan bül') the largest city of Turkey, located on both sides of the Bosporus. It was formerly called Constantinople and, in ancient times, Byzantium. Pop., 5,475,982.

It·a·ly (it'ə lē) a country in southern Europe, on the Mediterranean. Capital, Rome. Area, 116,303 sq. mi. (301,225 sq. km.). Pop., 57,500,000.

Ivory Coast, a country in western Africa, on the Gulf of Guinea. Official name: **Côte d'Ivoire**. Capital, Yamassoukro. Area, 123,847 sq. mi. (320,764 sq. km.). Pop., 11,300,000.

I·wo Ji·ma (ē'wə jē'mə) an island in the northwestern Pacific, captured from Japan by the United States in 1945 during World War II and returned to Japan in 1968.

Iz·mir (iz'mîr) a port city in western Turkey, on the Aegean. Pop., 1,489,772. Formerly, **Smyrna**.

Jack·son (jak'sən) the capital of Mississippi, in the central part of the state. Pop., 208,000.

Jack·son·ville (jak'sən vil') the largest city in Florida, a major seaport on the northeastern coast of the state. Pop., 610,000.

Jaf·fa (jaf'ə) a seaport on the Mediterranean coast of Israel, combined with Tel Aviv in 1950 as one city. In ancient times it was known as Joppa.

Jai·pur (jī'pùr) a city in northwestern India. Pop., 997,165.

Ja·kar·ta (jə kär'tə) also, **Dja·kar·ta**. the capital and largest city of Indonesia, a seaport on the northwestern coast of Java. Pop., 6,503,449.

Ja·mai·ca (jə mā'kə) an island country of the Greater Antilles, in the Caribbean south of Cuba. Capital, Kingston. Area, 4,244 sq. mi. (10,992 sq. km.). Pop., 2,480,000. —**Ja·mai'can**, *adj., n.*

James·town (jamz'toun') a village in southeastern Virginia, the first permanent English settlement in America, founded in 1607.

Jam·mu and Kashmir (jum'ü) see **Kashmir** (*def. 2*).

Ja·pan (jə pan') **1.** a country in the northern Pacific, off the eastern coast of Asia, consisting of a chain of islands. The four main islands are Hokkaido, Honshu, Kyushu, and Shikoku. Capital, Tokyo. Area, 143,706 sq. mi. (372,199 sq. km.). Pop., 123,000,000. **2. Sea of.** an arm of the Pacific separating Japan from the Asian mainland.

Ja·va (jä'və) a large island of Indonesia, in the Malay Archipelago. Area, 51,000 sq. mi. (132,090 sq. km.).

Jeb·el Mu·sa (jeb'əl mü'sä) a mountain in Ceuta, a Spanish enclave in northern Morocco. It was known to ancient geographers as one of the Pillars of Hercules. Height, 2,775 ft. (846 m.).

Jed·da (jed'ə) see **Jidda**.

Jef·fer·son City (jef'ər sən) the capital of Missouri, in the central part of the state. Pop., 33,619.

Jer·i·cho (jer'i kō') **1.** an ancient Palestinian city near the northern tip of the Red Sea. According to the Old Testament, it was miraculously captured by Joshua, whose soldiers toppled the walls of the city by sounding their trumpets. **2.** a town in the West Bank on the site of ancient Jericho. Pop., 10,200.

Jer·sey (jûr'zē) a British island in the English Channel, off the coast of France, the largest of the Channel Islands. Area, approx. 45 sq. mi. (117 sq. km.).

Jersey City, a port city in northeastern New Jersey, on the Hudson opposite New York City. Pop., 219,000.

Je·ru·sa·lem (jə rü'sə ləm) a historic city in central Palestine, the capital of Israel. It is a holy city for Jews, Christians, and Muslims. The old section of the city, controlled by Jordan from 1949 to 1967, was occupied and annexed by Israel in 1967. Pop., 446,500.

Jid·da (jid'ə) a port city in western Saudi Arabia, on the Red Sea, near Mecca. Pop., 1,300,000. Also, **Jedda**.

Ji·lin (jē'lin) a port city in northeastern China. Pop., 882,700. Also, **Kirin**.

Ji·nan (jē'nän') a city in eastern China. Pop., 1,430,000. Also, **Chinan, Tsinan**.

Jo·han·nes·burg (jō han'əs bûrg') a city in the Republic of South Africa, in the northeastern part of the country. Pop., 632,369.

Jop·pa (jop'ə) see **Jaffa**.

Jor·dan (jôr'dən) **1.** a country in southwestern Asia, east of and bordering Israel. Capital, Amman. Area, 37,738 sq. mi. (97,741 sq. km.). Pop., 4,120,000. Formerly, **Transjordan**. **2.** a river in southwestern Asia, flowing between the West Bank and Jordan into the Dead Sea. —**Jor·da·ni·an** (jôr dä'nē ən) *adj., n.*

Juá·rez (wär'ez) see **Ciudad Juárez**.

Ju·de·a (jü dē'ə) *also,* **Ju·dae·a**. the southern part of ancient Palestine, especially when it was under Roman rule. —**Ju·de'an,** *adj., n.*

Ju·neau (jü'nō) the capital of Alaska, a port city in the southeastern part of the state. Pop., 19,528.

K2, see **Godwin Austen, Mount**.

Ka·bul (kä'bùl) the capital and largest city of Afghanistan, in the east-central part of the country. Pop., 913,164.

Ka·la·ha·ri (kä'lə här'ē) a large desert region in the central part of southern Africa. Area, approx. 200,000 sq. mi. (518,000 sq. km.).

Ka·li·man·tan (kä'lē män'tän) the part of Borneo that belongs to Indonesia. Area, 212,378 sq. mi. (550,059 sq. km.).

Kam·pa·la (käm pä'lə) the capital and largest city of Uganda, in the southern part of the country. Pop., 458,503.

Kam·pu·che·a (kam'pù chē'ə) see **Cambodia**.

Ka·no (kä'nō) a city in north-central Nigeria. Pop., 475,000.

Kan·pur (kän'pùr) a city in north-central India, on the Ganges. Pop., 1,481,789. Formerly, **Cawnpore**.

Kan·sas (kan'zəs) a state in the west-central United States. Capital, Topeka. Area, 82,277 sq. mi. (213,097 sq. km.). Pop., 2,460,000. Abbreviations, **Kans., Kan.**; postal abbreviation, **KS** —**Kan'san,** *n.* ▲ *Kansas* comes from the French version of a Siouan name for an Indian tribe that lived in what is now northeastern Kansas. The name was later used for the river along that tribe's land, then for the territory where the river was located, part of which became the state.

Kansas City 1. a city in western Missouri. Pop., 441,000. **2.** a city in eastern Kansas that adjoins Kansas City, Missouri. Pop., 162,000.

Kao·hsiung (gou'shyüng') a seaport in southwestern Taiwan. Pop., 1,227,454.

Ka·ra·chi (kə rä'chē) the largest city and former capital of Pakistan, a port in the southern part of the country, on the Arabian Sea. Pop., 4,901,627.

Ka·raj (kä räj') a city in north-central Iran, west of Tehran. Pop., 526,000.

Ka·ra·ko·ram Range (kär'ə kôr'əm) *also,* **Ka·ra·ko·rum Range**. a mountain system in central Asia, extending from northern Pakistan and India to southern China; its highest peak is Mount Godwin Austen.

Karl–Marx–Stadt (kärl'märks'shtät') a city in southern East Germany. Pop., 315,452. Formerly, **Chemnitz**.

Karls·ruh·e (kärlz'rü'ə) *also,* **Carls·ruh·e**. a city in southwestern West Germany. Pop., 268,400.

---

at; āpe; fär; câre; end; mē; it; īce; pîerce; hot; ōld; sông, fôrk; oil; out; up; ūse; rüle; pùll; tûrn; chin; sing; shop; thin; **this**; hw in white; zh in treasure. The symbol ə stands for the unstressed vowel sound heard in about, taken, pencil, lemon, and circus.

Kar·nak (kär′nak) a village in Egypt, on the Nile, the site of a large group of ancient temples. Karnak is located on part of the site of ancient Thebes. Pop., 10,865.

Kash·mir (kash′mîr, kazh′mîr) *also,* **Cash·mere. 1.** an area in the extreme north of the Indian subcontinent, disputed by India and Pakistan, each of which occupies part of the territory. Area, 86,024 sq. mi. (222,802 sq. km.). **2.** that part of this area occupied by India. Official name: **Jammu and Kashmir.** Area, 53,500 sq. mi. (138,565 sq. km.).

Kat·man·du (kat′man dü′) *also,* **Kath·man·du.** the capital of Nepal, in the central part of the country. Pop., 235,160.

Ka·to·wi·ce (kat′ō vēt′sä) a city in southern Poland. Pop., 363,300.

Kau·ai (kou′ī, kə wī′) the northernmost of the main islands of Hawaii. Area, 549 sq. mi. (1,422 sq. km.).

Ka·wa·sa·ki (kä′wə sä′kē) a seaport in Japan, in the southeastern part of the island of Honshu. Pop., 1,040,802.

Ka·zakh·stan (kä′zäk stän′) a republic of the Soviet Union, in the Asian part of the country. Official name: **Kazakh Soviet Socialist Republic.** Area, 1,049,155 sq. mi. (2,717,311 sq. km.). Pop., 16,036,000.

Ka·zan (kə zän′) a city in the European part of the Soviet Union, near the Volga River. Pop., 1,057,000.

Ken·tuck·y (kən tuk′ē) a state in the east-central United States. Capital, Frankfort. Area, 40,410 sq. mi. (104,662 sq. km.). Pop., 3,729,000. Abbreviation, **Ky.;** postal abbreviation, **KY** —**Ken·tuck′i·an,** *adj., n.* ▲ *Kentucky* comes from an Iroquois word that probably meant "meadow land" or "level land." This name was also used for a river running through the land known by this name. The name was later given to a county that included this land and river, which was organized by the state of Virginia in 1776, and was kept when this county eventually became the state of Kentucky.

Ken·ya (ken′yə, kēn′yə) a country in eastern Africa. Capital, Nairobi. Area, 224,961 sq. mi. (582,649 sq. km.). Pop., 24,400,000. —**Ken′yan,** *adj., n.*

Ker·man·shah (kâr′män shä′) see **Bakhataran.**

Key West 1. an island off the coast of southwestern Florida, in the Gulf of Mexico, one of the westernmost Florida Keys. **2.** a port city on this island. Pop., 24,382.

Khar·kov (kär′kof) a city in the European Soviet Union, in the Ukraine. Pop., 1,567,000.

Khar·toum (kär tüm′) the capital of Sudan, a port at the confluence of the Blue Nile and White Nile, in the north-central part of the country. Pop., 476,218.

Khartoum North, a city in north-central Sudan, north of Khartoum, on the Nile. Pop., 341,146.

Khul·na (kül′nə) a city in southern Bangladesh, in the Ganges delta. Pop., 648,359.

Khy·ber Pass (kī′bər) a mountain pass connecting Pakistan and Afghanistan.

Kiel (kēl) a city in northern West Germany. Pop., 245,300.

Ki·ev (kē′ev, kē′ef) a city in the southwestern Soviet Union, the largest city of the Ukraine. Pop., 2,073,000.

Ki·ga·li (ki gä′lē) the capital of Rwanda, in the central part of the country. Pop., 156,700.

Ki·lau·e·a (kil′ō ā′ə) an active volcano on the island of Hawaii. Height, 4,090 ft. (1,247 m.).

Kil·i·man·ja·ro, Mount (kil′ə mən jär′ō) the highest mountain in Africa, in northeastern Tanzania near the Kenyan border. Height, 19,340 ft. (5,895 m.).

Kings·ton (kingz′tən) the capital and largest city of Jamaica, on the southeastern coast of the island. Pop., 586,930.

King·ston-u·pon-Hull (kingz′tən ə pôn′hul′, kingz′tən ə pon′hul′) see **Hull.**

Kings·town (kingz′toun′) the capital of St. Vincent and the Grenadines, located on the island of St. Vincent. Pop., 18,378.

Kin·ner·et, Lake (ki ner′ət) see **Galilee, Sea of.**

Kin·sha·sa (kin shä′sə) the capital and largest city of Zaire, a port on the Congo River in the western part of the country. Pop., 2,653,558.

Kir·ghi·zia (kir gē′zhə) a republic of the Soviet Union, in the Asian part of the country, bordering northwestern China. Official name: **Kirghiz Soviet Socialist Republic.** Area, 76,640 sq. mi. (198,498 sq. km.). Pop., 4,055,000. Also, **Kir·ghiz·stan** (kîr′gi stän′).

Ki·ri·ba·ti (kîr′i bä′tē) an island nation in the central Pacific Ocean. Capital, Bairiki. Land area, 277 sq. mi. (717 sq. km.). Pop., 67,000.

Ki·rin (kē′rin′) see **Jilin.**

Kir·kuk (kîr kük′) a city in northeastern Iraq. Pop., 535,000.

Kit·a·kyu·shu (kē′tä kū′shü) a city in Japan, at the northwestern tip of the island of Kyushu. Pop., 1,065,078.

Kitch·e·ner (kich′ə nər) a city in southern Ontario, Canada. Pop., 150,604.

Kitty Hawk, a village in northeastern North Carolina where the first successful airplane flight was made in 1903 by Wilbur and Orville Wright.

Ki·twe (kē′twā) a city in north-central Zambia. Pop., 207,500.

Klon·dike (klon′dīk) a noted gold-mining region in the west-central Yukon, Canada. Area, approx. 800 sq. mi. (2,070 sq. km.).

Knos·sos (nos′əs, kə nos′əs) *also,* **Cnos·sus.** an ancient city on the northern coast of Crete, a center of Minoan civilization.

Knox·ville (noks′vil) a city in eastern Tennessee, on the Tennessee River. Pop., 173,000.

Ko·be (kō′bē) a port city in Japan, on the southern coast of the island of Honshu. Pop., 1,367,390.

Ko·lo·ni·a (kə lō′nē ə) the capital of the Federated States of Micronesia. Pop., 5,549.

Kol·wez·i (kōl wez′ē) a city in southern Zaire. Pop., 201,382.

Ko·re·a (kə rē′ə) a former country in eastern Asia, divided into **North Korea** and **South Korea** since 1948. Area, 84,562 sq. mi. (219,016 sq. km.).

Ko·ror (kə rôr′) the capital of Palau. Pop., 6,222.

Kos·ci·us·ko, Mount (kos′ē us′kō) the highest mountain in Australia, in southeastern New South Wales. Height, 7,316 ft. (2,230 m.).

Ko·si·ce (kō′shi tsā) a city in eastern Czechoslovakia. Pop., 218,238.

Kra·ka·to·a (krak′ə tō′ə) an uninhabited volcanic island between Java and Sumatra, in Indonesia, noted as the site of a catastrophic volcanic eruption in 1883. Also, **Kra·ka·tau** (krak′ə tou′).

Kra·ków (krä′kou) *also,* **Crac·ow.** a city in southern Poland. Pop., 740,100.

Kras·no·yarsk (kraz′nə yärsk′) a city in the Soviet Union, in north-central Asia. Pop., 885,000.

Kre·feld (krā′feld) a city in western West Germany, on the Rhine. Pop., 217,000.

Krung Thep (krüng′ täp′) see **Bangkok.**

Kua·la Lum·pur (kwä′lə lùm pùr′) the capital of Malaysia, on the Malay Peninsula. Pop., 937,800.

Kui·by·shev (kwē′bə shef′) a city in the European Soviet Union, on the Volga River. Pop., 1,267,000. Formerly, **Samara.**

Ku·ma·si (kù mä′sē) a city in south-central Ghana. Pop., 348,880.

Kun·ming (kùn′ming′) a city in southwestern China. Pop., 1,080,000.

Kur·di·stan (kûr′də stan′) a highland region of Asia that includes parts of Iran, Iraq, Turkey, and Syria, and is inhabited chiefly by Kurds.

Kush (kùsh, kush) see **Cush.**

Ku·wait (kü wät′) **1.** a country in the northeastern part of the peninsula of Arabia. Capital, Kuwait. Area, 6,880 sq. mi. (17,819 sq. km.). Pop., 2,150,000. **2.** the capital of Kuwait. Pop., 44,335. —**Ku·wai·ti** (kü wā′tē) *adj., n.*

Kyo·to (kyō′tō) a city in the west-central part of the island of Honshu, Japan, the former capital of the country. Pop., 1,473,065.

Kyu·shu (kū′shü) the southernmost of the four main islands of Japan. Area, 14,114 sq. mi. (36,555 sq. km.).

Lab·ra·dor (lab′rə dôr′) **1.** a region in eastern Canada, on the Atlantic Ocean, part of the province of Newfoundland and Labrador. **2.** a peninsula in eastern Canada, between the Atlantic Ocean and Hudson Bay. It is divided between the province of Quebec and the province of Newfoundland and Labrador.

Lac·e·dae·mon (las′ə dē′mən) see **Sparta.** —**Lac·e·dae·mo·ni·an** (las′ə də mō′nē ən) *adj., n.*

La·do·ga, Lake (lä′də gə) the largest freshwater lake in Europe, in the northwestern Soviet Union.

La·gos (lä′gōs, lā′gos) the capital and chief port of Nigeria, in the southwestern part of the country. Pop., 1,404,000.

La Ha·ba·na (lä′ ä vä′nə) see **Havana.**

La·hore (lə hôr′) a city in northeastern Pakistan. Pop., 2,707,215.

Lake of the Woods, a lake on the border of Minnesota and the Canadian provinces of Manitoba and Ontario.

Lam·beth (lam′bəth) a borough in the southern part of Greater London, England. Pop., 245,700.

Lan·chow (län′jō′) see **Lanzhou.**

Lan·sing (lan′sing) the capital of Michigan, in the south-central part of the state. Pop., 129,000.

Lan·zhou (län′jō′) *also,* **Lan·chow.** a city in central China. Pop., 1,060,000.

La·os (lä′ōs, lā′os) a country in southeastern Asia, between northern Thailand and northern Vietnam. Capital, Vientiane. Area, 91,430 sq. mi. (236,804 sq. km.). Pop., 3,980,000.

La Paz (lə päz′) a city in western Bolivia, in the Andes, the seat of the government and administrative capital of the country. Pop., 992,592.

Lap·land (lap′land′) a region in northern Europe, including the northernmost sections of Norway, Sweden, and Finland and the northwestern Soviet Union. Area, approx. 150,000 sq. mi. (388,500 sq. km.).

La Pla·ta (lə plä′tə) a port city in eastern Argentina. Pop., 454,884.

La·re·do (lə rā′dō) a city in southern Texas. Pop., 117,000.

La Ro·ma·na (lä rō mä′nə) a city in the southeastern Dominican Republic. Pop., 120,391.

La·sa (lä′sə) see **Lhasa.**

Las Pal·mas (läs päl′məs) a port city in the Canary Islands. Pop., 366,454.

Las·sen Peak (las′ən) a volcano in northern California at the southern end of the Cascade Range. Height, 10,457 ft. (3,187 m.). Also, **Mount Lassen.**

Las Ve·gas (läs vā′gəs) a city in southeastern Nevada, noted as a tourist resort and gambling center. Pop., 192,000.

Latin America, the countries south of the United States in the Western Hemisphere in which the languages, such as Spanish or Portuguese, are of Latin origin. —**Latin American.**

Lat·vi·a (lat′vē ə) a republic of the Soviet Union, in the European part of the country, on the Baltic Sea. It was formerly an independent nation. Official name: **Latvian Soviet Socialist Republic.** Area, approx. 24,600 sq. mi. (63,700 sq. km.). Pop., 2,621,000.

Laur·a·sia (lô rā′zhə) a vast prehistoric northern continent believed to have included North America, Europe, and most of Asia; it is thought to have split up into the present continents in the Mesozoic era.

La·val (lə val′) a city in southern Quebec, Canada, near Montreal. Pop., 284,164.

Leav·en·worth (lev′ən wûrth′) a city in northeastern Kansas, the site of a federal prison. Pop., 54,809.

Leb·a·non (leb′ə non′) a country in southwestern Asia, on the eastern shore of the Mediterranean. Capital, Beirut. Area, 4,015 sq. mi. (10,399 sq. km.). Pop., 2,900,000. —**Leb·a·nese** (leb′ə nēz′, leb′ə nēs′) *adj., n.*

Leeds (lēdz) a city in north-central England. Pop., 710,500.

Lee·ward Islands (lē′wərd) a Caribbean island group forming the northern part of the Lesser Antilles. Land area, 1,260 sq. mi. (3,263 sq. km.).

Le Ha·vre (lə hävr′ə, lə hä′vər) a port city in northern France, at the mouth of the Seine. Pop., 199,388. Also, **Havre.**

Leices·ter (les′tər) a city in central England. Pop., 282,900.

Leip·zig (līp′zig) a city in southern East Germany. Pop., 553,660.

Lem·berg (lem′bûrg) see **Lvov.**

Le·na (lē′nə) a river in the Soviet Union, flowing through east-central Siberia to the Arctic Ocean. Length, 2,734 mi. (4,399 km.).

Len·in·grad (len′in grad′) a historic city in the northwestern Soviet Union, the chief Soviet port on the Baltic Sea. The former capital of Russia, it was earlier known as St. Petersburg and later as Petrograd. Pop., 4,901,000.

Le·ón (lā ōn′) **1.** a region and former kingdom in northwestern Spain. **2.** a city in central Mexico. Pop., 593,000.

Le·so·tho (lə sō′tō) a country in southern Africa, entirely surrounded by the Republic of South Africa. Capital, Maseru. Area, 11,720 sq. mi. (30,355 sq. km.). Pop., 1,690,000.

Lesser Antilles, an island group of the West Indies southeast of Puerto Rico, including the Leeward Islands, the Windward Islands, Barbados, Trinidad, Tobago, and the Virgin Islands.

Le·vant (lə vant′) a region bordering the eastern shore of the Mediterranean, including the present-day countries of Greece, Turkey, Syria, Lebanon, Israel, and Egypt and the islands in the eastern Mediterranean.

Lex·ing·ton (lek′sing tən) **1.** a town in northeastern Massachusetts, the site of the first battle of the American Revolution, on April 19, 1775. Pop., 29,479. **2.** a city in north-central Kentucky. Pop., 213,000.

Lha·sa (lä′sə) *also,* **La·sa.** the capital of Tibet, in western China. Pop., 105,897.

Li·be·ri·a (lī bir′ē ə) a country on the west coast of Africa, founded in 1822 by freed slaves from the United States. Capital, Monrovia. Area, 43,000 sq. mi. (111,370 sq. km.). Pop., 2,490,000. —**Li·be·ri·an,** *adj., n.*

Li·bre·ville (lē′brə vil′) the capital and largest city of Gabon, on the northwestern coast of the country. Pop., 235,700.

Lib·y·a (lib′ē ə) a country on the Mediterranean coast of northern Africa. Capital, Tripoli. Area, 679,362 sq. mi. (1,759,548 sq. km.). Pop., 4,180,000. —**Lib′y·an,** *adj., n.*

Liech·ten·stein (lik′tən stīn′) a small country in central Europe, between Austria and Switzerland. Capital, Vaduz. Area, 62 sq. mi. (161 sq. km.). Pop., 29,000.

Li·ège (lē ezh′) a city in eastern Belgium. Pop., 207,496.

Li·long·we (li lông′wā) the capital of Malawi, in the west-central part of the country. Pop., 103,000.

at; āpe; fär; câre; end; mē; it; īce; pîerce; hot; ōld; sông, fôrk; oil; out; up; ūse; rüle; pùll; tûrn; chin; sing; shop; thin; this; hw in white; zh in treasure. The symbol ə stands for the unstressed vowel sound heard in about, taken, pencil, lemon, and circus.

Li·ma (lē′mə) the capital and chief city of Peru, in the west-central part of the country. Pop., 371,122.

Lin·coln (ling′kən) the capital of Nebraska, in the southeastern part of the state. Pop., 183,000.

Linz (lints) a city in northern Austria, on the Danube. Pop., 199,910.

Lis·bon (liz′bən) the capital, largest city, and chief seaport of Portugal, in the western part of the country. Pop., 807,937.

Lith·u·a·nia (lith′ü ā′nē ə) a republic of the Soviet Union, in the northwestern part of the country, on the Baltic Sea. It was formerly an independent country. Official name: **Lithuanian Soviet Socialist Republic.** Area, 25,175 sq. mi. (65,203 sq. km.). Pop., 3,603,000.

Little Bighorn, a river in northern Wyoming and southern Montana, near the site of the battle in which General George Custer and his entire body of troops were killed by American Indians in 1876. Length, 90 mi. (145 km.).

Little Rock, the capital and largest city of Arkansas, in the central part of the state. Pop., 181,000.

Liv·er·pool (liv′ər pūl′) a port city in western England. Pop., 491,500.

Li·vo·ni·a (lə vō′nē ə) a city in southeastern Michigan. Pop., 101,000.

Lju·blja·na (lē ü′blē ä′nə) a city in northwestern Yugoslavia. Pop., 305,211.

Łódź (lüj, lodz) a city in central Poland, southwest of Warsaw. Pop., 847,900.

Loire (lwär) the longest river of France, flowing from the south-central part of the country into the Bay of Biscay. Length, 625 mi. (1,006 km.).

Lo·mas de Za·mo·ra (lō′mäs də zə môr′ə) a city in eastern Argentina. Pop., 508,620.

Lo·mé (lō mā′) the capital and largest city of Togo. Pop., 369,926.

Lon·don (lun′dən) **1.** the capital and largest city of the United Kingdom and of the Commonwealth of Nations, in southeastern England, on the Thames. Pop., 6,767,500. Also, **Greater London. 2. City of.** a small section of London, on the north bank of the Thames, that is the financial and commercial center of the city. **3.** a city in southeastern Canada, in Ontario. Pop., 269,140.

Lon·don·der·ry (lun′dən der′ē) a port city in northwestern Northern Ireland. Pop., 68,000. Also, **Derry.**

Long Beach, a seaport and resort city in southwestern California. Pop., 396,000.

Long Island, a long, narrow island in southeastern New York State, south of Connecticut. Area, 1,682 sq. mi. (4,356 sq. km.).

Long Island Sound, an arm of the Atlantic, separating Connecticut from Long Island.

Lon·gueuil (lông gāl′) a city on the St. Lawrence River in southern Quebec, Canada. Pop., 125,441.

Los Al·a·mos (lôs al′ə mōs′) an unincorporated community in north-central New Mexico, a major U.S. center for atomic research. Pop., 11,039.

Los An·ge·les (lôs an′jə ləs, lôs an′jə lēz′) the chief port and largest city of California, in the southwestern part of the state. Pop., 3,259,000.

Louang·phra·bang (lwäng′ prə bäng′) a city in northern Laos, on the Mekong, the former royal capital of Laos. Pop., 43,000.

Lou·i·si·an·a (lü ē′zē an′ə) a state in the southern United States, on the Gulf of Mexico and the Mississippi River. Capital, Baton Rouge. Area, 47,752 sq. mi. (123,678 sq. km.). Pop., 4,501,000. Abbreviation, **La.**; postal abbreviation, **LA** —**Lou·i′si·an′an, Lou·i′si·an′i·an,** adj., n.

▲ When the French explorer La Salle claimed the Mississippi valley for France, he named it *Louisiane* after King Louis XIV. The area later became known as Louisiana and was sold to the United States. The name eventually came to be limited to what is now the state.

Lou·is·ville (lü′ē vil′) the largest city in Kentucky, a port on the Ohio in the northern part of the state. Pop., 286,000.

Lourdes (lùrd) a town in southwestern France, the site of a Roman Catholic shrine. Pop., 17,425.

Lou·ren·ço Mar·ques (lə ren′sō mär kes′) see **Maputo.**

Low Countries, a region of northwestern Europe consisting of the countries of the Netherlands, Belgium, and Luxembourg.

Lower California, see **Baja California.**

Lu·an·da (lü an′də) the capital and largest city of Angola, a port on the northeastern coast of the country. Pop., 1,200,000.

Lub·bock (lub′ək) a city in northwestern Texas. Pop., 186,000.

Lü·beck (lü′bek) a port city in northeastern West Germany. Pop., 211,000.

Lu·bum·ba·shi (lù′büm bä′shē) a city in southeastern Zaire. Pop., 543,268.

Luck·now (luk′nou) a city in north-central India. Pop., 895,721.

Lu·da (lü′dä) see **Dalian** (def. 1).

Lu·sa·ka (lü sä′kə) the capital and largest city of Zambia, in the south-central part of the country. Pop., 535,830.

Lu·shun (lü′shün′) a former city and seaport in northeastern China, now part of the municipality of Dalian. Pop., 40,000. Formerly, **Port Arthur.**

Lux·em·bourg (luk′səm bûrg′) also, **Lux·em·burg. 1.** a small country in western Europe, bordering France, Belgium, and West Germany. Capital, Luxembourg. Area, 998 sq. mi. (2,585 sq. km.). Pop., 362,000. **2.** the capital and chief city of Luxembourg. Pop., 78,900.

Lux·or (luk′sər) a city in Egypt, on the Nile River, noted for the ancient temples and burial grounds found nearby. It is on the site of ancient Thebes. Pop., 77,578.

Lvov (lə vof′) a city in the southwestern part of the Soviet Union, in the Ukraine. Pop., 753,000. Also, *German,* **Lemberg;** *Polish,* **Lwów** (lə vüf′).

Ly·all·pur (lī′əl pùr′) see **Faisalabad.**

Lyd·i·a (lid′ē ə) an ancient country in western Asia Minor. —**Lyd′i·an,** adj., n.

Ly·on (lē ōn′) a city in east-central France. Pop., 413,095.

Ma·cao (mə kou′) also, **Ma·cau. 1.** a Portuguese overseas territory on the southern coast of China. It will return to Chinese control in 1999. Area, 7 sq. mi. (18 sq. km.). Pop., 462,000. **2.** a seaport in this territory. Pop., 422,730.

Ma·cas·sar (mə kas′ər) see **Ujung Pandang.**

Mac·e·do·ni·a (mas′i dō′nē ə) **1.** an ancient kingdom north of Greece, the center of the empire created by Alexander the Great. Also, **Mac·e·don** (mas′i don′). **2.** a historic region in southeastern Europe, including parts of Greece, Yugoslavia, and Bulgaria. **3.** the Yugoslav section of this region, a constituent republic of Yugoslavia. Area, 9,930 sq. mi. (25,719 sq. km.). Pop., 1,912,257.

Mac·ken·zie (mə ken′zē) a river in northwestern Canada, flowing into the Arctic Ocean. Length, 2,635 mi. (4,240 km.).

Ma·con (mā′kən) a city in central Georgia. Pop., 118,000.

Mad·a·gas·car (mad′ə gas′kər) an island country in the Indian Ocean, east of southern Africa. Capital, Antananarivo. Area, 226,658 sq. mi. (587,044 sq. km.). Pop., 11,200,000. Formerly, **Malagasy Republic.**

Ma·dei·ra (mə dîr′ə, mə dâr′ə) **1.** a Portuguese island group in the Atlantic off the coast of Morocco. Land area, approx. 323 sq. mi. (837 sq. km.). Pop., 252,844. Also, **Madeira Islands. 2.** the largest island in this group. Area, approx. 286 sq. mi. (741 sq. km.). **3.** a large river in northwestern Brazil, one of the principal tributaries of the Amazon. Length, 2,100 mi. (3,379 km.).

Mad·i·son (mad′ə sən) the capital of Wisconsin, in the south-central part of the state. Pop., 176,000.

Ma·dras (mə dras′) a port city in southeastern India, on the Bay of Bengal. Pop., 3,276,622.

Ma·drid (mə drid′) the capital and largest city of Spain, in the central part of the country. Pop., 3,188,297.

Ma·du·rai (mad′yŭ rī′) a city in southern India. Pop., 820,891. Formerly, **Ma·du·ra** (mə dŭr′ə).

Mag·de·burg (mag′də bûrg′) a port city in west-central East Germany, on the Elbe River. Pop., 288,965.

Ma·gel·lan, Strait of (mə jel′ən) a strait at the southern tip of mainland South America, linking the Atlantic and the Pacific.

Main (mīn, män) a river flowing west through southwestern West Germany into the Rhine. Length, 325 mi. (523 km.).

Maine (mān) a state in the northeastern United States, on the Atlantic. Capital, Augusta. Area, 33,265 sq. mi. (86,156 sq. km.). Pop., 1,173,000. Abbreviation, **Me.**; postal abbreviation, **ME** —**Main′er,** *n.* ▲ *Maine* comes from the term "the main" (also spelled "the maine"), which means "the mainland." It was used by explorers of the coast of northern New England to distinguish the mainland from the many islands along the coast.

Ma·jor·ca (mə jôr′kə, mä yôr′kə) the largest of the Balearic Islands, in the western Mediterranean. Area, 1,350 sq. mi. (3,497 sq. km.). Also, **Mallorca.**

Ma·jur·o (mə jŭr′ō) an atoll in the Marshall Islands, the site of the capital. Pop., 11,791.

Ma·kas·sar (mə kas′ər) see **Ujung Pandang.**

Ma·la·bo (mə lä′bō) the capital of Equatorial Guinea. Pop., 30,710. Formerly, **Santa Isabel.**

Má·la·ga (mal′ə gə) a port city in southern Spain. Pop., 503,251.

Mal·a·ga·sy Republic (mal′ə gas′ē) see **Madagascar.**

Ma·la·wi (mə lä′wē) **1.** a landlocked country in southeastern Africa. Capital, Lilongwe. Area, 45,747 sq. mi. (118,485 sq. km.). Pop., 7,930,000. **2. Lake.** see **Nyasa, Lake.**

Ma·lay·a (mə lä′ə) a former nation in southeastern Asia, on the Malay Peninsula, now part of Malaysia. Area, 50,806 sq. mi. (131,588 sq. km.).

Malay Archipelago (mä′lā) a large island group between southeastern Asia on the north and Australia and New Guinea on the south, including the Philippines, most of Indonesia, and part of Malaysia. Also, **East Indies.**

Malay Peninsula, a long, narrow peninsula in southeastern Asia, including Malaya and part of Thailand.

Ma·lay·sia (mə lä′zhə) a country in southeastern Asia, divided by the South China Sea, consisting of Malaya on the west and Sarawak and Sabah on the east. Capital, Kuala Lumpur. Area, 128,430 sq. mi. (332,634 sq. km.). Pop., 17,000,000. —**Ma·lay′sian,** *adj.,* *n.*

Mal·dives (môl′dēvz, mal′dīvz) a country of about 2,000 islands in the Indian Ocean, southwest of India. Capital, Male. Land area, 115 sq. mi. (298 sq. km.). Pop., 207,000. Also, **Mal·dive Islands** (môl′dēv, mal′dīv).

Ma·le (mä′lā) the capital of the Maldives. Pop., 46,334.

Ma·li (mä′lē) a large, landlocked country in western Africa. Capital, Bamako. Area, 479,000 sq. mi. (1,240,610 sq. km.). Pop., 9,100,000.

Ma·llor·ca (mä yôr′kə) see **Majorca.**

Malm·ö (mal′mō) a port city in southwestern Sweden. Pop., 229,936.

Mal·ta (môl′tə) **1.** a country consisting of an island group in the Mediterranean, south of the Italian island of Sicily. Capital, Valletta. Land area, 122 sq. mi. (316 sq. km.). Pop., 393,000. Also, **Mal·tese Islands** (môl tēz′, môl tēs′). **2.** the chief island of this country. Area, 95 sq. mi. (246 sq. km.).

Mal·vi·nas (mal vē′nəs) see **Falkland Islands.**

Man, Isle of (man) an island in the Irish Sea, administered by the United Kingdom. Area, 221 sq. mi. (572 sq. km.). Pop., 64,282.

Ma·na·gua (mə nä′gwə) the capital and largest city of Nicaragua, in the southwestern part of the country. Pop., 644,588.

Ma·na·ma (mə nam′ə) the capital of Bahrain. Pop., 108,684.

Ma·nas·sas (mə nas′əs) a town in northeastern Virginia, near which the two battles of Bull Run took place during the Civil War.

Ma·naus (mə nous′) a city in western Brazil. Pop., 834,541.

Man·ches·ter (man′ches′tər, man′chə stər) **1.** a city in southern New Hampshire. Pop., 90,936. **2.** a city in northwestern England. Pop., 451,100.

Man·chu·kuo (man′chü′kwō′) a puppet state consisting principally of Manchuria, established by Japan in 1932 and lasting until 1945.

Man·chu·ri·a (man chŭr′ē ə) a historic region in northeastern China. Area, 413,000 sq. mi. (1,069,670 sq. km.).

Man·da·lay (man′də lā′) a city in central Burma. Pop., 532,895.

Man·hat·tan (man hat′ən) an island and borough of New York City, the financial, commercial, and cultural center of the city. Area, 23 sq. mi. (60 sq. km.).

Ma·nil·a (mə nil′ə) the capital and largest city of the Philippines. Pop., 1,630,485.

Man·i·to·ba (man′i tō′bə) a province in south-central Canada. Capital, Winnipeg. Area, 251,000 sq. mi. (650,090 sq. km.). Pop., 1,071,000.

Man·i·za·les (man′ə zal′əs) a city in west-central Colombia. Pop., 275,220.

Mann·heim (man′hīm) a port city in south-central West Germany, on the Rhine. Pop., 295,200.

Ma·pu·to (mə pü′tō) the capital of Mozambique, in the southern part of the country. Pop., 903,621. Formerly, **Lourenço Marques.**

Mar·a·cai·bo (mar′ə kī′bō) **1.** a port city in northwestern Venezuela, near the Caribbean Sea. Pop., 929,000. **2. Lake.** a lake in northwestern Venezuela.

Ma·ra·cay (mär′ə kī′) a city in northern Venezuela. Pop., 355,000.

Mar·a·thon (mar′ə thon′) the plain in Greece, northeast of Athens, where the Athenians defeated the Persians in battle in 490 B.C.

Mar del Pla·ta (mär′del plä′tə) a city in east-central Argentina, on the Atlantic. Pop., 414,696.

Mar·i·an·a Islands (mär′e an′ə) a volcanic island group in the western Pacific, divided into Guam and the Northern Mariana Islands. Land area, 453 sq. mi. (1,173 sq. km.). Also, **Mar·i·an·as** (môr′ē an′əz).

Mar·i·time Provinces (mar′i tīm′) the Canadian provinces of New Brunswick, Nova Scotia, and Prince Edward Island. Also, **Mar·i·times** (mar′i tīmz′).

Mark·ham (mär′kəm) a town in southern Ontario, Canada. Pop., 114,597.

Mar·ma·ra, Sea of (mär′mər ə) *also,* **Sea of Mar·mo·ra.** a sea between the European and Asian parts of Turkey, connected with the Black Sea by the Bosporus and with the Aegean Sea by the Dardanelles.

Marne (märn) a river in east-central France. Length, 326 mi. (525 km.).

Mar·ra·kesh (mar′ə kesh′) *also,* **Mar·ra·kech.** a city in central Morocco. Pop., 439,728.

---

at; āpe; fär; câre; end; mē; it; īce; pierce; hot; ōld; sông, fôrk; oil; out; up; ūse; rüle; pull; tûrn; chin; sing; shop; thin; this; hw in white; zh in treasure. The symbol ə stands for the unstressed vowel sound heard in about, taken, pencil, lemon, and circus.

Mar·seilles (mär sā′) *also*, **Mar·seille**. the chief seaport of France, on the Mediterranean. Pop., 874,436.

Mar·shall Islands (mär′shəl) a group of Pacific islands administered by the United States as part of the Trust Territory of the Pacific Islands. Capital, Majuro. Land area, approx. 70 sq. mi. (180 sq. km.). Pop., 38,000.

Mar·tha's Vineyard (mär′thəz) an island off the Massachusetts coast. Land area, approx. 100 sq. mi. (260 sq. km.).

Mar·ti·nique (mär′tə nēk′) a French island in the Caribbean. Area, approx. 425 sq. mi. (1,100 sq. km.). Pop., 330,000.

Mar·y·land (mer′ə lənd) a state in the eastern United States. Capital, Annapolis. Area, 10,460 sq. mi. (27,091 sq. km.). Pop., 4,463,000. Abbreviation, **Md.**; postal abbreviation, **MD** —**Mar′y·land·er**, *n*. ▲ The state of Maryland was named for Henrietta Maria (1609–1669), the Roman Catholic queen of King Charles I of England. Charles had given the land as a grant to Lord Baltimore (Cecilius Calvert, 1605?–1675), who founded a colony where Roman Catholics could settle.

Mas·e·ru (maz′ə rü′) the capital of Lesotho. Pop., 14,686.

Mash·had (mə shad′) a city in northeastern Iran. Pop., 1,130,000. Also, **Me·shed**.

Mas·sa·chu·setts (mas′ə chü′sits) a state in the northeastern United States. Capital, Boston. Area, 8,284 sq. mi. (21,456 sq. km.). Pop., 5,832,000. Abbreviation, **Mass.**; postal abbreviation, **MA** ▲ *Massachusetts* comes from an Algonquian word meaning "at the big hill," referring to the Blue Hills near Boston. It was originally the name of an Indian village located in this area. The English settlers applied it also to the tribe living in this village and to the bay. The name was used for the Massachusetts Bay Colony, which was later united with the Plymouth colony and Maine in the colony of Massachusetts, which eventually became the state.

Mat·ter·horn (mat′ər hôrn′) a steep, jagged mountain peak in the Alps, on the border between Switzerland and Italy.

Mau·i (mou′ē) the second largest island of Hawaii. Area, 728 sq. mi. (1,886 sq. km.).

Mau·na Ke·a (mou′nə kā′ə) an extinct volcano in the northwestern part of the island of Hawaii. Height, 13,796 ft. (4,205 m.).

Mau·na Lo·a (mou′nə lō′ə) the largest known active volcano in the world, on the island of Hawaii. Height, 13,680 ft. (4,170 m.).

Mau·ri·ta·ni·a (môr′i tā′nē ə) a country on the northwestern coast of Africa. Capital, Nouakchott. Area, 397,955 sq. mi. (1,030,703 sq. km.). Pop., 2,140,000. —**Mau′ri·ta′ni·an**, *adj.*, *n.*

Mau·ri·tius (mô rish′əs) an island country in the western Indian Ocean, east of Madagascar. Capital, Port Louis. Area, 788 sq. mi. (2,041 sq. km.). Pop., 1,120,000.

Ma·yotte (mä yot′) an island in the Indian Ocean, northwest of Madagascar, a French overseas territory. Area, 145 sq. mi. (376 sq. km.). Pop., 67,138.

Mba·bane (bä bän′) the capital of Swaziland, in the western part of the country. Pop., 30,000.

Mbu·ji-Ma·yi (bü′jē mī′ē) a city in southern Zaire. Pop., 423,363. Formerly, **Bakwanga**.

Mc·Kin·ley, Mount (mə kin′lē) the highest mountain in North America, in south-central Alaska. Height, 20,320 ft. (6,194 m.).

Mec·ca (mek′ə) a city in western Saudi Arabia, near the Red Sea, the birthplace of Muhammad. Pop., 550,000.

Me·dan (mā dän′) a city in Indonesia, on the northeastern coast of the island of Sumatra. Pop., 1,378,955.

Me·del·lín (med′ə lēn′) a city in west-central Colombia. Pop., 1,473,351.

Me·di·a (mē′dē ə) an ancient kingdom in northwestern Persia.

Me·di·na (mə dē′nə) a city in western Saudi Arabia, site of Muhammad's tomb. Pop., 290,000.

Med·i·ter·ra·ne·an (med′i tə rā′nē ən) **1.** a large, almost landlocked arm of the Atlantic between southern Europe, western Asia, and northern Africa. Also, **Mediterranean Sea. 2. the Mediterranean.** a region consisting of this sea and the countries in and around it. —**Med′·i·ter·ra′ne·an**, *adj.*

Mek·nès (mek nes′) a city in northwestern Morocco. Pop., 319,783.

Me·kong (mā′kong′) a river in southeastern Asia, flowing southeastward from western China into the South China Sea. Length, 2,600 mi. (4,183 km.).

Mel·a·ne·sia (mel′ə nē′zhə) one of the three major divisions of the Pacific islands, east of Australia.

Mel·bourne (mel′bərn) a port city in southeastern Australia, the capital of the state of Victoria. Pop., 2,578,759.

Me·li·lla (mə lē′yə) a port city on the Mediterranean, a Spanish enclave in northern Morocco. Pop., 56,247.

Mem·phis (mem′fis) **1.** the largest city in Tennessee, in the southwestern part of the state. Pop., 653,000. **2.** a city in ancient Egypt, on the west bank of the Nile.

Mé·ri·da (mer′i də) a city in southeastern Mexico, on the Yucatán Peninsula. Pop., 400,142.

Me·sa (mā′sə) a city in south-central Arizona. Pop., 251,000.

Me·shed (mə shed′) see **Mashhad**.

Mes·o·po·ta·mi·a (mes′ə pə tā′mē ə) a historic region in southwestern Asia, between the Tigris and Euphrates rivers, a center of ancient civilization. —**Mes′o·po·ta′mi·an**, *adj.*, *n.*

Mes·si·na (mə sē′nə) **1.** a port city in the northeastern part of the Italian island of Sicily. Pop., 267,264. **2. Strait of.** a narrow strait between Italy and Sicily.

Met·air·ie (met′ə rē) a city in southeastern Louisiana. Pop., 164,160.

Mex·i·ca·li (mek′si kal′ē) a city in northern Mexico, in Baja California on Mexico's border with the United States. Pop., 341,559.

Mex·i·co (mek′si kō′) **1.** a country in North America, south of and bordering the southwestern United States. Capital, Mexico City. Area, 761,605 sq. mi. (1,972,557 sq. km.). Pop., 87,000,000. **2. Gulf of.** an arm of the Atlantic, between the United States and Mexico.

Mexico City, the capital and largest city of Mexico, in the southern part of the country. Pop., 9,373,400.

Mi·am·i (mī am′ē) a resort and port city in southeastern Florida. Pop., 374,000.

Miami Beach, a resort city in southeastern Florida, just east of Miami. Pop., 96,298.

Mich·i·gan (mish′i gən) **1.** a state in the north-central United States. Capital, Lansing. Area, 58,527 sq. mi. (151,585 sq. km.). Pop., 9,145,000. Abbreviation, **Mich.**; postal abbreviation, **MI 2. Lake.** the third largest of the Great Lakes. It lies between Michigan and Wisconsin. —**Mich′i·gan′der, Mich·i·ga·ni·an** (mish′i gā′nē ən), **Mich′i·gan·ite′**, *n*. ▲ *Michigan* is the French version of an Algonquian phrase that meant "big water" or "great lake," referring to Lake Michigan. This name was given to a territory east of the lake in 1805, which later became part of the state.

Mi·cro·ne·sia (mī′krə nē′zhə) **1.** one of the three major divisions of the Pacific islands, north of Melanesia. **2.** see **Federated States of Micronesia**.

Middle East, a region that includes Egypt and the Arab countries of southwestern Asia, as well as Israel, Turkey, and Iran, and sometimes Algeria, Tunisia, Morocco, Libya, and Sudan. Also, **Mideast. —Middle Eastern**.

Middle West, a region of the north-central United States, the major agricultural area of the country. Area, 765,530 sq. mi. (1,982,723 sq. km.). Also, **Midwest. —Middle Western**.

Mid·east (mid′ēst′) see **Middle East.**

Mid·way Islands (mid′wā′) a small island group in the north-central Pacific, administered by the United States. Pop., 2,000.

Mid·west (mid′west′) see **Middle West.** —**Mid′west′ern,** adj. —**Mid′west′ern·er,** n.

Mi·lan (mə lan′) a city in northern Italy, the leading commercial and industrial center of the country. Pop., 1,515,233.

Mil·wau·kee (mil wô′kē) a city in southeastern Wisconsin, on Lake Michigan. Pop., 605,000.

Min·ne·ap·o·lis (min′ē ap′ə lis) the largest city in Minnesota, in the southeastern part of the state. Pop., 357,000.

Min·ne·so·ta (min′ə sō′tə) a state in the north-central United States. Capital, St. Paul. Area, 84,402 sq. mi. (218,601 sq. km.). Pop., 4,214,000. Abbreviation, **Minn.;** postal abbreviation, **MN** —**Min′ne·so′tan,** adj., n. ▲ *Minnesota* was a Siouan name for a river in the southern part of the state and meant "water the color of the sky" or "cloudy water." Congress applied the name in 1847 to the territory where the river was located, part of which later became the state.

Minsk (minsk) a city in the eastern Soviet Union. Pop., 1,510,000.

Miq·ue·lon (mik′ə lon′) see **St. Pierre and Miquelon.**

Mis·kolc (mish′kōlts) a city in northeastern Hungary. Pop., 211,660.

Mis·sis·sip·pi (mis′ə sip′ē) **1.** the principal river of the United States, flowing from northern Minnesota to the Gulf of Mexico. Length, 2,348 mi. (3,778 km.). **2.** a state in the southern United States. Capital, Jackson. Area, 47,689 sq. mi. (123,515 sq. km.). Pop., 2,625,000. Abbreviation, **Miss.;** postal abbreviation, **MS** —**Mis′sis·sip′pi·an,** adj., n. ▲ *Mississippi* comes from two Algonquian words meaning "big river," "great water," or "father of the waters." French explorers carried the name from the Great Lakes region to the mouth of the Mississippi River. In 1798, Congress applied it to a southern territory east of the river, part of which later became part of the state.

Mis·sou·ri (mi zŏŏr′ē, mi zŏŏr′ə) **1.** a large river in the United States, flowing from Montana to the Mississippi just north of St. Louis. Length, 2,315 mi. (3,725 km.). **2.** a state in the central United States. Capital, Jefferson City. Area, 69,697 sq. mi. (180,515 sq. km.). Pop., 5,066,000. Abbreviation, **Mo.;** postal abbreviation, **MO** —**Mis·sour′i·an,** adj., n. ▲ *Missouri* is an Algonquian word meaning "people of the big canoes." It was the name of a Sioux tribe living near the mouth of the Missouri River at the time of French exploration. The name was transferred from the tribe to the river, and later to the territory where the river was located, part of which became the state.

Mitch·ell, Mount (mich′əl) the highest mountain in the eastern United States, in western North Carolina. Height, 6,684 ft. (2,037 m.).

Mo·bile (mō bēl′, mō′bēl) a port city in southwestern Alabama. Pop., 203,000.

Mo·de·na (mō′də nə) a city in northern Italy. Pop., 178,190.

Mo·des·to (mə des′tō) a city in central California. Pop., 133,000.

Mo·ga·di·shu (mog′ə dish′ü) the capital of Somalia, in the southeastern part of the country, on the Indian Ocean. Pop., 500,000.

Mo·ja·ve Desert (mō hä′vē) also, **Mo·ha·ve Desert.** a desert in southeastern California. Area, approx. 15,000 sq. mi. (38,850 sq. km.).

Mol·da·vi·a (mol dā′vē ə) a republic of the Soviet Union, in the European part of the country, bordering Romania. Official name: **Moldavian Soviet Socialist Republic.** Area, approx. 13,000 sq. mi. (33,670 sq. km.). Pop., 4,142,000. —**Mol·da′vi·an,** adj., n.

Mo·lo·kai (mō′lə kī′) the fifth largest island of Hawaii. Area, 261 sq. mi. (676 sq. km.).

Mo·lo·tov (mol′ə tôf′) see **Perm.**

Mom·ba·sa (mom bä′sä) the principal port city of Kenya, on the Indian Ocean. Pop., 425,600.

Mon·a·co (mon′ə kō′, mə nä′kō) **1.** a small country in southern Europe, on the Mediterranean Sea. Capital, Monaco. Area, 0.6 sq. mi. (1.6 sq. km.). Pop., 28,000. **2.** the capital of this country. Pop., 1,700. Also, **Mon·a·co-Ville** (mon′ə kō vil′).

Mon·go·li·a (mong gō′lē ə) **1.** a vast area in east-central Asia, extending from northern China to Siberia, including Inner Mongolia and the country of Mongolia. Area, approx. 1,000,000 sq. mi. (2,590,000 sq. km.). **2.** a country in central Asia, bordered by the Soviet Union and China. Official name: **Mongolian People's Republic.** Capital, Ulan Bator. Area, 604,250 sq. mi. (1,565,008 sq. km.). Pop., 2,130,000. Formerly, *(def. 2),* **Outer Mongolia.**

Mo·non·ga·he·la (mə nong′gə hē′lə) a river in northern West Virginia and southwestern Pennsylvania, joining the Allegheny at Pittsburgh to form the Ohio River. Length, 128 mi. (206 km.).

Mon·ro·vi·a (mon rō′vē ə) the capital and largest city of Liberia, on the Atlantic. Pop., 243,243.

Mon·tan·a (mon tan′ə) a state in the northwestern United States. Capital, Helena. Area, 147,046 sq. mi. (380,849 sq. km.). Pop., 819,000. Abbreviation, **Mont.;** postal abbreviation, **MT** —**Mon·tan′an,** adj., n. ▲ *Montana* comes from a word meaning "mountainous" in Spanish and Latin. It was originally the name of a town near Pike's Peak in what is now Colorado. The name was suggested for a new territory being organized during the Civil War, but that area came to be called *Idaho* instead. In 1864, the name *Montana* was given to a new territory to the east of Idaho.

Mont Blanc (mont′ blangk′) the highest mountain in the Alps, on the French-Italian border. Height, 15,771 ft. (4,807 m.).

Mon·te Car·lo (mon′tē kär′lō) a resort town in Monaco, on the Mediterranean, site of a famous gambling casino. Pop., 10,000.

Mon·te·ne·gro (mon′tə nē′grō) a republic of Yugoslavia, on the Adriatic, formerly an independent kingdom. Area, approx. 5,333 sq. mi. (13,812 sq. km.). Pop., 584,310. —**Mon′te·ne′grin,** adj., n.

Mon·ter·rey (mon′tə rā′) a city in northeastern Mexico. Pop., 1,090,009.

Mon·te·vi·de·o (mon′tə vi dā′ō) the capital of Uruguay, in the southern part of the country, on the Río de la Plata. Pop., 1,237,227.

Mont·gom·er·y (mont gum′ə rē) the capital of Alabama, in the central part of the state. Pop., 194,000.

Mont·pel·ier (mont pēl′yər) the capital of Vermont, in the central part of the state. Pop., 8,241.

Mont·re·al (mon′trē ôl′) the largest city of Canada, in southern Quebec on the St. Lawrence River. Pop., 1,015,420.

Mont·ser·rat (mont′sə rat′) a British island in the West Indies, one of the Leeward islands. Area, 40 sq. mi. (104 sq. km.). Pop., 12,000.

Mo·ra·vi·a (mô rā′vē ə) a historic region in central Czechoslovakia. Area, approx. 10,000 sq. mi. (25,900 sq. km.). Pop., 4,016,897.

Mo·roc·co (mə rok′ō) a country in northwestern Africa,

---

at; āpe; fär; câre; end; mē; it; īce; pîerce; hot; ōld; sông, fôrk; oil; out; up; ūse; rüle; pŭll; tûrn; chin; sing; shop; thin; this; hw in white; zh in treasure. The symbol ə stands for the unstressed vowel sound heard in about, taken, pencil, lemon, and circus.

on the Atlantic and the Mediterranean. Capital, Rabat. Area, 172,410 sq. mi. (446,542 sq. km.). Pop., 24,100,000.

Mo·ron (mô rōn′) a city in eastern Argentina. Pop., 596,769.

Mo·ro·ni (mô rō′nē) the capital of the Comoros. Pop., 20,112.

Mos·cow (mos′kou) the capital and largest city of the Soviet Union, in the western part of the country. Pop., 8,703,000.

Mo·sul (mō sül′) a city in northern Iraq, on the Tigris River. Pop., 570,926. Also, **Al Mawsil.**

Mount Ver·non (vûr′nən) the home and burial place of George Washington, on the Potomac in Virginia, near Washington, D.C.

Mo·zam·bique (mō′zəm bēk′) a country in southeastern Africa. Capital, Maputo. Area, 308,642 sq. mi. (799,383 sq. km.). Pop., 15,500,000.

Muk·den (mùk′den′) see **Shenyang.**

Mul·tan (mùl tän′) a city in northeastern Pakistan. Pop., 696,316.

Mu·nich (mū′nik) a city in southern West Germany. Pop., 1,266,100.

Mün·ster (mùn′stər) a city in northwestern West Germany. Pop., 273,000.

Mur·mansk (mùr mänsk′) a port city in the northwestern Soviet Union. Pop., 419,000.

Mur·ray (mùr′ē) a river rising near Mount Kosciusko in New South Wales, Australia, and flowing west to the Indian Ocean near Adelaide. Length, 1,609 mi. (2,589 km.).

Mus·cat (mus′kat) the capital of Oman, in the northern part of the country. Pop., 30,000.

Muscat and Oman, see **Oman.**

My·ce·nae (mī sē′nē) an ancient city in southern Greece.

Na·ga·sa·ki (nä′gə sä′kē) a city in Japan, on the western coast of the island of Kyushu. On August 9, 1945, the second atomic bomb used in World War II was dropped on this city. Pop., 447,091.

Na·go·ya (nə goi′ə) a city in Japan, on the southern coast of the island of Honshu. Pop., 2,087,902.

Nag·pur (näg′pùr) a city in central India. Pop., 1,219,461.

Nai·ro·bi (nī rō′bē) the capital of Kenya, in the southern part of the country. Pop., 1,103,600.

Na·mib·i·a (nə mib′ē ə) a territory on the southwestern coast of Africa, administered by the Republic of South Africa. Capital, Windhoek. Area, 318,252 sq. mi. (824,273 sq. km.). Pop., 1,740,000. Formerly, **South-West Africa.**

Nan·chang (nän′jäng′) a city in southeastern China. Pop., 1,088,800.

Nan·jing (nän′jing′) a city in eastern China, on the Yangtze River. It is a former capital of the country. Pop., 2,250,000. Also, **Nan·king** (nän′king′).

Nantes (nants) a port city in western France, in the region of Brittany. Pop., 240,539.

Nan·tuck·et (nan tuk′it) an island off the southern coast of Cape Cod, Massachusetts. Area, 50 sq. mi. (130 sq. km.).

Na·ples (nā′pəlz) a port city on the southwestern coast of Italy. Pop., 1,206,010.

Nar·ra·gan·sett Bay (nar′ə gan′sit) a large inlet of the Atlantic, in eastern Rhode Island.

Nash·ville (nash′vil′) the capital of Tennessee, in the central part of the state. Pop., 474,000.

Nas·sau (nas′ô) the capital and largest city of the Bahamas. Pop., 135,000.

Na·tal (nə tal′) a port city in northeastern Brazil, on the Atlantic. Pop., 512,241.

Nationalist China, see **Taiwan.**

Na·u·ru (nä ü′rü) a small island country in the central Pacific, northeast of Australia. Area, approx. 8 sq. mi. (21 sq. km.). Pop., 8,000. —**Na·u′ru·an,** adj., n.

Na·varre (nə vär′) a historic region and former kingdom located in the western Pyrenees. It included parts of southwestern France and northern Spain.

Naz·a·reth (naz′ər əth) a town in Galilee, in northern Israel, where Jesus spent his youth. Pop., 46,300.

Ndja·me·na (ən jä′mə nə) the capital of Chad, in the west-central part of the country. Pop., 402,000. Formerly, **Fort-Lamy.**

Ndo·la (ən dō′lə) a city in north-central Zambia. Pop., 250,490.

Near East, a region usually regarded as including the countries of southwestern Asia and northeastern Africa, and sometimes the Balkans.

Ne·bras·ka (nə bras′kə) a state in the central United States. Capital, Lincoln. Area, 77,355 sq. mi. (200,349 sq. km.). Pop., 1,598,000. Abbreviations, **Nebr., Neb.;** postal abbreviation, **NE** —**Ne·bras′kan,** adj., n. ▲ Nebraska, meaning "flat water," comes from a Siouan name for the Platte River. Although the river's name was changed, the Indian name was used for the territory where the river was located, part of which later became the state.

Ne·pal (nə pôl′, nə päl′) a country in central Asia, bounded by India and Tibet. Capital, Katmandu. Area, 56,827 sq. mi. (147,182 sq. km.). Pop., 18,100,000.

Ness, Loch (nes) a lake in northwestern Scotland, said to be the home of an enormous sea creature known as the Loch Ness monster.

Neth·er·lands, the (neth′ər ləndz) a country in northwestern Europe, on the North Sea. Capital, Amsterdam. Seat of government, The Hague. Area, 16,133 sq. mi. (41,784 sq. km.). Pop., 14,700,000. Also, **Holland.** —**Neth·er·land·er** (neth′ər lan′dər) n.

Netherlands Antilles, a Dutch island group in the southern Caribbean. Land area, 309 sq. mi. (800 sq. km.). Pop., 221,000.

Netherlands East Indies, a group of islands off the southeastern coast of Asia, formerly controlled by the Netherlands, now part of Indonesia.

Net·za·hual·có·yotl (net′sə wäl kə yō′təl) a city in south-central Mexico, near Mexico City. Pop., 1,341,230.

Ne·vad·a (nə vad′ə, nə vä′də) a state in the western United States. Capital, Carson City. Area, 110,561 sq. mi. (286,353 sq. km.). Pop., 963,000. Abbreviation, **Nev.;** postal abbreviation, **NV** —**Ne·vad′an,** adj., n. ▲ Nevada comes from the Spanish word nevada, meaning "snowy" or "snow-covered." Spanish explorers gave this name to the Sierra Nevada, the mountains that extend from eastern California to the southwestern corner of Nevada. The state takes its name from these mountains.

Ne·vis (nē′vis) see **St. Kitts-Nevis.**

New Amsterdam, the capital of the Dutch colony of New Netherland. A town on the lower tip of Manhattan, it was taken by the British in 1664 and renamed New York.

New·ark (nü′ərk, nū′ərk) a city in northeastern New Jersey, near New York City. Pop., 316,000.

New Brunswick, a province of Canada, in the eastern part of the country. Capital, Fredericton. Area, 28,354 sq. mi. (73,437 sq. km.). Pop., 710,422.

New Cal·e·do·nia (kal′i dō′nē ə) a French island territory in the southern Pacific, east of Australia. Area, 7,366 sq. mi. (19,078 sq. km.). Pop., 162,000.

New·cas·tle (nü′kas′əl, nū′kas′əl) **1.** a port city in northeastern England, noted for its coal and shipbuilding industries. Pop., 282,200. Also, **Newcastle-upon-Tyne** (tīn). **2.** a port city in New South Wales, in southeastern Australia. Pop., 258,972.

New Delhi, the capital of India, in the north-central part of the country. Pop., 273,036.

New England, a region of the northeastern United States that includes Maine, New Hampshire, Vermont, Massachusetts, Rhode Island, and Connecticut. —**New Englander.**

New·found·land (nü′fənd lənd, nü′fənd lənd) **1.** an island off the east coast of Canada, part of Newfoundland and Labrador. Area, 43,359 sq. mi. (112,300 sq. km.). **2.** see **Newfoundland and Labrador.**

Newfoundland and Labrador, the easternmost province of Canada, consisting of the island of Newfoundland and the mainland area of Labrador. Capital, St. John's. Area, 156,185 sq. mi. (404,519 sq. km.). Pop., 568,349.

New France, a former territory in North America, explored and settled by the French from 1609 to 1763.

New Guinea, the second largest island in the world (after Greenland), in the western Pacific, north of Australia. Area, approx. 342,000 sq. mi. (885,780 sq. km.).

New Hamp·shire (hamp′shər) a state in the northeastern United States. Capital, Concord. Area, 9,279 sq. mi. (24,033 sq. km.). Pop., 1,027,000. Abbreviation, **N.H.**; postal abbreviation, **NH** —**New Hamp′shir·ite′.** ▲ *New Hampshire* was originally the name given to an area of land granted to the Englishman John Mason (1586–1635) for settlement. Mason named it after his home county of Hampshire in England.

New Ha·ven (hā′vən) a city in southern Connecticut. Pop., 123,000.

New Hebrides, see **Vanuatu.**

New Jersey, a state in the eastern United States. Capital, Trenton. Area, 7,787 sq. mi. (20,168 sq. km.). Pop., 7,619,000. Abbreviation, **N.J.**; postal abbreviation, **NJ** —**New Jer′sey·ite′.** ▲ New Jersey was named after the British island of Jersey in the English Channel. Sir George Carteret (1610?–1680), one of the colony's original proprietors, came from Jersey.

New Mexico, a state in the southwestern United States. Capital, Santa Fe. Area, 121,593 sq. mi. (314,926 sq. km.). Pop., 1,479,000. Abbreviations, **N. Mex., N.M.**; postal abbreviation, **NM** —**New Mexican.** ▲ *New Mexico* is an exact translation from the earlier Spanish name *Nuevo Mejico.* The Spanish explorer Francisco de Ibarra (1539?–1575) gave the territory this name to entice settlers with the promise that it would be as rich a land as Mexico. The name *Mexico* was derived from the name of an Aztec god.

New Neth·er·land (neth′ər lənd) a Dutch colony in North America from 1624 to 1664 that consisted of parts of present-day New York, New Jersey, and Connecticut.

New Or·le·ans (ôr′lē ənz, ôr′lənz, ôr lēnz′) a city in southeastern Louisiana, a port on the Mississippi. Pop., 554,000.

New·port News (nü′pôrt′, nü′pôrt′) a port city in southeastern Virginia. Pop., 162,000.

New South Wales, a state of Australia, in the southeastern part of the country. Capital, Sydney. Area, 309,433 sq. mi. (801,431 sq. km.). Pop., 5,406,900.

New Windsor, see **Windsor** (*def.* 1).

New York (yôrk) **1.** a state in the eastern United States. Capital, Albany. Area, 49,108 sq. mi. (127,190 sq. km.). Pop., 17,772,000. Abbreviation, **N.Y.**; postal abbreviation, **NY** Also, **New York State. 2.** the largest city and a major port of the United States, in southern New York State. Pop., 7,263,000. Also, **New York City.** —**New York′er.** ▲ The city of New York was called New Amsterdam when it was first settled by the Dutch. When the English took it and the colony of New Netherland from the Dutch, King Charles II gave them to his brother James, duke of York and Albany (later King James II), who kept the word *New* from the name *New Amsterdam* but renamed it after his duchy of York. The colony, which later became a state, was also given the name *New York* at the same time.

New York Bay, a bay of the Atlantic, south of New York City, at the mouth of the Hudson River.

New York State Barge Canal, a toll-free system of

canals in New York. It links the Hudson with Lakes Ontario, Erie, and Champlain.

New Zea·land (zē′lənd) an island country in the southern Pacific, east of Australia. Capital, Wellington. Area, 103,787 sq. mi. (268,808 sq. km.). Pop., 3,440,000. —**New Zea′land·er.**

Ni·ag·a·ra (nī ag′rə, nī ag′ər ə) **1.** a short river on which the Niagara Falls is located, flowing from Lake Erie into Lake Ontario. **2.** see **Niagara Falls.**

Niagara Falls 1. a waterfall on the Niagara River, between the United States and Canada. **2.** a city in western New York, located on the Niagara River at the falls, noted as a tourist center. Pop., 71,384. **3.** a city in southern Ontario, Canada, opposite Niagara Falls, New York. Pop., 72,107.

Nia·mey (nyä mā′) the capital and largest city of Niger, in the southwestern part of the country. Pop., 399,100.

Nic·a·ra·gua (nik′ə rä′gwə) the largest country of Central America. Capital, Managua. Area, 50,200 sq. mi. (130,018 sq. km.). Pop., 3,750,000. —**Nic′a·ra′guan,** *adj., n.*

Nice (nēs) a resort city in southeastern France, on the Mediterranean. Pop., 337,085.

Nic·o·si·a (nik′ə sē′ə) the capital of Cyprus, in the central part of the country. Pop., 48,221.

Ni·ger (nī′jər) **1.** a landlocked country in western Africa. Capital, Niamey. Area, 489,200 sq. mi. (1,267,028 sq. km.). Pop., 6,900,000. **2.** a river flowing from western Africa into the Gulf of Guinea. Length, 2,600 mi. (4,183 km.).

Ni·ge·ri·a (nī jîr′ē ə) a country in western Africa, on the Gulf of Guinea. Capital, Lagos. Area, 356,669 sq. mi. (923,773 sq. km.). Pop., 109,000,000. —**Ni·ge′ri·an,** *adj., n.*

Nile (nīl) the longest river in the world, flowing through east-central and northeastern Africa to the Mediterranean. Length, 4,150 mi. (6,677 km.).

Nin·e·veh (nin′ə və) the capital of ancient Assyria. It lay on the east bank of the Tigris River, in what is now northern Iraq.

Niš (nēsh) *also,* **Nish.** a city in eastern Yugoslavia. Pop., 643,470.

Ni·u·e (nē ü′ā) an island in the southern Pacific, a possession of New Zealand. Land area, 102 sq. mi. (264 sq. km.). Pop., 3,600.

Nor·folk (nôr′fək) a city in southeastern Virginia. Pop., 275,000.

Norfolk Island, an Australian island in the southern Pacific. Land area, 14 sq. mi. (36 sq. km.). Pop., 2,175.

Nor·man·dy (nôr′mən dē) a historic region and former province in northwestern France, bordering the English Channel. Area, 11,820 sq. mi. (30,614 sq. km.).

North America, the third largest continent, consisting of all the land between the Atlantic and Pacific oceans north of the Panama-Colombia border, including Mexico, the continental United States, and Canada. Area, approx. 9,362,000 sq. mi. (24,247,580 sq. km.). Pop., 423,000,000. —**North American.**

North Carolina, a state in the southeastern United States, on the Atlantic. Capital, Raleigh. Area, 52,669 sq. mi. (136,413 sq. km.). Pop., 6,333,000. Abbreviation, **N.C.**; postal abbreviation, **NC** —**North Car·o·lin·i·an** (kar′-ə lin′ē ən). ▲ North Carolina was formed from the northern part of the English colony of Carolina. In gratitude for

---

at; āpe; fär; câre; end; mē; it; īce; pîerce; hot; ōld; sông, fôrk; oil; out; up; ūse; rüle; pull; tûrn; chin; sing; shop; thin; this; hw in white; zh in treasure. The symbol ə stands for the unstressed vowel sound heard in about, taken, pencil, lemon, and circus.

the grant of land from Charles I in 1629, the proprietor gave the colony the name *Carolana*, which means "from Charles." The spelling was later changed to *Carolina* by King Charles II when he granted the unsettled colony to a group of noblemen in 1663.

North Dakota, a state in the north-central United States. Capital, Bismarck. Area, 70,702 sq. mi. (183,118 sq. km.). Pop., 679,000. Abbreviations, **N. Dak., N.D.**; postal abbreviation, **ND** —**North Dakotan.** ▲ North Dakota was once the northern section of the Dakota Territory, which derived its name from the Dakota Indians. The Dakota were a western branch of the Sioux, and the name *Dakota* is a Siouan word meaning "allied tribes."

Northern Ireland, a political division of the United Kingdom, occupying the northeast corner of the island of Ireland. Capital, Belfast. Area, 5,452 sq. mi. (14,121 sq. km.). Pop., 1,566,800.

Northern Mariana Islands, a group of 16 islands in the western Pacific, administered by the United States as part of the Trust Territory of the Pacific Islands. Capital, Saipan. Land area, 244 sq. mi. (632 sq. km.). Pop., 22,000. Also, **Northern Marianas.**

Northern Territory, a territory in the north-central part of Australia. Capital, Darwin. Area, 523,620 sq. mi. (1,356,176 sq. km.). Pop., 138,800.

North Island, the smaller of the two main islands of New Zealand. Area, 44,281 sq. mi. (114,688 sq. km.).

North Korea, a country occupying the northern part of the Korean peninsula. Official name: **Democratic People's Republic of Korea.** Capital, Pyongyang. Area, 46,540 sq. mi. (120,539 sq. km.). Pop., 22,400,000.

North Sea, a large arm of the Atlantic, between Great Britain and continental Europe.

North Slope, a region of northern Alaska bordering the Arctic Ocean, the site of rich oil deposits.

North Vietnam, see **Vietnam.**

Northwest Territories, an administrative division of Canada, in the northern part of the country. Capital, Yellowknife. Area, 1,304,903 sq. mi. (3,379,699 sq. km.). Pop., 52,238.

Northwest Territory, a U.S. territory organized in 1787, consisting of the land between the Ohio and Mississippi rivers that now forms Illinois, Indiana, Michigan, Ohio, Wisconsin, and part of Minnesota.

North York, a city in southern Ontario, Canada. Pop., 556,297.

Nor·way (nôr'wā') a country in northern Europe occupying the western and northernmost part of the Scandinavian peninsula. Capital, Oslo. Area, 125,057 sq. mi. (323,898 sq. km.). Pop., 4,170,000.

Nor·we·gian Sea (nôr wē'jən) the part of the Arctic Ocean east of Greenland and Iceland and west of Norway.

Not·ting·ham (not'ing əm) a city in central England. Pop., 279,400.

Nouak·chott (nwäk'shot') the capital of Mauritania, in the western part of the country. Pop., 150,000.

No·va I·gua·çu (nō'və ē'gwä sü') a city in southeastern Brazil. Pop., 1,324,639.

No·va Sco·tia (nō'və skō'shə) a province of Canada, in the southeastern part of the country. Capital, Halifax. Area, 21,425 sq. mi. (55,491 sq. km.). Pop., 873,199.

No·vi Sad (nō'vē säd') a city in northeastern Yugoslavia, on the Danube. Pop., 257,685.

No·vo·si·birsk (nō'və sə bîrsk') a city in the south-central Soviet Union. Pop., 1,405,000.

Nu·bi·a (nü'bē ə, nü'bē ə) an ancient country in what is now southern Egypt and northern Sudan.

Nu·ku·a·lo·fa (nü'kü ə lō'fə) the capital and chief port of Tonga. Pop., 21,745.

Nu·rem·berg (nùr'əm bûrg') a city in southern West Germany where prominent Nazis were tried for war crimes after World War II. Pop., 466,100.

Nuuk (nük) the capital and largest city of Greenland,

located on the southwestern coast. Pop., 10,972. Formerly, **Godthåb.**

Ny·as·a, Lake (nī as'ə) a large lake in southeastern Africa. Also, **Lake Malawi.**

O·a·hu (ō ä'hü) the third largest island of Hawaii. Honolulu is located on Oahu. Area, 593 sq. mi. (1,536 sq. km.).

Oak·land (ōk'lənd) a city in western California, on San Francisco Bay opposite San Francisco. Pop., 357,000.

Ob (ob) a river in western Siberia, in the Soviet Union, flowing northwest and north to the Arctic Ocean. Length, 2,500 mi. (4,023 km.).

O·ber·hau·sen (ō'bər hou'zən) a city in northwestern West Germany. Pop., 223,000.

O·ce·an·i·a (ō'shē an'ē ə) the islands of the Pacific, including Melanesia, Micronesia, and Polynesia, and sometimes including Australia, New Zealand, New Guinea, and the Malay Archipelago. Also, **O·ce·an·i·ca** (ō'shē-an'i kə). —**O'ce·an'i·an,** *adj., n.*

O·des·sa (ō des'ə) a port city on the Black Sea in the southwestern Soviet Union, in the Ukraine. Pop., 1,132,000.

Og·bo·mo·sho (og'bə mō'shō) a city in southwestern Nigeria. Pop., 514,400.

O·hi·o (ō hī'ō) **1.** a state in the north-central United States. Capital, Columbus. Area, 41,330 sq. mi. (107,045 sq. km.). Pop., 10,752,000. Postal abbreviation, **OH 2.** a river in the east-central United States, flowing from Pittsburgh southwest into the Mississippi. Length, 981 mi. (1,578 km.). —**O·hi'o·an,** *adj., n.* ▲ Ohio was an Iroquoian name meaning "fine, great, beautiful river." Settlers used the name for the district around the Ohio River. It was later given to a territory north of the river, part of which became the state.

O·khotsk, Sea of (ō kotsk') an arm of the Pacific, on the east coast of the Soviet Union.

O·ki·na·wa (ō'kə nä'wə) a Japanese island in the Pacific, occupied by the United States from 1945 to 1972. It was the site of a major battle of World War II in 1945. Area, 454 sq. mi. (1,176 sq. km.). Pop., 993,300.

O·kla·ho·ma (ō'klə hō'mə) a state in the south-central United States. Capital, Oklahoma City. Area, 69,856 sq. mi. (180,927 sq. km.). Pop., 3,305,000. Abbreviation, **Okla.**; postal abbreviation, **OK** —**O'kla·ho'man,** *adj., n.* ▲ In an Indian treaty of 1866, the Choctaw used *Oklahoma*, meaning "red people," to designate their lands. The name was borrowed for a railroad station at the present site of Oklahoma City and was adopted later for the territory that became the state.

Oklahoma City, the capital of Oklahoma, in the central part of the state. Pop., 446,000.

Old·ham (ōl'dəm) a city in central England, near Manchester. Pop., 220,000.

Olives, Mount of, a mountain east of Jerusalem. The garden of Gethsemane is at the foot of this mountain. Also, **Ol·i·vet** (ol'ə vet').

O·lym·pi·a (ō lim'pē ə) **1.** the capital of Washington, in the western part of the state. Pop., 27,447. **2.** a plain in southwestern Greece, site of the ancient Olympic games.

O·lym·pus, Mount (ō lim'pəs) a mountain in northeastern Greece that, in Greek mythology, was regarded as the home of the twelve major gods.

O·ma·ha (ō'mə hä') a city in eastern Nebraska. Pop., 349,000.

O·man (ō män') a country in Asia, located on the southeastern coast of the peninsula of Arabia. Capital, Muscat. Area, 82,030 sq. mi. (212,458 sq. km.). Pop., 1,410,000. Formerly, **Muscat and Oman.**

Om·dur·man (om'dùr män') a city in north-central Sudan, on the Nile. Pop., 526,287.

Omsk (omsk) a city in the central Soviet Union. Pop., 1,124,000.

On·tar·i·o (on târ'ē ō) **1. Lake.** the smallest and easternmost of the Great Lakes, between New York and

Canada. **2.** a province of Canada, in the southeastern part of the country, north of the Great Lakes. Capital, Toronto. Area, 412,582 sq. mi. (1,068,587 sq. km.). Pop., 9,113,515. **3.** a city in southern California. Pop., 114,000. —**On·tar′i·an,** *adj., n.*

O·por·to (ō pôr′tō) a port city in northwestern Portugal. Pop., 327,368. Also, **Porto.**

O·ran (ô ran′) a port city in northwestern Algeria, on the Mediterranean. Pop., 663,504. Also, **Ouahran, Wahran.**

Or·ange (ôr′inj, or′inj) a city in southern California. Pop., 101,000.

O·ran·je·stad (ô rän′jə stat′) the capital of Aruba. Pop., 19,800.

Or·e·gon (ôr′i gon′, ôr′i gən) a state in the northwestern United States, on the Pacific. Capital, Salem. Area, 97,073 sq. mi. (251,419 sq. km.). Pop., 2,698,000. Abbreviations, **Oreg., Ore.;** postal abbreviation, **OR** —**Or·e·go·ni·an** (ôr′i gō′nē ən) *n.* ▲ The origin of the name *Oregon* is not definitely known. One theory is that it came from a mistake made by a French mapmaker. He wrote the word *Ouisconsink* (an Indian name for the Wisconsin River) as *Ouariconsint,* with *Ouaricon* on one line and *sint* on the next. According to the theory, the first part of the name, *Ouaricon,* then became associated with a legendary river flowing into the Pacific Ocean. The name for this river changed several times until it became *Oregon.* The explorers who discovered what is now called the Columbia River thought that it was the legendary Oregon River. Oregon later became the name of the state bordering on this river on the south.

O·ri·no·co (ôr′ə nō′kō) a large river in South America, flowing through Venezuela into the Atlantic. Length, 1,600 mi. (2,574 km.).

Ork·ney Islands (ôrk′nē) a group of islands off the northern coast of Scotland. Land area, 376 sq. mi. (974 sq. km.).

Or·lan·do (ôr lan′dō) a city in east-central Florida. Pop., 146,000.

Or·lé·ans (ôr′lē ənz) a historic city in north-central France, on the Loire. It was saved by Joan of Arc from an English siege in 1429, during the Hundred Years War. Pop., 102,710.

O·sa·ka (ō sä′kə) a port city in Japan, on the southwest coast of the island of Honshu. Pop., 2,648,180.

O·sas·co (ú säs′kù) a city in southwestern Brazil. Pop., 594,249.

Osh·a·wa (osh′ə wə) a city in southern Ontario, Canada, on Lake Ontario. Pop., 123,651.

O·si·jek (ō′sē yek′) a city in northern Yugoslavia. Pop., 867,646.

Os·lo (os′lō, oz′lō) the capital and principal city of Norway, in the southeastern part of the country. Pop., 449,395.

Os·tra·va (ôs′trə və) a city in north-central Czechoslovakia. Pop., 325,431.

Os·wie·cim (osh vyen′tsim) see **Auschwitz.**

Ot·ta·wa (ot′ə wə) the capital of Canada, in the southeastern part of the country, in Ontario. Pop., 300,762.

Oua·ga·dou·gou (wä′gə dü′gü) the capital of Burkina Faso, in the central part of the country. Pop., 442,223.

Ouah·ran (wä rän′) see **Oran.**

Ox·ford (oks′fərd) a city in south-central England, on the Thames. Pop., 114,400.

Ox·nard (oks′närd) a city in southern California. Pop., 127,000.

O·zark Mountains (ō′zärk) a low, hilly area in southern Missouri, northern Arkansas, and northeastern Oklahoma. Also, **O·zarks** (ō′zärks).

Pa·cif·ic (pə sif′ik) an ocean bordered by North and South America on the east and by Asia and Australia on the west, the largest body of water in the world. Also, **Pacific Ocean.** —**Pa·cif′ic,** *adj.*

Pacific Islands, Trust Territory of the, a U.S. trust territory of more than 2,100 islands in the Pacific, including the Northern Mariana Islands, Marshall Islands, Palau, and the Federated States of Micronesia. Land area, 717 sq. mi. (1,857 sq. km.). Pop., 169,000.

Pad·u·a (paj′ü ə) a city in northeastern Italy. Pop., 225,769.

Pa·go Pa·go (päng′ō päng′ō, päng′gō päng′gō, pä′gō pä′gō) the capital of American Samoa. Pop., 3,075. Also, **Pango Pango.**

Pa·ki·stan (pak′ə stan′) a country in southern Asia. Capital, Islamabad. Area, 310,724 sq. mi. (804,775 sq. km.). Pop., 110,000,000.

Pa·lau (pä lou′) a group of Pacific islands administered by the United States as part of the Trust Territory of the Pacific Islands. Capital, Koror. Land area, 171 sq. mi. (443 sq. km.). Pop., 14,000. Also, **Belau.**

Pa·lem·bang (pä′ləm bäng′) a city in Indonesia, in the southern part of the island of Sumatra. Pop., 787,187.

Pa·ler·mo (pə lâr′mō) the largest city of Sicily, a port in the northwestern part of the island. Pop., 719,755.

Pal·es·tine (pal′ə stīn′) **1.** a region in southwestern Asia between the Mediterranean Sea and the Jordan River. In biblical times it was the land of the Jews. Also, **Holy Land. 2.** a former territory in this region, placed under a British mandate following World War I. It was divided into Israel, the Jordanian-controlled West Bank, and the Egyptian-controlled Gaza Strip in 1949. Israel has occupied all of Palestine since 1967. —**Pal·es·tin·i·an** (pal′ə stin′ē ən) *adj., n.*

Pa·mirs (pä mîrz′) a mountain range in central Asia, extending from northeastern Afghanistan through the southern Soviet Union to eastern China.

Pan·a·ma (pan′ə mä′) **1. Isthmus of.** a narrow strip of land connecting North and South America. **2.** a country on the Isthmus of Panama. Capital, Panama. Area, 29,762 sq. mi. (77,084 sq. km.). Pop., 2,370,000. **3.** the capital of Panama, a port on the Pacific coast. Pop., 413,992. Also (def. 3), **Panama City.** —**Pan·a·ma·ni·an** (pan′ə mä′nē ən) *adj., n.*

Panama Canal, a ship canal across the Isthmus of Panama, connecting the Atlantic and Pacific oceans.

Panama Canal Zone, see **Canal Zone.**

Panama City, see **Panama** (def. 3).

Pan·ge·a (pan jē′ə) *also,* **Pan·gae·a.** a huge prehistoric continent that is believed to have included all of the earth's present-day continents; it is thought to have broken up about 200 million years ago into the continents of Gondwanaland and Laurasia.

Pang·o Pang·o (päng′ō päng′ō, päng′gō päng′gō) see **Pago Pago.**

Papal States, a territory in central Italy ruled by the popes from 755 to 1870.

Pap·u·a New Guinea (pap′ü ə, pä′pü ä′) a country in the southwestern Pacific consisting of the eastern part of New Guinea, the Bismarck Archipelago, and various nearby islands. Capital, Port Moresby. Land area, 178,704 sq. mi. (462,843 sq. km.). Pop., 3,860,000.

Par·a·guay (par′ə gwā′, par′ə gwī′) **1.** a country in south-central South America. Capital, Asunción. Area, 157,048 sq. mi. (406,754 sq. km.). Pop., 4,120,000. **2.** the principal river of this country, flowing south from Brazil through Paraguay into the Paraná River. Length, 1,610 mi. (2,590 km.). —**Par·a·guay·an,** *adj., n.*

Par·a·mar·i·bo (par′ə mar′ə bō) the capital of Suriname,

---

at; āpe; fär; câre; end; mē; it; īce; pîerce; hot; ōld; sông, fôrk; oil; out; up; ūse; rüle; pùll; tûrn; chin; sing; shop; thin; **this**; hw in white; zh in treasure. The symbol ə stands for the unstressed vowel sound heard in about, taken, pencil, lemon, and circus.

a port in the northern part of the country. Pop., 67,905.

Pa·ra·ná (par'ə nä') a river in South America, flowing south through Brazil, Paraguay, and Argentina into the Río de la Plata. Length, 2,796 mi. (4,499 km.).

Par·is (par'is) the capital and largest city of France, in the north-central part of the country, on the Seine. Pop., 2,176,243.

Par·nas·sus, Mount (pär nas'əs) a mountain in southern Greece, held to be sacred to Apollo and the Muses in Greek mythology. —**Par·nas'si·an,** *adj.*

Pas·a·de·na (pas'ə dē'nə) **1.** a city in southern California. Pop., 130,000. **2.** a city in southeastern Texas. Pop., 118,000.

Pat·a·go·ni·a (pat'ə gō'nē ə) a region in southern Argentina, between the Andes and the Atlantic. Area, 300,000 sq. mi. (777,000 sq. km.). —**Pat'a·go'ni·an,** *adj., n.*

Pat·er·son (pat'ər sən) a city in northeastern New Jersey. Pop., 139,000.

Pat·na (put'nə) a city in eastern India, on the Ganges. Pop., 776,371.

Pearl City, a city in Hawaii, on the island of Oahu. Pop., 42,575.

Pe·cos (pā'kəs) a river flowing from northern New Mexico southeast through Texas into the Rio Grande. Length, 735 mi. (1,183 km.).

Pei·ping (bā'ping') see **Beijing.**

Pe·king (pē'king') see **Beijing.**

Pel·o·pon·ne·sus (pel'ə pə nē'səs) *also,* **Pel·o·pon·ne·sos.** a peninsula in southern Greece between the Ionian and Aegean seas. —**Pel·o·pon·ne·sian** (pel'ə pə nē'zhən), *adj., n.*

Pem·ba (pem'bə) an island in the Indian Ocean, off the eastern coast of Africa, part of Tanzania. Area, 380 sq. mi. (984 sq. km.).

Penn·syl·va·nia (pen'səl vān'yə) a state in the eastern United States. Capital, Harrisburg. Area, 45,308 sq. mi. (117,348 sq. km.). Pop., 11,888,000. Abbreviations, **Pa., Penn.**; postal abbreviation, **PA** —**Penn'syl·va'ni·an,** *adj., n.* ▲ *Pennsylvania,* usually translated as "Penn's woods," was the name coined by Charles II for the land he granted to William Penn to found a colony. The name is a combination of Penn's family name and the Latin word *silva* meaning "forest, woods."

Pe·o·ri·a (pē ôr'ē ə) a city in north-central Illinois. Pop., 110,000.

Perm (pûrm) a city in the west-central Soviet Union. Pop., 1,066,000. Formerly, **Molotov.**

Per·sia (pûr'zhə, pûr'shə) **1.** a great ancient empire of southwestern Asia, extending from Egypt to the Indus River at its height in the sixth and fifth centuries B.C. Also, **Persian Empire. 2.** see **Iran.**

Persian Gulf, a shallow body of water between Iran and Arabia.

Perth (pûrth) the capital of Western Australia, a city in southwestern Australia, near the Indian Ocean. Pop., 809,035.

Pe·ru (pə rü') a country on the western coast of South America. Capital, Lima. Area, 496,225 sq. mi. (1,285,223 sq. km.). Pop., 21,800,000.

Pe·sha·war (pə shä'wər) a city in northwestern Pakistan, near the Khyber Pass. Pop., 506,896.

Pet·ro·grad (pet'rə grad') see **Leningrad.**

Phil·a·del·phi·a (fil'ə del'fē ə) a city in southeastern Pennsylvania, on the Delaware River. Pop., 1,643,000.

Phil·ip·pines (fil'ə pēnz', fil'ə pēnz') an island country in the western Pacific, southeast of China. Capital, Manila. Land area, 115,800 sq. mi. (299,922 sq. km.). Pop., 59,700,000. Also, **Phil·ip·pine Islands** (fil'ə pēn').

Phi·lis·ti·a (fə lis'tē ə) the land of the ancient Philistines, on the southwestern coast of Palestine.

Phnom Penh (pə nom'pen') the capital and largest city of Cambodia, an inland port in the south-central part of the country. Pop., 400,000. Also, **Pnompenh.**

Phoe·ni·cia (fə nē'shə) an ancient district on the eastern Mediterranean coast, in the area that is now Lebanon.

Phoe·nix (fē'niks) the capital and largest city of Arizona, in the south-central part of the state. Pop., 894,000.

Pied·mont (pēd'mont) a region of the eastern United States, extending from northern New Jersey to central Alabama and sloping seaward from the Appalachian Mountains to the Atlantic coastal plain.

Pierre (pîr) the capital of South Dakota, in the central part of the state. Pop., 11,973.

Pike's Peak (pīks) a mountain of the Rocky Mountains, in central Colorado. Height, 14,110 ft. (4,301 m.).

Pillars of Hercules, the Rock of Gibraltar and the mountain of Jebel Musa, located on opposite sides of the eastern end of the Strait of Gibraltar.

Pi·rae·us (pī rē'əs, pə rā'əs) the principal seaport of Greece, and port of nearby Athens, in the eastern part of the country. Pop., 196,389.

Pi·sa (pē'zə) a city in central Italy. Pop., 104,384.

Pit·cairn Island (pit'kârn) a small British island in the southern Pacific, uninhabited until 1790, when it was settled by mutineers from the HMS *Bounty.* Area, 2 sq. mi. (5 sq. km.). Pop., 60.

Pitts·burgh (pits'bûrg) a city in southwestern Pennsylvania, the leading center of U.S. iron and steel production. Pop., 387,000.

Platte (plat) a river flowing from central Nebraska into the Missouri. Length, 310 mi. (499 km.).

Plov·div (plov dif') a city in south-central Bulgaria. Pop., 373,235.

Plym·outh (plim'əth) **1.** a town in southeastern Massachusetts, on the Atlantic, settled in 1620 by the Pilgrims. Pop., 7,232. **2.** a seaport in southwestern England, on the English Channel. Pop., 253,400.

Pnom·penh (nom'pen') see **Phnom Penh.**

Po·ca·tel·lo (pō'kə tel'ō) a city in southeastern Idaho. Pop., 46,340.

Po·land (pō'lənd) a country in central Europe, on the Baltic Sea. Capital, Warsaw. Area, 120,725 sq. mi. (312,678 sq. km.). Pop., 38,300,000.

Pol·y·ne·sia (pol'ə nē'zhə) one of the three main divisions of the Pacific islands, in the central and southern part of the Pacific, east of Melanesia and Micronesia.

Po·mo·na (pə mō'nə) a city in southwestern California. Pop., 116,000.

Pom·peii (pom pā') a partially excavated ancient city in southwestern Italy, near Naples. It was buried by the eruption of Mount Vesuvius in A.D. 79. —**Pom·pei'an,** *adj., n.*

Pon·ce (pon sā') a port city in southern Puerto Rico. Pop., 161,739.

Poo·na (pü'nə) a city in western India. Pop., 1,203,351.

Port Ar·thur (är'thər) see **Lushun.**

Port–au–Prince (pôrt'ō prins') the capital of Haiti, in the southwestern part of the country, on the Caribbean. Pop., 557,000.

Port E·lis·a·beth (i liz'ə bəth) a port city on the southern coast of the Republic of South Africa. Pop., 272,844.

Port·land (pôrt'lənd) **1.** the largest city and chief port of Maine, in the southwestern part of the state. Pop., 61,572. **2.** the largest city and chief port of Oregon, in the northwestern part of the state. Pop., 388,000.

Port Lou·is (lü'is, lü'ē) the capital and largest city of Mauritius. Pop., 136,323.

Port Mores·by (môrz'bē) the capital of Papua New Guinea, in the southeastern part of New Guinea. Pop., 123,624.

Por·to (pôr'tō) see **Oporto.**

Pôr·to A·le·gre (pôr'tō ə lā'grə) a port city in southern Brazil. Pop., 1,275,483.

Port-of-Spain (pôrt'əv spān') *also,* **Port of Spain.** the capital and chief port of Trinidad and Tobago, in the northwestern part of the island of Trinidad. Pop., 65,906.

Por·to–No·vo (pôr′tō nō′vō) the capital of Benin, in the southeastern part of the country. Pop., 144,000.

Por·to Ri·co (pôr′tə rē′kō) see **Puerto Rico.**

Ports·mouth (pôrts′məth) a port city and naval base in southeastern Virginia. Pop., 111,000.

Port Sudan, a city in northeastern Sudan, a port on the Red Sea. Pop., 206,727.

Por·tu·gal (pôr′chə gəl) a country in southwestern Europe, in the western part of the Iberian Peninsula, on the Atlantic. Capital, Lisbon. Area, 35,672 sq. mi. (92,390 sq. km.). Pop., 10,500,000.

Po·sen (pō′zən) see **Poznań.**

Po·to·mac (pə tō′mək) a river in the eastern United States, flowing through West Virginia, Virginia, and Maryland to the Chesapeake Bay. Length, 285 mi. (459 km.).

Pots·dam (pots′dam) a city in central East Germany, site of a meeting of the heads of the three major Allied governments after World War II. Pop., 139,497.

Poz·nań (pōz′nan) a city in western Poland. Pop., 575,100. Also, *German*, **Posen.**

Prague (präg) the capital and largest city of Czechoslovakia, in the western part of the country. Pop., 1,189,828.

Prai·a (prī′ə) the capital of Cape Verde. Pop., 37,480.

Pre·to·ri·a (pri tôr′ē ə) the administrative capital of the Republic of South Africa, in the northeastern part of the country. Pop., 443,059.

Prince Ed·ward Island (ed′wərd) the smallest province of Canada, consisting of an island in the Gulf of St. Lawrence. Capital, Charlottetown. Area, 2,184 sq. mi. (5,657 sq. km.). Pop., 126,646.

Prov·i·dence (prov′i dəns) the capital and largest city of Rhode Island, in the eastern part of the state. Pop., 157,000.

Pro·vo (prō′vō) a city in north-central Utah. Pop., 74,108.

Prus·sia (prush′ə) a former state in northern Germany, formally dissolved in 1947 and divided among East and West Germany, Poland, and the Soviet Union.

Pueb·la (pweb′lə) a city in central Mexico. Pop., 835,759.

Pueb·lo (pweb′lō) a city in south-central Colorado. Pop., 101,000.

Puer·to Ri·co (pwer′tō rē′kō, pôr′tə rē′kō) an island in the West Indies, a commonwealth of the United States. Capital, San Juan. Area, 3,515 sq. mi. (9,104 sq. km.). Pop., 3,610,000. Abbreviation, **P.R.**; postal abbreviation, **PR** Also, **Porto Rico. —Puer′to Ri′can.**

Pu·get Sound (pū′jit) an inlet of the Pacific, extending into the northwestern part of the state of Washington.

Pu·rus (pu rus′) a river in South America, flowing through Peru and Brazil into the Amazon. Length, 1,900 mi. (3,057 km.).

Pu·san (pū′sän′) the chief port of South Korea, on the southeastern coast of the country. Pop., 3,160,300.

Pyong·yang (pyung′yäng′) the capital of North Korea, in the west-central part of the country. Pop., 1,700,000.

Pyr·e·nees (pir′ə nēz′) a mountain range in southwestern Europe extending along the border of France and Spain from the Bay of Biscay to the Mediterranean Sea. **—Pyr′-e·ne′an,** *adj.*

Qa·cen·ti·na (kä′sen tē′nə) see **Constantine.**

Qa·tar (kä′tər) a country in southwestern Asia, on the Persian Gulf coast of the peninsula of Arabia. Capital, Doha. Area, 4,250 sq. mi. (11,008 sq. km.). Pop., 395,000.

Qing·dao (ching′dou′) *also,* **Tsingtao.** a seaport in eastern China. Pop., 1,250,000.

Qom (kùm) *also,* **Qum.** a city in north-central Iran. Pop., 424,000.

Que·bec (kwi bek′) **1.** the largest province of Canada, in the eastern part of the country. Capital, Quebec. Area, 594,860 sq. mi. (1,540,687 sq. km.). Pop., 6,540,276. **2.** the capital of this province, a port city on the St. Lawrence River in southeastern Canada. Pop., 164,580.

Queens (kwēnz) the largest borough of New York City. Area, 115 sq. mi. (298 sq. km.).

Queens·land (kwēnz′lənd) a state of Australia, in the northeastern part of the country. Capital, Brisbane. Area, 667,000 sq. mi. (1,727,530 sq. km.). Pop., 2,505,300.

Que·zon City (kā′zon) a city north of Manila in the Philippines. It was the capital of the country from 1948 to 1976. Pop., 1,165,865.

Qui·to (kē′tō) the capital of Ecuador, in the north-central part of the country, in the Andes. Pop., 1,093,278.

Qum (kùm) see **Qom.**

Ra·bat (rə bät′) the capital of Morocco, in the northern part of the country. Pop., 518,616.

Ra·leigh (rô′lē) the capital of North Carolina, in the central part of the state. Pop., 180,000.

Ran·goon (rang gün′) the capital and chief port of Burma, in the southern part of the country. Pop., 2,458,712.

Re·ci·fe (rə sē′fə) a port city in northeastern Brazil, on the Atlantic. Pop., 1,289,627.

Red China, see **China** (*def. 1*).

Red River, a river flowing from southwestern Oklahoma, across the southern United States, into the Mississippi. Length, 1,270 mi. (2,043 km.).

Red Sea, a narrow sea between Arabia and northeastern Africa, opening into the Gulf of Aden.

Re·gi·na (rə jē′nə) a city in southern Canada, the capital of Saskatchewan. Pop., 175,064.

Re·no (rē′nō) a city in western Nevada. Pop., 110,000.

Ré·u·nion (rē ūn′yən) a mountainous island in the Indian Ocean, east of Madagascar. It is a French possession. Area, 970 sq. mi. (2,512 sq. km.). Pop., 564,000.

Rey·kja·vik (rā′kyə vēk′) the capital and largest city of Iceland, in the southwestern part of the country. Pop., 88,745.

Rhine (rīn) a river flowing from eastern Switzerland through West Germany and the Netherlands to the North Sea. Length, 700 mi. (1,126 km.).

Rhine·land (rīn′land′) a region in the westernmost part of West Germany, along the Rhine.

Rhode Island (rōd) a state in the northeastern United States, the smallest state in the country. Capital, Providence. Area, 1,212 sq. mi. (3,139 sq. km.). Pop., 975,000. Abbreviation, **R.I.**; postal abbreviation, **RI —Rhode Islander.** ▲ Rhode Island was named for the island of *Rhodes* in the Aegean Sea. In 1524, the Italian navigator Giovanni Verrazano (1485?–1528?) gave this name to what is now called Block Island because he thought it resembled the Aegean island. In 1630, the Dutch referred to a *Roodt Evlandt,* or "red island," in this area, which may also have influenced the name. Roger Williams, the founder of the colony of Rhode Island, transferred the name to another island that lay off the coast of the colony. Eventually the name came to include the entire colony, which later became the state.

Rhodes (rōdz) **1.** a Greek island in the southeastern Aegean Sea, off the coast of Turkey. Area, 542 sq. mi. (1,404 sq. km.). **2.** a port city on this island. The Colossus of Rhodes, one of the Seven Wonders of the World, stood by the entrance to its harbor during the third century B.C. Pop., 40,392.

Rho·de·sia (rō dē′zhə) see **Zimbabwe.**

Rhône (rōn) a river flowing generally southwestward from central Switzerland through southeastern France into the Mediterranean. Length, 500 mi. (805 km.).

Rich·mond (rich′mənd) **1.** the capital of Virginia, a port city in the eastern part of the state. Pop., 218,000. **2.** a

---

at; āpe; fär; câre; end; mē; it; īce; pîerce; hot; ōld; sông, fôrk; oil; out; up; ūse; rüle; pùll; tûrn; chin; sing; shop; thin; **th**is; hw in white; zh in treasure. The symbol ə stands for the unstressed vowel sound heard in about, taken, pencil, lemon, and circus.

borough of New York City, consisting of Staten Island. Area, 62 sq. mi. (161 sq. km.). **3.** a city in southwestern British Columbia, Canada. Pop., 108,492.

Ri·ga (rē′gə) a port city in the western Soviet Union, on the Baltic Sea. Pop., 890,000.

Ri·o de Ja·nei·ro (rē′ō dä zhə när′ō) a port city in southeastern Brazil, the former capital of the country. Pop., 5,615,149.

Rí·o de la Pla·ta (rē′ō dä lä plä′tə) the estuary of the Paraná and Uruguay rivers, between Uruguay and Argentina. Length, 225 mi. (362 km.).

Ri·o Grande (rē′ō grand′, rē′ō grän′dē) a river flowing from southwestern Colorado into the Gulf of Mexico and forming the border between Texas and Mexico. Length, 1,885 mi. (3,033 km.).

Riv·er·side (riv′ər sīd′) a city in southwestern California. Pop., 197,000.

Riv·i·er·a (riv′ē âr′ə) a narrow strip of land along the Mediterranean coasts of Italy, France, and Monaco.

Ri·yadh (rē yäd′) the capital of Saudi Arabia, in the east-central part of the country. Pop., 1,250,000.

Ro·a·noke (rō′ə nōk′) a city in southwestern Virginia. Pop., 102,000.

Roch·es·ter (roch′es tər, roch′ə stər) a city in western New York, on Lake Ontario. Pop., 236,000.

Rock·ford (rok′fərd) a city in northern Illinois. Pop., 136,000.

Rocky Mountains, a mountain system in the western United States and Canada, extending from central New Mexico to northern Alaska. Also, **Rock·ies** (rok′ēz).

Ro·ma·ni·a (rō mā′nē ə) a country in southeastern Europe, in the northeastern part of the Balkan Peninsula. Capital, Bucharest. Area, 91,700 sq. mi. (237,503 sq. km.). Pop., 23,700,000. Also, **Roumania, Rumania.**

Rome (rōm) the capital of Italy, on the Tiber, the former capital and center of the Roman Empire and the ancient Roman republic. Pop., 2,826,488.

Ro·sa·ri·o (rō zär′ē ō′) a port city in east-central Argentina, on the Paraná. Pop., 938,120.

Ro·seau (rō zō′) the capital of Dominica. Pop., 9,348.

Ros·tock (ros′tok) a port city in northern East Germany, near the Baltic coast. Pop., 244,400.

Ros·tov (ros′tôf) a port city in the southwestern Soviet Union, on the Don River. Pop., 993,000.

Rot·ter·dam (rot′ər dam′) a port city in the southwestern Netherlands, near the North Sea. Pop., 571,372.

Rou·ma·ni·a (rü mā′nē ə) see **Romania.**

Ru·bi·con (rü′bi kon′) a small stream in north-central Italy that formed the northern boundary of the ancient Roman republic. Julius Caesar's crossing of the Rubicon in 49 B.C. began a civil war in Rome that led to his dictatorship.

Ruhr (rür) **1.** a river in northwestern Germany, a tributary of the Rhine. Length, 146 mi. (235 km.). **2.** a coal mining and industrial region along this river.

Ru·ma·ni·a (rü mā′nē ə) see **Romania.**

Run·ny·mede (run′ē mēd′) a meadow on the Thames, near London, where King John signed the Magna Carta on June 15, 1215.

Rush·more, Mount (rush′môr′) a mountain in western South Dakota, on the side of which are carved huge heads of Washington, Jefferson, Lincoln, and Theodore Roosevelt. Height, 6,200 ft. (1,890 m.).

Rus·sia (rush′ə) **1.** see **Union of Soviet Socialist Republics. 2.** a former empire in eastern Europe and northern Asia ruled by the czars. Its capital was St. Petersburg. The Russian Revolution, in 1917, ended the rule of the czars and led to the founding of the Union of Soviet Socialist Republics. **3.** see **Russian Soviet Federated Socialist Republic.**

Russian Soviet Federated Socialist Republic, the largest republic of the Soviet Union, comprising more than three-quarters of the country's area. Area, 6,592,850

sq. mi. (17,075,482 sq. km.). Pop., 144,027,000. Also, **Russia, Soviet Russia.**

Rwan·da (rü än′də) a landlocked country in east-central Africa. Capital, Kigali. Area, 10,169 sq. mi. (26,338 sq. km.). Pop., 6,940,000.

Ryu·kyu Islands (rē ü′kü) a Japanese island chain in the western Pacific, extending in an arc from Kyushu, Japan, to Taiwan. The largest of the group is Okinawa. Area, 1,800 sq. mi. (4,662 sq. km.).

Saar·land (sär′land′, zär′land′) a state of West Germany, in the western part of the country. Area, 991 sq. mi. (2,567 sq. km.). Pop., 1,081,100. Also, **Saar** (sär, zär).

Sa·bah (sä′bə) a state of Malaysia, in the northeastern part of the island of Borneo. Area, 29,347 sq. mi. (76,009 sq. km.). Pop., 1,011,046.

Sac·ra·men·to (sak′rə men′tō) **1.** the capital of California, in the central part of the state, on the Sacramento River. Pop., 324,000. **2.** a river flowing from northern California into San Francisco Bay. Length, 382 mi. (615 km.).

Sa·fa·qis (sä fä′kis) see **Sfax.**

Sa·har·a (sə har′ə, sə här′ə) a desert in northern Africa, the largest in the world. Area, 3,000,000 sq. mi. (7,770,000 sq. mi.). Also, **Sahara Desert.**

Sa·hel (sə hel′) a semiarid region in northern Africa south of the Sahara desert, extending from Senegal to Sudan.

Sai·gon (sī gon′) see **Ho Chi Minh City.**

Saint, see **St.** for place names beginning with the word "Saint."

Sai·pan (sī pan′) the capital of the Northern Mariana Islands, an island in the western Pacific. Area, approx. 71 sq. mi. (184 sq. km.). Pop., 17,182.

Sa·kai (sä′kī′) a seaport in Japan, in the southern part of the island of Honshu. Pop., 810,106.

Sak·ha·lin (sak′ə lēn′, sak′ə lēn′) a large island of the Soviet Union, in the western Pacific, just off the eastern coast of Siberia. Area, 29,498 sq. mi. (76,400 sq. km.).

Sa·lem (sā′ləm) **1.** the capital of Oregon, in the northwestern part of the state. Pop., 89,235. **2.** a historic city in eastern Massachusetts, the site of seventeenth-century witchcraft trials. Pop., 38,220.

Salis·bur·y (sôlz′ber′ē, sôlz′bə rē) see **Harare.**

Sa·lo·ni·ka (sə lon′i kə) a port city in northern Greece, known in ancient times as **Thessalonica.** Pop., 406,413.

Salt Lake City, the capital and largest city of Utah, in the northern part of the state. Pop., 158,000.

Sal·va·dor (sal′və dôr′) **1.** see **El Salvador. 2.** a port city on the eastern coast of Brazil, north of Rio de Janeiro. Pop., 1,811,367.

Sa·ma·ra (sə mär′ə) see **Kuibyshev.**

Sa·mar·i·a (sə mâr′ē ə, sə mar′ē ə) **1.** in the Bible, an ancient region west of the Jordan. **2.** the main city of this region.

Sa·mo·a (sə mō′ə) an island group in the southern Pacific, divided politically into Western Samoa and American Samoa. Land area, 1,173 sq. mi. (3,038 sq. km.).

Sa·na (sä nä′) the capital and largest city of Yemen, in the central part of the country. Pop., 277,818.

San An·to·ni·o (san′ an tō′nē ō′) a city in south-central Texas. Pop., 914,000.

San Ber·nar·di·no (san′ bûr′nər dē′nō) a city in southern California. Pop., 139,000.

San Cris·tó·bal (san′ kris tō′bəl) a city in western Venezuela, near the Colombian border. Pop., 280,000.

San Di·e·go (san′ dē ā′gō) a port city in southern California, at the Mexican border. Pop., 1,015,000.

Sandwich Islands see **Hawaiian Islands.**

San Fran·cis·co (san′ frən sis′kō) a port city in western California, on the Pacific. Pop., 749,000.

San Francisco Bay, an inlet of the Pacific, on the central coast of California.

San Joa·quin (san′ wä kēn′) a river in central California, flowing westward to the mouth of the Sacramento. Length, 350 mi. (563 km.).

San Jo·se (san′ hō zā′) a city in western California. Pop., 712,000.

San Jo·sé (san′ hō zā′) the capital and largest city of Costa Rica, in the central part of the country. Pop., 241,464.

San Juan (san hwän′) the capital of Puerto Rico, a port in the northeastern part of the island. Pop., 424,600.

San Jus·to (san jùs′tō) a city in eastern Argentina. Pop., 941,499.

San Ma·ri·no (san′ mə rē′nō) **1.** a small country in southern Europe, near the Adriatic, completely surrounded by Italy. Capital, San Marino. Area, 23 sq. mi. (60 sq. km.). Pop., 22,000. **2.** the capital of this country.

San Mi·guel de Tu·cu·mán (san′ mi gel′ də tü′kəmän′) see **Tucumán.**

San Pe·dro Su·la (san pā′drō sü′lə) a city in northwestern Honduras. Pop., 397,200.

San Sal·va·dor (san sal′və dôr′) **1.** the capital and largest city of El Salvador, in the central part of the country. Pop., 445,100. **2.** an island in the central Bahamas, southeast of Miami, Florida, believed to be the first landing place of Columbus in the New World. Area, 60 sq. mi. (155 sq. km.).

San·ta An·a (san′tə an′ə) a city in southern California. Pop., 237,000.

San·ta Bar·bar·a Islands (san′tə bär′bər ə; bär′brə) an island group off the southern coast of California.

Santa Catalina, one of the Santa Barbara Islands, a resort noted for its beaches and fishing. Also, **Catalina, Catalina Island.**

San·ta Cruz (san′tə krüz′) a city in central Bolivia. Pop., 441,717.

San·ta Fe (san′tə fā′) the capital of New Mexico, in the north-central part of the state. Pop., 75,360.

San·ta Fé (san′tə fā′) a city in eastern Argentina. Pop., 291,966.

San·ta Is·a·bel (san′tə iz′ə bel′) see **Malabo.**

San·ti·a·go (san′tē ä′gō) the capital and largest city of Chile, in the central part of the country. Pop., 425,924.

Santiago de Cuba, a port city in southeastern Cuba. Pop., 326,066.

Santiago de los Ca·ba·lle·ros (də lôs kä′bə yâr′ōs) a city in the northern Dominican Republic. Pop., 318,000.

San·to An·dré (san′tù än drā′) a city in southern Brazil. Pop., 637,010.

San·to Do·min·go (san′tō də ming′gō) the capital and largest city of the Dominican Republic, on the southern coast of the country. Pop., 1,657,000.

San·tos (san′təs) a port city in southeastern Brazil, on the Atlantic. Pop., 476,102.

São Ber·nar·do do Cam·po (soun′ bər när′dù dù käm′pù) a city in southeastern Brazil. Pop., 565,620.

São Fran·cis·co (soun′ frän sēs′kù) a river in South America, flowing through eastern Brazil to the Atlantic. Length, 1,800 mi. (2,896 km.).

São Gon·ça·lo (soun′ gún sä′lù) a city in southeastern Brazil. Pop., 731,061.

São Lu·is (soun′ lü ēs′) a city in northern Brazil. Pop., 564,434.

São Pau·lo (sou pou′lō, soun pou′lù) the largest city in Brazil, in the southeastern part of the country. Pop., 10,099,086.

São To·mé (soun′ tù mā′) the capital and largest city of São Tomé and Príncipe. Pop., 17,380.

São Tomé and Prín·ci·pe (prēn′si pā′) an island country located off the west coast of Africa, in the Gulf of Guinea. Capital, São Tomé. Land area, 372 sq. mi. (963 sq. km.). Pop., 108,000.

Sap·po·ro (sə pôr′ō) a city in Japan, in the western part of the island of Hokkaido. Pop., 1,401,757.

Sar·a·gos·sa (sar′ə gos′ə) a city in northeastern Spain. Pop., 590,750. Also, **Zaragoza.**

Sa·ra·je·vo (sar′ə yä′vō) *also,* **Sa·ra·ye·vo, Se·ra·jevo.** a city in central Yugoslavia, where the assassination of the Austrian Archduke Francis Ferdinand took place in 1914, leading to the outbreak of World War I. Pop., 448,500.

Sa·ra·tov (sä rä′tôf) a city in the southwestern Soviet Union, on the Volga River. Pop., 908,000.

Sa·ra·wak (sə rä′wäk) a state of Malaysia, in the northwestern part of the island of Borneo. Area, 48,250 sq. mi. (124,968 sq. km.). Pop., 1,307,582.

Sa·ra·ye·vo (sar′ə yä′vō) see **Sarajevo.**

Sar·din·i·a (sär din′ē ə) an Italian island in the Mediterranean, west of Italy. Area, 9,196 sq. mi. (23,818 sq. km.). —**Sar·din′i·an,** *adj., n.*

Sar·gas·so Sea (sär gas′ō) an oval-shaped part of the north-central Atlantic, between the West Indies and the Azores, noted for its abundance of floating seaweed.

Sas·katch·e·wan (sas kach′ə won′) a province of Canada, in the western part of the country. Capital, Regina. Area, 251,700 sq. mi. (651,903 sq. km.). Pop., 1,010,198.

Sas·ka·toon (sas′kə tün′) a city in south-central Saskatchewan, Canada. Pop., 177,641.

Sa·u·di Arabia (sä ü′dē) a country in southwestern Asia, occupying most of the peninsula of Arabia. Capital, Riyadh. Area, 830,000 sq. mi. (2,149,700 sq. km.). Pop., 13,500,000.

Sa·van·nah (sə van′ə) **1.** a port city in southeastern Georgia. Pop., 147,000. **2.** a river in the southeastern United States, flowing into the Atlantic, forming most of the border between South Carolina and Georgia. Length, 314 mi. (505 km.).

Scan·di·na·vi·a (skan′də nā′vē ə) **1.** a region in northern Europe, consisting of Norway, Sweden, and Denmark, and sometimes Iceland or Finland. **2.** a large peninsula of northern Europe, divided between Norway and Sweden.

Scar·bor·ough (skär′bûr′ō, skär′bur′ō) a city in southern Ontario, Canada. Pop., 484,676.

Scot·land (skot′lənd) a division of the United Kingdom, north of England. Capital, Edinburgh. Area, 30,415 sq. mi. (78,775 sq. km.). Pop., 5,121,000.

Scotts·dale (skots′dāl′) a city in south-central Arizona. Pop., 111,000.

Sea Islands, an island chain in the southeastern United States, along the Atlantic coast of South Carolina, Georgia, and northern Florida.

Se·at·tle (sē at′əl) a port city in western Washington, on Puget Sound. Pop., 486,000.

Seine (sān) a river flowing from eastern France northward into the English Channel. Length, 485 mi. (780 km.).

Se·ma·rang (sə mär′äng) a port city in Indonesia, on the northern coast of the island of Java. Pop., 1,026,671.

Sen·e·gal (sen′i gôl′, sen′i gäl′) **1.** a country in western Africa, on the Atlantic. Capital, Dakar. Area, 75,750 sq. mi. (196,193 sq. km.). Pop., 7,180,000. **2.** a river in western Africa, on the southern border of the Sahara, flowing into the Atlantic. Length, 1,000 mi. (1,609 km.).

Sen·e·gam·bi·a (sen′i gam′bē ə) a confederation of Senegal and Gambia, formed in 1982.

Seoul (sōl) the capital and largest city of South Korea, in the northwestern part of the country. Pop., 8,366,800.

Se·ra·je·vo (ser′ə yä′vō) see **Sarajevo.**

Ser·bia (sûr′bē ə) the largest republic of Yugoslavia, in the eastern part of the country, formerly an independent

---

at; āpe; fär; câre; end; mē; it; īce; pîerce; hot; ōld; sông, fôrk; oil; out; up; ūse; rüle; pùll; tûrn; chin; sing; shop; thin; this; hw in white; zh in treasure. The symbol ə stands for the unstressed vowel sound heard in about, taken, pencil, lemon, and circus.

country. Area, 34,116 sq. mi. (88,360 sq. km.). Pop., 9,313,677.

Se·ville (sə vil′) a city in southwestern Spain. Pop., 653,833.

Sey·chelles (sā shel′) an island country in the western Indian Ocean, northeast of Madagascar. Land area, 175 sq. mi. (453 sq. km.). Capital, Victoria. Pop., 87,000.

Sfax (sfäks) a port city in northeastern Tunisia. Pop., 231,911. Also, **Safaqis**.

Shang·hai (shang′hī′) the chief port and largest city of China, in the eastern part of the country, near the mouth of the Yangtze River. Pop., 6,980,000.

Shatt–al–Ar·ab (shat′al ar′əb) a channel flowing southeast along the Iran-Iraq border into the Persian Gulf, formed by the confluence of the Tigris and Euphrates rivers. Length, 120 mi. (193 km.).

She·ba (shē′bə) in the Bible, the name of an ancient country in southwestern Arabia.

Shef·field (shef′ēld) a city in northern England. Pop., 538,700.

Shen·an·do·ah (shen′ən dō′ə) a river flowing through northern Virginia into the Potomac. Length, 55 mi. (88 km.).

Shen·yang (shun′yäng′) a city in northeastern China. Pop., 3,250,000. Formerly, **Mukden**.

Sher·wood Forest (shûr′wùd′) an ancient royal forest of central England, known as the legendary home of Robin Hood.

Shet·land Islands (shet′lənd) an island group off northern Scotland, in the Atlantic. Area, 550 sq. mi. (1,425 sq. km.).

Shi·jia·zhuang (shu′jyä′jwäng′) a city in northeastern China. Pop., 1,127,800.

Shi·ko·ku (shi kō′kü) the smallest of the four main islands of Japan. Area, 7,049 sq. mi. (18,257 sq. km.).

Shi·raz (shi räz′) a city in southwestern Iran. Pop., 800,000.

Shreve·port (shrēv′pôrt′) a city in northwestern Louisiana. Pop., 220,000.

Shu·bra al–Khay·mah (shü′brə al kā′mə) a city in northern Egypt. Pop., 515,500.

Si·am (sī am′) see **Thailand**.

Si·an (sē′än′) see **Xian**.

Si·be·ri·a (sī bîr′ē ə) a region of the Soviet Union, extending from the Ural Mountains to the Pacific. Area, 5,000,000 sq. mi. (12,950,000 sq. km.).

Sic·i·ly (sis′ə lē) an Italian island in the Mediterranean, off the southwestern tip of Italy. Area, 9,831 sq. mi. (25,462 sq. km.).

Si·er·ra Le·o·ne (sē er′ə lē ō′nē) a country on the western coast of Africa. Capital, Freetown. Area, 27,699 sq. mi. (71,740 sq. km.). Pop., 3,890,000.

Si·er·ra Ma·dre (sē er′ə mä′drā) a mountain system in eastern and western Mexico.

Si·er·ra Ne·vad·a (sē er′ə nə vad′ə, sē er′ə nə vä′də) a mountain range in eastern California.

Si·le·sia (si lē′zhə) a historic region in southwestern Poland and northern Czechoslovakia. —**Si·le′sian**, adj., n.

Si·nai (sī′nī) **1.** a triangular desert area in northeastern Egypt, extending south from the Mediterranean to the northern end of the Red Sea. Also, **Sinai Peninsula**. **2. Mount.** in the Bible, the mountain on which Moses received the Ten Commandments.

Sin·ga·pore (sing′ə pôr′) **1.** an island off the southern tip of the Malay Peninsula. **2.** a small country comprising this island and adjacent islets. Capital, Singapore. Area, 224 sq. mi. (580 sq. km.). Pop., 2,670,000. **3.** the capital and largest city of this country. Pop., 2,413,900.

Sin·ui·ju (shin′wē′jü′) a city in western North Korea, on the Yalu River. Pop., 300,000.

Sioux Falls (sü) a city in southeastern South Dakota. Pop., 81,343.

Skop·je (skôp′yä) a city in southern Yugoslavia. Pop., 506,547. Also, **Skop·lje** (skop′lyä).

Slo·va·ki·a (slō vä′kē ə) a historic region in eastern Czechoslovakia. Area, 18,800 sq. mi. (48,692 sq. km.).

Slo·ve·ni·a (slō vē′nē ə) a republic of Yugoslavia, in the northwestern part of the country. Area, approx. 7,820 sq. mi. (20,254 sq. km.).

Smoky Mountains, see **Great Smoky Mountains**.

Smyr·na (smûr′nə) see **Izmir**.

Snake River, a river in the northwestern United States, the principal tributary of the Columbia River. Length, 1,038 mi. (1,670 km.).

Society Islands, a French island group in the east-central Pacific, northeast of New Zealand. The largest island of the group is Tahiti. Land area, 636 sq. mi. (1,647 sq. km.). Pop., 142,129.

Sod·om (sod′əm) in the Bible, a city near the Dead Sea which, along with the nearby city of Gomorrah, was destroyed by fire from heaven because of the wickedness of the inhabitants.

So·fi·a (sō′fē ə) the capital of Bulgaria, in the western part of the country. Pop., 1,093,752.

So·li·hull (sō′li hul′) a city in central England, near Birmingham. Pop., 201,900.

Sol·o·mon Islands (sol′ə mən) an island country in the southwestern Pacific, east of Papua New Guinea. Capital, Honiara. Land area, 10,983 sq. mi. (28,446 sq. km.). Pop., 315,000.

So·ma·lia (sō mäl′yə) a country in eastern Africa, on the Indian Ocean and Gulf of Aden. Capital, Mogadishu. Area, 246,201 sq. mi. (637,661 sq. km.). Pop., 5,060,000.

South Africa, Republic of, a country in southern Africa, on the Atlantic and Indian oceans. Administrative capital, Pretoria; judicial capital, Bloemfontein; legislative capital, Cape Town. Area, 472,359 sq. mi. (1,223,410 sq. km.). Pop., 35,800,000.

South America, the fourth largest continent in the world, in the Western Hemisphere. Area, 6,884,000 sq. mi. (17,829,560 sq. km.). Pop., 291,000,000.

South·amp·ton (south hamp′tən) a port city on the southern coast of England. Pop., 202,200.

South Australia, a state in south-central Australia. Capital, Adelaide. Area, 380,070 sq. mi. (984,381 sq. km.). Pop., 1,352,900.

South Bend, a city in northern Indiana. Pop., 107,000.

South Carolina, a state in the southeastern United States, on the Atlantic. Capital, Columbia. Area, 31,113 sq. mi. (80,583 sq. km.). Pop., 3,377,000. Abbreviation, **S.C.**; postal abbreviation, **SC** —**South Car·o·lin·i·an** (kar′ə lin′ē ən). ▲ South Carolina was formed from the southern part of the English colony of Carolina. In gratitude for the grant of land from King Charles I in 1629, the proprietor gave the colony the name *Carolana,* which means "from Charles." The spelling was later changed to *Carolina* by King Charles II when he granted the unsettled colony to a group of noblemen in 1663.

South China Sea, a part of the Pacific, bounded by southeastern China, Vietnam, the Malay Peninsula, Borneo, and the Philippines.

South Dakota, a state in the north-central United States. Capital, Pierre. Area, 77,116 sq. mi. (199,730 sq. km.). Pop., 708,000. Abbreviations, **S. Dak., S.D.**; postal abbreviation, **SD** —**South Dakotan.** ▲ South Dakota was once the southern part of the Dakota Territory. The territory was named for a western branch of the Sioux Indians that lived in this region. The name *Dakota* means "allied tribes."

Southeast Asia, a region of Asia that includes the countries of Brunei, Burma, Cambodia, Indonesia, Laos, Malaysia, Philippines, Singapore, Thailand, and Vietnam.

Southern Yemen, a country on the southern coast of the peninsula of Arabia, bordered on the north by Saudi Arabia and Yemen. Official name: **People's Democratic**

Republic of Yemen. Capital, Aden. Area, 111,075 sq. mi. (287,684 sq. km.). Pop., 2,410,000.

South Island, the larger of the two main islands of New Zealand. Area, 58,093 sq. mi. (150,461 sq. km.).

South Korea, a country occupying the southern part of the Korean peninsula. Official name: **Republic of Korea.** Capital, Seoul. Area, 38,022 sq. mi. (98,477 sq. km.). Pop., 44,100,000.

South Sea Islands, the islands of the southern Pacific; Oceania.

South Seas, the seas south of the equator, especially the southern Pacific.

South Vietnam, see **Vietnam.**

South-West Africa, see **Namibia.**

So·vi·et Russia (sō′vē et′) **1.** see **Union of Soviet Socialist Republics. 2.** see **Russian Soviet Federated Socialist Republic.**

Soviet Union, see **Union of Soviet Socialist Republics.**

So·we·to (sə wē′tō) a black African township in the Republic of South Africa, in the Johannesburg metropolitan area. Pop., 868,580.

Spain (spān) a country in southwestern Europe, on the Iberian Peninsula. Capital, Madrid. Area, 194,885 sq. mi. (504,752 sq. km.). Pop., 39,500,000.

Spanish America, the countries south of the United States in which the chief language is Spanish, including Mexico, Central America except Belize, South America except Brazil and the Guianas, and Cuba and other islands in the West Indies.

Spanish Main, 1. formerly, the mainland of Spanish America, especially the northern coast of South America from the mouth of the Orinoco River to the Isthmus of Panama. **2.** that part of the Caribbean Sea through which Spanish merchant ships traveled in colonial times, a former haunt of pirates.

Spanish Sahara, see **Western Sahara.**

Spar·ta (spär′tə) an ancient city-state in southern Greece, noted for the austerity of its life and the stern discipline and military effectiveness of its soldiers.

Split (split) a port city in western Yugoslavia. Pop., 235,922.

Spo·kane (spō kan′) a city in eastern Washington. Pop., 173,000.

Spring·field (spring′fēld′) **1.** the capital of Illinois, in the central part of the state. Pop., 100,000. **2.** a city in southwestern Massachusetts, on the Connecticut River. Pop., 149,000. **3.** a city in southwestern Missouri. Pop., 139,000.

Sri Lan·ka (srē läng′kə, shrē läng′kə) an island country in the Indian Ocean, east of the southern tip of India. Capital, Colombo. Area, 25,332 sq. mi. (65,610 sq. km.). Pop., 17,200,000. Formerly, **Ceylon. —Sri Lan′kan.**

Sta·lin·grad (stä′lin grad′) see **Volgograd.**

Stam·ford (stam′fərd) a city in southwestern Connecticut. Pop., 101,000.

Stat·en Island (stat′ən) an island southwest of Manhattan, in New York City, forming the borough of Richmond.

St. Au·gus·tine (ô′gə stēn′) a historic city in northeastern Florida, the oldest continuously inhabited city in the United States. Pop., 11,985.

St. Cath·a·rines (kath′ər inz, kath′rinz) a city in southeastern Canada, in Ontario. Pop., 123,455.

St. Chris·to·pher (kris′tə fər) see **St. Kitts-Nevis.**

St. Croix (kroi) the largest and southernmost of the Virgin Islands. It belongs to the United States. Area, 82 sq. mi. (212 sq. km.).

Sterling Heights, a city in southeastern Michigan. Pop., 112,000.

St. É·tienne (ā tyen′) a city in southeastern France. Pop., 220,070.

Stet·tin (shte tēn′) see **Szczecin.**

St. George's (jôr′jiz) the capital and largest city of Grenada. Pop., 7,500.

St. He·le·na (hə lē′nə) a small British island in the southern Atlantic, the site of Napoleon Bonaparte's exile from 1815 until his death in 1821. Area, 47 sq. mi. (122 sq. km.). Pop., 5,564.

St. Hel·ens, Mount (hel′ənz) an active volcano in the southwestern part of the state of Washington, in the Cascade Range. Height, 8,364 ft. (2,549 m.).

St. John (jon) the largest city in New Brunswick, Canada, located on the Bay of Fundy. Pop., 76,381.

St. John's (jonz) **1.** the capital of Antigua and Barbuda. Pop., 24,359. **2.** the capital of Newfoundland and Labrador, a port on the southeastern coast of Newfoundland. Pop., 96,216.

St. Kitts–Ne·vis (kits′nē′vis, kits′nev′is) a West Indian island nation made up of two of the Leeward Islands, St. Kitts (also called St. Christopher) and Nevis. Land area, 101 sq. mi. (262 sq. km.). Capital, Basseterre. Pop., 48,000.

St. Law·rence (lôr′əns) **1.** a river in North America flowing from Lake Ontario northeast into the Gulf of St. Lawrence. It is the chief outlet of the Great Lakes. Length, 800 mi. (1,287 km.). **2. Gulf of.** an arm of the Atlantic, on the eastern coast of Canada, at the mouth of the St. Lawrence River.

St. Lawrence Seaway, an inland waterway in east-central North America, connecting the Atlantic with the Great Lakes.

St. Lou·is (lü′is, lü′ē) a city in eastern Missouri, on the Mississippi. Pop., 426,000.

St. Lu·cia (lü′shə) a West Indian island nation, one of the Windward Islands. Capital, Castries. Area, 238 sq. mi. (616 sq. km.). Pop., 135,000.

Stock·holm (stok′hōm, stok′hōlm) the capital and largest city of Sweden, on the eastern coast of the country. Pop., 659,030.

Stock·ton (stok′tən) a city in central California. Pop., 183,000.

Stoke-on-Trent (stōk′ôn trent′, stōk′on trent′) a city in west-central England. Pop., 248,700.

St. Paul (pôl) the capital of Minnesota, in the southeastern part of the state, on the Mississippi opposite Minneapolis. Pop., 264,000.

St. Pe·ters·burg (pē′tərz bûrg′) **1.** see **Leningrad. 2.** a city in west-central Florida, on the Gulf of Mexico. Pop., 239,000.

St. Pierre and Mi·que·lon (pyâr; mik′ə lon′, mik′ə-lon′) a French department in the northern Atlantic, south of Newfoundland, made up of St. Pierre, Miquelon, and several smaller islands. Land area, 93 sq. mi. (241 sq. km.). Pop., 6,000.

Stras·bourg (stras′bûrg′) a city in northeastern France, on the Rhine. Pop., 248,712.

Strat·ford-on-A·von (strat′fərd ôn ā′von, strat′fərd on ā′von) a town in central England, noted as the birthplace, home, and burial place of William Shakespeare. Pop., 20,800. Also, **Stratford.**

St. Tho·mas (tom′əs) the westernmost of the Virgin Islands. It belongs to the United States. Area, 32 sq. mi. (83 sq. km.).

Stutt·gart (stut′gärt, stůt′gärt) a city in southwestern West Germany. Pop., 561,200.

St. Vin·cent and the Grenadines (vin′sənt) a West Indian island nation in the Windward Islands, made up of St. Vincent and the northern islands of the Grenadines

at; āpe; fär; câre; end; mē; it; īce; pîerce; hot; ōld; sông, fôrk; oil; out; up; ūse; rüle; půll; tûrn; chin; sing; shop; thin; this; hw in white; zh in treasure. The symbol ə stands for the unstressed vowel sound heard in about, taken, pencil, lemon, and circus.

1147

group. Capital, Kingstown. Land area, 150 sq. mi. (389 sq. km.). Pop., 108,000.

Su·cre (sü′krā) the legal capital of Bolivia, in the southern part of the country. Pop., 86,609.

Su·dan (sü dan′) **1.** a country in northwestern Africa, on the southern border of Egypt. Capital, Khartoum. Area, 967,500 sq. mi. (2,505,825 sq. km.). Pop., 24,200,000. **2.** a region extending across Africa from the Atlantic to Ethiopia and south from the Sahara to the central and western tropical forests. Much of the Sudan is semiarid grassland.

Su·ez (sü ez′) **1.** a port city in northeastern Egypt, at the southern entrance of the Suez Canal. Pop., 254,000. **2.** see **Suez Canal.**

Suez Canal, a canal in northeastern Egypt, connecting the Mediterranean and Red seas.

Su·la·we·si (sü′lə wä′sē) a large island in central Indonesia, east of the island of Borneo. Area, approx. 72,000 sq. mi. (186,480 sq. km.). Formerly, **Celebes.**

Su·ma·tra (sü mä′trə) the westernmost island of Indonesia, a large island south of the Malay Peninsula. Area, 182,860 sq. mi. (473,607 sq. km.).

Su·mer (sü′mər) an ancient country in southern Mesopotamia.

Sun·der·land (sun′dər lənd) a port city in northeastern England, on the North Sea. Pop., 298,800.

Sun·ny·vale (sun′e vāl′) a city in western California. Pop., 112,000.

Superior, Lake, the largest and northernmost of the Great Lakes, on the U.S.-Canadian border.

Su·ra·ba·ja (sūr′ə bä′yə) *also,* **Su·ra·ba·ya.** a port city of Indonesia, on the northeast coast of the island of Java. Pop., 2,027,913.

Su·rat (sü rat′) a city in western India. Pop., 776,583.

Su·ri·name (sūr′ə näm′) a country on the northeastern coast of South America. Capital, Paramaribo. Area, 63,037 sq. mi. (163,266 sq. km.). Pop., 397,000. Formerly, **Su·ri·nam** (sūr′ə näm′).

Sus·que·han·na (sus′kwə han′ə) a river flowing through New York, Pennsylvania, and Maryland into the Chesapeake Bay. Length, 444 mi. (714 km.).

Su·va (sü′və) the capital of Fiji. Pop., 74,000.

Su·wan·nee (sə won′ē) a river in Florida and Georgia, flowing into the Gulf of Mexico. Length, 386 mi. (621 km.). Also, **Swanee.**

Sval·bard (sväl′bärd′) a Norwegian island group in the Arctic Ocean, north of Norway. Land area, approx. 24,000 sq. mi. (62,150 sq. km.). Pop., 3,942.

Sverd·lovsk (sverd lôfsk′) a city in the west-central Soviet Union. Pop., 1,316,000.

Swa·nee (swä′nē), see **Suwannee.**

Swa·zi·land (swä′zē land′) a landlocked country in southeastern Africa. Capital, Mbabane. Area, 6,704 sq. mi. (17,363 sq. km.). Pop., 736,000.

Swe·den (swē′dən) a country in northern Europe, on the eastern part of the Scandinavian peninsula. Capital, Stockholm. Area, 170,250 sq. mi. (440,948 sq. km.). Pop., 8,320,000.

Switz·er·land (swit′sər lənd) a landlocked, mountainous country in central Europe. Capital, Bern. Area, 15,943 sq. mi. (41,292 sq. km.). Pop., 6,390,000.

Syd·ney (sid′nē) the largest city and chief port of Australia, on the eastern coast of the country. It is the capital of New South Wales. Pop., 2,876,508.

Syr·a·cuse (sir′ə kūs′) **1.** a city in central New York. Pop., 161,000. **2.** a port city in the southeastern part of the Italian island of Sicily, in ancient times a leading Greek city. Pop., 116,755.

Syr·i·a (sîr′ē ə) **1.** a country in southwestern Asia. Capital, Damascus. Area, 71,498 sq. mi. (185,180 sq. km.). Pop., 12,200,000. **2.** an ancient country at the eastern end of the Mediterranean, roughly consisting of what is now Syria, Lebanon, Israel, and some adjacent areas.

Szcze·cin (shche′tsēn) a port city in northwestern Poland. Pop., 392,300. Formerly, **Stettin.**

Ta·briz (tä brēz′) a city in northwestern Iran. Pop., 852,000.

Ta·co·ma (tə kō′mə) a city in western Washington, on Puget Sound. Pop., 159,000.

Ta·dzhik·i·stan (tə jik′ə stan′) a republic of the Soviet Union, in the south-central part of the country, bordering Afghanistan and China. Official name: **Tadzhik Soviet Socialist Republic.** Area, 55,250 sq. mi. (143,098 sq. km.). Pop., 4,643,000.

Tae·gu (tī′gü′) a city in southeastern South Korea. Pop., 1,607,500.

Ta·hi·ti (tə hē′tē) the largest of the Society Islands, in French Polynesia, midway between Australia and South America. Area, 402 sq. mi. (1,041 sq. km.). Pop., 115,820.

Ta·if (tä′if) see **At Taif.**

Tai·pei (tī′pā′) *also,* **Tai·peh.** the capital of Taiwan, in the northern part of the island. Pop., 2,270,983.

Tai·wan (tī′wän′) an island country in the western Pacific, east of Mainland China, seat of the Nationalist government of China since 1949. Official name: **Republic of China.** Capital, Taipei. Area, 13,885 sq. mi. (35,962 sq. km.). Pop., 20,400,000. Also, **Nationalist China.**

Tai·yu·an (tī′ ü än′) a city in northern China. Pop., 1,390,000.

Tal·ca·hua·no (tal′kə wä′nō) a port city in central Chile, on the Pacific. Pop., 220,910.

Tal·la·has·see (tal′ə has′ē) the capital of Florida, in the northwestern part of the state. Pop., 119,000.

Tam·pa (tam′pə) a port city in western Florida. Pop., 278,000.

Ta·na·na·rive (tə nan′ə rēv′) see **Antananarivo.**

Tan·gan·yi·ka (tan′gən yē′kə) **1.** a former country in eastern Africa, now part of Tanzania. **2. Lake.** a lake in east-central Africa, lying between Zaire, Tanzania, and Zambia. It is the longest freshwater lake in the world.

Tan·gier (tan jîr′) a port city in northern Morocco, on the Strait of Gibraltar. Pop., 266,346.

Tan·ta (tän′tə) a city in north-central Egypt, in the Nile delta. Pop., 364,700.

Tan·za·ni·a (tan′zə nē′ə) a country in east-central Africa, formed in 1964 by the merger of the former countries of Tanganyika and Zanzibar. Capitals, Dodoma and Dar es Salaam. Area, 364,900 sq. mi. (945,091 sq. km.). Pop., 26,000,000.

Ta·ra·bu·lus (tə rab′ə ləs) see **Tripoli** *(defs. 2 and 3).*

Ta·ran·to (tär′ən tō′) a port city in southeastern Italy, on the Ionian Sea. Pop., 241,386.

Ta·ra·wa (tə rä′wə) an atoll in the Pacific island country of Kiribati, site of the capital of Bairiki.

Tash·kent (täsh kent′) a city in the south-central Soviet Union. Pop., 2,073,000.

Tas·ma·ni·a (taz mā′nē ə) an island state of Australia, off the southeastern coast of the mainland. Capital, Hobart. Area, 26,215 sq. mi. (67,897 sq. km.). Pop., 437,300.

Tas·man Sea (taz′mən) the part of the Pacific between southeastern Australia and New Zealand.

Tbi·li·si (tə bə lē′sē) a city in the southwestern Soviet Union. Pop., 1,174,000. Formerly, **Tiflis.**

Te·gu·ci·gal·pa (tə gü′si gal′pə) the capital of Honduras, in the south-central part of the country. Pop., 597,500.

Teh·ran (te rän′, te ran′) *also,* **Te·he·ran.** the capital and largest city of Iran, in the north-central part of the country. Pop., 5,700,000.

Tel A·viv (tel′ə vēv′) a city in west-central Israel, on the Mediterranean, combined with Jaffa in 1950. Official name: **Tel Aviv-Jaffa.** Pop., 323,400.

Tem·pe (tem′pē) a city in south-central Arizona. Pop., 136,000.

Ten·nes·see (ten′ə sē′) **1.** a state in the southeastern United States. Capital, Nashville. Area, 42,144 sq. mi. (109,153 sq. km.). Pop., 4,803,000. Abbreviation, **Tenn.**;

postal abbreviation, **TN 2.** a river in the southeastern United States, flowing through Tennessee, Alabama, and Kentucky into the Ohio River. Length, 652 mi. (1,049 km.). —**Ten'nes·se'an**, *adj., n.* ▲ *Tennessee* comes from the Cherokee name for the tribe's ancient capital. This name was given to a nearby stream, and the English settlers extended its application to the Tennessee River, into which the stream flows. A county of North Carolina established in this area took its name from the river, and the territory in which the county was located adopted the name when it was admitted as a state in 1796.

Te·noch·ti·tlán (te nôch'tē tlän') the capital of the ancient Aztec empire, on the site of present-day Mexico City.

Té·touan (tā twän') a port city in northern Morocco, on the Mediterranean. Pop., 199,615.

Tex·as (tek'səs) a state in the south-central United States, bordering Mexico and the Gulf of Mexico. Capital, Austin. Area, 266,807 sq. mi. (691,030 sq. km.). Pop., 16,685,000. Abbreviation, **Tex.;** postal abbreviation, **TX** —**Tex'an**, *adj., n.* ▲ *Texas* comes from an American Indian word meaning "friends." Spanish explorers applied the term to Indians living in the eastern part of Texas, and the Spanish, and later the Mexicans, used it as the official name of that region. The name was retained when Texas declared itself independent of Mexico and, later, when it became a U.S. state.

Thai·land (tī'land') a country in southeastern Asia. Capital, Bangkok. Area, 198,115 sq. mi. (513,118 sq. km.). Pop., 54,800,000. Formerly, **Siam.**

Thames (temz) a river in southern England, flowing east through London to the North Sea. Length, 210 mi. (338 km.).

Thebes (thēbz) **1.** an ancient Egyptian city on the Nile, a former capital of Egypt. The site, now occupied in part by Luxor and Karnak, is renowned for its tombs and ruins. **2.** one of the leading city-states of ancient Greece, northwest of Athens. —**The'ban**, *adj., n.*

Ther·mop·y·lae (thər mop'ə lē') a mountain pass in central Greece, site of a battle in 480 B.C. between the Greeks and Persians.

Thes·sa·lon·i·ca (thes'ə lon'i kə) see **Salonika.**

Thim·bu (tim'bü) the capital of Bhutan, in the western part of the country. Pop., 8,982. Also, **Thim·phu** (tim'pü).

Thousand Islands, a group of about 1,700 small islands in the United States and Canada, in the St. Lawrence River.

Thunder Bay, a port city in southwestern Ontario, Canada, located on an inlet at the western end of Lake Superior. Pop., 112,272.

Tian·jin (tyän'jin') a port city in northeastern China. Pop., 5,380,000. Also, **Tientsin.**

Ti·ber (tī'bər) a river flowing southward from north-central Italy, through Rome, into the Tyrrhenian Sea. Length, 247 mi. (397 km).

Ti·be·ri·as, Lake (tī bîr'ē əs) see **Galilee, Sea of.**

Ti·bet (ti bet') an autonomous region in southwestern China, north of the Himalayas. Prior to 1950 it was an independent nation ruled by the Dalai Lama. Capital, Lhasa. Area, 471,660 sq. mi. (1,221,599 sq. km.). Pop., 1,990,000.

Ti·con·de·ro·ga (tī'kon də rō'gə) a village and historic fort on Lake Champlain, in northeastern New York. Pop., 2,938.

Tien·tsin (tyen'tsin') see **Tianjin.**

Tier·ra del Fue·go (tyer'ə del fwā'gō) an archipelago at the southern tip of South America, divided between Chile and Argentina. Land area, approx. 27,500 sq. mi. (71,200 sq. km.).

Tif·lis (tif'lis) see **Tbilisi.**

Ti·gris (tī'gris) a river in southwestern Asia, flowing from eastern Turkey to southeastern Iraq, where it joins the Euphrates to form the Shatt-al-Arab. Length, 1,180 mi. (1,899 km.).

Ti·jua·na (tē'ə wä'nə, tē wä'nə) a resort city in northwestern Mexico, on the U.S. border. Pop., 429,500.

Tim·buk·tu (tim'buk tü') a town in western Africa, in Mali, a great trade and cultural center in the twelfth through fifteenth centuries. Pop., 19,166.

Ti·mi·şoa·ra (tē'mē shwä'rə) a city in western Romania, near the Yugoslav border. Pop., 325,272.

Ti·mor (tē'môr) an Indonesian island southwest of Sulawesi and north of Australia. The western part formerly belonged to the Netherlands, and the eastern part to Portugal. Area, 13,094 sq. mi. (33,913 sq. km.).

Ti·ra·në (ti rä'nə) *also,* **Ti·ra·na.** the capital and largest city of Albania, in the central part of the country. Pop., 198,000.

Ti·ti·ca·ca, Lake (tit'i kä'kə) the largest lake in South America, in the Andes, in southeastern Peru and western Bolivia.

To·ba·go (tə bā'gō) an island of the Lesser Antilles, near Venezuela, forming part of the country of Trinidad and Tobago. Area, 116 sq. mi. (300 sq. km.).

To·bruk (tō'brūk) *also,* **Tu·bruq.** a port city in northeastern Libya, on the Mediterranean. Pop., 71,800.

To·go (tō'gō) a country in western Africa on the Gulf of Guinea, between Ghana and Benin. Capital, Lomé. Area, 21,925 sq. mi. (56,786 sq. km.). Pop., 3,350,000.

To·ke·lau (tō'kə lou') a group of three atolls administered by New Zealand, in the southern Pacific. Land area, approx. 5 sq. mi. (13 sq. km.). Pop., 1,572.

To·ky·o (tō'kyō) the capital and largest city of Japan, in the east-central part of the island of Honshu. Pop., 8,351,893.

To·le·do (tə lē'dō) **1.** a port city in northwestern Ohio, on Lake Erie. Pop., 341,000. **2.** a historic city in central Spain. Pop., 40,700.

Ton·ga (tong'gə) a country consisting of three groups of islands in the southwestern Pacific. Capital, Nukualofa. Land area, 270 sq. mi. (700 sq. km.). Pop., 117,000. Also, **Tonga Islands.**

Ton·kin, Gulf of (ton'kin', tong'kin') an arm of the South China Sea, bordered by Vietnam and China.

To·pe·ka (tə pē'kə) the capital of Kansas, in the northeastern part of the state. Pop., 119,000.

To·ron·to (tə ron'tō) the capital and largest city of Ontario, in the southeastern part of Canada, on Lake Ontario. Pop., 612,289.

Tor·rance (tôr'əns) a city in southern California. Pop., 136,000.

Tor·re·ón (tôr'ē ōn') a city in northern Mexico, northwest of Mexico City. Pop., 328,086.

Tou·louse (tü lüz') a city in southern France. Pop., 347,995.

Tours (tùr) a city in west-central France. In A.D. 732 Charles Martel defeated the Moors in a battle near here. Pop., 132,209.

Tra·fal·gar, Cape (trə fal'gər) a cape in southwestern Spain, on the Atlantic, the site of a naval battle on October 21, 1805, in which the fleets of France and Spain were defeated by a British fleet led by Horatio Nelson.

Trans·jor·dan (trans jôr'dən) see **Jordan** *(def. 1).*

Tran·syl·va·ni·a (tran'səl vā'nē ə) a historic region in central Romania. Area, approx. 24,000 sq. mi. (62,160 sq. km.).

---

at; āpe; fär; câre; end; mē; it; īce; pîerce; hot; ōld; sông, fôrk; oil; out; up; ūse; rüle; pùll; tûrn; chin; sing; shop; thin; this; hw in white; zh in treasure. The symbol ə stands for the unstressed vowel sound heard in about, taken, pencil, lemon, and circus.

Tren·ton (tren′tən) the capital of New Jersey, in the western part of the state, on the Delaware River. Pop., 92,124

Tri·este (trē est′) a port city in northeastern Italy, at the head of the Adriatic Sea. Pop., 244,506.

Trin·i·dad (trin′i dad′) one of the Lesser Antilles, off the coast of Venezuela, part of the country of Trinidad and Tobago. Area, 1,864 sq. mi. (4,828 sq. km.).

Trinidad and Tobago, a country consisting of the West Indian islands of Trinidad and Tobago. Capital, Port-of-Spain. Land area, 1,980 sq. mi. (5,128 sq. km.). Pop., 1,260,000.

Trip·o·li (trip′ə lē) **1.** a region on the northern coast of Africa, now in western Libya, once a major base for the Barbary pirates. **2.** the capital and largest city of Libya, a port in the northeastern part of the country, on the Mediterranean. Pop., 858,500. **3.** a port city in northern Lebanon, on the Mediterranean Sea. Pop., 198,000. Also (*defs. 2 and 3*), **Tarabulus.** —**Tri·pol·i·tan** (tri pol′i tən) *adj., n.*

Troy (troi) an ancient city and stronghold in northwestern Asia Minor, near the mouth of the Dardanelles. Excavations and archaeological research have shown that it was actually settled nine times. The seventh of these cities was the scene of the Trojan War. Also, **Ilium.**

Tru·ji·llo (trü hē′ō) a city in northwestern Peru. Pop., 202,469.

Tsi·nan (jē′nän′) see **Jinan.**

Tu·bruq (tü′brŭk) see **Tobruk.**

Tuc·son (tü′son) a city in southeastern Arizona, noted as a health and tourist resort. Pop., 359,000.

Tu·cu·mán (tü′kə män′) a city in northwestern Argentina. Pop., 392,751. Also, **San Miguel de Tucumán.**

Tul·sa (tul′sə) a city in northeastern Oklahoma, on the Arkansas River. Pop., 374,000.

Tu·nis (tü′nis, tū′nis) the capital and largest city of Tunisia, in the northern part of the country. Pop., 596,654.

Tu·ni·sia (tü nē′zhə, tū nē′zhə) a country on the northern coast of Africa, on the Mediterranean. Capital, Tunis. Area, 63,170 sq. mi. (163,610 sq. km.). Pop., 7,730,000. —**Tu·ni′sian,** *adj., n.*

Tu·rin (tür′in, tyür′in) a city in northwestern Italy. Pop., 1,035,383.

Tur·key (tûr′kē) a country in western Asia and southeastern Europe. Capital, Ankara. Area, 300,948 sq. mi. (779,455 sq. km.). Pop., 53,600,000.

Turk·men Republic (tûrk′men) the southernmost republic of the Soviet Union, bordering Iran and Afghanistan. Official name: **Turkmen Soviet Socialist Republic.** Area, approx. 188,450 sq. mi. (488,100 sq. km.). Pop., 3,271,000. Also, **Turk·me·nia** (tûrk mē′nē ə), **Turk·me·ni·stan** (tûrk′mə nə stan′).

Turks and Cai·cos Islands (tûrks; kā′kəs) a British island group of the West Indies, located south of the Bahamas. Land area, 166 sq. mi. (430 sq. km.). Pop., 8,000.

Tu·va·lu (tù vä′lü) an island country in the central Pacific. Capital, Funafuti. Land area, approx. 10 sq. mi. (26 sq. km.). Pop., 8,000.

Tyre (tīr) a town on the Mediterranean coast of Lebanon, the principal seaport of ancient Phoenicia and an important commercial center of the ancient world.

Tyr·rhe·ni·an Sea (ti rē′nē ən) the part of the Mediterranean between Italy and the islands of Sicily, Sardinia, and Corsica.

U·fa (ü fä′) a city in the west-central Soviet Union. Pop., 1,077,000.

U·gan·da (ü gan′də, ü gän′də) a landlocked country in east-central Africa. Capital, Kampala. Area, 93,104 sq. mi. (241,139 sq. km.). Pop., 17,800,000.

U·jung Pan·dang (ü jüng′ pän däng′) the largest city and chief port of the island of Sulawesi, in Indonesia. Pop., 709,038. Formerly, **Macassar, Makassar.**

U·kraine (ü krān′) a republic of the Soviet Union, in the southwestern part of the country, on the Black Sea. Official name: **Ukrainian Soviet Socialist Republic.** Area, approx. 233,000 sq. mi. (603,470 sq. km.). Pop., 50,973,000.

U·lan Ba·tor (ü′län bä′tôr) *also,* **U·laan Baa·tar.** the capital and largest city of the country of Mongolia, in the northeastern part of the country. Pop., 488,200.

Ul·ster (ul′stər) see **Northern Ireland.**

Union of Soviet Socialist Republics, the largest country in the world in area, extending from eastern Europe to the northeastern coast of Asia. It is divided into fifteen constituent republics. Capital, Moscow. Area, 8,649,540 sq. mi. (22,402,309 sq. km.). Pop., 289,000,000. Also, **Soviet Union, Russia, Soviet Russia.**

United Arab Emirates, a country composed of seven sheikdoms on the east-central coast of the peninsula of Arabia. Capital, Abu Dhabi. Area, 32,380 sq. mi. (83,864 sq. km.). Pop., 1,530,000.

United Arab Republic **1.** the former name of the republic of Egypt, from 1961 to 1971. **2.** the former name of the union of Egypt and Syria, from 1958 to 1961.

United Kingdom **1.** a country in northwestern Europe, composed of England, Scotland, Wales, and Northern Ireland. Capital, London. Area, 92,214 sq. mi. (238,834 sq. km.). Pop., 56,200,000. **2.** from 1801 to 1922, a country composed of England, Scotland, Wales, and all of Ireland. Also, **Great Britain.**

United States, a country mainly in North America, consisting of fifty states, the District of Columbia, and several territories. Capital, Washington, D.C. Area, 3,618,770 sq. mi. (9,372,614 sq. km.). Pop., 246,000,000. Also, **United States of America, America.**

Upper Vol·ta (vōl′tə) see **Burkina Faso.**

Ur (ûr) a city of ancient Sumer in southern Mesopotamia, on the Euphrates.

U·ral Mountains (yür′əl) a mountain system extending north to south in the east-central Soviet Union, forming part of the traditional boundary between Europe and Asia. Also, **Urals.**

Ural River, a river rising in the southern Ural Mountains and flowing into the Caspian Sea. It forms part of the traditional boundary between Europe and Asia. Also, **Ural.**

Urals (yür′əlz) see **Ural Mountains.**

U·ru·guay (yür′ə gwā′, ür′ə gwī′) **1.** a country on the southeastern coast of South America, between Brazil and Argentina. Capital, Montevideo. Area, 68,536 sq. mi. (177,508 sq. km.). Pop., 3,100,000. **2.** a river in southeastern South America, flowing between Brazil and Uruguay on the east and Argentina on the west. It empties into the Río de la Plata. Length, 1,000 mi. (1,609 km.).

U·tah (ü′tô, ü′tä) a state in the western United States. Capital, Salt Lake City. Area, 84,899 sq. mi. (219,888 sq. km.). Pop., 1,665,000. Abbreviation, **Ut.**; postal abbreviation, **UT** —**U·tah·an** (ü′tôn, ü′tän) *adj., n.* ▲ *Utah* comes from the Spanish pronunciation of *Ute,* the name of a Shoshone tribe that lived in what is now Colorado and Utah. The tribal name may have meant "the people" in the Shoshone language. The American explorer John Frémont used the name *Utah* to refer also to a lake south of the Great Salt Lake and the river flowing into that lake. Congress organized the territory in which the lake was located in 1850 and named it *Utah,* and part of the territory later became the state.

U·trecht (ü′trekt) a historic city in the central Netherlands. Pop., 229,933.

Uz·bek·i·stan (ùz bek′i stan′) a republic of the Soviet Union, in Central Asia. Official name: **Uzbek Soviet Socialist Republic.** Area, approx. 172,740 sq. mi. (447,400 sq. km.). Pop., 18,479,000.

Va·duz (vä′düts) the capital of Liechtenstein. Pop., 4,927.

Va·len·ci·a (və len′sē ə, və len′shə) **1.** a port city in eastern Spain. Pop., 751,734.   **2.** a city in northern Venezuela. Pop., 523,000.

Val·let·ta (və let′ə) the capital of Malta. Pop., 14,013.

Valley Forge,   a village in southeastern Pennsylvania where George Washington and his army camped during the winter of 1777–1778.

Val·pa·rai·so (val′pə rī′zō) a port city in central Chile. Pop., 267,025.

Van·cou·ver (van kü′vər)   **1.** a city in southwestern British Columbia, Canada. Pop., 431,147.   **2.** an island of British Columbia. Area, 12,408 sq. mi. (32,137 sq. km.).

Van·u·a·tu (van′ü ä′tü) a country in the southwestern Pacific. Capital, Vila. Land area, 4,706 sq. mi. (12,189 sq. km.). Pop., 159,000. Formerly, **New Hebrides.**

Va·ra·na·si (və rä′nə sē) a Hindu holy city on the Ganges, in northeastern India. Pop., 708,647. Formerly, **Benares.**

Vat·i·can City (vat′i kən) an independent state ruled by the pope and located within Rome. Pop., 1,000.

Ven·e·zue·la (ven′ə zwā′lə, ven′ə zwē′lə) a country in northern South America, on the Caribbean. Capital, Caracas. Area, 352,145 sq. mi. (912,056 sq. km.). Pop., 19,200,000. —**Ven′e·zue′lan,** adj., n.

Ven·ice (ven′is) a port city in northeastern Italy, on 118 islets in the Adriatic. Pop., 334,107.

Verde, Cape (vûrd) the westernmost point of Africa, a peninsula on the coast of Senegal.

Ver·mont (vər mont′) a state in the northeastern United States. Capital, Montpelier. Area, 9,614 sq. mi. (24,900 sq. km.). Pop., 541,000. Abbreviation, **Vt.;** postal abbreviation, **VT** —**Ver·mont′er,** n. ▲ The area now called Vermont was known by the English as "Green Mountain," and the name *Vermont* was probably suggested by *Vert Mont,* which is the French translation of the English name.

Ver·sailles (vâr sī′, vər sī′) a historic city in north-central France, just southwest of Paris. It is the site of the magnificent palace of Louis XIV. Pop., 91,494.

Ve·su·vi·us, Mount (və sü′vē əs) an active volcano in southern Italy. Height, 4,190 ft. (1,277 m.).

Vicks·burg (viks′bûrg) a port city in western Mississippi, on the Mississippi River. Vicksburg was besieged and captured by Union forces in 1863. Pop., 25,434.

Vic·to·ri·a (vik tôr′ē ə)   **1.** a state of Australia, in the southeastern part of the country. Capital, Melbourne. Area, 87,884 sq. mi. (227,620 sq. km.). Pop., 4,075,500.   **2. Lake,** a lake in east-central Africa, the largest of the continent. Also, **Victoria Ny·an·za** (nī an′zə).   **3.** the capital of British Columbia, Canada, on the southern tip of Vancouver Island. Pop., 66,303.   **4.** the capital of the Seychelles. Pop., 23,000.

Vi·en·na (vē en′ə) the capital and largest city of Austria, on the Danube River. Pop., 1,489,153.

Vien·tiane (vyen tyän′) the capital and largest city of Laos. Pop., 174,200.

Vi·et·nam (vē′et näm′) also, **Vi·et Nam.** a country in southeastern Asia, divided from 1954 to 1975 into North Vietnam and South Vietnam. Capital, Hanoi. Area, 127,242 sq. mi. (329,557 sq. km.). Pop., 64,800,000.

Vi·la (vē′lə) the capital of Vanuatu. Pop., 13,067.

Vir·gin·ia (vər jin′yə) a state in the eastern United States. Capital, Richmond. Area, 40,767 sq. mi. (105,587 sq. km.). Pop., 5,787,000. Abbreviation, **Va.;** postal abbreviation, **VA** —**Vir·gin′ian,** adj., n. ▲ *Virginia* comes from the title "the *Virgin* Queen," given to Queen Elizabeth I because she never married. The colony of Virginia was founded during her reign.

Virginia Beach,   a resort city in southeastern Virginia, on the Atlantic. Pop., 333,000.

Vir·gin Islands (vûr′jin) an island group of the Caribbean, the westernmost of the Lesser Antilles. It is divided politically between the United States and Great Britain. Land area, approx. 192 sq. mi. (497 sq. km.).

Vlad·i·vos·tok (vlad′ə vos′tok) a port city in the southeasternmost Soviet Union. Pop., 608,000.

Vol·ga (vol′gə) a river in the European Soviet Union. Length, 2,194 mi. (3,530 km.).

Vol·go·grad (vol′gə grad′) a port city in the southwestern Soviet Union, on the Volga River. Formerly known as Stalingrad, the city was the scene of a major Soviet victory over the Germans in World War II. Pop., 981,000.

Wa·co (wā′kō) a city in east-central Texas. Pop., 105,000.

Wah·ran (wä rän′) see **Oran.**

Wake Island,   an atoll in the Pacific, administered by the United States. Land area, 3 sq. mi. (8 sq. km.).

Wales (wālz) a division of the United Kingdom, west of and bordering England. Area, 8,019 sq. mi. (20,769 sq. km.). Pop., 2,821,000.

War·ren (wôr′ən, wor′ən) a city in southeastern Michigan. Pop., 150,000.

War·saw (wôr′sô) the capital and largest city of Poland, in the east-central part of the country. Pop., 1,659,400.

War·wick (wôr′wik) a city in central Rhode Island. Pop., 87,123.

Wash·ing·ton (wô′shing tən, wosh′ing tən)   **1.** the capital of the United States, lying between Maryland and northern Virginia and occupying the District of Columbia. Pop., 626,000. Also, **Washington, D.C.   2.** a state in the northwestern United States, on the Pacific. Capital, Olympia. Area, 68,139 sq. mi. (176,480 sq. km.). Pop., 4,462,000. Abbreviation, **Wash.;** postal abbreviation, **WA   3. Mount.** the highest mountain in New England, in northern New Hampshire. Height, 6,288 ft. (1,917 m.). —**Wash·ing·to·ni·an** (wô′shing tō′nē ən, wosh′ing tō′nē ən) adj., n. (defs. 1, 2). ▲ In 1853, Congress named a new territory *Washington* after George *Washington.* The name was kept when the territory became a state.

Wa·ter·bur·y (wô′tər ber′ē, wô′tər bə rē) a city in western Connecticut. Pop., 103,266.

Wa·ter·loo (wô′tər lü′) a village in central Belgium, scene of the final defeat of Napoleon Bonaparte, on June 18, 1815, by a combined army of English, Dutch, and Prussians. Pop., 24,536.

Wel·ling·ton (wel′ing tən) the capital of New Zealand, on the southwestern tip of North Island. Pop., 133,200.

West Bank,   an area in the Middle East, west of the Jordan River, formerly part of Palestine. Annexed by Jordan in 1950, it has been occupied by Israel since 1967. Area, approx. 3,300 sq. mi. (8,500 sq. km.).

West Berlin,   the part of the city of Berlin belonging to West Germany. It is located in north-central East Germany. Pop., 1,860,004.

Western Australia,   a state occupying the western part of Australia. Capital, Perth. Area, 975,290 sq. mi. (2,526,001 sq. km.). Pop., 1,382,500.

Western Sahara,   a territory on the northwestern coast of Africa, claimed by Morocco and by a political group based in Algeria. Capital, El Aaiún. Area, 102,700 sq. mi. (265,993 sq. km.). Pop., 168,000. Formerly, **Spanish Sahara.**

Western Samoa,   an island country in the southern Pacific, east of Australia, consisting of the western islands of Samoa. Capital, Apia. Land area, 1,097 sq. mi. (2,841 sq. km.). Pop., 168,000.

West Germany,   a country in north-central Europe. Official name: **Federal Republic of Germany.** Capital, Bonn. Area, 96,030 sq. mi. (248,718 sq. km.). Pop., 60,400,000.

West In·dies (in′dēz) an archipelago extending from

at; āpe; fär; câre; end; mē; it; īce; pîerce; hot; ōld; sông, fôrk; oil; out; up; ūse; rüle; pull; tûrn; chin; sing; shop; thin; this; hw in white; zh in treasure. The symbol ə stands for the unstressed vowel sound heard in about, taken, pencil, lemon, and circus.

1151

Florida to the coast of Venezuela, separating the Caribbean from the Atlantic. It consists of the Greater Antilles, the Lesser Antilles, and the Bahamas. —**West Indian.**

West·min·ster (west′min′stər) a borough in the central part of Greater London. Pop., 184,100.

West Pakistan, one of two former provinces of Pakistan. In 1971, the other former province, East Pakistan, became the independent country of Bangladesh. The country of Pakistan now consists of what was the province of West Pakistan.

West Point, a military reserve in southeastern New York State, site of the United States Military Academy.

West Virginia, a state in the eastern United States. Capital, Charleston. Area, 24,232 sq. mi. (62,761 sq. km.). Pop., 1,918,000. Abbreviation, **W. Va.**; postal abbreviation, **WV** —**West Virginian.** ▲ West Virginia was originally part of the state of Virginia. The people in Virginia's western counties decided to form their own government during the Civil War and chose the name *West Virginia.*

White·horse (hwīt′hôrs′, wīt′hôrs′) a city in northwestern Canada, capital of the Yukon. Pop., 15,199.

White Nile, a river in eastern Africa, flowing northward through Uganda and Sudan to Khartoum, where it joins the Blue Nile. Length, 1,180 mi. (1,899 km.).

White Russia, see **Byelorussia.**

Whit·ney, Mount (hwit′nē, wit′nē) a mountain of the Sierra Nevada, in eastern California. Height, 14,494 ft. (4,418 m.).

Wich·i·ta (wich′i tô′) the largest city in Kansas, in the south-central part of the state. Pop., 289,000.

Wil·liams·burg (wil′yəmz bûrg′) a historic town in southeastern Virginia. Pop., 9,870.

Wil·ming·ton (wil′ming tən) the largest city of Delaware, a port in the northern part of the state. Pop., 70,195.

Wind·hoek (vint′hŏk′) the capital of Namibia, in the central part of the territory. Pop., 97,000.

Wind·sor (win′zər) **1.** a city in southern England, southwest of London, on the Thames. It is the site of Windsor Castle. Pop., 28,300. Also, **New Windsor. 2.** a city in southern Ontario, Canada. Pop., 193,111.

Wind·ward Islands (wind′wərd) a Caribbean island group forming the southern part of the Lesser Antilles. Land area, approx. 1,412 sq. mi. (3,657 sq. km.).

Win·ni·peg (win′ə peg′) **1.** a city in southern Canada, the capital and largest city of Manitoba. Pop., 594,551. **2. Lake.** a lake in south-central Manitoba.

Win·ston–Sa·lem (win′stən sā′ləm) a city in north-central North Carolina. Pop., 148,000.

Wis·con·sin (wis kon′sin) a state in the north-central United States, bordering Lake Michigan on the east. Capital, Madison. Area, 56,153 sq. mi. (145,436 sq. km.). Pop., 4,785,000. Abbreviation, **Wis.**; postal abbreviation, **WI** —**Wis·con·sin·ite′,** *n.* ▲ *Wisconsin* comes from the French form of an Algonquian word meaning "at the big (or long) river" or, perhaps, "gathering of waters," referring to a river with this name in central Wisconsin.

Worces·ter (wùs′tər) a city in central Massachusetts. Pop., 158,000.

Wroc·law (vrots′läf) a city in southwestern Poland. Pop., 637,200. Formerly, **Breslau.**

Wu·chang (wü′chäng′) a former city in east-central China, now part of Wuhan.

Wu·han (wü′hän′) a metropolis in east-central China, formed by the merger of the cities of Hankou, Hanyang, and Wuchang. Pop., 3,400,000.

Wy·o·ming (wī ō′ming) a state in the western United States. Capital, Cheyenne. Area, 97,809 sq. mi. (253,325 sq. km.). Pop., 507,000. Abbreviation, **Wyo.**; postal abbreviation, **WY** —**Wy·o·ming·ite′,** *n.* ▲ *Wyoming* comes from an Algonquian word meaning "at the big plains" or "flat area between mountains."

Xi·an (sē′än′) *also,* **Si·an.** a city in east-central China. Pop., 1,730,000.

Ya·mas·sou·kro (yä′mä sü′krō) the capital of the Ivory Coast, in the central part of the country. Pop., 70,000.

Yang·tze (yäng′tsē′) *also,* **Yang·tse.** the longest river in China. Length, 3,915 mi. (6,299 km.). Also, **Chang, Chang Jiang.**

Ya·oun·dé (yä ün dā′) the capital of Cameroon, in the south-central part of the country. Pop., 561,000.

Yel·low·knife (yel′ō nīf′) the capital and largest city of the Northwest Territories, Canada. Pop., 10,923.

Yellow River, see **Huang He.**

Yellow Sea, a shallow arm of the Pacific, between northeastern China and North and South Korea.

Yel·low·stone National Park (yel′ō stōn′) a national park in northwestern Wyoming and neighboring sections of Montana and Idaho.

Yem·en (yem′ən) **1.** a country in the southwestern part of the peninsula of Arabia, on the Red Sea. Official name: **Yemen Arab Republic.** Capital, Sana. Area, 75,300 sq. mi. (195,027 sq. km.). Pop., 7,700,000. **2. People's Democratic Republic of.** see **Southern Yemen.**

Ye·re·van (yer′ə vän′) a city in the southwestern Soviet Union. Pop., 1,148,000.

Yo·ko·ha·ma (yō′kə hä′mə) a port city in east-central Japan, on the island of Honshu. Pop., 2,773,674.

Yon·kers (yong′kərz) a city in southeastern New York. Pop., 186,000.

York·town (yôrk′toun′) a historic town in southeastern Virginia, scene in 1781 of the last major battle of the American Revolution.

Yo·sem·i·te Falls (yō sem′i tē) waterfalls in Yosemite National Park, among the world's highest. Height, 2,425 ft. (739 m.).

Yosemite National Park, a national park in east-central California.

Youngs·town (yungz′toun′) a city in northeastern Ohio. Pop., 105,000.

Yu·ca·tán (ū′kə tan′) a peninsula in southeastern Mexico and northeastern Central America, between the Gulf of Mexico and the Caribbean. It was the center of Mayan civilization. Area, 70,000 sq. mi. (181,300 sq. km.).

Yu·go·sla·vi·a (ū′gō slä′vē ə) a country in southeastern Europe, on the eastern shore of the Adriatic. Capital, Belgrade. Area, 98,766 sq. mi. (255,804 sq. km.). Pop., 23,800,000. —**Yu′go·sla′vi·an,** *adj., n.*

Yu·kon (ū′kon) a territory in northwestern Canada. Capital, Whitehorse. Area, 207,076 sq. mi. (536,327 sq. km.). Pop., 23,504.

Za·greb (zä′greb) a city in northwestern Yugoslavia. Pop., 768,700.

Za·ire (zä îr′) **1.** a country in central Africa. Capital, Kinshasa. Area, 905,568 sq. mi. (2,345,421 sq. km.). Pop., 33,800,000. Formerly, **Democratic Republic of the Congo. 2.** see **Congo** (*def. 1*).

Zam·bi·a (zam′bē ə) a landlocked country in south-central Africa. Capital, Lusaka. Area, 290,586 sq. mi. (752,618 sq. km.). Pop., 7,640,000.

Zan·zi·bar (zan′zə bär′) **1.** an island in the Indian Ocean, off the eastern coast of Africa, part of Tanzania. Area, 640 sq. mi. (1,658 sq. km.). **2.** a former country consisting of the islands of Zanzibar and Pemba.

Za·ra·go·za. (zar′ə gō′zə) see **Saragossa.**

Zar·qa (zär′kə) *also,* **Zar·ka.** see **Az Zarqa.**

Zheng·zhou (jung′jō′) a city in eastern China. Pop., 1,000,000. Also, **Chengchow.**

Zim·bab·we (zim bäb′wē, zim bäb′wä) a landlocked country in south-central Africa. Capital, Harare. Area, 150,873 sq. mi. (390,761 sq. km.). Pop., 10,100,000.

Zu·rich (zůr′ik) the largest city in Switzerland, in the northern part of the country. Pop., 351,545.

*C*ontents

*W*riter's Resources

THE WRITING PROCESS

Writing is an important skill, not only in your studies and your schoolwork but in all parts of life. When you write a story or a report, or a note to a friend, you want your readers to understand what you are trying to say. You can help make sure they will understand by thinking like your readers. What do they need to know? Are you telling them enough? Can they understand how your ideas are related or connected?

PREWRITING STRATEGIES

You can use some strategies, or plans, to get ready to write. Some prewriting strategies you can use are listed below.

- **BRAINSTORMING** is thinking about a topic or problem and writing down all the ideas that come to your mind. You can brainstorm by yourself, with a partner, or with a small group.

- **CLUSTERING** is another way to organize your ideas for writing. When you cluster your ideas, you put them into groups. A clustering model like the one below can help you plan.

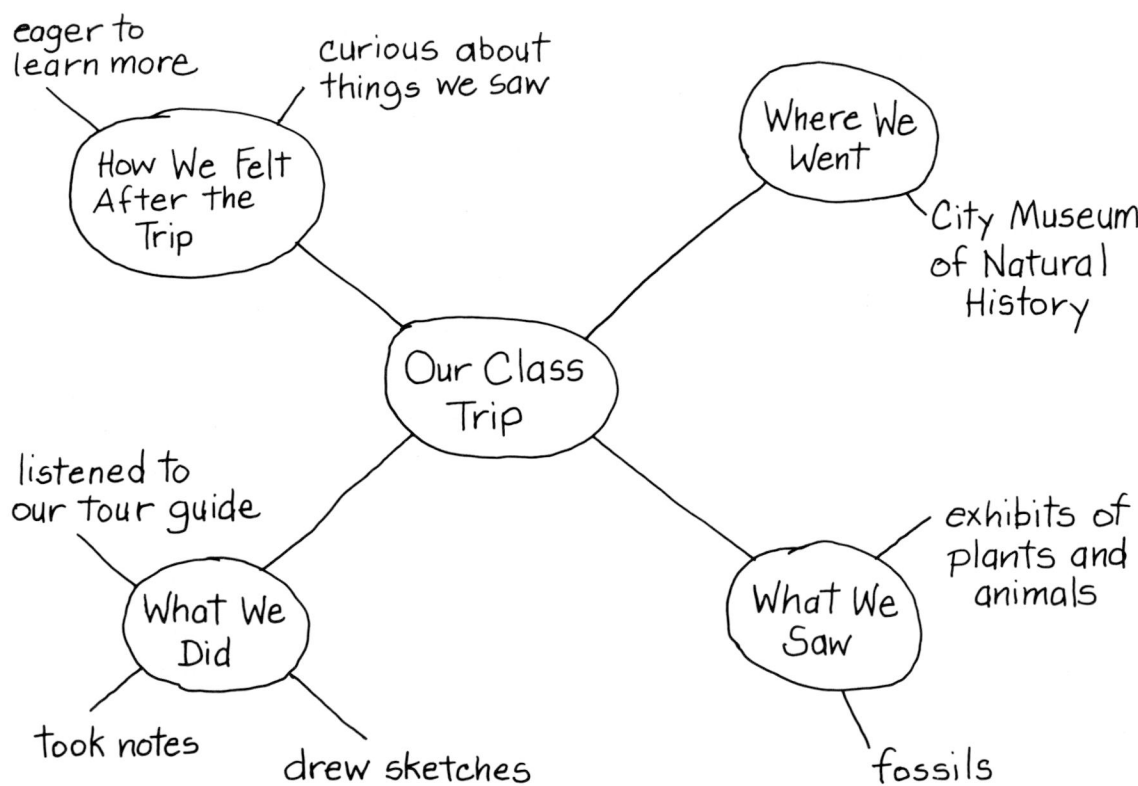

- **TIME LINES** can help you organize events that happen in a certain order, or sequence. You can also use a time line to show the steps in a process.

Gandhi	
1869	born
1888	went to England to study law
1893	went to South Africa
1914	left Africa and returned to India
1919	staged first nonviolent demonstration in India
1924	elected president of Indian National Congress

- **CHARTING** is a way to organize your ideas about a topic.

  The headings for a chart will be different for different kinds of writing. You might use the following chart, for example, when getting ready to write a persuasive paragraph.

Opinions	Reasons

- **OUTLINING** is a useful strategy for getting ready to write longer pieces such as research reports. When you outline, you give a summary by listing main ideas and important details. In the final report, each main idea becomes a paragraph.

  Report Topic
  I.   Introduction
  II. Main Idea
       A. Detail
       B. Detail
  III. Main Idea
       A. Detail
       B. Detail
       C. Detail
  IV. Conclusion

- **FREEWRITING** is a strategy you can use to get your thoughts down on paper as quickly as possible. The purpose of freewriting is to get some words, phrases, and sentences on paper. Reading your freewriting will help you find the ideas you can write more about.

- **LISTING** is a strategy you can use to organize ideas or events in their order of importance.

  Why I Need to Go to College
  1. It will help me get a good job.
  2. I will find out about different careers.
  3. I will learn about important ideas.
  4. I will get a chance to learn about computers.

WRITING PROCESS CHECKLISTS

Writing is a process. Like other processes, writing involves certain steps. Prewriting is just the first step in the writing process. The steps that make up the complete writing process are:

1. Prewriting
2. Writing a First Draft
3. Revising
4. Proofreading
5. Publishing

Asking yourself some key questions as you go through the steps of the writing process can help you write clearly. Use the checklists that follow as you complete the steps in *your* writing process. If you refer to the checklists often enough, you will soon be able to think of the questions yourself.

Prewrite
Checklist for Prewriting

1. What type of writing am I going to do? What are some of the characteristics of this type of writing?
2. What is my purpose for writing? Who will be my audience?
3. How can I use a prewriting strategy to think of a topic and formulate ideas?
4. What other materials can I use as sources of ideas? How can I use these ideas?
5. How can I best state the main idea of my topic to make the purpose of my writing known? What details can I offer to support my main idea?

Write a First Draft
Checklist for Writing a First Draft

1. Do I have my audience in mind as I write? Have I selected words that my audience will understand?
2. Does my topic sentence state the main idea of my paragraph in a general way? In what way will it capture the reader's interest?
3. How does each supporting sentence relate to the topic sentence? Does it expand on the main idea?
4. How does my closing sentence set a boundary for the paragraph by restating the topic sentence, stating an opinion, or providing a final thought?

Revise
Checklist for Revising

1. Have I shared my writing with someone who could comment on it? How can I incorporate that person's suggestions?
2. Could I revise my topic sentence to state the main idea more precisely? Do my detail sentences support the main idea?
3. How may I rearrange sentences for maximum clarity and effectiveness? Would it improve my sentences to break up, combine, or expand them?
4. Are there any descriptive words I would like to add to make my writing more vivid and colorful? What transition words have I used to show the relationship of ideas?
5. How can I rephrase my closing sentence for greater effect? Does my paragraph reflect my purpose and audience?

Proofread

Checklist for Proofreading

1. What errors in spelling can I find and correct by checking the dictionary?
2. What adjustments should I make in grammar and punctuation? Have I capitalized all necessary words? Does each subject agreee with its verb? Are subject and object pronouns correct?
3. Have I indented my paragraph?
4. Is my handwriting neat and easy to read?

Publish

Suggestions for Sharing

How shall I share my writing with my audience? Which of the following ideas is most appropriate?

- Publish a class book, magazine, or newspaper
- Create a bulletin board display
- Read aloud to an audience
- Perform a skit or other type of demonstration
- Illustrate as a poster
- Record as part of an oral history

PROOFREADING MARKS		
Mark	**Meaning**	**Example**
¶	indent	¶The beach is lovely in summer. The sand is warm and the water cool.
∧	add this	love I to dig in the sand.
(Sp)	spelling	My mother enjoys the ocean breze. (Sp) [breeze]
⬭	move this	The lifeguard for sharks watches.
ℐ	take this out	Where is my suntan oil lotion?
≡	capital letter	after swimming I feel hungry.
/	lower-case letter	I wish the Summer would never end.

THESAURUS

A **thesaurus** is a reference tool that can be very useful in your writing. It provides synonyms for many common words. Synonyms are words that mean almost the same thing.

The thesaurus can help you choose more interesting words and more exact words. For example, you may write this sentence:

Perry **ran** to the nearest fire alarm.

Ran is not a very interesting word, and it says very little about Perry. If you looked up the word *run* in the thesaurus, you will find these words: *dash, race, scurry, sprint.* Using one of these words would make your sentence more interesting and more exact.

USING THE THESAURUS

The words in a thesaurus are listed in alphabetical order. You look up words in a thesaurus as you do in a dictionary. If the word is listed in the thesaurus, you will find an entry.

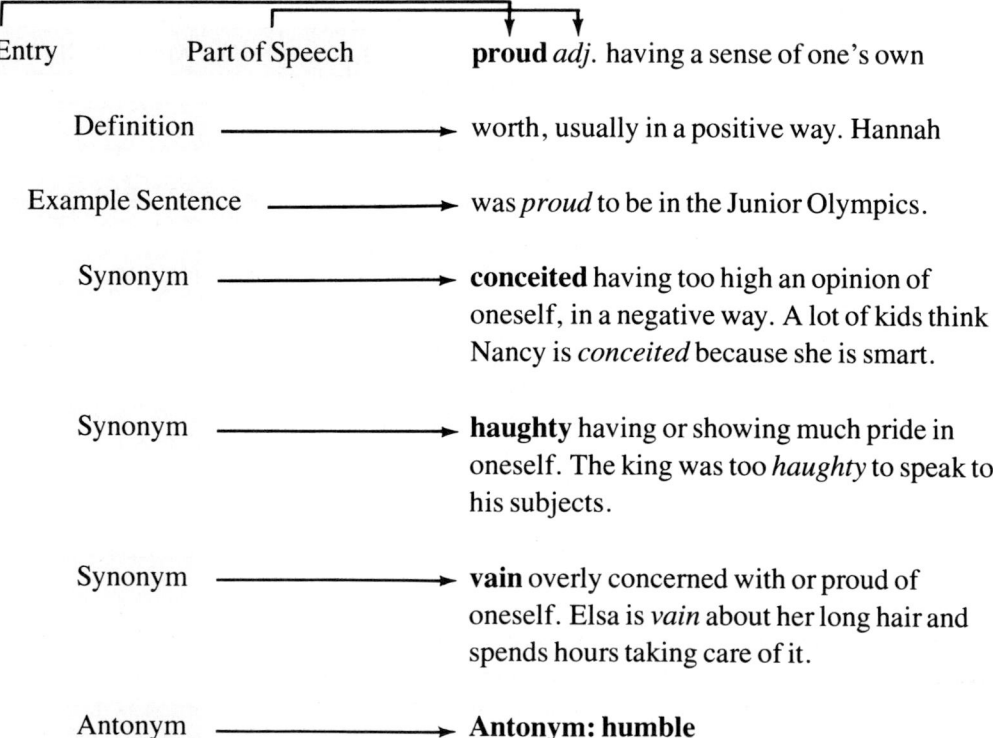

Main Entry — Part of Speech — **proud** *adj.* having a sense of one's own

Definition → worth, usually in a positive way. Hannah

Example Sentence → was *proud* to be in the Junior Olympics.

Synonym → **conceited** having too high an opinion of oneself, in a negative way. A lot of kids think Nancy is *conceited* because she is smart.

Synonym → **haughty** having or showing much pride in oneself. The king was too *haughty* to speak to his subjects.

Synonym → **vain** overly concerned with or proud of oneself. Elsa is *vain* about her long hair and spends hours taking care of it.

Antonym → **Antonym: humble**

A

allow *See* **let**.

angry *adj.* feeling or showing anger. Cal's lie made Fay *angry*.
> **enraged** filled with rage; angry beyond control. The *enraged* animal attacked the hunters.
> **furious** extremely angry. Dad was *furious* that we got home so late.
> **incensed** filled with anger. Leah was *incensed* by Barb's remark.
> **resentful** feeling bitter or indignant. Is he *resentful* about coming in second in the contest?

awful *adj.* causing fear, dread, or awe. Ana gave an *awful* shriek.
> **dreadful** causing great fear or unhappiness. I had a *dreadful* nightmare.
> **frightful** causing fright. He wore a *frightful* mask.
> **horrible** arousing feelings of horror. What a *horrible* sight!
> **terrible** causing terror or awe. Other dinosaurs ran from the *terrible* tyrannosaurus.

B

beautiful *adj.* full of beauty; having qualities that are pleasing. Look at that *beautiful* magnolia tree.
> **attractive** appealing or pleasing, but not in an exceptional way. Tom is an *attractive* man.
> **gorgeous** extremely beautiful or richly colored. She wore a *gorgeous* red silk dress.
> **lovely** beautiful in a soothing or peaceful way. He played a *lovely* tune.
> **pretty** pleasing or attractive, often said of something small or dainty. Canaries are *pretty* birds.
> **Other synonyms: stunning, striking, appealing**
> **Antonyms: ugly, hideous, unattractive**

big *adj.* of great size. This is a *big* room
> **enormous** much greater than the usual size. I have an *enormous* amount of homework tonight.
> **gigantic** like a giant in size. The 747 is a *gigantic* airplane.
> **huge** extremely big. The explosion tore a *huge* hole in the wall.
> **large** of great size; big. German shepherds are usually *large* dogs.
> **Other synonyms: monstrous, massive, titanic**
> **Antonyms:** *See* **little**.

bright *adj.* filled with light; shining. The room is *bright*.
> **brilliant** shining or sparkling with light. She wore *brilliant* diamond earrings.
> **glistening** shining or sparkling with reflected light. Moonlight danced across the *glistening* water.
> **luminous** giving off light. *Luminous* fireflies lit the sky.
> **shiny** reflecting brightly. The bear had *shiny* eyes.
> **Antonyms: dark, dull**

C

cheap *adj.* low in price; inferior in quality or value. She bought a *cheap* dress for the party.
> **gaudy** tastelessly bright or ornate. He wore a *gaudy* red tie.
> **inexpensive** low in price. Fruit is *inexpensive* in the summer.
> **Antonym: expensive**

cold *adj.* having a low temperature; lacking warmth or heat. It's *cold* in this room.
> **chilly** uncomfortably cool. It was a gray and *chilly* November day.
> **frigid** extremely cold. A *frigid* wind was blowing from the north.
> **icy** very cold. He enjoyed a tall, *icy* glass of milk with his lunch.
> **Antonyms:** *See* **hot**.

cry *v.* to shed tears. The little boy *cried* when he fell.
> **bawl** to cry loudly. As soon as she woke up, the baby began to *bawl*.
> **sob** to cry with short gasps. Lynn *sobbed* for hours when Button died.
> **weep** to show grief, joy, or other strong emotions by crying. Safe at last, Tony *wept* with relief.
> **whine** to make a high-pitched, mournful or irritating cry of pain or distress. The new puppy *whined* all night.
> **Antonyms:** *See* **laugh**.

do/happy

D

do *v.* carry out. We will *do* our skit right after the piano solo.
achieve to reach an intended result. He *achieved* most of his goals for the year.
contrive to bring about, especially with difficulty or planning. I'm sure I can *contrive* to be there.
perform to carry out to completion. Ms. Lewis asked her aide to *perform* a difficult task.

dry *adj.* not wet; free of moisture. Our swimsuits were *dry* in no time.
arid dry as a result of having little rainfall. Parts of the southwestern United States are quite *arid*.
desiccated completely dried up. After a month without rain, the garden was *desiccated*.
parched dried out by heat. A cool drink relieved her *parched* throat.
Antonym: wet

F

fast *adj.* moving or done with speed. He is a *fast* reader.
quick done in a very short time. Mrs. Mann made a *quick* phone call.
rapid with great speed. We had to make some *rapid* decisions.

speedy characterized by rapid motion. We started late, but a *speedy* taxi got us there on time.
swift moving with great speed. Be careful of the *swift* current.
Antonym: slow

funny *adj.* causing laughter. All the party guests wore *funny* hats.
amusing causing smiles or enjoyment. The old pictures were *amusing* to look at.
comical causing laughter through actions. The frolicking dog was a *comical* sight.
humorous funny or joking. Aunt Lou told us a *humorous* story.
hilarious very funny; causing noisy laughter. That Marx Brothers movie has some *hilarious* scenes.

G

get *v.* to go for and return with. Will you *get* me a drink of water?
acquire to come into possession of. The collector *acquired* many famous paintings.
earn to gain through effort. I need to *earn* some money.
obtain to get as one's own, often with some difficulty. You must *obtain* your parent's permission.
procure to purchase or get hold of through effort. He *procured* the supplies.

give *v.* to turn over possession or control of; to make a present of. Please *give* this note to Amelia.
confer to give as an honor. The club *conferred* an award on Jaime.
contribute to give or supply in common with others. Will you *contribute* to the Animal Fund?
grant to give in response to a request. The queen said, "I will *grant* your wish."
present to give in a formal way, usually something of value. The author *presented* her book to the library.
Antonyms: *See* **take**.

H

happy *adj.* having or showing pleasure. "I am *happy* to be here," the speaker began.
gay full of joy and fun. Colored lights made the yard look *gay*.
glad feeling or expressing joy or pleasure. Henry was *glad* to be able to help Mrs. Corelli.
joyful very happy; filled with joy. "It's a girl!" was the *joyful* announcement.
merry happy and cheerful. We always have a *merry* time together.
pleased satisfied or content. Are you *pleased* with your new haircut?
Other synonyms: delighted, contented, ecstatic
Antonyms: *See* **sad**.

hot *adj.* having a high temperature; having much heat. The sun is *hot*.
fiery as hot as fire; burning. Mickey had a *fiery* sunburn.
scalding hot enough to burn, often said of liquids. Don't touch that *scalding* water!
scorching intensely hot, enough to cause burning or drying. The *scorching* sun killed the grass.
tepid slightly warm; lukewarm. We bathed the wound in *tepid* water.
torrid extremely hot, often said of weather. Light-colored clothes are the best for *torrid* regions.
Other synonyms: blistering, blazing
Antonyms: *See* **cold.**

I

interesting *adj.* arousing or holding interest or attention. History is an *interesting* subject.
captivating capturing and holding attention by beauty or excellence. Dolley Madison is said to have been a *captivating* woman.
fascinating causing and holding interest through a special quality or charm. Kerry has had some *fascinating* adventures.
inspiring having a rousing effect; arousing interest. Nate gave an *inspiring* speech.
Antonyms: dull, boring

L

large *See* **big.**

laugh *v.* to make the sounds and facial movements that show amusement. Dale makes me *laugh*.
chortle to chuckle gleefully. "I fooled you!" Andy *chortled*.
chuckle to laugh softly, especially to oneself. Something she was reading made Liz *chuckle*.
giggle to laugh in a silly, high-pitched, or nervous way. Rudy *giggled* at the silly songs.
guffaw to laugh loudly. Theo *guffawed* when I told him.
snicker to laugh slyly, in a mocking way. William *snickered* at the newspaper ad.
Antonyms: *See* **cry.**

let *v.* to give permission to. Will your parents *let* you sleep over?
allow to grant permission to or for, often in relation to rules. No one is *allowed* to visit him.
permit to allow (a person) to do something. Please *permit* me to ask a question.
Antonyms: deny, refuse, forbid

look *v.* to see with one's eyes. Let me *look* at the map with you.
glance to look quickly. Jim *glanced* at the headlines.

peer to look closely. I *peered* into the fog but saw nothing.
regard to look at attentively. The children *regarded* the new boy with curiosity.
stare to look at for a long time. People *stared* at the woman's strange outfit.
Other synonyms: behold, discern, inspect, scan; *see also* **see.**

M

mean *adj.* lacking kindness or understanding. I warned Ike not to be *mean* to that dog.
cruel willing to cause pain or suffering to others. The boy was often *cruel* to smaller children.
nasty resulting from hate. Linda said some *nasty* things about me.
selfish concerned only about oneself. Howie was *selfish* and kept the best piece for himself.
spiteful filled with ill feelings toward others. Why is Sharon being so *spiteful* today?
Antonyms: *See* **nice.**

N

neat *adj.* orderly. She is good about keeping her bedroom clean and *neat*.

new/quiet

meticulous extremely careful about details. Andy is *meticulous* about his appearance.

tidy neat and clean. Outside the cottage door the man had planted a *tidy* little garden.

well-groomed carefully dressed and groomed. Anna manages to look *well-groomed* even in blue jeans.

Antonyms: messy, untidy, sloppy

new *adj.* having just come into being, use, or possession. What color is your family's *new* car?

fresh new or seeming new and unaffected by time or use. Get me a *fresh* head of lettuce.

innovative new in approach or method. The company's *innovative* techniques made production easier.

modern having to do with the present time; up-to-date. *Modern* homes depend on electricity.

novel new and unusual. Henry is full of *novel* ideas.

recent referring to a time just before the present. The Chous are *recent* immigrants to this country.

Antonyms: See old.

nice *adj.* agreeable or pleasing. The new teacher is *nice*.

agreeable to one's liking; pleasant. He was quite *agreeable*.

gentle mild and kindly in manner. The veterinarian was a *gentle* woman.

kind gentle and friendly; good-hearted. An old woman with a *kindly* face answered the door.

pleasant agreeable and friendly. Ellie had a *pleasant* chat with her best friend.

sweet having or marked by agreeably mild, kind, or pleasing qualities. Their son is a *sweet* little boy.

Antonyms: *See* mean.

O

old *adj.* having lived or existed for a long time. The *old* house was badly in need of repairs.

aged having grown old. Her *aged* grandmother is still very active.

ancient of great age; very old; of times long past. The car is *ancient*, but it runs well.

hoary white or gray with age. Great-uncle Joe ran his fingers through his *hoary* beard.

Other synonyms: archaic, elder, venerable, senior, antique

Antonyms: young; *see also* **new**.

P

proud *adj.* having a sense of one's own worth, usually in a positive way. Hannah was *proud* to be in the Junior Olympics.

conceited having too high an opinion of oneself, in a negative way. A lot of kids think Nancy is *conceited* because she is smart.

haughty having or showing much pride in oneself. The king was too *haughty* to speak with his subjects.

vain overly concerned with or proud of oneself. Elsa is *vain* about her long hair and spends hours taking care of it.

Antonym: humble

Q

quiet *adj.* with little or no noise. We heard the cat's *quiet* footsteps in the hall.

calm free of excitement. When giving first aid, try to keep the victim *calm*.

peaceful calm; undisturbed. The house seemed very *peaceful* after the children left for school.

serene not disturbed or troubled. Just seeing her *serene* face was somehow reassuring.

silent completely quiet; without noise. The courtroom was *silent* as we waited for the verdict.

still without sound or movement; silent. Be *still* so I can hear the news.

tranquil of a calm or peaceful nature. We spent a *tranquil* morning at the lake.

Antonyms: loud, noisy

R

rich *adj.* having great wealth. The Duchess is a *rich* woman.

affluent wealthy; prosperous. These expensive stores are geared toward *affluent* customers.

opulent showing wealth. Their *opulent* mansion even had silver doorknobs.

wealthy having many material goods or riches. Mr. Harris's successful invention made him a *wealthy* man.

Antonym: poor

rude *adj.* not polite; ill-mannered. The salesperson was *rude* to me.

discourteous without good manners. It was *discourteous* of her to start eating without the rest of us.

impolite not showing good manners. Dan was so *impolite* that Mrs. Fisk never invited him back.

insolent offensively rude or arrogant. "Why do you want to know?" was Clyde's *insolent* reply.

uncouth lacking social polish or culture. Margie was surprised by her friend's *uncouth* behavior.

Antonyms: polite, courteous

S

sad *adj.* feeling or showing unhappiness or sorrow. Beth was *sad* because her friend was sick.

depressed feeling low. The bad news made Michelle feel *depressed*.

downcast low in spirits. Why does Bob look so *downcast*?

miserable extremely unhappy. The boy was *miserable* about missing the school play.

wretched very unhappy; deeply distressed. Ellen felt *wretched* when she realized how mean she had been.

Antonyms: *See* happy.

scared *adj.* afraid; alarmed. He is *scared* to move to a new city.

afraid feeling fear, often in a continuing way or for a long time. Many people are *afraid* of snakes.

fearful filled with fear. Cruel treatment made the dog *fearful*.

frightened scared, often suddenly or for a short time. The *frightened* deer ran back into the woods.

terrified extremely scared; filled with terror. Lucy is *terrified* of thunderstorms.

Other synonyms: petrified, aghast, awestricken

see *v.* to receive information, impressions, etc. through use of the eyes. Did you *see* the parade?

observe to watch and notice. The police are trained to *observe* details.

perceive to become aware of through sight or other senses. Do you *perceive* anything unusual?

view to see or look at, usually for some purpose. Tourists climb the tower to *view* the landscape. *See also* **look.**

shy *adj.* uncomfortable in the presence of others. We saw a *shy* little face peeking out at us.

bashful easily embarrassed. Ben is *bashful* and turns red when the teacher calls on him.

demure quiet and modest, sometimes in an artificial way. Ann acts *demure* whenever boys are around.

retiring avoiding society or publicity. The poet became more *retiring* as he got older.

timid showing a lack of courage; easily frightened. The *timid* boy spoke in a tiny voice.

Antonym: bold

strange *adj.* differing from the usual or the ordinary. Do you hear something *strange*?

bizarre strikingly out of the ordinary; startlingly odd. Some of the costumes were quite *bizarre*.

odd not expected or appropriate. What an *odd* thing to say!

peculiar strange or odd, but in an interesting or curious way. Listen to this *peculiar* story.

weird strange or odd in a frightening or mysterious way. *Weird* noises were coming from one of the carnival tents; *see also* **unusual.**

take/want

T

take *v.* to bring into one's hands or possession. Please *take* some of these delicious apples.
grab to take roughly or suddenly. Children must learn not to *grab*.
seize to take suddenly and by force. The police officer *seized* the robber's gun.
snatch to take suddenly and quickly, often in secret. A man tried to *snatch* Myra's purse.
Antonyms: *See* **give**.

thin *adj.* not fat. She is not fat, but she is not *thin* either.
lean with little or no fat, but often strong. Being *lean* helps a greyhound run fast.
skinny very thin, in a way that suggests poor health. How can Saul eat so much and stay so *skinny*?
slim thin, in a good or healthy way. People who want to be *slim* need a healthful diet.
Antonyms: fat, plump, chubby

U

unusual *adj.* not usual, common, or ordinary. We've had *unusual* weather for this time of year.
exceptional much above average in quality or ability. Jesse is an *exceptional* student.

extraordinary very unusual; beyond the ordinary. No one should miss this *extraordinary* event.
rare seldom happening, seen, or found. Tornadoes are *rare* in the Northeast.
uncommon not happening often. It is *uncommon* to have such a big crowd.
unique having no equal or match; one of a kind. Many of the museum's specimens are *unique*.
Other synonyms: abnormal, queer, singular, irregular; *see also* **strange**.
Antonyms: usual, common

upset *adj.* feeling uneasy; distressed. Walt gets *upset* whenever he loses a chess game.
anxious uneasy or fearful of what may happen. Are you *anxious* about tomorrow's test?
concerned troubled or worried. The teacher became *concerned* when Vera began to fail in her work.
disturbed in an unsettled state of mind. Maria was *disturbed* by the news about her aunt.
nervous emotionally tense or restless; apprehensive or fearful. Carl was *nervous* about his upcoming interview.
worried uneasy or troubled about something. I was late, and my parents were quite *worried*.
Other synonyms: agitated, distraught

W

walk *v.* to move or travel on foot at a normal, comfortable speed. Harry and Lynn *walk* to school.
amble to walk at a relaxed, leisurely pace. Jerry *ambled* across the lawn.
march to walk with regular steps. The kindergartners were learning to *march* to music.
stride to walk with long steps, usually with purpose. The principal *strode* down the hall.
stroll to walk in a relaxed or leisurely manner. The couple *strolled* through the museum.
strut to walk in a vain or very proud way. We knew Stan had won by the way he *strutted* into the room.
Other synonyms: ramble, saunter, hike, parade, tread, step, pace

want *v.* to have a desire or wish for. Lauren *wanted* a new bicycle.
crave to want badly. I *crave* a good, crunchy apple.
desire to have a strong wish for. The reporter *desired* an interview.
wish to have a longing for. We *wish* we could go, too.
yearn to feel a strong and deep desire. The sailors *yearned* for the sight of land.

SPELLING HELPS

In your writing, it is very important to spell every word correctly. Otherwise, the meaning of what you write may not be clear. Follow the steps below to help improve your spelling.

1. Learn some basic spelling rules.
2. Learn to spell some commonly misspelled words.
3. Learn to spell words by syllable.
4. Check your work carefully when you have finished writing.
5. Whenever you have a question about how a word should be spelled, check the spelling in your dictionary.

VOWEL SOUNDS

Sometimes the way you pronounce a word can help you spell the word correctly.

Words with *ie* and *ei*. Spell the word with *ie* when the word has the long *e* sound except after *c*. Examples: **believe, ceiling, deceit, perceive, relief, shield.**

Spell the word with *ei* when the word does not have the long *e* vowel sound, especially if the word has the long *a* sound. Examples: **eighty, neigh, sleigh, weight.** There are some exceptions to this rule: **either, friend, seize, weird.**

PLURAL NOUNS

Sometimes when you make a noun plural, the spelling of the word changes. Here are some rules to help you spell these words correctly.

Adding *es*. If the word ends in *ch, s, sh, x,* or *z*, add *es*.

wrench/wrenches	**suffix/suffixes**
genius/geniuses	**buzz/buzzes**

Changing *f* to *v*. For most words ending in *f* or *fe*, change the *f* to *v* when adding *s* or *es*.

sheaf/sheaves	**life/lives**	**self/selves**

There are some exceptions to this rule, such as **roof/roofs, chief/chiefs.**

Words ending in *o*. For most words that end in *o* following a vowel, add *s* to form the plural.

studio + s = studios   cameo + s = cameos

For most words that end in *o* following a consonant, add *es*.

zero + es = zeroes   potato + es = potatoes
halo + es = haloes   echo + es = echoes

For words from the Italian language that refer to music, add *s*.

piano + s = pianos   solo + s = solos

Irregular nouns. Some words become plural in irregular ways.

ox/oxen   child/children   mouse/mice
tooth/teeth   goose/geese

Some words stay the same when singular or plural, as in: **sheep, deer, series.**

Compound nouns. To form the plural of a compound made up of a noun and modifiers, usually joined by hyphens, make the noun plural.

attorneys general   brothers-in-law   presidents-elect

The plural forms of some compound nouns are irregular.

ten-year-olds   drive-ins

INFLECTIONAL ENDINGS

With many kinds of words, if you add an ending such as *es, ed, ing, er,* or *est,* the spelling of the word may change. Here are some rules.

Changing *y* to *i*. If the word ends in a consonant and *y*, change the *y* to *i* before any ending that does not begin with *i*.

tally + es = tallies   hurry + ed = hurried
skinny + est = skinniest   bury + ed = buried

However, for most words that end in a vowel and *y,* keep the *y* when adding an ending. Example: **overjoy + ed = overjoyed.**

Doubling the final consonant. In most cases, if a one-syllable word ends in one vowel and one consonant, double the consonant when adding an ending that begins with a vowel.

skip + ed = skipped   grim + er = grimmer
chop + ing = chopping   thin + est = thinnest

For most two-syllable words ending in one vowel and one consonant, double the consonant only if the accent is on the second syllable:

prefer + ed = preferred   **compel + ing = compelling**

Silent *e*. If the word ends in a silent *e,* drop the *e* when adding an ending that begins with a vowel.

sure + er = surer   **strive + ing = striving**
lame + est = lamest   **graze + ed = grazed**

PREFIXES AND SUFFIXES

When a prefix is added to a word, the spelling of the word stays the same.

bi + weekly = biweekly   **sub + marine = submarine**
fore + warn = forewarn   **im + possible = impossible**

When a suffix is added to a word, the spelling of the word may change. If the word ends in a silent *e,* drop the *e* when adding a suffix that begins with a vowel.

reptile + ian = reptilian   **future + ist = futurist**

However, for most words ending in silent *e,* keep the *e* when adding a suffix that begins with a consonant.

shame + less = shameless **side + ward = sideward**
prince + ly = princely   **state + hood = statehood**

WORDS OFTEN CONFUSED

There are many pairs of words that sound alike, or similar, but are spelled differently and have different meanings. Knowing what these words mean will help you choose—and spell—the correct word when you use it in your writing. Here are some examples. If you do not know what these words mean, look them up in the dictionary.

affect/effect	complement/compliment	council/counsel
accept/except	stationary/stationery	weather/whether
capital/capitol	principal/principle	cellar/seller

GRAMMAR, MECHANICS, USAGE HANDBOOK

   This handbook is a reference you can use when you revise your writing or when you want to check a rule of grammar, capitalization, punctuation, or usage. The **Grammar** section describes sentences and parts of speech. The **Mechanics** section gives rules for capitalization and punctuation. The **Usage** section gives rules that will help you use language effectively and write correctly.

GRAMMAR
SENTENCES
   A **sentence** is a group of words that expresses a complete thought. A **sentence fragment** is a group of words that does not express a complete thought.

Sentence:	Jet pilots train in small airplanes.
Sentence Fragments:	The airplanes at smaller airports.
	Flew quickly away.

   There are four kinds of sentences. A **declarative** sentence makes a statement and ends with a period. An **interrogative** sentence has the form of a question and ends with a question mark. An **exclamatory** sentence expresses strong feeling and ends with an exclamation mark. An **imperative** sentence gives a command or makes a request and ends with a period.

Declarative:	Leah went to the museum.
Interrogative:	Did she see any interesting paintings?
Exclamatory:	What a beautiful painting!
Imperative:	Tell me all about it.

   Every sentence has a subject and a predicate. The **complete subject** names whom or what the sentence is about. The **simple subject** is the main word or group of words in the complete subject. The **complete predicate** tells what action the subject does. The **simple predicate** is the main word or group of words in the complete predicate.

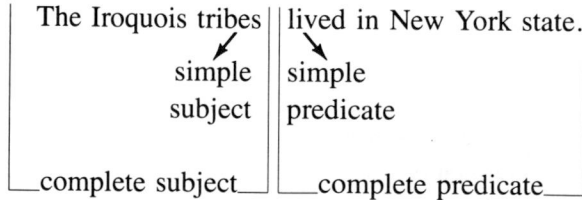

The Iroquois tribes | lived in New York state.
         simple | simple
         subject | predicate

complete subject | complete predicate

A **compound subject** has two or more simple subjects with the same predicate, joined by *and* or *or: Joe* and *Beth* play chess.

A **compound predicate** has two or more verbs with the same subject, joined by *and, but,* or *or:* People *stood* and *clapped* their hands.

A **simple sentence** has one subject part and one predicate part and can stand alone. When a simple sentence becomes part of another sentence, it is called an **independent clause. A compound sentence** has two or more independent clauses.

> **Simple Sentence:** Marco went to the stadium.
> **Compound Sentence:** Marco went to the stadium, and Julie went to the movie theater.

A **complex sentence** is a sentence that has an independent clause and a subordinate clause. A **subordinate clause** is a group of words with a subject and a predicate that cannot stand alone as a sentence.

> **Complex Sentences:** After we had dinner, we sat by the fire.
> Sam was frightened when the lights went out.

COMBINING SENTENCES

Avoid repeating words in short, choppy sentences by combining sentences. Sentences can be combined by joining the subjects, joining the predicates, or joining other words.

> **Combining Subjects:** Mary went skiing. Joel went skiing.
> *Mary and Joel went skiing.*
> **Combining Predicates:** Pierre went skating. Pierre went sledding.
> *Pierre went skating and sledding.*
> **Combining Other Words:** The woods were cold. The woods were covered with snow.
> *The woods were cold and covered with snow.*

RUN-ON SENTENCES

A run-on sentence is a sentence that contains too many complete thoughts. Run-on sentences should be divided into short, clear sentences.

> **Incorrect:** Mark took singing lessons he learned about breathing.
> **Correct:** Mark took singing lessons. He learned about breathing.

MECHANICS

RULES FOR CAPITALIZATION

1. Capitalize the first word of a sentence or a direct quotation.

The country of Canada extends across North America.

Duane said, "About 25 million people live in Canada."

2. Capitalize the first word in the salutation and in the closing of a letter.

Dear Sherry,   Yours truly,

3. Capitalize a person's name, a person's initials, and titles that appear before a person's name.

| John Cabot | S.D. Thompson | Dr. Turner |
| Captain Hudson | Mary C. Larson | Ms. Kelly |

Capitalize abbreviations of academic degrees that follow a person's name and the abbreviations *Jr.* and *Sr.*

W. F. Buckley, **Jr.**   Linda Tsang, **M.D.**   Henry Lake, **Ph.D.**

4. Capitalize words that show family relationships when used as titles or substitutes for a person's name, but not when they are preceded by a possessive noun or pronoun.

Aunt Beth   In 1987, Father got a new job.

his aunt, Tony's aunt   My father got a new job.

5. Capitalize the pronoun *I*.

Jody and **I** went to see Mr. Wilkins.

6. Capitalize all important words in the names of cities, states, countries, continents, bodies of water, and geographical features.

| Cheyenne, Wyoming | Mexico | Europe |
| Atlantic Ocean | Gulf of St. Lawrence | Hudson Bay |

7. Capitalize the names of sections of the country and the compass points when they refer to a specific part of the country.

New England   the Midwest   the East Coast

8. Capitalize the names of streets and highways, bridges, buildings, and monuments.

| Hyde Street | Hollywood Freeway | Route 17 |
| Empire State Building | Washington Monument | Bay Bridge |

9. Capitalize the names of celestial bodies, but not *sun* or *moon*. Capitalize *Earth* when preceded by *the*.

Mercury   North Star   Pluto

10. Capitalize the names of clubs, organizations, businesses, institutions, and political parties.

Girl Scouts   Franklin Middle School   Democrats
Capital Industries   the American Red Cross

11. Capitalize brand (or trade) names.

Wheaties   Downhome cookies

12. Capitalize the names of historical events, periods of time, and documents.

Mexican Revolution   **Bronze Age**   Constitution

13. Capitalize the names of days of the week, months of the year, and holidays. Do not capitalize the names of the seasons.

Monday   August   Thanksgiving **D**ay   winter

14. Capitalize all important words in the title of a book, play, short story, poem, essay, article, film, TV series, song, magazine, newspaper, and chapter of a book.

A Wrinkle in Time   **Star Trek**
Miami Herald   "Billie Jean"

15. Capitalize the names of ethnic groups, nationalities, languages, and proper adjectives formed from the names of ethnic groups and nationalities.

Mexican art   Italian food   Latin
Native American crafts   the French   Chinese

RULES FOR PUNCTUATION

End Punctuation

1. Use a period at the end of a declarative or imperative sentence, after an abbreviation, and after a person's initials.

Dr. Milton works at the I.J. Stone Hospital.

2. Use a question mark at the end of an interrogative sentence.

Where does Dr. Milton work?

3. Use an exclamation point (exclamation mark) at the end of an exclamatory sentence and after an interjection.

Wow! What a wonderful invention!

Commas

1. Use commas to separate three or more items in a series.

Ms. Bethune served as a teacher, adviser, and administrator.
She lived, studied, and worked in the South.

2. Use commas to separate two or more adjectives.

Marty found a smooth, glassy rock.

3. Use a comma to separate the name of the day from the date, the month and day from the year, and after the year.

Kathy was born on Monday, June 6, 1976.

I met her on August 12, 1987, at the shopping mall.

4. Use a comma to separate the name of a city and state and after the state. Do not use a comma between the state and ZIP code.

Our address is 27 Green Street, Ann Arbor, MI 48104.

We are going to Baton Rouge, Louisiana, in the spring.

5. Use a comma to set off *too* when used to mean *also*.

Kathy Sullivan is a famous astronaut, too.

6. Use a comma or a pair of commas to set off an abbreviated title or degree after a person's name.

The first American woman to travel in space was Sally Ride, Ph.D.

7. Use a comma after the salutation of a friendly letter and after the closing of a friendly or business letter.

Dear Tina,   Yours truly,   Best wishes,

8. Use a comma before *and, but,* or *or* to separate simple sentences in a compound sentence.

She was born in Ghana, but she lives in London.

9. Use a comma to show a pause after an introductory word, phrase, or clause.

Yes, he won the election.

For a number of years, she served as the director.

Drawing on her wide experience, she became a capable leader.

Because she was late for work, Phyllis ran out the door.

10. Use commas to set off a noun of direct address, an appositive if it is not essential to the meaning of a sentence, and words that interrupt the flow of thought in a sentence.

You should have studied the candidates, Derek.

Well, Ms. Jansen, did you finish your homework?

Jill Newsome, a friend of mine, was hired as the new editor.

Mayor Carnes, of course, will be re-elected.

11. Use a comma after a conjunctive adverb, such as *however, moreover, therefore, nevertheless,* and *furthermore.*

She was concerned; however, there was nothing she could do.

Semicolons

1. Use a semicolon to join the parts of a compound sentence when a coordinating conjunction is not used.

   Albert Einstein made many discoveries in science; his work changed scientific thought.

2. Use a semicolon before a conjunctive adverb, such as *however.*

   Einstein was born in Germany; however, he grew up in Switzerland.

Colons

1. Use a colon to separate the hour and the minute when you write the time of day.

   His train left Princeton at 10:15 A.M.

2. Use a colon after the salutation of a business letter.

   Dear Madam: Dear Ms. Santiago: Dear Sirs:

3. Use a colon to introduce a list of items at the end of a sentence.

   Mr. Braun ordered the following: paint, lacquer, brushes, and turpentine.

Quotation Marks

1. Use quotation marks before and after a direct quotation and with a divided quotation. Use a comma or commas to separate the quotation from the rest of the sentence.

   "Sojourner Truth was born a slave," said Garret.

   "She was the first black woman," he explained, "to speak out against slavery."

2. Place a period inside closing quotation marks. Place a question mark or exclamation point (exclamation mark) inside the quotation marks only when it is part of the quotation.

   Mrs. Yu said, "Sojourner Truth preached concern for others."

   "What a great woman she was!" Jan exclaimed.

3. Use quotation marks to enclose the title of a short story, essay, poem, song, magazine, or newspaper article, and chapter from a book.

   Short Story: "The Open Boat"   Song: "Yesterday"

Italics

Use italics (underlining) to set off the title of a book, play, film, TV series, magazine, or newspaper.

Book: *Charlotte's Web*   Magazine: *Cobblestone*

Apostrophes

1. Use an apostrophe + **s** to form the possessive of a singular noun or the possessive of a plural noun that does not end in **s**.

> the girl**'s** hat   the men**'s** club

2. Use an apostrophe to form the possessive of a plural noun that ends in **s**.

> the girls**'** hats   the cities**'** mayors

3. Use an apostrophe in a contraction to signal that a letter or letters have been omitted.

> it + is = **it's**   we + are = **we're**   did + not = **didn't**

USAGE

SUBJECT-VERB AGREEMENT

A subject and its verb must agree in number. A singular subject takes a singular form of the verb. A plural subject takes a plural form.

> A **mountain rises** sharply.   The **mountains rise** sharply.

When a prepositional phrase comes between the subject and the verb, be sure that the verb agrees with the subject.

> A **park** in the islands **contains** molten lava.
> The **parks** of Hawaii **contain** volcanoes.

In sentences beginning with *Here* or *There*, *Here* or *There* is never the subject. Look for the subject after the verb.

> There **is** a lush **forest** on the slopes.
> Here in the trees **live** many tropical **birds.**

An indefinite pronoun does not refer to a specific person, place, or thing. Some indefinite pronouns are singular, such as *anybody, anyone, everyone, much, neither, nobody,* and *something.* These pronouns take a singular verb.

> **Everyone wants** to go on the picnic.

Some indefinite pronouns are plural, such as *both, few, many,* and *several.* These pronouns take a plural verb.

> **Many** of the picnickers **want** sandwiches.

Still other indefinite pronouns may be either singular or plural. A word in a prepositional phrase usually shows whether these pronouns are singular or plural.

Most of the food **is** ready.
All of the sandwiches **are** made.

A compound subject joined by *and* or by *both . . . and* takes a plural verb.

Both the wildlife **and** the scenery attract visitors.

When a compound subject is joined by *or, nor, either . . . or,* or *neither . . . nor,* its verb agrees with the part of the subject closest to it.

An eagle **or a hawk soars** in the sky.
Neither bad weather **nor rough trails discourage** us.

SUBJECT AND OBJECT PRONOUNS

A subject pronoun can be used as the subject of a sentence or as a predicate noun. Subject pronouns include: **I, you, he, she, it, we, they.**

Subject:	**I** like canaries.
	She and **I** enjoy the birds' songs.
Predicate Noun:	The captain is **she.**
	The players are **they.**

Object pronouns are used as direct objects, indirect objects, and objects of prepositions. Object pronouns include: **me, you, him, her, it, us, them.**

Direct Object:	Marsha liked **them** very much.
Indirect Object:	My classmates gave **me** pats on the back.
Object of a Preposition:	The captain gave a speech to **them.**

Avoid mistakes in the use of pronouns in compound subjects and compound objects.

Correct:	**You and I** will feed the finches.
Incorrect:	**You and me** will feed the finches.
Correct:	She gave the presents to **you and me.**
Incorrect:	She gave the presents to **you and I.**

*R*eader's Resources

The dictionary is a helpful resource. If you want to find the meaning of a word, you would look in the dictionary. There are also many other kinds of resources that can help you find different kinds of information. You can find these resources in a library.

ALMANAC

An **almanac** is a single-volume reference book. A new edition is usually published every year. The almanac provides information on current events, and it gives facts, figures, and brief information on a great variety of subjects. It is a good place to look for a short, quick answer to a specific question or to find out about certain things that have happened in the last year. For example, if you wanted to know who won the World Series in 1987, you could find the answer in an almanac. What is the tallest building in the United States? Who was elected to the Senate from Nebraska in 1984? These are the kinds of questions you can use the almanac to answer.

Two of the best known almanacs are the *World Almanac and Book of Facts* and the *Information Please Almanac*.

To locate information in an almanac, you must use the index. To find the right pages, you must know what word or topic to look under. Think of the key word or words in the question you want to answer. For example, if you wanted to know the population of the capital city of Australia, you would look under *Australia*. There you would find subtopics, such as *Ambassadors*, *Area*, and *Cities (population)*.

In some cases, you may look up a topic and find a cross-reference. For example, if you wanted to know who won the Olympic gold medals in figure skating in 1984, you might look under *Figure skating*. There you would find the subtopic *Figure—Olympic records (1908–1988)*.

ATLAS

An **atlas** is a book of maps. The title of the atlas tells you what parts of the world are included in the maps. A **world atlas**, for example, has maps of all parts of the world. A **United States atlas** has maps of the United States. Most atlases offer a variety of information about places by including maps that show land and water forms, boundaries, roads, annual rainfall, etc. There are also specialized atlases with historical maps, religious maps, road maps, and so on.

To find information in an atlas, you use the index. It lists every place name that appears on a map and the page on which the map can be found. It also tells where to find each place on a specific map by indicating latitude and longitude or by giving the letter-number coordinates on the map.

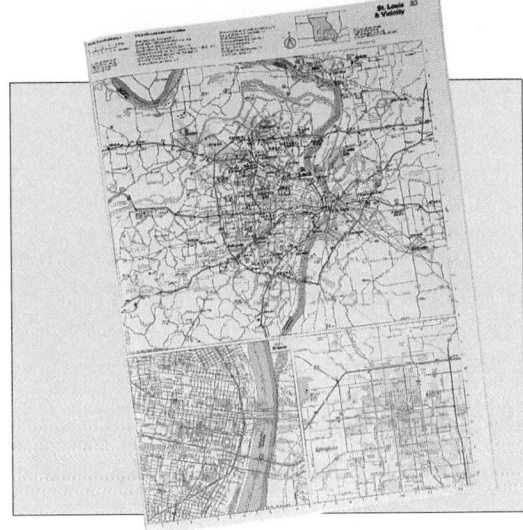

Atlases are most useful for answering questions about places that can be found on maps. For example, where is the Persian Gulf? How far is Beijing from Moscow? What major rivers flow through the United States?

ENCYCLOPEDIA

An **encyclopedia** is a book or set of books with articles on a large variety of subjects: people, places, events, ideas, and general topics. Many encyclopedias have a number of volumes and an index. The articles in the encyclopedia help you find information on a topic beginning with a specific letter of the alphabet.

When you want to find the answer to a question, you must look for the key word or words in the question. For example, if you wanted to find out which parts of North America were settled by the Apaches, you should look for information under *Apaches*.

In most encyclopedias, the last volume is an index of all the places where a specific topic is discussed. For example, you may find information on George Washington in the volume that covers the letter *W*. By using the index, you would discover that information on George Washington also appears in other articles in other volumes. For each topic, the index lists the volumes which contain information and the page numbers where the information in each volume can be found.

In addition, most encyclopedias publish a **yearbook** that gives information about things that have happened since the set of encyclopedias was printed. If you want information about an event that happened in 1990, for example, and your encyclopedia was published in 1988, you could probably find the information in the encyclopedia yearbook.

SPECIAL DICTIONARIES

The *Macmillan School Dictionary* is an abridged, or desk, dictionary. It includes the most commonly used words in the English language. But there are several other kinds of dictionaries, for different purposes. An **unabridged dictionary** includes almost all of the words in a language. A **biographical dictionary** is a list of famous persons. **Foreign language** dictionaries often translate words from one language to another.

There are also dictionaries of synonyms, slang, and rhyming words. And many libraries have dictionaries of music, science, mythology, computer terms, and other special subjects.

When you need specific information that you can't find in your desk dictionary, you must decide what kind of dictionary to use. For example, if you wanted to know what Englishmen of the Middle Ages used a *glaive* for, you could look in an unabridged dictionary. If you wanted to know who Washington Irving was and what he did, you could look in a biographical dictionary.

CARD CATALOG

When you need information that cannot be found in a reference book, such as a dictionary or encyclopedia, you can go to the library and find the information in other ways. One useful source is the **card catalog**, which contains information about the books in the library. The information is usually printed on small, separate cards arranged alphabetically in a cabinet. (Some libraries have a book form of the card catalog or a computer data base, but the information and how it is arranged are much the same.)

For every nonfiction book in the library, there are three cards: an **author card**, a **title card**, and a **subject card**. All three cards contain the same information arranged in different ways. The cards are filed in alphabetical order in the drawers of the cabinet. Here are examples of the three cards.

Author Card

```
539    Jackson, Annabel C.
Ja
       A Lot of Hot Air. Baltimore: Sky
       High Publishers, Inc., 1988.
       276 p.: il.

       Describes types of hot air balloons
       and how they work.
```

Title Card

```
       A Lot of Hot Air.

539    Jackson, Annabel C.
Ja
       A Lot of Hot Air. Baltimore: Sky
       High Publishers, Inc., 1988.
       276 p.: il.

       Describes types of hot air balloons
       and how they work.
```

Subject Card

```
       SPORTS—HOT AIR BALLOONING

539    Jackson, Annabel C.
Ja
       A Lot of Hot Air. Baltimore: Sky
       High Publishers, Inc., 1988.
       276 p.: il.

       Describes types of hot air balloons
       and how they work.
```

Each card gives the author (or editor), the title, the place and date of publication, and the name of the publisher. The card also has a **call number** in the upper left-hand corner. This number tells you where the book is located in the library. It consists of a Dewey Decimal classification number and the initial two letters of the author's last name. The call number on all three cards is the same.

If you know the author of a book, you can look for the author card. An author card lists the author's last name first. If you know the title of a book, you can look for the title card. This card lists the title first. If you are looking for books on a particular subject, you can look up the subject card. For example, if you want to find a book about the Civil War, you can look under *Civil War*. There you will find a card for every book in the library about the Civil War.

Many catalog cards also provide other information. A card may indicate the number of pages in the book and the use of illustrations (il.) or photographs. It may also include a brief description of the content of the book.

READERS' GUIDE TO PERIODICAL LITERATURE

The card catalog is quite helpful for finding books in the library. If you want to find magazine articles on a particular subject, however, you would use a different kind of resource. The most widely used guide of this kind is the **Readers' Guide to Periodical Literature**. It lists articles published in more than 150 magazines. Author and subject entries are listed together in a single alphabetical list. The listing gives the name of the magazine, the date, and the page numbers.

Some libraries provide this information on microfilm instead, and some libraries use a computerized system called *Magazine Index*. Both of these systems work in much the same way as the *Readers' Guide*.

If you wanted to find magazine articles about national parks in the United States, for example, you would look under *National Parks*. There you would find a listing of all the articles written about national parks in different magazines. The articles would be arranged alphabetically by title. The listing might look like this example.

National Parks
See also
Campgrounds
Fire ravages Yellowstone. J. Murray. il.
   The Far West 24:31–33   Ag 12 '88
Going to Yosemite. M. Perkins il
   California 10:12–15   Je 28 '88

This example lists two articles about national parks. Each entry gives the name of the article, the first initial and the last name of the author, and an indication that the article is illustrated. It also gives the name of the magazine in which the article appeared, the volume and page numbers, and the date of publication. The note *See also* means that other articles related to this subject are listed under other topics, such as "Campgrounds."

You might also be interested in finding articles written by a certain author, such as William F. Buckley, Jr. or Erma Bombeck. You could look under *Buckley, William F., Jr.* or *Bombeck, Erma* and find a listing of all the articles written by the author during a given year.

The *Readers' Guide to Periodical Literature* has a bound volume for every year. In addition, a small paperbound volume of the *Readers' Guide* is published every two weeks, every month, and every three months (quarterly). At the end of each year, all these "temporary" volumes are compiled in one bound volume for the whole year.

When you use the *Readers' Guide*, you may use it in one of two ways. You can look in each yearly volume under a certain topic, such as *Space Exploration*, and find listings of all the articles written about this topic. Or, if you want to find articles on a specific event, you would look in the volume covering the date of the event. For example, if you wanted to read articles about the first landing on the moon, you would look for the volume of the *Readers' Guide* that covers July, 1969.

If you wanted information about something that happened in the past year, you could look in the quarterly or monthly publications. For example, articles about an event that happened in February of this year would be listed in the quarterly volume for January-March.

MULTIMEDIA RESOURCES

Most libraries also have other materials which are not books or magazines. Some of these resources are described below. Check with your own library to see what kinds of nonprint materials may be available.

The **vertical file** is a collection of pamphlets, clippings, pictures, and other materials. It usually has current materials that will eventually be discarded. All materials in the vertical file are arranged alphabetically by subject, and the materials for each subject are kept in labeled folders in a special cabinet or in

marked boxes. The index for the vertical file tells what subjects you will find there.

Audiovisual materials are electronic media with sound and/or pictures. These usually include records, listening tapes, videotapes, filmstrips, and so on. The library usually has an index or listing of these materials.

Computers are available at some libraries, and the library often provides software programs for using the computer. The software might include video games, educational programs, and "how-to" materials for learning how to do something.

Many libraries also have **microfilm** and **microfiche** equipment. Both microfilm and microfiche are used to store reproductions of books, magazines, newspapers, indexes, and other kinds of materials. Microfilm, a film containing miniature photographs, works like a filmstrip. Microfiche also has miniature photographs of printed matter but is in sheet form, not film form. A sheet of microfiche contains rows of pages of printed matter. Both types of media require the use of a special machine for viewing.

Time Line of United States History

Many groups of American Indians had been living in North America for thousands of years before European explorers arrived.

1492 Christopher Columbus leaves Spain, seeking to find a sea route to the Far East, but he lands in San Salvador. Europeans honor him as the discoverer of America.

1513 Ponce de Léon explores and names Florida and claims it for Spain.

1565 Spaniards found St. Augustine on the Atlantic Coast in Florida. It is the oldest city in the U.S.

1585 The settlement by the English on Roanoke Island begins. This is their first attempt to begin colonizing North America, and it later proves unsuccessful.

1607 A group of about one hundred English colonists found Jamestown, the first permanent British settlement in North America.

1610 Santa Fe, in the area that would later become New Mexico, is founded by the Spanish.

1620 The Pilgrims found Plymouth Colony in Massachusetts. It is the second permanent British settlement in North America.

1625 New Amsterdam, later named New York, is founded by the Dutch.

1636 Harvard, the first North American college, is founded.

1647 Massachusetts establishes first public school system.

1673 Father Jacques Marquette and fur trader Louis Jolliet explore the upper Mississippi.

1718 San Antonio, in what would later become Texas, is founded by the Spanish.

1733 Georgia becomes the thirteenth colony. Each colony has its own governing body, but all are under the rule of Britain.

1750 The first Conestoga wagons carry pioneers and freight to new settlements in the West.

1754 French and Indian War begins.

1763 Britain defeats France in the French and Indian War and gains control of a large section of the country. Because the war has cost the British a great deal, they increase taxes on the colonists.

1773 Colonists dump cargo of tea on British ships into Boston Harbor (the Boston Tea Party) in protest to buying tea from British East India Company.

1775 The Revolutionary War between the colonists and Great Britain begins at Lexington and Concord.

1776 On July 4, the colonists adopt the Declaration of Independence and form the United States of America.

1781 The Americans defeat the British at Yorktown, Virginia, in the last major battle of the Revolutionary War.

1787 The Northwest Ordinance is passed, outlining provisions that allow a territory to become a state.

The Founding Fathers write the Constitution.

1789 George Washington is elected the nation's first President.

1791 The Bill of Rights goes into effect. It guarantees civil liberties to every citizen.

1793 Eli Whitney invents the cotton gin. His invention helps to make the U.S. the world's largest cotton producer.

1803 The Louisiana Purchase doubles the size of the U.S. The government buys the land from France for $15 million.

1811 Work begins on the Cumberland Road, which starts the national system of transportation in the U.S.

1812-1815 British interference in American shipping and the practice of forcing American seamen into service on British ships results in the War of 1812.

1820 The Missouri Compromise temporarily settles disagreements about slavery by defining areas in which slavery is forbidden.

1823 The Monroe Doctrine declares North and South America off limits to European interference.

1825 The Erie Canal opens, providing a water route from the Atlantic Ocean to the Great Lakes.

1837 Samuel F. B. Morse demonstrates the first successful telegraph in the U.S.

1846 The Mexican War begins.

1848 Victory in the Mexican War gives the U.S. new territory in the West, including what would later become California, Utah, Texas, New Mexico, Nevada, and parts of other states.

Lucretia Coffin Mott and Elizabeth Cady Stanton meet with a group of women at Seneca Falls, NY, to inaugurate the women's rights movement.

The discovery of gold in California starts a Gold Rush.

1857 The Dred Scott decision denies citizen rights to slaves and rules the Missouri Compromise unconstitutional.

1860-1861 Eleven Southern states leave the Union in disagreement with the North about slavery and states' rights to form the Confederate States of America.

1861 The Civil War begins when Confederate troops fire on Fort Sumter in Charleston, South Carolina.

1863 The Emancipation Proclamation is signed by President Lincoln. The proclamation declares freedom for all slaves in Confederate-held territory.

President Lincoln describes the meaning of the Civil War in his Gettysburg Address.

1865 The Civil War ends when General Lee surrenders to General Grant at Appomattox Court House, Virginia.

Louisiana Purchase

ELIZABETH STANTON

LUCRETIA MOTT

EQUALITY

1879
1914
1929
1939
1960s
1876
1908
1927
1945
1958

1865-1870 The Thirteenth Amendment to the Constitution outlaws slavery; the Fourteenth gives citizenship to former slaves; the Fifteenth opens voting to all men, regardless of race.

1867 The United States buys Alaska from Russia for a little more than $7 million.

1869 The first transcontinental railroad is completed when a golden spike joins the Central Pacific and Union Pacific railroads near Ogden, Utah.

1876 Alexander Graham Bell invents the telephone.

1879 Thomas Alva Edison invents the electric light bulb.

1886 The American Federation of Labor is formed. It calls for better wages and working conditions and for employers to talk and bargain with their workers.

1898 The U.S. defeats Spain in the Spanish-American War. Under the terms of the peace treaty, the U.S. receives Guam, Puerto Rico, and the Philippines.

1903 The Wright Brothers make the first successful airplane flight.

1908 Henry Ford brings out the Model T automobile and demonstrates the value of the assembly line.

1914 The first ship travels through the Panama Canal.

World War I begins.

1920 The Nineteenth Amendment to the Constitution gives women the right to vote.

1927 The first solo transatlantic flight flown by Charles Lindbergh helps to start the Air Age.

1929 A stock market crash brings financial ruin to thousands and starts the Great Depression.

1933 The New Deal program to end the Depression begins under President Franklin D. Roosevelt. Many government public work projects provide work and wages for the unemployed.

1939 World War II begins.

1941-1945 After the bombing of Pearl Harbor, the U.S. joins the Allies in World War II. War against Japan, Germany, and Italy is declared.

1945 The United Nations is founded.

1950-1953 The U.S. joins with other members of the United Nations in trying to help restore peace in Korea.

1958 The U.S. creates the National Aeronautics and Space Administration (NASA) in response to challenge posed by Soviets, who launch *Sputnik I* into outer space.

U.S. launches *Explorer I*.

1960s Civil rights organizations become active in demanding civil rights for African Americans, Hispanic Americans, American Indians, and other minorities.

1962 John Glenn is the first American to orbit the Earth.

1963

1965

1968

1969

1979

1976

1981

1986

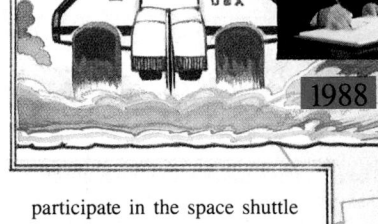

1987

1988

1990

1963 Martin Luther King, Jr., leads civil rights march in Washington, D.C.
President Kennedy is assassinated.

1965 U.S. sends troops to Vietnam to support South Vietnam in its effort to remain independent.

1968 Martin Luther King, Jr., is assassinated.

1969 Astronauts Neil A. Armstrong and Edwin Aldrin are the first people to walk on the moon.

1970 Clean Air Act is passed, and the Environmental Protection Agency is created.

1972 SALT I treaty, limiting nuclear arms, is signed.
President Nixon visits China, becoming the first American President to do so.
Break-in at Democratic National Committee headquarters is the first of a series of events leading to a loss of confidence in President Nixon.

1973 U.S. involvement in the Vietnam War ends.

1974 President Nixon resigns.

1976 The Bicentennial of the signing of the Declaration of Independence is celebrated.

1979 Full diplomatic relations are established between the U.S. and China. U.S. ends diplomatic relations with The Republic of China in Taiwan.
President Carter, Israeli Prime Minister Begin, and Egyptian President Sadat sign Camp David peace agreements.
President Carter and Soviet President Brezhnev sign SALT II treaty.
Iranians seize U.S. embassy in Tehran and take more than 60 Americans hostage.

1980 U.S. military mission to rescue hostages in Iran fails.

1981 American hostages in Iran are freed after 444 days of captivity.
Columbia, the first reusable space shuttle, is launched by the U.S.
Sandra O'Connor is the first woman associate justice of the U.S. Supreme Court.

1985 U.S.—Soviet Summit takes place in Geneva, Switzerland.

1986 U.S. space shuttle, *Challenger,* explodes, killing all onboard including Christa McAuliffe—the first teacher to participate in the space shuttle program.

1987 President Reagan and General Secretary Gorbachev meet for summit meeting in Washington, D.C., and sign treaty to reduce the size of U.S. and Soviet nuclear arsenals.

1988 U.S. space shuttle *Discovery* is launched thirty-two months after the *Challenger* tragedy.

1990 International Literacy Year.

*S*tates of the United States

ALABAMA

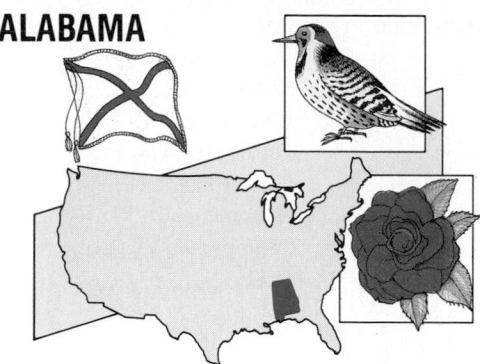

U.S. Postal Abbreviation	AL
Capital	Montgomery
Population	4,083,000
Area	51,609 (sq. mi.)
	133,667 (sq. km)
State Nicknames	Yellowhammer State; Heart of Dixie; Cotton State
State Flower	Camellia
State Bird	Yellowhammer
Year Admitted to Union	1819
Order of Admission	22

ALASKA

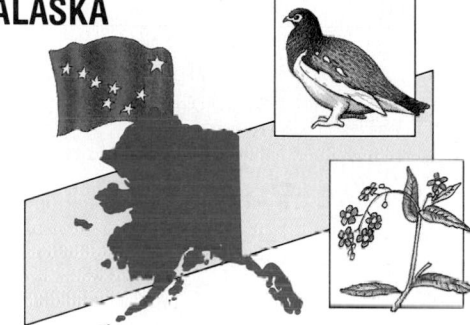

U.S. Postal Abbreviation	AK
Capital	Juneau
Population	525,000
Area	586,412 (sq. mi.)
	1,518,800 (sq. km)
State Nickname	The Last Frontier
State Flower	Forget-Me-Not
State Bird	Willow Ptarmigan
Year Admitted to Union	1959
Order of Admission	49

ARIZONA

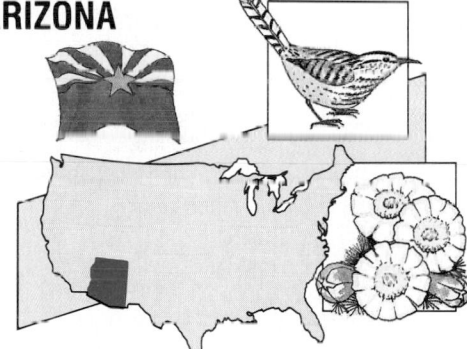

U.S. Postal Abbreviation	AZ
Capital	Phoenix
Population	3,386,000
Area	113,909 (sq. mi.)
	295,023 (sq. km)
State Nickname	Grand Canyon State
State Flower	Blossom of the Saguaro Cactus
State Bird	Cactus Wren
Year Admitted to Union	1912
Order of Admission	48

ARKANSAS

U.S. Postal Abbreviation	AR
Capital	Little Rock
Population	2,388,000
Area	53,104 (sq. mi.)
	137,539 (sq. km)
State Nickname	Land of Opportunity
State Flower	Apple Blossom
State Bird	Mockingbird
Year Admitted to Union	1836
Order of Admission	25

CALIFORNIA

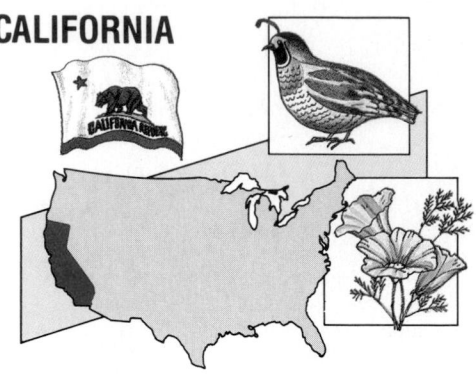

U.S. Postal Abbreviation	CA
Capital	Sacramento
Population	27,663,000
Area	158,706 (sq. mi.)
	411,013 (sq. km)
State Nickname	Golden State
State Flower	Golden Poppy
State Bird	California Valley Quail
Year Admitted to Union	1850
Order of Admission	31

COLORADO

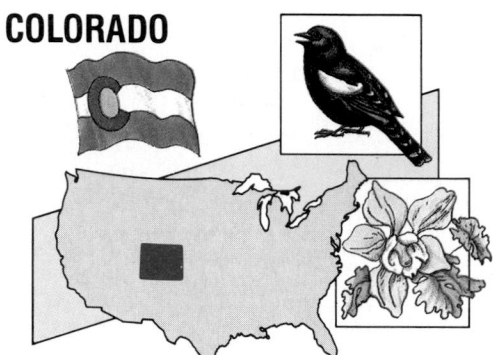

U.S. Postal Abbreviation	CO
Capital	Denver
Population	3,296,000
Area	104,247 (sq. mi.)
	269,998 (sq. km)
State Nickname	Centennial State
State Flower	Rocky Mountain Columbine
State Bird	Lark Bunting
Year Admitted to Union	1876
Order of Admission	38

CONNECTICUT

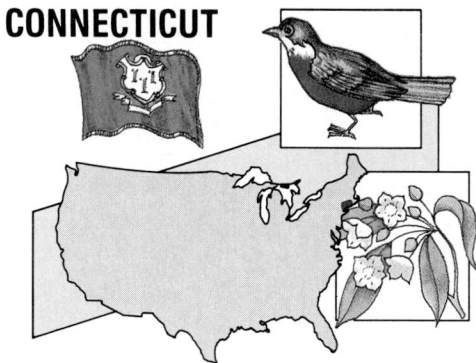

U.S. Postal Abbreviation	CT
Capital	Hartford
Population	3,211,000
Area	5,009 (sq. mi.)
	12,973 (sq. km)
State Nicknames	Constitution State; Nutmeg State
State Flower	Mountain Laurel
State Bird	Robin
Year Admitted to Union	1788
Order of Admission	5

DELAWARE

U.S. Postal Abbreviation	DE
Capital	Dover
Population	644,000
Area	2,057 (sq. mi.)
	5,328 (sq. km)
State Nicknames	First State; Diamond State
State Flower	Peach Blossom
State Bird	Blue Hen Chicken
Year Admitted to Union	1787
Order of Admission	1

FLORIDA

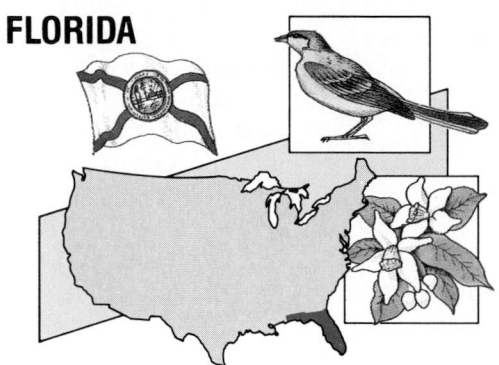

U.S. Postal Abbreviation	FL
Capital	Tallahassee
Population	12,023,000
Area	58,560 (sq. mi.)
	151,670 (sq. km)
State Nickname	Sunshine State
State Flower	Orange Blossom
State Bird	Mockingbird
Year Admitted to Union	1845
Order of Admission	27

GEORGIA

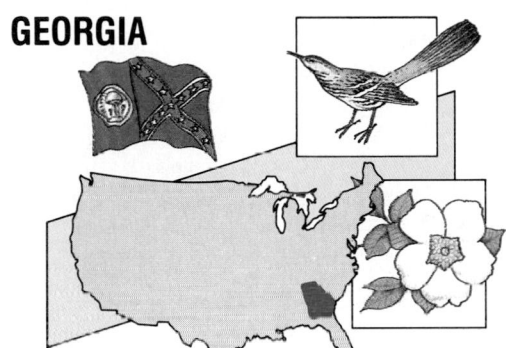

U.S. Postal Abbreviation	GA
Capital	Atlanta
Population	6,222,000
Area	58,876 (sq. mi.)
	152,488 (sq. km)
State Nicknames	Empire State of the South;
	Peach State; Goober State
State Flower	Cherokee Rose
State Bird	Brown Thrasher
Year Admitted to Union	1788
Order of Admission	4

HAWAII

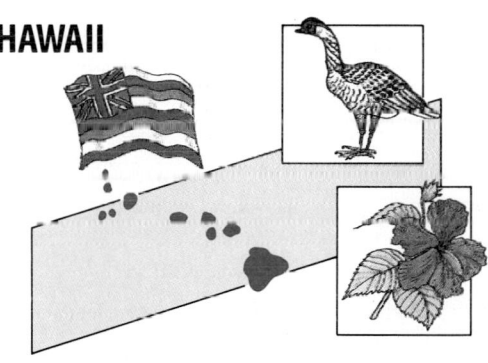

U.S. Postal Abbreviation	HI
Capital	Honolulu
Population	1,083,000
Area	6,450 (sq. mi.)
	16,705 (sq. km)
State Nickname	Aloha State
State Flower	Hibiscus
State Bird	Nene (Hawaiian Goose)
Year Admitted to Union	1959
Order of Admission	50

IDAHO

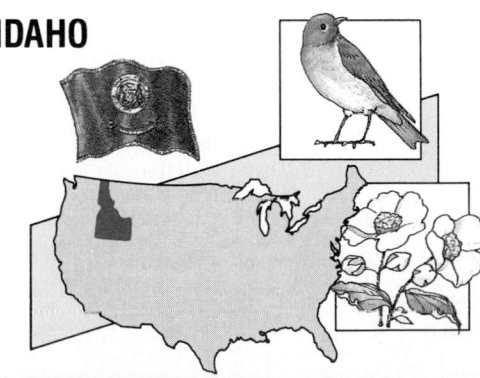

U.S. Postal Abbreviation	ID
Capital	Boise
Population	998,000
Area	83,557 (sq. mi.)
	216,412 (sq. km)
State Nickname	Gem State
State Flower	Mock Orange
State Bird	Mountain Bluebird
Year Admitted to Union	1890
Order of Admission	43

ILLINOIS

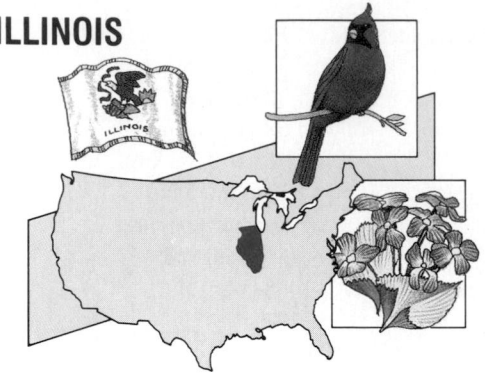

U.S. Postal Abbreviation	IL
Capital	Springfield
Population	11,582,000
Area	56,400 (sq. mi.)
	146,075 (sq. km)
State Nicknames	Prairie State; Land of Lincoln
State Flower	Violet
State Bird	Cardinal
Year Admitted to Union	1818
Order of Admission	21

INDIANA

U.S. Postal Abbreviation	IN
Capital	Indianapolis
Population	5,531,000
Area	36,291 (sq. mi.)
	93,993 (sq. km)
State Nickname	Hoosier State
State Flower	Peony
State Bird	Cardinal
Year Admitted to Union	1816
Order of Admission	19

IOWA

U.S. Postal Abbreviation	IA
Capital	Des Moines
Population	2,834,000
Area	56,290 (sq. mi.)
	145,790 (sq. km)
State Nickname	Hawkeye State
State Flower	Wild Rose
State Bird	Eastern Goldfinch
Year Admitted to Union	1846
Order of Admission	29

KANSAS

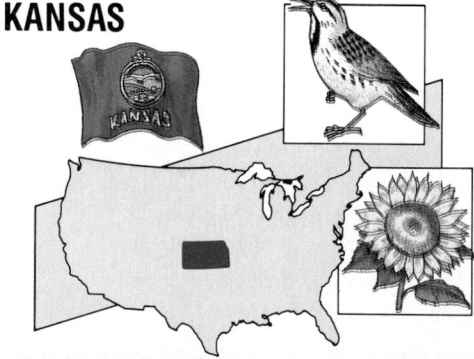

U.S. Postal Abbreviation	KS
Capital	Topeka
Population	2,476,000
Area	82,264 (sq. mi.)
	213,063 (sq. km)
State Nickname	Sunflower State
State Flower	Sunflower
State Bird	Western Meadowlark
Year Admitted to Union	1861
Order of Admission	34

KENTUCKY

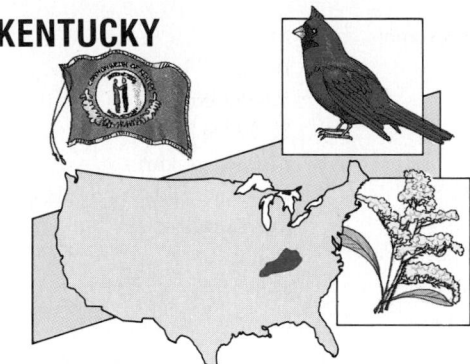

U.S. Postal Abbreviation	KY
Capital	Frankfort
Population	3,727,000
Area	40,409 (sq. mi.)
	104,623 (sq. km)
State Nickname	Bluegrass State
State Flower	Goldenrod
State Bird	Cardinal
Year Admitted to Union	1792
Order of Admission	15

LOUISIANA

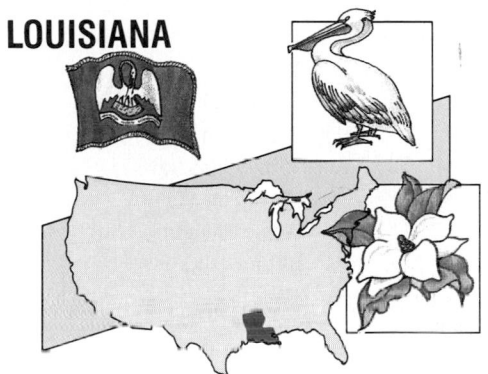

U.S. Postal Abbreviation	LA
Capital	Baton Rouge
Population	4,461,000
Area	48,523 (sq. mi.)
	125,674 (sq. km)
State Nickname	Pelican State
State Flower	Magnolia
State Bird	Brown Pelican
Year Admitted to Union	1812
Order of Admission	18

MAINE

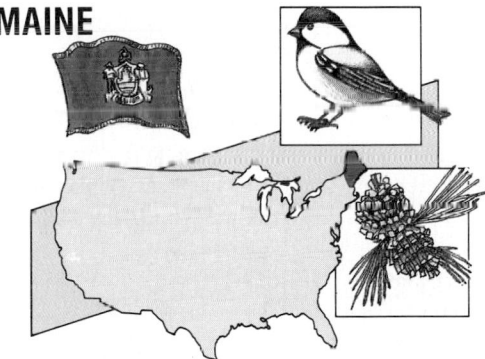

U.S. Postal Abbreviation	ME
Capital	Augusta
Population	1,187,000
Area	33,215 (sq. mi.)
	86,026 (sq. km)
State Nickname	Pine Tree State
State Flower	White Pine Cone and Tassel
State Bird	Chickadee
Year Admitted to Union	1820
Order of Admission	23

MARYLAND

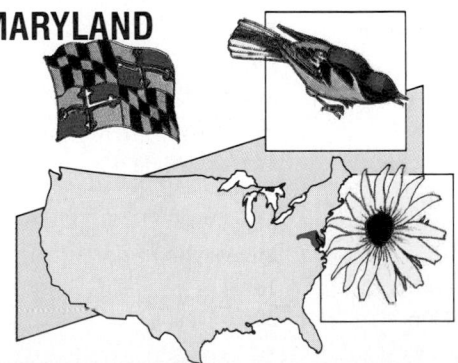

U.S. Postal Abbreviation	MD
Capital	Annapolis
Population	4,535,000
Area	10,577 (sq. mi.)
	27,394 (sq. km)
State Nicknames	Old Line State; Free State
State Flower	Black-Eyed Susan
State Bird	Baltimore Oriole
Year Admitted to Union	1788
Order of Admission	7

MASSACHUSETTS

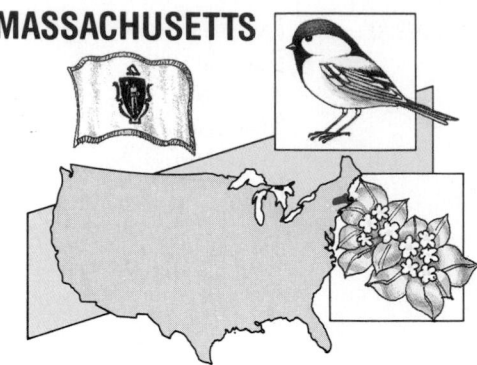

U.S. Postal Abbreviation	MA
Capital	Boston
Population	5,855,000
Area	8,257 (sq. mi.)
	21,386 (sq. km)
State Nicknames	Bay State; Old Colony State
State Flower	Mayflower
State Bird	Chickadee
Year Admitted to Union	1788
Order of Admission	6

MICHIGAN

U.S. Postal Abbreviation	MI
Capital	Lansing
Population	9,200,000
Area	58,216 (sq. mi.)
	150,779 (sq. km)
State Nickname	Wolverine State
State Flower	Apple Blossom
State Bird	Robin
Year Admitted to Union	1837
Order of Admission	26

MINNESOTA

U.S. Postal Abbreviation	MN
Capital	St. Paul
Population	4,246,000
Area	84,068 (sq. mi.)
	217,735 (sq. km)
State Nicknames	North Star State; Gopher State
State Flower	Pink and White Lady's Slipper
State Bird	Common Loon
Year Admitted to Union	1858
Order of Admission	32

MISSISSIPPI

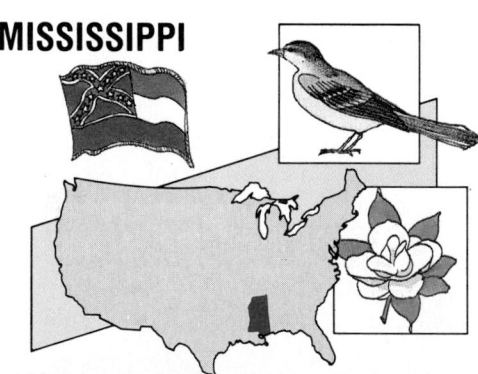

U.S. Postal Abbreviation	MS
Capital	Jackson
Population	2,625,000
Area	47,716 (sq. mi.)
	123,584 (sq. km)
State Nickname	Magnolia State
State Flower	Magnolia
State Bird	Mockingbird
Year Admitted to Union	1817
Order of Admission	20

MISSOURI

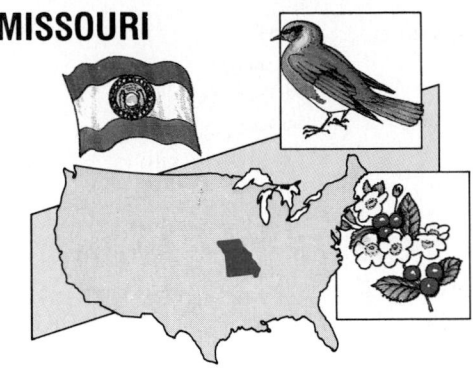

U.S. Postal Abbreviation	MO
Capital	Jefferson City
Population	5,103,000
Area	69,686 (sq. mi.)
	180,486 (sq. km)
State Nickname	Show Me State
State Flower	Hawthorn
State Bird	Bluebird
Year Admitted to Union	1821
Order of Admission	24

MONTANA

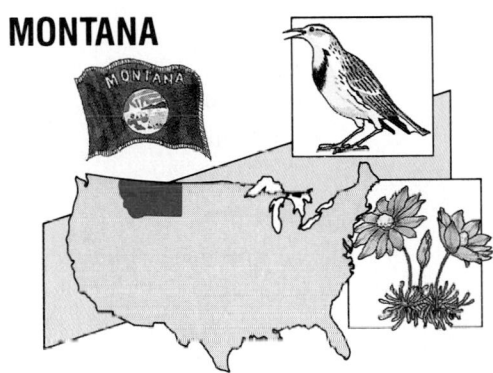

U.S. Postal Abbreviation	MT
Capital	Helena
Population	809,000
Area	147,138 (sq. mi.)
	381,086 (sq. km)
State Nickname	Treasure State
State Flower	Bitterroot
State Bird	Western Meadowlark
Year Admitted to Union	1889
Order of Admission	41

NEBRASKA

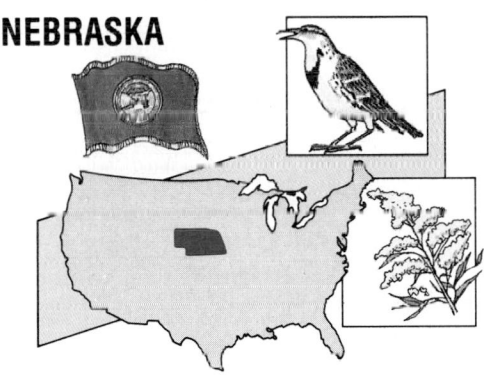

U.S. Postal Abbreviation	NE
Capital	Lincoln
Population	1,594,000
Area	77,227 (sq. mi.)
	200,017 (sq. km)
State Nickname	Cornhusker State
State Flower	Goldenrod
State Bird	Western Meadowlark
Year Admitted to Union	1867
Order of Admission	37

NEVADA

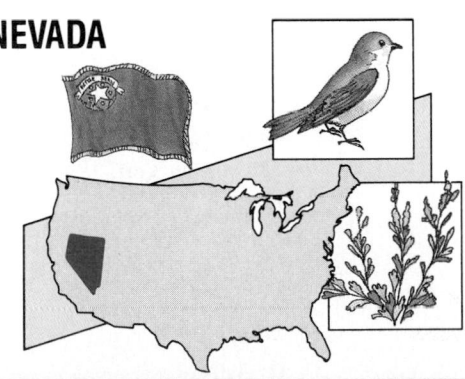

U.S. Postal Abbreviation	NV
Capital	Carson City
Population	1,007,000
Area	110,540 (sq. mi.)
	286,297 (sq. km)
State Nicknames	Silver State; Sagebrush State
State Flower	Sagebrush
State Bird	Mountain Bluebird
Year Admitted to Union	1864
Order of Admission	36

NEW HAMPSHIRE

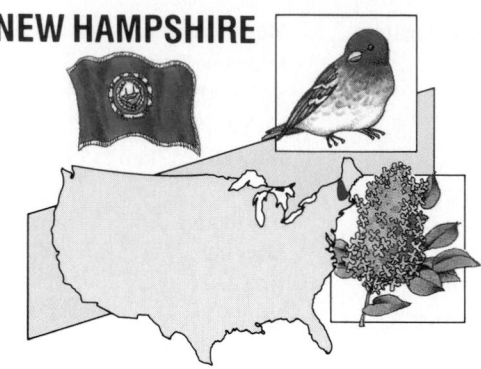

U.S. Postal Abbreviation	NH
Capital	Concord
Population	1,057,000
Area	9,304 (sq. mi.)
	24,097 (sq. km)
State Nickname	Granite State
State Flower	Purple Lilac
State Bird	Purple Finch
Year Admitted to Union	1788
Order of Admission	9

NEW JERSEY

U.S. Postal Abbreviation	NJ
Capital	Trenton
Population	7,672,000
Area	7,836 (sq. mi.)
	20,295 (sq. km)
State Nickname	Garden State
State Flower	Purple Violet
State Bird	Eastern Goldfinch
Year Admitted to Union	1787
Order of Admission	3

NEW MEXICO

U.S. Postal Abbreviation	NM
Capital	Sante Fe
Population	1,500,000
Area	121,666 (sq. mi.)
	315,113 (sq. km)
State Nickname	Land of Enchantment
State Flower	Yucca
State Bird	Roadrunner
Year Admitted to Union	1912
Order of Admission	47

NEW YORK

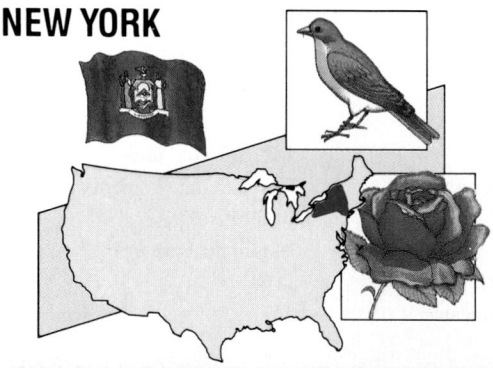

U.S. Postal Abbreviation	NY
Capital	Albany
Population	17,825,000
Area	49,576 (sq. mi.)
	128,401 (sq. km)
State Nickname	Empire State
State Flower	Rose
State Bird	Bluebird
Year Admitted to Union	1788
Order of Admission	11

NORTH CAROLINA

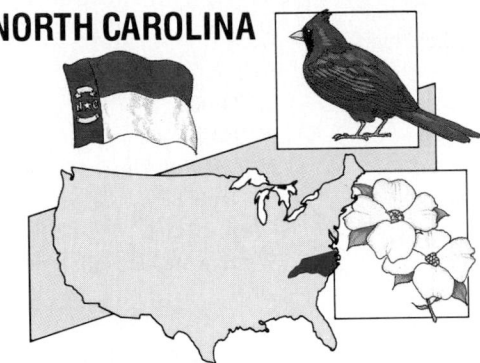

U.S. Postal Abbreviation	NC
Capital	Raleigh
Population	6,413,000
Area	52,586 (sq. mi.)
	136,197 (sq. km)
State Nickname	Tar Heel State
State Flower	Dogwood
State Bird	Cardinal
Year Admitted to Union	1789
Order of Admission	12

NORTH DAKOTA

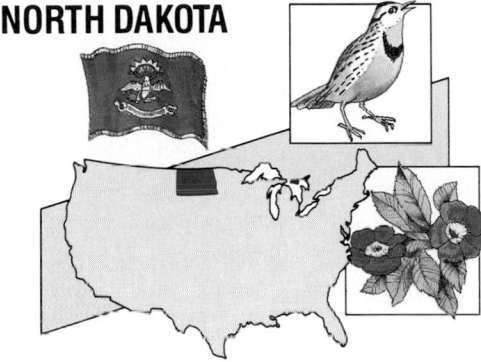

U.S. Postal Abbreviation	ND
Capital	Bismarck
Population	672,000
Area	70,665 (sq. mi.)
	183,022 (sq. km)
State Nicknames	Flickertail State; Sioux State
State Flower	Wild Prairie Rose
State Bird	Western Meadowlark
Year Admitted to Union	1889
Order of Admission	39

OHIO

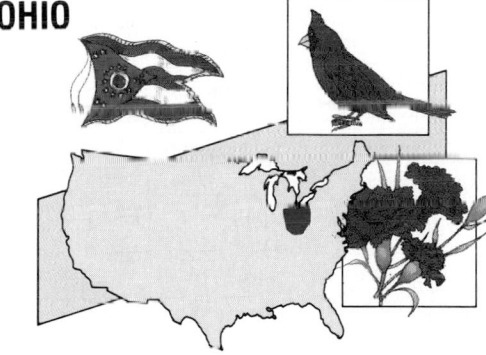

U.S. Postal Abbreviation	OH
Capital	Columbus
Population	10,784,000
Area	41,222 (sq. mi.)
	106,764 (sq. km)
State Nickname	Buckeye State
State Flower	Scarlet Carnation
State Bird	Cardinal
Year Admitted to Union	1803
Order of Admission	17

OKLAHOMA

U.S. Postal Abbreviation	OK
Capital	Oklahoma City
Population	3,272,000
Area	69,919 (sq. mi.)
	181,089 (sq. km)
State Nickname	Sooner State
State Flower	Mistletoe
State Bird	Scissor-Tailed Flycatcher
Year Admitted to Union	1907
Order of Admission	46

OREGON

U.S. Postal Abbreviation	OR
Capital	Salem
Population	2,724,000
Area	96,981 (sq. mi.)
	251,180 (sq. km)
State Nickname	Beaver State
State Flower	Oregon Grape
State Bird	Western Meadowlark
Year Admitted to Union	1859
Order of Admission	33

PENNSYLVANIA

U.S. Postal Abbreviation	PA
Capital	Harrisburg
Population	11,936,000
Area	45,333 (sq. mi.)
	117,412 (sq. km)
State Nickname	Keystone State
State Flower	Mountain Laurel
State Bird	Ruffed Grouse
Year Admitted to Union	1787
Order of Admission	2

RHODE ISLAND

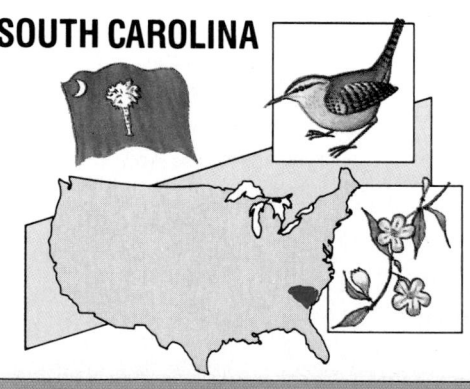

U.S. Postal Abbreviation	RI
Capital	Providence
Population	986,000
Area	1,214 (sq. mi.)
	3,144 (sq. km)
State Nickname	Ocean State
State Flower	Violet
State Bird	Rhode Island Red
Year Admitted to Union	1790
Order of Admission	13

SOUTH CAROLINA

U.S. Postal Abbreviation	SC
Capital	Columbia
Population	3,425,000
Area	31,055 (sq. mi.)
	80,432 (sq. km)
State Nickname	Palmetto State
State Flower	Yellow Jessamine
State Bird	Carolina Wren
Year Admitted to Union	1788
Order of Admission	8

SOUTH DAKOTA

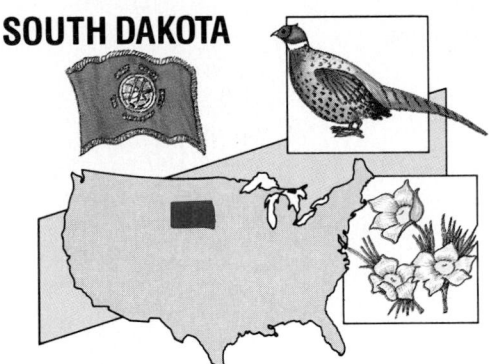

U.S. Postal Abbreviation	SD
Capital	Pierre
Population	709,000
Area	77,047 (sq. mi.)
	199,551 (sq. km)
State Nicknames	Sunshine State; Coyote State
State Flower	Pasqueflower
State Bird	Ring-Necked Pheasant
Year Admitted to Union	1889
Order of Admission	40

TENNESSEE

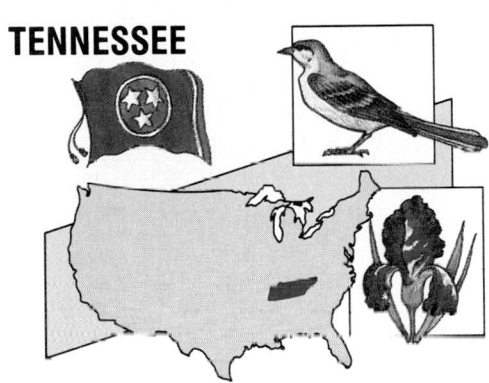

U.S. Postal Abbreviation	TN
Capital	Nashville
Population	4,855,000
Area	42,244 (sq. mi.)
	109,411 (sq. km)
State Nickname	Volunteer State
State Flower	Iris
State Bird	Mockingbird
Year Admitted to Union	1796
Order of Admission	16

TEXAS

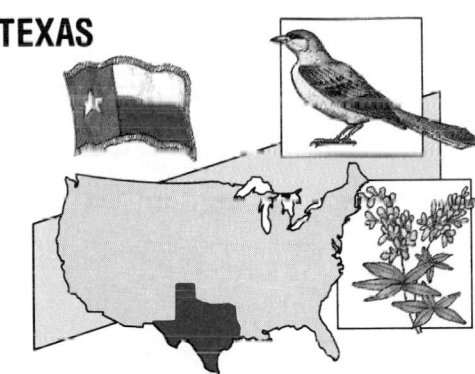

U.S. Postal Abbreviation	TX
Capital	Austin
Population	16,789,000
Area	267,338 (sq. mi.)
	692,402 (sq. km)
State Nickname	Lone Star State
State Flower	Bluebonnet
State Bird	Mockingbird
Year Admitted to Union	1845
Order of Admission	28

UTAH

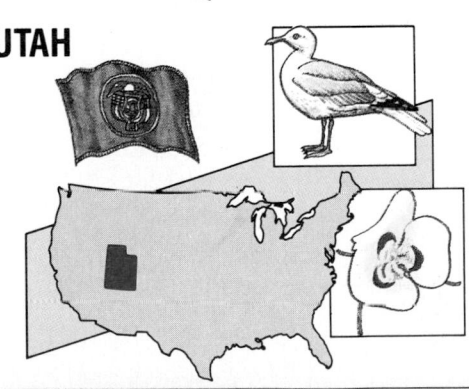

U.S. Postal Abbreviation	UT
Capital	Salt Lake City
Population	1,680,000
Area	84,916 (sq. mi.)
	219,931 (sq. km)
State Nickname	Beehive State
State Flower	Sego Lily
State Bird	Sea Gull
Year Admitted to Union	1896
Order of Admission	45

VERMONT

U.S. Postal Abbreviation	VT
Capital	Montpelier
Population	548,000
Area	9,609 (sq. mi.)
	24,887 (sq. km)
State Nickname	Green Mountain State
State Flower	Red Clover
State Bird	Hermit Thrush
Year Admitted to Union	1791
Order of Admission	14

VIRGINIA

U.S. Postal Abbreviation	VA
Capital	Richmond
Population	5,904,000
Area	40,817 (sq. mi.)
	105,716 (sq. km)
State Nickname	Old Dominion
State Flower	Dogwood
State Bird	Cardinal
Year Admitted to Union	1788
Order of Admission	10

WASHINGTON

U.S. Postal Abbreviation	WA
Capital	Olympia
Population	4,538,000
Area	68,192 (sq. mi.)
	176,616 (sq. km)
State Nickname	Evergreen State
State Flower	Rhododendron
State Bird	Willow Goldfinch
Year Admitted to Union	1889
Order of Admission	42

WEST VIRGINIA

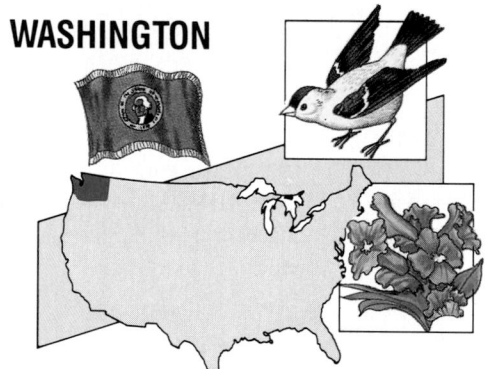

U.S. Postal Abbreviation	WV
Capital	Charleston
Population	1,897,000
Area	24,181 (sq. mi.)
	62,628 (sq. km)
State Nickname	Mountain State
State Flower	Rhododendron
State Bird	Cardinal
Year Admitted to Union	1863
Order of Admission	35

WISCONSIN

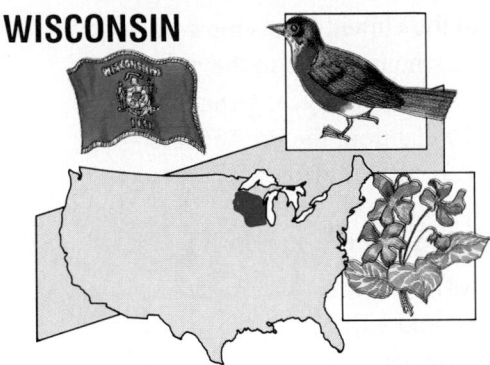

U.S. Postal Abbreviation	WI
Capital	Madison
Population	4,807,000
Area	56,154 (sq. mi.)
	145,438 (sq. km)
State Nickname	Badger State
State Flower	Wood Violet
State Bird	Robin
Year Admitted to Union	1848
Order of Admission	30

WYOMING

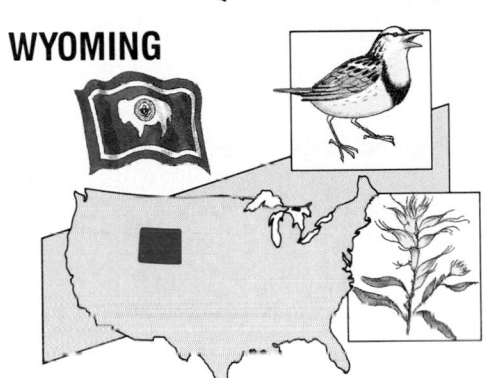

U.S. Postal Abbreviation	WY
Capital	Cheyenne
Population	490,000
Area	97,914 (sq. mi.)
	253,596 (sq. km)
State Nickname	Equality State
State Flower	Indian Paintbrush
State Bird	Meadowlark
Year Admitted to Union	1890
Order of Admission	44

*P*residents of the United States

According to the Constitution, the President of the United States must be a natural-born citizen of at least 35 years of age who has lived in the United States for 14 years. The President may serve two 4-year terms, but not more than two. On January 20 following the election, the President is inaugurated. On that day, the President takes this oath of office:

> "I do solemnly swear (or affirm) that I
> will faithfully execute the office of
> President of the United States, and will
> to the best of my ability, preserve,
> protect, and defend the Constitution of
> the United States."

The Presidents of the United States are listed below and on the pages that follow.

In Office: 1789–1797
Age When Inaugurated: 57
Political Party: Federalist
Native State: Virginia
Vice President: John Adams
First Lady: Martha Dandridge
　　　　　　 Washington

GEORGE WASHINGTON (1732–1799)

In Office: 1797–1801
Age When Inaugurated: 61
Political Party: Federalist
Native State: Massachusetts
Vice President: Thomas Jefferson
First Lady: Abigail Smith Adams

JOHN ADAMS (1735–1826)

In Office: 1801–1809
Age When Inaugurated: 57
Political Party: Democratic-Republican
Native State: Virginia
Vice Presidents: Aaron Burr (1801–1805)
　　George Clinton (1805–1809)
No First Lady in his Administration

THOMAS JEFFERSON (1743–1826)

In Office: 1809–1817
Age When Inaugurated: 57
Political Party: Democratic-Republican
Native State: Virginia
Vice Presidents:
　　George Clinton (1809–1812)
　　Elbridge Gerry (1813–1814)
First Lady: Dolley Payne Madison

JAMES MADISON (1751–1836)

In Office: 1817–1825
Age When Inaugurated: 58
Political Party: Democratic-Republican
Native State: Virginia
Vice President: Daniel D. Tompkins
First Lady: Elizabeth Kortright Monroe

JAMES MONROE (1758–1831)

In Office: 1825–1829
Age When Inaugurated: 57
Political Party: Democratic-Republican
Native State: Massachusetts
Vice President: John C. Calhoun
First Lady: Louisa Johnson Adams

JOHN QUINCY ADAMS (1767–1848)

In Office: 1829–1837
Age When Inaugurated: 61
Political Party: Democratic
Native State: South Carolina
Vice Presidents:
    John C. Calhoun (1829–1832)
    Martin Van Buren (1833–1837)
No First Lady in his Administration

ANDREW JACKSON (1767–1845)

In Office: 1837–1841
Age When Inaugurated: 54
Political Party: Democratic
Native State: New York
Vice President: Richard M. Johnson
No First Lady in his Administration

MARTIN VAN BUREN (1782–1862)

In Office: 1841 (one month)
Age When Inaugurated: 68
Political Party: Whig
Native State: Virginia
Vice President: John Tyler*
First Lady: Anna Symmes Harrison

WILLIAM HENRY HARRISON (1773–1841)

In Office: 1841–1845
Age When Inaugurated: 51
Political Party: Whig
Native State: Virginia
No Vice President in his Administration
First Ladies:
    Letitia Christian Tyler (1841–1842)
    Julia Gardiner Tyler (1844–1845)

JOHN TYLER (1790–1862)

In Office: 1845–1849
Age When Inaugurated: 49
Political Party: Democratic
Native State: North Carolina
Vice President: George M. Dallas
First Lady: Sarah Childress Polk

JAMES K. POLK (1795–1849)

In Office: 1849–1850
Age When Inaugurated: 64
Political Party: Whig
Native State: Virginia
Vice President: Millard Fillmore*
First Lady: Margaret Smith Taylor

ZACHARY TAYLOR (1784–1850)

*Succeeded from the vice-presidency on the death of the President.

In Office: 1850–1853
Age When Inaugurated: 50
Political Party: Whig
Native State: New York
No Vice President in his Administration
First Lady: Abigail Powers Fillmore

MILLARD FILLMORE (1800–1874)

In Office: 1853–1857
Age When Inaugurated: 48
Political Party: Democratic
Native State: New Hampshire
Vice President: William R. King (1853)
First Lady: Jane Appleton Pierce

FRANKLIN PIERCE (1804–1869)

In Office: 1857–1861
Age When Inaugurated: 65
Political Party: Democratic
Native State: Pennsylvania
Vice President: John C. Breckinridge
No First Lady in his Administration

JAMES BUCHANAN (1791–1868)

In Office: 1861–1865
Age When Inaugurated: 52
Political Party: Republican
Native State: Kentucky
Vice Presidents:
    Hannibal Hamlin (1861–1865)
    Andrew Johnson* (1865)
First Lady: Mary Todd Lincoln

ABRAHAM LINCOLN (1809–1865)

In Office: 1865–1869
Age When Inaugurated: 56
Political Party: Democratic
Native State: North Carolina
No Vice President in his Administration
First Lady: Eliza McCardle Johnson

ANDREW JOHNSON (1808–1875)

In Office: 1869–1877
Age When Inaugurated: 46
Political Party: Republican
Native State: Ohio
Vice Presidents:
    Schuyler Colfax (1869–1873)
    Henry Wilson (1873–1875)
First Lady: Julia Dent Grant

ULYSSES S. GRANT (1822–1885)

In Office: 1877–1881
Age When Inaugurated: 54
Political Party: Republican
Native State: Ohio
Vice President: William A. Wheeler
First Lady: Lucy Webb Hayes

RUTHERFORD B. HAYES (1822–1893)

In Office: 1881 (6 months)
Age When Inaugurated: 49
Political Party: Republican
Native State: Ohio
Vice President: Chester A. Arthur*
First Lady: Lucretia Rudolph Garfield

JAMES A. GARFIELD (1831–1881)

*Succeeded from the vice presidency on the death of the President.

In Office: 1881–1885
Age When Inaugurated: 50
Political Party: Republican
Native State: Vermont
No Vice President in his
    Administration
No First Lady in his Administration

CHESTER A. ARTHUR (1829–1886)

In Office: 1885–1889
Age When Inaugurated: 47
Political Party: Democratic
Native State: New Jersey
Vice President:
    Thomas A. Hendricks (1885)
First Lady: Frances Folsom Cleveland

• GROVER CLEVELAND (1837–1908)

In Office: 1889–1893
Age When Inaugurated: 55
Political Party: Republican
Native State: Ohio
Vice President: Levi P. Morton
First Lady: Caroline Scott Harrison

BENJAMIN HARRISON (1833–1901)

In Office: 1893–1897
Age When Inaugurated: 56
Political Party: Democratic
Native State: New Jersey
Vice President:
    Adlai E. Stevenson (1893–1897)
First Lady: Frances Folsom Cleveland

GROVER CLEVELAND (1837–1908)

In Office: 1897–1901
Age When Inaugurated: 54
Political Party: Republican
Native State: Ohio
Vice Presidents:
    Garret A. Hobart (1897–1899)
    Theodore Roosevelt* (1901)
First Lady: Ida Saxton McKinley

WILLIAM McKINLEY (1843–1901)

In Office: 1901–1909
Age When Inaugurated: 42
Political Party: Republican
Native State: New York
Vice President: Charles W. Fairbanks
    (1905–1909)
First Lady: Edith Carow Roosevelt

THEODORE ROOSEVELT (1858–1919)

In Office: 1909–1913
Age When Inaugurated: 51
Political Party: Republican
Native State: Ohio
Vice President: James S. Sherman
    (1909–1912)
First Lady: Helen Herron Taft

WILLIAM HOWARD TAFT (1857–1930)

In Office: 1913–1921
Age When Inaugurated: 56
Political Party: Democratic
Native State: Virginia
Vice President: Thomas R. Marshall
First Ladies:
    Ellen Louise Wilson (1913–1914)
    Edith Bolling Wilson (1915–1921)

WOODROW WILSON (1856–1924)

•Cleveland was elected for a second term after Benjamin Harrison.

*Succeeded from the vice presidency on the death of the President.

In Office: 1921–1923
Age When Inaugurated: 56
Political Party: Republican
Native State: Ohio
Vice President: Calvin Coolidge*
First Lady: Florence Kling Harding

WARREN G. HARDING (1865–1923)

In Office: 1923–1929
Age When Inaugurated: 51
Political Party: Republican
Native State: Vermont
Vice President: Charles G. Dawes
    (1925–1929)
First Lady: Grace Goodhue Coolidge

CALVIN COOLIDGE (1872–1933)

In Office: 1929–1933
Age When Inaugurated: 54
Political Party: Republican
Native State: Iowa
Vice President: Charles Curtis
First Lady: Lou Henry Hoover

HERBERT HOOVER (1874–1964)

In Office: 1933–1945
Age When Inaugurated: 51
Political Party: Democratic
Native State: New York
Vice Presidents: John N. Garner (1933–1941)
    Henry A. Wallace (1941–1945)
    Harry S. Truman* (1945)
First Lady: Anna Eleanor Roosevelt

FRANKLIN DELANO ROOSEVELT (1882–1945)

In Office: 1945–1953
Age When Inaugurated: 60
Political Party: Democratic
Native State: Missouri
Vice President: Alben W. Barkley
    (1949–1953)
First Lady: Elizabeth (Bess) W. Truman

HARRY S. TRUMAN (1884–1972)

In Office: 1953–1961
Age When Inaugurated: 62
Political Party: Republican
Native State: Texas
Vice President: Richard M. Nixon
First Lady: Marie (Mamie) Doud
    Eisenhower

DWIGHT D. EISENHOWER (1890–1969)

In Office: 1961–1963
Age When Inaugurated: 43
Political Party: Democratic
Native State: Massachusetts
Vice President: Lyndon B. Johnson*
First Lady: Jacqueline Bouvier Kennedy

JOHN F. KENNEDY (1917–1963)

In Office: 1963–1969
Age When Inaugurated: 55
Political Party: Democratic
Native State: Texas
Vice President: Hubert H. Humphrey
First Lady: Claudia (Lady Bird) Taylor
    Johnson

LYNDON BAINES JOHNSON (1908–1973)

*Succeeded from the vice presidency on the death of the President.

In Office: 1969–1974
Age When Inaugurated: 56
Political Party: Republican
Native State: California
Vice Presidents:
  Spiro T. Agnew (1969–1973)
  Gerald R. Ford** (1973–1974)
First Lady: Patricia (Pat) Ryan Nixon

RICHARD M. NIXON (1913–)

In Office: 1974–1977
Age When Inaugurated: 61
Political Party: Republican
Native State: Nebraska
Vice President: Nelson A. Rockefeller
First Lady: Elizabeth (Betty) B. Ford

GERALD R. FORD (1913–)

In Office: 1977–1981
Age When Inaugurated: 52
Political Party: Democratic
Native State: Georgia
Vice President: Walter F. Mondale
First Lady: Rosalynn Smith Carter

JAMES EARL CARTER (1924–)

In Office: 1981–1989
Age When Inaugurated: 69
Political Party: Republican
Native State: Illinois
Vice President: George Bush
First Lady: Nancy Davis Reagan

RONALD W. REAGAN (1911–)

In Office: 1989–
Age When Inaugurated: 64
Political Party: Republican
Native State: Massachusetts
Vice President: James
     Danforth Quayle
First Lady: Barbara Pierce Bush

GEORGE BUSH (1924–)

**Succeeded from the vice presidency on the resignation of the President.

PACIFIC OCEAN

CANADA

120°W

110°W

100°W

Seattle
WASHINGTON
★Olympia
Spokane

River

Great Falls

Grand Forks

NORTH DAKOTA

Portland
Columbia
★Salem

Helena ★

MONTANA

Bismarck ★
Fargo

•Eugene

IDAHO

OREGON

★Boise

Billings

Pierre ★

Snake   River

SOUTH DAKOTA

40°N

Pocatello

WYOMING

Sioux Falls

NEVADA

Great Salt Lake

Ogden

Salt Lake City

Casper

NEBRASKA

Reno
★Carson City

Provo

Cheyenne ★

Platte   River

Lincoln ★

San Francisco
•Oakland
San Jose

Sacramento

UTAH

Denver
COLORADO

KANSAS

Colorado Springs
Pueblo

Arkansas R.

CALIFORNIA

Las Vegas

Colorado   River

Santa Fe

Oklahoma City ★

Los Angeles
Long Beach

ARIZONA

Albuquerque

OKLAHOMA

San Diego

Phoenix

NEW MEXICO

30°N

Tucson

Dallas

120°W

110°W

El Paso

TEXAS

Kauai
Oahu Honolulu
Molokai
HAWAII Maui
PACIFIC OCEAN
20°N
160°W
Hilo
Hawaii

0   100 Miles
0   100 Kilometers

ARCTIC OCEAN
SOVIET UNION
170°W   150°W
70°N
ALASKA
Nome
Yukon   River
Arctic Circle
Fairbanks
Anchorage   CANADA
60°N
Juneau

San Antonio

Austin

Rio Grande

MEXICO

50°N

Gulf of Alaska

170°E

PACIFIC OCEAN

170°W

150°W

130°W

100°W

0   250   500 Miles
0   250   500   750 Kilometers

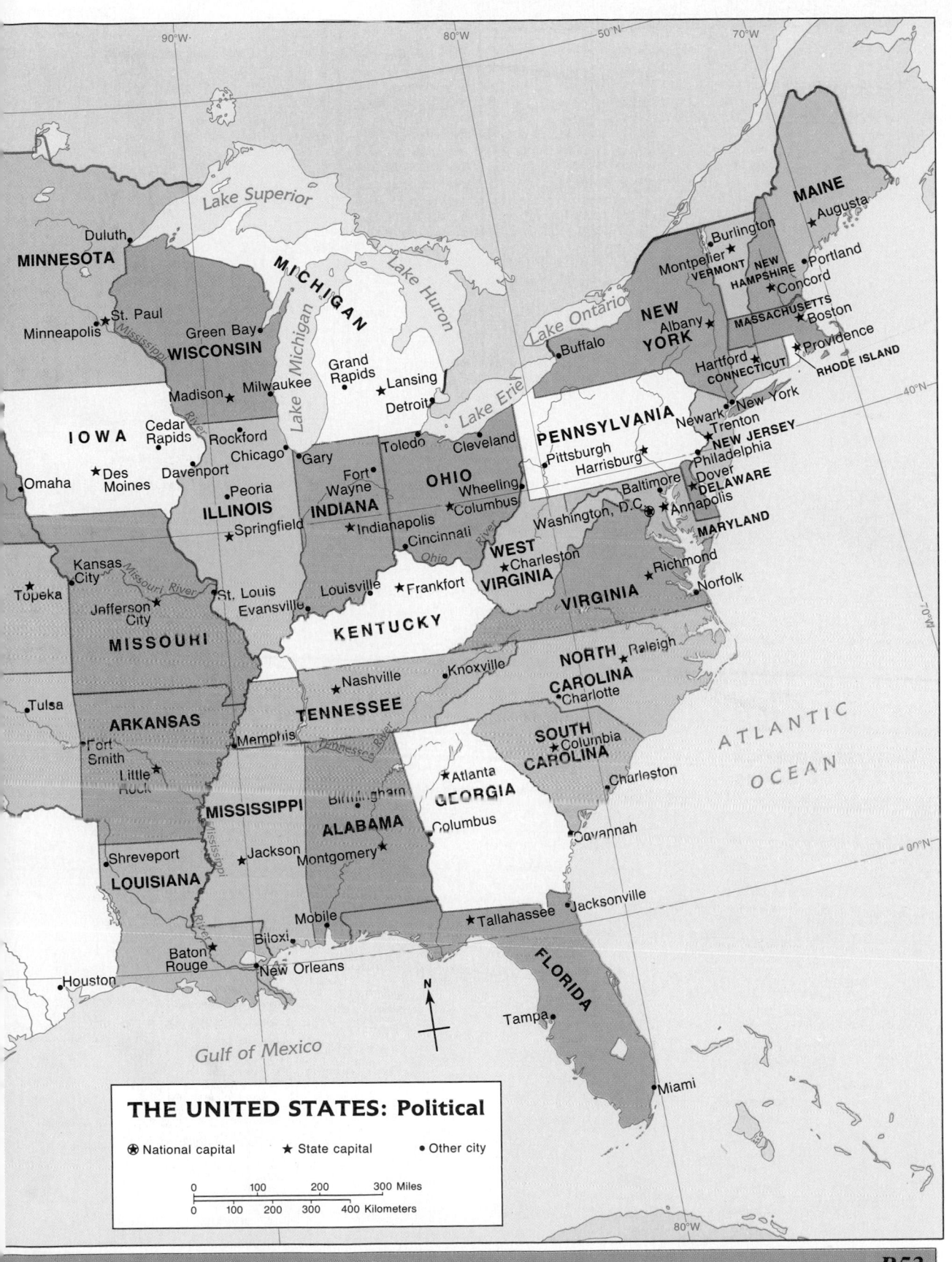

THE UNITED STATES: Political

⊗ National capital   ★ State capital   ● Other city

```
0        100        200        300 Miles
0    100   200   300   400 Kilometers
```

THE WORLD
Political

ARCTIC OCEAN

180° 160°W 140°W 120°W 100°W 80°W 60°W 40°

80°N

GREENLAND (DENMARK)

Arctic Circle

ALASKA (U.S.)

60°N

CANADA

NORTH AMERICA

PACIFIC OCEAN

40°N

UNITED STATES

AZORES (PORT.)

BERMUDA (U.K.)

MIDWAY ISLANDS (U.S.)

Tropic of Cancer

See inset below

ATLANTIC OCEAN

MEXICO

20°N

HAWAII (U.S.)

CAPE VERDE

Caribbean Sea

VENEZUELA GUYANA
SURINAME
COLOMBIA FRENCH GUIANA

0° Equator

GALAPAGOS ISLANDS (ECUADOR)

ECUADOR

SOUTH AMERICA

PERU

BRAZIL

WESTERN SAMOA
AMERICAN SAMOA (U.S.)

BOLIVIA

TONGA

20°S

FRENCH POLYNESIA (FR.)

PARAGUAY

Tropic of Capricorn

EASTER ISLAND (CHILE)

CHILE

URUGUAY

ARGENTINA

40°S

PACIFIC OCEAN

FALKLAND ISLANDS (U.K.)

Central America and West Indies

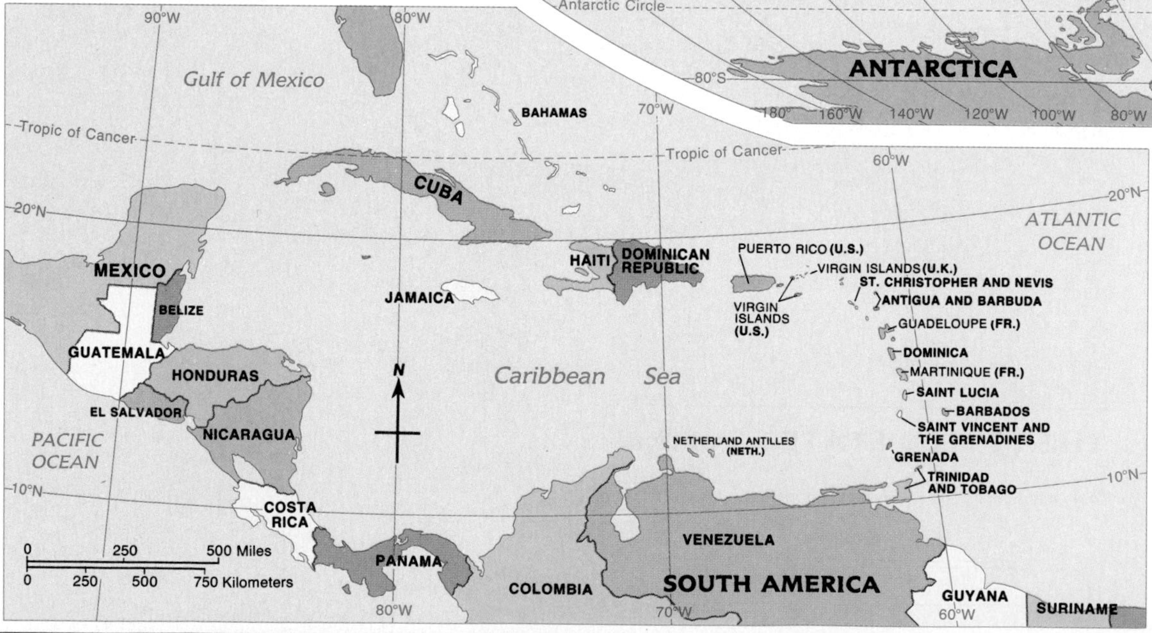

60°S

Antarctic Circle

80°S

ANTARCTICA

180° 160°W 140°W 120°W 100°W 80°W 60°W 40°W

90°W 80°W 70°W 60°W 20°N

Gulf of Mexico

BAHAMAS

ATLANTIC OCEAN

Tropic of Cancer

Tropic of Cancer

20°N

CUBA

DOMINICAN REPUBLIC

PUERTO RICO (U.S.)

MEXICO

HAITI

VIRGIN ISLANDS (U.K.)
ST. CHRISTOPHER AND NEVIS

BELIZE

JAMAICA

VIRGIN ISLANDS (U.S.)

ANTIGUA AND BARBUDA

GUADELOUPE (FR.)

GUATEMALA

HONDURAS

Caribbean Sea

DOMINICA

MARTINIQUE (FR.)

SAINT LUCIA

EL SALVADOR

BARBADOS

NICARAGUA

SAINT VINCENT AND THE GRENADINES

PACIFIC OCEAN

NETHERLAND ANTILLES (NETH.)

GRENADA

TRINIDAD AND TOBAGO

10°N

COSTA RICA

10°N

0 250 500 Miles

PANAMA

VENEZUELA

0 250 500 750 Kilometers

COLOMBIA

SOUTH AMERICA

GUYANA

SURINAME

80°W 70°W 60°W

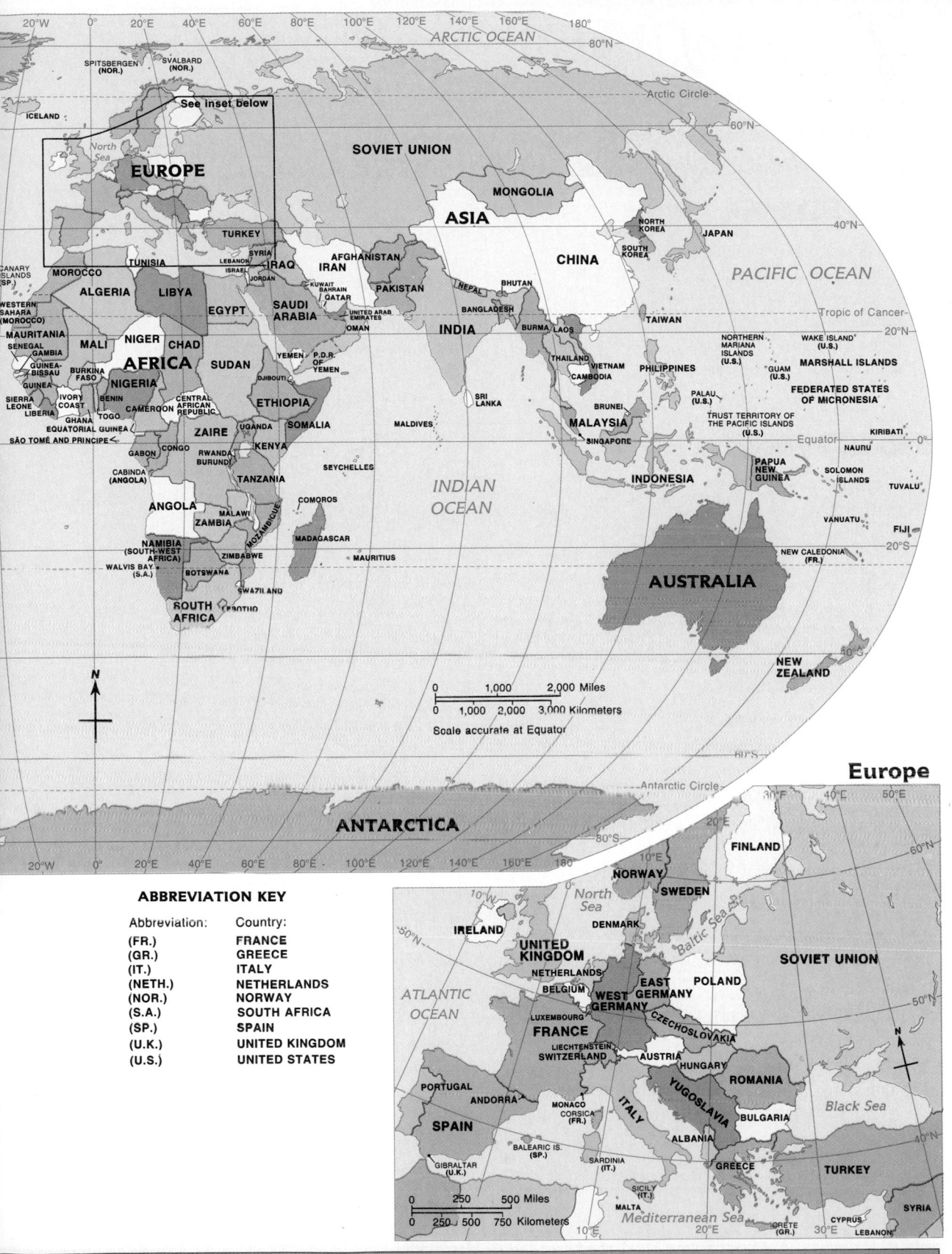

ARCTIC OCEAN

SPITSBERGEN (NOR.) SVALBARD (NOR.)

See inset below

ICELAND

North Sea

EUROPE

SOVIET UNION

MONGOLIA

ASIA

NORTH KOREA JAPAN

TURKEY

SOUTH KOREA

CANARY ISLANDS (SP.)

MOROCCO TUNISIA

SYRIA IRAQ IRAN AFGHANISTAN

LEBANON ISRAEL JORDAN

CHINA

ALGERIA LIBYA

EGYPT

SAUDI ARABIA

KUWAIT BAHRAIN QATAR UNITED ARAB EMIRATES OMAN

PAKISTAN

NEPAL BHUTAN

BANGLADESH

TAIWAN

PACIFIC OCEAN

Tropic of Cancer

WESTERN SAHARA (MOROCCO)

MAURITANIA

SENEGAL GAMBIA GUINEA-BISSAU GUINEA

MALI NIGER CHAD

AFRICA SUDAN

YEMEN P.D.R. OF YEMEN DJIBOUTI

INDIA BURMA LAOS

THAILAND VIETNAM PHILIPPINES

CAMBODIA

NORTHERN MARIANA ISLANDS (U.S.)

WAKE ISLAND (U.S.)

GUAM (U.S.)

MARSHALL ISLANDS

SIERRA LEONE IVORY COAST GHANA LIBERIA BENIN TOGO

BURKINA FASO

NIGERIA

CAMEROON CENTRAL AFRICAN REPUBLIC

EQUATORIAL GUINEA

SÃO TOMÉ AND PRÍNCIPE

ETHIOPIA

SRI LANKA

MALAYSIA

BRUNEI

SINGAPORE

PALAU (U.S.)

TRUST TERRITORY OF THE PACIFIC ISLANDS (U.S.)

FEDERATED STATES OF MICRONESIA

Equator

KIRIBATI

NAURU

GABON CONGO

ZAIRE

UGANDA SOMALIA

RWANDA BURUNDI KENYA

MALDIVES

SEYCHELLES

INDONESIA

PAPUA NEW GUINEA

SOLOMON ISLANDS

TUVALU

CABINDA (ANGOLA)

TANZANIA

INDIAN OCEAN

ANGOLA MALAWI ZAMBIA

COMOROS

MOZAMBIQUE

MADAGASCAR

MAURITIUS

VANUATU

NEW CALEDONIA (FR.)

FIJI

20°S

NAMIBIA (SOUTH-WEST AFRICA)

WALVIS BAY (S.A.)

BOTSWANA

ZIMBABWE

SWAZILAND

SOUTH AFRICA LESOTHO

AUSTRALIA

N

0 1,000 2,000 Miles
0 1,000 2,000 3,000 Kilometers
Scale accurate at Equator

NEW ZEALAND

40°S

60°S

Antarctic Circle

ANTARCTICA

80°S

20°W 0° 20°E 40°E 60°E 80°E 100°E 120°E 140°E 160°E 180°

Europe

FINLAND

NORWAY SWEDEN

North Sea Baltic Sea

IRELAND DENMARK

SOVIET UNION

UNITED KINGDOM

NETHERLANDS

BELGIUM EAST GERMANY POLAND

WEST GERMANY

LUXEMBOURG CZECHOSLOVAKIA

ATLANTIC OCEAN

FRANCE

LIECHTENSTEIN SWITZERLAND AUSTRIA HUNGARY

N

PORTUGAL ANDORRA

MONACO CORSICA (FR.)

ITALY

YUGOSLAVIA ROMANIA

SPAIN

BALEARIC IS. (SP.)

SARDINIA (IT.)

ALBANIA

BULGARIA

Black Sea

GIBRALTAR (U.K.)

GREECE

TURKEY

0 250 500 Miles
0 250 500 750 Kilometers

SICILY (IT.)

MALTA

Mediterranean Sea

CRETE (GR.)

CYPRUS

SYRIA

LEBANON

Tables of Weights and Measures and

UNITS FOR MEASURING LENGTH, WIDTH, HEIGHT, DEPTH, AND DISTANCE

METRIC UNITS

1 centimeter (cm) = 10 millimeters (mm)
1 decimeter (dm) = 10 centimeters
1 meter (m) = 100 centimeters
1 dekameter (dam) = 10 meters
1 hectometer (hm) = 100 meters
1 kilometer (km) = 1,000 meters

*A penny is about 1 millimeter in thickness.
A stack of ten pennies is about 1 centimeter in
height.*

CUSTOMARY UNITS

1 foot (ft.) = 12 inches (in.)
1 yard (yd.) = 3 feet
1 mile (mi.) = 1,760 yards = 5,280 feet

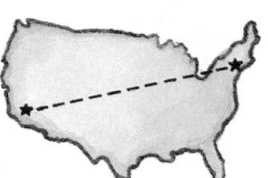

*The distance from New York City to Los Angeles is
about 3,000 miles.*

CONVERSION TABLE

Unit	Conversion Number	Unit	Conversion Number
1 inch	= 2.54 centimeters	1 yard	= 0.914 meter
1 centimeter	= 0.3937 inch	1 meter	= 1.0936 yards
1 foot	= 0.3048 meter	1 mile	= 1.609 kilometers
1 meter	= 3.2808 feet	1 kilometer	= 0.621 mile

CONVERSION FORMULA

To convert metric units to customary units or
customary units to metric units, use the following formula:

Metric to Customary: Metric Unit × *Conversion Number = Customary Unit
Example: 12 inches × 2.54 (conversion number) = 30.48
      12 inches = 30.48 centimeters
Customary to Metric: Customary Unit × *Conversion Number = Metric Unit
Example: 6 centimeters × 0.3937 (conversion number) = 2.36
      6 centimeters = 2.36 inches

*See Conversion Tables

Conversion Tables

UNITS FOR MEASURING MASS OR WEIGHT

METRIC UNITS

1 gram (g)   = 1,000 milligrams (mg)
1 kilogram (kg) = 1,000 grams
1 metric ton (t) = 1,000 kilograms

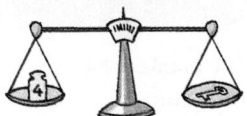

A key weighs about 4 grams.

CUSTOMARY UNITS

1 pound (lb.) = 16 ounces (oz.)
1 ton (tn.) = 2,000 pounds

A car weighs about 1 ton.

CONVERSION TABLE

Unit	Conversion Number
1 ounce	= 28.35 grams
1 gram	= 0.0353 ounce
1 pound	= 0.4536 kilogram
1 kilogram	= 2.2 pounds
1 ton	= 907.2 kilograms
1 kilogram	= 0.001 ton

A bag of potatoes weighs about 5 pounds;
2,268 grams; or 2.268 kilograms.

UNITS FOR MEASURING TEMPERATURE

METRIC UNITS

Celsius (C)
Freezing Point of Water = 0°C
Boiling Point of Water = 100°C
Normal Body Temperature = 37°C

CUSTOMARY UNITS

Fahrenheit (F.)
Freezing Point of Water = 32°F.
Boiling Point of Water = 212°F.
Normal Body Temperature = 98.6°F.

CONVERSION FORMULA

To convert Celsius to Fahrenheit or Fahrenheit to Celsius, use the following formula:

Celsius to Fahrenheit:
Celsius unit × 1.8; then add 32.
Example: 20° × 1.8 = 36 + 32 = 68°
       20°C = 68°F.

Fahrenheit to Celsius:
Fahrenheit unit − 32; then divide by 1.8.
Example: 80° − 32 = 48 ÷ 1.8 = 26.6°
       80°F. = 26.6°C

UNITS FOR MEASURING CAPACITY

METRIC UNITS

1 liter (L)   = 1,000 milliliters (mL)
1 kiloliter (kL) = 1,000 liters

A large soda bottle holds 2 liters.

CUSTOMARY UNITS

Liquid Measure
1 cup (c.) = 8 fluid ounces (oz.)
1 pint (pt.) = 2 cups
1 quart (qt.) = 2 pints
1 gallon (gal.) = 4 quarts

Dry Measure
2 pints = 1 quart
8 quarts = 1 peck (pk.)
4 pecks = 1 bushel (bu.)

LIQUID VOLUME CONVERSION TABLE

Unit	Conversion Number
1 fluid ounce	= 29.57 milliliters
1 milliliter	= 0.0338 fluid ounce
1 quart	= 0.946 liter
1 liter	= 1.057 quarts
1 gallon	= 3.785 liters
1 liter	= 0.264 gallon

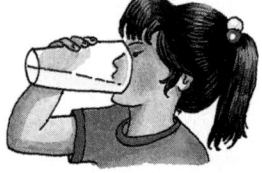

An average drinking glass holds about 10 ounces of lemonade.

DRY MEASURE CONVERSION TABLE

Unit	Conversion Number
1 dry quart	= 1.101 liters
1 liter	= 0.908 dry quart
1 peck	= 8.810 liters
1 liter	= 0.114 peck
1 bushel	= 35.24 liters
1 liter	= 0.028 bushel

A peck of peaches

A bushel of apples

UNITS FOR MEASURING AREA

METRIC UNITS

1 square meter (m²) = 10,000 square centimeters (cm²)

1 square centimeter (1 cm²)

CUSTOMARY UNITS

1 square foot (ft.²) = 144 square inches (in.²)
1 square yard (yd.²) = 9 square feet
1 acre (a.) = 43,560 square feet = 4,840 square yards

CONVERSION TABLE

Unit	Conversion Number
1 square inch	= 6.45 square centimeters
1 square centimeter	= 0.155 square inch
1 square foot	= 0.093 square meter
1 square meter	= 10.76 square feet
1 square yard	= 0.836 square meter

A small rug has an area of about 300 square centimeters.

Unit	Conversion Number
1 square meter	= 1.196 square yards
1 square mile	= 2.59 square kilometers
1 square kilometer	= 0.386 square mile

UNITS FOR MEASURING VOLUME

METRIC UNITS

1 cubic meter (m³) = 1,000,000 cubic centimeters (cm³)

1 cubic centimeter (1 cm³)

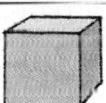

CUSTOMARY UNITS

1 cubic foot (ft.³) = 1,728 cubic inches
1 cubic yard (yd.³) = 27 cubic feet

CONVERSION TABLE

Unit	Conversion Number
1 cubic inch	= 16.387 cubic centimeters
1 cubic centimeter	= 0.061 cubic inch
1 cubic yard	= 0.765 cubic meter
1 cubic meter	= 1.31 cubic yards
1 cubic foot	= 0.028 cubic meter
1 cubic meter	= 35.315 cubic feet

A small box has a volume of about 600 cubic centimeters.

Geometric Figures

The word *geometry* comes from two Greek words meaning "to measure the earth." Probably the first use of geometry was measuring land to set up boundaries. From the Greek and Latin languages come many of the words still used today to describe geometric figures. For example, the word *angle* comes from a Greek word for *knee.* Can you guess why?

The word *triangle* is made from the word *angle* and the prefix *tri-,* which means "three." A triangle has three angles. There are several different kinds of **triangles.**

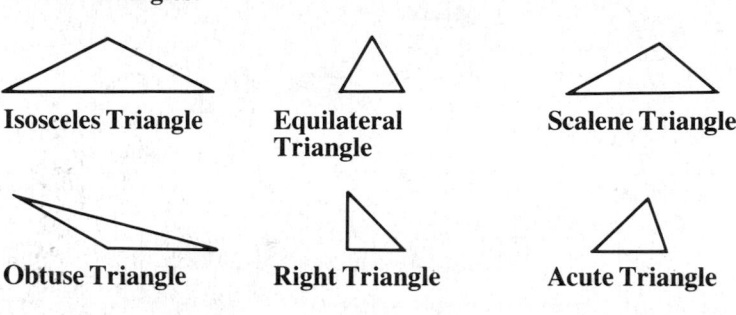

Isosceles Triangle   Equilateral Triangle   Scalene Triangle

Obtuse Triangle   Right Triangle   Acute Triangle

Quadrilaterals are four-sided figures. *Quad* comes from a Latin word meaning "four." *Lateral* comes from a Latin word meaning "side." There are several different kinds of quadrilaterals.

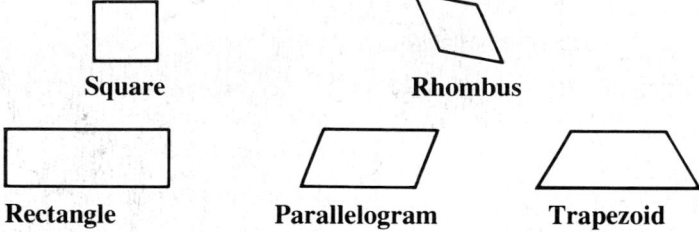

Square   Rhombus

Rectangle   Parallelogram   Trapezoid

A five-sided figure is called a **pentagon.** *Penta* means "five" and *gon* means "angle." A pentagon has five angles. You can figure out what many other geometric figures look like by referring to the chart below.

Numerical Prefix	Meaning	Numerical Prefix	Meaning
uni-	one	hexa-	six
bi-	two	sept-	seven
tri-	three	octa-, octo-	eight
quad-, quadri-, ⎤	four	nona-	nine
tetra- ⎦		deca-, deka-	ten
penta-	five	poly-, multi-	many

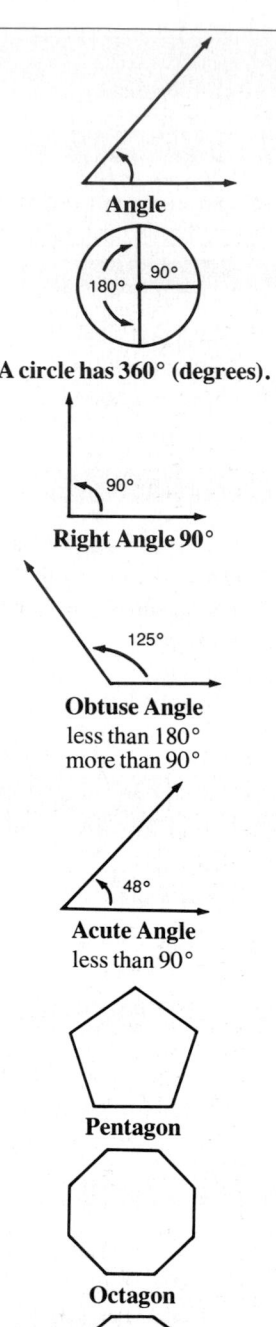

Angle

A circle has 360° (degrees).

Right Angle 90°

Obtuse Angle
less than 180°
more than 90°

Acute Angle
less than 90°

Pentagon

Octagon

Decagon

The Solar System

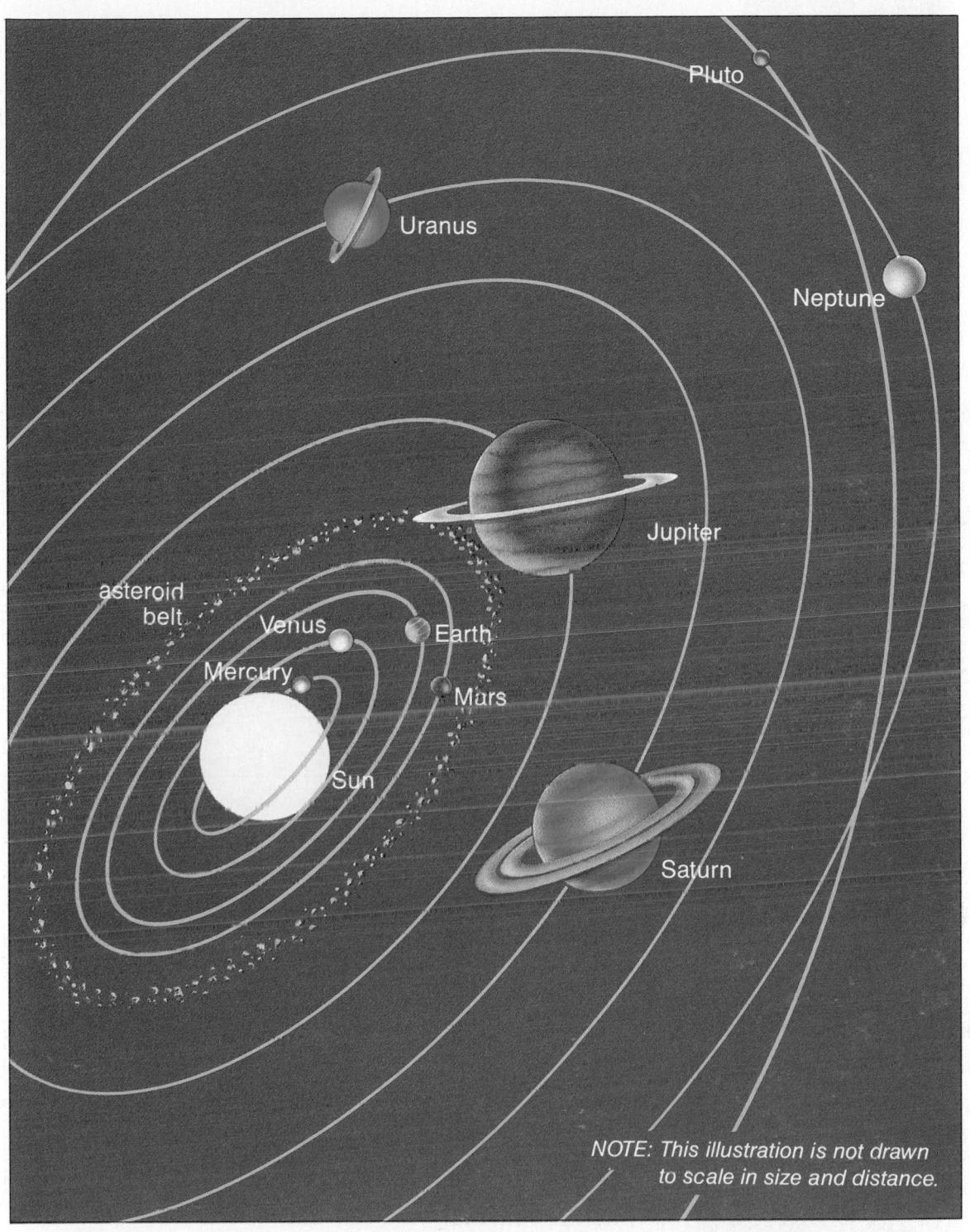

Pluto

Uranus

Neptune

Jupiter

asteroid belt

Venus

Earth

Mercury

Mars

Sun

Saturn

NOTE: This illustration is not drawn to scale in size and distance.

PLANET	AVERAGE DISTANCE FROM SUN	PERIOD OF ROTATION	PERIOD OF REVOLUTION
 MERCURY	36,000,000 mi. (57,900,000 km)	59 days	88 days

FACTS *Mercury has no atmosphere to protect it from the rays of the sun. The side facing the sun becomes very hot. The side facing away from the sun becomes very cold. Mercury has no moons.*

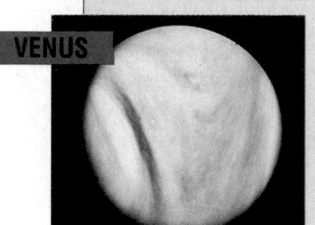 VENUS	67,250,000 mi. (108,230,000 km)	243 days	225 days

FACTS *Venus has a thick, cloudy atmosphere, made largely of carbon dioxide. The atmosphere produces a "greenhouse" effect, trapping heat near its surface. Temperatures may reach 878°F. (470°C). Venus has no moons.*

 EARTH	93,000,000 mi. (150,000,000 km)	23 hrs./56 mins.	365 days

FACTS *Earth is rich in oxygen, water, and nitrogen. It is the only planet that is known to support life. The Earth has one moon.*

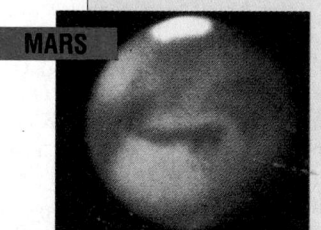 MARS	141,700,000 mi. (228,000,000 km)	24 hrs./37 mins.	687 days

FACTS *Mars has a thin atmosphere and reddish-brown, desertlike regions on its surface. Like the Earth, it has a tilted axis. As a result, it has changes in seasons as it revolves around the sun. Mars has two moons.*

 JUPITER	483,700,000 mi. (778,400,000 km)	9 hrs./55 mins.	12 years

FACTS *Jupiter's atmosphere has colored bands of clouds. The Great Red Spot resembles a large hurricane and seems to consist of spinning masses of gases. Jupiter has a single, faint ring and 17 known moons. One moon has active volcanoes.*

PLANET	AVERAGE DISTANCE FROM SUN	PERIOD OF ROTATION	PERIOD OF REVOLUTION

SATURN

	AVERAGE DISTANCE FROM SUN	PERIOD OF ROTATION	PERIOD OF REVOLUTION
	885,200,000 mi. (1,424,600,000 km)	10 hrs./39 mins.	29.5 years

FACTS *Saturn has a complex ring system. Each ring is made up of smaller rings of ice and rock particles. Saturn has at least 22 known moons.*

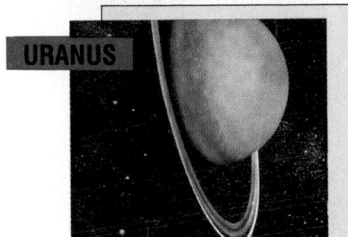

URANUS

	1,781,000,000 mi. (2,866,900,000 km)	17 hours	84.1 years

FACTS *Uranus's greenish color is a result of its thick atmosphere. Uranus has several dark rings and at least 15 known moons.*

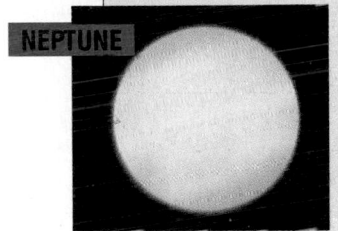

NEPTUNE

	2,788,000,000 mi. (4,486,100,000 km)	18-20 hours	165 years

FACTS *Neptune is similar in size and color to Uranus. It has three known moons. One moon, Triton, is one of the largest moons in the solar system.*

PLUTO

	3,660,000,000 mi. (5,890,000,000 km)	6 days	248 years

FACTS *Pluto, the smallest planet, is about the size of Earth's moon. It may well be the coldest planet, with temperatures ranging from −342° to −369°F. (−208° to −223°C). Pluto has one known moon.*

NOTE: The planets are not shown to scale in size.

PLANET	AVERAGE DISTANCE FROM SUN	PERIOD OF ROTATION	PERIOD OF REVOLUTION
 **SATURN**	885,200,000 mi. (1,424,600,000 km)	10 hrs./39 mins.	29.5 years

FACTS *Saturn has a complex ring system. Each ring is made up of smaller rings of ice and rock particles. Saturn has at least 22 known moons.*

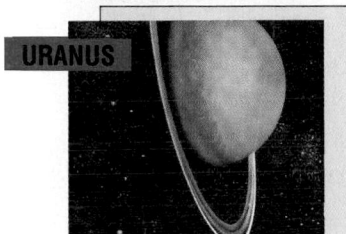 **URANUS**	1,781,000,000 mi. (2,866,900,000 km)	17 hours	84.1 years

FACTS *Uranus's greenish color is a result of its thick atmosphere. Uranus has several dark rings and at least 15 known moons.*

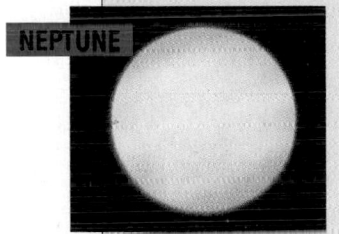 **NEPTUNE**	2,788,000,000 mi. (4,486,100,000 km)	18–20 hours	165 years

FACTS *Neptune is similar in size and color to Uranus. It has three known moons. One moon, Triton, is one of the largest moons in the solar system.*

 **PLUTO**	3,660,000,000 mi. (5,890,000,000 km)	6 days	248 years

FACTS *Pluto, the smallest planet, is about the size of Earth's moon. It may well be the coldest planet, with temperatures ranging from −342° to −369°F. (−208° to −223°C). Pluto has one known moon.*

NOTE: The planets are not shown to scale in size.

*I*nside the Earth

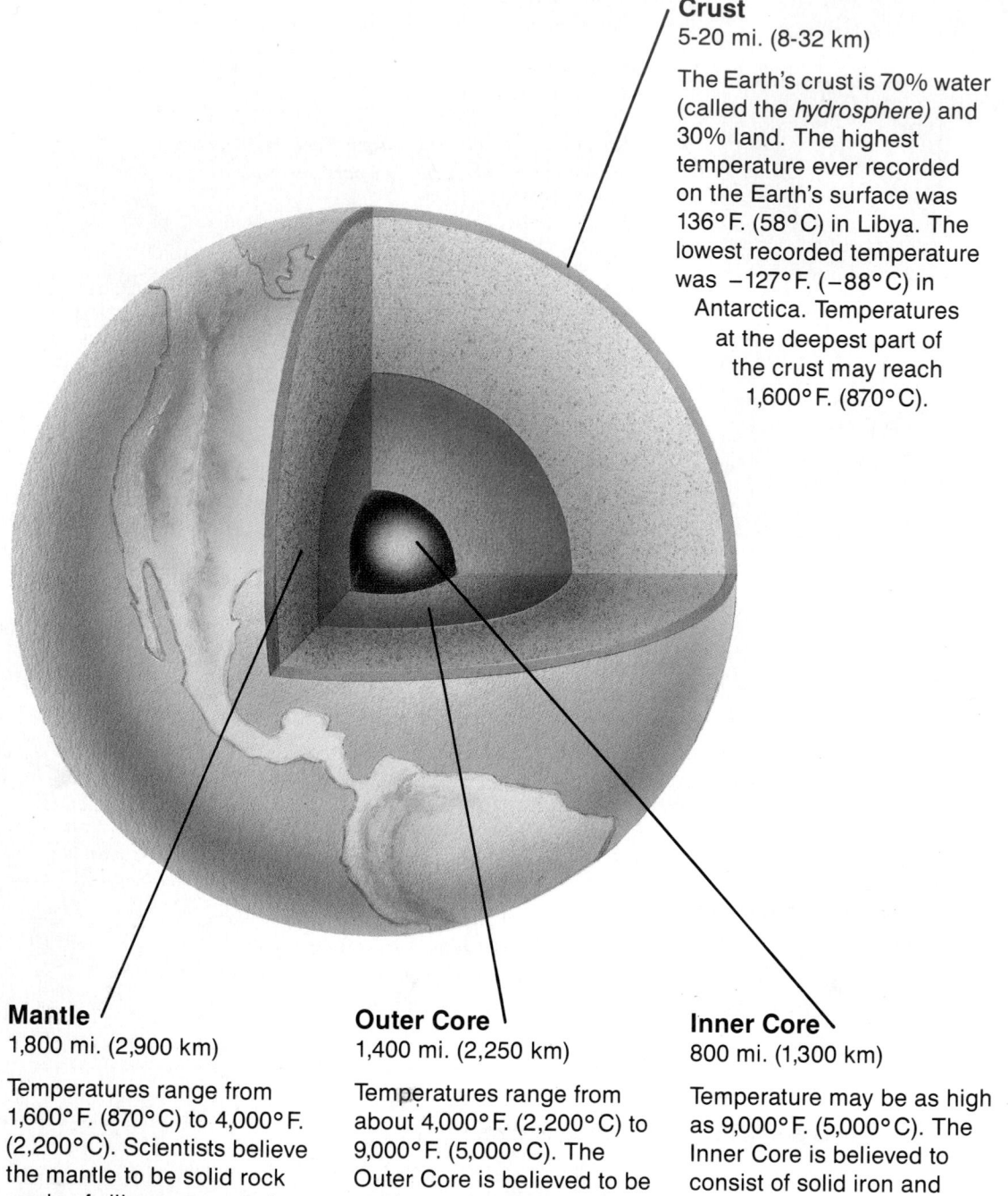

Crust
5-20 mi. (8-32 km)

The Earth's crust is 70% water (called the *hydrosphere*) and 30% land. The highest temperature ever recorded on the Earth's surface was 136°F. (58°C) in Libya. The lowest recorded temperature was −127°F. (−88°C) in Antarctica. Temperatures at the deepest part of the crust may reach 1,600°F. (870°C).

Mantle
1,800 mi. (2,900 km)

Temperatures range from 1,600°F. (870°C) to 4,000°F. (2,200°C). Scientists believe the mantle to be solid rock made of silicon, oxygen, iron, and magnesium.

Outer Core
1,400 mi. (2,250 km)

Temperatures range from about 4,000°F. (2,200°C) to 9,000°F. (5,000°C). The Outer Core is believed to be made up of melted iron and nickel.

Inner Core
800 mi. (1,300 km)

Temperature may be as high as 9,000°F. (5,000°C). The Inner Core is believed to consist of solid iron and nickel.